2020 HARRIS ADVERTISING

The **2020 Harris Directories** provides you with the most up-to-date information on the region's most prominent companies. Through offering you multiple ways to look up any specific business within the area, important data can easily be located.
. For reliability and assurance, Harris directories are the source for all pertinent information for all companies in there state.

To **Highlight** your company and get the most exposure necessary you can now get full page color advertisements inserted in the front of the book. This gives your company a step up showing all your company's information while remaining competitive with the larger companies. These ad pages are supplied by you and can showcase your company logo's, shareholder letters or any other information you would like the thousands of readers who use the Harris Directories to see.

You also get **complimentary** books highlighting your company's information and you can also purchase extra books at a 40% discount.

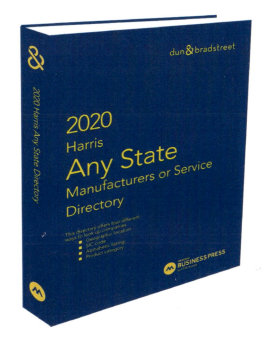

Plan 1

$1,500

1 full page 4 color ad. (Supplied by you)

3 free books (Additional books can be purchased at a 40% discount of regular price)

Plan 2

$2,100

2 full page 4 color ads. (Supplied by you)

5 free books (Additional books can be purchased at a 40% discount of regular price)

Plan 3

$4,000

4 full page color ads. (Supplied by you)

10 Free Book (Additional books can be purchased at 40% discount off original costs)

For additional information or to order please contact

Thomas Wecera at 212-413-7726 thomas.wecera@mergent.com

2020 Oklahoma
Directory of Manufacturers and Processors

Published September 2020 next update September 2021

WARNING: Purchasers and users of this directory may not use this directory to compile mailing lists, other marketing aids and other types of data, which are sold or otherwise provided to third parties. Such use is wrongful, illegal and a violation of the federal copyright laws.

CAUTION: Because of the many thousands of establishment listings contained in this directory and the possibilities of both human and mechanical error in processing this information, Mergent Inc. cannot assume liability for the correctness of the listings or information on which they are based. Hence, no information contained in this work should be relied upon in any instance where there is a possibility of any loss or damage as a consequence of any error or omission in this volume.

Publisher
Mergent Inc.
444 Madison Ave
New York, NY 10022

©Mergent Inc All Rights Reserved
2020 Mergent Business Press
ISSN 1080-2614
ISBN 978-1-64141-642-9

TABLE OF CONTENTS

Explanatory Notes 4
User's Guide to Listings 6

Geographic Section
County/City Cross-Reference Index 9
Firms Listed by Location City 11

Standard Industrial Classification (SIC) Section
SIC Alphabetical Index 397
SIC Numerical Index 399
Firms Listed by SIC 401

Alphabetic Section
Firms Listed by Firm Name 513

Product Section
Product Index 659
Firms Listed by Product Category 675

SUMMARY OF CONTENTS

Number of Companies 11,809
Number of Decision Makers 17,648
Minimum Number of Employees 1

EXPLANATORY NOTES

How to Cross-Reference in This Directory

Sequential Entry Numbers. Each establishment in the Geographic Section is numbered sequentially (G-0000). The number assigned to each establishment is referred to as its "entry number." To make cross-referencing easier, each listing in the Geographic, SIC, Alphabetic and Product Sections includes the establishment's entry number. To facilitate locating an entry in the Geographic Section, the entry numbers for the first listing on the left page and the last listing on the right page are printed at the top of the page next to the city name.

Source Suggestions Welcome

Although all known sources were used to compile this directory, it is possible that companies were inadvertently omitted. Your assistance in calling attention to such omissions would be greatly appreciated. A special form on the facing page will help you in the reporting process.

Analysis

Every effort has been made to contact all firms to verify their information. The one exception to this rule is the annual sales figure, which is considered by many companies to be confidential information. Therefore, estimated sales have been calculated by multiplying the nationwide average sales per employee for the firm's major SIC/NAICS code by the firm's number of employees. Nationwide averages for sales per employee by SIC/NAICS codes are provided by the U.S. Department of Commerce and are updated annually. All sales—sales (est)—have been estimated by this method. The exceptions are parent companies (PA), division headquarters (DH) and headquarter locations (HQ) which may include an actual corporate sales figure—sales (corporate-wide) if available.

Types of Companies

Descriptive and statistical data are included for companies in the entire state. These comprise manufacturers, machine shops, fabricators, assemblers and printers. Also identified are corporate offices in the state.

Employment Data

The employment figure shown in the Geographic Section includes male and female employees and embraces all levels of the company: administrative, clerical, sales and maintenance. This figure is for the facility listed and does not include other plants or offices. It should be recognized that these figures represent an approximate year-round average. These employment figures are broken into codes A through G and used in the Product and SIC Sections to further help you in qualifying a company. Be sure to check the footnotes on the bottom of pages for the code breakdowns.

GEOGRAPHIC SECTION
Companies sorted by city in alphabetical order
In-depth company data listed

STANDARD INDUSTRIAL CLASSIFICATIONS
Alphabetical index of classifcation descriptions
Numerical index of classifcation descriptions
Companies sorted by SIC product groupings

ALPHABETIC SECTION
Company listings in alphabetical order

PRODUCT INDEX
Product categories listed in alphabetical order

PRODUCT SECTION
Companies sorted by product and manufacturing service classifications

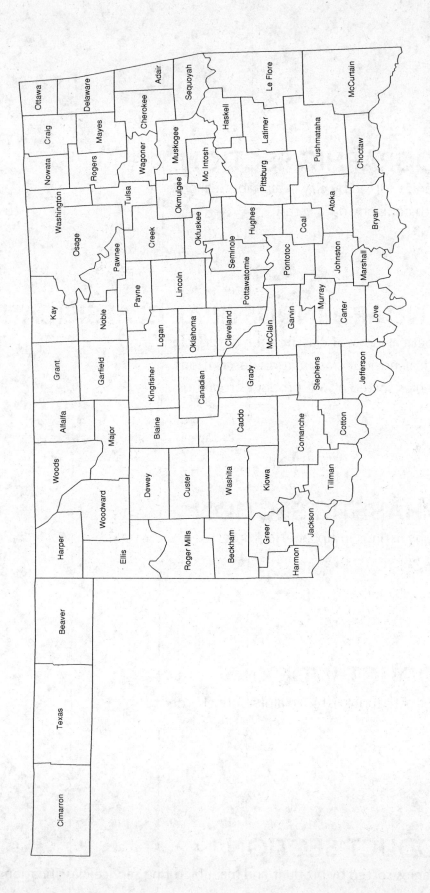

COUNTY/CITY CROSS-REFERENCE INDEX

Adair
- Proctor .... (G-7939)
- Stilwell .... (G-8779)
- Watts .... (G-11356)
- Westville .... (G-11480)

Alfalfa
- Carmen .... (G-1272)
- Cherokee .... (G-1413)
- Goltry .... (G-3248)
- Helena .... (G-3434)
- Jet .... (G-3741)

Atoka
- Atoka .... (G-395)
- Caney .... (G-1262)
- Lane .... (G-3870)

Beaver
- Balko .... (G-432)
- Beaver .... (G-538)
- Forgan .... (G-3169)
- Knowles .... (G-3841)
- Turpin .... (G-11181)

Beckham
- Carter .... (G-1281)
- Elk City .... (G-2780)
- Erick .... (G-3085)
- Sayre .... (G-8337)

Blaine
- Canton .... (G-1265)
- Geary .... (G-3216)
- Longdale .... (G-4123)
- Okeene .... (G-5258)
- Southard .... (G-8588)
- Watonga .... (G-11339)

Bryan
- Achille .... (G-1)
- Bennington .... (G-563)
- Bokchito .... (G-750)
- Caddo .... (G-1232)
- Calera .... (G-1238)
- Cartwright .... (G-1282)
- Colbert .... (G-1785)
- Durant .... (G-2200)
- Hendrix .... (G-3438)
- Mead .... (G-4365)

Caddo
- Anadarko .... (G-199)
- Apache .... (G-217)
- Binger .... (G-606)
- Carnegie .... (G-1273)
- Cement .... (G-1370)
- Cyril .... (G-1975)
- Eakly .... (G-2278)
- Fort Cobb .... (G-3171)
- Gracemont .... (G-3254)
- Hinton .... (G-3520)
- Hydro .... (G-3631)
- Lookeba .... (G-4128)

Canadian
- Calumet .... (G-1245)
- El Reno .... (G-2695)
- Mustang .... (G-4760)
- Piedmont .... (G-7752)
- Union City .... (G-11220)
- Yukon .... (G-11688)

Carter
- Ardmore .... (G-233)
- Fox .... (G-3190)
- Healdton .... (G-3407)
- Lone Grove .... (G-4114)
- Ratliff City .... (G-8048)
- Springer .... (G-8621)
- Wilson .... (G-11531)

Cherokee
- Cookson .... (G-1849)
- Hulbert .... (G-3623)
- Park Hill .... (G-7639)
- Peggs .... (G-7713)
- Tahlequah .... (G-8848)
- Welling .... (G-11466)

Choctaw
- Boswell .... (G-757)
- Fort Towson .... (G-3183)
- Grant .... (G-3258)
- Hugo .... (G-3602)
- Sawyer .... (G-8334)
- Soper .... (G-8587)

Cimarron
- Boise City .... (G-747)

Cleveland
- Lexington .... (G-4034)
- Moore .... (G-4483)
- Newalla .... (G-4804)
- Noble .... (G-4875)
- Norman .... (G-4894)
- Oklahoma City .... (G-5278)

Coal
- Coalgate .... (G-1774)

Comanche
- Cache .... (G-1223)
- Chattanooga .... (G-1389)
- Elgin .... (G-2774)
- Fletcher .... (G-3160)
- Fort Sill .... (G-3182)
- Lawton .... (G-3880)
- Medicine Park .... (G-4370)

Cotton
- Temple .... (G-8932)
- Walters .... (G-11299)

Craig
- Big Cabin .... (G-601)
- Vinita .... (G-11247)
- Welch .... (G-11462)

Creek
- Bristow .... (G-762)
- Depew .... (G-2010)
- Drumright .... (G-2049)
- Kellyville .... (G-3761)
- Kiefer .... (G-3775)
- Mannford .... (G-4174)
- Mounds .... (G-4607)
- Oilton .... (G-5241)
- Sapulpa .... (G-8244)
- Tulsa .... (G-9244)

Custer
- Arapaho .... (G-224)
- Butler .... (G-1220)
- Clinton .... (G-1735)
- Custer City .... (G-1973)
- Thomas .... (G-8940)
- Weatherford .... (G-11385)

Delaware
- Colcord .... (G-1789)
- Eucha .... (G-3094)
- Grove .... (G-3259)
- Jay .... (G-3677)
- Kansas .... (G-3754)

Dewey
- Camargo .... (G-1251)
- Fay .... (G-3156)
- Leedey .... (G-4028)
- Seiling .... (G-8349)
- Taloga .... (G-8907)
- Vici .... (G-11240)

Ellis
- Arnett .... (G-387)
- Gage .... (G-3210)
- Shattuck .... (G-8420)

Garfield
- Bison .... (G-607)
- Covington .... (G-1868)
- Drummond .... (G-2046)
- Enid .... (G-2900)
- Garber .... (G-3212)
- Kremlin .... (G-3851)
- Lahoma .... (G-3856)
- Waukomis .... (G-11359)

Garvin
- Elmore City .... (G-2893)
- Lindsay .... (G-4042)
- Maysville .... (G-4254)
- Paoli .... (G-7637)
- Pauls Valley .... (G-7648)
- Stratford .... (G-8804)
- Wynnewood .... (G-11664)

Grady
- Alex .... (G-129)
- Amber .... (G-196)
- Bradley .... (G-760)
- Chickasha .... (G-1426)
- Minco .... (G-4475)
- Ninnekah .... (G-4867)
- Pocasset .... (G-7774)
- Rush Springs .... (G-8119)
- Tuttle .... (G-11184)
- Verden .... (G-11237)

Grant
- Lamont .... (G-3864)
- Manchester .... (G-4167)
- Medford .... (G-4369)
- Nash .... (G-4803)
- Pond Creek .... (G-7889)
- Wakita .... (G-11297)

Greer
- Granite .... (G-3257)
- Mangum .... (G-4170)
- Willow .... (G-11530)

Harmon
- Hollis .... (G-3563)

Harper
- Buffalo .... (G-1212)
- Laverne .... (G-3876)

Haskell
- Keota .... (G-3772)
- Kinta .... (G-3832)
- Mc Curtain .... (G-4267)
- Stigler .... (G-8628)
- Whitefield .... (G-11516)

Hughes
- Atwood .... (G-428)
- Holdenville .... (G-3549)
- Lamar .... (G-3862)
- Stuart .... (G-8825)
- Wetumka .... (G-11489)

Jackson
- Altus .... (G-140)
- Blair .... (G-696)
- Duke .... (G-2079)
- Eldorado .... (G-2773)
- Elmer .... (G-2892)
- Martha .... (G-4251)
- Olustee .... (G-7531)

Jefferson
- Grady .... (G-3255)
- Ringling .... (G-8081)
- Waurika .... (G-11362)

Johnston
- Coleman .... (G-1792)
- Mannsville .... (G-4195)
- Milburn .... (G-4463)
- Mill Creek .... (G-4465)
- Ravia .... (G-8072)
- Tishomingo .... (G-8961)

Kay
- Blackwell .... (G-673)
- Braman .... (G-761)
- Kaw City .... (G-3756)
- Newkirk .... (G-4846)
- Ponca City .... (G-7789)
- Tonkawa .... (G-8970)

Kingfisher
- Cashion .... (G-1285)
- Dover .... (G-2038)
- Hennessey .... (G-3442)
- Kingfisher .... (G-3783)
- Loyal .... (G-4130)
- Okarche .... (G-5242)

Kiowa
- Hobart .... (G-3541)
- Lone Wolf .... (G-4122)
- Mountain Park .... (G-4626)
- Mountain View .... (G-4627)
- Roosevelt .... (G-8116)
- Snyder .... (G-8581)

Latimer
- Red Oak .... (G-8073)
- Talihina .... (G-8905)
- Wilburton .... (G-11518)

Le Flore
- Arkoma .... (G-385)
- Bokoshe .... (G-752)
- Cameron .... (G-1254)
- Heavener .... (G-3425)
- Hodgen .... (G-3548)
- Howe .... (G-3599)
- Pocola .... (G-7779)
- Poteau .... (G-7896)
- Shady Point .... (G-8414)
- Spiro .... (G-8613)
- Wister .... (G-11547)

Lincoln
- Agra .... (G-124)
- Carney .... (G-1279)
- Chandler .... (G-1372)
- Davenport .... (G-1978)
- Meeker .... (G-4374)
- Prague .... (G-7920)
- Sparks .... (G-8589)
- Stroud .... (G-8808)
- Wellston .... (G-11468)

Logan
- Coyle .... (G-1904)
- Crescent .... (G-1907)
- Guthrie .... (G-3295)
- Marshall .... (G-4250)
- Mulhall .... (G-4637)

Love
- Burneyville .... (G-1216)
- Leon .... (G-4033)
- Marietta .... (G-4199)
- Overbrook .... (G-7538)

Major
- Ames .... (G-198)
- Chester .... (G-1420)
- Cleo Springs .... (G-1712)
- Fairview .... (G-3132)
- Meno .... (G-4387)
- Ringwood .... (G-8083)

Marshall
- Kingston .... (G-3824)
- Lebanon .... (G-4027)
- Madill .... (G-4144)

Mayes
- Adair .... (G-107)
- Chouteau .... (G-1558)
- Ketchum .... (G-3774)
- Langley .... (G-3871)
- Locust Grove .... (G-4103)
- Mazie .... (G-4264)
- Pryor .... (G-7940)
- Rose .... (G-8117)
- Salina .... (G-8133)
- Spavinaw .... (G-8591)
- Strang .... (G-8803)

Mcclain
- Blanchard .... (G-698)
- Byars .... (G-1222)
- Goldsby .... (G-3244)
- Newcastle .... (G-4818)

COUNTY/CITY CROSS-REFERENCE

	ENTRY #
Purcell	(G-8002)
Washington	(G-11332)
Wayne	(G-11365)

Mccurtain
Broken Bow	(G-1182)
Eagletown	(G-2274)
Haworth	(G-3404)
Idabel	(G-3636)
Millerton	(G-4473)
Smithville	(G-8578)
Valliant	(G-11222)
Watson	(G-11355)

Mcintosh
Checotah	(G-1391)
Eufaula	(G-3097)

Murray
Davis	(G-1979)
Sulphur	(G-8826)

Muskogee
Fort Gibson	(G-3172)
Haskell	(G-3397)
Muskogee	(G-4639)
Oktaha	(G-7530)
Porum	(G-7895)
Warner	(G-11307)

Noble
Morrison	(G-4603)
Perry	(G-7725)
Red Rock	(G-8079)

Nowata
Delaware	(G-2008)
Nowata	(G-5209)

Okfuskee
Boley	(G-756)
Okemah	(G-5263)
Paden	(G-7632)
Weleetka	(G-11463)

Oklahoma
Arcadia	(G-226)
Bethany	(G-571)
Choctaw	(G-1527)
Del City	(G-1994)
Edmond	(G-2282)
Harrah	(G-3373)
Jones	(G-3742)
Luther	(G-4131)
Midwest City	(G-4437)
Nichols Hills	(G-4854)
Nicoma Park	(G-4866)
Oklahoma City	(G-5326)
Spencer	(G-8594)
Tinker Afb	(G-8953)
Warr Acres	(G-11309)
Wheatland	(G-11515)

Okmulgee
Beggs	(G-548)
Henryetta	(G-3499)
Morris	(G-4596)
Okmulgee	(G-7491)

Osage
Barnsdall	(G-434)
Burbank	(G-1214)
Fairfax	(G-3118)
Foraker	(G-3168)
Hominy	(G-3573)
Pawhuska	(G-7676)
Shidler	(G-8524)
Wynona	(G-11678)

Ottawa
Afton	(G-113)
Bernice	(G-565)
Bluejacket	(G-746)
Fairland	(G-3123)
Miami	(G-4388)
North Miami	(G-5206)
Picher	(G-7751)
Quapaw	(G-8027)
Wyandotte	(G-11660)

Pawnee
Cleveland	(G-1714)
Jennings	(G-3739)
Pawnee	(G-7699)
Terlton	(G-8937)

Payne
Cushing	(G-1922)
Glencoe	(G-3219)
Perkins	(G-7714)
Ripley	(G-8099)
Stillwater	(G-8651)
Yale	(G-11681)

Pittsburg
Alderson	(G-127)
Bache	(G-429)
Canadian	(G-1260)
Hartshorne	(G-3389)
Indianola	(G-3651)
Kiowa	(G-3837)
Krebs	(G-3849)
Mc Alester	(G-4265)
McAlester	(G-4268)
Quinton	(G-8035)
Wardville	(G-11306)

Pontotoc
Ada	(G-2)
Allen	(G-132)
Fittstown	(G-3158)
Francis	(G-3191)
Roff	(G-8107)
Stonewall	(G-8797)

Pottawatomie
Asher	(G-389)
Earlsboro	(G-2279)
Macomb	(G-4141)
Maud	(G-4252)
McLoud	(G-4352)
Saint Louis	(G-8131)
Shawnee	(G-8426)
Tecumseh	(G-8909)
Wanette	(G-11305)

Pushmataha
Antlers	(G-212)
Clayton	(G-1708)
Rattan	(G-8071)
Tuskahoma	(G-11183)

Roger Mills
Cheyenne	(G-1423)
Crawford	(G-1905)
Durham	(G-2273)
Hammon	(G-3372)
Reydon	(G-8080)
Sweetwater	(G-8847)

Rogers
Catoosa	(G-1293)
Chelsea	(G-1399)
Claremore	(G-1573)
Inola	(G-3652)
Oologah	(G-7532)
Talala	(G-8895)

Seminole
Bowlegs	(G-759)
Konawa	(G-3842)
Sasakwa	(G-8329)
Seminole	(G-8353)
Wewoka	(G-11497)

Sequoyah
Gore	(G-3250)
Marble City	(G-4197)
Muldrow	(G-4630)
Roland	(G-8113)
Sallisaw	(G-8136)
Vian	(G-11238)

Stephens
Comanche	(G-1832)
Duncan	(G-2083)
Foster	(G-3185)
Loco	(G-4102)
Marlow	(G-4220)
Velma	(G-11235)

Texas
Goodwell	(G-3249)
Guymon	(G-3344)
Hooker	(G-3595)
Texhoma	(G-8939)
Tyrone	(G-11218)

Tillman
Frederick	(G-3192)
Grandfield	(G-3256)
Tipton	(G-8957)

Tulsa
Bixby	(G-608)
Broken Arrow	(G-807)
Collinsville	(G-1798)
Glenpool	(G-3228)
Jenks	(G-3688)
Owasso	(G-7540)
Sand Springs	(G-8156)
Skiatook	(G-8529)
Sperry	(G-8604)
Tulsa	(G-9054)

Wagoner
Broken Arrow	(G-1107)
Coweta	(G-1869)
Okay	(G-5256)
Porter	(G-7892)
Wagoner	(G-11274)

Washington
Bartlesville	(G-443)
Copan	(G-1851)
Dewey	(G-2012)
Ochelata	(G-5233)
Ramona	(G-8043)

Washita
Bessie	(G-568)
Burns Flat	(G-1218)
Canute	(G-1266)
Cordell	(G-1852)
Corn	(G-1866)
Dill City	(G-2034)
Foss	(G-3184)
Rocky	(G-8104)
Sentinel	(G-8409)

Woods
Alva	(G-173)
Dacoma	(G-1976)
Freedom	(G-3205)
Waynoka	(G-11370)

Woodward
Mooreland	(G-4585)
Sharon	(G-8417)
Woodward	(G-11552)

GEOGRAPHIC SECTION

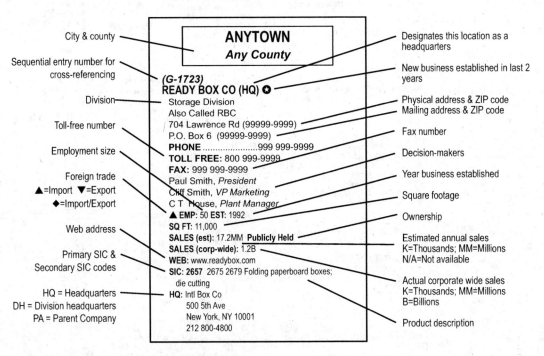

See footnotes for symbols and codes identification.
- This section is in alphabetical order by city.
- Companies are sorted alphabetically under their respective cities.
- To locate cities within a county refer to the County/City Cross Reference Index.

IMPORTANT NOTICE: It is a violation of both federal and state law to transmit an unsolicited advertisement to a facsimile machine. Any user of this product that violates such laws may be subject to civil and criminal penalties which may exceed $500 for each transmission of an unsolicited facsimile. Harris InfoSource provides fax numbers for lawful purposes only and expressly forbids the use of these numbers in any unlawful manner.

Achille
Bryan County

(G-1)
SOUTHERN COOKER
Also Called: Southern Style Custom Cookers
117 Hwy 78 (74720)
P.O. Box 146 (74720-0146)
PHONE..................580 283-3982
Gary Robinson, *Owner*
EMP: 3 **EST:** 1994
SALES (est): 132K **Privately Held**
SIC: 3631 Barbecues, grills & braziers (outdoor cooking)

Ada
Pontotoc County

(G-2)
3 CS TEES LLC
16045 County Road 1590 (74820-0160)
PHONE..................405 208-1320
EMP: 2
SALES (est): 89.2K **Privately Held**
SIC: 2759 Screen printing

(G-3)
ADA COCA COLA BOTTLING COMPANY
Also Called: Coca-Cola
1205 Cradduck Rd (74820-8439)
P.O. Box 1607 (74821-1607)
PHONE..................580 427-2000
Thomas B Crabtree, *President*
Frank R Crabtree Jr, *Vice Pres*
Agnes Lane, *Vice Pres*
Mike Ohmstede, *Vice Pres*
David Pinley, *Prdtn Mgr*
EMP: 100 **EST:** 1905
SQ FT: 37,500
SALES (est): 30.6MM **Privately Held**
WEB: www.adacocacola.com
SIC: 2086 Bottled & canned soft drinks

(G-4)
ADA ENERGY CEMENTING LLC
13710 County Road 1550 (74820-0867)
PHONE..................580 436-5228
William J Maloy, *Principal*
EMP: 2
SALES (est): 177.6K **Privately Held**
SIC: 1389 Cementing oil & gas well casings

(G-5)
ADA ENERGY SERVICE LLC
Also Called: Ada Drilling
13710 County Road 1550 (74820-0867)
PHONE..................580 436-5228
William Maloy,
Daniel Schlachter,
EMP: 75
SALES (est): 8.2MM **Privately Held**
SIC: 1382 Oil & gas exploration services

(G-6)
ADA IRON AND WELDING LLC (PA)
13655 County Road 1570 (74820-0190)
PHONE..................580 332-6694
Darren Gregory,
Tressa McGinty,
Mike Pinley,
EMP: 7
SALES (est): 1.2MM **Privately Held**
SIC: 3441 Fabricated structural metal

(G-7)
AMERICANA ENERGY COMPANY INC
106 N Main St (74820-9574)
P.O. Box 1527 (74821-1527)
PHONE..................580 310-0084
Bill G Cantrell, *President*
EMP: 4
SQ FT: 6,000
SALES (est): 250K **Privately Held**
SIC: 1311 Crude petroleum production

(G-8)
AMT DIVERSIFIED CNSTR INC
12157 County Road 3570 (74820-0616)
PHONE..................580 279-6250
Angelique Wescott, *COO*
EMP: 7
SQ FT: 2,300
SALES (est): 850K **Privately Held**
SIC: 3699 Particle accelerators, high voltage

(G-9)
APEX COMPOSITES INC
414 Chamber Loop (74820-2254)
PHONE..................580 436-6444
Jeff Landredeth, *President*
Tracy Hatton, *Mfg Staff*
EMP: 55
SQ FT: 70,000
SALES (est): 7.5MM
SALES (corp-wide): 173.9MM **Privately Held**
SIC: 3728 Aircraft assemblies, subassemblies & parts
HQ: Apex Engineering International, L.L.C.
1804 W 2nd St N
Wichita KS 67203
316 262-1494

(G-10)
APP-SOLUTE INNOVATIONS LLC
1016 S Mississippi Ave (74820-8474)
PHONE..................580 453-0055
EMP: 2
SALES (est): 56.5K **Privately Held**
SIC: 7372 Prepackaged software

(G-11)
BARRETT OIL COMPANY
820 Egypt Rd (74820-0664)
P.O. Box 1806 (74821-1806)
PHONE..................580 436-1896
Glen Barrett, *Owner*
Janet Barrett, *Co-Owner*
EMP: 1
SALES (est): 170K **Privately Held**
SIC: 1311 Crude petroleum production; natural gas production

(G-12)
BOADIE L ANDERSON QUARRIES INC
Also Called: Boadie Anderson Quarries
504 Rosedale Rd (74820-9222)
P.O. Box 1648 (74821-1648)
PHONE..................580 436-2100
Edwin R Anderson, *President*
Judy Anderson, *Corp Secy*
Boadie Anderson II, *Vice Pres*
John Anderson, *Vice Pres*
▲ **EMP:** 20 **EST:** 1968
SQ FT: 20,200

Ada - Pontotoc County (G-13)

SALES (est): 2.6MM **Privately Held**
SIC: 3281 Monuments, cut stone (not finishing or lettering only)

(G-13)
BROKEN ARROW ELECTRIC SUP INC
300 Arlington St Ste 7 (74820-2249)
PHONE..................580 436-1470
Mike Hayes, *Branch Mgr*
EMP: 2
SALES (corp-wide): 138.8MM **Privately Held**
SIC: 5082 5063 3699 Construction & mining machinery; electrical supplies; electrical equipment & supplies
PA: Broken Arrow Electric Supply, Inc.
2350 W Vancouver St
Broken Arrow OK 74012
918 258-3581

(G-14)
BROWN OIL TOOLS INC
275 Seabrook Rd (74820-1006)
P.O. Box 2634 (74821-2634)
PHONE..................580 436-0002
David Brown, *President*
EMP: 2
SALES (est): 340.6K **Privately Held**
SIC: 5082 1389 Oil field equipment; oil field services

(G-15)
BUCK CREEK HOMES CNSTR INC
15070 County Road 3539 (74820-0861)
PHONE..................580 272-0102
Cheryl A Cotten, *President*
Gary Cotten, *Vice Pres*
EMP: 12
SALES (est): 1.7MM **Privately Held**
SIC: 1521 3281 General remodeling, single-family houses; altars, cut stone

(G-16)
C & H TOOL & MACHINE INC
Also Called: C & H Bit Company
1904 N Broadway Ave (74820-1419)
PHONE..................580 332-1929
EMP: 1
SALES (corp-wide): 1.5MM **Privately Held**
SIC: 3533 Oil & gas field machinery
PA: C & H Tool & Machine, Inc.
1000 Lonnie Abbott Blvd
Ada OK 74820
580 332-1929

(G-17)
C & H TOOL & MACHINE INC (PA)
Also Called: C & H Bit Company
1000 Lonnie Abbott Blvd (74820-1843)
P.O. Box 481 (74821-0481)
PHONE..................580 332-1929
Rodney Haynes, *President*
Ronda Willis, *Manager*
Sherry Haynes, *Admin Sec*
▲ EMP: 13
SQ FT: 1,700,000
SALES (est): 1.5MM **Privately Held**
SIC: 3533 5999 5084 Oil & gas field machinery; alcoholic beverage making equipment & supplies; oil refining machinery, equipment & supplies

(G-18)
CAMMOND INDUSTRIES LLC
1920 A St (74820-2803)
PHONE..................580 332-9300
Bruce Andrews, *CEO*
Connor Haines, *CFO*
EMP: 10
SQ FT: 50,000
SALES: 1.5MM **Privately Held**
SIC: 3531 3523 Construction machinery; farm machinery & equipment

(G-19)
CANTRELL ENERGY CORPORATION
2313 N Broadway Ave (74820-1068)
PHONE..................580 332-4710
Mike Cantrell, *President*
EMP: 2

SQ FT: 3,000
SALES (est): 431.3K **Privately Held**
SIC: 1382 Oil & gas exploration services

(G-20)
CHARLES D MAYHUE
114 S Broadway Ave (74820-5800)
P.O. Box 1488 (74821-1488)
PHONE..................580 436-6500
Charles D Mayhue, *Owner*
EMP: 2
SALES (est): 190K **Privately Held**
SIC: 1382 8111 Oil & gas exploration services; legal services

(G-21)
CHICKASAW NATION
Also Called: Oklahoma Optical
1005 N Country Club Rd (74820-2847)
PHONE..................580 332-2796
Floyd Gurley, *Manager*
EMP: 1 **Privately Held**
SIC: 3229 9131 Optical glass;
PA: Chickasaw Nation
520 Arlington St
Ada OK 74820
580 436-2603

(G-22)
CHICKASAW PRESS
1020 N Mississippi Ave (74820-2212)
PHONE..................580 436-7282
EMP: 1 EST: 2018
SALES (est): 37.5K **Privately Held**
SIC: 2741 Miscellaneous publishing

(G-23)
CHOCTAW MANUFACTURING & DEV CO
1324 Cradduck Rd (74820-8442)
PHONE..................580 310-6021
Steven Benefield, *President*
EMP: 1
SALES (est): 37.5K **Privately Held**
SIC: 2741 Miscellaneous publishing

(G-24)
CLEARVIEW INTERNATIONAL
1415 Sunrise Ln (74820-4249)
PHONE..................580 332-2384
EMP: 2
SALES (est): 65.5K **Privately Held**
SIC: 1389 Oil/Gas Field Services

(G-25)
CLINCO MFG LLC
4161 County Road 1570 (74820-4154)
PHONE..................580 759-3434
Clint Welch, *Mng Member*
Julie Welch, *Mng Member*
EMP: 7
SALES: 127K **Privately Held**
SIC: 5051 3444 3353 Aluminum bars, rods, ingots, sheets, pipes, plates, etc.; sheet metalwork; aluminum sheet & strip

(G-26)
COAL OIL & GAS COMPANY
201 E Cottage St (74820-2256)
P.O. Box 8 (74821-0008)
PHONE..................580 332-6170
Silvia Harrell, *Partner*
Tom Loffland, *Partner*
Barbara L Middleton, *Partner*
Max Roberson, *Partner*
Ruth Stacey, *Partner*
EMP: 6 EST: 1955
SALES (est): 661.1K **Privately Held**
SIC: 1311 Crude petroleum production

(G-27)
CORPO COMMISSION OK
Also Called: Oil & Gas Conservation Div
1318 Cradduck Rd (74820-8442)
PHONE..................580 332-3441
J R Stewart, *Branch Mgr*
EMP: 17 **Privately Held**
WEB: www.occeweb.com
SIC: 1389 9199 Oil field services; general government administration;
HQ: Corporation Commission, Oklahoma
2101 N Lincoln Blvd # 480
Oklahoma City OK 73105

(G-28)
D C IGNITION CO INC
412 W Main St (74820-5408)
P.O. Box 884 (74821-0884)
PHONE..................580 332-0878
Jim Price, *President*
Walter Stokes, *Vice Pres*
Brenda Price, *Treasurer*
EMP: 8
SQ FT: 2,125
SALES (est): 667.5K **Privately Held**
SIC: 7538 3694 5531 5015 Engine repair; engine electrical equipment; generators, automotive & aircraft; automotive & home supply stores; motor vehicle parts, used; relays & industrial controls

(G-29)
DALE P JACKSON
Also Called: Sooner Millwork
222 E 9th St (74820-5104)
PHONE..................580 332-1988
Dale Jackson, *Owner*
EMP: 12
SALES (est): 857.9K **Privately Held**
SIC: 2541 2851 2521 2434 Cabinets, except refrigerated: show, display, etc.: wood; paints & allied products; wood office furniture; wood kitchen cabinets; millwork; cabinet & finish carpentry

(G-30)
DANDEE DONUTS
109 S Mississippi Ave (74820-6632)
PHONE..................580 332-7700
Bobby Bunyard, *Owner*
EMP: 4
SALES (est): 83.9K **Privately Held**
SIC: 5461 2052 2051 Bakeries; cookies & crackers; bread, cake & related products

(G-31)
DAYLIGHT DONUTS
300 S Mississippi Ave (74820-6637)
PHONE..................580 279-6560
Jim P Leon, *Owner*
Teresa Leon, *Owner*
EMP: 5
SALES (est): 177.4K **Privately Held**
SIC: 5461 2051 Doughnuts; doughnuts, except frozen

(G-32)
DOLESE BROS CO
1727 N Mississippi Ave (74820-1610)
PHONE..................580 332-0820
Tony Welton, *Manager*
EMP: 10
SALES (corp-wide): 8.5MM **Privately Held**
SIC: 3273 5082 Ready-mixed concrete; contractors' materials
PA: Dolese Bros. Co.
20 Nw 13th St
Oklahoma City OK 73103
405 235-2311

(G-33)
DOUG STRICKLAND
Also Called: Superior Sign Shop
930 Industrial Blvd (74820)
P.O. Box 1186 (74821-1186)
PHONE..................580 436-1010
Doug Strickland, *Owner*
Eric Strickland, *Foreman/Supr*
EMP: 3
SALES (est): 15.9K **Privately Held**
SIC: 3993 Signs & advertising specialties

(G-34)
EVERY NOOK & CRANNY
110 E Main St (74820-5602)
PHONE..................580 332-3899
Anita Bolin, *Principal*
EMP: 1
SALES (est): 76K **Privately Held**
SIC: 3421 Table & food cutlery, including butchers'

(G-35)
FLEX-N-GATE OKLAHOMA LLC
1 General St (74820-2858)
PHONE..................580 272-6700
Justin Lacy, *Plant Mgr*
Doug Suits, *Engineer*
Nathan Matzkvech, *Executive*

Shahid R Khan,
Keith Bittle, *Maintence Staff*
▲ EMP: 320
SQ FT: 12,000
SALES (est): 99.3MM
SALES (corp-wide): 3.3B **Privately Held**
SIC: 3714 Motor vehicle parts & accessories
PA: Flex-N-Gate Llc
1306 E University Ave
Urbana IL 61802
217 384-6600

(G-36)
FORSTER & SON INC
1900 B St (74820-2831)
PHONE..................580 332-6020
John Forster, *President*
Sue Lynn Forster, *Corp Secy*
EMP: 3 EST: 1937
SQ FT: 44,000
SALES (est): 111.6K **Privately Held**
SIC: 3556 3441 3523 3541 Flour mill machinery; fabricated structural metal; elevators, farm; machine tools, metal cutting type

(G-37)
FRANK T FLEET INC
920 N Mississippi Ave (74820-2210)
P.O. Box 729 (74821-0729)
PHONE..................580 332-1422
Frank T Fleet, *President*
EMP: 2
SQ FT: 1,000
SALES (est): 245K **Privately Held**
SIC: 1311 Crude petroleum production; natural gas production

(G-38)
FRONTIER ELEVATOR INC
731 Kerr Research Dr (74820-9709)
PHONE..................888 421-9400
Chad King, *CPA*
Ralph Dean, *Associate*
EMP: 4
SQ FT: 16,500
SALES (est): 259K **Privately Held**
SIC: 2048 Feed supplements

(G-39)
GARRETT EDUCATIONAL CORP
Also Called: Garrett Book Co
130 E 13th St (74820-6512)
P.O. Box 1588 (74821-1588)
PHONE..................580 332-6884
Lionel H Garrett, *President*
John H Garrett, *Vice Pres*
EMP: 35
SQ FT: 10,500
SALES (est): 7.4MM **Privately Held**
WEB: www.garrettbooks.com
SIC: 5192 2731 Books; books: publishing only

(G-40)
GENERAL AVI MODIFICATIONS INC
Also Called: Gami
2800 Airport Rd Hngr A (74820-1900)
PHONE..................580 436-4833
Tim Roehl, *President*
George W Braly, *Corp Secy*
▲ EMP: 20
SQ FT: 18,000
SALES (est): 3.8MM **Privately Held**
WEB: www.gami.com
SIC: 3728 Aircraft parts & equipment

(G-41)
GEORGE W SMITH SALVAGE CITY
12521 State Highway 3w (74820-1707)
PHONE..................580 332-2250
Georgie Smith, *President*
Robbie Smith, *Vice Pres*
EMP: 6
SALES: 290K **Privately Held**
WEB: www.adatowingservice.com
SIC: 3531 Automobile wrecker hoists

GEOGRAPHIC SECTION
Ada - Pontotoc County (G-71)

(G-42)
GIFFORD MONUMENT WORKS INC (PA)
900 N Broadway Ave (74820-2035)
P.O. Box 1927, Wylie TX (75098-1927)
PHONE.................................580 332-1271
Nick Kurz, *VP Opers*
Holly Morgan, *Office Mgr*
Judy Kurz, *Technology*
▲ **EMP:** 10
SALES (est): 1.3MM **Privately Held**
WEB: www.giffordmonument.com
SIC: 5999 1542 3272 Monuments, finished to custom order; mausoleum construction; monuments & grave markers, except terrazo

(G-43)
GLOBE MFG COMPANY-OK LLC
2000 B St (74820-2833)
PHONE.................................580 272-9400
Donald D Welch II, *President*
Geroge E Freese III, *Vice Pres*
Robert A Freese, *Vice Pres*
EMP: 40
SALES (est): 2MM
SALES (corp-wide): 1.4B **Publicly Held**
SIC: 2311 Firemen's uniforms: made from purchased materials
HQ: Globe Holding Company Llc
37 Loudon Rd
Pittsfield NH 03263

(G-44)
GLORIA CORP INC
830 N Broadway Ave (74820-2034)
P.O. Box 297 (74821-0297)
PHONE.................................580 332-4050
James H Kemp, *President*
Elizabeth Brown, *Vice Pres*
Winnie Hobbs, *Admin Sec*
EMP: 6
SQ FT: 1,800
SALES (est): 680K **Privately Held**
SIC: 1311 Crude petroleum production

(G-45)
GRAYSON INVESTMENTS LLC
19264 State Rte 1 E (74820)
PHONE.................................580 421-9770
Kevin Cantrell, *President*
EMP: 9
SALES (est): 1.1MM **Privately Held**
SIC: 2869 Fuels

(G-46)
GURLEY CUSTOM WOODWORK
219 S Johnston St (74820)
PHONE.................................580 235-3350
Braden Gurley, *Principal*
EMP: 1
SALES (est): 54.1K **Privately Held**
SIC: 2431 Millwork

(G-47)
HANSONS STONE & LANDSCAPE
2129 1/2 Woodland Dr (74820-4461)
PHONE.................................580 310-0071
EMP: 3
SALES (est): 90.5K **Privately Held**
SIC: 1411 Dimension stone

(G-48)
HOLCIM (US) INC
Also Called: Ada Plant
14500 County Road 1550 (74820-7400)
PHONE.................................580 332-1512
Ramakrishnan Kaliappen, *Project Mgr*
James Quaid, *Maint Spvr*
Christine Bragge, *Opers-Prdtn-Mfg*
Theresa Hammons, *QC Mgr*
Norberto Vargas, *Engineer*
EMP: 120
SALES (corp-wide): 4.5B **Privately Held**
WEB: www.holcim.us
SIC: 3241 Cement, hydraulic
HQ: Holcim (Us) Inc.
8700 W Bryn Mawr Ave
Chicago IL 60631

(G-49)
HOLCIM (US) INC
Also Called: Clarksville Plant
14500 County Road 1550 (74820-7400)
P.O. Box 67, Clarksville MO (63336-0067)
PHONE.................................573 242-3571
EMP: 190
SALES (corp-wide): 4.5B **Privately Held**
WEB: www.holcim.us
SIC: 3241 5032 Cement, hydraulic; cement
HQ: Holcim (Us) Inc.
8700 W Bryn Mawr Ave
Chicago IL 60631

(G-50)
IN-TELE COMMUNICATION LLC
111 W Main St (74820-5401)
PHONE.................................580 272-0303
Jeremy Young, *Principal*
EMP: 2
SALES (est): 159.9K **Privately Held**
SIC: 3669 1731 Burglar alarm apparatus, electric; telephone & telephone equipment installation

(G-51)
INKANA PUBLISHING
406 Winchester Ave (74820-1147)
PHONE.................................937 760-8446
Traci Schafer, *Principal*
EMP: 1
SALES (est): 37.5K **Privately Held**
SIC: 2741 Miscellaneous publishing

(G-52)
J BS WELDING INC
Also Called: J B Welding
120 Armory Rd (74820-1432)
P.O. Box 2599 (74821-2599)
PHONE.................................580 332-6194
JB Bolin Jr, *President*
Leaann Taylor, *Admin Sec*
EMP: 15
SQ FT: 4,000
SALES (est): 2.4MM **Privately Held**
SIC: 7692 Welding repair

(G-53)
JET TECH INTERIORS INC
10729 County Road 3600 (74820-0078)
PHONE.................................580 310-2610
David Stokes, *President*
EMP: 3
SALES: 90K **Privately Held**
SIC: 1799 3728 Renovation of aircraft interiors; aircraft parts & equipment

(G-54)
JOBRI LLC
Also Called: Pleasing Ptnts/Bttrbody Cmpny/
305 Lake Dr (74820-4219)
PHONE.................................580 925-3500
Brian Gourley, *Partner*
Joan Gourley, *CFO*
Johnathan Hulme, *
◆ **EMP:** 13
SALES (est): 2MM **Privately Held**
WEB: www.jobri.com
SIC: 5712 3842 2392 Furniture stores; orthopedic appliances; household furnishings

(G-55)
KELLY LOYD
Also Called: Snapbacks & Flatbills
17525 County Road 3545 (74820-7934)
PHONE.................................405 740-2345
Kelly Loyd, *Owner*
EMP: 1 EST: 2015
SALES (est): 43.7K **Privately Held**
SIC: 2253 Hats & headwear, knit

(G-56)
KINDRICK CO PRTG & COPYING SVC
Also Called: Kindrick & Co Prtg & Copy Svc
1320 Cradduck Rd (74820-8442)
PHONE.................................580 332-1022
Doug Kindrick, *President*
EMP: 2
SQ FT: 5,000
SALES (est): 471K **Privately Held**
SIC: 2752 7334 2791 2789 Commercial printing, offset; photocopying & duplicating services; typesetting; bookbinding & related work; commercial printing

(G-57)
LAKE OIL COMPANY INC
111 N Turner St (74820-5242)
P.O. Box 1505 (74821-1505)
PHONE.................................580 332-1737
R W Young, *Principal*
Nolan Young, *Vice Pres*
EMP: 1
SALES (est): 120K **Privately Held**
SIC: 1311 Crude petroleum production; natural gas production; crude petroleum & natural gas production

(G-58)
LAWRENCE WELDING LLC
804 E Main St (74820-5616)
PHONE.................................580 272-3294
EMP: 1
SALES (est): 25K **Privately Held**
SIC: 7692 Welding repair

(G-59)
LEACHCO INC
130 E 10th St (74820-5109)
P.O. Box 717 (74821-0717)
PHONE.................................580 436-1142
Clyde E Leach, *President*
Jamie Leach, *Vice Pres*
Ada Valles, *Admin Asst*
▲ **EMP:** 49
SQ FT: 38,000
SALES (est): 14.3MM **Privately Held**
SIC: 2392 Cushions & pillows

(G-60)
LEDDY CONSTRUCTION
Also Called: Madden's Buildings
3421 N Broadway Ave (74820-1001)
P.O. Box 1871 (74821-1871)
PHONE.................................580 332-3056
Spencer Leddy, *Owner*
Donna Leddy, *Principal*
EMP: 3
SALES (est): 345.8K **Privately Held**
SIC: 1542 3448 Nonresidential construction; prefabricated metal buildings

(G-61)
LOPORCHIO SILK SCREEN
Also Called: Loporchios Silk Screening
731 S Oak Ave (74820-7665)
PHONE.................................323 258-6459
Steve Loporchio, *Owner*
EMP: 2
SALES (est): 185K **Privately Held**
SIC: 2759 Screen printing

(G-62)
MAGIC TS
Also Called: Magic T'S T-Shirts
407 Nw J A Rchardson Loop (74820-2057)
PHONE.................................580 332-6675
Patty Allen, *Owner*
Clifford Allen, *Co-Owner*
EMP: 3
SALES: 200K **Privately Held**
SIC: 5699 2396 2759 Sports apparel; automotive & apparel trimmings; screen printing

(G-63)
MANUFACTURING JACK LLC RAM
13655 County Road 1570 (74820-0190)
PHONE.................................580 332-6694
Mike Pinley, *President*
Tressa McGinty, *Admin Sec*
EMP: 60
SALES (est): 10.5MM **Privately Held**
SIC: 3441 Fabricated structural metal

(G-64)
MC ALESTER FOOD WAREHOUSE
Also Called: Nickel Saver
1601 N Broadway Ave (74820-1403)
PHONE.................................580 436-4302
Evert Wall, *Manager*
EMP: 80
SQ FT: 65,000
SALES (corp-wide): 12MM **Privately Held**
SIC: 5411 5992 2051 Grocery stores, independent; florists; bread, cake & related products
PA: Mc Alester Food Warehouse, Inc
601 E Wyandotte Ave
Mcalester OK

(G-65)
MICHAEL FEEZEL
Also Called: United Energy Exploration
808 E Main St (74820-5622)
P.O. Box 2449 (74821-2449)
PHONE.................................580 332-5544
EMP: 6
SALES (est): 560K **Privately Held**
SIC: 1382 Oil And Gas Exploration

(G-66)
MILTON DONAGHEY
224 N Rennie St (74820-5123)
P.O. Box 2539 (74821-2539)
PHONE.................................580 332-1551
Milton Donaghey, *Owner*
Kelley Donaghey, *Co-Owner*
EMP: 5 EST: 1918
SQ FT: 3,200
SALES (est): 294.7K **Privately Held**
SIC: 3599 7692 Machine shop, jobbing & repair; welding repair

(G-67)
MJS FENCE WELDING
17302 County Road 3540 (74820-1547)
PHONE.................................580 320-1620
Michael Jordan, *Principal*
EMP: 1
SALES (est): 75.9K **Privately Held**
SIC: 7692 Welding repair

(G-68)
MOTHER EARTH ECO ENTPS LLC
17814 County Road 1499 Ct (74820-4740)
PHONE.................................785 250-8706
Michael Roberts,
Rebecca Roberts,
EMP: 2 EST: 2010
SALES (est): 76.3K **Privately Held**
WEB: www.motherearthco.com
SIC: 7349 8744 7342 2842 Janitorial service, contract basis; ; disinfecting services; sanitation preparations, disinfectants & deodorants; medical apparatus & supplies

(G-69)
N P T INC
Also Called: Nprocess Technology
227 E 26th St (74820-8305)
PHONE.................................580 399-0306
Stanley Townsend, *President*
EMP: 2
SALES (est): 191K **Privately Held**
SIC: 3625 Motor controls, electric

(G-70)
NATIONAL COATING MFG INC
Also Called: Flex-Kote
13707 County Road 3500 (74820-3344)
PHONE.................................580 332-8751
Jerry Wilcher, *President*
EMP: 14
SQ FT: 13,600
SALES (est): 3.3MM **Privately Held**
SIC: 2851 1721 2891 Coating, air curing; painting & paper hanging; adhesives & sealants

(G-71)
NEWMANS ELECTRIC MOTOR REPAIR
18032 County Road 1558 (74820-1402)
PHONE.................................580 310-0151
Brad Newman, *President*
Cheri Newman, *Vice Pres*
EMP: 4
SALES: 250K **Privately Held**
SIC: 5063 7694 5999 Motors, electric; electric motor repair; engine & motor equipment & supplies

Ada - Pontotoc County (G-72)

(G-72)
NEWSPAPER HOLDING INC
Also Called: Ada Evening News
116 N Broadway Ave (74820-5004)
P.O. Box 489 (74821-0489)
PHONE..................................580 332-4433
Lone Beasley, *Manager*
EMP: 50 Privately Held
SIC: 2711 2752 Newspapers: publishing only, not printed on site; commercial printing, lithographic
HQ: Newspaper Holding, Inc.
 425 Locust St
 Johnstown PA 15901
 814 532-5102

(G-73)
OKLAHOMA BASIC ECONOMY CORP
2313 N Broadway Ave (74820-1068)
P.O. Box 1608 (74821-1608)
PHONE..................................580 332-4710
Mike Cantrell, *President*
Judy Brooks, *Corp Secy*
Linda Cantrell, *Vice Pres*
EMP: 11
SQ FT: 2,500
SALES (est): 1.3MM
SALES (corp-wide): 55.1MM Privately Held
SIC: 1311 Crude petroleum production; natural gas production
PA: Pontotoc Production
 100 E 13th St
 Ada OK
 580 436-6100

(G-74)
PALM VAULT CO INC
401 Arlington St (74820-2201)
P.O. Box 1244 (74821-1244)
PHONE..................................580 332-7565
Larry Hill, *President*
EMP: 5
SALES (est): 654.3K Privately Held
SIC: 3272 Burial vaults, concrete or pre-cast terrazzo

(G-75)
POWER LIFT FNDTN RPR OK INC
120 Armory Rd (74820-1432)
PHONE..................................580 332-8282
William B Bowlen, *President*
EMP: 20
SQ FT: 2,000
SALES (est): 3.2MM Privately Held
SIC: 3441 1741 Fabricated structural metal; foundation & retaining wall construction

(G-76)
PRINTING SOLUTIONS INC
205 Arlington St (74820-2226)
PHONE..................................580 421-6446
Crystal Bigham, *President*
EMP: 3
SALES (est): 184.2K Privately Held
SIC: 2759 Commercial printing

(G-77)
PRO WALK MANUFACTURING COMPANY
1115 W Main St (74820-5423)
PHONE..................................580 332-5516
Gary Tate, *President*
EMP: 8
SQ FT: 9,000
SALES (est): 1MM Privately Held
SIC: 3462 Horseshoes

(G-78)
PRUITT COMPANY OF ADA INC
Also Called: Pruitt Care
402 E 12th St (74820-6602)
PHONE..................................580 332-3523
Dexter Pruitt, *President*
Tammy Pruitt, *Corp Secy*
EMP: 20
SQ FT: 22,000
SALES (est): 5MM Privately Held
SIC: 5085 5093 3599 5599 Welding supplies; ferrous metal scrap & waste; machine shop, jobbing & repair; utility trailers; medical equipment rental; fabricated structural metal

(G-79)
RACCOON TECHNOLOGIES INC
130 N Country Club Rd (74820-4317)
PHONE..................................580 399-9126
EMP: 2 EST: 2016
SALES (est): 74.1K Privately Held
WEB: www.raccoontech.com
SIC: 3861 Photographic equipment & supplies

(G-80)
RD ROOFING AND CARPENTRY
11025 County Road 3502 (74820-5518)
PHONE..................................580 341-0607
Ryan Temple, *Owner*
EMP: 8
SALES (est): 80K Privately Held
SIC: 1761 3423 Roof repair; carpenters' hand tools, except saws: levels, chisels, etc.

(G-81)
RED RIVER SPECIALTIES LLC
1906 N Broadway Ave (74820-1410)
P.O. Box 806 (74821-0806)
PHONE..................................580 436-0883
Philip Lawrence, *Branch Mgr*
EMP: 3
SALES (corp-wide): 10.1MM Privately Held
SIC: 2879 Insecticides, agricultural or household
HQ: Red River Specialties, Llc
 1324 N Hearne Ave Ste 120
 Shreveport LA 71107

(G-82)
RLC HOLDING CO INC
Also Called: Cummins Construction Co
4 Miles N Ada (74821)
P.O. Box 2690 (74821-2690)
PHONE..................................580 332-3080
Denny Buchanan, *Manager*
EMP: 20 Privately Held
WEB: www.cumminsasphalt.com
SIC: 1611 5032 2951 Concrete construction: roads, highways, sidewalks, etc.; brick, stone & related material; asphalt paving mixtures & blocks
PA: Rlc Holding Co Inc
 1420 W Chestnut Ave
 Enid OK 73703

(G-83)
ROBERSON OIL CO INC
Also Called: Roberson, David A
201 E Cottage St (74820-2256)
P.O. Box 8 (74821-0008)
PHONE..................................580 332-6170
David A Roberson II, *President*
EMP: 4
SQ FT: 1,500
SALES (est): 370K Privately Held
SIC: 1311 Crude petroleum production; crude petroleum & natural gas production

(G-84)
ROBERT R CANTRELL
11330 County Road 3560 (74820-4707)
P.O. Box 1433 (74821-1433)
PHONE..................................580 332-9495
Robert R Cantrell, *Owner*
EMP: 12
SALES (est): 1.2MM Privately Held
SIC: 1381 Directional drilling oil & gas wells

(G-85)
SHARPSHOOTERS INC
12698 State Highway 3w (74820-1708)
PHONE..................................580 332-3109
Glen Jones, *President*
Jim C Sharp, *President*
Barbara Enewzy, *Treasurer*
Beulah Sharp, *Treasurer*
Deanna Jones, *Admin Sec*
EMP: 4
SALES (est): 321.5K Privately Held
SIC: 1389 Perforating well casings; well logging

(G-86)
SHELLEY BENEFIELD
Also Called: Grayson Creek
9085 County Road 3510 (74820-3506)
PHONE..................................580 436-0296
Shelley Benefield, *Principal*
EMP: 3
SALES (est): 233.4K Privately Held
SIC: 3537 2421 Dollies (hand or power trucks), industrial except mining; furniture dimension stock, softwood

(G-87)
SHERRELL STEEL LLC
12625 State Highway 19 (74820-1751)
PHONE..................................580 436-4322
D E Sherrell,
EMP: 10
SALES (est): 980K Privately Held
SIC: 3312 Rods, iron & steel: made in steel mills

(G-88)
SIGN SOURCE
531 N Broadway Ave (74820-3401)
PHONE..................................580 436-1323
Ann Janda, *Owner*
EMP: 2
SALES (est): 100K Privately Held
SIC: 3993 5999 Signs & advertising specialties; banners

(G-89)
SNYDERS STUCCO AND STONE
6065 State Highway 99n (74820-0398)
PHONE..................................580 421-9747
Ronnie Snyder, *Principal*
EMP: 1
SALES (est): 74.7K Privately Held
SIC: 3299 Stucco

(G-90)
SOLO CUP OPERATING CORPORATION
401 Ne Richardson Loop (74820-1607)
PHONE..................................580 436-1500
Truitt McCarty, *Plant Mgr*
James Drawbaugh, *Facilities Mgr*
Randy Golden, *Engineer*
Jack Kinkade, *Controller*
Sid Smith, *Branch Mgr*
EMP: 150
SALES (corp-wide): 965.8MM Privately Held
SIC: 3089 2656 3421 Cups, plastic, except foam; plates, plastic; plastic containers, except foam; straws, drinking: made from purchased material; cutlery
HQ: Solo Cup Operating Corporation
 500 Hogsback Rd
 Mason MI 48854
 800 248-5960

(G-91)
SPENCER MACHINE WORKS LLC
224 N Rennie St (74820-5123)
P.O. Box 2539 (74821-2539)
PHONE..................................580 332-1551
Spencer Mach, *Owner*
EMP: 1
SALES (est): 33.4K Privately Held
WEB: www.spencermachineworks.com
SIC: 7692 1389 Welding repair; grading oil & gas well foundations

(G-92)
TANK MASTERS
120 Armory Rd (74820-1432)
PHONE..................................580 332-3325
JB Bolin Jr, *President*
EMP: 2
SALES (est): 135.6K Privately Held
SIC: 1389 Oil field services

(G-93)
TECHNOLOGY MANAGEMENT INC
Also Called: National Petro Chem
529 Seabrook Rd (74820-1030)
P.O. Box 1602 (74821-1602)
PHONE..................................580 332-8615
Tom Hampton, *President*
Mark Southerland, *Corp Secy*
EMP: 11
SQ FT: 4,200
SALES (est): 1.5MM
SALES (corp-wide): 1.2B Publicly Held
SIC: 2899 Chemical supplies for foundries
HQ: Reef Services, Llc
 1515 W Sam Houston Pkwy N
 Houston TX 77043

(G-94)
THREE B LAND & CATTLE COMPANY
201 W 14th St (74820-6415)
PHONE..................................580 332-9480
Mack M Braly, *Partner*
George W Braly, *Partner*
John Braly, *Partner*
EMP: 3 EST: 1973
SALES (est): 200.3K Privately Held
SIC: 1311 Crude petroleum production

(G-95)
TORNADO ALLEY TURBO INC
300 Airport Rd (74820-1901)
PHONE..................................580 332-3510
Tim Roehl, *President*
George Braly, *Corp Secy*
EMP: 60
SQ FT: 42,000
SALES (est): 8MM Privately Held
WEB: www.tatparts.com
SIC: 3728 3724 Aircraft parts & equipment; aircraft engines & engine parts

(G-96)
TRIBAL CONSORTIUM INC
6950 County Road 3610 (74820-2152)
P.O. Box 391 (74821-0391)
PHONE..................................580 332-1134
Zachary Vogt, *President*
Bryant Vogt, *Corp Secy*
EMP: 6
SALES (est): 25K Privately Held
SIC: 3531 Construction machinery

(G-97)
TRUE ENERGY SERVICES LLC (DH)
329 S Rennie St (74820-6536)
P.O. Box 2570 (74821-2570)
PHONE..................................580 421-9808
Robert Cantrell, *Mng Member*
Kevin Cantrell, *Mng Member*
Mike Feezel, *Mng Member*
EMP: 5 EST: 2007
SALES (est): 1.2MM
SALES (corp-wide): 140.9MM Publicly Held
WEB: www.trueenergyservices.com
SIC: 1382 Aerial geophysical exploration oil & gas
HQ: The North American Coal Corporation
 5340 Legacy Dr Ste 300
 Plano TX 75024
 972 448-5400

(G-98)
TRUE STEEL LLC
19380 County Road 1590 (74820-0681)
PHONE..................................580 310-0595
Greg Perry, *President*
Melissa Perry,
EMP: 20
SQ FT: 20,000
SALES (est): 4.7MM Privately Held
SIC: 3444 1761 Metal housings, enclosures, casings & other containers; roofing, siding & sheet metal work

(G-99)
TRUEVINE OPERATING LLC
2612 Arlington St (74820-2905)
P.O. Box 1422 (74821-1422)
PHONE..................................580 427-7919
Mike E Flowers, *Administration*
EMP: 2

SALES (est): 223.8K **Privately Held**
SIC: **1389** Gas field services

(G-100)
UNITED FUELS ENERGY
301 N Broadway Ave (74820-5007)
PHONE.................................580 332-5222
EMP: 4
SALES (est): 312.9K **Privately Held**
SIC: **2869** Mfg Industrial Organic Chemicals

(G-101)
VASSAL WELL SERVICES LLC
808 E Main St (74820-5622)
P.O. Box 817 (74821-0817)
PHONE.................................580 279-1579
EMP: 15 EST: 2005
SALES (est): 910K **Privately Held**
SIC: **1381** Oil/Gas Well Drilling

(G-102)
VOGT SHEET METAL
10140 State Highway 99n (74820-1128)
PHONE.................................580 332-2454
Shelldon Vogt, *Owner*
EMP: 1
SALES (est): 99K **Privately Held**
SIC: **1711 3444** Warm air heating & air conditioning contractor; sheet metalwork

(G-103)
WADDELL VINEYARDS LLC
11533 County Road 3570 (74820-0610)
PHONE.................................580 421-6933
EMP: 2
SALES (est): 69.2K **Privately Held**
SIC: **2084** Wines

(G-104)
WATKINS CABINET DOORS LLC
416 E Broadway (74820-0373)
PHONE.................................580 320-6301
EMP: 2
SALES (est): 135.5K **Privately Held**
SIC: **2434** Mfg Wood Kitchen Cabinets

(G-105)
WE-GO PERFORATORS INC (PA)
Also Called: Arrow We Go Perforators
8717 County Road 3470 (74820-3513)
PHONE.................................580 332-1346
Marshall Bracken, *President*
EMP: 4 EST: 1957
SQ FT: 1,600
SALES (est): 1.8MM **Privately Held**
SIC: **1389** Oil field services

(G-106)
WHIT INDUSTRIES
1312 Willow Brook St (74820-8509)
PHONE.................................405 343-1181
William Laxton, *Principal*
EMP: 1 EST: 2017
SALES (est): 73.3K **Privately Held**
SIC: **3999** Manufacturing industries

Adair
Mayes County

(G-107)
BLUE COYOTE WINERY
9564 N 429 Rd (74330-2696)
PHONE.................................918 785-4727
Jacque Schulze, *Owner*
EMP: 1
SALES (est): 103.1K **Privately Held**
WEB: www.bluecoyotewinery.com
SIC: **2084** Wines

(G-108)
COYOTE RUN VINEYARD LLC
9564 N 429 Rd (74330-2696)
PHONE.................................918 785-4727
Jackie Schulz, *Principal*
EMP: 3
SALES (est): 150.8K **Privately Held**
SIC: **2084** Wines

(G-109)
HENSON MANUFACTURING & SLS INC
612 E Main St (74330-2229)
P.O. Box 398 (74330-0398)
PHONE.................................918 785-2153
William Henson, *President*
Judy Henson, *Vice Pres*
EMP: 28
SQ FT: 12,000
SALES (est): 5.3MM **Privately Held**
SIC: **3599** Machine shop, jobbing & repair

(G-110)
HUBBARD
412 W Main St (74330)
PHONE.................................918 785-2000
EMP: 3 EST: 2010
SALES (est): 240K **Privately Held**
SIC: **2048** Mfg Prepared Feeds

(G-111)
QUALITY LINE TRUSS INC
434557 E 350 Rd (74330-2622)
PHONE.................................918 783-5227
Walt Barlass, *President*
EMP: 7
SQ FT: 10,000
SALES (est): 480K **Privately Held**
SIC: **2439** Trusses, wooden roof

(G-112)
TRECE INC (PA)
7569 Highway 28 W (74330-2817)
P.O. Box 129 (74330-0129)
PHONE.................................918 785-3061
Bill W Lingren, *President*
Donna Lingren, *Principal*
Wes Petersen, *Controller*
Marcia Flocks, *Accountant*
Vincent Chebny, *Manager*
◆ EMP: 17
SQ FT: 6,800
SALES (est): 4.3MM **Privately Held**
SIC: **3829** Measuring & controlling devices

Afton
Ottawa County

(G-113)
BOAT FLOATERS IND LLC
E Hgwy 85 (74331)
PHONE.................................918 256-3330
Phil Woodall, *Owner*
Shane Littlefield, *Manager*
EMP: 15
SALES (est): 1.1MM **Privately Held**
SIC: **3536** Boat lifts

(G-114)
CABINET DOORS UNLIMITED
55450 E Highway 59 (74331-2712)
P.O. Box 597 (74331-0597)
PHONE.................................918 257-5765
Gale Rider, *Owner*
EMP: 10
SALES: 340K **Privately Held**
SIC: **2434 2431** Wood kitchen cabinets; millwork

(G-115)
COPY BOX INC
Also Called: C B I
56414 E 230 Rd (74331-2898)
PHONE.................................918 257-8000
Don Russell, *President*
Jason Russell, *Vice Pres*
Monica Russell, *Vice Pres*
Josh Russell, *Sales Staff*
EMP: 12
SALES: 910K **Privately Held**
SIC: **2752** Commercial printing, offset

(G-116)
CREATIVE STITCHES BY C S
50991 E 243 Rd (74331-6434)
P.O. Box 3538 (74331-3538)
PHONE.................................918 418-9049
EMP: 1
SALES (est): 53K **Privately Held**
SIC: **2395** Embroidery & art needlework

(G-117)
GRAND LAKE DETAIL LLC
450672 E 338 Rd (74331-8121)
PHONE.................................918 257-2174
Joseph Sikes,
Marilyn Sikes,
EMP: 2
SALES: 6K **Privately Held**
SIC: **3732** Boat building & repairing

(G-118)
GTSA MANUFACTURING INC
Also Called: Afton Manufacturing
1 S Maple Ave (74331)
P.O. Box 2 (74331-0002)
PHONE.................................918 257-4269
George E May III, *President*
Tricia May, *Admin Sec*
EMP: 7
SQ FT: 500
SALES (est): 750K **Privately Held**
SIC: **3599** Machine shop, jobbing & repair

(G-119)
NUTTING CUSTOM TRIKES
21507 S Highway 69 (74331-3016)
PHONE.................................918 257-8795
Doug Nutting, *Principal*
EMP: 2
SALES (est): 203.6K **Privately Held**
SIC: **3011** Motorcycle tires, pneumatic

(G-120)
ROBERT MRRSON AUTOCAD SVCS LLC
28805 S 563 Rd (74331-8040)
PHONE.................................918 257-4622
Robert Morrison, *Principal*
EMP: 1
SALES (est): 122K **Privately Held**
SIC: **3441** Fabricated structural metal

(G-121)
SIGNS BY SIKORSKI
55015 E 70th Rd (74331)
PHONE.................................918 257-5164
Kathi Sikorski, *Owner*
EMP: 1
SALES (est): 53K **Privately Held**
SIC: **3993** Signs & advertising specialties

(G-122)
SLOW HAND MANUFACTURING LLC
32128 Pine Vly (74331-6406)
P.O. Box 964, Ketchum (74349-0964)
PHONE.................................580 618-0867
Gary Michael, *Principal*
EMP: 2
SALES (est): 143.3K **Privately Held**
SIC: **3999** Manufacturing industries

(G-123)
TREES OIL CO
56351 E 307 Rd (74331-4600)
PHONE.................................918 257-5050
EMP: 2
SALES (est): 97.4K **Privately Held**
SIC: **1311** Crude petroleum production

Agra
Lincoln County

(G-124)
CALLIE OIL COMPANY LLC
344442 E 790 Rd (74824-6317)
PHONE.................................918 521-9292
Rory Jett, *Mng Member*
EMP: 1
SALES (est): 126.5K **Privately Held**
SIC: **1382** Oil & gas exploration services

(G-125)
KOLB TYPE SERVICE INCORPORATED
Also Called: Kolb's Printing & Type Service
3009 S Ripley Rd (74824-6226)
P.O. Box 183, Edmond (73083-0183)
PHONE.................................405 341-0984
Marilyn Kolb Hinton, *President*
EMP: 2 EST: 1950
SQ FT: 5,100
SALES (est): 113.7K **Privately Held**
SIC: **2791 2759** Typesetting; commercial printing

(G-126)
LAND RUN ALPACAS
780596 S Highway 18 (74824-1015)
PHONE.................................405 226-9005
Sheila Robinson, *Principal*
EMP: 2 EST: 2015
SALES (est): 138.5K **Privately Held**
WEB: www.landrunalpacas.com
SIC: **2231** Alpacas, mohair: woven

Alderson
Pittsburg County

(G-127)
ARCHROCK INC
401 E Hwy 270 (74522)
PHONE.................................918 558-2216
EMP: 1 **Publicly Held**
SIC: **1389** Gas compressing (natural gas) at the fields
PA: Archrock, Inc.
    9807 Katy Fwy Ste 100
    Houston TX 77024

(G-128)
SELECT ENERGY SERVICES LLC
Also Called: Impact Energy Services
104 9th St (74522)
PHONE.................................918 302-0069
Josh Ingram, *Branch Mgr*
EMP: 59
SALES (corp-wide): 1.2B **Publicly Held**
SIC: **1389** Oil field services
HQ: Select Energy Services, Llc
    1820 N I 35
    Gainesville TX 76240
    940 668-1818

Alex
Grady County

(G-129)
ALEX ARMS AND INSTRUCTION LLC
606 W G Ave (73002)
PHONE.................................405 351-0806
Frederic D Spencer, *CEO*
EMP: 2
SALES (est): 169.3K **Privately Held**
SIC: **3484 8331** Guns (firearms) or gun parts, 30 mm. & below; skill training center

(G-130)
DON WILMUT
Also Called: Longhorn Express
705 S Main St (73002)
PHONE.................................405 785-9192
Don Wilmut, *Owner*
EMP: 4
SALES (est): 260.1K **Privately Held**
SIC: **2741** Miscellaneous publishing

(G-131)
DRP WELDING MET BUILDINGS LLC
2498 County Road 1400 (73002-2215)
PHONE.................................405 344-6582
Donnie Ryan Palmer, *Principal*
EMP: 2
SALES (est): 43.7K **Privately Held**
SIC: **7692** Welding repair

Allen
Pontotoc County

(G-132)
ALLEN ADVOCATE
Also Called: Robinson, Bill & Dayna
101 W Broadway (74825)
P.O. Box 465 (74825-0465)
PHONE.................................580 857-2687

Allen - Pontotoc County (G-133)

GEOGRAPHIC SECTION

Bill Robinson, *Owner*
EMP: 2
SALES (est): 134.5K **Privately Held**
SIC: 2711 Newspapers, publishing & printing

(G-133)
ALLEN CAMPER MFG COMPANY INC
Also Called: Idle Time Rv Sales & Service
29981 State Highway 1e (74825-7413)
PHONE...................580 857-2177
Tom Peay, *President*
David Peay, *Vice Pres*
Doug Peay, *Vice Pres*
Dale Peay, *Treasurer*
Susie Snider, *Manager*
EMP: 40 **EST:** 1958
SQ FT: 50,000
SALES (est): 4.8MM **Privately Held**
WEB: www.allencampermfg.com
SIC: 3792 3714 5561 Campers, for mounting on trucks; camping trailers & chassis; motor vehicle parts & accessories; recreational vehicle dealers; campers (pickup coaches) for mounting on trucks; travel trailers: automobile, new & used

(G-134)
ED PRENTICE
7581 County Road 3700 (74825-6958)
PHONE...................580 857-2713
Ed Prentice, *Owner*
EMP: 1 **EST:** 1975
SALES (est): 100K **Privately Held**
SIC: 1311 Crude petroleum production

(G-135)
JPS CREATIONS
Also Called: Pillow Walks
414 4th St (74825-8125)
PHONE...................580 892-3455
Joe Powell, *Owner*
EMP: 2
SALES (est): 135.8K **Privately Held**
SIC: 2339 Women's & misses' accessories

(G-136)
KAZE LLC
28561 County Road 1470 (74825-6204)
PHONE...................580 857-2707
Kim Crossley, *CEO*
EMP: 4
SALES (est): 200K **Privately Held**
SIC: 3674 Random access memory (RAM)

(G-137)
PRE MC INC
304 E Broadway (74825)
P.O. Box 416 (74825-0416)
PHONE...................580 857-2408
Danny McDougal, *President*
Robert A Hammonds, *Corp Secy*
EMP: 3
SQ FT: 480
SALES (est): 300K **Privately Held**
SIC: 1311 Crude petroleum production; natural gas production

(G-138)
ROCKY TOP WINERY LLC
7569 E West 148 (74825)
PHONE...................580 857-2869
Wilma Harden, *Mng Member*
Bobby Harden,
EMP: 2 **EST:** 2013
SALES (est): 82.5K **Privately Held**
SIC: 2084 7299 5921 Wines; facility rental & party planning services; wine

(G-139)
WHITE DOVE SMALL ENGINES
28396 State Highway 1e (74825-7412)
PHONE...................580 857-2201
EMP: 2
SALES (est): 138.2K **Privately Held**
SIC: 3519 Internal combustion engines

Altus
Jackson County

(G-140)
ALTUS PRINT SHIP
1701 Falcon Rd (73521-4511)
PHONE...................580 482-6855
EMP: 2
SALES (est): 110K **Privately Held**
SIC: 2752 Commercial Printing, Lithographic

(G-141)
ALTUS PRINTING CO INC
421 W Broadway St (73521-3827)
P.O. Box 596 (73522-0596)
PHONE...................580 482-2020
Matt Litsch, *President*
Ronda Litsch, *Treasurer*
EMP: 7
SQ FT: 4,000
SALES: 600K **Privately Held**
SIC: 2752 2791 2789 Lithographing on metal; commercial printing, offset; typesetting; bookbinding & related work

(G-142)
ALTUS READY-MIX INC
710 S Jackson St (73521-6215)
PHONE...................580 482-3418
Steve Rohde, *Principal*
EMP: 16
SALES: 46K **Privately Held**
WEB: www.evans-assoc.com
SIC: 3273 5032 5211 Ready-mixed concrete; brick, stone & related material; lumber & other building materials

(G-143)
ARCHER-DANIELS-MIDLAND COMPANY
Also Called: ADM
701 S Lee St (73521-4429)
P.O. Box 978 (73522-0978)
PHONE...................580 482-7100
James Geary, *Branch Mgr*
EMP: 6
SALES (corp-wide): 64.6B **Publicly Held**
SIC: 2041 Flour & other grain mill products
PA: Archer-Daniels-Midland Company
77 W Wacker Dr Ste 4600
Chicago IL 60601
312 634-8100

(G-144)
BAR-S FOODS CO
500 S Bar S Blvd (73521-5800)
P.O. Box 793 (73522-0793)
PHONE...................580 821-5700
Don Bohnsack, *Plant Mgr*
EMP: 142 **Privately Held**
SIC: 2013 2015 Sausages & other prepared meats; poultry slaughtering & processing
HQ: Bar-S Foods Co.
5090 N 40th St Ste 300
Phoenix AZ 85018
602 264-7272

(G-145)
BOEING AROSPC OPERATIONS INC
320 N 6th St (73523-5010)
P.O. Box 478 (73522-0478)
PHONE...................580 481-3306
Jim Temple, *Principal*
Randy Pitz, *Network Mgr*
EMP: 775
SALES (corp-wide): 76.5B **Publicly Held**
SIC: 3721 Aircraft
HQ: Boeing Aerospace Operations, Inc.
6001 S A Depo Blvd Ste E
Oklahoma City OK 73150
405 622-6000

(G-146)
BOEING AROSPC OPERATIONS INC
515 S 7th St (73523-5323)
PHONE...................580 480-4040
EMP: 99

SALES (corp-wide): 76.5B **Publicly Held**
SIC: 3721 Aircraft
HQ: Boeing Aerospace Operations, Inc.
6001 S A Depo Blvd Ste E
Oklahoma City OK 73150
405 622-6000

(G-147)
BOEING COMPANY
1608 Cleveland St (73521-4708)
P.O. Box 478 (73522-0478)
PHONE...................580 482-0354
Charles Adair, *Branch Mgr*
EMP: 895
SALES (corp-wide): 76.5B **Publicly Held**
WEB: www.boeing.com
SIC: 3721 Airplanes, fixed or rotary wing
PA: The Boeing Company
100 N Riverside Plz
Chicago IL 60606
312 544-2000

(G-148)
CITY OF ALTUS
Also Called: City Altus Water & Sewer Dept
300 E Commerce St (73521-3916)
PHONE...................580 481-2270
Bob Stephenson, *Director*
EMP: 10 **Privately Held**
SIC: 3589 9111 Water treatment equipment, industrial; mayors' offices
PA: City Of Altus
509 S Main St
Altus OK 73521
580 481-2210

(G-149)
CIVITAS MEDIA LLC
Also Called: Altus Times
218 W Commerce St (73521-3810)
P.O. Box 578 (73522-0578)
PHONE...................580 482-1221
Matt Moran, *Branch Mgr*
EMP: 17
SQ FT: 7,000
SALES (corp-wide): 1.6MM **Privately Held**
SIC: 2759 2711 Publication printing; newspapers: publishing only, not printed on site
PA: Civitas Media Llc
200 W Beech St
Durant OK 74701
580 634-2152

(G-150)
CMG OPERATIONS LLC
212 E Broadway St (73521-5504)
PHONE...................580 477-0880
EMP: 1 **EST:** 2011
SALES (est): 54K **Privately Held**
SIC: 3421 Mfg Cutlery

(G-151)
COTTON CANDI CREATIONS LLC
927 E Broadway St (73521-5518)
PHONE...................580 471-6550
Michelle Coe, *Administration*
EMP: 2 **EST:** 2010
SALES (est): 188.8K **Privately Held**
WEB: www.cottoncandicreations.com
SIC: 2064 Candy & other confectionery products

(G-152)
CUSTOM GRAPHICS
521 N Main St (73521-3109)
PHONE...................580 477-4597
Loren Ahrens, *Owner*
Merrill Ahrens, *Co-Owner*
EMP: 2
SQ FT: 2,000
SALES (est): 184.3K **Privately Held**
SIC: 2759 Screen printing

(G-153)
DALE ROGERS TRAINING CTR INC
Altus Air Force Base (73522)
PHONE...................580 481-6170
Marvin Berg, *Branch Mgr*
EMP: 50

SALES (corp-wide): 19.5MM **Privately Held**
SIC: 8249 3999 Vocational schools; plaques, picture, laminated
PA: Dale Rogers Training Center, Inc.
2501 N Utah Ave
Oklahoma City OK 73107
405 946-4489

(G-154)
DO IT BEST HARDWARE
500 N Market Rd (73521-3661)
PHONE...................580 482-8898
Shery Finley, *President*
EMP: 6 **EST:** 1975
SQ FT: 27,000
SALES (est): 545.7K **Privately Held**
SIC: 2439 Trusses, wooden roof

(G-155)
EVANS & ASSOCIATES ENTPS INC
Also Called: Altus Ready Mix
710 S Jackson St (73521-6215)
P.O. Box 1128 (73522-1128)
PHONE...................580 482-3418
Steve Rohde, *Branch Mgr*
EMP: 15
SALES (corp-wide): 100.1MM **Privately Held**
WEB: www.evans-assoc.com
SIC: 3273 5032 5211 Ready-mixed concrete; gravel; sand, construction; stone, crushed or broken; sand & gravel
PA: Evans & Associates Enterprises, Inc.
3320 N 14th St
Ponca City OK 74601
580 765-6693

(G-156)
FARMERS UNION CO-OPERATIVE GIN
Also Called: Humphreys Coop
2109 Afthalt Rd (73521)
PHONE...................580 482-5136
James Allen, *Manager*
EMP: 9
SALES (corp-wide): 7.2MM **Privately Held**
SIC: 2875 Fertilizers, mixing only
PA: Farmers Union Co-Operative Gin
20964 E County Road 1696
Altus OK 73521
580 738-5274

(G-157)
HELENA AGRI-ENTERPRISES LLC
20369 E County Road 158 (73521-8218)
P.O. Box 814 (73522-0814)
PHONE...................580 477-0986
Johnny Hamilton, *Enginr/R&D Mgr*
EMP: 11 **Privately Held**
WEB: www.helenaagri.com
SIC: 2879 4225 Pesticides, agricultural or household; general warehousing
HQ: Helena Agri-Enterprises, Llc
255 Schilling Blvd # 300
Collierville TN 38017
901 761-0050

(G-158)
HORIZON WELL SERVICING LLC
300 Pintail Cir (73521-9553)
PHONE...................580 482-7500
Will C Nordman, *Administration*
Will Nordman,
EMP: 2
SALES (est): 99.4K **Privately Held**
SIC: 1389 Oil field services

(G-159)
JOHN PATRICK RAYMOND
Also Called: Jr Custom Welding & Repair
21 Constitution Ave (73521-1003)
PHONE...................580 481-0869
John Raymond, *Owner*
EMP: 1 **EST:** 2016
SALES (est): 28.9K **Privately Held**
SIC: 7692 Welding repair

GEOGRAPHIC SECTION
Alva - Woods County (G-191)

(G-160)
KENNYS SIGN GRAPHX-ETCHIHG IN
Also Called: Kenny's Graphx
1000 N Park Ln (73521-4522)
PHONE..................580 477-4250
Kenny Burnett,
EMP: 1
SALES (est): 140.4K Privately Held
SIC: 3993 Electric signs

(G-161)
KWP WELDING & FABRICATION LLC
1025 Darla Ave (73521-6807)
PHONE..................580 471-7238
Kyle Williamson, Mng Member
EMP: 2 EST: 2017
SALES (est): 33.6K Privately Held
SIC: 7692 Welding repair

(G-162)
MLB WELDING LLC
2112 N Canary Ln (73521-1414)
PHONE..................580 481-0852
Monte Brown, Principal
EMP: 1
SALES (est): 124.2K Privately Held
SIC: 3496 Gas welding rods

(G-163)
MOBONOTO AUTOMOTIVE LLC
400 W Broadway St (73521-3870)
PHONE..................580 480-0410
Wilfredo Mobonoto, Mng Member
EMP: 3 EST: 2009
SALES (est): 211.7K Privately Held
SIC: 5411 7513 2396 Convenience stores; truck rental & leasing, no drivers; automotive & apparel trimmings

(G-164)
NELCO DEFENSE LLC
220 Buena Vista St (73521-1104)
PHONE..................580 471-7992
Cody Nelson,
Kramer Nelson,
EMP: 3
SALES (est): 170.8K Privately Held
SIC: 3812 Defense systems & equipment

(G-165)
OK-1 MANUFACTURING CO
709 S Veterans Dr (73521-5833)
PHONE..................580 482-0891
EMP: 2 EST: 2016
SALES (est): 48K Privately Held
SIC: 3999 Mfg Misc Products

(G-166)
PAK ELECTRIC INC (PA)
Also Called: Kay Electric
1101 W Broadway St (73521-4196)
P.O. Box 635 (73522-0635)
PHONE..................580 482-1757
Hershel Kay, President
Barbara Kay, Corp Secy
Greg Kay, Vice Pres
Jeff Kay, Vice Pres
EMP: 11
SQ FT: 15,000
SALES (est): 6.1MM Privately Held
WEB: www.kayelectricaltus.com
SIC: 5063 7694 3599 7692 Electrical supplies; electric motor repair; machine shop, jobbing & repair; welding repair

(G-167)
R & R LAWNCARE & CLEANING
2104 N Robin St (73521-1740)
PHONE..................580 480-1953
Annette Erickson, Partner
EMP: 2
SALES (est): 131.1K Privately Held
SIC: 3523 Farm machinery & equipment

(G-168)
SEWFLY EMBROIDERY
2000 E Tamarack Rd # 607 (73521-9766)
P.O. Box 594 (73522-0594)
PHONE..................580 477-1957
Susan Davidson, Owner
EMP: 1
SALES: 15K Privately Held
SIC: 2395 Embroidery products, except schiffli machine

(G-169)
STEVENS & SONS LLC
Also Called: Yellow Rose Firing Range
113 S Main St (73521-3127)
PHONE..................580 482-4142
Jerry Stevens,
EMP: 2
SALES (est): 121.4K Privately Held
SIC: 3484 Small arms

(G-170)
TURBINES INC
15935 Us Highway 283 (73521-8374)
P.O. Box 933 (73522-0933)
PHONE..................580 477-3067
Bruce Briggs, President
Dezi Halmi, Vice Pres
Barry Ellison, Engineer
Shane Bonds, Cust Mgr
Mark Stokes, Technology
EMP: 30 EST: 1975
SQ FT: 15,000
SALES (est): 30MM Privately Held
WEB: www.turbinesinc.com
SIC: 3824 Fluid meters & counting devices

(G-171)
VINTAGE REVIVAL INC
313 Falcon Rd (73521-2513)
PHONE..................580 379-9060
Jacqueline Smiley, President
EMP: 4
SALES (est): 438.9K Privately Held
SIC: 3911 Jewelry, precious metal

(G-172)
WHAT PRINT NOW
1705 Oxford Dr (73521-4767)
PHONE..................580 649-7996
EMP: 2
SALES (est): 83.9K Privately Held
SIC: 2752 Commercial printing, lithographic

Alva
Woods County

(G-173)
ALVA CONCRETE INC
44223 Harmon Rd (73717-1309)
P.O. Box 601 (73717-0601)
PHONE..................580 327-2281
Jerry Evans, Manager
Raymond Jackobson, Manager
EMP: 300 EST: 1963
SALES (est): 27.6MM Privately Held
WEB: www.evans-assoc.com
SIC: 3273 5032 Ready-mixed concrete; sand, construction; gravel

(G-174)
ALVA MONUMENT WORKS INC (PA)
724 E Oklahoma Blvd (73717-3348)
P.O. Box 426 (73717-0426)
PHONE..................580 327-0626
E V Sams, President
EMP: 8
SQ FT: 2,000
SALES (est): 870K Privately Held
WEB: www.alvamonument.com
SIC: 5999 3281 Monuments, finished to custom order; cut stone & stone products

(G-175)
ARYSTA LIFE SCIENCE TECHNOLOGY
19940 County Road 480 (73717-5052)
PHONE..................580 871-2316
EMP: 2
SALES (est): 83K Privately Held
SIC: 3295 Mfg Minerals-Ground/Treated

(G-176)
BAKER HUGHES A GE COMPANY LLC
3000 College Blvd (73717-5045)
PHONE..................580 327-2162
Hughes Baker, Manager
EMP: 84
SALES (corp-wide): 23.8B Publicly Held
SIC: 1389 Oil field services
HQ: Baker Hughes Holdings Llc
17021 Aldine Westfield Rd
Houston TX 77073
713 439-8600

(G-177)
BAKER MANUFACTURING INC
602 Hart St Apt 103 (73717-3401)
PHONE..................580 327-0234
Bobby S Baker, President
EMP: 12
SQ FT: 30,000
SALES (est): 146.8K Privately Held
SIC: 3523 Plows, agricultural: disc, moldboard, chisel, listers, etc.

(G-178)
BLOOM ELECTRIC SERVICES LLC
46457 Howe Rd (73717-1133)
PHONE..................580 327-2345
EMP: 18
SALES (corp-wide): 26.7MM Privately Held
SIC: 3699 Mfg Electrical Equipment/Supplies
PA: Bloom Electric Services Llc
9525 W Reno Ave
Oklahoma City OK 73102
405 491-5500

(G-179)
BLUE CANVAS LLC
1043 8th St (73717-3119)
PHONE..................580 327-3406
Calvin Graybill, Administration
EMP: 1
SALES (est): 57.4K Privately Held
SIC: 2211 Canvas

(G-180)
CARDON TRAILERS
913 5th St (73717-2719)
PHONE..................580 327-0701
EMP: 1
SQ FT: 12,000
SALES: 250K Privately Held
SIC: 3523 Mfg Farm Machinery/Equipment

(G-181)
DBR CONSTRUCTION SERVICES INC
Also Called: D B R Construction
1704 Oklahoma Blvd (73717-1833)
P.O. Box 93 (73717-0093)
PHONE..................580 327-4335
Renita Heinrichs, President
EMP: 3
SALES (est): 425.2K Privately Held
SIC: 1389 Pipe testing, oil field service

(G-182)
GLENN SCHLARB WELDING
1322 Mill St (73717-1446)
PHONE..................580 327-3832
Elizabeth Schlarb, Owner
EMP: 2 EST: 1966
SQ FT: 1,600
SALES (est): 75.9K Privately Held
SIC: 7692 2514 Welding repair; metal household furniture

(G-183)
IOFINA NATURAL GAS
19940 County Road 480 (73717-5052)
PHONE..................580 871-2316
EMP: 2
SALES (est): 62.6K Privately Held
SIC: 3295 Minerals, ground or treated

(G-184)
LARIAT SERVICES INC
2300 E Oklahoma Blvd (73717-4018)
PHONE..................580 977-5050
Truck Daniels, Superintendent
EMP: 4
SALES (corp-wide): 266.8MM Publicly Held
WEB: www.lariatservices.com
SIC: 8999 1382 Actuarial consultant; oil & gas exploration services
HQ: Lariat Services, Inc.
123 Robert S Kerr Ave
Oklahoma City OK 73102
405 753-5500

(G-185)
LARRY WILCOXSON
44934 Jefferson Rd (73717-5032)
PHONE..................580 327-2110
Larry Wilcoxson, Principal
EMP: 1
SALES (est): 49.3K Privately Held
SIC: 7692 Welding repair

(G-186)
MARTIN BROADCASTING CORP
Also Called: Newsgram
620 Choctaw St (73717-1626)
PHONE..................580 327-1510
Lynn Martin, President
Marione Martin, Corp Secy
EMP: 35
SQ FT: 4,000
SALES (est): 2MM Privately Held
SIC: 2711 Newspapers, publishing & printing

(G-187)
MEYER ELECTRIC MOTOR SERVICE
Hwy 281 N (73717)
PHONE..................580 327-1399
Kenny Meyer, Owner
Sherrill Meyer, Co-Owner
EMP: 2
SALES (est): 90.5K Privately Held
SIC: 7694 Electric motor repair

(G-188)
PLANE PLASTICS LTD
Also Called: Vantage Plane Plastics
3161 College Blvd (73717-5003)
P.O. Box 400 (73717-0400)
PHONE..................580 327-1565
Paul Roy, CEO
Eric Clack, President
Andrea Alpinieri Glover, CFO
EMP: 42
SALES (est): 7.3MM
SALES (corp-wide): 63.6MM Privately Held
SIC: 3728 Aircraft parts & equipment
PA: Vantage Associates Inc.
900 Civic Center Dr
National City CA 91950
619 477-6940

(G-189)
PONY BOY LURES
600 Mimosa Dr (73717-3332)
PHONE..................580 327-1233
Delbert Rhodes, Principal
EMP: 2
SALES (est): 217.4K Privately Held
SIC: 3949 Lures, fishing: artificial

(G-190)
PREMIER AEROSPACE SVCS & TECH
1601 Oklahoma Blvd (73717-1816)
P.O. Box 604 (73717-0604)
PHONE..................580 327-3706
Scott Brown, President
EMP: 5 EST: 2007
SALES (est): 300K Privately Held
WEB: www.premieraerostore.com
SIC: 3728 Aircraft parts & equipment

(G-191)
SANDRIDGE ENERGY INC
2300 E Oklahoma Blvd (73717-4018)
PHONE..................580 430-4500
Lindsay Seaman, Branch Mgr
EMP: 1
SALES (corp-wide): 266.8MM Publicly Held
WEB: www.sandridgeenergy.com
SIC: 1311 Crude petroleum production
PA: Sandridge Energy, Inc.
123 Robert S Kerr Ave
Oklahoma City OK 73102
405 429-5500

Alva - Woods County (G-192) — GEOGRAPHIC SECTION

(G-192)
SPEEDYS TS & MORE LLC
29864 County Road 452 (73717-1156)
PHONE..................580 748-0067
Chere J Williams,
EMP: 1
SALES (est): 86K **Privately Held**
SIC: 2396 5136 5137 5651 Screen printing on fabric articles; men's & boys' clothing; women's & children's clothing; family clothing stores

(G-193)
SPORTS & STRESS MARKETING
1710 College Blvd B (73717-3414)
P.O. Box 493 (73717-0493)
PHONE..................580 327-3463
EMP: 4
SQ FT: 2,500
SALES (est): 110K **Privately Held**
SIC: 2834 Mfg Metabolic Enhancers

(G-194)
TARGA PPLINE MID-CONTINENT LLC
38348 Craig Rd (73717-1209)
PHONE..................580 435-2267
Arnie Krush, *Branch Mgr*
EMP: 24 **Publicly Held**
SIC: 1389 Processing service, gas
HQ: Targa Pipeline Mid-Continent Llc
 110 W 7th St Ste 2300
 Tulsa OK 74119
 918 574-3500

(G-195)
VALUE ADDED PRODUCTS
2101 College Blvd (73717-9733)
PHONE..................580 327-0400
Dirk Merle, *CEO*
Bob Baker, *President*
Myron Bradt, *Principal*
Richard Kutz, *Prdtn Mgr*
Rudy Smith-Dunn, *Warehouse Mgr*
EMP: 60
SQ FT: 10,000
SALES (est): 13MM **Privately Held**
SIC: 2041 Doughs, frozen or refrigerated

Amber
Grady County

(G-196)
HURLEY WELDING LLC
104 Holly (73004-9727)
PHONE..................405 224-7332
EMP: 1
SALES (est): 51K **Privately Held**
SIC: 7692 Welding Repair

(G-197)
TURNER WELDING INC
Also Called: Turner Welding and Steel Sups
1496 County Road 1280 (73004-5509)
PHONE..................405 224-3867
Dale Turner, *President*
Tina Johnson, *Admin Sec*
EMP: 14
SQ FT: 3,200
SALES (est): 2.5MM **Privately Held**
SIC: 7692 Welding repair

Ames
Major County

(G-198)
MOI OIL & GAS INC
274410 E County Road 56 (73718-2315)
P.O. Box 1 (73718-0001)
PHONE..................580 753-4266
Brent Hajek, *President*
EMP: 2
SALES (est): 180K **Privately Held**
SIC: 1382 Oil & gas exploration services

Anadarko
Caddo County

(G-199)
ANADARKO PUBLISHING CO
117 E Broadway St (73005)
P.O. Box 548 (73005-0548)
PHONE..................405 247-3331
Joe McBride, *President*
EMP: 20 EST: 1901
SQ FT: 7,000
SALES: 857K **Privately Held**
SIC: 2711 Newspapers, publishing & printing

(G-200)
APEX INC (PA)
117 S 1st St (73005-3551)
P.O. Box 804 (73005-0804)
PHONE..................405 247-7377
Greg Wallace, *President*
Micky Bottom, *Treasurer*
Sheri Hammons, *Exec Dir*
Anne Pemberton, *Director*
Randi Clift, *Admin Sec*
EMP: 40
SQ FT: 6,000
SALES (est): 1.1MM **Privately Held**
SIC: 8331 7389 8361 2389 Sheltered workshop; sewing contractor; residential care for the handicapped; men's miscellaneous accessories

(G-201)
CKENERGY ELECTRIC CO OP INC
311 W Petree Rd (73005-5657)
PHONE..................405 247-3041
EMP: 3
SALES (est): 53.5K **Privately Held**
SIC: 4911 3699 Distribution, electric power; electrical equipment & supplies

(G-202)
DOLESE BROS CO
1800 S Mission St (73005)
P.O. Box 1059 (73005-1059)
PHONE..................405 247-2564
Dwayne Coy, *Manager*
EMP: 3
SALES (corp-wide): 8.5MM **Privately Held**
SIC: 3273 5211 5032 Ready-mixed concrete; masonry materials & supplies; stone, crushed or broken
PA: Dolese Bros. Co.
 20 Nw 13th St
 Oklahoma City OK 73103
 405 235-2311

(G-203)
ENTWINED VINES WINERY LLC
17134 County Road 1340 (73005-2455)
PHONE..................405 320-0452
John Foster, *Owner*
EMP: 2
SALES (est): 102.9K **Privately Held**
SIC: 2084 Wines

(G-204)
FANCY DANCER LEATHER DESIGNS
302 W Alabama Ave (73005-4848)
PHONE..................405 247-7030
Cara Purdy, *Owner*
EMP: 2
SALES (est): 50K **Privately Held**
SIC: 3366 Copper foundries

(G-205)
PERFORMANCE SCREEN PRINTING
401 E Central Blvd (73005-3619)
PHONE..................405 247-9891
Kim Linkin, *Owner*
Kim Shook, *Owner*
EMP: 1 EST: 1991
SALES (est): 78.8K **Privately Held**
SIC: 2759 2396 Screen printing; automotive & apparel trimmings

(G-206)
REDTAIL INDUSTRIES LLC
131 E Central Blvd (73005-3419)
PHONE..................405 933-6654
Anthony Oberhauser, *Principal*
EMP: 2 EST: 2018
SALES (est): 66.1K **Privately Held**
SIC: 3999 Manufacturing industries

(G-207)
TROPHIES N THINGS
121 W Broadway St (73005-2805)
PHONE..................405 247-9771
Carolyn Myers, *President*
EMP: 3
SQ FT: 1,400
SALES: 100K **Privately Held**
SIC: 5999 3914 3479 5947 Trophies & plaques; trophies; engraving jewelry silverware, or metal; gift shop; signs & advertising specialties; marking devices

(G-208)
UNAMI LLC
1617 Industrial Rd (73005-9592)
PHONE..................405 320-5696
Jerry Kennedy, *Director*
EMP: 2
SQ FT: 30,000
SALES (est): 816.5K **Privately Held**
SIC: 3648 1541 8711 1611 Lighting equipment; industrial buildings & warehouses; renovation, remodeling & repairs: industrial buildings; engineering services; highway & street maintenance; telephone/video communications; computer related maintenance services

(G-209)
WICHITA INDUSTRIES
1503 S Mission St Ste 4 (73005-5816)
P.O. Box 682 (73005-0682)
PHONE..................405 933-2162
Vanessa Vance, *Owner*
EMP: 1
SALES (est): 46K **Privately Held**
SIC: 3999 Manufacturing industries

(G-210)
WOODS AND WATERS HOLDINGS LLC
Also Called: Woods Waters Winery Vineyards
17153 Cty Rd 1380 (73005)
P.O. Box 51, Cyril (73029-0051)
PHONE..................405 347-3000
EMP: 11
SALES (est): 493.8K **Privately Held**
SIC: 2084 Mfg Wines/Brandy/Spirits

(G-211)
WOODS WTERS WNERY VNEYARDS LLC (PA)
17153 County Road 1380 (73005-2419)
PHONE..................405 247-3000
Elena Pound,
Robert Pound,
EMP: 5
SALES: 210K **Privately Held**
SIC: 2084 Wines

Antlers
Pushmataha County

(G-212)
4 M WELDING SERVICES INC
185885 Us Highway 271 (74523-4266)
PHONE..................580 298-9809
Jinmy Morehead, *Principal*
EMP: 1
SALES (est): 42.8K **Privately Held**
SIC: 7692 Welding repair

(G-213)
ANTLERS ROOF-TRUSS & BLDRS SUP
Also Called: Antlers Roof & Truss Co
1010 Ne 5th St (74523-2807)
PHONE..................580 298-3560
Tommy Jones, *President*
Misty Alford, *Corp Secy*
Jackie Jones, *Vice Pres*
EMP: 8
SQ FT: 5,000
SALES (est): 1.9MM **Privately Held**
SIC: 5211 2439 Lumber & other building materials; trusses, wooden roof

(G-214)
BIG 3 WOODYARD INC
Hc 67 (74523)
P.O. Box 646 (74523-0646)
PHONE..................580 298-6123
EMP: 1
SALES (est): 132.2K **Privately Held**
SIC: 3743 Train Maintenance Cars

(G-215)
CHOCTAW MFG DEF CONTRS INC (DH)
209 Sw 7th St (74523-3834)
PHONE..................580 298-2203
Stephen Benefield, *CEO*
Gary Batton, *Chairman*
Keith Briem, *Vice Pres*
Cynthia Briscoe, *Vice Pres*
Bob Henry, *Vice Pres*
EMP: 6
SALES (est): 25.4MM **Privately Held**
SIC: 2448 3441 Wood pallets & skids; fabricated structural metal
HQ: Choctaw Global, Llc
 20 Sandstone Rd
 Durant OK 74701
 580 200-0927

(G-216)
HARPERS WELDING
1207 Se 3rd St (74523-4232)
PHONE..................580 298-7165
Neil Harper, *Owner*
EMP: 1
SALES (est): 33.6K **Privately Held**
SIC: 7692 Welding repair

Apache
Caddo County

(G-217)
APACHE NEWS
120 E Evans Ave (73006)
P.O. Box 778 (73006-0778)
PHONE..................580 588-3862
Joyel Wright, *Owner*
Joye Wright, *Partner*
Stanley Wright, *Co-Owner*
EMP: 2 EST: 1901
SQ FT: 1,000
SALES: 60K **Privately Held**
SIC: 2711 2759 2752 Newspapers: publishing only, not printed on site; commercial printing; commercial printing, lithographic

(G-218)
BEAVERS HIGH PRESSURE WSHG LLC
15989 Nw Allison Rd (73006-8321)
P.O. Box 83 (73006-0083)
PHONE..................580 512-3530
Mitchell Beavers, *Mng Member*
EMP: 1
SALES: 30K **Privately Held**
SIC: 7299 3589 Miscellaneous personal service; high pressure cleaning equipment

(G-219)
JENKINS QUARY
616 W Evans Ave (73006-9197)
PHONE..................580 588-3020
EMP: 9 EST: 1999
SALES (est): 380K **Privately Held**
SIC: 1422 Crushed/Broken Limestone

(G-220)
MOBETTA
104 E Evans Ave (73006)
PHONE..................580 588-9222
Maury Tate, *President*
Mary Kay Turner, *Corp Secy*
EMP: 2
SQ FT: 2,000

GEOGRAPHIC SECTION

Ardmore - Carter County (G-251)

SALES (est): 382.8K **Privately Held**
SIC: 5136 5137 5699 2335 Shirts, men's & boys' blouses; shirts, custom made; women's, juniors' & misses' dresses; men's & boys' furnishings; men's & boys' suits & coats

(G-221)
RATH INC
Also Called: Kittys Chicken
908 E Apache Trail Rd (73006-9282)
PHONE 580 588-3064
Jerry E Rath, *CEO*
Katherine Rath, *Principal*
EMP: 18
SQ FT: 12,000
SALES (est): 2MM **Privately Held**
SIC: 2015 Chicken, processed

(G-222)
SANDRA CROW
45200 County Street 2540 (73006-9529)
PHONE 580 588-2321
EMP: 1
SALES (est): 25K **Privately Held**
SIC: 7692 Welding repair

(G-223)
THOMAS CABINET COMPANY
128 S Hillside Rd (73006-9117)
P.O. Box 165 (73006-0165)
PHONE 580 588-9231
EMP: 2
SALES (est): 100K **Privately Held**
SIC: 2434 Mfg Wood Kitchen Cabinets

Arapaho
Custer County

(G-224)
JOHNSON SIGNS INC
10057 N 2250 Rd (73620-2113)
PHONE 580 323-6454
Lee Johnson, *President*
Deann Johnson, *President*
EMP: 4
SALES (est): 436.9K **Privately Held**
SIC: 3993 1799 Signs & advertising specialties; sign installation & maintenance

(G-225)
MCAMIS FUR COMPANY
209 S 14th St (73620)
P.O. Box 292 (73620-0292)
PHONE 580 323-5961
Charles McAmis, *Owner*
EMP: 3
SALES (est): 128.8K **Privately Held**
SIC: 3999 Furs

Arcadia
Oklahoma County

(G-226)
ACCURATE BLINDS
13450 E Timberwood Ln (73007-7407)
PHONE 405 396-8583
David Daws, *Principal*
EMP: 4
SALES (est): 238.8K **Privately Held**
SIC: 2431 Blinds (shutters), wood

(G-227)
ALLENS TRUCKING & WELDING SVC
14585 E Old Highway 66 (73007-7918)
P.O. Box 239 (73007-0239)
PHONE 405 341-8066
Allen Smith, *President*
EMP: 1
SALES (est): 67.1K **Privately Held**
SIC: 7692 4214 Welding repair; local trucking with storage

(G-228)
B & A PRODUCING LLC
4700 N Westminster Rd (73007-7815)
PHONE 405 664-3628
Michael Felice,
EMP: 1

SALES: 110K **Privately Held**
SIC: 1389 Oil & gas field services

(G-229)
GHOST TOWN PRESS
13100 E Old Highway 66 (73007-7909)
PHONE 405 396-2166
EMP: 2
SALES (est): 92.1K **Privately Held**
WEB: www.66maps.com
SIC: 2741 Miscellaneous publishing

(G-230)
HARPER WELDING DESIGN LLC
11316 E 15th St (73007-6801)
PHONE 405 396-8558
Durwin Harper, *Mng Member*
EMP: 1
SALES: 75K **Privately Held**
SIC: 7692 Welding repair

(G-231)
MODULAR SERVICES COMPANY
12501 E Coffee Creek Rd (73007-7636)
PHONE 405 521-9923
EMP: 2
SALES (est): 90.4K **Privately Held**
SIC: 2599 Mfg Furniture/Fixtures

(G-232)
WESTFALL INDUSTRIES INC
10233 Beaupre Dr (73007-5803)
PHONE 520 744-2330
Marla Westfall, *President*
EMP: 4
SALES (est): 216.3K **Privately Held**
SIC: 3999 Manufacturing industries

Ardmore
Carter County

(G-233)
3M IMTEC CORPORATION
2401 N Commerce St (73401-1280)
PHONE 800 879-9799
Chuck Dehler, *President*
Dr M K Patterson Jr, *Senior VP*
Stephen Hadwin, *Vice Pres*
▲ **EMP:** 150
SQ FT: 16,000
SALES (est): 10.6MM
SALES (corp-wide): 32.1B **Publicly Held**
SIC: 3843 Dental materials
PA: 3m Company
 3m Center
 Saint Paul MN 55144
 651 733-1110

(G-234)
4 K KUSTOMZ DESIGNS & SIGNS
904 S Commerce St (73401-5003)
PHONE 580 226-2259
EMP: 1 **EST:** 2017
SALES (est): 46K **Privately Held**
SIC: 3993 Signs & advertising specialties

(G-235)
AARON LANCE BUTLER
3792 Countyline Rd (73401-8988)
PHONE 580 220-7715
Aaron Butler, *Principal*
EMP: 4
SALES (est): 218.3K **Privately Held**
SIC: 2711 Newspapers, publishing & printing

(G-236)
AC NUTRITION LP
100 Mill St Se (73401-7031)
P.O. Box 2006 (73402-2006)
PHONE 580 223-3900
Ann Baskett, *Branch Mgr*
EMP: 12
SALES (corp-wide): 33.5MM **Privately Held**
WEB: www.acnutrition.com
SIC: 2048 Livestock feeds
HQ: Ac Nutrition, Lp
 158 N Main St
 Winters TX 79567

(G-237)
ACTION PETROLEUM SERVICES CORP
1001 Timber Grv (73401-9282)
PHONE 580 223-6544
Raymond E Pletcher, *President*
Donna M Pletcher, *Corp Secy*
EMP: 2
SALES (est): 344.2K **Privately Held**
SIC: 4212 7699 1389 Local trucking, without storage; oil burner repair service; lease tanks, oil field: erecting, cleaning & repairing

(G-238)
AMETHYST RESEARCH INCORPORATED
123 Case Cir (73401-0643)
PHONE 580 657-2575
Terry Golding, *CEO*
Mangal Dhoubhadel, *Research*
Jiayi Shao, *Program Mgr*
EMP: 12
SALES (est): 1.8MM **Privately Held**
SIC: 3674 Semiconductors & related devices

(G-239)
AMIGOS SALSA (PA)
1009 S Rockford Rd (73401-3432)
PHONE 580 224-0667
Marty Currier, *Owner*
EMP: 2
SALES: 187.9K **Privately Held**
SIC: 2099 Ready-to-eat meals, salads & sandwiches

(G-240)
AMIGOS SALSA
3334 S Commerce St (73401-3737)
PHONE 580 224-1424
Marty Currier, *Branch Mgr*
EMP: 4 **Privately Held**
SIC: 2099 Food preparations
PA: Amigo's Salsa
 1009 S Rockford Rd
 Ardmore OK 73401

(G-241)
ANDREAE TEAM INC
3550 Cypert Way (73401-3707)
P.O. Box 2538 (73402-2538)
PHONE 580 223-9334
Robert Andreae, *President*
Patrick Hayoun, *Vice Pres*
Jack Riley, *Treasurer*
Glenn Burns, *Admin Sec*
▼ **EMP:** 10
SQ FT: 1,000
SALES (est): 2.2MM **Privately Held**
SIC: 3564 Air cleaning systems

(G-242)
ANGEL DELITE INC
1019 Republic St (73401-4554)
PHONE 580 223-9777
Linda F Miller, *President*
EMP: 2
SALES (est): 100K **Privately Held**
SIC: 3999 Candles

(G-243)
ARBUCKLE MOUNTAIN TOWER CORP
10 W Main St Ste 418 (73401-6515)
P.O. Box 1754 (73402-1754)
PHONE 580 223-3408
Fred Chapman Jr, *President*
Joann Chapman, *Principal*
EMP: 4
SALES: 15K **Privately Held**
SIC: 3441 0291 Tower sections, radio & television transmission; livestock farm, general

(G-244)
ARBUCKLE WIRELINE LLC
2214323 Us Hwy 701 (73401)
P.O. Box 817, Lone Grove (73443-0817)
PHONE 580 226-4001
Steven McBride,
Gerry Connor,
EMP: 2
SQ FT: 1,500

SALES: 2MM **Privately Held**
SIC: 1389 Oil field services

(G-245)
ARDMORE CONSTRUCTION SUP INC
Also Called: ACS
506 S Washington St (73401-7047)
PHONE 580 223-2322
Mark Ellis, *President*
EMP: 9
SQ FT: 18,000
SALES: 1MM **Privately Held**
SIC: 2431 2439 5231 5198 Doors, combination screen-storm, wood; trim, wood; windows & window parts & trim, wood; trusses, wooden roof; paint; paints

(G-246)
ARDMORE DRAGWAY
3801 Springdale Rd (73401-0213)
PHONE 580 226-7811
EMP: 2
SALES (est): 87.2K **Privately Held**
SIC: 3715 Truck trailers

(G-247)
ARDMORE INC
225 Harryette Pl (73401-5243)
PHONE 405 201-1288
Travis Williams, *Principal*
Barbara Selby, *Opers Mgr*
Christy Morris, *Administration*
EMP: 3
SALES (est): 108K **Privately Held**
WEB: www.ardmoreite.com
SIC: 2711 Newspapers, publishing & printing

(G-248)
ARDMORE OPTICAL CO
Also Called: Dr G W Clay Optomotrist
226 W Main St (73401-6316)
P.O. Box 1848 (73402-1848)
PHONE 580 223-8676
Garland Clay, *Owner*
Mary Lockwood, *Manager*
EMP: 3 **EST:** 1964
SQ FT: 2,160
SALES (est): 229.9K **Privately Held**
SIC: 8042 3851 Offices & clinics of optometrists; ophthalmic goods

(G-249)
ARDMORE PROD & EXPLORATION
Also Called: Ardmore Drilling
301 W Main St Ste 415 (73401-6322)
P.O. Box 1988 (73402-1988)
PHONE 580 223-2292
Chuck Teacle, *President*
Andrew T Smith, *Vice Pres*
Charlie Ammons, *Prdtn Mgr*
Katherine Smith, *Advt Staff*
Robby Short, *Manager*
EMP: 6
SALES (est): 881K **Privately Held**
SIC: 1311 1381 Crude petroleum production; natural gas production; drilling oil & gas wells

(G-250)
ASSOCIATED RESEARCH INC
801 Hailey St Sw (73401-5113)
PHONE 580 223-4773
William Long, *Principal*
Carl Barnes, *Info Tech Mgr*
EMP: 8 **EST:** 2008
SALES (est): 647.7K **Privately Held**
WEB: www.asresearch.com
SIC: 3825 Instruments to measure electricity

(G-251)
ATLAS ROOFING CORPORATION
Gypsum and Roofing Division
2300 P St Ne (73401)
P.O. Box 2416 (73402-2416)
PHONE 580 226-3283
Robert Moore, *Opers-Prdtn-Mfg*
L Keith Williams, *Persnl Mgr*
EMP: 125 **Privately Held**
SIC: 3086 2952 Insulation or cushioning material, foamed plastic; roofing materials

Ardmore - Carter County (G-252)

HQ: Atlas Roofing Corporation
802 Highway 19 N Ste 190
Meridian MS 39307
601 484-8900

(G-252)
BALERO
1 Valero Way (73401-1615)
P.O. Box 188 (73402-0188)
PHONE..............................580 221-6202
Ron Downing, *Manager*
EMP: 2 **EST:** 2014
SALES (est): 99.9K **Privately Held**
SIC: 3312 Blast furnaces & steel mills

(G-253)
BARBARA J MCGINNIS
Also Called: Uniforms Etc
717 N Commerce St (73401-3914)
PHONE..............................580 226-7675
Barbara J McGinnis, *President*
EMP: 2 **EST:** 1998
SQ FT: 1,500
SALES (est): 350K **Privately Held**
WEB: www.uniformsetcok.com
SIC: 5699 2326 Uniforms; medical & hospital uniforms, men's

(G-254)
BBR OIL CORP (PA)
Also Called: Fractal Oil & Gas
10 W Main St Ste 212 (73401-6515)
PHONE..............................580 223-2887
Lloyd Biddick Jr, *President*
Michael Biddick, *Vice Pres*
EMP: 5
SQ FT: 1,600
SALES (est): 60K **Privately Held**
SIC: 1311 Crude petroleum production

(G-255)
BEANE DEVELOPMENT CORP
Also Called: Brad's Western & Work Wear
132 Holiday Dr (73401-2513)
PHONE..............................580 222-1150
Brad Beane, *President*
Melonie Beane, *Vice Pres*
EMP: 4
SALES (est): 500K **Privately Held**
SIC: 2326 Work apparel, except uniforms

(G-256)
BEETLE PLASTICS LLC (HQ)
601 Beetle Dr (73401-1192)
P.O. Box 1569 (73402-1569)
PHONE..............................580 389-5421
Larry Brown, *Mng Member*
EMP: 20
SALES (est): 3.5MM
SALES (corp-wide): 50MM **Privately Held**
SIC: 3089 3084 Plastic & fiberglass tanks; ducting, plastic; plastics pipe
PA: Midwest Cooling Towers Inc.
1156 E Highway 19
Chickasha OK 73018
405 224-4622

(G-257)
BLUE BONNET FEEDS LP
100 Mill St Se (73401-7031)
P.O. Box 2006 (73402-2006)
PHONE..............................580 223-3010
Arnne Surnar, *Partner*
EMP: 70
SQ FT: 2,000
SALES (est): 63.2K **Privately Held**
SIC: 2048 2047 Livestock feeds; feed supplements; dry pet food (except dog & cat); dog & cat food

(G-258)
BLUE ROCK OIL & GAS LLC
235 Stanton Rd (73401-1369)
PHONE..............................580 229-5697
Colton Allen, *Principal*
EMP: 2
SALES (est): 77.7K **Privately Held**
SIC: 1389 Oil & gas field services

(G-259)
BLUE SAIL PUBLISHING INC
1405 4th Ave Nw (73401-2708)
P.O. Box 6271, Aurora IL (60598-0271)
PHONE..............................630 851-4731
D McNees, *Principal*
EMP: 2
SALES (est): 139.1K **Privately Held**
SIC: 2741 Miscellaneous publishing

(G-260)
BRADLEY WELDING & MACHINE
3500 S Commerce St (73401-3728)
P.O. Box 1653 (73402-1653)
PHONE..............................580 223-2250
Ed Bradley, *Owner*
EMP: 1
SALES (est): 91.7K **Privately Held**
SIC: 3599 7692 Machine shop, jobbing & repair; welding repair

(G-261)
BUTTONS AUTO ELECTRICAL SUPPLY
28 S Commerce St (73401-3925)
PHONE..............................580 223-3855
Larry Hatley, *President*
Mary Cottrell, *Corp Secy*
Glen Hatley, *Vice Pres*
EMP: 5
SQ FT: 2,000
SALES (est): 350K **Privately Held**
SIC: 3694 5013 3625 3621 Motors, starting: automotive & aircraft; alternators, automotive; automotive supplies & parts; relays & industrial controls; motors & generators

(G-262)
C & J MINERALS LLC
1805 Stanley St Sw (73401-3241)
P.O. Box 2192 (73402-2192)
PHONE..............................580 504-4048
Joel Wellmitz, *Mng Member*
Christian O'Donnell, *Mng Member*
EMP: 1
SALES (est): 122.6K **Privately Held**
SIC: 1382 6799 Oil & gas exploration services; commodity investors

(G-263)
CANDLES BY ME
815 A St Nw (73401-5937)
PHONE..............................580 798-5200
Holden Dylan Roberts, *Manager*
EMP: 1
SALES (est): 39.6K **Privately Held**
SIC: 3999 Candles

(G-264)
CHADDICK & ASSOCIATES INC
Also Called: Office Concepts
2421 Autumn Run Ste E (73401-2278)
PHONE..............................580 223-1202
Hans Chaddick, *President*
Dana Chaddick, *Vice Pres*
Ranea Lynch, *Mktg Dir*
EMP: 12
SQ FT: 7,500
SALES (est): 2MM **Privately Held**
SIC: 3661 5044 5943 5045 Facsimile equipment; copying equipment; stationery stores; printers, computer; office machine rental, except computers; systems engineering consultant, ex. computer or professional

(G-265)
CHARLES DALE KELLER
Also Called: Keller Custom Cabinets & Trim
1922 Knox Rd Apt 404 (73401-0810)
PHONE..............................940 597-1763
Charles D Keller, *Owner*
EMP: 2
SALES (est): 166K **Privately Held**
SIC: 2434 Wood kitchen cabinets

(G-266)
CHASTON OIL & GAS LLC
100 W Main St (73401-6414)
PHONE..............................580 226-2640
Kermit Mc Kinney, *Principal*
EMP: 2
SALES (est): 200.4K **Privately Held**
SIC: 1382 6211 6282 Oil & gas exploration services; mineral, oil & gas leasing & royalty dealers; investment advice

(G-267)
CLEMENT ELEC
550 S Washington St (73401-7047)
PHONE..............................580 223-6500
T Clements, *Owner*
EMP: 2 **EST:** 2007
SALES (est): 393.2K **Privately Held**
SIC: 3699 Electrical equipment & supplies

(G-268)
CLEMENTS SAND GRAVEL & EXCAVAT
9363 State Highway 199 (73401-7671)
PHONE..............................580 465-4191
J C Clements, *Principal*
EMP: 3
SALES (est): 239.9K **Privately Held**
SIC: 1442 Construction sand & gravel

(G-269)
COLSTON CORPORATION
Also Called: Colston Building
10 W Main St Ste 406 (73401-6515)
PHONE..............................580 223-1309
Bob Colston, *President*
Ronnie Colston, *Vice Pres*
Leah Colston, *Treasurer*
Lisa Wallace, *Admin Sec*
EMP: 2 **EST:** 1975
SALES (est): 442.3K **Privately Held**
SIC: 6512 1311 Commercial & industrial building operation; crude petroleum & natural gas

(G-270)
COULTER OIL FIELD SERVICES LLC
567 Pinewood Trails Dr (73401-0666)
PHONE..............................580 504-0813
Brian Coulter, *Owner*
EMP: 4 **EST:** 2012
SALES (est): 246.2K **Privately Held**
SIC: 1389 Roustabout service

(G-271)
DA VINCI BROOM LLC
710 Franklin Ct (73401-1063)
PHONE..............................580 224-1424
Gordon Currier, *President*
▲ **EMP:** 3
SALES (est): 175.4K **Privately Held**
SIC: 3991 7389 Push brooms;

(G-272)
DANIEL P WOLLASTON
Also Called: American Pirate Screen
6 W Main St (73401-6514)
PHONE..............................580 768-4694
Dainiel P Wollaston, *Owner*
EMP: 2
SALES (est): 120K **Privately Held**
SIC: 2759 Screen printing

(G-273)
DARR LIFT MAIN LINE
266 Case Cir (73401-0602)
PHONE..............................580 657-6337
Cory Hodges, *Principal*
EMP: 2
SALES (est): 276.1K **Privately Held**
WEB: www.darrjcb.com
SIC: 3537 Forklift trucks

(G-274)
DAUBE COMPANY
5 S Commerce St Ste 21 (73401-3996)
P.O. Box 38 (73402-0038)
PHONE..............................580 223-7403
Carol D Simms, *President*
Keith Crites, *Vice Pres*
Sam Daube, *Vice Pres*
Richard S Simms, *Treasurer*
EMP: 17
SQ FT: 5,000
SALES (est): 2.2MM **Privately Held**
SIC: 1311 Crude petroleum production; natural gas production

(G-275)
DAVENPORT OILFIELD SERVICES
3075 Meridian Rd (73401-8721)
PHONE..............................580 465-0314
Chanse Davenport, *Principal*
EMP: 3
SALES (est): 284.5K **Privately Held**
SIC: 1389 Oil field services

(G-276)
DAVID W POTTS LAND EXPLORATION
301 W Main St Ste 545 (73401-6335)
P.O. Box 692 (73402-0692)
PHONE..............................580 226-3633
David W Potts, *President*
EMP: 4
SALES (est): 328.1K **Privately Held**
SIC: 1382 Oil & gas exploration services

(G-277)
DAY CONCRETE BLOCK COMPANY
1401 Monroe St Ne (73401-2121)
P.O. Box 844 (73402-0844)
PHONE..............................580 223-3317
Roger Day, *President*
Rod Day, *Vice Pres*
EMP: 18 **EST:** 1959
SQ FT: 600
SALES (est): 2.5MM **Privately Held**
SIC: 3271 3273 Blocks, concrete or cinder: standard; ready-mixed concrete

(G-278)
DEHART COMPANY
115 4th Ave Sw (73401-4908)
P.O. Box 914 (73402-0914)
PHONE..............................580 223-7792
John W Dehart, *Owner*
Charles Swindale, *Partner*
EMP: 2
SQ FT: 2,500
SALES (est): 181.8K **Privately Held**
SIC: 1311 Crude petroleum production

(G-279)
DOLESE BROS CO
115 N Plainview Rd (73401-0737)
PHONE..............................580 223-2243
Tony Bosolo, *Branch Mgr*
EMP: 16
SALES (corp-wide): 8.5MM **Privately Held**
SIC: 3273 Ready-mixed concrete
PA: Dolese Bros. Co.
20 Nw 13th St
Oklahoma City OK 73103
405 235-2311

(G-280)
DOLESE BROS CO
164 Dolese Rd (73401-7577)
PHONE..............................580 226-8737
Alvin Brown, *Manager*
EMP: 23
SALES (corp-wide): 8.5MM **Privately Held**
SIC: 5032 1422 Stone, crushed or broken; crushed & broken limestone
PA: Dolese Bros. Co.
20 Nw 13th St
Oklahoma City OK 73103
405 235-2311

(G-281)
DUNLAP & COMPANY
100 W Main St (73401-6414)
P.O. Box 1888 (73402-1888)
PHONE..............................580 223-8181
Thomas F Dunlap, *Partner*
Nancy Dunlap, *Partner*
EMP: 3 **EST:** 1976
SQ FT: 6,000
SALES (est): 262.4K **Privately Held**
SIC: 1311 0212 Crude petroleum production; beef cattle except feedlots

(G-282)
EJ USA INC
Also Called: Ejiw Ardmore Foundry
270 Redwing Rd (73401-7786)
PHONE..............................231 536-2261
Russell Douthit, *Safety Mgr*
Nickolas Parnell, *Engineer*
Todd Ingalls, *Manager*
Murray Pearson, *Maintence Staff*
EMP: 250 **Privately Held**
WEB: www.eastjordancity.org
SIC: 3321 3322 Gray iron castings; malleable iron foundries

GEOGRAPHIC SECTION

Ardmore - Carter County (G-315)

HQ: Ej Usa, Inc.
301 Spring St
East Jordan MI 49727
800 874-4100

(G-283)
ELECTRIC MOTOR SERVICE COMPANY
808 K St Nw (73401-4002)
PHONE..........................580 223-8940
Donald Callaway, *Owner*
Belinda Callaway, *Co-Owner*
EMP: 2
SQ FT: 3,200
SALES: 100K **Privately Held**
SIC: 5063 7694 3621 Motors, electric; armature rewinding shops; motors & generators

(G-284)
ELITE WOOD CREATIONS LLC
15 W Broadway St (73401-6224)
PHONE..........................580 220-1153
EMP: 2
SALES (est): 111.3K **Privately Held**
SIC: 2431 Millwork

(G-285)
EMBROIDERY BY STACIE
42 Sonora St (73401-7283)
PHONE..........................580 656-5232
EMP: 1
SALES (est): 58.5K **Privately Held**
SIC: 2395 Embroidery & art needlework

(G-286)
ERGON ARDMORE
2500 Refinery Rd (73401-1669)
PHONE..........................580 223-8010
Chuck Ellsworth, *Principal*
Gregg Lewis, *Facilities Mgr*
Jesus Martinez, *Facilities Mgr*
Wendell Nolan, *Sales Staff*
EMP: 3 EST: 2010
SALES (est): 306.3K **Privately Held**
WEB: www.ergonasphalt.com
SIC: 2951 Asphalt paving mixtures & blocks

(G-287)
ERIK ROBINS
Also Called: Erik Robins Woodworks
237 Killarney Lake Rd (73401-1454)
PHONE..........................580 371-1470
Erik Robins, *Owner*
EMP: 1
SALES (est): 56.2K **Privately Held**
SIC: 2411 Wooden logs

(G-288)
FARRIER LIVINGSTON TECHNOLOGY
7300 Myall Rd (73401-8741)
PHONE..........................580 657-3469
Craig Livingston, *Owner*
EMP: 3
SALES (est): 207.5K **Privately Held**
SIC: 6512 2899 Nonresidential building operators; rosin sizes

(G-289)
FIBRE REDUCTION INC
112 2nd Ave Se (73401-6249)
PHONE..........................580 223-3401
Susan Trumble, *President*
▲ EMP: 3
SQ FT: 15,000
SALES (est): 230K **Privately Held**
WEB: www.fibrereduction.com
SIC: 3089 3533 Plastic processing; oil & gas field machinery

(G-290)
FLANDERS CORPORATION
Also Called: Flanders of Oklahoma
3500 Flanders Dr (73401-4512)
PHONE..........................580 223-1853
Harry L Smith Jr, *CEO*
EMP: 6 **Privately Held**
SIC: 3569 Filters
HQ: Flanders Corporation
531 Flanders Filter Rd
Washington NC 27889

(G-291)
FLANDERS OF OKLAHOMA
3500 Flanders Dr (73401-4512)
PHONE..........................580 223-5730
Harry Smith, *CEO*
Brenda Davis, *Exec VP*
▲ EMP: 150
SALES (est): 8MM **Privately Held**
SIC: 3564 Filters, air: furnaces, air conditioning equipment, etc.
HQ: Flanders Corporation
531 Flanders Filter Rd
Washington NC 27889

(G-292)
FREELANCE OPERATIONS INC
5605 Prairie Valley Rd (73401-0631)
P.O. Box 1564 (73402-1564)
PHONE..........................580 226-7051
Mike Hathorn, *President*
Jimmie Hathorn, *Systems Mgr*
EMP: 4
SQ FT: 2,000
SALES (est): 250K **Privately Held**
SIC: 3699 Welding machines & equipment, ultrasonic

(G-293)
GALAXIE SIGN CO
414 A St Ne (73401-6934)
PHONE..........................580 226-2944
Montey Boatright, *Owner*
EMP: 5
SQ FT: 7,000
SALES (est): 350K **Privately Held**
SIC: 3993 Signs, not made in custom sign painting shops

(G-294)
GARRISON BACKHOE LLC
4204 12th Ave Nw (73401-9580)
PHONE..........................580 465-2014
Terry Garrison, *Principal*
EMP: 1
SALES (est): 60K **Privately Held**
SIC: 3531 Backhoes

(G-295)
GARY LAND SERVICES INC
10 W Main St Ste 401 (73401-6515)
P.O. Box 1182 (73402-1182)
PHONE..........................580 226-9808
Roger D Gary, *Owner*
EMP: 2
SALES (est): 211.6K **Privately Held**
SIC: 1382 Oil & gas exploration services

(G-296)
GATEHUSE MDIA OKLA HLDINGS INC
117 W Broadway St (73401-6226)
PHONE..........................585 598-0030
Garrett J Cummings,
EMP: 1
SALES (est): 76.4K
SALES (corp-wide): 1.8B **Publicly Held**
SIC: 2711 Commercial printing & newspaper publishing combined
PA: Gannett Co., Inc.
7950 Jones Branch Dr
Mc Lean VA 22102
703 854-6000

(G-297)
GOURLEY ROYALTY COMPANY LLC
1112 S Rockford Rd (73401-3437)
PHONE..........................580 223-8783
Dorothy N Gourley, *Principal*
EMP: 1 EST: 2010
SALES (est): 61K **Privately Held**
WEB: www.gourleyoilandgas.com
SIC: 1382 Oil & gas exploration services

(G-298)
GRIFFIN OIL PROPERTIES LLC
1320 W Broadway St (73401-2838)
PHONE..........................580 226-0461
Clara Jones, *Owner*
EMP: 2
SALES (est): 136.8K **Privately Held**
SIC: 1311 Crude petroleum production

(G-299)
H C RUSTIN CORPORATION
1948 Cooper Dr (73401-9099)
PHONE..........................580 224-2672
EMP: 2
SALES (corp-wide): 2.2B **Publicly Held**
SIC: 3273 Ready-mixed concrete
HQ: H. C. Rustin Corporation
50 E Main St
Durant OK 74701
580 924-3260

(G-300)
HALL & ANDERSON SERVICES INC
14867 Us Highway 70 (73401-8780)
P.O. Box 1407, Lone Grove (73443-1407)
PHONE..........................580 319-5624
Brittney Hall, *President*
EMP: 30 EST: 2012
SQ FT: 1,200
SALES (est): 2.9MM **Privately Held**
SIC: 1389 Oil field services

(G-301)
HANGER PRSTHETCS & ORTHO INC
1109 Walnut Dr (73401-2354)
PHONE..........................580 226-7900
Tom Kirk, *CEO*
EMP: 50
SALES (corp-wide): 1.1B **Publicly Held**
SIC: 3842 Surgical appliances & supplies
HQ: Hanger Prosthetics & Orthotics, Inc.
10910 Domain Dr Ste 300
Austin TX 78758
512 777-3800

(G-302)
HARRELL EXPLORATION
5 S Commerce St Ste 32 (73401-3932)
PHONE..........................580 226-8887
James Harrell, *Principal*
EMP: 2
SALES (est): 153.5K **Privately Held**
SIC: 1382 Oil & gas exploration services

(G-303)
HEWITT MINERAL CORP
10 W Main St Ste 522 (73401-6515)
P.O. Box 1388 (73402-1388)
PHONE..........................580 223-3619
Janes Dolman, *President*
Bridger Cox, *Vice Pres*
EMP: 4
SALES (est): 193.6K **Privately Held**
WEB: www.hewittmineral.com
SIC: 1381 5172 Drilling oil & gas wells; fuel oil

(G-304)
HEWITT MINERAL CORPORATION
10 W Main St (73401-6516)
P.O. Box 1388 (73402-1388)
PHONE..........................580 223-6565
William Dolman, *President*
EMP: 5
SALES (est): 114.8K **Privately Held**
SIC: 3295 Minerals, ground or treated

(G-305)
HODGES MATERIALS INC
1401 Monroe St.Ne (73401-2121)
P.O. Box 844 (73402-0844)
PHONE..........................580 223-3317
Roger Day, *President*
EMP: 20
SQ FT: 4,000
SALES (est): 2.6MM **Privately Held**
SIC: 3273 Ready-mixed concrete

(G-306)
HOLDEN ENERGY CORP (PA)
301 W Main St Ste 600 (73401-6322)
P.O. Box 1703 (73402-1703)
PHONE..........................580 226-3960
Harold Holden, *President*
Sue Rushing, *Controller*
EMP: 32 **EST:** 1977
SQ FT: 1,200
SALES (est): 1.1MM **Privately Held**
SIC: 1389 1382 1311 Oil field services; oil & gas exploration services; crude petroleum production; natural gas production

(G-307)
HU DON MANUFACTURING CO INC
159 C St Se (73401-8031)
PHONE..........................580 223-7333
David Miller, *President*
Theresa Miller, *Vice Pres*
EMP: 11
SALES (est): 750K **Privately Held**
SIC: 3444 3564 Ventilators, sheet metal; blowers & fans

(G-308)
INDUSTRIAL SERVICE PROVIDERS (PA)
619 Interstate Dr (73401-9338)
PHONE..........................580 319-7417
Daniel Perry, *CEO*
Cliff Nichols, *COO*
Brecklyn Constant, *CFO*
EMP: 10
SALES (est): 8MM **Privately Held**
SIC: 3589 1711 1731 Commercial cooking & foodwarming equipment; heating & air conditioning contractors; general electrical contractor

(G-309)
J T WELDING
53 Walnut Hill St (73401-9659)
PHONE..........................580 504-3862
EMP: 1
SALES (est): 25K **Privately Held**
SIC: 7692 Welding repair

(G-310)
JAG FUELS COMPANY INC
2744 Brock Rd (73401-7282)
P.O. Box 720, Lone Grove (73443-0720)
PHONE..........................580 465-3256
John Miller Sr, *Officer*
EMP: 6
SALES (est): 727.7K **Privately Held**
SIC: 2869 Fuels

(G-311)
JAMES B READ OPERATING INC
5 A St Sw Ste 300 (73401-6518)
P.O. Box 638 (73402-0638)
PHONE..........................580 226-0055
James B Read, *President*
EMP: 2
SALES (est): 221.5K **Privately Held**
SIC: 1311 Crude petroleum production; natural gas production

(G-312)
JAMES S JIM VANWAY
303 C St Sw (73401-4924)
P.O. Box 2593 (73402-2593)
PHONE..........................580 223-8962
James Vanway, *Owner*
EMP: 1
SALES (est): 111.9K **Privately Held**
SIC: 1382 Oil & gas exploration services

(G-313)
JEFFS OPTACLE
2617 N Commerce St Ste C (73401-1391)
PHONE..........................580 223-5999
Linda Montgomery, *Partner*
EMP: 2
SALES (est): 127.3K **Privately Held**
SIC: 3851 Glasses, sun or glare

(G-314)
JERRY ELLIS
275 Woodstock Ln (73401-8494)
PHONE..........................580 223-5649
Jerry Ellis, *Principal*
EMP: 1
SALES (est): 30.2K **Privately Held**
SIC: 7692 Welding repair

(G-315)
JIM FORD SIGN CO
672 Dove Ln (73401-7468)
PHONE..........................580 223-8880
Jim Ford, *Owner*
EMP: 1
SALES (est): 80K **Privately Held**
SIC: 3993 Signs & advertising specialties

Ardmore - Carter County (G-316)

(G-316)
JOHNNY L RUTH (PA)
Also Called: Ardmore Photo Copy Rproduction
11 W Main St (73401-6513)
P.O. Box 134 (73402-0134)
PHONE...................................580 223-3061
Johnny L Ruth, *Owner*
EMP: 7
SQ FT: 3,000
SALES (est): 350K **Privately Held**
WEB: www.ardmorephotocopy.com
SIC: 7334 5049 2752 Blueprinting service; drafting supplies; engineers' equipment & supplies; commercial printing, lithographic

(G-317)
JOHNSON KENDALL CNSTR CO
Also Called: Kj's Const Co
1410 Kings Rd (73401-8838)
PHONE...................................580 223-5954
Kendall Johnson, *Owner*
EMP: 1
SALES (est): 106.9K **Privately Held**
SIC: 2434 Wood kitchen cabinets

(G-318)
JOHNSON OTEY PROPERTIES INC
5 A St Sw (73401-6518)
P.O. Box 248 (73402-0248)
PHONE...................................580 226-8425
Tom Dunlap, *President*
Paul Pitts, *Vice Pres*
EMP: 2
SALES (est): 348.5K **Privately Held**
SIC: 6792 1389 Oil leases, buying & selling on own account; cementing oil & gas well casings

(G-319)
JONES-KALKMAN MINERAL CO
425 1st Ave Sw (73401-4725)
P.O. Box 2327 (73402-2327)
PHONE...................................580 223-3101
Joe Kalkman, *Owner*
EMP: 1
SALES (est): 78.8K **Privately Held**
SIC: 1311 Crude petroleum production

(G-320)
KARL AMANNS TRUCKING
1520 Dogwood Rd (73401-8588)
PHONE...................................580 226-2082
Karl Amanns, *Owner*
EMP: 1 EST: 1974
SALES (est): 68K **Privately Held**
SIC: 3537 Industrial trucks & tractors

(G-321)
KEITH F WALKER OIL GAS CO LLC (PA)
219 Stanley St Sw (73401-6305)
P.O. Box 1725 (73402-1725)
PHONE...................................580 223-1575
Allan Stacey, *CEO*
Mark Crain, *Manager*
Dale Walker, *Supervisor*
Keith F Walker, *Supervisor*
EMP: 4
SQ FT: 3,000
SALES (est): 4.9MM **Privately Held**
SIC: 1311 Crude petroleum production; natural gas production

(G-322)
KINGERY DRILLING COMPANY INC (PA)
210 W Broadway St (73401-6229)
P.O. Box 1588 (73402-1588)
PHONE...................................580 223-6823
David K Little, *President*
Doug Little, *Vice Pres*
Steve Rhines, *Admin Sec*
EMP: 6 EST: 1948
SQ FT: 5,000
SALES (est): 1.6MM **Privately Held**
WEB: www.kingerydrilling.com
SIC: 1311 Crude petroleum production

(G-323)
LABEL STABLE INC
102 W Main St (73401-6414)
PHONE...................................580 223-2037
Sam Matheny, *President*
Diana Matheny, *Vice Pres*
EMP: 5
SQ FT: 1,500
SALES (est): 400K **Privately Held**
SIC: 7336 2396 2395 Silk screen design; automotive & apparel trimmings; pleating & stitching

(G-324)
LEMCO ENTERPRISES INC
3204 Hale Rd (73401-3740)
P.O. Box 1407 (73402-1407)
PHONE...................................580 226-7808
Aaron Midden, *President*
EMP: 9
SQ FT: 43,000
SALES (est): 893.4K **Privately Held**
SIC: 7389 3841 Product sterilization service; surgical & medical instruments

(G-325)
LIBERTY MINERALS LLC (PA)
1405 4th Ave Nw (73401-2708)
PHONE...................................405 317-8107
Micah Ogden, *Vice Pres*
Tommy D Ogden, *Administration*
EMP: 6
SALES (est): 2.3MM **Privately Held**
WEB: www.libertymineralsllc.com
SIC: 1381 Drilling oil & gas wells

(G-326)
MACHINE PARTS & TOOL
Also Called: Mpt
620 Happy Trails Rd (73401-8391)
PHONE...................................580 389-5346
Darrell Driskill, *Owner*
Garland Driskill, *MIS Dir*
EMP: 1
SALES (est): 199K **Privately Held**
SIC: 5084 3599 3533 Oil well machinery, equipment & supplies; machine shop, jobbing & repair; oil & gas field machinery

(G-327)
MARK HENDRIX WELDING LLC
998 Memorial Rd (73401-8710)
PHONE...................................580 657-3716
Pauline Hendrix, *Owner*
EMP: 1
SALES (est): 85.9K **Privately Held**
SIC: 7692 Welding repair

(G-328)
MARTIN HOUSE CANDLE COMPANY
786 Comet Rd (73401-7438)
PHONE...................................580 504-1699
EMP: 1 EST: 2017
SALES (est): 39.6K **Privately Held**
SIC: 3999 Candles

(G-329)
MATIN HOUSE CANDLE COMPANY
4735 State Highway 199 (73401-0561)
PHONE...................................580 490-6500
EMP: 1 EST: 2015
SALES (est): 43.6K **Privately Held**
SIC: 3999 Candles

(G-330)
METAL BUILDING SERVICES
300 Case Cir (73401-0603)
PHONE...................................580 657-3339
Roy Neil, *Owner*
EMP: 6
SALES (est): 382.5K **Privately Held**
SIC: 3441 Fabricated structural metal

(G-331)
MICHELIN NORTH AMERICA INC
1101 Michelin Rd (73401-1085)
P.O. Box 1867 (73402-1867)
PHONE...................................580 226-1200
Mark Bruegel, *Plant Mgr*
Andy Hutson, *Engineer*
Todd Peacock, *Engineer*
Bernard Jarrousse, *Finance*
Gary Rheingans, *Manager*
EMP: 90
SALES (corp-wide): 1.1B **Privately Held**
SIC: 3011 Automobile tires, pneumatic
HQ: Michelin North America, Inc.
1 Parkway S
Greenville SC 29615
864 458-5000

(G-332)
MIDWEST COOLING TOWERS INC
601 Beetle Dr (73401-1192)
PHONE...................................580 389-5421
EMP: 1
SALES (corp-wide): 50MM **Privately Held**
SIC: 2499 Cooling towers, wood or wood & sheet metal combination
PA: Midwest Cooling Towers Inc.
1156 E Highway 19
Chickasha OK 73018
405 224-4622

(G-333)
MLB CONSULTING LLC
620 General Dr Ste 5 (73401-9233)
PHONE...................................580 504-8810
Andrea Wiseman, *Office Mgr*
EMP: 80
SALES (corp-wide): 6.4MM **Privately Held**
SIC: 1389 Oil consultants
PA: Mlb Consulting Llc
213 N Jefferson Ave
Elk City OK 73644
580 225-2717

(G-334)
MODESTO VINYL LETTERING INC
Also Called: Modesto Signs
604 W Broadway St (73401-4523)
PHONE...................................580 223-4262
John Sneltver, *President*
EMP: 4
SALES (est): 420.9K **Privately Held**
SIC: 3993 Signs & advertising specialties

(G-335)
MORE BOOM COMPANY
1823 Stanley St Sw (73401-3241)
PHONE...................................580 226-5303
Scott Dillon, *Manager*
EMP: 6 EST: 1999
SALES (est): 397.9K **Privately Held**
WEB: www.moreboom.com
SIC: 3531 Ladder ditchers, vertical boom or wheel

(G-336)
MORGAN DRILLING CO
Also Called: Lake Country Drilling
2308 Foxden Rd (73401-7772)
P.O. Box 1807, Lone Grove (73443-1807)
PHONE...................................580 657-3659
Max Morgan, *Owner*
EMP: 1 EST: 1971
SALES (est): 249.1K **Privately Held**
SIC: 1382 1781 Oil & gas exploration services; water well drilling

(G-337)
NEDLEY PUBLISHING CO
1045 15th Ave Nw (73401-1810)
P.O. Box 1565 (73402-1565)
PHONE...................................580 223-5980
Paula Reiter, *Manager*
EMP: 10
SALES (est): 969.8K **Privately Held**
WEB: www.nedleyhealthsolutions.com
SIC: 2731 Book publishing

(G-338)
OKLAHOMA PRIME ENERGY LLC
301 W Main St Ste 430 (73401-6322)
P.O. Box 1468 (73402-1468)
PHONE...................................580 226-2373
Craig Watkins, *Mng Member*
EMP: 4
SALES (est): 808.1K **Privately Held**
SIC: 1389 Gas field services; oil field services

(G-339)
ONLINE PACKAGING
575 Waterplant Rd (73401-9778)
PHONE...................................580 389-5373
Connie Denison, *Principal*
EMP: 1
SALES (est): 199.1K **Privately Held**
WEB: www.onlinepackaging.org
SIC: 2621 Wrapping & packaging papers

(G-340)
ORR OIL & GAS E & P INC
5 S Commerce St (73401-3937)
P.O. Box 915 (73402-0915)
PHONE...................................580 224-9290
Rick Orr, *President*
EMP: 2
SALES (est): 204.9K **Privately Held**
SIC: 1382 Oil & gas exploration services

(G-341)
OVERLAND FEDERAL LLC
534 Us Highway 77 (73401-2085)
P.O. Box 1947 (73402-1947)
PHONE...................................469 269-2303
Johnathan McAlister, *CFO*
Lionel Sullivan, *Info Tech Mgr*
EMP: 10
SQ FT: 1,100
SALES (est): 330.9K **Privately Held**
SIC: 1771 1611 2951 Concrete work; highway & street construction; asphalt paving mixtures & blocks

(G-342)
OVERLAND MATERIALS AND MFG INC
534 Us Highway 77 (73401-2085)
P.O. Box 1947 (73402-1947)
PHONE...................................580 223-8432
Michael S Voorhes, *President*
EMP: 20 EST: 1999
SQ FT: 5,000
SALES: 4MM
SALES (corp-wide): 42.4MM **Privately Held**
SIC: 2951 Asphalt paving mixtures & blocks
PA: Overland Corporation
534 Us Highway 77
Ardmore OK 73401
580 223-8432

(G-343)
PAK OILFIELD SERVICES LLC
179 Stone Bridge Ln (73401-5656)
PHONE...................................580 504-7049
Pepper Vanbuskirk, *Administration*
EMP: 2 EST: 2017
SALES (est): 109.4K **Privately Held**
SIC: 1389 Oil field services

(G-344)
PARK DENTAL RESEARCH CORP
2401 N Commerce St Ste D (73401-1311)
PHONE...................................580 226-0410
Ronald Bulard, *President*
EMP: 11 EST: 1974
SQ FT: 1,500
SALES (est): 628.3K **Privately Held**
WEB: www.parkdentalresearch.com
SIC: 3841 Surgical & medical instruments

(G-345)
PHILIP H BREWER
2236 Deese Rd (73401-7398)
PHONE...................................580 657-8029
Philip Brewer, *Principal*
EMP: 1
SALES (est): 57.7K **Privately Held**
SIC: 2741 Miscellaneous publishing

(G-346)
PLETCHER OIL COMPANY
473 Gateway Rd (73401-6517)
PHONE...................................580 657-4221
Donna Pletcher, *Partner*
Jack Pletcher, *Partner*
Myrna Pletcher, *Partner*
Raymond Pletcher, *Principal*
EMP: 2
SALES (est): 188.6K **Privately Held**
SIC: 1311 Crude petroleum production

(G-347)
PRONTO PRINT INC
1020 N Washington St (73401-6737)
PHONE...................................580 223-1612

GEOGRAPHIC SECTION
Ardmore - Carter County (G-377)

Stan Daugherty, *President*
Robert Rogers, *President*
Brandy Rogers, *Admin Sec*
EMP: 7
SQ FT: 500
SALES: 250K **Privately Held**
SIC: 2752 2791 2789 Commercial printing, offset; typesetting; bookbinding & related work

(G-348)
QUINTIN LITTLE COMPANY INC
2007 N Commerce St (73401-1268)
P.O. Box 1509 (73402-1509)
PHONE............................580 226-7600
Jud Little, *President*
Andrew Jackson, *General Mgr*
Chad Craddack, *Corp Secy*
Tracy Yarbrough, *Property Mgr*
Mike Vanlandingham, *Supervisor*
EMP: 32 **EST:** 1935
SQ FT: 6,000
SALES (est): 8.1MM **Privately Held**
SIC: 1311 Crude petroleum production; natural gas production

(G-349)
RESORT RV
26 Kingfisher Rd (73401-1396)
PHONE............................580 465-4428
Ron Elmore, *Principal*
EMP: 2
SALES (est): 114.5K **Privately Held**
SIC: 3792 Travel trailers & campers

(G-350)
ROCKLAND OIL CO
310 W Main St Ste 309 (73401-6319)
P.O. Box 1625 (73402-1625)
PHONE............................580 223-0960
John R North II, *President*
Susan Bisco, *Vice Pres*
Janice Rosenthal, *Vice Pres*
Eulela Cavins, *Admin Sec*
Tommy Craighead, *Admin Sec*
EMP: 6
SQ FT: 2,500
SALES (est): 556.4K **Privately Held**
SIC: 1311 Crude petroleum production

(G-351)
ROLCO ENERGY SERVICES LLC
308 Case Cir (73401-0603)
PHONE............................580 657-2602
EMP: 3
SALES (est): 48.7K **Privately Held**
WEB: www.rolcoenergyservices.com
SIC: 4911 1389 Electric services; oil & gas field services

(G-352)
RUBY INDUSTRIAL TECH LLC
2601 Crossroads Dr (73401-2574)
PHONE............................580 223-9301
Greg Reeve, *Branch Mgr*
EMP: 4
SALES (corp-wide): 735.6MM **Privately Held**
SIC: 3443 Boilers: industrial, power, or marine
PA: Ruby Industrial Technologies, Llc
1 Vision Way
Bloomfield CT 06002
860 687-5000

(G-353)
SEMMATERIALS LP
2500 Refinery Rd (73401-1669)
PHONE............................580 223-8010
Bobby Moore Jr, *Branch Mgr*
EMP: 7 **Publicly Held**
SIC: 2951 Asphalt paving mixtures & blocks
HQ: Semmaterials, L.P.
6520 S Yale Ave Ste 700
Tulsa OK 74136
918 524-8100

(G-354)
SIGN GYPSIES ARDMORE LLC
135 Chaparral St (73401-9467)
PHONE............................512 644-6976
Terri Garza, *Principal*
EMP: 1
SALES (est): 46K **Privately Held**
SIC: 3993 Signs & advertising specialties

(G-355)
SMITH CONSTRUCTION INC
2720 Refinery Rd (73401-1670)
P.O. Box 5214 (73403-0214)
PHONE............................580 226-2159
Bob Smith, *Owner*
EMP: 20
SQ FT: 1,000
SALES (est): 1.1MM **Privately Held**
SIC: 1389 Lease tanks, oil field: erecting, cleaning & repairing; oil field services

(G-356)
SOUTHSTAR ENERGY CORP
301 W Main St Ste 500 (73401-6322)
PHONE............................580 223-1553
Scott Holden, *President*
EMP: 2
SQ FT: 4,000
SALES (est): 150K **Privately Held**
SIC: 1389 Oil field services

(G-357)
SOUTHWEST SILICON TECH CORP
18 Interstate Dr (73401-9425)
PHONE............................580 223-5058
Robert Weeks, *CEO*
Harald Mynster, *Vice Pres*
Kelly Burke, *Treasurer*
Lynnea Hackney, *Human Res Mgr*
EMP: 35
SQ FT: 30,000
SALES (est): 7.3MM **Privately Held**
SIC: 3674 Silicon wafers, chemically doped

(G-358)
SPARTAN RESOURCES LLC
216 1st Ave Sw (73401-6310)
P.O. Box 2266 (73402-2266)
PHONE............................580 226-2400
Phil Martin, *Manager*
EMP: 4
SALES (corp-wide): 839.1K **Privately Held**
SIC: 1382 Oil & gas exploration services
PA: Spartan Resources L.L.C.
4013 Nw Expwy St Ste 690
Oklahoma City OK 73116
405 843-0420

(G-359)
SPREKELMEYER PRINTING COMPANY
12 C St Sw (73401-6314)
P.O. Box 1627 (73402-1627)
PHONE............................580 223-5100
Donald Black Jr, *Owner*
Black Don, *Sales Staff*
Marianna Bennett, *Office Mgr*
Jason Sears, *Graphic Designe*
EMP: 9
SQ FT: 9,000
SALES (est): 500K **Privately Held**
WEB: www.sprekelmeyer.com
SIC: 2752 2791 2789 2759 Commercial printing, offset; typesetting; bookbinding & related work; commercial printing

(G-360)
SPRING DRILLING CORP
911 W Broadway St (73401-4567)
P.O. Box 1788 (73402-1788)
PHONE............................580 226-3800
Harry A Spring, *President*
EMP: 4
SALES (est): 392K **Privately Held**
SIC: 1381 Drilling oil & gas wells

(G-361)
SPRING HARRY A GEOLOGICAL ENGR
Also Called: Engineering Consultant
911 W Broadway St (73401-4567)
PHONE............................580 226-1910
Harry A Spring, *Owner*
EMP: 4
SQ FT: 1,200
SALES (est): 276.3K **Privately Held**
SIC: 8711 1311 Consulting engineer; crude petroleum production

(G-362)
SSB PRODUCTION LLC
Also Called: Bigbie, Bane CPA
1505 N Commerce St # 201 (73401-1863)
P.O. Box 998 (73402-0998)
PHONE............................580 226-7000
Bane Bigbie,
Jess Storts Jr,
EMP: 3
SALES (est): 360K **Privately Held**
SIC: 1311 Crude petroleum & natural gas

(G-363)
STANTON SAND & GRAVEL INC
1887 Memorial Rd (73401-6665)
PHONE............................580 229-3353
Brent Perkins, *Owner*
EMP: 2
SALES (est): 70.6K **Privately Held**
SIC: 1442 Construction sand & gravel

(G-364)
SUGAR PILLS APPAREL
202 E Main St (73401-7017)
PHONE............................580 277-0231
Josh Boyd, *Owner*
EMP: 4
SALES (est): 210.6K **Privately Held**
SIC: 2732 Book printing

(G-365)
T C CRAIGHEAD & COMPANY
310 W Main St Ste 311 (73401-6319)
P.O. Box 576 (73402-0576)
PHONE............................580 223-7470
Tommy C Craighead, *President*
Tommy Don Craighead, *Vice Pres*
Mel Van Craighead, *Vice Pres*
Billye Joy Craighead, *Treasurer*
Lana Jayne Martin, *Assistant*
EMP: 15
SALES: 20MM **Privately Held**
SIC: 1311 6792 Crude petroleum production; oil leases, buying & selling on own account

(G-366)
TDP ENERGY COMPANY LLC
16 E St Se (73401-8038)
P.O. Box 849 (73402-0849)
PHONE............................580 226-6700
John D Gibbs, *Mng Member*
Diane Allen,
EMP: 14
SALES (est): 10.9MM **Privately Held**
SIC: 1382 Oil & gas exploration services

(G-367)
TEXOMA SHEDS
1411 4th Ave Nw (73401-2708)
PHONE............................580 223-0000
EMP: 2
SALES (est): 127.2K **Privately Held**
SIC: 3448 Prefabricated metal buildings

(G-368)
THUNDER OIL & GAS LLC
911 W Broadway St (73401-4567)
P.O. Box 1788 (73402-1788)
PHONE............................580 226-3800
EMP: 3
SALES (est): 290.6K **Privately Held**
SIC: 1382 Oil & gas exploration services

(G-369)
THURMOND-MCGLOTHLIN LLC
34 Broadlawn Vlg (73401)
PHONE............................580 223-9632
Phil Floyd, *Manager*
EMP: 8
SALES (corp-wide): 38.4MM **Privately Held**
SIC: 1389 Gas field services
PA: Thurmond-Mcglothlin, Llc
1428 N Banks St
Pampa TX 79065
806 665-5700

(G-370)
TJK MOLDED PRODUCTS LLC (PA)
1649 Fernwood Rd (73401-8693)
PHONE............................409 200-1007
Ken Klingbail, *CEO*
Tim Klingbail, *Mfg Mgr*
EMP: 10
SQ FT: 15,000
SALES: 1.5MM **Privately Held**
WEB: www.tjkmp.com
SIC: 3061 Mechanical rubber goods

(G-371)
TJK MOLDED PRODUCTS LLC
1405 4th Ave Nw Ste 103 (73401-2708)
PHONE............................409 200-1007
Ken Klingbail, *CEO*
EMP: 1
SALES (corp-wide): 1.5MM **Privately Held**
SIC: 3061 Mechanical rubber goods
PA: Tjk Molded Products, Llc
1649 Fernwood Rd
Ardmore OK 73401
409 200-1007

(G-372)
TNT SAND & GRAVEL LLC
7189 Prairie Valley Rd (73401-0653)
PHONE............................580 277-0640
Eric Taliaferro, *Administration*
E Taliaferro, *Administration*
EMP: 3
SALES (est): 299.1K **Privately Held**
SIC: 1442 Construction sand & gravel

(G-373)
TPI PETROLEUM INC
E Hwy 33 Byp (73401)
P.O. Box 188 (73402-0188)
PHONE............................580 221-6288
Martin Hawkins, *Branch Mgr*
EMP: 200
SALES (corp-wide): 108.3B **Publicly Held**
SIC: 2911 1311 Petroleum refining; crude petroleum & natural gas
HQ: Tpi Petroleum, Inc
6000 N Loop 1604 W
San Antonio TX 78249
210 592-2000

(G-374)
TRIPLEDEE DRILLING CO INC (PA)
Also Called: State Oil Company
100 W Main St (73401-6414)
P.O. Box 1888 (73402-1888)
PHONE............................580 223-8181
Thomas F Dunlap, *President*
Nancy Dunlap, *Admin Sec*
EMP: 6 **EST:** 1951
SQ FT: 6,000
SALES (est): 1MM **Privately Held**
WEB: www.tripledeeoperating.com
SIC: 1311 Crude petroleum production; natural gas production

(G-375)
TRIPOWER RESOURCES LLC
16 E St Sw Ste 200 (73401-4750)
P.O. Box 849 (73402-0849)
PHONE............................580 226-6700
John D Gibbs, *Mng Member*
Diane Allen,
EMP: 13
SQ FT: 13,440
SALES (est): 9.9MM **Privately Held**
SIC: 1311 Crude petroleum production

(G-376)
US FERROICS LLC
123 Case Cir (73401-0643)
PHONE............................601 763-1058
EMP: 2
SALES (est): 106K **Privately Held**
SIC: 3559 Special industry machinery

(G-377)
VALERO REFINING-TEXAS LP
718 Cameron St (73401)
PHONE............................580 223-0534
Charlene Archibeque, *Principal*
Patrick Williams, *Engineer*
Charles Gay, *Manager*
EMP: 205
SALES (corp-wide): 108.3B **Publicly Held**
SIC: 2911 Gasoline blending plants

Ardmore - Carter County (G-378)

HQ: Valero Refining-Texas, L.P.
1 Valero Way
San Antonio TX 78249
210 345-2000

(G-378)
VAN EATON C W
Also Called: Vaneaton & Vaneaton
108 D St Sw (73401)
P.O. Box 1356 (73402-1356)
PHONE..................580 223-4374
C W Van Eaton, *Owner*
EMP: 2
SALES (est): 127.2K **Privately Held**
SIC: 1311 Crude petroleum production

(G-379)
WALLIS PRINTING INC
28 N Washington St (73401-7013)
PHONE..................580 223-7473
Steve Hoke, *President*
Susan Pilgrim, *Vice Pres*
EMP: 4
SQ FT: 3,500
SALES: 250K **Privately Held**
SIC: 2752 2796 2791 2789 Commercial printing, offset; platemaking services; typesetting; bookbinding & related work; commercial printing; automotive & apparel trimmings

(G-380)
WESOK DRILLING CORP
911 W Broadway St (73401-4567)
PHONE..................580 226-2450
EMP: 2 **EST:** 2013
SALES (est): 120K **Privately Held**
SIC: 3541 Mfg Machine Tools-Cutting

(G-381)
WEST VALBEL CORPORATION
10 W Main St (73401-6516)
P.O. Box 428 (73402-0428)
PHONE..................580 223-3494
Gerome M Westheimer Sr, *President*
Gerome M Westheimer Jr, *Vice Pres*
EMP: 3
SQ FT: 500
SALES (est): 300K **Privately Held**
SIC: 1311 Crude petroleum production; natural gas production

(G-382)
WILDHORSE OIL & GAS CORP
301 W Main St Ste 540 (73401-6322)
P.O. Box 1604 (73402-1604)
PHONE..................580 223-0936
S Neil Sisson Jr, *Principal*
EMP: 2
SALES (est): 180K **Privately Held**
SIC: 1311 Crude petroleum & natural gas

(G-383)
XTO ENERGY INC
15948 Us Highway 77 (73401-6946)
PHONE..................580 653-3200
Mark Reichardt, *Engineer*
Dan Johns, *Branch Mgr*
EMP: 78
SALES (corp-wide): 264.9B **Publicly Held**
SIC: 1311 Crude petroleum production
HQ: Xto Energy Inc.
110 W 7th St
Fort Worth TX 76102

(G-384)
ZKC WELDING
538 Case Cir (73401-0659)
P.O. Box 994, Lone Grove (73443-0994)
PHONE..................580 220-7685
Steve Ellis,
EMP: 11
SALES (est): 2.1MM **Privately Held**
SIC: 3441 Fabricated structural metal

Arkoma
Le Flore County

(G-385)
H ROCKIN INDUSTRIES INC
113 Oak St (74901-4007)
PHONE..................479 285-1766
Jeff Humphreville, *CEO*
EMP: 3
SALES (est): 240K **Privately Held**
SIC: 3999 Manufacturing industries

(G-386)
MANN SOLVENTS INC
100 Phoenix Ave (74901-4019)
P.O. Box 6764, Fort Smith AR (72906-6764)
PHONE..................918 626-3733
EMP: 4
SQ FT: 4,000
SALES (est): 335.8K **Privately Held**
SIC: 2851 5198 Mfg Paints/Allied Products Whol Paints/Varnishes

Arnett
Ellis County

(G-387)
ELLIS COUNTY CAPITAL
Also Called: Gage Record
323 E Renfrow Ave (73832)
P.O. Box 236 (73832-0236)
PHONE..................580 885-7788
Jerry Denson, *Partner*
Anita Kay Denson, *Partner*
EMP: 2 **EST:** 1982
SQ FT: 2,500
SALES: 100K **Privately Held**
SIC: 2711 2752 2791 2789 Newspapers: publishing only, not printed on site; commercial printing, offset; typesetting; bookbinding & related work; commercial printing

(G-388)
QES PRESSURE CONTROL LLC
14658 Us Highway 60 (73832-1793)
PHONE..................580 885-7885
Mark Clingenpeel, *Branch Mgr*
EMP: 30
SALES (corp-wide): 1.1B **Privately Held**
WEB: www.quintanaenergyservices.com
SIC: 1381 Drilling oil & gas wells
HQ: Qes Pressure Control Llc
4500 Se 59th St
Oklahoma City OK 73135

Asher
Pottawatomie County

(G-389)
GEORGE B HUGHES
43138 Tooley Rd (74826-3601)
P.O. Box 165 (74826-0165)
PHONE..................405 784-5575
George Hughes, *Owner*
Nancy Hughes, *Co-Owner*
EMP: 2
SALES (est): 231.4K **Privately Held**
SIC: 1381 Drilling oil & gas wells

(G-390)
HOLT TRAILER MFG & SALES LLC
901 Us Highway 177 (74826-6601)
PHONE..................405 784-2233
Jennifer Holt, *Mng Member*
EMP: 10
SQ FT: 13,500
SALES (est): 1MM **Privately Held**
SIC: 3799 5599 Trailers & trailer equipment; utility trailers

(G-391)
MARCY A SHARP
41423 Saint Louis Rd (74826-4219)
PHONE..................405 615-9879
Marcy A Sharp, *Principal*
EMP: 1
SALES (est): 141.6K **Privately Held**
SIC: 3553 Woodworking machinery

(G-392)
MICHAEL ALLAN SHARP
Also Called: More Than Wood Sawmill
41423 Saint Louis Rd (74826-4219)
PHONE..................405 615-3771
Michael Sharp, *Owner*
EMP: 2
SALES (est): 179.1K **Privately Held**
SIC: 3553 Woodworking machinery

(G-393)
OKLAHOMA AZTEC CO INC
44701 Tooley Rd (74826-3602)
PHONE..................405 784-2475
Richmond H Hill, *President*
Bryan Hill, *Vice Pres*
Connie Spicer, *Admin Sec*
EMP: 7
SQ FT: 700
SALES (est): 1.1MM **Privately Held**
SIC: 5211 1442 Sand & gravel; construction sand & gravel

(G-394)
PERK DYNAMICS LLC
37500 Us Highway 177 (74826-6615)
PHONE..................405 585-2520
John Sharpley,
EMP: 6 **EST:** 2011
SQ FT: 3,000
SALES (est): 400K **Privately Held**
SIC: 7372 Business oriented computer software

Atoka
Atoka County

(G-395)
A & B PRINTING & OFFICE SUPPLY
1397 S Mississippi Ave (74525-3225)
PHONE..................580 889-5103
Robert Benson, *Owner*
Lois Benson, *Co-Owner*
EMP: 2
SALES (est): 70K **Privately Held**
SIC: 5943 2752 2791 Office forms & supplies; lithographing on metal; typesetting

(G-396)
ARTWORKS
467 E A St (74525-2025)
P.O. Box 402, Coalgate (74538-0402)
PHONE..................580 927-9094
Lee N Jackson, *Owner*
EMP: 1
SALES (est): 29K **Privately Held**
SIC: 3993 Signs & advertising specialties

(G-397)
ATOKA TRAILER AND MFG LLC
677 S Jefferson Hwy (74525-6864)
P.O. Box 569 (74525-0569)
PHONE..................580 889-7270
Caleb Eaves, *Sales Staff*
Ronny Eaves, *Mng Member*
Billy Eaves,
EMP: 33
SQ FT: 80,000
SALES (est): 6.6MM **Privately Held**
SIC: 3715 Semitrailers for truck tractors

(G-398)
ATOKA WELDING & FABRICATION
477 N Jefferson Hwy (74525-6817)
PHONE..................580 889-2534
James Herring, *Principal*
EMP: 2
SALES (est): 159K **Privately Held**
SIC: 7692 Welding repair

(G-399)
B & B LOG & LUMBER CO INC
8592 E Highway 3 (74525-4807)
PHONE..................580 889-2438
Ray Belcher, *President*
▲ **EMP:** 14
SALES (est): 1MM **Privately Held**
SIC: 5031 5082 2426 2411 Lumber: rough, dressed & finished; construction & mining machinery; hardwood dimension & flooring mills; logging

(G-400)
BOXEL LLC
3216 Nw Industrial Rd (74525-4382)
PHONE..................580 239-0819
Jonathan Inglis, *Opers Mgr*
James Lahman, *Officer*
EMP: 1
SALES (est): 214.2K **Privately Held**
SIC: 5211 3444 Closets, interiors & accessories; sheet metalwork

(G-401)
C-ALL MANUFACTURING INC
Also Called: Nuttall Trailers
472 S Jefferson Hwy (74525-9468)
P.O. Box 236 (74525-0236)
PHONE..................580 889-3351
Carl Henderson, *President*
EMP: 21
SQ FT: 100,000
SALES (est): 3.8MM **Privately Held**
SIC: 3715 Truck trailers

(G-402)
CHARLES TIGERT WELDING SH
151 W Highway 7 (74525-4213)
PHONE..................580 889-3558
EMP: 1 **EST:** 2010
SALES (est): 43K **Privately Held**
SIC: 7692 Welding Repair

(G-403)
CHOCTAW MFG & DEV CORP
Also Called: Choctaw Nation Fabricators
357 N Hill Rd (74525)
PHONE..................580 326-8365
Stephen R Benefield, *Branch Mgr*
EMP: 75 **Privately Held**
SIC: 3441 Fabricated structural metal
HQ: Choctaw Manufacturing & Development Corp.
203 Choctaw Industrial Dr
Hugo OK 74743
580 326-8365

(G-404)
D&S DIRTWORK AND SMALL EQP
3351 E Allison Rd (74525-7282)
PHONE..................580 485-8933
Robert S Richie, *Manager*
EMP: 1
SALES (est): 71.4K **Privately Held**
SIC: 3531 Rakes, land clearing: mechanical

(G-405)
DIAMOND ATTACHMENTS LLC
4381 S Mississippi Ave A (74525-6810)
PHONE..................580 889-3366
Pat Loftis, *Owner*
Ronnie Cochran, *Owner*
Shirley Gregory, *Admin Sec*
EMP: 45 **EST:** 2006
SALES (est): 7MM **Privately Held**
WEB: www.diamondattachments.com
SIC: 7353 3531 Heavy construction equipment rental; backhoes, tractors, cranes, plows & similar equipment

(G-406)
DIAMOND MANUFACTURING INC
Also Called: Diamond Catchment
2801 S Mkokippi Ave Ste A (74525)
P.O. Box 270 (74525-0270)
PHONE..................580 889-6202
Ronnie J Cochran, *President*
Pat Loftis, *Vice Pres*
Craig Cochran, *Info Tech Mgr*
EMP: 50
SQ FT: 25,000
SALES (est): 9MM **Privately Held**
SIC: 3531 3545 Construction machinery attachments; machine tool accessories

(G-407)
DIAMOND WELDING MFG
Highway 69 S (74525)
PHONE..................580 889-7767
EMP: 1
SALES (est): 55.9K **Privately Held**
SIC: 7692 Welding Repair

(G-408)
DOLESE BROS CO
2791 N Highway 69 (74525-3515)
PHONE..................580 889-6033
Robert Stellwell, *Manager*

EMP: 3
SALES (corp-wide): 8.5MM **Privately Held**
SIC: 3273 Ready-mixed concrete
PA: Dolese Bros. Co.
20 Nw 13th St
Oklahoma City OK 73103
405 235-2311

(G-409)
EAVES MANUFACTURING INC
677 S Jefferson Hwy (74525-6864)
PHONE.................580 889-3530
EMP: 1
SALES (est): 39.6K **Privately Held**
SIC: 3999 Manufacturing industries

(G-410)
EAVES STONES PRODUCTS
Also Called: Quality Stone
925 W 13th St (74525-3403)
P.O. Box 419 (74525-0419)
PHONE.................580 889-7858
David Eaves, *Partner*
Larry Eaves, *Partner*
Ray Eaves, *Partner*
EMP: 12
SQ FT: 4,400
SALES (est): 1.4MM **Privately Held**
SIC: 3272 3281 1411 Building stone, artificial: concrete; cut stone & stone products; dimension stone

(G-411)
EDDIE BROWN
718 W 13th St (74525-3711)
PHONE.................580 889-1506
Eddie Brown, *Owner*
Debbie Brown, *Owner*
EMP: 13
SALES: 500K **Privately Held**
SIC: 6512 5999 7692 Nonresidential building operators; monuments & tombstones; welding repair

(G-412)
EVANS TOOL CO INC
301 S Bond St (74525-4059)
PHONE.................580 889-5770
Thomas Evans, *President*
Caleen Evans, *Vice Pres*
EMP: 2
SALES (est): 156.3K **Privately Held**
SIC: 3423 Hand & edge tools

(G-413)
HWS HAMILTON WELDING SVC LLC
6757 S Sawmill Rd (74525-4150)
PHONE.................580 889-1725
Garrett Hamilton, *Principal*
EMP: 1
SALES (est): 33.6K **Privately Held**
SIC: 7692 Welding repair

(G-414)
HYATT LADONA
9398 S Sawmill Rd (74525-4176)
PHONE.................580 889-0199
Ladona Hyatt, *Owner*
EMP: 1
SALES (est): 54.8K **Privately Held**
SIC: 2254 Knit underwear mills

(G-415)
HYDRO-LINK CONTAINMENT LLC
4757 S Crestview Rd (74525-4665)
PHONE.................580 889-4701
Tony Shawn Hauff, *Principal*
EMP: 6
SALES (est): 936.2K **Privately Held**
SIC: 3443 Reactor containment vessels, metal plate

(G-416)
JONES & JACKSON CABINETS
551 N Texhoma Ave (74525-1730)
PHONE.................580 889-8978
Dave Jackson, *Owner*
EMP: 1
SALES (est): 118.3K **Privately Held**
SIC: 2434 Wood kitchen cabinets

(G-417)
K&R BACKHOE AND DIRT SVCS LLC
4618 E Boggy Depot Rd (74525-4657)
PHONE.................580 239-8630
James Ridgway, *Principal*
EMP: 1 **EST:** 2016
SALES (est): 60K **Privately Held**
SIC: 3531 Backhoes

(G-418)
KOBE EXPRESS LLC (PA)
544 N Hickory St (74525-1689)
PHONE.................580 889-2420
Tina La, *Principal*
EMP: 4
SALES (est): 343.2K **Privately Held**
SIC: 2741 Miscellaneous publishing

(G-419)
MID-AMERICA INDUS COATINGS LLC
4757 S Crestview Rd (74525-4665)
PHONE.................580 239-9003
Casey Hauff, *Principal*
Marcus Logan, *Opers Mgr*
Jared Hauff, *Manager*
EMP: 5
SALES (est): 230.9K **Privately Held**
WEB: www.midaic.com
SIC: 3479 Coating of metals & formed products

(G-420)
MULLINS SIGN SHOP
2700 S Mississippi Ave (74525-4064)
PHONE.................580 889-4772
Jimmy Mullins, *Principal*
EMP: 1
SALES (est): 60K **Privately Held**
SIC: 3993 Electric signs

(G-421)
PRESS GO
107 N Ohio Ave (74525-2051)
P.O. Box 1302 (74525-6302)
PHONE.................580 889-2399
EMP: 2 **EST:** 2010
SALES (est): 72K **Privately Held**
SIC: 2741 Misc Publishing

(G-422)
PRUITT OIL COMPANY LLC
1171 S Mississippi Ave (74525-2867)
P.O. Box 58 (74525-0058)
PHONE.................580 889-2413
Larry Pruitt, *President*
Katie Pruitt, *Corp Secy*
EMP: 4
SQ FT: 5,000
SALES (est): 910.5K **Privately Held**
SIC: 2911 2869 Oils, fuel; fuels

(G-423)
SHOPS OF STANDING ROCK INC
Also Called: R & B Sports
2783 S Mississippi Ave (74525-4019)
P.O. Box 1466 (74525-6466)
PHONE.................580 364-0834
Robb Alberta, *President*
EMP: 5
SQ FT: 10,000
SALES (est): 556.3K **Privately Held**
SIC: 2396 2395 Screen printing on fabric articles; embroidery & art needlework

(G-424)
SOUTHEAST MACHINE INC
4375 S Mississippi Ave (74525-6810)
P.O. Box 270 (74525-0270)
PHONE.................580 889-6418
Ronnie J Cochran, *President*
Randy Thompson, *General Mgr*
Pat Loftis, *Vice Pres*
Jason Thompson, *Prdtn Mgr*
EMP: 20
SQ FT: 25,500
SALES (est): 3.4MM **Privately Held**
SIC: 3599 Machine shop, jobbing & repair

(G-425)
TOP O TEXAS OILFIELD SERVICES
1353 W Highway 7 (74525-4215)
PHONE.................806 662-5206
Jerrod Imeo, *Branch Mgr*
EMP: 1 **Privately Held**
WEB: www.topotexas.net
SIC: 1389 Oil field services
PA: Top O Texas Oilfield Services Ltd
408 S Price Rd
Pampa TX 79065

(G-426)
TRINITY SCRNPRNTNG/DMOND AWRDS
5692 S Mockingbird Ln (74525-6860)
PHONE.................580 364-3752
EMP: 2
SALES (est): 83.9K **Privately Held**
SIC: 2752 Commercial printing, lithographic

(G-427)
WILLOW CREEK CO LLC
5563 S Katy Rd (74525-7423)
PHONE.................580 239-9549
Shannon Wilson, *Principal*
EMP: 2
SALES (est): 115.1K **Privately Held**
SIC: 3999 Candles

Atwood
Hughes County

(G-428)
BROWNS SAWMILL
4361 N 377 (74827-9724)
PHONE.................918 617-7935
William H Brown, *Co-Owner*
William L Brown, *Co-Owner*
Melissa Jennings, *Office Mgr*
EMP: 5
SALES (est): 248.2K **Privately Held**
SIC: 2421 Custom sawmill; specialty sawmill products

Bache
Pittsburg County

(G-429)
BAKER PETROLITE INC
2491 N Highway 69 Byp (74501)
PHONE.................918 302-0490
James Oden, *Principal*
EMP: 2
SALES (est): 137.2K **Privately Held**
SIC: 1389 Oil field services

(G-430)
DURA-LINE CORPORATION
10 Steven Taylor Blvd (74501-8603)
PHONE.................918 302-0330
David Leeper, *Manager*
EMP: 49 **Privately Held**
SIC: 3084 Plastics pipe
HQ: Dura-Line Corporation
11400 Parkside Dr Ste 300
Knoxville TN 37934
865 218-3460

(G-431)
DUTTON WELDING & CONSTRUC
2831 N Main St (74501-2629)
P.O. Box 3201, McAlester (74502-3201)
PHONE.................918 420-5688
EMP: 5
SALES (est): 502.7K **Privately Held**
SIC: 7692 Welding repair

Balko
Beaver County

(G-432)
INTEGRITY TRCKG CNSTR SVCS INC
Rr 2 Box 17 (73931-9611)
Rural Route Box 17
PHONE.................580 361-2387
Larry R Zielke, *President*
Matt Underdown, *Vice Pres*
EMP: 23
SALES (est): 2.9MM **Privately Held**
SIC: 1389 1611 Oil field services; gravel or dirt road construction

(G-433)
WATONGA CHEESE PLANT
Rr 2 Box 114 (73931-9657)
PHONE.................580 623-5915
Kasey Cowan, *Owner*
EMP: 8
SQ FT: 8,000
SALES: 200K **Privately Held**
SIC: 5451 2022 Cheese; cheese, natural & processed

Barnsdall
Osage County

(G-434)
BAKER HGHES OLFLD OPRTIONS LLC
601 S 5th St (74002)
PHONE.................918 847-3296
C Kelley, *Branch Mgr*
EMP: 5 **Privately Held**
SIC: 1389 Oil field services
PA: Baker Hughes Oilfield Operations Llc
2001 Rankin Rd
Houston TX 77073

(G-435)
BAKER PETROLITE LLC
New Phase Technologies
800 Birch Lake Rd (74002-5230)
P.O. Box 669 (74002-0669)
PHONE.................918 847-2522
Frank Trailor, *Branch Mgr*
EMP: 125
SQ FT: 7,000 **Privately Held**
SIC: 2911 2842 2821 Mineral waxes, natural; specialty cleaning, polishes & sanitation goods; plastics materials & resins
HQ: Baker Petrolite Llc
12645 W Airport Blvd
Sugar Land TX 77478
281 276-5400

(G-436)
BARNSDALL MEAT PROCESSORS INC
34 Florence Ave (74002-5193)
PHONE.................918 847-2814
Eddie Spears, *President*
Branden Spears, *Vice Pres*
Barbara Spears, *Admin Sec*
EMP: 2
SALES (est): 166.2K **Privately Held**
SIC: 2011 5421 5147 2013 Meat packing plants; meat markets, including freezer provisioners; meats, fresh; sausages & other prepared meats

(G-437)
JBK WELL SERVICE LLC
8689 State Highway 11 (74002-5104)
PHONE.................918 695-6062
Joe Bob Kelley,
EMP: 13
SALES (est): 266.2K **Privately Held**
SIC: 1381 Drilling oil & gas wells

(G-438)
MARMAC RESOURCES COMPANY
S Of Hwy 99 E 11 Jct (74002)
PHONE.................918 846-2293
Paul Hopkins, *Manager*
EMP: 4
SALES (corp-wide): 50K **Privately Held**
SIC: 1381 Drilling oil & gas wells
PA: Marmac Resources Company
5143 W Sunset Blvd
Los Angeles CA
323 666-1916

(G-439)
PERFORMANCE OPERATING CO LLC
3993 State Hiwy 123 (74002)
P.O. Box 628 (74002-0628)
PHONE.................918 847-3830

Barnsdall - Osage County (G-440)

J Scott Ducharme,
Dan Carone,
EMP: 15
SALES (est): 3.2MM **Privately Held**
SIC: 1311 Crude petroleum production

(G-440)
PERFORMANCE PETROLEUM CO
Ne Cor Intrs Hwy 11123 (74002)
P.O. Box 628 (74002-0628)
PHONE..................................918 847-2531
J Scott Ducharme, *President*
Dan Carone, *Vice Pres*
EMP: 45
SQ FT: 1,200
SALES (est): 8.3MM **Privately Held**
SIC: 1311 Crude petroleum & natural gas production

(G-441)
SMITH PETROLEUM LLC
401 W Main St (74002)
P.O. Box 134 (74002-0134)
PHONE..................................918 638-1301
Andy Smith,
EMP: 4
SQ FT: 6,000
SALES: 400K **Privately Held**
SIC: 1389 Pumping of oil & gas wells; oil field services

(G-442)
WARREN AMERICAN OIL COMPANY
7326 County Road 2420 (74002-5064)
PHONE..................................918 846-2294
EMP: 1
SALES (corp-wide): 4.3MM **Privately Held**
SIC: 1311 Crude petroleum & natural gas production
PA: Warren American Oil Company
6585 S Yale Ave Ste 800
Tulsa OK 74136
918 481-7990

Bartlesville
Washington County

(G-443)
4K SPOOLING BANDING SALES & SE
1740 Se Washington Blvd (74006-6713)
PHONE..................................918 766-0001
Shelley Coster, *Owner*
EMP: 10
SALES (est): 1.5MM **Privately Held**
SIC: 1389 Bailing, cleaning, swabbing & treating of wells

(G-444)
ABB INC
Also Called: Total Flow Products Div
7051 Industrial Blvd (74006-6036)
PHONE..................................918 338-4888
Bob Rutledge, *Manager*
EMP: 140
SALES (corp-wide): 27.9B **Privately Held**
SIC: 3823 3625 3571 Controllers for process variables, all types; relays & industrial controls; electronic computers
HQ: Abb, Inc.
305 Gregson Dr
Cary NC 27511

(G-445)
ALL AMERICAN WROUGHT IRON
525 S Choctaw Ave (74003-4021)
PHONE..................................918 213-9949
Donna Campos, *Principal*
EMP: 1
SALES (est): 42.8K **Privately Held**
SIC: 3269 Pottery products

(G-446)
AMERICAN FIBER INDUSTRIES
1560 Industrial Blvd (74006-6035)
PHONE..................................918 335-6100
Juana Martinez, *Principal*
EMP: 2
SALES (est): 131.5K **Privately Held**
SIC: 3999 Manufacturing industries

(G-447)
AMERICAN ZINC RECYCLING CORP
Also Called: Equidae
Hwy 123 (74005)
P.O. Box 579 (74005-0579)
PHONE..................................918 336-7100
Tom Johnson, *Branch Mgr*
EMP: 52 **Privately Held**
SIC: 3339 2819 1031 Zinc refining (primary), including slabs & dust; industrial inorganic chemicals; lead & zinc ores
HQ: American Zinc Recycling Corp.
4955 Stbnvlle Pike Ste 40
Pittsburgh PA 15205

(G-448)
ARCHITECTURAL FABRICATORS INC
1034 Ne Washington Blvd (74006-1221)
PHONE..................................918 331-0393
Mike Proctor, *President*
Howard Gilbert, *Vice Pres*
Andrew Proctor, *Vice Pres*
Jennifer Weabe, *Manager*
EMP: 25
SQ FT: 12,000
SALES (est): 5.1MM **Privately Held**
SIC: 3444 Metal flooring & siding

(G-449)
ARTISTIC APPAREL
401 S Dewey Ave Ste 212 (74003-3537)
PHONE..................................918 338-0038
Greg Barber, *Principal*
EMP: 2
SALES (est): 168K **Privately Held**
SIC: 2759 5621 5949 Screen printing; women's clothing stores; sewing, needlework & piece goods

(G-450)
BANGS
128 W 2nd St (74003-2603)
PHONE..................................918 338-2339
Kimberly Vander, *Principal*
EMP: 2
SALES (est): 116.7K **Privately Held**
SIC: 3999 Hair curlers, designed for beauty parlors

(G-451)
BARTLESVILLE CUSTOM CABINETS
398681 W 2400 Rd (74006-0243)
PHONE..................................918 440-5981
Brandon Hough, *Manager*
EMP: 1
SALES (est): 99K **Privately Held**
SIC: 2434 Wood kitchen cabinets

(G-452)
BARTLESVILLE PRINT SHOP
120 E 2nd St (74003-2601)
PHONE..................................918 336-6070
R H Geurin, *Owner*
EMP: 4
SQ FT: 5,600
SALES (est): 250K **Privately Held**
SIC: 2752 2791 2789 2396 Commercial printing, offset; typesetting; bookbinding & related work; automotive & apparel trimmings

(G-453)
BARTLESVILLE REDI-MIX INC
1500 Tuxedo Blvd (74006-4111)
P.O. Box 30, Ponca City (74602-0030)
PHONE..................................580 765-6693
Lloyd I Evans, *President*
Jackie E Boahn, *Vice Pres*
Glen E Nickles, *Vice Pres*
Linda J Brown, *Treasurer*
Andy Roberts, *Advisor*
EMP: 10
SQ FT: 2,000
SALES: 52.7K
SALES (corp-wide): 100.1MM **Privately Held**
SIC: 3273 Ready-mixed concrete
PA: Evans & Associates Enterprises, Inc.
3320 N 14th St
Ponca City OK 74601
580 765-6693

(G-454)
BIOSPEC PRODUCTS INC
280 N Virginia Ave (74003-2438)
P.O. Box 788 (74005-0788)
PHONE..................................918 336-3363
T R Hopkins, *President*
Sharon Hopkins, *Vice Pres*
EMP: 7
SALES (est): 1.2MM **Privately Held**
SIC: 3821 3829 Laboratory equipment: fume hoods, distillation racks, etc.; measuring & controlling devices

(G-455)
BISON MATERIALS LLC
1800 W 14th St (74003-3717)
PHONE..................................918 333-2266
Spencer Hopper, *Info Tech Mgr*
Spencer G Hopper,
EMP: 8
SALES (est): 1.1MM **Privately Held**
SIC: 1411 Limestone, dimension-quarrying

(G-456)
BLAINE EXPLORATION LTD
1821 Arbor Dr (74006-7004)
PHONE..................................918 333-2115
Blaine Hanks, *President*
EMP: 1
SALES (est): 143.6K **Privately Held**
SIC: 1382 Oil & gas exploration services

(G-457)
BMC ENTERPRISE LLC
3365 County Road 2706 (74003-1294)
P.O. Box 293 (74005-0293)
PHONE..................................918 336-4431
EMP: 3
SALES (est): 225K **Privately Held**
SIC: 1389 Oil/Gas Field Services

(G-458)
BULLSEYE OPERATING LLC
301 Se Adams Blvd (74003-3613)
P.O. Box 518 (74005-0518)
PHONE..................................918 336-7898
Robert M Kane,
EMP: 1
SALES (est): 285.5K **Privately Held**
WEB: www.bullseyeoperating.com
SIC: 1311 Crude petroleum production

(G-459)
BYFIELD WELDING
3401 Kansas Ln (74006-1247)
PHONE..................................918 333-8100
Toll Free:..................................888
Robert Byfield, *Owner*
EMP: 1
SQ FT: 2,000
SALES (est): 106.8K **Privately Held**
SIC: 7692 Welding repair

(G-460)
CG DISTRIBUTORS
2145 Mountain Dr (74003-6956)
PHONE..................................918 336-8882
Gordon Fletcher, *Owner*
EMP: 2
SALES: 12K **Privately Held**
SIC: 3999 Manufacturing industries

(G-461)
CHARLES F DOORNBOS REVOCABLE T
105 1/2 Se Frank Phillips (74003-3519)
PHONE..................................918 336-0611
EMP: 3
SALES (est): 222.6K **Privately Held**
SIC: 1311 Crude petroleum production

(G-462)
CHEVRON PHILLIPS CHEM CO LP
105 Ptc (74004-0001)
PHONE..................................918 977-6846
Bill Fisher, *Engineer*
Mark Haney, *Manager*
EMP: 200
SALES (corp-wide): 8.3B **Privately Held**
SIC: 2821 Plastics materials & resins
HQ: Chevron Phillips Chemical Company Lp
10001 Six Pines Dr
The Woodlands TX 77380
832 813-4100

(G-463)
CHEVRON PHILLIPS CHEM CO LP
Highway 60 & 123 (74004-0001)
PHONE..................................918 661-3317
Steve Saterlee, *Manager*
Daniel Adler, *Technician*
EMP: 250
SALES (corp-wide): 8.3B **Privately Held**
SIC: 2821 Plastics materials & resins
HQ: Chevron Phillips Chemical Company Lp
10001 Six Pines Dr
The Woodlands TX 77380
832 813-4100

(G-464)
CHEW COAST & SONS
401280 W 2460 Dr (74006-0407)
PHONE..................................918 333-3318
Dean Coast, *Partner*
David Coast, *Partner*
Mike Coast, *Partner*
EMP: 3 **EST:** 1979
SALES (est): 227.9K **Privately Held**
SIC: 1311 Crude petroleum production

(G-465)
CHIC GALLERIA PUBLICATIONS
628 Chestnut Ct (74003-6018)
PHONE..................................918 671-2379
Beth Anderson, *Chief*
EMP: 1
SALES (est): 44.8K **Privately Held**
WEB: www.chicgalleria.com
SIC: 2741 Miscellaneous publishing

(G-466)
CLOVERLEAF BAKING CO
4712 Ne Wisconsin St (74006-1955)
PHONE..................................612 708-8196
Jennifer Francis, *Principal*
EMP: 4
SALES (est): 196.4K **Privately Held**
SIC: 2051 Bread, cake & related products

(G-467)
CONOCOPHILLIPS
Also Called: Phillips 66
315 S Johnstone Ave (74003-6617)
P.O. Box 840, Owasso (74055-0840)
PHONE..................................918 977-6002
EMP: 473
SALES (corp-wide): 36.6B **Publicly Held**
SIC: 2911 Petroleum refining
PA: Conocophillips
925 N Eldridge Pkwy
Houston TX 77079
281 293-1000

(G-468)
CONOCOPHILLIPS COMPANY
315 S Johnstone Ave (74003-6617)
P.O. Box 2200 (74005-2200)
PHONE..................................281 293-1000
Eric Reich, *Manager*
Cynthia Crow, *Agent*
David Bratcher, *Supervisor*
Mark Nel, *Technology*
Casper Naegle, *Director*
EMP: 23
SALES (corp-wide): 36.6B **Publicly Held**
SIC: 5541 1382 Filling stations, gasoline; oil & gas exploration services
HQ: Conocophillips Company
925 N Eldridge Pkwy
Houston TX 77079
281 293-1000

(G-469)
COPPER CUP IMAGES
117 W 5th St Ste 410 (74003-6615)
P.O. Box 485 (74005-0485)
PHONE..................................918 337-2781
Melissa Green, *Partner*
Frederick Green, *Partner*
EMP: 6

GEOGRAPHIC SECTION

Bartlesville - Washington County (G-502)

SALES (est): 422.9K **Privately Held**
WEB: www.coppercupimages.com
SIC: 2759 7336 Commercial printing; commercial art & graphic design

(G-470)
CUNNINGHAM GRAPHICS INC
1209 Sw Frank Phllips Blv (74003-3206)
PHONE..................................918 337-9100
Vince Cunningham, *President*
Karla Cunningham, *Vice Pres*
EMP: 3
SALES (est): 400K **Privately Held**
SIC: 7336 2396 Graphic arts & related design; automotive & apparel trimmings

(G-471)
CUSTOM LEA SAD & COWBOY DECOR
Also Called: Yocham Custom Saddlery
401300 Us Highway 60 (74006-0118)
PHONE..................................918 335-2277
Rick S Yocham, *Owner*
Rhonda Yocham, *Co-Owner*
EMP: 5
SQ FT: 5,700
SALES: 400K **Privately Held**
SIC: 3199 5941 2512 Equestrian related leather articles; saddlery & equestrian equipment; upholstered household furniture

(G-472)
CUSTOM MOLDING SERVICES INC
3509 Minnesota St (74006-1208)
P.O. Box 2407 (74005-2407)
PHONE..................................918 333-4872
Gerald Smith, *President*
William Johnson, *President*
Catherine Johnson, *Treasurer*
Timothy Miller, *Director*
EMP: 6
SALES (est): 801.5K **Privately Held**
SIC: 3089 Injection molding of plastics

(G-473)
DAVID GREENS OFFICE
2407 Nowata Pl Ste 304 (74006-4700)
P.O. Box 117 (74005-0117)
PHONE..................................918 335-3855
David L Greens, *Owner*
EMP: 6
SALES (est): 413.5K **Privately Held**
SIC: 1382 Oil & gas exploration services

(G-474)
DAVID L GREENE INC
2407 Nowata Pl Ste 304 (74006-4700)
PHONE..................................918 335-3855
David Greens, *Principal*
EMP: 3
SALES (est): 308K **Privately Held**
SIC: 1311 Crude petroleum production

(G-475)
DAVIS OIL CO
399232 W 1800 Rd (74006-0121)
PHONE..................................918 333-5871
Thelma Davis, *Owner*
EMP: 1
SALES (est): 98.7K **Privately Held**
SIC: 1311 Crude petroleum production

(G-476)
E E SEWING INC
2377 London Ln (74006-7410)
PHONE..................................918 214-5343
EMP: 3
SALES (est): 127.2K **Privately Held**
SIC: 3399 Primary metal products

(G-477)
EAGLE GRAPHICS
1000 Ne Washington Blvd (74006-1221)
P.O. Box 626, Dewey (74029-0626)
PHONE..................................918 335-7777
Shannon Swan, *Owner*
EMP: 2
SALES (est): 89.7K **Privately Held**
SIC: 3993 Signs & advertising specialties

(G-478)
EATON BUILDING CONTRACTORS
3820 Se Kentucky St Ste 6 (74006-2551)
PHONE..................................918 273-9191
EMP: 2 EST: 2017
SALES (est): 88.3K **Privately Held**
SIC: 3625 Mfg Relays/Industrial Controls

(G-479)
ECONO BIOGASOLINE CORPORATION
414 Se Wash Blvd Ste 215 (74006-2428)
PHONE..................................918 347-5408
Fred Simila, *President*
Lisa Simila, *Corp Secy*
EMP: 2
SALES (est): 133.2K **Privately Held**
SIC: 2911 Gasoline

(G-480)
ELQUI INTERNATIONAL LTD CO
Also Called: Sign & Banner Express
330 Sw Watson Ave (74003-3400)
PHONE..................................918 335-5002
James W Reali,
Hanny Basso,
▲ EMP: 4
SQ FT: 2,000
SALES (est): 422.7K **Privately Held**
SIC: 3993 2399 Signs, not made in custom sign painting shops; banners, pennants & flags

(G-481)
EMBRODRED MNOGRAMS DESIGNS LLC
137 Ne Washington Blvd (74006-1635)
PHONE..................................918 335-5055
Chrystal Brown, *Mng Member*
EMP: 1 EST: 1997
SALES (est): 76.8K **Privately Held**
WEB: www.embroideredbartlesville.com
SIC: 2395 Embroidery products, except schiffli machine

(G-482)
EXCEL PARALUBES LLC
411 S Keeler Ave (74003-6620)
PHONE..................................800 527-3236
EMP: 5
SALES (est): 462.7K **Privately Held**
SIC: 2869 Olefins

(G-483)
FIRST THOUGHT INC
Also Called: Recognition Place
114 Se Frank Phllips Blvd (74003-3518)
PHONE..................................918 336-3322
Kevin Bryan, *President*
EMP: 3
SQ FT: 2,000
SALES (est): 180K **Privately Held**
WEB: www.recognitionplace.net
SIC: 5199 5099 5947 5999 Advertising specialties; gifts & novelties; signs, except electric; gift, novelty & souvenir shop; trophies & plaques; signs & advertising specialties

(G-484)
FOX NORTHEASTERN OIL GAS CORP
Also Called: Jim's Used Oilfield Equipment
1723 W Hensley Blvd (74003-2226)
PHONE..................................918 331-7791
Jim Fox, *Principal*
EMP: 1
SALES (est): 175.3K **Privately Held**
SIC: 1311 5082 Crude petroleum & natural gas; oil field equipment

(G-485)
FRANKS SIGNS
746 Ne Washington Blvd (74006-1245)
PHONE..................................918 335-9715
Frank Martin, *Owner*
EMP: 2
SALES (est): 78.1K **Privately Held**
SIC: 3993 Signs & advertising specialties

(G-486)
GATEWAY RESOURCES USA INC
1821 Arbor Dr (74006-7004)
PHONE..................................918 333-2115
Blaine Hanks, *President*
Cindy Hanks, *Vice Pres*
EMP: 2
SALES (est): 355.8K **Privately Held**
SIC: 1382 Oil & gas exploration services

(G-487)
GOLDTECHS INC
1525 Saddle Ln Ste B (74006-5745)
P.O. Box 3912 (74006-3912)
PHONE..................................918 856-9059
Marty Carver, *President*
EMP: 2
SALES (est): 163.1K **Privately Held**
SIC: 7372 Application computer software

(G-488)
GRAVEL ROAD LLC
3820 Silver Lake Vw (74006-7341)
PHONE..................................918 766-6368
Jennifer Brewington, *Principal*
EMP: 3
SALES (est): 171.3K **Privately Held**
SIC: 1442 Construction sand & gravel

(G-489)
HANGER PRSTHETCS & ORTHO INC
Also Called: Green Cntry Orthtic Prsthetics
1904 Se Washington Blvd (74006-6736)
PHONE..................................918 333-6900
Bill Dunham, *Manager*
EMP: 3
SALES (corp-wide): 1.1B **Publicly Held**
SIC: 3842 5999 Limbs, artificial; braces, elastic; orthopedic & prosthesis applications
HQ: Hanger Prosthetics & Orthotics, Inc.
10910 Domain Dr Ste 300
Austin TX 78758
512 777-3800

(G-490)
HEARTBEAT DESIGNS LLC
3383 State St Ste 100 (74003)
PHONE..................................918 333-0833
Michael Lott,
EMP: 1
SALES: 125K **Privately Held**
SIC: 2759 Screen printing

(G-491)
HEATWAVE SUPPLY INC
332 Ne Katherine Ave (74006-1512)
PHONE..................................918 333-6363
J Barber, *Principal*
EMP: 3
SALES (corp-wide): 20.5MM **Privately Held**
SIC: 5074 3432 Plumbing fittings & supplies; plumbing fixture fittings & trim
PA: Heatwave Supply, Inc.
6529 E 14th St
Tulsa OK 74112
918 838-9841

(G-492)
HELMCO MANUFACTURING INC
Hwy 123 Sw 14th Lkout Ave (74003)
P.O. Box 1602 (74005-1602)
PHONE..................................918 336-4757
William Whitchurch, *President*
EMP: 6
SALES (est): 616.5K **Privately Held**
SIC: 3541 Milling machines

(G-493)
HIGHWAY MAN SIGNS LLC
1037 Ne Washington Blvd (74006-1222)
PHONE..................................918 534-9100
Kenneth Sutherland, *Mng Member*
EMP: 6
SALES (est): 256.4K **Privately Held**
SIC: 3993 Signs & advertising specialties

(G-494)
HILL STEEL CORPORATION
1800 W 14th St (74003-3717)
P.O. Box 1235 (74005-1235)
PHONE..................................918 336-2430
Calvin Hill, *President*
EMP: 22
SQ FT: 63,000
SALES (est): 1.9MM **Privately Held**
SIC: 3443 Dumpsters, garbage

(G-495)
HOWES LTG & WIN BLINDS LLC
627 Se Wilshire Ave (74006-8427)
PHONE..................................918 791-4101
EMP: 2
SALES (est): 133.7K **Privately Held**
SIC: 2591 Window blinds

(G-496)
HUSKY PORTABLE CONTAINMENT CO
7202 Se International Ct (74006)
P.O. Box 3404 (74006-3404)
PHONE..................................918 333-2000
Jay Claeys, *President*
Pam Claeys, *Vice Pres*
▲ EMP: 25
SQ FT: 20,000
SALES: 2.8MM **Privately Held**
SIC: 3569 0851 3443 Firefighting apparatus & related equipment; forestry services; fire fighting services, forest; tanks for tank trucks, metal plate; tanks, lined: metal plate; liners/lining

(G-497)
INMAN WELL SERVICE
23530 N 4025 Rd (74006-0434)
PHONE..................................918 440-3151
Robert E Inman, *Owner*
Cody Inman, *Co-Owner*
EMP: 3
SALES (est): 254.1K **Privately Held**
SIC: 1389 Oil field services

(G-498)
IRON HORSE METAL WORKS
3908 Minnesota St (74006-1211)
PHONE..................................918 333-8877
Michelle Bordner, *Principal*
EMP: 2
SALES (est): 177K **Privately Held**
SIC: 5039 3446 1799 1542 Construction materials; architectural metalwork; sandblasting of building exteriors; nonresidential construction

(G-499)
J B WELDING
806 Belmont Rd (74006-8917)
PHONE..................................918 574-1806
Jim Brashear, *Owner*
Melissa Brashear, *Manager*
EMP: 1
SALES: 130K **Privately Held**
SIC: 7692 Welding repair

(G-500)
K C WELDING & MACHINE CORP
428 W 8th St (74003-4401)
P.O. Box 1497 (74005-1497)
PHONE..................................918 336-4560
Michael Conover, *President*
Richard Conover, *Vice Pres*
EMP: 4
SQ FT: 10,000
SALES (est): 855.1K **Privately Held**
WEB: www.kcwelding.com
SIC: 7692 Welding repair

(G-501)
KEEPSAKE CANDLES INC
263 County Road 3022 (74003-7173)
PHONE..................................918 336-0351
Alice A Ririe, *President*
Katherine Ririe, *Vice Pres*
Otis Edward Ririe, *Treasurer*
Karen Ririe, *Admin Sec*
EMP: 11
SQ FT: 6,200
SALES (est): 1MM **Privately Held**
SIC: 3999 5999 Candles; candle shops

(G-502)
KELEHER OUTDOOR ADVERTISING CO
523 S Virginia Ave (74003-3340)
P.O. Box 1361 (74005-1361)
PHONE..................................918 333-8855

Bartlesville - Washington County (G-503)

Dan J Keleher, *President*
EMP: 13
SQ FT: 2,500
SALES (est): 1.2MM **Privately Held**
WEB: www.keleheroutdoor.com
SIC: 7312 3993 Billboard advertising; signs & advertising specialties

(G-503)
KM METAL POLISHING
5915 Baylor Dr (74006-8910)
PHONE..................................918 397-2221
Kevin Marshall, *Principal*
EMP: 2
SALES (est): 74.4K **Privately Held**
SIC: 2842 Metal polish

(G-504)
KNOX LABORATORY SERVICES INC
2232 Se Wash Blvd Ste 203 (74006-7142)
PHONE..................................918 331-9982
Jennifer Lopp, *Branch Mgr*
EMP: 2
SALES (est): 100K
SALES (corp-wide): 1.5MM **Privately Held**
SIC: 2899
PA: Knox Laboratory Services, Inc
   5640 S Memorial Dr
   Tulsa OK 74145
   918 622-5669

(G-505)
LAYS CUSTOM WELDING LLC
300 S Quapaw Ave (74003-4326)
PHONE..................................918 766-5227
Tyler Lay, *Administration*
EMP: 1
SALES (est): 52.1K **Privately Held**
SIC: 7692 Welding repair

(G-506)
LEATHER OUR WAY
249 County Road 3309 (74003-1667)
PHONE..................................918 214-2036
EMP: 1
SALES (est): 60.8K **Privately Held**
SIC: 3172 Personal leather goods

(G-507)
M & BJ FARM & MACHINE LLC
403260 W 2380 Dr (74006-0425)
PHONE..................................918 333-0430
Jay Malcolm, *Mng Member*
Barbara Joyce Malcolm,
EMP: 2
SALES: 34K **Privately Held**
SIC: 0139 3599 Hay farm; machine shop, jobbing & repair

(G-508)
MARANATHA INDUSTRIES LLC
526 S Seminole Ave (74003-3335)
PHONE..................................918 336-1221
Scott Ecklund, *Principal*
EMP: 2
SALES (est): 119.6K **Privately Held**
WEB: www.sescocp.com
SIC: 3999 Manufacturing industries

(G-509)
MATRIX PRINT & PROMO LLC
1006 Arbor Dr (74006-7806)
P.O. Box 3351 (74006-3351)
PHONE..................................918 994-1943
Harry Beeman, *Principal*
EMP: 3
SALES (est): 173.7K **Privately Held**
SIC: 2752 Promotional printing, lithographic

(G-510)
MCELYEA CUSTOM WOODWORKING LLC
1207 May Ln (74006-5628)
PHONE..................................918 332-7651
EMP: 1
SALES (est): 54.1K **Privately Held**
SIC: 2431 Millwork

(G-511)
MERRICK PRINTING
4006 Fairview Rd (74006-7105)
PHONE..................................918 876-6264
Doris Merrick, *Owner*
Enos L Merrick, *Manager*
EMP: 2
SQ FT: 2,600
SALES (est): 113K **Privately Held**
SIC: 2759 2752 Letterpress printing; screen printing; commercial printing, lithographic

(G-512)
METAL GOODS MANUFACTURING CO
Also Called: McAbery Acquistion
309 W Hensley Blvd (74003-2514)
P.O. Box 2096 (74005-2096)
PHONE..................................918 336-4282
Buz McAbery, *President*
Harley Gray, *Vice Pres*
Dianne McCarty, *Vice Pres*
Charles Staudinger, *QC Mgr*
EMP: 15 **EST:** 1939
SQ FT: 12,800
SALES (est): 2.8MM **Privately Held**
WEB: www.metalgoodsmfg
SIC: 3821 3829 3545 3494 Laboratory apparatus & furniture; measuring & controlling devices; machine tool accessories; valves & pipe fittings

(G-513)
NELL GAVIN LLC
1524 Mountain Rd (74003-6935)
PHONE..................................972 935-6692
EMP: 1
SALES (est): 39.7K **Privately Held**
SIC: 3269 Pottery products

(G-514)
OILTECH MANUFACTURING DIV LLC
2601 E Durham Rd (74006-0025)
PHONE..................................918 534-3568
EMP: 1
SALES (est): 39.6K **Privately Held**
SIC: 3999 Manufacturing industries

(G-515)
PAUL WRECKER SERVICE
731 Ne Washington Blvd (74006-1216)
PHONE..................................918 333-9685
EMP: 3
SALES (est): 140K **Privately Held**
SIC: 3711 Mfg Motor Vehicle/Car Bodies

(G-516)
PHILLIPS 66 SPECTRUM CORP
411 S Keeler Ave (74003-6670)
P.O. Box 9000 (74005-9000)
PHONE..................................918 977-7909
Chuck Rorhs, *Manager*
EMP: 15
SALES (corp-wide): 28.8MM **Privately Held**
SIC: 2992 5172 2911 Lubricating oils; lubricating oils & greases; oils, lubricating
PA: Phillips 66 Spectrum Corporation
   3010 Briarpark Dr
   Houston TX 77042
   281 293-6600

(G-517)
PHILLIPS PRCSION MACHINING LLC
1321 Industrial Blvd (74006-6030)
PHONE..................................918 914-2131
Mark Phillips,
EMP: 18
SALES (est): 650K **Privately Held**
SIC: 3449 Bars, concrete reinforcing: fabricated steel

(G-518)
PUBLIC SAFETY-DRIVERS LICENSE
1816 W Hensley Blvd (74003-2237)
PHONE..................................918 336-0604
Roger Duncan, *Principal*
EMP: 2
SALES (est): 103.9K **Privately Held**
SIC: 3469 Automobile license tags, stamped metal

(G-519)
QES PRESSURE PUMPING LLC
155 County Rd (74003)
PHONE..................................918 338-0808
Mike Littlepage, *General Mgr*
EMP: 37
SALES (corp-wide): 1.1B **Privately Held**
WEB: www.cows.bz
SIC: 1389 Oil field services
HQ: Qes Pressure Pumping Llc
   1322 S Grant Ave
   Chanute KS 66720
   620 431-9210

(G-520)
QUANTUM TRADING TECHNOLOGIES
401 S Dewey Ave Ste 503 (74003-3517)
PHONE..................................918 876-3921
Ryan Jones, *Principal*
EMP: 4
SALES (est): 306.4K **Privately Held**
SIC: 7372 Application computer software

(G-521)
RAINBOW OIL & GAS INC
5800 Harvard Dr (74006-8843)
PHONE..................................918 335-2188
Steven W Schrag, *President*
EMP: 1
SALES (est): 74.2K **Privately Held**
SIC: 1311 Crude petroleum & natural gas production

(G-522)
REAL CABINETS
717 W 5th St (74003-3310)
PHONE..................................918 336-0255
Randy Stringer, *Partner*
Tim Vaughn, *Partner*
EMP: 2
SALES (est): 186.8K **Privately Held**
SIC: 2434 Wood kitchen cabinets

(G-523)
ROY PUTNAM
2733 Oxford Ct (74006-7326)
PHONE..................................918 333-5642
Roy Putnam, *Owner*
EMP: 1
SALES (est): 59.9K **Privately Held**
SIC: 2911 Oils, fuel

(G-524)
SARVAM SOLUTIONS CORPORATION
6105 Nowata Rd 4 (74006-6010)
PHONE..................................918 346-9502
Sarvam Solutions, *President*
EMP: 1
SALES (est): 61.7K **Privately Held**
SIC: 8711 2835 Petroleum, mining & chemical engineers; microbiology & virology diagnostic products

(G-525)
SCHLUMBERGER TECHNOLOGY CORP
Reda Pump Division of TRW
509 W Hensley Blvd (74003-2518)
PHONE..................................918 661-2000
Billy Winter, *Electrical Engi*
Bud Missel, *Branch Mgr*
EMP: 100 **Publicly Held**
SIC: 1389 Oil field services
HQ: Schlumberger Technology Corp
   300 Schlumberger Dr
   Sugar Land TX 77478
   281 285-8500

(G-526)
SCHMOLDT ENGINEERING SERVICES
526 S Seminole Ave (74003-3300)
PHONE..................................918 336-1221
Terence R Wilken, *President*
Ronald M Fields, *Vice Pres*
Randy Crouch, *Engineer*
EMP: 12 **EST:** 1946
SQ FT: 3,900
SALES (est): 1.3MM **Privately Held**
WEB: www.sescocp.com
SIC: 8711 2899 2851 Engineering services; chemical preparations; paints & allied products

(G-527)
SERVICE PIPE & SUPPLY COMPANY
389 Cr 3007 (74003-1217)
PHONE..................................918 336-8433
Kumar Krishnan, *President*
K Vasudevan, *Shareholder*
EMP: 20
SQ FT: 45,000
SALES (est): 2.8MM **Privately Held**
SIC: 3599 2542 Machine shop, jobbing & repair; partitions & fixtures, except wood

(G-528)
SHARPS MACHINE SHOP
103 N Kaw Ave (74003-2422)
PHONE..................................918 336-2516
EMP: 1
SALES (est): 50K **Privately Held**
SIC: 3599 7629 Mfg Industrial Machinery Electrical Repair

(G-529)
SUPCO INC
101 N Johnstone Ave (74003-2621)
PHONE..................................918 336-5075
J Randall Judd, *President*
EMP: 150 **EST:** 1999
SQ FT: 300,000
SALES (est): 5.3MM **Privately Held**
SIC: 3599 3321 Machine shop, jobbing & repair; ductile iron castings; gray iron castings

(G-530)
SUPERIOR COMPANIES INC (PA)
Also Called: Supco
101 N Johnstone Ave (74003-2621)
PHONE..................................918 336-5075
J Randall Judd, *President*
Richard K Harris, *Principal*
W L Rippetoe, *Principal*
Glen B Webster, *Principal*
EMP: 150 **EST:** 1957
SQ FT: 300,000
SALES (est): 27.6MM **Privately Held**
SIC: 3599 3321 Machine shop, jobbing & repair; ductile iron castings; gray iron castings

(G-531)
SUPERIOR DYNMICS FBRCATION LLC ◆
1800 W 14th St (74003-3717)
PHONE..................................918 698-9846
Jason Tackett,
EMP: 2 **EST:** 2019
SALES (est): 96.6K **Privately Held**
SIC: 3498 Coils, pipe: fabricated from purchased pipe

(G-532)
THOMAS WELDING
5711 Harvard Dr (74006-8842)
PHONE..................................918 214-7657
Brodie Alvin Thomas, *Principal*
EMP: 1
SALES (est): 25K **Privately Held**
SIC: 7692 Welding repair

(G-533)
TREASURES CUSTOM JEWELRY
2245 Se Wash Blvd Ste D (74006-7141)
PHONE..................................918 333-1311
Scott Clark, *Owner*
EMP: 7
SALES (est): 676.8K **Privately Held**
SIC: 3911 5944 Jewelry, precious metal; jewelry stores

(G-534)
WASHINGTONS WELDING LLC
1340 S Virginia Ave (74003-4408)
PHONE..................................918 336-2111
Michael Washington, *Principal*
EMP: 2 **EST:** 2010
SALES (est): 174.7K **Privately Held**
SIC: 7692 Welding repair

GEOGRAPHIC SECTION

Bennington - Bryan County (G-564)

(G-535)
WILDWOOD FINE CABINET DOORS
211 Ne Debell Ave (74006-1606)
PHONE.................918 331-0007
Sue Sanders, *Owner*
EMP: 2
SQ FT: 3,249
SALES (est): 40K **Privately Held**
SIC: 2434 Wood kitchen cabinets

(G-536)
WKD ASSOCIATES
401 S Dewey Ave (74003-3514)
PHONE.................918 336-9865
EMP: 2
SALES (est): 120K **Privately Held**
SIC: 3537 Mfg Industrial Trucks/Tractors

(G-537)
WRB REFINING LP
411 S Keeler Ave (74003-6620)
P.O. Box 8575 (74005-8575)
PHONE.................918 977-6600
EMP: 28 **Privately Held**
SIC: 2911 Petroleum refining
PA: Wrb Refining Lp
  2331 Citywest Blvd
  Houston TX 77042

Beaver
Beaver County

(G-538)
ARKHOMA TRANSPORTS INC
724 W 4th St (73932)
PHONE.................580 651-2682
Tex Gross, *Branch Mgr*
EMP: 2
SALES (corp-wide): 2.2MM **Privately Held**
SIC: 1389 Fishing for tools, oil & gas field; chemically treating wells
PA: Arkhoma Transports Inc
  102 S Juniper St
  Perryton TX 79070
  806 435-2380

(G-539)
BACAS OILFIELD SERVICES LLC
615 Douglas Ave (73932-9644)
PHONE.................580 461-8458
Uriel Baca,
EMP: 2 EST: 2016
SALES (est): 248.4K **Privately Held**
SIC: 1389 Oil field services

(G-540)
C & W CONSTRUCTION INC (PA)
1 Fourth Mile E Of Bevr (73932)
P.O. Box 784 (73932-0784)
PHONE.................580 625-4520
Calvin Madsen, *President*
Cindy Madsen, *Corp Secy*
Garland Pillars, *Vice Pres*
EMP: 16
SQ FT: 2,500
SALES: 1MM **Privately Held**
SIC: 1389 Construction, repair & dismantling services

(G-541)
JOE BRENT LANSDEN
Also Called: Herald Democrat, The
108 Douglas Ave (73932-9620)
P.O. Box 490 (73932-0490)
PHONE.................580 625-3241
Brent Lansden, *Partner*
Joe Lansden, *Partner*
EMP: 4
SQ FT: 3,750
SALES (est): 237.7K **Privately Held**
SIC: 2711 2752 Job printing & newspaper publishing combined; commercial printing, lithographic

(G-542)
MIDWEST READY MIX
Also Called: Midwest Ready Mix Concrete
20 Avenue G (73932)
P.O. Box 806 (73932-0806)
PHONE.................580 625-4477
Phillip Howard, *Owner*
Marcy Howard, *COO*
EMP: 2
SALES (est): 124.2K **Privately Held**
SIC: 3273 Ready-mixed concrete

(G-543)
PARTNERS OILFIELD SERVICES LLC
1 Mile South Of Beaver (73932)
P.O. Box 165 (73932-0165)
PHONE.................580 625-2239
Blaine Snyder, *Owner*
Bob Snyder, *Owner*
Ronnie Morrison, *Opers Mgr*
EMP: 10
SALES (est): 650K **Privately Held**
SIC: 1389 Testing, measuring, surveying & analysis services

(G-544)
PLATEAU ENERGY SERVICES LLC
1 M S Of Bevr E 4 10 Snto (73932)
Rural Route 170
PHONE.................580 625-3618
Lisa Renshaw, *Treasurer*
Randall Renshaw, *Mng Member*
EMP: 11
SALES: 954K **Privately Held**
SIC: 3563 7389 Air & gas compressors;

(G-545)
PVR MIDSTREEM LLC
Rr 2 Box 82 (73932-9660)
P.O. Box 82 (73932-0082)
PHONE.................580 837-5265
Ricky Littlefield, *Principal*
EMP: 16
SALES (est): 817.6K **Privately Held**
SIC: 1321 Natural gas liquids

(G-546)
RAMON & BENNETT ROUSTABOUT
107 Douglas Ave (73932-9617)
P.O. Box 9 (73932-0009)
PHONE.................580 625-4092
Ramon Castillo, *President*
Rhonda Bennett, *Owner*
EMP: 20
SALES (est): 2.3MM **Privately Held**
SIC: 1389 Roustabout service

(G-547)
REGENCY GAS
8 Miles E Of Forgan Hwy (73932)
P.O. Box 967 (73932-0967)
PHONE.................580 487-3862
Lanese Jentrey, *President*
EMP: 2
SALES (est): 172.7K **Privately Held**
SIC: 1382 Oil & gas exploration services

Beggs
Okmulgee County

(G-548)
AHC FABRICATION CO INC
1585 Highway 16 (74421-3076)
PHONE.................918 267-5052
Joe Cestore, *Principal*
EMP: 3
SALES (est): 327.6K **Privately Held**
SIC: 3433 Heating equipment, except electric

(G-549)
BALES CUSTOM WOODWORK INC
7100 Seay Rd (74421-3122)
PHONE.................918 277-6612
Christopher L Bales, *Principal*
EMP: 1

SALES (est): 70.8K **Privately Held**
SIC: 2431 Woodwork, interior & ornamental

(G-550)
CALLIDUS TECHNOLOGIES LLC
2499 Highway 16 (74421-2981)
PHONE.................918 267-4920
Jim Single, *Manager*
EMP: 100
SALES (corp-wide): 36.7B **Publicly Held**
SIC: 8734 3564 3433 2899 Testing laboratories; blowers & fans; heating equipment, except electric; chemical preparations
HQ: Callidus Technologies, L.L.C.
  7130 S Lewis Ave Ste 500
  Tulsa OK 74136

(G-551)
DONERITE WELDING
5410 Harreld Rd (74421-2588)
PHONE.................918 304-9594
Tenisha Tate, *Principal*
EMP: 1
SALES (est): 33.8K **Privately Held**
SIC: 7692 Welding repair

(G-552)
ECONOFAB PIPING INC
8255 Highway 16 (74421-2892)
PHONE.................918 267-5901
Billy Hamilton, *President*
▲ EMP: 10
SQ FT: 17,000
SALES (est): 780K **Privately Held**
SIC: 3446 Architectural metalwork

(G-553)
FIRST IMPRESSION PRTG CO INC (PA)
11 E Main (74421)
P.O. Box 667 (74421-0667)
PHONE.................918 749-5446
Albert E Fuqua, *President*
Kenneth Fuqua, *Vice Pres*
Marjie Fuqua, *Admin Sec*
EMP: 5
SALES (est): 277K **Privately Held**
SIC: 2752 2796 2791 2789 Lithographing on metal; platemaking services; typesetting; bookbinding & related work; commercial printing; automotive & apparel trimmings

(G-554)
FIRST IMPRESSION PRTG CO INC
Also Called: Terrico Printing
111 E Main St (74421)
P.O. Box 667 (74421-0667)
PHONE.................918 749-5446
EMP: 2
SALES (corp-wide): 277K **Privately Held**
SIC: 2752 Lithographic Commercial Printing
PA: The First Impression Printing Co Inc
  11 E Main
  Beggs OK 74421
  918 749-5446

(G-555)
FIRST IMPRESSIONS INC
Also Called: Terrico Advertising
111 E Main St (74421)
P.O. Box 801 (74421-0801)
PHONE.................918 267-4642
Al Fuqua, *President*
Margie Fuqua, *Corp Secy*
Ken Fuqua, *Vice Pres*
EMP: 3
SQ FT: 3,000
SALES (est): 188.3K **Privately Held**
SIC: 3993 Signs & advertising specialties

(G-556)
GAME CHANGING IMAGE LLC
6843 N 120 Rd (74421-3197)
PHONE.................918 289-3392
David Lee Tenison, *Mng Member*
Saundra Tenison, *Mng Member*
Brian Hardrick, *Manager*
John Metcalf, *Manager*
Gabe Rodriguez, *Manager*
EMP: 2

SALES: 71K **Privately Held**
SIC: 3993 Signs & advertising specialties

(G-557)
GENESIS METAL CORPORATION
8255 Highway 16 (74421-2892)
PHONE.................918 267-5901
Deborah Ziegler, *President*
Sid Ziegler, *Managing Dir*
Chris Ziegler, *Info Tech Mgr*
Tiffany Lampkins, *Admin Asst*
EMP: 19
SALES (est): 4.5MM **Privately Held**
SIC: 3443 Fabricated plate work (boiler shop)

(G-558)
INTEGRITY RAIL SERVICES INC
7828 Highway 16 (74421-3038)
PHONE.................918 267-3761
Thomas Holdaway, *Principal*
Rodney Cargil, *Principal*
Tina Bradshaw, *Parts Mgr*
EMP: 8 EST: 2012
SALES (est): 961.1K **Privately Held**
SIC: 3743 Locomotives & parts

(G-559)
ROSE ROCK RESOURCES INC (PA)
5060 N 240 Rd (74421-3058)
PHONE.................918 752-0511
Jeffery Andrews, *President*
EMP: 2
SQ FT: 1,200
SALES (est): 479.4K **Privately Held**
SIC: 1382 Oil & gas exploration services

(G-560)
SAMSON PUBLISHING COMPANY LLC
11024 Ferguson Rd (74421-2280)
PHONE.................918 344-7416
EMP: 2
SALES (est): 61.8K **Privately Held**
SIC: 2741 Miscellaneous publishing

(G-561)
SINGING WIRE CEDAR
12250 Grimes Rd (74421-2170)
PHONE.................918 607-8643
Dangete McDonald, *Owner*
EMP: 3
SQ FT: 1,200
SALES: 125K **Privately Held**
SIC: 2421 Lumber: rough, sawed or planed

(G-562)
SWEARINGEN MACHINE SHOP INC
71216 E (74421)
P.O. Box 622 (74421-0622)
PHONE.................918 267-4308
Jack Swearingen, *President*
Retta Swearingen, *Corp Secy*
Bruce Swearingen, *Vice Pres*
EMP: 3
SQ FT: 3,600
SALES: 250K **Privately Held**
SIC: 3599 Crankshafts & camshafts, machining; oil filters, internal combustion engine, except automotive

Bennington
Bryan County

(G-563)
EMERT ENTERPRISES LLC
326 E Valliant St (74723-3446)
PHONE.................580 495-5511
Mason Emert,
EMP: 1
SALES: 40K **Privately Held**
SIC: 2396 Screen printing on fabric articles

(G-564)
MASTER WORKS
36613 Us Highway 70 (74723-1830)
P.O. Box 167 (74723-0167)
PHONE.................580 847-2273
Russell Cook, *Owner*
Larry Tom, *Manager*

EMP: 7
SALES (est): 594.5K **Privately Held**
SIC: 5099 3931 Musical instruments; musical instruments

Bernice
Ottawa County

(G-565)
HYDROHOIST BOAT LIFTS
453265 E Highway 85a (74331-6472)
PHONE..................................918 256-8125
Joe Cox, *Principal*
EMP: 2
SALES (est): 197.1K **Privately Held**
SIC: 3536 Boat lifts

(G-566)
HYDROHOIST MARINE GROUP INC
453265 E Highway 85a (74331-6472)
PHONE..................................918 256-8775
Joe Cox, *President*
EMP: 5
SALES (corp-wide): 29.3MM **Privately Held**
SIC: 3536 Boat lifts
PA: Hydrohoist Marine Group, Inc.
915 W Blue Starr Dr
Claremore OK 74017
918 341-6811

(G-567)
JERRYS DOCK CONSTRUCTION INC
321 Hwy 85 A (74331)
P.O. Box 3777, Afton (74331-3777)
PHONE..................................918 256-3390
Chad Crouse, *President*
Tony Haskins, *Opers Staff*
Cola Crouse, *Treasurer*
EMP: 15
SQ FT: 195,000
SALES (est): 4.5MM **Privately Held**
SIC: 1629 3441 Dock construction; fabricated structural metal

Bessie
Washita County

(G-568)
GRANNAS LLC
412 Main St (73622-2017)
PHONE..................................580 337-6360
Connie Miller,
Farrell Miller,
EMP: 13
SQ FT: 6,000
SALES (est): 2.2MM **Privately Held**
SIC: 2032 Soups & broths: canned, jarred, etc.

(G-569)
HARRISON GYPSUM LLC
Also Called: Acg Materials
1113 Main St (73622-2001)
P.O. Box 100 (73622-0100)
PHONE..................................580 337-6371
Randy Wenninger, *Manager*
EMP: 20
SALES (corp-wide): 1.7B **Publicly Held**
SIC: 3275 Gypsum products
HQ: Harrison Gypsum, Llc
1550 Double C Dr
Norman OK 73069
405 366-9500

(G-570)
S AND J FOODS LLC
Also Called: Granna's
412 Main St (73622-2017)
P.O. Box 225 (73622-0225)
PHONE..................................580 337-6360
James Bennight, *Principal*
EMP: 28
SQ FT: 10,000
SALES (est): 1.7MM **Privately Held**
SIC: 2099 Emulsifiers, food

Bethany
Oklahoma County

(G-571)
A 1 MASTER PRINT INC
Also Called: Hooper Printing
8302 Nw 39th Expy (73008-3011)
PHONE..................................405 787-0505
Randy Struble, *President*
Mike Holmes, *Sr Corp Ofcr*
Suzanne Struble, *Vice Pres*
Donald Wiseman, *Human Res Mgr*
Buddy Johnson, *Administration*
EMP: 3
SQ FT: 4,000
SALES (est): 330K **Privately Held**
SIC: 2752 2791 2789 Commercial printing, offset; typesetting; bookbinding & related work

(G-572)
ALLEN VINEYARDS LLC
6708 Nw 39th Expy (73008-2647)
PHONE..................................405 240-7147
EMP: 2
SALES (est): 80K **Privately Held**
SIC: 2084 Wines

(G-573)
CLASSIC CUSTOM PLATING COMPANY
3709 N Peniel Ave (73008-3440)
PHONE..................................405 787-3075
Robert Posey, *Owner*
EMP: 2
SQ FT: 2,720
SALES (est): 110K **Privately Held**
SIC: 3471 Plating of metals or formed products

(G-574)
CUSTOM MONOGRAMS & LETTERING
7801 Nw 23rd St (73008-4947)
PHONE..................................405 495-8586
Ron Kuykendall, *President*
EMP: 3
SQ FT: 1,400
SALES (est): 230K **Privately Held**
SIC: 7389 7336 2752 2396 Textile & apparel services; silk screen design; commercial printing, lithographic; automotive & apparel trimmings

(G-575)
DALE KREIMEYER CO
3211 N Wilburn Ave (73008-3736)
PHONE..................................405 789-9499
Dale Kreimeyer, *Owner*
EMP: 2
SALES: 150K **Privately Held**
SIC: 5013 5015 3089 Automobile glass; automotive parts & supplies, used; windshields, plastic

(G-576)
DOVETAIL ENTERPRISES LLC
6417 Nw 31st St (73008-4111)
PHONE..................................405 476-3953
James Miller, *Principal*
EMP: 2
SALES (est): 51.3K **Privately Held**
SIC: 2499 Wood products

(G-577)
E LYLE JOHNSON INC (PA)
7100 Nw 63rd St Ste 1703 (73008-5008)
PHONE..................................405 470-2047
James A Johnson, *President*
James E Johnson, *President*
Louise Trammel, *Corp Secy*
EMP: 2
SQ FT: 1,000
SALES (est): 739.8K **Privately Held**
SIC: 1311 6512 Crude petroleum & natural gas; nonresidential building operators

(G-578)
GAMEDAY SCREEN PRTG PROMOTIONS
5008 N Rockwell Ave (73008-2432)
PHONE..................................405 637-8577
EMP: 2
SALES (est): 92.3K **Privately Held**
SIC: 2759 Screen printing

(G-579)
GARYS GUNS
30th Terr St (73008)
PHONE..................................405 789-6896
Gary Funderburg, *Owner*
Sheryl Funderburg, *Co-Owner*
EMP: 2
SALES: 50K **Privately Held**
SIC: 5941 3484 Firearms; small arms

(G-580)
GOLD SHOP CUSTOM JEWELERS
7005 Nw 50th St (73008-2437)
PHONE..................................405 789-2919
Rick Funderburg, *Owner*
EMP: 1
SALES (est): 40K **Privately Held**
SIC: 5944 3911 Jewelry, precious stones & precious metals; jewelry, precious metal

(G-581)
HAYNES WELDING SERVICE INC
7921 Nw 39th St (73008-3149)
PHONE..................................337 380-7126
EMP: 1
SALES (est): 25K **Privately Held**
SIC: 7692 Welding repair

(G-582)
INDUSTRIAL POWER WASH INC
7608 Nw 40th St (73008-3113)
PHONE..................................405 787-9274
Robert Milburn, *President*
EMP: 1
SALES (est): 82K **Privately Held**
SIC: 7211 3589 Power laundries, family & commercial; car washing machinery

(G-583)
INKLING DESIGN
5508 N Rockwell Ave Ste B (73008-2059)
PHONE..................................405 495-5575
Brian AB Neeley, *Owner*
EMP: 1
SQ FT: 18,230
SALES: 100K **Privately Held**
SIC: 7336 2396 Silk screen design; automotive & apparel trimmings

(G-584)
J W COMPANIES (PA)
3709 N Grant Ave (73008-3543)
PHONE..................................405 789-2460
Joe Wade, *Partner*
Carol Wade, *Partner*
EMP: 3
SQ FT: 1,500
SALES (est): 392.9K **Privately Held**
SIC: 2759 5199 Screen printing; advertising specialties

(G-585)
KEY TO NATURES BLESSINGS LLC
8282 Nw 39th Expy (73008-3009)
PHONE..................................405 603-8200
Lynn Key, *Mng Member*
EMP: 3
SQ FT: 1,500
SALES (est): 121.8K **Privately Held**
SIC: 2051 Cakes, bakery: except frozen

(G-586)
LEVELOPS INC
7000 Nw 39th St (73008-3352)
PHONE..................................405 602-8040
Sid Helms, *CEO*
Bryan Albrecht, *Vice Pres*
EMP: 40
SALES (est): 4.8MM **Privately Held**
SIC: 1382 Oil & gas exploration services

(G-587)
MAMMOTH MANUFACTURING INC
591 Philip J Rhoads Ave (73008)
PHONE..................................405 820-8301
Jason Mullen, *CEO*
EMP: 2
SALES (est): 151.3K **Privately Held**
SIC: 2241 3599 Hose fabric, tubular; flexible metal hose, tubing & bellows

(G-588)
MCSMITH CREATIONS LLC
5508 N Rockwell Ave Ste B (73008-2051)
PHONE..................................405 596-2301
Jeff Smith,
EMP: 1 **EST:** 2013
SALES: 175K **Privately Held**
SIC: 2395 Art goods for embroidering, stamped: purchased materials

(G-589)
META SPECIAL AEROSPACE LLC
5600 Philip J Rhoads Ave (73008-7012)
PHONE..................................405 516-3357
Armand Paliotta, *Principal*
EMP: 6
SALES (est): 989.2K **Privately Held**
SIC: 3812 Search & navigation equipment

(G-590)
MICHAEL AND MARY SEEVER
7119 Nw 45th St (73008-2311)
PHONE..................................405 808-2494
Michael Seever, *Principal*
EMP: 2
SALES: 50K **Privately Held**
SIC: 3231 Products of purchased glass

(G-591)
MISSION TRANSPORTATION LLC
7200 Nw 63rd St (73008-5002)
PHONE..................................405 694-4755
Robert P Billy II, *Principal*
Jeff Morton, *CFO*
Mark Lacroix, *Manager*
EMP: 99
SALES: 3MM **Privately Held**
SIC: 3724 4522 4581 Aircraft engines & engine parts; air transportation, non-scheduled; air passenger carriers, non-scheduled; aircraft maintenance & repair services

(G-592)
PRAIRIE GRAPHICS & SPORTSWEAR
6600 Nw 36th St Ste A (73008-3456)
PHONE..................................405 789-0028
Charles Rayshell, *Owner*
EMP: 1
SQ FT: 3,250
SALES (est): 83.4K **Privately Held**
SIC: 5699 2396 Miscellaneous apparel & accessories; automotive & apparel trimmings

(G-593)
RAY HARRINGTON DRAPERIES
6710 Nw 29th St (73008-4730)
PHONE..................................405 789-6710
Orlan Ray Harrington, *Owner*
EMP: 2 **EST:** 1968
SALES: 50K **Privately Held**
SIC: 2221 1799 5719 2392 Draperies & drapery fabrics, manmade fiber & silk; drapery track installation; window shades; venetian blinds; household furnishings; curtains & draperies

(G-594)
SHOFNER CUSTOM WOOD
7804 Nw 33rd St (73008-3621)
PHONE..................................405 787-5768
Janie Shofner, *Principal*
EMP: 2 **EST:** 2010
SALES (est): 226.8K **Privately Held**
SIC: 2431 Millwork

(G-595)
SOUTHWIND AVIATION SUPPLY LLC
5700 N Rockwell Ave (73008-2052)
PHONE..................................405 491-0500
Sandi Chuck, *Controller*
George S Andrews, *Mng Member*
Gary Henricksen, *Mng Member*
Justin Nalley, *Mng Member*
Ron Shrum, *Mng Member*
EMP: 8

GEOGRAPHIC SECTION

Bixby - Tulsa County (G-627)

SQ FT: 2,500
SALES: 300K **Privately Held**
SIC: 3728 Aircraft parts & equipment

(G-596)
STARLINE INC
5412 N Rockwell Ave (73008-2038)
PHONE 405 495-8274
Kristen Latham, *President*
Tracy Latham, *Principal*
Paul Harris, *Engineer*
Joe Howsden, *Engineer*
EMP: 12
SQ FT: 25,000
SALES (est): 3.1MM **Privately Held**
SIC: 3728 Aircraft assemblies, subassemblies & parts

(G-597)
STEVEOS CUSTOM WOOD-WORK LLC
5202 N Rockwell Ave (73008-2034)
P.O. Box 2955, Dillon CO (80435-2955)
PHONE 405 532-1863
Steve Norman, *Owner*
EMP: 1
SALES (est): 56.7K **Privately Held**
SIC: 2431 Millwork

(G-598)
TBK INDUSTRIES LLC
6656 Nw 39th Expy Ste 101 (73008-2704)
P.O. Box 1159 (73008-1159)
PHONE 405 789-6940
Steven Glass, *Mng Member*
Helen Glass,
EMP: 3
SQ FT: 900
SALES (est): 162K **Privately Held**
SIC: 3086 Ice chests or coolers (portable), foamed plastic

(G-599)
TURBINE AIRCRAFT SERVICES LLC
7101 Mllonaire Dr Bethany (73008)
PHONE 405 491-8995
Michael Harbison,
Terri Harbison,
EMP: 5
SQ FT: 12,000
SALES (est): 1MM **Privately Held**
SIC: 4581 5599 3728 Aircraft servicing & repairing; aircraft instruments, equipment or parts; aircraft parts & equipment

(G-600)
WESNER PUBLICATIONS COMPANY
Also Called: Tribune-Review
6728 Nw 38th St (73008-3360)
P.O. Box 40 (73008-0040)
PHONE 405 789-1962
Gloria Quiad, *Managing Prtnr*
EMP: 10 **Privately Held**
WEB: www.cordellbeacon.com
SIC: 2711 Newspapers: publishing only, not printed on site
PA: Wesner Publications Company
115 E Main St
Cordell OK 73632

Big Cabin
Craig County

(G-601)
CIMCO INDUSTRIES LLC
32207 S Highway 69 (74332-8537)
PHONE 918 783-5500
EMP: 2
SALES (est): 85.6K **Privately Held**
SIC: 3498 Piping systems for pulp paper & chemical industries

(G-602)
DECAL SHOP
432332 E 330 Rd (74332-8607)
PHONE 918 783-5206
Tammy Fetter, *Owner*
EMP: 1
SALES (est): 103.7K **Privately Held**
SIC: 2759 Screen printing

(G-603)
EXPRESS METAL FABRICATORS INC
32207 S Highway 69 (74332-8537)
PHONE 918 783-5129
Dale Williams, *Manager*
▲ **EMP:** 90
SALES (est): 7.6MM **Privately Held**
SIC: 3441 3567 3443 Fabricated structural metal; industrial furnaces & ovens; fabricated plate work (boiler shop)

(G-604)
FOUR STATE MEAT PROCESSING LLC
440439 E 320 Rd (74332-8030)
PHONE 918 783-5556
Cindy Greenwood, *Mng Member*
Dallas Greenwood,
Gary Greenwood,
EMP: 15
SALES (est): 1.7MM **Privately Held**
SIC: 2011 Meat packing plants

(G-605)
SAM YEOMAN
Also Called: Yeomans Mch Sp & Auto Parts
287 W Main St (74332-5004)
P.O. Box 112 (74332-0112)
PHONE 918 783-5608
Sam Yeoman, *Owner*
EMP: 3
SALES (est): 212.6K **Privately Held**
SIC: 3599 Machine shop, jobbing & repair

Binger
Caddo County

(G-606)
GUNTER PEANUT CO
401 S Broadway (73009)
P.O. Box H (73009-0508)
PHONE 405 656-2398
Robert Gunter, *Owner*
EMP: 25
SALES (est): 3.5MM **Privately Held**
SIC: 5159 2068 Peanuts (bulk), unroasted; salted & roasted nuts & seeds

---
Bison
Garfield County

(G-607)
BISON WELDING LLC
16128 S Van Burren (73720)
PHONE 580 758-3359
Larry Kokojan, *Mng Member*
EMP: 3
SALES (est): 574.6K **Privately Held**
SIC: 3449 7692 Bars, concrete reinforcing: fabricated steel; welding repair

---
Bixby
Tulsa County

(G-608)
AFG ACQUISITION GROUP LLC (PA)
Also Called: American Foundry Group
14602 S Grant St (74008-3714)
PHONE 918 366-4401
Philip Harper, *President*
Jogi Makhani, *Vice Pres*
David Standridge, *Purch Mgr*
Jim Vandeventer, *Controller*
Susan Tackett, *Human Res Dir*
EMP: 273
SQ FT: 120
SALES (est): 78.9MM **Privately Held**
SIC: 3324 Steel investment foundries

(G-609)
AGE STONE MANUFACTURING
19473 S Harvard Ave (74008-5807)
PHONE 918 366-3270
Joe Rider, *President*
EMP: 8
SALES (est): 1.1MM **Privately Held**
SIC: 3272 Fireplace & chimney material: concrete

(G-610)
ALLISON ALLISON INC
11822 S 96th East Pl (74008-1772)
PHONE 918 344-1768
Darren Allison, *President*
EMP: 1
SALES (est): 120K **Privately Held**
SIC: 3441 Fabricated structural metal

(G-611)
ARCADIA PRINTING OF TULSA INC
14956 S Grant St (74008-3834)
PHONE 918 622-1875
Rick Ellis, *President*
Wanda Ellis, *Vice Pres*
Ryan Ellis, *Sales Staff*
EMP: 4
SQ FT: 5,000
SALES (est): 489.3K **Privately Held**
SIC: 2752 Commercial printing, offset

(G-612)
ARROWHEAD TRUCK EQUIPMENT INC
12300 S Mingo Rd (74008-2141)
P.O. Box 459 (74008-0459)
PHONE 918 224-5570
David Justin Doak, *President*
Kimberly D Doak, *Admin Sec*
EMP: 8
SALES (est): 1.5MM **Privately Held**
SIC: 3713 Truck & bus bodies

(G-613)
AVIATION TRAINING DEVICES INC
613 W Needles Ave (74008-4131)
P.O. Box 777 (74008-0777)
PHONE 918 366-6680
Roger Ganner, *President*
EMP: 10
SQ FT: 13,000
SALES (est): 1.5MM **Privately Held**
SIC: 3728 3812 3699 2531 Aircraft training equipment; search & navigation equipment; electrical equipment & supplies; public building & related furniture

(G-614)
BEYOND BLINDS LLC
9622 E 117th Pl S (74008-1700)
PHONE 918 935-6317
Jennifer Sanford, *Principal*
EMP: 1
SALES (est): 57.3K **Privately Held**
SIC: 2591 Window blinds

(G-615)
BIXBY FABCO INC
8900 E 171st St S (74008-6400)
PHONE 918 366-3446
Tom Rash, *President*
Russell Rash, *Vice Pres*
EMP: 15
SALES (est): 3MM **Privately Held**
SIC: 3441 Fabricated structural metal

(G-616)
BY-WELD INDUSTRIES INC
7900 E 148th St S (74008)
P.O. Box 760 (74008-0760)
PHONE 918 366-4850
Robert Fuqua, *President*
EMP: 15
SQ FT: 12,500
SALES (est): 1.2MM **Privately Held**
SIC: 3441 Fabricated structural metal

(G-617)
CMG INTERNATIONAL LLC
Also Called: Cmgi
11811 S 96th East Pl (74008-1783)
PHONE 918 493-5888
Don Maney, *Mng Member*
EMP: 2 **EST:** 2012
SALES (est): 201.6K **Privately Held**
SIC: 2541 Table or counter tops, plastic laminated

(G-618)
COPPER ACCENTS BY JERRY
12808 S Memorial Dr # 107 (74008-2596)
PHONE 918 724-8473
Jerry Mulkey, *Owner*
EMP: 4
SALES (est): 430.7K **Privately Held**
WEB: www.copperaccentsbyjerry.com
SIC: 3444 Sheet metalwork

(G-619)
CUPCAKES BY LU
12681 S 88th East Ave (74008-2496)
PHONE 918 671-0599
Bruno Teles, *Principal*
EMP: 4
SALES (est): 189.6K **Privately Held**
SIC: 2051 Bread, cake & related products

(G-620)
DOUGLAS ROSE CUSTOM TAILORING
Also Called: Douglass Rose Custom Clothing
17115 E 176th St S (74008-7328)
PHONE 918 366-6002
Douglas Rose, *President*
Cindy Rose, *Vice Pres*
EMP: 2
SALES (est): 161K **Privately Held**
SIC: 2311 Tailored suits & formal jackets

(G-621)
ETCHED IN STONE
8303 E 111th St S Ste A (74008-2457)
PHONE 918 369-0500
James Hartlep, *Principal*
▲ **EMP:** 4 **EST:** 2007
SALES (est): 377K **Privately Held**
SIC: 3479 Etching & engraving

(G-622)
FAIRWAY E&P LLC
14322 S 50th East Ave (74008-3759)
PHONE 918 284-5322
Winfred Kopczynski,
EMP: 2 **EST:** 2016
SALES (est): 109K **Privately Held**
SIC: 1311 Natural gas production

(G-623)
FLOATINGMATS LLC
13330 S 19th St (74008-1010)
PHONE 918 504-8586
Jay James Rogers, *Administration*
EMP: 4
SALES (est): 320.1K **Privately Held**
SIC: 3949 Sporting & athletic goods

(G-624)
FURRS CUSTOM WOODWORK
18237 S 132nd East Ave (74008-7761)
PHONE 918 406-7021
Jason Furr, *Principal*
EMP: 2
SALES (est): 119.7K **Privately Held**
SIC: 2431 Millwork

(G-625)
G & D INDUSTRIES INC
11448 S 99th East Ave (74008-2221)
PHONE 918 369-2648
Greg Alleva, *President*
Dianne Alleva, *Vice Pres*
EMP: 2
SALES: 350K **Privately Held**
SIC: 3088 3053 Bathroom fixtures, plastic; gaskets, packing & sealing devices

(G-626)
G C BROACH CO
11323 S 109th East Ave (74008-2865)
PHONE 918 369-4320
Larry T Totten, *Principal*
EMP: 2
SALES (est): 183.6K **Privately Held**
SIC: 3541 Machine tools, metal cutting type

(G-627)
GALLEY LLC
12626 S Memorial Dr (74008-2655)
PHONE 918 794-2700
Scott Anderson, *President*
Lori East, *Accounting Mgr*
Gabby Vonigas, *Marketing Staff*

Bixby - Tulsa County (G-628)

David Kotowsky,
Roger Schollmier,
EMP: 8
SALES: 5MM **Privately Held**
WEB: www.thegalley.com
SIC: 3431 Sinks: enameled iron, cast iron or pressed metal

(G-628)
GARBAGE TO GARDEN COMPOST INC
8617 E 132nd St S (74008-3308)
PHONE..............................918 260-4463
Callie Escue, *Director*
EMP: 2
SALES (est): 99.3K **Privately Held**
SIC: 2875 Compost

(G-629)
GUARDIAN INTERLOCK SYSTEMS
8311 E 111th St S Ste G (74008-2464)
PHONE..............................918 369-9935
EMP: 2
SALES (est): 104.2K **Privately Held**
SIC: 3829 Breathalyzers

(G-630)
GYPSY TWANG PUBLISHING
14578 S Gary Pl (74008-7611)
PHONE..............................918 398-3116
EMP: 1
SALES (est): 37.5K **Privately Held**
SIC: 2741 Miscellaneous publishing

(G-631)
H&H RETAIL SERVICES LLC
Also Called: H&H Printer Services
12816 S Memorial Dr # 110 (74008-2592)
P.O. Box 330225, Tulsa (74133-0225)
PHONE..............................918 369-4055
Eric Hartman, *Mng Member*
G Renee Hartman,
EMP: 11
SALES (est): 3.1MM **Privately Held**
SIC: 2893 5085 7699 5999 Printing ink; ink, printers'; printing trades machinery & equipment repair; alcoholic beverage making equipment & supplies

(G-632)
HOLLIDAY SAND GRAVEL CO LLC
14389 S Mingo Rd (74008-3536)
P.O. Box 606 (74008-0606)
PHONE..............................918 369-8850
Mark Thompson, *Principal*
EMP: 3
SALES (est): 162.7K **Privately Held**
SIC: 1442 Construction sand & gravel

(G-633)
HOW TO BUILD A FLAGSTONE PATIO
12300 S Mingo Rd (74008-2141)
PHONE..............................405 478-1200
EMP: 2
SALES (est): 62.6K **Privately Held**
SIC: 3281 Flagstones

(G-634)
IDEALIST SOFTWARE LLC
18003 S 72nd East Ave (74008-7006)
PHONE..............................918 609-4364
EMP: 1
SALES (est): 77K **Privately Held**
SIC: 7372 Prepackaged Software Services

(G-635)
INFINITY HOME SOLUTIONS LLC
12806 S Memorial Dr # 113 (74008-2589)
PHONE..............................918 704-8014
EMP: 2 **EST:** 2010
SALES (est): 180K **Privately Held**
SIC: 5099 3651 7929 Video & audio equipment; home entertainment equipment, electronic; entertainment service

(G-636)
J B HOT OIL AND STEAM CO INC
18134 S Harvard Ave (74008-5601)
PHONE..............................918 366-3872
John Bittle, *President*
EMP: 2
SALES (est): 200.3K **Privately Held**
SIC: 1389 Oil field services

(G-637)
JALEX LLC
6583 E 122nd St S (74008-2729)
PHONE..............................405 627-7856
Jean Ann Lundeen, *Mng Member*
EMP: 1 **EST:** 2014
SALES: 41.8K **Privately Held**
SIC: 1382 Oil & gas exploration services

(G-638)
JASON M HAAG
Also Called: Edge One Signs
8230 E 111th Pl S Ste C (74008-2454)
PHONE..............................918 369-1805
Jason Hag, *Owner*
EMP: 1
SALES (est): 81.3K **Privately Held**
SIC: 3993 Signs, not made in custom sign painting shops

(G-639)
KEVIN DAVIS COMPANY
9919 E 46th Pl (74008)
P.O. Box 656 (74008-0656)
PHONE..............................918 280-0717
Kevin Davis, *Owner*
EMP: 2
SQ FT: 1,224
SALES (est): 146K **Privately Held**
SIC: 3536 Hoists, cranes & monorails

(G-640)
KING CBD DISTRIBUTING LLC
9012 E 138th St S (74008-3919)
PHONE..............................918 698-7118
Marcus King, *Principal*
EMP: 2 **EST:** 2017
SALES (est): 94.6K **Privately Held**
SIC: 3999

(G-641)
KING PROPERTIES INC
14 N Armstrong St (74008-4446)
P.O. Box 10 (74008-0010)
PHONE..............................918 366-6868
Donald Stephens, *President*
EMP: 1
SALES (est): 96.8K **Privately Held**
SIC: 1311 Crude petroleum production

(G-642)
LITTA SOLUTIONS LLC
14242 E 208th St S (74008-7719)
PHONE..............................918 845-4854
Loren Green,
Irina Green,
EMP: 2
SALES (est): 110.9K **Privately Held**
SIC: 1389 3589 Oil field services; servicing machines, except dry cleaning, laundry: coin-oper.

(G-643)
MASTER MACHINE
16552 S 129th East Ave (74008-7110)
P.O. Box 905 (74008-0905)
PHONE..............................918 366-4855
George Roberts, *Owner*
EMP: 1
SALES (est): 143.5K **Privately Held**
SIC: 3549 Metalworking machinery

(G-644)
MC MACHINING INC
16416 S 129th East Ave (74008-7153)
PHONE..............................918 521-8945
Henry McClain, *President*
Dani McClain, *Vice Pres*
EMP: 2
SALES: 75K **Privately Held**
SIC: 3599 Machine shop, jobbing & repair

(G-645)
MIRACLE RECREATION EQP CO
14221 S Urbana Ave (74008-3791)
PHONE..............................918 299-1415
Clay Carter, *Manager*
EMP: 1 **Publicly Held**
SIC: 3949 Playground equipment
HQ: Miracle Recreation Equipment Company
878 E Us Highway 60
Monett MO 65708
888 458-2752

(G-646)
MONROE GRAY LLC (PA)
122 W Breckenridge Ave (74008-4437)
PHONE..............................918 813-6588
Jenny Collier,
EMP: 2
SALES: 621K **Privately Held**
SIC: 5621 7372 Women's clothing stores; application computer software

(G-647)
NATURAL STONE INTERIORS
611 W Breckenridge Ave (74008-4458)
PHONE..............................918 851-3451
Edward Swanson,
Angela Swanson,
EMP: 10
SALES: 719.7K **Privately Held**
SIC: 7389 1743 3281 Interior design services; marble installation, interior; granite, cut & shaped

(G-648)
NEW DAY CREATIONS LLC
12345 S Memorial Dr # 120 (74008-2569)
PHONE..............................918 576-9619
Jun LI, *Mng Member*
EMP: 1
SALES (est): 62.1K **Privately Held**
SIC: 3089 Synthetic resin finished products

(G-649)
NMB MANUFACTURING LLC
8453 E 151st St S (74008-4317)
PHONE..............................918 943-6633
Dennis Nuley, *President*
Robert Barnett, *Vice Pres*
Rick Martin, *Vice Pres*
EMP: 17
SQ FT: 1,000
SALES (est): 5.4MM **Privately Held**
SIC: 2911 Oils, fuel

(G-650)
OKLAHOMA SLF-DEFENSE CARRY LLC
10317 E 112th Pl S (74008-3236)
PHONE..............................918 814-0122
EMP: 2
SALES (est): 138.9K **Privately Held**
SIC: 3812 Defense systems & equipment

(G-651)
PAINT HANDY LLC
8303 E 111th St S Ste E (74008-2457)
PHONE..............................918 734-3422
Maria Eugenia Cantu, *Purch Mgr*
Federico Yanez,
Samuel Guzman,
EMP: 9
SALES (est): 961K **Privately Held**
SIC: 2851 Paints & allied products

(G-652)
PAPERWORK COMPANY
11 E Dawes Ave (74008-4414)
PHONE..............................918 369-1014
Jim Kirkpatrick, *President*
Tom Daniels, *Shareholder*
Ray Odom, *Shareholder*
EMP: 10 **EST:** 1975
SQ FT: 12,000
SALES (est): 1.6MM **Privately Held**
SIC: 2752 5112 2796 Commercial printing, offset; stationery & office supplies; office supplies; platemaking services

(G-653)
REX B BENWAY
16401 S Yale Ave (74008-5126)
PHONE..............................918 366-3626
Rex B Benway, *Owner*
EMP: 2
SALES (est): 132.3K **Privately Held**
SIC: 1389 Oil consultants

(G-654)
ROBINOWITZ OIL COMPANY
419 W Main St (74008)
PHONE..............................918 557-1544
EMP: 7
SALES (est): 321.7K **Privately Held**
SIC: 1382 Oil/Gas Exploration Services

(G-655)
RON SHANKS RACING ENTERPRISES
15303 E 161st St S (74008-7265)
PHONE..............................918 366-6050
Ronald Shanks, *President*
EMP: 1
SQ FT: 3,200
SALES (est): 153.5K **Privately Held**
SIC: 3711 3714 Automobile assembly, including specialty automobiles; motor vehicle parts & accessories

(G-656)
RV SMART PRODUCTS LLC
14759 S Grant St (74008-3703)
PHONE..............................575 513-1712
Mike Bakker, *Owner*
Chad Whittington, *CFO*
Mike Bakker Sr, *Director*
EMP: 2
SQ FT: 3,000
SALES: 150K **Privately Held**
SIC: 3714 Motor vehicle parts & accessories

(G-657)
S&S CUSTOM WOOD MOLDINGS LLC (PA)
14625 S Grant St (74008-3705)
P.O. Box 576 (74008-0576)
PHONE..............................214 995-8710
Terry Seabolt, *Mng Member*
▲ **EMP:** 15
SQ FT: 24,000
SALES (est): 2.1MM **Privately Held**
SIC: 2431 Moldings, wood: unfinished & prefinished

(G-658)
SIGNATURE GRAPHICS CORP
11110 S 82nd East Pl D (74008-2470)
PHONE..............................918 294-3485
Patti Ledford, *President*
Jerry Ledford, *Vice Pres*
Pam Brown, *Manager*
EMP: 7
SALES: 390K **Privately Held**
SIC: 2752 5947 3993 2791 Commercial printing, offset; novelties; signs & advertising specialties; typesetting; bookbinding & related work

(G-659)
SIMAIR LTD
613 W Needles Ave (74008-4131)
P.O. Box 777 (74008-0777)
PHONE..............................918 366-6680
Roger L Ganner, *Principal*
EMP: 10
SQ FT: 13,500
SALES: 3MM **Privately Held**
SIC: 3599 Machine shop, jobbing & repair

(G-660)
SOLAR VIEW LLC
18622 S 62nd East Ave (74008-5739)
PHONE..............................918 366-6413
Harry Barbour,
EMP: 3
SALES (est): 80K **Privately Held**
SIC: 5023 3812 1799 5999 Window shades; air traffic control systems & equipment, electronic; window treatment installation; miscellaneous retail stores

(G-661)
SONNY MAC INDUSTRIES INC (PA)
Also Called: Hotrod City USA
12806 S Memorial Dr (74008-2589)
P.O. Box 470988, Tulsa (74147-0988)
PHONE..............................918 261-8446
Sonny McMillan, *President*
Claudette McMillan, *Admin Sec*
EMP: 12
SQ FT: 3,000

GEOGRAPHIC SECTION

Blackwell - Kay County (G-692)

SALES: 500K **Privately Held**
SIC: 3714 Motor vehicle transmissions, drive assemblies & parts

(G-662)
SOUTH MANUFACTURING INC
11640 S Memorial Dr (74008-2033)
PHONE...................918 894-5255
John S Coombs, *President*
Monica L Coombs, *Vice Pres*
Donna S Harrison, *Treasurer*
EMP: 4 EST: 1965
SQ FT: 9,000
SALES (est): 572.3K **Privately Held**
SIC: 3844 X-ray apparatus & tubes

(G-663)
SPARKS GREG OPERATING CO
8307 E 111th St S Ste N (74008-2461)
P.O. Box 985, Vinita (74301-0985)
PHONE...................918 633-8807
Gregory Sparks, *Owner*
EMP: 10
SQ FT: 1,000
SALES (est): 750K **Privately Held**
SIC: 1382 Oil & gas exploration services

(G-664)
SPEER CUSHION CO
9513 E 117th St S (74008-1819)
PHONE...................970 854-2911
Deb Dusenbury, *President*
EMP: 8 EST: 1957
SQ FT: 40,000
SALES (est): 833.7K **Privately Held**
WEB: www.speercushion.com
SIC: 2393 2399 Cushions, except spring & carpet: purchased materials; seat covers, automobile

(G-665)
STELLAR ART PUBLISHING INC
5765 E 140th St S (74008-4126)
PHONE...................918 277-3325
David Lemon, *Principal*
EMP: 2
SALES (est): 92.4K **Privately Held**
SIC: 2741 Miscellaneous publishing

(G-666)
TOWNSEND MARKETING INC
8315 E 111th St S Ste J (74008-2466)
PHONE...................918 496-9222
Perry K Townsend, *Principal*
Jamie Townsend, *Corp Secy*
EMP: 8
SQ FT: 1,600
SALES (est): 1MM **Privately Held**
SIC: 2396 5699 5199 Stamping fabric articles; T-shirts, custom printed; advertising specialties

(G-667)
TULSA CASTING INC
15250 S 76th East Ave (74008-4164)
PHONE...................918 366-1272
Greg Folz, *President*
Peggy Folz, *Corp Secy*
George Folz, *Vice Pres*
EMP: 7
SALES: 550K **Privately Held**
SIC: 3272 Concrete products, precast

(G-668)
TULSA TURBINES
8303 E 111th St S Ste Q (74008-2458)
PHONE...................918 960-8918
EMP: 2
SALES (est): 115.1K **Privately Held**
SIC: 3728 Aircraft parts & equipment

(G-669)
V W CASEY INDUSTRIES LLC
8312 E 132nd St S (74008-3313)
PHONE...................918 369-5205
Virgil Casey, *Principal*
EMP: 2
SALES (est): 81.4K **Privately Held**
SIC: 3599 Industrial machinery

(G-670)
VERSATECH INDUSTRIES INC
14750 S Grant St (74008-3704)
PHONE...................918 366-7400
Gene Randall, *Owner*
EMP: 8

SQ FT: 1,200
SALES (est): 766K **Privately Held**
SIC: 3663 7373 3829 3671 Television broadcasting & communications equipment; computer integrated systems design; measuring & controlling devices; electron tubes; household audio & video equipment; relays & industrial controls

(G-671)
WATKINS SAND CO
Also Called: Watkins Trucking & Sand
14376 S Mingo Rd (74008-3536)
P.O. Box 687 (74008-0687)
PHONE...................918 369-5238
Frank Watkins, *President*
Adrion Watkins, *Corp Secy*
Euwin Watkins, *Vice Pres*
EMP: 30 EST: 1965
SALES (est): 2.2MM **Privately Held**
SIC: 1442 Common sand mining

(G-672)
WESMAR RACING ENGINES INC
14502 S Lewis Ave (74008-3622)
PHONE...................918 366-7222
Robert E Westphal, *President*
Daniel Gentrup, *Treasurer*
EMP: 8
SQ FT: 4,800
SALES (est): 1.2MM **Privately Held**
SIC: 3714 Motor vehicle engines & parts

Blackwell
Kay County

(G-673)
ACID INC
Also Called: A. J. Acid
421 N 20th St (74631-2466)
P.O. Box 758 (74631-0758)
PHONE...................580 363-5413
Ashley Newsome, *President*
Jeff Newsome, *Vice Pres*
EMP: 30
SALES (est): 2.1MM **Privately Held**
SIC: 1389 Acidizing wells

(G-674)
BIG DIPPER HOT OIL SERVICE
1005 S O St (74631-6409)
PHONE...................580 363-0168
Richard Denton, *President*
EMP: 4
SALES (est): 411.3K **Privately Held**
SIC: 1389 Oil field services

(G-675)
BLACKWELL WIND
220 N 20th St (74631-2421)
PHONE...................580 363-0553
EMP: 2
SALES (est): 88.1K **Privately Held**
SIC: 2711 Newspapers, publishing & printing

(G-676)
BOSTD AMERICA LLC
510 N 25th St (74631-2402)
PHONE...................580 670-0594
Stephen Valero,
EMP: 35
SALES (est): 3MM **Privately Held**
SIC: 3083 Laminated plastics plate & sheet

(G-677)
CALL
307 Wildwood Ln (74631-4425)
PHONE...................580 789-0074
EMP: 2
SALES (est): 123.7K **Privately Held**
SIC: 3949 Sporting & athletic goods

(G-678)
CFM CORPORATION
102 S 29th St (74631-3604)
P.O. Box 549 (74631-0549)
PHONE...................580 363-2850
Kurt Ack, *President*
EMP: 15
SALES (est): 1.9MM **Privately Held**
SIC: 3321 Gray iron castings

(G-679)
CROWN OIL FIELD SERVICES LLC
2103 Ridgeway Rd (74631-3649)
PHONE...................580 363-0269
EMP: 2
SALES (est): 99K **Privately Held**
SIC: 1389 Oil/Gas Field Services

(G-680)
CUPID FOUNDATIONS INC
318 N 29th St (74631-2408)
PHONE...................580 363-1935
David Welsch, *President*
Thomas Richardosn, *Vice Pres*
Gary Foreman, *MIS Dir*
EMP: 125
SALES (corp-wide): 68.6MM **Privately Held**
SIC: 2342 Brassieres; girdles & panty girdles
PA: Cupid Foundations, Inc.
475 Park Ave S Manhattan
New York NY 10022
212 686-6224

(G-681)
DEMCO OIL & GAS COMPANY
1335 S 6th St (74631-4203)
PHONE...................580 363-4223
Dennis Kahle, *President*
Elston Kenneth Kahle, *Vice Pres*
EMP: 1 EST: 1978
SALES (est): 421.9K **Privately Held**
SIC: 1311 5531 Crude petroleum production; natural gas production; automotive parts

(G-682)
DREAMERS SCREEN PRINT AND MORE
105 S Main St (74631-2942)
PHONE...................580 761-4376
Darcy Leach, *Principal*
EMP: 2
SALES (est): 83.9K **Privately Held**
SIC: 2752 Commercial printing, lithographic

(G-683)
HMT LLC
1545 W Doolin Ave (74631-1302)
PHONE...................580 363-8800
Tommy Wilhelm, *Sales Executive*
EMP: 1
SALES (corp-wide): 112.7MM **Privately Held**
WEB: www.hmttank.com
SIC: 7699 3443 7389 1791 Tank repair; fuel tanks (oil, gas, etc.): metal plate; industrial & commercial equipment inspection service; storage tanks, metal: erection
PA: Hmt Llc
19241 David Memorial Dr # 150
Shenandoah TX 77385
281 681-7000

(G-684)
JB OIL FIELD SERVICES
421 N 20th St (74631-2466)
P.O. Box 326, Lamont (74643-0326)
PHONE...................580 363-3030
Ross Whitehead, *Principal*
EMP: 2
SALES (est): 525K **Privately Held**
SIC: 1389 Oil field services

(G-685)
KICE INDUSTRIES INC
Also Called: CFM
102 S 29th St (74631-3604)
P.O. Box 549 (74631-0549)
PHONE...................580 363-2850
Toll Free:...................888
David Kice, *President*
EMP: 50
SALES (corp-wide): 36.1MM **Privately Held**
SIC: 3444 3559 Sheet metalwork; foundry machinery & equipment
PA: Kice Industries, Inc.
5500 N Mill Heights Dr
Park City KS 67219
316 744-7148

(G-686)
KINGS WELL SERVICE
4008 W Doolin Ave (74631-9512)
P.O. Box 323 (74631-0323)
PHONE...................580 363-3912
King D Goff, *Owner*
EMP: 14 EST: 1981
SALES (est): 1MM **Privately Held**
SIC: 1389 Oil field services

(G-687)
LEWIS COUNTY PRESS LLC
Also Called: Blackwell Journal-Tribune
523 S Main St (74631-3934)
P.O. Box 760 (74631-0760)
PHONE...................580 363-3370
Tina Anderson, *Mng Member*
EMP: 5 EST: 2015
SALES (est): 156.6K **Privately Held**
SIC: 2711 5192 5963 Newspapers: publishing only, not printed on site; newspapers; newspapers, home delivery, not by printers or publishers

(G-688)
LOS ANGELES BOILER WORKS INC
Also Called: La Boiler Works
707 N 20th St (74631-2414)
P.O. Box 948 (74631-0948)
PHONE...................580 363-1312
Paul E Clark, *President*
Randall H Schaller, *Admin Sec*
EMP: 36
SQ FT: 100,000
SALES (est): 8.3MM **Privately Held**
WEB: www.laboiler.com
SIC: 3498 3443 3494 3444 Pipe fittings, fabricated from purchased pipe; tanks, standard or custom fabricated: metal plate; vessels, process or storage (from boiler shops): metal plate; valves & pipe fittings; sheet metalwork

(G-689)
MANILA FOODS
110 S Main St (74631-2943)
PHONE...................580 262-9900
EMP: 2
SALES (est): 110K **Privately Held**
SIC: 2032 Mfg Canned Specialties

(G-690)
SCHATZ PUBLISHING GROUP LLC
Also Called: Schatz Strategy Group
11950 W Highland Ave (74631-6511)
PHONE...................580 628-4607
Sheree Lewis,
Hiyan Sisson, *Graphic Designe*
Sherrie Schatz,
EMP: 17
SQ FT: 1,400
SALES: 1.5MM **Privately Held**
SIC: 2741 Miscellaneous publishing

(G-691)
SHEBESTER BECHTEL INC (PA)
605 N 29th St (74631-2439)
P.O. Box 311 (74631-0311)
PHONE...................580 363-4124
R C Bechtel, *President*
Bob Blue, *Exec VP*
Brad Bechtel, *Vice Pres*
Bruce Dale, *CFO*
Chris Tucker, *Human Res Dir*
EMP: 70
SQ FT: 3,000
SALES (est): 41.1MM **Privately Held**
SIC: 1389 Oil field services

(G-692)
SOONER STATE PATTERN WORKS
2701 W Dewey St (74631-2470)
PHONE...................580 363-1543
Rick Bullessfeld, *President*
EMP: 7
SQ FT: 7,500
SALES (est): 590K **Privately Held**
SIC: 3543 Foundry patternmaking

Blackwell - Kay County

(G-693)
SOUTHWEST CORSET CORPORATION
Also Called: Southwest Cupid
318 N 29th St (74631-2408)
P.O. Box 700 (74631-0700)
PHONE..................580 363-1935
David Welsh, *Manager*
EMP: 230
SALES (corp-wide): 7.3MM **Privately Held**
WEB: www.cupidintimates.com
SIC: 5812 2341 Eating places; women's & children's underwear
PA: Southwest Corset Corporation
318 N 29th St
Blackwell OK 74631
212 686-6224

(G-694)
TRI RESOURCES INC
Also Called: Dynegy
14500 W Adobe Rd (74631-6856)
P.O. Box 391 (74631-0391)
PHONE..................580 363-0243
EMP: 2
SALES (corp-wide): 8.6B **Publicly Held**
SIC: 1321 Natural Gas Liquids Production
HQ: Tri Resources Inc.
1000 Louisiana St # 4300
Houston TX 77002
713 584-1000

(G-695)
WRIGHTS MACHINE SHOP
2245 S Main St (74631-6752)
P.O. Box 876 (74631-0876)
PHONE..................580 363-1740
Darin Wright, *Owner*
EMP: 2
SALES (est): 110K **Privately Held**
SIC: 3599 7692 3544 Machine shop, jobbing & repair; welding repair; special dies, tools, jigs & fixtures

Blair
Jackson County

(G-696)
LEISURE LANE HANDICRAFTS
115 W 9th (73526)
P.O. Box 321 (73526-0321)
PHONE..................580 563-2747
Larry W Paxton, *Owner*
EMP: 2 **EST:** 1977
SALES (est): 103.8K **Privately Held**
SIC: 3944 Craft & hobby kits & sets

(G-697)
PETZOLD BUILDINGS LLC
15319 Us Highway 283 (73526)
P.O. Box 475 (73526-0475)
PHONE..................580 563-2818
Talyan Petzold,
David Petzold,
EMP: 11 **EST:** 2001
SALES: 801K **Privately Held**
SIC: 3448 Buildings, portable: prefabricated metal

Blanchard
Mcclain County

(G-698)
30 CENT PRINT LLC
7406 N Council Rd (73010-8017)
PHONE..................469 408-8968
Tommy Brooks, *Principal*
EMP: 2
SALES (est): 90.4K **Privately Held**
SIC: 2752 Commercial printing, lithographic

(G-699)
ABMI INC
211 Sw 6th St (73010-5205)
PHONE..................405 485-9608
EMP: 2
SALES (est): 88.9K **Privately Held**
SIC: 3089 Plastics products

(G-700)
ACCURATE MACHINE WORKS INC
1266 County Street 2964 (73010-3026)
PHONE..................405 615-4983
Dustin Sandlin, *President*
EMP: 10
SALES: 400K **Privately Held**
SIC: 3728 3711 Aircraft assemblies, sub-assemblies & parts; automobile assembly, including specialty automobiles

(G-701)
BJS OILFIELD CNSTR INC
722 W Veterans Mem Hwy (73010-8946)
P.O. Box 696 (73010-0696)
PHONE..................405 485-3390
Billy Graham, *President*
Frank White, *Vice Pres*
Vanessa Tedder,
EMP: 46
SQ FT: 3,750
SALES (est): 6.2MM **Privately Held**
SIC: 1389 Servicing oil & gas wells; building oil & gas well foundations on site

(G-702)
BLANCHARD NEWS PUBLISHING
220 N Main (73010-5701)
P.O. Box 60 (73010-0060)
PHONE..................405 485-2311
Ross Coyle, *President*
EMP: 5
SQ FT: 1,000
SALES (est): 385.8K **Privately Held**
SIC: 2711 2791 Newspapers: publishing only, not printed on site; typesetting

(G-703)
C & C BACKHOE & TRACTOR INC
2313 County Road 1214 (73010-2814)
PHONE..................405 392-4699
Ronnie D Conner, *Principal*
EMP: 2
SALES (est): 173.8K **Privately Held**
SIC: 3531 Backhoes

(G-704)
CANVASS LLC
1429 Bradford Pl (73010-8216)
PHONE..................580 284-7896
David George, *Info Tech Mgr*
Phong Hoang,
EMP: 1 **EST:** 2012
SALES (est): 50K **Privately Held**
SIC: 7372 Application computer software; business oriented computer software

(G-705)
CAREL PUMPING
1007 Summer Oaks Dr (73010-9751)
PHONE..................405 485-3495
Glenda Carel, *Partner*
John Carel, *Partner*
EMP: 2
SALES (est): 168.7K **Privately Held**
SIC: 1381 Drilling oil & gas wells

(G-706)
CENTERPIECE CUSTOM WDWKG LLC
8418 Shadow Lake Dr (73010-4026)
PHONE..................405 387-9312
David Bryon Jones, *Owner*
EMP: 1
SALES (est): 54.1K **Privately Held**
SIC: 2431 Millwork

(G-707)
CLASSIC CHISEL CABINET SHOP
2280 County Road 1247 (73010-3010)
PHONE..................405 387-2216
Kerry Alexander, *Owner*
EMP: 2
SALES (est): 250.5K **Privately Held**
SIC: 3553 Cabinet makers' machinery

(G-708)
CRAFTY MANATEES LLC
938 Timber Xing (73010-8711)
PHONE..................405 630-5415
Kris Stowers, *Principal*
EMP: 3
SALES (est): 126.5K **Privately Held**
SIC: 2759 Screen printing

(G-709)
DEANGEL FARMS & WINERY LLC
3041 S County Line Ave (73010-3909)
PHONE..................405 996-0914
Frank Deangelis, *Principal*
EMP: 2
SALES (est): 110.5K **Privately Held**
SIC: 2084 Wines

(G-710)
DEREKS PIT LLC
922 S Rockwell Ave (73010-5041)
PHONE..................405 485-2562
Patsy Raper, *Owner*
EMP: 1
SALES: 95K **Privately Held**
SIC: 1442 Sand mining

(G-711)
DEVILBISS CORING SERVICE INC
2373 County Road 1207 (73010-2806)
PHONE..................405 392-2515
Elizabeth Devilbiss, *President*
Virgil Devilbiss, *Vice Pres*
EMP: 2
SALES (est): 167.5K **Privately Held**
SIC: 1389 Oil field services

(G-712)
DODCO OF OKLAHOMA LLC
1041 Parrish Pl (73010-3488)
PHONE..................405 314-1757
Leslie Dodd, *Principal*
EMP: 5
SALES (est): 349.6K **Privately Held**
SIC: 3496 Miscellaneous fabricated wire products

(G-713)
ECONOLITE CONTROL PRODUCTS INC
Rr 5 Box 977 (73010-9805)
P.O. Box 3 (73010-0003)
PHONE..................405 485-2230
Steve Outon, *Manager*
EMP: 1
SALES (corp-wide): 70MM **Privately Held**
SIC: 3669 Traffic signals, electric
PA: Econolite Control Products, Inc.
1250 N Tustin Ave
Anaheim CA 92807
714 630-3700

(G-714)
ELITE POLISHING CO
114 Nw 3rd St (73010-5713)
P.O. Box 971 (73010-0971)
PHONE..................405 371-5780
Samuel Thomas, *Principal*
EMP: 2
SALES (est): 126.6K **Privately Held**
WEB: www.elitepolishingco.com
SIC: 3599 Machine shop, jobbing & repair

(G-715)
H & M ENERGY SERVICES LLC
200 Sheperds Way (73010-7209)
P.O. Box 1523 (73010-1523)
PHONE..................405 428-0740
Natheniel Hacker, *President*
EMP: 7
SALES (est): 335.4K **Privately Held**
SIC: 1389 Servicing oil & gas wells

(G-716)
INFINITY SCREENPRINTING LLC
1899 Doc Bar Ave (73010-9503)
PHONE..................405 485-3203
Richard Smalley, *Principal*
EMP: 2
SALES (est): 165.9K **Privately Held**
SIC: 2759 Screen printing

(G-717)
JACK SPRAGUE
1035 County Street 2982 (73010-4440)
PHONE..................405 367-7655
Jack Sprague, *Principal*
EMP: 1
SALES (est): 93.8K **Privately Held**
SIC: 3531 Backhoes

(G-718)
JONES POWER PRODUCTS LLC
3415 Hunters Ridge Ln (73010-5535)
P.O. Box 220, Wayne (73095-0220)
PHONE..................405 485-2019
Jones Power,
Steve Jones,
EMP: 3 **EST:** 2009
SALES: 450K **Privately Held**
WEB: www.jonespowerproducts.com
SIC: 3999 Barber & beauty shop equipment

(G-719)
L & S SEAMLESS GUTTERING INC
834 S County Line Rd (73010-2907)
P.O. Box 999 (73010-0999)
PHONE..................405 392-4487
Sally Linam, *President*
EMP: 2
SALES (est): 296.4K **Privately Held**
SIC: 3444 1521 1761 Gutters, sheet metal; culverts, flumes & pipes; single-family home remodeling, additions & repairs; roofing, siding & sheet metal work; roofing & gutter work

(G-720)
LUTHER INDUSTRIES LLC
2450 County Road 1341 (73010-3655)
PHONE..................405 819-0346
James Luther, *Mng Member*
EMP: 1 **EST:** 2015
SALES: 200K **Privately Held**
SIC: 3444 1711 Sheet metalwork; plumbing, heating, air-conditioning contractors

(G-721)
MARCUM WELDING SERVICE
14148 State Highway 74b (73010-4647)
PHONE..................405 485-9340
EMP: 2
SALES (est): 72K **Privately Held**
SIC: 7692 Welding Contractor

(G-722)
MATADOR PROCESSING LLC
1820 N Council Aka Hwy 76 (73010)
PHONE..................405 485-3567
Betty Wood, *President*
Ron Diggs, *Vice Pres*
EMP: 32
SQ FT: 35,000
SALES (est): 6.8MM **Privately Held**
SIC: 2099 Food preparations

(G-723)
MIDWEST PERFORMANCE PACK INC
1820 N Council (73010)
P.O. Box 2200 (73010-2200)
PHONE..................405 485-3567
Chris Allensworth, *President*
EMP: 23
SALES (est): 1.2MM **Privately Held**
SIC: 3556 Smokers, food processing equipment

(G-724)
MIKES WELDING SERVICE
7756 N County Line Ave (73010-7130)
PHONE..................405 387-3782
Michael Parrish, *Owner*
EMP: 1
SALES (est): 40K **Privately Held**
SIC: 7692 Welding repair

(G-725)
PARKS OIL TOOLS LLC
703 S Tyler Ave (73010-7564)
P.O. Box 1217 (73010-1217)
PHONE..................405 485-9515
Roger Parks, *Mng Member*
EMP: 3
SQ FT: 3,000
SALES: 700K **Privately Held**
SIC: 1389 Oil field services

GEOGRAPHIC SECTION

Boley - Okfuskee County (G-756)

(G-726)
PAUL G PENNINGTON INDUSTRIES (PA)
2325 Fox Ln (73010-6626)
P.O. Box 358, Newcastle (73065-0358)
PHONE..................................405 392-2317
Paul Greg Pennington, *Owner*
Greg Pennington, *Owner*
EMP: 8
SQ FT: 10,000
SALES: 500K **Privately Held**
SIC: 3599 7692 3444 5084 Machine shop, jobbing & repair; welding repair; sheet metalwork; industrial machinery & equipment

(G-727)
PESTCO INC
606 N Monroe Ave (73010-6000)
P.O. Box 1777 (73010-1777)
PHONE..................................405 485-8060
Travece Clarque, *Owner*
EMP: 1
SALES (est): 58.4K **Privately Held**
SIC: 2393 Cushions, except spring & carpet: purchased materials

(G-728)
PRINT PLUS OK LLC
314 Nw 7th St (73010-8920)
PHONE..................................405 371-5365
EMP: 2
SALES (est): 83.9K **Privately Held**
SIC: 2752 Commercial printing, lithographic

(G-729)
RAMCO PACKERS
Hwy 76 S (73010)
P.O. Box 353 (73010-0353)
PHONE..................................405 485-8804
Walter Ott, *Owner*
EMP: 4
SALES (est): 280K **Privately Held**
SIC: 1389 Servicing oil & gas wells

(G-730)
RANK INDUSTRIES LLC
10808 270th St (73010-4109)
PHONE..................................405 308-0503
Michaela Gordy, *Principal*
EMP: 2 EST: 2016
SALES (est): 124.5K **Privately Held**
SIC: 3999 Manufacturing industries

(G-731)
RECOIL ENERGY RENTAL LLC
8177 Skyline Dr (73010-9498)
PHONE..................................405 650-1373
James C Cathey,
EMP: 1
SALES (est): 41K **Privately Held**
SIC: 1389 Roustabout service

(G-732)
RECOIL OILFIELD SERVICES LLC
8177 Skyline Dr (73010-9498)
PHONE..................................405 227-4198
Matthew Kopf, *Mng Member*
EMP: 135 EST: 2016
SALES: 3MM **Privately Held**
WEB: www.recoiloilfieldservices.com
SIC: 1389 Oil field services

(G-733)
REDRHINO LLC
547 Chippingham Ln (73010-4055)
PHONE..................................405 740-5132
EMP: 2
SALES (est): 77.4K **Privately Held**
SIC: 3489 Ordnance & accessories

(G-734)
RIVER BEND INDUSTRIES LLC
1700 Crystal Lk (73010-1197)
PHONE..................................405 703-2758
Adam Wallace, *VP Opers*
Bethany Clements, *Controller*
Will Irvin, *Sales Staff*
Buddy Cooper, *Manager*
Larry J Wallace,
EMP: 108

SALES: 35MM **Privately Held**
SIC: 3441 Building components, structural steel

(G-735)
SUNRISE SYSTEMS
2126 County Road 1386 (73010-4209)
P.O. Box 1623, Chickasha (73023-1623)
PHONE..................................405 222-3816
Ken Ferrara, *Owner*
EMP: 1
SALES (est): 109.5K **Privately Held**
SIC: 3629 Electronic generation equipment

(G-736)
SUPERIOR STAINLESS INC
1076 S Sara Rd (73010-6643)
PHONE..................................405 387-3414
Ray Adams, *President*
Sherlene Adams, *Corp Secy*
EMP: 8
SALES (est): 1.2MM **Privately Held**
SIC: 3469 Kitchen fixtures & equipment: metal, except cast aluminum

(G-737)
TEALS WELDING INC
2093 County Road 1400 (73010-4212)
PHONE..................................405 756-0615
Brent J Teal, *Owner*
EMP: 1
SALES (est): 44.8K **Privately Held**
SIC: 7692 Welding repair

(G-738)
TREND TO TREND WREATHS
2309 County Road 1268 (73010-3125)
PHONE..................................405 503-8992
Amy Roe, *Principal*
EMP: 3
SALES (est): 109.9K **Privately Held**
SIC: 3999 Wreaths, artificial

(G-739)
TROGLIN TANK GAUGE SVCS LLC
125 Prairie Hawk Ln (73010-5047)
PHONE..................................806 275-0010
Ronnie Troglin, *Mng Member*
EMP: 1
SALES (est): 129.7K **Privately Held**
SIC: 1389 Haulage, oil field

(G-740)
TSB WELDING LLC
1510 Ladderback Ln (73010-5030)
PHONE..................................405 485-4274
Haley Dawn Brown, *Principal*
EMP: 1
SALES (est): 25K **Privately Held**
SIC: 7692 Welding repair

(G-741)
TURNING POINT INDUSTRIES INC
3180 Greystone Dr (73010-7218)
P.O. Box 1805 (73010-1805)
PHONE..................................405 401-3930
Patrick S Kemery, *President*
Aaron Zike, *Vice Pres*
EMP: 60
SALES (est): 224.5K **Privately Held**
SIC: 3599 Machine shop, jobbing & repair

(G-742)
VANHOOSE WOOD CREATIONS
1514 Jacy Ln (73010-9023)
PHONE..................................405 443-0454
EMP: 2 EST: 2012
SALES (est): 98.2K **Privately Held**
SIC: 2431 Millwork

(G-743)
VICTORS ELECTRIC MOTOR S
23822 State Highway 76 (73010-3728)
PHONE..................................405 344-7339
Victor Unsell, *Principal*
EMP: 2
SALES (est): 97.5K **Privately Held**
SIC: 7694 Electric motor repair

(G-744)
VICTORY GARDEN HOMESTEAD LLC
1058 County Street 2965 (73010-4408)
PHONE..................................405 306-0308
Jeff Golinghorst,
EMP: 1
SALES (est): 27.9K **Privately Held**
SIC: 0252 2011 5148 2452 Chicken eggs; beef products from beef slaughtered on site; fresh fruits & vegetables; chicken coops, prefabricated, wood; market garden

(G-745)
WHITE BFFALO CSTM WDWRK RNVTIO ✪
5005 Eagle Nest Dr (73010-3378)
PHONE..................................405 387-3278
EMP: 2 EST: 2019
SALES (est): 85.2K **Privately Held**
SIC: 2431 Millwork

Bluejacket
Ottawa County

(G-746)
VIP MANUFACTURING CORPORATION
13356 S 4440th Rd (74333)
P.O. Box 62 (74333-0062)
PHONE..................................918 244-2131
Mike Mitchell, *President*
EMP: 1
SALES (est): 58.4K **Privately Held**
SIC: 3728 Bodies, aircraft

Boise City
Cimarron County

(G-747)
MESA BLACK PUBLISHING LLC
Also Called: Boise City News
105 W Main St (73933)
P.O. Box 278 (73933-0278)
PHONE..................................580 544-2222
Charles F David,
Charles Fankllin,
EMP: 3
SQ FT: 4,000
SALES (est): 273.6K **Privately Held**
WEB: www.boisecitynews2.wordpress.com
SIC: 2711 2759 2752 2796 Commercial printing & newspaper publishing combined; letterpress printing; screen printing; commercial printing, offset; platemaking services; typesetting; bookbinding & related work

(G-748)
NO MANS LAND FOODS LLC
Also Called: No Mans Land Beef Jerky
1016 E Main St (73933)
P.O. Box 163 (73933-0163)
PHONE..................................580 297-5142
Peter Dillingham, *Mng Member*
Paul Allen,
Clint Beagaley,
Belinda Gardner,
Marvin B Simth,
EMP: 60
SALES: 8MM **Privately Held**
SIC: 2013 Snack sticks, including jerky: from purchased meat

(G-749)
TRACI RAE WOOLMAN
Also Called: Wkp Compost
118 W Main St (73933)
P.O. Box 548 (73933-0548)
PHONE..................................580 544-2521
Traci Rae Woolman, *Owner*
William W Woolman, *Co-Owner*
EMP: 5 EST: 2013
SQ FT: 15,000
SALES: 250K **Privately Held**
SIC: 2875 Compost

Bokchito
Bryan County

(G-750)
CIMARRON MACHINE INC
1740 Dodson School Rd (74726-2224)
PHONE..................................972 658-7051
Charles A Smith, *President*
Joann Smith, *Treasurer*
EMP: 2
SALES (est): 175.9K **Privately Held**
SIC: 3599 Machine shop, jobbing & repair

(G-751)
SIGN INNOVATIONS INC
Also Called: Scare Innovations
27490 Us 70 (74726)
Rural Route 1 Box 4
PHONE..................................214 234-1614
Charla Whittington, *President*
Keith Whittington, *Vice Pres*
EMP: 2
SALES (est): 12.5K **Privately Held**
SIC: 3993 Signs & advertising specialties

Bokoshe
Le Flore County

(G-752)
C & B FABRICATORS INC
29717 Church House Rd (74930-2169)
P.O. Box 96 (74930-0096)
PHONE..................................918 760-6508
Charles Bailey, *President*
Charles E Bailey Jr, *President*
EMP: 1
SALES (est): 225.7K **Privately Held**
SIC: 3312 Structural shapes & pilings, steel

(G-753)
F & F PRODUCTION EQP SVCS LLC
Also Called: P.E.S.
25640 Winding Trail Rd (74930-2560)
PHONE..................................479 414-2772
Daniel Fout,
Jamie Fout,
EMP: 2
SALES (est): 137.2K **Privately Held**
SIC: 1382 Geological exploration, oil & gas field

(G-754)
ROCK PRODUCERS INC
24275 Mine Rd (74930)
P.O. Box 568 (74930-0568)
PHONE..................................918 969-2100
Daryl Jackson, *President*
Kevin Jackson, *Corp Secy*
EMP: 20
SQ FT: 1,000
SALES: 2MM **Privately Held**
SIC: 1429 Sandstone, crushed & broken-quarrying

(G-755)
TRUSTY WILLOW LLC
21637 Carters Lake Rd (74930-2599)
PHONE..................................253 241-0520
Britnee Stearman, *Principal*
EMP: 1
SALES (est): 51.9K **Privately Held**
SIC: 2869 9511 Butyl alcohol, butanol; alcohols, industrial: denatured (non-beverage); ethyl alcohol, ethanol; isopropyl alcohol, isopropanol; waste management agencies

Boley
Okfuskee County

(G-756)
WILLIAMS RANCH WELDING LLC
367103 Us Highway 62 (74829-3005)
PHONE..................................405 509-0289

Willie Williams Jr, *Mng Member*
EMP: 2
SALES (est): 27.2K **Privately Held**
SIC: 7692 Welding repair

Boswell
Choctaw County

(G-757)
KERR-BILT TRAILERS JL INC
491 E 2060 Rd (74727-9239)
PHONE..................................580 566-1200
John Kerr, *President*
EMP: 11 **EST:** 2011
SALES: 1.4MM **Privately Held**
WEB: www.kerrbilt.com
SIC: 5599 3715 Utility trailers; truck trailers

(G-758)
TRIPLE D MACHINE INC
406 6th St (74727-2072)
P.O. Box 479 (74727-0479)
PHONE..................................580 566-2284
James Dickson, *President*
Joyce Pomeroy, *General Mgr*
EMP: 25
SQ FT: 18,000
SALES (est): 4.2MM **Privately Held**
SIC: 3599 Machine shop, jobbing & repair

Bowlegs
Seminole County

(G-759)
KAY PRODUCTION CO INC
35833 Hi Way 59 E (74830)
P.O. Box 115 (74830-0115)
PHONE..................................405 398-4254
Dick Kay, *President*
Diana Kay, *Corp Secy*
EMP: 4
SALES: 1.2MM **Privately Held**
SIC: 1311 Crude petroleum & natural gas

Bradley
Grady County

(G-760)
BLACKJACK EXPRESS LLC
3507 County Street 2920 (73011-9758)
PHONE..................................405 462-7410
Conie Barrington,
EMP: 1
SALES (est): 222.3K **Privately Held**
SIC: 4213 2741 Trucking, except local; miscellaneous publishing

Braman
Kay County

(G-761)
OK CONTRACT SERVICES LLC
Also Called: Superior Vegetation Solutions
11587 W Indian Rd (74632-9162)
PHONE..................................918 352-5369
Miranda McDaniels, *Mng Member*
EMP: 4
SALES (est): 270.4K **Privately Held**
SIC: 0721 1382 1389 0851 Crop spraying services; geological exploration, oil & gas field; gas field services; pest control services, forest; weed control services before planting

Bristow
Creek County

(G-762)
A-1 MACHINE WORKS INC
624 Industrial Rd (74010-9701)
PHONE..................................918 367-2788
Jim McDaniel, *President*

Catherine McDaniel, *Corp Secy*
EMP: 5
SQ FT: 3,000
SALES (est): 500K **Privately Held**
SIC: 3599 5088 Machine shop, jobbing & repair; transportation equipment & supplies

(G-763)
ADVANCED WELDING & EXCAV LLC
20304 W Highway 66 (74010-2690)
PHONE..................................918 306-2061
Landon Carr,
EMP: 1 **Privately Held**
SIC: 1389 Oil & gas field services

(G-764)
APPLE STREET INC
119 W 6th Ave (74010-2840)
PHONE..................................918 367-9898
EMP: 2
SALES (est): 89.5K **Privately Held**
SIC: 3571 Mfg Electronic Computers

(G-765)
BETHEL WELDING METAL BUILDING
30515 W Highway 66 (74010-4045)
PHONE..................................918 367-5776
Harley Bethel, *Owner*
EMP: 2
SALES (est): 103.2K **Privately Held**
SIC: 7692 Welding repair

(G-766)
BISHOP BROTHERS
Also Called: Bishop Tadoli Products
113 W 5th Ave (74010-2824)
P.O. Box 814 (74010-0814)
PHONE..................................918 367-2270
Eddie Bishop, *Owner*
Pam Schook, *Manager*
EMP: 5
SQ FT: 5,000
SALES: 200K **Privately Held**
WEB: www.bishoptaboli.com
SIC: 5149 2099 Baking supplies; food preparations

(G-767)
BOB POUND DRILLING INC
Also Called: B & D Oil Co
121 W 6th Ave (74010-2801)
P.O. Box 984 (74010-0984)
PHONE..................................918 367-6262
Robert M Pound, *President*
Don Pound, *Vice Pres*
Maxine Pound, *Admin Sec*
EMP: 17
SQ FT: 4,500
SALES (est): 1.6MM **Privately Held**
SIC: 1381 1382 Drilling oil & gas wells; oil & gas exploration services

(G-768)
BRISTOW 800 KELLY LLC
800 S Kelly Ave (74010-4001)
PHONE..................................248 268-3289
Kirk Bruce, *Principal*
EMP: 1
SALES (est): 41.5K **Privately Held**
SIC: 2499 Wood products

(G-769)
BRISTOW HOT OIL & STEAM SVC
18708 S 337th West Ave (74010-2127)
P.O. Box 1083 (74010-1083)
PHONE..................................918 367-2121
Jame Gee, *President*
Ramona Gee, *Vice Pres*
EMP: 3
SALES (est): 150K **Privately Held**
SIC: 1389 Servicing oil & gas wells

(G-770)
BTM TECHNOLOGIES INC
21825 S 401st West Ave (74010-8437)
PHONE..................................918 857-2855
Mark Beach, *President*
EMP: 3 **EST:** 1998
SALES (est): 199.2K **Privately Held**
SIC: 3829 Thermometers & temperature sensors

(G-771)
BUG RIGHT
637 S Maple St (74010-3318)
P.O. Box 1048 (74010-1048)
PHONE..................................918 367-9792
Paul Goss, *Owner*
EMP: 1
SALES (est): 98.9K **Privately Held**
SIC: 2879 Agricultural chemicals

(G-772)
CALVIN HEATERS
21640 S 417th West Ave (74010-8711)
P.O. Box 576 (74010-0576)
PHONE..................................918 367-7011
Thomas B Calvin, *Partner*
Donald R Calvin, *Partner*
EMP: 2
SALES (est): 175.2K **Privately Held**
SIC: 3433 Unit heaters, domestic

(G-773)
CONFEDERITE WELDING LLC
508 W 10th Ave (74010-1804)
PHONE..................................918 407-1635
EMP: 1 **EST:** 2011
SALES (est): 48K **Privately Held**
SIC: 7692 Welding Repair

(G-774)
CONSOLDTED TRBINE SPCLISTS LLC
24323 S 385th West Ave (74010-5089)
P.O. Box 596 (74010-0596)
PHONE..................................918 367-9665
Joseph Brostmeyer, *CEO*
Johnny Grant, *President*
EMP: 6 **EST:** 2012
SQ FT: 3,200
SALES (est): 1.3MM **Publicly Held**
SIC: 3724 Turbines, aircraft type
PA: Kratos Defense & Security Solutions, Inc.
10680 Treena St Ste 600
San Diego CA 92131

(G-775)
DANNYS OILFIELD SERVICES INC
605 E 5th Ave (74010-3121)
P.O. Box 633 (74010-0633)
PHONE..................................918 645-1651
Danny Hanks, *Administration*
EMP: 1 **EST:** 2010
SALES (est): 68.8K **Privately Held**
SIC: 1389 Oil field services

(G-776)
DUNLAP WELL SERVICE INC
21 W First St (74010)
P.O. Box 837 (74010-0837)
PHONE..................................918 367-2660
Kerry Dunlap, *President*
Sam Dunlap, *Corp Secy*
Chris Dunlap, *Vice Pres*
EMP: 3
SALES (est): 300.1K **Privately Held**
SIC: 1389 Oil field services

(G-777)
FALCON OIL PROPERTIES
Hwy 66 And Turner Tpke (74010)
P.O. Box 988 (74010-0988)
PHONE..................................918 367-5596
Wiley Cox, *Partner*
EMP: 1
SALES (est): 140.7K **Privately Held**
SIC: 1311 Crude petroleum production; natural gas production

(G-778)
FISHER AG ENTERPRISES INC
Also Called: Fisher's Eggs & Grain
14 Mi S E Of Town (74010)
PHONE..................................918 367-6382
Ernest B Fisher, *President*
David Fisher, *Vice Pres*
Mark Fisher, *Treasurer*
Helen C Fisher, *Admin Sec*
EMP: 14
SALES (est): 4.4MM **Privately Held**
SIC: 5191 5144 0191 2048 Feed; eggs; general farms, primarily crop; prepared feeds

(G-779)
ILLINOIS REFINING CO
210 E 9th Ave (74010-2516)
P.O. Box 749 (74010-0749)
PHONE..................................918 367-5562
George W Krumme, *President*
Robert Krumme, *Vice Pres*
EMP: 2 **EST:** 1921
SQ FT: 9,400
SALES: 500K **Privately Held**
SIC: 1311 Crude petroleum production

(G-780)
IRON HORSE ROUSTABOUT SVCS LLC
34251 W 161st St S (74010-2542)
PHONE..................................918 352-8586
Brittney Nichole Bishop, *Administration*
EMP: 2
SALES (est): 89.6K **Privately Held**
SIC: 1389 Roustabout service

(G-781)
J B WOODWORKING
17525 S 273rd West Ave (74010-2277)
PHONE..................................918 760-2399
Ed Beaver, *President*
EMP: 2
SALES (est): 176.2K **Privately Held**
SIC: 2431 Millwork

(G-782)
JEFFERY W MATLOCK
35000 W Highway 66 (74010-9335)
P.O. Box 1016 (74010-1016)
PHONE..................................918 367-9828
Jeffery Matlock, *Owner*
EMP: 2
SALES (est): 143.6K **Privately Held**
SIC: 3441 Building components, structural steel

(G-783)
JIM WATKINS
109 S Main St (74010-2802)
PHONE..................................918 367-5575
Jim Watkins, *Principal*
EMP: 1
SALES (est): 65.4K **Privately Held**
SIC: 3993 Signs & advertising specialties

(G-784)
JULY GAS LTD LIABILITY CO
27301 W 201st St S (74010-2236)
PHONE..................................918 367-2831
Dwight M Blansett, *Administration*
EMP: 2
SALES (est): 118.7K **Privately Held**
SIC: 2911 Gases & liquefied petroleum gases

(G-785)
KEVIN BANKS
Also Called: Banks Son Backhoe & Dumptruck
1020 E Tejon Ave (74010-3915)
PHONE..................................918 230-2142
Kevin Banks, *Principal*
EMP: 1
SALES (est): 105.2K **Privately Held**
SIC: 3531 Backhoes

(G-786)
KIMBERLING CITY PUBLISHING CO
Also Called: Bristow News
112 W 6th Ave (74010-2810)
P.O. Box 840 (74010-0840)
PHONE..................................918 367-2282
Don Stumner, *President*
Francis Stipe, *President*
Robbie Mangum, *Advt Staff*
Sharan Reagan, *Manager*
Dee Eslick, *Admin Asst*
EMP: 5 **EST:** 1948
SQ FT: 5,000
SALES (est): 468.6K **Privately Held**
WEB: www.bristownews.com
SIC: 2752 2711 Commercial printing, offset; newspapers: publishing only, not printed on site

GEOGRAPHIC SECTION

Broken Arrow - Tulsa County (G-818)

(G-787)
KRUMME OIL COMPANY LLP
210 E 9th Ave (74010-2516)
P.O. Box 749 (74010-0749)
PHONE..............................918 367-5562
Robert B Krumme, *Managing Prtnr*
EMP: 14
SQ FT: 9,000
SALES (est): 1.1MM **Privately Held**
SIC: **1311** Crude petroleum production

(G-788)
LARRYS WELDING SERVICE
31653 S 193rd West Ave (74010-3198)
PHONE..............................918 267-4091
Larry Story, *Principal*
Duane Yoder, *Med Doctor*
EMP: 1
SALES (est): 49.6K **Privately Held**
SIC: **7692** Welding repair

(G-789)
NAFCOAT INC
20963 W Highway 16 (74010-3284)
PHONE..............................918 367-9606
EMP: 2 EST: 2012
SALES (est): 74K **Privately Held**
SIC: **3479** Coating/Engraving Service

(G-790)
NUYAKA CREEK WINERY LLC
35230 S 177th West Ave (74010-3031)
PHONE..............................918 756-8485
James W Jones,
Diane Jones,
EMP: 2
SALES (est): 134.4K **Privately Held**
SIC: **2084** Wines

(G-791)
OKLAHOMA COMM ON CONSMR CR
Also Called: District 1
115 W 6th Ave (74010-2801)
PHONE..............................918 367-3396
Terry Grooms, *District Mgr*
EMP: 15 **Privately Held**
SIC: **1382** 9199 Oil & gas exploration services; general government administration
HQ: Oklahoma Common Consumer Credit
3613 Nw 56th St Ste 240
Oklahoma City OK 73112

(G-792)
PARKLINE SYSTEMS CORPORATION
Also Called: Parkline Arrow
23630 S 369th West Ave (74010-4359)
P.O. Box 1260 (74010-1260)
PHONE..............................918 367-5523
Howard Westerman Jr, *President*
EMP: 35 EST: 1976
SQ FT: 40,000
SALES (est): 5MM **Privately Held**
SIC: **3829** Measuring & controlling devices

(G-793)
PETERS OIL & GAS
33820 W 261st St S (74010-3998)
PHONE..............................405 315-6378
EMP: 2
SALES (est): 152.8K **Privately Held**
SIC: **1389** Oil & gas field services

(G-794)
POWELLS WATERWELL PUMP AND SUP
46427 W 154th (74010)
P.O. Box 1151 (74010-1151)
PHONE..............................918 637-9150
Jess Powell, *Owner*
EMP: 1
SALES: 8K **Privately Held**
SIC: **3533** Water well drilling equipment

(G-795)
RAJON LLC
Also Called: Vertical Aerospace
23800 S 369th West Ave (74010-3957)
PHONE..............................918 367-5487
Jon Werthen,
EMP: 65
SQ FT: 226,000
SALES (est): 19.8MM **Privately Held**
SIC: **3728** Aircraft parts & equipment

(G-796)
SHELLBACK WOODWORKS ✪
321 E 5th Ave (74010-3011)
PHONE..............................918 851-3992
Ray-Dean Canfield, *Principal*
EMP: 1 EST: 2019
SALES (est): 54.1K **Privately Held**
SIC: **2431** Millwork

(G-797)
SUPERIOR TOOL SERVICES INC
26400 S Highway 48 (74010-3963)
P.O. Box 725 (74010-0725)
PHONE..............................918 640-5503
Danny Joslen, *President*
Pam Joslen, *Vice Pres*
EMP: 2
SALES (est): 274.8K **Privately Held**
SIC: **7699** 1389 Industrial tool grinding; oil field services

(G-798)
SWEET PUFFS LLC
Also Called: Main Street Vapors
214 S Main St (74010-2831)
PHONE..............................918 367-9544
Ronda Mc Brayer, *General Mgr*
EMP: 2
SALES (est): 143.7K **Privately Held**
SIC: **3634** Cigarette lighters, electric

(G-799)
TIMCO BLASTING & COATINGS (PA)
200 N Main St (74010-2408)
PHONE..............................918 367-1700
Anthony Don Jolley, *CEO*
Tim Farley, *President*
Beverly Farley, *Office Mgr*
EMP: 24 EST: 1989
SQ FT: 2,500
SALES (est): 6MM **Privately Held**
WEB: www.timcoblastingandcoating.com
SIC: **1799** 7532 1446 1794 Paint & wallpaper stripping; truck painting & lettering; industrial sand; excavation work

(G-800)
TIMCO BLASTING & COATINGS
34081 W 241st St S (74010-5093)
PHONE..............................918 605-1179
A Don Jolley, *CEO*
Tim Farley, *Manager*
EMP: 10
SALES (corp-wide): 6MM **Privately Held**
SIC: **1799** 7532 1446 1794 Paint & wallpaper stripping; truck painting & lettering; industrial sand; excavation work
PA: Timco Blasting & Coatings, Inc
200 N Main St
Bristow OK 74010
918 367-1700

(G-801)
TIMCO BLASTING & COATINGS
31188 S Highway 48 (74010-4847)
PHONE..............................918 605-1179
A Don Jolley, *CEO*
Tim Farley, *Manager*
EMP: 1
SALES (corp-wide): 6MM **Privately Held**
SIC: **1799** 7532 1446 1794 Paint & wallpaper stripping; truck painting & lettering; industrial sand; excavation work
PA: Timco Blasting & Coatings, Inc
200 N Main St
Bristow OK 74010
918 367-1700

(G-802)
UNITHERM FOOD SYSTEMS LLC (PA)
502 Industrial Rd (74010-9763)
PHONE..............................918 367-0197
Mark Smith, *CEO*
David Howard, *President*
Amanda Howard, *Corp Secy*
Bryan Gray, *Manager*
▲ EMP: 50
SQ FT: 50,000
SALES (est): 13.8MM **Privately Held**
SIC: **3556** Food products machinery

(G-803)
VARNERS EQP SLS & SVC LLC
921 S Roland St (74010-9554)
PHONE..............................918 367-3800
Joey Varner, *Owner*
EMP: 1
SALES (est): 191.4K **Privately Held**
SIC: **3531** Tractors, crawler

(G-804)
W E O C INC
121 E 6th Ave (74010-3038)
P.O. Box 1146 (74010-1146)
PHONE..............................918 367-5918
Stan Earnhardt, *Principal*
EMP: 2
SALES (est): 112.8K **Privately Held**
SIC: **1389** Oil & gas field services

(G-805)
WAYLAND WOODWORKS LLC
18668 S 344th West Ave (74010-2172)
PHONE..............................918 799-6196
Michael Bryan Wayland, *Owner*
EMP: 2
SALES (est): 85.2K **Privately Held**
SIC: **2431** Millwork

(G-806)
WITTY IDEAS INC
115 S Main St (74010-2802)
PHONE..............................918 367-9528
Randy Witty, *President*
EMP: 2
SQ FT: 3,097
SALES (est): 178.3K **Privately Held**
SIC: **2759** 2396 Screen printing; automotive & apparel trimmings

Broken Arrow
Tulsa County

(G-807)
3G SIGN INC
3304 W Galveston Pl (74012-3255)
PHONE..............................918 630-5976
Thomas L Feller, *Principal*
EMP: 2
SALES (est): 119.1K **Privately Held**
SIC: **3993** Signs & advertising specialties

(G-808)
A & E FRAME MFG INC
1113 E Memphis St (74012-5806)
P.O. Box 140310 (74014-0003)
PHONE..............................918 251-3343
Rodney Pearson, *President*
Bobbie Pearson, *Vice Pres*
EMP: 9
SQ FT: 6,500
SALES (est): 1.8MM **Privately Held**
SIC: **3599** Machine shop, jobbing & repair

(G-809)
A G EQUIPMENT COMPANY
3401 W Albany St (74012-1174)
PHONE..............................918 250-7386
Henry G Ash, *CEO*
Kent Bright, *President*
Keith Miller, *Vice Pres*
Douglas Bassett, *CFO*
Doug Hillin, *Sales Staff*
◆ EMP: 520 EST: 1979
SQ FT: 650,000
SALES: 364.4MM **Privately Held**
SIC: **3563** 5084 Air & gas compressors; industrial machine parts

(G-810)
A SIGN OF SURPRISE
709 Magnolia Ct (74011-8607)
PHONE..............................918 607-0747
April Bever, *Principal*
EMP: 2
SALES (est): 109.8K **Privately Held**
SIC: **3993** Signs & advertising specialties

(G-811)
A-Z MANUFACTURING LLC
1116 E Memphis St (74012-5805)
PHONE..............................918 258-2900
Ronnie McMurray, *Mng Member*
EMP: 8
SALES (est): 938.4K **Privately Held**
SIC: **3999** Manufacturing industries

(G-812)
ACCESS OPTICS LLC
2201 N Maple Ave (74012-0529)
PHONE..............................918 294-1234
Robert Hogrefe,
John Hannam,
Pamela Hogrefe,
Tamara Redmond,
◆ EMP: 26
SQ FT: 10,000
SALES (est): 4.3MM **Privately Held**
SIC: **3841** 3827 Surgical & medical instruments; lenses, optical: all types except ophthalmic

(G-813)
ACURA NEON INC
Also Called: Acura Sign
1801 N Willow Ave (74012-9161)
PHONE..............................918 252-2258
Kenneth C Ellison, *CEO*
Mir Khezri, *President*
Starla Khezri, *Corp Secy*
Mehdi Khezri, *Vice Pres*
EMP: 36
SQ FT: 25,000
SALES (est): 5.1MM **Privately Held**
SIC: **3993** 1799 Neon signs; sign installation & maintenance

(G-814)
ADDITIVE SYSTEMS INC (PA)
Also Called: A S I
407 S Main St (74012-4146)
PHONE..............................918 357-3433
Robert Roggendorff, *President*
Linda Roggendorff, *Corp Secy*
Matt Pitman, *Vice Pres*
Shae Roggendorff, *Vice Pres*
Belinda Short, *Human Res Mgr*
EMP: 11
SQ FT: 10,000
SALES (est): 7MM **Privately Held**
SIC: **3561** Pump jacks & other pumping equipment

(G-815)
ADVANCED IMAGING RESOURCES CO
1761 N Aspen Ave (74012-1197)
PHONE..............................918 609-5250
EMP: 6 EST: 1991
SALES (est): 459K **Privately Held**
SIC: **3845** Mfg Electromedical Equipment

(G-816)
ADVANCED MEDICAL INSTRS INC (PA)
Also Called: AMI
3061 W Albany St (74012-1104)
PHONE..............................918 250-0566
Gary Kinley, *President*
Peter Dorflinger, *Corp Secy*
Leo Suchor, *Controller*
▲ EMP: 121
SQ FT: 28,000
SALES (est): 22MM **Privately Held**
SIC: **3841** 3672 3845 Diagnostic apparatus, medical; blood pressure apparatus; printed circuit boards; electromedical equipment

(G-817)
AERO AUTOMATION LLC
5621 W Austin St (74011-1577)
PHONE..............................918 251-0987
Tommy Worth,
EMP: 10
SALES (est): 1.1MM **Privately Held**
SIC: **3728** Aircraft parts & equipment

(G-818)
AERO DYNAMICS
905 S 11th St (74012-5727)
PHONE..............................918 258-0290
Steve Hamm, *Owner*
EMP: 10
SQ FT: 6,500
SALES (est): 1.1MM **Privately Held**
SIC: **3599** 3812 3714 Machine shop, jobbing & repair; search & navigation equipment; motor vehicle parts & accessories

Broken Arrow - Tulsa County (G-819)   **GEOGRAPHIC SECTION**

(G-819)
AERON GROUP LLC
1901 N Willow Ave (74012-9108)
PHONE..................................918 294-1167
Jason Miller, *Sales Executive*
Joel Miller, *Mng Member*
Leslie Miller, *Info Tech Dir*
Jamie Terry, *Info Tech Dir*
EMP: 14
SQ FT: 30,000
SALES (est): 2.3MM **Privately Held**
WEB: www.aerongroup.com
SIC: 3444 Sheet metal specialties, not stamped

(G-820)
AGAPE INC
1608 W Gulfport St (74011-4256)
PHONE..................................918 455-9516
Teddy Pledger, *President*
Daryl M Pledger, *Vice Pres*
Frances P Pledger, *Vice Pres*
Ted W Pledger, *Vice Pres*
Elaine Pledger, *Treasurer*
EMP: 2
SALES (est): 279.7K **Privately Held**
SIC: 1311 Crude petroleum & natural gas

(G-821)
AJS TEES INC
18700 E 94th St (74012-7217)
PHONE..................................918 455-6751
John Kosir, *President*
Anita Kosir, *Vice Pres*
EMP: 2
SQ FT: 2,000
SALES (est): 75K **Privately Held**
SIC: 2339 5137 Women's & misses' outerwear; sportswear, women's & children's

(G-822)
ALAN THOMPSON SIGNS
1516 W Phoenix Pl (74011-1606)
PHONE..................................918 808-3976
Alan Randal Thompson, *Principal*
EMP: 2 EST: 2015
SALES (est): 81.9K **Privately Held**
WEB: www.alanthompsonsigns.com
SIC: 3993 Signs & advertising specialties

(G-823)
ALFA LAVAL INC
Air Cooled Exchangers Ace
1201 S 9th St (74012-5810)
PHONE..................................918 251-7477
EMP: 3 **Privately Held**
SIC: 3443 Heat exchangers: coolers (after, inter), condensers, etc.
HQ: Alfa Laval Inc.
5400 Intl Trade Dr
Richmond VA 23231
866 253-2528

(G-824)
ALFA LAVAL INC
1030 E Nashville St (74012)
PHONE..................................918 251-7477
EMP: 2 **Privately Held**
SIC: 3491 3821 3433 3569 Industrial valves; laboratory apparatus & furniture; heating equipment, except electric; assembly machines, non-metalworking; refrigeration & heating equipment
HQ: Alfa Laval Inc.
5400 Intl Trade Dr
Richmond VA 23231
866 253-2528

(G-825)
ALFA LVAL A CLED EXCHNGERS INC
1201 S 9th St (74012-5810)
PHONE..................................918 251-7477
EMP: 2 EST: 2012
SALES (est): 190K **Privately Held**
SIC: 3491 3433 Mfg Industrial Valves Mfg Heating Equipment-Nonelectric

(G-826)
ALLYS DISCOUNT SCRUBS
115 E El Paso St (74012-4122)
PHONE..................................918 935-1359
EMP: 1
SALES (est): 46.5K **Privately Held**
SIC: 2211 Scrub cloths

(G-827)
ANCHOR STONE CO
14311 S 129th East Ave (74011-7451)
PHONE..................................918 872-8449
EMP: 1
SALES (corp-wide): 81.4MM **Privately Held**
WEB: www.anchor-stone.com
SIC: 1422 Crushed & broken limestone
PA: Anchor Stone Co.
4124 S Rockford Ave # 201
Tulsa OK 74105
918 599-7255

(G-828)
ANDERSON RT INDUSTRIES LLC
2316 S Kalanchoe Ave (74012-0934)
PHONE..................................918 607-5150
Anderson Robert, *Principal*
EMP: 2
SALES (est): 119.7K **Privately Held**
SIC: 3999 Manufacturing industries

(G-829)
ANGEL WELDING SERVICE LLC
1732 S 6th St (74012-6533)
PHONE..................................918 706-2237
Carl Angel, *Principal*
EMP: 1
SALES (est): 46K **Privately Held**
SIC: 7692 Welding repair

(G-830)
APOLLO ENGINEERING COMPANY
809 W Elgin St (74012-2426)
P.O. Box 2050 (74013-2050)
PHONE..................................918 251-6780
Jon A Carnell, *President*
EMP: 6
SQ FT: 6,000
SALES (est): 711.5K **Privately Held**
SIC: 3599 3494 3533 Gasoline filters, internal combustion engine, except auto; line strainers, for use in piping systems; oil & gas field machinery

(G-831)
AQUA ECO ENVIRONMENTAL SVCS
4004 W Twin Oaks Pl (74011-1219)
PHONE..................................952 300-0456
Brian Foster, *CEO*
Robert Warwick, *CEO*
Angus Martin, *COO*
EMP: 4
SALES (est): 192.6K **Privately Held**
SIC: 3589 7389 Water treatment equipment, industrial;

(G-832)
ARCTIC BLENDS CORPORATION
2409 N Aspen Ave (74012-1142)
PHONE..................................918 455-2079
Richard Douglas, *President*
EMP: 2
SALES (est): 140K **Privately Held**
SIC: 2087 Concentrates, drink

(G-833)
ARROWHEAD PRECAST LLC
1701 E Houston St (74012-4432)
PHONE..................................918 995-2227
Cecil Casinger, *Opers Mgr*
Molly Pickering, *Purch Mgr*
Tony Roberts, *QC Mgr*
Stephanie Wade, *Controller*
Whitney Swift, *Human Res Mgr*
EMP: 85
SALES (est): 17.4MM **Privately Held**
SIC: 3271 3272 Blocks, concrete: landscape or retaining wall; concrete products, precast; concrete stuctural support & building material; prestressed concrete products
PA: Napco Precast, Llc
6949 Low Bid Ln
San Antonio TX 78250

(G-834)
ARTISAN CUSTOM CABINETRY INC
2709 W Detroit St (74012-2108)
PHONE..................................918 645-3874
Barry South, *Principal*
EMP: 4
SALES (est): 378.9K **Privately Held**
SIC: 2434 Wood kitchen cabinets

(G-835)
ARTISAN DESIGN INC
808 S 9th St (74012-5707)
P.O. Box 2433 (74013-2433)
PHONE..................................918 251-9795
Robert Sheldon Padawer, *President*
Denise Pelt, *Manager*
EMP: 6
SQ FT: 7,480
SALES (est): 563.4K **Privately Held**
SIC: 2499 Decorative wood & woodwork

(G-836)
ASPEN FLOW CONTROL LLC
5128 S 95th E Ave Ste C (74012)
P.O. Box 140238 (74014-0002)
PHONE..................................918 933-5617
Larry Forester, *Owner*
EMP: 3
SALES (est): 320K **Privately Held**
WEB: www.aspenflow.com
SIC: 3592 Valves

(G-837)
AVIATIONS SIMULATIONS INC
415 E Houston St (74012-4303)
PHONE..................................918 251-6880
Jon Werthen, *President*
EMP: 4
SALES (est): 309.4K **Privately Held**
SIC: 3441 Fabricated structural metal

(G-838)
AWESOME APPAREL PRINTING
4412 W Oakridge St (74012-8822)
PHONE..................................918 402-3672
Don Jones, *Manager*
EMP: 2
SALES (est): 143.3K **Privately Held**
SIC: 2752 Commercial printing, lithographic

(G-839)
B & L PRINTING INC
Also Called: Royal Printing & Copy Center
400 S Elm Pl Ste A (74012-4058)
PHONE..................................918 258-6655
Bill Scrimsher, *President*
Linda Scrimsher, *Corp Secy*
Mike Scrimsher, *Vice Pres*
EMP: 5
SQ FT: 1,850
SALES (est): 830K **Privately Held**
WEB: www.royalprintba.com
SIC: 2752 7334 2791 2789 Lithographing on metal; photocopying & duplicating services; typesetting; bookbinding & related work; variety stores

(G-840)
B BROTHERS MANUFACTURING LLC
1293 E Kenosha St (74012-2008)
PHONE..................................918 625-9583
Ilya Bogoslov,
EMP: 1 EST: 2018
SALES (est): 39.6K **Privately Held**
SIC: 3999 Manufacturing industries

(G-841)
B P S INC
Also Called: Burns Pressure Systems
304 N Walnut Ave (74012-2351)
PHONE..................................918 258-7554
Jim Burns, *President*
Mike Burns, *Vice Pres*
EMP: 4
SQ FT: 5,000
SALES (est): 553.8K **Privately Held**
SIC: 3491 Industrial valves

(G-842)
BA MANUFACTURING LLC
405 S 9th Ave (74012-4411)
PHONE..................................239 246-3606
EMP: 1
SALES (est): 67.6K **Privately Held**
SIC: 3444 Sheet metalwork

(G-843)
BAKER HGHES OLFLD OPRTIONS LLC
Also Called: Baker Oil Tools
3000 N Hemlock Cir (74012-1113)
PHONE..................................918 455-3000
Greg Perry, *Opers-Prdtn-Mfg*
EMP: 338
SQ FT: 115,000 **Privately Held**
SIC: 1389 Oil field services
PA: Baker Hughes Oilfield Operations Llc
2001 Rankin Rd
Houston TX 77073

(G-844)
BEEFYS BEASTRO FOOD SVC LLC
3201 S 1st St (74012-7946)
PHONE..................................580 491-0325
Phillip Teufel, *President*
EMP: 2 EST: 2016
SALES (est): 115.9K **Privately Held**
SIC: 2599 7389 Food wagons, restaurant;

(G-845)
BEEMAN PRODUCTS CO INC
2228 W Oakridge St (74012-4727)
PHONE..................................918 251-1432
James D Beeman, *President*
Tom Cheatham, *Vice Pres*
Elizabeth Beeman, *Admin Sec*
EMP: 5
SQ FT: 20,000
SALES: 1MM **Privately Held**
SIC: 5039 3446 1752 Architectural metalwork; architectural metalwork; floor laying & floor work

(G-846)
BERRYHILL ORNAMENTAL IRON LLC
550 S 12th St (74012-4419)
PHONE..................................918 258-6531
Darin Berryhill, *Principal*
EMP: 3
SALES (est): 287.7K **Privately Held**
SIC: 1799 3446 Fence construction; architectural metalwork; railings, bannisters, guards, etc.: made from metal pipe; fences or posts, ornamental iron or steel; ornamental metalwork

(G-847)
BEST COMPANIES (PA)
4212 W Wichita St (74012-9118)
PHONE..................................918 280-8066
Kevin L Best, *President*
Todd Best, *President*
Amy Best, *Corp Secy*
EMP: 4
SQ FT: 5,000
SALES (est): 570.3K **Privately Held**
SIC: 3271 Architectural concrete: block, split, fluted, screen, etc.

(G-848)
BETHS BAGS AND MORE LLC
12220 E 131st St S (74011-5428)
PHONE..................................918 451-7346
Beth Kern,
EMP: 1
SALES (est): 69.1K **Privately Held**
SIC: 2393 Textile bags

(G-849)
BICI LLC
4108 N Pine Ave (74012-0472)
PHONE..................................918 625-8811
Dan Ward,
EMP: 2 EST: 2013
SALES (est): 133.3K **Privately Held**
SIC: 2899 Water treating compounds

(G-850)
BICO DRILLING TOOLS INC
13675 E 61st St (74012-1118)
PHONE..................................918 872-9983
Mark Gregoli, *Branch Mgr*
EMP: 6

GEOGRAPHIC SECTION
Broken Arrow - Tulsa County (G-880)

SALES (corp-wide): 2.6MM **Privately Held**
WEB: www.bicodrilling.com
SIC: 3533 Oil field machinery & equipment
HQ: Bico Drilling Tools, Inc
4667 Kennedy Commerce Dr
Houston TX 77032

(G-851)
BILL KITE SALES
5309 S Hickory Ave (74011-4600)
PHONE 918 806-2958
EMP: 1
SALES (est): 41K **Privately Held**
SIC: 3944 Kites

(G-852)
BILLY SIMS BARBEQUE LLC
Also Called: Barbeque Brew Trading Company
2427 W Kenosha St (74012-8964)
PHONE 918 258-1978
Jeff Jackson, *Mng Member*
EMP: 35
SALES (est): 930.7K **Privately Held**
SIC: 5812 2033 Barbecue restaurant; barbecue sauce: packaged in cans, jars, etc.

(G-853)
BLACKHAWK INDUSTRIAL DIST INC (PA)
Also Called: Duncan Industrial Solutions
1501 Sw Expressway Dr (74012-1773)
PHONE 918 610-4700
John Mark, *CEO*
Derek Upson, *General Mgr*
Mark Sommers, *Vice Pres*
Annette Strba, *Buyer*
Bob Koch, *Accountant*
◆ EMP: 153
SQ FT: 30,000
SALES (est): 337.6MM **Privately Held**
SIC: 5085 3561 5084 Industrial supplies; pumps & pumping equipment; industrial machinery & equipment

(G-854)
BOBS VACUUM SEWING REPAIR
15702 E 101st St (74011-1823)
PHONE 918 378-1844
Bob Smith, *Owner*
EMP: 1
SALES (est): 41.3K **Privately Held**
SIC: 3635 Household vacuum cleaners

(G-855)
BORDON DAVID & ASSOCIATES LLC
Also Called: Bordon Books
1408 W Glendale St (74011-6217)
PHONE 918 495-3508
David Bordon, *Owner*
EMP: 6
SALES (est): 486.7K **Privately Held**
SIC: 2731 Book publishing

(G-856)
BROKEN ARROW POWDR COATING INC (PA)
2051 Sw Expressway Dr (74012-1117)
P.O. Box 3637 (74013-3637)
PHONE 918 251-2192
Mike Boyce, *President*
Tommy Thompson, *Corp Secy*
Shane Vaughn, *Vice Pres*
EMP: 45
SALES (est): 4.7MM **Privately Held**
SIC: 3479 3471 Coating of metals & formed products; plating & polishing

(G-857)
BROKEN ARROW POWDR COATING INC
2501 Sw Express Way Dr (74012)
P.O. Box 3637 (74013-3637)
PHONE 918 258-1017
Tommy Thompson, *Branch Mgr*
EMP: 25
SALES (est): 1.9MM
SALES (corp-wide): 4.7MM **Privately Held**
SIC: 3479 Coating of metals & formed products

PA: Broken Arrow Powder Coating, Inc.
2051 Sw Expressway Dr
Broken Arrow OK 74012
918 251-2192

(G-858)
BROKEN ARROW QUALITY LUBE
1031 N 9th St (74012-2843)
P.O. Box 1887, Catoosa (74015-1887)
PHONE 918 258-5823
Jeff Brandstetter, *Principal*
EMP: 2
SALES (est): 129.1K **Privately Held**
WEB: www.brokenarrowok.gov
SIC: 2992 Lubricating oils

(G-859)
BROKEN ARROW WOODWORKS
2021 W Detroit St (74012-3616)
PHONE 918 893-6763
Doug Humphrey, *President*
EMP: 13
SALES (est): 1.5MM **Privately Held**
WEB: www.brokenarrowwoodworks.com
SIC: 2434 Wood kitchen cabinets

(G-860)
BUILDERS FIRSTSOURCE INC
12215 E 61st St (74012-9115)
PHONE 918 459-6872
Paul Vaughn, *Branch Mgr*
EMP: 70
SALES (corp-wide): 7.2B **Publicly Held**
SIC: 2439 Structural wood members
PA: Builders Firstsource, Inc.
2001 Bryan St Ste 1600
Dallas TX 75201
214 880-3500

(G-861)
C & D MANUFACTURING CO INC
601 S 10th St (74012-4424)
PHONE 918 251-8535
Jerry Moudy, *President*
Lisbeth Moudy, *Treasurer*
EMP: 4
SQ FT: 6,000
SALES (est): 524.1K **Privately Held**
SIC: 3599 Machine shop, jobbing & repair

(G-862)
CAMERON GLASS INC
Also Called: Camglass
3550 W Tacoma St (74012-1176)
PHONE 918 254-6000
Jim K Cameron, *President*
▲ EMP: 100
SALES (est): 22.2MM **Privately Held**
SIC: 3231 Tempered glass: made from purchased glass

(G-863)
CANE ADVERTISING LLC
812 W Elgin St (74012-2425)
PHONE 918 806-6817
Drew Dyer, *Principal*
EMP: 4
SALES (est): 352K **Privately Held**
WEB: www.canetshirtcompany.com
SIC: 2759 Screen printing

(G-864)
CANVAS SKY STUDIOS LLC
1501 W Detroit St (74012-3619)
PHONE 917 514-9632
Tommy Robinson, *Principal*
EMP: 2
SALES (est): 69.7K **Privately Held**
SIC: 2211 Canvas

(G-865)
CHAMBERS SIGNS
828 N Ash Ave (74012-2507)
PHONE 918 251-6513
Larry Chambers, *Manager*
EMP: 1
SQ FT: 840
SALES (est): 90.7K **Privately Held**
SIC: 7389 3993 Lettering service; sign painting & lettering shop; signs & advertising specialties

(G-866)
CHANDLER INSTRUMENTS CO LLC (HQ)
Also Called: Ametek-Chandler Instruments
2001 N Indianwood Ave (74012-1162)
P.O. Box 470710, Tulsa (74147-0710)
PHONE 918 250-7200
Daniel J Skinner, *President*
Robert S Foit, *Vice Pres*
David Duda, *Opers Mgr*
Tom Steele, *Design Engr*
William J Burke, *Treasurer*
◆ EMP: 90
SQ FT: 65,000
SALES (est): 16MM
SALES (corp-wide): 5.1B **Publicly Held**
WEB: www.chandlerengineering.com
SIC: 3823 3829 Industrial instrmnts msrmnt display/control process variable; measuring & controlling devices
PA: Ametek, Inc.
1100 Cassatt Rd
Berwyn PA 19312
610 647-2121

(G-867)
CHEAPER TS INC
821 W Freeport St (74012-2408)
PHONE 918 615-6262
Janna Wynne, *Owner*
Don Winn, *COO*
EMP: 3
SALES (est): 247.5K **Privately Held**
SIC: 2759 Screen printing

(G-868)
CHEROKEE ARCHTECTURAL MTLS LLC
1100 E Houston St (74012-4406)
PHONE 918 258-5700
Debra Lyons, *Manager*
Stuart Gibbs,
Geene Hayges, *Admin Sec*
EMP: 19
SQ FT: 9,000
SALES (est): 202.6K **Privately Held**
SIC: 2431 Staircases, stairs & railings

(G-869)
CJ HILL INC
2333 W Wichita St (74012-1016)
PHONE 918 251-1164
Cheryl J Hill, *President*
Jerry L Hill, *Principal*
William R Moss, *Principal*
Tilman E Pool, *Principal*
Connie Rice, *Purchasing*
EMP: 47 EST: 1977
SQ FT: 9,000
SALES (est): 7.5MM **Privately Held**
SIC: 3599 Machine shop, jobbing & repair

(G-870)
CLIFTTON WALLCOVERING
1611 S Magnolia Ave (74012-9007)
PHONE 918 638-4454
Darrell Clifton, *Owner*
EMP: 1
SALES (est): 89K **Privately Held**
SIC: 2211 Upholstery, tapestry & wall coverings: cotton

(G-871)
COMMUNICATION GRAPHICS INC
Also Called: Comgraphx
1765 N Juniper Ave (74012-1455)
PHONE 918 258-6502
Dave Cleveland, *President*
Andrew Terrell, *Associate*
▲ EMP: 100
SQ FT: 50,000
SALES (est): 16.5MM **Privately Held**
SIC: 2759 Screen printing; decals: printing

(G-872)
COMMUNITY PUBLISHERS INC
510 W Atlanta St (74012-7004)
PHONE 918 259-7500
Steve Trolinger, *Principal*
EMP: 4
SALES (est): 282.6K **Privately Held**
SIC: 2741 Miscellaneous publishing

(G-873)
COMPUTER TECHNOLOGY SOLTN
1825 S Umbrella Ct (74012-6115)
PHONE 918 607-2136
Earl Hay, *Partner*
EMP: 1
SALES (est): 500K **Privately Held**
SIC: 7372 Business oriented computer software

(G-874)
CONTINENTAL BATTERY COMPANY
509 N Redbud Ave Ste G (74012-2383)
PHONE 918 259-0662
Tom Fabian, *Branch Mgr*
EMP: 42
SALES (corp-wide): 79MM **Privately Held**
SIC: 3691 Storage batteries
PA: Continental Battery Company
4919 Woodall St
Dallas TX 75247
214 631-5701

(G-875)
CONTROL DEVICES INC
Also Called: C D I
1801 N Juniper Ave (74012-6662)
PHONE 918 258-6068
Tony Farque, *President*
Laverne Farque, *Corp Secy*
Eric Farque, *Vice Pres*
Jason Farque, *Vice Pres*
EMP: 40
SQ FT: 30,000
SALES (est): 9.5MM **Privately Held**
SIC: 3823 Controllers for process variables, all types

(G-876)
CONTROL DEVICES INTL INC
1801 N Juniper Ave (74012-6662)
PHONE 918 258-6068
Jason Farque, *Vice Pres*
Margaret Farque,
EMP: 1
SALES (est): 66.6K **Privately Held**
SIC: 1389 Pipe testing, oil field service

(G-877)
COOL GREEN ROOFING SUPPLY LLC
712 S 8th St (74012-5539)
PHONE 918 860-7525
Vladimir Galushkin, *Partner*
Eduard Mishkov, *Manager*
EMP: 9
SALES (est): 1.2MM **Privately Held**
SIC: 5031 5033 3444 Trim, sheet metal; roofing, asphalt & sheet metal; metal roofing & roof drainage equipment; downspouts, sheet metal

(G-878)
COOLING PRODUCTS INC
500 N Pecan Ave (74012-2333)
P.O. Box 470523, Tulsa (74147-0523)
PHONE 918 251-8588
Stephen L Chalmers, *CEO*
Chris Burk, *Corp Secy*
James Carter, *COO*
EMP: 45
SQ FT: 6,000
SALES (est): 12.7MM **Privately Held**
WEB: www.coolprod.com
SIC: 3443 Air coolers, metal plate

(G-879)
CROCHETANGEL
8316 S Kalanchoe Ave (74011-7808)
PHONE 918 282-3056
Paula Judd, *Principal*
EMP: 1
SALES (est): 40.9K **Privately Held**
SIC: 2399 Hand woven & crocheted products

(G-880)
CSI AEROSPACE INC
2020 W Detroit St Ste 1 (74012-3627)
PHONE 918 258-1290
Luis Morell, *CEO*
Eric Mendelson, *Ch of Bd*

Broken Arrow - Tulsa County (G-881)

Andrew Feeley, *Vice Pres*
Chris Feeley, *Vice Pres*
Christopher Feeley, *Vice Pres*
▼ **EMP:** 85
SALES (est): 15MM **Publicly Held**
SIC: 3728 Aircraft parts & equipment
HQ: Flight Support Group Inc
161 Turnberry Cir
New Smyrna FL 32168
954 987-4000

(G-881)
CUSTOM AUTOMOTIVE MFG
1116 E Memphis St (74012-5805)
PHONE.................................918 258-2900
John Nimmo, *President*
Peggy Nimmo, *Treasurer*
EMP: 11
SQ FT: 9,000
SALES (est): 337.5K **Privately Held**
SIC: 7699 3713 3544 Customizing services; truck & bus bodies; special dies, tools, jigs & fixtures

(G-882)
CUSTOM SHUTTERS INC
1904 W Albany St (74012-1410)
PHONE.................................918 924-3489
EMP: 3
SALES (est): 162.1K **Privately Held**
SIC: 3442 Shutters, door or window: metal

(G-883)
CYCLONIC VALVE COMPANY
2349 W Vancouver St (74012-1183)
PHONE.................................918 317-8200
Garrett Graves, *CEO*
John Graves, *President*
Luke Gastgeb, *Sales Staff*
Sarah Graves, *Admin Sec*
▲ **EMP:** 26
SQ FT: 25,000
SALES (est): 9.5MM **Privately Held**
SIC: 3491 3533 3494 3492 Industrial valves; oil & gas field machinery; valves & pipe fittings; fluid power valves & hose fittings; industrial supplies

(G-884)
CYMSTAR LLC (PA)
1700 W Albany St Ste 500 (74012-1482)
PHONE.................................918 251-8100
John Corder, *CEO*
Chris Carpenter, *Principal*
Derrick Ball, *Site Mgr*
Michael Hitz, *Engineer*
Dan Hoar, *Engineer*
EMP: 246
SQ FT: 50,000
SALES: 96.8MM **Privately Held**
SIC: 3699 3728 Flight simulators (training aids), electronic; aircraft parts & equipment

(G-885)
CYTEC INDUSTRIAL MTLS OK INC
2514 N Hemlock Cir (74012-1128)
PHONE.................................918 252-3922
EMP: 4
SALES (corp-wide): 13.8MM **Privately Held**
SIC: 2295 Buckram: varnished, waxed & impregnated
HQ: Cytec Industrial Materials (Ok) Inc.
5350 S 129th East Ave
Tulsa OK 74134

(G-886)
DA/PRO RUBBER INC (PA)
601 N Poplar Ave (74012-2379)
P.O. Box 470175, Tulsa (74147-0175)
PHONE.................................918 258-9386
C B Daubenberger, *President*
Walter Sanders, *COO*
Thomas Mason, *Vice Pres*
Harold Sosner, *Vice Pres*
Al Martin, *Plant Mgr*
▲ **EMP:** 200 **EST:** 1961
SQ FT: 30,000
SALES (est): 69.2MM **Privately Held**
WEB: www.daprorubber.com
SIC: 3069 Molded rubber products

(G-887)
DASHSKIN LLC
606 N Redbud Ave (74012-2345)
PHONE.................................918 940-8900
EMP: 1
SALES (est): 59.2K **Privately Held**
SIC: 3999 Manufacturing industries

(G-888)
DATRAN CORPORATION
4211 W Wichita St (74012-9119)
PHONE.................................918 307-2200
John Rathbone, *President*
EMP: 8
SQ FT: 10,000
SALES (est): 1.3MM **Privately Held**
SIC: 3678 Electronic connectors

(G-889)
DAVID LACY
Also Called: D & S Surveying
1233 S Aspen Ct (74012-4702)
PHONE.................................918 519-1873
David Lacy, *Owner*
EMP: 1
SALES (est): 44.2K **Privately Held**
SIC: 1389 Testing, measuring, surveying & analysis services

(G-890)
DK MACHINE INC
820 W Elgin St (74012-2425)
PHONE.................................918 251-1034
David King, *President*
EMP: 1
SQ FT: 3,200
SALES (est): 150K **Privately Held**
SIC: 3599 7692 Custom machinery; welding repair

(G-891)
DOUBLE J PRODUCTION LLC
601 Meadowood Dr (74011-8614)
PHONE.................................918 691-4060
Craig H Ford,
EMP: 1 **EST:** 2013
SALES (est): 61K **Privately Held**
SIC: 1382 Oil & gas exploration services

(G-892)
EAGLE RIVER ENERGY CORPORATION
3701 S Orange Cir (74011-1103)
PHONE.................................918 494-8928
Mark Godsey, *President*
EMP: 2
SQ FT: 2,300
SALES (est): 1.4MM **Privately Held**
SIC: 1311 Crude petroleum production; natural gas production

(G-893)
EAGLECREST AVIATION LLC
54 Cedar Ridge Rd (74011-1101)
PHONE.................................918 249-0980
EMP: 1
SALES (est): 126.9K **Privately Held**
SIC: 5599 3721 Ret Misc Vehicles Mfg Aircraft

(G-894)
ECO INCORPORATED
3101 N Hemlock Cir 110f (74012-1125)
PHONE.................................918 258-5002
Ray Tarwater, *President*
John Sullivan, *Vice Pres*
EMP: 6 **EST:** 1980
SQ FT: 3,000
SALES (est): 39.3K **Privately Held**
SIC: 3443 3441 Economizers (boilers); heat exchangers, condensers & components; fabricated structural metal

(G-895)
ECO 2007 LLC
3101 N Hemlock Cir 110f (74012-1103)
PHONE.................................918 258-5002
Ray Tarwater, *Mng Member*
EMP: 6
SQ FT: 3,000
SALES (est): 911.4K **Privately Held**
SIC: 3443 3441 Economizers (boilers); fabricated structural metal

(G-896)
ELI LILLY AND COMPANY
Also Called: Elanco Animal Health
3611 W Boston Ct (74012-9458)
PHONE.................................918 250-6848
Mark Declirk, *Manager*
Cristine Morris, *Manager*
EMP: 2
SALES (corp-wide): 22.3B **Publicly Held**
SIC: 2834 Pharmaceutical preparations
PA: Eli Lilly And Company
1 Lilly Corporate Ctr
Indianapolis IN 46285
317 276-2000

(G-897)
ELITE CREATIVE SOLUTIONS LLC
Also Called: Eco Elite
2502 N Hemlock Cir (74012-1128)
PHONE.................................918 994-5435
Paul Foegelle, *Vice Pres*
John Alber, *VP Sales*
Angela Starr-Grom, *Accounts Exec*
John Foegelle, *Mng Member*
EMP: 40
SQ FT: 50,000
SALES (est): 7.1MM **Privately Held**
SIC: 3955 2759 Print cartridges for laser & other computer printers; flexographic printing

(G-898)
EMPIRE LASER & METAL WORK LLC
4151 W Albany St (74012-1276)
PHONE.................................918 584-6232
Yvonne Plante, *Bookkeeper*
Vincent Crow, *Manager*
Steven E Etter,
EMP: 11
SQ FT: 7,000
SALES (est): 2.2MM **Privately Held**
WEB: www.empirelaserandmetalwork.com
SIC: 3444 Sheet metal specialties, not stamped

(G-899)
ENEREX INC
1217 E Houston St (74012-4405)
P.O. Box 1744 (74013-1744)
PHONE.................................918 258-3573
Robert M Mason, *President*
Marion Mason, *Corp Secy*
EMP: 1
SQ FT: 600
SALES (est): 190.3K **Privately Held**
SIC: 3443 Economizers (boilers)

(G-900)
ENERFIN INC
1217 E Houston St (74012-4405)
P.O. Box 282 (74013-0282)
PHONE.................................918 258-3571
Robert Mason, *President*
Marion Mason, *Corp Secy*
EMP: 4
SQ FT: 13,500
SALES (est): 608.3K **Privately Held**
SIC: 3469 3443 3621 Tube fins, stamped metal; heat exchangers, plate type; motors & generators

(G-901)
ENGINES ALIVE
1637 S Birch Ave (74012-5408)
PHONE.................................918 406-8149
Nathan Kinsey, *Principal*
EMP: 2
SALES (est): 183.3K **Privately Held**
SIC: 3519 Internal combustion engines

(G-902)
ENVIRO VALVE (US) INC
807 N Sycamore Ave (74012-2350)
PHONE.................................918 251-6103
Wayne Thomson, *President*
Hanna Battenfield, *Marketing Mgr*
EMP: 1
SALES (est): 203K **Privately Held**
SIC: 3491 Industrial valves

(G-903)
EXTRACT TOUCH-UP LLC
505 E Reno Pl (74012-8488)
PHONE.................................918 639-4011
Miguel Solorzano, *Administration*
EMP: 3
SALES (est): 207.2K **Privately Held**
SIC: 2836 Extracts

(G-904)
F&D INDUSTRIES LLC
4800 W Houston St (74012-4666)
PHONE.................................918 461-0447
EMP: 2
SALES (est): 128.5K **Privately Held**
SIC: 3999 Manufacturing industries

(G-905)
FACTOR 1 RACING INC
805 W Freeport St (74012-2408)
PHONE.................................918 258-7223
Sharrie McDougal, *President*
Sharrie Mc Dougal, *Corp Secy*
EMP: 5
SQ FT: 4,000
SALES (est): 1MM **Privately Held**
SIC: 3711 5013 3714 Automobile bodies, passenger car, not including engine, etc.; motor vehicle supplies & new parts; motor vehicle parts & accessories

(G-906)
FAST SIGNS
Also Called: Fastsigns
927 N Elm Pl (74012-1642)
PHONE.................................918 251-0330
Ashley Beaker, *Principal*
EMP: 2
SALES (est): 196.4K **Privately Held**
WEB: www.fastsigns.com
SIC: 3993 5099 Signs & advertising specialties; signs, except electric

(G-907)
FENIX OUTFITTERS
904 S Main St (74012-5531)
PHONE.................................918 259-0099
Daniel Housley, *Principal*
Denise Housley, *Sales Staff*
EMP: 2
SALES (est): 169.5K **Privately Held**
WEB: www.fenixoutfitters.com
SIC: 3949 Sporting & athletic goods

(G-908)
FINISH LINE MACHINING LLC
800 S 12th St (74012-5717)
PHONE.................................918 258-2944
Scott Sawyer, *Mng Member*
EMP: 2
SALES (est): 168.4K **Privately Held**
SIC: 3599 Machine shop, jobbing & repair

(G-909)
FIREPRO FIRE PROTECTION SVC
4812 N Poplar Ave (74012-0256)
P.O. Box 141112 (74014-0011)
PHONE.................................918 857-1513
Darrin Kallenberger, *Owner*
EMP: 1
SALES: 10K **Privately Held**
SIC: 7389 5099 3999 Building inspection service; fire extinguishers; fire extinguishers, portable

(G-910)
FLIGHTSAFETY INTERNATIONAL INC
Also Called: Simulation Systems Division
700 N 9th St (74012-2847)
P.O. Box 160 (74013-0160)
PHONE.................................918 259-4000
Nidal Sammur, *Engineer*
Tom Amburn, *Controller*
Winston Perez, *Marketing Mgr*
David Maclean, *Marketing Staff*
Susan Baker, *Manager*
EMP: 650
SALES (corp-wide): 327.2B **Publicly Held**
SIC: 4789 3812 Space flight operations, except government; search & navigation equipment

GEOGRAPHIC SECTION
Broken Arrow - Tulsa County (G-942)

HQ: Flightsafety International Inc.
Marine A Trml Lgrdia Arpr
Flushing NY 11371
718 565-4100

(G-911)
FLOWMATICS INC
2342 W Vancouver St (74012-1159)
PHONE.................................918 259-3740
EMP: 1
SALES (corp-wide): 1.1MM **Privately Held**
SIC: 3494 Mfg Valves/Pipe Fittings
PA: Flowmatics Inc
1507 Willow Crest Dr
Richardson TX 75081
972 480-8700

(G-912)
FORGED BY CREATION LLC
822 W Elgin St (74012-2425)
PHONE.................................918 798-0051
Britt Mansfield,
EMP: 6
SQ FT: 3,000
SALES (est): 612.1K **Privately Held**
WEB: www.forgedbycreation.com
SIC: 3281 Table tops, marble

(G-913)
FORKLIFT PARTS AND SERVICE LLC
305 N Redbud Ave (74012-2381)
PHONE.................................918 251-5119
Walter Lee Kannady, *Owner*
EMP: 2 **EST:** 2018
SALES (est): 111.3K **Privately Held**
SIC: 3537 Forklift trucks

(G-914)
FREEDOM RUBBER LLC
3081 W Albany St Ste 103 (74012-1148)
PHONE.................................918 250-4673
Brian Ray, *Mng Member*
EMP: 4
SQ FT: 3,000
SALES (est): 1MM **Privately Held**
SIC: 3053 Gaskets, all materials

(G-915)
FREEMAN PRODUCTS INC (PA)
1912 W Kenosha St (74012-8999)
PHONE.................................918 258-8861
William D Freeman, *Ch of Bd*
D Duane Freeman, *President*
Alan Semenito, *Corp Secy*
▲ **EMP:** 25 **EST:** 1978
SQ FT: 42,000
SALES (est): 10.5MM **Privately Held**
SIC: 5032 3275 Drywall materials; acoustical plaster, gypsum

(G-916)
GARYS WELDING INC
312 E Washington St (74012-7123)
PHONE.................................918 688-2058
Gary Kolpek, *President*
EMP: 1
SALES (est): 82.9K **Privately Held**
SIC: 7692 Welding repair

(G-917)
GAS DEVELOPMENT CORPORATION
Also Called: Sable Exploration
908 S 11th St (74012-5726)
PHONE.................................918 523-9090
Kirt Fryer, *President*
Deanna Wilson, *Accountant*
EMP: 5
SALES (est): 770.8K **Privately Held**
SIC: 1382 Oil & gas exploration services

(G-918)
GENRAL ENQURIES
3081 W Albany Ste 111 (74012-1148)
PHONE.................................918 749-1301
EMP: 2
SALES (est): 90.5K **Privately Held**
SIC: 2752 Commercial printing, offset

(G-919)
GLOBAL FLOW PRODUCTS LLC
Also Called: American Wheatley
2701 W Concord St (74012-1110)
PHONE.................................866 267-1379
Dan Llewelyen, *Mng Member*
EMP: 3
SALES (corp-wide): 20.2MM **Privately Held**
SIC: 3443 Boiler shop products: boilers, smokestacks, steel tanks
HQ: Global Flow Products, L.L.C.
2701 W Concord St
Broken Arrow OK 74012
918 317-0401

(G-920)
GOLDEN BRONZE INC
Also Called: J Davids Jeweler
613 N Aspen Ave (74012-2222)
PHONE.................................918 251-6300
Joel Wiland, *Owner*
Kendra Wiland, *Co-Owner*
EMP: 6
SQ FT: 3,760
SALES (est): 1.4MM **Privately Held**
SIC: 5944 3911 Jewelry, precious stones & precious metals; jewelry, precious metal

(G-921)
GRAPHIC RSOURCES REPRODUCTIONS
Also Called: Graphic Resources Reproduction
4251 W Albany St (74012-1233)
PHONE.................................918 461-0303
Verna Roberts, *President*
Kenneth Roberts, *Exec VP*
Sean Roberts, *Vice Pres*
EMP: 10
SQ FT: 5,000
SALES (est): 1.3MM **Privately Held**
SIC: 5999 5131 5734 3829 Drafting equipment & supplies; flags & banners; printers & plotters: computers; plotting instruments, drafting & map reading; video tape or disk reproduction; blueprint reproduction machines & equipment

(G-922)
GREGORY DEE SPAHN TRUST
7305 S 2nd St (74011-3547)
P.O. Box 27, Hartshorne (74547-0027)
PHONE.................................405 826-6777
Nicole Fitzpatrick,
Kara Jordan,
Greg Spahn,
Logan Spahn,
Morgan Spahn,
EMP: 6
SALES (est): 139.2K **Privately Held**
SIC: 0219 3523 General livestock; planting, haying, harvesting & processing machinery

(G-923)
GREYFOX INDUSTRIES LLC
1805 N 14th St (74012-9350)
PHONE.................................918 830-1144
Steven Aryan, *Administration*
EMP: 2
SALES (est): 68K **Privately Held**
SIC: 3999 Barber & beauty shop equipment

(G-924)
GRISHAM SERVICES INCORPORATED
800 S 11th St (74012-5701)
PHONE.................................918 307-7635
Jim Grisham, *President*
Pam Grisham, *Vice Pres*
Klaus Larrieu, *Manager*
Mindy Smith, *Manager*
▲ **EMP:** 16
SQ FT: 6,000
SALES (est): 9.5MM **Privately Held**
SIC: 1389 Oil field services

(G-925)
GYPSY MOON STUDIOS
1412 W Kenosha St (74012-8959)
PHONE.................................918 251-7188
EMP: 2

SALES (est): 161.7K **Privately Held**
SIC: 3861 Sound recording & reproducing equipment, motion picture

(G-926)
HAMPTON SOFTWARE DEVELOPMENT L
4704 W El Paso St (74012-7266)
PHONE.................................918 607-5307
Bill Hampton, *Principal*
EMP: 5
SALES (est): 213.2K **Privately Held**
SIC: 7372 Prepackaged software

(G-927)
HELP HOUSING
945 N Elm Pl (74012-1642)
PHONE.................................918 258-7252
Peter Updike, *Principal*
EMP: 3
SALES (est): 132.3K **Privately Held**
SIC: 3229 Cooking utensils, glass or glass ceramic

(G-928)
HILLENBURG OIL CO LLC (PA)
Also Called: Hill Pipe and Supply
11600 S Lynn Lane Rd (74011-4021)
PHONE.................................918 455-4444
Harold A Hillenburg Jr, *Owner*
Danny D Hillenburg, *Owner*
EMP: 9
SQ FT: 3,600
SALES (est): 1.8MM **Privately Held**
SIC: 1311 5084 Crude petroleum production; oil well machinery, equipment & supplies

(G-929)
HILTI INDUSTRIES INC
305 S 2nd St (74012-4159)
PHONE.................................918 251-7788
Lance Young, *Principal*
EMP: 3
SALES (est): 231K **Privately Held**
SIC: 3999 Manufacturing industries

(G-930)
HINDMAN METAL FABRICATORS
6998 S 145th East Ave (74012-9522)
PHONE.................................918 251-3949
EMP: 2
SALES (est): 181.2K **Privately Held**
SIC: 3444 Mfg Sheet Metalwork

(G-931)
HOEL MACHINE MFG INC
2220 N Yellowood Ave (74012-9102)
PHONE.................................918 294-8895
Mike Hoel, *President*
EMP: 6 **EST:** 1989
SQ FT: 4,000
SALES (est): 800K **Privately Held**
WEB: www.hoelmachine.com
SIC: 3469 Machine parts, stamped or pressed metal

(G-932)
HUMPS N HORNS BULL RIDING NEWS
3004 S Birch Ave (74012-7821)
P.O. Box 34172, Fort Worth TX (76162-4172)
PHONE.................................918 872-9713
EMP: 4
SALES (est): 438.9K **Privately Held**
SIC: 7311 5994 2711 Advertising agencies; magazine stand; newspapers, publishing & printing

(G-933)
IGG LLC
913 S Willow Ave (74012-4572)
PHONE.................................918 607-3032
Martin Lewis, *Mng Member*
EMP: 1
SALES: 25K **Privately Held**
SIC: 3944 7389 Board games, puzzles & models, except electronic;

(G-934)
IMPACT SCREEN PRINTING
720 W Elgin St (74012-2401)
PHONE.................................918 258-8337
Kenneth Foster, *Owner*

EMP: 2
SALES (est): 110K **Privately Held**
SIC: 7336 2396 Silk screen design; automotive & apparel trimmings

(G-935)
INDUSTRIAL TRCTR PARTS CO INC
Also Called: Industrial Tractor Parts Tulsa
2251 N Indianwood Ave (74012-1165)
PHONE.................................918 258-6580
Jerry Maggio, *Manager*
EMP: 4
SALES (corp-wide): 16.2MM **Privately Held**
SIC: 3531 Construction machinery
PA: Industrial Tractor Parts Co., Inc.
2815 14th St
Long Island City NY 11102
718 721-6661

(G-936)
INGERSOLL-RAND AIR SOLUTIO
6613 S Birch Ave (74011-6821)
PHONE.................................918 451-9747
EMP: 1 **EST:** 2008
SALES (est): 85K **Privately Held**
SIC: 3131 Mfg Footwear Cut Stock

(G-937)
INKED CUSTOM PRINTING
2234 W Houston St Ste A (74012-3519)
PHONE.................................918 872-6544
Vincent Ponteri, *Principal*
EMP: 3
SALES (est): 362.3K **Privately Held**
SIC: 2752 Commercial printing, offset

(G-938)
INLAND MANUFACTURING LLC
2701 W Montgomery St (74012-7498)
PHONE.................................918 697-4436
Sandra Brumley, *Principal*
EMP: 3
SALES (est): 150.8K **Privately Held**
SIC: 3999 Manufacturing industries

(G-939)
INTEGRATED TRAINING & MFG TECH
1300 E Fort Worth St (74012-4416)
PHONE.................................918 893-2225
EMP: 3
SALES (est): 161.6K **Privately Held**
SIC: 3999 Manufacturing industries

(G-940)
INTERACTIVE CAD SERVICES INC
2101 N Yellowood Ave (74012-9105)
PHONE.................................918 251-4470
Howard Yee, *President*
David Smith, *Vice Pres*
Dan Belcher, *Info Tech Mgr*
EMP: 6
SQ FT: 2,000
SALES (est): 705.1K **Privately Held**
SIC: 8711 7389 3679 Consulting engineer; drafting service, except temporary help; electronic circuits

(G-941)
JACOBSON FABRICATION INC
1500 N Poplar Ave (74012-1417)
PHONE.................................918 251-1181
Steven Jacobson, *President*
EMP: 6
SALES (est): 372.9K **Privately Held**
SIC: 3999 Manufacturing industries

(G-942)
JAMES MATTHEWS FORD LLC
Also Called: Jim Norton Ford
1101 Sw Expressway Dr (74012-1751)
PHONE.................................918 251-3673
James Matthews, *President*
Mike Couch, *Sales Staff*
Karen McGrath, *Admin Sec*
James Morton,
EMP: 25
SALES (est): 8.5MM **Privately Held**
SIC: 5511 3711 7538 Automobiles, new & used; motor vehicles & car bodies; general automotive repair shops

Broken Arrow - Tulsa County (G-943)

(G-943)
JAPA CORP
1304 W Phoenix St (74011-1835)
PHONE..................918 893-6763
Humphrey Douglas, *Administration*
EMP: 2 **EST:** 2011
SALES (est): 179.9K **Privately Held**
SIC: 2431 Millwork

(G-944)
JET SET SCREEN PRINTING I
2107 W Greeley St (74012-2326)
PHONE..................918 294-1053
EMP: 2
SALES (est): 169.5K **Privately Held**
SIC: 2752 Commercial printing, lithographic

(G-945)
JIREH SOFTWARE INC
3901 W South Park Blvd (74011-1247)
PHONE..................918 294-8240
EMP: 2 **EST:** 2010
SALES (est): 99K **Privately Held**
SIC: 7372 Prepackaged Software Services

(G-946)
JLM2 LLC
Also Called: Custom EMB & More By Rose
816 W Elgin St (74012-2425)
PHONE..................918 258-0239
Heidi Weber, *Mng Member*
Hillary Wright,
EMP: 4 **EST:** 2017
SQ FT: 2,400
SALES: 240K **Privately Held**
SIC: 2395 Embroidery products, except schiffli machine

(G-947)
JM MANUFACTURING
1712 E Edgewater St (74012-7961)
PHONE..................918 261-2816
Jim Miller, *Principal*
EMP: 3
SALES (est): 210.4K **Privately Held**
WEB: www.jrmanufacturing.com
SIC: 3999 Manufacturing industries

(G-948)
JNL EQUIPMENT
1721 N 10th St (74012-9381)
PHONE..................918 286-1951
Lloyd Walker, *Owner*
EMP: 1
SALES (est): 85.6K **Privately Held**
SIC: 3823 Industrial instrmnts msrmnt display/control process variable

(G-949)
JOHNNY BLAYLOCK
12106 E 131st St S (74011-5429)
PHONE..................918 639-5951
Johnny Blaylock, *Principal*
EMP: 1
SALES (est): 50.6K **Privately Held**
SIC: 7699 7692 Miscellaneous automotive repair services; welding repair

(G-950)
JOMAGA HOUSE
4520 S Redbud Ave (74011-3954)
P.O. Box 1233 (74013-1233)
PHONE..................918 455-0794
Terri Kalfas, *President*
Goerge Kalfas, *Corp Secy*
EMP: 2
SALES (est): 113.6K **Privately Held**
SIC: 2731 Pamphlets: publishing & printing

(G-951)
JTS WOODWORKS LLC
700 W Fredericksburg St (74011-6407)
PHONE..................918 640-1791
Joshua Breedlove, *Principal*
EMP: 1 **EST:** 2013
SALES (est): 108.2K **Privately Held**
SIC: 2431 Millwork

(G-952)
JUST DOUGH IT LLC
11375 E 61st St (74012-1264)
P.O. Box 140414 (74014-0004)
PHONE..................918 455-0770
Brenda Chapman, *Mng Member*
EMP: 3
SALES (est): 295.2K **Privately Held**
WEB: www.justdoughit.com
SIC: 3999 Advertising display products

(G-953)
JW NUTRITIONAL LLC
1607 S Main St (74012-5604)
PHONE..................214 221-0404
Sharon Windrix, *Accounts Mgr*
EMP: 5
SALES (corp-wide): 25.5MM **Privately Held**
SIC: 2023 Dietary supplements, dairy & non-dairy base
PA: Jw Nutritional, Llc
   601 Century Pkwy Ste 300
   Allen TX 75013
   214 221-0404

(G-954)
KAONOHI WOODWORKS
1009 W Decatur St (74011-6025)
PHONE..................918 893-4661
Jonathan Bell, *Principal*
EMP: 1
SALES (est): 54.1K **Privately Held**
SIC: 2431 Millwork

(G-955)
KDL PRINT PRODUCTION SVCS LLC
3801 W Urbana St (74012-6144)
PHONE..................918 254-8150
Karen Lesikar, *Principal*
EMP: 1 **EST:** 2010
SALES (est): 91.4K **Privately Held**
WEB: www.williams.com
SIC: 2752 Commercial printing, lithographic

(G-956)
KI INC
118 S Main St (74012-4139)
PHONE..................918 289-0200
EMP: 2
SALES (est): 90.4K **Privately Held**
SIC: 2599 Furniture & fixtures

(G-957)
KING SCREENS
2103 W Greeley St (74012-2326)
PHONE..................918 845-0004
EMP: 3
SALES (est): 228.5K **Privately Held**
SIC: 2759 Screen printing

(G-958)
KING VALVE CO INC
304 N Redbud Ave (74012-2339)
PHONE..................918 251-0369
Leon Hayden, *Principal*
Scott Pennington, *Business Mgr*
Brian Davidson, *Manager*
EMP: 7
SALES (est): 791.5K **Privately Held**
SIC: 3592 Valves

(G-959)
KINKOS INC
732 W New Orleans St # 150 (74011-1849)
PHONE..................303 449-9247
Gary Kusin, *CEO*
EMP: 2
SALES (est): 73.2K **Privately Held**
SIC: 2759 Commercial printing

(G-960)
KOSMOI LLC
221 S Yellowood Ave (74012-8638)
PHONE..................918 520-7822
Faith Raymer, *Owner*
Carolyn Beason, *Partner*
Kerie Moore, *Partner*
EMP: 2
SALES (est): 218.5K **Privately Held**
SIC: 3961 Costume jewelry

(G-961)
L3 COMM AMI INSTRUMENTS
1914 W Reno St Ste A (74012-1473)
PHONE..................212 697-1111
EMP: 3

SALES (est): 272.9K **Privately Held**
WEB: www.l-3com.com
SIC: 3812 Search & navigation equipment

(G-962)
L3 TECHNOLOGIES INC
Also Called: L3 AMI
3724 W Vancouver St (74012-2424)
PHONE..................918 258-0707
Ron Falk, *Vice Pres*
Mark Hymer, *Electrical Engi*
James Grant, *Manager*
EMP: 200
SALES (corp-wide): 6.8B **Publicly Held**
SIC: 3699 Electrical equipment & supplies
HQ: L3 Technologies, Inc.
   600 3rd Ave Fl 34
   New York NY 10016
   212 697-1111

(G-963)
L6 INC (PA)
Also Called: Total Valve Systems
1300 E Memphis St (74012-5800)
P.O. Box 1957 (74013-1957)
PHONE..................918 251-5791
Mike Lybarger, *President*
Michael A Lybarger, *President*
Laura Powell, *Opers Staff*
Judson Smalley, *Engineer*
Gary Stell, *Sales Mgr*
▲ **EMP:** 30
SQ FT: 56,000
SALES (est): 5.8MM **Privately Held**
SIC: 3491 5085 Industrial valves; valves & fittings

(G-964)
LATHEM TOOL AND MACHINE INC
701 S 11th St A (74012-5723)
PHONE..................918 724-6655
Douglas Lathem, *President*
EMP: 2
SQ FT: 4,500
SALES: 200K **Privately Held**
SIC: 3544 Special dies, tools, jigs & fixtures

(G-965)
LEATHER DOCTOR
501 S 10th St (74012-4422)
PHONE..................918 271-4600
Thomas Mills, *Owner*
EMP: 1
SALES: 50K **Privately Held**
SIC: 3199 Leather goods

(G-966)
LENNOX NAS
2301 N Sweet Gum Ave (74012-2399)
PHONE..................405 370-7001
EMP: 2
SALES (est): 146.5K **Privately Held**
SIC: 3585 Refrigeration & heating equipment

(G-967)
LIFES ADULT DAY SERVICES
3106 S Juniper Ave (74012-7712)
PHONE..................918 664-9000
Bill Major, *Principal*
EMP: 2
SALES (est): 62.9K **Privately Held**
SIC: 2711 Newspapers

(G-968)
MAVERICK MACHINERY LLC
2301 N Aspen Ave (74012-1182)
PHONE..................918 584-2504
EMP: 1
SALES (est): 57.6K **Privately Held**
SIC: 3366 Machinery castings: brass

(G-969)
MCELROY MANUFACTURING INC
311 S Redwood Ave (74012-4540)
PHONE..................918 254-7182
Jim M Craig, *Principal*
EMP: 2
SALES (est): 134.4K **Privately Held**
SIC: 3999 Manufacturing industries

(G-970)
MERE MINERALS
1313 W Quinton St (74011-8254)
PHONE..................918 902-3156
Yhannah Cormier, *Owner*
EMP: 1
SALES (est): 82.5K **Privately Held**
SIC: 2844 Toilet preparations

(G-971)
MERIDIAN BRICK LLC
Also Called: Boral Bricks Studio
225 N Aspen Ave (74012-2203)
PHONE..................918 258-7533
Joe Eischen, *Manager*
EMP: 4
SALES (corp-wide): 441MM **Privately Held**
SIC: 5211 3251 3255 Brick; brick & structural clay tile; clay refractories
PA: Meridian Brick Llc
   6455 Shiloh Rd D
   Alpharetta GA 30005
   770 645-4500

(G-972)
MICHAEL A PHILLIPS
Also Called: Commercial Electronics
801 N 15th St (74012-2838)
PHONE..................918 251-0925
Michael A Phillips, *Owner*
EMP: 2
SQ FT: 10,000
SALES: 1MM **Privately Held**
SIC: 5999 7629 3674 Communication equipment; electrical repair shops; semiconductors & related devices

(G-973)
MICROFRAME CORP
604 S 12th St (74012-4404)
P.O. Box 1700 (74013-1700)
PHONE..................918 258-4839
Bob McCullough, *President*
Gwen McCullough, *Treasurer*
EMP: 15
SALES (est): 2.9MM **Privately Held**
SIC: 3663 3873 Pagers (one-way); watches, clocks, watchcases & parts

(G-974)
MIDWEST AUTOMOTIVE FAS LLC
1704 W Baton Rouge Cir (74011-5803)
P.O. Box 6 (74013-0006)
PHONE..................918 520-6904
Michael Murray,
Grady Murray,
EMP: 2
SALES (est): 110K **Privately Held**
SIC: 3965 Fasteners

(G-975)
MIKES WELDING
18819 E 141st St (74011-3701)
PHONE..................918 455-7227
Michael Shieldnight, *Owner*
EMP: 1
SALES (est): 73.4K **Privately Held**
SIC: 1799 7692 3446 Welding on site; welding repair; architectural metalwork

(G-976)
MILITARY PARTS PLUS INC (PA)
2320 W Mobile Pl (74011-8264)
PHONE..................918 232-1581
Robert Swanfeld, *President*
EMP: 2
SQ FT: 7,500
SALES: 750K **Privately Held**
SIC: 3566 Speed changers, drives & gears

(G-977)
MILLER PUMP SYSTEMS INC
6301 S 5th St (74011-9003)
PHONE..................918 455-4556
Alan Miller, *President*
EMP: 4 **EST:** 1996
SALES (est): 381.9K **Privately Held**
SIC: 1389 Pumping of oil & gas wells

(G-978)
MILTECH LAB SERVICES INC
2225 W Atlanta St Ste B (74012-6702)
PHONE..................918 251-4436

GEOGRAPHIC SECTION
Broken Arrow - Tulsa County (G-1011)

Toney Miller, *President*
EMP: 1
SALES (est): 168.8K **Privately Held**
SIC: 3821 8734 8731 Laboratory apparatus & furniture; testing laboratories; commercial physical research

(G-979)
MITCHELL OIL COMPANY
900 W Vandever Blvd (74012-7667)
PHONE.................918 652-9175
Cecil Mitchell, *Owner*
EMP: 1
SALES (est): 85.3K **Privately Held**
SIC: 1381 Drilling oil & gas wells

(G-980)
MOM HUSTLE TEE CO ✪
4001 S Ash Ave (74011-2616)
PHONE.................417 658-6450
Marissa Bailey, *Principal*
EMP: 2 **EST:** 2019
SALES (est): 73.2K **Privately Held**
SIC: 2759 Screen printing

(G-981)
MONUMENTAL ROCKS
1001 S Desert Palm Ave (74012-8802)
PHONE.................918 240-8398
John Hidalgo, *Principal*
EMP: 3
SALES (est): 114.6K **Privately Held**
SIC: 3272 Monuments & grave markers, except terrazo

(G-982)
MOSLEY
2916 N Hickory Ave (74012-0860)
PHONE.................918 407-6619
Allison Mosely, *Principal*
EMP: 4
SALES (est): 284.1K **Privately Held**
SIC: 3569 General industrial machinery

(G-983)
MPL MANUFACTURING LLC
13555 S 129th East Ave (74011-7454)
PHONE.................918 630-9944
David Yonce, *Principal*
EMP: 2 **EST:** 2017
SALES (est): 68.7K **Privately Held**
SIC: 3999 Manufacturing industries

(G-984)
NAKED WOOD WORKS
509 N Redbud Ave Ste E (74012-2383)
PHONE.................918 864-0229
EMP: 2
SALES (est): 59.5K **Privately Held**
SIC: 2431 Millwork

(G-985)
NATIVE AMERICAN CAPITAL LLC
1932 S Desert Palm Ave (74012-6133)
PHONE.................918 289-7489
EMP: 2
SALES (est): 120K **Privately Held**
SIC: 5961 8748 1382 Catalog And Mail-Order Houses

(G-986)
NATURES LIGHT LLC
2420 S Sowegel Ave (74012)
PHONE.................925 209-1766
Charis Miller, *Mng Member*
EMP: 2
SALES (est): 88.8K **Privately Held**
SIC: 2844 Toilet preparations

(G-987)
NETPRO INDUSTRIES INC
2604 S Beech Ave (74012-7303)
PHONE.................918 630-3201
EMP: 1
SALES (est): 111.1K **Privately Held**
WEB: www.netproi.com
SIC: 3999 Manufacturing industries

(G-988)
NEW TIMES TECHNOLOGIES INC
2600 W Albany St Ste A (74012-1463)
PHONE.................918 872-9600
Renato Almeida, *President*
EMP: 80
SALES (est): 3.5MM **Privately Held**
SIC: 3949 5045 Sporting & athletic goods; computer software

(G-989)
NORTHWOOD PUBLISHING LLC
507 W Los Angeles Pl (74011-4838)
PHONE.................918 451-9388
Kimberly D Prescott, *Principal*
EMP: 1
SALES (est): 81.4K **Privately Held**
SIC: 2741 Music book & sheet music publishing

(G-990)
NUPOCKET LLC
3400 W Washington St (74012-9001)
PHONE.................918 850-1903
Linda Neal, *Mng Member*
Linda Harper,
EMP: 10
SALES: 30K **Privately Held**
SIC: 5099 3172 Mobile home parts & accessories; vanity cases

(G-991)
O C & ASSOCIATES INC
509 N Walnut Ave Ste C (74012-2321)
PHONE.................918 251-0971
Oscar Gnaedig, *President*
EMP: 2
SALES (est): 160.8K **Privately Held**
SIC: 3089 Injection molding of plastics

(G-992)
OCONNELL WOODWORKS LLC
2100 S Aster Ave (74012-6066)
PHONE.................918 805-7233
Jonathan O'Connell, *Principal*
EMP: 2
SALES (est): 85.2K **Privately Held**
SIC: 2431 Millwork

(G-993)
OILFIELD IMPROVEMENTS INC
1902 N Yellowood Ave (74012-9163)
PHONE.................918 250-5584
Hughes A Coston Sr, *CEO*
Hughes A Coston Jr, *President*
Pat F Coston, *CFO*
EMP: 5
SQ FT: 10,000
SALES: 1.2MM **Privately Held**
SIC: 3533 8711 3498 Oil field machinery & equipment; engineering services; fabricated pipe & fittings

(G-994)
OKLAHOMA SAFETY EQP CO INC (DH)
Also Called: Oseco
1701 W Tacoma St (74012-1449)
P.O. Box 1327 (74013-1327)
PHONE.................918 258-5626
Bryan Sanderlin, *President*
Rob Barcik, *Vice Pres*
Darren Doyle, *Vice Pres*
Taylor Garren, *Vice Pres*
Mark Holt, *Vice Pres*
EMP: 112
SQ FT: 31,791
SALES (est): 17.2MM
SALES (corp-wide): 1.5B **Privately Held**
WEB: www.oseco.com
SIC: 3499 3491 Aerosol valves, metal; pressure valves & regulators, industrial
HQ: Halma Holdings Inc.
  11500 Northlake Dr # 306
  Cincinnati OH 45249
  513 772-5501

(G-995)
OSIYO MEDALS INC
1801 N Indianwood Ave (74012-1149)
PHONE.................918 258-4717
Stuart Gibs, *Principal*
Stuart Gibbs, *Principal*
Mike Quinton, *Principal*
▼ **EMP:** 10
SALES (est): 1.8MM **Privately Held**
SIC: 3446 Ornamental metalwork

(G-996)
PACCAR INC
800 E Dallas St (74012-4300)
PHONE.................918 251-8511
Brennan Gourdie, *Division Mgr*
EMP: 215
SALES (corp-wide): 24.1B **Publicly Held**
SIC: 3531 Winches
PA: Paccar Inc
  777 106th Ave Ne
  Bellevue WA 98004
  425 468-7400

(G-997)
PAIGE 1 PUBLISHING
12350 E 138th St S (74011-7600)
PHONE.................918 706-4359
J Jones, *Principal*
EMP: 1
SALES (est): 36.1K **Privately Held**
SIC: 2731 Book publishing

(G-998)
PARAGON FILMS INC (PA)
3500 W Tacoma St (74012-1164)
PHONE.................918 250-3456
Darin W Tang, *CEO*
Rolly Cochlin, *COO*
Brian K Stock, *Exec VP*
Robert Cochlin, *Vice Pres*
Alex Jech, *Vice Pres*
◆ **EMP:** 135
SQ FT: 140,000
SALES (est): 25.4MM **Privately Held**
SIC: 3081 Polyethylene film

(G-999)
PATRIOT WLDG & FABRICATION LLC
305 N Redbud Ave (74012-2381)
PHONE.................918 600-7147
Ryan Pluss, *Principal*
EMP: 1
SALES (est): 72.9K **Privately Held**
SIC: 7692 Welding repair

(G-1000)
PATTISON METAL FAB INC
701 N 15th St (74012-2835)
PHONE.................918 251-9967
Karyn Pattison, *President*
EMP: 25 **EST:** 2000
SQ FT: 10,000
SALES: 2.9MM **Privately Held**
SIC: 3441 1761 Fabricated structural metal; sheet metalwork

(G-1001)
PATTISON PRECISION PRODUCTS
701 N 15th St (74012-2835)
PHONE.................918 251-9967
Raymond Pattison, *President*
EMP: 30
SQ FT: 70,000
SALES (est): 4.7MM **Privately Held**
SIC: 3599 Machine shop, jobbing & repair

(G-1002)
PENNY SHEET METAL LLC
1910 W Detroit St (74012-3614)
P.O. Box 691255, Tulsa (74169-1255)
PHONE.................918 251-6911
Ric Penny, *Mng Member*
EMP: 11
SQ FT: 3,000
SALES: 313K **Privately Held**
SIC: 3444 1761 Sheet metalwork; architectural sheet metal work; gutter & downspout contractor

(G-1003)
PERSONAL EXPRESSIONS
1129 S Tamarack Ave (74012-4640)
PHONE.................918 406-4581
Linda Palkowski, *Owner*
John Palkowski, *Co-Owner*
EMP: 1
SALES: 250K **Privately Held**
SIC: 2395 Embroidery products, except schiffli machine

(G-1004)
PETNET SOLUTIONS INC
2341 W Albany St Ste H (74012-1458)
PHONE.................918 259-0899
Ronnie Cipple, *Branch Mgr*
EMP: 4
SALES (corp-wide): 96.9B **Privately Held**
SIC: 2835 Radioactive diagnostic substances
HQ: Petnet Solutions, Inc.
  810 Innovation Dr
  Knoxville TN 37932
  865 218-2000

(G-1005)
PETROLAB LLC (HQ)
2001 N Indianwood Ave (74012-1163)
PHONE.................918 459-7170
Dave Zapico, *Manager*
Eric Swertfeger, *Manager*
EMP: 6
SQ FT: 30,000
SALES: 5MM
SALES (corp-wide): 5.1B **Publicly Held**
SIC: 3621 3823 3824 5084 Motors & generators; industrial instrmnts msrmnt display/control process variable; fluid meters & counting devices; measuring & testing equipment, electrical
PA: Ametek, Inc.
  1100 Cassatt Rd
  Berwyn PA 19312
  610 647-2121

(G-1006)
PHIL SINGLETARY CO INC
500 S 12th St (74012-4419)
PHONE.................918 258-7733
Craig Singletary, *President*
John Craig Singletary, *Vice Pres*
EMP: 6
SQ FT: 6,000
SALES: 557.6K **Privately Held**
SIC: 3599 3533 Machine shop, jobbing & repair; oil & gas field machinery

(G-1007)
PINE COVE JERKY LLC
431 Stone Wood Dr (74012-1026)
PHONE.................918 872-1138
Benjamin Dye, *Principal*
EMP: 3 **EST:** 2017
SALES (est): 213.4K **Privately Held**
SIC: 2013 Snack sticks, including jerky: from purchased meat

(G-1008)
PLANTATION SHUTTER CO
304 N Redbud Ave (74012-2339)
PHONE.................817 703-1091
Alan Wallace, *Principal*
EMP: 3 **EST:** 2018
SALES (est): 180.7K **Privately Held**
SIC: 3442 Shutters, door or window: metal

(G-1009)
PREMIER VALVE GROUP
1401 W Plymouth St (74012-0417)
PHONE.................918 519-4309
EMP: 1
SALES: 350K **Privately Held**
SIC: 3491 Mfg Industrial Valves

(G-1010)
PRINT HAPPY LLC
1015 E Lansing St (74012-2074)
PHONE.................918 270-1300
Scott Brown, *Principal*
EMP: 2 **EST:** 2014
SALES (est): 149.9K **Privately Held**
SIC: 2752 Commercial printing, lithographic

(G-1011)
PRINT N COPY INC
Also Called: Ambiance Graphics
921 N Elm Pl (74012-1642)
PHONE.................918 258-8200
Dean Hartshorne, *President*
EMP: 2
SQ FT: 1,200
SALES: 300K **Privately Held**
WEB: www.printncopytulsa.com
SIC: 2752 2791 2789 Commercial printing, offset; typesetting; bookbinding & related work

Broken Arrow - Tulsa County (G-1012)

(G-1012)
PROSTHETICS BY WADE
12920 S 126th East Ave (74011-5615)
PHONE..................918 850-7544
Joseph Bognuda, *Principal*
EMP: 3
SALES (est): 167.5K **Privately Held**
SIC: 3842 Prosthetic appliances

(G-1013)
PROTEGE ENERGY III LLC
4509 S Yellow Pine Ave (74011-5616)
PHONE..................918 286-2457
Martin L Thalken, *Principal*
EMP: 1
SALES (corp-wide): 500K **Privately Held**
SIC: 1382 Oil & gas exploration services
PA: Protege Energy Iii Llc
    2200 S Utica Pl Ste 400
    Tulsa OK 74114
    918 728-3092

(G-1014)
PURE MOUNTAIN
108 E El Paso St (74012-4121)
PHONE..................918 254-2225
EMP: 3
SALES (est): 117.9K **Privately Held**
SIC: 2086 Bottled & canned soft drinks

(G-1015)
PUT ON YOUR ARMOR INC
1000 E Memphis St (74012-5803)
P.O. Box 703131, Tulsa (74170-3131)
PHONE..................918 259-5000
Jim Schmidt, *Principal*
EMP: 2
SALES: 21.3K **Privately Held**
SIC: 2759 Commercial printing

(G-1016)
QUALITY MACHINING OF BROKEN
12320 E 126th St S (74011-5400)
PHONE..................918 294-1434
EMP: 3
SALES (est): 399.3K **Privately Held**
SIC: 3599 Mfg Industrial Machinery

(G-1017)
QUALITY MACHINING INC
12320 E 126th St S (74011-5400)
PHONE..................918 294-1434
EMP: 15
SQ FT: 4,000
SALES (est): 847K **Privately Held**
SIC: 3599 Job Machine Shop

(G-1018)
R & R ENGINEERING CO INC
12585 E 61st St (74012-9117)
P.O. Box 700005, Tulsa (74170-0005)
PHONE..................918 252-2571
Wayne B Rumley, *President*
Warren Rumley, *Treasurer*
Jim Hammers, *Manager*
EMP: 50
SQ FT: 50,000
SALES (est): 9MM **Privately Held**
WEB: www.coolersbyrr.com
SIC: 3443 Heat exchangers, condensers & components; heat exchangers: coolers (after, inter), condensers, etc.

(G-1019)
RACF INDUSTRIES INC
102 W Norman St (74012-1943)
PHONE..................918 258-1290
Ron Feeley, *President*
Christopher Feeley, *Vice Pres*
Andrew Feeley, *Admin Sec*
EMP: 3
SALES (est): 209.8K **Privately Held**
SIC: 3999 Barber & beauty shop equipment

(G-1020)
RAILROAD SGNLING SOLUTIONS INC
1103 E Houston St (74012-4426)
PHONE..................918 973-1888
Rachel Stayton,
EMP: 4
SALES (est): 505.6K **Privately Held**
SIC: 4789 5088 3743 3669 Transportation services; transportation equipment & supplies; railroad equipment; communications equipment; fabricated structural metal

(G-1021)
RAPID APPLICATION GROUP LLC
13105 E 61st St Ste A (74012-1192)
PHONE..................918 760-1242
Terry Hill,
EMP: 2 EST: 2017
SALES: 100K **Privately Held**
SIC: 2821 7389 Plasticizer/additive based plastic materials;

(G-1022)
RAR WOOD WORKS LLC
2612 S Walnut Ave (74012-7561)
PHONE..................205 233-2920
Rachael Arrington, *Owner*
EMP: 1
SALES (est): 51.1K **Privately Held**
SIC: 2431 Millwork

(G-1023)
RAXTER LLC
3820 W El Paso St (74012-4514)
PHONE..................918 706-7987
Michael Farney, *Principal*
Kevin Wilson, *Sales Staff*
EMP: 2
SALES (est): 213.2K **Privately Held**
SIC: 3714 Motor vehicle parts & accessories

(G-1024)
RCP PRINT SOLUTIONS
1018 N 6th St (74012-2038)
P.O. Box 3434 (74013-3434)
PHONE..................918 341-1950
Dennis Compton, *President*
EMP: 2 EST: 2012
SALES (est): 188.1K **Privately Held**
SIC: 2752 Commercial printing, offset

(G-1025)
RCP PRINTING
1018 N 6th St (74012-2038)
P.O. Box 3434 (74013-3434)
PHONE..................918 341-1950
Curtis Cole, *Owner*
EMP: 3 EST: 1986
SQ FT: 2,775
SALES (est): 112.8K **Privately Held**
SIC: 2752 Commercial printing, offset

(G-1026)
RDS MANUFACTURING
304 N Redbud Ave (74012-2339)
PHONE..................918 251-0369
EMP: 1 EST: 2018
SALES (est): 39.6K **Privately Held**
SIC: 3999 Manufacturing industries

(G-1027)
RDS MANUFACTURING INC
4217 W Seattle St (74012-9113)
PHONE..................918 459-5100
Roy D Sturgeon, *President*
Sheri Smith, *Corp Secy*
EMP: 130
SQ FT: 110,000
SALES (est): 26.2MM **Privately Held**
SIC: 3599 Machine shop, jobbing & repair

(G-1028)
REALTIME AUTOMATION INC
1401 W Detroit St (74012-3610)
PHONE..................918 249-9217
Douglas J McAllister, *President*
Jose Cosa, *Vice Pres*
EMP: 7
SALES (est): 400K **Privately Held**
SIC: 3625 Relays & industrial controls

(G-1029)
REASOR ENTERPRISES
Also Called: Reasor Fiberglass
1600 S Fir Ave (74012-6323)
P.O. Box 2014 (74013-2014)
PHONE..................918 633-1746
Michael Reasor, *Owner*
Melloria Reasor, *Co-Owner*
EMP: 4 EST: 2012
SALES (est): 180K **Privately Held**
SIC: 3089 7389 Plastic & fiberglass tanks;

(G-1030)
REMWOOD PRODUCTS CO
501 N Redbud Ave Ste G (74012-2382)
P.O. Box 35305, Tulsa (74153-0305)
PHONE..................918 251-8399
Sterling Woody, *President*
Joanne Woody, *Corp Secy*
A H Woody, *Vice Pres*
EMP: 3
SQ FT: 3,000
SALES: 139.9K **Privately Held**
SIC: 2841 Soap & other detergents

(G-1031)
RICHARD BOLUSKY
3500 W Tacoma St (74012-1164)
PHONE..................918 381-5694
EMP: 4
SALES (est): 250.1K **Privately Held**
SIC: 2673 Mfg Bags-Plastic/Coated Paper

(G-1032)
RISE MANUFACTURING LLC
1605 E Lola St (74012)
PHONE..................918 994-6240
Matt Torres, *President*
Cassie Smith, *Accountant*
Brian Torres, *Manager*
EMP: 23 EST: 2012
SQ FT: 55,000
SALES (est): 6.8MM **Privately Held**
SIC: 3441 3443 3721 3498 Fabricated structural metal; tanks, standard or custom fabricated: metal plate; aircraft; fabricated pipe & fittings; small arms

(G-1033)
RITBERGER INC
523 E Madison St (74012-2042)
PHONE..................918 271-3895
Gary Ritberger, *President*
EMP: 5
SALES: 310K **Privately Held**
SIC: 3523 Greens mowing equipment

(G-1034)
RIVERSIDE OPERATIONS GROUP LLC
1700 W Albany St Ste 100 (74012-1481)
PHONE..................918 908-9480
Donn Campbell, *Mng Member*
Cody Brooks,
EMP: 22
SALES: 5MM **Privately Held**
SIC: 1611 3532 Concrete construction: roads, highways, sidewalks, etc.; drills (portable), rock

(G-1035)
RL HUDSON & COMPANY (PA)
Also Called: Rl Hudson
2000 W Tacoma St (74012-1442)
PHONE..................918 259-6600
Rick L Hudson, *CEO*
Mike McNulty, *Vice Pres*
Ross Parmley, *Vice Pres*
James R Podesta, *Vice Pres*
Ray Podesta, *Vice Pres*
◆ EMP: 110 EST: 1980
SQ FT: 108,000
SALES: 46.3MM **Privately Held**
WEB: www.rlhudson.com
SIC: 5085 3089 Rubber goods, mechanical; molding primary plastic

(G-1036)
ROBINSON MANUFACTURING CO
604 S 10th St (74012-4418)
PHONE..................918 251-0353
Thomas A Tejeda, *President*
Rico Tejeda, *General Mgr*
EMP: 6
SQ FT: 6,000
SALES (est): 1.3MM **Privately Held**
SIC: 3569 Centrifuges, industrial

(G-1037)
ROCKING CHAIR ENTERPRISES LLC
4328 S Dogwood Ave (74011-1524)
PHONE..................918 455-3744
Pamela K Hawkins,
Edward C Hawkins,
Edward Hawkins,
▼ EMP: 2
SALES: 232K **Privately Held**
SIC: 2741 Music, sheet: publishing & printing

(G-1038)
ROWDY HANGER
2218 W Houston St (74012-3500)
PHONE..................918 804-7375
Rowdy Williams, *Principal*
EMP: 3
SALES (est): 152.4K **Privately Held**
SIC: 3842 Braces, orthopedic

(G-1039)
RUBBER & GASKET CO AMER INC
Also Called: R G A Rubber & Gasket Co Amer
1751 N Indianwood Ave (74012-1100)
PHONE..................918 249-2069
John Zimmerman, *Manager*
EMP: 8 **Privately Held**
SIC: 3599 Flexible metal hose, tubing & bellows
PA: Rubber & Gasket Company Of America, Inc.
    3905 E Progress St
    North Little Rock AR 72114

(G-1040)
RUSSELECTRIC INC
1215 E Houston St (74012-4405)
PHONE..................918 251-7877
Larry Hopper, *Manager*
EMP: 80
SALES (corp-wide): 96.9B **Privately Held**
SIC: 3613 Switchgear & switchgear accessories
HQ: Russelectric Inc.
    99 Industrial Park Rd
    Hingham MA 02043
    781 749-6000

(G-1041)
RWDESIGN PUBLISHING ●
828 W Midway St (74012-2404)
PHONE..................918 924-8865
Rose Wenning, *Principal*
EMP: 1 EST: 2019
SALES (est): 37.5K **Privately Held**
SIC: 2741 Miscellaneous publishing

(G-1042)
S COKER CUSTOM WOODWORKS
731 W Freeport St (74012-2406)
PHONE..................918 638-3443
EMP: 4 EST: 2010
SALES (est): 214.3K **Privately Held**
SIC: 2431 Millwork

(G-1043)
SAW SWAN SERVICE INC
2200 N Yellowood Ave (74012-9102)
PHONE..................918 249-3821
Michael Swan, *President*
Ann Swan, *Corp Secy*
EMP: 3
SQ FT: 1,500
SALES (est): 270K **Privately Held**
WEB: www.swansaw.com
SIC: 3425 Saw blades for hand or power saws

(G-1044)
SAWDUST LTD
509 N Walnut Ave Ste A (74012-2321)
P.O. Box 386 (74013-0386)
PHONE..................918 809-3456
Rick Vaughan, *Owner*
EMP: 3
SALES (est): 258.7K **Privately Held**
SIC: 2439 1521 Structural wood members; patio & deck construction & repair

GEOGRAPHIC SECTION
Broken Arrow - Tulsa County (G-1081)

(G-1045)
SCRAPWORX
1430 W Kenosha St (74012-8959)
PHONE..................918 259-9547
Debbie Thomas, *Owner*
EMP: 1
SALES (est): 46.4K **Privately Held**
SIC: 2782 Blankbooks & looseleaf binders

(G-1046)
SEAL SUPPORT SYSTEMS INC
Also Called: Lube Power
432 N Pecan Ave (74012-2331)
PHONE..................918 258-6484
Dave Eubanks, *Vice Pres*
EMP: 10
SALES (corp-wide): 10.8B **Privately Held**
SIC: 2891 3443 Adhesives & sealants; fabricated plate work (boiler shop)
HQ: Seal Support Systems, Inc.
141 Shafer Dr
Romeo MI

(G-1047)
SEAPORT SOFTWARE INC
3700 W Iola St (74012-2146)
PHONE..................918 258-8611
Clell L Beavers, *President*
EMP: 5
SALES (est): 377.4K **Privately Held**
SIC: 7372 Prepackaged software

(G-1048)
SECURE SCREEN LLC
3101 W Albany St (74012-1146)
PHONE..................918 294-4444
Brian Smidt, *Principal*
EMP: 7
SALES (est): 559.3K **Privately Held**
SIC: 2431 Blinds (shutters), wood

(G-1049)
SEW GLAM MONOGRAM LLC
6227 S Date Pl (74011-4156)
PHONE..................918 606-2644
Holly Hansen, *Principal*
EMP: 1
SALES (est): 41.6K **Privately Held**
SIC: 2395 Embroidery & art needlework

(G-1050)
SIGN DEZIGNS
317 E New Orleans St (74011-2640)
PHONE..................918 688-3660
C Gehrke, *Principal*
EMP: 2
SALES (est): 159.9K **Privately Held**
SIC: 3993 Signs & advertising specialties

(G-1051)
SILVERSTONE LLC
740 W Elgin St (74012-2401)
PHONE..................918 373-2437
EMP: 2
SALES (est): 146.9K **Privately Held**
SIC: 2752 Commercial printing, lithographic

(G-1052)
SIMPLY SCENTSATIONAL
925 W Quincy St (74012-6631)
PHONE..................918 691-8027
EMP: 2
SALES (est): 118K **Privately Held**
SIC: 2844 Toilet preparations

(G-1053)
SINISTER SAND SPORTS
2013 W Detroit St (74012-3616)
PHONE..................918 521-3736
Joshua Burrup, *Principal*
EMP: 6 EST: 2011
SALES (est): 921.7K **Privately Held**
SIC: 3465 Body parts, automobile: stamped metal

(G-1054)
SOLAR TURBINES INCORPORATED
4217 W Seattle St (74012-9113)
PHONE..................918 459-5100
Roydean Sturgeon, *President*
EMP: 8
SALES (corp-wide): 53.8B **Publicly Held**
SIC: 3511 Turbines & turbine generator sets
HQ: Solar Turbines Incorporated
2200 Pacific Hwy
San Diego CA 92101
619 544-5000

(G-1055)
SOUTH EDGE
7850 S Elm Pl (74011-4342)
PHONE..................918 286-4936
Ronald Purvis, *Principal*
EMP: 4
SALES (est): 368.2K **Privately Held**
SIC: 2599 Bar, restaurant & cafeteria furniture

(G-1056)
SOUTHLAND AWARDS & SIGNS
914 S Nyssa Pl (74012-5860)
PHONE..................918 691-9141
Angela Davis, *Principal*
EMP: 2 EST: 2009
SALES (est): 164.1K **Privately Held**
SIC: 3993 Signs & advertising specialties

(G-1057)
SPRAY MAGNIFIQUE LLC
2509 W Iola St (74012-2238)
PHONE..................918 613-6284
EMP: 3
SALES (est): 298.4K **Privately Held**
SIC: 3563 Air & gas compressors

(G-1058)
SPRINGCREST DRAPERY CENTER
2004 W Nashville St (74012-4828)
PHONE..................918 258-5644
Lennis Robertson, *Owner*
EMP: 2 EST: 1978
SALES (est): 131.5K **Privately Held**
SIC: 5714 2391 Drapery & upholstery stores; curtains & draperies

(G-1059)
SSI TECHNOLOGIES INC
8405 S 7th St (74011-8833)
PHONE..................918 451-6160
Janie Kleibert, *Principal*
EMP: 2
SALES (est): 145.2K **Privately Held**
SIC: 2752 Commercial printing, lithographic

(G-1060)
STAR CORRAL
Also Called: Artesan Design
808 S 9th St (74012-5707)
P.O. Box 2433 (74013-2433)
PHONE..................918 251-9795
EMP: 1 EST: 2005
SALES (est): 41.7K **Privately Held**
SIC: 2395 Pleating/Stitching Services

(G-1061)
STAR JEWELERS INC
120 S Main St (74012-4139)
PHONE..................918 251-9236
Dale Brake, *President*
Kelli Mitchell, *Corp Secy*
Danny Brake, *Vice Pres*
Shelba Brake, *Vice Pres*
EMP: 8 EST: 1973
SQ FT: 2,000
SALES (est): 1MM **Privately Held**
SIC: 5944 3911 Jewelry, precious stones & precious metals; jewelry, precious metal

(G-1062)
STICKEM FISHING LURES LTD
9 Royal Dublin Ln (74011-1127)
PHONE..................918 636-6179
Scott Hood, *President*
EMP: 1
SALES (est): 99.5K **Privately Held**
SIC: 3949 Lures, fishing: artificial

(G-1063)
STITCHIN STITCHES
118 E Jackson St (74012-5507)
PHONE..................918 251-9696
Oliver Reiff, *Principal*
EMP: 1

SALES (est): 54.9K **Privately Held**
SIC: 2395 Embroidery & art needlework

(G-1064)
STONE WAREHOUSE
9251 S Garnett Rd (74012-6055)
PHONE..................918 250-0800
Bud Burnes, *Owner*
EMP: 13
SALES (est): 701K **Privately Held**
SIC: 3272 Stone, cast concrete

(G-1065)
STONEWOOD VISION SOURCE
433 Stone Wood Dr (74012-1026)
PHONE..................918 994-4450
Scott Hibbets, *Owner*
Terry Sloan, *Assistant VP*
EMP: 3 EST: 2011
SALES (est): 411.4K **Privately Held**
SIC: 3851 5995 Contact lenses; optical goods stores

(G-1066)
SUES MONOGRAMMING
12829 E 133rd St S (74011-7432)
PHONE..................918 455-1011
Sue Arnold, *Owner*
EMP: 1
SALES (est): 58.9K **Privately Held**
SIC: 2395 Embroidery & art needlework

(G-1067)
SULLINS INTERNATIONAL INC
801 E Jackson Pl (74012-5522)
PHONE..................918 258-5460
Fred Carr, *President*
James Brown, *Vice Pres*
EMP: 3 EST: 1978
SQ FT: 3,000
SALES (est): 325.2K **Privately Held**
SIC: 3844 Radiographic X-ray apparatus & tubes

(G-1068)
SWC
604 N Redbud Ave (74012-2345)
PHONE..................918 251-2679
Randy Schmitz, *CFO*
EMP: 1
SALES (est): 54.3K **Privately Held**
SIC: 3496 Miscellaneous fabricated wire products

(G-1069)
SWIFT ECKRICH INC
1901 W Iola St (74012-2330)
PHONE..................918 258-4565
Alan Edwards, *Principal*
EMP: 2
SALES (est): 192.6K **Privately Held**
SIC: 3556 Meat processing machinery

(G-1070)
TACTICAL ELEC MILITARY SUP LLC (PA)
2200 N Hemlock Ave (74012-1122)
PHONE..................866 541-7996
Tim Thornton, *Mng Member*
◆ EMP: 44
SQ FT: 23,000
SALES (est): 10.5MM **Privately Held**
SIC: 3699 3827 3651 3663 Fire control or bombing equipment, electronic; gun sights, optical; video camera-audio recorders, household use; transmitting apparatus, radio or television

(G-1071)
TARGET COMPLETIONS LLC
1700 N Indianwood Ave (74012-1133)
PHONE..................918 872-6115
Michael Sommers, *Partner*
Jessica Foster, *Purchasing*
Travis Noorigian, *Purchasing*
Jo Clark, *Sales Staff*
Kevin Clark, *Sales Staff*
EMP: 4
SALES (est): 774.9K **Privately Held**
WEB: www.targetcompletions.com
SIC: 1389 Oil field services

(G-1072)
TCAACP LLC
511 S Aspen Ave (74012-2296)
PHONE..................918 251-6655
Gayle Abney, *Partner*
Digi Field, *Partner*
EMP: 2
SALES (est): 100K **Privately Held**
SIC: 2834 Solutions, pharmaceutical

(G-1073)
TEXAS REFINERY CORP
2205 W Canton Pl (74012-7334)
PHONE..................918 455-6881
Richard Tanner, *Principal*
EMP: 3 EST: 2010
SALES (est): 228.9K **Privately Held**
SIC: 3559 Refinery, chemical processing & similar machinery

(G-1074)
TIER LVEL THRADS STUFF SCREEN
1904 W Iola St Ste 106 (74012-2449)
PHONE..................918 808-7290
EMP: 2
SALES (est): 73.2K **Privately Held**
SIC: 2759 Letterpress & screen printing

(G-1075)
TIGER TOWN TEES
309 N Aspen Ave (74012-2207)
PHONE..................918 409-4282
Galen Engel, *Principal*
Lisa Engel, *Principal*
EMP: 3
SALES (est): 172.2K **Privately Held**
WEB: www.tulsatshirtshop.com
SIC: 2759 Screen printing

(G-1076)
TIGERS EXPRESS
701 S 9th St (74012-4413)
PHONE..................918 251-0118
Maily T Lam, *Owner*
EMP: 2
SALES (est): 139.6K **Privately Held**
SIC: 2741 Miscellaneous publishing

(G-1077)
TIMOTHY PUBLISHING SERVICES
3409 W Gary St (74012-7588)
PHONE..................918 924-6246
EMP: 1 EST: 2013
SALES (est): 41.3K **Privately Held**
SIC: 2741 Miscellaneous publishing

(G-1078)
TITANIUM NUTRITION LLC
1301 Oakwood Dr (74011-8221)
PHONE..................918 697-1012
Angie Zimmer, *Principal*
EMP: 4
SALES (est): 133K **Privately Held**
SIC: 3356 Titanium

(G-1079)
TRANE US INC
2201 N Willow Ave (74012-9192)
PHONE..................918 250-5522
EMP: 8 **Privately Held**
SIC: 3585 Refrigeration & heating equipment
HQ: Trane U.S. Inc.
3600 Pammel Creek Rd
La Crosse WI 54601
608 787-2000

(G-1080)
TRANE US INC
2205 N Willow Ave Ste A (74012-9189)
PHONE..................855 200-0072
EMP: 2 **Privately Held**
SIC: 3585 Refrigeration & heating equipment
HQ: Trane U.S. Inc.
3600 Pammel Creek Rd
La Crosse WI 54601
608 787-2000

(G-1081)
TRANE US INC
2201 N Willow Ave Ste A (74012-9193)
PHONE..................405 787-2237

Broken Arrow - Tulsa County (G-1082)

Mike Presson, *Manager*
Ryan Rodriguez, *Manager*
EMP: 25 **Privately Held**
SIC: 3585 Refrigeration & heating equipment
HQ: Trane U.S. Inc.
3600 Pammel Creek Rd
La Crosse WI 54601
608 787-2000

(G-1082)
TRAVIS QUALITY PDTS & SLS INC
1404 W Detroit St (74012-3609)
P.O. Box 7 (74013-0007)
PHONE.................................918 251-0115
Michael Travis, *President*
Kathy Travis, *Corp Secy*
EMP: 9
SQ FT: 11,000
SALES (est): 1.1MM **Privately Held**
SIC: 3569 3823 Filters & strainers, pipeline; primary elements for process flow measurement

(G-1083)
TRENARY PUBLISHING LLC
1100 S Yellowood Ave (74012-8806)
PHONE.................................918 607-3280
EMP: 1
SALES (est): 41.3K **Privately Held**
SIC: 2741 Miscellaneous publishing

(G-1084)
TRI STATE INDUSTRIAL
314 N Redbud Ave (74012-2339)
PHONE.................................918 286-8110
Gary Allison, *Owner*
EMP: 12
SALES (est): 514.1K **Privately Held**
SIC: 1389 Gas field services

(G-1085)
TULSA SCREEN PRINTING
1310 N Elm Pl (74012-1609)
PHONE.................................918 488-1331
EMP: 2 **EST:** 2017
SALES (est): 83.9K **Privately Held**
SIC: 2752 Commercial printing, lithographic

(G-1086)
TULSA SIGNS
2437 N Aspen Ave (74012-1142)
PHONE.................................918 251-6262
Keith Hough, *Owner*
EMP: 3
SALES (est): 211.1K **Privately Held**
SIC: 3993 Signs, not made in custom sign painting shops

(G-1087)
TULSAT CORPORATION
1221 E Houston St (74012-4405)
PHONE.................................918 251-2887
David E Chymiak, *President*
Scott Francis, *Corp Secy*
Kenneth A Chymiak, *Vice Pres*
EMP: 75
SALES (est): 32.6MM **Privately Held**
SIC: 5063 5065 3663 Antennas, receiving, satellite dishes; electronic parts & equipment; space satellite communications equipment; cable television equipment

(G-1088)
UNIVERSAL WELDING SERVICE
7401 S Birch Ave (74011-6837)
PHONE.................................918 455-3241
Ronald Reed, *Principal*
EMP: 1
SALES (est): 48.8K **Privately Held**
SIC: 7692 Welding repair

(G-1089)
URBAN WORM COMPOST LLC
3112 W Pittsburg Pl (74012-9067)
PHONE.................................918 557-9255
Micah Robert Barker, *Principal*
EMP: 2
SALES (est): 74.4K **Privately Held**
SIC: 2875 Compost

(G-1090)
VAULT MANAGEMENT INC
1805 W Detroit St (74012-3613)
PHONE.................................918 258-7782
Keith Lindenberg, *President*
Cherisa Lindenberg, *Vice Pres*
EMP: 6
SQ FT: 16,000
SALES (est): 750K **Privately Held**
SIC: 3572 Computer storage devices

(G-1091)
VENTURE INDUSTRIES INC
1812 W Phoenix Pl (74011-1624)
PHONE.................................918 557-8789
Aaron Ashworth, *Principal*
EMP: 2
SALES (est): 121.1K **Privately Held**
SIC: 3999 Barber & beauty shop equipment

(G-1092)
WATERS EDGE WINERY ON ROSE
116 S Main St (74012-4139)
PHONE.................................918 286-0086
EMP: 4 **EST:** 2018
SALES (est): 329K **Privately Held**
SIC: 2084 Wines

(G-1093)
WEBREADY SOFTWARE INC
Also Called: Jacckson Techinical
200 S Desert Palm Ave (74012-8716)
PHONE.................................918 808-8465
Tim M Jackson, *CEO*
EMP: 3
SALES (est): 144.4K **Privately Held**
SIC: 7372 Prepackaged software

(G-1094)
WERCO AVIATION INC
415 E Houston St (74012-4303)
PHONE.................................918 251-6880
Jon Werthen, *CEO*
EMP: 1
SALES (est): 154.4K **Privately Held**
SIC: 3441 Fabricated structural metal

(G-1095)
WERCO MANUFACTURING INC
415 E Houston St (74012-4303)
PHONE.................................918 251-6880
Jon Werthen, *President*
Theda Werthen, *Corp Secy*
EMP: 50
SQ FT: 80,000
SALES (est): 8.8MM **Privately Held**
SIC: 3599 3441 3444 3446 Machine shop, jobbing & repair; fabricated structural metal; sheet metalwork; ornamental metalwork; special dies, tools, jigs & fixtures; aircraft parts & equipment

(G-1096)
WESCO ENTERPRISES INC
1907 W Detroit St (74012-3626)
PHONE.................................918 449-1081
Ralph Byerlee, *President*
EMP: 3
SALES: 400K **Privately Held**
SIC: 3844 Radiographic X-ray apparatus & tubes; therapeutic X-ray apparatus & tubes

(G-1097)
WILKINSON MFG CO
808 S 8th St (74012-5541)
PHONE.................................918 258-8282
Stephen Wilkinson, *Principal*
EMP: 8
SQ FT: 8,043
SALES (est): 875.4K **Privately Held**
SIC: 3999 Manufacturing industries

(G-1098)
WILSDORF MANUFACTURING LLC
11409 E 130th St S (74011-5242)
PHONE.................................918 369-5824
Ray Wilsdorf, *Principal*
EMP: 2
SALES (est): 129.5K **Privately Held**
SIC: 3999 Manufacturing industries

(G-1099)
WITTER MARKETING INC
11716 E 133rd St S (74011-7430)
PHONE.................................918 369-8639
Tony Witter, *President*
EMP: 2
SALES (est): 180.9K **Privately Held**
SIC: 2389 Apparel & accessories

(G-1100)
WOHALI OUTDOORS LLC (PA)
2466 W New Orleans St (74011-1590)
PHONE.................................918 343-3800
Jonathan Brocksmith, *Mng Member*
Jt Griffin,
▲ **EMP:** 12
SALES (est): 16MM **Privately Held**
WEB: www.arcoutdoors.com
SIC: 2211 2385 3949 Apparel & outerwear fabrics, cotton; waterproof outerwear; fishing equipment; hunting equipment

(G-1101)
WOLTJER ENGINES
805 W Elgin St (74012-2426)
PHONE.................................918 258-0598
Carl Woltjer, *Partner*
Carl Wesley Woltjer, *Partner*
EMP: 5
SALES (est): 636.5K **Privately Held**
WEB: www.woltjerengines.com
SIC: 7538 3519 Engine rebuilding: automotive; internal combustion engines

(G-1102)
WOODWRIGHT WOODWORKING LLC
2518 S Gardenia Pl (74012-0904)
PHONE.................................918 254-6577
James Douglas Lewis, *Principal*
EMP: 1
SALES (est): 54.1K **Privately Held**
SIC: 2431 Millwork

(G-1103)
XIT SYSTEMS INC
803 E Jackson Pl (74012-5522)
PHONE.................................918 259-9071
James E Brown, *President*
Fred Carr, *Corp Secy*
EMP: 3
SALES (est): 361.2K **Privately Held**
SIC: 3844 X-ray apparatus & tubes

(G-1104)
ZEPHYR SOUTHWEST ORNA LLC
600 S 10th St (74012-4423)
P.O. Box 2075 (74013-2075)
PHONE.................................918 251-4133
Stuart Gibbs,
Pamela Gibbs,
EMP: 38
SQ FT: 8,000
SALES (est): 1.1MM **Privately Held**
SIC: 1799 3446 3231 Ornamental metal work; architectural metalwork; products of purchased glass

(G-1105)
ZETA
1814 W Tacoma St (74012-1406)
PHONE.................................918 664-8200
Mary Oconnell Esq, *Marketing Staff*
EMP: 2
SALES (est): 88.3K **Privately Held**
WEB: www.xeta.com
SIC: 3661 Telephone & telegraph apparatus

(G-1106)
ZOE STUDIOS LLC
920 S Lions Ave (74012-8423)
PHONE.................................918 258-4073
Bruce Halstad, *Mng Member*
EMP: 2
SALES (est): 97.7K **Privately Held**
SIC: 3861 Sound recording & reproducing equipment, motion picture

Broken Arrow
Wagoner County

(G-1107)
3G PRINTING
3000 E Knoxville St (74014-2817)
P.O. Box 140331 (74014-0003)
PHONE.................................918 346-0035
James Camper, *Principal*
EMP: 2
SALES (est): 83.9K **Privately Held**
SIC: 2752 Commercial printing, lithographic

(G-1108)
ALLEGIANT PRECAST LLC
10763 S 257th East Ave (74014-3961)
PHONE.................................918 486-6227
Daniel Simon,
EMP: 17
SQ FT: 3,000
SALES: 2.1MM **Privately Held**
SIC: 3272 Burial vaults, concrete or precast terrazzo; concrete products, precast

(G-1109)
APERGY ARTFL LIFT SYSTEMS LLC
19425 E 54th St S (74014-1603)
PHONE.................................918 396-0558
EMP: 2
SALES (est): 685.6K
SALES (corp-wide): 1.1B **Publicly Held**
SIC: 1389 Testing, measuring, surveying & analysis services
PA: Championx Corporation
2445 Tech Frest Blvd Bldg
The Woodlands TX 77381
281 403-5772

(G-1110)
APERGY ESP SYSTEMS LLC (HQ)
19425 E 54th St S (74014-1603)
PHONE.................................918 396-0558
Robert Livingston,
▲ **EMP:** 55
SQ FT: 15,000
SALES (est): 41.8MM
SALES (corp-wide): 1.1B **Publicly Held**
WEB: www.apergy.com
SIC: 1389 5084 Pumping of oil & gas wells; servicing oil & gas wells; pumps & pumping equipment
PA: Championx Corporation
2445 Tech Frest Blvd Bldg
The Woodlands TX 77381
281 403-5772

(G-1111)
AUTO-TURN MANUFACTURING INC
9800 S 219th East Ave (74014-5911)
PHONE.................................918 451-4511
Garry Shotton, *President*
EMP: 50
SQ FT: 25,000
SALES (est): 9.7MM **Privately Held**
SIC: 3599 Machine shop, jobbing & repair

(G-1112)
B-MAC WELDING SERVICE ✦
8424 S 353rd East Ave (74014-7567)
PHONE.................................918 370-0921
Richard Fuller, *Principal*
EMP: 1 **EST:** 2019
SALES (est): 32.6K **Privately Held**
SIC: 7692 Welding repair

(G-1113)
BLUE BELL CREAMERIES LP
8201 E Highway 51 (74014-2900)
PHONE.................................918 258-5100
Marty Kilgore, *Branch Mgr*
EMP: 259
SALES (corp-wide): 964.8MM **Privately Held**
SIC: 2024 5143 Ice cream, packaged: molded, on sticks, etc.; dairy based frozen desserts; ice cream & ices

PA: Blue Bell Creameries, L.P.
1101 S Blue Bell Rd
Brenham TX 77833
979 836-7977

(G-1114)
BUSH PUBLISHING
20232 E 43rd St S (74014-1582)
PHONE.................................901 468-8388
Margo Bush, *Principal*
EMP: 1 **EST:** 2017
SALES (est): 50.6K **Privately Held**
SIC: 2741 Miscellaneous publishing

(G-1115)
C O HANOVER BKA
20602 E 81st St S (74014-2935)
PHONE.................................918 251-8571
Carlos Conerly, *Principal*
EMP: 11
SALES (est): 1.7MM **Privately Held**
SIC: 3563 Air & gas compressors

(G-1116)
C&S DESIGN
20600 E 111th St S (74014-4063)
PHONE.................................918 455-8137
Carol Hawkins, *Partner*
James Hawkins, *Partner*
EMP: 2
SALES (est): 109.4K **Privately Held**
SIC: 2397 Schiffli machine embroideries

(G-1117)
CORD & PLEAT DESIGN INC
24212 E Highway 51 (74014-3473)
PHONE.................................918 622-7676
Marilie W Smock, *President*
Brian L Smock, *Vice Pres*
EMP: 2
SALES (est): 151.6K **Privately Held**
SIC: 2391 Curtains & draperies

(G-1118)
COWANS MILLWORK INC
24620 E 91st St S (74014-7801)
PHONE.................................918 357-3725
Perry Cowan, *President*
▲ **EMP:** 1
SALES (est): 145.9K **Privately Held**
SIC: 2491 Structural lumber & timber, treated wood

(G-1119)
D & B PROCESSING LLC
9750 S 219th East Ave (74014-5909)
P.O. Box 141290 (74014-0013)
PHONE.................................918 619-6452
Doug Burgess, *Owner*
EMP: 16
SALES: 17.3MM **Privately Held**
SIC: 5051 3541 Steel; plasma process metal cutting machines

(G-1120)
DANIEL W DUENSING
Also Called: Danco Machine
3404 E Jersey St (74014-8707)
PHONE.................................417 781-1850
EMP: 2
SALES: 120K **Privately Held**
SIC: 3469 Mfg Metal Stampings

(G-1121)
DAVENPORTS WELDING
10210 S 257th East Ave (74014-3947)
PHONE.................................918 855-9593
Chris Davenport, *Manager*
EMP: 1
SALES (est): 54K **Privately Held**
WEB: www.davenportswelding.com
SIC: 7692 Welding repair

(G-1122)
DELCO LLC
9107 S 241st East Ave (74014-7802)
PHONE.................................918 527-8058
Patrick Delehanty, *Mng Member*
EMP: 1 **EST:** 2016
SALES (est): 202.5K **Privately Held**
SIC: 3542 Machine tools, metal forming type

(G-1123)
DYNAMIC BRANDS INC
7223 S 285th East Pl (74014-5462)
PHONE.................................918 630-7083
Brian Hester, *President*
EMP: 2
SALES (corp-wide): 6.5MM **Privately Held**
WEB: www.dynamicbrandsok.com
SIC: 2084 Wines, brandy & brandy spirits
PA: Dynamic Brands, Inc.
4157 S 72nd East Ave
Tulsa OK 74145
918 630-7083

(G-1124)
E-TECH INC
20701 E 81st St S Ste 103 (74014-2960)
PHONE.................................918 665-1930
James H Tighe II, *President*
Mike Giangreco, *Purch Mgr*
Mark Tighe, *Treasurer*
Judd Johns, *Finance Mgr*
Darren Stephenson, *Sales Engr*
▼ **EMP:** 24
SQ FT: 8,000
SALES (est): 6.9MM **Privately Held**
SIC: 3443 Fabricated plate work (boiler shop)

(G-1125)
EASLEYS PERFORMANCE WEAR INC
6818 S 245th East Ave (74014-7631)
PHONE.................................918 357-2400
DEA Ann Easley, *President*
Kevin Easley, *Corp Secy*
EMP: 4
SQ FT: 2,500
SALES (est): 458.9K **Privately Held**
SIC: 2389 Costumes

(G-1126)
EN-FAB CORP
8200 S 202nd East Ave (74014-2907)
P.O. Box 727 (74013-0727)
PHONE.................................918 251-9647
George A McMillen, *President*
EMP: 12
SQ FT: 17,000
SALES (est): 1.7MM **Privately Held**
SIC: 2439 Trusses, wooden roof

(G-1127)
FRIENDS WELDING
20219 E 83rd St S (74014-2908)
P.O. Box 1234, Haskell (74436-1234)
PHONE.................................918 482-1544
Fred Friend, *Owner*
EMP: 3
SALES (est): 82.7K **Privately Held**
SIC: 7692 3441 Welding repair; fabricated structural metal

(G-1128)
GASOLINE ALLEY CLASSICS INC
9820 Swan Dr (74014-7923)
PHONE.................................918 806-1000
Michael Jones, *President*
Larry Dunn, *Vice Pres*
Bob McCray, *Treasurer*
EMP: 3
SALES (est): 50K **Privately Held**
SIC: 5961 3999 Collectibles & antiques, mail order; miniatures

(G-1129)
H&A SHIRT CAFE CSTM SCREEN PRT
7839 S Townsend Ave (74014-6909)
PHONE.................................918 357-1115
Allen Henfrey, *President*
EMP: 3
SALES (est): 98K **Privately Held**
SIC: 2759 Screen printing

(G-1130)
HAMILTON INDUSTRIES LLC
8112 S Winwood Ln (74014-3443)
PHONE.................................918 357-3862
Steve Hamilton, *Principal*
EMP: 3 **EST:** 2009
SALES (est): 208.8K **Privately Held**
SIC: 3999 Manufacturing industries

(G-1131)
HANDY & HARMAN
21808 E Highway 51 (74014-5940)
PHONE.................................918 258-1566
Kurt Campbell, *Prdtn Mgr*
Jessie Nunes, *Production*
Ron Short, *Opers-Prdtn-Mfg*
Glen Bryan, *Controller*
EMP: 30
SQ FT: 6,000
SALES (corp-wide): 1.5B **Publicly Held**
SIC: 5162 3498 Plastics materials; fabricated pipe & fittings
HQ: Handy & Harman
C/O Steel Partners
New York NY 10022
212 520-2300

(G-1132)
HI-TEC INDUSTRIES OK LLC
19701 E 91st St S (74014-6500)
P.O. Box 212 (74013-0212)
PHONE.................................918 455-7141
Don Cypert, *General Mgr*
Gary Keel,
Nedra Keel,
EMP: 10
SQ FT: 22,500
SALES: 2.3MM
SALES (corp-wide): 33.3MM **Privately Held**
SIC: 3599 Machine shop, jobbing & repair
PA: Hi-Tec Industries Inc
1000 Ave Ne
Portage La Prairie MB R1N 0
204 239-4270

(G-1133)
HORTON WORLD SOLUTIONS LLC
5971 S 301st East Ave (74014-8410)
PHONE.................................817 821-8320
Melissa Ripley, *Accountant*
David Oberle, *Mng Member*
Terry Horton,
SQ FT: 40,000
SALES: 40MM **Privately Held**
SIC: 3531 Construction machinery

(G-1134)
HOUSTON BROTHERS INC
Also Called: Hbi
19465 E 131st St S (74014-4509)
P.O. Box 639, Bixby (74008-0639)
PHONE.................................918 449-1175
Marty Houston, *President*
Bob Richardson, *Vice Pres*
EMP: 2
SALES (est): 200K **Privately Held**
SIC: 2879 Agricultural chemicals

(G-1135)
INK SPOT TTTOO BDY PERCING LLC
27108 E 82nd St S (74014-6119)
PHONE.................................918 637-2897
Joe L Martin, *Administration*
EMP: 2
SALES (est): 173K **Privately Held**
SIC: 2752 Commercial printing, offset

(G-1136)
JOE MARTIN
Also Called: Make Ready Mobiles
27108 E 82nd St S (74014-6119)
PHONE.................................918 850-2776
Joe Martin, *Principal*
Joe L Martin, *Principal*
EMP: 4
SALES (est): 338.6K **Privately Held**
SIC: 3273 Ready-mixed concrete

(G-1137)
LAFAVER FIBERGLASS CORPORATION
Also Called: La Faver Fiberglass Supply
19955 E Highway 51 (74014-2355)
PHONE.................................918 258-4845
Bob Lafaver, *President*
Patricia Lafaver, *Vice Pres*
EMP: 4
SQ FT: 14,000
SALES (est): 393.7K **Privately Held**
SIC: 3713 Truck bodies & parts

(G-1138)
LAVISHEA LLC
4103 S 193rd East Ave (74014-8000)
PHONE.................................303 805-0805
Nancy Reinhard,
EMP: 2
SALES (est): 116.9K **Privately Held**
SIC: 2844 Toilet preparations

(G-1139)
M&M CUSTOM WELDING
29350 E 19th St S (74014-4934)
PHONE.................................918 231-0829
EMP: 2
SALES (est): 40.2K **Privately Held**
SIC: 7692 Welding repair

(G-1140)
MAGNUM AERO INC
8256 Wright Pl (74014-3049)
PHONE.................................918 357-2376
Roger Johnson, *Principal*
Michael A Smith, *Principal*
EMP: 3 **EST:** 2000
SALES (est): 217.4K **Privately Held**
SIC: 3728 Refueling equipment for use in flight, airplane

(G-1141)
MANUFACTURING SOLUTIONS LLC
20665 E 46th St S (74014-8760)
PHONE.................................918 951-0750
Kevin Porter, *President*
Franchesca Porter,
EMP: 2
SALES: 200K **Privately Held**
SIC: 3452 7389 Cotter pins, metal;

(G-1142)
MBS MANUFACTURING INC
26319 E Highway 51 (74014-3920)
PHONE.................................918 521-6865
EMP: 1
SALES (est): 39.6K **Privately Held**
SIC: 3999 Manufacturing industries

(G-1143)
MFG SOLUTIONS LLC
9806 S 236th East Ave (74014-6859)
PHONE.................................918 232-3503
Dustin Carter,
EMP: 4 **EST:** 2015
SALES (est): 192.2K **Privately Held**
SIC: 3541 Numerically controlled metal cutting machine tools

(G-1144)
MOLDED PRODUCTS INCORPORATED
21920 E 96th St S (74014-5903)
PHONE.................................918 254-9061
David N Clonts, *President*
Rustin Garland, *Prdtn Mgr*
EMP: 27
SQ FT: 12,000
SALES (est): 5.7MM **Privately Held**
SIC: 3069 Molded rubber products

(G-1145)
MORNING FAX
24010 Lamb Ter (74014-3069)
PHONE.................................918 357-5245
EMP: 3 **EST:** 1998
SALES: 110K **Privately Held**
SIC: 2721 2741 Periodicals-Publishing/Printing Misc Publishing

(G-1146)
NEWSPAPER SALES LLC
27109 E 82nd St S (74014-6114)
PHONE.................................918 357-5070
Michael S Detherage, *Principal*
EMP: 3
SALES (est): 127.3K **Privately Held**
SIC: 2711 Newspapers, publishing & printing

(G-1147)
ON SITE WELDING & FABRICATION
20219 E 83rd St S (74014-2908)
PHONE.................................918 706-3339
Chris Enevolbsen, *Principal*
EMP: 1 **EST:** 2003

Broken Arrow - Wagoner County (G-1148)

SALES (est): 35.8K **Privately Held**
SIC: 7692 Welding repair

(G-1148)
PACCAR
4841 S 197th East Ave (74014-1382)
PHONE..................................918 810-3810
Dan Maloney, *Principal*
EMP: 2
SALES (est): 133K **Privately Held**
WEB: www.paccar.com
SIC: 3711 Truck & tractor truck assembly

(G-1149)
PRINT HAPPY FUNDRAISING
21440 E 39th Pl S (74014-8791)
PHONE..................................918 355-4368
Mike Sisco, *Principal*
EMP: 2 EST: 2017
SALES (est): 103.5K **Privately Held**
SIC: 2752 Commercial printing, lithographic

(G-1150)
PSS ENTERPRISES LLC
508 S 62nd St (74014-2668)
PHONE..................................918 928-7971
Scott Levy, *Principal*
EMP: 2
SALES (est): 176.1K **Privately Held**
SIC: 3714 Motor vehicle parts & accessories

(G-1151)
QUALITY STEEL COATINGS INC
7528 E Galveston Pl (74014-7052)
P.O. Box 141303 (74014-0013)
PHONE..................................918 269-9104
EMP: 2 EST: 2017
SALES (est): 112.2K **Privately Held**
SIC: 3479 Metal coating & allied service

(G-1152)
RAM MACHINE PRODUCTS LLC
9818 S 219th East Ave (74014-5911)
PHONE..................................918 455-5555
Dave Goodell, *President*
EMP: 15 EST: 1978
SALES (est): 2.7MM **Privately Held**
WEB: www.rammachineproducts.com
SIC: 3599 Machine shop, jobbing & repair

(G-1153)
RCW WELDING SERVICES LLC
29606 E 68th St S (74014-5437)
PHONE..................................918 852-4775
Raul Cisneros, *Principal*
EMP: 8
SALES (est): 88.7K **Privately Held**
SIC: 7692 Welding repair

(G-1154)
REFRACTORY ANCHORS INC
Also Called: R A I
9836 S 219th East Ave (74014-5911)
PHONE..................................918 455-8485
Randy Buchman, *President*
Charlie Fell, *Vice Pres*
Jed Dunn, *Prdtn Mgr*
Joyce Arnold, *Controller*
◆ EMP: 22
SQ FT: 14,300
SALES (est): 8.4MM **Privately Held**
WEB: www.rai-1.com
SIC: 3312 3452 3297 Blast furnaces & steel mills; bolts, nuts, rivets & washers; nonclay refractories

(G-1155)
REHOBOTH ROBES
400 N Forest Ridge Blvd (74014-2758)
PHONE..................................918 357-1529
Ouida Lewis, *Principal*
EMP: 2
SALES (est): 121.9K **Privately Held**
SIC: 3999 Manufacturing industries

(G-1156)
RELYASSIST LLC
4059 S 213th East Ave (74014-8723)
P.O. Box 141252 (74014-0012)
PHONE..................................918 260-6517
Frances Honeycutt, *CEO*
EMP: 1

SALES (est): 52.3K **Privately Held**
SIC: 3085 5049 Plastics bottles; laboratory equipment, except medical or dental

(G-1157)
ROCK OIL CO
27089 E 89th St S (74014-6106)
PHONE..................................918 357-1188
Darryl Simmons, *Principal*
EMP: 3 EST: 2001
SALES (est): 158.6K **Privately Held**
SIC: 2079 Edible fats & oils

(G-1158)
ROYAL TOGA INDUSTRIES LLC
10355 S 261st East Ave (74014-3880)
PHONE..................................405 641-1643
EMP: 2 EST: 2017
SALES (est): 172.3K **Privately Held**
SIC: 3999 Manufacturing industries

(G-1159)
S4F INC
4804 S 194th East Ave (74014-8067)
PHONE..................................888 390-2224
Sam Pfanstiel, *Ch of Bd*
Terry L Clark, *Principal*
Kirk Murdoch, *Info Tech Mgr*
EMP: 1
SALES (est): 62.7K **Privately Held**
SIC: 7372 Application computer software

(G-1160)
SAFECO MANUFACTURING INC
21200 E 91st St S (74014-5902)
P.O. Box 1046, Tulsa (74101-1046)
PHONE..................................918 455-0100
Harvey D Grimes, *President*
EMP: 15
SQ FT: 12,000
SALES (est): 1.5MM **Privately Held**
SIC: 3441 3443 3498 3564 Fabricated structural metal; fabricated plate work (boiler shop); fabricated pipe & fittings; blowers & fans; metalworking machinery; valves & pipe fittings

(G-1161)
SCREEN TECH INTL LTD CO
26319 E Highway 51 (74014-3920)
PHONE..................................918 234-0010
Matt Peters, *President*
Scott Crawford, *Plant Mgr*
Kaleb Files, *Sales Staff*
EMP: 12 EST: 2010
SALES (est): 1.2MM **Privately Held**
SIC: 3469 3315 Machine parts, stamped or pressed metal; steel wire & related products

(G-1162)
SDH MANUFACTURE LLC
29500 E 68th St S (74014-5436)
PHONE..................................918 407-1065
EMP: 2 EST: 2008
SALES (est): 140K **Privately Held**
SIC: 3599 Mfg Industrial Machinery

(G-1163)
SHANE LEE DUVALL
Also Called: Mark 4 Technologies
22333 E 66th St S (74014-6614)
PHONE..................................918 960-0506
Shane Duvall, *Owner*
EMP: 3
SALES (est): 163.5K **Privately Held**
SIC: 7372 7371 7373 Application computer software; custom computer programming services; software programming applications; office computer automation systems integration

(G-1164)
SIGN SOLUTIONS
15534 S 193rd East Ave (74014-8028)
PHONE..................................918 449-9439
Peter Gerner, *Principal*
EMP: 2 EST: 2011
SALES (est): 125.5K **Privately Held**
WEB: www.oksignsolutions.com
SIC: 3993 Signs & advertising specialties

(G-1165)
SMITH PRECISION PRODUCTS LLC
7150 S 305th East Ave (74014-6042)
PHONE..................................918 691-5797
Steven Smith, *President*
Nikole Siegel Smith, *Accounts Mgr*
EMP: 2 EST: 2011
SALES (est): 139.9K **Privately Held**
SIC: 3452 7389 Bolts, nuts, rivets & washers;

(G-1166)
SOFTWARE PERFECTION LLC
30175 E 36th St S (74014-8335)
PHONE..................................918 266-8883
EMP: 1
SALES (est): 57.5K **Privately Held**
SIC: 7372 Prepackaged Software Services

(G-1167)
STEEL SYSTEMS PLUS INC
10540 S 213th East Ave (74014-3682)
PHONE..................................918 286-7947
Leon Dazey, *Principal*
EMP: 3
SALES (est): 220.7K **Privately Held**
SIC: 3842 Welders' hoods

(G-1168)
STUDYLAMP SOFTWARE LLC
7529 S Shelby Ln (74014-2538)
P.O. Box 140478 (74014-0004)
PHONE..................................918 357-1946
Brandon Staggs, *Administration*
EMP: 2
SALES (est): 182.6K **Privately Held**
WEB: www.studylamp.com
SIC: 7372 Prepackaged software

(G-1169)
T S I L C
Also Called: Treatment Systems
7420 E Forest Ridge Blvd (74014-6982)
PHONE..................................918 357-5992
Jim Chittenden, *President*
EMP: 2
SALES (est): 1MM **Privately Held**
SIC: 3589 5074 Water treatment equipment, industrial; water purification equipment

(G-1170)
TEDDY HALL
Also Called: Hallco
20937 E 37th Pl S (74014-1209)
PHONE..................................918 355-3822
Teddy Hall, *Owner*
EMP: 2
SALES (est): 155.8K **Privately Held**
SIC: 3599 Machine & other job shop work

(G-1171)
TERAC CONTROLS INC
Also Called: Terac Manufacturing
9600 S 219th East Ave (74014-5941)
P.O. Box 470206, Tulsa (74147-0206)
PHONE..................................918 622-6818
Jack D Angleton, *President*
Lisa Angleton, *Corp Secy*
EMP: 25
SQ FT: 25,000
SALES (est): 5.1MM **Privately Held**
SIC: 3613 Control panels, electric; switchgear & switchgear accessories

(G-1172)
THUNDERBOLT MACHINE SERVICES
24787 E 51st St S (74014-7122)
PHONE..................................918 357-2294
Thomas A Garrard, *Owner*
EMP: 1 EST: 1997
SALES (est): 73.5K **Privately Held**
SIC: 3599 Machine shop, jobbing & repair; barber & beauty shop equipment

(G-1173)
TRIPLE T WELDING
10875 S 209th East Ave (74014-3552)
PHONE..................................918 449-0037
EMP: 2 EST: 2010
SALES (est): 80K **Privately Held**
SIC: 7692 Welding Repair

(G-1174)
TRUCK BODIES & EQP INTL INC
6112 New Sapulpa Rd (74014)
PHONE..................................918 355-6842
Robert Sewell, *Manager*
EMP: 1
SALES (corp-wide): 1.2B **Publicly Held**
SIC: 3715 Truck trailers
HQ: Truck Bodies & Equipment International, Inc.
1 Independence Plz # 820
Birmingham AL 35209

(G-1175)
TULSA METAL FAB INC
9805 S 219th East Ave (74014-5912)
PHONE..................................918 451-7150
Bill Friend, *President*
Edith Friend, *Manager*
EMP: 11 EST: 1980
SQ FT: 5,000
SALES (est): 2.2MM **Privately Held**
SIC: 3441 Fabricated structural metal

(G-1176)
WEINGARTNER RACING LLC
20211 E 45th St S (74014-8752)
PHONE..................................918 520-3480
Eric Weingartner,
EMP: 2
SALES (est): 137.9K **Privately Held**
WEB: www.wengines.com
SIC: 3714 Cylinder heads, motor vehicle

(G-1177)
WHITE SHELL LLC
Also Called: Asset Weapon Manufacturing
11233 S 212th East Ave (74014-5109)
PHONE..................................918 978-2767
Derek H Shelton, *President*
EMP: 2
SALES (est): 88.6K **Privately Held**
SIC: 3999 Manufacturing industries

(G-1178)
WOODCREST LITHO INC
24814 E 71st St S (74014-7623)
P.O. Box 141108 (74014-0011)
PHONE..................................918 357-1676
Jim Woodring, *President*
EMP: 15
SQ FT: 5,000
SALES (est): 1MM **Privately Held**
SIC: 2752 Lithographing on metal

(G-1179)
ZEECO INC (HQ)
22151 E 91st St S (74014-3250)
PHONE..................................918 258-8551
Darton Zink, *CEO*
Liz Mattiuzzo, *Business Mgr*
Michael Abner, *Engineer*
Tim Ediger, *Engineer*
Maddie Harrison, *Engineer*
◆ EMP: 249
SQ FT: 100,000
SALES (est): 167.3MM **Privately Held**
WEB: www.zeeco.com
SIC: 3433 Gas burners, industrial

(G-1180)
ZEECO USA LLC (PA)
22151 E 91st St S (74014-3250)
PHONE..................................918 258-8551
Darton Zink, *President*
▼ EMP: 20
SQ FT: 100,000
SALES (est): 155.3MM **Privately Held**
SIC: 3433 Gas burners, industrial

(G-1181)
ZIEGLERS BOB PORTABLE BLDG SLS
10295 S State Highway 51 (74014-3969)
PHONE..................................918 486-4462
Bob Ziegler, *Owner*
EMP: 1
SALES (est): 65.7K **Privately Held**
SIC: 3448 4212 Buildings, portable: prefabricated metal; moving services

GEOGRAPHIC SECTION

Broken Bow
Mccurtain County

(G-1182)
ALLENS WELDING SERVICE
100 Silvey Rd (74728-5514)
PHONE............................580 584-2375
Derald Allen, *Owner*
EMP: 2
SALES (est): 73.9K **Privately Held**
SIC: 7692 Welding repair

(G-1183)
ANDERSON LOGGING LLC
155 Freesia Rd (74728-5986)
PHONE............................580 584-9898
Drew Anderson, *Administration*
EMP: 6
SALES (est): 214.9K **Privately Held**
SIC: 2411 Logging

(G-1184)
B & P LOGGING LLC
1111 Pleasant Valley Rd (74728-5971)
PHONE............................580 584-6718
Christopher Pratt, *Principal*
EMP: 2
SALES (est): 81.7K **Privately Held**
SIC: 2411 Logging

(G-1185)
BELL TIMBER INC
7316 Craig Rd (74728-6247)
PHONE............................580 584-6902
EMP: 3 **EST:** 2015
SALES (est): 238.2K **Privately Held**
SIC: 2499 Wood products

(G-1186)
BRAYS CABINET SHOP
2078 E Us Highway 70 (74728-6886)
PHONE............................580 584-6771
Kenneth C Bray, *Owner*
EMP: 4 **EST:** 1971
SALES (est): 283.9K **Privately Held**
SIC: 2541 2434 Table or counter tops, plastic laminated; wood kitchen cabinets

(G-1187)
BROKENBOW BOAT CENTER
Highway 259 S (74728)
PHONE............................580 584-5428
Mike Snow, *Principal*
EMP: 1
SALES (est): 97.3K **Privately Held**
SIC: 3732 Boat building & repairing

(G-1188)
COPYPASTA PUBLISHING
904 N Park Dr (74728-2148)
PHONE............................580 236-4071
Jordan Jones, *Principal*
EMP: 1
SALES (est): 37.5K **Privately Held**
SIC: 2741 Miscellaneous publishing

(G-1189)
DOMINANCE INDUSTRIES INC
Also Called: Pan Pacific Products
610 W State Highway 3 A (74728-6634)
PHONE............................580 584-6247
Edward McDonald, *CEO*
Philip Ling, *President*
▲ **EMP:** 147
SALES (est): 24.1MM
SALES (corp-wide): 2.1B **Publicly Held**
SIC: 2493 Fiberboard, other vegetable pulp
PA: Masonite International Corporation
201 N Franklin St Ste 300
Tampa FL 33602
800 895-2723

(G-1190)
FISH TALE WINERY
17 Oak Leaf Ln (74728-6602)
PHONE............................580 494-6115
Linda King, *Principal*
EMP: 2
SALES (est): 107.9K **Privately Held**
WEB: www.fishtaleswine.com
SIC: 2084 Wines

(G-1191)
GIRLS GONE WINE
471 Old Broken Bow Hwy (74728-5919)
PHONE............................580 494-6243
Chandra Rickey, *Principal*
EMP: 25 **EST:** 2010
SALES (est): 2.4MM **Privately Held**
SIC: 2084 Wines

(G-1192)
HUBER ENGINEERED WOODS LLC
1070 W State Highway 3 (74728-6736)
PHONE............................580 584-7000
Ricky Franklin, *Branch Mgr*
EMP: 43
SALES (corp-wide): 860.2MM **Privately Held**
SIC: 2493 3613 Reconstituted wood products; panel & distribution boards & other related apparatus
HQ: Huber Engineered Woods Llc
10925 David Taylor Dr # 3
Charlotte NC 28262
800 933-9220

(G-1193)
JAMES JEREMY BURCHAM
247 Ogden Rd (74728-6021)
PHONE............................580 420-3243
James J Burcham, *Owner*
EMP: 7
SALES (est): 671K **Privately Held**
SIC: 2411 Logging

(G-1194)
JM HUBER CORPORATION
1070 W State Highway 3 (74728-6736)
P.O. Box 1250 (74728-1250)
PHONE............................580 584-7002
Ed Milburn, *Manager*
EMP: 150
SALES (corp-wide): 860.2MM **Privately Held**
SIC: 1455 Kaolin & ball clay
PA: J.M. Huber Corporation
499 Thornall St Ste 8
Edison NJ 08837
732 549-8600

(G-1195)
KAREN E HOPSON
413 Darlene Dr (74728-1525)
PHONE............................580 584-7221
Karen E Hopson, *Principal*
EMP: 3
SALES (est): 206.5K **Privately Held**
SIC: 2411 Logging camps & contractors

(G-1196)
KEITH LYONS
Also Called: Broken Bow Redimix
1300 S Park Dr (74728-5716)
PHONE............................580 584-3360
Keith Lyons, *Owner*
Shawn Lyons, *Plant Mgr*
EMP: 10
SALES: 1MM **Privately Held**
SIC: 3273 3272 Ready-mixed concrete; concrete products

(G-1197)
KNOTTED ROPE WINERY LLC
85 N Lukfata Trail Rd (74728-7025)
PHONE............................918 839-1464
Julie A McDaniel, *Owner*
EMP: 2
SALES (est): 60.2K **Privately Held**
SIC: 2084 Wines

(G-1198)
MARTIN MARIETTA MATERIALS INC
Also Called: Broken Bow Sand & Gravel
500 River Rock Rd (74728)
P.O. Box 36 (74728-0036)
PHONE............................580 835-7311
Rick Gray, *Branch Mgr*
EMP: 7 **Publicly Held**
SIC: 1422 Crushed & broken limestone
PA: Martin Marietta Materials Inc
2710 Wycliff Rd
Raleigh NC 27607

(G-1199)
MCCURTAIN COUNTY NEWS INC
Also Called: Broken Bow
108 N Broadway St (74728-3934)
P.O. Box 179, Idabel (74745-0179)
PHONE............................580 584-6210
Gwen Willingham, *General Mgr*
EMP: 17
SALES (est): 904.4K
SALES (corp-wide): 1.3MM **Privately Held**
SIC: 2711 Newspapers: publishing only, not printed on site
PA: Mccurtain County News Inc
107 S Central Ave
Idabel OK 74745
580 286-3321

(G-1200)
MCFARLAND CASCADE
305 Silvey Rd (74728-5517)
PHONE............................580 584-3511
Bren Titman, *Office Mgr*
EMP: 1
SALES (est): 143.9K **Privately Held**
SIC: 2439 Timbers, structural: laminated lumber

(G-1201)
MCFARLAND CASCADE HOLDINGS INC
611 N Bock St (74728-2711)
P.O. Box 1165 (74728-1165)
PHONE............................580 584-2272
Alan Payne, *Owner*
EMP: 1
SALES (corp-wide): 1.6B **Privately Held**
SIC: 2491 5031 Wood preserving; lumber, plywood & millwork
HQ: Mcfarland Cascade Holdings, Inc.
1640 E Marc St
Tacoma WA 98421
253 572-3033

(G-1202)
MORGAN HAULING
1550 Morgan Rd (74728-6136)
PHONE............................580 420-3265
Joe Ray Morgan, *Owner*
EMP: 2
SALES (est): 104.6K **Privately Held**
SIC: 3531 Construction machinery

(G-1203)
PRIMO REDIMIX LLC
9627 N Us Highway 259 (74728-6681)
PHONE............................580 494-7649
Carissa Watson, *Mng Member*
EMP: 15
SALES (est): 2.1MM **Privately Held**
SIC: 3273 Ready-mixed concrete

(G-1204)
SCOTTS WLDG & FABRICATION LLC
7087 W State Highway 3 (74728-6146)
PHONE............................580 236-2990
Michael Dickerson, *Principal*
EMP: 1 **EST:** 2016
SALES (est): 39.6K **Privately Held**
SIC: 3999 Manufacturing industries

(G-1205)
SHAWN GIBSON
Also Called: Shawn Gibson Logging
N Hwy 259 1/4 W Sweethome (74728)
PHONE............................580 584-5537
Shawn Gibson, *Owner*
EMP: 20
SALES: 7.4MM **Privately Held**
SIC: 2411 Logging camps & contractors

(G-1206)
SILVER CREEK LOGGING
Hc 72 Box 737 (74728)
P.O. Box 425, Pickens (74752-0425)
PHONE............................580 241-7717
Mel Baggs, *Owner*
EMP: 9
SALES (est): 490.2K **Privately Held**
SIC: 2411 Logging camps & contractors

(G-1207)
SORRELS VENTURES LLC
2168 Belpine Loop (74728-6378)
PHONE............................903 556-2941
Nathaniel Sorrels,
EMP: 1 **EST:** 2015
SALES (est): 62.4K **Privately Held**
SIC: 2752 Promotional printing, lithographic

(G-1208)
SOUTHERN BOYS CLAY GRAVEL LLC
211 Mountain Goat Trl (74728-7048)
PHONE............................580 584-6711
Candi Scott, *Principal*
EMP: 2
SALES (est): 66K **Privately Held**
SIC: 1442 Construction sand & gravel

(G-1209)
T J CONSTRUCTION
8041 N Us Highway 259 (74728-6640)
PHONE............................580 494-6500
EMP: 1
SALES (est): 75.4K **Privately Held**
SIC: 7692 5039 1521 Welding Repair Whol Construction Materials Single-Family House Construction

(G-1210)
TAG AGENT
32 Main St (74728-3972)
PHONE............................580 584-2892
Jannete McCoy, *Owner*
EMP: 4 **EST:** 2010
SALES (est): 241.8K **Privately Held**
SIC: 3469 Automobile license tags, stamped metal

(G-1211)
TYSON FOODS INC
Hwy 259 S (74728)
P.O. Box 220 (74728-0220)
PHONE............................580 584-9191
Gilbert Mitchell, *Manager*
Alex Wade, *Executive*
EMP: 800
SALES (corp-wide): 42.4B **Publicly Held**
SIC: 2015 0751 Poultry, processed; poultry services
PA: Tyson Foods, Inc.
2200 W Don Tyson Pkwy
Springdale AR 72762
479 290-4000

Buffalo
Harper County

(G-1212)
DRY FABRICATION AND WELDING
405 N Hoy St (73834)
P.O. Box 395 (73834-0395)
PHONE............................580 735-2958
Ray Yauk, *President*
EMP: 20
SALES (est): 252.6K **Privately Held**
SIC: 7692 Welding repair

(G-1213)
HARPER COUNTY JOURNAL
3 W Turner Ave (73834)
PHONE............................580 735-2526
Mark Anderson, *Owner*
EMP: 2 **EST:** 1904
SQ FT: 3,500
SALES (est): 85.8K **Privately Held**
SIC: 2711 5942 Newspapers: publishing only, not printed on site; books, religious

Burbank
Osage County

(G-1214)
CEJA CORPORATION
Rr 1 (74633)
PHONE............................918 648-5215
Don Carpenter, *Branch Mgr*
EMP: 20

SALES (corp-wide): 25MM **Privately Held**
SIC: **1311** Crude petroleum production
PA: Ceja Corporation
1437 S Boulder Ave # 1250
Tulsa OK 74119
918 496-0770

(G-1215)
OK CASTING
1716 Remington Rd (74633-2370)
PHONE..................918 648-5300
Gary Smith, *Manager*
EMP: 2
SALES (est): 117.9K **Privately Held**
SIC: **3999** Manufacturing industries

Burneyville
Love County

(G-1216)
ENERGY EQUIP SALES CO
72 Golf Club Dr (73430-9764)
PHONE..................580 276-5900
Richard Moore, *Owner*
EMP: 3
SALES (est): 100.7K **Privately Held**
WEB: www.energyequipco.com
SIC: **3559** Sewing machines & hat & zipper making machinery

(G-1217)
MITCHELL T WIDLER
Also Called: Widler Welding
10434 Brug Hartman Rd (73430-2114)
Rural Route 73 Box 288 (73430)
PHONE..................501 860-3738
EMP: 1 EST: 2012
SALES (est): 36K **Privately Held**
SIC: **7692** Welding Repair

Burns Flat
Washita County

(G-1218)
BOBBY K BIRDWELL
300 Bryan (73624)
PHONE..................580 799-2357
Bobby Birdwell, *Principal*
EMP: 2 EST: 2008
SALES (est): 91.9K **Privately Held**
SIC: **3599** Machine shop, jobbing & repair

(G-1219)
MARYS TAG OFFICE
312 State Rt 44 (73624)
PHONE..................580 562-4745
Mary Cook, *Principal*
EMP: 2
SALES (est): 138.9K **Privately Held**
SIC: **3469** Automobile license tags, stamped metal

Butler
Custer County

(G-1220)
ARTHUR CRAIG
Also Called: Craig Welding
20945 E 850 Rd (73625-5055)
PHONE..................580 488-3398
Arthur Craig, *Owner*
EMP: 1
SALES: 75K **Privately Held**
SIC: **7692** Welding repair

(G-1221)
MARKWEST HYDROCARBON INC
8718 N 2120 Rd (73625-5021)
PHONE..................580 664-5282
Jason Palmer, *Manager*
EMP: 20
SALES (corp-wide): 9B **Publicly Held**
SIC: **1321** Natural gas liquids

HQ: Markwest Hydrocarbon, L.L.C.
1515 Arapahoe St
Denver CO 80202
303 290-8700

Byars
Mcclain County

(G-1222)
DYWY SPOOLING LLC
38601 110th St (74831-7955)
PHONE..................405 469-4148
Scottie Webster, *Principal*
EMP: 5
SALES (est): 392.6K **Privately Held**
SIC: **1389** Bailing, cleaning, swabbing & treating of wells

Cache
Comanche County

(G-1223)
A BOLT ELECTRIC
13806 Sw Pecan Rd (73527-3239)
PHONE..................580 510-0123
EMP: 2
SALES (est): 150K **Privately Held**
SIC: **3699** Mfg Electrical Equipment/Supplies

(G-1224)
BEST MOLD TECHNOLOGY LLC
17069 Sw Lee Blvd (73527-3013)
PHONE..................405 659-1991
Brad Seaton, *Principal*
EMP: 2
SALES (est): 81.4K **Privately Held**
SIC: **3599** Industrial machinery

(G-1225)
CACHE TIMES
518 W C Ave (73527-9491)
P.O. Box 3, Lawton (73502-0003)
PHONE..................580 429-8200
Tommy Hawthorne, *Owner*
EMP: 4
SQ FT: 4,130
SALES (est): 300K **Privately Held**
SIC: **7313** **2711** Newspaper advertising representative; newspapers

(G-1226)
E & D ENTERPRISES
1249 Nw Airport Rd (73527-4813)
PHONE..................580 512-1806
Ed Wiese, *Owner*
EMP: 1
SALES: 15K **Privately Held**
SIC: **3524** Lawn & garden equipment

(G-1227)
JOSHUA OIL & GAS LLC
14646 Sw Bishop Rd (73527-4737)
PHONE..................620 672-5505
EMP: 2
SALES (est): 65.5K **Privately Held**
SIC: **1389** Oil & gas field services

(G-1228)
KENCAN FLOWBACK LLC
21501 Sw Coombs Rd (73527-4916)
PHONE..................580 429-8913
Kenneth Colvin, *Principal*
EMP: 2 EST: 2016
SALES (est): 81.9K **Privately Held**
SIC: **1311** Crude petroleum & natural gas

(G-1229)
LANCO SERVICES LLC
15016 Sw Lee Blvd (73527-3249)
P.O. Box 6370, Lawton (73506-0370)
PHONE..................580 429-6526
Tommy Landis, *President*
Thomas Riley Landis III, *Vice Pres*
EMP: 24
SQ FT: 30,000

SALES: 3.5MM **Privately Held**
SIC: **5083** 5999 5531 3599 Agricultural machinery & equipment; farm equipment parts & supplies; farm equipment & supplies; automotive parts; machine shop, jobbing & repair; farm machinery repair; testing laboratories

(G-1230)
PATRICIA MCKAY
Also Called: McKay's Interior Design Center
6 Mountain View Dr (73527-9226)
PHONE..................580 355-2739
Patricia McKay, *Owner*
EMP: 2
SALES (est): 100K **Privately Held**
SIC: **2391** 7389 2512 2392 Draperies, plastic & textile: from purchased materials; interior decorating; upholstered household furniture; household furnishings; draperies; mini blinds

(G-1231)
SOPHISTICATED SWEETS INC
514 W C Ave (73527)
PHONE..................580 704-8038
Brooke Secoy, *President*
Martin Secoy, *Vice Pres*
EMP: 2
SQ FT: 2,800
SALES (est): 62.3K **Privately Held**
SIC: **2051** 3556 5149 Cakes, bakery: except frozen; pies, bakery: except frozen; ovens, bakery; crackers, cookies & bakery products

Caddo
Bryan County

(G-1232)
COLE INDUSTRIAL SERVICES INC
12469 S Woodside Dr (74729-5465)
PHONE..................580 775-0949
Ted R Cole, *President*
EMP: 3
SALES (est): 254.7K **Privately Held**
SIC: **3429** 7389 Cabinet hardware;

(G-1233)
DIANE E DEAN
Also Called: Blue River Valley Winery
3633 Sawmill Rd (74729)
PHONE..................580 775-4203
Diane Dean, *Owner*
EMP: 1
SALES (est): 73K **Privately Held**
SIC: **2084** Wines

(G-1234)
EFFICIENT FUEL SOLUTIONS LLC
350 Nails Crossing Rd (74729-2718)
P.O. Box 557 (74729-0557)
PHONE..................713 466-1400
EMP: 5
SALES (est): 325.5K **Privately Held**
SIC: **2869** Fuels

(G-1235)
FINCHER & SON PIPE & STEEL
Also Called: Fincher & Son Steel Buildings
13289 S Chisolm Rd (74729-5478)
PHONE..................580 889-6778
Jonathan Fincher, *Owner*
Doyle Fincher, *Owner*
EMP: 8
SQ FT: 10,000
SALES: 1MM **Privately Held**
SIC: **3448** Prefabricated metal buildings

(G-1236)
JOA INC
Also Called: J & A Peanut
605 Buffalo St (74729-1112)
P.O. Box 426 (74729-0426)
PHONE..................580 367-2616
John Nail, *President*
Marry and Nail, *Treasurer*
EMP: 6
SALES (est): 641.3K **Privately Held**
SIC: **2068** Nuts: dried, dehydrated, salted or roasted

(G-1237)
TEXOMA MATERIALS
1975 Bandit Trl (74729-3003)
PHONE..................580 367-2339
Fax: 580 367-2322
EMP: 2
SALES (est): 100K **Privately Held**
SIC: **1429** Crushed/Broken Stone

Calera
Bryan County

(G-1238)
BLUE RIVER VENTURES INC
Also Called: Blue River Tractors
8087 Hwy 69 75 (74730)
PHONE..................580 920-0111
EMP: 1
SALES (corp-wide): 1.5MM **Privately Held**
SIC: **3523** Tractors, farm
PA: Blue River Ventures Inc
4710 W Highway 70
Durant OK 74701

(G-1239)
CAPROCK COUNTRY ENTPS INC
Also Called: Gas Turbine Applications
19550 State Road 78 (74730-4810)
P.O. Box 369 (74730-0369)
PHONE..................580 924-1647
Wayne Metcolfaf, *President*
Mark Blake, *Manager*
EMP: 11
SQ FT: 18,500
SALES (est): 1.9MM **Privately Held**
SIC: **7699** 3511 Compressor repair; engine repair & replacement, non-automotive; gas turbine generator set units, complete

(G-1240)
JERRY BEAGLEY BRAIDING COMPANY
3569 Carley Creek Rd (74730-4814)
P.O. Box 207 (74730-0207)
PHONE..................580 924-4995
Jerry Beagley, *President*
EMP: 2
SALES: 170K **Privately Held**
SIC: **2241** 2221 3199 Narrow fabric mills; broadwoven fabric mills, manmade; equestrian related leather articles

(G-1241)
KT PLASTICS INC
132 Gantry Ln (74730)
P.O. Box 363 (74730-0363)
PHONE..................580 434-5655
Kenny Townsend, *President*
Faye Boydstun, *CFO*
Faye Boydstun, *CFO*
Sidni Rains, *Info Tech Mgr*
▲ EMP: 20
SQ FT: 9,600
SALES: 2.3MM **Privately Held**
SIC: **3053** 3082 3599 Gaskets & sealing devices; rods, unsupported plastic; tubes, unsupported plastic; machine shop, jobbing & repair

(G-1242)
ONESOURCE LLC
11 W Main St (74730-1515)
PHONE..................580 434-6250
Tony Hudgins, *Principal*
EMP: 3
SALES (est): 491.7K **Privately Held**
SIC: **5912** 2834 8082 Drug stores & proprietary stores; pharmaceutical preparations; home health care services

(G-1243)
PEANUT PRODUCTS CO INC
Also Called: Peanut Shoppe, The
26 Spivey Dr (74730-4314)
P.O. Box 1197, Durant (74702-1197)
PHONE..................580 296-4888
Robert V Armstrong, *President*
Bernon Armstrong, *Treasurer*
Marla Ballard, *Admin Sec*
EMP: 15 EST: 1979

GEOGRAPHIC SECTION

Canute - Washita County (G-1271)

SALES (est): 2.3MM **Privately Held**
SIC: **2064** 5159 2099 5441 Nuts, candy covered; peanuts (bulk), unroasted; peanut butter; candy, nut & confectionery stores; salted & roasted nuts & seeds

(G-1244)
PIONEER SPORT FLOORS LLC
166 Allison Rd (74730-4727)
P.O. Box 447 (74730-0447)
PHONE..................214 460-6921
Alvin Stalford, *Mng Member*
EMP: 5
SALES: 200K **Privately Held**
SIC: **2426** 1771 7389 Flooring, hardwood; flooring contractor;

Calumet
Canadian County

(G-1245)
CARLS BACKHOE & ROUSTABOUT
15692 N Heaston Rd (73014-9000)
PHONE..................405 893-7212
Carl Carter, *Principal*
EMP: 2
SALES (est): 250K **Privately Held**
SIC: **1389** Roustabout service

(G-1246)
ENOGEX SERVICES CORPORATION
18005 W 192nd St (73014-9003)
PHONE..................405 893-2267
Hollis Capenter, *Manager*
EMP: 20
SQ FT: 1,200
SALES (corp-wide): 12.3B **Publicly Held**
SIC: **1321** Natural gas liquids production
HQ: Enogex Services Corporation
515 Central Park Dr # 408
Oklahoma City OK 73105
405 525-7788

(G-1247)
MO MONEY MINERALS LLC
824 N Calumet Rd (73014-8854)
PHONE..................405 262-2457
Christy Fees, *Principal*
EMP: 2
SALES (est): 84.3K **Privately Held**
SIC: **3259** Structural clay products

(G-1248)
SAND HILL VINEYARDS LLC
12767 N Courtney Rd (73014-9029)
PHONE..................405 760-1268
Andrew Snyder, *Mng Member*
EMP: 5
SALES: 1MM **Privately Held**
SIC: **2084** Wine cellars, bonded: engaged in blending wines

(G-1249)
SJH WELDING & BACKHOE LLC
18210 N Red Rock Rd (73014-9026)
P.O. Box 180 (73014-0180)
PHONE..................405 833-8353
Wambui Esther, *Principal*
EMP: 2
SALES (est): 171.6K **Privately Held**
SIC: **3531** Backhoes

(G-1250)
SUPERIOR OIL AND GAS CO
844 S Walbaum Rd (73014-8528)
PHONE..................405 884-2069
Bill J Sparks, *President*
Gayla McCoy, *Corp Secy*
Dan Lloyd Jr, *Vice Pres*
EMP: 3
SQ FT: 3,000
SALES (est): 280K **Privately Held**
SIC: **1382** Oil & gas exploration services

Camargo
Dewey County

(G-1251)
CAMARGO JACKS BACKHOE SERVICE
Hwy 34 S And Black St (73835)
P.O. Box 48 (73835-0048)
PHONE..................580 926-3378
Mike Fairchild, *President*
Mike Myers, *Vice Pres*
EMP: 5
SALES (est): 800K **Privately Held**
SIC: **1389** Oil field services; roustabout service; pumping of oil & gas wells

(G-1252)
GASTON SERVICES INC
217239 E 750 Rd (73835-2046)
PHONE..................580 328-5647
Jane Gaston, *President*
Scott Gaston, *Partner*
EMP: 3
SALES (est): 248.8K **Privately Held**
SIC: **1389** Oil field services

(G-1253)
JACKS BACKHOE SERVICE
Also Called: Jacks Backhoe & Roustabout Svc
Hwy 34 In Town (73835)
PHONE..................580 926-3378
Jackie L Salisbury, *President*
EMP: 4
SALES (est): 293.1K **Privately Held**
SIC: **1389** 1794 Roustabout service; excavation work

Cameron
Le Flore County

(G-1254)
ATLAS RESOURCE PARTNERS LP
27404 Walls Rd (74932-2465)
PHONE..................918 654-3702
Fax: 918 654-3725
EMP: 15 **Privately Held**
SIC: **1311** Crude Petroleum/Natural Gas Production

(G-1255)
CAROLYNS CHEESECAKE HOUSE
27444 State Highway 112 (74932-2598)
PHONE..................918 839-5757
Carolyn Pennel, *Principal*
EMP: 1
SALES (est): 57.3K **Privately Held**
SIC: **2591** Window blinds

(G-1256)
CORNERSTONE QUARRIES INC
16511 Mckeown Rd (74932-2634)
PHONE..................918 647-2117
Bill Peterson, *President*
EMP: 7
SALES (est): 331.8K **Privately Held**
SIC: **1411** Dimension stone

(G-1257)
EASTERN OKLA FABRICATION INC
27355 State Highway 112 (74932-2562)
PHONE..................918 654-7344
Ray Finchum, *Owner*
Ross Ridenour, *Sr Project Mgr*
EMP: 6
SQ FT: 15,000
SALES (est): 1.4MM **Privately Held**
SIC: **3496** 7692 Miscellaneous fabricated wire products; welding repair

(G-1258)
KULLY CHAHA NATIVE STONE LLC
13253 Duboise Rd (74932-2380)
P.O. Box 220 (74932-0220)
PHONE..................918 654-3005

Dennis Waren,
EMP: 4
SALES (est): 751.5K **Privately Held**
WEB: www.kullychahastone.com
SIC: **1481** Mine & quarry services, non-metallic minerals

(G-1259)
WELL COMPLETIONS INC
16578 Knot Hole Rd (74932-2555)
P.O. Box 94, Poteau (74953-0094)
PHONE..................918 654-3030
Rodney Evans, *President*
Shelva Evans, *Corp Secy*
EMP: 30
SQ FT: 120
SALES (est): 4MM **Privately Held**
SIC: **1389** 4213 Oil & gas wells: building, repairing & dismantling; servicing oil & gas wells; heavy hauling

Canadian
Pittsburg County

(G-1260)
BUCKYS WELDING
112 N Erie St (74425-5019)
PHONE..................918 339-4187
Steven Ponnequin, *Principal*
EMP: 1 EST: 2012
SALES (est): 67.4K **Privately Held**
SIC: **7692** Welding repair

(G-1261)
CANADIAN TOWN OF INC
Also Called: Canadian Pwa
2 Blocks North Of Po (74425)
P.O. Box 255 (74425-0255)
PHONE..................918 339-2517
Danny Arterberry, *Mayor*
EMP: 2 **Privately Held**
SIC: **9224** 3443 Fire department, not including volunteer; ; dumpsters, garbage
PA: Canadian Town Of Inc
302 Tignor St
Canadian OK 74425
918 339-2517

Caney
Atoka County

(G-1262)
RB CNSTR MET FABRICATION LLC
2436 E Folsom Rd (74533-2506)
PHONE..................580 367-5039
Rick Bagby, *Principal*
EMP: 4
SALES (est): 497.5K **Privately Held**
SIC: **3499** Fabricated metal products

(G-1263)
TEXHOMA LIMESTONE
1102 S Highway 69 75 Rd (74533)
PHONE..................580 889-8808
Left Wilson, *Principal*
EMP: 3
SALES (est): 160K **Privately Held**
SIC: **1411** 5032 5211 Dimension stone; building stone; stone, crushed or broken; lime & plaster

(G-1264)
TOM MCBRIDE MANUFACTURING
100 E Smith St (74533)
P.O. Box 209 (74533-0209)
PHONE..................580 239-9020
Tom McBride, *Principal*
EMP: 1
SALES (est): 51.5K **Privately Held**
SIC: **3999** Manufacturing industries

Canton
Blaine County

(G-1265)
GILCHRIST CONSTRUCTION INC
102 W Main St (73724)
P.O. Box 206 (73724-0206)
PHONE..................580 886-2540
Carol Gilchrist, *President*
Charles Gilchrist, *Vice Pres*
Sherry Mc Donald, *Treasurer*
Jean Howard, *Admin Sec*
EMP: 8
SALES (est): 1.7MM **Privately Held**
SIC: **1389** Oil & gas wells: building, repairing & dismantling

Canute
Washita County

(G-1266)
BARELAS WELDING
10930 N 2090 Rd (73626-2651)
PHONE..................580 497-7485
Carlos Barela, *Owner*
EMP: 1
SALES (est): 70K **Privately Held**
SIC: **3548** 7389 Arc welding generators, alternating current & direct current;

(G-1267)
CHRIST CENTERED CARRIERS LLC
11579 N 2080 Rd (73626-6708)
P.O. Box 217, Leedey (73654-0217)
PHONE..................417 850-8137
Timothy Bradford, *Mng Member*
EMP: 20 EST: 2010
SQ FT: 5,000
SALES: 600K **Privately Held**
SIC: **4226** 1389 Oil & gasoline storage caverns for hire; roustabout service

(G-1268)
JACKSON WELDING & MACHINE
124 Willard (73626)
P.O. Box 370 (73626-0370)
PHONE..................580 472-3631
Shelby Jackson, *Partner*
EMP: 2
SALES (est): 176.1K **Privately Held**
SIC: **1522** 7692 Residential construction; welding repair

(G-1269)
KOS MACHINE LLC
Also Called: Kos Engineering & Machine
500 Willard St (73626)
P.O. Box 133 (73626-0133)
PHONE..................580 799-5042
James M Kos, *Mng Member*
EMP: 3
SALES (est): 153.8K **Privately Held**
SIC: **3599** Machine shop, jobbing & repair

(G-1270)
SCHONES BUTCHER SHOP & MARKET
Old Hwy 66 (73626)
PHONE..................580 472-3300
Ray Shones, *Owner*
Cathy Shones, *Co-Owner*
EMP: 4
SALES: 200K **Privately Held**
SIC: **3556** 2011 Meat processing machinery; meat packing plants

(G-1271)
STOUTS WELDING
20778 E 1160 Rd (73626-2633)
PHONE..................580 243-9116
Chris Stout, *Owner*
EMP: 6
SALES (est): 140K **Privately Held**
SIC: **7692** Automotive welding

Carmen
Alfalfa County

(G-1272)
CARMEN NATURAL GAS MEASUREMENT
417 N Central Ave (73726-2402)
PHONE..................................580 987-2778
Harvey Curry, *Owner*
EMP: 1
SALES (est): 40K **Privately Held**
SIC: 1389 Measurement of well flow rates, oil & gas

Carnegie
Caddo County

(G-1273)
CARNEGIE CONCRETE COMPANY
Also Called: Tng Construction
Hwy 9 W (73015)
PHONE..................................580 654-1208
Larry Graceson, *President*
Gary Campbell, *President*
Mitchell Young, *General Mgr*
EMP: 5
SQ FT: 2,500
SALES (est): 340K **Privately Held**
SIC: 3273 Ready-mixed concrete

(G-1274)
CARNEGIE HERALD
14 W Main St (73015)
P.O. Box 129 (73015-0129)
PHONE..................................580 654-1443
Donald Cooper, *Owner*
Lori Cooper, *Co-Owner*
EMP: 2
SQ FT: 2,500
SALES: 200K **Privately Held**
WEB: www.carnegieherald.com
SIC: 2711 2752 5999 2796 Newspapers: publishing only, not printed on site; commercial printing, lithographic; trophies & plaques; platemaking services; typesetting

(G-1275)
CARNEGIE PRECAST INC
Also Called: Carnegie Pre-Cast Septic Tanks
33129 State Highway 58 (73015-9797)
PHONE..................................580 654-1718
Charles Pettit, *President*
EMP: 10
SALES (est): 713K **Privately Held**
SIC: 7699 3272 1711 Septic tank cleaning service; concrete products, precast; septic system construction

(G-1276)
GARY MACE
Hwy 9 E (73015)
PHONE..................................580 654-2660
Gary Mace, *Owner*
EMP: 1
SALES (est): 98.2K **Privately Held**
SIC: 3499 Fabricated metal products

(G-1277)
KNL SCREENPRINTING
20 E 4th St (73015-9410)
P.O. Box H (73015-0996)
PHONE..................................580 654-5394
Kandice Williams, *Owner*
EMP: 2
SALES (est): 85.5K **Privately Held**
SIC: 2396 Screen printing on fabric articles

(G-1278)
S AND W EMBROIDERY
26 W Main St (73015)
PHONE..................................580 654-2929
Kelly Williams, *Owner*
Orval Williams, *Co-Owner*
EMP: 3
SALES (est): 144.1K **Privately Held**
SIC: 2395 Embroidery & art needlework

Carney
Lincoln County

(G-1279)
PERKINS SAND LLC
335754 E 794 Rd (74832-4843)
PHONE..................................405 240-7870
James E Kinder,
EMP: 2
SALES: 200K **Privately Held**
SIC: 1442 Construction sand mining

(G-1280)
SLYDER ENERGY SOLUTIONS LLC
901 S Neva St (74832)
P.O. Box 467, Chandler (74834-0467)
PHONE..................................405 258-3608
Frank Williams, *President*
EMP: 1
SALES: 393.3K **Privately Held**
SIC: 3714 Hydraulic fluid power pumps for auto steering mechanism

Carter
Beckham County

(G-1281)
ELK VALLEY WOODWORKING INC
12334 N 2000 Rd (73627-3717)
PHONE..................................580 486-3337
Bruce Cain, *President*
Roger Cain, *President*
Annise Cain, *Corp Secy*
Joe Cain, *Vice Pres*
EMP: 3
SQ FT: 11,400
SALES (est): 130K **Privately Held**
SIC: 2431 5999 3993 Ornamental woodwork: cornices, mantels, etc.; woodwork, interior & ornamental; trophies & plaques; signs & advertising specialties

Cartwright
Bryan County

(G-1282)
D & D STUD WELDING LLC PROJ
1242 Boat Club Rd (74731-1311)
P.O. Box 58 (74731-0058)
PHONE..................................888 965-4155
EMP: 1
SALES (est): 55.2K **Privately Held**
SIC: 7692 Welding Repair

(G-1283)
DAVID DOLLAR
Also Called: D & D Stud Welding
1463 4th Ave (74731-2213)
P.O. Box 58 (74731-0058)
PHONE..................................580 965-4155
EMP: 6
SALES (est): 260K **Privately Held**
SIC: 7692 Welding Services

(G-1284)
GREENLAMPS USA LLC
107 Red Oak Rd (74731-8400)
PHONE..................................580 775-2883
James Proctor, *Administration*
EMP: 2 **EST:** 2015
SALES (est): 127.4K **Privately Held**
SIC: 3648 Lighting equipment

Cashion
Kingfisher County

(G-1285)
BIG LEAGUE OIL AND GAS LLC
26761 E 870 Rd (73016-1657)
PHONE..................................405 433-9908
Michael Peterman,
EMP: 2
SALES (est): 90.6K **Privately Held**
SIC: 1389 Oil field services

(G-1286)
D AND L MACHINE INC
1 123a (73016)
PHONE..................................405 433-2233
Donald E Herman, *President*
Liz Herman, *Admin Sec*
EMP: 1
SALES (est): 234.3K **Privately Held**
SIC: 3544 Special dies, tools, jigs & fixtures

(G-1287)
DADDY RUSS CUSTOMS & WLDG LLC
16562 W Camp Dr (73016-9500)
PHONE..................................405 623-9709
Russell Thompson, *Administration*
EMP: 1
SALES (est): 58.4K **Privately Held**
SIC: 7692 Welding repair

(G-1288)
FUELS MARKETING INC
19550 Lakeview Dr (73016-9506)
PHONE..................................405 433-9935
EMP: 1 **EST:** 2007
SALES (est): 105.3K **Privately Held**
SIC: 2869 Fuels

(G-1289)
MACKELLAR INC
74 S County Line Rd (73016)
P.O. Box 18298, Oklahoma City (73154-0298)
PHONE..................................405 433-2658
Lawrence Scheihing, *Manager*
EMP: 14
SALES (corp-wide): 40.1MM **Privately Held**
SIC: 1389 Servicing oil & gas wells
PA: Mackellar, Inc
  809 Nw 57th St
  Oklahoma City OK
  405 848-2877

(G-1290)
MIDWEST ENTERPRISES INC
17980 W Prairie Grove Rd (73016-9679)
PHONE..................................405 433-2419
Ollen Rising, *President*
Naomi Rising, *Corp Secy*
EMP: 2
SALES (est): 180.3K **Privately Held**
SIC: 1311 Crude petroleum production; natural gas production

(G-1291)
MILOT JAMES RESIDENCE CNSTR
16371 W Forrest Hills Rd (73016-9793)
PHONE..................................405 433-2661
James Milot, *Owner*
EMP: 1
SALES (est): 117.6K **Privately Held**
SIC: 1521 2599 2511 General remodeling, single-family houses; cabinets, factory; wood household furniture

(G-1292)
ONPOINT MANUFACTURING
25586 N 2980 Rd (73016-1747)
PHONE..................................580 284-5431
EMP: 2
SALES (est): 110.4K **Privately Held**
SIC: 3999 Manufacturing industries

Catoosa
Rogers County

(G-1293)
ADVANCE RES CHEM & MFG LLC
5010 Skiatook Rd (74015-3050)
PHONE..................................918 266-6789
Dayal Meshri, *Principal*
▲ **EMP:** 6 **EST:** 2006
SALES (est): 726.2K **Privately Held**
SIC: 2819 Industrial inorganic chemicals

(G-1294)
ADVANCE RESEARCH CHEMICALS INC
1110 Keystone Ave (74015-3051)
PHONE..................................918 266-6789
Dayal T Meshri, *President*
Sanjay D Meshri, *Senior VP*
Jagdish Prajapati, *Plant Mgr*
Harpreet Bhinhar, *Purchasing*
Gautam Andotra, *Engineer*
◆ **EMP:** 75
SQ FT: 160,442
SALES (est): 25.9MM **Privately Held**
SIC: 2819 Industrial inorganic chemicals

(G-1295)
AIR PRODUCTS AND CHEMICALS INC
1115 Keystone Ave (74015-3021)
PHONE..................................918 266-8800
Mac Anderson, *Manager*
EMP: 30
SALES (corp-wide): 8.9B **Publicly Held**
WEB: www.airproducts.com
SIC: 2819 2813 Industrial inorganic chemicals; industrial gases
PA: Air Products And Chemicals, Inc.
  7201 Hamilton Blvd
  Allentown PA 18195
  610 481-4911

(G-1296)
AMARILLO CSTM FIXS CO INC OKLA
25905 E Admiral Pl (74015-5727)
PHONE..................................918 266-7752
Larry Ogden, *President*
Wayne Hargrave, *Vice Pres*
EMP: 14
SQ FT: 30,000
SALES: 5MM **Privately Held**
SIC: 2542 Partitions & fixtures, except wood

(G-1297)
AMERICAN ANGLER PUBLICATIONS
800 S Cherokee St C (74015-3304)
PHONE..................................918 364-4210
EMP: 2 **EST:** 2011
SALES (est): 167.5K **Privately Held**
SIC: 2759 Publication printing

(G-1298)
API METALLURGICAL
18501 E Admiral Pl (74015-2818)
PHONE..................................918 266-4130
John Phillips, *President*
EMP: 2
SALES (est): 124.3K **Privately Held**
SIC: 7692 Welding repair

(G-1299)
AZZ INC
5101 Bird Creek Ave (74015-3003)
PHONE..................................918 379-0090
EMP: 32
SALES (corp-wide): 1B **Publicly Held**
SIC: 3479 Galvanizing of iron, steel or end-formed products
PA: Azz Inc.
  3100 W 7th St Ste 500
  Fort Worth TX 76107
  817 810-0095

(G-1300)
B&M METALWORKS INC
Also Called: B&M Metal Works
25912 E Admiral Pl (74015-5780)
PHONE..................................918 266-5103
William E Brownlow Jr, *President*
Denise M Brownlow, *Corp Secy*
EMP: 4
SQ FT: 12,500
SALES (est): 580.3K **Privately Held**
SIC: 3441 Fabricated structural metal

(G-1301)
BEMIS COMPANY INC
905 W Verderiges (74015)
PHONE..................................918 739-4907
Luis Bogran, *Manager*
EMP: 35

GEOGRAPHIC SECTION

Catoosa - Rogers County (G-1329)

SALES (corp-wide): 524.7K **Privately Held**
SIC: **3086** Packaging & shipping materials, foamed plastic
HQ: Bemis Company, Inc.
2301 Industrial Dr
Neenah WI 54956
920 727-4100

(G-1302)
BERRY CUSTOM PRINTING LLC
7 S 276th East Ave (74015-5532)
PHONE 918 266-3732
EMP: **2** EST: 2012
SALES (est): 93K **Privately Held**
SIC: **2752** Lithographic Commercial Printing

(G-1303)
BKEP MATERIALS LLC
5645 E Channel Rd (74015-3048)
PHONE 918 266-1606
Larry Brewer, *Principal*
EMP: **6**
SALES (est): 528.7K **Privately Held**
SIC: **3732** Motorboats, inboard or outboard: building & repairing

(G-1304)
BLM EQUIPMENT & MFG CO INC
100 S Shawnee St (74015-2153)
P.O. Box 418 (74015-0418)
PHONE 918 266-5282
Edward Michaels, *President*
Brenda Michaels, *Corp Secy*
EMP: **10**
SQ FT: 9,200
SALES (est): 3.2MM **Privately Held**
SIC: **3563** 3561 3443 3441 Air & gas compressors; pumps, oil well & field; industrial vessels, tanks & containers; fabricated structural metal

(G-1305)
BOXCO TRIM CABINETS
10105 E 576 Rd (74015-6409)
PHONE 918 266-4030
EMP: **1** EST: 2010
SALES (est): 58K **Privately Held**
SIC: **2434** Mfg Wood Kitchen Cabinets

(G-1306)
BRENNTAG SOUTHWEST INC
5702 E Channel Rd (74015-3013)
PHONE 918 266-2951
Joel Spellings, *Branch Mgr*
EMP: **25**
SALES (corp-wide): 14.1B **Privately Held**
WEB: www.brenntagsouthwest.com
SIC: **5169** 2869 2842 2841 Industrial chemicals; industrial organic chemicals; specialty cleaning, polishes & sanitation goods; soap & other detergents
HQ: Brenntag Southwest, Inc.
610 Fisher Rd
Longview TX 75604
972 218-3500

(G-1307)
BURTCO ENTERPRISES LLC
25910 E 19th St (74015-4587)
PHONE 918 857-1293
Raymond Burtner, *Principal*
EMP: **1** EST: 2017
SALES (est): 73.3K **Privately Held**
SIC: **2273** Carpets & rugs

(G-1308)
CARC INC
104 W Elm St (74015-2415)
PHONE 918 266-1341
Dennis Benton, *President*
Shellie Benton, *Admin Sec*
EMP: **4**
SQ FT: 3,200
SALES (est): 457.6K **Privately Held**
SIC: **7538** 7549 7539 5531 General automotive repair shops; inspection & diagnostic service, automotive; electrical services; automobile air conditioning equipment, sale, installation; radio broadcasting & communications equipment

(G-1309)
CCL ACQUISITION LLC
Also Called: Custom Components & Logistics
19722 E Admiral Pl (74015-3238)
P.O. Box 1710 (74015-1710)
PHONE 918 739-4400
Sandra Brumley, *Vice Pres*
Sarah Reitz, *Cust Mgr*
Tim Brumley,
Rick Wilson, *Maintence Staff*
EMP: **53**
SALES (est): 10MM **Privately Held**
SIC: **3444** 3469 3544 Sheet metalwork; boxes: tool, lunch, mail, etc.: stamped metal; special dies, tools, jigs & fixtures

(G-1310)
CHEROKEE NATION BUSINESSES LLC (HQ)
Also Called: CNB
777 W Cherokee St (74015-3235)
PHONE 918 384-7474
Shawn Slaton, *CEO*
David Mullen, *President*
Ryan Wasmus, *President*
Adam Soerries, *Engineer*
Doug Evans, *CFO*
EMP: **280**
SQ FT: 10,000
SALES: 1.1B **Privately Held**
SIC: **3728** 5085 5088 Aircraft parts & equipment; fasteners, industrial: nuts, bolts, screws, etc.; transportation equipment & supplies
PA: The Cherokee Nation
17675 S Muskogee Ave
Tahlequah OK 74464
918 453-5000

(G-1311)
CLAW MANUFACTURING LLC
19801 E Pine St (74015-3300)
PHONE 918 739-4848
Wally Thrun, *Manager*
EMP: **3**
SALES (est): 363.8K **Privately Held**
SIC: **3999** Manufacturing industries

(G-1312)
CNRW DEFENSE SERVICE
777 W Cherokee St (74015-3235)
PHONE 706 545-5088
EMP: **3** EST: 2018
SALES (est): 271.6K **Privately Held**
SIC: **3812** Defense systems & equipment

(G-1313)
CONTINENTAL OIL & REFINING CO
E Of City (74015)
P.O. Box 831 (74015-0831)
PHONE 918 266-4420
EMP: **3** EST: 2010
SALES (est): 224.5K **Privately Held**
SIC: **1311** Crude petroleum & natural gas

(G-1314)
CSI
8455 E 590 Rd (74015-6422)
PHONE 319 274-5005
EMP: **2**
SALES (est): 90K **Privately Held**
SIC: **3679** Electronic components

(G-1315)
DAVID LOGAN
Also Called: American Badge & Engraving
3510 Crestview Ln (74015-5973)
P.O. Box 33132, Tulsa (74153-1132)
PHONE 918 739-4231
David Logan, *Owner*
EMP: **1**
SALES (est): 49.3K **Privately Held**
SIC: **7389** 5999 5199 3993 Engraving service; miscellaneous retail stores; badges; signs & advertising specialties; plastics products

(G-1316)
DIAMOND P FORREST PRODUCTS CO
10707 E 590 Rd (74015-6376)
PHONE 918 266-2478
JW Powers, *President*
J W Powers, *President*
Linda Powers, *Admin Sec*
EMP: **10**
SQ FT: 6,000
SALES (est): 2.2MM **Privately Held**
SIC: **5031** 2421 2426 5261 Lumber: rough, dressed & finished; sawmills & planing mills, general; hardwood dimension & flooring mills; lawnmowers & tractors; lumber products; saws & sawing equipment

(G-1317)
ELITE MANUFACTURING LLC
Also Called: Double D Horse Stalls
950 Verdigris Pkwy (74015-3061)
P.O. Box 1740 (74015-1740)
PHONE 918 266-1077
Rick Dean, *Mng Member*
David Franklin,
EMP: **6**
SALES (est): 1.2MM **Privately Held**
SIC: **3441** Fabricated structural metal

(G-1318)
ENVIRONMATE INC
16171 Redbud Dr (74015-6301)
PHONE 817 707-5282
Randy Mosley, *President*
EMP: **1**
SALES: 165K **Privately Held**
SIC: **4959** 2833 Environmental cleanup services; organic medicinal chemicals: bulk, uncompounded

(G-1319)
ERGON INC
5850 Arkansas Rd (74015-3046)
PHONE 918 266-7070
Thomas L Kivisto, *Principal*
David Belcher, *Plant Mgr*
Irby Summerlin, *Project Engr*
Rusty Easterling, *Manager*
Richard Henke, *Manager*
EMP: **10**
SALES (corp-wide): 897.8MM **Privately Held**
WEB: www.ergon.com
SIC: **2911** Gases & liquefied petroleum gases
PA: Ergon, Inc.
2829 Lakeland Dr Ste 2000
Flowood MS 39232
601 933-3000

(G-1320)
FORTIS SOLUTIONS GROUP
19014 E Admiral Pl (74015-2861)
PHONE 918 258-8321
EMP: **6**
SALES (est): 878.4K **Privately Held**
SIC: **2759** Commercial printing

(G-1321)
HERMANN JERMEY
Also Called: Trickser Native Apparel Co
17823 E Brady St (74015-2838)
PHONE 918 200-2604
EMP: **1**
SALES (est): 47.7K **Privately Held**
SIC: **2759** Screen printing

(G-1322)
HUGHES LUMBER COMPANY
5615 Bird Creek Ave (74015-3006)
PHONE 918 266-9100
Zach Smith, *Branch Mgr*
EMP: **9**
SALES (corp-wide): 30.4MM **Privately Held**
SIC: **5211** 3442 2431 Lumber products; metal doors, sash & trim; millwork
PA: Hughes Lumber Company
5611 Bird Creek Ave
Catoosa OK 74015
918 266-9140

(G-1323)
IPSCO TUBULARS INC
Also Called: Ipsco Tubulars OK
5610 Bird Creek Ave (74015-3005)
PHONE 918 384-6400
Joel Mastervich, *Vice Pres*
Inside Source, *Branch Mgr*
Paul Phelps, *Manager*
EMP: **105**
SALES (corp-wide): 183.7K **Privately Held**
SIC: **3498** 3312 Pipe sections fabricated from purchased pipe; blast furnaces & steel mills
HQ: Ipsco Tubulars Inc.
10120 Houston Oaks Dr
Houston TX 77064

(G-1324)
JB METAL FABRICATION
9878 E 570 Rd (74015-6277)
P.O. Box 1063 (74015-1063)
PHONE 918 266-3228
Jerry Boyle, *Owner*
EMP: **1**
SALES (est): 108.1K **Privately Held**
SIC: **3441** Fabricated structural metal

(G-1325)
JH NEWTON LLC
29343 S 4130 Rd (74015-6219)
PHONE 918 636-0423
Jeffrey Newton, *President*
EMP: **1**
SALES: 100K **Privately Held**
SIC: **3728** Aircraft parts & equipment

(G-1326)
KELVION INC
Kelvion Phe
990 Keystone Ave (74015-3041)
PHONE 918 416-9058
Paul Suwanachat, *Plant Mgr*
EMP: **21** **Privately Held**
SIC: **3443** Fabricated plate work (boiler shop)
HQ: Kelvion Inc.
5202 W Channel Rd
Catoosa OK 74015
918 266-9200

(G-1327)
KELVION INC (DH)
Also Called: Thermal Solutions
5202 W Channel Rd (74015-3017)
PHONE 918 266-9200
Christine O'Connor, *President*
Eric Peters, *Transportation*
Sergio Fernandes, *CFO*
Terry Willis, *Human Res Mgr*
Brian Steinke, *Manager*
◆ EMP: **237**
SQ FT: 241,876
SALES (est): 5.8MM **Privately Held**
SIC: **3443** Heat exchangers: coolers (after, inter), condensers, etc.
HQ: Kelvion Holding Gmbh
Meesmannstr. 103
Bochum 44807
234 980-0

(G-1328)
KLOECKNER METALS CORPORATION
5250 Bird Creek Ave (74015-3004)
PHONE 918 266-1666
Bailey Lashley, *Sales Staff*
Gary Freeman, *Manager*
EMP: **23**
SALES (corp-wide): 6.9B **Privately Held**
SIC: **5051** 3312 Steel; aluminum bars, rods, ingots, sheets, pipes, plates, etc.; blast furnaces & steel mills
HQ: Kloeckner Metals Corporation
500 Colonial Center Pkwy # 500
Roswell GA 30076

(G-1329)
KLOECKNER METALS CORPORATION
Steel Coil Services
5151 Skiatook Rd (74015-3023)
PHONE 918 660-2050
Bob King, *Manager*
EMP: **20**
SALES (corp-wide): 6.9B **Privately Held**
SIC: **3498** 5051 4225 Coils, pipe: fabricated from purchased pipe; metals service centers & offices; iron & steel (ferrous) products; general warehousing & storage
HQ: Kloeckner Metals Corporation
500 Colonial Center Pkwy # 500
Roswell GA 30076

Catoosa - Rogers County (G-1330)

(G-1330)
KOCH INDUSTRIES INC
5850 Arkansas Rd (74015-3046)
PHONE.................................918 266-7070
Josh Labounty, *Engineer*
Johnny Roe, *Branch Mgr*
EMP: 6
SALES (corp-wide): 48.9B **Privately Held**
SIC: 2951 Asphalt paving mixtures & blocks
PA: Koch Industries, Inc.
4111 E 37th St N
Wichita KS 67220
316 828-5500

(G-1331)
LINDE ENGINEERING N AMER LLC
Also Called: Linde Engineering Americas
945 Keystone Ave (74015-3041)
PHONE.................................918 266-5700
Fred Hage, *Business Mgr*
Becky Ford, *Human Res Mgr*
Susan Meyer, *Benefits Mgr*
Mark Alexion, *Nat'l Sales Mgr*
Doug Houston, *Branch Mgr*
EMP: 28 **Privately Held**
SIC: 3567 3444 Incinerators, metal: domestic or commercial; sheet metalwork
HQ: Linde Engineering North America Llc
6100 S Yale Ave Ste 1200
Tulsa OK 74136
918 477-1424

(G-1332)
LMI AEROSPACE INC
5270 Skiatook Rd (74015-3082)
PHONE.................................918 271-0207
EMP: 2
SALES (est): 190.5K **Privately Held**
SIC: 3728 Aircraft parts & equipment

(G-1333)
LMI FINISHING INC
Also Called: LMI Distributing
5270 Skiatook Rd (74015-3082)
PHONE.................................918 379-0899
Jim Chris, *Branch Mgr*
EMP: 5
SALES (est): 554.1K **Privately Held**
WEB: www.lmiaerospace.com
SIC: 3728 Aircraft parts & equipment

(G-1334)
LPS SPECIALTY PRODUCTS INC
Also Called: Lps Specialty Tubing
5505 Bird Creek Ave (74015-3022)
PHONE.................................918 893-5486
Darrill Scott, *General Mgr*
▲ **EMP:** 1 **EST:** 2012
SALES (est): 198.2K **Privately Held**
SIC: 3317 Steel pipe & tubes

(G-1335)
LUXFER-GTM TECHNOLOGIES LLC
5785 Bird Creek Ave (74015-3008)
PHONE.................................918 439-4248
Pete Anderson, *Branch Mgr*
EMP: 10
SALES (est): 1.6MM
SALES (corp-wide): 3.6MM **Privately Held**
SIC: 3443 Fabricated plate work (boiler shop)
PA: Gtm Technologies, Llc
1619 Shattuck Ave
Berkeley CA 94709
415 856-0570

(G-1336)
MACHINING TECHNOLOGIES OF OK
2003 N 193rd East Ave (74015-9503)
PHONE.................................918 266-1700
Jeanine Curtis, *President*
EMP: 6
SALES (est): 836.6K **Privately Held**
SIC: 3599 Machine shop, jobbing & repair

(G-1337)
MAJESTIC MARBLE & GRANITE
2930 N S Highway 167 (74015-2357)
P.O. Box 1313 (74015-1313)
PHONE.................................918 266-1121
Fax: 918 266-6747
EMP: 22
SALES (est): 2MM **Privately Held**
SIC: 3281 3949 2541 2434 Mfg Cut Stone/Products Mfg Sport/Athletic Goods Mfg Wood Partitions/Fixt

(G-1338)
MARTIN THOMAS ENTERPRISES INC
Also Called: MEI Labels
19014 E Admiral Pl (74015-2861)
PHONE.................................918 739-4015
Lynn Higgs, *CEO*
Jo Anna Oakes, *Accounting Mgr*
EMP: 90
SQ FT: 45,000
SALES (est): 15.8MM **Privately Held**
SIC: 2672 2759 Labels (unprinted), gummed: made from purchased materials; commercial printing

(G-1339)
MATRIX SERVICE INC
Also Called: Tank Division
5725 Kaw Lake Rd (74015-3036)
PHONE.................................918 425-3106
Mark Fillman, *Branch Mgr*
Clint Green, *Director*
EMP: 49
SALES (corp-wide): 1.4B **Publicly Held**
SIC: 3443 Tanks, standard or custom fabricated: metal plate
HQ: Matrix Service Inc.
5100 E Skelly Dr Ste 100
Tulsa OK 74135

(G-1340)
MCCASKILL MACHINING & REPAIR
24454 S Keetonville Rd (74015-3418)
PHONE.................................918 266-5186
Mark McCaskill, *President*
Jackie McCaskill, *Vice Pres*
EMP: 2
SQ FT: 1,500
SALES: 100K **Privately Held**
SIC: 7539 3542 Machine shop, automotive; machine tools, metal forming type

(G-1341)
MID-CONTINENT FUEL CO INC
5550 E Channel Rd (74015-3009)
PHONE.................................918 266-1923
Chris Mouchka, *Principal*
EMP: 3
SALES (est): 224.4K **Privately Held**
SIC: 2869 Fuels

(G-1342)
NATURAL GAS SERVICES GROUP INC
5725 Bird Creek Ave (74015-3008)
PHONE.................................918 266-3330
Paul Hensley, *Branch Mgr*
EMP: 120
SALES (corp-wide): 78.4MM **Publicly Held**
SIC: 3533 3563 Gas field machinery & equipment; air & gas compressors
PA: Natural Gas Services Group, Inc.
508 W Wall St Ste 550
Midland TX 79701
432 262-2700

(G-1343)
NEWTON DESIGN LLC
26015 E Admiral Pl (74015-5743)
PHONE.................................918 266-6205
Jeanessa Marler, *Director*
Jeffrey H Newton,
Dustin L Reynolds,
Timothy T Taylor,
EMP: 60
SQ FT: 44,000
SALES: 16.7MM **Privately Held**
SIC: 3728 3699 Aircraft training equipment; electrical equipment & supplies

(G-1344)
NEWTON DESIGN LLC
26015 E Admiral Pl (74015-5743)
PHONE.................................918 381-3012
EMP: 2
SALES (est): 144.1K **Privately Held**
SIC: 3728 3699 Mfg Aircraft Parts/Equipment Mfg Electrical Equipment/Supplies

(G-1345)
P & K MACHINE INC
401 N Cherokee St (74015-2020)
PHONE.................................918 266-7815
Phillip Mills, *President*
Kimberly Mills, *Vice Pres*
EMP: 2
SALES (est): 80K **Privately Held**
SIC: 3599 Machine shop, jobbing & repair

(G-1346)
PECHINEY PLASTIC PACKAGING
905 Verdigris Pkwy (74015-3062)
PHONE.................................918 739-4900
Luis Bogran, *Principal*
EMP: 4
SALES (est): 419K **Privately Held**
SIC: 5162 2621 Plastics materials & basic shapes; wrapping & packaging papers

(G-1347)
R & S MANUFACTURING
3010 N Highway 167 (74015-9501)
PHONE.................................918 266-2266
Ronald Appleman, *Owner*
▲ **EMP:** 4
SQ FT: 3,000
SALES: 700K **Privately Held**
SIC: 3599 1799 Machine & other job shop work; welding on site

(G-1348)
RACEWAY ELECTRIC INC
119 N Cherokee St (74015-2014)
PHONE.................................918 629-4252
Toby Bue, *Owner*
EMP: 10
SALES (est): 1.3MM **Privately Held**
SIC: 3644 Raceways

(G-1349)
REINFORCED EARTH COMPANY
5101 Bird Creek Ave Ste A (74015-3003)
PHONE.................................918 379-0090
David Wuellner, *Manager*
EMP: 24
SALES (corp-wide): 18.3MM **Privately Held**
WEB: www.reinforcedearth.com
SIC: 5032 3547 Concrete & cinder building products; galvanizing lines (rolling mill equipment)
HQ: The Reinforced Earth Company
12001 Sunrise Valley Dr # 400
Reston VA 20191
703 547-8797

(G-1350)
REINFORCING SERVICES INC
5101 Bird Creek Ave (74015-3003)
PHONE.................................918 379-0090
Ron Pallini, *President*
Earl Williams, *Controller*
EMP: 15
SQ FT: 40,000
SALES (est): 2.3MM
SALES (corp-wide): 1B **Publicly Held**
SIC: 3449 3547 Bars, concrete reinforcing: fabricated steel; galvanizing lines (rolling mill equipment)
PA: Azz Inc.
3100 W 7th St Ste 500
Fort Worth TX 76107
817 810-0095

(G-1351)
SCREW COMPRESSION SYSTEMS INC
Also Called: S C S
5725 Bird Creek Ave (74015-3008)
PHONE.................................918 266-3330
Paul Hensley, *President*
Tony Vohjesus, *Vice Pres*
▲ **EMP:** 120 **EST:** 1997
SQ FT: 22,000
SALES (est): 14.7MM
SALES (corp-wide): 78.4MM **Publicly Held**
WEB: www.ngsgi.com
SIC: 3563 3533 Air & gas compressors; gas field machinery & equipment
PA: Natural Gas Services Group, Inc.
508 W Wall St Ste 550
Midland TX 79701
432 262-2700

(G-1352)
SEMMATERIALS LP
5645 E Channel Rd (74015-3048)
PHONE.................................918 266-1606
Pat Wisdom, *Manager*
EMP: 7 **Publicly Held**
SIC: 2951 Asphalt paving mixtures & blocks
HQ: Semmaterials, L.P.
6520 S Yale Ave Ste 700
Tulsa OK 74136
918 524-8100

(G-1353)
SERVA GROUP LLC
1045 Keystone Ave (74015-3035)
PHONE.................................918 266-0700
Billy Hart, *Prdtn Mgr*
Rhawnie Simons, *Senior Buyer*
Sheila Spearman, *Cust Mgr*
Bobby Wayman, *Branch Mgr*
Jan Bartos, *Supervisor*
EMP: 20 **Privately Held**
SIC: 3533 Oil field machinery & equipment
HQ: Serva Group Llc
1500 Fisher Rd Ste A
Wichita Falls TX 76305

(G-1354)
SOONER NEON
202 Waterford St (74015-2060)
PHONE.................................918 269-5250
EMP: 3
SALES (est): 123.2K **Privately Held**
SIC: 2813 Neon

(G-1355)
SPECIALTY MACHINING INC
19100 E Pine St (74015-2221)
P.O. Box 523 (74015-0523)
PHONE.................................918 266-3626
Jim Elam, *President*
Oneita Elam, *Treasurer*
EMP: 4
SQ FT: 2,100
SALES (est): 470.5K **Privately Held**
SIC: 3599 Machine shop, jobbing & repair

(G-1356)
TMK IPSCO INTERNATIONAL LLC
5610 Bird Creek Ave (74015-3005)
PHONE.................................918 384-6400
James Montgomery, *Plant Mgr*
Lea Smith, *Purchasing*
Kamran Ahmadov, *Controller*
Carl Beck, *Manager*
Don Burgardt, *Manager*
EMP: 9
SALES (corp-wide): 183.7K **Privately Held**
SIC: 3316 Cold finishing of steel shapes
HQ: Tmk Ipsco International, L.L.C.
10120 Houston Oaks Dr
Houston TX 77064
281 949-1023

(G-1357)
TOWER COMPONENTS INC
4730 N 193rd East Ave (74015-9505)
P.O. Box 595 (74015-0595)
PHONE.................................918 379-0769
Clifford Lee Clyma, *President*
Faye Jane Clyma, *Corp Secy*
Kevin L Clyma, *Vice Pres*
EMP: 45
SQ FT: 30,000
SALES: 7.5MM **Privately Held**
SIC: 3441 Tower sections, radio & television transmission

GEOGRAPHIC SECTION

Chandler - Lincoln County (G-1386)

(G-1358)
TRANSCONTINENTAL HOLDING CORP
905 Verdigris Pkwy (74015-3062)
PHONE.................................918 739-4907
Rusty Bryant, *Manager*
EMP: 13
SALES (corp-wide): 2.2B **Privately Held**
SIC: 2673 Bags: plastic, laminated & coated
HQ: Transcontinental Holding Corp.
8600 W Bryn Mawr Ave
Chicago IL 60631

(G-1359)
TRANSCONTINENTAL US LLC
905 Verdigris Pkwy (74015-3062)
PHONE.................................918 739-4906
Luis Bogran, *Plant Mgr*
EMP: 53
SALES (corp-wide): 2.2B **Privately Held**
SIC: 2673 Bags: plastic, laminated & coated
HQ: Transcontinental Us Llc
8600 W Bryn Mawr Ave
Chicago IL 60631
773 877-3300

(G-1360)
TURNAIR FAB LLC
28102 E Admiral Pl (74015-5748)
PHONE.................................918 379-0796
Jimmie Turner, *Owner*
Linda Turner, *CFO*
EMP: 5
SALES: 500K **Privately Held**
SIC: 3569 Lubrication equipment, industrial

(G-1361)
UMICORE AUTOCAT USA INC
1301 W Main Pkwy (74015-2560)
PHONE.................................918 266-8923
Bernard K Terhune III, *Manager*
EMP: 57
SALES (corp-wide): 3.7B **Privately Held**
SIC: 2819 Industrial inorganic chemicals
HQ: Umicore Autocat Usa Inc.
2347 Commercial Dr
Auburn Hills MI 48326
248 340-9328

(G-1362)
UMICORE PRECIOUS METALS
1305 W Main Pkwy (74015-2560)
◆ **EMP:** 23 **EST:** 2013
SQ FT: 700,000
PHONE.................................918 266-1400
SALES: 5MM
SALES (corp-wide): 3.7B **Privately Held**
SIC: 2899 Chemical supplies for foundries
PA: Umicore
Rue Du Marais 31
Bruxelles 1000
222 771-11

(G-1363)
VERSUM MATERIALS US LLC
1115 Keystone Ave (74015-3021)
PHONE.................................918 379-7101
Thomas M Willer, *Branch Mgr*
EMP: 40
SALES (corp-wide): 17.8B **Privately Held**
SIC: 2842 2891 3569 Ammonia, household; adhesives; gas producers, generators & other gas related equipment; gas separators (machinery); separators for steam, gas, vapor or air (machinery)
HQ: Versum Materials Us, Llc
8555 S River Pkwy
Tempe AZ 85284
602 282-1000

(G-1364)
WEBCO INDUSTRIES INC
307 Waterford St (74015-5990)
PHONE.................................865 388-5001
David Foster, *Branch Mgr*
EMP: 2
SALES (corp-wide): 480.7MM **Privately Held**
SIC: 3312 Tubes, steel & iron
PA: Webco Industries, Inc.
9101 W 21st St
Sand Springs OK 74063
918 245-2211

(G-1365)
WEILERT ENTERPRISES INC
Also Called: Viking Packing Specialists
5505 Bird Creek Ave (74015-3022)
PHONE.................................918 252-5515
David Weilert, *President*
▲ **EMP:** 48 **EST:** 2000
SALES (est): 23.7MM **Privately Held**
SIC: 5113 2449 Containers, paper & disposable plastic; wood containers

(G-1366)
WESTWAY FEED PRODUCTS LLC
5450 E Channel Rd (74015-3049)
PHONE.................................918 266-5911
Jeremy Degroot, *Manager*
EMP: 6
SALES (corp-wide): 8.1B **Privately Held**
SIC: 2048 Prepared feeds
HQ: Westway Feed Products Llc
365 Canal St Ste 2929
New Orleans LA 70130
504 934-1850

(G-1367)
WOODWORK PRODUCTIONS LLC
18441 Woodcrest Ln (74015-2222)
PHONE.................................918 639-3167
Tom Connell,
EMP: 1
SALES: 500K **Privately Held**
SIC: 2434 1751 Wood kitchen cabinets; window & door installation & erection

(G-1368)
WOOLSLAYER COMPANIES INC
Also Called: Lee C Moore
5002 Bird Creek Ave (74015-3011)
PHONE.................................918 523-9191
Thomas L Wingerter, *CEO*
Joseph P Woolslayer, *Ch of Bd*
Dwayne Vogt, *President*
Melissa D Herring, *Senior VP*
Harold H Kalich, *Director*
▼ **EMP:** 125
SALES (est): 25.3MM **Privately Held**
SIC: 8711 3533 1381 Designing: ship, boat, machine & product; oil & gas field machinery; oil field machinery & equipment; service well drilling

(G-1369)
WORTHINGTON INDUSTRIES INC
5215 Arkansas Rd (74015-3002)
PHONE.................................614 438-3048
EMP: 2
SALES (corp-wide): 3.7B **Publicly Held**
SIC: 3316 Strip steel, cold-rolled: from purchased hot-rolled
PA: Worthington Industries, Inc.
200 W Wlson Bridge Rd
Worthington OH 43085
614 438-3210

Cement
Caddo County

(G-1370)
WAPCO INC
605 N Main St (73017)
P.O. Box 240 (73017-0240)
PHONE.................................405 489-3212
Terry Brisco, *President*
Bobby Brisco, *Vice Pres*
EMP: 9
SQ FT: 1,200
SALES (est): 687K **Privately Held**
SIC: 4212 1389 Petroleum haulage, local; oil field services

(G-1371)
WHITES ROUSTABOUT SERVICE INC
401 E 5th St (73017)
P.O. Box 515 (73017-0515)
PHONE.................................405 489-7126
Loren White, *President*
EMP: 2

SALES (est): 419.4K **Privately Held**
SIC: 1389 Roustabout service

Chandler
Lincoln County

(G-1372)
12 ACRE WOODWORK LLC
338378 E Cedar Canyon Rd (74834-9020)
PHONE.................................405 328-0655
EMP: 2
SALES (est): 149.7K **Privately Held**
SIC: 2431 Millwork

(G-1373)
ADVANCE GRAPHICS & PRINTING
1113 Manvel Ave (74834-3855)
PHONE.................................405 258-0796
Jim Tuttle, *President*
EMP: 4
SQ FT: 6,000
SALES (est): 500K **Privately Held**
SIC: 2752 2796 2791 2789 Commercial printing, offset; platemaking services; typesetting; bookbinding & related work; commercial printing

(G-1374)
ALAN L BUCK
Also Called: Psa
960812 S Highway 18 (74834-4222)
PHONE.................................405 401-9372
Alan L Buck, *Owner*
EMP: 5
SALES: 1MM **Privately Held**
SIC: 1389 Gas field services; oil field services

(G-1375)
APPLI-FAB CUSTOM COATING
913 Woods Ter (74834-3426)
PHONE.................................405 235-7039
EMP: 8
SQ FT: 5,000
SALES (est): 478.7K **Privately Held**
SIC: 1389 3533 2891 2851 Oil/Gas Field Services Mfg Oil/Gas Field Mach Mfg Adhesives/Sealants Mfg Paints/Allied Prdts

(G-1376)
BLACK STAR MANUFACTURING LLC
930290 S Highway 18 (74834)
PHONE.................................405 315-3336
Tyler Scheller,
EMP: 1
SALES (est): 39.6K **Privately Held**
SIC: 3999 Manufacturing industries

(G-1377)
BUCKEYE EXPLORATION COMPANY
417 Manvel Ave (74834-2044)
P.O. Box 334 (74834-0334)
PHONE.................................405 258-5428
Jerry Spalvieri, *President*
EMP: 8
SALES (est): 2.5MM **Privately Held**
SIC: 1382 Oil & gas exploration services

(G-1378)
DAVENPORT ROUSTABOUT SERVICE
349358 E 910 Rd (74834-6648)
PHONE.................................918 377-2987
Russell Norman, *President*
James Norman, *President*
EMP: 3
SQ FT: 2,500
SALES (est): 994K **Privately Held**
SIC: 1389 Roustabout service; oil field services

(G-1379)
E H PUBLISHING INC
109 Clador Dr (74834-1413)
PHONE.................................405 258-0877
Christine Ayers, *VP Mktg*
Gary Schroeder, *Manager*
EMP: 1 **Privately Held**
SIC: 2741 Miscellaneous publishing

PA: E H Publishing, Inc.
111 Speen St Ste 200
Framingham MA 01701

(G-1380)
HILAND DAIRY FOODS COMPANY LLC
1100 Thunderbird Rd (74834-1000)
P.O. Box 219 (74834-0219)
PHONE.................................405 258-3100
Jacob Sims, *General Mgr*
Angela Nunn, *Human Resources*
James Roberson, *Branch Mgr*
EMP: 400
SALES (corp-wide): 1.7B **Privately Held**
WEB: www.hilanddairy.com
SIC: 2026 2024 0241 Milk & cream, except fermented, cultured & flavored; ice cream & frozen desserts; milk production
HQ: Hiland Dairy Foods Company., Llc
1133 E Kearney St
Springfield MO 65803
417 862-9311

(G-1381)
JACOBS LADDER CAMPS & RETREAT
880876 S 3390 Rd (74834-5418)
P.O. Box 308 (74834-0308)
PHONE.................................405 258-5176
Todd Vinson, *President*
Derin Carr, *Program Dir*
EMP: 2
SALES (est): 149.1K **Privately Held**
WEB: www.jlcamps.com
SIC: 3446 Ladders, for permanent installation: metal

(G-1382)
JON A BELONOIK
Also Called: Jon's Cabinet Shop
213 E 1st St (74834-2205)
PHONE.................................405 258-4131
Jon Beloncik, *Owner*
EMP: 2
SALES (est): 164.2K **Privately Held**
SIC: 2434 Wood kitchen cabinets

(G-1383)
KING SCREEN CO
109 W 11th St (74834-3611)
P.O. Box 195 (74834-0195)
PHONE.................................405 258-0416
Randall D King, *Owner*
EMP: 3 **EST:** 1979
SQ FT: 1,875
SALES (est): 110K **Privately Held**
SIC: 2396 Screen printing on fabric articles

(G-1384)
LARRY SHERMAN OIL LLC
340604 E 870 Rd (74834-8988)
P.O. Box 391 (74834-0391)
PHONE.................................405 258-0816
Larry Sherman, *President*
EMP: 3
SALES (est): 192.5K **Privately Held**
SIC: 1311 Crude petroleum production

(G-1385)
LINCOLN COUNTY PUBLISHING CO
Also Called: Lincoln County News, The
718 Manvel Ave (74834-2843)
P.O. Box 248 (74834-0248)
PHONE.................................405 258-1818
Stephen Mathis, *President*
Dawn Mathis, *Office Mgr*
EMP: 12
SQ FT: 3,100
SALES: 450K **Privately Held**
SIC: 2711 2791 Newspapers, publishing & printing; typesetting

(G-1386)
SHERMAN OIL AND GAS COMPANY
820 Manvel Ave (74834-3806)
P.O. Box 571 (74834-0571)
PHONE.................................405 258-5932
Larry Sherman, *President*
Allen Sherman, *President*
Mary Ann Moore, *Corp Secy*
Bobby Sherman, *Vice Pres*
EMP: 6

SQ FT: 1,000
SALES (est): 650.5K **Privately Held**
SIC: **1311** Crude petroleum production; natural gas production

(G-1387)
SMITH PUMP SUPPLY
Also Called: Smith Pump & Supply
709 Manvel Ave (74834-2842)
PHONE..................405 258-0834
William P Smith, *Owner*
EMP: 3
SQ FT: 1,500
SALES: 350K **Privately Held**
SIC: **5084** 1389 Pumps & pumping equipment; oil field services

(G-1388)
SPECIALTY SALES ASSOCIATES
840481 S 3420 Rd (74834-1486)
PHONE..................405 495-1136
Henry Pederson, *President*
EMP: 2
SQ FT: 600
SALES (est): 800K **Privately Held**
SIC: **3441** Building components, structural steel

Chattanooga
Comanche County

(G-1389)
COUNTY OF TILLMAN
204 3rd St (73528-2683)
P.O. Box 160 (73528-0160)
PHONE..................580 597-3097
Ricky Stracker, *Branch Mgr*
EMP: 3 **Privately Held**
SIC: **3823** 9511 Water quality monitoring & control systems;
PA: County Of Tillman
201 N Main St
Frederick OK 73542
580 335-3421

(G-1390)
L & L SALES LLC
404 3rd St (73528-2678)
P.O. Box 185, Marlow (73055-0185)
PHONE..................580 658-3739
Thomas E Linam, *Principal*
EMP: 1
SALES (est): 110.3K **Privately Held**
SIC: **3648** Lighting equipment

Checotah
Mcintosh County

(G-1391)
CHECOTAH W T J SHOPPE INC
212 Miles Ave (74426-5246)
PHONE..................918 473-2819
Joan Housely, *Owner*
Virgil E Housely, *Owner*
EMP: 2
SALES (est): 110K **Privately Held**
SIC: **5944** 5999 3993 Jewelry stores; trophies & plaques; signs & advertising specialties

(G-1392)
D & C TOOL GRINDING INC
114500 Dogwood Gln (74426-2482)
PHONE..................918 689-9799
Dean Wilborn, *President*
Richard Myers, *Superintendent*
Heather Wilborn, *Treasurer*
Gary Creekmore, *Human Res Dir*
Billie Been, *Sales Staff*
EMP: 4
SQ FT: 5,000
SALES (est): 508K **Privately Held**
SIC: **3545** Cutting tools for machine tools

(G-1393)
FIDGETS OILFIELD SERVICES LLC
2213 N Broadway St (74426-5309)
PHONE..................918 473-2765
Jeff McPeak, *Mng Member*

Clint Walker,
EMP: 2
SQ FT: 1,200
SALES (est): 681.4K **Privately Held**
WEB: www.fidgetsoilfieldservices.com
SIC: **1389** Oil field services

(G-1394)
HENDERSON TRUSS INCORPORATED
423225 E 1100 Rd (74426-1230)
P.O. Box 166, Eufaula (74432-0166)
PHONE..................918 473-5573
Charles J Henderson, *President*
Charles Henderson, *President*
EMP: 12
SQ FT: 25,000
SALES (est): 1.4MM **Privately Held**
SIC: **2439** 5211 Trusses, except roof: laminated lumber; trusses, wooden roof; roofing material

(G-1395)
HTS MANUFACTURING CORPORATION
317 W Gentry Ave (74426-2441)
PHONE..................918 318-0280
EMP: 1
SALES (est): 39.6K **Privately Held**
SIC: **3999** Manufacturing industries

(G-1396)
KATAHDIN CEDAR LOG HOMES OK
109930 Highway 150 (74426-5592)
PHONE..................918 473-7020
Ed Davis, *Owner*
EMP: 1 **EST:** 1999
SALES (est): 79.4K **Privately Held**
WEB: www.cedarloghomesofokla.com
SIC: **2452** Log cabins, prefabricated, wood

(G-1397)
MCINTOSH COUNTY DEMOCRAT
300 S Broadway St Ste D (74426-4800)
P.O. Box 385 (74426-0385)
PHONE..................918 473-2313
Dale Davenport, *Principal*
EMP: 5
SALES (est): 145.5K **Privately Held**
SIC: **2711** Newspapers: publishing only, not printed on site

(G-1398)
OPTIONS INC (PA)
1129 White Stag Ave (74426-2246)
PHONE..................918 473-2614
Donna Cuningham, *Director*
EMP: 13
SALES: 1.2MM **Privately Held**
SIC: **8331** 2759 2396 Vocational rehabilitation agency; commercial printing; automotive & apparel trimmings

Chelsea
Rogers County

(G-1399)
A WALKER ELECTRIC
7134 N 426 (74016)
PHONE..................918 232-6023
Jereme Walker, *Principal*
EMP: 3
SALES (est): 270.4K **Privately Held**
SIC: **3842** Walkers

(G-1400)
AAA GALVANIZING CHELSEA INC
6022 S Industrial Dr (74016-2003)
PHONE..................918 789-9333
Gary Pomrenke, *President*
EMP: 20
SALES (est): 2.4MM
SALES (corp-wide): 1B **Publicly Held**
SIC: **3479** Galvanizing of iron, steel or end-formed products
PA: Azz Inc.
3100 W 7th St Ste 500
Fort Worth TX 76107
817 810-0095

(G-1401)
AEROSTAR INTERNATIONAL INC
5869 S Ernest Pk Indus Rd (74016-4114)
P.O. Box 992, Claremore (74018-0992)
PHONE..................918 789-3000
EMP: 9
SQ FT: 15,000
SALES (est): 1.5MM **Privately Held**
SIC: **3499** 3544 3728 3449 Mfg Misc Fab Metal Prdts Mfg Dies/Tools/Jigs/Fixt Mfg Aircraft Parts/Equip Mfg Misc Structural Mtl

(G-1402)
BILL STOCKTON WELDING LLC
441 W 7th St (74016-1635)
P.O. Box 138 (74016-0138)
PHONE..................918 697-7750
EMP: 1
SALES (est): 39K **Privately Held**
SIC: **7692** Welding repair

(G-1403)
BWS WLDING FABRICTION SVCS LLC
21500 E 340 Rd (74016-9313)
P.O. Box 2 (74016-0002)
PHONE..................918 789-3094
Troy Bowman, *Mng Member*
Janet Bowman,
EMP: 2
SALES (est): 204.8K **Privately Held**
SIC: **7692** 7699 Welding repair; antique repair & restoration, except furniture, automobiles

(G-1404)
E E SEWING INC
21601 E 340 Rd (74016-9301)
PHONE..................918 789-5881
Luke Cowles, *President*
Effie L Cowles, *Admin Sec*
EMP: 31
SQ FT: 27,000
SALES (est): 4MM **Privately Held**
SIC: **2259** 2392 Curtains & bedding, knit; household furnishings

(G-1405)
H S MILAM
341 W 6th St (74016-1637)
PHONE..................918 789-2666
H S Milam, *Principal*
EMP: 3
SALES (est): 172.9K **Privately Held**
SIC: **1311** Crude petroleum & natural gas

(G-1406)
JUST BEE CANDLES AND MORE LLC
8495 N 4270 Rd (74016-5491)
PHONE..................918 557-5145
Ricki Woodruff, *Principal*
EMP: 2 **EST:** 2017
SALES (est): 62.5K **Privately Held**
SIC: **3999** Candles

(G-1407)
K G MACHINE
21571 E 340 Rd (74016-9313)
PHONE..................918 789-2228
Kenneth Gray, *Owner*
EMP: 3
SALES (est): 280K **Privately Held**
SIC: **3599** 7692 3544 Machine shop, jobbing & repair; welding repair; special dies, tools, jigs & fixtures

(G-1408)
O & L RESOURCES INC
400 E 1st St (74016-2403)
P.O. Box 46 (74016-0046)
PHONE..................918 789-5553
Dennis Owens, *President*
Brenda Owens, *Admin Sec*
EMP: 6
SQ FT: 1,800
SALES (est): 500K **Privately Held**
SIC: **3812** Radar systems & equipment

(G-1409)
PARKS CUSTOM CABINETS LLC
7454 S Highway 28 (74016-5134)
PHONE..................918 789-2694

Bruce Park, *Owner*
EMP: 7
SQ FT: 5,600
SALES (est): 544.2K **Privately Held**
SIC: **1751** 2434 Cabinet building & installation; wood kitchen cabinets

(G-1410)
QUALITY GALVANIZING
6022 S Industrial Dr (74016-2003)
PHONE..................918 789-9333
Laxman Aljeria, *President*
EMP: 2
SALES (est): 237.8K
SALES (corp-wide): 1B **Publicly Held**
SIC: **3479** Galvanizing of iron, steel or end-formed products
PA: Azz Inc.
3100 W 7th St Ste 500
Fort Worth TX 76107
817 810-0095

(G-1411)
REPORTER PUBLISHING CO INC
Also Called: Chelsea Reporter, The
245 W 6th St (74016-1833)
P.O. Box 6 (74016-0006)
PHONE..................918 789-2331
Linda Lord, *President*
John Lord, *Vice Pres*
EMP: 3 **EST:** 1927
SQ FT: 2,100
SALES (est): 215.2K **Privately Held**
SIC: **2711** Newspapers, publishing & printing

(G-1412)
SAMCO POLISHING INC
Ew 34 W Of Hwy 66 (74016)
P.O. Box 67 (74016-0067)
PHONE..................918 789-5541
August K Doner, *President*
Sammie Doner, *President*
Billie Doner, *Vice Pres*
Carrie Bucher, *MIS Staff*
Carie Doner, *Shareholder*
EMP: 10
SQ FT: 20,000
SALES (est): 1.5MM **Privately Held**
SIC: **3089** 3599 3544 Injection molding of plastics; machine shop, jobbing & repair; forms (molds), for foundry & plastics working machinery

Cherokee
Alfalfa County

(G-1413)
AGUEVENT INDUSTRIES
820 S Oklahoma Ave (73728-3555)
PHONE..................580 748-0710
Micheal Cox, *Principal*
EMP: 2
SALES (est): 102.5K **Privately Held**
SIC: **3999** Manufacturing industries

(G-1414)
BRIANS HOT OIL SERVICE
32660 State Highway 8 (73728-5808)
PHONE..................580 431-2070
Aaron Ream, *President*
EMP: 3
SALES (est): 138.3K **Privately Held**
SIC: **1311** Crude petroleum & natural gas

(G-1415)
BURLINGTON WELDING LLC
1101 Industrial Blvd (73728-3909)
PHONE..................580 596-3381
R L Wilson, *Mng Member*
EMP: 2
SALES (est): 410.8K **Privately Held**
WEB: www.diamondwcorrals.com
SIC: **7692** Welding repair

(G-1416)
DUANE WAUGH
Also Called: Oilfield Services
N Of Town (73728)
PHONE..................580 596-2485
Duane Waugh, *Owner*
Carolyn Waugh, *Admin Sec*
EMP: 1 **EST:** 1973

SALES (est): 157K **Privately Held**
SIC: **1389** 5082 Oil field services; pumping of oil & gas wells; servicing oil & gas wells; oil field equipment

(G-1417)
JACK EXPLORATION INC
409 S Kansas Ave (73728-2520)
PHONE..................580 621-3679
Alan Watson, *Principal*
EMP: 1
SALES (corp-wide): 700.9K **Privately Held**
SIC: **1381** Directional drilling oil & gas wells
PA: Jack Exploration, Inc
  812 W 11th St
  Sulphur OK 73086
  580 622-2310

(G-1418)
LARRY D HAMMER
Also Called: Cherokee Publishing
216 S Grand Ave (73728-2030)
P.O. Box 245 (73728-0245)
PHONE..................580 596-3344
Heather Gilley, *Branch Mgr*
EMP: 4
SALES (corp-wide): 488.5K **Privately Held**
WEB: www.fairviewrepublican.com
SIC: **2711** 2759 2752 Newspapers: publishing only, not printed on site; commercial printing; commercial printing, lithographic
PA: Larry D Hammer
  112 N Main St
  Fairview OK 73737
  580 227-2100

(G-1419)
SMITH ENERGY SERVICES
201 E 2nd St (73728-2003)
PHONE..................580 596-2104
EMP: 1
SALES (est): 65.5K **Privately Held**
SIC: **1389** Oil/Gas Field Services

Chester
Major County

(G-1420)
MICHAEL NELSON
Also Called: Nelson's Pumping Service
228070 E County Road 56 (73838-2281)
PHONE..................580 922-5074
Michael Nelson, *Owner*
EMP: 1
SALES: 60K **Privately Held**
SIC: **1382** Oil & gas exploration services

(G-1421)
STEVEN CAMPBELL
Also Called: Campbell Metalworks
237289 E County Road 58 (73838-2232)
PHONE..................580 764-3469
Steve Campbell, *Owner*
EMP: 4
SALES (est): 144.8K **Privately Held**
SIC: **3541** Plasma process metal cutting machines

(G-1422)
WESTERN GAS RESOURCES INC
225695 E County Road 53 (73838-3811)
PHONE..................580 764-3397
Gary Eyer, *Principal*
EMP: 1
SALES (corp-wide): 21.2B **Publicly Held**
SIC: **2911** Gases & liquefied petroleum gases
HQ: Western Gas Resources, Inc.
  1099 18th St
  Denver CO 80202

Cheyenne
Roger Mills County

(G-1423)
CHEYENNE STAR
422 E Broadway Ave (73628)
P.O. Box 250 (73628-0250)
PHONE..................580 497-3324
Melanie Cole, *Owner*
EMP: 2
SALES (est): 115.9K **Privately Held**
SIC: **2711** Newspapers: publishing only, not printed on site

(G-1424)
GLENNA F KIRK
19450 E 1100 Rd (73628)
P.O. Box 576 (73628-0576)
PHONE..................580 497-3435
Glenna Kirk, *Owner*
EMP: 1
SALES: 120K **Privately Held**
SIC: **1382** Oil & gas exploration services

(G-1425)
HI PRO FEEDS INC
402 N Ll Males (73628)
P.O. Box 529 (73628-0529)
PHONE..................580 497-2219
Dean Prevost, *CEO*
EMP: 12
SALES (est): 1.5MM **Privately Held**
SIC: **2048** Prepared feeds

Chickasha
Grady County

(G-1426)
A B N G INC
402 W Chickasha Ave # 200 (73018-2504)
P.O. Box 926 (73023-0926)
PHONE..................405 222-0024
Je Epperson II, *President*
Bd Epperson, *Vice Pres*
Kathy Ibsen, *Manager*
EMP: 11
SALES (est): 576.5K **Privately Held**
SIC: **1311** Crude petroleum & natural gas

(G-1427)
ALANS BENCHWORKS CO
510 S 4th St (73018-3405)
PHONE..................405 222-1181
Alan Robbins, *Owner*
EMP: 1
SQ FT: 600
SALES (est): 79.5K **Privately Held**
SIC: **5944** 3915 3911 7631 Jewelry, precious stones & precious metals; jewelers' materials & lapidary work; jewelry, precious metal; jewelry repair services

(G-1428)
AMERICAN TANK GAUGE INC
1801 W Carolina Ave (73018-6905)
PHONE..................405 224-7881
Jerry Morris, *President*
Fran Morris, *Owner*
EMP: 10
SALES (est): 550K **Privately Held**
SIC: **1389** Oil field services; measurement of well flow rates, oil & gas

(G-1429)
ANNS QUICK PRINT CO INC
320 W Chickasha Ave (73018-2653)
PHONE..................405 222-1871
Julius Haroldson, *President*
Ann Haroldson, *Corp Secy*
EMP: 5
SQ FT: 3,500
SALES (est): 565.1K **Privately Held**
SIC: **2752** 3993 2791 2789 Commercial printing, offset; signs, not made in custom sign painting shops; typesetting; bookbinding & related work; commercial printing

(G-1430)
ANYTIME PROPANE LLC
124 Mockingbird Ln (73018-5114)
PHONE..................405 417-0222
James Clark,
EMP: 15 EST: 2013
SQ FT: 5,000
SALES (est): 256K **Privately Held**
WEB: www.anytimepropane.com
SIC: **7699** 3581 Vending machine repair; automatic vending machines

(G-1431)
APACHE CORPORATION
1710 Charles Allen Blvd (73018-1635)
PHONE..................405 222-5040
Dee Young, *Vice Pres*
Jim Branstool, *Manager*
EMP: 30
SALES (corp-wide): 6.4B **Publicly Held**
SIC: **1311** Crude petroleum production
PA: Apache Corporation
  2000 Post Oak Blvd # 100
  Houston TX 77056
  713 296-6000

(G-1432)
ARCHITECTURAL GRAPHICS INC
104 S 2nd St (73018-3608)
PHONE..................757 427-1900
Kelli Smith, *Branch Mgr*
EMP: 6
SALES (corp-wide): 188.8MM **Privately Held**
SIC: **3993** Signs, not made in custom sign painting shops
PA: Architectural Graphics, Inc.
  2655 International Pkwy
  Virginia Beach VA 23452
  800 877-7868

(G-1433)
ATLAS TUCK CONCRETE INC
Chisholm Trail Concrete,
3401 S 4th St (73018-7505)
PHONE..................405 224-5005
EMP: 6
SALES (est): 1.4B **Publicly Held**
WEB: www.us-concrete.com
SIC: **3273** Ready-mixed concrete
HQ: Atlas-Tuck Concrete, Inc.
  2112 W Bois D Arc Ave
  Duncan OK 73533
  580 255-1716

(G-1434)
B & S ROUSTABOUTS LLC
1224 S 18th St (73018-3926)
PHONE..................405 779-0842
Bruce Anderson,
EMP: 5 EST: 2012
SALES (est): 707.7K **Privately Held**
SIC: **1389** Roustabout service

(G-1435)
B&P DETAILING LLC
301 W Oklahoma St 19 (73018-2479)
PHONE..................405 684-7730
Preston Shoemake, *Mng Member*
EMP: 4
SALES: 100K **Privately Held**
SIC: **3713** Truck bodies & parts

(G-1436)
BAD BOY SIGNS GRAPHIC
1426 S 4th St (73018-5817)
PHONE..................405 224-2059
Manuel Rangel, *Partner*
EMP: 54
SALES (est): 3.2MM **Privately Held**
SIC: **3993** 2759 Signs & advertising specialties; screen printing

(G-1437)
BADGETT CORPORATION
4009 S 4th St (73018-7517)
P.O. Box 730 (73023-0730)
PHONE..................405 224-4138
Gary L Badgett, *President*
Gerald H Badgett Sr, *Vice Pres*
Julie Sinn, *Vice Pres*
Tim Sinn, *Vice Pres*
Brandon Armstrong, *Plant Mgr*
▲ EMP: 70 EST: 1923

SQ FT: 57,000
SALES (est): 19.7MM **Privately Held**
WEB: www.badgetts.com
SIC: **3494** 3451 Valves & pipe fittings; screw machine products

(G-1438)
BAILEYS WELDING & MACHINE LLC
3601 State Highway 92 (73018-7015)
P.O. Box 1285 (73023-1285)
PHONE..................405 224-6611
Rusty Bailey, *Mng Member*
EMP: 10
SQ FT: 8,000
SALES (est): 1.1MM **Privately Held**
SIC: **7692** 3443 Welding repair; industrial vessels, tanks & containers

(G-1439)
BAITY SCREW PRODUCTS INC
302 N Genevieve St (73018)
P.O. Box 1367 (73023-1367)
PHONE..................405 222-1520
Richard C Pace, *President*
James S Pace, *Co-Owner*
EMP: 48
SQ FT: 36,000
SALES (est): 8.9MM **Privately Held**
WEB: www.baityscrewmachine.com
SIC: **3599** Machine shop, jobbing & repair

(G-1440)
BOB LOWE FARM MACHINERY INC
1524 E Choctaw Ave (73018-9428)
PHONE..................405 224-6500
Robert Lowe Jr, *President*
Elizabeth Lowe, *Admin Sec*
EMP: 19
SALES: 4.8MM **Privately Held**
WEB: www.lowefarm.com
SIC: **5083** 5999 7699 3524 Agricultural machinery & equipment; farm machinery; farm machinery repair; lawn & garden tractors & equipment; lawn & garden mowers & accessories; lawn & garden equipment

(G-1441)
BOBS SIGN COMPANY
404 S 29th St Rm 203 (73018-2526)
PHONE..................580 467-3646
Peggy J Crutcher, *President*
EMP: 1
SALES (est): 60.4K **Privately Held**
SIC: **3993** Signs & advertising specialties

(G-1442)
BRADFORD BORING LLC
897 County Road 1405 (73018-8111)
PHONE..................405 922-9344
Scott Bradford,
EMP: 2
SALES (est): 232K **Privately Held**
SIC: **3545** Diamond cutting tools for turning, boring, burnishing, etc.

(G-1443)
BRADLEY MACHINE & DESIGN L L C
816 N 18th St (73018-1637)
P.O. Box 663 (73023-0663)
PHONE..................405 224-2223
Stacy McCrackin, *Mng Member*
Rebecca McCrackin,
EMP: 14 EST: 1980
SALES: 1.8MM **Privately Held**
SIC: **3599** Machine shop, jobbing & repair

(G-1444)
BRI-CHEM SUPPLY CORP LLC
715 N Industrial Blvd (73018)
PHONE..................405 200-5466
EMP: 2
SALES (corp-wide): 68.8MM **Privately Held**
SIC: **3533** Oil & gas field machinery
HQ: Bri-Chem Supply Corp. Llc.
  9351 Grant St Ste 380
  Thornton CO 80229
  720 236-1012

Chickasha - Grady County (G-1445)

(G-1445)
C & R PRINT SHOP INC (PA)
420 W Dakota Ave (73018-3436)
PHONE................................405 224-7921
Craig McClennen, *President*
Teresa McClennen, *Vice Pres*
Jessica Crocker, *Accounts Exec*
Amy Trotter, *Director*
EMP: 6 EST: 1974
SQ FT: 4,000
SALES (est): 752.2K **Privately Held**
SIC: **2752** 2759 2796 2791 Commercial printing, offset; letterpress printing; platemaking services; typesetting; bookbinding & related work

(G-1446)
CAN-OK OIL FIELD SERVICES INC
887 County Road 1405 (73018-8111)
PHONE................................405 222-2474
Rick Bellinger, *President*
EMP: 35
SALES (est): 7MM **Privately Held**
WEB: www.can-ok.com
SIC: **1389** 5084 7353 Oil field services; oil well machinery, equipment & supplies; oil field equipment, rental or leasing

(G-1447)
CARBON ECONOMY LLC
2281 County Street 2920 (73018-8096)
PHONE................................405 222-4244
Marvin Chauncey,
EMP: 10
SQ FT: 4,000
SALES (est): 1.2MM **Privately Held**
SIC: **3731** Drilling & production platforms, floating (oil & gas)

(G-1448)
CARBON ECONOMY LLC
2400 S 29th St (73018-9683)
PHONE................................405 222-9399
Streetman Foy, *Manager*
EMP: 2
SALES (est): 98.5K **Privately Held**
SIC: **1389** Oil field services

(G-1449)
CHICKASHA MANUFACTURING CO INC
5501 S 4th St (73018-9604)
PHONE................................405 224-0229
Larry Lewis, *President*
Glenn McNatt, *Vice Pres*
Jennifer Jones, *QC Mgr*
Linda Freeman, *Info Tech Mgr*
EMP: 36
SQ FT: 99,200
SALES (est): 6.8MM **Privately Held**
WEB: www.chickashamfg.com
SIC: **3599** Machine shop, jobbing & repair

(G-1450)
CIMARRON TRAILERS INC
Also Called: CM Aluminum Trailers
1442 Highway 62 (73018-8666)
P.O. Box B (73023-0756)
PHONE................................405 222-4800
Ben Janssen, *President*
EMP: 120
SQ FT: 64,000
SALES (est): 17.5MM
SALES (corp-wide): 119MM **Privately Held**
SIC: **3799** Horse trailers, except fifth-wheel type; trailers & trailer equipment
PA: Folience, Inc.
500 3rd Ave Se
Cedar Rapids IA 52401
319 398-8211

(G-1451)
CRAIGS OKLAHOMA PRIDE LLC
Also Called: Oklahoma Pride Mfg
1301 S 3rd St (73018-4730)
PHONE................................405 224-6410
Chad Craig, *Mng Member*
EMP: 9 EST: 2015
SQ FT: 30,000
SALES: 950K **Privately Held**
SIC: **3523** Cattle feeding, handling & watering equipment; trailers & wagons, farm

(G-1452)
DOLESE BROS CO
3028 W Country Club Rd (73018-7404)
P.O. Box 828 (73023-0828)
PHONE................................405 235-1515
Joe Shelton, *Branch Mgr*
EMP: 10
SQ FT: 1,250
SALES (corp-wide): 8.5MM **Privately Held**
SIC: **3273** Ready-mixed concrete
PA: Dolese Bros. Co.
20 Nw 13th St
Oklahoma City OK 73103
405 235-2311

(G-1453)
DR PEPPER-ROYAL CROWN BTLG CO
205 W Kansas Ave (73018-3654)
P.O. Box 368 (73023-0368)
PHONE................................405 224-1260
Steve Gerdes, *President*
Jean Gerdes, *Corp Secy*
EMP: 19 EST: 1927
SQ FT: 10,000
SALES: 2MM **Privately Held**
SIC: **2086** Soft drinks: packaged in cans, bottles, etc.

(G-1454)
DUNCAN OVERHEAD DOOR
513 W Choctaw Ave (73018-2433)
PHONE................................405 222-0748
Scott Want, *Principal*
EMP: 8
SALES (est): 1.1MM **Privately Held**
SIC: **3679** Electronic components

(G-1455)
DUSTERS & SPRAYERS SUPPLY INC
2163 Highway 81 (73018-8302)
P.O. Box 766 (73023-0766)
PHONE................................405 224-1201
Buddy Hector, *President*
Roberty Nobotny, *General Mgr*
Robert Novotny, *Manager*
Kay Bush, *Admin Sec*
EMP: 11 EST: 1951
SQ FT: 85,000
SALES (est): 1.8MM **Privately Held**
WEB: www.dustersandsprayers.com
SIC: **3728** Aircraft body assemblies & parts

(G-1456)
EMC
1728 Frisco Ave (73018-1600)
PHONE................................405 320-5675
EMP: 4
SALES (est): 275.4K **Privately Held**
SIC: **3572** Computer storage devices

(G-1457)
FENIMORE MANUFACTURING INC
900 N 18th St (73018-1639)
P.O. Box 1287 (73023-1287)
PHONE................................405 224-2637
Steve Smith, *President*
Barry Rhodes, *Vice Pres*
Mike McDonald, *Plant Mgr*
Janice Smith, *Asst Treas*
Jeanice McDonald, *Admin Sec*
EMP: 13 EST: 1955
SQ FT: 20,000
SALES (est): 1.5MM **Privately Held**
WEB: www.fenimoremfg.com
SIC: **3555** Bookbinding machinery

(G-1458)
FORD ENERGY CORPORATION
2802 S 4th St (73018-7208)
P.O. Box 906 (73023-0906)
PHONE................................405 224-3620
James F Ford, *President*
Rick Ford, *Vice Pres*
EMP: 5
SQ FT: 2,000
SALES: 150K **Privately Held**
SIC: **1311** Crude petroleum production; natural gas production

(G-1459)
FORUM ENERGY TECHNOLOGIES INC
1175 State Highway 19 (73018-8401)
PHONE................................405 224-5779
Kevin Kendall, *Branch Mgr*
EMP: 82 **Publicly Held**
SIC: **3533** Gas field machinery & equipment
PA: Forum Energy Technologies, Inc.
10344 Sam Houston Park Dr # 300
Houston TX 77064

(G-1460)
FTS INTERNATIONAL SERVICES LLC
2500 Highway 62 W (73018-6113)
PHONE................................405 574-3900
Mark Bozich, *Branch Mgr*
EMP: 11 **Publicly Held**
WEB: www.ftsi.com
SIC: **3561** 8711 Pumps & pumping equipment; chemical engineering
HQ: Fts International Services, Llc
777 Main St Ste 2900
Fort Worth TX 76102
817 850-1008

(G-1461)
GB ENERGY INC
124 S 4th St (73018-3401)
PHONE................................405 224-8634
B Thomas, *Principal*
EMP: 5
SALES (est): 326K **Privately Held**
SIC: **1389** 1382 Oil & gas field services; oil & gas exploration services

(G-1462)
GERALDS WELDING FABRICATION
150 Quail Rd (73018-2490)
P.O. Box 249 (73023-0249)
PHONE................................405 222-5510
Gayla Brown, *President*
Gerald Brown, *Vice Pres*
EMP: 15
SALES (est): 2.1MM **Privately Held**
SIC: **7692** Welding repair

(G-1463)
GREEN BAY PACKAGING INC
1800 Charles Allen Blvd (73018-1627)
PHONE................................405 222-2306
Matt Johnson, *Maint Spvr*
Jory Gromer, *Manager*
EMP: 22
SQ FT: 85,000
SALES (corp-wide): 1.3B **Privately Held**
WEB: www.gbpcoated.com
SIC: **2653** 5113 Boxes, corrugated: made from purchased materials; corrugated & solid fiber boxes
PA: Green Bay Packaging Inc.
1700 N Webster Ave
Green Bay WI 54302
920 433-5111

(G-1464)
GREGS WLDG & BACKHOE SVC INC
1388 E Highway 19 (73018-9331)
P.O. Box 1803 (73023-1803)
PHONE................................405 222-1004
Greg Seibold, *President*
EMP: 15
SQ FT: 7,000
SALES (est): 869.9K **Privately Held**
SIC: **7692** Welding repair

(G-1465)
GRYPHON OILFIELD SOLUTIONS
479 E Highway 19 (73018-8172)
PHONE................................405 446-8065
EMP: 2
SALES (est): 128.4K **Privately Held**
SIC: **1389** Oil field services

(G-1466)
H & B MACHINE & MANUFACTURING
1003 Quail Ln (73018-2487)
PHONE................................405 224-0006
Henry Bickerstaff, *Owner*
EMP: 10
SALES (est): 1.3MM **Privately Held**
SIC: **3599** Machine shop, jobbing & repair; machine & other job shop work

(G-1467)
H ROCKN INC
106 Rosewood Dr (73018-7730)
PHONE................................405 323-6593
Kim Hawthorn, *President*
Janet Hawthorn, *Treasurer*
EMP: 2
SALES: 273K **Privately Held**
SIC: **1381** Drilling oil & gas wells

(G-1468)
HART FEEDS INC
2301 W Country Club Rd (73018-7601)
PHONE................................405 224-0102
Richard Hart Sr, *President*
EMP: 5
SQ FT: 24,000
SALES (est): 1.5MM **Privately Held**
SIC: **0723** 4213 3599 2048 Feed milling custom services; trucking, except local; machine shop, jobbing & repair; prepared feeds

(G-1469)
HART TRAILER LLC
3909 S 4th St (73018-7509)
P.O. Box C (73023-0757)
PHONE................................405 224-3634
Anthony Hart, *President*
Kay Hart, *Vice Pres*
Jon Drummond, *Purch Agent*
EMP: 75
SQ FT: 112,000
SALES (est): 12MM **Privately Held**
WEB: www.harttrailer.com
SIC: **3715** Trailers or vans for transporting horses

(G-1470)
HERMETIC SWITCH INC (PA)
Also Called: Hsi Sensing
3100 S Norge Rd (73018-6169)
PHONE................................405 224-4046
David Posey, *CEO*
Ryan Posey, *Vice Pres*
Travis Posey, *Vice Pres*
Barbara Mandrell, *Opers Mgr*
Kim Kellogg, *Prdtn Mgr*
▼EMP: 107
SQ FT: 60,000
SALES (est): 47.6MM **Privately Held**
WEB: www.hsisensing.com
SIC: **3679** 3823 3613 Electronic switches; industrial instrmnts msrmnt display/control process variable; switchgear & switchboard apparatus

(G-1471)
INTEGRATED FLUID SYSTEMS
3 Honda Ln (73018-1624)
PHONE................................405 418-2897
EMP: 2 EST: 2013
SALES (est): 109.9K **Privately Held**
SIC: **1389** Oil field services

(G-1472)
IRONMAN WELDING & MFG LLC
203 Christopher Dr (73018-7103)
PHONE................................580 464-3478
Myron Ladymon, *Principal*
EMP: 1
SALES (est): 27.6K **Privately Held**
SIC: **7692** Welding repair

(G-1473)
J C PETROLEUM INC
3010 S 4th St (73018-7256)
P.O. Box 1433 (73023-1433)
PHONE................................405 222-1412
John Donnellan, *President*
EMP: 3
SQ FT: 1,000
SALES (est): 405.1K **Privately Held**
SIC: **1311** Crude petroleum production

(G-1474)
JACMAC ENERGY CORP
114 Mockingbird Ln (73018-5114)
PHONE................................405 224-1284
Michael McCaughtry, *President*

GEOGRAPHIC SECTION

Chickasha - Grady County (G-1506)

Craig Mc Caughtry, *Corp Secy*
James Mc Caughtry, *Vice Pres*
EMP: 5
SALES (est): 200K **Privately Held**
SIC: 1311 Natural gas production

(G-1475)
JAYS JEWELRY
327 W Chickasha Ave Ste 1 (73018-2673)
PHONE 405 224-9021
Jason D Jarnagin, *Owner*
EMP: 5
SALES (est): 850K **Privately Held**
SIC: 5944 3911 Jewelry, precious stones & precious metals; jewelry, precious metal

(G-1476)
JEROCO INC
2908 Lacey Dr (73018-7342)
P.O. Box 395 (73023-0395)
PHONE 405 222-1179
Robert Jernigan, *President*
EMP: 5
SALES (est): 353.7K **Privately Held**
SIC: 1382 Oil & gas exploration services

(G-1477)
KECHI ENERGY LLC
3010 S 4th St (73018-7256)
P.O. Box 1433 (73023-1433)
PHONE 405 222-1412
John Donnellan, *Mng Member*
EMP: 3
SALES: 250K **Privately Held**
SIC: 1311 Crude petroleum production; natural gas production

(G-1478)
KELMAR OIL CO
Mid First Bank Bldg 606 (73018)
P.O. Box 1435 (73023-1435)
PHONE 405 222-2364
Daniel Sparks, *President*
James Sparks, *Vice Pres*
EMP: 3
SQ FT: 2,000
SALES (est): 338.6K **Privately Held**
SIC: 1382 Oil & gas exploration services

(G-1479)
KENNETH PACE
Also Called: Batie Screw Machine Products
124 Bowerwood Dr (73018-7704)
P.O. Box 1367 (73023-1367)
PHONE 405 222-1426
Richard Pace, *Owner*
EMP: 45
SALES (est): 5MM **Privately Held**
SIC: 3451 Screw machine products

(G-1480)
KUYKENDALL WELDING LLC
1711 S 15th St (73018-5421)
P.O. Box 1451 (73023-1451)
PHONE 405 905-0389
Adam Kuykendall, *CEO*
EMP: 1 **EST:** 2014
SALES (est): 30.3K **Privately Held**
SIC: 7692 3589 3479 1799 Welding repair; sandblasting equipment; painting of metal products; welding on site

(G-1481)
LEMANS MANUFACTURING INC
1301 S 3rd St (73018-4730)
P.O. Box 1352 (73023-1352)
PHONE 405 224-6410
Leman A Spoon, *President*
Louise Spoon, *Vice Pres*
EMP: 18
SQ FT: 10,000
SALES (est): 2.8MM **Privately Held**
SIC: 3523 Cattle feeding, handling & watering equipment; trailers & wagons, farm

(G-1482)
M-I LLC
110 S Grand Ave (73018-2002)
P.O. Box B (73023-0756)
PHONE 405 224-4170
Roger Ross, *Manager*
EMP: 27 **Publicly Held**
SIC: 1389 Oil field services
HQ: M-I L.L.C.
5950 N Course Dr
Houston TX 77072
281 561-1300

(G-1483)
MCDONALD SAFETY ANCHOR INC
520 S 7th St (73018-3310)
PHONE 405 574-4151
Ron McDonald, *President*
Sandra McDonald, *Corp Secy*
EMP: 1
SALES: 50K **Privately Held**
SIC: 1389 Oil field services

(G-1484)
MERITOR INC
700 N Industrial Blvd (73018-1625)
P.O. Box 988 (73023-0988)
PHONE 405 224-8600
Paul Rogers, *Branch Mgr*
EMP: 11 **Publicly Held**
SIC: 3714 Motor vehicle parts & accessories
PA: Meritor, Inc.
2135 W Maple Rd
Troy MI 48084

(G-1485)
METAL FINISHING OF CHICKASHA
Also Called: Metal Finishings
402 N 6th St (73018-2426)
PHONE 405 224-6703
Keith Caraway, *President*
Connie Caraway, *Admin Sec*
EMP: 14
SQ FT: 25,000
SALES (est): 1.5MM **Privately Held**
WEB: www.metalfinishok.com
SIC: 3471 Electroplating of metals or formed products

(G-1486)
MIDWEST COOLING TOWERS INC (PA)
1156 E Highway 19 (73018-6347)
PHONE 405 224-4622
Terry Ogburn, *President*
Larry Brown, *Principal*
◆ **EMP:** 170
SQ FT: 100,000
SALES: 50MM **Privately Held**
SIC: 2499 2452 Cooling towers, wood or wood & sheet metal combination; prefabricated wood buildings

(G-1487)
MIDWESTERN PET FOODS INC
913 N 9th St (73018-1817)
PHONE 405 224-2691
Edward Cooper, *Branch Mgr*
EMP: 10
SALES (corp-wide): 24.1MM **Privately Held**
SIC: 2047 2048 Dog food; cat food; prepared feeds
PA: Midwestern Pet Foods Inc
9634 Hedden Rd
Evansville IN 47725
812 867-7466

(G-1488)
MIKE MCGILLS CARPET INC
Also Called: Carpet Market
426 W Chickasha Ave (73018-2410)
PHONE 405 222-0899
William J Pate, *President*
EMP: 4
SALES (est): 470K **Privately Held**
SIC: 2273 Floor coverings: paper, grass, reed, coir, sisal, jute, etc.

(G-1489)
MIKES FAMOUS BEEF JERKY
102 W Kansas Ave (73018-3653)
PHONE 405 414-7501
EMP: 3
SALES (est): 144.2K **Privately Held**
SIC: 2013 Snack sticks, including jerky; from purchased meat

(G-1490)
MORRIS WELDING
1644 County Road 1380 (73018-8053)
PHONE 580 486-3474
Ron Morris, *Principal*
EMP: 2
SALES (est): 100.2K **Privately Held**
SIC: 7692 Welding repair

(G-1491)
MUSICK WELDING LLC
4401 S 16th St (73018-9664)
PHONE 405 274-1766
EMP: 1
SALES (est): 28.1K **Privately Held**
SIC: 7692 Welding repair

(G-1492)
NICOLA ACQUISITIONS LLC
709 W Country Club Rd (73018-7259)
PHONE 405 224-0061
Charles Nicola, *Principal*
EMP: 2
SALES (est): 147.3K **Privately Held**
SIC: 3721 Aircraft

(G-1493)
OAK TREE SALES
1103 N Industrial Blvd (73018-1626)
P.O. Box 712 (73023-0712)
PHONE 405 224-9332
Steven Unruh, *Owner*
EMP: 3
SQ FT: 6,000
SALES (est): 242K **Privately Held**
SIC: 2434 5251 5031 7699 Wood kitchen cabinets; builders' hardware; tools, power; lumber: rough, dressed & finished; power tool repair; cabinet & finish carpentry

(G-1494)
OLSON PACKAGING SERVICE
2500 Highway 62 W (73018-6113)
PHONE 405 224-5577
Alberto Martinez, *Principal*
EMP: 1
SALES (est): 79.9K **Privately Held**
WEB: www.olsonpackaging.com
SIC: 2631 Container, packaging & boxboard

(G-1495)
OP NAIL
1716 S 1st St (73018-6011)
PHONE 405 222-1829
Deo Duong, *Owner*
EMP: 4
SALES (est): 329K **Privately Held**
SIC: 2844 Manicure preparations

(G-1496)
OUACHITA EXPLORATION INC
Also Called: Abng
402 W Chickasha Ave # 200 (73018-2504)
P.O. Box 926 (73023-0926)
PHONE 405 222-0024
J E Epperson Sr, *Ch of Bd*
Joseph E Epperson II, *President*
Douglas Epperson, *Vice Pres*
EMP: 5 **EST:** 1974
SQ FT: 10,000
SALES: 1.3MM **Privately Held**
SIC: 1311 1381 Crude petroleum production; natural gas production; drilling oil & gas wells

(G-1497)
OVER 60 LLC
4007 Hickory Stick Dr (73018-7801)
PHONE 405 224-0711
James M Palmer, *Principal*
EMP: 1
SALES (est): 55.5K **Privately Held**
SIC: 2759 Commercial printing

(G-1498)
PAINT ON CANVAS
624 W Chickasha Ave (73018-2414)
PHONE 405 574-6689
Carrie Chavers, *Principal*
EMP: 1
SALES (est): 70.7K **Privately Held**
WEB: www.paintoncanvas.net
SIC: 2211 Canvas

(G-1499)
PARADISE DOUGHNUTS
Also Called: Snyder's Doughnuts
601 S 4th St (73018-3459)
PHONE 405 224-2907
Lance Snyder, *Owner*
EMP: 2
SALES (est): 81.1K **Privately Held**
SIC: 5461 2051 Doughnuts; doughnuts, except frozen

(G-1500)
PRAIRIE ROSE PROCESSING INC
830 County Road 1310 (73018-7919)
PHONE 405 224-6429
Phillip Schmitt, *President*
EMP: 7 **EST:** 1997
SALES (est): 140K **Privately Held**
SIC: 2011 2013 Meat packing plants; sausages & other prepared meats

(G-1501)
RICHARDS PRINTING CO
2200 S 29th St (73018-8200)
PHONE 405 224-8640
Danny King, *Owner*
June Welch, *Admin Sec*
EMP: 3
SQ FT: 2,100
SALES (est): 290.5K **Privately Held**
SIC: 2752 Commercial printing, offset

(G-1502)
RIDE CONTROL LLC
Also Called: Gabriel Ride Control Products
700 N Industrial Blvd (73018-1625)
P.O. Box 988 (73023-0988)
PHONE 800 251-5932
Rodney Bolinger, *General Mgr*
EMP: 400 **Privately Held**
SIC: 3714 Tie rods, motor vehicle
HQ: Ride Control, Llc
39300 Country Club Dr
Farmington Hills MI 48331

(G-1503)
ROYAL FILTER MANUFACTURING CO
4327 S 4th St (73018-9336)
PHONE 405 224-0229
Gary McNatt, *President*
Glenn McNatt, *President*
Gary Mc Natt, *Principal*
EMP: 29
SALES (est): 6MM **Privately Held**
SIC: 3569 3714 3564 Filters, general line: industrial; motor vehicle parts & accessories; filters, air: furnaces, air conditioning equipment, etc.

(G-1504)
RT MANUFACTURING LLC
501 W Michigan Ave (73018-2471)
P.O. Box 1508 (73023-1508)
PHONE 405 222-7180
Mary B Dimmitt,
Debra Hamilton,
Troy Rodgers,
EMP: 17
SQ FT: 1,800
SALES: 9MM **Privately Held**
SIC: 3441 Fabricated structural metal

(G-1505)
S KAT EMBROIDERY & QUILTING
3119 S 9th St (73018-7263)
PHONE 405 200-6283
Katherine Hopkins, *Partner*
Rodney Hopkins, *Partner*
EMP: 2
SALES (est): 90.7K **Privately Held**
SIC: 2611 Kraft (sulfate) pulp

(G-1506)
SAMMYS SIGNS LLC
925 Vermont St (73018-1700)
PHONE 405 320-1156
Sammy Rainer, *Principal*
EMP: 1
SALES (est): 49.4K **Privately Held**
SIC: 3993 Signs & advertising specialties

Chickasha - Grady County (G-1507)

(G-1507)
SENTRY MANUFACTURING COMPANY
1201 Crystal Park (73018-1766)
P.O. Box 1212 (73023-1212)
PHONE..................................202 262-0225
William Guy Sr, *President*
Dana Guy, *Treasurer*
EMP: 25
SQ FT: 13,000
SALES (est): 2MM **Privately Held**
SIC: 3679 Quartz crystals, for electronic application

(G-1508)
SERVICE TECH COOLG TOWERS LLC
801 S 29th St (73018-9602)
PHONE..................................405 222-0722
Kelly Boyd,
Becca Boyd,
EMP: 15
SALES: 2MM **Privately Held**
WEB: www.stct.biz
SIC: 3443 Cooling towers, metal plate

(G-1509)
SHERIDAN PRODUCTION CO LLC
1656 County Street 2780 (73018-8229)
PHONE..................................405 453-7860
Roger Burns, *Manager*
EMP: 6
SALES (est): 288.2K **Privately Held**
SIC: 1382 Oil & gas exploration services

(G-1510)
SHOWTEK
727 Reding Rd (73018-7126)
P.O. Box 1391 (73023-1391)
PHONE..................................405 222-0632
Andrew Reding, *President*
Martin Reding, *Manager*
EMP: 1 **EST:** 1980
SALES (est): 124.7K **Privately Held**
SIC: 3648 3999 Lighting equipment; stage hardware & equipment, except lighting

(G-1511)
SIMER PALLET RECYCLING INC
3000 Industrial Blvd (73018)
P.O. Box 1189 (73023-1189)
PHONE..................................405 224-8583
Newton Dale Simer II, *President*
Heather Simer, *Vice Pres*
Wanda Simer, *Vice Pres*
EMP: 11
SQ FT: 16,000
SALES: 975K **Privately Held**
SIC: 2448 Pallets, wood

(G-1512)
SMALL POTATO TEES LLC
2402 S 13th St (73018-6728)
PHONE..................................405 264-6330
Leslie Neal, *Principal*
EMP: 2 **EST:** 2018
SALES (est): 129.2K **Privately Held**
SIC: 2759 Screen printing

(G-1513)
STAR WELL SERVICES INC
5401 Glenwood Dr (73018-7370)
PHONE..................................405 222-4606
Aaron Spears, *CEO*
EMP: 15 **EST:** 2000
SALES (est): 871K **Privately Held**
WEB: www.starwellservices.com
SIC: 1389 Oil field services

(G-1514)
SUPERIOR FEDERAL BANK
1927 S 4th St (73018-5949)
PHONE..................................405 224-1021
Tammy Taylor, *Principal*
EMP: 1
SALES (est): 95.7K **Privately Held**
SIC: 3578 Automatic teller machines (ATM)

(G-1515)
TAYLOR & SONS FARMS INC
2222 County Street 2900 (73018-7970)
PHONE..................................405 222-0751
Russell Taylor, *President*
Scott Taylor, *Vice Pres*
Terry Taylor, *Treasurer*
Nancy Taylor, *Admin Sec*
EMP: 7
SQ FT: 38,000
SALES (est): 1.4MM **Privately Held**
SIC: 5051 0191 3523 3496 Pipe & tubing, steel; steel; general farms, primarily crop; farm machinery & equipment; miscellaneous fabricated wire products; manufactured hardware (general)

(G-1516)
TAYLOR & SONS PIPE AND STL INC
2479 County Street 2865 (73018-8085)
PHONE..................................405 222-0751
Russell Taylor, *President*
Scott Taylor, *Vice Pres*
EMP: 15
SALES (est): 13.3MM **Privately Held**
SIC: 5051 3317 Steel; steel pipe & tubes

(G-1517)
TERRY TYLOR WLDG FBRCATION LLC
2489 County Street 2865 (73018-8085)
PHONE..................................405 205-2964
Bonnie L Taylor, *Principal*
EMP: 2
SALES (est): 181.2K **Privately Held**
SIC: 3448 1799 Prefabricated metal buildings; welding on site

(G-1518)
TRACE OIL
2931 County Street 2773 (73018-8133)
PHONE..................................405 222-4449
Tom Harris, *Owner*
EMP: 3
SALES (est): 484.1K **Privately Held**
SIC: 1311 Crude petroleum production

(G-1519)
UNION HILL ELECTRIC LLC
1232 County Road 1390 (73018-8105)
PHONE..................................405 222-1068
Karen Willoughby, *Mng Member*
Jeff Willoughby,
EMP: 7
SALES (est): 981.7K **Privately Held**
SIC: 1731 3621 Electrical work; electric motor & generator parts

(G-1520)
UNIT CORP
4413 S 4th St (73018-9662)
PHONE..................................405 222-6441
EMP: 2
SALES (est): 119.9K **Privately Held**
SIC: 1382 Oil & gas exploration services

(G-1521)
W & W CUSTOM CABINETS
102 Todd Estate Dr (73018-5118)
PHONE..................................405 222-1410
Bob Wilson, *Owner*
EMP: 2
SALES (est): 70K **Privately Held**
SIC: 1751 2434 5211 5031 Cabinet & finish carpentry; wood kitchen cabinets; cabinets, kitchen; kitchen cabinets

(G-1522)
WASHITA VALLEY WEEKLY
920 S 4th St (73018-4632)
PHONE..................................405 224-7467
EMP: 2
SALES (est): 45.4K **Privately Held**
SIC: 2711 Newspapers, publishing & printing

(G-1523)
WASHITA WLDG & FABRICATION LLC
115 N 29th St (73018-9792)
PHONE..................................405 779-0140
EMP: 2 **EST:** 2018
SALES (est): 106.7K **Privately Held**
SIC: 7692 Welding repair

(G-1524)
WESTERN IRON WORKS LLC
1691 Highway 62 (73018-8671)
PHONE..................................405 779-1961
Marvin Igo,
EMP: 1 **EST:** 2010
SALES (est): 196.5K **Privately Held**
SIC: 3499 Fabricated metal products

(G-1525)
WRIGHT WATER CORPORATION
Also Called: Culligan
1001 S 3rd St (73018-4721)
PHONE..................................405 224-1839
Sean Wright, *President*
EMP: 6 **EST:** 1968
SQ FT: 2,800
SALES (est): 1MM **Privately Held**
SIC: 3589 Swimming pool filter & water conditioning systems

(G-1526)
WYOMING CASING SERVICE IN
401 E Highway 19 (73018-8172)
PHONE..................................701 456-0136
EMP: 2
SALES (est): 137K **Privately Held**
SIC: 1389 Oil field services

Choctaw
Oklahoma County

(G-1527)
ASSOCIATED PLASTICS LLC
2675 Plant Dr (73020)
P.O. Box 918, Nicoma Park (73066-0918)
PHONE..................................405 390-0406
Merl Medcalf,
EMP: 9
SQ FT: 25,000
SALES (est): 940K **Privately Held**
SIC: 3089 Injection molding of plastics

(G-1528)
BARNETT JAMES
Also Called: Twisted B Industries
15301 Se 33rd St (73020-5900)
PHONE..................................405 833-4052
James N Barnett, *Principal*
EMP: 1
SALES (est): 63K **Privately Held**
SIC: 3999 Manufacturing industries

(G-1529)
BARNETTS
915 Oak Park Dr (73020-7558)
PHONE..................................405 390-3026
Robert Barnett, *Owner*
EMP: 1
SALES: 50K **Privately Held**
SIC: 3599 Machine shop, jobbing & repair

(G-1530)
BEES KNEES TEES
245 Woodlake Dr (73020-7313)
PHONE..................................405 370-2132
Mallory Marler, *Principal*
EMP: 2
SALES (est): 92.1K **Privately Held**
SIC: 2759 Screen printing

(G-1531)
BLAZE SKATEBOARDS LLC
4100 Maxine Dr (73020-5977)
PHONE..................................405 391-3838
Kameron Clark, *Principal*
EMP: 1
SALES (est): 47K **Privately Held**
SIC: 3949 Skateboards

(G-1532)
BM
1618 Mill Creek Blvd (73020-7191)
PHONE..................................405 388-3999
Richard Barringer, *Owner*
EMP: 1
SALES: 100K **Privately Held**
SIC: 3728 Aircraft parts & equipment

(G-1533)
CBD4HELP LLC
601 S Henney Rd (73020-7122)
PHONE..................................405 206-9672
Stephanie Jean Sowell, *Owner*
EMP: 2 **EST:** 2017
SALES (est): 78.9K **Privately Held**
SIC: 3999

(G-1534)
COMPUTER SOLUTIONS + LLC (PA)
Also Called: Georges Gun Shop
12228 Ne 23rd St (73020-8732)
PHONE..................................405 259-9603
George Dykes,
Karen Dykes,
EMP: 2
SQ FT: 1,200
SALES (est): 215.5K **Privately Held**
SIC: 5734 5045 3652 Modems, monitors, terminals & disk drives: computers; printers & plotters: computers; personal computers; printers, computer; magnetic tape (audio): prerecorded

(G-1535)
CREATIVE PINS
1147 Whisper Ln (73020-8052)
PHONE..................................405 390-2038
Valerie Davie, *Owner*
EMP: 1
SALES (est): 55.1K **Privately Held**
SIC: 3951 Meter pens

(G-1536)
D J WELDING
15232 Se 104th St (73020-4048)
PHONE..................................405 386-4620
EMP: 1 **EST:** 2010
SALES (est): 57K **Privately Held**
SIC: 7692 Welding Repair

(G-1537)
DC INDUSTRIES
5320 Hart Ln (73020-9622)
PHONE..................................405 923-0815
Dave Colangelo, *Principal*
EMP: 1 **EST:** 2017
SALES (est): 39.6K **Privately Held**
SIC: 3999 Manufacturing industries

(G-1538)
DEJAY OIL & GAS INC
13700 Ne 50th St (73020-9650)
PHONE..................................405 390-0906
EMP: 2
SALES (est): 109.2K **Privately Held**
SIC: 1389 Oil/Gas Field Services

(G-1539)
DIE HARD PROPERTIES LLC
14458 Autumn Dr (73020-6214)
PHONE..................................405 769-3145
Ray Males, *Administration*
EMP: 2
SALES (est): 157.9K **Privately Held**
SIC: 3544 Special dies & tools

(G-1540)
DRILLWORX DIRECTIONAL DRLG LLC
16533 Se 89th St (73020-3900)
P.O. Box 6342, Moore (73153-0342)
PHONE..................................405 386-3380
Kim Winsett, *Administration*
EMP: 3
SALES (est): 385.9K **Privately Held**
SIC: 1381 Directional drilling oil & gas wells

(G-1541)
EMERALD ISLE OF MIDWEST INC
3891 N Choctaw Rd (73020-9029)
PHONE..................................405 802-0092
Timothy Kearns, *President*
EMP: 3
SQ FT: 2,000
SALES (est): 359.1K **Privately Held**
SIC: 3086 Insulation or cushioning material, foamed plastic

(G-1542)
EXCELL PRODUCTS INC
2500 Enterprise Blvd (73020-8400)
PHONE..................................405 390-4491
Merle Medcalf, *President*
Suzanne Medcalf, *Corp Secy*
Krista Myers, *Vice Pres*
Jenny Nowka, *Treasurer*
Jim Nowka, *Sales Mgr*
◆ **EMP:** 27
SQ FT: 39,000

GEOGRAPHIC SECTION

SALES (est): 7.7MM **Privately Held**
SIC: 3993 Signs & advertising specialties

(G-1543)
FROZEN MESA WINERY LLC
16322 Sandstone Cir (73020-8290)
PHONE..................405 281-5962
Tejay Botchlet, *Owner*
EMP: 2
SALES (est): 88.2K **Privately Held**
SIC: 2084 Wines

(G-1544)
HIS PUBLISHING LLC
15210 Scottsdale Ln (73020-5809)
PHONE..................405 390-0518
John Dillinger,
EMP: 2 EST: 2010
SALES: 20K **Privately Held**
SIC: 2741 Miscellaneous publishing

(G-1545)
HOPPIS INTERIORS
540 S Choctaw Rd (73020-7181)
PHONE..................405 390-2963
Ethel Hoppis, *Owner*
▲ EMP: 3 EST: 1969
SALES (est): 273.7K **Privately Held**
SIC: 5714 2392 2391 Draperies; household furnishings; curtains & draperies

(G-1546)
J&S OVERHEAD DOOR & GATE LLC
274 Murray Dr (73020-2410)
PHONE..................405 249-0779
Jason Crawford,
EMP: 2
SALES (est): 30K **Privately Held**
SIC: 3442 Metal doors, sash & trim

(G-1547)
JANS DIGITZING & EMB LLC
15023 Scottsdale Ln (73020-5804)
PHONE..................970 587-2834
Janet Eperry, *Owner*
EMP: 1
SALES (est): 77.8K **Privately Held**
SIC: 2395 Embroidery & art needlework

(G-1548)
JBR SOFTWARE DEVELOPMENT LLC
17550 Tall Oak Rd (73020-6954)
PHONE..................405 872-8561
James Bailey Roberts, *Principal*
EMP: 2
SALES (est): 56.5K **Privately Held**
SIC: 7372 Prepackaged software

(G-1549)
LAUGHING RABBIT SOAP
12732 Se 38th St (73020-6177)
PHONE..................405 737-7413
Charlotte Hayer, *Owner*
EMP: 1 EST: 1989
SALES (est): 77.2K **Privately Held**
SIC: 2841 Soap: granulated, liquid, cake, flaked or chip

(G-1550)
LINDSAY WOODWORKS
13290 Ne 36th St (73020-9104)
PHONE..................405 370-9712
Michael Lindsay, *Owner*
EMP: 2
SALES (est): 142.8K **Privately Held**
SIC: 2431 Millwork

(G-1551)
LOTHROP TECHNOLOGIES INC
Also Called: Enviro-Tech Products
17171 Se 29th St (73020-6453)
PHONE..................405 390-3499
Linwood Lothrop, *President*
Joyce Lothrop, *Vice Pres*
EMP: 3
SQ FT: 4,500
SALES: 400K **Privately Held**
SIC: 3499 Magnets, permanent: metallic

(G-1552)
NICNIK WOODWORKS
8617 Mercato St (73020-2058)
PHONE..................703 474-7994
Nick Janik, *Principal*
EMP: 2
SALES (est): 85.2K **Privately Held**
SIC: 2431 Millwork

(G-1553)
OKLAHOMA CEMENT SOLUTIONS LLC
13133 Chinkapin Oak Pl (73020-2006)
PHONE..................214 802-1527
Dan Richwine,
EMP: 5
SALES (est): 230.7K **Privately Held**
SIC: 3531 Bituminous, cement & concrete related products & equipment

(G-1554)
RTA SYSTEMS INCORPORATED (PA)
14260 Whippoorwill Vis (73020-7027)
P.O. Box 721985, Norman (73070-8510)
PHONE..................405 388-6802
Bill Johnson, *President*
Geoff Mitchell, *Vice Pres*
EMP: 8
SALES (est): 860.5K **Privately Held**
SIC: 2834 Medicines, capsuled or ampuled

(G-1555)
STORM HAVEN ALPACA LLC
2301 S Peebly Rd (73020-6318)
PHONE..................405 391-2767
George Storm, *Principal*
EMP: 1 EST: 2010
SALES (est): 72.5K **Privately Held**
SIC: 2231 Alpacas, mohair: woven

(G-1556)
TRB INDUSTRIES LLC
700 N Peebly Rd (73020-7440)
PHONE..................405 990-4159
Tracy Brown Brown, *Principal*
EMP: 2
SALES (est): 98.6K **Privately Held**
SIC: 3999 Manufacturing industries

(G-1557)
WHORTON WELDING
14113 Se 29th St (73020-6507)
PHONE..................405 610-6545
EMP: 1
SALES (est): 25K **Privately Held**
SIC: 7692 Welding repair

Chouteau
Mayes County

(G-1558)
BEAUCHAMP CABINETS CSTM HOMES
2682 W 600 (74337-6310)
PHONE..................918 476-5532
Lewis Beauchamp, *Owner*
EMP: 2
SALES (est): 105.7K **Privately Held**
SIC: 2521 2517 2434 Wood office furniture; wood television & radio cabinets; vanities, bathroom: wood

(G-1559)
CADET MANUFACTURING INC
Also Called: Cadet Truck Bodies
1125 E Main St (74337-3819)
PHONE..................918 476-8159
Guy L Holden, *Incorporator*
Patsy E Holden, *Incorporator*
EMP: 32
SQ FT: 45,000
SALES (est): 8.6MM **Privately Held**
WEB: www.cadettruckbodies.com
SIC: 3713 Truck bodies (motor vehicles); truck bodies & parts

(G-1560)
CHOUTEAU FUELS COMPANY
8142 Highway 412b (74337-6027)
PHONE..................405 249-8273
EMP: 3 EST: 2016
SALES (est): 237.8K **Privately Held**
SIC: 2869 Fuels

(G-1561)
CHOUTEAU PALLET
10451 S 430 (74337-5356)
PHONE..................918 476-6098
EMP: 4
SALES (est): 205.7K **Privately Held**
SIC: 2448 Pallets, wood & wood with metal

(G-1562)
DOVER PRODUCTS INC
5321 W 570 (74337-6163)
PHONE..................918 476-5688
Jamie Dover, *Owner*
EMP: 6
SQ FT: 4,000
SALES: 250K **Privately Held**
SIC: 1711 3272 3523 Septic system construction; concrete products; concrete products used to facilitate drainage; farm machinery & equipment

(G-1563)
EASTERN ETCHING & MFG
420 E Loy St (74337-2824)
PHONE..................918 476-6007
Frank Clark, *Principal*
EMP: 2
SALES (est): 74.8K **Privately Held**
SIC: 3999 Manufacturing industries

(G-1564)
HEATER SPECIALISTS LLC
303 S Main St (74337-5388)
P.O. Box 426 (74337-0426)
PHONE..................918 476-8670
John Anderson, *Manager*
EMP: 20
SALES (est): 1.1MM
SALES (corp-wide): 66.5MM **Privately Held**
SIC: 3443 Industrial vessels, tanks & containers
HQ: Heater Specialists, L.L.C.
3171 N Toledo Ave
Tulsa OK 74115
918 835-3126

(G-1565)
HOLLANDS MOBILE HOMES
116 N 2nd St (74337)
P.O. Box 168 (74337-0168)
PHONE..................918 476-5663
Billie Holland, *Owner*
EMP: 1
SALES: 20K **Privately Held**
SIC: 7519 2451 Mobile home rental, except on site; mobile homes

(G-1566)
HUMPS N HRNS BULL RDNG NWS LLC
Also Called: Humps N Horns Bull Riding News
105 E Orr St (74337-3239)
P.O. Box 34172, Fort Worth TX (76162-4172)
PHONE..................918 476-8213
Rita Williams,
EMP: 3
SALES (est): 200.7K **Privately Held**
SIC: 2711 Newspapers, publishing & printing

(G-1567)
INDUSTRIAL ENTERPRISE INC
65 Lakeside Dr (74337)
P.O. Box 497 (74337-0497)
PHONE..................918 476-5907
Thomas E Hickok, *President*
Steve Maham, *Vice Pres*
Denise Maham, *Treasurer*
EMP: 12 EST: 1963
SQ FT: 48,000
SALES (est): 1.8MM **Privately Held**
SIC: 3599 5084 7692 Machine shop, jobbing & repair; metalworking machinery; metalworking tools (such as drills, taps, dies, files); welding repair

(G-1568)
NBS FABRICATION
13537 S 4328 (74337-6119)
PHONE..................918 527-5211
Nick Smith, *Principal*
EMP: 1 EST: 2010
SALES (est): 78.2K **Privately Held**
SIC: 7692 Welding repair

(G-1569)
PERKINS CABINET TRIM
11207 S 432 (74337-6088)
PHONE..................918 476-6567
Mark Perkins, *Principal*
EMP: 1
SALES (est): 111.4K **Privately Held**
SIC: 2434 Wood kitchen cabinets

(G-1570)
SOONER STATE SPRING MFG CO
Also Called: Jackson Powder Coating
9799 S 432 (74337-6084)
P.O. Box 406 (74337-0406)
PHONE..................918 476-5707
Martin Jackson, *President*
Zachary Jackson, *Vice Pres*
Sylvia Jackson, *Admin Sec*
EMP: 6
SQ FT: 6,000
SALES (est): 512.4K **Privately Held**
SIC: 3496 3495 3469 Wire fasteners; wire springs; ornamental metal stampings

(G-1571)
STEPHEN POORBOY
Also Called: Bristol Field Services
31875 E 668 Rd (74337-5582)
PHONE..................918 373-5073
Stephen Poorboy, *Owner*
EMP: 3
SQ FT: 1,500
SALES (est): 187.8K **Privately Held**
SIC: 3431 7539 Metal sanitary ware; machine shop, automotive

(G-1572)
THOMPSONS CUSTOM BUTCHER BARN
6878 W 590 (74337-5409)
PHONE..................918 476-5508
Paul Thompson, *Owner*
Debbie Thompson, *Vice Pres*
EMP: 8
SQ FT: 4,500
SALES (est): 513.4K **Privately Held**
SIC: 0751 5421 5147 2013 Slaughtering: custom livestock services; meat & fish markets; meats, fresh; sausages & other prepared meats; meat packing plants

Claremore
Rogers County

(G-1573)
52 STONE
17520 S 4150 Rd (74017-3691)
PHONE..................918 798-9952
Hugh Anglin, *Principal*
EMP: 3
SALES (est): 212.6K **Privately Held**
SIC: 3272 Cast stone, concrete

(G-1574)
A&B HOME IMPROVEMENT
10595 E Second St (74019-5465)
PHONE..................918 341-7410
Bill Self, *Principal*
EMP: 2
SALES (est): 168.1K **Privately Held**
SIC: 1521 1761 3089 General remodeling, single-family houses; siding contractor; windows, plastic

(G-1575)
ACME MANUFACTURING CORPORATION (PA)
Also Called: Fastcurbs
6532 Tower Ln (74019-4373)
PHONE..................918 266-3097
Scott C Lewis, *Ch of Bd*
Hal Lewis, *President*
Blair Williams, *Vice Pres*
David Bridgewater, *Plant Mgr*
Sandy Crase, *Train & Dev Mgr*
EMP: 30
SQ FT: 22,000

Claremore - Rogers County (G-1576)

SALES (est): 3.4MM **Privately Held**
SIC: **3444** 3354 2952 Gutters, sheet metal; ventilators, sheet metal; aluminum extruded products; asphalt felts & coatings

(G-1576)
ACME MANUFACTURING CORPORATION
Mistop
6532 Tower Ln (74019-4373)
PHONE..................................800 647-8671
Hal Lewis, *President*
EMP: 1
SALES (corp-wide): 3.4MM **Privately Held**
SIC: **3444** Sheet metalwork
PA: Acme Manufacturing Corporation
    6532 Tower Ln
    Claremore OK 74019
    918 266-3097

(G-1577)
AERIAL DRONES OF OKLAHOMA LLC
26460 Arrowood Dr (74019-2920)
PHONE..................................918 694-6523
Carl Boggs, *Principal*
EMP: 2
SALES (est): 105.9K **Privately Held**
SIC: **3721** Motorized aircraft

(G-1578)
AIR-X-HEMPHILL LLC
401 E Lowry Rd (74017-3542)
PHONE..................................918 283-9220
J Alumbaugh, *Human Res Dir*
Angela Mort, *Office Mgr*
EMP: 9 EST: 2015
SALES (est): 329.5K **Privately Held**
SIC: **3443** Fabricated plate work (boiler shop)

(G-1579)
ALL AMERICAN FIRE SYSTEMS INC
21125 E 480 Rd (74019-3999)
PHONE..................................918 341-6977
Harry Troyer, *President*
Melinda Troyer, *Treasurer*
EMP: 10
SQ FT: 1,000
SALES (est): 1.7MM **Privately Held**
SIC: **1711** 3569 7382 Fire sprinkler system installation; sprinkler systems, fire: automatic; fire alarm maintenance & monitoring

(G-1580)
ALL DECKED OUT
24103 S Highway 66 # 89 (74019-0289)
PHONE..................................918 313-9691
Jeff Brock, *Principal*
EMP: 2 EST: 2016
SALES (est): 103.6K **Privately Held**
SIC: **2892** Explosives

(G-1581)
ALL-STAR TROPHIES & RIBBON MFG
Also Called: All Star Trophy Mfg
911 W Will Rogers Blvd (74017-5040)
PHONE..................................918 283-2200
Deric Brock, *Owner*
EMP: 2
SQ FT: 5,000
SALES (est): 195.4K **Privately Held**
SIC: **3499** 5611 2759 3993 Trophies, metal, except silver; clothing, sportswear, men's & boys'; screen printing; signs & advertising specialties; automotive & apparel trimmings; trophies & plaques

(G-1582)
ANCHOR EXPLORATION OF OKLAHOMA
17007 S 4102 Rd (74017-9442)
P.O. Box 35082, Tulsa (74153-0082)
PHONE..................................918 605-1005
Bruce D Locke, *President*
Larry M Locke, *Vice Pres*
EMP: 3 EST: 1981
SALES (est): 242.4K **Privately Held**
WEB: www.anchorexploration.com
SIC: **1382** Oil & gas exploration services

(G-1583)
APOLLO METAL SPECIALTIES INC
Also Called: Apollo Metal Specialities
2605 S Highway 66 (74019-5521)
PHONE..................................918 341-7650
Daniel C Pilgrim, *President*
Renee Pilgrim, *Corp Secy*
EMP: 15
SQ FT: 25,000
SALES (est): 3.3MM **Privately Held**
SIC: **3441** 7692 3444 Fabricated structural metal; welding repair; sheet metalwork

(G-1584)
AW SPECIALTIES LLC
18985 S 4210 Rd (74017-1715)
P.O. Box 1107 (74018-1107)
PHONE..................................918 798-9272
John Wagoner, *President*
EMP: 5 EST: 2012
SALES (est): 457K **Privately Held**
WEB: www.awspecialties.com
SIC: **3443** 1799 Fabricated plate work (boiler shop); sandblasting of building exteriors

(G-1585)
AXH AIR-COOLERS LLC
401 E Lowry Rd (74017-3542)
PHONE..................................918 283-9200
Ken Jones,
◆ EMP: 5
SQ FT: 143,000
SALES (est): 95.3MM **Privately Held**
SIC: **3443** Heat exchangers: coolers (after, inter), condensers, etc.
PA: Air-X-Limited
    2230 E 49th St Ste D
    Tulsa OK 74105
    918 743-6111

(G-1586)
AZTEC NE OVERHEAD DOOR INC
221 N Owalla Ave (74017-3922)
PHONE..................................918 341-7502
Thomas Olari, *President*
EMP: 4
SQ FT: 3,350
SALES (est): 367.3K **Privately Held**
SIC: **1751** 7699 5211 3699 Garage door, installation or erection; garage door repair; garage doors, sale & installation; door opening & closing devices, electrical

(G-1587)
BACCO INC
20318 E 103rd St N (74019-5709)
PHONE..................................918 344-3670
John C Wyatt, *Principal*
EMP: 8 EST: 2014
SALES (est): 1MM **Privately Held**
SIC: **3444** Metal ventilating equipment

(G-1588)
BAKER CENTRILIFT CABLE INC
Also Called: Centrilift A Baker Hughes Co
200 W Stuart Roosa Dr (74017-3028)
PHONE..................................713 439-8600
Louis Moncada, *Principal*
▲ EMP: 14
SALES (est): 1.3MM
SALES (corp-wide): 23.8B **Publicly Held**
SIC: **1389** Oil field services
HQ: Baker Hughes Holdings Llc
    17021 Aldine Westfield Rd
    Houston TX 77073
    713 439-8600

(G-1589)
BAKER HGHES OLFLD OPRTIONS LLC
2210 El Anderson Blvd (74017-2126)
PHONE..................................918 341-9600
Aj Ingersoll, *Principal*
EMP: 1 **Privately Held**
SIC: **1381** Drilling oil & gas wells
PA: Baker Hughes Oilfield Operations Llc
    2001 Rankin Rd
    Houston TX 77073

(G-1590)
BAKER HGHES OLFLD OPRTIONS LLC
Also Called: Lowry Baker Hughes
844 W Lowry Rd (74017-2116)
PHONE..................................918 283-7911
EMP: 2
SALES (est): 101.4K **Privately Held**
SIC: **1389** Oil & gas field services

(G-1591)
BAKER HGHES OLFLD OPRTIONS LLC
Baker Hughes Centrilift
200 W Stuart Roosa Dr (74017-3028)
PHONE..................................918 341-9600
Wil Faubel, *President*
EMP: 400 **Privately Held**
SIC: **1389** Oil field services
PA: Baker Hughes Oilfield Operations Llc
    2001 Rankin Rd
    Houston TX 77073

(G-1592)
BAKER HUGHES A GE COMPANY LLC
844 W Lowry Rd (74017-2116)
PHONE..................................918 283-1957
Kristi Franks, *Buyer*
Denise Harold, *Engineer*
Dustin Lester, *Branch Mgr*
EMP: 49
SALES (corp-wide): 23.8B **Publicly Held**
SIC: **1389** Oil field services
HQ: Baker Hughes Holdings Llc
    17021 Aldine Westfield Rd
    Houston TX 77073
    713 439-8600

(G-1593)
BASDEN STEEL-OKLAHOMA LLC
15151 S Highway 66 (74017-2659)
PHONE..................................918 341-9468
Bruce Basden, *Principal*
EMP: 25
SALES: 2.4MM **Privately Held**
SIC: **3441** Fabricated structural metal
PA: Renfro Street Holdings, Ltd.
    645 E Renfro St
    Burleson TX 76028

(G-1594)
BEAN COUNTER INC
2601 Holly Rd (74017-8539)
PHONE..................................918 925-9667
EMP: 3
SALES (est): 155K **Privately Held**
SIC: **3131** Counters

(G-1595)
BELLOFRAM CORPORATION
Belgas FM
900 N Owalla Ave (74017-3809)
PHONE..................................918 965-1964
A B Siemer, *Ch of Bd*
EMP: 3
SALES (corp-wide): 125.2MM **Privately Held**
WEB: www.marshbellofram.com
SIC: **3621** Motors & generators
PA: Bellofram Corporation
    8019 Ohio River Blvd
    Newell WV 26050
    304 387-1200

(G-1596)
BILLS ELECTRIC INC
24704 S Highway 66 (74019-2407)
PHONE..................................918 341-4414
EMP: 2
SALES (est): 97.2K **Privately Held**
SIC: **3699** 1731 Electrical equipment & supplies; electrical work

(G-1597)
BLUE ARC METAL SPECIALTIES
505 W Lowry Rd (74017-2148)
PHONE..................................918 341-3903
Mike O'Dell, *Principal*
EMP: 2

SALES (est): 401.7K **Privately Held**
WEB: www.bluearcms.com
SIC: **3548** 1799 2899 Spot welding apparatus, electric; welding on site; fluxes: brazing, soldering, galvanizing & welding

(G-1598)
BLUEARC WELDING LLC
4805 E Ranch Rd (74019-0142)
PHONE..................................918 341-0629
John Chastain, *Principal*
EMP: 1
SALES (est): 45.5K **Privately Held**
SIC: **7692** Welding repair

(G-1599)
BOXING BEAR LLC
10010 E Pin Oak Ln (74019-0301)
PHONE..................................918 606-9991
Jeff Mitchell, *Principal*
EMP: 2
SALES (est): 83.9K **Privately Held**
SIC: **2752** Commercial printing, lithographic

(G-1600)
BUTAPHALT PRODUCTS LLC
25615 Briar Dr (74019-4512)
P.O. Box 549, Catoosa (74015-0549)
PHONE..................................918 740-7290
Dennis Duane Krivohlavek,
EMP: 2
SALES (est): 90.7K **Privately Held**
SIC: **2952** Asphalt felts & coatings

(G-1601)
C & C MACHINE INC
904 W 1st St (74017-5426)
PHONE..................................918 342-1950
Doug Conder, *President*
Iona Conder, *Admin Sec*
EMP: 6
SQ FT: 5,000
SALES: 500K **Privately Held**
WEB: www.condermachine.com
SIC: **3599** Machine shop, jobbing & repair

(G-1602)
CD SERVICES
12062 Branch Rd (74017-1717)
PHONE..................................918 341-1032
Gary Davis, *Owner*
EMP: 2
SALES (est): 84K **Privately Held**
SIC: **2741** Miscellaneous publishing

(G-1603)
CENTRAL STATES CRANE HOIST LLC (PA)
518 N J M Davis Blvd A (74017-5615)
P.O. Box 294 (74018-0294)
PHONE..................................918 341-2320
Gator Greenwill,
EMP: 10
SALES (est): 3MM **Privately Held**
SIC: **3536** 7389 Cranes, overhead traveling; crane & aerial lift service

(G-1604)
CENTRAL STATES CRANE HOIST LLC
415 N Owalla Ave Ste A (74017-5860)
PHONE..................................918 341-2320
Gregory Todd,
EMP: 3
SALES (corp-wide): 3MM **Privately Held**
SIC: **3536** Hoists, cranes & monorails
PA: Central States Crane & Hoist Llc
    518 N J M Davis Blvd A
    Claremore OK 74017
    918 341-2320

(G-1605)
CENTRAL VALVE BODY
15551 S Highway 66 (74017-2658)
PHONE..................................918 341-0266
Shannon Lester, *Owner*
Donny Lester, *Co-Owner*
EMP: 4
SALES: 180K **Privately Held**
SIC: **3592** Valves

GEOGRAPHIC SECTION
Claremore - Rogers County (G-1639)

(G-1606)
CITY OF CLAREMORE
2060 S Highway 66 (74019-4513)
PHONE..................918 342-2490
EMP: 1 **Privately Held**
SIC: 3469 Automobile license tags, stamped metal
PA: City Of Claremore
104 S Muskogee Ave
Claremore OK 74017
918 341-2365

(G-1607)
CLACO ENTERPRISES
24605 S 4150 Rd (74019-5499)
PHONE..................918 343-0276
Carl Ayers, *Owner*
EMP: 2
SQ FT: 2,500
SALES (est): 110K **Privately Held**
SIC: 3599 Machine shop, jobbing & repair

(G-1608)
CLAREMORESIGNS COM
514 N J M Davis Blvd (74017-5615)
PHONE..................918 965-1233
EMP: 1
SALES (est): 71.4K **Privately Held**
SIC: 3993 Signs & advertising specialties

(G-1609)
CONTECH ENTERPRISES LLC (PA)
Also Called: Aci Mfg
14241 E 450 Rd (74017-3469)
PHONE..................918 341-6232
Ben Compton, *President*
▼ **EMP:** 10
SALES: 1.9MM **Privately Held**
SIC: 3564 3444 Filters, air; furnaces, air conditioning equipment, etc.; sheet metalwork

(G-1610)
CONTECH MFG INC
14241 E 450 Rd (74017-3469)
PHONE..................918 341-6232
Joe Conder, *President*
Greg Conder, *Vice Pres*
EMP: 5
SQ FT: 7,000
SALES (est): 700K
SALES (corp-wide): 1.9MM **Privately Held**
SIC: 3599 3444 Machine shop, jobbing & repair; sheet metalwork
PA: Contech Enterprises, Llc
14241 E 450 Rd
Claremore OK 74017
918 341-6232

(G-1611)
CUSTOM UPHOLSTERY
1618 N Chambers Ter (74017-2617)
PHONE..................918 342-3489
Edward Martinez, *Owner*
EMP: 1 **EST:** 2009
SALES: 45K **Privately Held**
SIC: 7641 3731 7537 Upholstery work; lighters, marine: building & repairing; automotive transmission repair shops

(G-1612)
DARK OPS DESIGNS
26520 Foxen Dr (74019-7529)
PHONE..................918 269-0049
Cody Schreck, *Principal*
EMP: 2 **EST:** 2016
SALES (est): 73.4K **Privately Held**
SIC: 3484 Small arms

(G-1613)
DBMAC 50 INC
Also Called: Bob's Printing
117 W Blue Starr Dr (74017-4226)
P.O. Box 1425 (74018-1425)
PHONE..................918 342-5590
Bob McCuistian, *President*
Julie McCuistian, *Corp Secy*
EMP: 3
SALES: 500K **Privately Held**
SIC: 2759 2791 2789 2752 Commercial printing; typesetting; bookbinding & related work; commercial printing, lithographic

(G-1614)
DESIGN MY SIGNS OK LLC
605 N Lynn Riggs Blvd (74017-5632)
PHONE..................918 923-0175
EMP: 1
SALES (est): 46K **Privately Held**
SIC: 3993 Signs & advertising specialties

(G-1615)
EAGLE RESOURCES INC
8202 E 485 Rd (74019-5398)
PHONE..................918 342-5733
Thomas Oly, *President*
EMP: 1
SQ FT: 560
SALES (est): 70K **Privately Held**
SIC: 1311 Crude petroleum production; natural gas production

(G-1616)
EMCO LLC
Also Called: Emco Springs
24625 Amah Pkwy (74019-4316)
P.O. Box 1065 (74018-1065)
PHONE..................918 342-3488
Cathy Mathews, *Purch Mgr*
Rebecca Meier,
Betty Pearcy,
David M Pearcy,
EMP: 80
SQ FT: 62,000
SALES (est): 30.5MM **Privately Held**
WEB: www.emcoind.com
SIC: 3493 Steel springs, except wire

(G-1617)
EMCO INDUSTRIES LLC
Also Called: Emco Spring
24625 Amah Pkwy (74019-4316)
PHONE..................918 342-3488
Cathy Mathews, *Buyer*
Taylor Jones, *Mng Member*
Bill Boydston, *Maintence Staff*
▲ **EMP:** 65 **EST:** 1991
SALES (est): 10.3MM **Privately Held**
SIC: 3495 Wire springs

(G-1618)
F C WITT ASSOCIATES LTD
Also Called: Witt Lining Systems
2211 El Anderson Blvd (74017-2119)
P.O. Box 488 (74018-0488)
PHONE..................918 342-0083
Jacqueline Witt, *CEO*
Andrew Hotchkies, *President*
Michelle Hotchkies, *Vice Pres*
EMP: 12
SQ FT: 38,000
SALES (est): 2.1MM **Privately Held**
SIC: 3081 Polyvinyl film & sheet

(G-1619)
FALCON AUDIO VIDEO INC (PA)
Also Called: Falcon Audio Video East
13560 E 463 Rd (74017-1083)
PHONE..................918 272-3969
Porter Falcon, *President*
EMP: 4
SQ FT: 2,400
SALES (est): 900K **Privately Held**
SIC: 3651 Audio electronic systems

(G-1620)
FIELDCO INC
9155 E Misty Dr (74019-1084)
PHONE..................918 266-1815
J L Field, *CEO*
EMP: 2
SALES (est): 112.7K **Privately Held**
SIC: 3544 Dies, steel rule

(G-1621)
FINISH LINE OF OKLAHOMA INC
15593 E 523 Rd (74019-3737)
PHONE..................918 341-8291
Lorrie Dahnke, *President*
▲ **EMP:** 5
SQ FT: 1,600
SALES (est): 633.6K **Privately Held**
SIC: 3199 5191 2321 Riding crops; equestrian equipment; men's & boys' furnishings

(G-1622)
FISH TALES LURE COMPANY LLC
24103 S Highway 66 (74019-0289)
PHONE..................918 814-6241
Cheri Doyle, *Principal*
EMP: 2
SALES (est): 98.8K **Privately Held**
SIC: 3949 Sporting & athletic goods

(G-1623)
FREEDOM MANUFACTURING LLC
24055 Amah Pkwy (74019-4302)
PHONE..................918 283-1520
EMP: 4
SQ FT: 3,000
SALES (est): 250K **Privately Held**
SIC: 3451 3599 Mfg Scrw Machine Products Mfg Industrial Machinery

(G-1624)
FROMAN WLDG U0026 FBRCTION INC
8032 E 480 Rd (74017-5269)
PHONE..................918 798-1050
Andrew Ehlmann, *Vice Pres*
Alex Nanna, *Project Mgr*
Lance Allen Froman, *Administration*
EMP: 1 **EST:** 2017
SALES (est): 81.8K **Privately Held**
WEB: www.fromanwelding.com
SIC: 7692 Welding repair

(G-1625)
GALAXY CHEMICALS LLC
6472 Tower Ln (74019-4500)
PHONE..................918 379-0820
Tariq Mahmood, *President*
Jason Mahmood, *Info Tech Mgr*
▲ **EMP:** 10
SQ FT: 10,518
SALES (est): 1.5MM **Privately Held**
SIC: 2899 2869 2819 Chemical preparations; industrial organic chemicals; industrial inorganic chemicals

(G-1626)
GLOBAL SEALCOATING INC
9603 Alawhe Dr (74019-4366)
PHONE..................918 283-2040
EMP: 2
SALES (est): 132.5K **Privately Held**
SIC: 2952 Asphalt felts & coatings

(G-1627)
GRAY EAGLE INDUSTRIES LLC
18974 E 480 Rd (74019-4194)
PHONE..................918 230-6652
Jay Floyd Bennett, *Administration*
EMP: 2 **EST:** 2012
SALES (est): 143.4K **Privately Held**
SIC: 3999 Manufacturing industries

(G-1628)
GREEN COUNTRY COMPRSR SVC LLC
11974 E 530 Rd (74019-5498)
PHONE..................918 906-6343
Ashley Piguet, *Mng Member*
EMP: 4
SALES (est): 577.9K **Privately Held**
SIC: 3563 Air & gas compressors

(G-1629)
GRETCHEN CAGLE PUBLICATIONS
1199 W Country Club Rd (74017-7124)
P.O. Box 2104 (74018-2104)
PHONE..................918 342-1080
EMP: 2
SALES (est): 98K **Privately Held**
SIC: 2731 8412 Books-Publishing/Printing Museum/Art Gallery

(G-1630)
GTS INDUSTRIES LLC
Also Called: GTS Ind.
1607 Forest Hill Dr (74017-9436)
PHONE..................918 706-2525
Greg Todd,
EMP: 2
SALES (est): 70.5K **Privately Held**
SIC: 3999 Manufacturing industries

(G-1631)
HEATH TECHNOLOGIES LLC
2405 S Hwy 66 (74017)
PHONE..................918 342-3222
Rodney Heath, *Mng Member*
Joel Burr,
Gary Schildt,
EMP: 35 **EST:** 2007
SALES (est): 5.1MM **Privately Held**
SIC: 3731 Drilling & production platforms, floating (oil & gas)

(G-1632)
HEJIN WALDRAN
Also Called: K & M Outfitters
9583 E Highway 88 (74017-0753)
PHONE..................918 408-3500
Hejin Waldran, *President*
EMP: 1
SALES (est): 50.9K **Privately Held**
SIC: 5963 7389 3537 3715 Direct selling establishments; ; industrial trucks & tractors; trucks, tractors, loaders, carriers & similar equipment; forklift trucks; truck trailers; truck farm

(G-1633)
HELTON CUSTOM KNIVES LLC
18633 S Fern Pl (74019-2869)
PHONE..................918 230-1773
Billy Helton, *Principal*
EMP: 2
SALES (est): 108.7K **Privately Held**
SIC: 3423 Hand & edge tools

(G-1634)
HENDERSON ORNAMENTAL IRON
2001 College Park Rd (74017-2006)
PHONE..................918 341-1089
Milton Henderson, *Owner*
EMP: 1
SALES (est): 84.4K **Privately Held**
SIC: 3446 Architectural metalwork

(G-1635)
HOOTY CREEK ALPACAS
23005 S Hooty Creek Rd (74019-2145)
PHONE..................918 284-5025
EMP: 2
SALES (est): 94.5K **Privately Held**
WEB: www.hootycreekalpacas.com
SIC: 2231 Alpacas, mohair: woven

(G-1636)
HOT ROD MACHINE TOOL LLC
13052 S Pine Ave (74017-0772)
PHONE..................918 508-1043
Allen Schuler, *President*
Kc Counce, *Vice Pres*
EMP: 2
SALES (est): 85.2K **Privately Held**
SIC: 3545 Machine tool accessories

(G-1637)
HOUSE OF TROPHIES
127 W Blue Starr Dr (74017-4226)
PHONE..................918 341-2111
Leslie George, *Owner*
EMP: 2
SALES (est): 87.8K **Privately Held**
SIC: 5999 3993 3499 3479 Trophies & plaques; signs & advertising specialties; fabricated metal products; metal coating & allied service; plastics products; automotive & apparel trimmings

(G-1638)
HY-H MANUFACTURING CO INC
Also Called: Hydro Hoist
915 W Blue Starr Dr (74017-2802)
PHONE..................918 341-6811
Joe Cox, *Manager*
▼ **EMP:** 40
SQ FT: 3,696
SALES (est): 9MM **Privately Held**
SIC: 3536 3534 Boat lifts; elevators & moving stairways

(G-1639)
HYPOWER INC
24012 Amah Pkwy (74019-4302)
PHONE..................918 341-6811
Michael Webber, *President*
Todd Elson, *Principal*

Claremore - Rogers County (G-1640)

EMP: 9
SALES (est): 1.2MM **Privately Held**
SIC: 3643 Current-carrying wiring devices

(G-1640)
INDUSTRIAL COATINGS OKLAHOMA
903 Star St (74017-4418)
PHONE..........................918 638-5606
Roy Jones, *Owner*
EMP: 2 EST: 2014
SALES (est): 155.4K **Privately Held**
SIC: 3479 Metal coating & allied service

(G-1641)
INDUSTRIAL ELECTRONICS REPAIR
Also Called: B & S Light Industries
24905 S Highway 66 (74019-2479)
PHONE..........................918 342-1160
Richard Young, *President*
Mike Young, *Vice Pres*
EMP: 20
SQ FT: 32,000
SALES: 1.5MM **Privately Held**
SIC: 3625 3679 7389 Industrial controls: push button, selector switches, pilot; electronic circuits; design, commercial & industrial

(G-1642)
INLAND MANUFACTURING LLC
6852 E Highway 20 (74019-0117)
PHONE..........................918 342-5733
EMP: 4
SQ FT: 7,500
SALES (est): 283.9K **Privately Held**
SIC: 3679 Mfg Electric Cable Systems

(G-1643)
JFJ INDUSTRIES INC
Also Called: Auto Pride
2301 El Anderson Blvd (74017-2121)
P.O. Box 1428 (74018-1428)
PHONE..........................918 342-2453
Joel F Jones, *President*
Ruby Jones, *Corp Secy*
David J Jones, *Vice Pres*
David Jones, *VP Sales*
EMP: 5
SQ FT: 8,750
SALES (est): 187.4K **Privately Held**
WEB: www.jfjind.com
SIC: 3728 Aircraft parts & equipment

(G-1644)
JIM GRIFFITH CUSTOM JEWELER
3207 Club St (74019-4987)
PHONE..........................918 342-0151
EMP: 1
SALES (est): 74K **Privately Held**
SIC: 5944 7631 3911 Ret Jewelry Watch/Clock/Jewelry Repair Mfg Precious Metal Jewelry

(G-1645)
JOHNSON WOODCRAFT
16210 S 4110 Rd (74017-9422)
PHONE..........................918 693-2388
EMP: 2
SALES (est): 129.2K **Privately Held**
SIC: 2511 Wood household furniture

(G-1646)
JORDAN WELDING & FABRICATION
14325 S 4170 Rd (74017-6840)
PHONE..........................918 346-7243
Michael Jordan, *Principal*
EMP: 1
SALES (est): 34.5K **Privately Held**
SIC: 7692 Welding repair

(G-1647)
K & B MACHINING INC
24055 Amah Pkwy (74019-4302)
PHONE..........................918 343-2620
Kevin Knight, *President*
Terri Webb, *Office Mgr*
Brian Knight, *Admin Sec*
EMP: 15
SQ FT: 2,500
SALES (est): 3.2MM **Privately Held**
WEB: www.k-bmachining.com
SIC: 3599 Machine shop, jobbing & repair

(G-1648)
K & D MANUFACTURING
816 W 1st St (74017-5412)
PHONE..........................918 923-6422
Dana Burd, *Officer*
EMP: 3
SALES (est): 213.2K **Privately Held**
SIC: 3999 Manufacturing industries

(G-1649)
KLASSEN ENTERPRISES INC
Also Called: Printing Plus
910 N J M Davis Blvd (74017-4043)
P.O. Box 2622 (74018-2622)
PHONE..........................918 342-1850
Mary Klassen, *President*
EMP: 9
SALES (est): 764K **Privately Held**
SIC: 2759 Commercial printing

(G-1650)
KNOCK ON WOOD CUSTOM
501 W Lowry Rd (74017-2115)
PHONE..........................918 261-6948
EMP: 1
SALES (est): 58.4K **Privately Held**
SIC: 2431 Millwork

(G-1651)
LOVE AIR CONDITIONING
Also Called: Love Heating & AC
122 W Will Rogers Blvd (74017-7017)
PHONE..........................918 341-0508
Timothy W Fleetwood, *Owner*
Julie Fleetwood, *Co-Owner*
EMP: 6 EST: 1949
SQ FT: 9,000
SALES (est): 421.2K **Privately Held**
WEB: www.loveairconditioning.com
SIC: 1711 3444 Warm air heating & air conditioning contractor; sheet metalwork

(G-1652)
MAD DOGS EMPORIUM
103 N Cherokee Ave (74017-7019)
PHONE..........................918 283-4480
EMP: 2
SALES (est): 124.9K **Privately Held**
SIC: 3931 Musical instruments

(G-1653)
MCMILLIAN WELDING LLC
25010 Singletree Ln (74019-3319)
PHONE..........................918 521-6886
Joshua McMillian,
EMP: 1
SALES (est): 76.4K **Privately Held**
SIC: 7692 Welding repair

(G-1654)
MICHELANGELO PROPERTIES LLC
16881 S 4200 Rd (74017-0967)
PHONE..........................918 341-4771
Michael J Howard,
EMP: 2
SALES (est): 109.5K **Privately Held**
SIC: 2731 Book publishing

(G-1655)
MIKET ADS INC
218 N Missouri Ave (74017-6807)
PHONE..........................918 341-2992
Mike Kedzior, *President*
EMP: 3
SALES (est): 200K **Privately Held**
SIC: 3993 5999 Signs & advertising specialties; banners

(G-1656)
MIKETADS INC
218 N Missouri Ave (74017-6807)
PHONE..........................918 341-2992
Mike Kedzior, *President*
EMP: 4
SQ FT: 2,600
SALES: 300K **Privately Held**
SIC: 3993 Signs & advertising specialties

(G-1657)
MITCHELLS SAUSAGE ROLLS
9459 Alawhe Dr (74019-4376)
PHONE..........................918 342-5852
Farron Mitchell, *Owner*
EMP: 2
SALES: 900K **Privately Held**
SIC: 2051 Cakes, bakery: except frozen

(G-1658)
MOSTMACHINE LLC
327 S Cherokee Ave (74017-8032)
PHONE..........................918 706-0393
Wayne Most, *Principal*
Ralph Wayne Most, *Mng Member*
EMP: 1
SALES: 150K **Privately Held**
SIC: 3599 Industrial machinery

(G-1659)
NEGATIVE ONE-EIGHTY
24747 S Highway 66 (74019-2480)
PHONE..........................918 852-2332
Roy Kulp, *Mng Member*
EMP: 6
SALES (est): 906.1K **Privately Held**
SIC: 3563 Air & gas compressors

(G-1660)
NEGATIVE ONE-EIGHTY CRYOGENIC
24747 S Highway 66 Unit A (74019-2480)
PHONE..........................918 261-7748
Roy Kulp, *CEO*
EMP: 2
SQ FT: 1,000
SALES (est): 110.8K **Privately Held**
SIC: 3563 Air & gas compressors

(G-1661)
NEWSPAPER HOLDING INC
Also Called: Claremore Daily Progress
315 W Will Rogers Blvd (74017-7021)
P.O. Box 248 (74018-0248)
PHONE..........................918 341-1101
EMP: 29 **Privately Held**
SIC: 2711 7313 Newspapers: publishing only, not printed on site; newspaper advertising representative
HQ: Newspaper Holding, Inc.
425 Locust St
Johnstown PA 15901
814 532-5102

(G-1662)
NEWSPAPER SERVICES
521 S Pine St (74017-4724)
PHONE..........................918 283-1564
EMP: 2
SALES (est): 71K **Privately Held**
SIC: 2711 Newspapers-Publishing/Printing

(G-1663)
NORTHEAST TCHNLGY CTR-CLRMORE
1901 N Highway 88 (74017-2209)
PHONE..........................918 342-8066
Rick Reimer, *Principal*
Melissa Oversahs, *Director*
Paula Reed, *Advisor*
EMP: 25
SALES (est): 1.4MM **Privately Held**
SIC: 7372 Educational computer software

(G-1664)
NUT HOUSE
26677 S Highway 66 (74019-2400)
PHONE..........................918 266-1604
Mike Emerson, *President*
EMP: 2
SALES (est): 147.6K **Privately Held**
SIC: 2099 2066 2051 5441 Almond pastes; chocolate & cocoa products; bread, cake & related products; nuts

(G-1665)
NXTNANO LLC
2201 El Anderson Blvd (74017-2119)
PHONE..........................918 923-4824
Justin Volpe, *General Mgr*
EMP: 30
SQ FT: 165,000
SALES: 3MM **Privately Held**
SIC: 2297 Nonwoven fabrics

(G-1666)
OFFICES ETC
Also Called: Office Everything
436 S Lynn Riggs Blvd (74017-7812)
PHONE..........................918 342-1501
Marv Gregory, *Owner*
EMP: 3
SALES (est): 238.5K **Privately Held**
SIC: 2759 5943 Commercial printing; office forms & supplies

(G-1667)
ON BEAT GOES
Also Called: CD and More
9652 E Shadowview Dr (74017-1484)
PHONE..........................918 342-5654
Nancy Goggins, *Owner*
Benny Bolen, *Co-Owner*
EMP: 2
SALES (est): 95K **Privately Held**
SIC: 3652 Compact laser discs, prerecorded

(G-1668)
PELCO STRUCTURAL LLC
1501 N Industrial Blvd (74017-2845)
PHONE..........................918 283-4004
Phil Albert, *President*
Kasey Scott, *Vice Pres*
Kelly Scott, *Vice Pres*
James Sutphen, *Vice Pres*
EMP: 72
SQ FT: 192,000
SALES (est): 42.6MM **Privately Held**
SIC: 3441 Fabricated structural metal

(G-1669)
PEMCO INC
15201 S Highway 66 (74017-2662)
PHONE..........................918 341-7500
Daniel Dyches, *Owner*
Andy Holt, *Sales Staff*
EMP: 3 EST: 2010
SALES (est): 265.1K **Privately Held**
WEB: www.pemcofab.com
SIC: 3842 Welders' hoods

(G-1670)
PHILLIPS PRINTING CO
7363 E Ridgeview Way (74019-2394)
PHONE..........................918 266-3373
Jesse Phillips, *Owner*
EMP: 2
SALES (est): 123.2K **Privately Held**
SIC: 2752 Commercial printing, offset

(G-1671)
PLAY 2 WIN ATHLETICS
514 N J M Davis Blvd (74017-5615)
PHONE..........................918 341-9500
Jeff Losornio, *Owner*
EMP: 7
SQ FT: 1,200
SALES: 275K **Privately Held**
SIC: 2395 5137 5661 5699 Embroidery products, except schiffli machine; sportswear, women's & children's; footwear, athletic; T-shirts, custom printed; screen printing

(G-1672)
PLUM GOLD JEWELERS & DESIGNERS
418 S Lynn Riggs Blvd (74017-7866)
PHONE..........................918 341-4716
Randy Smith, *Owner*
EMP: 3 EST: 1974
SQ FT: 1,600
SALES (est): 235.7K **Privately Held**
SIC: 5944 5094 3911 Jewelry, precious stones & precious metals; jewelry; jewelry, precious metal

(G-1673)
PRAXAIR DISTRIBUTION INC
5101 Sw Alliance Dr (74017)
PHONE..........................918 266-3210
Billy Joe Byrd, *Branch Mgr*
EMP: 35 **Privately Held**
SIC: 3585 2813 Refrigeration & heating equipment; refrigeration equipment, complete; carbon dioxide

HQ: Praxair Distribution, Inc.
10 Riverview Dr
Danbury CT 06810
203 837-2000

(G-1674)
PRINT SHOP
910 N J M Davis Blvd (74017-4043)
P.O. Box 2622 (74018-2622)
PHONE 918 342-3993
Mary Claussen, *Owner*
EMP: 8
SALES (est): 630.4K **Privately Held**
SIC: 2759 2796 2791 2789 Commercial printing; platemaking services; typesetting; bookbinding & related work; commercial printing, lithographic

(G-1675)
PROCESS EQUIPMENT MFG CO
15151 S Highway 66 (74017-2659)
PHONE 817 710-2826
EMP: 4
SALES (est): 327.4K **Privately Held**
SIC: 3443 Mfg Fabricated Plate Work

(G-1676)
PROMOS ADVERTISING PDTS INC
224 E 8th St (74017-7237)
PHONE 918 343-9675
Debbie Long, *Owner*
EMP: 5
SALES (est): 140K **Privately Held**
SIC: 5999 2759 Trophies & plaques; commercial printing

(G-1677)
QUALITY TRUSS CO INC
14852 E 530 Rd (74019-2583)
PHONE 918 543-2077
Richard Brown, *President*
Roberta Brown, *Corp Secy*
Rocky Brown, *Vice Pres*
EMP: 4
SALES: 750K **Privately Held**
SIC: 2439 Trusses, wooden roof

(G-1678)
RAM DESIGN INC
24454 S Orange Cv (74019-0273)
PHONE 918 342-4051
Richard A McGuire, *President*
Linda McGuire, *Vice Pres*
EMP: 2 **EST:** 1988
SALES (est): 154.3K **Privately Held**
WEB: www.ramdesigninc.net
SIC: 2426 Hardwood dimension & flooring mills

(G-1679)
READING EQUIPMENT & DIST LLC
2800 N Lynn Riggs Blvd (74017-3387)
PHONE 918 283-2999
Mark Robinson, *President*
EMP: 32
SALES (corp-wide): 1.2B **Privately Held**
SIC: 3713 3443 Truck bodies (motor vehicles); fabricated plate work (boiler shop)
HQ: Reading Equipment & Distribution, Llc
1363 Bowmansville Rd
Bowmansville PA 17507
717 445-6746

(G-1680)
RELIABLE MANUFACTURING CORP
9688 Alawhe Dr (74019-4366)
PHONE 918 341-1966
John Brumley, *President*
Kevin Brumley, *Vice Pres*
EMP: 8
SALES (est): 600K **Privately Held**
SIC: 3599 Machine shop, jobbing & repair

(G-1681)
REYNOLDS CUSTOM WOODWORKS
9488 E Mulberry Ln (74019-0262)
PHONE 918 595-5988
Shane Reynolds, *Principal*
EMP: 1
SALES (est): 54.1K **Privately Held**
SIC: 2431 Millwork

(G-1682)
RHODES PRINTING
1820 N Sioux Ave (74017-3133)
PHONE 918 965-1005
EMP: 2
SALES (est): 80.6K **Privately Held**
SIC: 2759 Screen printing

(G-1683)
RIVAL INNVTION SURFC ENGRG LLC
18307 S Quail Meadow Dr (74017-2750)
PHONE 918 978-7001
Joe Holmes,
EMP: 2
SALES (est): 180K **Privately Held**
SIC: 3724 Aircraft engines & engine parts

(G-1684)
ROTATIONAL TECHNOLOGIES INC
Also Called: Rotek
915 W Blue Starr Dr (74017-2802)
P.O. Box 1560 (74017-1560)
PHONE 918 343-1350
Michael Webber, *CEO*
Ron Liebl, *Principal*
EMP: 10 **EST:** 1990
SQ FT: 42,000
SALES (est): 1.6MM **Privately Held**
WEB: www.rotomoldusa.com
SIC: 3089 Injection molding of plastics

(G-1685)
SOLID ROCK CUSTOM FLOORING
14309 E 500 Rd (74019-1871)
PHONE 918 833-2884
EMP: 3
SALES: 85K **Privately Held**
SIC: 3996 Hard Surface Floor Coverings, Nec

(G-1686)
SOONER PALLET SERVICES INC
18215 Quail Creek Rd (74017-0918)
P.O. Box 518 (74018-0518)
PHONE 918 342-9663
Scott Foster, *President*
Lisa Foster, *Corp Secy*
EMP: 8
SALES (est): 1MM **Privately Held**
SIC: 2448 Pallets, wood

(G-1687)
SPACEBAR PUBLISHING LLC
8133 E 485 Rd (74019-5397)
PHONE 918 852-6311
EMP: 1
SALES (est): 37.5K **Privately Held**
SIC: 2741 Miscellaneous publishing

(G-1688)
STRIKE AN ARC WLDG FBRCTION LL
19496 Helt Rd (74017-3500)
PHONE 918 407-7964
David Shook, *Principal*
EMP: 1
SALES (est): 28.1K **Privately Held**
SIC: 7692 Welding repair

(G-1689)
STRIPER TINTING
4763 E 486 Rd (74019-5003)
PHONE 918 636-4043
Nathan Wiggin, *Principal*
EMP: 1 **EST:** 1996
SALES (est): 50.1K **Privately Held**
SIC: 3211 Window glass, clear & colored

(G-1690)
SWAN BROTHERS DAIRY INC
938 E 5th St (74017-6300)
PHONE 918 341-2069
Harley Swan Jr, *President*
Dorthy Swan, *Treasurer*
Diane Swan Williamson, *Manager*
EMP: 7 **EST:** 1900
SQ FT: 4,200
SALES (est): 860K **Privately Held**
WEB: www.swandairy.com
SIC: 2022 0241 2026 Natural cheese; dairy farms; fluid milk

(G-1691)
TANK & FUEL SOLUTIONS LLC
14800 S 4220 Rd (74017-0710)
P.O. Box 1709 (74018-1709)
PHONE 918 960-4361
Johnny M Wells, *Principal*
EMP: 2
SALES (est): 319.2K **Privately Held**
SIC: 5172 7694 4959 5171 Service station supplies, petroleum; motor repair services; environmental cleanup services; petroleum bulk stations & terminals; electric & other services combined; diesel fuels

(G-1692)
THOMAS APPRAISAL SERVICE
Also Called: Thomas Companies
18303 S 4200 (74017)
P.O. Box 1305 (74018-1305)
PHONE 918 341-5860
Richard Thomas, *Owner*
EMP: 3
SALES (est): 190K **Privately Held**
SIC: 3531 Construction machinery

(G-1693)
TOP SECRET CASE LLC
25567 Blackberry Blvd (74019-2740)
PHONE 918 521-0601
Luke Miller, *Mng Member*
EMP: 2
SALES (est): 150K **Privately Held**
SIC: 3523 Farm machinery & equipment

(G-1694)
TRIAD PERSONAL DEFENSE LLC
18833 S 4185 Rd (74017-0975)
PHONE 918 443-7803
Bill Hooker, *Principal*
EMP: 3
SALES (est): 165.9K **Privately Held**
SIC: 3812 Defense systems & equipment

(G-1695)
TRUBEND SYSTEMS INC
15505 E 520 Rd (74019-2139)
PHONE 918 342-3373
EMP: 2
SQ FT: 500
SALES (est): 160K **Privately Held**
SIC: 3699 Mfg Electrical Equipment/Supplies

(G-1696)
UNIQUELY YOURS LLC
411 N Owalla Ave Ste B (74017-5862)
PHONE 918 283-2228
Sandie Bowls, *Principal*
EMP: 3
SALES (est): 326.6K **Privately Held**
SIC: 2254 Shirts & t-shirts (underwear), knit

(G-1697)
UNITED AXLE
24850 Amah Pkwy (74019)
PHONE 918 344-1157
EMP: 3 **EST:** 2018
SALES (est): 341.8K **Privately Held**
WEB: www.unitedaxle.com
SIC: 3552 3312 Spindles, textile; pipes & tubes

(G-1698)
UNITED UTLTIES SPECIALISTS LLC
17211 S 4170 Rd (74017-3466)
P.O. Box 2145 (74018-2145)
PHONE 918 342-0840
Brain Green,
Todd Hindman,
EMP: 20
SALES: 3.3MM **Privately Held**
SIC: 3321 Water pipe, cast iron

(G-1699)
V5 CONTRACTING LLC
20632 E 440 Rd (74017-0571)
PHONE 918 720-4675
EMP: 2

SALES: 1K **Privately Held**
SIC: 1761 1442 1794 7692 Roofing/Siding Contr Construction Sand/Gravel Excavation Contractor Welding Repair Plumbing/Heat/Ac Contr

(G-1700)
VALMONT INDUSTRIES INC
Also Called: Valmont Coatings
25055 Alliance Dr (74019-4372)
PHONE 918 266-2800
Pete Smith, *Vice Pres*
Dan Cavanaugh, *Controller*
Kyle Uptmor, *Manager*
EMP: 100
SALES (corp-wide): 2.7B **Publicly Held**
WEB: www.valmont.com
SIC: 3441 Fabricated structural metal
PA: Valmont Industries, Inc.
1 Valmont Plz Ste 500
Omaha NE 68154
402 963-1000

(G-1701)
VANN METAL PRODUCTS INC
74754 Amah Pkwy (74017)
P.O. Box 254 (74018-0254)
PHONE 918 341-0469
EMP: 5
SQ FT: 4,800
SALES (est): 340K **Privately Held**
SIC: 3444 7692 3441 Mfg Sheet Metalwork Welding Repair Structural Metal Fabrication

(G-1702)
VINEYARD PLATING & SUP CO TX
2211 El Anderson Blvd (74017-2119)
P.O. Box 488 (74018-0488)
PHONE 918 342-0083
F C Witt, *President*
Jacqueline Witt, *Vice Pres*
▼ **EMP:** 15
SQ FT: 22,400
SALES: 850K **Privately Held**
SIC: 3081 Polyvinyl film & sheet

(G-1703)
W C BRADLEY CO
Also Called: Zebco
6505 Tower Ln (74019-4429)
PHONE 918 379-6238
Jeff N Moore, *Manager*
EMP: 7
SALES (corp-wide): 230.3MM **Privately Held**
SIC: 2048 Fish food
PA: W. C. Bradley Co.
1017 Front Ave
Columbus GA 31901
706 571-7000

(G-1704)
WALKE BROTHERS MEATS INC
9815 E 520 Rd Unit B (74019-0834)
PHONE 918 341-3236
John Walke, *President*
Bill Walke, *Vice Pres*
EMP: 8
SALES (est): 893.2K **Privately Held**
SIC: 2011 2013 7299 5421 Meat packing plants; sausages & other prepared meats; butcher service, processing only; meat markets, including freezer provisioners

(G-1705)
WYNN WYNN MEDIA
2105 Walnut Hill Ln (74019-3703)
P.O. Box 4, Welch (74369-0004)
PHONE 918 283-1834
Jeane Wynn, *Owner*
Tyson Wynn, *Vice Pres*
EMP: 2
SALES (est): 102.7K **Privately Held**
SIC: 2731 Books: publishing only

(G-1706)
XS WELDING COMPANY LLC
16144 E 460 Rd (74017-5356)
PHONE 918 346-2550
Chris Schiesel, *Administration*
EMP: 1 **EST:** 2015
SALES (est): 27.6K **Privately Held**
SIC: 7692 Welding repair

Claremore - Rogers County (G-1707)

(G-1707)
YONA MFG SOLUTIONS LLC
1102 N Oklahoma Ave (74017-6464)
PHONE.................................918 698-9713
Debra Lea Leipzig, *Owner*
EMP: 2
SALES (est): 103.6K **Privately Held**
SIC: 3999 Manufacturing industries

Clayton
Pushmataha County

(G-1708)
CLUBBS WOOD ART
60 Rte Hc 60 Box 33 6 Box (74536)
PHONE.................................918 569-4401
Justin Clubb, *Owner*
EMP: 5 EST: 1988
SALES: 90K **Privately Held**
SIC: 2499 Wood products

(G-1709)
DOS OKIES SIGNS & GRAPHICS
436 S 6th St (74536-5068)
P.O. Box 262 (74536-0262)
PHONE.................................918 569-7292
Crystal Russell, *Owner*
EMP: 1
SALES (est): 46K **Privately Held**
SIC: 3993 Signs & advertising specialties

(G-1710)
OUTLAW INDUSTRIES LLC
168344 N 4280 Rd (74536-5509)
PHONE.................................918 569-7555
Dusty Kirkes, *Principal*
EMP: 2
SALES (est): 58.5K **Privately Held**
SIC: 3999 Manufacturing industries

(G-1711)
WILL ROBINSON LOGGING LLC
171272 N 4250 Rd (74536-3205)
PHONE.................................918 569-4248
EMP: 2 EST: 2013
SALES (est): 120K **Privately Held**
SIC: 2411 Logging

Cleo Springs
Major County

(G-1712)
TIM SCOGGINS
Also Called: Scoggins Production Co
Highway 8 (73729)
PHONE.................................580 438-2476
Timothy Scoggins, *Owner*
EMP: 2
SALES (est): 124.1K **Privately Held**
SIC: 1389 Building oil & gas well foundations on site; derrick building, repairing & dismantling

(G-1713)
TROY HULETT
252334 E County Road 39 (73729-1087)
PHONE.................................580 922-5298
Troy Hulett, *Owner*
EMP: 2 EST: 2014
SALES (est): 147.7K **Privately Held**
SIC: 1381 Service well drilling

Cleveland
Pawnee County

(G-1714)
300 PSI INC
Also Called: Division Harris Mud Chem Inc
51249 E Highway 64 (74020-4043)
PHONE.................................918 358-5713
Todd Harris, *President*
Ken Harris, *Vice Pres*
EMP: 3
SALES (est): 199.8K **Privately Held**
SIC: 1389 Oil field services

(G-1715)
AMERICAN-CHIEF CO
Also Called: Cleveland American, The
212 S Broadway St (74020-4617)
P.O. Box 68 (74020-0068)
PHONE.................................918 358-2553
Rustin Ferguson, *Manager*
EMP: 7
SALES (corp-wide): 907.5K **Privately Held**
WEB: www.pawneenation.org
SIC: 2711 2752 Newspapers, publishing & printing; commercial printing, lithographic
PA: American-Chief Co
558 Illinois St
Pawnee OK 74058
918 762-2552

(G-1716)
ANSON MEMORIAL CO
606 N Division St (74020-2224)
PHONE.................................918 358-2504
Ron Anson, *Owner*
Debra Anson, *Principal*
EMP: 2
SALES (est): 110K **Privately Held**
SIC: 3281 7389 Tombstone engraving; cut stone & stone products

(G-1717)
BILL SNEED OILFIELD
607 Miami St Nw (74020-1007)
PHONE.................................918 358-3487
Bill Sneed, *Owner*
EMP: 3
SALES (est): 204.3K **Privately Held**
SIC: 1381 Drilling oil & gas wells

(G-1718)
CARNES PETROLEUM CORPORATION
1315 W Caddo St (74020-4050)
P.O. Box 29 (74020-0029)
PHONE.................................918 358-2541
Carl S Carnes, *President*
C Dwain Carnes, *President*
EMP: 5
SQ FT: 2,600
SALES (est): 563.9K **Privately Held**
SIC: 1311 Crude petroleum production; natural gas production

(G-1719)
CASA DOSA
Hwy 64 (74020)
PHONE.................................918 243-7277
Sandy Ford, *Owner*
EMP: 2
SALES (est): 125.6K **Privately Held**
SIC: 2399 Horse & pet accessories, textile

(G-1720)
CLEVELAND LEASE SERVICE INC
119 N Broadway St (74020-3809)
P.O. Box 597 (74020-0597)
PHONE.................................918 358-2791
Barry Sparks, *President*
Lori Sparks, *Admin Sec*
EMP: 15
SQ FT: 5,000
SALES (est): 3MM **Privately Held**
SIC: 1389 Oil field services

(G-1721)
DADDY HINKLES INC
2000 W Caddo St (74020-4100)
PHONE.................................918 358-2129
David Southard, *President*
Jo Rice, *Corp Secy*
EMP: 7 EST: 1994
SQ FT: 8,000
SALES: 930K **Privately Held**
WEB: www.daddyhinkles.com
SIC: 2035 5149 Pickles, sauces & salad dressings; spices & seasonings

(G-1722)
DAVIS PIPE TESTING COMPANY
Se Of City (74020)
P.O. Box 270 (74020-0270)
PHONE.................................918 358-5272
Frank L Davis, *Owner*
EMP: 17
SQ FT: 1,500
SALES (est): 1.2MM **Privately Held**
SIC: 1389 Pipe testing, oil field service

(G-1723)
FERGUSON & FERGUSON
Also Called: Clevand Newspaper
212 S Broadway St (74020-4617)
P.O. Box 68 (74020-0068)
PHONE.................................918 358-2553
Larry Ferguson, *Partner*
Rusty Ferguson, *Partner*
EMP: 4
SALES (est): 652.3K **Privately Held**
SIC: 2711 Newspapers, publishing & printing

(G-1724)
ICES CORPORATION
50152 Highway Dr (74020-7148)
P.O. Box 141446, Broken Arrow (74014-0014)
PHONE.................................918 358-5446
Mike Mills, *President*
Sandy Mills, *Admin Sec*
EMP: 25
SQ FT: 60,000
SALES (est): 5MM **Privately Held**
SIC: 3728 Aircraft assemblies, subassemblies & parts

(G-1725)
J&K MACHINING INC
1232 E Scenic Blf (74020-5709)
PHONE.................................918 243-7936
Jon De Cou, *Owner*
EMP: 1
SALES (est): 197.6K **Privately Held**
SIC: 3569 3541 3559 3449 General industrial machinery; machine tools, metal cutting type; special industry machinery; miscellaneous metalwork

(G-1726)
K & S HOTSHOT SERVICES LLC
998 W Oak Grove Rd (74020-3766)
PHONE.................................918 899-2649
EMP: 4
SALES (est): 190.6K **Privately Held**
SIC: 1389 Hot shot service

(G-1727)
MOKU LLC
110 E Delaware St (74020-4816)
PHONE.................................918 398-8479
James Gramblin, *President*
EMP: 3
SQ FT: 3,000
SALES (est): 254.3K **Privately Held**
SIC: 3851 Eyeglasses, lenses & frames

(G-1728)
NATURAL GAS COMMPRESSION CORP
102 N Elm St (74020)
P.O. Box 65 (74020-0065)
PHONE.................................918 243-7500
Jeff Phillips, *President*
EMP: 5 EST: 1984
SALES (est): 388.9K **Privately Held**
SIC: 1381 Drilling oil & gas wells

(G-1729)
NELSON EXPLORATION CORP
1567 S Timber Rd (74020-5725)
PHONE.................................405 853-6933
Patricia Nelson, *CEO*
EMP: 3
SALES (est): 330.7K **Privately Held**
SIC: 1311 1382 Crude petroleum production; natural gas production; oil & gas exploration services

(G-1730)
OKLAHOMA CELLULOSE INC
Also Called: Hughes Electric
733 N Cimarron Valley Rd (74020)
P.O. Box 193 (74020-0193)
PHONE.................................918 706-5279
Phil Hughes, *President*
Julia Hughes, *Vice Pres*
EMP: 7 EST: 2001
SALES (est): 1.1MM **Privately Held**
SIC: 1389 Oil field services

(G-1731)
OSAGE WIRELINE SERVICE INC
2 Miles S Of Cy On Hwy 64 (74020)
P.O. Box 490 (74020-0490)
PHONE.................................918 358-5155
Roger A Couffer, *Principal*
EMP: 6 EST: 1979
SQ FT: 3,200
SALES (est): 550K **Privately Held**
SIC: 1389 Oil field services

(G-1732)
R & M FLEET SERVICE INC
543 N Meadowood Pl (74020-3563)
PHONE.................................918 367-9326
Robert McQuary, *President*
EMP: 3
SQ FT: 36,000
SALES (est): 1.8MM **Privately Held**
SIC: 3533 7538 Oil field machinery & equipment; general truck repair

(G-1733)
S-T MAGI
53195 S 36700 Rd (74020-6486)
PHONE.................................918 358-2312
Robert Kilgore, *Partner*
John Kilgore, *Partner*
EMP: 2
SALES (est): 84.8K **Privately Held**
SIC: 7692 3533 3444 Welding repair; oil & gas field machinery; sheet metalwork

(G-1734)
SPESS DRILLING COMPANY (PA)
Also Called: Prairie Supply Co
200 S Broadway St (74020-4617)
PHONE.................................918 358-5831
Frank Spess, *Partner*
Carol Spess, *Partner*
Paul Spess, *Partner*
EMP: 12 EST: 1929
SALES (est): 2.1MM **Privately Held**
SIC: 1311 5084 5511 Crude petroleum production; natural gas production; oil well machinery, equipment & supplies; automobiles, new & used; pickups, new & used; vans, new & used

Clinton
Custer County

(G-1735)
A W POOL INC
Hwy 183 (73601)
PHONE.................................580 323-3454
Arvil W Pool, *President*
Mary Ruth Pool, *Corp Secy*
Keith Pool, *Vice Pres*
Winston Pool, *Vice Pres*
EMP: 9 EST: 1952
SQ FT: 1,800
SALES (est): 1MM **Privately Held**
SIC: 1781 3599 7692 Water well drilling; machine shop, jobbing & repair; welding repair

(G-1736)
ACE COMPLETIONS OK
1717 S 28th St (73601-5608)
PHONE.................................580 547-4088
EMP: 2
SALES (est): 88.7K **Privately Held**
SIC: 1389 Oil field services

(G-1737)
ACE NDT LLC
1430 S 14th St (73601-9723)
PHONE.................................580 323-8601
EMP: 2
SALES (est): 72K **Privately Held**
SIC: 1389 Oil field services

(G-1738)
BAKER HUGHES A GE COMPANY LLC
1620 S 13th St (73601-9502)
PHONE.................................580 323-4541
EMP: 2
SALES (corp-wide): 23.8B **Publicly Held**
SIC: 1389 Oil field services

GEOGRAPHIC SECTION

Clinton - Custer County (G-1766)

HQ: Baker Hughes Holdings Llc
17021 Aldine Westfield Rd
Houston TX 77073
713 439-8600

(G-1739)
BAKER PETROLITE LLC
1620 S 13th St (73601-9502)
PHONE.................580 323-4541
Jose Jacquez, *Branch Mgr*
EMP: 87 **Privately Held**
SIC: **1389** Oil field services
HQ: Baker Petrolite Llc
12645 W Airport Blvd
Sugar Land TX 77478
281 276-5400

(G-1740)
BAR-S FOODS CO
200 Locust Ave (73601-4148)
P.O. Box 339 (73601-0339)
PHONE.................580 331-1628
Ed Appel, *Manager*
EMP: 550 **Privately Held**
WEB: www.bar-s.com
SIC: **2013** 2015 Sausages & other prepared meats; poultry, processed
HQ: Bar-S Foods Co.
5090 N 40th St Ste 300
Phoenix AZ 85018
602 264-7272

(G-1741)
CDL CONSTRUCTION LLC
1642 Vanessa Dr (73601-5623)
PHONE.................580 323-2847
Charles Harris, *Mng Member*
Deana Harris,
EMP: 30
SALES (est): 2MM **Privately Held**
SIC: **1389** Oil field services

(G-1742)
CHAMPION DRILLING FLUIDS INC
Also Called: AES Drilling Fluids
3940 Custer Ave (73601-9131)
PHONE.................580 323-0044
J D Rambo, *Principal*
John M Traw, *Principal*
Donald A Pape, *Manager*
▲ EMP: 2
SALES (est): 166.1K **Privately Held**
SIC: **1389** Oil field services

(G-1743)
CIMAREX ENERGY CO
31990 I 40 Service Rd (73601)
PHONE.................580 330-0188
Geg McGee, *Branch Mgr*
EMP: 7
SALES (corp-wide): 2.3B **Publicly Held**
SIC: **1311** 1382 4924 Crude petroleum & natural gas production; oil & gas exploration services; natural gas distribution
PA: Cimarex Energy Co.
1700 N Lincoln St # 3700
Denver CO 80203
303 295-3995

(G-1744)
CLASSIC MARBLE DESIGN INC
3800 Sw Commerce (73601-3122)
PHONE.................580 323-4917
Toll Free:..............................888 -
John Russell, *President*
Bret Russell, *Vice Pres*
Stormie Hill, *Office Mgr*
EMP: 3
SALES: 1.6MM **Privately Held**
WEB: www.classicmarbledesign.com
SIC: **3281** 2434 Marble, building; cut & shaped; wood kitchen cabinets

(G-1745)
CLINTON DAILY NEWS COMPANY
Also Called: Clinton Daily News, The
522 Avant Ave (73601-3436)
PHONE.................580 323-5151
Rodney Sersoss, *President*
Carol Sander, *Corp Secy*
EMP: 18 EST: 1927
SQ FT: 7,000
SALES (est): 1.2MM **Privately Held**
WEB: www.clintondailynews.com
SIC: **2711** Commercial printing & newspaper publishing combined; newspapers, publishing & printing

(G-1746)
CLINTON ICE LLC
3750 Custer Ave (73601-9110)
P.O. Box 368 (73601-0368)
PHONE.................580 331-6060
Kathleen Davis, *Mng Member*
Tim Davis,
EMP: 18
SQ FT: 10,000
SALES: 2.2MM **Privately Held**
SIC: **2097** 5078 Manufactured ice; ice making machines

(G-1747)
DANLIN INDUSTRIES LLC (PA)
Also Called: Kel-Tech Mid-Con
801 Marshall Rd (73601-6020)
PHONE.................580 661-3248
Roger Floyd,
Doug Eyster,
Linda Floyd,
EMP: 200
SQ FT: 6,500
SALES (est): 32.9MM **Privately Held**
SIC: **3312** Chemicals & other products derived from coking

(G-1748)
DOLESE BROS CO
S Highway 183 (73601)
P.O. Box 875 (73601-0875)
PHONE.................580 323-1202
Jim Clymar, *Manager*
EMP: 3
SALES (corp-wide): 8.5MM **Privately Held**
SIC: **3273** 4212 Ready-mixed concrete; local trucking, without storage
PA: Dolese Bros. Co.
20 Nw 13th St
Oklahoma City OK 73103
405 235-2311

(G-1749)
DRIVER & SON WELDING SHOP
2 Miles N On Hwy 183 (73601)
P.O. Box 1656 (73601-1656)
PHONE.................580 323-1714
Kenneth Driver, *Owner*
Marciea Driver, *Co-Owner*
EMP: 3
SQ FT: 3,860
SALES (est): 131.5K **Privately Held**
SIC: **7692** Welding repair

(G-1750)
ENABLE OKLAHOMA INT TRANSM LLC
5 Mile E 1 And One Half S (73601)
PHONE.................580 323-7450
Mitch Kauk, *Manager*
EMP: 3
SALES (corp-wide): 12.3B **Publicly Held**
SIC: **1321** Natural gas liquids production
HQ: Enable Oklahoma Intrastate Transmission, Llc
499 W Sheridan Ave # 1500
Oklahoma City OK 73102
405 525-7788

(G-1751)
GOOD FILTER CO
505 Frisco Ave (73601-3441)
PHONE.................580 323-5200
Robert Haney, *Principal*
EMP: 1
SALES (est): 70.8K **Privately Held**
SIC: **3564** Filters, air: furnaces, air conditioning equipment, etc.

(G-1752)
HIRSCH3667 CORP
Also Called: Willco Hollow Metal
1749 S Highway 183 (73601-9533)
P.O. Box 1507 (73601-1507)
PHONE.................580 323-6966
EMP: 52
SALES (corp-wide): 11.9MM **Privately Held**
SIC: **3442** Mfg Hollow Metal Door Frames
PA: Hirsch3667 Corp
5700 Hannum Ave Ste 250
Culver City CA 90230

(G-1753)
INTEGRATED FLUID SYSTEMS LLC
22456 E 1078 Rd (73601-6003)
PHONE.................580 323-8431
EMP: 2 EST: 2011
SALES (est): 140K **Privately Held**
SIC: **1389** Oil/Gas Field Services

(G-1754)
JIGGS SMOKEHOUSE
10635 N 2230 Rd (73601-7747)
PHONE.................580 323-5641
Geoge Lawson, *Owner*
EMP: 2
SALES (est): 114.8K **Privately Held**
SIC: **5812** 2013 Barbecue restaurant; sausages & other prepared meats

(G-1755)
KINGFISHER RESOURCES INC
123 S 6th St (73601-3431)
P.O. Box 277 (73601-0277)
PHONE.................580 323-6097
Norb Rother, *President*
Don Rodolph, *Vice Pres*
EMP: 3
SQ FT: 1,000
SALES (est): 379.3K **Privately Held**
SIC: **1311** Crude petroleum production; natural gas production

(G-1756)
LEON KINDER
Also Called: Kinder's Shutter Shop
1514 Neptune Dr (73601-9706)
PHONE.................580 323-0365
Leon Kinder, *Owner*
EMP: 1 EST: 1996
SALES (est): 72K **Privately Held**
SIC: **2431** Window shutters, wood

(G-1757)
LINDERER PRINTING CO INC
221 Regency Dr (73601-3621)
P.O. Box 1313 (73601-1313)
PHONE.................580 323-2102
Jeff Linderer, *President*
Debbie Linderer, *Corp Secy*
Harold Linderer, *Vice Pres*
EMP: 10 EST: 1946
SQ FT: 8,800
SALES (est): 1MM **Privately Held**
SIC: **5943** 2752 2791 2789 Office forms & supplies; commercial printing, lithographic; typesetting; bookbinding & related work

(G-1758)
MARTINEZ FENCING CONSTRUCTION
301 N 4th St (73601-2817)
PHONE.................580 309-2046
Lucas Martinez, *Owner*
EMP: 15
SALES (est): 849.3K **Privately Held**
SIC: **1389** 1771 1799 1721 Construction, repair & dismantling services; concrete work; exterior concrete stucco contractor; fence construction; commercial painting; construction & civil engineering

(G-1759)
MORTON BUILDINGS INC
I40 W At Parkersburg Rd (73601)
P.O. Box 67 (73601-0067)
PHONE.................580 323-1172
Dean Taylor, *Branch Mgr*
Harold Hunter, *Manager*
EMP: 6
SALES (corp-wide): 462.5MM **Privately Held**
SIC: **5039** 3448 2452 Prefabricated buildings; prefabricated metal buildings; prefabricated wood buildings
PA: Morton Buildings, Inc.
252 W Adams St
Morton IL 61550
800 447-7436

(G-1760)
NABORS COMPLETION PROD SVCS CO
22096 Highway 73 (73601-2300)
PHONE.................580 323-0058
EMP: 39 **Privately Held**
SIC: **1389** Oil/Gas Field Services
HQ: Nabors Completion & Production Services Co.
515 W Greens Rd Ste 1170
Houston TX 77042
281 874-0035

(G-1761)
NEWPARK DRILLING FLUIDS LLC
Also Called: Mid Continent Completion
3600 S Hwy 183 (73601)
P.O. Box 1506 (73601-1506)
PHONE.................580 323-1612
Adam Cromer, *Manager*
EMP: 165
SALES (corp-wide): 820.1MM **Publicly Held**
SIC: **1389** Oil field services
HQ: Newpark Drilling Fluids Llc
21920 Merchants Way
Katy TX 77449

(G-1762)
NICHOLSON MONUMENT CO
638 N 6th St (73601-1914)
P.O. Box 275 (73601-0275)
PHONE.................580 323-7513
Darriel Nicholson, *Owner*
Doris Nicholson, *COO*
EMP: 6
SALES (est): 464.2K **Privately Held**
SIC: **3281** 5999 Monuments, cut stone (not finishing or lettering only); monuments, finished to custom order

(G-1763)
PEPSI COLA BTLG CLINTON OKLA
Also Called: Pepsi-Cola
712 Frisco Ave (73601-3321)
PHONE.................580 323-1666
Mark Nicholson, *President*
Debra Goucher, *Vice Pres*
EMP: 20 EST: 1938
SQ FT: 14,000
SALES (est): 450K **Privately Held**
WEB: www.clintonok.org
SIC: **2086** Carbonated soft drinks, bottled & canned

(G-1764)
RAYMOND L WEIL PBLICATIONS LLC
2717 Owen Dr (73601-5705)
PHONE.................580 323-4594
Raymond Weil, *Principal*
EMP: 1 **Privately Held**
SIC: **2741** Miscellaneous publishing

(G-1765)
RED COLLAR PET FOODS INC
1 Mars Rd (73601-9500)
PHONE.................580 323-3359
EMP: 100
SALES (corp-wide): 82.6MM **Privately Held**
SIC: **2047** Dog food
PA: Red Collar Pet Foods, Inc.
1550 W Mcewen Dr Ste 250
Franklin TN 37067
615 622-5259

(G-1766)
REDDY ICE CORPORATION
106 W Gary Blvd (73601-2802)
P.O. Box 368 (73601-0368)
PHONE.................580 323-3080
Tim Davis,
EMP: 30 **Privately Held**
WEB: www.reddyice.com
SIC: **2097** Manufactured ice
HQ: Reddy Ice Corporation
5720 Lyndon B Johnson Fwy # 200
Dallas TX 75240
214 526-6740

Clinton - Custer County (G-1767)

(G-1767)
SAMCO ANCHORS
22035 Highway 73 (73601-2300)
PHONE..................806 435-6870
Sam Tingelpon, *Owner*
Sam Tingelpon, *Owner*
EMP: 4
SALES (est): 296.9K **Privately Held**
SIC: 1389 Lease tanks, oil field: erecting, cleaning & repairing

(G-1768)
SECURITY METAL PRODUCTS CORP
1749 S Highway 183 (73601-9533)
P.O. Box 1507 (73601-1507)
PHONE..................580 323-6966
Dean Williams, *Branch Mgr*
EMP: 6
SALES (corp-wide): 9.3B **Privately Held**
SIC: 3442 Metal doors, sash & trim
HQ: Security Metal Products Corporation
5678 Concours
Ontario CA 91764
310 641-6690

(G-1769)
SOUTHWEST INTERIORS INC
Also Called: Custom Picture Framing
421 Frisco Ave (73601-3439)
P.O. Box 742 (73601-0742)
PHONE..................580 323-3050
Penny Carpenter, *President*
EMP: 2
SQ FT: 5,000
SALES: 60K **Privately Held**
WEB: www.swintandcertifiedtravel.4my-deals.com
SIC: 4724 2499 Travel agencies; picture & mirror frames, wood

(G-1770)
SPORTCHASSIS LLC
2300 S 13th St (73601-9529)
PHONE..................580 323-4100
Alan Aneshansley, *CEO*
EMP: 98
SQ FT: 300,000
SALES (est): 19.8MM **Privately Held**
SIC: 3711 Motor vehicles & car bodies

(G-1771)
TALL BOYS TOYS
2410 W Commerce Rd (73601-7734)
PHONE..................580 323-2765
Cindy Whitaker, *Owner*
EMP: 1 EST: 2010
SALES (est): 78.9K **Privately Held**
WEB: www.tallboystoys.com
SIC: 3715 5012 3799 5084 Truck trailers; trailers for passenger vehicles; trailers for trucks, new & used; horse trailers, except fifth-wheel type; trailers, industrial

(G-1772)
VANS TRAILER SALES
1012 Scissortail Dr (73601-5433)
PHONE..................580 323-3999
Van Lasley, *Principal*
EMP: 2
SALES (est): 149.6K **Privately Held**
SIC: 3799 Trailers & trailer equipment

(G-1773)
YIPPEE AY-O-K WINERY
420 S 3rd St (73601-4110)
PHONE..................580 515-8214
EMP: 2
SALES (est): 127K **Privately Held**
WEB: www.yippeeayok.com
SIC: 2084 Wines

Coalgate
Coal County

(G-1774)
A & W MACHINE LLC
1410 S Highway 75 (74538)
P.O. Box 211 (74538-0211)
PHONE..................580 927-1188
Greg Abales, *Partner*
Floyd Williamson, *Principal*
EMP: 7
SQ FT: 25,000
SALES (est): 1.3MM **Privately Held**
SIC: 3549 Metalworking machinery

(G-1775)
BOB LUMBER & GRAIN LLC
Also Called: B.O.B. Contracting
17301 Lake St (74538-5026)
P.O. Box 309 (74538-0309)
PHONE..................580 927-3168
Chuck Horton,
EMP: 12
SQ FT: 2,000
SALES (est): 1.6MM **Privately Held**
SIC: 4212 1389 5082 Lumber & timber trucking; oil field services; excavating machinery & equipment

(G-1776)
BRIAN RINGELS
Also Called: Arrow-R Construction
110 N Ada St (74538-4202)
PHONE..................580 927-6144
Brian Ringels, *Owner*
EMP: 1
SALES (est): 46.4K **Privately Held**
SIC: 7692 Welding repair

(G-1777)
CARDINAL MIDSTREAM LLC
17145 Coutry Rd 3790 (74538)
P.O. Box 430 (74538-0430)
PHONE..................580 927-2799
EMP: 2
SALES (est): 174K **Privately Held**
SIC: 1382 Oil & gas exploration services

(G-1778)
COALGATE RECORD REGISTER
Also Called: Coalgate Newspaper
602 E Lafayette Ave (74538-4018)
P.O. Box 327 (74538-0327)
PHONE..................580 927-2355
Bill Robinson, *Owner*
EMP: 3
SALES (est): 150K **Privately Held**
WEB: www.coalgaterecordregister.com
SIC: 2711 Newspapers: publishing only, not printed on site

(G-1779)
DU-ANN CO INC (PA)
Also Called: Priority Dodge
8 Mi W Of Town On Hwy 31 (74538)
P.O. Box 5 (74538-0005)
PHONE..................580 428-3315
Robert Dodge, *President*
EMP: 5
SQ FT: 4,000
SALES (est): 705.1K **Privately Held**
SIC: 3545 3823 Gauges (machine tool accessories); industrial instrmnts msrmnt display/control process variable

(G-1780)
H L CUSTOM PROCESSING
17208 County Road 3760 (74538-5311)
PHONE..................580 927-5408
EMP: 3
SALES (est): 175.6K **Privately Held**
SIC: 3471 Plating & polishing

(G-1781)
HEAVYBILT MFG INC
38038 Us Highway 75 (74538-5001)
PHONE..................580 927-3003
Steven T Cody, *President*
Shannon Whitehead, *Admin Asst*
EMP: 55
SALES: 1.5MM **Privately Held**
SIC: 3523 Crop storage bins

(G-1782)
M & W OILFIELD SERVICE LLC
Inman Rd Hwy 75 N (74538)
P.O. Box 366 (74538-0366)
PHONE..................580 927-2200
Albert Mowdy,
Agnes Faire,
Bobby Wardrope,
EMP: 4
SALES (est): 310K **Privately Held**
SIC: 1389 Oil field services

(G-1783)
RAWHIDE DIRT WORKS
37427 State Highway 31 (74538-3898)
PHONE..................580 367-5242
Josh Brecheen, *Principal*
EMP: 1
SALES (est): 49.1K **Privately Held**
WEB: www.rawhidedirtworks.com
SIC: 3111 Rawhide

(G-1784)
TEX STAR AG LLC
16774 County Road 3820 (74538-3838)
PHONE..................580 579-9877
Barbara Bonner-Stephens,
EMP: 1
SALES (est): 47.2K
SALES (corp-wide): 130.3K **Privately Held**
SIC: 2879 7389 Agricultural chemicals;
PA: Reata Group Llc
16774 County Road 3820
Coalgate OK 74538
580 579-9877

Colbert
Bryan County

(G-1785)
LEATHER GUNS & ETC
216 S Collins St (74733-2015)
P.O. Box 117 (74733-0117)
PHONE..................580 296-2616
William Weaver, *Owner*
Sylvia Weaver, *Co-Owner*
EMP: 10
SALES: 600K **Privately Held**
WEB: www.leathergunsetc.com
SIC: 2295 3484 Leather, artificial or imitation; guns (firearms) or gun parts, 30 mm. & below

(G-1786)
RV STATION LTD
411 Sherrard St (74733-2104)
PHONE..................888 466-1384
Christin Falcone, *Partner*
EMP: 2
SALES (corp-wide): 4.1MM **Privately Held**
WEB: www.rvstationbryan.com
SIC: 5511 3799 Automobiles, new & used; recreational vehicles
PA: Rv Station, Ltd.
4520 State Highway 6 S
College Station TX 77845
979 778-8000

(G-1787)
W&W ENTERPRISES
261 Elnora Ln (74733)
P.O. Box 342, Cartwright (74731-0342)
PHONE..................580 434-2736
Ronnie Wines, *Owner*
EMP: 1
SALES (est): 42.8K **Privately Held**
SIC: 7692 1794 1795 Welding repair; excavation work; wrecking & demolition work

(G-1788)
WELDCO MFG
350 S Franklin St (74733-2000)
PHONE..................580 296-1585
Jacob Pearson, *Owner*
EMP: 8
SALES (est): 1.6MM **Privately Held**
WEB: www.weldcomfg.com
SIC: 3399 3441 Primary metal products; fabricated structural metal

Colcord
Delaware County

(G-1789)
DORSSERS USA INC
3350 Highway 412 (74338-1438)
PHONE..................918 422-5881
Jeff Zimmer, *Treasurer*
EMP: 8
SALES (est): 1MM
SALES (corp-wide): 8MM **Privately Held**
SIC: 3532 Pellet mills (mining machinery)
PA: Dorssers Inc
29 Industrial Ave
Blenheim ON N0P 1
519 676-8113

(G-1790)
TALKING HANDS PUPPETS
10342 E 550 Rd (74338-2888)
PHONE..................918 868-5553
Sandy Solis, *Principal*
EMP: 1
SALES (est): 67.3K **Privately Held**
SIC: 3999 Furs

(G-1791)
TDS PORTABLE BUILDINGS LLC
21239 Us Highway 412 (74338-3526)
PHONE..................918 422-4009
Scot Nelson, *Mng Member*
Judy Maynard, *Manager*
EMP: 1
SALES (est): 171.8K **Privately Held**
WEB: www.tdsbuildings.com
SIC: 3448 Prefabricated metal buildings

Coleman
Johnston County

(G-1792)
A-1 INDUSTRIES LLC
12520 Ok Highway 48 S (73432-1226)
PHONE..................580 380-2328
EMP: 2
SALES (est): 59.2K **Privately Held**
SIC: 3999 Manufacturing industries

(G-1793)
CARDINAL FG MINERALS LLC
13030 E Swamp Creek Rd (73432)
PHONE..................580 367-2123
Sall Peck, *Partner*
Shau Bann, *Mng Member*
EMP: 25
SQ FT: 5,000
SALES (est): 4.8MM **Privately Held**
WEB: www.cardinalcorp.com
SIC: 2819 1442 Industrial inorganic chemicals; sand mining

(G-1794)
DOLESE BROS CO
13982 W Crusher Rd (73432-8852)
PHONE..................580 937-4889
Daryl Stevens, *Branch Mgr*
EMP: 19
SALES (corp-wide): 8.5MM **Privately Held**
SIC: 5032 5211 1422 Stone, crushed or broken; masonry materials & supplies; crushed & broken limestone
PA: Dolese Bros. Co.
20 Nw 13th St
Oklahoma City OK 73103
405 235-2311

(G-1795)
HARRISON ROOF TRUSS CO
Also Called: Coleman Roof Services
9240 Ok Highway 48 S (73432-1242)
PHONE..................580 937-4900
Mike Harrison, *Owner*
EMP: 5
SALES: 400K **Privately Held**
SIC: 2439 Trusses, wooden roof

(G-1796)
HOURGLASS TRANSPORT LLC
9805 Ok Highway 48 S (73432-1215)
PHONE..................580 937-4569
Paul Schanz, *Opers Mgr*
Billy White,
EMP: 7
SALES (est): 866.9K **Privately Held**
SIC: 3799 3231 Horse trailers, except fifth-wheel type; products of purchased glass

GEOGRAPHIC SECTION

Collinsville - Tulsa County (G-1828)

(G-1797)
NENOS HOMEMADE CANDLES LLC
13085 E Egypt Rd (73432-8572)
PHONE 580 367-9874
Melvin Eugene Morgan, *Principal*
EMP: 1
SALES (est): 39.6K **Privately Held**
SIC: 3999 Candles

Collinsville
Tulsa County

(G-1798)
ADC QUALITY MFG
12348 N 97th East Ave (74021-4817)
PHONE 918 808-2329
EMP: 2
SALES (est): 97.6K **Privately Held**
SIC: 3999 Manufacturing industries

(G-1799)
ALL ELECTRONIC AND MORE LLC
9742 E 182nd Pl N (74021-6013)
PHONE 918 557-5410
Bee Lor,
EMP: 7 EST: 2014
SALES: 443K **Privately Held**
SIC: 3679 3671 Electronic circuits; electron tubes

(G-1800)
ATLAS INSTRUMENT & MFG CO
16301 E 123rd St N (74021-5883)
PHONE 918 371-1976
Robert Guptill, *Owner*
Joyce Guptill, *Co-Owner*
EMP: 3
SALES: 500K **Privately Held**
SIC: 3599 3533 Machine shop, jobbing & repair; oil & gas field machinery

(G-1801)
B & B SHEET METAL HEAT & A INC
13217 N 91st East Ave (74021-3947)
P.O. Box 278 (74021-0278)
PHONE 918 371-1335
David Wilson, *President*
Clint Morgan, *Vice Pres*
EMP: 4
SQ FT: 1,800
SALES (est): 417.9K **Privately Held**
SIC: 3444 Sheet metalwork

(G-1802)
BASKINS MACHINED PRODUCTS LLC
12645 N 103rd East Ave (74021-4878)
PHONE 918 284-4298
Josh Baskins, *Partner*
Andrew Baskins, *Partner*
EMP: 2
SQ FT: 28,000
SALES (est): 350K **Privately Held**
SIC: 7389 3599 Metal cutting services; machine shop, jobbing & repair

(G-1803)
BIGFOOT PRINTS LLC
315 W Main St (74021-3305)
PHONE 918 805-0543
Michael Moreno, *Owner*
EMP: 6 EST: 2007
SQ FT: 2,400
SALES (est): 19.4K **Privately Held**
SIC: 2752 3993 Commercial printing, lithographic; letters for signs, metal

(G-1804)
BOB GENE MOORE
Also Called: Moore Oil & Gas
40401 N 4010 Rd (74021-6334)
PHONE 918 371-4381
Bob Gene Moore, *Owner*
EMP: 3
SQ FT: 2,400
SALES: 109K **Privately Held**
SIC: 1389 1311 6512 6514 Oil field services; crude petroleum production; natural gas production; nonresidential building operators; dwelling operators, except apartments; mobile home site operators

(G-1805)
CHARLES H COLPITT
Also Called: Colpitt Charles H Oil Prod
12328 N Sheridan Rd (74021-7107)
PHONE 918 371-2455
Charles H Colpitt, *Owner*
EMP: 5
SQ FT: 1,500
SALES (est): 417.8K **Privately Held**
SIC: 1311 Crude petroleum production; natural gas production

(G-1806)
COPPEDGE SEPTIC TANK
Highway 169 & 156th St N (74021)
PHONE 918 371-4549
Bob Coppedge, *Owner*
EMP: 1
SALES (est): 198.6K **Privately Held**
SIC: 5039 3272 5211 Septic tanks; concrete products; masonry materials & supplies

(G-1807)
CROSSROADS LED LLC
10710 E 119th Ct N (74021-5539)
PHONE 918 504-6595
Dana Stefanoff, *President*
Buddy Stefanoff, *Vice Pres*
EMP: 2
SQ FT: 1,200
SALES: 120K **Privately Held**
WEB: www.crossroadsled.com
SIC: 3646 Ornamental lighting fixtures, commercial

(G-1808)
DARLING INGREDIENTS INC
915 N 5th St (74021-2513)
P.O. Box 86 (74021-0086)
PHONE 918 371-2528
Mike Molini, *General Mgr*
EMP: 35
SQ FT: 12,500
SALES (corp-wide): 3.3B **Publicly Held**
WEB: www.darlingii.com
SIC: 2077 2048 Grease rendering, inedible; prepared feeds
PA: Darling Ingredients Inc.
5601 N Macarthur Blvd
Irving TX 75038
972 717-0300

(G-1809)
DEBORAH C MONTGOMERY
Also Called: Pleasant Expressions
15710 E 146th St N (74021-6896)
PHONE 918 527-9375
Deborah C Montgomery, *Owner*
EMP: 1
SALES (est): 41.7K **Privately Held**
SIC: 3999 Wreaths, artificial; artificial flower arrangements; sprays, artificial & preserved

(G-1810)
DIGITAL PRINTS PLUS INC
5966 E 138th St N (74021-5745)
P.O. Box 2894, Tulsa (74101-2894)
PHONE 918 520-7630
Jason Bachman, *President*
EMP: 2 EST: 2013
SQ FT: 2,500
SALES: 200K **Privately Held**
SIC: 2752 Commercial printing, offset

(G-1811)
H & H MUFFLER WHSE & MFG CO
Also Called: Quality Exhaust Sales
10301 E 126th St N (74021-3995)
P.O. Box 393 (74021-0393)
PHONE 918 371-9633
Rubin Hearn, *President*
Goldie Hearn, *Vice Pres*
Jeff Hearn, *Admin Sec*
EMP: 23
SQ FT: 30,000
SALES (est): 4.1MM **Privately Held**
SIC: 3714 Mufflers (exhaust), motor vehicle

(G-1812)
HART BROTHERS WELDING
Also Called: Hart, Elzie
17315 N Memorial Dr (74021-4282)
PHONE 918 697-5682
Elzie Hart, *Owner*
EMP: 2
SQ FT: 2,400
SALES (est): 119K **Privately Held**
SIC: 7692 3465 Welding repair; body parts, automobile: stamped metal

(G-1813)
HELEN MURPHY COLPITT TRUST
118 S 11th St (74021-3101)
P.O. Box 128 (74021-0128)
PHONE 918 371-9930
Helen Murphy, *Owner*
Mary Wood, *Bookkeeper*
EMP: 2
SQ FT: 265
SALES (est): 192.9K **Privately Held**
SIC: 1311 6799 Crude petroleum production; investors

(G-1814)
JOHNSON MACHINE INC
Also Called: Jmi
226 S 2nd St (74021-3303)
PHONE 918 371-7537
Robert Johnson, *President*
Gene Johnson, *Treasurer*
Tamara Johnson, *Admin Sec*
EMP: 20 EST: 1997
SALES: 2MM **Privately Held**
SIC: 3599 Machine shop, jobbing & repair

(G-1815)
LEWIS INDUSTRIES CORP
816 N 5th St (74021-2501)
P.O. Box 624 (74021-0624)
PHONE 918 371-2596
George E Lewis, *President*
EMP: 48
SQ FT: 20,000
SALES (est): 7.5MM **Privately Held**
SIC: 3498 3443 Fabricated pipe & fittings; fabricated plate work (boiler shop); vessels, process or storage (from boiler shops): metal plate

(G-1816)
LINN ENERGY LLC
216 N 20th St (74021-1605)
PHONE 281 605-4100
EMP: 2
SALES (est): 81.9K **Privately Held**
SIC: 1382 Oil & gas exploration services

(G-1817)
MULE HUNTING CLOTHES INC
19723 E 126th St N (74021-6269)
PHONE 601 856-5169
Michael T Franklin, *President*
Jim Ward, *Shareholder*
EMP: 2
SALES: 250K **Privately Held**
SIC: 2329 2339 Hunting coats & vests, men's; women's & misses' athletic clothing & sportswear

(G-1818)
MYSKEY WELDING
16718 N 137th East Ave (74021-4489)
PHONE 918 371-4906
EMP: 1
SALES (est): 56.5K **Privately Held**
SIC: 7692 Welding Repair

(G-1819)
OWASSO PRESSUREWASHING LLC
10956 E 176th St N (74021-4836)
PHONE 918 557-4059
Nicholas Eckerd, *Principal*
EMP: 5 EST: 2012
SALES: 500K **Privately Held**
WEB: www.powerwashingtulsa.com
SIC: 3589 High pressure cleaning equipment

(G-1820)
QUARTER MIDGETS OF AMERICA
310 S Avenue G (74021-3625)
P.O. Box 1070, Riverton IL (62561-1070)
PHONE 918 371-9410
Charles Cagle, *Principal*
EMP: 3
SALES (est): 167.7K **Privately Held**
SIC: 3131 Footwear cut stock

(G-1821)
RIVER INDUSTRIES LLC
12610 N Garnett Rd (74021-5473)
PHONE 918 406-8991
Jordan E Scott, *Mng Member*
EMP: 1
SALES: 50K **Privately Held**
SIC: 3499 Metal household articles

(G-1822)
ROCKIN DOLLS DENIM
10759 E 122nd St N (74021-5558)
PHONE 918 402-6151
EMP: 1
SALES (est): 54.2K **Privately Held**
SIC: 2211 Denims

(G-1823)
SALINA JOURNAL
17214 E 119th St N (74021-5145)
PHONE 785 822-1470
Jeanie Warner, *Executive*
EMP: 2
SALES (est): 71K **Privately Held**
SIC: 2711 Newspapers, publishing & printing

(G-1824)
SALLEE OIL CORP
2115 W Broadway St (74021)
P.O. Box 550 (74021-0550)
PHONE 918 371-2290
George L Sallee Jr, *President*
Delores A Sallee, *Corp Secy*
Gregory Sallee, *Vice Pres*
Lincoln Sallee, *Vice Pres*
Stan Sallee, *Vice Pres*
EMP: 6
SALES (est): 750K **Privately Held**
SIC: 1311 Crude petroleum production; natural gas production

(G-1825)
STITCH WITCH
2411 Black Jack Ct (74021-4063)
PHONE 918 371-3568
Terry Barwell, *Owner*
EMP: 1
SALES: 25K **Privately Held**
SIC: 2395 Embroidery & art needlework

(G-1826)
STOUT MANUFACTURING LLC
10903 E 166th St N (74021-4250)
PHONE 918 371-7700
Lori Stout, *Mng Member*
EMP: 3
SQ FT: 6,000
SALES: 180K **Privately Held**
SIC: 3599 Machine shop, jobbing & repair

(G-1827)
TIMES STAR
1122 W Main St Ste A (74021-3107)
PHONE 918 710-5740
EMP: 3
SALES (est): 110.6K **Privately Held**
SIC: 2711 Newspapers, publishing & printing

(G-1828)
VICTORY ENERGY OPERATIONS LLC (PA)
10701 E 126th St N (74021-3872)
PHONE 918 274-0023
John C Viskup Jr, *CEO*
Larry Edwards, *Ch of Bd*
Robert Williams, *COO*
Keith Brockman, *Production*
Thomas Dwyer, *Senior Buyer*
▼ EMP: 210
SQ FT: 100,000

Collinsville - Tulsa County (G-1829)

SALES (est): 84.6MM **Privately Held**
SIC: 3823 Boiler controls: industrial, power & marine type

(G-1829)
WILDCAT FIELD SERVICES LLC
123b N 14th St (74021-2209)
PHONE..................918 606-6217
Chris Rozzell, *Branch Mgr*
EMP: 3
SALES (corp-wide): 8MM **Privately Held**
SIC: 1389 Pipe testing, oil field service
PA: Field Wildcat Services Llc
8333 Douglas Ave Ste 300
Dallas TX 75225
214 363-8220

(G-1830)
WILNAT INCORPORATED
Also Called: Koons Gas Measurement
15332 N 149th East Ave (74021-6800)
PHONE..................918 640-0003
Benight Terry, *Principal*
Terry Benight, *Opers Mgr*
Shane Goossen, *Manager*
Steve Wood, *Manager*
EMP: 1
SALES (corp-wide): 217.5K **Privately Held**
WEB: www.kgmgas.com
SIC: 3823 Industrial instrmnts msrmnt display/control process variable
PA: Wilnat, Incorporated
10934 E 55th Pl
Tulsa OK 74146
918 794-9494

(G-1831)
WORSTELL OIL
10116 E 156th St N (74021-5918)
PHONE..................918 371-5425
Michael H Worstell, *Owner*
EMP: 4
SALES (est): 243.4K **Privately Held**
SIC: 1311 Crude petroleum production

Comanche
Stephens County

(G-1832)
3B INDUSTRIES INC
2 3b Rd St 3 (73529)
P.O. Box 37 (73529-0037)
PHONE..................580 439-8876
John Brown Sr, *President*
John Brown Jr, *Vice Pres*
William Brown, *Vice Pres*
EMP: 15
SQ FT: 15,000
SALES (est): 3.2MM **Privately Held**
SIC: 5999 3589 5169 Cleaning equipment & supplies; car washing machinery; detergents & soaps, except specialty cleaning

(G-1833)
ACCESSORIES-TO-GO
Also Called: Reba Tidwell Beck
212 Oak Main Ave (73529-1462)
PHONE..................580 467-7408
Reba Beck, *Owner*
EMP: 1
SALES: 25K **Privately Held**
SIC: 5621 5632 3171 5023 Ready-to-wear apparel, women's; teenage apparel; costume jewelry; women's handbags & purses; decorating supplies

(G-1834)
CHARLIES WELDING
401 Hickory Ave (73529-2637)
PHONE..................580 467-2266
Charlie Ralls, *Owner*
EMP: 1
SALES: 6K **Privately Held**
SIC: 7692 Welding repair

(G-1835)
COLT FERRELL INDUSTRIES LLC
273814 E 1810 Rd (73529-7236)
PHONE..................580 439-6106
EMP: 2

SALES (est): 135.7K **Privately Held**
SIC: 3999 Manufacturing industries

(G-1836)
COMANCHE BIT SERVICE INC
2 Miles North Hwy 81 (73529)
P.O. Box 267 (73529-0267)
PHONE..................580 439-6424
Jimmy Lynn Diehl, *President*
Beverly Diehl, *Vice Pres*
◆ EMP: 7
SQ FT: 5,000
SALES (est): 1.1MM **Privately Held**
SIC: 3533 7311 Bits, oil & gas field tools: rock; advertising agencies

(G-1837)
COMANCHE LEATHER WORKS INC
104a Village Mall (73529-2431)
PHONE..................580 439-6276
EMP: 2
SALES (est): 136K **Privately Held**
SIC: 3199 Leather goods

(G-1838)
COMANCHE SPORTS GROUP LLC
281645 E 1790 Rd (73529-7728)
PHONE..................580 439-5230
Nick Reed, *Owner*
EMP: 2
SALES (est): 67.9K **Privately Held**
SIC: 2711 Newspapers, publishing & printing

(G-1839)
COMANCHE TIMES
404 N Rodeo Dr (73529-1426)
P.O. Box 580 (73529-0580)
PHONE..................580 439-6500
Steven Bolton, *Owner*
EMP: 1
SALES (est): 61.2K **Privately Held**
SIC: 2711 Newspapers, publishing & printing

(G-1840)
CORNERSTONE LEATHER
179867 N 2800 Rd (73529-7769)
PHONE..................817 598-0367
James Chambers, *Principal*
EMP: 1
SALES (est): 59.9K **Privately Held**
SIC: 3199 Leather goods

(G-1841)
GRAHAM JEWELERS
219 Oak Main Ave (73529-1465)
P.O. Box 237 (73529-0237)
PHONE..................580 439-6680
John Graham, *Owner*
▲ EMP: 2
SQ FT: 1,400
SALES (est): 160K **Privately Held**
SIC: 5944 3911 Jewelry, precious stones & precious metals; jewelry, precious metal

(G-1842)
J C & J MACHINE & AUTO
9950 E 1880 Rd (73529-8901)
PHONE..................580 439-5919
Junior D Waller, *Owner*
EMP: 8 EST: 1996
SQ FT: 10,000
SALES (est): 400K **Privately Held**
SIC: 3599 Machine shop, jobbing & repair

(G-1843)
MYSTIK RIVER WOODWORKS
711 Church Ave (73529-1025)
PHONE..................580 606-0071
Roger Watters, *Principal*
EMP: 1
SALES (est): 54.1K **Privately Held**
SIC: 2431 Millwork

(G-1844)
PAULA GALLAHER
Also Called: Gallaher Printing
185939 N 2810 Rd (73529-4604)
PHONE..................580 439-6484
Paula Gallaher, *Principal*
EMP: 2

SALES (est): 96K **Privately Held**
SIC: 2752 Commercial printing, lithographic

(G-1845)
SAM S WELDING
274255 E 1800 Rd (73529-7100)
PHONE..................580 470-5725
EMP: 3
SALES (est): 62.9K **Privately Held**
SIC: 7692 Welding repair

(G-1846)
SHELBY TRAILER SERVICE LLC
282066 E 1790 Rd (73529-7722)
P.O. Box 148 (73529-0148)
PHONE..................580 252-2922
Ronnie Shelby, *Mng Member*
EMP: 5
SALES (est): 796.7K **Privately Held**
SIC: 3069 Rubber floor coverings, mats & wallcoverings

(G-1847)
VETERAN BAT COMPANY LLC
281645 E 1790 Rd (73529-7728)
PHONE..................580 439-5230
Nick Reed, *Principal*
EMP: 2 EST: 2016
SALES (est): 135.7K **Privately Held**
SIC: 3949 Sporting & athletic goods

(G-1848)
VOIGHT RONNIE LYNN LINDA GAIL
Also Called: Voight Manufacturing
7249 S 13th St (73529-7623)
PHONE..................580 251-9897
Ronnie L Voight, *Co-Owner*
EMP: 4
SALES (est): 52.4K **Privately Held**
SIC: 3599 Machine shop, jobbing & repair

Cookson
Cherokee County

(G-1849)
DAVIS WELDING DOCK SERV
33333 Highway 82 (74427-2205)
PHONE..................918 457-4071
Tony Davis, *Principal*
EMP: 1
SALES (est): 74.8K **Privately Held**
SIC: 7692 Welding repair

(G-1850)
DEEP BRANCH WINERY LLC
20827 W 887 Rd (74427-2370)
PHONE..................918 519-5490
EMP: 2
SALES (est): 119.6K **Privately Held**
SIC: 2084 Wines

Copan
Washington County

(G-1851)
MLB PORTABLE WELDING LLC
399551 W 400 Rd (74022-4915)
PHONE..................918 531-2414
Mike Beaston, *Principal*
EMP: 1
SALES (est): 25K **Privately Held**
SIC: 7692 Welding repair

Cordell
Washita County

(G-1852)
A1 HEAT AND AIR
222 E Main St (73632-4826)
P.O. Box 673 (73632-0673)
PHONE..................580 832-2605
Randy Olson, *Owner*
EMP: 3
SQ FT: 2,500

SALES (est): 326.5K **Privately Held**
SIC: 3585 Heating & air conditioning combination units

(G-1853)
ADAMS PRINTING
206 W Main St (73632-4830)
PHONE..................580 832-2123
EMP: 2
SQ FT: 2,500
SALES: 100K **Privately Held**
SIC: 2759 2791 2789 2752 Commercial Printing Typesetting Services Bookbinding/Related Work Lithographic Coml Print

(G-1854)
ALLURING LURES & TACKLE CO LLC
Also Called: Lead Babies
215 E Main St (73632-4825)
PHONE..................580 832-5177
Connie Slaughterback,
Dennis Slaughterback,
EMP: 2
SALES (est): 230K **Privately Held**
SIC: 5091 3949 Fishing tackle; sporting & athletic goods

(G-1855)
CAPROCK PLUNGERS LLC
100 Ne Mcclary Rd (73632)
P.O. Box 223 (73632-0223)
PHONE..................580 799-1387
Dale Selman, *Mng Member*
EMP: 13
SQ FT: 4,000
SALES (est): 1.3MM **Privately Held**
SIC: 1389 Lease tanks, oil field: erecting, cleaning & repairing

(G-1856)
CHEMPLEX ADVANCED MTLS LLC
200 N Mcclary St (73632-2216)
PHONE..................580 832-5288
Fred Chandler, *President*
EMP: 8
SALES (est): 895.5K **Privately Held**
SIC: 2819 Industrial inorganic chemicals

(G-1857)
DANNY LEE SIGNS
11973 N 2240 Rd (73632-3229)
PHONE..................580 832-5256
Danny Lee, *Owner*
EMP: 1
SALES (est): 62.5K **Privately Held**
SIC: 3993 Electric signs

(G-1858)
DOLESE BROS CO
106 S Grant St (73632-4833)
P.O. Box 875, Oklahoma City (73101-0875)
PHONE..................580 832-2720
Joe Shelton, *Manager*
EMP: 35
SALES (corp-wide): 8.5MM **Privately Held**
SIC: 3273 Ready-mixed concrete
PA: Dolese Bros. Co.
20 Nw 13th St
Oklahoma City OK 73103
405 235-2311

(G-1859)
FLOYD CRAIG COMPANY
404 S Market St (73632-5220)
PHONE..................580 832-2597
EMP: 2
SQ FT: 864
SALES (est): 115.5K **Privately Held**
SIC: 3999 3161 Mfg Misc Products Mfg Luggage

(G-1860)
GIBLET WELDING LLC
212 N Massingale Dr (73632-4631)
PHONE..................580 751-0104
Lee Christopher Giblet, *Principal*
EMP: 2
SALES (est): 43.7K **Privately Held**
SIC: 7692 Welding repair

GEOGRAPHIC SECTION

(G-1861)
KENNETH E JONES
Also Called: East Hill Car Wash
615 E Ollie St (73632-6060)
PHONE.................................580 832-2227
Kennth E Jones, *Partner*
EMP: 3
SALES (est): 240K **Privately Held**
SIC: 8011 3589 Offices & clinics of medical doctors; car washing machinery

(G-1862)
PRICE PRINTS INC
300 N Mcclary St (73632-2243)
PHONE.................................580 832-2492
Jim Price, *President*
Dana Price, *Admin Sec*
EMP: 11
SQ FT: 23,000
SALES: 300K **Privately Held**
SIC: 2759 Textile printing rolls: engraving

(G-1863)
ROGUE INDUSTRIAL LLC
311 W 7th St (73632-3000)
P.O. Box 555 (73632-0555)
PHONE.................................580 832-7060
Lester Lind,
EMP: 1
SALES (est): 50.4K **Privately Held**
SIC: 1382 Geological exploration, oil & gas field

(G-1864)
WELDING SHOP
202 W Main St (73632-4830)
PHONE.................................580 832-5545
Claude Duereksen, *President*
EMP: 6
SALES: 450K **Privately Held**
SIC: 3799 7692 Trailer hitches; welding repair

(G-1865)
WESNER PUBLICATIONS COMPANY (PA)
Also Called: Cordell Beacon The
115 E Main St (73632-4823)
P.O. Box 220 (73632-0220)
PHONE.................................580 832-3333
Brett Wesner, *President*
Zonelle Rainbolt, *Editor*
Scott Wesner, *Corp Secy*
EMP: 31
SALES (est): 1.9MM **Privately Held**
SIC: 2711 Newspapers: publishing only, not printed on site

Corn
Washita County

(G-1866)
BROOKS CUSTOM WELDING LLC
308 W Jefferson (73024-9611)
PHONE.................................580 343-2253
Michael A Brooks Jr, *Administration*
EMP: 1 EST: 2010
SALES (est): 33.9K **Privately Held**
SIC: 7692 Welding repair

(G-1867)
HIDDEN VALLEY MANUFACTURING
23849 Highway 152 (73024-3001)
PHONE.................................580 343-2303
Buddy Schmidt, *Partner*
EMP: 4
SQ FT: 4,000
SALES: 600K **Privately Held**
WEB: www.hiddenvalleymanufacturing.com
SIC: 3523 5083 Farm machinery & equipment; farm equipment parts & supplies

Covington
Garfield County

(G-1868)
TERRYS CONTRACT PUMPING
21625 E Wood Rd (73730-2103)
PHONE.................................580 554-2387
EMP: 2
SALES (est): 83.3K **Privately Held**
SIC: 1389 Pumping of oil & gas wells

Coweta
Wagoner County

(G-1869)
3G PRINTING
15389 S 273rd East Ave (74429-5342)
PHONE.................................918 284-9433
EMP: 2
SALES (est): 83.9K **Privately Held**
SIC: 2752 Commercial printing, lithographic

(G-1870)
A & H MANUFACTURING
11726 S 272nd East Ave (74429-4840)
PHONE.................................918 698-0987
EMP: 2
SALES (est): 87.1K **Privately Held**
SIC: 3999 Manufacturing industries

(G-1871)
ALFALFA DEHYDRATING PLANT INC
33090 E 211th St S (74429-3916)
PHONE.................................918 482-3267
Donald Cole, *President*
EMP: 2
SALES (est): 80.5K **Privately Held**
SIC: 2034 2048 Dehydrated fruits, vegetables, soups; prepared feeds

(G-1872)
BILL RATHBONE
Also Called: ABC Printing
304 N Broadway (74429-2604)
P.O. Box 982 (74429-0982)
PHONE.................................918 486-3028
Shawna Barrett, *Owner*
EMP: 2
SALES (est): 209.9K **Privately Held**
SIC: 2752 2759 2791 2789 Commercial printing, offset; commercial printing; typesetting; bookbinding & related work

(G-1873)
CALIBER WELDING INC
17018 Highway 51b (74429-3469)
P.O. Box 988 (74429-0988)
PHONE.................................918 486-1388
Troy Lichlyter, *Vice Pres*
EMP: 2 EST: 2008
SALES (est): 204.6K **Privately Held**
WEB: www.caliberwelding.com
SIC: 7692 Welding repair

(G-1874)
CARTER BF
31061 E 191st St S (74429-3795)
PHONE.................................918 486-7208
B F Carter, *Principal*
EMP: 2
SALES (est): 133K **Privately Held**
SIC: 3011 Tires & inner tubes

(G-1875)
COYOTE ENTERPRISES INC
27301 E 121st St S (74429-5937)
PHONE.................................918 486-8411
James R Goff, *President*
Cynthia Goff, *CFO*
▲ EMP: 10 EST: 1998
SALES (est): 2.2MM **Privately Held**
SIC: 3569 Blast cleaning equipment, dustless

(G-1876)
CUSTOM CATINGS OF BROKEN ARROW
27100 E 111th St S (74429-6496)
PHONE.................................918 258-0996
Edward Pearce, *President*
Margaret Pearce, *Corp Secy*
EMP: 4
SQ FT: 6,000
SALES (est): 676.5K **Privately Held**
SIC: 3479 Coating of metals & formed products

(G-1877)
CUSTOM WOOD WORKS
11741 S 305th East Ave (74429-6809)
PHONE.................................918 279-1333
Charles Stubblefield, *Principal*
EMP: 2
SALES (est): 187K **Privately Held**
SIC: 2431 Millwork

(G-1878)
D & G MACHINE
13746 S 337th East Ave (74429-3724)
PHONE.................................918 486-3501
Danny Farmer, *Owner*
EMP: 2
SALES (est): 173.5K **Privately Held**
SIC: 3599 Machine shop, jobbing & repair

(G-1879)
DC CHOPPERS LLC
30288 E 169th St S (74429-3870)
PHONE.................................918 791-1846
EMP: 2
SALES (est): 120.5K **Privately Held**
SIC: 3751 Motorcycles & related parts

(G-1880)
DOUBLE H FARMS INC
14279 S 385th East Ave (74429-8579)
PHONE.................................918 486-7635
David Hermesch, *President*
EMP: 3
SALES: 270K **Privately Held**
SIC: 0191 7692 General farms, primarily crop; welding repair

(G-1881)
EASTSIDE SEPTIC TANK
11614 S 272nd East Ave (74429)
PHONE.................................918 486-2290
Danny Hamilton, *Principal*
EMP: 3
SALES (est): 221.7K **Privately Held**
SIC: 3272 7699 Septic tanks, concrete; septic tank cleaning service

(G-1882)
ETCHED ORDNANCE LLC
26387 E 115th Pl S (74429-6431)
PHONE.................................918 855-8779
Nicholas Don Lenard, *Agent*
EMP: 2
SALES (est): 84.5K **Privately Held**
SIC: 3489 Ordnance & accessories

(G-1883)
GWS WELDING INC
16255 S 225th East Ave (74429-6605)
PHONE.................................918 527-5776
George Sheridan, *CEO*
EMP: 1
SQ FT: 1,619
SALES (est): 87.9K **Privately Held**
SIC: 7692 Welding repair

(G-1884)
HILLTOP TURF INC
14412 S State Highway 51 (74429-7685)
P.O. Box 249 (74429-0249)
PHONE.................................918 486-4482
EMP: 6
SALES (est): 311.8K **Privately Held**
SIC: 3999 Manufacturing Industries, Nec, Nsk

(G-1885)
HOLLIDAY SAND & GRAVEL CO
17402 S 305th East Ave (74429)
PHONE.................................918 486-1413
John Gipson, *President*
Grady Davis, *Manager*
EMP: 6
SALES (est): 343.1K **Privately Held**
SIC: 1442 Construction sand & gravel

(G-1886)
HUGHES EXPLORATION CONSULTING
13232 S 275th East Ave (74429-7057)
PHONE.................................918 486-3188
EMP: 1 EST: 1996
SALES (est): 73.3K **Privately Held**
SIC: 1382 Oil/Gas Exploration Services

(G-1887)
J BS DONUTS
13743 S State Highway 51 (74429-7103)
PHONE.................................918 486-4022
Antia Sanchez, *Owner*
Carol Foussel, *Partner*
EMP: 4
SALES (est): 282K **Privately Held**
SIC: 2051 Doughnuts, except frozen

(G-1888)
JACK CHARTIER WELDING LLC
16818 S 305th East Ave (74429-3732)
PHONE.................................918 486-2347
Jack Chartier, *Principal*
EMP: 1
SALES (est): 37.6K **Privately Held**
SIC: 7692 Welding repair

(G-1889)
JONES SPCLTY WLDG FBRCTION LLC
12066 S 257th East Ave (74429-5854)
PHONE.................................918 486-7740
Clayton Jones, *Principal*
EMP: 1
SALES (est): 38.1K **Privately Held**
SIC: 7692 Welding repair

(G-1890)
MASON ENTERPRISES GROUP LLC
14473 S 302nd East Ave B (74429-7851)
P.O. Box 492 (74429-0492)
PHONE.................................918 230-5782
Bryan Mason, *Principal*
EMP: 1
SALES (est): 160.2K **Privately Held**
SIC: 1542 1381 1711 Commercial & office building contractors; reworking oil & gas wells; plumbing, heating, air-conditioning contractors

(G-1891)
MELS ELECTRIC CONTRACTING
29827 E State Highway 51 (74429-7716)
PHONE.................................918 279-6036
EMP: 2
SALES (est): 122.9K **Privately Held**
WEB: www.electricalcontractorbrokenarrow.com
SIC: 5082 3699 General construction machinery & equipment; electrical equipment & supplies

(G-1892)
MTW POWDER COATING
11283 S 285th East Ave (74429-3314)
PHONE.................................918 638-4795
EMP: 2
SALES (est): 78.9K **Privately Held**
SIC: 3479 Metal coating & allied service

(G-1893)
PEARSON PUMPING INC
18505 Highway 51b (74429-3292)
PHONE.................................918 486-2386
Ron Pearson, *President*
Sharon Pearson, *Treasurer*
EMP: 1
SALES (est): 143.7K **Privately Held**
SIC: 1389 Oil field services

(G-1894)
PROFAB
Also Called: B & S Profab
29861 E State Highway 51 (74429-7716)
PHONE.................................918 486-4464
Steve Swaringim, *President*
Beverly Swaringim, *Vice Pres*
EMP: 2
SQ FT: 5,000

Coweta - Wagoner County (G-1895)

SALES (est): 250K **Privately Held**
SIC: 3621 7694 Electric motor & generator parts; armature rewinding shops

(G-1895)
RAFTER H BAR WELDING SVC LLC
121 N Broadway (74429-2601)
P.O. Box 553 (74429-0553)
PHONE..................................918 210-0175
Heath D Holmes, *Principal*
EMP: 1
SALES (est): 67.9K **Privately Held**
SIC: 7692 Welding repair

(G-1896)
RHODES PRINTING
207 N Broadway (74429-2603)
PHONE..................................918 445-7444
EMP: 2
SALES (est): 92.3K **Privately Held**
SIC: 2759 Screen printing

(G-1897)
SIGNS-N-MORE
27721 E 146th St S (74429-5391)
PHONE..................................918 760-5080
EMP: 1 EST: 2013
SALES (est): 69K **Privately Held**
WEB: www.oksignshop.com
SIC: 3993 Signs & advertising specialties

(G-1898)
STARFALL LLC
13142 S 267th East Ave (74429-5861)
PHONE..................................918 269-4364
Toni Napier, *Principal*
EMP: 2 EST: 2014
SALES (est): 134.1K **Privately Held**
WEB: www.starfallfab.com
SIC: 3999 Manufacturing industries

(G-1899)
TEEDS UP PRINTING
13779 S State Highway 51 (74429-7103)
PHONE..................................918 279-1018
Russell Andrews, *Principal*
EMP: 2
SALES (est): 88.6K **Privately Held**
WEB: www.teedupprinting.com
SIC: 2759 Publication printing

(G-1900)
TJ TROST LLC
14515 S 209th East Ave (74429-6302)
PHONE..................................918 269-1582
James H Beauchamp, *Incorporator*
EMP: 8
SALES (est): 495.5K **Privately Held**
SIC: 3999 Manufacturing industries

(G-1901)
TORNADO ALLEY OK STORM SHLTERS
11851 S State Highway 51 (74429-7123)
PHONE..................................918 706-1341
Dennis Trott, *Principal*
EMP: 2
SALES (est): 159K **Privately Held**
WEB: www.tornadoalleyok.com
SIC: 3448 Prefabricated metal buildings

(G-1902)
WINKLES WOODWORKS LTD
119 E Chestnut St (74429-2519)
PHONE..................................918 486-5022
Tom Widmar, *President*
EMP: 17
SQ FT: 6,000
SALES: 600K **Privately Held**
WEB: www.woodworksandantiques.com
SIC: 2511 2431 2521 Wood household furniture; porch work, wood; louver windows, glass, wood frame; wood office furniture

(G-1903)
ZIMMERMANS CUSTOM DESIGN INC
14048 S 302nd East Ave (74429-3089)
PHONE..................................918 486-4179
Jack Dean Zimmerman, *President*
Annette Zimmerman, *Vice Pres*
EMP: 3

SALES (est): 235K **Privately Held**
SIC: 2541 1799 Counter & sink tops; counter top installation

Coyle
Logan County

(G-1904)
SPANGLER FARM
11208 S Coyle Rd (73027-2307)
PHONE..................................405 466-2536
Donald Spangler, *Owner*
EMP: 1
SALES (est): 110K **Privately Held**
SIC: 3563 Air & gas compressors including vacuum pumps

Crawford
Roger Mills County

(G-1905)
GARY COBB WELDING LLC
18388 E 850 Rd (73638-6013)
PHONE..................................580 983-2499
Gary Cobb, *Principal*
EMP: 1
SALES (est): 56K **Privately Held**
SIC: 7692 Welding repair

(G-1906)
WAGON WHEEL PRODUCTION CO
8167 N 1815 Rd (73638-5000)
PHONE..................................580 983-2371
Jackie Castle, *Principal*
EMP: 4
SALES (est): 394K **Privately Held**
SIC: 1381 Drilling oil & gas wells

Crescent
Logan County

(G-1907)
ACIDIZING & CEMENTING SERVICE
Also Called: ACS
2 1/2 Mi S On Hwy 74 (73028)
P.O. Box 751 (73028-0751)
PHONE..................................405 969-3093
Lance Berry, *Owner*
EMP: 10
SQ FT: 3,500
SALES (est): 1.1MM **Privately Held**
SIC: 1389 Acidizing wells; cementing oil & gas well casings

(G-1908)
BOSTICK SERVICE CORPORATION
505 W Adams St (73028-8905)
P.O. Box 113 (73028-0113)
PHONE..................................405 969-2198
Mike Bostick, *President*
EMP: 3
SALES (est): 573.4K **Privately Held**
SIC: 1389 Oil field services

(G-1909)
CASSIDAY PUMPING SERVICE INC
11062 W County Road 71 (73028-9766)
PHONE..................................405 969-3374
Nathan Cassiday, *President*
EMP: 1
SALES (est): 64.7K **Privately Held**
SIC: 1389 Pumping of oil & gas wells

(G-1910)
CRESCENT READY MIX INC
14417 W Cooksey Rd (73028-8746)
PHONE..................................405 853-1599
Steven C Schwarz, *President*
Donna Schwarz, *Vice Pres*
EMP: 5
SQ FT: 2,000
SALES: 500K **Privately Held**
SIC: 3273 Ready-mixed concrete

(G-1911)
CUSTOM WOOD CREATIONS LLC
17068 W County Road 76 (73028-9572)
PHONE..................................405 517-8689
Larry Rogers, *Manager*
EMP: 4
SALES (est): 390.1K **Privately Held**
SIC: 2431 Millwork

(G-1912)
D AND R DIRECTIONAL DRILLING
13525 Cimarron Dr (73028-9292)
PHONE..................................405 208-1399
Robert C Snelson, *Principal*
EMP: 2 EST: 2012
SALES (est): 119.7K **Privately Held**
SIC: 1381 Directional drilling oil & gas wells

(G-1913)
DON SCOTT
Also Called: Mechanics Plus
200 E Adams St (73028-9156)
P.O. Box 701 (73028-0701)
PHONE..................................405 969-3649
Don Scott, *Owner*
EMP: 3
SALES (est): 900K **Privately Held**
SIC: 1389 Oil field services

(G-1914)
ENABLE OKLA INTRSTATE TRNSM LL
15400 W Cooksey Rd (73028-8739)
PHONE..................................405 969-3906
Kent Wilson, *Manager*
EMP: 17
SALES (corp-wide): 12.3B **Publicly Held**
SIC: 1311 Crude petroleum production
HQ: Enable Oklahoma Intrastate Transmission, Llc
499 W Sheridan Ave # 1500
Oklahoma City OK 73102
405 525-7788

(G-1915)
FOUR FEATHERS TRANSPORTS
15383 W County Road 71 (73028-9736)
PHONE..................................405 343-9799
Luke Yeahquo, *Owner*
EMP: 2
SALES (est): 145K **Privately Held**
SIC: 3531 Construction machinery

(G-1916)
GENIE WELL SERVICE INC
7507 N Meridian Ave (73028-9037)
P.O. Box 600 (73028-0600)
PHONE..................................405 969-2141
Kelli Navratil, *Manager*
EMP: 35
SALES (corp-wide): 5.9MM **Privately Held**
SIC: 1389 Oil field services
PA: Genie Well Service Inc
2424 E 21st St Ste 500
Tulsa OK

(G-1917)
KENNETH VALLIQUETTE INC
Rr 1 (73028)
PHONE..................................405 969-3317
Kenneth Valliquette, *President*
James Reed, *Pastor*
EMP: 1
SALES (est): 89.2K **Privately Held**
SIC: 1382 Oil & gas exploration services

(G-1918)
M AND V RESOURCES INC
108 N Grand (73028)
P.O. Box 772 (73028-0772)
PHONE..................................405 969-2338
Randy Mc Guire, *President*
EMP: 1
SALES (est): 116.1K **Privately Held**
SIC: 1311 Crude petroleum production

(G-1919)
R & D MUD LOGGING SERVICES LLP
602 S Pine St (73028-8932)
PHONE..................................405 969-2587
Robert Prescott, *Owner*
EMP: 2
SALES (est): 114.1K **Privately Held**
SIC: 2411 Logging camps & contractors

(G-1920)
TRACY TARRENT
Also Called: Trace Oil Co
7 Appleridge Rd (73028)
P.O. Box 707 (73028-0707)
PHONE..................................405 969-2343
Tracy Tarrent, *Owner*
EMP: 1
SALES (est): 300K **Privately Held**
SIC: 1389 Pumping of oil & gas wells

(G-1921)
TRI-LIFT SERVICES INC
5325 N Highway 74 (73028-9351)
PHONE..................................405 969-2069
Kevin Kegin, *COO*
Joey Thompson, *Vice Pres*
Randall Thompson, *Vice Pres*
EMP: 6
SALES (est): 860K **Privately Held**
SIC: 3533 5084 Oil & gas field machinery; oil well machinery, equipment & supplies

Cushing
Payne County

(G-1922)
AKL SERVICES
601 E Pine St (74023-2056)
P.O. Box 1564 (74023-1564)
PHONE..................................918 225-5533
Kenny Longbrake, *Owner*
Mary Longbrake, *Co-Owner*
EMP: 40
SQ FT: 15,000
SALES (est): 3.2MM **Privately Held**
SIC: 1389 Oil field services

(G-1923)
BASIC ENERGY SERVICES INC
7101 E Main St (74023-3062)
PHONE..................................918 225-0161
EMP: 1
SALES (est): 65.5K
SALES (corp-wide): 864MM **Publicly Held**
SIC: 1389 Oil And Gas Field Services, Nec, Nsk
PA: Basic Energy Services, Inc.
801 Cherry St Unit 2
Fort Worth TX 76102
817 334-4100

(G-1924)
BOB MC KINNEY & SONS
8807 N Norfolk (74023-5937)
PHONE..................................918 387-2401
Bob Mc Kinney Jr, *Owner*
EMP: 3
SALES (est): 58K **Privately Held**
SIC: 0751 2011 2013 2011 Slaughtering: custom livestock services; sausages & other prepared meats; meat packing plants

(G-1925)
CIMARRON GLASS LLC
Also Called: Cimarron Glass & Ovrhd Door Co
223 E Main St (74023-2641)
PHONE..................................918 225-6600
Freda Wulf, *Corp Secy*
Timothy Smith, *Mng Member*
Stan Akins, *Manager*
EMP: 6
SQ FT: 2,600
SALES (est): 744.6K **Privately Held**
SIC: 1793 1751 5231 5211 Glass & glazing work; garage door, installation or erection; glass; garage doors, sale & installation; doors & windows; furniture tops, glass: cut, beveled or polished

(G-1926)
COMPUTALOG WIRELINE INC
Rr 2 Box 2020 (74023-9802)
P.O. Box 591, Drumright (74030-0591)
PHONE..................................918 225-1187
Jerry L Delong, *President*
Janette Delong, *Corp Secy*
EMP: 6 **EST:** 1979
SQ FT: 2,000
SALES (est): 866.2K **Privately Held**
SIC: 1389 Perforating well casings; well logging

(G-1927)
CUSHING SCREEN PRINTING LLC
1024 E Leland St (74023-2032)
P.O. Box 1321 (74023-1321)
PHONE..................................646 267-3513
Marc Gilman, *Principal*
Heather D Stokes, *Principal*
EMP: 2
SALES (est): 140.4K **Privately Held**
SIC: 2752 Commercial printing, lithographic

(G-1928)
CUSTOM SIGNS
947 E Main St (74023-2837)
PHONE..................................918 225-2749
EMP: 2
SALES (est): 147.5K **Privately Held**
SIC: 3993 Signs & advertising specialties

(G-1929)
DCA INC
Also Called: D C A
1515 E Pine St (74023-9161)
PHONE..................................918 225-0346
Doug Carson, *CEO*
Mike Griffith, *President*
Sharon Kerr, *Human Res Mgr*
Jack Forsyth, *Admin Sec*
EMP: 32
SQ FT: 11,000
SALES (est): 9.8MM **Privately Held**
SIC: 5045 7372 7371 Computer peripheral equipment; computer software; prepackaged software; computer software systems analysis & design, custom

(G-1930)
DEEPROCK OIL OPERATING LLC
321 E Broadway St (74023-3337)
PHONE..................................918 225-7100
EMP: 3
SALES (est): 380.8K **Privately Held**
SIC: 1311 Crude petroleum & natural gas

(G-1931)
DEEPROCK TANK OPER COLO LLC
321 E Broadway St (74023-3337)
PHONE..................................918 225-7100
Glenn Collum, *CEO*
EMP: 23
SALES (est): 6MM **Privately Held**
SIC: 1321 Natural gas liquids

(G-1932)
DON WILSON PIPELINE CONSTRUCTI
780454 S Highway 99 (74023-6761)
PHONE..................................918 225-2786
Don Wilson, *CEO*
EMP: 3
SALES (est): 387.9K **Privately Held**
SIC: 3531 Backhoes, tractors, cranes, plows & similar equipment; excavation work

(G-1933)
ESECO-SPEEDMASTER
730 E Eseco Rd (74023-5505)
PHONE..................................918 225-1266
Arthur Kaminshine, *President*
Steven Holley, *Vice Pres*
Edward L Handlin, *CFO*
Jerome Kaminshine, *Treasurer*
EMP: 88
SQ FT: 52,000
SALES (est): 9.2MM **Privately Held**
WEB: www.eseco-speedmaster.com
SIC: 3442 3826 3861 Metal doors, sash & trim; analytical instruments; densitometers
PA: Speedmaster Inc
1 E Eseco Rd
Cushing OK 74023

(G-1934)
HARVEY KATES
Also Called: Harvey's Vacuum Service
920 E Maple St (74023-2820)
PHONE..................................918 225-2567
Harvey Kates, *Owner*
EMP: 2 **EST:** 1968
SALES (est): 96K **Privately Held**
SIC: 1389 Oil field services

(G-1935)
HEM MFG
7101 E Main St (74023-3062)
PHONE..................................918 225-4600
EMP: 3 **EST:** 2006
SALES (est): 100K **Privately Held**
SIC: 3999 Mfg Misc Products

(G-1936)
HOUGH OILFIELD SERVICE INC
Also Called: Hotco
711 W Cherry St (74023-3765)
P.O. Box 1603 (74023-1603)
PHONE..................................918 225-1851
David Hough, *President*
Linda Newton, *Corp Secy*
EMP: 20
SQ FT: 2,400
SALES: 3MM **Privately Held**
SIC: 1389 7359 5983 Fishing for tools, oil & gas field; tool rental; fuel oil dealers

(G-1937)
HUNTS WELDING SERVICE LLC
1306 W Dunkin Rd (74023-1949)
PHONE..................................806 339-4591
EMP: 1
SALES (est): 39.1K **Privately Held**
SIC: 7692 Welding repair

(G-1938)
INK MASTERS SCREEN PRINTING
1421 E Moses St (74023-3635)
PHONE..................................918 399-5220
Shannon D Wesson, *Principal*
EMP: 2
SALES (est): 101.5K **Privately Held**
SIC: 2752 Commercial printing, lithographic

(G-1939)
JIMS TRUCK CENTER
Also Called: Partical Rent A Car
601 N Steele Ave (74023-2655)
PHONE..................................918 225-1013
Jim Wilson, *Owner*
EMP: 3
SALES (est): 314.1K **Privately Held**
SIC: 7514 3713 7513 Rent-a-car service; automobile wrecker truck bodies; truck rental & leasing, no drivers

(G-1940)
K & W WELL SERVICE INC
Hwy 33 E 3 Miles (74023)
P.O. Box 511 (74023-0511)
PHONE..................................918 225-7855
Kenneth D Wood, *President*
Willy Boley, *Vice Pres*
EMP: 25
SALES (est): 3.1MM **Privately Held**
SIC: 1389 Oil field services

(G-1941)
KOBY OIL TOOLS LLC
900 N Little Ave (74023-2212)
PHONE..................................405 236-3551
Elisha Wooten,
EMP: 25
SALES (est): 3.8MM **Privately Held**
SIC: 3533 Bits, oil & gas field tools: rock

(G-1942)
LEDA GRIMM
Also Called: D & L Printing
742 E Main St (74023-2741)
PHONE..................................918 225-0507
Leda Grimm, *Owner*
EMP: 2
SQ FT: 2,500
SALES (est): 70K **Privately Held**
SIC: 2759 2791 2789 2752 Letterpress & screen printing; typesetting; bookbinding & related work; commercial printing, lithographic; automotive & apparel trimmings

(G-1943)
LONGBREAK WELDING SERVICE INC
5212 W Eseco Rd (74023-4884)
PHONE..................................918 223-5976
Eric Longbrake, *President*
EMP: 1
SALES (est): 75K **Privately Held**
SIC: 7692 Welding repair

(G-1944)
MARTIN TANK TRCK CSING PULLING
2626 N Little Ave (74023-2382)
P.O. Box 383 (74023-0383)
PHONE..................................918 225-2388
Kenneth Martin, *President*
EMP: 10
SALES (est): 920K **Privately Held**
SIC: 1389 4212 Running, cutting & pulling casings, tubes & rods; liquid haulage, local

(G-1945)
MELBRE SOUTHERN STITCHES LLC
501 S Linwood Ave (74023-4643)
PHONE..................................918 399-4966
Melanie Vier, *Principal*
EMP: 1
SALES (est): 34.5K **Privately Held**
SIC: 2395 Embroidery & art needlework

(G-1946)
MULLINS SALVAGE INC
7304 E Main St (74023-2935)
PHONE..................................918 352-9612
Brian Jones, *President*
Dana Jones, *Vice Pres*
EMP: 6
SALES (est): 2MM **Privately Held**
SIC: 5399 3411 Surplus & salvage goods; metal cans

(G-1947)
NELSON BACKHOE AND WELDING
1513 S Linwood Ave (74023-5311)
PHONE..................................918 399-3426
EMP: 1
SALES (est): 60K **Privately Held**
SIC: 3531 Backhoes

(G-1948)
NORTHRUP METALS LLC
322 W Grandstaff (74023)
PHONE..................................918 225-2100
William Arnth, *Mng Member*
EMP: 2
SALES (est): 100K **Privately Held**
SIC: 3471 Finishing, metals or formed products

(G-1949)
OKLAHOMA CEMENTING CUSHING LLC
1115 N Euchee Valley Rd (74023)
P.O. Box 590 (74023-0590)
PHONE..................................918 225-0688
JB Niccum,
EMP: 9 **EST:** 2014
SALES (est): 1.6MM **Privately Held**
SIC: 1389 Cementing oil & gas well casings

(G-1950)
PROFESSIONAL MARBLE COMPANY
802 E Brissy St (74023-2006)
PHONE..................................918 225-5364
Cecil Davidson, *President*
Betty Davidson, *Admin Sec*
EMP: 4
SQ FT: 3,600
SALES (est): 306K **Privately Held**
SIC: 3281 1743 3261 Marble, building: cut & shaped; marble installation, interior; vitreous plumbing fixtures

(G-1951)
QUAPAW COMPANY
7312 E Main St (74023-2935)
PHONE..................................918 225-0580
Brian Floyd, *General Mgr*
EMP: 15
SALES (corp-wide): 19MM **Privately Held**
SIC: 2951 1771 Asphalt paving mixtures & blocks; blacktop (asphalt) work
PA: The Quapaw Company
3224 N Perkins Rd
Stillwater OK
405 377-9240

(G-1952)
RCO FABRICATION LLC
8221 E 9th St (74023-6337)
PHONE..................................918 225-0708
James Randal, *Principal*
EMP: 3
SALES (est): 303.4K **Privately Held**
SIC: 3999 Manufacturing industries

(G-1953)
RDS OILFIELD SERVICE LLC
910 Whispering Oaks (74023-6467)
PHONE..................................918 521-9205
Roger Simon, *Mng Member*
EMP: 5
SALES: 300K **Privately Held**
SIC: 3533 Oil & gas field machinery

(G-1954)
REECE-ATS HOLDING LLC
613 N Euchee Vly (74023-2990)
P.O. Box 1311 (74023-1311)
PHONE..................................918 225-1010
Jerad Beeler, *Superintendent*
Nmk Brow, *Foreman/Supr*
Damon Green, *CFO*
EMP: 50
SALES (est): 19MM **Privately Held**
SIC: 3443 Industrial vessels, tanks & containers

(G-1955)
REID COMMUNICATIONS LLC
202 N Harrison Ave (74023-3302)
PHONE..................................918 285-5555
David Reid,
EMP: 7
SALES (est): 429.4K **Privately Held**
SIC: 2711 Newspapers: publishing only, not printed on site

(G-1956)
ROD PUMP CONSULTING LLC
2707 Schlegel 1st (74023-6203)
PHONE..................................918 306-2318
Ken Cupples, *President*
EMP: 5 **EST:** 2015
SQ FT: 2,000
SALES (est): 237.5K **Privately Held**
SIC: 3561 Pump jacks & other pumping equipment

(G-1957)
RUGGED ROUSTABOUT LLC
740384 S 3480 Rd (74023-5290)
P.O. Box 18734, Oklahoma City (73154-0734)
PHONE..................................918 225-0700
Kevin Glenn Rich,
EMP: 17
SALES (est): 1.3MM **Privately Held**
SIC: 1389 Roustabout service

(G-1958)
SEMGROUP CORPORATION
3710 N Little Ave (74023-1992)
PHONE..................................918 225-7758
Cecil Mooreland, *Terminal Mgr*
Oc Simpson, *Engineer*
EMP: 7 **Publicly Held**
SIC: 1311 Crude petroleum & natural gas production

Cushing - Payne County (G-1959)

HQ: Semgroup Corporation
6120 S Yale Ave Ste 1500
Tulsa OK 74136
918 524-8100

(G-1959)
SHOW AND TELL TIMES INC
1047 E Main St (74023-2839)
PHONE..................918 225-4111
John Johnston, *Principal*
EMP: 7
SQ FT: 2,000
SALES (est): 484.5K **Privately Held**
WEB: www.showntelltimes.com
SIC: 2741 Shopping news: publishing only, not printed on site

(G-1960)
SOUTHERN PLAINS ENRGY SVCS LLC
5405 S Country Club Rd (74023)
P.O. Box 1030 (74023-1030)
PHONE..................918 225-3570
Fredrick H Ahrberg,
EMP: 9
SALES (est): 510.5K **Privately Held**
WEB: www.southernplainsllc.com
SIC: 1389 Oil field services

(G-1961)
SPEEDMASTER INC (PA)
Also Called: E S E C O Speed Master
1 E Eseco Rd (74023-5531)
PHONE..................918 225-1266
Arthur Kaminshine, *President*
EMP: 56
SQ FT: 44,000
SALES (est): 9.2MM **Privately Held**
SIC: 3861 3442 Densitometers; metal doors, sash & trim

(G-1962)
STEWART STONE INC
1016 N Elm Creek Rd (74023)
PHONE..................918 225-2704
James Couch, *Superintendent*
EMP: 15
SALES (corp-wide): 3.6MM **Privately Held**
SIC: 1422 Cement rock, crushed & broken-quarrying
PA: Stewart Stone, Inc.
2003b E Main St
Cushing OK
918 285-5600

(G-1963)
SWEET MEMORIES BY HEATHER LLC
821 Holmes Ave (74023-4705)
PHONE..................360 608-1600
Heather Becher,
EMP: 1
SALES (est): 70.1K **Privately Held**
SIC: 2051 Bakery: wholesale or wholesale/retail combined

(G-1964)
TAYLOR INTERNATIONAL INC
8701 E Main (74023)
P.O. Box 1173, Drumright (74030-1173)
PHONE..................918 352-9511
Fax: 918 352-9834
EMP: 2
SQ FT: 1,500
SALES (est): 300K **Privately Held**
SIC: 1311 Oil & Gas Production

(G-1965)
V M I INC
1125 N Maitlen Dr (74023-2920)
PHONE..................918 225-7000
Tony Maitlen, *CEO*
Randy Maitlen, *President*
Peggy Maitlen, *Corp Secy*
Mason Maitlen, *Technology*
▼ EMP: 15 EST: 1972
SQ FT: 15,900
SALES (est): 3.9MM **Privately Held**
SIC: 3531 7353 Dredging machinery; earth moving equipment, rental or leasing

(G-1966)
VASSER MACHINE
2115 W Old Highway 33 (74023-6179)
PHONE..................918 225-2677
Wade Vassar, *Owner*
EMP: 1
SQ FT: 15,000
SALES (est): 92K **Privately Held**
SIC: 3534 3599 Automobile elevators; machine shop, jobbing & repair

(G-1967)
VICTORY ENERGY OPERATIONS LLC
1200 N Maitlen Dr (74023-2921)
PHONE..................918 225-2164
Stephanie Franklin, *Manager*
EMP: 20
SALES (corp-wide): 84.6MM **Privately Held**
SIC: 3823 Boiler controls: industrial, power & marine type
PA: Victory Energy Operations Llc
10701 E 126th St N
Collinsville OK 74021
918 274-0023

(G-1968)
W K LINDUFF INC
1101 S Thompson Ave (74023-5104)
P.O. Box 869 (74023-0869)
PHONE..................918 225-6000
Lisa Cooper, *President*
EMP: 3
SALES (est): 563.9K **Privately Held**
SIC: 5084 1389 Water pumps (industrial); oil field services

(G-1969)
WHEELS OF PAST
2320 S Agra Rd (74023-5866)
PHONE..................918 225-2250
Dennis Francis, *Owner*
EMP: 2
SALES (est): 146.5K **Privately Held**
SIC: 7532 3713 3711 Antique & classic automobile restoration; truck & bus bodies; motor vehicles & car bodies

(G-1970)
WILEY TRANSFORMER CO
6624 E Main St (74023-2954)
P.O. Box 1448 (74023-1448)
PHONE..................918 225-5772
Jack Wiley, *Owner*
EMP: 4
SQ FT: 4,124
SALES (est): 390K **Privately Held**
SIC: 5063 3612 Transformers, electric; transformers, except electric

(G-1971)
WILLIAMS MONUMENTS
1445 E Main St (74023-3041)
PHONE..................918 225-1344
Glenn B Williams II, *Owner*
Sue Williams, *Co-Owner*
EMP: 2
SQ FT: 3,800
SALES (est): 125K **Privately Held**
WEB: www.williamsmonumentsllc.com
SIC: 5999 3272 Monuments, finished to custom order; monuments, concrete

(G-1972)
WYATT EARP COMPANIES
112 S Highway 99 (74023-6250)
PHONE..................918 225-7770
Wyatt Earp, *President*
EMP: 3
SALES (est): 218.1K **Privately Held**
SIC: 3993 Signs & advertising specialties

Custer City
Custer County

(G-1973)
BACH WELDING & DIESEL SERVICE
409 N Main St (73639)
PHONE..................580 593-2599
Frank Bach, *Partner*
Terry Bach, *Partner*
EMP: 2 EST: 1946
SALES (est): 166.6K **Privately Held**
SIC: 7538 7549 7692 3519 Truck engine repair, except industrial; towing service, automotive; welding repair; internal combustion engines

(G-1974)
FORREST VALENTINE
8705 N 2220 Rd (73639-4112)
PHONE..................580 309-2190
Forrest Valentine, *Principal*
EMP: 2 EST: 2013
SALES (est): 162.6K **Privately Held**
SIC: 2431 Millwork

Cyril
Caddo County

(G-1975)
JAMES D JOHNSON
Also Called: Custom Products Company
Highway 8 (73029)
P.O. Box 210 (73029-0210)
PHONE..................580 464-3299
EMP: 1 EST: 1969
SALES (est): 100K **Privately Held**
SIC: 2512 Mfg Upholstered Household Furniture

Dacoma
Woods County

(G-1976)
PRINTING AND DESIGN
859 Main St (73731)
P.O. Box 127 (73731-0127)
PHONE..................580 871-2396
Donna L Williams, *Owner*
EMP: 1
SALES: 60K **Privately Held**
SIC: 2759 Commercial printing

(G-1977)
SNWELLSERVICE LLC
15314 County Road 490 (73731-1102)
PHONE..................580 430-9346
Myra Nettles, *Manager*
Stormy Nettles,
EMP: 1
SALES (est): 56.7K **Privately Held**
SIC: 1389 7389 Oil consultants;

Davenport
Lincoln County

(G-1978)
NEW ERA
Also Called: New ERA Newspaper
209 N Broadway St (74026)
P.O. Box 700 (74026-0700)
PHONE..................918 377-2259
Don Eugene Sporleder, *Owner*
EMP: 2
SQ FT: 2,750
SALES: 35K **Privately Held**
SIC: 2711 Newspapers: publishing only, not printed on site

Davis
Murray County

(G-1979)
CHADWICK PAPER INC
Also Called: Davis News, The
400 E Main St (73030-1908)
P.O. Box 98 (73030-0098)
PHONE..................580 369-2807
Sharon Chadwick, *President*
Richard Chadwick, *Vice Pres*
EMP: 2
SQ FT: 3,000
SALES: 175K **Privately Held**
WEB: www.davisnewspaper.net
SIC: 2711 5943 Newspapers: publishing only, not printed on site; office forms & supplies

(G-1980)
CHICKASAW NATION
Also Called: Bedr Fine Chocolates Factory
37 N Colbert Rd (73030-9338)
PHONE..................405 331-2300
Jerry Couch, *Branch Mgr*
EMP: 1 **Privately Held**
SIC: 2066 9131 Chocolate & cocoa products;
PA: Chickasaw Nation
520 Arlington St
Ada OK 74820
580 436-2603

(G-1981)
CITY OF DAVIS
Also Called: Turner Falls Park
227 E Main St (73030-1903)
PHONE..................580 369-2988
Tom Graham, *Manager*
EMP: 25 **Privately Held**
SIC: 2531 9111 Picnic tables or benches, park; mayors' offices
PA: City Of Davis
227 E Main St
Davis OK 73030
580 369-2917

(G-1982)
DOLESE BROS CO
Also Called: Dolese Trucking Co
Hwy 77 S (73030)
P.O. Box 9 (73030-0009)
PHONE..................580 369-2834
EMP: 35
SALES (corp-wide): 8.5MM **Privately Held**
SIC: 3273 Ready-mixed concrete
PA: Dolese Bros. Co.
20 Nw 13th St
Oklahoma City OK 73103
405 235-2311

(G-1983)
FORUM ENERGY TECHNOLOGIES INC
Also Called: Forum Flow Equipment
5015 Highway 7 W (73030-9697)
PHONE..................580 622-5058
EMP: 1 **Publicly Held**
SIC: 3533 Oil field machinery & equipment; drilling tools for gas, oil or water wells
PA: Forum Energy Technologies, Inc.
10344 Sam Houston Park Dr # 300
Houston TX 77064

(G-1984)
FORUM PRODUCTION EQUIPMENT
Also Called: Wood Flowline Products, L.L.C.
5015 Highway 7 W (73030-9697)
P.O. Box 1108, Sulphur (73086-8108)
PHONE..................580 622-5058
Tommy Bilbeck, *General Mgr*
EMP: 65
SALES (est): 15MM **Publicly Held**
SIC: 3533 Oil field machinery & equipment
PA: Forum Energy Technologies, Inc.
10344 Sam Houston Park Dr # 300
Houston TX 77064

(G-1985)
HANSON AGGREGATES WRP INC
6.5 Mles W Of I 35 On Hwy (73030)
PHONE..................580 369-3773
Tim Nickols, *Manager*
EMP: 29
SALES (corp-wide): 20.8B **Privately Held**
SIC: 1429 5032 Igneous rock, crushed & broken-quarrying; stone, crushed or broken
HQ: Hanson Aggregates Wrp, Inc.
1333 Campus Pkwy
Wall Township NJ 07753

GEOGRAPHIC SECTION

(G-1986)
JANTZ SUPPLY INC
309 W Main St (73030-1751)
P.O. Box 584 (73030-0584)
PHONE.................................580 369-5503
Kenneth F Jantz, *President*
▲ **EMP:** 30 **EST:** 1966
SQ FT: 15,000
SALES (est): 2.4MM **Privately Held**
SIC: 3546 5072 5251 Power-driven handtools; power handtools; tools, power

(G-1987)
K AND G SAND & GRAVEL LLC
5140 Sunshine Rd (73030-9370)
PHONE.................................580 369-2244
Gary Young, *Principal*
EMP: 3
SALES (est): 190K **Privately Held**
SIC: 1442 Construction sand & gravel

(G-1988)
MAC TRAILER OF OKLAHOMA INC
8304 Mckee Industrial Rd (73030-9410)
PHONE.................................817 900-2006
Mike Conny, *President*
Tina Crouse, *Superintendent*
Jenny Conny, *Corp Secy*
Bill Ogden, *CFO*
EMP: 5
SQ FT: 350,000
SALES (est): 244.7K **Privately Held**
SIC: 3715 5012 5013 5015 Truck trailers; trailers for trucks, new & used; truck bodies; motor vehicle supplies & new parts; motor vehicle parts, used; trailer repair
PA: Mac Trailer Manufacturing, Inc.
14599 Commerce St Ne
Alliance OH 44601

(G-1989)
MARTIN MARIETTA MATERIALS INC
Also Called: Mpi Davis Quarry
Hwy 7 W Interstate 35 (73030)
P.O. Box 147 (73030-0147)
PHONE.................................580 369-2706
Tim Lockridge, *Manager*
EMP: 34 **Publicly Held**
SIC: 1422 Crushed & broken limestone
PA: Martin Marietta Materials Inc
2710 Wycliff Rd
Raleigh NC 27607

(G-1990)
MCCABE INDUSTRIAL MINERALS
1444 Woodland Rd (73030)
P.O. Box 485 (73030-0485)
PHONE.................................580 369-3660
Shawn Parks, *Branch Mgr*
EMP: 10
SALES (corp-wide): 4.3MM **Privately Held**
SIC: 3295 2952 Roofing granules; asphalt felts & coatings
PA: Mccabe Industrial Minerals Inc
7225 S 85th East Ave # 400
Tulsa OK 74133
918 252-5090

(G-1991)
MELTON DENTAL LAB
Also Called: Melton, Bill
309 E Freeman Ave (73030-3347)
PHONE.................................580 369-2448
Bill Melton, *Owner*
EMP: 3
SALES (est): 100K **Privately Held**
SIC: 2869 8072 Laboratory chemicals, organic; dental laboratories

(G-1992)
PALLETS PLUS LLC
100 E Ferguson Ave (73030)
PHONE.................................580 513-4090
Charles Dodd,
EMP: 6
SALES: 200K **Privately Held**
SIC: 2448 Pallets, wood

(G-1993)
SEAL MASTERS INC
Also Called: Sealmaster
2244 Highway 77 S 134 (73030-9576)
PHONE.................................580 369-2393
Ron Gillihan, *President*
EMP: 20
SALES: 6MM **Privately Held**
SIC: 2951 Asphalt paving mixtures & blocks

Del City
Oklahoma County

(G-1994)
AEROCORE X LLC
4312 Se 31st St (73115-3402)
PHONE.................................405 669-8655
Chris Dofflemeyer, *CEO*
Jeff Kelly,
EMP: 6
SALES (est): 399.6K **Privately Held**
SIC: 3721 3443 Aircraft; heat exchangers, plate type

(G-1995)
AI SIGNS & WRAPS LLC
513 Howard Dr (73115-3809)
PHONE.................................405 531-6938
Byron Boyd, *Principal*
EMP: 1
SALES (est): 46K **Privately Held**
SIC: 3993 Signs & advertising specialties

(G-1996)
ALL SHEET METAL CO
5717 Se 70th St (73135-5800)
PHONE.................................405 733-0039
Les Unsell, *Partner*
Ken Haffner, *Partner*
EMP: 2
SALES (est): 190K **Privately Held**
SIC: 3444 Sheet metal specialties, not stamped

(G-1997)
GUN WORLD INC
3420 S Sunnylane Rd (73115-3535)
PHONE.................................405 670-5885
Mike Mathews, *Principal*
EMP: 2
SALES (est): 210.3K **Privately Held**
SIC: 3489 7699 3484 Guns, howitzers, mortars & related equipment; gunsmith shop; pistols or pistol parts, 30 mm. & below

(G-1998)
K9 MEDIA
3401 Vickie Dr (73115-4339)
PHONE.................................504 233-2576
Karintha Wheaton, *President*
EMP: 50
SALES (est): 1.2MM **Privately Held**
SIC: 2721 Magazines: publishing only, not printed on site

(G-1999)
LARRY BOBS WELDING LLC ✪
4712 Michael Dr (73115-3830)
PHONE.................................405 672-7224
Larry Judkins, *Principal*
EMP: 1 **EST:** 2019
SALES (est): 44.7K **Privately Held**
SIC: 7692 Welding repair

(G-2000)
MASTERMIND COMICS
4308 Se 12th St (73115-3020)
PHONE.................................315 308-0593
Jojo Williams, *CEO*
EMP: 4 **EST:** 2016
SALES (est): 157.9K **Privately Held**
SIC: 2721 Comic books: publishing & printing

(G-2001)
MEADOWBROOK OIL CORP OF OKLA
3612 Epperly Dr (73115-3608)
PHONE.................................405 672-0240
Judith Dean, *President*
Michael Dean, *Vice Pres*
John Dean, *Treasurer*
EMP: 6
SALES (est): 2MM **Privately Held**
SIC: 1311 6211 Crude petroleum production; natural gas production; mineral royalties dealers

(G-2002)
MTM RECOGNITION CORPORATION
3405 Se 29th St (73115-1609)
PHONE.................................405 670-4545
David Smith, *CEO*
Rick Bewley, *General Mgr*
Candy Kendrick, *Purchasing*
EMP: 238
SALES (corp-wide): 109MM **Privately Held**
SIC: 3911 3873 Jewelry, precious metal; watches, clocks, watchcases & parts
PA: Mtm Recognition Corporation
3201 Se 29th St
Oklahoma City OK 73115
405 609-6900

(G-2003)
NEXTGEN UAS TRANSPONDERS LLC
213 Howard Dr (73115-3803)
PHONE.................................405 637-7940
Roger Ray Coats, *Principal*
EMP: 2
SALES (est): 100.2K **Privately Held**
SIC: 3728 Aircraft parts & equipment

(G-2004)
OKLAHOMA SCHOOL OF WELDING
321 S Scott St (73115-1011)
PHONE.................................405 672-1841
EMP: 1
SALES (est): 17.5K **Privately Held**
SIC: 8299 7692 School/Educational Services Welding Repair

(G-2005)
PARKER KUSTOM WOODWORKING
4209 Angela Dr (73115-4409)
PHONE.................................405 414-2820
Gregory O Parker, *Administration*
EMP: 2
SALES (est): 119.9K **Privately Held**
SIC: 2431 Millwork

(G-2006)
PLUMB SQUARE CONSTRUCTION
3112 Del View Dr (73115-4268)
PHONE.................................405 619-9898
Calvin Stanford, *Owner*
EMP: 4
SALES (est): 288.1K **Privately Held**
SIC: 3448 Prefabricated metal buildings

(G-2007)
SOONER BINDERY INC
4335 Se 28th St Ste A (73115-3318)
PHONE.................................405 232-4764
Paul Strolle, *President*
EMP: 2 **EST:** 1997
SALES: 100K **Privately Held**
SIC: 2789 Binding only: books, pamphlets, magazines, etc.

Delaware
Nowata County

(G-2008)
LADDER ENERGY CO
Rr 1 (74027)
PHONE.................................918 467-3323
Tom Cochrane, *Principal*
EMP: 3
SALES (est): 315.6K **Privately Held**
SIC: 1382 Oil & gas exploration services

(G-2009)
TOP RIM TECHNOLOGY
319 E Delaware (74027)
PHONE.................................918 467-3617
EMP: 2 **EST:** 2002
SALES: 50K **Privately Held**
SIC: 7372 Prepackaged Software Services

Depew
Creek County

(G-2010)
BLUE STAR ACID SERVICE INC
25914 S 465th West Ave (74028)
P.O. Box 278 (74028-0278)
PHONE.................................918 324-5350
Larry Combs, *President*
Mike Prescott, *Vice Pres*
Judy Combs, *Admin Sec*
EMP: 8
SQ FT: 3,750
SALES (est): 800K **Privately Held**
SIC: 1389 Oil field services

(G-2011)
J & S FITTINGS INC
21284 Milfay Rd (74028-3499)
PHONE.................................918 324-5777
Jim Wilkerson, *President*
Donita Hope, *Corp Secy*
EMP: 5
SQ FT: 1,913
SALES: 400K **Privately Held**
SIC: 3089 Fittings for pipe, plastic

Dewey
Washington County

(G-2012)
ADAMS INVESTMENT COMPANY (PA)
Also Called: Central States Bus Forms Div
2500 Industrial Pkwy (74029-9702)
P.O. Box 9, Bartlesville (74005-0009)
PHONE.................................918 335-1234
Kenneth G Adams, *Ch of Bd*
Diana M Adams, *President*
David Baumann, *Principal*
Paul J Korte, *Principal*
Craig D Stover, *Principal*
▲ **EMP:** 85
SQ FT: 110,000
SALES (est): 86.2MM **Privately Held**
SIC: 2761 Manifold business forms

(G-2013)
ADAMS INVESTMENT COMPANY
Also Called: Central States Business Forms
2500 Industrial Pkwy (74029-9702)
P.O. Box 9 (74029-0009)
PHONE.................................918 661-2100
Kenneth Adams, *Owner*
Melissa Campbell, *Purch Mgr*
Katie Mullis, *Sales Staff*
Gwen Nichols, *Sales Staff*
EMP: 100
SALES (corp-wide): 86.2MM **Privately Held**
SIC: 2711 Job printing & newspaper publishing combined
PA: Adams Investment Company
2500 Industrial Pkwy
Dewey OK 74029
918 335-1234

(G-2014)
ALLTRA CORP
2300 Partridge Rd (74029)
PHONE.................................918 534-5100
EMP: 2
SALES (est): 97.8K **Privately Held**
SIC: 3548 8331 Welding apparatus; job training & vocational rehabilitation services

(G-2015)
ALLTRA CORPORATION
1600 Patridge Rd (74029-9700)
P.O. Box 370 (74029-0370)
PHONE.................................918 534-5100
Jon Arrowsmith, *President*
Jason Jones, *Purchasing*
Bruce Gwilliam, *Engineer*
Anton Steyn, *Engineer*
Jim Countryman, *Sales Engr*
EMP: 117

SQ FT: 100,000
SALES (est): 34MM **Privately Held**
SIC: **3548** 8331 Electric welding equipment; job training & vocational rehabilitation services

(G-2016)
APAC-CENTRAL
400251 W 1500 Rd (74029-4501)
P.O. Box 128 (74029-0128)
PHONE..................................918 534-1741
Clint Hays, *Executive*
EMP: 2
SALES (est): 66K **Privately Held**
SIC: **1429** Crushed & broken stone

(G-2017)
BLUCO INC
399258 W 1330 Dr (74029-4217)
PHONE..................................800 535-0135
John Rountree, *Principal*
EMP: 1
SALES (est): 54.1K **Privately Held**
SIC: **3548** Electric welding equipment

(G-2018)
BRATCO OPERATING COMPANY
399258 W 1330 Dr (74029-4217)
P.O. Box 279 (74029-0279)
PHONE..................................918 534-2322
John Rountree, *President*
Jeff Meszaros, *President*
Jeff M Meszaros, *Exec Dir*
EMP: 16
SQ FT: 560
SALES (est): 2.4MM **Privately Held**
SIC: **1311** 4493 Crude petroleum production; marinas

(G-2019)
CUTS CUSTOM BUTCHERING LLC
Highway 75 (74029)
P.O. Box 577 (74029-0577)
PHONE..................................918 534-1382
Janet Peck, *Mng Member*
EMP: 8
SALES (est): 136.9K **Privately Held**
SIC: **2011** 2013 Meat packing plants; sausages & other prepared meats

(G-2020)
DIW ENGNEERING FABRICATION LLC
1220 Industrial Pkwy (74029-9747)
P.O. Box 158 (74029-0158)
PHONE..................................918 534-0001
Dick Scott, *General Mgr*
Joan Baughman, *Info Tech Mgr*
John Kane,
John D Kane,
EMP: 21
SQ FT: 30,000
SALES (est): 1.9MM **Privately Held**
WEB: www.diwfab.com
SIC: **1799** 3444 3446 3715 Ornamental metal work; sheet metalwork; architectural metalwork; truck trailers; mechanical engineering

(G-2021)
ENTRANSCO INC
112 N Delaware St (74029-2414)
PHONE..................................916 628-6835
James Kitchel, *CEO*
Doug L Lamb, *COO*
Todd E Wille, *CFO*
EMP: 6
SALES (est): 169.4K **Privately Held**
SIC: **1382** Oil & gas exploration services

(G-2022)
GREEN COUNTRY WIRELINE INC
8 3/4 Mi Ne On Road 11 (74029)
P.O. Box 13 (74029-0013)
PHONE..................................918 534-2107
Steve Harter, *President*
EMP: 2
SALES (est): 200K **Privately Held**
SIC: **1389** Oil field services

(G-2023)
HAYS TENT & AWNING
Also Called: Hays Awning
512 S Osage Ave (74029-2816)
PHONE..................................918 534-1663
Thomas Hays, *Owner*
EMP: 3 EST: 1971
SALES (est): 239.6K **Privately Held**
SIC: **5999** 2394 7699 3993 Canvas products; tarpaulins, fabric: made from purchased materials; liners & covers, fabric: made from purchased materials; awnings, fabric: made from purchased materials; awning repair shop; signs & advertising specialties

(G-2024)
HEM INDUSTRIES
13280 N 3990 Rd (74029-4212)
PHONE..................................918 534-0579
James A Herndon, *Owner*
EMP: 1
SQ FT: 3,000
SALES (est): 300K **Privately Held**
SIC: **3599** 3679 3451 Machine shop, jobbing & repair; electronic circuits; screw machine products

(G-2025)
HS FIELD SERVICES INC
397781 W 1400 Rd (74029-3970)
P.O. Box 605 (74029-0605)
PHONE..................................918 534-9121
Jum Shambles, *President*
EMP: 50
SALES (est): 7MM **Privately Held**
SIC: **1389** 8211 Servicing oil & gas wells; high school, junior or senior

(G-2026)
IMAGING CONCEPTS
516 E Don Tyler Ave (74029-2518)
PHONE..................................918 534-1761
Michael McCracken Jr, *Owner*
Shara McCracken, *Co-Owner*
EMP: 2 EST: 1997
SALES: 50K **Privately Held**
SIC: **2759** 2396 Screen printing; automotive & apparel trimmings

(G-2027)
L & M WELDING LLC
12700 N 3990 Rd (74029-4012)
PHONE..................................918 534-6864
Luke Nathaniel Gotwalt, *Owner*
EMP: 1
SALES (est): 25K **Privately Held**
SIC: **7692** Welding repair

(G-2028)
MCCABE ROUSTABOUT SERVICE
11783 Us Highway 75 (74029-3710)
P.O. Box 176 (74029-0176)
PHONE..................................918 534-3131
EMP: 2
SALES (est): 110K **Privately Held**
SIC: **1389** Oil/Gas Field Services

(G-2029)
OPS SALES COMPANY
14861 N 3980 Rd (74029-3947)
P.O. Box 189 (74029-0189)
PHONE..................................918 534-3760
Brian Kimrey, *President*
EMP: 3
SALES (est): 3MM **Privately Held**
SIC: **5051** 3259 3317 Pipe & tubing, steel; sewer pipe or fittings, clay; steel pipe & tubes

(G-2030)
QUARRY
Also Called: Quarry Custom Cultured Marble
2001 N Osage Ave (74029-1514)
P.O. Box 433 (74029-0433)
PHONE..................................918 534-2120
Steve L Williams, *Owner*
EMP: 2
SQ FT: 2,000
SALES (est): 165K **Privately Held**
SIC: **3089** 3431 2434 Composition stone, plastic; metal sanitary ware; wood kitchen cabinets

(G-2031)
ROBERT C BEARD
Also Called: Beard Production Co
423 E 9th St (74029-1648)
P.O. Box 490 (74029-0490)
PHONE..................................918 534-2020
Robert C Beard, *Owner*
EMP: 1
SQ FT: 5,500
SALES (est): 93.7K **Privately Held**
SIC: **1381** Drilling oil & gas wells

(G-2032)
RON GRIGGS BACKHOE & DUMP
600 W 9th St (74029-2015)
PHONE..................................918 440-1334
Ron Griggs, *President*
EMP: 2
SALES (est): 225K **Privately Held**
SIC: **3531** Backhoes

(G-2033)
SUPERIOR COMPANIES INC
Also Called: Superior Manufacturing
1000 E 14th St (74029-1715)
PHONE..................................918 534-0755
Barney Powell, *COO*
EMP: 70
SALES (corp-wide): 27.6MM **Privately Held**
SIC: **3799** 7692 3429 Trailers & trailer equipment; welding repair; manufactured hardware (general)
PA: Superior Companies, Inc.
101 N Johnstone Ave
Bartlesville OK 74003
918 336-5075

Dill City
Washita County

(G-2034)
CHRISTIANS WELDING SERVICE
201 N Rambo (73641-9525)
P.O. Box 6 (73641-0006)
PHONE..................................580 674-3384
Radford Christian, *Owner*
Eddie Christian, *Corp Secy*
EMP: 1
SALES (est): 78K **Privately Held**
SIC: **1799** 7692 Welding on site; welding repair

(G-2035)
DILL CITY EMBROIDERY
Highway 152 (73641)
PHONE..................................580 674-3989
Alma Black, *Owner*
EMP: 2
SALES (est): 75K **Privately Held**
SIC: **2241** Narrow fabric mills

(G-2036)
KNOWLES PERFORMANCE ENGINES
11828 N 2120 Rd (73641-4128)
PHONE..................................580 821-4825
EMP: 2
SALES (est): 107.4K **Privately Held**
SIC: **3569** General industrial machinery

(G-2037)
ROCKY FARMERS COOPERATIVE INC
Also Called: Western Producers Cooperative
702 S Rambo (73641-9578)
P.O. Box 128 (73641-0128)
PHONE..................................580 674-3356
Terry Shelton, *General Mgr*
EMP: 4
SALES (est): 521.9K
SALES (corp-wide): 4.7MM **Privately Held**
SIC: **5153** 2048 5191 0724 Grain elevators; prepared feeds; feed; cotton ginning
PA: Rocky Farmers Cooperative Inc
105 N Main St
Rocky OK 73661
580 666-2440

Dover
Kingfisher County

(G-2038)
BARKER MACHINE SHOP
Rr 1 (73734)
PHONE..................................405 828-4683
Scotty Barker, *Owner*
EMP: 1
SQ FT: 2,000
SALES (est): 114.4K **Privately Held**
SIC: **3599** 0111 Machine shop, jobbing & repair; wheat

(G-2039)
CWS WIRELINE LLC
600 S Hwy 81 (73734)
P.O. Box 340 (73734-0340)
PHONE..................................405 828-4225
Billy Matthews,
Dan Darling,
EMP: 25
SALES: 12MM **Privately Held**
SIC: **1389** Oil & gas wells: building, repairing & dismantling

(G-2040)
ISBELL INDUSTRIES LLC
10602 N 2850 Rd (73734-5819)
PHONE..................................405 828-7228
Seth Wade Isbell, *Principal*
EMP: 1 EST: 2018
SALES (est): 39.6K **Privately Held**
SIC: **3999** Manufacturing industries

(G-2041)
LIBERTY SWABBING INC
19762 E 700 Rd (73734-3434)
P.O. Box 175 (73734-0175)
PHONE..................................405 828-4427
Dave Ingle, *President*
Twila Ingle, *Corp Secy*
EMP: 2
SALES (est): 195.3K **Privately Held**
SIC: **1389** Swabbing wells; cleaning wells

(G-2042)
OREMUS PRESS & PUBLISHING
24212 E 680 Rd (73734-3411)
PHONE..................................405 368-4645
Jeremy Ingle, *Principal*
EMP: 1
SALES (est): 37.5K **Privately Held**
SIC: **2741** Miscellaneous publishing

(G-2043)
R M SWABBING LLC
17199 E 715 Rd (73734-3460)
PHONE..................................405 828-7213
Ricky D Matthews, *Principal*
EMP: 2
SALES (est): 139.1K **Privately Held**
SIC: **1389** Bailing, cleaning, swabbing & treating of wells

(G-2044)
RED FORK MFG LLC
11921 N 2850 Rd (73734-5822)
PHONE..................................405 368-7367
Greg Terrell, *Principal*
EMP: 2 EST: 2001
SALES (est): 283.5K **Privately Held**
SIC: **3523** Farm machinery & equipment

(G-2045)
STINEBRINGS CUSTOM PROCESSING
308 S Barr St (73734-9410)
PHONE..................................405 828-4247
Gary Stinebring, *Owner*
Teresa Stinebring, *Co-Owner*
EMP: 2
SALES: 195K **Privately Held**
SIC: **2011** Meat packing plants

GEOGRAPHIC SECTION

Drumright - Creek County (G-2076)

Drummond
Garfield County

(G-2046)
C M TRAILERS
11711 W Wood Rd (73735-1081)
PHONE.................................580 493-2301
Charles Mears, *Owner*
EMP: 3
SALES (est): 347.2K **Privately Held**
SIC: 3715 Semitrailers for truck tractors

(G-2047)
DSA DESIGNS LLC
Also Called: Inboard Hammock Light
9512 S Logan Rd (73735-1022)
PHONE.................................580 493-2723
Darrell Dwight Wanzer, *Administration*
EMP: 1
SALES (est): 83.6K **Privately Held**
SIC: 2399 Hammocks & other net products

(G-2048)
T AND L EMBROIDERY
418 Nebraska Ave (73735)
PHONE.................................580 493-2239
Tammy Sweetwood, *Principal*
EMP: 1
SALES (est): 40.3K **Privately Held**
SIC: 2395 Embroidery & art needlework

Drumright
Creek County

(G-2049)
5A ENTERPRISES INC
303 N Skinner Ave (74030-2852)
PHONE.................................918 260-8909
EMP: 1 **EST:** 2010
SALES (est): 49K **Privately Held**
SIC: 2741 Misc Publishing

(G-2050)
ALLAN BGHS WLDG ROUSTABOUT SVC
12589 S 486th West Ave (74030-5914)
PHONE.................................918 625-1712
Allan Baugh, *Principal*
EMP: 2
SALES (est): 147.6K **Privately Held**
SIC: 1389 Roustabout service

(G-2051)
BARNES OIL CO
10015 S 433rd West Ave (74030-5879)
PHONE.................................918 352-2308
Darrell Barnes, *Owner*
EMP: 1
SALES (est): 150K **Privately Held**
SIC: 1311 Crude petroleum production

(G-2052)
BEREXCO LLC
110 N Magnolia (74030-3434)
P.O. Box 231 (74030-0231)
PHONE.................................918 352-2588
Tomy Wessell, *Manager*
EMP: 12
SALES (corp-wide): 410.9MM **Privately Held**
SIC: 1311 Crude petroleum production; natural gas production
PA: Berexco Llc
2020 N Bramblewood St
Wichita KS 67206
316 265-3311

(G-2053)
BILLY CARROLL
10431 S 513th West Ave (74030-5450)
P.O. Box 362 (74030-0362)
PHONE.................................918 352-9228
EMP: 1 **EST:** 1987
SALES (est): 100K **Privately Held**
SIC: 0191 1311 General Crop Farm Crude Petroleum/Natural Gas Production

(G-2054)
CARGILL VALVE LLC
507 Griffith Ave (74030-5932)
P.O. Box 768 (74030-0768)
PHONE.................................918 352-2203
James Alcorn,
EMP: 7
SALES (est): 1MM **Privately Held**
SIC: 3592 Valves

(G-2055)
DELPHIA PUBLISHING LLC
129 E Broadway St (74030-3801)
PHONE.................................918 232-8709
EMP: 1
SALES (est): 54.8K **Privately Held**
SIC: 2741 Miscellaneous publishing

(G-2056)
DRUMRIGHT GUSHER INC
129 E Broadway St (74030-3801)
PHONE.................................918 352-2284
Darla Graves, *President*
Barbara Vice, *Principal*
EMP: 2
SALES (est): 145.9K **Privately Held**
SIC: 2711 Newspapers: publishing only, not printed on site

(G-2057)
DRUMRIGHT OILWELL SERVICES LLC
501 Ok 99 (74030)
P.O. Box 1114 (74030-1114)
PHONE.................................918 352-9646
David Shields,
EMP: 90
SALES (est): 5.8MM **Privately Held**
SIC: 1389 Servicing oil & gas wells

(G-2058)
DRUMRIGHT TAR
1103 E Broadway St (74030-3855)
PHONE.................................918 352-4000
Tony Thompson, *Principal*
EMP: 2
SALES (est): 146.2K **Privately Held**
SIC: 2865 Tar

(G-2059)
EARL-LE DOZER SERVICE LLC
51266 W Highway 33 (74030-5708)
P.O. Box 351 (74030-0351)
PHONE.................................918 352-2072
Truman Weaver,
Steve Weaver,
EMP: 55
SQ FT: 9,500
SALES (est): 6MM **Privately Held**
SIC: 1794 1622 1389 Excavation work; highway construction, elevated; oil field services

(G-2060)
GLIMP OIL COMPANY LLC
Se Of City (74030)
P.O. Box 391 (74030-0391)
PHONE.................................918 352-2978
Ella Glimp, *Owner*
Dale Glimp, *Mng Member*
EMP: 2 **EST:** 1954
SALES (est): 130K **Privately Held**
SIC: 1389 Oil field services

(G-2061)
HAUSNERS PRECAST CON PDTS INC
Also Called: Hausner's
505 Griffith Ave (74030-5932)
P.O. Box 32 (74030-0032)
PHONE.................................918 352-3479
John Hausner, *President*
EMP: 40
SQ FT: 11,880
SALES (est): 11.8MM **Privately Held**
SIC: 3272 Septic tanks, concrete; grease traps, concrete; concrete products, pre-cast

(G-2062)
IDEAL MACHINE & WELDING INC
405 N Harley Ave (74030-3005)
P.O. Box 1135 (74030-1135)
PHONE.................................918 352-3660
Dennis Tull, *President*
EMP: 8
SQ FT: 2,000
SALES (est): 442.8K **Privately Held**
SIC: 3599 7692 Machine shop, jobbing & repair; welding repair

(G-2063)
INDEPENDENT TRUCKING CO INC
902 N Smather Ave (74030-2240)
P.O. Box 271 (74030-0271)
PHONE.................................918 352-2539
Bob Shideler, *President*
Betty Shideler, *Corp Secy*
EMP: 19 **EST:** 1947
SQ FT: 6,800
SALES (est): 1.8MM **Privately Held**
SIC: 1389 4212 Oil field services; local trucking, without storage

(G-2064)
JA MARRS OIL CO INC
206 E Pine St (74030)
P.O. Box 1157 (74030-1157)
PHONE.................................918 352-2798
Cheryl Marrs, *Principal*
EMP: 4 **EST:** 2001
SALES (est): 666.3K **Privately Held**
SIC: 1381 Drilling oil & gas wells

(G-2065)
KEYSTONE GAS CORPORATION (PA)
101 E Broadway St (74030-3801)
P.O. Box 711 (74030-0711)
PHONE.................................918 352-2443
R A Sellers Jr, *Ch of Bd*
R A Sellers III, *President*
Jim Martin, *Principal*
L C Cobb, *Vice Pres*
James Martin Jr, *CFO*
EMP: 42
SQ FT: 2,850
SALES: 5MM **Privately Held**
SIC: 1382 Oil & gas exploration services

(G-2066)
KEYSTONE GAS CORPORATION
1106 N Smather Ave (74030-2259)
P.O. Box 711 (74030-0711)
PHONE.................................918 352-2443
Kevin Smith, *Manager*
EMP: 20
SALES (est): 2.3MM **Privately Held**
SIC: 1382 Oil & gas exploration services
PA: Keystone Gas Corporation
101 E Broadway St
Drumright OK 74030

(G-2067)
MR MFG
9931 S Highway 99 (74030-5779)
PHONE.................................918 352-4461
EMP: 7
SALES (est): 360K **Privately Held**
SIC: 3999 Mfg Misc Products

(G-2068)
O K PLUNGER SERVICE
Highway 33 W (74030)
P.O. Box 706 (74030-0706)
PHONE.................................918 352-4269
Vera Sherwood, *Owner*
Henry F Sherwood, *Co-Owner*
EMP: 3
SALES (est): 157.9K **Privately Held**
SIC: 1389 7692 3561 Oil field services; welding repair; pumps & pumping equipment

(G-2069)
OVERBILT TRAILER COMPANY
1115 E Broadway St (74030-3855)
P.O. Box 272 (74030-0272)
PHONE.................................918 352-4474
William G Schiffmacher, *President*
Shelly Schiffmacher, *Vice Pres*
▼ **EMP:** 20
SQ FT: 6,000
SALES (est): 4.9MM **Privately Held**
SIC: 3715 Truck trailers

(G-2070)
QUAPAW COMPANY INC
Hwy 33 2 One Half Mi E (74030)
P.O. Box 609, Stillwater (74076-0609)
PHONE.................................918 352-2533
Tom Kiser, *Manager*
EMP: 20
SQ FT: 4,000
SALES (corp-wide): 19MM **Privately Held**
SIC: 5032 2951 Paving materials; asphalt paving mixtures & blocks
PA: The Quapaw Company
3224 N Perkins Rd
Stillwater OK
405 377-9240

(G-2071)
SOONER TOOL COMPANY (PA)
1 Mile W Of City Hwy 33 (74030)
P.O. Box 311 (74030-0311)
PHONE.................................918 352-4440
Douglas Sparks, *President*
Doug Sparks, *President*
Laveta Jean Sparks, *Corp Secy*
EMP: 4
SALES (est): 1.3MM **Privately Held**
SIC: 1311 7359 Crude petroleum production; tool rental

(G-2072)
SUNOCO LOGISTICS PARTNERS LP
907 S Detroit (74030)
PHONE.................................918 352-9442
EMP: 3
SALES (est): 255.2K **Privately Held**
SIC: 1311 Crude Petroleum/Natural Gas Production

(G-2073)
SWEEPER METAL FABRICATORS CORP
Hwy 99 Truck Byp (74030)
PHONE.................................918 352-9180
Gerald Vann, *Branch Mgr*
EMP: 28
SALES (corp-wide): 4.6MM **Privately Held**
SIC: 3441 3442 2531 2522 Building components, structural steel; metal doors, sash & trim; public building & related furniture; office furniture, except wood; partitions & fixtures, except wood
PA: Sweeper Metal Fabricators Corp.
1240 E Broadway St
Drumright OK 74030
918 352-2133

(G-2074)
T & D FABRICATION INC
54440 W Highway 16 (74030-4452)
P.O. Box 135 (74030-0135)
PHONE.................................918 352-8031
Terry Martin, *President*
Denise Martin, *Vice Pres*
Charity Ellis, *Purch Mgr*
EMP: 20
SQ FT: 25,000
SALES (est): 3MM **Privately Held**
SIC: 3441 Fabricated structural metal

(G-2075)
THOMPSON PUMP COMPANY
409 E Federal St (74030-3817)
P.O. Box 152 (74030-0152)
PHONE.................................918 352-2117
Lance Campbell, *Manager*
EMP: 3
SQ FT: 1,800
SALES (corp-wide): 6.1MM **Privately Held**
WEB: www.thompsonpump.com
SIC: 3533 7699 Oil & gas field machinery; pumps & pumping equipment repair
PA: Thompson Pump Company
801 W 20th St
Okmulgee OK 74447
918 756-6164

(G-2076)
TIDAL SCHOOL WINERY
500 N Bristow Ave (74030-2402)
PHONE.................................918 352-4900
Gary Schroeder, *Principal*

EMP: 2
SALES (est): 118.5K **Privately Held**
SIC: 2084 5921 Wines; wine

(G-2077)
XTRA OIL FIELD & CNSTR CO
Also Called: X-Tra Oil Field Svcs & Cnstr
113 N Skinner Ave (74030-3232)
PHONE.....................918 352-3722
Ralph Bray, *Owner*
EMP: 8
SALES (est): 739.4K **Privately Held**
SIC: 1389 Oil field services

(G-2078)
YOUNG TOOL COMPANY LLC
49698 W Highway 33 (74030)
P.O. Box 1195 (74030-1195)
PHONE.....................918 352-2213
Kim Young, *President*
EMP: 4
SALES (est): 441.5K **Privately Held**
SIC: 1389 Oil field services

Duke
Jackson County

(G-2079)
AMERICAN GYPSUM COMPANY LLC
Highway 62 W (73532)
PHONE.....................580 679-3391
Dave House, *President*
▲ **EMP:** 225
SALES (est): 46.4MM
SALES (corp-wide): 1.3B **Publicly Held**
SIC: 3275 Gypsum products
PA: Eagle Materials Inc.
5960 Berkshire Ln Ste 900
Dallas TX 75225
214 432-2000

(G-2080)
TARACO ENTERPRISES LLC
101 W 2nd St (73532)
P.O. Box 367 (73532-0367)
PHONE.....................580 679-3956
Kit Ray-Lewis,
Debbie Lewis,
Kit Ray-Lewis,
EMP: 4
SQ FT: 2,800
SALES: 1MM **Privately Held**
SIC: 3499 Nozzles, spray: aerosol, paint or insecticide

(G-2081)
TWO TERRITORIES TRADING CO LLC
16249 State Highway 34 (73532-9406)
P.O. Box 254 (73532-0254)
PHONE.....................580 679-4701
Gayle Johnson, *Mng Member*
Joe R Johnson, *Mng Member*
EMP: 2
SALES (est): 47.2K **Privately Held**
SIC: 2033 Canned fruits & specialties

(G-2082)
WINDRUNNER ENERGY INC
19016 Us Highway 62 (73532-9433)
PHONE.....................580 841-0404
Chris Claussen, *Officer*
EMP: 2
SALES: 300K **Privately Held**
SIC: 3621 Windmills, electric generating

Duncan
Stephens County

(G-2083)
ATLAS CONCRETE INC (HQ)
2112 W Bois D Arc Ave (73533-2927)
PHONE.....................580 255-7280
Eugene Martinenu, *President*
Fallis A Beall, *President*
Nola Sue Beall, *Corp Secy*
Robert Beall, *Vice Pres*
Michael Harlan, *Vice Pres*
EMP: 2 **EST:** 1960
SQ FT: 2,000
SALES (est): 450.1K
SALES (corp-wide): 1.4B **Publicly Held**
SIC: 3273 Ready-mixed concrete
PA: U.S. Concrete, Inc.
331 N Main St
Euless TX 76039
817 835-4105

(G-2084)
ATLAS-TUCK CONCRETE INC (HQ)
2112 W Bois D Arc Ave (73533-2900)
P.O. Box 787 (73534-0787)
PHONE.....................580 255-1716
Eugene Martineau, *President*
Cristle Okelly, *General Mgr*
EMP: 5 **EST:** 1964
SQ FT: 2,000
SALES (est): 1.2MM
SALES (corp-wide): 1.4B **Publicly Held**
SIC: 3273 Ready-mixed concrete
PA: U.S. Concrete, Inc.
331 N Main St
Euless TX 76039
817 835-4105

(G-2085)
AXIS TECHNOLOGIES LLC
4895 W Plato Rd (73533-9094)
PHONE.....................580 467-4257
Brian Wilkerson, *Mng Member*
EMP: 8 **EST:** 2008
SALES (est): 948.9K **Privately Held**
SIC: 3533 Drilling tools for gas, oil or water wells; oil & gas drilling rigs & equipment

(G-2086)
B AND J BACKHOE AND CNSTR
177030 N 2950 Rd (73533-6880)
PHONE.....................580 467-4981
EMP: 2
SALES (est): 66K **Privately Held**
SIC: 3531 Backhoes

(G-2087)
BARTLING PUMPS & SUPPLIES LLC
4310 Ashland (73533-8956)
PHONE.....................580 444-2227
Marvin Todd Bartling, *Principal*
EMP: 2
SALES (est): 107.4K **Privately Held**
SIC: 3561 Pumps & pumping equipment

(G-2088)
BASIC ENERGY SERVICES INC
7302 N Hwy 81 (73533-8794)
PHONE.....................580 252-6200
EMP: 1
SALES (corp-wide): 567.2MM **Publicly Held**
SIC: 1389 Oil field services
PA: Basic Energy Services, Inc.
801 Cherry St Unit 2
Fort Worth TX 76102
817 334-4100

(G-2089)
BECHTELS HEAVY METAL WORKS LLC
1003 E Willow Ave (73533-7723)
PHONE.....................580 251-1412
Jerry Bechtel,
Laurie Bechtel,
EMP: 2
SALES: 100K **Privately Held**
SIC: 3569 Robots, assembly line: industrial & commercial

(G-2090)
BF MACHINE SHOP INC
1603 N 5th St (73533-3638)
P.O. Box 247 (73534-0247)
PHONE.....................580 255-6119
Larry Foster, *President*
Jason Foster, *Vice Pres*
EMP: 7
SALES: 1.8MM **Privately Held**
SIC: 3599 Machine shop, jobbing & repair

(G-2091)
BF MACHINES SHOP INC
1603 N 5th St (73533-3638)
P.O. Box 247 (73534-0247)
PHONE.....................580 255-5899
Benny W Wilson, *President*
Bryn Wilson, *Vice Pres*
EMP: 12
SQ FT: 8,500
SALES (est): 1.3MM **Privately Held**
SIC: 3599 3533 Machine shop, jobbing & repair; oil & gas field machinery

(G-2092)
BUD OIL INC
1032 W Main St Ste 100 (73533-4549)
P.O. Box 1970 (73534-1970)
PHONE.....................580 251-1378
Jerry Budowsky, *President*
Patti Budowsky, *Corp Secy*
EMP: 2
SALES (est): 424.5K **Privately Held**
SIC: 1311 Crude petroleum production

(G-2093)
BUTKIN OIL CO LLC (PA)
16 S 9th St Rm 306 (73533-4900)
P.O. Box 2090 (73534-2090)
PHONE.....................580 444-2561
Robert Butkin,
Tom Luetkemeyer,
EMP: 10
SQ FT: 1,000
SALES (est): 1.6MM **Privately Held**
SIC: 1311 Crude petroleum production

(G-2094)
C & C PERFORMANCE ENGINES
Also Called: Phil C Cook's & C Performance
1402 W Park Ave (73533-5351)
PHONE.....................580 252-4331
Phil Cook, *Owner*
EMP: 2
SQ FT: 1,500
SALES: 104K **Privately Held**
SIC: 3714 7538 5531 Rebuilding engines & transmissions, factory basis; general automotive repair shops; automotive & home supply stores

(G-2095)
C & R PRINT SHOP INC
1401 W Main St (73533-4330)
PHONE.....................580 255-5656
Karen Villarreal, *Branch Mgr*
EMP: 1
SALES (corp-wide): 752.2K **Privately Held**
WEB: www.candrprintshop.com
SIC: 2752 2759 Commercial printing, offset; letterpress printing
PA: C & R Print Shop Inc
420 W Dakota Ave
Chickasha OK 73018
405 224-7921

(G-2096)
C&Y CASEING PULLING CO INC
250 S Eastland Dr (73533)
P.O. Box 37 (73534-0037)
PHONE.....................580 255-4453
Keith Smith, *President*
EMP: 1 **EST:** 1965
SQ FT: 5,000
SALES: 250K **Privately Held**
SIC: 1311 Crude petroleum production

(G-2097)
CAMERON TECHNOLOGIES INC
Also Called: Measurement Systems
7000 Nix Dr (73533-4185)
PHONE.....................580 470-9600
Candi Mc Guire, *Financial Exec*
Ricky Alen, *Manager*
EMP: 22 **Publicly Held**
SIC: 3533 5084 Oil field machinery & equipment; oil well machinery, equipment & supplies
HQ: Cameron Technologies, Inc.
4646 W Sam Houston Pkwy N
Houston TX 77041

(G-2098)
CAPROCK INC
15 N 9th St Ste 208 (73533-4657)
P.O. Box 1341 (73534-1341)
PHONE.....................580 255-0831
William S Richardson, *President*
Margie Kennedy, *Vice Pres*
EMP: 2
SQ FT: 800
SALES (est): 182.7K **Privately Held**
SIC: 1311 Crude petroleum production

(G-2099)
COOK MACHINE COMPANY
3920 S 13th St (73533-9098)
PHONE.....................580 252-1699
Greg Cook, *President*
EMP: 30
SQ FT: 37,000
SALES (est): 2.1MM **Privately Held**
SIC: 7359 7363 7549 3429 Equipment rental & leasing; employee leasing service; automotive maintenance services; manufactured hardware (general)

(G-2100)
CRYOGAS SERVICES LLC
7024 N Highway 81 (73533-4001)
P.O. Box 488 (73534-0488)
PHONE.....................580 252-6200
Don Weaks,
EMP: 11
SALES (est): 509.6K **Privately Held**
SIC: 1389 Oil field services

(G-2101)
CRYSTALTECH INC
Also Called: Crystal Tech
1601 N 5th St (73533-3638)
P.O. Box 56 (73534-0056)
PHONE.....................580 252-8893
Charles Totty, *President*
▲ **EMP:** 4
SQ FT: 3,500
SALES (est): 500K **Privately Held**
WEB: www.crystaltechinc.com
SIC: 3674 3823 3533 Radiation sensors; industrial instrmnts msrmnt display/control process variable; oil & gas field machinery

(G-2102)
CUSTOM EXPRESSIGNZ
1306 W Sycamore Ave (73533-5034)
PHONE.....................580 252-2868
Terry Moore, *Owner*
EMP: 1
SALES (est): 56.1K **Privately Held**
SIC: 3993 Signs & advertising specialties

(G-2103)
DADS MACHINE & CUSTOM WELDING
105 E Bois D Arc Ave (73533-7573)
PHONE.....................580 470-8334
EMP: 1
SALES (est): 122K **Privately Held**
SIC: 3599 Machine Shop

(G-2104)
DASTAR INC
511 N 10th St (73533-4421)
PHONE.....................580 786-8833
David Nichols, *President*
EMP: 3
SALES (est): 164.8K **Privately Held**
SIC: 3341 Secondary precious metals

(G-2105)
DISTINCTIVE DECOR LLC
901 W Main St (73533-4617)
P.O. Box 957 (73534-0957)
PHONE.....................580 252-9494
Mary Edwards, *Cust Mgr*
Leigh McEntire,
EMP: 10
SALES (est): 996.8K **Privately Held**
SIC: 3229 5947 5311 Tableware, glass or glass ceramic; gift shop; department stores

(G-2106)
DMS TERMS & CONDITIONS
750 Ridley Rd (73533-7700)
PHONE.....................580 303-7500

GEOGRAPHIC SECTION

Duncan - Stephens County (G-2138)

EMP: 1
SALES (est): 39.6K **Privately Held**
SIC: 3999 Manufacturing industries

(G-2107)
DOLESE BROS CO
1109 S 2nd St (73533-7841)
PHONE.................580 255-3046
David Turner, *Manager*
EMP: 11
SALES (corp-wide): 8.5MM **Privately Held**
SIC: 3531 5211 4212 3273 Construction machinery; lumber & other building materials; local trucking, without storage; ready-mixed concrete
PA: Dolese Bros. Co.
20 Nw 13th St
Oklahoma City OK 73103
405 235-2311

(G-2108)
DREAM TEAM PROSTHETICS LLC
7111 Nix Dr (73533-4191)
PHONE.................580 255-2100
Chad Simpson,
Randy Richardson,
EMP: 3
SALES (est): 117.5K **Privately Held**
SIC: 3842 Surgical appliances & supplies

(G-2109)
DUNCAN BIT SERVICE INC
2501 S Highway 81 (73533-9769)
PHONE.................580 255-9787
Joseph Davis, *President*
Sharon Davis, *Vice Pres*
EMP: 17
SQ FT: 15,000
SALES (est): 4.4MM **Privately Held**
SIC: 5084 3545 Drilling bits; oil well machinery, equipment & supplies; drill bits, metalworking

(G-2110)
DUNCAN MACHINE PRODUCTS INC
1003 S 2nd St (73533-7825)
PHONE.................580 467-6784
Teri Billings, *President*
Christopher Billings, *Treasurer*
EMP: 28 EST: 2013
SQ FT: 27,000
SALES (est): 2.9MM **Privately Held**
SIC: 3599 3728 3484 Machine shop, jobbing & repair; aircraft parts & equipment; guns (firearms) or gun parts, 30 mm. & below

(G-2111)
DUNCAN MANNEQUIN INC
Also Called: Duncan Mannequin & Mfg
2525 S Highway 81 (73533-9769)
PHONE.................580 252-5915
Daron Duncan, *President*
EMP: 5
SQ FT: 1,200
SALES (est): 474.5K **Privately Held**
SIC: 3999 Mannequins

(G-2112)
DUNCAN MANUFACTURING INC
100 E Hwy 7 Receiving (73536-0001)
PHONE.................580 251-2137
▲ EMP: 6
SALES (est): 458.7K **Privately Held**
SIC: 3999 Manufacturing industries

(G-2113)
DUNCAN WOOD WORKS LLC
1225 W Park Ave (73533-5346)
P.O. Box 397, Comanche (73529-0397)
PHONE.................580 641-1190
Jennifer Whaley, *Mng Member*
EMP: 5
SALES: 1.9MM **Privately Held**
SIC: 2448 5199 Wood pallets & skids; baling of wood shavings for mulch

(G-2114)
DWW INC
750 Ridley Rd (73533-7700)
PHONE.................580 255-7886
Don Waller, *Principal*

EMP: 3
SALES (est): 88.7K **Privately Held**
SIC: 3599 Machine shop, jobbing & repair

(G-2115)
EASTLAND LAWN MOWER SERVICE
1105 S Highway 81 (73533-3009)
PHONE.................580 252-0077
Carl Merril, *Owner*
Curt Merrill, *Partner*
EMP: 3
SALES (est): 415.6K **Privately Held**
SIC: 5084 3546 5261 Engines, gasoline; saws & sawing equipment; lawnmowers & tractors

(G-2116)
EVANS WELDING LLC
615 E Willow Ave (73533-7715)
PHONE.................580 470-8111
Rickey J Smith, *Principal*
EMP: 2
SALES (est): 228.8K **Privately Held**
SIC: 7692 Welding repair

(G-2117)
EX-PRESS VAC LLC
1625 E Bois D Arc Ave (73533-7779)
PHONE.................580 606-0799
EMP: 2
SALES (est): 49K **Privately Held**
SIC: 2741 Miscellaneous publishing

(G-2118)
FLOTEK INDUSTRIES INC
3600 S 13th St (73533-9067)
PHONE.................580 252-5111
John Callihan, *Branch Mgr*
EMP: 1
SALES (corp-wide): 119.3MM **Publicly Held**
SIC: 3532 Drills & drilling equipment, mining (except oil & gas)
PA: Flotek Industries, Inc.
10603 W Sam Houston Pkwy
Houston TX 77064
713 849-9911

(G-2119)
G&J MEASUREMENT INC
2004 Townsend St (73533-3344)
PHONE.................580 560-3190
B R Gooden, *President*
EMP: 6
SALES: 91K **Privately Held**
SIC: 1321 4922 Natural gas liquids production; natural gas transmission

(G-2120)
GENESIS FINANCIAL SOFTWARE
15 N 9th St Ste 105 (73533-4657)
PHONE.................580 252-2594
Doug Morrow, *Principal*
Chad Rother, *Manager*
EMP: 2
SALES (est): 103.6K **Privately Held**
SIC: 7372 Application computer software

(G-2121)
HALLIBURTON COMPANY
Also Called: Halliburton Energy Services
100 E Halliburton Blvd (73536-0001)
PHONE.................580 251-4614
Lyn Ferguson, *Manager*
EMP: 20 **Publicly Held**
WEB: www.halliburton.com
SIC: 3533 3713 Oil field machinery & equipment; truck & bus bodies
PA: Halliburton Company
3000 N Sam Houston Pkwy E
Houston TX 77032

(G-2122)
HALLIBURTON COMPANY
Also Called: Halliburton Energy Services
1015 W Bois D Arc Ave (73533-4818)
P.O. Box 1431 (73534-1431)
PHONE.................580 251-3002
Tim Hunter, *Project Mgr*
Karla Shackelford, *Accounting Mgr*
Greg Bevans, *Supervisor*
Mike Gray, *Director*
Russell Rodgers, *Technician*

EMP: 200 **Publicly Held**
WEB: www.halliburton.com
SIC: 1389 3533 Well logging; oil & gas field machinery
PA: Halliburton Company
3000 N Sam Houston Pkwy E
Houston TX 77032

(G-2123)
HALLIBURTON COMPANY
Also Called: Halliburton Energy Services
1310 N Hwy 81 (73533-1722)
PHONE.................580 251-3379
Davy Davidson, *President*
EMP: 20 **Publicly Held**
WEB: www.halliburton.com
SIC: 1389 Oil field services
PA: Halliburton Company
3000 N Sam Houston Pkwy E
Houston TX 77032

(G-2124)
HALLIBURTON COMPANY
215 E Bois D Arc Ave (73533-7601)
PHONE.................580 251-2847
Michael Miller, *Manager*
EMP: 153 **Publicly Held**
SIC: 1389 1781 1381 Cementing oil & gas well casings; hydraulic fracturing wells; water well drilling; drilling oil & gas wells
PA: Halliburton Company
3000 N Sam Houston Pkwy E
Houston TX 77032

(G-2125)
HALLIBURTON COMPANY
Also Called: Halliburton Service Division
215 E Bois D Arc Ave (73533-7601)
PHONE.................405 278-9685
Sid Hunnicutt, *Branch Mgr*
EMP: 22 **Publicly Held**
SIC: 1389 Oil field services
PA: Halliburton Company
3000 N Sam Houston Pkwy E
Houston TX 77032

(G-2126)
HALLIBURTON COMPANY
1409 S 13th St 718 (73533-5376)
PHONE.................580 251-4421
EMP: 2 **Publicly Held**
SIC: 1389 Oil field services
PA: Halliburton Company
3000 N Sam Houston Pkwy E
Houston TX 77032

(G-2127)
HALLIBURTON COMPANY
Also Called: Halliburton Energy Services
215 E Bois D Arc Ave (73533-7601)
PHONE.................806 665-0005
Dennis Chambers, *Branch Mgr*
EMP: 140 **Publicly Held**
SIC: 1389 Oil field services
PA: Halliburton Company
3000 N Sam Houston Pkwy E
Houston TX 77032

(G-2128)
HALLIBURTON COMPANY
Also Called: Vann Systems
2600 S 2nd St (73536-0001)
P.O. Box 9000 (73534-9000)
PHONE.................580 251-3406
Jason Henry, *Manager*
Monty McElroy, *Manager*
EMP: 40 **Publicly Held**
SIC: 1389 Oil field services
PA: Halliburton Company
3000 N Sam Houston Pkwy E
Houston TX 77032

(G-2129)
HALLIBURTON COMPANY
1015 W Bois D Arcade Ave (73533)
P.O. Box 9000 (73534-9000)
PHONE.................580 251-3760
Joseph Wates, *Branch Mgr*
Ben Hoffman, *Technical Staff*
EMP: 87 **Publicly Held**
SIC: 1389 Oil field services
PA: Halliburton Company
3000 N Sam Houston Pkwy E
Houston TX 77032

(G-2130)
HOLLOWAY TECHNICAL SVCS LLC
7576 N Highway 81 Ste 12 (73533-3432)
P.O. Box 702, Marlow (73055-0702)
PHONE.................405 223-9352
Stephen Holloway,
EMP: 2
SALES (est): 73.5K **Privately Held**
SIC: 1731 3357 Fiber optic cable installation; fiber optic cable (insulated)

(G-2131)
INDUSTRIAL SPECIALTIES INC
508 And A Half S Hwy 81 (73533)
PHONE.................580 475-9088
Steve Thompson, *President*
EMP: 3
SALES (est): 372.9K **Privately Held**
SIC: 3492 Hose & tube fittings & assemblies, hydraulic/pneumatic

(G-2132)
JACK OIL COMPANY
1032 W Main St Ste 100 (73533-4549)
P.O. Box 237 (73534-0237)
PHONE.................580 255-2310
John Cornwell, *Owner*
Perry Cohen, *Partner*
Linda Cornwell, *Partner*
Anthony Fiorillo, *Partner*
Mike Fiorillo, *Partner*
EMP: 3 EST: 1981
SQ FT: 750
SALES (est): 385.1K **Privately Held**
SIC: 1311 Crude petroleum production; natural gas production

(G-2133)
JATH OIL CO (PA)
1202 N 10th St (73533-3832)
P.O. Box 400 (73534-0400)
PHONE.................580 252-5580
Tom H McCasland III, *President*
Chris K Fowler, *Vice Pres*
Chris F Cain, *VP Prdtn*
Noble Means, *Treasurer*
Johr R Braught, *Admin Sec*
EMP: 125
SALES (est): 33.6MM **Privately Held**
SIC: 1311 1382 Crude petroleum production; natural gas production; oil & gas exploration services

(G-2134)
JELKE SIGNS
1112 N 5th St (73533-5830)
PHONE.................580 252-2523
EMP: 1 EST: 1983
SALES (est): 52K **Privately Held**
SIC: 3993 Mfg Signs/Advertising Specialties

(G-2135)
JERRY D PIERCE
Also Called: J D'S Machine Shop
Rr 4 (73533)
PHONE.................580 252-5354
Jerry D Pierce, *Owner*
EMP: 2
SALES: 100K **Privately Held**
SIC: 3599 Machine shop, jobbing & repair

(G-2136)
JIM DID IT SIGNS
802 S 1st St (73533-7501)
PHONE.................580 255-5533
James R Deal, *Owner*
EMP: 2
SALES: 200K **Privately Held**
SIC: 3993 Signs & advertising specialties

(G-2137)
JONES MACHINE SHOP
1501 Shadybrook Ln (73533-1423)
PHONE.................580 255-5784
Fax: 580 255-6859
EMP: 3
SALES (est): 197K **Privately Held**
SIC: 3599 Machine Shop

(G-2138)
JONES MONUMENTS CO
701 W Willow Ave (73533-4951)
PHONE.................580 255-2276

Bill Crowdis, *President*
Opal Rives, *Treasurer*
EMP: 1
SQ FT: 1,000
SALES (est): 130K **Privately Held**
SIC: 5999 3281 Monuments, finished to custom order; monuments & tombstones; cut stone & stone products

(G-2139)
JONES OIL CO LLC
Also Called: Jones Oil Co The
16 S 9th St Rm 302 (73533-4995)
PHONE.................................580 255-9400
Thomas J Jones III, *Partner*
Janalyn Geurkink, *Partner*
Jo Ann Morrison, *Partner*
Judy Neville, *Partner*
EMP: 10
SQ FT: 1,000
SALES (est): 973.9K **Privately Held**
SIC: 1311 Crude petroleum production

(G-2140)
JUDY TOMLINSON
Also Called: Sunset Ridge Vineyard
755 Oakridge Dr (73533-2587)
PHONE.................................580 252-2559
Judy Tomlinson, *Owner*
Tiffany Schilling, *Co-Owner*
EMP: 2
SALES (est): 86.6K **Privately Held**
SIC: 2084 Wines

(G-2141)
KEYSTONE PRODUCTION CO
Also Called: Whitten, J D Jr
1730 W Camelback Rd (73533-9117)
PHONE.................................580 255-2162
Jerry D Whitten, *President*
EMP: 1
SALES (est): 135.1K **Privately Held**
SIC: 1382 Oil & gas exploration services

(G-2142)
KIESTER OPERATING COMPANY
1226 N Grand Blvd (73533-3738)
P.O. Box 705, Oklahoma City (73101-0705)
PHONE.................................580 255-4020
Michael Kiester, *President*
Elaine Kiester, *Corp Secy*
EMP: 6
SQ FT: 3,200
SALES (est): 75K **Privately Held**
SIC: 1389 Oil field services

(G-2143)
L E JONES DRILLING LLC
15 S 10th St Ste A (73533-4950)
P.O. Box 1185 (73534-1185)
PHONE.................................580 255-3532
Dixie Sparks, *Opers Staff*
Lance Jones, *Mng Member*
Becky Sanner, *Manager*
EMP: 4
SALES (est): 316.4K **Privately Held**
SIC: 1381 Drilling oil & gas wells

(G-2144)
L E JONES PRODUCTION CO (PA)
Also Called: L E Jones Production Company
15 S 10th St Ste A (73533-4950)
P.O. Box 1185 (73534-1185)
PHONE.................................580 255-1191
Lawayne E Jones, *Owner*
▲ **EMP:** 1
SQ FT: 2,000
SALES (est): 211.2K **Privately Held**
SIC: 1311 Crude petroleum production; natural gas production

(G-2145)
LATIGO DRILLING CORPORATION
4550 Odom Dr (73533-5230)
P.O. Box 2150 (73534-2150)
PHONE.................................580 255-1674
David K Moore, *President*
Ted Tucker, *Vice Pres*
EMP: 1
SQ FT: 500
SALES (est): 226.9K **Privately Held**
SIC: 1381 Drilling oil & gas wells

(G-2146)
LEDFORD OIL & GAS LLC
2206 Fairway Dr (73533-3210)
PHONE.................................580 467-0593
Jan Ledford, *Principal*
EMP: 2
SALES (est): 86K **Privately Held**
SIC: 1389 Oil & gas field services

(G-2147)
LEJONES OPERATING INC
15 S 10th St (73533-4962)
P.O. Box 1185 (73534-1185)
PHONE.................................580 255-3532
L Jones, *Principal*
EMP: 14
SALES (est): 1.3MM **Privately Held**
SIC: 1381 Drilling oil & gas wells

(G-2148)
LIBERTY BIT CO
7414 N Highway 81 (73533-8792)
P.O. Box 631, Marlow (73055-0631)
PHONE.................................580 255-6400
Wesley Balthrop, *President*
Tom Balthrop, *Vice Pres*
▲ **EMP:** 5
SQ FT: 12,500
SALES (est): 1.5MM **Privately Held**
WEB: www.libertybitco.com
SIC: 1381 Drilling oil & gas wells

(G-2149)
LYNNS AUTO PARTS AND MACHINE
1101 E Plato Rd (73533-3123)
PHONE.................................580 255-5190
Lynn Davenport, *President*
EMP: 9 **EST:** 1956
SQ FT: 5,000
SALES (est): 1MM **Privately Held**
SIC: 5013 5531 3599 Automotive supplies & parts; automotive parts; machine shop, jobbing & repair

(G-2150)
MACK ENERGY CO
1202 N 10th St (73533-3832)
P.O. Box 400 (73534-0400)
PHONE.................................580 252-5580
T H McCasland III, *President*
Chris Fowler, *Vice Pres*
Randy Smith, *Vice Pres*
Mike Lamascus, *Engineer*
Noble Means, *Treasurer*
EMP: 125
SQ FT: 10,000
SALES (est): 33.6MM **Privately Held**
SIC: 1311 1382 Crude petroleum production; natural gas production; oil & gas exploration services
PA: Jath Oil Co.
 1202 N 10th St
 Duncan OK 73533

(G-2151)
MAMMOTH MANUFACTURING
2000 N 5th St (73533-3317)
PHONE.................................580 252-4660
Keith Schoonover, *Owner*
EMP: 5
SALES (est): 290.8K **Privately Held**
SIC: 3599 Machine shop, jobbing & repair

(G-2152)
MARK CONDIT
Also Called: Sooner Welding Inspection
178884 N 2910 Rd (73533-1770)
PHONE.................................580 656-8028
Mark Condit, *Owner*
EMP: 1
SALES (est): 33.4K **Privately Held**
SIC: 7692 Welding repair

(G-2153)
MCCASLAND MERCANTILE LLC
905 W Peach Ave (73533-3853)
P.O. Box 400 (73534-0400)
PHONE.................................580 252-5580
EMP: 2
SALES (est): 86.1K **Privately Held**
SIC: 1311 Crude petroleum production

(G-2154)
METCOAT INC
1619 N 5th St (73533-3638)
P.O. Box 324 (73534-0324)
PHONE.................................580 255-6441
Warren Crook, *President*
EMP: 6
SQ FT: 6,500
SALES (est): 645.6K **Privately Held**
SIC: 3599 3471 Machine & other job shop work; plating & polishing

(G-2155)
MID CONTINENT LIFT AND EQP LLC
517 W Bois D Arc Ave (73533-7427)
P.O. Box 186 (73534-0186)
PHONE.................................580 255-3867
Matthew Rogers, *President*
EMP: 15
SQ FT: 36,000
SALES (est): 3.1MM **Privately Held**
SIC: 3537 1799 5084 7699 Forklift trucks; hydraulic equipment, installation & service; materials handling machinery; hydraulic equipment repair

(G-2156)
MONTGOMERY MATTRESS
Also Called: Montgomery Mattress Factory
5101 N Hwy 81 (73533-8971)
PHONE.................................580 255-8979
Rod Pinnell, *Owner*
EMP: 2
SQ FT: 6,600
SALES (est): 300K **Privately Held**
SIC: 2515 5712 Mattresses & bedsprings; mattresses

(G-2157)
MOWDY MACHINE INC
1245 Boren Rd (73533-4184)
P.O. Box 1422 (73534-1422)
PHONE.................................580 252-9333
Brad Mowdy, *President*
John Mowdy, *Principal*
Dale Mowdy, *Corp Secy*
EMP: 2
SQ FT: 3,000
SALES (est): 270K **Privately Held**
SIC: 3533 Oil & gas drilling rigs & equipment; oil field machinery & equipment

(G-2158)
NATIONAL OILWELL VARCO INC
Also Called: Hydra Rig
1200 E Highway 7 (73533-7752)
PHONE.................................580 251-6900
Mike Gist, *General Mgr*
Michael Roberson, *Prdtn Mgr*
Jay Albin, *Materials Mgr*
David Turkett, *Mfg Spvr*
Chris Maxey, *Purch Mgr*
EMP: 80
SALES (corp-wide): 8.4B **Publicly Held**
WEB: www.nov.com
SIC: 1389 Oil field services
PA: National Oilwell Varco, Inc.
 7909 Parkwood Circle Dr
 Houston TX 77036
 713 346-7500

(G-2159)
NEWSPAPER HOLDING INC
Also Called: Duncan Banner
1001 W Elm Ave (73533-4746)
PHONE.................................580 255-5354
Floyd Jernigan, *Principal*
EMP: 30 **Privately Held**
SIC: 2711 Newspapers, publishing & printing
HQ: Newspaper Holding, Inc.
 425 Locust St
 Johnstown PA 15901
 814 532-5102

(G-2160)
NEXTSTEP CUSTOM PRINTING
7126 S Hillside Dr (73533-2124)
PHONE.................................580 678-4331
Randall Staggs, *Principal*
EMP: 2

SALES (est): 83.9K **Privately Held**
SIC: 2752 Commercial printing, lithographic

(G-2161)
OILFIELD EQUIPMENT COMPANY
Also Called: Max Dubs & Machine
4 1/2 Mi W Twn Beach Rd (73533)
PHONE.................................405 850-1406
Mack L Kennedy, *Principal*
EMP: 6
SQ FT: 6,000
SALES: 1MM **Privately Held**
SIC: 5082 3498 3471 Oil field equipment; fabricated pipe & fittings; steel pipe & tubes

(G-2162)
OKLAHOMA SUPERIOR PLATING LLC
602 S 2nd St (73533-7576)
PHONE.................................580 252-2787
Phil Johnson, *Principal*
EMP: 5 **EST:** 2008
SALES (est): 505.4K **Privately Held**
SIC: 3471 Electroplating of metals or formed products

(G-2163)
PEDROS CSTM CABINETS TRIM LLC
205 N I St (73533-6843)
PHONE.................................580 656-3982
Richard Peddell, *Principal*
EMP: 2 **EST:** 2011
SALES (est): 185.7K **Privately Held**
SIC: 2434 Wood kitchen cabinets

(G-2164)
PERKINS ENERGY CO
903 W Peach Ave (73533-3853)
P.O. Box 878 (73534-0878)
PHONE.................................580 255-5400
Jerry P Roop, *Vice Pres*
Jerry Roop, *Vice Pres*
EMP: 6
SQ FT: 3,000
SALES (est): 700.3K **Privately Held**
SIC: 1311 Crude petroleum production

(G-2165)
PREMIER FABRICATORS LLC
1251 Mccurdy Rd (73533-4180)
PHONE.................................580 251-9525
Joshua Leffler, *Principal*
EMP: 6
SALES (est): 968.3K **Privately Held**
SIC: 3441 Fabricated structural metal

(G-2166)
RAPTOR OILFIELD CONTROLS LLC
7025 Nix Dr (73533-4185)
PHONE.................................580 251-9806
Wayne Handke, *Mng Member*
EMP: 6
SALES: 2.3MM **Privately Held**
SIC: 3533 Oil & gas drilling rigs & equipment

(G-2167)
RICK WOODTEN
715 W Main St (73533-4613)
PHONE.................................580 786-5050
EMP: 1
SALES (est): 39K **Privately Held**
SIC: 2499 Mfg Wood Products

(G-2168)
RICKS WELDING
615 E Willow Ave (73533-7715)
PHONE.................................580 470-8111
Fax: 580 470-8111
EMP: 1
SALES (est): 84.9K **Privately Held**
SIC: 7692 Welding Service

(G-2169)
RIDLEYS BUTCHER SHOP INC
416 W Main St (73533-7030)
PHONE.................................580 255-9330
Bill D Ridley, *President*
Brook Ridley, *Vice Pres*
Rita L Ridley, *Treasurer*

GEOGRAPHIC SECTION

Duncan - Stephens County (G-2199)

EMP: 4
SALES (est): 403K **Privately Held**
SIC: **5421** 5812 2013 Meat markets, including freezer provisioners; eating places; sausages & other prepared meats

(G-2170)
RIGHTWAY MFG SOLUTIONS LLC
5615 N Hwy 81 Unit 100 (73533-5757)
PHONE..................................580 252-2284
Richard Newman, *CEO*
Amy Bruns, *Purchasing*
Lorrie Colavito, *Accountant*
Jeremy Bruns, *Manager*
EMP: 37 EST: 2010
SQ FT: 26,800
SALES: 9.8MM **Privately Held**
WEB: www.rightwaymfgsolutions.com
SIC: **3545** 3451 Precision tools, machinists'; screw machine products

(G-2171)
ROCHELL MACHINE SHOP INC
Terry Rd & Old 81 (73534)
P.O. Box 1511 (73534-1511)
PHONE..................................580 252-1424
Jack Rochell, *Owner*
Fred Rochell, *Partner*
EMP: 4 EST: 1976
SQ FT: 5,000
SALES (est): 362K **Privately Held**
SIC: **3599** Machine shop, jobbing & repair

(G-2172)
ROSES CUSTOM
3930 Country Ests (73533-8767)
PHONE..................................580 252-9633
Rose Mc Donald, *Principal*
EMP: 2
SALES (est): 316.5K **Privately Held**
SIC: **3552** Embroidery machines

(G-2173)
SCHLUMBERGER TECHNOLOGY CORP
3445 Us 81 (73533)
PHONE..................................580 252-3355
EMP: 2 **Publicly Held**
SIC: **1389** Oil field services
HQ: Schlumberger Technology Corp
300 Schlumberger Dr
Sugar Land TX 77478
281 285-8500

(G-2174)
SCISSORTAIL GRAPHICS INC
Also Called: Scissortail Printing
117 S 10th St (73533-4901)
PHONE..................................580 255-2914
Phyllis C Baker, *President*
Joyce Meiki, *Principal*
EMP: 4 EST: 1987
SALES (est): 487K **Privately Held**
WEB: www.scissortailprinting.com
SIC: **2752** Commercial printing, offset

(G-2175)
SERVA GROUP LLC
3600b S 13th St (73533-9067)
PHONE..................................580 252-5111
John Callihan, *Branch Mgr*
EMP: 3 **Privately Held**
SIC: **3533** Oil field machinery & equipment
HQ: Serva Group Llc
1500 Fisher Rd Ste A
Wichita Falls TX 76305

(G-2176)
SHABBY CHICKS SMART CLEAN LLC
Also Called: Shabby Chicks Natural Product
8100 N Hwy 81 Ste 16 (73533-8764)
PHONE..................................405 414-8938
Amber Malcom, *Mng Member*
Jason Malcom,
EMP: 3
SQ FT: 1,200
SALES: 55K **Privately Held**
WEB: www.shabbychickcleaners.com
SIC: **2841** 2842 Textile soap; specialty cleaning, polishes & sanitation goods

(G-2177)
SIGN DEZIGNS LLC
603 S Highway 81 (73533-2914)
PHONE..................................580 656-0621
EMP: 2
SALES (est): 67.4K **Privately Held**
SIC: **3993** Signs & advertising specialties

(G-2178)
SMITH INTERNATIONAL INC
3445 N Hwy 81 Bldg J (73533-8903)
PHONE..................................580 252-3355
Rebecca Daffron, *Branch Mgr*
EMP: 3 **Publicly Held**
SIC: **5084** 1389 Drilling equipment, excluding bits; oil field services
HQ: Smith International, Inc.
1310 Rankin Rd
Houston TX 77073
281 443-3370

(G-2179)
SOLITAIRE HOLDINGS LLC
7232 Nickles Rd (73533)
PHONE..................................580 252-6060
D J Hogstad, *President*
EMP: 1
SALES: 24.3K **Privately Held**
SIC: **5271** 2452 Mobile homes; prefabricated wood buildings

(G-2180)
SOLITAIRE HOMES INC (PA)
7232 Nickles Rd (73533)
PHONE..................................580 252-6060
D J Hogstad, *President*
Helen I Elliott, *Corp Secy*
Matthew K Leitner, *Treasurer*
EMP: 40
SQ FT: 20,000
SALES (est): 29.3MM **Privately Held**
SIC: **5271** 2452 Mobile homes; prefabricated wood buildings

(G-2181)
SOUTHERN BOX COMPANY
908 W Main St (73533-4618)
PHONE..................................580 255-7969
Daniel Pool, *Owner*
Rick Smith, *Partner*
Bill Watts, *Manager*
EMP: 3
SQ FT: 4,000
SALES: 130K **Privately Held**
SIC: **2653** 5947 Boxes, corrugated: made from purchased materials; gift shop

(G-2182)
SOUTHERN MACHINE WORKS INC
907 E Bois D Arc Ave (73533-7670)
P.O. Box 1226 (73534-1226)
PHONE..................................580 255-6525
Frank W Burch II, *President*
Bradley Howard, *Vice Pres*
Jerrel Beck, *Foreman/Supr*
Casey Brooksher, *Production*
Heather Casteel, *Controller*
EMP: 28 EST: 1974
SQ FT: 14,000
SALES (est): 1.4MM **Privately Held**
WEB: www.southernmach.com
SIC: **3599** Machine shop, jobbing & repair

(G-2183)
SPECIAL EQUIPMENT MFG INC
3600 S 13th St (73533-9067)
PHONE..................................580 252-5111
Greg Hammes, *President*
Tom Collinsworth, *Vice Pres*
EMP: 50
SALES (est): 5.3MM **Privately Held**
SIC: **7353** 3561 Oil equipment rental services; pumps & pumping equipment

(G-2184)
STAGESTAND RANCH
Also Called: Edwards Trust
1214 N Hwy 81 Ste 116 (73533-1762)
P.O. Box 1348 (73534-1348)
PHONE..................................580 255-1161
Nelson Rice, *Owner*
Sally Rice, *Co-Owner*
EMP: 3
SQ FT: 1,500
SALES (est): 274.9K **Privately Held**
SIC: **1311** 0212 Crude petroleum production; beef cattle except feedlots

(G-2185)
STARLITE WELDING SUPPLIES
506 S Industrial Ave (73533-2938)
P.O. Box 1562 (73534-1562)
PHONE..................................580 252-8320
Mary Golay, *President*
EMP: 3 EST: 1982
SQ FT: 4,700
SALES (est): 500K **Privately Held**
SIC: **3549** 3543 Metalworking machinery; industrial patterns

(G-2186)
STOCKMANS SUPPLY COMPANY
Also Called: Stockmans Tack & Supply
3733 N Highway 81 (73533-9182)
PHONE..................................580 255-7762
Ed Morgan, *Owner*
EMP: 9
SQ FT: 20,000
SALES (est): 540K **Privately Held**
SIC: **5651** 5191 3111 5261 Family clothing stores; feed; saddlery leather; fountains, outdoor

(G-2187)
THINK ABILITY INC
1301 W Main St (73533-4328)
PHONE..................................580 252-8000
Robin Arter, *Exec Dir*
EMP: 158
SALES: 4.3MM **Privately Held**
SIC: **8331** 8052 8361 8322 Sheltered workshop; work experience center; intermediate care facilities; residential care for the handicapped; adult day care center; furniture stores; letterpress & screen printing

(G-2188)
THOMAS OIL TOOLS LLC
293833 E 1760 Rd (73533)
PHONE..................................580 252-4672
Danny Thomas, *Mng Member*
Dale Goodrich,
Rodney Thomas,
EMP: 9 EST: 2016
SQ FT: 1,600
SALES: 4MM **Privately Held**
SIC: **1382** Oil & gas exploration services

(G-2189)
TOOLBOX OIL GAS CONSULTING INC
1201 N 13th St (73533-3719)
PHONE..................................432 234-2067
Dustin McMahon, *President*
EMP: 1
SALES: 200K **Privately Held**
SIC: **1389** Measurement of well flow rates, oil & gas

(G-2190)
TRINITY TECHNOLOGIES LLC
1710 W Terry Rd (73533-9266)
P.O. Box 759 (73534-0759)
PHONE..................................580 475-0900
Matt Tucker, *Mng Member*
EMP: 12
SQ FT: 5,000
SALES (est): 2MM **Privately Held**
SIC: **5063** 3699 5065 7382 Fire alarm systems; security control equipment & systems; security control equipment & systems; fire alarm maintenance & monitoring

(G-2191)
VALCO INC (PA)
Also Called: Valco Manufacturing Company
1009 Boren Rd (73533-4182)
P.O. Box 2117, Oklahoma City (73101-2117)
PHONE..................................405 228-0932
Roger Valdez, *President*
Eric Samuelson, *COO*
Rogers Rober, *CFO*
Priscilla Plumlee, *Controller*
▲ EMP: 50
SALES: 7MM **Privately Held**
SIC: **3444** Sheet metalwork

(G-2192)
VERTIPRIME GOVERNMENT SVCS LLC
Also Called: Vertiprime Aerospace
7576 N Highway 81 (73533-3400)
PHONE..................................844 474-2600
Michael Morford,
EMP: 3
SALES (est): 196.3K **Privately Held**
SIC: **3721** 7371 Aircraft; software programming applications

(G-2193)
VERTIPRIME MOWDY MCH JV LLC
1245 Boren Rd (73533-4184)
PHONE..................................405 747-6668
Michael Morford, *Principal*
Brad Mowdy, *Principal*
EMP: 2
SALES (est): 86K **Privately Held**
SIC: **3728** Aircraft parts & equipment

(G-2194)
VINCENT ENTERPRISES INC
Also Called: Industrial Ignition Supply
3209 Lansbrook Ct (73533-2249)
PHONE..................................580 252-1322
Gordan Vincent, *President*
Betty Vincent, *Corp Secy*
EMP: 2
SQ FT: 5,800
SALES (est): 250K **Privately Held**
SIC: **5261** 1389 Lawnmowers & tractors; oil field services

(G-2195)
VIRIDIAN COFFEE LLC
1441 W Willow Duncan (73533)
PHONE..................................405 795-0773
Shay Hayes, *Mng Member*
EMP: 3 EST: 2014
SQ FT: 2,200
SALES (est): 71.1K **Privately Held**
SIC: **5812** 2095 Coffee shop; roasted coffee

(G-2196)
VVC DRY CLEANING & LAUNDRY
1015 W Oak Ave (73533-4537)
PHONE..................................580 255-2121
Valerie Cardinas, *Owner*
EMP: 8
SALES (est): 562.1K **Privately Held**
SIC: **2842** Laundry cleaning preparations

(G-2197)
WAJO CHEMICAL INC
15 S 10th St (73533-4962)
P.O. Box 1185 (73534-1185)
PHONE..................................580 255-1191
Lance E Jones, *President*
EMP: 2
SQ FT: 2,000
SALES (est): 160.5K **Privately Held**
SIC: **1389** Oil field services; chemically treating wells

(G-2198)
WETZEL PRODUCING COMPANY
Also Called: Lindzco
18 N 8th St (73533-4602)
PHONE..................................580 255-2929
EMP: 2 EST: 1951
SQ FT: 500
SALES: 1.3MM **Privately Held**
SIC: **1311** Oil Producer

(G-2199)
WILD OLIVES LLC
Also Called: Manufacturing/ Wholesaler
7 Miller Ave (73533)
PHONE..................................580 230-1231
Joanie Antholz,
EMP: 1
SALES (est): 113.1K **Privately Held**
SIC: **3842** Surgical appliances & supplies

Durant
Bryan County

(G-2200)
AERO COMPONENT REPAIR LLC
3625 W Arkansas St (74701-4555)
PHONE.....................................580 924-7999
William F Moskwa,
EMP: 10
SALES (est): 922.6K **Privately Held**
SIC: 7699 3724 3728 Aircraft & heavy equipment repair services; aircraft engines & engine parts; turbines, aircraft type; aircraft parts & equipment

(G-2201)
ALLIED STONE INC
2201 W Arkansas St (74701-5617)
P.O. Box 559 (74702-0559)
PHONE.....................................580 931-3388
Richard Rodriguez, *Warehouse Mgr*
Deana Ogle, *Human Res Mgr*
Ellen Wells, *Sales Staff*
Jennifer Roberts, *Office Mgr*
Charlie Wilson, *Branch Mgr*
EMP: 23 **Privately Held**
WEB: www.alliedstoneinc.com
SIC: 3281 Marble, building: cut & shaped; granite, cut & shaped
HQ: Allied Stone, Inc.
2405 Crown Rd
Dallas TX 75229
214 838-2225

(G-2202)
ANSIELS WELDING & CONSTRUCTIO
72 Moore Ln (74701-0233)
PHONE.....................................580 920-0573
David Ansiel, *Principal*
EMP: 1
SALES (est): 60.8K **Privately Held**
SIC: 7692 Welding repair

(G-2203)
AUTOMATIC GATE SYSTEMS OF OKLA
5580 Armstrong Rd (74701-2463)
PHONE.....................................580 920-8752
Jason Earles, *President*
Korbin Eppler, *Principal*
Ed Morenz, *Principal*
Garrett Earles, *Vice Pres*
EMP: 4
SALES (est): 447.3K **Privately Held**
SIC: 3446 3315 Gates, ornamental metal; fence gates posts & fittings: steel

(G-2204)
BANKS MOTOR CO
502 Bryan Dr (74701-3400)
P.O. Box 1543 (74702-1543)
PHONE.....................................580 924-8883
Mike Banks, *Owner*
Lynn Banks, *Co-Owner*
EMP: 1
SALES (est): 117.4K **Privately Held**
SIC: 3089 5521 Automotive parts, plastic; used car dealers

(G-2205)
BEST TRAILER PRODUCTS
301 S 22nd Ave (74701-5620)
PHONE.....................................580 931-3534
Ottis Hall, *Principal*
EMP: 2
SALES (est): 193.6K **Privately Held**
SIC: 3799 Trailers & trailer equipment

(G-2206)
BLUE RIVER VENTURES INC
Also Called: Blue River Tractors
4710 W Highway 70 (74701-5058)
PHONE.....................................580 920-0111
EMP: 4 EST: 2010
SALES: 1.6MM **Privately Held**
SIC: 3523 Mfg Farm Machinery/Equipment

(G-2207)
BOBRICK WASHROOM EQUIPMENT INC
Gamco Commercial Restroom ACC
1 Gamco Pl (74701-1910)
PHONE.....................................580 924-8066
Ketan Jain, *Division Mgr*
EMP: 17
SALES (corp-wide): 97.9MM **Privately Held**
SIC: 3261 Bathroom accessories/fittings, vitreous china or earthenware
HQ: Bobrick Washroom Equipment, Inc.
6901 Tujunga Ave
North Hollywood CA 91605
818 764-1000

(G-2208)
BODY CONNECTION LLC
322 1/2 N 3rd Ave (74701-4212)
PHONE.....................................580 745-9201
EMP: 2
SALES (est): 96K **Privately Held**
SIC: 3842 Mfg Surgical Appliances/Supplies

(G-2209)
BROKEN ARROW ELECTRIC SUP INC
3119 Westside Dr (74701-1822)
PHONE.....................................580 924-2237
Bruce Garner, *Principal*
EMP: 4
SALES (corp-wide): 138.8MM **Privately Held**
SIC: 5063 3699 Electrical supplies; electrical equipment & supplies
PA: Broken Arrow Electric Supply, Inc.
2350 W Vancouver St
Broken Arrow OK 74012
918 258-3581

(G-2210)
BRUCE PACKING COMPANY INC
1915 E Highway 70 (74701-7204)
PHONE.....................................503 874-3000
Glen Golomski, *President*
EMP: 4
SALES (corp-wide): 185.3MM **Privately Held**
SIC: 2013 Cooked meats from purchased meat
HQ: Bruce Packing Company, Inc.
380 S Pacific Hwy 99e
Woodburn OR 97071
503 874-3000

(G-2211)
CARDINAL GLASS INDUSTRIES INC
Also Called: Cardinal Fg Glass
515 Cardinal Pkwy (74701-8932)
PHONE.....................................580 924-2142
Wayne Atee, *Manager*
Larry Peck, *Executive*
EMP: 116
SALES (corp-wide): 1B **Privately Held**
SIC: 3231 Insulating glass: made from purchased glass
PA: Cardinal Glass Industries Inc
775 Pririe Ctr Dr Ste 200
Eden Prairie MN 55344
952 229-2600

(G-2212)
CARDINAL GLASS INDUSTRIES INC
Also Called: Cardinal F G Co
515 Cardinal Pkwy (74701-8932)
PHONE.....................................580 924-2142
Ron Erickson, *Materials Mgr*
Rich Valtieras, *Manager*
EMP: 200
SALES (corp-wide): 1B **Privately Held**
SIC: 3231 Products of purchased glass
PA: Cardinal Glass Industries Inc
775 Pririe Ctr Dr Ste 200
Eden Prairie MN 55344
952 229-2600

(G-2213)
CHEMTICA USA
2912 Enterprise Dr Ste A1 (74701-1963)
PHONE.....................................580 366-6799
Matthew Trump, *Principal*
Lilliana Gonzalez, *Info Tech Mgr*
EMP: 3 EST: 2008
SALES (est): 217.3K **Privately Held**
SIC: 3999 Manufacturing industries

(G-2214)
CHOCTAW TRAVEL PLAZA
4015 Choctaw Rd (74701-1988)
PHONE.....................................580 920-2186
EMP: 2
SALES (est): 81.9K **Privately Held**
SIC: 1311 Crude petroleum & natural gas

(G-2215)
CLASSIC OVERHEAD DOO
170 Fisher Station Rd (74701-6507)
PHONE.....................................580 931-0340
EMP: 1
SALES (est): 70K **Privately Held**
SIC: 2431 Mfg Millwork

(G-2216)
CLINT DODSON ENTERPRISES LLC
Also Called: Platinum Machine
301 S 21st Ave (74701-5645)
P.O. Box 1826 (74702-1826)
PHONE.....................................580 931-9410
Clint Dodson, *Principal*
EMP: 2
SALES (est): 346.3K **Privately Held**
WEB: www.platinummanufacturing.com
SIC: 3599 Industrial machinery

(G-2217)
CMC STEEL OKLAHOMA LLC
584 Old Highway 70 (74701-6094)
P.O. Box 1250 (74702-1250)
PHONE.....................................580 634-5092
Alan Jackson, *Principal*
EMP: 1
SALES (est): 83.4K
SALES (corp-wide): 5.8B **Publicly Held**
SIC: 3312 Stainless steel
PA: Commercial Metals Company
6565 N Macarthur Blvd # 800
Irving TX 75039
214 689-4300

(G-2218)
COMMERCIAL METALS COMPANY
Also Called: CMC Steel
584 Old Highway 70 (74701-6094)
P.O. Box 1250 (74702-1250)
PHONE.....................................580 634-5046
EMP: 2
SALES (corp-wide): 5.8B **Publicly Held**
SIC: 3312 Blast furnaces & steel mills
PA: Commercial Metals Company
6565 N Macarthur Blvd # 800
Irving TX 75039
214 689-4300

(G-2219)
CURTIS JEWELRY
Also Called: Personal Touch, The
207 W Main St (74701-5022)
PHONE.....................................580 924-0041
Albert Curtis, *Owner*
EMP: 4
SQ FT: 700
SALES (est): 200K **Privately Held**
SIC: 5944 5947 5632 3911 Jewelry, precious stones & precious metals; gift shop; costume jewelry; jewelry, precious metal; jewelry repair services

(G-2220)
DANDY DONUTS
111 N 8th Ave (74701-4755)
PHONE.....................................580 924-7872
Roger Thompson, *Owner*
Ann Thompson, *Co-Owner*
EMP: 5
SALES (est): 178.5K **Privately Held**
SIC: 5461 2051 Doughnuts; doughnuts, except frozen

(G-2221)
DAVID KEMPE
Also Called: Texhoma Truss
3805 W Main St (74701)
PHONE.....................................580 924-6798
David Kempe, *Owner*
EMP: 12
SALES (est): 1.1MM **Privately Held**
SIC: 2439 Trusses, wooden roof

(G-2222)
DAY IN SUN LANDSCAPING
757 Church Rd (74701-0849)
PHONE.....................................580 768-4986
EMP: 2
SALES (est): 76.3K **Privately Held**
SIC: 5083 3524 Cultivating machinery & equipment; lawn & garden mowers & accessories

(G-2223)
DAYTON PARTS LLC
Eagle Suspensions
1811 W Arkansas St (74701-5623)
PHONE.....................................580 931-9350
Shirley Robinson, *Vice Pres*
Rick Roy, *Plant Mgr*
Adrian Gill, *Engineer*
Cindy Ervin, *Human Res Mgr*
Mike Duffy, *Manager*
EMP: 55
SALES (corp-wide): 98.4MM **Privately Held**
SIC: 3493 Leaf springs: automobile, locomotive, etc.
PA: Dayton Parts, Llc
490 Railroad Ave
Shiremanstown PA 17011
717 255-8500

(G-2224)
DOLESE BROS CO
3305 N Washington Ave (74701-1640)
PHONE.....................................580 924-4944
Roger Dolese, *Branch Mgr*
EMP: 2
SALES (corp-wide): 8.5MM **Privately Held**
WEB: www.dolese.com
SIC: 3273 Ready-mixed concrete
PA: Dolese Bros. Co.
20 Nw 13th St
Oklahoma City OK 73103
405 235-2311

(G-2225)
DURANT
142 W Main St (74701-5008)
PHONE.....................................580 920-2069
Jeffrey Duane Ross, *Principal*
EMP: 2
SALES (est): 223K **Privately Held**
WEB: www.durantdemocrat.com
SIC: 3949 Bowling alleys & accessories

(G-2226)
DURANT IRON & METAL INC
11 W Locust St (74701-3900)
P.O. Box 563 (74702-0563)
PHONE.....................................580 924-0595
James Clark, *President*
William Clark, *Vice Pres*
EMP: 21
SALES (est): 5.4MM **Privately Held**
SIC: 5051 3341 Cast iron pipe; pipe & tubing, steel; secondary nonferrous metals

(G-2227)
DURANT PLASTICS & MFG
301 Gerlach Dr (74701-2557)
PHONE.....................................580 745-9430
Gary Neely, *Principal*
EMP: 2
SALES (est): 342.2K **Privately Held**
SIC: 3089 Injection molding of plastics

(G-2228)
DURANT PRINTING
401 N 3rd Ave (74701-4117)
PHONE.....................................580 924-2271
Chris Allen, *Administration*
EMP: 4
SALES (est): 258.5K **Privately Held**
SIC: 2752 Commercial printing, offset

GEOGRAPHIC SECTION
Durant - Bryan County (G-2259)

(G-2229)
EMERALD QUEST
2015 W Liveoak St (74701-3435)
PHONE.................................580 920-5917
Joey McWilliams, *Owner*
EMP: 2
SALES: 70K **Privately Held**
SIC: 2741

(G-2230)
ETS-LINDGREN INC
1016 Waldron Dr (74701-1912)
PHONE.................................580 434-7490
Jon Hall, *Regl Sales Mgr*
Doug Bailey, *Manager*
EMP: 45 **Publicly Held**
WEB: www.ets-lindgren.com
SIC: 4225 3444 3442 3296 General warehousing & storage; sheet metalwork; metal doors, sash & trim; mineral wool
HQ: Ets-Lindgren Inc.
1301 Arrow Point Dr
Cedar Park TX 78613
512 531-6400

(G-2231)
GRAY & SONS SAWMILL & SUP LLC
44 Sawmill Rd (74701-1001)
PHONE.................................580 924-2941
Brandon Gray,
EMP: 5
SALES: 500K **Privately Held**
SIC: 2421 Sawmills & planing mills, general

(G-2232)
GRAYS SAWMILL INC
44 Sawmill Rd (74701-1001)
PHONE.................................580 924-2941
Bryant E Gray, *President*
Chad Gray, *Vice Pres*
EMP: 12 **EST:** 1946
SALES (est): 1.2MM **Privately Held**
WEB: www.grayssawmill.com
SIC: 2421 2426 Lumber: rough, sawed or planed; hardwood dimension & flooring mills

(G-2233)
GRICES AUTOMOTIVE MACHINE SHOP
Also Called: Grice's Machine Shop
2501 Rodeo Rd (74701-1935)
PHONE.................................580 924-1006
EMP: 1
SALES (est): 79K **Privately Held**
SIC: 3599 5531 3714 Mfg Industrial Machinery Ret Auto/Home Supplies Mfg Motor Vehicle Parts/Accessories

(G-2234)
GURLEY TROY MATTINGLY
28 W Ward Rd (74701-9329)
PHONE.................................580 924-3042
Gurley T Mattingly, *Principal*
EMP: 2
SALES (est): 166.3K **Privately Held**
SIC: 3537 Trucks, tractors, loaders, carriers & similar equipment

(G-2235)
H C RUSTIN CORPORATION (HQ)
Also Called: Rustin Concrete
50 E Main St (74701-5962)
P.O. Box 449 (74702-0449)
PHONE.................................580 924-3260
Philip Rustin, *President*
Barton Rustin, *Exec VP*
Barton L Rustin, *Vice Pres*
Stuart Rustin, *Vice Pres*
Bethany Hanna, *Accounting Mgr*
EMP: 30
SQ FT: 6,000
SALES (est): 32.9MM
SALES (corp-wide): 2.2B **Publicly Held**
WEB: www.rustinconcrete.com
SIC: 3273 5211 Ready-mixed concrete; concrete & cinder block
PA: Summit Materials, Inc.
1550 Wynkoop St Ste 300
Denver CO 80202
303 893-0012

(G-2236)
ICON CONSTRUCTION INC
2917 Big Lots Rd (74701-2172)
PHONE.................................580 931-3806
James Bell, *President*
EMP: 10 **Privately Held**
SIC: 2452 Prefabricated wood buildings
PA: Icon Construction, Inc.
2917 Big Lots Rd
Durant OK 74701

(G-2237)
ICON MANUFACTURING LLC
2917 Big Lots Rd Ste B (74701-2172)
PHONE.................................903 819-9091
Rodney Whitworth,
EMP: 5
SALES (est): 150.7K **Privately Held**
SIC: 3999 Manufacturing industries

(G-2238)
IMAGINE DURANT INC
215 N 4th Ave (74701-4353)
PHONE.................................580 380-0743
EMP: 4
SALES: 97.6K **Privately Held**
SIC: 2711 Newspapers, publishing & printing

(G-2239)
INTERNATIONAL SFTWR CONS INC (PA)
Also Called: ISC Computers
402 N 1st Ave (74701-4114)
P.O. Box 1059 (74702-1059)
PHONE.................................580 924-1231
Lawrence Wilcox, *CEO*
Steve Wilcox, *President*
EMP: 6
SQ FT: 1,500
SALES (est): 766.5K **Privately Held**
SIC: 5734 7372 7378 Computer software & accessories; software, computer games; prepackaged software; computer maintenance & repair

(G-2240)
JC FAB LLC
1325 Highway 78 S (74701-2393)
P.O. Box 1662 (74702-1662)
PHONE.................................580 920-0878
J Scott Crain, *Mng Member*
▲ EMP: 15
SQ FT: 50,000
SALES (est): 2.5MM **Privately Held**
SIC: 3444 3443 Forming machine work, sheet metal; fabricated plate work (boiler shop)

(G-2241)
KOBE EXPRESS LLC
1428 W University Blvd (74701-3106)
PHONE.................................580 920-0444
Tina La, *Branch Mgr*
EMP: 1 **Privately Held**
SIC: 2752 Commercial printing, lithographic
PA: Kobe Express Llc
544 N Hickory St
Atoka OK 74525

(G-2242)
L AND A FILTRATION LLC
2467 Folsom Rd (74701-1806)
PHONE.................................580 380-2976
Lane Cormier, *Principal*
EMP: 4
SALES (est): 325.8K **Privately Held**
SIC: 1381 Service well drilling

(G-2243)
LANE VICTORY SCREEN PRINTING
316 W Main St (74701-5025)
P.O. Box 1391 (74702-1391)
PHONE.................................580 924-3556
David Lane, *Mng Member*
Jennifer Jones,
EMP: 4
SALES: 150K **Privately Held**
SIC: 2759 2395 Screen printing; embroidery & art needlework

(G-2244)
MORRIS MONUMENTS
1517 Cemetery Rd (74701-6735)
PHONE.................................580 924-1323
James Ray Morris, *Owner*
Ethel Morris, *Co-Owner*
EMP: 4 **EST:** 1941
SALES (est): 180K **Privately Held**
SIC: 5999 3281 Monuments, finished to custom order; cut stone & stone products

(G-2245)
NOLAN AVIONICS LLC
8 Waldron Dr (74701-1900)
PHONE.................................580 924-5507
Michael Koval,
EMP: 3
SQ FT: 600
SALES (est): 200K **Privately Held**
SIC: 3721 Aircraft

(G-2246)
NOLAN ENTERPRISES
8 Waldron Dr Hngr 24-C (74701-1900)
PHONE.................................580 924-5507
Larry Nolan, *Owner*
EMP: 4
SALES: 250K **Privately Held**
SIC: 3728 Aircraft parts & equipment

(G-2247)
POTTER INDUSTRIES
503 E Georgia St (74701-6703)
PHONE.................................580 775-8580
David Potter, *Principal*
EMP: 2
SALES (est): 67.8K **Privately Held**
SIC: 3999 Manufacturing industries

(G-2248)
PRICES QUALITY PRINTING INC
Also Called: Price's Printing
401 N 3rd Ave (74701-4117)
PHONE.................................580 924-2271
Chris Allen, *President*
Shelly Allen, *Vice Pres*
EMP: 7 **EST:** 1957
SQ FT: 6,000
SALES: 700K **Privately Held**
WEB: www.pricesprinting.com
SIC: 2752 2796 2791 2789 Commercial printing, offset; platemaking services; typesetting; bookbinding & related work

(G-2249)
PROFESSIONAL COMMUNICATIONS
3016 Quail Ridge Cir (74701-2533)
PHONE.................................580 745-9838
EMP: 1 **Privately Held**
WEB: www.pcibooks.com
SIC: 2741 Miscellaneous publishing
PA: Professional Communications Inc
1223 W Main St Unit 1427
Durant OK

(G-2250)
R & R SIGNS INC
1325 Highway 78 S (74701-2393)
P.O. Box 1662 (74702-1662)
PHONE.................................580 924-4363
William Remshardt, *President*
Jill Gordon, *President*
Marjorie Remshardt, *Corp Secy*
Steven Remshardt, *Vice Pres*
EMP: 3
SALES (est): 440.7K **Privately Held**
SIC: 7312 3993 Outdoor advertising services; signs & advertising specialties

(G-2251)
RED RIVER CUSTOM CAMO & HYDRO
3825 N 1st Ave (74701-2536)
PHONE.................................580 745-5262
EMP: 2
SALES (est): 110.8K **Privately Held**
SIC: 2752 Commercial printing, lithographic

(G-2252)
RIVER RIDGE LOGGING LLC
929 Hoover Rd (74701-7253)
PHONE.................................580 380-2948
Richardson Smith, *Principal*
EMP: 3
SALES (est): 173.8K **Privately Held**
SIC: 2411 Logging

(G-2253)
ROWLANDS PROC & CATTLE CO
Also Called: Tucker Slaughter House
524 Lee Ave (74701-5336)
PHONE.................................580 924-2560
Tom Rowland, *President*
John Rowland, *Treasurer*
EMP: 10
SQ FT: 3,600
SALES (est): 670K **Privately Held**
SIC: 2011 5421 2013 Meat packing plants; meat markets, including freezer provisioners; sausages & other prepared meats

(G-2254)
S & H ELECTRIC MOTOR SERVICE
1903 W Arkansas St (74701-5625)
PHONE.................................580 924-3514
Gary Dodd, *Owner*
EMP: 1
SQ FT: 2,500
SALES: 100K **Privately Held**
SIC: 5999 7694 Motors, electric; rebuilding motors, except automotive

(G-2255)
SCHOOLWARE INC
2912 Enterprise Dr Ste C1 (74701-1963)
P.O. Box 5250 (74702-5250)
PHONE.................................580 745-9100
Kathy Robinson, *President*
EMP: 1
SALES (est): 820K **Privately Held**
SIC: 7372 Educational computer software

(G-2256)
SELF AUTOMOTIVE & RACING INC
54 W Locust St (74701-3914)
PHONE.................................580 924-5866
Glenn Self, *President*
EMP: 5
SQ FT: 2,300
SALES (est): 387.4K **Privately Held**
SIC: 7549 7538 3714 High performance auto repair & service; general automotive repair shops; motor vehicle parts & accessories

(G-2257)
SIGN DEPOT
44 W Evergreen St (74701-4706)
P.O. Box 751 (74702-0751)
PHONE.................................580 931-9363
Ricky Campo, *CEO*
Ricky D Campo, *Partner*
Teresa Campo, *Partner*
Alexis Olguin, *Graphic Designe*
EMP: 13
SALES (est): 300K **Privately Held**
SIC: 3993 2759 Signs & advertising specialties; commercial printing

(G-2258)
SOUTH CENTRAL MACHINE
3376 S Mclean Rd (74701-9309)
PHONE.................................580 775-1623
Gary Dillingham, *Owner*
EMP: 1
SALES: 130K **Privately Held**
SIC: 2399 3532 Bandoleers; mining machinery

(G-2259)
SOUTHWEST PICKLING INC
68 Waldron Dr (74701-1900)
P.O. Box 1186 (74702-1186)
PHONE.................................580 924-6996
Roby Mersecchi, *President*
Joe Engle, *Vice Pres*
Marian Mersecchi, *Admin Sec*
EMP: 5
SALES: 600K **Privately Held**
SIC: 7699 3325 3471 Industrial equipment cleaning; steel foundries; plating & polishing

Durant - Bryan County (G-2260)

(G-2260)
STAHL/SCOTT FETZER COMPANY
92 Waldron Dr (74701-1900)
PHONE.................580 924-5575
David Bibb, *Manager*
EMP: 60
SALES (corp-wide): 327.2B **Publicly Held**
WEB: www.stahl.cc
SIC: 3715 Trailer bodies
HQ: Stahl/Scott Fetzer Company
3201 W Old Lincoln Way
Wooster OH 44691

(G-2261)
START RITE AUTO ELECTRIC INC (PA)
805 S 9th Ave (74701-6801)
P.O. Box 446, Calera (74730-0446)
PHONE.................580 924-7290
Martin Schein, *President*
Toni Schein, *Corp Secy*
EMP: 6
SQ FT: 1,500
SALES (est): 744.5K **Privately Held**
SIC: 7694 7539 Electric motor repair; electrical services

(G-2262)
STEELFAB TEXAS INC
446 Country Club Rd (74701-6707)
PHONE.................972 562-7720
Jim Reeves, *Owner*
EMP: 50
SALES (corp-wide): 445MM **Privately Held**
SIC: 3441 Fabricated structural metal
HQ: Steelfab Texas, Inc.
1600 Redbud Blvd Ste 208
Mckinney TX 75069
972 562-7720

(G-2263)
TETRACHEM SEAL COMPANY INC
9660 W Highway 70 (74701-8901)
P.O. Box 1225 (74702-1225)
PHONE.................580 924-1717
Dennis Bowen, *President*
Deann Shessield, *Corp Secy*
Betty Bowen, *Vice Pres*
Dee Ann Sheffield, *Office Mgr*
EMP: 12
SQ FT: 8,000
SALES (est): 2.1MM **Privately Held**
WEB: www.tetrachemseal.com
SIC: 2821 3053 Plastics materials & resins; gaskets, packing & sealing devices

(G-2264)
TEXOMA ENGRAVING LLC
Also Called: T Shirt & Signs
3509 W Arkansas St (74701-4562)
PHONE.................580 775-7333
Susan Chalk, *Mng Member*
Kevin Chalk,
EMP: 2
SQ FT: 4,000
SALES: 85K **Privately Held**
SIC: 2759 3479 3953 5699 Plateless engraving; letterpress & screen printing; etching & engraving; screens, textile printing; T-shirts, custom printed

(G-2265)
TEXOMA MFG LLC
3324 N 1st Ave (74701-2521)
P.O. Box 1662 (74702-1662)
PHONE.................580 920-0878
Scott Crain, *CEO*
EMP: 4
SALES (est): 245.7K **Privately Held**
SIC: 3999 Manufacturing industries

(G-2266)
TEXOMA MILLWRIGHT AND WLDG INC
1325 Se 3rd Ave (74701-6749)
P.O. Box 216, Calera (74730-0216)
PHONE.................580 931-9368
Michael Forbis, *President*
Relita Cayton, *Admin Sec*
EMP: 16

SALES (est): 2MM **Privately Held**
SIC: 7692 Welding repair

(G-2267)
TEXOMA PRINTING INC
Also Called: Choctaw Print Services
2712 Enterprise Dr (74701-2386)
P.O. Box 1667 (74702-1667)
PHONE.................580 924-1120
Ron Washer, *Vice Pres*
Russell Marcum, *Director*
Katlyn Dodds, *Graphic Designe*
EMP: 8
SQ FT: 1,500
SALES (est): 2.5MM **Privately Held**
WEB: www.texprintone.com
SIC: 2752 Commercial printing, offset
PA: Choctaw Nation Of Oklahoma
1802 Chukka Hina
Durant OK 74701
580 924-8280

(G-2268)
TEXOMA WHEELCHAIRS
1400 Bryan Dr (74701-2156)
PHONE.................855 924-2525
EMP: 2 EST: 2014
SALES (est): 77K **Privately Held**
SIC: 3842 Mfg Surgical Appliances/Supplies

(G-2269)
TILE SHOP LLC
1800 W Arkansas St (74701-5624)
PHONE.................580 920-1570
EMP: 13
SALES (corp-wide): 340.3MM **Publicly Held**
WEB: www.tileshop.com
SIC: 2891 Adhesives, paste
HQ: The Tile Shop Llc
14000 Carlson Pkwy
Plymouth MN 55441
763 541-1444

(G-2270)
TUBACEX DURANT INC
362 Country Club Rd (74701-6767)
PHONE.................724 646-4301
Javier Lorenzo, *President*
Doug Faber, *CFO*
Cathy J Brindza, *Accounts Mgr*
EMP: 3
SALES (est): 127.2K **Privately Held**
SIC: 3312 Stainless steel

(G-2271)
UNITED SEWING AGENCY INC
2929 W Main St (74701-4825)
PHONE.................580 924-6936
Dennis Hall, *President*
Wendy Gilmore, *Corp Secy*
Gayle Hall, *Vice Pres*
EMP: 8
SQ FT: 12,000
SALES (est): 628.3K **Privately Held**
SIC: 6163 3661 Mortgage brokers arranging for loans, using money of others; switching equipment, telephone

(G-2272)
WASTEQUIP MANUFACTURING CO LLC
101 Waldron Dr (74701-1903)
PHONE.................580 924-1575
EMP: 40 **Privately Held**
SIC: 3443 Mfg Fabricated Plate Work
HQ: Wastequip Manufacturing Company Llc
6525 Morrison Blvd # 300
Charlotte NC 28211

Durham
Roger Mills County

(G-2273)
SUM PROFESSIONALS INC
Also Called: S U M Professional
7725 N 1740 Rd (73642-4258)
PHONE.................580 983-2379
Charles W Hartley, *President*
Kevin Hartley, *Vice Pres*
Timmy Hartley, *Admin Sec*

EMP: 10
SALES (est): 525.3K **Privately Held**
SIC: 1389 Oil field services

Eagletown
Mccurtain County

(G-2274)
BRUCE HOPSON LOGGING INC
2300 Rd Stuffy Ln (74734)
P.O. Box 33 (74734-0033)
PHONE.................580 835-7145
Bruce Hopson, *President*
Gail Hopson, *Corp Secy*
Johnnie Hopson, *Corp Secy*
Brute Hopson, *Vice Pres*
EMP: 4 EST: 1990
SALES (est): 600K **Privately Held**
SIC: 2411 Logging camps & contractors

(G-2275)
HADLEY-KEENEY CHIPPING INC
3631 Cascade Creek Rd (74734-5076)
PHONE.................580 835-2645
Kelly Hadley, *President*
Angie Keeney, *Vice Pres*
EMP: 20
SALES (est): 2.3MM **Privately Held**
SIC: 3531 2411 Chippers: brush, limb & log; logging

(G-2276)
JAMES ROY HOPSON
Also Called: Roy Hopson Logging
555 Skipjack Rd (74734-5167)
P.O. Box 322 (74734-0322)
PHONE.................580 835-2288
EMP: 3
SALES (est): 361.8K **Privately Held**
SIC: 2411 Logging

(G-2277)
REX ROSS
Also Called: Rex Ross Logging
737 Tablerville Rd (74734)
P.O. Box 171 (74734-0171)
PHONE.................580 835-7244
Rex Ross, *Owner*
EMP: 1 EST: 2013
SALES (est): 126.9K **Privately Held**
SIC: 2411 Driving & booming timber

Eakly
Caddo County

(G-2278)
COUNTRY CONNECTION NEWS INC
315 Main St (73033)
P.O. Box 206 (73033-0206)
PHONE.................405 797-3648
Marilyn J Carney, *President*
Amanda Carney, *Vice Pres*
Russel Carney, *Treasurer*
EMP: 2
SALES (est): 138.8K **Privately Held**
SIC: 2711 Newspapers, publishing & printing

Earlsboro
Pottawatomie County

(G-2279)
CH MUFFLERS & WELDING LLC
35084 Highway 9 (74840-9027)
PHONE.................405 380-3877
EMP: 1
SALES (est): 40.8K **Privately Held**
SIC: 7692 Welding repair

(G-2280)
DIVERSIFIED GEOSYNTHETICS INC
49600 Highway 3e (74840-3545)
PHONE.................580 395-0041
Barry Thompson, *Branch Mgr*
EMP: 1

SALES (corp-wide): 2.4MM **Privately Held**
WEB: www.diversifiedgeo.com
SIC: 1389 Construction, repair & dismantling services
PA: Diversified Geosynthetics, Inc.
1101 N Harrison Ave Ste D
Shawnee OK 74801
405 214-0535

(G-2281)
KENS HOT OIL & STEAM SERVICE
35355 Highway 99a (74840-9038)
PHONE.................405 382-3052
Ken Howard, *Owner*
EMP: 2
SALES (est): 138.2K **Privately Held**
SIC: 1389 Oil field services

Edmond
Oklahoma County

(G-2282)
2B PUBLISHING LLC
2024 Turtlecreek Rd (73013-6611)
PHONE.................405 209-8465
Delores Chumley, *Principal*
EMP: 1
SALES (est): 37.5K **Privately Held**
SIC: 2741 Miscellaneous publishing

(G-2283)
2BY2 INDUSTRIES LLC
14710 Metro Plaza Blvd A (73013-1988)
P.O. Box 7987 (73083-7987)
PHONE.................877 234-6558
Stephen Shepherd, *Manager*
Stephen Shephard,
▲ EMP: 4
SQ FT: 2,000
SALES (est): 165.1K **Privately Held**
SIC: 3089 Fences, gates & accessories: plastic

(G-2284)
405 COATINGS LLC
3604 Ne 143rd St (73013-7201)
PHONE.................405 822-5095
Jason Cook, *Principal*
EMP: 3
SALES (est): 237.2K **Privately Held**
SIC: 2851 Paints & allied products

(G-2285)
4524 LLC
Also Called: Creative Marketing Promotion
3700 Bonaire Pl (73013-1773)
PHONE.................405 620-3711
Vance Harrison, *President*
EMP: 2
SALES (est): 188K **Privately Held**
SIC: 7336 2395 2396 Silk screen design; pleating & stitching; automotive & apparel trimmings

(G-2286)
4RV PUBLISHING LLC
2912 Rankin Ter (73013-5344)
P.O. Box 6482 (73083-6482)
PHONE.................405 225-7298
Vivian Zabel,
EMP: 4
SALES (est): 252.4K **Privately Held**
WEB: www.4rvpublishingllc.com
SIC: 2741 Miscellaneous publishing

(G-2287)
AARON WILLIS PRESIDENT
11780 S Sooner Rd (73034-8553)
PHONE.................405 219-9411
EMP: 2
SALES (est): 118.2K **Privately Held**
SIC: 3599 Machine shop, jobbing & repair

(G-2288)
ABLE WELDING
304 Longhorn Dr (73003-6318)
PHONE.................405 760-1442
Michael Renkus, *Owner*
EMP: 1
SALES (est): 20K **Privately Held**
SIC: 7692 Welding repair

GEOGRAPHIC SECTION
Edmond - Oklahoma County (G-2320)

(G-2289)
ADAIRS SLEEP WORLD INC
Also Called: Adair's Custom Upholstering
611 W Edmond Rd (73003-5624)
PHONE..............................405 341-9468
Robby Weeden, *President*
Shari Weeden, *Vice Pres*
Herb Kimball, *Shareholder*
EMP: 10
SQ FT: 15,000
SALES (est): 1.6MM **Privately Held**
SIC: 2515 7641 2395 2392 Mattresses & bedsprings; reupholstery; quilting, for the trade; household furnishings

(G-2290)
ADVANCED MICRO SOLUTIONS INC
Also Called: AMS
1709 S State St (73013-3633)
PHONE..............................405 562-0112
Thomas Douglas, *President*
Denise Payne, *Sales Staff*
Newberry Richard, *Technical Staff*
Sean Douglass, *Prgrmr*
EMP: 14
SQ FT: 3,360
SALES (est): 1.9MM **Privately Held**
SIC: 7372 Business oriented computer software

(G-2291)
AERO SOLUTIONS AND SERVICES
Also Called: Aero S2
14196 Meritage Dr (73034-2563)
PHONE..............................405 308-6788
Ronald Stencel, *Principal*
EMP: 1 EST: 2016
SALES (est): 60K **Privately Held**
SIC: 3728 3613 3724 Aircraft parts & equipment; aircraft landing assemblies & brakes; switchgear & switchboard apparatus; turbines, aircraft type

(G-2292)
AEXCO PETROLEUM INC
785 W Covell Rd Ste 125 (73003-2392)
PHONE..............................405 844-1991
Karl Holliman, *Manager*
EMP: 3
SALES (corp-wide): 2.9MM **Privately Held**
WEB: www.aexco.net
SIC: 1382 Oil & gas exploration services
PA: Aexco Petroleum, Inc.
1675 Broadway Ste 1900
Denver CO 80202
303 863-1110

(G-2293)
AGION PRESS
409 Woodhollow Trl (73012-4435)
P.O. Box 1052 (73083-1052)
PHONE..............................405 341-7477
Louis Parkhurst, *Principal*
EMP: 2
SALES (est): 156.8K **Privately Held**
WEB: www.agionpress.com
SIC: 2741 Miscellaneous publishing

(G-2294)
AKITA COMPRESSION SERVICES LLC
14701 Glenmark Dr (73013-1820)
PHONE..............................405 201-2677
Joe Vaughn, *Mng Member*
EMP: 4
SALES (est): 540K **Privately Held**
SIC: 1389 Gas compressing (natural gas) at the fields

(G-2295)
ALL AMERICAN EAR MOLD LABS
Also Called: All American Mold Labs
625 Enterprise Dr Ste 160 (73013-3762)
P.O. Box 25751, Oklahoma City (73125-0751)
PHONE..............................405 285-2411
Katie McKellips, *President*
Keith McKellits, *Treasurer*
Kerri Betterton, *Admin Sec*
EMP: 12
SALES: 1.7MM **Privately Held**
SIC: 3842 5047 Hearing aids; hearing aids

(G-2296)
ALLIED H2O INC
1004 Woodbury Dr (73034-6723)
PHONE..............................405 550-3085
Steve Stewart, *President*
EMP: 2
SALES: 500K **Privately Held**
SIC: 3523 Fertilizing, spraying, dusting & irrigation machinery

(G-2297)
ALLSBURY MARKETING & PUBG LLC
2017 Bradford Way (73003-4393)
PHONE..............................405 412-0809
Sherri Allsbury, *Principal*
EMP: 1
SALES (est): 37.5K **Privately Held**
SIC: 2741 Miscellaneous publishing

(G-2298)
ALPHA DENTAL STUDIOS
2300 S Broadway Ste 102 (73013-4065)
PHONE..............................405 359-2976
Hyeonmi Kim, *Owner*
EMP: 5
SALES (est): 730.9K **Privately Held**
SIC: 3821 Clinical laboratory instruments, except medical & dental

(G-2299)
ALPINE INC
3409 S Broadway Ste 600 (73013-4162)
PHONE..............................405 507-1111
EMP: 2
SALES (est): 81.9K **Privately Held**
SIC: 1382 Oil & gas exploration services

(G-2300)
ALWAYS DONE RIGHT LLC
2228 Nw 159th Ter (73013-7320)
P.O. Box 273, Guthrie (73044-0273)
PHONE..............................405 615-5955
Taleb Dixon, *Mng Member*
Kevin Dixon, *Mng Member*
Jason Seapon, *Mng Member*
EMP: 5
SALES (est): 467.9K **Privately Held**
SIC: 3444 Gutters, sheet metal

(G-2301)
AMEREX CORP
933 Nw 164th St Ste 3 (73013-1044)
PHONE..............................405 216-5548
EMP: 2
SALES (est): 169.4K **Privately Held**
SIC: 1382 Oil/Gas Exploration Services

(G-2302)
AMERICAN PETROLEUM & ENVRNMNTL
Also Called: American Petro & Enviromental
2240 Nw 164th St (73013-8801)
PHONE..............................405 513-6055
Saleem Nizami, *President*
EMP: 5
SALES: 1.2MM **Privately Held**
SIC: 1382 Oil & gas exploration services

(G-2303)
AMERITIES HOLDINGS LLC (PA)
933 Nw 164th St Ste 1 (73013-1044)
P.O. Box 6176 (73083-6176)
PHONE..............................405 359-3235
John McGinley,
EMP: 54
SALES (est): 10.8MM **Privately Held**
SIC: 3743 Railroad equipment, except locomotives

(G-2304)
AMERITIES SOUTH LLC (HQ)
933 Nw 164th St Ste 1 (73013-1044)
P.O. Box 6176 (73083-6176)
PHONE..............................405 359-3235
John McGinley,
EMP: 16
SQ FT: 1,500
SALES (est): 2.4MM
SALES (corp-wide): 10.8MM **Privately Held**
SIC: 3743 Railroad equipment, except locomotives
PA: Amerities Holdings, Llc
933 Nw 164th St Ste 1
Edmond OK 73013
405 359-3235

(G-2305)
AP JETWORKS LLC
Also.Called: Aerospace
4625 Spectacular Bid Ave (73025-2375)
PHONE..............................405 226-2583
Adam Pugh,
EMP: 2
SALES (est): 92.9K **Privately Held**
SIC: 3721 Aircraft

(G-2306)
APPLICATIONS FOR MEDICINE LLC
3013 Broken Bow Cir (73013-7815)
PHONE..............................405 330-7910
George Orza, *Mng Member*
EMP: 3
SALES: 750K **Privately Held**
SIC: 3842 Trusses, orthopedic & surgical

(G-2307)
ARBUCKLE ENTERPRISES INC
1620 E 19th St (73013-6619)
P.O. Box 5250 (73083-5250)
PHONE..............................405 359-2815
David Bohnert, *President*
Carlos Elwell, *Vice Pres*
EMP: 5
SQ FT: 4,200
SALES (est): 952.3K **Privately Held**
SIC: 1311 Crude petroleum production; natural gas production

(G-2308)
ARBUCKLE WIRELINE
4374 W Waterloo Rd (73025-1694)
P.O. Box 30293 (73003-0005)
PHONE..............................405 620-6739
Terry Conner, *Principal*
EMP: 2 EST: 2011
SALES (est): 188.7K **Privately Held**
SIC: 1389 Well logging

(G-2309)
ARCADIA OIL CORP
4910 Clipper Xing (73013)
PHONE..............................405 409-2013
Chad W Dobbins, *President*
EMP: 1
SALES (est): 97K **Privately Held**
SIC: 1389 Oil consultants

(G-2310)
ARROW DRILLING LLC
1004 Nw 139th Street Pkwy (73013-9791)
PHONE..............................405 749-7860
Craig Elder, *Mng Member*
Brad Pumphrey,
EMP: 40
SALES (est): 3.8MM **Privately Held**
SIC: 1381 Directional drilling oil & gas wells

(G-2311)
AUDIO LINK INC
3140 Waterloo Cir (73034-8903)
PHONE..............................405 359-0017
Henry Gresham, *President*
W C Gresham, *Principal*
EMP: 6
SALES (est): 350K **Privately Held**
SIC: 3532 3523 Feeders, ore & aggregate; farm machinery & equipment

(G-2312)
AUTO HAIL DAMAGE REPAIR
3825 Nw 166th St Ste A11 (73012-9229)
PHONE..............................405 696-6031
EMP: 2
SALES (est): 87.2K **Privately Held**
SIC: 3714 Motor vehicle parts & accessories

(G-2313)
AVALANCHE PRINT COMPANY
1105 S Fretz Ave (73003-5776)
PHONE..............................405 808-4229
Neil Phillips, *President*
Jackie Patterson-Phill, *Marketing Staff*
EMP: 5 EST: 2010
SALES (est): 23.2K **Privately Held**
WEB: www.avalancheprintcompany.com
SIC: 2752 Commercial printing, lithographic

(G-2314)
AZTEC MANUFACTURING CORP
6333 Boucher Dr (73034-9258)
PHONE..............................405 330-4888
Geary Wilson, *President*
Wayne Wilson, *Vice Pres*
Velma Wilson, *Admin Sec*
EMP: 9
SQ FT: 126,000
SALES (est): 1.1MM **Privately Held**
SIC: 3089 Molding primary plastic; injection molding of plastics

(G-2315)
BABB LAND & DEVELOPMENT
1900 E 15th St Ste 600b (73013-6691)
PHONE..............................405 340-1178
Rodney Babb, *Owner*
EMP: 3
SALES (est): 310.2K **Privately Held**
SIC: 1382 Oil & gas exploration services

(G-2316)
BANKERS ONLINE
2541 Flint Ridge Rd (73003-2442)
PHONE..............................888 229-8872
Mary Beth Guard, *Partner*
Carin Eisenhauer, *Partner*
George Milner, *Partner*
Michele Petry, *Partner*
EMP: 4 EST: 2012
SALES (est): 276.4K **Privately Held**
WEB: www.bankersonline.com
SIC: 2741 7389 Catalogs: publishing & printing;

(G-2317)
BARON EXPLORATION CO INC
107 S Broadway (73034-3843)
PHONE..............................405 341-1779
Chris Hoke, *President*
Charlene White, *Corp Secy*
EMP: 9 EST: 1978
SQ FT: 2,000
SALES (est): 1.2MM **Privately Held**
SIC: 1311 Crude petroleum production; natural gas production

(G-2318)
BARRETTS INC
Also Called: Barrett Jewelers
3224 S Boulevard (73013-5483)
PHONE..............................405 340-1519
Dennis Barrett, *President*
Elsie Barrett, *Corp Secy*
Ivan L Barrett, *Vice Pres*
EMP: 5
SALES (est): 150K **Privately Held**
SIC: 5944 3911 Jewelry, precious stones & precious metals; jewelry, precious metal

(G-2319)
BB2 LLC
Also Called: Bricktown Brewery
1150 E 2nd St (73034-5315)
PHONE..............................405 726-8300
EMP: 2 **Privately Held**
SIC: 2082 Malt beverages
PA: Bb2 Llc
1 N Oklahoma Ave
Oklahoma City OK 73104

(G-2320)
BEST BUILDING MATERIALS INC
14801 Bristol Park Blvd (73013-1892)
PHONE..............................405 755-0554
Todd Best, *Principal*
EMP: 2
SALES (est): 74.4K **Privately Held**
SIC: 2899 Chemical preparations

Edmond - Oklahoma County (G-2321) GEOGRAPHIC SECTION

(G-2321)
BIG PRODUCTIONS LLC
2844 Nw 159th St (73013-1234)
PHONE..............................405 513-6545
Lily Shangreaux,
Daniel Bigbee,
EMP: 2
SQ FT: 2,000
SALES: 90K **Privately Held**
SIC: 7819 2099 7389 Video tape or disk reproduction; seasonings & spices;

(G-2322)
BISBY CANDLES LLC
16209 Monarch Field Rd (73013-1185)
PHONE..............................918 408-5291
EMP: 2 EST: 2014
SALES (est): 147.4K **Privately Held**
WEB: www.shopbisby.com
SIC: 3999 Candles

(G-2323)
BIZ NETWORKS LLC
Also Called: Advanced Printing and Mktg
500 E 2nd St (73034-5303)
PHONE..............................405 348-6090
Syed Taha, *President*
Taha Syed, *Officer*
Rachel Giles, *Graphic Designe*
EMP: 3
SQ FT: 2,500
SALES (est): 434.9K **Privately Held**
SIC: 2752 Commercial printing, lithographic

(G-2324)
BLACK & PURYEAR PAINT MFG CO
1640 Oak Creek Dr (73034-5922)
PHONE..............................405 348-0447
Jon Furman Puryear, *President*
Laura Puryear, *Vice Pres*
Martha Puryear, *Admin Sec*
EMP: 5 EST: 1944
SQ FT: 7,200
SALES (est): 846.2K **Privately Held**
SIC: 2851 Paints & paint additives

(G-2325)
BLACK SWAN OIL & GAS
2513 S Kelly Ave Ste 200 (73013-6801)
PHONE..............................405 285-1996
Ian Yingling, *CEO*
Jason Kneedy, *Exec VP*
David Lalonde, *CFO*
EMP: 2
SALES (est): 121.9K **Privately Held**
SIC: 1382 Oil & gas exploration services

(G-2326)
BLEYTHING OIL & GAS LLC
14709 Bristol Park Blvd (73013-1894)
PHONE..............................405 535-0253
Jeff Bleything, *Owner*
EMP: 2 EST: 2017
SALES (est): 70.5K **Privately Held**
SIC: 1389 Oil & gas field services

(G-2327)
BLUEHAWK ENERGY INC
4000 Calm Waters Way (73034-1026)
PHONE..............................405 406-1580
David Scull, *President*
Benny Galloway, *CFO*
EMP: 3
SALES (est): 137.4K **Privately Held**
SIC: 1321 2869 2821 Natural gas liquids production; methyl alcohol, synthetic methanol; polypropylene resins, polyethylene resins

(G-2328)
BOELTE EXPLORATIONS LLC
16812 Conifer Ln (73012-0619)
PHONE..............................405 285-0063
Craig E Boelte, *Administration*
Craig Boelte, *Administration*
EMP: 2
SALES (est): 209.3K **Privately Held**
SIC: 1382 Oil & gas exploration services

(G-2329)
BOOK VILLAGES LLC
2800 Berrywood Cir (73034-6831)
PHONE..............................719 339-8048
Karen Pickering,
Ruth Marlene Hollis,
EMP: 2
SALES (est): 59.2K **Privately Held**
SIC: 2741 Miscellaneous publishing

(G-2330)
BOOLEAN INC
2701 Hidden Valley Rd (73013-6151)
PHONE..............................405 341-1499
Duane D Deaton, *President*
Connie Deaton, *Vice Pres*
EMP: 2
SALES (est): 164.6K **Privately Held**
SIC: 5734 7372 Software, business & non-game; prepackaged software

(G-2331)
BOUNCE DIAGNOSTICS INC
317 Antelope Trl (73012-4420)
PHONE..............................405 740-5889
Tom Collier, *Principal*
Wanda Collier, *CFO*
EMP: 5
SALES (est): 405.3K **Privately Held**
SIC: 2835 In vivo diagnostics

(G-2332)
BREXCO INC
900 Brook Frst (73034-7515)
PHONE..............................405 348-8124
Greg Browder, *President*
EMP: 1
SALES (est): 109.6K **Privately Held**
SIC: 1381 Drilling oil & gas wells

(G-2333)
BROOKLINE MINERALS LLC
36 W 8th St (73003-5767)
PHONE..............................405 359-0900
Ashford Gokel,
EMP: 1
SALES (est): 170K **Privately Held**
SIC: 1382 Oil & gas exploration services

(G-2334)
BUCKELEW ACCNTING SLUTIONS LLC
Also Called: Ba Solutions
2700 Morrison Trl (73012-6418)
PHONE..............................405 359-5887
Scott Buckelew,
EMP: 1
SALES (est): 89.9K **Privately Held**
WEB: www.ba-solutions.com
SIC: 8999 7372 Actuarial consultant; prepackaged software

(G-2335)
CABINET CURES OKLAHOMA LLC
129 W 1st St (73003-5508)
PHONE..............................405 285-5700
EMP: 4
SALES (est): 343.1K **Privately Held**
SIC: 2434 Mfg Wood Kitchen Cabinets

(G-2336)
CAGAN LAND SERVICES LLC
1900 S Broadway Ste B (73013-4066)
PHONE..............................405 757-4046
Wesley C Willits,
EMP: 1
SALES: 1MM **Privately Held**
SIC: 1382 Oil & gas exploration services

(G-2337)
CALEBS RESOURCES LLC
18801 Woody Creek Dr (73012-4109)
P.O. Box 6655 (73083-6655)
PHONE..............................405 330-8252
Lee McBay, *Principal*
Deborah McBay,
EMP: 2
SALES (est): 260K **Privately Held**
SIC: 1382 Geological exploration, oil & gas field

(G-2338)
CASCADE OIL LLC
1900 E 15th St Bldg 700 (73013-6610)
P.O. Box 888 (73083-0888)
PHONE..............................405 236-4554
Marlene Sanders, *Opers Staff*
Larry Nilsen, *Mng Member*
Carol Nilsen,
Christopher Nilsen,
RC Powell, *Sr Consultant*
EMP: 6
SQ FT: 1,200
SALES (est): 385K **Privately Held**
WEB: www.cascade-oil.com
SIC: 1311 Crude petroleum production; natural gas production

(G-2339)
CBD FARMACY LLC
617 N Oakridge Dr (73034-7114)
PHONE..............................405 697-5245
Daryl Holland, *Principal*
EMP: 1
SALES (est): 75.5K **Privately Held**
SIC: 3999

(G-2340)
CCS PUBLISHING LLC
1209 Rockwood Dr (73013-6048)
PHONE..............................405 359-0656
Thomas Rider, *President*
EMP: 3
SALES (est): 167.6K **Privately Held**
SIC: 2741 Miscellaneous publishing

(G-2341)
CEDAR GATE LLC
3508 French Park Dr Ste 1 (73034-7263)
PHONE..............................405 640-3235
Brian D Hill, *Principal*
EMP: 1
SALES (est): 58.4K **Privately Held**
WEB: www.thecedargate.com
SIC: 2741 Miscellaneous publishing

(G-2342)
CENTERMASS INDUSTRIES LLC
4817 Blackjack Ln (73034-8317)
PHONE..............................760 485-7405
Tyler Blevins, *Administration*
EMP: 2
SALES (est): 141.4K **Privately Held**
WEB: www.centermassindustries.wordpress.com
SIC: 3999 Manufacturing industries

(G-2343)
CFM INDUSTRIES LLC
508 Cloudview Pl (73003-1059)
PHONE..............................405 213-9557
EMP: 2
SALES (est): 79.7K **Privately Held**
SIC: 3999 Manufacturing industries

(G-2344)
CHANDLER WELL SERVICES LLC
10850 Hunters Pointe (73034-1608)
PHONE..............................817 673-8140
Gerald L Chandler Jr, *Mng Member*
Gerald Chandler Jr, *Mng Member*
EMP: 2
SALES: 400K **Privately Held**
SIC: 1389 Oil consultants

(G-2345)
CHARLES JONES
Also Called: Maverick Tarkets
825 W Simmons Rd (73034-8259)
PHONE..............................405 348-2187
Charles Jones, *Owner*
Beverly Jones, *Co-Owner*
EMP: 2
SALES (est): 107.6K **Privately Held**
SIC: 3949 1799 7389 Target shooting equipment; target systems installation;

(G-2346)
CHARLES WEATHERS WELDING
616 W Main St (73003-5347)
PHONE..............................405 341-2413
Charles Weathers, *Principal*
EMP: 1
SALES (est): 54K **Privately Held**
SIC: 7692 Welding repair

(G-2347)
CHEFTAIN ROYALTY COMPANY
1249 E 33rd St (73013-6307)
PHONE..............................405 767-1251
Kenneth Abernathy, *Principal*
EMP: 2
SALES (est): 161.8K **Privately Held**
SIC: 1382 Oil & gas exploration services

(G-2348)
CHERMAC ENERGY CORPORATION
2909 Nw 156th St (73013-2101)
P.O. Box 5446 (73083-5446)
PHONE..............................405 341-3506
Jaime McAlpine, *President*
Cheryl McAlpine, *CFO*
Cheryl L McAlpine, *Treasurer*
EMP: 15
SQ FT: 5,100
SALES (est): 2.4MM **Privately Held**
SIC: 1311 8711 Crude petroleum production; natural gas production; consulting engineer

(G-2349)
CHRISTIAN CHRONICLE INC
Also Called: Christian Chronicle, The
2801 E Memorial Rd # 102 (73013-6474)
P.O. Box 11000, Oklahoma City (73136-1100)
PHONE..............................405 425-5070
Lynn McMillon, *President*
Neil Arter, *Dean*
Phil Lewis, *Dean*
David Lowry, *Dean*
Kristen Alcon, *Vice Pres*
EMP: 7
SALES (est): 1.1MM **Privately Held**
SIC: 2711 Newspapers, publishing & printing

(G-2350)
CHRISTINA STOKES
Also Called: Bug Reaper Pest Control
1325 Northgate Ter (73013-4706)
PHONE..............................405 551-1017
Christina Stokes, *Owner*
EMP: 2
SALES (est): 105.2K **Privately Held**
SIC: 2879 7389 Exterminating products, for household or industrial use;

(G-2351)
CHROMATECH SCIENTIFIC CORP
3720 Harris Dr (73013-8076)
PHONE..............................405 370-4466
John Liton, *President*
EMP: 2
SALES (est): 163.7K **Privately Held**
SIC: 2879 7389 Agricultural chemicals;

(G-2352)
CIMARRON SCREEN PRINTING
Also Called: Edmond Screen Printing
13716 N Lincoln Blvd (73013-3401)
PHONE..............................405 755-8337
James W McTiernan, *Owner*
EMP: 4
SQ FT: 2,000
SALES (est): 254K **Privately Held**
SIC: 2759 2752 2396 Screen printing; commercial printing, lithographic; automotive & apparel trimmings

(G-2353)
CINDY NICKEL AESTHETICS
200 N Bryant Ave 100 (73034-6273)
PHONE..............................405 513-6690
Cindy Nickel, *Owner*
EMP: 1
SALES (est): 108.8K **Privately Held**
SIC: 3356 Nickel

(G-2354)
CINDY NICKEL INC
1816 Winding Ridge Rd (73034-1408)
PHONE..............................405 209-1444
Cindy Nickel, *Principal*
EMP: 4
SALES (est): 487.6K **Privately Held**
SIC: 3356 Nickel

(G-2355)
CJS CUSTOM APPAREL
2100 S Broadway (73013-4021)
PHONE..............................405 340-9677
EMP: 6

GEOGRAPHIC SECTION   Edmond - Oklahoma County (G-2386)

SALES (est): 597.7K **Privately Held**
WEB: www.cjs-embroidery.com
SIC: 2759 Screen printing

(G-2356)
CLAYTON HOMES INC
Also Called: Oakridge Estates
601 Vista Ln (73034-6365)
PHONE..................405 341-4479
Stephen Orr, *Manager*
EMP: 4
SALES (corp-wide): 327.2B **Publicly Held**
SIC: 2451 Mobile homes
HQ: Clayton Homes, Inc.
   5000 Clayton Rd
   Maryville TN 37804
   865 380-3000

(G-2357)
CLEARY PETROLEUM CORPORATION
10 N Broadway (73034-3729)
PHONE..................405 672-4544
Douglas B Cleary, *CEO*
William B Cleary, *Chairman*
George M Moore, *Exec VP*
Devin Giddens, *General Counsel*
EMP: 10
SQ FT: 6,700
SALES (est): 1.5MM **Privately Held**
SIC: 1381 Directional drilling oil & gas wells

(G-2358)
CLUBHOUSE TRAILER CO LLC
Also Called: Clubhouse Trailers
14625 Snta Fe Crssings Dr (73013-3446)
P.O. Box 2004 (73083-2004)
PHONE..................405 396-6747
Jeffrey D Hadley, *Mng Member*
Drew Taylor, *Mng Member*
EMP: 5 EST: 2016
SALES (est): 638.8K **Privately Held**
WEB: www.hadleydesign.com
SIC: 3715 3931 Trailer bodies; musical instruments

(G-2359)
CNHI LLC
Also Called: Edmond Sun
123 S Broadway (73034-3843)
P.O. Box 2470 (73083-2470)
PHONE..................405 341-2121
Stephanie Brackett, *Branch Mgr*
EMP: 50 **Privately Held**
SIC: 2711 7313 Newspapers: publishing only, not printed on site; newspaper advertising representative
HQ: Cnhi, Llc
   445 Dexter Ave Ste 7000
   Montgomery AL 36104

(G-2360)
COLUMBIA REHABILITATION SVCS
Also Called: Oklahoma Center For Athletes
301 S Bryant Ave Ste B100 (73034-5790)
PHONE..................405 359-2741
EMP: 9
SALES (est): 640K **Privately Held**
SIC: 3999 Mfg Misc Products

(G-2361)
COMBINED RESOURCES CORPORATION
1001 Medical Park Blvd (73013-3025)
P.O. Box 6118 (73083-6118)
PHONE..................405 341-7700
James V Collins, *President*
EMP: 6
SQ FT: 3,500
SALES (est): 745.6K **Privately Held**
SIC: 1311 Crude petroleum production; natural gas production

(G-2362)
COMPANY DE ROTH
2104 Hummingbird Ln (73034-6039)
PHONE..................405 348-3754
Ken Roth, *Owner*
EMP: 1

SALES (est): 108.4K **Privately Held**
WEB: www.company-de-roth.com
SIC: 3641 3648 Electric light bulbs, complete; lighting equipment

(G-2363)
COMPETITIVE ACTION SPORTS LLC
6000 Oak Tree Rd (73025-2625)
PHONE..................405 474-7777
Steve Zabel, *Mng Member*
◆ EMP: 1
SALES: 45K **Privately Held**
SIC: 3949 7389 Sporting & athletic goods;

(G-2364)
CONCEPT AIRCRAFT LLC
818 Hawthorne Pl (73003-5016)
PHONE..................405 620-1701
Anthony Windisch,
EMP: 1
SALES (est): 62.6K **Privately Held**
SIC: 3721 Aircraft

(G-2365)
CONTEMPORARY CABINETS INC
308 Westland Dr (73013-3731)
P.O. Box 127, Chandler (74834-0127)
PHONE..................405 330-4592
David Brownell, *President*
EMP: 90
SQ FT: 30,000
SALES (est): 15.3MM **Privately Held**
SIC: 2431 2541 2517 2434 Millwork; wood partitions & fixtures; wood television & radio cabinets; wood kitchen cabinets; millwork & lumber

(G-2366)
CONYER SIGNS
809 Nw 143rd St (73013-1945)
P.O. Box 5146 (73083-5146)
PHONE..................405 755-0061
Brenda Conyer, *Owner*
EMP: 1
SALES (est): 110K **Privately Held**
SIC: 3993 Signs & advertising specialties

(G-2367)
COOL BABY INC
16800 Kingsley Rd (73012-6849)
PHONE..................405 755-1100
EMP: 3 EST: 2010
SALES (est): 130K **Privately Held**
SIC: 2676 Mfg Sanitary Paper Products

(G-2368)
COUNTRY HOME MEAT COMPANY
2775 E Waterloo Rd (73034-8131)
PHONE..................405 341-0267
Robert Noll, *Owner*
Jessee Davis, *Plant Mgr*
EMP: 9 EST: 1956
SQ FT: 5,200
SALES (est): 887.6K **Privately Held**
WEB: www.countryhomemeats.com
SIC: 2011 5421 2013 Meat packing plants; meat markets, including freezer provisioners; sausages & other prepared meats

(G-2369)
CP ENERGY HOLDINGS LLC (PA)
317 Lilac Dr Ste 200 (73034-7283)
PHONE..................405 513-6006
Greg Piper, *President*
Les Harding, *COO*
Jackson Wise, *Senior VP*
Kyle Essmiller, *VP Admin*
Terry Bond, *Vice Pres*
EMP: 11
SALES (est): 24.2MM **Privately Held**
SIC: 3533 Oil & gas drilling rigs & equipment

(G-2370)
CP ENERGY LLC
317 Lilac Dr Ste 200 (73034-7283)
PHONE..................405 513-6006
Kyle Essmiller, *VP Admin*
Jim Crossen, *Vice Pres*
Stephen Mezo, *Opers Staff*

Justin Clapper, *Engineer*
Joseph Kieval, *Marketing Staff*
EMP: 14
SQ FT: 500
SALES (est): 9.4MM
SALES (corp-wide): 24.2MM **Privately Held**
WEB: www.cpenergy.com
SIC: 1382 Oil & gas exploration services
PA: Cp Energy Holdings, Llc
   317 Lilac Dr Ste 200
   Edmond OK 73034
   405 513-6006

(G-2371)
CRAIG ELDER OIL AND GAS LLC
1004 Nw 139th Street Pkwy (73013-9791)
P.O. Box 7267 (73083-7267)
PHONE..................405 917-7860
Craig Elder, *Mng Member*
EMP: 4
SQ FT: 3,000
SALES (est): 754.7K **Privately Held**
SIC: 1382 Geological exploration, oil & gas field

(G-2372)
CREATIVE SPACES
6400 Industrial Blvd (73034-9492)
PHONE..................405 341-8710
David Hansen, *Owner*
EMP: 4
SQ FT: 5,000
SALES (est): 1MM **Privately Held**
SIC: 2599 2517 2511 2434 Cabinets, factory; wood television & radio cabinets; wood household furniture; wood kitchen cabinets

(G-2373)
CREATIVESTITCH LLC
1312 Nw 172nd St (73012-9700)
PHONE..................405 664-1144
James Lucas, *Principal*
EMP: 1
SALES (est): 49.6K **Privately Held**
SIC: 2395 Embroidery & art needlework

(G-2374)
CROAN CUSTOM WOODWORKS LLC
134 W Lily Ln (73025-1019)
PHONE..................405 227-2067
Billy Croan, *Principal*
EMP: 4 EST: 2010
SALES (est): 244.3K **Privately Held**
SIC: 2431 Millwork

(G-2375)
CROSS ROLL INC (PA)
2604 Nw 159th St (73013-1204)
PHONE..................405 348-9663
Rick Machacek, *President*
Debbie Machacek, *Vice Pres*
EMP: 9
SALES: 600K **Privately Held**
SIC: 1389 Oil field services

(G-2376)
CROWN ENERGY TECHNOLOGY OKLA
6024 Nw 178th St (73012-8736)
PHONE..................405 348-9954
Rance Fisher, *President*
Randy Little, *General Mgr*
EMP: 45
SALES (est): 9.5MM **Privately Held**
SIC: 3533 7699 Drilling tools for gas, oil or water wells; gas appliance repair service

(G-2377)
CTSA LLC
Also Called: Dad's Guide To Wdw
14004 Pecan Hollow Ter (73013-7254)
PHONE..................405 478-3501
Carl Trent, *CEO*
Terri Trent, *COO*
EMP: 2 EST: 2012
SALES (est): 129K **Privately Held**
WEB: www.wdw-magazine.com
SIC: 2741 7389

(G-2378)
CUTTING EDGE SIGNS
3012 Aerie Dr (73013-7410)
PHONE..................918 688-1878
EMP: 2
SALES (est): 101.1K **Privately Held**
SIC: 3993 Mfg Signs/Advertising Specialties

(G-2379)
DARK PEEK TECHNOLOGIES LLC
2011 W Danforth Rd # 137 (73003-4685)
PHONE..................405 316-8551
James Chiles, *President*
EMP: 1
SALES (est): 128.1K **Privately Held**
SIC: 3812 5731 3647 Detection apparatus: electronic/magnetic field, light/heat; video cameras & accessories; dome lights, automotive

(G-2380)
DASA INVESTMENTS INC
1900 S Broadway (73034-4044)
P.O. Box 7498 (73083-7498)
PHONE..................405 820-7703
Cheryl Hacker, *President*
EMP: 4
SALES (est): 199.3K **Privately Held**
SIC: 1389 Oil consultants

(G-2381)
DAVID DODD INC
2701 Coltrane Pl Ste 6 (73034-6783)
P.O. Box 1756 (73083-1756)
PHONE..................405 216-5412
David Dodd, *President*
EMP: 2
SALES (est): 214.7K **Privately Held**
SIC: 1381 Directional drilling oil & gas wells

(G-2382)
DAVID KELSO WELDING
304 W Main St (73003-5341)
PHONE..................405 630-7108
David Kelso, *Owner*
EMP: 1
SALES (est): 80.3K **Privately Held**
SIC: 7692 Welding repair

(G-2383)
DAVIS HUDSON INC
2024 Woodland Rd (73013-6651)
P.O. Box 1028 (73083-1028)
PHONE..................405 203-0604
Davis Hudson, *President*
EMP: 3 EST: 1983
SALES (est): 100K **Privately Held**
SIC: 2079 Edible fats & oils

(G-2384)
DAYLIGHT DONUTS INC
400 S Santa Fe Ave (73003-6336)
PHONE..................405 359-9016
Andrew Lee, *Owner*
EMP: 1
SALES (est): 55.1K **Privately Held**
SIC: 5461 2051 Doughnuts; doughnuts, except frozen

(G-2385)
DCP MIDSTREAM LLC
2445 Nw 164th St (73013-8857)
PHONE..................405 705-7400
EMP: 11
SALES (corp-wide): 2.2B **Privately Held**
SIC: 1321 Natural Gas Liquids Production
PA: Dcp Midstream Llc
   370 17th St Ste 2500
   Denver CO 80202
   303 633-2900

(G-2386)
DDIECI MIDWEST LLC
3855 S Boulevard (73013-5498)
PHONE..................816 591-1350
Thomas Carder,
Joshua Fast Sr,
Sally Kulp Pecher,
EMP: 3
SQ FT: 1,800

Edmond - Oklahoma County (G-2387)   GEOGRAPHIC SECTION

SALES (est): 190.6K **Privately Held**
SIC: 3537 Trucks, tractors, loaders, carriers & similar equipment; aircraft loading hoists; cranes, industrial truck; forklift trucks

(G-2387)
DEACON RACE CARS
5419 Butte Rd (73025-2805)
PHONE..............................405 348-4419
Royce Deacon, *Principal*
EMP: 3
SALES (est): 298.8K **Privately Held**
SIC: 3711 Automobile assembly, including specialty automobiles

(G-2388)
DECORATIVE ROCK & STONE
501 S Broadway (73034-3851)
PHONE..............................405 341-8900
Ali Ghazansari, *Owner*
Donna K Ghazansari, *Admin Sec*
EMP: 8
SALES (est): 568.4K **Privately Held**
SIC: 5039 3272 Construction materials; stone, cast concrete

(G-2389)
DENNENY OIL AND GAS LLC
1201 River Chase Dr (73025-2195)
PHONE..............................405 229-4885
EMP: 2 **EST:** 2018
SALES (est): 70.5K **Privately Held**
SIC: 1389 Oil & gas field services

(G-2390)
DESIGN SYSTEMS INC
1800 Hardy Dr (73013-5106)
PHONE..............................405 341-7353
Patrick Young, *President*
EMP: 1
SALES (est): 92.2K **Privately Held**
SIC: 3822 Temperature controls, automatic

(G-2391)
DHS TEES
2421 Nw 161st St (73013-1299)
PHONE..............................405 397-0274
EMP: 2 **EST:** 2018
SALES (est): 73.2K **Privately Held**
SIC: 2759 Screen printing

(G-2392)
DOS TEES LLC
16720 N Pennsylvania Ave (73012-9053)
PHONE..............................405 323-2382
Andrea Arroyave, *Owner*
EMP: 2
SALES (est): 102K **Privately Held**
SIC: 2759 Screen printing

(G-2393)
DOUGLAS THOMPSON AUTO INC
Also Called: Doug's Automotive Garage
16120 Silverado Dr (73013-1455)
PHONE..............................405 330-6997
Douglas Thompson, *President*
Douglas Thompson Owens, *Manager*
Brenda Thompson, *Admin Sec*
EMP: 8
SQ FT: 8,000
SALES (est): 600K **Privately Held**
SIC: 7538 5014 5531 7513 General automotive repair shops; tires & tubes; automotive tires; truck rental & leasing, no drivers; axles, motor vehicle; universal joints, motor vehicle

(G-2394)
DPS PRINTING SERVICES INC
6121 Stonecreek Way (73025-2529)
P.O. Box 5578 (73083-5578)
PHONE..............................405 285-4614
EMP: 8
SQ FT: 10,000
SALES (est): 1MM **Privately Held**
SIC: 5943 5112 2759 Commercial Printing Ret Stationery Whol Stationery/Offc Sup

(G-2395)
DRAGONFLY PUBLISHING INC
2440 Twin Ridge Dr (73034-1934)
PHONE..............................405 359-6952

Terri Branson, *President*
Pat Gaines, *Senior Editor*
EMP: 2
SALES (est): 21.9K **Privately Held**
SIC: 2731 Book publishing

(G-2396)
DREYAR INDUSTRIES LLC
904 Oak Tree Dr (73025-2603)
PHONE..............................405 826-2454
Ashlee Boyce, *Owner*
EMP: 1
SALES (est): 39.6K **Privately Held**
SIC: 3999 Manufacturing industries

(G-2397)
DUGGANS ANN MARIE PRO SHOP
3501 S Boulevard (73013-5414)
PHONE..............................405 715-2695
Ann M Duggan, *Owner*
EMP: 1
SALES (est): 111.6K **Privately Held**
SIC: 3949 Bowling alleys & accessories

(G-2398)
EAGLE CHIEF MIDSTREAM LLC (PA)
2575 Kelley Pointe Pkwy # 340 (73013-2912)
PHONE..............................405 888-5585
Bob Firth, *President*
Brad Misialek, *Associate*
EMP: 20 **EST:** 2011
SQ FT: 2,800
SALES (est): 3.7MM **Privately Held**
SIC: 1382 Oil & gas exploration services

(G-2399)
EAST TEXAS EXPLORATION LLC
755 W Covell Rd Ste 100 (73003-2381)
PHONE..............................405 245-6568
Terry L Shyer,
EMP: 3 **EST:** 2012
SALES (est): 645.4K **Privately Held**
SIC: 1382 Oil & gas exploration services

(G-2400)
EDITORIAL ANNEX
3113 Carriage Park Ln (73003-2255)
PHONE..............................405 474-2114
Richard Crum, *Principal*
EMP: 2
SALES (est): 96.1K **Privately Held**
SIC: 2741 Miscellaneous publishing

(G-2401)
EDMOND COINS INC
3409 S Broadway Ste 650 (73013-4172)
PHONE..............................405 607-6800
Casey Tilford,
EMP: 1
SALES (est): 52.8K **Privately Held**
SIC: 3999 5961 Coins & tokens, non-currency; stamps, coins & other collectibles, mail order

(G-2402)
EDMOND GLASS
13778 N Lincoln Blvd (73013-3414)
PHONE..............................405 751-5900
Edmond Glass, *Principal*
EMP: 4
SALES (est): 196.6K **Privately Held**
SIC: 3211 Window glass, clear & colored

(G-2403)
EDMOND LIFE & LEISURE
107 S Broadway (73034-3843)
P.O. Box 164 (73083-0164)
PHONE..............................405 340-3311
Ray Hibbard, *Partner*
EMP: 12
SALES (est): 520.3K **Privately Held**
WEB: www.edmondlifeandleisure.com
SIC: 2711 Newspapers: publishing only, not printed on site

(G-2404)
EDMOND PRINTINGS
Also Called: Edmond Printing Co
13 S Broadway (73034-3739)
P.O. Box 765 (73083-0765)
PHONE..............................405 341-4330

Rhonda Wade, *President*
EMP: 4
SQ FT: 11,000
SALES (est): 200K **Privately Held**
WEB: www.apmok.com
SIC: 2752 5943 2791 2789 Commercial printing, offset; office forms & supplies; typesetting; bookbinding & related work; commercial printing

(G-2405)
EDMOND TROPHY CO
401 W 15th St (73013-3614)
PHONE..............................405 341-4631
Carolyn Flewelling, *Owner*
EMP: 3
SQ FT: 3,720
SALES (est): 174.9K **Privately Held**
SIC: 5999 2499 Trophies & plaques; trophy bases, wood

(G-2406)
EDMONDS FNEST MOLD DMAGE RMVAL
1708 S Broadway (73013-4013)
PHONE..............................405 509-9508
EMP: 2 **EST:** 2010
SALES (est): 110K **Privately Held**
SIC: 3544 Mfg Dies/Tools/Jigs/Fixtures

(G-2407)
EICHLER VALVE
11 Stony Trl (73034-7015)
PHONE..............................405 370-6891
Don Eichler, *Principal*
EMP: 2
SALES (est): 175.6K **Privately Held**
WEB: www.eichlervalve.com
SIC: 3491 Industrial valves

(G-2408)
EK EXPLORATION LLC
3501 French Park Dr Ste A (73034-7290)
PHONE..............................405 285-1220
Gary W Listen,
EMP: 5
SALES (est): 210.5K **Privately Held**
SIC: 1382 Oil & gas exploration services

(G-2409)
ELECTRONIC LABEL TECHNOLOGY
425 Centennial Blvd (73013-3732)
PHONE..............................812 875-2521
EMP: 2
SALES (est): 86.6K **Privately Held**
SIC: 3841 Surgical & medical instruments

(G-2410)
ELEMENT DESIGN & FABRICATION
1915 Genova Ct (73034-3485)
P.O. Box 4481, Parker CO (80134-1452)
PHONE..............................720 372-1940
Scott Krell, *President*
Brian Stamer, *CFO*
EMP: 5
SALES (est): 363.7K **Privately Held**
SIC: 3599 Machine & other job shop work

(G-2411)
ENDICO INC
2000 E 15th St Ste 450 (73013-6770)
P.O. Box 2552 (73083-2552)
PHONE..............................405 340-8009
James C Endicott, *President*
Laura Endicott, *Vice Pres*
EMP: 1
SALES (est): 1MM **Privately Held**
SIC: 1382 Oil & gas exploration services

(G-2412)
ENERGY AND ENVMTL SVCS INC
6701 Boucher Dr (73034-9211)
PHONE..............................405 285-8767
Troy Todd, *Director*
EMP: 1 **Privately Held**
SIC: 8744 5169 3479 1799 ; oil additives; painting, coating & hot dipping; corrosion control installation
PA: Energy And Environmental Services, Inc.
6300 Boucher Dr
Edmond OK 73034

(G-2413)
ENERGY AND ENVMTL SVCS INC (PA)
6300 Boucher Dr (73113-9258)
P.O. Box 14726, Oklahoma City (73113-0726)
PHONE..............................405 843-8996
Melvin Smith, *CEO*
Todd Jelinek, *Exec VP*
Ernestine Sell, *CFO*
Emma Gershon, *Executive Asst*
▲ EMP: 5
SQ FT: 2,300
SALES (est): 13.6MM **Privately Held**
SIC: 5169 3479 Chemicals & allied products; coating, rust preventive

(G-2414)
FIELDS JEWELRY INC
12 S Broadway (73034-3738)
P.O. Box 1463 (73083-1463)
PHONE..............................405 348-2802
Robert Fields, *President*
Carol Fields, *Corp Secy*
EMP: 6
SQ FT: 2,878
SALES (est): 214K **Privately Held**
SIC: 5944 3911 Jewelry, precious stones & precious metals; watches; earrings, precious metal; bracelets, precious metal; necklaces, precious metal; rings, finger: precious metal

(G-2415)
FIXTURES EXPRESS
3425 Cheyenne Dr (73013-6833)
PHONE..............................405 834-1633
Stephanie Burger, *Owner*
EMP: 1
SALES: 70K **Privately Held**
SIC: 3993 Signs & advertising specialties

(G-2416)
FLATROCK ENERGY ADVISERS
3856 S Boulevard Ste 210 (73013-5584)
PHONE..............................405 341-9993
Dennis Jaggi, *Partner*
EMP: 2
SALES (est): 198K **Privately Held**
SIC: 1382 Oil & gas exploration services

(G-2417)
FORD EXPLORATION INC
Also Called: Louis McKee Ford Living Trust
5 S Broadway Ste 200 (73034-3717)
PHONE..............................405 341-7502
Louis M Ford, *President*
EMP: 3
SQ FT: 5,800
SALES (est): 310.6K **Privately Held**
SIC: 1382 Oil & gas exploration services

(G-2418)
FOTI DIRECTIONAL LLC
4624 Crestmere Ln (73025-1267)
PHONE..............................352 848-5281
Gregory S Foti, *Owner*
EMP: 2
SALES (est): 146.1K **Privately Held**
SIC: 1381 Directional drilling oil & gas wells

(G-2419)
FOUR-O-ONE CORPORATION
14000 N Western Ave (73013-1977)
PHONE..............................405 848-0425
K W Throgmorton, *President*
EMP: 1
SQ FT: 2,000
SALES (est): 377.5K **Privately Held**
SIC: 1311 Crude petroleum production

(G-2420)
FRACTALSOFT LLC
19109 Saddle River Dr (73012-4123)
PHONE..............................405 330-3555
R Krishna, *Principal*
EMP: 1
SALES (est): 191.5K **Privately Held**
SIC: 1389 Oil field services

GEOGRAPHIC SECTION

Edmond - Oklahoma County (G-2455)

(G-2421)
FRANK K YOUNG OIL PROPERTIES
Also Called: Young, Frank K
1320 E 9th St Ste 6 (73034-5773)
P.O. Box 176, Oklahoma City (73101-0176)
PHONE..................................405 340-2500
Frank K Young, *Owner*
EMP: 2
SQ FT: 1,100
SALES (est): 179.1K Privately Held
WEB: www.frankkyoung.com
SIC: 1311 Crude petroleum production

(G-2422)
FREEDOM ENERGY LTD
1015 Waterwood Pkwy (73034-5327)
PHONE..................................405 285-2682
Alan W Jackson, *Principal*
EMP: 5
SALES (est): 293K Privately Held
SIC: 1382 Oil & gas exploration services

(G-2423)
FREEPOINT PIPE & SUPPLY INC
5624 Industrial Blvd (73034-9472)
P.O. Box 30660 (73003-0011)
PHONE..................................405 341-1913
Jim Meyer, *President*
Bracken Meyer, *Marketing Staff*
EMP: 4
SALES (est): 388.7K Privately Held
SIC: 1389 Oil field services

(G-2424)
FRIEDEL PETROLEUM CORPORATION
2817 Sweetbriar (73034-6554)
PHONE..................................405 359-1285
George Friedel, *President*
Michelle Freidel, *Admin Sec*
EMP: 2
SALES (est): 210K Privately Held
SIC: 1382 Oil & gas exploration services

(G-2425)
FROM HEART
1701 Westwood Ln (73013-6006)
PHONE..................................405 348-3009
Sherry Protes, *Owner*
Robert Protes, *Co-Owner*
EMP: 1
SALES (est): 47K Privately Held
SIC: 5947 2499 Gift, novelty & souvenir shop; wood products

(G-2426)
FRONTIER LAND SURVEYING LLC
600 W 18th St (73013-3631)
P.O. Box 7197 (73083-7197)
PHONE..................................405 285-0433
Kelly Farmer, *President*
Joseph Farmer,
Adam Hinds,
EMP: 14 EST: 2015
SALES (est): 636.2K Privately Held
SIC: 1389 8713 7389 Testing, measuring, surveying & analysis services; surveying services; photogrammetric engineering;

(G-2427)
FUNGO DESIGNS
629 Redstone Ave (73013-5915)
PHONE..................................405 348-9922
EMP: 2
SALES (est): 62.9K Privately Held
SIC: 2711 Newspapers-Publishing/Printing

(G-2428)
G P ENTERPRISES
Also Called: Gpe Competition Starters
2629 Broadway Ct (73013-4004)
PHONE..................................405 340-8986
Greg Porter, *Owner*
EMP: 2
SQ FT: 1,800
SALES (est): 75K Privately Held
SIC: 3621 3625 5531 Starters, for motors; relays & industrial controls; speed shops, including race car supplies

(G-2429)
GARY M LAKE & COMPANY
18700 Aerial Rd (73012-8208)
PHONE..................................405 340-6138
Gary M Lake, *President*
Chris Lake, *Vice Pres*
Pam Lake, *Treasurer*
EMP: 3
SALES (est): 340.1K Privately Held
SIC: 1311 Crude petroleum & natural gas

(G-2430)
GARY RUMSEY
33 Greenmore Dr (73034-7620)
PHONE..................................405 330-5732
Gary Rumsey, *Owner*
EMP: 1
SALES (est): 78.6K Privately Held
SIC: 1382 Oil & gas exploration services

(G-2431)
GARY UNDERWOOD
Also Called: Underwood, Gary Oil & Gas
2 E 11th St Ste 209 (73034-3989)
P.O. Box 3794 (73083-3794)
PHONE..................................405 341-0935
Gary Underwood, *Owner*
EMP: 1
SALES (est): 50K Privately Held
SIC: 1382 Oil & gas exploration services

(G-2432)
GATEWAY COM INC
1605 E 2nd St Ste 5 (73034-6340)
PHONE..................................405 787-0800
Denise Edwards, *President*
EMP: 4
SALES (est): 367.7K Privately Held
SIC: 3663 Cellular radio telephone

(G-2433)
GATEWAY DIRECTIONAL DRILLING
13911 N Harvey Ave (73013-2431)
PHONE..................................405 752-4230
Jimmy McGuire, *Owner*
EMP: 9
SALES (est): 855.2K Privately Held
WEB: www.gatewayok.com
SIC: 1381 Directional drilling oil & gas wells

(G-2434)
GEORGE MILLER
7321 Shannon Cir (73034-8151)
PHONE..................................405 341-4097
EMP: 1
SALES (est): 49.4K Privately Held
SIC: 3993 Mfg Signs/Advertising Specialties

(G-2435)
GH PRINTING SOLUTIONS INC
22900 Bailey Cir (73025-9743)
P.O. Box 20528, Oklahoma City (73156-0528)
PHONE..................................405 630-0609
William Powers, *President*
EMP: 2
SALES (est): 269.8K Privately Held
SIC: 2752 Commercial printing, offset

(G-2436)
GLACIER PETROLEUM CO OF OKLA
14000 N Western Ave (73013-1977)
PHONE..................................405 840-2625
Kit W Throgmorton, *President*
Ed H Hawes, *Vice Pres*
EMP: 8
SQ FT: 1,500
SALES (est): 1MM Privately Held
SIC: 1311 Crude petroleum production

(G-2437)
GLOVER SHEET METAL INC
2817 Perth Dr (73013-9022)
PHONE..................................405 619-7117
Darryl R Glover, *President*
Kris Boatright, *Manager*
EMP: 30
SQ FT: 10,000
SALES: 2.5MM Privately Held
SIC: 1711 1761 3444 Heating & air conditioning contractors; sheet metalwork; sheet metalwork

(G-2438)
GOLDEN TREND GAS GATHERING LLC
1004 Nw 139th Street Pkwy (73034-9791)
PHONE..................................405 749-7860
Craig Elder,
Melissa Elder,
EMP: 3
SALES (est): 185K Privately Held
SIC: 1382 Oil & gas exploration services

(G-2439)
GOOD LIFE CONCEPTS INC
23000 N May Ave (73025-9168)
PHONE..................................478 714-9114
Teresa Wurster, *Principal*
EMP: 1 EST: 2011
SALES (est): 130.8K Privately Held
SIC: 3993 Signs & advertising specialties

(G-2440)
GORE EXPLORATION LLC
1208 Mary Lee Ln (73034-5427)
P.O. Box 6, Seiling (73663-0006)
PHONE..................................580 922-4673
Leisa Gore, *Principal*
EMP: 2
SALES (est): 290.3K Privately Held
SIC: 1382 Oil & gas exploration services

(G-2441)
GRACE ALLEN DESIGN - CUSTOM
1329 Sims Ave (73013-6353)
PHONE..................................405 509-5164
EMP: 1
SALES (est): 57.3K Privately Held
SIC: 2591 Window blinds

(G-2442)
GRANDE OIL & GAS INC
19 W 1st St Ste 4 (73003-5553)
P.O. Box 2514 (73083-2514)
PHONE..................................405 348-8135
Al Swanson, *President*
Beverly Hayden, *Vice Pres*
EMP: 2 EST: 1998
SALES (est): 200K Privately Held
SIC: 1382 Oil & gas exploration services

(G-2443)
GRAVEL GROUP LLC
7601 Sunset Sail Ave (73034-8597)
PHONE..................................405 359-4932
EMP: 2
SALES (est): 66K Privately Held
SIC: 1442 Construction sand & gravel

(G-2444)
GREENBRIAR RESOURCES CORP
Also Called: Earth Data Graphics
2204 Tredington Way (73034-6462)
PHONE..................................405 348-7114
Gary King, *President*
Barbara King, *Corp Secy*
EMP: 2
SALES (est): 167.4K Privately Held
SIC: 1389 7379 8742 8999 Oil consultants; computer related consulting services; management consulting services; geological consultant

(G-2445)
GREG HALL OIL & GAS LLC
2940 Nw 156th St (73013-2102)
PHONE..................................405 330-6238
Tony Montalvo, *Human Resources*
EMP: 5
SALES (est): 717.9K Privately Held
WEB: www.ghog.co
SIC: 1382 Oil & gas exploration services

(G-2446)
GREY DOG INDUSTRIES LLC
528 Nw 170th St (73012-6706)
PHONE..................................405 926-0967
EMP: 2
SALES (est): 72.7K Privately Held
SIC: 3999 Manufacturing industries

(G-2447)
GROVES OIL INVESTMENTS
Also Called: Groves, James R
4312 Red Bud Pl (73013-7778)
PHONE..................................405 341-8828
James R Groves, *Owner*
EMP: 2
SALES (est): 183.4K Privately Held
SIC: 1382 Oil & gas exploration services

(G-2448)
GUEST PETROLEUM INCORPORATED
Also Called: Oil Office
1600 E 19th St Ste 204 (73013-6562)
P.O. Box 805 (73083-0805)
PHONE..................................405 341-8698
Robert Guest, *President*
David Guest, *Vice Pres*
Robin Guest, *Admin Sec*
EMP: 12
SQ FT: 1,600
SALES: 600K Privately Held
SIC: 1311 Crude petroleum production

(G-2449)
GUST MEDIA LLC
3126 S Boulevard Unit 139 (73013-5308)
PHONE..................................641 715-3900
Shawn Coughlin, *CEO*
EMP: 2
SALES (est): 78.8K Privately Held
SIC: 2741

(G-2450)
H & K SPECIFICATION & SLS LLC
633 Enterprise Dr Ste 160 (73013-3764)
PHONE..................................405 844-7456
Johnie Hamit, *Mng Member*
EMP: 10
SALES (est): 622.5K Privately Held
SIC: 3432 Plumbing fixture fittings & trim

(G-2451)
HARRIS DISCOUNT SUPPLIES INC
1318 Fretz Dr (73003-5871)
PHONE..................................847 726-3800
Deborah Delana, *President*
EMP: 4 EST: 1998
SALES (est): 234K Privately Held
WEB: www.harrisdiscount.com
SIC: 3843 Gold, dental; dental metal; orthodontic appliances

(G-2452)
HARTCO METAL PRODUCTS INC
6300 N Coltrane Rd (73034-9191)
PHONE..................................405 471-2784
Robert Miller, *President*
EMP: 1 EST: 2012
SALES: 30K Privately Held
SIC: 3312 7539 Tool & die steel; machine shop, automotive

(G-2453)
HAVARD INDUSTRIES LLC
Also Called: Hawk Ammo
704 Nw 139th St (73013-1911)
PHONE..................................405 888-0961
Jeffery Havard,
EMP: 1
SALES: 58.3K Privately Held
SIC: 2891 8748 3826 Epoxy adhesives; environmental consultant; analytical instruments

(G-2454)
HEARTLAND PRECIOUS METALS
307 E Danforth Rd Ste 150 (73034-4495)
PHONE..................................405 254-6870
EMP: 1
SALES (est): 57.6K Privately Held
SIC: 3339 Precious metals

(G-2455)
HENDRYX PRINTING BROKERAGE LLC
2725 Flagstone Ln (73003-2114)
PHONE..................................405 532-1255
Jean Hendryx, *Mng Member*
EMP: 1 EST: 2009

Edmond - Oklahoma County (G-2456)   GEOGRAPHIC SECTION

SALES (est): 124.5K **Privately Held**
SIC: 2752 Commercial printing, lithographic

(G-2456)
HNT WELDING & MACHINE
27 W 4th St (73003-5560)
PHONE 405 348-8249
EMP: 1
SALES: 86K **Privately Held**
SIC: 3599 7692 Mfg Industrial Machinery Welding Repair

(G-2457)
HOKE JAMES T JR OIL PRODUCER
107 S Broadway (73034-3843)
PHONE 405 341-1779
James Hoke Jr, *Owner*
EMP: 2
SALES (est): 150K **Privately Held**
SIC: 1311 Crude petroleum production; natural gas production

(G-2458)
HOT ROD HOT SHOT SERVICE INC
2104 W Glen Eagle (73025-1548)
PHONE 405 834-5591
Stephanie Johnson, *Principal*
EMP: 2 EST: 2010
SALES (est): 237.5K **Privately Held**
SIC: 1389 Hot shot service

(G-2459)
IMAGE PRINT & PROMO LLC
605 Aberdeen Rd (73025-2717)
P.O. Box 5578 (73083-5578)
PHONE 405 408-6763
Michael J Mudd, *Administration*
EMP: 2 EST: 2017
SALES (est): 100.1K **Privately Held**
WEB: www.muddprintandpromo.com
SIC: 2752 Commercial printing, lithographic

(G-2460)
INFINITE TOOL SYSTEMS INC
1009 Hunters Pointe Rd (73003-3517)
PHONE 405 205-4206
Larry Kirby, *Principal*
EMP: 2
SALES (est): 141K **Privately Held**
WEB: www.infinitetool.com
SIC: 3599 Machine shop, jobbing & repair

(G-2461)
INTEGRITY POWER SOLUTIONS LLC
2708 Cumberland Dr (73034-8372)
PHONE 918 925-9693
David Clarida, *President*
EMP: 3 EST: 2008
SALES: 900K **Privately Held**
SIC: 3511 7389 Gas turbine generator set units, complete;

(G-2462)
INTEGRITY TECH & SVCS LLC
15716 Hyde Parke Dr (73013-1364)
PHONE 405 482-9206
Steve Kuranoff, *President*
Kevin Harder, *Vice Pres*
John Springwater, *Vice Pres*
David Tiger, *Vice Pres*
EMP: 4
SALES (est): 189.6K **Privately Held**
SIC: 2842 2879 Sanitation preparations, disinfectants & deodorants; industrial plant disinfectants or deodorants; agricultural disinfectants

(G-2463)
INTERNATIONAL JOURNAL OF PH
Also Called: International Journal Phrm Com
122 N Bryant Ave Ste B4 (73034-6303)
PHONE 405 330-0094
Loyd Allen, *CEO*
Robert Scarborough, *President*
Mike Collins, *Corp Secy*
Pat Downing, *Vice Pres*
EMP: 10
SQ FT: 800

SALES (est): 1.5MM **Privately Held**
SIC: 2721 Trade journals: publishing & printing

(G-2464)
J & A HOT OILERS INC
9 W 9th St (73003-5770)
PHONE 405 341-7600
Christopher Anderson, *President*
Rod Ferguson, *Vice Pres*
EMP: 2
SALES (est): 160K **Privately Held**
SIC: 1389 Oil field services

(G-2465)
J C N PETROLEUM CORP
1625 E Coffee Creek Rd (73034-5804)
P.O. Box 3357 (73083-3357)
PHONE 405 341-8179
J C Conger Jr, *President*
EMP: 2
SALES (est): 220K **Privately Held**
SIC: 1311 Crude petroleum production; natural gas production

(G-2466)
J T G INDUSTRIES LLC
3324 Findhorn Dr (73034-8328)
PHONE 405 285-6627
John T Griffith III, *Principal*
EMP: 2
SALES (est): 116.7K **Privately Held**
SIC: 3999 Manufacturing industries

(G-2467)
JAK D UP TEES INC
301 W Waterloo Rd Bldg C (73025-1957)
PHONE 405 260-0007
Gayla Bonien, *President*
EMP: 10 EST: 2013
SALES (est): 1.1MM **Privately Held**
WEB: www.jakduptees.com
SIC: 2759 Screen printing

(G-2468)
JASARS ENTERPRISES INC
7416 Ne 133rd St (73003-7676)
PHONE 405 808-6460
James Joyce, *CEO*
EMP: 1
SALES: 75K **Privately Held**
SIC: 3452 Bolts, nuts, rivets & washers

(G-2469)
JETTA CORPORATION (PA)
425 Centennial Blvd (73013-3732)
PHONE 405 340-6661
Matt Peterson, *President*
Scott Davidson, *Plant Mgr*
Shaun Hembree, *Engineer*
Scott Craddick, *Technology*
Scott Yandell, *Technology*
EMP: 45
SQ FT: 45,000
SALES (est): 12.8MM **Privately Held**
SIC: 3088 Tubs (bath, shower & laundry), plastic

(G-2470)
JK INDUSTRIES INC
6250 Industrial Blvd (73034-9495)
P.O. Box 31987 (73003-0034)
PHONE 405 285-9800
William Jake Barnhart, *Principal*
EMP: 8
SALES (est): 31.3K **Privately Held**
WEB: www.jkirestoration.com
SIC: 3999 Atomizers, toiletry

(G-2471)
JM PUBLISHING LLC
101 W 5th St (73003-5515)
PHONE 405 684-0450
Jack McBride, *Owner*
EMP: 1
SALES (est): 37.5K **Privately Held**
SIC: 2741 Miscellaneous publishing

(G-2472)
JO SCO ENVIRONMENTAL
3027 Willowood Rd Ste 110 (73034-9725)
P.O. Box 895 (73083-0895)
PHONE 405 340-5499
Scott Lewis, *President*
EMP: 3 EST: 2009

SALES (est): 232.7K **Privately Held**
WEB: www.sco-jooilandgas.com
SIC: 1382 Oil & gas exploration services

(G-2473)
JOHN HENLEY CSTM CABINETS LLC
13909 N Everest Ave (73013-4713)
PHONE 405 535-9143
John Henley, *Principal*
EMP: 2 EST: 2015
SALES (est): 70.2K **Privately Held**
SIC: 2434 Wood kitchen cabinets

(G-2474)
JR SAND & GRAVEL INC
2825 Charleston Rd (73025-1628)
P.O. Box 31871 (73003-0032)
PHONE 405 474-8730
James E Kelm Jr, *President*
EMP: 4 EST: 2014
SQ FT: 3,200
SALES (est): 112.2K **Privately Held**
SIC: 1442 Construction sand & gravel

(G-2475)
JUICE BLENDZ CAFE
1200 W Covell Rd Ste 132 (73003-3554)
PHONE 405 285-0133
Annette Napp, *President*
EMP: 3 EST: 2013
SALES (est): 140.8K **Privately Held**
WEB: www.blenderscafe.com
SIC: 2023 Dietary supplements, dairy & non-dairy based

(G-2476)
JUST TWO PUBLISHING INC
Also Called: Brides of Oklahoma
14013 N Eastern Ave (73013-6593)
PHONE 405 607-2902
Ashley Murphy, *President*
Kami Huddleston, *Vice Pres*
Lauren Votaw, *Assistant*
EMP: 2
SQ FT: 3,000
SALES (est): 236.9K **Privately Held**
WEB: www.thebridesofoklahoma.com
SIC: 2721 5192 Magazines: publishing only, not printed on site; magazines

(G-2477)
K D TYPESETTING
14024 Choctaw Dr (73013-1626)
PHONE 405 302-0799
Kelly D Chanler, *Owner*
EMP: 1
SALES (est): 113.8K **Privately Held**
SIC: 2791 Typesetting

(G-2478)
KARIS GIFTS
1500 Turtlecreek Rd (73013-6605)
PHONE 405 330-6428
Beverly Cole, *Owner*
EMP: 3
SALES: 85K **Privately Held**
SIC: 3999 Christmas tree ornaments, except electrical & glass

(G-2479)
KEMMERLYS AIR PLUS
22106 Ole Barn Rd (73025-9624)
PHONE 405 348-2154
EMP: 3
SALES (est): 196.3K **Privately Held**
SIC: 3728 Military Aircraft Surplus

(G-2480)
KENMAR ENERGY SERVICES LLC
6288 Boucher Dr (73034-9257)
PHONE 405 844-2500
Mark Latham, *President*
Edward Cower, *Vice Pres*
EMP: 10 EST: 2009
SALES (est): 370K **Privately Held**
SIC: 0782 1389 Spraying services, lawn; lease tanks, oil field: erecting, cleaning & repairing

(G-2481)
KJM INDUSTRIES LLC
7090 Orchard Trl (73025-1681)
PHONE 405 340-1448

Jeff Maxwell, *Principal*
EMP: 2
SALES (est): 62.5K **Privately Held**
SIC: 3999 Manufacturing industries

(G-2482)
L & M EXPLORATION
1600 E 19th St (73013-6622)
PHONE 405 359-6060
Ron Mercer,
Mark Lawyer,
EMP: 2
SALES (est): 190.6K **Privately Held**
SIC: 1382 Oil & gas exploration services

(G-2483)
LASKA LLC
1212 Pine Oak Cir (73034-5470)
P.O. Box 3261 (73083-3261)
PHONE 405 820-7617
Michael Laska, *Partner*
Elizabeth Laska, *Partner*
EMP: 2
SALES: 110K **Privately Held**
SIC: 3089 Injection molding of plastics

(G-2484)
LEADERSHIP TRAINING ACADEMY
13800 Benson Rd Ste 206 (73013-6422)
PHONE 405 551-8059
EMP: 3 EST: 2011
SALES (est): 66K **Privately Held**
SIC: 8211 2899 Academy; salt

(G-2485)
LEGACY RESOURCES LLC
15625 Bald Cypress Cv (73013-1370)
PHONE 405 359-1080
Keith Berry, *Principal*
EMP: 2
SALES (est): 108.7K **Privately Held**
SIC: 1389 Pumping of oil & gas wells

(G-2486)
LEGEND ENTERPRISES INC
Also Called: Daylight Donuts
1700 S Kelly Ave Ste A (73013-3624)
PHONE 405 340-0410
Andrew Lee, *President*
EMP: 8
SALES (est): 212.9K **Privately Held**
SIC: 5461 2051 Doughnuts; doughnuts, except frozen

(G-2487)
LEVIATHAN APPLIED SCIENCES LLC
904 Posados Dr (73012-4248)
PHONE 405 315-1759
David Fozdar,
EMP: 1 EST: 2013
SALES (est): 129.6K **Privately Held**
SIC: 3826 7389 Laser scientific & engineering instruments;

(G-2488)
LIPSTICK CHICA
2249 Flint Ridge Rd (73003-2481)
PHONE 405 432-6399
Norma Ramirez, *Principal*
EMP: 2
SALES (est): 90K **Privately Held**
SIC: 2844 Lipsticks

(G-2489)
LITTRELL INDUSTRIES LLC
900 Jupiter Rd (73003-6025)
P.O. Box 7444 (73083-7444)
PHONE 405 637-8930
EMP: 2
SALES (est): 128.9K **Privately Held**
WEB: www.spcchelp.com
SIC: 3999 Manufacturing industries

(G-2490)
LM SOFTWARE INC
2008 Mill Creek Rd (73025-2830)
PHONE 405 630-4663
Larry Marks, *President*
EMP: 1
SALES (est): 98.4K **Privately Held**
SIC: 7372 Prepackaged software

GEOGRAPHIC SECTION

Edmond - Oklahoma County (G-2524)

(G-2491)
LOBAR OIL CO
3500 S Boulevard (73013-5486)
PHONE.....................405 330-7938
Carol Cole, *Principal*
EMP: 4
SALES (est): 447.5K **Privately Held**
SIC: 1311 Crude petroleum production

(G-2492)
LODESTONE LETTERPRESS LLC
116 W 10th Pl (73003-5755)
PHONE.....................405 269-9111
EMP: 2
SALES (est): 82.7K **Privately Held**
SIC: 2759 Letterpress printing

(G-2493)
LONESTAR GPHYSICAL SURVEYS LLC
Also Called: Lsgs
441 Fretz Ave (73003-5547)
PHONE.....................405 726-8626
EMP: 81
SALES (est): 13.2MM **Privately Held**
SIC: 1382 7389 Oil/Gas Exploration Services

(G-2494)
LONESTAR MSUREMENT CONTRLS INC
520 Harrier Hawk (73003-3181)
PHONE.....................972 653-0765
Robert H Fritz, *Director*
EMP: 3 EST: 2012
SALES (est): 251.7K **Privately Held**
SIC: 3823 Industrial instrmnts msrmnt display/control process variable

(G-2495)
LOS QUESITOS DE MAMA LLC
8020 Nw 159th St (73013-5800)
PHONE.....................312 276-2638
EMP: 1
SALES (est): 39.5K **Privately Held**
SIC: 2022 Mfg Cheese

(G-2496)
LOST RIVER OILFIELD SERVICES L
501 S Coltrane Rd Ste 1 (73034-6729)
PHONE.....................208 670-5787
Kirk Taylor, *Principal*
EMP: 5
SALES (est): 586.3K **Privately Held**
SIC: 1389 Oil field services

(G-2497)
LOUD GRAPHIC STUDIOS LLC
Also Called: Loud Gs
2417 Nw 162nd Ter (73013-1293)
PHONE.....................405 520-5349
Lardale Loud, *Agent*
Landon Loud,
EMP: 2
SALES (est): 129.9K **Privately Held**
SIC: 2721 7389 Comic books: publishing & printing;

(G-2498)
LOUIS SYSTEMS & PRODUCTS INC
8234 Gold Circle Dr (73025-9717)
P.O. Box 684 (73083-0684)
PHONE.....................405 285-0950
Gerald Barrett, *President*
EMP: 5
SQ FT: 4,800
SALES (est): 570K **Privately Held**
SIC: 3663 3651 Radio broadcasting & communications equipment; sound reproducing equipment

(G-2499)
M1 WOODWORKS
157 Barrett Pl (73003-5229)
PHONE.....................405 923-4144
Jace McDaniel, *Principal*
EMP: 1
SALES (est): 54.1K **Privately Held**
SIC: 2431 Millwork

(G-2500)
MAF SEISMIC LLC
4600 Avalon Pl (73034-4074)
PHONE.....................405 285-6444
Mark A Fortuna, *Principal*
EMP: 2 EST: 2016
SALES (est): 92.8K **Privately Held**
SIC: 1382 Seismograph surveys

(G-2501)
MAGNUS INDUSTRIES LLC
5608 Industrial Blvd (73034-9472)
P.O. Box 30415 (73003-0007)
PHONE.....................405 513-8295
Jeff McLaughlin, *Vice Pres*
Wayne Darce, *Mng Member*
EMP: 6
SALES (est): 2MM **Privately Held**
SIC: 3533 Oil & gas drilling rigs & equipment

(G-2502)
MALCHUS SKTBARD MNISTRIES ASSN
1035 Riley Rdg (73025-5504)
P.O. Box 6312 (73083-6312)
PHONE.....................405 615-6066
Jonathan Albarran, *Principal*
EMP: 1 EST: 2018
SALES (est): 47K **Privately Held**
SIC: 3949 Skateboards

(G-2503)
MANGUM BRICK
1409 Cedar Ridge Rd (73013-6057)
PHONE.....................405 410-4478
Jackie Sparkes, *Principal*
EMP: 2
SALES (est): 112.9K **Privately Held**
SIC: 3251 Brick & structural clay tile

(G-2504)
MARK STEVENS INDUSTRIES INC
2504 Nw 159th St (73013-1202)
P.O. Box 23443, Oklahoma City (73123-2443)
PHONE.....................405 948-1077
Mark Stevens, *President*
Rita Flora, *Vice Pres*
Connie Champlain, *Treasurer*
Heidi Finkhouse, *Director*
EMP: 99
SALES (est): 5.5MM **Privately Held**
SIC: 3652 3089 5192 Magnetic tape (audio): prerecorded; novelties, plastic; books, periodicals & newspapers

(G-2505)
MARKENIA FOODS LLC
125 Deer Creek Rd (73012-9318)
PHONE.....................405 751-8616
EMP: 3 EST: 2011
SALES (est): 80K **Privately Held**
SIC: 2099 Mfg Food Preparations

(G-2506)
MARKETING & EMBROIDERY MAGIC
3900 S Broadway Ste 6e (73013-4154)
PHONE.....................405 340-9677
Robert Merriman, *Owner*
EMP: 4
SALES (est): 194K **Privately Held**
SIC: 2395 Embroidery products, except schiffli machine

(G-2507)
MAXIM ENERGY CORP
721 S Boulevard (73034-4677)
P.O. Box 1570 (73083-1570)
PHONE.....................405 348-9669
Pat Wilsey, *President*
EMP: 3
SQ FT: 1,000
SALES (est): 430K **Privately Held**
SIC: 1382 1311 Oil & gas exploration services; crude petroleum production; natural gas production

(G-2508)
MCKINNEYS CUSTOM WELDING & FAB
1350 Echo Dr (73034-8160)
PHONE.....................405 341-6559
James L McKinney, *Administration*
EMP: 1 EST: 2011
SALES (est): 39.3K **Privately Held**
SIC: 7692 Welding repair

(G-2509)
MCMUR OIL AND GAS LLC
1643 Nw 164th Cir (73013-1681)
PHONE.....................405 834-2221
Brett Merrell, *Mng Member*
EMP: 1 EST: 2010
SALES (est): 250K **Privately Held**
SIC: 1382 Oil & gas exploration services

(G-2510)
MEADOWS OIL GAS CORP
609 S Kelly Ave Ste G3 (73003-7501)
PHONE.....................405 285-8500
Zach Meadows, *President*
Ralene Sword, *Technician*
EMP: 10
SALES (est): 1.1MM **Privately Held**
WEB: www.meadows-photography.com
SIC: 1382 Oil & gas exploration services

(G-2511)
MEDXPERT NORTH AMERICA LLC
609 S Kelly Ave Ste H1 (73003-7502)
PHONE.....................405 285-1671
Erhard Reisberg, *President*
EMP: 8
SALES (est): 794.3K **Privately Held**
WEB: www.medxpertna.com
SIC: 3841 Inhalation therapy equipment

(G-2512)
MENTAL NOTE LLC
Also Called: Book Distribution
401 W Covell Rd Apt 1334 (73003-2020)
PHONE.....................405 301-4182
Sharon Lewis,
EMP: 1
SALES (est): 49.4K **Privately Held**
SIC: 2741 Miscellaneous publishing

(G-2513)
MERCER PETROLEUM MANAGEMENT
Also Called: Mercer, Ronald G
1600 E 19th St Ste 102 (73013-6677)
PHONE.....................405 341-1110
Robert L Cox, *President*
Robert L Cox Jr, *Vice Pres*
EMP: 2
SQ FT: 3,000
SALES (est): 210K **Privately Held**
SIC: 1311 Crude petroleum & natural gas

(G-2514)
METCEL LLC
3901 Sea Ray Channel (73013-8763)
PHONE.....................405 334-7846
Amir Bhochhibhoya, *Principal*
EMP: 4
SALES (est): 516K **Privately Held**
SIC: 2679 Honeycomb core & board: made from purchased material

(G-2515)
METRO BUILDERS SUPPLY INC
220 Ne 150th St (73013-3420)
PHONE.....................405 751-8833
Troy Thompson, *Branch Mgr*
EMP: 41
SALES (corp-wide): 127.3MM **Privately Held**
SIC: 5064 3639 Electrical appliances, major; major kitchen appliances, except refrigerators & stoves
PA: Metro Builders Supply, Inc.
    5313 S Mingo Rd
    Tulsa OK 74146
    918 622-7692

(G-2516)
MEXCO ENERGY CORPORATION
1019 Waterwood Pkwy Ste E (73034-5329)
PHONE.....................405 330-4042
Fax: 405 330-8007
EMP: 1
SALES (corp-wide): 3.3MM **Publicly Held**
SIC: 1311 Crude Petroleum/Natural Gas Production
PA: Mexco Energy Corporation
    214 W Texas Ave Ste 1101
    Midland TX 79701
    432 682-1119

(G-2517)
MEZ WOODWORKS LLC
1700 Nw 164th Cir (73013-1675)
PHONE.....................405 589-5408
Sean Gomez, *Principal*
EMP: 1
SALES (est): 54.1K **Privately Held**
SIC: 2431 Millwork

(G-2518)
MIDWAY SERVICES LLC
5709 Lakewood Ridge Rd (73013-8439)
PHONE.....................405 820-8850
James Kirkland, *Mng Member*
EMP: 6
SALES (est): 600K **Privately Held**
SIC: 1389 Oil field services

(G-2519)
MIDWEST CLSSIC MOTORSPORTS LLC
6177 Boucher Dr (73034-9251)
PHONE.....................405 359-0050
Mike Finn, *Administration*
EMP: 2
SALES (est): 265.2K **Privately Held**
WEB: www.autorestorationoklahoma.com
SIC: 3713 Car carrier bodies

(G-2520)
MLB CONSULTING LLC
3075 Willowood Rd (73034-9725)
P.O. Box 3942 (73083-3942)
PHONE.....................405 285-8559
Mitchel Brown, *Mng Member*
EMP: 6 EST: 2014
SALES (est): 850.9K **Privately Held**
SIC: 1389 Cementing oil & gas well casings

(G-2521)
MOSTLY MISSILES
1404 Nw 141st St (73013-1610)
PHONE.....................405 808-4611
John Bolene, *Principal*
EMP: 2
SALES (est): 151.1K **Privately Held**
SIC: 3999 Manufacturing industries

(G-2522)
MUDD PRINT & PROMO LLC
1701 Signal Ridge Dr # 15 (73013-3787)
P.O. Box 5578 (73083-5578)
PHONE.....................405 501-6107
Leslie Mudd, *Principal*
Vincent Mudd, *Administration*
EMP: 2
SALES (est): 325.2K **Privately Held**
SIC: 2752 Commercial printing, lithographic

(G-2523)
MURAS ENERGY INC
25 Nw 144th Cir Ste B (73013-2470)
P.O. Box 5525 (73083-5525)
PHONE.....................405 751-0442
Raja Reddy, *President*
EMP: 12
SALES (est): 1.2MM **Privately Held**
SIC: 1389 Oil field services

(G-2524)
MYERS & MYERS INC
1616 E 19th St Ste 500 (73013-6627)
P.O. Box 1016 (73083-1016)
PHONE.....................405 341-5861
Gary Myers, *President*
Kerry Myers, *Corp Secy*
Glenn Myers, *Vice Pres*
EMP: 4

Edmond - Oklahoma County (G-2525)

SQ FT: 640
SALES (est): 3.5MM **Privately Held**
SIC: **1382** 1481 Oil & gas exploration services; mine exploration, nonmetallic minerals

(G-2525)
MYERS METALKRAFT LLC
1201 Allens Trl (73012-6409)
PHONE..................405 657-2084
Larry Myers, *Principal*
EMP: 1 EST: 2013
SALES (est): 47K **Privately Held**
SIC: **7692** Welding repair

(G-2526)
N O C SUPPLY INC
1326 S Fretz Ave (73003)
PHONE..................405 562-7070
Ryan Byers, *President*
Russell Newberry, *Vice Pres*
Joshua Newberry, *Treasurer*
EMP: 5
SALES (est): 1.1MM **Privately Held**
SIC: **3825** Network analyzers

(G-2527)
N2R MEDIA LLC
3126 S Boulevard Ste 127 (73013-5308)
PHONE..................405 301-0188
Tanner Ward,
EMP: 8
SALES: 500K **Privately Held**
SIC: **2741**

(G-2528)
NANCY W GRAVEL
4708 Blackjack Ln (73034-8316)
PHONE..................405 348-4409
Nancy Gravel, *Principal*
EMP: 3
SALES (est): 150K **Privately Held**
SIC: **1442** Construction sand & gravel

(G-2529)
NATIONAL SIGN MARKET
18409 Agua Dr (73012-9607)
PHONE..................405 821-8768
EMP: 1
SALES (est): 46K **Privately Held**
SIC: **3993** Mfg Signs/Advertising Specialties

(G-2530)
NATIVE REMEDY CBD LLC
5712 Industrial Blvd (73034-9473)
PHONE..................405 285-4050
EMP: 2
SALES (est): 74.6K **Privately Held**
SIC: **3999**

(G-2531)
NAVAJO COUNTY PUBLISHERS INC
1920 E 2nd St Apt 4011 (73034-6385)
PHONE..................928 524-6203
Matthew Barger, *Owner*
EMP: 10
SALES: 500K **Privately Held**
SIC: **2711** Newspapers: publishing only, not printed on site

(G-2532)
NELLIS VINEYARDS LLC
21204 Bogie Rd (73012-9518)
PHONE..................405 826-5279
Linda Nellis, *Principal*
EMP: 2
SALES (est): 190.7K **Privately Held**
SIC: **2084** Wines

(G-2533)
NEON CREATIVE LLC
801 Nw 189th Cir (73012-1230)
PHONE..................405 837-0178
Jennifer Kubes, *Principal*
EMP: 3
SALES (est): 123.2K **Privately Held**
SIC: **2813** Neon

(G-2534)
NESS ENERGY INTERNATIONAL
1900 E 15th St Bldg 600 (73013-6610)
PHONE..................405 285-1140
David Boyce, *Principal*
EMP: 2
SALES (est): 152.4K **Privately Held**
WEB: www.nessenergy.com
SIC: **1382** Oil & gas exploration services

(G-2535)
NESTLE PURINA PETCARE COMPANY
Also Called: Nestle Purina Factory
13900 N Lincoln Blvd (73013-3422)
PHONE..................405 751-4550
Bill Reiley, *Branch Mgr*
EMP: 100
SALES (corp-wide): 93.5B **Privately Held**
SIC: **2047** 2048 Dog food; prepared feeds
HQ: Nestle Purina Petcare Company
1 Checkerboard Sq
Saint Louis MO 63164
314 982-1000

(G-2536)
NEW PLAINS REVIEW
100 N University Dr (73034-5207)
PHONE..................405 974-5613
Shay Rahm, *Principal*
EMP: 1 EST: 2017
SALES (est): 53K **Privately Held**
SIC: **2741** Miscellaneous publishing

(G-2537)
NEW VISION CONSULTING GROUP
14711 Bristol Park Blvd (73013-1894)
P.O. Box 7135 (73083-7135)
PHONE..................405 796-7400
Kreg Decker, *President*
Shawn Rohrer, *Vice Pres*
EMP: 10
SQ FT: 4,000
SALES: 2MM **Privately Held**
SIC: **7372** 7371 Prepackaged software; custom computer programming services

(G-2538)
NOAHS PARK & PLAYGROUNDS LLC
14710 Metro Plaza Blvd A (73013-1988)
P.O. Box 7987 (73083-7987)
PHONE..................405 607-0714
Deann Shepherd, *Finance Mgr*
Shannon G Shephard, *Mng Member*
EMP: 10
SQ FT: 4,500
SALES (est): 3MM **Privately Held**
SIC: **1799** 3949 5941 Playground construction & equipment installation; playground equipment; playground equipment

(G-2539)
NOMAC DRILLING
16217 N May Ave (73013-8871)
PHONE..................405 242-4444
EMP: 2
SALES (est): 81.9K **Privately Held**
SIC: **1381** Oil/Gas Well Drilling

(G-2540)
NORTHERN ARIZONA NEWSPAPER
Also Called: Holbrook Tribune-News
1920 E 2nd St Apt 4011 (73034-6385)
PHONE..................928 524-6203
W Paul Barger, *President*
EMP: 10
SALES (corp-wide): 50MM **Privately Held**
WEB: www.winslowaz.gov
SIC: **2711** 7313 Newspapers: publishing only, not printed on site; newspaper advertising representative
HQ: Northern Arizona Newspaper, Inc
208 W First St
Winslow AZ

(G-2541)
NORTHPORT PRODUCTION CO INC
3501 French Park Dr Ste B (73034-7290)
P.O. Box 14545, Oklahoma City (73113-0545)
PHONE..................405 848-1212
John Vaughan, *Vice Pres*
EMP: 4
SALES (est): 485.1K **Privately Held**
SIC: **1311** Crude petroleum production; natural gas production

(G-2542)
NORTHWEST ALPACAS LTD
5804 Wilson Dr (73034-7717)
PHONE..................903 450-1999
EMP: 2 EST: 2018
SALES (est): 73.4K **Privately Held**
SIC: **2231** Broadwoven fabric mills, wool

(G-2543)
O K RESTAURANT SUPPLY
6176 Boucher Dr (73034-9251)
PHONE..................405 330-9932
David Hennessy, *Owner*
EMP: 3 EST: 1972
SQ FT: 7,000
SALES: 175K **Privately Held**
SIC: **3556** Food products machinery

(G-2544)
OCUBRITE LLC
14901 Carlingford Way (73013-1868)
PHONE..................405 250-2084
Yan Feng,
Jianxing MA,
EMP: 2
SALES (est): 135.3K **Privately Held**
SIC: **2833** Medicinals & botanicals

(G-2545)
OHANA OIL & GAS LLC
1800 Canyon Park Cir # 201 (73013-6678)
PHONE..................405 341-8822
EMP: 2 EST: 2017
SALES (est): 65.5K **Privately Held**
SIC: **1389** Oil & gas field services

(G-2546)
OILFIELD LEASE MAINTENANCE
2917 Cedarbend Ct (73003-2140)
PHONE..................405 348-1562
Richard D Buck Jr, *Owner*
EMP: 1
SALES (est): 110K **Privately Held**
SIC: **1389** Oil field services

(G-2547)
OKAY SEE LTD CO
4700 Nw 157th Ter (73013-8951)
PHONE..................405 562-3154
Blake Behrens, *Principal*
EMP: 2
SALES (est): 163.8K **Privately Held**
WEB: www.theokaysee.com
SIC: **2752** Commercial printing, lithographic

(G-2548)
OKC DUMPSTERS INC
14900 Kurdson Way (73013-2424)
PHONE..................405 640-4345
Roberts Jason, *Principal*
EMP: 4
SALES (est): 330.7K **Privately Held**
SIC: **3443** Dumpsters, garbage

(G-2549)
OKLAHOMA EMB SUP & DESIGN
13821 N Harvey Ave (73013-2448)
PHONE..................405 359-2741
Phil Newton, *President*
Mary Newton, *Vice Pres*
▲ EMP: 1
SALES (est): 98.7K **Privately Held**
WEB: www.embroideryonline.com
SIC: **2395** 7371 5045 Embroidery products, except schiffli machine; custom computer programming services; computers, peripherals & software

(G-2550)
OKLAHOMA FUEL ATHLETICS LLC
14712 Bristol Park Blvd (73013-1893)
PHONE..................405 286-3144
Tanya Brumbuth, *Mng Member*
EMP: 6
SALES (est): 675.1K **Privately Held**
WEB: www.oklahomafuelathletics.com
SIC: **2869** Fuels

(G-2551)
OKLAHOMA INDUSTRIAL SILVER
2700 Coltrane Pl Ste 6 (73034-6794)
P.O. Box 186 (73083-0186)
PHONE..................405 341-6021
Michael Hill, *President*
Marsha Kurtz, *Vice Pres*
EMP: 7
SALES (est): 600K **Privately Held**
SIC: **3339** 3341 Silver refining (primary); silver recovery from used photographic film

(G-2552)
OKLAHOMA MILLWORKS INC
2019 Ruoh Dr (73003)
P.O. Box 30190 (73003-0004)
PHONE..................405 282-4887
EMP: 2
SALES (est): 216.2K **Privately Held**
SIC: **3843** Cabinets, dental

(G-2553)
OKLAHOMA OIL GAS MANAGEMENT
1721 W 33rd St (73013-3833)
PHONE..................405 341-1856
EMP: 3
SALES (est): 125.9K **Privately Held**
SIC: **5541** 1382 Gasoline service stations; oil & gas exploration services

(G-2554)
OKT RESOURCES LLC
1900 E 15th St Ste 600c (73013-6691)
PHONE..................405 285-1140
David Boyce,
Taylor W Dillard,
EMP: 6
SQ FT: 3,000
SALES (est): 506.9K **Privately Held**
SIC: **1382** Oil & gas exploration services

(G-2555)
OKY INVESTMENTS INC
600 Nw 149th St (73013-1842)
PHONE..................405 850-4533
Robert E Partin, *President*
EMP: 1
SALES (est): 820.1K **Privately Held**
SIC: **1311** Crude petroleum & natural gas

(G-2556)
OLIVER & OLIVIA APPAREL
3825 Nw 166th St Ste C3 (73012-9237)
PHONE..................405 300-8906
Jill Snow, *President*
EMP: 20
SALES (est): 97.5K **Privately Held**
SIC: **5621** 2759 Ready-to-wear apparel, women's; commercial printing

(G-2557)
ON THE GO HOT SHOT SVCS LLC
612 Earl A Rodkey Dr (73003-4618)
PHONE..................405 471-2055
Jerry Childers, *Principal*
EMP: 2
SALES (est): 183.5K **Privately Held**
SIC: **1389** Hot shot service

(G-2558)
P F SERVICES LLC
921 Glacier Ln (73003-4658)
P.O. Box 30813 (73003-0014)
PHONE..................405 226-4871
Patrick Fitter,
EMP: 1
SALES: 50K **Privately Held**
SIC: **3822** Auto controls regulating residntl & coml environmt & applncs

(G-2559)
PAIA ELECTRONICS INC
3200 Teakwood Ln (73013-3709)
PHONE..................405 340-6300
John S Simonton Jr, *President*
Linda Simonton, *Treasurer*
Scott Lee, *Technical Staff*
EMP: 6
SQ FT: 2,500

GEOGRAPHIC SECTION

Edmond - Oklahoma County (G-2593)

SALES (est): 660K **Privately Held**
WEB: www.paia.com
SIC: **5961** 3679 8748 Mail order house; electronic circuits; systems analysis or design

(G-2560)
PALADIN GEOLOGICAL SVCS LLC
Also Called: Paladin Surface Logging
13832 Snta Fe Crssings Dr (73013-2512)
PHONE.....................405 463-3270
James Beard, *General Mgr*
Andrew Sneddon, *General Mgr*
David Milburn, *Engineer*
Julia Sessions, *Engineer*
Tisha Farr, *Accounts Mgr*
EMP: 11
SALES (est): 361K **Privately Held**
WEB: www.paladingeo.com
SIC: **2411** Logging

(G-2561)
PAPER CONCIERGE
1717 W 33rd St (73013-3863)
PHONE.....................405 286-3322
David Oliver, *CFO*
EMP: 2 EST: 2011
SALES (est): 200.7K **Privately Held**
SIC: **2679** Paperboard products, converted

(G-2562)
PARAGON PRODUCTION CO
1300 E 15th St Ste 100 (73013-5051)
PHONE.....................405 348-1116
Robert Harmon, *Owner*
EMP: 6
SQ FT: 4,096
SALES (est): 910K **Privately Held**
SIC: **1311** Crude petroleum production; natural gas production

(G-2563)
PARKERS CUSTOM HARDWOODS INC
17 N Fretz Ave (73003-5354)
PHONE.....................405 341-9663
Melody Parker, *President*
EMP: 3
SQ FT: 1,500
SALES: 150K **Privately Held**
SIC: **2517** Home entertainment unit cabinets, wood

(G-2564)
PARKERS WELDING CUSTOM WORK
309 W Main St (73003-5342)
PHONE.....................405 341-3344
Clyde Parker, *Partner*
Margie Parker, *Partner*
EMP: 1 EST: 1969
SQ FT: 2,600
SALES (est): 15K **Privately Held**
SIC: **7692** Welding repair

(G-2565)
PELCO PRODUCTS INC
320 W 18th St (73013-3628)
PHONE.....................405 340-3434
Philip Parduhn, *Principal*
Steve Parduhn, *Vice Pres*
▲ EMP: 125
SQ FT: 100,000
SALES (est): 30MM **Privately Held**
SIC: **3429** Manufactured hardware (general)

(G-2566)
PENTERRA SERVICES LLC
15314 N May Ave (73013-8864)
PHONE.....................405 726-2762
EMP: 6
SALES (corp-wide): 2.6MM **Privately Held**
SIC: **1389** Oil consultants
PA: Penterra Services, L.L.C.
1700 Kaliste Saloom Rd # 5
Lafayette LA 70508
337 706-8650

(G-2567)
PETRA SOLUTIONS LLC
4551 Hillside Ln (73025-1272)
PHONE.....................316 554-6586
Bradley Dale Horton,
EMP: 1
SALES (est): 41K **Privately Held**
SIC: **1389** Oil field services

(G-2568)
PICKLES OF EDMOND INC
921 E Danforth Rd (73034-5004)
PHONE.....................405 285-4342
Sohrab Ahadizadeh, *Principal*
EMP: 2
SALES (est): 145K **Privately Held**
SIC: **2035** Pickled fruits & vegetables

(G-2569)
PIERCE INDUSTRIES INC
21353 Backhorn Rd (73012-1109)
PHONE.....................405 923-4201
Marc Pierce, *Principal*
EMP: 2
SALES (est): 78.9K **Privately Held**
SIC: **3999** Manufacturing industries

(G-2570)
PIN EFX LLC
3801 Pawnee (73013-7722)
PHONE.....................405 341-9956
EMP: 3
SALES (est): 222.6K **Privately Held**
WEB: www.pinefx.com
SIC: **3452** Pins

(G-2571)
PINNACLE BUSINESS SYSTEMS INC (PA)
3824 S Boulevard Ste 200 (73013-5781)
P.O. Box 5530 (73083-5530)
PHONE.....................405 359-0121
Robert A Anderson, *CEO*
J Todd Cox, *Senior VP*
Darrel Davis, *Vice Pres*
Kirk Zaranti, *Vice Pres*
Matt Bergeson, *Engineer*
EMP: 20
SQ FT: 10,000
SALES (est): 16.7MM **Privately Held**
SIC: **7372** 5045 Prepackaged software; computers, peripherals & software

(G-2572)
PITNEY BOWES INC
3224 Teakwood Ln Ste 120 (73013-3781)
PHONE.....................405 341-3279
EMP: 2
SALES: 85.9K
SALES (corp-wide): 3.5B **Publicly Held**
SIC: **3579** Office Machines, Nec, Nsk
PA: Pitney Bowes Inc.
3001 Summer St Ste 3
Stamford CT 06905
203 356-5000

(G-2573)
POLYPIPE HDLG SPECIALISTS INC
Also Called: Midland Carriers
6992 E Waterloo Indus Rd (73034-8125)
P.O. Box 1225 (73083-1225)
PHONE.....................405 330-4733
Mike Mays, *President*
Michael Mays, *Manager*
Trevor Mays, *Manager*
EMP: 4 EST: 2007
SALES (est): 803.2K **Privately Held**
WEB: www.midlandoilfieldrentals.com
SIC: **3799** 5084 5599 Trailers & trailer equipment; petroleum industry machinery; utility trailers

(G-2574)
PRECISION PUNCH
2116 Castle Rock (73003-4704)
PHONE.....................405 340-7546
Bret Loftiss, *Owner*
EMP: 1
SALES (est): 56.8K **Privately Held**
SIC: **2395** Embroidery products, except schiffli machine

(G-2575)
PRINCO PRESS CORP
19525 Talavera Ln (73012-9757)
PHONE.....................405 760-6064
Ethan Han, *Owner*
▲ EMP: 5

SALES (est): 179K **Privately Held**
SIC: **2741** Miscellaneous publishing

(G-2576)
PRINT PARTY
4904 Butte Rd (73025-2817)
PHONE.....................405 206-2191
Kelly Dyvig, *Principal*
EMP: 2
SALES (est): 83.9K **Privately Held**
SIC: **2752** Commercial printing, lithographic

(G-2577)
PUEBLO MOTORS INC
Also Called: Invitation
14709 Glenmark Dr (73013-1820)
PHONE.....................520 297-3244
Sandy Childress, *President*
EMP: 2
SALES (est): 187.7K **Privately Held**
SIC: **2759** 7389 Invitations: printing;

(G-2578)
QUALGEN LLC
301 Enterprise Dr (73013-3918)
PHONE.....................405 551-8216
James Sipols, *Opers Staff*
Jules Dsouza, *Director*
Shaun Riney,
EMP: 25
SALES (est): 2.3MM **Privately Held**
WEB: www.qualgen.us
SIC: **2834** 5122 Pharmaceutical preparations; drugs, proprietaries & sundries

(G-2579)
QUALGEN LLC
301 Enterprise Dr (73013-3918)
PHONE.....................405 551-8216
Shaun Riney, *CEO*
EMP: 25
SALES (est): 4.1MM **Privately Held**
SIC: **2834** Pharmaceutical preparations

(G-2580)
QUEST LOOT LLC
509 Country Side Trl (73012-6632)
PHONE.....................405 609-4100
Timothy Layman, *CEO*
EMP: 3
SALES (est): 78.2K **Privately Held**
SIC: **7372** Application computer software

(G-2581)
R & J OIL AND GAS ROYALTY LLC
689 Outer Banks Way (73034-7589)
PHONE.....................405 562-3334
David Johnson, *Principal*
EMP: 2 EST: 2017
SALES (est): 76.5K **Privately Held**
SIC: **1389** Oil & gas field services

(G-2582)
R E BLAIK INC
1616 E 19th St Ste 201 (73013-6675)
PHONE.....................405 285-8000
Robert E Blaik, *President*
S G Williamson, *Vice Pres*
EMP: 4
SALES: 1MM **Privately Held**
SIC: **1311** Crude petroleum production; natural gas production

(G-2583)
R&D LABS LLC
2518 Countrywood Ln (73012-6433)
PHONE.....................405 875-9937
Devin Hayden-Young,
EMP: 2
SALES (est): 90.7K **Privately Held**
SIC: **2678** Stationery products

(G-2584)
RADIOTRONIX INC
2117 Shadow Lake Dr (73025-1713)
PHONE.....................405 794-7730
Philip L Engle, *President*
EMP: 30 EST: 2001
SQ FT: 12,000
SALES (est): 5MM **Privately Held**
SIC: **3577** Encoders, computer peripheral equipment

(G-2585)
RALSTON PURINA
13700 N Lincoln Blvd (73013-3401)
PHONE.....................405 751-4550
Jim Kerr, *Principal*
EMP: 2
SALES (est): 147.9K **Privately Held**
SIC: **2047** Dog & cat food

(G-2586)
RAVEN RESOURCES LLC
2575 Kelley Pointe Pkwy # 380 (73013-2906)
P.O. Box 721880, Oklahoma City (73172-2057)
PHONE.....................405 773-7340
EMP: 6
SQ FT: 3,000
SALES (est): 1.1MM **Privately Held**
SIC: **1311** Crude petroleum production

(G-2587)
RCCS WOODWORKING LLC
4625 Vista Valley Ln (73025-1187)
PHONE.....................405 694-9680
David Fish,
EMP: 1
SALES (est): 66.7K **Privately Held**
SIC: **2431** Woodwork, interior & ornamental

(G-2588)
RED DIRT WOOD WORKS LLC
109 E 21st St (73013-4335)
PHONE.....................918 640-5917
Joseph Rodrigues, *Principal*
EMP: 2 EST: 2015
SALES (est): 87.1K **Privately Held**
SIC: **2431** Millwork

(G-2589)
RED LAND ENERGY LLC
Also Called: Ok-Red Land Energy
1600 E 19th St Ste 103 (73013-6677)
PHONE.....................405 520-1205
Ronald R Mercer, *Manager*
EMP: 3 EST: 2012
SALES (est): 254.6K **Privately Held**
WEB: www.redskyland.com
SIC: **1382** Oil & gas exploration services

(G-2590)
RED RIVER OILFIELD SVCS LLC
19401 Stubblefield Ln (73012-3495)
P.O. Box 52907, Midland TX (79710-2907)
PHONE.....................405 802-4280
Rick Blankenship,
EMP: 2
SALES (est): 159.1K **Privately Held**
SIC: **1389** Oil field services

(G-2591)
RED ROCK FABRICATION
417 Westland Dr (73013-3719)
PHONE.....................405 602-4602
Mike Mc Daniels, *Principal*
EMP: 3
SALES (est): 436.1K **Privately Held**
SIC: **2541** Counter & sink tops

(G-2592)
REDSKY LAND LLC
1501 Renaissance Blvd (73013-3018)
P.O. Box 5936 (73083-5936)
PHONE.....................405 470-2015
John B Brogan, *Vice Pres*
Rick Dawson,
John Brogan,
EMP: 100
SALES (est): 5.2MM **Privately Held**
SIC: **1382** Oil & gas exploration services

(G-2593)
REFLECTION FOIL AND LTR PRESS
Also Called: Reflection Carl Mles Phtgraphy
3909 E 30th St (73013-7920)
PHONE.....................405 341-8660
Carl Miles, *President*
Marvin Miles, *CFO*
Melvin Adams, *Admin Sec*
EMP: 5

Edmond - Oklahoma County (G-2594)

SALES (est): 60K **Privately Held**
SIC: **2796** 3599 2759 Letterpress plates, preparation of; machine shop, jobbing & repair; commercial printing

(G-2594)
REFUNK MY JUNK INC
2520 Antelope Trl (73012-4421)
PHONE..................405 990-0707
Allison Griffith, *Principal*
EMP: 2
SALES (est): 233.9K **Privately Held**
WEB: www.refunkmyjunk.com
SIC: **3585** Coolers, milk & water: electric

(G-2595)
REGRID ENERGY LLC
528 Nw 141st St (73013-1917)
PHONE..................405 837-8707
Shawn Clark, *CEO*
EMP: 1
SALES (est): 56K **Privately Held**
SIC: **3699** Accelerating waveguide structures

(G-2596)
REID PRINTING INC
3120 S Boulevard (73013-5308)
PHONE..................405 348-0066
Laverna Reid, *President*
David Reid, *Vice Pres*
Dennis Reid, *Treasurer*
Christy Rice, *Technology*
EMP: 7
SQ FT: 3,200
SALES (est): 867.2K **Privately Held**
SIC: **2752** 2789 Commercial printing, offset; bookbinding & related work

(G-2597)
RESCUE LUMBER & WDWKG LLC
7801 Tangle Vine Dr (73034-8445)
PHONE..................405 650-4637
EMP: 1
SALES (est): 54.1K **Privately Held**
SIC: **2431** Millwork

(G-2598)
REXBO ENERGY CO
819 Sunny Brook Dr (73034-4852)
P.O. Box 2572 (73083-2572)
PHONE..................405 359-0458
EMP: 3 EST: 1998
SALES: 1.2MM **Privately Held**
SIC: **1311** Natural Gas Exploration & Production

(G-2599)
RHINO OIL & GAS INC
22906 Crossfield Ct (73025-1285)
PHONE..................405 657-2999
Fleharty Michael, *Principal*
EMP: 2
SALES (est): 158.3K **Privately Held**
SIC: **1382** Oil & gas exploration services

(G-2600)
RIGYARD PUBLICATIONS LLC
304 Carmel Valley Way (73025-2747)
PHONE..................405 330-1456
Robert Murray, *Principal*
EMP: 1
SALES (est): 69.3K **Privately Held**
SIC: **2741** Miscellaneous publishing

(G-2601)
RINGS ETC FINE JEWELRY
225 S Broadway (73034-3845)
PHONE..................405 359-7464
Roger Boulware, *Owner*
EMP: 2
SQ FT: 1,196
SALES (est): 130K **Privately Held**
SIC: **5944** 7631 3911 5094 Jewelry, precious stones & precious metals; jewelry repair services; jewelry, precious metal; precious metals

(G-2602)
ROBERT C BROOKS INC
12707 N Bryant Ave (73013-7506)
PHONE..................405 478-0260
Robert Brooks, *President*
EMP: 1

SALES (est): 45.1K **Privately Held**
SIC: **1389** Oil field services

(G-2603)
ROSE ROCK PETROLEUM LLC
1712 Nw 195th Cir (73012-3545)
PHONE..................405 212-6987
Aaron Anderson, *Principal*
EMP: 2 EST: 2016
SALES (est): 88.9K **Privately Held**
SIC: **1381** Drilling oil & gas wells

(G-2604)
ROSEROCK CREATIONS INC
13525 S Western Ave (73025-1670)
PHONE..................405 209-6005
Jeanne Paradise, *President*
EMP: 3
SALES (est): 169.5K **Privately Held**
SIC: **3269** Art & ornamental ware, pottery

(G-2605)
ROYAL IRONWORKS ◆
14801 Metro Plaza Blvd # 7 (73013-1996)
PHONE..................580 492-4265
Richard Queen, *Owner*
EMP: 2 EST: 2020
SALES (est): 88.9K **Privately Held**
SIC: **3446** Architectural metalwork

(G-2606)
RP WINDOW WASHING
625 Oak Springs Dr (73034-8777)
PHONE..................405 341-0065
Randall Poling, *Owner*
EMP: 1
SALES (est): 112K **Privately Held**
SIC: **2842** Window cleaning preparations

(G-2607)
RTPR LLC
Also Called: Real Time Pain Relief
129 W 1st St Ste A (73003-5509)
P.O. Box 798, Cabot AR (72023-0798)
PHONE..................877 787-7180
Lori Bhada, *Director*
Ronald Snodgrass,
Tim Flatt,
Roberta Snodgrass,
EMP: 4
SALES (est): 438.4K **Privately Held**
SIC: **2833** Medicinals & botanicals

(G-2608)
RUSSELL OIL INC
904 Nw 139th Street Pkwy (73013-9525)
PHONE..................405 752-7600
Leroy Holt, *President*
EMP: 4
SALES (est): 317.6K **Privately Held**
WEB: www.russelloil.com
SIC: **1382** Geophysical exploration, oil & gas field

(G-2609)
S & S WOODWORKS INC
2417 Horse Trail Rd (73012-4559)
PHONE..................405 627-8195
EMP: 2
SALES (est): 201.1K **Privately Held**
SIC: **2431** Millwork

(G-2610)
SALT SOOTHERS LLC (PA)
2702 Princeton Ave (73034-4103)
PHONE..................405 201-2020
Andrea Fredricks, *Co-Owner*
William Fredricks,
EMP: 2
SALES (est): 65K **Privately Held**
SIC: **2844** 2211 Bath salts; scrub cloths

(G-2611)
SANDOLLAR EXPLORATION CO LLC
2600 Still Meadow Rd (73013-6761)
P.O. Box 621 (73083-0621)
PHONE..................405 513-7715
E W Pollock, *Mng Member*
Eks Pollock, *Mng Member*
EMP: 2
SALES (est): 130.6K **Privately Held**
SIC: **1382** Oil & gas exploration services

(G-2612)
SANDY CHILDRESS INC
14709 Glenmark Dr (73013-1820)
PHONE..................405 748-4949
Sandy Childress, *President*
EMP: 2
SALES (est): 148.6K **Privately Held**
SIC: **2335** 5136 Wedding gowns & dresses; men's & boys' sportswear & work clothing

(G-2613)
SANGUINE GAS EXPLORATION LLC
3404 E 2nd St (73034-7211)
P.O. Box 3185 (73083-3185)
PHONE..................405 285-1904
Rich Hauschild, *Manager*
EMP: 6
SALES (corp-wide): 104.3MM **Privately Held**
SIC: **1382** Oil & gas exploration services
PA: Sanguine Gas Exploration, L.L.C.
110 W 7th St Ste 2700
Tulsa OK 74119
918 494-6070

(G-2614)
SEABOARD GAS COMPANY
107 S Broadway (73034-3843)
PHONE..................405 341-1779
Chris Hoke, *President*
J T Hoke, *Vice Pres*
EMP: 3
SQ FT: 2,000
SALES (est): 310K **Privately Held**
SIC: **1311** Crude petroleum production; natural gas production

(G-2615)
SEC PRODUCTION INC
3206 Teakwood Ln (73013-3709)
PHONE..................405 715-0088
Donald S Boyd, *CEO*
Margret Worthan, *Admin Sec*
EMP: 2
SQ FT: 1,600
SALES (est): 250K **Privately Held**
SIC: **1382** 1311 Oil & gas exploration services; crude petroleum production; natural gas production

(G-2616)
SEW MUCH FUN
5817 Dundee Ct (73025-2643)
PHONE..................405 359-1544
Jennifer Shipley, *Owner*
EMP: 1
SALES (est): 54K **Privately Held**
SIC: **2395** Embroidery & art needlework

(G-2617)
SEWCOOL EMBROIDERY LLC
8124 Ne 139th St (73013-8702)
PHONE..................405 326-2854
Michael Ballard, *Principal*
EMP: 1 EST: 2014
SALES (est): 31.2K **Privately Held**
SIC: **2395** Embroidery & art needlework

(G-2618)
SHADOWKAST SCREEN PRINTING LLC
2704 Nw 160th Ter (73013-1212)
PHONE..................405 808-5148
EMP: 2 EST: 2014
SALES (est): 141.5K **Privately Held**
SIC: **2752** Commercial printing, offset

(G-2619)
SHEBESTER BECHTEL INC
2948 Via Esperanza (73013-8934)
P.O. Box 270598, Oklahoma City (73137-0598)
PHONE..................405 513-8580
Terri Bechtel, *Branch Mgr*
EMP: 52
SALES (est): 2.1MM
SALES (corp-wide): 41.1MM **Privately Held**
WEB: www.sbiwellservice.com
SIC: **1389** Construction, repair & dismantling services; oil field services

PA: Shebester Bechtel, Inc
605 N 29th St
Blackwell OK 74631
580 363-4124

(G-2620)
SHIELDS OPERATING INC
411 W Waterloo Rd (73025-1997)
PHONE..................405 341-7607
John Shields, *Manager*
EMP: 1 **Privately Held**
SIC: **1311** 8999 Crude petroleum production; natural gas production; geological consultant
PA: Shields Operating, Inc.
312 S 16th St
Fort Smith AR 73118

(G-2621)
SIGNS TO GO LLC
3130 S Boulevard (73013-5371)
PHONE..................405 348-8646
Carolyn Haller, *Mng Member*
EMP: 5
SQ FT: 8,500
SALES (est): 662.2K **Privately Held**
SIC: **3993** 2796 5999 Signs, not made in custom sign painting shops; electric signs; platemaking services; decals

(G-2622)
SLAPSOK LLC
2309 Brenton Dr (73012-3633)
PHONE..................405 845-2299
Jeremy Cox,
EMP: 2 EST: 2017
SALES (est): 71.3K **Privately Held**
SIC: **2361** 2321 5136 5137 T-shirts & tops: girls', children's & infants'; men's & boys' dress shirts; shirts, men's & boys'; coordinate sets: women's, children's & infants'

(G-2623)
SOCCER WAVE LLC
16716 Crest Vly (73012-6802)
PHONE..................405 361-7813
Ben Mazloompour, *COO*
EMP: 4
SALES (est): 338.9K **Privately Held**
SIC: **3949** Sporting & athletic goods

(G-2624)
SOS POOLS
625 Evergreen St (73003-5727)
PHONE..................405 471-3792
Zach Teague, *Owner*
EMP: 1
SALES (est): 47K **Privately Held**
SIC: **3949** Sporting & athletic goods

(G-2625)
SOUTHERN OKIE LLC
2009 Bridgeview Blvd (73003-9007)
P.O. Box 30261 (73003-0005)
PHONE..................405 657-7765
Gina Hollingsworth, *President*
Mark Hollingsworth, *CFO*
EMP: 2
SALES: 40K **Privately Held**
SIC: **2033** Jams, jellies & preserves: packaged in cans, jars, etc.

(G-2626)
SPANISH LADY OIL CO
200 Shortgrass Rd (73003-3057)
P.O. Box 7103 (73083-7103)
PHONE..................405 659-3515
Gary Zellner, *CEO*
EMP: 2
SALES (est): 270K **Privately Held**
SIC: **1382** Oil & gas exploration services

(G-2627)
SPINNING STAR DESIGN
513 Joni Deanne Ct (73034-3033)
PHONE..................405 359-3965
Elizabeth Eagan, *Owner*
EMP: 1
SALES (est): 78.2K **Privately Held**
SIC: **7389** 2395 Design services; quilting & quilting supplies

GEOGRAPHIC SECTION

Edmond - Oklahoma County (G-2660)

(G-2628)
SPRING ENERGY CO
201 E Campbell St (73034-4524)
P.O. Box 2096 (73083-2096)
 PHONE.................................405 340-6811
Robert Spring, *President*
Jackie Spring, *Treasurer*
EMP: 2
SQ FT: 680
SALES (est): 267.2K **Privately Held**
SIC: 1382 Oil & gas exploration services

(G-2629)
SRM INC
4004a S Kelly Ave (73013-3800)
 PHONE.................................405 475-1746
Ben Hopcus, *Principal*
EMP: 490
SALES (corp-wide): 50.6MM **Privately Held**
SIC: 3273 Ready-mixed concrete
PA: Srm, Inc.
  1400 S Holly St
  Yukon OK 73099
  405 354-8824

(G-2630)
STARFALL PRESS LLC
6677 Valley Ridge Dr (73034-9543)
 PHONE.................................405 343-2369
Audrey Lindell Cunnyngham, *Principal*
EMP: 1
SALES (est): 37.5K **Privately Held**
SIC: 2741 Miscellaneous publishing

(G-2631)
STARS RESTAURANTS LLC (PA)
2941 Nw 156th St (73013-2101)
 PHONE.................................405 947-1396
James G Barrett, *Partner*
Holly Barrett, *Partner*
Morris J Hyde, *Partner*
EMP: 32
SQ FT: 600
SALES (est): 65.3MM **Privately Held**
WEB: www.starsdrivein.com
SIC: 6512 5812 1311 Commercial & industrial building operation; drive-in restaurant; crude petroleum production; natural gas production

(G-2632)
STEPHENS CUSTOM WOODWORKS
22399 Sutherly Farms Blvd (73025)
 PHONE.................................405 938-7065
Stephen Mullins, *Principal*
EMP: 1
SALES (est): 54.1K **Privately Held**
SIC: 2431 Millwork

(G-2633)
STITCHABELLA LLC
5008 Kelly Lakes Dr (73025-9798)
 PHONE.................................405 562-3316
Paula Jean Melendy, *Principal*
EMP: 1 EST: 2014
SALES (est): 64K **Privately Held**
SIC: 2395 Embroidery & art needlework

(G-2634)
STREAM-FLO USA LLC
5712 Industrial Blvd (73034-9473)
 PHONE.................................405 330-5504
EMP: 5 **Privately Held**
SIC: 3533 Mfg Oil/Gas Field Machinery
HQ: Stream-Flo Usa Llc
  3000 Synergy Blvd
  Kilgore TX 77064
  903 983-2992

(G-2635)
SYNAPTICGROOVE LLC
3601 Lea Ct (73013-8259)
 PHONE.................................405 205-6094
Benjamin Harrison,
EMP: 2 EST: 2013
SALES (est): 94.7K **Privately Held**
SIC: 3931 Guitars & parts, electric & non-electric

(G-2636)
TALL OAK WOODFORD LLC
2575 Kelley Pointe Pkwy # 340 (73013-2912)
 PHONE.................................405 888-5585
Ryan Lewellyn, *CEO*
EMP: 2 EST: 2016
SALES (est): 239.5K **Privately Held**
SIC: 1389 Pipe testing, oil field service; oil field services; pumping of oil & gas wells

(G-2637)
TEES FOR SOUL
507 S Coltrane Rd (73034-7152)
 PHONE.................................405 844-7685
EMP: 2 EST: 2011
SALES (est): 111.7K **Privately Held**
SIC: 2759 Screen printing

(G-2638)
TERRAQUEST CORPORATION
1015 Waterwood Pkwy Ste J (73034-5325)
 PHONE.................................405 359-0773
Michael Root, *President*
Elaine D Root, *Vice Pres*
Steven A Root, *Vice Pres*
EMP: 41
SQ FT: 5,400
SALES (est): 5.1MM **Privately Held**
SIC: 1382 6792 Oil & gas exploration services; oil leases, buying & selling on own account

(G-2639)
TGG PROSTHETICS ORTHOTICS LLC
125 E 3rd St Ste C (73034-3822)
 PHONE.................................405 285-5499
Richard Foster, *President*
EMP: 2 EST: 2015
SALES (est): 95K **Privately Held**
WEB: www.tggpo.com
SIC: 3842 Orthopedic appliances

(G-2640)
THINK SCREENPRINTING LLC
2713 Ne 129th St (73013-7455)
 PHONE.................................405 590-5131
Jason Shilling, *Principal*
EMP: 2
SALES (est): 83.9K **Privately Held**
SIC: 2752 Commercial printing, lithographic

(G-2641)
THUNDER CBD LLC
500 Seville Dr (73034-7180)
 PHONE.................................405 568-7235
EMP: 2
SALES (est): 97.7K **Privately Held**
SIC: 3999

(G-2642)
THUNDRBIRD RSOURCES EQUITY INC (PA)
6300 Oak Tree Cir (73025-2510)
 PHONE.................................405 600-0711
David Baggett, *CEO*
Michael J Rohleder, *President*
Gary D Jackson, *Exec VP*
Harry C Stahel Jr, *Exec VP*
James A Merrill, *CFO*
EMP: 16 EST: 1998
SALES (est): 11.9MM **Privately Held**
SIC: 1311 Crude petroleum production

(G-2643)
TILFORD PINSON EXPLORATION LLC
Also Called: Tpx
841 S Kelly Ave Ste 130 (73003-5672)
 PHONE.................................405 348-7201
Maxwell Tilford,
EMP: 10
SQ FT: 3,000
SALES (est): 1.7MM **Privately Held**
SIC: 1382 8999 Oil & gas exploration services; geological consultant

(G-2644)
TIRE SOFT LLC
3325 French Park Dr Ste 4 (73034-7265)
 PHONE.................................405 341-5070
Paul Anderson,
Lisa Anderson,
EMP: 2
SALES (est): 152.9K **Privately Held**
SIC: 7372 Business oriented computer software

(G-2645)
TK AERO INC
312 Saint James Dr (73034-6661)
 PHONE.................................405 359-8638
Thomas Kerstine, *President*
EMP: 1
SALES (est): 190K **Privately Held**
SIC: 5599 3465 Aircraft dealers; automotive stampings

(G-2646)
TOLAND & JOHNSTON INC
3324 French Park Dr Ste C (73034-7262)
P.O. Box 189 (73083-0189)
 PHONE.................................405 330-2006
Jerry L Johnston, *CEO*
Karen Supplee, *President*
Curtis Supplee, *Treasurer*
EMP: 3
SALES (est): 375.7K **Privately Held**
SIC: 1311 Crude petroleum production

(G-2647)
TOM-STACK LLC
2575 Kelley Pointe Pkwy (73013-2906)
 PHONE.................................405 888-5585
Ryan Lewellyn, *CEO*
Lindel Larison, *COO*
Max Myers, *CFO*
EMP: 19
SALES (est): 2.2MM
SALES (corp-wide): 6B **Publicly Held**
SIC: 1321 Natural gas liquids
HQ: Enlink Oklahoma Gas Proc Lp
  2501 Cedar Springs Rd
  Dallas TX 75201
  214 953-9500

(G-2648)
TOMCAT SPECIALTY OIL TOOLS LLC
6304 Blackberry Rd (73034-9416)
P.O. Box 30062 (73003-0002)
 PHONE.................................405 659-9222
Bob Weaver,
EMP: 3
SALES (est): 395.7K **Privately Held**
SIC: 3533 Drilling tools for gas, oil or water wells

(G-2649)
TOMPC LLC
2575 Kelley Pointe Pkwy (73013-2906)
 PHONE.................................405 888-5585
Ryan Lewellyn, *CEO*
Lindel Larison, *COO*
Max Myers, *CFO*
EMP: 21
SALES (est): 2.9MM
SALES (corp-wide): 6B **Publicly Held**
SIC: 1382 Oil & gas exploration services
HQ: Enlink Oklahoma Gas Proc Lp
  2501 Cedar Springs Rd
  Dallas TX 75201
  214 953-9500

(G-2650)
TONYS WELDING
6933 E Waterloo Rd (73034-1903)
 PHONE.................................405 996-6657
EMP: 1
SALES (est): 28.1K **Privately Held**
SIC: 7692 Welding repair

(G-2651)
TOTE4ME
1312 Nw 172nd St (73012-9700)
 PHONE.................................405 664-1144
James Christopher Lucas, *Mng Member*
EMP: 2
SALES (est): 72.9K **Privately Held**
SIC: 2515 Foundations & platforms

(G-2652)
TRANSPONDER KEY
15001 N Kelly Ave (73013-4139)
 PHONE.................................405 757-3199
EMP: 2
SALES (est): 89.1K **Privately Held**
SIC: 3429 Keys, locks & related hardware

(G-2653)
TRIOS OF OKLAHOMA LLC
10 N Grand Fork Dr (73034-4748)
P.O. Box 8753 (73083-8753)
 PHONE.................................918 760-2734
Betty C Ritchie,
EMP: 2
SALES (est): 176.9K **Privately Held**
SIC: 3471 Cleaning & descaling metal products

(G-2654)
TRUE NORTH MINISTRIES INC (PA)
14033 N Eastern Ave Fl 2 (73013-5586)
 PHONE.................................405 562-2986
Brad Montgomery, *Ch of Bd*
EMP: 4
SALES (est): 188K **Privately Held**
SIC: 8661 7372 Religious organizations; application computer software

(G-2655)
TRUMAN F LOGSDON
1616 E 19th St Ste 403 (73013-6628)
 PHONE.................................405 348-4504
EMP: 1
SQ FT: 1,000
SALES (est): 100K **Privately Held**
SIC: 1311 Crude Petroleum/Natural Gas Production

(G-2656)
TUBOSCOPE PIPELINE SVCS INC
Also Called: Tuboscope Vetco International
3600 S Kelly Ave (73013-3805)
 PHONE.................................405 478-2441
Andy Newsom, *Manager*
EMP: 19
SALES (corp-wide): 8.4B **Publicly Held**
SIC: 1389 Testing, measuring, surveying & analysis services
HQ: Tuboscope Pipeline Services Inc.
  2835 Holmes Rd
  Houston TX 77051

(G-2657)
UNITED PRODUCTION CO L L C
1001 Nw 139th Street Pkwy (73013-9792)
P.O. Box 5348 (73083-5348)
 PHONE.................................405 728-8900
Joseph Hamra Jr, *Mng Member*
EMP: 3
SALES (est): 708.2K **Privately Held**
SIC: 1311 Crude petroleum production; natural gas production

(G-2658)
URBAN OKIE CUSTOM WOODWORK
1000 W 15th St (73013-3026)
 PHONE.................................405 420-1176
Charles Freede, *Owner*
EMP: 1 EST: 2017
SALES (est): 54.1K **Privately Held**
SIC: 2431 Millwork

(G-2659)
URBAN OKIE CUSTOM WOODWORK LLC
1615 Ketch Pl (73003-3817)
 PHONE.................................405 635-7800
Tiffany Webb, *Principal*
EMP: 1
SALES (est): 54.1K **Privately Held**
SIC: 2431 Millwork

(G-2660)
US FLEET TRACKING LLC (PA)
2912 Nw 156th St (73013-2102)
 PHONE.................................405 726-9900
Justin McMillan, *Accounts Exec*
Richard Banks, *Sales Staff*
Jim Carman, *Sales Staff*
Sam Sims, *Pub Rel Dir*
Jerry Hunter, *Mng Member*
▲ **EMP:** 21
SQ FT: 18,000
SALES (est): 3.7MM **Privately Held**
SIC: 3953 Marking devices

Edmond - Oklahoma County (G-2661)

(G-2661)
USA INDUSTRIES OKLAHOMA INC
3126 S Boulevard Ste 208 (73013-5308)
PHONE..............................405 840-5577
Donald E Rogers, *President*
EMP: 2
SQ FT: 2,000
SALES: 50K **Privately Held**
SIC: 2395 Emblems, embroidered

(G-2662)
USEFUL PRODUCTS INC
Also Called: Body Buddy
1605 Kings Rd (73013-4323)
PHONE..............................405 715-2639
Shiolett Meier, *President*
Michelle Graves, *Vice Pres*
EMP: 3 EST: 1997
SALES (est): 338.5K **Privately Held**
WEB: www.bodybuddy.com
SIC: 2844 Face creams or lotions

(G-2663)
USFILTER
16208 Acoma Pl (73013-2025)
PHONE..............................405 359-7441
Curtis Cook, *Principal*
EMP: 2
SALES (est): 183.4K **Privately Held**
SIC: 3569 General industrial machinery

(G-2664)
V O INC
Also Called: OK Print and Promo
509 Clermont Dr (73003-3127)
PHONE..............................405 659-0654
Rita McGill, *President*
Dana Parsons, *President*
EMP: 2
SALES (est): 88.6K **Privately Held**
WEB: www.okprintandpromo.com
SIC: 2752 Commercial printing, offset

(G-2665)
VALIANT MIDSTREAM LLC
16420 Muirfield Pl (73013-9161)
PHONE..............................405 286-5580
Brandon J Webster, *CEO*
Zach N Gray, *CFO*
EMP: 3
SALES (est): 99.1K **Privately Held**
SIC: 1311 1382 Crude petroleum & natural gas production; oil & gas exploration services

(G-2666)
VALOR ENERGY SERVICES LLC (PA)
111 N Broadway Ste B (73034-3737)
P.O. Box 2078, Elk City (73648-2078)
PHONE..............................405 513-5043
Deak Harris, *CEO*
Darren L Skelton, *President*
David Jones, *COO*
EMP: 1 EST: 2016
SALES: 10MM **Privately Held**
SIC: 1389 Oil field services

(G-2667)
VAN EATON READY MIX INC
2547 E Waterloo Indus Rd (73034-6993)
P.O. Box 1058, Shawnee (74802-1058)
PHONE..............................405 844-2900
Mike Van Eaton, *Owner*
Cacy Eaton, *Vice Pres*
Cacy Vaneaton, *Executive*
EMP: 33 **Privately Held**
SIC: 3273 Ready-mixed concrete
PA: Van Eaton Ready Mix, Inc.
8 Timber Pond
Shawnee OK 74804

(G-2668)
VECTOR EXPLORATION INC
223 N Broadway (73034-3776)
P.O. Box 1327 (73083-1327)
PHONE..............................405 340-5373
Kenneth Hedrick, *President*
EMP: 3
SQ FT: 20,000
SALES (est): 1.5MM **Privately Held**
SIC: 1382 Oil & gas exploration services

(G-2669)
VERDAVIA PRESS LLC
208 Nw 142nd St (73013-1941)
PHONE..............................405 254-5030
Rodney E Stamps, *Agent*
EMP: 1
SALES (est): 37.5K **Privately Held**
SIC: 2741 Miscellaneous publishing

(G-2670)
VEREXCO INC
111 N Broadway (73034-3734)
P.O. Box 50 (73083-0050)
PHONE..............................405 341-4302
Boyd Ratliff, *President*
EMP: 3
SALES (est): 306.7K **Privately Held**
SIC: 1382 Oil & gas exploration services

(G-2671)
VIKING RAIN COVERS
1409 Devonshire Ct (73034-5721)
PHONE..............................405 359-1850
Mark Fryklund, *Owner*
EMP: 1
SALES (est): 63.7K **Privately Held**
SIC: 3089 Plastics products

(G-2672)
VINSON JAMES R LINDA F CO
2216 Red Elm Dr (73013-5610)
PHONE..............................405 478-1330
James Vinson, *Principal*
EMP: 2
SALES (est): 88.7K **Privately Held**
WEB: www.balcro.com
SIC: 2741 Miscellaneous publishing

(G-2673)
VINYL VIKINGS LLC
2101 Rambling Rd (73025-2309)
PHONE..............................405 260-9022
Tyler Hartgrove, *Principal*
EMP: 3 EST: 2016
SALES (est): 299.7K **Privately Held**
WEB: www.vinylvikings.com
SIC: 3993 Signs & advertising specialties

(G-2674)
VISUALS TECH SOLUTIONS LLC
2501 E Memorial Rd (73013-5525)
PHONE..............................913 526-1775
Russell McGuire, *Principal*
Austin McRay, *Marketing Staff*
EMP: 2
SALES (est): 80.9K **Privately Held**
SIC: 7379 3571 Computer related consulting services; electronic computers

(G-2675)
VITS SCREEN PRINTING
180 W 15th St Ste 180 # 180 (73013-3601)
PHONE..............................405 531-6012
EMP: 2
SALES (est): 83.9K **Privately Held**
SIC: 2752 Commercial printing, lithographic

(G-2676)
VUS FABRICS LLC
340 S Kelly Ave (73003-5630)
PHONE..............................405 330-9050
EMP: 2 EST: 2014
SALES (est): 147.4K **Privately Held**
SIC: 2391 Mfg Curtains/Draperies

(G-2677)
W F D OIL CORPORATION
16800 Conifer Ln (73012-0619)
PHONE..............................405 715-3130
Bill Dost, *President*
EMP: 4
SALES (est): 466.7K **Privately Held**
SIC: 1381 1311 Drilling oil & gas wells; crude petroleum & natural gas production

(G-2678)
W H BRAUM INC
Also Called: Braums Ice Cream & Dar Stores
2410 W Edmond Rd (73012-4562)
PHONE..............................405 340-9288
Michael Thornton, *Branch Mgr*
EMP: 23

SALES (corp-wide): 133.4MM **Privately Held**
SIC: 5451 5812 2024 5411 Ice cream (packaged); eating places; ice cream & frozen desserts; grocery stores
PA: W. H. Braum, Inc.
3000 Ne 63rd St
Oklahoma City OK 73121
405 478-1656

(G-2679)
WALLER EXPLORATION LLC
1616 E 19th St Ste 202 (73013-6675)
PHONE..............................405 359-2050
Bryan Waller, *Owner*
EMP: 1
SQ FT: 960
SALES: 300K **Privately Held**
SIC: 1382 Oil & gas exploration services

(G-2680)
WARHALL DESIGNS LLC
Also Called: Hom Kitchen Bath
14350 N Lincoln Blvd # 210 (73013-3444)
PHONE..............................405 330-0907
Greg Warlick, *CEO*
Joe Penhall, *President*
Stephanie Johnson, *Vice Pres*
Brittany Warlick, *CFO*
Sarah Waldron, *Manager*
EMP: 15
SQ FT: 2,000
SALES (est): 1.9MM **Privately Held**
SIC: 1743 3281 Marble installation, interior; cut stone & stone products

(G-2681)
WARNING AWARE LLC
1050 E 2nd St Ste 117 (73034-5313)
PHONE..............................405 300-8833
Seth Deckard, *CEO*
EMP: 1
SQ FT: 1,200
SALES (est): 43.6K **Privately Held**
SIC: 7372 Business oriented computer software

(G-2682)
WATERWOOD PARKWAY LLC
3820 Woodshadow Rd (73003-3046)
PHONE..............................405 341-5077
Brad Allred, *Principal*
EMP: 1
SALES (est): 59.6K **Privately Held**
SIC: 2499 Wood products

(G-2683)
WEHLU PRODUCERS INC
708 W 15th St (73013-3750)
PHONE..............................405 844-9487
James V Collins, *President*
EMP: 2
SALES (est): 230.9K **Privately Held**
SIC: 1311 Crude petroleum production; natural gas production

(G-2684)
WEST MATTISON PUBLISHING INC
Also Called: Mattison Ave
320 N Broadway Ste 201 (73034-3642)
PHONE..............................405 842-2266
EMP: 15
SALES (est): 600K **Privately Held**
SIC: 2731 2721 Books-Publishing/Printing Periodicals-Publishing/Printing

(G-2685)
WESTSTAR OIL AND GAS INC
1601 E 19th St (73013-6620)
PHONE..............................405 341-2338
Michael Krenger, *President*
David Phillips, *Corp Secy*
Don McNeill, *Vice Pres*
EMP: 2
SQ FT: 10,000
SALES (est): 2MM **Privately Held**
SIC: 1382 5084 Oil & gas exploration services; petroleum industry machinery

(G-2686)
WHISTLE STOP BEDDING & MORE (PA)
7205 Nw 210th St (73012-9563)
PHONE..............................405 620-5749

Jason Romine, *Principal*
EMP: 3
SALES (est): 141.7K **Privately Held**
SIC: 2392 Blankets, comforters & beddings

(G-2687)
WHITE SAIL ENERGY LLC
3024 Katie Ln (73013-9748)
PHONE..............................405 255-4669
Kyle Wilson, *Principal*
EMP: 2
SALES (est): 158.3K **Privately Held**
SIC: 1382 Oil & gas exploration services

(G-2688)
WHITEBOARD SOFTWARE LLC
1015 Waterwood Pkwy Ste F (73034-5325)
PHONE..............................405 408-3326
Robert Wright, *Principal*
EMP: 2 EST: 2016
SALES (est): 100K **Privately Held**
SIC: 7372 Prepackaged software

(G-2689)
WILSON II GEARY WAYNE
Also Called: Wilson Patriot
6333 Boucher Dr (73034-9258)
PHONE..............................405 330-4888
EMP: 2
SALES (est): 113.8K **Privately Held**
SIC: 3089 Tooling Injection Molding Custom

(G-2690)
WINZELER FAMILY LLC
709 Aberdeen Rd (73025-2719)
PHONE..............................405 218-2829
Richard D Winzeler, *President*
EMP: 1
SALES (est): 91.5K **Privately Held**
SIC: 1382 Oil & gas exploration services

(G-2691)
WK WINTERS & ASSOC
21 S Easy St (73012-4533)
PHONE..............................405 341-6571
W Winters, *Principal*
EMP: 5
SALES (est): 305.4K **Privately Held**
SIC: 7372 Prepackaged software

(G-2692)
WOODSHOP LTD
4425 Deason Dr (73013-8112)
PHONE..............................405 922-3789
James Blake, *Owner*
EMP: 1 EST: 1996
SALES (est): 85.3K **Privately Held**
SIC: 2511 Wood household furniture

(G-2693)
XPECT ENERGY SERVICES LLC
609 Westland Dr (73013-3726)
P.O. Box 7232 (73083-7232)
PHONE..............................405 641-7537
Garret Hunt, *CEO*
EMP: 10
SALES (est): 1.3MM **Privately Held**
WEB: www.xpectenergyservices.com
SIC: 1382 Oil & gas exploration services

(G-2694)
XZENO PRODUCTIONS
100 N University Dr (73034-5207)
PHONE..............................405 974-4016
Tewfic Kidess, *Owner*
EMP: 2
SALES (est): 73.1K **Privately Held**
SIC: 2721 Periodicals

El Reno
Canadian County

(G-2695)
AB SWABBING INCORPORATED
914 S Ellison Ave (73036-5226)
PHONE..............................219 765-3239
Shirley Galbreth, *Principal*
EMP: 2
SALES (est): 84K **Privately Held**
SIC: 1389 Bailing, cleaning, swabbing & treating of wells

GEOGRAPHIC SECTION

El Reno - Canadian County (G-2725)

(G-2696)
ALAN BEATY
Also Called: Trooper Trap
2409 S Dille Ave (73036-5917)
PHONE..................405 664-6768
Alan Beaty, *Owner*
EMP: 1
SALES (est): 106.7K **Privately Held**
SIC: 3699 Security devices

(G-2697)
ALEXCO MANUFACTURING LLC
1911 E Highway 66 (73036-6620)
PHONE..................405 274-4003
Mike Cooper, *Owner*
EMP: 2
SALES (est): 121.4K **Privately Held**
SIC: 3999 Manufacturing industries

(G-2698)
ALL DAY WELDING & FABRICATION
4503 N Highway 81 (73036-8909)
P.O. Box 786 (73036-0786)
PHONE..................405 550-2233
EMP: 1
SALES (est): 49.5K **Privately Held**
SIC: 7692 Welding repair

(G-2699)
ARKOS FIELD SERVICES LP
3705 S Choctaw Ave (73036-6737)
PHONE..................405 262-1548
EMP: 2 **EST:** 2016
SALES (est): 97.2K **Privately Held**
SIC: 1382 Oil & gas exploration services

(G-2700)
BAKERS SIGN & DESIGN
1315 S Shepard Ave (73036-6367)
PHONE..................405 262-5100
Ryan Baker, *Owner*
Brian Baker, *Owner*
EMP: 1
SALES (est): 82.8K **Privately Held**
SIC: 3993 Signs & advertising specialties

(G-2701)
BEST OIL FIELD SERVICE INC
Also Called: Best Oilfield Service
1901 E Highway 66 (73036-6620)
P.O. Box 1108 (73036-1108)
PHONE..................405 262-5060
Steve Williams, *President*
Belinda Williams, *Corp Secy*
EMP: 41
SQ FT: 1,343
SALES (est): 1MM **Privately Held**
SIC: 1629 1389 Oil refinery construction; oil field services

(G-2702)
BLACKSTONE CAPITAL PARTNERS SE
1021 S El Reno Ave (73036-3956)
PHONE..................424 355-5050
Ryan Arnold, *CFO*
EMP: 4
SALES (est): 156.9K **Privately Held**
SIC: 3272 Concrete products

(G-2703)
BRADY WELDING & MACHINE SHOP
4210 S Alfadale Rd (73036-9696)
PHONE..................405 262-3665
Blake Brady, *Opers Mgr*
Mike Brady, *Branch Mgr*
EMP: 1
SALES (corp-wide): 52.1MM **Privately Held**
SIC: 3599 Machine shop, jobbing & repair
PA: Brady Welding & Machine Shop Inc
 11991 Highway 76
 Healdton OK 73438
 580 229-1168

(G-2704)
C&J WELL SERVICES INC
201 Jensen Rd E (73036-6815)
PHONE..................405 234-9800
Chris Amanis, *Manager*
EMP: 30

SALES (corp-wide): 567.2MM **Publicly Held**
SIC: 1389 Mud service, oil field drilling
HQ: C&J Well Services, Inc.
 3990 Rogerdale Rd
 Houston TX 77042

(G-2705)
CENTURION PIPELINE LP
2301 S Evans Rd (73036-9283)
PHONE..................405 262-4750
Tom Brozovich, *Branch Mgr*
Kalpesh Patel, *Analyst*
EMP: 2
SALES (corp-wide): 275.2MM **Privately Held**
SIC: 1311 Crude petroleum & natural gas
HQ: Centurion Pipeline L.P.
 5 Greenway Plz Ste 110
 Houston TX 77046
 713 215-7000

(G-2706)
CIMAREX ENERGY CO
3503 Jensen Rd E (73036-9684)
PHONE..................405 262-2966
Dustin Lindley, *Superintendent*
Darlene Lutz, *Manager*
EMP: 15
SQ FT: 1,489
SALES (corp-wide): 2.3B **Publicly Held**
SIC: 1382 Oil & gas exploration services
PA: Cimarex Energy Co.
 1700 N Lincoln St # 3700
 Denver CO 80203
 303 295-3995

(G-2707)
CROSS SHADOWS INC
Also Called: Rainbow Studies International
1502 Ridgecrest Dr (73036-5600)
P.O. Box 759 (73036-0759)
PHONE..................405 262-9777
Billy F Hughey, *President*
Janice Hughey, *Corp Secy*
▲ **EMP:** 2
SALES (est): 203.2K **Privately Held**
SIC: 2731 5192 5942 Books: publishing only; books; books, religious

(G-2708)
CUSTOM WOOD CRAFT CONSTRUCTION
Also Called: Custom Woodcraft
2424 Sunset Dr (73036-2128)
PHONE..................405 262-5228
Marc J Stagg, *Owner*
EMP: 1
SQ FT: 1,000
SALES (est): 97.1K **Privately Held**
SIC: 2434 Wood kitchen cabinets

(G-2709)
CUTTING EDGE SIGNS & GRAPHICS
1302 S Choctaw Ave (73036-5508)
PHONE..................405 262-4300
Chris Bromlow, *Owner*
EMP: 2
SQ FT: 1,300
SALES (est): 167.3K **Privately Held**
SIC: 3993 Signs, not made in custom sign painting shops

(G-2710)
DAVID DAVIS
Also Called: Western Portable Building
16547 W Us Highway 66 (73036-9151)
PHONE..................405 354-6974
David Davis, *Owner*
EMP: 2
SALES (est): 167.8K **Privately Held**
SIC: 3448 2452 Buildings, portable: prefabricated metal; prefabricated wood buildings

(G-2711)
DELSON PROPERTIES LTD
Also Called: Heritage
2517 Sw Holloway St (73036-5778)
P.O. Box 1069 (73036-1069)
PHONE..................405 262-5005
David C Delana, *President*
Janice Delana, *Vice Pres*
Dale Crump, *Maint Mgr*
Judy Kamm, *Human Res Mgr*

Karen Lear, *Sales Staff*
EMP: 76 **EST:** 1974
SQ FT: 50,000
SALES (est): 16.9MM **Privately Held**
SIC: 7319 2759 Display advertising service; commercial printing

(G-2712)
DEXTER AXLE COMPANY
500 Se 27th St (73036-5708)
P.O. Box 790 (73036-0790)
PHONE..................405 262-1178
Chuck Winans, *Plant Mgr*
Tony Meyers, *Branch Mgr*
EMP: 150
SALES (corp-wide): 2.4B **Privately Held**
SIC: 3714 Axles, motor vehicle
HQ: Dexter Axle Company
 2900 Industrial Pkwy
 Elkhart IN 46516

(G-2713)
DOLESE BROS CO
305 Se 22nd St (73036-5729)
P.O. Box 1045 (73036-1045)
PHONE..................405 262-0226
Chase Choffman, *Manager*
EMP: 4
SALES (corp-wide): 8.5MM **Privately Held**
SIC: 3273 Ready-mixed concrete
PA: Dolese Bros. Co.
 20 Nw 13th St
 Oklahoma City OK 73103
 405 235-2311

(G-2714)
EL RENO BOWL INC
2412 Sunset Dr (73036-2128)
P.O. Box 397 (73036-0397)
PHONE..................405 262-3611
Charles Hale, *President*
Loreta Hale, *Admin Sec*
EMP: 8
SALES (est): 766K **Privately Held**
SIC: 3949 5812 Bowling alleys & accessories; American restaurant

(G-2715)
EL RENO TRIBUNE
801 Thompson Dr (73036-5402)
PHONE..................405 262-7231
EMP: 4
SALES (est): 19.2K **Privately Held**
WEB: www.elrenotribune.com
SIC: 2711 Newspapers, publishing & printing

(G-2716)
FHL HOT SHOT TRUCKING SERVICES
16905 Sw 29th St (73036-9681)
PHONE..................405 615-6658
Scott Deimel, *Principal*
EMP: 1 **EST:** 2014
SALES (est): 149.7K **Privately Held**
SIC: 1389 Hot shot service

(G-2717)
FLEXX WIRELINE SERVICES LLC
2729 M And K Ln (73036-9265)
P.O. Box 1292 (73036-1292)
PHONE..................405 990-1593
Londell McMillian,
Michael Burgener,
EMP: 3
SALES: 1MM **Privately Held**
SIC: 1382 Oil & gas exploration services

(G-2718)
GEMINI COATINGS INC (HQ)
421 Se 27th St (73036-5705)
P.O. Box 699 (73036-0699)
PHONE..................405 262-5710
David P Warren, *President*
Mike Green, *Sales Staff*
Jeffrey Thomas, *Manager*
Richard Ruiz, *Technical Staff*
Brian Hansen, *Director*
▲ **EMP:** 110
SQ FT: 100,000
SALES (est): 1.4MM
SALES (corp-wide): 1.6MM **Privately Held**
SIC: 2851 Lacquer: bases, dopes, thinner

PA: Gemini Industries, Inc.
 421 Se 27th St
 El Reno OK 73036
 405 262-5710

(G-2719)
GEMINI INDUSTRIES INC (PA)
Also Called: Gemini Coatings
421 Se 27th St (73036-5705)
P.O. Box 699 (73036-0699)
PHONE..................405 262-5710
David Warren, *President*
Patrick Clary, *Vice Pres*
Rob Doman, *Vice Pres*
Sal Malgari, *Vice Pres*
Jason Melton, *Vice Pres*
▲ **EMP:** 100
SQ FT: 100,000
SALES: 1.6MM **Privately Held**
WEB: www.gemini-coatings.com
SIC: 2851 7389 Lacquer: bases, dopes, thinner; packaging & labeling services

(G-2720)
GREAT PLAINS OILFLD RENTL LLC
3401 S Radio Rd (73036-9119)
PHONE..................405 422-2873
Rhone Prather, *Mng Member*
Mike Edwards, *Director*
Rick Treeman, *Director*
Trey Landry,
EMP: 894
SALES (est): 15.6MM
SALES (corp-wide): 2.4B **Publicly Held**
SIC: 1381 Drilling oil & gas wells
HQ: Seventy Seven Operating Llc
 777 Nw 63rd St
 Oklahoma City OK 73116
 405 608-7777

(G-2721)
GUARDIAN TUBULAR SERVICES INC
8208 E Us Highway 66 (73036-9118)
P.O. Box 850980, Yukon (73085-0980)
PHONE..................405 262-3800
Mark Lowe, *President*
EMP: 7
SALES (est): 459.2K **Privately Held**
SIC: 1389 Oil field services

(G-2722)
H & H SPECIALTY WELDING LLC
2727 M And K Ln (73036-9265)
PHONE..................479 322-1125
EMP: 1
SALES (est): 40.5K **Privately Held**
SIC: 7692 Welding repair

(G-2723)
HARDTIMES REAL BEEF JERKY INC
3533 Jensen Rd E (73036-9684)
P.O. Box 268, Stratford (74872-0268)
PHONE..................580 497-7695
JW Tennery, *President*
EMP: 20
SQ FT: 12,000
SALES: 2.7MM **Privately Held**
SIC: 2013 Prepared beef products from purchased beef

(G-2724)
HOUSE DOG INDUSTRIES LLC
701 Thompson Dr (73036-5403)
PHONE..................405 761-5576
Steve House, *President*
EMP: 1
SQ FT: 998
SALES (est): 39.5K **Privately Held**
SIC: 2047 5149 Dog food; dog food

(G-2725)
INSPIRED GIFTS & GRAPHICS LLC
Also Called: Igg Screen Printing
1605 E Us Highway 66 (73036-5769)
PHONE..................405 295-1669
Yvonne Bruner, *Mng Member*
EMP: 9

El Reno - Canadian County (G-2726)

SALES (est): 848.4K **Privately Held**
WEB: www.iggscreenprinting.com
SIC: **2759** 2752 2796 Commercial printing; screen printing; promotional printing; commercial printing, lithographic; platemaking services

(G-2726)
INTEGRITY PUMP & SUPPLY LLC
301 S Bickford Ave (73036-2767)
P.O. Box 758 (73036-0758)
PHONE..................405 422-2828
EMP: 1
SQ FT: 3,000
SALES: 200K **Privately Held**
SIC: **3586** 5084 Mfg Measuring/Dispensing Pumps Whol Industrial Equipment

(G-2727)
J SCOTT INC
Also Called: Oilfield Fresh Wtr Mud Dsposal
12215 Reuter Rd W (73036-8853)
PHONE..................405 262-5900
Jack C Scott, *President*
Mary L Scott, *Vice Pres*
EMP: 10
SALES (est): 801.3K **Privately Held**
SIC: **1389** Oil field services

(G-2728)
JADE FIRE LLC
2604 S Reno Ave (73036-5843)
PHONE..................405 295-7734
Micah Hurst,
EMP: 1
SALES: 36K **Privately Held**
SIC: **7372** 7389 Educational computer software;

(G-2729)
KACTUS ROSE LLC
6512 Foreman Rd E (73036-8601)
PHONE..................405 830-7551
Carry Lancaster, *President*
EMP: 1
SALES (est): 51.5K **Privately Held**
SIC: **2499** Decorative wood & woodwork

(G-2730)
KAISER-FRANCIS OIL COMPANY
4101 E Highway 66 (73036)
PHONE..................405 262-5511
George Kaiser, *Owner*
EMP: 5
SALES (corp-wide): 678.5MM **Privately Held**
SIC: **1311** Crude petroleum production
HQ: Kaiser-Francis Oil Company
   6733 S Yale Ave
   Tulsa OK 74136
   918 494-0000

(G-2731)
KEY ENERGY SERVICES INC
3801 Valley Park Dr Ste A (73036-6828)
PHONE..................405 262-1190
Dick Lario, *Principal*
EMP: 15
SALES (corp-wide): 413.8MM **Publicly Held**
WEB: www.keyenergy.com
SIC: **1389** Oil field services
PA: Key Energy Services, Inc.
   1301 Mckinney St Ste 1800
   Houston TX 77010
   713 651-4300

(G-2732)
KEY ENERGY SERVICES INC
4000 Valley Park Dr (73036-6817)
PHONE..................405 262-1231
M Pape, *Branch Mgr*
EMP: 46
SALES (corp-wide): 413.8MM **Publicly Held**
SIC: **1389** Servicing oil & gas wells
PA: Key Energy Services, Inc.
   1301 Mckinney St Ste 1800
   Houston TX 77010
   713 651-4300

(G-2733)
KINGFISHER PIPE SALES AND SVC
9016 Lehman Rd (73036-8514)
PHONE..................405 262-4422
Jimmy Redwine, *President*
EMP: 4
SQ FT: 7,560
SALES (est): 645.3K **Privately Held**
SIC: **3312** 7389 5051 Pipes, iron & steel; ; pipe & tubing, steel

(G-2734)
KIRKLAND EXPRESS LLC
2624 Homestead Dr (73036-2157)
PHONE..................405 312-3061
Terry Kirkland,
EMP: 2
SALES (est): 95.5K **Privately Held**
SIC: **3537** Trucks, tractors, loaders, carriers & similar equipment

(G-2735)
KIRKLIND GLOBAL INC
2719 M&K Ln (73036)
PHONE..................580 618-2527
Erik Gonzales, *President*
EMP: 2
SALES: 130K **Privately Held**
SIC: **3577** Printers, computer

(G-2736)
MATHENA INC (HQ)
3900 S Hwy 81 Service Rd (73036-6808)
PHONE..................405 422-3600
John Mathena, *President*
Greg Cantrell, *Vice Pres*
David Mathena, *Vice Pres*
Harold Mathena, *Vice Pres*
Trebor Nall, *Vice Pres*
EMP: 70
SQ FT: 10,000
SALES: 89MM
SALES (corp-wide): 3.4B **Privately Held**
SIC: **3699** 3822 Security control equipment & systems; surface burner controls, temperature
PA: Weir Group Plc(The)
   1 West Regent Street
   Glasgow G2 1R
   141 637-7111

(G-2737)
MCLEMORE MONUMENT SERVICES
5803 N Reformatory Rd (73036-9039)
PHONE..................405 788-0164
Josh McLemore, *Principal*
EMP: 3
SALES (est): 116.8K **Privately Held**
SIC: **3272** Monuments & grave markers, except terrazo

(G-2738)
MIDCENTRAL COMPLETION SERVICES
901 Se 35th St (73036-6821)
PHONE..................405 445-5979
EMP: 6
SALES (est): 512.2K **Privately Held**
SIC: **1389** Construction, repair & dismantling services

(G-2739)
MORAN EQUIPMENT
2614 Sunset Dr (73036-2171)
PHONE..................405 262-1422
EMP: 2 EST: 2017
SALES (est): 65.5K **Privately Held**
WEB: www.moranequipment.com
SIC: **1389** Grading oil & gas well foundations

(G-2740)
MRC GLOBAL (US) INC
2010 S Radio Rd (73036-8187)
PHONE..................405 491-7392
Ken Mitchell, *Manager*
EMP: 12 **Publicly Held**
WEB: www.mrcglobal.com
SIC: **1311** Crude petroleum & natural gas
HQ: Mrc Global (Us) Inc.
   1301 Mckinney St Ste 2300
   Houston TX 77010
   877 294-7574

(G-2741)
MYSTIC ROCK MINIATURES
16101 Sw 25th St (73036-6005)
PHONE..................817 845-1590
Diana Gilger, *Principal*
EMP: 2
SALES (est): 101.2K **Privately Held**
SIC: **3999** Miniatures

(G-2742)
NABORS WELL SERVICES LTD
4301 Us 66 E (73036)
PHONE..................405 262-6262
Dennis Jones, *Manager*
Joe Walstad, *Executive*
EMP: 20
SQ FT: 1,800 **Privately Held**
WEB: www.nabors.com
SIC: **1389** Oil field services
HQ: Nabors Well Services Ltd.
   515 W Greens Rd Ste 1200
   Houston TX 77067
   281 874-0035

(G-2743)
NOMAC DRILLING LLC (DH)
Also Called: Mid-States Oilfield Machine
3400 S Radio Rd (73036-9111)
P.O. Box 54366, Oklahoma City (73154-1366)
PHONE..................405 422-2754
Jerry Winchester, *CEO*
Jay Minmier, *President*
Karl Blanchard, *COO*
Jared Nance, *Project Mgr*
Cary Baetz, *CFO*
EMP: 1 EST: 2008
SALES (est): 2.3MM
SALES (corp-wide): 2.4B **Publicly Held**
WEB: www.nomacdrilling.com
SIC: **1381** Drilling oil & gas wells
HQ: Seventy Seven Operating Llc
   777 Nw 63rd St
   Oklahoma City OK 73116
   405 608-7777

(G-2744)
OKLAHOMA TOOL & MACHINE
401 E Foreman St (73036-2747)
P.O. Box 1363 (73036-1363)
PHONE..................405 262-2624
Steven Pickett, *Owner*
EMP: 6
SQ FT: 8,000
SALES (est): 350.6K **Privately Held**
SIC: **2048** Knife, saw & tool sharpening & repair

(G-2745)
PALOMA PARTNERS IV
221 N Rock Island Ave (73036-2730)
PHONE..................405 295-6755
EMP: 2
SALES (est): 112.7K **Privately Held**
SIC: **1311** Crude petroleum production

(G-2746)
PERFORMANCE TECHNOLOGIES LLC (DH)
3715 S Radio Rd (73036-9245)
P.O. Box 18837, Oklahoma City (73154-0837)
PHONE..................405 262-2441
Jerry Winchester, *CEO*
Bill Stanger, *President*
Karl Blanchard, *COO*
Cary Baetz, *CFO*
Jerry L Winchester,
EMP: 60
SQ FT: 100,000
SALES (est): 10.4MM
SALES (corp-wide): 2.4B **Publicly Held**
SIC: **1389** Pumping of oil & gas wells
HQ: Seventy Seven Operating Llc
   777 Nw 63rd St
   Oklahoma City OK 73116
   405 608-7777

(G-2747)
PERMIAN TANK & MFG INC
2309 E Highway 66 (73036-6627)
P.O. Box 1107 (73036-1107)
PHONE..................405 295-2525
Rod Richardson, *Manager*
EMP: 49
SALES (corp-wide): 122MM **Privately Held**
SIC: **3443** Tanks, standard or custom fabricated: metal plate
PA: Permian Tank & Manufacturing, Inc.
   2701 W Interstate 20
   Odessa TX 79766
   432 580-1050

(G-2748)
PREMIERE INC
4004 W 10th St (73036-7407)
PHONE..................405 262-1554
Dennis Bundy, *Administration*
EMP: 19 **Privately Held**
WEB: www.premiereinc.com
SIC: **1389** Oil field services
PA: Premiere, Inc.
   615 N Landry Dr
   New Iberia LA 70563

(G-2749)
QUICK START INC
3700 S Highway 81 Svc Rd (73036)
PHONE..................405 422-3135
Henry Swartz, *President*
Kay Harwick, *Vice Pres*
EMP: 10
SQ FT: 5,800
SALES: 600K **Privately Held**
SIC: **3612** Specialty transformers

(G-2750)
R360 OKLAHOMA LLC
12000 Reuter Rd W (73036-8963)
PHONE..................405 262-5900
Rick Felberg, *Principal*
EMP: 22 EST: 2012
SALES (est): 1MM
SALES (corp-wide): 5.3B **Privately Held**
SIC: **1389** Oil field services
HQ: Waste Connections Inc.
   3 Waterway Square Pl # 110
   The Woodlands TX 77380

(G-2751)
RAFTER H OPERATING LLC
219 N Bickford Ave (73036-2714)
P.O. Box 399 (73036-0399)
PHONE..................405 295-2100
Timothy Haley, *Mng Member*
EMP: 2
SQ FT: 2,000
SALES: 300K **Privately Held**
SIC: **1389** Cementing oil & gas well casings

(G-2752)
RED DIRT MSUREMENT CONTRLS LLC
2742 M And K Ln (73036-9265)
P.O. Box 885, Mustang (73064-0885)
PHONE..................405 422-5085
Clay Grissom, *Mng Member*
Dewayne Thompson, *Mng Member*
EMP: 23
SALES (est): 68.6K **Privately Held**
SIC: **1799** 1389 1623 Petroleum storage tank installation, underground; cementing oil & gas well casings; electric power line construction

(G-2753)
SCHLUMBERGER TECHNOLOGY CORP
Also Called: Dowell Schlumberger
560 Jensen Rd W (73036-6708)
PHONE..................405 422-8700
Steve Chisler, *Branch Mgr*
EMP: 155 **Publicly Held**
SIC: **1389** 1382 Oil field services; oil & gas exploration services
HQ: Schlumberger Technology Corp
   300 Schlumberger Dr
   Sugar Land TX 77478
   281 285-8500

(G-2754)
SCHLUMBERGER TECHNOLOGY CORP
Also Called: Dowell Schlumberger
560 Jensen Rd W (73036-6708)
PHONE..................580 225-0730
Fax: 580 225-2159
EMP: 150 **Privately Held**

GEOGRAPHIC SECTION

Elk City - Beckham County (G-2783)

SIC: **1389** Oil/Gas Field Services
HQ: Schlumberger Technology Corp
  100 Gillingham Ln
  Sugar Land TX 77478
  281 285-8500

(G-2755)
SEABOARD INTERNATIONAL INC
3900 S Highway 81 Svc Rd (73036)
P.O. Box 95995, Oklahoma City (73143-5995)
PHONE..................405 619-3099
Tom Hawkins, *Branch Mgr*
EMP: 22
SALES (corp-wide): 3.4B **Privately Held**
SIC: **3533** Oil field machinery & equipment
HQ: Seaboard International Inc.
  13815 South Fwy
  Houston TX 77047
  713 644-3535

(G-2756)
SELECT ENERGY SERVICES LLC
1900 Sw 27th St (73036-6100)
PHONE..................405 295-2566
Ron Rhines, *Branch Mgr*
EMP: 5
SALES (corp-wide): 1.2B **Publicly Held**
WEB: www.selectenergyservices.com
SIC: **1389** Oil field services
HQ: Select Energy Services, Llc
  1820 N I 35
  Gainesville TX 76240
  940 668-1818

(G-2757)
SHUR-CO LLC
Also Called: Shurco of Oklahoma
1604 E Us Highway 66 (73036-5779)
P.O. Box 713, Yankton SD (57078-0713)
PHONE..................405 262-7600
Stan Witt, *Manager*
EMP: 8 **Privately Held**
SIC: **3429** 5014 3713 2394 Motor vehicle hardware; truck tires & tubes; truck & bus bodies; canvas & related products
PA: Shur-Co, Llc
  2309 Shurlock St
  Yankton SD 57078

(G-2758)
SMOOTH LANDINGS LLC
2735 M And K Ln (73036-9265)
P.O. Box 850439, Yukon (73085-0439)
PHONE..................405 422-1822
Alan Keith Hadlock, *Principal*
EMP: 3
SALES (est): 252.1K **Privately Held**
WEB: www.smoothlandingsllc.com
SIC: **3728** Gears, aircraft power transmission

(G-2759)
SPINNAKER OIL COMPANY LLC
3675 S Alfadale Rd (73036-7322)
PHONE..................405 345-9556
Will Higginbotham, *Sales Mgr*
Miles Hagee, *Supervisor*
Cliff Leach, *Supervisor*
Mark Corwder,
EMP: 49
SALES (corp-wide): 19MM **Privately Held**
SIC: **1389** Mud service, oil field drilling
HQ: Spinnaker Oil Company Llc
  3040 Post Oak Blvd # 1450
  Houston TX 77056
  713 574-2240

(G-2760)
STATEWIDE ROUSTABOUTS INC
5910 N Radio Rd (73036-9000)
PHONE..................405 262-5934
EMP: 2 **EST:** 2012
SALES (est): 85K **Privately Held**
SIC: **1389** Oil/Gas Field Services

(G-2761)
TEG SOLUTIONS LLC (PA)
2490 Auction Pkwy (73036)
PHONE..................405 354-1951
Richard Anderson, *CEO*
EMP: 10
SQ FT: 5,000
SALES (est): 2.1MM **Privately Held**
WEB: www.tegsol.com
SIC: **1389** Oil field services

(G-2762)
TIMBERCREEK FLOWBACK & SAFETY
1708 E Woodson St (73036-3337)
PHONE..................405 694-7228
Jodee Nichols,
EMP: 1
SALES (est): 64.3K **Privately Held**
SIC: **3823** Industrial flow & liquid measuring instruments

(G-2763)
TRANS-TECH LLC
1600 Grider Ave (73036-5722)
P.O. Box 174 (73036-0174)
PHONE..................405 422-5000
Dale Cox,
Pamela Cox,
EMP: 10
SQ FT: 6,000
SALES (est): 620K **Privately Held**
SIC: **3993** 5199 Signs & advertising specialties; decals

(G-2764)
TRIBUNE CORP
Also Called: El Reno Tribune
102 E Wade St (73036-2742)
P.O. Box 9 (73036-0009)
PHONE..................405 262-5180
Ray T Dyer, *President*
Glen Miller, *Editor*
Erin Dyer, *Vice Pres*
Sean Dyer, *Treasurer*
Judy Hampton, *Advt Staff*
EMP: 22 **EST:** 1934
SQ FT: 9,000
SALES (est): 1.5MM **Privately Held**
WEB: www.elrenotribune.com
SIC: **2711** Commercial printing & newspaper publishing combined; newspapers, publishing & printing

(G-2765)
UNIVERSAL PRESSURE PUMPING INC
3715 S Radio Rd (73036-9245)
PHONE..................405 262-2441
Brian Davis, *Branch Mgr*
EMP: 350
SALES (corp-wide): 2.4B **Publicly Held**
SIC: **3511** Hydraulic turbines
HQ: Universal Pressure Pumping, Inc.
  6 Desta Dr Ste 4400
  Midland TX 79705

(G-2766)
UNIVERSAL TRLR HOLDINGS CORP
900 E Trail Blvd (73036-6339)
PHONE..................405 422-7238
Brett Hunter, *Plant Mgr*
Steven Esler, *Engineer*
David Walker, *Engineer*
Kenny Eagles, *Branch Mgr*
EMP: 1
SALES (corp-wide): 894.6MM **Privately Held**
SIC: **3715** Truck trailers
PA: Universal Trailer Holdings Corp.
  12800 University Dr # 300
  Fort Myers FL 33907

(G-2767)
VIKING PIPE AND SUPPLY LLC
1911 E Highway 66 (73036-6620)
P.O. Box 1518 (73036-1518)
PHONE..................405 262-9337
Jacobi Cooper, *Store Mgr*
Lindsay Judd, *Mktg Dir*
Mike Cooper,
Belinda Williams,
Steve Williams,
EMP: 1
SALES (est): 549.5K **Privately Held**
SIC: **1389** Oil field services

(G-2768)
WARRENS SCREEN PRTG EMB L L C
1307 Fairfax Ln (73036-5747)
PHONE..................405 422-3900
Danny Warren, *Principal*
EMP: 4
SALES (est): 380.7K **Privately Held**
WEB: www.warrensscreenprinting.com
SIC: **2752** Commercial printing, lithographic

(G-2769)
WEIR OIL GAS
3900 S Highway 81 Svc Rd (73036)
PHONE..................580 225-2381
Doice Lay, *President*
EMP: 2
SALES (est): 260.7K **Privately Held**
SIC: **1382** Oil & gas exploration services

(G-2770)
WET WILLIES SCREEN PRINT & CU
705 N Rock Island Ave (73036-1962)
PHONE..................405 262-6076
William Chadwick, *Owner*
EMP: 3
SQ FT: 6,000
SALES (est): 166.4K **Privately Held**
SIC: **2396** 5999 Screen printing on fabric articles; decals

(G-2771)
WHITETAIL BATH BOMBS
808 Allison Pl (73036-5411)
PHONE..................405 474-8017
Hannah Jones, *Principal*
EMP: 2
SALES (est): 74.4K **Privately Held**
SIC: **2844** Bath salts

(G-2772)
WOOD FINISHERS SUPPLY INC
Also Called: Wood Finishers Supply & Gemini
2300 Sw Holloway St (73036-5773)
P.O. Box 699 (73036-0699)
PHONE..................405 422-1025
Roger Woolery, *President*
Parrish Terry, *Vice Pres*
▼ **EMP:** 150
SQ FT: 5,000
SALES (est): 1.5MM
SALES (corp-wide): 1.6MM **Privately Held**
SIC: **2851** 2843 Stains: varnish, oil or wax; surface active agents
PA: Gemini Industries, Inc.
  421 Se 27th St
  El Reno OK 73036
  405 262-5710

Eldorado
Jackson County

(G-2773)
EL DORADO MANUFACTURING CO LLC
110 N Lloyd St (73537-9111)
PHONE..................580 318-2313
Barbara Ishmael, *Manager*
Raymond Green,
EMP: 3
SALES (est): 267K **Privately Held**
SIC: **3443** Plate work for the metalworking trade

Elgin
Comanche County

(G-2774)
AMBROSE WELDING LLC
13671 Ne Cornwallis Dr (73538-5008)
P.O. Box 589 (73538-0589)
PHONE..................580 704-0356
EMP: 1 **EST:** 2016
SALES (est): 63.1K **Privately Held**
SIC: **7692** Welding repair

(G-2775)
DOLESE BROS CO
Also Called: Richard Spur Plant
375 Nw Dolese Rd (73538-3054)
PHONE..................580 492-4771
Bryce Hoffman, *Manager*
EMP: 72
SALES (corp-wide): 8.5MM **Privately Held**
SIC: **3281** 1422 Limestone, cut & shaped; crushed & broken limestone
PA: Dolese Bros. Co.
  20 Nw 13th St
  Oklahoma City OK 73103
  405 235-2311

(G-2776)
HAUL AROUND
12714 Ne Townley Rd (73538-3713)
PHONE..................580 353-0808
James R Landoll, *Partner*
James J Landoll Sr, *Partner*
EMP: 4
SALES: 400K **Privately Held**
SIC: **3715** Truck trailers

(G-2777)
MARTY WATLEY
Also Called: Watley's Welding Service
108 Green Way (73538-8910)
P.O. Box 436 (73538-0436)
PHONE..................580 492-4859
Marty Watley, *Owner*
EMP: 1
SALES (est): 78.3K **Privately Held**
SIC: **1799** 7692 Welding on site; welding repair

(G-2778)
PRINT MASTER GENERAL LLC
13293 Ne Kleeman Rd (73538-3502)
PHONE..................580 442-2474
EMP: 2
SALES (est): 100K **Privately Held**
SIC: **2752** Commercial printing, lithographic

(G-2779)
ROY SLAGEL KENO
Also Called: Wildcat Welding & Fabrications
13883 Ne Townley Rd (73538-3704)
PHONE..................580 585-0283
Roy Slagle, *Owner*
EMP: 1
SALES (est): 62.1K **Privately Held**
SIC: **2899** Fluxes: brazing, soldering, galvanizing & welding

Elk City
Beckham County

(G-2780)
4AG MFG LLC
11110 N 1950 Rd (73644-2329)
PHONE..................580 821-9300
EMP: 1
SALES (est): 39.6K **Privately Held**
SIC: **3999** Manufacturing industries

(G-2781)
ACE HARDWARE
1210 S Main St (73644-6900)
PHONE..................580 225-0100
EMP: 2
SALES (est): 73.2K **Privately Held**
SIC: **5251** 2431 Hardware; millwork

(G-2782)
AES DRILLING FLUIDS
101 Falcon Rd Ste 8 (73644-9503)
PHONE..................580 225-3450
Martin Kelley, *Manager*
EMP: 2 **EST:** 2018
SALES (est): 65.5K **Privately Held**
SIC: **1389** Oil & gas field services

(G-2783)
AMERICAN MANIFOLD
102 Oilfield Rd (73644-9289)
PHONE..................580 225-1116
Rhonda Belcher, *Principal*
EMP: 5

Elk City - Beckham County (G-2784) — GEOGRAPHIC SECTION

SALES (est): 514.5K **Privately Held**
SIC: **1382** Oil & gas exploration services

(G-2784)
ARCHROCK INC
Also Called: Exterran
1306 Airport Indus Rd (73644-1923)
PHONE.....................580 225-2091
Steve Snyder, *Branch Mgr*
EMP: 16 **Publicly Held**
SIC: **1389** 5084 Gas compressing (natural gas) at the fields; compressors, except air conditioning
PA: Archrock, Inc.
9807 Katy Fwy Ste 100
Houston TX 77024

(G-2785)
BAKER HGHES OLFLD OPRTIONS LLC
521 Ed Tillery Ave (73644-2925)
PHONE.....................580 243-3424
Bob Davis, *Principal*
EMP: 2 **Privately Held**
SIC: **1389** Servicing oil & gas wells
PA: Baker Hughes Oilfield Operations Llc
2001 Rankin Rd
Houston TX 77073

(G-2786)
BECKS FORKLIFT SVC LLC
100 Ranch Rd (73644-9703)
P.O. Box 2069 (73648-2069)
PHONE.....................580 303-8038
Alan Beck, *Owner*
EMP: 2
SALES (est): 202K **Privately Held**
SIC: **3537** Forklift trucks

(G-2787)
BOBBY JOE CUDD COMPANY
S Highway 6 (73644)
P.O. Box 150, Fargo (73840-0150)
PHONE.....................580 515-3131
Bobby Joe Cudd, *Owner*
EMP: 1 EST: 1999
SALES (est): 98.9K **Privately Held**
SIC: **1389** Oil field services

(G-2788)
BURCH PRINTING CO
219 W Broadway Ave (73644-4741)
P.O. Box 906 (73648-0906)
PHONE.....................580 225-3270
Dean Burch, *Owner*
EMP: 3
SALES (est): 88K **Privately Held**
SIC: **2759** 2791 2789 2752 Commercial printing; typesetting; bookbinding & related work; commercial printing, lithographic

(G-2789)
BURNAM WELDING
610 S Van Buren Ave (73644-6722)
PHONE.....................580 821-0311
Jaymee Burnam, *Principal*
EMP: 1
SALES (est): 33.6K **Privately Held**
SIC: **7692** Welding repair

(G-2790)
C D ADKERSON CONSULTANT INC
2060 W 7th Pl (73644-5909)
P.O. Box 2036 (73648-2036)
PHONE.....................580 225-7860
C D Adkerson, *President*
EMP: 2
SALES (est): 162.7K **Privately Held**
SIC: **1389** Oil consultants

(G-2791)
CAMERON SOLUTIONS INC
Also Called: Natco
106 Robinson Pl (73644-1929)
P.O. Box 804 (73648-0804)
PHONE.....................580 821-0494
Brent Layman, *Branch Mgr*
EMP: 2 **Publicly Held**
SIC: **1389** Oil field services
HQ: Cameron Solutions Inc.
11210 Equity Dr Ste 100
Houston TX 77041
713 849-7500

(G-2792)
CANYON OILFIELD SERVICES LLC (PA)
11552 Highway 6 (73644-9722)
PHONE.....................580 225-7100
Michael Sloan, *President*
Roger Sloan, *Vice Pres*
Meggan Church, *Human Resources*
EMP: 37
SALES (est): 29.3MM **Privately Held**
SIC: **1389** Oil field services

(G-2793)
CASWELL CONSTRUCTION CO INC (PA)
113 Panel Rd (73644-9285)
P.O. Box 1886 (73648-1886)
PHONE.....................580 225-6833
Wayne Caswell, *President*
EMP: 66 EST: 1977
SQ FT: 3,750
SALES (est): 11.4MM **Privately Held**
SIC: **1623** 2951 3273 Underground utilities contractor; asphalt & asphaltic paving mixtures (not from refineries); ready-mixed concrete

(G-2794)
CHESAPEAKE ENERGY CORPORATION
501 S Eastern Ave (73644-9714)
PHONE.....................877 245-1427
Danny Rutledge, *Branch Mgr*
EMP: 50 **Publicly Held**
SIC: **1311** 1382 Crude petroleum production; oil & gas exploration services
PA: Chesapeake Energy Corporation
6100 N Western Ave
Oklahoma City OK 73118

(G-2795)
CONOCOPHILLIPS COMPANY
909 S Main St (73644-6707)
P.O. Box 987 (73648-0987)
PHONE.....................580 243-6000
Rod Weatherby, *Principal*
EMP: 18
SALES (corp-wide): 36.6B **Publicly Held**
WEB: www.conocophillips.com
SIC: **5541** 1311 Filling stations, gasoline; crude petroleum & natural gas
HQ: Conocophillips Company
925 N Eldridge Pkwy
Houston TX 77079
281 293-1000

(G-2796)
CRESCENT SERVICES LLC
200 Hughes Access Rd (73644-9146)
PHONE.....................580 225-4346
Scott Wharry, *Manager*
EMP: 85
SALES (corp-wide): 997.8MM **Privately Held**
SIC: **1389** Pipe testing, oil field service
PA: Crescent Services, L.L.C.
5721 Nw 132nd St
Oklahoma City OK 73142
405 603-1200

(G-2797)
CUDD PRESSURE CONTROL INC
6001 Oklahoma 6 (73644)
PHONE.....................580 243-5890
Keith Hulen, *Manager*
Bodie Goodspeed, *Manager*
EMP: 30
SALES (corp-wide): 1.2B **Publicly Held**
WEB: www.cuddenergyservices.com
SIC: **1389** Oil field services
HQ: Cudd Pressure Control, Inc.
2828 Tech Forest Blvd
The Woodlands TX 77381
832 295-5555

(G-2798)
CUDD PRESSURE CONTROL INC
900 S Merritt Rd (73644-2472)
P.O. Box 1801 (73648-1801)
PHONE.....................580 225-6922
Torrance Cowherd, *Parts Mgr*
Nelson Britton, *Manager*
EMP: 45
SALES (corp-wide): 1.2B **Publicly Held**
WEB: www.cuddenergyservices.com
SIC: **1389** 1382 Oil field services; oil & gas exploration services
HQ: Cudd Pressure Control, Inc.
2828 Tech Forest Blvd
The Woodlands TX 77381
832 295-5555

(G-2799)
CUSTOM CARBIDE APPLICATION LLC
19848 E 1160 Rd (73644-2314)
PHONE.....................580 799-5575
Finley James, *Administration*
EMP: 3
SALES (est): 199.7K **Privately Held**
SIC: **2819** Carbides

(G-2800)
DAVIS PRINTING COMPANY INC
217 S Jefferson Ave (73644-5737)
P.O. Box 867 (73648-0867)
PHONE.....................580 225-2902
Karsen Davis, *Vice Pres*
K Karsen Davis, *Vice Pres*
Kevin Davis, *Vice Pres*
Kenneth A Davis, *Admin Sec*
EMP: 5 EST: 1980
SQ FT: 3,000
SALES (est): 430K **Privately Held**
WEB: www.davisprintingco-ok.com
SIC: **2752** 2759 2791 2789 Commercial printing, offset; letterpress printing; typesetting; bookbinding & related work

(G-2801)
DAVIS SIGN CO
11112 N 1967 Rd (73644-6005)
PHONE.....................580 225-3121
Nancy Davis, *Partner*
Gary Davis, *Partner*
EMP: 3
SALES (est): 154.7K **Privately Held**
SIC: **3993** Signs & advertising specialties

(G-2802)
DBK CONTRACT PUMPING
20208 E 1070 Rd (73644-9401)
PHONE.....................580 225-2009
Kelly Gardner, *Partner*
EMP: 2
SALES (est): 136.3K **Privately Held**
SIC: **1389** Pumping of oil & gas wells

(G-2803)
DOLESE BROS CO
1201 S Pioneer Rd (73644-9286)
P.O. Box 390 (73648-0390)
PHONE.....................580 225-1247
James Irwin, *Manager*
EMP: 10
SALES (corp-wide): 8.5MM **Privately Held**
SIC: **3272** 3273 Concrete products; ready-mixed concrete
PA: Dolese Bros. Co.
20 Nw 13th St
Oklahoma City OK 73103
405 235-2311

(G-2804)
DR PEPPER BOTTLING CO ELK CITY
322 S Jefferson Ave (73644-5740)
PHONE.....................580 225-3186
James Schimdt, *General Mgr*
EMP: 14 EST: 1955
SQ FT: 12,000
SALES (est): 2.3MM **Privately Held**
WEB: www.drpepper.com
SIC: **2086** Soft drinks: packaged in cans, bottles, etc.

(G-2805)
DRILLING FLUIDS TECHNOLOGY
Also Called: DRILLING FLUIDS TECHNOLOGY INC
106 Panel Rd (73644-9285)
PHONE.....................580 225-1009
EMP: 3 **Privately Held**
WEB: www.dftonline.com

SIC: **8731** 1389 Biological research; construction, repair & dismantling services
PA: Drilling Fluids Technology, Inc.
202 S Main St
Booker TX 79005

(G-2806)
DYNA-TURN OF OKLAHOMA INC
116 Meadow Ridge Dr (73644-9732)
PHONE.....................580 243-1291
Douglas Schones, *President*
EMP: 14
SQ FT: 20,000
SALES (est): 2MM **Privately Held**
SIC: **3599** Machine shop, jobbing & repair

(G-2807)
ELK CITIAN
120 S Main St (73644-5744)
PHONE.....................580 799-0925
Derek Manning, *Principal*
EMP: 2
SALES (est): 133.2K **Privately Held**
SIC: **2711** Commercial printing & newspaper publishing combined

(G-2808)
ELK CITY DAILY NEWS INC
109 W Broadway Ave (73644-4739)
P.O. Box 1009 (73648-1009)
PHONE.....................580 225-3000
Larry R Wade, *President*
Mary Jane Wade, *Treasurer*
EMP: 19
SALES (est): 1.1MM **Privately Held**
WEB: www.ecdailynews.com
SIC: **2711** Commercial printing & newspaper publishing combined; newspapers, publishing & printing

(G-2809)
ELK CITY FORKLIFT SERVICE INC
19482 E 1140 Rd (73644-2306)
P.O. Box 631 (73648-0631)
PHONE.....................580 225-0855
Glen P Gifford, *President*
Dana Gifford, *Vice Pres*
EMP: 1 EST: 1976
SALES (est): 170.7K **Privately Held**
SIC: **1389** Oil field services

(G-2810)
ELK CITY SHEET METAL INC
Also Called: Elk City Sheet Metal Works
217 N Main St (73644-4753)
PHONE.....................580 225-5844
Johnny Ashley, *President*
Barbara Ashley, *Corp Secy*
EMP: 2
SQ FT: 2,500
SALES (est): 120K **Privately Held**
SIC: **1761** 7699 3444 Sheet metalwork; awning repair shop; sheet metalwork

(G-2811)
ENABLE MIDSTREAM PARTNERS LP
1316 Airport Indus Rd (73644-1923)
PHONE.....................580 225-7190
John Akingbola, *Engineer*
EMP: 5
SALES (corp-wide): 12.3B **Publicly Held**
SIC: **1311** Crude petroleum & natural gas
HQ: Enable Midstream Partners, Lp
211 N Robinson Ave # 150
Oklahoma City OK 73102

(G-2812)
ENERGES
610 S Van Buren Ave (73644-6722)
PHONE.....................580 339-8044
EMP: 2
SALES (est): 73.6K **Privately Held**
SIC: **1389** Oil field services

(G-2813)
EOG RESOURCES INC
105 Stout Dr (73644-1922)
P.O. Box 1669 (73648-1669)
PHONE.....................580 225-8314
Curby Boone, *Principal*
EMP: 11
SALES (corp-wide): 17.3B **Publicly Held**
SIC: **1382** Oil & gas exploration services

GEOGRAPHIC SECTION — Elk City - Beckham County (G-2845)

PA: Eog Resources, Inc.
1111 Bagby Sky Lbby 2
Houston TX 77002
713 651-7000

(G-2814)
FAIRMOUNT MINERALS
910 S Eastern Ave (73644-9718)
PHONE..................580 303-9160
EMP: 3
SALES (est): 156.2K **Privately Held**
SIC: 1446 Industrial sand

(G-2815)
FOURPOINT ENERGY LLC
501 S Eastern Ave (73644-9714)
PHONE..................580 225-8556
Bryce Kvasnicka, *Engineer*
Danny Rutledge, *Mng Member*
Jackie Carnes, *Consultant*
Dylan Dirickson, *Technician*
Roy Huerta, *Technician*
EMP: 2
SALES (est): 175.6K **Privately Held**
WEB: www.fourpointenergy.com
SIC: 1382 Oil & gas exploration services

(G-2816)
G & G STEAM SERVICE INC (PA)
Also Called: Galmor's
120 W 12th St (73644-6745)
P.O. Box 2199 (73648-2199)
PHONE..................580 225-4254
Steve Galmor, *President*
Jeff Klick, *CFO*
EMP: 185
SQ FT: 2,400
SALES (est): 30.6MM **Privately Held**
SIC: 1389 Servicing oil & gas wells; excavating slush pits & cellars

(G-2817)
GALMORS INC
120 W 12th St (73644-6745)
P.O. Box 2199 (73648-2199)
PHONE..................580 225-4254
Steve Galmor, *Principal*
EMP: 9
SALES (est): 2MM **Privately Held**
SIC: 1389 Servicing oil & gas wells

(G-2818)
GARDNERS GUNS & MFG LLC
1901 E 20th St (73644-7113)
P.O. Box 391 (73648-0391)
PHONE..................580 225-8884
Kelly Gardner, *Principal*
EMP: 1
SALES (est): 78.8K **Privately Held**
SIC: 3999 Atomizers, toiletry

(G-2819)
GBG EARTHMOVERS LLC
19338 Highway 6 (73644-2375)
P.O. Box 249 (73648-0249)
PHONE..................580 243-5662
Bobby Drinnon, *President*
EMP: 8
SALES (est): 210.3K **Privately Held**
SIC: 1389 1794 Construction, repair & dismantling services; excavation work

(G-2820)
GENES CUSTOMIZED TAGS & EMB
122 S Main St (73644-5744)
PHONE..................580 225-8247
Brenda Pittser, *Partner*
Gene Pittser, *Partner*
EMP: 2
SALES (est): 204.9K **Privately Held**
SIC: 3714 3429 2395 Motor vehicle parts & accessories; manufactured hardware (general); pleating & stitching

(G-2821)
GIVENS WRECKER SERVICE
1212 W 5th St (73644-5410)
PHONE..................580 225-0892
Ronny Givens, *Owner*
EMP: 2
SALES (est): 144.4K **Privately Held**
SIC: 3713 Automobile wrecker truck bodies

(G-2822)
HIGH PLAINS SERVICES INC
2615 W 20th St (73644-9257)
P.O. Box 1865 (73648-1865)
PHONE..................580 225-7388
L C Price, *President*
Christi Price, *Vice Pres*
Janice Mitchell, *Admin Sec*
EMP: 65 EST: 1978
SQ FT: 5,000
SALES (est): 10.4MM **Privately Held**
SIC: 7353 1389 Oil field equipment, rental or leasing; oil field services

(G-2823)
HMH PUBLISHING
161 Fairway Dr (73644-9791)
PHONE..................405 788-5589
EMP: 1
SALES (est): 37.5K **Privately Held**
SIC: 2741 Miscellaneous publishing

(G-2824)
HOSKINS WIRELINE LLC
1320 Airport Indus Rd (73644-1923)
P.O. Box 454 (73648-0454)
PHONE..................580 303-9101
Earl Hoskins,
Eugenia Hoskins,
EMP: 14
SALES (est): 2MM **Privately Held**
SIC: 1389 Oil field services

(G-2825)
HUTTON INC
19676 Route 66 N (73644-5000)
P.O. Box 1976 (73648-1976)
PHONE..................580 225-0225
Doug Hutton, *President*
Sharon Hutton, *Treasurer*
EMP: 18
SQ FT: 6,000
SALES: 8.5MM **Privately Held**
SIC: 1389 Oil field services

(G-2826)
INDUSTRIAL SPECIALTIES LLC
315 W 20th St (73644-6815)
PHONE..................580 303-9170
Butch Hodge, *Sales Mgr*
Eric Shepard, *Branch Mgr*
EMP: 1
SALES (corp-wide): 12.2MM **Privately Held**
SIC: 3533 Oil field machinery & equipment
PA: Industrial Specialties, Llc
3500 S Macarthur Blvd
Oklahoma City OK 73179
405 672-1221

(G-2827)
INNOVATIVE TECHNOLOGY LTD
105 Carter Rd (73644-9700)
P.O. Box 726 (73648-0726)
PHONE..................580 243-1559
R R Sorelle Jr, *President*
Bob Counts, *Principal*
James Chopping, *Vice Pres*
Robert Sorelle, *CFO*
EMP: 15
SQ FT: 8,000
SALES: 1.5MM **Privately Held**
WEB: www.itlpros.com
SIC: 5045 5734 8711 3571 Computers; computer & software stores; engineering services; electronic computers

(G-2828)
INTEGRATED PRODUCTION SERVICES
Also Called: Ips
1602 Enterprise Rd (73644-9765)
PHONE..................580 225-5667
Al Blackedge, *Manager*
EMP: 6
SALES (est): 644.1K **Privately Held**
SIC: 1389 Oil field services

(G-2829)
IRON GATE TUBULAR SERVICES
11118 N 1967 Rd (73644-6005)
PHONE..................580 303-9046
EMP: 2

SALES (est): 123.5K **Privately Held**
SIC: 1389 Oil field services

(G-2830)
JANET D REDD
202 Ramsey Dr. (73644-4932)
PHONE..................580 243-0595
Janet Redd, *Owner*
EMP: 1
SALES (est): 41.1K **Privately Held**
SIC: 2741 Miscellaneous publishing

(G-2831)
JANNING WELDING AND SUPPLY LLC
918 N Van Buren Ave (73644-2916)
PHONE..................580 225-6554
Matt Janning, *Sales Mgr*
Carol Ann Janning,
Mike Janning,
EMP: 13
SALES (est): 2.6MM **Privately Held**
SIC: 7692 Welding repair

(G-2832)
JESSE GRIFFITH REPAIRS ✪
101 E 20th St (73644-6901)
PHONE..................580 379-0790
EMP: 2 EST: 2019
SALES (est): 88.3K **Privately Held**
SIC: 3694 Engine electrical equipment

(G-2833)
JIMMY FUCHS
1019 S Main St (73644-6909)
PHONE..................580 225-7784
Jimmy Fuchs, *Principal*
EMP: 3
SALES (est): 245.3K **Privately Held**
SIC: 2836 Veterinary biological products

(G-2834)
JOSHUA JAMES LENNOX
710 E 7th St (73644-7205)
PHONE..................580 739-1050
EMP: 2
SALES (est): 79.9K **Privately Held**
SIC: 3585 Refrigeration & heating equipment

(G-2835)
KEY ENERGY SERVICES INC
3611 W 3rd St (73644-4503)
PHONE..................806 323-8361
Norman Anderson, *General Mgr*
EMP: 30
SALES (corp-wide): 413.8MM **Publicly Held**
SIC: 1389 Servicing oil & gas wells
PA: Key Energy Services, Inc.
1301 Mckinney St Ste 1800
Houston TX 77010
713 651-4300

(G-2836)
LANES WELDING LLC
1902 Bell Ave (73644-2226)
PHONE..................580 302-1279
EMP: 2
SALES (est): 79K **Privately Held**
SIC: 7692 Welding repair

(G-2837)
LEGEND ENERGY SERVICES LLC
2115 W 20th St (73644-9251)
PHONE..................580 225-4500
Rodney Rogers, *Branch Mgr*
EMP: 20
SALES (corp-wide): 150MM **Privately Held**
WEB: www.legendenergyservices.com
SIC: 1389 Cementing oil & gas well casings
PA: Legend Energy Services, Llc
5801 Broadway Ext Ste 210
Oklahoma City OK 73118
405 600-1204

(G-2838)
LIBERTY TRANSPORTATION LLC
Also Called: Whitson Services
522 N Van Buren Ave (73644-4261)
PHONE..................580 225-2784

Shannon Whitson, *Mng Member*
EMP: 1
SALES (est): 274.9K **Privately Held**
SIC: 1389 Oil field services

(G-2839)
LINLEY WELDING LLC
1216 Crestview Dr (73644-2817)
PHONE..................405 420-5968
Joshua Linley, *Owner*
EMP: 1
SALES (est): 45K **Privately Held**
SIC: 7692 Welding repair

(G-2840)
LUBRI FLANGE LLC
3511 S Highway 6 (73644-9785)
P.O. Box 781 (73648-0781)
PHONE..................580 303-9139
Bradley Britton, *Principal*
EMP: 8
SALES (est): 639.5K **Privately Held**
SIC: 1389 Oil field services

(G-2841)
LUCAS OIL & GAS SERVICE INC
Also Called: Measurement Control Specialist
1303 S Main St (73644-6912)
PHONE..................580 225-3006
Gary Lucas, *President*
Joe Allen, *VP Sales*
Sondra Allen, *Manager*
Tamera Lucas, *Admin Sec*
EMP: 8
SQ FT: 11,000
SALES (est): 1MM **Privately Held**
SIC: 1389 Servicing oil & gas wells

(G-2842)
M-1 MACHINE LLC
3833 W 3rd St (73644-4511)
P.O. Box 2176 (73648-2176)
PHONE..................580 225-6826
Aaron Long, *CEO*
Jamie Long, *CFO*
EMP: 4
SQ FT: 11,000
SALES (est): 403.7K **Privately Held**
SIC: 3599 Machine shop, jobbing & repair

(G-2843)
M-I LLC
100 S Monroe St Ste 9 (73644-5761)
P.O. Box 722 (73648-0722)
PHONE..................580 225-0104
EMP: 47 **Privately Held**
SIC: 3533 Mfg Oil/Gas Field Machinery
HQ: M-I L.L.C.
5950 N Course Dr
Houston TX 77072
281 561-1300

(G-2844)
M-I LLC
Also Called: M I Swaco
524 S Woodward St (73644-7201)
PHONE..................580 225-2482
Israel Mendoza, *Branch Mgr*
EMP: 8 **Publicly Held**
SIC: 1389 Oil field services
HQ: M-I L.L.C.
5950 N Course Dr
Houston TX 77072
281 561-1300

(G-2845)
MARKWEST ENERGY PARTNERS LP
905 S Eastern Ave (73644-9718)
PHONE..................580 225-5400
Frank M Semple, *Branch Mgr*
EMP: 7
SALES (corp-wide): 9B **Publicly Held**
WEB: www.markwest.com
SIC: 1311 Crude petroleum & natural gas
HQ: Markwest Energy Partners, L.P.
1515 Arapahoe St
Denver CO 80202
303 925-9200

Elk City - Beckham County (G-2846)

(G-2846)
MARKWEST OKLAHOMA GAS CO LLC
Also Called: Mark West
905 S Eastern Ave (73644-9718)
PHONE.................................580 225-5400
Jason Palmer, *Manager*
EMP: 50
SALES (corp-wide): 9B **Publicly Held**
SIC: **1382** 1311 Oil & gas exploration services; crude petroleum & natural gas
HQ: Markwest Oklahoma Gas Co Llc
1515 Arapahoe St Ste 1600
Denver CO 80202
303 925-9200

(G-2847)
MARTIN-DECKER TOTCO INC
Also Called: M/D Totco
990 S Merritt Rd (73644)
PHONE.................................580 225-8980
Billy Canon, *Store Mgr*
Armando O'Choa, *Manager*
Terri Pruitt, *Admin Asst*
EMP: 6
SALES (corp-wide): 8.4B **Publicly Held**
SIC: **1389** Oil field services
HQ: Martin-Decker Totco, Inc.
1200 Cypress Creek Rd
Cedar Park TX 78613

(G-2848)
MARTINEZ METAL BUILDINGS
3605 W Country Club Blvd (73644-4458)
PHONE.................................580 821-2780
Lucio Martinez, *Owner*
EMP: 4
SALES (est): 214.1K **Privately Held**
SIC: **3448** 1542 Buildings, portable: prefabricated metal; nonresidential construction

(G-2849)
MLB CONSULTING LLC (PA)
213 N Jefferson Ave (73644-4747)
PHONE.................................580 225-2717
Stacy Smith, *Production*
Mitchel Brown, *Mng Member*
Jim Barrow, *Consultant*
EMP: 6 EST: 2010
SALES (est): 6.4MM **Privately Held**
WEB: www.mlbconsultingusa.com
SIC: **1389** Oil consultants

(G-2850)
MORAN EQUIPMENT LLC
305 Industrial Pkwy (73644-1927)
P.O. Box 2232 (73648-2232)
PHONE.................................580 225-2575
Joshua Moran,
EMP: 23
SQ FT: 16,500
SALES: 12.3MM **Privately Held**
SIC: **1389** Oil field services

(G-2851)
MUD MIXERS LLC
201 W Broadway Ave # 203 (73644-4737)
PHONE.................................580 243-7826
Donald Sparks, *Principal*
EMP: 13
SALES (est): 1.5MM **Privately Held**
SIC: **1389** Cementing oil & gas well casings

(G-2852)
MUNOZ OILFIELD SERVICES LLC
103 Mary Dr (73644-1211)
PHONE.................................580 799-5857
John Anthony Munoz, *Principal*
EMP: 2
SALES (est): 94.1K **Privately Held**
SIC: **1389** Oil field services

(G-2853)
NABORS DRILLING TECH USA INC
100 Panel Rd (73644-9285)
PHONE.................................580 243-4000
Brian Merz, *Branch Mgr*
EMP: 111 **Privately Held**
WEB: www.nabors.com
SIC: **1389** Oil field services
HQ: Nabors Drilling Technologies Usa, Inc.
515 W Greens Rd Ste 1200
Houston TX 77067
281 874-0035

(G-2854)
NABORS DRILLING USA LP
1501 S Merritt Rd (73644-6882)
PHONE.................................580 225-0072
Fax: 580 225-0139
EMP: 4 **Privately Held**
SIC: **1381** Oil/Gas Well Drilling
HQ: Nabors Drilling Usa, Lp
515 W Greens Rd Ste 1200
Houston TX 77067
281 874-0035

(G-2855)
NATIONAL OILWELL VARCO INC
S Hwy 6 (73648)
PHONE.................................580 225-4136
Ron Morrow, *Principal*
EMP: 20
SALES (corp-wide): 8.4B **Publicly Held**
SIC: **1389** 1382 Oil field services; oil & gas exploration services
PA: National Oilwell Varco, Inc.
7909 Parkwood Circle Dr
Houston TX 77036
713 346-7500

(G-2856)
NEWMAN PRECISION
119 Rainbow Dr (73644-1623)
PHONE.................................580 339-0097
EMP: 2
SALES (est): 205.5K **Privately Held**
SIC: **3484** Rifles or rifle parts, 30 mm. & below

(G-2857)
OVINTIV EXPLORATION INC
2001 E 20th St (73644-7103)
PHONE.................................580 243-4101
Ken Edwards, *Manager*
EMP: 3
SALES (corp-wide): 8.5MM **Publicly Held**
SIC: **1479** Mineral pigment mining
HQ: Ovintiv Exploration Inc.
4 Waterway Square Pl # 100
The Woodlands TX 77380
281 210-5100

(G-2858)
OVINTIV MID-CONTINENT INC
106 Panel Rd (73644-9285)
P.O. Box 843 (73648-0843)
PHONE.................................580 243-4101
Ken Edwards, *Manager*
EMP: 30
SALES (corp-wide): 8.5MM **Publicly Held**
SIC: **1382** Oil & gas exploration services
HQ: Ovintiv Mid-Continent Inc,
101 E 2nd St
Tulsa OK 74103
918 582-2690

(G-2859)
PIONEER OILFIELD SERVICES INC
Also Called: Pioneer Services
2020 N Randall Ave (73644-1437)
PHONE.................................580 243-4000
Brian Merz, *President*
Janet Merz, *Vice Pres*
Butch Black, *Manager*
EMP: 20
SALES (est): 1.6MM **Privately Held**
SIC: **7353** 0131 1389 0111 Oil field equipment, rental or leasing; cotton; roustabout service; wheat

(G-2860)
POLAR INSULATED SHEDS OKLAH
112 Meadow Ridge Dr (73644-9732)
PHONE.................................580 799-2265
Michael Rogers, *President*
EMP: 4
SALES (est): 413.1K **Privately Held**
WEB: www.polarsheds.com
SIC: **3448** Buildings, portable: prefabricated metal

(G-2861)
POWELL SERVICES INC
Rr 2 Box 305 (73644-9802)
P.O. Box 6 (73648-0006)
PHONE.................................580 225-9017
Andy Blankenship, *President*
Steve Powell, *Vice Pres*
EMP: 9
SALES (est): 732K **Privately Held**
SIC: **1389** Roustabout service

(G-2862)
PRO FAB WELDING INC
11740 N 1970 Rd (73644-2339)
PHONE.................................405 470-8776
Leslie Dykes, *Owner*
EMP: 1 EST: 2013
SALES (est): 81.2K **Privately Held**
WEB: www.pro-fab-balebeds.com
SIC: **7692** Welding repair

(G-2863)
QES PRESSURE CONTROL LLC
2003 S Merritt Rd (73644-7603)
PHONE.................................580 243-6622
EMP: 90
SALES (corp-wide): 1.1B **Privately Held**
SIC: **1381** Drilling oil & gas wells
HQ: Qes Pressure Control Llc
4500 Se 59th St
Oklahoma City OK 73135

(G-2864)
R G ENTERPRISES
806 S Randall Ave (73644-6200)
PHONE.................................580 225-2260
Rick Pitman, *Principal*
EMP: 3
SALES (est): 132.5K **Privately Held**
SIC: **5999** 5947 5099 3993 Decals; gift, novelty & souvenir shop; signs, except electric; signs & advertising specialties

(G-2865)
RED BONE SERVICES LLC (HQ)
1700 Enterprise Rd (73644)
P.O. Box 887 (73648-0887)
PHONE.................................580 225-1200
Wes Marshal,
▲ EMP: 11
SQ FT: 10,000
SALES: 4.6MM
SALES (corp-wide): 544MM **Publicly Held**
SIC: **1389** Oil field services
PA: Klx Energy Services Holdings, Inc.
1300 Corporate Center Way
Wellington FL 33414
561 383-5100

(G-2866)
REDDIRT OILFIELD SERVICES
703 S Oliver Ave (73644-6654)
PHONE.................................580 665-9321
EMP: 2
SALES (est): 123.1K **Privately Held**
SIC: **1389** Oil field services

(G-2867)
REDIBUILT METAL PDTS & CNSTR
3830 W Highway 66 (73644-9237)
PHONE.................................580 225-2829
Neil Callahan, *Owner*
EMP: 1
SALES (est): 149.1K **Privately Held**
SIC: **1791** 3448 Structural steel erection; prefabricated metal buildings

(G-2868)
ROGER W BOONE
Also Called: Boone's Backhoe Services
11076 N 1960 Rd (73644-2613)
PHONE.................................580 799-0035
Roger W Boone, *Principal*
EMP: 4
SALES (est): 409K **Privately Held**
SIC: **3531** Backhoes

(G-2869)
ROLLING THUNDER OILFIELD
918 N Van Buren Ave (73644-2916)
PHONE.................................580 303-4587
Thomas Geoffrey, *Principal*
EMP: 2 EST: 2013
SALES (est): 354.8K **Privately Held**
SIC: **1389** Haulage, oil field

(G-2870)
ROVILL BIODIESEL SOLUTION LLC
220 Ridgecrest Dr Apt 80 (73644-9106)
PHONE.................................580 339-6815
Ronan D Villanueva, *President*
EMP: 5
SALES (est): 263.5K **Privately Held**
SIC: **2869** Fuels

(G-2871)
RPC INC
723 S Merritt Rd (73644-2470)
PHONE.................................580 225-0843
Dennis Shannon, *Manager*
EMP: 20
SALES (corp-wide): 1.2B **Publicly Held**
WEB: www.rpc.net
SIC: **1389** Oil field services
PA: Rpc, Inc.
2801 Buford Hwy Ne # 520
Brookhaven GA 30329
404 321-2140

(G-2872)
SAMSON RESOURCES COMPANY
320 Industrial Pkwy (73644-1927)
P.O. Box 310 (73648-0310)
PHONE.................................580 225-4272
Jim Gebhart, *Superintendent*
EMP: 25
SALES (corp-wide): 1.4B **Privately Held**
SIC: **1382** Oil & gas exploration services
HQ: Samson Resources Company
2 W 2nd St Ste 1500
Tulsa OK 74103
918 583-1791

(G-2873)
SMART OILFIELD SOLUTIONS LLC
11580 Highway 6 (73644)
PHONE.................................580 243-9571
EMP: 2
SALES (est): 81.9K **Privately Held**
SIC: **1382** Oil & gas exploration services

(G-2874)
SOLAR POWER & PUMP COMPANY LLC
Also Called: Sunrotor Solar Products
301 W 12th St (73644-6740)
PHONE.................................580 225-1704
Chris Culwell, *Sales Staff*
Nathan Smith, *Marketing Mgr*
Dennis W Austin, *Mng Member*
▲ EMP: 10
SQ FT: 10,125
SALES (est): 1.6MM **Privately Held**
SIC: **5084** 1623 4941 3561 Pumps & pumping equipment; pumping station construction; water supply; pumps & pumping equipment

(G-2875)
SPM FLOW CONTROL INC
1600 S Merritt Rd (73644-7601)
PHONE.................................580 225-1186
EMP: 138
SALES (corp-wide): 3.4B **Privately Held**
WEB: www.weir.co.uk
SIC: **3533** Oil & gas field machinery
HQ: S.P.M. Flow Control, Inc.
7601 Wyatt Dr
Fort Worth TX 76108
817 246-2461

(G-2876)
STALLION OILFIELD SERVICES LTD
319 Industrial Pkwy (73644-1927)
P.O. Box 10 (73648-0010)
PHONE.................................580 225-5800
Carl Farni, *Manager*
EMP: 40 **Privately Held**
SIC: **1389** Oil field services
HQ: Stallion Oilfield Services Ltd.
950 Corbindale Rd Ste 400
Houston TX 77024
713 528-5544

(G-2877)
STALLION OILFIELD SERVICES LTD
108 Oilfield Rd (73644-9289)
PHONE....................580 225-8990
Marian Miller, *General Mgr*
EMP: 40 **Privately Held**
SIC: 1389 Oil field services
HQ: Stallion Oilfield Services Ltd.
950 Corbindale Rd Ste 400
Houston TX 77024
713 528-5544

(G-2878)
STOUTS WELDING LLC
713 N Van Buren Ave (73644-3427)
PHONE....................580 339-8047
EMP: 1
SALES (est): 25K **Privately Held**
SIC: 7692 Welding repair

(G-2879)
SUB INDUSTRIES LLC
118 Mitchell Dr (73644-4812)
PHONE....................918 798-9712
Jesse Anne Dirickson, *Owner*
EMP: 1
SALES (est): 44.7K **Privately Held**
SIC: 3999 Manufacturing industries

(G-2880)
SUPER HEATERS LLC
1701 E 20th St (73644-7138)
P.O. Box 421328, Houston TX (77242-1328)
PHONE....................580 225-3196
Justin Hefley, *President*
Mark Hefley,
EMP: 10
SQ FT: 11,000
SALES (est): 3MM **Privately Held**
SIC: 1389 Oil field services
HQ: Metal Services Llc
148 W State St Ste 301
Kennett Square PA 19348

(G-2881)
TESTERS INC
Also Called: Haley Specialty Tools
100 Robinson Pl (73644-1929)
P.O. Box 83437, Oklahoma City (73148-1437)
PHONE....................580 243-0148
Charlie Haley, *Owner*
EMP: 2
SALES (corp-wide): 9.2MM **Privately Held**
WEB: www.haileytools.com
SIC: 1389 1382 Testing, measuring, surveying & analysis services; oil & gas exploration services
PA: Testers, Inc.
1661 Exchange Ave
Oklahoma City OK 73108
405 235-9911

(G-2882)
THRU TUBING SOLUTIONS INC
1501 E 20th St (73644-6903)
PHONE....................580 225-6977
Andy Ferguson, *Principal*
EMP: 15
SALES (corp-wide): 1.2B **Publicly Held**
SIC: 1389 Oil field services
HQ: Thru Tubing Solutions, Inc.
11515 S Portland Ave
Oklahoma City OK 73170
405 692-1900

(G-2883)
TLR WELL SERVICES INC
Hwy 6 & Lakeview Rd (73644)
P.O. Box 703 (73648-0703)
PHONE....................580 225-4096
Larry Odom, *President*
Sandi Odom, *Vice Pres*
EMP: 50
SQ FT: 12,000
SALES (est): 8.7MM **Privately Held**
SIC: 1389 Oil field services

(G-2884)
TOMS HOT SHOT SERVICE
Rr 4 Box 204a (73644-9804)
P.O. Box 1496 (73648-1496)
PHONE....................580 243-4300
Tom Suter, *President*
Debbie Suter, *Vice Pres*
EMP: 10
SALES (est): 657.9K **Privately Held**
SIC: 1389 Oil field services

(G-2885)
TRIGUARD OF OKLAHOMA
1701 E 20th St (73644-7138)
PHONE....................580 243-8015
Brad Whinery, *Owner*
EMP: 2
SALES (est): 91.3K **Privately Held**
SIC: 3272 Concrete products

(G-2886)
U S WEATHERFORD L P
Also Called: Weatherford Cementation
1505 S Main St (73644-6914)
PHONE....................580 225-8890
Durock Danner, *CEO*
EMP: 18 **Privately Held**
WEB: www.weatherford.com
SIC: 3533 Oil & gas field machinery
HQ: U S Weatherford L P
179 Weatherford Dr
Schriever LA 70395
985 493-6100

(G-2887)
VALOR ENERGY SERVICES LLC
120 W 12th St (73644-6745)
PHONE....................405 209-6081
EMP: 29
SALES (corp-wide): 10MM **Privately Held**
SIC: 1389 Servicing oil & gas wells
PA: Valor Energy Services, Llc
111 N Broadway Ste B
Edmond OK 73034
405 513-5043

(G-2888)
WEATHERFORD INTERNATIONAL LLC
Also Called: Weatherford Jar Repair
104 Harless (73644-9710)
P.O. Box 1616 (73648-1616)
PHONE....................580 225-1237
Ron Ayes, *Branch Mgr*
EMP: 13 **Privately Held**
WEB: www.weatherford.com
SIC: 1389 Oil field services
HQ: Weatherford International, Llc
2000 Saint James Pl
Houston TX 77056
713 693-4000

(G-2889)
WESTERN OKLA POWERTRAIN INC
19485 E 1130 Rd (73644-2298)
PHONE....................580 243-4501
Doug Mills, *President*
Angie Mills, *Admin Sec*
EMP: 3
SALES (est): 463.1K **Privately Held**
SIC: 3711 Motor vehicles & car bodies

(G-2890)
WESTERN SEAMLESS GUTTERING
2001 E Highway 66 (73644-1903)
PHONE....................580 225-7983
Donald Nichols, *Owner*
Criscilla Nichols, *Co-Owner*
EMP: 2
SALES (est): 50K **Privately Held**
SIC: 1761 3444 Gutter & downspout contractor; sheet metalwork

(G-2891)
YT WELDING LLC
19953 E 1070 Rd (73644-9373)
PHONE....................580 799-1984
Thomas W Berry, *Administration*
EMP: 1
SALES (est): 30.3K **Privately Held**
SIC: 7692 Welding repair

Elmer
Jackson County

(G-2892)
TCJ OILFIELD SERVICES LLC
237 Barr Ave (73539-1000)
PHONE....................580 687-4454
EMP: 2 **EST:** 2017
SALES (est): 81.7K **Privately Held**
SIC: 1389 Oil field services

Elmore City
Garvin County

(G-2893)
3L INDUSTRIES
104 S Missouri St (73433-9234)
P.O. Box 242 (73433-0242)
PHONE....................580 788-2122
Shalon McMillen, *Principal*
EMP: 2
SALES (est): 99.8K **Privately Held**
SIC: 3999 Manufacturing industries

(G-2894)
BIG IRON OILFIELD SERVICES
22650 Highway 29 (73433-8830)
P.O. Box 536 (73433-0536)
PHONE....................580 788-2247
Darrell Chapman, *Director*
EMP: 2
SALES (est): 7MM **Privately Held**
SIC: 3533 Oil field machinery & equipment

(G-2895)
DOOMSDAYTACTICALSOLUTIONS LLC ✪
27494 E County Road 1650 (73433-9499)
PHONE....................580 788-2412
EMP: 2 **EST:** 2019
SALES (est): 112.5K **Privately Held**
SIC: 3827 Optical instruments & lenses

(G-2896)
FORUM US INC
22568 Highway 29 (73433-8819)
PHONE....................580 788-2333
Brent Rennick, *Branch Mgr*
EMP: 75 **Publicly Held**
WEB: www.f-e-t.com
SIC: 3533 Oil field machinery & equipment
HQ: Forum Us, Inc.
10344 Sam Houston Park Dr
Houston TX 77064
713 351-7900

(G-2897)
STEVES CONSTRUCTION COMPANY
680 Pernell Pl (73433)
PHONE....................580 432-5398
Steve McConell, *Owner*
EMP: 4
SALES (est): 630.7K **Privately Held**
SIC: 1389 Oil field services

(G-2898)
TAPOIL INC
Hwy 2974 2 1/2 Miles N (73433)
P.O. Box 296 (73433-0296)
PHONE....................580 788-4576
Don Tapper, *President*
EMP: 1
SALES (est): 199.9K **Privately Held**
SIC: 1389 Servicing oil & gas wells

(G-2899)
WALTERS OIL
630 Pernell Pl (73433)
PHONE....................580 432-5294
Tim Johnson, *Owner*
EMP: 1
SALES (est): 90.7K **Privately Held**
SIC: 1389 Oil sampling service for oil companies

Enid
Garfield County

(G-2900)
A W BRUEGGEMANN COMPANY INC
412 N Independence St (73701-3116)
PHONE....................580 237-3857
Jennifer Branch, *President*
Stephanie Patterson, *Corp Secy*
Jeff Bruegemann, *Vice Pres*
EMP: 15
SQ FT: 7,500
SALES (est): 2.7MM **Privately Held**
WEB: www.awbrueggemann.com
SIC: 3599 Machine shop, jobbing & repair

(G-2901)
A W BUGERMAN COMPANY
Also Called: Branch"n Out
412 N Independence St (73701-3116)
PHONE....................580 237-3857
EMP: 3
SALES (est): 193.1K **Privately Held**
SIC: 3495 Mfg Wire Springs

(G-2902)
AARON CUSTOM CREATIONS
2700 N Van Buren St # 93 (73703-1714)
PHONE....................580 603-0467
Aaron Stewart, *Principal*
EMP: 2
SALES (est): 117.5K **Privately Held**
SIC: 2431 Millwork

(G-2903)
ABC SERVICES LLC
4805 E Chestnut Ave (73701-9425)
P.O. Box 3748 (73702-3748)
PHONE....................580 242-1015
Pete Dinsome, *Mng Member*
EMP: 1
SALES (est): 142K **Privately Held**
SIC: 1389 Oil field services

(G-2904)
ADM MILLING CO
1301 N 4th St (73701-2283)
P.O. Box 1388 (73702-1388)
PHONE....................580 237-8000
Kelvin Woods, *Manager*
EMP: 65
SALES (est): 1.5MM **Privately Held**
SIC: 2041 Flour & other grain mill products

(G-2905)
ADVANCE FOOD COMPANY INC (DH)
Also Called: Advancepierre Foods Holdings
221 W Oxford Ave (73701-1227)
PHONE....................800 969-2747
Greg Allen, *CEO*
Dan Lebrun, *Mfg Staff*
Wyatt Whittenburg, *Production*
Kim Brown, *Supervisor*
Lacie Taylor,
▲ **EMP:** 168
SALES (est): 123.1MM
SALES (corp-wide): 42.4B **Publicly Held**
SIC: 2013 2015 2099 Cooked meats from purchased meat; prepared beef products from purchased beef; prepared pork products from purchased pork; chicken, processed: cooked; chicken, processed: frozen; turkey, processed: cooked; turkey, processed: frozen; food preparations

(G-2906)
ADVANCE FOOD COMPANY INC
201 S Raleigh Rd (73701-7800)
PHONE....................580 237-6656
Janet Byrum, *Human Res Mgr*
EMP: 600
SALES (corp-wide): 42.4B **Publicly Held**
SIC: 2013 2015 Sausages & other prepared meats; poultry slaughtering & processing
HQ: Advance Food Company, Inc.
221 W Oxford Ave
Enid OK 73701
800 969-2747

Enid - Garfield County (G-2907)

(G-2907)
ADVANCEPIERRE FOODS INC
5110 Enterprise Blvd (73701-9711)
PHONE..................................800 969-2747
EMP: 14
SALES (est): 2MM Privately Held
SIC: 2099 Food preparations

(G-2908)
AIRCRAFT STRUCTURES INTL CORP
1026 S 66th St (73701-9660)
PHONE..................................580 242-5907
Mickey A Stowers, President
Sharen Preston, Officer
EMP: 25
SQ FT: 28,000
SALES (est): 3MM Privately Held
SIC: 4581 3728 Aircraft servicing & repairing; accumulators, aircraft propeller

(G-2909)
AJ PUBLISHERS LLC
117 N Washington St (73701-4019)
PHONE..................................580 234-0064
Art Reed, Principal
EMP: 2
SALES (est): 82K Privately Held
WEB: www.homeschoolwithsaxon.com
SIC: 2741 Miscellaneous publishing

(G-2910)
ARCHER-DANIELS-MIDLAND COMPANY
Also Called: ADM
1301 N 4th St (73701-2283)
P.O. Box 1388 (73702-1388)
PHONE..................................580 237-8000
Kelvin Woods, Branch Mgr
EMP: 65
SALES (corp-wide): 64.6B Publicly Held
WEB: www.adm.com
SIC: 2041 5149 Flour & other grain mill products; groceries & related products
PA: Archer-Daniels-Midland Company
77 W Wacker Dr Ste 4600
Chicago IL 60601
312 634-8100

(G-2911)
ARCHER-DANIELS-MIDLAND COMPANY
Also Called: ADM
2502 N 16th St (73701)
PHONE..................................580 233-3800
Cal Williams, Manager
EMP: 2
SALES (corp-wide): 64.6B Publicly Held
SIC: 2041 Flour & other grain mill products
PA: Archer-Daniels-Midland Company
77 W Wacker Dr Ste 4600
Chicago IL 60601
312 634-8100

(G-2912)
ARCHER-DANIELS-MIDLAND COMPANY
Also Called: ADM
2309 N 10th St Ste A (73701-8709)
PHONE..................................580 233-5100
Gary Sipe, Manager
EMP: 9
SALES (corp-wide): 64.6B Publicly Held
SIC: 2041 Flour & other grain mill products
PA: Archer-Daniels-Midland Company
77 W Wacker Dr Ste 4600
Chicago IL 60601
312 634-8100

(G-2913)
BANNER PIPELINE COMPANY LLC
302 N Independence St (73701-4097)
PHONE..................................580 233-8955
EMP: 3
SALES (est): 144.7K
SALES (corp-wide): 4.6B Publicly Held
SIC: 1311 Crude petroleum & natural gas
PA: Continental Resources, Inc.
20 N Broadway
Oklahoma City OK 73102
405 234-9000

(G-2914)
BARCLAY CONTRACT PUMPING
4030 S Highway 132 (73703-1094)
PHONE..................................580 541-7439
Jeannie Barclay, Principal
EMP: 2
SALES (est): 162.1K Privately Held
SIC: 1389 Pumping of oil & gas wells

(G-2915)
BB MACHINE & SUPPLY INC
Also Called: B B Machine & Supply
2317 N 11th St (73701-8720)
PHONE..................................580 237-8686
Bill Beebe, President
Carilyn Beebe, Corp Secy
Terry Beebe, Vice Pres
EMP: 8
SQ FT: 5,750
SALES (est): 1MM Privately Held
WEB: www.bbmachineok.com
SIC: 3599 5013 3568 Machine shop, jobbing & repair; motor vehicle supplies & new parts; automotive supplies & parts; power transmission equipment

(G-2916)
BETTER SIGN CO
1518 W Hudson Dr (73703-7925)
PHONE..................................580 242-9317
Lynn Jensen, Principal
EMP: 2
SALES (est): 143.1K Privately Held
SIC: 3993 Signs & advertising specialties

(G-2917)
BIG BUCKETS RATHOLE DRILLING
5915 Memorial Dr (73701)
P.O. Box 5252 (73702-5252)
PHONE..................................580 233-9850
Bob Thornton, President
Daryl Thornton, Vice Pres
Terry Rice, Treasurer
EMP: 4
SQ FT: 4,900
SALES (est): 550K Privately Held
SIC: 1381 Directional drilling oil & gas wells

(G-2918)
BIMBO BAKERIES USA INC
2620 N 11th St (73701-8755)
PHONE..................................580 234-1213
Donald Wilbourn, Manager
EMP: 6 Privately Held
SIC: 2051 Bakery: wholesale or wholesale/retail combined
HQ: Bimbo Bakeries Usa, Inc
255 Business Center Dr # 200
Horsham PA 19044
215 347-5500

(G-2919)
BMC PETROLEUM INC
1209 N 30th St (73701-2700)
PHONE..................................580 234-3725
Marlin Esau, President
EMP: 2
SALES (est): 157K Privately Held
SIC: 1389 Gas field services

(G-2920)
BO MC RESOURCES CORPORATION
901 The Trails West Loop (73703-6337)
P.O. Box 1765 (73702-1765)
PHONE..................................580 237-2324
Randall J Boehs, President
Steve Walker, Corp Secy
EMP: 5
SQ FT: 3,200
SALES (est): 620.3K Privately Held
SIC: 1311 6211 Crude petroleum production; natural gas production; oil & gas lease brokers

(G-2921)
BOGO ENERGY CORPORATION
4100 S Van Buren St (73701-8519)
PHONE..................................580 237-3756
Larry Wagner, Manager
EMP: 6 Privately Held
SIC: 1311 Crude petroleum production
PA: Bogo Energy Corporation
13933 Quail Pointe Dr
Oklahoma City OK 73134

(G-2922)
BRG PRODUCTION COMPANY
Also Called: Brg Petroleum
2414 S Monroe St (73701-8670)
PHONE..................................580 233-9302
B J Reid, Branch Mgr
EMP: 7
SALES (corp-wide): 8.5MM Privately Held
SIC: 1311 1389 Crude petroleum production; pumping of oil & gas wells
PA: Brg Production Company
7134 S Yale Ave Ste 600
Tulsa OK 74136
918 496-2626

(G-2923)
BUCKE-TEE LLC
1618 Indian Dr (73703-7015)
PHONE..................................580 747-9288
EMP: 2 EST: 2009
SALES (est): 177.7K Privately Held
WEB: www.bucketdriver.com
SIC: 3312 Fence posts, iron & steel

(G-2924)
BUY RITE SERVICES LLC
4511 N Van Buren Byp (73701-1837)
P.O. Box 392, Pond Creek (73766-0392)
PHONE..................................580 984-1008
Neil Deterding, Partner
Danielle Deterding, Partner
Shane Krittenbrink, Partner
EMP: 15
SQ FT: 9,000
SALES (est): 1.7MM Privately Held
SIC: 1389 Roustabout service

(G-2925)
CASTLE WLDG & FABRICATION LLC
1805 E Oklahoma Ave (73701-6360)
PHONE..................................580 747-0218
Rickey Castle, Owner
EMP: 1
SALES (est): 25K Privately Held
SIC: 7692 Welding repair

(G-2926)
CENTRAL CHEMICAL COMPANY
222 Crestwood (73701-6626)
P.O. Box 5865 (73702-5865)
PHONE..................................580 234-8245
Chris Scott, Owner
EMP: 4
SQ FT: 3,000
SALES: 385K Privately Held
WEB: www.sprayweeds.net
SIC: 1389 Oil field services

(G-2927)
CENTRAL MACHINE & TOOL COMPANY
1414 E Willow Rd (73701-8714)
P.O. Box 3909 (73702-3909)
PHONE..................................580 237-4033
Toll Free:..888
James R Parrish, Ch of Bd
EMP: 260
SALES (est): 18.1MM
SALES (corp-wide): 2.8MM Privately Held
WEB: www.ptcoupling.com
SIC: 3599 Machine shop, jobbing & repair
PA: Parrish Enterprises, Ltd.
1414 E Willow Rd
Enid OK 73701
580 237-4033

(G-2928)
CHAMPLIN EXPLORATION INC
201 N Grand St Ste 700 (73701-4138)
P.O. Box 3488 (73702-3488)
PHONE..................................580 233-1155
Herbert H Champlin, President
Clark Young, COO
Cheryl Briggs, Vice Pres
Sandy Greene, Bookkeeper
Cheryl Nickel, Manager
EMP: 7
SQ FT: 3,500
SALES: 5.2MM Privately Held
WEB: www.champlinexploration.com
SIC: 1311 Crude petroleum production; natural gas production

(G-2929)
CHAMPLIN FIREARMS INC
Woodring Airport 66th St (73701)
P.O. Box 3191 (73702-3191)
PHONE..................................580 237-7388
George Caswell, President
Muriel L Caswell, Vice Pres
EMP: 4
SQ FT: 3,200
SALES: 250K Privately Held
WEB: www.champlinarms.com
SIC: 5941 3484 Firearms; rifles or rifle parts, 30 mm. & below

(G-2930)
CIRRUS PRODUCTION COMPANY (PA)
201 N Grand St Ste 200 (73701-4138)
P.O. Box 5469 (73702-5469)
PHONE..................................580 237-0002
Peter Gill, Ch of Bd
Ray Gill, President
Michael Johnson, Vice Pres
Sheron Kindred, Vice Pres
Jim McCamey, Production
EMP: 7
SQ FT: 4,000
SALES (est): 1.5MM Privately Held
SIC: 1311 Crude petroleum production; natural gas production

(G-2931)
CLAYTON HOMES INC
902 Overland Trl (73703-6310)
PHONE..................................580 237-7094
Kenneth Bellar, Branch Mgr
EMP: 2
SALES (corp-wide): 327.2B Publicly Held
SIC: 2451 Mobile homes
HQ: Clayton Homes, Inc.
5000 Clayton Rd
Maryville TN 37804
865 380-3000

(G-2932)
CODY MUD COMPANY INC
1122 Briar Creek Rd (73703-2835)
P.O. Box 3368 (73702-3368)
PHONE..................................580 237-5347
Gary Flemming, President
Judy Fleming, Vice Pres
EMP: 2
SALES: 500K Privately Held
SIC: 1389 Oil field services

(G-2933)
COMPLETE ENERGY SERVICES INC
Also Called: Hamm & Phillips Services
302 N Independence St # 12 (73701-4097)
PHONE..................................580 249-3200
EMP: 3
SALES (est): 82.9K Privately Held
SIC: 1389 Oil field services

(G-2934)
COMPLETION OIL TOOLS LLC
1802 N Grand St (73701-1706)
P.O. Box 985 (73702-0985)
PHONE..................................580 478-6263
John Root, Owner
EMP: 1
SQ FT: 1,800
SALES: 250K Privately Held
SIC: 1389 Oil field services

(G-2935)
CROMWELLS INC
Also Called: Cromwells Press
302 E Maine Ave (73701-5746)
P.O. Box 1109 (73702-1109)
PHONE..................................580 234-6561
John L Cromwell, President
Justin Cromwell, Corp Secy
Elizabeth Glasser, Vice Pres
EMP: 4

GEOGRAPHIC SECTION

Enid - Garfield County (G-2967)

SALES (est): 900K Privately Held
SIC: 2752 7334 2791 2789 Commercial printing, offset; photocopying & duplicating services; typesetting; bookbinding & related work; commercial printing; newspapers

(G-2936)
CSI MEASUREMENT LLC
3730 Cactus Flts (73703-7303)
PHONE..................580 234-4979
Christi Staab Hristi, *Mng Member*
Christi Staab, *Mng Member*
EMP: 2
SALES (est): 192.6K Privately Held
WEB: www.csimeasurement.com
SIC: 1389 8734 Oil field services; calibration & certification

(G-2937)
CUMMINS CONSTRUCTION CO INC (HQ)
Also Called: Paving Materials Southern Okla
1420 W Chestnut Ave (73703-4307)
P.O. Box 748 (73702-0748)
PHONE..................580 233-6000
Robert L Cummins Jr, *President*
Ray Feightner Jr, *CFO*
Debbie Marshall, *Contract Mgr*
Ellen Le Peat, *Info Tech Dir*
Robert Wise, *Administration*
EMP: 50 EST: 1955
SQ FT: 4,500
SALES (est): 48MM Privately Held
WEB: www.cumminsasphalt.com
SIC: 1611 2951 Concrete construction: roads, highways, sidewalks, etc.; asphalt & asphaltic paving mixtures (not from refineries)

(G-2938)
D & S REFINISHING
1915 W Maine Ave (73703-5426)
PHONE..................580 233-4351
EMP: 1 EST: 1985
SALES (est): 46K Privately Held
SIC: 7641 2499 Reupholstery/Furniture Repair Mfg Wood Products

(G-2939)
DAMSEL IN DEFENSE
4209 Lexington Pl (73703-1337)
PHONE..................580 233-6609
Judy Stubblefield, *Principal*
EMP: 2
SALES (est): 97.7K Privately Held
SIC: 3812 Defense systems & equipment

(G-2940)
DESTIN CORPORATION
Rr 5 (73701-9805)
P.O. Box 2403 (73702-2403)
PHONE..................580 242-6627
Kenneth R Hollrah, *President*
Dee Ann Ediger, *Admin Sec*
EMP: 2
SALES: 100K Privately Held
SIC: 1311 Crude petroleum production; natural gas production

(G-2941)
DINKS MONOGRAMMING & EMB LLC
718 W Broadway Ave Ste 12 (73701-3819)
PHONE..................580 541-4371
Justin Locke, *Mng Member*
EMP: 1
SALES (est): 58.1K Privately Held
SIC: 2395 Embroidery & art needlework

(G-2942)
DOLESE BROS CO
805 W Southgate Rd (73701-8634)
P.O. Box 828 (73702-0828)
PHONE..................580 237-2650
Ray Terry, *Manager*
EMP: 8
SALES (corp-wide): 8.5MM Privately Held
WEB: www.dolese.com
SIC: 3273 Ready-mixed concrete
PA: Dolese Bros. Co.
    20 Nw 13th St
    Oklahoma City OK 73103
    405 235-2311

(G-2943)
DON L GERBRANDT
Also Called: Gerbrant Agency
3201 N Lincoln St (73703-1600)
PHONE..................580 234-3247
Don L Gerbrandt, *Principal*
EMP: 1
SALES: 87K Privately Held
SIC: 6331 3721 6321 Property damage insurance; aircraft; accident & health insurance

(G-2944)
DRISKILLS WELDING
717 N 30th St (73701-3787)
PHONE..................580 233-3093
Terry Driskill, *Owner*
EMP: 1
SQ FT: 320
SALES (est): 97.6K Privately Held
SIC: 3548 7692 Welding apparatus; welding repair

(G-2945)
DUBLIN PETROLEUM CORP
2500 N 11th St (73701-8722)
PHONE..................580 234-7718
Robert L Stallings Jr, *President*
Harvey Glasser MD, *Treasurer*
EMP: 5
SQ FT: 3,000
SALES (est): 246.3K Privately Held
SIC: 1311 Crude petroleum production; natural gas production

(G-2946)
DUNLAP MANUFACTURING
3022 N Van Buren St (73703-1732)
PHONE..................580 237-3434
EMP: 1
SALES (est): 47.3K Privately Held
SIC: 3999 Manufacturing industries

(G-2947)
DUNSWORTH MACHINE
701 N Independence St (73701-3161)
PHONE..................580 233-5812
Gary Dunsworth, *Owner*
EMP: 3
SALES (est): 200K Privately Held
SIC: 3599 7539 5531 Machine shop, jobbing & repair; machine shop, automotive; speed shops, including race car supplies

(G-2948)
EAGLE MARKETING
227 W Broadway Ave (73701-4017)
PHONE..................580 548-8186
Jason Maly, *Principal*
Cathy Nulph, *Accounts Exec*
EMP: 1
SALES (est): 119.1K Privately Held
SIC: 3555 Mats, advertising & newspaper

(G-2949)
ENID CBD COMPANY LLC
721 S Oakwood Rd (73703-6247)
PHONE..................580 297-5011
EMP: 2
SALES (est): 126.5K Privately Held
SIC: 3999

(G-2950)
ENID CONCRETE CO INC
621 W Birch Ave (73701-1681)
P.O. Box 1344 (73702-1344)
PHONE..................580 237-7766
Linda Brown, *President*
Larry Courier, *Vice Pres*
EMP: 300
SQ FT: 10,000
SALES (est): 27.5MM
SALES (corp-wide): 100.1MM Privately Held
SIC: 3273 Ready-mixed concrete
PA: Evans & Associates Enterprises, Inc.
    3320 N 14th St
    Ponca City OK 74601
    580 765-6693

(G-2951)
ENID DRILL SYSTEMS INC
1611 W Chestnut Ave (73703-4310)
PHONE..................580 234-5971
Espoir John, *Principal*
EMP: 2
SALES (est): 235.4K Privately Held
SIC: 3532 Mining machinery

(G-2952)
ENID ELECTRIC MOTOR SVC INC
Also Called: Harold's Vibration Control
3311 N 4th St (73701-6702)
PHONE..................580 234-8622
Richard Wallace, *President*
Darryl Wallace, *Vice Pres*
EMP: 15 EST: 1961
SQ FT: 8,000
SALES (est): 2.5MM Privately Held
SIC: 7694 5063 3621 Electric motor repair; motors, electric; motors & generators

(G-2953)
ENID INSULATION & SIDING INC
808 W Willow Rd (73701-1190)
PHONE..................580 237-5317
Don Carter, *President*
EMP: 9
SALES (est): 500K Privately Held
WEB: www.enidsiding.com
SIC: 5211 3442 Siding; windows, storm: wood or metal; storm doors or windows, metal

(G-2954)
ENID MACK SALES INC
5913 E Owen K Garriott Rd (73701-9499)
P.O. Box 5009 (73702-5009)
PHONE..................580 234-0043
Troy Phillips, *President*
Jill Phillips, *Treasurer*
EMP: 58
SQ FT: 46,400
SALES (est): 24.7MM Privately Held
SIC: 5511 5531 3533 7538 Trucks, tractors & trailers: new & used; truck equipment & parts; oil field machinery & equipment; truck engine repair, except industrial

(G-2955)
ENTERPRISE ICE INC
Also Called: Sturdevant Ice
416 S Independence St (73701-5630)
P.O. Box 823 (73702-0823)
PHONE..................580 237-4015
EMP: 5 EST: 1968
SQ FT: 5,000
SALES (est): 250K Privately Held
SIC: 2097 Mfg Ice

(G-2956)
EXTRAORDINARY WOODWORKS
4402 Oakcrest Ave (73703-3505)
PHONE..................801 995-0906
Jordan Eyre, *Principal*
EMP: 1
SALES (est): 54.1K Privately Held
SIC: 2431 Millwork

(G-2957)
FENCE SOLUTIONS INC
217 W Oxford Ave (73701-1227)
PHONE..................580 233-4600
Randy Breitenkamp, *President*
EMP: 7
SQ FT: 900
SALES (est): 550K Privately Held
SIC: 3496 1799 Fencing, made from purchased wire; fence construction

(G-2958)
FISHER WELDING
1618 N Van Buren St (73703-2513)
PHONE..................580 748-0445
EMP: 1
SALES (est): 25K Privately Held
SIC: 7692 Welding repair

(G-2959)
FREEDOM EMBROIDERY LLC
2918 Dona Kaye Dr (73701-4609)
PHONE..................580 540-8504
Shelley Rauh, *Principal*
EMP: 1
SALES (est): 36.7K Privately Held
SIC: 2395 Embroidery & art needlework

(G-2960)
G&J ENTERPRISES
2601 N 30th St (73701-8760)
PHONE..................580 237-2029
Jerry Beguin, *Principal*
EMP: 2
SALES (est): 77K Privately Held
SIC: 1389 Oil field services

(G-2961)
GARFIELD INC (PA)
Also Called: Garfield Equipment
500 W Southgate Rd (73701-8631)
PHONE..................580 242-6411
John Green, *President*
Jon R Ford, *Principal*
Marcia Weber, *Purch Mgr*
Trent Harris, *Sales Mgr*
▼ EMP: 27
SQ FT: 31,440
SALES (est): 5.9MM Privately Held
SIC: 3531 3523 Backhoes, tractors, cranes, plows & similar equipment; farm machinery & equipment

(G-2962)
GEFCO INC
2215 S Van Buren St (73703-8218)
P.O. Box 872 (73702-0872)
PHONE..................580 243-4141
Vince Trotta, *President*
Charles Cunningham, *Vice Pres*
Arnold Law, *Vice Pres*
Matt Gregston, *Safety Mgr*
John Lang, *Mfg Staff*
▼ EMP: 176
SALES (est): 63.8MM
SALES (corp-wide): 1.1B Publicly Held
SIC: 3533 Drilling tools for gas, oil or water wells
PA: Astec Industries, Inc.
    1725 Shepherd Rd
    Chattanooga TN 37421
    423 899-5898

(G-2963)
GOOD OIL COMPANY
Also Called: Compass Drilling
3801 N Oakwood Rd (73703-1438)
P.O. Box 3744 (73702-3744)
PHONE..................580 233-3899
Mike Good, *President*
Vaugnh Good, *Vice Pres*
EMP: 10
SALES (est): 890.2K Privately Held
SIC: 1311 Crude petroleum production; natural gas production

(G-2964)
GRAND AVENUE LIGHTING
323 S Grand St (73701-5658)
P.O. Box 842 (73702-0842)
PHONE..................580 237-4656
Scott Conrady, *Owner*
EMP: 2 EST: 2014
SALES (est): 204.5K Privately Held
SIC: 3648 Lighting equipment

(G-2965)
GUARD EXPLORATION PARTNERSHIP
502 S Fillmore St (73703-5703)
PHONE..................580 234-3229
EMP: 2 EST: 2011
SALES (est): 115.5K Privately Held
SIC: 1382 Oil & gas exploration services

(G-2966)
H & J SERVICES
3312 N 16th St (73701-6735)
PHONE..................580 237-4613
Harvey Miller, *President*
Mark Miller, *Vice Pres*
Matthew Miller, *Vice Pres*
Jackie Miller, *Treasurer*
EMP: 10
SALES (est): 1.5MM Privately Held
SIC: 1389 Oil field services

(G-2967)
HACKNEY LADISH INC
400 E Willow Rd (73701-1515)
PHONE..................580 237-4212
Jeremiah Jackson, *Sales Staff*
Randy Smith, *Manager*

Enid - Garfield County (G-2968)

EMP: 94
SALES (corp-wide): 327.2B Publicly Held
SIC: 3089 3441 3566 3548 Fittings for pipe, plastic; fabricated structural metal; speed changers, drives & gears; welding apparatus; valves & pipe fittings; flange, valve or pipe fitting forgings, nonferrous
HQ: Hackney Ladish, Inc.
708 S Elmira Ave
Russellville AR 72802

(G-2968)
HANGER PRSTHETCS & ORTHO INC
Also Called: Hanger Clinic
330 S 5th St Ste 102 (73701-5860)
PHONE.................................479 484-1620
Thomas Kirk PHD, CEO
EMP: 3
SALES (corp-wide): 1.1B Publicly Held
SIC: 3842 Limbs, artificial; braces, elastic
HQ: Hanger Prosthetics & Orthotics, Inc.
10910 Domain Dr Ste 300
Austin TX 78758
512 777-3800

(G-2969)
HANOR COMPANY OF WISCONSIN LLC
Also Called: Hanor Feed Mill
3025 S Van Buren St (73703-8356)
PHONE.................................580 237-3255
Phillip Sumner, Opers Dir
Fred C McCulley, Manager
Diane Stanberry, Manager
Joseph Bradford, CIO
Mark McCulley, CTO
EMP: 20 Privately Held
SIC: 2048 Prepared feeds
PA: The Hanor Company Of Wisconsin Llc
E4614 Us Hwy 14 And 60
Spring Green WI 53588

(G-2970)
HENRY GUNGOLL OPERATING INC
2208 W Willow Rd (73703-2405)
P.O. Box 6209 (73702-6209)
PHONE.................................580 234-2302
James H Gungoll, President
EMP: 4
SQ FT: 4,000
SALES (est): 390K Privately Held
SIC: 1311 Natural gas production; crude petroleum production

(G-2971)
HIGGINS WELDING
730 N Malone St (73701-3310)
PHONE.................................580 231-9211
Michael Higgins, Principal
EMP: 1
SALES (est): 27.6K Privately Held
SIC: 7692 Welding repair

(G-2972)
HILAND LP LLC (DH)
302 N Independence St # 100 (73701-4097)
PHONE.................................713 369-9000
Joseph L Griffin, President
Terry Strain, Maint Spvr
Angela Wood, Business Anlyst
Ron Hill, Director
Dan Davis, Contractor
EMP: 10
SALES (est): 1.3MM Publicly Held
SIC: 1321 Natural gas liquids production
HQ: Hiland Partners Holdings, Llc
1001 Louisiana St # 1000
Houston TX 77002
713 369-9000

(G-2973)
HODGDEN OPERATING COMPANY INC
1005 The Trails West Loop (73703-6339)
P.O. Box 3485 (73703-3485)
PHONE.................................580 233-2870
Larry Hodgden, President
Lawrence Hodgden, President
Michael Hodgen, Vice Pres
EMP: 4
SQ FT: 3,200

SALES (est): 441.8K Privately Held
SIC: 1311 Crude petroleum production; natural gas production

(G-2974)
HOTSY OF OK INC
1627 N Van Buren St (73703-2514)
PHONE.................................580 234-0608
Robert Skaggs, President
Billy Menasco, Vice Pres
Rodney Solomon, Sales Staff
Matt Holmes, Sales Associate
Kent Cook, Manager
EMP: 8
SQ FT: 5,500
SALES (est): 440K Privately Held
WEB: www.hotsyok.com
SIC: 5999 5084 3433 Cleaning equipment & supplies; plumbing & heating supplies; water purification equipment; cleaning equipment, high pressure, hand or steam; heating equipment, except electric

(G-2975)
HUSTON ENERGY CORPORATION
2414 Heritage Trl Ste B (73703-1697)
P.O. Box 5318 (73702-5318)
PHONE.................................580 233-6030
Michael W Huston, President
EMP: 5 EST: 1978
SALES (est): 616.7K Privately Held
WEB: www.hustonenergy.com
SIC: 1311 Crude petroleum production

(G-2976)
I AM DRILLING LLC
3521 Lisa Ln (73703-2915)
P.O. Box 6212 (73702-6212)
PHONE.................................580 234-2277
EMP: 2
SALES (est): 173.9K Privately Held
SIC: 3541 Drilling & boring machines

(G-2977)
INDEPENDENT DIESEL SERVICE
Also Called: Independent Diesel Parts & Svc
4524 E Market St (73701-9671)
P.O. Box 3336 (73703-3336)
PHONE.................................580 234-0435
Bretta Gillaspy, President
James Gillaspy, Corp Secy
EMP: 17
SALES (est): 2.5MM Privately Held
SIC: 7538 7699 5084 3519 Engine repair, except diesel: automotive; truck engine repair, except industrial; tractor repair; engines & parts, diesel; diesel, semi-diesel or duel-fuel engines, including marine; generator sets: gasoline, diesel or dual-fuel

(G-2978)
J & S OF ENID INC
1913 N 10th St (73701-8702)
P.O. Box 389 (73702-0389)
PHONE.................................580 237-6152
Jerry Dunkin, President
Sandra Dunkin, Corp Secy
Everett Dunkin, Vice Pres
EMP: 23
SQ FT: 1,500
SALES (est): 1.1MM Privately Held
SIC: 1389 1382 Running, cutting & pulling casings, tubes & rods; well plugging & abandoning, oil & gas; oil & gas exploration services

(G-2979)
JACK WARNER FIREWORKS
Southgate Rd (73702)
P.O. Box 1412 (73702-1412)
PHONE.................................580 234-3827
Melody Manahan, Principal
EMP: 3
SALES (est): 309K Privately Held
SIC: 2899 Fireworks

(G-2980)
JANES MACHINE SHOP LLC
421 S Grand St (73701-5660)
PHONE.................................580 237-4434
Dustin Janes, Mng Member
EMP: 2

SALES (est): 200K Privately Held
SIC: 3559 Automotive related machinery

(G-2981)
JANICE SUE DANIEL (PA)
Also Called: Enid Packing Co
2424 N Madison St (73701-2129)
P.O. Box 734 (73702-0734)
PHONE.................................580 237-2695
Janice Sue Daniel, Owner
EMP: 8
SQ FT: 4,000
SALES (est): 750K Privately Held
SIC: 5421 2011 Meat markets, including freezer provisioners; meat packing plants

(G-2982)
JANICE SUE DANIEL
Also Called: Big Country Meat Market
606 W Willow Rd (73701-2104)
P.O. Box 734 (73702-0734)
PHONE.................................580 233-8666
Carl Lightfield, Owner
EMP: 7
SALES (est): 281.8K
SALES (corp-wide): 750K Privately Held
SIC: 5421 2013 2011 Meat markets, including freezer provisioners; sausages & other prepared meats; meat packing plants
PA: Janice Sue Daniel
2424 N Madison St
Enid OK 73701
580 237-2695

(G-2983)
JEAN JACQUES PERODEAU GUNMAKER
Woodring Airport 66th St (73701)
P.O. Box 3191 (73702-3191)
PHONE.................................580 237-7388
Jean Jacques Perodeau, Owner
EMP: 1 EST: 1995
SALES (est): 63.7K Privately Held
SIC: 3484 Guns (firearms) or gun parts, 30 mm. & below

(G-2984)
JERRY DUNKIN WELL SERVICES
1913 N 10th St (73701-8702)
P.O. Box 389 (73702-0389)
PHONE.................................580 237-6152
Jerry Dunkin, President
Sandra Dunkin, Treasurer
EMP: 4
SALES (est): 755.8K Privately Held
SIC: 1389 Oil field services

(G-2985)
JERRY SANNER OIL PROPERTIES
1202 W Willow Rd Ste B (73703-2530)
P.O. Box 5942 (73702-5942)
PHONE.................................580 233-2442
Jerry D Sanner, President
Jerry Horner, Vice Pres
Nettie Horner, Admin Sec
EMP: 3
SALES (est): 2MM Privately Held
SIC: 1311 Crude petroleum production; natural gas production

(G-2986)
JM OILFIELD SERVICES INC
1502 Oakhill Cir (73703-3113)
P.O. Box 2046, Gonzales TX (78629-1546)
PHONE.................................501 589-4044
John McClung, President
EMP: 20
SQ FT: 1,800
SALES (est): 2MM Privately Held
SIC: 1389 Oil field services

(G-2987)
JOEL BUMPUS
Also Called: J & J Machine
4520 N 4th St (73701-6503)
P.O. Box 621 (73702-0621)
PHONE.................................580 237-5305
Joel Bumpus, Owner
EMP: 1
SQ FT: 3,000

SALES: 100K Privately Held
SIC: 3599 7692 Machine shop, jobbing & repair; welding repair

(G-2988)
JOS LAMERTON WOODWORKING LLC
2020 Willow Run (73703-1421)
PHONE.................................580 336-8448
Joseph Lamerton,
EMP: 1
SQ FT: 2,000
SALES (est): 116.7K Privately Held
SIC: 2511 Wood household furniture

(G-2989)
JS OILFIELD SERVICES LLC
807 W Cherokee Ave (73701-5407)
PHONE.................................580 542-7822
James Driskell, Principal
EMP: 2
SALES (est): 197.8K Privately Held
SIC: 1389 Oil field services

(G-2990)
K & J WELDING LLC
1418 Beverly Dr (73703-7713)
P.O. Box 5734 (73702-5734)
PHONE.................................580 541-2200
Kenny Gilbreath, Principal
EMP: 2
SALES (est): 104.9K Privately Held
SIC: 7692 Welding repair

(G-2991)
K & S PUMPING UNIT REPAIR INC
722 Morningside Pl (73701-9688)
PHONE.................................580 237-7343
Joy Koon, President
EMP: 11
SALES (est): 1.7MM Privately Held
SIC: 3561 Pumps & pumping equipment

(G-2992)
K3 LLC
1323 W Poplar Ave (73703)
PHONE.................................580 231-2040
Jennifer Kelley,
Shannon Kelley,
EMP: 4
SALES (est): 273.6K Privately Held
SIC: 1389 Pipe testing, oil field service

(G-2993)
KALAMAR INC
1405 E Willow Rd (73701-8714)
PHONE.................................580 242-5121
Larry Martin, President
Katherine Martin, Corp Secy
EMP: 14
SQ FT: 114,200
SALES: 3MM Privately Held
SIC: 1389 7353 Fishing for tools, oil & gas field; oil field equipment, rental or leasing

(G-2994)
KELLEY SHEPARD WELDING
2658 Rock Island Blvd (73701-1343)
PHONE.................................580 234-3280
Kelley Shepard, Owner
EMP: 2
SALES (est): 89.1K Privately Held
SIC: 7692 Welding repair

(G-2995)
KLINE SIGN LLC
3005 S Van Buren St (73703-8356)
PHONE.................................580 237-0732
Joe Kline,
Sheri Kline,
EMP: 3
SQ FT: 2,000
SALES: 250K Privately Held
SIC: 3993 Electric signs

(G-2996)
KOCH FERTILIZER ENID LLC
1619 S 78th St (73701-9588)
PHONE.................................580 249-4870
Chase Koch, President
Vanessa Bertucci, Credit Staff
▲ EMP: 520

GEOGRAPHIC SECTION
Enid - Garfield County (G-3026)

SALES (est): 133.9MM
SALES (corp-wide): 48.9B **Privately Held**
SIC: 2873 Nitrogenous fertilizers
HQ: Koch Ag & Energy Solutions, Llc
  4111 E 37th St N
  Wichita KS 67220
  316 828-5500

(G-2997)
KOCH INDUSTRIES INC
1619 S 78th St (73701-9588)
PHONE..................580 233-3900
Wayne Aholt, *Persnl Mgr*
Roger Morris, *Branch Mgr*
EMP: 83
SALES (corp-wide): 48.9B **Privately Held**
WEB: www.kochind.com
SIC: 2873 Anhydrous ammonia
PA: Koch Industries, Inc.
  4111 E 37th St N
  Wichita KS 67220
  316 828-5500

(G-2998)
L & B PIPE & FABRICATION INC
10801 Bluestem Dr (73701-6907)
PHONE..................580 234-0712
EMP: 2 EST: 2003
SALES (est): 140K **Privately Held**
SIC: 1389 Oil/Gas Field Services

(G-2999)
LEGENDS HAIR STUDIO
1014 N Van Buren St (73703-3303)
PHONE..................580 237-5524
Roy D Ward, *Owner*
EMP: 2
SALES (est): 113.5K **Privately Held**
SIC: 2844 Hair preparations, including shampoos

(G-3000)
LUCKINBILL INC (PA)
Also Called: Mechanical Contractors
304 E Broadway Ave (73701-4102)
P.O. Box 186 (73702-0186)
PHONE..................580 233-2026
Dennis Luckinbill, *President*
Trevor Miller, *General Mgr*
Anna Sue Luckinbill, *Corp Secy*
JC Vincent, *Vice Pres*
Hector Covarrubias, *Safety Dir*
▲ EMP: 90 EST: 1939
SQ FT: 26,000
SALES (est): 42.8MM **Privately Held**
WEB: www.luckinbill.com
SIC: **1711** 1623 7692 1731 Plumbing contractors; warm air heating & air conditioning contractor; refrigeration contractor; oil & gas pipeline construction; sewer line construction; water main construction; underground utilities contractor; welding repair; general electrical contractor

(G-3001)
LYNNS MACHINE INC
3616 E Market St (73701-9675)
P.O. Box 1224 (73702-1224)
PHONE..................580 234-2051
Lynn Kvasnicka, *President*
Viola Kvasnicka, *Treasurer*
EMP: 10
SQ FT: 6,000
SALES (est): 1.6MM **Privately Held**
SIC: 3599 Machine shop, jobbing & repair

(G-3002)
M & M ELECTRIC
11219 W Fox Dr (73703-8128)
PHONE..................580 233-8999
Marty McNaughton, *President*
EMP: 6
SALES (est): 884.2K **Privately Held**
SIC: **1389** 1731 Oil field services; general electrical contractor

(G-3003)
M D SPOONEMORE WELDING
5306 N 16th St (73701-6722)
PHONE..................580 233-9596
M D Spoonemore, *Owner*
EMP: 1
SALES (est): 41.3K **Privately Held**
SIC: 7692 Welding repair

(G-3004)
MACKELLAR SERVICES INC
1101 Sooner Trend (73701-9442)
PHONE..................580 237-9383
EMP: 9
SALES (corp-wide): 49.6MM **Privately Held**
SIC: 1389 Oil Field Service Specializing In Well Workover
HQ: Mackellar Services Inc
  7100 N Classen Blvd # 100
  Oklahoma City OK 73116
  405 848-2877

(G-3005)
MARIA RAES INC
2517 N Van Buren St (73703-1711)
PHONE..................580 242-3342
Mary Buthman, *President*
Mark Buthman, *Corp Secy*
EMP: 3
SQ FT: 1,000
SALES (est): 50K **Privately Held**
SIC: **5499** 2099 2035 2033 Gourmet food stores; food preparations; pickles, sauces & salad dressings; canned fruits & specialties

(G-3006)
MARK CROMWELL INC
119 N Washington St (73701-4019)
P.O. Box 5436 (73702-5436)
PHONE..................580 233-7992
Mark Cromwell, *President*
EMP: 1
SALES (est): 140K **Privately Held**
SIC: 1382 Oil & gas exploration services

(G-3007)
MARSAU ENTERPRISES INC
1209 N 30th St (73701-2700)
PHONE..................580 233-3910
Marlin Esau, *President*
Rob Niles, *Vice Pres*
EMP: 600
SQ FT: 8,800
SALES: 100MM **Privately Held**
SIC: 1389 Oil field services

(G-3008)
MARTIN JACOB WELDING LLC
1717 N Adams St (73701-2579)
PHONE..................580 747-1031
EMP: 1 EST: 2012
SALES (est): 25K **Privately Held**
SIC: 7692 Welding repair

(G-3009)
MARY REALLY NICE THINGS
1126 Hillcrest Dr (73701-7779)
PHONE..................580 237-1177
Mary Lou, *Owner*
Leon Walters, *Co-Owner*
EMP: 2
SALES (est): 74K **Privately Held**
SIC: 3961 Costume jewelry

(G-3010)
MAVERICK BROS RESOURCES LLC
1710 W Willow Rd (73703-2438)
P.O. Box 392 (73702-0392)
PHONE..................580 233-4701
Bret Brickman, *Principal*
Doug Pethoud, *Manager*
EMP: 7
SALES (est): 1MM **Privately Held**
SIC: 1382 Oil & gas exploration services

(G-3011)
MCLENDON WELDING LLC
5405 Fountain Head Dr (73703-5927)
PHONE..................580 304-5187
Richard McLendon, *Principal*
EMP: 1 EST: 2015
SALES (est): 27.6K **Privately Held**
SIC: 7692 Welding repair

(G-3012)
METCO INC
Also Called: Metco Provers
1522 S Imo Rd (73703-6062)
PHONE..................580 233-3127
Richard Oller, *President*
Karla Oller, *Admin Sec*
EMP: 2
SALES (est): 244.1K **Privately Held**
SIC: 1389 Testing, measuring, surveying & analysis services

(G-3013)
MID-CONTINENT PACKAGING INC
1200 N 54th St (73701-9407)
PHONE..................580 234-5200
Mark Epstein, *President*
Andrew Epstein, *Vice Pres*
Lawrence Epstein, *Vice Pres*
Steven Epstein, *Vice Pres*
Tom Otto, *Plant Mgr*
EMP: 65
SQ FT: 174,000
SALES (est): 17.6MM
SALES (corp-wide): 38MM **Privately Held**
SIC: **4783** 2899 Packing goods for shipping; chemical preparations
PA: Alden - Leeds, Inc.
  55 Jacobus Ave Ste 1
  Kearny NJ 07032
  973 589-3544

(G-3014)
MITCHELL IRONWORKS INC
3825 E Willow Rd (73701-9439)
PHONE..................580 237-7925
Roger Mitchell, *President*
Tim Reed, *Corp Secy*
Rebecca Mitchell, *Vice Pres*
EMP: 1
SALES (est): 156.7K **Privately Held**
SIC: **1799** 3523 3446 Fence construction; windmills for pumping water, agricultural; architectural metalwork

(G-3015)
MOHAWK INDUSTRIES
2504 W Owen K Garriott Rd (73703-5223)
PHONE..................214 309-4652
EMP: 2
SALES (est): 51.2K **Privately Held**
SIC: 2273 Finishers of tufted carpets & rugs

(G-3016)
MUNGER AND KROUT INC
Also Called: Downtown Threads
101 S Grand St (73701-5654)
PHONE..................580 237-7060
Vicki Brown, *President*
Vonda Benton, *Vice Pres*
David Brown, *Vice Pres*
Manda Munger, *Graphic Designe*
EMP: 12
SALES: 600K **Privately Held**
SIC: **2396** 2395 Screen printing on fabric articles; embroidery & art needlework

(G-3017)
MUSTANG FUEL CORPORATION
3214 N 42nd St (73701-9403)
PHONE..................580 446-5552
Mark Biel, *Manager*
EMP: 1
SALES (corp-wide): 107.7MM **Privately Held**
SIC: 1389 Processing service, gas
PA: Mustang Fuel Corporation
  9800 N Oklahoma Ave
  Oklahoma City OK 73114
  405 884-2092

(G-3018)
NEWSPAPER HOLDING INC
Also Called: Enid News and Eagle, The
227 W Broadway Ave (73701-4017)
P.O. Box 1192 (73702-1192)
PHONE..................580 233-6600
Gloria Fletcher, *Administration*
EMP: 51 **Privately Held**
WEB: www.tribdem.com
SIC: **2711** 2752 Newspapers: publishing only, not printed on site; commercial printing, lithographic
HQ: Newspaper Holding, Inc.
  425 Locust St
  Johnstown PA 15901
  814 532-5102

(G-3019)
NORTH AMERCN PRECISION CAST CO
1414 E Willow Rd (73701-8714)
P.O. Box 1407, Columbus MS (39703-1407)
PHONE..................580 237-4033
James R Parrish, *President*
EMP: 68
SALES (est): 8.7MM
SALES (corp-wide): 2.8MM **Privately Held**
SIC: 3324 Commercial investment castings, ferrous
PA: Parrish Enterprises, Ltd.
  1414 E Willow Rd
  Enid OK 73701
  580 237-4033

(G-3020)
NORTH AMRCN ARSPC HOLDINGS LLC
4002 Twilight Ave (73703-3615)
PHONE..................316 644-2553
Ken Brooks, *Principal*
Mark Seaver, *Principal*
EMP: 100 EST: 2016
SALES (est): 3.2MM **Privately Held**
SIC: 3728 Accumulators, aircraft propeller

(G-3021)
NORTH AMRCN BRINE RSOURCES LLC
2415 S Garland Rd (73703-7369)
PHONE..................405 828-7123
Bruce Baverka,
EMP: 2
SALES (est): 170.1K **Privately Held**
SIC: 2834 Iodine, tincture of

(G-3022)
NORTHWEST PRINTING INC
120 N Independence St (73701-4001)
PHONE..................580 234-0953
Fred Alexander, *President*
EMP: 2
SQ FT: 2,000
SALES (est): 282.7K **Privately Held**
SIC: **2752** 2791 2789 Commercial printing, offset; typesetting; bookbinding & related work

(G-3023)
OASIS RV CENTER LLC
1610 N Van Buren St (73703-2513)
PHONE..................580 233-9400
Brad Mendenhall, *Mng Member*
EMP: 5
SALES (est): 393.8K **Privately Held**
SIC: 3799 Recreational vehicles

(G-3024)
OIL TOOLS RENTALS INC
1029 N 54th St (73701-5016)
PHONE..................580 242-1140
EMP: 19 EST: 1979
SQ FT: 8,000
SALES (est): 1.6MM **Publicly Held**
SIC: 1389 Oil/Gas Field Services
HQ: Complete Energy Services, Inc.
  1001 La St Ste 2900
  Houston TX 77002
  713 654-2200

(G-3025)
OILFIELD DSTRBTONS SPCLSTS LLC
4025 Shady Ln (73701-1806)
PHONE..................580 237-1237
Brad Chegwidden, *Opers Mgr*
Kelly M Forell,
EMP: 4 EST: 2014
SALES (est): 210.3K **Privately Held**
WEB: www.ods-us.com
SIC: 1389 Oil field services

(G-3026)
ONE GRAND CENTER
201 N Grand St Ste 700 (73701-4138)
PHONE..................580 234-6600
Herbert Champlin, *Principal*
EMP: 2
SALES (est): 191.2K **Privately Held**
SIC: 1382 Oil & gas exploration services

Enid - Garfield County (G-3027) — GEOGRAPHIC SECTION

(G-3027)
OUT ON A LIMB MFG LLC
5710 N Us Highway 81 (73701-9748)
PHONE 580 541-3794
Matt Garis, *Mng Member*
EMP: 2
SQ FT: 400
SALES: 150K **Privately Held**
SIC: 3949 Hunting equipment

(G-3028)
OVERSTREET BUILDING & SUPPLY
2613 Mcgill Dr (73703-3121)
PHONE 580 234-5666
Kim R Overstreet, *President*
Cheryl Overstreet, *Vice Pres*
EMP: 2
SQ FT: 2,700
SALES: 200K **Privately Held**
SIC: 2439 Trusses, wooden roof

(G-3029)
P-T COUPLING COMPANY (HQ)
1414 E Willow Rd (73701-8714)
P.O. Box 3909 (73702-3909)
PHONE 580 237-4033
James R Parrish, *President*
Jerry A Parrish, *Vice Pres*
Linda Petr, *Buyer*
Debby Roggow, *Purchasing*
Walter Boeckman, *Engineer*
◆ EMP: 42
SALES (est): 53.6MM
SALES (corp-wide): 2.8MM **Privately Held**
WEB: www.ptcoupling.com
SIC: 3429 Manufactured hardware (general)
PA: Parrish Enterprises, Ltd.
1414 E Willow Rd
Enid OK 73701
580 237-4033

(G-3030)
PARRISH ENTERPRISES
Also Called: Punch-Lok Co
3005 N Emerson St (73701-1368)
P.O. Box 3909 (73702-3909)
PHONE 580 233-4757
Matt Parrish, *Principal*
▲ EMP: 99
SALES: 950K **Privately Held**
SIC: 3429 Clamps, couplings, nozzles & other metal hose fittings

(G-3031)
PARRISH ENTERPRISES LTD (PA)
Also Called: Central Machine & Tools
1414 E Willow Rd (73701-8714)
P.O. Box 3909 (73702-3909)
PHONE 580 237-4033
James R Parrish, *President*
Terry Johnson, *General Mgr*
Terry D Johnson, *Corp Secy*
Jerry D Koehn, *Vice Pres*
Jerry Parrish, *Vice Pres*
▲ EMP: 250
SQ FT: 170,000
SALES: 2.8MM **Privately Held**
SIC: 3429 3599 3324 3949 Clamps & couplings, hose; machine shop, jobbing & repair; steel investment foundries; fishing equipment; rods & rod parts, fishing

(G-3032)
PDQ PRINTING LLC
131 E Maine Ave (73701-5741)
PHONE 580 233-3241
Richard L Combs, *Owner*
EMP: 5
SQ FT: 2,500
SALES (est): 735.8K **Privately Held**
SIC: 2752 Commercial printing, offset

(G-3033)
PDQLIPPRINTS LLC
131 E Maine Ave (73701-5741)
PHONE 580 233-3241
Darlene Combs, *Mng Member*
EMP: 2
SALES (est): 73.1K **Privately Held**
SIC: 2721 Magazines: publishing & printing

(G-3034)
PELAGIC TANK LLC
301 S 54th St (73701-5022)
P.O. Box 351 (73702)
PHONE 580 856-2182
Mike Shores, *Mng Member*
Mark Houser,
EMP: 110 EST: 2011
SALES (est): 14.5MM **Privately Held**
WEB: www.pelagictank.com
SIC: 3795 Tanks & tank components

(G-3035)
PETTITT WIRELINE SERVICE LLC
5710 N Us Highway 81 (73701-9748)
PHONE 580 234-0550
Ken Pettitt, *Principal*
EMP: 2
SALES (est): 105.3K **Privately Held**
SIC: 1389 Oil field services

(G-3036)
PIONEER PRECISION MACHINE SHOP
4502 E Market St (73701-9671)
PHONE 580 233-1670
Ed Clements, *President*
Susie Clements, *Vice Pres*
EMP: 13
SQ FT: 10,000
SALES (est): 1.5MM **Privately Held**
SIC: 3599 7692 Machine shop, jobbing & repair; welding repair

(G-3037)
PRECISION WIRELINE LLC
2402 S Monroe St (73701-8670)
PHONE 580 233-0033
Tim Winfield, *Mng Member*
Keith Boyles,
EMP: 10
SALES (est): 965.8K **Privately Held**
WEB: www.precisionwirelineservice.com
SIC: 1389 Removal of condensate gasoline from field (gathering) lines; oil field services

(G-3038)
PREMIER CHEM & OILFLD SUP LLC
302 N Independence St # 1500 (73701-4097)
PHONE 405 893-2321
Tim Haley, *President*
EMP: 19
SALES (est): 6.2MM **Privately Held**
SIC: 2869 5084 Industrial organic chemicals; pumps & pumping equipment

(G-3039)
PRODUCTION STRING SERVICES
1410 S Van Buren St (73703-7853)
P.O. Box 349 (73702-0349)
PHONE 580 747-4017
EMP: 6
SALES (est): 404.8K **Privately Held**
SIC: 1389 Oil field services

(G-3040)
PUNCH-LOK CO
3001 N 4th St (73701-1372)
P.O. Box 3909 (73702-3909)
PHONE 580 233-4757
James R Parrish, *President*
Jerry Koehn, *Vice Pres*
Matt Parrish, *Vice Pres*
EMP: 20
SQ FT: 16,000
SALES: 5.5MM
SALES (corp-wide): 2.8MM **Privately Held**
SIC: 3429 3494 3492 Clamps & couplings, hose; valves & pipe fittings; fluid power valves & hose fittings
PA: Parrish Enterprises, Ltd.
1414 E Willow Rd
Enid OK 73701
580 237-4033

(G-3041)
RABID
2302 W Willow Rd (73703-2416)
PHONE 580 234-3632

Michael Koehn, *Administration*
EMP: 2
SALES (est): 151.8K **Privately Held**
SIC: 2499 Trophy bases, wood

(G-3042)
RAMBLER ENERGY SERVICES INC
114 E Broadway Ave # 207 (73701-4127)
P.O. Box 3447 (73702-3447)
PHONE 580 242-7447
Rodney Ylitalo, *President*
EMP: 29
SQ FT: 700
SALES (est): 1.9MM **Privately Held**
SIC: 1389 1382 Oil field services; oil & gas exploration services

(G-3043)
RANGER RENTALS LLC
723 W Randolph Ave Ste 8 (73701-3827)
P.O. Box 2026 (73702-2026)
PHONE 580 541-4242
Dana Foster,
Ken Foster,
EMP: 2 EST: 2012
SQ FT: 300
SALES (est): 127.4K **Privately Held**
SIC: 1389 Oil field services

(G-3044)
REAGENT CHEMICAL & RES INC
5520 E Market St (73701-9755)
PHONE 580 233-1024
Bruce Mitchell, *Manager*
EMP: 4
SALES (corp-wide): 517MM **Privately Held**
SIC: 2819 3949 Sulfur, recovered or refined, incl. from sour natural gas; targets, archery & rifle shooting
PA: Reagent Chemical & Research, Inc.
115 Rte 202
Ringoes NJ 08551
908 284-2800

(G-3045)
RECLAIMED OIL & GAS PRPTS LLC
2421 Rockwood Rd (73703-1409)
PHONE 580 234-8085
Dean Pitchford, *Principal*
EMP: 2
SALES (est): 94.3K **Privately Held**
SIC: 1311 Crude petroleum production

(G-3046)
REDZONE COIL TUBING LLC
1201 Sooner Trend (73701-9455)
PHONE 580 237-3663
Waylin Ott, *Branch Mgr*
EMP: 6
SALES (corp-wide): 832.9MM **Publicly Held**
SIC: 1389 Construction, repair & dismantling services
HQ: Redzone Coil Tubing, Llc
203 S 1st St
Lufkin TX 75901
936 632-2645

(G-3047)
RESOURCES OPERATING COMPANY
2428 Wagon Trl (73703-1628)
PHONE 580 237-7744
R L Rogers, *President*
EMP: 3
SALES (est): 264.3K
SALES (corp-wide): 479K **Privately Held**
SIC: 1311 Crude petroleum production
PA: Rogers Resources Inc
2428 Wagon Trl
Enid OK 73703
580 237-7744

(G-3048)
RLC HOLDING CO INC (PA)
Also Called: Cummins Construction Company
1420 W Chestnut Ave (73703-4307)
P.O. Box 748 (73702-0748)
PHONE 580 233-6000
Robert L Cummins, *Ch of Bd*
Ray Feightner Jr, *CFO*
Willa Jane Cummins, *Shareholder*

Pam Cummins, *Admin Sec*
EMP: 80
SQ FT: 4,500
SALES (est): 48MM **Privately Held**
SIC: 2951 Asphalt & asphaltic paving mixtures (not from refineries)

(G-3049)
ROBINSON WELDING LLC
5105 Ridgeview Ave (73703-4622)
PHONE 580 278-9363
Curt Robinson, *Principal*
EMP: 1
SALES (est): 631.2K **Privately Held**
SIC: 7692 Welding repair

(G-3050)
ROGERS RESOURCES INC (PA)
2428 Wagon Trl (73703-1628)
PHONE 580 237-7744
R Rogers, *President*
Dorothy J Rogers, *Corp Secy*
Robert G Rogers, *Treasurer*
EMP: 2
SALES (est): 479K **Privately Held**
SIC: 1311 Crude petroleum production; natural gas production

(G-3051)
ROMAYNE - BAKER OIL & GAS LTD
108 N Washington St (73701-4020)
P.O. Box 3607 (73702-3607)
PHONE 580 237-1626
Romayne Baker Jr, *Partner*
EMP: 1
SQ FT: 500
SALES (est): 86.3K **Privately Held**
SIC: 1311 Crude petroleum production; natural gas production

(G-3052)
ROWE WIRELINE SERVICES LLC
3801 Whippoorwill Ln (73703-1480)
PHONE 580 541-5086
Robert Rowe,
EMP: 4
SALES (est): 258.6K **Privately Held**
SIC: 1381 Drilling oil & gas wells

(G-3053)
RUSCO PLASTICS
3125 Chisholm Trl (73701-1237)
PHONE 580 234-1596
Eveline Allen, *Owner*
EMP: 2
SALES (est): 87K **Privately Held**
SIC: 7389 3953 3089 Engraving service; marking devices; plastics products

(G-3054)
RUSSELL CHEMICAL SALES & SVC
901 Sooner Trend (73701-9445)
PHONE 580 234-2100
Bob Russell, *President*
Virginia Russell, *Treasurer*
Sarah Roberts, *Admin Sec*
EMP: 9
SQ FT: 7,500
SALES: 1MM **Privately Held**
SIC: 5169 2899 Industrial chemicals; chemical preparations

(G-3055)
SHEBESTER BECHTEL INC
4210 S Van Buren St (73703-8521)
PHONE 580 242-4876
Thomas Fletcher, *President*
EMP: 43
SALES (est): 1.4MM
SALES (corp-wide): 41.1MM **Privately Held**
SIC: 1389 Oil field services
PA: Shebester Bechtel, Inc
605 N 29th St
Blackwell OK 74631
580 363-4124

(G-3056)
SIGNS ON A DIME
1212 W Oklahoma Ave (73703-5861)
PHONE 580 237-3078
Angela Stone, *Principal*
EMP: 2

SALES (est): 117.3K **Privately Held**
SIC: 3993 Signs & advertising specialties

(G-3057)
SILVER ARC WELDING INC
3809 E Willow Rd (73701-9439)
P.O. Box 3366 (73702-3366)
PHONE.................................580 234-2209
Thomas Silver, *President*
Misty Silver, *Vice Pres*
EMP: 8
SALES (est): 1.6MM **Privately Held**
SIC: 7692 Welding repair

(G-3058)
SOONER PUBLISHING INC
412 N Van Buren St (73703-4453)
PHONE.................................580 233-8400
Danny Means, *Principal*
EMP: 4
SALES (est): 425.8K **Privately Held**
SIC: 2741 Miscellaneous publishing

(G-3059)
SOONER SWABBING SERVICES INC
2120 W Willow Rd (73703-2403)
PHONE.................................580 233-4347
Tony McKaig, *Principal*
EMP: 2
SALES (est): 102.9K **Privately Held**
SIC: 1389 Bailing, cleaning, swabbing & treating of wells

(G-3060)
SPARKS AEROSPACE LLC
3501 Elm Pl (73703-3759)
PHONE.................................580 234-7972
James Sparks, *Principal*
EMP: 2
SALES (est): 97.1K **Privately Held**
SIC: 3721 Aircraft

(G-3061)
SPECIALTY PLASTICS INC
2302 N 11th St (73701-8720)
PHONE.................................580 237-1018
J R Parrish, *President*
Jerry Koehn, *Corp Secy*
Jim Reed, *Vice Pres*
EMP: 10
SQ FT: 10,000
SALES (est): 1.4MM
SALES (corp-wide): 2.8MM **Privately Held**
SIC: 3089 Molding primary plastic
PA: Parrish Enterprises, Ltd.
1414 E Willow Rd
Enid OK 73701
580 237-4033

(G-3062)
STAR INDUSTRIES
1721 N Grand St (73701-1733)
PHONE.................................580 977-4576
Larry Latta, *Owner*
EMP: 2
SALES (est): 117.9K **Privately Held**
SIC: 1389 Oil & gas field services

(G-3063)
STRIDE WELL SERVICE INC
205 W Maple Ave Ste 600 (73701-4021)
PHONE.................................405 375-4129
Ron Boyd, *Branch Mgr*
EMP: 2 **Publicly Held**
SIC: 1389 Servicing oil & gas wells
HQ: Stride Well Service Inc.
615 E Ponca St
Lindsay OK 73052
580 242-7300

(G-3064)
SUMMIT ESP LLC
103 S 42nd St (73701-9421)
PHONE.................................918 392-7820
John Kenner, *President*
EMP: 2 **Publicly Held**
SIC: 3585 Heat pumps, electric
HQ: Summit Esp, Llc
835 W 41st St
Tulsa OK 74107

(G-3065)
TITAN FENCE COMPANY
5110 E Market St (73701-9687)
PHONE.................................580 237-3412
Warren Brown, *Principal*
EMP: 2
SALES (est): 265.5K **Privately Held**
SIC: 3496 Miscellaneous fabricated wire products

(G-3066)
TRADE MARK SIGNS
1610 N Van Buren St (73703-2513)
PHONE.................................580 242-7446
Chris Erickson, *Owner*
EMP: 3
SALES (est): 120K **Privately Held**
SIC: 3993 Signs & advertising specialties

(G-3067)
TRINITY GAS CORPORATION (PA)
201 N Grand St Ste 700 (73701-4138)
P.O. Box 3488 (73702-3488)
PHONE.................................580 233-1155
Joanne Champlin, *President*
Dave Meara, *Corp Secy*
Clark Young, *Vice Pres*
Alvin Solomon, *Manager*
EMP: 7
SQ FT: 1,500
SALES (est): 1.1MM **Privately Held**
SIC: 1311 Natural gas production

(G-3068)
TUMBLEWEED CREEK COTTAGE
112 N Independence St (73701-4001)
PHONE.................................580 242-2767
Gina Malaska, *Principal*
EMP: 2
SALES (est): 235.8K **Privately Held**
SIC: 2782 5621 Scrapbooks; women's clothing stores

(G-3069)
UNION VALLEY PETROLEUM CORP
10422 Pinto Ln (73701-6932)
PHONE.................................580 237-3959
Paul Youngblood, *President*
Gayla Youngblood, *Vice Pres*
EMP: 3
SALES (est): 346.6K **Privately Held**
SIC: 1311 Crude petroleum production; natural gas production

(G-3070)
UNIQUE DESIGNS STUDIO MORE LLC
1814 N Grand St (73701-1706)
PHONE.................................580 237-0034
Billie Neathery,
EMP: 2
SALES (est): 227.4K **Privately Held**
SIC: 2759 Screen printing

(G-3071)
WAGGONER OIL & GAS
3114 Wren Ln (73703-1570)
PHONE.................................580 234-0030
William Waggoner, *Principal*
EMP: 2
SALES (est): 95.5K **Privately Held**
SIC: 1382 Oil & gas exploration services

(G-3072)
WAKO LLC
5606 N Us Highway 81 (73701-9759)
PHONE.................................580 234-3434
Rex Bland, *Ch of Bd*
Wayne Bland, *President*
Shane Bland, *General Mgr*
Jeff Unruh, *Vice Pres*
Diana Bland, *Treasurer*
▲ EMP: 50 EST: 1961
SQ FT: 36,000
SALES: 7MM **Privately Held**
WEB: www.wakollc.com
SIC: 3523 Fertilizing machinery, farm

(G-3073)
WALTER BAKER
1510 N Tyler St (73701-4464)
PHONE.................................580 233-7820
Walter L Baker, *Owner*
EMP: 1
SALES (est): 73.1K **Privately Held**
SIC: 1231 Anthracite mining

(G-3074)
WARD PETROLEUM CORPORATION (PA)
502 S Fillmore St (73703-5703)
P.O. Box 1187 (73702-1187)
PHONE.................................580 234-3229
Lew O Ward, *Ch of Bd*
William C Ward, *President*
Richard Tozzi, *Vice Pres*
Mark Jopling, *Opers Mgr*
Richard R Tozzi, *Treasurer*
EMP: 86
SQ FT: 12,000
SALES (est): 50.2MM **Privately Held**
WEB: www.wardpetroleum.com
SIC: 1382 Oil & gas exploration services

(G-3075)
WASHITA VALLEY ENTERPRISES INC
4411 Shady Ln (73701-1840)
PHONE.................................580 540-9277
EMP: 2
SALES (est): 73.6K **Privately Held**
SIC: 1389 Oil field services

(G-3076)
WD SALES INC
3520 Edgewater Dr (73703-1405)
P.O. Box 49 (73702-0049)
PHONE.................................580 237-1220
Warren L Duffy, *President*
EMP: 15
SALES: 1.5MM **Privately Held**
SIC: 2434 Wood kitchen cabinets

(G-3077)
WEEKS WELDING LLC
3502 N Grant St (73703-1612)
PHONE.................................918 931-1167
Susan Michelle Weeks, *Principal*
EMP: 1 EST: 2012
SALES (est): 49.8K **Privately Held**
SIC: 7692 Welding repair

(G-3078)
WELLSTAR DOWNHOLE SERVICES LLC
2504 W Owen K Garriott Rd # 301 (73703-5223)
PHONE.................................580 542-6982
Paul Wilcoxen, *Principal*
EMP: 1
SALES (est): 129.3K **Privately Held**
SIC: 1389 Construction, repair & dismantling services

(G-3079)
WHITING PETROLEUM CORPORATION
418 Chisholm Crk (73701-6548)
PHONE.................................580 234-5554
EMP: 124
SALES (corp-wide): 3B **Publicly Held**
SIC: 1311 Oil And Gas Exploration And Production
PA: Whiting Petroleum Corporation
1700 Broadway Ste 2300
Denver CO 80203
303 837-1661

(G-3080)
WILLIAMS WATER WELL CO
700 Applewood (73701-6511)
PHONE.................................405 250-8531
Terrill Bryan Williams, *Owner*
EMP: 1
SQ FT: 2,400
SALES: 600K **Privately Held**
SIC: 1389 Mud service, oil field drilling

(G-3081)
WINE PRESS ✪
3604 W Owen K Garriott Rd (73701-4911)
PHONE.................................580 540-8913
EMP: 1 EST: 2019
SALES (est): 37.5K **Privately Held**
SIC: 2741 Miscellaneous publishing

(G-3082)
WINFIELD SOLUTIONS LLC
3225 E Willow Rd (73701-9434)
PHONE.................................580 237-2456
Randy Elunkett, *Principal*
EMP: 3
SALES (corp-wide): 6B **Privately Held**
SIC: 5191 2048 8742 Chemicals, agricultural; feed concentrates; business consultant
HQ: Winfield Solutions, Llc
1080 County Road F W
Saint Paul MN 55126

(G-3083)
WORD EXPLORATION LP
502 S Fillmore St (73703-5703)
P.O. Box 1187 (73702-1187)
PHONE.................................580 234-3229
William Ward, *Partner*
EMP: 59 EST: 1995
SALES (est): 1.5MM
SALES (corp-wide): 50.2MM **Privately Held**
SIC: 1382 Oil & gas exploration services
PA: Ward Petroleum Corporation
502 S Fillmore St
Enid OK 73703
580 234-3229

(G-3084)
WRIGHT LEASE SERVICES
1116 Quail Ridge Rd (73703-2850)
P.O. Box 602 (73702-0602)
PHONE.................................806 857-9116
Jeff Wright, *President*
EMP: 3 EST: 2013
SALES (est): 150K **Privately Held**
SIC: 1389 Oil consultants

Erick
Beckham County

(G-3085)
BADGER MINING CORPORATION
12353 N 1760 Rd (73645-5521)
PHONE.................................608 864-1157
Andy Elbaker, *Manager*
EMP: 2
SALES (corp-wide): 503.4MM **Privately Held**
SIC: 1446 Industrial sand
PA: Badger Mining Corporation
409 S Church St
Berlin WI 54923
920 361-2388

(G-3086)
CARL ABLA
Also Called: Abla Bulldozer Service
202 Ne Boundry Rd (73645-3800)
PHONE.................................580 526-3267
Carl Abla, *Owner*
EMP: 1
SALES (est): 102.2K **Privately Held**
SIC: 3531 Bulldozers (construction machinery)

(G-3087)
HEXT TRUCKING LLC
17871 E 1200 Rd (73645-4512)
PHONE.................................580 821-6150
J'Lene Holley,
EMP: 3
SALES (est): 266K **Privately Held**
SIC: 1389 Haulage, oil field

(G-3088)
MACK SMOTHERMAN
Also Called: Macks Welding
101 N Sheb Wooley Ave (73645-4569)
P.O. Box 1203 (73645-1203)
PHONE.................................580 526-3089
Mack Smotherman, *Owner*
EMP: 1
SALES (est): 40.3K **Privately Held**
SIC: 7692 Welding repair

Erick - Beckham County (G-3089)

(G-3089)
MCINTYRE TRANSPORTS INC
Also Called: Tyler McIntyre
12248 N 1790 Rd (73645-5537)
P.O. Box 1 (73645-0001)
PHONE....................580 526-3121
Tyler McIntyre, *President*
EMP: 35
SQ FT: 5,000
SALES (est): 5.9MM **Privately Held**
SIC: 1389 Well plugging & abandoning, oil & gas

(G-3090)
NORTH WELDING AND CONSTRUCTION
17433 E 1190 Rd (73645-4502)
PHONE....................580 526-3260
Leah North, *Owner*
Ronnie North, *Co-Owner*
EMP: 1
SALES (est): 40.1K **Privately Held**
SIC: 7692 Welding repair

(G-3091)
OUTLAW OILFIELD SUPPLY LLC
12292 Highway 30 (73645-5029)
P.O. Box 564 (73645-0564)
PHONE....................580 526-3792
Brian Austin,
Jon Phillips,
EMP: 20
SALES (est): 2.8MM **Privately Held**
SIC: 5099 1389 7519 5983 Brass goods; cementing oil & gas well casings; trailer rental; fuel oil dealers

(G-3092)
RUSTYS WELDING & REPAIR
Old Hgwy 66 (73645)
PHONE....................580 526-3611
Rusty Austin, *Owner*
EMP: 2
SALES (est): 65K **Privately Held**
SIC: 7692 Welding repair

(G-3093)
WESTOAK INDUSTRIES INC
110 N Sheb Wooley Ave (73645-4569)
P.O. Box 1188 (73645-1188)
PHONE....................580 526-3221
Larry J Rosson, *President*
Stephanie Pennington, *Purchasing*
Deanna Moore, *Controller*
Gail Pritchard, *Sales Associate*
Judy Banick, *Manager*
▲ EMP: 31
SQ FT: 12,000
SALES (est): 6.9MM **Privately Held**
SIC: 3679 Electronic circuits; harness assemblies for electronic use: wire or cable

Eucha
Delaware County

(G-3094)
LONNIE WILLIAMS
Also Called: Williams Welding
4319 E 400 Rd (74342-3028)
PHONE....................918 253-4650
Lonnie Williams, *Owner*
EMP: 1
SALES (est): 70.2K **Privately Held**
SIC: 7692 Welding repair

(G-3095)
PAULS PALLET CO
37419 County Road 492 (74342-3296)
PHONE....................918 435-4321
EMP: 4
SALES (est): 273.8K **Privately Held**
SIC: 2448 Pallets, wood & wood with metal

(G-3096)
T&B WELDING LLC
4763 E 400 Rd (74342-3406)
PHONE....................918 253-4120
Tom Williams, *Administration*
EMP: 1 EST: 2016
SALES (est): 35.3K **Privately Held**
SIC: 7692 Welding repair

Eufaula
Mcintosh County

(G-3097)
ATWOOD WLDG CSTM FBRCATION LLC
116421 S 4110 Rd (74432-3432)
PHONE....................918 617-7522
EMP: 1 EST: 2012
SALES (est): 46.3K **Privately Held**
SIC: 7692 Welding repair

(G-3098)
CANOPIES PLUS INC
420331 Texanna Rd (74432-1206)
P.O. Box 1737 (74432-7037)
PHONE....................918 689-7077
Fax: 918 689-7251
EMP: 5
SQ FT: 12,280
SALES (est): 718.9K **Privately Held**
SIC: 3444 Mfg Sheet Metalwork

(G-3099)
CONCORDE RESOURCE CORPORATION
111 S Main St (74432-2875)
P.O. Box 841 (74432-0841)
PHONE....................918 689-9510
Gary Moores, *President*
J Mark Dobbs, *Vice Pres*
Kathleen Nickell, *Admin Sec*
EMP: 2
SQ FT: 1,000
SALES (est): 302.5K **Privately Held**
SIC: 4922 1382 1311 Natural gas transmission; oil & gas exploration services; crude petroleum production; natural gas production

(G-3100)
DOBBS & CROWDER INC
Also Called: Dobbs J Mark & Associates
111 S Main St (74432-2875)
P.O. Box 879 (74432-0879)
PHONE....................918 452-3211
Jeff Herrick, *President*
EMP: 5
SALES (est): 227.6K **Privately Held**
SIC: 8111 7231 2394 7539 General practice attorney, lawyer; manicurist, pedicurist; canvas & related products; wheel alignment, automotive; contract haulers; video recorders, players, disc players & accessories

(G-3101)
FORESEE READY-MIX CONCRETE INC (PA)
710 S Main St (74432-3304)
P.O. Box 246 (74432-0246)
PHONE....................918 689-3951
Thomas A Foresee, *President*
Kathy Turner, *Vice Pres*
EMP: 15 EST: 1950
SQ FT: 1,000
SALES (est): 1MM **Privately Held**
SIC: 3273 3272 Ready-mixed concrete; septic tanks, concrete

(G-3102)
FOUR WINDS FIELD SERVICES LLC
413299 E 1210 Rd (74432-5682)
PHONE....................918 568-1143
Tom McIntosh, *Owner*
EMP: 1
SALES (est): 28.4K **Privately Held**
SIC: 7692 Welding repair

(G-3103)
JOSH LEEPER
Also Called: CL Installation
121316 S 4083 Rd (74432-3392)
PHONE....................918 618-2215
Josh Leeper, *Owner*
EMP: 1
SALES: 15K **Privately Held**
SIC: 3663 Mobile communication equipment

(G-3104)
LAKELIFE INDUSTRIES LLC
139 N Main St (74432-2425)
PHONE....................918 618-6201
Amanda S Reeb, *Principal*
EMP: 1 EST: 2016
SALES (est): 58.6K **Privately Held**
SIC: 3999 Manufacturing industries

(G-3105)
MV PIPELINE COMPANY
111 S Main St (74432-2875)
PHONE....................918 689-5600
Eddie Harper, *President*
EMP: 2
SALES (est): 73.6K **Privately Held**
SIC: 1389 Oil & gas field services

(G-3106)
NORTHFORK AUTO REPAIR
Highway 69 (74432)
PHONE....................918 689-3589
Tim Stokes, *Owner*
EMP: 1
SALES (est): 125.8K **Privately Held**
SIC: 3732 7538 Boat building & repairing; general automotive repair shops

(G-3107)
NORTHFORK MARINE MANUFACTURING
417797 E 1145 Rd (74432-3494)
PHONE....................918 689-9309
EMP: 1
SALES (est): 49.9K **Privately Held**
SIC: 3999 Manufacturing industries

(G-3108)
OHANA MANUFACTURING LLC
116785 S 4214 Rd (74432-5751)
P.O. Box 328 (74432-0328)
PHONE....................918 490-9053
Mike Miller, *Owner*
EMP: 2
SALES (est): 84.3K **Privately Held**
SIC: 3999 Manufacturing industries

(G-3109)
PROBUILT SPINCASTING LLC
Also Called: Probuilt Manufacturing
420267 E 1140 Rd (74432-5471)
PHONE....................918 617-9053
Shannon Cure, *Co-Owner*
Mark Cure, *Co-Owner*
James Couch, *General Counsel*
EMP: 7 EST: 2017
SALES (est): 289.7K **Privately Held**
SIC: 3339 Babbitt metal (primary)

(G-3110)
RIO VISTA OPERATING LLC
120702 S 4104 Rd (74432-3372)
PHONE....................918 689-5600
Ian Dothwell, *CEO*
EMP: 79
SQ FT: 2,200
SALES: 5MM **Privately Held**
SIC: 1382 Oil & gas exploration services

(G-3111)
ROCKIN L-H ASPARAGUS FARMS
111800 S 4120 Rd (74432-5653)
PHONE....................918 689-5086
Lee Henry, *Owner*
Sharon Henry, *Owner*
EMP: 2
SQ FT: 1,500
SALES (est): 98.4K **Privately Held**
SIC: 0161 2032 Asparagus farm; canned specialties

(G-3112)
SAILING HORSE ENTERPRISES LLC
412887 Highway 9 (74432-3341)
P.O. Box 859 (74432-0859)
PHONE....................918 618-4824
Rick Gibbens, *Owner*
Debi Givvens, *Owner*
EMP: 2
SALES (est): 130K **Privately Held**
SIC: 0172 2084 Grapes; wines

(G-3113)
SHAWN SCHAEFFER
Also Called: SDS Services
414938 E 1203 Rd (74432-5692)
PHONE....................918 689-6781
Shawn Schaeffer, *Owner*
EMP: 1
SALES (est): 76.8K **Privately Held**
SIC: 2879 Fungicides, herbicides

(G-3114)
SOONER SWAGE & COATING CO INC
Hc 62 Box A3 (74432-9601)
PHONE....................918 689-7142
William K Fisher, *President*
Joanne Jacobs, *Corp Secy*
Richard Menees, *Vice Pres*
EMP: 5
SALES (est): 273.8K **Privately Held**
SIC: 5085 3533 3498 Industrial fittings; oil & gas field machinery; fabricated pipe & fittings

(G-3115)
SPORTEES
139 N Main St (74432-2425)
PHONE....................918 618-6201
EMP: 2
SALES (est): 97.5K **Privately Held**
SIC: 2759 Screen printing

(G-3116)
SUPERIOR STEEL BLDG MFG LLC
710 Birkes Rd (74432-4002)
PHONE....................918 689-9745
EMP: 1
SALES (est): 42.9K **Privately Held**
SIC: 3999 Manufacturing industries

(G-3117)
WAYNE WINKLER
Also Called: Superior Steel Buildings Mfg
710 Birkes Rd (74432-4002)
PHONE....................918 689-9745
Wayne Winkler, *Owner*
EMP: 3
SALES (est): 124.8K **Privately Held**
SIC: 3441 Building components, structural steel

Fairfax
Osage County

(G-3118)
FAIRFAX CHIEF
100 N 2nd St (74637-2009)
PHONE....................918 642-3814
Ida Roberts, *Owner*
EMP: 1
SALES (est): 78.6K **Privately Held**
SIC: 2711 Newspapers, publishing & printing

(G-3119)
JAMES CASE
Also Called: Custom Metal Fab
3248 Fairfax Lake Rd (74637-5056)
P.O. Box 697, Barnsdall (74002-0697)
PHONE....................918 846-2884
EMP: 2 EST: 2000
SALES: 60K **Privately Held**
SIC: 3448 Fabricated Metal Buildings

(G-3120)
LINN OPERATING LLC
10599 County Road 5451 (74637-5142)
PHONE....................918 642-1265
EMP: 2
SALES (est): 159.3K **Privately Held**
SIC: 1382 Oil & gas exploration services

(G-3121)
SECURE OPERATIONS GROUP LLC
39 Little Star Dr (74637-5224)
PHONE....................918 642-3444
Johnny L McAlpine, *Mng Member*
EMP: 2

GEOGRAPHIC SECTION

Fairview - Major County (G-3151)

SALES (est): 75.9K **Privately Held**
WEB: www.secureoperationsgroup.com
SIC: **1389** Construction, repair & dismantling services

(G-3122)
WOOTEN PUMPING SERVICE
Also Called: Wooten Ranch
192 Littlechief Ranch Rd (74637-5154)
PHONE.................................918 642-5312
Sam Wooten, *Owner*
EMP: 3
SALES (est): 146.8K **Privately Held**
SIC: **1389** Oil field services

Fairland
Ottawa County

(G-3123)
CMS WELDING & FABRICATION
21150 S Highway 125 (74343-2539)
PHONE.................................918 676-3133
EMP: 1
SALES (est): 25K **Privately Held**
SIC: **7692** Welding repair

(G-3124)
DIGITAL INTERFACE LLC
19600S S 609 Rd (74343-2164)
PHONE.................................405 201-5070
Howard Panter,
EMP: 1 EST: 2011
SALES (est): 57.6K **Privately Held**
SIC: **8748** 7373 3674 Systems analysis & engineering consulting services; systems engineering, computer related; local area network (LAN) systems integrator; integrated circuits, semiconductor networks, etc.

(G-3125)
INDUSTRIAL MANUFACTURING INC
Also Called: I M I
57530 E Highway 59 (74343-2340)
P.O. Box 451778, Grove (74345-1778)
PHONE.................................918 787-5500
Don Williams, *President*
Christine Williams, *Corp Secy*
EMP: 5
SQ FT: 12,000
SALES (est): 400K **Privately Held**
SIC: **3599** Machine shop, jobbing & repair

(G-3126)
MAHURIN GENERAL REPAIR LLC
1799 Taft Hwy 125 (74343)
P.O. Box 305 (74343-0305)
PHONE.................................918 676-3855
John Looper, *Owner*
EMP: 1
SALES (est): 59.3K **Privately Held**
SIC: **7692** Welding repair

(G-3127)
OTTAWA COUNTY DISTRICT 3
7 S Main St (74343-4915)
P.O. Box 737 (74343-0737)
PHONE.................................918 676-3227
Russell Gurls, *Manager*
Russell Earls, *Commissioner*
EMP: 12
SALES (est): 1.8MM **Privately Held**
SIC: **3531** Road construction & maintenance machinery

(G-3128)
RANDY WYRICK
58495 E 160 Rd (74343-2748)
PHONE.................................918 848-0117
Randy Wyrick, *Owner*
EMP: 1
SALES (est): 118.3K **Privately Held**
SIC: **2711** Newspapers, publishing & printing

(G-3129)
SILHOUETTE SHOP
57301 E Highway 59 (74343-2317)
PHONE.................................918 257-6143
Ron Wagner, *Owner*
EMP: 1

SALES (est): 97.4K **Privately Held**
SIC: **7692** Welding repair

(G-3130)
SIMMONS FOODS INC
1010 Industrial Park (74343-2926)
P.O. Box 749 (74343-0749)
PHONE.................................918 676-3285
Brad Johnston, *Vice Pres*
Vince Lett, *Branch Mgr*
EMP: 14
SALES (corp-wide): 1.7B **Privately Held**
SIC: **2015** Poultry slaughtering & processing
PA: Simmons Foods, Inc.
    601 N Hico St
    Siloam Springs AR 72761
    479 524-8151

(G-3131)
SPARKS MTAL DSIGN FBRCTION LLC
21100 S 625 Rd (74343-2278)
PHONE.................................918 676-5112
Michael Allen Hopkins, *Owner*
EMP: 1
SALES (est): 54.3K **Privately Held**
SIC: **3499** Fabricated metal products

Fairview
Major County

(G-3132)
BASIC ENERGY SERVICES INC
Hwy 60 N 2/5 Mi (73737)
PHONE.................................580 227-3144
Chad Durdin, *Branch Mgr*
EMP: 30
SALES (corp-wide): 567.2MM **Publicly Held**
SIC: **1389** Oil field services
PA: Basic Energy Services, Inc.
    801 Cherry St Unit 2
    Fort Worth TX 76102
    817 334-4100

(G-3133)
BRAMCO INC
513 N Main St (73737-1200)
PHONE.................................580 227-2345
Marva Morris, *President*
Marva Marten, *Corp Secy*
Bradley J Martens, *Vice Pres*
Sandy Fitzsimmons, *Purchasing*
EMP: 10
SQ FT: 20,000
SALES (est): 1.9MM **Privately Held**
SIC: **3713** 3523 Truck & bus bodies; balers, farm: hay, straw, cotton, etc.

(G-3134)
DANIEL R WILLITS OFFICES
120 N Main St (73737-1621)
P.O. Box 70 (73737-0070)
PHONE.................................580 227-2592
Mr Daniel R Willits, *Owner*
EMP: 6
SALES (est): 345K **Privately Held**
SIC: **1382** Oil & gas exploration services

(G-3135)
ENVIRNMNTAL TCHNCIANS OKLA LLC
3 And A Half Mile N (73737)
PHONE.................................580 227-2521
Harold Hamm, *Owner*
EMP: 1
SALES (corp-wide): 496.1K **Privately Held**
SIC: **1389** Oil field services
PA: Environmental Technicians Of Oklahoma Llc
    302 N Independence St # 11
    Enid OK 73701
    580 242-1876

(G-3136)
GREEN VALLEY ENTERPRISES INC
Also Called: Fairview Ready Mix
201 W Central St (73737-2017)
P.O. Box 306 (73737-0306)
PHONE.................................580 227-4938

Dean Gilchrist, *President*
Artalea Gilchrist, *Treasurer*
EMP: 5
SQ FT: 200
SALES: 400K **Privately Held**
WEB: www.greenvalleyinc.org
SIC: **3273** Ready-mixed concrete

(G-3137)
HAMMER HOBY
Also Called: Artistic Printing
112 N Main St (73737-1621)
P.O. Box 497 (73737-0497)
PHONE.................................580 227-2100
Hoby Hammer, *Owner*
EMP: 6 EST: 1979
SQ FT: 4,000
SALES (est): 409.7K **Privately Held**
SIC: **2752** 2759 2791 2789 Commercial printing, offset; letterpress printing; typesetting; bookbinding & related work

(G-3138)
JOHN KENNEDY WELDING LLC
56526 S County Road 256 (73737-7623)
PHONE.................................580 227-2300
John Kennedy, *Owner*
EMP: 1 EST: 2017
SALES (est): 30K **Privately Held**
SIC: **7692** Welding repair

(G-3139)
L&S FUELS LLC
120 Cedar Springs Rd (73737)
P.O. Box 554 (73737-0554)
PHONE.................................580 227-0999
Danny Lawrence, *Mng Member*
EMP: 3
SALES (est): 228.6K **Privately Held**
SIC: **2869** Fuels

(G-3140)
LARRY D HAMMER (PA)
Also Called: Jet Vistor
112 N Main St (73737-1621)
P.O. Box 497 (73737-0497)
PHONE.................................580 227-2100
Phyllis Hammer, *Owner*
EMP: 11 EST: 1961
SQ FT: 3,125
SALES (est): 488.5K **Privately Held**
WEB: www.fairviewrepublican.com
SIC: **2711** 2752 2791 2789 Job printing & newspaper publishing combined; commercial printing, lithographic; typesetting; bookbinding & related work; commercial printing

(G-3141)
LEVIATHAN INC
1925 Industrial Blvd (73737)
PHONE.................................580 227-3105
Shane Bode, *President*
William Shane Bode, *Vice Pres*
Lori Lynn Bode, *Admin Sec*
EMP: 5
SQ FT: 7,500
SALES (est): 971K **Privately Held**
SIC: **7692** Welding repair

(G-3142)
MARTENS MACHINE SHOP
1414 N Main St (73737-2710)
PHONE.................................580 227-2734
Paul A Martens, *Owner*
EMP: 6
SQ FT: 6,000
SALES (est): 523.1K **Privately Held**
SIC: **3599** Machine shop, jobbing & repair

(G-3143)
MOBILE PRODUCTS INC
201 W Oklahoma Ave (73737-9659)
PHONE.................................580 227-3711
Donald Collins, *President*
Randall Swiftt, *Principal*
◆ EMP: 7
SALES (est): 10MM **Publicly Held**
SIC: **3537** Lift trucks, industrial: fork, platform, straddle, etc.
HQ: Collins Industries, Inc.
    15 Compound Dr
    Hutchinson KS 67502
    620 663-5551

(G-3144)
MOBLIE PRODUCTS INC
201 W Oklahoma Ave (73737-9602)
PHONE.................................580 227-3711
Geral Gurka, *President*
Jim Sery, *Vice Pres*
EMP: 102
SQ FT: 70,000
SALES (est): 7.6MM **Publicly Held**
SIC: **3537** Tractors, used in plants, docks, terminals, etc.: industrial; forklift trucks
HQ: Collins Industries, Inc.
    15 Compound Dr
    Hutchinson KS 67502
    620 663-5551

(G-3145)
PENDPAC INCORPORATED
124 E Broadway Ste 4 (73737-2123)
P.O. Box 2785, Oshkosh WI (54903-2785)
PHONE.................................418 831-8250
Steve Degeorge, *President*
Terry Hill, *General Mgr*
Rob Gnatovich, *COO*
Jim Scali, *Controller*
Paul Butcher, *Sales Engr*
EMP: 75
SQ FT: 50,000
SALES (est): 11MM **Privately Held**
SIC: **3713** Garbage, refuse truck bodies

(G-3146)
PLYMOUTH VALLEY CELLARS INC
57442 S County Road 255 (73737-5655)
PHONE.................................580 227-0348
EMP: 2
SALES (est): 110.7K **Privately Held**
WEB: www.plymouthvalleycellars.com
SIC: **2084** Wines

(G-3147)
PROGRESSIVE WINDOWS INC
Rr 2 Box 296 (73737-9802)
P.O. Box 296 (73737-0296)
PHONE.................................580 227-9915
Larry Kliewer, *President*
Jerome Haines, *General Mgr*
Jay Kliewer, *Corp Secy*
EMP: 8
SALES (est): 119.7K **Privately Held**
SIC: **2824** Vinyl fibers

(G-3148)
RANGE ENERGY SERVICES COMPANY
Also Called: Range Production Co
253632 E County Road 49 (73737-5707)
P.O. Box 1 (73737-0001)
PHONE.................................580 227-3762
EMP: 17
SALES (corp-wide): 2.6B **Publicly Held**
SIC: **1311** 4953 Oil & Gas Production & Water Hauling & Disposal
HQ: Range Energy Services Company
    5600 N May Ave Ste 350
    Oklahoma City OK 73112

(G-3149)
RED BUD RESOURCES
120 N Main St (73737-1621)
P.O. Box 70 (73737-0070)
PHONE.................................580 227-2592
Daniel Willits, *Principal*
EMP: 2
SALES (est): 99K **Privately Held**
SIC: **1389** Gas field services

(G-3150)
SAGE BRUSH JUNCTION
15154 Highway 60 (73737-4652)
PHONE.................................580 227-3434
EMP: 2 EST: 2012
SALES (est): 167.9K **Privately Held**
SIC: **2311** Tuxedos: made from purchased materials

(G-3151)
SAND CREEK CUSTOM CABINETS LLC
314 N 4th Ave (73737-1605)
PHONE.................................580 822-1269
Eric Nightingale, *Principal*
EMP: 2

Fairview - Major County (G-3152)

SALES (est): 152.4K **Privately Held**
WEB: www.sandcreekwoodworks.com
SIC: 2434 Wood kitchen cabinets

(G-3152)
STOCKTON TRANSPORTS INC
253920 E County Road 49 (73737-5763)
P.O. Box 554 (73737-0554)
PHONE..................580 227-3793
Bill Stockton, *President*
Carole Stockton, *Treasurer*
EMP: 6
SQ FT: 5,000
SALES: 1MM **Privately Held**
SIC: 1389 Oil field services

(G-3153)
TIM METZ
707 S 13th Ave (73737-2528)
PHONE..................580 227-2456
Tim Metz, *Owner*
EMP: 1 **EST:** 1993
SALES (est): 75.4K **Privately Held**
SIC: 3592 Valves

(G-3154)
TODD J NIGHTENGALE
17557 Highway 8 (73737-7601)
PHONE..................580 227-2646
Todd Nightengale, *Principal*
EMP: 1
SALES (est): 87.1K **Privately Held**
SIC: 2842 Specialty cleaning preparations

(G-3155)
WALDON EQUIPMENT LLC
201 W Oklahoma Ave (73737-9602)
PHONE..................580 227-3711
Merle Patzkowsky, *Mng Member*
▲ **EMP:** 15
SQ FT: 70,000
SALES (est): 2.4MM **Privately Held**
SIC: 3531 Backhoes, tractors, cranes, plows & similar equipment

Fay
Dewey County

(G-3156)
DS WELDING
Block 1 Box 210 (73646)
PHONE..................580 623-4104
Dennis Houk, *Owner*
EMP: 1
SALES (est): 63K **Privately Held**
SIC: 7692 1799 Welding repair; athletic & recreation facilities construction

(G-3157)
IRONMAN WELDING MACHINE
81594 Wild Goose Cir (73646-4662)
PHONE..................580 791-3091
Blayne Barnes, *Principal*
EMP: 1
SALES (est): 62.5K **Privately Held**
SIC: 7692 Welding repair

Fittstown
Pontotoc County

(G-3158)
FITTSTONE INC
County Rd 1670 (74842)
P.O. Box 279 (74842-0279)
PHONE..................580 777-2808
Randy Jennings, *President*
EMP: 30
SALES (est): 1.7MM **Privately Held**
SIC: 3281 Stone, quarrying & processing of own stone products

(G-3159)
JENNINGS STONE COMPANY INC
Also Called: Fittstone
17330 County Road 1670 (74842)
P.O. Box 279 (74842-0279)
PHONE..................580 777-2880
Randy Jennings, *President*
Beverly Jennings, *Corp Secy*

EMP: 26
SQ FT: 1,800
SALES: 6.7MM **Privately Held**
SIC: 4212 1422 Local trucking, without storage; crushed & broken limestone

Fletcher
Comanche County

(G-3160)
AINSWORTH WELDING
14647 Ne Cline Rd (73541-4708)
P.O. Box 573, Marlow (73055-0573)
PHONE..................580 512-7874
EMP: 1
SALES (est): 47.3K **Privately Held**
SIC: 7692 Welding repair

(G-3161)
BUILT BETTER ENTERPRISES LLC
Also Called: Hoswel
410 Us Highway 277 (73541)
PHONE..................580 492-5227
Jogay Renshaw, *CEO*
Jerry I Renshaw, *Principal*
EMP: 9
SALES (est): 1.1MM **Privately Held**
WEB: www.bbe-hoswel.com
SIC: 3715 3523 3499 5083 Truck trailers; farm machinery & equipment; strapping, metal; livestock equipment; agricultural equipment repair services

(G-3162)
GEORGIA-PACIFIC LLC
16850 Ne 135th St (73541-2530)
PHONE..................580 549-7100
Dexter Stockstill, *Principal*
EMP: 124
SALES (corp-wide): 48.9B **Privately Held**
SIC: 2653 Boxes, corrugated: made from purchased materials
HQ: Georgia-Pacific Llc
133 Peachtree St Nw
Atlanta GA 30303
404 652-4000

(G-3163)
JOHN SAMUT-TAGLIAFERRO
Also Called: Samut Welding
15801 Ne North Dr (73541-9451)
PHONE..................580 284-6058
John Samut-Tagliaferro, *Principal*
EMP: 1
SALES (est): 60.2K **Privately Held**
SIC: 7692 Welding repair

(G-3164)
MY MAN TEES LLC
20077 Ne Wolf Rd (73541-3716)
PHONE..................580 695-9474
Dominic Pawlowski, *Principal*
EMP: 2
SALES (est): 77.5K **Privately Held**
SIC: 2759 Screen printing

(G-3165)
OKLAHOMA METAL CREATIONS LLC
10185 Ne Wolf Rd (73541-3870)
PHONE..................580 917-5434
Thorsten Littau, *President*
EMP: 1 **EST:** 2016
SALES (est): 145K **Privately Held**
SIC: 1799 3231 5999 3446 Ornamental metal work; ornamental glass: cut, engraved or otherwise decorated; stained glass: made from purchased glass; trophies & plaques; architectural metalwork; prefabricated building erection, industrial; gaskets, packing & sealing devices

(G-3166)
PHILIP R ECKART
8166 Ne Watts Rd (73541-3642)
PHONE..................580 917-3882
Philip R Eckart, *Owner*
EMP: 1
SALES: 500K **Privately Held**
SIC: 3444 Sheet metalwork

(G-3167)
SCHMIDT FARMS AT STRLNG RIDGE
133 Ne Grandview St (73541)
PHONE..................580 919-2111
Sherry Schmidt, *General Ptnr*
Michael Schmidt, *General Ptnr*
EMP: 5
SALES (est): 188.1K **Privately Held**
SIC: 0214 0252 2841 7389 Goat farm; chicken eggs; textile soap;

Foraker
Osage County

(G-3168)
GARRISON WELDING
Also Called: Charles Garrison
135 County Road 4657 (74652-5127)
PHONE..................918 331-6336
Charles Garrison, *Owner*
EMP: 1
SALES (est): 66.7K **Privately Held**
SIC: 7692 Welding repair

Forgan
Beaver County

(G-3169)
COOPER CONTRACT PUMPING SVC
Rr 1 Box 101 (73938-9766)
P.O. Box 1 (73938-0001)
PHONE..................580 487-3552
Jerry Cooper, *President*
EMP: 3
SALES (est): 162.2K **Privately Held**
SIC: 1389 Oil field services

(G-3170)
H 5 C PUMPING INC
621 Main (73938)
P.O. Box 86 (73938-0086)
PHONE..................580 487-3869
Johnnie Hoover, *President*
Margie Hoover, *Vice Pres*
Mary Hoover, *Treasurer*
EMP: 1
SALES (est): 60K **Privately Held**
SIC: 1389 Pumping of oil & gas wells

Fort Cobb
Caddo County

(G-3171)
FORT COBB LOCKER PLANT
100 Mopope St (73038)
PHONE..................405 643-2355
Bobby Dyer, *Owner*
Colleen Dyer, *Co-Owner*
EMP: 7
SQ FT: 4,800
SALES (est): 415.5K **Privately Held**
SIC: 2011 5963 Meat packing plants; direct selling establishments

Fort Gibson
Muskogee County

(G-3172)
AMERICAN SWAT SOLUTIONS LLC
5472 N 55th St E (74434-4403)
PHONE..................405 568-1413
Joshua Brown, *CEO*
Joshua Johns, *President*
Dustin Hopkins, *Vice Pres*
EMP: 3
SALES (est): 200.7K **Privately Held**
SIC: 3541 Machine tools, metal cutting type

(G-3173)
ARTUR BOOKBINDING INTL
Also Called: Bible & Books Repair Center
100 N Jackson St (74434-8614)
P.O. Box 1806 (74434-1806)
PHONE..................918 478-4888
Zbigeinew Niebieszczanski, *Owner*
EMP: 2
SALES (est): 146.3K **Privately Held**
SIC: 2789 2657 Binding only: books, pamphlets, magazines, etc.; folding paperboard boxes

(G-3174)
BURROW CONSTRUCTION LLC
Also Called: BCI Barn Builders
101 Leaning Tree Rd (74434-7611)
PHONE..................800 766-5793
Evan Gobdel, *CEO*
Terry D Burrow, *Partner*
Wendy Qualls, *Controller*
▲ **EMP:** 50
SQ FT: 33,000
SALES (est): 6.7MM **Privately Held**
SIC: 3325 1542 2439 2452 Rolling mill rolls, cast steel; agricultural building contractors; trusses, wooden roof; farm buildings, prefabricated or portable: wood

(G-3175)
JOHNSON SERVICE COMPANY
Also Called: Kpj Enterprises
8199 W 800 Rd (74434)
P.O. Box 1394, Muskogee (74402-1394)
PHONE..................918 869-7147
Kenneth Johnson, *Owner*
EMP: 1
SQ FT: 4,000
SALES (est): 22.9K **Privately Held**
SIC: 7694 Hermetics repair

(G-3176)
MOLLYCODDLED HASH SLINGER LLC
118 Se Railroad (74434)
PHONE..................918 236-1196
Melissa Wedman,
EMP: 2 **EST:** 2016
SALES: 150K **Privately Held**
SIC: 2064 5441 Candy & other confectionery products; confectionery

(G-3177)
NEO SIGN COMPANY
23761 N 7 Mile Rd (74434-6248)
PHONE..................918 456-1959
Tammy Brown, *Principal*
EMP: 1 **EST:** 2008
SALES (est): 34K **Privately Held**
SIC: 5949 5099 2759 Sewing, needlework & piece goods; signs, except electric; screen printing

(G-3178)
SONBURST GRAPHICS LLC
116 W Poplar (74434)
PHONE..................918 478-8600
Tonya Cooper,
Denise Bain,
EMP: 1 **EST:** 2008
SALES (est): 63.8K **Privately Held**
WEB: www.sonburstgraphics.com
SIC: 5999 5949 5099 3993 Banners, flags, decals & posters; sewing, needlework & piece goods; signs, except electric; signs & advertising specialties

(G-3179)
SUNFLOWER EMBROIDERY LLC
1404 Richmond Dr (74434-6391)
PHONE..................918 869-9646
Barry Moses, *Principal*
EMP: 1
SALES (est): 33.7K **Privately Held**
SIC: 2395 Embroidery & art needlework

(G-3180)
TIGERS DEN BY DREAMCATCHER
131 S Lee St (74434-8749)
P.O. Box 1022 (74434-1022)
PHONE..................918 478-4873
Amber Wright, *Mng Member*
EMP: 2

SALES (est): 101.2K **Privately Held**
SIC: 2396 5699 Screen printing on fabric articles; shirts, custom made; T-shirts, custom printed

(G-3181)
TRACK PRODUCTS
101 E Railroad St S (74434-8969)
P.O. Box 1084 (74434-1084)
PHONE..................918 231-9960
EMP: 2
SALES (est): 180K **Privately Held**
SIC: 3465 Mfg Automotive Stampings

Fort Sill
Comanche County

(G-3182)
UPS STORE 6206
1712 Macomb Rd Ste 300 (73503-4544)
PHONE..................580 248-7800
John Cherry, *Manager*
Robyn Cherry,
EMP: 3
SALES (est): 221.3K **Privately Held**
SIC: 7389 2759 Mailbox rental & related service; commercial printing; post cards, picture: printing; business forms: printing; menus: printing

Fort Towson
Choctaw County

(G-3183)
MT DESIGNS
194541 N 4360 Rd (74735-2204)
PHONE..................580 317-3921
Marty Montague, *Partner*
Teresa Montague, *Partner*
EMP: 2
SALES (est): 120.2K **Privately Held**
SIC: 3993 Letters for signs, metal

Foss
Washita County

(G-3184)
SYDCO SYSTEM INC (PA)
10879 Highway 44 (73647)
P.O. Box 9 (73647-0009)
PHONE..................405 350-3161
Sydney Gonzales, *President*
EMP: 11
SQ FT: 7,500
SALES (est): 2.1MM **Privately Held**
SIC: 7353 3533 Oil field equipment, rental or leasing; oil field machinery & equipment

Foster
Stephens County

(G-3185)
DUNNS TANK SERVICE INC
300637 State Highway 29 (73434-1119)
PHONE..................580 465-1687
James T Dunn, *President*
EMP: 25
SALES (est): 2.7MM **Privately Held**
SIC: 1389 Haulage, oil field

(G-3186)
MARSAU
161909 State Highway 76 (73434-1715)
PHONE..................580 432-5000
Justin Henry, *President*
EMP: 2
SALES (est): 107.3K **Privately Held**
SIC: 1389 Oil field services

(G-3187)
MOES PORTABLE STEAM CO INC
28252 N County Road 3070 (73434-9792)
PHONE..................580 432-5467
Wayne Owens, *President*
Caroline Owens, *Vice Pres*
Alissa Coles, *Treasurer*
Alissa Owens, *Treasurer*
Stacy Roady, *Admin Sec*
EMP: 4
SALES (est): 325.9K **Privately Held**
SIC: 1389 Servicing oil & gas wells

(G-3188)
OKLA CASING CO
27244 Highway 76 (73434-9770)
PHONE..................580 432-5311
EMP: 2 **EST:** 2010
SALES (est): 94K **Privately Held**
SIC: 1389 Oil/Gas Field Services

(G-3189)
T & C CONSTRUCTION
Oklahoma 76 (73434)
PHONE..................580 432-5413
Tim Mc Connell, *Owner*
EMP: 3
SALES (est): 293.3K **Privately Held**
SIC: 1389 Construction, repair & dismantling services

Fox
Carter County

(G-3190)
CANFIELD MACHINE INC
16096 Oklahoma 76 (73435)
P.O. Box 237 (73435-0237)
PHONE..................580 673-2185
Dennis Canfield, *President*
EMP: 3
SALES (est): 280K **Privately Held**
WEB: www.canfieldsci.com
SIC: 3599 Machine shop, jobbing & repair

Francis
Pontotoc County

(G-3191)
REAGENT CHEMICAL & RES INC
201 W 5th St (74844)
P.O. Box 59 (74844-0059)
PHONE..................580 436-4100
David Piercy, *Branch Mgr*
EMP: 18
SALES (corp-wide): 517MM **Privately Held**
SIC: 2819 3949 Sulfur, recovered or refined, incl. from sour natural gas; targets, archery & rifle shooting
PA: Reagent Chemical & Research, Inc.
    115 Rte 202
    Ringoes NJ 08551
    908 284-2800

Frederick
Tillman County

(G-3192)
CHRISTY COLLINS INC
18149 County Road Ns 234 (73542-9486)
PHONE..................580 305-0001
Christy Collins, *President*
EMP: 4
SALES (est): 475K **Privately Held**
SIC: 7311 8742 7389 7372 Advertising consultant; marketing consulting services; music & broadcasting services; application computer software

(G-3193)
GREEN ROOM STUDIOS
521 N 12th St (73542-3405)
PHONE..................580 335-5689
Larry Greer, *Owner*
EMP: 2
SALES (est): 67.3K **Privately Held**
SIC: 5999 3952 Art dealers; boards, drawing, artists'

(G-3194)
IRON COWBOY WELDING LLC
22325 State Highway 5 (73542-9424)
PHONE..................580 335-2900
EMP: 1 **EST:** 2014
SALES (est): 37.4K **Privately Held**
SIC: 7692 Welding repair

(G-3195)
KINDER EQUIPMENT LLC
22146 County Road Ew 183 (73542-9374)
PHONE..................580 335-2363
Toby Dale Kinder, *Principal*
EMP: 1 **EST:** 2017
SALES (est): 66K **Privately Held**
SIC: 3531 Construction machinery

(G-3196)
LANEY MFG INC
1007 Rebecca Rd (73542-2423)
PHONE..................580 335-2363
Evelyn Laney, *President*
Terri Gray, *Vice Pres*
Teresa Kinder, *Treasurer*
EMP: 6
SQ FT: 25,000
SALES (est): 1.5MM **Privately Held**
SIC: 3531 Graders, road (construction machinery)

(G-3197)
NEW TONGS
715 S Main St (73542-6805)
PHONE..................580 335-3030
Yan Yen, *Principal*
EMP: 2
SALES (est): 144.9K **Privately Held**
SIC: 1389 Construction, repair & dismantling services

(G-3198)
RED RIVER GUNSMITHING LLC
112 N Main St (73542-5427)
PHONE..................580 770-1911
Billy Underwood, *Principal*
EMP: 3
SALES (est): 168.9K **Privately Held**
SIC: 3489 Ordnance & accessories

(G-3199)
ROCKY L EMMONS & JUDY E SPRAG
18417 Ste Hwy 54 (73542)
PHONE..................580 305-1940
EMP: 1
SALES (est): 112.9K **Privately Held**
SIC: 5083 3713 4221 3523 Farm implements; farm truck bodies; farm product warehousing & storage; farm machinery & equipment; farm animals

(G-3200)
SHOWSTRING USA INC
1000 S Main St (73542-6814)
PHONE..................580 335-7171
Duane Baudino, *President*
EMP: 3
SALES (est): 236.3K **Privately Held**
SIC: 2395 Embroidery products, except schiffli machine; embroidery & art needlework

(G-3201)
SMITH WELDING CO
503 S 8th St (73542-6603)
PHONE..................580 335-7521
Burnis Smith, *Owner*
EMP: 3 **EST:** 1975
SALES (est): 60K **Privately Held**
WEB: www.smithsfencingok.com
SIC: 7692 Welding repair

(G-3202)
TAGS 2 GO
102 W Grand Ave (73542-5436)
PHONE..................580 335-7474
Linda Hasting, *Owner*
EMP: 1
SALES (est): 77.5K **Privately Held**
SIC: 3469 Automobile license tags, stamped metal

(G-3203)
WASINGER WASINGER
Also Called: Ke-Fab Manufacturing
17972 County Road Ns 222 (73542-9265)
PHONE..................580 335-3490
Keith Wasinger, *Owner*
EMP: 4
SALES (est): 250K **Privately Held**
SIC: 1791 7692 Structural steel erection; welding repair

(G-3204)
WESTERN HULL SACKING INC
Rr 2 (73542)
P.O. Box 1041 (73542-1041)
PHONE..................580 335-2144
Ray Walker, *President*
Kent Walker, *Vice Pres*
Virginia Walker, *Treasurer*
▲ **EMP:** 5
SQ FT: 12,500
SALES (est): 1MM **Privately Held**
WEB: www.westernhull.com
SIC: 2899 2823 Drilling mud; cellulosic manmade fibers

Freedom
Woods County

(G-3205)
CARGILL INCORPORATED
27565 County Road 110 (73842-3851)
P.O. Box 167 (73842-0167)
PHONE..................580 621-3246
Todd Reasons, *Plant Mgr*
Eric Augspurper, *Opers Mgr*
Mick Berning, *Mfg Staff*
Michelle Schroeder, *Branch Mgr*
EMP: 27
SALES (corp-wide): 113.4B **Privately Held**
SIC: 2899 Salt
PA: Cargill, Incorporated
    15407 Mcginty Rd W
    Wayzata MN 55391
    952 742-7575

(G-3206)
FREEDOM CALL LLC
512 Main St (73842)
PHONE..................580 621-3578
Donna Hodgson,
EMP: 4
SALES (est): 100K **Privately Held**
SIC: 2711 Newspapers, publishing & printing

(G-3207)
KOG PRODUCTION LLC
1121 Tumbleweed Ln Po (73842-4223)
P.O. Box 123 (73842-0123)
PHONE..................580 621-3510
Susan Kinkel,
EMP: 1
SALES (est): 45.1K **Privately Held**
SIC: 1389 Servicing oil & gas wells

(G-3208)
NIXON MATERIALS COMPANY
511 Sandbur Ln (73842)
PHONE..................580 621-3297
C R Nixon, *President*
Tana Nixon, *Partner*
EMP: 1 **EST:** 1966
SALES (est): 101.5K **Privately Held**
SIC: 3273 0191 3443 3355 Ready-mixed concrete; general farms, primarily crop; fabricated plate work (boiler shop); aluminum rolling & drawing

(G-3209)
STANSBERRY WELDING INC
5 Miles Ne On Hwy 64 (73842)
P.O. Box 93, Alva (73717-0093)
PHONE..................580 621-3211
Bruce Stansberry, *President*
Dixie Stansberry, *Vice Pres*
EMP: 6
SALES (est): 363.5K **Privately Held**
SIC: 1799 7692 Welding on site; welding repair

Gage
Ellis County

(G-3210)
GAGE LOCKER SERVICE
611 N Main St (73843)
P.O. Box 183 (73843-0183)
PHONE.................................580 923-7661
Gary Wolfington, *Owner*
EMP: 1
SALES (est): 141.1K **Privately Held**
SIC: 2011 Meat packing plants

(G-3211)
RUSSELL W MACKEY
Rr 1 Box 17 (73843-9706)
Rural Route Box 17
PHONE.................................580 571-7595
EMP: 1
SALES (est): 87K **Privately Held**
SIC: 1389 Oil And Gas Well Pumping

Garber
Garfield County

(G-3212)
DOUBLE S TANK TRUCK SERVICE
Garber Rd (73738)
P.O. Box 262 (73738-0262)
PHONE.................................580 863-5231
Paul Holt, *President*
Terry Stubblefield, *Corp Secy*
EMP: 4
SQ FT: 2,400
SALES (est): 300K **Privately Held**
SIC: 1389 Oil field services; haulage, oil field

(G-3213)
F W GRUBB OILFIELD SERVICE
Corner Of Rlrad Apache St (73738)
P.O. Box 186 (73738-0186)
PHONE.................................580 863-2395
Forrest W Grubb, *President*
Patricia Grubb, *Corp Secy*
Alan Grubb, *Vice Pres*
EMP: 3
SALES (est): 210K **Privately Held**
SIC: 1389 Haulage, oil field

(G-3214)
HAYDEN BETCHAN WELDING LLC
1309 S Knox Rd (73738-0569)
PHONE.................................580 863-5372
Hayden Betchan, *Owner*
EMP: 1
SALES (est): 25K **Privately Held**
SIC: 7692 Welding repair

(G-3215)
MIKE DEEDS WELDING LLC
21715 E Centennial Rd (73738-0206)
PHONE.................................580 863-2339
Michael Deeds, *Owner*
EMP: 1
SALES (est): 38.9K **Privately Held**
SIC: 7692 Welding repair

Geary
Blaine County

(G-3216)
GEARY STAR
114 W Main St (73040-2418)
P.O. Box 176 (73040-0176)
PHONE.................................405 884-2424
Elisa Bingham, *Owner*
EMP: 3
SALES (est): 79.8K **Privately Held**
SIC: 2711 2791 2752 Newspapers: publishing only, not printed on site; typesetting; commercial printing, lithographic

(G-3217)
PEAK OILFIELD SERVICES
26460 Highway 281 Spur (73040)
PHONE.................................405 884-2379
EMP: 2
SALES (est): 100.3K **Privately Held**
SIC: 1389 Oil field services

(G-3218)
WORKHORSE INDUSTRIES LLC
93497 N 2630 Rd (73040-4344)
PHONE.................................405 884-2023
Darren Lynn Base, *Agent*
EMP: 1
SALES (est): 39.6K **Privately Held**
SIC: 3999 Manufacturing industries

Glencoe
Payne County

(G-3219)
CIRCLE V ENERGY SERVICES LLC
10000 E Yost Rd (74032-3049)
PHONE.................................405 614-0891
Terry D Vigil, *Administration*
EMP: 9 **EST:** 2014
SALES (est): 618.9K **Privately Held**
SIC: 1389 1381 Construction, repair & dismantling services; drilling oil & gas wells

(G-3220)
D&P WELDING CORP
12520 E Airport Rd (74032-3149)
PHONE.................................405 624-0170
Patricia Goosman, *Principal*
EMP: 1
SALES (est): 37.7K **Privately Held**
SIC: 7692 Welding repair

(G-3221)
DEWITT TRUCKING & EXCAVATION
4601 N West Point Rd (74032-3114)
PHONE.................................580 669-2534
David Dewitt, *Co-Owner*
Sylvia Dewitt, *Co-Owner*
EMP: 8
SALES (est): 1.6MM **Privately Held**
WEB: www.dewittok.com
SIC: 1389 4212 Construction, repair & dismantling services; local trucking, without storage

(G-3222)
GLENCOE MANUFACTURING CO
Also Called: Glencoe Mfg Roofg Installation
401 S Excel Ave (74032)
P.O. Box 161 (74032-0161)
PHONE.................................580 669-2555
Jack Burnett, *Owner*
EMP: 11 **EST:** 1971
SQ FT: 14,000
SALES (est): 1.5MM **Privately Held**
SIC: 2899 3599 5812 1742 Insulating compounds; machine shop, jobbing repair; eating places; plastering, drywall & insulation

(G-3223)
HAKEN DOZER SERVICE
14004 E Richmond Rd (74032-3129)
PHONE.................................580 669-2211
Irvin Haken, *Owner*
Lois Haken, *Co-Owner*
EMP: 2
SALES (est): 150K **Privately Held**
SIC: 1794 1711 1622 1389 Excavation work; septic system construction; highway construction, elevated; oil field services

(G-3224)
HOT ROD SHIRTS & STUFF
6800 N Rose Rd (74032-1403)
PHONE.................................580 669-2531
Kelly Horton, *Owner*
EMP: 1
SALES (est): 73.1K **Privately Held**
SIC: 5531 2759 Automotive parts; screen printing

(G-3225)
OKLAHOMA HAND POURS
10309 E Tower Ests (74032-3240)
PHONE.................................580 669-2520
Jim Valentine, *Owner*
EMP: 15
SALES (est): 1.3MM **Privately Held**
SIC: 3089 Injection molding of plastics

(G-3226)
PIONEER METAL & LAND SVCS LLC
14509 E Mcelroy (74032-3208)
PHONE.................................405 612-3575
Leonard Ellis, *Principal*
EMP: 1
SALES (est): 42.7K **Privately Held**
SIC: 7692 1791 Welding repair; building front installation metal

(G-3227)
WECKTEES
7311 E Airport Rd (74032-5102)
PHONE.................................580 747-5363
Reggie Weckstein, *Principal*
EMP: 2 **EST:** 2016
SALES (est): 90.5K **Privately Held**
SIC: 2759 Screen printing

Glenpool
Tulsa County

(G-3228)
ABCO STEEL INC
643 W 138th St (74033-3438)
P.O. Box 249 (74033-0249)
PHONE.................................918 322-3435
A B Mainard, *President*
Patricia Mainard, *Corp Secy*
EMP: 12
SQ FT: 17,000
SALES (est): 1.8MM **Privately Held**
SIC: 3312 3441 Blast furnaces & steel mills; fabricated structural metal

(G-3229)
AIR INSPIRED HOME MEDICAL
519i E 141st St (74033)
PHONE.................................918 299-3037
Beth Peters,
Bruce Arnette,
EMP: 12
SQ FT: 1,200
SALES (est): 1.1MM **Privately Held**
SIC: 3842 Respiratory protection equipment, personal

(G-3230)
AMERICAN TS
15072 S Dogwood St (74033-3567)
PHONE.................................918 288-6682
Randy Fulbright, *Owner*
EMP: 8
SALES (est): 456.2K **Privately Held**
WEB: www.americantsonline.com
SIC: 2395 Embroidery products, except schiffli machine

(G-3231)
BOYDS CSTM TRIM CABINETRY LLC
1459 E 138th St (74033-3178)
PHONE.................................918 724-7033
Rob Boyd, *Owner*
EMP: 2
SALES (est): 153.7K **Privately Held**
SIC: 2434 Wood kitchen cabinets

(G-3232)
CUSTOM DRAWERS AND CABINETRY
1243 E 142nd St (74033-3730)
PHONE.................................918 322-9819
EMP: 1 **EST:** 2011
SALES (est): 74K **Privately Held**
SIC: 3553 Mfg Woodworking Machinery

(G-3233)
DUNLAP DRILLING PRODUCING INC
16950 S 9th West Ave (74033-4206)
PHONE.................................918 237-0015
Jennifer Dunlap, *Principal*
EMP: 4
SALES (est): 347.3K **Privately Held**
SIC: 1381 Drilling oil & gas wells

(G-3234)
EUROCRAFT LTD
16052 S Broadway St (74033-5242)
PHONE.................................918 322-5500
Johann Skaftason, *President*
▲ **EMP:** 25
SQ FT: 22,000
SALES (est): 3.9MM **Privately Held**
SIC: 3281 2541 5999 5032 Cut stone & stone products; counter & sink tops; monuments & tombstones; marble building stone; counter top installation

(G-3235)
H-V MANUFACTURING COMPANY (PA)
138th & Hwy 75 (74033)
PHONE.................................918 291-2108
Marice Hodges, *President*
EMP: 16
SQ FT: 7,200
SALES (est): 2.7MM **Privately Held**
SIC: 3533 Oil & gas field machinery

(G-3236)
JC HOT SHOT SERVICES INC
13827 S Elm St (74033-2716)
PHONE.................................918 782-7922
Charles Segress, *Principal*
EMP: 2 **EST:** 2018
SALES (est): 65.5K **Privately Held**
SIC: 1389 Hot shot service

(G-3237)
KAYDAWN MANUFACTURING CO INC
5224 W 151st St (74033)
PHONE.................................918 321-5017
EMP: 3
SALES (est): 200K **Privately Held**
SIC: 3315 3496 3446 Mfg Steel Wire/Related Products Mfg Misc Fabricated Wire Products Mfg Architectural Metalwork

(G-3238)
MC CONNELLS SYSTEMS
15089 S Yukon Ave (74033-4340)
PHONE.................................918 322-5426
Robert Mc Connell, *Owner*
EMP: 2 **EST:** 1998
SALES (est): 100K **Privately Held**
SIC: 3571 Mainframe computers

(G-3239)
MRW TECHNOLOGIES INC
2301 W 171st St S (74033-5000)
PHONE.................................918 827-6030
Robert L Rawlings, *President*
Andrew Rosander, *Project Engr*
EMP: 24
SALES (est): 5.1MM **Privately Held**
SIC: 2899 1389 Oxidizers, inorganic; construction, repair & dismantling services

(G-3240)
PARNEL BIOGAS INC
13701 S Hwy 75 (74033)
PHONE.................................918 294-3868
Jeff Parker, *CEO*
Kevin Godwin, *Vice Pres*
EMP: 12 **EST:** 1999
SQ FT: 3,000
SALES (est): 2.8MM **Privately Held**
WEB: www.parnelbiogas.com
SIC: 3822 Auto controls regulating residntl & coml environmt & applncs

(G-3241)
PREMIER STEEL SERVICES LLC
16420 S Highway 75 (74033-5254)
PHONE.................................918 227-0110
J Paul Miller, *Accountant*
Andy Vanaman, *Mng Member*
EMP: 30
SALES (est): 12.3MM **Privately Held**
SIC: 3441 Fabricated structural metal

GEOGRAPHIC SECTION

Grove - Delaware County (G-3268)

(G-3242)
T & L FOUNDRY INC
515 W 138th St (74033-3440)
P.O. Box 279 (74033-0279)
PHONE..................918 322-3310
Bill Covington, *President*
Deanna Covington, *Vice Pres*
Tony Chadwick, *Manager*
EMP: 75
SQ FT: 50,000
SALES (est): 12.3MM Privately Held
SIC: 3366 Copper foundries

(G-3243)
TTS EMBROIDERYS PLUS
14915 Courtney Ln (74033-3590)
PHONE..................918 770-3515
EMP: 1 EST: 2010
SALES (est): 52K Privately Held
SIC: 2395 Pleating/Stitching Services

Goldsby
Mcclain County

(G-3244)
BRANDON HYDE
Also Called: Hyde Sand & Gravel
490 W Chestnut Rd (73093-9143)
PHONE..................405 919-4520
Brandon Hyde, *Principal*
EMP: 3
SALES (est): 153.3K Privately Held
SIC: 1442 Construction sand & gravel

(G-3245)
M E KLEIN & ASSOCIATES INC
143 Airport Rd (73093-4663)
P.O. Box 721436, Norman (73070-8106)
PHONE..................405 288-2804
Mark E Klein, *President*
EMP: 4
SQ FT: 2,000
SALES (est): 959.9K Privately Held
SIC: 1382 Geophysical exploration, oil & gas field

(G-3246)
SAGE PREMIUM DENIM BAR ✪
2538 S Ladd Ave (73093-9214)
PHONE..................405 288-1503
EMP: 1 EST: 2019
SALES (est): 46.5K Privately Held
WEB: www.sagepremiumdenimbar.com
SIC: 2211 Denims

(G-3247)
TOWN OF GOLDSBY
Also Called: TOWN HALL
100 E Center Rd (73093-9112)
PHONE..................405 288-6675
Sandy Jenkins, *Principal*
Cindy Andrews, *Mayor*
Glenn Berglan, *Mayor*
Virgie Andrews, *Treasurer*
EMP: 15
SQ FT: 1,712
SALES (est): 2.3MM Privately Held
WEB: www.townofgoldsby.com
SIC: 2899 1629 Water treating compounds; waste disposal plant construction

Goltry
Alfalfa County

(G-3248)
NORTHWEST TRUSS
Hwy 45 Newell St (73739)
PHONE..................580 496-2420
Gene Kuepfer, *Owner*
EMP: 2
SALES: 225K Privately Held
SIC: 2439 Structural wood members

Goodwell
Texas County

(G-3249)
PANHANDLE CORROSION LLC
717 Jackson St (73939)
P.O. Box 716 (73939-0716)
PHONE..................580 651-3208
Trey Fankhouser,
EMP: 1
SALES (est): 45.1K Privately Held
SIC: 1389 1799 Oil consultants; corrosion control installation

Gore
Sequoyah County

(G-3250)
INDEPENDENCE RACE WORKS & FABG
Also Called: Irw
306 Ray Fine Dr (74435-2031)
PHONE..................918 489-2353
Heath Orabanec, *Owner*
EMP: 2
SALES: 12K Privately Held
SIC: 7692 Welding repair

(G-3251)
SEQUOYAH FUELS CORPORATION
I-40 Hwy 10 (74435)
P.O. Box 610 (74435-0610)
PHONE..................918 489-5511
John Ellis, *President*
James N Blue, *Owner*
EMP: 7
SALES: 9.9MM Privately Held
SIC: 2819 Industrial inorganic chemicals
HQ: General Atomics
3550 General Atomics Ct
San Diego CA 92121
858 455-2810

(G-3252)
SOUTER LIMESTONE AND MNRL LLC
445501 E 987 Rd (74435)
P.O. Box 359 (74435-0359)
PHONE..................918 489-5589
William Cooper, *President*
EMP: 11
SALES (est): 345.3K Privately Held
SIC: 1429 1422 Riprap quarrying; crushed & broken limestone; agricultural limestone, ground; lime rock, ground; limestones, ground

(G-3253)
ZERO HOUR INDUSTRIES INC
97791 S 4433 Rd (74435-5330)
PHONE..................918 685-0235
Christopher Huitt, *Principal*
EMP: 2
SALES (est): 137.6K Privately Held
SIC: 3999 Manufacturing industries

Gracemont
Caddo County

(G-3254)
TY SLEMP DAKOTA
25100 County Road 1260 (73042-9465)
PHONE..................405 933-2078
Dakota Ty Slemp, *Principal*
EMP: 1 EST: 2018
SALES (est): 50.3K Privately Held
SIC: 7692 Welding repair

Grady
Jefferson County

(G-3255)
DON DENNIS
Also Called: Dennis Ranch
423 N Main (73569)
PHONE..................580 662-3163
Billy Dennis, *Owner*
Donald Dennis, *Owner*
EMP: 2 EST: 1948
SALES (est): 174.3K Privately Held
WEB: www.dennniscattlecompany.com
SIC: 1311 0212 Crude petroleum production; beef cattle except feedlots

Grandfield
Tillman County

(G-3256)
BULLDOG JERKY CO
Also Called: Josefy, Jerry
503 W 2nd St (73546-9457)
PHONE..................580 479-5542
Jerry Josefy, *Owner*
Carla Josefy, *Owner*
EMP: 2
SALES (est): 8K Privately Held
SIC: 5147 2013 Meats, cured or smoked; beef, dried: from purchased meat

Granite
Greer County

(G-3257)
WHM GRANITE PRODUCTS INC (PA)
Also Called: Willis Granite Products
900 Quarry Dr (73547)
PHONE..................580 535-2184
William R Willis, *CEO*
Ellen L Willis, *President*
Brenda Willis-Hickerson, *Exec VP*
Linda Morris, *Vice Pres*
Karen Willis-Harrison, *Manager*
EMP: 17 EST: 1944
SQ FT: 3,200
SALES: 1.2MM Privately Held
WEB: www.willisgranite.com
SIC: 3281 5999 7389 1411 Monuments, cut stone (not finishing or lettering only); granite, cut & shaped; monuments & tombstones; tombstone engraving; dimension stone

Grant
Choctaw County

(G-3258)
KELLEY RETHA
Also Called: Kelleyo
1705 N 4290 Rd (74738-9731)
PHONE..................580 317-7483
Retha Kelley, *Owner*
EMP: 3
SALES (est): 122.6K Privately Held
SIC: 2541 Store & office display cases & fixtures

Grove
Delaware County

(G-3259)
BELDEN RUSSELL ELECT CO
63201 E 290 Rd (74344-7552)
PHONE..................918 791-9600
Chris Karleskint, *Principal*
EMP: 2
SALES (est): 135.8K Privately Held
SIC: 5063 3699 3634 1731 Electrical supplies; electrical equipment & supplies; electric housewares & fans; general electrical contractor

(G-3260)
CELLFILL LLC
802 Industrial Road C (74344-4109)
P.O. Box Pobox 451023 (74345)
PHONE..................918 787-2355
EMP: 6
SALES (est): 407.7K Privately Held
SIC: 3272 Sewer pipe, concrete

(G-3261)
CIMARRON DOCS BAR-B-QUE CHILI
61890 E 346 Rd (74344)
PHONE..................918 787-7881
EMP: 2 EST: 2010
SALES (est): 83K Privately Held
SIC: 2099 Food Preparations, Nec, Nsk

(G-3262)
CONCESSIONS MFG CO LLC
34320 S 620 Rd (74344-0453)
PHONE..................918 786-5100
Howard Turrel,
Susan E Turrel,
EMP: 8
SALES (est): 1.6MM Privately Held
WEB: www.kettlepopcorn.net
SIC: 3589 3321 Popcorn machines, commercial; gray & ductile iron foundries

(G-3263)
CONTROL PRODUCTS UNLIMITED INC
24570 S 647 Rd (74344-4414)
PHONE..................918 786-1801
Kelly Zini, *President*
Karen Still-Zini, *Admin Sec*
EMP: 2
SALES (est): 104.2K Privately Held
SIC: 3823 7389 Water quality monitoring & control systems;

(G-3264)
CP INDUSTRIES INC
500 Industrial Rd (74344-4102)
PHONE..................918 468-2230
Elaine Pollett, *President*
EMP: 9
SALES (est): 200K Privately Held
SIC: 3365 Aluminum foundries

(G-3265)
D C JONES MACHINE CO
Also Called: Jones, D C Machine Co
818 Industrial Rd (74344-4106)
PHONE..................918 786-6855
Steve Jones, *Owner*
EMP: 3
SQ FT: 10,500
SALES (est): 350K Privately Held
SIC: 3469 3728 3533 Machine parts, stamped or pressed metal; aircraft parts & equipment; oil & gas field machinery

(G-3266)
DYNAMIC MACHINE
2001 E Industrial 5 Rd (74344-4101)
PHONE..................918 791-1114
Doug Morgan, *President*
EMP: 2
SQ FT: 2,400
SALES: 140K Privately Held
SIC: 3429 Aircraft hardware

(G-3267)
EMPIRE PLUMBING CONTRS LLC
307 N 3rd St (74344-3104)
P.O. Box 453273 (74345-3273)
PHONE..................918 320-1427
Jelly Sapp,
EMP: 2
SALES (est): 151.7K Privately Held
SIC: 1711 3432 2842 Plumbing contractors; plumbers' brass goods: drain cocks, faucets, spigots, etc.; drain pipe solvents or cleaners

(G-3268)
FERRA AEROSPACE INC
64353 E 290 Rd (74344-7912)
PHONE..................918 787-2220
Unknown Branch, *Manager*
EMP: 13

Grove - Delaware County (G-3269)

SALES (corp-wide): 2.8MM **Privately Held**
SIC: 3728 Aircraft parts & equipment
PA: Ferra Aerospace, Inc.
64353 E 290 Rd
Grove OK 74344
918 787-2220

(G-3269)
FERRA AEROSPACE INC (PA)
Also Called: Ferra Holdings Limited
64353 E 290 Rd (74344-7912)
PHONE..................................918 787-2220
Jerry Cook, *President*
David Rogers, *CFO*
Jon Klugh, *Controller*
EMP: 6
SQ FT: 43,000
SALES (est): 2.8MM **Privately Held**
SIC: 3721 Aircraft

(G-3270)
FIRST IMPRESSION CUSTOM EMB
Also Called: Custom Embriodary
62311 E 252 Rd (74344-7467)
PHONE..................................918 787-4182
Carol Goodwin, *Partner*
Bob Goodwin, *Partner*
EMP: 2
SALES (est): 99K **Privately Held**
SIC: 2395 Embroidery products, except schiffli machine

(G-3271)
FRACDOGS
28860 S 595 Cir (74344-7752)
PHONE..................................918 786-9797
EMP: 1
SALES (est): 85K **Privately Held**
SIC: 1389 Oil/Gas Field Services

(G-3272)
GRAND RIVER CHRONICLE-GROVE
1627 S Main St (74344-5368)
PHONE..................................918 786-8722
EMP: 3
SALES (est): 144.2K **Privately Held**
SIC: 2711 Newspapers-Publishing/Printing

(G-3273)
GREENLURE LLC
2633 Shasten St (74344-4905)
PHONE..................................918 786-9156
EMP: 2
SALES (est): 104.9K **Privately Held**
SIC: 3949 Sporting & athletic goods

(G-3274)
HOMETOWN BOTTLED WATER LLC
Also Called: Hometown Water
63651 E 290 Rd (74344-7547)
P.O. Box 450367 (74345-0367)
PHONE..................................918 786-4426
Tim Sievert, *Partner*
EMP: 5
SALES (est): 384.6K **Privately Held**
SIC: 2086 Pasteurized & mineral waters, bottled & canned

(G-3275)
J N B INC
Also Called: J T Jewelers
62042 E 278 Rd (74344-7545)
PHONE..................................918 786-6311
John Blevins, *President*
EMP: 3
SQ FT: 1,200
SALES (est): 450K **Privately Held**
SIC: 5944 7631 3911 Jewelry stores; jewelry repair services; jewelry, precious metal

(G-3276)
JACOB MANUFACTURING INC
Also Called: Jacobs Manufacturing
499 Industrial Road A (74344-4100)
PHONE..................................918 787-6606
Michael Jacobs, *President*
Stephanie Shoffner, *Office Mgr*
EMP: 4
SALES: 600K **Privately Held**
SIC: 2221 Fiberglass fabrics

(G-3277)
JAG MACHINE INC
340 Industrial Road A (74344-4104)
PHONE..................................918 791-0004
Jim Gibbs, *President*
Janie A Gibbs, *Vice Pres*
EMP: 12
SQ FT: 4,800
SALES: 1.2MM **Privately Held**
SIC: 3365 Aerospace castings, aluminum

(G-3278)
LAND & LAKE ELECTRIC LLC
29530 S 585 Trl (74344-7943)
PHONE..................................918 791-1731
Claude C Oliver IV, *Administration*
EMP: 1
SALES (est): 62.2K **Privately Held**
SIC: 7694 Electric motor repair

(G-3279)
LOST TREASURE INC
5500 Us Highway 59 (74344-3708)
PHONE..................................918 786-2182
Lee Harris, *President*
EMP: 8
SQ FT: 12,000
SALES (est): 658.9K **Privately Held**
SIC: 2721 Magazines: publishing only, not printed on site

(G-3280)
MALONES CNC MACHINING INC
2015 E Industrial 5 Rd (74344-4101)
PHONE..................................918 786-7313
Donald E Malone, *President*
Bryan Brasher, *Opers Mgr*
Debra M Malone, *Treasurer*
Angele Catherine Schulte, *Human Res Mgr*
Monica Marcial, *Manager*
EMP: 40
SQ FT: 21,000
SALES: 4.6MM **Privately Held**
SIC: 3599 Machine shop, jobbing & repair

(G-3281)
NOTE-ABLE WORKSHOP LLC
4600 Us Highway 59 (74344-4229)
PHONE..................................918 801-2725
EMP: 2 EST: 2018
SALES (est): 140.8K **Privately Held**
SIC: 2431 Millwork

(G-3282)
NOTE-ABLE WORKSHOP LLC
24501 S 613 Rd (74344-0151)
PHONE..................................918 801-2725
EMP: 2
SALES (est): 137.7K **Privately Held**
SIC: 2431 Millwork

(G-3283)
NUCLEIC PRODUCTS LLC
63225 E 290 Rd (74344-7552)
PHONE..................................818 419-9176
Paula Rochelle,
EMP: 3
SALES (est): 91.3K **Privately Held**
SIC: 2023 Dietary supplements, dairy & non-dairy based

(G-3284)
ORIZON ARSTRCTURES - GROVE INC
Also Called: Precision Machine & Mfg
500 Industrial Rd (74344-4102)
PHONE..................................918 786-9094
Keith Martin, *General Mgr*
▲ EMP: 90
SQ FT: 140,000
SALES (est): 44MM
SALES (corp-wide): 74.6MM **Privately Held**
WEB: www.precisionaerogroup.com
SIC: 3441 3724 Fabricated structural metal; aircraft engines & engine parts
PA: Orizon Aerostructures, Llc
1200 Main St Ste 4000
Kansas City MO 64105
816 788-7800

(G-3285)
PHILS ORNAMENTAL IRON INC
10732 Us Highway 59 (74344-4511)
PHONE..................................918 786-2979
Phillip Endicott, *President*
Wanda Endicott, *Admin Sec*
EMP: 4
SQ FT: 10,000
SALES (est): 210K **Privately Held**
SIC: 3446 3444 Ornamental metalwork; sheet metalwork

(G-3286)
PRIDE PLATING INC
Also Called: Valence Surface Technologies
2900 E Highway 10 (74344-4119)
P.O. Box 845324, Dallas TX (75284-5324)
PHONE..................................918 786-6111
Ronald Lay, *President*
Dale Sorrels, *Engineer*
Jack Shumaker, *Supervisor*
Maria Rodriguez, *Clerk*
EMP: 80
SQ FT: 30,000
SALES (est): 11.1MM **Privately Held**
SIC: 3471 Finishing, metals or formed products; anodizing (plating) of metals or formed products

(G-3287)
RUSTIC REHAB
3633 Us Highway 59 (74344-3705)
PHONE..................................918 314-6647
Barb Barnes, *President*
EMP: 3
SALES (est): 149.4K **Privately Held**
SIC: 1799 5999 2339 3911 Home/office interiors finishing, furnishing & remodeling; miscellaneous retail stores; women's & misses' athletic clothing & sportswear; jewelry apparel; antiques; essential oils

(G-3288)
SIMMONS FOODS INC
69605 E 300 Rd (74344-7616)
PHONE..................................918 791-0010
Angela Newman, *President*
EMP: 1
SALES (est): 64.4K **Privately Held**
SIC: 2015 Poultry slaughtering & processing

(G-3289)
SOLTOW BUSINESS SUPPLY (PA)
810 Industrial Rd (74344-4106)
PHONE..................................918 786-4465
Frances Soltow, *Owner*
EMP: 2
SQ FT: 2,000
SALES (est): 370.1K **Privately Held**
SIC: 5943 2752 Office forms & supplies; commercial printing, lithographic

(G-3290)
TWO K ENTERPRISES LLC
Also Called: Party Station
1400 Kayla St (74344-4922)
PHONE..................................918 964-7004
T Jennifer Kent, *Mng Member*
Tennille Jennifer Kent, *Mng Member*
EMP: 2
SALES: 500K **Privately Held**
SIC: 5947 1389 Party favors; oil consultants

(G-3291)
VANS PRINTING SERVICE
423 S Hazel St (74344-7052)
PHONE..................................918 786-9496
Harvey Hicks, *Owner*
EMP: 4 EST: 1974
SQ FT: 3,000
SALES (est): 499.8K **Privately Held**
SIC: 2752 2791 Lithographing on metal; typesetting

(G-3292)
WATER TANK SERVICE
66500 E 255 Rd (74344-6145)
PHONE..................................918 786-7850
Gary Hall, *President*
EMP: 4
SALES (est): 312.5K **Privately Held**
SIC: 3443 Water tanks, metal plate

(G-3293)
WAYNE BURT MACHINE
Also Called: Burt, Wayne Machine Shop
510 Industrial Rd (74344-4102)
PHONE..................................918 786-4415
Wayne E Burt, *Owner*
EMP: 8
SQ FT: 19,000
SALES (est): 750K **Privately Held**
SIC: 3599 3429 7692 3548 Machine shop, jobbing & repair; clamps, metal; welding repair; welding apparatus; machine tools, metal cutting type; fabricated structural metal

(G-3294)
WRIGHT WAY SCREEN PRINTING
25890 S 621 Rd (74344-7481)
PHONE..................................918 787-7898
Robbi Wright, *Principal*
EMP: 2
SALES (est): 141.8K **Privately Held**
SIC: 2759 Screen printing

Guthrie
Logan County

(G-3295)
1014 INDUSTRIES LLC
8500 S Anderson Rd (73044-9150)
PHONE..................................405 831-5351
Corey Eaton, *Principal*
EMP: 1
SALES (est): 42.8K **Privately Held**
SIC: 3999 Manufacturing industries

(G-3296)
ADVANCE ROUSTABOUT SVCS LLC
3101 S Anderson Rd (73044-9435)
PHONE..................................405 612-0781
EMP: 2
SALES (est): 79.8K **Privately Held**
SIC: 1389 Roustabout service

(G-3297)
ARMSTRONG PRODUCTS INC
500 E Industrial Rd (73044-6827)
P.O. Box 979 (73044-0979)
PHONE..................................405 282-7584
Gary Armstrong Sr, *President*
Deborah Brewer, *Treasurer*
EMP: 5 EST: 1974
SQ FT: 10,000
SALES: 1MM **Privately Held**
SIC: 3446 3354 Stairs, staircases, stair treads: prefabricated metal; aluminum extruded products

(G-3298)
B B FIBERGLASS LLC
11501 Cory Rd (73044-8125)
PHONE..................................405 755-5895
Bobby Padack, *Mng Member*
EMP: 2 EST: 1994
SALES (est): 150K **Privately Held**
SIC: 2221 3544 Fiberglass fabrics; special dies, tools, jigs & fixtures

(G-3299)
BECKS FARM EQUIPMENT INC
3650 Ne Highway 33 (73044-9692)
PHONE..................................405 282-1196
Ray E Beck, *President*
Jacob Beck, *Sales Staff*
Brian Williams, *Assistant*
EMP: 8
SALES: 2.7MM **Privately Held**
WEB: www.becksfarmequipment.com
SIC: 5083 1311 0111 0212 Farm implements; crude petroleum production; natural gas production; wheat; beef cattle except feedlots

(G-3300)
BODY BILLBOARDS
Also Called: Body Billboards & Trophies Too
2403 S Division St Ste G (73044-6031)
PHONE..................................405 282-9922
Jack Rhinehart, *Owner*
EMP: 2

GEOGRAPHIC SECTION

Guthrie - Logan County (G-3333)

SALES (est): 155.8K **Privately Held**
SIC: 2261 7336 Screen printing of cotton broadwoven fabrics; silk screen design

(G-3301)
BOSTICK SERVICES CORPORATION
12700 W Highway 33 Ste 4 (73044-9876)
P.O. Box 536, Crescent (73028-0536)
PHONE..................................405 260-0306
Mike Bostick, *President*
EMP: 18
SALES (est): 4.1MM **Privately Held**
SIC: 1389 Oil field services

(G-3302)
BULLDOG ENERGY SERVICES LLC (PA)
6000 E College Ave (73044-9446)
PHONE..................................405 919-9950
Joshua Smith, *Partner*
Steve Smith, *Partner*
Robyn Smith, *Principal*
EMP: 3
SALES: 100K **Privately Held**
SIC: 1389 Oil field services

(G-3303)
BURGESS MANUFACTURING OKLA INC
1250 Roundhouse Rd (73044-4700)
P.O. Box 237 (73044-0237)
PHONE..................................405 282-1913
Bob Burgess, *President*
EMP: 23 EST: 1970
SQ FT: 21,000
SALES (est): 4.1MM **Privately Held**
SIC: 2448 2449 Pallets, wood; food containers, wood; wirebound

(G-3304)
C C MCMILLIN & COMPANY INC
6 Miles North On Hwy 77 (73044)
P.O. Box 546 (73044-0546)
PHONE..................................405 282-3637
Calvin Mays, *President*
EMP: 2
SQ FT: 1,200
SALES (est): 189.1K **Privately Held**
SIC: 1311 Crude petroleum production; natural gas production

(G-3305)
C V WEST LLC
1831 S May Ave (73044-9842)
PHONE..................................623 363-3529
Rod Bartram, *Principal*
EMP: 2 EST: 2012
SALES (est): 110.3K **Privately Held**
SIC: 7692 Welding repair

(G-3306)
CALVIN MAYS OILFIELD SVCS INC
201 W County Road 72 (73044-9737)
PHONE..................................405 282-6664
Calvin R Mays, *President*
Denna Mays, *Corp Secy*
EMP: 19 EST: 1976
SQ FT: 1,200
SALES: 2MM **Privately Held**
SIC: 1389 5082 Oil field services; oil field equipment

(G-3307)
CANARY CUSTOMS
3704 S Pine St (73044-6900)
PHONE..................................405 293-6429
Jason Canary, *President*
EMP: 1 EST: 2017
SALES (est): 30K **Privately Held**
SIC: 7692 Welding repair

(G-3308)
CIMARRON AEROSPACE LLC
120 Highway 74 (73044-9665)
PHONE..................................405 260-0990
Michael Burnett, *Opers Staff*
EMP: 2
SALES (est): 245.3K **Privately Held**
SIC: 3599 Machine shop, jobbing & repair

(G-3309)
CLARK MTAL BLDNGS FBRCATION LL
11332 Coyote Run (73044-2093)
PHONE..................................580 695-4915
Jeremy Clark, *Principal*
EMP: 1 EST: 2017
SALES (est): 54.3K **Privately Held**
SIC: 3499 Fabricated metal products

(G-3310)
COOK ROUSTABOUT LLC
6574 S Kelly Ave (73044-7316)
PHONE..................................405 410-7951
Sylvia R Stewart, *Owner*
EMP: 2
SALES (est): 65.5K **Privately Held**
SIC: 1389 Roustabout service

(G-3311)
DOLESE BROS CO
Also Called: Dolese Sand Plant
5740 N Hway 77 (73044)
P.O. Box 39 (73044-0039)
PHONE..................................405 282-2153
Brandon Wells, *Plant Mgr*
Jerry Taylor, *Plant Mgr*
EMP: 5
SALES (corp-wide): 8.5MM **Privately Held**
SIC: 3273 Ready-mixed concrete
PA: Dolese Bros. Co.
  20 Nw 13th St
  Oklahoma City OK 73103
  405 235-2311

(G-3312)
EARLSBORO ENERGIES CORP
7424 S Westminster Rd (73044-8969)
PHONE..................................405 282-5007
Roger Sloan, *Vice Pres*
EMP: 2
SALES (est): 81.9K **Privately Held**
SIC: 1382 Oil & gas exploration services

(G-3313)
FORTRESS WHITETAILS
2951 S Post Rd (73044-9058)
PHONE..................................405 401-5533
Jason Hirzel, *Partner*
EMP: 1
SQ FT: 1,500
SALES (est): 95.3K **Privately Held**
SIC: 2411 Logging

(G-3314)
FORUM US INC
Also Called: Forum Production Equipment
3110 W Noble Ave (73044-8729)
PHONE..................................405 260-7800
Tylar K Schmitt, *President*
EMP: 2 **Publicly Held**
SIC: 1382 Oil & gas exploration services
HQ: Forum Us, Inc.
  10344 Sam Houston Park Dr
  Houston TX 77064
  713 351-7900

(G-3315)
FUEL HAULERS LLC
210 N Buffalo Ave (73044-9430)
PHONE..................................405 830-3385
EMP: 3
SALES (est): 158.8K **Privately Held**
SIC: 2869 Fuels

(G-3316)
GUTHRIE GUTHRIE HOME CH INC ✪
116 Sw 19th St (73044-4023)
PHONE..................................405 600-8254
Armin Smith, *Administration*
EMP: 2 EST: 2019
SALES (est): 83.2K **Privately Held**
SIC: 3544 Special dies, tools, jigs & fixtures

(G-3317)
H2 SERVICES LLC
4700 Highway 105 (73044-8635)
P.O. Box 1310 (73044-1310)
PHONE..................................405 388-9049
Craig Hamilton, *Mng Member*
EMP: 25 EST: 2014
SQ FT: 300

SALES (est): 1.8MM **Privately Held**
SIC: 1389 7359 Oil field services; business machine & electronic equipment rental services

(G-3318)
HANEY JOHN
Also Called: C & J Son Machine Shop
1501 S Post Rd (73044-9481)
PHONE..................................405 282-2839
John Haney, *Owner*
EMP: 2
SALES (est): 111.3K **Privately Held**
SIC: 3599 Machine shop, jobbing & repair

(G-3319)
JAY HICKMAN WELDING INC
2002 Polly Pl (73044-6012)
PHONE..................................405 205-7136
EMP: 1
SALES (est): 25K **Privately Held**
SIC: 7692 Welding repair

(G-3320)
JEFFRIES PUMPING SERVICE INC
525 Broadway (73044-8761)
PHONE..................................580 628-2769
Chet F Jeffries, *President*
Kay Jeffries, *Treasurer*
EMP: 10
SALES (est): 1.4MM **Privately Held**
SIC: 1381 Drilling oil & gas wells

(G-3321)
K AND G INVESTMENTS INC
8924 Morningside Rd (73044-8516)
PHONE..................................401 396-9280
EMP: 1
SALES (est): 41K **Privately Held**
SIC: 3961 Costume jewelry

(G-3322)
LADYBUGS AND LOLLIPOPS LLC
11274 Kim Cir (73044-8033)
PHONE..................................405 919-8555
EMP: 2
SALES (est): 70.4K **Privately Held**
SIC: 2064 Candy And Other Confectionery Products

(G-3323)
LOGAN COUNTY ASPHALT CO
2905 Commerce Blvd (73044-5531)
PHONE..................................405 282-3711
Don McBride, *President*
Tim McBride, *Vice Pres*
Sue Smith, *Admin Sec*
EMP: 20
SQ FT: 6,750
SALES: 2.7MM **Privately Held**
WEB: www.logancountyasphalt.com
SIC: 2951 1611 Asphalt & asphaltic paving mixtures (not from refineries); surfacing & paving

(G-3324)
MIDCO FABRICATORS INC
3110 W Noble Ave (73044-8729)
PHONE..................................405 282-6667
J B Valentine, *President*
Belinda Whatley, *Principal*
William Bowen, *Vice Pres*
EMP: 40 EST: 1991
SQ FT: 71,000
SALES (est): 42.6K **Privately Held**
SIC: 3533 3564 3444 3443 Oil field machinery & equipment; blowers & fans; sheet metalwork; fabricated plate work (boiler shop)

(G-3325)
MIDWEST PUBLISHING CO
100 E College Ave (73044-1810)
P.O. Box 818 (73044-0818)
PHONE..................................405 282-1890
Loren L Jones, *Owner*
EMP: 2 EST: 1973
SQ FT: 2,400

SALES: 210K **Privately Held**
SIC: 2752 2759 2791 2789 Lithographing on metal; commercial printing; typesetting; bookbinding & related work; book publishing; automotive & apparel trimmings

(G-3326)
MZMOUZE EMBROIDERY CREAT LLP
215 S 17th St (73044-4009)
PHONE..................................405 696-6545
Terrianne Lowe, *Principal*
EMP: 1
SALES (est): 31.2K **Privately Held**
SIC: 2395 Embroidery & art needlework

(G-3327)
OBRIEN OIL CORPORATION
201 W Oklahoma Ave # 233 (73044-3144)
PHONE..................................405 282-6500
Edward O'Brien, *President*
EMP: 3
SALES (est): 370.1K **Privately Held**
SIC: 1382 Oil & gas exploration services

(G-3328)
OKIE ROASTERS LLC
1540 Debbie Dr (73044-4434)
PHONE..................................405 699-2007
McKenna Hampton,
EMP: 1
SALES (est): 39.5K **Privately Held**
SIC: 2095 Roasted coffee

(G-3329)
OKLAHOMA HOME CENTERS INC
Also Called: Ace Lumber & Building Supply
5103 S Division St (73044-7078)
P.O. Box 1406 (73044-1406)
PHONE..................................405 260-7625
William Van Sant, *President*
William Marscharka, *Vice Pres*
EMP: 47
SQ FT: 30,000
SALES (est): 9.1MM **Privately Held**
WEB: www.ohcsupply.com
SIC: 2421 5031 5063 5074 Building & structural materials, wood; lumber: rough, dressed & finished; electrical apparatus & equipment; plumbing & hydronic heating supplies; hardware

(G-3330)
OKLAHOMA MILLWORKS INC
2019 Ruhl Dr (73044-6014)
PHONE..................................405 282-4887
Kyle Copeland, *President*
EMP: 55
SQ FT: 35,000
SALES (est): 5.5MM **Privately Held**
SIC: 2434 Wood kitchen cabinets

(G-3331)
OKRUSTICWOODWORKS
5424 Fawn Run (73044-1108)
PHONE..................................405 562-0371
Craig Kelley, *Principal*
EMP: 2
SALES (est): 110K **Privately Held**
SIC: 2431 Millwork

(G-3332)
P /MASTERS C INC
1700 E Seward Rd (73044-9114)
PHONE..................................405 293-9777
Terry Langley, *President*
Charlotte Langley, *Corp Secy*
EMP: 27
SQ FT: 10,000
SALES (est): 9MM **Privately Held**
SIC: 1389 Oil field services

(G-3333)
QUALITY IN COUNTERS INC
6611 Central Rd (73044-7744)
PHONE..................................405 664-2744
Teara Whitaker, *Principal*
EMP: 3
SALES (est): 225.8K **Privately Held**
SIC: 3131 Counters

Guthrie - Logan County (G-3334) — GEOGRAPHIC SECTION

(G-3334)
RADIAL ENGINES LTD
Also Called: Vintage Aero Parts
11701 W Forrest Hills Rd (73044-9428)
PHONE.....................................405 433-2263
Stephen Curry, *President*
Sandra Curry, *Vice Pres*
◆ EMP: 18
SQ FT: 6,500
SALES: 2MM **Privately Held**
SIC: 3724 Aircraft engines & engine parts

(G-3335)
RAYS PORTABLE WELDING
2750 Browne Ave (73044-9227)
PHONE.....................................405 282-3218
EMP: 1
SALES: 29K **Privately Held**
SIC: 7692 1799 0782 Welding Repair Trade Contractor Lawn/Garden Services

(G-3336)
SALLEE MEAT PROCESSING INC
7901 S Sooner Rd (73044-7809)
PHONE.....................................405 282-1241
Pat Sallee, *Owner*
EMP: 5
SALES (est): 266.6K **Privately Held**
SIC: 2011 2013 Meat packing plants; sausages & other prepared meats

(G-3337)
SEW N SAW
9924 S Kelly Ave (73044-3529)
PHONE.....................................405 282-2241
Gary Cornforth, *Partner*
EMP: 2 EST: 1989
SALES (est): 110K **Privately Held**
SIC: 3171 Purses, women's

(G-3338)
SHARP CUTS CUSTOM CABINETS
1418 Chapco Dr (73044-6924)
PHONE.....................................405 282-3657
EMP: 1 EST: 2017
SALES (est): 53.7K **Privately Held**
SIC: 2434 Wood kitchen cabinets

(G-3339)
STEWART INDUSTRIES INTL LLC (PA)
120 Highway 74 (73044-9665)
P.O. Box 1458 (73044-1458)
PHONE.....................................405 260-0990
Katherine S Stewart, *CEO*
Tom Stewart, *President*
David Watson, *CFO*
Tina Fischer, *Human Res Dir*
Jeff Goodwin, *Manager*
EMP: 12 EST: 1993
SQ FT: 114,000
SALES: 4MM **Privately Held**
WEB: www.siiair.com
SIC: 3728 3769 Aircraft assemblies, sub-assemblies & parts; guided missile & space vehicle parts & auxiliary equipment

(G-3340)
WESTERN MOBILE GLASS MIRROR
424 Sigma Pl (73044-6096)
PHONE.....................................913 764-7444
EMP: 2
SALES: 86K **Privately Held**
SIC: 3751 Motorcycles, bicycles & parts

(G-3341)
WOLHER COMPANY
Also Called: Wohler
509 W Oklahoma Ave (73044-2897)
PHONE.....................................405 282-6210
Kenneth Wohler, *Owner*
EMP: 3
SQ FT: 2,450
SALES (est): 200K **Privately Held**
SIC: 5712 2434 2521 Cabinet work, custom; wood kitchen cabinets; wood office furniture

(G-3342)
ZECO MACHINE INCORPORATED
1800 E Seward Rd (73044-9111)
P.O. Box 876 (73044-0876)
PHONE.....................................405 282-3313
Tony Ziegelgruber, *President*
Teresa Russell, *Accounting Mgr*
EMP: 28
SQ FT: 12,000
SALES (est): 4.1MM **Privately Held**
SIC: 3599 1799 Machine shop, jobbing & repair; welding on site

(G-3343)
ZIVKO AERONAUTICS INC
502 Airport Rd Hngr 6 (73044-6802)
PHONE.....................................405 282-1330
William Zivko, *CEO*
Judith A Zivko, *President*
Eric Zivko, *Mfg Staff*
▲ EMP: 30
SQ FT: 21,500
SALES (est): 5.7MM **Privately Held**
SIC: 3728 8711 Aircraft assemblies, sub-assemblies & parts; aviation &/or aeronautical engineering

---

Guymon
Texas County

(G-3344)
ALAN DAVIS
Also Called: Davis Welding
3054 Ne Hwy 54 (73942)
P.O. Box 1301, Hooker (73945-1301)
PHONE.....................................580 651-9961
Alan Davis, *Owner*
EMP: 2
SALES (est): 53.2K **Privately Held**
SIC: 7692 Welding repair

(G-3345)
CAERUS OPERATING LLC
1009 Ne 4th St Ste B (73942-5425)
P.O. Box 1947 (73942-1947)
PHONE.....................................580 468-3527
EMP: 1 **Privately Held**
SIC: 1382 Oil/Gas Exploration Services
PA: Caerus Operating Llc
   1001 17th St Ste 1600
   Denver CO 80202

(G-3346)
CNHI LLC
Also Called: Guymon Daily Herald
515 N Ellison St (73942-4311)
P.O. Box 19 (73942-0019)
PHONE.....................................580 338-3355
Allison Gipe, *Branch Mgr*
EMP: 17 **Privately Held**
WEB: www.cnhi.com
SIC: 2711 2796 2791 Newspapers: publishing only, not printed on site; platemaking services; typesetting
HQ: Cnhi, Llc
   445 Dexter Ave Ste 7000
   Montgomery AL 36104

(G-3347)
D GALA
707 N Main St (73942-4016)
PHONE.....................................580 468-4980
EMP: 5
SALES (est): 160K **Privately Held**
SIC: 3161 Mfg Luggage

(G-3348)
DEWIND CO
810 Ne 6th St (73942-4520)
PHONE.....................................580 338-3271
B Chon, *Manager*
EMP: 9 **Privately Held**
SIC: 3511 Turbines & turbine generator sets
HQ: Dewind Co.
   2201 W Royal Ln Ste 200
   Irving TX 75063
   469 420-9886

(G-3349)
GUYMON EXTRACTS INC
3001 Tumbleweed Dr (73942-6015)
PHONE.....................................580 338-2624
Yoshihisa Inoguchi, *President*
EMP: 40
SQ FT: 12,000
SALES (est): 6.6MM **Privately Held**
SIC: 2038 Frozen specialties
PA: Riken Vitamin Co., Ltd.
   2-9-18, Kandamisakicho,
   Chiyoda-Ku TKY 101-0

(G-3350)
GUYMON MOTOR PARTS INC
Also Called: NAPA Auto Parts
1313 Ne Highway 54 (73942-4565)
P.O. Box 1429 (73942-1429)
PHONE.....................................580 338-3316
Jerry Wing, *President*
EMP: 40
SQ FT: 20,000
SALES (est): 1.7MM **Privately Held**
SIC: 5531 3599 Automobile & truck equipment & parts; machine shop, jobbing & repair

(G-3351)
GUYMON SAFETY LANE
203 N Crumley St (73942-4820)
PHONE.....................................580 338-6960
Fred Cox, *Owner*
EMP: 2
SALES (est): 300K **Privately Held**
SIC: 3714 7538 Motor vehicle parts & accessories; general automotive repair shops

(G-3352)
J & J OIL TOOLS LLC
Rr 2 Box 106a (73942-9618)
PHONE.....................................580 523-1995
Jamie A Jones,
EMP: 5
SALES (est): 322.5K **Privately Held**
SIC: 1389 Construction, repair & dismantling services

(G-3353)
J-A-G CONSTRUCTION COMPANY
913 Ne 14th St (73942-3309)
PHONE.....................................580 338-3188
Chris Pierce, *Manager*
EMP: 5
SALES (corp-wide): 32.8MM **Privately Held**
SIC: 3273 5211 Ready-mixed concrete; masonry materials & supplies
PA: J-A-G Construction Company
   11257 109 Rd
   Dodge City KS 67801
   620 225-0061

(G-3354)
KEY ENERGY SERVICES INC
2202 Yucca Blvd (73942-6027)
PHONE.....................................580 338-0664
Kelly Kuriyama, *General Mgr*
EMP: 60
SALES (corp-wide): 413.8MM **Publicly Held**
SIC: 1389 1382 Construction, repair & dismantling services; oil & gas exploration services
PA: Key Energy Services, Inc.
   1301 Mckinney St Ste 1800
   Houston TX 77010
   713 651-4300

(G-3355)
M&M HOT OIL SERVICE LLC
102 S Ellison St (73942-4842)
PHONE.....................................580 651-1746
Margartia Martinez, *Principal*
EMP: 1
SALES (est): 120.1K **Privately Held**
SIC: 1389 Oil field services

(G-3356)
MITRE BOX FRAME SHOP
507 N Main St (73942-4317)
PHONE.....................................580 338-2319
Thomas D Jarvis, *Owner*
EMP: 1 EST: 1977
SQ FT: 1,000
SALES (est): 68.5K **Privately Held**
SIC: 2499 Picture frame molding, finished

(G-3357)
MUD HAULERS LLC
102 S East St (73942-5371)
P.O. Box 1326 (73942-1326)
PHONE.....................................580 338-3830
Don R Winter, *Mng Member*
EMP: 2
SALES (est): 165.2K **Privately Held**
SIC: 1389 Mud service, oil field drilling

(G-3358)
OXY INC
2810 Tumbleweed Dr (73942)
P.O. Box 277 (73942-0277)
PHONE.....................................580 338-6593
Jim Costner, *Branch Mgr*
EMP: 9
SALES (corp-wide): 21.2B **Publicly Held**
SIC: 1311 Crude petroleum production; natural gas production
HQ: Oxy Inc.
   5 Greenway Plz Ste 2400
   Houston TX 77046
   713 215-7000

(G-3359)
PANHANDLE CONSTRUCTION SVCS
Hwy 64 Rd T (73942)
P.O. Box 62 (73942-0062)
PHONE.....................................580 338-7667
Darrel Livesay, *President*
Deanna Rodman, *Corp Secy*
EMP: 19
SALES: 1.1MM **Privately Held**
SIC: 1389 1623 Oil field services; oil & gas pipeline construction

(G-3360)
PANHANDLE PRINTING
315 Ne 4th St (73942-4838)
Rural Route 2 Box 61 (73942-9602)
PHONE.....................................580 338-1633
Larry Stump, *Owner*
EMP: 2
SALES (est): 326.9K **Privately Held**
SIC: 2752 Commercial printing, offset

(G-3361)
PETES SIGNS
805 N Quinn St (73942-3815)
PHONE.....................................580 338-2266
George Peterson, *Owner*
Pete Peterson, *Owner*
EMP: 1
SALES (est): 83.4K **Privately Held**
SIC: 3993 Signs, not made in custom sign painting shops

(G-3362)
SEABOARD CORPORATION
Also Called: Seaboard Energy Guymon
3291 Desert Rd (73942-1430)
PHONE.....................................580 468-3790
EMP: 3
SALES (corp-wide): 6.8B **Publicly Held**
SIC: 2011 Pork products from pork slaughtered on site
PA: Seaboard Corporation
   9000 W 67th St
   Merriam KS 66202
   913 676-8800

(G-3363)
SEABOARD FARMS INC
2801 Hurliman Rd (73942-6024)
PHONE.....................................580 338-4900
Darrell Hill, *Mfg Staff*
EMP: 50
SALES (corp-wide): 6.8B **Publicly Held**
SIC: 2011 Meat packing plants
HQ: Seaboard Farms, Inc.
   424 N Main St Ste 200
   Guymon OK 73942

(G-3364)
SEABOARD FARMS INC
2700 Ne 28th St (73942-6000)
PHONE.....................................580 338-3311
Stan Scott, *General Mgr*
Mike Newkirk, *Manager*
Richard B Sappington, *Technical Staff*

GEOGRAPHIC SECTION

Hartshorne - Pittsburg County (G-3395)

Raymond Quintero, *IT/INT Sup*
Jennifer C Nelson, *Director*
EMP: 15
SALES (corp-wide): 6.8B **Publicly Held**
SIC: 0213 2013 Hogs; sausages & other prepared meats
HQ: Seaboard Farms, Inc.
   424 N Main St Ste 200
   Guymon OK 73942

(G-3365)
SEABOARD FOODS LLC
2801 Hurliman Rd (73942-6024)
PHONE.................................580 338-4900
Tom Faught, *Superintendent*
Rod Burnaman, *Branch Mgr*
EMP: 4
SALES (corp-wide): 6.8B **Publicly Held**
SIC: 0213 2011 Hogs; pork products from pork slaughtered on site
HQ: Seaboard Foods Llc
   9000 W 67th St Ste 200
   Shawnee Mission KS 66202
   913 261-2600

(G-3366)
SIMS ELECTRIC OF OKLAHOMA INC
1104 S East St (73942-5726)
P.O. Box 1387 (73942-1387)
PHONE.................................580 338-8932
Mark Dunham, *President*
Cindy Taylor, *Manager*
EMP: 15
SALES: 550K **Privately Held**
SIC: 1389 Oil field services

(G-3367)
SUZLON WIND ENERGY CORPORATION
507 Sw Highway 54 (73942-5100)
PHONE.................................580 468-2641
Tony Graham, *Branch Mgr*
EMP: 6 **Privately Held**
SIC: 3511 Turbines & turbine generator sets
HQ: Suzlon Wind Energy Corporation
   8750 W Bryn Mawr Ave # 300
   Chicago IL 60631
   773 328-5077

(G-3368)
TORTILLA VELASQUEZ
409 Ne 4th St (73942-4840)
PHONE.................................580 468-6753
Tereso Velasquez, *Owner*
EMP: 3
SALES (est): 30K **Privately Held**
SIC: 2099 Tortillas, fresh or refrigerated

(G-3369)
TRUNCH BULL SERVICE LLC
3235 Ne Highway 54 (73942-5143)
PHONE.................................580 468-1501
Martin Montelongo, *Mng Member*
EMP: 15 **EST:** 2016
SALES (est): 2.5MM **Privately Held**
SIC: 7692 Welding repair

(G-3370)
WESTAIR GAS & EQUIPMENT LP
502 Ne 4th St (73942-5373)
P.O. Box 701 (73942-0701)
PHONE.................................580 338-6449
Jesse Gonzalez, *Sales/Mktg Mgr*
EMP: 3 **Privately Held**
SIC: 3548 5084 5169 Welding apparatus; industrial machinery & equipment; chemicals & allied products
HQ: Westair Gas & Equipment, Lp
   4258 S Treadaway Blvd
   Abilene TX 79602
   325 670-0444

(G-3371)
WILSON WELDING WORKS LLC
3101 Tumbleweed Dr (73942-6016)
PHONE.................................580 338-7345
Jerry Alan,
Lanny Wilson,
EMP: 10
SALES (est): 1MM **Privately Held**
SIC: 7692 1799 Welding repair; welding on site

Hammon
Roger Mills County

(G-3372)
THOMASS WELDING
20062 E 950 Rd (73650-5029)
PHONE.................................580 821-0843
EMP: 1
SALES (est): 49.1K **Privately Held**
SIC: 7692 Welding repair

Harrah
Oklahoma County

(G-3373)
A&M AEROSPACE LLC
1877 Church Ave (73045-9750)
PHONE.................................405 323-6428
Marvin Pitman, *Principal*
EMP: 5
SALES (est): 120.5K **Privately Held**
SIC: 3721 Aircraft

(G-3374)
BE CUSTOM COATINGS
329483 E 1000 Rd (73045-7906)
PHONE.................................405 205-9347
Ben Cowart, *Principal*
EMP: 2
SALES (est): 103.6K **Privately Held**
SIC: 3479 Metal coating & allied service

(G-3375)
CEDAR RDGE RCORDING STUDIO LLC
2129 N Dobbs Rd (73045-9149)
PHONE.................................405 651-5961
George Dykes, *Principal*
EMP: 1
SALES (est): 44.6K
SALES (corp-wide): 215.5K **Privately Held**
SIC: 5734 5045 3652 Modems, monitors, terminals & disk drives: computers; printers & plotters: computers; personal computers; printers, computer; magnetic tape (audio): prerecorded
PA: Computer Solutions + , Llc
   12228 Ne 23rd St
   Choctaw OK 73020
   405 259-9603

(G-3376)
DIG-IT BACKHOE TRCTR SVCS LLC
1035 Timberidge Rd (73045-8831)
PHONE.................................405 921-2623
EMP: 1
SALES (est): 66K **Privately Held**
SIC: 3531 Backhoes

(G-3377)
DOLESE BROS CO
21500 E Reno Ave (73045-9514)
PHONE.................................405 454-2478
Bill Schlittler, *Branch Mgr*
EMP: 2
SALES (corp-wide): 8.5MM **Privately Held**
WEB: www.dolese.com
SIC: 3273 Ready-mixed concrete
PA: Dolese Bros. Co.
   20 Nw 13th St
   Oklahoma City OK 73103
   405 235-2311

(G-3378)
GRACE FIBRGLS & COMPOSITES LLC
9677 N Harrah Rd (73045-8928)
PHONE.................................405 233-3203
Rodney Thompson,
EMP: 3
SALES: 300K **Privately Held**
SIC: 2821 Molding compounds, plastics

(G-3379)
JOSHUA PROMOTIONS
2335 Janene St (73045-6555)
PHONE.................................405 590-8894
Jimmy Holbrook, *Owner*
EMP: 2
SALES (est): 73.2K **Privately Held**
SIC: 2759 Commercial printing

(G-3380)
MARTINEZ INDUSTRIES LLC
21213 Se 37th St (73045-6136)
PHONE.................................405 503-4020
Matthew Ray Martinez, *Owner*
EMP: 2
SALES (est): 117.2K **Privately Held**
SIC: 3999 Manufacturing industries

(G-3381)
MENZ PRINTING SERVICE LLC
20922 Se 29th St (73045-6439)
PHONE.................................405 620-3673
EMP: 2
SALES (est): 83.9K **Privately Held**
SIC: 2752 Commercial printing, lithographic

(G-3382)
OKIE DOKIE CBD DISPENSARY LLC
20107 Ne 23rd St (73045-9116)
PHONE.................................405 454-5040
EMP: 1
SALES (est): 39.6K **Privately Held**
SIC: 3999

(G-3383)
OKLAHOMA ACADEMY PUBLISHING
18509 Ne 63rd St (73045-8550)
PHONE.................................405 454-6211
Daniel Arroyo, *Director*
EMP: 1 **EST:** 2015
SALES (est): 40.3K **Privately Held**
SIC: 2731 Book publishing

(G-3384)
REDNECK FIREARMS INC
19891 Se 15th St (73045-6389)
PHONE.................................405 650-6605
George Bridges, *President*
EMP: 2
SALES: 250K **Privately Held**
SIC: 3484 Small arms

(G-3385)
S E A Y MANUFACTURING LLC
20747 Prairie Hills Dr (73045-9608)
PHONE.................................405 454-2328
Bobby Seay, *Principal*
Shelley Seay,
EMP: 2
SALES (est): 170K **Privately Held**
SIC: 3312 Hot-rolled iron & steel products

(G-3386)
SWEET SAP EXTRACTS INC
9120 N Harrah Rd (73045-9043)
PHONE.................................405 205-8706
John Walker, *Owner*
EMP: 2
SALES (est): 74.4K **Privately Held**
SIC: 2836 Extracts

(G-3387)
TOWN & COUNTRY WELDING LLC
21800 Martin Rd (73045-7665)
PHONE.................................405 664-5361
EMP: 1
SALES (est): 54.1K **Privately Held**
SIC: 7692 Welding repair

(G-3388)
TRILOGY HORSE INDUSTRIES INC
2169 Copperidge Ln (73045-6595)
P.O. Box 1102 (73045-1102)
PHONE.................................405 248-1010
Jack Owen, *President*
Nancy Owen, *Principal*
EMP: 4
SALES (est): 220K **Privately Held**
SIC: 3949 Treadmills

Hartshorne
Pittsburg County

(G-3389)
3R WELDING
7564 Nw Bowers Rd (74547-1428)
PHONE.................................918 839-8945
Joe Ramirez, *Principal*
EMP: 1
SALES (est): 28.2K **Privately Held**
SIC: 7692 Welding repair

(G-3390)
CHARLES SERVICE STATION LLC
14365 E Us Highway 270 (74547-5302)
P.O. Box 100 (74547-0100)
PHONE.................................918 297-3308
Jerimiah D Foreman, *Mng Member*
Jeremiah D Foreman, *Mng Member*
EMP: 2 **EST:** 1959
SQ FT: 2,460
SALES: 360K **Privately Held**
SIC: 5541 7538 3011 Filling stations, gasoline; general automotive repair shops; tires & inner tubes

(G-3391)
DOLESE BROS CO
S Of Hartshorne (74547)
P.O. Box 1009 (74547-1009)
PHONE.................................918 297-2376
Alfred Smith, *Manager*
EMP: 2
SALES (corp-wide): 8.5MM **Privately Held**
SIC: 3273 Ready-mixed concrete
PA: Dolese Bros. Co.
   20 Nw 13th St
   Oklahoma City OK 73103
   405 235-2311

(G-3392)
KESC ENTERPRISES LLC
1008 Pennsylvania Ave (74547-3644)
P.O. Box 1011 (74547-1011)
PHONE.................................918 297-2501
Richard C Lerblance, *CEO*
EMP: 5
SQ FT: 800
SALES: 150K **Privately Held**
SIC: 2819 Fuels & radioactive compounds

(G-3393)
MASS BROTHERS INC
Also Called: Buffalo Creek
1116 Lehigh Ave (74547-3826)
P.O. Box 738 (74547-0738)
PHONE.................................918 527-3753
Steve Mass, *President*
EMP: 6
SQ FT: 6,000
SALES: 217.1K **Privately Held**
SIC: 2511 2434 Wood household furniture; wood kitchen cabinets

(G-3394)
NEWSPAPER HOLDING INC
Also Called: Hartshorne Sun
1101 Pennsylvania Ave (74547-3833)
PHONE.................................918 297-2544
Jim Nicholson, *Branch Mgr*
EMP: 38 **Privately Held**
SIC: 2711 Newspapers: publishing only, not printed on site
HQ: Newspaper Holding, Inc.
   425 Locust St
   Johnstown PA 15901
   814 532-5102

(G-3395)
SMITH & SMITH CONSTRUCTION
2624 Hartshorne Lake Rd (74547-5036)
PHONE.................................918 297-5062
Terri Smith, *Partner*
EMP: 5
SALES (est): 298.8K **Privately Held**
SIC: 3548 7389 Electrodes, electric welding;

Hartshorne - Pittsburg County (G-3396)

GEOGRAPHIC SECTION

(G-3396)
WILLIAM PETTIT
Also Called: Pettit Motor Co
800 Pennsylvania Ave (74547-3640)
P.O. Box 390 (74547-0390)
PHONE.....................918 297-2564
William O Pettit, *Owner*
EMP: 15
SQ FT: 3,000
SALES (est): 870K **Privately Held**
SIC: 1311 5511 0272 0212 Crude petroleum & natural gas; automobiles, new & used; horse farm; beef cattle except feedlots

Haskell
Muskogee County

(G-3397)
EASTERN MANUFACTURING INC
100 E South Pr (74436)
P.O. Box 727 (74436-0727)
PHONE.....................918 482-1544
James Brewer, *President*
Kaled Brewer, *Vice Pres*
EMP: 8
SALES (est): 1.5MM **Privately Held**
SIC: 3549 Metalworking machinery

(G-3398)
HASKELL NEWS
108 E Main St (74436)
PHONE.....................918 482-5619
Julie Arrowood, *Owner*
EMP: 1 **EST:** 1930
SALES (est): 101.1K **Privately Held**
SIC: 2711 Job printing & newspaper publishing combined

(G-3399)
JIM HAYNES
Also Called: Jim Haynes Oil Company
4280 N 320 Rd (74436-8803)
PHONE.....................918 733-2517
Jim Haynes, *Owner*
EMP: 1 **Privately Held**
SIC: 1389 1311 Servicing oil & gas wells; crude petroleum production; natural gas production
PA: Jim Haynes

Okmulgee OK

(G-3400)
RYAN MANUFACTURING INC
19212 Oklahoma 104 (74436)
Rural Route 2 Box 1b (74436-9611)
PHONE.....................918 482-6512
Michael Ryan, *Principal*
Steve Rogers, *Principal*
Scott Ryan, *Principal*
EMP: 6
SALES (est): 439.2K **Privately Held**
SIC: 3599 Machine shop, jobbing & repair

(G-3401)
SPARKS PLATING COMPANY
201 N Broadway (74436)
P.O. Box 1148 (74436-1148)
PHONE.....................918 482-5080
Lonnie Sparks, *Partner*
Kevin Sparks, *Partner*
EMP: 2
SALES (est): 199.2K **Privately Held**
SIC: 3471 Electroplating of metals or formed products

(G-3402)
WH INTERNATIONAL CASTING LLC
117 E Airport Rd (74436)
PHONE.....................562 521-0727
Donald Hu, *President*
EMP: 2
SALES (corp-wide): 287.4MM **Privately Held**
SIC: 3321 Gray & ductile iron foundries
HQ: Wh International Casting, Llc
14821 Artesia Blvd
La Mirada CA 90638
562 521-0727

(G-3403)
WILLIE DEWAYNE BROWN
Also Called: Mega Tek Steel Fabricators
2315 Haskell Blvd (74436)
P.O. Box 670 (74436-0670)
PHONE.....................918 482-1115
Willie Dewayne Brown, *Owner*
EMP: 10
SALES (est): 925K **Privately Held**
SIC: 3441 Fabricated structural metal

Haworth
Mccurtain County

(G-3404)
HARRISON LOGGING LC
3161 Ferguson Rd (74740-5085)
PHONE.....................580 245-2179
Mh Harrison Jr, *Mng Member*
Bettie Harrison,
EMP: 7
SALES (est): 350K **Privately Held**
SIC: 2411 Logging camps & contractors

(G-3405)
LLOYD PROVENCE LOGGING
998 Geode Hill Rd (74740-5675)
PHONE.....................580 245-1170
EMP: 1
SALES (est): 71K **Privately Held**
SIC: 2411 Logging

(G-3406)
TUNNELL CHANCE
174 Log Spur Rd (74740-5673)
PHONE.....................580 245-2422
Chance Tunnell, *Principal*
EMP: 3 **EST:** 2013
SALES (est): 159K **Privately Held**
SIC: 2411 Logging

Healdton
Carter County

(G-3407)
ASSOCIATED WIRE LINE SVCS INC
203 Apple St (73438)
PHONE.....................580 229-0731
Robert Johnston, *President*
Robert Johnston Jr, *Vice Pres*
Velma Johnston, *Vice Pres*
EMP: 18
SALES (est): 968.3K **Privately Held**
WEB: www.associatedwireline.com
SIC: 1389 Oil field services

(G-3408)
BRADY WELDING & MACHINE SHOP (PA)
11991 Highway 76 (73438)
P.O. Box 788 (73438-0788)
PHONE.....................580 229-1168
William H Brady, *Ch of Bd*
Mike Brady, *President*
David Brady, *Vice Pres*
Sterling Foster, *Vice Pres*
Jana Strange, *Admin Sec*
EMP: 62
SQ FT: 6,000
SALES (est): 52.1MM **Privately Held**
WEB: www.bradywelding.com
SIC: 1389 3599 4213 Construction, repair & dismantling services; machine shop, jobbing & repair; liquid petroleum transport, non-local

(G-3409)
CAULUMET ORE CO
824 Convict Hill Rd (73438-4441)
PHONE.....................580 673-2815
J Graves, *Principal*
EMP: 2
SALES (est): 170.4K **Privately Held**
SIC: 2911 Petroleum refining

(G-3410)
CHAPARRAL ENERGY INC
824 Convict Hill Rd (73438-4441)
PHONE.....................580 673-2815
Jo Atnip, *Manager*
EMP: 20 **Publicly Held**
SIC: 1311 Crude petroleum production; natural gas production
PA: Chaparral Energy, Inc.
701 Cedar Lake Blvd
Oklahoma City OK 73114

(G-3411)
CITATION OIL & GAS CORP
4597 Texas St (73438-2906)
P.O. Box 190 (73438-0190)
PHONE.....................580 229-1756
Dale McCurry, *Branch Mgr*
EMP: 35
SALES (corp-wide): 283.5MM **Privately Held**
SIC: 1311 Crude petroleum production; natural gas production
PA: Citation Oil & Gas Corp.
14077 Cutten Rd
Houston TX 77069
281 891-1000

(G-3412)
DARK HORSE OIL FIELD SVCS LLC
13152 Highway 76 (73438-1703)
PHONE.....................580 229-0626
Carey Powell, *Principal*
EMP: 3
SALES (est): 445.6K **Privately Held**
SIC: 5172 1389 Crude oil; oil & gas field services

(G-3413)
DAVID SMITH
189 Golf Course Rd (73438-3161)
PHONE.....................580 229-1195
David Smith, *Principal*
EMP: 2
SALES (est): 65.5K **Privately Held**
SIC: 1389 Oil & gas field services

(G-3414)
HILTON HERALD CORP OKLAHOMA
Also Called: Healdton Herald
11204 Highway 76 (73438-1724)
P.O. Box 250 (73438-0250)
PHONE.....................580 229-0132
Christi Blakemore, *President*
EMP: 3 **EST:** 1917
SQ FT: 6,250
SALES (est): 206.6K **Privately Held**
SIC: 2711 2752 Newspapers, publishing & printing; commercial printing, offset

(G-3415)
HOTROD WELDING
10837 Highway 76 (73438-1717)
PHONE.....................580 229-0888
EMP: 2
SALES (est): 103.7K **Privately Held**
SIC: 7692 Welding Repair

(G-3416)
J FLETCHER DERRELL
Also Called: Fletcher Welding
27970 State Highway 53 (73438-6106)
PHONE.....................580 673-2489
EMP: 1
SALES (est): 40.9K **Privately Held**
SIC: 7692 Welding Repair

(G-3417)
JOHN WARD WELDING
4065 Inwood Rd (73438-6017)
PHONE.....................580 673-2127
John Ward, *Owner*
EMP: 1
SALES (est): 62K **Privately Held**
SIC: 7692 Welding repair

(G-3418)
KINGERY DRILLING COMPANY INC
1217 W Like Rd (73438)
P.O. Box 789 (73438-0789)
PHONE.....................580 229-0716
Bruce Ayles, *Manager*
EMP: 8

SALES (corp-wide): 1.6MM **Privately Held**
SIC: 1311 Crude petroleum production; natural gas production
PA: Kingery Drilling Company, Inc.
210 W Broadway St
Ardmore OK 73401
580 223-6823

(G-3419)
MITCHELLS TANK TRUCK SERVICE
12546 Highway 76 (73438-1741)
P.O. Box 457 (73438-0457)
PHONE.....................580 229-1880
Glen Mitchell, *President*
Beverly Mitchell, *Vice Pres*
EMP: 4
SALES (est): 231.6K **Privately Held**
SIC: 1389 Oil field services

(G-3420)
OIL WELL CEMENTERS INC (PA)
189 Golf Course Rd (73438-3161)
PHONE.....................580 229-1776
Sherri Blevins, *President*
David Smith, *Corp Secy*
Jim Darling, *Vice Pres*
EMP: 10 **EST:** 1978
SQ FT: 1,000
SALES (est): 2.3MM **Privately Held**
SIC: 1389 Cementing oil & gas well casings

(G-3421)
PROCHEM ENERGY SERVICES INC
9396 Highway 76 (73438-1688)
P.O. Box 268 (73438-0268)
PHONE.....................580 465-1737
John Turner, *President*
EMP: 11
SALES: 1.3MM **Privately Held**
WEB: www.prochemes.com
SIC: 1389 Construction, repair & dismantling services

(G-3422)
SUTHERLAND WELL SERVICE INC (PA)
S On Hwy 76 (73438)
P.O. Box 400 (73438-0400)
PHONE.....................580 229-1338
Scott Sutherland, *President*
EMP: 54 **EST:** 1945
SQ FT: 3,600
SALES (est): 5.2MM **Privately Held**
SIC: 1389 1311 Oil field services; crude petroleum production; natural gas production

(G-3423)
TRI PRODUCTION INC
Hwy 76 S (73438)
PHONE.....................580 229-1280
Joe W Davis, *President*
Patsy Davis, *Corp Secy*
EMP: 2
SQ FT: 500
SALES (est): 163.8K **Privately Held**
SIC: 1311 Crude petroleum production

(G-3424)
WITHERS TRUCKING CO
3 1/2 S On S W 8th St (73438)
P.O. Box 831 (73438-0831)
PHONE.....................580 668-2320
Buddy Withers, *Owner*
EMP: 1
SALES (est): 200K **Privately Held**
SIC: 4212 3273 Dump truck haulage; ready-mixed concrete

Heavener
Le Flore County

(G-3425)
BC FIELD SERVICES INC
13006 526th St (74937-8825)
PHONE.....................918 839-0490
Jesse Palmer, *President*
Kendra Palmer, *Vice Pres*
EMP: 2

GEOGRAPHIC SECTION

Hennessey - Kingfisher County (G-3457)

SALES (est): 65.5K **Privately Held**
SIC: 1389 Gas field services

(G-3426)
BUCKY MCGEE LOGGING
24178 Independence Rd (74937)
PHONE..................918 635-0909
EMP: 2
SALES (est): 81.7K **Privately Held**
SIC: 2411 Logging

(G-3427)
DOUBLE H WELDING
Highway 59 N Frrest Hl Rd (74937)
P.O. Box 366 (74937-0366)
PHONE..................918 653-2289
Roger Himes, *Owner*
Ruby Himes, *Manager*
EMP: 1
SQ FT: 4,800
SALES (est): 50K **Privately Held**
SIC: 1791 7692 Structural steel erection; welding repair

(G-3428)
DUKE MANUFACTURING
907 W Highway 270 (74937-9408)
PHONE..................918 653-3404
EMP: 3
SALES (est): 130K **Privately Held**
SIC: 3999 Mfg Misc Products

(G-3429)
HEAVENER LEDGER
507 E 1st St (74937-3203)
P.O. Box 38 (74937-0038)
PHONE..................918 653-2425
James Johnson, *Partner*
Bobby Johnson, *Treasurer*
EMP: 4 EST: 1947
SQ FT: 4,000
SALES (est): 150K **Privately Held**
WEB: www.heavenerledger.com
SIC: 2711 2759 2791 2789 Newspapers: publishing only, not printed on site; letterpress printing; typesetting; bookbinding & related work; commercial printing, lithographic

(G-3430)
MIMIC MANUFACTURING LLC
102 Pitchford Ln (74937-7489)
PHONE..................918 653-7161
EMP: 6
SALES (est): 43.6K **Privately Held**
SIC: 3999 Manufacturing industries

(G-3431)
O K FOODS INC
Hwy 128 E (74937)
P.O. Box 1119, Fort Smith AR (72902-1119)
PHONE..................918 653-1640
Ricky Bryan, *Branch Mgr*
EMP: 3300 **Privately Held**
SIC: 2048 Poultry feeds
HQ: O. K. Foods, Inc.
4601 N 6th St
Fort Smith AR 72904
479 783-4186

(G-3432)
O K FOODS INC
1000 Old Pike Rd (74937-7425)
P.O. Box 158 (74937-0158)
PHONE..................918 653-2819
B J Shaw, *Manager*
EMP: 900 **Privately Held**
SIC: 2015 Poultry, processed
HQ: O. K. Foods, Inc.
4601 N 6th St
Fort Smith AR 72904
479 783-4186

(G-3433)
TAG AGENT
103 E Avenue C (74937-2603)
P.O. Box 686 (74937-0686)
PHONE..................918 653-2236
Charlotte Moody, *Principal*
EMP: 2
SALES (est): 119.2K **Privately Held**
SIC: 3469 Automobile license tags, stamped metal

Helena
Alfalfa County

(G-3434)
HUNGERFORD OIL & GAS INC
3rd Main St (73741)
P.O. Box 118 (73741-0118)
PHONE..................580 852-3288
Ken Allen Hungerford, *President*
Marilyn Hungerford, *Corp Secy*
Kip Hungerford, *Vice Pres*
EMP: 1
SALES (est): 216.4K **Privately Held**
SIC: 1382 Oil & gas exploration services

(G-3435)
MCCOLLUM CUSTOM CABINETS
6411 County Road 650 (73741-4227)
PHONE..................580 548-5851
Lydel McCollum, *Principal*
EMP: 2
SALES (est): 115.7K **Privately Held**
SIC: 2434 Wood kitchen cabinets

(G-3436)
NORMAN KOEHN
Also Called: Norman's Welding & Repair
103 W 2nd St (73741)
P.O. Box 588 (73741-0588)
PHONE..................580 852-3260
Norman Koehn, *Owner*
EMP: 1
SALES (est): 75K **Privately Held**
SIC: 7692 7699 Welding repair; agricultural equipment repair services

(G-3437)
TIMBERLAKE TRUSSWORKS LLC
12177 State Highway 58 (73741-4126)
P.O. Box 58 (73741-0058)
PHONE..................580 852-3660
Mahlon Boehs, *President*
EMP: 6
SALES (est): 253.6K **Privately Held**
SIC: 2439 5031 Trusses, wooden roof; structural assemblies, prefabricated: wood

Hendrix
Bryan County

(G-3438)
ANITA AND HAROLD SPEED
Also Called: Silver Dollar Grocery Store
725 Carpenters Bluff Rd (74741-1210)
PHONE..................580 838-2297
Anita Speed, *Owner*
Harold Speed, *Owner*
EMP: 3
SALES (est): 175K **Privately Held**
SIC: 5411 3949 Grocery stores; fishing tackle, general

(G-3439)
ARMOUR PEST CONTROL LLC
117 Kemp Rd (74741-1225)
PHONE..................918 489-5734
Johnnie M Sears, *Manager*
EMP: 2
SALES (est): 50K **Privately Held**
SIC: 2879 Agricultural chemicals

(G-3440)
HAROLD SPEED JR
Also Called: Silver Dollar Custom Boats
635 Carpenters Bluff Rd (74741-1212)
PHONE..................580 838-2578
Harold Speed Jr, *Owner*
Rose Speed, *Bookkeeper*
EMP: 2
SALES (est): 110K **Privately Held**
SIC: 3732 Motorized boat, building & repairing; houseboats, building & repairing

(G-3441)
WARREN WEST
2297 Kemp Rd (74741-1815)
PHONE..................580 838-2173
Warren West, *Owner*
EMP: 1
SALES (est): 66.6K **Privately Held**
SIC: 7692 Welding repair

Hennessey
Kingfisher County

(G-3442)
AC OIL & GAS LLC
21505 E 630 Rd (73742-6206)
PHONE..................405 919-8088
EMP: 2
SALES (est): 130.4K **Privately Held**
SIC: 1389 Oil & gas field services

(G-3443)
ACTION PIPE AND SUPPLY INC
400 W Jack Choate Ave (73742-1031)
PHONE..................405 853-7170
Randy Holder, *Partner*
Kenny Bateman, *Partner*
Tom Holder, *Partner*
EMP: 6
SALES (est): 343.3K **Privately Held**
SIC: 1389 Oil field services

(G-3444)
ADVANTAGE SUPPLEMENTS LLC
Also Called: Shoberts Feed Supplements
4597 N 2830 Rd (73742-6507)
P.O. Box 823 (73742-0823)
PHONE..................866 226-9613
Chad Charmasson, *Mng Member*
Amy Charmasson,
EMP: 2 EST: 2015
SALES (est): 62.3K **Privately Held**
SIC: 2048 Mineral feed supplements

(G-3445)
ANNA LIGHTLE
Also Called: Lightle Sand & Construction Co
Rr 3 (73742-9803)
P.O. Box 242 (73742-0242)
PHONE..................405 853-4530
Anna Lightle, *Owner*
EMP: 9
SALES (est): 200K **Privately Held**
SIC: 1442 1794 Sand mining; gravel mining; excavation work

(G-3446)
BECK RESOURCES INCORPORATED
Hwy 81 N (73742)
P.O. Box 175 (73742-0175)
PHONE..................405 853-2736
Terry Beck, *President*
William H Beck, *Chairman*
Tracy Beck, *Corp Secy*
Tim Beck, *Exec VP*
EMP: 35
SQ FT: 12,400
SALES (est): 6.8MM **Privately Held**
SIC: 1389 1311 Pumping of oil & gas wells; crude petroleum production

(G-3447)
BOB & SON OIL CO INC
2 One Hlf Mile S On Hwy81 (73742)
P.O. Box 124 (73742-0124)
PHONE..................405 853-6261
Bobby Dean Pitchford Jr, *President*
Terry Pitchford, *Admin Sec*
EMP: 2
SALES (est): 224K **Privately Held**
SIC: 1311 Crude petroleum production; natural gas production

(G-3448)
CAPSTONE OIL & GAS INC (PA)
S Cemetary Rd (73742)
PHONE..................405 853-7170
Randy Holder, *President*
Tom Holder, *Vice Pres*
EMP: 4
SALES (est): 1.4MM **Privately Held**
SIC: 1382 Oil & gas exploration services

(G-3449)
CAPSTONE OIL & GAS INC
Also Called: Pronto Chemical Co
Cemetary Rd (73742)
PHONE..................405 853-7168
Randy Holder, *President*
EMP: 1
SALES (corp-wide): 1.4MM **Privately Held**
SIC: 1389 Oil field services
PA: Capstone Oil & Gas, Inc
S Cemetary Rd
Hennessey OK 73742
405 853-7170

(G-3450)
CHRISTYS QUILTS
7939 E 590 Rd (73742-6504)
PHONE..................405 853-2155
Christy Hladik, *Owner*
EMP: 1
SALES: 8K **Privately Held**
SIC: 7299 2395 Quilting for individuals; embroidery & art needlework

(G-3451)
CIMARRON TANK SERVICE
420 E 3rd St (73742-1605)
PHONE..................405 853-6523
EMP: 1
SALES (est): 52.5K **Privately Held**
SIC: 3088 Mfg Plastic Plumbing Fixtures

(G-3452)
COPELAND HOT OIL SERVICE LLC
526 N Oak Ave (73742-1232)
P.O. Box 184 (73742-0184)
PHONE..................405 853-2179
Vickie Pruitt, *Mng Member*
EMP: 5 EST: 1999
SALES (est): 1MM **Privately Held**
SIC: 1389 Oil field services

(G-3453)
COWBOY COMPOST
17067 E 672 Rd (73742-6000)
PHONE..................405 853-0462
Richard James Schmidt, *Principal*
EMP: 2
SALES (est): 74.4K **Privately Held**
SIC: 2875 Compost

(G-3454)
COWBOY PMPG UNIT SLS REPR LLC
600 W Jack Choate Ave (73742)
P.O. Box 698 (73742-0698)
PHONE..................405 853-7170
Tom Holder,
EMP: 3
SALES (est): 158.8K **Privately Held**
SIC: 1389 Pumping of oil & gas wells

(G-3455)
CRIS CHOATE WELDING INC
432 N Oak Ave (73742-1230)
PHONE..................405 853-2792
Cris Choate, *Principal*
EMP: 1
SALES (est): 64.1K **Privately Held**
SIC: 7692 Welding repair

(G-3456)
D & T SWABBING & WELL SERVICE
Rr 3 (73742)
P.O. Box 124 (73742-0124)
PHONE..................405 853-7045
B Dean Pitchford Jr, *President*
Terry Pitchford, *Corp Secy*
Clara Lee Pitchford, *Vice Pres*
EMP: 3
SALES (est): 210.8K **Privately Held**
SIC: 1389 Swabbing wells

(G-3457)
DANLIN INDUSTRIES CORP
431 W Oklahoma St (73742-1312)
PHONE..................405 853-2559
EMP: 2 EST: 2013
SALES (est): 108.9K **Privately Held**
SIC: 1382 Oil & gas exploration services

Hennessey - Kingfisher County (G-3458)

(G-3458)
DIXIE WIRELINE
7248 Us Highway 81 (73742-7504)
PHONE................................405 853-5402
Phil Duncan, *Principal*
EMP: 2 **EST:** 2000
SALES (est): 116.7K **Privately Held**
SIC: 1389 Removal of condensate gasoline from field (gathering) lines

(G-3459)
EAT IT UP LLC
114 S Main St (73742-1403)
PHONE................................405 853-2313
Tracey Solis, *Principal*
EMP: 4
SALES (est): 393.8K **Privately Held**
SIC: 2599 Bar, restaurant & cafeteria furniture

(G-3460)
ENERGY METER SYSTEMS LLC
Also Called: E M S
1161 S Main St (73742-1754)
PHONE................................405 853-4976
Ken Hudgeons, *President*
Jack Chisum, *Vice Pres*
Chris Irigoyen, *Sales Staff*
Gavin Nailon, *Sales Staff*
Penny McEachern, *Admin Sec*
EMP: 40
SQ FT: 10,000
SALES (est): 11.2MM **Privately Held**
SIC: 3823 3533 Industrial instrmnts msrmnt display/control process variable; gas field machinery & equipment

(G-3461)
FLUID LIFT INC
Hwy 81 S (73742)
P.O. Box 241 (73742-0241)
PHONE................................405 853-6876
Alan Heath, *President*
Becky Heath, *Principal*
EMP: 1
SALES (est): 77.2K **Privately Held**
SIC: 1389 Oil field services

(G-3462)
GILLILAND FLUID CORPORATION
Rr 1 (73742)
P.O. Box 275 (73742-0275)
PHONE................................405 853-7188
Ron Gilliam, *President*
Barabara Gilliam, *Admin Sec*
EMP: 2
SALES (est): 276.9K **Privately Held**
SIC: 1389 Oil field services

(G-3463)
GILLILAND OIL & GAS INC
601 N Cheyenne St (73742-1153)
P.O. Box 305 (73742-0305)
PHONE................................405 853-7116
Steve Gilliland, *President*
Cheryl Gilliland, *Vice Pres*
EMP: 11
SALES (est): 2.3MM **Privately Held**
SIC: 1311 Crude petroleum production

(G-3464)
GRIFFIN RESOURCES
805 E Jack Choate Ave (73742-9655)
PHONE................................405 853-4688
Patrick S Griffin, *Principal*
Patrick Griffin, *Principal*
EMP: 4
SALES (est): 234.5K **Privately Held**
SIC: 1311 Crude petroleum production

(G-3465)
HARDIN IGNITION INC
Also Called: Hardin Ignition Magneto Shop
210 S Main St (73742-1405)
P.O. Box 246 (73742-0246)
PHONE................................405 853-4324
Randy Hardin, *President*
Sandra Hardin, *Corp Secy*
EMP: 2
SQ FT: 3,300
SALES: 250K **Privately Held**
SIC: 7699 3429 Battery service & repair; manufactured hardware (general)

(G-3466)
HENNESSEY CLIPPER
117 S Main St (73742-1402)
P.O. Box 338 (73742-0338)
PHONE................................405 853-4888
William B Walter, *Owner*
Barbara Walter, *Owner*
EMP: 5 **EST:** 1954
SQ FT: 3,000
SALES (est): 236.6K **Privately Held**
WEB: www.hennesseyclipper.com
SIC: 2711 2752 Job printing & newspaper publishing combined; commercial printing, offset

(G-3467)
HENNESSEY READY MIX CONCRETE
507 S Dunlap St (73742-1721)
P.O. Box 501 (73742-0501)
PHONE................................405 853-4473
Christopher Harris, *President*
Mike Schwarz, *Vice Pres*
Katherine Schwarz, *Admin Sec*
EMP: 1 **EST:** 1955
SALES (est): 600K **Privately Held**
SIC: 3273 Ready-mixed concrete

(G-3468)
HENRY & SON ROUSTABOUTS LLC
13533 E 630 Rd (73742-6671)
PHONE................................580 747-8400
EMP: 2
SALES (est): 151.9K **Privately Held**
SIC: 1389 Roustabout service

(G-3469)
JIMS WELDING SERVICE
S 81 Hwy (73742)
PHONE................................405 853-4522
Jim Hawk, *Owner*
EMP: 1
SALES (est): 59.5K **Privately Held**
SIC: 7692 Welding repair

(G-3470)
KEY ENERGY SERVICES INC
Hwy 81 (73742)
PHONE................................405 853-4327
Jim Dillon, *Branch Mgr*
Mich Broghton, *Manager*
EMP: 54
SALES (corp-wide): 413.8MM **Publicly Held**
WEB: www.keyenergy.com
SIC: 1389 Servicing oil & gas wells
PA: Key Energy Services, Inc.
1301 McKinney St Ste 1800
Houston TX 77010
713 651-4300

(G-3471)
KIRKPATRICK OIL COMPANY INC
Hwy 81 (73742)
P.O. Box 86 (73742-0086)
PHONE................................405 853-2922
Wyatt Scoles, *Manager*
EMP: 4
SALES (corp-wide): 16MM **Privately Held**
SIC: 1311 Crude petroleum production
PA: Kirkpatrick Oil Company, Inc.
1001 W Wilshire Blvd # 202
Oklahoma City OK 73116
405 840-2882

(G-3472)
LIGHTNING SERVICES INC
708 E 4th St (73742-1626)
P.O. Box 295 (73742-0295)
PHONE................................405 853-6669
Eugene Smith, *President*
SEC-Tr Ruby Smith, *Corp Secy*
Tina Smith, *Vice Pres*
EMP: 1 **EST:** 1977
SALES (est): 105.1K **Privately Held**
SIC: 1389 Oil field services

(G-3473)
LONGHORN SERVICE COMPANY LLC
S Cemetery Rd (73742)
P.O. Box 698 (73742-0698)
PHONE................................405 853-7170
Jill N Skufca,
Randy Holder,
EMP: 50
SQ FT: 3,000
SALES (est): 14.4MM **Privately Held**
SIC: 1389 Oil field services

(G-3474)
LORRAINE OIL CO INC
2760 Us Highway 81 (73742-7514)
P.O. Box 175 (73742-0175)
PHONE................................405 853-2715
EMP: 3
SALES (est): 168K **Privately Held**
SIC: 1311 Crude petroleum production

(G-3475)
M S WELDING FABRICATION
Rr 1 (73742)
PHONE................................405 368-7451
Micheal Semrad, *Owner*
EMP: 1
SALES (est): 49.4K **Privately Held**
SIC: 7692 Welding repair

(G-3476)
MAVERICK OIL TOOLS LLC
600 N Cheyenne St (73742-1152)
PHONE................................405 853-5524
Jacob Weaver,
EMP: 2
SALES: 250K **Privately Held**
SIC: 3533 Oil & gas drilling rigs & equipment

(G-3477)
MELS CONSTRUCTION INC
1216 S Main St (73742-1745)
PHONE................................405 853-4621
Melvin E Franks Jr, *President*
Connie Franks, *Corp Secy*
EMP: 8 **EST:** 1970
SALES (est): 599.4K **Privately Held**
SIC: 4212 1389 Local trucking, without storage; roustabout service

(G-3478)
OK SWABBING INC
400 E Jack Taute Ave (73742)
P.O. Box 835 (73742-0835)
PHONE................................405 853-6953
Harold W Caulder, *President*
Wayne Caulder, *President*
Dona Caulder, *Admin Sec*
EMP: 2
SALES (est): 323.1K **Privately Held**
SIC: 1311 Crude petroleum production

(G-3479)
PERKS WELDING LLC
8384 E 600 Rd (73742-6691)
PHONE................................405 853-6848
Terry Choate, *Principal*
EMP: 1 **EST:** 2009
SALES (est): 45.3K **Privately Held**
SIC: 7692 Welding repair

(G-3480)
R & S SWABBING INC
318 S Oak Ave (73742-1610)
P.O. Box 116 (73742-0116)
PHONE................................405 853-5445
Reydecol Najera, *President*
EMP: 8
SALES (est): 1.7MM **Privately Held**
SIC: 1389 7389 Bailing, cleaning, swabbing & treating of wells;

(G-3481)
RANGER OILFIELD SERVICES CORP
1801 N Hwy 81 (73742)
P.O. Box 594 (73742-0594)
PHONE................................405 853-7279
Tim Beck, *President*
Terry Beck, *Vice Pres*
EMP: 40
SQ FT: 7,200
SALES (est): 8.1MM **Privately Held**
SIC: 1389 Haulage, oil field; oil field services

(G-3482)
RAYCO PARAFFIN SERVICE INC
S Metro Rd (73742)
P.O. Box 21 (73742-0021)
PHONE................................405 853-2055
Imogene Scruggs, *President*
Terri Renee Scruggs, *Corp Secy*
Arlan Ray Scruggs, *Vice Pres*
EMP: 4
SALES (est): 389.6K **Privately Held**
SIC: 1389 3599 Swabbing wells; machine shop, jobbing & repair

(G-3483)
ROYAL SIGNS LLC
7177 Us Highway 81 (73742-6005)
PHONE................................918 507-3303
EMP: 2
SALES (est): 144.2K **Privately Held**
SIC: 3993 Signs & advertising specialties

(G-3484)
SEIGER WELDING LLC ◆
2443 Us Highway 81 (73742-7515)
PHONE................................405 853-7237
Joshua E Seiger, *Principal*
EMP: 1 **EST:** 2019
SALES (est): 39.8K **Privately Held**
SIC: 7692 Welding repair

(G-3485)
SHAW WIRELINE LLC
501 S Arapaho St (73742-1714)
PHONE................................405 853-2168
EMP: 2
SALES (est): 65.5K **Privately Held**
SIC: 1389 Removal of condensate gasoline from field (gathering) lines

(G-3486)
SINGER OIL COMPANY LLC
203 Exxon Rd (73742)
P.O. Box 307 (73742-0307)
PHONE................................405 853-6807
Richard B Singer,
Goepz Schuppan,
EMP: 5
SALES (est): 832.9K **Privately Held**
SIC: 1311 Crude petroleum production; natural gas production

(G-3487)
SIRRAH INVESTMENTS
12707 E 630 Rd (73742-6668)
PHONE................................405 853-4909
Mike Harris, *Owner*
EMP: 1 **EST:** 1997
SALES (est): 78.8K **Privately Held**
SIC: 1389 Oil field services

(G-3488)
SJL OIL AND GAS INC
Highway 81 S (73742)
P.O. Box 655 (73742-0655)
PHONE................................405 853-2044
Fax: 405 853-2215
EMP: 50
SQ FT: 6,000
SALES (est): 3.1MM **Privately Held**
SIC: 1389 Oil Field Well Services

(G-3489)
SJL WELL SERVICE LLC
7553 Us Highway 81 (73742-7525)
P.O. Box 655 (73742-0655)
PHONE................................405 853-2044
Mark Bishop,
EMP: 1
SALES (est): 65.4K
SALES (corp-wide): 832.9MM **Publicly Held**
WEB: www.sjlwellservice.com
SIC: 1389 Servicing oil & gas wells
HQ: Beckman Production Services, Inc.
3786 Beebe Rd
Kalkaska MI 49646
231 258-9524

(G-3490)
SNUFFYS OILFIELD SERVICES
8528 N 2830 Rd (73742-6511)
PHONE................................405 368-9333

GEOGRAPHIC SECTION

Henryetta - Okmulgee County (G-3519)

Warren L McConnell, *President*
Margie McConnell, *President*
Warren L McConnell, *President*
Margie McConnell, *Principal*
EMP: 2
SQ FT: 150
SALES (est): 350K **Privately Held**
SIC: 1382 Oil & gas exploration services

(G-3491)
TAMCO PLUNGER & LIFT INC
Hwy 81 S (73742)
P.O. Box 2365, Enid (73702-2365)
PHONE..................405 853-6195
Gerald Moore, *President*
Inez Moore, *Corp Secy*
Gorma Rose, *Vice Pres*
EMP: 5
SQ FT: 1,500
SALES (est): 436.1K **Privately Held**
SIC: 1389 Oil field services

(G-3492)
TERRYS PUMP & SUPPLY INC
112 N Main St (73742-1003)
P.O. Box 56 (73742-0056)
PHONE..................405 853-6550
Terry Berkenbile, *President*
EMP: 1
SQ FT: 5,000
SALES (est): 136.3K **Privately Held**
SIC: 1389 Oil field services

(G-3493)
THURMOND-MCGLOTHLIN LLC
Hwy 81 S (73742)
P.O. Box 744 (73742-0744)
PHONE..................405 853-2248
David Cofer, *Manager*
EMP: 8
SALES (corp-wide): 38.4MM **Privately Held**
SIC: 1389 Testing, measuring, surveying & analysis services
PA: Thurmond-Mcglothlin, Llc
1428 N Banks St
Pampa TX 79065
806 665-5700

(G-3494)
TURNER RESOURCES INC
105 E Exxon Rd Hwy 81 (73742)
P.O. Box 775 (73742-0775)
PHONE..................405 853-6275
Mannie Turner, *President*
Billie Turner, *Vice Pres*
Shirley Turner, *Treasurer*
Kathleen Turner, *Admin Sec*
EMP: 5
SALES: 750K **Privately Held**
SIC: 1311 Crude petroleum production

(G-3495)
TWENTY-TWENTY OIL & GAS CO
115 S Main St (73742-1402)
P.O. Box 247 (73742-0247)
PHONE..................405 853-4607
Hayden Hobbs, *President*
EMP: 3
SALES (est): 410K **Privately Held**
SIC: 1311 Crude petroleum production; natural gas production

(G-3496)
WEATHERFORD ARTIFICIA
Also Called: Leamco Ruthco Division
Hwy 81 S (73742)
PHONE..................405 853-7181
Bill Long, *Manager*
EMP: 15 **Privately Held**
SIC: 1389 Oil field services
HQ: Weatherford Artificial Lift Systems, Llc
2000 Saint James Pl
Houston TX 77056
713 836-4000

(G-3497)
WEATHERFORD INTERNATIONAL LLC
34th St 557 (73742)
PHONE..................405 853-7127
Josh Pitts, *General Mgr*
Sally Witzke, *Branch Mgr*
EMP: 5 **Privately Held**
SIC: 3533 Oil & gas field machinery

HQ: Weatherford International, Llc
2000 Saint James Pl
Houston TX 77056
713 693-4000

(G-3498)
WEAVER ENERGY CORPORATION
600 N Cheyenne St (73742-1152)
PHONE..................405 853-6068
Tony Weaver, *President*
Lisa Weaver, *Admin Sec*
EMP: 5
SALES (est): 790K **Privately Held**
SIC: 1311 Crude petroleum production

Henryetta
Okmulgee County

(G-3499)
ANCHOR GLASS CONTAINER CORP
601 E Bollinger Rd (74437-6604)
PHONE..................918 652-9631
Andy Bealko, *Principal*
Ellis Glover, *Site Mgr*
Cheryl Scott, *Human Res Mgr*
William Patrick, *Executive*
EMP: 425 **Privately Held**
SIC: 3221 Glass containers
PA: Anchor Glass Container Corporation
3001 N Rocky Point Dr E # 300
Tampa FL 33607

(G-3500)
BROWN PRINTING CO INC
407 W Trudgeon St (74437-4027)
P.O. Box 400 (74437-0400)
PHONE..................918 652-9611
Jim Lollis, *Manager*
Gladys Lollis, *Admin Sec*
EMP: 5
SQ FT: 4,865
SALES (est): 350K **Privately Held**
SIC: 2759 5112 2791 2789 Commercial printing; business forms; typesetting; bookbinding & related work; commercial printing, lithographic

(G-3501)
CNHI LLC
Also Called: Henryetta Free Lance
302 W Main St (74437-4240)
P.O. Box 848 (74437-0848)
PHONE..................918 652-3311
Valerie Rice, *Systems Mgr*
EMP: 5 **Privately Held**
SIC: 2711 2791 Newspapers: publishing only, not printed on site; typesetting
HQ: Cnhi, Llc
445 Dexter Ave Ste 7000
Montgomery AL 36104

(G-3502)
COALTON ROAD ENTERPRISES LLC
Also Called: Coaltons Shavings & Feed
13755 Coalton Rd (74437-7486)
P.O. Box 39, Schulter (74460-0039)
PHONE..................918 652-0474
Bryan Teague,
EMP: 1 **EST:** 2007
SALES: 1.3MM **Privately Held**
SIC: 2844 5999 5261 Shaving preparations; feed & farm supply; garden supplies & tools

(G-3503)
COX MOTOR CO HENRYETTA LLC
1007 N 5th St (74437-1627)
PHONE..................918 652-0202
James Cox, *Principal*
EMP: 2
SALES (est): 177.5K **Privately Held**
SIC: 3711 Cars, electric, assembly of

(G-3504)
DESERT INDUSTRIAL X RAY LP
902 E Robertson Hwy (74437-7630)
PHONE..................918 650-0018
Scott Harvey, *Manager*

EMP: 2
SALES (est): 163.1K **Privately Held**
SIC: 3844 X-ray apparatus & tubes

(G-3505)
DRUMRIGHT OIL WELL SERVIC
1501 W Main St (74437-3905)
PHONE..................918 704-0252
EMP: 1 **EST:** 2010
SALES (est): 52.4K **Privately Held**
SIC: 1389 Oil/Gas Field Services

(G-3506)
FIRETECH AUTOMATIC SPRINKLERS
12745 New Lake Rd (74437-8247)
P.O. Box 700 (74437-0700)
PHONE..................918 633-3773
Alvin Pharris, *President*
EMP: 2
SALES (est): 170K **Privately Held**
SIC: 3569 Sprinkler systems, fire: automatic

(G-3507)
G & H DECOY INC
601 N Highway 75 (74437-8007)
P.O. Box 1208 (74437-1208)
PHONE..................918 652-3314
Richard S Gazalski, *President*
EMP: 80
SQ FT: 100,000
SALES (est): 7.8MM **Privately Held**
WEB: www.ghdecoys.com
SIC: 3949 3089 Decoys, duck & other game birds; blow molded finished plastic products

(G-3508)
HENRYETTA PALLET COMPANY
999 E Industry Rd (74437-8019)
P.O. Box 157 (74437-0157)
PHONE..................918 652-9897
Rodnay Maynard, *President*
Rodney Maynard, *President*
Lucretia Maynard, *Corp Secy*
April Gray, *Admin Sec*
EMP: 50
SQ FT: 450
SALES (est): 7.3MM **Privately Held**
SIC: 5031 4953 2448 Pallets, wood; refuse systems; wood pallets & skids

(G-3509)
J & F OIL CO
22420 S 250 Rd (74437-7531)
P.O. Box 464 (74437-0464)
PHONE..................918 652-7957
James Jenkins, *President*
EMP: 2
SALES (est): 258.9K **Privately Held**
SIC: 1311 Crude petroleum production

(G-3510)
J & M MACHINE SHOP INC
Also Called: Skd Craft Embroidery
511 E Gum St (74437-2035)
PHONE..................918 650-0074
Sharon Dameron, *President*
Mike Dameron, *Vice Pres*
EMP: 2 **EST:** 1996
SQ FT: 1,650
SALES (est): 125K **Privately Held**
SIC: 3599 Machine shop, jobbing & repair

(G-3511)
JOSHUA COAL COMPANY
205 Perryman Rd (74437-7455)
PHONE..................918 652-3023
Alan Churchill, *Owner*
EMP: 1
SALES (est): 200K **Privately Held**
SIC: 1221 Bituminous coal surface mining

(G-3512)
MIKE BAILEY MOTORS INC
Hwy 75 & Industrial (74437)
P.O. Box 1120 (74437-1120)
PHONE..................918 652-9637
Mike Bailey, *President*
EMP: 16
SQ FT: 5,000
SALES (est): 5.3MM **Privately Held**
SIC: 5511 3465 7389 Automobiles, new & used; body parts, automobile: stamped metal; drive-a-way automobile service

(G-3513)
MORTON GRINDING WORKS
25980 S 290 Rd (74437-7432)
PHONE..................918 652-8550
Ray Morton, *Owner*
EMP: 3
SALES (est): 202.1K **Privately Held**
SIC: 3533 7692 Oil field machinery & equipment; welding repair

(G-3514)
P W MANUFACTURING COMPANY INC
610 High St (74437-2850)
PHONE..................918 652-4981
Judy Allen, *President*
Judy Wainwright, *Partner*
EMP: 5
SQ FT: 3,500
SALES (est): 470.3K **Privately Held**
SIC: 3429 3496 Animal traps, iron or steel; miscellaneous fabricated wire products

(G-3515)
PARKER HANNIFIN CORPORATION
26220 S 220 Rd (74437-1916)
P.O. Box 128 (74437-0128)
PHONE..................918 652-7364
Michael Brown, *President*
▲ **EMP:** 14
SALES (est): 3MM
SALES (corp-wide): 14.3B **Publicly Held**
SIC: 3443 Industrial vessels, tanks & containers
PA: Parker-Hannifin Corporation
6035 Parkland Blvd
Cleveland OH 44124
216 896-3000

(G-3516)
PERMOCAST INC
Hwy 75 N (74437)
P.O. Box 837 (74437-0837)
PHONE..................918 652-8812
Richard W Doyle, *President*
Janis D Doyle, *Vice Pres*
EMP: 7 **EST:** 1977
SQ FT: 7,000
SALES (est): 899.1K **Privately Held**
SIC: 3365 3544 Aluminum foundries; special dies, tools, jigs & fixtures

(G-3517)
WATSONS MACHINE SHOP
28885 S 196 Rd (74437-6832)
P.O. Box 8 (74437-0008)
PHONE..................918 652-3414
Jesse Watson, *Owner*
Melanie Watson, *Co-Owner*
EMP: 1 **EST:** 2001
SQ FT: 4,800
SALES (est): 729K **Privately Held**
SIC: 3599 Machine shop, jobbing & repair

(G-3518)
WHITLOCK SAW MILL
Rick Hill Addition (74437)
P.O. Box 239 (74437-0239)
PHONE..................918 652-4410
William D Whitlock, *Owner*
EMP: 4 **EST:** 1943
SQ FT: 860
SALES (est): 432.3K **Privately Held**
SIC: 2421 Sawmills & planing mills, general

(G-3519)
YOU ARE HERE CURRICULUM
910 N 14th St (74437-2414)
PHONE..................918 650-8586
EMP: 2
SALES (est): 78.7K **Privately Held**
SIC: 2741 Miscellaneous publishing

Hinton
Caddo County

(G-3520)
ALICE KIDD LLC
2318 N Broadway Blvd (73047-9479)
P.O. Box 130 (73047-0130)
PHONE..................................405 401-4391
Kendra Kimble, *Mng Member*
EMP: 1
SALES (est): 89.7K **Privately Held**
SIC: 2911 Petroleum refining

(G-3521)
ANADARKO DOZER AND TRCKG LLC
3 1/2 Miles S On Hwy 281 (73047)
P.O. Box 935 (73047-0935)
PHONE..................................405 542-3297
Jay Wyatt, *Branch Mgr*
EMP: 1
SALES (corp-wide): 7.3MM **Privately Held**
SIC: 1389 Oil field services
PA: Anadarko Dozer And Trucking, L.L.C.
1121 S Main St
Elk City OK 73644
580 243-0466

(G-3522)
ANSON DESIMONE
Also Called: Beav's Machine Shop
20350 State Highway 37 (73047-2329)
PHONE..................................610 433-1299
J C Carroll, *President*
Larry Desimone, *Principal*
Anson Desimone, *Principal*
Vonda Carroll, *Corp Secy*
EMP: 2 EST: 2010
SALES: 30K **Privately Held**
SIC: 3599 Machine shop, jobbing & repair

(G-3523)
DOUGHERTY FORESTRY MFG LTD
211 W Canyon Run (73047-9646)
PHONE..................................405 542-3520
Patrick Dougherty, *Partner*
Dolan Dougherty, *Partner*
Michael Dougherty, *Partner*
EMP: 17
SQ FT: 27,000
SALES (est): 950K **Privately Held**
SIC: 3699 5083 3531 Electrical equipment & supplies; farm & garden machinery; forestry related equipment; construction machinery attachments

(G-3524)
ECO-TECH INC
1212 S Broadway Ave (73047-9374)
PHONE..................................405 542-6483
Donnie Entz, *President*
EMP: 10
SALES (est): 421.6K **Privately Held**
SIC: 1389 Cementing oil & gas well casings

(G-3525)
ENCORE CNSTR SOLUTIONS LLC
31200 I 40 Service Rd 3 (73047-9754)
PHONE..................................405 542-3316
Danny Wright,
Libby Wright,
EMP: 15
SALES: 3MM **Privately Held**
SIC: 1389 Construction, repair & dismantling services

(G-3526)
ENTZ GROUND STERILANT INC
910 S Broadway (73047)
PHONE..................................405 542-3174
EMP: 2
SALES (est): 191K **Privately Held**
SIC: 1389 Oil Field Chemical Services

(G-3527)
ENTZ OILFIELD CHEMICALS INC (PA)
S Hwy 281 (73047)
PHONE..................................405 542-3174
Donnie Entz, *President*
EMP: 11
SQ FT: 3,600
SALES (est): 2.9MM **Privately Held**
SIC: 1389 5169 Servicing oil & gas wells; oil additives

(G-3528)
FIRST RESPONSE SOLUTIONS LLC
13400 S Maple Rd (73047-2007)
P.O. Box 1128, El Reno (73036-1128)
PHONE..................................405 284-6430
EMP: 2
SALES (est): 151.3K **Privately Held**
SIC: 3825 Integrating electricity meters

(G-3529)
GRAF-X LLC
109 W Main St (73047)
P.O. Box 447 (73047-0447)
PHONE..................................405 542-6631
Tisha Bender, *CEO*
EMP: 2
SALES (est): 174.5K **Privately Held**
SIC: 3993 2759 Signs & advertising specialties; commercial printing; screen printing

(G-3530)
JEDD INDUSTRIES
5905 S Methodist Rd (73047-2240)
P.O. Box 1017 (73047-1017)
PHONE..................................580 339-1500
EMP: 2
SALES (est): 135K **Privately Held**
WEB: www.jeddindustries.com
SIC: 3999 Manufacturing industries

(G-3531)
JUDA ENTERPRISES LLC
1106 N Broadway (73047)
PHONE..................................405 542-3975
Gary Dennis, *President*
Lisa Dennis,
EMP: 6 EST: 1997
SALES (est): 684.6K **Privately Held**
SIC: 3524 Grass catchers, lawn mower

(G-3532)
MARTIN WELDING SERVICE INC
16533 State Highway 37 (73047-2324)
PHONE..................................405 623-5361
Shawna Martin, *Principal*
EMP: 1
SALES (est): 52.1K **Privately Held**
SIC: 7692 Welding repair

(G-3533)
MIDCON COMPRESSION LLC
325 W Canyon Run (73047-9758)
PHONE..................................405 542-6280
EMP: 7 **Publicly Held**
SIC: 3563 Air & gas compressors
HQ: Midcon Compression, L.L.C.
6100 N Western Ave
Oklahoma City OK 73118
405 935-4159

(G-3534)
MURRAY SERVICES INC
3209 N Vernon Ave (73047-9247)
P.O. Box 1019 (73047-1019)
PHONE..................................405 542-3069
Steve Murray, *President*
Cody Bristow, *Technology*
EMP: 28
SALES (est): 6.8MM **Privately Held**
SIC: 3533 Oil field machinery & equipment

(G-3535)
RAZOR OILFIELD SERVICES LLC
3520 N Vernon Ave (73047)
P.O. Box 39 (73047-0039)
PHONE..................................405 661-0008
Brandon Hill, *Mng Member*
Cassidy Hioo, *Mng Member*
Marty Long, *Mng Member*
EMP: 14

SQ FT: 1,000
SALES: 1MM **Privately Held**
SIC: 1389 Oil field services

(G-3536)
S & S WELDING LLC
10761 Juniper St (73047-1201)
PHONE..................................405 496-1452
Scott Duetksen, *Manager*
EMP: 1 EST: 2013
SALES (est): 36.1K **Privately Held**
SIC: 7692 Welding repair

(G-3537)
STAR INDUSTRIES INC
Also Called: H & H Manufacturing and Distrg
124 W Main St (73047-9160)
P.O. Box 339 (73047-0339)
PHONE..................................405 542-3041
Scott Hudson, *President*
EMP: 5 EST: 2001
SQ FT: 5,500
SALES: 850K **Privately Held**
SIC: 3589 Car washing machinery; servicing machines, except dry cleaning, laundry: coin-oper.; high pressure cleaning equipment

(G-3538)
TETRA TECHNOLOGIES INC
31970 I 40 Service Rd (73047-9658)
PHONE..................................405 542-5461
Richard O Brien, *Vice Pres*
Ronnie Thompson, *Branch Mgr*
EMP: 6
SALES (corp-wide): 1B **Publicly Held**
WEB: www.tetratec.com
SIC: 8731 1389 Biological research; construction, repair & dismantling services
PA: Tetra Technologies, Inc.
24955 Interstate 45
The Woodlands TX 77380
281 367-1983

(G-3539)
VINCES LEASE SERVICE
321 N Noble Ave (73047-9025)
P.O. Box 556 (73047-0556)
PHONE..................................405 542-3908
Vince Mayorga, *Owner*
EMP: 12 EST: 1997
SALES (est): 584.7K **Privately Held**
SIC: 1389 Oil field services

(G-3540)
WILD WEST CREATIONS
28789 Reuter Rd W (73047-2260)
PHONE..................................405 542-6507
Karen Lanier, *Principal*
EMP: 1 EST: 2010
SALES (est): 83.5K **Privately Held**
SIC: 2431 Millwork

Hobart
Kiowa County

(G-3541)
DEMOCRAT CHIEF PUBLISHING CO
407 S Main St (73651-4017)
PHONE..................................580 726-3333
Joe Hancock, *President*
Neville Hancock, *Treasurer*
EMP: 9 EST: 1901
SQ FT: 6,750
SALES (est): 264K **Privately Held**
SIC: 2711 Newspapers, publishing & printing

(G-3542)
DOUBLE DIAMND WLDG FABRICATION
401 S Washington St (73651-4025)
PHONE..................................580 445-4524
EMP: 1 EST: 2015
SALES (est): 52.7K **Privately Held**
SIC: 7692 Welding repair

(G-3543)
LLOYD EDGE
902 W 11th St (73651-5435)
PHONE..................................580 726-2905
Lloyd Edge, *Owner*

EMP: 3
SALES (est): 191.4K **Privately Held**
SIC: 3561 0111 0139 Pumps & pumping equipment; wheat; hay farm

(G-3544)
ROCKING P SALES & SERVICES LLC
101 N Highland Ave (73651-4402)
PHONE..................................580 530-0028
Kevin Parmenter, *Mng Member*
EMP: 2
SALES (est): 266.8K **Privately Held**
SIC: 1389 0213 Oil field services; hogs

(G-3545)
S&F WELDING AND MFG LLC
22406 E 1430 Rd (73651-1664)
PHONE..................................580 341-0790
Ben Ross Horton, *Owner*
EMP: 1
SALES (est): 29.2K **Privately Held**
SIC: 3999 Manufacturing industries

(G-3546)
SEARCHLIGHT INC JEFFERSON
215 S Jefferson St (73651-3623)
PHONE..................................580 752-4374
EMP: 2 EST: 2017
SALES (est): 88.3K **Privately Held**
SIC: 3648 Searchlights

(G-3547)
TOOLS AND TROUBLESHOOTING
425 S Main St (73651-4017)
PHONE..................................580 726-5290
Phil Fischer, *President*
Phillip Fischer, *President*
EMP: 2
SQ FT: 13,500
SALES: 328K **Privately Held**
WEB: www.tntmold.com
SIC: 3544 Dies, plastics forming

Hodgen
Le Flore County

(G-3548)
BROTHER BUILT WELDING
21866 Pipe Springs Rd (74939-3083)
PHONE..................................918 385-1767
EMP: 1
SALES (est): 38.1K **Privately Held**
SIC: 7692 Welding repair

Holdenville
Hughes County

(G-3549)
AIRCRAFT POWER SERVICE INC
Airport Rd Hngr 1 Hanger 1 (74848)
P.O. Box 1036 (74848-1036)
PHONE..................................405 379-2407
Larry Lau, *President*
EMP: 2
SQ FT: 20,000
SALES (est): 300K **Privately Held**
SIC: 4581 3728 Aircraft servicing & repairing; aircraft parts & equipment

(G-3550)
BROWNS MEAT PROCESSING
7925 E 137 Rd (74848-9000)
PHONE..................................405 379-2979
Mark Brown, *Owner*
EMP: 1 EST: 1997
SALES (est): 86.1K **Privately Held**
SIC: 2011 Meat packing plants

(G-3551)
CENTRAL METAL FINISHING LLC
1006 Airport Rd (74848-2002)
PHONE..................................405 379-5252
Brandon Boyd, *Mng Member*
EMP: 24

GEOGRAPHIC SECTION

Hominy - Osage County (G-3582)

SALES (est): 442.8K **Privately Held**
SIC: 3471 Polishing, metals or formed products; electroplating & plating; decorative plating & finishing of formed products

(G-3552)
DEANS CASING SERVICE
222 W Main St (74848-3232)
P.O. Box 787 (74848-0787)
PHONE..................................405 379-3495
Dean Goforth, *Owner*
EMP: 16
SQ FT: 800
SALES (est): 1.4MM **Privately Held**
SIC: 1389 Oil field services

(G-3553)
DJF SERVICES INC
3231 N 3715 Rd (74848)
P.O. Box 150 (74848-0150)
PHONE..................................405 380-7273
Donald J Flint, *President*
Kathy Flint, *President*
EMP: 8
SQ FT: 1,500
SALES (est): 2.1MM **Privately Held**
SIC: 1382 1311 Oil & gas exploration services; crude petroleum & natural gas production

(G-3554)
HOLDENVILLE NEWS
112 S Creek St (74848-3226)
P.O. Box 751 (74848-0751)
PHONE..................................405 379-5411
Joe Templeton, *Persnl Mgr*
Tammy White, *Manager*
EMP: 5
SALES (est): 120K **Privately Held**
SIC: 2711 Newspapers, publishing & printing

(G-3555)
L C D EMBROIDERY
322 S Hinckley St (74848-5044)
PHONE..................................405 379-6083
Linda Clark, *Owner*
EMP: 1
SALES (est): 34K **Privately Held**
SIC: 2395 7336 Embroidery & art needlework; commercial art & graphic design

(G-3556)
LEMA PETROLEUM INC
111 N Oak St (74848-3213)
P.O. Box 957 (74848-0957)
PHONE..................................405 379-6678
Michael Majors, *President*
EMP: 4
SQ FT: 800
SALES (est): 473.9K **Privately Held**
SIC: 1311 5172 Crude petroleum production; natural gas production; petroleum brokers

(G-3557)
LEWIS PRINTING & OFFICE SUPPLY
Also Called: Robinson Publishing Company
114 N Broadway St (74848-3248)
P.O. Box 30 (74848-0030)
PHONE..................................405 379-5124
Bill Robinson, *Owner*
Dianna Brannan, *Editor*
Tracy Goza, *Editor*
Wanda Utterback, *Editor*
Dayna Robinson, *Co-Owner*
EMP: 10 EST: 1929
SQ FT: 2,100
SALES (est): 100K **Privately Held**
SIC: 2752 5943 Tickets, lithographed; office forms & supplies

(G-3558)
PALUCA PETROLEUM INC
225 Kingsberry Rd (74848-9201)
P.O. Box 2 (74848-0002)
PHONE..................................405 379-5656
Doug Humpries, *President*
Pam Humpries, *Treasurer*
Doug Humphreys,
EMP: 2 EST: 1995
SALES (est): 532.6K **Privately Held**
WEB: www.palucapetroleum.com
SIC: 1382 Oil & gas exploration services

(G-3559)
PIERCO PETROLEUM INC
225 Kingsberry Rd (74848-9201)
PHONE..................................405 379-0038
EMP: 2
SQ FT: 1,000
SALES (est): 180K **Privately Held**
SIC: 1382 Oil/Gas Exploration Services

(G-3560)
SPECIAL PARTS MFG INC
Also Called: Chaffin Manufacturing
1001 S Echo St (74848-9436)
P.O. Box 975 (74848-0975)
PHONE..................................405 379-3343
Kernek McDonald, *President*
George Brown, *Vice Pres*
EMP: 25
SALES (est): 4.6MM **Privately Held**
SIC: 3599 Machine shop, jobbing & repair; custom machinery

(G-3561)
TYSON FOODS INC
201 Kingsberry Rd (74848-9201)
PHONE..................................405 379-7241
Stan Everett, *Manager*
EMP: 25
SALES (corp-wide): 42.4B **Publicly Held**
SIC: 2011 Meat packing plants
PA: Tyson Foods, Inc.
2200 W Don Tyson Pkwy
Springdale AR 72762
479 290-4000

(G-3562)
WEBBER KATHRYN
Also Called: Embroidery For You
7749 Highway 270 (74848-6409)
PHONE..................................405 379-3872
Kathryn Webber, *Owner*
EMP: 2
SALES (est): 74K **Privately Held**
SIC: 2395 Embroidery & art needlework

Hollis
Harmon County

(G-3563)
ALLEN SIGNS
305 W Washington St (73550-4207)
PHONE..................................580 688-2985
Jack Allen, *Owner*
EMP: 1
SALES (est): 48.7K **Privately Held**
SIC: 3993 Signs & advertising specialties

(G-3564)
DEANS MACHINE & WELDING INC
Also Called: Dean's Motor Co
1122 E Broadway St (73550-4408)
PHONE..................................580 688-3374
Dean Crenshaw, *President*
EMP: 2 EST: 1973
SQ FT: 4,600
SALES (est): 150K **Privately Held**
SIC: 3523 7692 Farm machinery & equipment; welding repair

(G-3565)
HOLLIS COTTON OIL MILL INC
201 S Glover St (73550)
PHONE..................................580 688-3394
Paul H Horton, *President*
Sammy Horton, *Vice Pres*
EMP: 15
SQ FT: 1,500
SALES (est): 3.1MM **Privately Held**
SIC: 2048 Livestock feeds

(G-3566)
J C SHEET METAL
202 N 4th St (73550)
PHONE..................................580 688-9527
Jesse Cantu, *Owner*
EMP: 1
SALES (est): 67.9K **Privately Held**
SIC: 7692 Welding repair

(G-3567)
MCALLISTER FARMS
17362 E 1560 Rd (73550-7509)
PHONE..................................580 512-9009
Michael McAlister, *Partner*
Karrie McAlister, *Partner*
EMP: 2 EST: 2015
SALES (est): 254K **Privately Held**
SIC: 6111 2026 Farmers Home Administration; farmers' cheese

(G-3568)
SNIDER FARMS PEANUT BARN LLC
15651 N 1730 Rd (73550-7019)
PHONE..................................580 471-3470
Stephanie Snider, *Principal*
Jamie Lee Snider, *Principal*
EMP: 2 EST: 2006
SQ FT: 1,000
SALES (est): 255.3K **Privately Held**
WEB: www.sniderfarmspeanutbarn.com
SIC: 2099 Peanut butter

(G-3569)
TARHAY LLC
16091 N 1720 Rd (73550-7018)
P.O. Box 127 (73550-0127)
PHONE..................................940 655-4210
Jonathan Manney, *President*
EMP: 1
SALES (est): 180K **Privately Held**
SIC: 1389 Servicing oil & gas wells

(G-3570)
TONIS STITCHES-N-STUFF INC
210 W Broadway St (73550-4204)
PHONE..................................580 688-2697
Toni Hawkins, *President*
EMP: 3
SALES (est): 214.8K **Privately Held**
SIC: 2395 Embroidery products, except schiffli machine

(G-3571)
WESTERN FIBERS INC
1601 E Broadway St 62e (73550-4437)
P.O. Box 745 (73550-0745)
PHONE..................................509 679-4786
Paul Horton, *President*
Kathy Robinson, *Vice Pres*
EMP: 21 EST: 1977
SQ FT: 9,500
SALES: 2MM **Privately Held**
SIC: 3296 3531 Mineral wool insulation products; construction machinery

(G-3572)
WRIGHT COMFORT SOLUTIONS INC (PA)
Also Called: Wrights Heating & Air
302 W Broadway St (73550-4206)
PHONE..................................580 688-3586
Kellie Wright, *President*
Jimmy Wright, *Vice Pres*
EMP: 6
SQ FT: 11,000
SALES (est): 2MM **Privately Held**
SIC: 1711 3444 Warm air heating & air conditioning contractor; refrigeration contractor; sheet metalwork

Hominy
Osage County

(G-3573)
ACOTT OIL OPERATIONS
604 N Katy Ave (74035-1026)
P.O. Box 575 (74035-0575)
PHONE..................................918 885-2736
Melvin E Acott II, *Owner*
EMP: 4
SALES (est): 300K **Privately Held**
SIC: 1311 Crude petroleum production

(G-3574)
AMERICAN MACHINING COMPANY LLC
9646 State Highway 99 (74035-6796)
P.O. Box 106 (74035-0106)
PHONE..................................918 885-6194
Joe Prosenick, *Mng Member*
David Bevard,
Ronald Mitchel,
EMP: 7
SQ FT: 40,000
SALES: 900K **Privately Held**
SIC: 3599 Machine shop, jobbing & repair

(G-3575)
AMERICAN-CHIEF CO
Hominy News Progress
115 W Main St (74035-1031)
P.O. Box 38 (74035-0038)
PHONE..................................918 885-2101
Ramona Brown, *Manager*
Christy Buckner, *MIS Dir*
EMP: 3
SALES (corp-wide): 907.5K **Privately Held**
SIC: 2711 2791 Newspapers, publishing & printing; typesetting
PA: American-Chief Co
558 Illinois St
Pawnee OK 74058
918 762-2552

(G-3576)
BECKHAM AND BUTLER
1124 S Price Ave (74035-6006)
PHONE..................................918 885-4406
David Butler, *Partner*
EMP: 3
SALES (est): 325.5K **Privately Held**
SIC: 1311 Crude petroleum production

(G-3577)
BOB CLEMISHIRE OIL CO
2 Miles N (74035)
P.O. Box 558 (74035-0558)
PHONE..................................918 885-4755
Garon Clemishire, *Owner*
EMP: 2 EST: 1970
SALES (est): 185.7K **Privately Held**
SIC: 1311 Crude petroleum production

(G-3578)
BOBBY PRATER
199 Pope Rd (74035-6678)
PHONE..................................918 885-4864
Bobby Prater, *Owner*
EMP: 1
SALES (est): 69.2K **Privately Held**
SIC: 1389 Pumping of oil & gas wells

(G-3579)
BOJE OIL CO
Also Called: Metzger Oil Tools
203 E Main St (74035-1511)
P.O. Box 127 (74035-0127)
PHONE..................................918 885-2456
Frank Metzger Jr, *Partner*
David Metzger, *Partner*
EMP: 2
SQ FT: 6,700
SALES: 300K **Privately Held**
SIC: 1311 Crude petroleum production

(G-3580)
BURROWS
Hominy Rd (74035)
P.O. Box 74, Wynona (74084-0074)
PHONE..................................918 846-2245
Leroy Burrows, *Owner*
EMP: 1
SALES (est): 89.8K **Privately Held**
SIC: 3731 Drilling & production platforms, floating (oil & gas)

(G-3581)
CRD OIL CORP
401 N Price Ave (74035-1009)
P.O. Box 392 (74035-0392)
PHONE..................................918 885-4527
Ralph Dooling, *Principal*
EMP: 1
SALES (est): 130K **Privately Held**
SIC: 1389 Lease tanks, oil field: erecting, cleaning & repairing

(G-3582)
DUNLAP OIL TOOLS
300 E Main St (74035-1514)
P.O. Box 651 (74035-0651)
PHONE..................................918 885-6353
Mike Dunlap, *Owner*
EMP: 3
SQ FT: 3,000

Hominy - Osage County (G-3583)

SALES (est): 200K **Privately Held**
SIC: 1389 Oil field services

(G-3583)
FALCON FIELD SERVICE INC
150 County Road 1705 (74035)
P.O. Box 146 (74035-0146)
PHONE...............................918 885-2244
Darrell Brown, *President*
Terri Brown, *Corp Secy*
Don Brown, *Vice Pres*
EMP: 30
SQ FT: 2,400
SALES: 700K **Privately Held**
SIC: 1389 Oil field services

(G-3584)
FISHER WIRELINE SERVICES INC
Also Called: Great Guns Logging
11402 County Rd 1701 (74035)
P.O. Box 237 (74035-0237)
PHONE...............................918 885-6564
Gerald Fisher, *President*
Karen Carone, *Corp Secy*
Brenda Fisher, *Vice Pres*
EMP: 5
SQ FT: 4,800
SALES (est): 627.2K **Privately Held**
SIC: 1389 Oil field services

(G-3585)
GLOBAL OILFIELD SERVICES INC
10912 State Highway 99 (74035-6789)
PHONE...............................918 885-4024
Stuart Stence, *Branch Mgr*
EMP: 11 **Publicly Held**
SIC: 3561 Pumps, domestic: water or sump
HQ: Global Oilfield Services, Inc.
  2150 Town Square Pl # 410
  Sugar Land TX 77479

(G-3586)
HOMINY TAG AGENCY
113 W Main St (74035-1031)
PHONE...............................918 885-9955
Connie Brown, *Owner*
Connnie Brown, *Principal*
EMP: 2
SALES (est): 115.3K **Privately Held**
SIC: 7389 3469 Legal & tax services; automobile license tags, stamped metal

(G-3587)
HOPPERS WELDING
606 S Haines Ave (74035-4056)
PHONE...............................918 885-6978
EMP: 1
SALES (est): 32.6K **Privately Held**
SIC: 7692 Welding Repair

(G-3588)
HORTON TOOL COMPANY
215 W Main St (74035-1033)
P.O. Box 453 (74035-0453)
PHONE...............................918 885-6941
Dale Horton, *President*
Janett Horton, *Corp Secy*
EMP: 12
SQ FT: 11,250
SALES: 500K **Privately Held**
SIC: 1389 Oil field services

(G-3589)
HORTON TOOL CORPORATION
108 N Katy Ave (74035-1016)
P.O. Box 453 (74035-0453)
PHONE...............................918 885-6941
Janice Horton, *President*
EMP: 2
SALES (est): 1.5MM **Privately Held**
SIC: 1389 Oil field services

(G-3590)
JOHN C PARKS II ENERGY LLC
1616 County Road 5245 (74035-6656)
PHONE...............................918 885-6197
John C Parks, *Principal*
EMP: 5 EST: 2012
SALES (est): 235.1K **Privately Held**
SIC: 1382 Oil & gas exploration services

(G-3591)
L & J WELDING & MACHINE SVC
214 N Eastern Ave (74035-1504)
P.O. Box 506 (74035-0506)
PHONE...............................918 885-6666
Keith Hutchinson, *Owner*
EMP: 1
SALES (est): 96.1K **Privately Held**
SIC: 7692 3599 7629 Welding repair; machine shop, jobbing & repair; electrical repair shops

(G-3592)
METZGER OIL TOOLS INC
203 E Main St (74035-1511)
P.O. Box 127 (74035-0127)
PHONE...............................918 885-2456
David Metzger, *President*
Sherry Ridge, *Pathologist*
EMP: 2
SQ FT: 5,660
SALES (est): 151.6K **Privately Held**
WEB: www.ocic.k12.ok.us
SIC: 1389 5085 7353 1311 Oil field services; tools; oil field equipment, rental or leasing; crude petroleum production

(G-3593)
NOSS MACHINE
1715 Boston Pool Rd (74035-6696)
PHONE...............................918 358-3804
David L Noss Jr, *Owner*
EMP: 2 EST: 1995
SQ FT: 2,500
SALES (est): 156K **Privately Held**
WEB: www.nossmachine.com
SIC: 3469 5571 Machine parts, stamped or pressed metal; motorcycle dealers

(G-3594)
TUX HARD SHOP
1104 S Price Ave (74035-6006)
PHONE...............................918 885-2970
Tim Tucker, *Owner*
Phil Stevens, *General Mgr*
EMP: 2 EST: 1966
SQ FT: 7,000
SALES (est): 200K **Privately Held**
SIC: 5084 7694 5261 Oil well machinery, equipment & supplies; electric motor repair; lawn & garden equipment

Hooker
Texas County

(G-3595)
ARCHER-DANIELS-MIDLAND COMPANY
Also Called: ADM
Rr 1 Box 65 (73945-9739)
Rural Route Box 65
PHONE...............................580 652-3761
Sean Cravan, *Branch Mgr*
EMP: 9
SALES (corp-wide): 64.6B **Publicly Held**
SIC: 2041 Flour & other grain mill products
PA: Archer-Daniels-Midland Company
  77 W Wacker Dr Ste 4600
  Chicago IL 60601
  312 634-8100

(G-3596)
ARCHER-DANIELS-MIDLAND COMPANY
98-37 Mile (73945)
PHONE...............................580 652-2623
EMP: 2
SALES (corp-wide): 64.6B **Publicly Held**
SIC: 2041 Flour & other grain mill products
PA: Archer-Daniels-Midland Company
  77 W Wacker Dr Ste 4600
  Chicago IL 60601
  312 634-8100

(G-3597)
HITCH ENTERPRISES INC
Also Called: Hitch Mills
2 Miles North Of Optima (73945)
Rural Route 1 Box 53 (73945-9733)
PHONE...............................580 338-6510
Terry Campbell, *Manager*
EMP: 3
SALES (corp-wide): 44.5MM **Privately Held**
SIC: 2048 Feed supplements
PA: Hitch Enterprises, Inc.
  309 Northridge Cir
  Guymon OK 73942
  580 338-8575

(G-3598)
HOOKER ADVANCE & OFFICE SUPPLY
108 W Glaydas (73945)
P.O. Box 367 (73945-0367)
PHONE...............................580 652-2476
Sheila Blankenship, *Owner*
EMP: 3 EST: 1904
SQ FT: 2,125
SALES (est): 236.1K **Privately Held**
SIC: 2752 5112 5021 2711 Commercial printing, lithographic; office supplies; office furniture; newspapers

Howe
Le Flore County

(G-3599)
RONS DISCOUNT LUMBER INC
Also Called: Portable Building Sales
37850 Us Highway 59 (74940)
P.O. Box 233 (74940-0233)
PHONE...............................918 658-3857
Ronny J Blake, *President*
Jason Blake, *Principal*
EMP: 81
SQ FT: 6,000
SALES (est): 22.8MM **Privately Held**
SIC: 2452 5211 3448 Prefabricated buildings, wood; lumber & other building materials; prefabricated metal buildings

(G-3600)
VALLEY STONE INC
19782 Gardenhire Rd (74940-7010)
PHONE...............................918 647-2388
Johnny M Webb, *President*
Donna Webb, *Corp Secy*
EMP: 15
SALES (est): 3MM **Privately Held**
SIC: 3281 Stone, quarrying & processing of own stone products

(G-3601)
WISTER LAKE FEED INC
25096 Nobles Rd (74940-3160)
PHONE...............................918 655-7954
John Davis, *President*
EMP: 2
SALES (est): 124.4K **Privately Held**
SIC: 2048 5999 5191 Cereal-, grain-, & seed-based feeds; feed & farm supply; animal feeds

Hugo
Choctaw County

(G-3602)
B&T WELDING SERVICES LLC
1666 E 2060 Rd (74743-8807)
PHONE...............................580 326-4760
EMP: 1
SALES (est): 46K **Privately Held**
SIC: 7692 Welding repair

(G-3603)
BILLBOARDS ETC INC
3004 Deer Run (74743-1040)
PHONE...............................580 326-1660
Rebecca Thurman, *President*
EMP: 1
SALES (est): 122.7K **Privately Held**
SIC: 3993 Signs & advertising specialties

(G-3604)
BUFFALO EXAMINER
1410 E Jefferson St (74743-5404)
P.O. Box 481 (74743-0481)
PHONE...............................580 326-3926
John Brewer, *Principal*
EMP: 3
SALES (est): 105.7K **Privately Held**
WEB: www.examinernewspaper.net
SIC: 2711 Newspapers, publishing & printing

(G-3605)
CD INDUSTRYS CORPORATION
1705 Bearden Spring Rd (74743-2412)
PHONE...............................580 317-8448
Chris Methvin, *CEO*
EMP: 3
SALES (est): 233K **Privately Held**
SIC: 1799 3299 Home/office interiors finishing, furnishing & remodeling; brackets, architectural: plaster

(G-3606)
CHOCTAW DEFENSE MFG LLC
203 Choctaw Industrial Dr (74743-4253)
PHONE...............................580 326-8365
Terry Lanham, *President*
Cynthia Briscoe, *Vice Pres*
EMP: 50 **Privately Held**
SIC: 3711 Universal carriers, military, assembly of
HQ: Choctaw Defense Manufacturing Llc
  3 Skyway Dr
  Mcalester OK 74501
  918 426-2871

(G-3607)
CHOCTAW MFG & DEV CORP (DH)
203 Choctaw Industrial Dr (74743-4253)
PHONE...............................580 326-8365
Stephen Benefield, *CEO*
Keith Briem, *Vice Pres*
Cynthia Briscoe, *Vice Pres*
Bob Henry, *Vice Pres*
Derrick Loveless, *Vice Pres*
EMP: 60
SQ FT: 70,000
SALES (est): 24.3MM **Privately Held**
SIC: 3441 3471 3444 Fabricated structural metal; plating & polishing; sheet metalwork
HQ: Choctaw Global, Llc
  20 Sandstone Rd
  Durant OK 74701
  580 200-0927

(G-3608)
CHOCTAW MFG DEF CONTRS INC
203 Choctaw Industrial Dr (74743-4253)
P.O. Box 1210, Durant (74702-1210)
PHONE...............................580 326-8365
EMP: 15 **Privately Held**
WEB: www.choctawdefense.com
SIC: 2448 3441 Wood pallets & skids; fabricated structural metal
HQ: Choctaw Manufacturing Defense Contractors, Inc.
  209 Sw 7th St
  Antlers OK 74523

(G-3609)
CHOCTAW MFG DEF CONTRS INC
101 Ed Perry Rd (74743-5647)
PHONE...............................580 326-8365
John Uvodich, *President*
EMP: 5 **Privately Held**
SIC: 2449 Wood containers
HQ: Choctaw Manufacturing Defense Contractors, Inc.
  209 Sw 7th St
  Antlers OK 74523

(G-3610)
CHOCTAW NATION OF OKLAHOMA
Choctaw Nation Finishing Co
203 Choctaw Industrial Dr (74743-4253)
PHONE...............................580 326-8365
Leslie Johnson, *Manager*
EMP: 100 **Privately Held**
SIC: 3444 1721 3599 Sheet metalwork; industrial painting; chemical milling job shop
PA: Choctaw Nation Of Oklahoma
  1802 Chukka Hina
  Durant OK 74701
  580 924-8280

GEOGRAPHIC SECTION

Idabel - Mccurtain County (G-3640)

(G-3611)
HANGER PRSTHETCS & ORTHO INC
103 S Broadway St (74743-4417)
PHONE....................580 326-6661
EMP: 7
SALES (corp-wide): 1.1B Publicly Held
WEB: www.hanger.com
SIC: 3842 Surgical appliances & supplies
HQ: Hanger Prosthetics & Orthotics, Inc.
10910 Domain Dr Ste 300
Austin TX 78758
512 777-3800

(G-3612)
HUGO PUBLISHING COMPANY
Also Called: Hugo Daily News
128 E Jackson St (74743-4035)
PHONE....................580 326-3311
Stan Stamper, *President*
Judy Stamper, *Treasurer*
EMP: 8
SQ FT: 7,000
SALES (est): 1.1MM Privately Held
WEB: www.hugonews.com
SIC: 5943 2752 2711 Office forms & supplies; commercial printing, lithographic; newspapers, publishing & printing

(G-3613)
HUGO SASH & DOOR INC
Old Highway 70 W (74743)
P.O. Box 775 (74743-0775)
PHONE....................580 326-5569
Keith Shoneberger, *President*
Chris Shoneberger, *Vice Pres*
EMP: 19 EST: 1973
SQ FT: 7,500
SALES (est): 1.9MM Privately Held
SIC: 5211 2431 Millwork & lumber; doors, wood

(G-3614)
HUGO WYRICK LUMBER
Also Called: Wyrick Lumber Hugo
Old Hwy 70 W (74743)
P.O. Box 30, Atoka (74525-0030)
PHONE....................580 326-5569
Edward Wyrick, *President*
Hugo Wyrick, *Principal*
EMP: 42
SALES (est): 1.6MM Privately Held
SIC: 2421 2426 2431 2434 Sawmills & planing mills, general; hardwood dimension & flooring mills; millwork; wood kitchen cabinets; hardwood veneer & plywood

(G-3615)
JAMES PORTER SHORTY
Also Called: Porters Custom Meat Processing
2321 E 2000 Rd (74743-4300)
PHONE....................580 326-0592
James Shorty Porter, *Owner*
James Porter, *Owner*
EMP: 4
SALES (est): 126K Privately Held
SIC: 2026 Milk processing (pasteurizing, homogenizing, bottling)

(G-3616)
KOPPS ON RUN LLC
2689 Us Highway 70 (74743-1605)
PHONE....................580 326-9400
Jeffrey B Kopp, *Owner*
EMP: 4
SALES (est): 394.2K Privately Held
SIC: 2899

(G-3617)
P-AMERICAS LLC
Also Called: Pepsico
200 Pepsi Cola Ave (74743-5631)
PHONE....................580 326-8333
Mike Park, *Manager*
EMP: 8
SALES (corp-wide): 67.1B Publicly Held
SIC: 2086 Carbonated soft drinks, bottled & canned
HQ: P-Americas Llc
1 Pepsi Way
Somers NY 10589
336 896-5740

(G-3618)
PEPSI-COLA METRO BTLG CO INC
200 Pepsi Cola Ave (74743-5631)
PHONE....................580 326-8333
Mike Park, *Manager*
EMP: 127
SALES (corp-wide): 67.1B Publicly Held
SIC: 2086 Carbonated soft drinks, bottled & canned
HQ: Pepsi-Cola Metropolitan Bottling Company, Inc.
1111 Westchester Ave
White Plains NY 10604
914 767-6000

(G-3619)
PINK PETALS FLOWERS GIFTS LLC
401 E Bluff St (74743-3827)
PHONE....................580 317-8200
Toni Smith,
EMP: 3
SALES (est): 238.5K Privately Held
SIC: 2679 Gift wrap, paper: made from purchased material

(G-3620)
RICHARDS WELDING SERVICE LLC
667 N 4180 Rd (74743-1028)
P.O. Box 166, Broken Bow (74728-0166)
PHONE....................580 584-2831
Monty Richards, *Owner*
EMP: 2
SALES (est): 67K Privately Held
SIC: 7692 Welding repair

(G-3621)
SOUTHWEST FABRICATORS INC
503 S Industrial Blvd (74743-4201)
PHONE....................580 326-3589
Troy Minyard, *President*
EMP: 15
SQ FT: 6,000
SALES (est): 2.1MM Privately Held
SIC: 3441 3523 Fabricated structural metal; farm machinery & equipment

(G-3622)
WALLACE PRINTING COMPANY
509 S 10th St (74743-4820)
PHONE....................580 326-6323
Roy Wallace, *President*
EMP: 2
SALES (est): 147.6K Privately Held
SIC: 2754 5943 2791 2789 Commercial printing, gravure; office forms & supplies; typesetting; bookbinding & related work; commercial printing; commercial printing, lithographic

Hulbert
Cherokee County

(G-3623)
DYLANS PRECISION STAINLESS LLC
13509 E 655 Rd (74441-3440)
PHONE....................918 207-9149
Dylan Benard,
EMP: 2
SALES: 450K Privately Held
SIC: 3084 Plastics pipe

(G-3624)
KEMP STONE INC
Also Called: Quarry
17801 Highway 80 (74441-1916)
P.O. Box 949, Pryor (74362-0949)
PHONE....................918 772-3366
James Kemp, *Branch Mgr*
EMP: 4
SALES (corp-wide): 10MM Privately Held
SIC: 1422 Crushed & broken limestone
PA: Kemp Stone, Inc.
1050 E 520
Pryor OK 74361
918 825-3370

(G-3625)
NDN INK WORKS LLC
418 W Main St (74441-2113)
PHONE....................918 708-9250
Lee Peterson,
EMP: 2
SALES (est): 85.8K Privately Held
SIC: 2899 Ink or writing fluids

(G-3626)
NORWOOD CUSTOM CABINETS
20181 S 410 Rd (74441-2897)
PHONE....................918 478-2462
Lonnie Bowlin, *Owner*
EMP: 5
SALES (est): 358.8K Privately Held
SIC: 2434 Wood kitchen cabinets

(G-3627)
OG SAWMILL
13065 E 645 Rd (74441-3256)
PHONE....................918 598-3464
Jerry Faglie, *Owner*
Walter Faglie, *Co-Owner*
EMP: 9
SALES (est): 822.5K Privately Held
SIC: 2421 Sawmills & planing mills, general

(G-3628)
SPRING HOLLOW FEED MILL INC
13243 W Killabrew Rd (74441-3713)
PHONE....................918 453-9933
Buck George, *President*
EMP: 9
SALES (est): 1.4MM Privately Held
SIC: 2048 5999 Livestock feeds; feed & farm supply

(G-3629)
TACTICAL POWER SYSTEMS CORP
19375 S Coos Thompson Rd (74441-2703)
PHONE....................207 864-5528
Robert Freihoff-Lewin, *President*
Deni Freihoff-Lewin, *Treasurer*
EMP: 20
SALES (est): 2.1MM Privately Held
SIC: 3613 Switchgear & switchgear accessories

(G-3630)
WACKY LOGGING LLC
7919 N 450 Rd (74441-3493)
PHONE....................918 457-9393
EMP: 3
SALES (est): 98.8K Privately Held
SIC: 2411 Logging camps & contractors

Hydro
Caddo County

(G-3631)
KARLIN COMPANY
10111 Old 66 Rd (73048-9792)
PHONE....................405 542-6991
Bob Karlin, *President*
Jane Karlin, *Corp Secy*
Almeda Karlin, *Vice Pres*
EMP: 2
SALES (est): 429.2K Privately Held
SIC: 5032 5211 3273 1781 Sand, construction; gravel; sand & gravel; ready-mixed concrete; water well drilling

(G-3632)
L & K SEED & MANUFACTURING CO
246432 E 990 Rd (73048-1000)
PHONE....................405 663-2758
Lonnie Slagell, *Owner*
EMP: 3
SALES: 200K Privately Held
SIC: 7692 7538 Welding repair; general automotive repair shops

(G-3633)
NUTOPIA NUTS & MORE
206 W Main St (73048-8755)
P.O. Box 62 (73048-0062)
PHONE....................405 663-2330
Ronald Johnson, *President*
Judy Pitt, *Corp Secy*
EMP: 5 EST: 1940
SQ FT: 16,800
SALES (est): 510K Privately Held
WEB: www.nutopianuts.com
SIC: 5159 5812 4225 6512 Peanuts (bulk), unroasted; American restaurant; miniwarehouse, warehousing; commercial & industrial building operation; salted & roasted nuts & seeds; candy & other confectionery products

(G-3634)
RODNEY BROOKS WELDING LLC
5138 County Road 1040 (73048-9574)
PHONE....................405 663-2256
Rodney Brooks, *Principal*
EMP: 1 EST: 2015
SALES (est): 33.7K Privately Held
SIC: 7692 Welding repair

(G-3635)
TATES FLOW BACK LLC
711 N Hunt Ave (73048-8619)
PHONE....................405 663-2179
Eddie D Tate, *Principal*
EMP: 2
SALES (est): 121.7K Privately Held
SIC: 1382 Oil & gas exploration services

Idabel
Mccurtain County

(G-3636)
ABCO PRINTING & OFFICE SUPPLY
Also Called: Abco Printing & Office Sups
5 Se Washington St (74745-4633)
PHONE....................580 286-7575
Phyllis Butler, *Owner*
Don Butler, *Partner*
Phyliss Butler, *Partner*
EMP: 2
SALES (est): 255.7K Privately Held
SIC: 5943 2752 2791 2789 Office forms & supplies; commercial printing, offset; typesetting; bookbinding & related work; commercial printing

(G-3637)
FLOORING OUTFITTERS
501 Ne Lincoln Rd (74745-8127)
PHONE....................580 286-3030
Weylin Routh, *Principal*
EMP: 1
SALES (est): 110.1K Privately Held
SIC: 2426 Flooring, hardwood

(G-3638)
HONEYGROVE MACHINE
382 White Rock Rd (74745-6130)
PHONE....................580 420-3260
James W Stout, *Owner*
Donna Stout, *Owner*
EMP: 3
SALES (est): 200K Privately Held
SIC: 3599 5083 Machine shop, jobbing & repair; farm & garden machinery

(G-3639)
MADDIE & CO
1409 Garfield St (74745-8011)
PHONE....................580 212-9539
EMP: 2 EST: 2014
SALES (est): 132.2K Privately Held
SIC: 3915 Jewelers' materials & lapidary work

(G-3640)
MARTIN MARIETTA MATERIALS INC
Also Called: Idabel Plant
4401 Ne Lincoln Rd (74745-2411)
P.O. Box 386 (74745-0386)
PHONE....................580 286-3290
Scotty Gerbes, *Manager*
EMP: 7 Publicly Held
SIC: 1422 Crushed & broken limestone
PA: Martin Marietta Materials Inc
2710 Wycliff Rd
Raleigh NC 27607

Idabel - Mccurtain County

(G-3641)
MCCULLOUGH PRINTING
301 Nw Lincoln Rd (74745)
P.O. Box 1168 (74745-1168)
PHONE..................580 286-7681
Rodney McCullough, *Owner*
EMP: 2
SQ FT: 2,400
SALES: 200K **Privately Held**
SIC: 2752 2791 2789 Commercial printing, offset; typesetting; bookbinding & related work

(G-3642)
MCCURTAIN COUNTY NEWS INC (PA)
Also Called: McCurtain Daily Gazette
107 S Central Ave (74745-4847)
P.O. Box 179 (74745-0179)
PHONE..................580 286-3321
Bruce Willingham, *President*
Doris Gwen Willingham, *Vice Pres*
Gwen Willingham, *Administration*
EMP: 17
SQ FT: 6,750
SALES (est): 1.3MM **Privately Held**
SIC: 2711 2741 Newspapers: publishing only, not printed on site; job printing & newspaper publishing combined; shopping news: publishing only, not printed on site

(G-3643)
MIXON BROTHERS WOOD PRSV CO
1202 Nw 16th St (74745)
P.O. Box 327 (74745-0327)
PHONE..................580 286-9494
Gary Mixon, *President*
Bob Mixon, *Vice Pres*
EMP: 15 EST: 1947
SALES (est): 1.8MM **Privately Held**
WEB: www.mixonbros.com
SIC: 2491 2411 Posts, treated wood; logging

(G-3644)
PROFESSIONAL METAL WORKS INC
1100 Ne Avenue B (74745-9621)
PHONE..................580 584-7890
James Akers, *Principal*
Melissa Akers, *Principal*
EMP: 5
SALES (est): 331.1K **Privately Held**
SIC: 3441 Fabricated structural metal

(G-3645)
SETCO INC
Also Called: Setco Solid Tire & Rim
1803 Nw Seminole Ave (74745-6176)
P.O. Box 809 (74745-0809)
PHONE..................580 286-6531
Buck Hill, *President*
Duane Birdsong, *Administration*
Gary Branson, *Maintence Staff*
EMP: 98
SQ FT: 4,356,000
SALES (est): 32.1MM **Privately Held**
SIC: 3011 Tire sundries or tire repair materials, rubber

(G-3646)
SOUTHEAST TIMES
Also Called: Southeastern Oklahoma Pubg Co
110 S Central Ave (74745-4848)
PHONE..................580 286-2628
Jerry Ellis, *Owner*
Matt Miller, *Manager*
EMP: 3
SALES (est): 184.8K **Privately Held**
WEB: www.southeastasiantimes.com
SIC: 2711 Newspapers, publishing & printing

(G-3647)
SOUTHEAST TIRE INC
Also Called: Setco Solid Tire & Rim
1803 Nw Seminole Ave (74745-6176)
P.O. Box 809 (74745-0809)
PHONE..................580 286-6531
Giles Hill III, *President*
Duane Birdsong, *Manager*
Janice L Long, *Info Tech Mgr*

Tracey Lacy, *Admin Asst*
▲ EMP: 80
SALES (est): 10.5MM **Privately Held**
WEB: www.setcosolidtire.com
SIC: 3011 3714 Tires, cushion or solid rubber; motor vehicle parts & accessories

(G-3648)
STUART BEVERLY &
Also Called: Something Special
1449 Se Washington St (74745-3447)
PHONE..................580 286-5586
Fax: 580 286-3347
EMP: 3
SQ FT: 1,500
SALES: 200K **Privately Held**
SIC: 5947 4822 2759 Ret Gifts/Novelties Telegraph Communications Commercial Printing

(G-3649)
T-SHIRTS UNLIMITED
2103 E Washington St B (74745-7862)
PHONE..................580 286-5223
Bernadine Dempsey, *Partner*
David Dempsey, *Partner*
EMP: 2
SALES: 65K **Privately Held**
SIC: 5699 2396 T-shirts, custom printed; automotive & apparel trimmings

(G-3650)
TUFFROOTS LLC
6909 Old 21 Rd (74745-3100)
PHONE..................580 728-0000
Shane Dewayne Tabor, *Mng Member*
EMP: 7
SALES: 33K **Privately Held**
SIC: 2392 Household furnishings

Indianola
Pittsburg County

(G-3651)
C&S MARINE LLC
4335 Choate Prairie Rd (74442-5135)
P.O. Box 51 (74442-0051)
PHONE..................918 429-2758
Sheena Mathis, *Co-Owner*
Christopher Mathis, *Co-Owner*
EMP: 8
SALES (est): 214.3K **Privately Held**
SIC: 7692 Welding repair

Inola
Rogers County

(G-3652)
BRENDA RIGGS
Also Called: Riggs Tag Agency
5 E Commercial St (74036-9426)
P.O. Box 1281 (74036-1281)
PHONE..................918 543-3530
Brenda Riggs, *Owner*
EMP: 1
SALES (est): 95.7K **Privately Held**
SIC: 2679 Tags, paper (unprinted): made from purchased paper

(G-3653)
CEFCO INC
16313 E 590 Rd (74036-2027)
P.O. Box 429 (74036-0429)
PHONE..................918 543-8415
Danny M Parris, *President*
Martha Parris, *Vice Pres*
EMP: 2
SQ FT: 2,470
SALES: 120K **Privately Held**
SIC: 3841 3829 3821 Physiotherapy equipment, electrical; measuring & controlling devices; laboratory apparatus & furniture

(G-3654)
CISPER WELDING INC
36250 S 4220 Rd (74036-6048)
P.O. Box 946, Locust Grove (74352-0946)
PHONE..................918 543-2321
Clint Cisper, *Owner*
EMP: 5

SALES (est): 650.7K **Privately Held**
WEB: www.cisperwelding.com
SIC: 7692 Welding repair

(G-3655)
CISPER WELDING OF OKLAHOMA
15681 E 590 Rd (74036-3222)
P.O. Box 946, Locust Grove (74352-0946)
PHONE..................918 543-7755
Clint Cisper, *Principal*
EMP: 3
SALES (est): 465.4K **Privately Held**
SIC: 7692 Welding repair

(G-3656)
COMBOTRONICS INC
2800 Lock And Dam Rd (74036-9353)
PHONE..................918 543-3300
John Monroe Kerr, *President*
Mary Kerr, *Corp Secy*
EMP: 25
SQ FT: 22,000
SALES (est): 4.6MM **Privately Held**
SIC: 3531 7629 Road construction & maintenance machinery; electronic equipment repair

(G-3657)
CYPRESS SCENTS
17405 Tracy Rd (74036-3621)
PHONE..................918 629-8610
EMP: 2
SALES (est): 119.9K **Privately Held**
SIC: 2844 Toilet preparations

(G-3658)
EVENING GLOW CANDLES
9371 W 600 Rd (74036-3592)
PHONE..................918 543-2990
Verna Jantz, *Owner*
Harvey Jantz, *Co-Owner*
EMP: 2
SALES: 66K **Privately Held**
SIC: 3999 Candles

(G-3659)
GRAHAMS BAKERY & CAFE
25 N Broadway (74036-9413)
PHONE..................918 543-4244
Marvin Graham, *Principal*
EMP: 4
SALES (est): 206.4K **Privately Held**
SIC: 2051 Bakery products, partially cooked (except frozen)

(G-3660)
GS SPECIALTIES
36895 S 4215 Rd (74036-5608)
PHONE..................918 230-1295
Greg Esau, *Principal*
EMP: 1
SALES (est): 49.9K **Privately Held**
SIC: 7692 Welding repair

(G-3661)
HFE PROCESS INC
490 Summerlin Dr (74036-3059)
PHONE..................918 663-9083
Ken Ward, *President*
Vicky Ward, *Treasurer*
EMP: 7
SQ FT: 8,000
SALES (est): 1.3MM **Privately Held**
SIC: 3561 Pumps, domestic: water or sump

(G-3662)
HOWDY SIGNS
16644 E Kings Pl (74036-5182)
PHONE..................918 543-2854
EMP: 1 EST: 2010
SALES (est): 48K **Privately Held**
SIC: 3993 Mfg Signs/Advertising Specialties

(G-3663)
HURST AEROSPACE INC
21247 E 630 Rd (74036-5756)
P.O. Box 1855, Tulsa (74101-1855)
PHONE..................918 543-6527
Vernon W Hurst, *President*
EMP: 5
SQ FT: 5,000

SALES (est): 754.4K **Privately Held**
SIC: 3365 3769 Aluminum & aluminum-based alloy castings; guided missile & space vehicle parts & auxiliary equipment

(G-3664)
L & S MACHINING
191 Kayo Mullen (74036-5353)
PHONE..................918 543-6628
Leonerd Stephens, *Owner*
EMP: 2
SALES (est): 187.6K **Privately Held**
SIC: 3599 Machine shop, jobbing & repair

(G-3665)
M W MACHINING AND WELDING INC
18455 E 640 Rd (74036-6079)
P.O. Box 613 (74036-0613)
PHONE..................918 543-8431
Jerod Getzfried, *President*
EMP: 4
SALES (est): 280K **Privately Held**
SIC: 7692 Welding repair

(G-3666)
MADEWELL MACHINE WORKS COMPANY
30205 S 4230 Rd (74036-5120)
PHONE..................918 543-2904
Billy D Madewell, *President*
Darlene K Madewell, *Corp Secy*
EMP: 5
SALES: 450K **Privately Held**
SIC: 3599 3451 Machine shop, jobbing & repair; screw machine products

(G-3667)
MARTEK INC
32848 S 4230 Rd (74036-6138)
PHONE..................918 543-6477
Dwayne Martin, *President*
Dave Martin, *Manager*
EMP: 3 EST: 1992
SALES (est): 162K **Privately Held**
SIC: 7372 Business oriented computer software

(G-3668)
O S R INC
14265 E 590 Rd (74036-3448)
PHONE..................281 422-7206
Dale Powell, *Principal*
EMP: 3
SALES (est): 309.4K **Privately Held**
WEB: www.ossrs.com
SIC: 3398 Metal heat treating

(G-3669)
ONSITE STRESS RELIEVING SVC
14265 E 590 Rd (74036-3448)
PHONE..................918 234-1222
Richea Powell, *President*
Karen Powell, *Vice Pres*
Harvey Wilde, *Treasurer*
EMP: 45
SALES (est): 4.6MM **Privately Held**
SIC: 3398 Metal heat treating

(G-3670)
OSR SERVICES LP
14265 E 590 Rd (74036-3448)
PHONE..................918 234-1222
Karen Powell, *Branch Mgr*
EMP: 15
SALES (corp-wide): 8.1MM **Privately Held**
SIC: 3398 Metal heat treating
PA: Osr Services, Lp
2315 W Main St
Baytown TX 77520
281 422-7206

(G-3671)
PARFAB FIELD SERVICES LLC
15615 E 590 Rd (74036-3222)
PHONE..................918 543-6310
Jeff Ricketts, *Vice Pres*
Greg Dooley, *Safety Mgr*
Chris Weatherford, *QC Mgr*
Johnny Smith, *Controller*
Alvin Moore,
◆ EMP: 9

▲ = Import ▼ = Export
◆ = Import/Export

GEOGRAPHIC SECTION

Jenks - Tulsa County (G-3703)

SALES (est): 3.8MM Privately Held
SIC: 3559 Petroleum refinery equipment

(G-3672)
PARFAB INDUSTRIES LLC (PA)
15615 E 590 Rd (74036-3222)
PHONE..................................918 543-6310
Dale Williams, *President*
Patrick Guest, *President*
Judy Kelly, *Manager*
Chris Weatherford, *Manager*
Tommy Thompson, *Admin Sec*
▲ EMP: 79 EST: 2001
SQ FT: 59,650
SALES (est): 18.3MM Privately Held
WEB: www.parfabindustries.com
SIC: 3444 Pipe, sheet metal

(G-3673)
PLASMA SOLUTIONS 1
28644 S 4240 Rd (74036-5117)
P.O. Box 321 (74036-0321)
PHONE..................................918 543-2178
Corey Calico, *Principal*
EMP: 3
SALES (est): 99K Privately Held
SIC: 2836 Plasmas

(G-3674)
TR TACK SUPPLY
29022 S 4230 Rd (74036-5162)
PHONE..................................918 543-4095
David Philips, *Owner*
Kathy Philips, *Co-Owner*
EMP: 2
SALES (est): 100.6K Privately Held
SIC: 2399 5159 Horse & pet accessories, textile; horses

(G-3675)
TURN & BURN WELDING INC
30184 Gale Ave (74036-5442)
PHONE..................................918 543-7224
Fred A Davis, *Principal*
EMP: 1
SALES (est): 35.3K Privately Held
SIC: 7692 Welding repair

(G-3676)
UNRAU MEAT CO INC
9415 W 590 Rd (74036-5988)
PHONE..................................918 543-8245
Steve Unrau, *President*
EMP: 6
SQ FT: 4,000
SALES (est): 560.3K Privately Held
SIC: 2011 2013 Beef products from beef slaughtered on site; pork products from pork slaughtered on site; sausages & other prepared meats

Jay
Delaware County

(G-3677)
3 RIVERS WLDG FABRICATION LLC
25372 State Highway 20 (74346-3617)
PHONE..................................918 589-2300
Ronald A Haver, *Principal*
EMP: 1
SALES (est): 46.9K Privately Held
SIC: 7692 Welding repair

(G-3678)
AST STORAGE LLC
1082 E Monroe Ave (74346-2920)
P.O. Box 329 (74346-0329)
PHONE..................................918 208-0100
Darrel Robertson, *Chairman*
John Farris, *COO*
Lynn Ball, *Sales Staff*
EMP: 10
SALES (est): 897.1K Privately Held
SIC: 3443 Farm storage tanks, metal plate

(G-3679)
BLACK GOLD
104 S Main St (74346-2803)
PHONE..................................918 253-3344
EMP: 2
SALES (est): 73.2K Privately Held
SIC: 2759 Commercial printing

(G-3680)
DELAWARE COUNTY JOURNAL INC
254 N 5th St (74346)
P.O. Box 1050 (74346-1050)
PHONE..................................918 253-4322
Peter M Crow, *President*
Carol A Crow, *Co-Owner*
EMP: 2 EST: 1947
SQ FT: 1,200
SALES (est): 154.3K Privately Held
WEB: www.grandlakenews.com
SIC: 2711 Newspapers, publishing & printing

(G-3681)
FREE RANGER LLC
1st & Dial St (74346)
P.O. Box 318, West Liberty IA (52776-0318)
PHONE..................................918 253-4223
Blake Evans, *Mng Member*
EMP: 110 EST: 2015
SALES (est): 8.1MM Privately Held
SIC: 2015 Chicken, slaughtered & dressed

(G-3682)
LIBERTY FREE RANGE POULTRY LLC
Also Called: Crystal Lake Farms
234 E Dial St (74346-2806)
P.O. Box 318, West Liberty IA (52776-0318)
PHONE..................................319 627-6000
Gerald Lessard, *President*
Kathryn Rippentrop, *Treasurer*
EMP: 150
SALES (est): 3.9MM Privately Held
SIC: 2015 Chicken slaughtering & processing

(G-3683)
MOUNTAIN TOP MACHINE INC
35999 S 568 Rd (74346-5149)
PHONE..................................918 787-5510
Gerald Grivna, *President*
EMP: 1
SALES (est): 149.6K Privately Held
SIC: 3443 3444 Metal parts; forming machine work, sheet metal

(G-3684)
OKLAHOMA STATE UNIVERSITY
Also Called: Oklahoma Co Op
38267 Us Hwy 59 (74346)
P.O. Box 1020 (74346-1020)
PHONE..................................918 253-4332
Jason Holemback, *Director*
EMP: 10
SALES (corp-wide): 904MM Privately Held
SIC: 2721 8743 Statistical reports (periodicals); publishing & printing; public relations services
PA: Oklahoma State University
    401 Whitehurst Hall
    Stillwater OK 74078
    405 744-5000

(G-3685)
R & L MECHANICS & WELDING
Also Called: R&L Custom Cycles
804 S 17th St (74346-3924)
PHONE..................................918 253-4734
EMP: 1
SQ FT: 2,400
SALES (est): 30K Privately Held
SIC: 7539 1799 7692 Automotive Repair Trade Contractor Welding Repair

(G-3686)
TRIPLE DS NEON SIGNS LLC
55801 E 350 Rd (74346-6447)
PHONE..................................817 447-2830
Yvonne Daniels, *Principal*
EMP: 1
SALES (est): 46K Privately Held
SIC: 3993 Neon signs

(G-3687)
WALR CORP
2010 W Cedar St (74346-3804)
P.O. Box 1137 (74346-1137)
PHONE..................................918 253-4773
EMP: 6

SALES (est): 450K Privately Held
SIC: 3949 Mfg Sporting/Athletic Goods

Jenks
Tulsa County

(G-3688)
ADVANCED CRATIVE SOLUTIONS INC
Also Called: ACS Design Services
321 E 112th St S (74037-2020)
PHONE..................................918 519-3651
Charles Strohm, *President*
Angela Strohm, *Admin Sec*
EMP: 2
SQ FT: 4,900
SALES (est): 149K Privately Held
WEB: www.wirelesssensorsystems.com
SIC: 8711 3823 Electrical or electronic engineering; industrial instrmnts msrmnt display/control process variable

(G-3689)
ASHTON GAS GATHERING LLC
1030 W Main St (74037-3525)
PHONE..................................918 291-3200
James Haber, *Owner*
EMP: 2
SALES (est): 120K Privately Held
SIC: 1389 Servicing oil & gas wells

(G-3690)
BEAN CHRIS OIL & GAS SERVICE
Also Called: Chris Bean Lcnsed Glgist 284
543 W 112th Ct S (74037-3209)
PHONE..................................918 298-1569
EMP: 1
SALES (est): 88.5K Privately Held
SIC: 1382 Oil/Gas Exploration Services

(G-3691)
BETTER SOUND HEARING AID SVC
807 E A St Ste 117 (74037-4308)
PHONE..................................918 995-2222
Michi Dyke, *Bd of Directors*
EMP: 1
SALES (corp-wide): 106.9K Privately Held
SIC: 3842 Hearing aids
PA: Better Sound Hearing Aid Service
    1601 W Okmulgee St Ste C
    Muskogee OK 74401
    918 683-1234

(G-3692)
BLUE VALLEY ENERGY CORP
12222 S 2nd St (74037-2872)
P.O. Box 668, Blue Springs MO (64013-0668)
PHONE..................................918 298-1032
Phillip D Robinson, *CEO*
EMP: 2
SALES (est): 208.7K Privately Held
SIC: 1382 Oil & gas exploration services

(G-3693)
BOLT IT HYDRAULIC SOLUTIONS
Also Called: Hytorc Central
2807 W Main St (74037-3493)
PHONE..................................918 296-0202
EMP: 12 EST: 2011
SALES (est): 5.1MM Privately Held
SIC: 5072 3559 Whol Hardware Mfg Misc Industry Machinery

(G-3694)
BOXING BEAR LLC
1006 W D St (74037-2506)
PHONE..................................918 606-9991
Jeff Mitchell, *Administration*
EMP: 2 EST: 2012
SALES (est): 162.4K Privately Held
SIC: 2752 Commercial printing, lithographic

(G-3695)
BROWER OIL & GAS CO INC
505 E Main St (74037-4136)
P.O. Box 2009 (74037-2009)
PHONE..................................918 298-7200
Joe D Brower, *President*
Ruth Fagin Brower, *Corp Secy*
EMP: 6
SALES (est): 1.3MM Privately Held
SIC: 1311 Crude petroleum production; natural gas production

(G-3696)
BY HIM INDUSTRIES LLC
507 E E St (74037-3326)
P.O. Box 535 (74037-0535)
PHONE..................................918 406-0593
EMP: 1
SALES (est): 61.8K Privately Held
SIC: 3999 Manufacturing industries

(G-3697)
C&K INC
12522 S 13th Pl (74037-3629)
PHONE..................................918 299-6307
EMP: 8
SALES (est): 253.1K Privately Held
SIC: 2024 Mfg Ice Cream/Frozen Desert

(G-3698)
CB PRINTING AND MORE LLC
12505 S 13th Pl (74037-3648)
P.O. Box 850224, Yukon (73085-0224)
PHONE..................................405 488-7107
Carmell Lonnita Best, *Administration*
EMP: 2 EST: 2013
SALES (est): 149.9K Privately Held
SIC: 2752 Commercial printing, lithographic

(G-3699)
CLEARWTER ENTPS LLC NTURAL GAS
1914 W C St (74037-2367)
PHONE..................................918 296-7007
EMP: 1
SALES (est): 61K Privately Held
SIC: 1311 Crude petroleum & natural gas

(G-3700)
CONCORDE RESOURCES CORPORATION
1030 W Main St (74037-3525)
PHONE..................................918 291-3200
James M C Haver, *President*
EMP: 2
SALES (est): 348K Privately Held
SIC: 1389 Servicing oil & gas wells

(G-3701)
CONTINENTAL WIRE CLOTH LLC (PA)
11240 S James Ave (74037-1722)
PHONE..................................918 794-0334
George Martinez,
Bill Babcock,
Matt Lopez,
Richard Martinez,
▼ EMP: 2
SQ FT: 37,500
SALES (est): 6.6MM Privately Held
SIC: 3496 Miscellaneous fabricated wire products

(G-3702)
CRITICAL INFRASTRUCTUR
11258 S Franklin Ave (74037-2420)
P.O. Box 1316 (74037-1316)
PHONE..................................918 640-9301
Benny Alvarado, *Principal*
EMP: 3
SALES (est): 142.8K Privately Held
SIC: 3812 Search & navigation equipment

(G-3703)
DOUBLE C OIL AND GAS LLC
11204 S 26th West Ave (74037-6946)
PHONE..................................918 518-5047
Christopher Donald Crain, *Owner*
EMP: 2
SALES (est): 99.7K Privately Held
SIC: 1389 Oil & gas field services

(G-3704)
DP MANUFACTURING INC (PA)
11135 S James Ave (74037-1731)
P.O. Box 1130 (74037-1130)
PHONE.....................918 250-2450
Steve Oden, *President*
Mark Balam, *CFO*
Loren Armstrong, *Admin Sec*
▲ **EMP:** 175
SQ FT: 100,000
SALES (est): 11.3MM **Privately Held**
SIC: 3531 3547 Winches; road construction & maintenance machinery; rolling mill machinery

(G-3705)
EVERYDAY FOODS LLC
412 N Juniper St (74037-2551)
PHONE.....................918 299-7939
Anthony Todd Khoury, *Principal*
EMP: 3
SALES (est): 167.3K **Privately Held**
SIC: 2099 Food preparations

(G-3706)
GENREAL COMPRESSOR INC
395 W K Pl (74037-2949)
PHONE.....................918 209-5499
EMP: 3
SALES (est): 230.4K **Privately Held**
SIC: 3563 Air & gas compressors

(G-3707)
INDUSTRIAL CITY PRESS
103 E F St (74037-3126)
PHONE.....................918 299-2767
Luther Pilant III, *Principal*
EMP: 1
SALES (est): 51K **Privately Held**
SIC: 2741 Miscellaneous publishing

(G-3708)
INTEGRTED LOCK SEC SYSTEMS LLC
1239 W 111th St S (74037-2085)
PHONE.....................918 232-3436
Vince Blocker,
EMP: 3
SQ FT: 1,000
SALES: 500K **Privately Held**
SIC: 3429 Security cable locking system

(G-3709)
INVISIBLE ELEMENT LLC
12203 S 4th St (74037-4944)
PHONE.....................918 296-7562
Jason Christopher Yang, *Administration*
EMP: 3 **EST:** 2014
SALES (est): 237.9K **Privately Held**
SIC: 2819 Industrial inorganic chemicals

(G-3710)
JM DEFENSE & AROSPC SVCS LLC
2405 W 108th St S (74037-1707)
PHONE.....................918 298-2766
James A Porter, *Administration*
EMP: 1
SALES (est): 119.5K **Privately Held**
SIC: 3812 Defense systems & equipment

(G-3711)
JMJ PETROLEUM INC
2914 W 117th St S (74037-2882)
PHONE.....................918 209-5913
Will Roy, *Principal*
EMP: 2
SALES (est): 99K **Privately Held**
SIC: 1381 Drilling oil & gas wells

(G-3712)
KETCHUM GROUP LLC
12228 S 18th Ave E (74037-3657)
P.O. Box 551 (74037-0551)
PHONE.....................918 407-2228
Richard Ketchum, *Mng Member*
EMP: 1 **EST:** 2015
SALES: 415K **Privately Held**
SIC: 3449 1791 Bars, concrete reinforcing; fabricated steel; structural steel erection

(G-3713)
KIMBERLY-CLARK CORPORATION
13219 S Kimberly Clark Pl (74037)
P.O. Box 3000 (74037-3000)
PHONE.....................918 366-5000
Julia Bahldman, *Manager*
EMP: 281
SALES (corp-wide): 18.4B **Publicly Held**
SIC: 2621 2676 Sanitary tissue paper; infant & baby paper products
PA: Kimberly-Clark Corporation
351 Phelps Dr
Irving TX 75038
972 281-1200

(G-3714)
L Z WILLIAMS ENERGY INC
513 W Main St (74037-3750)
PHONE.....................918 296-3555
Len Z Williams, *CEO*
EMP: 2 **EST:** 1991
SALES (est): 147K **Privately Held**
SIC: 1382 Oil & gas exploration services

(G-3715)
LAHOMA PRODUCTION INC
240 1/2 St Se (74037)
P.O. Box 487 (74037-0487)
PHONE.....................918 298-2227
Larry Brown, *Owner*
EMP: 4 **EST:** 2010
SALES (est): 294.8K **Privately Held**
SIC: 3533 Oil & gas field machinery

(G-3716)
MCGONIGAL TED OIL AND WELL SVC
124 N 6th St (74037-4115)
PHONE.....................918 299-5250
Ted McGonigal, *Owner*
Ruby McGonigal, *Co-Owner*
EMP: 3
SALES (est): 294.3K **Privately Held**
SIC: 1311 Crude petroleum production

(G-3717)
MOBILE PC MANAGER LLC
606 E 119th St S (74037-3693)
PHONE.....................574 551-4521
EMP: 1
SALES (est): 31.2K **Privately Held**
SIC: 2395 Pleating & stitching

(G-3718)
MONOGRAM HUT
124 N Cedar St (74037-3739)
PHONE.....................214 707-4196
EMP: 1
SALES (est): 31.2K **Privately Held**
SIC: 2395 Embroidery & art needlework

(G-3719)
OKLAHOMA PROMO LLC
512 W 127th Pl S (74037-4405)
PHONE.....................918 248-8145
Shannon Thompson, *Mng Member*
Todd Fimple, *Mng Member*
EMP: 3
SALES (est): 361.1K **Privately Held**
SIC: 5199 2759 Advertising specialties; promotional printing

(G-3720)
ONEFIRE AEROSPACE SERVICES
Also Called: Padgett Machine
300 Riverwalk Ter Ste 280 (74037-5626)
PHONE.....................918 794-8804
Mike Payne, *Principal*
Sharon Bertram, *Principal*
Mark Morelli, *Principal*
EMP: 15
SALES (est): 1MM **Privately Held**
SIC: 3721 Aircraft

(G-3721)
ORTHOTICS PROS INC
11709 S Ivy St (74037-5051)
PHONE.....................918 296-3567
Daniel Thies, *President*
Roanne Thies, *Vice Pres*
EMP: 2
SALES (est): 30K **Privately Held**
SIC: 3842 Orthopedic appliances

(G-3722)
PATRICIA LYONS
Also Called: Pilcrow & Caret
12530 S Ash Ave (74037-4998)
PHONE.....................850 445-4782
Trish Lyons, *Owner*
EMP: 1
SALES: 5K **Privately Held**
SIC: 2741 7389 7338 Miscellaneous publishing; ; editing service; proofreading service

(G-3723)
PRECISION BIOMEDICAL SVCS INC
10712 S Gum St (74037-5079)
PHONE.....................918 671-8091
Michael E Macoubrie, *Principal*
EMP: 1
SALES (est): 540K **Privately Held**
SIC: 3841 7352 Surgical & medical instruments; medical equipment rental

(G-3724)
QUALITY CABINET COMPANY
817 N Elm St (74037-2975)
P.O. Box 55 (74037-0055)
PHONE.....................918 299-2721
David Grounds, *President*
EMP: 9
SQ FT: 10,350
SALES (est): 855K **Privately Held**
WEB: www.qualitycabinetsjenks.com
SIC: 2434 Wood kitchen cabinets

(G-3725)
RAY COMPUTER SERVICES INTL INC
381 E Main St (74037-4132)
P.O. Box 417 (74037-0417)
PHONE.....................918 299-7262
Luke Goodwin, *President*
EMP: 1
SALES (est): 72.1K **Privately Held**
SIC: 7372 Business oriented computer software

(G-3726)
RESCO ENTERPRISES INC
1917 W C St (74037-2367)
P.O. Box 882 (74037-0882)
PHONE.....................918 298-0052
Ronald E Smith, *President*
Judy Hudgins, *Admin Sec*
EMP: 9
SQ FT: 800
SALES (est): 941.5K **Privately Held**
SIC: 1521 1522 1382 New construction, single-family houses; apartment building construction; oil & gas exploration services

(G-3727)
SCENTS IN SOY NATURALS
105 E Main St (74037-3954)
PHONE.....................918 269-8322
EMP: 2
SALES (est): 86.7K **Privately Held**
SIC: 2844 Toilet preparations

(G-3728)
SOUTH TULSA HOT SHOT SVCS LLC
724 W 108th Pl S (74037-2482)
PHONE.....................918 299-7373
Mark Davis, *Principal*
EMP: 2
SALES (est): 65.5K **Privately Held**
SIC: 1389 Hot shot service

(G-3729)
STITCH BOOM BA LLC
12523 S 18th Cir E (74037-3658)
PHONE.....................918 518-5859
Connye Rene Adib Yazdi, *Principal*
EMP: 1
SALES (est): 50.8K **Privately Held**
SIC: 2395 Embroidery & art needlework

(G-3730)
STITCHSUMM LLC
161 W M St (74037-2148)
PHONE.....................918 201-2148
Bo Sherri Summers, *Principal*
EMP: 1
SALES (est): 33.7K **Privately Held**
SIC: 2395 Embroidery & art needlework

(G-3731)
SUGARWOOD DIGITAL PRINTING
706 W 119th Pl S (74037-4243)
PHONE.....................918 378-5771
Blake Ferguson, *Principal*
EMP: 2
SALES (est): 120.7K **Privately Held**
SIC: 2752 Commercial printing, offset

(G-3732)
T R TACK SUPPLY
636 W Main St (74037)
PHONE.....................918 299-5880
Andrew L Phillips, *Partner*
Gary Phillips, *Mfg Staff*
EMP: 4
SQ FT: 1,800
SALES (est): 220K **Privately Held**
SIC: 3199 Harness or harness parts

(G-3733)
TATCO METALS INC
2025 W 121st St S (74037-6907)
PHONE.....................918 853-4663
Tommy J McCord, *Principal*
EMP: 3
SALES (est): 206.7K **Privately Held**
SIC: 3369 Nonferrous foundries

(G-3734)
TEAM SPIRIT SALES
502 E Main St (74037-4137)
P.O. Box 1145 (74037-1145)
PHONE.....................918 296-5620
Tonia Van, *Principal*
EMP: 3 **EST:** 2013
SALES (est): 263.1K **Privately Held**
SIC: 2339 Women's & misses' outerwear

(G-3735)
TEREX MINING
302 W 120th St S (74037-3234)
PHONE.....................918 296-0530
Grossman Bob, *Principal*
EMP: 2
SALES (est): 223.4K **Privately Held**
SIC: 3531 Construction machinery

(G-3736)
TULSA WINCH INC (DH)
Also Called: T W G
11135 S James Ave (74037-1731)
P.O. Box 1130 (74037-1130)
PHONE.....................918 298-8300
Arjun Mirdha, *President*
Jeff Blan, *Production*
David McCarthy, *Engineer*
Liesl Glass, *Asst Controller*
Beth Glover, *Sales Staff*
▲ **EMP:** 150
SQ FT: 76,000
SALES (est): 31.3MM
SALES (corp-wide): 7.1B **Publicly Held**
SIC: 3531 3566 Winches; gears, power transmission, except automotive
HQ: Dover Energy, Inc.
691 N Squirrel Rd Ste 250
Auburn Hills MI 48326
248 836-6700

(G-3737)
WAGON WHEEL ARKLATEX LLC
100 S Riverfront Dr Ste 4 (74037-5661)
PHONE.....................918 528-1060
James Redfearn, *CEO*
EMP: 1
SALES (est): 87.9K **Privately Held**
SIC: 3533 Oil & gas field machinery

(G-3738)
WAGON WHEEL EXPLORATION LLC
100 Suth Rvrfront Dr Ste (74037)
PHONE.....................918 746-7477
James Redfearn, *CEO*
EMP: 5
SALES (est): 279.3K **Privately Held**
SIC: 1389 Construction, repair & dismantling services

Jennings
Pawnee County

(G-3739)
DAVCO FAB INC
921 N Main St (74038)
P.O. Box 361 (74038-0361)
PHONE..................918 757-2504
David L Frick, *President*
Josephine Gomez, *Principal*
Linda S Frick, *Vice Pres*
David Russel, *Treasurer*
Rebeca Hewitt, *Admin Sec*
EMP: 25 **EST:** 1982
SQ FT: 12,000
SALES (est): 6.6MM **Privately Held**
SIC: 3533 3443 3441 Oil field machinery & equipment; fabricated plate work (boiler shop); fabricated structural metal

(G-3740)
TOMS TREE SVC & BACKHOE
43851 W 61st St S (74038-2749)
PHONE..................918 865-4861
Tom Maness, *Owner*
EMP: 1 **EST:** 1999
SALES (est): 92.7K **Privately Held**
SIC: 3531 Backhoes

Jet
Alfalfa County

(G-3741)
BAYWEST EMBROIDERY
23958 Cottonwood Ln (73749-4939)
PHONE..................580 626-4728
Kim McClain, *Owner*
EMP: 1
SALES (est): 64.3K **Privately Held**
SIC: 2395 2752 2397 Decorative & novelty stitching, for the trade; commercial printing, lithographic; schiffli machine embroideries

Jones
Oklahoma County

(G-3742)
BLUE & GOLD SAUSAGE INC
10101 N Hiwassee Rd (73049-7438)
P.O. Box 657 (73049-0657)
PHONE..................405 399-2954
Donald Ramsey, *President*
Willadean Ramsey, *Corp Secy*
EMP: 7
SQ FT: 6,000
SALES (est): 1MM **Privately Held**
SIC: 2013 Sausages from purchased meat; prepared beef products from purchased beef

(G-3743)
COMPUTER ASSISTANCE
10413 N Indian Meridian (73049-7918)
PHONE..................405 399-2422
Laith Ryals, *Partner*
Blaine Ryals, *Partner*
EMP: 2
SALES (est): 190K **Privately Held**
SIC: 7372 Prepackaged software

(G-3744)
DESIGNS AND SIGNS BY JILLIAN
9131 N Midwest Blvd (73049-5823)
PHONE..................405 409-1522
Jill Jennings, *Principal*
EMP: 1
SALES (est): 46K **Privately Held**
SIC: 3993 Signs & advertising specialties

(G-3745)
ERIC ADAMS TRIM
402 Beebe St (73049-7518)
P.O. Box 30 (73049-0030)
PHONE..................405 570-5931
Eric Adams Trim, *Principal*
EMP: 3

SALES (est): 338.3K **Privately Held**
SIC: 2499 Decorative wood & woodwork

(G-3746)
GEMINI WOODWORKS
421 Sw 6th St (73049-7563)
PHONE..................405 630-8586
Heather Lea Dunaway, *Owner*
EMP: 1
SALES (est): 53.2K **Privately Held**
SIC: 2431 Millwork

(G-3747)
GPS WOODWORKS LLC
6501 Deer Creek Trl (73049-9614)
PHONE..................405 399-2369
Peter Lippold, *Principal*
EMP: 1 **EST:** 2016
SALES (est): 67K **Privately Held**
SIC: 2431 Millwork

(G-3748)
IXZIBIT
11120 Ne 141st St (73049-8718)
PHONE..................405 413-2260
Jeremiah Smith, *Principal*
EMP: 2
SALES (est): 86.8K **Privately Held**
WEB: www.ixzibit.com
SIC: 3993 Signs & advertising specialties

(G-3749)
JR ALPACAS LLC
13301 N Douglas Blvd (73049-3448)
PHONE..................405 771-2636
John Robinson, *Principal*
Janice Robinson, *Cust Mgr*
EMP: 5
SALES (est): 408.7K **Privately Held**
WEB: www.justrightalpacas.com
SIC: 2231 Alpacas, mohair: woven

(G-3750)
LAKE ICE LLC
13604 Silver Meadows Rd (73049-8313)
PHONE..................405 882-7227
Billyjack Grider, *Mng Member*
EMP: 1
SALES (est): 65.8K **Privately Held**
SIC: 3569 Ice crushers (machinery)

(G-3751)
PANTHERA ROUSTABOUT SVCS LLC
1601 Brook Bank Dr (73049-4931)
PHONE..................405 826-8466
Manuel Deleon III, *Administration*
EMP: 2
SALES (est): 165.3K **Privately Held**
SIC: 1389 Roustabout service

(G-3752)
SOY CANDLE COTTAGE LLC
Also Called: Botanicu
8500 E Memorial Rd (73049-3431)
PHONE..................405 519-6827
Leann Jenkins, *Principal*
Gary Spencer, *Director*
EMP: 2
SALES (est): 190.4K **Privately Held**
SIC: 3999 Candles

(G-3753)
TAYLORMADE CBNTRY CNTRTOPS LLC
9205 Nyswonger Rd (73049-6615)
PHONE..................405 227-4063
EMP: 2
SALES (est): 150K **Privately Held**
SIC: 2434 Wood kitchen cabinets

Kansas
Delaware County

(G-3754)
BORN AGAIN PEWS
5750 S 545 Rd (74347-1499)
PHONE..................918 868-7613
Rex Blisard, *Owner*
EMP: 12
SQ FT: 15,000
SALES (est): 1.2MM **Privately Held**
SIC: 2531 Pews, church

(G-3755)
STONE MILL INC
740 State Highway 10 (74347-1602)
PHONE..................918 812-4438
Susan Spring, *President*
Steve Koskey, *Vice Pres*
EMP: 11 **EST:** 2008
SALES (est): 1.8MM **Privately Held**
WEB: www.stonemillproducts.com
SIC: 3272 Building stone, artificial: concrete

Kaw City
Kay County

(G-3756)
BLUE SKY OIL FIELD SVCS LLC
116 Oak Dr (74641-9321)
P.O. Box 403, Shidler (74652-0403)
PHONE..................580 491-2349
EMP: 2 **EST:** 2013
SALES (est): 97.5K **Privately Held**
WEB: www.blueskycleanair.com
SIC: 1389 Oil field services

(G-3757)
CENTURY PRODUCTS LLC
306 N Cosden (74641)
PHONE..................908 793-3382
Jay Fagan,
EMP: 9
SQ FT: 7,500
SALES (est): 421.3K **Privately Held**
SIC: 3523 Cattle feeding, handling & watering equipment

(G-3758)
JB FABRICATION
709 Morgan Sq (74641)
P.O. Box 282 (74641-0282)
PHONE..................580 716-7524
EMP: 1
SQ FT: 1,200
SALES (est): 36.8K **Privately Held**
SIC: 7692 7389 Welding Repair

(G-3759)
KAW NATION SOLUTIONS LLC
698 Grandview Dr (74641-6000)
PHONE..................405 365-8900
EMP: 1
SALES (est): 55.9K **Privately Held**
SIC: 3999 Mfg Misc Products

(G-3760)
YANDELL FIRE INVESTIGATIONS
11 Acker Hill Rd (74641-9607)
PHONE..................580 269-2414
Tim Andale, *CEO*
EMP: 2
SALES (est): 13K **Privately Held**
SIC: 3699 Fire control or bombing equipment, electronic

Kellyville
Creek County

(G-3761)
CHEROKEE WELDING INDUSTRIES
14643 N Maple Dr (74039-4606)
P.O. Box 31 (74039-0031)
PHONE..................918 247-6122
Sam Nelson, *President*
June Nelson, *Corp Secy*
EMP: 1
SQ FT: 1,914
SALES (est): 32K **Privately Held**
SIC: 7692 Welding repair

(G-3762)
CORNELIUS OIL INC
Also Called: Cornelius Peteroleum
21301 W 191st St S (74039-8930)
P.O. Box 459 (74039-0459)
PHONE..................918 247-6743
Randall Cornelius, *President*
EMP: 2
SQ FT: 1,200

SALES (est): 833.7K **Privately Held**
SIC: 1311 5172 Crude petroleum production; natural gas production; petroleum brokers

(G-3763)
COUNTRY CRAFTS
236 And A Half W Buffalo (74039)
PHONE..................918 247-6144
Gene Hall, *Owner*
EMP: 1
SALES (est): 34.5K **Privately Held**
SIC: 2499 Wood products

(G-3764)
CUTTING EDGE ROBOTIC TECH LLC
50 E Buffalo St (74039-3621)
P.O. Box 787 (74039-0787)
PHONE..................918 247-6012
Jason Boatman,
EMP: 5
SALES (est): 1.5MM **Privately Held**
SIC: 3541 8999 Plasma process metal cutting machines; technical manual preparation

(G-3765)
HERO FLARE LLC
14842 N Maple Dr (74039-4428)
PHONE..................512 772-5744
David Giles, *President*
Craig Rosencutter, *Vice Pres*
Michael Giles, *Project Mgr*
Chris Osse, *Engineer*
EMP: 25
SQ FT: 25,000
SALES (est): 4.4MM **Privately Held**
SIC: 2899 Flares; flares, fireworks & similar preparations

(G-3766)
K & K MANUFACTURING INC
19155 W 141st St S (74039-4208)
PHONE..................918 247-2871
Sandra Scott, *CEO*
L Ketchum, *President*
Mikel Ketchum, *Owner*
EMP: 8
SALES (est): 726K **Privately Held**
SIC: 3599 Machine shop, jobbing & repair

(G-3767)
SCHLUMBERGER TECHNOLOGY CORP
Also Called: Kellyville Training Center
16879 W 141st St S (74039-4623)
PHONE..................918 247-1300
Richard Van Dertuin, *Principal*
Jennifer Sloan, *Administration*
EMP: 45
SQ FT: 48,198 **Publicly Held**
SIC: 1389 Oil field services
HQ: Schlumberger Technology Corp
  300 Schlumberger Dr
  Sugar Land TX 77478
  281 285-8500

(G-3768)
TRIDON COMPOSITES INC
18987 W Highway 66 (74039-3710)
P.O. Box 549 (74039-0549)
PHONE..................918 742-0426
Brian Kaupke, *President*
Dale Frates, *Corp Secy*
EMP: 11
SALES (est): 900K **Privately Held**
SIC: 3949 Rods & rod parts, fishing

(G-3769)
WEBCO INDUSTRIES INC
Webco Specialty Metal Division
18256 W Highway 66 (74039-4222)
PHONE..................918 865-6215
Stuart Keeton, *General Mgr*
EMP: 1
SALES (corp-wide): 480.7MM **Privately Held**
SIC: 3317 Steel pipe & tubes
PA: Webco Industries, Inc.
  9101 W 21st St
  Sand Springs OK 74063
  918 245-2211

Kellyville - Creek County (G-3770)

(G-3770)
WILDCAT MACHINE INC
19083 W Highway 66 (74039-4228)
PHONE.................................918 247-4220
Michael A Reiter, *President*
Maranell Reiter, *Vice Pres*
EMP: 6
SQ FT: 4,000
SALES (est): 410K **Privately Held**
SIC: 3599 Machine shop, jobbing & repair

(G-3771)
WILLIAMS MCHNING SPCALISTS INC
18750 W 141st St S (74039-4630)
PHONE.................................918 247-1719
Steve Williams, *President*
EMP: 13
SALES (est): 1.7MM **Privately Held**
WEB: www.williamsms.com
SIC: 3599 Machine shop, jobbing & repair

Keota
Haskell County

(G-3772)
HICKMANS WELDING
20337 N County Road 4560 (74941-6693)
PHONE.................................918 966-3783
EMP: 1 EST: 2008
SALES (est): 84K **Privately Held**
SIC: 7692 Welding Repair

(G-3773)
ROCKING H WELDING LLC
40824 E County Road 1240 (74941-6477)
PHONE.................................918 966-3882
Joshua Hurst, *Principal*
EMP: 1
SALES (est): 53.8K **Privately Held**
SIC: 7692 Welding repair

Ketchum
Mayes County

(G-3774)
KOLE INC
Also Called: Willow Park Marina
Grand Lake Of Cherokee (74349)
P.O. Box 120 (74349-0120)
PHONE.................................918 782-3001
Rick Bausher, *President*
EMP: 4
SQ FT: 9,460
SALES (est): 326K **Privately Held**
SIC: 3732 4493 Boat building & repairing; marine basins

Kiefer
Creek County

(G-3775)
ADVANCE OIL CORPORATION
14504 S Highway 75a (74041-4105)
P.O. Box 701835, Tulsa (74170-1835)
PHONE.................................918 321-9034
David Cox, *President*
EMP: 5
SQ FT: 3,700
SALES (est): 796.4K **Privately Held**
SIC: 3569 Gas producers, generators & other gas related equipment

(G-3776)
BRIDGE CRANE SPECIALISTS LLC (PA)
14536 Hwy 75 Alternate (74041)
P.O. Box 940 (74041-0940)
PHONE.................................918 321-3953
Russell Rooker, *President*
▲ EMP: 35
SQ FT: 5,000
SALES (est): 7.4MM **Privately Held**
SIC: 3536 Hoists, cranes & monorails

(G-3777)
CLARK SIGNS INC
306 N Main (74041-5108)
PHONE.................................918 291-3411
Mark Clark, *President*
Kevin Clark, *Vice Pres*
Lajan Clark, *Admin Sec*
EMP: 3
SALES (est): 288.3K **Privately Held**
SIC: 3993 Signs, not made in custom sign painting shops

(G-3778)
DEXXON INC
732 E Indiana (74041-4541)
P.O. Box 348 (74041-0348)
PHONE.................................918 321-9331
Ira E Rongey Jr, *Principal*
EMP: 7
SALES (est): 680K **Privately Held**
SIC: 1389 Construction, repair & dismantling services

(G-3779)
DRESSER-RAND SERVICES LLC
Also Called: Dresser-Rand Arrow
14963 S 49th Ave W (74041)
P.O. Box 579 (74041-0579)
PHONE.................................918 321-3690
EMP: 3 **Privately Held**
SIC: 1389 Oil/Gas Field Services

(G-3780)
HYPERION ENERGY LP
14530 S 49th West Ave (74041-5510)
PHONE.................................918 321-3350
Wade Ashlock, *Manager*
EMP: 7 **Privately Held**
SIC: 1389 Oil field services
PA: Hyperion Energy Lp
   12377 Merit Dr Ste 1200
   Dallas TX 75251

(G-3781)
RAMEYS WELDING & ROUSTABOUT
Also Called: Ramey Oil
11 S A St (74041)
P.O. Box 699 (74041-0699)
PHONE.................................918 321-3156
Lense Ramey Jr, *President*
Ruth Ramey, *Treasurer*
EMP: 9 EST: 1973
SALES (est): 841.4K **Privately Held**
SIC: 1389 5084 Oil field services; oil well machinery, equipment & supplies

(G-3782)
TULSA TRENCHLESS INC
4457 W 151st St S (74041-4581)
P.O. Box 880 (74041-0880)
PHONE.................................918 321-3330
Trevor A Young, *President*
Lynne Young, *Corp Secy*
EMP: 2
SALES: 54.4K
SALES (corp-wide): 23.3MM **Privately Held**
SIC: 3541 Drilling & boring machines
PA: Tulsa Rig Iron, Inc.
   4457 W 151st St S
   Kiefer OK 74041
   918 321-3330

Kingfisher
Kingfisher County

(G-3783)
33 - WELDING COMPANY
123 N 11th St (73750-2526)
PHONE.................................405 375-4468
Claude Lann, *Owner*
EMP: 3
SQ FT: 11,200
SALES: 200K **Privately Held**
SIC: 7692 1799 Welding repair; welding on site

(G-3784)
ALTMAN ENGINEERING INC
1 Mile N On Hwy 81 (73750)
P.O. Box 747 (73750-0747)
PHONE.................................405 368-7889
Steven Altman, *President*
EMP: 1
SALES (est): 98.9K **Privately Held**
SIC: 1389 Oil field services

(G-3785)
BLAIR OIL CO INC
219 N 6th St (73750-2714)
P.O. Box 1213 (73750-1213)
PHONE.................................405 263-4445
Kent Blair, *President*
EMP: 1
SALES (est): 250K **Privately Held**
SIC: 1311 Crude petroleum production

(G-3786)
BRISCOE OIL CO
406 N Main St (73750-2322)
PHONE.................................405 375-3700
Leonard Briscoe, *Owner*
EMP: 8
SALES (est): 720K **Privately Held**
SIC: 1311 Crude petroleum production

(G-3787)
BROWN & BORELLI INC
N Hwy 81 (73750)
P.O. Box 747 (73750-0747)
PHONE.................................405 375-5788
Steven Altman, *President*
EMP: 6 EST: 1962
SQ FT: 3,100
SALES (est): 714.9K **Privately Held**
SIC: 1311 Crude petroleum production; natural gas production

(G-3788)
CHEESE FACTORY LLC
701 Starlite Dr (73750-4929)
PHONE.................................405 375-4004
Shavone Whipple,
EMP: 4
SALES (est): 293.9K **Privately Held**
SIC: 2022 Natural cheese

(G-3789)
CHESAPEAKE OPERATING LLC
2110 S Main St (73750-4618)
PHONE.................................405 375-6755
Larry Settle, *Branch Mgr*
EMP: 17 **Publicly Held**
SIC: 1311 Crude petroleum production
HQ: Chesapeake Operating, L.L.C.
   6100 N Western Ave
   Oklahoma City OK 73118

(G-3790)
CHESAPEAKE OPERATING LLC
15446 E 770 Rd (73750-6249)
PHONE.................................405 375-6755
EMP: 17 **Publicly Held**
SIC: 1311 Crude petroleum production
HQ: Chesapeake Operating, L.L.C.
   6100 N Western Ave
   Oklahoma City OK 73118

(G-3791)
CIMARRON MACHINE WORKS INC
9 Miles East Highway 33 (73750)
P.O. Box 1138 (73750-1138)
PHONE.................................405 375-6452
Garry Lafave, *President*
▼ EMP: 3
SQ FT: 3,600
SALES: 200K **Privately Held**
SIC: 3599 Machine shop, jobbing & repair

(G-3792)
CONNIE PIRPLE
Also Called: Thirty Three Welding
123 N 11th St (73750-2526)
PHONE.................................405 375-4468
Connie Pirple, *Owner*
EMP: 5
SQ FT: 10,000
SALES (est): 100K **Privately Held**
SIC: 7692 3441 Welding repair; fabricated structural metal

(G-3793)
CORP COMM OIL & GAS DIV
101 S 6th St (73750-3209)
P.O. Box 1107 (73750-1107)
PHONE.................................405 375-5570
Tony Cupp, *Principal*
EMP: 2 EST: 2002
SALES (est): 135.3K **Privately Held**
SIC: 1382 Oil & gas exploration services

(G-3794)
CRANDALL AND SANDERS INC
Also Called: Crandall Sanders Plbg Elec Eng
110 N Main St (73750-2738)
P.O. Box 537 (73750-0537)
PHONE.................................405 375-3242
Steven Sanders, *President*
Vicki Sanders, *Corp Secy*
EMP: 9 EST: 1918
SQ FT: 2,500
SALES (est): 1.6MM **Privately Held**
SIC: 5074 5063 3648 Plumbing & hydronic heating supplies; electrical supplies; reflectors for lighting equipment: metal

(G-3795)
D AND M RESOURCES INC
1617 Anna Pl (73750-4603)
PHONE.................................405 375-4602
Don Shilling, *Owner*
EMP: 2
SALES: 400K **Privately Held**
SIC: 1475 Apatite mining

(G-3796)
DSIGNZ CUSTOM SCREEN PRINTING
108 W Miles Ave (73750-2646)
P.O. Box 326 (73750-0326)
PHONE.................................405 375-6806
Kim Siegel, *Owner*
EMP: 1
SALES (est): 78.1K **Privately Held**
SIC: 3953 Screens, textile printing

(G-3797)
FAST FUEL LLC
100 Mitchell Blvd (73750-4820)
PHONE.................................405 375-6666
EMP: 3 EST: 2013
SALES (est): 222K **Privately Held**
SIC: 2869 Fuels

(G-3798)
GEORGE E CHRISTIAN
Also Called: Christian Cheese Factory
13th And Airport Rd (73750)
PHONE.................................405 375-6711
George E Christian, *Principal*
EMP: 4 EST: 2001
SALES (est): 227.4K **Privately Held**
SIC: 2022 Cheese, natural & processed

(G-3799)
GOODEN STUDIOS
123 W Thompson Dr (73750-4323)
PHONE.................................405 375-3432
John Gooden, *Owner*
EMP: 2
SALES: 400K **Privately Held**
SIC: 8999 3089 3081 Sculptor's studio; plastic containers, except foam; plastic film & sheet

(G-3800)
HAMIL SERVICE LLC
15748 Beverly Dr (73750-6500)
PHONE.................................405 375-3815
Larry Hamil, *Mng Member*
Rosana Hamil,
EMP: 10
SALES (est): 745.8K **Privately Held**
SIC: 4213 1389 Automobiles, transport & delivery; cementing oil & gas well casings

(G-3801)
HILL METAL INC
Also Called: Hill Metal & Supply
421 N 4th St (73750-2328)
PHONE.................................405 375-6284
Carol Hill, *President*
Ray Hill, *Vice Pres*
Lynda Kremeier, *Manager*
EMP: 7

SALES (est): 1.4MM **Privately Held**
SIC: 5051 3444 3443 Steel; bins, prefabricated sheet metal; fabricated plate work (boiler shop)

(G-3802)
J & D POTTER OIL LLC
1203 W Fay Ave (73750-3832)
PHONE...................................405 375-6303
Jess Potter, *Mng Member*
Donna Potter,
EMP: 4 EST: 1981
SALES (est): 260K **Privately Held**
SIC: 1389 Construction, repair & dismantling services

(G-3803)
K B MACHINE & WELDING INC
Un Known (73750)
PHONE...................................405 375-5888
Kerry Stitt, *President*
EMP: 1
SALES (est): 125K **Privately Held**
SIC: 7692 Welding repair

(G-3804)
KINGFISHER COUNTY DRIVERS
101 S Main St Ste 4 (73750-3241)
P.O. Box 11415, Oklahoma City (73136-0415)
PHONE...................................405 375-3711
EMP: 2 EST: 2007
SALES (est): 110K **Privately Held**
SIC: 3469 Mfg Metal Stampings

(G-3805)
KINGFISHER NEWSPAPER INC
Also Called: Kingfisher Times & Free Press
323 N Main St (73750-2749)
P.O. Box 209 (73750-0209)
PHONE...................................405 375-3220
Gary Reid, *President*
Barry Reid, *Vice Pres*
EMP: 8 EST: 1889
SQ FT: 2,500
SALES (est): 200K **Privately Held**
WEB: www.kingfisherpress.net
SIC: 2711 Newspapers: publishing only, not printed on site

(G-3806)
KINGFISHER OFFICE SUPPLY INC
Also Called: Central Supply
317 N Main St (73750-2749)
P.O. Box 209 (73750-0209)
PHONE...................................405 375-3404
Gary Reid, *President*
Barry Reid, *Vice Pres*
Mary Reid, *Admin Sec*
EMP: 5
SQ FT: 2,500
SALES (est): 834.8K **Privately Held**
SIC: 2752 5044 5021 2791 Commercial printing, offset; office equipment; office furniture; typesetting; bookbinding & related work; office forms & supplies

(G-3807)
L C B RESOURCES
406 N Main St (73750-2322)
PHONE...................................405 375-3718
Leonard Brisco, *Owner*
EMP: 2
SALES (est): 133.1K **Privately Held**
SIC: 1311 Crude petroleum production

(G-3808)
MAC OIL & GAS
104 W Chisholm Dr (73750-4341)
PHONE...................................405 375-5619
EMP: 2
SALES (est): 96K **Privately Held**
SIC: 5172 1389 Whol Petroleum Products Oil/Gas Field Services

(G-3809)
NEOMANUFACTURING LLC
202 N 6th St Apt 4 (73750-2713)
PHONE...................................405 605-6581
Justin Mecklenburg, *Mng Member*
EMP: 30
SALES (est): 1MM **Privately Held**
SIC: 3644 Insulators & insulation materials, electrical

(G-3810)
PAPPE COURT JR OFFICE
204 N Main St (73750-2739)
P.O. Box 688 (73750-0688)
PHONE...................................405 375-5450
Court Pappe Jr, *Owner*
EMP: 1
SQ FT: 1,000
SALES (est): 93K **Privately Held**
SIC: 1311 Crude petroleum production; natural gas production

(G-3811)
PONY EXPRESS PRINTING LLC
103 N 6th St (73750-2712)
PHONE...................................405 375-5064
John Coughlan,
Melody Coughlan,
EMP: 2
SALES (est): 100K **Privately Held**
SIC: 2759 2791 2789 2752 Commercial printing; typesetting; bookbinding & related work; commercial printing, lithographic

(G-3812)
RED PLAINS OIL & GAS LLC
508 W Chisholm Dr (73750-4347)
PHONE...................................405 375-3377
Joe Markus, *Principal*
EMP: 1
SALES (est): 114.1K **Privately Held**
SIC: 1311 Crude petroleum production

(G-3813)
RIVIERA OPERATING LLC
Also Called: Linn Energy
Rr 24 Box B (73750)
PHONE...................................405 375-6065
Nick Lovelady, *Branch Mgr*
EMP: 20
SALES (corp-wide): 479.7MM **Publicly Held**
SIC: 1311 Crude petroleum production
HQ: Riviera Operating, Llc
    600 Travis St Ste 5100
    Houston TX 77002

(G-3814)
SIGN OF TIMES
Also Called: Conrady, Jeffery L
305 Seay Ave (73750-4226)
P.O. Box 984 (73750-0984)
PHONE...................................405 375-4717
Jeff Conrady, *Principal*
EMP: 2
SALES: 75K **Privately Held**
SIC: 3993 Signs & advertising specialties

(G-3815)
SISK CONSTRUCTION CO
1009 S Main St (73750-4417)
P.O. Box 676 (73750-0676)
PHONE...................................405 375-5318
William Sisk, *Owner*
EMP: 5
SQ FT: 2,000
SALES (est): 411.3K **Privately Held**
SIC: 1623 1389 Oil & gas pipeline construction; oil field services

(G-3816)
SOONER TREND EXPLORATION INC
1202 Regency Ct (73750-4252)
P.O. Box 71 (73750-0071)
PHONE...................................405 375-3405
Jim Gazin, *President*
Anne Gazin, *Admin Sec*
EMP: 2
SALES (est): 200K **Privately Held**
SIC: 1311 Crude petroleum production; natural gas production

(G-3817)
TERRA STAR INC (PA)
1515 S 7th St Ste 300 (73750-4317)
P.O. Box 744 (73750-0744)
PHONE...................................405 200-1336
Brad Wittrock, *President*
EMP: 43 EST: 2014
SQ FT: 4,000
SALES (est): 12.6MM **Privately Held**
SIC: 1389 Cementing oil & gas well casings

(G-3818)
TONYS ELECTRIC INC
102 E Schroeder Dr (73750)
P.O. Box 593 (73750-0593)
PHONE...................................405 375-4103
Allen Ludwig, *President*
EMP: 2
SQ FT: 6,250
SALES (est): 218.3K **Privately Held**
SIC: 7539 7694 1731 7699 Electrical services; electric motor repair; general electrical contractor; engine repair & replacement, non-automotive

(G-3819)
TRITAN MFG LLC
1512 S 10th St (73750-4306)
PHONE...................................405 375-3332
Jim Perdue, *Mng Member*
EMP: 2
SALES (est): 162.7K **Privately Held**
SIC: 3715 Truck trailers

(G-3820)
WAY-WEAR LLC
15276 E 770 Rd (73750-6247)
PHONE...................................405 410-8367
Hiawatha Newton, *President*
Hiawatha K Newton, *Owner*
EMP: 5
SALES (est): 10K **Privately Held**
SIC: 7336 7374 2396 Silk screen design; computer graphics service; screen printing on fabric articles

(G-3821)
WHEELER & SONS OIL AND GAS
406 N Main St (73750-2322)
PHONE...................................405 375-4613
Jack Wheeler, *Owner*
EMP: 8
SALES (est): 423.5K **Privately Held**
SIC: 1311 Crude petroleum production

(G-3822)
WILSON & WILSON
804 Clark Dr (73750-3800)
PHONE...................................405 375-5194
James W Wilson, *Owner*
EMP: 1
SALES (est): 70.6K **Privately Held**
SIC: 1389 Servicing oil & gas wells

(G-3823)
WORLD ENERGY RESOURCES INC
6th & Miles St (73750)
PHONE...................................405 375-6484
Randy Mecklenburg, *President*
EMP: 6
SALES (est): 294.3K **Privately Held**
SIC: 1382 2731 Oil & gas exploration services; textbooks: publishing only, not printed on site

Kingston
Marshall County

(G-3824)
BETTY E JESTER
Also Called: Gainsville Pallet Company
16939 Haircut Rd (73439-5605)
PHONE...................................580 564-9396
Betty Jester, *Owner*
EMP: 1
SALES (est): 101.3K **Privately Held**
SIC: 2448 Pallets, wood & wood with metal

(G-3825)
BRIER CREEK FURN WORKS LLC
20112 Highway 32 (73439-8111)
PHONE...................................903 327-5602
Curtis Oliver,
EMP: 1
SALES (est): 39.6K **Privately Held**
SIC: 3999 Manufacturing industries

(G-3826)
CAN-DO-CANDLES
11968 Thompson Rd (73439-5318)
P.O. Box 1764 (73439-1764)
PHONE...................................580 564-2816
EMP: 2
SALES (est): 75.6K **Privately Held**
SIC: 3999 Candles

(G-3827)
FIVE A TRAILERS AND EQUIPMENT
Hwy 70 N (73439)
P.O. Box 10 (73439-0010)
PHONE...................................580 564-2973
Donnie Allen, *President*
EMP: 4
SQ FT: 6,000
SALES: 150K **Privately Held**
SIC: 3799 7539 5599 Boat trailers; trailer repair; utility trailers

(G-3828)
FORBES ENTERPRISES INC
6300 Hummingbird Ln (73439-9175)
PHONE...................................580 564-2599
Allen Forbes, *President*
Stacey Forbes, *Treasurer*
EMP: 5
SQ FT: 3,100
SALES: 150K **Privately Held**
SIC: 3449 Miscellaneous metalwork

(G-3829)
KNAPE FABRICATION & WLDG LLC
13299 Cliff Rd (73439-7201)
PHONE...................................580 564-3107
Rowdy D Knape, *Principal*
EMP: 1 EST: 2018
SALES (est): 41.9K **Privately Held**
SIC: 7692 Welding repair

(G-3830)
OKIE NEWTS WELDING
401 Highway 70 N (73439-8235)
P.O. Box 1212 (73439-1212)
PHONE...................................580 564-4724
Lloyd D Newton, *Principal*
EMP: 2
SALES (est): 124.1K **Privately Held**
SIC: 7692 Welding repair

(G-3831)
TIP TOP PROP SHOP
Hc 72 Box 235 (73439)
PHONE...................................580 564-3712
John Ward, *Owner*
EMP: 1
SALES (est): 89.6K **Privately Held**
SIC: 3732 3559 7699 Boat building & repairing; special industry machinery; boat repair

Kinta
Haskell County

(G-3832)
BATES INSTRUMENTATION LLC
30949 S Cnty Rd Ste 4330 (74552)
P.O. Box 371, Stigler (74462-0371)
PHONE...................................918 441-7178
Kendrick Bates, *President*
EMP: 16
SALES: 1.1MM **Privately Held**
WEB: www.batesinst.com
SIC: 3823 Pressure measurement instruments, industrial

(G-3833)
BEAR PRODUCTIONS INC
30451 W Sans Bois Rd (74552)
P.O. Box 142 (74552-0142)
PHONE...................................918 768-3364
Allen King, *President*
Roy Lynn King, *Corp Secy*
Boyd King, *Vice Pres*
EMP: 18
SQ FT: 1,500
SALES (est): 2.3MM **Privately Held**
SIC: 1311 Natural gas production

Kinta

(G-3834)
BEAVER CREEK INDUSTRIES LLC
31078 W County Road 1270 (74552-3025)
PHONE..................918 469-2779
Kristin Butler-Hamlin, *Principal*
EMP: 1
SALES (est): 39.6K **Privately Held**
SIC: 3999 Manufacturing industries

(G-3835)
NRG WIRELINE LLC
203 N King St (74552-3200)
PHONE..................918 768-3210
Amber Myers, *Office Mgr*
James Myers,
EMP: 18
SALES: 650K **Privately Held**
SIC: 1389 Testing, measuring, surveying & analysis services; bailing, cleaning, swabbing & treating of wells; well logging; fishing for tools, oil & gas field

(G-3836)
SHELTON SANITATION
31387 Scr 4330 (74552)
P.O. Box 26 (74552-0026)
PHONE..................918 469-3498
David Shelton, *Owner*
EMP: 1
SALES (est): 92.1K **Privately Held**
SIC: 3443 Dumpsters, garbage

Kiowa
Pittsburg County

(G-3837)
DAVIDS TRADING YARD
16918 Taft Us Hwy 69 (74553)
P.O. Box 25 (74553-0025)
PHONE..................918 432-5671
David Rudrow, *Owner*
EMP: 1
SALES (est): 213.7K **Privately Held**
SIC: 3523 Farm machinery & equipment

(G-3838)
HUTSON WELDING SERVICES LLC
268 Haynes Ln (74553-5115)
PHONE..................918 470-3673
Henry Dale Hutson, *Principal*
EMP: 1
SALES (est): 41K **Privately Held**
SIC: 7692 Welding repair

(G-3839)
KIOWA POWER PARTNERS LLC
Milepost 69 Hwy 69 S (74553)
P.O. Box 430 (74553-0430)
PHONE..................918 432-5117
Robert Hope, *Branch Mgr*
EMP: 34
SALES (corp-wide): 117.6MM **Privately Held**
SIC: 3621 Generators & sets, electric
PA: Kiowa Power Partners, Llc
 14302 Fnb Pkwy
 Omaha NE 68154
 402 691-9500

(G-3840)
LARRYS WELDING SERVICE
Also Called: Sorrels, Larry
5 Miles South On Hwy 131 (74553)
P.O. Box 219 (74553-0219)
PHONE..................918 432-5787
Larry Sorrels, *Owner*
EMP: 1
SALES: 60K **Privately Held**
SIC: 1799 7692 Welding on site; welding repair

Knowles
Beaver County

(G-3841)
UNIBRIDGE SYSTEMS INC (PA)
4th & Oklahoma St (73844)
Rural Route 8
PHONE..................580 934-3211
Joe Hamilton, *President*
Kerry Hamilton, *Principal*
Terry D Mundell, *Vice Pres*
Linda Hester, *Admin Sec*
EMP: 40
SQ FT: 30,000
SALES (est): 7.4MM **Privately Held**
SIC: 3596 Railroad track scales; truck (motor vehicle) scales

Konawa
Seminole County

(G-3842)
AKERMAN DRILLING INC
111 S Broadway St (74849-2243)
P.O. Box 25 (74849-0025)
PHONE..................580 925-3938
William J Akerman, *President*
William Akerman, *President*
Judy Akerman, *Corp Secy*
EMP: 50
SALES: 3.3MM **Privately Held**
SIC: 1381 Drilling oil & gas wells

(G-3843)
BILLY JACK SHARBER OPER LLC
Seminole County (74849)
P.O. Box 71 (74849-0071)
PHONE..................405 382-5740
Bill Sharber,
EMP: 2
SALES (est): 446.3K **Privately Held**
SIC: 1382 Oil & gas exploration services

(G-3844)
DARRELLS DRILLING INC
N Of City On Hwy 9 A (74849)
P.O. Box 68 (74849-0068)
PHONE..................580 925-3854
Darrell Mackey, *President*
Linda Brown, *Corp Secy*
EMP: 5
SQ FT: 6,000
SALES (est): 603.4K **Privately Held**
SIC: 1381 Drilling oil & gas wells

(G-3845)
DUCK BROTHERS DOZER & TRUCKING
34826 Ew 1420 (74849)
P.O. Box 127 (74849-0127)
PHONE..................580 925-3509
Gary L Duck, *President*
June Duck, *Admin Sec*
Robert Duck, *Admin Sec*
EMP: 5
SALES (est): 925.8K **Privately Held**
SIC: 3531 Dozers, tractor mounted: material moving

(G-3846)
HERRIMAN OILFIELD SERVICES
13998 Ns 3520 (74849-6005)
PHONE..................580 925-2144
Sarah Herriman, *Principal*
EMP: 1
SALES (est): 127.9K **Privately Held**
SIC: 1389 Oil field services

(G-3847)
KATHY TIM LOWERY
35037 Ew 1370 (74849-5301)
PHONE..................580 925-2171
Kathy Lowery, *Principal*
EMP: 2
SALES (est): 131.3K **Privately Held**
SIC: 1389 Oil field services

(G-3848)
SOONER SCALE INC
14082 Ns 3500 (74849-4908)
PHONE..................580 925-2176
Steve McFadden, *CEO*
EMP: 10 EST: 2001
SALES (est): 737.2K **Privately Held**
SIC: 3596 Truck (motor vehicle) scales

Krebs
Pittsburg County

(G-3849)
CUDD PRESSURE CONTROL INC
Also Called: Cudd Energy Services
405 A Highway 270 E (74554)
P.O. Box 970 (74554-0970)
PHONE..................918 423-0160
Larry Turney, *Branch Mgr*
EMP: 40
SALES (corp-wide): 1.2B **Publicly Held**
SIC: 1389 Oil field services
HQ: Cudd Pressure Control, Inc.
 2828 Tech Forest Blvd
 The Woodlands TX 77381
 832 295-5555

(G-3850)
FLOW TESTING INC
1125 W Washington Ave (74554)
P.O. Box 601 (74554-0601)
PHONE..................918 423-0017
Mike Sossamon, *President*
Linda Sossamon, *Vice Pres*
EMP: 25
SQ FT: 8,000
SALES (est): 2.1MM **Privately Held**
SIC: 1389 Oil field services

Kremlin
Garfield County

(G-3851)
ENTERPRISE GRAIN COMPANY LLC (PA)
Po Box 68 (73753-0068)
P.O. Box 68
PHONE..................580 874-2286
Tiffany Walton, *Office Admin*
EMP: 7
SALES (est): 2MM **Privately Held**
SIC: 3523 Driers (farm): grain, hay & seed

(G-3852)
GRAY MUD DISPOSAL
14701 N Garland Rd (73753-0294)
PHONE..................580 635-2225
EMP: 2
SALES (est): 100K **Privately Held**
SIC: 1389 Oil/Gas Field Services

(G-3853)
KREMLIN WELDING & FABRICATION
Main St (73753)
P.O. Box 147 (73753-0147)
PHONE..................580 874-2522
Wayne Schoeling, *Owner*
EMP: 6
SQ FT: 8,000
SALES: 500K **Privately Held**
SIC: 3715 7692 3537 Truck trailers; welding repair; industrial trucks & tractors

(G-3854)
OXBOW CALCINING LLC
11826 N 30th St (73753-0189)
PHONE..................580 874-2201
Scott Hoard, *Principal*
Dan Rosendale, *Plant Mgr*
Mike Bloss, *Maintence Staff*
EMP: 19 EST: 2003
SALES (est): 5.5MM
SALES (corp-wide): 446.2MM **Privately Held**
WEB: www.oxbow.com
SIC: 2911 Petroleum refining
PA: Oxbow Carbon & Minerals Holdings, Inc.
 1601 Forum Pl Ste 1400
 West Palm Beach FL 33401
 561 907-5400

(G-3855)
STITCHIN ACRES
7618 W Keowee Rd (73753-0401)
PHONE..................405 740-6035
EMP: 1
SALES (est): 31.2K **Privately Held**
SIC: 2395 Embroidery & art needlework

Lahoma
Garfield County

(G-3856)
KANOKA RIDGE SERVICES
340 E Lahoma Rd (73754)
PHONE..................580 302-1561
Chance Cecil, *Manager*
EMP: 4
SALES (est): 222.9K **Privately Held**
SIC: 3545 Drill bits, metalworking

(G-3857)
KIRKS CONTRACT PUMPING
1228 Ridge Pl (73754-9698)
PHONE..................580 541-6405
Bob Kirk, *Owner*
EMP: 1 EST: 2011
SALES (est): 75.8K **Privately Held**
SIC: 1389 Pumping of oil & gas wells

(G-3858)
MCCARTNEY WELDING LLC
121 Anthony Dr (73754-1003)
P.O. Box 33 (73754-0033)
PHONE..................580 542-2564
Ross McCartney, *Principal*
EMP: 2
SALES (est): 184.9K **Privately Held**
SIC: 7692 Welding repair

(G-3859)
PLAINVIEW WINERY
Also Called: Papa Har's Pickles
321 W Lahoma Rd (73754)
PHONE..................580 796-2902
Con Pekrul, *Owner*
EMP: 1
SALES: 150K **Privately Held**
SIC: 2084 2035 Wines; pickles, sauces & salad dressings

(G-3860)
RAUH OILFIELD SERVICES CO
1622 S Higway 132 (73754)
P.O. Box 421 (73754-0421)
PHONE..................580 796-2128
J Rauh, *Owner*
EMP: 4 EST: 2012
SALES (est): 421.3K **Privately Held**
SIC: 1389 Oil field services

(G-3861)
T&M ROUSTABOUT SERVICES LLC
101 Oklahoma St (73754-1011)
PHONE..................580 796-2478
Toby Ging, *Principal*
EMP: 2
SALES (est): 207.9K **Privately Held**
SIC: 1389 Roustabout service

Lamar
Hughes County

(G-3862)
BLINKERS & SILKS UNLIMITED INC
8697 E Broadway (74850-9251)
PHONE..................405 463-0391
Anita Schmitt, *President*
Mike Schmitt, *Corp Secy*
Karen Rood, *Vice Pres*
Nancy Wyckoff, *Vice Pres*
EMP: 5

GEOGRAPHIC SECTION

Lawton - Comanche County (G-3892)

SALES: 185K **Privately Held**
SIC: 3111 5191 Saddlery leather; saddlery

(G-3863)
BLOODS LOGGING & LAND SVCS LLC
9116 E 130 Rd (74850-9219)
PHONE..................405 314-4275
Danny Blood, *Owner*
EMP: 2
SALES (est): 81.7K **Privately Held**
SIC: 2411 Logging

Lamont
Grant County

(G-3864)
CASING CREWS INCORPORATED
307 N Main (74643)
P.O. Box 158 (74643-0158)
PHONE..................580 388-4567
Cody Darling, *President*
EMP: 90
SALES (est): 5.8MM **Privately Held**
SIC: 1389 4789 Oil field services; cargo loading & unloading services

(G-3865)
D E M OPERATIONS INC
16489 County Road 1060 (74643-5010)
P.O. Box 1 (74643-0001)
PHONE..................580 388-4315
Don E Muegge, *President*
Clay Muegge, *Vice Pres*
Chad Muegge, *Treasurer*
Bonnie Muegge, *Admin Sec*
EMP: 3 EST: 1973
SALES (est): 669K **Privately Held**
SIC: 1311 0111 Crude petroleum production; wheat

(G-3866)
DARLING OIL CORP
307 N Main (74643)
P.O. Box 158 (74643-0158)
PHONE..................580 388-4567
Dan E Darling, *President*
Dan Darling, *President*
Lexi Pierce, *Corp Secy*
EMP: 3
SALES (est): 2.7MM **Privately Held**
SIC: 1381 Drilling oil & gas wells

(G-3867)
DARLING OIL CORPORATION
317 N Main St (74643)
P.O. Box 158 (74643-0158)
PHONE..................580 388-6681
Lexy J Pierce, *Corp Secy*
EMP: 3
SQ FT: 1,100
SALES (est): 523.1K **Privately Held**
SIC: 1311 Crude petroleum production; natural gas production

(G-3868)
DOUBLE R OILFIELD SERVICES LLC
307 N Main (74643)
P.O. Box 158 (74643-0158)
PHONE..................580 388-4567
EMP: 2
SALES (est): 106.4K **Privately Held**
SIC: 1389 Oil field services

(G-3869)
J-B OILFIELD SERVICES LLC
1227 Main (74643)
P.O. Box 326 (74643-0326)
PHONE..................580 388-4484
Ross Whitehead,
EMP: 16
SALES (est): 3.5MM **Privately Held**
SIC: 1389 Oil field services

Lane
Atoka County

(G-3870)
ARTHUR CREWS LOGGING
7669 S Double Springs Rd (74555-6035)
PHONE..................580 889-7757
Arthur B Crews, *Principal*
EMP: 3
SALES (est): 279K **Privately Held**
SIC: 2411 Logging camps & contractors

Langley
Mayes County

(G-3871)
LAKEWOOD CABINETRY INC
Hwy 82 (74350)
P.O. Box 388 (74350-0388)
PHONE..................918 782-2203
Doug Olson, *President*
Brandy Olson, *Admin Sec*
EMP: 10
SQ FT: 25,000
SALES (est): 1.7MM **Privately Held**
SIC: 2431 2434 Millwork; wood kitchen cabinets

(G-3872)
LONGS EXCAVATING
Second & Osage (74350)
P.O. Box 251 (74350-0251)
PHONE..................918 782-2235
Ray Long, *Owner*
EMP: 1
SALES (est): 73K **Privately Held**
SIC: 3446 1611 Architectural metalwork; concrete construction: roads, highways, sidewalks, etc.

(G-3873)
NEWELL MANUFACTURING
39026 S Hwy 82 (74350)
PHONE..................918 782-1900
EMP: 5
SALES (est): 236.6K **Privately Held**
SIC: 3949 Manufacturing

(G-3874)
PRECISION MFG & DESIGN
Also Called: Precision Mfg. & Design
1690 N 3rd St (74350)
P.O. Box 250 (74350-0250)
PHONE..................918 782-2723
Leonard Kauffman, *President*
EMP: 20
SQ FT: 16,000
SALES (est): 2.3MM **Privately Held**
SIC: 3599 7692 Machine shop, jobbing & repair; welding repair

(G-3875)
WAVE ON FLAGS AND BANNERS LLC
2165 N 3rd St (74350)
P.O. Box 356, Claremore (74018-0356)
PHONE..................918 782-3330
Devone Chezem, *President*
Jan Chezem, *CFO*
EMP: 2
SALES (est): 261.9K **Privately Held**
SIC: 5131 5999 2399 Flags & banners; banners, flags, decals & posters; banners, pennants & flags

Laverne
Harper County

(G-3876)
CIRCLE D MEAT
S County Line Rd (73848)
PHONE..................580 921-5500
Dan O Hair, *Owner*
EMP: 5
SALES (est): 324.8K **Privately Held**
SIC: 2011 2013 Meat packing plants; sausages & other prepared meats

(G-3877)
FOAM UNIT INC
172 Ns 19 2 Ew (73848)
P.O. Box 442 (73848-0442)
PHONE..................580 921-3366
Allen Barby, *CEO*
EMP: 1
SALES (est): 86.1K **Privately Held**
SIC: 1381 Drilling oil & gas wells

(G-3878)
GENERAL INC
N Edge Of City (73848)
P.O. Box 504 (73848-0504)
PHONE..................580 921-3365
Dwight Freeman, *President*
EMP: 30
SALES (est): 4MM **Privately Held**
SIC: 1389 Oil field services

(G-3879)
LEADER TRIBUNE
Also Called: Golden Plaines Publishing
205 S Broadway (73848)
P.O. Box 370 (73848-0370)
PHONE..................580 921-3391
Mark Anderson, *Owner*
EMP: 2
SALES (est): 98.4K **Privately Held**
SIC: 2711 Newspapers, publishing & printing

Lawton
Comanche County

(G-3880)
1TR3 PUBLISHING LLC
1213 Nw Arlington Ave (73507-6538)
PHONE..................580 350-9280
EMP: 1
SALES (est): 37.5K **Privately Held**
SIC: 2741 Miscellaneous publishing

(G-3881)
A PRIOR PUBLISHING
146 Nw Red Bud Rd (73507-8479)
PHONE..................903 882-5019
EMP: 2 EST: 2011
SALES (est): 80K **Privately Held**
SIC: 2741 Misc Publishing

(G-3882)
A-OK RUBBER STAMP
Also Called: A-O K Rubber Stamp Co
701 Nw 17th St Ste D (73507-5136)
P.O. Box 505 (73502-0505)
PHONE..................580 357-2822
La Ray Lemons, *Owner*
EMP: 2
SALES (est): 106.8K **Privately Held**
SIC: 3953 Embossing seals & hand stamps

(G-3883)
ACCU-TURN MACHINE LLC
Also Called: Ralph Lynn Szatkowski
3817 Nw Welch Rd (73507-7238)
PHONE..................580 704-8876
Ralph Szatkowski, *Principal*
EMP: 1 EST: 2012
SALES (est): 115K **Privately Held**
SIC: 3599 3541 Crankshafts & camshafts, machining; turret lathes

(G-3884)
ACCURATE FENCE CONTRUCTION LLC
6905 Se Lee Blvd (73501-3501)
PHONE..................580 591-3717
Colten Glover, *President*
EMP: 5
SALES (est): 170.5K **Privately Held**
SIC: 1799 3272 7692 Fence construction; concrete products; welding repair

(G-3885)
AFFINITEE GRAPHICS
502 Nw Sheridan Rd (73505-6505)
P.O. Box 124, Apache (73006-0124)
PHONE..................580 861-2253
EMP: 3

SALES (est): 190.3K **Privately Held**
WEB: www.affiniteegraphics.com
SIC: 2759 Screen printing

(G-3886)
ALBRIGHT STEEL AND WIRE CO
320 Se J Ave (73501-2465)
P.O. Box 2221 (73502-2221)
PHONE..................580 357-3596
Randy Martin, *Manager*
EMP: 7
SALES (corp-wide): 9.2MM **Privately Held**
SIC: 3291 5051 3498 3315 Abrasive metal & steel products; steel; tube fabricating (contract bending & shaping); wire & fabricated wire products
PA: Albright Steel And Wire Company
    12 S Virginia Ave
    Oklahoma City OK 73106
    405 232-7526

(G-3887)
AMERICAN PHOENIX INC
5201 Sw 11th St (73501-9532)
PHONE..................580 248-1488
Larry Mellott, *Branch Mgr*
EMP: 132 **Privately Held**
WEB: www.apimix.net
SIC: 3069 Medical & laboratory rubber sundries & related products
PA: American Phoenix, Inc.
    5500 Wayzata Blvd # 1010
    Golden Valley MN 55416

(G-3888)
ANDERSON WELDING
1440 Nw 40th St (73505-3601)
PHONE..................580 355-9806
Kent Anderson, *Owner*
Gayle Anderson, *Principal*
EMP: 2
SALES (est): 51.4K **Privately Held**
SIC: 7692 Welding repair

(G-3889)
ANESTHESIA SERVICES
7602 Nw Micklegate Blvd (73505-4133)
PHONE..................580 536-7150
Beth Allgood, *Owner*
EMP: 1
SALES (est): 121.4K **Privately Held**
SIC: 3841 Anesthesia apparatus

(G-3890)
ANTHONY W LAYTON CPO
Also Called: Layton, Tony Clinic
15 Sw B Ave (73501-4006)
PHONE..................580 353-8885
Anthony W Layton, *Owner*
Nicole Barnes, *Med Doctor*
EMP: 7
SQ FT: 5,000
SALES (est): 519.8K **Privately Held**
SIC: 3842 5999 Limbs, artificial; braces, orthopedic; medical apparatus & supplies

(G-3891)
ARROW SIGN COMPANY INC
1344 Se 1st St (73501-5793)
PHONE..................580 353-2227
Brian K Jester, *President*
Jones Jester, *Corp Secy*
Stephen L Jester, *Vice Pres*
Bryan Jester, *Sales Staff*
EMP: 19 EST: 1956
SQ FT: 23,000
SALES: 2MM **Privately Held**
WEB: www.arrowsign.com
SIC: 3993 Signs, not made in custom sign painting shops

(G-3892)
ATLAS TUCK CONCRETE INC
Also Called: US Concrete
1601 S Sheridan (73501)
P.O. Box 7049 (73506-1049)
PHONE..................580 355-8241
Frank Walker, *Branch Mgr*
EMP: 13
SALES (corp-wide): 1.4B **Publicly Held**
WEB: www.us-concrete.com
SIC: 3273 Ready-mixed concrete

Lawton - Comanche County (G-3893)　　　GEOGRAPHIC SECTION

HQ: Atlas-Tuck Concrete, Inc.
2112 W Bois D Arc Ave
Duncan OK 73533
580 255-1716

(G-3893)
ATRUE INDUSTRIES LLC
7126 Nw Birch Pl (73505-4241)
PHONE..................800 782-5440
Curtis Williams, *Owner*
EMP: 2
SALES (est): 117.3K **Privately Held**
SIC: 3999 Manufacturing industries

(G-3894)
B & B HAYBEDS
1903 Ne 60th St (73507-9766)
PHONE..................580 357-5083
Wanda McKelvey, *Treasurer*
EMP: 3
SALES: 50K **Privately Held**
SIC: 2515 Mattresses & bedsprings

(G-3895)
B & L INDUSTRIES INC
2802 Nw Liberty Ave (73505-5224)
PHONE..................580 591-1880
Jerry Sivers, *Owner*
EMP: 3 EST: 1984
SALES (est): 236.3K **Privately Held**
SIC: 3999 Manufacturing industries

(G-3896)
BAR-S FOODS CO
802 Sw Goodyear Blvd (73505-9797)
PHONE..................580 510-3300
Don Bohnsack, *Branch Mgr*
Tammy Knizek, *Administration*
EMP: 290 **Privately Held**
SIC: 3556 2013 Meat processing machinery; sausages & other prepared meats
HQ: Bar-S Foods Co.
5090 N 40th St Ste 300
Phoenix AZ 85018
602 264-7272

(G-3897)
BERRY MACHINE & TOOL COMPANY
1002 Sw Goodyear Blvd (73505-9718)
PHONE..................580 536-4382
Darrell Berry, *President*
Judith L Berry, *Corp Secy*
Judith Berry, *Treasurer*
EMP: 2
SQ FT: 17,500
SALES (est): 229.2K **Privately Held**
SIC: 3599 Machine shop, jobbing & repair

(G-3898)
BLACKHAWK SAFETY LLC
129 Landon Ln (73507-9366)
PHONE..................580 574-1271
Dustin Hilliary,
Clayton Landers,
EMP: 5
SQ FT: 2,200
SALES (est): 197.7K **Privately Held**
SIC: 1389 Oil field services

(G-3899)
BOYLES & ASSOCIATES INC
1908 Sw F Ave (73501-4767)
P.O. Box 6594 (73506-0594)
PHONE..................580 353-7056
Mattie Boyles, *President*
Elaine Boyles, *Corp Secy*
Melodye Dees, *Vice Pres*
EMP: 8
SQ FT: 4,800
SALES (est): 1.4MM **Privately Held**
SIC: 1542 6552 1311 Commercial & office building contractors; subdividers & developers; crude petroleum production

(G-3900)
BRAD MCKINZIE
Also Called: Pro-Grass By University Center
902 Sw 38th St (73505-7021)
PHONE..................580 355-3810
EMP: 3
SALES (est): 200K **Privately Held**
SIC: 3999 Mfg Misc Products

(G-3901)
BRIMS & ACCESSORIES
3801 Nw Cache Rd Ste 33 (73505-3742)
PHONE..................580 357-2746
Rose Duckett, *President*
EMP: 2
SALES (est): 135.5K **Privately Held**
WEB: www.brimsandaccessories.com
SIC: 2389 Apparel & accessories

(G-3902)
C & J PRINTING CO
217 Sw C Ave (73501-4648)
PHONE..................580 355-3099
Clayton Snodgrass, *Owner*
Richard Matthys, *Owner*
EMP: 4
SQ FT: 3,600
SALES (est): 125K **Privately Held**
WEB: www.candjprinting.com
SIC: 2752 2759 2796 2791 Lithographing on metal; letterpress printing; platemaking services; typesetting; bookbinding & related work

(G-3903)
C D CONNECTIONS
Also Called: C D Exchange
2316 W Gore Blvd (73505-6313)
PHONE..................580 248-6410
Barbara Nottingham, *Owner*
EMP: 4
SALES (est): 100K **Privately Held**
SIC: 3679 5735 Liquid crystal displays (LCD); compact discs

(G-3904)
CLASSIC CARPETS LAWTON INC
1302 Sw Sheridan Rd (73505-8605)
P.O. Box 6642 (73506-0642)
PHONE..................580 713-0653
Francis Baxter, *President*
David Baxter, *Vice Pres*
EMP: 8
SQ FT: 2,500
SALES: 1.1MM **Privately Held**
SIC: 2273 3253 Carpets & rugs; ceramic wall & floor tile

(G-3905)
CLASSIC COLLECTN INTERIORS INC
Also Called: Classic Collection, The
838 Se 1st St (73501-2401)
P.O. Box 7573 (73506-1573)
PHONE..................580 351-0024
Cheri Harrison, *President*
EMP: 3
SQ FT: 2,000
SALES: 565K **Privately Held**
SIC: 7389 2591 Interior design services; mini blinds

(G-3906)
CLEAN CANVAS LASER TATTOO REMO
1301 Nw 40th St (73505-3656)
PHONE..................580 919-5466
EMP: 1
SALES (est): 46.5K **Privately Held**
SIC: 2211 Canvas

(G-3907)
CLEARCO WINDOW CLEANING LLC
201 Sw 46th St (73505-6841)
PHONE..................580 248-9547
Daremy Gleaves, *Principal*
EMP: 3
SALES (est): 225.1K **Privately Held**
WEB: www.clearcowindows.com
SIC: 7217 2391 7349 Carpet & upholstery cleaning; curtains & draperies; window cleaning

(G-3908)
CMG OPERATIONS LLC
8 Se Lee Blvd (73501-2469)
PHONE..................580 353-2835
EMP: 1 EST: 2011
SALES (est): 75K **Privately Held**
SIC: 3421 Mfg Cutlery

(G-3909)
COMANCHE NATION PUB INFO OFF
584 Nw Bingo Rd (73507-1214)
PHONE..................580 492-3381
Jolene Schonchin, *Director*
EMP: 4
SALES (est): 179.4K **Privately Held**
SIC: 2711 Newspapers, publishing & printing

(G-3910)
CONWAY CUSTOM MARBLE CO
202 Se Park Ave (73501-5433)
PHONE..................580 357-3757
Patrick Joe Conway Jr, *Owner*
Lowell Powell, *Plant Mgr*
EMP: 6
SQ FT: 5,000
SALES (est): 515.3K **Privately Held**
SIC: 3281 5713 5023 Marble, building: cut & shaped; floor covering stores; floor coverings

(G-3911)
COUNTY OF COMANCHE
Also Called: Comanche County Tag Agency
902 Sw 38th St (73505-7021)
PHONE..................580 355-3810
Pamela White, *Manager*
EMP: 5 **Privately Held**
SIC: 9621 6411 7299 2679 Motor vehicle licensing & inspection office, government; insurance agents, brokers & service; personal document & information services; tags, paper (unprinted): made from purchased paper
PA: County Of Comanche
315 Sw 5th St
Lawton OK 73501

(G-3912)
CP AEROSPACE LLC
2202 Se 165th St (73501-5807)
PHONE..................580 355-5064
Christopher Pittman, *Principal*
EMP: 2
SALES (est): 110.9K **Privately Held**
SIC: 3721 Aircraft

(G-3913)
CPLP LLC
Also Called: Henderhan Recognition Award
212 Se Park Ave (73501-5433)
P.O. Box 7272 (73506-1272)
PHONE..................580 355-5515
Sharon Henderhan, *Mng Member*
EMP: 7
SALES (est): 736.8K **Privately Held**
SIC: 2759 Commercial printing

(G-3914)
CUSTOM VINYL SIGNS BY CHAS
1722 Jesse L Davenport St (73501-7244)
PHONE..................580 351-4058
EMP: 1
SALES (est): 46K **Privately Held**
SIC: 3993 Signs & advertising specialties

(G-3915)
CUSTOM WOOD CREATIONS
507 Ne Carver Ave (73507-5912)
PHONE..................580 512-6994
EMP: 2 EST: 2012
SALES (est): 122.8K **Privately Held**
SIC: 2431 Millwork

(G-3916)
CUSTOM YARMUCK SCRAP PROC LLC
907 Sw Rr St (73501)
PHONE..................580 354-9134
Charles M Baker,
EMP: 6
SALES (est): 410K **Privately Held**
SIC: 2611 Pulp mills, mechanical & recycling processing

(G-3917)
DALE MILLER GROUP LLC (PA)
102 Se B Ave (73501-5442)
PHONE..................580 353-4600
Dale Miller, *Mng Member*
EMP: 4

SALES (est): 9MM **Privately Held**
SIC: 3441 Joists, open web steel: long-span series

(G-3918)
DEBBIE DO EMB & SCREEN PRTG
207 Sw H Ave (73501-5326)
PHONE..................580 353-2606
Debbie Levick, *Owner*
EMP: 4
SALES: 225K **Privately Held**
SIC: 7299 2395 Quilting for individuals; embroidery products, except schiffli machine

(G-3919)
DESIGNS BY LEX LLC
7 Sw D Ave (73501-4619)
PHONE..................580 280-2557
Alexsas Rhodes, *President*
EMP: 1
SALES (est): 62.9K **Privately Held**
SIC: 2099 8742 Food preparations; planning consultant

(G-3920)
DUNLAW OPTICAL LABS INC
1313 Sw A Ave (73501-3895)
P.O. Box 314 (73502-0314)
PHONE..................580 355-8410
Dennis Foster, *President*
Dr John Barnes Jr, *Vice Pres*
Dr Robert Miller, *Treasurer*
Dr Donald C Rice, *Admin Sec*
EMP: 19
SQ FT: 3,000
SALES (est): 2.1MM
SALES (corp-wide): 1.7MM **Privately Held**
SIC: 5048 3851 3229 Ophthalmic goods; ophthalmic goods; pressed & blown glass
HQ: Essilor Laboratories Of America, Inc.
13515 N Stemmons Fwy
Dallas TX 75234
972 241-4141

(G-3921)
DYNOMITE CUSTOM SCREENS LLC
1421 Nw Great Plains Blvd E (73505-2843)
PHONE..................844 396-6648
Steven White,
EMP: 1
SQ FT: 250
SALES: 245K **Privately Held**
SIC: 3442 Screens, window, metal

(G-3922)
EPPINGERS
2106 One Half Nw Fort Sil (73507)
PHONE..................580 248-1442
EMP: 1 EST: 2010
SALES (est): 54K **Privately Held**
SIC: 3421 Mfg Cutlery

(G-3923)
ERGON A E LAWTON
9301 Sw Koch St (73505-9693)
PHONE..................580 536-0098
Sean Randall, *Principal*
EMP: 3
SALES (est): 299.8K **Privately Held**
WEB: www.ergonasphalt.com
SIC: 2951 Asphalt paving mixtures & blocks

(G-3924)
EVANS & ASSOC UTILITY SVCS
2208 Sw F Ave (73501-4766)
PHONE..................580 351-1800
EMP: 3
SALES (est): 99.1K **Privately Held**
SIC: 7692 1794 1623 Welding repair; excavation work; underground utilities contractor

(G-3925)
FAIRWIND LLC
6862 Nw Meers Porter Hl (73507-7706)
PHONE..................580 492-5209
Danny Tendall, *Business Anlyst*
Sonia Whitewolf, *Office Mgr*
Brett Bain, *Mng Member*
Lance Bowman, *Officer*

GEOGRAPHIC SECTION

Lawton - Comanche County (G-3956)

Brian Edwards,
EMP: 20 **EST:** 2008
SQ FT: 10,000
SALES: 100K **Privately Held**
WEB: www.fairwindllc.com
SIC: 7699 5169 2869 4939 Cleaning services; industrial chemicals; industrial organic chemicals; combination utilities

(G-3926)
FANCY STITCH
1421 Nw Great Plains Blvd A (73505-2856)
PHONE..................580 699-2112
Yong Trisdale, *Principal*
EMP: 1
SALES (est): 100.9K **Privately Held**
SIC: 2395 Embroidery products, except schiffli machine

(G-3927)
FASTSIGNS OF LAWTON
301 Se Wallock St (73501-5449)
PHONE..................580 595-9101
EMP: 1
SALES (est): 55K **Privately Held**
SIC: 3993 Signs & advertising specialties

(G-3928)
FATUTYI ADESHOLA
7301 Sw Lee Blvd Apt 602 (73505-0428)
PHONE..................785 424-4208
Adeshola Fatutyi, *Owner*
EMP: 1
SALES: 5K **Privately Held**
SIC: 2676 Napkins, sanitary: made from purchased paper

(G-3929)
FINITY ENTERPRISES INC
Also Called: Finity Marketing Group
605 Sw E Ave (73501-4511)
PHONE..................580 699-2640
Chuck Morgan, *President*
EMP: 3
SALES (est): 150.5K **Privately Held**
WEB: www.finitydigitalmarketing.com
SIC: 2741

(G-3930)
FRENCH OIL
2401 Se 45th St (73501-9454)
PHONE..................580 248-3131
M Blake French, *Partner*
Therman French, *Partner*
EMP: 3
SALES (est): 476.6K **Privately Held**
SIC: 1311 Crude petroleum & natural gas

(G-3931)
FROG PRINTING & AWARDS CTR LLC
1005 Sw F Ave (73501-4548)
PHONE..................580 678-1114
Robert S Henderson, *Mng Member*
EMP: 3 **EST:** 2016
SALES (est): 107.2K **Privately Held**
WEB: www.frogprintingandawardcenter.com
SIC: 2759 3499 2851 Screen printing; trophies, metal, except silver; vinyl coatings, strippable

(G-3932)
FT SILL TEES & EMBROIDERY
2609 Nw Sheridan Rd (73505-2217)
PHONE..................580 248-8484
Kevin Quarterman, *Principal*
EMP: 2
SALES (est): 91.2K **Privately Held**
SIC: 2395 Embroidery products, except schiffli machine; embroidery & art needlework

(G-3933)
FUEL INC
1620 Se Indiana Ave (73501-8345)
PHONE..................580 583-5202
Douglas Christian, *Principal*
EMP: 3
SALES (est): 226.1K **Privately Held**
SIC: 2869 Fuels

(G-3934)
GAME KING
2332 W Gore Blvd (73505-6313)
PHONE..................580 250-0707
Brent John, *Owner*
EMP: 6
SQ FT: 2,000
SALES (est): 439.3K **Privately Held**
SIC: 3944 5731 Video game machines, except coin-operated; video recorders, players, disc players & accessories

(G-3935)
GOODWILL INDUSTRIES OF SW
1210 Sw Summit Ave (73501-4900)
PHONE..................580 355-2163
James Cruz, *President*
EMP: 2
SALES (est): 279.2K **Privately Held**
SIC: 3999 Manufacturing industries

(G-3936)
GRACE POWER LLC
Also Called: Red Wolf Customs
8645 Nw 4 Mile Rd (73507-8145)
PHONE..................512 228-9049
Jessica Wolf,
EMP: 2
SQ FT: 1,100
SALES (est): 103.4K **Privately Held**
SIC: 7699 3613 4911 Precision instrument repair; control panels, electric; distribution boards, electric; distribution, electric power

(G-3937)
GUARDIAN INTERLOCK OF UTAH
4120 Nw Currell Dr (73505-4944)
PHONE..................580 357-8583
Ted Mason, *President*
EMP: 3
SALES (corp-wide): 412K **Privately Held**
SIC: 3711 5012 Cars, electric, assembly of; automobiles & other motor vehicles
PA: Guardian Interlock Of Utah
7163 S 2340 E
Salt Lake City UT 84121
800 499-0994

(G-3938)
H G JENKINS CONSTRUCTION LLC
1630 Sw Railroad St (73501-8526)
P.O. Box 706 (73502-0706)
PHONE..................580 355-9822
James Jenkins, *President*
Sharon Jenkins, *Treasurer*
EMP: 30 **EST:** 1963
SQ FT: 3,000
SALES (est): 6.3MM **Privately Held**
WEB: www.hgjenkinsconstruction.com
SIC: 1611 1794 7353 3531 Highway & street paving contractor; excavation & grading, building construction; heavy construction equipment rental; asphalt plant, including gravel-mix type

(G-3939)
HARRY A LIPPERT JR
Also Called: Eagle Web Design
1717 Nw Ozmun Ave (73507-1046)
P.O. Box 6073 (73506-0073)
PHONE..................512 705-1248
Harry Lippert, *Owner*
EMP: 3 **EST:** 2014
SALES (est): 109.3K **Privately Held**
SIC: 7371 1522 3172 7389 Custom computer programming services; residential construction; leather cases;

(G-3940)
IMPERIAL INC
815 Se 2nd St (73501-2412)
PHONE..................580 357-8300
Paul Tins, *President*
EMP: 17
SALES (corp-wide): 78.3MM **Privately Held**
SIC: 2095 5962 Roasted coffee; sandwich & hot food vending machines
PA: Imperial, L.L.C.
2020 N Mingo Rd
Tulsa OK 74116
918 437-1300

(G-3941)
INDIAN NATIONS FIBEROPTICS INC
Also Called: Indian Nations Fiber Optics
9 Sw 21st St (73501-4109)
PHONE..................580 355-2300
Jack Hestor, *Manager*
EMP: 1
SALES (est): 79.7K **Privately Held**
SIC: 3661 7359 Fiber optics communications equipment; mobile communication equipment rental
PA: Indian Nations Fiberoptics, Inc.
124 W Vinita Ave
Sulphur OK 73086

(G-3942)
IRON COWBOY WELDING LLC
25 Baylee Creek Cir (73501-5565)
PHONE..................580 301-3423
EMP: 1
SALES (est): 25K **Privately Held**
SIC: 7692 Welding repair

(G-3943)
J & W ELECTRIC MOTOR COMPANY
19 Se F Ave (73501-5411)
P.O. Box 503 (73502-0503)
PHONE..................580 357-7504
John Bennight, *Owner*
EMP: 4
SQ FT: 4,500
SALES: 242K **Privately Held**
SIC: 7694 Electric motor repair

(G-3944)
J B GRANITE COUNTERTOPS
2413 Nw 28th St (73505-1924)
PHONE..................580 771-6894
EMP: 2
SALES (est): 62.6K **Privately Held**
SIC: 3281 Granite, cut & shaped

(G-3945)
JMZ SOFTWARE LLC
6926 Sw Forest Ave (73505-6630)
PHONE..................580 284-9551
James Taylor, *Principal*
EMP: 2
SALES (est): 124.3K **Privately Held**
SIC: 7372 Prepackaged software

(G-3946)
JOHNSONM3 LLC
Also Called: Happy Carpet Cleaning
6732 Nw Eisenhower Dr (73505-5306)
PHONE..................580 353-5550
Lynn Johnson,
EMP: 3
SALES (est): 75.6K **Privately Held**
SIC: 7217 2842 Carpet & furniture cleaning on location; specialty cleaning preparations

(G-3947)
K E FISCHER LLC
2512 Sw 38th St (73505-8431)
P.O. Box 2428 (73502-2428)
PHONE..................580 353-2862
Heinrich Holzmann, *CEO*
Simone Theis, *CFO*
▲ **EMP:** 8
SQ FT: 2,000
SALES (est): 1.1MM **Privately Held**
SIC: 3545 5084 7629 Cutting tools for machine tools; industrial machinery & equipment; electrical repair shops

(G-3948)
K-DUB LLC
Also Called: Lawton Ice Co
106 Se D Ave (73501-5477)
PHONE..................580 353-6899
Kelly Walker,
Kent Walker,
EMP: 6
SQ FT: 3,500
SALES (est): 240K **Privately Held**
SIC: 5199 2097 5999 Ice, manufactured or natural; manufactured ice; ice

(G-3949)
KIMBRO FURNITURE LLC
1303 Ne 75th St (73507-9743)
PHONE..................580 351-7304
EMP: 2 **EST:** 2017
SALES (est): 90.4K **Privately Held**
SIC: 2599 Furniture & fixtures

(G-3950)
KINGDOM PRINTING
1328 Nw Elm Ave (73507-5211)
PHONE..................580 512-3789
Jesi Lemos, *Principal*
EMP: 2 **Privately Held**
SIC: 2752 Commercial printing, lithographic

(G-3951)
KP DESIGNS LLC
1521 Nw 31st St (73505-3882)
PHONE..................865 776-7769
Crystal Kaye Green, *Owner*
EMP: 1
SALES (est): 37.5K **Privately Held**
SIC: 2741 Miscellaneous publishing

(G-3952)
L & L MACHINE SHOP
Also Called: Joanie's Upholstery
2802 E Gore Blvd (73501-6106)
PHONE..................580 357-3560
Pat Landoll, *Partner*
Laura Landoll, *Partner*
Paul Landoll, *Partner*
Peter Landoll, *Partner*
EMP: 4
SQ FT: 2,880
SALES (est): 429.8K **Privately Held**
SIC: 3599 7641 Machine shop, jobbing & repair; reupholstery

(G-3953)
L W DUNCAN PRINTING INC
Also Called: Lw Duncan Printing
1312 Nw Lawton Ave (73507-4056)
PHONE..................580 355-6229
L W Duncan, *President*
Jessica Duncan, *Vice Pres*
Mike Duncan, *Vice Pres*
Barbara Duncan, *Treasurer*
EMP: 8 **EST:** 1953
SQ FT: 4,500
SALES (est): 975.3K **Privately Held**
SIC: 2791 2789 2752 Typesetting; bookbinding & related work; lithographing on metal

(G-3954)
LAWTON BRACE & LIMB CO INC
Also Called: Bill's Family Shoe Store
2724 W Gore Blvd (73505-6380)
PHONE..................580 353-5525
Josephine Layton, *President*
Harry W Layton, *Treasurer*
EMP: 3
SQ FT: 3,200
SALES (est): 328.3K **Privately Held**
WEB: www.ladonsys.com
SIC: 5999 3842 Orthopedic & prosthesis applications; orthopedic appliances

(G-3955)
LAWTON COUNCIL OF THE BLIND
7127 Nw Ash Ave (73505-4504)
PHONE..................580 536-1650
EMP: 1
SALES (est): 57.3K **Privately Held**
SIC: 2591 Window blinds

(G-3956)
LAWTON MACHINE & WELDING WORKS
Also Called: Lawton Machine and Wldg Work
611 Se 2nd St (73501-2408)
P.O. Box 147 (73502-0147)
PHONE..................580 355-4678
Carol Knowles, *President*
Robert Knowels, *President*
Robert Knowles, *Vice Pres*
EMP: 6 **EST:** 1947
SQ FT: 5,000
SALES (est): 636.3K **Privately Held**
SIC: 3599 7692 5085 Machine shop, jobbing & repair; welding repair; bearings

Lawton - Comanche County (G-3957)   GEOGRAPHIC SECTION

(G-3957)
LAWTON MEAT PROCESSING
603 Se F Ave (73501-5489)
P.O. Box 441 (73502-0441)
PHONE................................580 353-6448
Cecilia Scott, *Owner*
EMP: 4
SALES: 150K **Privately Held**
SIC: 2011 Meat packing plants

(G-3958)
LAWTON MEDIA INC
21 Nw 44th St (73505-6321)
P.O. Box 2069 (73502-2069)
PHONE................................580 355-8920
James Cottingham, *CFO*
Mike Owensby, *Manager*
EMP: 135
SALES (est): 4.3MM **Privately Held**
SIC: 2711 Newspapers, publishing & printing

(G-3959)
LAWTON NEWSPAPERS LLC
Also Called: Lawton Constitution, The
102 Sw 3rd St (73501-4031)
P.O. Box 2069 (73502-2069)
PHONE................................580 585-5115
Michael Cross, *Superintendent*
Kayla Durham, *Executive*
David Stringer,
Brad W Burgess,
EMP: 65 **EST:** 1910
SQ FT: 90,000
SALES (est): 9.9MM
SALES (corp-wide): 138.9MM **Privately Held**
WEB: www.swoknews.com
SIC: 2711 Newspapers, publishing & printing
PA: Southern Newspapers, Inc.
5701 Woodway Dr Ste 131
Houston TX 77057
713 266-5481

(G-3960)
LAWTON RC RACEWAY LLC
7807 Se Lee Blvd (73501-5978)
PHONE................................580 595-0814
Ian Milton Jefferson, *Principal*
EMP: 4
SALES (est): 348.8K **Privately Held**
SIC: 3644 Raceways

(G-3961)
LAWTON TRANSIT MIX INC (HQ)
2208 Sw F Ave (73501-4766)
P.O. Box 144 (73502-0144)
PHONE................................580 353-6900
Linda J Brown, *President*
Steve Rohde, *Vice Pres*
EMP: 25 **EST:** 1946
SQ FT: 25,000
SALES (est): 2.9MM
SALES (corp-wide): 100.1MM **Privately Held**
WEB: www.evans-assoc.com
SIC: 3273 5032 Ready-mixed concrete; sand, construction; gravel
PA: Evans & Associates Enterprises, Inc.
3320 N 14th St
Ponca City OK 74601
580 765-6693

(G-3962)
LAWTON WINDOW CO INC
Also Called: Rusty's Ornamental Iron, Co
604 Sw Sheridan Rd (73505-1527)
PHONE................................580 353-4655
Lance Butemeyer, *President*
Brad Butemeyer, *Vice Pres*
Maris Butemeyer, *Admin Sec*
EMP: 3 **EST:** 1956
SALES (est): 455.4K **Privately Held**
SIC: 3442 3312 1793 1751 Screens, window, metal; storm doors or windows, metal; bar, rod & wire products; glass & glazing work; carpentry work

(G-3963)
LAZY B WELDING AND MET ART LLC
4108 Nw Currell Dr (73505-4944)
PHONE................................580 512-8778
EMP: 2 **EST:** 2018

SALES (est): 43.2K **Privately Held**
SIC: 7692 Welding repair

(G-3964)
LLC SEARCHLIGHT
5802 Nw Elm Ave (73505-4624)
PHONE................................580 699-2971
EMP: 2 **EST:** 2015
SALES (est): 88.3K **Privately Held**
SIC: 3648 Searchlights

(G-3965)
LOCKHEED MARTIN CORPORATION
528 Sw D Ave 402 (73501)
PHONE................................580 357-5060
EMP: 2
SALES (est): 86K **Publicly Held**
SIC: 3721 Aircraft
PA: Lockheed Martin Corporation
6801 Rockledge Dr
Bethesda MD 20817

(G-3966)
LOCKHEED MARTIN CORPORATION
1614 W Gore Blvd 2 (73501-3611)
PHONE................................580 355-0581
John E Donahue, *Manager*
EMP: 2 **Publicly Held**
SIC: 3812 Search & navigation equipment
PA: Lockheed Martin Corporation
6801 Rockledge Dr
Bethesda MD 20817

(G-3967)
M SHAWN ANDERSON RPH PC
5366 Nw Cache Rd Ste 1 (73505-3353)
PHONE................................580 595-9500
Shawn Anderson, *Principal*
EMP: 8
SALES (est): 1MM **Privately Held**
WEB: www.andersonpharmacyandaccents.com
SIC: 2836 Vaccines & other immunizing products

(G-3968)
MADDEN STEEL BUILDINGS LAWTON
502 Sw Mckinley Ave (73501-8534)
PHONE................................580 357-1699
Scott Westfall, *President*
Luann Westfall, *Treasurer*
EMP: 5
SQ FT: 4,000
SALES (est): 495.2K **Privately Held**
SIC: 1541 3448 3443 Industrial buildings, new construction; prefabricated metal buildings; fabricated plate work (boiler shop)

(G-3969)
MATHESON TRI-GAS INC
1302 Sw 112th St (73505-9566)
PHONE................................580 536-2965
James Marshall, *Branch Mgr*
EMP: 11 **Privately Held**
WEB: www.mathesongas.com
SIC: 5084 2813 Welding machinery & equipment; safety equipment; nitrogen
HQ: Matheson Tri-Gas, Inc.
150 Allen Rd Ste 302
Basking Ridge NJ 07920
908 991-9200

(G-3970)
MILLER WELDING & SUPPLY
4700 Nw Wolf Rd (73507-8836)
PHONE................................580 492-5464
Dale Miller, *Owner*
Yolanda Miller, *Owner*
EMP: 6
SALES (est): 353K **Privately Held**
SIC: 3441 Fabricated structural metal

(G-3971)
MILLERS MARBLE AND GRANITE
19106 Se Woodlawn Rd (73501-5653)
PHONE................................580 357-1348
EMP: 1
SALES (est): 36.3K **Privately Held**
SIC: 3281 Mfg Cut Stone/Products

(G-3972)
MO PUBLISHING LLC
30 Nw Sandy Trail Ln (73505-9558)
PHONE................................580 284-3719
EMP: 1
SALES (est): 37.5K **Privately Held**
SIC: 2741 Miscellaneous publishing

(G-3973)
MONOGRAMS ELITE INC
2422 Sw Jefferson Ave (73505-8612)
PHONE................................580 353-1635
Ima J Scruggs, *President*
Richard Scruggs, *Vice Pres*
EMP: 2
SQ FT: 2,000
SALES (est): 35K **Privately Held**
SIC: 7299 2262 2395 Stitching services; screen printing: manmade fiber & silk broadwoven fabrics; embroidery products, except schiffli machine

(G-3974)
MULBERRY TREE GRAPHICS
5527 Nw Eisenhower Dr (73505-5826)
PHONE................................580 248-3194
EMP: 1
SALES (est): 34.4K **Privately Held**
SIC: 2395 3999 3952 Pleating/Stitching Services Mfg Misc Products Mfg Lead Pencils/Art Goods

(G-3975)
NACOLS JEWELRY
3801 Nw Cache Rd Ste 33 (73505-3742)
PHONE................................580 355-4280
EMP: 8
SALES (est): 607.3K **Privately Held**
SIC: 5944 7631 3479 Ret Jewelry Watch/Clock/Jewelry Repair Coating/Engraving Service

(G-3976)
NORTHROP CORP
1 Sw 11th St (73501-3842)
PHONE................................580 536-9191
Tom Vise, *President*
Meredith Mazza, *President*
EMP: 1
SALES (est): 137.2K **Privately Held**
SIC: 3812 Defense systems & equipment

(G-3977)
O H S N INC
201 Se Lee Blvd (73501-2474)
P.O. Box 2037 (73502-2037)
PHONE................................580 248-1299
EMP: 48
SQ FT: 15,000
SALES (est): 3.7MM **Privately Held**
SIC: 2011 Meat Packing Plant

(G-3978)
OLD TOWN N CANDLES LAWTON OK
611 Nw Bell Ave (73507-6834)
PHONE................................580 678-7608
EMP: 1
SALES (est): 39.6K **Privately Held**
SIC: 3999 Candles

(G-3979)
OMER DISTRIBUTORS LLC
2323 Nw Nottingham Rd (73505-3105)
PHONE................................580 695-3211
Da Jeong Choi, *CFO*
Da Jeong Cook Choi, *CFO*
EMP: 1
SALES (est): 39.3K **Privately Held**
SIC: 7389 5199 3949 ; general merchandise, non-durable; sporting & athletic goods

(G-3980)
PEABODYS PRINTING & A BRUSH SP
Also Called: Peabodys Prtg & Airbrush Sp
709 Sw Lee Blvd (73501-5714)
PHONE................................580 248-8317
Marline Simington, *Owner*
Lamarr Simington, *Owner*
EMP: 2

SALES: 24K **Privately Held**
SIC: 2759 2796 2791 2789 Screen printing; platemaking services; typesetting; bookbinding & related work; automotive & apparel trimmings; chart & graph design

(G-3981)
PEARL PETROLEUM INC
3202 Se 165th St (73501-5821)
PHONE................................580 355-6477
Leonard Middleton, *President*
Valerie Middleton, *Corp Secy*
EMP: 2
SALES (est): 197.9K **Privately Held**
SIC: 1381 Drilling oil & gas wells

(G-3982)
PEPPER CREEK FARMS INC
1002 Sw Ard St (73505-9660)
PHONE................................580 536-1300
Susan Weissman, *President*
Marshall Weissman, *Vice Pres*
▲ **EMP:** 6
SQ FT: 5,000
SALES (est): 687.6K **Privately Held**
SIC: 2033 2035 2099 2087 Jams, jellies & preserves: packaged in cans, jars, etc.; pickles, sauces & salad dressings; food preparations; flavoring extracts & syrups

(G-3983)
PEPSI-COLA METRO BTLG CO INC
209 Se Simpson St (73501-5402)
PHONE................................580 585-6281
Joe Dabney, *Manager*
EMP: 42
SALES (corp-wide): 67.1B **Publicly Held**
SIC: 2086 Carbonated soft drinks, bottled & canned
HQ: Pepsi-Cola Metropolitan Bottling Company, Inc.
1111 Westchester Ave
White Plains NY 10604
914 767-6000

(G-3984)
POLISH KITCHEN LLC
2801 Se 165th St (73501-5808)
PHONE................................580 583-5970
Claude Lamoreux, *Mng Member*
EMP: 4 **EST:** 2017
SALES (est): 116.1K **Privately Held**
SIC: 2032 Chinese foods: packaged in cans, jars, etc.

(G-3985)
PRO-FEIL MKTG SOLUTIONS LLC
301 Se Wallock St (73501-5449)
P.O. Box 3361 (73502-3361)
PHONE................................580 595-9101
Mathew Feil, *Mng Member*
EMP: 9
SQ FT: 2,880
SALES (est): 800K **Privately Held**
SIC: 3993 Signs & advertising specialties; electric signs; advertising artwork

(G-3986)
PROUD VETERANS INTL LTD
Also Called: Pvintl
2325 Sw Pennsylvania Ave (73505-0935)
P.O. Box 478, Maize KS (67101-0478)
PHONE................................316 209-8701
EMP: 9
SALES (est): 401.8K **Privately Held**
SIC: 5063 1793 3842 Whol Electrical Equip Glass/Glazing Contractor Mfg Surgical Appliances

(G-3987)
R & J ALUMINUM PRODUCTS
Also Called: A & A Aluminum
1415 Nw Taylor Ave (73503-7871)
PHONE................................580 355-1809
Kenney Hinkle, *Partner*
Mable Hinkle, *Partner*
EMP: 3
SALES (est): 40K **Privately Held**
SIC: 1799 1761 1751 3444 Awning installation; gutter & downspout contractor; siding contractor; window & door (prefabricated) installation; sheet metalwork

GEOGRAPHIC SECTION
Lawton - Comanche County (G-4017)

(G-3988)
R MEYERS ENTERPRISES
2402 Sw Lee Blvd Unit 2 (73505-8309)
PHONE.....................580 917-7554
Richard Meyers, *Owner*
EMP: 1
SALES: 92K **Privately Held**
SIC: 3843 Dental equipment & supplies

(G-3989)
RAYTHEON COMPANY
1 Sw 11th St Ste 290 (73501-3850)
PHONE.....................580 351-6966
Donna McCullough, *Branch Mgr*
EMP: 132
SALES (corp-wide): 77B **Publicly Held**
SIC: 3812 Radar systems & equipment
HQ: Raytheon Company
870 Winter St
Waltham MA 02451
781 522-3000

(G-3990)
RED FALCON LLC
6302 Sw Oakmont (73505-9024)
PHONE.....................580 647-2152
Jesse Cross, *President*
EMP: 2
SALES (est): 90.2K **Privately Held**
SIC: 3721 Aircraft

(G-3991)
RED LINE WELDING AND SERVICES
2395 Se 45th St (73501-6509)
PHONE.....................580 591-3162
EMP: 1
SALES (est): 50.1K **Privately Held**
SIC: 7692 Welding repair

(G-3992)
REDNECK CANDLES AND GIFTS
6908 Nw Sprucewood Dr (73505-5314)
PHONE.....................405 492-8987
Sara Williams, *Principal*
EMP: 2
SALES (est): 48K **Privately Held**
SIC: 3999 Candles

(G-3993)
REPUBLIC PAPERBOARD CO LLC
8801 Sw Lee Blvd (73505-9764)
PHONE.....................580 510-2200
Lisa McGregor, *President*
Daniel Frenette,
Brian Sibley,
▲ **EMP:** 120
SQ FT: 500,000
SALES (est): 48.4MM
SALES (corp-wide): 1.3B **Publicly Held**
SIC: 2631 Paperboard mills
PA: Eagle Materials Inc.
5960 Berkshire Ln Ste 900
Dallas TX 75225
214 432-2000

(G-3994)
RIGHT MIX
12 Sw River Bend Rd (73505-9582)
PHONE.....................580 704-8904
Carlo Messina, *Principal*
EMP: 2
SALES (est): 243.8K **Privately Held**
SIC: 3273 Ready-mixed concrete

(G-3995)
RITA S NICAR
10956 Nw 4 Mile Rd (73507-8814)
PHONE.....................580 492-4521
Rita Nicar, *Owner*
EMP: 1
SALES (est): 22K **Privately Held**
SIC: 3942 7389 Dolls & stuffed toys;

(G-3996)
SEMMATERIALS LP
9301 Sw Koch St (73505-9693)
PHONE.....................580 536-0098
Bobby Moore, *Branch Mgr*
EMP: 7 **Publicly Held**
SIC: 2951 Asphalt paving mixtures & blocks
HQ: Semmaterials, L.P.
6520 S Yale Ave Ste 700
Tulsa OK 74136
918 524-8100

(G-3997)
SIGNS BY DALE INC
202 Se B Ave (73501-5440)
PHONE.....................479 518-3744
Dale L Robinson, *Owner*
EMP: 4
SALES (est): 299.7K **Privately Held**
SIC: 3993 Signs & advertising specialties

(G-3998)
SILVER-LINE PLASTICS CORP
8801 Sw Neal Blvd (73505-9583)
PHONE.....................828 252-8755
Steven Mock, *Mfg Staff*
Randy Rutledge, *Manager*
Tony Morton, *Technology*
EMP: 31
SALES (corp-wide): 155.7MM **Privately Held**
WEB: www.slpipe.com
SIC: 3084 Plastics pipe
PA: Silver-Line Plastics Corp
900 Riverside Dr
Asheville NC 28804
828 252-8755

(G-3999)
SMEAC GROUP INTERNATIONAL LLC
121 Melodie Ln (73507-7162)
PHONE.....................580 574-4092
Jon Peters, *Owner*
EMP: 2
SALES (est): 79.1K **Privately Held**
SIC: 1389 8741 7376 0782 Grading oil & gas well foundations; office management; computer facilities management; lawn & garden services; data processing & preparation

(G-4000)
SOUTHERN PLAINS CABLE LLC
22937 State Highway 58 (73507-6008)
P.O. Box 165, Medicine Park (73557-0165)
PHONE.....................580 529-5000
Dean Pennello, *CFO*
Dustin Hilliary,
EMP: 2
SALES (est): 224.4K **Privately Held**
SIC: 3663 Radio & TV communications equipment

(G-4001)
SOUTHWEST READY MIX (PA)
800 Se 1st St (73501-2401)
PHONE.....................580 248-4709
JC Grayson,
EMP: 10
SQ FT: 40,000
SALES: 13.7MM **Privately Held**
SIC: 3273 Ready-mixed concrete

(G-4002)
SOUTHWEST READY MIX
Also Called: Southwest Readymix
8 Se I Ave (73501-2449)
PHONE.....................580 355-2093
Mitchell Young, *Manager*
EMP: 25
SALES (corp-wide): 13.7MM **Privately Held**
SIC: 3273 5211 Ready-mixed concrete; masonry materials & supplies
PA: Southwest Ready Mix
800 Se 1st St
Lawton OK 73501
580 248-4709

(G-4003)
SRIFUSION LLC
5406 Nw Wilfred Dr (73505-3127)
P.O. Box 7751 (73506-1751)
PHONE.....................774 238-7466
Vidyasagar Katta,
EMP: 3

SALES (est): 129.5K **Privately Held**
SIC: 7379 7372 7371 Computer related consulting services; prepackaged software; business oriented computer software; computer software systems analysis & design, custom; computer software development & applications; software programming applications

(G-4004)
STANTONS APPAREL INC
Also Called: Stanton's Custom Prints
3708 Sw J Ave (73505-6900)
P.O. Box 1433 (73502-1433)
PHONE.....................580 353-1777
Stanton Ward, *President*
EMP: 6
SQ FT: 5,000
SALES: 300K **Privately Held**
SIC: 2759 Screen printing

(G-4005)
STERLING PROPERTIES
9910 E Gore Blvd (73501-9601)
PHONE.....................580 357-6095
John Sterling, *President*
EMP: 2
SALES: 120K **Privately Held**
SIC: 2992 Lubricating oils

(G-4006)
SUFRANK CORPORATION
Also Called: Larrance Steel & Door
102 Se B Ave (73505-5442)
PHONE.....................580 353-4600
Frank Parrish, *President*
EMP: 40 **EST:** 1920
SQ FT: 44,200
SALES (est): 9MM **Privately Held**
WEB: www.larrancesteel.com
SIC: 3441 3443 5031 Joists, open web steel; long-span series; tanks, lined: metal plate; doors & windows
PA: The Dale Miller Group Llc
102 Se B Ave
Lawton OK 73501
580 353-4600

(G-4007)
SULLIVANS GRADING & SOD
4728 Se Tinney Rd (73501-5593)
PHONE.....................580 591-2868
Russell Sullivan,
Caresse Sullivan,
EMP: 2 **EST:** 2014
SALES (est): 201K **Privately Held**
SIC: 1629 3523 7389 Land leveling; grounds mowing equipment;

(G-4008)
SUSAN SECOR
Also Called: Susan's Framing
1609 Sw Sandra Cir (73505-8503)
PHONE.....................580 510-0060
Susan Secor, *Owner*
EMP: 2
SALES (est): 81.8K **Privately Held**
SIC: 5999 3999 Art, picture frames & decorations; framed artwork

(G-4009)
SYNERGY MAINTENANCE LLC
6104 Nw Ferris Ave (73505-5702)
PHONE.....................580 574-7355
Sang Lee, *Business Mgr*
Jeong Lee,
EMP: 2
SALES (est): 148.8K **Privately Held**
SIC: 2311 2321 2322 2325 Men's & boys' uniforms; uniform shirts: made from purchased materials; nightwear, men's & boys': from purchased materials; underwear, men's & boys': made from purchased materials; slacks, dress: men's, youths' & boys'; trousers, dress (separate): men's, youths' & boys'; work uniforms; medical & hospital uniforms, men's; knickers, dress (separate): men's & boys'; shirt & slack suits: men's, youths' & boys'

(G-4010)
T & G CONSTRUCTION INC
800 Se 1st St (73502-2498)
P.O. Box 1557 (73502-1557)
PHONE.....................580 355-6655

John C Grayson, *President*
Jodie Reece, *Vice Pres*
Angela Reece, *Admin Sec*
EMP: 110
SQ FT: 4,000
SALES: 38.1MM **Privately Held**
SIC: 1611 2951 4212 5032 Highway & street paving contractor; asphalt & asphaltic paving mixtures (not from refineries); local trucking, without storage; sand, construction; gravel

(G-4011)
T2T STORM SHELTERS
2201 Se Flower Mound Rd (73501-6315)
PHONE.....................580 512-4890
Jared Turner, *Principal*
EMP: 2
SALES (est): 114.6K **Privately Held**
SIC: 3531 Backhoes

(G-4012)
TEXOMA ORTHTICS PRSTHTICS PLLC
Also Called: Texoma O & P
1915 W Gore Blvd Ste 1 (73501-3661)
PHONE.....................580 699-8690
Nicholas Chelenza III, *Partner*
Connie Chelenza,
EMP: 3
SALES (est): 308.8K **Privately Held**
WEB: www.texomaoandp.com
SIC: 5999 3842 Artificial limbs; supports: abdominal, ankle, arch, kneecap, etc.

(G-4013)
TKING ENERGY SOLUTIONS LLC
671 Ne Addiebeth Rd (73507)
PHONE.....................740 827-4599
FL Pete Evans, *Accountant*
Justin Evans, *Sales Mgr*
Charles Zukerman, *Manager*
Tyler Zukerman,
EMP: 1 **EST:** 2018
SALES (est): 41K **Privately Held**
SIC: 1389 Construction, repair & dismantling services

(G-4014)
TRAILING EDGE TECHNOLOGIES
Also Called: Sounds Impossible
7109 Nw Birch Pl (73505-4515)
PHONE.....................580 536-0559
Scott Hoffman, *President*
Mark Norman, *Vice Pres*
Peggy Hoffman, *Treasurer*
EMP: 3
SALES (est): 222.5K **Privately Held**
WEB: www.tetinc.net
SIC: 3648 Stage lighting equipment

(G-4015)
TWISTED OKIE WELDING LLC
2302 Ne 9th St (73507-1801)
PHONE.....................580 335-1494
Gage Calvin,
Cole Powers,
EMP: 2
SALES (est): 40.6K **Privately Held**
SIC: 7692 7389 Automotive welding;

(G-4016)
ULTRA TECH ULTRA TECH
105 Sw 2nd St (73501-4028)
PHONE.....................580 351-1220
Cristy Chancler, *Owner*
EMP: 2 **EST:** 2018
SALES (est): 69.9K **Privately Held**
SIC: 3471 Plating & polishing

(G-4017)
VICS TELECOMMUNICATIONS
387 Sunset St (73507-8849)
PHONE.....................580 512-0313
Vic Menendez Jr, *Partner*
EMP: 2
SALES: 50K **Privately Held**
SIC: 3661 Telephone & telegraph apparatus

Lawton - Comanche County (G-4018) GEOGRAPHIC SECTION

(G-4018)
WALKERS POWDER COATING LLC
804 Se 135th St (73501-9559)
PHONE...................580 355-5000
Clint Walker, *Owner*
Hank Walker, *Principal*
EMP: 1
SALES (est): 70K **Privately Held**
SIC: 3399 3479 Powder, metal; etching & engraving

(G-4019)
WALKERS SIGN COMPANY
804 Se 135th St (73501-9559)
PHONE...................580 353-7446
Clint Walker, *Owner*
EMP: 1
SALES (est): 69.9K **Privately Held**
SIC: 3993 Signs & advertising specialties

(G-4020)
WALTER SHPMAN DSBLITY SSI CSES
605 W Gore Blvd (73501-3727)
PHONE...................580 280-4727
EMP: 1
SALES (est): 77K **Privately Held**
SIC: 3523 Farm machinery & equipment

(G-4021)
WARNER JWLY BOX DISPLAY CO LLC
1002 Sw Ard St (73505-9660)
PHONE...................580 536-8885
Marshall Weissman, *President*
Debbie Galie, *Vice Pres*
Deborah Galie, *Vice Pres*
Mark Tortolani, *VP Sales*
▲ EMP: 85 EST: 1904
SQ FT: 65,000
SALES (est): 13.2MM **Privately Held**
WEB: www.warnerusa.com
SIC: 3172 3086 3993 2657 Cases, jewelry; packaging & shipping materials, foamed plastic; signs & advertising specialties; folding paperboard boxes

(G-4022)
WICHITA RACEWAY PARK
1709 Nw Lake Ave (73507-6454)
PHONE...................580 704-0341
Andrew D Vanover, *Principal*
EMP: 3 EST: 2013
SALES (est): 245.7K **Privately Held**
SIC: 3644 Raceways

(G-4023)
WILLIAM B FINLEY
Also Called: Finley Welding and Fencing
4916 Nw Wolf Rd (73507-8869)
PHONE...................580 512-7573
Brock Finley, *Owner*
EMP: 1 EST: 2014
SALES (est): 69.7K **Privately Held**
SIC: 3315 Chain link fencing

(G-4024)
XCEL OFFICE SOLUTIONS LLC
500 N Merridian (73501)
PHONE...................580 595-9235
Michael Reed, *Branch Mgr*
EMP: 5
SALES (corp-wide): 2.6MM **Privately Held**
WEB: www.xceloffice.com
SIC: 3861 Photocopy machines
PA: Xcel Office Solutions, Llc
   304 N Meridian Ave Ste 18
   Oklahoma City OK 73107
   405 748-4222

(G-4025)
ZLB BIO SERVICES
1216 Nw Sheridan Rd (73505-5210)
PHONE...................580 248-4851
EMP: 2
SALES (est): 74.4K **Privately Held**
SIC: 2836 Plasmas

(G-4026)
ZOO TOO
2002 Sw Lee Blvd (73501-5623)
PHONE...................580 250-1088
Joyce Peters, *Owner*
EMP: 2
SALES (est): 130.2K **Privately Held**
SIC: 2064 Candy bars, including chocolate covered bars

Lebanon
Marshall County

(G-4027)
ROPER PRODUCT
411 Hagood Rd (73440)
P.O. Box 254 (73440-0254)
PHONE...................580 795-2293
Cesil Roper, *Principal*
EMP: 1
SALES (est): 104.6K **Privately Held**
SIC: 2394 Canvas & related products

Leedey
Dewey County

(G-4028)
ENOS KAUK
203737 E 820 Rd (73654-6619)
PHONE...................580 488-3375
Enos Kauk, *Owner*
EMP: 1
SALES (est): 158K **Privately Held**
SIC: 1389 Oil field services

(G-4029)
LYNNS WELDING LLC
20185 Highway 47 (73654-6024)
PHONE...................580 488-3587
Lynn Blackketter,
EMP: 5 EST: 1993
SALES (est): 470K **Privately Held**
SIC: 1799 7692 Welding on site; welding repair

(G-4030)
PROFAB WELDING INC
601 S Main (73654)
PHONE...................580 488-2020
Leslie Dykes, *Owner*
Robin Dykes, *Vice Pres*
EMP: 4
SALES (est): 900K **Privately Held**
SIC: 7692 Welding repair

(G-4031)
SCOTT CRAIG CONSULTING LLC
203476 E 720 Rd (73654-6064)
PHONE...................580 571-4199
Scott Craig,
EMP: 1
SALES (est): 240K **Privately Held**
SIC: 1389 Oil consultants

(G-4032)
TRIPLE M
75000 N 2090 Rd (73654-6071)
PHONE...................580 488-3468
Wesley Medzler, *Managing Prtnr*
EMP: 1
SALES (est): 85K **Privately Held**
SIC: 1389 Pumping of oil & gas wells

Leon
Love County

(G-4033)
COATING SOLUTION
16288 Grassbur Rd (73441-9627)
PHONE...................580 276-5432
Donna Cox, *Owner*
EMP: 2
SALES (est): 137.1K **Privately Held**
WEB: www.fusionrecoating.com
SIC: 3479 Coating of metals & formed products

Lexington
Cleveland County

(G-4034)
CANADIAN RVER VNYRDS WNERY LLC
7050 Slaughterville Rd (73051-9408)
PHONE...................405 872-5565
William Layman, *Mng Member*
William Latman, *Mng Member*
Gene Coifton,
Charles Dicious,
EMP: 5
SQ FT: 1,652
SALES (est): 64.4K **Privately Held**
SIC: 2084 0172 Wines; grapes

(G-4035)
HILLTOP CUSTOM PROCESSING
11651 Duffy Rd (73051-7205)
PHONE...................405 527-7048
Phillip Marino, *Owner*
EMP: 2
SALES (est): 90.4K **Privately Held**
SIC: 2011 7299 2013 Meat packing plants; butcher service, processing only; sausages & other prepared meats

(G-4036)
KENS ADVERTISING
11400 Bryant Rd (73051-7316)
PHONE...................405 527-6030
Kenneth D Anderson, *Owner*
EMP: 1 EST: 1970
SALES (est): 113.7K **Privately Held**
SIC: 2759 Trading stamps; printing

(G-4037)
KILGORE WELDING INC
6851 Slaughterville Rd (73051-9433)
PHONE...................405 872-9677
Kyle Kilgore, *President*
EMP: 1
SALES (est): 47.9K **Privately Held**
SIC: 7692 Welding repair

(G-4038)
OUTBACK LABORATORIES
13110 Us Highway 77 (73051)
P.O. Box 1300 (73051-1300)
PHONE...................405 527-6355
EMP: 2
SALES (est): 140.6K **Privately Held**
WEB: www.outbacklabs.com
SIC: 2844 Toilet preparations

(G-4039)
PAIGE PUBLISHING
518 Se 6th St (73051-8746)
PHONE...................405 527-3245
Orville Comer, *Owner*
EMP: 2
SALES (est): 62.4K **Privately Held**
SIC: 2741 2731 Miscellaneous publishing; book publishing

(G-4040)
TRUPRODUCTS LLC
8700 Banner Rd (73051-7702)
PHONE...................405 830-0151
Steve Easom, *Principal*
EMP: 2
SALES (est): 94.8K **Privately Held**
SIC: 3965 Fasteners, buttons, needles & pins

(G-4041)
ZR WELDING LLC
11800 Duffy Rd (73051-7206)
PHONE...................405 602-4164
Zachery Robinson, *Administration*
EMP: 1 EST: 2015
SALES (est): 64.1K **Privately Held**
SIC: 7692 Welding repair

Lindsay
Garvin County

(G-4042)
3D CABINETRY LLC
12381 Sycamore Ct (73052-7922)
PHONE...................405 488-5604
EMP: 2
SALES (est): 94.9K **Privately Held**
SIC: 2434 Wood kitchen cabinets

(G-4043)
ANADARKO PETROLEUM CORPORATION
804 W Cherokee St (73052-4018)
PHONE...................405 756-4347
Wyett Yates, *Manager*
EMP: 35
SALES (corp-wide): 21.2B **Publicly Held**
SIC: 1382 Oil & gas exploration services
HQ: Anadarko Petroleum Corporation
   1201 Lake Robbins Dr
   The Woodlands TX 77380
   832 636-1000

(G-4044)
APRIL OILFIELD SERVICES
10414 N County Road 3010 (73052-9723)
PHONE...................405 756-5688
Brandy Aprill, *Principal*
EMP: 1
SALES (est): 117.9K **Privately Held**
SIC: 1389 Oil field services

(G-4045)
B & B TOOL CO INC
Hwy 76 N (73052)
P.O. Box 729 (73052-0729)
PHONE...................405 756-4530
Robert D Poteet, *President*
Jo Ann Poteet, *Corp Secy*
EMP: 7
SQ FT: 10,000
SALES (est): 735.1K **Privately Held**
SIC: 1389 4212 Oil field services; petroleum haulage, local

(G-4046)
BAKER HGHES OLFLD OPRTIONS LLC
Centrilift
Industrial Hts (73052)
PHONE...................405 756-3384
Rodger Conner, *Branch Mgr*
EMP: 9 **Privately Held**
SIC: 1389 Oil field services
PA: Baker Hughes Oilfield Operations Llc
   2001 Rankin Rd
   Houston TX 77073

(G-4047)
BASIC ENERGY SERVICES INC
401 Se 4th St (73052-6413)
P.O. Box 129 (73052-0129)
PHONE...................405 756-1820
Austin O'Neil, *Manager*
EMP: 30
SALES (corp-wide): 567.2MM **Publicly Held**
SIC: 1389 Oil field services
PA: Basic Energy Services, Inc.
   801 Cherry St Unit 2
   Fort Worth TX 76102
   817 334-4100

(G-4048)
BENNETT CONSTRUCTION
505 Se 4th St (73052-6415)
PHONE...................405 756-1918
EMP: 2
SALES (est): 139.6K **Privately Held**
SIC: 1522 1521 1389 Residential construction; single-family housing construction; oil & gas field services

(G-4049)
BLAZER OILFIELD SERVICES LLC
414 E Cherokee St (73052-4416)
PHONE...................405 756-4800
Frank Wells,
EMP: 20

GEOGRAPHIC SECTION

Lindsay - Garvin County (G-4079)

SALES (est): 1.6MM **Privately Held**
SIC: **1389** 1381 Oil consultants; drilling oil & gas wells

(G-4050)
BLUESTEM GAS SERVICES LLC
4655 County Street 2970 (73052-8011)
PHONE..................580 658-6530
Donna Hilderbrand, *Principal*
EMP: 15
SALES (est): 432.3K
SALES (corp-wide): 8.2B **Publicly Held**
SIC: **1389** Oil consultants
HQ: Williams Partners L.P.
1 Williams Ctr
Tulsa OK 74172

(G-4051)
BRICKMAN FAST LINE
1001 Se 4th St (73052-7452)
P.O. Box 56, Okeene (73763-0056)
PHONE..................405 756-1665
Freddy Gutierrez, *Manager*
EMP: 2
SALES (est): 130.4K **Privately Held**
WEB: www.brickmanoil.com
SIC: **1389** Oil & gas field services

(G-4052)
BS OIL COMPANY
801 Nw 4th St (73052-3205)
P.O. Box 589 (73052-0589)
PHONE..................405 756-8357
Thomas D Blankenship, *Owner*
Thomas Blankenship, *Owner*
EMP: 1
SALES (est): 134.7K **Privately Held**
SIC: **1389** Servicing oil & gas wells

(G-4053)
C C & R CONSTRUCTION INC
14357 180th St (73052-3415)
P.O. Box 277 (73052-0277)
PHONE..................405 756-4710
Chester Dean, *President*
Robert Whitworth, *Vice Pres*
EMP: 8
SALES (est): 598.5K **Privately Held**
SIC: **1389** Roustabout service

(G-4054)
C-STAR MFG INC
13801 120th St (73052-3371)
P.O. Box 277 (73052-0277)
PHONE..................405 756-1530
Brandon Connor, *President*
Jessica Conner, *Vice Pres*
EMP: 4 EST: 2016
SALES (est): 322K **Privately Held**
SIC: **1542** 3533 Nonresidential construction; oil & gas field machinery

(G-4055)
CABLE PRINTING CO INC
117 S Main St (73052-5631)
P.O. Box 768 (73052-0768)
PHONE..................405 756-4045
Darrell Cable, *President*
Gina Cable, *Vice Pres*
EMP: 12
SQ FT: 7,375
SALES (est): 1.7MM **Privately Held**
SIC: **2752** 2711 2791 2759 Commercial printing, offset; newspapers: publishing only, not printed on site; typesetting; commercial printing

(G-4056)
CHESAPEAKE OPERATING LLC
1407 Nw 4th St (73052)
PHONE..................405 756-8700
Mark Fields, *Manager*
EMP: 40 **Publicly Held**
SIC: **1311** Crude petroleum production
HQ: Chesapeake Operating, L.L.C.
6100 N Western Ave
Oklahoma City OK 73118

(G-4057)
CUDD ENERGY SERVICES
Also Called: Cudd Pressure Control
1210 Nw 4th St (73052)
P.O. Box 39 (73052-0039)
PHONE..................405 756-4344
EMP: 5
SALES (est): 312.9K **Privately Held**
SIC: **1389** Oil field services

(G-4058)
CUDD PRESSURE CONTROL INC
1210 Se 4th St (73052)
PHONE..................405 756-4337
Ken Miller, *Branch Mgr*
Brian Jones, *Manager*
EMP: 40
SALES (corp-wide): 1.2B **Publicly Held**
WEB: www.cuddenergyservices.com
SIC: **1389** 1382 Oil field services; oil & gas exploration services
HQ: Cudd Pressure Control, Inc.
2828 Tech Forest Blvd
The Woodlands TX 77381
832 295-5555

(G-4059)
DAVIS MACHINE SHOP INC
901 State Hwy 76 N (73052)
P.O. Box 674 (73052-0674)
PHONE..................405 756-3055
Lillie M Davis, *President*
Lea Ann Springman, *Corp Secy*
Cheryl Doyal, *Senior VP*
Lillie Davis, *Export Mgr*
EMP: 15
SQ FT: 7,000
SALES: 2.2MM **Privately Held**
SIC: **3533** Oil field machinery & equipment

(G-4060)
DESIGN IT
Also Called: Design-It Advertising
304 S Main St (73052-5636)
PHONE..................405 756-3635
Renee Taylor, *Owner*
EMP: 2
SQ FT: 1,500
SALES (est): 176.6K **Privately Held**
SIC: **7336** 2396 2395 2759 Silk screen design; automotive & apparel trimmings; pleating & stitching; screen printing

(G-4061)
EVAN & SONS INC
512 Industrial Park (73052-9510)
P.O. Box 466 (73052-0466)
PHONE..................405 756-2704
Evan Flood, *President*
Cindy Flood, *Vice Pres*
Chris Flood, *Admin Sec*
EMP: 6 EST: 1997
SQ FT: 2,500
SALES: 650K **Privately Held**
WEB: www.evan.org
SIC: **1389** Construction, repair & dismantling services

(G-4062)
EXCO RESOURCES INC
Also Called: Exco Midcontinent Division
804 W Cherokee St (73052-4018)
PHONE..................405 756-4347
G W Reeve, *Manager*
EMP: 4
SALES (corp-wide): 394MM **Privately Held**
SIC: **1382** Oil & gas exploration services
PA: Exco Resources, Inc.
12377 Merit Dr Ste 1700
Dallas TX 75251
214 368-2084

(G-4063)
FREDS RAT HOLE SERVICE INC
211 Ne 3rd St (73052-4408)
P.O. Box 741 (73052-0741)
PHONE..................405 756-4300
Mike Davis, *President*
Mary Davis, *Vice Pres*
EMP: 16
SQ FT: 11,427
SALES (est): 2.8MM **Privately Held**
SIC: **1389** 1781 Oil field services; water well drilling

(G-4064)
GREG TUCKER CONSTRUCTION
Also Called: Tucker Construction Co
915 Se 4th St (73052-7417)
P.O. Box 442 (73052-0442)
PHONE..................405 756-3958
Greg Tucker, *Owner*
EMP: 22
SALES (est): 4.4MM **Privately Held**
SIC: **1389** 1799 1623 Oil field services; welding on site; pipeline construction

(G-4065)
GULFPORT ENERGY CORPORATION
401 Industrial Park (73052-9005)
PHONE..................405 756-0060
Coby Wynn, *Branch Mgr*
EMP: 10
SALES (corp-wide): 1.3B **Publicly Held**
SIC: **1311** Crude petroleum & natural gas production
PA: Gulfport Energy Corporation
3001 Quail Springs Pkwy
Oklahoma City OK 73134
405 252-4600

(G-4066)
HASSLER HOT OIL SERVICE LLC
202 Se 4th St (73052-5616)
P.O. Box 580 (73052-0580)
PHONE..................405 756-0448
Greg Adams, *President*
EMP: 2
SALES (est): 95K **Privately Held**
SIC: **1389** Oil field services

(G-4067)
HOMER RINEHART COMPANY (PA)
15914 Hwy 19 (73052)
P.O. Box 32 (73052-0032)
PHONE..................405 756-2785
Daniel Evans, *President*
Bobby Bruton, *Vice Pres*
Bonnie Rinehart, *Treasurer*
EMP: 60 EST: 1977
SQ FT: 2,500
SALES (est): 8.5MM **Privately Held**
SIC: **1389** Oil field services; roustabout service

(G-4068)
HOMER RINEHART COMPANY
Highway 19 E (73052)
P.O. Box 32 (73052-0032)
PHONE..................405 756-2785
Bobby Bruton, *Manager*
EMP: 50
SALES (corp-wide): 8.5MM **Privately Held**
SIC: **1389** Oil field services
PA: Homer Rinehart Company
15914 Hwy 19
Lindsay OK 73052
405 756-2785

(G-4069)
HYBRID TOOL SOLUTIONS LLC
12509 State Highway 76 (73052-7902)
PHONE..................405 756-1408
Belo Kellam,
Leslie Howell,
Red Kennedy,
EMP: 6
SALES (est): 327.9K **Privately Held**
WEB: www.hybridtool.com
SIC: **1381** Drilling oil & gas wells

(G-4070)
KELLY BLAKE WELDING INC
15453 E County Road 1554 (73052-9399)
PHONE..................405 756-0868
Kelly Blake, *Principal*
EMP: 1
SALES (est): 69K **Privately Held**
SIC: **7692** Welding repair

(G-4071)
KEY ENERGY SERVICES INC
Also Called: Hydra-Walk
603 Industrial Park (73052-9012)
PHONE..................405 756-3347
Kent Toleman, *Branch Mgr*
EMP: 18
SALES (corp-wide): 413.8MM **Publicly Held**
SIC: **1389** Oil field services
PA: Key Energy Services, Inc.
1301 Mckinney St Ste 1800
Houston TX 77010
713 651-4300

(G-4072)
L & O PUMP AND SUPPLY INC
201 Se 3rd St (73052-5609)
PHONE..................405 756-3877
John Bradford, *President*
Robert Holman, *Manager*
EMP: 2
SALES (est): 151.7K **Privately Held**
SIC: **1389** Oil field services

(G-4073)
LEGENDS VINEYARD & WINERY
12955 Meridian Ave (73052-3516)
PHONE..................405 823-8265
Bob Sirpless, *Owner*
Deborah Sirpless, *Owner*
EMP: 4
SALES (est): 191K **Privately Held**
SIC: **2084** Wines

(G-4074)
LINDSEY WEBB PRESS
305 S Main St (73052-5635)
P.O. Box 248 (73052-0248)
PHONE..................405 756-9551
Mark Gillam, *Owner*
EMP: 8
SALES (est): 583.1K **Privately Held**
SIC: **2741** Miscellaneous publishing

(G-4075)
NABORS WELDING & SUPPLIES INC
202 W Cherokee St (73052-4210)
P.O. Box 774 (73052-0774)
PHONE..................405 756-8198
Mark Nabors, *President*
EMP: 5
SQ FT: 4,000
SALES: 1.5MM **Privately Held**
SIC: **3548** 5999 7692 Welding apparatus; welding supplies; welding repair

(G-4076)
PARKER & PARSLEY PETROLEUM
302 W Pawnee St (73052-7222)
PHONE..................405 756-1912
EMP: 6
SALES (corp-wide): 1.1MM **Privately Held**
SIC: **4911** 1382 Electric services; oil & gas exploration services
PA: Parker & Parsley Petroleum
30191 N County Road 3120
Elmore City OK 73433
580 788-2885

(G-4077)
POTEET OIL CO INC (PA)
Hwy 76 N (73052)
P.O. Box 516 (73052-0516)
PHONE..................405 756-4530
Robert Poteet, *President*
Joanne Poteet, *Vice Pres*
EMP: 2
SQ FT: 900
SALES (est): 619.1K **Privately Held**
SIC: **1381** Drilling oil & gas wells

(G-4078)
QUALITY TANK MANUFACTURING
202 Se 4th St (73052-5616)
PHONE..................405 756-1188
Elizabet Picklesime, *Principal*
EMP: 2
SALES (est): 80.9K **Privately Held**
SIC: **1389** Oil field services

(G-4079)
RALPH M THOMAS
Also Called: Lindsay Gauge & Instrument
109 Nw 2nd St (73052-4201)
P.O. Box 366 (73052-0366)
PHONE..................405 756-4426
Ralph M Thomas, *Owner*
EMP: 3
SQ FT: 1,800

Lindsay - Garvin County (G-4080)

SALES (est): 446.4K **Privately Held**
SIC: **3533** 5084 Oil field machinery & equipment; industrial machinery & equipment

(G-4080)
REEF SERVICES LLC
Hwy 76 N (73052)
PHONE..............................405 756-4747
Alicia Holley, *Manager*
EMP: 20
SALES (corp-wide): 1.2B **Publicly Held**
SIC: **3533** Oil & gas drilling rigs & equipment
HQ: Reef Services, Llc
   1515 W Sam Houston Pkwy N
   Houston TX 77043

(G-4081)
S & H TANK SERVICE INC
Also Called: S&H Tank Service of Oklahoma
103 W Cherokee St (73052-4207)
P.O. Box 773 (73052-0773)
PHONE..............................405 756-3121
Jerry Sublette, *President*
Sharon Sublette, *Corp Secy*
Jason Sublette, *Vice Pres*
EMP: 26 EST: 1979
SQ FT: 3,000
SALES (est): 5.1MM **Privately Held**
SIC: **1389** 4212 Oil field services; local trucking, without storage

(G-4082)
S & H TANK SERVICE OF OKLAHOMA
Hwy 76 N (73052)
P.O. Box 773 (73052-0773)
PHONE..............................405 756-3121
Jerry Sublette, *President*
Sharon Sublette, *Corp Secy*
EMP: 18
SQ FT: 3,000
SALES (est): 951.3K **Privately Held**
SIC: **1389** 4212 Oil field services; local trucking, without storage

(G-4083)
SHERIDAN PRODUCTION CO LLC
804 W Cherokee St (73052-4018)
PHONE..............................405 756-4347
Larry Brinlee, *President*
EMP: 61 **Privately Held**
WEB: www.sheridanproduction.com
SIC: **1382** Oil & gas exploration services
PA: Sheridan Production Company Llc
   1360 Post Oak Blvd # 2500
   Houston TX 77056

(G-4084)
SHOPPER NEWS NOTE
Also Called: Smith Office Supply
318 S Main St (73052-5636)
P.O. Box 8 (73052-0008)
PHONE..............................405 756-3169
Gary M Smith, *Owner*
A Harriet Smith, *Corp Secy*
Holly Belknap, *Vice Pres*
William Belknap, *Manager*
EMP: 10
SQ FT: 3,400
SALES (est): 660K **Privately Held**
SIC: **5943** 2741 2791 Office forms & supplies; shopping news: publishing only, not printed on site; typesetting

(G-4085)
SILVERBACK PUMP & ANCHOR LLC
207 Ne 4th St (73052-4431)
P.O. Box 709 (73052-0709)
PHONE..............................405 756-1148
Robert Holman, *Partner*
James C Smith,
EMP: 1
SALES (est): 201.7K **Privately Held**
SIC: **3561** Pumps & pumping equipment

(G-4086)
SPEARHEAD SERVICES
708 Se 4th St (73052-7414)
PHONE..............................405 756-8615
EMP: 2

SALES (est): 83.6K **Privately Held**
SIC: **1389** Oil field services

(G-4087)
STREAM LINE
903 Se 3rd St (73052-7411)
PHONE..............................405 756-4422
EMP: 3
SALES (est): 211.4K **Privately Held**
SIC: **1311** Crude Petroleum/Natural Gas Production

(G-4088)
STRIDE WELL SERVICE INC (DH)
615 E Ponca St (73052-7431)
P.O. Box 3907, Enid (73702-3907)
PHONE..............................580 242-7300
Ron Boyd, *President*
Nancy Allred, *Corp Secy*
Mike Mayer, *Vice Pres*
EMP: 13 EST: 1981
SQ FT: 500
SALES (est): 21MM **Publicly Held**
SIC: **1389** Servicing oil & gas wells; oil & gas wells: building, repairing & dismantling; swabbing wells
HQ: Complete Energy Services, Inc.
   1001 La St Ste 2900
   Houston TX 77002
   713 654-2200

(G-4089)
STRONG SERVICE LP
601 Nw 4th St (73052-3201)
PHONE..............................405 756-1716
EMP: 2 EST: 2018
SALES (est): 120.8K **Privately Held**
SIC: **1389** Oil field services

(G-4090)
SUPER FLOW TESTERS INC
400 Industrial Park Ste A (73052)
P.O. Box 643 (73052-0643)
PHONE..............................405 756-8795
Joey Williams, *President*
Jimmy Kennedy, *Vice Pres*
EMP: 25
SALES (est): 1.6MM **Privately Held**
SIC: **1389** Oil field services

(G-4091)
SWABBING JOHNS LLC
Hwy 76 N (73052)
P.O. Box 222 (73052-0222)
PHONE..............................405 756-8141
Barbara Martin, *Principal*
Steven J Smith,
EMP: 19
SALES (est): 976.5K **Privately Held**
SIC: **1389** Swabbing wells

(G-4092)
SWABBING JOHNS INC
Hwy 76 N (73052)
P.O. Box 458 (73052-0458)
PHONE..............................405 756-8141
John Chappell, *President*
Ula Chappell, *Corp Secy*
EMP: 12
SALES (est): 1.4MM **Privately Held**
SIC: **1389** Oil field services

(G-4093)
T&T FORKLIFT SERVICE INC
G Brown Ave (73052)
P.O. Box 623 (73052-0623)
PHONE..............................405 756-3451
Kent Toleman, *President*
Nita Toleman, *Admin Sec*
EMP: 5
SQ FT: 8,000
SALES (est): 670.1K **Privately Held**
SIC: **1799** 4213 1389 Dock equipment installation, industrial; trucking, except local; oil field services

(G-4094)
TONY GOSNELL OPERATING
4148 County St (73052)
P.O. Box 833 (73052-0833)
PHONE..............................405 756-8091
Tony Gosnell, *Owner*
EMP: 2
SALES (est): 365.1K **Privately Held**
SIC: **3561** Pumps, oil well & field

(G-4095)
U S WEATHERFORD L P
1 2 Mile N Hwy 76 (73052)
PHONE..............................405 756-4331
EMP: 18 **Privately Held**
WEB: www.weatherford.com
SIC: **3533** Oil & gas field machinery
HQ: U S Weatherford L P
   179 Weatherford Dr
   Schriever LA 70395
   985 493-6100

(G-4096)
U S WEATHERFORD L P
Hwy 76 N 1/2 Mile (73052)
PHONE..............................405 756-4389
Eddie Yance, *Branch Mgr*
EMP: 17 **Privately Held**
SIC: **1389** Oil field services
HQ: U S Weatherford L P
   179 Weatherford Dr
   Schriever LA 70395
   985 493-6100

(G-4097)
VICKERS CONSTRUCTION INC
1102 Cherokee Pl (73052-5036)
P.O. Box 249 (73052-0249)
PHONE..............................405 756-4386
Steve Vickers, *President*
EMP: 58
SQ FT: 8,000
SALES (est): 14.2MM **Privately Held**
SIC: **1629** 1389 Oil refinery construction; oil field services

(G-4098)
VITRUVIAN II WOODFORD LLC
401 Industrial Park (73052-9005)
PHONE..............................405 428-2491
EMP: 2
SALES (est): 242.1K **Privately Held**
SIC: **1382** Oil & gas exploration services

(G-4099)
WASHITA FLOW TESTERS INC
Hwy 76 N (73052)
P.O. Box 813 (73052-0813)
PHONE..............................405 756-3397
Jerry Algeo, *President*
Michelle Algeo, *Vice Pres*
EMP: 57
SQ FT: 3,600
SALES (est): 2.1MM **Privately Held**
SIC: **1389** Oil field services

(G-4100)
WEBSTER DRILLING SERVICES LLC
13817 May Ave (73052-3502)
PHONE..............................405 517-5585
Steven Webster,
EMP: 1
SALES (est): 114.6K **Privately Held**
SIC: **1389** Oil & gas field services

(G-4101)
YANDELLS WELL SERVICE
610 Se 4th St (73052-6418)
P.O. Box 311 (73052-0311)
PHONE..............................405 756-3407
Tim C Yandell, *Partner*
James Nathan, *Partner*
Nathan Yandell, *Partner*
EMP: 3
SQ FT: 1,152
SALES (est): 280.2K **Privately Held**
SIC: **1389** Oil field services

Loco
Stephens County

(G-4102)
KETA OIL RURAL
610 5th St (73442-1815)
PHONE..............................580 537-2443
EMP: 2
SALES (est): 97K **Privately Held**
SIC: **1389** Oil And Gas Field Services, Nec, Nsk

Locust Grove
Mayes County

(G-4103)
ABLE INTERIOR CONTRACTOR LLC
5420 E 580 Rd (74352)
P.O. Box 825 (74352-0825)
PHONE..............................918 605-2887
Charles Roach, *President*
EMP: 10
SALES (est): 701.3K **Privately Held**
SIC: **3446** Partitions & supports/studs, including accoustical systems

(G-4104)
BILL GLASS
Also Called: Glass, Bill Studio
8934 S 446 (74352-9360)
PHONE..............................918 479-8884
Bill Glass Jr, *Owner*
EMP: 1
SALES (est): 61.3K **Privately Held**
SIC: **3952** Colors, artists': water & oxide ceramic glass

(G-4105)
C & H RANCH
Also Called: C & H Accounting
7 Mi E & 3 1/2 Mi S # 312 (74352)
PHONE..............................918 479-8460
Marry Coffelt, *Owner*
EMP: 2 EST: 1975
SALES: 150K **Privately Held**
SIC: **0212** 2048 8721 5999 Beef cattle except feedlots; mineral feed supplements; accounting, auditing & bookkeeping; farm equipment & supplies

(G-4106)
EXPRESS METAL FABRICATORS LLC
9490 E Highway 412 (74352-9134)
PHONE..............................918 622-1420
EMP: 322
SALES (est): 17.4MM
SALES (corp-wide): 24.1MM **Privately Held**
SIC: **3441** Structural Metal Fabrication
PA: Express Group Holdings Llc
   10810 E 45th St Ste 401
   Tulsa OK 74146
   918 622-1420

(G-4107)
FTDM INVESTMENTS LLC
Also Called: Jer-Co Industries
14302 S 442 Rd (74352-1836)
PHONE..............................918 598-3430
Gary Brixey, *QC Mgr*
Debbie Duniphin, *Personnel Exec*
Frank Rush, *Mng Member*
EMP: 80 EST: 1981
SQ FT: 62,650
SALES (est): 24.1MM **Privately Held**
SIC: **3441** 3533 3462 Building components, structural steel; oil & gas field machinery; iron & steel forgings

(G-4108)
GILMORE WELDING & TRACTOR SVC
10371 S 437 (74352-7655)
PHONE..............................918 479-6224
James C Gilmore, *Owner*
EMP: 1
SALES (est): 68.2K **Privately Held**
SIC: **7692** Welding repair

(G-4109)
HOLMAN MANUFACTURING
302 E Main St (74352)
P.O. Box 548 (74352-0548)
PHONE..............................918 479-5861
Jimmy L Holman, *Partner*
Sidney Holman, *Partner*
EMP: 10 EST: 1968
SQ FT: 9,500
SALES (est): 500K **Privately Held**
SIC: **3599** 7692 3444 Machine shop, jobbing & repair; welding repair; sheet metalwork

GEOGRAPHIC SECTION

Luther - Oklahoma County (G-4140)

(G-4110)
HOSS MARINE PROPULSION INC
Also Called: Hoss Marine Propellers
Highway 82 (74352)
P.O. Box 367 (74352-0367)
PHONE..................918 479-5167
Glen Bostic, *President*
David Lee Bostic, *Corp Secy*
Shirley Bostic, *Vice Pres*
EMP: 3
SQ FT: 2,300
SALES (est): 200K **Privately Held**
WEB: www.hossprops.com
SIC: 3519 Outboard motors

(G-4111)
IRON POST WINERY LLC
9797 Se 560 Dr (74352-6175)
PHONE..................918 479-3600
Mark E O Hinson, *Principal*
EMP: 2
SALES (est): 68.6K **Privately Held**
SIC: 2084 Wines

(G-4112)
MACHINING SPECIALISTS INC
224 Sw 629 (74352-5600)
PHONE..................918 386-2387
Phillip Scheulen, *President*
EMP: 2
SALES: 75K **Privately Held**
SIC: 3599 Machine shop, jobbing & repair

(G-4113)
WESTERN FRONTIER LLC
6968 E 610 Rd (74352-2080)
PHONE..................918 760-4977
Jerry Rush,
EMP: 24
SALES (est): 9.7MM **Privately Held**
SIC: 3441 Fabricated structural metal

Lone Grove
Carter County

(G-4114)
AUTO CHLOR SERVICES LLC
131 E Case Cir (73443)
PHONE..................580 657-4482
Jonathan Herald, *Branch Mgr*
Perry Eastman,
EMP: 3
SALES (est): 249.6K **Privately Held**
WEB: www.autochlor.com
SIC: 3589 Dishwashing machines, commercial

(G-4115)
BIG RIVER SALES INC
Also Called: Big River Sales & Mfg
Hc 62 Box 3 (73443)
P.O. Box 45 (73443-0045)
PHONE..................580 657-4950
Jimmie P Hockersmith, *President*
Larry White, *Owner*
Jamie Smith, *Vice Pres*
Edna Hockersmith, *Treasurer*
EMP: 9
SALES (est): 1.2MM **Privately Held**
SIC: 3443 5051 3444 Metal parts; metals service centers & offices; sheet metalwork

(G-4116)
COUNTY OF CARTER
Also Called: Cater County District 3
Hwy 70 (73443)
P.O. Box 970 (73443-0970)
PHONE..................580 657-4050
Dale Ott, *Commissioner*
EMP: 13 **Privately Held**
SIC: 3531 Road construction & maintenance machinery
PA: County Of Carter
107 1st Ave Sw Ste A
Ardmore OK 73401
580 223-8162

(G-4117)
KLEEN OILFIELD SERVICES CO
Hwy 70 W (73443)
P.O. Box 574 (73443-0574)
PHONE..................580 657-3967
Lonnie Knowles, *Manager*
EMP: 16 **Privately Held**
SIC: 1389 Construction, repair & dismantling services
PA: Kleen Oilfield Services Co.
177855 Ncr 3030
Velma OK 73491

(G-4118)
LONE GROVE LEDGER
Also Called: Quality Prtg & Graphic Design
Hwy 70 W (73443)
P.O. Box 577 (73443-0577)
PHONE..................580 657-6492
Gary Hicks, *Owner*
EMP: 5
SALES (est): 277.9K **Privately Held**
SIC: 2711 Newspapers, publishing & printing

(G-4119)
PRICE WELDING AND SUPPLY
Hc 62 Box 39c (73443)
PHONE..................580 668-3057
Billy J Price, *Owner*
EMP: 2
SALES (est): 110K **Privately Held**
SIC: 7692 5084 Welding repair; welding machinery & equipment

(G-4120)
S & T ROSE INC
192 Rounsaville Ave (73443-6374)
PHONE..................580 657-4906
Shane Rose, *President*
EMP: 1 EST: 2013
SALES (est): 73.1K **Privately Held**
SIC: 1389 7389 Oil consultants;

(G-4121)
STRAITLINE INC
11899 Prairie Valley Rd (73443-6326)
PHONE..................405 263-4604
Jerry Walker, *President*
EMP: 11
SALES (est): 1.2MM **Privately Held**
SIC: 3429 Builders' hardware

Lone Wolf
Kiowa County

(G-4122)
WHITETAIL WELL TESTING LLC
13574 N 2040 Rd (73655-4402)
P.O. Box 86, Carter (73627-0086)
PHONE..................580 225-4200
Tracey Stewart, *Owner*
EMP: 14
SALES (est): 2.1MM **Privately Held**
WEB: www.whitetailwell.com
SIC: 1389 Oil field services

Longdale
Blaine County

(G-4123)
FRENCHS BLUE RIVER CNSTR
19 E 7th St (73755)
P.O. Box 250 (73755-0250)
PHONE..................580 274-3444
Wendall French, *President*
EMP: 10
SQ FT: 1,200
SALES (est): 800K **Privately Held**
SIC: 1389 Oil field services

(G-4124)
HOSKINS GYPSUM COMPANY LLC
4959 S Hwy 58 (73755)
P.O. Box 243 (73755-0243)
PHONE..................580 274-3446
Jody Hysell, *COO*
Devon Miller, *CFO*
Jessie Hoskins,
EMP: 15 EST: 2010
SQ FT: 5,000
SALES (est): 8MM **Privately Held**
SIC: 1429 4212 Grits mining (crushed stone); riprap quarrying; animal & farm product transportation services

(G-4125)
KELLY LABS
103 S Oak (73755)
PHONE..................682 367-8743
Kelly Labs, *Owner*
EMP: 5
SALES (est): 197.1K **Privately Held**
SIC: 3523 7389 Grounds mowing equipment;

(G-4126)
RANDYS BACKHOE SERVICE
2382 State Highway 58 (73755-5890)
PHONE..................580 227-0561
EMP: 1
SALES (est): 60K **Privately Held**
SIC: 3531 Backhoes

(G-4127)
RED CEDAR CREATIONS
249839 E County Road 58 (73755-5829)
PHONE..................580 227-3198
Brett Howerton, *Owner*
Bret Howerton, *Owner*
Zara Howerton, *Co-Owner*
EMP: 3
SQ FT: 5,000
SALES (est): 110K **Privately Held**
SIC: 2499 Decorative wood & woodwork

Lookeba
Caddo County

(G-4128)
DAVID PIATT
Also Called: Cobra Welding
12101 County Road 1110 (73053-5436)
PHONE..................405 542-6974
William David Piatt II, *Principal*
EMP: 2
SALES (est): 173.1K **Privately Held**
SIC: 7692 Welding repair

(G-4129)
HOUSE T SHIRT & SILK SCREENING
111 N Second St (73053)
P.O. Box 135 (73053-0135)
PHONE..................405 457-6321
Becca Clausan, *Owner*
EMP: 3
SALES (est): 30K **Privately Held**
SIC: 3552 2396 Silk screens for textile industry; automotive & apparel trimmings

Loyal
Kingfisher County

(G-4130)
COOPER CREEK MANUFACTURING INC
Rr 1 Box 97a (73756-9737)
PHONE..................405 729-4446
Richard E Meyer, *President*
Claudia L Meyer, *Corp Secy*
EMP: 2
SALES (est): 220K **Privately Held**
SIC: 3713 Truck & bus bodies

Luther
Oklahoma County

(G-4131)
66 SIGN AND LIGHT LLC
15455 E Coffee Creek Rd (73054-9134)
PHONE..................405 445-9212
Juliana McCollom, *Administration*
EMP: 1 EST: 2009
SALES (est): 113.3K **Privately Held**
SIC: 3993 Signs, not made in custom sign painting shops

(G-4132)
B ROWDY RNCH MET FBRCATION LLC
22120 N Dobbs Rd (73054-9222)
PHONE..................405 973-5976
Mark Dunn, *Principal*
EMP: 2
SALES (est): 72K **Privately Held**
WEB: www.browdyranch.com
SIC: 3499 Fabricated metal products

(G-4133)
BACKHOE SERVICES OKLAHOMA LLC
9687 Oak Pond Dr (73054-9684)
PHONE..................405 356-2712
Beth Gritte, *Principal*
EMP: 2
SALES (est): 176K **Privately Held**
SIC: 3531 Backhoes

(G-4134)
BETHS BAUBLES AND BITS
17910 N Harrah Rd (73054-8928)
PHONE..................405 659-3841
Elizabeth Lafave, *Owner*
EMP: 2
SALES (est): 57.7K **Privately Held**
SIC: 2711 Newspapers, publishing & printing

(G-4135)
LUTHER MILL AND FARM SUPPLY
300 N Ash St (73054-9050)
P.O. Box 187 (73054-0187)
PHONE..................405 277-3221
Danny Roy, *President*
EMP: 5
SQ FT: 5,000
SALES (est): 1.1MM **Privately Held**
SIC: 5191 2048 4221 Feed; seeds: field, garden & flower; fertilizer & fertilizer materials; prepared feeds; grain elevator, storage only

(G-4136)
MYERS WELDING LLC
18220 E Highway 66 (73054-9135)
PHONE..................405 277-3202
Douglas John Myers, *Principal*
EMP: 1
SALES (est): 33.7K **Privately Held**
SIC: 7692 Welding repair

(G-4137)
RELF UPHOLSTERY
10975 N Luther Rd (73054-9472)
PHONE..................405 454-3295
Carolyn Relf, *Owner*
EMP: 1
SALES: 6K **Privately Held**
SIC: 2512 Upholstered household furniture

(G-4138)
SOUTHERN BELLES CANDLE CO LLC
329425 E 950 Rd (73054-9585)
PHONE..................405 200-5986
Donita Roby, *Principal*
EMP: 1
SALES (est): 48K **Privately Held**
SIC: 3999 Candles

(G-4139)
TRIANGULAR SILT DIKE CO INC
18505 E Highway 66 (73054-8809)
P.O. Box 370 (73054-0370)
PHONE..................405 277-7015
Gary Roach, *President*
Jason Roach, *Vice Pres*
EMP: 7
SQ FT: 25,000
SALES: 2.5MM **Privately Held**
SIC: 3541 Electrical discharge erosion machines

(G-4140)
TWISS SUEONS WINERY INC
Also Called: Tres Suenos
19691 E Charter Oak Rd (73054-9516)
P.O. Box 482 (73054-0482)
PHONE..................405 277-7089
Richard Kennedy, *President*

EMP: 50
SALES (est): 3.4MM **Privately Held**
SIC: 2084 Wines

Macomb
Pottawatomie County

(G-4141)
DAVIS MORGAN INTERNATIONAL
31365 Rattlesnake Hill Rd (74852-8014)
PHONE.................................405 598-2380
Sandra A Davis, *Principal*
EMP: 3
SALES: 180K **Privately Held**
SIC: 2013 Beef, dried: from purchased meat

(G-4142)
JUST PLANT IT LLC
Also Called: Just Plant It Grnhse & Nurs
20301 Palomino Way (74852-8808)
PHONE.................................405 226-3111
Doug Moller,
EMP: 1
SQ FT: 8,000
SALES (est): 132.7K **Privately Held**
SIC: 3523 Windmills for pumping water, agricultural

(G-4143)
MID AMERICA HYDRO TECH
36376 Anderson Rd (74852-5709)
PHONE.................................405 598-1772
Douglas G Swinney, *Owner*
EMP: 6 EST: 2009
SALES (est): 533.2K **Privately Held**
SIC: 3589 Water treatment equipment, industrial

Madill
Marshall County

(G-4144)
B & B BUTLERS CUSTOM PROCESS
N Of City (73446)
PHONE.................................580 795-2667
Shirley Butler, *Owner*
EMP: 3
SALES (est): 166.4K **Privately Held**
SIC: 0751 2013 2011 Slaughtering: custom livestock services; sausages & other prepared meats; meat packing plants

(G-4145)
CITY MACHINE SHOP
409 E Main St (73446-2244)
PHONE.................................580 795-2282
Richard Conley, *Owner*
EMP: 3
SALES (est): 136.8K **Privately Held**
SIC: 3599 Machine shop, jobbing & repair

(G-4146)
DOLESE BROS CO
401 S 4th St (73446-3824)
PHONE.................................580 795-3549
Eugene Early, *Manager*
EMP: 19
SALES (corp-wide): 8.5MM **Privately Held**
WEB: www.dolese.com
SIC: 3273 Ready-mixed concrete
PA: Dolese Bros. Co.
    20 Nw 13th St
    Oklahoma City OK 73103
    405 235-2311

(G-4147)
FREEMAN ICE LLC
Rr 3 Box 30n (73446-8922)
P.O. Box 804 (73446-0804)
PHONE.................................580 263-0021
William Freeman,
EMP: 6
SALES (est): 516.1K **Privately Held**
SIC: 2097 Manufactured ice

(G-4148)
GODFREY OIL PROPERTIES (PA)
901 E Main St (73446-1831)
P.O. Box 200 (73446-0200)
PHONE.................................580 795-3087
Peter Godfrey, *President*
EMP: 10
SQ FT: 1,500
SALES (est): 1.4MM **Privately Held**
SIC: 1311 Crude petroleum production; natural gas production

(G-4149)
HARTINS WELDING
7376 Four Corners Rd (73446-8527)
PHONE.................................580 795-5594
EMP: 1
SALES (est): 44.8K **Privately Held**
SIC: 7692 Welding repair

(G-4150)
J & I MANUFACTURING INC
16967 Highway 99c (73446-6612)
P.O. Box 549 (73446-0549)
PHONE.................................580 795-7377
James H Williams, *President*
Tina Williams, *Vice Pres*
EMP: 20
SQ FT: 28,000
SALES (est): 5.2MM **Privately Held**
SIC: 3713 5051 Truck bodies (motor vehicles); steel

(G-4151)
J PRICE ENERGY SERVICES LLC
221 Plaza (73446-2250)
P.O. Box 485 (73446-0485)
PHONE.................................580 795-6106
EMP: 10
SALES (est): 1.9MM **Privately Held**
SIC: 1389 Construction, repair & dismantling services

(G-4152)
JBW VENTURES LLC
Also Called: S & H Trailer
200 County Rd (73446-2232)
P.O. Box 766 (73446-0766)
PHONE.................................580 795-5577
Jeff Jackson,
Melissa Bellittini,
Urian Weaver,
EMP: 75
SALES (est): 7.6MM **Privately Held**
SIC: 3715 Truck trailers

(G-4153)
M & R WIRE WORKS INC
1320 Smiley Rd (73446)
P.O. Box 651 (73446-0651)
PHONE.................................580 795-4290
Greg Moore, *President*
EMP: 8
SALES (est): 796.3K **Privately Held**
SIC: 3315 3496 Wire & fabricated wire products; miscellaneous fabricated wire products

(G-4154)
MADILL GAS PROCESSING CO LLC
3449 Neafus Rd (73446-6672)
PHONE.................................580 795-7396
Bob Jackson, *Principal*
EMP: 12
SALES (est): 1.2MM **Privately Held**
SIC: 1311 Crude petroleum & natural gas production
PA: Carrera Gas Companies, L.L.C.
    6120 S Yale Ave Ste 1640
    Tulsa OK 74136

(G-4155)
MARSHALL COUNTY PUBLISHING CO
Also Called: Madill Record, The
211 Plaza (73446-2250)
P.O. Box 529 (73446-0529)
PHONE.................................580 795-3355
John D Montgomery, *President*
Grace E Montgomery, *Vice Pres*
Sandee Westmoreland, *Librarian*
Sherry Codner, *Manager*
Mark Codner, *Admin Sec*

EMP: 11 EST: 1929
SQ FT: 2,250
SALES (est): 631.3K **Privately Held**
WEB: www.madillrecord.net
SIC: 2711 3993 2752 Commercial printing & newspaper publishing combined; signs & advertising specialties; commercial printing, lithographic

(G-4156)
MH SIGNS LLC
15762 W Highway 70 (73446-8167)
PHONE.................................580 795-2925
Amanda Arnold, *President*
EMP: 2
SQ FT: 3,200
SALES: 300K **Privately Held**
SIC: 3993 Signs & advertising specialties

(G-4157)
MID AMERICAN STL & WIRE CO LLC
1327 Smiley Rd (73446-9608)
P.O. Box 296 (73446-0296)
PHONE.................................580 795-2559
Shannon Strecker, *Plant Mgr*
Lori Littrell, *Production*
Mark Littrell, *Manager*
Boyd Lane, *Consultant*
Chris Dudley, *Technology*
▲ EMP: 25
SALES (est): 14.9MM **Privately Held**
SIC: 3317 Steel pipe & tubes

(G-4158)
MINOR PRINTING COMPANY
1201 Wiggs Ave (73446)
P.O. Box 249 (73446-0249)
PHONE.................................580 795-3745
Mike Minor, *Owner*
EMP: 1 EST: 1975
SALES: 35K **Privately Held**
SIC: 2759 2752 2791 2789 Advertising literature: printing; commercial printing, lithographic; typesetting; bookbinding & related work

(G-4159)
NEW VISION MANUFACTURING LLC
1000 N Industrial Rd (73446)
P.O. Box 654, Ada (74821-0654)
PHONE.................................580 677-9937
Lynn Hoppe,
EMP: 120
SALES (est): 94.6K **Privately Held**
SIC: 3799 Recreational vehicles

(G-4160)
OKLAHOMA STEEL & WIRE CO INC (PA)
Also Called: OK Brand
1042 S 1st St (73446)
P.O. Box 220 (73446-0220)
PHONE.................................580 795-7311
Craig Moore, *Ch of Bd*
Colleen Moore, *Corp Secy*
Brett James, *Safety Dir*
Jay Combs, *Plant Mgr*
Jerry Brown, *Transportation*
◆ EMP: 241
SQ FT: 170,000
SALES (est): 74.6MM **Privately Held**
SIC: 3496 Fencing, made from purchased wire; concrete reinforcing mesh & wire

(G-4161)
RED RIVER COLD STORAGE LLC
600 E Industrial Rd (73446-1520)
P.O. Box 617 (73446-0617)
PHONE.................................580 795-9948
James Swanson, *President*
EMP: 7
SQ FT: 101,000
SALES (est): 893.6K **Privately Held**
SIC: 4222 2068 Warehousing, cold storage or refrigerated; nuts: dried, dehydrated, salted or roasted

(G-4162)
SAVAGE EQUIPMENT INCORPORATED
1020 N Industrial Rd (73446-1521)
PHONE.................................580 795-3394

Basil Savage, *President*
Francis Savage, *Corp Secy*
Basil W Savage, *Engineer*
◆ EMP: 25
SQ FT: 15,000
SALES (est): 8.4MM **Privately Held**
SIC: 3523 Harvesters, fruit, vegetable, tobacco, etc.

(G-4163)
SPARLIN HOT OIL SERVICE INC
Hwy 99 3 Main St Ne (73446)
P.O. Box 615 (73446-0615)
PHONE.................................580 795-2513
Butch Sparlin, *Officer*
EMP: 4
SALES (est): 350K **Privately Held**
SIC: 1389 Oil field services

(G-4164)
SPORTS CENTER
502 N 1st St (73446-1408)
PHONE.................................580 795-2993
John Raper, *Owner*
EMP: 1
SALES (est): 47K **Privately Held**
SIC: 3949 Sporting & athletic goods

(G-4165)
SUTHERLAND WELL SERVICE INC
1300 Industrial Blvd (73446)
P.O. Box 400, Healdton (73438-0400)
PHONE.................................580 795-5525
Vidal Rodriguez, *Manager*
EMP: 9
SALES (corp-wide): 5.2MM **Privately Held**
SIC: 1389 Servicing oil & gas wells
PA: Sutherland Well Service Inc
    S On Hwy 76
    Healdton OK 73438
    580 229-1338

(G-4166)
W - W TRAILER MFRS INC
Hwy 199 W (73446)
P.O. Box 807 (73446-0807)
PHONE.................................580 795-5571
H G Watkins, *President*
Mary Watkins, *Corp Secy*
▲ EMP: 190
SQ FT: 245,000
SALES (est): 39.4MM **Privately Held**
WEB: www.wwtrailer.com
SIC: 3799 3537 3715 Horse trailers, except fifth-wheel type; industrial trucks & tractors; truck trailers

Manchester
Grant County

(G-4167)
KLOEFKORN ENTPS LTD PARTNR
Main & Hwy 132 (73758)
P.O. Box 36 (73758-0036)
PHONE.................................580 694-2292
Ron Kloefkorn, *Mng Member*
Aaron Kloefkorn,
Jacque Kloefkorn,
Talotta Kloefkorn,
EMP: 5 EST: 1998
SQ FT: 10,000
SALES: 250K **Privately Held**
SIC: 3462 0111 Chains, forged steel; wheat

(G-4168)
LANIE FARMS
80574 Mcclain Rd (73758-5027)
PHONE.................................580 694-2259
Lanie Farms, *Owner*
EMP: 1
SALES (est): 68.6K **Privately Held**
SIC: 2041 Granular wheat flour

(G-4169)
RIEGER HAY & WELDING
Rr 1 Box 125a (73758)
PHONE.................................580 985-3608
Bradley Rieger, *Owner*
EMP: 2

SALES (est): 136.4K **Privately Held**
SIC: 3548 Welding apparatus

Mangum
Greer County

(G-4170)
DEAN PRINTING
Also Called: Dean's Printing
210 E Lincoln St (73554-4216)
PHONE.................................580 782-3777
Sharon Dean, *Owner*
EMP: 2
SALES (est): 142.5K **Privately Held**
SIC: 2752 2791 2396 Commercial printing, offset; typesetting; automotive & apparel trimmings

(G-4171)
GAMBILL OILFIELD SERVICES LLC
324 E Cleveland St (73554-4427)
PHONE.................................580 471-1451
Brian Gambill, *Principal*
EMP: 2
SALES (est): 119.8K **Privately Held**
SIC: 1389 Oil field services

(G-4172)
MB HOLDINGS LLC
Also Called: Mangum Brick Company
2316 N Louis Tittle Ave (73554)
PHONE.................................580 782-2324
Jed Winters, *President*
Jewett Scott Jr, *President*
Twila Scott, *Corp Secy*
Joe M Johnson, *Vice Pres*
Ron Gay, *Advt Staff*
EMP: 55 EST: 1907
SQ FT: 15,000
SALES (est): 7.5MM **Privately Held**
WEB: www.mangumbrick.com
SIC: 3251 5211 Brick clay: common face, glazed, vitrified or hollow; lumber & other building materials

(G-4173)
PAXTON PUBLISHING CO
Also Called: Mangum Star News
121 S Oklahoma Ave (73554-4274)
PHONE.................................580 782-3321
Casey Paxton, *Owner*
Karla Paxton, *General Mgr*
EMP: 4
SQ FT: 5,000
SALES (est): 210.5K **Privately Held**
SIC: 2711 Newspapers: publishing only, not printed on site; newspapers, publishing & printing

Mannford
Creek County

(G-4174)
ANDY CROSS ROUSTABOUT SVC LLC
10718 S 337th West Ave (74044-6057)
PHONE.................................918 906-1240
Andy Cross, *Principal*
EMP: 2
SALES (est): 187.6K **Privately Held**
SIC: 1389 Roustabout service

(G-4175)
BROACH SPECIALIST INC
3051 Speck Wright Rd (74044-2876)
PHONE.................................480 840-1375
Roy Gerhard, *President*
Lisa Gerhard, *Vice Pres*
EMP: 4
SQ FT: 5,408
SALES (est): 160.7K **Privately Held**
WEB: www.broachspecialist.com
SIC: 3545 Broaches (machine tool accessories)

(G-4176)
C&S WELDING & FABRICATION INC
169 Greenwood Ave (74044-3453)
PHONE.................................918 282-4122
Douglas Meier, *Principal*
EMP: 1
SALES (est): 103.7K **Privately Held**
SIC: 7692 Welding repair

(G-4177)
CARDINAL HEALTH 200 LLC
400 Foster Rd (74044-3034)
PHONE.................................918 865-4727
John Briceland, *Principal*
Bill Morgan, *Branch Mgr*
EMP: 146
SALES (corp-wide): 145.5B **Publicly Held**
SIC: 5047 3841 Medical equipment & supplies; surgical & medical instruments
HQ: Cardinal Health 200, Llc
3651 Birchwood Dr
Waukegan IL 60085

(G-4178)
CAREFUSION CORPORATION
400 Foster Rd (74044-3034)
PHONE.................................918 865-4727
Greg Coney, *Director*
EMP: 160
SALES (corp-wide): 17.2B **Publicly Held**
SIC: 3316 3841 Cold finishing of steel shapes; surgical & medical instruments; needles, suture
HQ: Carefusion Corporation
3750 Torrey View Ct
San Diego CA 92130

(G-4179)
CIMARRON RIVER OPERATION CORP
3725 Speck Wright Rd (74044-2704)
P.O. Box 289 (74044-0289)
PHONE.................................918 633-2911
Harold Colpitt, *President*
Tamara Colpitt, *Admin Sec*
EMP: 3
SALES (est): 297.4K **Privately Held**
SIC: 1311 7389 Crude petroleum & natural gas;

(G-4180)
CRAMER FENCE COMPANY
93 Lake Country (74044-9522)
P.O. Box 522 (74044-0522)
PHONE.................................918 865-4529
Jimmy Cramer, *Owner*
EMP: 3
SALES (est): 126.9K **Privately Held**
SIC: 3446 1799 Fences, gates, posts & flagpoles; athletic & recreation facilities construction

(G-4181)
DL HARMER AND COMPANY LLC
44 N Basin Rd (74044-3444)
P.O. Box 435 (74044-0435)
PHONE.................................918 865-6993
Debbie Larson,
EMP: 11
SALES (est): 1.7MM **Privately Held**
SIC: 3634 5084 Radiators, electric; oil well machinery, equipment & supplies

(G-4182)
HIGH FIVE GRAPHICS
3904 Keystone Loop (74044)
PHONE.................................918 636-3312
Randall Faith,
EMP: 1
SALES (est): 46.5K **Privately Held**
SIC: 2759 7389 Screen printing;

(G-4183)
J F MACHINE LLC
6810 N Three Fnger Bay Rd (74044-3750)
PHONE.................................918 865-5855
EMP: 2
SALES (est): 81.4K **Privately Held**
SIC: 3599 Industrial machinery

(G-4184)
KIRKPATRICK WELDING
37723 W Highway 51 (74044-2800)
PHONE.................................918 865-2672
Alvin Kirkpatrick, *Owner*
EMP: 1
SALES (est): 42.2K **Privately Held**
SIC: 7692 Welding repair

(G-4185)
KYRA GUFFEY LLC
33778 W 51st St S (74044-6331)
PHONE.................................210 867-1374
Kyra Guffey, *Principal*
EMP: 2 EST: 2017
SALES (est): 104.8K **Privately Held**
SIC: 3724 Aircraft engines & engine parts

(G-4186)
MAGGARD SUPPLY AND OIL CO INC
Hwy 48 S (74044)
P.O. Box 1407 (74044-1407)
PHONE.................................918 865-4333
EMP: 1 EST: 1966
SQ FT: 1,500
SALES (est): 190K **Privately Held**
SIC: 1311 Oil Producer

(G-4187)
N & S FLAME SPRAY LLC
2158 S Highway 48 (74044-3303)
P.O. Box 39 (74044-0039)
PHONE.................................918 865-4737
Donna Norris, *Mng Member*
Raymond Norris,
EMP: 20
SQ FT: 9,437
SALES (est): 2.5MM **Privately Held**
SIC: 3599 3568 3533 Machine shop, jobbing & repair; power transmission equipment; oil & gas field machinery

(G-4188)
NOBLE RESOURCES INC
134 Evans Ave B (74044-3152)
P.O. Box 570 (74044-0570)
PHONE.................................918 865-3301
Stan Noble, *President*
Romanza Spess, *Vice Pres*
EMP: 3
SALES (est): 376.2K **Privately Held**
SIC: 1381 Drilling oil & gas wells

(G-4189)
OAKES WLDG & FABRICATION LLC
169 Greenwood Ave (74044-3453)
P.O. Box 601 (74044-0601)
PHONE.................................918 865-2356
Jerry Oakes, *CEO*
EMP: 9
SQ FT: 10,000
SALES (est): 1MM **Privately Held**
SIC: 1799 7692 Welding on site; welding repair

(G-4190)
PRO-FAB INDUSTRIES INC
2235 N Hwy 48 (74044)
P.O. Box 550 (74044-0550)
PHONE.................................918 865-7590
David Claybrook, *President*
Sharon Claybrook, *Corp Secy*
Jerry Claybrook, *Vice Pres*
EMP: 20
SQ FT: 13,000
SALES (est): 3MM **Privately Held**
SIC: 3498 3443 Fabricated pipe & fittings; fabricated plate work (boiler shop)

(G-4191)
R N J INC
34289 W Highway 51 (74044)
PHONE.................................918 865-2781
Jaquita Gilreath, *President*
EMP: 20 EST: 1980
SALES (est): 2.4MM **Privately Held**
WEB: www.rockinjhorsestalls.com
SIC: 3715 Trailers or vans for transporting horses

(G-4192)
TOWN & COUNTRY HARDWARE
104 Industrial Dr (74044-3096)
P.O. Box 805 (74044-0805)
PHONE.................................918 865-2888
Jim Bowling, *President*
EMP: 3 EST: 1977
SQ FT: 2,500
SALES (est): 352.9K **Privately Held**
SIC: 5251 0782 1389 Builders' hardware; lawn & garden services; oil field services

(G-4193)
UNITED CABLE TOOL & SUPPLY LLC
34679 W 31st St S (74044)
P.O. Box 1321 (74044-1321)
PHONE.................................918 760-9012
Marion McClaran,
EMP: 1
SALES (est): 150.3K **Privately Held**
WEB: www.unitedcabletool.com
SIC: 3533 Water well drilling equipment

(G-4194)
WEBCO INDUSTRIES INC
501 Foster Rd (74044-3074)
PHONE.................................918 865-6215
Stuart Keeton, *Vice Pres*
Gary Atwell, *Engineer*
Amber Hatten, *Human Res Dir*
Darren Monk, *Manager*
EMP: 140
SALES (corp-wide): 480.7MM **Privately Held**
SIC: 3317 Steel pipe & tubes
PA: Webco Industries, Inc.
9101 W 21st St
Sand Springs OK 74063
918 245-2211

Mannsville
Johnston County

(G-4195)
CUSTER ENTERPRISES INC
Also Called: Mannsville AG Center
450 W Broadway (73447-1212)
P.O. Box 488 (73447-0488)
PHONE.................................580 371-9588
Aaron Custer, *President*
EMP: 11
SALES (est): 4MM **Privately Held**
SIC: 5191 2048 2899 Chemicals, agricultural; fertilizer & fertilizer materials; cereal-, grain-, & seed-based feeds; drilling mud

(G-4196)
TUMBLEWEED EMBROIDERY AND SCRE
14000 S Church Rd (73447-1124)
PHONE.................................580 371-9742
ERA Mercer, *Owner*
Bobby Mercer, *Vice Pres*
Jammie Williams, *Vice Pres*
EMP: 1
SALES (est): 67.8K **Privately Held**
SIC: 2395 Embroidery & art needlework

Marble City
Sequoyah County

(G-4197)
POLYCOR OKLAHOMA INC
97065 S 4610 Rd (74945-9701)
PHONE.................................770 735-2611
EMP: 3
SALES (est): 130.2K **Privately Held**
SIC: 1411 Limestone, dimension-quarrying

(G-4198)
US LIME COMPANY - ST CLAIR
98054 S 4610 Rd (74945)
P.O. Box 160 (74945-0160)
PHONE.................................918 775-4466
Robb Graves, *Vice Pres*
EMP: 63

Marietta - Love County (G-4199)

SALES (est): 8.4MM
SALES (corp-wide): 419.3K **Publicly Held**
SIC: **1422** Crushed & broken limestone
HQ: United States Lime & Minerals, Inc.
5429 Lbj Fwy Ste 230
Dallas TX 75240
972 991-8400

Marietta
Love County

(G-4199)
BARRICHEM INC
Putman Rd (73448)
P.O. Box 365 (73448-0365)
PHONE..................580 276-3125
Bernon Berrick, *President*
EMP: 1 EST: 1990
SALES (est): 85K **Privately Held**
WEB: www.barricheminc.com
SIC: **1389** Oil field services

(G-4200)
BILLY MCGILL
17987 Buckeye Ln (73448-2087)
PHONE..................580 220-7097
Billy McGill, *Principal*
EMP: 1
SALES (est): 64.6K **Privately Held**
SIC: **3531** Backhoes

(G-4201)
BUCKS DIRECTIONAL DRILLING
1201 N Highway 77 (73448-7101)
Rr # 1 Box 762
PHONE..................580 276-2238
EMP: 2 EST: 2012
SALES (est): 96K **Privately Held**
SIC: **1381** Oil/Gas Well Drilling

(G-4202)
CHICKASAW ENERGY SOLUTIONS LLC
Also Called: Chickasaw Network Services
601 N Brentwood Ave (73448-2120)
PHONE..................580 276-3306
Kent Foster, *Manager*
EMP: 45
SALES (est): 10.8MM **Privately Held**
SIC: **3443** Tanks, standard or custom fabricated: metal plate

(G-4203)
CHICKASAW NATION INDS INC
Also Called: Cni
601 Ne 2nd St (73448)
P.O. Box 70 (73448-0070)
PHONE..................580 276-3305
Carl Cooper, *CFO*
Kent Foster, *Manager*
Aaron Duck, *Director*
Marvin E Mitchell, *Director*
Steve Woods, *Director*
EMP: 60 **Privately Held**
SIC: **3535** Conveyors & conveying equipment
HQ: Chickasaw Nation Industries, Inc.
2600 John Saxon Blvd # 100
Norman OK 73071
405 253-8200

(G-4204)
CHOATE PUBLISHING INC
Also Called: Marietta Monitor
104 W Main St (73448-2832)
P.O. Box 330 (73448-0330)
PHONE..................580 276-3255
H Willis Choate III, *President*
Norene Choate, *Corp Secy*
Wilma Choate, *Vice Pres*
EMP: 11
SQ FT: 7,500
SALES (est): 510K **Privately Held**
SIC: **2711** 2752 2789 Newspapers: publishing only, not printed on site; commercial printing, offset; bookbinding & related work

(G-4205)
CNI MANUFACTURING LLC
Also Called: Innovationone, LLC
601 N Brentwood Ave (73448-2120)
PHONE..................580 276-3306
Kent Foster, *Mng Member*
EMP: 3
SALES (est): 19.9MM **Privately Held**
SIC: **3499** Machine bases, metal
HQ: Chickasaw Nation Industries, Inc.
2600 John Saxon Blvd # 100
Norman OK 73071
405 253-8200

(G-4206)
DONUT SHOP
401 S Highway 77 (73448-3448)
PHONE..................580 276-3910
Ratana Hent, *Owner*
EMP: 2 EST: 2001
SALES (est): 156.7K **Privately Held**
SIC: **2051** 5812 5461 Doughnuts, except frozen; eating places; bakeries

(G-4207)
FEHR FOODS INC
600 N Highway 77 (73448-2200)
PHONE..................580 276-4100
Steve Fehr, *President*
EMP: 50
SALES (est): 6.1MM **Privately Held**
SIC: **2052** Cookies

(G-4208)
LATTIMORE MATERIALS COMPANY LP
4 Miles N 2 Miles Wof Bac (73448)
P.O. Box 556 (73448-0556)
PHONE..................580 276-4631
Fax: 580 276-1511
EMP: 13
SALES (corp-wide): 19.7B **Privately Held**
SIC: **1442** Construction Sand/Gravel
HQ: Lattimore Materials Company Lp
15900 Dooley Rd
Addison TX 75001
972 221-4646

(G-4209)
MARIETTA FILTRA SYSTEMS
601 N Brentwood Ave (73448-2120)
P.O. Box 70 (73448-0070)
PHONE..................580 276-3306
EMP: 8
SALES (est): 1.2MM **Privately Held**
SIC: **3535** Conveyors & conveying equipment

(G-4210)
MARIETTA TAG AGENCY
112 W Main St Ste J10 (73448-2847)
PHONE..................580 276-2101
EMP: 2
SALES (est): 88.3K **Privately Held**
SIC: **3699** Electrical equipment & supplies

(G-4211)
ROBERTSONS HAMS INC
110 Wanda St (73448-1208)
PHONE..................580 276-3395
Clay B Robertson, *President*
Betty J Robertson, *Corp Secy*
Rob B Robertson, *Vice Pres*
EMP: 17
SQ FT: 24,000
SALES (est): 2.4MM **Privately Held**
WEB: www.beefjerkynow.com
SIC: **2011** 2013 Cured meats from meat slaughtered on site; smoked meats from purchased meat

(G-4212)
SEW STYLISH EMBROIDERY LLC
10748 Red Oaks Rd (73448-7247)
P.O. Box 482 (73448-0482)
PHONE..................580 238-8797
EMP: 1
SALES (est): 40.4K **Privately Held**
SIC: **2395** Embroidery & art needlework

(G-4213)
TASLER PALLET INC
Also Called: T P I
9196 Peanut Rd (73448-7282)
PHONE..................580 276-9800
Mark Greufe, *President*
Holley Greufe, *Vice Pres*
EMP: 14
SALES (est): 2.1MM **Privately Held**
SIC: **2448** Pallets, wood

(G-4214)
TEXAS TRANSCO INC
10118 Mink Ln (73448-8500)
PHONE..................903 857-9136
Bobby Price, *President*
EMP: 2
SALES (est): 65.5K **Privately Held**
SIC: **1389** Oil field services

(G-4215)
TOMMY HIGLE PUBLISHERS
9052 Aztec Rd (73448-2049)
P.O. Box 416 (73448-0416)
PHONE..................580 276-5136
Tommy Higle, *Owner*
Virgina Higle, *Co-Owner*
▲ EMP: 8
SALES (est): 624.5K **Privately Held**
SIC: **2731** 8661 2791 2752 Books: publishing & printing; religious organizations; typesetting; commercial printing, lithographic

(G-4216)
U S WEATHERFORD L P
1000 N Highway 77 (73448-7106)
PHONE..................580 276-5362
Terry Willis, *Branch Mgr*
EMP: 250 **Privately Held**
SIC: **3498** Fabricated pipe & fittings
HQ: U S Weatherford L P
179 Weatherford Dr
Schriever LA 70395
985 493-6100

(G-4217)
UNCOMMON TOUCH
Hc 67 Box 189b (73448-9410)
PHONE..................580 276-9936
Lee Totzke, *Owner*
EMP: 2
SALES (est): 270K **Privately Held**
SIC: **3999** Wreaths, artificial

(G-4218)
WELL SOLUTIONS INC
13658 Sinclair Ln (73448-7337)
P.O. Box 127, Hennepin (73444-0127)
PHONE..................580 775-2373
David Sinclair, *CEO*
EMP: 4
SALES (est): 272.8K **Privately Held**
SIC: **1389** Measurement of well flow rates, oil & gas

(G-4219)
WJ WELDING LLC
801 W Main St (73448-2845)
PHONE..................580 465-4120
Lenny Walker, *Mng Member*
EMP: 1 EST: 2011
SALES (est): 47.5K **Privately Held**
SIC: **7692** Welding repair

Marlow
Stephens County

(G-4220)
ADVANCED PUMPING UNIT SERVICE
Also Called: Advanced Pumpin Unit Service
3812 Highway 29 (73055-1296)
P.O. Box 83 (73055-0083)
PHONE..................580 658-2050
Bill Craft,
EMP: 9
SALES: 1.2MM **Privately Held**
SIC: **1389** Oil field services

(G-4221)
ANYTHING CANVAS LLC
280906 E 1640 Rd (73055-1727)
PHONE..................580 658-9330
Renee Childress,
EMP: 4 EST: 2016
SALES (est): 107.4K **Privately Held**
SIC: **2211** Canvas

(G-4222)
B&L SMOKED MEATS
263 N Scott Rd (73055-3881)
PHONE..................580 641-1677
Lynne Littrell, *Principal*
EMP: 2 EST: 2016
SALES (est): 74.4K **Privately Held**
SIC: **2013** Smoked meats from purchased meat

(G-4223)
BIG TIME DESIGNS SCREEN PRTG
408 N 9th St (73055-1820)
PHONE..................580 658-5000
EMP: 2 EST: 2012
SALES (est): 88K **Privately Held**
SIC: **2752** Lithographic Commercial Printing

(G-4224)
CABLE MEAT CENTER INC
1316 S Broadway St (73055-3885)
P.O. Box 527 (73055-0527)
PHONE..................580 658-6646
Tom Wheat, *President*
EMP: 18
SQ FT: 12,000
SALES (est): 4.3MM **Privately Held**
SIC: **5147** 5421 2032 2013 Meats, fresh; meat markets, including freezer provisioners; canned specialties; sausages & other prepared meats; meat packing plants

(G-4225)
CESI CHEMICAL INC
1004 S Plainsman Rd (73055-8600)
PHONE..................580 658-6608
Jerry Dumas, *President*
◆ EMP: 487 EST: 2000
SALES (est): 112.3MM
SALES (corp-wide): 119.3MM **Publicly Held**
WEB: www.flotekind.com
SIC: **2087** Flavoring extracts & syrups
PA: Flotek Industries, Inc.
10603 W Sam Houston Pkwy
Houston TX 77064
713 849-9911

(G-4226)
CUTTING EDGE MACHINE INC
115 E Main St (73055-2206)
P.O. Box 352 (73055-0352)
PHONE..................580 658-5036
Warren John, *Principal*
EMP: 8
SALES (est): 689.2K **Privately Held**
SIC: **3364** 3317 3313 Brass & bronze diecastings; steel pipe & tubes; alloys, additive, except copper: not made in blast furnaces

(G-4227)
D-A WELDING & FAB LLC
10705 Highway 29 (73055-1285)
PHONE..................580 641-1189
David Maxwell, *Administration*
EMP: 1
SALES (est): 83.9K **Privately Held**
SIC: **7692** Welding repair

(G-4228)
DENNIS WELDING
Nw Of City (73055)
PHONE..................580 658-5669
Terry W Dennis, *Owner*
EMP: 1 EST: 1978
SALES (est): 45.5K **Privately Held**
SIC: **7692** Welding repair

(G-4229)
DORIANS FOODS INC
1020 County Road 1586 (73055-6612)
PHONE..................580 658-3022
Verlon J Coffee, *President*

▲ = Import ▼=Export
◆ =Import/Export

Joyce Giles, *Treasurer*
EMP: 2
SQ FT: 1,748
SALES (est): 159.6K **Privately Held**
SIC: 2035 2033 Relishes, fruit & vegetable; pickles, vinegar; jellies, edible, including imitation: in cans, jars, etc.; jams, including imitation: packaged in cans, jars, etc.

(G-4230)
DRONE 1 AERIAL LLC
280075 Hlavaty Rd (73055-5520)
PHONE..........................580 704-7223
EMP: 2
SALES (est): 116.1K **Privately Held**
SIC: 3721 Motorized aircraft

(G-4231)
ELROY MACHINE INC
4414 E York Rd (73055-1548)
PHONE..........................580 658-6725
EMP: 3
SALES: 100K **Privately Held**
SIC: 3599 Job Shop

(G-4232)
EMJO OPERATIONS INC
4754 County Street 2950 (73055-5804)
PHONE..........................580 658-6457
Joyce Harrison, *President*
Emmett Harrison, *Corp Secy*
EMP: 3
SALES: 250K **Privately Held**
SIC: 1389 Oil field services

(G-4233)
FLOTEK CHEMISTRY LLC
1004 S Plainsman Rd (73055-8600)
PHONE..........................713 849-9911
John W Chisholm, *Ch of Bd*
EMP: 1
SALES (est): 437.1K
SALES (corp-wide): 119.3MM **Publicly Held**
SIC: 2819 Chemicals, high purity: refined from technical grade
PA: Flotek Industries, Inc.
    10603 W Sam Houston Pkwy
    Houston TX 77064
    713 849-9911

(G-4234)
JACK MANGUM
Also Called: Mangum Equipment Company
1106 S 9th St (73055)
PHONE..........................580 658-2700
Jack Mangum, *Owner*
EMP: 7
SALES (est): 420.5K **Privately Held**
SIC: 5999 3585 Farm equipment & supplies; refrigeration & heating equipment

(G-4235)
MADER WELDING
816 W Clampitt Rd (73055)
PHONE..........................580 658-3593
EMP: 1
SALES (est): 58.7K **Privately Held**
SIC: 7692 Welding Repair

(G-4236)
PLAINSMAN TECHNOLOGY INC (HQ)
1004 S Plainsman Rd (73055-8600)
PHONE..........................580 658-6608
Karen L Johnson, *President*
J D Pittman, *Vice Pres*
Clayde Ravun, *Vice Pres*
Claudette Walters, *Treasurer*
EMP: 10
SQ FT: 13,600
SALES (est): 2.5MM
SALES (corp-wide): 119.3MM **Publicly Held**
SIC: 5169 2899 2869 Chemicals & allied products; chemical preparations; industrial organic chemicals
PA: Flotek Industries, Inc.
    10603 W Sam Houston Pkwy
    Houston TX 77064
    713 849-9911

(G-4237)
POTIONS BY PIER LLC
163352 6 Mile Rd (73055-7034)
PHONE..........................580 658-2900
Pier Jones, *Principal*
EMP: 2
SALES (est): 139.2K **Privately Held**
SIC: 2833 Drugs & herbs: grading, grinding & milling

(G-4238)
PRECISION ENGRG & MCH WORKS
219 N Railroad St (73055-2239)
PHONE..........................580 658-9193
Gary Graham, *President*
Keenan Graham, *Vice Pres*
Kim Graham, *Admin Sec*
EMP: 6
SALES: 1.1MM **Privately Held**
SIC: 8711 3599 Engineering services; machine shop, jobbing & repair

(G-4239)
PSF SERVICES LLC
109 W Cherokee St (73055-2653)
PHONE..........................707 386-8805
Brendon Davis,
Clint Gann,
EMP: 2
SQ FT: 2,000
SALES (est): 73.4K **Privately Held**
SIC: 3451 3452 3533 Screw machine products; bolts, nuts, rivets & washers; oil field machinery & equipment

(G-4240)
REHME MFG INC
100 E Cherokee St (73055-2817)
PHONE..........................580 658-2414
Mark L Rehme, *President*
EMP: 11
SALES (est): 1.5MM **Privately Held**
SIC: 5999 3999 Miscellaneous retail stores; manufacturing industries

(G-4241)
REVIEW PRINTING COMPANY INC
Also Called: Marlow Review
316 W Main St (73055-2442)
P.O. Box 153 (73055-0153)
PHONE..........................580 658-6657
Michael Sterns, *President*
John Hruby, *President*
Joshua Sterns, *Vice Pres*
Mike Stearns, *Manager*
V Kimbrough, *MIS Dir*
EMP: 12
SALES (est): 673.9K **Privately Held**
SIC: 2711 2752 2791 2789 Newspapers, publishing & printing; commercial printing, offset; typesetting; bookbinding & related work

(G-4242)
SOONER ENERGY SERVICES INC (HQ)
1004 S Plainsman Rd (73055-8600)
PHONE..........................405 579-3200
Gwen Bristow, *President*
Michelle Adams, *Bd of Directors*
▲ EMP: 6
SQ FT: 5,000
SALES (est): 4.3MM
SALES (corp-wide): 119.3MM **Publicly Held**
SIC: 2819 2899 2842 Industrial inorganic chemicals; chemical preparations; specialty cleaning, polishes & sanitation goods
PA: Flotek Industries, Inc.
    10603 W Sam Houston Pkwy
    Houston TX 77064
    713 849-9911

(G-4243)
SOUTHWEST LATEX LLC
210 Jones St (73055-1106)
PHONE..........................405 420-0018
Anthony Skahill, *Mng Member*
EMP: 5
SQ FT: 6,000
SALES: 400K **Privately Held**
SIC: 2822 Synthetic rubber

(G-4244)
TAPTEC MANUFACTURING LLC
913 Silverwood (73055-3860)
PHONE..........................580 467-5142
EMP: 1
SALES (est): 39.6K **Privately Held**
SIC: 3999 Manufacturing industries

(G-4245)
TERRACO PRODUCTION LEASING LLC
842 County Road 1610 (73055-6415)
PHONE..........................580 658-3000
Donnie McCaleb, *Principal*
EMP: 3
SALES (est): 291.3K **Privately Held**
SIC: 1389 Oil field services

(G-4246)
VERNON SHEET METAL
1010 Black Rd (73055-5235)
PHONE..........................580 658-6778
Vernon E Belk, *Owner*
EMP: 4
SALES (est): 170K **Privately Held**
SIC: 3444 Sheet metalwork

(G-4247)
WILCO MACHINE & FAB INC
1326 S Broadway St (73055-3885)
P.O. Box 48 (73055-0048)
PHONE..........................580 658-6993
Kris Boles, *CEO*
Brad Boles, *President*
Sue Boles, *Corp Secy*
Anthony Chandler, *Vice Pres*
David McCauley, *Vice Pres*
EMP: 275
SQ FT: 55,000
SALES (est): 52.5MM
SALES (corp-wide): 8.4B **Publicly Held**
SIC: 3533 Oil & gas field machinery
PA: National Oilwell Varco, Inc.
    7909 Parkwood Circle Dr
    Houston TX 77036
    713 346-7500

(G-4248)
WILSON PINSTAR CO
284539 E 1690 Rd (73055-0032)
P.O. Box 2 (73055-0002)
PHONE..........................580 255-5899
Ben Wilson, *Principal*
EMP: 5 EST: 2008
SALES (est): 329.6K **Privately Held**
WEB: www.wilsonpinstar.com
SIC: 1389 Oil field services

(G-4249)
WOODY CREEK RANCH
Rr 4 Box 59 (73055-9429)
PHONE..........................580 658-5448
EMP: 1
SALES (est): 75.8K **Privately Held**
SIC: 1381 Oil/Gas Well Drilling

Marshall
Logan County

(G-4250)
EARNHEART CRESCENT LLC
12782 W County Road 60 (73056-9756)
PHONE..........................888 536-8703
EMP: 2
SALES (est): 90.7K **Privately Held**
SIC: 2911 Oils, fuel

Martha
Jackson County

(G-4251)
FARMERS COOP GIN OF MARTHA
304 N Walnut St (73556)
P.O. Box 250 (73556-0250)
PHONE..........................580 266-3222
Pat Wallace, *President*
EMP: 9

SALES (est): 1.2MM **Privately Held**
SIC: 2429 Cooperage stock products: staves, headings, hoops, etc.

Maud
Pottawatomie County

(G-4252)
GILLHAM OIL & GAS INC
Also Called: Gillham Oil Co
301 E Wanda Jackson Blvd (74854)
PHONE..........................405 997-8549
Paul Gillham, *President*
EMP: 1
SQ FT: 2,000
SALES (est): 223.2K **Privately Held**
SIC: 6211 1381 Oil royalties dealers; drilling oil & gas wells

(G-4253)
WALTMAN OIL & GAS
46659 Romulus Rd (74854-2602)
PHONE..........................405 374-2694
Britt Waltman, *Owner*
EMP: 2
SALES (est): 115.8K **Privately Held**
SIC: 1389 Pumping of oil & gas wells

Maysville
Garvin County

(G-4254)
BACKWOODS WELDING INC
23396 E County Road 1520 (73057-9736)
PHONE..........................405 642-5199
EMP: 1
SALES (est): 25K **Privately Held**
SIC: 7692 Welding repair

(G-4255)
BURFORD CORP (HQ)
11284 Highway 74 (73057-9669)
P.O. Box 748 (73057-0748)
PHONE..........................405 867-4467
Fred Springer, *President*
Clay Miller, *Vice Pres*
Andrew Beaulieu, *Manager*
Josh Hughes, *Manager*
David Bergman, *Technical Staff*
◆ EMP: 87 EST: 1961
SQ FT: 32,000
SALES: 20MM
SALES (corp-wide): 2.9B **Publicly Held**
WEB: www.burford.com
SIC: 3556 Bakery machinery; packing house machinery
PA: The Middleby Corporation
    1400 Toastmaster Dr
    Elgin IL 60120
    847 741-3300

(G-4256)
CASEING CREWS INC
300 6th St (73057-9684)
PHONE..........................405 867-1500
Mark Fielding, *Office Mgr*
EMP: 2 EST: 2013
SALES (est): 112K **Privately Held**
SIC: 1389 Oil field services

(G-4257)
DARRELL LEWIS
Also Called: Lewis, Darrell Welding
Rr 2 Box 146 (73057)
P.O. Box 141 (73057-0141)
PHONE..........................405 867-5768
Darrell Lewis, *Owner*
EMP: 2
SALES (est): 180K **Privately Held**
SIC: 7692 7299 1799 Welding repair; personal item care & storage services; welding on site

(G-4258)
DEVINEY CONTRACT PUMPING LLC
12607 N County Road 3110 (73057-9473)
PHONE..........................405 428-2192
EMP: 2

Maysville - Garvin County (G-4259) GEOGRAPHIC SECTION

SALES (est): 125.5K **Privately Held**
SIC: 1389 Pumping of oil & gas wells

(G-4259)
DEVINEY PARAFFIN SCRAPING
Rr 2 (73057)
P.O. Box 246 (73057-0246)
PHONE....................405 867-5945
David Deviney, *Owner*
EMP: 2
SALES (est): 150.7K **Privately Held**
SIC: 1389 Oil field services

(G-4260)
IN HIS NAME SCREENPRINTING LLC
24260 E County Road 1560 (73057-9766)
PHONE....................405 756-8911
Dylan Kinard, *Principal*
EMP: 3
SALES (est): 192.8K **Privately Held**
SIC: 2759 Screen printing

(G-4261)
MAYSVILLE PUBLISHING CO
Also Called: Maysville News
402 Williams (73057-3683)
P.O. Box 617 (73057-0617)
PHONE....................405 867-4457
Kenneth Wood, *Owner*
EMP: 6
SQ FT: 1,000
SALES (est): 215.1K **Privately Held**
WEB: www.gcnews-star.com
SIC: 2711 Newspapers: publishing only, not printed on site

(G-4262)
UNIQUE WOOD WORKS INC
13877 Sooner Ave (73057-3737)
PHONE....................405 249-6615
Pedro Fuentes, *President*
EMP: 2
SALES (est): 108.8K **Privately Held**
SIC: 2431 Millwork

(G-4263)
WOODS PUMPING SERVICE INC
13612 State Highway 74 (73057-3720)
PHONE....................405 449-3485
Michael Welch, *President*
Than Maynard, *Principal*
EMP: 7
SQ FT: 1,500
SALES (est): 770K **Privately Held**
SIC: 1389 Oil field services

Mazie
Mayes County

(G-4264)
JACKSON CLIP CO INC
2 And A Half Mile W (74337)
P.O. Box 1150, Chouteau (74337-1150)
PHONE....................918 476-8331
EMP: 196
SALES (est): 28.5MM
SALES (corp-wide): 9.7MM **Privately Held**
SIC: 3315 Steel Wire And Related Products, Nsk
PA: Glass Operating Group, L.L.C.
200 E 6th St
Newkirk OK 74647
580 362-6221

Mc Alester
Pittsburg County

(G-4265)
OVINTIV EXPLORATION INC
5111 S Highway 69 (74501)
PHONE....................918 420-5086
Mike Cannon, *Manager*
EMP: 3
SALES (corp-wide): 8.5MM **Publicly Held**
SIC: 1311 Crude petroleum & natural gas production

HQ: Ovintiv Exploration Inc.
4 Waterway Square Pl # 100
The Woodlands TX 77380
281 210-5100

(G-4266)
SOONER COCA-COLA BOTTLING CO
1610 E Van Buren Ave (74501)
P.O. Box 176, McAlester (74502-0176)
PHONE....................918 423-0911
Ron Hutto, *President*
Tommy Browning, *President*
Mary Nell Hamilton, *Manager*
Pat Pennington, *Admin Sec*
EMP: 9
SALES (est): 1.1MM **Privately Held**
SIC: 2086 5499 Bottled & canned soft drinks; soft drinks

Mc Curtain
Haskell County

(G-4267)
A & M BLAYLOCK CNSTR & PARTS
S 7 St (74944)
P.O. Box 156, McCurtain (74944-0156)
PHONE....................918 945-7081
Nilford Blaylock, *President*
EMP: 8
SALES (est): 737.4K **Privately Held**
SIC: 1389 1799 Oil field services; antenna installation

McAlester
Pittsburg County

(G-4268)
7 UP BOTTLE
4107 W Highway 31 (74501-8646)
PHONE....................918 426-0310
EMP: 3
SALES (est): 141.7K **Privately Held**
SIC: 2086 Bottled & canned soft drinks

(G-4269)
ALWAYS WELDING
32 E Morris Ave (74501-3051)
PHONE....................918 426-9353
Mark Sanders, *Owner*
EMP: 2
SALES (est): 99.2K **Privately Held**
SIC: 7692 Welding repair

(G-4270)
ANCHOR AUTO & WELDING REPR LLC
8 W Tyler Ave (74501-3606)
PHONE....................918 426-7662
Mike Nolan, *Mng Member*
EMP: 3 **EST:** 2013
SALES (est): 257.5K **Privately Held**
SIC: 7538 7692 General automotive repair shops; welding repair

Mcalester
Pittsburg County

(G-4271)
BAKER HUGHES A GE COMPANY LLC
2375 S George Nigh Expy (74501)
PHONE....................918 302-0490
EMP: 2
SALES (corp-wide): 23.8B **Publicly Held**
SIC: 1389 Oil field services
HQ: Baker Hughes Holdings Llc
17021 Aldine Westfield Rd
Houston TX 77073
713 439-8600

McAlester
Pittsburg County

(G-4272)
BAKER HUGHES INCORPORATED
2491 Highway 69 Byp (74501)
PHONE....................918 426-6585
EMP: 87
SALES (corp-wide): 24.5B **Publicly Held**
SIC: 3533 Mfg Oil/Gas Field Machinery
PA: Baker Hughes Incorporated
2929 Allen Pkwy Ste 2100
Houston TX 77073
713 439-8600

(G-4273)
BARGAIN JOURNAL
Also Called: Morgn Graphic Design
126 E Choctaw Ave (74501-5024)
PHONE....................918 426-5500
Barbara Morgan, *Owner*
EMP: 5
SALES (est): 346.4K **Privately Held**
SIC: 2759 2711 Commercial printing; newspapers

(G-4274)
BERRY GLOBAL INC
349 Taylor Indus Pk Rd (74501-6974)
PHONE....................812 424-2904
Scott Wagoner, *Plant Mgr*
Terry Lanham, *Branch Mgr*
Vanessa Thompson, *Clerk*
EMP: 13 **Publicly Held**
SIC: 3089 Bottle caps, molded plastic
HQ: Berry Global, Inc.
101 Oakley St
Evansville IN 47710

(G-4275)
BERRY GLOBAL INC
349 Taylor Indus Prk Rd (74501-6974)
PHONE....................918 426-4800
Glen Hamilton, *Plant Engr*
Scott Wagoner, *Branch Mgr*
EMP: 198 **Publicly Held**
SIC: 3089 3081 Bottle caps, molded plastic; unsupported plastics film & sheet
HQ: Berry Global, Inc.
101 Oakley St
Evansville IN 47710

(G-4276)
BIG V FEEDS INC
Also Called: Big V Feeds
1621 E Electric Ave (74501-3859)
P.O. Box 943 (74502-0943)
PHONE....................918 423-1565
William L Verner, *President*
Dan Boatright, *Principal*
Christine Verner, *Principal*
Mike Verner, *Vice Pres*
John Allford, *Opers Mgr*
▲ **EMP:** 90
SQ FT: 75,000
SALES (est): 37MM **Privately Held**
WEB: www.bigvfeeds.com
SIC: 2047 2048 2041 Dog & cat food; prepared feeds; flour & other grain mill products

(G-4277)
BPM LLC
Also Called: Bullseye Precision Mfg
403 Edgewood Dr (74501-7529)
PHONE....................405 761-0911
Joseph Capers, *Principal*
EMP: 1
SALES (est): 57.6K **Privately Held**
SIC: 3999 Manufacturing industries

(G-4278)
BRUFFETT ELECTRIC
1803 Cardinal Ln (74501-7504)
PHONE....................918 426-1875
Timothy Bruffett, *Owner*
EMP: 1 **EST:** 1986
SALES (est): 91.1K **Privately Held**
SIC: 1389 Oil field services

(G-4279)
CENTERPINT ENRGY RSOURCES CORP
4262 E Us Highway 270 (74501-6392)
PHONE....................580 512-5903
Play Basden, *Branch Mgr*
EMP: 2
SALES (corp-wide): 12.3B **Publicly Held**
SIC: 4924 1311 Natural gas distribution; crude petroleum & natural gas
HQ: Centerpoint Energy Resources Corp.
1111 Louisiana St
Houston TX 77002
713 207-1111

(G-4280)
CHARLES KOMAR & SONS INC
Also Called: Seamprufe
400 W Chickasaw Ave (74501-5237)
P.O. Box 1227 (74502-1227)
PHONE....................918 423-3535
Gerald Calaway, *Vice Pres*
Joe King, *Director*
EMP: 263
SQ FT: 140,000
SALES (corp-wide): 283.9MM **Privately Held**
WEB: www.komarbrands.com
SIC: 2341 2384 2339 Panties: women's, misses', children's & infants'; women's & children's undergarments; nightgowns & negligees: women's & children's; robes & dressing gowns; women's & misses' outerwear
PA: Charles Komar & Sons, Inc.
90 Hudson St Fl 9
Jersey City NJ 07302
212 725-1500

Mcalester
Pittsburg County

(G-4281)
CHARLES KOMAR & SONS INC
10 Komar Dr (74501)
PHONE....................918 423-1227
EMP: 1
SALES (corp-wide): 160.6MM **Privately Held**
SIC: 2341 Mfg Women's/Youth Underwear
PA: Charles Komar & Sons, Inc.
90 Hudson St
Jersey City NJ 07302
212 725-1500

McAlester
Pittsburg County

(G-4282)
CHOC BREWING COMPANY INC
125 S Main St Ste 220 (74501-5363)
PHONE....................918 302-3002
EMP: 2
SALES (est): 62.3K **Privately Held**
SIC: 2082 Malt beverages

(G-4283)
CHOCTAW DEFENSE MFG LLC (DH)
3 Skyway Dr (74501-7610)
PHONE....................918 426-2871
Sean Lenardo, *President*
EMP: 9
SQ FT: 230,000
SALES (est): 11.9MM **Privately Held**
SIC: 3711 Universal carriers, military, assembly of
HQ: Choctaw Global, Llc
20 Sandstone Rd
Durant OK 74701
580 200-0927

▲ = Import ▼=Export
◆ =Import/Export

GEOGRAPHIC SECTION

McAlester - Pittsburg County (G-4313)

McAlester
Pittsburg County

(G-4284)
CHOCTAW DEFENSE MUNITIONS LLC
1 Skyway Dr Mcalester (74501)
PHONE..................918 426-7871
Sean Lenardo, *President*
Scott Callaway, *President*
EMP: 1
SALES (est): 100.8K **Privately Held**
SIC: 3482 Small arms ammunition
HQ: Choctaw Global, Llc
  20 Sandstone Rd
  Durant OK 74701
  580 200-0927

McAlester
Pittsburg County

(G-4285)
CHOCTAW GLOBAL LLC
3 Skyway Dr Ste 103 (74501-7610)
PHONE..................918 426-2871
Stephen Benefield, *Branch Mgr*
EMP: 1
SQ FT: 25,000 **Privately Held**
SIC: 3715 Truck trailers
HQ: Choctaw Global, Llc
  20 Sandstone Rd
  Durant OK 74701
  580 200-0927

(G-4286)
CHOCTAW MFG DEF CONTRS INC
Also Called: Choctaw Defense
3 Skyway Dr (74501-7610)
PHONE..................918 426-2871
John Uvodich, *President*
EMP: 5 **Privately Held**
SIC: 2448 3441 Wood pallets & skids; fabricated structural metal
HQ: Choctaw Manufacturing Defense Contractors, Inc.
  209 Sw 7th St
  Antlers OK 74523

McAlester
Pittsburg County

(G-4287)
CRANDELL SALVAGE INCORPORATED
904 Old Highway 69 (74501)
PHONE..................918 429-0001
Randy Crandell, *President*
Tammy Jones, *Admin Sec*
EMP: 15
SALES (est): 2.9MM **Privately Held**
SIC: 3537 Trucks: freight, baggage, etc.: industrial, except mining

McAlester
Pittsburg County

(G-4288)
CRAWFORD GRANITE WORKS
Rr 6 Box 5 (74501)
PHONE..................918 423-3020
Derek Shaw, *Owner*
EMP: 4
SALES: 220K **Privately Held**
SIC: 3281 Marble, building: cut & shaped

(G-4289)
CREATIVE BLESSINGS
2755 Krebs Lake Rd (74501-2684)
PHONE..................918 302-0734
Alissa Carmany, *Owner*
EMP: 1
SALES (est): 41.5K **Privately Held**
SIC: 3944 Craft & hobby kits & sets

(G-4290)
CUSTOM SCREEN PRINTERS
502 E Wyandotte Ave (74501-5466)
P.O. Box 1950 (74502-1950)
PHONE..................918 423-3696
Cindy Cumbie, *Owner*
EMP: 1
SALES (est): 69.3K **Privately Held**
SIC: 5699 2396 Customized clothing & apparel; automotive & apparel trimmings

(G-4291)
DAVIS INSULATED BUILDING INC
Also Called: Davis Pakeing Co and Bldg Stor
1539 S Main St (74501-7035)
PHONE..................918 423-2636
Lonnie Davis, *President*
EMP: 1
SALES (corp-wide): 4MM **Privately Held**
WEB: www.davisbuildings.com
SIC: 3448 5211 Buildings, portable: prefabricated metal; lumber & other building materials
PA: Davis Insulated Building Inc
  300 Sw A St
  Stigler OK 74462
  918 967-2042

(G-4292)
DB WIRELINE SERVICES INC
12558 W Us Highway 270 (74501-5562)
PHONE..................918 389-5038
Jimmy Dean, *President*
Glen Dale Brown, *Vice Pres*
EMP: 4 EST: 2010
SQ FT: 3,500
SALES: 420K **Privately Held**
SIC: 1389 Oil field services; gas field services

(G-4293)
DIANE BARCHEERS
Also Called: Scipio Creek Livestock Feed
821 Byington School Rd (74501-5784)
PHONE..................918 649-0440
Diane Barcheers, *Principal*
EMP: 3
SALES (est): 170K **Privately Held**
SIC: 2048 Livestock feeds

(G-4294)
DOLESE BROS CO
1620 S George Nigh Expy (74501-7411)
P.O. Box 1162 (74502-1162)
PHONE..................918 423-1061
James Roberts, *Manager*
EMP: 6
SALES (corp-wide): 8.5MM **Privately Held**
SIC: 3273 Ready-mixed concrete
PA: Dolese Bros. Co.
  20 Nw 13th St
  Oklahoma City OK 73103
  405 235-2311

(G-4295)
ERIC TURNER
Also Called: Independent Machine
820 N Main St (74501-4141)
PHONE..................918 423-7330
Eric Turner, *Owner*
EMP: 2
SALES (est): 120K **Privately Held**
SIC: 3444 Sheet metalwork

(G-4296)
EURECAT U S INCORPORATED
100 Steven Taylor Blvd (74501)
PHONE..................918 423-5800
EMP: 2
SALES (corp-wide): 2MM **Privately Held**
SIC: 2819 Catalysts, chemical
HQ: Eurecat U. S. Incorporated
  1331 Gemini St Ste 310
  Houston TX 77058
  281 218-0669

(G-4297)
FAMILY TREE CORPORATION
Also Called: Family Tree Oil & Gas
1000 E Seneca Ave (74501-6948)
PHONE..................307 850-4147
Rp Dykes, *Branch Mgr*
EMP: 1 **Privately Held**
SIC: 1389 Construction, repair & dismantling services
PA: Family Tree Corporation
  915 S Pearl St
  Denver CO 80209

(G-4298)
FIFTH QUARTER PRINTING LLC
224 S 3rd St (74501-5444)
PHONE..................918 471-9390
EMP: 2
SALES (est): 159K **Privately Held**
SIC: 2752 Commercial printing, lithographic

(G-4299)
FIRST CLASS OUTLET
1 E Chickasaw Ave (74501-5328)
P.O. Box 524 (74502-0524)
PHONE..................918 808-3405
Gaynel Kirkpatrick, *Owner*
EMP: 3 EST: 2015
SALES (est): 127.5K **Privately Held**
SIC: 2339 Women's & misses' outerwear

(G-4300)
FRANKLIN BAKING COMPANY LLC
Also Called: Flowers Bakery Outlet
460 S Main St (74501-5802)
PHONE..................918 423-2888
Greg Carter, *Manager*
EMP: 4
SALES (corp-wide): 4.1B **Publicly Held**
SIC: 2051 Bread, cake & related products
HQ: Franklin Baking Company, Llc
  500 W Grantham St
  Goldsboro NC 27530
  919 735-0344

(G-4301)
FREE SPIRIT EMBROIDERY
200 E Choctaw Ave (74501-5026)
PHONE..................918 429-4552
EMP: 1
SALES (est): 46.6K **Privately Held**
SIC: 2395 Pleating/Stitching Services

(G-4302)
GOURDIN CONSULTING LLC
153 High Point St (74501-7455)
PHONE..................918 207-9825
Bonnie Gourdin, *Principal*
EMP: 2
SALES (est): 68.2K **Privately Held**
SIC: 1389 Oil consultants

(G-4303)
HANGER PRSTHETCS & ORTHO INC
1611 N Strong Blvd (74501-3847)
PHONE..................918 423-1024
Terry Vanzandt, *Branch Mgr*
EMP: 3
SALES (corp-wide): 1.1B **Publicly Held**
SIC: 3842 Surgical appliances & supplies
HQ: Hanger Prosthetics & Orthotics, Inc.
  10910 Domain Dr Ste 300
  Austin TX 78758
  512 777-3800

McAlester
Pittsburg County

(G-4304)
HORIZON WELLTESTING LLC
3635 E Us Hwy 270 (74501)
P.O. Box 1469 (74502-1469)
PHONE..................918 429-1200
Michael Steele, *President*
EMP: 1 EST: 2011
SALES (est): 177K
SALES (corp-wide): 28.1MM **Publicly Held**
SIC: 1389 Oil field services
PA: Alpine 4 Technologies Ltd.
  2525 E Az Bltmore Cir
  Phoenix AZ 85016
  855 777-0077

McAlester
Pittsburg County

(G-4305)
HTW INC
Also Called: Weddle Signs
18 W Cherokee Ave (74501-5215)
PHONE..................918 423-4619
Darrin Weddle, *President*
EMP: 5
SALES (est): 390K **Privately Held**
SIC: 7389 3993 Lettering & sign painting services; signs & advertising specialties

(G-4306)
INFOCUS PRINT CO LLC
502 E Chickasaw Ave (74501-5305)
PHONE..................918 465-5572
EMP: 2
SALES (est): 104.1K **Privately Held**
SIC: 2752 Commercial printing, lithographic

(G-4307)
J & JS WDWRK HM DECOR & GIFTS
32 E Cherokee Ave (74501-5323)
PHONE..................918 420-9411
EMP: 1
SALES (est): 54.1K **Privately Held**
SIC: 2431 Millwork

(G-4308)
J&JS WOODWORK AND MORE
429 W Osage Ave (74501-6140)
PHONE..................918 429-9704
Jamie Ezell, *Principal*
EMP: 1
SALES (est): 54.1K **Privately Held**
SIC: 2431 Millwork

(G-4309)
JIM WOOD REFRIGERATION INC
200 E Wyandotte Ave (74501-5460)
PHONE..................918 426-3283
Jim Wood, *President*
Sandy Woodland, *Vice Pres*
EMP: 6 EST: 1983
SALES: 250K **Privately Held**
WEB: www.jimwoodrfg.com
SIC: 3585 Refrigeration & heating equipment

(G-4310)
KEY ENERGY SERVICES INC
142 Powell Rd (74501-4782)
PHONE..................918 302-0372
EMP: 2
SALES (corp-wide): 413.8MM **Publicly Held**
SIC: 1389 Servicing oil & gas wells
PA: Key Energy Services, Inc.
  1301 Mckinney St Ste 1800
  Houston TX 77010
  713 651-4300

(G-4311)
KOOL-BREEZ LLC
1507 N 1st St (74501-3540)
P.O. Box 846, Krebs (74554-0846)
PHONE..................918 715-3358
Shawn Smoot, *Owner*
EMP: 8
SALES: 1.6MM **Privately Held**
SIC: 3715 Truck trailers

(G-4312)
LAFES
3402 N Robin St (74501-2056)
PHONE..................918 423-5311
EMP: 1
SALES (est): 94K **Privately Held**
SIC: 3448 Mfg Prefabricated Metal Buildings

(G-4313)
LAKE COUNTRY BEVERAGE INC
4107 W Highway 31 (74501-8646)
PHONE..................918 426-0310
Howard Wise, *Principal*
EMP: 5 EST: 2010
SALES (est): 170.3K **Privately Held**
SIC: 2086 Bottled & canned soft drinks

McAlester - Pittsburg County (G-4314)   GEOGRAPHIC SECTION

(G-4314)
MANFORD OILFIELD SERVICES LLC
2257 Green Meadows Cir (74501-3245)
PHONE..................................918 424-3280
Mandy Parker, *Principal*
EMP: 2
SALES (est): 97.7K **Privately Held**
SIC: 1389 Oil field services

(G-4315)
MARKWEST ENRGY E TEXAS GAS LP
Also Called: Markwest Eastern
9725 W Us Highway 270 (74501-5552)
PHONE..................................918 389-5100
EMP: 7
SALES (corp-wide): 9B **Publicly Held**
SIC: 1382 Oil & gas exploration services
HQ: Markwest Energy East Texas Gas Company L.P.
    2448 E 81st St Ste 5400
    Tulsa OK 74137

(G-4316)
MCALESTER DEMOCRAT INC
500 S 2nd St (74501-5812)
P.O. Box 519 (74502-0519)
PHONE..................................918 423-1700
Ed Choate, *Publisher*
Amy Johns, *Principal*
Adrian O'Hanlon III, *Editor*
Corey Stolzenbach, *Editor*
EMP: 4
SALES (est): 232.5K **Privately Held**
SIC: 2711 Job printing & newspaper publishing combined

(G-4317)
MCALESTER MONUMENT CO INC
320 E Choctaw Ave (74501-5028)
PHONE..................................918 423-1647
Toll Free:.................................877
James A Stizza, *President*
Philip Stizza, *Admin Sec*
EMP: 3 EST: 1921
SQ FT: 4,000
SALES (est): 311.2K **Privately Held**
WEB: www.mcalestermonument.com
SIC: 5999 5032 3281 Monuments, finished to custom order; brick, stone & related material; cut stone & stone products

(G-4318)
MCCABE CRANE & SIGN
801 E Miami Ave (74501-6609)
PHONE..................................918 424-6381
Jared McCabe, *Owner*
EMP: 1
SALES (est): 120K **Privately Held**
WEB: www.mccabeledsigns.com
SIC: 3993 Signs & advertising specialties

(G-4319)
MCCRAYS MANUFACTURING CO
500 W Brewer Ave (74501-2035)
PHONE..................................918 426-1691
EMP: 3
SALES: 100K **Privately Held**
SIC: 7692 Welding Repair

(G-4320)
MEECO SULLIVAN LLC (PA)
1501 E Electric Ave (74501-3833)
P.O. Box 639, Warwick NY (10990-0639)
PHONE..................................918 423-6833
Steve Sullivan, *President*
Dan Adams, *Vice Pres*
Tonya Campbell, *Vice Pres*
Carmine Guido, *Vice Pres*
Bob Sullivan, *Vice Pres*
EMP: 19 EST: 2012
SALES (est): 20.4MM **Privately Held**
SIC: 3448 1629 Docks: prefabricated metal; dock construction

(G-4321)
MIA BELLA CANDLES
117 E South Ave (74501-6816)
PHONE..................................918 470-3862
EMP: 2
SALES (est): 66K **Privately Held**
SIC: 3999 Mfg Misc Products

(G-4322)
NATIONAL OILWELL VARCO INC
501 N George Nigh Expy (74501-8164)
PHONE..................................918 423-8000
Tracy Kelley, *Buyer*
Ashton Hackler, *Accountant*
Dale Riley, *Branch Mgr*
Kathie Covey, *Software Dev*
EMP: 7
SALES (corp-wide): 8.4B **Publicly Held**
WEB: www.nov.com
SIC: 3533 Oil & gas field machinery
PA: National Oilwell Varco, Inc.
    7909 Parkwood Circle Dr
    Houston TX 77036
    713 346-7500

(G-4323)
NATIONAL OILWELL VARCO INC
Also Called: Nov Rig Systems
401 Steven Taylor Blvd (74501-8639)
PHONE..................................918 423-8000
EMP: 5
SALES (corp-wide): 8.4B **Publicly Held**
SIC: 3561 Pumps, oil well & field
PA: National Oilwell Varco, Inc.
    7909 Parkwood Circle Dr
    Houston TX 77036
    713 346-7500

(G-4324)
NEWSPAPER HOLDING INC
Also Called: News Capital & Democrat
500 S 2nd St (74501-5812)
P.O. Box 987 (74502-0987)
PHONE..................................918 423-1700
John Tucker, *Manager*
EMP: 58 **Privately Held**
SIC: 2711 Newspapers, publishing & printing
HQ: Newspaper Holding, Inc.
    425 Locust St
    Johnstown PA 15901
    814 532-5102

(G-4325)
OK FIRE LLC
400 N Main St (74501-4606)
P.O. Box 729 (74502-0729)
PHONE..................................918 424-1808
Emory Dilbeck, *Principal*
EMP: 2
SALES (est): 148.9K **Privately Held**
SIC: 2899 3569 Fire retardant chemicals; foam charge mixtures; firefighting apparatus & related equipment; firehose equipment: driers, rack & reels; firehose, except rubber

(G-4326)
OLD TOWN WELDING SHOP
509 W Coal Ave (74501-2033)
PHONE..................................918 423-8506
EMP: 1
SALES (est): 56.6K **Privately Held**
SIC: 7539 1799 7692 Automotive Repair Shops, Nec

(G-4327)
OVINTIV EXPLORATION INC
5505 S Us Highway 69 (74501-6355)
PHONE..................................580 927-9064
Mike Cannon, *Manager*
EMP: 3
SALES (corp-wide): 8.5MM **Publicly Held**
WEB: www.theinnatrsf.com
SIC: 1311 Crude petroleum production
HQ: Ovintiv Exploration Inc.
    4 Waterway Square Pl # 100
    The Woodlands TX 77380
    281 210-5100

(G-4328)
PEPSI-COLA BTLG MCALESTER INC (PA)
1528 E Electric Ave (74501-3814)
PHONE..................................918 423-2360
Gerald Rogers, *CEO*
Zona M Rogers, *President*
Jeffrey Lozier, *Business Mgr*
Robert Rogers, *Sales Mgr*
Bill Tillman, *Sales Mgr*
EMP: 30

SQ FT: 16,000
SALES (est): 5.5MM **Privately Held**
WEB: www.pepsico.com
SIC: 2086 Carbonated soft drinks, bottled & canned

(G-4329)
PLAINS NITROGEN LLC
4997 W State Highway 31 (74501-6933)
PHONE..................................918 429-0041
Larry Hobgood, *Office Mgr*
EMP: 3
SALES (corp-wide): 129.8MM **Privately Held**
SIC: 1389 Oil field services
HQ: Plains Nitrogen Llc
    2601 Nw Expwy Ste 411w
    Oklahoma City OK

(G-4330)
POWERCO SEISMIC SERVICES LLC
3537 Mt Moriah (74501)
PHONE..................................918 424-3745
Bryan Powers, *Principal*
EMP: 1
SALES (est): 103.9K **Privately Held**
SIC: 1382 Seismograph surveys

(G-4331)
RAINBOW SPREME ASSMBLY I ORG
Also Called: INTERNATIONAL ORDER OF THE RAI
315 E Carl Albert Pkwy (74501-5043)
PHONE..................................918 423-1328
Barbara Russell, *Admin Sec*
EMP: 5
SALES: 775.3K **Privately Held**
SIC: 2389 8641 5192 5137 Regalia; fraternal associations; books, periodicals & newspapers; women's & children's clothing; men's & boys' clothing

(G-4332)
RED SEAL FEEDS LLC
1400 E Washington Ave (74501-4900)
PHONE..................................918 423-3710
EMP: 9
SALES: 1.8MM **Privately Held**
SIC: 2048 Mfg Prepared Feeds

McAlester
Pittsburg County

(G-4333)
ROGER KEY INC
2600 Standard Rd (74501)
PHONE..................................918 423-5420
Roger Key, *President*
Kevin Connor, *Vice Pres*
EMP: 8
SALES: 550K **Privately Held**
SIC: 3531 Bulldozers (construction machinery)

McAlester
Pittsburg County

(G-4334)
SE OKLAHOMA SCHOOL OF WELDING
1710 E College Ave (74501-4272)
P.O. Box 3848 (74502-3848)
PHONE..................................918 423-9353
William John Allen, *Administration*
EMP: 3
SALES (est): 122.6K **Privately Held**
SIC: 7692 Welding repair

(G-4335)
SIGNS BY JADE
Also Called: Custom Signs By Jade
343 E Choctaw Ave (74501-5027)
PHONE..................................918 423-0041
Jade Oldham, *Owner*
EMP: 2
SQ FT: 1,800
SALES (est): 145.3K **Privately Held**
SIC: 3993 Signs & advertising specialties

(G-4336)
SMALLWOOD BUILDING LLC
426 S Main St (74501-5802)
PHONE..................................918 424-9378
Brian West, *Principal*
EMP: 2
SALES (est): 55.2K **Privately Held**
SIC: 2499 Wood products

(G-4337)
SPIRIT AEROSYSTEMS INC
1900 E Electric Ave (74501-3889)
PHONE..................................918 423-6979
A J Vercelli, *Purchasing*
Joe Bass, *QA Dir*
K B Hicks, *Branch Mgr*
Drew Breese, *Info Tech Mgr*
Gary Mordecai, *Executive*
EMP: 175 **Publicly Held**
WEB: www.spiritaero.com
SIC: 3728 3812 3769 Aircraft parts & equipment; search & navigation equipment; guided missile & space vehicle parts & auxiliary equipment
HQ: Spirit Aerosystems, Inc.
    3801 S Oliver St
    Wichita KS 67210
    316 526-9000

(G-4338)
STANDARD MACHINE LLC
Also Called: Standard Machine & Wldg Works
5610 S Us Highway 69 (74501-6356)
P.O. Box 3246 (74502-3246)
PHONE..................................918 423-9430
Floyd D Cable,
Denson Cable,
EMP: 6 EST: 1976
SQ FT: 12,000
SALES (est): 1.5MM **Privately Held**
SIC: 7692 3599 7699 Welding repair; machine shop, jobbing & repair; hydraulic equipment repair

(G-4339)
STEP ENERGY SVCS HOLDINGS LTD
7319 E Us Highway 270 (74501-6457)
P.O. Box 330, Alderson (74522-0330)
PHONE..................................918 423-4300
Wayne Tucker, *President*
EMP: 21
SALES (corp-wide): 501.9MM **Privately Held**
SIC: 1389 3533 Oil consultants; well logging equipment
HQ: Step Energy Services Holdings Ltd.
    480 Wildwood Forest Dr
    Spring TX 77380

(G-4340)
THIRD ROCK CONSTRUCTION LLC
308 E Camp Loop (74501-8696)
PHONE..................................918 429-2011
Terry Kesler, *Principal*
EMP: 2
SALES (est): 111.9K **Privately Held**
SIC: 1429 Crushed & broken stone

(G-4341)
THRU TUBING SOLUTIONS INC
225 Sw Haileyville Ave (74501-6578)
PHONE..................................918 429-7700
Andrew Ferguson, *President*
EMP: 8
SALES (corp-wide): 1.2B **Publicly Held**
WEB: www.thrutubing.com
SIC: 1389 Oil field services
HQ: Thru Tubing Solutions, Inc.
    11515 S Portland Ave
    Oklahoma City OK 73170
    405 692-1900

(G-4342)
TITAN CHEMICAL
5034 E Us Highway 270 (74501-6482)
PHONE..................................918 420-5990
EMP: 8
SALES (est): 1.3MM **Privately Held**
SIC: 2869 Mfg Industrial Organic Chemicals

GEOGRAPHIC SECTION

(G-4343)
TRICAT INC
103 Taylar Rd (74501-1019)
P.O. Box 789 (74502-0789)
PHONE..................................918 423-5800
Carl Sandburg, *Manager*
EMP: 25
SALES (corp-wide): 2MM **Privately Held**
SIC: 2819 Catalysts, chemical
HQ: Tricat, Inc
 1331 Gemini St Ste 310
 Houston TX 77058

(G-4344)
TRIM RITE MOLDINGS INC
2303 N Main St (74501-3048)
PHONE..................................918 423-2525
Greg Shores, *President*
EMP: 5
SALES (est): 755.3K **Privately Held**
SIC: 2431 Millwork

(G-4345)
TURNEY BROS OILFLD SVCS & PP
401 Oklahoma Ave (74501-7386)
PHONE..................................918 470-6937
EMP: 50
SALES (est): 3.1MM **Privately Held**
SIC: 1389 Oil/Gas Field Services

(G-4346)
TWIN CITIES READY MIX INC (PA)
102 W Ashland Ave (74501-2004)
PHONE..................................918 423-8855
George C Schwarz, *President*
Gordon A Schwarz, *Corp Secy*
EMP: 40 EST: 1960
SQ FT: 1,000
SALES (est): 15.7MM **Privately Held**
SIC: 3273 Ready-mixed concrete

(G-4347)
TY GIAUDRONE
290 Baileys Bend Rd (74501-8692)
P.O. Box 310 (74502-0310)
PHONE..................................918 423-6499
Ty Giaudrone, *Principal*
EMP: 3
SALES (est): 264.4K **Privately Held**
SIC: 3721 Motorized aircraft

(G-4348)
UNITED STATES DEPT OF ARMY
Also Called: McAlester Army Ammun Plant
1 C Tree Rd (74501-9002)
PHONE..................................918 420-6642
Donald Shields, *General Mgr*
EMP: 900 **Publicly Held**
WEB: www.us.army.mil
SIC: 3482 9711 Small arms ammunition; Army;
HQ: The Army United States Department Of
 101 Army Pentagon
 Washington DC 20310

(G-4349)
WASHITA VALLEY ENTERPRISES INC
387 Alderson Rd (74501-2192)
P.O. Box 247 (74502-0247)
PHONE..................................918 429-0186
Tiffany Midgett, *Branch Mgr*
EMP: 100
SALES (corp-wide): 46.4MM **Privately Held**
SIC: 1389 Oil field services
PA: Washita Valley Enterprises, Inc.
 1705 Se 59th St
 Oklahoma City OK 73129
 405 670-5338

(G-4350)
WEBCOAT INC
Also Called: Visions Innovated Products
1801 E College Ave (74501-4275)
P.O. Box 3160 (74502-3160)
PHONE..................................918 426-5100
Bob Vevoda, *CEO*
Robert Webb, *CEO*
Denise Webb, *Corp Secy*
Brian Campbell, *CFO*
▲ EMP: 109

SQ FT: 82,000
SALES (est): 22.8MM **Privately Held**
SIC: 2514 Garden furniture, metal

(G-4351)
WHISPRING MDOWS VNYARDS WINERY
34 E Choctaw Ave (74501-5055)
PHONE..................................918 423-9463
Karen Stobaugh, *Principal*
EMP: 4
SALES (est): 303.9K **Privately Held**
SIC: 2084 Wines

McLoud
Pottawatomie County

(G-4352)
BLOCK SAND CO INC
329044 E 1070 Rd (74851-9709)
PHONE..................................405 391-2919
Dan Block, *President*
Frances Block, *Treasurer*
EMP: 25
SQ FT: 900
SALES (est): 7.9MM **Privately Held**
SIC: 5032 3273 4212 Sand, construction; ready-mixed concrete; local trucking, without storage

(G-4353)
BRIEFCASE SOLUTIONS LTD LLC
19006 Walker Rd (74851-9008)
PHONE..................................405 788-9250
Samantha Thomas, *Principal*
EMP: 2
SALES (est): 83K **Privately Held**
SIC: 3161 Briefcases

(G-4354)
BROKEN BONE VNYARDS WINERY LLC
1356 S Blackberry Dr (74851-8124)
PHONE..................................405 585-8319
EMP: 2
SALES (est): 77.4K **Privately Held**
SIC: 2084 Wines

(G-4355)
BRUNO IND LIVING AIDS INC
420 E Broadway Ave (74851-8147)
PHONE..................................405 964-5887
Marcie Bruno, *Principal*
EMP: 4
SALES (corp-wide): 105MM **Privately Held**
WEB: www.bruno.com
SIC: 3842 Technical aids for the handicapped
PA: Bruno Independent Living Aids, Inc.
 1780 Executive Dr
 Oconomowoc WI 53066
 262 953-5405

(G-4356)
C&H SAFETY PIN INC
35 Walker Ln (74851-8541)
P.O. Box 261, Newalla (74857-0261)
PHONE..................................405 386-3942
Cheryl Jennings, *President*
EMP: 5
SALES (est): 536.8K **Privately Held**
SIC: 3533 Oil field machinery & equipment

(G-4357)
CARL BRIGHT INC
3210 S Arena Rd (74851-8066)
PHONE..................................405 761-7129
Leslie Martin, *CEO*
Carl Bright, *Principal*
Karyn Bright, *Admin Sec*
EMP: 5
SQ FT: 3,000
SALES (est): 601.8K **Privately Held**
WEB: www.carlbright.com
SIC: 3533 Oil & gas field machinery

(G-4358)
HMT MACHINING INCORPORATED
3108 S Arena Rd (74851-8005)
PHONE..................................405 964-2054
Robert Gardner, *Owner*
EMP: 3
SALES (est): 326.5K **Privately Held**
SIC: 3599 Machine shop, jobbing & repair

(G-4359)
LOCAL HOMETOWN PUBLISHING INC
17809 Deer Trl (74851-8549)
PHONE..................................405 273-3838
Neal Davis, *Principal*
EMP: 1 EST: 2012
SALES (est): 64.5K **Privately Held**
SIC: 2741 Miscellaneous publishing

(G-4360)
MAC PUBLISHING COMPANY LLC
333244 E 1070 Rd (74851-9631)
PHONE..................................405 964-3576
Mary Campbell, *Principal*
EMP: 2
SALES (est): 59.2K **Privately Held**
SIC: 2741 Miscellaneous publishing

(G-4361)
PENIELITE GGG PRESS
Also Called: Penielite Press
407 Jarman Dr (74851-8043)
PHONE..................................405 850-5795
Mark A Johnson, *CEO*
EMP: 4
SALES (est): 113.5K **Privately Held**
SIC: 2731 Books: publishing & printing

(G-4362)
PERCEPTIONS
1927 N Fishmarket Rd (74851-8313)
PHONE..................................405 964-7000
Roger Tuter, *Owner*
EMP: 5
SALES: 150K **Privately Held**
SIC: 2542 2541 Cabinets: show, display or storage: except wood; wood partitions & fixtures

(G-4363)
TORNADOS SCREEN PRINTING
1 Whispering Oaks Dr (74851-8134)
PHONE..................................405 964-5339
David Thompson, *Owner*
EMP: 2
SALES (est): 152.7K **Privately Held**
SIC: 3993 2759 Signs & advertising specialties; screen printing

(G-4364)
TRENDY TEES
305 Teri Ln (74851-8615)
PHONE..................................405 620-3673
Shelly Palmer, *Principal*
EMP: 2 EST: 2018
SALES (est): 99.9K **Privately Held**
SIC: 2759 Screen printing

Mead
Bryan County

(G-4365)
COLOR EXPRESS
121 Palmer Pt (73449-6341)
PHONE..................................214 384-0887
EMP: 2
SALES (est): 106.8K **Privately Held**
SIC: 2752 Commercial printing, offset

(G-4366)
HAUSNERS LIMITED
8883 Us 70 (73449-5523)
P.O. Box 1307, Durant (74702-1307)
PHONE..................................580 924-6988
Allen Hausner, *President*
Krystal Hausner, *Manager*
Linda Hausner, *Admin Sec*
EMP: 18 EST: 1954
SQ FT: 1,200

SALES: 2.5MM **Privately Held**
SIC: 3272 Septic tanks, concrete

(G-4367)
ROLL-OFFS OF AMERICA INC
Also Called: Roll-Offs USA
8567 Us Hwy 70 (73449)
P.O. Box 727, Durant (74702-0727)
PHONE..................................580 924-6355
Daniel J Hankey, *President*
Rod Donica, *Corp Secy*
Ray Jean Hankey, *Vice Pres*
EMP: 65
SQ FT: 150,000
SALES (est): 20.3MM **Privately Held**
SIC: 3469 Garbage cans, stamped & pressed metal

(G-4368)
THREE PRCENT FRRMS CATINGS LLC
2104 S Ranchette Rd (73449-5267)
PHONE..................................580 931-9908
Bobby Shults, *Principal*
Vonna Shults, *Officer*
Bobby Joe Shults, *Administration*
EMP: 2
SALES (est): 143.1K **Privately Held**
SIC: 3484 Guns (firearms) or gun parts, 30 mm. & below

Medford
Grant County

(G-4369)
S&W WELDING AND FABRICATION
311 N 3rd St (73759-1112)
PHONE..................................918 219-2565
Wendy Sherrod, *Principal*
EMP: 1
SALES (est): 25K **Privately Held**
SIC: 7692 Welding repair

Medicine Park
Comanche County

(G-4370)
EMERGENCY SITE PROTECTION LLC
191 W Lake Dr (73557-9000)
P.O. Box 244 (73557-0244)
PHONE..................................580 699-6386
Daryll Howell, *Managing Prtnr*
Michael William McCoy, *Principal*
EMP: 52
SALES (est): 11.1MM **Privately Held**
WEB: www.espsafetynet.com
SIC: 3713 Ambulance bodies

(G-4371)
TEXHOMA FIBER LLC
1 Big Rock Blvd (73557)
P.O. Box 171 (73557-0171)
PHONE..................................918 747-7000
EMP: 2
SALES (est): 98.2K **Privately Held**
SIC: 2298 Ropes & fiber cables

(G-4372)
WAID FORENSICS SCIENCE LLC
115 E Lake Dr (73557-9800)
P.O. Box 74 (73557-0074)
PHONE..................................580 574-8692
Margaret Waid, *President*
EMP: 1
SALES (est): 76.6K **Privately Held**
SIC: 3821 Laboratory apparatus, except heating & measuring

(G-4373)
WAID GROUP INC
115 E Lk Dr Mdcine Park Medicine (73557)
P.O. Box 74 (73557-0074)
PHONE..................................817 980-8985
Margaret C Waid, *President*
Charles Carter Waid, *Vice Pres*
EMP: 4

Meeker
Lincoln County

SALES: 304K **Privately Held**
WEB: www.amoebamath.com
SIC: **1389** 3999 Oil consultants; education aids, devices & supplies

(G-4374)
A T ROUSTABOUTS
43335 Curtis Dr (74855-5002)
PHONE..............................405 788-0735
EMP: 2
SALES (est): 65.5K **Privately Held**
SIC: **1389** Roustabout service

(G-4375)
ARROWPROP INC
106476 S 3440 Rd (74855-5573)
P.O. Box 610 (74855-0610)
PHONE..............................405 279-3833
Don Miller, *President*
Kay Miller, *Vice Pres*
EMP: 5
SQ FT: 11,000
SALES (est): 861.5K **Privately Held**
SIC: **3728** Aircraft parts & equipment

(G-4376)
CHESSER CONTRACT PUMPING LLC
9798 Musson Rd (74855-5210)
PHONE..............................405 820-7240
EMP: 2
SALES (est): 94K **Privately Held**
SIC: **1389** Pumping of oil & gas wells

(G-4377)
DANNY BOWEN
337215 E 1010 Rd (74855-5450)
PHONE..............................405 618-3377
Danny Bowen, *Principal*
EMP: 4
SALES (est): 285.9K **Privately Held**
SIC: **2741** Miscellaneous publishing

(G-4378)
LEWIS MANUFACTURING CO LLC
705 W Carl Hubbell Blvd (74855)
PHONE..............................405 279-2553
Caroll Harper, *Manager*
EMP: 37
SALES (corp-wide): 4.8MM **Privately Held**
WEB: www.lewismfg.com
SIC: **3199** 3533 Safety belts, leather; oil & gas field machinery
PA: Lewis Manufacturing Company, Llc
3601 S Byers Ave
Oklahoma City OK 73129
405 634-5401

(G-4379)
LINCOLN COUNTY BARN DIST NO 3
1408 Veteran Dr (74855)
P.O. Box 783 (74855-0783)
PHONE..............................405 279-3313
Pat McGinness, *Commissioner*
EMP: 22
SALES (est): 3MM **Privately Held**
SIC: **3531** Road construction & maintenance machinery

(G-4380)
MARK ARMITAGE
Also Called: Armitage Equipment
425 E Maker (74855)
P.O. Box 251 (74855-0251)
PHONE..............................405 279-2372
Mark Armitage, *Owner*
EMP: 2 EST: 1970
SALES (est): 261.4K **Privately Held**
SIC: **3523** Farm machinery & equipment

(G-4381)
MEEKER FOOTBALL PRESS BOX
214 E Carl Hubbell Blvd (74855-8400)
PHONE..............................405 279-1075
EMP: 1

SALES (est): 37.5K **Privately Held**
SIC: **2741** Miscellaneous publishing

(G-4382)
MIDWEST INDUSTRIES INC (PA)
614 W Carl Hubbell Blvd (74855)
P.O. Box 703 (74855-0703)
PHONE..............................405 279-3595
Michael Porter, *President*
Ross Coleman, *General Mgr*
Mary Porter, *Vice Pres*
Juanita Ward, *CFO*
EMP: 4
SQ FT: 20,000
SALES (est): 1.1MM **Privately Held**
SIC: **3499** Magnets, permanent: metallic

(G-4383)
MIDWEST INDUSTRIES INC
701 W Main St (74855)
P.O. Box 703 (74855-0703)
PHONE..............................405 279-2706
Ross Coleman, *Manager*
EMP: 12
SALES (corp-wide): 1.1MM **Privately Held**
SIC: **3264** Magnets, permanent: ceramic or ferrite
PA: Midwest Industries Inc
614 W Carl Hubbell Blvd
Meeker OK 74855
405 279-3595

(G-4384)
NATIVE CBD DISTRIBUTING
980998 S 3390 Rd (74855-7522)
PHONE..............................405 831-5270
Ron Cunningham, *Principal*
EMP: 1
SALES (est): 39.6K **Privately Held**
SIC: **3999**

(G-4385)
PREMIER BUSINESS SOLUTIONS LLC
Also Called: Premier Iron Works
344142 E 1000 Rd (74855-5427)
P.O. Box 897 (74855-0897)
PHONE..............................405 650-3131
Jeff Towler, *Vice Pres*
Lisa M Towler,
EMP: 4
SQ FT: 3,785
SALES (est): 495K **Privately Held**
SIC: **3449** Miscellaneous metalwork

(G-4386)
R A D WELDING (2)
Also Called: RAD Welding Svc
105366 S 3410 Rd (74855-9157)
PHONE..............................405 206-9434
EMP: 1
SALES (est): 61.6K **Privately Held**
SIC: **7692** Welding repair

Meno
Major County

(G-4387)
RICE WELDING INC
3 Miles So 1/2 Mile E # 12 (73760)
PHONE..............................580 776-2584
Cecil Rice, *Owner*
EMP: 6
SALES (est): 309.4K **Privately Held**
SIC: **1799** 1389 Welding on site; oil & gas wells: building, repairing & dismantling; oil field services

Miami
Ottawa County

(G-4388)
ACTION GRAPHICS PRINTING INC
3520 27th Ave Ne (74354-1518)
PHONE..............................918 540-3336
Kent Goul, *President*
EMP: 3

SALES (est): 433.1K **Privately Held**
SIC: **2752** Commercial printing, offset

(G-4389)
ACTION GRAPHICS PRTG & DESIGN
3520 27th Ave Ne (74354-1518)
P.O. Box 57, Commerce (74339-0057)
PHONE..............................918 540-3336
Kent Goul, *Owner*
EMP: 8
SALES (est): 615.1K **Privately Held**
SIC: **2752** Commercial printing, offset

(G-4390)
ALLEN SIGN STUDIO LLC
307 E Central Ave (74354-7004)
PHONE..............................918 542-1180
Kelly Witten, *Sales Staff*
Norm Cousatte, *Manager*
Colby Allen,
Debbie Allen,
EMP: 9
SQ FT: 9,250
SALES (est): 495K **Privately Held**
SIC: **3993** Electric signs

(G-4391)
BLITZ USA INC
Also Called: Kcc
309 N Main St (74354-5919)
P.O. Box 969 (74355-0969)
PHONE..............................918 676-3620
Rocky Flick, *President*
John R Elmburg, *Owner*
Larry Chrisco, *Vice Pres*
▲ EMP: 350
SQ FT: 125,000
SALES (est): 50.8MM **Privately Held**
WEB: www.blitzagency.com
SIC: **3085** 3999 3411 Plastics bottles; pet supplies; oil cans, metal

(G-4392)
COOK PROCESSING
2603 E St Sw (74354-9020)
PHONE..............................918 542-5796
Melvin Cook, *Owner*
EMP: 2
SQ FT: 3,880
SALES: 60K **Privately Held**
SIC: **2011** Meat packing plants

(G-4393)
CREATIVE ORNAMENTAL INC
58250 E 100 Rd (74354-3537)
PHONE..............................918 540-1600
Matthew Schumacher, *President*
John Scorse, *Corp Secy*
EMP: 5
SALES: 600K **Privately Held**
WEB: www.creativeornamental.com
SIC: **3441** Fabricated structural metal

(G-4394)
DARNELL SERVICES
506 S Main St (74354-8104)
PHONE..............................918 542-9236
Stephen Darnell, *Owner*
EMP: 3
SALES (est): 140K **Privately Held**
SIC: **7692** Welding repair

(G-4395)
DESERT MOON ENTERPRISES
826 K St Nw (74354-4223)
P.O. Box 1604 (74355-1604)
PHONE..............................918 540-0333
Jason Dye, *Owner*
EMP: 1
SALES (est): 69.6K **Privately Held**
SIC: **2499** 5051 7641 2511 Decorative wood & woodwork; metals service centers & offices; reupholstery & furniture repair; wood household furniture

(G-4396)
DISCOVERY PLASTICS LLC
3607 28th Ave Ne (74354-1496)
PHONE..............................918 540-2822
Kyle Cornwell, *Plant Mgr*
Helen Meeks, *Executive*
Thomas Paul,
▲ EMP: 100 EST: 2000
SQ FT: 59,600

SALES (est): 25.8MM **Privately Held**
SIC: **3089** Injection molding of plastics

(G-4397)
DON HUME COMPANY LLC
500 26th Ave Nw (74354-2208)
PHONE..............................918 542-6604
George Coen,
Gail Wiford,
EMP: 22
SALES (est): 741.9K **Privately Held**
SIC: **3199** Holsters, leather

(G-4398)
DON HUME LEATHERGOODS INC
500 26th Ave Nw (74354-2208)
PHONE..............................918 542-6604
Jerry Collins, *President*
Sharon Maxville, *Treasurer*
Shaniece Zinn, *Sales Mgr*
EMP: 80
SQ FT: 68,000
SALES: 3.1MM **Privately Held**
WEB: www.donhume.com
SIC: **3199** Mill strapping for textile mills, leather; leather belting & strapping; equestrian related leather articles

(G-4399)
DOUG LEE INGENUITY LLC
9201 S 650 Rd (74354-4113)
PHONE..............................918 542-4686
Douglas Lee, *Owner*
EMP: 4
SALES (est): 110K **Privately Held**
SIC: **3441** Fabricated structural metal

(G-4400)
E C BEIGHTS
Also Called: Classic Screen Printing
60151 E 66 Rd (74354-3544)
PHONE..............................918 674-2773
E C Beights, *Owner*
EMP: 1
SALES (est): 69K **Privately Held**
SIC: **2759** Labels & seals: printing

(G-4401)
EP SCIENTIFIC PRODUCTS LLC
520 N Main St (74354-4850)
PHONE..............................918 540-1507
Don Leggett,
Justin Wingo,
▲ EMP: 80
SALES (est): 15.4MM
SALES (corp-wide): 25.5B **Publicly Held**
SIC: **3826** Analytical instruments
HQ: Fisher Scientific Company Llc
300 Industry Dr
Pittsburgh PA 15275
724 517-1500

(G-4402)
EULITT WELDING
50300 E 120 Rd (74354-5531)
PHONE..............................918 542-2635
Gary Eulitt, *Owner*
Virginia Eulitt, *Co-Owner*
EMP: 1
SALES (est): 97.8K **Privately Held**
SIC: **7692** Welding repair

(G-4403)
EZ MAIL EXPRESS
1621 N Main St (74354-2720)
PHONE..............................918 542-2057
Jason Blevins, *Owner*
EMP: 2
SALES (est): 140.5K **Privately Held**
SIC: **2655** Fiber shipping & mailing containers

(G-4404)
FIVE STAR CUB CADET
58610 E 100 Rd (74354-3541)
PHONE..............................918 542-4070
Jay A Calan, *Owner*
Jaycee Calan, *Office Mgr*
EMP: 4
SALES (est): 342K **Privately Held**
SIC: **3523** Cabs, tractors & agricultural machinery

GEOGRAPHIC SECTION

Miami - Ottawa County (G-4434)

(G-4405)
FORTIFLEX INC
1410 Goodrich Blvd Ste A (74354-2830)
PHONE.................................918 540-3131
Melissa Roher, *General Mgr*
◆ EMP: 14
SALES (est): 2.2MM **Privately Held**
SIC: 3334 Primary aluminum

(G-4406)
G & G QUALITY SERVICES LLC
9902 S Highway 137 (74354-3822)
PHONE.................................918 961-0288
Gordon Williams Jr, *Mng Member*
Gordon Williams Sr,
EMP: 7 EST: 2013
SALES: 1.5MM **Privately Held**
SIC: 3533 Oil & gas field machinery

(G-4407)
GREGATH PUBLISHING COMPANY (PA)
Also Called: Mid-West Division
61101 E 140 Rd (74354-7417)
P.O. Box 505, Wyandotte (74370-0505)
PHONE.................................918 542-4148
Carrik Cook, *Owner*
Anna Gregath, *Owner*
EMP: 5
SALES (est): 702.6K **Privately Held**
SIC: 2791 2789 2731 Typesetting; bookbinding & related work; books: publishing & printing

(G-4408)
HOPKINS MANUFACTURING CORP
2400 Industrial Pkwy (74354-2212)
PHONE.................................918 961-8722
Jim Calcagno, *Branch Mgr*
Jennifer Jauert, *Analyst*
EMP: 18
SALES (corp-wide): 197.4MM **Privately Held**
SIC: 3089 Automotive parts, plastic
PA: Hopkins Manufacturing Corporation
428 Peyton St
Emporia KS 66801
620 342-7320

(G-4409)
J-M FARMS INC
7001 S 580 Rd (74354-6501)
PHONE.................................918 540-1567
Virgil Jurgensmeyer, *Ch of Bd*
Curtis Jurgensmeyer, *President*
Joseph Jurgensmeyer, *Exec VP*
Terry Jurgensmeyer, *Vice Pres*
EMP: 320
SQ FT: 156,000
SALES (est): 49.4MM **Privately Held**
SIC: 0182 2099 Mushrooms grown under cover; food preparations

(G-4410)
M & M CUSTOM BUTCHERING
54420 E 110 Rd (74354-6060)
PHONE.................................918 542-6421
Kenny Jordan, *Owner*
EMP: 2
SALES (est): 93.5K **Privately Held**
SIC: 7299 5421 2013 2011 Butcher service, processing only; meat & fish markets; sausages & other prepared meats; meat packing plants

(G-4411)
MAH INDUSTRIES LLC
429 K St Nw (74354-5445)
P.O. Box 575 (74355-0575)
PHONE.................................918 540-0656
Mark A Hestand,
Sheila Hestand,
EMP: 2
SALES (est): 115.1K **Privately Held**
SIC: 2844 Toilet preparations

(G-4412)
MARS PETCARE US INC
Also Called: Doane Pet Care
2020 6th Ave Se (74354-5302)
PHONE.................................918 540-0045
Mike Bontrager, *Manager*
EMP: 43

SALES (corp-wide): 38.5B **Privately Held**
WEB: www.williamsonchamber.com
SIC: 2047 Dog food
HQ: Mars Petcare Us, Inc.
2013 Ovation Pkwy
Franklin TN 37067
615 807-4626

(G-4413)
MIAMI ARMATURE WORKS INC
1925 N Main St (74354-2133)
PHONE.................................918 542-2443
Corbin Helmick, *President*
Mary Jane Helmick, *Vice Pres*
EMP: 3
SQ FT: 4,000
SALES (est): 300K **Privately Held**
SIC: 7694 1731 Electric motor repair; general electrical contractor

(G-4414)
MIAMI DESIGNS
1601 N Main St (74354-2720)
P.O. Box 1525 (74355-1525)
PHONE.................................918 542-9553
J Leonard, *Principal*
EMP: 1
SALES (est): 45.3K **Privately Held**
SIC: 5949 2759 7336 Sewing & needlework; screen printing; graphic arts & related design

(G-4415)
MIAMI INDUSTRIAL SUPPLY & MFG
7251 S Highway 69a (74354-1007)
PHONE.................................918 542-6317
Terry Jurgensmeyer, *Ch of Bd*
Curtis Jurgensmeyer, *President*
Virgil Jurgensmeyer, *Vice Pres*
Pat Jurgensmeyer, *Admin Sec*
▲ EMP: 20
SQ FT: 6,000
SALES (est): 4.2MM **Privately Held**
SIC: 3549 5083 3523 3052 Metalworking machinery; agricultural machinery; farm machinery & equipment; rubber & plastics hose & beltings

(G-4416)
MIAMI MACHINE SHOP
135 D St Ne (74354-6320)
PHONE.................................918 542-1501
Bon Banober, *Partner*
Dennis Malloy, *Partner*
EMP: 2
SALES (est): 129K **Privately Held**
SIC: 3599 Machine shop, jobbing & repair

(G-4417)
MIAMI NEWSPAPERS INC
Also Called: Miami News-Record
14 1st Ave Nw (74354-6224)
P.O. Box 940 (74355-0940)
PHONE.................................918 542-5533
Jeremy Halbreich, *President*
James Ellis, *Editor*
Rebecca Branham, *Accounting Dir*
Bob Markham, *Director*
EMP: 31
SALES (est): 1.8MM **Privately Held**
WEB: www.miamiok.com
SIC: 2711 Newspapers, publishing & printing

(G-4418)
MILLER MFG GROUP
410 A St Ne (74354-4856)
PHONE.................................918 540-1600
Kathy Miller, *President*
EMP: 3
SQ FT: 5,000
SALES (est): 230K **Privately Held**
SIC: 3713 Truck tops

(G-4419)
MISACO SIGN & SCREEN PRINTING
424 Henley St (74354-5331)
PHONE.................................918 542-4188
Mike Willard, *Owner*
EMP: 6
SALES (est): 550.4K **Privately Held**
SIC: 3993 2759 2396 Signs, not made in custom sign painting shops; screen printing; automotive & apparel trimmings

(G-4420)
MISACO SIGN AND SCREEN PRTG
Also Called: MI SA Co Sign
424 Henley St (74354-5331)
PHONE.................................918 542-4188
EMP: 2
SALES (est): 73.4K **Privately Held**
SIC: 2261 Screen printing of cotton broadwoven fabrics

(G-4421)
MYPRINT
218 E Central Ave Ste D (74354-7013)
PHONE.................................918 542-7672
EMP: 1 EST: 2017
SALES (est): 61.6K **Privately Held**
SIC: 3993 Signs & advertising specialties

(G-4422)
N E O FABRICATION L L C
604 Henley St (74354-5356)
PHONE.................................918 541-9203
John Allemann, *Mng Member*
James Allemann, *Mng Member*
EMP: 21
SQ FT: 300,000
SALES (est): 5.1MM **Privately Held**
SIC: 3443 Dumpsters, garbage

(G-4423)
NEO CONCRETE & MATERIALS INC
Also Called: Miami Concrete
2840 G St Nw (74354-1940)
P.O. Box 598, North Miami (74358-0598)
PHONE.................................918 542-4456
Lloyd I Evans, *CEO*
EMP: 30
SALES (est): 3.3MM
SALES (corp-wide): 100.1MM **Privately Held**
SIC: 3273 Ready-mixed concrete
PA: Evans & Associates Enterprises, Inc.
3320 N 14th St
Ponca City OK 74601
580 765-6693

(G-4424)
OKLAHOMA LEATHER PRODUCTS INC
Also Called: Olpco
500 26th St Ave Nw (74354)
PHONE.................................918 542-6651
Richard G Platt, *Ch of Bd*
Michael Platt, *President*
Patricia Platt, *Shareholder*
EMP: 60 EST: 1974
SQ FT: 50,000
SALES (est): 8.1MM **Privately Held**
SIC: 3111 Accessory products, leather

(G-4425)
OLD SARGES ARMORY LLC
713 G St Nw (74354-4420)
PHONE.................................270 945-8324
Robert White,
EMP: 1
SALES (est): 60.4K **Privately Held**
SIC: 3484 Small arms

(G-4426)
OSAGE DOOR CO INC
7200 S 580th Rd (74354)
PHONE.................................918 542-7281
Randy Langford, *General Mgr*
EMP: 1
SALES (corp-wide): 6.7MM **Privately Held**
SIC: 2431 Door frames, wood
PA: Osage Door Co., Inc.
3249 E Ridgeview St
Springfield MO 65804
417 581-7571

(G-4427)
PAYTONS AUTO
817 D St Ne (74354-4830)
PHONE.................................918 540-2501
John Payton, *Co-Owner*
EMP: 5
SQ FT: 3,200

SALES (est): 453.1K **Privately Held**
SIC: 7538 3694 3625 General automotive repair shops; engine electrical equipment; relays & industrial controls

(G-4428)
PIONEER PRINTING INC
18 W Central Ave (74354-6831)
PHONE.................................918 542-5521
Thomas A Woods, *President*
Terry Woods, *Vice Pres*
Lillyan Woods, *Treasurer*
EMP: 9 EST: 1959
SQ FT: 6,700
SALES (est): 1.4MM **Privately Held**
SIC: 2752 5943 5044 5021 Letters, circular or form: lithographed; commercial printing, offset; office forms & supplies; office equipment; office furniture; bookbinding & related work; commercial printing

(G-4429)
RUSSELL BAKER RACING ENGINES
9295 S 490 Rd (74354-5576)
PHONE.................................918 533-3825
Russell Lee Baker, *Owner*
Bryan Baker, *Manager*
EMP: 4
SQ FT: 6,250
SALES (est): 383.9K **Privately Held**
SIC: 3519 Internal combustion engines

(G-4430)
SCEPTER MANUFACTURING LLC
404 26th Ave Nw (74354-2206)
PHONE.................................918 544-2222
Elaine Hook, *Finance*
Todd McClain, *Mng Member*
EMP: 60
SALES (est): 17.9MM
SALES (corp-wide): 515.7MM **Publicly Held**
SIC: 3089 Tubs, plastic (containers)
PA: Myers Industries, Inc.
1293 S Main St
Akron OH 44301
330 253-5592

(G-4431)
SOONER INDUSTRIES INC
Also Called: Sooner Printing
16 N Main St (74354-6323)
P.O. Box 550 (74355-0550)
PHONE.................................918 540-2422
Ron Forkum, *President*
Greg Forkum, *Corp Secy*
EMP: 9
SQ FT: 20,000
SALES (est): 1.1MM **Privately Held**
SIC: 2752 5943 5712 2791 Commercial printing, offset; office forms & supplies; office furniture; typesetting; bookbinding & related work; commercial printing

(G-4432)
THERMO FISHER SCIENTIFIC
520 N Main St (74354-4850)
PHONE.................................918 540-1507
Greg Johnson, *Manager*
EMP: 11
SALES (corp-wide): 25.5B **Publicly Held**
SIC: 3826 Analytical instruments
HQ: Thermo Fisher Scientific (Asheville) Llc
28 Schenck Pkwy Ste 400
Asheville NC 28803
828 658-2711

(G-4433)
TOTE ALONG INC
51701 E 110 Rd (74354-5574)
P.O. Box 1222 (74355-1222)
PHONE.................................918 542-6453
Bret Hays, *President*
EMP: 26
SALES (est): 2.6MM **Privately Held**
SIC: 3599 Custom machinery

(G-4434)
TRACKER MARINE LLC
Also Called: Tracker Marine Group
3807 Tahoe Way (74354-1900)
PHONE.................................918 541-2000
Ken Burroughs, *President*
Loren Smith, *Plant Mgr*

Miami - Ottawa County (G-4435)

▼ EMP: 3
SALES (est): 562.1K Privately Held
SIC: 3732 Boat building & repairing

(G-4435)
US WHIP INC
51701 E 110 Rd (74354-5574)
P.O. Box 1222 (74355-1222)
PHONE...................................918 542-6453
Bret Hays, *President*
Randy Devin, *Director*
▲ EMP: 30
SQ FT: 14,000
SALES (est): 4.6MM Privately Held
WEB: www.uswhip.com
SIC: 3199 Whipstocks

(G-4436)
WAX AND HIVE CANDLE LC
49721 E 95 Rd (74354-6070)
PHONE...................................918 542-6432
Leslie Swan, *Principal*
EMP: 1
SALES (est): 39.6K Privately Held
SIC: 3999 Candles

Midwest City
Oklahoma County

(G-4437)
CALICO INDUSTRIES LLC
211 Guy Dr (73110-3111)
PHONE...................................405 732-0638
Bob Baldwin, *Principal*
EMP: 2
SALES (est): 156.5K Privately Held
SIC: 3999 Manufacturing industries

(G-4438)
CASING POINT LLC
400 Buckboard Ln (73130-6812)
PHONE...................................405 245-9855
Tera Bisbee, *Bd of Directors*
EMP: 2
SALES (est): 121.6K Privately Held
SIC: 1389 Cementing oil & gas well casings

(G-4439)
EDEN PHARMACEUTICALS
7550 Se 15th St (73110-5426)
PHONE...................................405 455-7200
EMP: 3
SALES (est): 174K Privately Held
SIC: 2834 Pharmaceutical preparations

(G-4440)
ELYSIUM INDUSTRIES
710 Esther Ave (73130-2327)
PHONE...................................405 394-3087
Dana Drew, *Principal*
EMP: 1
SALES (est): 42.8K Privately Held
SIC: 3999 Manufacturing industries

(G-4441)
FRESH PROMISE FOODS INC
3416 Shadybrook Dr (73130-3851)
PHONE...................................561 703-4659
Joe E Poe Jr, *Ch of Bd*
EMP: 1
SALES (est): 1.5K Privately Held
SIC: 2086 Bottled & canned soft drinks; carbonated beverages, nonalcoholic: bottled & canned

(G-4442)
HOLLIS HOME MADE SALSA LLC
717 Small Oaks (73110-7451)
PHONE...................................405 464-6249
Tamar Prather, *Principal*
EMP: 3 EST: 2015
SALES (est): 123.7K Privately Held
SIC: 2099 Dips, except cheese & sour cream based

(G-4443)
IRONCLAD DEFENSE
437 W Fairchild Dr (73110-2906)
PHONE...................................405 413-9496
David Neely, *Principal*
EMP: 3

SALES (est): 145.3K Privately Held
SIC: 3812 Defense systems & equipment

(G-4444)
JAY INDUSTRIES LLC
9429 Se 29th St Trlr 133 (73130-7210)
PHONE...................................405 404-3242
Lacie Bullock, *Principal*
EMP: 1
SALES (est): 49.1K Privately Held
SIC: 3999 Manufacturing industries

(G-4445)
KIHOMAC INC
Also Called: Ki Ho Mltary Acqstion Cnslting
2801 Parklawn Dr Ste 500 (73110-4232)
PHONE...................................937 429-7744
Cynthia Morrison, *Director*
EMP: 99
SQ FT: 1,800
SALES (corp-wide): 50.9MM Privately Held
SIC: 3728 8711 7371 7376 Aircraft parts & equipment; engineering services; custom computer programming services; computer facilities management; research institute
PA: Kihomac, Inc.
    2100 Reston Pkwy Ste 310
    Reston VA 20191
    703 960-5450

(G-4446)
MATHERLY MECHANICAL CONTRS LLC
1520 Ocama Blvd (73110-7947)
P.O. Box 30889 (73140-3889)
PHONE...................................405 737-3488
Bill Moody, *Superintendent*
David Haney, *COO*
Mike Clark, *Vice Pres*
David Munson, *Vice Pres*
Dennis Wheeler, *Safety Dir*
EMP: 150
SQ FT: 15,000
SALES (est): 61.9MM Privately Held
WEB: www.matherlymech.com
SIC: 1711 3444 Mechanical contractor; sheet metalwork

(G-4447)
MOJO SPORTS LLC
6001 Se 15th St (73110-2619)
P.O. Box 563, Choctaw (73020-0563)
PHONE...................................405 390-8935
EMP: 12
SALES (est): 1.1MM Privately Held
SIC: 2754 Gravure Commercial Printing

(G-4448)
MOOG INC
Also Called: Aircraft Group
2501 Liberty Pkwy Ste 500 (73110-2858)
PHONE...................................405 732-0009
Tom Laird, *Manager*
EMP: 6
SQ FT: 10,000
SALES (corp-wide): 2.9B Publicly Held
SIC: 3721 Aircraft
PA: Moog Inc.
    400 Jamison Rd
    Elma NY 14059
    716 805-2604

(G-4449)
NICE PRINTING CO
9217 Forest Cove Cir (73130-3400)
PHONE...................................405 673-9437
EMP: 2
SALES (est): 83.9K Privately Held
SIC: 2752 Commercial printing, lithographic

(G-4450)
PSI MNFACTURING OPERATIONS LLC
8911 Se 29th St Ste B (73110-8308)
PHONE...................................561 747-6107
Gary P Prus,
EMP: 6
SALES (corp-wide): 1MM Privately Held
SIC: 3724 Aircraft engines & engine parts
PA: Psi Manufacturing Operations, Llc
    831 Jupiter Park Dr
    Jupiter FL 33458
    561 747-6107

(G-4451)
REDBUD WOODWORKS
9821 Lloyd Dr (73110-1522)
PHONE...................................316 765-4079
Benjamin Berryman, *Principal*
EMP: 1
SALES (est): 59.5K Privately Held
SIC: 2431 Millwork

(G-4452)
RUTHERFORD LTERARY GROUP L L C
1205 S Air Depot Blvd # 135 (73110-4807)
PHONE...................................405 623-9031
John Primo,
Jaz Primo, *Author*
EMP: 1
SALES: 12K Privately Held
WEB: www.jazprimo.com
SIC: 2731 Book publishing

(G-4453)
SIGN GYPSIES MIDWEST CITY LLC
12305 Jaycie Cir (73130-8464)
PHONE...................................405 259-9886
Tracey Kay, *Principal*
EMP: 1
SALES (est): 46K Privately Held
SIC: 3993 Signs & advertising specialties

(G-4454)
SILSBY MEDIA LLC
2425 S Douglas Blvd (73130-7115)
PHONE...................................405 733-9727
De Silsby, *Mng Member*
EMP: 3
SQ FT: 2,400
SALES: 150K Privately Held
SIC: 2752 2759 Commercial printing, lithographic; commercial printing

(G-4455)
SMC TECHNOLOGIES INC
1517 Ocama Blvd (73110-7946)
P.O. Box 18732, Oklahoma City (73154-0732)
PHONE...................................405 737-3740
Steve Bowersox, *President*
Callie Nelson, *Controller*
Steve Lile, *Technical Staff*
EMP: 10
SQ FT: 15,000
SALES (est): 1.1MM Privately Held
WEB: www.smc-technologies.com
SIC: 2841 2842 2899 Soap & other detergents; specialty cleaning, polishes & sanitation goods; water treating compounds

(G-4456)
STRATEGIC MISSION SYSTEMS LLC
2501 Liberty Pkwy Ste 200 (73110-2881)
PHONE...................................405 595-7243
Jack Boring,
EMP: 5
SALES (est): 215.2K Privately Held
SIC: 3721 Airplanes, fixed or rotary wing

(G-4457)
STROUP INDUSTRIES LLC
3629 Rolling Lane Cir (73110-1219)
PHONE...................................405 737-4170
C Brooks Stroup, *Principal*
EMP: 2
SALES (est): 89K Privately Held
SIC: 3999 Manufacturing industries

(G-4458)
STUDIO 180
7901 Ne 10th St Ste C223 (73110-3654)
PHONE...................................405 512-2404
Rosalyn Winters, *Principal*
EMP: 1
SALES (est): 149.4K Privately Held
SIC: 3999 Hair curlers, designed for beauty parlors

(G-4459)
TRIPLE B MEDIA LLC
9075 Harmony Dr (73130-6217)
PHONE...................................405 732-7577
Shawn Powell,
Jeff Johnson,
EMP: 5

SALES (est): 270.2K Privately Held
SIC: 2711 Newspapers: publishing only, not printed on site

(G-4460)
URBANE COMMERCIAL CONTRS LLC
12429 Goldsborough Rd (73130-4912)
PHONE...................................405 534-1677
Stephen Penton,
EMP: 2
SALES (est): 85.2K Privately Held
SIC: 2431 Millwork

(G-4461)
WHITECAPS INC
Also Called: Signs By Tomorrow
1932 S Air Depot Blvd (73110-5522)
PHONE...................................405 610-7007
Dale Hawkins, *President*
Gail Hawkins, *Vice Pres*
EMP: 3
SALES (est): 396.6K Privately Held
SIC: 3993 Signs & advertising specialties

(G-4462)
WOODALL WELDING
411 W Ercoupe Dr (73110-2904)
PHONE...................................405 736-0599
Greg Woodall, *Principal*
EMP: 1
SALES (est): 62K Privately Held
SIC: 7692 Welding repair

Milburn
Johnston County

(G-4463)
PATS WORLD
7100 E Egypt Rd (73450-9424)
PHONE...................................580 443-5751
Pat Gray, *Owner*
EMP: 2
SALES (est): 5K Privately Held
SIC: 3942 Miniature dolls, collectors'

(G-4464)
WASHITA REFRIGERATION & EQP CO
8725 S Callen Rd (73450-1025)
PHONE...................................800 235-9476
EMP: 22
SQ FT: 6,000
SALES (est): 3.9MM Privately Held
SIC: 5078 3585 7623 Whol Refrigeration Equipment/Supplies Mfg Refrigeration/Heating Equipment Refrigeration Service/Repair

Mill Creek
Johnston County

(G-4465)
3 C CATTLE FEEDERS INC
Also Called: Bear
103 E Main St (74856-5636)
P.O. Box 144 (74856-0144)
PHONE...................................580 384-3943
Fax: 580 384-3963
EMP: 10
SQ FT: 10,000
SALES: 1.4MM Privately Held
SIC: 3523 Mfg Farm Machinery/Equipment

(G-4466)
4V WELDING AND DOZER LLC
1191 Cyrus Harris Rd (74856-4800)
P.O. Box 123 (74856-0123)
PHONE...................................580 371-6524
EMP: 1
SALES (est): 25K Privately Held
SIC: 7692 Welding repair

(G-4467)
BUCKLEY POWDER COMPANY
Rr 1 (74856)
PHONE...................................580 384-5547
Steven Buckley, *Owner*
EMP: 10

GEOGRAPHIC SECTION

Moore - Cleveland County (G-4499)

SALES (est): 743.6K **Privately Held**
SIC: 3629 1081 Blasting machines, electrical; metal mining services

(G-4468)
MARTIN MARIETTA MATERIALS INC
11662 W Txi Mill Creek Rd (74856)
PHONE..................580 384-3574
Randal O'Billings, *Manager*
EMP: 2 **Publicly Held**
SIC: 3295 Magnesite, crude: ground, calcined or dead-burned
PA: Martin Marietta Materials Inc
2710 Wycliff Rd
Raleigh NC 27607

(G-4469)
MARTIN MARIETTA MATERIALS INC
Also Called: Mill Creek Quarry
7 Mi N Of Ravia Highway 1 (74856)
P.O. Box 86 (74856-0086)
PHONE..................580 384-5246
Dan Persyn, *Manager*
EMP: 35 **Publicly Held**
SIC: 1423 Crushed & broken granite
PA: Martin Marietta Materials Inc
2710 Wycliff Rd
Raleigh NC 27607

(G-4470)
NITRO LIFT HOLDINGS LLC
8980 Ok Highway 1 S (74856-5566)
PHONE..................405 620-3274
Vernon Daniels, *Principal*
John Beaver, *Principal*
Chase Daniels, *Principal*
Danny Daniels, *Principal*
EMP: 75
SALES (est): 844.7K **Privately Held**
SIC: 1389 Oil & gas field services

(G-4471)
NITRO LIFT TECHNOLOGIES LLC (PA)
8980 Ok Highway 1 S (74856-5566)
P.O. Box 81429, Lafayette LA (70598-1429)
PHONE..................580 371-3700
Bobby Fowler, *Opers Staff*
Luke Strong, *Sales Engr*
Danny Daniels, *Mng Member*
EMP: 100
SQ FT: 200,000
SALES (est): 30.4MM **Privately Held**
SIC: 2813 Nitrogen

(G-4472)
U S SILICA COMPANY
Also Called: Southwest Business Unit
Hwy 7 N (74856)
P.O. Box 36 (74856-0036)
PHONE..................580 384-5241
Jason Quigley, *Opers Mgr*
George Matthews, *Finance Other*
EMP: 70
SALES (corp-wide): 1.4B **Publicly Held**
SIC: 2819 Industrial inorganic chemicals
HQ: U. S. Silica Company
24275 Katy Fwy Ste 100
Katy TX 77494
301 682-0600

Millerton
Mccurtain County

(G-4473)
PHILLIPS & COMPANY
311 Nw Chickasaw St (74750)
PHONE..................714 663-6324
Howard Phillips, *Owner*
EMP: 1
SALES (est): 86.2K **Privately Held**
SIC: 2834 Pharmaceutical preparations

(G-4474)
QUILTS UNLIMITED
201 S Choctaw (74750)
P.O. Box 113 (74750-0113)
PHONE..................580 746-2770
Donna Whisenhunt, *Owner*
EMP: 1

SALES (est): 36.2K **Privately Held**
SIC: 2392 Comforters & quilts: made from purchased materials

Minco
Grady County

(G-4475)
A & J FABRICATORS INC
100 S 9th St (73059)
P.O. Box 296 (73059-0296)
PHONE..................405 352-4120
Jerry Mitchell, *President*
Sadie McCue, *Corp Secy*
Anala Mitchell, *Vice Pres*
EMP: 20
SQ FT: 6,000
SALES (est): 1MM **Privately Held**
SIC: 3441 Fabricated structural metal

(G-4476)
JIMS BACKHOE LLC
871 County Road 1170 (73059-8020)
PHONE..................405 352-5003
James V Rice, *Owner*
EMP: 2
SALES (est): 137.8K **Privately Held**
SIC: 3531 Backhoes

(G-4477)
MAINLINE INDUSTRIES
5015 Sw Clayton Rd (73059-7522)
EMP: 2
SALES (est): 20K **Privately Held**
SIC: 7692 Welding Repair

(G-4478)
OKLAHOMA FLDING CRTON PRTG INC
118 Nw Main St (73059)
P.O. Box 487 (73059-0487)
PHONE..................405 352-9920
Bruce Baade, *CEO*
Christy Baade, *Corp Secy*
John Snyder, *Opers Staff*
EMP: 14
SALES (est): 2.7MM **Privately Held**
SIC: 2759 5199 Commercial printing; packaging materials

(G-4479)
RONS WELDING SHOP
Hwy 81 N (73059)
P.O. Box 85 (73059-0085)
PHONE..................405 352-4331
Ronnie L Bass, *Owner*
EMP: 1
SALES (est): 150K **Privately Held**
SIC: 7692 Welding repair

(G-4480)
ROSS HONEY CO
1309 Sw 3rd St (73059-7524)
PHONE..................405 352-4125
Glenda Ross, *Owner*
EMP: 2
SALES (est): 130K **Privately Held**
SIC: 7389 2099 0279 Business services; food preparations; apiary (bee & honey farm)

(G-4481)
SHAWNEE MILLING COMPANY
Also Called: Minco Grain & Feed
826 Nw 3rd St (73059-2006)
P.O. Box 340 (73059-0340)
PHONE..................405 352-4336
Todd Reed, *Manager*
EMP: 4
SALES (corp-wide): 84.5MM **Privately Held**
SIC: 2041 2048 3523 5261 Flour: blended, prepared or self-rising; prepared feeds; farm machinery & equipment; nursery stock, seeds & bulbs; animal feeds; grain elevators
PA: Shawnee Milling Company
201 S Broadway Ave
Shawnee OK 74801
405 273-7000

(G-4482)
VERSER WELDING SERVICE
103 E 3rd St (73059)
P.O. Box 195 (73059-0195)
PHONE..................405 352-5048
Johnny Verser, *Owner*
EMP: 1
SALES: 43K **Privately Held**
SIC: 7692 Welding repair

Moore
Cleveland County

(G-4483)
ABBY CANDLES INC
Also Called: Abby Candles Fundraising
200 Se 19th St (73160-6053)
PHONE..................405 895-9957
James A Neal, *President*
EMP: 12
SQ FT: 4,000
SALES (est): 1.4MM **Privately Held**
SIC: 3999 Candles

(G-4484)
ACL COMBUSTION INC
228 Se 8th St (73160-6703)
P.O. Box 7528 (73153-1528)
PHONE..................405 310-2327
EMP: 9
SALES (est): 1.3MM **Privately Held**
SIC: 3823 Industrial instrmnts msrmnt display/control process variable

(G-4485)
ALLIED WIRELINE SERVICES LLC
13020 S Sunnylane Rd (73160-8806)
PHONE..................405 445-7135
Kent Hubbard, *Manager*
EMP: 35 **Privately Held**
SIC: 1389 Oil field services
PA: Allied Wireline Services, Llc
3200 Wilcrest Dr Ste 170
Houston TX 77042

(G-4486)
AMBERS CANDLE
821 Nw 23rd St Apt 21 (73160-1231)
PHONE..................405 492-3620
Amber Yeager, *Principal*
EMP: 1
SALES (est): 39.6K **Privately Held**
SIC: 3999 Candles

(G-4487)
AMERICAN DRONES LLC
1000 Sw 4th St (73160-2405)
PHONE..................405 308-0866
Darren Hensley, *Mng Member*
EMP: 3
SALES: 85K **Privately Held**
WEB: www.american-drones.com
SIC: 3728 7699 5092 Target drones; repair services; toys & hobby goods & supplies

(G-4488)
AMERICAN LOGO AND SIGN INC
2631 S I 35 Service Rd (73160)
PHONE..................405 799-1800
Rebecca Wells, *Manager*
EMP: 1
SQ FT: 9,444 **Privately Held**
SIC: 3993 1799 7336 Signs & advertising specialties; shoring & underpinning work; commercial art & graphic design
PA: American Logo And Sign, Inc
12501 N Santa Fe Ave
Oklahoma City OK 73114

(G-4489)
ANCILE INDUSTRIES
4309 Katie Ridge Dr (73160-6268)
PHONE..................405 990-5018
Joseph David Younger, *Owner*
EMP: 2 **EST:** 2016
SALES (est): 58.2K **Privately Held**
SIC: 3999 Manufacturing industries

(G-4490)
ANDRE ANDERSON
Also Called: Sb Wholesale
3300 Paul Dr (73160-0600)
P.O. Box 7852 (73153-1852)
PHONE..................405 642-3210
Ande Anderson, *Agent*
EMP: 1
SQ FT: 3,000
SALES (est): 89.6K **Privately Held**
SIC: 3695 Magnetic & optical recording media

(G-4491)
APPLE ART
1007 Sw 24th St (73170-7490)
PHONE..................405 691-4393
Steve Apple, *Owner*
EMP: 1
SALES (est): 20K **Privately Held**
SIC: 8999 7336 3993 Artist's studio; commercial art & graphic design; signs & advertising specialties

(G-4492)
APS OF OKLAHOMA LLC
Also Called: Fort Thunder Harley-Davidson
500 Sw 11th St Moore (73160-2545)
PHONE..................405 793-8877
EMP: 1
SALES (est): 100K **Privately Held**
SIC: 3751 Motorcycles & related parts

(G-4493)
ARCHER PRINTING INC
316 Se 6th St (73160-6715)
PHONE..................405 236-1607
Beverly Valentine, *President*
EMP: 8
SALES: 550K **Privately Held**
SIC: 2752 Commercial printing, offset

(G-4494)
ARES WEST WELDING LLC
1405 Nw 14th Pl (73170-1465)
PHONE..................405 534-6707
Ares West, *Principal*
EMP: 1
SALES (est): 36.8K **Privately Held**
SIC: 7692 Welding repair

(G-4495)
ARTILLERY NATION LLC
1505 Se 8th St (73160-8207)
PHONE..................405 606-5080
EMP: 1
SALES (est): 48.1K **Privately Held**
SIC: 3489 Ordnance & accessories

(G-4496)
AWNINGS UNIQUE
906 Ne 9th St (73160-6810)
PHONE..................405 249-2488
Nicole Gaither, *Corp Secy*
EMP: 2
SALES (est): 140K **Privately Held**
SIC: 2394 Canvas awnings & canopies

(G-4497)
BEAVERS INDEPENDENT PRINTE
3300 Michelle Ct (73160-7558)
PHONE..................405 205-5300
EMP: 2
SALES (est): 140K **Privately Held**
SIC: 2752 Lithographic Commercial Printing

(G-4498)
BLACK CAT SCREEN PRINTING LLC
2617 N Shields Blvd (73160-3302)
PHONE..................405 895-6635
Tim Bryant, *Owner*
EMP: 2
SALES (est): 145.1K **Privately Held**
WEB: www.blackcat-tshirts.com
SIC: 2759 Screen printing

(G-4499)
BLACK RIVER AEROSPACE LLC
1000 Ne 20th Pl (73160-6415)
PHONE..................386 212-3741
Melissa Kearby, *Principal*
EMP: 2

Moore - Cleveland County (G-4500)

SALES (est): 181.8K **Privately Held**
WEB: www.blackriveraerospace.com
SIC: 3721 Aircraft

(G-4500)
BOOMER FOUNDATIONS & PIERS
201 Se 1st St (73160-5903)
PHONE..............................405 799-6811
Shirley Wilson, *Principal*
EMP: 1
SALES (est): 60.5K **Privately Held**
SIC: 3271 Blocks, concrete: chimney or fireplace

(G-4501)
C & P AUTO ELECTRIC
815 S Sunnylane Rd (73160-9643)
P.O. Box 7094 (73153-1094)
PHONE..............................405 799-2083
Dewey Chenault, *Owner*
EMP: 3
SQ FT: 5,000
SALES (est): 130K **Privately Held**
SIC: 3694 Ignition apparatus, internal combustion engines; generators, automotive & aircraft; motors, starting: automotive & aircraft

(G-4502)
CALIBER COMPLETION SVCS LLC
2901 Pole Rd (73160-4110)
PHONE..............................405 385-3761
EMP: 2
SALES (est): 81.9K **Privately Held**
SIC: 1382 Oil & gas exploration services

(G-4503)
CAMERON TECHNOLOGIES INC
2101 S Broadway St (73160-6201)
PHONE..............................405 682-1661
Stephanie, *Branch Mgr*
EMP: 5 **Publicly Held**
SIC: 3533 Oil & gas field machinery
HQ: Cameron Technologies, Inc.
4646 W Sam Houston Pkwy N
Houston TX 77041

(G-4504)
CAMERON TECHNOLOGIES INC
Cameron Drilling Systems
2101 S Broadway St (73160-6201)
PHONE..............................405 703-8632
Edwardo Pacini, *Branch Mgr*
EMP: 40 **Publicly Held**
SIC: 1389 Oil field services
HQ: Cameron Technologies, Inc.
4646 W Sam Houston Pkwy N
Houston TX 77041

(G-4505)
CANADIAN PIPE & SUPPLY CO
233 Se 5th St (73160-6706)
PHONE..............................405 794-6825
Dickey Smith, *President*
EMP: 5
SQ FT: 6,000
SALES (est): 225.3K **Privately Held**
SIC: 1389 Oil field services

(G-4506)
CARPENTER CO
9401 Pole Rd Ste 100 (73160-9019)
PHONE..............................405 634-8124
Steve Garrison, *Manager*
EMP: 12
SALES (corp-wide): 1.8B **Privately Held**
SIC: 3086 Insulation or cushioning material, foamed plastic; carpet & rug cushions, foamed plastic; padding, foamed plastic
PA: Carpenter Co.
5016 Monument Ave
Richmond VA 23260
804 359-0800

(G-4507)
CATALOG SYSTEM INC
1316 Nw 7th Pl (73170-1106)
PHONE..............................405 808-1533
Robert Konrath, *President*
EMP: 1

SALES (est): 43.5K **Privately Held**
SIC: 7372 Application computer software; business oriented computer software; publishers' computer software

(G-4508)
CEDAR BUILT USA INC
2898 N Shields Blvd (73160-1001)
P.O. Box 2340, Chickasha (73023-2340)
PHONE..............................405 794-0811
EMP: 8
SALES (est): 1.1MM **Privately Held**
SIC: 2452 Prefabricated Wood Buildings

(G-4509)
COMPOUND SOFTWARE LLC
3600 S Bryant Ave (73160-8411)
PHONE..............................405 912-3301
Kimberly A McIntyre, *Principal*
EMP: 2 EST: 2012
SALES (est): 65K **Privately Held**
SIC: 7372 Prepackaged software

(G-4510)
COUNTERBATTERY PRESS LLC
2216 Ne 8th St (73160-8542)
PHONE..............................405 794-2885
Daniel Houston, *Principal*
EMP: 1
SALES (est): 44.8K **Privately Held**
SIC: 2741 Miscellaneous publishing

(G-4511)
COUNTRY LEISURE INC
3001 N Service Rd (73160-3239)
PHONE..............................405 799-7745
Rusty Britton, *President*
Reta Kling, *Vice Pres*
Bethanie Brietton, *CFO*
EMP: 50
SQ FT: 25,000
SALES (est): 9MM **Privately Held**
SIC: 3088 3949 Hot tubs, plastic or fiberglass; swimming pools, except plastic

(G-4512)
CROSBY CUSTOM WOODWORK
1016 Nw 8th St (73160-1808)
PHONE..............................405 802-9615
Allen Matthew, *Principal*
EMP: 2 EST: 2012
SALES (est): 168.5K **Privately Held**
SIC: 2431 Millwork

(G-4513)
DARRELL MONROE
Also Called: Dub's Sheet Metal
9700 S Sunnylane Rd G (73160-9207)
P.O. Box 7111 (73153-1111)
PHONE..............................405 793-2976
EMP: 12
SQ FT: 4,500
SALES (est): 1.1MM **Privately Held**
SIC: 3444 Sheet Metalwork, Nsk

(G-4514)
DAVIS THORPE CO LLC
216 Se 8th St (73160-6703)
PHONE..............................405 585-9823
Burke Thorpe,
Laura Emhoolah,
EMP: 2
SALES (est): 86K **Privately Held**
SIC: 3728 Aircraft parts & equipment

(G-4515)
DESTINY PETROLEUM LLC
2524 N Broadway St (73160)
PHONE..............................281 362-2833
Emad Elrafie, *CEO*
Jack Austin, *Vice Pres*
Ric Saalwachter, *VP Finance*
EMP: 10
SQ FT: 3,500
SALES: 5MM **Privately Held**
SIC: 1381 Drilling oil & gas wells

(G-4516)
DIAMOND DEE-LITE INC
Also Called: Diamond Dee-Lite Jewelry
308 Se 4th St (73160-6707)
PHONE..............................405 793-8166
Dee O'Dell, *President*
Teri O'Dell, *Admin Sec*
EMP: 9
SQ FT: 3,500

SALES (est): 875K **Privately Held**
SIC: 5944 7631 3915 3911 Jewelry, precious stones & precious metals; jewelry repair services; jewelers' materials & lapidary work; jewelry, precious metal

(G-4517)
DIVERSFIED WLDG FBRICATION LLC
Also Called: Willis Contruction
1825 Briarhill St (73160-6501)
PHONE..............................405 802-5487
Nathan Willis, *Mng Member*
EMP: 10
SALES (est): 690K **Privately Held**
SIC: 7692 Welding repair

(G-4518)
DOLESE BROS CO
310 Industrial Blvd (73160-6200)
P.O. Box 6158 (73153-0158)
PHONE..............................405 794-0546
Jim Towles, *Manager*
EMP: 35
SALES (corp-wide): 8.5MM **Privately Held**
SIC: 3273 Ready-mixed concrete
PA: Dolese Bros. Co.
20 Nw 13th St
Oklahoma City OK 73103
405 235-2311

(G-4519)
ELKOURI LAND SERVICES LLC
3116 White Cedar Dr (73160-1193)
PHONE..............................405 604-5580
Frank Elkouri,
EMP: 3
SALES (est): 216.7K **Privately Held**
SIC: 1389 Pumping of oil & gas wells

(G-4520)
ENDEAVOR LSER ETCHING ENGRV LL
617 Cross Timbers Dr (73160-6109)
PHONE..............................405 202-5921
EMP: 2
SALES (est): 105.5K **Privately Held**
SIC: 3699 Laser systems & equipment

(G-4521)
FADED CANVAS BARBER STUDIO
105 N Eastern Ave (73160-6957)
PHONE..............................405 735-7105
EMP: 1
SALES (est): 46.5K **Privately Held**
SIC: 2211 Canvas

(G-4522)
FAIRCHILD SIGNS
505 Messenger Ln (73160-5967)
PHONE..............................405 439-3100
EMP: 1 EST: 2017
SALES (est): 50.6K **Privately Held**
WEB: www.fairchildsigns.com
SIC: 3993 Signs & advertising specialties

(G-4523)
FINLEY DISCOUNT SIGN LIGH
1105 Teak Ct (73160-8345)
PHONE..............................405 445-8888
EMP: 2 EST: 2009
SALES (est): 91.6K **Privately Held**
SIC: 3993 Signs & advertising specialties

(G-4524)
FIRE SONG PUBLISHING
621 Sw 27th St (73160-5521)
PHONE..............................405 799-2799
Kevin McFarland, *Principal*
EMP: 3
SALES (est): 74K **Privately Held**
SIC: 2711 Newspapers

(G-4525)
GARIS INDUSTRIES LLC
106 N Santa Fe Ave (73160-2100)
PHONE..............................405 639-0319
Jeffrey Tyler Garis, *Principal*
EMP: 2
SALES (est): 107.9K **Privately Held**
SIC: 3999 Manufacturing industries

(G-4526)
GWIN INDUSTRIES INC
1017 Nw 25th St (73160-1125)
PHONE..............................405 795-4946
Jeremy A Gwin, *Administration*
EMP: 2
SALES (est): 74.4K **Privately Held**
SIC: 3999 Manufacturing industries

(G-4527)
HALLIBURTON COMPANY
9500 Pole Rd (73160-9025)
PHONE..............................405 231-1800
EMP: 20 **Publicly Held**
SIC: 1389 Oil field services
PA: Halliburton Company
3000 N Sam Houston Pkwy E
Houston TX 77032

(G-4528)
INKANA PUBLISHING LLC
4235 Macys Pl (73160-2879)
PHONE..............................937 725-1296
Traci Schafer, *Principal*
EMP: 1
SALES (est): 37.5K **Privately Held**
SIC: 2741 Miscellaneous publishing

(G-4529)
INKSPOT
216 W Main St (73160-5142)
PHONE..............................405 793-7200
Willie Fulmer, *Owner*
EMP: 4
SALES (est): 167.5K **Privately Held**
SIC: 2759 Screen printing

(G-4530)
JAMES A BRUMIT JR
Also Called: Jabjr Technology
1901 Se 13th St (73160-8007)
PHONE..............................405 924-9696
EMP: 1
SALES: 50K **Privately Held**
SIC: 3679 Mfg Electronic Components

(G-4531)
KG FAB
1004 Stadium Rd (73160-7946)
PHONE..............................405 912-9938
Keith Guisinger, *Owner*
EMP: 3
SALES: 100K **Privately Held**
SIC: 3496 Miscellaneous fabricated wire products

(G-4532)
KNOWLES MANUFACTURING & MCH
9600 S Sunnylane Rd Ste B (73160-9228)
PHONE..............................405 793-9339
John Knowles, *President*
K C Knowles, *Vice Pres*
Nicole Knowles, *Admin Sec*
EMP: 3
SQ FT: 10,000
SALES (est): 474.8K **Privately Held**
SIC: 3533 Oil field machinery & equipment

(G-4533)
LINDER SCREEN PRINTING
2418 N Moore Ave (73160-3327)
PHONE..............................405 558-1275
EMP: 2
SALES (est): 92.4K **Privately Held**
SIC: 2759 Screen printing

(G-4534)
LUX ILLUME LLC
2204 Se 8th St (73160-6769)
P.O. Box 7809 (73153-1809)
PHONE..............................405 618-4552
Nicole Nichols, *Principal*
EMP: 2
SALES (est): 128.6K **Privately Held**
SIC: 3999 Candles

(G-4535)
MAC INDUSTRIES INC
2119 N Eastern Ave (73160-5628)
PHONE..............................405 631-8553
Billy M Teague, *President*
Sam Teague, *Principal*
Zella Teague, *Corp Secy*
EMP: 3

SALES (est): 290K **Privately Held**
SIC: 3089 Injection molded finished plastic products

(G-4536)
MANUFCTRING CONTRACT SOLUTIONS
3113 White Cedar Dr (73160-1194)
PHONE.................................405 229-7639
Brad C Darby, *Principal*
EMP: 1
SALES (est): 82.9K **Privately Held**
SIC: 3999 Manufacturing industries

(G-4537)
MASTERCRAFT MILLWORK INC
811 S Sunnylane Rd Ste B (73160-9602)
PHONE.................................405 895-6050
Dariel Baeker, *Vice Pres*
EMP: 5
SALES (est): 250K **Privately Held**
SIC: 2431 5211 5046 2541 Millwork; millwork & lumber; store fixtures; wood partitions & fixtures; wood kitchen cabinets

(G-4538)
MATTOCKS PRINTING CO LLC
325 N Service Rd (73160-4942)
PHONE.................................405 794-2307
Kelley Mattocks, *Mng Member*
EMP: 6 EST: 1962
SQ FT: 3,000
SALES (est): 849.4K **Privately Held**
SIC: 2752 2759 2796 2791 Lithographing on metal; letterpress printing; platemaking services; typesetting; bookbinding & related work

(G-4539)
METER CHECK INC
2501 S I 35 Service Rd (73160-2777)
PHONE.................................405 790-0778
David Shults, *Sales Staff*
EMP: 7
SALES (corp-wide): 2.3MM **Privately Held**
SIC: 3823 Water quality monitoring & control systems
PA: Meter Check, Inc.
3501 S I 35 Service Rd
Oklahoma City OK 73129
405 790-0778

(G-4540)
MH WOODWORKING LLC
1704 Se 16th St (73160-8018)
PHONE.................................405 799-2661
Trey Martin, *Owner*
EMP: 1
SALES (est): 54.1K **Privately Held**
SIC: 2431 Millwork

(G-4541)
MIDSTATE TRAFFIC CONTROL INC
9215 S Shields Blvd (73160-1052)
PHONE.................................405 799-0313
Steve Weiis, *Manager*
EMP: 2
SALES (est): 155.1K **Privately Held**
SIC: 3669 Communications equipment

(G-4542)
MOLITOR DESIGN & CNSTR LLC
1404 Sw 25th St (73170-7554)
PHONE.................................405 802-8302
Eric Molitor, *CEO*
EMP: 1
SALES (est): 180.3K **Privately Held**
SIC: 1531 1542 1795 1799 Operative builders; commercial & office building, new construction; demolition, buildings & other structures; fence construction; prefabricated wood buildings

(G-4543)
MOORE PRINTING CO INC
604 S Classen Ave (73160-5401)
PHONE.................................417 866-6396
Kenneth Gunter Jr, *President*
Jeffrey K Gunter, *Vice Pres*
Kenneth Gunter Sr, *Shareholder*
EMP: 28
SQ FT: 15,000
SALES (est): 1.9MM **Privately Held**
WEB: www.mooreprinting.com
SIC: 2752 Commercial printing, offset

(G-4544)
NATIONAL OILWELL VARCO LP
9525b Pole Rd (73160-9006)
PHONE.................................405 677-2484
EMP: 1
SALES (corp-wide): 8.4B **Publicly Held**
SIC: 3533 Oil field machinery & equipment
HQ: National Oilwell Varco, L.P.
7909 Parkwood Circle Dr
Houston TX 77036
713 375-3700

(G-4545)
OKLAHOMA CUSTOM RUBBER CO
2117 N Lincoln Ave (73160-6316)
PHONE.................................405 634-3943
Oval Presley, *Owner*
EMP: 2
SQ FT: 6,000
SALES (est): 233.1K **Privately Held**
SIC: 5085 3061 Rubber goods, mechanical; mechanical rubber goods

(G-4546)
OKLAHOMA EMERGENCY GENERATOR S
2219 N Moore Ave (73160-3422)
P.O. Box 7912 (73153-1912)
PHONE.................................405 735-9888
Wayne Craney, *Counsel*
Jeff Cothren,
EMP: 1
SALES (est): 48.1K **Privately Held**
WEB: www.deq.ok.gov
SIC: 7629 5063 3621 Generator repair; generators; generators & sets, electric

(G-4547)
OKLAHOMA REP SALES INC
214 Ne 12th St Ste A (73160-5846)
PHONE.................................405 794-5200
Bruce Harkins, *Owner*
EMP: 2
SALES (est): 199.2K **Privately Held**
SIC: 3592 Valves

(G-4548)
OLD FARM PUBLISHING LLC
2119 Riverwalk Dr (73160-2700)
PHONE.................................405 237-1153
Terry Fritts, *Principal*
EMP: 1 EST: 2016
SALES (est): 40.1K **Privately Held**
WEB: www.oldfarmpublishing.com
SIC: 2741 Miscellaneous publishing

(G-4549)
OLH MOORE LLC
660 Sw 19th St Ste D (73160-5406)
PHONE.................................405 703-0250
Mandy Skitintheday, *Mng Member*
EMP: 7
SALES (est): 315.4K **Privately Held**
SIC: 2024 Yogurt desserts, frozen

(G-4550)
OPES INDUSTRIES LLC
4000 Turtle Crk (73160-9703)
P.O. Box 7438 (73153-1438)
PHONE.................................405 417-6223
Bryce Hays,
EMP: 2
SALES (est): 103.8K **Privately Held**
SIC: 3728 Aircraft parts & equipment

(G-4551)
PATS CUSTOM DRAPERIES
Also Called: Herbalife
2721 Little Ln (73160-4120)
PHONE.................................405 794-1019
Pat Burrough, *Owner*
EMP: 1
SALES (est): 91.1K **Privately Held**
SIC: 2391 5714 Curtains & draperies; draperies

(G-4552)
PAVING MATERIALS INC
Also Called: P M I
140 Industrial Blvd (73160-6208)
PHONE.................................405 799-9880
Craig Parker, *President*
EMP: 6
SALES (est): 2.1MM **Privately Held**
SIC: 5082 2951 5032 Pavers; asphalt paving mixtures & blocks; paving materials

(G-4553)
POWERHOUSE ELEC
601 Messenger Ln Ste B (73160-5977)
PHONE.................................405 735-6381
Randy Cox, *Principal*
EMP: 4
SALES (est): 208.5K **Privately Held**
SIC: 3699 Electrical equipment & supplies

(G-4554)
PRECISION PRINTING CORPORATION
2500 N Moore Ave (73160-3328)
PHONE.................................405 794-2500
Travis Gunter, *President*
Kelly Gunter, *Manager*
EMP: 2
SALES (est): 440K **Privately Held**
SIC: 2752 Commercial printing, offset

(G-4555)
PREMEIR COMPANIES INC
Also Called: Premier Catering
132 E Main St (73160-5104)
P.O. Box 7125 (73153-1125)
PHONE.................................405 895-7100
Randy Harms, *President*
EMP: 15
SQ FT: 8,000
SALES (est): 1.8MM **Privately Held**
SIC: 2099 Food preparations

(G-4556)
PRINT MONKEY LLC
114 N Broadway St (73160-5102)
PHONE.................................405 735-8999
EMP: 2
SALES (est): 110K **Privately Held**
SIC: 2752 Lithographic Commercial Printing

(G-4557)
PRODIGY CBD COMPANY LLC
811 Sw 19th St (73160-2889)
PHONE.................................405 378-2868
EMP: 2
SALES (est): 123.2K **Privately Held**
SIC: 3999

(G-4558)
Q B JOHNSON MFG INC
9000 S Sunnylane Rd (73160-9221)
P.O. Box 890120, Oklahoma City (73189-0120)
PHONE.................................405 677-6676
Lory L Johnson, *President*
Doris Johnson, *Principal*
Q B Johnson, *Principal*
Deborah Durbin, *Vice Pres*
Alexander Chuklin, *Engineer*
▼ EMP: 85
SQ FT: 20,000
SALES (est): 30.7MM **Privately Held**
WEB: www.qbjohnson.com
SIC: 3533 3398 Gas field machinery & equipment; metal heat treating

(G-4559)
RA GRAPHIX
214 Ne 12th St Ste C (73160-5846)
PHONE.................................405 703-3599
Scott Ashbrook, *Principal*
EMP: 2
SALES (est): 214.3K **Privately Held**
SIC: 2752 Commercial printing, offset

(G-4560)
RED DOG PRESS LLC
209 S Wyndemere Lakes Dr (73160-8139)
PHONE.................................405 703-2896
EMP: 1
SALES (est): 37.5K **Privately Held**
SIC: 2741 Miscellaneous publishing

(G-4561)
S M T VALVE LLC
405 Sw 145th St (73170-7298)
PHONE.................................405 512-4523
Ngo Michael, *Principal*
EMP: 2
SALES (est): 108.7K **Privately Held**
SIC: 3592 Valves

(G-4562)
SANDERS SAWMILL & FOREST PDTS
3020 N Eastern Ave (73160-9053)
PHONE.................................405 799-0899
EMP: 1
SALES (est): 57K **Privately Held**
SIC: 2421 Sawmill/Planing Mill

(G-4563)
SATTERLEE TEEPEES
Also Called: Satterlee, Louis
304 S Bristow Ave (73160-2225)
PHONE.................................405 255-6642
Louis Satterlee, *Owner*
EMP: 2
SALES (est): 20K **Privately Held**
SIC: 5941 3949 Playground equipment; playground equipment

(G-4564)
SCHLUMBERGER TECHNOLOGY CORP
Also Called: E & P Wire Line
2901 Pole Rd (73160-4110)
PHONE.................................405 306-8244
Barney O'Toole, *Branch Mgr*
EMP: 3 **Publicly Held**
SIC: 1389 Oil field services
HQ: Schlumberger Technology Corp
300 Schlumberger Dr
Sugar Land TX 77478
281 285-8500

(G-4565)
SCISSORTAIL DISTILLERY LLC
2318 N Moore Ave (73160-3320)
PHONE.................................405 326-5466
Garrett Janko, *Manager*
EMP: 1 EST: 2013
SQ FT: 2,500
SALES (est): 86.8K **Privately Held**
SIC: 2085 Ethyl alcohol for beverage purposes

(G-4566)
SCRIPTORIUM
313 Nw 2nd St (73160-5123)
PHONE.................................405 203-5943
EMP: 4
SALES (est): 240.5K **Privately Held**
WEB: www.scriptoriumdaily.com
SIC: 2741 Miscellaneous publishing

(G-4567)
SHOCKEY WELDING LLC
943 Nw 1st St (73160-2103)
PHONE.................................405 473-1783
Benjamin Shockey, *Principal*
EMP: 1 EST: 2017
SALES (est): 25K **Privately Held**
SIC: 7692 Welding repair

(G-4568)
SILEX LLC
9502 S Eastern Ave (73160-9015)
PHONE.................................844 239-4056
EMP: 2 EST: 2017
SALES (est): 113.9K **Privately Held**
SIC: 2899 Chemical preparations

(G-4569)
SILVER QUILL LLC
194 Ne 12th St Ste A (73160-4709)
PHONE.................................405 735-9191
Tammy Steele,
EMP: 6
SALES (est): 460K **Privately Held**
WEB: www.silver-quill.com
SIC: 2732 2789 Books: printing & binding; textbooks: printing & binding, not publishing; bookbinding & related work; rebinding books, magazines or pamphlets

Moore - Cleveland County (G-4570)

(G-4570)
SKYLINE DRCTONAL DRILLLING LLC
9620 Pole Rd (73160-9027)
PHONE................405 429-4050
Bobby Hayes, *Mng Member*
Darren Kline, *Mng Member*
EMP: 30
SALES (est): 5MM **Privately Held**
SIC: 1389 Oil field services

(G-4571)
SOONER CABINET & TRIM INC
208 S Ramblin Oaks Dr (73160-7828)
PHONE................405 820-2920
Robert M Taylor, *Principal*
Mike Taylor, *Principal*
EMP: 25
SALES (est): 1.7MM **Privately Held**
SIC: 1521 2434 2431 1751 General remodeling, single-family houses; wood kitchen cabinets; millwork; carpentry work

(G-4572)
SOONER MACHINE & EQUIPMENT CO
233 Se 5th St (73160-6706)
P.O. Box 94521, Oklahoma City (73143-4521)
PHONE................405 794-6833
Dickey G Smith, *President*
EMP: 3
SALES (est): 270K **Privately Held**
SIC: 3599 3444 Machine shop, jobbing & repair; sheet metalwork

(G-4573)
SPECIALTY COMPONENT MFG
2200 Pole Rd (73160-4239)
P.O. Box 50335, Midwest City (73140-5335)
PHONE................405 794-5535
Fax: 405 794-5519
EMP: 2
SQ FT: 5,000
SALES (est): 170K **Privately Held**
SIC: 3599 Machine Shop

(G-4574)
SSG INC
1700 S Broadway St Ste J (73160-5302)
PHONE................405 639-2056
EMP: 1 **Privately Held**
WEB: www.salonservicegroup.com
SIC: 7231 5087 3999 Beauty shops; beauty salon & barber shop equipment & supplies; barber & beauty shop equipment
PA: Ssg, Inc.
1520 E Evergreen St
Springfield MO 65803

(G-4575)
SUMMER COUCH WELDING LLC
128 Sw 15th St (73160-5323)
PHONE................405 408-3675
Summer Couch, *Principal*
EMP: 1
SALES (est): 54.9K **Privately Held**
SIC: 7692 Welding repair

(G-4576)
TEE FOR SOUL
2500 S Service Rd (73160-5543)
PHONE................405 237-3186
EMP: 2
SALES (est): 73.2K **Privately Held**
SIC: 2759 Screen printing

(G-4577)
TILLISON CABINET COMPANY LLC
137 Se 4th St (73160-5301)
PHONE................405 793-2940
Vickie Wolfe, *Manager*
Wes Tillison,
Shane Tillison,
EMP: 28
SALES (est): 2.9MM **Privately Held**
SIC: 2434 Wood kitchen cabinets

(G-4578)
TOPPS POWDER COATING
2132 Pole Rd (73160-4241)
PHONE................405 794-2900
Jeff Russel, *Owner*
Jim Moore, *Director*
EMP: 7
SALES (est): 1MM **Privately Held**
SIC: 7532 3479 3471 Top & body repair & paint shops; painting, coating & hot dipping; finishing, metals or formed products

(G-4579)
TRIPLE T PRINTING
116 N Broadway St (73160-5102)
PHONE................405 912-1212
Joi Tipton, *Owner*
EMP: 2
SALES (est): 222.5K **Privately Held**
SIC: 2752 Commercial printing, offset

(G-4580)
TWISTERS DISTILLERY
2322 N Moore Ave (73160-3320)
P.O. Box 23591, Oklahoma City (73123-2591)
PHONE................405 237-3499
EMP: 4 EST: 2012
SALES (est): 256.7K **Privately Held**
SIC: 2085 Mfg Distilled/Blended Liquor

(G-4581)
ULTIMATE CHEMICALS LLC
Also Called: Kevin Heidebrecht
821 Nw 27th St Ste A (73160-1079)
P.O. Box 7557 (73153-1557)
PHONE................405 703-2771
Kevin Heidebrecht,
EMP: 5 EST: 2010
SALES (est): 999.6K **Privately Held**
WEB: www.ultimatechemicals.com
SIC: 2819 2851 7699 Industrial inorganic chemicals; removers & cleaners; oil burner repair service

(G-4582)
ULTRA THIN INC
Also Called: Ultrathin Ribbons & Metals
1720 S Broadway St (73160-5356)
P.O. Box 7161 (73153-1161)
PHONE................405 794-7892
Joe Bryant, *President*
Dyanne L Bryant, *Manager*
▲ EMP: 26
SQ FT: 6,000
SALES (est): 1MM **Privately Held**
SIC: 2399 3911 2396 Military insignia, textile; medals, precious or semiprecious metal; automotive & apparel trimmings

(G-4583)
WOOD CREATIONS BY ROD LLC
2601 Crystal Dr (73160-5537)
PHONE................405 912-8099
Rodrigo Ferreira, *Principal*
EMP: 2
SALES (est): 185.9K **Privately Held**
WEB: www.woodcreationsbyrod.com
SIC: 2431 Millwork

(G-4584)
WORK ACTIVITY CENTER INC
203 E Main St (73160-5913)
PHONE................405 799-6911
Beverly Young, *Exec Dir*
Bryan Nash, *Director*
EMP: 46
SALES (est): 221.4K **Privately Held**
SIC: 3842 8322 8331 2789 Technical aids for the handicapped; individual & family services; job training & vocational rehabilitation services; bookbinding & related work

Mooreland
Woodward County

(G-4585)
AIR PRODUCTS AND CHEMICALS INC
28052 State Highway 50 (73852-5057)
PHONE................580 994-2732
Eddie Garcia, *Manager*
EMP: 15
SALES (corp-wide): 8.9B **Publicly Held**
SIC: 2813 Oxygen, compressed or liquefied
PA: Air Products And Chemicals, Inc.
7201 Hamilton Blvd
Allentown PA 18195
610 481-4911

(G-4586)
BY PRATHER INC
Also Called: Prather Cues
200 S Main St (73852-9000)
P.O. Box 7 (73852-0007)
PHONE................580 994-2414
Jeff Prather, *President*
Rhonda Prather, *Admin Sec*
EMP: 3
SQ FT: 2,500
SALES: 300K **Privately Held**
SIC: 3949 Billiard & pool equipment & supplies, general

(G-4587)
CSC INC (PA)
Also Called: Ruttman Printing
202 N Main St (73852-9217)
P.O. Box 137 (73852-0137)
PHONE................580 994-6110
Tim Schnoebelen, *President*
Tim Schnoebelen, *President*
Jeff Schnoebelen, *Vice Pres*
EMP: 8
SQ FT: 6,500
SALES: 450K **Privately Held**
SIC: 2711 2796 2791 2789 Commercial printing & newspaper publishing combined; platemaking services; typesetting; bookbinding & related work; commercial printing; commercial printing, lithographic

(G-4588)
CSC INC
Also Called: Ruttman Printing
202 N Main St (73852-9217)
P.O. Box 137 (73852-0137)
PHONE................580 256-2409
Fax: 580 256-4952
EMP: 1
SALES (corp-wide): 1.3MM **Privately Held**
SIC: 2752 Lithographic Commercial Printing
PA: Csc Inc
202 N Main St
Mooreland OK 73852
580 994-6110

(G-4589)
E & K OILFIELD SERVICES INC
604 Se 2nd St (73852-9040)
P.O. Box 872 (73852-0872)
PHONE................580 994-2442
Kim Aldridge, *President*
EMP: 2
SALES (est): 311.6K **Privately Held**
SIC: 1389 Oil field services

(G-4590)
EL PASO PROD OIL GAS TEXAS LP
3 Mi East On Hwy 412 (73852)
P.O. Box 47 (73852-0047)
PHONE................580 994-2171
Rod Savely, *Manager*
EMP: 20 **Publicly Held**
SIC: 1389 Gas compressing (natural gas) at the fields
HQ: El Paso Production Oil & Gas Texas, L.P.
1001 Louisiana St
Houston TX 77002
713 997-1000

(G-4591)
HARRISON GYPSUM LLC
Also Called: Acg Material
10930 Us Highway 412 (73852-5033)
PHONE................580 994-6048
Mark Hearrell, *Branch Mgr*
EMP: 30
SALES (corp-wide): 1.7B **Publicly Held**
SIC: 1499 4213 Gypsum mining; trucking, except local
HQ: Harrison Gypsum, Llc
1550 Double C Dr
Norman OK 73069
405 366-9500

(G-4592)
HARRISON GYPSUM LLC
Also Called: Allied Cstm Gyps Plasterworks
801 Sw 6th St (73852-9105)
P.O. Box 940 (73852-0940)
PHONE................580 994-6050
Mark Herald, *Branch Mgr*
EMP: 16
SALES (corp-wide): 1.7B **Publicly Held**
SIC: 1499 Gypsum mining
HQ: Harrison Gypsum, Llc
1550 Double C Dr
Norman OK 73069
405 366-9500

(G-4593)
PROVEN TORQUE LLC
9949 Us Highway 412 (73852-5029)
P.O. Box 1037 (73852-1037)
PHONE................780 982-7597
Darren Larson, *Mng Member*
Dusty Testerman,
EMP: 4 EST: 2017
SALES (est): 167.4K **Privately Held**
SIC: 1389 Oil field services

(G-4594)
SAMPSON BROTHERS INC
822 S Laird St (73852-8918)
P.O. Box 268 (73852-0268)
PHONE................580 994-2464
Danny Sampson, *President*
EMP: 3
SALES (est): 208.1K **Privately Held**
SIC: 1389 Oil field services

(G-4595)
SPREAD TECH LLC
417 Sw 7th St (73852-7602)
PHONE................580 994-2506
Jeff McIntosh, *Mng Member*
EMP: 22
SQ FT: 2,800
SALES: 3.5MM **Privately Held**
SIC: 1389 Oil field services

Morris
Okmulgee County

(G-4596)
GMG OIL & GAS CORPORATION
15648 Banyan Rd (74445-2098)
PHONE................918 756-5308
John McChesney, *President*
Nancy McChesney, *Corp Secy*
Wanda McChesney, *Vice Pres*
EMP: 5
SALES (est): 283.9K **Privately Held**
SIC: 1382 Oil & gas exploration services

(G-4597)
KENKAY MACHINE
18550 Ash Rd (74445-2714)
P.O. Box 67 (74445-0067)
PHONE................918 733-2780
Mike Warren, *Owner*
EMP: 9
SALES (est): 875K **Privately Held**
SIC: 3599 Machine shop, jobbing & repair

(G-4598)
KIRK TANK TRUCKS INC
100 E Ozark St (74445-4832)
P.O. Box 146 (74445-0146)
PHONE................918 733-4503
Bill E Kirk, *President*
EMP: 6
SQ FT: 800
SALES (est): 541.9K **Privately Held**
SIC: 1389 Oil field services

(G-4599)
M & M MACHINING LLC
419 N 6th St (74445-2782)
P.O. Box 395 (74445-0395)
PHONE................918 733-1337
Sarah Amador, *CEO*
Justin Amador, *Vice Pres*
EMP: 6 EST: 2007
SQ FT: 5,000
SALES: 380K **Privately Held**
WEB: www.mandmmachining.com
SIC: 3599 Machine shop, jobbing & repair

(G-4600)
MORRIS NEWS
421 E Ozark St Ste A (74445-4853)
P.O. Box 113 (74445-0113)
PHONE..................................918 733-4898
El Thomson, *Owner*
Herman L Thomson, *Principal*
EMP: 2
SALES (est): 149.8K **Privately Held**
SIC: 2711 Newspapers, publishing & printing

(G-4601)
MORTON LEASES INC
16360 N 280 Rd (74445-2831)
PHONE..................................918 733-2331
Nelson Morton, *President*
Clara Morton, *Admin Sec*
EMP: 4
SALES (est): 474.2K **Privately Held**
SIC: 1389 Oil & gas field services

(G-4602)
RICK DAVIS
Also Called: Tri D Cattle Farming
800 S 1st St (74445-2460)
PHONE..................................918 733-4760
Rick Davis, *Partner*
EMP: 2
SALES (est): 38K **Privately Held**
SIC: 0212 1311 Beef cattle except feedlots; crude petroleum & natural gas

Morrison
Noble County

(G-4603)
HMAN GLOBAL SOLUTIONS LLC
301 Echo Ln (73061-9250)
PHONE..................................405 338-5348
Brian Heishman,
Melinda Heishman,
EMP: 1
SALES (est): 52.7K **Privately Held**
SIC: 7381 8299 7389 2892 Guard services; security guard service; educational services; explosives recovery or extraction services; explosives

(G-4604)
JP WELDING
22801 Independence (73061-9577)
PHONE..................................405 714-0232
Jared Petree, *Principal*
EMP: 2
SALES (est): 70.2K **Privately Held**
SIC: 7692 Welding repair

(G-4605)
JP WELDING FABRICATION
22851 County Road 230 (73061-9575)
PHONE..................................580 724-9104
Jared Petree, *Principal*
EMP: 1
SALES (est): 65.3K **Privately Held**
SIC: 7692 Welding repair

(G-4606)
WILDCAT WELDING LLC
405 W Highway 64 (73061)
P.O. Box 255 (73061-0255)
PHONE..................................405 714-2273
Billy Galloway,
Billy Joe Galloway Sr,
EMP: 1
SALES (est): 54.8K **Privately Held**
SIC: 7692 Welding repair

Mounds
Creek County

(G-4607)
AC MACHINE
324 E 8th St (74047-4188)
PHONE..................................918 827-6552
Dean Clark, *Owner*
EMP: 3
SALES (est): 100K **Privately Held**
SIC: 3544 Special dies & tools

(G-4608)
ACECO VALVE INC
2300 Alt 75 (74047-6160)
P.O. Box 339 (74047-0339)
PHONE..................................918 827-3669
Orvel Wolf, *President*
Pat Wolf, *Corp Secy*
EMP: 35
SQ FT: 16,500
SALES (est): 5.2MM **Privately Held**
SIC: 3599 3533 3494 Machine & other job shop work; oil & gas field machinery; valves & pipe fittings

(G-4609)
AMERICAN TS
Also Called: American Textile Screen Prtg
1205 Alt 75 (74047-4608)
PHONE..................................918 284-7685
Randy Fulbright, *Owner*
EMP: 3
SALES (est): 177.5K **Privately Held**
SIC: 2759 Screen printing

(G-4610)
BETHESDA BOYS RANCH (PA)
Also Called: Bethesda Adult Lf Training Ctr
17477 S 49th Ave W (74047)
P.O. Box 460 (74047-0460)
PHONE..................................918 827-6409
Donald Toops, *President*
Lourdes Toops, *Vice Pres*
Brian Miller, *Admin Sec*
EMP: 10
SQ FT: 46,100
SALES: 587.8K **Privately Held**
SIC: 3441 8361 Fabricated structural metal; juvenile correctional home

(G-4611)
CAMO GALZ CANDLES & MORE
8443 W 176th St S (74047-4186)
PHONE..................................918 399-0044
Phala D Speer, *Principal*
EMP: 1
SALES (est): 60.9K **Privately Held**
SIC: 3999 Candles

(G-4612)
D DIAMOND ENTERPRISES INC
6490 Creager Rd (74047-4621)
PHONE..................................918 827-4727
H David Ivans, *President*
EMP: 1
SALES (est): 675K **Privately Held**
SIC: 3441 Fabricated structural metal

(G-4613)
DONALD STANDRIDGE
4701 W 187th St S (74047-5437)
P.O. Box 716, Antlers (74523-0716)
PHONE..................................580 298-3760
Donald Standridge, *Principal*
EMP: 1
SALES (est): 109.1K **Privately Held**
SIC: 2411 Logging

(G-4614)
EXTENDED FIN
7219 Ferguson Rd (74047-6179)
P.O. Box 280 (74047-0280)
PHONE..................................918 827-4044
Bradley Veale, *Owner*
EMP: 6
SQ FT: 20,000
SALES: 2MM **Privately Held**
SIC: 3443 Heat exchangers, condensers & components

(G-4615)
EZ CARRIER LLC
975 Highway 75 (74047-4326)
PHONE..................................918 827-7876
Mark Givens, *Mng Member*
John Murphy,
EMP: 5 EST: 2008
SQ FT: 2,500
SALES: 300K **Privately Held**
WEB: www.ezcarrierusa.com
SIC: 5088 3441 Transportation equipment & supplies; fabricated structural metal

(G-4616)
GIVENS MANUFACTURING INC
Also Called: EZ Carrier
975 Highway 75 (74047-4326)
PHONE..................................888 302-2774
Mark Givens, *Owner*
EMP: 4
SALES (est): 130K **Privately Held**
SIC: 3496 3315 Miscellaneous fabricated wire products; steel wire & related products

(G-4617)
GSS SIGN & DESIGN LLC
17424 S Union Ave (74047-5460)
PHONE..................................918 827-6561
EMP: 15
SALES (est): 1.9MM **Privately Held**
WEB: www.globalsignsolutions.com
SIC: 3993 Signs & advertising specialties

(G-4618)
J & J MACHINE SHOP
7660 Adams Rd (74047-4224)
P.O. Box 159 (74047-0159)
PHONE..................................918 827-6892
Melvin E Jones Jr, *Owner*
Melvin Jones, *CIO*
EMP: 3
SQ FT: 1,900
SALES (est): 219.6K **Privately Held**
SIC: 3599 Machine shop, jobbing & repair

(G-4619)
JANDJ MACHINE SHOP LLC
7660 Adams Rd (74047-4224)
PHONE..................................918 827-6892
Shelia Fay Jones, *Administration*
EMP: 2
SALES (est): 137.6K **Privately Held**
SIC: 3599 Machine shop, jobbing & repair

(G-4620)
MEDCRAFT LLC
Also Called: Spsc
1312 Commercial Ave (74047)
PHONE..................................918 938-0642
Gregory Berenato, *CEO*
Matthew Davidson, *Opers Staff*
EMP: 4
SALES (est): 90K **Privately Held**
SIC: 2834 Pharmaceutical preparations

(G-4621)
MOUNDS PRINTING
17257 S 89th West Ave (74047-4127)
PHONE..................................918 827-6573
EMP: 2
SALES (est): 83.9K **Privately Held**
SIC: 2752 Commercial printing, lithographic

(G-4622)
PERSONAL DEFENSE LLC
15695 Hectorville Rd (74047-5311)
PHONE..................................918 345-0075
Christofer Orcutt, *Principal*
EMP: 3
SALES (est): 153K **Privately Held**
SIC: 3812 Defense systems & equipment

(G-4623)
PROCESS PRODUCTS & SERVICE CO
Also Called: Teletronics Co
1115 Commercial St (74047)
P.O. Box 581 (74047-0581)
PHONE..................................918 827-4998
Charles Summers, *President*
Rebecca J Summers, *Vice Pres*
EMP: 3
SQ FT: 2,500
SALES: 500K **Privately Held**
SIC: 3822 3823 3625 3533 Ignition controls for gas appliances & furnaces, automatic; industrial instrmnts msrmnt display/control process variable; relays & industrial controls; oil & gas field machinery

(G-4624)
RICK CRSSLIN BACKHOE DOZER SVC
7675 W 183rd St S (74047-4530)
PHONE..................................918 371-7956
EMP: 2 EST: 2012
SALES (est): 97K **Privately Held**
SIC: 3531 Mfg Construction Machinery

(G-4625)
TECHNOLOGY LICENSING CORP
Also Called: Global Sign Solutions
17424 S Union Ave (74047-5460)
PHONE..................................918 836-5597
Abolfazl Ahmadian, *President*
Amir Labbaf, *Prdtn Mgr*
Michael Worley, *Sales Staff*
EMP: 22
SQ FT: 24,000
SALES (est): 2.4MM **Privately Held**
WEB: www.globalsignsolutions.com
SIC: 3993 Electric signs

Mountain Park
Kiowa County

(G-4626)
JOHNSON WELDING
114 Spruce St (73559)
P.O. Box 70 (73559-0070)
PHONE..................................580 569-2231
Mark Johnson, *Owner*
Lillian De Etta Johnson, *Co-Owner*
EMP: 1
SQ FT: 3,200
SALES (est): 96.9K **Privately Held**
SIC: 3523 7692 3444 Farm machinery & equipment; welding repair; sheet metalwork

Mountain View
Kiowa County

(G-4627)
DOLESE BROS CO
Also Called: Cooperton Plant
Rr 2 (73062)
PHONE..................................580 639-2237
Rick Pelk, *Superintendent*
EMP: 45
SALES (corp-wide): 8.5MM **Privately Held**
WEB: www.dolese.com
SIC: 3273 Ready-mixed concrete
PA: Dolese Bros. Co.
20 Nw 13th St
Oklahoma City OK 73103
405 235-2311

(G-4628)
MOUNTAIN VIEW PRINTING COMPANY
Also Called: Mountain View News
319 Main St (73062-9557)
P.O. Box 488 (73062-0488)
PHONE..................................580 347-2231
Leon Hobbs, *President*
Jill Hobbs, *Corp Secy*
EMP: 2
SQ FT: 1,500
SALES (est): 209K **Privately Held**
SIC: 2711 Newspapers: publishing only, not printed on site; newspapers, publishing & printing

(G-4629)
RACKLEY WELDING
12827 N 2410 Rd (73062-6208)
PHONE..................................580 660-1176
Lyndall Rackley, *Owner*
EMP: 1
SALES: 85K **Privately Held**
SIC: 3699 Laser welding, drilling & cutting equipment

Muldrow
Sequoyah County

(G-4630)
AFFORDABLE BUILDINGS LLC
416 W Treat Rd (74948)
P.O. Box 2324 (74948-2324)
PHONE..................918 427-6005
Roger Wilson, *Principal*
EMP: 4
SALES (est): 475.2K **Privately Held**
WEB: www.affordablebuildings.biz
SIC: 3448 Carports: prefabricated metal

(G-4631)
B & W DIESEL & DRIVETRAIN INC
303 W Treat Rd (74948)
P.O. Box 350 (74948-0350)
PHONE..................918 427-7918
Walter Newell, *President*
Betty Newell, *Treasurer*
EMP: 5
SALES (est): 571.7K **Privately Held**
SIC: 7538 3714 5013 5521 Diesel engine repair: automotive; motor vehicle parts & accessories; body repair or paint shop supplies, automotive; used car dealers

(G-4632)
COOPER CONSULTING LLC
472440 E 1070 Rd (74948-6601)
P.O. Box 6521, Fort Smith AR (72906-6521)
PHONE..................918 427-7171
Bill Cooper, *CEO*
Elizabeth Cooper, *CFO*
EMP: 2 EST: 2011
SALES: 20K **Privately Held**
SIC: 2851 Removers & cleaners

(G-4633)
CRAWSON CORPORATION
110872 S 4760 Rd (74948)
PHONE..................918 427-8400
Gary Kindy Jr, *President*
Steve Waddell, *Engineer*
Janet Kindy, *Administration*
EMP: 10
SQ FT: 35,000
SALES: 450K **Privately Held**
SIC: 2431 Millwork

(G-4634)
MORRIS RICHARDSON
Also Called: Fairview Production Co
Rr 2 Box 135 (74948-9600)
P.O. Box 1995 (74948-1995)
PHONE..................918 427-7323
Morris Richardson, *Co-Owner*
John Elliott, *Co-Owner*
Miles Elliott, *Co-Owner*
EMP: 3
SALES: 500K **Privately Held**
SIC: 1389 Pumping of oil & gas wells

(G-4635)
O K FOODS INC
Also Called: O K Distributions and Trnsp
100 N Wilson Rock Rd (74948)
P.O. Box 810 (74948-0810)
PHONE..................918 427-7000
Russ Bragg, *President*
EMP: 400 **Privately Held**
WEB: www.okfoods.com
SIC: 5144 2099 2015 Poultry & poultry products; food preparations; poultry slaughtering & processing
HQ: O. K. Foods, Inc.
4601 N 6th St
Fort Smith AR 72904
479 783-4186

(G-4636)
SENDEE SALES INC
107 W Treat Rd (74948-2421)
P.O. Box 1230 (74948-1230)
PHONE..................918 427-3318
Farrell McGehee, *President*
Janet Taylor, *President*
Senna McGehee, *Admin Sec*
EMP: 20 EST: 1965
SQ FT: 8,000
SALES (est): 2.9MM **Privately Held**
WEB: www.sendeefurniture.com
SIC: 2512 Living room furniture: upholstered on wood frames

Mulhall
Logan County

(G-4637)
BRIDGE CREEK PUBLISHING CO
7676 W County Road 66 (73063-9711)
PHONE..................405 519-6982
Robert Brian, *Principal*
EMP: 2
SALES (est): 50K **Privately Held**
SIC: 2741 Miscellaneous publishing

(G-4638)
FAB TECH WELDING
17535 Bow Rd (73063-9690)
PHONE..................405 649-2322
EMP: 1 EST: 1989
SALES (est): 62K **Privately Held**
SIC: 7692 Welding Repair

Muskogee
Muskogee County

(G-4639)
A 1 ADVERTISING BY L & H
2601 N Main St (74401-4059)
PHONE..................918 348-2529
Kenny Lane, *Principal*
EMP: 2
SALES (est): 105.2K **Privately Held**
SIC: 5099 5085 3993 Signs, except electric; signmaker equipment & supplies; signs & advertising specialties

(G-4640)
AARON SON CUSTOM CABINETS
2001 Deer Run Cir (74403-8440)
PHONE..................918 537-2129
Aaron Poggenpohl, *Principal*
EMP: 1
SALES (est): 74.7K **Privately Held**
SIC: 2434 Wood kitchen cabinets

(G-4641)
ACE FENCE CO
2337 S Cherokee St (74403-8004)
PHONE..................918 682-7895
Bruce Hayes, *Owner*
EMP: 6
SALES (est): 521.5K **Privately Held**
SIC: 1799 3446 Fence construction; architectural metalwork

(G-4642)
ACME ENGINEERING AND MFG CORP (PA)
1820 N York St (74403-1451)
P.O. Box 978 (74402-0978)
PHONE..................918 682-7791
Edward Buddrus, *Ch of Bd*
Lee E Buddrus, *President*
Brian Combs, *Exec VP*
Forrest Hooks, *Exec VP*
Adam Sterne, *Exec VP*
◆ EMP: 430 EST: 1938
SQ FT: 358,020
SALES (est): 149MM **Privately Held**
WEB: www.acmefan.com
SIC: 3564 Filters, air: furnaces, air conditioning equipment, etc.

(G-4643)
ADVANTAGE CONTROLS LLC
4700 Harold Abitz Dr (74403-6246)
P.O. Box 1472 (74402-1472)
PHONE..................918 686-6211
Dan Morris, *CEO*
Jeff Oneal, *Vice Pres*
Jesse Dubroc, *Purch Mgr*
Dick Morris, *Research*
Melanie Grayson, *Accounting Mgr*
▲ EMP: 72
SQ FT: 33,500
SALES (est): 37.6MM **Privately Held**
SIC: 5084 3822 Instruments & control equipment; hydronic controls; thermostats, except built-in

(G-4644)
AFG ACQUISITION GROUP LLC
Also Called: American Foundry Group
612 S 45th St E (74403-6219)
P.O. Box 2328 (74402-2328)
PHONE..................918 683-5683
Jogi P Makhani, *Branch Mgr*
David Barks, *Manager*
EMP: 20
SALES (est): 4.6MM
SALES (corp-wide): 78.9MM **Privately Held**
SIC: 3441 Building components, structural steel
PA: Afg Acquisition Group L.L.C.
14602 S Grant St
Bixby OK 74008
918 366-4401

(G-4645)
ALL STATE ELECTRIC MOTORS INC
Also Called: All State Elc Mtr & Eqp Co
1730 N 11th St (74401-3515)
P.O. Box 1508 (74402-1508)
PHONE..................918 683-6581
Edward Rivard, *Manager*
EMP: 3
SALES (corp-wide): 600K **Privately Held**
SIC: 7694 5084 Electric motor repair; industrial machinery & equipment
PA: All State Electric Motors, Inc.
1839 Linwood Blvd
Oklahoma City OK 73106
405 232-1129

(G-4646)
ALL STEEL CARPORTS LLC
2500 S 32nd St (74401-2901)
PHONE..................918 683-1717
Ignacio Chavez, *Principal*
EMP: 3
SALES (est): 313.9K **Privately Held**
WEB: www.glcarports.com
SIC: 3448 Prefabricated metal buildings

(G-4647)
ALPHA OMEGA MLTARY/DEFENCE MFG
228 N K St (74403-5160)
PHONE..................918 816-6918
Kyle Brown, *Principal*
EMP: 1
SALES (est): 60.9K **Privately Held**
SIC: 3711 Military motor vehicle assembly

(G-4648)
ANSA COMPANY INC (PA)
1200 S Main St (74401-7800)
PHONE..................918 687-1664
Austin Iodice, *President*
John Iodice, *Exec VP*
EMP: 12
SQ FT: 23,000
SALES (est): 2.6MM **Privately Held**
SIC: 5137 3085 Baby goods; plastics bottles

(G-4649)
ARC RVALS WLDG FABRICATION LLC
5231 S 37th St E (74403-9126)
PHONE..................918 577-5066
Casey Conrad,
EMP: 1
SALES: 15K **Privately Held**
SIC: 1799 3441 Welding on site; fabricated structural metal

(G-4650)
ARKHOLA SAND & GRAVEL CO
3300 W 40th St N (74401-5425)
PHONE..................918 687-4771
Chuck Bledsoe, *Principal*
EMP: 3
SALES (est): 194.9K **Privately Held**
SIC: 1442 Construction sand & gravel

(G-4651)
B & B MACHINE
2810 S 24th St W (74401-8264)
PHONE..................918 686-9900
Brett Bible, *Owner*
EMP: 1
SALES (est): 139.4K **Privately Held**
SIC: 3599 Machine shop, jobbing & repair

(G-4652)
B SEW INN LLC (PA)
2530 Chandler Rd (74403-5003)
PHONE..................918 687-5762
Mary Hess, *Principal*
EMP: 9
SALES (est): 7.9MM **Privately Held**
SIC: 5722 3552 7371 Sewing machines; vacuum cleaners; embroidery machines; computer software systems analysis & design, custom

(G-4653)
BOBS AUTO ELECTRIC
1306 Gibson St (74403-2408)
PHONE..................918 687-3701
Bob Workman, *Owner*
EMP: 1
SALES (est): 100.7K **Privately Held**
SIC: 3694 Automotive electrical equipment

(G-4654)
BPI INC
Also Called: Sintertec Div
2551 Port Pl (74403-9219)
PHONE..................918 682-5044
Maurice Cook, *Manager*
EMP: 5
SALES (corp-wide): 18.9MM **Privately Held**
SIC: 2819 3297 Industrial inorganic chemicals; nonclay refractories
PA: B.P.I. (By-Product Industries), Inc.
612 S Trenton Ave
Pittsburgh PA 15221
412 371-8554

(G-4655)
BRIGGS RAINBOW BUILDINGS INC (PA)
Also Called: B R B Roofing & Manufacturing
3143 N 32nd St (74401-2264)
P.O. Box 308, Fort Gibson (74434-0308)
PHONE..................918 683-3695
Doss Briggs, *President*
Darlene Briggs, *Vice Pres*
Darla Briggs, *Treasurer*
EMP: 105
SQ FT: 10,000
SALES (est): 10.8MM **Privately Held**
SIC: 1761 1541 3444 Roofing contractor; steel building construction; sheet metalwork

(G-4656)
BYRD SIGNS & DESIGNS
Also Called: Ross C Byrd III Signs Designs
140 W 61st St S (74401-9010)
PHONE..................918 687-4219
Ross Byrd, *Owner*
EMP: 1
SALES (est): 48.6K **Privately Held**
SIC: 7532 3993 Truck painting & lettering; signs & advertising specialties

(G-4657)
C&M ENTERPRISES
4002 Jefferson St (74403-2851)
PHONE..................918 683-4456
Marlene Collins, *Owner*
Cecil R Collins, *Partner*
EMP: 2
SALES (est): 190K **Privately Held**
SIC: 3499 Fire- or burglary-resistive products

(G-4658)
CAPTIVE-AIRE SYSTEMS INC
4031 Tull Ave (74403-6224)
PHONE..................918 686-6717
Bill Cowen, *Manager*
EMP: 100
SALES (corp-wide): 389.2MM **Privately Held**
SIC: 5075 3444 Warm air heating & air conditioning; sheet metalwork

GEOGRAPHIC SECTION

Muskogee - Muskogee County (G-4687)

PA: Captive-Aire Systems, Inc.
4641 Paragon Park Rd # 104
Raleigh NC 27616
919 882-2410

(G-4659)
CENTRAL MORTAR AND GROUT LLC
1300 S 43rd St E (74403-6254)
PHONE..................918 683-3003
▲ EMP: 20
SQ FT: 50,000
SALES: 3MM Privately Held
SIC: 3255 Mfg Clay Refractories

(G-4660)
CHOSKA ALFALFA MILLS LLC
3505 Severs St (74403-1842)
PHONE..................918 687-5805
Don Cole, *Principal*
EMP: 2
SALES (est): 143.6K Privately Held
SIC: 2048 Prepared feeds

(G-4661)
CLAYTON HOMES INC
2235 N 32nd St (74401-2274)
PHONE..................918 686-0584
Jeff Curtsinger, *Sales Mgr*
John Inman, *Branch Mgr*
EMP: 21
SALES (corp-wide): 327.2B Publicly Held
SIC: 2451 Mobile homes
HQ: Clayton Homes, Inc.
5000 Clayton Rd
Maryville TN 37804
865 380-3000

(G-4662)
CORPORATE TO CAUSAL SCREEN
1305 N Main St (74401-4445)
P.O. Box 1091 (74402-1091)
PHONE..................918 686-6688
Don Wrightsman, *President*
Sonja Wrightsman, *Treasurer*
EMP: 7 EST: 1995
SALES (est): 647.3K Privately Held
WEB: www.corporatetocasual.com
SIC: 2759 Screen printing

(G-4663)
CORPORATE TO CSUAL SCREEN PRTG
1305 N Main St (74401-4445)
PHONE..................918 686-6688
Sonia Wrightsman, *Owner*
EMP: 3
SALES (est): 274.5K Privately Held
SIC: 2759 Screen printing

(G-4664)
CREATIVE APPAREL AND MORE INC
1116 W Broadway St (74401-6246)
PHONE..................918 682-1283
Connie Duncan, *Owner*
Carolyn Duncan, *Co-Owner*
EMP: 6
SALES (est): 355.8K Privately Held
SIC: 2395 2329 3993 2396 Embroidery products, except schiffli machine; men's & boys' sportswear & athletic clothing; signs & advertising specialties; automotive & apparel trimmings

(G-4665)
CREEK NATION FOUNDATION INC
3420 W Peak Blvd (74401-8829)
P.O. Box 580, Okmulgee (74447-0580)
PHONE..................918 683-1825
Farrell Kaaihue, *Manager*
EMP: 2
SALES: 720.4K Privately Held
SIC: 8351 3944 Child day care services; electronic games & toys

(G-4666)
CUSTOM SEATING INCORPORATED
341 S 41st St E (74403-6223)
PHONE..................918 682-4400

David W Wood, *Ch of Bd*
Charles Gresham, *President*
Harold Rose, *Senior VP*
Bill Fender, *Vice Pres*
William Fender, *Vice Pres*
▲ EMP: 200
SQ FT: 120,000
SALES (est): 60.8MM Privately Held
WEB: www.customseating.com
SIC: 3443 1799 2431 Fabricated plate work (boiler shop); fiberglass work; millwork; woodwork, interior & ornamental

(G-4667)
DIAMONDBACK STEEL COMPANY INC
419 S Cherokee St (74403-5408)
PHONE..................918 686-6340
Keith Wright, *President*
EMP: 30
SQ FT: 40,000
SALES (est): 6.6MM Privately Held
SIC: 3441 Fabricated structural metal

(G-4668)
DVM NUTRION PETS CORP INC
Also Called: Meatlovers
1410 S Cherokee St (74403)
PHONE..................918 686-6111
Ed Johnson, *President*
EMP: 18
SALES (est): 1.4MM Privately Held
SIC: 2048 Dry pet food (except dog & cat)

(G-4669)
EASTERN SHEET METAL CO INC
2301 N Main St (74401-4047)
P.O. Box 1554 (74402-1554)
PHONE..................918 687-6231
Frank Delmedico, *President*
EMP: 5
SQ FT: 12,000
SALES (est): 574.9K Privately Held
SIC: 1761 7699 3444 Sheet metalwork; tinsmithing, repair work; sheet metalwork

(G-4670)
EASTPOINTE INDUSTRIES INC
4020 Tull Ave (74403-6229)
PHONE..................918 683-2169
Johnny L Rhodes, *President*
Kevin Gajan, *Exec VP*
▼ EMP: 35
SQ FT: 25,000
SALES (est): 9MM Privately Held
SIC: 3599 Machine shop, jobbing & repair; machine & other job shop work

(G-4671)
EASTPOINTE MANUFACTURING CORP
4020 Tull Ave (74403-6229)
PHONE..................918 683-2169
Arthur R King, *President*
Kevin Gajan, *Vice Pres*
Randell Scott, *Vice Pres*
EMP: 43 EST: 1998
SQ FT: 20,000
SALES (est): 4MM Privately Held
SIC: 3441 3446 Fabricated structural metal; architectural metalwork

(G-4672)
EGRET OPERATING COMPANY INC
Also Called: Robinson, Kurt
124 S 4th St (74401-7013)
P.O. Box 1871 (74402-1871)
PHONE..................918 687-8665
Kurt Robinson, *President*
Cheryl Robinson, *Admin Sec*
EMP: 1
SALES (est): 140K Privately Held
SIC: 1382 Oil & gas exploration services

(G-4673)
ERGON ASPHALT & EMULSIONS INC
2501 Port Pl (74403-9219)
PHONE..................918 683-1732
Mike Dean, *Manager*
EMP: 11

SALES (corp-wide): 897.8MM Privately Held
SIC: 2951 Asphalt paving mixtures & blocks
HQ: Ergon Asphalt & Emulsions Inc
2829 Lakeland Dr Ste 2000
Flowood MS 39232
601 933-3000

(G-4674)
FRANKLIN DIGITAL INC
3103 S Cherokee Dr (74403-8054)
PHONE..................918 687-6149
Aimee Burroughs, *President*
Steven Farley, *President*
Donna Keck, *Treasurer*
Ronnie Franklin, *Admin Sec*
EMP: 10
SQ FT: 13,000
SALES: 8.7MM Privately Held
SIC: 2754 Commercial printing, gravure

(G-4675)
FRANKLIN GRAPHICS INC
3103 S Cherokee Dr (74403-8054)
PHONE..................918 687-6149
David Franklin, *President*
Ronnie Franklin, *Corp Secy*
EMP: 16 EST: 1974
SQ FT: 13,000
SALES (est): 4.3MM Privately Held
SIC: 2752 2796 2791 2789 Commercial printing, offset; platemaking services; typesetting; bookbinding & related work

(G-4676)
FRONTIER RESOURCE DEVELOPMENT
240 North St (74403-2131)
PHONE..................918 682-6571
EMP: 8
SALES (est): 609.6K Privately Held
SIC: 2448 Mfg Wood Pallets/Skids

(G-4677)
G & L METAL BUILDINGS
3246 N 32nd St (74401-2265)
PHONE..................918 687-1867
Christina Page, *Principal*
EMP: 2
SALES (est): 118.9K Privately Held
SIC: 3448 Prefabricated metal buildings

(G-4678)
GEORGIA-PACIFIC LLC
4901 Chandler Rd (74403-4945)
PHONE..................918 687-9800
Rob Shaw, *Opers Staff*
Eric Hanson, *Engineer*
Brian Scott, *Engineer*
Eric Speir, *Engineer*
Wayne Tiller, *Project Engr*
EMP: 50
SALES (corp-wide): 48.9B Privately Held
SIC: 3081 3089 Polyethylene film; extruded finished plastic products
HQ: Georgia-Pacific Llc
133 Peachtree St Nw
Atlanta GA 30303
404 652-4000

(G-4679)
GERDAU AMERISTEEL US INC
Steel Coating
2301a Anderson Dr (74403)
P.O. Box 1454 (74402-1454)
PHONE..................918 682-2600
Ernie Franklin, *Manager*
EMP: 10 Privately Held
SIC: 3441 3479 Building components, structural steel; coating of metals & formed products
HQ: Gerdau Ameristeel Us Inc.
4221 W Boy Scout Blvd # 600
Tampa FL 33607
813 286-8383

(G-4680)
GERDAU AMERISTEEL US INC
Muskogee Reinforcing Steel
1921 Anderson Dr (74403-2423)
PHONE..................918 682-7806
Ernie Franklin, *Manager*
EMP: 32 Privately Held
SIC: 3441 Building components, structural steel

HQ: Gerdau Ameristeel Us Inc.
4221 W Boy Scout Blvd # 600
Tampa FL 33607
813 286-8383

(G-4681)
GOLD RULE INDUSTRIES INC
627 Elgin St (74403-7528)
PHONE..................918 682-6500
Robert Stewart, *Principal*
EMP: 1 EST: 2012
SALES: 1.3MM Privately Held
WEB: www.goldenrulejobs.org
SIC: 3999 Manufacturing industries

(G-4682)
GRAHAM PACKAGING COMPANY LP
102 Kaad St (74401-4466)
P.O. Box 2518 (74402-2518)
PHONE..................918 680-7900
John Gross, *Manager*
EMP: 1 Publicly Held
SIC: 3089 Plastic containers, except foam
HQ: Graham Packaging Company, L.P.
700 Indian Springs Dr # 100
Lancaster PA 17601
717 849-8500

(G-4683)
GRIFFIN FOOD COMPANY
111 S Cherokee St (74403-5420)
P.O. Box 1928 (74402-1928)
PHONE..................918 687-6311
John W Griffin, *President*
John T Griffin, *Principal*
EMP: 60
SQ FT: 450,000
SALES (est): 7.7MM Privately Held
WEB: www.griffinfoods.com
SIC: 2033 2035 2087 2099 Jellies, edible, including imitation: in cans, jars, etc.; dressings, salad: raw & cooked (except dry mixes); mustard, prepared (wet); flavoring extracts & syrups; syrups
PA: Griffin Holdings, Inc.
111 S Cherokee St
Muskogee OK 74403

(G-4684)
GRIFFIN HOLDINGS INC (PA)
Also Called: Griffin Food
111 S Cherokee St (74403-5420)
P.O. Box 1928 (74402-1928)
PHONE..................918 687-6311
John W Griffin, *Ch of Bd*
Kelly Boyle, *Principal*
Marti Killingsworth, *Treasurer*
▲ EMP: 100
SQ FT: 175,000
SALES (est): 20.3MM Privately Held
SIC: 2099 Food preparations

(G-4685)
GRW INC
Also Called: Data Video Systems
3105 Azalea Park Dr (74401-2284)
P.O. Box 1413 (74402-1413)
PHONE..................918 681-3282
Gary Wilson, *President*
Dan Hobbs, *Vice Pres*
EMP: 10
SQ FT: 8,300
SALES (est): 1.8MM Privately Held
SIC: 3357 Fiber optic cable (insulated)

(G-4686)
H G FLAKE COMPANY INC
3007 Kimberlea Dr (74403-1610)
PHONE..................918 684-9004
H Flake, *Principal*
EMP: 2
SALES (est): 119.1K Privately Held
SIC: 3498 Pipe fittings, fabricated from purchased pipe

(G-4687)
HANGER PRSTHTICS ORTHOTICS INC
737 S 32nd St (74401-5014)
PHONE..................918 687-1855
Gary Massey, *General Mgr*
Terry Van Zandt, *General Mgr*
EMP: 4

SALES (corp-wide): 1.1B **Publicly Held**
WEB: www.hanger.com
SIC: 3842 Prosthetic appliances
HQ: Hanger Prosthetics & Orthotics, Inc.
10910 Domain Dr Ste 300
Austin TX 78758
512 777-3800

(G-4688)
HEANDERSON COMPANY
2025 Anderson Dr (74403-2439)
P.O. Box 1006 (74402-1006)
PHONE..................................918 687-4426
Herbert E Anderson Jr, *President*
Jesse Webb, *Prdtn Mgr*
Pat Salmon, *Purchasing*
Eric Anderson, *Engineer*
Annette McFarland, *Accounting Mgr*
EMP: 15
SQ FT: 12,800
SALES (est): 3.1MM **Privately Held**
WEB: www.heanderson.com
SIC: 3823 3561 3586 Industrial instrmnts msrmnt display/control process variable; pumps & pumping equipment; measuring & dispensing pumps

(G-4689)
HEAVENS SCENT CANDLE FACTORY
2410 N 32nd St (74401-2243)
PHONE..................................918 686-0243
Pam Velines, *Partner*
Doye Day, *Partner*
EMP: 2
SQ FT: 174,240
SALES (est): 130K **Privately Held**
SIC: 3999 5199 5999 Candles; candles; candle shops

(G-4690)
HENDERSON COFFEE CORP
Also Called: Monarch Foods, Inc.
3421 S 24th St W (74401-8902)
P.O. Box 175 (74402-0175)
PHONE..................................918 682-8751
Mark Plaster, *President*
Mark Truitt, *Vice Pres*
EMP: 40 EST: 1944
SQ FT: 19,500
SALES (est): 5.4MM
SALES (corp-wide): 56.9MM **Privately Held**
WEB: www.hendersoncoffee.com
SIC: 5149 5087 2095 Coffee, green or roasted; restaurant supplies; roasted coffee
PA: Ronnoco Coffee, Llc
618 S Boyle Ave
Saint Louis MO 63110
314 371-5050

(G-4691)
HOFFMAN PRINTING LLC
1409 W Shawnee St (74401-3409)
P.O. Box 1529 (74402-1529)
PHONE..................................918 682-8341
Lynn Hoffman, *Mng Member*
Carol Hoffman,
EMP: 17 EST: 1907
SQ FT: 17,500
SALES (est): 2.4MM **Privately Held**
WEB: www.hoffmanprinting.com
SIC: 2752 2759 2791 2789 Commercial printing, offset; commercial printing; typesetting; bookbinding & related work; book publishing; periodicals

(G-4692)
HOLLOWAYS BLUPRT & COPY SP INC
Also Called: Holloway's Blue Print Co
810 Eastside Blvd (74403-2231)
P.O. Box 1543 (74402-1543)
PHONE..................................918 682-0280
Jay Updike, *President*
EMP: 2
SALES (est): 206.4K **Privately Held**
SIC: 7334 2752 2396 Blueprinting service; commercial printing, lithographic; automotive & apparel trimmings

(G-4693)
HUNTER STEEL LLC
3704 River Bend Rd (74403-2335)
P.O. Box 1731 (74402-1731)
PHONE..................................918 684-9600
Douglas Jones, *Mng Member*
EMP: 4
SALES: 10MM **Privately Held**
SIC: 3317 Steel pipe & tubes

(G-4694)
IRON IMAGES
5010 Elm Grove Rd (74403-6562)
PHONE..................................918 685-1514
Jim Morris, *CEO*
EMP: 1
SALES (est): 27.6K **Privately Held**
SIC: 7692 Welding repair

(G-4695)
J & J COMPANY
5611 Sally Brown Rd (74403-6903)
PHONE..................................918 616-2169
Jeremy Hollifield, *Owner*
EMP: 2
SALES (est): 183K **Privately Held**
SIC: 3599 Machine shop, jobbing & repair

(G-4696)
JACK STOUT INC
Also Called: Superior Graphics & Signs
515 S Main St (74401-7843)
PHONE..................................918 781-1000
Jack Stout, *President*
Judi Stout, *Treasurer*
EMP: 9
SALES (est): 657.8K **Privately Held**
SIC: 3993 Electric signs

(G-4697)
JAMES P COMPTON
Also Called: Jimco Sign Company
4159 S 65th St E (74403-5221)
PHONE..................................918 682-3700
James P Compton, *Owner*
Vicki Compton, *Co-Owner*
EMP: 7
SQ FT: 2,400
SALES: 350K **Privately Held**
SIC: 3993 Signs & advertising specialties

(G-4698)
JAN L JOBE
Also Called: Action Imprints
107 S Edmond Pl (74403-5020)
PHONE..................................918 683-0404
Jan L Jobe, *Owner*
Gary D Jobe, *Co-Owner*
EMP: 2 EST: 1987
SALES (est): 99K **Privately Held**
SIC: 2396 Screen printing on fabric articles

(G-4699)
JCR EXPLORATION INC
Also Called: Herring Rowsey Properties
124 S 4th St Ste A (74401-7013)
P.O. Box 386 (74402-0386)
PHONE..................................918 682-8200
Jeffrey C Rowsey, *President*
EMP: 3
SALES (est): 355.1K **Privately Held**
SIC: 1382 Oil & gas exploration services

(G-4700)
JEREMY HART MUSIC INC
1213 S 64th St W (74401-4589)
PHONE..................................918 687-3605
Jeremy Hart, *President*
EMP: 1 EST: 2009
SALES (est): 51.1K **Privately Held**
WEB: www.jeremyandjaminhart.com
SIC: 2741 Miscellaneous publishing

(G-4701)
JOHNSON MARCUM OIL AND GAS LLC
1320 N Mill St Ste 128 (74402-2078)
PHONE..................................918 949-8901
Jeff Potts, *Mng Member*
EMP: 10
SALES: 550K **Privately Held**
SIC: 1311 Crude petroleum & natural gas production

(G-4702)
KENS HANDCRAFTED LEATHER GDS
1001 Georgia Pl (74403-7726)
PHONE..................................918 616-5804
EMP: 2 EST: 2014
SALES (est): 124.2K **Privately Held**
SIC: 3199 Leather goods

(G-4703)
KICK16 SKATEBOARDS LLC
1902 Quail Run (74403-8461)
PHONE..................................918 869-6206
Jonathon Vanderveer, *Principal*
EMP: 1
SALES (est): 53.8K **Privately Held**
SIC: 3949 Skateboards

(G-4704)
LAKE COUNTRY GRAPHICS INC
Also Called: Signs For The Times
1321 N Main St (74401-4445)
PHONE..................................918 682-8849
Gregory Joe Vanderveer, *CEO*
EMP: 3
SALES (est): 221.5K **Privately Held**
SIC: 3993 Signs & advertising specialties

(G-4705)
LARRY CAMPBELL OFC
2940 S York St (74403-8881)
PHONE..................................918 682-1209
Larry Campbell, *Principal*
EMP: 3 EST: 2009
SALES (est): 184.1K **Privately Held**
SIC: 3273 Ready-mixed concrete

(G-4706)
LEGENDARY LUBE AND OIL LLC
1619 Houston St (74403-3528)
PHONE..................................918 351-5312
Casey Ledbetter,
EMP: 3
SALES (est): 186.3K **Privately Held**
SIC: 2992 Lubricating oils & greases

(G-4707)
MARTYS DUMPTRUCK & BACKHOE SVC
1517 Out Of Bounds Dr (74403-8468)
PHONE..................................918 869-2051
EMP: 1 EST: 2016
SALES (est): 72.6K **Privately Held**
SIC: 3531 Backhoes

(G-4708)
MATHIS PRINTING INC
Also Called: Mathis Printing & Copy Center
109 S 5th St (74401-7502)
P.O. Box 1462 (74402-1462)
PHONE..................................918 682-2999
Rod Mathis, *President*
Sandra Mathis, *Vice Pres*
EMP: 3
SQ FT: 1,800
SALES (est): 250K **Privately Held**
SIC: 2752 Commercial printing, offset

(G-4709)
MCCAWLEY SERVICE
704 Kershaw Dr (74401-4544)
PHONE..................................918 484-2189
Brian McCawley, *Owner*
Ann McCawley, *Co-Owner*
EMP: 5
SALES (est): 330K **Privately Held**
SIC: 3448 Greenhouses: prefabricated metal

(G-4710)
MED-SOLVE LLC
4495 E Hancock St (74403-8949)
PHONE..................................918 684-4030
Arthur Hulbert, *Mng Member*
EMP: 10
SALES: 766.4K **Privately Held**
SIC: 7372 Prepackaged software

(G-4711)
MEDEXPERTS LLC
4495 E Hancock St (74403-8949)
PHONE..................................918 684-4030
Alan Cunningham,
Ken Doke,

EMP: 13
SALES: 500K **Privately Held**
SIC: 7372 Business oriented computer software

(G-4712)
MERIDIAN BRICK LLC
3101 W 53rd St S (74401-9001)
PHONE..................................918 687-6734
Dick Mathiny, *Branch Mgr*
EMP: 35
SALES (corp-wide): 441MM **Privately Held**
SIC: 3251 5211 3271 Brick & structural clay tile; brick; concrete block & brick
PA: Meridian Brick Llc
6455 Shiloh Rd D
Alpharetta GA 30005
770 645-4500

(G-4713)
METALS USA PLATES AND SHAP
2800 N 43rd St E (74403-1145)
PHONE..................................918 682-7833
Michelle Arnold, *Manager*
EMP: 50
SALES (corp-wide): 10.9B **Publicly Held**
SIC: 5051 3312 Steel; blast furnaces & steel mills
HQ: Metals Usa Plates And Shapes Southcentral, Inc.
101 E Illinois Ave
Enid OK 73701
580 233-0411

(G-4714)
MINERAL RESOURCE TECH INC
Also Called: Mrt - Muskogee Plant TP
4901 Chandler Rd (74403-4945)
PHONE..................................918 683-7671
Lee J Miller, *Branch Mgr*
EMP: 1 **Privately Held**
WEB: www.cemexusa.com
SIC: 3273 Ready-mixed concrete
HQ: Mineral Resource Technologies, Inc.
929 Gessner Rd Ste 1900
Houston TX 77024

(G-4715)
MORTON BUILDINGS INC
4021 Old Shawnee Rd (74403-2565)
P.O. Box 1388 (74402-1388)
PHONE..................................918 683-6668
James Jones, *Manager*
EMP: 20
SALES (corp-wide): 462.5MM **Privately Held**
WEB: www.mortonbuildings.com
SIC: 3448 5039 3441 2452 Buildings, portable: prefabricated metal; prefabricated structures; fabricated structural metal; prefabricated wood buildings; hardwood veneer & plywood
PA: Morton Buildings, Inc.
252 W Adams St
Morton IL 61550
800 447-7436

(G-4716)
MUSKOGEE MARBLE & GRANITE LLC (PA)
Also Called: Kelly Monument
1525 N York St (74403-1435)
P.O. Box 1528 (74402-1528)
PHONE..................................918 682-0064
Walden Key, *Owner*
Taylor Foster, *Mng Member*
EMP: 29
SQ FT: 10,600
SALES (est): 6.4MM **Privately Held**
SIC: 5999 5099 3281 Monuments, finished to custom order; monuments & tombstones; monuments & grave markers; cut stone & stone products

(G-4717)
MUSKOGEE READY MIX INC
4400 Callery Dr (74403-4961)
P.O. Box 1344 (74402-1344)
PHONE..................................918 682-3403
Glen Oliver, *President*
Tom Martin, *Business Mgr*
Michelle Oliver, *Corp Secy*
Jim Steele, *Vice Pres*
EMP: 15 EST: 1936

GEOGRAPHIC SECTION

Muskogee - Muskogee County (G-4747)

SQ FT: 15,000
SALES (est): 1.6MM **Privately Held**
WEB: www.muskogeereadymix.com
SIC: 3273 Ready-mixed concrete

(G-4718)
MUSTARD SEED SCREEN PRINTING
3620 S Country Club Rd (74403-9140)
PHONE.................918 687-6290
Barbara Cameron, *Owner*
EMP: 1
SQ FT: 1,728
SALES (est): 51.6K **Privately Held**
SIC: 2759 Screen printing

(G-4719)
NATIONAL OILWELL VARCO INC
Tubular Corporation of America
3820 Port Pl (74403-9209)
PHONE.................918 781-4436
Dave Weigel, *Manager*
EMP: 250
SALES (corp-wide): 8.4B **Publicly Held**
SIC: 3498 3398 3312 Fabricated pipe & fittings; metal heat treating; blast furnaces & steel mills
PA: National Oilwell Varco, Inc.
7909 Parkwood Circle Dr
Houston TX 77036
713 346-7500

(G-4720)
NATIVE AMERICAN MAINT SVCS INC
Also Called: Global Machine Company
2000 Anderson Dr (74403-2438)
P.O. Box 3266 (74402-3266)
PHONE.................918 682-5700
Paula Bennett, *CEO*
Jared Bennett, *Vice Pres*
Ryan Bennett, *Vice Pres*
Richard Bennett, *CFO*
EMP: 26
SALES (est): 5.6MM **Privately Held**
SIC: 3599 Machine shop, jobbing & repair

(G-4721)
NEWELL WOOD PRODUCTS
6290 Highway 69 (74402)
P.O. Box 2873 (74402-2873)
PHONE.................918 686-8060
Ed Newell, *Owner*
EMP: 12
SQ FT: 9,000
SALES (est): 1.2MM **Privately Held**
SIC: 2439 Trusses, wooden roof

(G-4722)
NEWSPAPER HOLDING INC
Also Called: Muskogee Phoenix
214 Wall St (74401-6644)
PHONE.................918 684-2922
Tina Frost, *President*
EMP: 11 **Privately Held**
SIC: 2711 Newspapers, publishing & printing
HQ: Newspaper Holding, Inc.
425 Locust St
Johnstown PA 15901
814 532-5102

(G-4723)
OKIE INK SCREENPRINTING LLC
7910 S 13th St E (74403-6796)
PHONE.................918 681-0736
EMP: 2 EST: 2017
SALES (est): 90.3K **Privately Held**
SIC: 2759 Screen printing

(G-4724)
OKLAHOMA INTERPAK INC
2424 N Main St (74401-4054)
P.O. Box 1777 (74402-1777)
PHONE.................918 687-1681
John Schilt, *President*
Linda Schilt, *Admin Sec*
EMP: 45
SQ FT: 32,500
SALES (est): 9.4MM **Privately Held**
WEB: www.okinterpak.com
SIC: 2621 2653 2631 2273 Packaging paper; corrugated & solid fiber boxes; paperboard mills; carpets & rugs

(G-4725)
OMNI VALVE COMPANY LLC
4520 Chandler Rd (74403-4928)
PHONE.................918 687-6100
Nanette Spencer, *Controller*
Michael Johnson, *Mng Member*
Robert Smith,
▲ EMP: 50
SQ FT: 23,000
SALES (est): 37.4MM **Privately Held**
SIC: 3491 Industrial valves

(G-4726)
OPTICAL WORKS CORPORATION
7259 Border Ave (74401-8624)
P.O. Box 1686 (74402-1686)
PHONE.................918 682-1806
James Coburn, *President*
Cynthia Coburn, *Shareholder*
▲ EMP: 19
SQ FT: 12,200
SALES (est): 3.1MM **Privately Held**
SIC: 3559 5049 Optical lens machinery; optical goods

(G-4727)
OPTRONICS INTERNATIONAL LLC
401 S 41st St E (74403-6233)
PHONE.................918 683-9514
Greg Bland, *Branch Mgr*
EMP: 22
SALES (corp-wide): 24.3MM **Privately Held**
SIC: 1731 7361 3648 3641 Lighting contractor; employment agencies; lighting equipment; electric lamps
PA: Optronics International, Llc
5115 S 122nd East Ave # 20
Tulsa OK 74146
918 286-1288

(G-4728)
ORDER HERE TULSA LLC
2217 Arline St (74401-5536)
PHONE.................888 633-9905
Kenneth Charles Mason, *President*
EMP: 2
SALES: 134K **Privately Held**
SIC: 2051 Bakery, for home service delivery

(G-4729)
OVERHEAD DOOR SOLUTIONS LLC
10648 S Highway 64 (74403-6572)
PHONE.................918 686-8847
Neal G Hill,
EMP: 5
SALES (est): 662.3K **Privately Held**
SIC: 3535 Overhead conveyor systems

(G-4730)
OWENS-BROCKWAY GLASS CONT INC
2401 Old Shawnee Rd (74403-1562)
P.O. Box 8 (74402-0008)
PHONE.................918 684-4526
Dennis Silvis, *Branch Mgr*
EMP: 210
SALES (corp-wide): 6.6B **Publicly Held**
WEB: www.o-i.com
SIC: 3221 Glass containers
HQ: Owens-Brockway Glass Container Inc.
1 Michael Owens Way
Perrysburg OH 43551

(G-4731)
PARAGON INDUSTRIES INC
4632 Harold Scoggins Dr (74403)
PHONE.................918 781-1430
Derek Wachob, *Manager*
EMP: 20
SALES (est): 2.1MM
SALES (corp-wide): 125MM **Privately Held**
WEB: www.paragonindinc.com
SIC: 3317 Steel pipe & tubes

PA: Paragon Industries, Inc.
3378 W Highway 117
Sapulpa OK 74066
918 291-4459

(G-4732)
PAULAURA CATTLE CO
1852 W 63rd St N (74403-4402)
P.O. Box 1407 (74402-1407)
PHONE.................918 682-6030
Laura Kershaw- Rodriguez, *Owner*
Paul Rodriguez, *Manager*
EMP: 3
SALES (est): 75K **Privately Held**
SIC: 1311 0212 Crude petroleum production; beef cattle except feedlots

(G-4733)
PECAN CREEK WINERY LLC
8510 Fern Mountain Rd (74401-7211)
PHONE.................918 683-1087
Bob Wickizer, *Principal*
EMP: 3
SALES (est): 133.7K **Privately Held**
WEB: www.pecancreekwinery.com
SIC: 2084 Wines

(G-4734)
PIVOT MEDICAL SOLUTIONS LLC
207 Lancelot Ct (74403-4860)
PHONE.................918 684-4030
Ken Doke,
EMP: 4
SALES (est): 206.4K **Privately Held**
SIC: 7372 Prepackaged software

(G-4735)
PJ INDUSTRIES INC
3007 River Oaks Dr (74403-2308)
PHONE.................918 682-8479
Pamela Littlefield, *Principal*
EMP: 1
SALES (est): 51.4K **Privately Held**
SIC: 3999 Manufacturing industries

(G-4736)
POWDER COATING OF MUSKOGEE
13 Tantalum Pl (74403-9297)
PHONE.................918 681-4494
Andrew Morris, *President*
Michael Eubanks, *Prdtn Mgr*
EMP: 5 EST: 2012
SALES: 120K **Privately Held**
WEB: www.muskogeepowdercoat.com
SIC: 1799 3441 Sandblasting of building exteriors; fabricated structural metal

(G-4737)
PRIME PALLET LLC (PA)
Also Called: Muskogee Pallet
921 S Cherokee St (74403-6349)
PHONE.................918 683-0907
Logan Littrell, *CEO*
EMP: 2
SQ FT: 150,000
SALES: 4MM **Privately Held**
SIC: 2448 Pallets, wood

(G-4738)
PROFESSIONAL PACKAGING INC
Also Called: Oklahoma Interpak
2424 N Main St (74401-4054)
P.O. Box 1891 (74402-1891)
PHONE.................918 682-9531
John A Schilt, *President*
▼ EMP: 25 EST: 1979
SQ FT: 32,500
SALES (est): 2.4MM **Privately Held**
SIC: 2653 3231 Partitions, corrugated: made from purchased materials; decorated glassware: chipped, engraved, etched, etc.

(G-4739)
PROFORM GROUP INC (PA)
4400 Don Cayo Dr (74403-9211)
PHONE.................918 682-8666
Richard Cocq, *Principal*
Klaus Reithofer, *Principal*
Yohan Jativa, *Plant Mgr*
Charles Ferguson, *Engineer*
Arnaldo Herrera, *CFO*

▲ EMP: 120
SQ FT: 150,000
SALES (est): 57.6MM **Privately Held**
SIC: 3713 Truck bodies (motor vehicles)

(G-4740)
QUALITY LIQUID FEEDS INC
Also Called: Southern Qlf
2530 Port Pl (74403-9219)
PHONE.................918 683-7215
Harvey Morgan, *Manager*
EMP: 5
SALES (corp-wide): 153.2MM **Privately Held**
SIC: 2048 Cereal-, grain-, & seed-based feeds
PA: Quality Liquid Feeds, Inc.
3586 State Road 23
Dodgeville WI 53533
608 935-2345

(G-4741)
QUALITY WOODWORKS INC
3451 Southern Heights Dr (74401-8800)
PHONE.................918 944-3314
Harold W Maxwell, *CEO*
EMP: 3
SALES (est): 151.9K **Privately Held**
SIC: 2431 Millwork

(G-4742)
RCR CONSTRUCTION
1918 N 11th St (74401-3507)
PHONE.................918 682-9033
EMP: 2
SALES (est): 66K **Privately Held**
SIC: 1442 Construction sand & gravel

(G-4743)
RECTOR FIRE WORKS
4751 S 32nd St W (74401-6402)
PHONE.................918 681-0513
Bill Rector, *Owner*
EMP: 4
SALES (est): 216.1K **Privately Held**
SIC: 2899 Fireworks

(G-4744)
REDDY ICE CORPORATION
541 N Cherokee St (74403-4113)
PHONE.................918 682-2471
Rick Barnes, *Manager*
EMP: 10 **Privately Held**
WEB: www.reddyice.com
SIC: 2097 Manufactured ice
HQ: Reddy Ice Corporation
5720 Lyndon B Johnson Fwy # 200
Dallas TX 75240
214 526-6740

(G-4745)
RONNIE NEVITT
Also Called: Carport City
1113 Fredonia St (74403-3413)
PHONE.................918 687-5284
Ronnie Nevitt, *Owner*
EMP: 1
SQ FT: 1,000
SALES (est): 82K **Privately Held**
SIC: 7532 5511 3448 Body shop, automotive; automobiles, new & used; carports: prefabricated metal

(G-4746)
ROYAL SIGN & GRAPHIC INC
103 Kaad St (74401-4458)
PHONE.................918 682-6151
Darcy Kent, *President*
EMP: 6
SQ FT: 11,000
SALES (est): 859.4K **Privately Held**
SIC: 3993 2759 Signs & advertising specialties; screen printing

(G-4747)
SEMMATERIALS LP
2501 Port Pl (74403-9219)
PHONE.................918 683-1732
Kenny Osburn, *Branch Mgr*
EMP: 7 **Publicly Held**
SIC: 2951 Asphalt paving mixtures & blocks
HQ: Semmaterials, L.P.
6520 S Yale Ave Ste 700
Tulsa OK 74136
918 524-8100

Muskogee - Muskogee County (G-4748) GEOGRAPHIC SECTION

(G-4748)
SHELTRED WORK-ACTIVITY PROGRAM
Also Called: Incor
920 N 43rd St E (74403-2861)
P.O. Box 622 (74402-0622)
PHONE..................918 683-8162
Edward Breen, *President*
EMP: 20
SQ FT: 6,000
SALES: 5.7MM **Privately Held**
SIC: 8322 8331 7349 3648 Association for the handicapped; sheltered workshop; janitorial service, contract basis; lighting equipment

(G-4749)
SHEPHERDS HEART MUSIC INC
7804 Fern Mountain Rd (74401-7201)
PHONE..................918 781-1200
Dennis Jernigan, *President*
EMP: 7
SALES (est): 481.5K **Privately Held**
SIC: 2741 Miscellaneous publishing

(G-4750)
SPENCER L ROSSON
Also Called: Rosson Wheel Service
526 W Okmulgee St (74401-7531)
PHONE..................918 682-4291
Spencer L Rosson, *Owner*
EMP: 2
SALES (est): 229K **Privately Held**
SIC: 7539 3272 Wheel alignment, automotive; concrete products, precast

(G-4751)
SZABO SZABI
Also Called: Szabo's Construction Services
1303 Sallie St (74403-6845)
PHONE..................918 697-5441
Szabi Szabo, *Owner*
EMP: 1
SALES (est): 43.6K **Privately Held**
SIC: 7692 7694 1799 0782 Welding repair; motor repair services; electric motor repair; erection & dismantling of forms for poured concrete; mowing services, lawn

(G-4752)
THREE RIVERS CUSTOM CABINETS
240 North St (74403-2131)
PHONE..................918 537-2311
Arturo Aguilar, *Principal*
EMP: 1
SALES (est): 53.7K **Privately Held**
SIC: 2434 Wood kitchen cabinets

(G-4753)
TOMMY NIX CDJR MUSKOGEE LLC
1711 W Shawnee St (74401-2288)
PHONE..................918 456-2541
Craig Cole, *Principal*
EMP: 2
SALES (est): 88.3K **Privately Held**
SIC: 3694 Alternators, automotive

(G-4754)
TRIDON OIL INC
Also Called: Ragan Petroleum
111 And A Half S York St (74403)
PHONE..................918 682-6801
Mark Gannaway, *President*
EMP: 2
SQ FT: 960
SALES (est): 204.3K **Privately Held**
SIC: 1311 Natural gas production

(G-4755)
TRINITY WOOD WORKS
7290 River Ridge Rd (74403-8249)
PHONE..................918 619-3959
Sheri Glasgow, *Principal*
EMP: 2
SALES (est): 103.8K **Privately Held**
SIC: 2431 Millwork

(G-4756)
TWIN CITIES READY MIX INC
2601 S 6th St (74401)
P.O. Box 1913 (74402-1913)
PHONE..................918 682-8181
Keith Price, *Manager*
EMP: 22
SALES (corp-wide): 15.7MM **Privately Held**
WEB: www.twincitiesreadymix.com
SIC: 3273 Ready-mixed concrete
PA: Twin Cities Ready Mix, Inc.
102 W Ashland Ave
Mcalester OK 74501
918 423-8855

(G-4757)
V M STAR
Also Called: Vallouret
3800 Port Pl (74403-9209)
PHONE..................918 781-4400
Gary Hauck, *General Mgr*
▲ EMP: 250
SALES (est): 2.2MM **Privately Held**
WEB: www.muskogeedevelopment.org
SIC: 3398 Metal heat treating

(G-4758)
V&S SCHULER TUBULAR PDTS LLC
420 Frankfort Ave (74403-6401)
PHONE..................918 687-7701
Werner Niehaus, *President*
Brian Miller, *Vice Pres*
EMP: 280
SALES (est): 48.9MM
SALES (corp-wide): 819.3MM **Privately Held**
SIC: 3441 Fabricated structural metal
HQ: Voigt & Schweitzer Llc
987 Buckeye Park Rd
Columbus OH 43207
614 449-8281

(G-4759)
YOUNGMAN ROCK INC (PA)
2401 S 6th St W (74401-8263)
P.O. Box 489 (74402-0489)
PHONE..................918 682-7070
Paul Glover, *President*
Craig Glover, *Vice Pres*
EMP: 11
SALES (est): 1.6MM **Privately Held**
SIC: 1423 8741 Crushed & broken granite; management services

Mustang
Canadian County

(G-4760)
ACE 1 WELDING AND INSPTN LLC
10400 Fawn Trail Rd (73064-5405)
PHONE..................405 408-5370
Jeff Henriques, *Principal*
EMP: 1
SALES (est): 59.3K **Privately Held**
SIC: 7692 Welding repair

(G-4761)
ANADARKO CONSULTANTS LTD
1450 N Azalea Way (73064-7215)
PHONE..................405 354-7788
EMP: 7
SALES (est): 546.3K
SALES (corp-wide): 115.9MM **Privately Held**
SIC: 1389 Oil/Gas Field Services
PA: Sanguine Gas Exploration, L.L.C.
110 W 7th St Ste 2700
Tulsa OK 74119
918 494-6070

(G-4762)
AUTOMTED MCHNING SOLUTIONS LLC
1208 E Highline Ln (73064-6406)
PHONE..................405 697-6234
Scott Gray, *Principal*
Angela Gray, *Principal*
EMP: 4
SALES (est): 185.2K **Privately Held**
SIC: 3599 Crankshafts & camshafts, machining

(G-4763)
B RAYE OIL ENVIRONMENTA
631 Hunters Way (73064-3621)
PHONE..................405 818-6996
Bobby Smith, *Principal*
EMP: 2 EST: 2010
SALES (est): 114.7K **Privately Held**
SIC: 1382 Oil & gas exploration services

(G-4764)
BAKER WELDING MFG CO
707 S Pleasant View Dr (73064-1120)
PHONE..................405 376-6017
Wayne Baker, *Principal*
EMP: 1
SALES (est): 57.7K **Privately Held**
SIC: 7692 Welding repair

(G-4765)
BARRY FENNEL LLC
631 N Edgewood Ter (73064-6151)
PHONE..................405 745-7645
Barry Fennel, *Owner*
EMP: 1
SALES (est): 71.1K **Privately Held**
SIC: 1389 Oil field services

(G-4766)
CARDINAL MIDSTREAM
1460 N Mustang Rd Ste 101 (73064-7272)
PHONE..................405 706-4161
Jshawna Hayes, *Principal*
EMP: 3
SALES (est): 170.4K **Privately Held**
SIC: 1382 Oil & gas exploration services

(G-4767)
CAVES HOT SHOT SERVICES LLC
220 N Pebble Creek Ter # 202 (73064-4148)
PHONE..................405 397-2569
Daniel W Cave, *President*
EMP: 2
SALES (est): 67.5K **Privately Held**
SIC: 1389 Hot shot service

(G-4768)
CHARLES ODELL
Also Called: Seal Tight Doors & Windows
9840 Sw 44th St (73064-9405)
PHONE..................405 745-3353
Charles O'Dell, *Owner*
EMP: 1
SQ FT: 1,500
SALES (est): 177.3K **Privately Held**
SIC: 5211 3442 1751 Doors, storm: wood or metal; storm doors or windows, metal; carpentry work

(G-4769)
DH CABINET AND TRIM INC
1350 N Bettys Way (73064-1720)
PHONE..................405 376-1709
Darrell Hibbs, *Administration*
EMP: 1
SALES (est): 59.1K **Privately Held**
SIC: 2434 Wood kitchen cabinets

(G-4770)
ELVIS S SESHIE
Also Called: Raven Services
11216 Sw 37th St (73064-9200)
PHONE..................405 887-3050
Elvis S Seshie, *Owner*
EMP: 8
SALES (est): 797.8K **Privately Held**
SIC: 5012 7349 7373 1389 Automobiles & other motor vehicles; janitorial service, contract basis; office cleaning or charring; value-added resellers, computer systems; servicing oil & gas wells; cementing oil & gas well casings; fire fighting, oil & gas field; computer related maintenance services

(G-4771)
FITZS WELDING LLC
627 S Shepherd Dr (73064-3221)
PHONE..................405 371-1167
EMP: 1 EST: 2014
SALES (est): 32.6K **Privately Held**
SIC: 7692 Welding repair

(G-4772)
FREEDOM RAILCAR SOLUTIONS LLC (PA)
250 S Castlerock Ln (73064-4584)
P.O. Box 358 (73064-0358)
PHONE..................405 256-6780
Kevin Goins, *President*
James McConnaughey, *Supervisor*
Tom Barnett, *Director*
EMP: 13
SALES: 750K **Privately Held**
SIC: 3743 Railway maintenance cars

(G-4773)
GIRLINGHOUSE UNLIMITED LLC
Also Called: Embroidme- Yukon
528 W State Highway 152 # 1 (73064-3654)
PHONE..................405 265-3330
Willie Girlinghouse, *Principal*
Angela Girlinghouse,
EMP: 6 EST: 2013
SQ FT: 2,300
SALES: 187K **Privately Held**
WEB: www.embroidme-yukon.com
SIC: 7389 5699 2759 Embroidering of advertising on shirts, etc.; ; customized clothing & apparel; T-shirts, custom printed; screen printing

(G-4774)
H&H SPECIALTY WELDING
717 E Lydia Ter (73064-4872)
P.O. Box 1294 (73064-8294)
PHONE..................479 252-1991
Jessica Hamilton, *Principal*
EMP: 1
SALES (est): 56.7K **Privately Held**
SIC: 7692 Welding repair

(G-4775)
HAIL TO WREATH
119 E Forster Ln (73064-4031)
PHONE..................405 659-2216
Brenda Hale, *Principal*
EMP: 3
SALES (est): 102.2K **Privately Held**
SIC: 3999 Wreaths, artificial

(G-4776)
HOSS CONSULTING SERV
13125 Sw 47th St (73064-7932)
PHONE..................405 324-5543
Gerald Hoss, *President*
EMP: 7
SALES: 750K **Privately Held**
SIC: 1389 Oil field services

(G-4777)
ICON ROOFING AND CNSTR LLC
1824 W Crossbow Way (73064-1260)
PHONE..................405 403-6615
Brad Bates, *CEO*
EMP: 8
SALES (est): 113.6K **Privately Held**
SIC: 2493 7389 Insulation & roofing material, reconstituted wood;

(G-4778)
INDUSTRIAL GASKET INC
720 S Sara Rd (73064-4305)
P.O. Box 270780, Oklahoma City (73137-0780)
PHONE..................405 376-9393
Albert Gray, *President*
▲ EMP: 41 EST: 1948
SQ FT: 65,000
SALES: 3MM **Privately Held**
WEB: www.igok.com
SIC: 3053 3469 Gaskets, all materials; metal stampings

(G-4779)
INKLAHOMA SCREEN PRTG & EMB
317 N Trade Center Ter # 2 (73064-4424)
PHONE..................405 206-0500
EMP: 2
SALES (est): 80.6K **Privately Held**
SIC: 2759 Letterpress & screen printing

GEOGRAPHIC SECTION

Newalla - Cleveland County (G-4814)

(G-4780)
KEY CUT EXPRESS
949 E State Highway 152 (73064-5119)
PHONE..................405 353-3026
EMP: 2
SALES (est): 97.8K **Privately Held**
SIC: 3429 Keys, locks & related hardware

(G-4781)
LADY LIGHTS & STAGE INC
7400 Country Ln (73064-9666)
PHONE..................405 376-0076
Christina Ogg, *President*
EMP: 1 EST: 1990
SALES (est): 100K **Privately Held**
SIC: 3648 Stage lighting equipment

(G-4782)
MELANIE MARGARET DENNIS
Also Called: Dennis Farms Soap Company
310 S Mustang Rd (73064-3416)
PHONE..................405 760-1978
EMP: 1
SALES (est): 44.9K **Privately Held**
SIC: 2841 Mfg Soap/Other Detergents

(G-4783)
MUSTANG MACHINES WORKS INC
1516 E State Highway 152 (73064-5858)
PHONE..................405 745-7545
Jerry Harris, *Principal*
Stacey Harris,
EMP: 4
SQ FT: 3,000
SALES (est): 343.6K **Privately Held**
SIC: 3599 Machine shop, jobbing & repair

(G-4784)
MUSTANG OPTICAL INC
123 N Mustang Rd (73064-3912)
PHONE..................405 376-0222
Kennith Butler, *President*
Lauren Butler, *Vice Pres*
EMP: 4
SQ FT: 1,745
SALES (est): 450.1K **Privately Held**
SIC: 5995 3851 Opticians; ophthalmic goods

(G-4785)
NANCE SOLUTIONS INC
5800 Sycamore Pond Dr (73064-3031)
PHONE..................918 804-9301
EMP: 3
SALES (est): 290.1K **Privately Held**
SIC: 1389 Oil & gas field services

(G-4786)
NATURAL CARE SOLUTION LLC
9716 S Gregory Rd (73064-9731)
PHONE..................405 919-1982
EMP: 3
SALES (est): 154.9K **Privately Held**
WEB: www.naturalcaresolution.com
SIC: 2834 Pharmaceutical preparations

(G-4787)
NEWS ENTERPRISES INC
Also Called: Mustang News, The
290 N Trade Center Ter (73064-4416)
P.O. Box 828 (73064-0828)
PHONE..................405 376-4571
Sean Dyer, *President*
EMP: 6
SQ FT: 8,500
SALES (est): 313.8K **Privately Held**
SIC: 2711 Newspapers: publishing only, not printed on site

(G-4788)
PINNACLE FUEL ADDITIVES LLC
535 W Geronimo Court Way (73064-3604)
PHONE..................405 658-3744
EMP: 2 EST: 2015
SALES (est): 180K **Privately Held**
SIC: 2911 Petroleum Refiner

(G-4789)
PIXEL PARK LLC
10712 Hinshaw Dr (73064-2968)
PHONE..................405 613-0924
Wendy Renee Reed, *Administration*
Wendy Reed, *Administration*
EMP: 2

SALES (est): 115.5K **Privately Held**
SIC: 2335 Wedding gowns & dresses

(G-4790)
RKK PRODUCTION COMPANY
5501 Stuart Dr (73064)
P.O. Box 295 (73064-0295)
PHONE..................405 376-2223
Gary Craighead, *President*
EMP: 4
SALES (est): 814.7K **Privately Held**
SIC: 1311 Crude petroleum production

(G-4791)
ROBERTSON ARMS & MUNITIONS CO
Also Called: Ramco
10700 Hames Blvd (73064-9408)
PHONE..................405 376-2360
Gordon Robertson, *Owner*
EMP: 1
SALES (est): 84.5K **Privately Held**
SIC: 3482 Small arms ammunition

(G-4792)
S & S FOODS INC
1209 E Highline Ln (73064-6406)
PHONE..................405 256-6557
Erick Womack, *President*
Laura Womack, *Treasurer*
EMP: 15
SQ FT: 12,000
SALES: 1MM **Privately Held**
SIC: 2032 5149 5499 Canned specialties; canned goods: fruit, vegetables, seafood, meats, etc.; dried fruit

(G-4793)
SIMPLIFIED DYNAMICS INC
1810 E Dowden Ln (73064-6545)
PHONE..................405 806-0767
Pam Scott, *President*
Lynn Scott, *Vice Pres*
EMP: 2
SALES (est): 150K **Privately Held**
SIC: 3599 Machine & other job shop work

(G-4794)
SKYVIEW PRODUCTS INC
305 S Spring Ln (73064-5869)
PHONE..................405 745-6064
EMP: 5
SQ FT: 6,000
SALES (est): 900K **Privately Held**
SIC: 3211 1761 1542 Flat Glass, Nsk

(G-4795)
SNUFFY SCENTS LLC
606 N Songbird Way (73064-2087)
PHONE..................405 850-6889
Stephanie Hannan,
EMP: 1
SALES (est): 52.5K **Privately Held**
SIC: 2844 Cosmetic preparations

(G-4796)
STITCH WIZARD
525 W Carson Dr (73064-3546)
PHONE..................405 816-6356
Sharon Gaddis, *Principal*
EMP: 1
SALES (est): 42.7K **Privately Held**
SIC: 2395 Embroidery & art needlework

(G-4797)
SUMMIT SAND & GRAVEL LLC
628 W State Highway 152 (73064-3607)
PHONE..................405 256-6029
Brad Fleenor, *Principal*
EMP: 3
SALES (est): 148.3K **Privately Held**
SIC: 1442 Construction sand & gravel

(G-4798)
TRIPLE T HOTSHOT
9524 Kickapoo Dr (73064-9620)
P.O. Box 1131 (73064-8131)
PHONE..................405 745-6698
Greg Huddleston, *Owner*
EMP: 2
SALES (est): 173.8K **Privately Held**
SIC: 1389 Oil field services

(G-4799)
U-CHANGE LOCK INDUSTRIES INC
Also Called: Security Solutions
1640 W State Highway 152 (73064-2050)
PHONE..................405 376-1600
Bill D Dillard, *President*
Mike Reding, *Business Mgr*
Krista Bruton, *Corp Secy*
Tom Todt, *Opers Staff*
EMP: 30 EST: 1972
SQ FT: 17,000
SALES (est): 8MM **Privately Held**
SIC: 3429 7389 5072 Locks or lock sets; brokers' services; security devices, locks

(G-4800)
VANDERBILT CABINET & TRIM
234 E Hillcrest Ln (73064-4007)
PHONE..................405 376-3876
Dennis Vanderbilt, *Owner*
EMP: 1
SALES (est): 122.5K **Privately Held**
WEB: www.vanderbiltcabinets.com
SIC: 2434 Wood kitchen cabinets

(G-4801)
WIEDENMANNS MACHINE SHOP
10601 S County Line Rd (73064)
PHONE..................405 745-2682
EMP: 3
SALES (est): 200K **Privately Held**
SIC: 3599 Machine Shop

(G-4802)
WIRE TWISTERS INC
1813 W Cedar Ridge Dr (73064-1248)
PHONE..................405 376-0052
Stanley Wyckoff, *Principal*
EMP: 2
SALES (est): 125.5K **Privately Held**
SIC: 3312 Wire products, steel or iron

Nash
Grant County

(G-4803)
HAWLEY HOT OIL LLC
24986 County Road 800 (73761-5025)
PHONE..................580 839-2416
Norman Neilson, *Principal*
EMP: 5
SALES (est): 384.5K **Privately Held**
SIC: 1389 Oil field services

Newalla
Cleveland County

(G-4804)
BILCO CONSTRUCTION INC
7810 Buckwood Rd (74857-7855)
PHONE..................405 386-5591
Billy Davison, *President*
Kathleen Davison, *Admin Sec*
EMP: 2
SALES (est): 400K **Privately Held**
SIC: 1522 2819 Residential construction; catalysts, chemical; tanning agents, synthetic inorganic; chemicals, reagent grade: refined from technical grade; chemicals, high purity: refined from technical grade

(G-4805)
BILL KOENIG
Also Called: Mr Bill Sign Design & Graphics
11409 Jeffery Rd (74857-8984)
PHONE..................405 386-7979
Bill Koenig, *Owner*
EMP: 2 EST: 1988
SALES: 80K **Privately Held**
SIC: 3993 Signs & advertising specialties

(G-4806)
C & H SAFETY PIN INC
18450 Post Oak Dr (74857-9193)
P.O. Box 261 (74857-0261)
PHONE..................405 949-5843
Harold E Jennings, *President*
Cheryl Jennings, *Admin Sec*

EMP: 2
SALES (est): 260.8K **Privately Held**
WEB: www.chsafetypin.com
SIC: 3533 2759 7692 Oil field machinery & equipment; screen printing; welding repair

(G-4807)
COZY CUB PRODUCTS LLP
19112 Newsom Rd (74857-8043)
PHONE..................405 386-2879
Christy Rixmann, *Managing Prtnr*
Doylene Bremarman, *Managing Prtnr*
EMP: 2
SALES (est): 92.5K **Privately Held**
SIC: 2392 Cushions & pillows

(G-4808)
DAVIS CABINET SHOP
21001 Se 59th St (74857-8315)
PHONE..................405 391-5527
Paul Davis, *Owner*
EMP: 1
SQ FT: 2,720
SALES (est): 105.1K **Privately Held**
SIC: 2434 Wood kitchen cabinets

(G-4809)
FREDS SIGN CO
14425 Melody Ln (74857-6802)
PHONE..................405 235-8696
Fred Self, *President*
Marlyn Self, *Vice Pres*
EMP: 2 EST: 1949
SALES (est): 130K **Privately Held**
SIC: 7389 3993 Sign painting & lettering shop; lettering service; signs & advertising specialties

(G-4810)
HALAQ INC
Also Called: Stabor Sporting Goods
19912 S Dobbs Rd (74857-8563)
P.O. Box 514 (74857-0514)
PHONE..................405 321-7293
EMP: 1
SALES (est): 121.6K **Privately Held**
SIC: 3644 5999 5199 3949 Mfg Nonconductv Wire Dvc Ret Misc Merchandise Whol Nondurable Goods Mfg Sport/Athletic Goods Whol Sporting Goods/Supp

(G-4811)
L&L MANUFACTURING
15000 Choctaw Hills Rd (74857-9326)
PHONE..................405 436-8929
Renee Parenica, *Principal*
EMP: 2
SALES (est): 78.9K **Privately Held**
SIC: 3999 Manufacturing industries

(G-4812)
LYLE S SIGN CONTRACTORS
11415 S Peebly Rd (74857-7887)
PHONE..................405 386-7443
EMP: 2 EST: 2010
SALES (est): 77K **Privately Held**
SIC: 3993 Mfg Signs/Advertising Specialties

(G-4813)
MAGNUM DIVERSIFIED SERVICES
5800 S Harrah Rd (74857-6510)
P.O. Box 380 (74857-0380)
PHONE..................405 391-9653
Scott Jones, *President*
EMP: 12
SQ FT: 2,500
SALES (est): 1MM **Privately Held**
SIC: 1389 Gas field services; oil field services

(G-4814)
MAYHEM CSTM FBRCATION WLDG LLC
19001 Wolf Dr (74857-6110)
PHONE..................405 406-5160
Adam Vardaman, *Officer*
EMP: 1
SALES (est): 72.7K **Privately Held**
SIC: 3449 Miscellaneous metalwork

Newalla - Cleveland County (G-4815)

(G-4815)
ML SIGN SERVICE LLC
11601 S Triple Rd (74857)
PHONE 405 386-4898
Leslie Novotny, *Principal*
EMP: 1
SALES (est): 58.8K **Privately Held**
SIC: 3993 Signs & advertising specialties

(G-4816)
SOONER FOOD GROUP LLC
15101 Se 139th St (74857-7834)
PHONE 703 791-9069
Andre Robertson, *Principal*
Damon House, *COO*
EMP: 2 EST: 2017
SALES (est): 55.9K **Privately Held**
SIC: 0211 2011 7389 Beef cattle feedlots; meat packing plants; beef products from beef slaughtered on site; boxed beef from meat slaughtered on site; meat by-products from meat slaughtered on site;

(G-4817)
TWO CREEKS FABRICATION
21245 Se 97th Pl (74857-2417)
PHONE 505 999-8798
Joseph Bolton, *President*
Matthew Larson, *Principal*
EMP: 2
SALES (est): 114.5K **Privately Held**
SIC: 3728 Wing assemblies & parts, aircraft

Newcastle
Mcclain County

(G-4818)
405 WELDING
521 Sw 5th St (73065-5553)
PHONE 405 413-5764
James Miller, *Principal*
EMP: 1
SALES (est): 31.6K **Privately Held**
SIC: 7692 Welding repair

(G-4819)
BRENTS DANA
1220 Bell Dr (73065-5540)
PHONE 405 640-1566
Dana Brents, *Principal*
EMP: 2
SALES (est): 183K **Privately Held**
SIC: 3531 Backhoes

(G-4820)
CANNON OILFIELD SERVICES
204 Naomi Ln Ste B (73065-4246)
PHONE 405 387-2644
EMP: 2
SALES (est): 103.9K **Privately Held**
WEB: www.cannonoilfield.com
SIC: 1389 Oil field services

(G-4821)
CHICKASAW NATION
Also Called: Newcastle Gaming
2457 Hwy 62 Service Rd (73065-6258)
PHONE 405 387-6013
James Calvert, *Branch Mgr*
Kari Robertson, *Manager*
EMP: 1 **Privately Held**
SIC: 3944 9131 Electronic games & toys;
PA: Chickasaw Nation
  520 Arlington St
  Ada OK 74820
  580 436-2603

(G-4822)
CIMARRON ENERGY INC
4190 S Harvey (73065)
PHONE 405 928-2940
John W Moore, *Branch Mgr*
EMP: 7
SALES (corp-wide): 416.9MM **Privately Held**
WEB: www.cimarronenergy.com
SIC: 1389 Oil field services
PA: Cimarron Energy Inc.
  1012 24th Ave Nw Ste 100
  Norman OK 73069
  405 928-7373

(G-4823)
CLOSET CONSIGNMENTS LLC
1208 N Main St (73065-4125)
PHONE 405 387-3100
Angela Burk, *Owner*
EMP: 1
SALES (est): 62.1K **Privately Held**
SIC: 2361 Girls' & children's dresses, blouses & shirts

(G-4824)
DOUG TROXELL
Also Called: Doug's Sand & Gravel
1000 Springlake Rd (73065-5879)
P.O. Box 627 (73065-0627)
PHONE 405 387-3574
Doug Troxell, *Owner*
EMP: 3
SALES (est): 264K **Privately Held**
SIC: 1442 Construction sand & gravel

(G-4825)
E J HIGGINS INTERIOR DESIGN
Also Called: Gene Higgins Interiors
2224 Nw 32nd St (73065-6431)
PHONE 405 387-3434
Gene Higgins, *Owner*
EMP: 1
SQ FT: 6,000
SALES (est): 84K **Privately Held**
SIC: 7389 2542 7641 2541 Interior designer; cabinets: show, display or storage: except wood; upholstery work; wood partitions & fixtures

(G-4826)
GARY MORGAN
3383 N Meridian Ave (73065-3634)
P.O. Box 1465 (73065-1465)
PHONE 405 387-4884
Gary Morgan, *Owner*
Gary R Morgan,
EMP: 1
SQ FT: 1,920
SALES (est): 70K **Privately Held**
SIC: 3851 Eyeglasses, lenses & frames; eyes, glass & plastic

(G-4827)
GILLIAM CATTLE
1937 Hwy 76 Newcastle (73065)
PHONE 405 392-4204
Thomas Gilliam, *Principal*
EMP: 1
SALES (est): 73.6K **Privately Held**
SIC: 3523 Farm machinery & equipment

(G-4828)
GJ LEATHER LLC
404 S Main St (73065-5406)
PHONE 405 795-2998
EMP: 2
SALES (est): 119.7K **Privately Held**
SIC: 3199 Leather goods

(G-4829)
GOODTIMES BEEF JERKY
3613 N Country Club Rd (73065-6310)
PHONE 405 387-5448
EMP: 6
SALES (est): 509.3K **Privately Held**
SIC: 2013 Snack sticks, including jerky: from purchased meat

(G-4830)
LANDMARK DESIGN & SIGN CORP
1411 N Main St (73065-4130)
P.O. Box 683 (73065-0683)
PHONE 405 387-3999
Wayne McDoulett, *President*
EMP: 3
SALES: 100K **Privately Held**
SIC: 3993 1799 Signs, not made in custom sign painting shops; sign installation & maintenance

(G-4831)
MID AMERICA VENDING INC
Also Called: Armstrong Manufacturing
811 Nw 36th St (73065-6354)
PHONE 405 387-4441
Fred Armstrong, *President*
EMP: 4
SALES (est): 342.7K **Privately Held**
SIC: 3999 Manufacturing industries

(G-4832)
MOMS HAULIN DADS DOZIN INC
2705 Nw 16th St (73065-5928)
PHONE 405 392-5508
Dorth Martin, *President*
EMP: 2
SALES (est): 125.3K **Privately Held**
SIC: 3589 Dirt sweeping units, industrial

(G-4833)
NEWCASTLE PACER INC
Also Called: Early Bird Express
120 Ne 2nd St Ste 102 (73065-4185)
P.O. Box 429 (73065-0429)
PHONE 405 387-5277
Clarence Wright, *General Mgr*
Robin Wilson, *Principal*
EMP: 9 EST: 1982
SALES (est): 270K **Privately Held**
WEB: www.newcastlepacer.com
SIC: 2711 2791 Newspapers: publishing only, not printed on site; typesetting

(G-4834)
OFFSHORE EXTREME
3060 Highway 62 Svc Rd (73065)
PHONE 405 387-2628
Greg Ward, *Principal*
EMP: 2 EST: 2008
SALES (est): 83K **Privately Held**
SIC: 3732 Boat building & repairing

(G-4835)
PENNINGTON INDUSTRIES
7512 E Hwy 37 Tuttle (73065)
PHONE 405 392-2317
Greg Pennington, *Owner*
EMP: 1
SALES (corp-wide): 500K **Privately Held**
SIC: 7692 3599 Welding repair; machine shop, jobbing & repair
PA: Paul G Pennington Industries
  2325 Fox Ln
  Blanchard OK 73010
  405 392-2317

(G-4836)
RANDYS CONSTRUCTION
800 Springlake Rd (73065-5823)
P.O. Box 734 (73065-0734)
PHONE 405 387-3568
Randy Arnold, *President*
EMP: 2
SALES (est): 175K **Privately Held**
SIC: 3273 1771 Ready-mixed concrete; concrete work

(G-4837)
REDWOOD COUNTRY SIGNS
2016 N Rockwell Ave (73065-6109)
PHONE 405 596-8737
EMP: 2
SALES (est): 104.5K **Privately Held**
SIC: 3993 Signs & advertising specialties

(G-4838)
RHINESTONE COWGIRL
200 N Main St (73065-4105)
PHONE 405 387-3111
Robin Fielder, *Owner*
EMP: 15
SALES (est): 642.5K **Privately Held**
SIC: 2759 Laser printing

(G-4839)
RIVERS EDGE COUNTERTOPS INC
3066 Highway 62 Svc Rd (73065)
P.O. Box 670 (73065-0670)
PHONE 405 387-2930
Jeremiah Rivers, *Owner*
EMP: 15
SALES (est): 1.9MM **Privately Held**
WEB: www.riversedgecountertops.com
SIC: 3281 Granite, cut & shaped

(G-4840)
SILVER CITY EXCAVATING LLC
613 S Portland Ave (73065-4338)
P.O. Box 178 (73065-0178)
PHONE 405 673-3062
EMP: 5
SALES (est): 869.1K **Privately Held**
SIC: 1389 Excavating slush pits & cellars

(G-4841)
SOLIDTECH ANIMAL HEALTH INC
812 Ne 24th St (73065-6359)
P.O. Box 790 (73065-0790)
PHONE 405 387-3300
Lloyd D Barker, *President*
Richard Hansen, *COO*
John M Coffey, *Vice Pres*
EMP: 12
SQ FT: 8,000
SALES (est): 2.4MM **Privately Held**
SIC: 2836 5122 Veterinary biological products; biologicals & allied products

(G-4842)
STARS STRIPES CONSTRUCTION
721 Grigsby St (73065-5908)
PHONE 405 387-4847
Dennis Strickland, *Owner*
Connie Strickland, *Co-Owner*
EMP: 1 EST: 1991
SALES: 49K **Privately Held**
SIC: 1389 Construction, repair & dismantling services

(G-4843)
SUB ZERO ICE SERVICES LLC
1840 S Highway 76 (73065-5003)
P.O. Box 1452 (73065-1452)
PHONE 405 387-2224
Drenda Bigham, *General Mgr*
Gerald Bigham, *Mng Member*
EMP: 4 EST: 2010
SALES: 100K **Privately Held**
SIC: 2097 5199 Manufactured ice; ice, manufactured or natural

(G-4844)
THRU TUBING SOLUTIONS
200 Ne 16th St (73065-6238)
PHONE 405 692-1900
EMP: 2
SALES (est): 65.5K **Privately Held**
SIC: 1389 Oil/Gas Field Services

(G-4845)
TROY WESNIDGE INC
2024 S Main St (73065-5341)
P.O. Box 2035, Chickasha (73023-2035)
PHONE 405 387-4720
Troy D Wesnidge Jr, *President*
Frank Wesnidge, *Vice Pres*
▼ EMP: 35
SQ FT: 44,000
SALES (est): 4.9MM **Privately Held**
SIC: 2511 2541 Wood household furniture; cabinets, lockers & shelving

Newkirk
Kay County

(G-4846)
C JOHNSTONE WELDING FABRICAT ◯
126 S Elm Ave (74647-4501)
PHONE 580 362-2400
Curtis Johnstone, *Owner*
EMP: 1 EST: 2019
SALES (est): 90.4K **Privately Held**
SIC: 3449 Bars, concrete reinforcing: fabricated steel

(G-4847)
DEWAYNES BBQ SAUCE CATERING
5700 W Adobe Rd (74647-8520)
PHONE 580 363-3394
De Wayne L Muret, *President*
Dewayne Muret, *President*
Scott Haknis, *Manager*
EMP: 2
SALES: 75K **Privately Held**
SIC: 2033 Barbecue sauce: packaged in cans, jars, etc.

GEOGRAPHIC SECTION

Noble - Cleveland County (G-4880)

(G-4848)
IMPERIAL MOLDING LLC
122 E 7th St Nwkirk Ok (74647)
PHONE................................580 362-3412
John Kelsey, *President*
EMP: 17
SALES (est): 298.7K **Privately Held**
SIC: 3089 Injection molding of plastics; plastic processing; buoys & floats, plastic; tubs, plastic (containers)

(G-4849)
IMPERIAL PLASTICS INC
101 N Chestnut Ave (74647-2203)
PHONE................................580 362-3412
Ernie Conley, *President*
Jamie Logan, *Admin Sec*
EMP: 15
SALES (est): 2.9MM **Privately Held**
SIC: 3089 Injection molding of plastics

(G-4850)
NEWKIRK HERALD JOURNAL
Also Called: Newkirk Herald Journal
121 N Main St (74647-2217)
P.O. Box 131 (74647-0131)
PHONE................................580 362-2140
Wayne White, *Editor*
Scott Cloud, *Administration*
EMP: 4
SQ FT: 3,500
SALES (est): 130K **Privately Held**
SIC: 2711 2752 Newspapers: publishing only, not printed on site; commercial printing, offset

(G-4851)
PRECISION ROTATIONAL MOLDING
600 S Main St (74647-6503)
PHONE................................580 362-3262
Ernest Conley, *President*
EMP: 6
SQ FT: 6,000
SALES (est): 781.7K **Privately Held**
SIC: 3089 Injection molding of plastics

(G-4852)
RICK LEAMING CONSTRUCTION LLC
Also Called: Leaming Manufacturing & Cnstr
4525 N Pleasant Vw (74647)
P.O. Box 432 (74647-0432)
PHONE................................580 362-2262
Rick Leaming, *Mng Member*
EMP: 3
SQ FT: 6,000
SALES (est): 591.5K **Privately Held**
SIC: 1761 7692 3556 3549 Sheet metalwork; welding repair; food products machinery; metalworking machinery

(G-4853)
STONEY POINT MINE
6901 E Brake Rd (74647-8208)
PHONE................................580 362-3916
EMP: 2
SALES (est): 88.6K **Privately Held**
SIC: 1481 Nonmetallic Mineral Services

Nichols Hills
Oklahoma County

(G-4854)
ADROIT SURGICAL LLC
7103 Nichols Rd (73120-1221)
PHONE................................425 577-2713
Nelish Vasan, *Mng Member*
Paul Hagen, *Mng Member*
EMP: 2 EST: 2010
SALES: 150K **Privately Held**
WEB: www.adroitsurgical.com
SIC: 3841 5047 Surgical & medical instruments; medical equipment & supplies

(G-4855)
BREAST & BDY THERMOGRAPHY CTR
6440 Avondale Dr 20035 (73116-6421)
PHONE................................405 596-8099
Susie Sturgeon, *Officer*
EMP: 2 EST: 2017
SALES (est): 73.2K **Privately Held**
SIC: 2759 Thermography

(G-4856)
BROWN PUBLISHING INC
Also Called: Wide Area Directory
1727 Dorchester Pl (73120-1007)
PHONE................................405 842-5089
Tom Brown, *Manager*
EMP: 1
SALES (est): 102.6K **Privately Held**
SIC: 2741 Directories: publishing & printing

(G-4857)
CHRISTIAN MARTIN LAVERY
Also Called: Martin Oil Properties
6421 Avondale Dr Ste 212 (73116-6428)
PHONE................................405 810-0900
Christian L Martin, *Owner*
Christian Martin, *Owner*
EMP: 1
SALES (est): 234.3K **Privately Held**
SIC: 1311 Crude petroleum production

(G-4858)
COLTER BAY LLC
1217 Glenbrook Ter (73116-5701)
PHONE................................405 842-7622
James Sykora,
EMP: 1
SALES (est): 78.3K **Privately Held**
SIC: 1382 Oil & gas exploration services

(G-4859)
DISCOVERSOFT DEVELOPMENT LLC
6602 Trenton Rd (73116-6011)
P.O. Box 12161, Oklahoma City (73157-2161)
PHONE................................405 840-1235
Tod Hardin, *Owner*
Leslie Hardin, *Owner*
EMP: 2
SALES: 108.8K **Privately Held**
SIC: 7372 Prepackaged software

(G-4860)
ENERGETIC MATERIALS
1604 Norwood Pl (73120-1212)
PHONE................................405 203-2859
Timothy Melton, *Owner*
EMP: 1
SALES (est): 91K **Privately Held**
SIC: 3724 Rocket motors, aircraft

(G-4861)
OAK HILL PETROLEUM CORPORATION
1611 Randel Rd (73116-5627)
PHONE................................405 842-1568
David Bertschinger, *President*
R O Bertschinger, *Vice Pres*
EMP: 3
SQ FT: 550
SALES (est): 310K **Privately Held**
SIC: 1311 Crude petroleum production

(G-4862)
PAULINE OIL AND GAS CO
1321 Sherwood Ln (73116-5631)
PHONE................................405 842-4213
Jerry Love, *Manager*
EMP: 3 EST: 2013
SALES (est): 179.1K **Privately Held**
SIC: 1311 Crude petroleum production

(G-4863)
SUGAR SISTERS LLC
2832 W Wilshire Blvd # 101 (73116-4018)
PHONE................................405 722-9266
EMP: 2 EST: 2013
SALES (est): 202.5K **Privately Held**
WEB: www.sugarsistersscrubs.com
SIC: 2844 Toilet preparations

(G-4864)
THINKWERX LLC
1609 Norwood Pl (73120-1211)
PHONE................................405 590-3937
Jim Greene, *Principal*
EMP: 1
SALES (est): 110.1K **Privately Held**
SIC: 3993 Signs & advertising specialties

(G-4865)
WORLD ARTS PRESS LLC
1716 Huntington Ave (73116-5511)
PHONE................................405 314-2578
EMP: 2
SALES (est): 110.4K **Privately Held**
SIC: 2741 Miscellaneous publishing

Nicoma Park
Oklahoma County

(G-4866)
BELL PRINTING AND ADVERTISING
2408 A N W Minster St (73066)
P.O. Box 788 (73066-0788)
PHONE................................405 769-6445
Carl Bell, *Partner*
EMP: 2
SQ FT: 2,000
SALES (est): 50K **Privately Held**
SIC: 2752 2791 2789 Commercial printing, offset; typesetting; bookbinding & related work

Ninnekah
Grady County

(G-4867)
BAILEY S MIKE WELDING INC
3513 County Street 2840 (73067-3036)
PHONE................................405 574-4489
EMP: 1
SALES (est): 25K **Privately Held**
SIC: 7692 Welding repair

(G-4868)
CLYDE WELDING SERVICE
3211 County Street 2850 (73067-3038)
PHONE................................405 222-1364
Clyde Bennett, *Owner*
Bonita Bennett, *Corp Secy*
EMP: 1
SALES: 100K **Privately Held**
SIC: 7692 7538 Welding repair; general truck repair

(G-4869)
DAVIS WELDING & FAB
3656 County Street 2850 (73067-4031)
PHONE................................405 779-5330
Jason Davis, *Principal*
EMP: 1
SALES (est): 38.1K **Privately Held**
SIC: 7692 Welding repair

(G-4870)
DOUGLAS A PHARR
Also Called: Farmer/Rancher
2972 County Street 2910 (73067-4051)
PHONE................................405 200-4983
Douglas A Parr, *Owner*
EMP: 4
SQ FT: 1,624
SALES (est): 227.2K **Privately Held**
SIC: 2048 Prepared feeds

(G-4871)
GERALDS WELDING 2
178 W Quail Rd (73067)
PHONE................................405 224-8510
Gayla Brown, *President*
EMP: 1
SALES (est): 68.2K **Privately Held**
SIC: 7692 Welding repair

(G-4872)
GRISWOLD TRUCKING RANDY
1398 County Road 1500 (73067-4027)
PHONE................................580 476-3590
Randy Griswold, *Owner*
▲ EMP: 1
SALES (est): 90.6K **Privately Held**
SIC: 1389 Pumping of oil & gas wells

(G-4873)
PRITCHARDS WELDING SERVICE
2525 W Highway 277 (73067-3834)
PHONE................................405 514-2360
Matthew Pritchard, *Principal*
EMP: 1
SALES (est): 27.6K **Privately Held**
SIC: 7692 Welding repair

(G-4874)
SS ROUSTABOUT SERVICES
3096 County Street 2800 (73067-4505)
P.O. Box 98 (73067-0098)
PHONE................................405 320-2183
EMP: 2
SALES (est): 65.5K **Privately Held**
SIC: 1389 Roustabout service

Noble
Cleveland County

(G-4875)
AARON OIL INC
17650 E Etowah Rd (73068-6310)
PHONE................................405 899-4138
J R Stark, *President*
Teresa Stark, *Vice Pres*
EMP: 2 EST: 2000
SALES: 540K **Privately Held**
SIC: 2911 7389 Oils, fuel;

(G-4876)
CHEVELLE WORLD INC
Also Called: Cheyenne Pickup Parts
9180 72nd St (73068-5508)
P.O. Box 926 (73068-0926)
PHONE................................405 872-3399
Henry Nunn, *President*
Kevin Anderson, *Chief*
Linda Nunn, *Vice Pres*
Heather Nunn, *Treasurer*
Roseanne Kittles, *Admin Sec*
EMP: 11
SQ FT: 8,000
SALES (est): 910K **Privately Held**
SIC: 5531 5013 3714 Automotive parts; automotive supplies & parts; motor vehicle parts & accessories

(G-4877)
CUSTOM MANUFACTURING & MAINT
Also Called: Custom Generator Power
427 S Front St (73068-9580)
P.O. Box 1623, Norman (73070-1623)
PHONE................................405 872-1000
Dick Couch, *President*
Sandra Couch, *Vice Pres*
EMP: 4
SQ FT: 3,400
SALES (est): 345.7K **Privately Held**
SIC: 1731 3825 5063 1389 General electrical contractor; test equipment for electronic & electric measurement; generators; oil field services

(G-4878)
DESIGN INTELLIGENCE INC LLC (PA)
Also Called: Dii
8901 72nd St (73068-5500)
PHONE................................405 307-0397
James L Grimsley,
EMP: 2
SALES (est): 567.9K **Privately Held**
SIC: 3761 3812 8731 Guided missiles & space vehicles, research & development; aircraft/aerospace flight instruments & guidance systems; commercial research laboratory

(G-4879)
EMR MACHINE
4224 Cemetery Rd (73068-8562)
PHONE................................405 361-7991
EMP: 2
SALES (est): 81.4K **Privately Held**
SIC: 3599 Machine shop, jobbing & repair

(G-4880)
FLAMING HOPE LLC
9850 E Maguire Rd (73068-7604)
PHONE................................405 924-4380
Kelly King, *Mng Member*
EMP: 2

Noble - Cleveland County (G-4881)

SALES (est): 67.6K **Privately Held**
SIC: 5812 2339 2389 5632 Steak & barbecue restaurants; women's & misses' accessories; men's miscellaneous accessories; apparel accessories

(G-4881)
GREEN RIVER OPERATING CO
201 Cemetery Rd (73068-8548)
PHONE..........................405 872-9616
David Bradshaw, *President*
EMP: 3
SALES (est): 220K **Privately Held**
SIC: 1389 Oil field services

(G-4882)
IRONWOLF MANUFACTURING LLC
9000 S Highway 77 (73068-5310)
PHONE..........................405 872-1890
Bruce Morain,
EMP: 17
SALES (est): 4.5MM **Privately Held**
SIC: 3531 Construction machinery

(G-4883)
JED WELDING AND FABRICATION
4300 Banner Rd (73068-5308)
PHONE..........................405 420-9062
Onur Dukes, *Owner*
EMP: 1
SALES (est): 35.4K **Privately Held**
WEB: www.jedwelding.com
SIC: 7692 Welding repair

(G-4884)
KODA WELDING LLC
4800 Memelou Ln (73068-8708)
PHONE..........................405 565-1867
EMP: 1
SALES (est): 25K **Privately Held**
SIC: 7692 Welding repair

(G-4885)
LIMBSAW COMPANY
340 N 84th St (73068-8852)
PHONE..........................580 272-3194
William F Casey, *Administration*
EMP: 4
SALES (est): 292K **Privately Held**
SIC: 2421 Sawmills & planing mills, general

(G-4886)
MMS LLC
Also Called: MMS Sales
1101 E Maguire Rd (73068-8432)
P.O. Box 1700 (73068-1700)
PHONE..........................405 872-3486
David Morris, *President*
Walter Morris, *Chairman*
▲ EMP: 3
SQ FT: 35,000
SALES (est): 370.1K **Privately Held**
SIC: 3845 Respiratory analysis equipment, electromedical

(G-4887)
NOBLE ACQUISITION LLC
Also Called: Dicaperl Minerals
312 W Chestnut (73068-8545)
PHONE..........................405 872-5660
Mark Dorman,
EMP: 4
SALES (est): 850.3K **Privately Held**
SIC: 1499 Perlite mining
HQ: Belmont Holdings Corp.
1 Bala Ave Ste 310
Bala Cynwyd PA 19004

(G-4888)
PRECISION WELDING MFG
4700 Brookwood Dr (73068-8450)
PHONE..........................405 872-3530
Tony Snow, *Owner*
EMP: 1
SALES (est): 42K **Privately Held**
SIC: 7692 Welding repair

(G-4889)
REACH WIRELINE
8530 Enterprise Ave (73068-1010)
PHONE..........................405 872-8828
EMP: 2

SALES (est): 65.5K **Privately Held**
SIC: 1389 Oil/Gas Field Services

(G-4890)
ROCKING RB QUARTER HORSES LLC
8301 E Etowah Rd (73068-8826)
PHONE..........................405 605-9458
EMP: 2
SALES (est): 119.1K **Privately Held**
SIC: 3944 Rocking horses

(G-4891)
SHARP METAL FABRICATORS INC
8401 156th St (73068-5238)
PHONE..........................405 899-4849
Ralph Pruitt, *President*
Suzanne Pruitt, *Vice Pres*
EMP: 10
SQ FT: 5,000
SALES (est): 500K **Privately Held**
SIC: 3443 3444 3498 Metal parts; sheet metalwork; fabricated pipe & fittings

(G-4892)
SOUTHSIDE POWDER COATING
9161 48th Ave Se (73068-5422)
PHONE..........................405 623-8557
Harold Ferguson, *Principal*
EMP: 2
SALES (est): 115.5K **Privately Held**
SIC: 3479 Metal coating & allied service

(G-4893)
VICTORY OIL FIELD SERVICES CO
11025 Bramblewood Ln (73068-7722)
PHONE..........................405 694-0468
Victor O Reyes, *Principal*
EMP: 2 EST: 2012
SALES (est): 116.3K **Privately Held**
SIC: 1389 Oil field services

Norman
Cleveland County

(G-4894)
A & Y ENTERPRISES INC
1100 N University Blvd (73069-7671)
PHONE..........................405 360-0307
EMP: 2
SQ FT: 2,000
SALES: 75K **Privately Held**
SIC: 1761 7692 Roofing/Siding Contractor Welding Repair

(G-4895)
A1 SCREEN PRINTING
Also Called: Underground Printing
102 W Eufaula St Ste 230 (73069-5686)
PHONE..........................405 701-6735
Barret White,
EMP: 1
SALES (est): 65.9K **Privately Held**
WEB: www.undergroundshirts.com
SIC: 2759 Screen printing

(G-4896)
ABBOTT LABORATORIES
404 Garland Ct (73072-5111)
PHONE..........................405 329-5513
Oliver Knoll, *Principal*
EMP: 764
SALES (corp-wide): 31.9B **Publicly Held**
SIC: 2834 Druggists' preparations (pharmaceuticals)
PA: Abbott Laboratories
100 Abbott Park Rd
Abbott Park IL 60064
224 667-6100

(G-4897)
ACTION PRINTING NORMAN INC
3400 Charleston Rd (73069-8307)
PHONE..........................405 364-3615
Steve Lindsay, *President*
Kathi Lindsay, *Treasurer*
Brad Smith, *Co-Mgr*
EMP: 25 EST: 1977
SQ FT: 3,500

SALES (est): 4.3MM **Privately Held**
SIC: 2752 Commercial printing, offset

(G-4898)
ACTIVE-ICE INC
3650 Classen Blvd (73071-1556)
PHONE..........................405 310-3880
Geoffrey D Wynn, *President*
▲ EMP: 18
SQ FT: 10,000
SALES: 2MM **Privately Held**
SIC: 3841 Inhalation therapy equipment

(G-4899)
ADVANCE RESEARCH & DEVELOPMENT
Also Called: Ardco
2285 Industrial Blvd (73069-8515)
PHONE..........................405 321-0550
Willie Rosseett, *President*
Robert Bearden, *CFO*
Nancy Burcham, *Sales Staff*
EMP: 9
SQ FT: 6,000
SALES: 715K **Privately Held**
SIC: 3672 8711 7629 Printed circuit boards; electrical or electronic engineering; electrical repair shops; circuit board repair

(G-4900)
ADVANCED COMFORT & ENERGY
2810 Broce Dr (73072-2405)
P.O. Box 2080, Blanchard (73010-2080)
PHONE..........................405 329-2237
Terry Taffar, *Principal*
EMP: 15
SALES (est): 1.6MM **Privately Held**
SIC: 8741 3272 Construction management; fireplaces, concrete

(G-4901)
ADVANCED PROCESSING TECH INC
Also Called: Avpro
405 Highland Pkwy (73069-7664)
P.O. Box 1696 (73070-1696)
PHONE..........................405 360-4848
Tom Rose, *President*
EMP: 7
SALES: 690K **Privately Held**
SIC: 3823 Controllers for process variables, all types

(G-4902)
AEROSPACE TRAINING SY
2600 John Saxon Blvd # 100 (73071-1167)
PHONE..........................405 253-8343
Terry McKenzie, *Partner*
Jimmy Ruth, *Partner*
EMP: 1 EST: 2013
SALES (est): 83K **Privately Held**
SIC: 3728 Aircraft parts & equipment

(G-4903)
ALICO EMBROIDERY ETC
222 Merkle Dr (73069-6428)
PHONE..........................405 321-2998
Ali Williams, *Owner*
EMP: 3
SALES (est): 89K **Privately Held**
SIC: 2395 Embroidery products, except schiffli machine

(G-4904)
ALS VACUUM REPAIR
336 Thompson Dr (73069-5249)
PHONE..........................405 550-8599
Al Fronko, *Owner*
EMP: 1
SALES (est): 56K **Privately Held**
SIC: 3635 Household vacuum cleaners

(G-4905)
AMAZING GRAZE LLC
2804 Belknap Ave (73072-6641)
PHONE..........................405 447-4893
Deborah Hicks,
EMP: 1
SALES (est): 92.2K **Privately Held**
SIC: 6799 1382 0291 Real estate investors, except property operators; oil & gas exploration services; general farms, primarily animals

(G-4906)
AMERICAN ENGRAVING & TROPHY
Also Called: American Stamp & Seal
2104 W Lindsey St (73069-4108)
PHONE..........................405 360-2744
Kelley Williams, *Partner*
Anthony Williams, *Partner*
EMP: 3
SQ FT: 1,850
SALES (est): 165K **Privately Held**
SIC: 5999 3953 Trophies & plaques; marking devices

(G-4907)
AMERICAN INTERNATIONAL LTD
Also Called: American Intl Flag Pole Map G
804 N Porter Ave (73071-6403)
PHONE..........................405 364-1776
Sally Alley, *Owner*
EMP: 2
SQ FT: 1,000
SALES (est): 83K **Privately Held**
SIC: 2499 5999 Flagpoles, wood; ladders & stepladders, wood; maps & charts; banners, flags, decals & posters

(G-4908)
AMERICAN IRON
2401 Oak Forest Dr (73071-6327)
PHONE..........................405 414-2629
EMP: 2
SALES (est): 88.9K **Privately Held**
SIC: 3446 Architectural metalwork

(G-4909)
ANATOLE PUBLISHING LLC
3613 24th Ave Se (73071-2987)
PHONE..........................405 609-0763
Thomas Lemke, *Principal*
EMP: 1
SALES (est): 37.5K **Privately Held**
SIC: 2741 Miscellaneous publishing

(G-4910)
ANTARES ENTERPRISES LLC
2715 Aspen Cir (73072-6834)
PHONE..........................405 329-4326
Claire McMurray, *Principal*
EMP: 2
SALES (est): 76.4K **Privately Held**
SIC: 3646 Commercial indusl & institutional electric lighting fixtures

(G-4911)
APEX405
1917 Atchison Dr (73069-8275)
PHONE..........................405 313-5145
EMP: 2
SALES (est): 67K **Privately Held**
SIC: 2321 Men's & boys' furnishings

(G-4912)
APOTHEM
733 Asp Ave Ste A (73069-4960)
PHONE..........................405 447-2345
Maria Porkka, *Owner*
EMP: 3
SALES (est): 361K **Privately Held**
SIC: 5136 5137 5699 5947 Shirts, men's & boys'; sportswear, women's & children's; T-shirts, custom printed; customized clothing & apparel; gift shop; embroidery products, except schiffli machine; regalia

(G-4913)
ARCHITECTURAL MODELS
2801 Meadow Ave (73072-7417)
PHONE..........................405 360-2828
Wiley White, *Owner*
EMP: 3
SALES (est): 120K **Privately Held**
SIC: 3299 3999 Architectural sculptures: gypsum, clay, papier mache, etc.; models, general, except toy

(G-4914)
ARCOSA ACG INC
1550 Double C Dr (73069-8288)
PHONE..........................405 366-9500
Paul Harrington, *CEO*
EMP: 1

▲ = Import ▼ = Export
◆ = Import/Export

GEOGRAPHIC SECTION

Norman - Cleveland County (G-4944)

SALES (est): 39.7K
SALES (corp-wide): 1.7B **Publicly Held**
SIC: 3295 Shale, expanded
HQ: Arcosa Materials, Inc.
1112 E Cpeland Rd Ste 500
Arlington TX 76011

(G-4915)
ARDELLAS FLOWERS INC (PA)
Also Called: Ardella's Pet & Garden Center
1016 Woods Ave (73069-7473)
PHONE..................405 321-6850
James R Loughmiller, *President*
Jayme Nurse, *Corp Secy*
Ardella Loughmiller, *Vice Pres*
EMP: 12
SQ FT: 3,500
SALES: 600K **Privately Held**
SIC: 5992 0181 5947 2759 Flowers, fresh; ornamental nursery products; greeting cards; invitation & stationery printing & engraving

(G-4916)
ARMADA LAND LC
1013 Greenway Cir (73072-6125)
PHONE..................405 210-7554
EMP: 2
SALES (est): 111K **Privately Held**
SIC: 1389 Oil field services

(G-4917)
ARROW ALLIANCE INDUSTRIES LLC
3100 84th Ave Se (73026-5708)
PHONE..................540 273-1548
EMP: 1
SALES (est): 39.6K **Privately Held**
SIC: 3999 Manufacturing industries

(G-4918)
ARROW OIL & GAS INC
2500 Mcgee Dr Ste 100 (73072-6723)
P.O. Box 722347 (73070-8776)
PHONE..................405 364-2601
Marshall S Brackin, *President*
Cole Brackin, *CFO*
EMP: 7 EST: 1977
SQ FT: 4,000
SALES (est): 1.3MM
SALES (corp-wide): 19.2MM **Privately Held**
SIC: 1311 Crude petroleum production; natural gas production
PA: Arrow Holding, Inc.
2500 Mcgee Dr Ste 100
Norman OK 73072
405 364-2601

(G-4919)
ARROWOOD COMPANIES
701 Wall St (73069-6360)
PHONE..................405 701-3673
Robert Arrowwood, *Owner*
EMP: 2 EST: 2011
SALES (est): 145.5K **Privately Held**
WEB: www.arrowoodholdings.com
SIC: 1382 Oil & gas exploration services

(G-4920)
ASK ME ABOUT SIGNS LLC
1005 N Flood Ave Ste 109 (73069-7659)
PHONE..................405 317-8157
EMP: 1 EST: 2015
SALES (est): 55.1K **Privately Held**
SIC: 3993 Signs & advertising specialties

(G-4921)
AVARA PHARMACEUTICAL TECH INC
Also Called: Avara Pharmaceutical Services
3300 Marshall Ave (73072-8064)
PHONE..................405 217-7670
Timothy Tyson, *CEO*
Paul Fioravanti, *CEO*
Andy Glanville, *CFO*
Keith Lyon, *CFO*
Josephine Maguire, *Manager*
▲ EMP: 180
SQ FT: 202,000
SALES (est): 90.7MM
SALES (corp-wide): 39.8MM **Privately Held**
SIC: 2834 Pharmaceutical preparations

PA: Avara Us Holdings Llc
101 Merritt 7
Norwalk CT 06851
203 655-1333

(G-4922)
AZIMUTH SPIRITS LLC
1126 Rambling Oaks Dr (73072-4134)
PHONE..................317 468-3931
Don Hornbeck,
EMP: 6
SALES: 1.5MM **Privately Held**
SIC: 2082 Malt liquors

(G-4923)
AZTEC BUILDING SYSTEMS INC
3361 Deskin Dr (73069-8294)
PHONE..................405 329-0255
William L Marley, *President*
Dirk W Marley, *Vice Pres*
Jeff Marley, *Vice Pres*
Jeffrey S Marley, *Vice Pres*
Joyce A Marley, *Vice Pres*
EMP: 42
SQ FT: 6,000
SALES: 12MM **Privately Held**
SIC: 1542 3448 Commercial & office building, new construction; prefabricated metal buildings

(G-4924)
B & B MACHINE OF NORMAN INC
17321 S Sunnylane Rd (73071-7943)
PHONE..................405 799-9878
Eugene Bruehl, *President*
Kelly Bruehl, *Treasurer*
EMP: 10
SQ FT: 7,500
SALES (est): 1.4MM **Privately Held**
SIC: 3599 Machine shop, jobbing & repair

(G-4925)
BAM JOURNAL LLC
333 N Sherry Ave (73069-6627)
PHONE..................405 307-8220
Mary B McLachlin, *Administration*
EMP: 3
SALES (est): 109.1K **Privately Held**
SIC: 2711 Newspapers, publishing & printing

(G-4926)
BBR OIL CORP
Also Called: Fractal
330 W Gray St Ste 305 (73069-7142)
PHONE..................405 366-8019
Joe Biddick, *Mng Member*
EMP: 2
SALES (est): 158.5K
SALES (corp-wide): 60K **Privately Held**
SIC: 1382 Oil & gas exploration services
PA: Bbr Oil Corp.
10 W Main St Ste 212
Ardmore OK 73401
580 223-2887

(G-4927)
BCRK LIMITED PARTNERSHIP
2004 Wyckham Pl (73072-3041)
PHONE..................405 321-0089
Chris Huston, *Principal*
EMP: 2
SALES (est): 91K **Privately Held**
SIC: 1389 Oil field services

(G-4928)
BEAVER FABRICATION INC
5757 York Dr (73069-9505)
PHONE..................405 360-0014
Virgil Votaw, *Owner*
EMP: 4
SALES (est): 484.6K **Privately Held**
SIC: 1629 4493 7692 Dock construction; boat yards, storage & incidental repair; welding repair

(G-4929)
BECCA VERMELIS
743 Terrace Pl (73069-5055)
PHONE..................405 701-1638
Becca Vermelis, *Principal*
EMP: 1
SALES (est): 91.4K **Privately Held**
WEB: www.realtorbecca.com
SIC: 2434 Wood kitchen cabinets

(G-4930)
BERGEY WINDPOWER COMPANY INC
2200 Industrial Blvd (73069-8516)
PHONE..................405 364-4212
Karl Bergey, *CEO*
Ken Craig, *Vice Pres*
Tod Hanley, *Engineer*
Britton Rife, *Sales Staff*
Michael Soriano, *Director*
◆ EMP: 33
SQ FT: 23,000
SALES (est): 7.4MM **Privately Held**
SIC: 3511 Turbines & turbine generator sets

(G-4931)
BILLS MARINE CANVAS UPHOLSTERY
717 N Crawford Ave (73069-7828)
PHONE..................405 306-2936
William Burrows, *Owner*
EMP: 1 EST: 2018
SALES (est): 46.5K **Privately Held**
SIC: 2211 Canvas

(G-4932)
BIO-CIDE INTERNATIONAL INC
Also Called: Warehouse
2650 Venture Dr (73069-8277)
PHONE..................405 364-1940
Neeraj Kajnna, *Opers-Prdtn-Mfg*
EMP: 8
SALES (corp-wide): 1.6MM **Privately Held**
SIC: 2869 2842 7342 Industrial organic chemicals; specialty cleaning, polishes & sanitation goods; disinfecting & deodorizing
PA: Bio-Cide International, Inc.
2650 Venture Dr
Norman OK 73069
800 323-1398

(G-4933)
BIODYNAMICS CORP
1809 Atchison Dr Ste B (73069-8299)
PHONE..................405 201-1289
Jay Portwood, *Principal*
EMP: 2
SALES (est): 166.2K **Privately Held**
SIC: 1389 Oil field services

(G-4934)
BIOMETRIC IDENTIFICATION SYSTE
Also Called: Safe Child IDS
311 Telstar St (73069-8634)
PHONE..................405 517-9641
Brandy White, *Mng Member*
Gina Mincey, *Consultant*
EMP: 1
SALES (est): 76.5K **Privately Held**
SIC: 3999 Buttons: Red Cross, union, identification

(G-4935)
BIORITE ACQUISITION CO LLC
Also Called: Biorite Nutritionals
1811 Industrial Blvd # 105 (73069-8519)
PHONE..................405 701-1515
Rocky Marshall, *President*
Linda Sue Marshall, *CFO*
EMP: 8 EST: 2016
SQ FT: 1,800
SALES: 1.6MM **Privately Held**
SIC: 2023 Dietary supplements, dairy & non-dairy based

(G-4936)
BLACK GOLD STONE RANCH LLC
4132 Castlerock Rd (73072-1764)
PHONE..................405 590-0700
Susan Stone,
EMP: 2 EST: 2012
SALES (est): 167.9K **Privately Held**
SIC: 1381 4212 6799 Drilling oil & gas wells; local trucking, without storage; real estate investors, except property operators

(G-4937)
BLUE STAR GAS CORP
1006 24th Ave Nw Ste 120 (73069-6344)
P.O. Box 720894 (73070-4694)
PHONE..................405 321-1397
David Swafford, *President*
Jon English, *Exec VP*
EMP: 2
SALES (est): 357.2K **Privately Held**
SIC: 1382 Oil & gas exploration services

(G-4938)
BLUSH BOUTIQUE INC
566 Buchanan Ave Ste E (73069-5793)
PHONE..................405 701-8600
Amanda Clark, *Principal*
EMP: 2
SALES (est): 120K **Privately Held**
SIC: 5621 2389 Boutiques; costumes

(G-4939)
BOOMER SOOIE LLC
1025 E Indian Hills Rd (73071-7944)
PHONE..................501 827-0269
William Fagan,
EMP: 50
SQ FT: 20,000
SALES (est): 1MM **Privately Held**
SIC: 1389 Servicing oil & gas wells

(G-4940)
BOYDS AUTO PARTS & MACHINE
Also Called: Boyds Racing Engines
1202 N Flood Ave (73069-7623)
PHONE..................405 329-3855
Louis C Boyd, *President*
Mildred M Boyd, *Corp Secy*
Terry Boyd, *Vice Pres*
Eric Casperson, *Vice Pres*
EMP: 11
SQ FT: 6,800
SALES: 1.2MM **Privately Held**
WEB: www.boydsracingengines.com
SIC: 3599 5531 3714 Machine shop, jobbing & repair; automotive parts; motor vehicle parts & accessories

(G-4941)
BOYER INDUSTRIES LLC
1801 Wheatland Pl (73071-1173)
PHONE..................405 310-3015
Zachary Boyer, *Owner*
EMP: 1
SALES (est): 63.6K **Privately Held**
SIC: 3999 Manufacturing industries

(G-4942)
BRIANS WELDING AND FABRICATION
2909 Pinecrest Ct (73071-6871)
PHONE..................405 412-7878
Brian Umana, *Principal*
EMP: 1
SALES (est): 42.8K **Privately Held**
SIC: 7692 Welding repair

(G-4943)
BROCE MANUFACTURING CO INC
205 E Main St (73069-1304)
P.O. Box 1187 (73070-1187)
PHONE..................405 579-4621
Terry Weimer, *Vice Pres*
Mike Gall, *Manager*
EMP: 4
SALES (corp-wide): 15.2MM **Privately Held**
SIC: 3711 Street sprinklers & sweepers (motor vehicles), assembly of
PA: Broce Manufacturing Co., Inc.
1460 S 2nd Ave
Dodge City KS 67801
620 227-8811

(G-4944)
BROKEN ARROW PRODUCTIONS INC
Also Called: Spectrum Distributing
3209 Broce Dr (73072-2453)
P.O. Box 722095 (73070-8586)
PHONE..................405 360-8702
William A Bodin, *President*
▲ EMP: 32 EST: 1968
SQ FT: 16,000

Norman - Cleveland County (G-4945)

GEOGRAPHIC SECTION

SALES (est): 3.1MM **Privately Held**
SIC: 2759 3652 3695 Commercial printing; pre-recorded records & tapes; magnetic & optical recording media

(G-4945)
BROMIDE INC
3200 Marshall Ave Ste 201 (73072-8032)
P.O. Box 720308 (73070-4231)
PHONE.................................405 360-2999
Kirk Reed, *Principal*
EMP: 4
SALES (est): 336.6K **Privately Held**
SIC: 1311 8999 Crude petroleum & natural gas production; earth science services

(G-4946)
BROWN METALS (PA)
3121 36th Ave Se (73026-1301)
PHONE.................................405 321-6866
Rick Brown, *Owner*
EMP: 3
SALES: 2.2MM **Privately Held**
SIC: 3341 5051 Silver recovery from used photographic film; aluminum bars, rods, ingots, sheets, pipes, plates, etc.

(G-4947)
BTO STRATEGIES & SOLUTIONS INC
3004 Pinelake St (73071-7136)
PHONE.................................405 473-8632
Carson J Wiens, *President*
EMP: 1
SALES (est): 49.1K **Privately Held**
SIC: 3812 Defense systems & equipment

(G-4948)
BUCHANAN BICYCLES INC
561 Buchanan Ave (73069-5709)
PHONE.................................405 364-5513
Eric Richardson, *President*
Dewayne Norvill, *Manager*
EMP: 4
SQ FT: 2,000
SALES (est): 412.4K **Privately Held**
WEB: www.buchananbikes.com
SIC: 5941 3751 7699 Bicycle & bicycle parts; frames, motorcycle & bicycle; bicycle repair shop

(G-4949)
BUTNER BROTHERS LLC
3540 Wellsite Dr (73069-8221)
PHONE.................................405 321-2322
Casey Butner, *Partner*
Shane Butner, *Partner*
David Cross, *Mng Member*
EMP: 3
SQ FT: 5,500
SALES: 600K **Privately Held**
SIC: 3443 3993 Fabricated plate work (boiler shop); neon signs

(G-4950)
C & L OIL AND GAS CORPORATION
1708 Topeka St (73069-8224)
PHONE.................................405 364-1950
Ron Arvine, *President*
Julie Arvine, *Corp Secy*
EMP: 4
SQ FT: 8,000
SALES (est): 400K **Privately Held**
SIC: 1311 Crude petroleum production; natural gas production

(G-4951)
CAMERA GUYS LLC
1005 N Flood Ave (73069-7656)
PHONE.................................405 310-0006
Justin Starr,
EMP: 1
SALES (est): 56K **Privately Held**
SIC: 3651 Video camera-audio recorders, household use

(G-4952)
CAMPUS RAGZ
3909 24th Ave Nw (73069-8229)
PHONE.................................405 329-3300
Hamp Baker, *Partner*
Curtis Dougherty, *Partner*
Lana Dougherty, *Partner*
EMP: 3

SALES (est): 176.1K **Privately Held**
SIC: 5699 2759 Customized clothing & apparel; screen printing

(G-4953)
CARDBOARD JUNKEEZ LLC
4104 Eden Ct (73072-8613)
PHONE.................................405 990-9443
EMP: 2
SALES (est): 156.7K **Privately Held**
SIC: 2631 Cardboard

(G-4954)
CEJCO INC
Also Called: Cej & Associates
3225 N Flood Ave (73069-8241)
PHONE.................................405 366-8256
Chris Griffith, *President*
Jay Brannon, *Sales Mgr*
Denise Lowery, *Marketing Staff*
EMP: 15
SQ FT: 5,000
SALES (est): 748.9K **Privately Held**
SIC: 7336 2395 Silk screen design; pleating & stitching

(G-4955)
CHC WELDING LLC
4700 Harrogate Dr (73072-3958)
PHONE.................................405 706-3367
Cameron H Clagg, *Administration*
EMP: 1 EST: 2012
SALES (est): 35.1K **Privately Held**
SIC: 7692 Welding repair

(G-4956)
CHRIS JOHNSON
Also Called: Action Signs & Banners
312 E Tonhawa St (73069-7240)
PHONE.................................405 364-3879
Chris Johnson, *Owner*
EMP: 1
SALES (est): 60K **Privately Held**
SIC: 3993 2399 Signs & advertising specialties; fabricated textile products

(G-4957)
CIMARRON ENERGY HOLDING CO LLC (HQ)
4190 S Harvey Ave (73072-9797)
PHONE.................................405 928-7373
Larry Holdge, *President*
EMP: 100
SALES (est): 61.4MM
SALES (corp-wide): 416.9MM **Privately Held**
SIC: 1389 Oil field services
PA: Cimarron Energy Inc.
  1012 24th Ave Nw Ste 100
  Norman OK 73069
  405 928-7373

(G-4958)
CITY ELECTRIC SUPPLY COMPANY
1900 Industrial Blvd (73069-8510)
PHONE.................................405 701-8544
EMP: 3
SALES (corp-wide): 1.3B **Privately Held**
SIC: 5063 4911 3699 1731 Electrical supplies; electric services; electrical equipment & supplies; electrical work
PA: City Electric Supply Company
  400 S Record St Ste 1250
  Dallas TX 75202
  214 865-6801

(G-4959)
CLARIOS
5005 York Rd N (73069)
PHONE.................................405 419-5400
Alex A Molinaroli, *CEO*
EMP: 1000 **Privately Held**
SIC: 3585 Refrigeration & heating equipment
HQ: Johnson Controls, Inc.
  5757 N Green Bay Ave
  Milwaukee WI 53209
  414 524-1200

(G-4960)
CLEARBAY SOFTWARE LLC
2904 Stonebridge Ct (73071-1704)
PHONE.................................405 310-9150
Matt T Luttrell, *Administration*

EMP: 2
SALES (est): 102.8K **Privately Held**
WEB: www.clearbaybounce.com
SIC: 7372 Prepackaged software

(G-4961)
CNI AVIATION ADVANTAGE A JOI
2600 John Saxon Blvd (73071-1166)
PHONE.................................405 253-8200
Susan Rogers, *Principal*
Mike Mitcheell, *Principal*
EMP: 1
SALES (est): 83.8K **Privately Held**
SIC: 3728 Aircraft parts & equipment

(G-4962)
COANDA COMPANY LLC
1000 Corbett Dr (73072-3726)
PHONE.................................214 601-4972
Nicole Bigbie,
Hunter Pemberton,
EMP: 3
SALES (est): 119.7K **Privately Held**
SIC: 3441 Fabricated structural metal

(G-4963)
COMMANDER AIRCRAFT CORPORATION
1600 Westheimer Dr (73069-8453)
PHONE.................................405 366-6454
EMP: 2
SALES (est): 270.5K **Privately Held**
SIC: 3721 Airplanes, fixed or rotary wing

(G-4964)
CONSTRUCTION SUPPLY HOUSE INC
Also Called: Concrete Supply House
1013 Hearthstone (73072-3972)
P.O. Box 721440 (73070-8110)
PHONE.................................405 214-9366
Greg Merlyn, *Mng Member*
▲ EMP: 5
SALES (est): 696.2K **Privately Held**
SIC: 3272 Concrete products

(G-4965)
COOLBODISPA
111 24th Ave Nw Ste 120-A (73069-6388)
PHONE.................................405 420-9785
EMP: 2
SALES (est): 74.4K **Privately Held**
SIC: 2844 Toilet preparations

(G-4966)
CORNER COPY & PRINTING LLC
770 Deans Row Ave (73069-7009)
PHONE.................................405 801-2020
Stephanie Odle, *Mng Member*
Mark Hamilton, *Mng Member*
EMP: 5
SQ FT: 1,500
SALES: 250K **Privately Held**
SIC: 7389 2396 2732 Printers' services: folding, collating; screen printing on fabric articles; books: printing & binding

(G-4967)
COUNTER CANTER INC
2500 Mcgee Dr Ste 147 (73072-6705)
PHONE.................................405 321-8326
EMP: 3 EST: 2011
SALES (est): 223.9K **Privately Held**
SIC: 3131 Counters

(G-4968)
CRADDUCK JOHN
Also Called: Cradduck Manufacturing Company
9004 E Franklin Rd (73026-6759)
PHONE.................................405 360-0251
John Cradduck, *President*
EMP: 1
SALES (est): 61.3K **Privately Held**
SIC: 5571 3751 Motorcycle parts & accessories; motorcycles, bicycles & parts

(G-4969)
CRIMSON HOT SHOT SERVICE LLC
1110 Missouri St (73071-4427)
PHONE.................................469 358-2005

EMP: 2
SALES (est): 65.5K **Privately Held**
SIC: 1389 Hot shot service

(G-4970)
CROSSLANDS A A RENT-ALL SLS CO
2451 E Imhoff Rd (73071-1106)
PHONE.................................405 366-8878
Joe Goodnoh, *Owner*
EMP: 2
SALES (corp-wide): 9.8MM **Privately Held**
SIC: 3531 Construction machinery
PA: Crossland's A & A Rent-All & Sales Co.
  15 Sw 29th St
  Oklahoma City OK 73109
  405 632-3393

(G-4971)
CRUCIBLE LLC
110 E Tonhawa St (73069-7238)
PHONE.................................405 579-2700
Mark Palmerton, *Mng Member*
EMP: 12
SALES (est): 816.2K **Privately Held**
WEB: www.thecruciblellc.com
SIC: 8999 3369 Art related services; non-ferrous foundries

(G-4972)
CUMMINS - ALLISON CORP
680 24th Ave Sw (73069-3913)
PHONE.................................405 321-1411
Doug Lane, *Manager*
EMP: 10
SALES (corp-wide): 3.2B **Publicly Held**
SIC: 3578 3519 Automatic teller machines (ATM); internal combustion engines
HQ: Cummins-Allison Corp.
  852 Feehanville Dr
  Mount Prospect IL 60056
  800 786-5528

(G-4973)
CURTISS-WRIGHT CORPORATION
1012 24th Ave Nw Ste 100 (73069-6493)
PHONE.................................405 515-8235
Andrew Masullo, *General Mgr*
EMP: 3
SALES (corp-wide): 2.4B **Publicly Held**
SIC: 3491 Industrial valves
PA: Curtiss-Wright Corporation
  130 Harbour Place Dr # 300
  Davidson NC 28036
  704 869-4600

(G-4974)
CUSTOM TIME & NEON CO INC
1809 Atchison Dr (73069-8299)
PHONE.................................405 364-9139
Don McDonald, *President*
EMP: 2
SQ FT: 11,000
SALES (est): 173.9K **Privately Held**
SIC: 3993 3873 Signs & advertising specialties; watches, clocks, watchcases & parts

(G-4975)
CYBER STITCHERY
2702 S Pickard Ave (73072-6924)
PHONE.................................405 329-6018
Dorthy Klippell, *Principal*
EMP: 2
SALES (est): 90.8K **Privately Held**
SIC: 3312 Blast furnaces & steel mills

(G-4976)
DEL NERO MANUFACTURING CO
4801 Pleasant Hill Ln (73026-2201)
P.O. Box 787 (73070-0787)
PHONE.................................405 364-4800
Kristin Del Nero, *CEO*
Philip Delnero, *President*
EMP: 2
SALES (est): 261K **Privately Held**
SIC: 3499 3444 7389 Locks, safe & vault: metal; sheet metal specialties, not stamped;

GEOGRAPHIC SECTION

Norman - Cleveland County (G-5011)

(G-4977)
DENNIS PETRILLA ENTERPRISES
813 E Mosier St (73071-6219)
PHONE..................405 364-4695
Dennis Petrilla, *Owner*
EMP: 2
SALES (est): 160K **Privately Held**
SIC: **1521** 3446 1751 Single-family housing construction; stairs, staircases, stair treads; prefabricated metal; cabinet & finish carpentry

(G-4978)
DHARMA INC
Also Called: Walker's Publishing
3750 W Main St Ste A (73072-4657)
PHONE..................405 366-1336
Marsha Walker, *President*
EMP: 3
SALES (est): 318.8K **Privately Held**
WEB: www.dharma-inc.com
SIC: **2721** Magazines: publishing & printing

(G-4979)
DICK HALL & ASSOCIATES
416 Terrace Pl (73069-5065)
PHONE..................405 202-4301
Richard Hall, *Mng Member*
EMP: 1 EST: 2001
SQ FT: 275
SALES (est): 86.5K **Privately Held**
SIC: **7372** Application computer software

(G-4980)
DIGITAL THEORY LLC
425 Golden Oaks Dr (73072-4311)
PHONE..................405 824-6460
Casey Butner, *Administration*
EMP: 1
SALES (est): 46K **Privately Held**
SIC: **3993** Signs & advertising specialties

(G-4981)
DIGITAL THEORY SIGNS
3540 Wellsite Dr (73069-8221)
PHONE..................405 438-0222
EMP: 1
SALES (est): 46K **Privately Held**
SIC: **3993** Signs & advertising specialties

(G-4982)
DOCO DEVELOPMENT CORP
2705 Poplar Ln (73072-6836)
P.O. Box 720443 (73070-4324)
PHONE..................405 321-7493
Pat Doherty, *President*
James Doherty, *President*
Brian Doherty, *Corp Secy*
Patrick Doherty, *Admin Sec*
EMP: 1
SQ FT: 6,000
SALES (est): 127.1K **Privately Held**
SIC: **1311** Crude petroleum production; natural gas production

(G-4983)
DREAM GREEN INTERNATIONAL LLC
133 24th Ave Nw 290 (73069-6320)
PHONE..................814 616-7800
EMP: 2
SALES (est): 66K **Privately Held**
SIC: **1411** 8712 1422 Trap rock, dimension-quarrying; architectural engineering; crushed & broken limestone
PA: Dream Green International Llc
32 W 8th St Ste No607
Erie PA 16501

(G-4984)
DUNCAN OIL & GAS INC
4604 Laurelbrook Ct (73072-3960)
PHONE..................405 360-2183
Dale Duncan, *Branch Mgr*
EMP: 1 **Privately Held**
SIC: **5172** 1382 Crude oil; oil & gas exploration services
PA: Duncan Oil & Gas Inc
23 E 9th St Ste 213
Shawnee OK 74801

(G-4985)
DUST CUTTER
3813 Danfield Ln (73072-3102)
PHONE..................405 615-7788
Bryan Vineyard, *CEO*
Jay Bird, *Sales Staff*
EMP: 20
SALES: 10MM **Privately Held**
SIC: **2086** Lemonade: packaged in cans, bottles, etc.

(G-4986)
EAGLE DRILLING LLC
1126 Rambling Oaks Dr (73072-4134)
PHONE..................405 447-8181
Rodney Thornton,
EMP: 9
SALES (est): 910K **Privately Held**
SIC: **1381** Drilling oil & gas wells

(G-4987)
EATON AND ASSOCIATES LLC
300 Victory Ct (73072-4363)
PHONE..................405 307-9631
EMP: 2 EST: 2017
SALES (est): 123.4K **Privately Held**
SIC: **3625** Relays & industrial controls

(G-4988)
EDEN CLINIC INC (PA)
1807 W Lindsey St (73069-4101)
P.O. Box 669 (73070-0669)
PHONE..................405 579-4673
Josh Wagner, *Chairman*
Mike Moran, *Treasurer*
Linda Wells, *Exec Dir*
Linda Cozadd, *Exec Dir*
Austin Manger, *Admin Sec*
EMP: 2
SALES (est): 338.3K **Privately Held**
WEB: www.edenclinic.tv
SIC: **8099** 8299 2835 8011 Physical examination & testing services; prenatal instruction; pregnancy test kits; medical centers; nurses & other medical assistants

(G-4989)
ELITE MEDIA GROUP LLC
Also Called: Blue Sky Digital Printing
2700 Technology Pl (73071-1127)
PHONE..................405 928-5800
Trent Lindmark,
EMP: 3
SALES (est): 348.3K **Privately Held**
WEB: www.blueskydigitalprinting.com
SIC: **3993** Signs & advertising specialties

(G-4990)
ELM CREEK GRAVEL LLC
Also Called: Ecowood Solutions
1529 24th Ave Sw (73072-5708)
PHONE..................405 360-7300
Jessica Bergen, *Vice Pres*
Blake Bergen, *Treasurer*
Susan Bergen, *Admin Sec*
EMP: 20
SALES (est): 1.8MM **Privately Held**
SIC: **1442** Construction sand & gravel

(G-4991)
ELSTER AMCO WATER INC
417 Misty Ridge Dr (73071-4121)
PHONE..................863 453-5336
Terri Rapoport, *Principal*
EMP: 2
SALES (est): 79.9K **Privately Held**
SIC: **3589** Service industry machinery

(G-4992)
ENERGY PARTNERS
1020 24th Ave Nw (73069-6341)
PHONE..................405 573-9064
EMP: 2
SALES (est): 104K **Privately Held**
SIC: **1382** Oil & gas exploration services

(G-4993)
EVANS ENTERPRISES INC (PA)
6707 N Interstate Dr (73069-9527)
P.O. Box 1088 (73070-1088)
PHONE..................405 631-1344
Sylynda J Thrash, *CEO*
Rusty Thrash, *President*
Dylan Baugh, *COO*
Evan Thrash, *Senior VP*
David Brantley, *Vice Pres*
▲ EMP: 120 EST: 1954
SQ FT: 47,000
SALES (est): 148.9MM **Privately Held**
WEB: www.goevans.com
SIC: **3625** 7629 7699 5084 Relays & industrial controls; electrical repair shops; industrial equipment services; controlling instruments & accessories; compressors, except air conditioning; cranes, industrial; motors & generators

(G-4994)
EVERYTHING WELDING & SAFETY IN
3451 N Flood Ave (73069-8240)
PHONE..................405 701-3711
EMP: 1 EST: 2017
SALES (est): 36.6K **Privately Held**
SIC: **7692** Welding repair

(G-4995)
EVES APPLE ✪
1107 W Apache St (73069-5408)
PHONE..................512 970-9016
Chloe Drake, *Principal*
EMP: 2 EST: 2019
SALES (est): 85.9K **Privately Held**
SIC: **3571** Personal computers (microcomputers)

(G-4996)
FANCY CAKES
404 W Main St (73069-1313)
PHONE..................405 701-3434
EMP: 5
SALES (est): 485.7K **Privately Held**
SIC: **2335** Womens, Juniors, And Misses Dresses

(G-4997)
FASCO MOTORS GROUP
2913 Se 44th St (73072-9623)
PHONE..................405 387-5560
Rich Asperheim, *Manager*
EMP: 2
SALES (est): 88.3K **Privately Held**
SIC: **3621** Motors & generators

(G-4998)
FASHIONABLE MEDICAL COVERS
121 Sandstone Dr (73071-2148)
PHONE..................405 414-1147
Tabatha Carney, *Owner*
EMP: 1
SALES: 0 **Privately Held**
SIC: **2393** Textile bags

(G-4999)
FASTSIGNS
900 24th Ave Nw (73069-6205)
PHONE..................405 701-2908
EMP: 3 EST: 2014
SALES (est): 213.3K **Privately Held**
SIC: **3993** Signs & advertising specialties

(G-5000)
FIREFLY CUSTOM LASER ENGRV LLC
2234 Ravenwood Ln (73071-7427)
PHONE..................405 664-4145
Timothy E Knighton,
EMP: 2
SALES (est): 98.4K **Privately Held**
SIC: **2759** Engraving

(G-5001)
FLAME CONTROL INC
1011 W Tecumseh Rd (73069-8301)
PHONE..................405 321-2535
Fax: 405 321-2535
EMP: 3
SQ FT: 2,200
SALES: 240K **Privately Held**
SIC: **3433** 5719 Mfg & Ret Fireplaces & Accessories

(G-5002)
FLOWERS BAKING CO DENTON LLC
5741 Huettner Ct (73069-9512)
PHONE..................405 366-2175
EMP: 3
SALES (corp-wide): 4.1B **Publicly Held**
SIC: **2051** Bread, cake & related products
HQ: Flowers Baking Co. Of Denton, Llc
4210 Edwards Rd
Denton TX 76208
940 383-5280

(G-5003)
FM2T WELDING LLC
3614 Stonebrook Dr (73072-9111)
PHONE..................405 837-8495
Carol Shelton, *Principal*
EMP: 1
SALES (est): 25K **Privately Held**
SIC: **7692** Welding repair

(G-5004)
FUDGENOMICS 101 LLC
1220 E Robinson St (73071-3602)
PHONE..................405 401-3832
EMP: 2
SALES (est): 93.2K **Privately Held**
SIC: **2064** Fudge (candy)

(G-5005)
FUNK
239 Crestmont Ave (73069-6603)
PHONE..................405 329-7571
EMP: 2
SALES: 500K **Privately Held**
SIC: **1382** Oil/Gas Exploration Services

(G-5006)
G M C OIL & GAS
2900 W Lindsey St (73072-5510)
PHONE..................405 701-5515
G Close, *Principal*
EMP: 2
SALES (est): 175.1K **Privately Held**
SIC: **1382** Oil & gas exploration services

(G-5007)
GENERAL AUTO SUPPLY INC
319 E Comanche St (73069-6008)
PHONE..................405 329-0772
Thomas F Ingram, *President*
Dixie Ingram, *Corp Secy*
Craig Ingram, *Vice Pres*
EMP: 1
SQ FT: 6,976
SALES (est): 120K **Privately Held**
SIC: **5531** 3694 3621 Automotive parts; alternators, automotive; starters, for motors

(G-5008)
GOLIATH PIPELINE AND CNSTR LLC
2116 138th Ave Se (73026-8705)
PHONE..................512 917-9313
Michael Forbes, *Managing Prtnr*
Monte McNew, *Partner*
EMP: 2
SALES: 500K **Privately Held**
SIC: **7692** 3545 Welding repair; machine tool accessories

(G-5009)
GRAHAM LABORATORIES
2033 24th Ave Sw (73072-6606)
P.O. Box 720236 (73070-4177)
PHONE..................405 329-4413
James Graham, *President*
Sharon Graham, *Admin Sec*
EMP: 2
SALES (est): 144.7K **Privately Held**
SIC: **3851** Contact lenses

(G-5010)
GREEN HORIZONS LLC
4700 168th Ave Ne (73026-8903)
PHONE..................405 364-9921
EMP: 2
SALES (est): 180K **Privately Held**
SIC: **2879** Mfg Agricultural Chemicals

(G-5011)
GRIPS ETC INC
3214 Bart Conner Dr (73072-2406)
PHONE..................405 447-2559
Ben H Faulk, *President*
▲ EMP: 56 EST: 1999
SALES (est): 4.1MM **Privately Held**
SIC: **5091** 3949 Gymnasium equipment; sporting & athletic goods

Norman - Cleveland County (G-5012)

(G-5012)
GUYS WISE
1200 W Main St (73069-6848)
PHONE................405 801-3339
Preston Miller, *Owner*
EMP: 2
SALES (est): 138.1K **Privately Held**
SIC: 3211 Window glass, clear & colored

(G-5013)
H & H CNSTR MET FBRICATION INC
1301 Quality Ave (73071-7962)
PHONE................405 701-1075
Tyson David Hopper, *President*
EMP: 28
SALES (est): 3.6MM **Privately Held**
SIC: 3441 Fabricated structural metal

(G-5014)
HAMMER CONSTRUCTION INC (PA)
4320 Adams Rd (73069-1007)
P.O. Box 721078 (73070-4830)
PHONE................405 310-3160
Shirley Hammer, *Principal*
Robby Moore, *Principal*
EMP: 120
SQ FT: 3,000
SALES (est): 57.6MM **Privately Held**
SIC: 1389 1794 Oil field services; excavation & grading, building construction

(G-5015)
HANSEN RESEARCH LLC
7510 E Lindsey St (73026-3941)
P.O. Box 89 (73070-0089)
PHONE................405 659-5079
Joel H Young, *Owner*
EMP: 1
SALES: 10K **Privately Held**
SIC: 8711 3429 Engineering services; manufactured hardware (general)

(G-5016)
HARD EDGE DESIGN INC
Also Called: Non Deplume
1007 N University Blvd (73069-7619)
PHONE................405 360-9714
Deborah Billingsely, *President*
Jeff Melton, *President*
Cathy Siler, *Supervisor*
EMP: 12
SQ FT: 20,000
SALES (est): 1.3MM **Privately Held**
SIC: 7389 2261 Advertising, promotional & trade show services; embroidering of advertising on shirts, etc.; screen printing of cotton broadwoven fabrics

(G-5017)
HARDEN METALWORKS LLC
3001 28th Ave Ne (73071-7805)
PHONE................405 812-2812
Steven Harden,
EMP: 1 EST: 2017
SALES (est): 39.6K **Privately Held**
SIC: 3999 Manufacturing industries

(G-5018)
HARRISON GYPSUM LLC (DH)
Also Called: Allied Custom Gypsum
1550 Double C Dr (73069-8288)
PHONE................405 366-9500
Paul Harrington, *President*
Scott Alexander, *Principal*
Paul Harrison, *Principal*
Kris Kinder, *Principal*
John Miller, *Principal*
▲ EMP: 18 EST: 1955
SALES (est): 263.4MM
SALES (corp-wide): 1.7B **Publicly Held**
WEB: www.acgmaterials.com
SIC: 1499 4213 Gypsum mining; trucking, except local
HQ: Harrison Gypsum Holdings, Llc
1550 Double C Dr
Norman OK 73069
405 366-9500

(G-5019)
HARRISON GYPSUM HOLDINGS LLC (DH)
1550 Double C Dr (73069-8288)
PHONE................405 366-9500
Paul Harrington, *President*
Bob Monaghan, *CFO*
EMP: 184
SALES (est): 264.7MM
SALES (corp-wide): 1.7B **Publicly Held**
SIC: 1499 Gypsum mining

(G-5020)
HEALTH ENGINEERING SYSTEM
2600 Technology Pl (73071-1100)
PHONE................405 329-6810
Rod Standridge, *Owner*
Jennifer Jenkins, *Mktg Dir*
▲ EMP: 3
SALES: 750K **Privately Held**
SIC: 3559 Special industry machinery

(G-5021)
HEISTER CUSTOM CABINETS INC
4915 W Tecumseh Rd (73072-1602)
PHONE................405 329-6318
Gary Heister, *Principal*
EMP: 2
SALES (est): 143.5K **Privately Held**
SIC: 2434 Wood kitchen cabinets

(G-5022)
HIGHLANDS PUBLISHING LLC
11201 Mystic Isle (73026-7205)
PHONE................405 596-8391
EMP: 1
SALES (est): 38.8K **Privately Held**
SIC: 2741 Miscellaneous publishing

(G-5023)
HILAND DAIRY FOODS COMPANY LLC
302 S Porter Ave (73071-5434)
P.O. Box 1248 (73070-1248)
PHONE................405 321-3191
Chris Shatley, *Plant Mgr*
Dean Mays, *Research*
Twila Rogers, *Loan Officer*
Ted Barlows, *Personnel Exec*
Randy Richison, *Branch Mgr*
EMP: 100
SALES (corp-wide): 1.7B **Privately Held**
SIC: 5143 2026 Dairy products, except dried or canned; fluid milk
HQ: Hiland Dairy Foods Company., Llc
1133 E Kearney St
Springfield MO 65803
417 862-9311

(G-5024)
HITACHI COMPUTER PDTS AMER INC (DH)
1800 E Imhoff Rd (73071-1200)
PHONE................405 360-5500
George Wilson, *President*
Randy Reynolds, *Treasurer*
▲ EMP: 350
SQ FT: 164,000
SALES (est): 84.7MM **Privately Held**
SIC: 3577 3572 7379 Computer peripheral equipment; computer storage devices; computer related consulting services
HQ: Hitachi Vantara Corporation
2535 Augustine Dr
Santa Clara CA 95054
408 970-1000

(G-5025)
HOLASEK OIL & GAS CO LLC
6378 Harold Way Ne (73026-3142)
PHONE................405 321-6663
G J Holasek, *Principal*
EMP: 2
SALES (est): 150K **Privately Held**
SIC: 1389 Oil & gas field services

(G-5026)
HOOPER PRINTING COMPANY INC (PA)
301 W Gray St (73069-7193)
PHONE................405 321-4288
Charles W Hooper, *President*
Randy Hooper, *Vice Pres*
EMP: 12 EST: 1950
SQ FT: 5,000
SALES (est): 500K **Privately Held**
SIC: 2752 2759 2791 2789 Commercial printing, offset; letterpress printing; typesetting; bookbinding & related work

(G-5027)
HOSS DIRECTIONAL SERVICE INC
1405 Jami Dr (73071-4400)
PHONE................405 822-0551
EMP: 2
SALES (est): 98.6K **Privately Held**
SIC: 1381 Directional drilling oil & gas wells

(G-5028)
I ENRG
1624 24th Ave Sw (73072-5709)
PHONE................405 360-4600
Rick Chapman, *President*
EMP: 1
SALES (est): 70.5K **Privately Held**
SIC: 1389 Oil & gas field services

(G-5029)
IBALL INSTRUMENTS LLC
3540 National Dr (73069-8222)
PHONE................405 366-6061
EMP: 12
SQ FT: 4,000
SALES (est): 2.5MM **Privately Held**
SIC: 3812 Mfg Search/Navigation Equipment

(G-5030)
IMMUNO-MYCOLOGICS INC
2701 Corporate Centre Dr (73069-2901)
PHONE................405 360-4669
Sean Bauman, *CEO*
Sharon J Bauman, *President*
Scott Bauman, *COO*
EMP: 17
SQ FT: 7,000
SALES (est): 3.2MM **Privately Held**
SIC: 3841 2835 Diagnostic apparatus, medical; in vitro & in vivo diagnostic substances

(G-5031)
IMMY AFRICA LLC
2701 Corporate Centre Dr (73069-2901)
PHONE................405 360-4669
Sean Bauman, *Mng Member*
EMP: 12 EST: 2017
SALES (est): 1.4MM **Privately Held**
SIC: 3841 Diagnostic apparatus, medical

(G-5032)
INFINITY RESOURCES COMPANY
2740 Washington Dr (73069-1000)
PHONE................405 701-3229
Brandon Stephens, *Principal*
EMP: 2
SALES (est): 167.7K **Privately Held**
SIC: 1382 Oil & gas exploration services

(G-5033)
INFO-SHARP LLC
1808 Parkridge Dr (73071-1301)
PHONE................520 204-5093
Ross Brown, *Partner*
Devin Welch, *Partner*
EMP: 2
SALES (est): 69.9K **Privately Held**
SIC: 7373 7372 7371 Systems engineering, computer related; application computer software; computer software writing services; computer software development; computer software systems analysis & design, custom

(G-5034)
INGELS VINEYARD LLC
2310 Ravenwood Ln (73071-7447)
PHONE................405 321-1008
Dorothy Ingels, *Owner*
EMP: 1
SALES (est): 56.9K **Privately Held**
SIC: 2084 Wines

(G-5035)
INTERNATIONAL GYMNAST MAGAZINE
Also Called: Paul Zirt & Associates
3214 Bart Conner Dr (73072-2406)
P.O. Box 721020 (73070-4788)
PHONE................405 447-9988
Paul Zirt, *President*
EMP: 6
SALES: 86.9K **Privately Held**
SIC: 2721 Magazines: publishing only, not printed on site

(G-5036)
INTUITION INC
Also Called: United Energy Technologies
613 Coopers Hawk Dr (73072-8125)
P.O. Box 1628 (73070-1628)
PHONE................405 361-8376
Bobby Jones III, *President*
Ryan Busler, *Vice Pres*
EMP: 4
SALES: 250K **Privately Held**
SIC: 3825 7389 Instruments to measure electricity;

(G-5037)
INVICTUS ENGRG CNSTR SVCS
800 W Rock Creek Rd # 115 (73069-8586)
PHONE................405 701-5622
Andrew Wade McPherson, *President*
EMP: 1
SALES (est): 138.5K **Privately Held**
SIC: 3569 8711 3669 Sprinkler systems, fire: automatic; fire protection engineering; fire alarm apparatus, electric; fire detection systems, electric

(G-5038)
ISLAND PALM LLC
2817 Cynthia Cir (73072-7456)
PHONE................405 321-1056
Gregory Buwick, *Principal*
EMP: 2
SALES (est): 78.2K **Privately Held**
SIC: 2084 Wines, brandy & brandy spirits

(G-5039)
J S WELDING
4000 48th Ave Nw (73072-1704)
PHONE................405 364-1362
Jerry Calvert, *Principal*
EMP: 1
SALES (est): 58.7K **Privately Held**
SIC: 7692 Welding repair

(G-5040)
J&A SERVICES CO INC
401 W Johnson St (73069-7632)
PHONE................405 833-4824
John Bottrell, *President*
EMP: 2
SALES (est): 150K **Privately Held**
SIC: 3531 Backhoe mounted, hydraulically powered attachments

(G-5041)
JAMES K ANDERSON INC (PA)
903 Chautauqua Ave (73069-4610)
P.O. Box 6546, Abilene TX (79608-6546)
PHONE................405 329-7414
James K Anderson, *President*
Becky Archey, *Vice Pres*
Jim Wick, *Admin Sec*
EMP: 3 EST: 1953
SALES (est): 179.5K **Privately Held**
SIC: 1311 1389 Crude petroleum production; natural gas production; roustabout service

(G-5042)
JCL & JFL OIL & GAS
1005 N Flood Ave (73069-7656)
P.O. Box 1228 (73070-1228)
PHONE................405 360-1620
Jim Logsdon, *Principal*
EMP: 2
SALES (est): 192.4K **Privately Held**
SIC: 1382 Oil & gas exploration services

(G-5043)
JET BLACK AIRCRAFT
2206 Research Park Blvd (73069-8542)
PHONE................405 310-6556
Michael Black, *President*

GEOGRAPHIC SECTION

Norman - Cleveland County (G-5077)

EMP: 9
SALES (est): 1.1MM **Privately Held**
SIC: **3599** Machine shop, jobbing & repair

(G-5044)
JOE DECKER SIGNS
3216 Dove Hollow Ln (73072-2968)
PHONE................................405 630-8691
EMP: 1 EST: 2018
SALES (est): 46K **Privately Held**
SIC: **3993** Signs & advertising specialties

(G-5045)
K A G U INC
Also Called: Anything Goes
3517 National Dr (73069-8261)
PHONE................................405 364-4637
Jerri Marquardt, *CEO*
Nizam Murshed, *Vice Pres*
EMP: 8
SQ FT: 900
SALES (est): 600K **Privately Held**
SIC: **2395** Embroidery & art needlework

(G-5046)
K G HILL COMPANY LLC
1857 Danfield Dr (73072-3000)
PHONE................................405 641-4190
Kenyon Hill,
EMP: 1
SALES (est): 39.6K **Privately Held**
SIC: **3999** Manufacturing industries

(G-5047)
K S OIL COMPANY INC
3100 S Berry Rd Ste 210 (73072-7480)
PHONE................................405 634-5115
Keith E Smith, *President*
EMP: 2
SQ FT: 1,500
SALES: 290K **Privately Held**
SIC: **1311** Crude petroleum production; natural gas production

(G-5048)
KEMAH OIL & GAS CO LLC
4600 Timberidge Cir (73072-1719)
PHONE................................405 364-3899
Martin Wernick, *Owner*
EMP: 2 EST: 2013
SALES (est): 65.5K **Privately Held**
SIC: **1389** Oil & gas field services

(G-5049)
KENT ENGINEERING INC
5 Burlington Pl (73072-3617)
PHONE................................405 364-2207
Kent Myers, *President*
EMP: 1
SALES (est): 101.5K **Privately Held**
SIC: **1389** Oil consultants

(G-5050)
KIAMICHI RESOURCES INC
4771 E Rock Creek Rd (73026-0622)
P.O. Box 95666, Oklahoma City (73143-5666)
PHONE................................405 364-8176
Cornelia P Suenram, *President*
John P Harkey, *Vice Pres*
Patrica Hacky, *Admin Sec*
EMP: 2
SQ FT: 7,000
SALES (est): 60K **Privately Held**
SIC: **1311** 3599 6799 5085 Crude petroleum production; machine shop, jobbing & repair; real estate investors, except property operators; filters, industrial

(G-5051)
KID TRAX
2345 Heatherfield Ln (73071-1450)
PHONE................................405 366-7982
Tracy Frost, *Owner*
EMP: 1
SALES (est): 57.8K **Privately Held**
SIC: **3999** Identification tags, except paper

(G-5052)
KING KOPY LLC
119 W Boyd St Ste 112 (73069-4858)
PHONE................................405 321-0202
Aisha Ali, *Owner*
EMP: 8
SQ FT: 1,000
SALES (est): 540K **Privately Held**
SIC: **3599** 2789 2759 Photocopying & duplicating services; bookbinding & related work; commercial printing

(G-5053)
KODA WELDING LLC
202 S Mercedes Dr (73069-5241)
PHONE................................405 443-9800
EMP: 1
SALES (est): 55.2K **Privately Held**
SIC: **7692** Welding repair

(G-5054)
L & C VENTURES LLC
530 Opportunity Dr (73071-7298)
P.O. Box 6147, Moore (73153-0147)
PHONE................................405 793-9353
EMP: 4
SALES (est): 237.1K **Privately Held**
SIC: **1799** 7692 Welding on site; welding repair

(G-5055)
L3HARRIS TECHNOLOGIES INC
600 W Rock Creek Rd (73069-8537)
PHONE................................405 573-2285
EMP: 53
SALES (corp-wide): 6.8B **Publicly Held**
SIC: **3812** Search & navigation equipment
PA: L3harris Technologies, Inc.
1025 W Nasa Blvd
Melbourne FL 32919
321 727-9100

(G-5056)
LAYLE COMPANY CORPORATION
Also Called: Lalye
110 S University Blvd (73069-5644)
PHONE................................405 329-5143
Marianne Raleigh, *President*
EMP: 3
SQ FT: 1,000
SALES (est): 180K **Privately Held**
SIC: **3953** 3089 7389 Marking devices; engraving of plastic; notary publics

(G-5057)
LEDETS WELDING SERVICE INC
8100 Bert Ln (73026-2930)
PHONE................................405 760-8935
Douglas J Ledet, *President*
Susan Ledet, *Principal*
EMP: 2
SALES (est): 307.8K **Privately Held**
SIC: **3548** Welding apparatus

(G-5058)
LIBERTY OPERATING INC
1827 Atchison Dr (73069-8225)
PHONE................................405 329-6200
Wayne McPherson, *President*
Wayne McPherson II, *Admin Sec*
EMP: 7
SQ FT: 3,000
SALES (est): 1.2MM **Privately Held**
SIC: **1311** Crude petroleum production; natural gas production

(G-5059)
LIGHTSTITCHING
4124 Moorgate Cir (73072-9773)
PHONE................................405 210-7645
Marie McCormick, *Principal*
EMP: 1
SALES (est): 33.7K **Privately Held**
SIC: **2395** Embroidery & art needlework

(G-5060)
LIV3DESIGN LLC
Also Called: Creative Printing
330 E Gray St (73069-7208)
P.O. Box 722075 (73070-8574)
PHONE................................432 296-1968
Al Reed, *Partner*
EMP: 4
SALES (est): 185.9K **Privately Held**
SIC: **2759** 2791 Business forms: printing; typesetting

(G-5061)
LW PUBLICATIONS
1100 Oak Tree Ave (73072-8035)
PHONE................................405 203-6740
EMP: 1 EST: 2017
SALES (est): 37.5K **Privately Held**
SIC: **2741** Miscellaneous publishing

(G-5062)
MADDENS PORTABLE BUILDINGS
1161 Bluestem (73069-9712)
PHONE................................405 799-4989
Clo Ellen Madden, *President*
Richard Madden, *Vice Pres*
Roy Madden, *Shareholder*
EMP: 25
SQ FT: 21,000
SALES (est): 3.9MM **Privately Held**
SIC: **3441** 3448 5211 Building components, structural steel; buildings, portable: prefabricated metal; prefabricated buildings

(G-5063)
MAGNUM ENERGY INC
3111 Broce Dr (73072-2403)
PHONE................................405 360-2784
Robert A Campbell, *President*
EMP: 2
SALES (est): 152.2K **Privately Held**
SIC: **1389** Oil field services

(G-5064)
MARPLE PETROLEUM LLC
412 Flint Ridge Ct (73072-4480)
P.O. Box 720666 (73070-4506)
PHONE................................405 360-2240
Todd Marple, *Mng Member*
Rhonda Marple,
EMP: 2
SALES (est): 300K **Privately Held**
SIC: **3533** Oil & gas field machinery

(G-5065)
MASONS PECANS & PEANUTS INC
4913 Se 44th St (73072-9799)
PHONE................................405 329-7828
Bret Mason, *President*
EMP: 7
SALES (est): 705.7K **Privately Held**
SIC: **5441** 5159 2068 2064 Nuts; candy; nuts, unprocessed or shelled only; pecan shellers; salted & roasted nuts & seeds; candy & other confectionary products; cookies & crackers

(G-5066)
MASSIVE GRAPHIC SCREEN PRTG
2895 Broce Dr (73072-2405)
PHONE................................405 364-3594
Kent Johnson, *President*
Kathy Johnson, *Vice Pres*
EMP: 12
SQ FT: 6,000
SALES (est): 850K **Privately Held**
SIC: **2261** 5136 2396 Screen printing of cotton broadwoven fabrics; sportswear, men's & boys'; automotive & apparel trimmings

(G-5067)
MCPHERSON IMPLEMENT INC
Also Called: McPherson Machine
I 35 Hwy 9 W (73072)
P.O. Box 654 (73070-0654)
PHONE................................405 321-6292
Tom K McPherson, *President*
Sylvia J McPherson, *Admin Sec*
EMP: 13 EST: 1953
SQ FT: 10,000
SALES (est): 1.3MM **Privately Held**
SIC: **3444** 1799 Sheet metalwork; welding on site

(G-5068)
MCWL INC
4510 Green Field Cir (73072-3131)
PHONE................................405 360-2277
Guy Prior, *President*
EMP: 1
SALES (est): 103.8K **Privately Held**
SIC: **1389** Oil field services

(G-5069)
MEDINA EXPLORATION INC
2600 Banburen St Ste 2636 (73072)
P.O. Box 722348 (73070-8777)
PHONE................................405 579-4200
Jerry Medina, *President*
EMP: 2
SALES (est): 153.8K **Privately Held**
SIC: **1382** Oil & gas exploration services

(G-5070)
MEMORABILIA CORNER
1312 Mckinley Ave (73072-6535)
PHONE................................405 321-8366
EMP: 2
SALES (est): 145.1K **Privately Held**
SIC: **3861** 5943 Mfg Photographic Equipment/Supplies Ret Stationery

(G-5071)
MERCURY SIGN AND BANNER
123 24th Ave Nw (73069-6320)
PHONE................................405 360-3303
Curt Willams, *President*
Stephen McCubbin, *Treasurer*
EMP: 3
SALES (est): 145.9K **Privately Held**
SIC: **3993** Signs & advertising specialties

(G-5072)
MERIDIAN CONTRACTING INC
Also Called: Meridian Contracting Co
17500 S Sooner Rd (73071-7916)
PHONE................................405 928-5959
Mark Sutton, *President*
Janis Harow, *Vice Pres*
EMP: 99 **Privately Held**
SIC: **1442** 1611 Construction sand mining; highway & street construction

(G-5073)
MERRELLS WELDING & ORNA IR
2219 60th Ave Ne (73026-0639)
PHONE................................405 321-7733
Dominick Merrell, *Partner*
Barney Merrell, *Partner*
Kemmy Merrell, *Partner*
EMP: 3 EST: 1944
SQ FT: 4,000
SALES: 160K **Privately Held**
SIC: **3446** 7692 Architectural metalwork; welding repair

(G-5074)
MG WELDING LLC
2829 Creekview Ter (73071-4711)
PHONE................................405 365-6416
Rae Gammon McKenzie, *Administration*
EMP: 1 EST: 2014
SALES (est): 71.7K **Privately Held**
SIC: **7692** Welding repair

(G-5075)
MID CONTINENT WELL LOG SVCS (PA)
717 26th Ave Nw (73069-6367)
PHONE................................405 360-7333
Guy Pryor, *Owner*
EMP: 9
SALES (est): 3MM **Privately Held**
SIC: **1389** Oil field services

(G-5076)
MJM RESOURCES INC
4003 Potomac Dr (73072-4500)
P.O. Box 722348 (73070-8777)
PHONE................................405 579-4455
Mike Rainer, *President*
EMP: 5
SQ FT: 1,500
SALES (est): 2MM **Privately Held**
SIC: **1311** Crude petroleum production; natural gas production

(G-5077)
MLTL ENTERPRISES LLC
Also Called: Signs Now 373
231 E Robinson St (73069-7814)
PHONE................................405 321-2224
Michael Hughes,
EMP: 6
SALES (est): 761.4K **Privately Held**
WEB: www.signsnow.com
SIC: **3993** Signs & advertising specialties

Norman - Cleveland County (G-5078)

(G-5078)
MONGREL EMPIRE PRESS LLC
133 24th Ave Nw (73069-6320)
PHONE...................405 459-0042
EMP: 1
SALES (est): 37.5K **Privately Held**
SIC: 2741 Miscellaneous publishing

(G-5079)
MONROE NATURAL GAS INC
501 Okmulgee St (73071-4624)
P.O. Box 5687 (73070-5687)
PHONE...................405 321-5647
Brent Maze, *Principal*
EMP: 2
SALES (est): 229.1K **Privately Held**
SIC: 1389 Pumping of oil & gas wells

(G-5080)
MONTGOMERY EXPLORATION COMPANY
Also Called: Minexco
2600 Van Buren St # 2636 (73072-5640)
P.O. Box 722348 (73070-8777)
PHONE...................405 232-1169
Jerry Medina, *Branch Mgr*
EMP: 2
SALES (corp-wide): 541.6K **Privately Held**
SIC: 1311 1382 Crude petroleum production; oil & gas exploration services
PA: Montgomery Exploration Company Ltd
2701 State St
Dallas TX 75204
214 742-1160

(G-5081)
MORROW WOOD PRODUCTS INC
6851 72nd Ave Ne (73026-2718)
PHONE...................405 579-5200
Wayne Morrow, *President*
EMP: 4
SQ FT: 4,800
SALES (est): 375K **Privately Held**
WEB: www.mwpcabinetdoors.com
SIC: 2434 Wood kitchen cabinets

(G-5082)
MPRESS CARDS
3405 Bright St (73072-1906)
PHONE...................405 590-5393
EMP: 2
SALES (est): 59.2K **Privately Held**
SIC: 2741 Miscellaneous publishing

(G-5083)
MRSDISH LLC
1025 E Indian Hills Rd (73071-7944)
PHONE...................405 447-3813
Stacey Riley, *Controller*
Tricia Covel,
EMP: 6
SALES (est): 191K **Privately Held**
SIC: 2389 Apparel & accessories

(G-5084)
NANO LIGHT
4625 Timberidge Cir (73072-1719)
PHONE...................405 579-5662
Zhisheng Shi, *Owner*
EMP: 1
SALES (est): 115.1K **Privately Held**
SIC: 3699 Laser systems & equipment

(G-5085)
NASH TACTICAL LLC
2716 Cimarron Dr (73071-1732)
PHONE...................405 589-6425
EMP: 2
SALES (est): 72.2K **Privately Held**
SIC: 3482 Small arms ammunition

(G-5086)
NATIVE DISTRIBUTING LLC
Also Called: Manufacturer
3300 Deskin Dr (73069-8293)
PHONE...................405 316-9223
Woody Bannister, *CEO*
EMP: 60
SALES (est): 68.5K **Privately Held**
SIC: 2023 3999 Dietary supplements, dairy & non-dairy based;

(G-5087)
NATIVE SPIRITS WINERY LLC
10500 E Lindsey St (73026-8245)
PHONE...................405 329-9942
Ric Vollmer, *Mng Member*
Staci Vollmer, *Master*
EMP: 2
SALES: 100K **Privately Held**
WEB: www.nativespiritswinery.com
SIC: 2084 5921 5182 Wines; wine; bottling wines & liquors

(G-5088)
NATURAL RESOURCES OPER LLC
1831 E Imhoff Rd Ste 100 (73071-1295)
PHONE...................405 997-3869
Curtis Harris,
▼ EMP: 15
SALES (est): 1.3MM **Privately Held**
SIC: 1382 Oil & gas exploration services

(G-5089)
NATURALOCK SOLUTIONS LLC
3201 Crystal Spring Dr (73072-1316)
PHONE...................405 812-9058
Gary Rayburn, *Mng Member*
Robert Maurer,
EMP: 5
SALES: 300K **Privately Held**
SIC: 2834 Pharmaceutical preparations

(G-5090)
NEW MOON VINEYARD
4717 Tanglewood Ct (73072-3118)
PHONE...................405 364-8655
Dennis Hutchison, *Administration*
EMP: 1 EST: 2014
SALES (est): 67.7K **Privately Held**
SIC: 2084 Wines

(G-5091)
NEWSPAPER HOLDING INC
Also Called: Norman Transcript
215 E Comanche St (73069-6007)
P.O. Box 1058 (73070-1058)
PHONE...................405 321-1800
Mark Millsat, *Principal*
EMP: 69 **Privately Held**
SIC: 2711 Commercial printing & newspaper publishing combined
HQ: Newspaper Holding, Inc.
425 Locust St
Johnstown PA 15901
814 532-5102

(G-5092)
NEXTTHOUGHT LLC
301 David Boren Ste 3030 (73072)
PHONE...................405 673-5588
Ken Parker, *CEO*
Jeffrey Meuhring, *President*
Michael Linville, *Manager*
EMP: 42
SALES (est): 962.7K **Privately Held**
SIC: 7372 Prepackaged software

(G-5093)
NITRO LIFT TECHNOLOGIES LLC
Also Called: Nitrogen Lifting Technologies
4009 S Harvey Ave (73072-9751)
PHONE...................405 618-3026
EMP: 1
SALES (corp-wide): 30.4MM **Privately Held**
SIC: 2813 Industrial gases
PA: Nitro Lift Technologies, L.L.C.
8980 Ok Highway 1 S
Mill Creek OK 74856
580 371-3700

(G-5094)
NORMAN COMPUTERS
916 W Main St (73069-6921)
PHONE...................405 292-9501
Mark Deaver, *Owner*
EMP: 10
SQ FT: 3,500
SALES (est): 875.8K **Privately Held**
SIC: 7372 5734 7371 7378 Prepackaged software; computer & software stores; computer software systems analysis & design, custom; computer maintenance & repair; computer integrated systems design

(G-5095)
NORTHSHORE CORP
2503 S Berry Rd (73072-6904)
PHONE...................405 329-8026
Gary Cox, *Principal*
EMP: 2
SALES (est): 150.2K **Privately Held**
SIC: 1382 Oil & gas exploration services

(G-5096)
NXT LVL WOODWORKING LLC
19421 8 A St (73026-9412)
PHONE...................405 613-6637
Joe Doiron, *Principal*
EMP: 1
SALES (est): 59.5K **Privately Held**
SIC: 2431 Millwork

(G-5097)
OCTAGON RESOURCES INC (PA)
Also Called: Hjd Gas
1831 E Imhoff Rd Ste 100 (73071-1295)
PHONE...................405 366-8885
G Curtis Harris, *President*
Max L Holloway, *Vice Pres*
Brian S Theriault, *Vice Pres*
▼ EMP: 10
SQ FT: 1,500
SALES (est): 3MM **Privately Held**
SIC: 1311 2911 Crude petroleum production; gases & liquefied petroleum gases

(G-5098)
OKLAHOMA BIOREFINING CORP
1611 Southern Heights Ave (73072-5756)
PHONE...................405 201-1824
Chris Simpson, *CEO*
EMP: 2
SALES: 50K **Privately Held**
SIC: 2869 Industrial organic chemicals

(G-5099)
OKLAHOMA COATING SPECIALISTS
1900 Robin Ridge Dr (73072-2832)
PHONE...................405 447-0448
Mike Bearrow, *Executive*
EMP: 2
SALES (est): 82.1K **Privately Held**
SIC: 3479 Coating of metals & formed products

(G-5100)
OKLAHOMA ELECTRIC COOPERATIVE (PA)
242 24th Ave Nw (73069-6371)
P.O. Box 1208 (73070-1208)
PHONE...................405 321-2024
Max Meek, *General Mgr*
Joe Bartram, *Vice Pres*
John Spencer, *Vice Pres*
Brad Keener, *Engineer*
Michael Preston O'Brien II, *CFO*
EMP: 98
SQ FT: 100,000
SALES: 128MM **Privately Held**
WEB: www.okcoop.org
SIC: 4911 2721 Distribution, electric power; periodicals

(G-5101)
OKLAHOMA TERRITORY LAND CO LLC
2007 Trailview Ct (73072-6654)
PHONE...................405 329-1142
Dwight N Johnson, *Mng Member*
EMP: 1
SALES (est): 120K **Privately Held**
SIC: 1382 7389 Oil & gas exploration services;

(G-5102)
OLIVER INDUSTRIES LLC
3901 24th Ave Se Apt 1 (73071-0807)
PHONE...................405 314-4423
EMP: 2 EST: 2015
SALES (est): 64.7K **Privately Held**
SIC: 3999 Manufacturing industries

(G-5103)
ORANGE OIL LLC
2401 Tee Cir Ste 203 (73069-6207)
PHONE...................405 701-3505
Eric Fleske, *Principal*
EMP: 2
SALES (est): 74.4K **Privately Held**
SIC: 2899 Orange oil

(G-5104)
ORIGINAL PRODUCTIONS PUBG LLC
612 Leopard Lily Dr (73069-9606)
PHONE...................405 420-9559
Blainton Storey, *Principal*
EMP: 1
SALES (est): 37.5K **Privately Held**
SIC: 2741 Miscellaneous publishing

(G-5105)
OTO-BIOMECHANICS LLC
201 Stephenson Pkwy # 130 (73072-2050)
PHONE...................405 325-6668
Marcus Brown, *Principal*
Chenkai Dai, *Principal*
Rong Gan, *Principal*
EMP: 3
SALES (est): 220.3K **Privately Held**
SIC: 3845 Electromedical equipment

(G-5106)
P & L WELDING AND FABRICATION
2021 Alameda St Apt 712 (73071-2223)
PHONE...................660 563-1775
Larry Myers, *Principal*
EMP: 1
SALES (est): 28.1K **Privately Held**
SIC: 7692 Welding repair

(G-5107)
P F BEELER LLC
1012 Nottingham Cir (73072-7522)
PHONE...................405 364-0799
Phil Beeler,
EMP: 2
SALES (est): 218.5K **Privately Held**
SIC: 1311 Crude petroleum production; natural gas production

(G-5108)
PAINT PROS INC
2009 Westbrooke Ter (73072-5845)
PHONE...................405 226-8898
Hugo Pike, *President*
EMP: 1
SALES (est): 90.8K **Privately Held**
SIC: 2851 Paints & allied products

(G-5109)
PASSION BERRI
1204 N Interstate Dr (73072-3354)
PHONE...................405 310-6669
Passion Berri, *Principal*
EMP: 4
SALES (est): 252.8K **Privately Held**
SIC: 2026 Yogurt

(G-5110)
PATTERNWORK VENEERING INC
303 E Main St (73069-1306)
P.O. Box 5027 (73070-5027)
PHONE...................405 447-1800
William Hall, *President*
Dan West, *Manager*
EMP: 3
SALES (est): 245.6K **Privately Held**
SIC: 2499 3083 Decorative wood & woodwork; laminated plastics plate & sheet

(G-5111)
PAUL PHILP GCHMICAL CONSLT LLC
4212 Brookfield Dr (73072-2896)
PHONE...................405 325-4469
Richard Philp, *Principal*
EMP: 1
SALES (est): 37.6K **Privately Held**
SIC: 8748 1389 Environmental consultant; oil consultants

Norman - Cleveland County (G-5145)

(G-5112)
PAUL ZIERT & ASSOCIATES INC (PA)
Also Called: International Gymnastic Mag
3214 Bart Conner Dr (73072-2406)
PHONE.................................405 364-5344
Paul Ziert, *President*
John Crumlish, *Editor*
Ben Fox, *Treasurer*
Christian Ivanov, *Director*
EMP: 55
SALES (est): 2.2MM **Privately Held**
SIC: 7999 5136 5137 2721 Gymnastic instruction, non-membership; sportswear, men's & boys'; sportswear, women's & children's; magazines: publishing only, not printed on site; sports clubs, managers & promoters; sporting & athletic goods

(G-5113)
PERMIAN SOFTWARE LLC
626 Cedarbrook Dr (73072-4221)
PHONE.................................405 329-6397
Will Hadgson, *Owner*
EMP: 2
SALES (est): 69.2K **Privately Held**
SIC: 7372 Prepackaged software

(G-5114)
PETRO SPEED INC
4900 Pullin Ln (73069-8116)
PHONE.................................405 364-6785
Philip E Gibson, *President*
EMP: 1 **EST:** 1982
SQ FT: 2,400
SALES (est): 154.5K **Privately Held**
SIC: 1311 8741 Crude petroleum production; management services

(G-5115)
PICKARD PROJECTS INC
Also Called: Dreams Reflected
545 S Pickard Ave (73069-5533)
PHONE.................................405 321-7072
Jerry Steele, *President*
Debbei Steele, *Corp Secy*
EMP: 4 **EST:** 1999
SALES (est): 220K **Privately Held**
SIC: 3429 Furniture builders' & other household hardware

(G-5116)
PINPOINT WIRE TECHNOLOGIES LLC
3505 N Interstate Dr (73069-8282)
PHONE.................................405 447-6900
EMP: 5 **EST:** 2015
SALES (est): 653.1K **Privately Held**
SIC: 3315 Wire & fabricated wire products

(G-5117)
PORT 40 INC
317 Towry Dr (73069-9607)
PHONE.................................405 360-9100
David C Kempf, *Principal*
EMP: 6
SALES (est): 555.7K **Privately Held**
WEB: www.port40.com
SIC: 3823 8744 3825 7371 Computer interface equipment for industrial process control; industrial process control instruments; facilities support services; instruments to measure electricity; custom computer programming services

(G-5118)
POWER SERVICES LLC
Also Called: Sooner Sandblasting
6700 103rd Ave Ne (73026-9735)
PHONE.................................405 677-7716
David Spaulding, *Mng Member*
EMP: 1
SALES (est): 68.6K **Privately Held**
SIC: 1799 1721 3471 Sandblasting of building exteriors; coating of metal structures at construction site; exterior cleaning, including sandblasting; industrial painting; sand blasting of metal parts

(G-5119)
PRAIRIE EXPLORATION CO
100 N Santa Fe Ave # 200 (73069-7101)
P.O. Box 720052 (73070-4036)
PHONE.................................405 360-7077
Vernon L Smith, *President*
Jane E Miller, *Treasurer*
EMP: 3
SQ FT: 2,000
SALES (est): 288.1K **Privately Held**
SIC: 1381 Drilling oil & gas wells
PA: L Smith Vernon & Associates Inc
3940 W Tecumseh Rd
Norman OK 73072

(G-5120)
PRAIRIE OIL & GAS
330 W Gray St Ste 180 (73069-7118)
PHONE.................................405 464-6060
EMP: 2
SALES (est): 160.7K **Privately Held**
WEB: www.prairieog.com
SIC: 1382 Oil & gas exploration services

(G-5121)
PRESCRIPTION CARE LLC
800 W Rock Creek Rd # 117 (73069-8586)
PHONE.................................405 310-9230
Emmanuel Torres, *Mng Member*
EMP: 3 **EST:** 2015
SALES: 700K **Privately Held**
SIC: 2834 5122 Proprietary drug products; drugs & drug proprietaries

(G-5122)
PRINTERS BINDERY INC
4417 Brookfield Dr (73072-2826)
PHONE.................................405 236-8423
Robert I Miller, *President*
Kelley Miller, *Treasurer*
EMP: 20 **EST:** 1958
SQ FT: 17,500
SALES (est): 1.5MM **Privately Held**
WEB: www.printersbinderyinc.net
SIC: 2789 Trade binding services

(G-5123)
PRO TEC ORTHOTICS COMPANY
4505 Beckett Ct (73072-3411)
PHONE.................................405 366-7688
Reed John, *Principal*
EMP: 3 **EST:** 2013
SALES (est): 231.6K **Privately Held**
WEB: www.protecorthotics.com
SIC: 3842 Orthopedic appliances

(G-5124)
PRODUCTIVE CLUTTER INC
Also Called: Suzy's Creations
753 Asp Ave (73069-4901)
PHONE.................................405 447-3839
Suzanne Cannon, *President*
John Cannon, *Vice Pres*
Dorothy Durkee, *Treasurer*
EMP: 3
SQ FT: 1,700
SALES (est): 200K **Privately Held**
SIC: 5947 7389 7219 2395 Gift shop; textile & apparel services; garment alteration & repair shop; embroidery products, except schiffli machine; screen printing

(G-5125)
PROFESSIONAL PRTG NORMAN LLC
913 Golden Eagle Dr (73072-8167)
PHONE.................................405 823-3383
EMP: 2
SALES (est): 189.9K **Privately Held**
SIC: 2752 Commercial printing, offset

(G-5126)
QUALITY BUILDINGS INC
714 E 34th St (73070)
PHONE.................................888 430-7721
EMP: 2 **EST:** 2006
SALES (est): 310K **Privately Held**
SIC: 3448 Mfg Prefabricated Metal Buildings

(G-5127)
QUALITY BUILDINGS INC
2450 W Robinson St (73069-6572)
P.O. Box 722217 (73070-8675)
PHONE.................................405 364-0516
Daniel Remington, *Principal*
EMP: 21
SALES (est): 5.1MM **Privately Held**
WEB: www.qbiusa.com
SIC: 3448 Buildings, portable: prefabricated metal

(G-5128)
RA JAC INC
1614 Wilshire Ave (73072-6037)
P.O. Box 720840 (73070-4656)
PHONE.................................405 701-5222
Jackie M Nelson, *President*
Mike Nelson, *Vice Pres*
Pamela Bowie, *Admin Sec*
EMP: 3
SALES (est): 330.1K **Privately Held**
SIC: 1381 Drilling oil & gas wells

(G-5129)
RAPID JACK SOLUTIONS INC
4101 Stonehurst St (73072-1791)
PHONE.................................405 203-3131
Bryan Bohnert, *President*
Charla Bohnert, *Treasurer*
EMP: 6 **EST:** 2012
SALES (est): 184.2K **Privately Held**
SIC: 7371 7372 8711 7389 Custom computer programming services; application computer software; engineering services; consulting engineer; drafting service, except temporary help

(G-5130)
RC CUSTOM WOODWORK
905 Eagle Cliff Dr (73072-8414)
PHONE.................................405 414-1162
Robert Buchanan, *Principal*
EMP: 1
SALES (est): 54.1K **Privately Held**
SIC: 2431 Millwork

(G-5131)
RELIANCE PRESSURE CONTROL
4845 Se 44th St (73072-9622)
P.O. Box 923, Chickasha (73023-0923)
PHONE.................................405 320-5074
EMP: 2 **EST:** 2014
SALES (est): 239.9K **Privately Held**
SIC: 1389 Oil field services

(G-5132)
RIVERSIDE RANCH LLC (PA)
2630 12th Ave Nw (73069-8535)
PHONE.................................405 360-7300
Tracey Parker, *Principal*
EMP: 16
SQ FT: 6,024
SALES (est): 2.3MM **Privately Held**
SIC: 2493 Fiberboard, other vegetable pulp

(G-5133)
ROCK CREEK WREATHS LLC
3025 Yosemite Dr (73071-2919)
PHONE.................................405 701-3421
Joanne Weatherford, *Principal*
EMP: 2 **EST:** 2014
SALES (est): 101K **Privately Held**
SIC: 3999 Wreaths, artificial

(G-5134)
ROGER MAGERUS
Also Called: Magerus Welding & Trucking
1602 Paso De Vaca Dr (73026-3530)
PHONE.................................405 364-7231
Roger Magerus, *Owner*
EMP: 1
SALES (est): 35K **Privately Held**
SIC: 7692 4119 Welding repair; local passenger transportation

(G-5135)
ROSEWOOD DESIGNS
2278 Industrial Blvd # 105 (73069-8583)
PHONE.................................405 329-0600
David Taylor, *Owner*
EMP: 2
SALES (est): 200K **Privately Held**
SIC: 3911 Jewelry, precious metal

(G-5136)
ROX EXPLORATION INC
2416 Palmer Cir (73069-6301)
PHONE.................................405 329-0009
Russ Oxsen, *President*
Linda G Oxsen, *Admin Sec*
EMP: 5
SQ FT: 1,604
SALES (est): 789.5K **Privately Held**
SIC: 1382 1311 Geological exploration, oil & gas field; crude petroleum production; natural gas production

(G-5137)
SAND RESOURCES LLC (PA)
3334 W Main St Pmb 154 (73072-4805)
PHONE.................................405 573-0242
Cecile Alexander, *CEO*
Gregory R Alexander, *President*
EMP: 3
SALES (est): 277.9K **Privately Held**
SIC: 1389 Pumping of oil & gas wells

(G-5138)
SCHULTZ ROOF TRUSS INC
1037 W Adkins Hill Rd (73072-9116)
PHONE.................................405 364-6530
Greg Schultz, *President*
Virginia Schultz, *Corp Secy*
EMP: 4
SQ FT: 6,000
SALES (est): 530.1K **Privately Held**
SIC: 2439 Trusses, wooden roof

(G-5139)
SCISSOR TAIL CUSTOM HOLSTER
1501 Morland Ave (73071-4606)
PHONE.................................405 595-6315
Daniel Petrilla, *Principal*
EMP: 2
SALES (est): 185.1K **Privately Held**
SIC: 3199 Holsters, leather

(G-5140)
SEDONA ENERGY LLC
4611 Churchill Downs Dr (73069-8202)
PHONE.................................405 973-7366
Kevin Ferdowsian, *Principal*
EMP: 2
SALES (est): 112K **Privately Held**
SIC: 1382 Oil & gas exploration services

(G-5141)
SEW GRAPHICS PLUS INC
1323 Spruce Dr (73072-6813)
PHONE.................................405 364-1707
EMP: 2
SALES: 100K **Privately Held**
SIC: 2752 2395 Lithographic Commercial Printing Pleating/Stitching Services

(G-5142)
SF WELDING AND BORING LLC
18501 Valley Dr (73026-9583)
PHONE.................................405 831-8602
EMP: 1
SALES (est): 25K **Privately Held**
SIC: 7692 Welding repair

(G-5143)
SHACK LITTLE GLASS
110 Lakeside Dr (73026-0721)
PHONE.................................405 364-2649
Martha Baldwin, *Owner*
EMP: 2
SALES (est): 131.3K **Privately Held**
SIC: 3231 Products of purchased glass

(G-5144)
SHAVE SOFTWARE LLC
1004 Bentbrook Pl (73072-4019)
PHONE.................................405 366-2168
Steve Jones, *Principal*
EMP: 2
SALES (est): 42.1K **Privately Held**
SIC: 7372 Prepackaged software

(G-5145)
SIGN LANGUAGE
220 N Crawford Ave (73069-7220)
PHONE.................................405 360-7500
Monty Jumper, *Owner*
EMP: 1
SALES (est): 82.5K **Privately Held**
SIC: 3993 5999 Signs, not made in custom sign painting shops; banners

Norman - Cleveland County (G-5146) — GEOGRAPHIC SECTION

(G-5146)
SIMPLY VINTAGE TEES LLC
3313 Valley Mdw (73071-3675)
PHONE..................405 239-0444
Melissa Parks, *Principal*
EMP: 2
SALES (est): 87.4K **Privately Held**
SIC: 2759 Screen printing

(G-5147)
SKYY SCREEN PRINTING
3920 W Indian Hills Rd (73072-1247)
PHONE..................405 412-4646
Hobi Haque, *Owner*
EMP: 1
SALES (est): 64.6K **Privately Held**
SIC: 2759 Letterpress & screen printing

(G-5148)
SLOW HAND MANUFACTURING L
980 Bluestem (73069-9709)
PHONE..................918 937-3046
EMP: 2
SALES (est): 84.3K **Privately Held**
SIC: 3999 Manufacturing industries

(G-5149)
SOO & ASSOCIATES
4029 Sam Gordon Dr (73072-4023)
PHONE..................405 397-5072
Samuel Osisanya, *Owner*
EMP: 1
SALES (est): 79.1K **Privately Held**
SIC: 1389 Oil consultants

(G-5150)
SOONER PRO ASSEMBLY
203 Keith St (73069-5923)
PHONE..................405 838-2838
Nick Hodgens, *Principal*
EMP: 1 EST: 2016
SALES (est): 39.6K **Privately Held**
SIC: 3999 Manufacturing industries

(G-5151)
SOONER SIGNS
2533 Hollywood Ave (73072-6727)
PHONE..................405 503-8902
Lindsey Francis, *Principal*
EMP: 1
SALES (est): 46K **Privately Held**
SIC: 3993 Signs & advertising specialties

(G-5152)
SOUTHWESTERN WIRE INC (PA)
3505 N Interstate Dr (73069-8282)
P.O. Box Cc (73070-7103)
PHONE..................405 447-6900
David Weinand, *President*
Steven Peters, *Exec VP*
Randy Gibbs, *Plant Mgr*
Robert Martella, *CFO*
Kathleen Moore, *Treasurer*
EMP: 130
SQ FT: 16,000
SALES (est): 52.5MM **Privately Held**
SIC: 3496 Miscellaneous fabricated wire products

(G-5153)
SPARK SOMETHING CANDLES LLC
1734 W Robinson St (73069-7392)
PHONE..................405 872-5673
EMP: 1
SALES (est): 39.6K **Privately Held**
SIC: 3999 Mfg Misc Products

(G-5154)
SSEC
3360 Allspice Run (73026-4540)
PHONE..................405 321-0916
EMP: 2 EST: 2011
SALES (est): 103.6K **Privately Held**
SIC: 3999 Manufacturing industries

(G-5155)
ST JOHN
9701 Brush Creek Rd (73026-8231)
PHONE..................405 364-1917
David Stjohn, *Principal*
EMP: 3 EST: 2011

SALES (est): 194K **Privately Held**
SIC: 2339 Women's & misses' outerwear

(G-5156)
STARLING ASSOC INC
1324 Brookside Dr (73072-6348)
PHONE..................405 740-8668
Kenneth Starling, *Chairman*
EMP: 1
SALES (est): 79.4K **Privately Held**
SIC: 7372 Prepackaged software

(G-5157)
STEDEN OIL CORP
330 W Gray St (73069-7129)
P.O. Box 720187 (73070-4144)
PHONE..................405 364-7611
Stephen Lunsford, *President*
EMP: 3
SALES: 250K **Privately Held**
SIC: 1382 Oil & gas exploration services

(G-5158)
STEWART TECH
1331 Quality Ave (73071-7962)
PHONE..................405 292-8214
EMP: 2
SALES (est): 207.8K **Privately Held**
SIC: 3599 Mfg Industrial Machinery

(G-5159)
STEWART TECH INCORPORATED
2112 Natchez Dr (73071-2024)
PHONE..................405 831-9316
David Stewart, *Owner*
Pam Stewart, *CFO*
EMP: 2
SQ FT: 7,000
SALES: 90K **Privately Held**
SIC: 3599 Machine shop, jobbing & repair

(G-5160)
STONEHOUSE MARKETING SVCS LLC
2039 Industrial Blvd (73069-8511)
PHONE..................405 360-5674
David Tucker, *COO*
Krista Moore, *Vice Pres*
Diane Tucker, *Sales Mgr*
Gena Copeland, *Accounts Mgr*
Michael Marooney, *Sales Staff*
▲ EMP: 70
SQ FT: 35,000
SALES (est): 22.3MM **Privately Held**
WEB: www.stonehousemarketing.com
SIC: 3089 2672 Identification cards, plastic; coated & laminated paper

(G-5161)
STRATA VIEW OPERATING LLC
1601 36th Ave Nw Ste 210 (73072-3269)
PHONE..................405 364-1613
Rodney D Thornton, *President*
EMP: 2
SALES (est): 146.4K **Privately Held**
SIC: 1389 Oil & gas field services

(G-5162)
STROP SHOPPE LLC
110 W Dale St (73069-8711)
PHONE..................775 557-8767
Jason Conkling, *Finance Dir*
Kali McLennan,
Sarah Croft, *Admin Sec*
Larry Barnett,
EMP: 3
SALES (est): 291.5K **Privately Held**
SIC: 2844 2841 Shaving preparations; lotions, shaving; soap & other detergents

(G-5163)
SUBLIME SIGNS LLC
912 N Flood Ave (73069-7642)
PHONE..................405 364-1700
Jason Jwells, *Mng Member*
EMP: 1
SALES: 90K **Privately Held**
SIC: 3993 8748 Signs, not made in custom sign painting shops; business consulting

(G-5164)
SUMMIT ENERGY SERVICES INC
1013 N University Blvd (73069-7619)
PHONE..................405 366-9999
EMP: 1
SALES (est): 35K **Privately Held**
SIC: 5947 1389 Ret Gifts/Novelties Oil/Gas Field Services

(G-5165)
SUMMIT ESP LLC
2720 Classen Blvd (73071-4016)
PHONE..................405 434-1257
John Kenner, *President*
Shamon Davis, *Administration*
EMP: 500 **Publicly Held**
SIC: 3585 Heat pumps, electric
HQ: Summit Esp, Llc
835 W 41st St
Tulsa OK 74107

(G-5166)
SWEETWATER EXPLORATION LLC
121 S Santa Fe Ave Ste A (73069-5636)
PHONE..................405 329-1967
David Millington,
EMP: 2
SQ FT: 1,000
SALES (est): 506.2K **Privately Held**
SIC: 1382 1311 Oil & gas exploration services; crude petroleum production; natural gas production

(G-5167)
SWINK WELDING LLC
4209 Snowy Owl Dr (73072-8403)
PHONE..................405 294-0114
EMP: 1
SALES (est): 32.3K **Privately Held**
SIC: 7692 Welding Repair

(G-5168)
SYLVAN CROFT WOODWORKS
7900 E Rock Creek Rd (73026-3165)
PHONE..................405 329-6668
Bill Johnson, *Principal*
EMP: 2
SALES (est): 161.8K **Privately Held**
SIC: 2431 Millwork

(G-5169)
T D CRAIGHEAD
Also Called: T D Crghead Oil Gas Invstments
100 N Santa Fe Ave # 100 (73069-7101)
P.O. Box 1707 (73070-1707)
PHONE..................405 329-2229
T D Craighead, *Owner*
EMP: 1
SALES (est): 68.2K **Privately Held**
SIC: 1389 Oil field services

(G-5170)
TAKEDA PHRMCEUTICALS N AMER IN
4405 Vincent St (73072-4473)
PHONE..................405 317-7495
Josh Calfy, *Principal*
Brody Onan, *District Mgr*
EMP: 3
SALES (est): 147.1K **Privately Held**
WEB: www.tpna.com
SIC: 2834 Pharmaceutical preparations

(G-5171)
TECHNICAL ENERGY SERVICES INC
6301 E Cedar Lane Rd (73026-5513)
P.O. Box 720069 (73070-4053)
PHONE..................405 329-8196
William Hicks, *President*
EMP: 1
SALES (est): 400K **Privately Held**
SIC: 1311 Crude petroleum & natural gas

(G-5172)
TELOS PAYMENT PROCESSING LLC
205 E Main St (73069-1304)
PHONE..................405 321-0474
Andrea L Worden Esq, *Principal*
EMP: 2

SALES (est): 109.6K **Privately Held**
WEB: www.telosprocessing.com
SIC: 7372 Prepackaged software

(G-5173)
TGV ROCKETS INC
2420 Springer Dr Ste 100 (73069-3965)
PHONE..................405 366-0779
Kent Ewing, *CTO*
EMP: 2
SALES (est): 77.4K **Privately Held**
SIC: 3812 Search & navigation equipment

(G-5174)
TITAN FUEL SYSTEMS LLC
2201 Tecumseh Dr (73069-1002)
PHONE..................405 788-2412
EMP: 2
SALES (est): 88.9K **Privately Held**
SIC: 3443 Fuel tanks (oil, gas, etc.): metal plate

(G-5175)
TONER EXPRESS
2624 Butler Dr (73069-5015)
PHONE..................405 517-8817
EMP: 2
SALES (est): 140.2K **Privately Held**
SIC: 2759 Commercial printing

(G-5176)
TOP QUALITY DOORS LLC
427 Highland Pkwy (73069-7647)
P.O. Box 720262 (73070-4196)
PHONE..................405 579-3667
Kelly Belvin, *Mng Member*
Selena Belvin, *Mng Member*
EMP: 4
SQ FT: 3,600
SALES: 550K **Privately Held**
SIC: 3446 Gates, ornamental metal

(G-5177)
TOTAL BEVERAGE SERVICES LLC
2451 Van Buren St (73072-5639)
PHONE..................405 366-1344
EMP: 1 **Privately Held**
SIC: 2086 Water, pasteurized: packaged in cans, bottles, etc.
PA: Total Beverage Services Llc
16301 N Rockwell Ave
Edmond OK 73013

(G-5178)
TOWNE PUBLISHING LLC
4017 Nw Pioneer Cir (73072-1222)
PHONE..................405 473-7436
Rebekah E Collins, *Principal*
EMP: 1
SALES (est): 37.5K **Privately Held**
SIC: 2741 Miscellaneous publishing

(G-5179)
TRACKUM INC
Also Called: Trackum Software
1525 Camden Way (73069-5306)
P.O. Box 6250, Moore (73153-0250)
PHONE..................405 799-4863
Christopher Collins, *President*
EMP: 3
SALES: 200K **Privately Held**
SIC: 7372 7371 Prepackaged software; computer software systems analysis & design, custom

(G-5180)
TRANS-TEL CENTRAL INC (PA)
2851 N Flood Ave (73069-8475)
PHONE..................405 447-5025
Carol Harper, *CEO*
Jay Elison, *CEO*
Audrey Pirtle, *President*
Bryan Shank, *President*
Jane Morgan, *Chairman*
▼ EMP: 104
SQ FT: 25,000
SALES (est): 28.2MM **Privately Held**
WEB: www.trans-tel.com
SIC: 1731 4813 1522 1623 Fiber optic cable installation; telephone/video communications; renovation, hotel/motel; communication line & transmission tower construction; industrial plant construction; mine development, nonmetallic minerals

▲ = Import ▼ = Export
◆ = Import/Export

GEOGRAPHIC SECTION   Nowata - Nowata County (G-5209)

(G-5181)
TRANSCRIPT PRESS INC
222 E Eufaula St (73069-6051)
P.O. Box 6440 (73070-6440)
PHONE.................................405 360-7999
Ron Minnix, *President*
Lori Kemmet, *Vice Pres*
Eric Wullich, *Plant Mgr*
Marcy Leonard, *Human Res Mgr*
Charles Bacon, *Marketing Staff*
EMP: 34
SQ FT: 60,000
SALES (est): 5.8MM **Privately Held**
SIC: 2752 2796 2791 2789 Commercial printing, offset; platemaking services; typesetting; bookbinding & related work

(G-5182)
TRANSMISSION CENTER
4015 60th Ave Ne (73026-0409)
PHONE.................................405 329-4620
Melvin Binson, *Owner*
EMP: 2
SALES (est): 171.6K **Privately Held**
SIC: 3714 7537 Transmissions, motor vehicle; automotive transmission repair shops

(G-5183)
TUXPRO SOFTWARE & DEVELOPMENT
517 Trinidad Dr (73072-5143)
PHONE.................................405 812-1334
Lanny Lamphere, *Principal*
EMP: 2
SALES (est): 60.4K **Privately Held**
SIC: 7372 Prepackaged software

(G-5184)
TWO SOCKS LLC
3914 Warwick Dr (73072-3217)
PHONE.................................405 535-4753
Gloria Mahaffey, *Principal*
EMP: 2
SALES (est): 73.4K **Privately Held**
SIC: 2252 Socks

(G-5185)
UNIVERSITY OF OKLAHOMA
Also Called: World Literature Today
3000 Chautauqua Ave # 111 (73072-7734)
PHONE.................................405 325-4531
Robert Condavis, *Branch Mgr*
EMP: 8
SALES (corp-wide): 754.6MM **Privately Held**
SIC: 2721 8221 Magazines: publishing & printing; university
PA: University Of Oklahoma
    660 Parrington Oval
    Norman OK 73019
    405 325-0000

(G-5186)
UNIVERSITY OF OKLAHOMA
Also Called: Ou Press
1005 Asp Ave Rm 117 (73019-1079)
PHONE.................................405 325-3189
Marielle Hoefnagels, *Editor*
John Drayton, *Director*
Lori Stevens, *Associate Dir*
EMP: 47
SALES (corp-wide): 754.6MM **Privately Held**
SIC: 8221 2731 University; book publishing
PA: University Of Oklahoma
    660 Parrington Oval
    Norman OK 73019
    405 325-0000

(G-5187)
UNIVERSITY OF OKLAHOMA
U of OK Press
4100 28th Ave Nw (73069-8218)
PHONE.................................405 325-3276
John Drayton, *Director*
EMP: 45
SALES (corp-wide): 754.6MM **Privately Held**
SIC: 8299 2731 Educational services; book publishing
PA: University Of Oklahoma
    660 Parrington Oval
    Norman OK 73019
    405 325-0000

(G-5188)
UNIVERSITY OF OKLAHOMA
Oklahoma Daily, The
860 Van Vleet Oval 149a (73019-2035)
PHONE.................................405 325-3666
Kathryn Stacy, *Manager*
Brian Ringer, *Director*
EMP: 150
SALES (corp-wide): 754.6MM **Privately Held**
SIC: 2711 8221 Newspapers; university
PA: University Of Oklahoma
    660 Parrington Oval
    Norman OK 73019
    405 325-0000

(G-5189)
UNIVERSITY OF OKLAHOMA PRESS
2800 Venture Dr (73069-8216)
PHONE.................................405 325-2000
EMP: 1
SALES (est): 37.5K **Privately Held**
SIC: 2741 Miscellaneous publishing

(G-5190)
UTEC CORPORATION LLC
222 E Eufaula St Ste 120 (73069-6048)
PHONE.................................405 928-7061
Suresh Subramanian, *Mng Member*
James C Stafford,
James Stafford,
David P Taylor,
EMP: 1
SALES (est): 209.5K **Privately Held**
SIC: 2892 1629 Explosives; blasting contractor, except building demolition
PA: Wimase International, Inc.
    222 E Eufaula St Ste 120
    Norman OK 73069
    405 928-7061

(G-5191)
VALIANT ARTFL LIFT SLTIONS LLC
5729 Huettner Ct (73069-9512)
PHONE.................................405 605-4567
EMP: 116
SALES (corp-wide): 15.9MM **Privately Held**
SIC: 3533 7353 Oil field machinery & equipment; oil field equipment, rental or leasing
PA: Valiant Artificial Lift Solutions, Llc
    1 Leadership Sq N
    Oklahoma City OK 73102
    405 605-4567

(G-5192)
VAN EATON READY MIX INC
17301 S Sunnylane Rd (73071-7917)
PHONE.................................405 912-4825
Jordan Everett, *Safety Mgr*
Pam Skeen, *Branch Mgr*
EMP: 26 **Privately Held**
WEB: www.vaneatonreadymix.com
SIC: 3273 Ready-mixed concrete
PA: Van Eaton Ready Mix, Inc.
    8 Timber Pond
    Shawnee OK 74804

(G-5193)
VAN EATON READY MIX INC
2905 Water View Ct (73071-4140)
PHONE.................................405 364-2028
John Vaneaton, *Branch Mgr*
EMP: 3 **Privately Held**
WEB: www.vaneatonreadymix.com
SIC: 3273 Ready-mixed concrete
PA: Van Eaton Ready Mix, Inc.
    8 Timber Pond
    Shawnee OK 74804

(G-5194)
VERNON L SMITH & ASSOC INC (PA)
3940 W Tecumseh Rd (73072-1707)
P.O. Box 720053 (73070-4037)
PHONE.................................405 360-3374
Vernon L Smith, *President*
Matthew Smith, *Vice Pres*
EMP: 9
SQ FT: 2,000
SALES (est): 1.3MM **Privately Held**
SIC: 1381 Drilling oil & gas wells

(G-5195)
VICKERS SAND AND GRAVEL
3976 S Harvey Ave (73072-9782)
P.O. Box 249, Lindsay (73052-0249)
PHONE.................................405 573-1989
Stephen F Vickers, *President*
EMP: 4 **EST:** 2014
SALES (est): 117K **Privately Held**
SIC: 1442 Construction sand & gravel

(G-5196)
VICTORTEES LLC
1860 W Robinson St Apt B (73069-7322)
PHONE.................................405 889-7763
EMP: 3
SALES (est): 119.6K **Privately Held**
SIC: 2759 Screen printing

(G-5197)
WE-GO PERFORATORS INC
Also Called: A&A Tank Truck
2500 Mackie Dr Ste 100 (73072)
P.O. Box 722588 (73070-8969)
PHONE.................................405 364-3618
Marshall Bracken, *Manager*
EMP: 5
SALES (corp-wide): 1.8MM **Privately Held**
SIC: 1389 Oil field services
PA: We-Go Perforators, Inc.
    8717 County Road 3470
    Ada OK 74820
    580 332-1346

(G-5198)
WEIBEE STEEL INC
5009 Se 44th St (73072-9715)
P.O. Box 721381 (73070-8063)
PHONE.................................405 360-7055
Mike Martin, *President*
Loanna Martin, *Corp Secy*
Jamie South, *Receptionist*
EMP: 10
SQ FT: 4,800
SALES (est): 2.3MM **Privately Held**
SIC: 3441 Building components, structural steel

(G-5199)
WESTWOOD PRINTING CENTER
2403 N Porter Ave (73071-7241)
PHONE.................................405 366-8961
EMP: 4
SQ FT: 1,500
SALES (est): 285.3K **Privately Held**
SIC: 2752 2796 2791 Commercial printing, offset; platemaking services; typesetting

(G-5200)
WFWOODWORKS LLC
1912 Grassland Dr (73072-2915)
PHONE.................................405 740-8920
Walter Fox, *Principal*
EMP: 1
SALES (est): 56.4K **Privately Held**
SIC: 2431 Millwork

(G-5201)
WINTER CREEK DRILLING LLC
2419 Wilcox Dr (73069-3956)
P.O. Box 720360 (73070-4265)
PHONE.................................405 321-1200
Phillip Chipwood, *Mng Member*
EMP: 1
SALES (est): 211.1K **Privately Held**
SIC: 1381 Drilling oil & gas wells

(G-5202)
WRANGLER AVIATION CORP
1700 Lexington Ave # 208 (73069-8433)
PHONE.................................405 364-5700
Joe W Davis, *President*
EMP: 1
SALES (est): 98K **Privately Held**
SIC: 3721 Aircraft

(G-5203)
XZUBE TEES
2848 Classen Blvd (73071-4059)
PHONE.................................405 249-9506
EMP: 2
SALES (est): 109.9K **Privately Held**
WEB: www.xzubetz.com
SIC: 2759 Screen printing

(G-5204)
YORK INTERNATIONAL CORPORATION
Also Called: Coleman Heating and AC
5005 York Dr (73069-9500)
PHONE.................................405 364-4040
Thomas Huntington, *Principal*
EMP: 94
SQ FT: 548,156 **Privately Held**
WEB: www.shumakerwilliams.com
SIC: 3585 Air conditioning units, complete: domestic or industrial
HQ: York International Corporation
    631 S Richland Ave
    York PA 17403
    717 771-7890

(G-5205)
YOUNG & NEW CENTURY LLC
3521 Glisten St (73072-1921)
PHONE.................................281 968-0718
Yang Wang, *Mng Member*
EMP: 2
SALES (est): 106K **Privately Held**
SIC: 3559 Electronic component making machinery

North Miami
Ottawa County

(G-5206)
COMMERCE PLASTICS INC
900 Main St (74358)
P.O. Box 21 (74358-0021)
PHONE.................................918 675-4506
Johnny Jones, *President*
EMP: 12
SQ FT: 6,240
SALES (est): 1.2MM **Privately Held**
SIC: 3089 Plastic processing

(G-5207)
PERFORMANCE MACHINE & INDUCTIO
Also Called: PMI
701 N Main St (74358)
P.O. Box 543 (74358-0543)
PHONE.................................918 542-8740
Rick Osborne, *President*
Herb Osborne, *Corp Secy*
Don Osborne, *Vice Pres*
EMP: 13
SALES: 730K **Privately Held**
SIC: 3599 5531 3714 Machine shop, jobbing & repair; automotive accessories; automotive parts; motor vehicle parts & accessories

(G-5208)
SCURLOCK INDUSTRIES MIAMI INC
600 Newman Rd (74358)
P.O. Box 257 (74358-0257)
PHONE.................................918 542-1884
James V Scurlock, *President*
Dean M Massey, *CFO*
EMP: 14
SALES (est): 2MM **Privately Held**
SIC: 3272 Pipe, concrete or lined with concrete

Nowata
Nowata County

(G-5209)
BRENNTAG SOUTHWEST INC
1 1/2 Mi N On Hwy 169 (74048)
PHONE.................................918 273-2265
Kevin Kessing, *President*
EMP: 40
SALES (corp-wide): 14.1B **Privately Held**
WEB: www.brenntagsouthwest.com
SIC: 5169 2899 2865 2842 Chemicals, industrial & heavy; chemical preparations; cyclic crudes & intermediates; specialty cleaning, polishes & sanitation goods; industrial inorganic chemicals; alkalies & chlorine

Nowata - Nowata County (G-5210)

HQ: Brenntag Southwest, Inc.
610 Fisher Rd
Longview TX 75604
972 218-3500

(G-5210)
CAPSTONE MUSIC COMPANY LTD
115 N Maple St (74048-2623)
PHONE..................918 273-1888
Suzanne M Hughes, *Principal*
EMP: 2
SALES (est): 143.1K **Privately Held**
SIC: 3993 Signs & advertising specialties

(G-5211)
COMMUNITY PUBLISHERS
Also Called: Nowata Printing Co West
Hwy 169th N (74048)
P.O. Box 472 (74048-0472)
PHONE..................918 273-1040
EMP: 30 EST: 2013
SALES (est): 1.8MM **Privately Held**
SIC: 2741 Misc Publishing

(G-5212)
D R TOPPING SADDLERY
1223 E Cherokee Ave (74048-3101)
PHONE..................918 273-2812
EMP: 4
SALES (est): 120K **Privately Held**
SIC: 3199 3429 Mfg Leather Goods Mfg Hardware

(G-5213)
DISAN ENGINEERING CORPORATION
101 Mohawk Dr (74048)
P.O. Box 632 (74048-0632)
PHONE..................918 273-1636
Billy G Brown, *President*
Sandra H Brown, *Corp Secy*
Susan Brown, *Exec VP*
Toby Lewis, *Vice Pres*
Cathy Templeton, *Property Mgr*
EMP: 30
SQ FT: 25,000
SALES (est): 5.3MM **Privately Held**
WEB: www.disancorp.com
SIC: 3669 Intercommunication systems, electric

(G-5214)
EQUIPMENT COMPANY
830 S Ash St (74048-4639)
P.O. Box 332 (74048-0332)
PHONE..................918 273-0240
Kenneth Parton, *Owner*
EMP: 1
SALES (est): 133.7K **Privately Held**
SIC: 3563 Air & gas compressors

(G-5215)
J & G TRUCKING
Rr 2 Box 202-10 (74048-9640)
PHONE..................918 693-4300
Jeff Plummer, *Owner*
EMP: 1
SALES (est): 105.3K **Privately Held**
SIC: 3531 Backhoes, tractors, cranes, plows & similar equipment

(G-5216)
J & S MACHINE & VALVE
125 Vinita Rd (74048-9442)
P.O. Box 152 (74048-0152)
PHONE..................918 273-1582
Mike Dunn, *Owner*
EMP: 3
SALES (est): 372.1K **Privately Held**
SIC: 3599 Machine shop, jobbing & repair

(G-5217)
J & S MACHINE & VALVE INC
131 Vinita Rd (74048)
P.O. Box 152 (74048-0152)
PHONE..................918 273-1582
Verla Smith, *President*
Mike Dan, *Vice Pres*
EMP: 23
SQ FT: 12,850
SALES (est): 4.8MM **Privately Held**
SIC: 3599 Machine shop, jobbing & repair

(G-5218)
K-H MACHINE SHOP
922 E Cherokee Ave (74048-3014)
PHONE..................918 273-1058
Becky Holinsworth, *Partner*
EMP: 2
SALES (est): 128.2K **Privately Held**
SIC: 3599 7692 Machine shop, jobbing & repair; welding repair

(G-5219)
MAJOR LEAGUE SPORTS LLC
347 N Ash St (74048-3000)
PHONE..................918 559-5030
Gregg Carter, *Owner*
EMP: 2 EST: 2011
SALES (est): 234.6K **Privately Held**
SIC: 3711 Motor vehicles & car bodies

(G-5220)
MC FERRONS QUALITY MEATS INC
Rr 1 Box 374 (74048-9703)
Rural Route Box 380 (74048-9742)
PHONE..................918 273-2892
Larry Mc Ferron, *President*
Linda Mc Ferron, *Vice Pres*
EMP: 10 EST: 1977
SALES: 1MM **Privately Held**
SIC: 2011 2013 Beef products from beef slaughtered on site; pork products from pork slaughtered on site; sausages & other prepared meats

(G-5221)
MILLERTIME MANUFACTURING LLC
Also Called: M T M Mfg
Rr 2 Box 354 (74048-9601)
Rural Route Box 354
PHONE..................918 273-2040
Bub Miller,
Valisa Miller,
▲ EMP: 6
SALES (est): 857.6K **Privately Held**
SIC: 3799 Trailers & trailer equipment

(G-5222)
NEOK PRODUCTION COMPANY
1223 E Cherokee Ave (74048-3101)
P.O. Box 428 (74048-0428)
PHONE..................918 273-5662
EMP: 3
SALES (est): 224.3K **Privately Held**
SIC: 1382 Oil & gas exploration services

(G-5223)
NMW INC
428 N Elm St (74048-2726)
PHONE..................918 273-2204
Rob Donald, *Principal*
◆ EMP: 2
SALES (est): 183.9K **Privately Held**
SIC: 3569 Filters

(G-5224)
OPS VALVES LLC
3.8 Miles (74048)
P.O. Box 208 (74048-0208)
PHONE..................918 273-3300
Bob Sudderth,
EMP: 7
SQ FT: 7,500
SALES: 1MM **Privately Held**
SIC: 3491 Industrial valves

(G-5225)
PAUL CLINTON HUGHES
Also Called: Universal Sign Company
115 N Maple St (74048-2623)
PHONE..................918 273-1888
Paul Hughes, *Owner*
EMP: 1
SALES (est): 84K **Privately Held**
SIC: 2759 3993 Commercial printing; signs & advertising specialties

(G-5226)
PEARCE QUINTON WELD
706 S Ash St (74048-4637)
PHONE..................918 559-3026
EMP: 2
SALES (est): 62.3K **Privately Held**
SIC: 7692 Welding repair

(G-5227)
RAWHIDE CUSTOM LEATHER
116 S Chase St (74048-4604)
PHONE..................918 273-0511
EMP: 3
SALES (est): 93K **Privately Held**
SIC: 3111 Leather Tanning/Finishing

(G-5228)
ROCKY TOP ENERGY LLC
701 E Modoc Ave (74048-3603)
P.O. Box 902 (74048-0902)
PHONE..................918 273-7444
Jim Staples, *Mng Member*
EMP: 2
SALES (est): 194.4K **Privately Held**
SIC: 1389 Building oil & gas well foundations on site

(G-5229)
SHADES OF COLOR
107 W Delaware Ave (74048-2616)
PHONE..................918 273-0001
Vicky Yirsa, *Principal*
EMP: 2
SALES (est): 123.5K **Privately Held**
SIC: 3999 Hair curlers, designed for beauty parlors

(G-5230)
STAR NOWATA
126 E Cherokee Ave (74048-2702)
P.O. Box 429 (74048-0429)
PHONE..................918 273-2446
Phillip Reid, *Principal*
Janet Carter, *Administration*
EMP: 4
SALES (est): 183.9K **Privately Held**
WEB: www.nowatastaronline.com
SIC: 2711 2791 Newspapers, publishing & printing; typesetting

(G-5231)
TED BRANHAM WELDING
Rr 2 Box 48-2 (74048-9630)
PHONE..................918 275-4431
Ted Branham, *Owner*
EMP: 1
SALES (est): 94.2K **Privately Held**
SIC: 7692 Welding repair

(G-5232)
WENDELL HICKS CONSTRUCTION
125 N Sycamore St (74048-2837)
PHONE..................918 520-9128
Wendell Hicks, *Owner*
EMP: 4 EST: 2016
SALES (est): 118.4K **Privately Held**
SIC: 3442 2431 Window & door frames; door shutters, wood

Ochelata
Washington County

(G-5233)
B A STEVENS
398887 W 2700 Rd (74051-2036)
PHONE..................918 695-4362
B A Stevens, *Principal*
EMP: 3
SALES (est): 257.2K **Privately Held**
SIC: 3412 Metal barrels, drums & pails

(G-5234)
DAVCO MANUFACTURING
724 County Road 2466 (74051-5104)
PHONE..................918 535-2360
David Hagan, *Partner*
John D Hagan, *Partner*
EMP: 12
SQ FT: 3,200
SALES: 350K **Privately Held**
SIC: 3412 3448 Barrels, shipping: metal; prefabricated metal buildings

(G-5235)
HENRYS WELDING AND FAB LLC
24521 N 3940 Rd (74051-2224)
PHONE..................918 535-2264
Genny Henry, *Principal*
EMP: 1
SALES (est): 33.4K **Privately Held**
SIC: 7692 Welding repair

(G-5236)
LATA GROUP
320 E Main St (74051-5017)
P.O. Box 360 (74051-0360)
PHONE..................918 535-2147
Michael Dennis, *President*
Dennis Hitzman, *President*
EMP: 15
SQ FT: 7,000
SALES (est): 1.4MM **Privately Held**
SIC: 1382 Oil & gas exploration services

(G-5237)
LUCAS METAL WORKS INC
396281 W 3000 Rd (74051-2446)
PHONE..................918 535-2726
J R Prather, *President*
Raymond Lucas, *Vice Pres*
Brian Inman, *Sales Staff*
Dona Miller, *Sales Staff*
EMP: 18
SQ FT: 25,000
SALES (est): 3.9MM **Privately Held**
SIC: 7692 Welding repair

(G-5238)
Q E M INC
Also Called: Quality Electric Motors
394640 Gap Rd (74051-2210)
PHONE..................918 534-2000
Fred Bishop, *President*
Dave Harvey, *Vice Pres*
EMP: 6
SALES (est): 1MM **Privately Held**
SIC: 5999 7694 Motors, electric; electric motor repair

(G-5239)
STITCH N SEW EMBROIDERY
27455 N 3979 Dr (74051-2064)
PHONE..................432 741-0433
Casey Tate, *Principal*
EMP: 1
SALES (est): 38.5K **Privately Held**
SIC: 2395 Embroidery & art needlework

(G-5240)
SWEET SCENT CANDLE
394661 W 2800 Rd (74051-2003)
PHONE..................918 535-3423
Tammy Pitts, *Manager*
EMP: 1 EST: 2014
SALES (est): 61.5K **Privately Held**
SIC: 3999 Candles

Oilton
Creek County

(G-5241)
TURNBOW TRAILERS INC
115 W Broadway St (74052)
P.O. Box 300 (74052-0300)
PHONE..................918 862-3233
Carl D Turnbow, *President*
Grace E Turnbow, *Corp Secy*
Dana Scott, *Vice Pres*
EMP: 12
SQ FT: 35,000
SALES: 2MM **Privately Held**
SIC: 3715 7539 7549 Trailers or vans for transporting horses; trailer repair; trailer maintenance

Okarche
Kingfisher County

(G-5242)
DIZZY LIZZY CUPCAKERY LLC
980 206th St Nw (73762-2505)
PHONE..................405 263-7667
Elizabeth Mary Schroeder, *Owner*
EMP: 4 EST: 2015
SALES (est): 171.3K **Privately Held**
SIC: 2051 Bread, cake & related products

▲ = Import ▼ = Export
◆ = Import/Export

GEOGRAPHIC SECTION

Okemah - Okfuskee County (G-5270)

(G-5243)
J & C WELDING CO INC
506 N 1st St (73762-8828)
P.O. Box 325 (73762-0325)
PHONE..................405 263-4967
Jim McCullough, *Owner*
EMP: 1
SALES (est): 85.1K Privately Held
SIC: 1799 7692 Welding on site; welding repair

(G-5244)
JEFF PARSON WELDING
28334 N 2860 Rd (73762-9225)
PHONE..................405 483-5770
Jeff Parson, *Manager*
EMP: 1
SALES (est): 68.1K Privately Held
SIC: 7692 Welding repair

(G-5245)
L & R PROPERTIES INC
114 N 4th St (73762)
P.O. Box 720840, Oklahoma City (73172-0840)
PHONE..................405 263-7404
Leroy Ussery, *President*
Verilie Faust, *Manager*
EMP: 2
SALES (est): 181.5K Privately Held
SIC: 1311 Crude petroleum & natural gas production

(G-5246)
MUEGGS HOT SHOT SERVICE LLC
210 Stroh Ave (73762-9201)
PHONE..................405 368-8362
John D Mueggenborg, *Administration*
EMP: 2
SALES (est): 71.8K Privately Held
SIC: 1389 Hot shot service

(G-5247)
NORTEK AIR SOLUTIONS LLC
Also Called: Temtrol
106 N Industrial Blvd (73762-9441)
PHONE..................405 263-7286
Andy Halko, *General Mgr*
Rick Osterholt, *Plant Mgr*
Kent Hallsten, *Buyer*
Kenny Bird, *Controller*
Steve Schulz, *Information Mgr*
EMP: 300
SALES (corp-wide): 11B Privately Held
SIC: 3585 3567 3498 Air conditioning units, complete: domestic or industrial; industrial furnaces & ovens; fabricated pipe & fittings
HQ: Nortek Air Solutions, Llc
8000 Phoenix Pkwy
O Fallon MO 63368
952 358-6600

(G-5248)
OEM SYSTEMS LLC
308 N Industrial Blvd (73762)
PHONE..................405 263-7529
Betty Borelli, *Director*
EMP: 5
SALES (corp-wide): 19MM Privately Held
SIC: 3537 Trucks, tractors, loaders, carriers & similar equipment
PA: O.E.M. Systems, L.L.C.
210 W Oklahoma Ave
Okarche OK 73762

(G-5249)
PARSONS WELDING INC
Also Called: Parson Welding
28334 N 2860 Rd (73762-9225)
P.O. Box 193, Tuttle (73089-0193)
PHONE..................405 263-7495
Jeff Parson, *Owner*
EMP: 1 EST: 2008
SALES (est): 87.8K Privately Held
WEB: www.parsonwelding.com
SIC: 7692 Welding repair

(G-5250)
QEP ENERGY COMPANY
600 W Oklahoma (73762)
PHONE..................405 263-4831
Dick Russell, *Branch Mgr*
EMP: 20
SALES (corp-wide): 1.2B Publicly Held
WEB: www.qepres.com
SIC: 1382 1311 Oil & gas exploration services; crude petroleum & natural gas production
HQ: Qep Energy Company
1050 17th St Ste 800
Denver CO 80265
303 672-6900

(G-5251)
SCHWEITZER GYPSUM & LIME (PA)
Also Called: 2r Schweitzer Farms
21139 N Calumet Rd (73762-2046)
PHONE..................405 263-7967
Rick Schweitzer, *Partner*
Ray Schweitzer, *Partner*
EMP: 2
SQ FT: 100
SALES (est): 250K Privately Held
SIC: 1422 1499 3274 Crushed & broken limestone; gypsum mining; lime

(G-5252)
SHAWNEE MILLING COMPANY
Also Called: Okarche Grain
20625 N Calumet Rd (73762-2044)
PHONE..................405 263-4566
Jim Grellner, *Manager*
EMP: 4
SALES (corp-wide): 84.5MM Privately Held
SIC: 2041 Flour & other grain mill products
PA: Shawnee Milling Company
201 S Broadway Ave
Shawnee OK 74801
405 273-7000

(G-5253)
STRAITLINE INC
108 N Industrial Blvd (73762-9441)
PHONE..................405 263-4604
Janice Flatt, *Principal*
EMP: 4
SALES (est): 402.6K Privately Held
SIC: 3429 Builders' hardware

(G-5254)
TEMTROL INC
106 N Industrial Blvd (73762-9441)
PHONE..................405 263-7286
Ambrose M Keyser, *Principal*
Inez B Keyser, *Principal*
Paul J Winger, *Principal*
Mike Whetstone, *Engineer*
Mike Wilczek, *Sales Engr*
EMP: 35
SALES (est): 10MM
SALES (corp-wide): 11B Privately Held
SIC: 3585 Air conditioning units, complete: domestic or industrial
HQ: Nortek, Inc.
8000 Phoenix Pkwy
O Fallon MO 63368

(G-5255)
TOWER CAFE INC
Also Called: Tower Inn
Hwy 81 S (73762)
P.O. Box 402 (73762-0402)
PHONE..................405 263-4853
Jana Hale, *Manager*
Dana Hubbard, *Manager*
Louise Hubbard, *Officer*
EMP: 10
SALES (est): 200K Privately Held
WEB: www.cinnamonrollbakery.com
SIC: 7011 5812 2051 Hotels; eating places; bread, cake & related products

Okay
Wagoner County

(G-5256)
APAC-CENTRAL INC
4997 State Hwy 251a (74446)
P.O. Box 50 (74446-0050)
PHONE..................918 683-1362
Tom Presnell, *Branch Mgr*
EMP: 11
SALES (corp-wide): 29.7B Privately Held
SIC: 2951 5032 1422 Asphalt paving mixtures & blocks; stone, crushed or broken; crushed & broken limestone
HQ: Apac-Central, Inc.
755 E Millsap Rd
Fayetteville AR 72703

(G-5257)
DIE TECH TOOL MACHINE
1000 S Hwy 251a (74446)
PHONE..................918 683-3422
Tommy Snider, *Partner*
Larry Hammack, *Partner*
EMP: 4
SALES (est): 330K Privately Held
SIC: 3544 2431 Special dies & tools; millwork

Okeene
Blaine County

(G-5258)
KAHN BACKHOE & TRENCHING
263584 E County Road 57 (73763-6307)
P.O. Box 162 (73763-0162)
PHONE..................580 541-6600
EMP: 1
SALES (est): 116.6K Privately Held
SIC: 3531 Backhoes

(G-5259)
MOUNTAIN COUNTRY FOODS LLC
201 Industrial Ave (73763-5001)
PHONE..................580 822-4130
Steve Gurley, *Parts Mgr*
Bill North, *Purchasing*
Terry Menlove, *QC Mgr*
Matt Dixon, *Branch Mgr*
Shawn Johnson, *Manager*
EMP: 20
SALES (corp-wide): 73.5MM Privately Held
WEB: www.mcfoods.com
SIC: 2048 2047 Dry pet food (except dog & cat); dog & cat food
PA: Mountain Country Foods, Llc
195 E 1600 N
Spanish Fork UT 84660
801 798-8634

(G-5260)
NORTHWEST MEASUREMENT
202 S Main St (73763-9110)
P.O. Box 526 (73763-0526)
PHONE..................580 822-3528
Douglas Barnes, *Owner*
EMP: 2
SQ FT: 5,000
SALES (est): 189.2K Privately Held
SIC: 1389 5084 0191 Pipe testing, oil field service; measuring & testing equipment, electrical; general farms, primarily crop

(G-5261)
OKEEN MOTEL
806 W Oklahoma (73763-9384)
P.O. Box 663 (73763-0663)
PHONE..................580 822-4491
Sherrie Beirigs, *Owner*
EMP: 3 EST: 1975
SALES (est): 177.7K Privately Held
SIC: 7011 2011 Motels; meat packing plants

(G-5262)
SHAWNEE MILLING COMPANY
Okeene Milling Co
302 W Oklahoma Ave (73763)
P.O. Box 1000 (73763-0790)
PHONE..................580 822-4415
Robert L Ford, *Manager*
EMP: 25
SALES (corp-wide): 84.5MM Privately Held
WEB: www.shawneemilling.com
SIC: 2041 Flour & other grain mill products
PA: Shawnee Milling Company
201 S Broadway Ave
Shawnee OK 74801
405 273-7000

Okemah
Okfuskee County

(G-5263)
AO INC
15 W Broadway St (74859-2614)
PHONE..................918 623-1711
Pam Kibby, *Principal*
EMP: 3
SALES (est): 30K Privately Held
SIC: 2821 Plastics materials & resins

(G-5264)
BECK ILLUMINATIONS LLC
Also Called: AMS
202 S 7th St (74859-3821)
PHONE..................918 623-2880
David Beck, *President*
EMP: 25
SQ FT: 40,000
SALES (est): 3.2MM Privately Held
SIC: 5065 3672 Electronic parts; printed circuit boards

(G-5265)
BINDER LEASING LLC
600 S Sertco Rd (74859-3224)
PHONE..................918 623-0526
Mikko Crouch, *Mng Member*
EMP: 1 EST: 2009
SALES (est): 82.2K Privately Held
SIC: 3563 Air & gas compressors

(G-5266)
CHASE INDUSTRIES INC
302 S Sertco Rd (74859-3216)
PHONE..................816 850-5323
Bob Chase, *President*
Mary Chase, *Corp Secy*
EMP: 5
SQ FT: 4,000
SALES (est): 200K Privately Held
SIC: 3599 Machine shop, jobbing & repair

(G-5267)
D & M OIL FLDS SVC CSING CREWS
Intersection Hwy48 & Hwy56 (74859)
P.O. Box 426 (74859-0426)
PHONE..................918 623-0492
Dewayne Wilson, *Owner*
Gale Wilson, *Admin Sec*
EMP: 5 EST: 1978
SALES (est): 381.2K Privately Held
SIC: 1389 Cementing oil & gas well casings; servicing oil & gas wells

(G-5268)
DEGGES OIL FIELD SERVICE
Also Called: Degge, Bill Oil Field Service
711 W Date St (74859-4432)
P.O. Box 269 (74859-0269)
PHONE..................918 623-1373
Betty Degge, *Partner*
Tim Degge, *Partner*
EMP: 1
SALES (est): 137.7K Privately Held
SIC: 1389 4212 Servicing oil & gas wells; local trucking, without storage

(G-5269)
FRASER OILFIELD SERVICE LLC
379060 E 1070 Rd (74859-5187)
PHONE..................918 716-0665
Lana Fraser,
EMP: 2
SALES (est): 79.1K Privately Held
SIC: 1389 Oil field services

(G-5270)
J & P MACHINE
E Of City (74859)
PHONE..................918 623-0005
Jerry McVeigh, *Owner*
EMP: 2
SALES (est): 135K Privately Held
SIC: 3599 Machine shop, jobbing & repair

Okemah - Okfuskee County

(G-5271)
OKEMAH LEADER
Also Called: Okemah News Leader
115 W Broadway St (74859-2616)
P.O. Box 191 (74859-0191)
PHONE..................918 623-0123
Robert G Mason, *President*
Lynn Thompson, *Editor*
Kenneth O Reid, *Vice Pres*
Joyce Mason, *Admin Sec*
EMP: 5 **EST:** 1975
SALES (est): 319.6K **Privately Held**
WEB: www.okemahnewsleader.com
SIC: 2711 Newspapers: publishing only, not printed on site

(G-5272)
OTA COMPRESSION LLC
401 E Columbia St (74859-2832)
PHONE..................918 623-9922
Josh Alaniz, *Vice Pres*
Thompson Speir, *Manager*
EMP: 114
SALES (corp-wide): 32.8MM **Privately Held**
SIC: 3533 Oil field machinery & equipment
PA: Ota Compression Llc
102 Decker Ct Ste 204
Irving TX 75062
972 831-1300

(G-5273)
PHAM THUY
517 S Woody Guthrie St (74859-4645)
PHONE..................918 623-0700
Thuy Pham, *Principal*
EMP: 2
SALES (est): 125.5K **Privately Held**
SIC: 2844 Manicure preparations

(G-5274)
PLATINUM CROSS WELDING INC
379054 E 1130 Rd (74859-4215)
P.O. Box 1279, Bristow (74010-1279)
PHONE..................918 623-9130
James Hays, *President*
Kyle Linaweaver, *Opers Staff*
EMP: 5 **EST:** 2010
SALES (est): 1MM **Privately Held**
SIC: 7692 Welding repair

(G-5275)
SEMINOLE OILFIELD SUPPLY
503 S 9th St (74859-4209)
PHONE..................918 623-9900
Mike Kahn, *President*
EMP: 2
SALES: 73K **Privately Held**
SIC: 1389 6531 Construction, repair & dismantling services; real estate agents & managers

(G-5276)
SERTCO INDUSTRIES INC (PA)
600 S Sertco Rd (74859-3224)
PHONE..................918 623-0526
Rick Crouch, *CEO*
Mikko C Crouch, *President*
Joe Harrington, *Vice Pres*
Tony Vaughn, *Vice Pres*
Beth Gray, *CFO*
▼ **EMP:** 41 **EST:** 1979
SQ FT: 18,249
SALES (est): 5.7MM **Privately Held**
SIC: 3728 Aircraft parts & equipment

(G-5277)
TUFF TROFF LLC
378181 E 1000 Rd (74859-5028)
PHONE..................918 623-6091
Greg Scott, *Partner*
EMP: 1 **EST:** 1996
SALES: 100K **Privately Held**
SIC: 3711 Motor vehicles & car bodies

Oklahoma City
Cleveland County

(G-5278)
ASSOCIATED STL FABRICATORS INC
14220 S Tulsa Dr (73170-9718)
PHONE..................405 787-5713
Harold Fike, *President*
Bill Ward, *Vice Pres*
Chris Anson, *Treasurer*
Connie Fike, *Admin Sec*
EMP: 35
SALES (est): 7.2MM **Privately Held**
SIC: 3441 Fabricated structural metal

(G-5279)
AWESOME ACRES PACAS PYRS
11800 S Hiwassee Rd (73165-8825)
PHONE..................405 990-8205
Michael Alpert, *Principal*
EMP: 2
SALES (est): 187.8K **Privately Held**
WEB: www.pacasnpyrs.com
SIC: 2211 Alpacas, cotton

(G-5280)
BILL DURBINS MOBILE HOME TRA
10550 Se 149th St (73165-7014)
PHONE..................405 799-3557
Billy Durbin, *Principal*
EMP: 2
SALES (est): 156.3K **Privately Held**
SIC: 2451 Mobile homes

(G-5281)
CINDYS STITCHING
2112 Abbeywood (73170-3205)
PHONE..................405 735-7126
EMP: 1
SALES (est): 44.7K **Privately Held**
WEB: www.stitchingcindys.com
SIC: 2395 Embroidery & art needlework

(G-5282)
CUSTOM 4 X 4 FABRICATION
11825 Se 109th St (73165-8602)
PHONE..................405 799-7599
Mike Houlett, *Owner*
EMP: 4
SALES (est): 125K **Privately Held**
WEB: www.custom4x4fabrication.com
SIC: 2211 Automotive fabrics, cotton

(G-5283)
DAN QUYEN NEWSPAPER
1320 Sw 116th Pl (73170-4460)
P.O. Box 892166 (73189-2166)
PHONE..................405 691-2522
Hoat Nguyen, *Owner*
EMP: 1
SALES (est): 73.4K **Privately Held**
SIC: 2711 Newspapers, publishing & printing

(G-5284)
DANCO INSPECTION SERVICE INC
1324 Sw 155th St (73170-9309)
PHONE..................405 691-5752
Dan Carter, *President*
EMP: 1
SALES (est): 344.8K **Privately Held**
SIC: 1389 Oil field services

(G-5285)
DARREN MCININCH
Also Called: Express Exterminators
14000 Sauna Ln (73165-6529)
PHONE..................405 912-8403
Darren Mcininch, *Owner*
EMP: 6 **EST:** 1997
SALES (est): 488.6K **Privately Held**
SIC: 2879 7342 Exterminating products, for household or industrial use; disinfecting & pest control services

(G-5286)
DISPLAY WITH HONOR WDWKG LLC
2724 Sw 115th St (73170-2630)
PHONE..................405 659-9894
Scott A Ferree, *Administration*
EMP: 2
SALES (est): 170.3K **Privately Held**
SIC: 2431 Millwork

(G-5287)
DRAKE MANUFACTURING INC
4601 Se 139th St (73165-7412)
PHONE..................405 799-8157
Bobby Boyd, *Principal*
EMP: 1
SALES (est): 39.6K **Privately Held**
SIC: 3999 Manufacturing industries

(G-5288)
DRONE MISFITS LLC
5816 Se 144th St (73165-1432)
PHONE..................918 810-0808
EMP: 2
SALES (est): 110.2K **Privately Held**
SIC: 3721 Motorized aircraft

(G-5289)
EARLYWINE PRESS LLC
3048 Sw 127th St (73170-2026)
PHONE..................405 820-8208
Jon Olin Roberts, *Owner*
EMP: 2
SALES (est): 59.2K **Privately Held**
SIC: 2741 Miscellaneous publishing

(G-5290)
ELEMENT FLEET CORPORATION
14312 Se 110th St (73165-8909)
PHONE..................405 799-4775
Glen Long, *Branch Mgr*
EMP: 3
SALES (corp-wide): 746.6MM **Privately Held**
SIC: 3999 Barber & beauty shop equipment
HQ: Element Fleet Corporation
940 Ridgebrook Rd
Sparks MD 21152
410 771-1900

(G-5291)
FLAMINGO MEDIA INC
12529 Crick Hollow Ct (73170-2074)
PHONE..................405 620-5889
Nathan Sowah, *CEO*
EMP: 1
SALES: 50K **Privately Held**
SIC: 2741

(G-5292)
GARY D ADAMS GEOLOGIST
2632 Sw 105th St (73170-2426)
P.O. Box 892517 (73189-2517)
PHONE..................405 691-5380
Gary D Adams, *Partner*
EMP: 2
SALES (est): 190K **Privately Held**
SIC: 1382 Oil & gas exploration services

(G-5293)
HEATHER HARJOCHEE
1213 Sw 105th St (73170-5217)
PHONE..................405 615-3273
Heather Harjochee, *Owner*
EMP: 1
SALES (est): 52.7K **Privately Held**
SIC: 3523 Harvesters, fruit, vegetable, tobacco, etc.

(G-5294)
HEINTZELMAN CONS & ROFING
9601 Bluewater Cir (73165-9653)
PHONE..................405 409-8954
EMP: 2
SALES (est): 196.7K **Privately Held**
SIC: 1521 3259 1761 1541 Single-Family House Cnst Mfg Structural Clay Prdt Roofing/Siding Contr Industrial Bldg Cnstn Mfg Reconstd Wood Prdts

(G-5295)
HERFF JONES LLC
541 Sw 154th Ct (73170-7551)
PHONE..................405 794-3764
Greg Sprayberry, *Representative*
EMP: 1
SALES (corp-wide): 1.1B **Privately Held**
SIC: 3911 Rings, finger: precious metal
HQ: Herff Jones, Llc
4501 W 62nd St
Indianapolis IN 46268
800 419-5462

(G-5296)
IDEAS MANUFACTURING INC
11821 S Walker Ave (73170-6407)
PHONE..................405 691-5525
Randall Long, *President*
Angie Long, *Vice Pres*
EMP: 2
SQ FT: 2,400
SALES (est): 334.4K **Privately Held**
SIC: 3561 8661 7692 3444 Industrial pumps & parts; religious organizations; welding repair; sheet metalwork

(G-5297)
JANSENS SOFTWARE
1112 Sw 132nd St (73170-6958)
PHONE..................405 692-4756
Jerry Jansen, *Principal*
EMP: 2 **EST:** 2008
SALES (est): 103.1K **Privately Held**
WEB: www.jansenssoftware.com
SIC: 7372 Prepackaged software

(G-5298)
K3 INDUSTRIES LLC
11617 Se 156th St (73165-6807)
PHONE..................205 568-1252
Mark Karazim, *Principal*
EMP: 2
SALES (est): 129.5K **Privately Held**
SIC: 3999 Manufacturing industries

(G-5299)
KELLEYS WELDING SERVICE INC
11505 S Miller Ave (73170-2627)
PHONE..................405 691-5515
Tim Kelley, *President*
Mary Kelley, *Admin Sec*
EMP: 2
SALES (est): 35K **Privately Held**
SIC: 7692 Welding repair

(G-5300)
KENNEDY RESTORATIONS LLC
150098 Kyle Dr Unit A (73170)
PHONE..................405 761-5303
Brad Kennedy,
EMP: 1 **EST:** 2013
SALES (est): 68K **Privately Held**
SIC: 3452 Washers

(G-5301)
KH PUBLISHING LLC
1436 Sw 129th St (73170-6999)
PHONE..................405 378-7539
Sonja K Watts, *Principal*
EMP: 1
SALES (est): 55.7K **Privately Held**
SIC: 2741 Miscellaneous publishing

(G-5302)
KINGSVIEW FREEWILL BAPTIST CH
14200 S May Ave (73170-5510)
PHONE..................405 692-1554
Kevin Daniels, *Pastor*
Tony Stokes, *CIO*
EMP: 1
SALES (est): 140K **Privately Held**
SIC: 2531 8661 Church furniture; Baptist Church

(G-5303)
LENOX LEASING LLC
16113 Raindust Dr (73170-3513)
PHONE..................405 664-5240
Nicholas Archibald, *Principal*
EMP: 2
SALES (est): 79.9K **Privately Held**
SIC: 3585 Refrigeration & heating equipment

GEOGRAPHIC SECTION

Oklahoma City - Oklahoma County (G-5338)

(G-5304)
LIFESAFER INTERLOCK
3424 Lakeside Dr (73160-2725)
PHONE..................800 634-3077
EMP: 2
SALES (est): 183.1K **Privately Held**
SIC: 3829 Measuring & controlling devices

(G-5305)
MARK A HOLKUM LLC
109 Sw 132nd St (73170-1438)
PHONE..................405 735-3463
Mark A Holkum,
EMP: 2 EST: 2013
SALES (est): 98.2K **Privately Held**
SIC: 1389 Oil consultants

(G-5306)
MICHAEL SHERRY ALPERT
11800 S Hiwassee Rd (73165-8825)
PHONE..................405 912-0062
Michael Alpert, *Principal*
EMP: 2 EST: 2007
SALES (est): 131.3K **Privately Held**
SIC: 2211 Alpacas, cotton

(G-5307)
MODERN COATINGS LLC
10600 S Pennsylvania Ave (73170-4256)
PHONE..................405 795-2633
EMP: 2 EST: 2013
SALES (est): 166.6K **Privately Held**
SIC: 3479 Metal coating & allied service

(G-5308)
NORMAN SUPPLY COMPANY
11901 S Portland Ave (73170-9708)
PHONE..................405 692-1191
Fax: 405 692-7382
EMP: 2 EST: 2008
SALES (est): 81K **Privately Held**
SIC: 5999 5074 3432 Ret Misc Merchandise Whol Plumbing Equipment/Supplies Mfg Plumbing Fixture Fittings

(G-5309)
NUTECH ENERGY ALLIANCE LTD
11301 Gateshead Dr (73170-3251)
PHONE..................405 388-4236
Alan Howard, *Branch Mgr*
EMP: 4
SALES (est): 189.4K
SALES (corp-wide): 14.8MM **Privately Held**
SIC: 1389 Oil field services
PA: Nutech Energy Alliance, Ltd.
4101 Interwood N Pkwy # 250
Houston TX 77032
281 812-4030

(G-5310)
P M GRAPHICS
11901 Se 157th St (73165-6808)
PHONE..................405 525-8789
EMP: 2
SALES (est): 145.1K **Privately Held**
SIC: 2759 Commercial Printing

(G-5311)
PRESSLEY PRESS N PROD FCILTY
13919 S Harvey Ave (73170)
PHONE..................405 752-5700
Colin Pressley, *Owner*
EMP: 2
SALES (est): 158K **Privately Held**
SIC: 2759 Commercial printing

(G-5312)
PRUETT CABINET AND TRIM LLC
13120 Turtle Creek Dr (73170-6805)
PHONE..................405 692-1552
James Pruett, *Administration*
EMP: 1
SALES (est): 80.1K **Privately Held**
SIC: 2434 Wood kitchen cabinets

(G-5313)
ROCK CREEK LAND AND ENERGY
15212 Bay Ridge Dr (73165-9756)
PHONE..................405 358-6090
EMP: 2
SALES (est): 150.5K **Privately Held**
SIC: 1382 Oil & gas exploration services

(G-5314)
RT MANUFACTURING CONCEPTS LLC
13233 Se 104th St (73165-9045)
PHONE..................405 388-3999
Richard Barringer, *Principal*
EMP: 1 EST: 2017
SALES (est): 47.3K **Privately Held**
SIC: 3999 Manufacturing industries

(G-5315)
SANTANA INC
13140 Eastvalley Rd (73170-1600)
PHONE..................405 826-8817
EMP: 3
SALES (est): 125K **Privately Held**
SIC: 1389 Oil/Gas Field Services

(G-5316)
SLEDGE ELECTRIC INC
10616 Fairway Ave (73170-2538)
PHONE..................405 793-4007
Jennifer Hamer, *President*
Dustin Hamer, *Vice Pres*
EMP: 2
SALES (est): 138.1K **Privately Held**
SIC: 3694 7299 Automotive electrical equipment; handyman service

(G-5317)
SNYDER PRINTING INC
Also Called: Snyder's Printing
10904 Gateshead Dr (73170-3238)
PHONE..................405 682-8880
Steve Snyder, *President*
Stacy Farley, *Vice Pres*
EMP: 19
SQ FT: 5,000
SALES (est): 1.9MM **Privately Held**
SIC: 2752 2791 2789 Commercial printing, offset; typesetting; bookbinding & related work

(G-5318)
STRAWBERRY VALLEY PRESS LLC
13601 Se 104th St (73165-9013)
PHONE..................405 237-1893
Gena Showalter, *Agent*
EMP: 2
SALES (est): 59.2K **Privately Held**
SIC: 2741 Miscellaneous publishing

(G-5319)
SUBTLEDEMON PUBLISHING LLC
12231 S May Ave (73170-4502)
PHONE..................405 670-3471
Walter Suttle, *Principal*
EMP: 2
SALES (est): 104K **Privately Held**
SIC: 2741 Miscellaneous publishing

(G-5320)
THRU TUBING SOLUTIONS INC (HQ)
11515 S Portland Ave (73170-9707)
PHONE..................405 692-1900
Andy Ferguson, *President*
Todd Graham, *District Mgr*
Justin Miller, *District Mgr*
Jeff Whitworth, *District Mgr*
Jenna Robertson, *Business Mgr*
EMP: 152 EST: 1997
SALES (est): 69.8MM
SALES (corp-wide): 1.2B **Publicly Held**
WEB: www.thrutubing.com
SIC: 1389 Oil field services
PA: Rpc, Inc.
2801 Buford Hwy Ne # 520
Brookhaven GA 30329
404 321-2140

(G-5321)
VANCO SYSTEMS
11308 Gateshead Dr (73170-3255)
P.O. Box 890540 (73189-0540)
PHONE..................405 692-4040
Howard Vanover, *Owner*
EMP: 3
SALES: 250K **Privately Held**
SIC: 5943 3861 Office forms & supplies; printing equipment, photographic

(G-5322)
VM WELDING LLC
13100 Cloverleaf Ln (73170-1127)
PHONE..................405 245-2833
EMP: 2
SALES (est): 37.6K **Privately Held**
SIC: 7692 Welding repair

(G-5323)
WILD HORSE DISTRUBUTING LLC
11816 Chelsea Chase (73170-3603)
PHONE..................405 691-0755
EMP: 2
SALES (est): 120K **Privately Held**
SIC: 7338 1389 Secretarial/Court Reporting Oil/Gas Field Services

(G-5324)
WILLIAM REED
Also Called: Quest
9500 Fendrych Dr (73165-9748)
PHONE..................405 912-8153
William Reed, *President*
EMP: 7
SALES (est): 763K **Privately Held**
SIC: 3423 Hand & edge tools

(G-5325)
WING-IT CONCEPTS
11324 S Shartel Ave (73170-5836)
PHONE..................405 691-8053
EMP: 1
SALES (est): 110.1K **Privately Held**
SIC: 3089 2221 Mfg Plastic Products Manmade Broadwoven Fabric Mill

Oklahoma City
Oklahoma County

(G-5326)
1 800 RADIATOR
4055 Nw 3rd St (73107-6607)
PHONE..................405 946-9800
Kerry Cooney, *Principal*
EMP: 3 EST: 2009
SALES (est): 264K **Privately Held**
WEB: www.1800radiatorokc.com
SIC: 5013 3714 Radiators; radiators & radiator shells & cores, motor vehicle

(G-5327)
12TH GATE PUBLISHING LLC
12216 Biltmore Dr (73173-7002)
PHONE..................405 735-7611
Brandon Trey Lewis, *Principal*
EMP: 1
SALES (est): 43.1K **Privately Held**
SIC: 2741 Miscellaneous publishing

(G-5328)
19TH HOLE
3401 Ne 36th St (73121-2009)
PHONE..................405 424-0520
Paul Hughes, *President*
EMP: 3
SALES (est): 184.2K **Privately Held**
SIC: 2085 Cocktails, alcoholic

(G-5329)
247 GRAPHX STUDIOS INC
325 S Scott St (73115-1011)
PHONE..................405 677-7775
Shawn J Graham, *President*
EMP: 5
SALES (est): 577.9K **Privately Held**
SIC: 3993 7389 Signs & advertising specialties; printing broker

(G-5330)
2911 LLC
Also Called: Signarama Okc
7111 S Western Ave (73139-2003)
PHONE..................405 631-2008
Rich Hess,
EMP: 5
SQ FT: 3,800
SALES (est): 183.4K **Privately Held**
SIC: 3993 Signs & advertising specialties

(G-5331)
4-STAR TRAILERS INC
10000 Nw 10th St (73127-7125)
P.O. Box 75395 (73147-0395)
PHONE..................405 324-7827
Kenneth R Waller, *President*
Caroline Waller, *Corp Secy*
Kenny Hobbs, *Vice Pres*
Bobby Key, *Prdtn Mgr*
Bobby McCormick, *Purchasing*
EMP: 250
SQ FT: 103,500
SALES (est): 49.2MM **Privately Held**
SIC: 3537 3444 3715 Industrial trucks & tractors; sheet metalwork; trailers or vans for transporting horses

(G-5332)
405 MAGAZINE INC
1613 N Broadway Ave (73103-4610)
PHONE..................405 604-2623
Tom Fraley, *Publisher*
Ronnie Morey, *Manager*
EMP: 2 EST: 2017
SALES (est): 176.2K **Privately Held**
WEB: www.405magazine.com
SIC: 5192 2741 Magazines; miscellaneous publishing

(G-5333)
405 PLASTICS & DISTRIBUTION
3201 N Santa Fe Ave (73118-8804)
PHONE..................405 562-8800
Richard Clements, *President*
EMP: 9
SQ FT: 22,000
SALES (est): 990K **Privately Held**
SIC: 3085 Plastics bottles

(G-5334)
405 R/C RACEWAY & HOBBIES LLC
2905 Nw 36th St (73112-6642)
PHONE..................405 503-0364
EMP: 4 EST: 2015
SALES (est): 213K **Privately Held**
SIC: 3644 Raceways

(G-5335)
405 SIGN AND LIGHTING LLC
9415 Peachtree Ln (73130-5036)
P.O. Box 95245 (73143-5245)
PHONE..................405 445-8888
Michael Brent Phillips, *Owner*
EMP: 1
SALES (est): 46K **Privately Held**
SIC: 3993 Signs & advertising specialties

(G-5336)
5 OVER GAMES LLC
2737 Nw 140th St Apt 503 (73134-6170)
PHONE..................405 928-5972
EMP: 2
SALES (est): 68.7K **Privately Held**
SIC: 7372 Prepackaged Software Services

(G-5337)
66 OILFIELD SERVICES LLC
7100 S Bryant Ave (73149-7200)
P.O. Box 892550 (73189)
PHONE..................405 735-6666
Jim E Frazier, *President*
Donald Woods, *COO*
Joseph R Wright, *Sales Mgr*
EMP: 1
SALES (est): 136K
SALES (corp-wide): 22.3MM **Privately Held**
SIC: 1389 Oil field services
PA: Sixty Six Oilfield Services, Inc.
3773 Howard Hughes Pkwy
Las Vegas NV

(G-5338)
89 ENERGY LLC
123 Nw 8th St (73102-5804)
PHONE..................405 600-6040
Jacob Hendrickson, *Controller*
John M Beaver, *Mng Member*
EMP: 15 EST: 2016
SALES (est): 1.3MM **Privately Held**
SIC: 1382 Oil & gas exploration services

Oklahoma City - Oklahoma County (G-5339)

(G-5339)
89 ENERGY II LLC
123 Nw 8th St (73102-5804)
PHONE.................405 600-6040
Jacob Hendrickson, *Controller*
John Mark Beaver,
EMP: 17
SALES (est): 418K **Privately Held**
SIC: 1382 Oil & gas exploration services

(G-5340)
8BIT CANVAS LLC
9818 Skylark Rd (73162-5660)
PHONE.................405 924-3298
EMP: 1 **EST:** 2013
SALES (est): 70K **Privately Held**
SIC: 2211 Canvas

(G-5341)
9800 NORTH OKLAHOMA LLC
9800 N Oklahoma Ave (73114-7406)
PHONE.................405 748-9400
Rand Phipps, *Principal*
EMP: 2
SALES (est): 132K **Privately Held**
SIC: 1382 Oil & gas exploration services

(G-5342)
A & B QUICK SIGNS LLC
6924 Melrose Ln Ste D (73127-6139)
P.O. Box 270512 (73137-0512)
PHONE.................405 789-7446
Leroy Melrose, *Owner*
EMP: 2
SALES (est): 150.6K **Privately Held**
SIC: 3993 Signs & advertising specialties

(G-5343)
A & R PLUMBING AND MECH LLC
3176 Nw Expwy Apt 313 (73112-4086)
PHONE.................405 808-0671
Alex Morales,
EMP: 7
SALES (est): 359.9K **Privately Held**
SIC: 3432 7389 Plastic plumbing fixture fittings, assembly;

(G-5344)
A B CURBS INC
6718 Ne 23rd St (73141-1012)
P.O. Box 418, Spencer (73084-0418)
PHONE.................405 427-1222
Diana Blackburn, *President*
Cory Blackburn, *Vice Pres*
EMP: 3
SQ FT: 3,000
SALES: 180K **Privately Held**
SIC: 3444 Sheet metalwork

(G-5345)
A FINLEY SIGN & LIGHTING CO
4712 S Blackwelder Ave (73119-5023)
PHONE.................405 413-5721
Steven Finley, *Principal*
EMP: 3
SALES (est): 234.8K **Privately Held**
SIC: 3993 Signs & advertising specialties

(G-5346)
A FULLER MEASURE
2300 Belleview Ter (73112-7741)
PHONE.................405 755-5036
Shenae Nicholson, *CEO*
EMP: 1
SALES (est): 33.3K **Privately Held**
SIC: 2731 Book publishing

(G-5347)
A P & R INDUSTRIES INC
Also Called: American Painting and Rmdlg
901 Nw 89th St (73114-2507)
PHONE.................405 702-7661
Erick Fletcher, *President*
EMP: 12 **EST:** 2010
SALES (est): 582.7K **Privately Held**
WEB: www.american-painting-remodeling.com
SIC: 1389 1521 1799 Construction, repair & dismantling services; single-family home remodeling, additions & repairs; general remodeling, single-family houses; patio & deck construction & repair; kitchen & bathroom remodeling

(G-5348)
A R T T CORP
Also Called: Artt Wood Mfg Co
1829 S May Ave (73108-4440)
PHONE.................405 681-0749
Tom L Davis, *Ch of Bd*
Dylan Davis, *Business Mgr*
Ann Starrett, *Corp Secy*
Steve Green, *Prdtn Mgr*
Autumn Langford, *Asst Mgr*
EMP: 8
SQ FT: 4,500
SALES (est): 1.2MM **Privately Held**
WEB: www.arttwood.com
SIC: 2431 3443 Porch columns, wood; staircases, stairs & railings; window shutters, wood; fabricated plate work (boiler shop)

(G-5349)
A&J MIXING
6101 Camille Ave (73149-5036)
PHONE.................405 946-1461
EMP: 2
SALES (est): 317.8K **Privately Held**
SIC: 3531 Construction machinery

(G-5350)
A-1 BACKHOE INC
4240 Sw 31st St (73119-1006)
PHONE.................405 863-7094
Christopher Campbell, *Principal*
EMP: 1
SALES (est): 130K **Privately Held**
SIC: 3531 Backhoes

(G-5351)
A-1 MSTER PRNTA/HOOPER PRTG SI
235 N Macarthur Blvd # 60 (73127-6624)
PHONE.................518 427-0282
EMP: 3
SALES (est): 54.1K **Privately Held**
SIC: 8011 7929 2752 Offices & clinics of medical doctors; entertainers & entertainment groups; commercial printing, lithographic

(G-5352)
A-1 SPECIALTIES
4905 Morris Ln (73112-6150)
PHONE.................405 942-1341
Veyda Burbridge, *Owner*
EMP: 1
SQ FT: 2,000
SALES (est): 120K **Privately Held**
SIC: 5199 3993 2672 Advertising specialties; signs & advertising specialties; coated & laminated paper

(G-5353)
A-1 SURE SHOT
Also Called: A-1 Sure Sht-Div Ptro Instrmen
1312 Se 25th St (73129-6434)
P.O. Box 96456 (73143-6456)
PHONE.................405 677-9800
Terry Tidwell, *Owner*
EMP: 10
SALES (est): 486.2K **Privately Held**
WEB: www.petroleuminstrumentsco.com
SIC: 1389 7699 3829 3823 Oil field services; repair services; measuring & controlling devices; industrial instrmnts msrmnt display/control process variable; power-driven handtools; oil field equipment

(G-5354)
AAA KOPY
709 S Air Depot Blvd A (73110-4816)
PHONE.................405 741-5679
Liequet Ali, *Owner*
EMP: 4
SALES: 750K **Privately Held**
SIC: 7334 2789 2759 Photocopying & duplicating services; bookbinding & related work; commercial printing

(G-5355)
AAE AUTOMATION INC
3021 S High Ave (73129-5025)
PHONE.................405 525-1100
EMP: 6
SALES: 1.3MM **Privately Held**
SIC: 3625 Mfg Relays/Industrial Controls

(G-5356)
AAR AIRCRAFT SERVICES INC
Also Called: AAR Aircraft Services - Okla
6611 S Meridian Ave # 59100 (73159-1111)
PHONE.................405 681-3000
James Patterson, *Vice Pres*
Robert Regan, *Vice Pres*
Don Ward, *Manager*
EMP: 40
SALES (corp-wide): 2B **Publicly Held**
SIC: 3728 Aircraft assemblies, subassemblies & parts
HQ: Aar Aircraft Services, Inc.
1100 N Wood Dale Rd
Wood Dale IL 60191
630 227-2000

(G-5357)
AAR AIRCRAFT SERVICES INC
6241 S Meridian Ave (73159)
PHONE.................405 218-3393
EMP: 3
SALES (est): 131.6K **Privately Held**
SIC: 3728 Aircraft parts & equipment

(G-5358)
ABC CHOPPERS LLC
1901 N Classen Blvd (73106-6015)
PHONE.................405 990-8641
EMP: 1
SALES (est): 54.6K **Privately Held**
SIC: 3751 Motorcycles & related parts

(G-5359)
ABUNDANT GRACE COMPANIES LLC (PA)
8801 S Kentucky Ave (73159-6214)
PHONE.................405 682-2589
Lori Packwood,
Karen Tingle,
EMP: 10
SALES (est): 703.7K **Privately Held**
SIC: 2741 7374 Miscellaneous publishing; data processing & preparation

(G-5360)
ACCELERATED PRODUCTION SVCS
9733 Nw 6th St (73127-7102)
PHONE.................405 603-7492
Jeff Whitney, *General Mgr*
EMP: 5 **EST:** 2012
SALES (est): 343.6K **Privately Held**
SIC: 1389 Oil field services

(G-5361)
ACCESS MIDSTREAM VENTURES LLC
6100 N Western Ave (73118-1044)
PHONE.................405 935-3500
J Mike Stice, *Principal*
EMP: 42
SALES (est): 3MM **Privately Held**
SIC: 1311 Crude petroleum & natural gas

(G-5362)
ACCESS MLP OPERATING LLC
600 N Western Ave (73106)
PHONE.................405 935-8000
Aubrey K McClendon, *CEO*
EMP: 119
SALES (est): 7.3MM
SALES (corp-wide): 8.2B **Publicly Held**
SIC: 1311 Crude petroleum & natural gas
HQ: Williams Partners L.P.
1 Williams Ctr
Tulsa OK 74101

(G-5363)
ACCORD UPHOLSTERY & FABRIC
Also Called: Accord Fabrics
2501 S Agnew Ave (73108-6219)
PHONE.................405 634-4070
Jim Chavez, *Owner*
EMP: 2
SQ FT: 6,200
SALES (est): 100K **Privately Held**
SIC: 7389 2599 Interior designer; hotel furniture

(G-5364)
ACE INFORMATION CO
319 S Scott St Ste A (73115-1015)
PHONE.................405 677-6747
Dennis Norton, *Owner*
EMP: 2 **EST:** 1992
SALES (est): 154.9K **Privately Held**
SIC: 2752 Commercial printing, offset

(G-5365)
ACE WELDING AND MECHANICAL LLC
4013 Nw 32nd St (73112-3323)
PHONE.................405 219-1490
EMP: 1
SALES (est): 35.4K **Privately Held**
SIC: 7692 Welding repair

(G-5366)
ACID SPECIALISTS LLC
14201 Caliber Dr Ste 300 (73134-1017)
PHONE.................432 617-2243
Oscar Dominguez, *Principal*
Larry P Noble,
EMP: 7
SALES (est): 305K **Privately Held**
SIC: 3297 2819 Cement refractories, non-clay; hydrofluoric acid

(G-5367)
ACME BRICK COMPANY
500 E Memorial Rd (73114-2285)
P.O. Box 5008, Edmond (73083-5008)
PHONE.................405 755-5010
John Steence, *Branch Mgr*
Tonya Pope, *Info Tech Dir*
EMP: 75
SALES (corp-wide): 327.2B **Publicly Held**
SIC: 3251 Structural brick & blocks
HQ: Acme Brick Company
3024 Acme Brick Plz
Fort Worth TX 76109

(G-5368)
ACO INC
1301 W Sheridan Ave (73106-5233)
PHONE.................405 239-6863
David J Asner, *President*
Patrick Brown, *Principal*
Keith R Tredway, *Principal*
Jerome Asner, *Shareholder*
EMP: 4
SQ FT: 83,000
SALES (est): 777.2K **Privately Held**
SIC: 3089 Injection molding of plastics

(G-5369)
ACP INC
1600 Sunset Ln (73127-3022)
PHONE.................405 249-8835
EMP: 2
SALES (est): 67.7K **Privately Held**
SIC: 2731 Book publishing

(G-5370)
AD TECH SIGNS INC
2000 S Santa Fe Ave (73109-1417)
PHONE.................405 236-0551
Blake Ballweber, *President*
EMP: 2
SQ FT: 5,000
SALES (est): 300K **Privately Held**
SIC: 3993 Electric signs

(G-5371)
AD TYPE INC
4401 Sw 23rd St 203 (73108-1750)
PHONE.................405 942-7951
David Graham, *President*
EMP: 2
SALES (est): 120K **Privately Held**
SIC: 2791 7336 Typesetting; graphic arts & related design

(G-5372)
ADCP INDUSTRIES LLC
2930 Nw 73rd St (73116-3224)
PHONE.................405 330-4728
Craig Parham, *Principal*
EMP: 2
SALES (est): 91K **Privately Held**
SIC: 3999 Manufacturing industries

GEOGRAPHIC SECTION

Oklahoma City - Oklahoma County (G-5404)

(G-5373)
ADEMCO INC
Also Called: ADI Global Distribution
3801 S Moulton Dr (73179-7644)
PHONE.................................405 681-4008
Dee Plumley, *Manager*
EMP: 8
SALES (corp-wide): 4.9B **Publicly Held**
SIC: 5063 3669 3822 Alarm systems; emergency alarms; auto controls regulating residntl & coml environmt & applncs
HQ: Ademco Inc.
1985 Douglas Dr N
Golden Valley MN 55422
800 468-1502

(G-5374)
ADJACENT CREATIONS LLC
4 Akin Dr (73149-1800)
P.O. Box 720393, Norman (73070-4289)
PHONE.................................405 819-6507
Carl Gilchrist,
EMP: 1
SALES (est): 43.5K **Privately Held**
SIC: 7371 7372 7389 Computer software systems analysis & design, custom; application computer software;

(G-5375)
ADKO INC
2221 S Eastern Ave (73129-7521)
PHONE.................................405 677-6507
Steve Adkins, *President*
Suzanne Adkins, *Vice Pres*
EMP: 2
SQ FT: 4,000
SALES (est): 245.5K **Privately Held**
WEB: www.adkoinc.com
SIC: 2899 3533 Drilling mud; oil & gas field machinery

(G-5376)
ADTEK SOFTWARE COMPANY
516 Nw 20th St (73103-1803)
PHONE.................................815 452-2345
Jerry Faw, *President*
EMP: 3
SALES (est): 241.6K **Privately Held**
SIC: 7372 Prepackaged software

(G-5377)
ADVANCE POLYBAG INC
4901 S I 35 Service Rd (73129-7017)
PHONE.................................405 677-8383
EMP: 4
SALES (est): 310.5K **Privately Held**
SIC: 2673 Bags: plastic, laminated & coated

(G-5378)
ADVANCED AIRCRAFT COATINGS (PA)
11020 Roxboro Ave (73162-2510)
PHONE.................................405 495-7545
Mike Buckley, *President*
Ron Stinson, *Senior VP*
EMP: 4
SQ FT: 3,200
SALES: 1.7MM **Privately Held**
SIC: 2851 Paints & allied products

(G-5379)
ADVANCED CHEMICAL TECH INC
Also Called: Act
9608 N Robinson Ave (73114-3612)
PHONE.................................405 843-2585
Kevin M Brown, *President*
Melissa Brown, *Corp Secy*
EMP: 6
SQ FT: 1,500
SALES (est): 1.3MM **Privately Held**
SIC: 2899 Chemical preparations

(G-5380)
ADVANCED DRAINAGE SYSTEMS
1418 E Reno Ave (73117-1812)
PHONE.................................405 272-1541
Shawn Crow, *Principal*
Jason Buck, *Site Mgr*
EMP: 4 **EST:** 2008
SALES (est): 450.1K **Privately Held**
WEB: www.ads-pipe.com
SIC: 3084 Plastics pipe

(G-5381)
ADVANCED FABRICATION SVCS LLC
1217 Sw 97th St (73139-2614)
PHONE.................................405 339-4867
Sean Sumpter, *CEO*
EMP: 2
SALES (est): 94.5K **Privately Held**
SIC: 3444 Sheet metalwork

(G-5382)
ADVANCED FOOT & ANKLE
1126 Sw 89th St (73139-9104)
PHONE.................................405 692-7114
Michael K Wilson, *Principal*
EMP: 5 **EST:** 2008
SALES (est): 383.5K **Privately Held**
SIC: 2252 Anklets (hosiery)

(G-5383)
ADVANCED GRAPHICS TECHNOLOGY
3201 S Western Ave (73109-2406)
P.O. Box 15113 (73155-5113)
PHONE.................................405 632-8600
Bruce Johnson, *Owner*
EMP: 2
SALES (est): 127.1K **Privately Held**
SIC: 5734 3955 Printers & plotters: computers; print cartridges for laser & other computer printers

(G-5384)
ADVANCED MCHNING SOLUTIONS LLC
Also Called: AMS
4703 Entp Dr Ste A (73128)
PHONE.................................405 208-8737
David Dennis, *Engineer*
Larry Hall, *Engineer*
Shontay Redden, *Asst Controller*
Jun Kwon, *Marketing Staff*
Mark Donovan, *Manager*
EMP: 2
SALES (est): 254.5K **Privately Held**
SIC: 3599 Machine shop, jobbing & repair

(G-5385)
ADVANCED PRESSURE INCORPORATED
10300 W Reno Ave (73127-7154)
P.O. Box 270323 (73137-0323)
PHONE.................................405 324-5600
Chris Graham, *President*
Dwight Deal, *Corp Secy*
Billy Woods, *Vice Pres*
EMP: 20
SQ FT: 30,000
SALES (est): 2MM **Privately Held**
SIC: 1389 Oil field services

(G-5386)
ADVANCED TECH SOLUTIONS LLC
1533 Sw 80th St (73159-5301)
PHONE.................................310 591-7163
Thomas Ordon,
EMP: 1
SALES (est): 140.9K **Privately Held**
SIC: 3641 Electric lamps

(G-5387)
ADVENTURE MANUFACTURING INC
4012 Sw 29th St (73119-1205)
PHONE.................................405 682-3833
Steve Manis, *President*
EMP: 9
SALES (est): 750K **Privately Held**
WEB: www.adventureinmetals.com
SIC: 3441 3444 Fabricated structural metal; sheet metalwork

(G-5388)
ADVERTISING SIGNS & AWNGS INC
Also Called: Amb Quick Sign Stores
6924 Melrose Ln (73127-6142)
P.O. Box 270512 (73137-0512)
PHONE.................................405 232-7446
Leroy Melrose, *President*
EMP: 5

SALES (est): 425.7K **Privately Held**
WEB: www.abokc.net
SIC: 3993 Signs & advertising specialties

(G-5389)
AEI CORP-OKLA
Also Called: American Electric Ignition Co
114 Nw 8th St (73102-5805)
P.O. Box 1945 (73101-1945)
PHONE.................................405 236-3551
Larry Hays, *President*
EMP: 7 **EST:** 1914
SQ FT: 11,000
SALES (est): 3.2MM **Privately Held**
SIC: 5063 3621 5084 Motors, electric; motors & generators; oil well machinery, equipment & supplies

(G-5390)
AERO COMPONENTS INC
535 Se 82nd St (73149-2926)
PHONE.................................405 631-6644
Danny Odom, *President*
EMP: 30 **EST:** 1981
SQ FT: 6,500
SALES (est): 7.1MM **Privately Held**
SIC: 3599 Machine shop, jobbing & repair

(G-5391)
AEROCHEM INC
212 N Falcon Dr (73127-7210)
PHONE.................................405 440-0380
EMP: 4
SQ FT: 10,000
SALES: 2.5MM **Privately Held**
SIC: 2851 Mfg Paints/Allied Products

(G-5392)
AEROCORP INTERNATIONAL LC
Also Called: Aci Machine & Engineering
8124 Sw 8th St Ste C (73128-4241)
PHONE.................................405 317-5844
Levi M Wilson,
EMP: 3
SALES: 500K **Privately Held**
SIC: 3728 Aircraft parts & equipment

(G-5393)
AEROSPACE PRODUCTS SE INC
621 N Robinson Ave # 550 (73102-9916)
PHONE.................................405 213-1034
David Evans, *President*
EMP: 16
SALES (est): 1.5MM **Privately Held**
SIC: 5088 3728 5085 Transportation equipment & supplies; aircraft parts & equipment; fasteners, industrial: nuts, bolts, screws, etc.

(G-5394)
AEROSPACE TRAINING
7919 Mid America Blvd (73135-6610)
PHONE.................................405 253-8343
Terry McKenzie, *Manager*
EMP: 2
SALES (est): 100.3K **Privately Held**
SIC: 3728 Aircraft parts & equipment

(G-5395)
AFFORDABLE DUMPSTER OK LLC
4113 Nw 52nd St (73112-2109)
PHONE.................................405 535-6644
Brian Meister, *Principal*
EMP: 3
SALES (est): 228.5K **Privately Held**
SIC: 3443 Dumpsters, garbage

(G-5396)
AFFORDABLE LEAK DETECTION
536 N Pennsylvania Ave (73107-6423)
PHONE.................................405 594-2341
EMP: 2
SALES (est): 113.3K **Privately Held**
SIC: 3599 Industrial machinery

(G-5397)
AFFORDABLE SIGNS & DECALS INC
952 N Macarthur Blvd (73127-5610)
PHONE.................................405 942-7059
David Story, *President*
Rebecca Story, *Vice Pres*

EMP: 2
SQ FT: 2,218
SALES (est): 201.4K **Privately Held**
SIC: 3993 2752 Signs, not made in custom sign painting shops; commercial printing, lithographic

(G-5398)
AGC INC
3300 W Reno Ave (73107-6132)
P.O. Box 18297 (73154-0297)
PHONE.................................913 451-8900
Charles Thomason, *Vice Pres*
EMP: 3
SALES (est): 88.5K **Privately Held**
SIC: 2721 Periodicals

(G-5399)
AGRIUM ADVANCED TECH US INC
5201 W Reno Ave Ste E (73127-6370)
PHONE.................................405 948-1084
Brett Davenport, *Manager*
EMP: 11
SALES (corp-wide): 20B **Privately Held**
SIC: 2873 Nitrogenous fertilizers
HQ: Agrium Advanced Technologies (U.S.) Inc.
2915 Rocky Mountain Ave # 400
Loveland CO 80538

(G-5400)
AGS LLC
Also Called: American Gaming Systems
308 Anthony Ave (73128-1116)
PHONE.................................405 605-8331
David B Lopez, *Branch Mgr*
EMP: 1 **Privately Held**
SIC: 3944 Electronic game machines, except coin-operated; video game machines, except coin-operated
PA: Ags Llc
5475 S Decatur Blvd # 100
Las Vegas NV 89118

(G-5401)
AIRGAS USA LLC
7248 Sw 29th St (73179-5212)
PHONE.................................405 745-2732
Tim Bennett, *Business Mgr*
Kyle Anderson, *Opers-Prdtn-Mfg*
EMP: 6
SQ FT: 16,800
SALES (corp-wide): 129.8MM **Privately Held**
SIC: 2813 5169 Industrial gases; oxygen
HQ: Airgas Usa, Llc
259 N Radnor Chester Rd
Radnor PA 19087
610 687-5253

(G-5402)
AIRGAS USA LLC
1225 W Reno Ave (73106-3205)
PHONE.................................405 235-0009
Tigger Archard, *Manager*
EMP: 7
SALES (corp-wide): 129.8MM **Privately Held**
SIC: 5169 5084 5085 2813 Industrial gases; gases, compressed & liquefied; carbon dioxide; dry ice; welding machinery & equipment; safety equipment; welding supplies; industrial gases; carbon dioxide; nitrous oxide; dry ice; carbon dioxide (solid); industrial inorganic chemicals; calcium carbide
HQ: Airgas Usa, Llc
259 N Radnor Chester Rd
Radnor PA 19087
610 687-5253

(G-5403)
AIRGO SYSTEMS
13616 Railway Dr (73114-2281)
PHONE.................................877 550-6111
EMP: 2 **EST:** 2015
SALES (est): 132.1K **Privately Held**
SIC: 3011 Tires And Inner Tubes, Nsk

(G-5404)
AIRGO SYSTEMS LLC
Also Called: Drov Technologies
8232 Sw 23rd Pl (73128-9527)
P.O. Box 3877, Edmond (73083-3877)
PHONE.................................405 346-5807

Tony Ingram, *Mng Member*
Peter Jankowski, *Manager*
Jim Hunter,
EMP: 15
SQ FT: 5,000
SALES (est): 2.2MM **Privately Held**
SIC: 3563 3669 7371 Tire inflators, hand or compressor operated; transportation signaling devices; software programming applications

(G-5405)
AL CAPONE LIMO CORP
8317 Nw 109th St (73162-3006)
PHONE.................................405 999-3335
Fuad Alhai Mahmound, *President*
EMP: 1
SALES: 36.4K **Privately Held**
SIC: 4119 7372 Limousine rental, with driver; application computer software

(G-5406)
AL PHARMA INC
7301 Broadway Ext Ste 110 (73116-9038)
PHONE.................................405 848-3299
Rebecca Johnson, *President*
H Warren Johnson, *Vice Pres*
EMP: 4
SALES (est): 156.7K **Privately Held**
SIC: 2834 Pharmaceutical preparations

(G-5407)
ALADDIN MANUFACTURING CORP
3121 Melcap Dr Ste B (73179)
PHONE.................................405 943-3037
EMP: 16
SALES (corp-wide): 7.8B **Publicly Held**
SIC: 2273 Mfg Carpets/Rugs
HQ: Aladdin Manufacturing Corporation
   160 S Industrial Blvd
   Calhoun GA 30701
   706 629-7721

(G-5408)
ALAN INDUSTRIES ONLINE
7612 Nw 14th Ter (73127-3115)
PHONE.................................405 787-1102
EMP: 2
SALES (est): 48K **Privately Held**
SIC: 3999 Manufacturing industries

(G-5409)
ALAN L LAMB
11900 N Penn Ave Ste 1c (73120-7839)
PHONE.................................405 755-2233
Alan Lamb, *Owner*
EMP: 3
SQ FT: 2,100
SALES (est): 286.7K **Privately Held**
SIC: 1311 Crude petroleum production; natural gas production

(G-5410)
ALBRIGHT STEEL AND WIRE CO (PA)
12 S Virginia Ave (73106-3038)
P.O. Box 2056 (73101-2056)
PHONE.................................405 232-7526
Trey Lewis, *President*
Leah A Beale, *Vice Pres*
Dewayne Ross, *Purchasing*
Mike Redding, *Branch Mgr*
EMP: 10
SQ FT: 2,000
SALES (est): 9.2MM **Privately Held**
WEB: www.albrightsteel.com
SIC: 5051 3351 3317 3316 Steel; sheets, galvanized or other coated; tubing, metal; reinforcement mesh, wire; copper rolling & drawing; steel pipe & tubes; cold finishing of steel shapes; blast furnaces & steel mills

(G-5411)
ALEX PALLETS
2716 S Central Ave (73129-1840)
PHONE.................................405 414-2710
EMP: 6
SALES (est): 343.4K **Privately Held**
SIC: 2448 Pallets, wood

(G-5412)
ALEX ROGERS
Also Called: Rogers Locker Plant
1925 Se 29th St (73129-7625)
PHONE.................................405 677-2306
Alex F Rogers, *Owner*
EMP: 1
SQ FT: 1,500
SALES (est): 168.6K **Privately Held**
WEB: www.hotlinksrus.com
SIC: 5147 4222 2013 2011 Meats, fresh; storage, frozen or refrigerated goods; sausages & other prepared meats; meat packing plants

(G-5413)
ALL STATE ELECTRIC MOTORS INC (PA)
1839 Linwood Blvd (73106-2625)
PHONE.................................405 232-1129
Louis F Retter, *Principal*
EMP: 5
SQ FT: 27,000
SALES: 600K **Privately Held**
WEB: www.allstateelectricmotors.com
SIC: 7694 Electric motor repair; rewinding stators

(G-5414)
ALL STATES PRODUCTION EQP CO (PA)
1128 Se 25th St (73129-6424)
P.O. Box 95287 (73143-5287)
PHONE.................................405 672-2323
Scot Lee, *President*
Bernice Lee, *Corp Secy*
EMP: 4 **EST:** 1973
SQ FT: 4,000
SALES (est): 2.3MM **Privately Held**
SIC: 5084 3533 Oil well machinery, equipment & supplies; oil & gas field machinery

(G-5415)
ALL THINGS BUGS LLC
2211 Snapper Ln (73130-6055)
PHONE.................................352 281-3643
Aaron Dossey,
EMP: 1
SALES (est): 118K **Privately Held**
SIC: 2023 Dietary supplements, dairy & non-dairy based

(G-5416)
ALL TOOLS CO INC
216 N Quapah Ave (73107-6690)
PHONE.................................405 942-6655
Robert M Henry, *President*
Gladys Henry, *Corp Secy*
Earl Henry, *Vice Pres*
EMP: 16
SQ FT: 22,000
SALES: 3MM **Privately Held**
SIC: 3469 Electronic enclosures, stamped or pressed metal

(G-5417)
ALLEGIANT ENERGY PRODUCTION &
1800 E Memorial Rd # 103 (73131-1827)
PHONE.................................405 550-2331
Michael A Trevino, *Principal*
Terry Reed, *Vice Pres*
EMP: 18
SALES (est): 755.7K **Privately Held**
SIC: 1389 Oil & gas wells: building, repairing & dismantling

(G-5418)
ALLEMAN TRIM & CABINETS
3800 Nw 28th St (73107-1304)
PHONE.................................405 942-7876
L Alleman, *Principal*
EMP: 2
SALES (est): 130K **Privately Held**
SIC: 2434 Wood kitchen cabinets

(G-5419)
ALLIANCE SEALANTS & WATERPROOF
1205 Se 44th St Ste 1 (73129-6860)
PHONE.................................405 627-9474
EMP: 3
SALES (est): 312K **Privately Held**
SIC: 2891 Sealants

(G-5420)
ALLIANCE STEEL INC
Also Called: Alliance Steel Bldg Systems
3333 S Council Rd (73179-4410)
PHONE.................................405 745-7500
Bill Cralley, *Principal*
Lisa Stewart, *Treasurer*
Mary McMullen, *Shareholder*
▲ **EMP:** 214
SQ FT: 323,570
SALES (est): 221.8MM
SALES (corp-wide): 267.5MM **Privately Held**
SIC: 5051 3448 Steel; prefabricated metal buildings
HQ: Associated Steel Group, Llc

   Nashville TN
   615 714-6234

(G-5421)
ALLIED FOAM FABRICATORS INC
902 N Ann Arbor Ave (73127-5827)
P.O. Box 270953 (73137-0953)
PHONE.................................405 946-0384
Earl W Deese, *President*
Kenneth A Deese, *Vice Pres*
EMP: 7
SQ FT: 15,000
SALES (est): 1.2MM **Privately Held**
SIC: 3086 Plastics foam products

(G-5422)
ALLSTATE SHEET METAL INC
8605 Gateway Ter (73149-3058)
PHONE.................................405 636-1914
William J Daniel, *President*
Val Daniel, *Corp Secy*
Juergen H Daniel, *Vice Pres*
EMP: 16 **EST:** 1981
SQ FT: 12,000
SALES (est): 4.8MM **Privately Held**
SIC: 3444 1711 Sheet metalwork; mechanical contractor

(G-5423)
ALOFT SOFTWARE LLC
2706 Nw 68th St (73116-4712)
PHONE.................................405 633-0250
Alonso Portillo,
EMP: 2
SALES (est): 113.1K **Privately Held**
SIC: 7372 Prepackaged software

(G-5424)
ALPHA CONCRETE PRODUCTS INC
10213 Ne 23rd St (73141-5211)
PHONE.................................405 769-7777
Russel Johnson, *President*
David Bacon, *President*
Jim Fox, *Corp Secy*
Linda Bacon, *Vice Pres*
EMP: 10
SQ FT: 20,000
SALES (est): 1.4MM **Privately Held**
SIC: 3272 3271 Floor slabs & tiles, precast concrete; furniture, garden: concrete; steps, prefabricated concrete; stone, cast concrete; concrete block & brick

(G-5425)
ALPHA RESEARCH & TECH INC
Also Called: Art
2601 Liberty Pkwy (73110-2855)
PHONE.................................405 733-1919
EMP: 1
SALES (corp-wide): 14.9MM **Privately Held**
SIC: 3571 Computer Systems Design Mfg And Integration
PA: Alpha Research & Technology, Inc.
   1107 Inv Blvd Ste 200
   El Dorado Hills CA 95762
   916 235-4400

(G-5426)
ALTEC INC
9920 W Reno Ave (73127-7139)
PHONE.................................405 577-6322
EMP: 1
SALES (corp-wide): 987MM **Privately Held**
SIC: 3531 Construction machinery

PA: Altec, Inc.
   210 Inverness Center Dr
   Birmingham AL 35242
   205 991-7733

(G-5427)
ALTERNTIVE GTHRMAL SLTIONS INC
3710 N Meridian Ave (73112-2818)
PHONE.................................405 948-0410
EMP: 1
SALES (est): 93K **Privately Held**
SIC: 3585 Mfg Refrigeration/Heating Equipment

(G-5428)
AMBASSADOR LIGHTING LLC
6701 N Prospect Ave (73111-7937)
PHONE.................................405 503-5726
EMP: 2 **EST:** 2015
SALES (est): 90.1K **Privately Held**
SIC: 3648 Lighting equipment

(G-5429)
AMBROSIA SWEET INC
1400 N Broadview Dr (73127-3159)
PHONE.................................405 816-2887
Angela McReynolds, *Administration*
EMP: 8
SALES (est): 501.6K **Privately Held**
SIC: 2051 Cakes, bakery: except frozen

(G-5430)
AMCON RESOURCES
Also Called: Amcon Resources & Engineering
5400 N Grand Blvd Ste 565 (73112-5688)
PHONE.................................405 236-4100
Alan Gann, *President*
EMP: 8
SALES (est): 1.2MM **Privately Held**
SIC: 1382 Oil & gas exploration services

(G-5431)
AMERICAN ACCESSIBILITY EQP SVC
1905 S Harvard Dr Ste C (73128-3049)
PHONE.................................405 631-4142
Steven Schmidt, *President*
Valerie Fox, *Principal*
EMP: 5
SQ FT: 3,000
SALES (est): 450K **Privately Held**
SIC: 3534 Elevators & moving stairways

(G-5432)
AMERICAN BANK SYSTEMS INC
Also Called: ABS
14000 Parkway Commons Dr (73134-6114)
P.O. Box 20668 (73156-0668)
PHONE.................................405 607-7000
James W Bruce Jr, *CEO*
Edwin B Cook, *President*
Jay Bruce, *Exec VP*
Joseph Jobby, *Vice Pres*
Elva Sears, *Vice Pres*
EMP: 42
SQ FT: 17,000
SALES: 4MM **Privately Held**
SIC: 2752 5045 8748 7372 Business forms, lithographed; computer software; business consulting; prepackaged software

(G-5433)
AMERICAN BOTTLING COMPANY
5200 Sw 36th St Ste 600 (73179-7810)
PHONE.................................405 680-5150
Dave Przygocki, *Principal*
EMP: 75 **Publicly Held**
SIC: 2086 Carbonated beverages, nonalcoholic: bottled & canned
HQ: The American Bottling Company
   5301 Legacy Dr
   Plano TX 75024

(G-5434)
AMERICAN CHORAL DIRECTORS ASSN (PA)
545 Couch Dr (73102-2207)
PHONE.................................405 232-8161
Marvin Meyer, *Controller*
Amanda Bumgarner, *Publications*
Trina Kopacka, *Corp Comm Staff*

GEOGRAPHIC SECTION

Oklahoma City - Oklahoma County (G-5463)

Sindy Hail, *Advt Staff*
Debbie Beckner, *Manager*
EMP: 14
SQ FT: 6,000
SALES: 5MM **Privately Held**
SIC: 8621 2721 Education & teacher association; trade journals: publishing only, not printed on site

(G-5435)
AMERICAN FENCE COMPANY INC
Also Called: American Fence and Carport
215 N Cooley Dr (73127-1051)
PHONE..................405 685-4800
Lance Wheeler, *President*
Dakota Wheeler, *Vice Pres*
Mike Markcum, *Opers Mgr*
EMP: 50
SQ FT: 6,000
SALES (est): 992.6K **Privately Held**
WEB: www.americanfenceok.com
SIC: 1799 3315 3446 3089 Core drilling & cutting; fence construction; fence gates posts & fittings: steel; fences, gates, posts & flagpoles; fences, gates & accessories: plastic

(G-5436)
AMERICAN INTELLECTUAL LLC
44 Nw 44th St (73118-7903)
PHONE..................405 605-2378
Jay Ridley,
EMP: 4
SALES (est): 412.2K **Privately Held**
SIC: 3499 Fabricated metal products

(G-5437)
AMERICAN INTRPRTIVE MONITORING
13401 Railway Dr (73114-2272)
PHONE..................405 841-7826
Daniel Lincoln, *President*
Amy Hall, *Office Mgr*
EMP: 7
SALES (est): 591.6K **Privately Held**
SIC: 3845 Patient monitoring apparatus

(G-5438)
AMERICAN LOGO AND SIGN INC (PA)
Also Called: Alas
12501 N Santa Fe Ave (73114-3804)
PHONE..................405 799-1800
Rebecca Wells, *President*
Diana F Jordan, *Corp Secy*
EMP: 15
SALES (est): 1.4MM **Privately Held**
SIC: 3993 1799 7336 5999 Signs & advertising specialties; sign installation & maintenance; commercial art & graphic design; banners

(G-5439)
AMERICAN MCHNING SOLUTIONS LLC
2618 S I 35 Svc Rd Ste 30 (73129)
PHONE..................405 606-7038
Donald Bishop, *Mng Member*
Brian Bishop,
EMP: 4
SALES (est): 323.2K **Privately Held**
SIC: 3599 Machine shop, jobbing & repair

(G-5440)
AMERICAN MILLWORK COMPANY INC
3650 Sw 29th St (73119-1499)
PHONE..................405 681-5347
David Culwell, *President*
Jim Culwell, *President*
Terri Culwell, *Corp Secy*
Whitney Culwell, *Admin Sec*
EMP: 30
SQ FT: 55,000
SALES (est): 3.8MM **Privately Held**
SIC: 1752 1743 2431 Carpet laying; tile installation, ceramic; millwork; trim, wood

(G-5441)
AMERICAN TISSUE INDUSTRIES LLC
50 N Council Rd (73127-4924)
PHONE..................562 207-6814
Lorainne Shackelford, *Purchasing*
Rizal Setiadi,
EMP: 14
1 EST: 2017
SALES (est): 22.3MM **Privately Held**
SIC: 2621 Towels, tissues & napkins: paper & stock
PA: Solaris Paper, Inc.
100 S Anaheim Blvd # 280
Anaheim CA 92805

(G-5442)
AMERIFLOW INC
Also Called: Ameriflow Energy Services
5749 Nw 132nd St (73142-4437)
PHONE..................405 603-1200
Bill Daniel, *Manager*
EMP: 9
SALES (est): 1.6MM **Privately Held**
SIC: 3823 Industrial flow & liquid measuring instruments

(G-5443)
AMERRIL ENERGY LLC
411 Nw 5th St (73102-3010)
PHONE..................770 856-2662
Ping He, *Manager*
EMP: 2
SALES (est): 81.9K **Privately Held**
SIC: 1382 Oil & gas exploration services
PA: Amerril Energy Llc
1116 S Walton Blvd # 205
Bentonville AR

(G-5444)
ANDREWS WELDING
Also Called: Dan Andrews Limited
13200 Se 74th St (73150-8101)
PHONE..................405 990-7326
Dan Andrews, *Owner*
EMP: 1
SALES (est): 118.4K **Privately Held**
SIC: 7692 Welding repair

(G-5445)
ANGEL EXPLORATION
3005 Nw 63rd St (73116-3603)
PHONE..................405 848-8360
Hugh Tullos, *President*
Robbie Tullos, *Corp Secy*
EMP: 3
SQ FT: 3,000
SALES (est): 173.3K **Privately Held**
SIC: 1389 1311 Oil field services; crude petroleum & natural gas

(G-5446)
ANGELA LYN SARABIA
1408 Sw 68th St (73159-3212)
PHONE..................405 808-8576
Angela Sarabia, *Owner*
Don Sarabia, *Co-Owner*
EMP: 2
SALES (est): 61.2K **Privately Held**
SIC: 2051 Bread, cake & related products

(G-5447)
ANNIE PRINTER
5412 Charwood Ln (73135-4354)
PHONE..................405 670-9640
Annie Printer, *Principal*
EMP: 2
SALES (est): 152.3K **Privately Held**
SIC: 2752 Commercial printing, lithographic

(G-5448)
ANTELOPE OIL TOOL MFG CO LLC
13808 S Macarthur Blvd (73173-8708)
PHONE..................405 691-2490
Bill Kelley, *CEO*
EMP: 2
SALES (est): 183.2K **Privately Held**
SIC: 3999 Manufacturing industries

(G-5449)
ANTIOCH OPERATING LLC
12 E California Ave # 200 (73104-2410)
PHONE..................405 236-0080
Kevin Dunnigton, *CEO*
EMP: 1
SALES (est): 281.6K **Privately Held**
SIC: 1382 Oil & gas exploration services

(G-5450)
ANTIQUE & ROD SHOP LLC
529 Se 59th St (73129-5641)
PHONE..................405 631-3544
Jim Ury,
EMP: 4
SQ FT: 10,000
SALES (est): 387.7K **Privately Held**
SIC: 5521 7699 3711 Antique automobiles; antique repair & restoration, except furniture, automobiles; chassis, motor vehicle

(G-5451)
APERGY ARTFL LIFT INTL LLC
Compressor Components Div
1315 Se 29th St (73129-6441)
PHONE..................405 677-3153
Lane Pate, *Branch Mgr*
EMP: 20
SALES (corp-wide): 1.1B **Publicly Held**
SIC: 1389 4225 5084 Oil field services; general warehousing; processing & packaging equipment
HQ: Apergy Artificial Lift International, Llc
2445 Tech Frest Blvd Ste
Spring TX 77381
281 403-5742

(G-5452)
API ENTERPRISES INC
4901 S I 35 Service Rd (73129-7017)
PHONE..................713 580-4800
Hiralal Chamdal, *President*
Janak Sheth, *President*
Hank D Nguyen, *Principal*
Tom Nguyen, *Vice Pres*
▲ **EMP:** 180
SALES (est): 93.4MM **Privately Held**
SIC: 2673 Plastic bags: made from purchased materials

(G-5453)
APOLLO EXPLORATION LLC
1001 Nw 63rd St Ste 100 (73116-7335)
P.O. Box 14779 (73113-0779)
PHONE..................405 286-0600
EMP: 3
SALES (est): 216.6K **Privately Held**
SIC: 1382 Oil & gas exploration services

(G-5454)
APOLLO ORNAMENTAL IRON LLC
5400 S Hattie Ave (73129-7324)
PHONE..................405 672-5377
Crystal Tyler, *Treasurer*
Joe Tyler, *Mng Member*
EMP: 26
SALES (est): 2.7MM
SALES (corp-wide): 10.4MM **Privately Held**
SIC: 3446 Ornamental metalwork
PA: Tyler Sheet Metal Inc.
5400 S Hattie Ave
Oklahoma City OK 73129
405 672-5344

(G-5455)
APPLIED INDUS COATINGS LLC
Also Called: Aic
13920 S Meridian Ave (73173-8804)
PHONE..................405 692-2249
Dennis Glasco, *CEO*
Brian Hurd, *Opers Staff*
Jay Hudson, *CFO*
▲ **EMP:** 42 **EST:** 2013
SALES: 1.9MM **Privately Held**
WEB: www.aicokc.com
SIC: 3471 Finishing, metals or formed products
PA: Rock Hill Capital Group, Llc
3737 Buffalo Speedway # 1800
Houston TX 77098

(G-5456)
APPLIED INDUS MACHINING INC
2601 Nw Expwy Ste 900e (73112-7237)
PHONE..................405 672-2222
Robert L Gilson, *Incorporator*
Mike Drain, *Admin Sec*
EMP: 65
SALES (est): 9.2MM **Privately Held**
WEB: www.aim-okc.com
SIC: 3599 Machine shop, jobbing & repair

(G-5457)
APPLIED INDUS MACHINING LLC
1930 Se 29th St (73129-7626)
PHONE..................405 672-2222
Robert Gilson, *President*
Mike Drain, *Admin Sec*
EMP: 115 **EST:** 1986
SALES (est): 16.6MM
SALES (corp-wide): 47.2MM **Privately Held**
SIC: 3599 Machine shop, jobbing & repair
PA: Argonaut Private Equity, L.L.C.
6733 S Yale Ave
Tulsa OK 74136
918 491-4538

(G-5458)
APPLIED OIL TOOLS LLC
1545 Se 29th St Ste A (73129-7601)
PHONE..................405 670-8665
EMP: 1
SALES (corp-wide): 345.6K **Privately Held**
SIC: 3949 Fishing equipment
PA: Applied Oil Tools, Llc
11410 Spring Cypress Rd
Tomball TX 77377
281 376-3784

(G-5459)
APSS INC
9500 Sw 15th St (73128-4813)
PHONE..................405 324-2071
Harold Poage, *President*
Michael Poage, *Corp Secy*
Darrin Hacker, *Vice Pres*
EMP: 1
SALES: 3MM **Privately Held**
SIC: 1382 7359 Oil & gas exploration services; equipment rental & leasing

(G-5460)
ARC DOCUMENT SOLUTIONS LLC
3631 Nw 23rd St (73107-2803)
PHONE..................405 943-0378
John Florer, *Manager*
EMP: 17
SALES (corp-wide): 382.4MM **Publicly Held**
WEB: www.riotcolor.com
SIC: 7334 2752 Blueprinting service; commercial printing, lithographic
HQ: Arc Document Solutions, Llc
6300 Gulfton St
Houston TX 77081
713 988-9200

(G-5461)
ARCADIA RESOURCES LP
301 Nw 63rd St Ste 600 (73116-7909)
P.O. Box 18756 (73154-0756)
PHONE..................405 608-5453
Scott Mueller, *Principal*
EMP: 100
SALES (est): 5.7MM **Privately Held**
SIC: 1382 Oil & gas exploration services

(G-5462)
ARCHITECTURAL METAL PANELS LLC
1616 S Lowery St (73129)
PHONE..................405 672-7407
Oshua L Edwards, *Mng Member*
EMP: 2
SALES (est): 88.9K **Privately Held**
SIC: 3448 Panels for prefabricated metal buildings

(G-5463)
ARINC INCORPORATED
Also Called: Airinc Aerospace
6015 S Portland Ave (73159-2229)
PHONE..................405 601-6000
Angela Allen, *Assistant VP*
Tim Putnam, *Technical Staff*
EMP: 14
SALES (corp-wide): 77B **Publicly Held**
WEB: www.arinc.com
SIC: 3728 Aircraft parts & equipment
HQ: Arinc Incorporated
2551 Riva Rd
Annapolis MD 21401
410 266-4000

Oklahoma City - Oklahoma County (G-5464)

(G-5464)
ARISTA
5221 Nw 5th St (73127-5801)
P.O. Box 272553 (73137-2553)
PHONE..................405 948-1500
Bruce Kerr, *Principal*
EMP: 1
SALES (est): 92K **Privately Held**
SIC: 2731 Book publishing

(G-5465)
ARK -RAMOS FNDRY MFG CO INC
Also Called: A R K Ramos Manufacturing Co
1321 S Walker Ave (73109-1345)
P.O. Box 26388 (73126-0388)
PHONE..................405 235-5505
Courtney Ramos-Finther, *CEO*
Beatrice Ramos, *CEO*
David Wommer, *President*
Dan Ramos, *Chairman*
Courtney Fincher, *Vice Pres*
EMP: 60
SQ FT: 30,000
SALES (est): 12.4MM **Privately Held**
WEB: www.arkramos.com
SIC: 3366 Castings (except die): brass; castings (except die): bronze

(G-5466)
ARMER & QUILLEN LLC
4127 Nw 122nd St Ste A (73120-8880)
PHONE..................405 842-3222
Jim Armer, *Managing Prtnr*
Brad Quillen,
EMP: 10
SALES (est): 595.2K **Privately Held**
SIC: 1389 Oil field services

(G-5467)
ARNOLD ELECTRIC INC
317 N Portland Ave Ste D (73107-6143)
PHONE..................405 605-1982
James M Ryals, *Branch Mgr*
EMP: 5 **Privately Held**
SIC: 3699 1731 Electrical equipment & supplies; electrical work
PA: Arnold Electric, Inc.
1424 E 3rd St
Tulsa OK 74120

(G-5468)
ARNOLD OIL PROPERTIES LLC
6816 N Robinson Ave (73116-9039)
PHONE..................405 842-1488
Blake Arnold,
Claude Arnold,
EMP: 11
SALES (est): 2.4MM **Privately Held**
SIC: 1311 1382 Crude petroleum production; natural gas production; oil & gas exploration services

(G-5469)
ARUZE GAMING AMERICA INC
6101 W Reno Ave Ste 400 (73127-6543)
PHONE..................405 301-8140
EMP: 4
SALES (corp-wide): 60MM **Privately Held**
SIC: 3999 Mfg Misc Products
PA: Aruze Gaming America, Inc.
745 Grier Dr
Las Vegas NV 89119
702 361-3166

(G-5470)
ASCENT RESOURCES - UTICA LLC
3501 Nw 63rd St (73116-2223)
PHONE..................405 608-5544
John Raymond,
John K Reinhart,
Ryan A Turner,
EMP: 100
SALES (est): 48.8MM
SALES (corp-wide): 163.7MM **Privately Held**
SIC: 1382 Oil & gas exploration services
PA: Ascent Resources Operating, Llc
3501 Nw 63rd St
Oklahoma City OK 73116
405 608-5544

(G-5471)
ASCENT RESOURCES OPERATING LLC (PA)
3501 Nw 63rd St (73116-2223)
P.O. Box 13678 (73113-1678)
PHONE..................405 608-5544
Jeff Fisher, *CEO*
Jeff Beck, *Superintendent*
Matthew Mroczkowski, *Superintendent*
Bob Kelly, *Senior VP*
Dale Cook, *Vice Pres*
EMP: 12
SALES (est): 163.7MM **Privately Held**
SIC: 1382 6719 Oil & gas exploration services; investment holding companies, except banks

(G-5472)
ASCENT RSRCES UTICA HLDNGS LLC
3501 Nw 63rd St (73116-2223)
PHONE..................405 608-5544
Jeffrey A Fisher, *CEO*
Amy Sanders, *Analyst*
EMP: 2 EST: 2013
SALES (est): 143.3K **Privately Held**
SIC: 1382 Oil & gas exploration services

(G-5473)
ASES LLC
Also Called: Field Aerospace
6400 Se 59th St (73135-5518)
PHONE..................405 219-3420
John Taylor, *Branch Mgr*
EMP: 245 **Privately Held**
SIC: 3721 3724 3728 8711 Motorized aircraft; air scoops, aircraft; military aircraft equipment & armament; aviation &/or aeronautical engineering
HQ: Ases, Llc
6015 S Portland Ave
Oklahoma City OK 73159

(G-5474)
ASES LLC (HQ)
Also Called: Field Aerospace
6015 S Portland Ave (73159-2229)
PHONE..................405 219-3400
John Mactaggart, *CEO*
V Magarian, *Ch of Bd*
Ray Ord, *Vice Pres*
John Taylor, *Vice Pres*
Darryl Devaney, *Engineer*
EMP: 247
SALES (est): 43.9MM **Privately Held**
SIC: 4581 3721 3724 3728 Aircraft maintenance & repair services; aircraft; motorized aircraft; air scoops, aircraft; fins, aircraft; aviation &/or aeronautical engineering

(G-5475)
ASHER OILFIELD SPECIALTY INC
1615 Se 37th St (73129-7912)
P.O. Box 95421 (73143-5421)
PHONE..................405 677-7868
Allen Vance, *President*
EMP: 8
SQ FT: 6,000
SALES (est): 2.1MM **Privately Held**
SIC: 7699 8742 1389 Pumps & pumping equipment repair; management consulting services; oil field services

(G-5476)
ASHER OILFIELD SPECIALTY INC
26 Ne 26th St (73105-2703)
P.O. Box 720944 (73172-0944)
PHONE..................405 568-3433
EMP: 5 EST: 2018
SALES (est): 276.8K **Privately Held**
SIC: 1389 Oil field services

(G-5477)
ASHLEY CAMERON BUILDING PRODS
2401 Sw 10th St (73108-2465)
PHONE..................405 236-0617
Don Edwards, *Principal*
EMP: 3 EST: 2010
SALES (est): 280.6K **Privately Held**
SIC: 3089 Plastics products

(G-5478)
ASSOCIATED TOOL & MACHINE CO
1126 Se 15th St (73129-6006)
PHONE..................405 670-4155
EMP: 3
SQ FT: 4,500
SALES (est): 220K **Privately Held**
SIC: 3544 Mfg Dies & Molds

(G-5479)
AT A GLANCE SOFTWARE LLC
3300 Nw 45th Ter (73112-5908)
PHONE..................405 601-3062
Wendy Sparkman, *Principal*
EMP: 2
SALES (est): 129.3K **Privately Held**
SIC: 7372 Prepackaged software

(G-5480)
ATC DRIVETRAIN LLC
9901 W Reno Ave (73127-7140)
P.O. Box 270180 (73137-0180)
PHONE..................405 577-9901
Greg Heald, *President*
◆ EMP: 1000
SQ FT: 150,000
SALES (est): 228.8MM **Privately Held**
SIC: 3714 4731 Motor vehicle transmissions, drive assemblies & parts; freight transportation arrangement

(G-5481)
ATC DRIVETRAIN LLC
4680 Nw 3rd St (73127-6408)
PHONE..................405 350-3600
EMP: 400
SALES (corp-wide): 47.4B **Publicly Held**
SIC: 3714 Mfg Motor Vehicle Parts/Accessories
HQ: Atc Drivetrain, Llc
9901 W Reno Ave
Oklahoma City OK 73127
405 350-3600

(G-5482)
ATC NEW TECHNOLOGIES
10001 Nw 2nd St (73127-7149)
PHONE..................405 577-9901
Monika Minarcin, *General Mgr*
Vicki Jones, *Accounts Mgr*
EMP: 20 EST: 2012
SQ FT: 5,000
SALES (est): 1.7MM **Privately Held**
SIC: 3629 Battery chargers, rectifying or nonrotating

(G-5483)
ATC TECHNOLOGY CORPORATION
Also Called: Drivetrain
9901 W Reno Ave (73127-7140)
PHONE..................405 577-9901
EMP: 600
SALES (corp-wide): 47.4B **Publicly Held**
SIC: 3714 Remfg Transmissions
HQ: Atc Technology Corporation
100 Papercraft Park
Pittsburgh PA 16066
412 820-3700

(G-5484)
ATCHLEY RESOURCES INC
13903 Quail Pointe Dr (73134-1002)
PHONE..................405 848-3331
Ronald W Atchley, *President*
Ronald Atchley Jr, *Vice Pres*
Wes Atchley, *Vice Pres*
EMP: 4
SQ FT: 1,500
SALES (est): 278.1K **Privately Held**
SIC: 1381 Reworking oil & gas wells

(G-5485)
ATLANTIC FBRICATION DESIGN LLC
Also Called: Boiler Repair Company
901 Se 29th St (73129-4835)
P.O. Box 94036 (73143-4036)
PHONE..................405 619-7607
Paul Stitt, *Owner*
Paul D Stitt, *Mng Member*
Mike Johnson, *Mng Member*
EMP: 8
SALES (est): 3.5MM **Privately Held**
SIC: 3441 Fabricated structural metal

(G-5486)
ATLAS ROCK BIT SERVICE INC
3901 Sw 113th St (73173-8387)
PHONE..................405 691-4848
Mike Waitman, *President*
▲ EMP: 16 EST: 1974
SQ FT: 2,500
SALES (est): 3.3MM **Privately Held**
SIC: 3533 Bits, oil & gas field tools: rock; water well drilling equipment

(G-5487)
ATTORNEY AND LEGAL PUBLICA
5609 Nw 110th St 11 (73162-5826)
PHONE..................405 728-0392
Charles Cantrell, *Principal*
EMP: 2
SALES (est): 133.5K **Privately Held**
SIC: 2741 Miscellaneous publishing

(G-5488)
AUCORA BREAKFAST BAR BACKYARD
1704 Nw 16th St (73106-2029)
PHONE..................405 609-8854
EMP: 2
SALES (est): 68.6K **Privately Held**
SIC: 2064 Breakfast bars

(G-5489)
AUDREY PARKS & ASSOCIATES LLC
101 Park Ave Ste 101 # 101 (73102-7201)
PHONE..................405 328-3186
Ashley Parker-Johnson,
EMP: 1
SALES (est): 188.4K **Privately Held**
SIC: 2621 Paper mills

(G-5490)
AUSTIN GAS PROPERTIES LLC
9609 Eagle Hill Dr (73162-6421)
PHONE..................405 229-2391
Ken Austin, *President*
EMP: 1
SALES (est): 86.5K **Privately Held**
SIC: 1389 Oil consultants

(G-5491)
AUTO WAY MANUFACTURING CO LLC
Also Called: Wayman Hugh Rev
3516 Nw 42nd St (73112-6354)
PHONE..................405 946-3516
Hugh Wayman, *Partner*
Betty Wayman, *Partner*
EMP: 2
SALES (est): 109.7K **Privately Held**
SIC: 3999 Manufacturing industries

(G-5492)
AUTOCRAFT INDUSTRIES ●
9901 W Reno Ave (73127-7140)
PHONE..................405 577-9901
EMP: 1 EST: 2019
SALES (est): 47.1K **Privately Held**
SIC: 3714 Motor vehicle parts & accessories

(G-5493)
AUTOCRAFT MATERIAL RECOVERY
10001 Nw 2nd St (73127-7149)
P.O. Box 270180 (73137-0180)
PHONE..................405 350-3800
Brett Dickson, *President*
Timothy Kendrick, *Production*
Dawn Cannom, *Director*
EMP: 5
SALES (est): 423.9K **Privately Held**
SIC: 3465 Body parts, automobile: stamped metal

(G-5494)
AUTOMATED GASKET COMPANY LLC
Also Called: Manufacturing
5706 Nw 5th St (73128-1230)
P.O. Box 270608 (73137-0608)
PHONE..................405 951-5301

GEOGRAPHIC SECTION

Oklahoma City - Oklahoma County (G-5522)

Terry M Brown, *President*
Ranndy Taylor, *Vice Pres*
Jim Bomgaars, *Engineer*
EMP: 13
SQ FT: 25,000
SALES (est): 2.4MM **Privately Held**
SIC: 3053 5085 Gaskets, all materials; gaskets

(G-5495)
AVENTURA TECHNOLOGIES INC
12330 Saint Andrews Dr (73120-8604)
PHONE.................631 300-4000
EMP: 1
SALES (corp-wide): 17.5MM **Privately Held**
SIC: 3577 Computer peripheral equipment
PA: Aventura Technologies, Inc.
 1 Lady Janes Way
 Northport NY 11768
 631 300-4000

(G-5496)
AWC INC
5600 Sw 36th St Ste A (73179-7815)
PHONE.................405 601-1090
Robert Alford, *CEO*
EMP: 1
SALES (corp-wide): 144.4MM **Privately Held**
SIC: 5063 3699 Electrical apparatus & equipment; electrical equipment & supplies
PA: Awc, Inc.
 6655 Exchequer Dr
 Baton Rouge LA 70809
 225 752-3939

(G-5497)
AWNIQUE
4400 Sw 36th St (73119-2412)
PHONE.................405 818-8032
EMP: 2
SALES (est): 84.5K **Privately Held**
SIC: 3444 Sheet metalwork

(G-5498)
AXIOM AUTOMOTIVE TECH INC
101 N Robinson Ave # 710 (73102-5504)
PHONE.................909 841-8200
Robert Loreaux, *President*
EMP: 2
SALES (est): 56.5K **Privately Held**
SIC: 7372 Prepackaged software

(G-5499)
B & B MEDICAL SERVICES INC (PA)
4045 Nw 64th St Ste 250 (73116-1732)
PHONE.................919 601-4756
Thomas Mirabile, *CEO*
William H Long, *Vice Pres*
Judy Franklin, *Opers Staff*
Barry Blackbird, *Manager*
William Espey, *Officer*
EMP: 20
SQ FT: 15,000
SALES (est): 10MM **Privately Held**
SIC: 7352 7699 5047 3841 Medical equipment rental; hospital equipment repair services; therapy equipment; surgical & medical instruments

(G-5500)
B & C MACHINE COMPANY INC
8301 Sw 3rd St (73128-4204)
PHONE.................405 787-8862
Maria Shrader, *President*
Sonia Hayes, *Corp Secy*
Scott Hayes, *Manager*
EMP: 15
SQ FT: 14,000
SALES (est): 2.3MM **Privately Held**
WEB: www.bcmachineco.com
SIC: 3599 3728 Machine shop, jobbing & repair; aircraft parts & equipment

(G-5501)
B & D EAGLE MACHINE SHOP
8124 Sw 8th St Ste A (73128-4241)
PHONE.................405 787-3232
EMP: 12
SALES (est): 530K **Privately Held**
SIC: 3599 Mfg Industrial Machinery

(G-5502)
B & R PUMP & EQUIPMENT INC
4001 S High Ave (73129-5241)
PHONE.................405 632-3051
Mike E Johnson, *President*
Karl L Rath, *Principal*
Larry W Barnhill, *Principal*
Phillip E Holmes, *Vice Pres*
EMP: 9
SQ FT: 16,000
SALES (est): 1MM **Privately Held**
SIC: 1389 Oil field services

(G-5503)
B & W EXPLORATION INC
6908 N Robinson Ave (73116-9041)
PHONE.................405 236-1807
Frederick M Black, *President*
Kirk Whitman, *Vice Pres*
EMP: 3
SQ FT: 3,700
SALES (est): 296.2K **Privately Held**
SIC: 1382 Oil & gas exploration services

(G-5504)
B B ROYALTY COMPANY
3300 S High Ave (73129-5128)
PHONE.................405 672-3381
EMP: 3
SALES (est): 131.3K **Privately Held**
SIC: 1311 Crude petroleum production

(G-5505)
B R POLK INC
5715 N Western Ave Ste C (73118-1239)
PHONE.................405 286-9666
Marjorie Polk, *President*
Tom W Klos, *Vice Pres*
Randel Polk, *Vice Pres*
Angie Klein, *Admin Sec*
EMP: 4 **EST:** 1957
SQ FT: 2,000
SALES (est): 688.2K **Privately Held**
SIC: 1311 1382 Crude petroleum production; natural gas production; oil & gas exploration services

(G-5506)
B&W OPERATING LLC
6908 N Robinson Ave (73116-9041)
PHONE.................405 236-1807
Frederick M Black,
Larry Fenity,
Kirk Whitman,
EMP: 8
SQ FT: 7,882
SALES (est): 799.9K **Privately Held**
SIC: 1382 Oil & gas exploration services

(G-5507)
BACHMAN SERVICES INC (HQ)
2220 S I 35 Service Rd (73129-6347)
P.O. Box 96265 (73143-6265)
PHONE.................405 677-8296
Patrick Williams, *President*
Harold L Smart, *Vice Pres*
Terry Hix, *Sales Staff*
Patrick S Williams, *Director*
▲ **EMP:** 27
SQ FT: 28,000
SALES: 80MM
SALES (corp-wide): 1.5B **Publicly Held**
WEB: www.bachmanservices.com
SIC: 2899 Chemical preparations
PA: Innospec Inc.
 8310 S Valley Hwy Ste 350
 Englewood CO 80112
 303 792-5554

(G-5508)
BADLANDS PETROLEUM LLC
2320 Nw 59th St (73112-7372)
PHONE.................303 921-2854
Ryan Rickett, *Principal*
EMP: 2
SALES (est): 90.1K **Privately Held**
SIC: 1381 Drilling oil & gas wells

(G-5509)
BAGS INC
1900 N Sooner Rd (73141-1226)
PHONE.................405 427-5473
Scott Currie, *President*
Harry O Currie, *Principal*
Joan Currie, *Principal*
Kevin McGehee, *Vice Pres*
▼ **EMP:** 40
SQ FT: 22,000
SALES (est): 10.1MM **Privately Held**
WEB: www.bags-inc.com
SIC: 2673 3081 Plastic bags: made from purchased materials; unsupported plastics film & sheet

(G-5510)
BAKER ENERGY SOLUTIONS LLC
11500 S Meridian Ave (73173-8228)
PHONE.................405 691-1202
Justin Baker, *President*
EMP: 3 **EST:** 2015
SALES (est): 90.1K **Privately Held**
SIC: 1381 Service well drilling

(G-5511)
BAKER HGHES OLFLD OPRTIONS INC
Also Called: Baker Oil Tools
12701 N Santa Fe Ave (73114-3805)
P.O. Box 1505, Fort Smith AR (72902-1505)
PHONE.................405 681-2175
EMP: 4
SALES (corp-wide): 9.8B **Publicly Held**
SIC: 1389 Sales And Gas Service
HQ: Baker Hughes Oilfield Operations Llc
 17021 Aldine Westfield Rd
 Houston TX 77073
 713 879-1000

(G-5512)
BAKER HGHES OLFLD OPRTIONS LLC
Also Called: Baker Atlas
12701 N Santa Fe Ave (73114-3805)
P.O. Box 186, Woodward (73802-0186)
PHONE.................580 256-3333
Marcus Baca, *Manager*
EMP: 50 **Privately Held**
WEB: www.bakerhughes.com
SIC: 1389 1382 Oil field services; well logging; seismograph surveys
PA: Baker Hughes Oilfield Operations Llc
 2001 Rankin Rd
 Houston TX 77073

(G-5513)
BAKER HGHES OLFLD OPRTIONS LLC
Also Called: Baker Hughes Inteq
6209 S Sooner Rd (73135-5607)
PHONE.................405 670-3354
Tom Rogers, *Regional Mgr*
EMP: 200 **Privately Held**
SIC: 1389 1382 Oil field services; oil & gas exploration services
PA: Baker Hughes Oilfield Operations Llc
 2001 Rankin Rd
 Houston TX 77073

(G-5514)
BAKER HUGHES A GE COMPANY LLC
Also Called: Energy Innovation Ctr N Amer
300 Ne 9th St (73104-1850)
PHONE.................518 387-7914
Todd Alhart, *Senior Mgr*
EMP: 9
SALES (corp-wide): 23.8B **Publicly Held**
SIC: 3724 Research & development on aircraft engines & parts
HQ: Baker Hughes Holdings Llc
 17021 Aldine Westfield Rd
 Houston TX 77073
 713 439-8600

(G-5515)
BAKER HUGHES A GE COMPANY LLC
12701 N Santa Fe Ave (73114-3805)
PHONE.................405 227-8471
EMP: 4
SALES (corp-wide): 23.8B **Publicly Held**
SIC: 3533 Oil & gas field machinery
HQ: Baker Hughes Holdings Llc
 17021 Aldine Westfield Rd
 Houston TX 77073
 713 439-8600

(G-5516)
BAKER HUGHES ELASTO SYSTEMS
6417 S Sooner Rd (73135-5611)
PHONE.................405 670-3354
Dirk Froehlich, *Principal*
Robert Robinson, *Manager*
▲ **EMP:** 10
SQ FT: 105,000
SALES (est): 1.1MM
SALES (corp-wide): 23.8B **Publicly Held**
SIC: 3061 3533 3498 3317 Oil & gas field machinery rubber goods (mechanical); oil & gas field machinery; fabricated pipe & fittings; steel pipe & tubes
HQ: Baker Hughes Holdings Llc
 17021 Aldine Westfield Rd
 Houston TX 77073
 713 439-8600

(G-5517)
BAKERS PRINTING CO INC
9014 N Western Ave (73114-2520)
P.O. Box 14204 (73113-0204)
PHONE.................405 842-6944
Kathi Powell, *President*
Carl Miles, *Vice Pres*
EMP: 7 **EST:** 1976
SQ FT: 6,000
SALES: 450K **Privately Held**
SIC: 2752 2791 2759 Letters, circular or form: lithographed; commercial printing, offset; typesetting; commercial printing

(G-5518)
BAKKEN HBT LP
100 Park Ave Ste 400 (73102-8002)
P.O. Box 779 (73101-0779)
PHONE.................405 516-8241
Steve Long, *Administration*
EMP: 3
SALES (est): 644.6K **Privately Held**
WEB: www.bakkenhbtlp.com
SIC: 1382 Oil & gas exploration services

(G-5519)
BALCO INC
Also Called: Balco Metalines
5551 Nw 5th St (73127-5811)
PHONE.................316 945-9328
Thomas Shupe, *Branch Mgr*
EMP: 50
SQ FT: 30,600
SALES (corp-wide): 385.8MM **Publicly Held**
SIC: 3446 3444 3443 Architectural metalwork; sheet metalwork; fabricated plate work (boiler shop)
HQ: Balco, Inc.
 2626 S Sheridan Ave
 Wichita KS 67217
 800 767-0082

(G-5520)
BALE CORPORATION
124 Nw 67th St (73116-8215)
PHONE.................405 848-8797
Charles R Bale, *President*
William E Owen, *Admin Sec*
EMP: 2 **EST:** 1969
SQ FT: 750
SALES (est): 226.1K **Privately Held**
SIC: 1311 Crude petroleum production

(G-5521)
BALLEWS ALUMINUM PRODUCTS INC
5405 Nw 5th St (73127-5809)
PHONE.................405 917-2225
Robert Nunnemaker, *Branch Mgr*
EMP: 3
SALES (corp-wide): 15.8MM **Privately Held**
SIC: 3354 Aluminum extruded products
PA: Ballew's Aluminum Products, Inc.
 2 Shelter Dr
 Greer SC 29650
 864 272-4453

(G-5522)
BALON CORPORATION
3245 S Hattie Ave (73129-6697)
PHONE.................405 677-3321
Phil Scaramucci, *President*
Domer Scaramucci Jr, *President*

Oklahoma City - Oklahoma County (G-5523)

GEOGRAPHIC SECTION

Kevin Spray, *Regional Mgr*
Dale Wilmoth, *Regional Mgr*
Shane Wold, *Regional Mgr*
▲ **EMP:** 850
SQ FT: 500,000
SALES (est): 227.4MM **Privately Held**
WEB: www.balon.com
SIC: 3491 3494 5085 Industrial valves; valves & pipe fittings; industrial supplies

(G-5523)
BALON VALVES
3700 W Eastern Ave (73129)
PHONE................405 670-8300
EMP: 2
SALES (est): 83K **Privately Held**
SIC: 3491 Industrial valves

(G-5524)
BANDON OIL & GAS GP LLC
123 Robert S Kerr Ave (73102-6406)
PHONE................405 429-5500
EMP: 3
SALES (est): 152.6K **Privately Held**
SIC: 1311 Crude petroleum & natural gas

(G-5525)
BANNERS SIGNS & BUSINESS CARDS ○
45 Ne 50th St (73105-1807)
PHONE................405 818-4371
EMP: 1 **EST:** 2019
SALES (est): 46K **Privately Held**
SIC: 3993 Signs & advertising specialties

(G-5526)
BARBARA CHAPLE
Also Called: Coop's Buttons
7030 W Wilshire Blvd (73132-5484)
PHONE................405 721-3758
Barbara Chaple, *Owner*
EMP: 5
SQ FT: 1,200
SALES (est): 343.5K **Privately Held**
SIC: 3993 Advertising novelties

(G-5527)
BARBOUR ENERGY CORPORATION
3111 Quail Springs Pkwy (73134-2609)
P.O. Box 13480 (73113-1480)
PHONE................405 848-7671
Jay Wayne Barbour, *President*
Laurie Barbour, *Vice Pres*
Teresa Porta, *Admin Sec*
EMP: 7 **EST:** 1979
SQ FT: 7,019
SALES (est): 1.1MM **Privately Held**
SIC: 1382 1311 Oil & gas exploration services; crude petroleum production; natural gas production

(G-5528)
BARON MANUFACTURING INC
3100 W I 44 Service Rd (73112-6242)
PHONE................405 947-3362
Don Perry, *President*
EMP: 5
SQ FT: 18,000
SALES: 500K **Privately Held**
SIC: 3679 3812 3728 Electronic circuits; search & navigation equipment; aircraft parts & equipment

(G-5529)
BATH & BODY WORKS LLC
2150 W Memorial Rd Ste A (73184-8045)
PHONE................405 748-3197
Rebecca Lynch, *Manager*
EMP: 20
SALES (corp-wide): 12.9B **Publicly Held**
SIC: 5999 2844 Perfumes & colognes; toilet preparations; toilet preparations
HQ: Bath & Body Works, Llc
7 Limited Pkwy E
Reynoldsburg OH 43068

(G-5530)
BATTERIES SOONER LLC
Also Called: Batteries Plus
4100 Will Rogers Pkwy # 300 (73108-2050)
PHONE................405 605-1237
Brandon Boocer, *Vice Pres*
EMP: 30

SALES (est): 4.7MM **Privately Held**
WEB: www.batteriesplus.com
SIC: 3621 5531 Generators for storage battery chargers; batteries, automotive & truck

(G-5531)
BAUMAN MACHINE INC
6600 Sw 44th St (73179-6412)
P.O. Box 526, Wheatland (73097-0526)
PHONE................405 745-3484
Mark McCarty, *President*
Troy Eplin, *Mfg Spvr*
Mike Edgar, *Sales Mgr*
Jonathan Barbour, *Supervisor*
Maggie Fields, *Admin Asst*
EMP: 32 **EST:** 1975
SQ FT: 21,000
SALES (est): 5.6MM **Privately Held**
WEB: www.baumanmachine.com
SIC: 3599 3533 Machine shop, jobbing & repair; oil & gas field machinery

(G-5532)
BAYS ENTERPRISES INC (PA)
228 Robert S Kerr Ave # 600 (73102-5217)
PHONE................405 235-2297
M Joe Bays, *President*
Lisa Ann Bays, *Admin Sec*
EMP: 2
SALES (est): 2.6MM **Privately Held**
SIC: 5084 1311 1381 Oil refining machinery, equipment & supplies; crude petroleum production; natural gas production; drilling oil & gas wells

(G-5533)
BAYS EXPLORATION INC
4005 Nw Expwy St Ste 600 (73116-1689)
PHONE................405 235-2297
M Joe Bays, *President*
Carlos Gonzalez, *Exploration*
EMP: 3
SQ FT: 3,500
SALES (est): 1.6MM
SALES (corp-wide): 2.6MM **Privately Held**
SIC: 1381 Drilling oil & gas wells
PA: Bays Enterprises Inc
228 Robert S Kerr Ave # 600
Oklahoma City OK 73102
405 235-2297

(G-5534)
BB2 LLC (PA)
Also Called: Bricktown Brewery
1 N Oklahoma Ave (73104-2413)
PHONE................405 232-2739
Jim Cowen, *Mng Member*
Jim Calen, *Mng Member*
EMP: 32
SQ FT: 30,000
SALES (est): 9.5MM **Privately Held**
SIC: 2082 Malt beverages

(G-5535)
BC STEEL BUILDINGS INC
9900 Nw 10th St (73127-7145)
PHONE................405 324-5100
Mary Weber, *President*
Rodney Laubach, *Corp Secy*
Dennis Hatch, *Vice Pres*
Karen Hatch, *Vice Pres*
Dennis Watson, *Engineer*
EMP: 65
SQ FT: 72,000
SALES (est): 15.5MM **Privately Held**
SIC: 3448 Prefabricated metal buildings

(G-5536)
BCE - MACH III LLC (PA)
14201 Wireless Way # 300 (73134-2521)
PHONE................405 252-8100
Tom L Ward, *Mng Member*
EMP: 83
SALES: 100MM **Privately Held**
SIC: 1311 Crude petroleum & natural gas production

(G-5537)
BCE-MACH II LLC
14201 Wireless Way # 300 (73134-2521)
PHONE................405 252-8100
Kevin White, *Principal*
Tom Ward, *Mng Member*
EMP: 86

SALES (est): 90.1K **Privately Held**
SIC: 1382 1311 Oil & gas exploration services; crude petroleum & natural gas production

(G-5538)
BCE-MACH LLC (PA)
14201 Wireless Way # 300 (73134-2521)
PHONE................405 252-8100
Tom Ward, *CEO*
EMP: 57
SQ FT: 30,000
SALES: 135MM **Privately Held**
SIC: 1382 Oil & gas exploration services

(G-5539)
BCEJ COMPANY
328 S Eagle Ln Ste D (73128-4224)
PHONE................405 470-3790
Jerry R Barton, *President*
Janice Barton, *Corp Secy*
EMP: 1
SALES: 750K **Privately Held**
SIC: 1389 Oil & gas wells: building, repairing & dismantling

(G-5540)
BEACON PUBLISHING CO INC
Also Called: Capitol Hill Beacon
124 Sw 25th St (73109-6020)
PHONE................405 232-4151
David Sellers, *President*
Gay Sellers, *Corp Secy*
EMP: 3 **EST:** 1905
SQ FT: 5,000
SALES (est): 212.7K **Privately Held**
SIC: 2711 Commercial printing & newspaper publishing combined

(G-5541)
BECSUL ENERGY INCORPORATED
6815 Nw 10th St Ste 1 (73127-4249)
PHONE................405 789-1061
Benny Bechtol, *President*
Greg Bechtol, *Vice Pres*
David Sullivan, *Treasurer*
EMP: 3
SQ FT: 1,000
SALES (est): 310K **Privately Held**
SIC: 1382 Oil & gas exploration services

(G-5542)
BEDFORD ENERGY INC
3555 Nw 58th St Ste 901 (73112-4731)
PHONE................405 820-2711
Bruce J Scambler, *President*
Ben Holland, *Corp Secy*
Jacob S Paine, *Vice Pres*
Donald G Kennedy, *Director*
Carl W Swan, *Director*
EMP: 7
SQ FT: 2,800
SALES (est): 561.1K **Privately Held**
SIC: 1382 Oil & gas exploration services

(G-5543)
BELL & MCCOY COMPANIES INC
719 N Shartel Ave (73102-1600)
PHONE................405 278-6909
Jason Shaver, *General Mgr*
Ashley Spring, *Opers Mgr*
EMP: 34
SALES (corp-wide): 34.2MM **Privately Held**
SIC: 5063 3699 Electrical supplies; electrical equipment & supplies
PA: Bell & Mccoy Companies, Inc.
4630 Nall Rd
Farmers Branch TX 75244
469 574-0300

(G-5544)
BELLA FORTE GLASS STUDIO LLC
1012 Nw 81st St (73114-1908)
PHONE................405 659-6169
Chris McGahan, *Principal*
EMP: 2
SALES (est): 149.4K **Privately Held**
WEB: www.bellaforteglass.com
SIC: 3229 Pressed & blown glass

(G-5545)
BELLOFRAM
Also Called: Whittle & Neher Company
2221 Se 69th St (73149-6003)
P.O. Box 96437 (73143-6437)
PHONE................405 677-7222
Larry Whittle, *President*
Jeff Smith, *General Mgr*
Brad Whittle, *Director*
EMP: 25
SQ FT: 3,000
SALES (est): 4.1MM **Privately Held**
SIC: 3491 Industrial valves

(G-5546)
BELLS AND WHISTLES
340 S Vermont Ave Ste 109 (73108-1038)
PHONE................405 470-8400
EMP: 2
SALES (est): 146.5K **Privately Held**
WEB: www.bellsandwhistlesokc.com
SIC: 3999 Whistles

(G-5547)
BELLWOOD PETROLEUM
4117 Nw 122nd St (73120-8869)
PHONE................405 254-3113
EMP: 2
SALES (est): 123.7K **Privately Held**
SIC: 1382 Oil & gas exploration services

(G-5548)
BELLYLOVE MATERNITY GIFTS
13104 Box Canyon Rd (73142-6202)
PHONE................405 818-3339
Suzanne Lee, *Principal*
EMP: 2
SALES (est): 90.9K **Privately Held**
SIC: 2339 Maternity clothing

(G-5549)
BENCHMARK 77 ENERGY
777 Nw 63rd St (73116-7601)
PHONE................405 239-3291
EMP: 2 **EST:** 2017
SALES (est): 113.2K **Privately Held**
SIC: 1382 Oil & gas exploration services

(G-5550)
BENCHMARK COMPLETIONS LLC
13800 S Macarthur Blvd (73173-8708)
PHONE................405 691-5659
Ryan Crow, *Branch Mgr*
EMP: 15
SALES (corp-wide): 8.1MM **Privately Held**
SIC: 3599 7692 5082 Machine & other job shop work; welding repair; oil field equipment
PA: Benchmark Completions Llc
1400 Woodloch Forest Dr
Spring TX 77380
281 537-8483

(G-5551)
BENJAMIN HARJO JR
1516 Nw 35th St (73118-3214)
PHONE................405 521-0246
Benjamin Harjo Jr, *Owner*
EMP: 1 **EST:** 1975
SALES (est): 52.7K **Privately Held**
SIC: 3952 Canvas board, artists'

(G-5552)
BENNIE PUBLICATIONS LLC
1809 S Grand Blvd (73108-4232)
PHONE................918 873-0250
Joelisha Rayvon Goggins, *Principal*
EMP: 1
SALES (est): 37.5K **Privately Held**
SIC: 2741 Miscellaneous publishing

(G-5553)
BENSON SOUND INC
Also Called: Benson Sound Lights & Video
5717 Se 74th St Ste F (73135-1105)
PHONE................405 610-7455
Larry R Benson, *President*
Linda Groves, *Corp Secy*
Diana Benson, *Exec VP*
Gary Duggan, *Engineer*
EMP: 9
SQ FT: 6,500

GEOGRAPHIC SECTION   Oklahoma City - Oklahoma County (G-5583)

SALES (est): 1.2MM **Privately Held**
SIC: 1731 7389 3695 Sound equipment specialization; computer installation; recording studio, noncommercial records; magnetic & optical recording media

(G-5554)
BEREDCO INC
2601 Nw Expwy Ste 1100e (73112-7250)
PHONE..................................405 858-2326
Bob Beren, *President*
Peter Wilson, *Agent*
EMP: 130
SQ FT: 3,000
SALES (est): 3.9MM **Privately Held**
SIC: 1382 Oil & gas exploration services

(G-5555)
BEREXCO LLC
2601 Nw Expwy Ste 1100e (73112-7250)
PHONE..................................405 848-1165
Evan Mayhew, *Vice Pres*
Pete Wilson, *Vice Pres*
Bob Burke, *Branch Mgr*
EMP: 2
SALES (corp-wide): 410.9MM **Privately Held**
WEB: www.berexco.com
SIC: 1382 Oil & gas exploration services
PA: Berexco Llc
    2020 N Bramblewood St
    Wichita KS 67206
    316 265-3311

(G-5556)
BERKSHIRE CORPORATION (PA)
Also Called: Holiday Car Care Center
1101 Se 26th St (73129-6463)
P.O. Box 652 (73101-0652)
PHONE..................................405 677-3391
Richard W Iman, *President*
J W McTiernan, *Corp Secy*
EMP: 3
SQ FT: 6,000
SALES (est): 638.5K **Privately Held**
WEB: www.berkshire.eu.com
SIC: 3589 7542 3563 2841 Car washing machinery; carwash, automatic; air & gas compressors; soap & other detergents

(G-5557)
BERRIDGE MFG DIST CTR
1400 Exchange Ave (73108-3015)
PHONE..................................405 248-7404
EMP: 1
SALES (est): 39.6K **Privately Held**
SIC: 3999 Manufacturing industries

(G-5558)
BERRYFIELDS CINNAMON ROLL LLC
3545 Nw 58th St (73112-4726)
PHONE..................................405 248-0777
Jonathan Buford,
EMP: 5 EST: 2015
SALES: 40K **Privately Held**
SIC: 2051 Bread, cake & related products

(G-5559)
BETA OIL COMPANY
Also Called: Beta Tex
4900 N Meridian Ave (73112-2221)
P.O. Box 12958 (73157-2958)
PHONE..................................405 601-3389
Steven C Holmes, *President*
Anita Holmes, *Admin Sec*
EMP: 5
SALES (est): 488.9K **Privately Held**
SIC: 1382 1311 Oil & gas exploration services; crude petroleum production; natural gas production

(G-5560)
BETTER POWER INC
7608 N Hudson Ave (73116-7717)
P.O. Box 13705 (73113-1705)
PHONE..................................405 753-1192
John Markland, *President*
EMP: 3
SQ FT: 26,000
SALES (est): 300K **Privately Held**
SIC: 3629 Power conversion units, a.c. to d.c.: static-electric

(G-5561)
BF BRANDT WELDING LLC
212 N Falcon Dr (73127-7210)
PHONE..................................405 657-4670
Burton Brandt, *Principal*
EMP: 1
SALES (est): 44.4K **Privately Held**
SIC: 7692 Welding repair

(G-5562)
BGR LLC
1020 E Grand Blvd (73129-8403)
PHONE..................................405 671-2000
Brazil Piper,
Britton F Piper,
CF Rick Piper,
Greg Piper,
Kay Piper,
EMP: 26
SALES (est): 3.3MM **Privately Held**
SIC: 3491 Industrial valves
PA: Piper International, Inc.
    1715 S Lowery St
    Oklahoma City OK 73129

(G-5563)
BIG D INDUSTRIES INC
5620 Sw 29th St (73179-7627)
P.O. Box 82219 (73148-0219)
PHONE..................................405 682-2541
Donald H Lees, *President*
Jidge Verity, *Vice Pres*
Todd Huffman, *Prdtn Mgr*
Wayne Yates, *Prdtn Mgr*
Mike Biggers, *Natl Sales Mgr*
▲ EMP: 30
SALES (est): 8.3MM **Privately Held**
WEB: www.bigdind.com
SIC: 2842 Deodorants, nonpersonal

(G-5564)
BIG GAS OIL LLC
4900 Richmond Sq Ste 300 (73118-2045)
P.O. Box 6213, Longview TX (75608-6213)
PHONE..................................405 763-9844
EMP: 3
SALES (est): 262.7K **Privately Held**
SIC: 1389 Oil & gas field services

(G-5565)
BIG RICKS JERKY LLC
9709 Lakeland Rd (73162-7436)
PHONE..................................405 414-9096
EMP: 2
SALES (est): 62.3K **Privately Held**
SIC: 2013 Snack sticks, including jerky: from purchased meat

(G-5566)
BILLIARDS & BAR STOOLS INC
Also Called: Amini's Galleria
525 W Memorial Rd (73114-2010)
PHONE..................................405 722-2400
Rosinna Gies, *Manager*
EMP: 10
SALES (est): 1.1MM
SALES (corp-wide): 5.5MM **Privately Held**
SIC: 2511 2514 Wood game room furniture; metal game room furniture
PA: Billiards & Bar Stools, Inc.
    7712 E 71st St
    Tulsa OK 74133
    918 254-6444

(G-5567)
BILLS WELDING COOP LLC
Also Called: Welding Co-Op, The
2000 Sw 15th St (73108-3218)
PHONE..................................405 370-6383
Kaleah Sellon,
EMP: 2
SQ FT: 8,000
SALES (est): 126.8K **Privately Held**
SIC: 3441 Building components, structural steel

(G-5568)
BILLS WELDING EQUIPMENT REPR
2006 Sw 15th St (73108-3218)
PHONE..................................405 232-4799
William Sellon, *CEO*
Janna Sellon, *Vice Pres*
EMP: 11

SQ FT: 10,000
SALES (est): 1.2MM **Privately Held**
SIC: 7692 Welding repair

(G-5569)
BIMBO BAKERIES USA INC
Also Called: Earthgrains Companies
1916 N Broadway Ave (73103-4408)
PHONE..................................405 556-2135
Mark Drozdowski, *Manager*
EMP: 400 **Privately Held**
SIC: 2051 Bakery: wholesale or wholesale/retail combined
HQ: Bimbo Bakeries Usa, Inc
    255 Business Center Dr # 200
    Horsham PA 19044
    215 347-5500

(G-5570)
BINGER OPERATIONS LLC
204 N Robinson Ave # 2300 (73102-7001)
PHONE..................................405 232-0201
Steve B Slawson, *Mng Member*
Steve Slawson, *Mng Member*
Joseph Sinner,
EMP: 3 EST: 1998
SALES (est): 234.1K **Privately Held**
WEB: www.slawsoncompanies.com
SIC: 1311 Crude petroleum production

(G-5571)
BINT EXPLORATION & DEVELOPMENT
5653 N Pennsylvania Ave (73112-7769)
PHONE..................................405 848-2113
Richard Sias, *Owner*
EMP: 2
SQ FT: 4,520
SALES (est): 180K **Privately Held**
SIC: 1382 Oil & gas exploration services

(G-5572)
BIOCORP TECHNOLOGIES INC
743 Nw 99th St (73114-5601)
PHONE..................................405 990-2350
Scot Sidwell, *Owner*
EMP: 2
SALES (est): 86.6K **Privately Held**
SIC: 3841 Surgical & medical instruments

(G-5573)
BIOSPHERE FUELS LLC
10601 N Penn Ave (73120-4108)
PHONE..................................713 332-5726
Douglas Stussi, *CEO*
▲ EMP: 5
SQ FT: 35,000
SALES (est): 300K **Privately Held**
SIC: 2869 Industrial organic chemicals

(G-5574)
BIOTECH PRODUCTS INC
1529 W Main St (73106-3013)
P.O. Box 82755 (73148-0755)
PHONE..................................405 235-7575
Steve Ochs, *President*
EMP: 7
SQ FT: 5,600
SALES: 800K **Privately Held**
SIC: 5169 5999 2899 Industrial chemicals; alcoholic beverage making equipment & supplies; anti-glare material

(G-5575)
BIPO INC
12225 Candy Tuft Ln (73162-1913)
P.O. Box 44056 (73144-1056)
PHONE..................................580 262-9640
Tom Blundell, *President*
Mike Mitchell, *Vice Pres*
Jan Blundell, *Admin Sec*
EMP: 50
SQ FT: 42,000
SALES (est): 5.9MM **Privately Held**
SIC: 3993 3944 Advertising novelties; games, toys & children's vehicles

(G-5576)
BIRDDOG SOFTWARE CORPORATION
8277 S Walker Ave (73139-9451)
PHONE..................................405 794-5950
Robin Zwirtz, *President*
Saul Ortiz, *Software Engr*
Jim Linger, *Technical Staff*

EMP: 17
SALES (est): 1.7MM **Privately Held**
SIC: 7372 Prepackaged software

(G-5577)
BISON ENERGY SERVICES LLC (PA)
210 Park Ave Ste 1350 (73102-5631)
PHONE..................................405 529-6577
North Whipple, *CEO*
EMP: 16
SALES (est): 299.8K **Privately Held**
SIC: 4212 1381 Moving services; drilling oil & gas wells

(G-5578)
BKEP CRUDE LLC
11501 S Intrstate 44 Svce (73173)
PHONE..................................405 278-6452
Mike Cockrell, *President*
Larry Hatley, *Vice Pres*
Alex Stallings, *CFO*
EMP: 350 EST: 2007
SALES (est): 9.6MM **Publicly Held**
SIC: 1311 Crude petroleum production
PA: Blueknight Energy Partners, L.P.
    6060 American Plz Ste 600
    Tulsa OK 74135

(G-5579)
BLACK BAYOU EXPLORATION LLC
1601 Nw Exprewoky 1200 (73118)
PHONE..................................405 753-5500
Julian M Bott,
EMP: 1
SALES (est): 939.6K
SALES (corp-wide): 266.8MM **Publicly Held**
SIC: 1311 Crude petroleum & natural gas
PA: Sandridge Energy, Inc.
    123 Robert S Kerr Ave
    Oklahoma City OK 73102
    405 429-5500

(G-5580)
BLACK BELT MAGAZINE 1000 LLC
1000 Century Blvd (73110-7961)
PHONE..................................405 732-5111
Michael Dillard, *Mng Member*
EMP: 2
SALES (est): 73.1K **Privately Held**
SIC: 2721 Magazines: publishing only, not printed on site

(G-5581)
BLACK CHRONICLE INC
Also Called: Black Chronicle Newspaper
1528 Ne 23rd St Ste A (73111-3200)
P.O. Box 17498 (73136-1498)
PHONE..................................405 424-4695
Russell Perry, *President*
Ranola Perry, *Vice Pres*
Myrtle Rucker, *Treasurer*
EMP: 11
SQ FT: 4,000
SALES: 550K **Privately Held**
SIC: 2711 Newspapers: publishing only, not printed on site

(G-5582)
BLACK THUNDER ROOFING LLC
305 Nw 5th St Unit 2131 (73102-3016)
PHONE..................................405 473-8028
Amanda Harrison, *Partner*
EMP: 2
SALES (est): 194.8K **Privately Held**
SIC: 2952 2621 2493 Mastic roofing composition; tar paper, roofing; building & roofing paper, felts & insulation siding; tar paper, building/roofing; insulation & roofing material, reconstituted wood

(G-5583)
BLACKROCK SERVICES LLC (PA)
5600 N May Ave Ste 137 (73112-4275)
PHONE..................................405 254-3939
Glen Major, *Principal*
Courtney Evans, *Accountant*
EMP: 3

Oklahoma City - Oklahoma County (G-5584)   GEOGRAPHIC SECTION

SALES (est): 12.7MM **Privately Held**
WEB: www.blackrocksvc.com
SIC: **1389** Gas field services

(G-5584)
BLAKE PRODUCTION COMPANY INC
1601 Nw Expressway # 777 (73118-1467)
PHONE.................................405 286-9800
Blake Vernon, *President*
EMP: 6
SQ FT: 2,200
SALES (est): 2.8MM **Privately Held**
SIC: **1311** Crude petroleum production; natural gas production

(G-5585)
BLAKES WESTSIDE TAG AGENCY
8400 Nw 76th St (73132-3943)
PHONE.................................918 446-1740
Billie Blake, *Principal*
EMP: 2
SALES (est): 144K **Privately Held**
SIC: **3469** Automobile license tags, stamped metal

(G-5586)
BLANKENSHIP BROTHERS INC
Also Called: Fastsigns
1401 S Meridian Ave (73108-1709)
PHONE.................................405 943-3278
Allen Blankenship, *Vice Pres*
EMP: 5
SALES (corp-wide): 4.1MM **Privately Held**
SIC: **3993** Signs & advertising specialties
PA: Blankenship Brothers Inc
    1401 S Meridian Ave A
    Oklahoma City OK 73108
    405 943-3278

(G-5587)
BLANKENSHIP BROTHERS INC (PA)
Also Called: Fastsigns
1401 S Meridian Ave A (73108-1709)
PHONE.................................405 943-3278
Alda Blankenship, *President*
Allen Blankenship, *Vice Pres*
EMP: 9
SQ FT: 2,000
SALES (est): 4.1MM **Privately Held**
SIC: **3993** 2759 5999 Signs & advertising specialties; commercial printing; banners

(G-5588)
BLANKENSHIP BROTHERS INC
Also Called: Fastsigns
2837 Nw 63rd St (73116-4809)
PHONE.................................405 848-7446
Karen McCasilin, *Manager*
EMP: 3
SALES (corp-wide): 4.1MM **Privately Held**
SIC: **3993** Signs & advertising specialties
PA: Blankenship Brothers Inc
    1401 S Meridian Ave A
    Oklahoma City OK 73108
    405 943-3278

(G-5589)
BLASTPRO MANUFACTURING INC
513 Beacon Pl (73127-5647)
PHONE.................................877 495-6464
EMP: 1 **Privately Held**
SIC: **3569** Blast cleaning equipment, dustless
PA: Blastpro Manufacturing, Inc.
    6021 Melrose Ln
    Oklahoma City OK 73127

(G-5590)
BLASTPRO MANUFACTURING INC (PA)
6021 Melrose Ln (73127-5527)
P.O. Box 270175 (73137-0175)
PHONE.................................405 491-6464
Michael Nelson, *Owner*
Les Smith, *COO*
Paul Robb, *Vice Pres*
Lisa Beals, *Purchasing*
Paul Jackson, *CFO*
▲ EMP: 35

SQ FT: 15,000
SALES (est): 8.1MM **Privately Held**
SIC: **3569** Blast cleaning equipment, dustless

(G-5591)
BLEVINS OIL FIELD
8117 Bourbon St (73128-4219)
PHONE.................................405 619-9909
Matt Blevins, *Exec Dir*
EMP: 4 EST: 2010
SALES (est): 310.9K **Privately Held**
WEB: www.blevinsoilfield.com
SIC: **1389** Oil field services

(G-5592)
BLEVINS OILFIELD SLS & SVC LLC
8117 Bourbon St (73128-4219)
PHONE.................................405 619-9909
James Blevins, *Principal*
Shawna Moore, *Principal*
EMP: 12
SALES (est): 393.6K **Privately Held**
SIC: **7699** 7694 Professional instrument repair services; caliper, gauge & other machinists' instrument repair; hydraulic equipment repair; motor repair services; electric motor repair

(G-5593)
BLUE MOUNTAIN MIDSTREAM LLC
14000 Quail Springs Pkwy # 5200 (73134-2620)
PHONE.................................281 377-8770
EMP: 2
SALES (corp-wide): 479.7MM **Publicly Held**
SIC: **1311** Crude petroleum & natural gas
HQ: Blue Mountain Midstream Llc
    600 Travis St Ste 1700
    Houston TX 77002
    281 377-8770

(G-5594)
BLUE SAGE STUDIOS
1218 N Western Ave (73106-6824)
PHONE.................................405 601-2583
Andrew M Boatman, *Principal*
EMP: 3
SALES (est): 189.5K **Privately Held**
SIC: **3229** Pressed & blown glass

(G-5595)
BLUMENTHAL COMPANIES LLC (PA)
301 S Western Ave (73109-1003)
PHONE.................................405 232-9557
Irving H Blumenthal Jr, *President*
David Blumenthal, *Vice Pres*
G Scott Blumenthal, *Vice Pres*
Kevin Blumenthal, *Vice Pres*
Kyle Chilton, *Manager*
▲ EMP: 40 EST: 1949
SQ FT: 250,000
SALES (est): 17.2MM **Privately Held**
SIC: **5013** 3714 Automotive engines & engine parts; transmissions, motor vehicle

(G-5596)
BLUMENTHAL COMPANIES LLC
Also Called: Blumenthal's Heavy Duty
504 Sw 4th St (73109-5102)
PHONE.................................405 232-9557
Irving Blumenthal, *Manager*
EMP: 7
SALES (corp-wide): 17.2MM **Privately Held**
SIC: **3714** Transmissions, motor vehicle
PA: The Blumenthal Companies L L C
    301 S Western Ave
    Oklahoma City OK 73109
    405 232-9557

(G-5597)
BOARD OF TRUSTEES OF THE TEACH
2500 N Lincoln Blvd # 500 (73105-4504)
PHONE.................................405 521-2387
Tom Spencer, *Exec Dir*
EMP: 38
SALES (est): 1.4MM **Privately Held**
SIC: **2759** Screen printing

(G-5598)
BOARDMAN LLC (PA)
Also Called: Boardman Co, The
1135 S Mckinley Ave (73108-7008)
PHONE.................................405 634-5434
Robby Hagemann, *President*
Roger Grommet, *Vice Pres*
James Hagemann, *CFO*
▲ EMP: 100
SQ FT: 140,000
SALES: 30MM **Privately Held**
SIC: **3441** Fabricated structural metal; fabricated structural metal for bridges; fabricated structural metal for ships; dam gates, metal plate

(G-5599)
BOB ALBAUER PORTABLE WELDING
5909 Nw 56th St (73122-6106)
PHONE.................................405 789-7999
EMP: 1
SALES (est): 84K **Privately Held**
SIC: **7692** 1799 Welding Repair Trade Contractor

(G-5600)
BOB BROOKS MOTOR COMPANY
Also Called: Precision Prts Remanufacturing
4411 Sw 19th St (73108-1771)
PHONE.................................405 681-2592
Bob Brooks, *President*
Mary Brooks, *Corp Secy*
Dan Brooks, *Vice Pres*
▲ EMP: 160 EST: 1963
SQ FT: 62,000
SALES (est): 28.7MM **Privately Held**
SIC: **3694** 5521 3625 Alternators, automotive; ignition apparatus & distributors; used car dealers; relays & industrial controls

(G-5601)
BOB HOWARD WHL PARTS DIST CTR
3501 N Santa Fe Ave (73118-8812)
PHONE.................................405 525-4400
Bob Howard, *Principal*
EMP: 4
SALES (est): 642.7K **Privately Held**
WEB: www.buypartsdirect.com
SIC: **5013** 3714 Automotive supplies & parts; motor vehicle parts & accessories

(G-5602)
BOBAY NUTRITION LLC
6313 Beaver Creek Rd (73162-3417)
PHONE.................................405 708-0407
Cody Bobay, *Principal*
EMP: 2
SALES (est): 73.2K **Privately Held**
SIC: **2741** Miscellaneous publishing

(G-5603)
BOBBY J DARNELL
2250 Nw 39th St Ste 100 (73112-8857)
PHONE.................................405 524-8891
Bobby Darnell, *Owner*
Julie Webb, *Manager*
EMP: 2 EST: 1960
SQ FT: 4,500
SALES (est): 150K **Privately Held**
SIC: **1311** Crude petroleum production; natural gas production

(G-5604)
BOBS WOOD WORKING
7313 S Klein Ave (73139-1923)
PHONE.................................405 632-4894
Bob Bishop, *Principal*
EMP: 2
SALES (est): 227.8K **Privately Held**
SIC: **2431** Millwork

(G-5605)
BODYCOTE THERMAL PROC INC
6924 S Eastern Ave (73149-5221)
PHONE.................................405 670-5710
Larry McCauley, *Engineer*
Barry Dunham, *Branch Mgr*
EMP: 13

SALES (corp-wide): 929.6MM **Privately Held**
WEB: www.bodycote.com
SIC: **3398** Metal heat treating
HQ: Bodycote Thermal Processing, Inc.
    12750 Merit Dr Ste 1400
    Dallas TX 75251
    214 904-2420

(G-5606)
BOEING AROSPC OPERATIONS INC
3000 Tower Dr Ste 604 (73115)
PHONE.................................405 610-3100
Robert Fortey, *Manager*
EMP: 12
SALES (corp-wide): 76.5B **Publicly Held**
SIC: **3721** Aircraft
HQ: Boeing Aerospace Operations, Inc.
    6001 S A Depo Blvd Ste E
    Oklahoma City OK 73150
    405 622-6000

(G-5607)
BOEING COMPANY
6001 S Air Depot Blvd (73135-5922)
PHONE.................................405 622-6000
Derek A McLuckey, *Branch Mgr*
EMP: 750
SALES (corp-wide): 76.5B **Publicly Held**
WEB: www.boeing.com
SIC: **3721** Aircraft
PA: The Boeing Company
    100 N Riverside Plz
    Chicago IL 60606
    312 544-2000

(G-5608)
BOEING COMPANY
1332 Sw 66th St (73159-3113)
PHONE.................................405 924-1385
Jr Davis, *Principal*
Chase Bartenhagen, *Engineer*
Ric Leist, *Engineer*
EMP: 895
SALES (corp-wide): 76.5B **Publicly Held**
WEB: www.boeing.com
SIC: **3721** Airplanes, fixed or rotary wing
PA: The Boeing Company
    100 N Riverside Plz
    Chicago IL 60606
    312 544-2000

(G-5609)
BOEING COMPANY
6001 S Air Depot Blvd (73135-5922)
PHONE.................................405 622-6206
L M Lackman, *Vice Pres*
EMP: 2000
SALES (corp-wide): 76.5B **Publicly Held**
SIC: **3721** Aircraft
PA: The Boeing Company
    100 N Riverside Plz
    Chicago IL 60606
    312 544-2000

(G-5610)
BOEING COMPANY
6001 S Air Depot Blvd (73135-5922)
PHONE.................................405 622-6720
EMP: 996
SALES (corp-wide): 76.5B **Publicly Held**
SIC: **3721** Airplanes, fixed or rotary wing
PA: The Boeing Company
    100 N Riverside Plz
    Chicago IL 60606
    312 544-2000

(G-5611)
BOEING COMPANY
6811 Se 59th St (73135-5530)
PHONE.................................405 618-2859
Ellen Anderson, *Branch Mgr*
EMP: 2
SALES (corp-wide): 76.5B **Publicly Held**
SIC: **3721** Aircraft
PA: The Boeing Company
    100 N Riverside Plz
    Chicago IL 60606
    312 544-2000

(G-5612)
BOEING COMPANY
601 S Air Depot Blvd (73110-4426)
PHONE.................................316 526-3272
Jeff Turner, *General Mgr*

EMP: 17
SALES (corp-wide): 76.5B **Publicly Held**
SIC: 3721 Aircraft
PA: The Boeing Company
100 N Riverside Plz
Chicago IL 60606
312 544-2000

(G-5613)
BOEING COMPANY
601 S Air Depot Blvd (73110-4426)
PHONE.................................316 977-2121
EMP: 25
SALES (corp-wide): 96.1B **Publicly Held**
SIC: 3721 Military
PA: The Boeing Company
100 N Riverside Plz
Chicago IL 60606
312 544-2000

(G-5614)
BOEING COMPANY
8121 Mid America Blvd (73135-6601)
PHONE.................................405 736-9227
Charlie Groh, *Engineer*
Stephen Herron, *Branch Mgr*
EMP: 996
SALES (corp-wide): 76.5B **Publicly Held**
SIC: 3721 Airplanes, fixed or rotary wing
PA: The Boeing Company
100 N Riverside Plz
Chicago IL 60606
312 544-2000

(G-5615)
BOGO ENERGY CORPORATION (PA)
13933 Quail Pointe Dr (73134-1002)
PHONE.................................405 840-1067
Richard D Bogert, *President*
Al Smiley, *CFO*
EMP: 6
SQ FT: 5,000
SALES: 2MM **Privately Held**
SIC: 1311 Crude petroleum production; natural gas production

(G-5616)
BOLEY ONE
1305 Ne 23rd St (73111-3001)
P.O. Box 11043 (73136-0043)
PHONE.................................405 301-7692
Richard Palmer, *Owner*
EMP: 1
SALES: 150K **Privately Held**
SIC: 2759 2284 Screen printing; embroidery thread

(G-5617)
BOOKS IN SIGHT INC
4141 Nw Expwy St Ste 110 (73116-1675)
P.O. Box 42467 (73123-3467)
PHONE.................................405 810-9501
Doug Manning, *President*
Barbara Manning, *Vice Pres*
EMP: 7
SALES (est): 829.9K **Privately Held**
SIC: 2741 Miscellaneous publishing

(G-5618)
BOONE OPERATING INC
709 Nw 54th St (73118-6014)
PHONE.................................405 879-2332
Bill Gwin, *President*
John P Gwin, *Vice Pres*
Beverly Gwin, *Admin Sec*
EMP: 2
SQ FT: 1,500
SALES: 1.2MM **Privately Held**
SIC: 1382 1381 Oil & gas exploration services; drilling oil & gas wells

(G-5619)
BORDEAUXS EMBROIDERY
6609 S Westminster Rd (73150-6007)
PHONE.................................405 227-0958
Anne Marie Bordeaux, *Principal*
EMP: 1
SALES (est): 33.7K **Privately Held**
SIC: 2395 Embroidery & art needlework

(G-5620)
BORDEN DAIRY COMPANY TEXAS LLC
316 N Western Ave (73106-7640)
PHONE.................................405 232-7955
Richard Vaughn, *Manager*
EMP: 8
SALES (corp-wide): 2MM **Privately Held**
SIC: 2026 Fluid milk
HQ: Borden Dairy Company Of Texas, Llc
5327 S Lamar St
Dallas TX 75215
214 565-0332

(G-5621)
BORETS US INC
400 N Macarthur Blvd (73127-6619)
PHONE.................................405 949-0031
EMP: 25 **Privately Held**
SIC: 3533 Mfg Oil/Gas Field Machinery
HQ: Borets U.S., Inc.
1600 N Garnett Rd
Tulsa OK 74116
918 439-7000

(G-5622)
BOSENDORFER OIL COMPANY
5311 S Drexel Ave (73119-5429)
PHONE.................................405 604-9025
EMP: 1
SALES: 75K **Privately Held**
SIC: 1382 1442 Oil/Gas Exploration Services Construction Sand/Gravel

(G-5623)
BRACE PLACE
409 E California Ave # 100 (73104-4226)
PHONE.................................405 858-5200
Chris Christainsen, *Principal*
EMP: 3
SALES (est): 285.3K **Privately Held**
SIC: 3842 Braces, orthopedic

(G-5624)
BRESHEARS ENTERPRISES INC
Also Called: Custom Stainless
20 N May Ave (73107)
PHONE.................................405 236-4523
Randy Breshears, *President*
Walt Breshears, *Corp Secy*
Dirk Breshears, *Vice Pres*
Edith Breshears, *Shareholder*
EMP: 12 EST: 1971
SALES (est): 2.2MM **Privately Held**
SIC: 3431 2541 5046 3556 Sinks: enameled iron, cast iron or pressed metal; counter & sink tops; restaurant equipment & supplies; food products machinery; sheet metalwork; wood household furniture

(G-5625)
BRETT EXPLORATION
1601 Nw Exprkway Ste 1300 (73118)
PHONE.................................405 842-2322
John A Brett III, *Owner*
EMP: 1
SALES (est): 87K **Privately Held**
SIC: 1382 Oil & gas exploration services

(G-5626)
BREWER MEDIA LLC
429 E California Ave (73104-4210)
PHONE.................................405 236-4143
EMP: 2
SALES (est): 62.3K **Privately Held**
SIC: 2082 Brewers' grain

(G-5627)
BRICKTOWN REAL ESTATE & DEVELO
429 E California Ave (73104-4210)
PHONE.................................405 236-4143
Brent Brewer, *Principal*
EMP: 5
SALES (est): 449.4K **Privately Held**
SIC: 2335 Wedding gowns & dresses

(G-5628)
BRIGHAM COMPANY LLC
2932 Nw 122nd St Ste 6 (73120-1955)
PHONE.................................405 843-2660
Vincent Brigham, *Owner*
EMP: 5

SALES (est): 446.4K **Privately Held**
SIC: 1382 Oil & gas exploration services

(G-5629)
BRITTON ELECTRIC MOTOR INC
1001 Nw 80th St (73114-1905)
PHONE.................................405 842-8357
Ron Frye, *President*
Debbie Frye, *Vice Pres*
EMP: 7
SQ FT: 7,000
SALES (est): 760K **Privately Held**
SIC: 7694 5063 3621 Rebuilding motors, except automotive; rewinding stators; electric motor repair; motors, electric; motors & generators

(G-5630)
BRITTON PRINTING
Also Called: Britton Printing & Copy Center
1337 W Britton Rd (73114-1305)
P.O. Box 14965 (73113-0965)
PHONE.................................405 840-3291
Gary Leiser, *Owner*
Jean A Leiser, *Co-Owner*
EMP: 3
SQ FT: 1,000
SALES (est): 190K **Privately Held**
SIC: 2752 2759 2791 2789 Commercial printing, offset; letterpress printing; typesetting; bookbinding & related work

(G-5631)
BRONCO MANUFACTURING
1501 Se 25th St (73129-7607)
PHONE.................................405 225-1909
EMP: 1
SALES (est): 75.4K **Privately Held**
SIC: 3999 Barber & beauty shop equipment

(G-5632)
BROOKS INDUSTRIES LLC
3015 Nw 18th St (73107-3907)
PHONE.................................405 305-9316
Dominique Brooks, *Principal*
EMP: 1 EST: 2018
SALES (est): 39.6K **Privately Held**
SIC: 3999 Manufacturing industries

(G-5633)
BROTHERS CONSTRUCTION AND ROUS
1523 Sw 30th St (73119-2205)
PHONE.................................405 602-3275
Jose Valdez, *Principal*
EMP: 2 EST: 2014
SALES (est): 88K **Privately Held**
SIC: 1389 Roustabout service

(G-5634)
BROW ART 23
1901 Nw Expressway (73118-1607)
PHONE.................................405 848-3346
Shazia Khan, *Owner*
EMP: 3
SALES (est): 178K **Privately Held**
WEB: www.browart23.com
SIC: 2273 Art squares

(G-5635)
BROWN EQUIPMENT CORPORATION
7000 S Walker Ave Apt 8 (73139-7201)
P.O. Box 6204, Moore (73153-0204)
PHONE.................................405 799-4000
Steve Brown, *President*
EMP: 2
SALES (est): 160K **Privately Held**
SIC: 3531 Construction machinery

(G-5636)
BROWNE BOTTLING CO INC (PA)
2712 Tealwood Dr (73120-1705)
PHONE.................................405 232-1158
Stephen B Browne, *Ch of Bd*
Stephen R Kerr, *Vice Pres*
EMP: 12
SALES (est): 63.3MM **Privately Held**
SIC: 2086 Soft drinks: packaged in cans, bottles, etc.

(G-5637)
BROWNS BAKERY INC
1100 N Walker Ave (73103-2624)
PHONE.................................405 232-0363
William Brown, *President*
Bill Brown, *President*
William N Brown Sr, *Vice Pres*
EMP: 25
SQ FT: 6,000
SALES (est): 1.2MM **Privately Held**
SIC: 5461 5149 2051 Bakeries; bakery products; bread, cake & related products

(G-5638)
BTG INC
3600 S Macarthur Blvd A (73179-7645)
PHONE.................................405 604-9145
K Huffman, *Assistant*
EMP: 2
SALES (est): 69.6K **Privately Held**
SIC: 2834 Pharmaceutical preparations

(G-5639)
BUFFALO INDUSTRIES
6812 Newman Dr (73162-7442)
PHONE.................................405 720-2324
Jon Heavener, *Principal*
EMP: 2
SALES (est): 127.4K **Privately Held**
SIC: 3999 Manufacturing industries

(G-5640)
BUILDBLOCK BLDG SYSTEMS LLC
9705 Broadway Ext Ste 150 (73114-6325)
PHONE.................................405 840-3386
Melissa Canoy, *COO*
Justin Nard, *Sales Staff*
Alfonso Nieves, *Sales Staff*
Isaiah Werner, *Marketing Staff*
Mike Garrett,
◆ EMP: 9
SALES (est): 2.2MM **Privately Held**
SIC: 3271 Blocks, concrete: insulating

(G-5641)
BUILDERS FIRSTSOURCE INC
7401 S Sooner Rd (73135-2613)
PHONE.................................405 321-2255
Greg Bush, *Sales Staff*
Dan Siofis, *Manager*
EMP: 30
SALES (corp-wide): 7.2B **Publicly Held**
SIC: 5031 2439 Lumber: rough, dressed & finished; structural wood members
PA: Builders Firstsource, Inc.
2001 Bryan St Ste 1600
Dallas TX 75201
214 880-3500

(G-5642)
BUILDING CONCEPTS LTD
9900 Nw 10th St (73127-7145)
PHONE.................................405 324-5100
Mary Weber, *President*
EMP: 3
SALES (est): 540K **Privately Held**
WEB: www.bcsteel.com
SIC: 3441 Fabricated structural metal

(G-5643)
BUILDINGS BY MADDEN LLC
Also Called: B B M
3220 E I 240 Service Rd (73135-1729)
PHONE.................................405 677-0466
Brian Satterfield, *Sales Staff*
Larry Wells, *Sales Executive*
EMP: 8
SQ FT: 20,000
SALES (est): 1.3MM **Privately Held**
SIC: 3448 Prefabricated metal buildings

(G-5644)
BULL DOG WELDING
1240 Sw 15th St (73108)
PHONE.................................405 412-8199
Sergio Delgado, *Principal*
EMP: 1 EST: 2009
SALES (est): 41.4K **Privately Held**
SIC: 7699 7692 1799 1389 Industrial equipment services; welding repair; sandblasting of building exteriors; construction, repair & dismantling services

Oklahoma City - Oklahoma County (G-5645)   GEOGRAPHIC SECTION

(G-5645)
BURLESON PUMP COMPANY
4207 S I 35 Service Rd (73129-6908)
P.O. Box 95166 (73143-5166)
PHONE..................................405 677-6881
Tom Whilden Jr, *President*
Jon West, *Sales Staff*
EMP: 5
SALES (est): 803.5K Privately Held
WEB: www.burlesonpump.com
SIC: 3561 Pumps & pumping equipment

(G-5646)
BURNS & MCDONNELL INC
615 N Hudson Ave Ste 200 (73102-3090)
PHONE..................................405 200-0300
Josh Evans, *General Mgr*
Kelly Nugent, *Engineer*
John Sullens, *Engineer*
EMP: 7
SALES (corp-wide): 3.3B Privately Held
SIC: 8712 8748 2211 Architectural services; business consulting; bed sheeting, cotton
PA: Burns & Mcdonnell, Inc.
9400 Ward Pkwy
Kansas City MO 64114
816 333-9400

(G-5647)
BURTON CONTROLS INC (PA)
11600 S Meridian Ave (73173-8230)
PHONE..................................405 692-7278
Steve Burton, *President*
Vera Burton, *Principal*
Ryan Overholt, *Principal*
Mike Nazworth, *Vice Pres*
Jason Shepherd, *Safety Mgr*
EMP: 23
SQ FT: 6,000
SALES (est): 2.6MM Privately Held
SIC: 1389 Oil field services

(G-5648)
BUSINESS CARDS & MORE
2920 N Pennsylvania Ave (73107-2551)
PHONE..................................405 235-9621
Richard Salamy, *Owner*
EMP: 3
SQ FT: 3,800
SALES (est): 160K Privately Held
SIC: 2759 Commercial printing

(G-5649)
BUSINESS RECORDS STORAGE LLC
5 Ne 12th St (73104-1421)
P.O. Box 2665 (73101-2665)
PHONE..................................405 232-7867
Dahl Luttrell, *President*
EMP: 23
SQ FT: 65,000
SALES (est): 1.7MM Privately Held
SIC: 5093 4226 3572 Waste paper; document & office records storage; computer storage devices

(G-5650)
BUZZI UNICEM USA INC P
4601 Ne 4th St (73117-7616)
PHONE..................................405 670-0677
Randy Louelland, *District Mgr*
EMP: 3
SALES (est): 246.6K Privately Held
WEB: www.buzziunicemusa.com
SIC: 3241 Portland cement

(G-5651)
BWB SIGN INC
Also Called: Lindmark Outdoor Advertising
115 E California Ave # 370 (73104-2456)
PHONE..................................405 292-3534
▲ EMP: 15
SALES (est): 1.4MM Privately Held
SIC: 3993 Mfg Sign

(G-5652)
BYERS PRODUCTS GROUP INC
9641 Nw 6th St (73127-7112)
P.O. Box 270366 (73137-0366)
PHONE..................................405 491-8550
Thomas Byers, *CEO*
Richard Byers, *President*
Thomas L Byers, *President*
Misty Bashaw, *Office Mgr*
▲ EMP: 5 EST: 2006
SALES (est): 859.7K Privately Held
SIC: 3448 3496 Screen enclosures; slings, lifting: made from purchased wire

(G-5653)
BYRUM ENTERPRISES INC
10201 Lyndon Rd (73120-4202)
PHONE..................................812 595-4598
EMP: 2
SALES (est): 56.5K Privately Held
SIC: 7372 Prepackaged software

(G-5654)
C & B PUMP REBUILDERS
8308 Sw 3rd St Ste D (73128-4243)
PHONE..................................405 789-4808
Greg Dobson, *Owner*
EMP: 1
SALES: 100K Privately Held
SIC: 3561 Pumps, domestic: water or sump

(G-5655)
C & C EQUIPMENT SPECIALIST INC (PA)
1141 Se Grand Blvd # 122 (73129-6756)
P.O. Box 95571 (73143-5571)
PHONE..................................405 677-3110
Cory Cole, *President*
EMP: 25
SQ FT: 5,000
SALES (est): 2.7MM Privately Held
SIC: 3533 Oil field machinery & equipment

(G-5656)
C & C WELDING & CONSTRUCTION
10812 Ne 16th St (73130-2106)
PHONE..................................405 769-4924
Kevin Vernon, *Principal*
EMP: 1
SALES (est): 61.2K Privately Held
SIC: 7692 Welding repair

(G-5657)
C & M PRECISION INC
5700 Sw 134th St (73173-8655)
PHONE..................................405 691-0984
Wayne Cowart, *President*
EMP: 10
SALES (est): 1.5MM Privately Held
SIC: 3599 Machine shop, jobbing & repair

(G-5658)
C & W SHOES OF GEORGIA INC
Also Called: Shoe Gallery
11950 N May Ave (73120-6808)
PHONE..................................405 755-7112
Doug Waggoner, *Manager*
EMP: 14 Privately Held
SIC: 3144 5661 Dress shoes, women's; men's shoes
PA: C & W Shoes Of Georgia, Inc.
606 Holcomb Bridge Rd # 130
Roswell GA 30076

(G-5659)
C JS JEWELERS
8200 S Western Ave (73139-2542)
PHONE..................................405 631-0555
Don Correll, *Owner*
John Johnson, *Partner*
EMP: 3
SQ FT: 6,000
SALES (est): 340.1K Privately Held
SIC: 5944 3911 Jewelry, precious stones & precious metals; jewelry, precious metal

(G-5660)
C L AND L INC
Also Called: Signs Now
7101 Nw Expressway # 100 (73132-1579)
PHONE..................................405 722-9427
Jennifer Lovelace, *President*
EMP: 5
SALES (est): 550.1K Privately Held
SIC: 3993 Signs & advertising specialties

(G-5661)
C M Y K COLOUR CORP
Also Called: Showtime Display & Graphics
706 N Villa Ave (73107-6418)
PHONE..................................405 270-0060
Don Werp, *President*
Bill Werp, *Admin Sec*
EMP: 6
SQ FT: 5,000
SALES (est): 530K Privately Held
SIC: 7335 5046 3993 Color separation, photographic & movie film; display equipment, except refrigerated; signs & advertising specialties

(G-5662)
C&D MACHINE TOOL SVC & PARTS
4225 Nw 48th St (73112-2285)
PHONE..................................405 943-6033
Donald Rittman, *President*
EMP: 1
SALES (est): 120K Privately Held
SIC: 3541 Machine tool replacement & repair parts, metal cutting types

(G-5663)
C&D VALVE LLC
201 Nw 67th St (73116-8247)
P.O. Box 13250 (73113-1250)
PHONE..................................405 843-5621
Lance Gill,
▲ EMP: 50
SQ FT: 10,000
SALES (est): 9.7MM Privately Held
SIC: 3585 Air conditioning equipment, complete

(G-5664)
C&J ENERGY SERVICES INC
9636 W Reno Ave (73127-2981)
PHONE..................................405 222-8304
Chris Amanis, *Branch Mgr*
EMP: 30
SALES (corp-wide): 1.8B Publicly Held
SIC: 1389 Oil field services
HQ: King Merger Sub Ii Llc
3990 Rogerdale Rd
Houston TX 77042
713 325-6000

(G-5665)
C2 INNOVATIVE TECHNOLOGIES INC
10200 Se 57th St (73150-4523)
P.O. Box 55555 (73155-0555)
PHONE..................................405 388-2357
Trina Channel, *President*
Anthony Channel, *Vice Pres*
EMP: 2
SALES (est): 3K Privately Held
SIC: 3651 Household audio & video equipment

(G-5666)
CABINETWORKS INC
239 Nw 95th St (73114-6156)
PHONE..................................405 286-1053
Gerald Miller, *CEO*
EMP: 4
SALES (est): 260.2K Privately Held
SIC: 2434 Wood kitchen cabinets

(G-5667)
CACTUS WELLHEAD LLC
5517 Sw 29th St (73179-7625)
PHONE..................................405 708-7200
EMP: 8
SALES (corp-wide): 628.4MM Publicly Held
SIC: 1389 Oil field services
HQ: Cactus Wellhead Llc
920 Mmrial Cy Way Ste 300
Houston TX 77024

(G-5668)
CADENCE ENERGY PARTNERS LLC
Also Called: Riley Exporation
29 E Reno Ave Ste 5 (73104-4238)
PHONE..................................405 485-8200
Bobby Riley, *Mng Member*
Mark Meyer,
EMP: 50
SALES (est): 2.6MM Privately Held
SIC: 1382 Oil & gas exploration services

(G-5669)
CAIRNS MANUFACTURING INC
2213 Sw 19th St (73108-6427)
P.O. Box 82065 (73148-0065)
PHONE..................................405 636-4063
Berry Wagner, *Principal*
EMP: 1 EST: 2008
SALES (est): 54.4K Privately Held
SIC: 3999 Manufacturing industries

(G-5670)
CAIRNS MANUFACTURING INC
Also Called: Best Pressure Cairns Mfg
4929 Nw 18th St (73127-2833)
PHONE..................................405 947-1350
Paul Cairns, *President*
EMP: 6
SQ FT: 3,000
SALES (est): 660K Privately Held
SIC: 3589 3441 High pressure cleaning equipment; fabricated structural metal

(G-5671)
CALAMITY JANES FUNK & JUNK INC
Also Called: Calamity Jane's Apparel
1537 W Main St (73106-3013)
PHONE..................................405 759-3383
Jazmine Farmer, *Principal*
EMP: 3
SALES (est): 178.3K Privately Held
WEB: www.calamityjanesapparel.com
SIC: 2253 T-shirts & tops, knit

(G-5672)
CALLAWAY EQUIPMENT & MFG
8417 Gateway Ter (73149-3052)
PHONE..................................405 632-1870
David Callaway, *President*
EMP: 15
SALES (est): 2.4MM Privately Held
SIC: 3533 Oil & gas field machinery

(G-5673)
CALS PLASTICS DESIGNS & FABG
4861 Se 29th St (73115-5003)
PHONE..................................405 670-1690
Cal Johnson, *Owner*
EMP: 2
SALES (est): 166.8K Privately Held
SIC: 3089 2541 Injection molding of plastics; wood partitions & fixtures

(G-5674)
CALUMET OIL CO
701 Cedar Lake Blvd (73114-7806)
PHONE..................................405 478-8770
James Graves, *Principal*
Mark Fischer, *Administration*
EMP: 3
SALES (est): 275.3K Privately Held
SIC: 1311 Crude petroleum production

(G-5675)
CALVERT COMPANY
Also Called: Calvert Investment Company
6301 N Wstn Ave Ste 110 (73118)
PHONE..................................405 848-2222
S Whitfield Lee, *President*
EMP: 2
SALES (est): 202.3K Privately Held
SIC: 1311 Crude petroleum production

(G-5676)
CAMERON INTERNATIONAL CORP
Cooper Cameron Valves
845 Se 29th St (73129-4829)
P.O. Box 94700 (73143-4700)
PHONE..................................405 631-1321
Check Wepfer, *Branch Mgr*
EMP: 325
SQ FT: 176,603 Publicly Held
WEB: www.c-a-m.com
SIC: 3491 Industrial valves
HQ: Cameron International Corporation
4646 W Sam Houston Pkwy N
Houston TX 77041

GEOGRAPHIC SECTION

Oklahoma City - Oklahoma County (G-5706)

(G-5677)
CAMERON INTERNATIONAL CORP
Also Called: CAM Surface Sys - Okc Plant
7500 Sw 29th St Bldg B (73179-5207)
PHONE.................................405 745-2715
Wally Pugsley, *Branch Mgr*
EMP: 160
SQ FT: 125,000 **Publicly Held**
SIC: 3533 3491 Oil field machinery & equipment; industrial valves
HQ: Cameron International Corporation
   4646 W Sam Houston Pkwy N
   Houston TX 77041

(G-5678)
CAMERON INTERNATIONAL CORP
6700 N Classen Blvd (73116-7312)
PHONE.................................405 843-5578
EMP: 49 **Publicly Held**
SIC: 3533 Mfg Oil/Gas Field Machinery
HQ: Cameron International Corporation
   4646 W Sam Houston Pkwy N
   Houston TX 77041

(G-5679)
CAMERON INTERNATIONAL CORP
8533 Sw 2nd St (73128-3602)
PHONE.................................405 789-8065
Eric Nechvatal, *Manager*
EMP: 49 **Publicly Held**
SIC: 3533 Oil & gas field machinery
HQ: Cameron International Corporation
   4646 W Sam Houston Pkwy N
   Houston TX 77041

(G-5680)
CAMERON SOLUTIONS INC
Also Called: Natco
1708 Se 25th St (73129-7612)
PHONE.................................405 677-8827
Jerry Martin, *Branch Mgr*
EMP: 13
SQ FT: 10,140 **Publicly Held**
SIC: 1389 5082 Oil field services; oil field equipment
HQ: Cameron Solutions Inc.
   11210 Equity Dr Ste 100
   Houston TX 77041
   713 849-7500

(G-5681)
CAMPAIGN TECHNOLOGIES PROFESSI
2601 Nw Expwy Ste 210w (73112-7253)
PHONE.................................405 286-2686
J Pierce, *Principal*
EMP: 2
SALES (est): 167.2K **Privately Held**
SIC: 3578 Accounting machines & cash registers

(G-5682)
CAMPBELL CRANE AND SERVICE LLC
4104 Nw 21st St (73107-2608)
PHONE.................................405 245-8983
Thomas Campbell,
EMP: 3
SALES (est): 235.4K **Privately Held**
SIC: 3536 7389 Hoists, cranes & monorails;

(G-5683)
CAN GLOBAL USA INC (PA)
4740 United Dr (73179-7954)
PHONE.................................405 261-0417
Sean Connors, *President*
Greg Connors, *Vice Pres*
EMP: 10
SQ FT: 11,800
SALES: 8MM **Privately Held**
SIC: 1381 Service well drilling

(G-5684)
CANAAN ENERGY CORP
211 N Robinson Ave N1000 (73102-7168)
PHONE.................................405 604-9200
Fax: 405 879-9587
EMP: 2 EST: 2011
SALES (est): 151.9K **Privately Held**
SIC: 1382 Oil/Gas Exploration Services

(G-5685)
CANAAN NATURAL GAS CORP (PA)
1101 N Broadway Ave # 300 (73103-4941)
PHONE.................................405 604-9300
John Penson, *CEO*
Leo E Woodard, *CEO*
John K Penton, *President*
Brent V Beebe, *Vice Pres*
Brent Beebe, *Vice Pres*
▼ EMP: 10
SQ FT: 16,392
SALES (est): 3.3MM **Privately Held**
SIC: 1311 Crude petroleum production; natural gas production

(G-5686)
CANADIAN GLOBAL MFG LTD
4740 United Dr (73179-7954)
PHONE.................................405 250-1785
Sean Connors, *Manager*
EMP: 5
SALES (corp-wide): 8.4MM **Privately Held**
SIC: 1389 Gas field services
PA: Canadian Global Manufacturing Ltd
   9050 Innovation Ave Se
   Calgary AB T3S 0
   403 294-9492

(G-5687)
CANFIELD RANCH ENERGY LLC
101 Park Ave Fl 5 (73102-7209)
PHONE.................................405 272-1080
EMP: 3
SALES (est): 117.3K **Privately Held**
SIC: 1381 Drilling oil & gas wells

(G-5688)
CANNON & REFERMAT LLC
Also Called: CANNON SPRING COMPANY
4601 N Walnut Ave (73105-2033)
PHONE.................................405 521-0636
Kerry Cannon, *President*
Michael Refermat, *Vice Pres*
EMP: 15 EST: 1974
SQ FT: 9,300
SALES: 1.1MM **Privately Held**
SIC: 3493 3495 Steel springs, except wire; wire springs

(G-5689)
CANNON RACECRAFT INC
Also Called: Springmaker
201 E Hill St (73105-4009)
PHONE.................................405 524-7223
Dianne Cannon, *President*
Kerry Cannon, *Vice Pres*
Tony Hawkins, *Co-Mgr*
EMP: 10
SALES (est): 1.6MM **Privately Held**
SIC: 3495 5531 3751 Wire springs; automotive & home supply stores; motorcycles, bicycles & parts

(G-5690)
CANYON LAKES WINERY LLC
7600 Nw 134th St (73142-6234)
PHONE.................................405 367-7291
EMP: 2
SALES (est): 107.7K **Privately Held**
SIC: 2084 Mfg.Wines/Brandy/Spirits

(G-5691)
CAPITAL BUSINESS FORMS INC
4600 N Cooper Ave (73118-7887)
PHONE.................................405 524-2010
Don Tucker Sr, *President*
EMP: 13
SQ FT: 31,000
SALES (est): 2.3MM **Privately Held**
SIC: 2752 2759 Business forms, lithographed; business forms: printing

(G-5692)
CAPITAL RISK MANAGEMENT CORP (PA)
6301 N Wstn Ave Ste 225 (73118)
PHONE.................................405 848-5420
John Stranger, *President*
Carol Trent, *Corp Secy*
EMP: 3
SQ FT: 3,220
SALES (est): 385.2K **Privately Held**
SIC: 1311 6722 Crude petroleum production; natural gas production; management investment, open-end

(G-5693)
CAPITOL ELECTRIC MTR REPR INC (PA)
2215 Sw 11th St (73108-2697)
PHONE.................................405 235-9638
Ron Harrison, *President*
Roland F Harrison, *Vice Pres*
EMP: 10 EST: 1964
SQ FT: 10,000
SALES (est): 1.4MM **Privately Held**
WEB: www.capitolelectricmtrs.com
SIC: 7694 Electric motor repair

(G-5694)
CAPITOL HILL GRAFFIX LLC
330 Sw 25th St (73109-5922)
PHONE.................................405 616-3050
Armando Lopez,
Anna Lopez,
EMP: 5 EST: 2000
SQ FT: 11,484
SALES (est): 275.3K **Privately Held**
SIC: 2759 Screen printing

(G-5695)
CAPITOL PAINT MANUFACTURING
722 Sw 23rd St (73109-1706)
P.O. Box 95186 (73143-5186)
PHONE.................................405 634-3383
Stanton Ballew, *President*
Annnn Ballew, *Corp Secy*
EMP: 8 EST: 1959
SQ FT: 20,000
SALES (est): 1MM **Privately Held**
WEB: www.capitolpaintmfg.com
SIC: 2851 Paints: oil or alkyd vehicle or water thinned; lacquer: bases, dopes, thinner

(G-5696)
CAPITOL TUBE CO INC
820 Sw 27th St (73109-2208)
PHONE.................................405 632-9901
Alvie Jefferys, *President*
Judy Jefferys, *Vice Pres*
Michael Jefferys, *Treasurer*
EMP: 8 EST: 1971
SQ FT: 40,000
SALES (est): 400K **Privately Held**
SIC: 2655 Tubes, fiber or paper: made from purchased material; cores, fiber: made from purchased material

(G-5697)
CARDINAL RIVER ENERGY CO
211 N Robinson Ave N200 (73102-7235)
PHONE.................................405 606-7481
Art L Swanson, *Ch of Bd*
Jay C Jimerson, *Owner*
Jim Allen, *Vice Pres*
Bob Woodside, *Vice Pres*
Brian Cardell, *CFO*
EMP: 6
SALES (est): 176.1K **Privately Held**
SIC: 1382 1381 Oil & gas exploration services; drilling oil & gas wells

(G-5698)
CARGILL INCORPORATED
2100 S Robinson Ave (73109-5943)
PHONE.................................405 270-7011
Barry Cooper, *Manager*
EMP: 60
SALES (corp-wide): 113.4B **Privately Held**
WEB: www.cargill.com
SIC: 2048 8742 Prepared feeds; management consulting services
PA: Cargill, Incorporated
   15407 Mcginty Rd W
   Wayzata MN 55391
   952 742-7575

(G-5699)
CARGILL INCORPORATED
2100 S Robinson Ave (73109-5943)
PHONE.................................405 236-0525
Michael Murphy, *Manager*
EMP: 26
SALES (corp-wide): 113.4B **Privately Held**
SIC: 5153 5191 2048 Grain & field beans; farm supplies; prepared feeds
PA: Cargill, Incorporated
   15407 Mcginty Rd W
   Wayzata MN 55391
   952 742-7575

(G-5700)
CARGILL HEAT TREAT LLC
1626 Se 40th St (73129-7908)
P.O. Box 95206 (73143-5206)
PHONE.................................405 510-3404
Steve Cargill, *Manager*
EMP: 6
SALES (est): 982K **Privately Held**
SIC: 3398 Metal heat treating

(G-5701)
CARL A NILSEN
Also Called: Cascade Oils
3904 E Reno Ave (73117-7220)
P.O. Box 888, Edmond (73083-0888)
PHONE.................................405 236-4554
Carl A Nilsen, *Owner*
Carl Nielsen, *Owner*
Marlene Sanders, *Admin Sec*
EMP: 4 EST: 1951
SALES (est): 344K **Privately Held**
SIC: 1311 Crude petroleum production

(G-5702)
CARL E GUNGOLL EXPLORATION LLC
6 Ne 63rd St Ste 300 (73105-1408)
P.O. Box 18466 (73154-0466)
PHONE.................................405 848-7898
Corry Woolington, *Manager*
Ramsey W Drake,
Marith Means, *Admin Asst*
Carol J Drake,
EMP: 16
SQ FT: 7,700
SALES (est): 4.9MM **Privately Held**
SIC: 1311 Crude petroleum production; natural gas production

(G-5703)
CARLISLE SANITARY MAINTENANCE
4711 E Hefner Rd (73131-6114)
PHONE.................................405 475-5600
Wes Foltz, *Principal*
EMP: 6
SALES (est): 924.1K **Privately Held**
SIC: 2842 8742 Sanitation preparations; restaurant & food services consultants

(G-5704)
CARLSONS RURAL MAILBOX CO
301 Se 54th St (73129-3811)
PHONE.................................405 632-7338
Ronald Carlson, *Owner*
EMP: 1
SQ FT: 2,094
SALES (est): 78K **Privately Held**
SIC: 3444 7389 3089 Mail chutes, sheet metal; mailbox rental & related service; plastic containers, except foam

(G-5705)
CAROLS SIGNS
Also Called: Carols Sgns/Hand Painted Vinyl
1910 N Post Rd (73141-4408)
PHONE.................................405 769-5521
Carol Long, *Owner*
EMP: 2
SALES (est): 140K **Privately Held**
SIC: 5999 3993 Banners; signs & advertising specialties

(G-5706)
CASADY N COMPANY LLC
2921 N Oklahoma Ave (73105-2728)
P.O. Box 5704, Edmond (73083-5704)
PHONE.................................405 528-4299
Thomas Casady, *Mng Member*
EMP: 9
SQ FT: 20,000
SALES (est): 1.3MM **Privately Held**
WEB: www.casadync.com
SIC: 3599 Machine shop, jobbing & repair

Oklahoma City - Oklahoma County (G-5707) GEOGRAPHIC SECTION

(G-5707)
CASS HOLDINGS LLC (PA)
311 Nw 122nd St Ste 100 (73114-7325)
PHONE...................................405 755-8448
Doug Frans,
Greg Edwards,
EMP: 24 **EST:** 1997
SQ FT: 5,000
SALES (est): 2.4MM **Privately Held**
WEB: www.cassholdings.com
SIC: 2851 2821 5162 Lacquers, varnishes, enamels & other coatings; plastics materials & resins; epoxy resins; polyesters; plastics materials & basic shapes

(G-5708)
CASS POLYMERS INC (PA)
311 Nw 122nd St Ste 100 (73114-7325)
PHONE...................................405 755-8448
Doug Frans, *President*
Mike Ward, *Vice Pres*
Barbara Webster, *Purchasing*
Janie Wythe, *Purchasing*
Jeff Kautz, *Accountant*
EMP: 20
SQ FT: 5,000
SALES (est): 11.5MM **Privately Held**
WEB: www.casspolymers.com
SIC: 2851 Lacquers, varnishes, enamels & other coatings

(G-5709)
CASTLE ROCK KITCHENS
3017 Castlerock Rd (73120-1820)
PHONE...................................405 751-1822
Patrice Brown, *Owner*
EMP: 1
SALES (est): 33.7K **Privately Held**
SIC: 5812 2066 2064 Eating places; chocolate & cocoa products; candy & other confectionery products

(G-5710)
CASTLEROCK RESOURCES INC
3333 Nw 63rd St Ste 102a (73116-3718)
PHONE...................................405 842-4249
Robert E Gonce Jr, *President*
Stephanie S Gonce, *Treasurer*
EMP: 3
SQ FT: 1,500
SALES: 700K **Privately Held**
SIC: 1311 Crude petroleum production; natural gas production

(G-5711)
CASTON ARCHITECTURAL MLLWK INC
6701 N Hudson Ave (73116-7917)
PHONE...................................405 843-6652
Dan Foltz, *President*
EMP: 45
SALES (est): 7.9MM **Privately Held**
SIC: 2431 Millwork

(G-5712)
CATCH 21
12505 Blue Sage Rd (73120-1905)
PHONE...................................617 227-0730
Judi Jones, *Principal*
EMP: 1
SALES (est): 35.1K **Privately Held**
SIC: 2731 Book publishing

(G-5713)
CATHEDRAL ENERGY SERVICES INC
4701 United Dr (73179-7954)
PHONE...................................405 261-6011
Hoyt Williams, *Representative*
EMP: 51
SALES (corp-wide): 13.2MM **Privately Held**
SIC: 1381 Directional drilling oil & gas wells
PA: Cathedral Energy Services Inc
  6622 Willow Brook Park
  Houston TX 77066
  303 825-1001

(G-5714)
CAVE MAN CHOPPERS
4001 Meadowview Dr (73115-2035)
PHONE...................................405 672-8008
EMP: 2 **EST:** 2010
SALES (est): 94K **Privately Held**
SIC: 3751 Mfg Motorcycles/Bicycles

(G-5715)
CBD EVERYTHING LLC
8404 S Hillcrest Ter (73159-5822)
PHONE...................................405 605-5634
Daniel Pratt, *Owner*
EMP: 2
SALES (est): 78.9K **Privately Held**
SIC: 3999

(G-5716)
CBHC RESOURCES INC
3000 Thorn Ridge Rd (73120-1924)
PHONE...................................405 905-9791
Jeremy Hammond, *President*
EMP: 1
SALES (est): 38.1K **Privately Held**
SIC: 8742 1311 Business planning & organizing services; crude petroleum & natural gas

(G-5717)
CBS ENERGY LLC
5753 Nw 132nd St (73142-4437)
PHONE...................................405 470-4644
Joy Hahn, *Principal*
EMP: 2
SALES (est): 267.1K **Privately Held**
SIC: 1382 Oil & gas exploration services

(G-5718)
CCCC INC
Also Called: Turner Electric Communications
1901 Oaks Way (73131-1298)
PHONE...................................405 230-0638
Thomas Turner, *President*
Carol Turner, *Vice Pres*
EMP: 17
SQ FT: 3,000
SALES (est): 1.2MM **Privately Held**
SIC: 1731 3825 General electrical contractor; electrical power measuring equipment

(G-5719)
CEI PIPELINE LLC
701 Cedar Lake Blvd (73114-7806)
PHONE...................................405 478-8770
Jim Miller, *Senior VP*
Mark A Fischer,
EMP: 1
SALES (est): 662K **Publicly Held**
SIC: 1389 Gas compressing (natural gas) at the fields
PA: Chaparral Energy, Inc.
  701 Cedar Lake Blvd
  Oklahoma City OK 73114

(G-5720)
CELERITY ORTHOTCS & PROSTHETCS
937 Sw 89th St (73139-9231)
PHONE...................................405 605-3030
Heather Anders, *Owner*
EMP: 2
SALES (est): 93.5K **Privately Held**
WEB: www.celerityprosthetics.com
SIC: 3842 Orthopedic appliances

(G-5721)
CELERITY PROSTHETICS LLC
8625 S Walker Ave (73139-9462)
PHONE...................................405 605-3030
Heather Anders, *Partner*
EMP: 1
SQ FT: 2,500
SALES (est): 137.6K **Privately Held**
SIC: 3842 Limbs, artificial; orthopedic appliances

(G-5722)
CEMENT SPECIALISTS LLC
14201 Caliber Dr Ste 300 (73134-1017)
PHONE...................................432 617-2243
Javier Urias, *Partner*
Larry P Noble,
EMP: 7
SALES (est): 2.4MM **Privately Held**
SIC: 1389 Oil field services

(G-5723)
CENTAUR RESOURCES INC
5500 Pulchella Ln (73142-6804)
PHONE...................................405 603-8800
Ernest G Brewer Jr, *President*
EMP: 5
SQ FT: 1,550
SALES (est): 2.2MM **Privately Held**
SIC: 1311 Crude petroleum production; natural gas production

(G-5724)
CENTEK INC
5500 Sw 36th St (73179-7813)
PHONE...................................405 219-3200
John Carnuccio, *President*
Gary Depew, *Plant Mgr*
Greg Delonais, *Plant Engr*
Barry Coats, *Controller*
Joe Markley, *Accountant*
▲ **EMP:** 29
SALES (est): 7.5MM **Privately Held**
WEB: www.centekgroup.com
SIC: 3533 8711 Drilling tools for gas, oil or water wells; professional engineer

(G-5725)
CENTRAL PARTS & MACHINE INC
219 Se 29th St (73129-2039)
PHONE...................................405 631-5460
Ronald E Raper, *President*
Karen C Raper, *Corp Secy*
Sheri Raper, *Vice Pres*
EMP: 4 **EST:** 1962
SQ FT: 6,000
SALES (est): 500K **Privately Held**
SIC: 5084 3599 Industrial machine parts; machine shop, jobbing & repair

(G-5726)
CENTRAL STTES SHRDDING SYSTEMS
13001 Green Valley Dr (73120-8856)
P.O. Box 21710 (73156-1710)
PHONE...................................405 752-8300
Karol Hill, *Principal*
EMP: 3
SALES (est): 230.6K **Privately Held**
SIC: 3559 Tire shredding machinery

(G-5727)
CENTRAL TEXAS EX METALWORK LLC
1501 Se 66th St Ste C (73149-5200)
PHONE...................................765 492-9058
EMP: 2
SALES (est): 73.4K **Privately Held**
SIC: 2241 Narrow fabric mills

(G-5728)
CENTURY LLC (PA)
Also Called: Century Martial Art Supply
1000 Century Blvd (73110-7961)
PHONE...................................405 732-2226
Chris Rooney, *Business Anlyst*
Natalie Wheeler, *Manager*
Lawrence Michael Dillard,
Steve Meston,
Wanda Munroe,
◆ **EMP:** 135
SQ FT: 455,000
SALES (est): 79.2MM **Privately Held**
SIC: 5091 3949 Sporting & recreation goods; sporting & athletic goods

(G-5729)
CENTURY PRINTING INC
2713 N Windsor Ter (73127-1928)
P.O. Box 12901 (73157-2901)
PHONE...................................405 942-7171
Cecil Sullivan, *Principal*
EMP: 2
SALES (est): 191.3K **Privately Held**
SIC: 2752 Commercial printing, offset

(G-5730)
CERALUSA LLC
7002 S Bryant Ave (73149-7208)
PHONE...................................405 455-7720
Bruce Bodger, *General Mgr*
Suzanne Bodger,
▲ **EMP:** 9
SALES (est): 692.5K **Privately Held**
SIC: 2899 Chemical preparations

(G-5731)
CERTIFIED MACHINE & DESIGN INC
2300 S High Ave (73129-4838)
PHONE...................................405 672-9607
Gary Scantlin, *President*
Rosa Scott, *Vice Pres*
EMP: 9
SQ FT: 1,500
SALES (est): 1.1MM **Privately Held**
WEB: www.certifiedmachine.com
SIC: 3599 Machine shop, jobbing & repair

(G-5732)
CFS BRANDS LLC (HQ)
Also Called: Carlisle Foodservice Products
4711 E Hefner Rd (73131-6114)
P.O. Box 53006 (73152-3006)
PHONE...................................405 475-5600
Trent Freiberg, *President*
Jeff Fisher, *Vice Pres*
Craig Frye, *Plant Mgr*
Tim Larson, *Plant Mgr*
Rex Shriner, *Plant Mgr*
◆ **EMP:** 290 **EST:** 1983
SQ FT: 150,000
SALES (est): 326.5MM **Privately Held**
WEB: www.carlislefsp.com
SIC: 3269 3089 Stoneware pottery products; plastic containers, except foam; plastic kitchenware, tableware & houseware
PA: Cfsp Acquisition Corp.
  4711 E Hefner Rd
  Oklahoma City OK 73131
  405 475-5600

(G-5733)
CFS BRANDS LLC
3421 N Lincoln Blvd (73105-5407)
PHONE...................................405 397-0103
EMP: 17
SALES (corp-wide): 326.5MM **Privately Held**
SIC: 3089 3269 Plastic containers, except foam; plastic kitchenware, tableware & houseware; stoneware pottery products
HQ: Cfs Brands, Llc
  4711 E Hefner Rd
  Oklahoma City OK 73131
  405 475-5600

(G-5734)
CFSP ACQUISITION CORP (PA)
4711 E Hefner Rd (73131-6114)
P.O. Box 53006 (73152-3006)
PHONE...................................405 475-5600
Trent Freiberg, *CEO*
EMP: 2
SALES (est): 326.5MM **Privately Held**
SIC: 3269 3089 Stoneware pottery products; plastic containers, except foam; plastic kitchenware, tableware & houseware

(G-5735)
CG PRINTING
1125 Ne 48th St (73111-5601)
PHONE...................................405 818-4371
Joe Gresham, *Principal*
EMP: 2 **EST:** 2017
SALES (est): 83.9K **Privately Held**
SIC: 2752 Commercial printing, lithographic

(G-5736)
CHALLENGER DOWNHOLE TOOLS INC
5353 S Hattie Ave (73129-7321)
PHONE...................................405 604-0096
EMP: 2 **EST:** 2018
SALES (est): 150.7K **Privately Held**
SIC: 1389 Oil field services

(G-5737)
CHAMPION DESIGNS & SYSTEMS LLC
701 Cedar Lake Blvd # 143 (73114-7806)
PHONE...................................405 888-8370
John Reilly, *Mng Member*
Zach Pate,
EMP: 2
SQ FT: 500

GEOGRAPHIC SECTION

Oklahoma City - Oklahoma County (G-5764)

SALES (est): 713.3K **Privately Held**
SIC: **5039** 5033 3272 Metal buildings; roofing, siding & insulation; roofing, asphalt & sheet metal; concrete structural support & building material

(G-5738)
CHAMPION OPCO LLC
417 Hudiburg Cir Ste A (73108-1004)
PHONE...................405 708-6858
Dale Holloway, *Branch Mgr*
EMP: 80
SALES (corp-wide): 589.9MM **Privately Held**
SIC: **3089** Window frames & sash, plastic
PA: Champion Opco, Llc
  12121 Champion Way
  Cincinnati OH 45241
  513 327-7338

(G-5739)
CHAPARRAL ENERGY INC (PA)
701 Cedar Lake Blvd (73114-7806)
PHONE...................405 478-8770
Charles Duginski, *President*
James M Miller, *Senior VP*
Justin Byrne, *Vice Pres*
Clint Calhoun, *Vice Pres*
Stephanie Carnes, *Vice Pres*
EMP: 63
SALES: 236.3MM **Publicly Held**
SIC: **1311** 1382 Crude petroleum production; natural gas production; oil & gas exploration services

(G-5740)
CHAPARRAL ENERGY LLC (HQ)
701 Cedar Lake Blvd (73114-7806)
PHONE...................405 478-8770
Mark Fischer, *CEO*
Earl Reynolds, *President*
Don Culpepper Jr, *Senior VP*
John D Wehrle, *Senior VP*
David R Winchester, *Senior VP*
EMP: 150
SQ FT: 90,000
SALES (est): 382.5MM **Publicly Held**
SIC: **1311** 1382 Crude petroleum production; natural gas production; oil & gas exploration services

(G-5741)
CHAPARRAL EXPLORATION LLC
701 Cedar Lake Blvd (73114-7806)
PHONE...................405 426-4449
James Miller, *Vice Pres*
Mark A Fischer,
EMP: 1 EST: 2008
SALES (est): 1.2MM **Publicly Held**
SIC: **1311** Crude petroleum production
PA: Chaparral Energy, Inc.
  701 Cedar Lake Blvd
  Oklahoma City OK 73114

(G-5742)
CHARLES E MORRISON CO
6914 N Classen Blvd (73116-7210)
PHONE...................405 840-1604
Fred Boross, *President*
Karen Boross, *Admin Sec*
EMP: 2 EST: 1937
SQ FT: 3,500
SALES (est): 63K **Privately Held**
SIC: **2759** 2752 Commercial printing; commercial printing, lithographic

(G-5743)
CHARLIE BEAN COFFEE LLC
4020 Will Rogers Pkwy # 900 (73108-2093)
PHONE...................405 376-4815
Joshua Mangus, *CEO*
Charles Mangus, *Mng Member*
Linda Mangus,
EMP: 15
SQ FT: 18,000
SALES (est): 1.8MM **Privately Held**
SIC: **2095** 5141 Roasted coffee; groceries, general line; food brokers

(G-5744)
CHARTER OAK PRODUCTION CO LLC (PA)
13929 Quail Pointe Dr (73134-1002)
PHONE...................405 286-0361
Lynn Barbara, *Opers Staff*
Joseph C Brevetti, *Mng Member*
Penny Dabbs, *Director*
EMP: 10
SQ FT: 5,000
SALES (est): 3.9MM **Privately Held**
SIC: **1382** Oil & gas exploration services

(G-5745)
CHASE ENTERPRISES INC
Also Called: Chappell Supply & Equipment
6509 W Reno Ave (73127-6510)
P.O. Box 270960 (73137-0960)
PHONE...................405 495-1722
Roy Chappell, *CEO*
Shyla Chappell, *Opers Staff*
Tracy Wagoner, *Auditing Mgr*
Judy Howell, *Human Res Mgr*
Christopher Casey, *Sales Staff*
◆ EMP: 57
SQ FT: 60,000
SALES (est): 17MM **Privately Held**
SIC: **5999** 5084 3563 Cleaning equipment & supplies; cleaning equipment, high pressure, sand or steam; spraying outfits: metals, paints & chemicals (compressor)

(G-5746)
CHECOS MACHINE SHOP & GENERAL
2115 Sw 42nd St (73119-3615)
PHONE...................405 680-0900
Sergio Frausto, *Administration*
EMP: 2
SALES (est): 146.5K **Privately Held**
SIC: **3599** Machine shop, jobbing & repair

(G-5747)
CHELINOS TORTILLA FACTORY (PA)
4320 S Walker Ave (73109-6940)
PHONE...................405 631-3188
Gina Gray, *Admin Sec*
EMP: 13
SALES (est): 2.7MM **Privately Held**
SIC: **2099** Tortillas, fresh or refrigerated

(G-5748)
CHEMICAL PRODUCTS INDS INC
7649 Sw 34th St (73179-4404)
PHONE...................405 745-2070
Floyd Farha, *CEO*
Jordan Flanigan, *CFO*
▲ EMP: 7
SQ FT: 25,000
SALES (est): 3MM **Privately Held**
SIC: **2842** 2899 Degreasing solvent; chemical preparations

(G-5749)
CHEMOIL ENERGY INC
4 E Sheridan Ave Ste 400 (73104-2514)
PHONE...................405 605-5436
Mike McGloughlin, *President*
Bram Boer, *Opers Staff*
Matt Hamilton, *CIO*
EMP: 300
SALES (est): 18.5MM **Privately Held**
WEB: www.chemoilenergy.biz
SIC: **1389** Oil field services

(G-5750)
CHEROKEE INDUSTRIES INC
Also Called: Cherokee Trailers
11301 S Interstate 44 Svc (73173-8311)
PHONE...................405 691-8222
Thomas M Welchel, *President*
Wanda Welchel, *Corp Secy*
EMP: 65
SQ FT: 60,000
SALES (est): 9.5MM **Privately Held**
SIC: **3715** Trailers or vans for transporting horses; demountable cargo containers

(G-5751)
CHESAPEAKE ENERGY CORPORATION (PA)
6100 N Western Ave (73118-1044)
P.O. Box 18496 (73154-0496)
PHONE...................405 848-8000
Robert D Lawler, *President*
William M Buergler, *Senior VP*
EMP: 1163
SALES: 8.6B **Publicly Held**
SIC: **1311** Crude petroleum production; natural gas production

(G-5752)
CHESAPEAKE ENERGY LA CORP
6100 N Western Ave (73118-1044)
PHONE...................405 848-8000
EMP: 2
SALES (est): 81.9K **Privately Held**
SIC: **1381** Drilling oil & gas wells

(G-5753)
CHESAPEAKE ENERGY MKTG LLC
6100 N Western Ave (73118-1044)
P.O. Box 18496 (73154-0496)
PHONE...................877 245-1427
Robert Doug Lawler, *President*
EMP: 111
SALES (est): 11.9MM **Publicly Held**
SIC: **1389** Gas field services
PA: Chesapeake Energy Corporation
  6100 N Western Ave
  Oklahoma City OK 73118

(G-5754)
CHESAPEAKE EXPLORATION LLC
6100 N Western Ave (73118-1044)
PHONE...................405 848-8000
Chesapeake Energy Corporation, *General Ptnr*
Jeffrey A Fisher, *Senior VP*
Thomas S Price, *Senior VP*
David Doland, *Opers Mgr*
Cody Bogle, *Engineer*
EMP: 362
SQ FT: 75,000
SALES (est): 42.8MM **Publicly Held**
WEB: www.chk.com
SIC: **1311** Crude petroleum production
PA: Chesapeake Energy Corporation
  6100 N Western Ave
  Oklahoma City OK 73118

(G-5755)
CHESAPEAKE LOUISIANA LP
6100 N Western Ave (73118-1044)
P.O. Box 18496 (73154-0496)
PHONE...................405 848-8000
Seth Barkocy, *Partner*
Chesapeake Energy Corporation, *General Ptnr*
Benjamin Dennis, *Foreman/Supr*
Zack Dimeo, *Foreman/Supr*
Clint Filson, *Foreman/Supr*
EMP: 450 EST: 1997
SQ FT: 75,000
SALES (est): 40.7MM **Publicly Held**
WEB: www.chk.com
SIC: **1311** Crude petroleum production
PA: Chesapeake Energy Corporation
  6100 N Western Ave
  Oklahoma City OK 73118

(G-5756)
CHESAPEAKE MIDSTREAM DEV LP
6100 N Western Ave (73118-1044)
P.O. Box 18496 (73154-0496)
PHONE...................405 935-8000
Robert Doug Lawler, *President*
Dominic J Vellosso Jr, *CFO*
EMP: 1
SALES (est): 2.8MM **Publicly Held**
SIC: **1311** Crude petroleum production
PA: Chesapeake Energy Corporation
  6100 N Western Ave
  Oklahoma City OK 73118

(G-5757)
CHESAPEAKE OPERATING LLC (HQ)
6100 N Western Ave (73118-1044)
P.O. Box 548806 (73154-8806)
PHONE...................405 848-8000
Robert Doug Lawler, *CEO*
Lauren Tenpenny, *Engineer*
Jessica Jones, *Accountant*
David Owen, *Agent*
Kesha Jones, *Analyst*
EMP: 1800
SQ FT: 504,000
SALES (est): 4.4B **Publicly Held**
SIC: **1311** 1389 4212 Crude petroleum production; natural gas production; building oil & gas well foundations on site; mud service, oil field drilling; local trucking, without storage

(G-5758)
CHEYENNE PETRO CO LTD PARTNR (PA)
14000 Quail Springs Parkw (73134)
PHONE...................405 936-6220
Bill Spurgeon, *President*
Stephen Ives, *Principal*
Terry Allen, *Opers Staff*
Randy Gasaway, *Engineer*
Danny Parks, *CFO*
EMP: 30 EST: 1983
SQ FT: 10,000
SALES (est): 44MM **Privately Held**
SIC: **1382** 1311 Oil & gas exploration services; crude petroleum production; natural gas production

(G-5759)
CHICKASAW DEFENSE SERVICES INC
6101 Camille Ave (73149-5036)
PHONE...................405 203-0144
Ronald Heald, *Co-Owner*
Carlton Dawson, *Co-Owner*
EMP: 3
SALES (est): 170.8K **Privately Held**
SIC: **8711** 1541 1711 1721 Building construction consultant; pharmaceutical manufacturing plant construction; plumbing, heating, air-conditioning contractors; residential painting; structural shapes & pilings, steel

(G-5760)
CHILD HEROES LLC
6802 Lancer Ln (73132-6032)
PHONE...................757 286-8181
Sharon Liddle,
▲ EMP: 3
SALES (est): 150K **Privately Held**
SIC: **2731** Book publishing

(G-5761)
CHK CLEVELAND TONKAWA LLC
6100 N Western Ave (73118-1044)
PHONE...................405 848-8000
Robert D Lawler, *CEO*
EMP: 1 EST: 2012
SALES (est): 73.8K **Publicly Held**
SIC: **1311** Crude petroleum production; natural gas production
PA: Chesapeake Energy Corporation
  6100 N Western Ave
  Oklahoma City OK 73118

(G-5762)
CHK LOUISIANA LLC
6100 N Western Ave (73118-1044)
PHONE...................405 935-7871
Archie W Dunham, *Principal*
EMP: 4
SALES (est): 276K **Privately Held**
WEB: www.chk.com
SIC: **1311** Crude petroleum production

(G-5763)
CHORUS LABS LLC
2205 Nw 57th St (73112-7303)
PHONE...................405 317-2942
Justin Briggs,
Matthew Sartin,
EMP: 2 EST: 2012
SALES (est): 110.4K **Privately Held**
SIC: **7372** 7389 Application computer software;

(G-5764)
CHROMALLOY GAS TURBINE LLC
Also Called: Chromalloy Oklahoma
2701 Liberty Pkwy Ste 305 (73110-2895)
PHONE...................845 359-4700
Connie Vansleet, *General Mgr*
EMP: 153
SQ FT: 100,000

Oklahoma City - Oklahoma County (G-5765)

SALES (corp-wide): 3.3B **Publicly Held**
SIC: 7699 5088 3728 Engine repair & replacement, non-automotive; aircraft engines & engine parts; aircraft parts & equipment
HQ: Chromalloy Gas Turbine Llc
3999 Rca Blvd
Palm Beach Gardens FL 33410
561 935-3571

(G-5765)
CIMARRON PALLET MFG CO
1430 W Sheridan Ave (73106-5236)
PHONE.................................405 228-0288
Earl Hooks Jr, *Owner*
EMP: 3
SALES (est): 269.3K **Privately Held**
SIC: 2448 Pallets, wood

(G-5766)
CIMARRON PIPELINE LLC
1601 Nw Expwy St Ste 777 (73118-1446)
PHONE.................................405 286-9797
Blake Berrenne, *Partner*
EMP: 4
SALES (est): 225.1K **Privately Held**
SIC: 1389 Oil & gas wells: building, repairing & dismantling

(G-5767)
CIRCLE 9 RESOURCES LLC
2308 Nw 54th St (73112-7757)
P.O. Box 249 (73101-0249)
PHONE.................................972 528-6773
EMP: 10 EST: 2013
SALES (est): 403.8K **Privately Held**
SIC: 1382 Oil/Gas Exploration Services

(G-5768)
CIS INVESTORS LLC
316 Nw 61st St (73118-7418)
PHONE.................................405 370-5812
EMP: 6
SALES (est): 245.6K **Privately Held**
SIC: 3571 Electronic computers

(G-5769)
CITATION OIL & GAS CORP
9400 Broadway Ext Ste 510 (73114-7444)
PHONE.................................405 681-9400
Rod Smith, *Production*
EMP: 11
SALES (corp-wide): 283.5MM **Privately Held**
SIC: 1382 Oil & gas exploration services
PA: Citation Oil & Gas Corp.
14077 Cutten Rd
Houston TX 77069
281 891-1000

(G-5770)
CITY CARBONIC LLC
406 Sw 4th St (73109-5306)
PHONE.................................405 239-2068
Louis Morgan, *CEO*
Amy Bruecks, *Managing Prtnr*
Amy Morgan Bruecks,
EMP: 6
SQ FT: 3,800
SALES (est): 1.4MM **Privately Held**
WEB: www.citycarbonic.com
SIC: 5169 5084 8734 2813 Industrial gases; industrial machinery & equipment; testing laboratories; industrial gases

(G-5771)
CJ GRAPHICS
636 Sw 59th St Ste B (73109-8204)
PHONE.................................405 636-0400
EMP: 2
SQ FT: 2,596
SALES (est): 86K **Privately Held**
SIC: 2791 2752 Typesetting Services Lithographic Commercial Printing

(G-5772)
CLARAS KITCHEN LLC
6036 Nw 59th St (73122-7129)
PHONE.................................229 669-1493
EMP: 4
SALES (est): 84K **Privately Held**
SIC: 2033 Mfg Canned Fruits/Vegetables

(G-5773)
CLARIOS
Also Called: Johnson Controls
4730 Sw 20th St (73128-3043)
PHONE.................................405 688-3730
Lenn Niblett, *Manager*
Rodney Smith, *Analyst*
Janelle Schmidt, *Representative*
EMP: 7 **Privately Held**
SIC: 2531 Seats, automobile
HQ: Johnson Controls, Inc.
5757 N Green Bay Ave
Milwaukee WI 53209
414 524-1200

(G-5774)
CLARK CREATIVE INDUSTRIES INC
1909 Colebrook Dr (73120-3903)
PHONE.................................405 473-8046
Phil Goss, *Principal*
EMP: 2
SALES (est): 136.9K **Privately Held**
SIC: 3999 Manufacturing industries

(G-5775)
CLARK ELLISON
Also Called: Ellison Clark Irevocable Trust
222 Ne 50th St (73105-1893)
PHONE.................................405 525-3583
Clark Ellison, *Owner*
EMP: 2
SQ FT: 3,474
SALES (est): 170K **Privately Held**
SIC: 1311 Crude petroleum & natural gas

(G-5776)
CLARK PRINTING INC
Also Called: Clark Printing & Tag Co
109 E Madison Ave (73105-3016)
P.O. Box 60144 (73146-0144)
PHONE.................................405 528-5396
Frank Clark, *President*
EMP: 5 EST: 1959
SQ FT: 1,440
SALES: 100K **Privately Held**
SIC: 2752 2791 2789 2759 Commercial printing, offset; typesetting; bookbinding & related work; commercial printing

(G-5777)
CLASSEN WHOLESALE OPTICAL INC
6600 N Olie Ave Ste C (73116-7339)
PHONE.................................405 842-1900
Bud Mayfield, *President*
Anna Verrier, *Vice Pres*
Karen Gremillion, *Treasurer*
EMP: 5
SQ FT: 1,700
SALES (est): 330K **Privately Held**
SIC: 3851 5995 5048 Eyeglasses, lenses & frames; optical goods stores; ophthalmic goods

(G-5778)
CLASSIC PRINTING INC
2464 Nw 39th St (73112)
PHONE.................................405 524-6889
Ron Harper, *President*
Bryan Harper, *Treasurer*
Dewayne Moates, *Sales Staff*
Kyle Lunsford, *Manager*
EMP: 16
SQ FT: 9,500
SALES (est): 2.7MM **Privately Held**
SIC: 2752 Commercial printing, offset

(G-5779)
CLASSIC TILE STONE & MBL LLC
117 W Wilshire Blvd (73116-9033)
PHONE.................................405 858-8453
Mark Hammond, *Mng Member*
Mike Hammond,
▲ EMP: 18 EST: 1998
SQ FT: 17,000
SALES: 2.4MM **Privately Held**
SIC: 3253 5032 3281 Ceramic wall & floor tile; marble building stone; cut stone & stone products

(G-5780)
CLAUDE V SANDERSON PROP
Also Called: Sanderson Signs
1113 N Western Ave (73106-6821)
PHONE.................................405 232-5878
Claude Sanderson, *Owner*
EMP: 1
SQ FT: 2,420
SALES (est): 76.7K **Privately Held**
SIC: 3993 Signs & advertising specialties

(G-5781)
CLEAR CHANNEL OUTDOOR INC
5205 N Santa Fe Ave (73118-7511)
PHONE.................................405 528-2683
Jim Tidwell, *Manager*
EMP: 30 **Publicly Held**
SIC: 7312 3993 Billboard advertising; signs & advertising specialties
HQ: Clear Channel Outdoor, Llc
4830 N Loop 160 W Ste 111
San Antonio TX 78249

(G-5782)
CLEAR2THERE LLC
4211 N Barnes Ave (73112-8814)
PHONE.................................405 605-8158
Craig L Steen, *President*
David Shafron, *Mng Member*
Tom Shafron, *CTO*
EMP: 2
SALES (est): 321K
SALES (corp-wide): 65.7MM **Privately Held**
SIC: 3651 Household audio & video equipment
PA: Earthbend, Llc
2904 W 10th St
Sioux Falls SD 57104
605 777-7005

(G-5783)
CLEMENTS FOODS CO (PA)
6601 N Harvey Pl (73116-7925)
P.O. Box 14538 (73113-0538)
PHONE.................................405 842-3308
Edward B Clements, *President*
Richard Meadors, *COO*
Tarland Beauchamp, *Plant Mgr*
John Miller, *Plant Mgr*
Terry Williams, *Warehouse Mgr*
EMP: 205 EST: 1953
SQ FT: 61,000
SALES: 75MM **Privately Held**
WEB: www.clementsfoods.com
SIC: 2035 Pickles, sauces & salad dressings

(G-5784)
CLEMENTS FOODS CO
Also Called: Clements Vinegar
6601 N Harvey Pl (73116-7925)
PHONE.................................405 842-3308
Louis Leflore, *Purchasing*
Denise Klause, *Human Res Mgr*
Louis Le Flore, *Branch Mgr*
EMP: 1
SALES (corp-wide): 75MM **Privately Held**
SIC: 2099 Vinegar
PA: Clements Foods Co.
6601 N Harvey Pl
Oklahoma City OK 73116
405 842-3308

(G-5785)
CLIMACOOL CORP (HQ)
15 S Virginia Ave (73106-3009)
P.O. Box 2055 (73101-2055)
PHONE.................................405 815-3000
Ross Miglio, *President*
Judy Linder, *Production*
Alicia Haan, *Manager*
EMP: 11
SQ FT: 25,000
SALES (est): 3MM
SALES (corp-wide): 2.3B **Privately Held**
SIC: 3585 Air conditioning equipment, complete
PA: Nibe Industrier Ab
Jarnvagsgatan 40
Markaryd 285 3
433 730-00

(G-5786)
CLIMATE CONTROL GROUP INC (HQ)
Also Called: LSB Strategic Accounts
7300 Sw 44th St (73179-4307)
PHONE.................................405 745-6858
Steve Golsen, *President*
EMP: 29
SALES (est): 421.4MM
SALES (corp-wide): 2.5B **Privately Held**
SIC: 3561 Pumps & pumping equipment
PA: Nibe Industrier Ab
Jarnvagsgatan 40
Markaryd 285 3
433 730-00

(G-5787)
CLIMATE MASTER INC (DH)
7300 Sw 44th St (73179-4307)
P.O. Box 2540 (73101-2540)
PHONE.................................405 745-6000
Dan Ellis, *President*
Todd Graf, *Vice Pres*
Mary Starrett, *Vice Pres*
Dean Drake, *Engineer*
Mike Shankle, *Engineer*
◆ EMP: 550
SQ FT: 426,000
SALES (est): 228.8MM
SALES (corp-wide): 2.5B **Privately Held**
SIC: 3585 Heat pumps, electric
HQ: The Climate Control Group Inc
7300 Sw 44th St
Oklahoma City OK 73179
405 745-6858

(G-5788)
CLIMATECRAFT INC
1427 Nw 3rd St (73106-5207)
PHONE.................................405 415-9230
Joe Cappello, *President*
Andrew Hillis, *Principal*
Bud White, *Vice Pres*
Preston Hall, *Plant Mgr*
Charles Baxa, *Purch Mgr*
▲ EMP: 140 EST: 1983
SALES (est): 52.6MM
SALES (corp-wide): 2.5B **Privately Held**
WEB: www.climatecraft.com
SIC: 3585 Air conditioning condensers & condensing units
HQ: The Climate Control Group Inc
7300 Sw 44th St
Oklahoma City OK 73179
405 745-6858

(G-5789)
CLINTS PORTABLE WELDING
3309 Se 59th St (73135-1607)
P.O. Box 95271 (73143-5271)
PHONE.................................405 834-4517
Clint Maynard, *President*
EMP: 4
SALES (est): 2.1MM **Privately Held**
SIC: 7692 Welding repair

(G-5790)
CLOSE CUSTOM CABINETS INC
440 W Britton Rd (73114-3510)
PHONE.................................405 840-8226
Robert J Vahlberg, *President*
EMP: 48
SQ FT: 20,000
SALES: 3MM **Privately Held**
SIC: 2522 2511 2434 Office cabinets & filing drawers: except wood; wood household furniture; wood kitchen cabinets

(G-5791)
CMD INC
2300 S High Ave (73129-4838)
PHONE.................................405 672-9607
Gary Scantlin, *Principal*
EMP: 1
SALES (est): 51.7K **Privately Held**
SIC: 3599 Machine shop, jobbing & repair

(G-5792)
CMI TEREX CORPORATION (HQ)
Also Called: Terex Roadbuilding
9528 W I 40 Service Rd (73128-7108)
PHONE.................................405 787-6020
Robert L Curtis, *Principal*
Earl G Morris, *Principal*
J S Wylie Jr, *Principal*
Thane A Swisher, *Vice Pres*

GEOGRAPHIC SECTION

Oklahoma City - Oklahoma County (G-5821)

George Ellis, *Vice Pres*
◆ **EMP: 1504 EST:** 1926
SQ FT: 635,000
SALES (est): 303.7MM
SALES (corp-wide): 4.3B **Publicly Held**
SIC: 3715 3596 3541 3444 Truck trailers; scales & balances, except laboratory; truck (motor vehicle) scales; industrial scales; machine tools, metal cutting type; sheet metalwork; asphalt paving mixtures & blocks; asphalt plant, including gravel-mix type
PA: Terex Corporation
200 Nyala Farms Rd Ste 2
Westport CT 06880
203 222-7170

(G-5793)
CMI TEREX CORPORATION
I-40 Morgan Rd (73128)
PHONE..................405 787-6020
Carl Hatton, *President*
EMP: 2
SALES (est): 279.9K **Privately Held**
SIC: 3531 Construction machinery

(G-5794)
CNC METAL SHAPE CNSTR LLC
1718 S Agnew Ave (73108-2443)
PHONE..................405 605-5500
Randon Lafuente, *CEO*
Manuel Cordova Quintero, *CFO*
EMP: 12
SQ FT: 300,000
SALES: 600K **Privately Held**
SIC: 3441 3533 Fabricated structural metal for bridges; oil & gas field machinery

(G-5795)
CNG SPECIALISTS LLC
1211 Se 29th St (73129-6439)
PHONE..................405 677-5400
Jim Faubion, *Principal*
EMP: 8
SALES (est): 1.1MM **Privately Held**
SIC: 3714 Motor vehicle parts & accessories

(G-5796)
CNS AUDIO VIDEO INC
400 S Vermont Ave Ste 100 (73108-1035)
PHONE..................405 256-8546
Brandon Lowder, *President*
EMP: 40
SALES (est): 74.6K **Privately Held**
SIC: 3651 Public address systems

(G-5797)
COARE BIOTECHNOLOGY INC
800 Research Pkwy (73104-3611)
PHONE..................405 227-0406
Eddie Bannerman-Menson, *Director*
EMP: 5
SALES (est): 450.2K **Privately Held**
SIC: 2836 Biological products, except diagnostic

(G-5798)
COAT PRO LLC
1603 Se 25th St (73129-7609)
PHONE..................405 672-0705
Gary McFarlane,
Jodie McDaniel,
EMP: 7
SALES (est): 828.5K **Privately Held**
SIC: 3479 Coating of metals & formed products

(G-5799)
COCKERELL ENERGY
3160 W Britton Rd (73120-2068)
PHONE..................405 463-7118
EMP: 2
SALES (est): 217.4K **Privately Held**
SIC: 1382 Oil & gas exploration services

(G-5800)
COJAC PORTABLE BUILDINGS INC (PA)
2820 W Reno Ave (73107-6846)
PHONE..................405 232-1229
Toll Free:..................888 -
Michael Jackson, *President*
Jimmy Jackson, *Vice Pres*
EMP: 20
SALES (est): 3.1MM **Privately Held**
SIC: 3448 Buildings, portable: prefabricated metal

(G-5801)
COJAC PORTABLE BUILDINGS INC
Also Called: Cojac Building Co
2820 W Reno Ave (73107-6846)
PHONE..................405 232-1229
John Stratton, *Branch Mgr*
EMP: 2
SALES (est): 195.5K
SALES (corp-wide): 3.1MM **Privately Held**
SIC: 3448 Prefabricated metal buildings
PA: Cojac Portable Buildings, Inc.
2820 W Reno Ave
Oklahoma City OK 73107
405 232-1229

(G-5802)
COLDREN ENTERPRISES CORP
Also Called: Accurate Tool & Die
1821 Nw 6th St (73106-2618)
PHONE..................405 239-2205
David Coldren, *President*
Tarey Coldren, *Vice Pres*
EMP: 9 **EST:** 1996
SQ FT: 4,500
SALES (est): 889.4K **Privately Held**
SIC: 3544 Special dies, tools, jigs & fixtures

(G-5803)
COLE DEFENSE LLC
413 W Britton Rd Apt 142 (73114-3532)
PHONE..................214 934-5473
Brycen Cole,
EMP: 4 **EST:** 2017
SALES (est): 199.4K **Privately Held**
SIC: 3812 Defense systems & equipment

(G-5804)
COMANCHE EXPLORATION CO LLC
Also Called: Comanche Resources
6520 N Western Ave (73116-7346)
PHONE..................405 755-5900
Robert Blair, *Mng Member*
EMP: 30
SALES (est): 9.7MM **Privately Held**
SIC: 1382 Oil & gas exploration services

(G-5805)
COMMERCIAL COATINGS OKLA LLC
1421 N Fordson Dr (73127-3231)
PHONE..................405 226-8739
EMP: 2 **EST:** 2010
SALES (est): 162.1K **Privately Held**
SIC: 3479 Metal coating & allied service

(G-5806)
COMMERCIAL SERVICES CORP
6619 S Western Ave Ste A (73139-1713)
PHONE..................405 634-8888
William F White, *President*
Janice Talley, *Vice Pres*
EMP: 19
SQ FT: 2,500
SALES (est): 2.7MM **Privately Held**
SIC: 3585 7349 Heating & air conditioning combination units; building maintenance, except repairs

(G-5807)
COMPADRES TRADING CO
40 Ne 46th St (73105-2011)
PHONE..................405 816-9911
Timothy Herbel, *President*
EMP: 4
SALES (est): 116.1K **Privately Held**
SIC: 2095 Coffee roasting (except by wholesale grocers)

(G-5808)
COMPASS ENERGY OPERATING LLC
204 N Robinson Ave # 1300 (73102-6831)
PHONE..................405 594-4141
Keri Mitchell, *Treasurer*
EMP: 75 **EST:** 2017
SALES (est): 50MM
SALES (corp-wide): 6.2MM **Privately Held**
SIC: 1311 Crude petroleum & natural gas production
PA: Compass Production Partners, Lp
204 N Robinson Ave # 1300
Oklahoma City OK 73102
405 594-4141

(G-5809)
COMPASS MANUFACTURING LLC
11935 N Intrstate 44 Svce (73173)
P.O. Box 18918 (73154-0918)
PHONE..................405 735-3518
Robert Doug Lawler, *CEO*
Alan D Lavenue, *President*
Domenic Dell'osso Jr, *CFO*
EMP: 2
SALES (est): 1.8MM **Publicly Held**
SIC: 5084 3533 Compressors, except air conditioning; oil & gas field machinery
HQ: Chesapeake Operating, L.L.C.
6100 N Western Ave
Oklahoma City OK 73118

(G-5810)
COMPASS PRODUCTION PARTNERS LP (PA)
204 N Robinson Ave # 1300 (73102-6831)
PHONE..................405 594-4141
Matthew Grubb, *CEO*
EMP: 75
SALES (est): 6.2MM **Privately Held**
SIC: 1389 Oil field services

(G-5811)
COMPLETE COOLING SYSTEMS INC
717 Sw 4th St (73109-5105)
PHONE..................405 272-0453
John Schneider, *President*
EMP: 2
SALES (est): 190.6K **Privately Held**
SIC: 3792 Travel trailers & campers

(G-5812)
COMPLETE GRAPHICS INC
Also Called: Complete Graphics Service
1010 Sw 3rd St (73109-1011)
P.O. Box 892717 (73189-2717)
PHONE..................405 232-8882
Thomas Vasquez, *President*
Lisa Vasquez, *Admin Sec*
EMP: 4
SQ FT: 5,000
SALES (est): 250K **Privately Held**
SIC: 7336 3993 2396 2395 Silk screen design; signs & advertising specialties; automotive & apparel trimmings; pleating & stitching

(G-5813)
COMPONENT SERVICES LP
8316 Sw 8th St (73128-4228)
PHONE..................405 787-7180
Carol Preble, *Principal*
Key Enterprises, *General Ptnr*
▼ **EMP:** 14
SALES (est): 2.2MM **Privately Held**
SIC: 3469 Metal stampings

(G-5814)
COMPRESSCO INC (HQ)
1313 Se 25th St (73129-6433)
PHONE..................405 677-0221
Ronald Foster, *President*
Gary Bridges, *Area Mgr*
Kevin Book, *Vice Pres*
Ted Garner, *Vice Pres*
Sheri Vanhooser, *Vice Pres*
▲ **EMP:** 69
SALES (est): 77.5MM
SALES (corp-wide): 1B **Publicly Held**
WEB: www.compressco.com
SIC: 3533 Gas field machinery & equipment
PA: Tetra Technologies, Inc.
24955 Interstate 45
The Woodlands TX 77380
281 367-1983

(G-5815)
COMPRESSCO INC
8224 Sw 3rd St (73128-4201)
PHONE..................405 787-2808
EMP: 2 **EST:** 2010
SALES (est): 140K **Privately Held**
SIC: 3563 Mfg Air/Gas Compressors

(G-5816)
COMPRESSCO PARTNERS SUB INC (DH)
101 Park Ave Ste 1200 (73102-7207)
PHONE..................405 677-0221
Ronald J Foster, *President*
EMP: 122
SALES (est): 28MM
SALES (corp-wide): 1B **Publicly Held**
SIC: 1389 3533 Oil field services; gas field machinery & equipment

(G-5817)
COMPTECH COMPUTER TECH INC
2601 Liberty Pkwy Ste 102 (73110-2855)
PHONE..................937 228-2667
Melissa Shaw, *Exec Dir*
EMP: 21
SALES (est): 436.1K **Privately Held**
SIC: 2741 Technical manual & paper publishing

(G-5818)
COMPUTER DLERS RCYCLERS GLOBL
Also Called: Cdr Global
615 W Wilshire Blvd # 11 (73116-7722)
PHONE..................405 749-7989
Damian Rodriguez, *President*
Marc Siemens, *Vice Pres*
Robert Brown, *CFO*
Richard Russell, *Mktg Dir*
Dalton Brown, *Representative*
◆ **EMP:** 45
SQ FT: 65,000
SALES (est): 12.3MM **Privately Held**
SIC: 5045 3571 Computers, peripherals & software; computers, digital, analog or hybrid

(G-5819)
CONCRETE PRODUCTS INC
Also Called: Central Pre Past
2107 Ne 10th St (73117-5029)
PHONE..................405 427-8686
David White, *President*
Audrey D King, *President*
EMP: 20
SQ FT: 20,000
SALES (est): 3.4MM **Privately Held**
SIC: 3272 Concrete stuctural support & building material

(G-5820)
CONNELLY READY-MIX CON LLC
Also Called: Connelly Paving Company
917 N Tulsa Ave Ste A (73107-6078)
P.O. Box 75450 (73147-0450)
PHONE..................405 943-8388
James A Connelly Jr, *President*
Philip Kierl, *Treasurer*
Lee Ann Fisher, *Admin Sec*
EMP: 100
SQ FT: 7,500
SALES (est): 10.9MM **Privately Held**
SIC: 3273 Ready-mixed concrete

(G-5821)
CONSOLIDATED BUILDERS SUPPLY
Also Called: C B S
1450 Exchange Ave (73108-3015)
P.O. Box 83349 (73148-1349)
PHONE..................405 631-3033
Charles Khoury, *President*
Kenny Smith, *Vice Pres*
Lee Dear, *Opers Mgr*
Michael Maloy, *Purchasing*
Travis Baker, *Sales Mgr*
EMP: 37
SQ FT: 27,300

Oklahoma City - Oklahoma County (G-5822)

GEOGRAPHIC SECTION

SALES (est): 15.3MM **Privately Held**
SIC: 5031 3442 Windows; doors; skylights, all materials; window & door frames

(G-5822)
CONTACT PROCESS PIPING
100 N Quapah Ave Ste D (73107-6631)
P.O. Box 271566 (73137-1566)
PHONE..................................405 948-9125
Jim Hensley, *President*
EMP: 4
SALES (est): 377.3K **Privately Held**
WEB: www.contactprocesspiping.com
SIC: 3556 Food products machinery

(G-5823)
CONTINENTAL RESOURCES INC (PA)
20 N Broadway (73102-9213)
P.O. Box 268836 (73126-8836)
PHONE..................................405 234-9000
Harold G Hamm, *Ch of Bd*
Jack H Stark, *President*
Patrick W Bent, *Senior VP*
Eric S Eissenstat, *Senior VP*
Gary E Gould, *Senior VP*
EMP: 144 **EST:** 1967
SALES: 4.6B **Publicly Held**
SIC: 1311 Crude petroleum production; natural gas production

(G-5824)
CONTINENTAL-BROKERS & CONS INC
Also Called: Roasters Exchange
1530 W Main St (73106-3014)
PHONE..................................405 232-1534
Dan D Jolliff, *President*
Kim C Hahn, *Principal*
Michael W Hahn, *Principal*
▲ **EMP:** 25
SQ FT: 40,000
SALES (est): 9.4MM **Privately Held**
WEB: www.roasters-exchange.com
SIC: 5046 3589 Coffee brewing equipment & supplies; coffee brewing equipment

(G-5825)
CONTINNTAL OIL GAS ENRGY NTWRK
7121 S Santa Fe Ave (73139-7509)
PHONE..................................214 636-2401
Danny Cooper, *Principal*
EMP: 2
SALES (est): 65.5K **Privately Held**
SIC: 1389 Oil & gas field services

(G-5826)
COOK COMPRESSION
6836 Pat Ave (73149-5215)
PHONE..................................405 677-3153
Thomas Reece, *Principal*
EMP: 10
SALES (corp-wide): 7.1B **Publicly Held**
WEB: www.cookcompression.com
SIC: 3563 Air & gas compressors
HQ: Cook Compression
11951 Spectrum Blvd
Houston TX 77047

(G-5827)
COOKS FENCE & IRON CO INC
3725 S Meridian Ave (73119-2421)
PHONE..................................405 681-2301
David Swanda, *President*
Susan Swanda, *Corp Secy*
EMP: 15
SQ FT: 5,000
SALES (est): 1.9MM **Privately Held**
SIC: 1799 3496 Fence construction; miscellaneous fabricated wire products

(G-5828)
COOPER CABINET SYSTEMS INC
4019 N Walnut Ave (73105-3748)
PHONE..................................405 528-7220
Bill Hyder, *President*
Mike Mitchell, *COO*
EMP: 70
SALES (est): 8.8MM **Privately Held**
SIC: 2434 Wood kitchen cabinets

(G-5829)
COOPER CABINETS INC
4019 N Walnut Ave (73105-3748)
PHONE..................................405 528-7220
Kay Acosta, *Principal*
EMP: 26
SALES (est): 883.3K **Privately Held**
SIC: 2434 Wood kitchen cabinets

(G-5830)
COOPER MACHINERY SERVICES INC
2216 Se 15th St (73129)
PHONE..................................713 354-4068
EMP: 200
SALES (corp-wide): 166.1MM **Privately Held**
SIC: 1389 Cementing oil & gas well casings
PA: Cooper Machinery Services, Inc.
16250 Port Nw
Houston TX 77041
713 354-1900

(G-5831)
COORSTEK
7700 S Bryant Ave (73149-7412)
PHONE..................................800 821-6110
EMP: 9
SALES (est): 1.2MM **Privately Held**
SIC: 3812 Aircraft control instruments

(G-5832)
COORSTEK INC
Also Called: Coorstek Oklahoma City
7700 S Bryant Ave (73149-7412)
PHONE..................................405 601-4371
Shawn Grubb, *Manager*
EMP: 310
SALES (corp-wide): 297.1MM **Privately Held**
SIC: 3264 3674 Porcelain electrical supplies; semiconductors & related devices
HQ: Coorstek, Inc.
14143 Denver West Pkwy # 400
Lakewood CO 80401
303 271-7000

(G-5833)
COPE PLASTICS INC
310 Ne 31st St (73105-4004)
PHONE..................................405 528-5697
Jennifer Read, *Marketing Staff*
Mike Bonin, *Branch Mgr*
EMP: 6
SALES (corp-wide): 246.9MM **Privately Held**
SIC: 3089 5162 Plastic processing; plastics materials & basic shapes
PA: Cope Plastics, Inc.
4441 Indl Dr
Alton IL 62002
618 466-0221

(G-5834)
COPY FAST PRINTING INC
3629 Nw 50th St (73112-5668)
PHONE..................................405 947-7468
Flint A Lalli, *President*
Lawana Lalli, *Principal*
EMP: 15
SQ FT: 5,000
SALES (est): 2.1MM **Privately Held**
SIC: 2752 2796 2791 2789 Commercial printing, offset; platemaking services; typesetting; bookbinding & related work

(G-5835)
CORESLAB STRUCTURES OKLA INC
817 Se 55th St (73129-5600)
P.O. Box 94787 (73143-4787)
PHONE..................................405 632-4944
Jerry Baker, *COO*
Dave Hellyer, *Exec VP*
Mario Franciosa, *Vice Pres*
Tony Tvarc, *Plant Mgr*
Dale Goodner, *Purchasing*
EMP: 210
SQ FT: 8,000

SALES (est): 48.9MM
SALES (corp-wide): 27.3MM **Privately Held**
SIC: 1791 3272 2439 Precast concrete structural framing or panels, placing of; concrete stuctural support & building material; building materials, except block or brick: concrete; structural wood members
HQ: Coreslab Holdings U S Inc
332 Jones Rd Suite 1
Stoney Creek ON
905 643-0220

(G-5836)
CORESLAB STRUCTURES OKLAHOMA
7000 S Sunnylane Rd (73135-1714)
P.O. Box 94787 (73143-4787)
PHONE..................................405 672-2325
Dave Clarke, *Principal*
Sean Morris, *Engineer*
Marissa Samaripa, *Design Engr*
Gary Miller, *Technology*
Art Richardson, *Executive*
EMP: 16
SQ FT: 9,426
SALES (est): 3.5MM
SALES (corp-wide): 27.3MM **Privately Held**
SIC: 3272 Concrete products
HQ: Coreslab Structures (Ont) Inc
205 Coreslab Dr
Dundas ON L9H 0
905 689-3993

(G-5837)
CORONADO PETROLEUM CORPORATION
105 N Hudson Ave Ste 800 (73102-4803)
PHONE..................................405 232-9700
James B Crawley, *President*
Fred Ferris, *Vice Pres*
Kim Hatfield, *Vice Pres*
EMP: 30 **EST:** 1980
SQ FT: 8,000
SALES (est): 1.5MM
SALES (corp-wide): 13.7MM **Privately Held**
SIC: 1311 Crude petroleum production; natural gas production
PA: Crawley Petroleum Corporation
105 N Hudson Ave Ste 800
Oklahoma City OK 73102
405 232-9700

(G-5838)
CORPO COMMISSION OK
Also Called: Petroleum Storage Tank Div
2101 N Lincoln Blvd # 480 (73105-4905)
P.O. Box 52000 (73152-2000)
PHONE..................................405 521-4683
Robin Strickland, *Chief*
Bryan Painter, *Corp Comm Staff*
Bill Taylor, *Supervisor*
Jeff Robertson, *Webmaster*
Angela Pierce, *Analyst*
EMP: 11 **Privately Held**
SIC: 1389 9199 Oil field services;
HQ: Corporation Commission, Oklahoma
2101 N Lincoln Blvd # 480
Oklahoma City OK 73105

(G-5839)
CORPORATE IMAGE APPAREL LLC
11100 Roxboro Ave # 2314 (73162-2543)
PHONE..................................405 659-8264
Robert Scheetz, *Mng Member*
EMP: 1
SALES: 60K **Privately Held**
SIC: 5621 2395 7389 Ready-to-wear apparel, women's; embroidery & art needlework;

(G-5840)
CORRUGATED SERVICES LP
7216 S Bryant Ave (73149-7204)
PHONE..................................405 672-1695
Charles Wuchter, *Manager*
EMP: 8
SALES (est): 1.4MM **Privately Held**
SIC: 2653 Corrugated & solid fiber boxes

(G-5841)
COUGAR DRILLING SOLUTIONS USA
9505 W Reno Ave (73127-2917)
P.O. Box 850189, Yukon (73085-0189)
PHONE..................................405 789-4945
EMP: 41
SALES (corp-wide): 6.6MM **Privately Held**
SIC: 3533 Mfg Oil/Gas Field Machinery
PA: Cougar Tool Inc
7319 17 St Nw
Edmonton AB
780 440-2400

(G-5842)
COUNCIL STAINLESS & SHTMTL
7918 Nw 10th St (73127-4417)
PHONE..................................405 787-4400
Robert D Wallace, *President*
Curtis Brown, *Vice Pres*
EMP: 6 **EST:** 1965
SQ FT: 6,000
SALES: 634K **Privately Held**
WEB: www.councilstainless.us
SIC: 3589 3444 Commercial cooking & foodwarming equipment; ducts, sheet metal

(G-5843)
COUNTERTOP WERKS INC
Also Called: F A Highly Counter Top Werks
3800 Nw 39th St (73112-2960)
PHONE..................................405 943-1988
Michael Shaw, *President*
EMP: 26 **EST:** 1946
SQ FT: 23,000
SALES: 1.5MM **Privately Held**
WEB: www.fahighleyokc.com
SIC: 2541 Counter & sink tops

(G-5844)
COUNTRSTRIKE LGHTNING PRTCTION
2421 Sw 90th Pl (73159-6840)
P.O. Box 890875 (73189-0875)
PHONE..................................405 863-8480
Brock Bishop, *Owner*
EMP: 4 **EST:** 2005
SALES (est): 299.3K **Privately Held**
WEB: www.cstrikelp.com
SIC: 3131 Counters

(G-5845)
COUPLING SPECIALTIES INC
1300 S Meridian Ave # 501 (73108-1759)
PHONE..................................281 457-2000
Richard Ridgeway, *President*
Isaac Satterwhite, *Vice Pres*
Cynthia Ridgeway, *Admin Sec*
EMP: 12
SQ FT: 28,921
SALES: 1.2MM **Privately Held**
SIC: 1389 3498 Oil field services; couplings, pipe: fabricated from purchased pipe

(G-5846)
COVERS PLUS INC
1200 Se 34th St Ste 1 (73129-6710)
PHONE..................................405 670-2221
Connie Woods, *President*
EMP: 6
SQ FT: 4,500
SALES: 280K **Privately Held**
SIC: 2394 3949 5999 Liners & covers, fabric: made from purchased materials; sporting & athletic goods; spas & hot tubs

(G-5847)
COVINGTON OIL CO INC
901 Nw 63rd St Ste 102 (73116-7622)
P.O. Box 54470 (73154-1470)
PHONE..................................405 842-8727
John Covington, *President*
Eugene Covington, *Vice Pres*
EMP: 2
SALES (est): 210K **Privately Held**
SIC: 1311 Crude petroleum production; natural gas production

GEOGRAPHIC SECTION
Oklahoma City - Oklahoma County (G-5877)

(G-5848)
COX MACHINE AND TOOL
Also Called: Cox Machine & Tool
5301 Sw 25th St (73128-5807)
PHONE..............................405 681-1445
Fax: 405 685-6445
EMP: 2
SQ FT: 6,250
SALES (est): 170K Privately Held
SIC: 3599 Job Shop

(G-5849)
CPK MANUFACTURING LLC
Also Called: Tower Tech
5400 Nw 5th St (73127-5810)
PHONE..............................405 290-7788
Matthew Solo, *Branch Mgr*
EMP: 35
SALES (corp-wide): 819.3MM Privately Held
SIC: 3089 Hardware, plastic
HQ: Cpk Manufacturing, Llc
214 Industrial Ln
Alum Bank PA 15521
814 839-4186

(G-5850)
CR STRIPES LTD CO
3636 Nw 51st St (73112-5611)
PHONE..............................405 946-8577
Karen Crane, *President*
Mary Arbuckle, *Partner*
EMP: 1
SALES (est): 98K Privately Held
SIC: 2759 2396 2395 Commercial printing; automotive & apparel trimmings; pleating & stitching

(G-5851)
CRANKSHAFT SERVICE COMPANY
4600 S Macarthur Blvd (73179-8005)
PHONE..............................405 685-7553
Kent Jones, *President*
EMP: 3
SALES (est): 181.8K Privately Held
SIC: 3581 7539 3541 Mechanisms for coin-operated machines; machine shop, automotive; machine tools, metal cutting type

(G-5852)
CRAWLEY PETROLEUM CORPORATION (PA)
105 N Hudson Ave Ste 800 (73102-4819)
PHONE..............................405 232-9700
James B Crawley, *Ch of Bd*
S Kim Hatfield, *President*
Laura Bazzell, *Chairman*
J Mike Drennen, *Vice Pres*
Fred Ferris, *Vice Pres*
▼ **EMP:** 129
SQ FT: 8,000
SALES (est): 13.7MM Privately Held
SIC: 1311 Crude petroleum production; natural gas production

(G-5853)
CREATIVE PULTRUSIONS INC
Tower Tech
11935 S Intrstate 44 Svc (73173)
PHONE..............................405 979-2141
EMP: 3
SALES (corp-wide): 819.3MM Privately Held
SIC: 3089 Hardware, plastic
HQ: Creative Pultrusions, Inc.
214 Industrial Ln
Alum Bank PA 15521
814 839-4186

(G-5854)
CREEKSIDE WOODWORKS
4421 N Barnes Ave (73112-8863)
PHONE..............................405 528-5432
Frank Arney, *Principal*
EMP: 2
SALES (est): 164.1K Privately Held
SIC: 2431 Millwork

(G-5855)
CRESCENT COMPANIES LLC
5749 Nw 132nd St (73142-4437)
PHONE..............................405 721-5511
EMP: 2
SALES (est): 240.8K
SALES (corp-wide): 1.2B Publicly Held
SIC: 1389 Pipe testing, oil field service
PA: Select Energy Services, Inc.
1233 West Loop S Ste 1400
Houston TX 77027
713 235-9500

(G-5856)
CRESCENT SERVICES LLC (PA)
5721 Nw 132nd St (73142-4437)
PHONE..............................405 603-1200
Nick Andrews, *COO*
Nick Hughes, *Exec VP*
Jeff Nelson, *Vice Pres*
Shawn Priddy, *Vice Pres*
Ryan Stover, *Vice Pres*
EMP: 85 **EST:** 2006
SQ FT: 12,200
SALES (est): 997.8MM Privately Held
WEB: www.crescentservices.net
SIC: 1389 Oil field services

(G-5857)
CRITICAL COMPONENTS INC
Also Called: Critical Components-Oil & Gas
2400 Purdue Dr (73128-1826)
PHONE..............................405 212-9166
Tim Frisby, *President*
Brandon Garcia, *Principal*
EMP: 2
SALES (est): 122.5K Privately Held
SIC: 1389 Oil & gas wells: building, repairing & dismantling

(G-5858)
CRM ENERGY INC
600 N Walker Ave Ste 201 (73102-3081)
P.O. Box 1148 (73101-1148)
PHONE..............................405 848-5420
John Stranger, *President*
Carol Trent, *Treasurer*
EMP: 2
SALES (est): 252.6K Privately Held
SIC: 1311 Crude petroleum production
PA: Capital Risk Management Corp
6301 N Wstn Ave Ste 225
Oklahoma City OK 73118

(G-5859)
CROSS TIMBERS OPERATING CO
Also Called: Xto Energy
210 Park Ave Ste 2350 (73102-5683)
PHONE..............................405 232-4011
Richard Culmer, *Facilities Mgr*
Matt Carathers, *Engineer*
Susan Garrett, *Engineer*
Jason Maly, *Engineer*
Kirk Ross, *Project Engr*
EMP: 39
SALES (corp-wide): 264.9B Publicly Held
SIC: 1311 Crude petroleum production
HQ: Cross Timbers Operating Company
810 Houston St Ste 2000
Fort Worth TX 76102
817 870-2800

(G-5860)
CROSSROAD HOLSTERS LLC
2216 Nw 118th St (73120-7806)
PHONE..............................405 317-7405
William R Couch, *Administration*
EMP: 1
SALES (est): 84.7K Privately Held
SIC: 3199 Holsters, leather

(G-5861)
CROWN ENERGY COMPANY
1117 Nw 24th St (73106-5615)
PHONE..............................405 526-0111
Randall D Holleyman, *President*
John R Snedegar, *Chairman*
Jerry Lee P E, *Senior VP*
John Hill, *Foreman/Supr*
Jess Eastwood, *Project Engr*
EMP: 26
SQ FT: 5,000
SALES (est): 10.5MM
SALES (corp-wide): 19.1B Publicly Held
SIC: 1381 Drilling oil & gas wells
PA: Fluor Corporation
6700 Las Colinas Blvd
Irving TX 75039
469 398-7000

(G-5862)
CROWN MIDSTREAM LLC
701 Cedar Lake Blvd 210 (73114-7806)
PHONE..............................405 753-1955
Debbie Lessert,
EMP: 2
SALES (est): 118.1K Privately Held
SIC: 3569 Gas producers (machinery)

(G-5863)
CROWN PAINT COMPANY (PA)
Also Called: Crown Paint Co.
1801 W Sheridan Ave (73106-3249)
PHONE..............................405 232-8580
John P Evans, *CEO*
Nick Nickelsen, *President*
Evelyn Faye Evans, *Corp Secy*
Victoria Nickelsen, *Vice Pres*
▼ **EMP:** 33
SQ FT: 61,500
SALES (est): 4.3MM Privately Held
WEB: www.crownpaintok.com
SIC: 2851 5231 Paints & paint additives; paint

(G-5864)
CRYSTAL RIVER OPERATING CO LLC
100 Park Ave Ste 400 (73102-8002)
PHONE..............................405 510-0440
EMP: 2 **EST:** 2017
SALES (est): 104.3K Privately Held
SIC: 1382 Oil & gas exploration services

(G-5865)
CUDD OPERATING CORP
Also Called: Cudd Holdings
6305 Waterford Blvd # 130 (73118-1122)
PHONE..............................405 841-1144
B Keaton Cudd III, *President*
EMP: 4
SALES (est): 459.9K Privately Held
SIC: 1389 Oil field services

(G-5866)
CUMMINGS OIL COMPANY
4917 N Portland Ave (73112-6113)
PHONE..............................405 948-1818
Sean Cummings, *President*
Brent Cummings, *Vice Pres*
Cindy Mitchener, *Manager*
EMP: 8 **EST:** 1972
SQ FT: 6,000
SALES (est): 1.4MM Privately Held
SIC: 1382 1311 Oil & gas exploration services; crude petroleum production; natural gas production

(G-5867)
CUMMINS ENTERPRISES INC
202 E Sheridan Ave (73104-4233)
PHONE..............................405 232-9022
Andrew V Cummins, *President*
Andrew C Cummins, *Treasurer*
Elizabeth Zaitz, *Comms Mgr*
EMP: 3
SQ FT: 900
SALES (est): 345.4K Privately Held
SIC: 6512 3519 Nonresidential building operators; internal combustion engines

(G-5868)
CUMMINS INC
5800 W Reno Ave (73127-6601)
PHONE..............................405 946-4481
Gary Long, *Parts Mgr*
Brett Minges, *Manager*
EMP: 343
SALES (corp-wide): 23.5B Publicly Held
WEB: www.cummins.com
SIC: 3519 Internal combustion engines
PA: Cummins Inc.
500 Jackson St
Columbus IN 47201
812 377-5000

(G-5869)
CUMMINS SOUTHERN PLAINS LLC
5800 W Reno Ave (73127-6601)
P.O. Box 270006 (73137-0006)
PHONE..............................405 946-4481
Robby Severance, *Sales Staff*
Richard Himes, *Manager*
EMP: 45
SALES (corp-wide): 23.5B Publicly Held
WEB: www.cummins-sp.com
SIC: 5084 7538 3519 Engines & parts, diesel; engine repair; internal combustion engines
HQ: Cummins Southern Plains Llc
600 N Watson Rd
Arlington TX 76011
817 640-6801

(G-5870)
CUPCAKES & SWEETS GALORE
8301 Willow Creek Blvd (73162-2022)
PHONE..............................405 641-7760
EMP: 4
SALES (est): 174.5K Privately Held
SIC: 2051 Bread, cake & related products

(G-5871)
CURZON OPERATING COMPANY LTD
4509 N Classen Blvd # 20 (73118-4836)
PHONE..............................405 235-8180
Robert Tucker, *Vice Pres*
EMP: 3
SALES (est): 157.4K Privately Held
SIC: 1311 Crude petroleum production

(G-5872)
CUSTOM CUTTING MILLWORK INC
3905 Amelia Ave (73112-2831)
PHONE..............................405 942-3196
Mark Todd, *President*
EMP: 11
SQ FT: 19,000
SALES (est): 1.2MM Privately Held
SIC: 2431 Millwork

(G-5873)
CUSTOM IDENTIFICATION PRODUCTS
Also Called: Burlane
3131 S Council Rd (73179-4497)
P.O. Box 270033 (73137-0033)
PHONE..............................405 745-1010
Eric Morris, *Manager*
John Pfoutz, *Manager*
▼ **EMP:** 6 **EST:** 1999
SALES (est): 991.4K Privately Held
SIC: 3069 3953 Rubber hardware; marking devices

(G-5874)
CUSTOM MANUFACTURING INC
4101 Sw 113th St (73173-8331)
PHONE..............................405 692-6311
Jamie Morton, *President*
Julie Moore, *Admin Sec*
EMP: 20
SQ FT: 30,000
SALES (est): 3.8MM Privately Held
SIC: 3412 1389 3443 3441 Metal barrels, drums & pails; construction, repair & dismantling services; tanks, standard or custom fabricated; metal plate; fabricated structural metal

(G-5875)
CUSTOM SOFTWARE SYSTEMS INC
2250 Nw 39th St Ste 103 (73112-8857)
PHONE..............................405 524-1919
Cindy Stevenson, *President*
EMP: 9
SALES (est): 401.2K Privately Held
SIC: 7372 Computer software development

(G-5876)
CUSTOM STORM SHELTERS LLC
7225 Nw 16th St (73127-3203)
PHONE..............................405 209-5525
Tim Ward, *Principal*
EMP: 2 **EST:** 2013
SALES (est): 247.7K Privately Held
WEB: www.customstormsheltersok.com
SIC: 3444 Sheet metalwork

(G-5877)
CUSTOM TILE & MARBLE INC
8220 N Western Ave (73114-1920)
PHONE..............................405 810-8515
Larry Waller, *President*

Oklahoma City - Oklahoma County (G-5878)

Paula Waller, *Vice Pres*
EMP: 11
SQ FT: 5,000
SALES (est): 1.1MM **Privately Held**
SIC: 3281 5032 Granite, cut & shaped; marble building stone

(G-5878)
CUSTOM UPHOLSTERY CONTRACTING
1209 W Main St (73106-7802)
PHONE 405 236-3505
Donald C Plugge, *President*
Larry Corwin, *Vice Pres*
EMP: 15
SALES (est): 830K **Privately Held**
SIC: 7641 2512 Upholstery work; upholstered household furniture

(G-5879)
CUSTOM WD FBERS CDAR MULCH LLC
616 N Macarthur Blvd (73127-5604)
PHONE 405 745-2270
EMP: 3 **EST:** 2016
SALES (est): 283.3K **Privately Held**
WEB: www.customwoodfibers.com
SIC: 2499 Wood products

(G-5880)
CUSTOMIZED FCTRY INTERIORS LLC
Also Called: Leatherseats.com
8320 S Shields Blvd (73149-3028)
PHONE 405 848-9999
Josh Joseph, *Principal*
EMP: 1 **EST:** 2002
SALES (est): 170.2K **Privately Held**
SIC: 7641 2396 Upholstery work; automotive & apparel trimmings; trimming, fabric

(G-5881)
CUTTING EDGE ARMS LLC
6840 Nw 11th St (73127-4252)
PHONE 405 603-6723
Gina May, *Principal*
EMP: 2
SALES (est): 179.1K **Privately Held**
WEB: www.cuttingedgearms.com
SIC: 3489 Guns, howitzers, mortars & related equipment

(G-5882)
CVR ENERGY
14000 Quail Springs Pkwy (73134-2620)
PHONE 405 286-0341
EMP: 2
SALES (est): 95.9K **Privately Held**
SIC: 1389 Oil field services

(G-5883)
CYTOVANCE BIOLOGICS INC
100 Ne 30th St (73105-2608)
PHONE 405 319-8310
Yan Wang, *CEO*
EMP: 2
SALES (corp-wide): 28.2MM **Privately Held**
SIC: 2834 Druggists' preparations (pharmaceuticals)
HQ: Cytovance Biologics, Inc.
800 Research Pkwy Ste 200
Oklahoma City OK 73104
405 319-8310

(G-5884)
D & B PRINTING INC
9124 S Walker Ave (73139-8508)
PHONE 405 632-0055
Tom Smith, *President*
EMP: 2
SALES (est): 107.9K **Privately Held**
SIC: 2759 2396 Screen printing; automotive & apparel trimmings

(G-5885)
D & D DESIGN & MFG INC
5701 S Rockwell St (73179-6633)
P.O. Box 129, Wheatland (73097-0129)
PHONE 405 745-2126
Nancy S Davidson, *President*
Robin Davidson, *Vice Pres*
EMP: 13
SQ FT: 5,600
SALES (est): 2.1MM **Privately Held**
SIC: 3444 Sheet metal specialties, not stamped

(G-5886)
D & J FILTER LTD LIABILITY CO
2320 S Portland Ave (73108-4827)
PHONE 405 376-5343
Don Ward, *Mng Member*
EMP: 7 **EST:** 2009
SALES (est): 560K **Privately Held**
SIC: 3569 Filters

(G-5887)
D & M STEEL MANUFACTURING
2320 S Agnew Ave (73108-6216)
PHONE 405 631-5027
David Blair, *President*
EMP: 7
SQ FT: 17,000
SALES (est): 550K **Privately Held**
SIC: 1799 5999 3496 3446 Ornamental metal work; safety supplies & equipment; miscellaneous fabricated wire products; architectural metalwork; metal doors, sash & trim

(G-5888)
D&R PROPERTY SERVICES INC
817 Se 88th St Ste 10 (73149-3095)
P.O. Box 15781 (73155-5781)
PHONE 405 677-2178
Deena Smith, *President*
Ron Smith, *Vice Pres*
EMP: 2
SALES (est): 250K **Privately Held**
SIC: 3589 High pressure cleaning equipment

(G-5889)
DAILY STOP
108 S Rockwell Ave (73127-6110)
PHONE 405 495-5556
EMP: 3
SALES (est): 111.1K **Privately Held**
SIC: 2711 Newspapers-Publishing/Printing

(G-5890)
DALE CASE HOMES INC ○
13424 Railway Dr (73114-2272)
PHONE 405 755-5055
EMP: 1 **EST:** 2019
SALES (est): 54.5K **Privately Held**
SIC: 3523 Farm machinery & equipment

(G-5891)
DALES MANUFACTURING CO
8717 S I 35 Service Rd (73149-3088)
PHONE 405 631-8988
Dale Bliss, *Owner*
Micheal Forehand, *Manager*
▲ **EMP:** 6
SQ FT: 8,000
SALES (est): 360K **Privately Held**
SIC: 3714 Motor vehicle parts & accessories

(G-5892)
DALLAS HERMETIC COMPANY INC
4101 Se 85th St (73135-6325)
PHONE 214 634-1744
Robert F Powell, *CEO*
Thomas W Dillard, *President*
Andrew Merrick, *Vice Pres*
Bob Powell, *VP Mktg*
EMP: 16
SQ FT: 23,800
SALES (est): 1.9MM
SALES (corp-wide): 1.6MM **Privately Held**
SIC: 3585 5075 Compressors for refrigeration & air conditioning equipment; air conditioning & ventilation equipment & supplies
PA: American Envircon Inc
8305 Sovereign Row
Dallas TX 75247
214 634-1744

(G-5893)
DALMARC ENTERPRISES INC
Also Called: Dalmarc Signs
4040 S I 35 Service Rd (73129-6905)
P.O. Box 95698 (73143-5698)
PHONE 405 942-8703

Phil Schwarz, *President*
Andrea Jean Hull, *Vice Pres*
Alana Faye Schwarz, *Treasurer*
Pam Young, *Executive*
Marlin Hull, *Admin Sec*
EMP: 56
SQ FT: 22,000
SALES (est): 7.7MM **Privately Held**
SIC: 3993 Electric signs

(G-5894)
DANDELION WELDING AND FABG LLC
7921 Nw 83rd St (73132-3357)
PHONE 405 431-8138
Daniel Tallbear, *Principal*
EMP: 1
SALES (est): 28.1K **Privately Held**
SIC: 7692 Welding repair

(G-5895)
DANNYS BOP LLC
727 N Morgan Rd (73127-7142)
PHONE 405 815-4041
Kristian Kos,
Dikran Tourian,
EMP: 75 **EST:** 2011
SALES (est): 3.1MM **Privately Held**
SIC: 1382 Oil & gas exploration services

(G-5896)
DANS CUSTOM AWNINGS LLC
3309 E Reno Ave (73117-6613)
PHONE 405 601-2703
William Smith,
Jennifer Smith,
EMP: 7
SALES: 500K **Privately Held**
WEB: www.danscustomawnings.com
SIC: 2394 Canvas awnings & canopies; canvas covers & drop cloths

(G-5897)
DANS CUSTOM CANVAS
545 Nw 33rd St (73118-7346)
PHONE 405 525-2419
EMP: 1 **EST:** 2013
SALES (est): 79K **Privately Held**
SIC: 2211 Cotton Broadwoven Fabric Mill

(G-5898)
DARNELL DRILLING INC
2250 Nw 39th St Ste 100 (73112-8895)
PHONE 405 524-8816
Bob J Darnell, *President*
July Webb, *Corp Secy*
Shirley Darnell, *Vice Pres*
EMP: 4 **EST:** 1975
SQ FT: 4,500
SALES (est): 420K **Privately Held**
SIC: 1311 Crude petroleum production; natural gas production

(G-5899)
DATA SYSTEMS CONSULTANTS
11332 Marbella Dr (73173-8154)
PHONE 405 445-0886
Dan Lessmann, *Owner*
Brandon Battle, *Director*
EMP: 3
SALES (est): 180K **Privately Held**
SIC: 7372 Prepackaged software

(G-5900)
DATALOG LWT INC
228 Nw 59th St (73118-7424)
PHONE 405 286-0418
Ian M Underdown, *Principal*
Gustavo Murillo, *Opers Mgr*
EMP: 8
SALES (corp-wide): 163.7MM **Privately Held**
SIC: 1389 Well logging
PA: Datalog Technology Inc
10707 50 St Se
Calgary AB T2C 3
403 243-2024

(G-5901)
DATEBOX INC OKC
7501 Sw 29th St (73179-5217)
PHONE 253 678-1173
EMP: 1
SALES (est): 37.5K **Privately Held**
SIC: 2741 Miscellaneous publishing

(G-5902)
DAVE BOLTON
Also Called: Mustang Land & Cattle Co
3413 Stone Brook Ct (73120-0812)
P.O. Box 56, Mustang (73064-0056)
PHONE 205 637-1402
Dave Bolton, *Owner*
EMP: 1 **EST:** 1997
SALES (est): 127.9K **Privately Held**
SIC: 1311 Natural gas production

(G-5903)
DAVID COMBS AUTO TRIM
813 Nw 8th St (73106-7205)
PHONE 405 799-7330
David Combs, *Owner*
EMP: 1
SALES (est): 50.5K **Privately Held**
SIC: 3999 7532 Parasols & frames: handles, parts & trimmings; top & body repair & paint shops

(G-5904)
DAVID MUZNY
Also Called: Muzny Sheet Metal Works
2148 Sw 46th St (73119-4913)
PHONE 405 681-7593
Dave Muzny, *Owner*
EMP: 2
SQ FT: 5,200
SALES (est): 200K **Privately Held**
SIC: 1761 3444 Sheet metalwork; sheet metalwork

(G-5905)
DAVIS CNSTR RCVERY SLTIONS LLC
7428 Nw 131st St (73142-2567)
PHONE 580 500-7527
Lemorris Davis, *Ch of Bd*
EMP: 10
SALES (est): 216.3K **Privately Held**
SIC: 1389 Construction, repair & dismantling services

(G-5906)
DAWSON GEOPHYSICAL COMPANY
1001 Nw 63rd St Ste 210 (73116-7335)
PHONE 405 848-7512
EMP: 15
SALES (corp-wide): 145.7MM **Publicly Held**
WEB: www.tgcseismic.com
SIC: 1382 Oil & gas exploration services
PA: Dawson Geophysical Company
508 W Wall St Ste 800
Midland TX 79701
432 684-3000

(G-5907)
DAWSON-MARKWELL EXPLORATION CO
1000 Sw 5th St (73109-1018)
P.O. Box 2446 (73101-2446)
PHONE 405 232-0418
Ed L Markwell Jr, *President*
Ed L Markwell III, *Vice Pres*
Joan Z Markwell, *Treasurer*
EMP: 3
SQ FT: 16,200
SALES (est): 420K **Privately Held**
SIC: 1311 Crude petroleum production; natural gas production

(G-5908)
DAYBREAK SCREEN PRINTING LLC
2525 Sw 102nd St (73159-7303)
P.O. Box 890452 (73189-0452)
PHONE 405 919-6386
Penny Dean, *Partner*
EMP: 2
SALES (est): 184.5K **Privately Held**
SIC: 2759 Screen printing

(G-5909)
DC CONSULTING INC
1408 Carltoe (73143)
PHONE 405 833-4856
Steve Lee, *President*
EMP: 2
SALES: 242K **Privately Held**
SIC: 1389 Oil consultants

GEOGRAPHIC SECTION

Oklahoma City - Oklahoma County (G-5937)

(G-5910)
DCI INDUSTRIES LLC
Also Called: Duracoatings
13920 S Meridian Ave (73173-8804)
PHONE..................405 947-2863
Dennis Glasco, *Opers Mgr*
Jay Hudson,
▲ **EMP:** 30 **EST:** 1974
SALES (est): 6.1MM **Privately Held**
SIC: 3471 Electroplating of metals or formed products

(G-5911)
DEAN JOHNSON
Also Called: Costume Fun House
4917 Nw 23rd St (73127-2313)
PHONE..................405 947-5736
Dean Johnson, *Owner*
EMP: 1
SQ FT: 3,000
SALES (est): 68.1K **Privately Held**
SIC: 5699 3999 7929 Costumes & wigs; magic equipment, supplies & props; entertainers & entertainment groups

(G-5912)
DEANS TYPESETTING SERVICE
7416 Broadway Ext Ste J (73116-9066)
PHONE..................405 842-7247
Sharon A Dean, *President*
Belphry Dean, *Admin Sec*
EMP: 3
SALES: 270K **Privately Held**
SIC: 2791 2754 Typesetting; business form & card printing, gravure

(G-5913)
DEAR JOHN DENIM INC
7316 Nw 120th St (73162-1513)
PHONE..................580 334-6637
EMP: 1
SALES (est): 46.5K **Privately Held**
SIC: 2211 Denims

(G-5914)
DEATSCHWERKS LLC
415 E Hill St (73105-4013)
PHONE..................405 217-0701
Mark Heinen, *Sales Staff*
David Reyna, *Sales Staff*
David Deatsch,
EMP: 8
SALES (est): 1.5MM **Privately Held**
SIC: 3714 Fuel pumps, motor vehicle

(G-5915)
DEBO DMNSONS LASER CUT ENGRAVE
7210 Broadway Ext Ste 203 (73116-9052)
PHONE..................405 843-9098
EMP: 2
SALES (est): 17.8K **Privately Held**
SIC: 3993 Mfg Signs/Advertising Specialties

(G-5916)
DECORATIVE ROCK & STONE INC
305 Tinker Diagonal St (73129-8239)
PHONE..................405 672-2564
Ali M Ghazanfari, *President*
Donna Ghazanfari, *Treasurer*
▲ **EMP:** 1
SQ FT: 4,500
SALES: 300K **Privately Held**
SIC: 5032 5999 1741 3915 Concrete & cinder building products; concrete products, pre-cast; stone masonry; jewelers' materials & lapidary work; cut stone & stone products

(G-5917)
DECORATOR DRAPERY MFG INC
428 N Ann Arbor Ave (73127-6310)
PHONE..................405 942-5613
Howard Watts, *President*
Mark Frederic Watts, *Vice Pres*
Michael Watts, *Opers Mgr*
EMP: 28 **EST:** 1978
SQ FT: 10,000
SALES (est): 2.6MM **Privately Held**
SIC: 2391 2392 Draperies, plastic & textile: from purchased materials; household furnishings

(G-5918)
DEE-JAY EXPLORATION
5909 Nw Expressway # 500 (73132-5172)
PHONE..................405 773-8500
Fax: 405 773-8818
EMP: 6
SQ FT: 2,700
SALES (est): 548.4K **Privately Held**
SIC: 1382 Oil And Gas Exploration Services

(G-5919)
DEEP WELL TUBULAR SERVICES INC
8080 Glade Ave Bldg B (73132-4236)
PHONE..................405 850-5826
James McKanna, *President*
EMP: 17
SQ FT: 3,000
SALES (est): 4.3MM **Privately Held**
SIC: 1389 7389 Oil field services;

(G-5920)
DEL TECHNICAL COATINGS INC
1801 W Reno Ave (73106-3217)
PHONE..................405 672-1431
Sean Childers, *President*
Bill Williams, *Vice Pres*
EMP: 20
SQ FT: 40,000
SALES (est): 3.3MM **Privately Held**
SIC: 2851 Paints & paint additives

(G-5921)
DEN-CON TOOL CO
5354 S I 35 Service Rd (73129-7026)
P.O. Box 96308 (73143-6308)
PHONE..................405 670-5942
Lawrence A Denny, *President*
Mark Seyfried, *Vice Pres*
◆ **EMP:** 12
SQ FT: 30,500
SALES (est): 3.1MM **Privately Held**
WEB: www.dencon.com
SIC: 3533 Oil & gas drilling rigs & equipment; oil field machinery & equipment

(G-5922)
DENNIS GROTHE WATER SVC
8112 Sw 8th St (73128-4210)
PHONE..................405 651-5353
Dennis Grothe, *Owner*
EMP: 2
SALES (est): 78.4K **Privately Held**
SIC: 2899 Chemical preparations

(G-5923)
DENNIS ROBERTS WELDING
2801 S Eastern Ave (73129-7654)
P.O. Box 94536 (73143-4536)
PHONE..................405 672-8285
Dennis C Roberts, *Owner*
EMP: 1
SALES (est): 69K **Privately Held**
SIC: 7692 Welding repair

(G-5924)
DENTCRAFT TOOLS
8118 Glade Ave (73132-4210)
PHONE..................405 495-0533
Sid Emmert, *Partner*
Sonya Emmert, *Partner*
Tj Tinga, *Engineer*
Justin Weaver, *Marketing Staff*
Brent Buck, *Manager*
EMP: 15
SALES (est): 3.3MM **Privately Held**
SIC: 3542 Machine tools, metal forming type

(G-5925)
DERMAMEDICS LLC
3000 United Founders Blvd # 145 (73112-4292)
PHONE..................405 319-8130
Bryan Fuller, *CEO*
Nila Murphy, *Director*
▲ **EMP:** 9
SALES (est): 1.1MM **Privately Held**
WEB: www.dermamedics.com
SIC: 2834 2841 Emulsions, pharmaceutical; soap & other detergents

(G-5926)
DESIGN READY CONTROLS INC
3512 S Lakeside Dr (73179-8400)
PHONE..................405 605-8234
EMP: 15 **Privately Held**
SIC: 5084 3613 3561 Industrial machinery & equipment; switchgear & switchboard apparatus; pumps & pumping equipment
PA: Design Ready Controls, Inc.
9325 Winnetka Ave N
Minneapolis MN 55445

(G-5927)
DESIRED SIZE
1148 Ne 5th Ter (73117-1405)
PHONE..................405 314-3704
Dinna Coleman, *Principal*
EMP: 2
SALES (est): 140K **Privately Held**
SIC: 2899 Sizes

(G-5928)
DEVON ENERGY CORPORATION
20 N Broadway Ave # 1500 (73102-8260)
PHONE..................405 235-7798
Ricky Tackett, *Superintendent*
Dan Werner, *Superintendent*
Rick White, *Vice Pres*
Adam Bryson, *Foreman/Supr*
Josh Caldwell, *Foreman/Supr*
EMP: 15
SALES (corp-wide): 6.2B **Publicly Held**
WEB: www.devonenergy.com
SIC: 1311 Natural gas production
PA: Devon Energy Corporation
333 W Sheridan Ave
Oklahoma City OK 73102
405 235-3611

(G-5929)
DEVON ENERGY CORPORATION (PA)
333 W Sheridan Ave (73102-5015)
PHONE..................405 235-3611
John Richels, *Ch of Bd*
Duane C Radtke, *Vice Ch Bd*
David A Hager, *President*
Lindsay Hill, *Principal*
Tony D Vaughn, *COO*
◆ **EMP:** 123
SALES: 6.2B **Publicly Held**
WEB: www.devonenergy.com
SIC: 1311 1382 Crude petroleum production; crude petroleum & natural gas production; oil & gas exploration services

(G-5930)
DEVON ENERGY CORPORATION (HQ)
Also Called: Debon Energy Oil & Gas
333 W Sheridan Ave (73102-5015)
PHONE..................405 235-3611
J M Lacey, *Senior VP*
Duke R Lidon, *Senior VP*
Marion J Moon, *Senior VP*
Darryl G Smette, *Senior VP*
William Taughn, *Senior VP*
EMP: 15
SALES (est): 5.1MM
SALES (corp-wide): 6.2B **Publicly Held**
SIC: 1311 Crude petroleum & natural gas
PA: Devon Energy Corporation
333 W Sheridan Ave
Oklahoma City OK 73102
405 235-3611

(G-5931)
DEVON ENERGY INTERNATIONAL CO (HQ)
20 N Broadway Ave # 1500 (73102-8296)
PHONE..................405 235-3611
Jeff Ritenour, *Vice Pres*
Travis Black, *Engineer*
Robert Kiesewetter, *Accountant*
Mike Dickey, *Manager*
Aaron Roark, *Manager*
EMP: 1000
SALES (est): 142.6MM
SALES (corp-wide): 6.2B **Publicly Held**
SIC: 2911 Gasoline
PA: Devon Energy Corporation
333 W Sheridan Ave
Oklahoma City OK 73102
405 235-3611

(G-5932)
DEVON ENERGY PRODUCTION CO LP (HQ)
333 W Sheridan Ave (73102-5015)
PHONE..................405 235-3611
John Richels, *Principal*
J Larry Nichols, *Chairman*
Ryan Rash, *Associate*
▲ **EMP:** 1300
SQ FT: 48,923
SALES (est): 3.9B
SALES (corp-wide): 6.2B **Publicly Held**
SIC: 1311 5172 Crude petroleum production; natural gas production; crude oil
PA: Devon Energy Corporation
333 W Sheridan Ave
Oklahoma City OK 73102
405 235-3611

(G-5933)
DEVON GAS SERVICES LP (HQ)
333 W Sheridan Ave (73102-5010)
PHONE..................405 235-3611
George P Mitchell, *Partner*
Liquid Energy Fuel Corporation, *Ltd Ptnr*
Mitchell Marketing Corporation, *Ltd Ptnr*
EMP: 1 **EST:** 1998
SALES (est): 240.5MM
SALES (corp-wide): 6.2B **Publicly Held**
WEB: www.devonenergy.com
SIC: 1382 Oil & gas exploration services
PA: Devon Energy Corporation
333 W Sheridan Ave
Oklahoma City OK 73102
405 235-3611

(G-5934)
DEVON GAS SERVICES LP
20 N Broadway (73102-9213)
PHONE..................405 228-7543
EMP: 3
SALES (est): 104.3K **Privately Held**
SIC: 1311 Crude petroleum production

(G-5935)
DEVON INDUSTRIES INC
Also Called: Devon Lube Center Equipment
7510 Melrose Ln (73127-5143)
P.O. Box 270514 (73137-0514)
PHONE..................405 943-3881
Mark Cawthon, *President*
Ann Cawthon, *Corp Secy*
Ken Miller, *Vice Pres*
Tim Roberts, *VP Sales*
Duncan Smith, *Sales Staff*
EMP: 20
SALES (est): 4MM **Privately Held**
SIC: 2542 Partitions & fixtures, except wood

(G-5936)
DEVON OEI OPERATING INC (HQ)
20 N Broadway (73102-9213)
PHONE..................405 235-3611
Michael Clapp, *Production*
Janice Dobbs, *Admin Sec*
Jennifer Reed, *Administration*
Allison Bailey, *Relations*
◆ **EMP:** 2000
SALES (est): 673.5MM
SALES (corp-wide): 6.2B **Publicly Held**
SIC: 4922 4924 1311 4613 Natural gas transmission; pipelines, natural gas; natural gas distribution; crude petroleum production; natural gas production; refined petroleum pipelines
PA: Devon Energy Corporation
333 W Sheridan Ave
Oklahoma City OK 73102
405 235-3611

(G-5937)
DEWEY CHEMICAL INC
5801 Broadway Ext Ste 305 (73118-7489)
PHONE..................405 848-8611
Kenichi Onishi, *President*
EMP: 1
SALES (est): 71.9K **Privately Held**
SIC: 2819 Iodine, elemental
PA: Toyota Tsusho Corporation
4-9-8, Meieki, Nakamura-Ku
Nagoya AIC 450-0

Oklahoma City - Oklahoma County (G-5938)

(G-5938)
DIAMOND GAME ENTERPRISES
6100 Nw 2nd St Ste 1600 (73127-6534)
PHONE...................405 789-5800
Brian Zimmer, *Manager*
EMP: 40
SALES (corp-wide): 298.7MM **Privately Held**
SIC: 3999 Slot machines
HQ: Diamond Game Enterprises
9340 Penfield Ave
Chatsworth CA 91311

(G-5939)
DIAMONDBACK E&P LLC
Also Called: Accounting Office
515 Central Park Dr (73105-1724)
PHONE...................432 221-7400
Travis D Stice, *President*
EMP: 45
SALES (corp-wide): 3.9B **Publicly Held**
SIC: 1311 Crude petroleum & natural gas
HQ: Diamondback E&P Llc
500 W Texas Ave Ste 1200
Midland TX 79701
866 531-3667

(G-5940)
DIAMONDBACK ENERGY INC
9400 Broadway Ext Ste 600 (73114-7423)
PHONE...................405 600-0711
Thomas Hawkins, *Vice Pres*
EMP: 1
SALES (corp-wide): 3.9B **Publicly Held**
SIC: 1381 Drilling oil & gas wells
PA: Diamondback Energy, Inc.
500 W Texas Ave Ste 1200
Midland TX 79701
432 221-7400

(G-5941)
DIAMONDBACK ENERGY SERVICES
14301 Caliber Dr Ste 200 (73134-1016)
PHONE...................405 242-4080
Arty Straehla, *CEO*
Mike Liddell, *Ch of Bd*
Grant Defehr, *COO*
Cale Coulter, *CFO*
EMP: 1
SALES (est): 507.9K **Privately Held**
SIC: 1389 Construction, repair & dismantling services; bailing, cleaning, swabbing & treating of wells; swabbing wells; well plugging & abandoning, oil & gas
PA: Wexford Capital, L.P.
411 W Putnam Ave Ste 125
Greenwich CT 06830

(G-5942)
DIAMONDBACK ENERGY SVCS LLC (HQ)
14201 Caliber Dr Ste 300 (73134-1017)
PHONE...................405 789-3499
Raty Straehla, *CEO*
EMP: 12
SALES (est): 4MM **Privately Held**
SIC: 1389 Detection & analysis service, gas

(G-5943)
DIANE OIL CO
47 Ne 37th St (73105-2513)
P.O. Box 60157 (73146-0157)
PHONE...................405 528-5100
Rich Wager, *President*
EMP: 2
SQ FT: 1,000
SALES: 215K **Privately Held**
SIC: 1389 Oil field services

(G-5944)
DIB 718 LLC
617 Nw 16th St (73103-2109)
PHONE...................405 525-2151
Torrey Butzer, *Owner*
EMP: 1
SALES (est): 87.5K **Privately Held**
SIC: 2874 Phosphatic fertilizers

(G-5945)
DIGI PRINT LLC (PA)
Also Called: Digital Print Communications
4222 N May Ave (73112-6271)
PHONE...................405 947-0099
Jim Aiken,
Kevin Ross,
EMP: 8
SQ FT: 5,000
SALES (est): 889.1K **Privately Held**
SIC: 2752 7336 2791 2789 Commercial printing, offset; commercial art & graphic design; typesetting; bookbinding & related work

(G-5946)
DIGII ID LLC
5534 N Portland Ave (73112-1907)
PHONE...................405 662-5504
Dequan Bizzell, *Principal*
EMP: 3 EST: 2014
SALES (est): 180K **Privately Held**
SIC: 7372 7389 Application computer software;

(G-5947)
DIGITAL DOCTOR
1950 Nw 16th St (73106-2033)
PHONE...................405 618-1416
EMP: 2 EST: 2017
SALES (est): 72.1K **Privately Held**
SIC: 7372 Prepackaged software

(G-5948)
DIRECT DOWNHOLE RENTALS LLC
Also Called: D D R
10005 S Penn Ave Ste C (73159-6924)
P.O. Box 940968, Houston TX (77094-7968)
PHONE...................281 531-8881
Michael Tanner, *Mng Member*
Brian Tanner,
EMP: 5
SALES (est): 304K **Privately Held**
SIC: 1389 Oil sampling service for oil companies

(G-5949)
DIRECTIONAL BORING INC
5001 N Pennsylvania Ave (73112-8883)
PHONE...................405 842-8850
EMP: 2 EST: 2017
SALES (est): 107.6K **Privately Held**
SIC: 1381 Directional drilling oil & gas wells

(G-5950)
DIRECTIONAL FLUID DISPOSALS
6801 Camille Ave (73149-5204)
PHONE...................405 626-3261
Ted Griffin, *General Mgr*
Bill Hare, *Principal*
Michelle Griffin, *Office Mgr*
EMP: 4
SALES (est): 213.4K **Privately Held**
WEB: www.directionalfluiddisposals.com
SIC: 1381 Directional drilling oil & gas wells

(G-5951)
DIVERSIFIED ENERGY SVCS LLC
3141 Nw 63rd St Ste 4 (73116-3701)
PHONE...................405 775-0414
Jason Werner, *Mng Member*
Craig Rocha,
Michael Werner,
EMP: 5
SQ FT: 1,600
SALES: 4.2MM **Privately Held**
SIC: 1382 Oil & gas exploration services

(G-5952)
DIVERSIFIED PLATING LTD
2109 W Sheridan Ave (73107-7035)
PHONE...................405 236-0545
Tom Hughes, *President*
Brian Hart, *Mfg Staff*
Marsha Pierce, *Admin Sec*
EMP: 5
SQ FT: 3,600
SALES (est): 586.5K **Privately Held**
SIC: 3471 Chromium plating of metals or formed products; electroplating of metals or formed products

(G-5953)
DIVINE THUMB INDUSTRIES INC
2112 Churchill Pl (73120-4802)
PHONE...................405 418-7855
Travis Chad Green, *Owner*
EMP: 1 EST: 2018
SALES (est): 39.6K **Privately Held**
SIC: 3999 Manufacturing industries

(G-5954)
DMN INC
Also Called: Dallas Morning News
1000 W Wilshire Blvd # 3 (73116-7030)
PHONE...................405 848-9401
Arnold Hamilton, *Branch Mgr*
EMP: 1 **Publicly Held**
SIC: 2711 Newspapers: publishing only, not printed on site
HQ: Dmn, Inc.
1954 Commerce St
Dallas TX 75201

(G-5955)
DOCUMENT CENTRE INC
333 W Wilshire Blvd Ste B (73116-7765)
PHONE...................405 879-1101
Charles Ashley, *CEO*
EMP: 3
SQ FT: 1,500
SALES: 280K **Privately Held**
SIC: 2752 Commercial printing, lithographic

(G-5956)
DOCUMENT IMGING NTWRK SLUTIONS
713 E Frolich Dr (73110-7816)
P.O. Box 50161, Midwest City (73140-5161)
PHONE...................405 818-3888
Jim Reilly, *Owner*
EMP: 4
SALES (est): 190K **Privately Held**
SIC: 2741 Technical manual & paper publishing

(G-5957)
DOLESE BROS CO (PA)
20 Nw 13th St (73103-4806)
P.O. Box 677 (73101-0677)
PHONE...................405 235-2311
Mark Helm, *President*
Joe Howell, *Manager*
Pam Pettigrew, *Manager*
Jared Ryker, *Manager*
Nik Pottala, *CIO*
▲ EMP: 150
SQ FT: 50,000
SALES: 8.5MM **Privately Held**
WEB: www.dolese.com
SIC: 3273 1422 1442 Ready-mixed concrete; crushed & broken limestone; construction sand mining

(G-5958)
DOLESE BROS CO
5600 W Reno Ave (73127-6634)
PHONE...................405 947-7085
Larry Braun, *Principal*
EMP: 1
SALES (corp-wide): 8.5MM **Privately Held**
WEB: www.dolese.com
SIC: 3273 Ready-mixed concrete
PA: Dolese Bros. Co.
20 Nw 13th St
Oklahoma City OK 73103
405 235-2311

(G-5959)
DOLESE BROS CO
4727 N Midwest Blvd (73141-9621)
PHONE...................405 795-9757
Glenn Thomas, *Branch Mgr*
EMP: 1
SALES (corp-wide): 8.5MM **Privately Held**
SIC: 3273 Ready-mixed concrete
PA: Dolese Bros. Co.
20 Nw 13th St
Oklahoma City OK 73103
405 235-2311

(G-5960)
DOLESE BROS CO
901 N Sooner Rd (73117)
P.O. Box 960144 (73196-0144)
PHONE...................405 672-4577
EMP: 1
SALES (corp-wide): 8.5MM **Privately Held**
SIC: 3273 Ready-mixed concrete
PA: Dolese Bros. Co.
20 Nw 13th St
Oklahoma City OK 73103
405 235-2311

(G-5961)
DOLESE BROS CO
10625 Se 29th St (73130-7719)
PHONE...................405 732-0909
Steve Ronde, *Branch Mgr*
EMP: 4
SALES (corp-wide): 8.5MM **Privately Held**
SIC: 3273 Ready-mixed concrete
PA: Dolese Bros. Co.
20 Nw 13th St
Oklahoma City OK 73103
405 235-2311

(G-5962)
DOLESE BROS CO
7100 S Sunnylane Rd (73135-1717)
P.O. Box 677 (73101-0677)
PHONE...................405 670-9626
Mike Stanley, *Manager*
EMP: 35
SALES (corp-wide): 8.5MM **Privately Held**
SIC: 3273 1422 1442 3272 Ready-mixed concrete; crushed & broken limestone; construction sand & gravel; concrete products; concrete block & brick
PA: Dolese Bros. Co.
20 Nw 13th St
Oklahoma City OK 73103
405 235-2311

(G-5963)
DOLESE BROS CO
120 N Lottie Ave (73117-1800)
PHONE...................405 232-1228
Roger Dolese, *Branch Mgr*
EMP: 16
SALES (corp-wide): 8.5MM **Privately Held**
SIC: 3273 Ready-mixed concrete
PA: Dolese Bros. Co.
20 Nw 13th St
Oklahoma City OK 73103
405 235-2311

(G-5964)
DOLESE BROS CO
24 N Mccormick St (73127-6621)
PHONE...................405 949-2278
Duane Coy, *Manager*
EMP: 20
SALES (corp-wide): 8.5MM **Privately Held**
SIC: 3273 Ready-mixed concrete
PA: Dolese Bros. Co.
20 Nw 13th St
Oklahoma City OK 73103
405 235-2311

(G-5965)
DOLPHIN BLUE PRODUCTION LLC
13120 N Macarthur Blvd (73142-3017)
PHONE...................405 285-5388
David Arms, *Mng Member*
John Clark,
David Pletcher,
EMP: 6 EST: 2000
SALES (est): 2.5MM **Privately Held**
SIC: 1382 Oil & gas exploration services

(G-5966)
DON YOUNG COMPANY INCORPORATED
901 Enterprise Ave Ste 13 (73128-1461)
PHONE...................405 947-2000
Jimmy Butenhoff, *Opers-Prdtn-Mfg*
EMP: 6

GEOGRAPHIC SECTION

Oklahoma City - Oklahoma County (G-5997)

SALES (corp-wide): 24.1MM **Privately Held**
SIC: 3442 Screens, window, metal; storm doors or windows, metal; metal doors
PA: Don Young Company Incorporated
8181 Ambassador Row
Dallas TX 75247
214 630-0934

(G-5967)
DONRAY PETROLEUM LLC
2525 Nw Expwy Ste 640 (73112-7275)
PHONE..................405 418-4348
Ray Corbitt,
EMP: 25
SALES: 6MM **Privately Held**
SIC: 1382 Oil & gas exploration services

(G-5968)
DOODLEBUGS ETC INC
625 Nw 18th St (73103-1824)
PHONE..................405 525-1248
Robyn Wray, *President*
Laura Jergensen, *Corp Secy*
EMP: 2
SALES (est): 5K **Privately Held**
SIC: 3942 3999 Dolls & stuffed toys; manufacturing industries

(G-5969)
DORMAKABA USA INC
701 N Ann Arbor Ave (73127-5822)
PHONE..................405 232-6761
Lance Parr, *Branch Mgr*
EMP: 5
SALES (corp-wide): 2.7B **Privately Held**
SIC: 3442 7629 Hangar doors, metal; electrical repair shops
HQ: Dormakaba Usa Inc.
100 Dorma Dr
Reamstown PA 17567
717 336-3881

(G-5970)
DOUBLE D FOODS INC
7300 Sw 29th St (73179-5201)
PHONE..................405 245-8909
Greg Cook, *Vice Pres*
Tom Matejka, *Controller*
Patty Anderson, *Finance*
EMP: 14
SALES (est): 1.4MM **Privately Held**
SIC: 2011 Meat packing plants

(G-5971)
DOUBLE LIFE CORPORATION
200 N Rockwell Ave (73127-6115)
PHONE..................405 789-7867
Phillip L Banta, *President*
Phillip Banta, *QA Dir*
Tim Coil, *CFO*
Timothy Coil, *CFO*
Brandi Harrison, *Sales Staff*
◆ EMP: 18
SQ FT: 43,000
SALES: 4.2MM **Privately Held**
SIC: 3533 5082 3531 Oil field machinery & equipment; oil field equipment; construction machinery

(G-5972)
DOUGLAS GROUP LLC
4625 Nw 35th St (73122-1331)
PHONE..................405 946-6853
Asa Douglas,
EMP: 1
SALES (est): 80.1K **Privately Held**
SIC: 1389 7389 Oil & gas field services;

(G-5973)
DOWNING WELLHEAD EQUIPMENT LLC (HQ)
2601 Nw Expwy Ste 900e (73112-7237)
PHONE..................405 486-7858
David Caudill, *Area Mgr*
Steve Kirksey, *Vice Pres*
Aaron Jaques, *Inv Control Mgr*
Peter Simms, *CFO*
Bryan Henderson, *Asst Controller*
▲ EMP: 35 EST: 1980
SQ FT: 29,000
SALES (est): 27.2MM
SALES (corp-wide): 47.2MM **Privately Held**
WEB: www.downingwell.com
SIC: 3533 7353 5084 7699 Oil field machinery & equipment; oil field equipment, rental or leasing; oil well machinery, equipment & supplies; industrial machinery & equipment repair
PA: Argonaut Private Equity, L.L.C.
6733 S Yale Ave
Tulsa OK 74136
918 491-4538

(G-5974)
DOWNING WELLHEAD EQUIPMENT LLC
8528 Sw 2nd St (73128-3601)
PHONE..................405 789-8182
EMP: 2
SALES (corp-wide): 47.2MM **Privately Held**
SIC: 3533 7353 Oil field machinery & equipment; oil field equipment, rental or leasing
HQ: Downing Wellhead Equipment, Llc
2601 Nw Expwy Ste 900e
Oklahoma City OK 73112
405 486-7858

(G-5975)
DOWNTOWN MUSIC BOX LLC
535 N Ann Arbor Ave (73127-6311)
PHONE..................405 232-2099
Michael Curzio,
EMP: 2
SALES (est): 210.2K **Privately Held**
SIC: 7389 7929 5736 3931 Music recording producer; musical entertainers; musical instrument stores; drums, parts & accessories (musical instruments); musical instruments parts & accessories; business training services

(G-5976)
DPM GROUP LLC
Also Called: Mercury Press, Okc Digital Sol
1910 S Nicklas Ave (73128-3051)
PHONE..................405 682-3468
Ronald Franklin, *CEO*
EMP: 19
SALES (est): 681.7K **Privately Held**
SIC: 2721 Magazines: publishing & printing

(G-5977)
DR CBD
2711 W Britton Rd Apt 85 (73120-4477)
PHONE..................832 216-3301
Robert Adams, *Principal*
EMP: 1
SALES (est): 44.7K **Privately Held**
SIC: 3999

(G-5978)
DR PEPPER SNAPPLE GROUP
5200 Sw 36th St Ste 600 (73179-7810)
PHONE..................405 680-5150
Jeff Bynum, *General Mgr*
EMP: 5
SALES (est): 275K **Privately Held**
SIC: 2086 Bottled & canned soft drinks

(G-5979)
DRAFT2DIGITAL LLC
9400 Broadway Ext Ste 410 (73114-7407)
PHONE..................405 708-7894
EMP: 1
SALES (est): 65.8K **Privately Held**
SIC: 2741 Miscellaneous publishing

(G-5980)
DRILLERS SERVICE CENTER INC
2620 S Central Ave (73129-1838)
P.O. Box 95282 (73143-5282)
PHONE..................405 631-3728
Dan Kern, *President*
Cheryl Kern, *Vice Pres*
Derek Kern, *Admin Sec*
EMP: 4
SQ FT: 4,500
SALES: 650K **Privately Held**
SIC: 5084 3533 7629 Oil well machinery, equipment & supplies; oil field machinery & equipment; electrical repair shops

(G-5981)
DRILLING TOOLS INTL INC
2525 S Ann Arbor Ave (73128-1847)
PHONE..................405 604-2763
Wayne Prejean, *President*
EMP: 13
SALES (est): 1MM **Privately Held**
SIC: 1389 Oil field services

(G-5982)
DRIPLOC INC
2213 Sw 19th St (73108-6427)
PHONE..................405 632-5810
Barry Wagner, *Principal*
Jennifer Ponder, *Sales Staff*
EMP: 11
SALES (est): 2.2MM **Privately Held**
SIC: 3443 Reactor containment vessels, metal plate

(G-5983)
DRIVIN PRINTING BY AARON
2701 Nw 63rd St (73116-4801)
PHONE..................405 609-9608
EMP: 2
SALES (est): 94.6K **Privately Held**
SIC: 2752 Commercial printing, lithographic

(G-5984)
DROV LLC
Also Called: Drov Technologies
13832 Wireless Way # 100 (73134-2519)
P.O. Box 3877, Edmond (73083-3877)
PHONE..................405 463-6562
Jay Thompson, *Vice Pres*
Chris Jornlin, *Director*
Joseph Cappello,
Marisol Cappello,
EMP: 12
SALES (est): 1.3MM **Privately Held**
SIC: 3714 5013 Motor vehicle parts & accessories; motor vehicle supplies & new parts

(G-5985)
DROVERS TRAIL LAND COMPANY LLC
500 N Broadway Ave # 350 (73102-6206)
P.O. Box 3315 (73101-3315)
PHONE..................405 702-6300
EMP: 6
SALES (est): 613.8K **Privately Held**
SIC: 1389 Oil consultants

(G-5986)
DUMPSTER SERVICE PLUS
4217 S May Ave Ste 1 (73119-3279)
PHONE..................405 417-3707
Kenny Murry, *Principal*
EMP: 4
SALES (est): 198.3K **Privately Held**
SIC: 3443 Dumpsters, garbage

(G-5987)
DUNCAN INC WALTER
100 Park Ave Ste 1200 (73102-8004)
PHONE..................405 272-1800
J Walter Duncan Jr, *President*
Jame W Duncan IV, *President*
Raymond P Duncan, *Vice Pres*
Vincent J Duncan, *Vice Pres*
EMP: 30
SQ FT: 14,000
SALES (est): 5.6MM **Privately Held**
SIC: 1311 1382 Crude petroleum production; natural gas production; oil & gas exploration services

(G-5988)
DUNCAN OIL PROPERTIES INC
100 Park Ave Ste 1200 (73102-8023)
PHONE..................405 272-1800
Walt Duncan IV, *President*
Shelly Hatch, *Corp Secy*
Nicholas V Duncan, *Vice Pres*
EMP: 35
SQ FT: 14,000
SALES (est): 3.3MM **Privately Held**
SIC: 1311 1382 Crude petroleum production; natural gas production; oil & gas exploration services

(G-5989)
DUNCAN TICKING INC (PA)
1421 Nw 23rd St (73106-3619)
PHONE..................405 528-5480
Peter Duncan, *President*
Linda Duncan, *Vice Pres*
▲ EMP: 10
SALES (est): 1.5MM **Privately Held**
WEB: www.duncanticking.com
SIC: 2211 Broadwoven fabric mills, cotton

(G-5990)
DURACOATINGS HOLDINGS LLC
13920 S Meridian Ave (73173-8804)
PHONE..................405 692-2249
Jay Hudson,
EMP: 100
SALES (est): 2.8MM **Privately Held**
SIC: 3471 3541 Electroplating & plating; grinding, polishing, buffing, lapping & honing machines

(G-5991)
DUSTYS JERKY LLC
628 Se 82nd St (73149-2915)
PHONE..................405 702-8016
Russell Fowler, *Administration*
EMP: 3
SALES (est): 137.3K **Privately Held**
WEB: www.dustysbeefjerky.com
SIC: 2013 Sausages & other prepared meats

(G-5992)
DYNOSAW INC
9008 N Walker Ave (73114-3538)
PHONE..................405 418-6060
Darrell Gibson, *CEO*
EMP: 2
SQ FT: 1,250
SALES (est): 135.9K **Privately Held**
SIC: 1751 2434 Cabinet & finish carpentry; finish & trim carpentry; vanities, bathroom: wood

(G-5993)
E ENVIRONMENTAL LLC
Also Called: Chemstation of Oklahoma
101 Ne 24th St (73105-3008)
PHONE..................405 604-0000
Heather Newcomb, *Office Mgr*
Cari Epperson, *Mng Member*
Doug Epperson, *Mng Member*
EMP: 7
SALES: 870K **Privately Held**
SIC: 2841 Soap & other detergents

(G-5994)
EAGLE APPLCTIONS SOLUTIONS LTD
2501 Ne 23rd St Ste A (73111-3512)
PHONE..................888 511-8720
Antoine Warfield, *CEO*
EMP: 2
SQ FT: 1,800
SALES: 100K **Privately Held**
SIC: 7372 Application computer software

(G-5995)
EAGLE IMAGING MANAGEMENT
3600 Nw 138th St Ste 102 (73134-2504)
PHONE..................405 286-4114
Rejeana M Younkin, *COO*
EMP: 2 EST: 2009
SALES (est): 214.1K **Privately Held**
WEB: www.eagleimagingok.com
SIC: 8741 2759 Business management; screen printing

(G-5996)
EAGLE ROCK COATINGS INC
6424 N Santa Fe Ave Ste B (73116-9119)
PHONE..................405 948-8900
Neil Stanek, *Owner*
EMP: 3
SALES (est): 293.2K **Privately Held**
SIC: 3479 Coating of metals & formed products

(G-5997)
EAGLES NEST WELDING
6408 Nw 24th St (73127-1407)
PHONE..................405 639-8650
Kevin Pratt, *President*

Oklahoma City - Oklahoma County (G-5998)   **GEOGRAPHIC SECTION**

EMP: 1
SALES (est): 60.5K Privately Held
SIC: 7692 Welding repair

(G-5998)
EARL BANNON
Also Called: B & B Sheet Metal
1221 N Portland Ave (73107-1517)
PHONE 405 236-8829
Earl Bannon, Owner
EMP: 2
SQ FT: 5,000
SALES: 90K Privately Held
SIC: 3444 Sheet metalwork

(G-5999)
EARLSBORO ENERGIES CORPORATION
3007 Nw 63rd St Ste 205 (73116-3605)
PHONE 405 848-2829
Steve Clark, President
EMP: 7
SALES (est): 1.6MM Privately Held
SIC: 1311 Crude petroleum production; natural gas production

(G-6000)
EASTERN OIL WELL SERVICES
5400 N Grand Blvd Ste 450 (73112-5678)
PHONE 405 947-1091
Charles Drimel, President
EMP: 6
SALES (est): 651.1K
SALES (corp-wide): 104.8MM Publicly Held
SIC: 1389 Oil field services
HQ: Prime Operating Company
9821 Katy Fwy Ste 1050
Houston TX 77024

(G-6001)
EASTON LAND SERVICES
6600 N Meridian Ave # 242 (73116-1426)
P.O. Box 720192 (73172-0192)
PHONE 405 842-1930
Montee Hoffman, President
EMP: 1
SALES (est): 143K Privately Held
SIC: 1382 Oil & gas exploration services

(G-6002)
EATON-QUADE COMPANY
Also Called: Eaton-Quade Plastics
1116 W Main St (73106-7827)
PHONE 405 236-4475
Barbara Swindell, President
Ryan Swindell, Principal
Doug Swindell, Vice Pres
EMP: 10
SALES (est): 1.3MM Privately Held
WEB: www.eatonquade.com
SIC: 3993 3089 Signs & advertising specialties; plastic processing

(G-6003)
ECAPITOL LLC
113 Nw 13th St Apt 101 (73103-4837)
P.O. Box 3366 (73101-3366)
PHONE 405 524-2833
Darwin Maxey, Principal
EMP: 2
SALES (est): 163.7K Privately Held
SIC: 7372 Publishers' computer software

(G-6004)
ECHO E&P LLC
120 Robert S Kerr Ave (73102-6439)
PHONE 405 753-4232
M Christian Kennedy, Mng Member
EMP: 80
SALES (est): 1.1MM
SALES (corp-wide): 41.7MM Privately Held
SIC: 1389 Oil consultants
PA: Echo Energy, Llc
120 Robert S Kerr Ave
Oklahoma City OK 73102
405 753-4232

(G-6005)
ECHO ENERGY LLC (PA)
120 Robert S Kerr Ave (73102-6439)
PHONE 405 753-4232
M Christian Kanady, CEO
Kyler Kanady, COO
Marshall Harris, Counsel
Matthew Palmer, Vice Pres
John Senger, Finance Mgr
EMP: 52
SALES (est): 41.7MM Privately Held
WEB: www.echoenergy.com
SIC: 1382 Oil & gas exploration services

(G-6006)
ECKROAT SEED CO
1106 N Martin L King Ave (73117)
P.O. Box 17610 (73136-1610)
PHONE 405 427-2484
Robert Anthony Eckroat, President
Donald W Eckroat, Vice Pres
EMP: 18
SQ FT: 30,000
SALES: 7MM Privately Held
WEB: www.eckroatseed.com
SIC: 2875 5153 5191 Fertilizers, mixing only; beans, inedible; seeds: field, garden & flower

(G-6007)
ECM CAR WASH LLC
Also Called: Swash Car Wash
325 W Memorial Rd (73114-2314)
PHONE 405 590-3252
Blake Belanger, Mng Member
EMP: 25
SALES (est): 941.6K Privately Held
SIC: 3589 Car washing machinery

(G-6008)
EDC AG PRODUCTS COMPANY LLC
3503 Nw 63rd St Ste 500 (73116-2238)
PHONE 405 235-4546
EMP: 52 EST: 2011
SALES (est): 54.7K
SALES (corp-wide): 365MM Publicly Held
SIC: 2819 2875 Inorganic acids, except nitric & phosphoric; fertilizers, mixing only
HQ: El Dorado Chemical Company Inc
3503 Nw 63rd St Ste 500
Oklahoma City OK 73116
405 235-4546

(G-6009)
EDDIE WARD
Also Called: Britton Welding & Automotive
737 Nw 92nd St (73114-2905)
PHONE 405 848-3283
Edward Ward, Owner
EMP: 1
SALES (est): 77.7K Privately Held
SIC: 7692 Welding repair

(G-6010)
EDINGER ENGINEERING INC
105 N Hudson Ave Ste 600 (73102-4817)
PHONE 405 232-6315
Mark McKinney, President
Craig Barbee, Vice Pres
EMP: 5 EST: 1954
SQ FT: 3,000
SALES (est): 661K Privately Held
SIC: 1382 1311 Oil & gas exploration services; crude petroleum production; natural gas production

(G-6011)
EDRIO OIL CO
13300 N Macarthur Blvd (73142-3021)
PHONE 405 621-1300
Carri Bell, President
EMP: 2
SALES (est): 163.8K Privately Held
SIC: 1382 Oil & gas exploration services

(G-6012)
EDS INC
2401 Nw 23rd St Ste 11 (73107-2480)
PHONE 405 416-6700
Mac Scott, Manager
EMP: 1
SALES (est): 116.6K Privately Held
SIC: 3421 Table & food cutlery, including butchers'

(G-6013)
EGR CONSTRUCTION INC
601 N Miller Blvd (73107-6358)
PHONE 405 943-0900
Darren Lister, President
Eddie Martz, Project Mgr
Hannah Hutchens, Human Res Mgr
Charles Attaway, Info Tech Mgr
EMP: 42
SALES (est): 13.6MM Privately Held
SIC: 2431 2426 Millwork; blanks, wood: bowling pins, handles, etc.

(G-6014)
EL CAPORA TORTILLERIA
4608 S May Ave (73119-4604)
PHONE 405 662-0427
EMP: 2 EST: 2014
SALES (est): 115.8K Privately Held
SIC: 2099 Tortillas, fresh or refrigerated

(G-6015)
EL DORADO CHEMICAL COMPANY (DH)
3503 Nw 63rd St Ste 500 (73116-2238)
P.O. Box 1373 (73101-1373)
PHONE 405 235-4546
Paul Rydlund, Senior VP
Larry Fitzwater, Senior VP
Phil Gough, Senior VP
Brian Lewis, Vice Pres
Robert Porter, Vice Pres
EMP: 4
SALES (est): 138MM
SALES (corp-wide): 365MM Publicly Held
SIC: 2819 2875 2892 Inorganic acids, except nitric & phosphoric; fertilizers, mixing only; explosives
HQ: Lsb Chemical L.L.C.
3503 Nw 63rd St Ste 500
Oklahoma City OK 73116
405 235-4546

(G-6016)
EL LATINO AMERICAN INC
8870 S Western Ave (73139-9221)
P.O. Box 22893 (73123-1893)
PHONE 405 632-1934
Phillip Condreay, President
EMP: 5
SALES (est): 294.9K Privately Held
SIC: 2711 Newspapers, publishing & printing

(G-6017)
EL NACIONAL
2328 S Harvey Ave (73109-5930)
PHONE 405 632-4531
Rosa King, President
EMP: 10
SALES (est): 565.2K Privately Held
SIC: 2711 Newspapers: publishing only, not printed on site

(G-6018)
EL NACIONAL NEWS INC
300 Sw 25th St (73109-5922)
PHONE 405 632-4531
Rosa King, President
▲ EMP: 3
SQ FT: 1,300
SALES (est): 150K Privately Held
SIC: 5994 2711 Newsstand; newspapers

(G-6019)
EL TORO RESOURCES LLC
14301 Caliber Dr Ste 200 (73134-1016)
PHONE 405 242-2777
John Walker, CEO
Shane Gray, Vice Pres
Tracey Chancellor, Vice Pres
EMP: 22
SQ FT: 9,000
SALES (est): 2.9MM Privately Held
SIC: 1382 Aerial geophysical exploration oil & gas

(G-6020)
ELAND ENERGY INC
2601 Nw Expressway St 1200w (73112-7272)
PHONE 405 840-9885
EMP: 10
SALES (corp-wide): 17.2MM Privately Held
SIC: 1382 Oil & gas exploration services
PA: Eland Energy, Inc.
16400 Dallas Pkwy Ste 100
Dallas TX 75248
214 368-6100

(G-6021)
ELASTECH TECHNOLOGIES LLC
200 N Rockwell Ave (73127-6115)
PHONE 405 470-1539
Tim Coil, Office Mgr
Les Banta, Mng Member
EMP: 5
SALES: 500K Privately Held
SIC: 2821 Plastics materials & resins

(G-6022)
ELECTRIC GREEN INC
2737 Nw 24th St (73107-2217)
PHONE 405 706-1683
David Nordahl, President
EMP: 1
SALES (est): 19.4K Privately Held
SIC: 3674 5074 1796 Solar cells; heating equipment & panels, solar; power generating equipment installation

(G-6023)
ELEMETAL
1000 Cornell Pkwy Ste 800 (73108-1800)
PHONE 405 605-2402
John Jackson, Principal
EMP: 1 EST: 2018
SALES (est): 57.6K Privately Held
SIC: 3339 Primary nonferrous metals

(G-6024)
ELEVATED CANDLES
2701 N Lyon Blvd (73107-1455)
PHONE 405 763-8223
Kevin Hall, Principal
EMP: 1
SALES (est): 43.6K Privately Held
SIC: 3999 Candles

(G-6025)
ELITE SIGN BROKERS
8921 Nw 85th St (73132-4079)
PHONE 405 200-6970
Angela C Gulikers, Principal
EMP: 2
SALES (est): 55.7K Privately Held
SIC: 3993 Signs & advertising specialties

(G-6026)
ELLIS CONSTRUCTION SPC LLC
12409 Holmboe Ave (73114-8114)
PHONE 405 848-4676
James Holmboe Jr, President
Andy Holmboe, Principal
Judith Holmboe, Treasurer
▲ EMP: 40
SQ FT: 36,000
SALES (est): 8MM Privately Held
SIC: 3444 3443 Concrete forms, sheet metal; fabricated plate work (boiler shop)

(G-6027)
ELLIS ENTERPRISES INC
5100 N Brookline Ave # 465 (73112-3623)
PHONE 405 917-5336
Dr John Ellis, CEO
Harold Massey, President
EMP: 4
SQ FT: 3,900
SALES (est): 352.7K Privately Held
SIC: 7372 2741 Operating systems computer software; miscellaneous publishing

(G-6028)
ELLIS MANUFACTURING CO INC
4803 N Cooper Ave (73118-7885)
PHONE 405 528-4671
Clay Holmboe, President
Blair Holmboe, Corp Secy
Troy Frost, Vice Pres
Brent Holmboe, Vice Pres
Lois Holmboe, Shareholder
▲ EMP: 5
SQ FT: 21,000
SALES (est): 1.2MM Privately Held
WEB: www.ellismanufacturing.com
SIC: 3531 Bituminous, cement & concrete related products & equipment

(G-6029)
EMBROIDERY CREATIONS
8117 Nw 118th St (73162-1113)
PHONE 405 728-1355
Sonnie Winfree, Principal

GEOGRAPHIC SECTION

Oklahoma City - Oklahoma County (G-6060)

EMP: 1
SALES (est): 52K **Privately Held**
WEB: www.embroiderycreations.com
SIC: 2395 Embroidery & art needlework

(G-6030)
EMC BEAUTY LLC
123 Ne 2nd St Apt 179 (73104-2254)
PHONE.................................316 655-8839
EMP: 2
SALES (est): 85.9K **Privately Held**
SIC: 3572 Computer storage devices

(G-6031)
EMC SERVICES LLC
1400 Sw 56th St (73119-6220)
PHONE.................................405 596-0050
Saul A Elizondo, *Principal*
EMP: 2 **EST:** 2016
SALES (est): 85.9K **Privately Held**
SIC: 3572 Computer storage devices

(G-6032)
EMERALD MANUFACTURING CORP
Also Called: Emerald Film System
515 E California Ave (73104-4212)
PHONE.................................405 235-3704
Ronald E Fine Jr, *CEO*
Shirley Fine, *President*
EMP: 4
SQ FT: 7,500
SALES (est): 1MM **Privately Held**
SIC: 3081 3565 Packing materials, plastic sheet; packaging machinery

(G-6033)
ENABLE OKLA INTRSTATE TRNSM LL (DH)
Also Called: Oge Energy
499 W Sheridan Ave # 1500 (73102-5000)
P.O. Box 24300 (73124-0300)
PHONE.................................405 525-7788
E Keith Mitchell, *President*
Stephen E Merrill, *COO*
Jon E Hanna, *Vice Pres*
Patricia D Horn, *Vice Pres*
John Laws, *Vice Pres*
EMP: 150
SQ FT: 59,000
SALES (est): 682.8MM
SALES (corp-wide): 12.3B **Publicly Held**
WEB: www.enogex.com
SIC: 4922 1321 4923 2911 Pipelines, natural gas; natural gas liquids production; gas transmission & distribution; petroleum refining

(G-6034)
ENCHANTED DELIGHTS LLC
Also Called: Cupcake-A-Licious
2322 Sw 48th St (73119-4817)
PHONE.................................405 202-5782
Amanda Bias-Daley, *Principal*
EMP: 1
SALES (est): 64.1K **Privately Held**
SIC: 2053 Cakes, bakery: frozen

(G-6035)
ENCOMPASS MEDIA LLC
1715 N Midwest Blvd (73141-1432)
PHONE.................................405 823-8081
Angela Rowe, *General Mgr*
Richard Rowe, *Principal*
EMP: 1
SALES (est): 30.3K **Privately Held**
SIC: 7221 7335 7812 8713 Photographic studios, portrait; aerial photography, except mapmaking; motion picture & video production; ; oil & gas exploration services

(G-6036)
ENER-CORR SOLUTIONS LLC
2136 Huntleigh Dr (73120-3807)
PHONE.................................405 509-9391
Ardie Rah, *President*
EMP: 1 **EST:** 2014
SALES (est): 77.2K **Privately Held**
SIC: 1389 Oil consultants

(G-6037)
ENERGAS CORP (PA)
800 Ne 63rd St Ste 300 (73105-6495)
PHONE.................................405 879-1752
George Shaw, *President*
Scott Shaw, *Treasurer*
EMP: 22
SQ FT: 4,500
SALES (est): 2.9MM **Privately Held**
SIC: 1311 Crude petroleum production; natural gas production

(G-6038)
ENERGY ANNASTIN
701 N Broadway Ave # 120 (73102-6050)
PHONE.................................405 810-5460
Kevin Ferdowsian, *Managing Prtnr*
EMP: 3
SALES (est): 268.1K **Privately Held**
SIC: 1382 Oil & gas exploration services

(G-6039)
ENERGY FINANCIAL AND PHYSCL LP
Also Called: Energy Financial & Physcl EFP
105 N Hudson Ave Ste 206 (73102-4801)
P.O. Box 3086 (73101-3086)
PHONE.................................405 702-4700
Mike Samis, *Managing Prtnr*
Bob Samis, *Partner*
Anthony Warren, *Partner*
EMP: 6
SALES (est): 49.6MM **Privately Held**
SIC: 1311 Natural gas production

(G-6040)
ENERLABS INC
6300 Nw Expressway (73132-5128)
PHONE.................................405 879-1752
George G Shaw, *President*
G Scott Shaw, *Vice Pres*
EMP: 2
SQ FT: 4,800
SALES (est): 165.7K **Privately Held**
SIC: 1382 1311 Oil & gas exploration services; crude petroleum & natural gas

(G-6041)
ENERQUEST OIL & GAS LLC
12368 Market Dr (73114-8136)
PHONE.................................405 478-3300
Matt Mollman, *COO*
Wm Dennison, *Opers Staff*
Tammy Smith, *Office Mgr*
Mark Singleton, *Executive*
Matthew Mollman,
EMP: 10
SQ FT: 7,200
SALES (est): 26.9MM **Privately Held**
WEB: www.enerquest.net
SIC: 1382 Oil & gas exploration services

(G-6042)
ENOGEX SERVICES CORPORATION (DH)
515 Central Park Dr # 408 (73105-1704)
P.O. Box 24300 (73124-0300)
PHONE.................................405 525-7788
Danny Haris, *President*
EMP: 9
SQ FT: 59,000
SALES (est): 6.3MM
SALES (corp-wide): 12.3B **Publicly Held**
SIC: 1321 Natural gas liquids production
HQ: Enable Oklahoma Intrastate Transmission, Llc
499 W Sheridan Ave # 1500
Oklahoma City OK 73102
405 525-7788

(G-6043)
ENVIA ENERGY OKLAHOMA CITY LLC
3500 N Sooner Rd (73141-9503)
PHONE.................................405 427-0790
EMP: 5
SALES (est): 586.4K **Privately Held**
SIC: 2911 Petroleum refining

(G-6044)
ENVIRNMENTAL TOXIN REMOVAL LLC
2410 W Memorial Rd (73134-8047)
PHONE.................................405 757-4099
EMP: 2 **Privately Held**
SIC: 2836 Toxins

(G-6045)
ENVIRO-CLEAN SERVICES L L C
Also Called: Enviro Clean
525 Central Park Dr # 500 (73105-1708)
P.O. Box 721090 (73172-1090)
PHONE.................................405 373-4545
Herschel Roberts, *CEO*
Gregory Meacham, *President*
Ken Murphy, *Principal*
Clint Lord, *CFO*
EMP: 24
SALES (est): 17.6MM **Privately Held**
SIC: 1389 7699 Oil field services; industrial equipment cleaning

(G-6046)
ENVIRONMENTAL COMPLIANCE LLC
Also Called: Wepadit
2333 Nw 3rd St (73107-6975)
PHONE.................................405 949-0103
Tracey Vanveckhoven, *Mng Member*
EMP: 15 **EST:** 2009
SQ FT: 6,000
SALES (est): 2MM **Privately Held**
WEB: www.wepadit.com
SIC: 3086 Padding, foamed plastic

(G-6047)
ENVIRONMENTAL REMEDIATION
4625 S Rockwell St (73179-6415)
PHONE.................................405 235-9999
Ken Duckworth, *Principal*
EMP: 2
SALES (est): 120.3K **Privately Held**
SIC: 2833 Botanical products, medicinal: ground, graded or milled

(G-6048)
EOG RESOURCES INC
14701 Hrtz Qail Sprng Pkw (73134-2646)
PHONE.................................405 246-3100
Tony Marando, *Manager*
EMP: 42
SALES (corp-wide): 17.3B **Publicly Held**
SIC: 1382 1311 Oil & gas exploration services; crude petroleum production
PA: Eog Resources, Inc.
1111 Bagby Sky Lbby 2
Houston TX 77002
713 651-7000

(G-6049)
EQUIPMENT TECHNOLOGY INC
Also Called: Etr Fabricators
341 Nw 122nd St (73114-7318)
PHONE.................................405 748-3841
Jim Neuberger, *President*
Donald Dick, *Plant Mgr*
Glenn Smith, *Mktg Dir*
Richard Dowdle, *Manager*
EMP: 12
SALES (est): 1.2MM **Privately Held**
SIC: 3713 Truck bodies (motor vehicles)

(G-6050)
ESCHER CORP
2932 Nw 122nd St Ste G (73120-1955)
P.O. Box 721952 (73172-1952)
PHONE.................................405 751-2893
Dale Smith, *President*
Wayne D Smith, *Vice Pres*
EMP: 3
SALES (est): 334.2K **Privately Held**
SIC: 8711 1311 Petroleum engineering; crude petroleum production; natural gas production

(G-6051)
ESPIRITU MIKI
Also Called: Lucas Trading Company
6025 Se 87th St (73135-6080)
PHONE.................................405 213-5167
EMP: 1
SALES (est): 81.6K **Privately Held**
SIC: 5047 2048 Whol Medical/Hospital Equipment Mfg Prepared Feeds

(G-6052)
ESTATE SALES BY GREG EARLES
12609 Redstone Ct (73142-2227)
PHONE.................................405 210-8472
EMP: 7

SALES: 96K **Privately Held**
SIC: 3993 Mfg Signs/Advertising Specialties

(G-6053)
ESTEE LAUDER COMPANIES INC
3030 Nw Expressway (73112-5474)
PHONE.................................405 949-9757
Mary Ann Smith, *Branch Mgr*
EMP: 4 **Publicly Held**
SIC: 2844 Toilet preparations
PA: The Estee Lauder Companies Inc
767 5th Ave Fl 1
New York NY 10153

(G-6054)
EUPHORIA OKC CBD LLC
1618 N Blackwelder Ave (73106-2055)
PHONE.................................405 412-2448
Christee Wittig, *Principal*
EMP: 2
SALES (est): 84.2K **Privately Held**
SIC: 3999

(G-6055)
EVANS COAL COMPANY
15008 Gaillardia Dr (73142-1834)
PHONE.................................405 202-3239
Karen Dahlren, *President*
EMP: 2
SALES (est): 231.7K **Privately Held**
SIC: 1241 Coal mining services

(G-6056)
EVERHART PUBLISHING LLC
2929 Fennel Rd (73128-1041)
PHONE.................................405 370-4850
Jeremy B Cunkle, *Owner*
EMP: 1
SALES (est): 38.8K **Privately Held**
SIC: 2741 Miscellaneous publishing

(G-6057)
EXCALIBUR CAST STONE LLC
1601 Sw 89th St Ste B400 (73159-6377)
PHONE.................................405 702-4314
David Steed,
EMP: 25
SALES (est): 2.4MM **Privately Held**
SIC: 3272 Cast stone, concrete

(G-6058)
EXCALIBUR STONEWORKS LLC
3820 Nw 39th St (73112-2960)
PHONE.................................405 702-4314
Joe Fergson,
EMP: 75
SALES (est): 7.6MM **Privately Held**
SIC: 3272 Cast stone, concrete

(G-6059)
EXECUTIVE COFFEE SERVICE CO (PA)
Also Called: Neighbors Quality House Coffee
11 Ne 11th St (73104-1417)
P.O. Box 54527 (73154-1527)
PHONE.................................405 236-3932
Fred Neighbors, *President*
Phil Huggard, *Vice Pres*
Max Boydston, *Purch Mgr*
Brad Ebert, *Engineer*
Todd Henson, *Accounts Exec*
▲ **EMP:** 65 **EST:** 1972
SQ FT: 102,000
SALES (est): 10.5MM **Privately Held**
SIC: 2095 2099 2066 7389 Coffee roasting (except by wholesale grocers); tea blending; cocoa & cocoa products; coffee service

(G-6060)
EXECUTIVE FORMS & SUPPLIES (PA)
3848 Nw 10th St (73107-6035)
P.O. Box 272128 (73137-2128)
PHONE.................................817 423-9088
Ron Skrasek, *President*
EMP: 2
SQ FT: 1,800
SALES: 500K **Privately Held**
SIC: 2759 5943 5112 Commercial printing; office forms & supplies; office supplies; computer & photocopying supplies

Oklahoma City - Oklahoma County (G-6061)

(G-6061)
EXIDE TECHNOLOGIES LLC
Also Called: Exide Battery
6000 Nw 2nd St Ste 100 (73127-6515)
PHONE..............................405 745-2511
Ron Choake, *Manager*
EMP: 10
SALES (corp-wide): 3.1B **Privately Held**
WEB: www.exide.com
SIC: 5013 5063 3629 Automotive batteries; tools & equipment, automotive; storage batteries, industrial; battery chargers, rectifying or nonrotating
PA: Exide Technologies, Llc
 13000 Drfeld Pkwy Bldg 20
 Milton GA 30004
 678 566-9000

(G-6062)
EXOK INC
6410 N Santa Fe Ave Ste B (73116-9120)
PHONE..............................405 840-9196
James Wallis, *President*
Steven D Bryant, *President*
James W Wallis, *President*
EMP: 5 EST: 1979
SQ FT: 2,000
SALES (est): 540.7K **Privately Held**
SIC: 1382 1311 Oil & gas exploration services; crude petroleum production; natural gas production

(G-6063)
EXPRESS ENERGY SVCS OPER LP
2704 S Meridian Ave (73108-1738)
PHONE..............................405 763-5850
Richard Swindle, *Manager*
EMP: 25
SALES (corp-wide): 770.4MM **Privately Held**
WEB: www.eeslp.com
SIC: 1389 Oil field services
PA: Express Energy Services Operating, Lp
 9800 Richmond Ave Ste 500
 Houston TX 77042
 713 625-7400

(G-6064)
EXPRESS LTG & SIGN MAINT LLC
4311 Sw 119th St (73173-8330)
PHONE..............................405 378-3838
Keith Hutton, *Owner*
EMP: 1
SALES (est): 173.2K **Privately Held**
SIC: 3993 Signs & advertising specialties

(G-6065)
EXPRO AMERICAS LLC
4404 Sw 134th St (73173-8326)
PHONE..............................405 378-6762
Russell Roeder, *Opers Staff*
Simirone Rapp, *Branch Mgr*
EMP: 26 **Privately Held**
SIC: 1389 Oil field services
HQ: Expro Americas, Llc
 1311 Brdfeld Blvd Ste 400
 Houston TX 77084

(G-6066)
F & F MACHINE SHOP INC
2115 Sw 42nd St (73119-3615)
PHONE..............................405 680-0900
EMP: 2
SALES (est): 142.8K **Privately Held**
SIC: 3599 Machine shop, jobbing & repair

(G-6067)
FABRIC FACTORY
1421 Nw 23rd St (73106-3619)
PHONE..............................405 521-1694
Peter Duncan, *Owner*
▲ EMP: 10
SALES (est): 330K **Privately Held**
SIC: 5949 5131 2511 Fabric stores piece goods; broadwoven fabrics; bed frames, except water bed frames: wood

(G-6068)
FABRICATING SPECIALISTS INC
1915 Se 29th St (73129-7625)
P.O. Box 94728 (73143-4728)
PHONE..............................405 476-1959
Brad Bartholomew, *President*
Susie Bartholomew, *Treasurer*
EMP: 10
SQ FT: 8,000
SALES (est): 990.1K **Privately Held**
SIC: 3561 3533 3444 3441 Pumps & pumping equipment; oil & gas field machinery; sheet metalwork; fabricated structural metal

(G-6069)
FAIRWAY ENERGY LLC
1601 Nw Expwy St Ste 777 (73118-1446)
PHONE..............................405 286-9796
Blake Vernon, *Owner*
EMP: 2
SALES (est): 267.5K **Privately Held**
SIC: 1382 Oil & gas exploration services

(G-6070)
FAKE BAKE LLC
Also Called: Toma's Tanning
210 W Wilshire Blvd C3 (73116-7748)
PHONE..............................405 843-9660
Joe Cooper, *Mng Member*
Mary Cooper,
EMP: 20
SQ FT: 3,000
SALES (est): 4.2MM **Privately Held**
SIC: 2819 4226 5122 Tanning agents, synthetic inorganic; special warehousing & storage; drugs, proprietaries & sundries

(G-6071)
FALCON FLOWBACK SERVICES LLC
1708 Se 25th St (73129-7612)
P.O. Box 180575, Fort Smith AR (72918-0575)
PHONE..............................405 563-0163
Christopher Cragg, *President*
EMP: 430
SALES (est): 253.9K **Privately Held**
SALES (corp-wide): 1B **Publicly Held**
SIC: 1389 Oil field services
HQ: Oil States Energy Services, L.L.C.
 333 Clay St Ste 2100
 Houston TX 77002
 713 425-2400

(G-6072)
FAR WEST DEVELOPMENT LLC
1410 Nw 44th St (73118-5002)
PHONE..............................405 557-1384
Kent E Phillips, *Mng Member*
EMP: 8
SALES (est): 874.2K **Privately Held**
SIC: 1389 Oil field services

(G-6073)
FARALLON PETROLEUM LLC
1425 Nw 37th St (73118-2802)
PHONE..............................405 225-1009
Jack Zedlitz, *Principal*
EMP: 2
SALES (est): 81.9K **Privately Held**
SIC: 1381 Drilling oil & gas wells

(G-6074)
FARMER BROS CO
Also Called: Farmers Brothers Coffee
13131 Broadway Ext (73114-2246)
PHONE..............................405 751-7222
David Tedesco, *Manager*
EMP: 8
SQ FT: 7,785
SALES (corp-wide): 595.9MM **Publicly Held**
SIC: 5149 2095 Coffee & tea; roasted coffee
PA: Farmer Bros. Co.
 1912 Farmer Brothers Dr
 Northlake TX 76262
 888 998-2468

(G-6075)
FARMERS ROYALTY COMPANY
3829 N Classen Blvd (73118-2870)
PHONE..............................405 521-9685
Henry F Gibson, *Administration*
EMP: 2
SALES (est): 159.4K **Privately Held**
SIC: 1311 Crude petroleum production

(G-6076)
FASHION GEAR DIV
7507 Sw 44th St (73179-4312)
PHONE..............................405 745-1991
Dan Johnson, *Principal*
EMP: 1
SALES (est): 44.7K **Privately Held**
SIC: 3999 Manufacturing industries

(G-6077)
FASHION SPORTS BY SIA INC
1300 Nw 23rd St (73106-3618)
PHONE..............................405 524-9990
Santi Kositchaiwat, *President*
EMP: 10
SQ FT: 3,900
SALES (est): 150K **Privately Held**
SIC: 5699 2395 Sports apparel; embroidery & art needlework

(G-6078)
FAT & HAPPY SERVICES INC
4001 Sw 113th St (73173-8309)
PHONE..............................405 834-5782
Roger Lindley, *President*
EMP: 1
SALES (est): 46.6K **Privately Held**
SIC: 1795 2448 3441 Wrecking & demolition work; wood pallets & skids; fabricated structural metal

(G-6079)
FATT HEDZ
2 W Memorial Rd (73114-2302)
PHONE..............................405 607-8484
EMP: 1
SALES (est): 82.5K **Privately Held**
SIC: 3911 Jewelry, Precious Metal

(G-6080)
FEDERAL SERVICES LLC
120 E Main St (73104-2408)
P.O. Box 2600 (73101-2600)
PHONE..............................405 239-7301
Alan N Loeffler,
EMP: 1
SALES (est): 23.7K **Privately Held**
SIC: 7699 3433 Oil burner repair service; burners, furnaces, boilers & stokers

(G-6081)
FEDERAL-MOGUL CHASSIS LLC
5600 S Hattie Ave (73129-7301)
PHONE..............................405 672-4500
Cindy Allen, *Accountant*
EMP: 14
SALES (corp-wide): 17.4B **Publicly Held**
SIC: 3711 Chassis, motor vehicle
HQ: Federal-Mogul Chassis Llc
 27300 W 11 Mile Rd
 Southfield MI 48034
 248 354-7700

(G-6082)
FERGUSON ENTERPRISES LLC
3950 Nw 3rd St (73107-6606)
PHONE..............................405 945-0107
EMP: 6
SALES (corp-wide): 20.7B **Privately Held**
WEB: www.ferguson.com
SIC: 5074 3432 Plumbing fittings & supplies; plumbing fixture fittings & trim
HQ: Ferguson Enterprises, Llc
 12500 Jefferson Ave
 Newport News VA 23602
 757 874-7795

(G-6083)
FG WELDING
3313 Sw 21st St (73108-4019)
PHONE..............................405 863-8210
EMP: 1
SALES (est): 32.6K **Privately Held**
SIC: 7692 Welding repair

(G-6084)
FIFE CORPORATION (DH)
222 W Memorial Rd (73114-2317)
P.O. Box 26508 (73126-0508)
PHONE..............................405 755-1600
Bruce E Ryan, *CEO*
Darcy Winter, *Managing Dir*
Greg Lechner, *District Mgr*
Doug Knudtson, *COO*
Marcel Hage, *Vice Pres*
▲ EMP: 140 EST: 1939
SQ FT: 100,000
SALES (est): 29MM
SALES (corp-wide): 2.9B **Privately Held**
WEB: www.maxcessintl.com
SIC: 3823 3625 Industrial instrmnts msrmnt display/control process variable; relays & industrial controls

(G-6085)
FIVE F PUBLISHING
4004 Twisted Trail Rd (73150-1910)
PHONE..............................405 732-1050
Ronald Fox, *Owner*
EMP: 1
SALES (est): 66.9K **Privately Held**
SIC: 2741 Miscellaneous publishing

(G-6086)
FIVE STAR STEEL INC
6412 Melrose Ln (73127-5536)
PHONE..............................405 787-7620
Ahmad Ghazanfari, *President*
EMP: 30
SQ FT: 52,000
SALES (est): 7.7MM **Privately Held**
SIC: 3441 Fabricated structural metal

(G-6087)
FJSP INC
13001 Twisted Oak Rd (73120-8928)
P.O. Box 721773, Norman (73070-8357)
PHONE..............................405 306-0735
Jack Ross, *CEO*
Caryn Ross, *Vice Pres*
EMP: 5
SALES (est): 109.1K **Privately Held**
SIC: 7375 7372 Remote data base information retrieval; application computer software

(G-6088)
FLANCO GASKET AND MFG INC
1010 Se 36th Grand Blvd (73129)
P.O. Box 96768 (73143-6768)
PHONE..............................405 672-7893
Bill Flanary, *Principal*
Mary L Flanary, *Vice Pres*
▼ EMP: 32 EST: 1973
SQ FT: 23,855
SALES (est): 5.9MM **Privately Held**
SIC: 3053 2891 3469 Gaskets, all materials; sealants; sealing compounds for pipe threads or joints; metal stampings

(G-6089)
FLATLANDS THREADING CO INC
1621 E Grand Blvd (73129-8416)
P.O. Box 94102 (73143-4102)
PHONE..............................405 677-7351
John Hager, *President*
Jim Hager, *Corp Secy*
EMP: 7 EST: 1980
SQ FT: 1,000
SALES (est): 520K **Privately Held**
SIC: 3498 Fabricated pipe & fittings

(G-6090)
FLETCHER LEWIS ENGINEERING
605 N Sweetgum Ave (73127-6237)
PHONE..............................405 840-5675
Fletcher Lewis, *President*
EMP: 2
SALES (est): 189.8K **Privately Held**
SIC: 8711 1389 Professional engineer; oil consultants

(G-6091)
FLEX-ABILITY CONCEPTS LLC
5500 W Reno Ave Ste 300 (73127-6378)
P.O. Box 7145, Edmond (73083-7145)
PHONE..............................405 996-5343
Frank Wheeler,
Dick Ninness,
Mark Ninness,
Dave Younge,
EMP: 9 EST: 1995
SQ FT: 60,000
SALES (est): 5.4MM **Privately Held**
SIC: 2452 Prefabricated wood buildings

GEOGRAPHIC SECTION

Oklahoma City - Oklahoma County (G-6123)

(G-6092)
FLOGISTIX LP (PA)
6529 N Classen Blvd (73116-7309)
PHONE....................405 536-0000
Brooks Mims Talton III, *CEO*
Justin Atkins, *District Mgr*
Dusty Myers, *Area Mgr*
Denis Baker, *Vice Pres*
Paul Munding, *Vice Pres*
EMP: 100
SALES (est): 28.7MM **Privately Held**
SIC: 3563 Air & gas compressors including vacuum pumps

(G-6093)
FLOWERS FOODS INC
301 N Rhode Island Ave (73117-3209)
PHONE....................405 270-7880
EMP: 2
SALES (corp-wide): 4.1B **Publicly Held**
SIC: 2051 Bread, cake & related products
PA: Flowers Foods, Inc
1919 Flowers Cir
Thomasville GA 31757
229 226-9110

(G-6094)
FLUID ART TECHNOLOGY LLC
Also Called: Fluidart
8100 N Clken Blvd Ste 115 (73114)
PHONE....................405 843-2009
Heather Vaughan, *Owner*
Joe Vaughan, *Co-Owner*
EMP: 4
SALES (est): 370K **Privately Held**
WEB: www.fluidart.com
SIC: 3569 5084 Filters; industrial machinery & equipment

(G-6095)
FLYWHEEL ENERGY LLC (PA)
621 N Robinson Ave # 400 (73102-9942)
PHONE....................405 702-6991
Danny Weingeist, *Mng Member*
David Iverson,
Mark Teshoian,
EMP: 3
SALES (est): 1MM **Privately Held**
SIC: 1311 Crude petroleum & natural gas

(G-6096)
FLYWHEEL ENERGY MANAGEMENT LLC
621 N Robinson Ave # 400 (73102-9942)
PHONE....................405 702-6991
Son Hoang, *Mng Member*
EMP: 55
SALES (est): 743.9K **Privately Held**
SIC: 1389 Oil & gas field services

(G-6097)
FLYWHEEL ENERGY OPERATING LLC (PA)
621 N Robinson Ave # 400 (73102-6232)
PHONE....................405 702-6991
Jeremy Fitzpatrick,
EMP: 7
SALES (est): 22.8MM **Privately Held**
SIC: 1311 Crude petroleum & natural gas

(G-6098)
FMC TECHNOLOGIES INC
Also Called: Wellhead Equipment Division
8624 Sw 2nd St (73128-3697)
PHONE....................405 787-6301
Everett Childress, *Branch Mgr*
EMP: 15
SQ FT: 15,000
SALES (corp-wide): 13.4B **Privately Held**
SIC: 3533 Oil & gas field machinery
HQ: Fmc Technologies, Inc.
11740 Katy Fwy Enrgy Twr
Houston TX 77079
281 591-4000

(G-6099)
FMC TECHNOLOGIES INC
Also Called: F M C Energy Systems
8624 Sw 2nd St (73128-3697)
PHONE....................405 972-1305
Rick Tatton, *Branch Mgr*
EMP: 11
SALES (corp-wide): 13.4B **Privately Held**
SIC: 3533 Oil field machinery & equipment
HQ: Fmc Technologies, Inc.
11740 Katy Fwy Enrgy Twr
Houston TX 77079
281 591-4000

(G-6100)
FMC TECHNOLOGIES INC
3400 Melcat Dr (73179-8418)
PHONE....................405 415-9532
EMP: 2
SALES (est): 95.5K **Privately Held**
SIC: 3533 Oil & gas field machinery

(G-6101)
FOCAL POINT INC
3417 Nw 42nd St (73112-6350)
PHONE....................405 942-2044
EMP: 2 EST: 1983
SALES (est): 130K **Privately Held**
SIC: 3961 Mfg Costume Jewelry

(G-6102)
FORMULATED MATERIALS LLC
Also Called: Smart Batch Systems
3010 Nw 149th St 100 (73134-1849)
PHONE....................405 310-1650
John Igo, *President*
Kim Yoder, *Controller*
EMP: 3
SALES (est): 116.6K **Privately Held**
SIC: 3559 Concrete products machinery

(G-6103)
FORREST LAWNS LANDSCAPES
3916 Nw 15th St (73107-4319)
PHONE....................405 397-4679
EMP: 2
SALES (est): 84K **Privately Held**
SIC: 5083 3524 Cultivating machinery & equipment; lawn & garden mowers & accessories

(G-6104)
FORTERRA PIPE & PRECAST LLC
6504 Interpace St (73135-4443)
PHONE....................405 677-8811
EMP: 5
SALES (corp-wide): 1.5B **Publicly Held**
SIC: 1771 3272 Concrete work; concrete products
HQ: Forterra Pipe & Precast, Llc
511 E John Carpenter Fwy
Irving TX 75062
469 458-7973

(G-6105)
FORUM ENERGY TECHNOLOGIES INC
Also Called: Forum Oilfield Technologies
1610 Se 66th St (73149-5236)
PHONE....................405 603-7198
Mason Fishback, *Plant Mgr*
Eric Vanderlugt, *Buyer*
Reagan Coy, *Manager*
EMP: 82 **Publicly Held**
WEB: www.f-e-t.com
SIC: 3533 Oil field machinery & equipment
PA: Forum Energy Technologies, Inc.
10344 Sam Houston Park Dr # 300
Houston TX 77064

(G-6106)
FORWARD OIL AND GAS INC
6801 Broadway Ext Ste 100 (73116-9037)
PHONE....................405 607-2247
Earl Ingram III, *President*
EMP: 1 EST: 1981
SQ FT: 1,200
SALES (est): 150K **Privately Held**
SIC: 1382 1311 3731 Oil & gas exploration services; crude petroleum production; natural gas production; drilling & production platforms, floating (oil & gas)

(G-6107)
FOSSIL CREEK ENERGY CORP
4216 N Portland Ave # 206 (73112-6387)
PHONE....................405 949-0880
Peter Massion, *President*
EMP: 3
SQ FT: 5,000
SALES (est): 436.8K **Privately Held**
SIC: 1382 1311 Oil & gas exploration services; crude petroleum production; natural gas production

(G-6108)
FOSTER JL WELDING LLC
3209 Sw 85th St (73159-6460)
PHONE....................405 686-6090
Jayson Foster, *Principal*
EMP: 1
SALES (est): 44.7K **Privately Held**
SIC: 7692 Welding repair

(G-6109)
FOXBOROUGH ENERGY COMPANY LLC
6501 Broadway Ext Ste 220 (73116-8246)
PHONE....................405 286-3526
Robert May, *Mng Member*
Joshua Brim,
EMP: 3
SQ FT: 2,000
SALES (est): 594.2K **Privately Held**
SIC: 1382 Oil & gas exploration services

(G-6110)
FRAC SPECIALISTS LLC
14201 Caliber Dr Ste 300 (73134-1017)
PHONE....................432 617-3722
Larry P Noble, *Mng Member*
▲ EMP: 13
SALES (est): 7.6MM **Privately Held**
SIC: 1389 Oil field services

(G-6111)
FRANK A HOGAN II TRANSPORT
3920 E Reno Ave (73117-7220)
PHONE....................405 889-4278
Frank A Hogan II, *Owner*
EMP: 6 EST: 2006
SQ FT: 100
SALES (est): 300K **Privately Held**
SIC: 3799 Automobile trailer chassis

(G-6112)
FRANKLIN ELECTRIC CO INC
301 N Macarthur Blvd (73127-6616)
PHONE....................405 947-2511
Todd Herrick, *Manager*
EMP: 4
SALES (corp-wide): 1.3B **Publicly Held**
WEB: www.franklinwater.com
SIC: 3561 Pumps, domestic: water or sump
PA: Franklin Electric Co., Inc.
9255 Coverdale Rd
Fort Wayne IN 46809
260 824-2900

(G-6113)
FRANKLIN ELECTRIC CO INC
301 N Macarthur Blvd (73127-6616)
PHONE....................501 455-1234
EMP: 471
SALES (corp-wide): 1.3B **Publicly Held**
SIC: 3621 3561 Motors, electric; electric motor & generator auxillary parts; pumps & pumping equipment; pumps, domestic: water or sump; pumps, oil well & field
PA: Franklin Electric Co., Inc.
9255 Coverdale Rd
Fort Wayne IN 46809
260 824-2900

(G-6114)
FRED JONES ENTERPRISES LLC (PA)
6200 Sw 29th St (73179-6800)
P.O. Box 25068 (73125-0068)
PHONE....................800 927-7845
Al Dearmon, *CEO*
Scott Weaver, *President*
Fred Jones Hall, *Chairman*
Kristi Edelman, *CFO*
David Holsted, *Admin Sec*
▲ EMP: 39
SQ FT: 250,000
SALES (est): 28.2MM **Privately Held**
SIC: 3714 7539 5731 Motor vehicle parts & accessories; electrical services; automotive sound system service & installation; sound equipment, automotive

(G-6115)
FRED M BUXTON
6402 N Santa Fe Ave Ste B (73116-9118)
PHONE....................405 840-4331
EMP: 2
SQ FT: 1,500
SALES (est): 150K **Privately Held**
SIC: 8711 1311 Engineering Services Crude Petroleum/Natural Gas Production

(G-6116)
FREESTYLE EMBROIDERY
5236 Coble St (73135-1512)
PHONE....................405 802-5838
Cornelia Chatman, *Principal*
EMP: 1
SALES (est): 37.3K **Privately Held**
SIC: 2395 Embroidery & art needlework

(G-6117)
FRENCH NAIL SPA LLC
1841 Belle Isle Blvd L3 (73118-4226)
PHONE....................405 843-2080
Tha Ho, *Owner*
EMP: 2
SALES (est): 148.3K **Privately Held**
SIC: 2844 Manicure preparations

(G-6118)
FRESH MONKEY FICTION LLC
11825 Blue Sage Rd (73120-5905)
PHONE....................405 751-3826
W Woodrow Murphy Sr,
William Woodrow Murphy Sr,
EMP: 1
SALES (est): 24.5K **Privately Held**
SIC: 5945 3944 Toys & games; games, toys & children's vehicles

(G-6119)
FRIGHT CASKET
3010 N Mckinley Ave (73106-3443)
PHONE....................405 602-1534
EMP: 1
SALES (est): 49.9K **Privately Held**
SIC: 3995 Burial caskets

(G-6120)
FRONTIER DRILLING LLC
13800 S Meridian Ave (73173-8803)
PHONE....................405 745-7700
EMP: 208 **Privately Held**
SIC: 1381 Drilling oil & gas wells
PA: Frontier Drilling Llc
4801 Richmond Sq
Oklahoma City OK 73118

(G-6121)
FRONTIER DRILLING LLC (PA)
4801 Richmond Sq (73118-2058)
PHONE....................405 745-7700
Glen Macalister, *Mng Member*
Shiela Michels, *Manager*
EMP: 90
SALES (est): 47MM **Privately Held**
SIC: 1381 Drilling oil & gas wells

(G-6122)
FRONTIER LOGGING CORPORATION
7221 Nw 3rd St (73127-6134)
PHONE....................405 787-3952
Francis L Weedon, *President*
Sybil Weedon, *Corp Secy*
EMP: 2
SQ FT: 1,300
SALES (est): 350K **Privately Held**
SIC: 1389 3531 8742 Well logging; logging equipment; management consulting services

(G-6123)
FRONTIER LOGISTICAL SVCS LLC
Also Called: Cone Solvents
600 N Bryant Ave (73117-6401)
P.O. Box 1238 (73101-1238)
PHONE....................405 232-4401
Brian Taylor, *General Mgr*
EMP: 7 **Privately Held**
WEB: www.frontierlogistical.com
SIC: 2911 Solvents
PA: Frontier Logistical Services Llc
2000 Richard Jones Rd # 1
Nashville TN 37215

Oklahoma City - Oklahoma County (G-6124)

GEOGRAPHIC SECTION

(G-6124)
FRONTTOBACK STUDIO LLC
10802 Quail Plaza Dr # 120 (73120-3116)
PHONE..................405 788-4400
Peter Kahuria, *CEO*
EMP: 1
SALES (est): 35.5K **Privately Held**
SIC: 7371 4813 2741 Software programming applications; ;

(G-6125)
FROST ENTERTAINMENT
Also Called: City Sentinel, The
434 Nw 18th St (73103-1906)
PHONE..................405 834-8484
Richard Grellner,
EMP: 1
SALES (est): 51.9K **Privately Held**
SIC: 2711 Newspapers

(G-6126)
FUNDOM ENTERPRISES INC
12 Ne 29th St (73105-2723)
PHONE..................405 557-0296
Doug Redleff, *President*
EMP: 7
SQ FT: 8,000
SALES (est): 1MM **Privately Held**
SIC: 3544 Special dies & tools

(G-6127)
FURSETH G N OIL & GAS PRODUCER
901 Nw 63rd St Ste 201 (73116-7627)
PHONE..................405 848-1232
G N Furseth, *Owner*
EMP: 1
SQ FT: 2,000
SALES (est): 100K **Privately Held**
SIC: 1311 Crude petroleum production; natural gas production

(G-6128)
FUTURE FOAM INC
1101 Metropolitan Ave (73108-2045)
PHONE..................405 948-0001
Reg Henderson, *Branch Mgr*
EMP: 30
SALES (corp-wide): 377.2MM **Privately Held**
SIC: 3086 Insulation or cushioning material, foamed plastic
PA: Future Foam, Inc.
1610 Avenue N
Council Bluffs IA 51501
712 323-9122

(G-6129)
G & S PRINTING INC
7706 Nw 3rd St Ste B (73127-6050)
P.O. Box 57111 (73157-7111)
PHONE..................405 789-6813
Gene Tarbox, *President*
Shirlene Tarbox, *Treasurer*
EMP: 2
SALES (est): 293.4K **Privately Held**
SIC: 2752 2796 2791 2789 Commercial printing, offset; platemaking services; typesetting; bookbinding & related work

(G-6130)
G & S SIGN SERVICES LLC
1019 E Grand Blvd (73129-8404)
PHONE..................405 604-3636
James Gleason, *Administration*
EMP: 8
SALES (est): 89.8K **Privately Held**
SIC: 3993 Signs & advertising specialties

(G-6131)
G E C ENTERPRISES
512 Country Club Ter (73110-3937)
PHONE..................405 740-9365
George Edward Cook, *Owner*
EMP: 2
SQ FT: 1,000
SALES (est): 120K **Privately Held**
SIC: 7692 Welding repair

(G-6132)
G L B EXPLORATION INC
7716 Melrose Ln (73127-6040)
PHONE..................405 787-0049
Glenn Blumstein, *President*
Debra Blumstein, *Admin Sec*
EMP: 4
SQ FT: 1,400
SALES (est): 1.2MM **Privately Held**
SIC: 1382 Oil & gas exploration services

(G-6133)
GADES SALES CO
7216 Nw 111th St (73162-2767)
PHONE..................405 720-6839
EMP: 2
SALES (est): 146.8K
SALES (corp-wide): 236.2K **Privately Held**
SIC: 3669 Mfg Communications Equipment
PA: Gade Sales Inc.
3524 S Maybrook Ave
Independence MO 64055
816 478-1120

(G-6134)
GAME TIME DESIGNS LLC
8000 S Shields Blvd (73149-1723)
PHONE..................405 702-1318
Philip Rapp,
EMP: 3 **EST:** 2012
SQ FT: 1,500
SALES (est): 186.3K **Privately Held**
SIC: 2759 Screen printing

(G-6135)
GAMEDAY SCREEN PRINTING
8717 Nw 73rd St (73132-3741)
PHONE..................405 570-0176
Brent Wetwiska, *Principal*
EMP: 2 **EST:** 2017
SALES (est): 89.6K **Privately Held**
SIC: 2752 Commercial printing, lithographic

(G-6136)
GARY L DEATON CORPORATION (PA)
2520 N Oklahoma Ave (73105-3023)
PHONE..................405 521-8811
Gary L Deaton, *President*
Edwina Deaton, *Vice Pres*
EMP: 1
SQ FT: 15,000
SALES (est): 335.5K **Privately Held**
SIC: 1382 1311 Oil & gas exploration services; crude petroleum & natural gas production

(G-6137)
GAYLAN ADAMS INC
13524 Railway Dr Ste E (73114-2258)
PHONE..................405 751-9668
Gaylan Adams, *President*
EMP: 1 **EST:** 1985
SALES (est): 140K **Privately Held**
SIC: 1382 Oil & gas exploration services

(G-6138)
GAYLY
1406 Nw 15th St (73106-4429)
PHONE..................405 496-0011
Ronald Shaffer, *Administration*
EMP: 2
SALES (est): 66.6K **Privately Held**
SIC: 2711 Newspapers, publishing & printing

(G-6139)
GAZETTE MEDIA INC
Also Called: Oklahoma Gazette
3701 N Shartel Ave (73118-7102)
P.O. Box 54649 (73154-1649)
PHONE..................405 528-6000
William P Bleakley, *President*
James Bengfort, *Publisher*
Jeffri-Lynn Dyer, *Corp Secy*
EMP: 50
SALES (est): 3.5MM **Privately Held**
SIC: 2711 Newspapers: publishing only, not printed on site; newspapers, publishing & printing

(G-6140)
GE OIL & GAS ESP INC (DH)
Also Called: E S P
5500 Se 59th St (73135-4530)
PHONE..................405 670-1431
Lorenzo Simonelli, *President*
Boris Aranovich, *Vice Pres*
Brian Sevin, *Vice Pres*
Damon Burkhart, *Engineer*
Scott Erler, *Engineer*
◆ **EMP:** 250
SQ FT: 81,412
SALES (est): 49.2MM
SALES (corp-wide): 95.2B **Publicly Held**
SIC: 7699 1389 7353 Pumps & pumping equipment repair; testing, measuring, surveying & analysis services; oil field equipment, rental or leasing
HQ: Ge Energy Manufacturing, Inc.
1333 West Loop S Ste 700
Houston TX 77027
713 803-0900

(G-6141)
GEAR EXCHANGE
3401 Nw 36th St (73112-6303)
PHONE..................405 606-3050
EMP: 2
SALES (est): 177.2K **Privately Held**
SIC: 3949 Sporting & athletic goods

(G-6142)
GEM ASSET ACQUISITION LLC
Also Called: Gemseal Pvments Pdts - Okla Cy
1628 S Kelham Ave (73129-7454)
PHONE..................405 200-1992
EMP: 43
SALES (corp-wide): 127.6MM **Privately Held**
SIC: 2951 Asphalt paving mixtures & blocks
PA: Gem Asset Acquisition Llc
3700 Arco Corprt Dr # 425
Charlotte NC 28273
704 225-3321

(G-6143)
GENESIS OIL TOOL INTERNATIONAL
5353 S Hattie Ave (73129-7321)
PHONE..................403 298-2430
EMP: 5
SALES (est): 263.8K **Privately Held**
SIC: 1389 Oil field services

(G-6144)
GEOLOG LLC
9412 Sw 33rd St (73179-1200)
PHONE..................405 745-2197
Greg Andersen,
EMP: 2
SALES (est): 100K **Privately Held**
SIC: 1389 Mud service, oil field drilling

(G-6145)
GEORGE TOWNSEND & CO INC
629 N Blackwelder Ave (73106-2634)
PHONE..................405 235-1387
William G Townsend, *President*
Barbara Dixson, *Corp Secy*
James F Mitchell, *Vice Pres*
EMP: 4
SQ FT: 2,400
SALES: 1MM **Privately Held**
WEB: www.gtandco.com
SIC: 5198 5169 3531 3471 Paints; sealants; pavers; sand blasting of metal parts

(G-6146)
GEORGIA-PACIFIC LLC
204 N Robinson Ave # 300 (73102-7001)
PHONE..................405 536-0070
Ali Bowie, *Principal*
Ken Webster, *Research*
EMP: 2
SALES (est): 100.5K **Privately Held**
SIC: 3275 Gypsum products

(G-6147)
GERDAU AMERISTEEL US INC
Also Called: Oklahoma City Reinforcing Stl
3200 Se 59th St (73135-1606)
PHONE..................405 677-9792
Ken Mowry, *Manager*
EMP: 17 **Privately Held**
SIC: 3441 Fabricated structural metal
HQ: Gerdau Ameristeel Us Inc.
4221 W Boy Scout Blvd # 600
Tampa FL 33607
813 286-8383

(G-6148)
GET A GRIP INC
5225 N Shartel Ave # 200 (73118-6064)
PHONE..................405 286-4778
Joe D Johnson, *President*
Bennett Anderson, *Vice Pres*
EMP: 2
SALES (est): 237.2K **Privately Held**
WEB: www.lilweggie.com
SIC: 3429 Clamps, metal

(G-6149)
GET PEOPLE MOVING LLC
4504 Gaylord Dr Apt D (73162-3906)
PHONE..................405 529-6033
Nathan Gardner, *Partner*
Maurice Haff,
EMP: 5
SALES (est): 279K **Privately Held**
SIC: 3842 Wheelchairs

(G-6150)
GH LAND CO
4216 N Portland Ave # 104 (73112-6363)
PHONE..................405 947-5500
Bill Holland, *Partner*
Tad Gocket, *Principal*
EMP: 5
SALES (est): 470K **Privately Held**
SIC: 1311 Crude petroleum & natural gas

(G-6151)
GHK COMPANY LLC
6305 Waterford Blvd # 470 (73118-1122)
PHONE..................405 858-9800
Terry Shyer, *President*
David M Schuermann, *Controller*
Brandi Kusiak, *Accountant*
Wade Kovash, *Manager*
Charles C Hefner, *Technology*
▲ **EMP:** 25
SQ FT: 10,000
SALES (est): 6.7MM **Privately Held**
SIC: 1311 Crude petroleum production; natural gas production

(G-6152)
GIBSONS TREASURES
Also Called: Cgshops
6001 N Brookline Ave # 1207 (73112-4256)
PHONE..................405 835-1109
Christopher Gibson, *Principal*
EMP: 2
SALES (est): 28.1K **Privately Held**
SIC: 5947 3578 5015 5963 Gift, novelty & souvenir shop; point-of-sale devices; automotive supplies, used; home related products, direct sales; catalog sales

(G-6153)
GIDEON STEEL PANEL COMPANY LLC
814 Overhead Dr (73128-1220)
PHONE..................405 942-7878
Corona David A, *Owner*
Russell Segelquist, *Sales Staff*
EMP: 16
SALES (est): 4.4MM **Privately Held**
SIC: 3448 Prefabricated metal buildings

(G-6154)
GIESECKE & DEVRIENT AMER INC
Also Called: Cash Dept
226 Dean A Mcgee Ave (73102-3413)
PHONE..................405 270-8400
Dwayne Boggs, *Vice Pres*
Bryan Cantrell, *Branch Mgr*
EMP: 100
SALES (corp-wide): 2.5B **Privately Held**
WEB: www.gi-de.com
SIC: 2672 Coated & laminated paper
HQ: Giesecke+Devrient Currency Technology America, Inc.
45925 Horseshoe Dr # 100
Dulles VA 20166
703 480-2000

(G-6155)
GILDED GATE
2617 Nw 61st St (73112-7118)
PHONE..................405 590-3139
Diane Foster, *Owner*
EMP: 1

SALES (est): 52.8K *Privately Held*
SIC: 2392 Household furnishings

(G-6156)
GLENN BRENTS SALES INC
2904 Mockingbird Ln (73110-3108)
PHONE...................405 733-4960
Patricia Derrick, *President*
Glenn Brents, *President*
EMP: 3 EST: 1977
SALES (est): 240K *Privately Held*
SIC: 1389 Building oil & gas well foundations on site

(G-6157)
GLENN TOOL INC
5940 Nw 5th St (73127-5648)
PHONE...................405 787-1400
David Glenn, *President*
Robert L Wheeler, *Vice Pres*
Kathy May, *Treasurer*
EMP: 59
SQ FT: 12,000
SALES (est): 5.2MM *Privately Held*
SIC: 3599 7692 Machine shop, jobbing & repair; welding repair

(G-6158)
GLENNS COMPETITION CHASSIS
423 N Douglas Blvd (73130-3203)
PHONE...................405 732-4603
Glenn Hagerman, *Owner*
EMP: 1
SQ FT: 4,500
SALES (est): 59K *Privately Held*
SIC: 3711 3714 Chassis, motor vehicle; motor vehicle parts & accessories

(G-6159)
GLITTER GEAR LLC
420 N Pennsylvania Ave (73107-6914)
PHONE...................405 321-4327
Toby Hammer, *Mng Member*
Jamie Hammer,
▲ EMP: 12
SQ FT: 2,500
SALES: 1.5MM *Privately Held*
SIC: 2335 Women's, juniors' & misses' dresses

(G-6160)
GLM ENERGY INC
5732 Nw 132nd St (73142-4430)
PHONE...................405 470-2873
Gary McGee, *Principal*
EMP: 6
SALES (est): 560.4K *Privately Held*
SIC: 1389 1382 Oil & gas field services; oil & gas exploration services

(G-6161)
GLOBAL OILFIELD SERVICES LLC (DH)
Also Called: Global Artificial Lift
6917 S Air Depot Blvd (73135-5907)
PHONE...................405 741-0163
Wayne Richards, *CEO*
Stuart Stence,
▲ EMP: 50
SALES (est): 14.7MM *Publicly Held*
SIC: 3561 7699 Pumps, domestic: water or sump; pumps & pumping equipment repair

(G-6162)
GLOBE MARKETING SERVICES INC
133 Nw 122nd St (73114-7214)
PHONE...................800 742-6787
Chuck B Hudson, *Senior VP*
EMP: 350
SALES (est): 60.6MM
SALES (corp-wide): 4.5B *Publicly Held*
SIC: 2752 Commercial printing, lithographic
HQ: Globe Life & Accident Insurance Company
100 N Broadway Ave 7
Oklahoma City OK 73102
972 540-5242

(G-6163)
GLORIA RAE TRAVEL ACCESSORIES
917 Nw 79th St (73114-1901)
P.O. Box 18252 (73154-0252)
PHONE...................405 848-1300
Gloria Archibald, *Principal*
EMP: 2
SALES (est): 102K *Privately Held*
SIC: 5199 4724 3499 Gifts & novelties; travel agencies; novelties & giftware, including trophies

(G-6164)
GOAT BEEF JERKY CO LLC
9617 Sw 18th St (73128-3002)
PHONE...................405 627-5096
EMP: 6
SALES (est): 353.3K *Privately Held*
SIC: 2013 Snack sticks, including jerky: from purchased meat

(G-6165)
GODDARDS READY MIX CON INC (PA)
Also Called: Goddard's Concrete
3101 Ne 10th St (73117-6414)
PHONE...................405 424-4383
Kelly Goddard, *President*
Wendy McEntire, *General Mgr*
EMP: 12 EST: 1951
SQ FT: 2,100
SALES: 3.5MM *Privately Held*
WEB: www.goddardconcrete.com
SIC: 3273 Ready-mixed concrete

(G-6166)
GODDARDS READY MIX CONCRETE
10100 Ne 10th St (73130-1704)
PHONE...................405 424-4383
Raymond Dallard, *Manager*
EMP: 5
SALES (corp-wide): 3.5MM *Privately Held*
WEB: www.goddardconcrete.com
SIC: 3273 Ready-mixed concrete
PA: Goddard's Ready Mix Concrete Inc.
3101 Ne 10th St
Oklahoma City OK 73117
405 424-4383

(G-6167)
GOFF ASSOCIATES INC
9608 S Allen Dr (73139-5303)
P.O. Box 19272 (73144-0272)
PHONE...................615 750-2900
Ben Goff, *Principal*
Teresa L Goff, *Principal*
EMP: 4
SALES (est): 280K *Privately Held*
SIC: 8748 2879 8742 6411 Business consulting; soil conditioners; management consulting services; insurance information & consulting services

(G-6168)
GOLD STAR GRAPHICS INC
8812 S Bryant Ave (73149-7610)
PHONE...................405 677-1529
Stan Guffey, *President*
Pam Guffey, *Corp Secy*
Lance Guffey, *Prdtn Mgr*
EMP: 15
SQ FT: 5,000
SALES (est): 1.1MM *Privately Held*
SIC: 2395 2396 Embroidery products, except schiffli machine; automotive & apparel trimmings

(G-6169)
GOLF CAR FACTORY
6922 Melrose Ln Ste A (73127-6143)
PHONE...................405 782-0460
EMP: 2
SALES (est): 92K *Privately Held*
SIC: 3949 5091 Mfg Sporting/Athletic Goods Whol Sporting/Recreational Goods

(G-6170)
GOLSEN PETROLEUM CORP
16 S Pennsylvania Ave (73107-7024)
P.O. Box 705 (73101-0705)
PHONE...................405 232-7033
Jack E Golsen, *President*
EMP: 10
SALES (est): 1MM *Privately Held*
SIC: 1311 6799 Crude petroleum production; natural gas production; investors

(G-6171)
GOOD PRINTING CO INC
1910 S Nicklas Ave (73128-3051)
PHONE...................405 235-9593
Steve Reagan, *President*
Kenneth Daughtery, *President*
EMP: 7 EST: 1959
SALES: 700K *Privately Held*
WEB: www.goodprinting.org
SIC: 2752 2791 2759 Commercial printing, offset; typesetting; commercial printing

(G-6172)
GOODWILL INDS CENTL OKLA INC (PA)
316 S Blackwelder Ave (73108-1418)
PHONE...................405 236-4451
Chris Daniels, *CEO*
Charlie Wright, *Ch of Bd*
Stephanie Bally, *Vice Pres*
Jenna Morey, *Vice Pres*
Traci Moses, *Vice Pres*
EMP: 75
SQ FT: 57,000
SALES: 32.7MM *Privately Held*
SIC: 8331 3714 3694 3672 Job training services; vocational training agency; motor vehicle parts & accessories; engine electrical equipment; printed circuit boards; blowers & fans; architectural metalwork

(G-6173)
GRA ENTERPRISES INC
Also Called: Lady Love Gifts
115 Nw 44th St (73118-7828)
P.O. Box 18252 (73154-0252)
PHONE...................405 848-1300
Gloria Archibald, *President*
Thomas A Archibald, *Vice Pres*
EMP: 8 EST: 1978
SQ FT: 16,000
SALES (est): 1MM *Privately Held*
SIC: 3161 3999 Luggage; novelties, bric-a-brac & hobby kits

(G-6174)
GRA SERVICES INTERNATIONAL LP
5540 Ne 2nd St (73117-8424)
PHONE...................405 672-8885
Doug Reeves, *Mng Member*
David Browning,
EMP: 5
SQ FT: 8,000
SALES: 1MM *Privately Held*
SIC: 2851 5169 Epoxy coatings; chemicals & allied products

(G-6175)
GRAIN AND GRIT WOODWORKS LLC
117 Sw 99th St (73139-8906)
PHONE...................405 250-6824
Seth David Coleman, *Owner*
EMP: 1
SALES (est): 39.9K *Privately Held*
SIC: 2431 Millwork

(G-6176)
GRAVLEY COMPANIES INC (PA)
3401 Nw Expressway (73112-4419)
PHONE...................405 842-1404
Brad Gravley, *President*
EMP: 4
SQ FT: 2,500
SALES (est): 1.2MM *Privately Held*
SIC: 2752 7334 Commercial printing, offset; photocopying & duplicating services

(G-6177)
GREAT PLAINS AUDIO
7127 Nw 3rd St (73127-6132)
PHONE...................405 789-0221
Bill Hanuschak, *Owner*
▲ EMP: 3
SALES (est): 280.4K *Privately Held*
SIC: 3651 Audio electronic systems

(G-6178)
GREAT PLAINS COCA COLA BTLG CO
Also Called: Coca-Cola
12112 Skyway Ave (73162-1001)
PHONE...................405 503-9328
Julie Z Duke, *Principal*
EMP: 2 EST: 2011
SALES (est): 127K *Privately Held*
SIC: 2086 Bottled & canned soft drinks

(G-6179)
GREAT PLAINS COCA COLA BTLG CO
Also Called: Coca-Cola
600 N May Ave (73107-6324)
P.O. Box 75220 (73147-0220)
PHONE...................405 280-2000
Don Bischoff, *Vice Pres*
EMP: 400 *Privately Held*
SIC: 2086 Bottled & canned soft drinks
HQ: Great Plains Coca-Cola Bottling Company
600 N May Ave
Oklahoma City OK 73107
405 280-2000

(G-6180)
GREAT PLAINS COCA-COLA BTLG CO (DH)
600 N May Ave (73107-6324)
PHONE...................405 280-2000
Don Bischoff, *President*
Henry W Browne Jr, *Exec VP*
Clayton Sliger, *CFO*
EMP: 100
SQ FT: 157,000
SALES (est): 110.9MM *Privately Held*
SIC: 2086 Bottled & canned soft drinks
HQ: Coca-Cola Southwest Beverages Llc
14185 Dallas Pkwy # 1300
Dallas TX 75254
214 902-2600

(G-6181)
GREAT PLAINS COCA-COLA BTLG CO
227 N Quapah Ave (73107-6613)
PHONE...................405 280-2700
John Compton, *Branch Mgr*
EMP: 200 *Privately Held*
SIC: 2086 Bottled & canned soft drinks
HQ: Great Plains Coca-Cola Bottling Company
600 N May Ave
Oklahoma City OK 73107
405 280-2000

(G-6182)
GREAT PLAINS DESIGN
3340 Nw 19th St (73107-3828)
PHONE...................405 943-9018
Joanne Vervinck, *Owner*
EMP: 1
SALES (est): 74.1K *Privately Held*
SIC: 2086 Bottled & canned soft drinks

(G-6183)
GREAT PLAINS REBAR LLC (PA)
13800 S Macarthur Blvd (73173-8708)
P.O. Box 892280 (73189-2280)
PHONE...................405 576-3270
Ken Mowery, *President*
Travis Ketter, *Vice Pres*
Brian Browning, *Engineer*
EMP: 14
SALES (est): 5.8MM *Privately Held*
SIC: 3441 Fabricated structural metal

(G-6184)
GREAT SALT PLAINS MIDSTREAM
14000 Quail Springs Pkwy (73134-2620)
PHONE...................405 608-8569
Rusty Rains, *CEO*
EMP: 2
SALES (est): 81.9K *Privately Held*
SIC: 1382 Oil & gas exploration services

Oklahoma City - Oklahoma County (G-6185)

GEOGRAPHIC SECTION

(G-6185)
GRECIAN MARBLE & GRANITE LLC
919 Nw 74th St (73116-7001)
PHONE 405 632-3802
Jesse Miller, *President*
EMP: 16
SALES: 1.5MM **Privately Held**
SIC: **1411** 3281 Granite dimension stone; granite, dimension-quarrying; marble, dimension-quarrying; marble, building: cut & shaped; granite, cut & shaped

(G-6186)
GREEN EDWARD DBA ED GREEN TRCK
3409 Lazy Ln Ste 4 (73115-1956)
PHONE 405 672-4522
Edward Green, *Owner*
EMP: 1
SALES (est): 135.9K **Privately Held**
SIC: **3537** Trucks, tractors, loaders, carriers & similar equipment

(G-6187)
GREEN OX PALLET TECHNOLOGY LLC
12352 Market Dr (73114-8136)
PHONE 720 276-8013
Roy Nuttall, *CEO*
Josh Herbeck, *Mng Member*
EMP: 7
SALES (est): 233.6K **Privately Held**
SIC: **2631** 5113 Cardboard; cardboard & products

(G-6188)
GREENLEAF ENERGY CORPORATION
101 Park Ave Ste 310 (73102-7201)
PHONE 405 239-7763
Rick Veal, *President*
EMP: 1
SALES (est): 117.2K **Privately Held**
SIC: **1382** Oil & gas exploration services

(G-6189)
GREENSTAR ENERGY LLC (PA)
101 Park Ave Ste 1000 (73102-7202)
PHONE 205 349-2852
Barbra Landreth, *Principal*
EMP: 3
SALES (est): 968.4K **Privately Held**
WEB: www.greenstarenergy.com
SIC: **1382** Oil & gas exploration services

(G-6190)
GREENSTAR ENERGY LLC
123 S Hudson Ave (73102-5020)
PHONE 405 604-0781
EMP: 2
SALES (est): 119.9K **Privately Held**
SIC: **1382** Oil & gas exploration services

(G-6191)
GREG RIEPL
200 N Harvey Ave Apt 404 (73102-4028)
PHONE 405 232-6818
Greg Riepl, *Owner*
EMP: 1
SALES (est): 47K **Privately Held**
SIC: **8999** 1382 Geological consultant; oil & gas exploration services

(G-6192)
GREGORY PRIZZELL P & R M INC
11317 Twisted Oak Rd (73120-5331)
PHONE 405 752-0782
Gregory R Frizzell, *Principal*
Greg Frizzell, *Principal*
EMP: 1
SALES: 121.1K **Privately Held**
SIC: **8661** 5942 2731 Religious organizations; books, religious; books: publishing & printing

(G-6193)
GULF EXPLORATION LLC
9701 Broadway Ext (73114-6316)
PHONE 405 840-3351
EMP: 10

SALES (est): 2MM **Privately Held**
SIC: **1382** 6792 Oil & gas exploration services; oil leases, buying & selling on own account

(G-6194)
GULFPORT ENERGY CORPORATION (PA)
3001 Quail Springs Pkwy (73134-2640)
PHONE 405 252-4600
David L Houston, *Ch of Bd*
David M Wood, *President*
Donnie G Moore, *COO*
Donnie Moore, *COO*
Zachary Simpson, *Counsel*
EMP: 82 EST: 1997
SQ FT: 120,000
SALES: 1.3B **Publicly Held**
WEB: www.gulfportenergy.com
SIC: **1382** Oil & gas exploration services

(G-6195)
GYRODATA INCORPORATED
421 S Eagle Ln (73128-4225)
PHONE 405 677-0200
Kevin Bales, *Branch Mgr*
EMP: 57
SALES (corp-wide): 416.5MM **Privately Held**
WEB: www.gyrodata.com
SIC: **1389** Oil field services
PA: Gyrodata Incorporated
    23000 Nw Lake Dr
    Houston TX 77095
    713 461-3146

(G-6196)
H & H ORNAMENTAL IRON
Also Called: H&H Ornamental Ironworks
2205 S Agnew Ave (73108-6213)
PHONE 405 634-0646
Art Mac, *President*
EMP: 9
SQ FT: 7,200
SALES (est): 750K **Privately Held**
SIC: **5211** 5039 3446 3441 Lumber & other building materials; architectural metalwork; architectural metalwork; fabricated structural metal

(G-6197)
H C E INC
Also Called: Keco Store
8100 Sw 15th St (73128-9594)
PHONE 405 745-2145
Chris White, *President*
Denver Neely, *Opers Mgr*
David Arney, *Prdtn Mgr*
▲ EMP: 50
SQ FT: 60,000
SALES (est): 12MM **Privately Held**
WEB: www.keco.com
SIC: **3089** Injection molding of plastics

(G-6198)
H K & S IRON CO
6801 S Council Rd (73169-2012)
PHONE 405 745-2761
Robert Whittall, *President*
Nick Allison, *Exec VP*
Brian Wallace, *Purchasing*
Beth King, *Shareholder*
Anola Merkle, *Admin Sec*
EMP: 30
SQ FT: 4,000
SALES (est): 8.6MM **Privately Held**
WEB: www.hksiron.com
SIC: **3441** 8711 Building components, structural steel; engineering services

(G-6199)
H PETRO R INC
5530 N Western Ave # 100 (73118-4003)
PHONE 405 242-4400
David Hanks, *Vice Pres*
EMP: 3
SALES (est): 121.3K **Privately Held**
SIC: **2911** Oils, fuel

(G-6200)
H&H AIRCRAFT INC
3828 Nw 67th St (73116-1813)
PHONE 405 833-3330
Robert Hensley, *CEO*
Phylis Hensley, *President*
EMP: 2 EST: 1999

SALES (est): 170.4K **Privately Held**
SIC: **3724** Aircraft engines & engine parts

(G-6201)
H-I-S PAINT MFG CO INC (PA)
Also Called: His Coatings
1801 W Reno Ave (73106-3248)
PHONE 405 232-2077
Joe T Cox, *President*
Sean Childers, *General Mgr*
Dorothy Cox, *Corp Secy*
Steve Bussjaeger, *Vice Pres*
J Kent Cox, *Vice Pres*
EMP: 30
SQ FT: 42,000
SALES: 22.8MM **Privately Held**
SIC: **2851** Paints, waterproof; paints: oil or alkyd vehicle or water thinned

(G-6202)
HAIKU CANDLES LLC
910 Nw 32nd St (73118-7245)
PHONE 405 528-5556
Hai Nguyen, *Principal*
EMP: 2
SALES (est): 68.7K **Privately Held**
SIC: **3999** Candles

(G-6203)
HAILEY ORDNANCE COMPANY
1661 Exchange Ave (73108-3018)
PHONE 405 813-0700
Stephen Hailey, *President*
Herbert Hailey, *Vice Pres*
EMP: 2 EST: 2013
SQ FT: 13,000
SALES (est): 162.5K **Privately Held**
SIC: **3482** 3484 3489 3599 Small arms ammunition; small arms; ordnance & accessories; machine & other job shop work

(G-6204)
HALE PUBLICATIONS
740 Sw 39th St (73109-3420)
PHONE 405 632-2450
Lewis Hale, *Owner*
EMP: 2
SALES: 9K **Privately Held**
SIC: **2731** 2741 Books: publishing only; pamphlets: publishing only, not printed on site; miscellaneous publishing

(G-6205)
HALL ENERGY
9225 Lake Hefner Pkwy # 200 (73120-2061)
PHONE 405 231-2490
Eva Whiten, *Principal*
EMP: 2
SALES (est): 173.3K **Privately Held**
WEB: www.hall-capital.com
SIC: **1389** Oil field services

(G-6206)
HALLIBURTON COMPANY
6917 S Air Depot Blvd (73135-5907)
PHONE 580 251-3420
EMP: 6 **Publicly Held**
SIC: **1389** Oil field services
PA: Halliburton Company
    3000 N Sam Houston Pkwy E
    Houston TX 77032

(G-6207)
HALLIBURTON COMPANY
210 Park Ave Ste 2000 (73102-5638)
PHONE 405 231-1800
Timothy Fields, *Foreman/Supr*
Robert Coronel, *Production*
David Carbajal, *Research*
Oscar Araujo, *Engineer*
David Tirther, *Sales & Mktg St*
EMP: 120 **Publicly Held**
SIC: **1389** 7353 1382 Oil field services; oil field equipment, rental or leasing; oil & gas exploration services
PA: Halliburton Company
    3000 N Sam Houston Pkwy E
    Houston TX 77032

(G-6208)
HALLIBURTON COMPANY
210 Park Ave Ste 1950 (73102-5644)
PHONE 405 552-8520
Bob Schuman, *Manager*
EMP: 20 **Publicly Held**

SIC: **1389** Oil field services
PA: Halliburton Company
    3000 N Sam Houston Pkwy E
    Houston TX 77032

(G-6209)
HALLIBURTON COMPANY
9800 W Reno Ave (73127-2969)
PHONE 405 805-2200
Travis Buchanan, *Manager*
EMP: 20 **Publicly Held**
SIC: **1389** Oil field services
PA: Halliburton Company
    3000 N Sam Houston Pkwy E
    Houston TX 77032

(G-6210)
HANDI-SAK INC
Also Called: Mohawk Materials
8300 Nw 3rd St (73127-7228)
PHONE 405 789-3001
Scott Waller, *President*
Pat Sutton, *Corp Secy*
EMP: 35
SQ FT: 27,000
SALES (est): 4.1MM **Privately Held**
SIC: **3272** Dry mixture concrete

(G-6211)
HANDLE LLC
2410 W Memorial Rd (73134-8047)
PHONE 405 822-9312
Meagan Pratt, *Principal*
EMP: 2
SALES (est): 147.7K **Privately Held**
SIC: **2499** Handles, wood

(G-6212)
HANDS DOWN SOFTWARE
516 Nw 20th St (73103-1803)
PHONE 405 844-6314
Robert Hanna, *President*
EMP: 2
SALES (est): 120K **Privately Held**
WEB: www.handsdownsoftware.com
SIC: **7372** Prepackaged software

(G-6213)
HANGER PRSTHETCS & ORTHO INC
4207 W Memorial Rd (73134-1761)
PHONE 405 525-4000
Sam Liang, *President*
Vinit Asar, *Principal*
Kevin Hill, *Manager*
EMP: 30
SALES (corp-wide): 1.1B **Publicly Held**
SIC: **3842** Surgical appliances & supplies
HQ: Hanger Prosthetics & Orthotics, Inc.
    10910 Domain Dr Ste 300
    Austin TX 78758
    512 777-3800

(G-6214)
HANSEN MILLWORK & TRIM INC
812 Sw 6th St (73109-1122)
PHONE 405 239-2564
James Hansen, *President*
Diana Hansen, *Admin Sec*
EMP: 20
SQ FT: 22,000
SALES: 1.5MM **Privately Held**
SIC: **2431** Millwork

(G-6215)
HARBISON-FISCHER INC
Also Called: Harbison-Fischer Sales Co
1606 S Jordan Ave (73129-7446)
PHONE 405 677-3393
Bill Maxi, *Manager*
EMP: 4
SQ FT: 6,312
SALES (corp-wide): 1.1B **Publicly Held**
SIC: **1389** Pumping of oil & gas wells
HQ: Harbison-Fischer, Inc.
    901 N Crowley Rd
    Crowley TX 76036
    817 297-2211

(G-6216)
HARBOR LIGHT HOSPICE LLC
1009 N Meridian Ave (73107-5732)
PHONE 405 949-1200
EMP: 12

Oklahoma City - Oklahoma County (G-6246)

SALES (est): 980K **Privately Held**
SIC: 1389 Oil/Gas Field Services

(G-6217)
HARD HAT SAFETY AND GLOVE LLC (PA)
6015 S I 35 Service Rd (73149-2101)
PHONE................................405 942-9500
Jay Blough, *General Mgr*
Tommy Jones, *Sales Staff*
EMP: 7
SALES (est): 950K **Privately Held**
SIC: 3842 5047 5099 7218 Personal safety equipment; industrial safety devices; first aid kits & masks; safety equipment & supplies; flame & heat resistant clothing supply; safety glove supply

(G-6218)
HARDING & SHELTON INC
12 E California Ave (73104-2410)
P.O. Box 1557 (73101-1557)
PHONE................................405 236-0080
Charles Harding, *President*
Alissa Patterson, *Office Admin*
EMP: 19
SALES (est): 3.3MM **Privately Held**
SIC: 1311 Crude petroleum production; natural gas production

(G-6219)
HARDWOOD INNOVATIONS INC
8025 N Wilshire Ct Ste C (73132-5424)
PHONE................................405 722-5588
Rick Kohn, *President*
Patty Kohn, *Treasurer*
Cathy Kohn, *Admin Sec*
EMP: 12
SQ FT: 5,400
SALES (est): 1.5MM **Privately Held**
SIC: 2499 2431 Decorative wood & woodwork; millwork

(G-6220)
HARRELL VERLAN W OIL & GAS CO
Also Called: Harrell Petroleum
101 Park Ave Ste 310 (73102-7201)
PHONE................................405 272-9345
Verlan W Harrell, *President*
EMP: 2
SALES: 160K **Privately Held**
SIC: 1311 Crude petroleum production; natural gas production

(G-6221)
HARWELL INDUSTRIES
100 N Quapah Ave Ste B (73107-6631)
P.O. Box 892874 (73189-2874)
PHONE................................405 948-7775
Terry Harwell, *Partner*
Corey Harwell, *Partner*
EMP: 4
SALES (est): 405.4K **Privately Held**
SIC: 3443 Metal parts

(G-6222)
HASCO CORPORATION
Also Called: Signfxr Sign Superstore
6220 S I 35 Service Rd (73149-2108)
PHONE................................405 524-6366
Bill Allen, *President*
EMP: 30
SQ FT: 30,000
SALES: 5.1MM **Privately Held**
SIC: 3993 Electric signs

(G-6223)
HASKELL LEMON CONSTRUCTION CO (PA)
3800 Sw 10th St (73108-2047)
P.O. Box 75608 (73147-0608)
PHONE................................405 947-6069
Kent Wert, *President*
Larry Lemon, *Corp Secy*
Bob Lemon, *Vice Pres*
Brian Wolf, *Plant Mgr*
Julie Hazen, *Opers Mgr*
EMP: 145
SQ FT: 20,000
SALES (est): 80.5MM **Privately Held**
SIC: 5032 1611 3272 2951 Paving materials; highway & street paving contractor; concrete products; asphalt paving mixtures & blocks

(G-6224)
HASKELL LEMON CONSTRUCTION CO
1400 Ne 2nd St (73117-1603)
PHONE................................405 236-2701
Larry Lemon, *President*
EMP: 6
SALES (corp-wide): 80.5MM **Privately Held**
SIC: 2951 Asphalt & asphaltic paving mixtures (not from refineries)
PA: Haskell Lemon Construction Co.
3800 Sw 10th St
Oklahoma City OK 73108
405 947-6069

(G-6225)
HAUS BIOCEUTICALS INC
755 Research Pkwy Ste 460 (73104-3657)
PHONE................................405 295-5257
Adam Payne, *CEO*
Casey Centola, *Manager*
Kelly Douglass, *Director*
Liz Sutton, *Director*
Philip Alex, *Shareholder*
▲ EMP: 7
SQ FT: 1,700
SALES (est): 1.3MM **Privately Held**
SIC: 2833 Drugs & herbs: grading, grinding & milling

(G-6226)
HAWKEYE FLEET SERVICES
924 S Morgan Rd (73128-7105)
PHONE................................405 495-9939
Dennis Thompson, *President*
EMP: 30
SALES (est): 3.8MM **Privately Held**
SIC: 3537 7538 Industrial trucks & tractors; general automotive repair shops

(G-6227)
HAWTHORNE RESOURCES
5225 N Shartel Ave (73118-6064)
PHONE................................405 840-1928
EMP: 1 EST: 2010
SALES (est): 93.3K **Privately Held**
SIC: 1382 Oil & gas exploration services

(G-6228)
HAZELWOOD INC
6801 Broadway Ext Ste 320 (73116-9090)
PHONE................................405 848-6884
James R Hazelwood Jr, *President*
Phyliss Whiteley, *Asst Sec*
EMP: 2
SALES (est): 220K **Privately Held**
SIC: 1311 Crude petroleum production; natural gas production

(G-6229)
HAZELWOOD PROD EXPLORATION LLC
6801 Broadway Ext Ste 320 (73116-9090)
PHONE................................405 848-6884
James R Hazelwood Sr,
EMP: 8 EST: 1977
SQ FT: 4,100
SALES (est): 952.9K **Privately Held**
SIC: 1311 1382 Crude petroleum production; natural gas production; oil & gas exploration services

(G-6230)
HAZLEWOOD OIL & GAS CO INC
5350 S Western Ave # 608 (73109-4533)
PHONE................................405 631-3532
Scott Hazlewood, *CEO*
Kyle Hazlewood, *Vice Pres*
EMP: 3
SQ FT: 2,000
SALES (est): 469.6K **Privately Held**
SIC: 1311 Crude petroleum production; natural gas production

(G-6231)
HB BRACKETS
6625 Sw 104th St (73169-5801)
PHONE................................405 745-4717
Marilyn Braymer, *Sales Associate*
EMP: 2
SALES (est): 110.6K **Privately Held**
SIC: 3471 Plating of metals or formed products

(G-6232)
HEART 2 HEART EMBROIDERY
5004 N Cromwell Ave (73112-6128)
PHONE................................405 401-7408
Brenda Styers, *Principal*
EMP: 1
SALES (est): 55.4K **Privately Held**
WEB: www.heart2heartembroiderycreations.net
SIC: 2395 Embroidery & art needlework

(G-6233)
HEARTLAND OIL & GAS LLC
7100 N Classen Blvd # 400 (73116-7101)
PHONE................................405 848-8099
EMP: 2 EST: 2016
SALES (est): 65.5K **Privately Held**
SIC: 1389 Oil & gas field services

(G-6234)
HEARTLAND TANK SERVICES
5200 S Hattie Ave (73129-7328)
PHONE................................800 774-3230
EMP: 5
SALES (est): 598.3K **Privately Held**
SIC: 3443 Fabricated plate work (boiler shop)

(G-6235)
HEFNER CO INC
1 Ne 2nd St Ste 207 (73104-2242)
P.O. Box 2177 (73101-2177)
PHONE................................405 236-4404
John Hefner, *President*
Brian Stanley, *Vice Pres*
EMP: 6
SALES (est): 1.1MM **Privately Held**
WEB: www.hefnerco.com
SIC: 1382 Oil & gas exploration services

(G-6236)
HELMERICH & PAYNE INTL DRLG CO
Also Called: H & P Drilling
5401 S Hattie Ave (73129-7323)
P.O. Box 95969 (73143-5969)
PHONE................................918 742-5531
John Baer, *Branch Mgr*
EMP: 500
SALES (corp-wide): 2.8B **Publicly Held**
SIC: 1381 Directional drilling oil & gas wells
HQ: Helmerich & Payne International Drilling Co Inc
1437 S Boulder Ave # 1400
Tulsa OK 74119
918 742-5531

(G-6237)
HELVEY INTERNATIONAL USA INC
330 Se 29th St (73129-1856)
PHONE................................405 203-0251
Michael Helvey, *President*
EMP: 47
SALES (est): 3.1MM **Privately Held**
SIC: 3532 Drills & drilling equipment, mining (except oil & gas)

(G-6238)
HENDERSHOT TOOL COMPANY (PA)
Also Called: Nov-Tuboscope-Machining Svcs
1008 Se 29th St (73129-6436)
P.O. Box 94444 (73143-4444)
PHONE................................405 677-3386
Edward Rubac, *President*
▲ EMP: 50
SQ FT: 30,000
SALES (est): 10.9MM **Privately Held**
WEB: www.nov.com
SIC: 3533 3599 1381 Oil field machinery & equipment; machine shop, jobbing & repair; drilling oil & gas wells

(G-6239)
HENDRIE RESOURCES LTD
Also Called: Roadrunner Apparel
4361 Nw 50th St Ste E (73112-2299)
PHONE................................405 948-4459
Don Hendrie, *President*
Dorothy Hendrie, *Corp Secy*
EMP: 3

SALES (est): 432.9K **Privately Held**
SIC: 1311 7299 5136 5137 Crude petroleum production; natural gas production; stitching, custom; sportswear, men's & boys'; sportswear, women's & children's

(G-6240)
HENLEY SEALANTS INC
200 N Wisconsin Ave (73117-3221)
P.O. Box 14236 (73113-0236)
PHONE................................405 235-7325
EMP: 3
SQ FT: 14,400
SALES (est): 330K **Privately Held**
SIC: 2891 2822 Mfg Adhesives/Sealants Mfg Synthetic Rubber

(G-6241)
HERBERT MALARKEY ROOFING CO
Also Called: Malarkey Roofing Products
3400 S Council Rd (73179-4407)
PHONE................................405 261-6900
Jay Kraft, *Manager*
EMP: 243
SALES (corp-wide): 158.5MM **Privately Held**
SIC: 3411 3354 3545 Metal cans; aluminum extruded products; cams (machine tool accessories)
PA: Herbert Malarkey Roofing Company
3131 N Columbia Blvd
Portland OR 97217
503 283-1191

(G-6242)
HERITAGE BURIAL PARK
4000 Sw 119th St (73173-8306)
PHONE................................405 692-5503
Steven Fuller, *Principal*
EMP: 3
SALES (est): 182.7K **Privately Held**
WEB: www.vondelsmithmortuary.com
SIC: 3272 Burial vaults, concrete or precast terrazzo

(G-6243)
HERNANDEZ PALLETS
2401 S Shartel Ave (73109-1722)
P.O. Box 19126 (73144-0126)
PHONE................................405 636-0503
Luis Hernandez, *Owner*
EMP: 3
SALES (est): 297.7K **Privately Held**
SIC: 2448 Pallets, wood

(G-6244)
HETRONIC INTERNATIONAL INC (PA)
3905 Nw 36th St (73112-2953)
PHONE................................405 946-3574
Max Heckl, *President*
Torsten Rempe, *Exec VP*
▲ EMP: 12
SALES (est): 2.7MM **Privately Held**
SIC: 3823 Industrial instrmnts msrmnt display/control process variable

(G-6245)
HETRONIC USA INC
Also Called: Hetronic International
3905 Nw 36th St (73112-2953)
PHONE................................405 946-3574
Torsten Rempe, *CEO*
EMP: 41
SQ FT: 9,000
SALES (est): 9.2MM
SALES (corp-wide): 1B **Publicly Held**
SIC: 3823 5065 7699 3625 Industrial instrmnts msrmnt display/control process variable; electronic parts & equipment; industrial equipment services; relays & industrial controls
PA: Methode Electronics, Inc
8750 W Bryn Mawr Ave # 1000
Chicago IL 60631
708 867-6777

(G-6246)
HIGH CALIPER GROWING INC
7000 N Robinson Ave (73116-9043)
PHONE................................405 842-7700
Kurt Reiger, *President*
Pamela W Harris, *Principal*
Michael E Joseph, *Principal*
Richard G Taft, *Principal*

Oklahoma City - Oklahoma County (G-6247)

Ralph Reiger, *Vice Pres*
▲ **EMP:** 55
SQ FT: 4,000
SALES (est): 13.9MM **Privately Held**
SIC: 2655 3081 Containers, liquid tight fiber: from purchased material; unsupported plastics film & sheet

(G-6247)
HIGH POINTE CONSTRUCTION
2256 Laneway Cir (73159-5828)
PHONE.................................405 685-8303
Clarence M Peake, *Owner*
EMP: 1
SALES (est): 74K **Privately Held**
SIC: 1799 1611 3441 Parking lot maintenance; surfacing & paving; tower sections, radio & television transmission

(G-6248)
HIGH ROLLERS EMPIRE LLC
11325 N Markwell Dr (73162-2349)
PHONE.................................405 535-3066
Trevor Burke,
James Tice,
EMP: 2 **EST:** 2015
SALES (est): 62.1K **Privately Held**
SIC: 7372 Application computer software

(G-6249)
HILLSHIRE BRANDS COMPANY
Cain's Coffee
13131 Broadway Ext (73114-2246)
P.O. Box 25009 (73125)
PHONE.................................405 751-7222
Scott Abbott, *Branch Mgr*
EMP: 225
SQ FT: 144,693
SALES (corp-wide): 42.4B **Publicly Held**
WEB: www.sterlingbay.com
SIC: 2095 2099 Roasted coffee; food preparations
HQ: The Hillshire Brands Company
400 S Jefferson St Fl 1
Chicago IL 60607
312 614-6000

(G-6250)
HINDERLITER HEAT TREATING INC
6924 S Eastern Ave (73149-5221)
PHONE.................................405 670-5710
Jeanne Clark, *Principal*
EMP: 3
SALES (est): 263.7K **Privately Held**
SIC: 3398 Metal heat treating

(G-6251)
HINKLE OIL AND GAS (PA)
5600 N May Ave Ste 295 (73112-4275)
PHONE.................................405 848-0924
Bill B Hinkle, *CEO*
Richard L Hinkle, *President*
Bruce Alan Hinkle, *Vice Pres*
David W Hinkle, *Vice Pres*
EMP: 15
SQ FT: 1,700
SALES (est): 2.9MM **Privately Held**
SIC: 8711 1311 Petroleum engineering; crude petroleum & natural gas production

(G-6252)
HIPSLEYS LITHO & PRTG CO LLC
313 Ne 36th St (73105-2507)
PHONE.................................405 528-2686
Robert Jackson, *Mng Member*
EMP: 4
SQ FT: 7,500
SALES: 400K **Privately Held**
SIC: 2752 2791 2789 2759 Business forms, lithographed; typesetting; bookbinding & related work; commercial printing

(G-6253)
HIS CONSTRUCTION
3400 S Kelley Ave (73129-5138)
PHONE.................................405 642-4306
Ken Davis, *Owner*
EMP: 2
SALES: 200K **Privately Held**
SIC: 3663 Satellites, communications

(G-6254)
HISCO INC
4320 N Cooper Ave (73118-8521)
P.O. Box 18481 (73154-0481)
PHONE.................................405 524-2700
Mark H Pierce, *President*
Lisa Pierce, *Admin Sec*
▲ **EMP:** 12
SALES (est): 2.5MM
SALES (corp-wide): 26.4MM **Privately Held**
SIC: 3423 5072 Shovels, spades (hand tools); hand tools
PA: Saunders Midwest Llc
29 E Madison St Ste 900
Chicago IL 60602
312 372-3690

(G-6255)
HITE PLASTICS INC (PA)
201 N Wisconsin Ave (73117-3222)
PHONE.................................405 297-9818
Ray Hite, *President*
Amber D Hite, *CFO*
EMP: 25
SALES (est): 5.4MM **Privately Held**
SIC: 4953 5093 3087 Recycling, waste materials; scrap & waste materials; custom compound purchased resins

(G-6256)
HOBBY SUPERMARKET INC
Also Called: H.S.
1301 W Sheridan Ave (73106-5233)
PHONE.................................405 239-6864
Esther Feiler, *President*
Sue Garcia, *General Mgr*
EMP: 20
SQ FT: 73,000
SALES (est): 3.3MM **Privately Held**
SIC: 2821 2656 Plastics materials & resins; sanitary food containers

(G-6257)
HOLLAND SERVICES LLC
1200 Nw 63rd St (73116-5712)
PHONE.................................405 842-9393
Steve Todd Holland, *President*
Steve Craig Holland, *Vice Pres*
EMP: 8 **EST:** 2012
SQ FT: 10,000
SALES (est): 2.6MM **Privately Held**
SIC: 1389 Oil field services

(G-6258)
HOLLRAH EXPLORATION COMPANY
8104 Nw 122nd St (73142-3303)
P.O. Box 721174 (73172-1174)
PHONE.................................405 773-5440
Terry L Hollrah, *President*
Elizabeth Hollrah, *Admin Sec*
EMP: 3
SQ FT: 3,000
SALES (est): 289.7K **Privately Held**
SIC: 1382 1311 Oil & gas exploration services; crude petroleum production

(G-6259)
HOMETOWN NRDGNSTCS-CLORADO LLC
11900 N Macarthur Blvd # 200 (73162-1801)
PHONE.................................405 286-1016
Paige Powell, *Office Mgr*
EMP: 5
SALES (est): 197.3K **Privately Held**
SIC: 8071 3829 Neurological laboratory; medical diagnostic systems, nuclear

(G-6260)
HONEST RONS GUITARS
1129 N May Ave (73107-5325)
PHONE.................................405 947-3683
Ron Lira, *Owner*
EMP: 1
SALES (est): 50K **Privately Held**
SIC: 3931 7699 Guitars & parts, electric & nonelectric; musical instrument repair services

(G-6261)
HONEYWELL INTERNATIONAL INC
804 W I 240 Service Rd (73139-4552)
PHONE.................................405 605-0101
EMP: 673
SALES (corp-wide): 36.7B **Publicly Held**
SIC: 3724 Aircraft engines & engine parts
PA: Honeywell International Inc.
300 S Tryon St
Charlotte NC 28202
704 627-6200

(G-6262)
HONING BY HARDY
2313 Sw 82nd St (73159-4900)
PHONE.................................405 919-3589
S J Hardy, *Principal*
EMP: 2
SALES (est): 163K **Privately Held**
SIC: 3599 Grinding castings for the trade

(G-6263)
HORNBEEK AND WADLEY
100 N Broadway Ave (73102-8614)
PHONE.................................405 604-2874
EMP: 3
SALES (est): 220.4K **Privately Held**
SIC: 1382 Oil & gas exploration services

(G-6264)
HORSEPOWER PRINTING INC
7113 Ashby Ter (73149-2735)
PHONE.................................405 631-3800
Tom Buttress, *Principal*
EMP: 6
SALES (est): 573.7K **Privately Held**
SIC: 2752 Commercial printing, offset

(G-6265)
HOSPITAL LINEN SERVICES LLC
2121 Sw 71st St (73159-2908)
PHONE.................................405 473-0422
Jonathan Howard, *President*
EMP: 1
SALES (est): 59.9K **Privately Held**
SIC: 3582 3589 7212 Dryers, laundry: commercial, including coin-operated; pressing machines, commercial laundry & drycleaning; servicing machines, except dry cleaning, laundry: coin-oper.; pickup station, laundry & drycleaning; retail agent, laundry & drycleaning

(G-6266)
HOUSE OF BEDLAM LLC
3100 S Meridian Ave (73119-1023)
PHONE.................................405 946-3100
Chris E Johnson, *President*
EMP: 3
SALES (est): 306.8K **Privately Held**
SIC: 2254 Shirts & t-shirts (underwear), knit

(G-6267)
HOUSING USA
6100 S Shields Blvd (73149-1220)
PHONE.................................405 631-3653
EMP: 2
SALES (est): 86.7K **Privately Held**
SIC: 2451 Mobile homes

(G-6268)
HOWMEDICA OSTEONICS CORP
1141 N Robinson Ave (73103-4929)
PHONE.................................405 230-1340
Debbie Carel, *Principal*
Paris Deadmon, *Marketing Staff*
Maurice Kasianko, *Manager*
EMP: 17
SALES (corp-wide): 14.8B **Publicly Held**
WEB: www.howmedica.com
SIC: 3841 Surgical & medical instruments
HQ: Howmedica Osteonics Corp.
325 Corporate Dr
Mahwah NJ 07430
201 831-5000

(G-6269)
HUB OIL & GAS INC
110 N Robinson Ave # 400 (73102-9035)
PHONE.................................405 236-3354
EMP: 1

SALES (est): 91K **Privately Held**
SIC: 1382 Oil/Gas Exploration Services

(G-6270)
HUBBARD INDUSTRIES LLC
2009 Nw 18th St (73106-1820)
PHONE.................................405 388-6798
Bryce Hubbard, *Principal*
EMP: 3
SALES (est): 146.4K **Privately Held**
SIC: 3999 Manufacturing industries

(G-6271)
HULEN OPERATING COMPANY
205 Nw 63rd St Ste 140 (73116-8209)
PHONE.................................405 848-5252
Randy P Pruitt, *CEO*
EMP: 8 **EST:** 1994
SQ FT: 1,700
SALES (est): 840K **Privately Held**
WEB: www.hulenoil.com
SIC: 1381 Drilling oil & gas wells

(G-6272)
HUNT JIM SALES & MFG
2809 N Sterling Ave (73127-1949)
PHONE.................................405 670-5663
James Hunt Jr, *President*
Dee Hunt, *Corp Secy*
EMP: 6
SQ FT: 16,000
SALES (est): 640K **Privately Held**
SIC: 3053 3469 Gaskets, all materials; metal stampings

(G-6273)
HUNTING TITAN INC
Also Called: Titan Specialties
8600 W Reno Ave (73127-2913)
PHONE.................................405 495-1322
Randy Kennedy, *Branch Mgr*
EMP: 43
SALES (corp-wide): 960MM **Privately Held**
WEB: www.hunting-intl.com
SIC: 3533 Oil field machinery & equipment
HQ: Hunting Titan, Inc.
11785 Highway 152
Pampa TX 79065
806 665-3781

(G-6274)
HUNTINGTON ENERGY LLC
908 Nw 71st St (73116-7402)
PHONE.................................405 840-9876
Robert Samis, *Mng Member*
David M Herritt,
EMP: 18
SALES (est): 6.7MM **Privately Held**
SIC: 1381 Drilling oil & gas wells

(G-6275)
HUNTON OIL AND GAS CORP
6416 N Santa Fe Ave (73116-9129)
P.O. Box 18191 (73154-0191)
PHONE.................................405 848-5545
Jim Crowley, *President*
Kevin Crowley, *Corp Secy*
Bryan Crowley, *Vice Pres*
EMP: 6
SQ FT: 2,200
SALES (est): 724.1K **Privately Held**
SIC: 1311 1382 Crude petroleum production; oil & gas exploration services

(G-6276)
HUSKY VENTURES INC
5800 Nw 135th St (73142-5938)
PHONE.................................405 600-9393
Charles Long, *President*
EMP: 1
SALES (est): 967.9K **Privately Held**
SIC: 1382 Oil & gas exploration services

(G-6277)
HUTCHINSON PRODUCTS COMPANY
3900 N Tulsa Ave (73112-2937)
P.O. Box 12066 (73157-2066)
PHONE.................................405 946-4403
G Patrick Hutchinson, *President*
Jim Johnston, *Vice Pres*
EMP: 28 **EST:** 1956
SQ FT: 10,800

GEOGRAPHIC SECTION

Oklahoma City - Oklahoma County (G-6307)

SALES: 848.8K **Privately Held**
WEB: www.hpcdoors.com
SIC: 2431 Doors, wood

(G-6278)
HYDRAULIC SPECIALISTS INC
Also Called: Hsi
12100 N Santa Fe Ave (73114-8109)
PHONE..........................405 752-7980
Keneth C Otto, *President*
Kenneth C Otto, *Vice Pres*
Bruce Huck, *Vice Pres*
◆ EMP: 20
SQ FT: 35,000
SALES (est): 4.9MM **Privately Held**
SIC: 3594 7699 3492 Motors: hydraulic, fluid power or air; hydraulic equipment repair; fluid power valves & hose fittings

(G-6279)
HYDROGEN ON DEMAND
425 W Wilshire Blvd (73116-7705)
PHONE..........................405 618-6644
EMP: 2
SALES (est): 82.3K **Privately Held**
SIC: 2813 Mfg Industrial Gases

(G-6280)
HYDROSTATIC ENGINEERS INC
2328 Se 13th St (73129-8125)
PHONE..........................405 677-7169
Ed Hailey, *President*
EMP: 6
SQ FT: 10,000
SALES (est): 472.4K **Privately Held**
SIC: 1389 Pipe testing, oil field service

(G-6281)
I CHEMEX CORPORATION (PA)
5700 N Portland Ave # 301 (73112-1668)
PHONE..........................405 947-0764
Beth Moxley, *Manager*
EMP: 5
SQ FT: 2,400
SALES (est): 6MM **Privately Held**
SIC: 2873 Nitrogenous fertilizers

(G-6282)
IAP WORLDWIDE SERVICES INC
5400 Se 44th St Ste B (73135-4032)
PHONE..........................321 784-7100
EMP: 19
SQ FT: 11,000
SALES (corp-wide): 525.1MM **Privately Held**
SIC: 8744 3728 7699 8711 Facilities support services; aircraft parts & equipment; professional instrument repair services; engineering services; marine reporting
HQ: Iap Worldwide Services, Inc.
7315 N Atlantic Ave
Cape Canaveral FL 32920

(G-6283)
ICANDEE REFINISHINGS LLC
8001 N Wilshire Ct Ste F (73132-5469)
PHONE..........................405 923-4956
Deangelo Sherfield, *Principal*
EMP: 4
SALES (est): 218.3K **Privately Held**
SIC: 2231 Refinishing cloth of wool, mohair or similar fabric

(G-6284)
ICE-T KING LLC
905 Nw 6th St (73106-7242)
PHONE..........................405 206-1185
Karlin Williamson, *CEO*
Michael Clark, *COO*
Tavanyia Davis-Williamson, *CFO*
EMP: 3 EST: 2014
SALES (est): 156.1K **Privately Held**
SIC: 2086 Tea, iced: packaged in cans, bottles, etc.

(G-6285)
ICEE COMPANY
2804 Purdue Dr (73128-5803)
PHONE..........................405 685-7739
Bennett Jerry, *Opers Mgr*
Cyril Windman, *Manager*
Hoffman Mark, *Manager*
Butler Kimberly, *Admin Sec*
EMP: 8

SALES (corp-wide): 1.1B **Publicly Held**
WEB: www.icee.com
SIC: 2037 Fruit juice concentrates, frozen
HQ: The Icee Company
265 Mason Rd
La Vergne TN 37086
800 426-4233

(G-6286)
ICX TECHNOLOGIES INC
800 Research Pkwy (73104-3611)
PHONE..........................703 678-2111
EMP: 2
SALES (est): 88.3K **Privately Held**
SIC: 3699 Mfg Electrical Equipment/Supplies

(G-6287)
ID SOLUTIONS LLC (PA)
3821 S Robinson Ave (73109-7004)
PHONE..........................405 677-8833
Andrew Njoo,
EMP: 11
SALES (est): 915.3K **Privately Held**
SIC: 2759 Screen printing

(G-6288)
IDEX CORPORATION
3805 Nw 36th St (73112-2983)
PHONE..........................405 609-1116
Art Lazloo, *Vice Pres*
Michael Chidester, *Opers Staff*
Mike Spidell, *Engineer*
Nikki McKeaigg, *Human Resources*
Richard Jones, *Marketing Staff*
EMP: 100
SALES (corp-wide): 2.4B **Publicly Held**
SIC: 3561 Pumps & pumping equipment
PA: Idex Corporation
1925 W Field Ct Ste 200
Lake Forest IL 60045
847 498-7070

(G-6289)
IFCO SYSTEMS
8812 Sheringham Dr (73132-4762)
PHONE..........................405 491-9300
EMP: 3
SALES (est): 126.8K **Privately Held**
SIC: 2448 Pallets, wood

(G-6290)
IFCO SYSTEMS US LLC (DH)
2211 S May Ave (73108-4437)
PHONE..........................405 681-8090
Karl Pohler, *CEO*
David Daut, *General Mgr*
Tammy Gainey, *Sales Staff*
Tran Nguyen, *Sales Staff*
Mike Reidy, *Manager*
▲ EMP: 28
SQ FT: 50,000
SALES (est): 10.1MM **Privately Held**
SIC: 2448 Pallets, wood
HQ: Chep (U.S.A.) Inc.
5897 Windward Pkwy
Alpharetta GA 30005
770 668-8100

(G-6291)
IGNITION SYSTEMS & CONTROLS
Also Called: ISC
3612 S Moulton Dr (73179-7608)
PHONE..........................405 682-3030
Martin Scasny, *Manager*
EMP: 11
SALES (corp-wide): 731.7MM **Privately Held**
SIC: 3694 3714 Engine electrical equipment; motor vehicle parts & accessories
HQ: Ignition Systems & Controls, Inc.
6300 W Highway 80
Midland TX 79706
432 697-6472

(G-6292)
IMAK INDUSTRIAL SOLUTIONS LLC
8816 S Hillcrest Dr (73159-6129)
PHONE..........................405 406-9778
Fred Barnett, *President*
EMP: 2

SALES (est): 239.7K **Privately Held**
SIC: 5085 3568 3562 Industrial supplies; power transmission equipment; ball & roller bearings

(G-6293)
IMPRESSIONS PRINTING A
2241 W I 44 Service Rd (73112-8885)
PHONE..........................405 722-2442
Jeff Summerford, *CEO*
John Braaten, *President*
Jason McWilliams, *Vice Pres*
Mike Stuart, *Vice Pres*
Scott Johnson, *Sales Mgr*
EMP: 40
SQ FT: 12,000
SALES (est): 7.3MM **Privately Held**
SIC: 2752 Commercial printing, offset

(G-6294)
IMPROVED CNSTR METHODS INC
4127 W Reno Ave (73107-6531)
P.O. Box 2001 (73101-2001)
PHONE..........................405 235-2609
Pat White, *Branch Mgr*
EMP: 3
SALES (corp-wide): 27.5MM **Privately Held**
SIC: 1623 3272 Sewer line construction; concrete products
PA: Improved Construction Methods, Inc.
1040 N Redmond Rd
Jacksonville AR 72076
501 404-4221

(G-6295)
INDIAN EXPLORATION COMPANY LLC
123 S Hudson Ave (73102-5020)
PHONE..........................405 231-2476
Rick Dunning,
EMP: 6
SALES (est): 1MM **Privately Held**
SIC: 1382 Oil & gas exploration services

(G-6296)
INDUSTRIAL CNTRLS SLUTIONS LLC
1005 Metropolitan Ave (73108-2031)
PHONE..........................405 601-0625
James D Bullard, *Mng Member*
James Allen,
EMP: 6
SQ FT: 5,500
SALES (est): 1.6MM **Privately Held**
SIC: 3613 Control panels, electric

(G-6297)
INDUSTRIAL COIL INC
Also Called: Industrial Coil Shop
4305 Beacon Dr (73179-7001)
PHONE..........................405 745-2030
Doug Kemp, *President*
Paula Pittman, *Corp Secy*
Ron Pittman, *Vice Pres*
Kelly Pittman, *Treasurer*
EMP: 17
SQ FT: 12,000
SALES (est): 5.4MM **Privately Held**
WEB: www.industrialcoil.net
SIC: 3621 Coils, for electric motors or generators

(G-6298)
INDUSTRIAL COMMERCIAL ENTP
3120 S Ann Arbor Ave (73179-7634)
PHONE..........................405 681-2991
EMP: 2
SALES (est): 112.4K **Privately Held**
SIC: 3589 Vacuum cleaners & sweepers, electric: industrial

(G-6299)
INDUSTRIAL MACHINE CO INC
Also Called: Imco
1546 W Reno Ave (73106-3212)
PHONE..........................405 236-5419
Peggy Manning, *President*
Don Manning, *Vice Pres*
EMP: 19
SQ FT: 1,344

SALES (est): 1.7MM **Privately Held**
SIC: 3599 7699 1623 7692 Machine shop, jobbing & repair; construction equipment repair; oil & gas pipeline construction; welding repair; electrical repair shops

(G-6300)
INDUSTRIAL RUBBER INC
11801 S Meridian Ave (73173-8235)
PHONE..........................405 632-9783
Paul A Chaney, *President*
Bill Bajema, *Vice Pres*
Mary Garrison, *Vice Pres*
▲ EMP: 50
SQ FT: 18,000
SALES (est): 12.8MM **Privately Held**
WEB: www.iri-oiltool.com
SIC: 3533 Oil field machinery & equipment

(G-6301)
INDUSTRIAL SIGNS & NEON INC
101 S Villa Ave (73107-7049)
PHONE..........................405 236-5599
Mark Kwitowski, *President*
David Kowals, *Exec VP*
Susan Greenway-Kwitowski, *Treasurer*
EMP: 16
SQ FT: 20,000
SALES (est): 980.6K **Privately Held**
SIC: 3993 Neon signs; letters for signs, metal

(G-6302)
INFINITEE BY MARS LLC
919 W Britton Rd (73114-2717)
PHONE..........................405 474-6505
Monserrat Randolph, *Mng Member*
EMP: 4
SALES (est): 169.3K **Privately Held**
SIC: 2741 Miscellaneous publishing

(G-6303)
INFINITY RESOURCES LLC
6301 Waterford Blvd (73118-1162)
PHONE..........................405 767-3519
Greg Myles, *Controller*
EMP: 2
SALES (est): 130.6K **Privately Held**
SIC: 1311 Crude petroleum & natural gas

(G-6304)
INGLESRUD CORP
Also Called: Milam Engineering
5104 N Francis Ave A600 (73118-6017)
P.O. Box 18759 (73154-0759)
PHONE..........................405 429-7928
Willaim T Milam Sr, *President*
Katherine Milam, *Corp Secy*
William Milam Jr, *Vice Pres*
EMP: 6
SQ FT: 1,200
SALES: 350K **Privately Held**
SIC: 8711 1381 1044 Aviation &/or aeronautical engineering; directional drilling oil & gas wells; silver ores

(G-6305)
INLAND MACHINE & WELDING CO
2133 Se 15th St (73129-8103)
P.O. Box 82745 (73148-0745)
PHONE..........................405 670-4355
Kathy Stapp, *President*
EMP: 20
SQ FT: 50,000
SALES (est): 2.5MM **Privately Held**
WEB: www.inlandmachineokc.com
SIC: 3599 7692 Machine shop, jobbing & repair; welding repair

(G-6306)
INNOCATIVE COMPUTING TECH
8524 S Wstn Ave Ste 114 (73139)
P.O. Box 892484 (73189-2484)
PHONE..........................405 255-4453
Mitch Hilger, *Principal*
EMP: 2
SALES (est): 108.1K **Privately Held**
SIC: 7372 Prepackaged software

(G-6307)
INNOVATIVE PRODUCTS INC
520 Beacon Pl (73127-5646)
PHONE..........................405 949-0040
Sam John, *President*

Oklahoma City - Oklahoma County (G-6308)

EMP: 25
SQ FT: 1,500
SALES: 250K **Privately Held**
SIC: **3821** 8711 Laboratory apparatus & furniture; engineering services

(G-6308)
INNOVEX DOWNHOLE SOLUTIONS INC
2709 S Ann Arbor Ave (73128-1851)
PHONE..............................405 491-2658
Tracy Yanbell, *Branch Mgr*
EMP: 4
SALES (corp-wide): 187MM **Privately Held**
SIC: **3317** Steel pipe & tubes
PA: Innovex Downhole Solutions, Inc.
4310 N Sam Houston Pkwy E
Houston TX 77032
281 602-7815

(G-6309)
INSIGNIA SIGNS INC
809 Se 83rd St (73149-3044)
P.O. Box 6323, Moore (73153-0323)
PHONE..............................405 631-5522
Christel Van Tuyle, *President*
Bret Van Tuyle, *Vice Pres*
EMP: 7 EST: 2001
SQ FT: 5,000
SALES (est): 1.1MM **Privately Held**
WEB: www.insigniasigns.com
SIC: **3993** Electric signs

(G-6310)
INSPIRATION LOGOS INC
1810 S Midwest Blvd (73110-5409)
PHONE..............................405 741-5646
Sherry Maupin, *President*
Steve Maupin, *Vice Pres*
EMP: 3
SQ FT: 1,400
SALES (est): 170K **Privately Held**
SIC: **2399** 2395 Emblems, badges & insignia; pleating & stitching

(G-6311)
INSTANT SIGNS INC
227 Nw 63rd St (73116-8221)
PHONE..............................405 848-8181
Jim Benson, *President*
Barbara Benson, *Corp Secy*
EMP: 2
SALES (est): 257.5K **Privately Held**
SIC: **3993** 5999 Signs, not made in custom sign painting shops; banners

(G-6312)
INSTINCT PERFORMANCE LLC
Also Called: Vima
7 Ne 6th St 30 (73104-1801)
PHONE..............................405 463-7300
Kelly Owen, *CEO*
EMP: 4
SALES (est): 255.1K **Privately Held**
SIC: **3949** 5731 Sporting & athletic goods; consumer electronic equipment

(G-6313)
INTEGRAL GEOPHYSICS INC
3037 Nw 63rd St Ste 158w (73116-3608)
PHONE..............................405 848-4573
Roberto Feige, *President*
EMP: 1
SALES: 150K **Privately Held**
SIC: **1382** Oil & gas exploration services

(G-6314)
INTEGRATED S MYCARE
5401 N Portland Ave A (73112-2121)
PHONE..............................405 605-0546
Craig Brown, *Mng Member*
EMP: 4
SALES: 1MM **Privately Held**
SIC: **7372** Application computer software

(G-6315)
INTEGRITY DIRECTIONAL SVCS LLC (PA)
119 N Robinson Ave # 400 (73102-4613)
PHONE..............................817 731-8881
Steve Boyd, *President*
Charlie Hodges, *Vice Pres*
Dwight Dickerson, *Director*
EMP: 12

SALES (est): 11.3MM **Privately Held**
SIC: **1381** Directional drilling oil & gas wells

(G-6316)
INTEGRITY RMDLG CNSTR SVCS LLC
708 Nw 25th St (73103-1426)
PHONE..............................405 754-9836
Ronald Tyler,
EMP: 1
SALES (est): 52.7K **Privately Held**
SIC: **1389** 1799 7389 Construction, repair & dismantling services; construction site cleanup;

(G-6317)
INTEGSENSE INC
3030 Nw Expwy Ste 200b (73112-5474)
PHONE..............................404 429-4780
Mehdi Alighanbari, *CEO*
Reza Abdolvand, *Principal*
EMP: 3
SALES (est): 148.1K **Privately Held**
SIC: **3841** Surgical & medical instruments

(G-6318)
INTERIOR DESIGNERS SUPPLY INC
Also Called: Design Resources
7720 N Robinson Ave B3 (73116-7734)
P.O. Box 2053 (73101-2053)
PHONE..............................405 521-1551
Michael D Smith, *President*
EMP: 12
SQ FT: 12,000
SALES (est): 1.5MM **Privately Held**
SIC: **2391** 2392 5131 5023 Curtains & draperies; bedspreads & bed sets: made from purchased materials; comforters & quilts: made from purchased materials; pillows, bed: made from purchased materials; drapery material, woven; upholstery fabrics, woven; venetian blinds; vertical blinds; window shades

(G-6319)
INTERNATIONAL ENVMTL CORP
Also Called: IEC
5000 W I 40 Service Rd (73128-1201)
PHONE..............................405 605-5024
Larry Jewel, *President*
Jim Brown, *President*
Larry Jewel, *President*
Dennis F Kloster, *President*
Kim Sabatino, *President*
◆ EMP: 236 EST: 1965
SQ FT: 190,000
SALES (est): 86.5MM
SALES (corp-wide): 2.5B **Privately Held**
WEB: www.iec-okc.com
SIC: **3585** Refrigeration & heating equipment
HQ: The Climate Control Group Inc
7300 Sw 44th St
Oklahoma City OK 73179
405 745-6858

(G-6320)
INTERNATIONAL PAPER COMPANY
4901 Westpoint Blvd (73179-4315)
PHONE..............................405 745-5800
Steve Dennehy, *General Mgr*
Charles Loyd, *Manager*
EMP: 70
SALES (corp-wide): 22.3B **Publicly Held**
WEB: www.internationalpaper.com
SIC: **2631** 2653 5113 Cardboard; corrugated & solid fiber boxes; corrugated & solid fiber boxes
PA: International Paper Company
6400 Poplar Ave
Memphis TN 38197
901 419-9000

(G-6321)
INTERNATIONAL PRO RODEO ASSN
Also Called: PRO RODEO WORLD
1412 S Agnew Ave (73108-2430)
P.O. Box 83377 (73148-1377)
PHONE..............................405 235-6540
Dale Yerigan, *President*
Annetta Abott, *Corp Secy*

Bonnie McBee, *COO*
Platon Macon, *Treasurer*
Amy L Duvall, *Director*
EMP: 8
SQ FT: 4,100
SALES: 1.5MM **Privately Held**
SIC: **8621** 2721 Professional membership organizations; periodicals

(G-6322)
INTERSTATE SUPPLY COMPANY
Also Called: ISC Surfaces LLC
5600 Sw 36th St Ste C (73179-7815)
PHONE..............................405 232-7141
Angela Sams, *Manager*
EMP: 46
SALES (corp-wide): 42.9MM **Privately Held**
WEB: www.iscsurfaces.com
SIC: **3996** Hard surface floor coverings
PA: Interstate Supply Company
9245 Dielman Indus Dr
Saint Louis MO 63132
314 994-7100

(G-6323)
INTERSTATE TRUCKER LTD
Also Called: Assistance Administration
1101 Sovereign Row Ste A (73108-1827)
P.O. Box 54438 (73154-1438)
PHONE..............................405 948-6576
J Keith Butler, *President*
EMP: 22
SALES (est): 2.4MM **Privately Held**
SIC: **8111** 8621 2741 General practice law office; professional membership organizations; newsletter publishing

(G-6324)
INTREPID DIRECTIONAL DRILLING
205 Nw 63rd St (73116-8254)
PHONE..............................405 607-0422
EMP: 2
SALES (est): 134.4K **Privately Held**
SIC: **1381** Oil/Gas Well Drilling

(G-6325)
IOCHEM CORPORATION (PA)
5801 Broadway Ext Ste 305 (73118-7489)
PHONE..............................405 848-8611
Yutaka Imaizumi, *President*
Kent Hood, *Exec VP*
Chuck Parr, *Vice Pres*
Craig Randolph, *Foreman/Supr*
Jerome Morrison, *Treasurer*
◆ EMP: 41
SQ FT: 2,753
SALES (est): 11.2MM **Privately Held**
SIC: **2819** Iodine, elemental

(G-6326)
IPS
7408 Nw 83rd St (73132-4292)
PHONE..............................405 722-0896
EMP: 3
SALES (est): 159.3K **Privately Held**
SIC: **1311** Crude petroleum production

(G-6327)
IRONCRAFT URBAN PRODUCTS LLC
5401 5405 Nw 5th St (73127)
PHONE..............................855 601-1647
Justin Hodges, *Mng Member*
EMP: 7
SQ FT: 15,000
SALES (est): 1MM **Privately Held**
SIC: **5712** 2514 3446 Customized furniture & cabinets; metal household furniture; architectural metalwork; stairs, staircases, stair treads: prefabricated metal; ornamental metalwork

(G-6328)
J & B GRAPHICS INC
1811 Nw 1st St (73106-3007)
PHONE..............................405 524-7446
Jackie Turner, *President*
Jackie Morris, *Co-Owner*
Tod Hutchinson, *Mfg Staff*
Myra Cleveland, *Graphic Designe*
EMP: 20
SQ FT: 10,000

SALES (est): 4.3MM **Privately Held**
SIC: **3993** 5087 Signs, not made in custom sign painting shops; engraving equipment & supplies

(G-6329)
J & D GEARING & MACHINING INC
1900 E Grand Blvd (73129-8421)
P.O. Box 95134 (73143-5134)
PHONE..............................405 677-7667
Dale Dixon, *President*
Melba Sue Sims, *Corp Secy*
Joel D Mahan, *Vice Pres*
EMP: 9 EST: 1978
SQ FT: 12,000
SALES: 642.4K **Privately Held**
SIC: **3599** 3462 3541 3568 Machine shop, jobbing & repair; gear & chain forgings; machine tools, metal cutting type; power transmission equipment

(G-6330)
J & J TUBULARS INC
14024 S Meridian Ave (73173-8805)
P.O. Box 613, Newcastle (73065-0613)
PHONE..............................405 691-2039
Sandra McMinn, *President*
EMP: 8
SQ FT: 3,500
SALES (est): 2.7MM **Privately Held**
SIC: **5051** 3498 Tubing, metal; tube fabricating (contract bending & shaping)

(G-6331)
J & L EXPLORATION LLC
6412 N Santa Fe Ave (73116-9114)
PHONE..............................405 842-6876
John O Cockerell, *Administration*
EMP: 2 EST: 2010
SALES (est): 109.3K **Privately Held**
SIC: **1382** Oil & gas exploration services

(G-6332)
J & M INVESTMENT
901 Nw 84th St (73114-2115)
P.O. Box 14801 (73113-0801)
PHONE..............................405 848-3755
Joan Maguire, *Partner*
Malcolm J Maguire, *General Ptnr*
EMP: 5
SALES (est): 409.6K **Privately Held**
SIC: **1311** 6531 Crude petroleum production; natural gas production; real estate agents & managers

(G-6333)
J & S WOODWORKING INC
1033 Se 40th St (73129-6827)
PHONE..............................405 619-9910
John Throckmorton, *Principal*
EMP: 2
SALES (est): 155K **Privately Held**
SIC: **2431** Millwork

(G-6334)
J A OIL FIELD MFG INC (PA)
2101 Se 67th St (73149-6002)
P.O. Box 95545 (73143-5545)
PHONE..............................405 672-2299
James Acquaye, *President*
Mina Acquaye, *Vice Pres*
Francis Bampoe, *Opers Mgr*
Dg Morris, *Opers Staff*
Adam Cardamon, *Sales Staff*
▲ EMP: 49
SQ FT: 14,600
SALES: 15.3MM **Privately Held**
WEB: www.jaoilfield.com
SIC: **7353** 7699 3533 Oil well drilling equipment, rental or leasing; industrial equipment services; oil & gas field machinery

(G-6335)
J C SHEET METAL FABRICATION
Also Called: JC Sheet Metal Fabrication
7233 Nw 3rd St (73127-6134)
PHONE..............................405 787-1902
John Collins, *Owner*
EMP: 1
SALES (est): 92.9K **Privately Held**
SIC: **1761** 3444 Sheet metalwork; sheet metalwork

GEOGRAPHIC SECTION

Oklahoma City - Oklahoma County (G-6368)

(G-6336)
J M A RESOURCES INC
1021 Nw Grand Blvd (73118-6039)
PHONE.................405 947-4322
Jeffrey J McDougall, *President*
EMP: 4
SQ FT: 2,500
SALES (est): 410K **Privately Held**
SIC: 1311 Crude petroleum production; natural gas production

(G-6337)
J P MACHINE & TOOL CO
1534 Se 29th St (73129-7618)
P.O. Box 95085 (73143-5085)
PHONE.................405 677-3341
Glenn E Berry, *President*
Syble Berry, *Corp Secy*
Patrick Berry, *Vice Pres*
EMP: 12 EST: 1936
SQ FT: 19,000
SALES (est): 2.4MM **Privately Held**
SIC: 3533 3494 Oil field machinery & equipment; valves & pipe fittings

(G-6338)
J R LUKEMAN & ASSOCIATES INC
3017 Hemingford Ln (73120-4321)
PHONE.................405 842-6548
John R Lukeman, *President*
EMP: 2
SALES (est): 180K **Privately Held**
SIC: 3441 3423 Floor jacks, metal; hand & edge tools

(G-6339)
J WALTER DUNCAN JR OIL INC
100 Park Ave Ste 1200 (73102-8004)
PHONE.................405 272-1800
Walter Duncan IV, *President*
EMP: 35
SQ FT: 7,000
SALES (est): 2.1MM **Privately Held**
SIC: 1311 1382 Crude petroleum production; natural gas production; oil & gas exploration services

(G-6340)
J&M STAINLESS FABRICATORS LTD
744 Sw 23rd St (73109-1706)
PHONE.................405 517-0875
Paula Morales, *Principal*
EMP: 2
SALES (est): 136.1K **Privately Held**
SIC: 3449 3446 2599 2514 Miscellaneous metalwork; architectural metalwork; restaurant furniture, wood or metal; serving carts & tea wagons: metal

(G-6341)
JACK HENRY & ASSOCIATES INC
4248 Highline Blvd (73108-2028)
PHONE.................405 947-6644
Gale Pace, *Principal*
EMP: 16
SALES (corp-wide): 1.5B **Publicly Held**
WEB: www.jackhenry.com
SIC: 8742 7372 Banking & finance consultant; prepackaged software
PA: Jack Henry & Associates, Inc.
663 W Highway 60
Monett MO 65708
417 235-6652

(G-6342)
JACK PRATT SCREEN-AD CO
409 Ne 40th St (73105-3700)
PHONE.................405 524-5551
Pauline F Pratt, *President*
Pete Penner, *COO*
Jack Pratt, *COO*
Jack S Pratt, *Vice Pres*
Monte Pratt, *Vice Pres*
▲ EMP: 17 EST: 1950
SQ FT: 8,000
SALES (est): 2.2MM **Privately Held**
WEB: www.jackpratt.com
SIC: 3993 Signs, not made in custom sign painting shops

(G-6343)
JACKSON HOLDINGS LLC
Also Called: Woody Candy Company
922 Nw 70th St (73116-7517)
PHONE.................405 842-8903
Brian Jackson, *Mng Member*
William A Jackson, *Mng Member*
EMP: 7
SALES (est): 786K **Privately Held**
SIC: 2064 Candy & other confectionery products

(G-6344)
JACMOR INC
8028 N May Ave Ste 202 (73120-4503)
PHONE.................405 843-0203
Laurence B Trachtenberg, *President*
EMP: 4
SALES (est): 338.7K **Privately Held**
SIC: 1311 Natural gas production; crude petroleum production

(G-6345)
JAF INDUSTRIES LLC
5909 Nw Expressway # 269 (73132-5161)
PHONE.................405 834-8362
Kenneth James Brown, *Principal*
EMP: 1
SALES (est): 39.6K **Privately Held**
SIC: 3999 Manufacturing industries

(G-6346)
JAGUAR METER SERVICE INC
1605 Se 37th St (73129-7912)
P.O. Box 96495 (73143-6495)
PHONE.................405 670-2327
Reggie Fleming, *President*
Rex Lewis, *Vice Pres*
EMP: 2
SQ FT: 2,400
SALES (est): 505.1K **Privately Held**
SIC: 5511 1389 Automobiles, new & used; testing, measuring, surveying & analysis services

(G-6347)
JAMES D PATE JR
3625 Goodger Dr Ste D (73112-1485)
PHONE.................405 942-3647
James D Pate Jr, *Owner*
EMP: 1
SQ FT: 4,728
SALES (est): 84.9K **Privately Held**
SIC: 1241 Exploration, anthracite mining

(G-6348)
JAMES H MILLIGAN ENTERPRISES
5400 N Grand Blvd Ste 545 (73112-5672)
PHONE.................405 525-8331
James H Milligan, *Owner*
Michael J Milligan, *Principal*
EMP: 7 EST: 1968
SQ FT: 3,000
SALES (est): 420K **Privately Held**
SIC: 1311 Crude petroleum production; natural gas production

(G-6349)
JAMES LAND RESIDUAL ASSETS LLC
11316 Cedar Hollow Rd (73162-3400)
PHONE.................405 842-2828
EMP: 2
SALES (est): 90.7K **Privately Held**
SIC: 2911 Residues

(G-6350)
JANKE PRODUCTS LLC
1600 Se 37th St (73129-7911)
P.O. Box 96362 (73143-6362)
PHONE.................405 677-3600
Janice Roberts, *President*
Ronald Roberts, *Vice Pres*
Ron Roberts, *Info Tech Mgr*
EMP: 12
SQ FT: 10,000
SALES (est): 1.7MM **Privately Held**
SIC: 3599 Machine shop, jobbing & repair

(G-6351)
JATCO INC
Also Called: Jatco Environmental Equipment
244 Nw 111th St (73114-6602)
PHONE.................405 755-4100
Jeff Hill, *President*
Scott Hill, *Vice Pres*
EMP: 20
SQ FT: 10,000
SALES (est): 7.3MM **Privately Held**
SIC: 3823 Industrial instrmnts msrmnt display/control process variable

(G-6352)
JEC OPERATING LLC
921 E Britton Rd (73114-7802)
PHONE.................405 235-4454
Mickey Raney, *VP Opers*
Russell V Johnson,
EMP: 4
SALES (est): 391.7K **Privately Held**
SIC: 1389 Oil field services

(G-6353)
JEC PRODUCTION LLC
921 W Britton Rd (73114-2717)
PHONE.................405 235-4454
Russel Johnson,
EMP: 3 EST: 2001
SALES (est): 240K **Privately Held**
SIC: 2911 Oils, fuel

(G-6354)
JEFF MC KENZIE & CO INC
630 W Sheridan Ave (73102-2410)
PHONE.................405 236-5848
Jeffrey F Mc Kenzie, *President*
Jeffrey F McKenzie, *President*
EMP: 3
SQ FT: 5,700
SALES: 205K **Privately Held**
SIC: 2759 2396 Screen printing; automotive & apparel trimmings

(G-6355)
JEFFREY C JAMES
6804 Newman Dr (73162-7442)
PHONE.................405 728-8145
C J James, *Owner*
EMP: 1
SALES (est): 67.1K **Privately Held**
SIC: 1389 Oil field services

(G-6356)
JEMISON DENNA
2624 W Park Pl (73107-5434)
PHONE.................405 922-7830
Denna Jemison, *Owner*
EMP: 1
SALES (est): 41.7K **Privately Held**
SIC: 2051 7389 Bakery products, partially cooked (except frozen);

(G-6357)
JERRY BENDORF TRUSTEE
3300 S High Ave (73129-5128)
P.O. Box 95638 (73143-5638)
PHONE.................405 840-9900
Jerry Bendorf, *Owner*
EMP: 1
SQ FT: 500
SALES (est): 100K **Privately Held**
SIC: 1311 6512 Crude petroleum production; natural gas production; nonresidential building operators

(G-6358)
JESCO PRODUCTS INC
304 N Meridian Ave Ste B (73107-6535)
P.O. Box 57506 (73157-7506)
PHONE.................405 943-1721
Ken Massey, *President*
K C Massey, *Vice Pres*
EMP: 5
SALES (est): 420K **Privately Held**
SIC: 3843 3291 Compounds, dental; abrasive products

(G-6359)
JESS HARRIS INC
2601 Nw Expwy Ste 200e (73112-7228)
PHONE.................405 840-3271
EMP: 3
SQ FT: 1,800
SALES (est): 272.3K **Privately Held**
SIC: 6211 1311 Security Broker & Dealer Crude Petroleum & Natural Gas Production

(G-6360)
JESTER INDUSTRIES INC
11212 Sturbridge Rd (73162-2162)
PHONE.................405 919-2013
Thomas J Jester, *Principal*
EMP: 1 EST: 2012
SALES (est): 171.6K **Privately Held**
SIC: 3999 Manufacturing industries

(G-6361)
JET PRINTING CO INC
7017 Se 15th St (73110-5123)
PHONE.................405 732-1262
Juanita Ruth Henthorn, *President*
EMP: 2 EST: 1952
SALES (est): 170K **Privately Held**
SIC: 2759 2752 2789 Letterpress printing; commercial printing, lithographic; bookbinding & related work

(G-6362)
JEWELL JORDAN PUBLISHING LLC (PA)
3212 Ne Overbrook Dr (73121-2853)
PHONE.................405 496-2672
Stephana Colbert,
EMP: 1 EST: 2014
SALES (est): 129.4K **Privately Held**
SIC: 2741 Miscellaneous publishing

(G-6363)
JIM ROTH
101 N Robinson Ave (73102-5504)
P.O. Box 18904 (73154-0904)
PHONE.................405 235-4100
Jim Roth, *Principal*
EMP: 3
SALES (est): 103.1K **Privately Held**
WEB: www.phillipsmurrah.com
SIC: 2711 Newspapers, publishing & printing

(G-6364)
JJS SECURITY CAMERAS INC
3717 Se 45th St (73135-2049)
PHONE.................405 408-6096
John M Jones, *President*
Wanda Jones, *Admin Sec*
EMP: 2
SALES (est): 147.6K **Privately Held**
SIC: 3699 7389 Security devices;

(G-6365)
JM PUBLICATIONS LLC
11305 N Markwell Dr (73162-2349)
PHONE.................405 639-9472
James Mitchell, *Principal*
EMP: 1
SALES (est): 37.5K **Privately Held**
SIC: 2741 Miscellaneous publishing

(G-6366)
JMA ENERGY COMPANY LLC
1021 Nw Grand Blvd (73118-6039)
PHONE.................405 418-2853
Jeffrey J McDougall, *President*
Richard Smith, *Property Mgr*
Lindsey Brock, *Manager*
Josh Cope, *Technology*
EMP: 50
SQ FT: 13,000
SALES (est): 26.4MM **Privately Held**
SIC: 1382 Oil & gas exploration services

(G-6367)
JMD PROPERTIES
1201 W Britton Rd (73114-1711)
P.O. Box 14426 (73113-0426)
PHONE.................405 848-5722
Joedan Trigg, *President*
EMP: 1
SALES (est): 143.6K **Privately Held**
SIC: 1382 Oil & gas exploration services

(G-6368)
JOHN M BEARD
12316 Saint Andrews Dr A (73120-8655)
PHONE.................405 751-2727
Barbara Beard, *Principal*
EMP: 3
SALES (est): 162.6K **Privately Held**
SIC: 1311 Crude petroleum production

Oklahoma City - Oklahoma County (G-6369)

(G-6369)
JOHN R LITTLE JR
2601 Kings Way (73120-3306)
PHONE.................................405 751-5227
John R Little Jr, *Owner*
EMP: 1
SALES (est): 68K **Privately Held**
SIC: 2421 Sawmills & planing mills, general

(G-6370)
JOHN R WARREN
Also Called: John R Warren Revocable Trust
50 Penn Pl 410 (73118-1900)
PHONE.................................405 843-9402
Fax: 405 848-8609
EMP: 6 EST: 1991
SALES: 1.6MM **Privately Held**
SIC: 1311 Crude Petroleum/Natural Gas Production

(G-6371)
JOHNNY L WINDSOR
Also Called: Okla Hi-Tech. Equipment
2624 Sw 102nd St (73159-7306)
PHONE.................................405 691-3083
Johnny L Windsory, *Owner*
EMP: 2
SALES (est): 27.5K **Privately Held**
SIC: 3482 Small arms ammunition

(G-6372)
JOHNS MANVILLE CORPORATION
812 N Bryant Ave (73117-6423)
PHONE.................................405 552-4115
Brian Olson, *Branch Mgr*
EMP: 40
SALES (corp-wide): 327.2B **Publicly Held**
SIC: 3296 Mineral wool
HQ: Johns Manville Corporation
717 17th St Ste 800
Denver CO 80202
303 978-2000

(G-6373)
JOHNSON BVLLE FINE JWLERS PAWN
9344 N May Ave (73120-4421)
PHONE.................................405 751-1216
Fax: 405 751-1257
EMP: 1
SQ FT: 8,800
SALES (est): 140K **Privately Held**
SIC: 3911 5944 5932 Mfg And Retails Jewelery And Pawn Shop

(G-6374)
JOHNSON CRATING SERVICES LLC
5354 S I 35 (73143)
P.O. Box 95147 (73143-5147)
PHONE.................................405 672-7964
Brandon Pellow,
EMP: 5
SQ FT: 30,500
SALES (est): 1MM **Privately Held**
SIC: 4783 2441 2449 Packing & crating; nailed wood boxes & shook; rectangular boxes & crates, wood

(G-6375)
JOHNSON EXPLORATION COMPANY
Also Called: Jec Operating
921 E Britton Rd (73114-7802)
PHONE.................................405 235-4454
Russell V Johnson III, *Ch of Bd*
Diane Mier, *Corp Secy*
Frank L Johnson, *Shareholder*
EMP: 1
SQ FT: 2,200
SALES (est): 130K **Privately Held**
SIC: 1311 Crude petroleum production; natural gas production

(G-6376)
JOHNSON PLASTICS PLUS - OKLA
6100 Nw 2nd St Ste 1600 (73127-6534)
PHONE.................................800 654-4150
EMP: 2

SALES (est): 156K **Privately Held**
WEB: www.johnsonplastics.com
SIC: 3993 Signs & advertising specialties

(G-6377)
JOHNSON WELL LOGGING INC
6112 N State St (73122-7430)
P.O. Box 32071 (73123-0271)
PHONE.................................405 721-5989
Lonnie I Johnson, *President*
EMP: 3
SALES: 405K **Privately Held**
SIC: 1389 Well logging

(G-6378)
JOHNSTON TEST CELL GROUP LLC
1300 Se Grand Blvd (73129-6716)
PHONE.................................405 604-2804
Joyce L Johnston,
Stephen E Johnston,
EMP: 7
SQ FT: 8,400
SALES (est): 1.3MM **Privately Held**
SIC: 3441 Fabricated structural metal

(G-6379)
JOLEN OPERATING COMPANY (PA)
100 N Broadway Ave # 2460 (73102-8614)
PHONE.................................405 235-8444
David Fleischaker, *President*
John Bryant, *Vice Pres*
Rhonda Carretero, *CFO*
Don Mc Combs, *General Counsel*
EMP: 10
SQ FT: 6,000
SALES (est): 1.4MM **Privately Held**
SIC: 1311 Crude petroleum production; natural gas production

(G-6380)
JOLEN PRODUCTION COMPANY (PA)
100 N Broadway Ave # 2460 (73102-8829)
P.O. Box 1178 (73101-1178)
PHONE.................................405 235-8444
David S Fleischaker, *President*
EMP: 6 EST: 1980
SQ FT: 5,000
SALES (est): 919.4K **Privately Held**
SIC: 1311 Crude petroleum production; natural gas production

(G-6381)
JONES ENERGY INC
8308 N May Ave Ste 100 (73120-4551)
PHONE.................................405 832-5100
EMP: 1
SALES (corp-wide): 236.3MM **Publicly Held**
SIC: 1311 Crude petroleum & natural gas
PA: Jones Energy, Inc.
14301 Caliber Dr Ste 110
Oklahoma City OK 73134
512 328-2953

(G-6382)
JONES ENERGY INC (PA)
14301 Caliber Dr Ste 110 (73134-1016)
PHONE.................................512 328-2953
Carl F Giesler Jr, *CEO*
Jonny Jones, *Ch of Bd*
Kirk Goehring, *COO*
Jeffrey Tanner, *Exec VP*
Jeff Tanner, *Vice Pres*
EMP: 22
SQ FT: 43,000
SALES: 236.3MM **Publicly Held**
SIC: 1311 Crude petroleum & natural gas production

(G-6383)
JONES ENERGY FINANCE CORP
14301 Caliber Dr Ste 110 (73134-1016)
PHONE.................................512 328-2953
Carl F Giesler Jr, *CEO*
EMP: 1
SALES (est): 83.7K
SALES (corp-wide): 236.3MM **Publicly Held**
SIC: 1311 Crude petroleum & natural gas

HQ: Jones Energy Holdings, Llc
14301 Caliber Dr Ste 110
Oklahoma City OK 73134
512 328-2953

(G-6384)
JONES ENERGY HOLDINGS LLC (HQ)
Also Called: Jones Energy Limited
14301 Caliber Dr Ste 110 (73134-1016)
PHONE.................................512 328-2953
Michael Dean, *Superintendent*
Craig M Fleming, *Exec VP*
Robert J Brooks, *Exec VP*
Jody Crook, *Senior VP*
Hal Hawthorne, *Senior VP*
EMP: 44
SALES: 83.6MM
SALES (corp-wide): 236.3MM **Publicly Held**
SIC: 1311 1382 Crude petroleum production; natural gas production; oil & gas exploration services
PA: Jones Energy, Inc.
14301 Caliber Dr Ste 110
Oklahoma City OK 73134
512 328-2953

(G-6385)
JORDAN SERVICES INC
3129 Brookhollow Rd (73120-5208)
PHONE.................................405 748-3997
Jack Jordan, *President*
EMP: 1
SALES (est): 63K **Privately Held**
SIC: 1381 Drilling oil & gas wells

(G-6386)
JOULLIAN VINEYARDS LTD (PA)
5653 N Pennsylvania Ave (73112-7769)
PHONE.................................405 848-4585
Richard L Sias, *President*
Jeanette Sias, *Vice Pres*
EMP: 50
SQ FT: 3,500
SALES (est): 4.8MM **Privately Held**
SIC: 2084 Wines

(G-6387)
JOURNAL RECORD
2300 N Lincoln Blvd (73105-4805)
PHONE.................................405 524-7777
Russell Ray, *Editor*
Shelly Sanderson, *Accounts Exec*
Laura Watts, *Accounts Exec*
EMP: 3 EST: 2017
SALES (est): 130.8K **Privately Held**
SIC: 2711 Newspapers, publishing & printing

(G-6388)
JOURNAL RECORD PUBLISHING CO
101 N Robinson Ave # 101 (73102-5500)
PHONE.................................405 278-2848
Mary Me'lon, *Vice Pres*
EMP: 60
SQ FT: 13,000
SALES (est): 885K
SALES (corp-wide): 514.1MM **Privately Held**
SIC: 2721 2711 Magazines: publishing only, not printed on site; newspapers
HQ: Dolan Llc
222 S 9th St Ste 2300
Minneapolis MN 55402

(G-6389)
JPS LLC
8401 Timberwood Ln (73135-6111)
PHONE.................................405 535-5136
Jon North, *CEO*
EMP: 1
SALES (est): 71.8K **Privately Held**
SIC: 2752 Commercial printing, lithographic

(G-6390)
JUAN MANZO CUSTOM REFINISHING
9215 N Western Ave (73114-2623)
P.O. Box 14765 (73113-0765)
PHONE.................................405 848-3843
Juan Manzo, *Owner*
EMP: 9 EST: 1976

SALES (est): 350K **Privately Held**
SIC: 7641 2511 5932 2426 Furniture refinishing; furniture repair & maintenance; wood household furniture; antiques; hardwood dimension & flooring mills

(G-6391)
JUNK N LESLIES TRUNK LLC
3429 Partridge Rd (73120-8906)
PHONE.................................405 748-6702
Leslie Michele Cockerell, *Principal*
EMP: 3
SALES (est): 150K **Privately Held**
SIC: 3161 Trunks

(G-6392)
JUSTICE
1901 Nw Expwy St Ste 2086 (73118-9217)
PHONE.................................405 842-7180
EMP: 2
SALES (est): 67K **Privately Held**
SIC: 2361 Girls' & children's dresses, blouses & shirts

(G-6393)
K AND E FABRICATION
6401 Se 74th St (73135-1085)
PHONE.................................405 635-8552
Eddie Kozak, *Principal*
Mike Eskina, *Principal*
EMP: 9
SALES (est): 1.2MM **Privately Held**
SIC: 3444 Sheet metalwork

(G-6394)
K2 BATH SALTS ONLINE
2613 Nw 35th St (73112-7637)
PHONE.................................405 445-4295
EMP: 2 EST: 2017
SALES (est): 81.8K **Privately Held**
SIC: 2844 Bath salts

(G-6395)
KAISER-FRANCIS OIL COMPANY
Also Called: Cactus Drilling Company
8300 Sw 15th St (73128-9515)
PHONE.................................405 577-5347
Ron Tyson, *Manager*
EMP: 15
SALES (corp-wide): 678.5MM **Privately Held**
WEB: www.kfoc.net
SIC: 1382 1311 Oil & gas exploration services; crude petroleum & natural gas
HQ: Kaiser-Francis Oil Company
6733 S Yale Ave
Tulsa OK 74136
918 494-0000

(G-6396)
KAMS INC
1831 Nw 4th Dr (73106-2699)
PHONE.................................405 232-3103
Bobby Joe Horton, *President*
David D Wilhoite, *Principal*
Roma Lynn Horton, *Corp Secy*
Jeffrey B Horton, *Vice Pres*
Clay Buchanan, *Info Tech Mgr*
▼ EMP: 18 EST: 1970
SQ FT: 30,000
SALES (est): 3.5MM **Privately Held**
SIC: 3599 3714 Crankshafts & camshafts, machining; motor vehicle parts & accessories

(G-6397)
KAR GLO TUFFY
2618 S I 35 Service Rd # 106 (73129-6401)
PHONE.................................405 631-4091
Bill Blaylock Sr, *Owner*
EMP: 1
SALES (est): 37K **Privately Held**
SIC: 2842 Specialty cleaning, polishes & sanitation goods

(G-6398)
KARCHMER PIPE & SUPPLY CO INC
2100 Ne 4th St (73117-4404)
P.O. Box 36688 (73136-2688)
PHONE.................................405 236-3568
Toll Free:.................................877 -
Anthony James, *President*
Kimberly Kretchmar, *Corp Secy*
Richard Irwin, *Vice Pres*

GEOGRAPHIC SECTION

Oklahoma City - Oklahoma County (G-6428)

EMP: 5
SQ FT: 5,000
SALES (est): 935.7K **Privately Held**
SIC: 3312 Pipes, iron & steel

(G-6399)
KAT INDUSTRIES INC
Also Called: Kat Machine
5209 Sw 23rd St (73128-1843)
PHONE................405 702-1387
Keith A Thompson, *President*
Jeff Thompson, *Opers Mgr*
Austin Lowry, *Design Engr*
EMP: 32 EST: 1997
SALES (est): 10MM **Privately Held**
WEB: www.katmachine.com
SIC: 3599 Machine shop, jobbing & repair

(G-6400)
KAT MACHINE INCORPORATED
5209 Sw 23rd St (73128-1843)
P.O. Box 270656 (73137-0656)
PHONE................405 702-1387
Keith Thompson, *President*
EMP: 12
SALES (est): 3MM **Privately Held**
SIC: 3599 Machine shop, jobbing & repair

(G-6401)
KATHYS KLOSET INC
Also Called: Kathy's Clothing
1209 Nw 23rd St (73106-3615)
PHONE................405 524-9447
Greg Travis, *Owner*
EMP: 3
SALES (est): 162.9K **Privately Held**
SIC: 3961 5944 5961 5621 Jewelry apparel, non-precious metals; jewelry stores; jewelry, mail order; ready-to-wear apparel, women's
PA: Kathy's Kloset Inc
530 Nw 27th St
Oklahoma City OK 73103

(G-6402)
KATHYS KLOSET INC (PA)
Also Called: Kathy's On Paseo
530 Nw 27th St (73103-1312)
PHONE................405 521-0055
Kathleen Jacobson, *President*
John Jacobson, *Vice Pres*
Craig Travis, *Vice Pres*
EMP: 10
SQ FT: 7,000
SALES: 250K **Privately Held**
SIC: 3961 5947 Jewelry apparel, non-precious metals; costume jewelry, ex. precious metal & semiprecious stones; gift shop

(G-6403)
KCR WELDING INC
108 Se 24th St (73129-1610)
PHONE................405 619-0068
Robert Wilkins, *President*
Christopher Wilkins, *Vice Pres*
EMP: 2 EST: 2005
SALES: 250K **Privately Held**
SIC: 7692 Welding repair

(G-6404)
KEEPA LLC
101 N Robinson Ave # 1000 (73102-5504)
PHONE................405 235-4968
Carolyn Frans, *Principal*
EMP: 2
SALES (est): 120.2K **Privately Held**
SIC: 1382 Oil & gas exploration services

(G-6405)
KENDOL RESOURCES LLC
3239 Elmwood Ave (73116-3003)
PHONE................405 627-3523
Kenneth Townsend, *Principal*
EMP: 2
SALES (est): 139.5K **Privately Held**
SIC: 1382 Oil & gas exploration services

(G-6406)
KEY ENERGY SERVICES INC
4334 Nw Expwy St Ste 235 (73116-1516)
PHONE................405 843-6854
EMP: 31

SALES (corp-wide): 413.8MM **Publicly Held**
WEB: www.keyenergy.com
SIC: 1381 Drilling oil & gas wells
PA: Key Energy Services, Inc.
1301 Mckinney St Ste 1800
Houston TX 77010
713 651-4300

(G-6407)
KEY ENERGY SERVICES INC
1328 Se 25th St (73129-6434)
PHONE................713 651-4300
EMP: 2
SALES (corp-wide): 413.8MM **Publicly Held**
SIC: 1389 Servicing oil & gas wells
PA: Key Energy Services, Inc.
1301 Mckinney St Ste 1800
Houston TX 77010
713 651-4300

(G-6408)
KEY MAGAZINE
25 S Oklahoma Ave Ste 112 (73104-2422)
PHONE................405 602-3300
Frank Sims, *Principal*
EMP: 3
SALES (est): 194.8K **Privately Held**
SIC: 2721 Magazines: publishing only, not printed on site

(G-6409)
KEYMIAEE AERO-TECH INC
Also Called: Aero Tech
1300 Ne 4th St Ste 2 (73117-2409)
P.O. Box 11565 (73136-0565)
PHONE................405 235-5010
Kellie Saiedi, *President*
Michael Saiedi, *Vice Pres*
EMP: 10
SQ FT: 18,000
SALES (est): 2.1MM **Privately Held**
SIC: 3441 3728 3444 3412 Fabricated structural metal; aircraft parts & equipment; sheet metalwork; metal barrels, drums & pails; metal cans

(G-6410)
KEYS N MORE
900 W Reno Ave (73106-3204)
PHONE................405 415-1797
EMP: 2
SALES (est): 74.9K **Privately Held**
SIC: 3429 Keys, locks & related hardware

(G-6411)
KEYS N MORE
7420 S Shields Blvd (73149-1517)
PHONE................405 415-2105
EMP: 2
SALES (est): 77.8K **Privately Held**
SIC: 3429 Keys, locks & related hardware

(G-6412)
KEYSTONE FLEX ADMNSTRATORS LLC
2932 Nw 122nd St Ste 1 (73120-1955)
P.O. Box 5502, Edmond (73083-5502)
PHONE................405 285-1144
Kim Linn, *President*
EMP: 4
SALES (est): 191.5K **Privately Held**
WEB: www.keystoneflex.com
SIC: 6411 7372 Insurance claim processing, except medical; application computer software

(G-6413)
KEYSTONE LABELS LLC
5501 Sw 29th St (73179-7625)
PHONE................405 631-2341
Mike West, *Mng Member*
EMP: 7
SQ FT: 5,000
SALES (est): 780.1K **Privately Held**
WEB: www.keystonelabels.com
SIC: 2759 Flexographic printing

(G-6414)
KEYSTONE ROCK & EXCAVATION LLC
777 Nw 63rd St (73116-7601)
P.O. Box 54962 (73154-1962)
PHONE................405 608-7777

Jerry Winchester, *CEO*
Jerry L Winchester,
EMP: 1 EST: 2010
SALES (est): 65.2K
SALES (corp-wide): 2.4B **Publicly Held**
SIC: 1411 Trap rock, dimension-quarrying
HQ: Seventy Seven Operating Llc
777 Nw 63rd St
Oklahoma City OK 73116
405 608-7777

(G-6415)
KEYSTONE TAPE & LABEL INC
5501 Sw 29th St (73179-7625)
PHONE................405 631-2341
Mike West, *President*
EMP: 8
SQ FT: 4,700
SALES: 650K **Privately Held**
SIC: 2672 Labels (unprinted), gummed: made from purchased materials; tape, pressure sensitive: made from purchased materials

(G-6416)
KHODY LAND & MINERALS COMPANY
210 Park Ave Ste 900 (73102-5643)
P.O. Box 3102, Tulsa (74101-3102)
PHONE................405 949-2221
Ronnie K Irani, *CEO*
EMP: 2
SALES (est): 493.4K **Privately Held**
SIC: 1382 Oil & gas exploration services

(G-6417)
KIMRAY INC (PA)
52 Nw 42nd St (73118-8590)
P.O. Box 18949 (73154-0949)
PHONE................405 525-6601
Garman Kimmell, *President*
Thomas A Hill, *General Mgr*
Mike Hendrix, *District Mgr*
Brian Larrison, *District Mgr*
Mark Roberts, *District Mgr*
EMP: 222 EST: 1948
SQ FT: 76,000
SALES (est): 93.7MM **Privately Held**
WEB: www.kimray.com
SIC: 3829 3533 3822 3612 Measuring & controlling devices; oil field machinery & equipment; auto controls regulating residntl & coml environmt & applncs; transformers, except electric; pumps & pumping equipment; industrial valves

(G-6418)
KIMRAY INC
4305 N Santa Fe Ave (73118-8518)
PHONE................405 525-4200
EMP: 2
SALES (est): 119.5K **Privately Held**
SIC: 3829 Measuring & controlling devices

(G-6419)
KING ENERGY LLC
7025 N Robinson Ave (73116-9044)
PHONE................405 463-0909
Randy Moore, *Mng Member*
EMP: 2
SQ FT: 800
SALES (est): 281.1K **Privately Held**
SIC: 1382 Oil & gas exploration services

(G-6420)
KING GRAPHICS INC
1821 Linwood Blvd (73106-2625)
P.O. Box 17, Wheatland (73097-0017)
PHONE................405 232-2369
Mike King, *President*
EMP: 7
SQ FT: 2,000
SALES (est): 300K **Privately Held**
SIC: 7336 2791 2752 Commercial art & graphic design; typesetting; commercial printing, lithographic

(G-6421)
KING VALVE INC
4015 Se 29th St (73115-2641)
P.O. Box 15478 (73155-5478)
PHONE................405 672-0046
Chester Clarence King, *President*
Patricia King, *Corp Secy*
EMP: 12
SQ FT: 4,000

SALES (est): 1.3MM **Privately Held**
SIC: 3533 3494 3491 5082 Oil field machinery & equipment; valves & pipe fittings; industrial valves; oil field equipment

(G-6422)
KINGFISHER MIDSTREAM LLC
1833 S Morgan Rd (73128-7004)
PHONE................281 655-3200
EMP: 3
SALES (corp-wide): 100MM **Privately Held**
SIC: 1389 Processing service, gas
HQ: Kingfisher Midstream, Llc
15021 Katy Fwy Ste 400
Houston TX 77094
281 655-3200

(G-6423)
KINGSTON FLOORING LLC
100 N Rockwell Ave Ste 76 (73127-6108)
PHONE................405 470-3494
EMP: 6
SALES: 1MM **Privately Held**
SIC: 2273 1771 Mfg Carpets/Rugs Concrete Contractor

(G-6424)
KINRICH
8604 N Classen Blvd (73114-2151)
PHONE................405 842-4307
Kenny Richards, *Partner*
Neil Richards, *Partner*
EMP: 2
SQ FT: 2,850
SALES: 60K **Privately Held**
SIC: 2273 Rugs, hand & machine made

(G-6425)
KIRBY - SMITH MACHINERY INC (PA)
6715 W Reno Ave (73127-6590)
P.O. Box 270300 (73137-0300)
PHONE................888 861-0219
Ed Kirby, *President*
Brian Burris, *Manager*
Michael Fuentes, *Manager*
JD Young, *Info Tech Mgr*
▲ EMP: 154
SQ FT: 18,000
SALES: 575.9MM **Privately Held**
SIC: 7353 5082 7692 Heavy construction equipment rental; road construction equipment; general construction machinery & equipment; welding repair

(G-6426)
KIRKPATRICK OIL COMPANY INC (PA)
1001 W Wilshire Blvd # 202 (73116-7017)
PHONE................405 840-2882
Mike Steele, *President*
Christian Kessee, *President*
George Drew, *Vice Pres*
John Gelders, *Vice Pres*
Stephen Nath, *Vice Pres*
EMP: 19
SQ FT: 50,376
SALES (est): 16MM **Privately Held**
SIC: 1311 Crude petroleum production; natural gas production

(G-6427)
KIZE CONCEPTS INC
1740 Nw 3rd St (73106-2811)
PHONE................405 226-0701
Jeff M Ragan, *CEO*
Dillon Schooley, *Security Dir*
EMP: 10 EST: 2013
SALES (est): 1.4MM **Privately Held**
WEB: www.kizeconcepts.com
SIC: 2099 Box lunches, for sale off premises

(G-6428)
KLEEN PRODUCTS INC
Also Called: Joe's Hand Cleaner
8136 Sw 8th St (73128-4210)
P.O. Box 852100, Yukon (73085-2100)
PHONE................405 495-1168
Kenneth Newman, *President*
Mike Newman, *Vice Pres*
Blake Newman, *Plant Mgr*
K Blake Newman, *Warehouse Mgr*
EMP: 10
SQ FT: 22,500

Oklahoma City - Oklahoma County (G-6429)

GEOGRAPHIC SECTION

SALES (est): 2.3MM **Privately Held**
WEB: www.joeskleenproducts.com
SIC: **2841** Soap & other detergents

(G-6429)
KLX ENERGY SERVICES LLC
10625 Nw 4th St (73127)
PHONE.....................................405 838-1230
EMP: 2
SALES (corp-wide): 544MM **Publicly Held**
SIC: **1389** Fishing for tools, oil & gas field
HQ: Klx Energy Services Llc
3040 Post Oak Blvd # 1500
Houston TX 77056
832 844-1015

(G-6430)
KMH ENTERPRISES INC
Also Called: Kmh Labs
7717 W Britton Rd (73132-1514)
PHONE.....................................405 722-4600
Mervyn Hackney, *President*
EMP: 1
SALES: 150K **Privately Held**
SIC: **2834** Pharmaceutical preparations

(G-6431)
KOAX CORP
510 N Indiana Ave (73106-2607)
P.O. Box 1535 (73101-1535)
PHONE.....................................405 235-7178
Barry H Golsen, *President*
Kristopher Simmons, *Administration*
▲ EMP: 65
SQ FT: 55,000
SALES (est): 17.5MM
SALES (corp-wide): 2.5B **Privately Held**
SIC: **3443** Heat exchangers, condensers & components
HQ: The Climate Control Group Inc
7300 Sw 44th St
Oklahoma City OK 73179
405 745-6858

(G-6432)
KOBY OIL COMPANY LLC
114 Nw 8th St (73102-5805)
P.O. Box 1945 (73101-1945)
PHONE.....................................405 236-3551
Jennifer Hays, *Vice Pres*
Larry Hays,
EMP: 4
SQ FT: 10,500
SALES (est): 1.1MM **Privately Held**
SIC: **1381** Drilling oil & gas wells

(G-6433)
KODIAK CORP
9500 Cedar Lake Ave (73114-7807)
PHONE.....................................405 478-1900
Ralph L Harvey, *President*
Robert R Hale, *Admin Sec*
EMP: 8
SALES (est): 600K **Privately Held**
SIC: **1389** **1382** Servicing oil & gas wells; oil & gas exploration services

(G-6434)
KONECRANES INC
3208 E I 240 Service Rd (73135-1729)
PHONE.....................................405 208-8808
Gary Fisher, *Manager*
EMP: 5
SALES (corp-wide): 3.6B **Privately Held**
SIC: **3536** Hoists, cranes & monorails
HQ: Konecranes, Inc.
4401 Gateway Blvd
Springfield OH 45502

(G-6435)
KRATOS UNMNNED ARIAL SYSTEMS I
7501 Sw 29th St Ste 200 (73179-5214)
PHONE.....................................405 248-9545
Peter Pepaj, *Branch Mgr*
EMP: 6 **Publicly Held**
SIC: **3089** Pallets, plastic
HQ: Kratos Unmanned Aerial Systems, Inc.
5381 Raley Blvd
Sacramento CA 95838
916 431-7977

(G-6436)
KUSTOM GRAPHICS
1223 Sw 59th St (73109-4906)
PHONE.....................................405 635-8009
Arturo Rodriquez, *Owner*
EMP: 1
SALES (est): 85.1K **Privately Held**
SIC: **3993** Signs & advertising specialties

(G-6437)
KUSTOM SIGNS
1223 Sw 59th St (73109-4906)
PHONE.....................................405 635-8009
EMP: 1
SALES (est): 46K **Privately Held**
SIC: **3993** Signs & advertising specialties

(G-6438)
L & L WELDING INC
4201 S High Ave (73129-5427)
PHONE.....................................405 631-4939
Lee Steeds, *President*
EMP: 1
SQ FT: 1,500
SALES (est): 80K **Privately Held**
SIC: **7692** Welding repair

(G-6439)
L I B VENTURES COMPANY INC
5821 Nw Grand Blvd Ste B (73118-1203)
P.O. Box 12958 (73157-2958)
PHONE.....................................405 659-8800
William C Bradford Sr, *President*
Lucille I Bradford, *Vice Pres*
Anita M Holmes, *Treasurer*
William C Bradford Jr, *Admin Sec*
EMP: 3
SALES (est): 320K **Privately Held**
SIC: **1311** Crude petroleum production; natural gas production

(G-6440)
L M R GENERAL CONTRACTING LLC
3801 S Eastern Ave (73129-7923)
P.O. Box 54885 (73154-1885)
PHONE.....................................405 605-6547
Laure Resides,
Devin Resides,
EMP: 4
SALES (est): 481.5K **Privately Held**
SIC: **2851** Paints & allied products

(G-6441)
L S MARANN PUBLISHING
2608 Abbey Rd (73120-3403)
P.O. Box 20514 (73156-0514)
PHONE.....................................405 751-9369
Mary Anne Puckett, *Owner*
EMP: 1
SALES (est): 66K **Privately Held**
SIC: **2741** Miscellaneous publishing

(G-6442)
L3 TECHNOLOGIES INC
6700 Se 59th St (73135-5524)
PHONE.....................................405 601-0874
Wayne Beckler, *Branch Mgr*
EMP: 5
SALES (corp-wide): 6.8B **Publicly Held**
SIC: **3699** Flight simulators (training aids), electronic
HQ: L3 Technologies, Inc.
600 3rd Ave Fl 34
New York NY 10016
212 697-1111

(G-6443)
LA-Z-BOY INCORPORATED
3400 W Memorial Rd (73120-0911)
PHONE.....................................405 417-5704
EMP: 2
SALES (corp-wide): 1.7B **Publicly Held**
SIC: **2512** Upholstered household furniture
PA: La-Z-Boy Incorporated
1 Lazboy Dr
Monroe MI 48162
734 242-1444

(G-6444)
LA-Z-BOY INCORPORATED
3738 W Reno Ave (73107-6622)
PHONE.....................................405 951-1437
Desiree Garrett, *Sales Staff*
EMP: 2

SALES (corp-wide): 1.7B **Publicly Held**
SIC: **2512** Upholstered household furniture
PA: La-Z-Boy Incorporated
1 Lazboy Dr
Monroe MI 48162
734 242-1444

(G-6445)
LAFARGE NORTH AMERICA INC
2728 Sw 20th St (73108-2402)
PHONE.....................................405 686-0320
Larry Gilmore, *Manager*
EMP: 3
SALES (corp-wide): 4.5B **Privately Held**
SIC: **3273** Ready-mixed concrete
HQ: Lafarge North America Inc.
8700 W Bryn Mawr Ave
Chicago IL 60631
773 372-1000

(G-6446)
LAKESIDE WOMENS IMAGING
10900 Hefner Pointe Dr # 501 (73120-5082)
PHONE.....................................405 418-0302
EMP: 2
SALES (est): 186.5K **Privately Held**
SIC: **3829** Medical diagnostic systems, nuclear

(G-6447)
LAMAR ENTERPRISES INC
Also Called: Marathon Electric Co
4300 W River Park Dr (73108-1730)
P.O. Box 271565 (73137-1565)
PHONE.....................................405 682-5511
Larry Stanley, *President*
EMP: 20
SQ FT: 28,000
SALES (est): 3.8MM **Privately Held**
SIC: **3612** **7629** Transformers, except electric; electrical equipment repair, high voltage

(G-6448)
LANSING BUILDING PRODUCTS INC
500 N Ann Arbor Ave (73127-6312)
PHONE.....................................405 943-2493
Joe West, *Principal*
EMP: 8
SALES (corp-wide): 356.7MM **Privately Held**
WEB: www.lansingbp.com
SIC: **5211** **3089** Siding; windows, plastic
PA: Lansing Building Products, Llc
2221 Edward Holland Dr
Richmond VA 23230
804 266-8893

(G-6449)
LARIAT SERVICES INC (HQ)
Also Called: Chapparal Drilling Fluids
123 Robert S Kerr Ave (73102-6406)
P.O. Box 108827 (73101-8827)
PHONE.....................................405 753-5500
James D Bennett, *Principal*
Glen Cantwell, *Manager*
▲ EMP: 26
SALES (est): 834.3MM
SALES (corp-wide): 266.8MM **Publicly Held**
SIC: **1382** Oil & gas exploration services
PA: Sandridge Energy, Inc.
123 Robert S Kerr Ave
Oklahoma City OK 73102
405 429-5500

(G-6450)
LASER SOURCE LLC (PA)
7925 N Hudson Ave Ste C (73114-3133)
P.O. Box 16181 (73113-2181)
PHONE.....................................405 843-2528
James Bell, *Partner*
Mike Bell, *Partner*
Juan A Morales, *Partner*
EMP: 12 EST: 1995
SQ FT: 2,800
SALES (est): 1.9MM **Privately Held**
WEB: www.lasersource.net
SIC: **3955** Print cartridges for laser & other computer printers

(G-6451)
LASER SOURCE LLC
4937 Nw 29th St (73127-1756)
PHONE.....................................405 330-4442
Michael Bell, *Partner*
EMP: 9
SALES (corp-wide): 1.9MM **Privately Held**
WEB: www.lasersource.net
SIC: **3955** Print cartridges for laser & other computer printers
PA: Laser Source, L.L.C.
7925 N Hudson Ave Ste C
Oklahoma City OK 73114
405 843-2528

(G-6452)
LASSER INC
3244 Nw Grand Blvd (73116-3019)
PHONE.....................................405 842-4010
John Vance, *President*
EMP: 3
SALES (est): 504.4K **Privately Held**
SIC: **1382** Oil & gas exploration services

(G-6453)
LASSO OIL & GAS LLC
14313 N May Ave Ste 100 (73134-5003)
PHONE.....................................405 753-5300
Frank Harrison, *Principal*
EMP: 1
SALES (est): 170K **Privately Held**
SIC: **1382** Oil & gas exploration services

(G-6454)
LAST DITCH INDUSTRIES LLC
744 Culbertson Dr (73105-8412)
PHONE.....................................405 609-2317
Christopher S Dorr, *Principal*
EMP: 1
SALES (est): 46.2K **Privately Held**
SIC: **3999** Manufacturing industries

(G-6455)
LASTING IMPRESSIONS GIFTS INC
Also Called: Cordray Candle Company
3900 S Noma Rd (73150-2802)
PHONE.....................................405 732-2401
EMP: 2
SALES: 310K **Privately Held**
SIC: **3999** **5023** **5999** Mfg Misc Products Whol Homefurnishings Ret Misc Merchandise

(G-6456)
LATEESHA D HUNTER PC
1230 Sw 89th St Ste A (73139-9106)
P.O. Box 12742 (73157-2742)
PHONE.....................................405 534-2200
Lateesha Hunter, *Principal*
EMP: 2
SALES (est): 159.6K **Privately Held**
WEB: www.lateeshahunter.com
SIC: **2759** Screen printing

(G-6457)
LAVI WASH
9124 N Council Rd (73132-1347)
PHONE.....................................405 470-0895
EMP: 2 EST: 2008
SALES (est): 139.3K **Privately Held**
SIC: **3589** Car washing machinery

(G-6458)
LBR SMITH LLC
2205 S Agnew Ave (73108-6213)
PHONE.....................................405 601-7051
Adam White, *Vice Pres*
EMP: 2
SALES (est): 178.6K **Privately Held**
SIC: **3441** Fabricated structural metal

(G-6459)
LBZ PRINTS
11941 N Pennsylvania Ave (73120-7826)
PHONE.....................................405 905-1607
Travis Zackery, *Principal*
EMP: 2
SALES (est): 83.9K **Privately Held**
SIC: **2752** Commercial printing, lithographic

GEOGRAPHIC SECTION

Oklahoma City - Oklahoma County (G-6487)

(G-6460)
LDS BUILDING SPECIALTIES LLC
5229 Nw 5th St Ste A (73127-5802)
PHONE..............................405 917-9901
Strider Outlander, *General Mgr*
Doug Daniels, *Sales Staff*
Tony Struthers, *Sales Staff*
Ron Barrus,
EMP: 6
SQ FT: 12,000
SALES (est): 930.4K **Privately Held**
SIC: 2431 5251 Doors, wood; windows & window parts & trim, wood; builders' hardware

(G-6461)
LEAM DRILLING SYSTEMS LLC
9733 Nw 4th St (73127-2951)
P.O. Box 11938, New Iberia LA (70562-1938)
PHONE..............................405 440-9376
Willie Girlinghouse, *Manager*
EMP: 14
SALES (corp-wide): 13.2MM **Privately Held**
WEB: www.leam.net
SIC: 1381 Drilling oil & gas wells
PA: Leam Drilling Systems Llc
3114 W Old Spanish Trl
New Iberia LA 70560
337 367-3552

(G-6462)
LEASEHOLD MANAGEMENT CORP (PA)
1141 Se Grand Blvd # 101 (73129-6756)
PHONE..............................405 670-5535
Bill E Sidwell, *President*
Lela Sidwell, *Treasurer*
EMP: 4
SQ FT: 1,500
SALES (est): 1.6MM **Privately Held**
SIC: 1311 Crude petroleum production

(G-6463)
LEDETS WELDING SERVICE INC
4725 Se 59th St (73135-4418)
PHONE..............................405 610-2299
EMP: 1 **EST:** 2014
SALES (est): 87.8K **Privately Held**
WEB: www.ledetwelding.com
SIC: 7692 Welding repair

(G-6464)
LEGEND ENERGY SERVICES LLC (PA)
5801 Broadway Ext Ste 210 (73118-7491)
PHONE..............................405 600-1264
Trey Ingram, *CEO*
Matt Goodson, *COO*
Joe Orosco, *Opers Mgr*
Frankie Goad, *Foreman/Supr*
Josh Pruett, *CFO*
EMP: 20
SQ FT: 8,400
SALES: 150MM **Privately Held**
WEB: www.legendenergyservices.com
SIC: 1389 Oil field services

(G-6465)
LEGGETT & PLATT INCORPORATED
Also Called: Leggett & Platt 0004
6828 Melrose Ln (73127-6299)
PHONE..............................405 787-1212
Mike Powelson, *Treasurer*
EMP: 7
SQ FT: 73,596
SALES (corp-wide): 4.7B **Publicly Held**
WEB: www.leggett.com
SIC: 2515 Bedsprings, assembled
PA: Leggett & Platt, Incorporated
1 Leggett Rd
Carthage MO 64836
417 358-8131

(G-6466)
LEONARD SKODAK DISTRIBUTORS
Also Called: Watkins Products
2516 N Adams Ave (73127-1528)
PHONE..............................405 787-8044
Leonard Skodac, *Owner*
Marlene Payton, *Owner*
EMP: 1
SALES (est): 65.6K **Privately Held**
SIC: 2836 Extracts

(G-6467)
LETICA CORPORATION
7428 Sw 29th St (73179-5202)
PHONE..............................405 745-2781
Tony Gose, *Human Res Mgr*
Thomas Scott, *Manager*
EMP: 105
SQ FT: 81,228 **Publicly Held**
SIC: 3089 Plastic containers, except foam
HQ: Letica Corporation
52585 Dequindre Rd
Rochester Hills MI 48307
248 652-0557

(G-6468)
LETTERING EXPRESS
241 W Wilshire Blvd Ste A (73116-7742)
PHONE..............................405 260-9022
EMP: 2
SALES (est): 83.9K **Privately Held**
SIC: 2752 Commercial printing, lithographic

(G-6469)
LETTERING EXPRESS OK INC
2130 W Reno Ave (73107-7028)
PHONE..............................405 235-8999
Charlie Trujillo, *CEO*
Richard Braun, *Principal*
Justin Lombardi, *Principal*
Brett Newman, *Graphic Designe*
EMP: 30
SALES (est): 1.7MM **Privately Held**
SIC: 7389 3993 Lettering service; signs & advertising specialties

(G-6470)
LEWIS FRICTION PRODUCTS LLC
3601 S Byers Ave (73129-2438)
P.O. Box 95089 (73143-5089)
PHONE..............................405 634-5401
Charles A Lewis,
Andrew Lewis,
Tom Lewis,
▲ **EMP:** 10
SALES: 800K **Privately Held**
SIC: 3533 Oil & gas field machinery

(G-6471)
LEWIS MANUFACTURING CO LLC (PA)
3601 S Byers Ave (73129-2438)
P.O. Box 95089 (73143-5089)
PHONE..............................405 634-5401
Hilda Lewis, *President*
Charles A Lewis, *Vice Pres*
Kristen Del Nero, *Controller*
Lynn Manning, *Manager*
▲ **EMP:** 7
SQ FT: 1,500
SALES (est): 4.8MM **Privately Held**
WEB: www.lewismfg.com
SIC: 3533 3315 3199 Oil field machinery & equipment; steel wire & related products; safety belts, leather

(G-6472)
LIBERTY TRANSMISSION PARTS (HQ)
Also Called: Wdks
301 N Western Ave (73106-7639)
PHONE..............................405 236-8749
David Neal, *President*
EMP: 3
SQ FT: 35,000
SALES (est): 1.5MM **Privately Held**
SIC: 5531 3714 Batteries, automotive & truck; motor vehicle transmissions, drive assemblies & parts

(G-6473)
LIBERTY TRANSMISSION PARTS
Also Called: Macho Muffler
701 Sw 89th St (73139-9335)
PHONE..............................405 634-3450
Danny Miller, *Manager*
EMP: 5
SQ FT: 6,400 **Privately Held**
SIC: 3714 7537 Motor vehicle transmissions, drive assemblies & parts; automotive transmission repair shops
HQ: Liberty Transmission Parts
301 N Western Ave
Oklahoma City OK 73106
405 236-8749

(G-6474)
LIFE LIFT SYSTEMS INC
2805 S Purdue Ave (73128)
PHONE..............................904 635-8231
Levi Wilson, *CEO*
EMP: 12
SQ FT: 12,000
SALES: 4MM **Privately Held**
SIC: 2514 2392 5712 Beds, including folding & cabinet, household: metal; pillows, bed: made from purchased materials; beds & accessories

(G-6475)
LIFETONE TECHNOLOGY INC
755 Research Pkwy Ste 125 (73104-3631)
P.O. Box 18122 (73154-0122)
PHONE..............................405 200-1555
Cindy Sewell, *Principal*
Elizabeth Norris, *Engineer*
EMP: 4
SALES (est): 337.9K **Privately Held**
SIC: 5063 3669 Electrical apparatus & equipment; emergency alarms

(G-6476)
LIGHTHOUSE GRAPHICS
212 Corona Dr (73149-1926)
PHONE..............................405 635-0022
Joseph Assifuah, *Owner*
EMP: 2 **EST:** 2015
SALES (est): 151.3K **Privately Held**
SIC: 2759 Screen printing

(G-6477)
LILLIAN STRICKLER LIGHTING
617 Nw 23rd St (73103-1415)
P.O. Box 23233 (73123-2233)
PHONE..............................405 528-4476
Norma Bagley, *President*
EMP: 4
SQ FT: 3,600
SALES (est): 498.1K **Privately Held**
WEB: www.lillianstrickler.com
SIC: 5719 3645 Lamps & lamp shades; residential lighting fixtures

(G-6478)
LINCOLN ELECTRIC HOLDINGS INC
3860 Harmon Ave (73179-8604)
PHONE..............................405 681-0183
Alvin Bennett, *Branch Mgr*
EMP: 9
SALES (corp-wide): 3B **Publicly Held**
SIC: 3548 2813 Arc welding generators, alternating current & direct current; electrodes, electric welding; industrial gases
PA: Lincoln Electric Holdings, Inc.
22801 Saint Clair Ave
Cleveland OH 44117
216 481-8100

(G-6479)
LINE X PRTCTIVE CTNGS OKLA LLC
4928 W I 40 Service Rd (73128-1203)
PHONE..............................405 232-4994
Paul Reber,
Melanie Reber,
EMP: 13
SQ FT: 9,000
SALES (est): 860K **Privately Held**
SIC: 7699 2891 Tank repair & cleaning services; adhesives & sealants

(G-6480)
LINEAR HEALTH SCIENCES LLC
5333 Wisteria Dr (73142-1818)
PHONE..............................415 388-2794
Ryan Dennis, *CEO*
Daniel Clark, *COO*
EMP: 3
SALES (est): 189.8K **Privately Held**
SIC: 3841 IV transfusion apparatus

(G-6481)
LINN ENERGY INC
14000 Quail Springs Pkwy # 5000 (73134-2619)
PHONE..............................405 241-2100
Don Davis, *General Mgr*
Donald Davis, *Engineer*
Bill Shanahan, *Manager*
Kevin Davis, *Analyst*
EMP: 71
SALES (corp-wide): 517.8MM **Privately Held**
SIC: 1311 Crude petroleum & natural gas
HQ: Linn Energy, Inc.
600 Travis St
Houston TX 77002
281 840-4000

(G-6482)
LIQUEFIED PETRO GAS BD OKLA
3815 N Santa Fe Ave # 117 (73118-8528)
PHONE..............................405 521-2458
Bill Glass, *Administration*
Carolline Inman, *Admin Sec*
Lisa Burlingame, *Administration*
EMP: 10
SALES (est): 1MM **Privately Held**
SIC: 2911 9199 Petroleum refining;
HQ: Executive Office Of The State Of Oklahoma
2300 N Lincoln Blvd
Oklahoma City OK 73105

(G-6483)
LITTLE GIANT PUMP COMPANY LLC
301 N Macarthur Blvd (73127-6616)
P.O. Box 12010 (73157-2010)
PHONE..............................405 947-2511
Todd W Herrick, *Mng Member*
Ted Foti,
Norman Heidebrecht,
Daryl McDonald,
James Nicholson,
◆ **EMP:** 500 **EST:** 1940
SQ FT: 395,000
SALES (est): 79.3MM
SALES (corp-wide): 1.3B **Publicly Held**
WEB: www.franklin-electric.com
SIC: 3561 Pumps, domestic: water or sump; cylinders, pump
PA: Franklin Electric Co., Inc.
9255 Coverdale Rd
Fort Wayne IN 46809
260 824-2900

(G-6484)
LK CBD LLC
8117 N Classen Blvd (73114-2135)
PHONE..............................405 220-3502
EMP: 2
SALES (est): 89.4K **Privately Held**
SIC: 3999

(G-6485)
LOCKDOWN LTD CO
Also Called: Industrial Metal Fab and Sup
301 Nw 70th St Ste B (73116-7805)
PHONE..............................405 605-6161
Scott Jones IV,
EMP: 12
SQ FT: 6,500
SALES: 1MM **Privately Held**
SIC: 3699 3444 Security devices; hoods, range: sheet metal

(G-6486)
LOCKHEED MARTIN
F35 Ppe Oak Holow Industr (73149)
PHONE..............................405 606-3988
EMP: 2
SALES (est): 97.1K **Privately Held**
SIC: 3721 Aircraft

(G-6487)
LOCKHEED MARTIN CORPORATION
4243 Will Rogers Pkwy (73108-2039)
PHONE..............................405 917-3863
EMP: 430 **Publicly Held**
SIC: 3721 Research & development on aircraft by the manufacturer

PA: Lockheed Martin Corporation
6801 Rockledge Dr
Bethesda MD 20817

(G-6488)
LOFLAND CO
2101 S Villa Ave (73108-6046)
PHONE..................................405 631-9555
EMP: 2
SALES (est): 86.6K **Privately Held**
SIC: 3441 Structural Metal Fabrication

(G-6489)
LOGIC ENERGY SOLUTIONS LLC
3939 N Walnut Ave (73105-3746)
P.O. Box 2718 (73101-2718)
PHONE..................................405 601-9037
John Moore, *CEO*
Trey Moore, *President*
EMP: 2 EST: 2012
SALES (est): 412K **Privately Held**
SIC: 3589 1389 Water treatment equipment, industrial; oil field services

(G-6490)
LOGISTICS MANAGEMENT COMPANY
7626 Sw 89th St (73169-3717)
PHONE..................................405 633-1201
Kris Kelley, *Owner*
EMP: 1 EST: 2017
SALES (est): 55.3K **Privately Held**
SIC: 3711 5012 7389 Automobile assembly, including specialty automobiles; automobile bodies, passenger car, not including engine, etc.; automobiles & other motor vehicles; automobile auction; commercial vehicles;

(G-6491)
LONDON MONTIN HARBERT INC
6303 Waterford Blvd # 220 (73118-1119)
PHONE..................................405 879-1900
Fax: 405 879-1966
EMP: 5
SALES (est): 530K **Privately Held**
SIC: 1382 Oil/Gas Exploration Services

(G-6492)
LONE STAR INDUSTRIES INC
4601 Ne 4th St (73117-7616)
PHONE..................................405 670-0677
Don Prater, *Manager*
EMP: 3
SQ FT: 8,542
SALES (corp-wide): 395.5MM **Privately Held**
WEB: www.buzziunicemusa.com
SIC: 3241 Portland cement
HQ: Lone Star Industries Inc
10401 N Meridian St # 120
Indianapolis IN 46290
317 706-3314

(G-6493)
LOPEZ FOODS INC
9500 Nw 4th St (73127-2961)
PHONE..................................405 499-0131
EMP: 260
SALES (corp-wide): 324MM **Privately Held**
WEB: www.lopezfoods.com
SIC: 2013 Prepared beef products from purchased beef; sausages from purchased meat; bacon, side & sliced: from purchased meat
PA: Lopez Foods, Inc.
3817 Nw Expwy Ste 900
Oklahoma City OK 73112
405 789-7500

(G-6494)
LOPEZ FOODS INC (PA)
3817 Nw Expwy Ste 900 (73112-1487)
PHONE..................................405 789-7500
Ed Sanchez, *CEO*
James D English, *COO*
Jim Edwards, *Assistant VP*
Kevin Nanke, *Vice Pres*
Chance Vorpahl, *Export Mgr*
EMP: 20 EST: 1989
SALES (est): 324MM **Privately Held**
SIC: 2013 2011 Prepared beef products from purchased beef; sausages from purchased meat; bacon, side & sliced: from purchased meat; meat packing plants

(G-6495)
LOPEZ FOODS INC
9500 Nw 4th St (73127-2961)
PHONE..................................405 789-7500
Don Lopez, *Owner*
Michelle Wagner, *Human Res Mgr*
EMP: 500
SALES (corp-wide): 324MM **Privately Held**
SIC: 2013 Prepared beef products from purchased meat; bacon, side & sliced: from purchased meat
PA: Lopez Foods, Inc.
3817 Nw Expwy Ste 900
Oklahoma City OK 73112
405 789-7500

(G-6496)
LORTZ R MICHAEL OFFICE
200 N Harvey Ave Ste 617 (73102-4005)
PHONE..................................405 236-3230
R Michael Lortz, *Owner*
EMP: 1
SALES (est): 91K **Privately Held**
SIC: 1382 Oil & gas exploration services

(G-6497)
LOUD CITY PHARMACEUTICAL
9113 Ne 23rd St (73141-3011)
PHONE..................................405 259-9014
EMP: 3
SALES (est): 162K **Privately Held**
SIC: 2834 Pharmaceutical preparations

(G-6498)
LSB CHEMICAL LLC (HQ)
3503 Nw 63rd St Ste 500 (73116-2238)
P.O. Box 754 (73101-0754)
PHONE..................................405 235-4546
Mark Behrman, *President*
John Diesch, *Exec VP*
Michael Foster, *General Counsel*
◆ EMP: 12
SALES (est): 161.3MM
SALES (corp-wide): 365MM **Publicly Held**
SIC: 2819 2873 2892 Sulfuric acid, oleum; nitric acid; ammonium nitrate, ammonium sulfate; explosives
PA: Lsb Industries, Inc.
3503 Nw 63rd St Ste 500
Oklahoma City OK 73116
405 235-4546

(G-6499)
LSB INDUSTRIES INC (PA)
3503 Nw 63rd St Ste 500 (73116-2238)
PHONE..................................405 235-4546
Richard W Roedel, *Ch of Bd*
Mark T Behrman, *President*
John Burns, *Exec VP*
John H Diesch, *Exec VP*
John Diesch, *Exec VP*
EMP: 29
SALES: 365MM **Publicly Held**
WEB: www.lsbindustries.com
SIC: 2873 Nitrogenous fertilizers; ammonia & ammonium salts; ammonium nitrate, ammonium sulfate

(G-6500)
LUCAS HOLDINGS LLC
Also Called: Lucas Color Card
4900 N Santa Fe Ave (73118-7912)
PHONE..................................405 524-1811
Ron Ferguson, *President*
Michael Blake, *Mfg Mgr*
Russell Walker, *Sales Mgr*
Kevin Doke, *Sales Staff*
Mindy Wilson, *Manager*
◆ EMP: 50
SQ FT: 30,000
SALES: 10MM **Privately Held**
SIC: 3699 5065 5199 Security control equipment & systems; security control equipment & systems; cards, plastic: unprinted

(G-6501)
LUFKIN INDUSTRIES LLC
2300 S I 35 Service Rd (73129-6466)
P.O. Box 95205 (73143-5205)
PHONE..................................405 677-0567
Jeff Weaver, *Manager*
EMP: 10
SQ FT: 10,500
SALES (corp-wide): 95.2B **Publicly Held**
SIC: 5084 3462 Pumps & pumping equipment; gear & chain forgings
HQ: Lufkin Industries, Llc
601 S Raguet St
Lufkin TX 75904
936 634-2211

(G-6502)
LURE PROMO
8520 Nw 118th St (73162-1034)
PHONE..................................405 664-3415
EMP: 1
SALES (est): 47K **Privately Held**
SIC: 3949 Sporting & athletic goods

(G-6503)
LUTHER SIGN CO
4425 Sw 34th St (73119-2405)
P.O. Box 950117 (73195-0117)
PHONE..................................405 681-6535
Bob Luther, *President*
EMP: 3 EST: 1977
SQ FT: 7,000
SALES (est): 418.4K **Privately Held**
SIC: 7389 3993 Sign painting & lettering shop; signs & advertising specialties

(G-6504)
LUXE KITCHEN & BATH
219 W Wilshire Blvd 101a (73116-7767)
P.O. Box 165, Coyle (73027-0165)
PHONE..................................405 471-5577
Bill Livingston, *Principal*
EMP: 2
SALES (est): 175.5K **Privately Held**
WEB: www.luxeok.com
SIC: 3429 Cabinet hardware

(G-6505)
M & D OILFIELD SERVICES
1607 Se 25th St (73129-7609)
PHONE..................................405 677-5720
Melvin Carr, *Owner*
EMP: 1
SALES (est): 200K **Privately Held**
SIC: 1389 5082 Oil field services; oil field equipment

(G-6506)
M & M FABRICATION & SERVICE
1033 Se 36th St (73129)
P.O. Box 95363 (73143-5363)
PHONE..................................405 677-1982
Boyd Mankin, *President*
Carolyn Mankin, *Corp Secy*
EMP: 4
SQ FT: 4,000
SALES (est): 581.3K **Privately Held**
SIC: 3533 3444 Oil field machinery & equipment; sheet metalwork

(G-6507)
M L S OIL PROPERTIES
12101 N Macarthur Blvd # 171 (73162-1800)
PHONE..................................405 720-8867
Michael Sias, *Owner*
EMP: 3
SALES (est): 229.5K **Privately Held**
SIC: 1382 Oil & gas exploration services

(G-6508)
M M ENERGY INC
13927 Qail Pinte Dr Ste A (73134)
PHONE..................................405 463-3355
EMP: 2
SALES (est): 150.9K **Privately Held**
SIC: 1389 Construction, repair & dismantling services

(G-6509)
M P READY MIX INC
5800 S High Ave (73129-5614)
PHONE..................................405 631-6814
Mike Hill, *Manager*
EMP: 3 **Privately Held**
WEB: www.srmokc.com

SIC: 3273 Ready-mixed concrete
PA: M P Ready Mix Inc
1400 Holly Ave
Yukon OK 73099

(G-6510)
M-D BUILDING PRODUCTS INC (PA)
4041 N Santa Fe Ave (73118-8512)
P.O. Box 25188 (73125-0188)
PHONE..................................405 528-4411
Loren A Plotkin, *CEO*
Richard Gaugler, *Chairman*
Ryan Plotkin, *COO*
Kipp Collins, *Exec VP*
Larry Sanford, *Exec VP*
◆ EMP: 500 EST: 1919
SQ FT: 481,000
SALES (est): 248MM **Privately Held**
WEB: www.mdteam.com
SIC: 3442 Weather strip, metal; moldings & trim, except automobile: metal

(G-6511)
M-D PLASTICS GROUP
4041 N Santa Fe Ave (73118-8512)
PHONE..................................503 981-3726
Breanna Kirtley, *Principal*
EMP: 3
SALES (est): 179.4K **Privately Held**
SIC: 3089 Injection molding of plastics

(G-6512)
M-O MASONRY LLC
413 Sw 64th Pl (73139-7009)
PHONE..................................405 219-4220
EMP: 2
SALES (est): 62.3K **Privately Held**
SIC: 2024 Yogurt desserts, frozen

(G-6513)
MABELS FASHION ALTERATION
5603 S Western Ave (73109-4512)
PHONE..................................405 605-4558
EMP: 1
SALES (est): 50.2K **Privately Held**
SIC: 2299 Jute & flax textile products

(G-6514)
MACH RESOURCES LLC
14201 Wireless Way # 300 (73134-2521)
P.O. Box 54525 (73154-1525)
PHONE..................................405 252-8100
Tom L Ward, *CEO*
EMP: 40
SALES (est): 273.9K **Privately Held**
SIC: 1382 Geological exploration, oil & gas field

(G-6515)
MACKELLAR SERVICES INC (HQ)
7100 N Classen Blvd # 100 (73116-7151)
PHONE..................................405 848-2877
James P Mackellar Jr, *President*
EMP: 6
SQ FT: 2,800
SALES (est): 6.1MM
SALES (corp-wide): 40.1MM **Privately Held**
SIC: 1389 Servicing oil & gas wells
PA: Mackellar, Inc
809 Nw 57th St
Oklahoma City OK
405 848-2877

(G-6516)
MAESE WELDING SERVICE LLC
2513 Pine Ave (73128-3038)
PHONE..................................405 606-4619
EMP: 1 EST: 2014
SALES (est): 53K **Privately Held**
SIC: 7692 Welding Repair

(G-6517)
MAGNAT-FAIRVIEW LLC
222 W Memorial Rd (73114-2300)
PHONE..................................413 593-5742
James Kolodziej, *Engineer*
Sean Parnell, *Engineer*
Lou Bargatti, *Design Engr*
Bill Blackak, *Manager*
Denis Laflamme, *Manager*
EMP: 15 EST: 2017

GEOGRAPHIC SECTION

Oklahoma City - Oklahoma County (G-6545)

SALES: 8MM
SALES (corp-wide): 2.9B Privately Held
SIC: 3599 3554 Machine shop, jobbing & repair; paper industries machinery
HQ: Maxcess Americas, Inc.
222 W Memorial Rd
Oklahoma City OK 73114
405 755-1600

(G-6518)
MAMMOTH ENERGY PARTNERS LLC (PA)
14201 Caliber Dr Ste 300 (73134-1017)
PHONE.................................405 265-4600
Arty Straehla, CEO
Mammoth E LLC, General Ptnr
Mark Layton, CFO
Randy Ransom, Technology
EMP: 18
SALES: 359.9MM Publicly Held
SIC: 1381 1389 Drilling oil & gas wells; construction, repair & dismantling services; oil field services

(G-6519)
MAMMOTH ENERGY SERVICES INC (HQ)
14201 Caliber Dr Ste 300 (73134-1017)
PHONE.................................405 608-6007
Arty Straehla, CEO
Marc McCarthy, Ch of Bd
Mark Layton, CFO
Desirae Morrison, Manager
EMP: 12 EST: 2016
SALES: 625MM
SALES (corp-wide): 359.9MM Publicly Held
SIC: 1389 Construction, repair & dismantling services; oil field services
PA: Mammoth Energy Partners Llc
14201 Caliber Dr Ste 300
Oklahoma City OK 73134
405 265-4600

(G-6520)
MAR-K SPECIALIZED MFG INC
6625 W Wilshire Blvd (73132-5449)
PHONE.................................405 721-7945
David Hill, CEO
Mark Sharp, Human Res Mgr
EMP: 31 EST: 1977
SQ FT: 31,895
SALES (est): 4.9MM Privately Held
SIC: 3465 Body parts, automobile: stamped metal; moldings or trim, automobile: stamped metal

(G-6521)
MARATHON OIL COMPANY
7301 Nw Expressway # 225 (73132-1501)
P.O. Box 68, Houston TX (77001-0068)
PHONE.................................318 624-0874
Mike Wiskosske, Branch Mgr
Bruce Mc Ininch, Manager
Adam Traylor, Supervisor
Jody Harryman, Technician
EMP: 20
SALES (corp-wide): 5.1B Publicly Held
SIC: 5541 2911 Gasoline service stations; liquefied petroleum gases, LPG
HQ: Marathon Oil Company
5555 San Felipe St B1
Houston TX 77056
713 629-6600

(G-6522)
MARDAV INDUSTRIES CO LLC
3030 Nw Expwy Ste 200 (73112-5466)
PHONE.................................855 248-2220
EMP: 1
SALES (est): 50.5K Privately Held
SIC: 3999 Manufacturing industries

(G-6523)
MAREXCO INC
3033 Nw 63rd St Ste 151 (73116-3639)
P.O. Box 21598 (73156-1598)
PHONE.................................405 286-5657
James Lorenz, Principal
EMP: 2
SALES (est): 160.9K Privately Held
SIC: 1382 Oil & gas exploration services

(G-6524)
MARIE ANASTASIA LABS INC
Also Called: Diabetic Pure Skin Therapy
6520 N Western Ave # 100 (73116-7334)
PHONE.................................405 840-0123
EMP: 7
SQ FT: 2,000
SALES (est): 500K Privately Held
SIC: 2834 Pharmaceutical Preparations

(G-6525)
MARIE THIERREY LUCINDA
Also Called: Made By ME Publications
414 Betty Ln (73110-2110)
PHONE.................................405 623-9431
Lucinda Marie Thierry, Owner
EMP: 1
SALES (est): 66.5K Privately Held
SIC: 2741 Miscellaneous publishing

(G-6526)
MARK C BLAKLEY
Also Called: Mark's Sand & Gravel
9200 S Villa Ave (73159-6745)
PHONE.................................405 245-3606
Mark C Blakley, Principal
EMP: 3
SALES (est): 159K Privately Held
SIC: 1442 Construction sand & gravel

(G-6527)
MARK HOLLOWAY INC
100 S Vermont Ave (73107-6526)
PHONE.................................405 833-7947
Graydon P Sheen, President
Andy Sheen, Vice Pres
EMP: 3 EST: 1955
SQ FT: 7,000
SALES (est): 300K Privately Held
SIC: 1311 Crude petroleum production; natural gas production

(G-6528)
MARK W MCGUFFEE INC (PA)
Also Called: Dgmi.com
11408 N Grove Ave (73162-3529)
PHONE.................................405 603-8113
Mark W McGuffee, President
Mark McGuffee, President
EMP: 1 EST: 1995
SQ FT: 2,400
SALES (est): 212.2K Privately Held
SIC: 2759 Commercial printing

(G-6529)
MARLIN OIL CORPORATION
9500 Cedar Lake Ave (73114-7896)
P.O. Box 14630 (73113-0630)
PHONE.................................405 478-1900
Ralph L Harvey, President
Larry Gordon, Vice Pres
Robert Hale, Treasurer
EMP: 22 EST: 1972
SQ FT: 7,500
SALES (est): 2.3MM Privately Held
SIC: 1311 Crude petroleum production; natural gas production

(G-6530)
MARPRO LABEL INC
1612 Se Grand Blvd Ste A (73129-7800)
P.O. Box 96888 (73143-6888)
PHONE.................................405 672-3344
Robert Spencer, President
Steven Spencer, Vice Pres
EMP: 5
SQ FT: 6,000
SALES (est): 367.5K Privately Held
SIC: 2759 2672 Labels & seals: printing; coated & laminated paper

(G-6531)
MARSHALL MINERALS LLC
2825 Nw Grand Blvd Apt 23 (73116-4024)
PHONE.................................405 848-5715
EMP: 2 EST: 2018
SALES (est): 92.6K Privately Held
SIC: 2048 Prepared feeds

(G-6532)
MARTIN BIONICS INNOVATIONS LLC
214 E Main St (73104-4221)
P.O. Box 2391 (73101-2391)
PHONE.................................405 850-2069
Jay Martin, President
EMP: 1
SALES (est): 63.6K Privately Held
SIC: 8731 3559 Commercial physical research; robots, molding & forming plastics

(G-6533)
MARTIN MARIETTA MATERIALS INC
8524 S Wstn Ave Ste 118 (73139)
PHONE.................................405 799-7799
Deanna Loveland, Manager
EMP: 2 Publicly Held
SIC: 1422 Crushed & broken limestone
PA: Martin Marietta Materials Inc
2710 Wycliff Rd
Raleigh NC 27607

(G-6534)
MARTINDALE CONSULTANTS INC
Also Called: Complete Computer Company
4242 N Meridian Ave (73112-2457)
PHONE.................................405 728-3003
Patrick Martindale, President
Jean Martindale, Treasurer
Todd Attalla, Manager
Laura Rowe Melman, Exec Dir
EMP: 39
SQ FT: 1,100
SALES (est): 1.5MM Privately Held
SIC: 8742 1389 Management consulting services; oil consultants

(G-6535)
MASCOTS ETC INC
7212 Walnut Creek Dr (73142-2519)
PHONE.................................405 722-3406
Marjorie Ainsworth, President
Steve Ainsworth, Vice Pres
EMP: 1
SALES (est): 83.6K Privately Held
SIC: 2389 Costumes

(G-6536)
MASON PIPE & SUPPLY COMPANY
3212 Nw 50th St (73112-5325)
PHONE.................................405 942-6926
Larry Triplett, President
EMP: 5
SALES (est): 890K Privately Held
SIC: 5082 1389 Oil field equipment; well plugging & abandoning, oil & gas

(G-6537)
MAVERICK TECHNOLOGIES LLC
2800 Purdue Dr (73128-5803)
PHONE.................................405 680-0100
Lawrence Kincheloe, Engineer
Bill Bennett,
Michael Baker,
Bruce Davis,
Jim Delbridge,
EMP: 12
SQ FT: 5,000
SALES (est): 2.8MM Privately Held
SIC: 3629 3699 Power conversion units, a.c. to d.c.: static-electric; electrical equipment & supplies

(G-6538)
MAXCESS AMERICAS INC (DH)
Also Called: Fife
222 W Memorial Rd (73114-2300)
PHONE.................................405 755-1600
Odd Joergenrud, CEO
Greg Jehlik, President
Doug Knudtson, COO
Scott Braun, Engineer
Hengzhi Yao, Engineer
▲ EMP: 5
SALES: 100MM
SALES (corp-wide): 2.9B Privately Held
SIC: 3554 3565 Paper industries machinery; packaging machinery

(G-6539)
MAXCESS INTERNATIONAL CORP (DH)
222 W Memorial Rd (73114-2300)
P.O. Box 26508 (73126-0508)
PHONE.................................405 755-1600
Thomas Varner, District Mgr
Marcel Hage, Vice Pres
Tom Herold, Vice Pres
Karen Delong, Mfg Dir
Jacquelyn Adams, Buyer
◆ EMP: 4
SQ FT: 100,000
SALES (est): 192.3MM
SALES (corp-wide): 2.9B Privately Held
SIC: 3554 3565 6719 Paper industries machinery; packaging machinery; investment holding companies, except banks
HQ: Maxcess International Holding Corp.
222 W Memorial Rd
Oklahoma City OK 73114
405 755-1600

(G-6540)
MAXCESS INTL HOLDG CORP (DH)
222 W Memorial Rd (73114-2300)
PHONE.................................405 755-1600
Odd Joergenrud, CEO
Doug Knudtson, COO
Sean Craig, Vice Pres
Dave Hawkins, CFO
EMP: 8
SALES (est): 214.2MM
SALES (corp-wide): 2.9B Privately Held
SIC: 3554 3565 6719 Paper industries machinery; packaging machinery; investment holding companies, except banks
HQ: Wh Acquisitions, Inc.
800 Concar Dr Ste 100
San Mateo CA 94402
650 358-5000

(G-6541)
MAXIMUS EXPLORATION LLC
13903 Quail Pointe Dr (73134-1002)
PHONE.................................405 239-2829
Gregg McDonald, Exploration
EMP: 6 EST: 2011
SALES (est): 537K Privately Held
SIC: 1382 Geological exploration, oil & gas field

(G-6542)
MAXX MACHINE INC
3940 Sw 113th St (73173-8387)
P.O. Box 890232 (73189-0232)
PHONE.................................405 692-8300
Don Workman, President
EMP: 10
SQ FT: 19,000
SALES (est): 1.4MM Privately Held
WEB: www.maxxmachine.com
SIC: 3599 Machine shop, jobbing & repair

(G-6543)
MAYCO INC
3501 E Reno Ave (73117-6611)
P.O. Box 94070 (73143-4070)
PHONE.................................405 677-5969
Dwight Brown, President
Tom Hughes, VP Sales
Robert Wheeler, Manager
Aaron Youngblood, Shareholder
EMP: 48
SALES (est): 13MM Privately Held
SIC: 3321 3533 3498 3494 Cast iron pipe & fittings; oil & gas field machinery; fabricated pipe & fittings; valves & pipe fittings; oil field equipment

(G-6544)
MAZZELLA CO
301 S Eagle Ln (73128-4222)
PHONE.................................405 423-6283
EMP: 5
SALES (est): 493.7K Privately Held
SIC: 3496 Miscellaneous fabricated wire products

(G-6545)
MCCLARIN PLASTICS LLC
3949 Nw 36th St (73112-2953)
PHONE.................................877 912-6297
Jerry Armstrong, President
EMP: 22
SALES (corp-wide): 64MM Privately Held
SIC: 3089 Plastic containers, except foam
PA: Mcclarin Plastics, Llc.
15 Industrial Dr
Hanover PA 17331
717 637-2241

Oklahoma City - Oklahoma County (G-6546)

GEOGRAPHIC SECTION

(G-6546)
MCCURDY AND ASSOCIATES LLC
11300 N Penn Ave Apt 175 (73120-7775)
PHONE..................................405 317-4178
Kathie McCurdy, *Mng Member*
EMP: 2
SALES: 100K **Privately Held**
SIC: 3993 7389 Signs & advertising specialties;

(G-6547)
MCDERMOTT ELECTRIC LLC
328 S Eagle Ln Ste F (73128-4224)
P.O. Box 1898, Bethany (73008-1898)
PHONE..................................405 603-4665
EMP: 13
SALES (est): 3MM **Privately Held**
SIC: 3699 Mfg Electrical Equipment/Supplies

(G-6548)
MCKINLEY HARDWOODS LLC
1815 S Agnew Ave (73108-2444)
P.O. Box 82215 (73148-0215)
PHONE..................................800 522-3305
Mike McKinley, *President*
Scott Jackson, *Vice Pres*
McKinley Hardwoods,
EMP: 8
SALES (est): 1MM **Privately Held**
SIC: 3949 Sporting & athletic goods

(G-6549)
MCLANE FOODSERVICE DIST INC
Also Called: Mbm
1301 Se 89th St (73149-4604)
PHONE..................................405 632-0118
Dennis Sandlin, *Manager*
EMP: 250
SALES (corp-wide): 327.2B **Publicly Held**
SIC: 5147 5141 5046 2013 Meat brokers; food brokers; commercial cooking & food service equipment; sausages & other prepared meats
HQ: Mclane Foodservice Distribution, Inc.
2641 Meadowbrook Rd
Rocky Mount NC 27801
252 985-7200

(G-6550)
MCMURTRY CABINET SHOP
1429 Sw 54th St (73119-6211)
PHONE..................................405 627-3275
William McMurtry, *Owner*
EMP: 1
SALES (est): 75K **Privately Held**
SIC: 5712 2431 Cabinet work, custom; millwork

(G-6551)
MD-ADVANTAGES LLC
5300 Ryan Dr (73135-4324)
PHONE..................................405 996-6125
William O'Donnell, *CEO*
EMP: 1
SALES (est): 110K **Privately Held**
SIC: 2599 7389 Hospital furniture, except beds;

(G-6552)
ME OIL CO
105 N Hudson Ave Ste 310 (73102-4801)
PHONE..................................405 232-9541
Don Waggoner, *President*
Mark Waggoner, *Vice Pres*
Helen Stroz, *Admin Sec*
EMP: 3
SALES (est): 230K **Privately Held**
SIC: 1389 Oil consultants

(G-6553)
ME3 COMMUNICATIONS COMPANY LLC
Also Called: Kxok TV
13121 Box Canyon Rd (73142-6203)
PHONE..................................405 834-8992
Jack Mills,
EMP: 1
SALES (est): 120K **Privately Held**
SIC: 3663 Radio & TV communications equipment

(G-6554)
MECHANICAL SALES OKLAHOMA INC
5229 Nw 5th St Ste B (73127-5802)
PHONE..................................405 681-1971
Cheryl Carry, *President*
Brad L Carry, *Vice Pres*
Mark Miller, *Branch Mgr*
▲ EMP: 7
SQ FT: 7,500
SALES (est): 1.5MM **Privately Held**
SIC: 3585 Parts for heating, cooling & refrigerating equipment

(G-6555)
MEDIA RESOURCES INC
Also Called: Media Technology
3731 Sw 29th St (73119-1248)
PHONE..................................405 682-4400
Tom Hale, *President*
Rocco Santoro, *Principal*
Betty Hickman, *Vice Pres*
Susan Codding, *Sales Staff*
▼ EMP: 22
SQ FT: 36,000
SALES (est): 3.7MM **Privately Held**
SIC: 2679 2657 Paper products, converted; paperboard backs for blister or skin packages

(G-6556)
MEDIA TECHNOLOGY INCORPORATED
3731 Sw 29th St (73119-1248)
PHONE..................................405 682-4400
Betty Hickman, *President*
Rocco Santoro, *Vice Pres*
EMP: 25
SQ FT: 24,000
SALES (est): 3.2MM **Privately Held**
SIC: 2761 5111 5112 7389 Manifold business forms; printing & writing paper; business forms; design services

(G-6557)
MEDICAL CSMTC ELCTRLYSIS CLNIC
9809 Lakeshore Dr (73120-2221)
PHONE..................................405 755-7599
Patty Peters, *Owner*
EMP: 1
SALES (est): 31.5K **Privately Held**
SIC: 7231 3634 Depilatory salon, electrolysis; massage machines, electric, except for beauty/barber shops

(G-6558)
MEDLINE INDUSTRIES
8001 Sw 47th St Ste B (73179-4604)
PHONE..................................405 745-9977
EMP: 3 EST: 2009
SALES (est): 68.5K **Privately Held**
SIC: 3999 Barber & beauty shop equipment

(G-6559)
MEDTRONIC USA INC
14000 Quail Springs Pkwy (73134-2620)
PHONE..................................405 302-5301
Attebery Curtis, *Sales Staff*
Brad Hawley, *Sales Staff*
Frank Klaus, *Manager*
Justin Fuller, *Director*
EMP: 17 **Privately Held**
WEB: www.medtronic.com
SIC: 3841 Surgical & medical instruments
HQ: Medtronic Usa, Inc.
710 Medtronic Pkwy
Minneapolis MN 55432
763 514-4000

(G-6560)
MEDUNISON LLC
701 Ne 10th St Ste 302 (73104-5033)
PHONE..................................405 271-9900
David Kendrick, *President*
Mary Mikelk, *Vice Pres*
Derek Degrace, *Manager*
Wesley Wilkey, *Info Tech Mgr*
EMP: 45 EST: 2000
SALES (est): 2.8MM **Privately Held**
WEB: www.medunison.com
SIC: 7371 7372 Computer software development; software programming applications; prepackaged software; business oriented computer software

(G-6561)
MEL ROBINSON
Also Called: Mr Windshield Repair
21 Ne 65th St (73105-1234)
PHONE..................................405 843-7529
Mel Robinson, *Owner*
EMP: 1
SALES: 50K **Privately Held**
SIC: 3231 Windshields, glass: made from purchased glass

(G-6562)
MELODY HOUSE INC
819 Nw 92nd St (73114-2701)
PHONE..................................405 840-3383
Stephen Fite, *President*
Gladys Lecrone, *Shareholder*
EMP: 5 EST: 1964
SQ FT: 4,500
SALES: 709.2K **Privately Held**
SIC: 3652 Master records or tapes, preparation of; magnetic tape (audio): prerecorded

(G-6563)
MELTON CO INC
Also Called: Major Lab Mfg
4408 N Sewell Ave (73118-8005)
PHONE..................................405 524-2281
Fax: 405 524-2281
EMP: 7
SALES (corp-wide): 5.5MM **Privately Held**
SIC: 2514 2522 2515 Mfg Metal Household Furn Mfg Nonwood Office Furn Mfg Mattress/Bedsprings
PA: Melton Co., Inc
4408 N Sewell Ave
Oklahoma City OK
405 235-7481

(G-6564)
MEMORIAL AUTO SUPPLY INC
709 N Morgan Rd (73127-7159)
PHONE..................................405 324-5400
Rex Crumpton, *Owner*
EMP: 10
SALES (corp-wide): 4.4MM **Privately Held**
SIC: 3519 3599 Diesel engine rebuilding; machine shop, jobbing & repair
PA: Memorial Auto Supply, Inc.
6303 S 40th West Ave
Tulsa OK
918 446-1828

(G-6565)
MENTORHOPE LLC
Also Called: Mentorhope Publishing
5915 Nw 23rd St (73127-1251)
PHONE..................................405 752-0940
Tom Haste,
EMP: 1
SALES (est): 65.1K **Privately Held**
SIC: 2731 Book publishing

(G-6566)
MERCER VALVE CO INC (PA)
9609 Nw 4th St (73127-2962)
P.O. Box 270970 (73137-0970)
PHONE..................................405 470-5213
Richard Taylor, *President*
Derek Bryant, *Mfg Mgr*
Beau Bellard, *Opers Staff*
Reanna Patton, *Mfg Staff*
Amanda Morriss, *Production*
▼ EMP: 44
SQ FT: 10,000
SALES (est): 46.3MM **Privately Held**
SIC: 3494 3491 Valves & pipe fittings; industrial valves

(G-6567)
MERIDIAN BRICK LLC
Also Called: Boral Bricks Studio
2912 W Hefner Rd (73120-6204)
PHONE..................................405 749-9900
Ben Griswold, *Manager*
EMP: 4
SALES (corp-wide): 441MM **Privately Held**
SIC: 5211 3251 3255 Brick; brick & structural clay tile; clay refractories
PA: Meridian Brick Llc
6455 Shiloh Rd D
Alpharetta GA 30005
770 645-4500

(G-6568)
MERIDIAN PRESS PUBLICATIONS
2932 Nw 122nd St Ste H (73120-1955)
PHONE..................................405 751-2342
John Orban, *Principal*
EMP: 1
SALES (est): 121.9K **Privately Held**
WEB: www.meridianpress.com
SIC: 2731 2721 Books: publishing only; periodicals

(G-6569)
MERRITTS MONOGRAMS LLC
2608 Nw 69th St (73116-4716)
PHONE..................................918 346-2757
Jack Merritt, *Principal*
EMP: 1
SALES (est): 60.1K **Privately Held**
SIC: 2395 Embroidery & art needlework

(G-6570)
MESH NETWORKS LLC
6701 Broadway Ext Ste 310 (73116-8213)
PHONE..................................832 230-8074
Martin Scheid, *President*
Donald H Kelly, *Principal*
Richard Heath, *Vice Pres*
Leon Hubby, *Vice Pres*
EMP: 5 EST: 2006
SALES (est): 550.7K **Privately Held**
WEB: www.themeshnetworks.com
SIC: 7372 Business oriented computer software

(G-6571)
MESQUITE MINERALS INC
6801 Broadway Ext Ste 300 (73116-9037)
PHONE..................................405 848-7551
Cameron R McLain, *CEO*
EMP: 2
SALES (est): 104.6K **Privately Held**
SIC: 3295 Minerals, ground or otherwise treated

(G-6572)
METAL BUILDINGS INC
7000 S Eastern Ave (73149-5223)
P.O. Box 95998 (73143-5998)
PHONE..................................405 672-7676
W H Braum, *President*
A R Ginn, *President*
Greg Byers, *Manager*
W Anthony Bostwick, *Officer*
Mary Braum, *Officer*
EMP: 35
SALES (est): 5.8MM **Privately Held**
SIC: 3448 Prefabricated metal buildings

(G-6573)
METAL CHECK INC
5700 S High Ave (73129-5612)
PHONE..................................405 636-1916
Diana Salazar, *President*
EMP: 10
SQ FT: 1,200
SALES (est): 1.9MM **Privately Held**
SIC: 4953 3341 Recycling, waste materials; secondary nonferrous metals

(G-6574)
METAL CONTAINER CORPORATION
3713 Harmon Ave (73179-8620)
PHONE..................................405 680-3140
Robert Deguilio, *Mfg Staff*
Louis Lackey, *Engineer*
Patrick Voeller, *Engineer*
Mike Vanhorn, *Manager*
EMP: 130
SQ FT: 127,912
SALES (corp-wide): 1.5B **Privately Held**
SIC: 3411 Can lids & ends, metal
HQ: Metal Container Corporation
3636 S Geyer Rd Ste 100
Saint Louis MO 63127
314 577-2000

GEOGRAPHIC SECTION
Oklahoma City - Oklahoma County (G-6604)

(G-6575)
METALTECH INC
7700 Melrose Ln (73127-6002)
P.O. Box 270664 (73137-0664)
PHONE.....................405 659-9911
Derick Stephens, *President*
Dale Stevens, *Vice Pres*
Tri Le, *Manager*
EMP: 12
SALES: 750K **Privately Held**
WEB: www.metaltechinc.com
SIC: 3444 1721 Sheet metal specialties, not stamped; industrial painting

(G-6576)
METAVANTE HOLDINGS LLC
1200 Sovereign Row (73108-1823)
PHONE.....................800 554-8095
EMP: 6
SALES (corp-wide): 6.6B **Publicly Held**
SIC: 3578 Mfg Calculating Equipment
HQ: Metavante Holdings, Llc
    601 Riverside Ave
    Jacksonville FL 32204
    904 438-6000

(G-6577)
METHENY CONCRETE PRODUCTS INC
504 N Sunnylane Rd (73117)
PHONE.....................405 947-5566
EMP: 32
SALES (corp-wide): 19.2MM **Privately Held**
SIC: 3273 Ready-mixed concrete
PA: Metheny Concrete Products Inc
    1617 S Lowery St
    Oklahoma City OK 73129
    405 947-5566

(G-6578)
METHENY CONCRETE PRODUCTS INC (PA)
1617 S Lowery St (73129-8343)
PHONE.....................405 947-5566
Richard Metheny, *President*
Matt Metheny, *Assistant VP*
Randy Dunn, *Vice Pres*
Connie Metheny, *Vice Pres*
Debbie McFall, *Financial Exec*
EMP: 55
SQ FT: 18,000
SALES (est): 19.2MM **Privately Held**
SIC: 3273 Ready-mixed concrete

(G-6579)
METRO FAMILY MAGAZINE
Also Called: Inprint Publishing
318 Nw 13th St (73103-3709)
PHONE.....................405 601-2081
Sarah Taylor, *President*
Lindsay Cuomo, *Editor*
Erin Page, *Editor*
Callie Collins, *Mktg Dir*
Kathy Alberty, *Manager*
EMP: 8
SALES: 650K **Privately Held**
WEB: www.metrofamilymagazine.com
SIC: 2721 Magazines: publishing only, not printed on site

(G-6580)
METRO PORTABLE BUILDINGS
8201 S Shartel Ave (73139-9315)
PHONE.....................405 921-5688
Frank A Hogan II, *Principal*
EMP: 2 EST: 2010
SALES (est): 127.2K **Privately Held**
SIC: 3448 Buildings, portable: prefabricated metal

(G-6581)
METRO PUBLISHING LLC
Also Called: Oklahoma City's Nursing Times
4501 N Classen Blvd # 10 (73118-4822)
P.O. Box 239, Mustang (73064-0239)
PHONE.....................405 631-5100
Amanda Miller, *Advt Staff*
Steven R Eldridge,
EMP: 4
SALES: 600K **Privately Held**
SIC: 2711 Newspapers, publishing & printing

(G-6582)
MEWBOURNE OIL COMPANY
211 N Robinson Ave N2000 (73102-7186)
PHONE.....................405 235-6374
Tony D Phillips, *Manager*
EMP: 10
SALES (corp-wide): 458.1MM **Privately Held**
WEB: www.mewbourne.net
SIC: 1382 Oil & gas exploration services
HQ: Mewbourne Oil Company
    3620 Old Bullard Rd
    Tyler TX 75701
    903 561-2900

(G-6583)
MFG UNLIMITED LLC
3101 S Council Rd (73179-4497)
PHONE.....................405 788-9567
EMP: 1 EST: 2018
SALES (est): 39.6K **Privately Held**
SIC: 3999 Manufacturing industries

(G-6584)
MFP PETROLEUM LTD PARTNERSHIP
Also Called: Warren, Robert H & Assoc
430 Nw 5th St Ste A (73102-3011)
PHONE.....................405 728-5588
Joe Warren, *Managing Prtnr*
Robt H Warren,
EMP: 3
SQ FT: 2,000
SALES (est): 205.8K **Privately Held**
SIC: 1311 Crude petroleum production; natural gas production

(G-6585)
MICAHEL A SLEEM
6303 N Portland Ave (73112-1467)
PHONE.....................405 947-6288
Michael A Sleem, *Principal*
EMP: 2
SALES (est): 148.1K **Privately Held**
SIC: 1382 Oil & gas exploration services

(G-6586)
MICCO AIRCRAFT COMPANY INC
1302 Nw 84th St (73114-1529)
PHONE.....................918 336-4700
EMP: 20
SALES: 1,000K **Privately Held**
SIC: 3728 3724 Aircraft Manufacturing And Service

(G-6587)
MICHAEL GIPSON LLC
Also Called: G2solutions
4820 Casper Dr (73111-6266)
PHONE.....................405 819-6349
Michael Gipson, *Principal*
EMP: 1
SALES (est): 57.4K **Privately Held**
SIC: 2522 Office desks & tables: except wood

(G-6588)
MID CONTINENT MINERALS INC
120 N Robinson Ave 1350w (73102-7509)
PHONE.....................405 272-0204
EMP: 1 EST: 1992
SALES (est): 140K **Privately Held**
SIC: 1382 Oil/Gas Exploration Services

(G-6589)
MID-AMERICA MIDSTREAM GAS
6100 N Western Ave (73118-1044)
P.O. Box 18955 (73154-0955)
PHONE.....................405 935-8000
Aubrey K McClendon, *CEO*
J Michael Stice, *President*
Steven Dixon, *Senior VP*
Douglas Jacobson, *Senior VP*
Domenic J Dell'osso Jr, *CFO*
EMP: 1
SALES (est): 189.1K **Publicly Held**
SIC: 1311 Natural gas production
HQ: Semgas Lp
    880 Plainview Rd
    Sherman TX 75092

(G-6590)
MID-AMERICAN OIL CO INC
6801 Broadway Ext Ste 300 (73116-9037)
PHONE.....................405 848-7551
Mason McLain, *President*
Jerry Crow, *Corp Secy*
R T McLain, *Vice Pres*
EMP: 8
SALES (est): 528.7K **Privately Held**
SIC: 1311 Crude petroleum production; natural gas production

(G-6591)
MID-CENTRAL ENERGY SVCS LLC
727 N Morgan Rd (73127-7142)
PHONE.....................405 815-4041
Nick Armoudian,
Antranik Armoudian,
EMP: 99
SQ FT: 4,500
SALES (est): 37.8MM **Privately Held**
SIC: 1389 Servicing oil & gas wells

(G-6592)
MID-CON DATA SERVICES INC
13431 Broadway Ext # 115 (73114-2224)
PHONE.....................405 478-1234
Randal Allen, *President*
Donald Jones, *Vice Pres*
Ronald Mantel, *Admin Sec*
EMP: 20
SQ FT: 16,800
SALES (est): 2.7MM **Privately Held**
SIC: 1382 7375 7389 4226 Seismograph surveys; information retrieval services; document & office record destruction; document & office records storage

(G-6593)
MID-STATES OILFIELD MCH LLC
6501 Interpace St (73135-4444)
PHONE.....................405 605-5656
Dona Badger, *Office Mgr*
Kayla Wallis,
EMP: 20
SALES (est): 1.6MM **Privately Held**
SIC: 1389 Oil field services

(G-6594)
MIDAMERICA WATER TECHNOLOGIES
8003 N Wilshire Ct Ste E (73132-5470)
P.O. Box 720715 (73172-0715)
PHONE.....................405 613-0250
Gary Arnold, *President*
Jimmy Barton, *Vice Pres*
EMP: 3
SALES (est): 468.5K **Privately Held**
WEB: www.midamericawatertech.com
SIC: 2899 3589 5084 Desalter kits, sea water; sewage & water treatment equipment; pollution control equipment, water (environmental)

(G-6595)
MIDCO SAND PUMP MANUFACTURING
1200 Se 34th St Ste 44 (73129-6700)
PHONE.....................405 824-2620
EMP: 2
SALES (est): 118K **Privately Held**
SIC: 3999 Manufacturing industries

(G-6596)
MIDCON MIDSTREAM LP
123 Robert S Kerr Ave (73102-6406)
PHONE.....................405 429-5500
EMP: 1
SALES (est): 91.5K
SALES (corp-wide): 266.8MM **Publicly Held**
SIC: 1311 Crude petroleum production
PA: Sandridge Energy, Inc.
    123 Robert S Kerr Ave
    Oklahoma City OK 73102
    405 429-5500

(G-6597)
MIDLAND VINYL PRODUCTS INC
Also Called: Mvp
11607 N Santa Fe Ave A (73114-8110)
PHONE.....................405 755-4972
Gwynn McDowell, *President*
Mike McDowell, *Vice Pres*
EMP: 5
SQ FT: 4,500
SALES (est): 914K **Privately Held**
SIC: 2824 3446 Vinyl fibers; fences, gates, posts & flagpoles

(G-6598)
MIDSTATE MFG & MKTG INC
12501 N Santa Fe Ave (73114-3804)
PHONE.....................405 751-6227
Steve E Wells, *President*
Len Scantling, *Exec VP*
Travis Rucker, *Vice Pres*
Dianna Jordan, *Treasurer*
Heather Esau, *Controller*
EMP: 30
SQ FT: 14,000
SALES (est): 6.5MM **Privately Held**
SIC: 3441 Fabricated structural metal

(G-6599)
MIDWEST BAKERS SUPPLY CO INC
2716 Nw 10th St (73107-5410)
PHONE.....................405 942-3489
Jane Schmitz, *President*
Susan Hoefer, *Vice Pres*
EMP: 4
SALES (est): 540K **Privately Held**
SIC: 5046 5149 2099 2087 Bakery equipment & supplies; flavourings & fragrances; food preparations; flavoring extracts & syrups

(G-6600)
MIDWEST CITY PUB SCHOOLS I-52
Also Called: Miid Del Print Shop
607 W Rickenbacker Dr (73110-5650)
PHONE.....................405 739-1665
Ron Starns, *Principal*
EMP: 3
SALES (corp-wide): 122.4MM **Privately Held**
SIC: 2621 Printing paper
PA: Midwest City Public Schools I-52
    7217 Se 15th St
    Oklahoma City OK 73110
    405 737-4461

(G-6601)
MIDWEST COPY AND PRINTING
7031 E Reno Ave (73110-4442)
PHONE.....................405 737-8311
Fereidoun Saabat, *Owner*
EMP: 3
SALES (est): 170K **Privately Held**
SIC: 2752 Commercial printing, offset

(G-6602)
MIDWEST DECALS LLC
6001 Sw 12th St Apt 1328 (73128-1885)
PHONE.....................405 787-8747
Max M Muller Jr, *President*
Max Muller Jr, *Mng Member*
EMP: 5 EST: 1972
SALES (est): 1.4MM **Privately Held**
SIC: 2752 3993 2396 Decals, lithographed; signs & advertising specialties; automotive & apparel trimmings

(G-6603)
MIDWEST FABRICATORS LLC
10521 N Garnett St (73116-6009)
PHONE.....................405 755-7799
Nathan Dills, *Mng Member*
EMP: 8
SALES (est): 1.3MM **Privately Held**
WEB: www.acpsheetmetal.com
SIC: 3444 Sheet metal specialties, not stamped

(G-6604)
MIDWEST MACHINE & COMPRSR CO
601 Se 29th St (73129-4713)
P.O. Box 94311 (73143-4311)
PHONE.....................405 634-5454
Henry E Malone Jr, *President*
Beverly Benham, *Corp Secy*
EMP: 8
SQ FT: 13,000

Oklahoma City - Oklahoma County (G-6605)

SALES (est): 500K **Privately Held**
SIC: 3599 Custom machinery; machine shop, jobbing & repair

(G-6605)
MIDWEST MED ISTPES NCLEAR PHRM
5401 N Portland Ave # 330 (73112-2121)
PHONE.....................405 604-4438
George Chacko, *Principal*
EMP: 4
SALES (est): 310.3K **Privately Held**
SIC: 2834 Pharmaceutical preparations

(G-6606)
MIDWEST PUBLICATION
500 N Meridian Ave (73107-5700)
PHONE.....................405 948-6506
EMP: 1 EST: 2017
SALES (est): 37.5K **Privately Held**
SIC: 2741 Miscellaneous publishing

(G-6607)
MIKE PUNG
Also Called: Mikes Custom Woodworking
1108 Loftin Dr (73130-1308)
PHONE.....................405 736-6282
Mike Pung, *Owner*
EMP: 1
SALES: 200K **Privately Held**
SIC: 2431 1521 Ornamental woodwork: cornices, mantels, etc.; new construction, single-family houses

(G-6608)
MILAMAR COATINGS LLC (HQ)
Also Called: Milamar/Polymax
311 Nw 122nd St Ste 100 (73114-7325)
PHONE.....................405 755-8448
James Panebianco, *Principal*
EMP: 15
SQ FT: 33,000
SALES (est): 4.3MM
SALES (corp-wide): 11.5MM **Privately Held**
SIC: 3479 Coating of metals & formed products
PA: Cass Polymers, Inc.
311 Nw 122nd St Ste 100
Oklahoma City OK 73114
405 755-8448

(G-6609)
MILL CREEK LUMBER & SUPPLY CO
5251 W Reno Ave Ste E (73127-6365)
PHONE.....................405 947-7227
Adam James, *Branch Mgr*
EMP: 65
SALES (corp-wide): 163.4MM **Privately Held**
SIC: 3442 1771 5031 5211 Casements, aluminum; flooring contractor; lumber, plywood & millwork; lumber & other building materials
PA: Mill Creek Lumber & Supply Company Inc
6974 E 38th St
Tulsa OK 74145
918 794-3600

(G-6610)
MILLBRAE ENERGY LLC
770 E Britton Rd (73114-7705)
PHONE.....................405 286-1941
EMP: 7
SALES (est): 655.8K **Privately Held**
SIC: 1381 Drilling Oil And Gas Wells, Nsk
PA: Millbrae Energy Llc
500 W Putnam Ave Ste 400
Greenwich CT 06830

(G-6611)
MILLENNIAL TECHNOLOGIES LLC
6701 N Bryant Ave (73121-4402)
PHONE.....................405 478-4351
David R High, *President*
EMP: 1
SQ FT: 20,000
SALES (est): 82.2K **Privately Held**
SIC: 3845 Electrotherapeutic apparatus

(G-6612)
MILLENNIUM PROD EXPLRTION CORP
229 S Eagle Ln (73128-4209)
PHONE.....................405 495-3311
Monty Hott, *President*
EMP: 1
SALES (est): 95.4K **Privately Held**
SIC: 1382 Oil & gas exploration services

(G-6613)
MILLS ENTERPRISES INC
Also Called: Mills Roof Truss Co
2709 Sw 52nd St (73119-5611)
PHONE.....................405 236-4470
EMP: 9
SQ FT: 12,000
SALES: 1.3MM **Privately Held**
SIC: 2439 Mfg Wood Roof & Floor Trusses

(G-6614)
MILTON NICHOLS INC
Also Called: Tunbridge Enterprises
232 N Tunbridge Rd (73130-4916)
PHONE.....................405 769-2216
Milton Nichols, *President*
EMP: 1
SALES (est): 89.9K **Privately Held**
SIC: 1382 Oil & gas exploration services

(G-6615)
MINERAL RESOURCES COMPANY
20 N Broadway (73102-9213)
PHONE.....................405 234-9000
EMP: 2 EST: 2018
SALES (est): 788K
SALES (corp-wide): 4.6B **Publicly Held**
SIC: 1311 Crude petroleum & natural gas
PA: Continental Resources, Inc.
20 N Broadway
Oklahoma City OK 73102
405 234-9000

(G-6616)
MINICK MATERIALS COMPANY (PA)
326 N Council Rd (73127-4930)
PHONE.....................405 789-2068
Kenneth Minick, *President*
Curtis Watson, *General Mgr*
Sam Minick, *Vice Pres*
Jason Huffaker, *Opers Mgr*
Steve Pavick, *Store Mgr*
▲ EMP: 24
SQ FT: 4,000
SALES (est): 8.4MM **Privately Held**
WEB: www.minickmaterials.com
SIC: 5211 5261 5032 5191 Sand & gravel; top soil; sand, construction; gravel; stone, crushed or broken; soil, potting & planting; construction sand & gravel

(G-6617)
MINUTEMAN PRESS
300 N Ann Arbor Ave (73127-6308)
PHONE.....................405 942-5595
Pat Patterson, *Owner*
Craig Collins, *Sales Staff*
EMP: 5
SQ FT: 2,400
SALES (est): 590.5K **Privately Held**
SIC: 2752 2791 2789 Commercial printing, lithographic; typesetting; bookbinding & related work

(G-6618)
MIRACLE PRODUCTION INC
Also Called: Poage Sand & Dirt
9500 Sw 15th St (73128-4813)
P.O. Box 850680, Yukon (73085-0680)
PHONE.....................405 324-2216
Harold Poage, *President*
EMP: 10
SALES (est): 1.5MM **Privately Held**
SIC: 4214 1311 Local trucking with storage; crude petroleum production

(G-6619)
MISSON FLUID KING OIL FIELD
1501 Se 25th St (73129-7607)
PHONE.....................405 670-8771
Jack Adams, *Principal*
EMP: 2

SALES (est): 93.5K **Privately Held**
SIC: 1389 Oil field services

(G-6620)
MOBILE HIGHTECH
Also Called: Mht Luxury Alloys
1001 Enterprise Ave Ste 9 (73128-1464)
PHONE.....................405 942-4600
Ed Nance, *General Mgr*
EMP: 3
SALES (est): 375.9K **Privately Held**
SIC: 3312 Blast furnaces & steel mills

(G-6621)
MOBILE LASER FORCES
10009 Ne 23rd St (73141-5207)
PHONE.....................405 259-9300
Carolyn Herman, *Principal*
EMP: 2 EST: 2008
SALES (est): 177.8K **Privately Held**
WEB: www.mobilelaserforces.com
SIC: 3652 Compact laser discs, prerecorded

(G-6622)
MOBILE MINI INC
14120 S Meridian Ave (73173-8806)
PHONE.....................405 682-9333
Brett Gillefpie, *Branch Mgr*
EMP: 30
SALES (corp-wide): 612.6MM **Publicly Held**
SIC: 3448 3537 Buildings, portable: prefabricated metal; industrial trucks & tractors
PA: Mobile Mini, Inc.
4646 E Van Buren St # 400
Phoenix AZ 85008
480 894-6311

(G-6623)
MOBILITY LIVING INC
1215 Se 44th St (73129-6813)
PHONE.....................405 672-7237
Cody Craft, *President*
Brady Chafey, *Manager*
Curtis Morgan,
EMP: 6
SQ FT: 888
SALES (est): 570K **Privately Held**
SIC: 7699 5999 5712 5661 Mattress renovating & repair shop; medical apparatus & supplies; beds & accessories; shoes, orthopedic; medical equipment & supplies; wheelchair lifts

(G-6624)
MOE MARK OF EXCELLENCE LLC
1112 Nw 5th St (73106-7430)
PHONE.....................405 650-9898
Mark E Danford, *Principal*
EMP: 2 EST: 2012
SALES (est): 162.8K **Privately Held**
SIC: 2752 Commercial printing, offset

(G-6625)
MOEDER OIL & GAS LLC
14208 Gaillardia Pl (73142-1820)
PHONE.....................405 286-9192
Randy Moeder Moeder, *Administration*
EMP: 2
SALES (est): 130.2K **Privately Held**
SIC: 1382 Oil & gas exploration services

(G-6626)
MONKEY CHASE BANANA LLC
Also Called: Sightglass
1705 Dublin Rd (73120-3905)
PHONE.....................405 706-5551
Brian Christian Jarod,
EMP: 3
SALES (est): 269.3K **Privately Held**
SIC: 3585 1711 Heating & air conditioning combination units; heating & air conditioning contractors; ventilation & duct work contractor

(G-6627)
MONTICELLO CABINETS DOORS INC
512 Sw 3rd St (73109-5026)
PHONE.....................405 228-4900
Mark Gardner, *Owner*
EMP: 9

SALES (est): 24.4K **Privately Held**
SIC: 2434 Wood kitchen cabinets

(G-6628)
MONTY L HOTT PRODUCTION CORP
7925 N Wilshire Ct (73132-5467)
PHONE.....................405 495-3311
Monty L Hott, *President*
Annette Hott, *Admin Sec*
EMP: 3
SALES (est): 430K **Privately Held**
SIC: 1311 Crude petroleum production

(G-6629)
MOON CHEMICAL PRODUCTS CO
409 N Ann Arbor Ave (73127-6309)
PHONE.....................405 602-6678
Moon Choi, *Principal*
EMP: 1
SALES (corp-wide): 16.1MM **Privately Held**
WEB: www.moonchemical.com
SIC: 2899 Chemical preparations
PA: Moon Chemical Products Co.
8112 Sw 8th St
Oklahoma City OK 73128
405 787-2310

(G-6630)
MOONDOG PUZZLES LLC
2748 Nw Grand Blvd (73116-4004)
PHONE.....................405 286-6881
Martha Wooldridge, *Principal*
EMP: 1 EST: 2017
SALES (est): 41K **Privately Held**
SIC: 3944 Puzzles

(G-6631)
MOWER PARTS INC
Also Called: SMITH DISTRIBUTING
4110 Nw 10th St (73107-5802)
PHONE.....................405 947-6484
Glen Smith, *President*
Randal Smith, *Corp Secy*
Donald Smith, *Vice Pres*
Sandra Smith, *Shareholder*
EMP: 20
SQ FT: 30,000
SALES: 4MM **Privately Held**
SIC: 5083 3694 Lawn & garden machinery & equipment; battery charging alternators & generators

(G-6632)
MSI INSPECTION SERVICE LLC
1306 Sovereign Row (73108-1825)
P.O. Box 271435 (73137-1435)
PHONE.....................405 265-2121
Kim Harless, *Manager*
EMP: 3 EST: 2009
SALES (est): 271.3K **Privately Held**
SIC: 7389 1389 Inspection & testing services; oil field services

(G-6633)
MTM RECOGNITION LLC
3501 Se 29th St (73115-2631)
PHONE.....................405 670-4545
Didi Desmore, *Principal*
EMP: 3
SALES (est): 259.6K **Privately Held**
WEB: www.mtmcoinsource.com
SIC: 3914 Silverware & plated ware

(G-6634)
MTM RECOGNITION CORPORATION (PA)
3201 Se 29th St (73115-1605)
P.O. Box 15659 (73155-5659)
PHONE.....................405 609-6900
Dave Smith, *CEO*
Roger Mashore, *President*
Jeff Weis, *Governor*
Darrel Davis, *Vice Pres*
Monica Finley, *Vice Pres*
▲ EMP: 456
SQ FT: 350,000
SALES (est): 102.8MM **Privately Held**
SIC: 3911 3873 2499 2389 Jewelry, precious metal; watches, clocks, watchcases & parts; trophy bases, wood; men's miscellaneous accessories; trophies, metal, except silver; typesetting

GEOGRAPHIC SECTION   Oklahoma City - Oklahoma County (G-6663)

(G-6635)
MULTIGRAPHIC DESIGN
3517 Ridglea Ct (73115-1831)
PHONE..............................405 672-8201
Moses Sogunro, *Owner*
EMP: 3
SALES (est): 160K **Privately Held**
SIC: 3993 Advertising artwork

(G-6636)
MURPHY PRODUCTS INC
2512 Exchange Ave (73108-2438)
PHONE..............................405 842-7177
Harry Murphy, *President*
Roy Caldwell, *General Mgr*
EMP: 1
SQ FT: 20,000
SALES (est): 150K **Privately Held**
WEB: www.murphyproducts.com
SIC: 3523 5191 Turf & grounds equipment; fertilizer & fertilizer materials

(G-6637)
MUSICWARE PRESS
409 Sw 64th St (73139-7039)
PHONE..............................405 627-1894
William Ware, *Principal*
EMP: 2
SALES (est): 56.3K **Privately Held**
SIC: 2741 Miscellaneous publishing

(G-6638)
MUSKIE PROPPANT LLC (DH)
14201 Caliber Dr Ste 300 (73134-1017)
PHONE..............................405 233-3558
Kevin Offel,
EMP: 5
SALES (est): 24.5MM
SALES (corp-wide): 359.9MM **Publicly Held**
SIC: 1442 Sand mining
HQ: Mammoth Energy Services, Inc.
  14201 Caliber Dr Ste 300
  Oklahoma City OK 73134
  405 608-6007

(G-6639)
MUSTANG EXTREME ENVIRONMENTAL
2425 S Ann Arbor Ave (73128-1845)
PHONE..............................405 681-1800
Wade Holt, *Branch Mgr*
EMP: 12 **Privately Held**
SIC: 1389 Oil field services
PA: Mustang Extreme Environmental Services Llc
  5049 Edwards Ranch Rd # 2
  Fort Worth TX 76109

(G-6640)
MUSTANG FUEL CORPORATION
Also Called: Mustang Gas Proc In Texas
9800 N Oklahoma Ave (73114-7406)
PHONE..............................405 748-9400
E Carey Joullian IV, *Ch of Bd*
EMP: 45
SALES (corp-wide): 107.7MM **Privately Held**
SIC: 2911 Petroleum refining
PA: Mustang Fuel Corporation
  9800 N Oklahoma Ave
  Oklahoma City OK 73114
  405 884-2092

(G-6641)
MUSTANG FUEL CORPORATION (PA)
9800 N Oklahoma Ave (73114-7406)
PHONE..............................405 884-2092
Carey Joullian IV, *Ch of Bd*
E Carey Joullian IV, *Ch of Bd*
Rand Phipps, *Senior VP*
Stephanie McCarty, *Director*
David Salter, *Director*
▲ EMP: 80
SQ FT: 30,000
SALES (est): 107.7MM **Privately Held**
SIC: 1311 4923 Crude petroleum production; natural gas production; gas transmission & distribution

(G-6642)
MUSTANG GAS PRODUCTS LLC
9800 N Oklahoma Ave (73114-7406)
PHONE..............................405 748-9400

Carey Joullian IV,
J Paul Belflower,
Carrie Brower,
M Scott Chapline,
Rand Phipps,
EMP: 40
SALES (est): 6.2MM
SALES (corp-wide): 107.7MM **Privately Held**
SIC: 1382 Oil & gas exploration services
PA: Mustang Fuel Corporation
  9800 N Oklahoma Ave
  Oklahoma City OK 73114
  405 884-2092

(G-6643)
MUSTANG TIMES
4557 W Memorial Rd (73142-2013)
PHONE..............................405 606-1023
EMP: 2
SALES (est): 62.9K **Privately Held**
SIC: 2711 Newspapers: publishing only, not printed on site

(G-6644)
MUSTANG VENTURES COMPANY
13439 Broadway Ext (73114-2256)
PHONE..............................405 748-9400
E Carey Joullian IV, *President*
M Scott Chapline, *CFO*
Rand Phipps, *Admin Sec*
EMP: 1
SQ FT: 33,000
SALES (est): 132.9K
SALES (corp-wide): 107.7MM **Privately Held**
SIC: 1382 Oil & gas exploration services
PA: Mustang Fuel Corporation
  9800 N Oklahoma Ave
  Oklahoma City OK 73114
  405 884-2092

(G-6645)
N A BLASTRAC INC
13201 N Santa Fe Ave (73114-2232)
PHONE..............................405 478-3440
Brian Mackenzie, *CEO*
Steve Klugherz, *President*
Donna Wettlaufer, *Opers Mgr*
Grant Phillips, *Purchasing*
Stephen Boothe, *Engineer*
▲ EMP: 54
SQ FT: 80,000
SALES (est): 19.5MM
SALES (corp-wide): 44.5MM **Privately Held**
SIC: 3569 3531 5085 Blast cleaning equipment, dustless; construction machinery; abrasives
PA: Blastrac Global, Inc.
  222 Greystone Rd
  Evergreen CO 80439
  405 478-3440

(G-6646)
NABORS DRILLING TECH USA INC
10100 Nw 10th St (73127-7127)
PHONE..............................405 324-8081
Robert Hill, *Branch Mgr*
EMP: 20
SQ FT: 728 **Privately Held**
WEB: www.nabors.com
SIC: 1381 Drilling oil & gas wells
HQ: Nabors Drilling Technologies Usa, Inc.
  515 W Greens Rd Ste 1200
  Houston TX 77067
  281 874-0035

(G-6647)
NABORS DRILLING TECH USA INC
5500 S Rockwell St (73179-6609)
PHONE..............................405 745-3457
Dean Sherrill, *Manager*
EMP: 20 **Privately Held**
SIC: 1381 Directional drilling oil & gas wells
HQ: Nabors Drilling Technologies Usa, Inc.
  515 W Greens Rd Ste 1200
  Houston TX 77067
  281 874-0035

(G-6648)
NAFTA MUD INC
4324 Nw Expressway 202 (73116)
PHONE..............................405 751-6261
John Stover, *President*
EMP: 3
SALES (est): 275.9K **Privately Held**
SIC: 1389 Mud service, oil field drilling; oil field services

(G-6649)
NAFTA MUD LLC (PA)
4334 Nw Expwy St Ste 202 (73116-1515)
PHONE..............................405 751-6261
John Stover, *Mng Member*
EMP: 4
SQ FT: 2,500
SALES (est): 8MM **Privately Held**
SIC: 1389 Mud service, oil field drilling

(G-6650)
NANCY DALRYMPLE
Also Called: Shepprds Retreat Bed Breakfast
1949 Nw 14th St (73106-2017)
PHONE..............................405 525-7544
EMP: 1 EST: 2009
SALES (est): 44K **Privately Held**
SIC: 7011 2411 Hotel/Motel Operation Logging

(G-6651)
NANNA NETWORKS LLC
3324 Green Wing Ct (73120-5014)
PHONE..............................405 833-3329
Ramey Redden,
EMP: 1
SALES (est): 53K **Privately Held**
SIC: 3825 Network analyzers

(G-6652)
NANOMED TARGETING SYSTEMS INC
4901 Richmond Sq Ste 103 (73118-2000)
PHONE..............................646 641-4747
Alex Harel, *CEO*
Kenneth Dormer, *Principal*
EMP: 2
SALES (est): 29.3K **Privately Held**
SIC: 3841 Surgical & medical instruments

(G-6653)
NARCOMEY LLC
150 Sw 10th St (73109)
P.O. Box 2137, Edmond (73083-2137)
PHONE..............................405 473-1350
Don Narcomey,
EMP: 1
SQ FT: 1,000
SALES (est): 34K **Privately Held**
SIC: 7999 1799 2521 7389 Art gallery, commercial; office furniture installation; wood office furniture; interior design services

(G-6654)
NASH CUSTOM CABINETS
8329 Sw 92nd Cir (73169-2707)
PHONE..............................405 919-7711
EMP: 2
SALES (est): 148.6K **Privately Held**
SIC: 2434 Wood kitchen cabinets

(G-6655)
NATIONAL BUMPER & PLATING
Also Called: National Quality Cooling Pdts
717 Sw 4th St (73109-5100)
PHONE..............................405 235-1535
Gary Schneider, *President*
Charlotte Schneider, *Corp Secy*
EMP: 7 EST: 1971
SQ FT: 20,000
SALES (est): 650K **Privately Held**
SIC: 3714 Motor vehicle parts & accessories

(G-6656)
NATIONAL OILWELL VARCO INC
6602 Newcastle Rd (73179-7201)
P.O. Box 94853 (73143-4853)
PHONE..............................405 745-6850
Jeremy Taypen, *President*
Kyle Crick, *District Mgr*
Jason Nightengale, *District Mgr*
Mark Boyes, *Vice Pres*

Susan Southerland, *Opers Mgr*
EMP: 70
SALES (corp-wide): 8.4B **Publicly Held**
WEB: www.nov.com
SIC: 3533 Oil & gas field machinery
PA: National Oilwell Varco, Inc.
  7909 Parkwood Circle Dr
  Houston TX 77036
  713 346-7500

(G-6657)
NATIONAL OILWELL VARCO INC
1008 Se 29th St (73129-6436)
PHONE..............................405 677-3386
EMP: 90
SALES (corp-wide): 8.4B **Publicly Held**
SIC: 3533 Oil & gas field machinery
PA: National Oilwell Varco, Inc.
  7909 Parkwood Circle Dr
  Houston TX 77036
  713 346-7500

(G-6658)
NATIONAL OILWELL VARCO INC
6440 Sw 44th St (73179-8007)
PHONE..............................713 346-7500
Bill Kellum, *Manager*
EMP: 2
SALES (corp-wide): 8.4B **Publicly Held**
SIC: 3594 Pumps, hydraulic power transfer
PA: National Oilwell Varco, Inc.
  7909 Parkwood Circle Dr
  Houston TX 77036
  713 346-7500

(G-6659)
NATIONAL SEATING MOBILITY INC
3401 N May Ave Ste B (73112-6953)
PHONE..............................918 856-3000
EMP: 2 **Privately Held**
SIC: 3842 Wheelchairs
PA: National Seating & Mobility, Inc.
  302 Innovation Dr 500
  Franklin TN 37067

(G-6660)
NATIONAL SEATING MOBILITY INC
3401 N May Ave (73112-6952)
PHONE..............................405 896-3680
EMP: 2 **Privately Held**
SIC: 3842 Wheelchairs
PA: National Seating & Mobility, Inc.
  302 Innovation Dr 500
  Franklin TN 37067

(G-6661)
NATIVE EXPLORATION MNRL LLC
909 Nw 63rd St (73116-7605)
PHONE..............................405 603-5520
EMP: 2
SALES (est): 81.9K **Privately Held**
SIC: 1382 Oil & gas exploration services

(G-6662)
NATIVE EXPLRATION HOLDINGS LLC
909 Nw 63rd St (73116-7605)
PHONE..............................405 603-5520
Aaron Borgan, *COO*
Chris Flenthrope, *Vice Pres*
Toby Fullbright, *Vice Pres*
Lindsey Walton, *Vice Pres*
Lane Gibbs,
EMP: 2
SALES (est): 81.9K **Privately Held**
SIC: 1382 Oil & gas exploration services

(G-6663)
NATIVE EXPLRTION OPERATING LLC
921 Nw 63rd St (73116-7605)
P.O. Box 18108 (73154-0108)
PHONE..............................405 603-5520
Lane Gibbs,
Matt Whitaker,
EMP: 3
SALES (est): 358.6K **Privately Held**
SIC: 1382 Oil & gas exploration services

Oklahoma City - Oklahoma County (G-6664)

(G-6664)
NATURE CREATIONS
1901 Nw Expressway (73118-1607)
PHONE 405 848-2605
EMP: 2
SALES (est): 103.3K **Privately Held**
SIC: 3911 Jewelry, precious metal

(G-6665)
NCI GROUP INC
Also Called: Metal Building Components Mbci
7000 S Eastern Ave (73149-5223)
P.O. Box 95998 (73143-5998)
PHONE 405 672-7676
Cody Rodden, *Manager*
EMP: 30
SQ FT: 60,410
SALES (corp-wide): 4.8B **Publicly Held**
SIC: 3448 3444 Buildings, portable: prefabricated metal; prefabricated metal components; metal roofing & roof drainage equipment
HQ: Nci Group, Inc.
10943 N Sam Huston Pkwy W
Houston TX 77064
281 897-7788

(G-6666)
NDC SYSTEMS
5420 Nw 112th St (73162-3701)
PHONE 405 722-1101
EMP: 2 EST: 2010
SALES (est): 138.1K **Privately Held**
SIC: 3829 Measuring & controlling devices

(G-6667)
NECO INDUSTRIES INC
3345 S Ann Arbor Ave (73179-7619)
PHONE 405 682-3003
Rudolph Nevez, *President*
Trent Nevez, *Vice Pres*
EMP: 23
SQ FT: 30,000
SALES: 2MM **Privately Held**
SIC: 3365 Aerospace castings, aluminum

(G-6668)
NEEDHAM ROYALTY COMPANY LLC
722 N Broadway Ave (73102-6007)
PHONE 405 297-0177
EMP: 3
SALES (est): 382.8K **Privately Held**
SIC: 1382 Oil & gas exploration services

(G-6669)
NEOINSULATION LLC
3900 E I 240 Scc Rd (73135)
PHONE 405 605-6518
EMP: 6 EST: 2014
SALES (est): 742.3K **Privately Held**
SIC: 2822 Neoprene, chloroprene

(G-6670)
NEON MOORE AND SIGN
3501 Se 89th St (73135-6217)
PHONE 405 672-6277
Kenny Moore, *Partner*
Nola Moore, *Partner*
EMP: 2
SQ FT: 2,000
SALES (est): 200K **Privately Held**
SIC: 3993 Electric signs; neon signs

(G-6671)
NEWS OK LLC
100 W Main St Ste 100 # 100 (73102-9007)
PHONE 405 475-4000
Kelly Dyer, *General Mgr*
EMP: 16
SALES (est): 964.8K **Privately Held**
SIC: 3577 Data conversion equipment, media-to-media: computer

(G-6672)
NEWVIEW OKLAHOMA INC (PA)
501 N Douglas Ave (73106-5007)
PHONE 405 232-4364
Gene N Steely, *Engineer*
Ben Knolles, *Info Tech Dir*
Christian Gorshing, *Info Tech Mgr*
Lauren White, *Exec Dir*
Brandi Bynum, *Director*
EMP: 88
SQ FT: 300,000
SALES: 34.2MM **Privately Held**
SIC: 8399 2421 3599 Council for social agency; kiln drying of lumber; machine & other job shop work

(G-6673)
NEXT GENERATION
1533 Se 66th St (73149-5209)
PHONE 405 606-4455
EMP: 2
SALES (est): 110K **Privately Held**
SIC: 3949 Mfg Sporting/Athletic Goods

(G-6674)
NEXT-GEN WIND LLC
210 Park Ave Ste 2820 (73102-5644)
PHONE 405 948-1556
Robert Hefner, *Sls & Mktg Exec*
Scott Calhoon,
EMP: 1
SALES (est): 132.2K **Privately Held**
SIC: 3511 Turbines & turbine generator sets

(G-6675)
NEXTSTREAM HEAVY OIL LLC
300 Ne 9th St (73104-1850)
PHONE 405 808-5435
Jacob Gibson,
EMP: 8
SALES (est): 340K
SALES (corp-wide): 475.3K **Privately Held**
SIC: 2813 2911 Industrial gases; gasoline
PA: Nextstream Growth I, Llc
300 Ne 9th St
Oklahoma City OK 73104
405 924-1452

(G-6676)
NG DISCOVERY LLC
5121 Gaillardia Corp Pl (73142-1873)
PHONE 405 945-0940
Douglas Dowd, *Mng Member*
EMP: 2
SALES (est): 487.1K **Privately Held**
SIC: 1382 Oil & gas exploration services

(G-6677)
NIAGARA BOTTLING LLC
500 N Sara Rd (73127)
PHONE 909 230-5000
EMP: 3
SALES (corp-wide): 230.9MM **Privately Held**
SIC: 2086 Water, pasteurized: packaged in cans, bottles, etc.
PA: Niagara Bottling, Llc
1440 Bridgegate Dr
Diamond Bar CA 91765
909 230-5000

(G-6678)
NICHOLS HILLS PUBLISHING CO
Also Called: Friday Newspaper
10801 Quail Plaza Dr (73120-3118)
P.O. Box 20340 (73156-0340)
PHONE 405 755-3311
Vicky Courley, *Ch of Bd*
Vicky Gourley, *President*
EMP: 12
SALES (est): 720.6K **Privately Held**
SIC: 2711 Commercial printing & newspaper publishing combined

(G-6679)
NICHOLS LAND SERVICES INC
1025 N Broadway Ave (73102-5811)
PHONE 405 840-1344
Lyman Nichols Jr, *President*
Lyman Nichols Sr, *Vice Pres*
EMP: 2
SQ FT: 2,500
SALES (est): 244.9K **Privately Held**
WEB: www.nicholsenergyservices.com
SIC: 1382 Oil & gas exploration services

(G-6680)
NICKEL 8 LLC
1200 Nw 63rd St (73116-5712)
PHONE 405 721-7945
EMP: 2
SALES (est): 102.5K **Privately Held**
SIC: 3356 Nonferrous rolling & drawing

(G-6681)
NIGHTOWL PUBLICATIONS MAIN OFF
10216 Mantle Dr (73162-4518)
PHONE 405 603-8130
Gordon Walker, *Principal*
EMP: 2
SALES (est): 153.2K **Privately Held**
WEB: www.nightowlpubco.com
SIC: 2721 Magazines: publishing only, not printed on site

(G-6682)
NINE ENERGY SERVICE
2817 S Ann Arbor Ave (73128-1853)
PHONE 405 601-5336
Paul Butero, *CEO*
Christopher Payson, *Vice Pres*
Ann Fox, *CFO*
EMP: 2 EST: 2014
SALES (est): 110K **Privately Held**
SIC: 1389 Construction, repair & dismantling services

(G-6683)
NINE WEST HOLDINGS INC
Also Called: Kasper
1901 Nw Exprkway Ste 1017 (73118)
PHONE 405 810-8568
EMP: 8
SALES (corp-wide): 2.2B **Privately Held**
SIC: 2337 Mfg Women's/Misses' Suits/Coats
PA: Nine West Holdings, Inc.
1411 Broadway Fl 15
New York NY 10018
212 642-3860

(G-6684)
NONOVELS PRESS LLC
6213 Se 80th St (73135-7009)
PHONE 325 721-2577
Alexander Deville, *Principal*
EMP: 1 EST: 2016
SALES (est): 43.8K **Privately Held**
SIC: 2741 Miscellaneous publishing

(G-6685)
NORRISEAL-WELLMARK INC
1903 Se 29th St (73129-7625)
PHONE 405 672-6660
Luis Gomez, *CEO*
Vince Cipresso, *Vice Pres*
John Miller, *CFO*
◆ EMP: 100
SQ FT: 55,582
SALES (est): 26MM
SALES (corp-wide): 1.1B **Publicly Held**
WEB: www.norrisealwellmark.com
SIC: 3533 Oil field machinery & equipment; gas field machinery & equipment
HQ: Apergy Artificial Lift International, Llc
2445 Tech Frest Blvd Ste
Spring TX 77381
281 403-5742

(G-6686)
NORTEK AIR SOLUTIONS LLC
4841 N Sewell Ave (73118-7820)
PHONE 405 525-6546
Burke Lucas, *Engineer*
Kim Osborn, *Engineer*
Carlita Wheeler, *Enginr/R&D Asst*
Rick Brown, *Natl Sales Mgr*
Chukwudi Igweze, *Sales Staff*
EMP: 300
SALES (corp-wide): 11B **Privately Held**
SIC: 3585 Air conditioning units, complete: domestic or industrial; heating equipment, complete
HQ: Nortek Air Solutions, Llc
8000 Phoenix Pkwy
O Fallon MO 63368
952 358-6600

(G-6687)
NORTEK AIR SOLUTIONS LLC
5510 Sw 29th St (73179-7626)
PHONE 405 594-2811
Michael Mayhew, *Branch Mgr*
EMP: 79
SALES (corp-wide): 11B **Privately Held**
SIC: 3585 Air conditioning equipment, complete

HQ: Nortek Air Solutions, Llc
8000 Phoenix Pkwy
O Fallon MO 63368
952 358-6600

(G-6688)
NORTH STAR PUBLISHING LLC
Also Called: Printing
6801 Sandlewood Dr (73132-3910)
PHONE 405 415-2400
Barry Martin, *President*
Tim Shanahan, *Vice Pres*
Rosemary Martin,
EMP: 53
SQ FT: 60,000
SALES (est): 9.8MM **Privately Held**
SIC: 2752 2789 2796 Commercial printing, offset; bookbinding & related work; platemaking services

(G-6689)
NORTHROP GRUMMAN SYSTEMS CORP
6400 Se 59th St Ste A (73135-5518)
PHONE 405 739-7875
Ronald Naylor, *Branch Mgr*
Brian Pitts, *Software Engr*
EMP: 80 **Publicly Held**
SIC: 3812 Aircraft/aerospace flight instruments & guidance systems
HQ: Northrop Grumman Systems Corporation
2980 Fairview Park Dr
Falls Church VA 22042
703 280-2900

(G-6690)
NORTHROP GRUMMAN SYSTEMS CORP
6401 S Air Depot Blvd (73135-5911)
PHONE 405 737-3300
Jeremy Hemeon, *Project Mgr*
Greg Hazeldine, *Engineer*
Derek Nightingale, *Engineer*
Brandon Edmonds, *Program Mgr*
John Mackey, *Program Mgr*
EMP: 310 **Publicly Held**
SIC: 3721 Airplanes, fixed or rotary wing; research & development on aircraft by the manufacturer
HQ: Northrop Grumman Systems Corporation
2980 Fairview Park Dr
Falls Church VA 22042
703 280-2900

(G-6691)
NORTHROP GRUMMAN SYSTEMS CORP
Also Called: Northrop Grumman Integrated
5600 Liberty Pkwy Ste 101 (73110-2801)
PHONE 405 733-1208
R Stuart Scannell, *Director*
EMP: 185 **Publicly Held**
SIC: 3721 5599 Aircraft; aircraft, self-propelled
HQ: Northrop Grumman Systems Corporation
2980 Fairview Park Dr
Falls Church VA 22042
703 280-2900

(G-6692)
NORTHWEST OIL GAS EXPLRTN
125 Park Ave Ste LI (73102-9110)
PHONE 405 974-0165
Kevin Burshears, *Principal*
David Burshears, *Administration*
EMP: 2
SALES (est): 90.1K **Privately Held**
SIC: 1382 Oil & gas exploration services

(G-6693)
NORTHWEST ROYALTY LLC
125 Park Ave Ste LI (73102-9110)
PHONE 405 241-9707
EMP: 2
SALES (est): 216.3K **Privately Held**
SIC: 1382 Oil & gas exploration services

(G-6694)
NORTHWEST RUBBER
3501 Melcat Dr Ste B (73179-8445)
PHONE 405 681-2667
Greg Bean, *Branch Mgr*

GEOGRAPHIC SECTION

Oklahoma City - Oklahoma County (G-6724)

▲ EMP: 1 EST: 2009
SALES (est): 119.8K **Privately Held**
SIC: 3069 Hard rubber & molded rubber products

(G-6695)
NORTHWEST TRANSFORMER CO INC
8 Sw 29th St (73109-6200)
PHONE.................................405 636-1454
Gene Stanley, *President*
Allan Shipman, *Vice Pres*
EMP: 34 EST: 1977
SQ FT: 4,000
SALES (est): 3.5MM **Privately Held**
SIC: 7629 3612 Electrical equipment repair, high voltage; transformers, except electric

(G-6696)
NORVILLE OIL CO LLC
901 E Britton Rd (73114-7802)
PHONE.................................405 286-9100
Robert Harris,
EMP: 5 EST: 1945
SQ FT: 2,000
SALES (est): 648.1K **Privately Held**
SIC: 1311 Crude petroleum production; natural gas production

(G-6697)
NOSLEY SCOOP LLC
14301 Caliber Dr Ste 110 (73134-1016)
PHONE.................................512 328-2953
Carl F Giesler Jr,
EMP: 1
SALES (est): 117.9K
SALES (corp-wide): 236.3MM **Publicly Held**
SIC: 1311 Crude petroleum & natural gas
HQ: Nosley Assets, Llc
    14301 Caliber Dr Ste 110
    Oklahoma City OK 73134
    512 328-2953

(G-6698)
NOV DOWNHOLE
6602 Newcastle Rd (73179-7201)
PHONE.................................405 688-5000
Carlos Flores, *Principal*
EMP: 5
SALES (est): 319.5K **Privately Held**
SIC: 1389 Construction, repair & dismantling services

(G-6699)
NOV TUBOSCOPE INC
1800 Se 44th St (73129-7918)
PHONE.................................405 677-8889
Mateus Monteiro, *Controller*
Vonda Kellum, *Sales Staff*
Bryan Jensen, *Marketing Staff*
EMP: 6 EST: 2010
SALES (est): 189.2K **Privately Held**
WEB: www.nov.com
SIC: 1389 Testing, measuring, surveying & analysis services

(G-6700)
NOVALCO INC
130 Ne 31st St (73105-2623)
PHONE.................................405 528-2711
Bryan Pease, *President*
Ed Knowles, *VP Opers*
Terry Nowell, *Manager*
EMP: 11
SALES (est): 1.6MM **Privately Held**
SIC: 2431 5031 Doors & door parts & trim, wood; doors

(G-6701)
NOVO OIL & GAS
1001 W Wilshire Blvd # 2 (73116-7004)
PHONE.................................405 286-4391
EMP: 2
SALES (est): 239.3K **Privately Held**
SIC: 1382 Oil & gas exploration services

(G-6702)
NOVO OIL & GAS LLC
105 N Hudson Ave Ste 500 (73102-4802)
PHONE.................................405 609-1625
Tim Fahler, *CEO*
Justin Christofferson, *Exec VP*
John Zimmerman, *CFO*
David Avery, *VP Finance*
Kiley Mixon, *Office Mgr*
EMP: 12
SALES (est): 2.8MM **Privately Held**
SIC: 1382 Oil & gas exploration services

(G-6703)
NUESTRA COMUNIDAD
2524 Sw 44th St (73119-3414)
P.O. Box 850161, Yukon (73085-0161)
PHONE.................................405 685-3822
Franco Tevallos, *Owner*
EMP: 1
SQ FT: 1,234
SALES (est): 81.3K **Privately Held**
SIC: 2711 Newspapers: publishing only, not printed on site

(G-6704)
NYE INVESTMENT CO LLC
9520 N May Ave Ste 320 (73120-2722)
PHONE.................................405 923-7155
EMP: 2
SALES (est): 81.9K **Privately Held**
SIC: 1382 Oil & gas exploration services

(G-6705)
NYE OIL CO
Also Called: Nye J Marshall
5805 Nw Grand Blvd Ste C (73118-1203)
PHONE.................................405 843-6609
Jay Marshall Nye, *President*
EMP: 3
SALES (est): 233.9K **Privately Held**
SIC: 1311 Crude petroleum production

(G-6706)
O2 CONCEPTS LLC (PA)
6303 Waterford Blvd # 150 (73118-1119)
PHONE.................................877 867-4008
Cory Smith, *CEO*
Kate Forgione, *Vice Pres*
Lindsay Payer, *Vice Pres*
▲ EMP: 33
SALES (est): 17.4MM **Privately Held**
WEB: www.o2-concepts.com
SIC: 2813 5085 Oxygen, compressed or liquefied; oxygen therapy equipment

(G-6707)
OAK TREE NATURAL RESOURCES LLC
10900 Hefner Pointe Dr # 401 (73120-5082)
PHONE.................................405 775-0987
Melvin Scoggin,
EMP: 150
SQ FT: 2,600
SALES (est): 4.8MM **Privately Held**
SIC: 1382 Oil & gas exploration services

(G-6708)
OAKLEY INC
1901 Nw Expwy St Ste 1045 (73118-1640)
PHONE.................................405 843-5447
EMP: 2
SALES (corp-wide): 1.7MM **Privately Held**
SIC: 3851 Ophthalmic goods
HQ: Oakley, Inc.
    1 Icon
    Foothill Ranch CA 92610
    949 951-0991

(G-6709)
OATSKC GRANOLA COMPANY LLC
6 Ne 63rd St Ste 220 (73105-1401)
PHONE.................................405 834-6159
Judd W McDonald, *Principal*
EMP: 1 EST: 2016
SALES (est): 52.6K **Privately Held**
SIC: 2043 Granola & muesli, except bars & clusters

(G-6710)
OCTAGON RESOURCES INC
6801 Broadway Ext Ste 204 (73116-9037)
PHONE.................................405 842-3322
EMP: 8
SALES (corp-wide): 3.4MM **Privately Held**
SIC: 2911 Petroleum Refiner
PA: Octagon Resources Inc
    1831 E Imhoff Rd Ste 100
    Norman OK 73071
    405 366-8885

(G-6711)
OCTAPHARMA PLASMA
2962 Sw 59th St (73119-6402)
PHONE.................................405 686-9226
EMP: 2 EST: 2017
SALES (est): 81.4K **Privately Held**
SIC: 2836 Plasmas

(G-6712)
ODOR CONTROL ENTPS TEXAS INC
Also Called: A Grease Catch
1610 Se 37th St (73129-7911)
P.O. Box 890189 (73189-0189)
PHONE.................................405 670-5600
Steve White, *President*
David White, *Vice Pres*
Helen White, *Treasurer*
EMP: 10
SQ FT: 4,500
SALES (est): 1.2MM **Privately Held**
SIC: 3714 Cleaners, air, motor vehicle

(G-6713)
OERLIKON BLZERS CATING USA INC
7124 Sw 29th St Ste 101 (73179-5229)
PHONE.................................405 745-1026
Joe Holmes, *President*
EMP: 9
SALES (corp-wide): 2.6B **Privately Held**
SIC: 3479 Coating of metals & formed products
HQ: Oerlikon Balzers Coating Usa Inc.
    1700 E Golf Rd Ste 200
    Schaumburg IL 60173
    847 619-5541

(G-6714)
OFS INC
Also Called: Oklahoma Ferrious Services
4901 Ne 23rd St (73121-6814)
P.O. Box 124, Spencer (73084-0124)
PHONE.................................405 424-1101
Don Cox, *President*
Richard Olney, *VP Accounting*
Carrie Carpenter, *Admin Sec*
EMP: 12
SALES (est): 3.8MM **Privately Held**
SIC: 2899 Water treating compounds

(G-6715)
OGP ENERGY L P
Also Called: Garbrecht, Robt A
211 N Robinson Ave N1520 (73102-7234)
PHONE.................................405 235-9571
Robert Garbrecht, *Partner*
Ted Collins,
Paul Nickens,
EMP: 2
SALES (est): 225.4K **Privately Held**
SIC: 1311 Crude petroleum production; natural gas production

(G-6716)
OH KEYS
14101 N Pennsylvania Ave (73134-6051)
PHONE.................................405 529-5202
Angie Messner, *Owner*
EMP: 2
SALES (est): 100.3K **Privately Held**
SIC: 3429 Keys, locks & related hardware

(G-6717)
OH KEYS
9001 S May Ave (73159-6601)
PHONE.................................405 378-5674
EMP: 2
SALES (est): 73.4K **Privately Held**
SIC: 3429 Keys, locks & related hardware

(G-6718)
OIL PRO INDUSTRIES
3536 S Meridian Ave (73119-2418)
PHONE.................................405 323-6988
EMP: 1
SALES (est): 39.6K **Privately Held**
SIC: 3999 Manufacturing industries

(G-6719)
OIL STATES ENERGY SERVICES LLC
3120 Melcat Dr (73179-8442)
PHONE.................................405 702-6536
EMP: 8
SALES (corp-wide): 1B **Publicly Held**
SIC: 3533 5082 Oil field machinery & equipment; construction & mining machinery
HQ: Oil States Energy Services, L.L.C.
    333 Clay St Ste 2100
    Houston TX 77002
    713 425-2400

(G-6720)
OIL STATES ENERGY SERVICES LLC
5300 Sw 33rd St (73179-8444)
PHONE.................................405 686-1001
Davin Grassmann, *Branch Mgr*
EMP: 50
SALES (corp-wide): 1B **Publicly Held**
SIC: 3533 5082 Oil field machinery & equipment; oil field equipment
HQ: Oil States Energy Services, L.L.C.
    333 Clay St Ste 2100
    Houston TX 77002
    713 425-2400

(G-6721)
OIL STATES INDUSTRIES INC
Also Called: Oil States Piper Valves
1020 E Grand Blvd (73129-8403)
PHONE.................................405 671-2000
Allan Smith, *Human Res Mgr*
EMP: 80
SALES (corp-wide): 1B **Publicly Held**
SIC: 1389 3061 3561 3533 Oil & gas wells: building, repairing & dismantling; oil field services; oil & gas field machinery rubber goods (mechanical); pumps & pumping equipment; drilling tools for gas, oil or water wells
HQ: Oil States Industries, Inc.
    7701 S Cooper St
    Arlington TX 76001

(G-6722)
OIL-LAW RECORDS CORPORATION
8 Nw 65th St (73116-9199)
PHONE.................................405 840-1631
Brad McPherson, *President*
Kerry E Master, *COO*
Paul Lamb, *CTO*
Dennis E Carpenter JD, *Officer*
D Paul Lamb, *Officer*
EMP: 25
SQ FT: 6,000
SALES (est): 2.7MM **Privately Held**
WEB: www.oil-law.com
SIC: 1382 Oil & gas exploration services

(G-6723)
OILAB INC
Also Called: Environmental Tstg & Oil Lab
4619 N Santa Fe Ave (73118-7905)
PHONE.................................405 528-8378
Russel Britain, *President*
Jorge Gamarra, *Manager*
EMP: 7
SQ FT: 7,500
SALES (est): 618.6K **Privately Held**
SIC: 1389 8731 8734 Testing, measuring, surveying & analysis services; oil field services; environmental research; testing laboratories

(G-6724)
OILFIELD TECHNICAL SVCS LLC
7412 Nw 83rd St (73132-4275)
PHONE.................................405 603-4288
Dustin Smith, *Principal*
Jay Pearman, *Electrical Engi*
Julie Smith, *Manager*
Lyndee Wright, *Admin Asst*
EMP: 1
SALES (est): 424.6K **Privately Held**
SIC: 1389 Oil field services

Oklahoma City - Oklahoma County (G-6725)

(G-6725)
OILWELL TECH & ENHANCEMENT
3030 Nw Expressway (73112-5474)
PHONE................405 202-9720
EMP: 2
SALES (est): 100.8K Privately Held
SIC: 1382 Oil & gas exploration services

(G-6726)
OKC ALLERGY SUPPLIES INC
1005 Sw 2nd St (73109-1006)
PHONE................405 235-1451
Michael Moulton, Principal
EMP: 90
SALES: 14MM
SALES (corp-wide): 5B Privately Held
SIC: 2834 Pharmaceutical preparations
HQ: Alk-Abello, Inc.
1700 Royston Ln
Round Rock TX 78664
512 251-0037

(G-6727)
OKC BOYS OF LEATHER
3612 Altadena Ave (73112-7846)
PHONE................318 564-0312
Nate Benner, Principal
EMP: 2
SALES (est): 100.3K Privately Held
SIC: 3199 Leather goods

(G-6728)
OKC ENERGY CORPORATION
10804 Quail Plaza Dr # 100 (73120-3100)
PHONE................405 330-5586
EMP: 2
SQ FT: 1,400
SALES (est): 210K Privately Held
SIC: 1311 Oil & Gas Production

(G-6729)
OKC FABRIC MARKET
10956 N May Ave (73120-6202)
PHONE................405 531-0546
EMP: 1
SALES (est): 46.5K Privately Held
SIC: 2221 Apparel & outerwear fabric, manmade fiber or silk

(G-6730)
OKC SODA CO LLC
6516 Westrock Dr (73132-2007)
PHONE................405 628-9543
Michael Crowder, Managing Prtnr
Michael S Noonan, Managing Prtnr
EMP: 2
SALES: 300K Privately Held
SIC: 2611 Soda pulp

(G-6731)
OKIE FERMENTS
44 Ne 51st St Ste A (73105-1898)
PHONE................405 310-9724
Okie Ferments, Owner
EMP: 1
SALES (est): 48.9K Privately Held
SIC: 2033 Canned fruits & specialties

(G-6732)
OKIEWOOD LLC
3817 Nw 51st Pl (73112-2051)
PHONE................405 245-5257
Sean Eaton, Principal
EMP: 1
SALES (est): 41.5K Privately Held
SIC: 2499 Wood products

(G-6733)
OKKI INDUSTRIES LLC
2925 Chapel Hill Rd (73120-4430)
PHONE................405 204-6357
Nelson L Bolen, Owner
EMP: 2
SALES (est): 271.1K Privately Held
SIC: 1382 Oil & gas exploration services

(G-6734)
OKLAHOMA AAA PALLET COMPANY (PA)
1901 S Skyline Dr (73129-6053)
PHONE................405 670-1414
Jim Crowe, President
Sean Crowe, Vice Pres
EMP: 50
SQ FT: 30,000
SALES (est): 3.2MM Privately Held
SIC: 2448 Pallets, wood

(G-6735)
OKLAHOMA ASSN OF ELC COOP
Also Called: Oklahoma Living Publication
2325 E I 44 Service Rd (73111-8219)
P.O. Box 54309 (73154-1309)
PHONE................405 478-1455
Christopher Meyers, CEO
EMP: 20 EST: 1942
SALES: 5.9MM Privately Held
SIC: 8611 2711 2796 2791 Public utility association; newspapers; platemaking services; typesetting

(G-6736)
OKLAHOMA BANKERS
Also Called: Oba
643 Ne 41st St (73105-7231)
P.O. Box 18246 (73154-0246)
PHONE................405 424-5252
Roger Beverage, President
Myrna Smith, COO
Janis Reeser, Exec VP
Margo Ward, Vice Pres
Leann Jackson, CFO
EMP: 23
SQ FT: 14,000
SALES: 3.1MM Privately Held
SIC: 8611 2711 Trade associations; bankers' organization, advisory services; newspapers

(G-6737)
OKLAHOMA BAR FOUNDATION INC
1901 N Lincoln Blvd (73105-4900)
P.O. Box 53036 (73152-3036)
PHONE................405 416-7000
John Parsley, President
John M Williams, Director
EMP: 30
SALES: 1.9MM Privately Held
SIC: 8621 2721 8111 Bar association; periodicals; legal services

(G-6738)
OKLAHOMA BINDERY INC
2832 W Lindley Ave (73107-6816)
PHONE................405 235-4802
Gayle Ballard, President
Kelly Ballard, Corp Secy
Doris Ballard, Vice Pres
EMP: 7 EST: 1976
SALES: 240K Privately Held
SIC: 2789 Binding only: books, pamphlets, magazines, etc.

(G-6739)
OKLAHOMA CITY BLAZERS
119 N Robinson Ave (73102-4617)
PHONE................405 543-2922
Brad Lund, Principal
Eric Rodgers, Comms Dir
EMP: 2
SALES (est): 83.9K Privately Held
SIC: 2752 Commercial printing, lithographic

(G-6740)
OKLAHOMA CITY FREQUENCY
5201 Se 56th St (73135-4505)
PHONE................405 887-7115
EMP: 1
SALES (est): 46K Privately Held
SIC: 3993 Mfg Signs/Advertising Specialties

(G-6741)
OKLAHOMA CITY HERALD
7416 Broadway Ext (73116-9069)
PHONE................405 842-7827
John Pettis, Principal
EMP: 1
SALES (est): 70.2K Privately Held
WEB: www.okcherald.org
SIC: 2711 Commercial printing & newspaper publishing combined; newspapers, publishing & printing

(G-6742)
OKLAHOMA CITY SHUTTER CO INC
210 S Alliance Blvd (73128-3609)
PHONE................405 787-1234
Jesse Lentz, President
EMP: 15
SQ FT: 800
SALES (est): 1MM Privately Held
SIC: 5211 2431 Door & window products; millwork

(G-6743)
OKLAHOMA CITY STEEL LLC
100 Se 17th St (73129-1203)
P.O. Box 94905 (73143-4905)
PHONE................405 235-2300
Bryan Wells, Mng Member
EMP: 8 EST: 2001
SQ FT: 25,000
SALES (est): 1.4MM Privately Held
WEB: www.okcsteel.net
SIC: 3441 Fabricated structural metal

(G-6744)
OKLAHOMA COMMUNITY TV LLC
7401 N Kelley Ave (73111-8420)
PHONE................405 808-2509
Steve Foerster, Principal
EMP: 4
SALES (est): 355.1K Privately Held
SIC: 3663 Radio & TV communications equipment

(G-6745)
OKLAHOMA CONTAINER CORP
9545 N I 35 Service Rd (73131-5220)
PHONE................405 842-8300
Corey Williams, CEO
Misty Williams, Admin Sec
EMP: 2
SALES (est): 293.3K Privately Held
SIC: 3715 Demountable cargo containers

(G-6746)
OKLAHOMA ENVELOPE COMPANY LLC
5621 W Reno Ave Ste B (73127-6632)
PHONE................405 946-2169
Patricia A Sparks,
Wayne Sparks,
EMP: 14
SQ FT: 27,700
SALES (est): 2.5MM Privately Held
SIC: 2759 Commercial printing

(G-6747)
OKLAHOMA EQUIPMENT MFG PDT
2401 Purdue Dr (73128-1831)
PHONE................405 491-6484
Rex Davidson, Owner
Eva Davidson, Co-Owner
EMP: 6
SQ FT: 3,000
SALES: 300K Privately Held
SIC: 3599 Bellows, industrial: metal

(G-6748)
OKLAHOMA EXECUTIVE PRINTING
1017 S Meridian Ave (73108-1701)
PHONE................405 948-8136
Nick Kakish, President
Sam Baker, Vice Pres
EMP: 3
SQ FT: 2,400
SALES: 750K Privately Held
SIC: 2752 2796 2791 Commercial printing, offset; platemaking services; typesetting

(G-6749)
OKLAHOMA FOUNDATION FOR DIGES
711 Stanton L Young Blvd (73104-5023)
PHONE................405 271-4602
Kay Springer, Exec Dir
Paige Ross,
EMP: 15
SALES (est): 800.7K Privately Held
SIC: 3721 Research & development on aircraft by the manufacturer

(G-6750)
OKLAHOMA GROCERS ASSOCIATION
25 Ne 52nd St (73105-1825)
PHONE................405 525-9419
Ron Edgmon, President
EMP: 11
SQ FT: 9,000
SALES: 80.8K Privately Held
SIC: 8611 2721 Trade associations; periodicals

(G-6751)
OKLAHOMA HIGH PRFMCE POLSG
117 N Council Rd Ste B (73127-4988)
PHONE................405 787-8388
EMP: 2 EST: 1995
SALES (est): 120K Privately Held
SIC: 3471 Plating/Polishing Service

(G-6752)
OKLAHOMA HOT SHOT SERVICE
1225 Se 29th St (73129-6439)
PHONE................405 605-0464
Daniel Baldwin, Principal
EMP: 1 EST: 2010
SALES (est): 124.3K Privately Held
SIC: 1389 Hot shot service

(G-6753)
OKLAHOMA LOGO SIGNS INC
4334 Nw Expwy St Ste 169 (73116-1515)
PHONE................405 840-1550
Jeremy Tilton, General Mgr
EMP: 8 EST: 2001
SALES (est): 779.3K Publicly Held
WEB: www.oklahoma.interstatelogos.com
SIC: 7312 3993 Outdoor advertising services; signs & advertising specialties
HQ: Interstate Logos, L.L.C.
16560 Old Perkins Rd
Baton Rouge LA 70810

(G-6754)
OKLAHOMA MACHINE GUNS LLC
615 W Wilshire Blvd Ste 1 (73116-7722)
P.O. Box 54925 (73154-1925)
PHONE................405 418-4867
Larry Hazelwood,
EMP: 2 EST: 2011
SQ FT: 500
SALES (est): 80.8K Privately Held
SIC: 3484 Guns (firearms) or gun parts, 30 mm. & below

(G-6755)
OKLAHOMA NEWSPAPER
Also Called: The Oklahoman Online
100 W Main St Ste 100 # 100 (73102-9007)
P.O. Box 25125 (73125-0125)
PHONE................405 475-3989
Christy Everest, President
EMP: 18
SALES (est): 841.7K Privately Held
SIC: 2711 Newspapers: publishing only, not printed on site
HQ: The Oklahoma Publishing Company Of Oklahoma
100 W Main St Ste 100 # 100
Oklahoma City OK 73102

(G-6756)
OKLAHOMA NEWSPAPER FOUNDATION
3601 N Lincoln Blvd (73105-5411)
PHONE................405 499-0020
Lisa Potts, Exec Dir
EMP: 20
SALES: 57.3K Privately Held
SIC: 2711 Newspapers, publishing & printing

(G-6757)
OKLAHOMA NTRY SVC A DIV OF M-
3627 Nw 50th St (73112-5605)
PHONE................405 948-8900
EMP: 1 EST: 2017
SALES (est): 37.5K Privately Held
SIC: 2741 Miscellaneous publishing

GEOGRAPHIC SECTION

Oklahoma City - Oklahoma County (G-6787)

(G-6758)
OKLAHOMA PROPANE GAS ASSN
4200 N Lindsay Ave (73105-7226)
PHONE.................405 424-1775
Roger Luke, *President*
Richard Hess, *Exec Dir*
EMP: 2
SALES: 133.5K **Privately Held**
SIC: 1321 2721 Propane (natural) production; periodicals

(G-6759)
OKLAHOMA PUBLISHING CO OF OKLA
Also Called: Distribution Systems Oklahoma
3901 N Harvard Ave (73122-2510)
P.O. Box 25125 (73125-0125)
PHONE.................405 475-3585
Larry Unruh, *General Mgr*
Carol Davis, *Credit Staff*
EMP: 40 **Privately Held**
SIC: 2711 6512 7375 5192 Newspapers, publishing & printing; nonresidential building operators; data base information retrieval; books, periodicals & newspapers
HQ: The Oklahoma Publishing Company Of Oklahoma
100 W Main St Ste 100 # 100
Oklahoma City OK 73102

(G-6760)
OKLAHOMA PUBLISHING COMPANY
7015 N Robinson Ave (73116-9044)
PHONE.................405 475-4040
Bekki Liles, *Principal*
EMP: 1
SALES (est): 37.5K **Privately Held**
SIC: 2741 Miscellaneous publishing

(G-6761)
OKLAHOMA RESTAURANT ASSN
3800 N Portland Ave (73112-2994)
PHONE.................405 942-8181
Jim Hopper, *President*
Robert Clift, *President*
Debra Bailey, *CFO*
Theresa Martin, *Manager*
Elizabeth Sanchez,
EMP: 15 **EST:** 1933
SQ FT: 7,500
SALES: 1.5MM **Privately Held**
SIC: 8611 2721 Merchants' association; periodicals

(G-6762)
OKLAHOMA SIGN COMPANY
5913 Se 67th St (73135-1739)
PHONE.................405 620-6716
Jeremiah Phillips, *Principal*
EMP: 2
SALES (est): 100K **Privately Held**
SIC: 3993 Signs & advertising specialties

(G-6763)
OKLAHOMA SOC PROF ENGINEERS
201 Ne 27th St Rm 125 (73105)
PHONE.................405 528-1435
Tommy Lear, *Treasurer*
Sheri Boeckman, *Exec Dir*
Sheri P BBA, *Exec Dir*
Marcia Bates, *Director*
John McElhenney, *Director*
EMP: 1
SQ FT: 2,000
SALES: 14.8K **Privately Held**
SIC: 8621 8641 2721 Professional membership organizations; civic social & fraternal associations; periodicals

(G-6764)
OKLAHOMA VISUAL GRAPHICS LLC
Also Called: Fastsigns
1401 S Meridian Ave (73108-1709)
PHONE.................405 943-3278
Michael Graves, *Principal*
EMP: 23
SALES (est): 642.8K **Privately Held**
SIC: 3993 Signs & advertising specialties

(G-6765)
OKLAHOMAN MEDIA COMPANY
100 W Main St Ste 100 # 100 (73102-9007)
P.O. Box 25125 (73125-0125)
PHONE.................405 475-3311
Gary Pierson, *CEO*
Christopher Reen, *President*
Todd Fraser, *Production*
Ed Oakley, *Accountant*
Trina Robinson, *Accounts Exec*
EMP: 15
SALES (est): 1MM **Privately Held**
SIC: 2711 Newspapers, publishing & printing

(G-6766)
OKLAND OIL COMPANY (PA)
110 N Robinson Ave # 400 (73102-9022)
PHONE.................405 236-3046
Steven Wetwiska, *President*
Mark Clay, *Vice Pres*
Cindy Jacobs, *Human Resources*
Rebecca Wetwiska, *Admin Sec*
Janice Fisher, *Assistant*
EMP: 20
SQ FT: 10,000
SALES: 7.2MM **Privately Held**
SIC: 1382 1311 7375 Oil & gas exploration services; crude petroleum production; natural gas production; data base information retrieval

(G-6767)
OKLUMA LLC
434 Nw 35th St (73118-8627)
PHONE.................580 716-1343
Jeff Sapp, *Principal*
EMP: 2 **EST:** 2015
SALES (est): 88.3K **Privately Held**
SIC: 3648 3676 Flashlights; electronic resistors

(G-6768)
OKSTYLE PUBLISHING LLC
220 W Wilshire Blvd F2 (73116-7774)
PHONE.................405 816-3338
EMP: 1
SALES (est): 40K **Privately Held**
SIC: 2741 Miscellaneous publishing

(G-6769)
OLD EPP INC
2425 S Ann Arbor Ave (73128-1845)
PHONE.................866 408-2837
EMP: 2
SALES (corp-wide): 62.7MM **Privately Held**
SIC: 3083 Laminated plastics plate & sheet
HQ: Old Epp, Inc.
360 Epic Circle Dr
Fairmont WV 26554
304 534-3600

(G-6770)
OLD INC
901 Nw 63rd St Ste 100 (73116-7622)
PHONE.................405 840-3017
Christopher J Dobbins, *President*
Kelly Wismer, *Vice Pres*
EMP: 2
SALES (est): 306K **Privately Held**
SIC: 1382 Oil & gas exploration services

(G-6771)
OLD WORLD IRON
8405 Mantle Ave (73132-4243)
PHONE.................405 722-0008
Todd Miller, *Owner*
EMP: 5
SALES (est): 579.3K **Privately Held**
SIC: 3446 Architectural metalwork

(G-6772)
OLMEVA USA LLC
1211 Se 29th St (73129-6439)
PHONE.................405 677-5400
EMP: 2 **EST:** 2015
SALES (est): 160.5K **Privately Held**
SIC: 3714 Motor vehicle parts & accessories

(G-6773)
OLYMPIA OIL INC
4808 Rose Rock Dr (73111-5406)
P.O. Box 7088, Edmond (73083-7088)
PHONE.................405 726-8400
Andrew Faulkner, *President*
EMP: 8 **EST:** 1979
SALES (est): 1.2MM **Privately Held**
SIC: 1311 Crude petroleum production; natural gas production

(G-6774)
OMADA INTERNATIONAL LLC
910 N Morgan Rd (73127-7143)
PHONE.................405 495-2131
Jim Hoover, *CEO*
EMP: 170
SALES (est): 48.2K **Privately Held**
SIC: 3812 Aircraft/aerospace flight instruments & guidance systems

(G-6775)
OMEGA OPTICAL CO LP
Also Called: Team Duffens Optical
713 Nw 119th St (73114)
PHONE.................405 703-4133
Ray Osborn, *Branch Mgr*
EMP: 27 **Privately Held**
SIC: 3851 5048 5049 Eyeglasses, lenses & frames; contact lenses; ophthalmic goods; frames, ophthalmic; lenses, ophthalmic; optical goods
PA: Omega Optical Co Lp
13515 N Stemmons Fwy
Dallas TX 75234

(G-6776)
OMG TOOLING INC
8000 Sw 8th St (73128-4248)
PHONE.................405 789-4774
Olie Gerardi, *President*
EMP: 9
SQ FT: 25,000
SALES (est): 1.4MM **Privately Held**
SIC: 3544 Industrial molds

(G-6777)
OMNI LLC
Also Called: Nexus Alliance Editorial &
3105 Huntleigh Dr (73120-2211)
PHONE.................405 246-9252
Kell Miller-Arrow, *Mng Member*
Mary Brown Miller,
EMP: 2
SQ FT: 3,000
SALES (est): 152.2K **Privately Held**
SIC: 2711 5112 Newspapers, publishing & printing; stationery & office supplies; computer & photocopying supplies; laserjet supplies

(G-6778)
ONEDOC MANAGED PRINT SVCS LLC
6505 Nw 114th St (73162-2928)
PHONE.................405 633-3050
Kevin Morris, *CEO*
EMP: 7
SALES (est): 2MM **Privately Held**
SIC: 5044 5045 7359 2759 Photocopy machines; typewriters; computers; business machine & electronic equipment rental services; office machine rental, except computers; commercial printing

(G-6779)
OPTIONONE LLC
14000 N Portland Ave (73134-4003)
PHONE.................405 548-4848
Jeff Wills, *COO*
Susan Schwarz, *Vice Pres*
Tom Garrett, *VP Bus Dvlpt*
Rebecca McReynolds, *VP Finance*
Heather Yancey, *Cert Phar Tech*
EMP: 20
SALES (est): 5.3MM **Privately Held**
SIC: 2834 8082 Pharmaceutical preparations; home health care services

(G-6780)
OPUBCO DEVELOPMENT CO
100 W Main St Ste 100 # 100 (73102-9025)
PHONE.................405 475-3311
Christy Everest, *CEO*
EMP: 50
SALES (est): 3MM **Privately Held**
SIC: 2711 Newspapers
HQ: The Oklahoma Publishing Company Of Oklahoma
100 W Main St Ste 100 # 100
Oklahoma City OK 73102

(G-6781)
ORDER-MATIC ELECTRONICS CORP
340 S Eckroat St (73129-8208)
P.O. Box 30469, Midwest City (73140-3469)
PHONE.................405 672-1487
Robert Powell, *CEO*
Jon Cervone, *Buyer*
Danny B Webb, *CFO*
John Derscha, *Business Anlyst*
Stevie Cunningham, *Marketing Staff*
EMP: 116 **EST:** 1956
SQ FT: 130,000
SALES (est): 24.6MM **Privately Held**
WEB: www.ordermatic.com
SIC: 3578 3669 3577 3993 Point-of-sale devices; intercommunication systems, electric; computer peripheral equipment; signs & advertising specialties

(G-6782)
ORTCO INC
1317 Se 25th St (73129-6433)
P.O. Box 94127 (73143-4127)
PHONE.................405 670-2803
Bill Newton, *Ch of Bd*
Carole Newton, *President*
Terri Church, *Vice Pres*
Diana McDowell, *Treasurer*
EMP: 26 **EST:** 1955
SQ FT: 20,000
SALES (est): 5.9MM **Privately Held**
SIC: 3533 Oil field machinery & equipment

(G-6783)
ORTHWEIN PETROLEUM
925 E Britton Rd (73114-7802)
P.O. Box 14180 (73113-0180)
PHONE.................405 478-7663
Richard Orthwein, *President*
EMP: 2
SALES (est): 280K **Privately Held**
SIC: 1382 Oil & gas exploration services

(G-6784)
OSAGE LAND COMPANY
1800 Cyn Pk Cir Ste 201 (73156)
P.O. Box 20772 (73156-0772)
PHONE.................405 946-8402
EMP: 13
SALES (est): 275K **Privately Held**
SIC: 1389 1381 8742 Whol Petroleum Products

(G-6785)
OSAGE OIL AND GAS PROPERTY
9520 N May Ave Ste 301 (73120-2735)
PHONE.................405 841-7600
James Dedine, *President*
Carmen Gomez, *Technician*
EMP: 3
SALES (est): 263.3K **Privately Held**
SIC: 1382 Oil & gas exploration services

(G-6786)
OSCIUM
5909 Nw Expressway # 269 (73132-5185)
PHONE.................719 695-0600
Mathew Lee, *Manager*
EMP: 1
SALES (est): 39.6K **Privately Held**
SIC: 3999 Manufacturing industries

(G-6787)
OSTEEN MEAT SPECIALTIES INC
2126 N Broadway Ave (73103-4310)
PHONE.................405 236-1952
Jim O Steen, *CEO*
Rick O Steen, *President*
June O Steen, *Corp Secy*
EMP: 60
SQ FT: 1,600

Oklahoma City - Oklahoma County (G-6788)

GEOGRAPHIC SECTION

SALES (est): 16.6MM **Privately Held**
SIC: **5147** 5144 2015 2013 Meats, fresh; poultry: live, dressed or frozen (unpackaged); poultry slaughtering & processing; sausages & other prepared meats

(G-6788)
OTC PETROLEUM CORPORATION
3244 Nw Grand Blvd (73116-3019)
PHONE..................................405 840-2255
John A Vance, *President*
EMP: 3
SALES (est): 317.3K **Privately Held**
SIC: **1382** 1311 Oil & gas exploration services; crude petroleum production; natural gas production

(G-6789)
OWEN OIL TOOLS LP
9616 Nw 6th St (73127-7111)
PHONE..................................405 495-4441
Hank Mayfield, *Regional Mgr*
Jamey Lindsey, *Technical Staff*
EMP: 5
SALES (corp-wide): 700.8MM **Privately Held**
SIC: **1389** Oil field services
HQ: Owen Oil Tools Lp
12001 County Road 1000
Godley TX 76044
817 551-0540

(G-6790)
OWENS CORNING SALES LLC
3400 Ne 4th St (73117-6407)
PHONE..................................405 235-2491
Pat Ryan, *Manager*
EMP: 12
SQ FT: 1,500 **Publicly Held**
SIC: **3296** Mineral wool
HQ: Owens Corning Sales, Llc
1 Owens Corning Pkwy
Toledo OH 43659
419 248-8000

(G-6791)
P D I INC
105 N Hudson Ave Ste 800 (73102-4803)
PHONE..................................405 232-9700
James B Crawley, *President*
Kim Hatfield, *Vice Pres*
Hatfield S K, *Vice Pres*
Donna Covington, *Admin Sec*
Mary Crawley, *Admin Sec*
EMP: 26
SQ FT: 9,378
SALES (est): 1.7MM
SALES (corp-wide): 13.7MM **Privately Held**
SIC: **1311** Crude petroleum production; natural gas production
PA: Crawley Petroleum Corporation
105 N Hudson Ave Ste 800
Oklahoma City OK 73102
405 232-9700

(G-6792)
PACCAR INC
5700 S Council Rd (73179-5000)
PHONE..................................405 745-3006
Kathy Horn, *Branch Mgr*
EMP: 40
SALES (corp-wide): 24.1B **Publicly Held**
SIC: **3711** Motor vehicles & car bodies
PA: Paccar Inc
777 106th Ave Ne
Bellevue WA 98004
425 468-7400

(G-6793)
PACIFIC POWER GROUP LLC
Also Called: Pacific Power Products
4253 Will Rogers Pkwy (73108-2039)
PHONE..................................405 685-4630
EMP: 5
SALES (corp-wide): 18.1MM **Privately Held**
SIC: **3519** 5084 Diesel engine rebuilding; engines & parts, diesel
HQ: Pacific Power Group, Llc
805 Broadway St Ste 700
Vancouver WA 98660
360 887-7400

(G-6794)
PAL-SERV OKLAHOMA CITY LLC
1432 W Main St (73106-5226)
PHONE..................................405 672-1155
Jacob Folmar, *Plant Mgr*
James R Norris, *Mng Member*
Russell B Bunker,
Roland W Burgess Jr,
Jackey D Foster,
EMP: 40
SALES: 900K **Privately Held**
WEB: www.pal-serv.com
SIC: **2448** Pallets, wood

(G-6795)
PALEO INC
6303 N Portland Ave # 203 (73112-1411)
PHONE..................................405 942-1546
Doug Summers, *President*
L L Summers, *Corp Secy*
Harold L Summers, *Vice Pres*
EMP: 5
SQ FT: 1,700
SALES (est): 590K **Privately Held**
SIC: **1311** Crude petroleum production; natural gas production

(G-6796)
PALLET LIQUIDATIONS OKC LLC
12017 Brookhollow Rd (73120-5502)
PHONE..................................405 843-0402
David Portman, *Principal*
EMP: 4
SALES (est): 159.6K **Privately Held**
SIC: **2448** Pallets, wood & wood with metal

(G-6797)
PALLET LOGISTICS OF AMERICA
1901 S Skyline Dr (73129-6053)
PHONE..................................405 670-1414
James Crow, *Principal*
EMP: 2 EST: 2008
SALES (est): 269.2K **Privately Held**
WEB: www.plofa.com
SIC: **2448** Pallets, wood

(G-6798)
PANHANDLE OIL AND GAS INC (PA)
5400 N Grand Blvd Ste 300 (73112-5672)
PHONE..................................405 948-1560
Chad L Stephens, *CEO*
Lonnie J Lowry, *Vice Pres*
Freda R Webb, *Vice Pres*
Ralph D'Amico, *CFO*
EMP: 12
SALES: 66MM **Publicly Held**
SIC: **1382** Oil & gas exploration services

(G-6799)
PANHANDLE OILFIELD SERVICE COM (PA)
Also Called: Panhandle Pipe Supply
14000 Quail Springs Pkwy # 300 (73134-2600)
P.O. Box 1256, Liberal KS (67905-1256)
PHONE..................................405 608-5330
Tim Long, *CEO*
Ty Williams, *Regional Mgr*
Carrie Hensley, *Vice Pres*
Jake Abney, *Sales Staff*
Tanner Long, *Marketing Staff*
EMP: 65
SALES (est): 111.5MM **Privately Held**
SIC: **1389** 7389 4212 5082 Oil & gas wells: building, repairing & dismantling; oil field services; inspection & testing services; local trucking, without storage; oil field equipment; excavation work

(G-6800)
PANHANDLE ROYALTY CO
5400 N Grand Blvd Ste 300 (73112-5672)
PHONE..................................405 945-6100
Michael Kauffman, *President*
EMP: 3
SALES (est): 171.1K **Privately Held**
WEB: www.panhandleoilandgas.com
SIC: **1311** 4925 6792 Crude petroleum production; gas production and/or distribution; oil royalty traders

(G-6801)
PANTHER DRILLING SYSTEMS LLC
14301 Caliber Dr Ste 220 (73134-1037)
PHONE..................................405 896-9300
James Steed, *Principal*
EMP: 32
SALES (est): 1.9MM **Privately Held**
SIC: **1381** Directional drilling oil & gas wells

(G-6802)
PAPER PLUS
290 S Quadrum Dr (73108-1101)
PHONE..................................405 948-1120
Kathy Williams, *Branch Mgr*
EMP: 4 **Privately Held**
SIC: **2611** Pulp manufactured from waste or recycled paper
PA: Paper Plus
6600 Governors Lake Pkwy
Peachtree Corners GA

(G-6803)
PARAGON PRESS INC
3029 S Ann Arbor Ave (73179-7636)
PHONE..................................405 681-5757
Paul Bull, *President*
Joyce Bull, *Vice Pres*
Kelton Spears, *Treasurer*
EMP: 6
SQ FT: 12,160
SALES (est): 959.1K **Privately Held**
SIC: **2752** Commercial printing, offset

(G-6804)
PARAMOUNT BUILDING PDTS LLC
6924 Nw 80th St (73132-4212)
PHONE..................................405 470-5073
EMP: 2
SALES (est): 113.5K **Privately Held**
SIC: **5031** 2431 Composite board products, woodboard; millwork

(G-6805)
PARWEST LAND EXPLORATION INC
2601 Nw Expwy Ste 707w (73112-7240)
PHONE..................................405 843-1917
Peter Ferraro, *President*
EMP: 3
SQ FT: 1,000
SALES (est): 476.2K **Privately Held**
SIC: **1382** Oil & gas exploration services

(G-6806)
PASCHALL LAND MANAGEMENT
6424 N Santa Fe Ave Ste A (73116-9119)
PHONE..................................405 842-1391
Susan Paschall, *Owner*
EMP: 4
SALES: 500K **Privately Held**
SIC: **1389** Construction, repair & dismantling services

(G-6807)
PASEO POTTERY
3017 Paseo (73103-1020)
PHONE..................................405 525-3017
Collin Rosebrook, *Owner*
Rita Rosebrook, *Co-Owner*
EMP: 2
SALES (est): 120K **Privately Held**
SIC: **5719** 3269 Pottery; pottery cooking & kitchen articles

(G-6808)
PASTA PIZZAZ INC
8121 N Classen Blvd Ste C (73114-2154)
PHONE..................................405 848-9966
Robert G Knobbe, *President*
Robert Knobbe, *President*
Cathy Meyer, *Vice Pres*
EMP: 4
SALES: 160K **Privately Held**
SIC: **2098** 5812 Noodles (e.g. egg, plain & water), dry; Italian restaurant

(G-6809)
PATHINNOVATION LLC
133 Lake Aluma Dr (73121-3401)
PHONE..................................405 475-9726
Peng Xiao Cong,
EMP: 1
SALES (est): 106.1K **Privately Held**
SIC: **3841** Surgical & medical instruments

(G-6810)
PATS MACHINE
2229 Sw 42nd St (73119-3520)
PHONE..................................405 681-1050
Pat Gabrish, *Owner*
EMP: 2
SALES (est): 110K **Privately Held**
SIC: **3599** Machine shop, jobbing & repair

(G-6811)
PATS PHASE II HAIR & NAIL SLN
120 N Robinson Ave B38e (73102-7509)
PHONE..................................405 232-4746
Pat Beckner, *Principal*
EMP: 2
SALES (est): 66K **Privately Held**
SIC: **1481** Nonmetallic mineral services

(G-6812)
PAUL E KLOBERDANZ
100 N Broadway Ave # 3150 (73102-8614)
P.O. Box 57756 (73157-7756)
PHONE..................................405 947-5570
Paul E Kloberdanz, *Owner*
EMP: 2
SQ FT: 1,500
SALES (est): 184.6K **Privately Held**
SIC: **1311** Crude petroleum production; natural gas production

(G-6813)
PAYCOM SOFTWARE INC (PA)
7501 W Memorial Rd (73142-1404)
PHONE..................................405 722-6900
Chad Richison, *Ch of Bd*
John McManamey, *Business Mgr*
Jon Evans, *COO*
Jessica Eibel, *Counsel*
Christopher Dingess, *Exec VP*
EMP: 96
SQ FT: 250,000
SALES: 737.6MM **Publicly Held**
SIC: **7371** 7372 8721 Custom computer programming services; computer software development & applications; prepackaged software; payroll accounting service

(G-6814)
PAYROCK II LLC
3200 Quail Springs Pkwy (73134-2604)
PHONE..................................405 608-8077
Chad Ford, *Exec VP*
Mike Brown, *Vice Pres*
Lindsey McCarty, *Vice Pres*
Steve Henley, *VP Opers*
Trey Roper, *CFO*
EMP: 2
SALES (est): 72K **Privately Held**
SIC: **1389** Oil field services

(G-6815)
PAYZONE COMPLETION SVCS LLC
837 Se 82nd St (73149-2928)
PHONE..................................405 772-7184
Calvin White, *CEO*
David Droke, *President*
Jk Meador, *Director*
EMP: 75
SALES: 25MM
SALES (corp-wide): 79MM **Privately Held**
WEB: www.payzonecompletionservices.com
SIC: **1389** Construction, repair & dismantling services
PA: White's Energy Services, Llc
46005 S County Road 202
Woodward OK 73801
580 254-3766

(G-6816)
PEAK OPERATING LLC
1601 Nw Expwy St Ste 1600 (73118-1420)
PHONE..................................405 343-7590
EMP: 3
SALES (est): 299.1K **Privately Held**
SIC: **1382** Oil & gas exploration services

GEOGRAPHIC SECTION

Oklahoma City - Oklahoma County (G-6849)

(G-6817)
PEAKE FUEL SOLUTIONS LLC
6100 N Western Ave (73118-1044)
P.O. Box 54894 (73154-1894)
PHONE..................................405 935-8000
Robert Doug Lawler, *CEO*
Domenic J Dell'osso Jr, *CFO*
EMP: 3
SALES (est): 251.1K **Privately Held**
SIC: 1311 Crude petroleum production

(G-6818)
PEARL ENERGY GROUP LLC
9201 Via Del Vis (73131-5803)
PHONE..................................281 799-7459
Justin Bruner, *Mng Member*
EMP: 2
SALES: 250K **Privately Held**
SIC: 1389 Cementing oil & gas well casings

(G-6819)
PEDESTAL OIL COMPANY INC
204 N Robinson Ave # 1700 (73102-6810)
P.O. Box 1522 (73101-1522)
PHONE..................................405 236-8596
Dave Singer, *President*
Janice Y Singer, *Corp Secy*
George Singer, *Vice Pres*
EMP: 15
SQ FT: 3,000
SALES (est): 2.1MM **Privately Held**
SIC: 1311 Crude petroleum production; natural gas production

(G-6820)
PEGLEG PUBLISHING LLC
1612 Nw 20th St (73106-3821)
PHONE..................................405 618-7740
EMP: 1
SALES (est): 37.5K **Privately Held**
WEB: www.peglegpublishing.com
SIC: 2741 Miscellaneous publishing

(G-6821)
PEL COMPANY LLC
2805 N Windsor Ter (73127-1930)
PHONE..................................405 816-6553
Jacob N Bollig, *Principal*
Jacob Bollig, *Principal*
Cody Boswell, *Principal*
Michelle Marshall, *Principal*
Thomas Weston, *Principal*
EMP: 4
SALES (est): 123.8K **Privately Held**
SIC: 2499 Wood products

(G-6822)
PELCO PRODUCTS INC
1025 Nw Grand Blvd (73118-6039)
PHONE..................................405 842-6978
Tom Holbrook, *Principal*
EMP: 2
SALES (est): 73.4K **Privately Held**
SIC: 3429 Manufactured hardware (general)

(G-6823)
PELICAN ENERGY LLC
301 Nw 63rd St Ste 600 (73116-7909)
PHONE..................................405 418-8000
Aubrey McClendon, *Principal*
Marika Johnson, *Treasurer*
EMP: 2 EST: 2012
SALES (est): 216.5K **Privately Held**
SIC: 1311 Crude petroleum & natural gas production

(G-6824)
PENN MACHINE INC
8513 Sw 2nd St (73128-3602)
PHONE..................................405 789-0084
Jeff Hall, *President*
EMP: 17
SQ FT: 5,000
SALES (est): 4MM **Privately Held**
SIC: 3533 3569 Oil field machinery & equipment; assembly machines, non-metalworking

(G-6825)
PENN-OK GATHERING SYSTEMS INC
Also Called: Meade Energy
5605 N Classen Blvd (73118-4015)
PHONE..................................405 843-1544
James C Meade, *President*
Virginia A Mead, *President*
EMP: 20
SQ FT: 6,000
SALES (est): 2.6MM **Privately Held**
SIC: 1382 Oil & gas exploration services

(G-6826)
PENNER ENERGY INC
3336 Rock Hollow Rd (73120-1930)
PHONE..................................405 751-7504
Frederic J Penner, *President*
Jennifer F Penner, *Corp Secy*
EMP: 1
SALES (est): 140K **Privately Held**
SIC: 1311 Crude petroleum production; natural gas production

(G-6827)
PENNMARK ENERGY LLC
2601 Nw Expwy Ste 1200w (73112-7285)
P.O. Box 57132 (73157-7132)
PHONE..................................405 840-9885
Richard Klingenberg, *Mng Member*
EMP: 1
SALES (est): 73.7K **Privately Held**
SIC: 1382 Oil & gas exploration services

(G-6828)
PERFECT PITCH MUSIC
412 Nw 23rd St (73103-1508)
PHONE..................................405 521-8088
Floyd Hanes, *Manager*
EMP: 2
SALES (est): 86.6K **Privately Held**
SIC: 3841 Surgical & medical instruments

(G-6829)
PERFORMANCE COATINGS INC
201 E Hill St (73105-4009)
PHONE..................................405 525-9790
Chuck Simpson, *President*
Barbara Newell, *Executive*
EMP: 7
SQ FT: 11,000
SALES (est): 512.2K **Privately Held**
SIC: 3479 2816 Aluminum coating of metal products; inorganic pigments

(G-6830)
PERFORMANCE SURFACES LLC
821 W Wilshire Blvd (73116-7021)
PHONE..................................405 463-0505
Kent Hoffman, *CEO*
John Conners, *President*
EMP: 7
SALES (est): 1MM **Privately Held**
SIC: 1752 3949 Floor laying & floor work; track & field athletic equipment

(G-6831)
PERISCOPE LEGAL
128 W Hefner Rd (73114-6629)
PHONE..................................405 418-4155
EMP: 2
SALES (est): 126.1K **Privately Held**
SIC: 3827 Periscopes

(G-6832)
PERKINS SOUTH PLAINS INC
4253 Will Rogers Pkwy (73108-2039)
PHONE..................................405 685-4630
Troy Luebecke, *Branch Mgr*
EMP: 46
SALES (corp-wide): 731.7MM **Privately Held**
SIC: 3561 Pumps & pumping equipment
HQ: Perkins South Plains, Inc.
6300 W Highway 80
Midland TX 79706
432 563-9602

(G-6833)
PERMIAN RESOURCES HOLDINGS LLC (PA)
301 Nw 63rd St (73116-7907)
PHONE..................................405 418-8000
Jeffrey Mobley, *CEO*

Thomas Ferguson, *Managing Prtnr*
Jerrald J Straton, *COO*
Laura Manwell, *Treasurer*
EMP: 7
SALES (est): 37.8MM
SALES (corp-wide): 37.4MM **Privately Held**
SIC: 6799 1382 Investors; oil & gas exploration services

(G-6834)
PERRY BROADCASTING COMPANY
1528 Ne 23rd St Ste A (73111-3260)
PHONE..................................405 427-5877
Kevin Perry, *General Mgr*
Johnny Moore, *Sales Mgr*
EMP: 10 **Privately Held**
SIC: 2711 Commercial printing & newspaper publishing combined
PA: Perry Broadcasting Company, Inc
1457 Ne 23rd St
Oklahoma City OK 73111

(G-6835)
PETRO SOURCE CONSULTANTS
2400 Nw 120th St (73120-7403)
PHONE..................................405 751-0474
Dennis Fraiser, *Owner*
EMP: 3
SALES (est): 195.8K **Privately Held**
SIC: 1389 Oil consultants

(G-6836)
PETROLEUM ELASTOMERS
1400 Se 25th St (73129-7606)
PHONE..................................405 672-0900
Jason Phelps, *Principal*
EMP: 3 EST: 2011
SALES (est): 128.6K **Privately Held**
WEB: www.fogt.com
SIC: 1389 Oil field services

(G-6837)
PETROLEUM INSTRUMENTS CO INC
1312 Se 25th St (73129-6434)
P.O. Box 94314 (73143-4314)
PHONE..................................405 670-6200
Terry Tidwell, *President*
Pam Pugsley, *Corp Secy*
Pam Tidwell, *Corp Secy*
Ed Tidwell, *Vice Pres*
EMP: 12 EST: 1978
SALES (est): 1MM **Privately Held**
SIC: 7699 7353 3533 Industrial machinery & equipment repair; oil field equipment, rental or leasing; oil & gas field machinery

(G-6838)
PETROLEUM STRATEGIES UNLIMITED
13120 Box Canyon Rd (73142-6202)
PHONE..................................405 720-0200
EMP: 14
SALES (est): 1MM **Privately Held**
SIC: 1382 Oil/Gas Exploration Services

(G-6839)
PFPP LP
Also Called: Randall Reed Ford
2800 W I 44 Service Rd (73112-3722)
PHONE..................................405 946-3381
Robert Wilson, *Manager*
EMP: 75 EST: 2012
SALES (est): 13.4MM **Privately Held**
SIC: 5511 3713 3715 Automobiles, new & used; vans, new & used; pickups, new & used; truck beds; truck trailer chassis

(G-6840)
PG13 GRAPHICS & DESIGN LLC
8324 Picnic Ln (73127-3025)
PHONE..................................405 720-8002
Eldon Harding, *Owner*
EMP: 2
SALES (est): 110K **Privately Held**
SIC: 3993 Signs & advertising specialties

(G-6841)
PHELPS SCULPTURE STUDIO
3 N Ellison Ave (73106-7801)
PHONE..................................405 752-9512
David L Phelps, *Owner*

EMP: 3
SALES (est): 152K **Privately Held**
SIC: 3299 3269 Architectural sculptures: gypsum, clay, papier mache, etc.; pottery products

(G-6842)
PHIL-GOOD PRODUCTS INC
3500 W Reno Ave (73107-6191)
PHONE..................................405 942-5527
Peggy Phillips, *President*
Tim Cassil, *Exec VP*
Rose Sutcliffe, *QC Mgr*
John Tate, *Manager*
Barbara Decastro, *Exec Dir*
▲ EMP: 30 EST: 1959
SQ FT: 20,000
SALES (est): 7.2MM **Privately Held**
WEB: www.philgood.com
SIC: 3089 Injection molding of plastics

(G-6843)
PHOENIX DESIGN & MFG LLC
6215 Aluma Valley Dr (73121-1415)
P.O. Box 891915 (73189-1915)
PHONE..................................405 418-4858
Stephnie Erickson, *Office Mgr*
Leslie C Barnhart,
▲ EMP: 6 EST: 2008
SALES (est): 1.1MM **Privately Held**
WEB: www.phoenixdesignmfg.com
SIC: 3444 Sheet metal specialties, not stamped

(G-6844)
PHOENIX GROUP HOLDING COMPANY
5725 Sw 21st St (73128-1837)
PHONE..................................405 948-7788
Denny Hight, *President*
EMP: 10
SQ FT: 2,400
SALES (est): 1.3MM **Privately Held**
SIC: 8748 7699 3845 3822 Environmental consultant; waste cleaning services; electromedical equipment; auto controls regulating residntl & coml environmt & applncs; blowers & fans

(G-6845)
PHOENIX INDUSTRIES LLC
6517 N May Ave (73116-4838)
PHONE..................................405 848-1688
Arthur Gordon, *President*
EMP: 4
SALES (est): 416.3K **Privately Held**
SIC: 5944 3911 Jewelry stores; jewelry, precious metal

(G-6846)
PHOENIX TRADE PUBLICATION
3108 Nw 54th St (73112-5309)
PHONE..................................405 948-6555
Bruce Sankey, *Principal*
EMP: 3
SALES (est): 215.5K **Privately Held**
SIC: 2721 Magazines: publishing only, not printed on site

(G-6847)
PHYSICAL HOME DEFENSE
10316 Greenbriar Pl Ste 7 (73159-7649)
PHONE..................................405 819-0939
Paul Palmer, *Principal*
EMP: 3
SALES (est): 145.5K **Privately Held**
SIC: 3812 Defense systems & equipment

(G-6848)
PIGEON DEBUT
3341 Sw 49th St (73119-4330)
PHONE..................................405 686-0412
EMP: 2 EST: 2010
SALES (est): 110K **Privately Held**
SIC: 2721 Periodicals-Publishing/Printing

(G-6849)
PINNACLE ENERGY SERVICES LLC (PA)
9420 Cedar Lake Ave (73114-7809)
PHONE..................................405 810-9151
John Dick,
Brian Simmons, *Analyst*
EMP: 8

Oklahoma City - Oklahoma County (G-6850)

SALES (est): 1.5MM **Privately Held**
SIC: **1389** 8711 Oil field services; engineering services

(G-6850)
PINPOINT MONOGRAMS INC
280 S Quadrum Dr (73108-1101)
P.O. Box 270426 (73137-0426)
PHONE.....................405 228-0600
Paula Prestridge, *President*
Bobby Prestridge, *Vice Pres*
Keri Prestridge, *Admin Sec*
Sheryl Farrell, *Graphic Designe*
EMP: 10
SQ FT: 11,000
SALES (est): 1.1MM **Privately Held**
SIC: **2395** 7299 2396 Embroidery & art needlework; embroidery products, except schiffli machine; stitching services; automotive & apparel trimmings

(G-6851)
PINSON WELL LOGGING
25 N Cooley Dr (73127-1026)
P.O. Box 31564, Edmond (73003-0027)
PHONE.....................405 604-5036
Bill Pinson, *Manager*
EMP: 2 EST: 2011
SALES (est): 267.3K **Privately Held**
WEB: www.pinsonwelllogging.com
SIC: **1389** Oil field services

(G-6852)
PIONEER WIRELINE SERVICES
1535 Se 25th St (73129-7607)
PHONE.....................405 601-8755
EMP: 2 EST: 2016
SALES (est): 101.8K **Privately Held**
SIC: **1389** Oil & gas field services

(G-6853)
PIPES PLUS LLC
920 N Meridian Ave (73107-5731)
PHONE.....................405 942-7473
Darla Kyles, *Mng Member*
EMP: 1
SALES: 119K **Privately Held**
SIC: **3088** Plastics plumbing fixtures

(G-6854)
PIRANHA PROPPANT LLC
14201 Caliber Dr Ste 200 (73134-1017)
PHONE.....................715 642-4192
EMP: 5
SALES (est): 596.8K **Privately Held**
SIC: **1382** Oil & gas exploration services

(G-6855)
PLAINS NITROGEN LLC
2601 Nw Exprkway Ste 411w (73112)
PHONE.....................405 418-8426
David Wright, *Owner*
EMP: 2
SALES (corp-wide): 129.8MM **Privately Held**
SIC: **1389** Oil field services
HQ: Plains Nitrogen Llc
    2601 Nw Expwy Ste 411w
    Oklahoma City OK

(G-6856)
PLATT ENERGY CORPORATION
11600 Broadway Ext # 250 (73114-6609)
PHONE.....................405 840-5081
George Platt, *President*
Michael Platt, *Vice Pres*
Steve Cottom, *CFO*
EMP: 5
SALES (est): 630K **Privately Held**
SIC: **1311** 6552 Crude petroleum production; natural gas production; subdividers & developers

(G-6857)
PLOW TECHNOLOGIES LLC
8925 Nw 10th St (73127-2919)
P.O. Box 851012, Yukon (73085-1012)
PHONE.....................405 265-6072
Jeremy Peterson, *Engineer*
Mohammad Khaled, *Electrical Engi*
Atlee Hickerson, *Marketing Staff*
Scott Murphy, *Mng Member*
Chad Edwards, *Manager*
EMP: 22 EST: 2011
SQ FT: 2,000
SALES (est): 8.1MM **Privately Held**
WEB: www.plowtech.net
SIC: **1382** Oil & gas exploration services

(G-6858)
PML EXPLORATION SERVICES LLC
5600 Se 11th St (73128)
PHONE.....................405 606-2701
Jim Fletcher, *Branch Mgr*
EMP: 50
SALES (corp-wide): 8MM **Privately Held**
SIC: **1389** Mud service, oil field drilling
PA: Pml Exploration Services Llc
    19059 Champion Forest Dr # 103
    Spring TX 77379
    405 606-2701

(G-6859)
PNG OPERATION
5704 Nw 132nd St (73142-4430)
PHONE.....................405 470-4333
Steve Prentice, *Principal*
EMP: 2
SQ FT: 2,832
SALES (est): 143.3K **Privately Held**
SIC: **1381** 8711 8748 Drilling oil & gas wells; petroleum engineering; business consulting

(G-6860)
POGUE MACHINE INC
3700 S High Ave (73129-5236)
P.O. Box 96145 (73143-6145)
PHONE.....................405 677-9397
Tommy Pogue, *President*
Sid Pogue, *Vice Pres*
EMP: 5 EST: 1956
SQ FT: 12,000
SALES: 600K **Privately Held**
SIC: **3599** 5013 Machine shop, jobbing & repair; motorcycle parts

(G-6861)
POINT TO POINT SOFTWARE
8901 S Anderson Rd (73150-6905)
PHONE.....................405 869-9921
EMP: 2 EST: 2004
SALES (est): 120K **Privately Held**
SIC: **7372** Prepackaged Software Services

(G-6862)
POINTER WADDELL & ASSOCIATES
5400 N Grand Blvd Ste 560 (73112-5680)
PHONE.....................405 942-5600
EMP: 2
SALES (est): 74.4K **Privately Held**
SIC: **2844** Toilet Preparations

(G-6863)
POMCO INC (PA)
17 Se 55th St (73129-3605)
P.O. Box 94607 (73143-4607)
PHONE.....................405 677-8859
Paul Nunley, *President*
Billie Jo Nunley, *Corp Secy*
Curtis Wayne Sanders, *Vice Pres*
Wayne Sanders, *Vice Pres*
Judy Sanders, *Shareholder*
EMP: 19
SQ FT: 13,000
SALES (est): 2.8MM **Privately Held**
SIC: **3561** 5085 Pumps & pumping equipment; gaskets

(G-6864)
PORTMAN MINERALS LLC
2424 Nw 55th Pl (73112-7723)
PHONE.....................405 843-4063
William Portman, *Principal*
EMP: 2
SALES (est): 171K **Privately Held**
SIC: **1311** Crude petroleum production

(G-6865)
POST OAK OIL CO
13300 N Macarthur Blvd (73142-3021)
PHONE.....................405 621-1300
Bruce M Bell, *CEO*
Carri A Bell, *Principal*
EMP: 4
SQ FT: 3,600
SALES (est): 371.5K **Privately Held**
SIC: **1311** Crude petroleum production; natural gas production

(G-6866)
POST-TENSION SERVICES OF OKLA
209 Nw 111th St (73114-6603)
PHONE.....................405 751-1582
Matthew Barlow, *Mng Member*
EMP: 13
SALES (est): 2.1MM **Privately Held**
SIC: **5051** 3449 Forms, concrete construction (steel); bars, concrete reinforcing: fabricated steel

(G-6867)
POTOCO LLC
1141 N Robinson Ave # 301 (73103-4929)
PHONE.....................405 600-3065
Darwin Maxey, *Principal*
EMP: 2
SALES (est): 153.8K **Privately Held**
SIC: **1382** Oil & gas exploration services

(G-6868)
POWDER COATINGS PLUS LLC
Also Called: Industrial Powder Coatings
513 N Indiana Ave (73106-2606)
PHONE.....................405 232-5707
Jim Sizemore, *General Mgr*
Karen Jones Phillpott, *Principal*
Bob Jones, *Mng Member*
Dan B Jones,
Robert S Jones,
EMP: 10
SQ FT: 33,000
SALES (est): 1.2MM **Privately Held**
WEB: www.ipc-sw.com
SIC: **3479** Coating of metals & formed products

(G-6869)
POWER EQUIPMENT & ENGRG INC (PA)
1739 W Main St (73106-3091)
PHONE.....................405 235-0531
Jon K Stallings, *President*
Bill Jones, *Sales Mgr*
Terry Choate, *Sales Staff*
Dan Ellis, *Sales Staff*
Terry Johnston, *Sales Staff*
EMP: 21
SQ FT: 22,000
SALES (est): 5.8MM **Privately Held**
WEB: www.pe-ei.com
SIC: **3714** Motor vehicle parts & accessories

(G-6870)
POWERHOUSE RESOURCES INTL INC
6 Ne 6th St (73104-1802)
PHONE.....................405 232-7474
Linda Mandel, *CEO*
Juan Velez, *Opers Staff*
Patricia Stover, *Finance*
Trish Stover, *Finance*
EMP: 59
SQ FT: 16,000
SALES (est): 6.3MM **Privately Held**
SIC: **4581** 3559 Aircraft maintenance & repair services; automotive maintenance equipment

(G-6871)
POWERTRAIN COMPANY LLC
400 S Lee Ave (73109-5025)
PHONE.....................703 419-0104
Joe Holinsworth, *Owner*
EMP: 2
SALES (est): 205.2K **Privately Held**
SIC: **3714** Motor vehicle parts & accessories

(G-6872)
PPM MANUFACTURING LLC
3333 Nw 63rd St Ste 104 (73116-3710)
PHONE.....................405 843-4448
Robert Monnet,
EMP: 6
SALES (est): 217K **Privately Held**
SIC: **3999** Manufacturing industries

(G-6873)
PRAIRIE GYPSIES INC
411 Nw 30th St (73118-8600)
PHONE.....................405 525-3013
Claudia Goodnight, *Corp Secy*
Debbie Leland, *Vice Pres*
EMP: 7 EST: 1994
SQ FT: 3,000
SALES (est): 324.4K **Privately Held**
WEB: www.prairiegypsies.com
SIC: **5812** 2033 Caterers; carry-out only (except pizza) restaurant; jams, jellies & preserves: packaged in cans, jars, etc.

(G-6874)
PRATT INDUSTRIES USA INC
305 N Rockwell Ave (73127-6116)
P.O. Box 270715 (73137-0715)
PHONE.....................405 787-3500
Tracy Baade, *General Mgr*
Kelle L Oliphant, *Sales Staff*
Kevin Brown, *Executive*
Paul Clark,
EMP: 267 **Privately Held**
WEB: www.prattindustries.com
SIC: **2653** 2441 3412 Boxes, corrugated: made from purchased materials; boxes, wood; metal barrels, drums & pails
PA: Pratt Industries, Inc.
    1800 Sarasot Bus Pkwy Ne S
    Conyers GA 30013

(G-6875)
PRATT WHTNEY MLTARY AFTRMRKET
Also Called: P&W Wrhuse Lgstic Srvices-Okc
8120 Mid America Blvd # 3 (73135-6613)
PHONE.....................405 622-2561
Carl McCoy, *Manager*
EMP: 3
SALES (est): 264.9K **Privately Held**
SIC: **3724** Aircraft engines & engine parts

(G-6876)
PRATT WHTNEY MLTARY AFTRMRKET
Also Called: Pratt Whtney Mltary Aftrmrket
2701 Liberty Pkwy Ste 301 (73110-2895)
PHONE.....................405 737-4851
Sam Anderson, *General Mgr*
Steven M Hurley, *General Mgr*
▲ EMP: 6
SALES (est): 1.3MM
SALES (corp-wide): 77B **Publicly Held**
SIC: **3724** Aircraft engines & engine parts
PA: Raytheon Technologies Corporation
    870 Winter St
    Waltham MA 02451
    781 522-3000

(G-6877)
PRECAST TRTMNT SOLUTIONS LLC
13525 Se 74th St (73150-8000)
PHONE.....................405 455-5303
Leslie J Vise, *Principal*
EMP: 3
SALES (est): 267K **Privately Held**
SIC: **3272** Precast terrazo or concrete products

(G-6878)
PRECIOUS MEMORIES BY M L
3801 Quail Dr (73121-4043)
PHONE.....................405 427-7007
Mary Howard, *Owner*
EMP: 1
SQ FT: 300
SALES (est): 51.7K **Privately Held**
SIC: **2051** Cakes, bakery: except frozen

(G-6879)
PRECISE TOOL & MACHINE COMPANY
8124 Sw 8th St Ste E (73128-4241)
PHONE.....................405 495-2001
Brian Faldo, *Partner*
Barry Litchfield, *Partner*
EMP: 6
SQ FT: 6,400
SALES (est): 723.7K **Privately Held**
SIC: **3544** Special dies & tools

GEOGRAPHIC SECTION

Oklahoma City - Oklahoma County (G-6908)

(G-6880)
PRECISION ANODIZING INC
800 804 Se 82nd St (73149)
PHONE..............................405 631-2079
Noel Rosser, *President*
Susan Rosser, *Corp Secy*
Kenneth Rosser, *Vice Pres*
EMP: 10 **EST:** 1978
SQ FT: 10,500
SALES (est): 1.1MM **Privately Held**
SIC: 3471 Electroplating of metals or formed products

(G-6881)
PRECISION DRIVE LTD INC
6201 Sw 15th St (73128-2002)
P.O. Box 82274 (73148-0274)
PHONE..............................405 495-1344
Gradyn F Avritt, *President*
T A Mace, *Vice Pres*
EMP: 3 **EST:** 1977
SQ FT: 4,800
SALES: 400K **Privately Held**
SIC: 3714 7539 Drive shafts, motor vehicle; automotive repair shops

(G-6882)
PRECISION METAL FORMING LLC
7000 S Bryant Ave (73149-7208)
PHONE..............................405 677-3777
Bill Clark, *Mng Member*
Ken Clark,
EMP: 30
SQ FT: 20,000
SALES (est): 2.9MM **Privately Held**
SIC: 3479 Coating of metals & formed products

(G-6883)
PRECISION SHELTERS
13612 Gentry Dr (73142-4202)
PHONE..............................405 936-0900
Jonathan Epps, *Principal*
EMP: 14
SALES (est): 3.2MM **Privately Held**
WEB: www.precisionshelters.com
SIC: 3442 Screen & storm doors & windows

(G-6884)
PREMIER ENERGY LLC
3700 N Classen Blvd # 220 (73118-2872)
PHONE..............................405 286-0615
J Carter Hines, *President*
Wilbur A Dennison, *Vice Pres*
Luke M Curley,
EMP: 3 **EST:** 1979
SQ FT: 1,119
SALES (est): 598.5K
SALES (corp-wide): 2.7MM **Privately Held**
SIC: 1382 Oil & gas exploration services
PA: Amer-Tex Energy, Inc
  6801 Broadway Ext Ste 316
  Oklahoma City OK
  405 840-0018

(G-6885)
PREMIER METAL FINISHING INC
640 N Meridian Ave (73107-5725)
P.O. Box 82785 (73148-0785)
PHONE..............................405 947-0200
Cliff Mareill, *Principal*
EMP: 6
SQ FT: 21,415
SALES (est): 625.9K **Privately Held**
SIC: 1799 3471 3479 Sandblasting of building exteriors; electroplating & plating; hot dip coating of metals or formed products

(G-6886)
PREMIER PRINTING
Also Called: Premier Printing & Stamp
320 Sw 89th St (73139-8516)
PHONE..............................405 632-1132
Shirley Eyler, *Owner*
Steven Ralph Eyler, *Partner*
EMP: 6
SALES (est): 200K **Privately Held**
SIC: 2711 2752 2791 2789 Commercial printing & newspaper publishing combined; commercial printing, lithographic; typesetting; bookbinding & related work; commercial printing

(G-6887)
PREMIERCRAFT INCORPORATED
1316 Se Grand Blvd (73129-6716)
PHONE..............................405 600-9339
David Hammond, *President*
Christine Hammond, *Vice Pres*
Crystal Repose, *Manager*
EMP: 19 **EST:** 2007
SALES (est): 3.6MM **Privately Held**
WEB: www.premiercraf93398888-362992.hibustudio.com
SIC: 3449 3446 Miscellaneous metalwork; architectural metalwork

(G-6888)
PRENTICE NAPIER & GREEN INC
Also Called: Png Operating Company
14000 Quail Springs Pkwy (73134-2620)
P.O. Box 721424 (73172-1424)
PHONE..............................405 752-7680
Steve Prentice, *President*
Dennis Napier, *Vice Pres*
Russell Green, *Admin Sec*
EMP: 11
SQ FT: 2,000
SALES (est): 1.3MM **Privately Held**
SIC: 1311 1382 8711 Crude petroleum production; natural gas production; oil & gas exploration services; petroleum engineering

(G-6889)
PRESLEY OPERATING LLC
101 Park Ave Ste 670 (73102-7220)
PHONE..............................405 526-3000
Travis Boughdadly, *Mng Member*
Cecilia Demille-Presley,
EMP: 2
SALES (est): 72K **Privately Held**
SIC: 1389 Oil & gas wells: building, repairing & dismantling

(G-6890)
PRESS
1610 N Gatewood Ave (73106-2057)
PHONE..............................405 464-6181
Joey Morris, *Principal*
EMP: 1
SALES (est): 37.5K **Privately Held**
SIC: 2741 Miscellaneous publishing

(G-6891)
PRESSBURG LLC (HQ)
Also Called: Roan Resources, Inc.
14701 Hrtz Qail Sprng Pkw (73134-2646)
PHONE..............................405 896-8050
Gregory A Augsburger, *CEO*
EMP: 2
SALES: 517.8MM **Privately Held**
SIC: 1311 Crude petroleum & natural gas
PA: Citizen Energy Operating, Llc
  320 S Boston Ave Ste 900
  Tulsa OK 74103
  918 949-4680

(G-6892)
PRIME CONDUIT INC
6500 Interpace St (73135-4443)
PHONE..............................405 670-6132
Lisa Denham, *Buyer*
Thomas Matejka, *Financial Exec*
Christine Disanto, *Business Anlyst*
Pete Clement, *Manager*
Blair Girard, *Maintence Staff*
EMP: 23 **Privately Held**
SIC: 2821 3084 Polyvinyl chloride resins (PVC); plastics pipe
PA: Prime Conduit, Inc.
  23240 Chagrin Blvd # 405
  Beachwood OH 44122

(G-6893)
PRIME OPERATING COMPANY
5400 N Grand Blvd Ste 360 (73112-5637)
PHONE..............................405 947-1091
Shawn Lemons, *District Mgr*
Norman Styers, *Accountant*
Steven Blair, *Manager*
EMP: 9

SALES (corp-wide): 104.8MM **Publicly Held**
SIC: 6519 1389 Real property lessors; construction, repair & dismantling services
HQ: Prime Operating Company
  9821 Katy Fwy Ste 1050
  Houston TX 77024

(G-6894)
PRIMEENERGY CORPORATION
Also Called: Prime Operating
5400 N Grand Blvd Ste 450 (73112-5678)
PHONE..............................405 942-2897
EMP: 14
SALES (corp-wide): 144.5MM **Publicly Held**
SIC: 1311 1382 Crude Petroleum/Natural Gas Production Oil/Gas Exploration Services
PA: Primeenergy Corporation
  9821 Katy Fwy
  Houston TX 77024
  713 735-0000

(G-6895)
PRIMEENERGY CORPORATION
Also Called: Southwest Oil Field Cnstr
5400 N Grand Blvd Ste 450 (73112-5678)
PHONE..............................405 375-5203
Robert Pool, *Manager*
EMP: 40
SALES (corp-wide): 104.8MM **Publicly Held**
SIC: 1311 1389 Crude petroleum & natural gas; oil field services
PA: Primeenergy Corporation
  9821 Katy Fwy Ste 1050
  Houston TX 77024
  713 735-0000

(G-6896)
PRINGLE PUBLICATIONS CORP
1601 Nw Expressway (73118-1467)
PHONE..............................405 848-4859
Laura N Pringle, *Principal*
EMP: 1
SALES (est): 60.8K **Privately Held**
SIC: 2741 Miscellaneous publishing

(G-6897)
PRINT FINISHING SYSTEMS INC
7116 Nw 79th St (73132-4281)
PHONE..............................405 232-1750
Thomas Hughes, *President*
Dustin Hughes, *Vice Pres*
Chris Johnstonbaugh, *Sales Mgr*
▲ **EMP:** 9
SALES (est): 1.5MM **Privately Held**
SIC: 3555 Printing trade parts & attachments; bookbinding machinery; collating machines for printing & bookbinding

(G-6898)
PRINT IMAGING GROUP LLC
607 N Western Ave (73106-7413)
PHONE..............................405 235-4888
Jim Everett,
Beth Everett,
EMP: 20
SQ FT: 4,500
SALES (est): 2.1MM **Privately Held**
SIC: 2752 4226 2759 2396 Business forms, lithographed; document & office records storage; commercial printing; automotive & apparel trimmings

(G-6899)
PRINT MONKEY LLC
9300 S Pennsylvania Ave (73159-6918)
P.O. Box 891834 (73189-1834)
PHONE..............................405 249-6926
Jeffery Lane,
EMP: 1
SALES (est): 123.4K **Privately Held**
SIC: 2752 Commercial printing, lithographic

(G-6900)
PRINTERS OF OKLAHOMA LLC
1601 N Portland Ave (73107-1525)
PHONE..............................405 943-8855
Ben Murphy, *Vice Pres*
Awet Tsehaye, *Mng Member*
EMP: 5
SQ FT: 5,250

SALES (est): 762.9K **Privately Held**
SIC: 2752 2789 Commercial printing, offset; bookbinding & related work

(G-6901)
PRINTING CENTER
1423 Sw 59th St (73119-7211)
PHONE..............................405 681-5303
John Mombaini, *Owner*
EMP: 1
SALES (est): 127.7K **Privately Held**
SIC: 2752 2791 2789 Commercial printing, offset; typesetting; bookbinding & related work

(G-6902)
PRO DARTS INC
Also Called: All Music Games
1500 Linwood Blvd (73106-5024)
PHONE..............................405 232-3552
John Thompson, *CEO*
EMP: 3
SALES (est): 274.2K **Privately Held**
SIC: 3944 Darts & dart games

(G-6903)
PRO DIRECTIONAL
2908 S Ann Arbor Ave (73128-1854)
PHONE..............................405 200-1450
EMP: 2
SALES (est): 107.3K **Privately Held**
SIC: 1389 Oil field services

(G-6904)
PRO OILFIELD SERVICES LLC
2704 S Meridian Ave (73108-1738)
PHONE..............................405 778-8844
EMP: 1
SALES (corp-wide): 229.6MM **Privately Held**
SIC: 1389 Oil field services
PA: Pro Oilfield Services, Llc
  840 Gessner Rd Ste 875
  Houston TX 77024
  281 496-5810

(G-6905)
PRO PALLETS
2228 Sw 20th St (73108-6430)
PHONE..............................405 679-8076
Hector Fernando, *Principal*
EMP: 3
SALES (est): 119.9K **Privately Held**
SIC: 2448 Pallets, wood

(G-6906)
PRO STAINLESS & SHTMTL LLC
Also Called: Council Stainless and Shtmtl
7918 Nw 10th St (73127-4417)
PHONE..............................405 787-4400
Chad Pritchett,
Mike Ruhl,
EMP: 9
SALES (est): 1MM **Privately Held**
SIC: 3444 3446 2514 Sheet metalwork; architectural metalwork; ornamental metalwork; metal household furniture

(G-6907)
PRO TECHNICS INTERNATIONAL
4300 Sw 33rd St (73119-1017)
PHONE..............................405 680-5560
Rj Ware, *District Mgr*
EMP: 2
SALES (est): 94.1K **Privately Held**
SIC: 1389 Oil field services

(G-6908)
PRO-FAB LLC
Also Called: Omada International OK Cy Div
910 N Morgan Rd (73127-7143)
PHONE..............................405 495-2131
Geina Dilbeck, *Vice Pres*
Mike Duty, *Vice Pres*
Cory Welscher, *Vice Pres*
Marty Stephenson, *Controller*
Tim Fleming, *Manager*
▲ **EMP:** 130
SQ FT: 195,000
SALES: 26.5MM
SALES (corp-wide): 48.2MM **Privately Held**
WEB: www.profab.com
SIC: 3728 3599 Aircraft parts & equipment; machine shop, jobbing & repair

Oklahoma City - Oklahoma County (G-6909)

GEOGRAPHIC SECTION

PA: Omada International, Llc
14513 32nd St E
Sumner WA 98390
425 242-5400

(G-6909)
PRODUCERS COOPERATIVE OIL MILL
2500 S Council Rd (73128-9506)
PHONE.................................405 232-7555
Austin Rose, *Branch Mgr*
EMP: 3
SALES (corp-wide): 18.4MM **Privately Held**
SIC: 2074 Cottonseed oil, cake or meal
PA: Producers Cooperative Oil Mill
6 Se 4th St
Oklahoma City OK 73129
405 232-7555

(G-6910)
PRODUCTION ENGINE & PUMP INC
3115 Se 67th St (73135-1701)
P.O. Box 94421 (73143-4421)
PHONE.................................405 672-3644
Chris Cunningham, *President*
Rick Hoegger, *Vice Pres*
Pam Hoegger, *Treasurer*
Sharon Cunningham, *Admin Sec*
EMP: 11
SQ FT: 6,000
SALES (est): 2.2MM **Privately Held**
WEB: www.productionengineandpump.com
SIC: 3519 7699 Gas engine rebuilding; pumps & pumping equipment repair

(G-6911)
PROGRESS LIGHTING
1217 Sovereign Row Ste 10 (73108-1890)
PHONE.................................405 949-2550
Phyliss Eudy, *Principal*
EMP: 1
SALES (est): 80.7K **Privately Held**
SIC: 3645 5063 Residential lighting fixtures; lighting fixtures

(G-6912)
PROGRESSIVE INDUSTRIES INC
816 Nw 70th St (73116-7512)
PHONE.................................405 843-0597
Greg Caldwell, *President*
EMP: 3
SQ FT: 3,600
SALES: 300K **Privately Held**
SIC: 2499 Spools, reels & pulleys: wood

(G-6913)
PROGRESSIVE STAMPING LLC
Also Called: Progrssive Stmping Fabrication
5500 W Reno Ave Ste 300 (73127-6378)
PHONE.................................405 996-5347
David Younge, *Mng Member*
Mark Ninness,
Romaeyn Ninness,
Frank Wheeler,
EMP: 23
SQ FT: 99,000
SALES (est): 5MM **Privately Held**
SIC: 3469 Stamping metal for the trade

(G-6914)
PROJECT 3810 LLC
11132 Blue Stem Back Rd (73162-4919)
PHONE.................................405 834-7418
Vicki Langford, *Principal*
EMP: 3
SALES (est): 225.3K **Privately Held**
SIC: 7389 1541 3999 Office facilities & secretarial service rental; industrial buildings & warehouses; manufacturing industries

(G-6915)
PROMO PRINT 4 U LLC
4220 Nw 23rd St (73107-2640)
PHONE.................................405 259-6721
Chris Heide, *Mng Member*
EMP: 1
SALES: 50K **Privately Held**
SIC: 2396 7389 2262 Fabric printing & stamping; advertising, promotional & trade show services; ; overprinting: man-made fiber & silk broadwoven fabrics

(G-6916)
PROPAK LOGISTICS INC
11300 Partnr Dr Ste C (73131)
PHONE.................................405 694-4441
Dirk Phippen, *Branch Mgr*
EMP: 60 **Privately Held**
SIC: 2448 Pallets, wood
PA: Propak Logistics, Inc.
1100 Garrison Ave
Fort Smith AR 72901

(G-6917)
PROPHECY IN NEWS
1145 W I 240 Service Rd B100 (73139-2134)
P.O. Box 7000 (73153-7000)
PHONE.................................405 634-1234
Jerry R Church, *President*
Linda Church, *Corp Secy*
Jerry J Church Jr, *Vice Pres*
EMP: 12 EST: 1978
SQ FT: 7,000
SALES: 4.1MM **Privately Held**
WEB: www.prophecyinthenews.com
SIC: 3861 Reproduction machines & equipment

(G-6918)
PROTECHNICS OKC CHEMICAL OFF
4307 Sw 34th St (73119-2402)
PHONE.................................405 601-3078
Bill Waters, *Manager*
EMP: 4 EST: 2009
SALES (est): 172.6K **Privately Held**
SIC: 1389 Oil field services

(G-6919)
PS TEES LLC
1104 Ne 5th St (73117-1410)
PHONE.................................405 694-7979
Peter L Roberson, *Owner*
EMP: 2
SALES (est): 54K **Privately Held**
SIC: 2759 Screen printing

(G-6920)
PTL PROP SOLUTIONS LLC
6100 N Western Ave (73118-1044)
PHONE.................................405 848-8000
EMP: 1
SALES (est): 132.8K
SALES (corp-wide): 2.4B **Publicly Held**
SIC: 1321 Natural gas liquids
HQ: Seventy Seven Energy Llc
777 Nw 63rd St
Oklahoma City OK 73116
405 608-7777

(G-6921)
PUNT & PUCKLE LLC
7201 S Klein Ave (73139-1921)
PHONE.................................719 358-1419
Terry N Blount, *Principal*
David Gerrells, *Principal*
EMP: 2
SALES (est): 88.3K **Privately Held**
SIC: 3648 Lighting equipment

(G-6922)
PURE CANNA CBD
127 Nw 16th St (73103-3406)
PHONE.................................405 628-5119
Jeremy Dalatri, *Principal*
EMP: 1
SALES (est): 46.2K **Privately Held**
SIC: 3999

(G-6923)
PURE PROTEIN LLC
655 Research Pkwy Ste 556 (73104-6278)
PHONE.................................405 271-3838
Thomas A Harlan, *CEO*
R A Tony Taylor, *Managing Dir*
Dawn Boos, *Principal*
EMP: 5
SQ FT: 1,800
SALES (est): 600K **Privately Held**
SIC: 2836 Vaccines & other immunizing products

(G-6924)
PURE TRANSPLANT SOLUTIONS LLC
655 Research Pkwy Ste 556 (73104-6278)
PHONE.................................512 697-8144
Blair Duncan,
EMP: 2
SALES (est): 180K **Privately Held**
SIC: 2834 Pharmaceutical preparations

(G-6925)
PURINA ANIMAL NUTRITION LLC
1108 Nw 3rd St (73106-7416)
PHONE.................................405 232-6171
Bryan Rebold, *Manager*
EMP: 35
SALES (corp-wide): 6B **Privately Held**
SIC: 2048 Prepared feeds
HQ: Purina Animal Nutrition Llc
100 Danforth Dr
Gray Summit MO 63039

(G-6926)
PURINA MILLS LLC
1108 Nw 3rd St (73106-7498)
PHONE.................................405 232-6171
Ron Duevel, *Branch Mgr*
EMP: 48
SQ FT: 73,409
SALES (corp-wide): 6B **Privately Held**
WEB: www.purinamills.com
SIC: 2048 Prepared feeds
HQ: Purina Mills, Llc
555 Maryvle Univ Dr 200
Saint Louis MO 63141

(G-6927)
PURPOSE PUBLISHING
3600 Ne 50th St (73121-5007)
PHONE.................................405 808-1332
Stacy Johnson, *Owner*
EMP: 1 EST: 2018
SALES (est): 37.5K **Privately Held**
SIC: 2741 Miscellaneous publishing

(G-6928)
PV PUBLISHING INC
5030 N May Ave 353 (73112-6010)
PHONE.................................405 409-1799
Dan Parks, *Principal*
EMP: 2
SALES (est): 139.1K **Privately Held**
SIC: 2741 Miscellaneous publishing

(G-6929)
PYFI TECHNOLOGIES
1113 W Wilshire Blvd (73116-6106)
PHONE.................................405 816-8685
Andy Payne, *CEO*
EMP: 1
SALES (est): 29.2K **Privately Held**
SIC: 7371 7382 3822 8748 Computer software systems analysis & design, custom; computer software writers, freelance; confinement surveillance systems maintenance & monitoring; building services monitoring controls, automatic; systems analysis or design

(G-6930)
QES PRESSURE CONTROL LLC (HQ)
Also Called: Great White Well Control
4500 Se 59th St (73135-3326)
PHONE.................................405 605-2700
Ronnie Roles, *Mng Member*
EMP: 80
SQ FT: 140,000
SALES (est): 552.7MM
SALES (corp-wide): 1.1B **Privately Held**
SIC: 1389 Oil field services
PA: Quintana Energy Services Lp
1415 La St Ste 2900
Houston TX 77002
832 518-4094

(G-6931)
QP BROADWAY EXT
401 W Wilshire Blvd (73116-7759)
PHONE.................................405 843-9820
EMP: 2
SALES (est): 90.5K **Privately Held**
SIC: 2752 Offset & photolithographic printing

(G-6932)
QUAD/GRAPHICS INC
6801 S Air Depot Blvd (73135-5905)
PHONE.................................405 264-4341
Keith Newman, *Principal*
EMP: 20
SALES (corp-wide): 3.9B **Publicly Held**
SIC: 2752 Commercial printing, offset
PA: Quad/Graphics Inc.
N61w23044 Harrys Way
Sussex WI 53089
414 566-6000

(G-6933)
QUAD/GRAPHICS INC
6801 S Sunnylane Rd (73135-1712)
PHONE.................................405 264-4000
Jeff Doescher, *Controller*
Ryan Ware, *Sales Mgr*
Roberto Ramirez, *Branch Mgr*
EMP: 400
SALES (corp-wide): 3.9B **Publicly Held**
SIC: 2752 Commercial printing, offset
PA: Quad/Graphics Inc.
N61w23044 Harrys Way
Sussex WI 53089
414 566-6000

(G-6934)
QUAIL CREEK OIL CORPORATION (PA)
Also Called: Quail Creek Companies
13831 Quail Pointe Dr (73134-1021)
PHONE.................................405 755-7419
Don Dahlgren, *President*
Thomas Biery, *Vice Pres*
Linda Biery, *Treasurer*
Alice Dahlgren, *Admin Sec*
EMP: 25 EST: 1981
SALES (est): 7.7MM **Privately Held**
SIC: 1311 Crude petroleum production; natural gas production

(G-6935)
QUAIL CREEK PRODUCTION COMPANY
13831 Quail Pointe Dr (73134-1021)
PHONE.................................405 755-7419
Eric Dahlgren, *Principal*
EMP: 3
SALES (est): 445.9K **Privately Held**
SIC: 1311 Crude petroleum production

(G-6936)
QUALITY MACHINE SERVICES INC
8412 Sw 8th St (73128-4238)
PHONE.................................405 495-4962
Tom A Lewis, *President*
EMP: 10
SQ FT: 3,000
SALES (est): 2MM **Privately Held**
SIC: 3533 Oil field machinery & equipment

(G-6937)
QUALITY METAL FINISHING INC
15 Sw 25th St (73109-6017)
PHONE.................................405 236-1155
Sandra Wilkins, *President*
Ray Rossler, *Vice Pres*
Michelli Wilkins, *Treasurer*
Tamara Rossler, *Admin Sec*
EMP: 15 EST: 1970
SQ FT: 5,500
SALES (est): 1.4MM **Privately Held**
SIC: 3471 Electroplating of metals or formed products

(G-6938)
QUALITY WHOLESALE MILLWORK INC
2320 S May Ave (73108-4436)
P.O. Box 82881 (73148-0881)
PHONE.................................405 681-6575
Freddie Baker, *President*
Anthony Baker, *Corp Secy*
Ronald Baker, *Vice Pres*
Alex Keller, *Manager*
▲ EMP: 6
SQ FT: 20,000
SALES (est): 1.4MM **Privately Held**
SIC: 2431 5031 Doors, wood; lumber, plywood & millwork

GEOGRAPHIC SECTION
Oklahoma City - Oklahoma County (G-6966)

(G-6939)
QUANTUM BUILDS COMPANY
14616 Brinklee Way (73142-7850)
PHONE.................................727 504-1628
EMP: 2
SALES (est): 85.9K Privately Held
SIC: 3572 Computer storage devices

(G-6940)
QUANTUM FORMS CORPORATION (PA)
6000 Nw 2nd St Ste 300 (73127-6515)
PHONE.................................918 665-1320
Terry M Davis, President
Jeff Simpsen, Vice Pres
Tom Tomlinson, Vice Pres
EMP: 13
SALES (est): 5.4MM Privately Held
SIC: 5112 2752 2789 2396 Business forms; commercial printing, lithographic; bookbinding & related work; automotive & apparel trimmings

(G-6941)
QUEST CHEROKEE LLC (HQ)
5901 N Western Ave # 200 (73118-1253)
PHONE.................................405 371-1653
EMP: 5 EST: 2003
SQ FT: 10,000
SALES (est): 6.6MM
SALES (corp-wide): 83.5MM Publicly Held
SIC: 1382 1381 Oil/Gas Exploration Services Oil/Gas Well Drilling
PA: Postrock Energy Corporation
210 Park Ave
Oklahoma City OK 73102
405 600-7704

(G-6942)
QUEST ENERGY PARTNERS LP
210 Park Ave Ste 2750 (73102-5641)
PHONE.................................405 600-7704
EMP: 1
SALES: 147.9MM
SALES (corp-wide): 83.5MM Publicly Held
SIC: 1382 Oil/Gas Exploration Services
PA: Postrock Energy Corporation
210 Park Ave
Oklahoma City OK 73102
405 600-7704

(G-6943)
QUEST MIDSTREAM PARTNERS LP
210 Park Ave Ste 2750 (73102-5641)
PHONE.................................405 702-7410
EMP: 60
SALES (est): 2.4MM
SALES (corp-wide): 83.5MM Publicly Held
SIC: 1382 Oil/Gas Exploration Services
PA: Postrock Energy Corporation
210 Park Ave
Oklahoma City OK 73102
405 600-7704

(G-6944)
QUICK CHARGE CORPORATION
1032 Sw 22nd St (73109-1637)
PHONE.................................405 634-2120
Raymond R Santilli Jr, President
EMP: 25
SQ FT: 15,000
SALES (est): 2.6MM
SALES (corp-wide): 3.6MM Privately Held
SIC: 3629 3612 3679 Battery chargers, rectifying or nonrotating; power conversion units, a.c. to d.c.: static-electric; specialty transformers; power supplies, all types: static
PA: Sanco Enterprises Inc
1032 Sw 22nd St
Oklahoma City OK 73109
405 634-2120

(G-6945)
QUIK PRINT OKLAHOMA CITY INC (PA)
3403 Nw Expressway (73112-4419)
PHONE.................................405 840-3275
Brad Gravley, General Mgr
EMP: 22
SQ FT: 2,500
SALES (est): 4MM Privately Held
SIC: 2752 Commercial printing, offset

(G-6946)
QUIK-PRINT OF OKLAHOMA CITY (PA)
Also Called: Quik Print
3401 Nw Expressway St (73112-4939)
PHONE.................................405 842-1404
Brad Gravley, President
Marie Gravley, Corp Secy
Mark Little, Vice Pres
Matt Warner, Prdtn Mgr
Rex Hankins, Accounts Exec
EMP: 5 EST: 1976
SQ FT: 2,500
SALES (est): 4.9MM Privately Held
SIC: 2752 7334 2791 2789 Commercial printing, offset; photocopying & duplicating services; typesetting; bookbinding & related work; commercial printing

(G-6947)
QUIK-PRINT OF OKLAHOMA CITY
Also Called: Quik-Print 1405
7206 N Western Ave (73116-7118)
PHONE.................................405 843-9820
T Fritsch Michael Moore, Manager
EMP: 4
SALES (corp-wide): 4.9MM Privately Held
SIC: 2752 2789 Commercial printing, offset; bookbinding & related work
PA: Quik-Print Of Oklahoma City, Inc
3401 Nw Expressway St
Oklahoma City OK 73112
405 842-1404

(G-6948)
QUIK-PRINT OF OKLAHOMA CITY
119 N Robinson Ave # 100 (73102-4613)
PHONE.................................405 232-7579
Brian Fritze, Manager
EMP: 5
SALES (corp-wide): 4.9MM Privately Held
SIC: 2752 7334 Commercial printing, offset; photocopying & duplicating services
PA: Quik-Print Of Oklahoma City, Inc
3401 Nw Expressway St
Oklahoma City OK 73112
405 842-1404

(G-6949)
QUIK-PRINT OF OKLAHOMA CITY
Also Called: Quik Print
4233 Charter Ave (73108-2023)
PHONE.................................405 943-3222
Mark Little, VP Opers
Matt Warner, Prdtn Mgr
Bart Thomas, Manager
EMP: 7
SALES (corp-wide): 4.9MM Privately Held
SIC: 2759 2791 2752 7336 Commercial printing; typesetting; commercial printing, lithographic; commercial art & graphic design
PA: Quik-Print Of Oklahoma City, Inc
3401 Nw Expressway St
Oklahoma City OK 73112
405 842-1404

(G-6950)
QUIK-PRINT OF OKLAHOMA CITY
3403 Nw Expwy (73112-4419)
PHONE.................................405 840-3275
Leo Menke, Manager
EMP: 5
SALES (corp-wide): 4.9MM Privately Held
SIC: 2752 7334 4215 2789 Commercial printing, offset; photocopying & duplicating services; courier services, except by air; bookbinding & related work; commercial printing; die-cut paper & board
PA: Quik-Print Of Oklahoma City, Inc
3401 Nw Expressway St
Oklahoma City OK 73112
405 842-1404

(G-6951)
QUIK-PRINT OF OKLAHOMA CITY
406 Nw 23rd St (73103-1508)
PHONE.................................405 528-7976
Brad Gravley, President
Jay Hardon, Branch Mgr
EMP: 3
SALES (corp-wide): 4.9MM Privately Held
SIC: 2752 7334 2789 2759 Commercial printing, offset; photocopying & duplicating services; bookbinding & related work; commercial printing
PA: Quik-Print Of Oklahoma City, Inc
3401 Nw Expressway St
Oklahoma City OK 73112
405 842-1404

(G-6952)
QUIK-PRINT OF OKLAHOMA CITY
10637 N May Ave (73120-2612)
PHONE.................................405 751-5315
James Johnson, Manager
EMP: 4
SALES (corp-wide): 4.9MM Privately Held
SIC: 2752 Commercial printing, offset
PA: Quik-Print Of Oklahoma City, Inc
3401 Nw Expressway St
Oklahoma City OK 73112
405 842-1404

(G-6953)
QUIKRETE COMPANIES LLC
Quikrete of Oklahoma
8000 Melrose Ln (73127-4832)
PHONE.................................405 787-2050
James Hodges, Plant Mgr
Don Martin, Manager
Cleo Nunley, Director
EMP: 25 Privately Held
WEB: www.quikrete.com
SIC: 3273 3255 3087 2899 Ready-mixed concrete; clay refractories; custom compound purchased resins; chemical preparations; nonclay refractories
HQ: The Quikrete Companies Llc
5 Concourse Pkwy Ste 1900
Atlanta GA 30328
404 634-9100

(G-6954)
QUINQUE OPERATING COMPANY
908 Nw 71st St (73116-7402)
PHONE.................................405 840-9876
Steven J Goetzinger, President
Mike Jones, Corp Secy
David Herritt, Vice Pres
EMP: 3
SALES: 230K Privately Held
SIC: 1389 Servicing oil & gas wells

(G-6955)
QUINTELLA PRINTING COMPANY INC
130 Se 44th St Ste 300 (73129-2872)
PHONE.................................405 631-6566
Martin Sandersfield, President
Joann Sandersfield, Treasurer
EMP: 7 EST: 1973
SALES (est): 1MM Privately Held
SIC: 2752 2796 Commercial printing, offset; platemaking services

(G-6956)
QUSES
Also Called: Quses Manufacturing
1224 Nw 4th St (73106-7402)
PHONE.................................817 829-1086
Alexander Marko, Principal
Katrina Marko, Principal
EMP: 33
SALES (est): 1.1MM Privately Held
SIC: 3714 Motor vehicle body components & frame; bumpers & bumperettes, motor vehicle

(G-6957)
R & L ENDEAVORS LLC
6912 Lakepointe Dr (73116-1627)
PHONE.................................405 826-8226
Ray Leuffer,
Leah Brashear,
EMP: 5
SALES (est): 392.4K Privately Held
SIC: 3322 Malleable iron foundries

(G-6958)
R & W MACHINE SHOP INC
6209 S Shields Blvd (73149-1221)
PHONE.................................405 632-4020
Richard E Williams Sr, President
Richard E Williams Jr, Vice Pres
Mary Williams, Admin Sec
EMP: 4
SQ FT: 5,000
SALES (est): 492K Privately Held
SIC: 3599 7692 Machine shop, jobbing & repair; welding repair

(G-6959)
R AND P CABINETRY LLC
540 Nw 42nd St (73118-7002)
PHONE.................................405 230-0495
Richard C Hauser Jr, Mng Member
EMP: 2
SALES: 100K Privately Held
SIC: 2434 2431 Wood kitchen cabinets; blinds (shutters), wood

(G-6960)
R B WATKINS INC
617 S Margene Dr (73130-4226)
PHONE.................................405 732-9969
Jim Rogers, President
Wes Watkins, Vice Pres
EMP: 15
SALES (est): 1.5MM Privately Held
SIC: 3825 Transformers, portable: instrument

(G-6961)
R C TAYLOR COMPANIES INC
5661 N Classen Blvd (73118-4015)
PHONE.................................405 840-2700
R Clark Taylor Sr, President
Michel Willam Taylor, Vice Pres
EMP: 3
SQ FT: 2,200
SALES (est): 900K Privately Held
SIC: 1311 Crude petroleum production; natural gas production

(G-6962)
R D DAVIS & ASSOCIATES INC
13212 N Mcarthur Blvd A (73142-3019)
PHONE.................................405 720-2882
Randy Davis, President
EMP: 7
SALES (est): 455.3K Privately Held
SIC: 1382 Oil & gas exploration services

(G-6963)
R E G ENERGY
3333 Nw 63rd St (73116-3722)
PHONE.................................405 842-4249
Robert E Gonce Jr, Owner
EMP: 3
SQ FT: 1,000
SALES (est): 220K Privately Held
SIC: 1311 Crude petroleum production; natural gas production

(G-6964)
R&C INDUSTRIES LLC
2113 N Gatewood Ave (73106-3816)
PHONE.................................405 640-7239
Rick Hunter, Principal
EMP: 1
SALES (est): 36K Privately Held
SIC: 3999 Manufacturing industries

(G-6965)
RAIL MASTERS LLC
7301 Broadway Ext Ste 228 (73116-9038)
PHONE.................................405 840-1019
Chris Smith, Principal
EMP: 1
SALES (est): 66.3K Privately Held
SIC: 3462 Iron & steel forgings

(G-6966)
RAINBO SERVICE CO (PA)
1839 Se 25th St (73129-7613)
PHONE.................................405 677-5353
Jim Robinson, President
EMP: 7

Oklahoma City - Oklahoma County (G-6967)

SALES (est): 931.9K **Privately Held**
SIC: 1389 Haulage, oil field

(G-6967)
RAINBOW CREATIONS
3252 N Nesbitt Ave (73112-3378)
PHONE..............................405 942-6207
Tim Holder, *Owner*
Susan O Holder, *Co-Owner*
EMP: 2
SALES: 50K **Privately Held**
SIC: 2389 Apparel & accessories

(G-6968)
RAINBOW PENNANT INC
148 Ne 48th St (73105-2021)
PHONE..............................405 524-1577
Glenn Spunaugle, *President*
Shirley Spunaugle, *Vice Pres*
EMP: 22 **EST:** 1957
SQ FT: 24,000
SALES (est): 2.5MM **Privately Held**
WEB: www.rpmflags.com
SIC: 2399 5131 5949 Flags, fabric; tape, textile; fabric, remnants

(G-6969)
RAMIIISOL VINEYARDS LLC
6305 Waterford Blvd (73118-1122)
PHONE..............................405 858-9800
Steven W Blaine, *Administration*
EMP: 2 **EST:** 2016
SALES (est): 89.1K **Privately Held**
SIC: 2084 Wines

(G-6970)
RAMOS PLATING CO
1320 S Walker Ave (73109-1325)
PHONE..............................405 232-4300
Edward A Ramos, *President*
Don Ramos, *Vice Pres*
EMP: 6
SQ FT: 4,500
SALES: 250K **Privately Held**
SIC: 3471 Electroplating of metals or formed products

(G-6971)
RAMSEY PROPERTY MANAGEMENT LLC
2932 Nw 122nd St Ste 4 (73120-1955)
PHONE..............................405 302-6200
Stephen Nichols, *Managing Prtnr*
Steven E Nicholas, *Mng Member*
Sandra Shaver, *Admin Mgr*
EMP: 2 **EST:** 1981
SQ FT: 7,000
SALES (est): 259.7K **Privately Held**
WEB: www.ramseyllc.com
SIC: 8748 1311 Business consulting; crude petroleum production; natural gas production

(G-6972)
RANGE RSURCES-MIDCONTINENT LLC
5600 N May Ave Ste 100 (73112-4275)
PHONE..............................405 810-7359
EMP: 106
SQ FT: 96,000
SALES (est): 3.4MM
SALES (corp-wide): 1.1B **Publicly Held**
SIC: 1321 Natural Gas Liquids Production
PA: Range Resources Corporation
   100 Throckmorton St # 1200
   Fort Worth TX 76102
   817 870-2601

(G-6973)
RATE MY WELDER
131 Dean A Mcgee Ave (73102-6418)
PHONE..............................405 400-0109
EMP: 1
SALES (est): 25K **Privately Held**
SIC: 7692 Welding repair

(G-6974)
RAY LU PETROLEUM LLC
5300 N Bryant Ave (73121-1607)
PHONE..............................405 424-4006
V Cloer, *Vice Pres*
V Ray Cloer Jr,
EMP: 7
SQ FT: 5,000
SALES (est): 767.8K **Privately Held**
SIC: 1311 Crude petroleum production; natural gas production

(G-6975)
RAYDON EXPLORATION INC
1601 Nw Expwy St Ste 1300 (73118-1462)
PHONE..............................405 478-8585
Steve Raybourn, *President*
Tom R Gray, *Exec VP*
Tom Gray, *Vice Pres*
Janet Muschinske, *Treasurer*
EMP: 7
SQ FT: 2,000
SALES (est): 1.4MM **Privately Held**
SIC: 1311 Crude petroleum production; natural gas production

(G-6976)
RBC BEARINGS INCORPORATED
R B C Oklahoma
5001 Sw 20th St (73128-1413)
PHONE..............................405 236-2666
Janice Horn, *Purch Agent*
David Pirog, *Branch Mgr*
EMP: 34
SALES (corp-wide): 727.4MM **Publicly Held**
SIC: 3562 Ball & roller bearings
PA: Rbc Bearings Incorporated
   102 Willenbrock Rd
   Oxford CT 06478
   203 267-7001

(G-6977)
RC WELDING & FAB LLC
9701 Lakeshore Dr (73120-2219)
PHONE..............................580 216-1274
Mayra Chavez, *Principal*
EMP: 1 **EST:** 2017
SALES (est): 40.9K **Privately Held**
SIC: 7692 Welding repair

(G-6978)
RDNJ LLC
Also Called: A-Tech Paving
500 N Vickie Dr (73117-7802)
P.O. Box 2865, Edmond (73083-2865)
PHONE..............................405 418-4741
Jay Doyle, *CEO*
EMP: 9 **EST:** 2011
SALES (est): 178K **Privately Held**
SIC: 3271 2951 1794 Paving blocks, concrete; asphalt paving mixtures & blocks; excavation work

(G-6979)
READY READING GLASSES INC
Also Called: Reading Glasses To Go
9223 N Pennsylvania Pl (73120-1516)
PHONE..............................405 840-4440
Jan Russo, *Manager*
EMP: 2 **Privately Held**
WEB: www.readingglasses.com
SIC: 3851 Ophthalmic goods
PA: Ready Reading Glasses, Inc.
   1003 Dragon St
   Dallas TX

(G-6980)
REAGAN RESOURCES INC
2601 Nw Expwy Ste 801w (73112-7244)
P.O. Box 57053 (73157-7053)
PHONE..............................405 848-2707
William Reagan, *President*
Jim Davis, *Vice Pres*
Jane Reagan, *Treasurer*
Bonnie Swearingen, *Accountant*
Eddie Wu, *IT/INT Sup*
EMP: 5
SALES (est): 1.1MM **Privately Held**
SIC: 1382 Oil & gas exploration services

(G-6981)
REBEL OIL COMPANY
6500 N Classen Blvd (73116-7310)
PHONE..............................405 848-2208
William H Headrick, *President*
Terry Lee Bradley, *Vice Pres*
Linda Lee Carpenter, *Vice Pres*
Dana Teepe, *Treasurer*
EMP: 6
SQ FT: 3,500
SALES (est): 1.1MM **Privately Held**
SIC: 1311 Crude petroleum production; natural gas production

(G-6982)
REBEL SIGN COMPANY LLC
7109 W Hefner Rd G2525 (73162-4535)
PHONE..............................405 456-9253
EMP: 1
SALES (est): 46K **Privately Held**
SIC: 3993 Signs & advertising specialties

(G-6983)
RED BLUFF RESOURCES OPER LLC
3030 Nw Expwy Ste 650 (73112-5447)
PHONE..............................405 605-8360
Timothy Haddican, *CEO*
Brian Exline, *Vice Pres*
Craig Stephenson, *Vice Pres*
Adam Swink, *Controller*
EMP: 6 **EST:** 2015
SALES (est): 131.9K **Privately Held**
SIC: 1382 Oil & gas exploration services

(G-6984)
RED DIRT WREATHS & THINGS
4036 Nw 60th St (73112-1410)
PHONE..............................918 809-3973
Paula Chupack, *Principal*
EMP: 3 **EST:** 2018
SALES (est): 132.3K **Privately Held**
SIC: 3999 Wreaths, artificial

(G-6985)
RED EARTH FARM STORE INC
2301 E I 44 Service Rd (73111-8219)
PHONE..............................405 478-3424
Zoe Midyett, *President*
EMP: 10
SALES (est): 930.1K **Privately Held**
WEB: www.clipclophorses.com
SIC: 2399 Horse harnesses & riding crops, etc.; non-leather

(G-6986)
RED MOUNTAIN ENERGY LLC
5901 N Western Ave # 200 (73118-1262)
PHONE..............................405 842-4500
Tony Say, *President*
Max Holloway, *Exec VP*
Lanny Holman, *Exec VP*
Brad Kemp, *Vice Pres*
Koray Bakir, *CFO*
EMP: 19
SALES (est): 7.3MM **Privately Held**
SIC: 1321 Butane (natural) production

(G-6987)
RED MOUNTAIN OPERATING LLC
5901 N Western Ave # 200 (73118-1262)
PHONE..............................405 842-9200
Koray Bakir, *CFO*
EMP: 2 **EST:** 2015
SALES (est): 102.1K **Privately Held**
SIC: 1321 Butane (natural) production

(G-6988)
RED RIVER PRINTING CORP
5300 Sw 23rd St (73128-1827)
PHONE..............................405 685-1794
James P Youngs, *President*
EMP: 12 **EST:** 2000
SQ FT: 12,000
SALES (est): 1.2MM **Privately Held**
SIC: 2752 Commercial printing, offset

(G-6989)
RED RIVER SOFTWARE LLC
11100 Roxboro Ave # 2303 (73162-2543)
PHONE..............................405 728-8102
John Killiany, *Principal*
EMP: 2
SALES (est): 93.9K **Privately Held**
SIC: 7372 Prepackaged software

(G-6990)
RED ROCKS RESOURCES LLC
Also Called: Red Rocks Oil & Gas Operating
1321 N Robinson Ave (73103-4821)
PHONE..............................405 600-3065
EMP: 11 **EST:** 2010
SALES (est): 1.3MM **Privately Held**
SIC: 1382 Oil & gas exploration services

(G-6991)
REDBACK COIL TUBING LLC (HQ)
14201 Caliber Dr Ste 300 (73134-1017)
PHONE..............................405 265-4600
Phil Lancaster, *CEO*
EMP: 30
SALES (est): 12.4MM **Privately Held**
SIC: 1382 Oil & gas exploration services
PA: Redback Energy Services Llc
   14201 Caliber Dr Ste 300
   Oklahoma City OK 73134
   405 265-4608

(G-6992)
REDBACK ENERGY SERVICES LLC (PA)
14201 Caliber Dr Ste 300 (73134-1017)
PHONE..............................405 265-4608
Phil Lancaster, *CEO*
Tommy McDonnel, *Opers Mgr*
Mark Layton, *CFO*
Darren Skelton, *Manager*
Donald Straley, *Supervisor*
EMP: 32
SALES (est): 12.4MM **Privately Held**
SIC: 3535 Conveyors & conveying equipment

(G-6993)
REDBUD SOIL COMPANY LLC
4217 Nw 144th Ter (73134-1712)
PHONE..............................405 476-0429
EMP: 4
SALES (est): 368.6K **Privately Held**
SIC: 2879 Insecticides & pesticides

(G-6994)
REDDY ICE CORPORATION
5525 Sw 29th St (73179-7625)
PHONE..............................405 681-2892
Brian Rakett, *Manager*
EMP: 20
SQ FT: 20,578 **Privately Held**
WEB: www.reddyice.com
SIC: 2097 Manufactured ice
HQ: Reddy Ice Corporation
   5720 Lyndon B Johnson Fwy # 200
   Dallas TX 75240
   214 526-6740

(G-6995)
REDHAWK PRESSURE CONTROL LLC
5400 N Grand Blvd Ste 210 (73112-5707)
PHONE..............................405 605-1958
Glenn Patterson, *COO*
EMP: 12
SALES (est): 997.5K **Privately Held**
SIC: 1382 Oil & gas exploration services

(G-6996)
REDLAND RESOURCES INC
6001 Nw 23rd St (73127-1253)
PHONE..............................405 789-7104
Allan Thrower, *President*
Leroy Buck, *Vice Pres*
EMP: 3
SQ FT: 2,200
SALES (est): 563.3K **Privately Held**
SIC: 1311 Crude petroleum production; natural gas production

(G-6997)
REDLAND SHEET METAL INC
7500 Melrose Ln (73127-5143)
PHONE..............................405 673-7107
Henry Adams, *Owner*
Tammy Adams, *Co-Owner*
EMP: 6
SALES (est): 713.7K **Privately Held**
SIC: 3444 1761 Sheet metal specialties, not stamped; roofing, siding & sheet metal work

(G-6998)
REEL POWER INDUSTRIAL INC (HQ)
Also Called: Tulsa Power
5101 S Council Rd Ste 100 (73179-4832)
PHONE..............................405 609-3326
Tom Frey, *CEO*
Tim Blythe, *Vice Pres*
Joe Henry, *Vice Pres*
Don Moreau, *Vice Pres*

GEOGRAPHIC SECTION

Oklahoma City - Oklahoma County (G-7027)

Michael Spence, *Vice Pres*
▲ EMP: 79
SQ FT: 98,000
SALES (est): 27.9MM
SALES (corp-wide): 42.9MM **Privately Held**
SIC: 3533 3357 Oil & gas drilling rigs & equipment; aluminum wire & cable
PA: Reel Power International Corp.
5101 S Council Rd Ste 100
Oklahoma City OK 73179
405 609-3326

(G-6999)
REEL POWER INTERNATIONAL CORP (PA)
5101 S Council Rd Ste 100 (73179-4832)
PHONE.................................405 609-3326
Tom Frey, *CEO*
Frank Pados, *Ch of Bd*
Matt Rohwer, *CFO*
EMP: 10
SQ FT: 98,000
SALES (est): 42.9MM **Privately Held**
SIC: 3353 Plates, aluminum

(G-7000)
REEL POWER WIRE & CABLE INC
Also Called: Tulsa Power
5101 S Council Rd Ste 100 (73179-4832)
PHONE.................................918 584-1000
Mike Spence, *President*
EMP: 45
SALES (corp-wide): 42.9MM **Privately Held**
SIC: 3533 3357 Oil & gas drilling rigs & equipment; aluminum wire & cable
HQ: Reel Power Industrial Inc.
5101 S Council Rd Ste 100
Oklahoma City OK 73179
405 609-3326

(G-7001)
REFLECTIVE EDGE SCREENPRINTING
200 N Ann Arbor Ave (73127-6306)
PHONE.................................405 917-7837
Doug Holloway, *President*
Kirk Weber, *Vice Pres*
EMP: 7
SQ FT: 12,000
SALES (est): 550K **Privately Held**
SIC: 2759 2396 Screen printing; automotive & apparel trimmings

(G-7002)
REGENCY LABELS INC
4303 Sw 44th St (73119-2857)
PHONE.................................405 682-3460
Blake Wright, *President*
EMP: 20
SQ FT: 10,000
SALES: 2.7MM **Privately Held**
SIC: 2679 2672 2671 5199 Tags & labels, paper; coated & laminated paper; packaging paper & plastics film, coated & laminated; decals; labels; flexographic printing

(G-7003)
REGGIE ADUDELL
Also Called: Aduddlls Altrnators Starters U
820 Sw 23rd St (73109-1708)
PHONE.................................405 631-9002
Reggie Audell, *Owner*
EMP: 1
SQ FT: 3,056
SALES (est): 124.1K **Privately Held**
SIC: 3694 3714 Alternators, automotive; motor vehicle parts & accessories

(G-7004)
REID MANUFACTURING LLC
212 N Ann Arbor Ave (73127-6306)
PHONE.................................405 606-7006
Bryce Reid, *CEO*
EMP: 1
SALES (est): 286.4K **Privately Held**
SIC: 2434 1751 Wood kitchen cabinets; cabinet & finish carpentry; cabinet building & installation

(G-7005)
RELEVANT PRODUCTS LLC
407 Ne 48th St (73105-3316)
PHONE.................................405 524-5250
Terry Marczewski, *COO*
Don Hazlewood, *Mfg Spvr*
Michael Davilman, *Mng Member*
Rebecca Lewis,
▲ EMP: 27
SQ FT: 10,000
SALES (est): 3.2MM **Privately Held**
SIC: 2331 2396 T-shirts & tops, women's: made from purchased materials; automotive & apparel trimmings

(G-7006)
RELIANCE MFG SOLUTIONS LLC
13509 Railway Dr (73114-2230)
PHONE.................................405 640-9660
Brent Merrell,
EMP: 1
SALES (est): 106.4K **Privately Held**
SIC: 3533 3484 Oil & gas field machinery; gas field machinery & equipment; oil field machinery & equipment; guns (firearms) or gun parts, 30 mm. & below

(G-7007)
RENT-A-CRANE INC
8020 Sw 74th St (73169-2202)
PHONE.................................405 745-2318
Gary Rohlmeier, *CEO*
EMP: 2 EST: 2014
SALES (est): 234.8K **Privately Held**
SIC: 7353 3541 Cranes & aerial lift equipment, rental or leasing; electrical discharge erosion machines

(G-7008)
RENT-A-CRANE OF OKLA INC
8020 Sw 74th St (73169-2202)
P.O. Box 553, Wheatland (73097-0553)
PHONE.................................405 745-2318
Gary Rohlmeier, *CEO*
Keith Rohlmeier, *Corp Secy*
EMP: 15
SQ FT: 7,000
SALES (est): 3MM **Privately Held**
SIC: 7353 3541 Cranes & aerial lift equipment, rental or leasing; electrical discharge erosion machines

(G-7009)
RESERVE PETROLEUM COMPANY
6801 Broadway Ext Ste 300 (73116-9037)
PHONE.................................405 848-7551
Kyle L McLain, *Ch of Bd*
Cameron R McLain, *President*
James L Tyler, *Treasurer*
EMP: 9
SALES: 6.6MM **Privately Held**
SIC: 1311 Crude petroleum production

(G-7010)
RESONANCE INC
Also Called: Digital Design
4025 Nw 36th St (73112-2903)
PHONE.................................405 239-2800
Jassa Langford, *President*
Vicki Langford, *Vice Pres*
◆ EMP: 20
SQ FT: 7,200
SALES (est): 3.1MM **Privately Held**
SIC: 5999 3651 Audio-visual equipment & supplies; amplifiers: radio, public address or musical instrument

(G-7011)
RESOURCE MFG
4334 Nw Expressway (73116-1578)
PHONE.................................405 842-0999
Kurt Loeffelholz, *Principal*
EMP: 3
SALES (est): 179K **Privately Held**
SIC: 3999 Manufacturing industries

(G-7012)
REVEILLE ENERGY INNOVATION LLC
9940 W Reno Ave (73127-7139)
PHONE.................................405 577-6438
Brent Storts, *President*
Jeremy Beard, *Vice Pres*
Rion Westfall, *Vice Pres*
◆ EMP: 32
SQ FT: 25,000
SALES: 2MM **Privately Held**
SIC: 1382 Oil & gas exploration services

(G-7013)
REYNOLDS & SONS NEON STUDIO
1201 Nw 38th St (73118-5425)
P.O. Box 54702 (73154-1702)
PHONE.................................405 525-6366
Katherin Reynolds, *President*
EMP: 2
SALES (est): 217.6K **Privately Held**
SIC: 3993 Neon signs

(G-7014)
RFG PETRO SYSTEMS LLC
6724 Pat Ave (73149-5212)
PHONE.................................941 487-7524
Mike Hickey, *Business Mgr*
EMP: 8
SALES (corp-wide): 2.3MM **Privately Held**
WEB: www.rfgpetrosystems.com
SIC: 3533 Bits, oil & gas field tools: rock
PA: Petro Rfg Systems Llc
32 S Osprey Ave Ste 1
Sarasota FL 34236
941 487-7524

(G-7015)
RICHARD B COLLINS
Also Called: Collins Copier Service
3009 Cashion Pl (73112-6929)
PHONE.................................405 947-6349
Richard Collins, *Owner*
EMP: 1
SALES (est): 84.2K **Privately Held**
SIC: 3861 Photocopy machines

(G-7016)
RICHARD DOUGLAS CO
220 S Alliance Ct (73128-3610)
P.O. Box 60, Mustang (73064-0060)
PHONE.................................405 577-6626
Doug Allen, *President*
Richard Poling, *Vice Pres*
EMP: 9 EST: 1996
SQ FT: 10,000
SALES (est): 1.2MM **Privately Held**
SIC: 2434 Wood kitchen cabinets

(G-7017)
RICHARD EXPLORATION CO INC
4141 Nw Expwy St Ste 343 (73116-1675)
PHONE.................................405 840-0101
James Richard, *Owner*
Barbara Richard, *Vice Pres*
Cindy Robertson, *Admin Sec*
EMP: 5 EST: 1970
SALES (est): 447.9K **Privately Held**
SIC: 1311 Crude petroleum production; natural gas production

(G-7018)
RICHARD VALLEJOS WELDING SER
2144 Sw 82nd St (73159-4924)
PHONE.................................405 688-0804
Richard Vallejo, *Owner*
EMP: 1
SALES (est): 99.2K **Privately Held**
SIC: 7692 Welding repair

(G-7019)
RICHLAND RESOURCES CORPORATION (PA)
917 Cedar Lake Blvd (73114-7813)
P.O. Box 10317, Midwest City (73140-1317)
PHONE.................................405 732-0045
Donnie M Hughes, *President*
Keystone Hughes, *Vice Pres*
Rick Taber, *Vice Pres*
Djuana Davis, *Accounting Mgr*
EMP: 11
SQ FT: 2,000
SALES (est): 2.8MM **Privately Held**
SIC: 1311 Crude petroleum production; natural gas production

(G-7020)
RICK KNIGHT
1106 S Robinson Ave (73109-5728)
PHONE.................................405 232-4954
Rick Knight, *Principal*
EMP: 3
SALES (est): 166.1K **Privately Held**
SIC: 3993 Signs & advertising specialties

(G-7021)
RICKS RIG SERVICE
1200 S Eastern Ave (73129-6031)
PHONE.................................405 619-9193
Rick Cagle, *Principal*
EMP: 6
SALES (est): 316.8K **Privately Held**
SIC: 1381 Drilling oil & gas wells

(G-7022)
RICKS ROD REEL SVC-HIGH
4901 Nw 58th St (73122-7503)
PHONE.................................405 823-7581
Rick Rowan, *Manager*
EMP: 2 EST: 2015
SALES (est): 115K **Privately Held**
SIC: 3499 Fabricated metal products

(G-7023)
RIDDLE CORPORATION
6301 Paschall Ct (73132-5622)
P.O. Box 21053 (73156-1053)
PHONE.................................405 728-7504
David B Glass, *President*
Joydell Lane, *Admin Sec*
EMP: 2
SALES (est): 210K **Privately Held**
SIC: 1382 Oil & gas exploration services

(G-7024)
RILEY EXPLORATION LLC
29 E Reno Ave Ste 5 (73104-4238)
PHONE.................................405 485-8200
Kevin Riley,
Bobby D Riley,
Corey N Riley,
EMP: 63
SALES (est): 17.9MM **Privately Held**
SIC: 1382 Oil & gas exploration services

(G-7025)
RILEY EXPLORATION GROUP LLC (PA)
29 E Reno Ave Ste 5 (73104-4238)
PHONE.................................405 485-8200
Bobby Riley, *CEO*
Corey Riley, *President*
James Doherty Jr, *Exec VP*
David Lalonde, *CFO*
EMP: 11
SALES (est): 70.6MM **Privately Held**
WEB: www.rileyexplorationgroup.com
SIC: 1382 Oil & gas exploration services

(G-7026)
RILEY EXPLRATION - PERMIAN LLC (PA)
29 E Reno Ave Ste 500 (73104-4231)
PHONE.................................405 415-8699
Bobby D Riley, *Ch of Bd*
Kevin Riley, *COO*
James J Doherty Jr, *Exec VP*
Jeffrey M Gutman, *CFO*
EMP: 9
SALES: 11.7MM **Privately Held**
SIC: 1382 1389 1321 Oil & gas exploration services; oil field services; natural gas liquids production

(G-7027)
RILEY PERMIAN OPERATING CO LLC
29 E Reno Ave Ste 5 (73104-4238)
PHONE.................................405 415-8699
Kevin Riley,
Bobby Riley,
Corey Riley,
EMP: 29
SALES (est): 3.6MM
SALES (corp-wide): 11.7MM **Privately Held**
SIC: 1382 Oil & gas exploration services
PA: Riley Exploration - Permian, Llc
29 E Reno Ave Ste 500
Oklahoma City OK 73104
405 415-8699

Oklahoma City - Oklahoma County (G-7028)   GEOGRAPHIC SECTION

(G-7028)
RINKER MATERIALS CONCRETE PIPE
6200 Sw 44th St (73179-8003)
PHONE....................405 745-3404
Martha Butler, *Principal*
EMP: 5
SALES (est): 816K **Privately Held**
SIC: 3272 Concrete products

(G-7029)
RIVER ROCK ENERGY LLC
211 N Robinson Ave S1525 (73102-7101)
PHONE....................405 606-7481
Jay Jimerson, *Mng Member*
EMP: 75
SALES (est): 180MM **Privately Held**
SIC: 1382 Oil & gas exploration services

(G-7030)
RKB WOODWORKS
10020 S Allen Dr (73139-5406)
PHONE....................405 919-4149
Kandice Baker, *Principal*
EMP: 1 EST: 2016
SALES (est): 54.1K **Privately Held**
SIC: 2431 Millwork

(G-7031)
ROADRUNNER PRESS
122 Nw 32nd St (73118-8824)
PHONE....................405 524-6205
Jeanne Devlin, *Editor*
EMP: 2
SALES (est): 142.4K **Privately Held**
SIC: 2741 Miscellaneous publishing

(G-7032)
ROAN RESOURCES LLC (DH)
14701 Hrtz Qail Sprng Pkw (73134-2646)
PHONE....................405 241-2271
Tony Maranto, *President*
Nick Cupp, *Opers Staff*
David Detrixhe, *Production*
Jeff Haddock, *Engineer*
Alan Pfortmiller, *Senior Engr*
EMP: 30
SALES (est): 58.3MM
SALES (corp-wide): 517.8MM **Privately Held**
SIC: 1382 Oil & gas exploration services
HQ: Pressburg, Llc
    14701 Hrtz Qail Sprng Pkw
    Oklahoma City OK 73134
    405 896-8050

(G-7033)
ROBBINS & MYERS INC
Also Called: R & M Energy System
2100 E Grand Blvd (73129-8425)
PHONE....................405 672-6793
Bob Neal, *Manager*
EMP: 7
SALES (corp-wide): 8.4B **Publicly Held**
SIC: 3561 Pumps & pumping equipment
HQ: Robbins & Myers, Inc.
    10586 N Highway 75
    Willis TX 77378
    936 890-1064

(G-7034)
ROBERT L SCOTT CO
Also Called: Rock Riverer Investments
101 Park Ave Ste 620 (73102-7201)
PHONE....................405 235-5345
Robert L Scott, *Owner*
EMP: 4 EST: 1960
SQ FT: 2,000
SALES (est): 389.2K **Privately Held**
SIC: 1382 Oil & gas exploration services

(G-7035)
ROBERT M COBB OILFIELD EQP SLS
Also Called: Robert M Cobb Oil Feld Eqp Sls
4201 S High Ave (73129-5427)
P.O. Box 57497 (73157-7497)
PHONE....................405 840-2902
Robert Cobb, *Owner*
EMP: 1
SALES: 5MM **Privately Held**
SIC: 5084 1389 Drilling equipment, excluding bits; oil & gas wells: building, repairing & dismantling

(G-7036)
ROBERT S CARGILE
10633 Quail Run Rd (73130-7058)
PHONE....................405 732-7915
Robert S Cargile, *Owner*
EMP: 1
SALES: 75K **Privately Held**
SIC: 1389 Construction, repair & dismantling services

(G-7037)
ROBERT SMITH
Also Called: Roadrunner Marketing
5030 N May Ave Ste 315 (73112-6010)
P.O. Box 2286 (73101-2286)
PHONE....................405 722-5188
Robert Smith, *Owner*
EMP: 1
SALES: 245K **Privately Held**
SIC: 3993 Signs & advertising specialties

(G-7038)
ROBERTS STEP-LITE SYSTEMS INC
8100 Sw 15th St (73128-9594)
PHONE....................800 654-8268
James R Roberts, *President*
EMP: 8
SALES (est): 1.2MM **Privately Held**
SIC: 3648 3645 Lighting equipment; residential lighting fixtures

(G-7039)
ROBERTSON-CECO II CORPORATION
8600 S I 35 Service Rd (73149-3100)
P.O. Box 94910 (73143-4910)
PHONE....................405 636-2010
Doug Clark, *Vice Pres*
Joe Edge, *Branch Mgr*
Don Weatherly, *Manager*
EMP: 225
SALES (corp-wide): 4.8B **Publicly Held**
WEB: www.robertson-cecoii.mfgpages.com
SIC: 3448 Buildings, portable: prefabricated metal
HQ: Robertson-Ceco Ii Corporation
    10943 N Sam Huston Pkwy W
    Houston TX 77064

(G-7040)
ROBERTSON-CECO II CORPORATION
Also Called: Star Building Systems
8600 S Interstate 35 (73149-3100)
PHONE....................405 636-2010
Joe Edge, *Manager*
EMP: 179
SALES (corp-wide): 4.8B **Publicly Held**
SIC: 3448 Prefabricated metal buildings
HQ: Robertson-Ceco Ii Corporation
    10943 N Sam Huston Pkwy W
    Houston TX 77064

(G-7041)
ROBYN HOLDINGS LLC
Also Called: Robyn Promotions & Printing
7717 W Britton Rd (73132-1514)
PHONE....................405 722-4600
Mervyn Hackney, *President*
Amy Ehl, *Supervisor*
EMP: 25
SQ FT: 14,000
SALES (est): 4.3MM **Privately Held**
SIC: 2759 5199 3993 2752 Promotional printing; business forms: printing; advertising specialties; signs & advertising specialties; commercial printing, lithographic

(G-7042)
ROCK ISLAND EXPLORATION LLC
500 W Main St Apt 200 (73102-2210)
PHONE....................405 232-7077
Paul Cox, *President*
EMP: 1
SALES (est): 132.5K **Privately Held**
SIC: 1382 Oil & gas exploration services

(G-7043)
ROCKET COLOR INC
Also Called: Rocket Color Copies
6905 N May Ave (73116-3238)
PHONE....................405 842-6001
Barney Semtner, *President*
Michael Carter, *Vice Pres*
Miranda Samford, *Graphic Designe*
EMP: 7
SQ FT: 2,500
SALES (est): 700K **Privately Held**
SIC: 2752 7334 Commercial printing, offset; photocopying & duplicating services

(G-7044)
ROCKET SCIENCE LABS INC
14300 S Rockwell Ave (73173-8521)
P.O. Box 891552 (73189-1552)
PHONE....................972 454-0412
Mitchel Paddyaker, *CEO*
EMP: 5
SALES (est): 365.1K **Privately Held**
SIC: 2899 Corrosion preventive lubricant

(G-7045)
ROCKIN WOOD LLC
700 Se 59th St (73129-5646)
PHONE....................405 673-5171
Tyelinda Baumgardner, *Principal*
EMP: 2
SALES (est): 185.5K **Privately Held**
SIC: 2431 Millwork

(G-7046)
ROCKY MOUNTAIN PROD CO LLC
7250 Nw Expressway (73132-1534)
P.O. Box 720455 (73172-0455)
PHONE....................405 720-2000
Charles Travis Henderson,
Coy Burgess,
EMP: 3
SALES: 300K **Privately Held**
SIC: 8742 1311 Industrial consultant; crude petroleum & natural gas

(G-7047)
ROHM-BOLSTER MFG CO LLC
Also Called: Victory Shooting Steel
8324 John Robert Dr (73135-6071)
PHONE....................405 274-6915
Jerry Bolster,
EMP: 2
SALES (est): 80.5K **Privately Held**
SIC: 3999 Manufacturing industries

(G-7048)
ROLLETT MFG INC
4101 Woodnoll St (73121-6467)
PHONE....................405 427-9707
EMP: 3
SQ FT: 1,200
SALES (est): 150K **Privately Held**
SIC: 7219 3549 Laundry/Garment Services Mfg Metalworking Machinery

(G-7049)
ROSS DUB COMPANY INC
6300 Melrose Ln (73127-5534)
P.O. Box 270066 (73137-0066)
PHONE....................405 495-3611
W A Dub Ross, *Ch of Bd*
W Mike Ross, *President*
Jerry Cravens, *Principal*
W A Ross, *Principal*
Dorothy Ross, *Corp Secy*
EMP: 20 EST: 1971
SQ FT: 30,000
SALES (est): 5.1MM **Privately Held**
SIC: 3317 3444 3312 Steel pipe & tubes; sheet metalwork; blast furnaces & steel mills

(G-7050)
ROSS PRINTING LLC
Also Called: Digiprint
4222 N May Ave (73112-6271)
PHONE....................405 947-0099
Stephen Ross, *Mng Member*
Kevin Ross,
EMP: 5
SALES (est): 5.5MM **Privately Held**
WEB: www.digiprintcom.com
SIC: 2752 Commercial printing, offset

(G-7051)
ROWMARK LLC
Also Called: Bur-Lane
6100 W Reno Ave (73127-6507)
PHONE....................405 787-4542
John Morris, *President*
EMP: 36
SALES (corp-wide): 46.5MM **Privately Held**
SIC: 5099 5087 5162 3953 Rubber stamps; engraving equipment & supplies; plastics products; marking devices; printing trades machinery
PA: Rowmark Llc
    5409 Hamlet Dr
    Findlay OH 45840
    419 425-8974

(G-7052)
ROYAL CUP INC
901 Enterprise Ave Ste 8a (73128-1425)
PHONE....................405 943-6088
Dan Cavaness, *Branch Mgr*
EMP: 5
SALES (corp-wide): 296.5MM **Privately Held**
SIC: 2095 5149 2099 Roasted coffee; groceries & related products; soft drinks; tea blending
PA: Royal Cup Inc.
    160 Cleage Dr
    Birmingham AL 35217
    205 849-5836

(G-7053)
ROYAL PRESTIGE JEALPA
2612 Sw 44th St (73119-3337)
PHONE....................405 602-5371
Carlos Padilla, *Principal*
EMP: 4 EST: 2007
SALES (est): 249.4K **Privately Held**
SIC: 3469 Kitchen fixtures & equipment, porcelain enameled

(G-7054)
ROYAL PRINTING CO INC
1830 Nw 4th Dr (73106-2613)
PHONE....................405 235-8581
Kelley Thomas, *President*
Phillip A Thomas, *Vice Pres*
Ali Sevier, *Marketing Staff*
Thomas Kelley, *Executive*
EMP: 13
SQ FT: 13,600
SALES (est): 2MM **Privately Held**
WEB: www.royalprintingco.com
SIC: 2759 2752 Commercial printing; lithographing on metal

(G-7055)
ROYALOK ROYALTY LLC
Also Called: Okla Royalty
6601 Briarcreek Dr (73162-7425)
P.O. Box 42284 (73123-3284)
PHONE....................405 721-9771
Roy E Cooper, *Mng Member*
EMP: 4
SALES (est): 225K **Privately Held**
SIC: 1311 Crude petroleum production; natural gas production

(G-7056)
ROYCE DUBLIN INC
4509 N Classen Blvd # 200 (73118-4836)
PHONE....................219 324-7995
EMP: 2
SALES (est): 81.9K **Privately Held**
SIC: 1382 Oil & gas exploration services

(G-7057)
RS FUEL LLC
3300 W Memorial Rd (73120-0924)
P.O. Box 14009 (73113-0009)
PHONE....................405 748-4277
Kevin Oblander, *Mng Member*
EMP: 9
SALES (est): 1MM **Privately Held**
WEB: www.rsfuelok.com
SIC: 2869 Fuels

(G-7058)
RTS ENERGY SERVICES LLC
14201 Caliber Dr Ste 300 (73134-1017)
PHONE....................432 617-2243
EMP: 12 EST: 2016
SALES (est): 2.3MM **Privately Held**
SIC: 1382 Oil & gas exploration services

(G-7059)
RUBBER MOLD COMPANY
6200 S Bryant Ave (73149-7022)
PHONE....................405 673-7177
Joe Robertson, *Owner*

GEOGRAPHIC SECTION

Oklahoma City - Oklahoma County (G-7090)

▼ EMP: 10
SQ FT: 2,400
SALES (est): 1MM Privately Held
SIC: 3069 Molded rubber products

(G-7060)
RUFFEL LANCE OIL & GAS CORP
210 Park Ave Ste 2150 (73102-5632)
PHONE.................405 239-7036
Lance Ruffel, *President*
Matha Wilkerson, *Corp Secy*
Jim Trepagnier, *Vice Pres*
EMP: 14
SQ FT: 3,800
SALES (est): 3.7MM Privately Held
SIC: 1311 Crude petroleum production; natural gas production

(G-7061)
RUFNEX OILFIELD SERVICES LLC
3120 S Meridian Ave (73119-1023)
PHONE.................405 741-8322
Micheal Holland, *Principal*
EMP: 9 EST: 2013
SALES (est): 636.7K Privately Held
SIC: 1389 Oil field services

(G-7062)
RUPTURE PIN TECHNOLOGY
Also Called: Bucklingtin Pen Technology
8230 Sw 8th St (73128-4212)
PHONE.................405 789-1884
Julian Taylor, *President*
Alok Dange, *Engineer*
▼ EMP: 27
SQ FT: 12,000
SALES (est): 9MM Privately Held
SIC: 3491 Pressure valves & regulators, industrial

(G-7063)
RVA
13904 Quailbrook Dr (73134-1718)
PHONE.................405 608-0744
Sandeet Shah, *Principal*
EMP: 7
SALES (est): 544K Privately Held
SIC: 3851 Ophthalmic goods

(G-7064)
S & S PROMOTIONS INC
1717 S Pennsylvania Ave (73108-7608)
PHONE.................405 631-6516
Steve Saak, *President*
Bill Gibson, *Prdtn Mgr*
Jeff Barry, *Research*
Ron Cawthon, *Human Res Mgr*
Todd Williamson, *VP Sales*
EMP: 35
SQ FT: 15,000
SALES (est): 4.9MM Privately Held
SIC: 2759 Screen printing

(G-7065)
S & S TEXTILE INC
2400 S Western Ave (73109-1733)
PHONE.................405 632-9928
Becky Goodrich, *President*
Scott Warren, *General Mgr*
Jerry Goodrich, *Vice Pres*
EMP: 15
SQ FT: 6,000
SALES (est): 1.1MM Privately Held
SIC: 2396 3993 2395 Screen printing on fabric articles; signs & advertising specialties; pleating & stitching

(G-7066)
S S & L OIL AND GAS PROPERTIES
Also Called: Oustanding Lady Oil & Gas,
5700 Nw 135th St Ste 200 (73142-5940)
PHONE.................405 603-6996
EMP: 3
SQ FT: 4,036
SALES (est): 286.8K Privately Held
SIC: 1382 Oil & Gas Exploration

(G-7067)
S&S PROFESSIONAL POLISHING LLC
129 Se 27th St (73129-2009)
PHONE.................405 631-7087
Sebastian Silva, *Principal*
EMP: 3
SALES (est): 143.7K Privately Held
SIC: 3471 Polishing, metals or formed products

(G-7068)
S&S STAR OPERATING LLC
13182 N Macarthur Blvd (73142-3017)
PHONE.................817 676-1638
Meghan Davis, *Principal*
EMP: 7
SALES (est): 923.4K Privately Held
SIC: 1389 Grading oil & gas well foundations

(G-7069)
S&S&D TRUCKING LLC
6128 Se 86th St (73135-6266)
PHONE.................405 365-3535
Dana Shackleford, *Partner*
EMP: 1
SALES (est): 104.8K Privately Held
SIC: 3728 Aircraft parts & equipment

(G-7070)
SAAN WORLD LLC
2324 N Macarthur Blvd (73127-2208)
PHONE.................405 494-1282
Pegus Thomas, *
EMP: 1
SALES (est): 69.4K Privately Held
SIC: 7335 2759 Commercial photography; promotional printing

(G-7071)
SABER INDUSTRIES
2601 Nw Expressway (73112-7272)
PHONE.................405 382-3975
David Luster, *Principal*
EMP: 3
SALES (est): 224K Privately Held
SIC: 3999 Manufacturing industries

(G-7072)
SAFETYCO LLC
3200 N May Ave Ste 112 (73112-6948)
PHONE.................405 603-3306
EMP: 1
SALES (est): 266.4K Privately Held
SIC: 5099 7389 2759 Whol Durable Goods Business Services Commercial Printing

(G-7073)
SAGEBRUSH PIPELINE LLC
1601 Nw Expressway (73118-1467)
PHONE.................405 753-5500
Wallace Jordan, *
EMP: 2
SALES (est): 1.8MM
SALES (corp-wide): 266.8MM Publicly Held
SIC: 1311 4924 Natural gas production; natural gas distribution
PA: Sandridge Energy, Inc.
123 Robert S Kerr Ave
Oklahoma City OK 73102
405 429-5500

(G-7074)
SAM DEE CUSTOM DRAPERIES
Also Called: San-Dee's Custom Draperies
6700 Sears Ter (73149-2404)
PHONE.................405 631-6128
Sandy Shockley, *Owner*
EMP: 2
SALES (est): 165.1K Privately Held
SIC: 2391 5714 Draperies, plastic & textile: from purchased materials; draperies

(G-7075)
SANCO ENTERPRISES INC (PA)
Also Called: Quick Charge
1032 Sw 22nd St (73109-1637)
PHONE.................405 634-2120
Raymond R Santilli, *President*
Clark John, *Plant Mgr*
EMP: 35
SQ FT: 15,000
SALES (est): 3.6MM Privately Held
WEB: www.quickcharge.com
SIC: 3629 3089 Electronic generation equipment; battery chargers, rectifying or nonrotating; injection molded finished plastic products

(G-7076)
SANCO PRODUCTS INC
Also Called: Quickcharge
1032 Sw 22nd St (73109-1637)
PHONE.................405 634-2120
Raymond R Santilli Jr, *President*
▲ EMP: 5
SQ FT: 25,000
SALES (est): 421.4K
SALES (corp-wide): 3.6MM Privately Held
SIC: 3089 Injection molding of plastics
PA: Sanco Enterprises Inc
1032 Sw 22nd St
Oklahoma City OK 73109
405 634-2120

(G-7077)
SAND POINT LLC
5909 Nw Expressway # 540 (73132-5155)
PHONE.................405 728-2111
Frank Hill, *Principal*
EMP: 2
SALES (est): 177.7K Privately Held
SIC: 1382 Oil & gas exploration services

(G-7078)
SANDRIDGE CO2 LLC
123 Robert S Kerr Ave (73102-6406)
P.O. Box 548807 (73154-8807)
PHONE.................405 429-5500
James D Bennett, *
EMP: 3
SALES (est): 136.5K Privately Held
SIC: 1311 Crude petroleum production

(G-7079)
SANDRIDGE ENERGY INC (PA)
123 Robert S Kerr Ave (73102-6406)
PHONE.................405 429-5500
Carl F Giesler Jr, *President*
Alicia Towler, *Manager*
Tim Heskett, *Director*
Alice Triana, *Receptionist*
EMP: 163
SALES (est): 266.8MM Publicly Held
SIC: 1311 Crude petroleum production

(G-7080)
SANDRIDGE EXPLORATION PROD LLC
123 Robert S Kerr Ave (73102-6406)
PHONE.................405 429-5734
James D Bennett, *CFO*
Matthew K Grubb, *
EMP: 1
SALES (est): 939.6K
SALES (corp-wide): 266.8MM Publicly Held
SIC: 1311 Crude petroleum production
PA: Sandridge Energy, Inc.
123 Robert S Kerr Ave
Oklahoma City OK 73102
405 429-5500

(G-7081)
SANDRIDGE OFFSHORE LLC
1601 Nw Expwy St Ste 1600 (73118-1420)
PHONE.................405 429-5500
Lisa Klein, *Principal*
EMP: 3
SALES (est): 382.2K Privately Held
SIC: 1311 Crude petroleum production

(G-7082)
SANDRIDGE OPERATING COMPANY
Also Called: Alsate Management and Inv Co
123 Robert S Kerr Ave (73102-6406)
PHONE.................405 753-5500
Malone Mitchell, *President*
John Suter, *COO*
Lance J Galvin, *Senior VP*
R Scott Griffin, *Senior VP*
Bill H Masino, *Senior VP*
EMP: 250
SQ FT: 20,000
SALES (est): 234.9MM
SALES (corp-wide): 266.8MM Publicly Held
WEB: www.sandridgeenergy.com
SIC: 1311 Crude petroleum production

PA: Sandridge Energy, Inc.
123 Robert S Kerr Ave
Oklahoma City OK 73102
405 429-5500

(G-7083)
SANDSTONE ENRGY ACQSTIONS CORP
101 N Robinson Ave # 810 (73102-5504)
P.O. Box 2532 (73101-2532)
PHONE.................405 239-2150
Greg D Byran, *President*
EMP: 7
SALES (est): 586.7K Privately Held
SIC: 1311 Crude petroleum & natural gas production

(G-7084)
SARA OIL & GAS INC
6016 Kingsbridge Dr (73162-3208)
PHONE.................405 721-2117
Paul Kelly, *President*
EMP: 2
SALES (est): 210K Privately Held
SIC: 1382 Oil & gas exploration services

(G-7085)
SASCO INC
Also Called: Sasco Rental Tools and Mch Sp
2101 S Eastern Ave (73129-7519)
P.O. Box 95246 (73143-5246)
PHONE.................405 670-3230
Kelly Meadows, *President*
Billy W Meadows, *Corp Secy*
EMP: 17
SQ FT: 8,000
SALES: 1.5MM Privately Held
SIC: 3533 7692 5082 Oil field machinery & equipment; welding repair; oil field equipment

(G-7086)
SAUNDERS INDUSTRIES LLC
8401 Mantle Ave (73132-4243)
PHONE.................405 728-3555
J Saunders, *Principal*
EMP: 2
SALES (est): 104.2K Privately Held
SIC: 3999 Manufacturing industries

(G-7087)
SAXET ENERGY
4205 Nw 146th Ter (73134-1753)
PHONE.................405 752-9544
Donald Henderson, *CEO*
EMP: 1
SALES (est): 92K Privately Held
SIC: 1389 Pumping of oil & gas wells

(G-7088)
SB CONSULTING LLC
Also Called: Sb Directional Services
5135 Sw 29th St (73179-8452)
PHONE.................405 926-7177
Scott Burch, *Mng Member*
EMP: 12 EST: 2014
SALES: 14MM Privately Held
SIC: 1381 Drilling oil & gas wells

(G-7089)
SCHLUMBERGER TECHNOLOGY CORP
10546 Nw 10th St (73127-7157)
PHONE.................405 789-1515
Steve Davis, *Branch Mgr*
EMP: 139 Publicly Held
SIC: 1389 Oil field services
HQ: Schlumberger Technology Corp
300 Schlumberger Dr
Sugar Land TX 77478
281 285-8500

(G-7090)
SCHLUMBERGER TECHNOLOGY CORP
5200 W I 40 Service Rd (73128-1200)
PHONE.................405 942-0002
EMP: 20 Publicly Held
SIC: 1389 Oil field services
HQ: Schlumberger Technology Corp
300 Schlumberger Dr
Sugar Land TX 77478
281 285-8500

Oklahoma City - Oklahoma County (G-7091)

(G-7091)
SCHOELLER BLECKMAN ENERGY
1901 Se 22nd St (73129-7515)
PHONE 405 672-4407
EMP: 4
SALES (est): 180.9K **Privately Held**
SIC: 3494 Plumbing & heating valves

(G-7092)
SCHWARZ ASPHALT LLC
8251 W Reno Ave (73127-7202)
PHONE 405 789-7203
Gene Schwarz,
Charles Schwarz,
Philip Schwarz,
EMP: 20
SQ FT: 2,000
SALES (est): 5.8MM **Privately Held**
SIC: 2952 Asphalt felts & coatings

(G-7093)
SCHWARZ SAND
7475 Sw 15th St (73128-9510)
PHONE 405 789-7914
Phillip Schwarz, *Principal*
EMP: 2
SALES (est): 169.4K **Privately Held**
SIC: 3272 Concrete products

(G-7094)
SCISSORTAIL TEES
8000 S Shields Blvd (73149-1723)
PHONE 405 706-6371
EMP: 2
SALES (est): 96.3K **Privately Held**
SIC: 2759 Screen printing

(G-7095)
SCOTT GREER SALES INC
1818 Se 22nd St (73129-7514)
P.O. Box 94656 (73143-4656)
PHONE 405 670-4654
Scott Greer, *President*
Marsha Greer, *Corp Secy*
EMP: 2
SQ FT: 2,000
SALES (est): 669.2K **Privately Held**
SIC: 1389 Oil field services

(G-7096)
SCOTT MANUFACTURING LLC
900 E Grand Blvd (73129-8401)
PHONE 405 949-2728
Harold Scott, *Manager*
EMP: 20
SALES (corp-wide): 43.9MM **Privately Held**
SIC: 7389 3644 3296 3086 Personal service agents, brokers & bureaus; insulators & insulation materials, electrical; mineral wool; plastics foam products
HQ: Scott Manufacturing, Llc
1573 State Route 136 W
Henderson KY 42420
270 831-2037

(G-7097)
SCOTT MANUFACTURING OF KY
900 E Grand Blvd (73129-8401)
PHONE 405 949-2728
Harold Scott, *Manager*
EMP: 21
SALES (corp-wide): 43.9MM **Privately Held**
SIC: 3296 Fiberglass insulation
HQ: Scott Manufacturing Of Kentucky Llc
1573 State Route 136 W
Henderson KY 42420
270 831-2037

(G-7098)
SCOTT SABOLICH PROSTHETICS & R (PA)
10201 Broadway Ext (73114-6217)
PHONE 405 841-6800
Kyle Wagner, *Med Doctor*
Scott Sabolich, *Mng Member*
EMP: 20
SQ FT: 21,000
SALES (est): 2.6MM **Privately Held**
SIC: 3842 5999 Prosthetic appliances; orthopedic & prosthesis applications

(G-7099)
SCOTTS PRINTING & COPYING INC
801 N Western Ave (73106-7235)
PHONE 405 236-0821
Scott Usher, *President*
Brad Balding, *Opers Mgr*
Gower Tony, *Cust Mgr*
EMP: 11
SALES: 1.7MM **Privately Held**
WEB: www.scottsprinting.org
SIC: 2752 Commercial printing, offset

(G-7100)
SCRAP MANAGEMENT OKLAHOMA INC
5200 Se 59th St (73135-4536)
PHONE 405 677-7000
Kenneth Burgess, *Ch of Bd*
Nicholas Hayes, *President*
Jerrit Burgess, *Vice Pres*
EMP: 13
SQ FT: 40,000
SALES (est): 3MM **Privately Held**
SIC: 5093 3443 Metal scrap & waste materials; metal parts

(G-7101)
SCUDDER SERVICE & SUPPLY INC
4410 Sw 34th St (73119-2406)
PHONE 405 232-6069
Russell Benton, *President*
EMP: 5
SQ FT: 1,100
SALES (est): 895.8K **Privately Held**
SIC: 3625 5065 Control circuit devices, magnet & solid state; security control equipment & systems

(G-7102)
SEAGATE TECHNOLOGY LLC
10321 W Reno Ave (73127-7136)
PHONE 405 324-3000
Jeffrey Brobst, *Vice Pres*
Jason Roles, *Opers Mgr*
Beverly Kang, *Opers Staff*
Gary Ness, *Opers Staff*
Jay Loven, *Engrg Dir*
EMP: 400 **Privately Held**
WEB: www.seagatetechnology.com
SIC: 3572 Disk drives, computer
HQ: Seagate Technology Llc
47488 Kato Rd
Fremont CA 94538
800 732-4283

(G-7103)
SEAGATE TECHNOLOGY LLC
401 E Memorial Rd Ste 500 (73114-2287)
PHONE 800 732-4283
Jeff Allen, *Vice Pres*
EMP: 1500 **Privately Held**
WEB: www.seagate.com
SIC: 3572 Disk drives, computer
HQ: Seagate Technology Llc
47488 Kato Rd
Fremont CA 94538
800 732-4283

(G-7104)
SEAL COMPANY ENTERPRISES INC
100 Ne 34th St (73105-2610)
PHONE 405 947-3307
Jim Whorton, *Manager*
EMP: 9
SALES (corp-wide): 15.2MM **Privately Held**
WEB: www.sealcompany.com
SIC: 3053 3061 Gaskets, packing & sealing devices; mechanical rubber goods
PA: Seal Company Enterprises, Inc.
1550 N 105th East Ave
Tulsa OK 74116
918 836-0441

(G-7105)
SEAL SEISMIC SERVICE LLC
6905 W Wilshire Blvd (73132-5423)
PHONE 405 603-2121
Don Seal, *President*
EMP: 2 EST: 2015
SALES (est): 128.1K **Privately Held**
SIC: 1382 Seismograph surveys

(G-7106)
SELECT COATINGS INC
2517 S Vermont Ave (73108-1051)
PHONE 405 745-9011
Jeff Pearson, *President*
Perry Robb, *Vice Pres*
EMP: 11
SALES (est): 585.6K **Privately Held**
SIC: 2851 Shellac (protective coating)

(G-7107)
SEMASYS INC
Also Called: Central Sales Promo
130 Ne 50th St (73105-1857)
P.O. Box 53444 (73152-3444)
PHONE 405 525-2335
Richard Darnell, *Vice Pres*
Nancy Moreland, *Vice Pres*
Marla Wagner, *Sales Staff*
EMP: 48
SQ FT: 111,400
SALES (corp-wide): 38.6MM **Privately Held**
SIC: 2262 3993 2759 2542 Screen printing; manmade fiber & silk broadwoven fabrics; signs & advertising specialties; commercial printing; partitions & fixtures, except wood; automotive & apparel trimmings
HQ: Semasys, Inc.
4480 Blalock Rd
Houston TX 77041
713 869-8331

(G-7108)
SEMGROUP CORPORATION
3030 Nw Expwy Ste 1100 (73112-5449)
PHONE 405 945-6300
Benjamin Olszewski, *Controller*
Pete Schwiering, *Branch Mgr*
EMP: 40 **Publicly Held**
SIC: 1311 Crude petroleum production
HQ: Semgroup Corporation
6120 S Yale Ave Ste 1500
Tulsa OK 74136
918 524-8100

(G-7109)
SENOX CORPORATION
1340 Metropolitan Ave (73108-2042)
PHONE 405 948-7464
Ken Ayers, *Branch Mgr*
EMP: 6
SALES (corp-wide): 54.9MM **Privately Held**
WEB: www.senox.com
SIC: 3442 Metal doors, sash & trim
PA: Senox Corporation
15409 Long Vista Dr
Austin TX 78728
512 251-3333

(G-7110)
SENTRY PUMP UNITS INTL LLC
4101 S High Ave (73129-5243)
PHONE 405 635-1800
Jerry Lordo,
EMP: 2 EST: 2007
SALES (est): 230K **Privately Held**
SIC: 3561 Pumps & pumping equipment

(G-7111)
SEQUOIA NATURAL RESOURCES LLC
6900 N Classen Blvd (73116-7210)
PHONE 405 463-0355
Jim Jones, *Principal*
EMP: 2
SALES (est): 153.5K **Privately Held**
SIC: 1382 1389 Oil & gas exploration services; oil & gas field services

(G-7112)
SEVENTY SEVEN ENERGY LLC (HQ)
Also Called: Seventy Seven Energy Inc.
777 Nw 63rd St (73116-7601)
PHONE 405 608-7777
Andy Hendricks, *CEO*
Clarence Foster, *Superintendent*
Drew Parker, *Regional Mgr*
Karl Blanchard, *COO*
Jerry Townley, *VP Opers*
EMP: 56
SALES (est): 520.3MM
SALES (corp-wide): 2.4B **Publicly Held**
SIC: 1389 Hydraulic fracturing wells; gas compressing (natural gas) at the fields
PA: Patterson-Uti Energy, Inc.
10713 W Sam Houston Pkwy
Houston TX 77064
281 765-7100

(G-7113)
SEVENTY SEVEN OPERATING LLC (DH)
777 Nw 63rd St (73116-7601)
P.O. Box 18856 (73154-0856)
PHONE 405 608-7777
Jerry L Winchester, *President*
Karl Blanchard, *COO*
Cary Baetz, *CFO*
EMP: 53
SALES (est): 467.1MM
SALES (corp-wide): 2.4B **Publicly Held**
SIC: 3533 1389 Drill rigs; hydraulic fracturing wells; gas compressing (natural gas) at the fields
HQ: Seventy Seven Energy Llc
777 Nw 63rd St
Oklahoma City OK 73116
405 608-7777

(G-7114)
SHANE BRALWEY WELDING LLC
9714 Sw 17th St (73128-1020)
PHONE 936 201-9072
Shane Brawley, *Principal*
EMP: 1
SALES (est): 25K **Privately Held**
SIC: 7692 Welding repair

(G-7115)
SHARED SERVICES
3433 Nw 56th St Ste 560 (73112-4420)
PHONE 405 947-0344
Teese Mullings, *Manager*
EMP: 2
SALES (est): 86.6K **Privately Held**
SIC: 3841 Surgical & medical instruments

(G-7116)
SHAW INDUSTRIES GROUP INC
4601 Nw 3rd St (73127-6400)
PHONE 405 917-5117
Micah Hotchkiss, *Branch Mgr*
EMP: 8
SALES (corp-wide): 327.2B **Publicly Held**
SIC: 3999 Barber & beauty shop equipment
HQ: Shaw Industries Group, Inc.
616 E Walnut Ave
Dalton GA 30721
800 446-9332

(G-7117)
SHEBESTER BECHTEL INC
400 S Jernivan Blvd (73128)
P.O. Box 270598 (73137-0598)
PHONE 405 577-2700
Robert Ingram, *Manager*
EMP: 44
SQ FT: 2,500
SALES (est): 1.6MM
SALES (corp-wide): 41.1MM **Privately Held**
WEB: www.sbiwellservice.com
SIC: 1389 Oil field services
PA: Shebester Bechtel, Inc
605 N 29th St
Blackwell OK 74631
580 363-4124

(G-7118)
SHEEN INCORPORATED
Also Called: Carousel Kids
2625 W Country Club Dr (73116-4216)
PHONE 405 848-0881
Vickie Sheen, *President*
EMP: 1
SQ FT: 2,000
SALES (est): 78.5K **Privately Held**
SIC: 3944 Games, toys & children's vehicles

GEOGRAPHIC SECTION

Oklahoma City - Oklahoma County (G-7152)

(G-7119)
SHEET METAL CONTRACTORS ASSN
3801 Willow Springs Ave (73112-2944)
PHONE.................................405 848-3683
Michael Clarke, *President*
Dean Myers, *Exec VP*
Kyle Bellman, *Vice Pres*
EMP: 2
SQ FT: 3,000
SALES: 74.6K **Privately Held**
SIC: 2721 Periodicals

(G-7120)
SHELBURNE OIL COMPANY
901 Nw 63rd St Ste 201 (73116-7627)
PHONE.................................405 843-1352
Gerald N Furseth, *President*
Betty A Furseth, *Corp Secy*
Sam Furseth, *Vice Pres*
Sherry Furseth, *Vice Pres*
EMP: 2 EST: 1932
SQ FT: 1,600
SALES (est): 210K **Privately Held**
SIC: 1311 Crude petroleum production; natural gas production

(G-7121)
SHERRI BURCH
Also Called: Sherri's Fashions & Accesories
768 N Main Ave (73116)
PHONE.................................405 720-9021
Sherri Burch, *Owner*
Robert Burch, *Co-Owner*
EMP: 1
SALES (est): 150K **Privately Held**
SIC: 5137 2389 Women's & children's clothing; men's miscellaneous accessories

(G-7122)
SHES HAPPY HAIR OKC LLC
1618 Nw 23rd St Ste A (73106-3613)
PHONE.................................405 328-3464
EMP: 4 EST: 2014
SALES (est): 133K **Privately Held**
SIC: 5813 7389 3999 Saloon; styling, wigs; wigs, including doll wigs, toupees or wiglets

(G-7123)
SHIELDS OPERATING INC (PA)
5661 N Classen Blvd (73118-4015)
PHONE.................................479 785-1222
Patrick E Shields, *President*
Timothy M Shields, *Admin Sec*
EMP: 7
SALES (est): 1.3MM **Privately Held**
SIC: 1382 Oil & gas exploration services

(G-7124)
SHORTRUNCDR
1810 Ne 67th St (73111-7951)
P.O. Box 950195 (73195-0195)
PHONE.................................405 602-5555
Lateef Lee, *Owner*
EMP: 1
SALES (est): 85K **Privately Held**
SIC: 3679 Liquid crystal displays (LCD)

(G-7125)
SHORTYS HATTERY
1007 S Agnew Ave (73108-2421)
PHONE.................................405 232-4287
Lavonna Kooger, *President*
EMP: 2
SALES (est): 193.1K **Privately Held**
SIC: 2353 Hats & caps

(G-7126)
SHUTTERS UNLIMITED LTD
900 Nw 85th St (73114-2129)
P.O. Box 14431 (73113-0431)
PHONE.................................405 843-7762
Mike Vandeveire, *President*
Charlie Calahan, *Vice Pres*
EMP: 14
SQ FT: 6,000
SALES (est): 1.7MM **Privately Held**
SIC: 2431 Window shutters, wood

(G-7127)
SIDES SCREENPRINTING MORE LLC
350 S Vermont Ave Ste 216 (73108-1022)
PHONE.................................580 772-8888
Sherry Sides,
Tommy Sides,
EMP: 5
SALES (est): 502.6K **Privately Held**
SIC: 2396 7336 Screen printing on fabric articles; silk screen design

(G-7128)
SIERRA HAMILTON LLC
3101 S Lakeside Dr (73179-8427)
PHONE.................................405 843-5566
EMP: 3 **Privately Held**
SIC: 1382 8711 Oil & gas exploration services; petroleum, mining & chemical engineers
HQ: Sierra Hamilton Llc
900 Threadneedle St # 150
Houston TX 77079
713 956-0956

(G-7129)
SIERRA MADERA CO2 PIPELINE LLC
1601 Nw Expwy St (73118-1467)
PHONE.................................405 753-5500
EMP: 1
SALES (est): 701.9K
SALES (corp-wide): 266.8MM **Publicly Held**
SIC: 1311 Crude petroleum & natural gas
PA: Sandridge Energy, Inc.
123 Robert S Kerr Ave
Oklahoma City OK 73102
405 429-5500

(G-7130)
SIERRA RESOURCES INC
5121 Gaillardia Corp Pl (73142-1873)
PHONE.................................405 946-2242
Tod Sanger, *President*
Scott Rund, *Vice Pres*
EMP: 24
SALES (est): 1.9MM **Privately Held**
SIC: 1382 Oil & gas exploration services

(G-7131)
SIGN A RAMA INC
Also Called: Sign-A-Rama
7111 S Western Ave (73139-2003)
PHONE.................................405 631-2008
John Bird, *Branch Mgr*
EMP: 5 **Privately Held**
SIC: 3993 Signs & advertising specialties
HQ: Sign A Rama Inc.
2121 Vista Pkwy
West Palm Beach FL 33411
561 640-5570

(G-7132)
SIGN INNOVATIONS LLC
1333 Se 38th St (73129-6912)
PHONE.................................405 840-1151
Mitch Stoker, *General Ptnr*
Michael Gipson, *Sales Staff*
Mark Hansen,
▲ EMP: 2
SQ FT: 10,000
SALES (est): 190K **Privately Held**
SIC: 3993 2752 Signs, not made in custom sign painting shops; decals, lithographed

(G-7133)
SIGN OF LIES LLC
3821 Nw 17th St (73107-3719)
PHONE.................................405 618-9695
Mark Stevenson, *Principal*
EMP: 1 EST: 2016
SALES (est): 46K **Privately Held**
SIC: 3993 Signs & advertising specialties

(G-7134)
SIGN SERVICE
8308 Sw 3rd St Ste B (73128-4243)
PHONE.................................405 495-0700
Carl Martin, *Owner*
Lori Martin, *Co-Owner*
EMP: 5
SQ FT: 3,000
SALES (est): 421.5K **Privately Held**
SIC: 3993 Electric signs

(G-7135)
SIGN UP FOR EMAILS
415 Couch Dr (73102-2214)
PHONE.................................405 236-3100
EMP: 1
SALES (est): 52K **Privately Held**
SIC: 3993 Signs & advertising specialties

(G-7136)
SIGN-A-RAMA OF OK INC
7111 S Western Ave (73139-2003)
PHONE.................................405 631-2008
John Bird, *President*
EMP: 5
SALES (est): 151.6K **Privately Held**
SIC: 3993 Signs & advertising specialties

(G-7137)
SIGNS AND T-SHIRTS OKLAHOMA CY
8805 S Western Ave (73139-9206)
PHONE.................................405 600-7080
EMP: 1
SALES (est): 46K **Privately Held**
SIC: 3993 Signs & advertising specialties

(G-7138)
SIGNTEC SIGNS DISTINCTION INC
4805 Nw 10th St (73127-5815)
PHONE.................................405 745-7555
Bradley W Codding, *President*
Ryan Codding, *Sales Mgr*
EMP: 6
SALES: 700K **Privately Held**
SIC: 3993 Electric signs

(G-7139)
SILAS SALSA COMPANY LLC
2340 W Britton Rd (73120-4903)
PHONE.................................469 556-9762
Aaron Hart,
Damon Clay,
Paul Clay,
EMP: 2
SALES (est): 62.3K **Privately Held**
WEB: www.silassalsa.com
SIC: 2032 Mexican foods: packaged in cans, jars, etc.

(G-7140)
SILVER CLIFF RESOURSE
3112 Nw 62nd St (73112-4225)
PHONE.................................405 842-8698
Gary Kunzler, *Owner*
EMP: 1
SALES (est): 75.2K **Privately Held**
SIC: 1389 Oil & gas field services

(G-7141)
SIMS AUTOMOTIVE INC
1628 Nw 6th St (73106-5099)
PHONE.................................405 235-1621
William Sims, *President*
Jordan Sims, *Shareholder*
EMP: 1
SQ FT: 35,000
SALES (est): 128.4K **Privately Held**
SIC: 3599 Machine shop, jobbing & repair

(G-7142)
SINE QUA NON LLC
9105 Oakmont Dr (73131-7239)
PHONE.................................405 478-2539
Walter C Parrish, *Administration*
EMP: 2
SALES (est): 137K **Privately Held**
SIC: 2084 Wines

(G-7143)
SINGER BROS
204 N Robinson Ave # 1700 (73102-6810)
P.O. Box 1522 (73101-1522)
PHONE.................................405 236-8596
David Singer, *Branch Mgr*
EMP: 6
SALES (corp-wide): 835.2K **Privately Held**
SIC: 1311 Oil shale mining

PA: Singer Bros
4124 S Rockford Ave # 101
Tulsa OK 74105
918 582-6237

(G-7144)
SIX S ENERGY GROUP LLC
2617 Nw 61st St (73112-7118)
P.O. Box 20474 (73156-0474)
PHONE.................................405 819-8053
Ralph Simon II, *Mng Member*
EMP: 1
SALES: 1.3MM **Privately Held**
SIC: 1382 7389 Oil & gas exploration services;

(G-7145)
SJB LININGS LLC
410 S Eagle Ln (73128-4225)
PHONE.................................405 225-3829
David Oberfield, *Mng Member*
EMP: 4
SALES (est): 373.3K **Privately Held**
SIC: 3533 Oil field machinery & equipment

(G-7146)
SKIS TEES
1014 Nw 1st St (73106-7642)
PHONE.................................405 239-7547
Marc Chorkey, *Owner*
EMP: 1
SALES (est): 126.3K **Privately Held**
SIC: 3993 Signs & advertising specialties

(G-7147)
SKM GRAPHICS & SIGNS
4601 S Shields Blvd (73129-3207)
PHONE.................................405 636-1911
Sharon K McBride, *Owner*
EMP: 1
SQ FT: 2,250
SALES (est): 93K **Privately Held**
SIC: 3993 Signs & advertising specialties

(G-7148)
SKYROCK INDUSTRIES LLC
12101 N Macarthur Blvd (73162-1800)
PHONE.................................660 525-7482
Lisa Eckhardt, *Principal*
EMP: 2 EST: 2016
SALES (est): 103.3K **Privately Held**
SIC: 3999 Manufacturing industries

(G-7149)
SKYSLATE SIGNS
1116 Ne 5th Ter (73117-1405)
PHONE.................................405 818-0838
Ryann Jenkins, *CEO*
Erik Gransberg, *President*
EMP: 10 EST: 2015
SALES (est): 353.1K **Privately Held**
SIC: 3993 7389 Signs & advertising specialties;

(G-7150)
SMA SURFACE LOGGING LLC
8224 Nw 92nd St (73132-1316)
PHONE.................................405 301-3375
EMP: 3 EST: 2014
SALES (est): 205.8K **Privately Held**
SIC: 2411 Logging

(G-7151)
SMART SHELTERS INC
4000 S I 35 Service Rd (73129-6905)
PHONE.................................405 702-7775
Robin Hood, *Office Mgr*
EMP: 19 EST: 2011
SALES (est): 3.9MM **Privately Held**
WEB: www.smartsheltersinc.com
SIC: 3442 Screen & storm doors & windows

(G-7152)
SMARTSIGNS LLC
905 Nw 74th St (73116-7001)
PHONE.................................405 659-5003
Joshua Holt, *Mng Member*
Elizabeth Holt, *Mng Member*
EMP: 2 EST: 2016
SALES (est): 111K **Privately Held**
SIC: 3993 Signs & advertising specialties

Oklahoma City - Oklahoma County (G-7153)

GEOGRAPHIC SECTION

(G-7153)
SMICO MANUFACTURING CO INC
6101 Camille Ave (73149-5036)
PHONE...................405 946-1461
Eric Heald, *President*
Randall Stoner, *CFO*
Zack Martin, *Sales Staff*
Cody German, *Director*
EMP: 45
SQ FT: 46,600
SALES: 15.2MM **Privately Held**
SIC: **3569** Sifting & screening machines

(G-7154)
SMITH & NEPHEW INC
76 S Meridian Ave (73107-6512)
PHONE...................405 917-8500
Curtis Lesniewski, *Facilities Mgr*
William Kimbro, *Opers Staff*
Nick Ritchey, *Production*
Sharrell Fossler, *Buyer*
Zakia Beattie, *Purchasing*
EMP: 110
SALES (corp-wide): 4.9B **Privately Held**
SIC: **5047** 3841 Medical equipment & supplies; surgical & medical instruments
HQ: Smith & Nephew, Inc.
7135 Goodlett Farms Pkwy
Cordova TN 38016
901 396-2121

(G-7155)
SMITH INTERNATIONAL INC
Also Called: Smith Drilling & Completions
6912 S Bryant Ave (73149-7210)
PHONE...................405 670-7200
Robert Owens, *Manager*
EMP: 50 **Publicly Held**
WEB: www.smithcodevelopment.com
SIC: **1389** Oil field services
HQ: Smith International, Inc.
1310 Rankin Rd
Houston TX 77073
281 443-3370

(G-7156)
SMURFIT KAPPA
7216 S Bryant Ave (73149-7204)
PHONE...................405 672-1695
Paul Beyer, *Manager*
EMP: 4 EST: 2014
SALES (est): 416K **Privately Held**
SIC: **2653** Boxes, corrugated: made from purchased materials

(G-7157)
SMURFIT KAPPA NORTH AMER LLC
7216 S Bryant Ave (73149-7204)
PHONE...................405 672-1695
Charles Wuchter, *Manager*
EMP: 450 **Privately Held**
SIC: **2653** Boxes, corrugated: made from purchased materials
HQ: Smurfit Kappa North America Llc
125 E John Carpenter Fwy # 925
Irving TX 75062
800 306-8326

(G-7158)
SOLUTIONS LUCID GROUP LLC
Also Called: Solutions Lighting
701 Ne 15th St 11 (73104-4613)
P.O. Box 121, Newcastle (73065-0121)
PHONE...................405 476-4332
Sheveron Glover,
▲ EMP: 2
SALES (est): 203.7K **Privately Held**
SIC: **3648** 7379 Lighting equipment; computer related maintenance services

(G-7159)
SOLUTIONWARE LTD
10400 Vineyard Blvd Ste F (73120-3830)
PHONE...................405 843-0809
Doug Hall, *President*
Dave Mc Reynolds, *Vice Pres*
Randy Overholt, *Vice Pres*
Joe Baumgardner, *Sales Mgr*
Tim Cole, *Manager*
EMP: 20
SQ FT: 3,900
SALES (est): 892.7K **Privately Held**
SIC: **7372** Application computer software

(G-7160)
SON SIGNS OKC ◎
350 S Vermont Ave Ste 204 (73108-1022)
PHONE...................405 830-2536
EMP: 1 EST: 2019
SALES (est): 46K **Privately Held**
WEB: www.sonsignsokc.com
SIC: **3993** Signs & advertising specialties

(G-7161)
SOONER DENIM INC
2817 Sw 88th St (73159-5618)
PHONE...................405 641-4720
Morton Dan, *Principal*
EMP: 2
SALES (est): 124.9K **Privately Held**
SIC: **2211** Denims

(G-7162)
SOONER PRINT IMAGING
900 Nw 6th St (73106-7243)
PHONE...................405 272-0600
Robert Elliott, *Principal*
EMP: 2
SALES (est): 109.9K **Privately Held**
SIC: **2752** Commercial printing, offset

(G-7163)
SOONER READY MIX
8420 S Bryant Ave (73149-7618)
PHONE...................405 670-3300
Greg Kilmer, *Principal*
EMP: 2
SALES (est): 101.3K **Privately Held**
SIC: **5211** 1771 3273 Cement; concrete work; ready-mixed concrete

(G-7164)
SOONER READY MIX LLC
13996 S Macarthur Blvd (73173-8710)
PHONE...................405 692-5595
Shirley Wilson, *Mng Member*
John Scott,
EMP: 25
SQ FT: 840
SALES (est): 3.6MM **Privately Held**
WEB: www.soonerreadymix.net
SIC: **3273** Ready-mixed concrete

(G-7165)
SOONER SCALE INC
2428 Sw 14th St (73108-2410)
P.O. Box 82386 (73148-0386)
PHONE...................405 236-3566
Steve E McFadden, *President*
McFadden Shane, *Sales Mgr*
EMP: 12 EST: 1974
SQ FT: 7,000
SALES: 500K **Privately Held**
SIC: **3596** 7699 Industrial scales; scale repair service

(G-7166)
SOONER STATE GRAPHICS & SIGNS
1909 Breakers West Blvd (73128-7014)
PHONE...................405 837-5226
EMP: 1
SALES (est): 50.6K **Privately Held**
SIC: **3993** Signs & advertising specialties

(G-7167)
SOONER STEEL AND TRUSS LLC
Also Called: Sooner Steel & Truss
801 S Agnew Ave (73108-2655)
PHONE...................405 232-5542
George Hughs, *President*
EMP: 1
SALES (est): 94.1K **Privately Held**
SIC: **3441** Fabricated structural metal

(G-7168)
SOONER WIPING RAGS LLC
301 N Rhode Island Ave # 109 (73117-3207)
PHONE...................405 670-3100
Brock Shumny, *Mng Member*
Emilee Shumny,
◆ EMP: 12
SALES: 2MM **Privately Held**
WEB: www.oklahomawipers.com
SIC: **2299** 5093 5999 Textile mill waste & remnant processing; waste paper & cloth materials; cleaning equipment & supplies

(G-7169)
SORB TECHNOLOGY INC
Also Called: Renal Solutions
3631 Sw 54th St (73119-4275)
P.O. Box 44500 (73144-4500)
PHONE...................405 682-1993
Pete Decomo, *President*
Preston Thompson, *Senior VP*
EMP: 22
SQ FT: 40,000
SALES (est): 3.4MM
SALES (corp-wide): 19.3B **Privately Held**
SIC: **3841** Medical instruments & equipment, blood & bone work
HQ: Renal Solutions, Inc.
770 Commonwealth Dr
Warrendale PA 15086
724 772-6900

(G-7170)
SOTHWESTERN EXPLORATION CONS
6305 Waterford Blvd # 405 (73118-1122)
PHONE...................405 767-0041
Stephan Eisner, *Principal*
EMP: 2 EST: 2009
SALES (est): 138.8K **Privately Held**
SIC: **1382** Oil & gas exploration services

(G-7171)
SOUTHERN INTERNATIONAL INC
4200 Perimeter Center Dr # 205 (73112-2310)
PHONE...................405 943-5288
Perry L Moore, *Ch of Bd*
Terry Brittenham, *President*
EMP: 13
SQ FT: 5,000
SALES (est): 927.1K **Privately Held**
SIC: **1389** Oil consultants

(G-7172)
SOUTHERN RESOURCES INC
4509 N Classen Blvd # 201 (73118-4836)
PHONE...................405 601-1322
Robert Tucker, *President*
EMP: 6
SQ FT: 2,500
SALES (est): 1.7MM **Privately Held**
SIC: **1382** 1311 Oil & gas exploration services; crude petroleum production; natural gas production

(G-7173)
SOUTHWEST CNSTR NEWS SVC (PA)
3616 Nw 58th St (73112-4409)
P.O. Box 57090 (73157-7090)
PHONE...................405 948-7474
Edwin O Minx, *President*
Mark Minx, *Vice Pres*
EMP: 2
SALES (est): 508.8K **Privately Held**
WEB: www.swcnews.com
SIC: **2711** 2752 Newspapers: publishing only, not printed on site; commercial printing, lithographic

(G-7174)
SOUTHWEST ELECTRIC CO (PA)
6503 Se 74th St (73135-1100)
P.O. Box 82639 (73148-0639)
PHONE...................800 364-4445
Roy Townsdin, *CEO*
Keith Nesbit, *President*
Howard Eaton, *Vice Pres*
John Maravich, *Vice Pres*
Jason Price, *Vice Pres*
EMP: 30
SQ FT: 35,000
SALES (est): 68MM **Privately Held**
SIC: **3825** 3612 Transformers, portable: instrument; specialty transformers

(G-7175)
SOUTHWEST ELECTRIC CO
Also Called: Power Transformer
6501 Se 74th St (73135-1100)
P.O. Box 82639 (73148-0639)
PHONE...................405 733-4700
Bruce Forsyth, *General Mgr*
EMP: 150

SALES (corp-wide): 68MM **Privately Held**
SIC: **7629** 3612 Electrical equipment repair, high voltage; transformers, except electric
PA: Southwest Electric Co.
6503 Se 74th St
Oklahoma City OK 73135
800 364-4445

(G-7176)
SOUTHWEST ENGINEERING
Also Called: Armorvault
729 Se 29th St (73129-4827)
PHONE...................405 634-2841
Mark Webb, *Owner*
EMP: 4
SQ FT: 6,000
SALES: 125K **Privately Held**
SIC: **3499** 8711 Safes & vaults, metal; engineering services

(G-7177)
SOUTHWESTERN STY & BNK SUP INC
4500 N Santa Fe Ave (73118-7999)
P.O. Box 18697 (73154-0697)
PHONE...................405 525-9411
Robert L Allee, *President*
Gary Newton, *General Mgr*
Barbara Allee, *Corp Secy*
Dick Robberson, *Vice Pres*
Gina Hammer, *Production*
EMP: 92 EST: 1921
SQ FT: 71,000
SALES (est): 13.3MM **Privately Held**
WEB: www.southwesternbanksuppliesok.com
SIC: **2752** 5712 5112 6512 Commercial printing, offset; office furniture; stationery & office supplies; nonresidential building operators

(G-7178)
SOUTHWSTERN GROUP OF COMPANIES
Also Called: Southwestern Stationary Bnk Sup
4500 N Santa Fe Ave (73118-7902)
P.O. Box 18697 (73154-0697)
PHONE...................405 525-9411
Don Miles, *President*
Robert Allie, *President*
Barbara Allie, *Corp Secy*
Patrick Livingston, *Vice Pres*
Dick Robertson, *Vice Pres*
EMP: 51
SQ FT: 70,000
SALES (est): 6.9MM **Privately Held**
SIC: **2759** 7331 Publication printing; mailing service

(G-7179)
SPARTAN RESOURCES LLC (PA)
4013 Nw Expwy St Ste 690 (73116-1697)
P.O. Box 2266, Ardmore (73402-2266)
PHONE...................405 843-0420
Fermon G Johnson, *Vice Pres*
Scott Stone, *Mng Member*
EMP: 4
SALES (est): 839.1K **Privately Held**
SIC: **1382** Oil & gas exploration services

(G-7180)
SPECIALTY ADVERTISING CO INC
1400 N Mcmillan Ave (73127-3049)
PHONE...................405 495-3838
Dewayne Orr, *President*
EMP: 3
SQ FT: 1,200
SALES (est): 296.5K **Privately Held**
SIC: **2759** Promotional printing

(G-7181)
SPECTRUM PAINT COMPANY INC
Also Called: Spectrum Paint & Decorating
709 Nw 36th St (73118-7316)
PHONE...................405 525-6519
Wayne Hay, *Store Mgr*
Jeff Burger, *Manager*
EMP: 4

GEOGRAPHIC SECTION

Oklahoma City - Oklahoma County (G-7215)

SALES (corp-wide): 152.9MM **Privately Held**
WEB: www.spectrumpaint.com
SIC: **5231** 5198 2851 Paint; paints; paints & allied products
PA: Spectrum Paint Company, Inc.
15247 E Skelly Dr
Tulsa OK 74116
918 398-2188

(G-7182)
SPELLER OIL CORPORATION
3535 Nw 58th St Ste 900 (73112-4889)
PHONE.................................405 942-7869
W Thomas Speller, *President*
EMP: 12 EST: 1976
SQ FT: 2,400
SALES (est): 1.3MM **Privately Held**
SIC: **1311** Crude petroleum production; natural gas production

(G-7183)
SPELLER PETROLEUM CORPORATION
3535 Nw 58th St Ste 900 (73112-4825)
PHONE.................................405 942-7869
William Thomas Speller, *President*
EMP: 7
SQ FT: 2,500
SALES (est): 1.2MM **Privately Held**
SIC: **4923** 1311 Gas transmission & distribution; crude petroleum production; natural gas production

(G-7184)
SPIERS NEW TECHNOLOGIES INC (PA)
1500 Se 89th St (73149-4607)
PHONE.................................405 464-2200
Dirk Spiers, *President*
James Greenberger, *Corp Secy*
Brian Enis, *Opers Staff*
Chad Kirby, *Senior Mgr*
EMP: 45
SALES (est): 9.9MM **Privately Held**
SIC: **3691** Storage batteries

(G-7185)
SPIERS NEW TECHNOLOGIES INC
3228 N Santa Fe Ave (73118-8805)
PHONE.................................405 605-8066
Brian Enis, *Director*
EMP: 22
SALES (corp-wide): 9.9MM **Privately Held**
SIC: **3691** Storage batteries
PA: Spiers New Technologies Inc.
1500 Se 89th St
Oklahoma City OK 73149
405 464-2200

(G-7186)
SPIRAL EXPLORATION LLC
1609 N Blackwelder Ave (73106-2061)
PHONE.................................330 936-4689
Trevor Adler, *Principal*
EMP: 2
SALES (est): 117.6K **Privately Held**
SIC: **1311** Crude petroleum production

(G-7187)
SPOR ENTERPRISES INC
5600 Hardy Dr (73179-6638)
PHONE.................................405 745-9888
Steve Spore, *President*
Maryann Tayalor, *Admin Sec*
EMP: 6
SQ FT: 4,000
SALES (est): 570K **Privately Held**
SIC: **3599** 3577 3545 Machine shop, jobbing & repair; computer peripheral equipment; machine tool accessories

(G-7188)
SPRAGUES BACKHOE LLC
8424 Nw 92nd St (73132-1103)
PHONE.................................405 600-4905
Jack Sprague, *Principal*
EMP: 1
SALES (est): 132.9K **Privately Held**
SIC: **3531** Backhoes

(G-7189)
SPURLOCK CO SATELLITE MAPPING
6017 1/2 Nw 16th St 3 (73127-2603)
PHONE.................................405 495-8628
EMP: 1
SALES: 70K **Privately Held**
SIC: **1389** Oil/Gas Field Services

(G-7190)
SRH LIGHTING LLC
2328 Nw 12th St (73107-5606)
PHONE.................................405 604-9414
EMP: 2 EST: 2015
SALES (est): 62.9K **Privately Held**
SIC: **3993** Mfg Signs/Advertising Specialties

(G-7191)
SRITE MECHANICAL LLC
2704 Nw 65th St (73116-4602)
PHONE.................................405 308-3182
Tom Srite, *Owner*
EMP: 1 EST: 2008
SALES (est): 104.1K **Privately Held**
SIC: **3599** Machine shop, jobbing & repair

(G-7192)
STANDARD PRINTING CO INC
905 Nw 74th St (73116-7046)
PHONE.................................405 840-0001
Sam Salamy, *President*
Karen Salamy, *Vice Pres*
Elizabeth Salamy, *Admin Sec*
EMP: 9
SQ FT: 4,000
SALES (est): 800K **Privately Held**
SIC: **2752** 2791 2789 Commercial printing, offset; typesetting; bookbinding & related work

(G-7193)
STAR BUILDING SYSTEMS INC
8600 S I 35 Service Rd A (73149-3100)
PHONE.................................405 636-2010
David Alexander, *President*
Dan Smith, *District Mgr*
Dan Dekalb, *Plant Mgr*
Trevor Cornelsen, *Engineer*
Matthew Dotta, *Engineer*
▼ EMP: 44
SALES (est): 10MM **Privately Held**
SIC: **3448** Prefabricated metal buildings

(G-7194)
STAR PIPE SERVICE INC
7100 S Bryant Ave (73149-7200)
PHONE.................................405 672-6688
Glenn Houck, *President*
EMP: 12
SALES (est): 1.4MM **Privately Held**
SIC: **1389** Oil field services

(G-7195)
STAR ROYALTY CO
13112 Oakcliff Rd (73120-8900)
PHONE.................................405 748-5070
Mike Starcevich, *President*
EMP: 2
SALES (est): 81.9K **Privately Held**
SIC: **1382** Oil & gas exploration services

(G-7196)
STATION 7
5900 W Memorial Rd (73142-2027)
PHONE.................................405 470-4317
EMP: 4
SALES (est): 295.1K **Privately Held**
SIC: **2869** Fuels

(G-7197)
STATON INC
3310 S Brunson St (73119-1035)
PHONE.................................405 605-3765
David Staton, *Principal*
EMP: 6
SALES (est): 1MM **Privately Held**
SIC: **3799** Wheelbarrows

(G-7198)
STEALTH MFG
3204 Nw 66th St (73116-3410)
PHONE.................................405 843-1954
EMP: 5

SALES (est): 160K **Privately Held**
SIC: **3949** Mfu Muliti Sport Puncho

(G-7199)
STEEL QUEEN INC
1740 Nw 5th St (73106-2615)
PHONE.................................405 949-1664
Christine Powers, *President*
EMP: 6
SQ FT: 12,000
SALES (est): 670K **Privately Held**
SIC: **3444** Sheet metalwork

(G-7200)
STEEL WELDING INC
5600 N Tulsa Ave (73112-2172)
PHONE.................................405 789-5713
Allen Jenkins, *President*
Marc Shanbour, *Vice Pres*
EMP: 2
SALES (est): 86.3K **Privately Held**
SIC: **7692** Welding repair

(G-7201)
STEELEY D UPSHAW PUBG LLC
3730 Newport St (73112-6330)
PHONE.................................405 948-7802
Steeley D Upshaw, *Owner*
EMP: 1 EST: 2018
SALES (est): 37.5K **Privately Held**
SIC: **2741** Miscellaneous publishing

(G-7202)
STEPHENS & JOHNSON OPER CO
6100 S Hattie Ave (73149-2106)
PHONE.................................405 619-1866
EMP: 2
SALES (est): 89.6K **Privately Held**
SIC: **1389** Oil consultants

(G-7203)
STEPHENS OIL & GAS EXPLORATION
3555 Nw 58th St Ste 1000 (73112-4723)
PHONE.................................214 773-5898
A Masters, *Director*
EMP: 2
SALES (est): 73.6K **Privately Held**
SIC: **1389** Oil & gas field services

(G-7204)
STEVES BINDERY SERVICE INC
1000 N Virginia Dr (73107-5741)
PHONE.................................405 946-2183
Steve Smith, *President*
Wensdae Smith, *VP Admin*
EMP: 6
SQ FT: 16,000
SALES (est): 851.8K **Privately Held**
SIC: **2752** Commercial printing, offset

(G-7205)
STINGER WLLHEAD PROTECTION INC (HQ)
4301 Will Rogers Pkwy # 600 (73108-1835)
PHONE.................................405 702-6575
Bob McGuire, *President*
Alfred Neustaedter, *Corp Secy*
▼ EMP: 16
SQ FT: 8,650
SALES (est): 88.1MM
SALES (corp-wide): 1B **Publicly Held**
SIC: **1389** Oil field services
PA: Oil States International, Inc.
333 Clay St Ste 4620
Houston TX 77002
713 652-0582

(G-7206)
STINGER WLLHEAD PROTECTION INC
Also Called: Oil State
3300 S Ann Arbor Ave (73179-7618)
PHONE.................................405 684-2940
Danny Artherholt, *Manager*
EMP: 35
SALES (corp-wide): 1B **Publicly Held**
SIC: **1389** Oil field services
HQ: Stinger Wellhead Protection, Incorporated
4301 Will Rogers Pkwy # 600
Oklahoma City OK 73108
405 702-6575

(G-7207)
STINGRAY CMNTING ACIDIZING LLC
14201 Caliber Dr Ste 300 (73134-1017)
PHONE.................................432 617-2243
EMP: 2
SALES (est): 187.3K **Privately Held**
SIC: **1382** Oil & gas exploration services

(G-7208)
STINGRAY PRESSURE PUMPING LLC
14201 Caliber Dr Ste 200 (73134-1017)
PHONE.................................405 242-4998
Bob Maughmer, *Branch Mgr*
EMP: 222
SALES (corp-wide): 130.1MM **Privately Held**
SIC: **1382** Oil & gas exploration services
PA: Stingray Pressure Pumping Llc
42739 National Rd
Belmont OH 43718
405 648-4177

(G-7209)
STITCH N PRINT
450 N Rockwell Ave (73127-6119)
PHONE.................................405 789-8862
Scott Colston, *President*
EMP: 10
SALES: 750K **Privately Held**
SIC: **2759** Screen printing

(G-7210)
STITCHED BY SHAYNA
3112 N Bartell Rd (73121-6634)
PHONE.................................405 708-8614
Shayna Watson, *Principal*
EMP: 1
SALES (est): 31.2K **Privately Held**
SIC: **2395** Embroidery & art needlework

(G-7211)
STONE CREEK OPERATING LLC
6301 Waterford Blvd # 115 (73118-1130)
PHONE.................................405 395-4313
David R Fitzell, *President*
Jarred Tarkington, *Vice Pres*
EMP: 4
SQ FT: 2,000
SALES (est): 265.4K **Privately Held**
SIC: **1382** Oil & gas exploration services

(G-7212)
STONE OAK OPERATING LLC
10900 Hefner Pointe Dr (73120-5082)
PHONE.................................888 606-4744
EMP: 2
SALES (est): 179.4K **Privately Held**
SIC: **1382** Oil & gas exploration services

(G-7213)
STORM SF NGRND TRND SHLTRS NC
6101 Camille Ave (73149-5036)
PHONE.................................405 606-2563
Erick Heald, *President*
EMP: 65 EST: 2012
SALES (est): 14.4MM **Privately Held**
SIC: **3441** Fabricated structural metal

(G-7214)
STRATA MINERALS INC
12028 N Pennsylvania Ave (73120-7827)
P.O. Box 21055 (73156-1055)
PHONE.................................405 722-3227
Craig Tirey, *President*
EMP: 3
SQ FT: 1,500
SALES: 5MM **Privately Held**
SIC: **1311** Crude petroleum production

(G-7215)
STREAM ENERGY
8241 S Walker Ave Ste C (73139-9401)
PHONE.................................405 272-1080
Mike Phillips, *Principal*
EMP: 2
SALES (est): 195.9K **Privately Held**
SIC: **1382** Oil & gas exploration services

Oklahoma City - Oklahoma County (G-7216)

(G-7216)
STREAM ENERGY INC (PA)
101 Park Ave Ste 500 (73102-7201)
P.O. Box 950605 (73195-0605)
PHONE..................405 272-1080
James Waldrup III, *Incorporator*
Davis A Cates, *Incorporator*
Steven Dobbs, *Incorporator*
EMP: 18
SQ FT: 5,800
SALES (est): 2.4MM **Privately Held**
SIC: 1311 Crude petroleum production; natural gas production

(G-7217)
STREBEL CREEK VINEYARD
11521 N Macarthur Blvd (73162-3508)
PHONE..................405 720-7779
Gary Strebel, *Principal*
EMP: 3
SALES (est): 222.4K **Privately Held**
SIC: 2084 Wines

(G-7218)
STUDS UNLIMITED LLC
809 S Agnew Ave Ste D (73108-2600)
PHONE..................214 683-8012
George Hughes,
EMP: 6
SALES (est): 872.4K **Privately Held**
SIC: 3441 Building components, structural steel

(G-7219)
STURGEON ACQUISITIONS LLC (DH)
14201 Caliber Dr Ste 300 (73134-1017)
PHONE..................405 608-6007
Patrick McConnell, *CEO*
EMP: 4
SALES (est): 18.3MM
SALES (corp-wide): 359.9MM **Publicly Held**
SIC: 1382 6719 Oil & gas exploration services; investment holding companies, except banks
HQ: Mammoth Energy Services, Inc.
14201 Caliber Dr Ste 300
Oklahoma City OK 73134
405 608-6007

(G-7220)
SUANS INC
4716 Dove Tree Ln (73162-1919)
P.O. Box 211 (73101-0211)
PHONE..................405 413-1751
Suan Grant, *CEO*
EMP: 1
SALES (est): 96.6K **Privately Held**
SIC: 2033 Jams, jellies & preserves: packaged in cans, jars, etc.

(G-7221)
SUBURBAN CABINET SHOP
128 Se 21st St (73129-1225)
P.O. Box 36504 (73136-2504)
PHONE..................405 231-3110
Tip Hale, *Owner*
Brent Hale, *Co-Owner*
Jeff Hays, *Opers Mgr*
EMP: 50
SQ FT: 9,600
SALES (est): 3.9MM **Privately Held**
WEB: www.suburbancabinetshop.com
SIC: 2434 Wood kitchen cabinets

(G-7222)
SULLIVAN WELDING
1706 Everglade Ct (73128-7002)
PHONE..................405 301-6034
Shelby Pryor, *Principal*
EMP: 1 **EST:** 2017
SALES (est): 28.2K **Privately Held**
SIC: 7692 Welding repair

(G-7223)
SUMMIT MACHINE TOOL LLC
518 N Indiana Ave (73106-2607)
PHONE..................405 235-2075
Bruce Smith, *President*
Steven Golsen, *Vice Pres*
Dan Cazacu, *Technical Mgr*
Linda Rappaport, *Treasurer*
Jason Bringaze, *Sales Staff*
▲ **EMP:** 15 **EST:** 1955
SQ FT: 55,000
SALES: 11MM **Privately Held**
WEB: www.summitmt.com
SIC: 3599 Machine shop, jobbing & repair

(G-7224)
SUMMIT OIL COMPANY INC
7011 N Robinson Ave (73116-9044)
PHONE..................405 842-7896
Jason Goss, *President*
Lana Llewellyn, *Office Admin*
EMP: 1
SQ FT: 2,200
SALES (est): 178.8K **Privately Held**
SIC: 1311 Crude petroleum production

(G-7225)
SUNBELT INDUSTRIES INC
8017 N Walker Ave (73114-2144)
P.O. Box 14948 (73113-0948)
PHONE..................405 843-1275
Charles Musgrave III, *President*
Pam Hardy, *Opers Mgr*
Craig Masse, *Manager*
▲ **EMP:** 9
SQ FT: 40,000
SALES (est): 2.5MM **Privately Held**
SIC: 3291 2819 Abrasive products; industrial inorganic chemicals

(G-7226)
SUNWEST MUD
6601 S I 35 Service Rd (73149-2303)
PHONE..................405 631-2101
EMP: 2
SALES (est): 125.3K **Privately Held**
SIC: 1389 Oil/Gas Field Services

(G-7227)
SUPER SIGNS & PRINTING LLC
2838 Guilford Ln (73120-4401)
PHONE..................405 842-7070
James Henrichs, *Principal*
EMP: 2
SALES (est): 152.3K **Privately Held**
SIC: 2752 Commercial printing, lithographic

(G-7228)
SUPERIOR ENERGY SERVICES LLC
Also Called: Completion Services
7408 Nw 83rd St Ste E (73132-4293)
PHONE..................405 722-0896
EMP: 44 **Publicly Held**
SIC: 1389 Well plugging & abandoning, oil & gas; oil field services
HQ: Superior Energy Services, L.L.C.
203 Commission Blvd
Lafayette LA 70508
337 714-4545

(G-7229)
SUPERIOR NEON CO INC
Also Called: Superior Sign Company
2515 N Oklahoma Ave (73105-3018)
PHONE..................405 528-5515
Dan Lorant, *President*
James E Wood, *Corp Secy*
EMP: 24
SQ FT: 7,500
SALES (est): 2.2MM **Privately Held**
SIC: 3993 Neon signs

(G-7230)
SUPPLYONE OKLAHOMA CITY INC (HQ)
3801 Nw 3rd St (73107-6603)
PHONE..................405 947-7373
Bill Leith, *CEO*
Steve Maness, *President*
Jack Keeney, *Corp Secy*
Randy Clonts, *Vice Pres*
Tere Williams, *CFO*
EMP: 120
SALES: 29.2MM
SALES (corp-wide): 327.1MM **Privately Held**
SIC: 2653 5199 3565 Boxes, corrugated: made from purchased materials; packaging materials; packaging machinery
PA: Supplyone Holdings Company, Inc.
11 Campus Blvd Ste 150
Newtown Square PA 19073
484 582-5005

(G-7231)
SURFACE MOUNT DEPOT INC
Also Called: Ted Davis Enterprise
6003 Nw 5th St (73127-5643)
PHONE..................405 789-0670
Joe Kane, *Manager*
EMP: 5 **Privately Held**
SIC: 3089 Automotive parts, plastic
PA: Surface Mount Depot, Inc.
4001 Will Rogers Pkwy
Oklahoma City OK 73108

(G-7232)
SURFACE MOUNT DEPOT INC (PA)
Also Called: SMD
4001 Will Rogers Pkwy (73108-2035)
PHONE..................405 948-8763
Ted Davis, *President*
Scott Blass, *Purch Mgr*
Diane Ezell, *Purch Mgr*
Susan Titus, *Purch Agent*
Minhtri Nguyen, *Engineer*
EMP: 75
SQ FT: 35,000
SALES (est): 17.4MM **Privately Held**
SIC: 3679 2298 Electronic circuits; cable, fiber

(G-7233)
SUSAN L CHUNG CHIRPRTR
7213 Nw 111th Ter (73162-2608)
PHONE..................405 773-8225
Richard Gant, *Principal*
EMP: 3
SALES (est): 160.1K **Privately Held**
SIC: 3443 Fabricated plate work (boiler shop)

(G-7234)
SWC PRODUCTION INC
210 Park Ave Ste 2820 (73102-5644)
PHONE..................405 948-1559
Scott Calhoon, *President*
Alison Calhoon, *Admin Sec*
EMP: 4
SALES (est): 651.4K **Privately Held**
SIC: 1382 Oil & gas exploration services

(G-7235)
SWEET ORGANIC SCRUBS & MORE
1529 Ne 34th St (73111-4801)
PHONE..................203 465-2683
Kenya D Escobar, *Administration*
EMP: 2
SALES (est): 120K **Privately Held**
SIC: 2844 Toilet preparations

(G-7236)
SWEETIESRITE BAKING
2201 Nw 35th St (73112-7945)
PHONE..................405 400-6581
Dalinda Long, *Owner*
EMP: 2
SALES: 15K **Privately Held**
SIC: 2051 Bakery, for home service delivery

(G-7237)
SWIFT WINDS INDUSTRIES LLC
400 N Walker Ave Ste 125 (73102-1891)
PHONE..................405 600-9112
EMP: 1
SALES (est): 39.6K **Privately Held**
SIC: 3999 Manufacturing industries

(G-7238)
SWIFTWATER ENERGY SERVICES LLC
9211 Lake Hefner Pkwy # 200 (73120-2066)
PHONE..................405 820-7612
EMP: 4
SALES (est): 722.5K **Privately Held**
SIC: 1389 6531 Impounding & storing salt water, oil & gas field; real estate leasing & rentals

(G-7239)
SYNERGEX INC (PA)
3705 W Memorial Rd # 1401 (73134-1512)
PHONE..................405 748-5050
Ron James, *President*
Gary Garbacz, *Vice Pres*
Sharon Garbacz, *Treasurer*
Linda S James, *Admin Sec*
EMP: 27
SQ FT: 6,000
SALES (est): 4.4MM **Privately Held**
SIC: 1311 Crude petroleum production; natural gas production

(G-7240)
T & E MOBILE SERVICE INC
5325 S Madera St (73129-9347)
PHONE..................405 990-4022
Tommy Edmonson, *President*
Julie Farmer, *Principal*
Jackie Edmonson, *Corp Secy*
Adeina Edmonson, *Vice Pres*
EMP: 6
SALES (est): 12.2K **Privately Held**
SIC: 3599 7538 Machine & other job shop work; general truck repair

(G-7241)
T A H SOFTWARE SYSTEMS
Also Called: Tah Software Systems
3400 Ne 115th St (73131-4801)
PHONE..................405 478-3962
Thomas Hamilton, *Owner*
EMP: 1
SALES (est): 82K **Privately Held**
SIC: 7372 Prepackaged software

(G-7242)
T A T INC
Also Called: T A T Oil Co
2910 N Macarthur Blvd (73127-1628)
PHONE..................405 942-0489
William TSE, *President*
Tom TSE, *Corp Secy*
John TSE, *Vice Pres*
EMP: 7
SQ FT: 1,500
SALES (est): 500K **Privately Held**
SIC: 1382 1311 Oil & gas exploration services; crude petroleum production; natural gas production

(G-7243)
T C WHILDEN CONSULTING INC (PA)
4207 S Prospect (73129)
P.O. Box 95166 (73143-5166)
PHONE..................405 677-6881
Tom Whilden Jr, *President*
EMP: 17
SQ FT: 5,000
SALES (est): 3.3MM **Privately Held**
SIC: 3561 7699 Pumps, oil well & field; pumps & pumping equipment repair

(G-7244)
T J CAMPBELL CONSTRUCTION CO (PA)
Also Called: Campbell Asphalt
6900 S Sunnylane Rd (73135-1713)
P.O. Box 15129 (73155-5129)
PHONE..................405 672-6800
Joanna Campbell, *President*
O Flynn Sewell, *Vice Pres*
EMP: 145 **EST:** 1978
SQ FT: 10,200
SALES (est): 72.2MM **Privately Held**
SIC: 1611 2951 Highway & street paving contractor; asphalt & asphaltic paving mixtures (not from refineries)

(G-7245)
T K EXPLORATION CO
204 N Robinson Ave # 2350 (73102-6812)
PHONE..................405 239-7006
Robert R Klabzuba, *President*
Raymond M Timpanelli, *Vice Pres*
EMP: 2
SQ FT: 1,300
SALES: 1MM **Privately Held**
SIC: 1382 Oil & gas exploration services

(G-7246)
T K STANLEY INC
6504 Sw 29th St Bldg B (73179-6024)
PHONE..................405 745-3479
Stephen Farrar, *President*
EMP: 2
SALES (corp-wide): 590MM **Privately Held**
SIC: 1389 Oil field services

GEOGRAPHIC SECTION

Oklahoma City - Oklahoma County (G-7278)

PA: T. K. Stanley, Inc.
4025 Highway 35 N
Columbia MS 39429
601 735-2855

(G-7247)
T3 ENERGY LLC
11900 N Macarthur Blvd (73162-1801)
PHONE 405 677-8051
EMP: 2
SALES (est): 81.7K **Privately Held**
SIC: 1389 Oil field services

(G-7248)
TAG OKC INC
5201 S Meridian Ave Ste 5 (73119-5109)
PHONE 405 685-7728
Wendell Steward Jr, *Principal*
EMP: 6
SALES (est): 364.3K **Privately Held**
SIC: 3743 Railroad equipment

(G-7249)
TALON/LPE LTD
5909 Nw Expressway G185 (73132-5198)
PHONE 806 467-0607
EMP: 1
SALES (corp-wide): 24.7MM **Privately Held**
SIC: 1381 8748 Drilling oil & gas wells; environmental consultant
PA: Talon/Lpe, Ltd.
921 N Bivins St
Amarillo TX 79107
806 467-0607

(G-7250)
TAM COMPLETION SYSTEMS INC
6809 Camille Ave (73149-5204)
PHONE 405 601-7564
EMP: 3 **EST:** 2017
SALES (est): 342.9K **Privately Held**
SIC: 3533 Oil & gas field machinery

(G-7251)
TAMI WHEELER LLC
741 Sw 101st St (73139-5403)
PHONE 405 759-2239
Tami J Wheeler, *Principal*
EMP: 1
SALES: 94.4K **Privately Held**
SIC: 1389 Oil consultants

(G-7252)
TAOS EXPLORATION
6412 N Santa Fe Ave (73116-9114)
PHONE 405 840-5398
Robert Hunt, *Owner*
EMP: 1
SALES (est): 92K **Privately Held**
SIC: 1382 Oil & gas exploration services

(G-7253)
TAPSTONE ENERGY LLC
100 E Main St Ste 101 (73104-2416)
P.O. Box 1608 (73101-1608)
PHONE 405 702-1600
Tom Ward, *Mng Member*
Jennifer Higgins, *Analyst*
EMP: 34
SQ FT: 16,000
SALES (est): 47.2MM **Privately Held**
WEB: www.tapstoneenergy.com
SIC: 1382 Oil & gas exploration services

(G-7254)
TARHEEL OIL & GAS LLC
9116 Woodrock Dr (73169-3700)
PHONE 405 823-9965
Tiffany Rhodes, *Principal*
EMP: 2
SALES (est): 65.5K **Privately Held**
SIC: 1389 Oil & gas field services

(G-7255)
TAXES PRINT SHOP
511 Ne 31st St (73105-4007)
PHONE 405 521-3165
Gene Washam, *Principal*
EMP: 2 **EST:** 2010
SALES (est): 163.8K **Privately Held**
SIC: 2752 Commercial printing, lithographic

(G-7256)
TAYLOR ACCOUNTING SYSTEMS
3401 Nw 36th St (73112-6303)
P.O. Box 12636 (73157-2636)
PHONE 405 949-9898
Dean Talyor, *Owner*
Dean Talyor, *Principal*
EMP: 1
SALES (est): 87.1K **Privately Held**
SIC: 7372 Prepackaged software

(G-7257)
TAYLOR CUSTOM CUES
4619 Nw 10th St (73127-5919)
PHONE 405 317-3298
Kent Taylor, *Principal*
EMP: 1
SALES (est): 128.5K **Privately Held**
SIC: 3949 Sporting & athletic goods

(G-7258)
TAYLOR FOAM INC
370 N Rockwell Ave (73127-6117)
PHONE 405 787-5811
Bryan J Taylor, *President*
Jason Taylor, *Vice Pres*
Nancy Taylor, *Vice Pres*
EMP: 9
SQ FT: 25,000
SALES (est): 1.6MM **Privately Held**
SIC: 3081 3086 Unsupported plastics film & sheet; ice chests or coolers (portable), foamed plastic; packaging & shipping materials, foamed plastic

(G-7259)
TAYLOR FRAC LLC (DH)
14201 Caliber Dr Ste 300 (73134-1017)
PHONE 405 293-4208
Patrick McConnell, *CEO*
Nathan Lisowski,
Drew McDougall,
EMP: 22
SALES (est): 8.5MM
SALES (corp-wide): 359.9MM **Publicly Held**
WEB: www.taylorfrac.com
SIC: 1446 Silica sand mining
HQ: Sturgeon Acquisitions Llc
14201 Caliber Dr Ste 300
Oklahoma City OK 73134
405 608-6007

(G-7260)
TAYLOR RESOURCES
3001 Quail Creek Rd (73120-1915)
PHONE 405 850-2283
Leland D Taylor, *President*
EMP: 1
SALES (est): 130K **Privately Held**
SIC: 1381 Drilling oil & gas wells

(G-7261)
TE-RAY ENERGY INC
Also Called: Te-Ray Resources
13208 N Macarthur Blvd (73142-3019)
PHONE 405 232-4121
EMP: 4
SQ FT: 5,000
SALES (est): 900.4K **Privately Held**
SIC: 1382 Oil & Gas Exploration And Production

(G-7262)
TE-RAY RESOURCES INC
13208 N Macarthur Blvd (73142-3019)
PHONE 405 792-7486
EMP: 2
SALES (est): 341.2K **Privately Held**
SIC: 1382 Oil/Gas Exploration Services

(G-7263)
TED DAVIS ENTERPRISES INC
4001 Will Rogers Pkwy (73108-2035)
PHONE 405 948-8673
Jason Hammonds, *CFO*
EMP: 10
SQ FT: 35,000
SALES (est): 1.1MM **Privately Held**
SIC: 3599 3471 Machine shop, jobbing & repair; plating & polishing

(G-7264)
TED SMITH
Also Called: Ted Smith Wire Rope Spooling
4004 S Highland Park Dr (73129-8541)
P.O. Box 96876 (73143-6876)
PHONE 405 677-8402
Steve Smith, *Owner*
Kim Smith, *Co-Owner*
EMP: 2
SALES (est): 229.7K **Privately Held**
SIC: 1389 Oil field services

(G-7265)
TEES Q USBS LLC
Also Called: Wholesale
6600 N Meridian Ave # 160 (73116-1427)
P.O. Box 17405 (73136-1405)
PHONE 405 414-3264
Demetrius Jones, *CEO*
EMP: 2
SALES (est): 78.4K **Privately Held**
SIC: 2759 Screen printing

(G-7266)
TEMPLAR ENERGY LLC (DH)
4700 Gaillardia Pkwy # 200 (73142-1839)
PHONE 405 548-1200
Brian A Simmons, *CEO*
Charles Sledge, *Ch of Bd*
Joe Pukaite, *CFO*
EMP: 7
SALES (est): 16.5MM
SALES (corp-wide): 708.6K **Privately Held**
SIC: 1382 Oil & gas exploration services

(G-7267)
TEMPLAR OPERATING LLC
4700 Gaillardia Pkwy # 200 (73142-1839)
PHONE 405 548-1200
Chris McCormick, *Vice Pres*
David D Le Norman, *Mng Member*
Crystal Nance, *Analyst*
Brian A Simmons,
EMP: 14
SALES (est): 16.3MM
SALES (corp-wide): 708.6K **Privately Held**
SIC: 1382 1321 1311 Oil & gas exploration services; natural gas liquids; crude petroleum & natural gas
HQ: Templar Energy Llc
4700 Gaillardia Pkwy # 200
Oklahoma City OK 73142
405 548-1200

(G-7268)
TENDERETTE STEAK CO INC
Also Called: Tendertte Old Fashioned Mt Mkt
2200 S Central Ave (73129-1498)
PHONE 405 634-5655
Thomas Albertson, *President*
EMP: 13
SQ FT: 3,382
SALES (est): 2.2MM **Privately Held**
SIC: 5147 2011 Meats, fresh; meat packing plants

(G-7269)
TEREX CRANES
9528 W I 40 Service Rd (73128-7108)
PHONE 405 491-2006
EMP: 8
SALES (est): 147.6K **Privately Held**
SIC: 3531 Backhoes, tractors, cranes, plows & similar equipment

(G-7270)
TEREX USA LLC
9528 W 140 Service Rd (73128)
PHONE 405 787-6020
EMP: 16
SALES (est): 3MM **Privately Held**
SIC: 3531 Construction machinery

(G-7271)
TERRA PILOT MWD TOOLS LLC
5 N Cooley Dr (73127-1026)
PHONE 405 603-2200
Karl Spring, *President*
Lynn Kemp, *Manager*
EMP: 10 **EST:** 2011
SALES: 5MM **Privately Held**
WEB: www.terrapilotmwd.com
SIC: 1389 Oil field services

(G-7272)
TERRY BUILDING CO INC
7621 S Shields Blvd (73149-1629)
PHONE 405 634-5777
Terry Koneckney, *President*
Don Morris, *Opers Mgr*
Susan Heard, *Treasurer*
EMP: 18
SQ FT: 6,000
SALES (est): 5MM **Privately Held**
SIC: 3448 Panels for prefabricated metal buildings

(G-7273)
TESTERS INC (PA)
Also Called: Hailey Spcalty Tls Div Testers
1661 Exchange Ave (73108-3087)
P.O. Box 83437 (73148-1437)
PHONE 405 235-9911
Herbert Hailey, *President*
Stephen Hailey, *Vice Pres*
EMP: 32
SQ FT: 9,000
SALES (est): 9.2MM **Privately Held**
WEB: www.haileytools.com
SIC: 3533 1389 Oil & gas field machinery; testing, measuring, surveying & analysis services

(G-7274)
TETHEREX PHARMACEUTICALS CORP
840 Research Pkwy Ste 516 (73104-3633)
PHONE 405 206-7843
Scott Rollins, *CEO*
Russell Rother, *Exec VP*
Richard Alvarez, *Vice Pres*
David Falconer, *Vice Pres*
Nick Stefanko, *Program Mgr*
EMP: 7
SQ FT: 6,000
SALES (est): 404.8K **Privately Held**
SIC: 2834 Drugs acting on the gastrointestinal or genitourinary system

(G-7275)
TETRA TECHNOLOGIES INC
119 N Robinson Ave # 700 (73102-4613)
PHONE 405 606-8600
Mohamed Nazari, *Branch Mgr*
EMP: 2
SALES (corp-wide): 1B **Publicly Held**
SIC: 2819 Brine
PA: Tetra Technologies, Inc.
24955 Interstate 45
The Woodlands TX 77380
281 367-1983

(G-7276)
TETRA TECHNOLOGIES INC
101 Park Ave Ste 1200 (73102-7207)
PHONE 405 677-0221
James P Rounsavall Jr, *Branch Mgr*
EMP: 2
SALES (corp-wide): 1B **Publicly Held**
SIC: 3533 Gas field machinery & equipment
PA: Tetra Technologies, Inc.
24955 Interstate 45
The Woodlands TX 77380
281 367-1983

(G-7277)
TEXAS ALUMINUM INDUSTRIES
2221 Se 69th St (73149-6003)
PHONE 405 677-6767
Debra Lowery, *Principal*
EMP: 1
SALES (est): 86.2K **Privately Held**
SIC: 3999 Manufacturing industries

(G-7278)
THERAPY FOR DOGS INC
3001 Pine Ridge Rd (73120-5930)
PHONE 405 314-7655
Gordon Gearn, *President*
Greg Gross, *Admin Sec*
EMP: 3
SQ FT: 1,500
SALES: 200K **Privately Held**
SIC: 3999 Pet supplies

Oklahoma City - Oklahoma County (G-7279) — GEOGRAPHIC SECTION

(G-7279)
THERMACLIME LLC
3503 Nw 63rd St Ste 500 (73116-2238)
P.O. Box 754 (73101-0754)
PHONE..................405 235-4546
Jack E Golsen,
Michael Adams,
Heidi L Brown,
John Carver,
Kristy Carver,
EMP: 31
SALES (est): 6.4MM
SALES (corp-wide): 365MM **Publicly Held**
SIC: 2819 5075 Industrial inorganic chemicals; warm air heating & air conditioning
PA: Lsb Industries, Inc.
3503 Nw 63rd St Ste 500
Oklahoma City OK 73116
405 235-4546

(G-7280)
THERMACLIME TECHNOLOGIES INC
5000 Interstate 40 W (73101)
PHONE..................405 778-6682
Steven J Golsen, *President*
Stephen F Rendon, *Vice Pres*
Betty Brown, *Controller*
EMP: 127
SALES (est): 35.8MM
SALES (corp-wide): 2.3B **Privately Held**
SIC: 3585 Heating equipment, complete
HQ: The Climate Control Group Inc
7300 Sw 44th St
Oklahoma City OK 73179
405 745-6858

(G-7281)
THERMAL SOLUTIONS MFG
717 Sw 4th St (73109-5105)
PHONE..................405 272-0453
John Schneider, *Principal*
EMP: 2
SALES (est): 147.4K **Privately Held**
SIC: 3714 Motor vehicle parts & accessories

(G-7282)
THERMAL SPECIALTIES LLC
5001 Sw 20th St (73128-1413)
PHONE..................405 681-4400
Alvin Bruce, *Branch Mgr*
EMP: 5
SALES (corp-wide): 29.1MM **Privately Held**
SIC: 3398 Metal heat treating
PA: Thermal Specialties, Llc
6314 E 15th St
Tulsa OK 74112
918 836-4800

(G-7283)
THOMAS H SCOTT WESTERN LLC
Also Called: AAMCO Transm Total Car Care
8817 S Western Ave (73139-9203)
PHONE..................405 632-6860
Thomas Scott,
EMP: 2
SALES (est): 210K **Privately Held**
SIC: 3714 3519 7537 Transmissions, motor vehicle; gas engine rebuilding; automotive transmission repair shops

(G-7284)
THOMCO CABINET CO
2650 Nw 13th St (73107-4812)
PHONE..................405 627-1445
EMP: 2
SALES (est): 202.9K **Privately Held**
SIC: 2434 Wood kitchen cabinets

(G-7285)
THUNDER ROAD MAGAZINE OKLAHOMA
2940 Nw 34th St (73112-6608)
P.O. Box 1864, Stillwater (74076-1864)
PHONE..................405 612-3844
Tracy McLaughlin, *Partner*
EMP: 2
SALES (est): 183.7K **Privately Held**
SIC: 2721 Magazines: publishing only, not printed on site

(G-7286)
TIETSORT LLC
1500 Ne 4th St Ste 100 (73117-3003)
PHONE..................405 664-7353
Christopher Tietsort, *CEO*
EMP: 1 **EST:** 2016
SALES (est): 83.6K **Privately Held**
SIC: 1791 3211 Building front installation metal; flat glass; strengthened or reinforced glass; tempered glass; insulating glass, sealed units

(G-7287)
TIGER MOUNTAIN GAS & OIL
4305 Nw 46th St (73112-2435)
PHONE..................405 605-1181
Lester L Cowden Jr,
EMP: 2
SALES (est): 121K **Privately Held**
SIC: 1389 Oil & gas field services

(G-7288)
TILE & DESIGN CONCEPTS INC
310 W Wilshire Blvd (73116-7704)
PHONE..................405 842-8551
Kathy Reed, *President*
Bill K Reed, *Vice Pres*
▲ **EMP:** 20
SQ FT: 18,000
SALES (est): 3.7MM **Privately Held**
SIC: 5032 3281 5211 Ceramic wall & floor tile; cut stone & stone products; tile, ceramic

(G-7289)
TILLEY OIL & GAS INC
12311 N May Ave (73120-1943)
PHONE..................405 608-4970
EMP: 2
SALES (est): 219K **Privately Held**
SIC: 5172 1311 Crude oil; crude petroleum & natural gas production

(G-7290)
TILMAN WOODWORKS LLC
2904 N Harvard Ave (73127-1946)
PHONE..................405 441-3324
EMP: 1 **EST:** 2018
SALES (est): 54.1K **Privately Held**
SIC: 2431 Millwork

(G-7291)
TIM CARLTON PROSTHETICS INC
9414 Westgate Rd Ste B (73162-6215)
PHONE..................405 721-7570
Tim Carlton, *President*
EMP: 3
SALES (est): 300K **Privately Held**
SIC: 3842 Limbs, artificial

(G-7292)
TIMBER RIDGE SPRAY FOAM
8401 N Walker Ave (73114-3316)
PHONE..................405 608-5995
Jeffrey Bartlett, *Principal*
EMP: 3
SALES (est): 384.6K **Privately Held**
SIC: 3086 Plastics foam products

(G-7293)
TIPTOP ENERGY PROD US LLC
3817 Nw Expwy Ste 950 (73112-1488)
PHONE..................405 821-0796
Hosne ARA Doly, *President*
EMP: 8 **EST:** 2013
SALES (est): 503.8K **Privately Held**
SIC: 1389 Oil consultants
HQ: Sinopec International Petroleum Exploration And Production Corporation
Sinopec Building, Jia No.6,Huixin East Street, Chaoyang District
Beijing 10002
106 916-5136

(G-7294)
TITANIUM PHOENIX INC
1205 S Air Depot Blvd (73110-4807)
PHONE..................405 305-1304
Pepsi Caligone, *CEO*
EMP: 4 **EST:** 2011
SALES (est): 244.8K **Privately Held**
WEB: www.titanium-phoenix.com
SIC: 2339 5999 5699 5611 Women's & misses' accessories; women's & misses' athletic clothing & sportswear; miscellaneous retail stores; customized clothing & apparel; clothing accessories: men's & boys'; clothing & apparel carrying cases

(G-7295)
TJ SERVICES LLC
1300 Se Grand Blvd (73129-6716)
PHONE..................405 596-5124
Teresa Johnston,
EMP: 1 **EST:** 2009
SALES (est): 54.9K **Privately Held**
SIC: 3441 1541 Fabricated structural metal; industrial buildings & warehouses

(G-7296)
TLP ENERGY LLC
4747 Gaillardia Pkwy # 100 (73142-1881)
PHONE..................405 241-1800
David D Le Norman,
EMP: 2
SALES (est): 230K **Privately Held**
SIC: 1382 Oil & gas exploration services

(G-7297)
TMG SERVICE COMPANY LLC
8000 Se Linda Ln (73149-2920)
PHONE..................405 213-4317
Shawn Thomas, *President*
Brian Thomas, *Vice Pres*
Kyle Hill, *Opers Mgr*
Scott Brown, *CFO*
Josh Payne, *Sales Staff*
EMP: 25
SALES (est): 422.6K **Privately Held**
SIC: 1389 Gas field services

(G-7298)
TMW SYSTEMS INC
4300 Highline Blvd (73108-1830)
PHONE..................405 602-6055
Mohanraj Veni, *Branch Mgr*
EMP: 2
SALES (corp-wide): 3.2B **Publicly Held**
WEB: www.tmwsystems.com
SIC: 7372 Business oriented computer software
HQ: Tmw Systems, Inc.
6085 Parkland Blvd
Mayfield Heights OH 44124
216 831-6606

(G-7299)
TO DIGITAL MEDIA LLC
1915 N Classen Blvd (73106-6005)
PHONE..................405 639-8219
Ashley Jones, *Manager*
Alfred Lennox,
EMP: 2
SALES (est): 80.6K **Privately Held**
SIC: 2759 Commercial printing

(G-7300)
TO MARKET LLC
1131 Entp Ave Ste 5a (73128)
PHONE..................405 236-2878
Phil Wexler, *Principal*
▲ **EMP:** 3
SALES (est): 415.2K **Privately Held**
SIC: 3299 Ceramic fiber

(G-7301)
TOKLAHOMA LLC
300 Smmit Ridge Dr Apt A4 (73114)
PHONE..................580 402-1243
Mason Camp,
EMP: 2 **Privately Held**
SIC: 3911 Cigar & cigarette accessories

(G-7302)
TOM BENNETT MANUFACTURING
Also Called: Bennett's Decal & Label
18 Ne 48th St (73105-2019)
PHONE..................405 528-5671
Joe Thomas, *Owner*
EMP: 10
SQ FT: 15,800
SALES (est): 580K **Privately Held**
WEB: www.decalandlabel.com
SIC: 2752 3993 2791 2671 Decals, lithographed; signs & advertising specialties; typesetting; packaging paper & plastics film, coated & laminated; automotive & apparel trimmings

(G-7303)
TONY NEWCOMB SPORTSWEAR INC (PA)
Also Called: Newcomb T Shirts and Promos
1824 Linwood Blvd (73106-2626)
PHONE..................405 232-0022
Frank Newcomb, *President*
EMP: 2 **EST:** 1972
SQ FT: 6,000
SALES: 100K **Privately Held**
SIC: 2759 2396 2395 Screen printing; automotive & apparel trimmings; embroidery & art needlework

(G-7304)
TOPCO OILSITE PRODUCTS USA INC (HQ)
8200 W Reno Ave (73127-7201)
P.O. Box 12213, Odessa TX (79768-2213)
PHONE..................405 491-8521
EMP: 12
SALES (est): 2.6MM
SALES (corp-wide): 53.8MM **Privately Held**
WEB: www.topcooilsite.com
SIC: 1381 Drilling oil & gas wells
PA: Topco Oilsite Products Ltd
9519 28 Ave Nw
Edmonton AB T6N 0
800 222-6448

(G-7305)
TORTILLERIA AZTECA INC
2400 Sw 29th St (73119-2004)
PHONE..................405 632-5382
Jorge Islas, *President*
Alma Islas, *Admin Sec*
EMP: 8
SQ FT: 3,000
SALES (est): 1.1MM **Privately Held**
SIC: 2099 Tortillas, fresh or refrigerated

(G-7306)
TORTILLERIA LUPITA INC
235 Sw 25th St Ste D (73109-5927)
PHONE..................405 232-2760
Elias Pando, *President*
EMP: 4
SALES (est): 200K **Privately Held**
SIC: 2096 Tortilla chips

(G-7307)
TORUS PRESSURE CONTROL LLC
1715 S Lowery St (73129-8317)
P.O. Box 94520 (73143-4520)
PHONE..................405 670-4456
Greg Piper, *Corp Secy*
Britt Piper,
Rick Piper,
EMP: 36
SQ FT: 10,000
SALES (est): 2.6MM **Privately Held**
SIC: 3822 Pressure controllers, air-conditioning system type
HQ: Piper Oilfield Products Ltd. Co.
1715 S Lowery St
Oklahoma City OK 73129
405 670-4456

(G-7308)
TOTAL HOME CONTROLS INC
10925 Rowlett Ave (73150-2808)
PHONE..................405 736-0191
Scott Anderson, *President*
Kimberly Anderson, *Vice Pres*
EMP: 3
SALES (est): 217.5K **Privately Held**
SIC: 7382 3699 Security systems services; security control equipment & systems

(G-7309)
TOTAL PUMP AND SUPPLY LLC
2800 S High Ave (73129-4814)
PHONE..................405 670-0333
Delora Lassiter,

GEOGRAPHIC SECTION

Oklahoma City - Oklahoma County (G-7340)

Bobby Bowles,
Henry Lanoy,
Ed Lassiter,
EMP: 4
SALES (est): 1.1MM **Privately Held**
SIC: 3561 Pumps & pumping equipment

(G-7310)
TOTAL RESTAURANT INTERIORS
3936 E I 240 Service Rd (73135-1722)
P.O. Box 96414 (73143-6414)
PHONE..........................405 535-6348
Laura Batchelor, *Administration*
EMP: 8
SALES (est): 79.7K **Privately Held**
SIC: 2599 Bar, restaurant & cafeteria furniture

(G-7311)
TOTAL ROD CONCEPTS INC
7001 S Eastern Ave (73149-5224)
PHONE..........................405 677-0585
Douglas Branch, *Principal*
EMP: 2
SALES (est): 195K **Privately Held**
SIC: 1389 Oil field services

(G-7312)
TOWER SEALANTS LLC
4041 N Santa Fe Ave (73118-8512)
PHONE..........................405 528-4411
EMP: 15
SALES (est): 4.9MM **Privately Held**
SIC: 2891 Mfg Adhesives/Sealants

(G-7313)
TOYKO TOYS
3805 Nw 57th St (73112-2011)
PHONE..........................405 204-7462
EMP: 3
SALES (est): 114.3K **Privately Held**
SIC: 3944 Games, toys & children's vehicles

(G-7314)
TRADE TRUCKING LLC
2316 Nw 32nd St (73112-7818)
PHONE..........................405 443-5375
Israel Zapata, *Mng Member*
EMP: 1
SALES (est): 41K **Privately Held**
SIC: 1389 Servicing oil & gas wells

(G-7315)
TRANE US INC
3450 S Macarthur Blvd B (73179-7638)
PHONE..........................405 943-6600
EMP: 2 **Privately Held**
SIC: 3585 Refrigeration & heating equipment
HQ: Trane U.S. Inc.
3600 Pammel Creek Rd
La Crosse WI 54601
608 787-2000

(G-7316)
TRANE US INC
305 Hudiburg Cir (73108-1008)
PHONE..........................405 787-2237
Wendell Rames, *Branch Mgr*
EMP: 40 **Privately Held**
SIC: 3585 Refrigeration & heating equipment
HQ: Trane U.S. Inc.
3600 Pammel Creek Rd
La Crosse WI 54601
608 787-2000

(G-7317)
TRANSELEARN
10333 Buccaneer Dr (73159-6037)
PHONE..........................405 922-4595
Hung Tran, *Owner*
EMP: 1
SALES: 59K **Privately Held**
SIC: 7372 Prepackaged software

(G-7318)
TRANSFER CSES CLTCHES DFFRNTAL
301 S Western Ave (73109-1027)
PHONE..........................405 232-9557
EMP: 1

SALES (est): 54.5K **Privately Held**
SIC: 3523 Farm machinery & equipment

(G-7319)
TRANSTATE CASTINGS INC
1424 Nw 1st St (73106-5204)
PHONE..........................405 232-3936
Jeffrey Carter, *President*
Bonny Keene, *Corp Secy*
EMP: 7
SQ FT: 7,500
SALES (est): 690K **Privately Held**
SIC: 3363 3366 3365 Aluminum die-castings; bronze foundry; aluminum foundries

(G-7320)
TRC ROD SERVICES OF OKLAHOMA
7001 S Eastern Ave (73149-5224)
PHONE..........................405 677-0585
Bob Payne, *President*
Don Heck, *Vice Pres*
EMP: 15
SQ FT: 1,200
SALES (est): 2MM
SALES (corp-wide): 14.6MM **Privately Held**
SIC: 1389 3312 Pipe testing, oil field service; blast furnaces & steel mills
HQ: American Rodco Inc
1400 Woodloch Forest Dr # 170
The Woodlands TX 77380

(G-7321)
TREBLE SERVICES LLC
4329 Nw 18th St (73107-3627)
PHONE..........................405 401-1217
Jennifer Godinez, *CEO*
EMP: 3
SALES (est): 161.9K **Privately Held**
SIC: 2515 7378 7812 Mattresses & bedsprings; computer maintenance & repair; motion picture & video production

(G-7322)
TREEHOUSE VAPOR CO LLC
Also Called: Flagship Vapor Company
8101 Nw 10th St Ste D (73127-2953)
PHONE..........................405 601-6867
C Lance Kimball, *Mng Member*
Christopher Kimball, *Mng Member*
Michael Taylor,
Spencer Vernon,
EMP: 6
SALES: 670K **Privately Held**
SIC: 2131 Chewing tobacco

(G-7323)
TRI-STATE CON FOUNDATIONS LLC
7608 N Harvey Ave (73116-7715)
PHONE..........................405 341-3043
Gary E Allison, *Mng Member*
EMP: 25
SALES (est): 4.2MM **Privately Held**
SIC: 3271 Brick, concrete

(G-7324)
TRI-STATE ELEC CONTRS LLC
7608 N Harvey Ave (73116-7715)
PHONE..........................405 341-3043
EMP: 2
SALES (est): 206.7K **Privately Held**
SIC: 3694 1731 Automotive electrical equipment; general electrical contractor

(G-7325)
TRIAD ENERGY INC (PA)
6 Ne 63rd St Ste 220 (73105-1401)
PHONE..........................405 842-4312
William M McDonald, *President*
Thomas S Stapleton, *Vice Pres*
EMP: 18 EST: 1981
SALES (est): 4.1MM **Privately Held**
SIC: 1382 Oil & gas exploration services

(G-7326)
TRIAD OPERATING CORPORATION
6 Ne 63rd St Ste 220 (73105-1401)
PHONE..........................405 842-4312
Mike McDonald, *President*
EMP: 11

SALES (est): 708.5K
SALES (corp-wide): 4.1MM **Privately Held**
SIC: 1311 Crude petroleum & natural gas
PA: Triad Energy Inc.
6 Ne 63rd St Ste 220
Oklahoma City OK 73105
405 842-4312

(G-7327)
TRIANGLE PUMP COMPONENTS INC
1600 Se 23rd St (73129-7661)
PHONE..........................405 672-6900
Dana Miller, *Manager*
EMP: 16 **Privately Held**
SIC: 3494 3561 5084 Valves & pipe fittings; pumps & pumping equipment; pumps & pumping equipment
PA: Triangle Pump Components Inc
3644 W Highway 67
Cleburne TX 76033

(G-7328)
TRIBALCOM WRLESS SOLUTIONS LLC
100 N Broadway Ave # 2550 (73102-8614)
PHONE..........................405 274-7245
John Fryrear, *CEO*
Gina Gray, *COO*
EMP: 5
SALES (est): 216K **Privately Held**
SIC: 3663 4812 4813 Cellular radio telephone; radio telephone communication; cellular telephone services; local & long distance telephone communications; data telephone communications

(G-7329)
TRICON UNLMITED CNSTR SVCS LLC
3917 Nw 16th St (73107-4326)
PHONE..........................405 473-9186
Nathan Langley, *Principal*
EMP: 2 EST: 2011
SALES (est): 114.8K **Privately Held**
SIC: 3272 Concrete products

(G-7330)
TRILLIUM TRNSP FUELS LLC (PA)
Also Called: Trillium CNG
10601 N Pennsylvania Ave (73120-4108)
PHONE..........................800 920-1166
Gregory M Love,
Frank C Love,
Jennifer L Meyer,
Douglas J Stussi,
EMP: 17 EST: 2011
SALES (est): 14.7MM **Privately Held**
SIC: 2999 Waxes, petroleum: not produced in petroleum refineries

(G-7331)
TRILLIUM TRNSP FUELS LLC
10601 N Pennsylvania Ave (73120-4108)
P.O. Box 26210 (73126-0210)
PHONE..........................405 302-6500
EMP: 7
SALES (corp-wide): 14.7MM **Privately Held**
SIC: 2999 Waxes, petroleum: not produced in petroleum refineries
PA: Trillium Transportation Fuels, Llc
10601 N Pennsylvania Ave
Oklahoma City OK 73120
800 920-1166

(G-7332)
TRILOGY HORSE IND
2840 Linda Ln (73115-5012)
PHONE..........................405 248-1010
EMP: 2
SALES (est): 160.7K **Privately Held**
SIC: 3949 Sporting & athletic goods

(G-7333)
TRIMARK LABS
Also Called: Pdrx Pharmaceutica
727 N Ann Arbor Ave (73127-5822)
PHONE..........................405 942-3289
Jack McCall, *CEO*
Kathy Horton, *Sales Staff*
Joe Surette, *Sales Staff*
EMP: 4

SALES (est): 253.5K **Privately Held**
SIC: 2834 Pharmaceutical preparations

(G-7334)
TRINITY INDUSTRIES INC
2100 S Pennsylvania Ave (73108-7609)
PHONE..........................405 629-1213
EMP: 8
SALES (corp-wide): 3B **Publicly Held**
SIC: 3999 Atomizers, toiletry
PA: Trinity Industries, Inc.
2525 N Stemmons Fwy
Dallas TX 75207
214 631-4420

(G-7335)
TRINITY TANK CAR INC
2100 S Pennsylvania Ave (73108-7609)
PHONE..........................405 629-1226
W Wallace, *President*
EMP: 10
SALES (corp-wide): 3B **Publicly Held**
WEB: www.trin.net
SIC: 3743 Tank freight cars & car equipment
HQ: Trinity Tank Car, Inc.
2525 N Stemmons Fwy
Dallas TX 75207

(G-7336)
TRIO DI VINO LLC
Also Called: Waters Edge Winery
712 N Broadway Ave (73102-6007)
PHONE..........................405 494-1954
Adam Edwards,
Roger Cude,
Sarah Edwards,
EMP: 10
SALES (est): 1.4MM **Privately Held**
SIC: 5182 2084 Wine; wine cellars, bonded: engaged in blending wines

(G-7337)
TRIPLE ELITE LLC
5717 Se 74th St Ste C (73135-1105)
PHONE..........................405 610-5200
Evan Luttrell, *Owner*
EMP: 2 EST: 2015
SALES (est): 197.3K **Privately Held**
SIC: 2759 Screen printing

(G-7338)
TRIUMPH RESOURCES INC
701 Cedar Lake Blvd (73114-7806)
PHONE..........................405 478-8770
Mark Fischer, *President*
EMP: 3
SALES (est): 481.6K **Publicly Held**
SIC: 1382 Oil & gas exploration services
HQ: Chaparral Energy, L.L.C.
701 Cedar Lake Blvd
Oklahoma City OK 73114
405 478-8770

(G-7339)
TRONOX INCORPORATED
Tronox Pigments
3301 Nw 150th St (73134-2009)
PHONE..........................405 775-5000
Dave Hinshaw, *Branch Mgr*
EMP: 63
SALES (corp-wide): 2.9MM **Privately Held**
SIC: 2819 Industrial inorganic chemicals
HQ: Tronox Incorporated
1 Stamford Plz
Stamford CT 06901
203 705-3800

(G-7340)
TRONOX LLC
3301 Nw 150th St (73134-2009)
P.O. Box 268859 (73126-8859)
PHONE..........................405 775-5000
Jeffry N Quinn, *President*
Jean-Francois Turgeon, *COO*
Timothy C Carlson, *CFO*
◆ EMP: 2000
SALES (est): 228.8MM
SALES (corp-wide): 2.9MM **Privately Held**
SIC: 2819 2816 Inorganic acids, except nitric & phosphoric; titanium dioxide, anatase or rutile (pigments)

Oklahoma City - Oklahoma County (G-7341)   GEOGRAPHIC SECTION

HQ: Tronox Worldwide Llc
3301 Nw 150th St
Oklahoma City OK 73134
405 775-5000

(G-7341)
TRONOX PIGMENTS LLC
3301 Nw 150th St (73134-2009)
PHONE..................405 775-5000
Mary Mikkelson, *Principal*
EMP: 1
SALES (est): 592.5K **Privately Held**
SIC: **2819** Sodium compounds or salts, inorg., ex. refined sod. chloride

(G-7342)
TRONOX US HOLDINGS INC (DH)
3301 Nw 150th St (73134-2009)
PHONE..................405 775-5000
Tom Casey, *CEO*
Trevor Arran, *Senior VP*
Michael J Foster, *Senior VP*
Greg Pilcher, *Senior VP*
John D Romano, *Senior VP*
◆ EMP: 23
SALES (est): 644MM
SALES (corp-wide): 2.9MM **Privately Held**
SIC: **2816** 2819 5198 Titanium dioxide, anatase or rutile (pigments); sulfuric acid, oleum; colors & pigments

(G-7343)
TRONOX WORLDWIDE LLC (DH)
3301 Nw 150th St (73134-2009)
PHONE..................405 775-5000
Mary Mikkelson, *Mng Member*
▼ EMP: 14
SALES (est): 228.8MM
SALES (corp-wide): 2.9MM **Privately Held**
SIC: **2819** 2816 Inorganic acids, except nitric & phosphoric; white pigments; titanium dioxide, anatase or rutile (pigments)
HQ: Tronox Incorporated
1 Stamford Plz
Stamford CT 06901
203 705-3800

(G-7344)
TROPICAL MINERALS INC
11032 Quail Creek Rd (73120-6219)
PHONE..................405 236-2700
EMP: 2
SALES (est): 94.9K **Privately Held**
SIC: **1382** Oil & gas exploration services

(G-7345)
TSALTA CORPORATION
Also Called: Tsalta Oil
821 W Wilshire Blvd (73116-7021)
PHONE..................405 607-4141
Kent Hoffman, *President*
Don Baker, *Admin Sec*
EMP: 2
SALES (est): 210K **Privately Held**
SIC: **1311** Crude petroleum production; natural gas production

(G-7346)
TSDR LLC
Also Called: Spin Doctor, The
1712 Nw 5th St (73106-2615)
PHONE..................405 823-1518
Deborah Clark, *Principal*
EMP: 1 EST: 2009
SQ FT: 5,000
SALES (est): 156.5K **Privately Held**
WEB: www.theokspindoctor.com
SIC: **3553** Shapers, woodworking machines

(G-7347)
TSIG LLC
7608 N Harvey Ave (73116-7715)
PHONE..................405 463-7700
David Mayfield, *Principal*
EMP: 2
SALES (est): 108.5K **Privately Held**
SIC: **7539** 3629 Electrical services; capacitors & condensers

(G-7348)
TUFF SHED INC
1250 E Reno Ave (73117-1808)
PHONE..................405 272-1011
EMP: 1
SALES (corp-wide): 292.4MM **Privately Held**
SIC: **2452** Prefabricated wood buildings
PA: Tuff Shed, Inc.
1777 S Harrison St # 600
Denver CO 80210
303 753-8833

(G-7349)
TULAROSA INC
6424 N Santa Fe Ave Ste A (73116-9119)
PHONE..................405 848-0408
Mark Cogburn, *President*
EMP: 3 EST: 2001
SQ FT: 1,119
SALES (est): 320K **Privately Held**
SIC: **3533** Oil & gas field machinery

(G-7350)
TULSA WORLD CAPITOL BUREAU
State Capital Bldg Rm 430 (73105)
PHONE..................405 528-2465
Jill Worley, *Principal*
Susan Ellerbach, *Principal*
EMP: 1
SALES (est): 78.9K **Privately Held**
SIC: **2711** Newspapers, publishing & printing

(G-7351)
TURBULATOR COMPANY LLC
8705 Gateway Ter (73149-3063)
PHONE..................405 820-3026
Jackie D McHenry,
EMP: 13
SALES (est): 2.3MM **Privately Held**
SIC: **3491** Industrial valves

(G-7352)
TURNER OIL & GAS PROPERTIES (PA)
3232 W Britton Rd Ste 200 (73120-2035)
PHONE..................405 752-8000
Calvin Turner Jr, *President*
EMP: 2
SQ FT: 2,000
SALES (est): 501.9K **Privately Held**
SIC: **1382** Oil & gas exploration services

(G-7353)
TWISTED OAK FOODS LLC
5209 Nw 111th Ter (73162-3713)
PHONE..................405 720-7059
Brian Hill, *Owner*
EMP: 3
SALES (est): 196K **Privately Held**
SIC: **2099** Food preparations

(G-7354)
TYLER ENTERPRISES
5101 S Shields Blvd (73129-3217)
PHONE..................405 616-5500
Robert Denegri, *Owner*
EMP: 1
SALES (est): 112.4K
SALES (corp-wide): 17.8MM **Privately Held**
SIC: **3663** Radio & TV communications equipment
PA: Tyler Media Group Inc
5101 S Shields Blvd
Oklahoma City OK 73129
405 616-5500

(G-7355)
TYLER SIGNS LLC
5107 S Shields Blvd (73129-3217)
PHONE..................405 631-5174
Matt Hinkle, *Principal*
▲ EMP: 5
SALES (est): 576.3K **Privately Held**
SIC: **3993** Signs, not made in custom sign painting shops

(G-7356)
U BIG TS DESIGNS INC
905 Nw 6th St Ste 100 (73106-7242)
PHONE..................405 401-4327
Christopher Nubine, *President*

Kuinten Rucker, *Vice Pres*
Michael Lamey, *Treasurer*
EMP: 3
SALES (est): 143.8K **Privately Held**
SIC: **2759** 2331 5699 2752 Letterpress & screen printing; T-shirts & tops, women's: made from purchased materials; T-shirts, custom printed; poster & decal printing, lithographic; screen printing on fabric articles

(G-7357)
U S WEATHERFORD L P
6525 N Meridian Ave # 201 (73116-1420)
PHONE..................918 465-2311
Fax: 918 465-2159
EMP: 35 **Privately Held**
SIC: **1389** Oil/Gas Field Services
HQ: U S Weatherford L P
2000 Saint James Pl
Houston TX 70395
713 693-4000

(G-7358)
ULTERRA DRILLING TECH LP
13913 Qail Pinte Dr Ste A (73134)
PHONE..................405 751-6212
Chad Huckaby, *Branch Mgr*
EMP: 4 **Privately Held**
WEB: www.ulterra.com
SIC: **1389** Oil field services
HQ: Ulterra Drilling Technologies, Lp
201 Main St Ste 1660
Fort Worth TX 76102

(G-7359)
ULTRA BOTANICA LLC
120 Ne 26th St (73105-2705)
PHONE..................405 694-4175
Josh Bellieu, *Sales Staff*
Adam Payne, *Mng Member*
Bryan Frank,
Israel Hannah,
Robert Turner,
EMP: 4
SQ FT: 15,000
SALES (est): 271.4K **Privately Held**
SIC: **2023** 2048 2834 Dietary supplements, dairy & non-dairy based; feed supplements; powders, pharmaceutical

(G-7360)
UNION BREWERS
Also Called: Brewers Union
520 N Meridian Ave (73107-5723)
PHONE..................405 604-8989
EMP: 4 EST: 2018
SALES (est): 212.1K **Privately Held**
SIC: **2082** Beer (alcoholic beverage)

(G-7361)
UNIQUE PRINTING INC (PA)
1625 Broadview Cir (73127-3142)
PHONE..................405 842-3966
Marcia Keele, *Admin Sec*
EMP: 7
SQ FT: 6,000
SALES (est): 879.3K **Privately Held**
SIC: **2752** 2791 2789 Commercial printing, offset; typesetting; bookbinding & related work

(G-7362)
UNIT DRILLING CO
7101 Sw 29th St (73179-5213)
PHONE..................281 446-6889
David Case, *Vice Pres*
Keith Rowekamp, *Vice Pres*
Jane Sounny, *Admin Sec*
EMP: 45
SALES (est): 6.2MM **Privately Held**
SIC: **1381** Drilling oil & gas wells

(G-7363)
UNIT DRILLING COMPANY
Also Called: Unit Texas Drilling
7101 Sw 29th St (73179-5213)
PHONE..................405 745-4948
Tracey Hindman, *Branch Mgr*
EMP: 125
SALES (corp-wide): 674.6MM **Privately Held**
SIC: **1381** Redrilling oil & gas wells
HQ: Unit Drilling Company
8200 S U Dr
Tulsa OK 74132

(G-7364)
UNIT DRILLING COMPANY
7101 Sw 29th St (73179-5213)
PHONE..................405 745-4948
Fax: 405 745-2136
EMP: 15
SALES (est): 2MM **Privately Held**
SIC: **1381** Oil/Gas Well Drilling

(G-7365)
UNIT TEXAS DRILLING LLC
7101 Sw 29th St (73179-5213)
PHONE..................281 446-6889
John Cromling, *Senior VP*
EMP: 9
SALES (est): 864.4K **Privately Held**
SIC: **1381** Drilling oil & gas wells

(G-7366)
UNITED ENGINES MANUFACTURE
1545 Se 29th St (73129-7601)
PHONE..................405 601-9861
Kevin Sheldon, *Principal*
EMP: 3
SALES (est): 304.8K **Privately Held**
SIC: **3519** Internal combustion engines

(G-7367)
UNITED FORD
1231 Sovereign Row Ste A2 (73108-1831)
PHONE..................405 813-7300
Jim Butler, *Manager*
▼ EMP: 4
SALES (est): 370.4K **Privately Held**
SIC: **3714** Motor vehicle parts & accessories

(G-7368)
UNITED FUELS & ENERGY
533 N Portland Ave (73107-6111)
PHONE..................405 945-7400
EMP: 3
SALES (est): 247.7K **Privately Held**
SIC: **2869** Mfg Industrial Organic Chemicals

(G-7369)
UNITED HOLDINGS LLC (HQ)
5 N Mccormick St Ste 200 (73127-6626)
PHONE..................405 947-3321
Kirk Waite, *Controller*
Bill Moore,
Dave Grage,
EMP: 4
SALES (est): 252.5MM
SALES (corp-wide): 2.8B **Publicly Held**
SIC: **5084** 5013 7538 7537 Engines & parts, diesel; automotive supplies & parts; diesel engine repair: automotive; automotive transmission repair shops; fabricated structural metal
PA: Kirby Corporation
55 Waugh Dr Ste 1000
Houston TX 77007
713 435-1000

(G-7370)
UNITED LAND CO LLC
6801 Broadway Ext Ste 105 (73116-9068)
P.O. Box 590, Washington (73093-0590)
PHONE..................405 840-2666
Peter Scott, *Principal*
EMP: 2
SALES (est): 253.7K **Privately Held**
SIC: **1382** Geological exploration, oil & gas field

(G-7371)
UNITED MILLWORK INC
1718 E Grand Blvd (73129-8417)
PHONE..................405 670-3999
Lowell Lassiter, *President*
EMP: 4
SQ FT: 4,000
SALES (est): 200K **Privately Held**
SIC: **1751** 2517 2511 2434 Finish & trim carpentry; wood television & radio cabinets; wood household furniture; wood kitchen cabinets; millwork & lumber

GEOGRAPHIC SECTION

Oklahoma City - Oklahoma County (G-7401)

(G-7372)
UNIVERSAL PRESSURE PUMPING INC
777 Nw 63rd St (73116-7601)
PHONE..............................405 608-7346
EMP: 3
SALES (corp-wide): 2.4B **Publicly Held**
SIC: 1389 Hydraulic fracturing wells
HQ: Universal Pressure Pumping, Inc.
6 Desta Dr Ste 4400
Midland TX 79705

(G-7373)
UP N SMOKE III
4424 Se 44th St (73135-3123)
PHONE..............................405 609-1702
David Alvarado, *Principal*
EMP: 1
SALES (est): 67.5K **Privately Held**
SIC: 3999 Cigarette & cigar products & accessories

(G-7374)
UPPER ROOM
5909 Nw Expressway # 365 (73132-5149)
EMP: 3 **EST:** 2010
SALES (est): 58K **Privately Held**
SIC: 3131 Mfg Footwear Cut Stock

(G-7375)
US ROD MANUFACTURING LLC
13212 N Macarthur Blvd (73142-3019)
P.O. Box 54679 (73154-1679)
PHONE..............................636 359-9947
EMP: 1
SALES (est): 39.6K **Privately Held**
SIC: 3999 Manufacturing industries

(G-7376)
US SHOTBLAST PARTS & SVC CORP
207 Nw 59th St (73118-7403)
P.O. Box 14725 (73113-0725)
PHONE..............................405 842-6766
Brad Roberts, *President*
Jerry Roberts, *Vice Pres*
EMP: 4
SQ FT: 6,000
SALES (est): 634.3K **Privately Held**
SIC: 3559 Metal finishing equipment for plating, etc.

(G-7377)
USA COMPRESSION
14504 Hrtz Qail Sprng Pkw (73134-2629)
PHONE..............................405 790-0300
Tina Kipp, *Manager*
EMP: 5
SALES (est): 718.5K **Privately Held**
SIC: 1389 Gas compressing (natural gas) at the fields

(G-7378)
USA COMPRESSION PARTNERS LLC
14504 Hertz Quail Spgs Pa (73134-2629)
PHONE..............................405 234-3850
Tina Kipp, *Branch Mgr*
EMP: 6
SALES (corp-wide): 698.3MM **Publicly Held**
SIC: 1389 Gas compressing (natural gas) at the fields
HQ: Usa Compression Partners, Llc
111 Congress Ave Ste 2400
Austin TX 78701
512 369-1380

(G-7379)
USA METAL FABRICATION LLC
1838 Nw 1st St Unit C (73106-3008)
PHONE..............................918 845-6500
EMP: 1
SALES (est): 54.3K **Privately Held**
SIC: 3499 Fabricated metal products

(G-7380)
USA SCREEN PRTG & EMB CO INC
101 S Mickey Mantle Dr (73104-2480)
PHONE..............................405 946-3100
Chris Johnson, *President*
Shelli Johnson, *Corp Secy*
EMP: 50

SALES (est): 5.8MM **Privately Held**
SIC: 2396 2395 Screen printing on fabric articles; pleating & stitching

(G-7381)
USA-BOPS LLC
9910 W Reno Ave (73127-7139)
PHONE..............................405 265-2988
Larry Grigsby, *Principal*
EMP: 6
SALES (est): 1MM **Privately Held**
SIC: 3533 Oil & gas drilling rigs & equipment

(G-7382)
USHER CORPORATION
1 N Hudson Ave Ste 190 (73102)
PHONE..............................405 495-2125
Scott Usher, *President*
Denise Usher, *Vice Pres*
EMP: 9
SQ FT: 7,000
SALES: 1.6MM **Privately Held**
SIC: 2759 5112 2796 2791 Commercial printing; stationery & office supplies; platemaking services; typesetting; bookbinding & related work; commercial printing, lithographic

(G-7383)
V J STONE LLC
3244 Nw Grand Blvd (73116-3019)
PHONE..............................405 840-2255
John Van, *Mng Member*
EMP: 5
SALES (est): 440K **Privately Held**
SIC: 3281 Stone, quarrying & processing of own stone products

(G-7384)
V&H COATINGS CO
500 Se 14th St (73129-4317)
PHONE..............................405 819-4163
Humberto Virgen, *Principal*
EMP: 5
SALES (est): 353K **Privately Held**
SIC: 3272 Concrete products

(G-7385)
VADOVATIONS INC
1333 Cornell Pkwy (73108-1809)
PHONE..............................405 601-5520
John B Jenkins, *Principal*
EMP: 20
SALES (est): 4.4MM
SALES (corp-wide): 1.9B **Privately Held**
SIC: 3845 Electromedical equipment
PA: Integris Health, Inc.
3300 Nw Expressway
Oklahoma City OK 73112
405 949-6066

(G-7386)
VALCO INC
4524 Enterprise Pl (73128-1421)
P.O. Box 2117 (73101-2117)
PHONE..............................405 228-0932
Roger Valdez, *President*
EMP: 30
SALES (est): 3.1MM
SALES (corp-wide): 7MM **Privately Held**
SIC: 3728 3444 3769 Aircraft body & wing assemblies & parts; sheet metalwork; guided missile & space vehicle parts & auxiliary equipment
PA: Valco, Inc.
1009 Boren Rd
Duncan OK 73533
405 228-0932

(G-7387)
VALIANT ARTFL LIFT SLTIONS LLC (PA)
Also Called: Valiant Artfl Lift Systems
1 Leadership Sq N (73102)
PHONE..............................405 605-4567
David Divine, *Engineer*
Jay Jones, *Senior Engr*
Christopher Moak, *CFO*
Kathleen White, *Human Res Dir*
Austin Degraaf, *Sales Staff*
EMP: 22
SQ FT: 5,641

SALES (est): 15.9MM **Privately Held**
SIC: 3533 7353 Oil field machinery & equipment; oil field equipment, rental or leasing

(G-7388)
VAM USA LLC
7424 Nw 84th St (73132-4271)
PHONE..............................405 720-2200
Judson Wallace, *President*
EMP: 5
SALES (corp-wide): 2.6MM **Privately Held**
SIC: 3312 Pipes & tubes
HQ: Vam Usa, Llc
4424 W Sam Houston Pkwy N S
Houston TX 77041

(G-7389)
VAN EATON READY MIX INC
401 N Council Rd (73127-4990)
PHONE..............................405 789-1795
EMP: 26 **Privately Held**
SIC: 3273 Ready-mixed concrete
PA: Van Eaton Ready Mix, Inc.
8 Timber Pond
Shawnee OK 74804

(G-7390)
VANCE BROTHERS INC
4908 N Bryant Ave (73121-1823)
P.O. Box 36297 (73136-2297)
PHONE..............................405 427-1389
Greg Fuller, *Manager*
EMP: 5
SQ FT: 13,000
SALES (corp-wide): 50.9MM **Privately Held**
SIC: 2951 5033 2952 Asphalt & asphaltic paving mixtures (not from refineries); asphalt felts & coating; asphalt felts & coatings
PA: Vance Brothers, Inc.
5201 Brighton Ave
Kansas City MO 64130
816 923-4325

(G-7391)
VANS INC
1901 Nw Expwy St Ste 2009 (73118-9233)
PHONE..............................405 843-5286
EMP: 10
SALES (corp-wide): 10.4B **Publicly Held**
WEB: www.vans.com
SIC: 3021 Canvas shoes, rubber soled
HQ: Vans, Inc.
1588 S Coast Dr
Costa Mesa CA 92626
855 909-8267

(G-7392)
VANS INC
7628 W Reno Ave Ste 100 (73127-7211)
PHONE..............................405 787-9992
EMP: 10
SALES (corp-wide): 10.4B **Publicly Held**
WEB: www.vans.com
SIC: 3021 Canvas shoes, rubber soled
HQ: Vans, Inc.
1588 S Coast Dr
Costa Mesa CA 92626
855 909-8267

(G-7393)
VARCO LP
1800 Se 44th St (73129-7918)
PHONE..............................405 677-8889
Bryan Brewster, *Principal*
EMP: 9
SALES (corp-wide): 8.4B **Publicly Held**
WEB: www.nov.com
SIC: 1389 Oil field services
HQ: Varco, L.P.
2835 Holmes Rd
Houston TX 77051
713 799-5272

(G-7394)
VARCO LP
3216 Aluma Valley Dve (73121)
PHONE..............................405 478-3400
Johnny Chapman, *Manager*
EMP: 32
SQ FT: 7,032

SALES (corp-wide): 8.4B **Publicly Held**
SIC: 1389 Testing, measuring, surveying & analysis services
HQ: Varco, L.P.
2835 Holmes Rd
Houston TX 77051
713 799-5272

(G-7395)
VARCO INC
Also Called: Vintage Accessory Reproduction
8200 S Anderson Rd (73150-6704)
PHONE..............................405 732-1637
Jack H Nievar, *President*
EMP: 1
SQ FT: 4,000
SALES (est): 199K **Privately Held**
SIC: 3714 Motor vehicle engines & parts

(G-7396)
VENTANA EXPLORATION & PROD LLC
13832 Wireless Way # 100 (73134-2519)
PHONE..............................405 754-5000
Jack C Rawdon, *President*
Greg McMahan, *Vice Pres*
Heather Powell, *Vice Pres*
Ashley Rose, *Controller*
Diana Rawdon, *Director*
EMP: 11
SALES: 8.4MM **Privately Held**
SIC: 1382 Oil & gas exploration services

(G-7397)
VENTURA LLC (PA)
6100 N Western Ave (73118-1044)
PHONE..............................405 418-0300
Ravi Ramdas, *Manager*
Tony Say,
Lance Peterson,
Jim Roop,
EMP: 2
SQ FT: 2,538
SALES (est): 1.8MM **Privately Held**
SIC: 2911 Gasoline

(G-7398)
VERDE INDUSTRIES LLC
9213 Sunnymeade Pl (73120-4422)
PHONE..............................405 413-5599
Anthony Greene, *Principal*
EMP: 1
SALES (est): 39.6K **Privately Held**
SIC: 3999 Manufacturing industries

(G-7399)
VERITRIS GROUP INC
2828 Nw 57th St Ste 207 (73112-7091)
PHONE..............................580 713-4927
Devon Dunham, *Ch of Bd*
Laura Maeker,
EMP: 4 **EST:** 2012
SALES (est): 157.3K **Privately Held**
SIC: 7373 4813 8742 7372 Office computer automation systems integration; ; ; management information systems consultant; business oriented computer software

(G-7400)
VICTORY GLASS CO INC
2404 S Robinson Ave (73109-5949)
P.O. Box 94524 (73143-4524)
PHONE..............................405 232-5114
David McClurg, *President*
EMP: 4 **EST:** 1950
SQ FT: 13,500
SALES (est): 450K **Privately Held**
SIC: 1793 3231 Glass & glazing work; products of purchased glass

(G-7401)
VISION ENERGY GROUP LLC
5600 N May Ave Ste 137 (73112-4275)
PHONE..............................405 848-3933
Lisa Williams, *Principal*
EMP: 4
SALES (est): 186.2K **Privately Held**
SIC: 1382 Oil & gas exploration services
HQ: Praxair, Inc.
10 Riverview Dr
Danbury CT 06810
203 837-2000

Oklahoma City - Oklahoma County (G-7402)

(G-7402)
VISION PRINT PPG
9717 Nw 10th St Trlr 103 (73127-7440)
PHONE................405 519-4047
Shane Carman, *Principal*
EMP: 2
SALES (est): 83.9K **Privately Held**
SIC: 2752 Commercial printing, lithographic

(G-7403)
VITOL INC
201 Nw 10th St Ste 105 (73103-3931)
PHONE................405 228-8100
Trent Carter, *Marketing Staff*
Stewart Terry, *Branch Mgr*
EMP: 3
SALES (corp-wide): 8.2MM **Privately Held**
SIC: 1382 Oil & gas exploration services
HQ: Vitol Inc.
2925 Richmond Ave Ste 11
Houston TX 77098

(G-7404)
VM ARKOMA STACK LLC
14612 Hertz Quail Spg (73134-2643)
PHONE................405 286-5580
Brandon Webster, *Mng Member*
EMP: 2
SALES: 81.9K **Privately Held**
SIC: 1311 Natural gas production

(G-7405)
VMEBUS INTL TRADE ASSN
Also Called: Vita
9100 Paseo Del Vita (73131-8220)
PHONE................480 577-1916
Ray Alderman, *Manager*
Steve Edwards, *Manager*
Dean Holman, *Manager*
Bill Kehret, *Manager*
Jerald Gipper, *Exec Dir*
EMP: 3
SALES (est): 630.9K **Privately Held**
SIC: 8611 2741 2731 Trade associations; catalogs: publishing only, not printed on site; pamphlets: publishing only, not printed on site

(G-7406)
VOX PRINTING INCORPORATED (PA)
4000 E Britton Rd (73131-5244)
PHONE................800 654-8437
Laverna Reid, *CEO*
David Reid, *President*
Dennis P Reid, *Vice Pres*
Robert Reid, *Vice Pres*
EMP: 75
SQ FT: 65,000
SALES: 15MM **Privately Held**
SIC: 2752 Commercial printing, offset

(G-7407)
W & W ASCO STEEL LLC (HQ)
1730 W Reno Ave (73106-3216)
PHONE................405 235-3621
Rick Cooper, *CEO*
Burt Cooper, *Ch of Bd*
Steven Richardson, *President*
Ken Price, *Vice Pres*
Terry Rieken, *Vice Pres*
EMP: 6
SALES (est): 1MM
SALES (corp-wide): 72.4MM **Privately Held**
SIC: 3441 Building components, structural steel
PA: Wwsc Holdings Corp.
1730 W Reno Ave
Oklahoma City OK 73106
405 235-3621

(G-7408)
W & W ELECTRIC MOTOR SERVICE
24 Se 29th St (73129-2036)
PHONE................405 634-3776
John Winkler, *President*
Elizabeth Winkler, *Treasurer*
EMP: 5
SQ FT: 7,500
SALES (est): 350K **Privately Held**
SIC: 7694 Electric motor repair

(G-7409)
W A WATERMAN AND CO INC
8101 S Walker Ave Ste B (73139-9406)
PHONE................405 632-5631
W A Waterman, *CEO*
Dave B Marshall, *Corp Secy*
EMP: 3
SALES (est): 207.7K **Privately Held**
SIC: 1389 Oil field services

(G-7410)
W E INDUSTRIES INC
Also Called: Bear Safes
4500 Nw 16th St (73127-2502)
PHONE................405 949-0222
David Walker, *President*
Carol Walker, *Vice Pres*
EMP: 7
SQ FT: 8,000
SALES (est): 1.1MM **Privately Held**
SIC: 3499 Safes & vaults, metal

(G-7411)
W R WESTERN COMPANY INC (PA)
4915 Nw 10th St (73127-5703)
P.O. Box 1157, Bethany (73008-1157)
PHONE................405 605-5586
Karma Auger, *President*
Charles Auger, *General Mgr*
Thomas Auger, *Manager*
EMP: 8 EST: 1967
SQ FT: 10,000
SALES (est): 1.6MM **Privately Held**
WEB: www.wrwestern.com
SIC: 3199 Equestrian related leather articles

(G-7412)
W&W STEEL ERECTORS LLC
1730 W Reno Ave (73106-3216)
PHONE................405 235-3621
Rick Cooper, *CEO*
Bert Cooper, *Ch of Bd*
Charles Dougherty, *President*
J Patrick Hare, *CFO*
Joe Rolston, *Asst Sec*
EMP: 1
SALES (est): 16.5MM
SALES (corp-wide): 9B **Publicly Held**
SIC: 3441 Fabricated structural metal
HQ: Wwsc Holdings, Llc
1730 W Reno Ave
Oklahoma City OK 73106

(G-7413)
W&W-AFCO STEEL LLC (DH)
1730 W Reno Ave (73106-3216)
P.O. Box 25369 (73125-0369)
PHONE................405 235-3621
Richard W Cooper, *President*
John Rogers, *CFO*
EMP: 300
SALES (est): 129.7MM
SALES (corp-wide): 9B **Publicly Held**
SIC: 3441 Fabricated structural metal

(G-7414)
WALKER RESOURCES INC
12308 Val Verde Dr (73142-5400)
PHONE................405 751-5357
James P Walker, *President*
EMP: 3
SALES (est): 320.2K **Privately Held**
SIC: 1311 Crude petroleum & natural gas production

(G-7415)
WALKER STAMP & SEAL CO
Also Called: Walker Companies
121 Nw 6th St (73102-6026)
P.O. Box 177 (73101-0177)
PHONE................405 235-5319
Kenny Walker, *President*
Natalie Schwenn, *Corp Secy*
Kathy Walker, *Vice Pres*
EMP: 20
SQ FT: 12,000
SALES (est): 2.8MM **Privately Held**
WEB: www.walkercompanies.com
SIC: 3953 5199 3993 Embossing seals & hand stamps; seal presses, notary & hand; stencils, painting & marking; advertising specialties; signs, not made in custom sign painting shops

(G-7416)
WALKER WOODS INC
Also Called: Walker Unlimited
14201 N Kentucky Ave # 308 (73134-3427)
PHONE................208 266-1601
David Walker, *President*
EMP: 1
SALES (est): 124.2K **Privately Held**
SIC: 2411 Logging

(G-7417)
WALL COLMONOY CORPORATION
4700 Se 59th St (73135-4419)
PHONE................405 672-1361
Brian Martin, *Business Mgr*
John Sturch, *Vice Pres*
John R Sturch, *Branch Mgr*
Dawn Vanderpool, *Manager*
EMP: 39
SQ FT: 23,519
SALES (corp-wide): 58.1MM **Privately Held**
WEB: www.wallcolmonoy.com
SIC: 3724 3728 3714 Exhaust systems, aircraft; aircraft parts & equipment; motor vehicle parts & accessories
HQ: Wall Colmonoy Corporation
101 W Girard Ave
Madison Heights MI 48071
248 585-6400

(G-7418)
WALRUS AUDIO LLC
7801 N Robinson Ave D8 (73116-7725)
PHONE................405 254-4118
Colt Westbrook, *President*
EMP: 12
SALES (est): 57.9K **Privately Held**
SIC: 5999 3931 Audio-visual equipment & supplies; musical instruments

(G-7419)
WARD PETROLEUM CORPORATION
14000 Quail Springs Pkwy # 5000 (73134-2619)
P.O. Box 144 (73101-0144)
PHONE................405 242-4188
EMP: 1
SALES (corp-wide): 50.2MM **Privately Held**
SIC: 5172 1382 Petroleum products; oil & gas exploration services
PA: Ward Petroleum Corporation
502 S Fillmore St
Enid OK 73703
580 234-3229

(G-7420)
WARD WOOD PRODUCTS INC
5401 Sw 33rd St (73179-7617)
PHONE................405 681-5522
Scott Ward, *President*
EMP: 84
SALES (est): 8.9MM **Privately Held**
SIC: 2434 Wood kitchen cabinets

(G-7421)
WARREN PRODUCTS INC
Also Called: Warren, Bill, Office Products
1233 Sovereign Row Ste B1 (73108-1832)
P.O. Box 14067 (73113-0067)
PHONE................405 947-5676
Bill Warren, *President*
Jeff Warren, *COO*
EMP: 16
SQ FT: 6,000
SALES (est): 5.2MM **Privately Held**
SIC: 5112 5712 2752 Office supplies; office furniture; commercial printing, offset

(G-7422)
WARREN RAMSEY INC
Also Called: First Circle
218 Ne 38th St (73105-2530)
PHONE................405 528-2828
Sally Chapline, *President*
John Chapline, *Vice Pres*
EMP: 8
SQ FT: 9,000
SALES: 400K **Privately Held**
WEB: www.firstcircle.net
SIC: 7389 5712 5713 5714 Interior designer; furniture stores; custom made furniture, except cabinets; floor covering stores; draperies; antiques; upholstered household furniture

(G-7423)
WARWICK ENERGY GROUP LLC (PA)
900 W Wilshire Blvd (73116-7024)
PHONE................405 607-3400
Katherine Richard, *CEO*
Doug Bellis, *Vice Pres*
Andrew Cullen, *Vice Pres*
Jessica Tompkins, *Vice Pres*
Jennifer Horrigan, *Opers Staff*
EMP: 10 EST: 2010
SALES (est): 4.8MM **Privately Held**
SIC: 1311 Crude petroleum production

(G-7424)
WARWICK ENERGY GROUP LLC
6608 N Western Ave 417 (73116-7326)
P.O. Box 417 (73101)
PHONE................972 351-2740
EMP: 25
SALES (corp-wide): 4.8MM **Privately Held**
SIC: 1311 Crude petroleum & natural gas
PA: Warwick Energy Group Llc
900 W Wilshire Blvd
Oklahoma City OK 73116
405 607-3400

(G-7425)
WARWICK ENERGY INV GROUP LLC
2802 W Country Club Dr (73116-4221)
PHONE................405 607-3400
Katherine Richard, *CEO*
Doug Bellis, *Vice Pres*
Andrew Cullen, *Vice Pres*
Ian Yingling, *Vice Pres*
EMP: 50
SALES (est): 1.2MM **Privately Held**
SIC: 1311 Crude petroleum & natural gas

(G-7426)
WASHITA VALLEY ENTERPRISES
5605 S Eastern Ave (73129-9266)
PHONE................405 568-4525
EMP: 2
SALES (est): 72K **Privately Held**
SIC: 1389 Oil field services

(G-7427)
WASHITA VALLEY ENTERPRISES INC (PA)
1705 Se 59th St (73129-7315)
P.O. Box 94160 (73143-4160)
PHONE................405 670-5338
Tiffany Midgett, *President*
Joe Midgett, *Vice Pres*
EMP: 75 EST: 1975
SQ FT: 8,000
SALES (est): 46.4MM **Privately Held**
SIC: 4212 1389 Petroleum haulage, local; testing, measuring, surveying & analysis services

(G-7428)
WD DISTRIBUTING CO INC (PA)
807 Se 83rd St (73149-3044)
P.O. Box 95972 (73143-5972)
PHONE................405 634-3603
Jerry Dawkins, *President*
Steve Daman, *Principal*
Lee Dawkins, *Principal*
Robert Smith, *Principal*
Craig Tucker, *Business Mgr*
EMP: 15
SQ FT: 60,000
SALES (est): 5.2MM **Privately Held**
SIC: 7629 3545 Electronic equipment repair; machine tool accessories

(G-7429)
WEATHERFORD ARTIFICIA
Also Called: Leamco Ruthco Division
2836 Se 15th St (73129-8449)
PHONE................405 677-2410
Freddy Elkins, *Manager*

GEOGRAPHIC SECTION

Oklahoma City - Oklahoma County (G-7459)

EMP: 9 Privately Held
SIC: 1389 Oil field services
HQ: Weatherford Artificial Lift Systems, Llc
2000 Saint James Pl
Houston TX 77056
713 836-4000

(G-7430)
WEATHERFORD INTERNATIONAL LLC
857 S Scott St (73115-1344)
PHONE 405 773-1100
Trace Watson, *Safety Mgr*
Shauna Alden, *Mfg Staff*
Bryan Clawson, *Sales Staff*
Roger McBay, *Branch Mgr*
Kenneth Gaston, *Supervisor*
EMP: 23 Privately Held
WEB: www.weatherford.com
SIC: 3498 3533 Fabricated pipe & fittings; oil field machinery & equipment
HQ: Weatherford International, Llc
2000 Saint James Pl
Houston TX 77056
713 693-4000

(G-7431)
WEATHERFORD INTERNATIONAL LLC
7725 W Reno Ave Ste 220 (73127-9712)
PHONE 405 773-1100
Chris Scroggins, *Sales Staff*
Greg Bird, *Branch Mgr*
EMP: 23 Privately Held
SIC: 1389 Oil field services
HQ: Weatherford International, Llc
2000 Saint James Pl
Houston TX 77056
713 693-4000

(G-7432)
WEATHERFORD INTERNATIONAL LLC
717 N Morgan Rd Ste 69 (73127-7142)
PHONE 405 577-5590
Nick Croskey, *Branch Mgr*
Joe Hall, *Manager*
EMP: 23 Privately Held
SIC: 3533 Oil & gas field machinery
HQ: Weatherford International, Llc
2000 Saint James Pl
Houston TX 77056
713 693-4000

(G-7433)
WEATHERFORD INTERNATIONAL LLC
2800 S Meridian Ave (73108-1736)
PHONE 940 683-8393
EMP: 30
SALES (corp-wide): 210.8B **Publicly Held**
SIC: 3533 Petroleum Refiner
HQ: Weatherford International, Llc
2000 Saint James Pl
Houston TX 77056
713 693-4000

(G-7434)
WEATHERFORD INTERNATIONAL LLC
808 Se 84th St (73149-3045)
PHONE 405 619-7238
EMP: 10 Privately Held
SIC: 3533 Old Field Equipment
HQ: Weatherford International, Llc
2000 Saint James Pl
Houston TX 77056
713 693-4000

(G-7435)
WENTWORTH OPERATING CO
11900 N Macarthur Blvd E1 (73162-1863)
PHONE 405 341-6122
J Gerald Knol, *President*
A Richard Tiehen, *Vice Pres*
EMP: 15
SALES (est): 1.7MM **Privately Held**
SIC: 1382 8721 Oil & gas exploration services; certified public accountant

(G-7436)
WENZEL DOWNHOLE TOOLS US INC
100 S Cooley Dr (73127-1035)
PHONE 405 787-4145
EMP: 8
SALES (est): 791.3K **Privately Held**
SIC: 3533 Oil & gas field machinery

(G-7437)
WEST WORLDWIDE SERVICES INC
5500 W Reno Ave Ste 500 (73127-6318)
PHONE 405 601-9877
EMP: 2
SQ FT: 50,000
SALES (est): 202.4K
SALES (corp-wide): 1MM **Privately Held**
SIC: 3011 Mfg Tires/Inner Tubes
PA: West Worldwide Services, Inc.
26378 289th Pl
Adel IA 50003
515 202-8424

(G-7438)
WESTENERGY
5651 N Classen Blvd # 200 (73118-4028)
PHONE 405 607-6604
Corbin H West, *Managing Prtnr*
Corbin West, *Managing Prtnr*
Dail West, *Principal*
Melissa Crain, *Finance*
EMP: 3
SALES (est): 345.4K **Privately Held**
WEB: www.westenergy.com
SIC: 1382 Oil & gas exploration services

(G-7439)
WESTERN INDUSTRIES CORPORATION (PA)
5500 S Hattie Ave (73129-7326)
PHONE 405 419-3100
James P Robertson, *President*
Thomas Wang, *General Prtnr*
Claudia Robertson, *Vice Pres*
Michelle Southerland, *Administration*
▲ **EMP:** 145
SALES (est): 41MM **Privately Held**
SIC: 3086 2449 Packaging & shipping materials, foamed plastic; wood containers

(G-7440)
WESTERN OIL AND GAS DEV CORP
420 Nw 13th St Ste 200 (73103-3775)
PHONE 405 235-4590
Frank Bannister, *President*
Bill Hodges, *Engineer*
EMP: 12
SQ FT: 4,000
SALES (est): 2.3MM **Privately Held**
SIC: 1311 Crude petroleum production; natural gas production

(G-7441)
WESTERN PLASTICS LLC
1819 Nw 5th St (73106-2616)
PHONE 405 235-7272
Vic Nicholson, *Plant Mgr*
Robert Plummer, *Sales Staff*
Sheryl Gipson,
▼ **EMP:** 15
SALES (est): 2.1MM **Privately Held**
SIC: 3089 Injection molding of plastics

(G-7442)
WESTERN WEB ENVELOPE CO INC (PA)
3711 Sw 29th St (73119-1248)
P.O. Box 83246 (73148-1246)
PHONE 405 682-0207
David Perkins, *President*
Billie H Smith, *Corp Secy*
Vicki Perkins, *Vice Pres*
EMP: 12
SQ FT: 12,000
SALES (est): 1.5MM **Privately Held**
SIC: 2759 2741 2677 Envelopes: printing; miscellaneous publishing; envelopes

(G-7443)
WESTPORT OIL COMPANY INC
5800 Nw 135th St (73142-5938)
PHONE 405 239-2829

Gregg McDonald, *President*
EMP: 1
SALES (est): 135.3K **Privately Held**
SIC: 1382 Oil & gas exploration services

(G-7444)
WHEELER FRRIS WHL PARTNERS LLC
223 S Walker Ave (73109-5047)
PHONE 405 206-6612
Blair Humphreys, *Administration*
EMP: 2 EST: 2016
SALES (est): 113.2K **Privately Held**
SIC: 3599 Ferris wheels

(G-7445)
WHITE OPERATING COMPANY
1627 Sw 96th St (73159-7136)
P.O. Box 95669 (73143-5669)
PHONE 405 735-8419
Lloyd White, *President*
Vickie White, *Corp Secy*
EMP: 3
SQ FT: 1,200
SALES (est): 462.4K **Privately Held**
SIC: 1311 Crude petroleum production; natural gas production

(G-7446)
WHITEMAN INDUSTRIES INC
2601 Nw Expressway (73112-7272)
P.O. Box 670249, Dallas TX (75367-0249)
PHONE 405 879-0077
Jack Whiteman, *President*
Kent Mauk, *President*
W W Whiteman Jr Trust, *Shareholder*
Dana Powell, *Admin Sec*
EMP: 1
SQ FT: 1,200
SALES (est): 154.4K **Privately Held**
SIC: 1311 Crude petroleum production; natural gas production

(G-7447)
WHITES WELDING
5400 N Grand Blvd (73112-5692)
PHONE 405 942-7070
EMP: 1
SALES (est): 25K **Privately Held**
SIC: 7692 Welding repair

(G-7448)
WHITNEY PRATT
3000 S Douglas Blvd (73150-1003)
PHONE 405 610-2612
Fred Mullis, *Principal*
EMP: 2 EST: 2014
SALES (est): 144.6K **Privately Held**
SIC: 3724 Aircraft engines & engine parts

(G-7449)
WHORTON WELDING INC
14220 Se 76th Pl (73150-2000)
PHONE 405 664-7123
Laura Whorton, *Principal*
EMP: 2 EST: 2012
SALES (est): 140.3K **Privately Held**
SIC: 7692 Welding repair

(G-7450)
WICHO LEATHER CREATIONS LLC
6209 Greenwood Ln (73132-5629)
PHONE 405 885-8644
Consuelo Delgado, *Administration*
EMP: 2 EST: 2012
SALES (est): 153.9K **Privately Held**
SIC: 3199 Leather goods

(G-7451)
WILBERT FUNERAL SERVICES INC
Oklahoma Wilbert Vaults
345 W Hefner Rd (73114-6728)
P.O. Box 14429 (73113-0429)
PHONE 405 752-9033
Kevin Wales, *Manager*
Kay Le May, *Manager*
EMP: 20
SALES (corp-wide): 9B **Publicly Held**
WEB: www.greensborowilbert.com
SIC: 5044 3272 Vaults & safes; concrete products

HQ: Wilbert Funeral Services, Inc.
10965 Granada Ln Ste 300
Overland Park KS 66211
913 345-2120

(G-7452)
WILD WELL CONTROL INC
6125 W Reno Ave Ste 300 (73127-6522)
PHONE 405 686-0330
EMP: 4 Publicly Held
SIC: 1389 Fire fighting, oil & gas field
HQ: Wild Well Control, Inc.
2202 Oil Center Ct
Houston TX 77073
281 784-4700

(G-7453)
WILDMAN MANUFACTURING INC
301 N Virginia Ave (73106-2821)
PHONE 405 235-1264
David C Wildman, *President*
Orville L Wildman, *Corp Secy*
Catherine E Wildman, *Vice Pres*
Craig Wildman, *Vice Pres*
Jennifer Wildman, *Vice Pres*
EMP: 11 EST: 1945
SQ FT: 13,000
SALES (est): 1.3MM **Privately Held**
WEB: www.wildmanmfg.com
SIC: 3533 3599 Oil field machinery & equipment; machine & other job shop work

(G-7454)
WILLIAM B HUGOS
909 Nw 71st St (73116-7401)
PHONE 405 810-0909
William B Hugos, *Owner*
EMP: 1
SALES (est): 83.5K **Privately Held**
SIC: 1382 Oil & gas exploration services

(G-7455)
WILLIAM CLOUD OIL
12008 Quail Creek Rd (73120-5408)
PHONE 405 751-8422
William Cloud, *Owner*
EMP: 2
SALES (est): 133.1K **Privately Held**
SIC: 1311 Crude petroleum production

(G-7456)
WILLYS FABRICATING & WLDG LLC
1813 Nw 36th St (73118-3228)
PHONE 405 250-1250
David S Mitchell, *Administration*
EMP: 1
SALES (est): 62K **Privately Held**
SIC: 7692 Welding repair

(G-7457)
WILSHIRE CABINET & COMPANY LLC
320 W Wilshire Blvd (73116-7704)
PHONE 405 286-6282
Robert Henderson,
EMP: 1
SALES (est): 176.8K **Privately Held**
WEB: www.wilshirecabinetco.com
SIC: 2434 Wood kitchen cabinets

(G-7458)
WILSON ELECTRIC MOTOR SVC INC
2208 S Agnew Ave (73108-6214)
PHONE 405 636-1515
Herb Wilson, *President*
EMP: 15 EST: 1979
SQ FT: 15,000
SALES: 1.8MM **Privately Held**
SIC: 7694 7629 5063 Rebuilding motors, except automotive; generator repair; motors, electric; generators

(G-7459)
WILSPEC TECHNOLOGIES INC (PA)
4801 S Council Rd (73179-4812)
PHONE 405 495-8989
Larry N Wilhelm, *President*
Christin Goines, *Vice Pres*
Owen Wickenkamp, *Project Mgr*
Rob Edwards, *Facilities Mgr*

Oklahoma City - Oklahoma County (G-7460)

Hubbard Andrew, *Engineer*
▲ **EMP:** 25
SALES (est): 9.6MM **Privately Held**
SIC: 5063 3592 Electrical apparatus & equipment; valves

(G-7460)
WINDS OF HEARTLAND
3625 Goodger Dr Ste C (73112-1485)
PHONE.................................405 947-8558
R M Lacava, *President*
Catherine Lacava, *Owner*
EMP: 2
SALES (est): 123.8K **Privately Held**
SIC: 5499 2834 Health foods; medicines, capsuled or ampuled

(G-7461)
WISHON WELDING LLC
7408 Nw 131st St (73142-2512)
PHONE.................................405 808-4673
Justin Wishon, *Principal*
EMP: 1
SALES (est): 28.1K **Privately Held**
SIC: 7692 Welding repair

(G-7462)
WOOD CREATIONS BY ROD LLC
215 N Western Ave (73106-7637)
PHONE.................................405 235-2222
EMP: 4
SALES (est): 372.2K **Privately Held**
SIC: 2431 Mfg Millwork

(G-7463)
WOOD OIL COMPANY
5400 N Grand Blvd Ste 300 (73112-5672)
PHONE.................................405 948-1560
Michael Coffman, *President*
EMP: 18 **EST:** 1919
SQ FT: 6,000
SALES (est): 1.1MM **Privately Held**
WEB: www.panhandleoilandgas.com
SIC: 1311 Crude petroleum production; natural gas production

(G-7464)
WOOD PIPE SERVICE INC
8400 S Bryant Ave (73149-7618)
P.O. Box 96322 (73143-6322)
PHONE.................................405 672-6097
Fax: 405 677-5681
EMP: 6
SQ FT: 5,000
SALES: 500K **Privately Held**
SIC: 3498 5082 7629 Mfg Fabricated Pipe/Fittings Whol Construction/Mining Equipment Electrical Repair

(G-7465)
WOODFORD EXPRESS LLC
301 Nw 63rd St 200 (73116-7907)
PHONE.................................405 437-0857
Richard Marshall, *Mng Member*
EMP: 11
SALES (est): 2.7MM
SALES (corp-wide): 291.4K **Privately Held**
SIC: 1321 Fractionating natural gas liquids
HQ: Xplorer Midstream Llc
301 Nw 63rd St Ste 200
Oklahoma City OK 73116
918 237-5885

(G-7466)
WOODSHOP CSTM CBINETS TRIM LLC
20 Sw 66th St (73139-7317)
PHONE.................................405 673-7139
Felix Herrera, *Owner*
EMP: 1
SALES (est): 62.6K **Privately Held**
SIC: 2434 Wood kitchen cabinets

(G-7467)
WOODSTOCK SAWMILL & TIMBERS CO
1117 Exchange Ave (73108-1425)
PHONE.................................405 673-7966
EMP: 3
SALES (est): 139.4K **Privately Held**
SIC: 2421 Sawmills & planing mills, general

(G-7468)
WOODY CANDY COMPANY INC
922 Nw 70th St (73116-7519)
PHONE.................................405 842-8903
Claude S W'Oody Jr, *President*
Claude S Woody Jr, *President*
EMP: 6 **EST:** 1975
SQ FT: 19,000
SALES (est): 782.4K **Privately Held**
WEB: www.woodycandycompany.com
SIC: 2064 Candy & other confectionery products

(G-7469)
WORLD IMPORTS AT WHOLESALE INC
3935 W Reno Ave (73107-6600)
P.O. Box 891510 (73189-1510)
PHONE.................................405 947-7710
Danny Chabino, *President*
EMP: 7
SQ FT: 13,000
SALES (est): 915.3K **Privately Held**
SIC: 2519 Household furniture, except wood or metal; upholstered

(G-7470)
WORLD ORGANIZATION CHINA PNTRS (PA)
2700 N Portland Ave (73107-1508)
PHONE.................................405 521-1234
Pat Dickerson, *Director*
EMP: 24
SALES (est): 180.5K **Privately Held**
SIC: 2721 Periodicals

(G-7471)
WORLD TRADING COMPANY INC
6754 Melrose Ln (73127-6212)
PHONE.................................405 787-1982
Sohail Ahmed, *President*
Kiran Sohail Ahmed, *Senior VP*
Umair Ahmed, *Senior VP*
▲ **EMP:** 2500
SQ FT: 20,000
SALES (est): 19.3MM **Privately Held**
SIC: 2299 Linen fabrics

(G-7472)
WORLD WATER WORKS INC
4000 Sw 113th St (73173-8322)
P.O. Box 892050 (73189-2050)
PHONE.................................405 943-9000
Prashant Mitta, *CFO*
◆ **EMP:** 75
SQ FT: 55,000
SALES (est): 16.1MM
SALES (corp-wide): 21.6MM **Privately Held**
SIC: 3589 Water treatment equipment, industrial
PA: World Water Works Holdings Inc.
4000 Sw 113th St
Oklahoma City OK 73173
800 607-7873

(G-7473)
WORLD WATER WORKS HOLDINGS INC (PA)
4000 Sw 113th St (73173-8322)
P.O. Box 892050 (73189-2050)
PHONE.................................800 607-7873
Mark Fosshage, *CEO*
Kyle Booth, *Exec VP*
Daniel Dair, *Vice Pres*
Scott Poe, *Vice Pres*
Don Burks, *Project Mgr*
EMP: 4
SQ FT: 55,000
SALES (est): 21.6MM **Privately Held**
SIC: 6719 3589 Investment holding companies, except banks; water treatment equipment, industrial

(G-7474)
WRITERS RESEARCH GROUP LLC
Also Called: Wrg Management Services
8801 S Kentucky Ave (73159-6214)
PHONE.................................405 682-2589
Karen Tingle, *CEO*
Lori Packwood, *President*
EMP: 10

SALES: 1.7MM **Privately Held**
SIC: 2741 7338 8732 7374 Miscellaneous publishing; formal writing services; research services, except laboratory; data processing service
PA: Abundant Grace Companies, Llc
8801 S Kentucky Ave
Oklahoma City OK 73159

(G-7475)
WTL OIL LLC
14201 Caliber Dr Ste 300 (73134-1017)
PHONE.................................405 608-6007
Rick Westfall,
EMP: 60
SQ FT: 20,000
SALES (est): 27MM
SALES (corp-wide): 359.9MM **Publicly Held**
WEB: www.wtloil.com
SIC: 1389 Oil field services
HQ: Mammoth Energy Services, Inc.
14201 Caliber Dr Ste 300
Oklahoma City OK 73134
405 608-6007

(G-7476)
WWSC HOLDINGS LLC (DH)
1730 W Reno Ave (73106-3216)
PHONE.................................405 235-3621
Rick Cooper, *President*
J Patrick Hare, *Exec VP*
EMP: 12
SALES (est): 816.5MM
SALES (corp-wide): 9B **Publicly Held**
SIC: 3441 Fabricated structural metal
HQ: Alleghany Capital Corporation
1411 Broadway Fl 34
New York NY 10018
212 752-1356

(G-7477)
WYERS WELDING
4024 N Barr Ave (73122-3422)
P.O. Box 341, Tyrone (73951-0341)
PHONE.................................580 854-6277
Francis Wyer, *Principal*
EMP: 1
SALES (est): 43.4K **Privately Held**
SIC: 7692 Welding repair

(G-7478)
XPLORER MIDSTREAM LLC (HQ)
301 Nw 63rd St Ste 200 (73116-7913)
PHONE.................................918 237-5885
Joe Griffin, *CEO*
Derek Gipson, *CFO*
EMP: 12
SALES (est): 2.7MM
SALES (corp-wide): 291.4K **Privately Held**
SIC: 4924 1311 Natural gas distribution; crude petroleum & natural gas; crude petroleum & natural gas production
PA: Intensity Midstream Llc
320 S Boston Ave Ste 705
Tulsa OK 74103
918 949-9098

(G-7479)
YESTER YEAR CAROUSEL
4949 N Coltrane Rd (73121-1806)
PHONE.................................405 427-5863
EMP: 2
SALES (est): 89K **Privately Held**
SIC: 2499 Mfg Carousel Horses

(G-7480)
YORK INTERNATIONAL CORPORATION
257 N Harvard Ave (73127-6404)
PHONE.................................405 942-9675
Billy Lusby, *Branch Mgr*
EMP: 94 **Privately Held**
SIC: 3585 Refrigeration & heating equipment
HQ: York International Corporation
631 S Richland Ave
York PA 17403
717 771-7890

(G-7481)
YORK METAL FABRICATORS INC
Also Called: Ymf
27 Ne 26th St (73105-2702)
P.O. Box 18149 (73154-0149)
PHONE.................................405 528-7495
Evelyn York, *CEO*
David York, *President*
Grant York, *Opers Mgr*
Dedra Runyan, *Treasurer*
EMP: 25
SQ FT: 15,000
SALES (est): 5.3MM **Privately Held**
WEB: www.yorkmetal.com
SIC: 3446 3444 3441 Railings, prefabricated metal; sheet metalwork; fabricated structural metal

(G-7482)
YOUNG BROTHERS INC
Also Called: Southwest Tile Distributor
100 N Classen Blvd (73106-7625)
PHONE.................................405 272-0821
Dean Young, *President*
Drew Carter, *Vice Pres*
Mike Pybas, *Project Mgr*
Kyle Matheson, *Warehouse Mgr*
Christie Roberts, *Sales Staff*
EMP: 40
SQ FT: 13,000
SALES: 4.9MM **Privately Held**
WEB: www.youngbrosinc.com
SIC: 1743 5032 3281 Tile installation, ceramic; marble installation, interior; ceramic wall & floor tile; marble building stone; table tops, marble

(G-7483)
YUKON DRILLING FLUID INC
9500 Sw 15th St (73128-4813)
P.O. Box 850680, Yukon (73085-0680)
PHONE.................................405 324-8876
Harold Poage, *Owner*
EMP: 6
SALES (est): 500K **Privately Held**
SIC: 1311 Crude petroleum & natural gas

(G-7484)
YUKON MANUFACTURING INC
3900 Ne Plum Creek Cir (73131-1510)
PHONE.................................918 850-3131
Ken Brack, *CEO*
EMP: 5
SALES (est): 769.5K **Privately Held**
SIC: 3679 Electronic components

(G-7485)
Z SIGNS INC
2101 S Missouri Ave (73129-7531)
PHONE.................................405 670-1416
Ronnie Zwirtz, *President*
Denise Zwirtz, *Vice Pres*
EMP: 10 **EST:** 1985
SALES (est): 1.2MM **Privately Held**
SIC: 3993 Signs, not made in custom sign painting shops

(G-7486)
ZEPHYR OPERATING CO LLC
Also Called: Zephyr Operating Company
5225 N Shartel Ave # 200 (73118-6064)
PHONE.................................405 286-4771
David Johnson, *Mng Member*
Carl Lang,
EMP: 5
SALES (est): 935.8K **Privately Held**
SIC: 1311 Crude petroleum production; natural gas production

(G-7487)
ZLB BEHRING
716 Nw 23rd St (73103-1418)
PHONE.................................405 521-9204
Daniel Wind, *Principal*
EMP: 2
SALES (est): 228.8K **Privately Held**
SIC: 2836 Plasmas

(G-7488)
ZOE HOMES LLC
4320 Nw 63rd St (73116-1505)
PHONE.................................405 550-3563
Darnell Seawright, *CEO*
Ladonna Seawright, *President*

EMP: 2
SQ FT: 300
SALES (est): 210.5K **Privately Held**
SIC: 3444 1799 7699 Metal roofing & roof drainage equipment; fence construction; boiler & heating repair services; plastics products repair

(G-7489)
ZOOP-CORP
2512 Ashley Dr (73120-3516)
PHONE..........................405 239-8184
Andy Zupan, *President*
Alicia Zupan, *Vice Pres*
EMP: 5
SALES: 25K **Privately Held**
WEB: www.zoopcorp.com
SIC: 3423 Leaf skimmers or swimming pool rakes

(G-7490)
ZZW GLOBAL INC
11300 N Pennsylvania Ave (73120-7781)
PHONE..........................405 985-8759
Christopher Poston, *Principal*
EMP: 2
SALES (est): 65.5K **Privately Held**
SIC: 1389 Oil & gas field services

Okmulgee
Okmulgee County

(G-7491)
3T OIL & GAS LLC
13099 Old Highway 75 (74447-6580)
PHONE..........................918 758-3269
Megan Matthews, *Principal*
EMP: 2
SALES (est): 65.5K **Privately Held**
SIC: 1389 Oil & gas field services

(G-7492)
ABBOTT INDUSTRIES INC (PA)
Also Called: Covington Aircrafts
12801 Highway 75 (74447-6516)
P.O. Box 1344 (74447-1344)
PHONE..........................918 756-8320
Paul W Abbott, *President*
Aaron Abbott, *Exec VP*
Luke Abbot, *Vice Pres*
Rob Seeman, *Opers Mgr*
Ron Hollis, *QC Mgr*
▲ **EMP:** 55
SALES (est): 10.3MM **Privately Held**
SIC: 3724 Aircraft engines & engine parts

(G-7493)
AIRWOLF FILTER CORP
12801 Highway 75 (74447-6516)
P.O. Box 1337 (74447-1337)
PHONE..........................918 561-8696
Aaron Abbott, *Exec VP*
EMP: 3
SALES (est): 142.6K
SALES (corp-wide): 10.3MM **Privately Held**
SIC: 3564 Filters, air: furnaces, air conditioning equipment, etc.
PA: Abbott Industries, Inc.
12801 Highway 75
Okmulgee OK 74447
918 756-8320

(G-7494)
AXIOM METAL SOLUTIONS LLC
1900 N Wood Dr (74447-7966)
PHONE..........................918 361-5982
Geoffrey Brewer,
Alexander Andre,
EMP: 2 **EST:** 2014
SQ FT: 60,000
SALES: 30K **Privately Held**
SIC: 8711 3444 Mechanical engineering; sheet metalwork

(G-7495)
BRADEN CARCO GEARMATIC WINCH
1204 W 20th St (74447-4202)
PHONE..........................918 756-4400
Amir Weiseerg, *CEO*
EMP: 2

SALES (est): 121.2K **Privately Held**
SIC: 3714 Motor vehicle parts & accessories

(G-7496)
BULLET FENCE SYSTEMS LLC
1001 E 20th St (74447-6029)
PHONE..........................918 777-3973
Ronald Goedecke, *Mng Member*
EMP: 2 **EST:** 2015
SALES: 80K **Privately Held**
WEB: www.bulletfence.com
SIC: 1799 3312 Fence construction; fence posts, iron & steel

(G-7497)
CAMPBELL SPECIALTY CO INC
1604 W 4th St (74447-2428)
P.O. Box 833 (74447-0833)
PHONE..........................918 756-3640
Ronald Campbell, *President*
Jeneane Campbell, *Vice Pres*
Carolyn Campbell, *Treasurer*
Glenn Campbell, *Admin Sec*
▼ **EMP:** 15
SQ FT: 40,000
SALES: 450K **Privately Held**
WEB: www.campbellspecialtyco.info
SIC: 3429 Pulleys metal

(G-7498)
CP KELCO US INC
Also Called: JM Huber
1200 W 20th St (74447-4202)
PHONE..........................918 758-2600
Tommy Wittman, *Superintendent*
Arthur Mullen, *Safety Mgr*
Jaime Gregory, *Purch Mgr*
Jamie Gregory, *Buyer*
Bruce Drake, *Engineer*
EMP: 23
SALES (corp-wide): 860.2MM **Privately Held**
WEB: www.cpkelco.com
SIC: 2899 Sizes
HQ: Cp Kelco U.S., Inc.
3100 Cumberland Blvd Se
Atlanta GA 30339
678 247-7300

(G-7499)
DK&K ENERGY LLC
501 S Seminole Ave (74447-4933)
PHONE..........................540 395-2400
Miranda Carman, *President*
EMP: 2
SALES (est): 87.1K **Privately Held**
SIC: 1389 Oil consultants

(G-7500)
DLUBAK GLASS COMPANY
Also Called: Dlubak Galss
1018 W 14th St (74447)
P.O. Box 459 (74447-0459)
PHONE..........................918 752-0226
Dale Hassinger, *Engineer*
Rick Carr, *Manager*
EMP: 10
SALES (corp-wide): 8.5MM **Privately Held**
WEB: www.dlubak.com
SIC: 3229 3231 Pressed & blown glass; products of purchased glass
PA: Dlubak Glass Company
789 County Highway 330
Upper Sandusky OH 43351
419 209-0908

(G-7501)
EMP INCORPORATED
5030 N Wood Dr (74447-9742)
PHONE..........................918 756-5767
Don Crawdford, *President*
EMP: 8
SALES (est): 785.5K **Privately Held**
WEB: www.rotaryscraper.com
SIC: 3599 Machine shop, jobbing & repair

(G-7502)
FRANK PRIEGEL CO
Also Called: Priegel Real Estate
907 E 6th St (74447-4702)
P.O. Box 818 (74447-0818)
PHONE..........................918 756-3161
Frank Priegel, *Owner*
EMP: 2

SQ FT: 2,600
SALES (est): 193K **Privately Held**
SIC: 1311 6531 Crude petroleum production; real estate brokers & agents

(G-7503)
GASTON H L III OIL PROPERTIES
114 N Grand Ave (74447-4013)
P.O. Box 212 (74447-0212)
PHONE..........................918 758-0008
H L Gaston III, *Owner*
EMP: 1
SALES (est): 128.7K **Privately Held**
SIC: 1382 Oil & gas exploration services

(G-7504)
GENERAL MANUFACTURER INC (PA)
Also Called: General Clamp and Tong
701 W 4th St (74447-3154)
P.O. Box 220 (74447-0220)
PHONE..........................918 756-3067
W R Tipsword, *President*
Nancy T Trainor, *Corp Secy*
Betty T Tipsword, *Vice Pres*
▲ **EMP:** 11 **EST:** 1912
SQ FT: 40,000
SALES (est): 1.6MM **Privately Held**
WEB: www.generalmfr.com
SIC: 3533 3441 Oil field machinery & equipment; fabricated structural metal

(G-7505)
GILL OPERATING COMPANY
Also Called: Gill Royalty
209 W 7th St (74447-5010)
P.O. Box 697 (74447-0697)
PHONE..........................918 756-1873
Jet Gill, *Vice Pres*
John K Gill, *Vice Pres*
EMP: 1 **EST:** 1945
SQ FT: 970
SALES (est): 120K **Privately Held**
SIC: 1311 Crude petroleum production

(G-7506)
GOPRINTS
15499 Ash Rd (74447-6673)
PHONE..........................918 798-0643
Carla Brown, *Owner*
EMP: 1
SALES (est): 72.1K **Privately Held**
SIC: 2759 Commercial printing

(G-7507)
GV AEROSPACE LLC
1007 Oakwood Dr (74447-7862)
PHONE..........................214 972-5055
Andrew McNinch,
EMP: 1
SALES (est): 71.6K **Privately Held**
SIC: 3728 Aircraft parts & equipment

(G-7508)
H & H XRAY
1113 N Griffin Ave (74447-2514)
PHONE..........................918 752-0966
Scott Powders, *Manager*
EMP: 2
SALES (est): 118.9K **Privately Held**
SIC: 3844 X-ray apparatus & tubes

(G-7509)
H-V MANUFACTURING COMPANY
2950 N Wood Dr (74447-7999)
P.O. Box 373, Glenpool (74033-0373)
PHONE..........................918 756-9620
Jimmy Warren, *Manager*
EMP: 4
SALES (corp-wide): 2.7MM **Privately Held**
SIC: 3479 3568 3429 Etching & engraving; power transmission equipment; manufactured hardware (general)
PA: H-V Manufacturing Company
138th & Hwy 75
Glenpool OK 74033
918 291-2108

(G-7510)
JOHNNY APPLE SEED STORE
320 S Wood Dr (74447-5230)
PHONE..........................918 304-2055

EMP: 3
SALES (est): 138.5K **Privately Held**
SIC: 5148 3571 Fresh fruits & vegetables; personal computers (microcomputers)

(G-7511)
KECK OIL & GAS LLC
15485 Old Morris Hwy (74447-8516)
PHONE..........................918 756-6688
Patricia Jill Keck, *Principal*
EMP: 2
SALES (est): 98.9K **Privately Held**
SIC: 1389 Oil & gas field services

(G-7512)
KIMBERLING CITY PUBLISHING CO
Also Called: Okmulgee Daily Times
320 W 6th St (74447-5018)
PHONE..........................918 756-3600
Darrell Sumner, *President*
EMP: 20
SALES: 1.5MM **Privately Held**
SIC: 2711 Newspapers, publishing & printing

(G-7513)
LIBERTY PARTNERS INC
812 W 9th St (74447-4521)
PHONE..........................918 756-6474
Martha Diaz, *CEO*
Jesus Diaz, *Engineer*
EMP: 14
SQ FT: 12,000
SALES (est): 610K **Privately Held**
SIC: 7389 8734 1799 3728 Design, commercial & industrial; testing laboratories; renovation of aircraft interiors; military aircraft equipment & armament; aircraft assemblies, subassemblies & parts

(G-7514)
LONNIE B NICKELS JR
450 Alder Rd (74447-9239)
PHONE..........................918 756-3426
Lonnie B Nickels Jr, *Principal*
EMP: 3
SALES (est): 182.5K **Privately Held**
SIC: 3356 Nickel

(G-7515)
MCADAMS ENERGY LLC
1406 E 10th St (74447-5222)
PHONE..........................918 758-0308
R McAdams, *Principal*
EMP: 2
SALES (est): 80.7K **Privately Held**
SIC: 1389 Oil & gas field services

(G-7516)
MID-CONTINENT CONCRETE CO INC
Also Called: Midcontinent Concrete Co
13449 Birch Rd (74447-7262)
PHONE..........................918 758-0200
Carrie Waddle, *General Mgr*
EMP: 5 **Privately Held**
SIC: 3273 Ready-mixed concrete
HQ: Mid-Continent Concrete Company, Inc.
431 W 23rd St
Tulsa OK 74107

(G-7517)
NEWTON EQUIPMENT LLC
Also Called: Stewart Martin Equipment
12751 Highway 75 (74447-6571)
P.O. Box 38 (74447-0038)
PHONE..........................918 756-3560
Joey Newton, *Owner*
EMP: 14
SALES (est): 2.4MM **Privately Held**
SIC: 3524 5083 Lawn & garden equipment; farm & garden machinery

(G-7518)
OKMULGEE AUTOMOTIVE MACHINE SP
205 N Alabama Ave (74447-3108)
PHONE..........................918 756-5861
George Jackson, *Owner*
EMP: 1
SQ FT: 1,000
SALES (est): 130.2K **Privately Held**
SIC: 3599 Machine shop, jobbing & repair

Okmulgee - Okmulgee County (G-7519)

(G-7519)
OKMULGEE MONUMENTS INC
Also Called: Martin Monument Co
2200 S Wood Dr (74447)
P.O. Box 1535 (74447-1535)
PHONE..................................918 756-6619
James McClendon, *President*
James Mc Clendon, *President*
Shari Mc Clendon, *Admin Sec*
Shari McClendon, *Admin Sec*
EMP: 4
SQ FT: 20,000
SALES (est): 411.7K **Privately Held**
SIC: 5999 3281 Monuments, finished to custom order; cut stone & stone products

(G-7520)
OKMULGEE READY MIX CONCRETE CO
300 N Comanche Ave (74447-3429)
P.O. Box 340 (74447-0340)
PHONE..................................918 756-6005
Kelly P Harlan, *CEO*
Fred C Harlan, *President*
Maryland Saint, *Assistant VP*
Don Ledford, *Vice Pres*
EMP: 11
SQ FT: 905
SALES: 1MM **Privately Held**
SIC: 3273 Ready-mixed concrete

(G-7521)
PACCAR INC
1204 W 20th St (74447-4202)
P.O. Box 550 (74447-0550)
PHONE..................................918 756-4400
Mike Talley, *Branch Mgr*
EMP: 50
SALES (corp-wide): 24.1B **Publicly Held**
SIC: 3711 Motor vehicles & car bodies
PA: Paccar Inc
 777 106th Ave Ne
 Bellevue WA 98004
 425 468-7400

(G-7522)
POLYVISION CORPORATION
4301 N Wood Dr (74447-9780)
PHONE..................................918 756-7392
Mike Dunn, *Branch Mgr*
Steve Putnam, *Maintence Staff*
EMP: 11 **Privately Held**
SIC: 2521 Tables, office: wood
PA: Polyvision Corporation
 10700 Abbotts Bridge Rd # 100
 Johns Creek GA 30097

(G-7523)
PRINT THIS
813 E 6th St (74447-4701)
PHONE..................................918 693-5581
EMP: 2
SALES (est): 83.9K **Privately Held**
SIC: 2752 Commercial printing, lithographic

(G-7524)
RAYMAC CORP
1015 E 13th St (74447-6035)
PHONE..................................918 752-0002
EMP: 2
SALES (est): 123K **Privately Held**
SIC: 2844 Toilet preparations

(G-7525)
REPAIR PROCESSES INC
Also Called: RPI
5401 N Wood Dr (74447-9781)
PHONE..................................918 758-0863
Larry Pryor, *President*
William T Burke Jr, *Principal*
Curt Been, *Vice Pres*
Glenn Moten, *Vice Pres*
Mike McCampbell, *Sales Staff*
EMP: 17
SALES (est): 6.2MM **Privately Held**
WEB: www.rpiengines.com
SIC: 5084 5082 3625 7699 Engines, gasoline; oil field equipment; relays & industrial controls; engine repair & replacement, non-automotive

(G-7526)
STAUDT JEWELERS
Also Called: O K Staudt Jewelers
113 W 6th St (74447-5015)
PHONE..................................918 756-0517
Ruth G Staudt, *Owner*
EMP: 2
SALES (est): 160K **Privately Held**
SIC: 5944 7631 3961 3911 Jewelry, precious stones & precious metals; jewelry repair services; pearl restringing; costume jewelry, ex. precious metal & semi-precious stones; jewelry, precious metal

(G-7527)
THOMPSON PUMP COMPANY (PA)
801 W 20th St (74447-4255)
P.O. Box 310 (74447-0310)
PHONE..................................918 756-6164
James R Thompson Jr, *President*
Juanita Thompson, *Director*
◆ EMP: 19 EST: 1935
SQ FT: 8,500
SALES (est): 6.1MM **Privately Held**
WEB: www.thompsonpump.com
SIC: 3561 3533 Pumps, oil well & field; oil & gas field machinery

(G-7528)
TORBETT PRINTING CO & OFF SUP
Also Called: Torbett Prntg Co
109 N Morton Ave (74447-7318)
P.O. Box 456 (74447-0456)
PHONE..................................918 756-5789
Fax: 918 756-2707
EMP: 2 EST: 1926
SQ FT: 3,500
SALES (est): 130K **Privately Held**
SIC: 2752 5943 2796 2791 Lithographic Coml Print Ret Stationery Platemaking Services Typesetting Services Bookbinding/Related Work

(G-7529)
WADLEY BILL & SON DRILLING CO
11461 Smith Rd (74447-8934)
PHONE..................................918 756-4650
Bill A Wadley Jr, *Partner*
EMP: 2 EST: 1965
SQ FT: 10,000
SALES (est): 237.7K **Privately Held**
SIC: 1311 0212 4212 Crude petroleum production; beef cattle except feedlots; dump truck haulage

Oktaha
Muskogee County

(G-7530)
BRADLEY STEPHEN BROWN
Also Called: Wildkat Manufacturing
101379 S 4190 Rd (74450-0017)
P.O. Box 754, Checotah (74426-0754)
PHONE..................................918 639-1853
Bradley Brown, *Owner*
EMP: 1
SALES (est): 33K **Privately Held**
SIC: 3999 Manufacturing industries

Olustee
Jackson County

(G-7531)
DON MOODY FARM
302 E 6th St (73560)
PHONE..................................580 648-2489
Don Moody, *Owner*
EMP: 1
SALES (est): 103.4K **Privately Held**
SIC: 3531 Bulldozers (construction machinery)

Oologah
Rogers County

(G-7532)
ABSOLUTE WELDING INC
220 E Nelms St (74053-3015)
P.O. Box 1177 (74053-1177)
PHONE..................................918 923-7300
Gina Quinby, *Principal*
EMP: 1
SALES (est): 65.4K **Privately Held**
SIC: 7692 Welding repair

(G-7533)
KXD DEFENSE AND ARMAMENT
13096 Horseshoe Bnd (74053-4164)
PHONE..................................918 813-3841
EMP: 3
SALES (est): 153K **Privately Held**
SIC: 3812 Defense systems & equipment

(G-7534)
LAKE OOLOGAH LEADER LLC
109 S Maple St (74053-3299)
P.O. Box 1175 (74053-1175)
PHONE..................................918 443-2428
John M Wylie II,
Faith Wylie,
EMP: 5
SQ FT: 900
SALES (est): 100K **Privately Held**
WEB: www.oologah.net
SIC: 2711 Newspapers: publishing only, not printed on site

(G-7535)
OKLAHOMA SCREEN MFG LLC (PA)
Also Called: Precision Screen Manufacturing
7287 E Highway 88 (74053-6389)
P.O. Box 1234 (74053-1234)
PHONE..................................918 443-6500
Joel Anglin, *Mng Member*
EMP: 10
SQ FT: 24,500
SALES (est): 5.5MM **Privately Held**
SIC: 3496 Screening, woven wire: made from purchased wire

(G-7536)
STREATER INDUSTRIES LLC
15102 S 4060 Rd (74053-3728)
PHONE..................................918 346-3247
Staci Streater, *Principal*
EMP: 2
SALES (est): 111K **Privately Held**
SIC: 3999 Manufacturing industries

(G-7537)
WS MFG LLC
12745 S Old Highway 169 (74053-3062)
P.O. Box 781 (74053-0781)
PHONE..................................918 443-2773
EMP: 3 EST: 2012
SALES (est): 299.5K **Privately Held**
SIC: 3999 Manufacturing industries

Overbrook
Love County

(G-7538)
BLUE RIVER VENTURES INC
360 Lodge Rd (73453-8010)
PHONE..................................580 798-4810
EMP: 1
SALES (corp-wide): 1.5MM **Privately Held**
SIC: 3523 Farm machinery & equipment
PA: Blue River Ventures Inc
 4710 W Highway 70
 Durant OK 74701

(G-7539)
SPRAYFOAM BANKS & COATINGS
574 Abner Rd (73453-2244)
PHONE..................................580 490-6308
James Banks, *Principal*
EMP: 2
SALES (est): 69.9K **Privately Held**
SIC: 3479 Metal coating & allied service

Owasso
Tulsa County

(G-7540)
A STITCH OF ART
16403 E 89th St N (74055-5625)
PHONE..................................918 638-2511
EMP: 1
SALES (est): 63.8K **Privately Held**
SIC: 2395 Embroidery products, except schiffli machine

(G-7541)
ADVANCED MACHINING & FABG
11212 E 112th St N (74055-4227)
PHONE..................................918 664-5410
Kim Parrish, *President*
Steve Shortess, *Principal*
Glenn Steven Shortness, *Chairman*
Jason Adkins, *Opers Staff*
Jeff Rogers, *Engineer*
EMP: 30
SALES (est): 5.1MM **Privately Held**
SIC: 3599 Machine shop, jobbing & repair

(G-7542)
AEGEOS OILFIELD TECHNOLOGY LLC
9503 N 137th East Ct (74055-4578)
PHONE..................................918 906-4328
EMP: 2 EST: 2015
SALES (est): 83.5K **Privately Held**
SIC: 1311 Crude petroleum & natural gas

(G-7543)
AFFORDABLE RESTORATIONS LLC
Also Called: R Collins Woodwork
16201 E 91st St N (74055-8301)
P.O. Box 226, Disney (74340-0226)
◆ PHONE..................................918 609-5399
Rick Collins,
EMP: 5
SALES (est): 328.5K **Privately Held**
SIC: 2599 Cabinets, factory

(G-7544)
ANCHOR PAINT MFG CO
401 E 2nd Ave (74055-3208)
PHONE..................................918 272-0880
Ralph Mills, *Vice Pres*
Scott Ross, *Manager*
Brandon Cochran, *Manager*
EMP: 2
SALES (corp-wide): 25MM **Privately Held**
WEB: www.anchorpaint.com
SIC: 2851 5231 Paints & allied products; paint
PA: Anchor Paint Mfg. Co.
 6707 E 14th St
 Tulsa OK 74112
 918 836-4626

(G-7545)
ANVIL HOUSE PUBLISHERS LLC
10208 E 89th St N (74055-6799)
PHONE..................................918 760-8991
Larry Johnson, *Owner*
EMP: 1
SALES (est): 72.4K **Privately Held**
WEB: www.anvilhousebooks.com
SIC: 2741 2731 Miscellaneous publishing; book publishing

(G-7546)
AS DESIGNS LLC
Also Called: Architectural Sign Designs
202 E 5th Ave (74055-3452)
P.O. Box 1502 (74055-1502)
PHONE..................................918 381-2390
Ryan Neurohr, *Mng Member*
EMP: 4
SALES: 350K **Privately Held**
SIC: 2499 Signboards, wood

GEOGRAPHIC SECTION

Owasso - Tulsa County (G-7578)

(G-7547)
BEEKMANN ENTERPRISES
8606 E 96th St N (74055-6726)
PHONE..................................918 272-7197
Fred E Beekmann, *Owner*
EMP: 1
SALES (est): 72.7K **Privately Held**
SIC: 3429 Aircraft hardware

(G-7548)
BERKSHIRE HATHAWAY INC
Also Called: Owasso Reporter
202 E 2nd Ave Ste 101 (74055-3131)
PHONE..................................918 272-1155
Charles Cagle, *Manager*
EMP: 5
SALES (corp-wide): 327.2B **Publicly Held**
SIC: 2711 Commercial printing & newspaper publishing combined
PA: Berkshire Hathaway Inc.
  3555 Farnam St Ste 1140
  Omaha NE 68131
  402 346-1400

(G-7549)
BRACELETS FOR BABY
8820 N 127th East Ave (74055-5016)
PHONE..................................918 625-0088
Tracie Ward, *Principal*
EMP: 2 EST: 2011
SALES (est): 105.4K **Privately Held**
SIC: 3961 Bracelets, except precious metal

(G-7550)
BUDGGET INDUSTRIES INC
8 S Atlanta St Unit A (74055-3123)
PHONE..................................918 272-6255
Fax: 918 272-0990
EMP: 2 EST: 2010
SALES (est): 110K **Privately Held**
SIC: 3999 Mfg Misc Products

(G-7551)
CAMCAST CORP
11231 N Memorial Dr (74055-6517)
PHONE..................................918 371-9966
Ed Campbell, *President*
Debbi Green, *Project Mgr*
EMP: 115
SALES (est): 5MM **Privately Held**
SIC: 8711 3369 3365 3324 Engineering services; nonferrous foundries; aluminum foundries; steel investment foundries; gray & ductile iron foundries

(G-7552)
CENTRIFUGAL CASTING MCH CO INC
Also Called: Ccmco
7744 N Owasso Expy Ste A (74055-3331)
P.O. Box 947, Tulsa (74101-0901)
PHONE..................................918 835-7323
Megan Harris, *President*
Susan Mc Kee, *Facilities Mgr*
Mindy Coonis, *Purch Mgr*
EMP: 4 EST: 1980
SQ FT: 1,700
SALES (est): 600K **Privately Held**
WEB: www.ccmcotulsa.com
SIC: 3559 Foundry machinery & equipment

(G-7553)
CHEYENNE PRODUCTS LLC
8818 N 176th East Ave (74055-5678)
PHONE..................................918 639-8583
Debbie Crump, *Owner*
David Crump, *Principal*
EMP: 2
SALES: 12.5MM **Privately Held**
SIC: 3499 Machine bases, metal

(G-7554)
CONSTIEN AND ASSOCIATES INC
7750 N Owasso Expy Ste A (74055-3338)
PHONE..................................918 272-9099
Vernon Constien, *President*
Dorothy Constien, *Vice Pres*
EMP: 6

SALES (est): 555.1K **Privately Held**
WEB: www.candalab.com
SIC: 1389 Testing, measuring, surveying & analysis services

(G-7555)
COPPER KILN LLC
122 S Main St (74055-3108)
PHONE..................................918 272-5200
EMP: 3 EST: 2012
SALES (est): 333.1K **Privately Held**
SIC: 3559 Kilns

(G-7556)
CORPORATE IMAGE INC
10305 E 94th Ct N (74055-7217)
PHONE..................................918 516-8376
Travis Hunnicutt, *President*
EMP: 3 EST: 1998
SALES (est): 405K **Privately Held**
SIC: 2395 3993 2326 2759 Embroidery products, except schiffli machine; signs & advertising specialties; work apparel, except uniforms; letterpress & screen printing;

(G-7557)
CROPPINSVILLE
208 W 17th St (74055-4629)
PHONE..................................405 521-2711
Alice Gower, *Principal*
EMP: 2
SALES (est): 126.8K **Privately Held**
WEB: www.croppinsville.com
SIC: 3469 Metal stampings

(G-7558)
CUTTING EDGE TECHNOLOGIES LLC
8913 N 151st East Ave (74055-8494)
PHONE..................................918 284-6069
John S Guilfoyle, *Mng Member*
Michael Leipzig, *Manager*
EMP: 1
SALES: 1MM **Privately Held**
SIC: 7371 3532 8742 Software programming applications; mining machinery; manufacturing management consultant

(G-7559)
DAVID W AND ABBE BELCHER
9508 N 139th East Ct (74055-4571)
PHONE..................................918 376-9816
Abbe Belcher, *Principal*
EMP: 3
SALES (est): 221.2K **Privately Held**
SIC: 2834 Pharmaceutical preparations

(G-7560)
DBR PUBLISHING CO LLC (PA)
18706 E Stonebridge Dr (74055-7715)
P.O. Box 470303, Tulsa (74147-0303)
PHONE..................................918 250-1984
Beverly Armstrong,
Debra Cash,
David Dahme,
Susan Dahme,
EMP: 20
SALES (est): 3.3MM **Privately Held**
SIC: 2759 2752 2741 Calendars: printing; commercial printing, lithographic; miscellaneous publishing

(G-7561)
DELENDA LLC
10005 E 100th Pl N (74055-6499)
PHONE..................................918 409-1313
Jollinus Salehy, *Principal*
EMP: 1
SALES (est): 40.7K **Privately Held**
SIC: 7372 7389 Application computer software;

(G-7562)
DON TOOKER
Also Called: J T Industries
15510 E 87th Pl N (74055-9409)
P.O. Box 250307, Plano TX (75025-0307)
PHONE..................................972 742-8515
Don Tooker, *Owner*
▲ EMP: 4
SALES: 893K **Privately Held**
SIC: 3674 Semiconductors & related devices

(G-7563)
DOWNTOWN PUB
Also Called: Vault
106 S Atlanta St (74055-3122)
P.O. Box 1854 (74055-1854)
PHONE..................................918 274-8202
Jerry Grigar, *Owner*
EMP: 10
SALES (est): 223.5K **Privately Held**
SIC: 5812 3272 Grills (eating places); burial vaults, concrete or precast terrazzo

(G-7564)
DUNBAR EVENT SIGNS INC
Also Called: Eventsigns.biz
9204 N 96th East Ave (74055-3014)
P.O. Box 52641, Tulsa (74152-0641)
PHONE..................................918 607-9254
Robert J Dunbar, *Vice Pres*
EMP: 2
SALES (est): 196.7K **Privately Held**
SIC: 3993 Signs & advertising specialties

(G-7565)
FABRICO INC
408 W 2nd Ave (74055-3128)
P.O. Box 331 (74055-0331)
PHONE..................................918 274-9329
Ken Robinson, *President*
Albert Keemp, *Vice Pres*
Selene Robinson, *Treasurer*
Darrell Nichols, *Manager*
EMP: 7
SQ FT: 40,000
SALES (est): 874.9K **Privately Held**
SIC: 3441 Fabricated structural metal

(G-7566)
FASTSIGNS
8751 N 117th East Ave D (74055-2098)
PHONE..................................918 376-7870
Sherri Menefee, *Principal*
EMP: 2 EST: 2016
SALES (est): 72.6K **Privately Held**
WEB: www.fastsigns.com
SIC: 3993 Signs & advertising specialties

(G-7567)
FEATHERSTON PUBLISHING LLC
7504 E 84th St N (74055-7419)
PHONE..................................918 289-7877
Featherston Todd, *Principal*
Bonnie Marcis, *Associate*
EMP: 1
SALES (est): 82.9K **Privately Held**
SIC: 2741 Miscellaneous publishing

(G-7568)
FELKINS ENTERPRISES LLC
Also Called: Sav-On Printing & Signs
9924 N Garnett Rd (74055-6463)
PHONE..................................918 272-3456
Marvin Felkin, *Mng Member*
EMP: 2
SQ FT: 1,200
SALES (est): 335.4K **Privately Held**
SIC: 2752 2791 2759 Commercial printing, offset; typesetting; bookbinding & related work; commercial printing

(G-7569)
FIN-X INC
402 W 2nd Ave (74055-3128)
P.O. Box 1048 (74055-1048)
PHONE..................................918 272-9546
Allen Robinson, *President*
Doris Robinson, *Vice Pres*
Ken Robinson, *Treasurer*
◆ EMP: 25
SQ FT: 44,000
SALES (est): 2.6MM **Privately Held**
SIC: 3443 Air coolers, metal plate

(G-7570)
FLARE INDUSTRIES
15008 E 89th St N (74055-8443)
PHONE..................................918 376-7811
EMP: 2
SALES (est): 96.2K **Privately Held**
SIC: 2899 Flares

(G-7571)
GRAPHICS ETC
6905 N 129th East Ave (74055-7147)
PHONE..................................918 274-4744
Cindee Treat, *Owner*
EMP: 1
SALES (est): 71.2K **Privately Held**
SIC: 7336 2791 2752 Graphic arts & related design; typesetting; commercial printing, lithography

(G-7572)
GREENHILL MATERIALS LLC
14701 E Hwy 266 (74055)
PHONE..................................918 274-6560
Shawn Roberts, *Manager*
EMP: 10
SQ FT: 1,103
SALES (est): 1MM
SALES (corp-wide): 103.6MM **Privately Held**
SIC: 1499 Precious stones mining
PA: Sherwood Construction Co., Inc.
  3219 W May St
  Wichita KS 67213
  316 943-0211

(G-7573)
HACKER INDUSTRIES LLC
Also Called: Milestones Learning Center
11505 E 76th St N (74055-3606)
PHONE..................................918 272-6607
Steven Hacker,
EMP: 12
SALES (est): 329.6K **Privately Held**
SIC: 3999 Manufacturing industries

(G-7574)
HOSPICE PHARMACY PROVIDERS LLC
9213 N 98th East Ct (74055-6947)
PHONE..................................918 633-6229
Sherry Crockett, *Mng Member*
EMP: 4 EST: 2011
SALES (est): 399.4K **Privately Held**
SIC: 2834 Pharmaceutical preparations

(G-7575)
INTEGRITY MACHINE SOURCE LLC
15405 E 114th St N (74055-5259)
PHONE..................................918 230-9657
John Freeny, *President*
EMP: 1
SQ FT: 3,663
SALES (est): 51.2K **Privately Held**
SIC: 3452 Bolts, nuts, rivets & washers

(G-7576)
INVICTUS PERSONAL DEFENSE LLC
9117 N 137th East Ave (74055-4536)
PHONE..................................918 605-1165
Robert A Jerome, *Principal*
EMP: 2
SALES (est): 181K **Privately Held**
SIC: 3812 Defense systems & equipment

(G-7577)
J E SHAFFER CO
8410 N 66th East Ave (74055-8518)
PHONE..................................918 582-1752
D M Stallcup, *President*
J R Lukeman, *Corp Secy*
EMP: 3
SQ FT: 1,500
SALES (est): 366.3K **Privately Held**
SIC: 3533 3531 Oil field machinery & equipment; construction machinery

(G-7578)
JAMESSED INC
Also Called: C and C Manufacturing
14411 E 56th St N (74055-7535)
PHONE..................................918 272-6775
James Wilson, *President*
Bill Bott, *Corp Secy*
Debra Wilson, *Vice Pres*
EMP: 3
SQ FT: 1,200
SALES (est): 323.1K **Privately Held**
SIC: 3599 Machine shop, jobbing & repair

Owasso - Tulsa County (G-7579) GEOGRAPHIC SECTION

(G-7579)
JBS GRAPHIC REPAIR
7918 N 120th East Ave (74055-3514)
P.O. Box 226 (74055-0226)
PHONE..................918 272-3522
John Bartley, *Owner*
EMP: 1
SALES (est): 68.6K **Privately Held**
SIC: 2759 Commercial printing

(G-7580)
JERRY WOODS PORTABLE WELDING
209 E 4th Ave (74055-3443)
PHONE..................918 272-6424
EMP: 1
SALES (est): 62.1K **Privately Held**
SIC: 7692 1799 Welding Repair Trade Contractor

(G-7581)
JOHN LANKFORD
Also Called: Lankford Welding
11505 E 112th Pl N (74055-6328)
P.O. Box 1504 (74055-1504)
PHONE..................918 855-4417
John Lankford, *Principal*
EMP: 1 EST: 2012
SALES (est): 48.5K **Privately Held**
SIC: 7692 Welding repair

(G-7582)
JOSTENS INC
7762 N Owasso Expy B (74055-3338)
PHONE..................918 274-7047
Tim Bowman, *Manager*
EMP: 20
SALES (corp-wide): 1.4B **Privately Held**
SIC: 3911 Rings, finger: precious metal
HQ: Jostens, Inc.
7760 France Ave S Ste 400
Minneapolis MN 55435
952 830-3300

(G-7583)
KMAC MANUFACTURING LLC
13809 E 87th St N (74055-2073)
PHONE..................918 272-6856
Kale William Macormic, *Owner*
EMP: 1
SALES (est): 29.2K **Privately Held**
SIC: 3999 Manufacturing industries

(G-7584)
KORMONDY ENTERPRISES INC
Also Called: National Steak & Poultry
301 E 5th Ave (74055-3450)
PHONE..................918 274-8787
Dave Albright, *CEO*
Steven A Kormondy, *President*
Eric Renfrow, *Opers Staff*
EMP: 325
SQ FT: 80,000
SALES (est): 85.6MM **Privately Held**
SIC: 2015 2013 Poultry slaughtering & processing; prepared beef products from purchased beef

(G-7585)
LEWIS OIL & GAS INC
10704 E 99th St N (74055-6440)
PHONE..................918 272-1278
Lioyd D Lewis, *Principal*
EMP: 2 EST: 2001
SALES (est): 107.9K **Privately Held**
SIC: 1389 Oil & gas field services

(G-7586)
LIBERTY PATTERNS INC
105 E 3rd St (74055-3100)
PHONE..................918 234-1037
EMP: 2 EST: 2011
SALES (est): 85K **Privately Held**
SIC: 3543 Mfg Industrial Patterns

(G-7587)
LINDA SULLIVAN
9901 N 114th East Ct (74055-4350)
PHONE..................918 629-7223
Linda Stritzke Sullivan, *Owner*
EMP: 1
SALES (est): 63.1K **Privately Held**
SIC: 1389 Oil consultants

(G-7588)
LOUVER & EQUIPMENT MFRS INC
Also Called: Lemi
7007 N 115th East Ave (74055-3641)
P.O. Box 449 (74055-0449)
PHONE..................918 272-5600
Lance Huneryager, *President*
Angela Huneryager, *Admin Sec*
EMP: 10
SQ FT: 7,500
SALES (est): 1.3MM **Privately Held**
SIC: 3442 Metal doors, sash & trim

(G-7589)
MAJETTA TRACTOR & BACKHOE INC
107 W 4th Ave (74055-3435)
PHONE..................918 272-7861
EMP: 1
SALES (est): 60K **Privately Held**
SIC: 3531 Mfg Construction Machinery

(G-7590)
MASTER MOVERS INCORPORATED
Also Called: Dennis Beyer Consulting
9030 N Memorial Dr Ste A (74055-6716)
PHONE..................918 408-1490
Dennis Beyer, *Principal*
EMP: 1
SALES (est): 52K **Privately Held**
SIC: 8999 1389 7389 Lecturing services; oil consultants; fire fighting, oil & gas field; fire protection service other than forestry or public

(G-7591)
MINGO AEROSPACE LLC
8141 N 116th East Ave (74055-2647)
PHONE..................918 272-7371
Jimmy Newman, *Vice Pres*
Todd Addis, *Opers Mgr*
Daniel Atkinson, *QC Mgr*
Brian Emery, *VP Sales*
Rene Witten, *Mng Member*
EMP: 19
SQ FT: 10,000
SALES (est): 2MM **Privately Held**
WEB: www.mingoaero.com
SIC: 3324 8711 Aerospace investment castings, ferrous; engineering services

(G-7592)
MINGO AEROSPACE LLC
8121 N 116th Ave (74055)
PHONE..................918 272-7371
EMP: 1
SALES (est): 57.6K **Privately Held**
SIC: 3324 Aerospace investment castings, ferrous

(G-7593)
MINGO MANUFACTURING INC
8091 N 115th East Ave (74055-3628)
P.O. Box 30 (74055-0030)
PHONE..................918 272-1151
Terry Ingle, *President*
Ray Witten, *Vice Pres*
Brad Saunders, *Purch Mgr*
▲ EMP: 48
SQ FT: 35,000
SALES (est): 12.4MM **Privately Held**
WEB: www.mingomanufacturing.com
SIC: 3533 Oil field machinery & equipment

(G-7594)
MORA MORA MEDIA LLC
Also Called: Aaron Atencio Photography
18390 E Red Fox Trl (74055-8331)
PHONE..................918 231-6651
Aaron Atencio,
EMP: 1
SALES (est): 59.4K **Privately Held**
SIC: 3861 Photographic equipment & supplies

(G-7595)
MWD SERVICES LLC
8404 E 80th St N (74055-6907)
PHONE..................918 698-6109
Mathew W Dossett, *Principal*
EMP: 2
SALES (est): 108K **Privately Held**
SIC: 1389 Oil field services

(G-7596)
NATIONAL STEAK PROCESSORS LLC
Also Called: National Steak and Poultry
301 E 5th Ave (74055-3450)
PHONE..................918 274-8787
Bill Hampton, *Vice Pres*
Susan Early, *Purchasing*
Amanda Mulanax, *Sales Staff*
Faustino Gomez, *VP Mktg*
Linda Snow, *Marketing Staff*
EMP: 53
SALES (est): 14.4MM **Privately Held**
SIC: 2013 Sausages & other prepared meats

(G-7597)
OKIE DOUGH LLC
9119 N 153rd East Ave (74055-5029)
PHONE..................580 606-0142
Dena Hudson, *Principal*
EMP: 2
SALES (est): 77.7K **Privately Held**
SIC: 2045 Prepared flour mixes & doughs

(G-7598)
OKLAHOMA SPECIALTIES INC
7007 N 115th East Ave (74055-3641)
P.O. Box 455 (74055-0455)
PHONE..................918 272-0931
Charles Helscel Jr, *President*
Toby Brewer, *General Mgr*
EMP: 6 EST: 1997
SALES: 1.3K **Privately Held**
WEB: www.osiforge.com
SIC: 3462 Flange, valve & pipe fitting forgings, ferrous

(G-7599)
ORIZON ARSTRCTRES - OWASSO INC
Also Called: Caudill Components, LLC
209 E 5th Ave (74055-3434)
PHONE..................918 274-9094
John Jurick, *General Mgr*
Keith Martin, *CFO*
◆ EMP: 284
SQ FT: 43,000
SALES (est): 13.7MM **Privately Held**
SIC: 3724 Aircraft engines & engine parts
PA: Technical Industries, Inc.
336 Pinewoods Rd
Torrington CT 06790

(G-7600)
OWASSO GLASS
304 S Birch St (74055-3433)
P.O. Box 450 (74055-0450)
PHONE..................918 272-4490
Joshua Foote, *Owner*
Kaite Foote, *Co-Owner*
EMP: 2
SALES (est): 173.7K **Privately Held**
SIC: 1793 7536 5231 3231 Glass & glazing work; automotive glass replacement shops; glass; furniture tops, glass: cut, beveled or polished

(G-7601)
PARKERVILLE USA EMB & MORE
7890 N Owasso Expy (74055-3336)
PHONE..................918 636-0048
Shawn Parker, *Principal*
EMP: 1
SALES (est): 33.1K **Privately Held**
SIC: 2395 Embroidery & art needlework

(G-7602)
PASSION RACING ENGINES
14911 E 94th St N (74055-5019)
PHONE..................918 232-3950
James Smart, *Principal*
EMP: 2
SALES (est): 146.8K **Privately Held**
SIC: 3751 Motorcycles & related parts

(G-7603)
PINS-N-NEEDLES BY SANDRA
11901 E 113th Pl N (74055-6349)
PHONE..................918 270-0204
Sandra Phillippe, *Principal*
EMP: 2
SALES (est): 64.6K **Privately Held**
SIC: 3965 Pins & needles

(G-7604)
PRINT PEOPLE USA
11259 N 177th East Ave (74055-6054)
PHONE..................918 346-2560
Misty Jones, *Principal*
EMP: 4
SALES (est): 266.5K **Privately Held**
SIC: 2752 Commercial printing, lithographic

(G-7605)
PURE CREATIVITY LLC
Also Called: Pure Republic
7160 Bluebird Ct (74055-5524)
P.O. Box 458 (74055-0458)
PHONE..................918 272-3152
Eric Rutherford, *CEO*
Joseph Burns, *Vice Pres*
EMP: 4
SALES (est): 160K **Privately Held**
SIC: 2052 Cookies & crackers

(G-7606)
RAGTOPS ATHLETICS INC
9100 N Garnett Rd Ste Dd (74055-4400)
PHONE..................918 274-3575
EMP: 3 EST: 2001
SALES (est): 250K **Privately Held**
SIC: 5941 2759 Ret Sporting Goods/Bicycles Commercial Printing

(G-7607)
RESPONDAIR UAS LLC
9101 N 130th East Ave (74055-4748)
PHONE..................918 899-2113
Gabriel A Graveline, *Principal*
EMP: 3 EST: 2016
SALES (est): 244.1K **Privately Held**
WEB: www.respondair.com
SIC: 3728 Aircraft parts & equipment

(G-7608)
ROADRUNNER PORTABLE BUILDINGS
6835 N 115th East Ave (74055-3901)
PHONE..................918 272-7788
Danny Mashburn, *Owner*
EMP: 2
SALES (est): 214.4K **Privately Held**
SIC: 3448 2452 Buildings, portable: prefabricated metal; prefabricated wood buildings

(G-7609)
ROSEMON MARTIN LLC
17892 E 101st Pl N (74055-7743)
PHONE..................918 272-7145
Rosemon Martin, *Owner*
EMP: 3
SALES (est): 98.1K **Privately Held**
SIC: 2711 Newspapers, publishing & printing

(G-7610)
SAFE HARBOR DOCKS INC
302 E 5th Ave (74055-3446)
PHONE..................918 376-2756
Kelly Lawrence, *President*
EMP: 7
SQ FT: 10,000
SALES (est): 50K **Privately Held**
SIC: 2499 Floating docks, wood

(G-7611)
SAFE HARBOR PRODUCTS LLC
7845 E 86th St N (74055-6944)
P.O. Box 1256 (74055-1256)
PHONE..................918 376-2756
Ron Lawrence, *President*
EMP: 5
SQ FT: 2,017
SALES: 250K **Privately Held**
SIC: 2499 Floating docks, wood

(G-7612)
SANDMAN SPORTS
11809 E 81st St N (74055-2668)
PHONE..................918 272-0862
Douglas Gross, *Owner*
EMP: 1
SALES (est): 63.2K **Privately Held**
SIC: 3482 Small arms ammunition

GEOGRAPHIC SECTION

(G-7613)
SARA SMITH INC
8254 N 128th East Ave (74055-6232)
PHONE..................918 272-3076
EMP: 1
SALES (est): 39.6K **Privately Held**
SIC: 3999 Manufacturing industries

(G-7614)
SC CANDLES
13314 E 89th St N (74055-4777)
PHONE..................469 855-2823
Staci McGarrah, *Principal*
EMP: 2
SALES (est): 62.5K **Privately Held**
SIC: 3999 Candles

(G-7615)
SCHOCK MANUFACTURING LLC
6901 N 115th East Ave (74055-3639)
PHONE..................918 609-3600
Gene Schockemoehl, *CEO*
Scott Schockemoehl, *President*
EMP: 25
SQ FT: 70,000
SALES: 6.4MM **Privately Held**
SIC: 3511 Gas turbine generator set units, complete

(G-7616)
SENTIENT INDUSTRIES INC
8406 N 156th East Ave (74055-7372)
PHONE..................918 770-0770
EMP: 1 EST: 2009
SALES (est): 47K **Privately Held**
SIC: 3999 Mfg Misc Products

(G-7617)
SHIRT NUTZ LLC
10226 N 151st East Ave (74055-4868)
PHONE..................918 900-2362
Michael Moe, *CEO*
EMP: 2
SALES (est): 102K **Privately Held**
SIC: 2759 Screen printing

(G-7618)
SOUTHERN PLASTICS LLC
408 W 2nd Ave (74055-3128)
PHONE..................918 274-6767
Ken Robinson,
EMP: 6
SALES (est): 1MM **Privately Held**
SIC: 3089 Injection molding of plastics

(G-7619)
STANDARD SUPPLY CO INC
Also Called: NAPA Auto Parts
6602b N Owasso Expy (74055)
PHONE..................918 272-5014
Bill E Breese, *President*
Bill D Farley, *Vice Pres*
Lee Klahr, *Admin Sec*
EMP: 5
SQ FT: 1,500
SALES: 500K **Privately Held**
WEB: www.standardlawnandgarden.com
SIC: 3524 Lawn & garden equipment

(G-7620)
STORM ROOFING & CNSTR LLC
19450 E 72nd St N (74055-8238)
PHONE..................918 688-0165
Erick Maupin, *Principal*
EMP: 2
SALES (est): 228.9K **Privately Held**
WEB: www.stormroofers.com
SIC: 1521 3444 5033 1761 Single-family housing construction; metal roofing & roof drainage equipment; roofing, asphalt & sheet metal; roofing & gutter work; roofing contractor

(G-7621)
SUENO DESIGNS
16518 E 93rd St N (74055-8310)
PHONE..................918 809-3027
Clydeen Lowman, *Owner*
EMP: 1 EST: 2001
SALES (est): 64.5K **Privately Held**
SIC: 7389 3911 Design services; jewelry, precious metal

(G-7622)
SUMMIT ENERGY EXPLORATIONS LLC
8198 N 70th East Ave (74055-5041)
PHONE..................918 396-3020
Shannon Potts, *Mng Member*
EMP: 1
SALES (est): 88.2K **Privately Held**
SIC: 1382 Oil & gas exploration services

(G-7623)
THERMAL SPECIALTIES LLC
10116 E 93rd St N (74055-6830)
PHONE..................970 532-3796
Myers Mitchell, *Branch Mgr*
EMP: 3
SALES (corp-wide): 29.1MM **Privately Held**
WEB: www.tsi-aic.com
SIC: 3398 Metal heat treating
PA: Thermal Specialties, Llc
6314 E 15th St
Tulsa OK 74112
918 836-4800

(G-7624)
THOMPSONS METAL COATING
15358 E 91st St N (74055-5005)
PHONE..................918 272-5711
David Thompson, *Owner*
Debbie Thompson, *Co-Owner*
EMP: 2
SALES (est): 157.3K **Privately Held**
SIC: 3479 Coating of metals & formed products

(G-7625)
TOTAL CONTROL SYSTEM INC
7524 N 119th East Ave (74055-3703)
PHONE..................918 810-4004
David Berg, *Administration*
EMP: 2
SALES (est): 250.1K **Privately Held**
WEB: www.tcsusa.biz
SIC: 3699 Electrical equipment & supplies

(G-7626)
TOURKICK LLC
12324 E 86th St N (74055-2543)
PHONE..................918 409-2543
Clifford Paulick, *Principal*
EMP: 2
SALES (est): 141.1K **Privately Held**
SIC: 8742 7371 7389 2759 Marketing consulting services; custom computer programming services; advertising, promotional & trade show services; promotional printing

(G-7627)
TULSA ASPHALT LLC
14901 E 66th St N (74055-7688)
P.O. Box 9159, Tulsa (74157-0159)
PHONE..................918 445-2684
William E Smith,
Carol Smith,
EMP: 12
SQ FT: 2,500
SALES (est): 2.1MM **Privately Held**
SIC: 2911 Asphalt or asphaltic materials, made in refineries

(G-7628)
TULSA INDUSTRIAL MFG LLC
8410 N 66th East Ave (74055-8518)
PHONE..................918 640-3802
Terry Hall, *Principal*
EMP: 1
SALES (est): 39.6K **Privately Held**
SIC: 3999 Manufacturing industries

(G-7629)
TULSA ORNAMENTAL IRON WORKS
101 E 21st St (74055-4417)
PHONE..................918 274-7253
David Shields, *Owner*
EMP: 4 EST: 1956
SQ FT: 1,000
SALES (est): 190K **Privately Held**
SIC: 3446 Architectural metalwork

(G-7630)
WITTEN COMPANY INC
Also Called: Witten Fasteners
8199 N 116th East Ave (74055-2647)
P.O. Box 269 (74055-0269)
PHONE..................918 272-9567
Donald W Witten, *President*
Sheryl Kay Witten, *Corp Secy*
Kirk Brewster, *Mfg Mgr*
EMP: 20
SQ FT: 12,600
SALES (est): 4.1MM **Privately Held**
SIC: 3728 3452 3599 Aircraft parts & equipment; bolts, nuts, rivets & washers; machine shop, jobbing & repair

(G-7631)
WOODS PRECISION PRODUCTS INC
11501 N 109th East Ave (74055-4205)
P.O. Box 74 (74055-0074)
PHONE..................918 272-9541
Jerry Fidler, *President*
EMP: 45
SQ FT: 27,000
SALES (est): 6.9MM **Privately Held**
SIC: 3599 Machine shop, jobbing & repair

Paden
Okfuskee County

(G-7632)
B B SAND AND GRAVEL
36827 Ew 1090 (74860)
P.O. Box 120 (74860-0120)
PHONE..................405 944-1163
Danney Bailey, *Principal*
EMP: 4
SALES (est): 252.6K **Privately Held**
SIC: 1442 Construction sand & gravel

(G-7633)
BAILEY PRODUCTION COMPANY
95146 N 3630 Rd (74860-7152)
PHONE..................405 932-5293
Leon Bailey, *Owner*
Judy Bailey, *Co-Owner*
EMP: 7
SALES: 400K **Privately Held**
WEB: www.baileys5starpecans.com
SIC: 1381 1382 Drilling oil & gas wells; oil & gas exploration services

(G-7634)
CIRCLE K STEEL BLDG CNSTR LLC
359071 Us Highway 62 (74860-9359)
PHONE..................405 932-4664
Frank Kornelsen, *Mng Member*
Bob Kornelsen, *Manager*
EMP: 13
SALES (est): 1.6MM **Privately Held**
SIC: 1541 3448 Steel building construction; panels for prefabricated metal buildings

(G-7635)
D SIGNS & WONDERS LLC
108 E 9th St (74860)
PHONE..................405 932-4585
David McNabb, *Owner*
EMP: 15
SQ FT: 1,800
SALES (est): 4.5MM **Privately Held**
SIC: 3993 5099 Signs & advertising specialties; signs, except electric

(G-7636)
MOCCASIN TRAIL COMPANY
359188 E 1090 Rd (74860-7175)
PHONE..................405 380-8221
EMP: 1
SALES (est): 49.1K **Privately Held**
WEB: www.mtcshooting.com
SIC: 3149 Moccasins

Paoli
Garvin County

(G-7637)
ALAN WARE
Also Called: Ware's The Bucks
12954 Highway 77 (73074-9654)
PHONE..................918 658-5267
Alan Ware, *Owner*
EMP: 1
SALES: 8K **Privately Held**
SIC: 2043 Corn, hulled: prepared as cereal breakfast food

(G-7638)
NATURES RX INC
62 Rr 1 (73074)
P.O. Box 445 (73074-0445)
PHONE..................405 484-7302
Roger Elder, *President*
▲ EMP: 4
SALES (est): 214.1K **Privately Held**
SIC: 2023 5912 Dietary supplements, dairy & non-dairy based; drug stores

Park Hill
Cherokee County

(G-7639)
A & A WELDING
36275 S Cherokee Dr (74451-2137)
PHONE..................918 772-0418
EMP: 1
SALES (est): 43.9K **Privately Held**
SIC: 7692 Welding repair

(G-7640)
ARKHOLA SAND & GRAVEL CO TAHLE
350 W Arkhola St (74451)
PHONE..................918 456-6121
Jerry W Goodson, *Principal*
EMP: 3
SALES (est): 146.2K **Privately Held**
SIC: 1442 Construction sand & gravel

(G-7641)
CRACO TRUSS POST FRAME SUP LLC
30257 S Sizemore Rd (74451-2041)
PHONE..................918 457-1111
Steven Crawford Jr, *Principal*
EMP: 4
SALES (est): 666.8K **Privately Held**
WEB: www.cracotruss.com
SIC: 2439 Trusses, wooden roof

(G-7642)
ENVIRO CLEAN
19150 E Flournory Rd (74451-4145)
PHONE..................918 207-9779
Ken Caughman, *Owner*
EMP: 1
SALES (est): 53.7K **Privately Held**
SIC: 2434 Wood kitchen cabinets

(G-7643)
HINSCO INC
22518 Highway 82 (74451-4086)
PHONE..................918 456-2138
Linda Harris, *President*
EMP: 2
SALES (est): 182.1K **Privately Held**
SIC: 3599 Machine shop, jobbing & repair

(G-7644)
HYDROGEN TECHNOLOGIES INC
15803 W Deer Run Rd (74451-2374)
P.O. Box 595, Tahlequah (74465-0595)
PHONE..................918 645-3430
Sheryl Mabie, *President*
EMP: 3
SALES (est): 222.5K **Privately Held**
SIC: 3714 Motor vehicle parts & accessories

Park Hill - Cherokee County (G-7645)

(G-7645)
LAKE TENKILLER HBR WTR PLANT
14977 W Forest Rd (74451-2081)
PHONE.................................918 457-4811
Tom O'Neil, *Director*
EMP: 2 EST: 1978
SALES (est): 247.3K **Privately Held**
WEB: www.laketenkillerharbor.com
SIC: **5074** 3589 Water heaters, except electric; water treatment equipment, industrial

(G-7646)
RED WIND TRAINING
Also Called: Red Wind Simulations
22349 E 843 Rd (74451-2831)
PHONE.................................918 822-0605
Don Berry, *Owner*
EMP: 2
SALES (est): 126.6K **Privately Held**
SIC: **7372** Prepackaged software

(G-7647)
ZIESE PRODUCTS INC
23374 E 878 Rd (74451-2907)
PHONE.................................918 457-5457
Richard Ziese, *President*
Sean Ziese, *Vice Pres*
Jason Santana, *Manager*
Ginger Ziese, *Admin Sec*
EMP: 20
SQ FT: 6,000
SALES (est): 3.5MM **Privately Held**
SIC: **3599** Machine shop, jobbing & repair

Pauls Valley
Garvin County

(G-7648)
4M WELDING INC
Rr 3 (73075)
PHONE.................................405 484-7293
EMP: 5
SALES: 500K **Privately Held**
SIC: **7692** Welding Repair

(G-7649)
ACCELATED ARTFL LIST SYSTEMS
20310 Hwy 77 (73075)
PHONE.................................405 207-9449
Brandon English, *General Mgr*
EMP: 12 EST: 2013
SALES (est): 550K **Privately Held**
SIC: **3561** Pumps & pumping equipment

(G-7650)
BEMIS COMPANY INC
Also Called: Bemis-Pauls Valley
200 N Indian Meridian Rd (73075-9102)
PHONE.................................405 207-2200
Allen Ubanks, *Plant Mgr*
Louis Bogran, *Plant Mgr*
EMP: 250
SALES (corp-wide): 524.7K **Privately Held**
SIC: **2671** 3565 Paper coated or laminated for packaging; thermoplastic coated paper for packaging; packaging machinery
HQ: Bemis Company, Inc.
2301 Industrial Dr
Neenah WI 54956
920 727-4100

(G-7651)
BLACKHAWK WIRELINE SERVICES
1110 W Royal Oaks Rd (73075-5328)
P.O. Box 640 (73075-0640)
PHONE.................................405 238-2929
Paul Carter, *President*
Julie Carter, *Corp Secy*
EMP: 5 EST: 1998
SALES (est): 1MM **Privately Held**
SIC: **1389** Oil field services

(G-7652)
BLOOMIN CRAZY LDSCP FLRAL DSIG
401 S Chickasaw St (73075-4219)
PHONE.................................405 238-3416
Melissa Koesler, *Principal*
EMP: 2
SALES (est): 111.1K **Privately Held**
SIC: **5261** 5191 2875 Lawn & garden equipment; fertilizer & fertilizer materials; compost

(G-7653)
CHRIS GREEN GREENS CONSTRUCT
15569 N County Road 3240 (73075-8728)
PHONE.................................405 207-0690
Chris Green, *Principal*
EMP: 2
SALES: 224K **Privately Held**
SIC: **1521** 7692 2514 7699 Single-family housing construction; welding repair; metal household furniture; tank repair

(G-7654)
CNHI LLC
Also Called: Pauls Valley Daily Democrat
108 S Willow St (73075-3834)
P.O. Box 790 (73075-0790)
PHONE.................................405 238-6464
Banks Dishmon, *Manager*
EMP: 10 **Privately Held**
SIC: **2711** Newspapers: publishing only, not printed on site
HQ: Cnhi, Llc
445 Dexter Ave Ste 7000
Montgomery AL 36104

(G-7655)
COVERCRAFT INDUSTRIES LLC (PA)
100 Enterprise (73075-9100)
PHONE.................................405 238-9651
Robert Lichtmann, *Ch of Bd*
Martin Lichtmann, *President*
Charlotte Lichtmann, *Corp Secy*
Adam Johnson, *Facilities Mgr*
Amanda McCarty, *Buyer*
◆ EMP: 147
SQ FT: 115,000
SALES (est): 116.6MM **Privately Held**
WEB: www.covercraft.com
SIC: **2394** Liners & covers, fabric: made from purchased materials

(G-7656)
DAYS WOOD PRODUCTS INC
220 S Earl St (73075-4221)
PHONE.................................405 238-6477
Fax: 405 238-6143
EMP: 15
SQ FT: 25,000
SALES (est): 940K **Privately Held**
SIC: **2511** 2541 2521 Mfg Wood Household Furn Mfg Wood Partitions/Fixt Mfg Wood Office Furn Mfg Wood Household Furn

(G-7657)
DIAMOND R WIRELINE LLC
2901 W Royal Oaks Rd (73075-5326)
PHONE.................................405 361-7933
Christy Fuller, *Principal*
EMP: 5 EST: 2009
SALES (est): 374.1K **Privately Held**
WEB: www.diamondrranch.biz
SIC: **1389** Removal of condensate gasoline from field (gathering) lines

(G-7658)
EDWARDS CANVAS INC
17499 Highway 77 (73075-8741)
P.O. Box 180 (73075-0180)
PHONE.................................405 238-7551
Clayton J Edwards, *President*
Tina A Frost, *Manager*
Amy Pogue Storey, *Manager*
EMP: 42
SQ FT: 25,000
SALES: 2.7MM **Privately Held**
SIC: **2394** Tarpaulins, fabric: made from purchased materials; canvas covers & drop cloths; awnings, fabric: made from purchased materials

(G-7659)
FIELDS INC
100 Fields Row (73075-9600)
P.O. Box 7 (73075-0007)
PHONE.................................405 238-7381
Chris Field, *President*
Jenny Wallace, *Corp Secy*
EMP: 25 EST: 1922
SQ FT: 25,000
SALES (est): 6.5MM **Privately Held**
WEB: www.fieldspv.com
SIC: **2053** Pies, bakery: frozen

(G-7660)
HINKLE PRINTING & OFFICE SUP
110 E Paul Ave (73075-3419)
PHONE.................................405 238-9308
Edward Strickland, *President*
Jo Ann Patton, *Corp Secy*
Bruce L Patton, *Vice Pres*
EMP: 8
SQ FT: 7,500
SALES (est): 850K **Privately Held**
WEB: www.hinklespv.com
SIC: **2752** 5943 2791 2789 Commercial printing, offset; office forms & supplies; typesetting; bookbinding & related work

(G-7661)
JACKS CNSTR & BACKHOE SVC
Rr 1 Box 268 (73075)
PHONE.................................405 238-3569
Alvie Jack, *President*
EMP: 3
SALES (est): 571.4K **Privately Held**
SIC: **3531** Backhoes

(G-7662)
JOHNSONS SPRING CREST DRPERY C
301 W Paul Ave (73075-3222)
PHONE.................................405 238-7341
Leon Johnson, *President*
Marita Johnson, *Vice Pres*
EMP: 4
SALES (est): 130K **Privately Held**
SIC: **5714** 2391 2591 Draperies; draperies, plastic & textile: from purchased materials; drapery hardware & blinds & shades

(G-7663)
KELLEY PRINTING
202 S Chickasaw St (73075-4235)
PHONE.................................405 238-4848
Howard Kelley, *Owner*
EMP: 1 EST: 1997
SALES (est): 65K **Privately Held**
SIC: **2759** 2791 2789 2752 Commercial printing; typesetting; bookbinding & related work; commercial printing, lithographic

(G-7664)
L A JACOBSON INC (PA)
Also Called: Jacobson Ready Mixed Concrete
102 E Bethlehem Rd (73075)
P.O. Box 130 (73075-0130)
PHONE.................................405 238-9313
Dean Jacobson, *Ch of Bd*
Terry Jacobson, *President*
Lucas Jacobson, *General Mgr*
Lewis Jacobson, *Co-President*
Marilyn Hubbard, *Treasurer*
EMP: 26 EST: 1945
SQ FT: 5,000
SALES: 6.6MM **Privately Held**
WEB: www.lajacobson.com
SIC: **3273** Ready-mixed concrete

(G-7665)
LARIO OIL & GAS COMPANY
3 Mi W Of Pauls Vly (73075)
P.O. Box 1052 (73075-1052)
PHONE.................................405 238-5609
Larry Parks, *Branch Mgr*
EMP: 3
SALES (corp-wide): 63.6MM **Privately Held**
SIC: **1311** Crude petroleum production
HQ: Lario Oil & Gas Company
301 S Market St
Wichita KS 67202
316 265-5611

(G-7666)
MAC MACHINE
17509 Highway 77 (73075-8679)
PHONE.................................405 238-7280
Jim Mc Gregor, *Owner*
EMP: 5
SQ FT: 6,000
SALES (est): 413.1K **Privately Held**
SIC: **3469** 7692 3444 Machine parts, stamped or pressed metal; welding repair; sheet metalwork

(G-7667)
MARSH OIL & GAS CO
111 N Chickasaw St (73075-3415)
P.O. Box 726 (73075-0726)
PHONE.................................405 238-9660
Susan Agee, *Vice Pres*
EMP: 3 EST: 2009
SALES (est): 218.2K **Privately Held**
SIC: **1311** Crude petroleum production

(G-7668)
NEW ERA SIGNS LLC
501 N Pecan St (73075-2431)
PHONE.................................405 926-2050
Jose Mendoza, *Owner*
EMP: 1
SALES (est): 50.6K **Privately Held**
SIC: **3993** Signs & advertising specialties

(G-7669)
OILFIELD R T
30980 E County Road 1585 (73075-9603)
PHONE.................................405 238-2026
EMP: 2 EST: 2014
SALES (est): 113.1K **Privately Held**
SIC: **1311** Crude petroleum & natural gas

(G-7670)
PC NET
1700 S Chickasaw St (73075-6804)
P.O. Box 537 (73075-0537)
PHONE.................................405 238-2001
James Kelly, *Owner*
James R Kelly, *Owner*
EMP: 1 EST: 1987
SALES (est): 97.3K **Privately Held**
WEB: www.k-softinc.com
SIC: **7372** Business oriented computer software

(G-7671)
PLUMMER ENERGY INC
17808 N County Road 3190 (73075-8663)
PHONE.................................405 238-9132
Larry T Plummer, *President*
Glenda Plummer, *Vice Pres*
EMP: 2
SALES: 639K **Privately Held**
SIC: **2911** 7389 Oils, fuel;

(G-7672)
STICH THIS AND MORE
123 E Grant Ave (73075-3496)
PHONE.................................405 207-9922
Brenda Jones, *Owner*
EMP: 2
SALES (est): 172K **Privately Held**
SIC: **2752** Commercial printing, lithographic

(G-7673)
SUBMERSIBLE TECHNICAL PRODUCTS
Also Called: Weatherford Submersible
2301 S Highway 77 (73075-9725)
PHONE.................................405 850-4091
EMP: 15
SALES (corp-wide): 1.3MM **Privately Held**
SIC: **3731** Submersible marine robots, manned or unmanned
PA: Submersible Technical Products, Inc
1600 N Garnett Rd
Tulsa OK
432 697-1900

(G-7674)
WELCHS WRECKER
Also Called: Welchs Twing Rcovery Trck Auto
2001 W Airline Rd (73075-9658)
P.O. Box 932 (73075-0932)
PHONE.................................405 238-6194
Otis Welch, *Owner*

GEOGRAPHIC SECTION

Pawnee - Pawnee County (G-7707)

EMP: 3
SALES (est): 250.3K **Privately Held**
SIC: 3711 Wreckers (tow truck), assembly of

(G-7675)
YELLOW BIRD COMMUNICATION
619 N Pine St (73075-2217)
P.O. Box 973 (73075-0973)
PHONE..................................405 238-6260
Suzanne Blake, *Owner*
EMP: 1
SALES (est): 41K **Privately Held**
SIC: 2731 Book publishing

Pawhuska
Osage County

(G-7676)
ALLEN BROTHERS FEED
129 E 5th St (74056-5201)
P.O. Box 1269 (74056-1269)
PHONE..................................918 287-4379
James Allen, *Owner*
EMP: 2
SQ FT: 16,200
SALES (est): 178.8K **Privately Held**
WEB: www.allenbrosfeed.com
SIC: 2048 5191 Prepared feeds; seeds: field, garden & flower

(G-7677)
BASIC ENERGY SERVICES INC
99 Oklahoma Ave (74056)
PHONE..................................918 287-3388
EMP: 1
SALES (corp-wide): 567.2MM **Publicly Held**
SIC: 1389 Oil field services
PA: Basic Energy Services, Inc.
801 Cherry St Unit 2
Fort Worth TX 76102
817 334-4100

(G-7678)
BRONZE HORSE INC
4 Old Highway 99 (74056)
PHONE..................................918 287-4433
John Free, *President*
Cindy Free, *Manager*
EMP: 4
SQ FT: 2,450
SALES: 400K **Privately Held**
SIC: 3366 Castings (except die): bronze

(G-7679)
BUFFALO NICKEL INDUSTRIES LLC
136 E 6th St (74056-4204)
PHONE..................................918 287-3899
Thomas Ryan, *Principal*
EMP: 1
SALES (est): 114.5K **Privately Held**
SIC: 3356 Nickel

(G-7680)
BUFFALO NICKEL PRESS
136 E 6th St (74056-4204)
PHONE..................................918 287-3899
Ryan Redcorn,
EMP: 3
SALES (est): 178.4K **Privately Held**
SIC: 2741 Miscellaneous publishing

(G-7681)
CEDAR CHEST
134 E 6th St (74056-4204)
P.O. Box 255 (74056-0255)
PHONE..................................918 287-9129
EMP: 2 EST: 2011
SALES (est): 114.6K **Privately Held**
SIC: 2511 Cedar chests

(G-7682)
CHAPARRAL ENERGY INC
447 State Highway 99 (74056-9745)
PHONE..................................918 287-2977
Pete Kelly, *Superintendent*
EMP: 11 **Publicly Held**
SIC: 1311 Crude petroleum production

PA: Chaparral Energy, Inc.
701 Cedar Lake Blvd
Oklahoma City OK 73114

(G-7683)
CRANE MACHINERY REPAIR
48176 State Highway 99 (74056-6545)
PHONE..................................918 349-2264
Michael Crane, *Owner*
EMP: 1
SALES (est): 41.8K **Privately Held**
SIC: 7692 Welding repair

(G-7684)
CSC OIL CO
Also Called: CSC Oil Company
2803 Cleo Ln (74056-2047)
P.O. Box 808 (74056-0808)
PHONE..................................918 287-1138
EMP: 1
SALES (est): 140K **Privately Held**
SIC: 1311 Crude Petroleum/Natural Gas Production

(G-7685)
FREDRICK F DRUMMOND
100 W Main St (74056-4149)
P.O. Box 1599 (74056-1599)
PHONE..................................918 287-4400
Fredrick F Drummond, *Owner*
EMP: 4
SALES (est): 1MM **Privately Held**
SIC: 0211 1311 Beef cattle feedlots; crude petroleum production

(G-7686)
ISLAND DISC GOLF COURSE
22005 State Highway 99 (74056-9798)
PHONE..................................541 337-8668
Avery Jenkins, *Principal*
EMP: 1
SALES (est): 49.1K **Privately Held**
SIC: 3149 Moccasins

(G-7687)
JAMES A TAYLOR
Also Called: RMR Energy
22005 State Highway 99 (74056-9798)
PHONE..................................918 724-3121
James A Taylor, *Principal*
EMP: 5
SALES (est): 238.5K **Privately Held**
SIC: 1389 7389 Oil field services;

(G-7688)
LARRY CHINN OIL
138 County Road 3304 (74056-9317)
PHONE..................................918 336-4269
Larry Chinn, *Owner*
EMP: 1
SALES: 450K **Privately Held**
SIC: 1311 Crude petroleum production

(G-7689)
MOORES HARDWARE AND HOME CTR
Also Called: Handy Grocery
521 E Main St (74056-5221)
PHONE..................................918 287-4458
Terry Moore, *Owner*
EMP: 6
SALES (est): 739.6K **Privately Held**
SIC: 2426 5251 Lumber, hardwood dimension; hardware

(G-7690)
NDN ENTERPRISES LLC
134 E 6th St (74056-4204)
PHONE..................................703 772-6635
Celeste Beaupre, *Mng Member*
Julie O'Keefe,
Roxanne Reed,
EMP: 3 EST: 2013
SALES (est): 133.3K **Privately Held**
SIC: 4225 2339 8331 8742 General warehousing & storage; women's & misses' athletic clothing & sportswear; job training & vocational rehabilitation services; management consulting services; business consultant

(G-7691)
OSAGE COUNTY TREASURER
611 Grandview Ave (74056-4201)
P.O. Box 1569 (74056-1569)
PHONE..................................918 287-3101
Joyce Hathcoat, *Manager*
EMP: 1
SALES (est): 81.8K **Privately Held**
SIC: 2741

(G-7692)
OSAGE SURVEYING SERVICE
100 W Main St Ste 210 (74056-4141)
PHONE..................................918 287-4029
Alan Altman, *Owner*
EMP: 3 EST: 1937
SALES (est): 222.2K **Privately Held**
SIC: 1311 8713 Crude petroleum production; surveying services

(G-7693)
OSAGE TRADING CO INC (PA)
153 John Dahl Ave (74056-2517)
P.O. Box 1360 (74056-1360)
PHONE..................................918 287-4544
Paul Mays III, *President*
EMP: 3
SALES (est): 20.8MM **Privately Held**
SIC: 2131 5993 Smoking tobacco; tobacco stores & stands

(G-7694)
REEF SERVICES LLC
876 Old Highway 99 (74056-5856)
PHONE..................................918 287-3850
EMP: 5
SALES (corp-wide): 1.2B **Publicly Held**
SIC: 3533 Oil & gas drilling rigs & equipment
HQ: Reef Services, Llc
1515 W Sam Houston Pkwy N
Houston TX 77043

(G-7695)
SELL WELL SERVICING COMPANY
N Of Cy On E 21st St (74056)
P.O. Box 1139 (74056-1139)
PHONE..................................918 287-1711
Eugene Sell, *Owner*
EMP: 1
SQ FT: 1,200
SALES (est): 139.3K **Privately Held**
SIC: 1311 Crude petroleum production

(G-7696)
SHORT OIL CO YARD
N Of City (74056)
PHONE..................................918 287-2925
Mark Short, *Principal*
EMP: 3
SALES (est): 166.2K **Privately Held**
SIC: 1311 Crude petroleum production

(G-7697)
WACHTMAN-SCHROEDER
Also Called: W & S Oil Co
2400 Mckenzie Rd (74056-9431)
P.O. Box 1138 (74056-1138)
PHONE..................................918 287-3122
Henry C Watchman Jr, *Partner*
Henry C Wachtman Jr, *Partner*
EMP: 4 EST: 1952
SALES (est): 329.3K **Privately Held**
SIC: 1311 8742 Crude petroleum & natural gas; industrial & labor consulting services

(G-7698)
WYATTS OIL CORP
731 W 6th St (74056-4011)
P.O. Box 344 (74056-0344)
PHONE..................................918 287-4285
Rick Wyatt, *Principal*
EMP: 2
SALES (est): 277K **Privately Held**
SIC: 3569 Gas producers, generators & other gas related equipment

Pawnee
Pawnee County

(G-7699)
AMERICAN-CHIEF CO (PA)
Also Called: Hominy News Progress
558 Illinois St (74058-2036)
P.O. Box 370 (74058-0370)
PHONE..................................918 762-2552
Larry R Ferguson, *Principal*
EMP: 6 EST: 1931
SQ FT: 3,800
SALES (est): 907.5K **Privately Held**
WEB: www.pawneenation.org
SIC: 2711 5112 2754 Newspapers: publishing only, not printed on site; office supplies; job printing, gravure

(G-7700)
BENSON MINERAL GROUP INC
Nw Of City (74058)
PHONE..................................918 762-3651
Phillip Kempton, *Opers-Prdtn-Mfg*
EMP: 9
SALES (corp-wide): 2.9MM **Privately Held**
SIC: 1311 Crude petroleum production
PA: Benson Mineral Group Inc
1560 Broadway Ste 1900
Denver CO 80202
303 863-3500

(G-7701)
BLACKBURN OIL & GAS INC
49651 S 360 Rd (74058-5142)
PHONE..................................918 688-1067
Justin Blackburn, *President*
Stacy Blackburn, *Corp Secy*
EMP: 2
SALES (est): 270K **Privately Held**
SIC: 1311 Crude petroleum & natural gas

(G-7702)
BOB G WELDING
1221 Harrison St (74058-4098)
PHONE..................................918 510-4769
Bob Gilliland, *Principal*
EMP: 1
SALES (est): 41.6K **Privately Held**
SIC: 7692 Welding repair

(G-7703)
COOPER WRECKER SERVICE
52500 S 34900 Rd (74058-3829)
PHONE..................................918 639-7381
Mark Cooper, *Owner*
EMP: 1
SALES (est): 20K **Privately Held**
SIC: 3713 7699 Automobile wrecker truck bodies; locksmith shop

(G-7704)
EVE BREATHE
53100 S 34800 Rd (74058-3809)
PHONE..................................918 454-2866
Cherri Richardson, *Owner*
EMP: 3
SALES (est): 186.4K **Privately Held**
SIC: 2048 Feed supplements

(G-7705)
J J CUSTOM FIRE
1300 N Sewell Dr (74058-1001)
PHONE..................................918 762-2102
Ray Potter, *Principal*
EMP: 2
SALES (est): 87.2K **Privately Held**
SIC: 3711 Motor vehicles & car bodies

(G-7706)
MALONE CONTRACT PUMPING INC
51575 E 45 (74058)
PHONE..................................918 767-2450
Lesley Malone, *Administration*
EMP: 2
SALES (est): 186.8K **Privately Held**
SIC: 1389 Pumping of oil & gas wells

(G-7707)
PAWNEE MILLWORKS LLC
51752 E 43 Rd (74058-1050)
PHONE..................................918 767-2565

Pawnee - Pawnee County (G-7708)

Heather Higgins, *Mng Member*
Charles Edwards,
JC Higgins,
EMP: 7
SQ FT: 900
SALES: 670K **Privately Held**
SIC: 1751 2431 Cabinet & finish carpentry; millwork

(G-7708)
PAWNEE READY MIX INC
2000 S 9th St (74058)
P.O. Box 93 (74058-0093)
PHONE..................918 762-3437
Thelma Rogers, *President*
EMP: 2
SQ FT: 288
SALES (est): 230K **Privately Held**
SIC: 5211 3273 Concrete & cinder block; ready-mixed concrete

(G-7709)
PIE IN SKY PUBLISHING CO LLC
415 Denver St (74058-3544)
PHONE..................918 762-3310
Suzanne Spears, *Principal*
EMP: 1
SALES (est): 8.8K **Privately Held**
SIC: 2741 Miscellaneous publishing

(G-7710)
QUAPAW COMPANY INC
Also Called: Quapaw Rock Co
45551 S 354 Rd (74058-1553)
PHONE..................918 767-2985
David Weaver, *Manager*
EMP: 20
SALES (corp-wide): 19MM **Privately Held**
SIC: 1411 1422 Dimension stone; crushed & broken limestone
PA: The Quapaw Company
3224 N Perkins Rd
Stillwater OK
405 377-9240

(G-7711)
STOCKMANS MILL & GRAIN INC
600 Kansas St (74058-2008)
P.O. Box 340 (74058-0340)
PHONE..................918 762-3459
William G Webb, *President*
Darrell Skidgel, *Vice Pres*
N W Skidgel Jr, *Treasurer*
EMP: 7 **EST:** 1943
SQ FT: 1,600
SALES: 740K **Privately Held**
SIC: 2041 5191 2875 2048 Grain mills (except rice); farm supplies; feed; seeds: field, garden & flower; fertilizers, mixing only; prepared feeds

(G-7712)
TECHTROL INC
1310 N Sewell Dr (74058-1001)
P.O. Box 336 (74058-0336)
PHONE..................918 762-1050
William Ardrey, *President*
Joyce Ardrey, *Corp Secy*
EMP: 25 **EST:** 1995
SQ FT: 10,000
SALES (est): 2.8MM **Privately Held**
WEB: www.techtrol-usa.com
SIC: 3823 8711 Industrial instrmnts msrmnt display/control process variable; engineering services

Peggs
Cherokee County

(G-7713)
SPENCERS CUSTOM CABINETS
Hwy 82 (74452)
P.O. Box 112 (74452-0112)
PHONE..................918 598-3208
Ed Spencer, *Partner*
EMP: 7
SALES (est): 856.8K **Privately Held**
SIC: 2434 Wood kitchen cabinets

Perkins
Payne County

(G-7714)
A-1 BACKHOE
12203 S Sangre Rd (74059-4184)
PHONE..................405 547-5452
Ricky Triplett, *Principal*
EMP: 3
SALES (est): 269.5K **Privately Held**
SIC: 3531 Backhoes

(G-7715)
BETTER BUILT BARNS
11809 S Washington (74059-4070)
PHONE..................405 547-2066
Ernest Strubhar, *Owner*
EMP: 7
SALES (est): 836.2K **Privately Held**
SIC: 2452 Prefabricated wood buildings

(G-7716)
DURNAL CONSTRUCTION LLC
12415 S Fairgrounds (74059-3959)
P.O. Box 820 (74059-0820)
PHONE..................405 413-5458
Lane Durnal,
Jenny Durnal,
EMP: 5
SALES: 610K **Privately Held**
SIC: 1799 3448 7692 7389 Welding on site; fence construction; prefabricated metal buildings; welding repair;

(G-7717)
FLOWCO ENERGY SERVICE LLC
605b Methodist Ave (74059-9111)
PHONE..................405 385-1062
Armando Covarrubias, *CEO*
Robert Dixon, *President*
EMP: 3
SALES (est): 153.1K **Privately Held**
SIC: 1389 Construction, repair & dismantling services; pipe testing, oil field service; oil consultants; roustabout service

(G-7718)
HYDRO FOAM TECHNOLOGY INC
4321 E 122nd St (74059-3741)
P.O. Box 7 (74059-0007)
PHONE..................405 547-5800
Dennis Fagan, *President*
Terry Fagan, *Vice Pres*
EMP: 14
SQ FT: 8,000
SALES (est): 3.5MM **Privately Held**
SIC: 5082 3533 Oil field equipment; oil field machinery & equipment

(G-7719)
LANCE EASLEY
Also Called: Easley Welding
330135 E 760 Rd (74059-3266)
PHONE..................405 269-1415
Lance Easley, *Principal*
EMP: 1 **EST:** 2012
SALES (est): 34.6K **Privately Held**
SIC: 7692 Welding repair

(G-7720)
LIGHTFOOT READY MIX LLC
332469 E 780 Rd (74059-8807)
PHONE..................405 714-5539
EMP: 2
SALES (est): 117.3K **Privately Held**
SIC: 1442 1771 Construction Sand/Gravel Concrete Contractor

(G-7721)
RALPHS PACKING COMPANY
500 W Freeman Ave (74059-2200)
P.O. Box 249 (74059-0249)
PHONE..................405 547-2464
Gary Crane, *President*
Sue Blackburn, *Treasurer*
Tess Crane, *Admin Sec*
EMP: 37
SQ FT: 9,800
SALES (est): 5.2MM **Privately Held**
WEB: www.ralphspacking.com
SIC: 2011 5142 Meat packing plants; packaged frozen goods; vegetables, frozen

(G-7722)
SMITHS BACKHOE AND UTILITY
1190 S Fairgrounds (74059)
PHONE..................405 202-7056
James Smith, *Owner*
EMP: 4
SALES (est): 399K **Privately Held**
SIC: 3531 Backhoes

(G-7723)
STRING UP MACHINE INC
10819 S Rose Rd (74059-3660)
PHONE..................936 349-0419
EMP: 2
SALES (est): 152.5K **Privately Held**
SIC: 3599 Machine shop, jobbing & repair

(G-7724)
TECH INC
511 E Highway 33 (74059-4129)
P.O. Box 525 (74059-0525)
PHONE..................405 547-8324
Jay Littau, *President*
Roger Gilbert, *Corp Secy*
EMP: 10
SQ FT: 7,500
SALES: 1MM **Privately Held**
SIC: 3544 3089 3086 5063 Forms (molds), for foundry & plastics working machinery; industrial molds; molding primary plastic; plastics foam products; electrical supplies

Perry
Noble County

(G-7725)
5R SERVICES
26700 County Road 110 (73077-9255)
PHONE..................580 370-0222
Kristen Rodebush, *Principal*
EMP: 1
SALES (est): 49.3K **Privately Held**
SIC: 7692 Welding repair

(G-7726)
ANVIL LAND AND PROPERTIES INC
1959 W Fir St (73077-5803)
P.O. Box 66 (73077-0066)
PHONE..................580 336-4402
Edwin Malzahn, *President*
Rick Johnson, *Corp Secy*
Donald Malzahn, *Vice Pres*
EMP: 4
SQ FT: 20,000
SALES (est): 953.7K
SALES (corp-wide): 3.1B **Publicly Held**
SIC: 6512 2353 2329 Nonresidential building operators; hats, caps & millinery; men's & boys' sportswear & athletic clothing
HQ: The Charles Machine Works Inc
1959 W Fir St
Perry OK 73077
580 572-2693

(G-7727)
BIG J TANK TRUCK SERVICE INC
1705 N 15th St (73077-1238)
PHONE..................580 336-3501
Scott Johnson, *President*
Mike Johnson, *Vice Pres*
EMP: 8
SALES (est): 510K **Privately Held**
SIC: 3713 7353 Tank truck bodies; oil field equipment, rental or leasing

(G-7728)
CHARLES MACHINE WORKS INC (HQ)
1959 W Fir St (73077-5803)
P.O. Box 1902 (73077-1900)
PHONE..................580 572-2693
Rick Johnson, *CEO*
Cliff Coffin, *General Mgr*
Roger Layne, *Principal*
Chris Gambrell, *Regional Mgr*
Anthony Wayne, *Vice Pres*
▼ **EMP:** 1900
SQ FT: 923,000
SALES: 760MM
SALES (corp-wide): 3.1B **Publicly Held**
WEB: www.ditchwitch.com
SIC: 3531 3541 3829 3546 Construction machinery; drilling & boring machines; measuring & controlling devices; power-driven handtools
PA: The Toro Company
8111 Lyndale Ave S
Bloomington MN 55420
952 888-8801

(G-7729)
CUSTOM MSER LVSTK PRE MIX WHSE
Also Called: Custom Mser Lvstk Pre-Mix Whse
9 Memorial Dr (73077)
PHONE..................580 336-2053
Carl Conrad, *Owner*
EMP: 2
SALES (est): 94.5K **Privately Held**
SIC: 2048 Feed supplements

(G-7730)
DON BETCHAN
19401 County Road 70 (73077-8908)
PHONE..................580 336-5954
Don Betchan, *Owner*
EMP: 1
SALES (est): 70K **Privately Held**
SIC: 1389 Pumping of oil & gas wells

(G-7731)
DUANE DURKEE PUMPING SVC
1916 Lake View Dr (73077-1308)
PHONE..................405 820-3256
Duane Durkee, *Owner*
EMP: 1
SALES (est): 65K **Privately Held**
SIC: 1389 Oil field services

(G-7732)
E-Z DRILL INC (PA)
610 Cedar St (73077-6615)
P.O. Box 517, Stillwater (74076-0517)
PHONE..................405 372-0121
Rick Walstad, *President*
EMP: 5
SQ FT: 30,000
SALES (est): 7.3MM **Privately Held**
SIC: 3531 Construction machinery

(G-7733)
E-Z DRILL INC
321 Ash St (73077-7801)
PHONE..................580 336-9874
Frank Douglas, *Branch Mgr*
EMP: 39
SALES (corp-wide): 7.3MM **Privately Held**
SIC: 3531 Concrete gunning equipment
PA: E-Z Drill, Inc.
610 Cedar St
Perry OK 73077
405 372-0121

(G-7734)
GERALD W DAVIDSON LLC
Also Called: Davidson Oil
621 Delaware St (73077-6609)
P.O. Box 782 (73077-0782)
PHONE..................580 336-9303
Gene Davidson, *Mng Member*
EMP: 1 **EST:** 1954
SALES (est): 214.3K **Privately Held**
SIC: 1311 Crude petroleum production; natural gas production

(G-7735)
GERONIMO MANUFACTURING INC
612 Cedar St (73077-6615)
P.O. Box 109 (73077-0109)
PHONE..................580 336-5707
Gerald Baldwin, *Manager*
EMP: 1 **Privately Held**
SIC: 3199 3842 Safety belts, leather; surgical appliances & supplies

GEOGRAPHIC SECTION

Piedmont - Canadian County (G-7765)

PA: Geronimo Manufacturing Inc
3717 Nw 63rd St Ste 160
Oklahoma City OK 73116

(G-7736)
HORIZON SMOKER COMPANY
Also Called: Horizon Smokers
802 N 15th St (73077-4000)
P.O. Box 737 (73077-0737)
PHONE..................580 336-2400
Roger Davidson, *President*
Steve Thomas, *Office Mgr*
EMP: 12
SALES (est): 1.9MM **Privately Held**
SIC: 3631 Barbecues, grills & braziers (outdoor cooking)

(G-7737)
J & J SOLUTIONS LLC
6990 Independence (73077-9187)
P.O. Box 44 (73077-0044)
PHONE..................580 336-3050
James Votaw, *Principal*
Larry Paschall, *Purch Agent*
Jim Votaw,
▲ **EMP:** 55
SQ FT: 4,000
SALES (est): 14.6MM **Privately Held**
SIC: 1389 Oil field services

(G-7738)
JIMS JEWELRY DESIGN
Also Called: Jim's Jewelry Design
320 N 1st St (73077-6804)
PHONE..................580 336-4066
James F Skluzacek, *Owner*
EMP: 1
SALES (est): 68K **Privately Held**
SIC: 5944 3911 Jewelry stores; jewelry, precious metal

(G-7739)
L M S PRODUCTS INC
Also Called: Larry's Machine Shop
6500 Independence 164 (73077-9174)
P.O. Box 31 (73077-0031)
PHONE..................580 336-3555
Larry Jarrett, *President*
Daniel Jarrett, *Vice Pres*
Carole Jarrett, *Admin Sec*
▲ **EMP:** 9
SQ FT: 12,000
SALES (est): 1.4MM **Privately Held**
SIC: 3599 3533 Machine shop, jobbing & repair; oil & gas field machinery

(G-7740)
LAMAMCO DRILLING COMPANY
13250 Deer Rdg (73077-8831)
PHONE..................580 336-3524
EMP: 3
SALES (est): 240K **Privately Held**
SIC: 1311 1382 1389 Crude Petroleum/Natural Gas Production Oil/Gas Exploration Services Oil/Gas Field Services

(G-7741)
PERRY DAILEY JOURNAL INC
714 Delaware St (73077-6425)
P.O. Box 311 (73077-0311)
PHONE..................580 336-2222
Phillip Reid, *President*
EMP: 9
SQ FT: 5,000
SALES (est): 564.2K **Privately Held**
WEB: www.pdjnews.com
SIC: 2711 Newspapers, publishing & printing

(G-7742)
PERRY READY MIX INC
910 Ash St (73077-6235)
P.O. Box 856 (73077-0856)
PHONE..................580 336-5575
Lloyd I Evans, *Principal*
EMP: 300
SALES (est): 24.6MM
SALES (corp-wide): 100.1MM **Privately Held**
SIC: 3273 Ready-mixed concrete
PA: Evans & Associates Enterprises, Inc.
3320 N 14th St
Ponca City OK 74601
580 765-6693

(G-7743)
RN CONCRETE PRODUCTS
4600 Independence (73077-9137)
PHONE..................405 564-3020
Richard Crow, *Principal*
EMP: 2
SALES (est): 409.1K **Privately Held**
SIC: 3272 Concrete products, precast

(G-7744)
RUPP DRILLING INC
1701 Parklane St (73077-1236)
P.O. Box 946 (73077-0946)
PHONE..................580 336-4717
Robert Rupp, *President*
Dorothy Rupp, *Corp Secy*
EMP: 2 **EST:** 1949
SALES (est): 184.3K **Privately Held**
SIC: 1381 Drilling oil & gas wells

(G-7745)
SOUTHERN PLAINS ENRGY SVCS LLC
13200 John Wayne (73077-9375)
PHONE..................580 336-7444
Rory Jett, *President*
EMP: 14
SALES (est): 2MM **Privately Held**
SIC: 1389 Servicing oil & gas wells

(G-7746)
SPLASH MARINE LLC
Also Called: Buster Boats
321 Ash St (73077-7801)
PHONE..................580 336-9874
Frank Douglas, *Manager*
EMP: 2
SALES (corp-wide): 680.6K **Privately Held**
SIC: 3732 5551 Fishing boats: lobster, crab, oyster, etc.: small; boat dealers
PA: Splash Marine, Llc
4615 W Lakeview Rd
Stillwater OK

(G-7747)
STILLWATER MILLING COMPANY LLC
Also Called: A & M Feeds
205 Gene Taylor St (73077-6618)
PHONE..................580 369-2354
Amy Shenold, *Manager*
EMP: 11
SALES (corp-wide): 100.7MM **Privately Held**
SIC: 5191 2875 5153 Feed; fertilizers, mixing only; grain elevators
PA: Stillwater Milling Company, Llc
512 E 6th Ave
Stillwater OK 74074
405 372-2766

(G-7748)
SUBSITE LLC
Also Called: Subsite Electronics
1950 W Fir St (73077-5803)
P.O. Box 66 (73077-0066)
PHONE..................580 572-3700
Tiffany Sewell-Howard, *President*
Robert Raymond, *Mfg Mgr*
Brad Marshall, *Research*
Jeff Hollas, *Engineer*
Brian McRae, *Engineer*
▼ **EMP:** 200
SQ FT: 37,500
SALES: 46MM
SALES (corp-wide): 3.1B **Publicly Held**
SIC: 3546 7371 Power-driven handtools; computer software development & applications
HQ: The Charles Machine Works Inc
1959 W Fir St
Perry OK 73077
580 572-2693

(G-7749)
THREE SANDS OIL INC
633 Delaware St (73077-6635)
P.O. Box 853 (73077-0853)
PHONE..................580 336-2410
Harry Hughes, *President*
Tim Dolezal, *Corp Secy*
EMP: 4
SQ FT: 10,000
SALES (est): 440K **Privately Held**
SIC: 1311 Crude petroleum production; natural gas production

(G-7750)
WHITEROCK OIL & GAS LLC
202 E Tower Ave (73077-2615)
PHONE..................580 307-5565
EMP: 2
SALES (est): 144.3K **Privately Held**
SIC: 1389 Oil & gas field services

Picher
Ottawa County

(G-7751)
TEETERS ASPHALT & MATERIALS
57221 E 30th Rd (74360)
P.O. Box 414, Quapaw (74363-0414)
PHONE..................918 673-1243
Steven Teeter, *Partner*
Roy Teeter, *Partner*
Steve Teeter, *Partner*
EMP: 5
SQ FT: 400
SALES: 1MM **Privately Held**
SIC: 2951 Paving mixtures

Piedmont
Canadian County

(G-7752)
A1 QUALITY WELDING
Also Called: A-1 Quality Welding Service
108 L And M Dr Sw (73078-9341)
PHONE..................405 373-0066
Wayne Waggoner, *Owner*
EMP: 2
SALES (est): 92.5K **Privately Held**
SIC: 7692 Welding repair

(G-7753)
AIRLOCK POOL COVERS INC
5703 Ridgeroad Dr Nw (73078-9727)
PHONE..................405 373-4040
Dwaine Phillips, *Principal*
EMP: 3 **EST:** 2008
SALES (est): 148K **Privately Held**
SIC: 3443 Airlocks

(G-7754)
AMERICAN STREET ROD CO
428 Ash Ne (73078-8519)
PHONE..................405 373-0376
Terry Harris, *Owner*
EMP: 3 **EST:** 1986
SALES (est): 291.3K **Privately Held**
SIC: 3711 Automobile assembly, including specialty automobiles

(G-7755)
BARAY ENTERPRISES INC
Also Called: Nance Precast Concrete Pdts
5601 Washington Ave E (73078-8817)
P.O. Box 116 (73078-0116)
PHONE..................405 373-1800
Randy A Nance, *President*
Ray Nance, *Vice Pres*
Stanley R Nance II, *Vice Pres*
Travis Stanley, *Project Mgr*
Brandon Gauthe, *Sales Mgr*
EMP: 30
SQ FT: 10,000
SALES (est): 7.3MM **Privately Held**
SIC: 3272 3271 Manhole covers or frames, concrete; blocks, concrete: landscape or retaining wall

(G-7756)
BELL & KINLEY COMPANY
13248 Nw Expressway (73078-8918)
PHONE..................405 373-5356
Eric Bell, *Partner*
J L Kinley, *Partner*
EMP: 3
SQ FT: 450
SALES (est): 270K **Privately Held**
SIC: 1311 Crude petroleum production; natural gas production

(G-7757)
CHESHIRE PORTABLE WELDING
13001 N Cemetery Rd (73078)
PHONE..................405 373-4669
Kent Cheshire, *Principal*
EMP: 4 **EST:** 2001
SALES (est): 362.1K **Privately Held**
SIC: 3441 Fabricated structural metal

(G-7758)
COOKS CONTACT WELDING INC
Also Called: Cook's Portable Shop Welding
14832 Nw Expressway (73078-9336)
PHONE..................405 373-0059
Richard Cook, *Owner*
EMP: 1
SALES (est): 78.8K **Privately Held**
SIC: 7692 Welding repair

(G-7759)
DAILY DENTAL SOLUTIONS INC
1213 Piedmont Rd N # 108 (73078-9709)
P.O. Box 594 (73078-0594)
PHONE..................405 373-3299
Katherine Jackson, *President*
EMP: 3
SALES (est): 180K **Privately Held**
SIC: 2711 Newspapers, publishing & printing

(G-7760)
DOLESE BROS CO
6013 Edmond Rd Ne (73078-9733)
PHONE..................405 373-2102
Roger Dolese, *Owner*
EMP: 5
SALES (corp-wide): 8.5MM **Privately Held**
SIC: 3273 Ready-mixed concrete
PA: Dolese Bros. Co.
20 Nw 13th St
Oklahoma City OK 73103
405 235-2311

(G-7761)
ENVIRO LOG OPERATING LLC
15305 N Richland Rd (73078-9451)
P.O. Box 598 (73078-0598)
PHONE..................405 834-1417
Mike Mayfield,
EMP: 2
SALES (est): 295.5K **Privately Held**
SIC: 1389 Oil field services

(G-7762)
HALL PAINTING AND WALL CVG
3555 Washington Ave E (73078-0029)
PHONE..................405 373-2724
M J Hall, *Owner*
EMP: 1
SALES (est): 94K **Privately Held**
SIC: 3081 Floor or wall covering, unsupported plastic

(G-7763)
HEARTLAND ENERGY OPTIONS LLC
Also Called: Heartland Mobility
4981 Moffat Rd Nw (73078-8162)
PHONE..................405 600-6009
Justin Steckman, *General Mgr*
EMP: 7
SQ FT: 12,750
SALES (est): 407.5K **Privately Held**
SIC: 3716 7532 3711 Recreational van conversion (self-propelled), factory basis; van conversion; ambulances (motor vehicles), assembly of

(G-7764)
J&C INDUSTRIES INC
3582 Southridge Ln Ne (73078-4265)
PHONE..................405 473-7834
Jimmy Maness, *Principal*
EMP: 2
SALES (est): 92.6K **Privately Held**
SIC: 3999 Manufacturing industries

(G-7765)
JD SUPPLY & MFG
5974 Tracy Ln (73078-9048)
PHONE..................405 517-3745
Keith Welch, *Owner*
EMP: 2

Piedmont - Canadian County (G-7766)

SALES (est): 131.5K **Privately Held**
SIC: 3728 5088 Aircraft parts & equipment; aircraft & parts

(G-7766)
KOHNS DOORS & WOODWORKING LLC
1608 Rolling Ct Nw (73078-9300)
P.O. Box 306 (73078-0306)
PHONE..................405 596-8245
Raymond L Kohn, *Administration*
EMP: 1
SALES (est): 158.1K **Privately Held**
SIC: 2431 Millwork

(G-7767)
NAYFA PUBLICATIONS INC
Also Called: Piedmont-Surrey Gazette
414 Piedmont Rd N Ste A (73078-9545)
PHONE..................405 373-1616
Paula Nayfa, *Principal*
EMP: 2
SALES (est): 12.2K **Privately Held**
SIC: 2711 Newspapers: publishing only, not printed on site

(G-7768)
PEAK CEMENT PIEDMONT
1823 Susanna Rd Ne (73078-6807)
PHONE..................405 373-2086
Duane Peak, *Owner*
EMP: 1 EST: 1973
SALES (est): 56.1K **Privately Held**
SIC: 3241 Natural cement

(G-7769)
RBS PET PRODUCTS
320 Piedmont Rd N (73078-9525)
P.O. Box 547 (73078-0547)
PHONE..................405 373-0235
William Means, *Owner*
EMP: 3
SQ FT: 3,000
SALES (est): 190K **Privately Held**
SIC: 3999 2047 5199 Pet supplies; dog & cat food; pet supplies

(G-7770)
SKYKAE KREATIONS
3336 Smokey Bend Rdg (73078-9384)
PHONE..................405 250-4055
Chad Walker, *Principal*
EMP: 1
SALES (est): 71.1K **Privately Held**
WEB: www.skykae.com
SIC: 2431 Millwork

(G-7771)
SNEAKY TS SALSA LLC
1011 Buchanan Ave (73078-8062)
PHONE..................405 323-7244
Joseph Hargus, *Administration*
EMP: 3
SALES (est): 146K **Privately Held**
SIC: 2099 Dips, except cheese & sour cream based

(G-7772)
SUPERIOR SOLUTIONS WELDING & F
1251 Golden Hills Ln (73078-8068)
PHONE..................405 623-0104
Joshua Galliher,
EMP: 2
SALES (est): 74.4K **Privately Held**
SIC: 2899 7389 Fluxes: brazing, soldering, galvanizing & welding;

(G-7773)
VALOR INDUSTRIES LLC
12005 Nw 135th St (73078-8988)
PHONE..................580 301-3805
Justin Rosalez, *Principal*
EMP: 2 EST: 2018
SALES (est): 87.2K **Privately Held**
SIC: 3999 Manufacturing industries

Pocasset
Grady County

(G-7774)
BAROID DRILLING FLUIDS
300 S Main St (73079-9517)
P.O. Box 934 (73079-0934)
PHONE..................405 459-6611
Carrie Farmer, *Principal*
EMP: 2
SALES (est): 131.4K **Privately Held**
SIC: 1389 Oil field services

(G-7775)
CLEARPOINT CHEMICALS LLC
131 E Cardinal St (73079-9522)
PHONE..................405 320-1719
Jemar Williams, *Manager*
EMP: 2
SALES (corp-wide): 15.7MM **Privately Held**
SIC: 1389 Oil field services
PA: Clearpoint Chemicals Llc
18300 Scenic Highway 98 F
Fairhope AL 36532
251 929-1772

(G-7776)
HALLIBURTON COMPANY
Also Called: Halliburton Energy Services
Hwy 81 N (73079)
P.O. Box 934 (73079-0934)
PHONE..................405 459-6611
Carrie Farmer, *Manager*
EMP: 8 **Publicly Held**
SIC: 5084 1389 Industrial machinery & equipment; oil field services
PA: Halliburton Company
3000 N Sam Houston Pkwy E
Houston TX 77032

(G-7777)
HALLIBURTON COMPANY
300 N Main St (73079)
P.O. Box 934 (73079-0934)
PHONE..................405 459-6611
EMP: 4 **Publicly Held**
SIC: 1389 Oil field services
PA: Halliburton Company
3000 N Sam Houston Pkwy E
Houston TX 77032

(G-7778)
RICHARD WELDING
240 Adams Cir (73079-9511)
PHONE..................405 459-6717
EMP: 1
SALES (est): 35.9K **Privately Held**
SIC: 7692 Welding repair

Pocola
Le Flore County

(G-7779)
412 COMICS LLC
707 Howard St (74902-3535)
PHONE..................479 414-0891
Franklin Fentress, *CEO*
EMP: 1
SALES (est): 34.5K **Privately Held**
SIC: 2731 7389 Books: publishing only;

(G-7780)
AMERICAN SIGNWORX
203 N Pocola Blvd (74902-3126)
PHONE..................479 650-4562
Wes Lashley, *Owner*
EMP: 4 EST: 2015
SALES (est): 280K **Privately Held**
SIC: 3993 2759 Signs & advertising specialties; screen printing

(G-7781)
BRENTS WELDING LLC
900 Gregory Ave (74902-1831)
PHONE..................918 413-1318
Brent H Bingley, *Principal*
EMP: 1
SALES (est): 50K **Privately Held**
SIC: 7692 Welding repair

(G-7782)
CENTRAL GLASS PRODUCTS INC
405 W Hamon Ave (74902-3702)
PHONE..................918 436-2401
Glynn Underwood, *President*
Dewayne Underwood, *Vice Pres*
EMP: 15
SQ FT: 50,000
SALES (est): 500K **Privately Held**
SIC: 3231 Products of purchased glass

(G-7783)
JOHNSON CONTROLS
1507b Highway 112 N (74902-3319)
PHONE..................918 626-3773
Dave Garraat, *Manager*
EMP: 5 **Privately Held**
SIC: 3669 Emergency alarms
HQ: Johnson Controls Fire Protection Lp
6600 Congress Ave
Boca Raton FL 33487
561 988-7200

(G-7784)
PARKER ENERGY SERVICES CO
401 Rose Dr (74902-3379)
PHONE..................918 626-4982
EMP: 2
SALES (est): 90K **Privately Held**
SIC: 1389 Oil field services

(G-7785)
PEROXYCHEM LLC
900 Highway 112 N (74902-3340)
PHONE..................918 626-8020
Randall Davidson, *Technical Staff*
EMP: 11
SALES (corp-wide): 2.6B **Privately Held**
SIC: 2819 Peroxides, hydrogen peroxide; sodium & potassium compounds, exc. bleaches, alkalies, alum.
HQ: Peroxychem Llc
1 Cmmrce Sq 2005 Mkt St
Philadelphia PA 19103
267 422-2400

(G-7786)
SPRAY-RITE INC
201 Durham (74902-3220)
P.O. Box 10063, Fort Smith AR (72917-0063)
PHONE..................479 648-3351
Michael C Rusin, *President*
Michael Rusin, *Vice Pres*
▲ EMP: 50 EST: 1977
SQ FT: 150,000
SALES: 7.1MM **Privately Held**
SIC: 3471 3479 3599 Electroplating & plating; coloring & finishing of aluminum or formed products; coating of metals & formed products; painting of metal products; machine & other job shop work

(G-7787)
STAN-MEL INDUSTRIES INC
Also Called: Garner Packaging
1 Archery Ln (74902-3258)
PHONE..................918 436-0056
Melissa Garner, *President*
EMP: 35
SALES: 6MM **Privately Held**
SIC: 2653 Corrugated boxes, partitions, display items, sheets & pad

(G-7788)
SWEETENS PRFMCE MACHINING INC
2701 S Pocola Blvd (74902)
PHONE..................918 436-9882
Shawn Sweeten, *Owner*
Maranda Sweeten, *Owner*
EMP: 3
SALES (est): 390.6K **Privately Held**
SIC: 3599 Machine shop, jobbing & repair

Ponca City
Kay County

(G-7789)
24 7 MACHINERY LLC
3417 W North Ave (74601-7721)
PHONE..................580 762-8965
Anthony Wyatt, *Principal*
EMP: 2
SALES (est): 238.6K **Privately Held**
SIC: 3569 General industrial machinery

(G-7790)
A & E SATELLITES
100 N 2nd St (74601-4320)
PHONE..................580 363-0931
Allen Kendle, *Owner*
EMP: 5
SALES: 70K **Privately Held**
SIC: 3651 Home entertainment equipment, electronic

(G-7791)
A PLUS PRINTING
119 N 3rd St (74601-4338)
PHONE..................580 765-7752
Mike Culver, *Partner*
Donna Culver, *Partner*
EMP: 4
SALES (est): 260K **Privately Held**
SIC: 2759 2791 2789 2752 Commercial printing; typesetting; bookbinding & related work; commercial printing, lithographic

(G-7792)
A PLUS PRINTING LLC
1113 Rosedale Dr (74604-4630)
PHONE..................580 765-7752
EMP: 2
SALES (est): 107.8K **Privately Held**
SIC: 2752 Commercial printing, offset

(G-7793)
ADVANTAGE GRAPHICS
7981 W Hubbard Rd (74601-8106)
PHONE..................580 363-5734
Dave Powell, *Owner*
EMP: 1
SALES (est): 63.5K **Privately Held**
SIC: 3993 Signs & advertising specialties

(G-7794)
AIR SYSTEM COMPONENTS INC
900 Darr Park Dr Bldg 1 (74601)
PHONE..................580 762-7521
Dain Web, *Branch Mgr*
EMP: 460 **Privately Held**
WEB: www.airsysco.com
SIC: 3585 Air conditioning equipment, complete
HQ: Air System Components, Inc.
605 Shiloh Rd
Plano TX 75074
972 212-4888

(G-7795)
AIRGAS USA LLC
1124 N Waverly St (74601-2128)
PHONE..................580 767-1313
John Rayburn, *Manager*
EMP: 10
SALES (corp-wide): 129.8MM **Privately Held**
SIC: 5085 3548 2813 Industrial supplies; welding apparatus; industrial gases
HQ: Airgas Usa, Llc
259 N Radnor Chester Rd
Radnor PA 19087
610 687-5253

(G-7796)
ANSTINE-MUSGROVE
204 E Grand Ave (74601-4317)
P.O. Box 391 (74602-0391)
PHONE..................580 762-6355
Marvin Musgrove, *President*
Bob Anstine, *Partner*
EMP: 1
SALES (est): 126.3K **Privately Held**
SIC: 1311 Crude petroleum production

GEOGRAPHIC SECTION

Ponca City - Kay County (G-7827)

(G-7797)
APPLAUSE APPAREL
1404 N Pecan Rd (74604-4131)
PHONE..................................580 762-1349
William Ken, *Owner*
Suzanne Ken, *Owner*
EMP: 2
SALES (est): 141.7K **Privately Held**
SIC: 2389 5699 Apparel & accessories; miscellaneous apparel & accessories

(G-7798)
ARCHEIN AEROSPACE LLC
2501 N Waverly St (74601-1122)
PHONE..................................682 499-2150
Michael Kaufhold,
Shelley Wombacher, *Admin Sec*
Kyle Barker,
Rich Cole Chair,
Robert D Moreau,
EMP: 21 **EST:** 2016
SQ FT: 35,000
SALES (est): 2MM **Privately Held**
SIC: 3728 7363 8711 8742 Research & dev by manuf., aircraft parts & auxiliary equip; pilot service, aviation; aviation &/or aeronautical engineering; marketing consulting services; business consulting

(G-7799)
BACK ALLEY BREWERS & MORE LLC
218 E Central Ave (74601)
PHONE..................................580 716-2571
Travis Megee, *Principal*
EMP: 5
SALES (est): 289.7K **Privately Held**
SIC: 2082 Malt beverages

(G-7800)
BLISS INDUSTRIES LLC (PA)
900 E Oakland Ave (74601-7683)
P.O. Box 910 (74602-0910)
PHONE..................................580 765-7787
Paul Gill, *President*
Rick Bliss, *President*
Chad Cook, *President*
Lee Hosey, *President*
Greg Alles, *Principal*
EMP: 73
SQ FT: 37,000
SALES (est): 17MM **Privately Held**
SIC: 3541 Milling machines

(G-7801)
BMI MANAGEMENT INC
Also Called: Resthaven & Sunset
1901 E Hubbard Rd (74604-1210)
PHONE..................................580 762-5659
Steve Houston, *President*
EMP: 5
SALES (est): 239K **Privately Held**
SIC: 6553 3272 Real property subdividers & developers, cemetery lots only; concrete products

(G-7802)
BRAUDRICK PRINTERY
211 N 2nd St (74601-4323)
PHONE..................................405 762-2054
Roger Hall, *Owner*
EMP: 2 **EST:** 2017
SALES (est): 83.9K **Privately Held**
SIC: 2752 Commercial printing, lithographic

(G-7803)
BURGESS TOOL & CUTTER GRINDING
1812 Potomac Dr (74601-2331)
PHONE..................................580 765-0954
EMP: 4 **EST:** 1998
SALES (est): 180K **Privately Held**
SIC: 3599 3545 3544 Mfg Industrial Machinery Mfg Machine Tool Accessories Mfg Dies/Tools/Jigs/Fixtures

(G-7804)
C & R OLFLD PNTG RUSTABOUT SVC
Also Called: C & R Oilfield Service
808 Monument Rd (74604-3917)
PHONE..................................620 272-6699
Cliff Oller, *President*
EMP: 4

SALES (est): 449.6K **Privately Held**
SIC: 1389 1321 Oil field services; liquefied petroleum gases (natural) production

(G-7805)
CENTERLINE INC
2110 N Ash St (74601-1105)
PHONE..................................580 762-5451
Mike Engster, *CEO*
Stephan Engster, *Vice Pres*
Jeff Williams, *Opers Mgr*
Janell Sherrill, *Controller*
Martin Engster, *VP Sales*
▼ **EMP:** 20
SQ FT: 10,000
SALES (est): 3.9MM **Privately Held**
SIC: 3599 Machine & other job shop work

(G-7806)
CLARENCE & LOIS PARKER
300 S Silverdale Ln (74604-7314)
PHONE..................................580 765-8188
Clarence Parker, *Principal*
EMP: 2
SALES (est): 127.4K **Privately Held**
SIC: 2711 Newspapers, publishing & printing

(G-7807)
COMPUSIGN VINYL GRAPHICS
2704 Canterbury Ave (74604-4314)
PHONE..................................580 762-4930
Tom Pardee, *President*
EMP: 1
SALES (est): 61.8K **Privately Held**
SIC: 7336 3993 2542 Graphic arts & related design; signs & advertising specialties; partitions & fixtures, except wood

(G-7808)
CONOCO INC
100 S Pine St (74601)
PHONE..................................580 767-3456
Frankie Wood Black, *Principal*
EMP: 8
SALES (est): 1.2MM **Privately Held**
SIC: 2911 Petroleum refining

(G-7809)
CONTINENTAL CARBON COMPANY
1006 E Oakland Ave (74601-7675)
PHONE..................................580 763-8100
Gary Tipton, *Opers Mgr*
Janet Handwerk, *Safety Mgr*
John Luton, *Mfg Staff*
Asish Adhikary, *Manager*
EMP: 119 **Privately Held**
SIC: 2895 3624 Carbon black; carbon & graphite products
HQ: Continental Carbon Company
  16850 Park Row
  Houston TX 77084
  281 647-3700

(G-7810)
COOKSHACK INC
2405 Sykes Blvd (74601-1111)
PHONE..................................580 765-3669
Stuart Powell, *CEO*
Ed De Aguiar Jr, *Vice Pres*
Mark Ellis, *Treasurer*
Donna Ellis, *Admin Sec*
▼ **EMP:** 30 **EST:** 1957
SQ FT: 11,000
SALES (est): 9.1MM **Privately Held**
SIC: 3556 Smokers, food processing equipment

(G-7811)
CREATIVE CABINETS
126 E Hartford Ave (74601-1507)
PHONE..................................580 762-9500
Dale Conner, *Owner*
EMP: 5
SALES (est): 158K **Privately Held**
SIC: 2434 Wood kitchen cabinets

(G-7812)
CREATIVE MONOGRAMMING EMB
108 N 2nd St (74601-4320)
PHONE..................................580 762-6694
Jennifer Glenn, *Owner*
EMP: 2

SALES (est): 211.3K **Privately Held**
SIC: 3552 Embroidery machines

(G-7813)
CSE BLISS MANUFACTURING LLC
1415 W Summit Ave (74601-3030)
P.O. Box 910 (74602-0910)
PHONE..................................580 749-4895
Rick Bliss,
Martin Berardi,
EMP: 8
SALES (est): 305K
SALES (corp-wide): 8.5MM **Privately Held**
SIC: 3549 Cutting & slitting machinery
PA: Mber Ventures, Inc.
  61 Depot St
  Buffalo NY 14206
  716 855-1555

(G-7814)
CUSTOM MECHANICAL EQUIPMENT
Also Called: C M E
2101 Hall Blvd (74601-2116)
PHONE..................................262 642-9803
Richard Pitz, *President*
EMP: 27
SALES (est): 4.7MM **Privately Held**
SIC: 1711 3585 Mechanical contractor; air conditioning condensers & condensing units

(G-7815)
CUSTOM POWDER COATING & DUSTLE
2101 Hall Blvd (74601-2116)
PHONE..................................580 382-8000
EMP: 2 **EST:** 2016
SALES (est): 97.7K **Privately Held**
SIC: 3479 Metal coating & allied service

(G-7816)
D & P TANK SERVICE INC (PA)
3833 Highway 60 (74604-5584)
P.O. Box 987 (74602-0987)
PHONE..................................580 762-4526
George W Pease III, *President*
Brad Irons, *Corp Secy*
Rod Hartness, *Vice Pres*
EMP: 6
SQ FT: 2,500
SALES (est): 4.3MM **Privately Held**
WEB: www.dptank.com
SIC: 7349 1389 Cleaning service, industrial or commercial; haulage, oil field

(G-7817)
D & P TANK SERVICE INC
1000 S Pine St (74601-7509)
P.O. Box 987 (74602-0987)
PHONE..................................580 762-4526
Brad Irons, *Branch Mgr*
EMP: 30
SALES (est): 1MM
SALES (corp-wide): 4.3MM **Privately Held**
SIC: 1389 Haulage, oil field
PA: D & P Tank Service, Inc.
  3833 Highway 60
  Ponca City OK 74604
  580 762-4526

(G-7818)
D & S DISTRIBUTING
520 N Elm St (74601-3913)
PHONE..................................580 763-3773
Susan Emery, *Principal*
EMP: 2
SALES (est): 14K **Privately Held**
SIC: 3843 Dental equipment & supplies

(G-7819)
DANCEY-MEADOR PUBLISHING CO
118 N Oak St (74601-4238)
PHONE..................................580 762-9359
Dean Meador, *President*
EMP: 3

SALES (est): 1.2MM **Privately Held**
SIC: 7311 7374 7371 2741 Advertising agencies; computer graphics service; software programming applications; miscellaneous publishing; commercial printing, lithographic

(G-7820)
DIG IT ROCKS LLC
638 E Furguson Ave (74601-8011)
P.O. Box 2557 (74602-2557)
PHONE..................................580 362-6211
Eddie Whitfield, *Principal*
EMP: 1 **EST:** 2001
SALES (est): 78.8K **Privately Held**
SIC: 1222 Underground mining, semibituminous

(G-7821)
DOLESE BROS CO
1300 W Cowboy Hill Rd (74601-7825)
P.O. Box 84 (74602-0084)
PHONE..................................580 761-0022
Jeffery Lewis, *Branch Mgr*
EMP: 5
SALES (corp-wide): 8.5MM **Privately Held**
SIC: 3273 Ready-mixed concrete
PA: Dolese Bros. Co.
  20 Nw 13th St
  Oklahoma City OK 73103
  405 235-2311

(G-7822)
DORADA POULTRY LLC
Also Called: Dorada Foods
2000 Hall Blvd (74601-2107)
PHONE..................................580 718-4700
Ed Sanchez, *Mng Member*
EMP: 26
SALES (est): 8.8MM **Privately Held**
WEB: www.lopezfoods.com
SIC: 2015 Chicken slaughtering & processing

(G-7823)
DR PEPPER CO
1200 N Union St (74601-2559)
P.O. Box 1783 (74602-1783)
PHONE..................................580 765-6468
EMP: 2
SALES (est): 58.3K **Privately Held**
SIC: 2086 Soft drinks: packaged in cans, bottles, etc.

(G-7824)
DRIVER EXAMINER DIV
1015 W South Ave (74601-5910)
PHONE..................................580 762-1728
Bill Griesel, *Principal*
EMP: 3
SALES (est): 126.1K **Privately Held**
SIC: 2711 Newspapers, publishing & printing

(G-7825)
ENCOMPASS TOOL & MACHINE INC
2402 Sykes Blvd (74601-1179)
PHONE..................................580 762-5800
Paul Maples, *President*
EMP: 37
SQ FT: 20,000
SALES (est): 3.8MM **Privately Held**
SIC: 3544 Forms (molds), for foundry & plastics working machinery

(G-7826)
ENGRAVING DESIGNS LLC
7879 Lake Rd (74604-7249)
PHONE..................................580 763-4228
EMP: 2
SALES (est): 85K **Privately Held**
SIC: 2759 Commercial printing

(G-7827)
EVANS & ASSOCIATES CNSTR CO
3320 N 14th St (74601-1036)
P.O. Box 30 (74602-0030)
PHONE..................................580 765-6693
Linda Brown, *President*
Glen Nickles, *Exec VP*
EMP: 100 **EST:** 1960
SQ FT: 10,000

Ponca City - Kay County (G-7828)   GEOGRAPHIC SECTION

SALES (est): 11MM
SALES (corp-wide): 100.1MM Privately Held
WEB: www.evans-assoc.com
SIC: 1611 2951 1623 Highway & street paving contractor; asphalt paving mixtures & blocks; water, sewer & utility lines
PA: Evans & Associates Enterprises, Inc.
3320 N 14th St
Ponca City OK 74601
580 765-6693

(G-7828)
EVANS & ASSOCIATES ENTPS INC (PA)
3320 N 14th St (74601-1036)
P.O. Box 30 (74602-0030)
PHONE...................580 765-6693
Linda Brown, *President*
Jimmie Bentley, *Vice Pres*
Bruce Evans, *Vice Pres*
Lee Evans, *Vice Pres*
Glen Nickles, *Vice Pres*
EMP: 30
SQ FT: 10,000
SALES (est): 100.1MM Privately Held
SIC: 5032 2951 1442 1611 Brick, stone & related material; asphalt & asphaltic paving mixtures (not from refineries); construction sand mining; gravel mining; highway & street paving contractor; ready-mixed concrete; crude petroleum production; natural gas production

(G-7829)
EVANS ASPHALT CO INC (HQ)
3320 N 14th St (74601-1036)
P.O. Box 30 (74602-0030)
PHONE...................580 765-6693
Linda Brown, *President*
Lloyd L Evans, *Vice Pres*
EMP: 7 **EST:** 1978
SQ FT: 5,000
SALES (est): 1.4MM
SALES (corp-wide): 100.1MM Privately Held
SIC: 3273 Ready-mixed concrete
PA: Evans & Associates Enterprises, Inc.
3320 N 14th St
Ponca City OK 74601
580 765-6693

(G-7830)
GARY SMITH
Also Called: Legend Lighting
2501 N Ash St (74601-1114)
PHONE...................580 762-7575
Gary Smith, *Owner*
▲ **EMP:** 12
SQ FT: 16,000
SALES (est): 667.7K Privately Held
SIC: 3646 3645 Chandeliers, commercial; chandeliers, residential

(G-7831)
GRAPHIX XPRESS
512 N 1st St (74601-4145)
PHONE...................580 765-7324
Fax: 580 765-5807
EMP: 2
SALES (est): 87K Privately Held
SIC: 2396 3993 5199 5136 Screen Printing Mfg Vinyl Signs Whol Advertising Specialities Team Uniforms And Graphic Design Services

(G-7832)
GREENWOOD GROUP INC
2117 N Waverly St (74601-1102)
PHONE...................580 762-2580
Charles Greenwood, *President*
Chuck Greenwood, *Manager*
EMP: 4 Privately Held
SIC: 3721 Aircraft
PA: Greenwood Group, Inc.
2117 N Waverly St
Ponca City OK 74601

(G-7833)
GREER OIL COMPANY
724 Monument Rd (74604-3931)
PHONE...................580 762-6355
Tom Greer, *Partner*
Welema Greer, *Partner*
EMP: 3

SALES (est): 222.5K Privately Held
SIC: 1311 Crude petroleum production; natural gas production

(G-7834)
HAUB OIL AND GAS LLC
135 Road Runner Dr (74604-5169)
PHONE...................580 765-3585
Frederick Haub, *Owner*
EMP: 3
SALES (est): 163.2K Privately Held
SIC: 1311 Crude petroleum & natural gas

(G-7835)
HEAD COUNTRY INC
2116 N Ash St (74601-1105)
PHONE...................580 762-1227
David Gladstone, *Ch of Bd*
Jessica Clement, *Associate*
EMP: 16
SALES (est): 2.5MM Privately Held
SIC: 2032 Canned specialties

(G-7836)
HOLICK FAMILY LLC
201 S Oak St (74601-5136)
PHONE...................580 765-3209
EMP: 2
SALES (est): 90.4K Privately Held
SIC: 2541 Wood partitions & fixtures

(G-7837)
INDUSTRIAL EQUIPMENT SERVICES
Also Called: I E S Raglin
1809 Princeton Ave (74604-2000)
PHONE...................580 765-5544
Larry Raglin, *Owner*
Diana Henry, *Office Mgr*
EMP: 1
SALES (est): 400K Privately Held
SIC: 1389 Oil & gas wells: building, repairing & dismantling

(G-7838)
IVERS WELDING AND MACHINE SHOP
715 S 1st St (74601-6234)
PHONE...................580 765-4882
Greg Ivers, *Owner*
EMP: 1 **EST:** 1971
SQ FT: 4,000
SALES (est): 50K Privately Held
SIC: 7692 Welding repair

(G-7839)
JASON AND RICKY LLC
1415 W Summit Ave (74601-3030)
P.O. Box 1332 (74602-1332)
PHONE...................580 749-4895
Rick Bliss, *CEO*
Jason Bliss, *President*
▼ **EMP:** 2 **EST:** 2016
SALES (est): 183.8K Privately Held
SIC: 3549 Cutting & slitting machinery

(G-7840)
JOHNDROW HOME IMPROVEMENT
Also Called: Johndrow Termite & Pest Ctrl
710 S 1st St (74601-6233)
P.O. Box 1847 (74602-1847)
PHONE...................580 762-4000
James Johndrow, *Owner*
EMP: 1
SALES (est): 100K Privately Held
SIC: 7342 5211 3442 Termite control; windows, storm: wood or metal; metal doors, sash & trim

(G-7841)
JUPITER SULPHUR LLC
200 Jupiter Pkwy (74601-7692)
PHONE...................580 762-1130
Doug McCleary,
EMP: 5 **EST:** 1999
SALES (est): 968.8K Privately Held
SIC: 2819 Industrial inorganic chemicals
HQ: Tessenderlo Kerley, Inc.
2255 N 44th St Ste 300
Phoenix AZ 85008
602 889-8300

(G-7842)
K & C MANUFACTURING INC
1025 N Waverly St (74601-2232)
P.O. Box 63, Newkirk (74647-0063)
PHONE...................580 362-2979
Kirk Brown, *Owner*
Walter Kirk Brown, *Principal*
Angela Steiner, *CFO*
EMP: 5
SALES (est): 865.9K Privately Held
SIC: 3089 Injection molding of plastics

(G-7843)
KB ENTERPRISE LLC
3408 Crown St (74604-1309)
PHONE...................580 789-0119
Kelsey Wagner,
EMP: 1
SALES (est): 106K Privately Held
SIC: 3429 Aircraft & marine hardware, inc. pulleys & similar items

(G-7844)
LEGACY SIGNS
2208 W South Ave (74601-8643)
PHONE...................580 762-2288
Casey E McClaskey, *Owner*
EMP: 1
SALES (est): 46K Privately Held
SIC: 3993 Signs & advertising specialties

(G-7845)
LINDSAY MANUFACTURING INC (PA)
Also Called: Valet
3 Darr Park Dr (74601-1185)
P.O. Box 1708 (74602-1708)
PHONE...................580 762-2457
Winston Lindsay, *CEO*
Edward W Lindsay Jr, *President*
Paul J Seeley, *Corp Secy*
Edward W Lindsay Sr, *Vice Pres*
Kim Wade, *Purchasing*
▲ **EMP:** 49 **EST:** 1956
SQ FT: 120,000
SALES (est): 7.4MM Privately Held
WEB: www.lindsaymfg.com
SIC: 3635 3589 Electric sweeper; vacuum cleaners & sweepers, electric: industrial

(G-7846)
LOCAL TELEPHONE DIRECTORY
118 N Oak St Ste 4 (74601-4238)
PHONE...................580 762-9359
Dean Meador, *President*
Ron Sweigert, *Vice Pres*
EMP: 5
SALES: 900K Privately Held
SIC: 2741 Directories, telephone: publishing only, not printed on site

(G-7847)
M J & H FABRICATION INC
Also Called: MJ&h Fabrication
2120 Hall Blvd (74601-2115)
PHONE...................580 749-5339
Gary Harvey, *President*
EMP: 10
SALES (est): 21.1MM Privately Held
SIC: 3443 Tank towers, metal plate

(G-7848)
MCDONALD ELECTRIC UTILITY SVCS
904 S Waverly St (74601)
PHONE...................580 767-8845
EMP: 7
SALES (est): 520K Privately Held
SIC: 3699 Mfg Electrical Equipment/Supplies

(G-7849)
MERTZ MANUFACTURING INC
1701 N Waverly St (74601-2141)
P.O. Box 150 (74602-0151)
PHONE...................580 762-5646
Bob Hengen, *Plant Mgr*
Marilyn Dewey, *Purch Mgr*
Lindy Merz, *Purchasing*
Roy Heath, *Engrg Dir*
Robert Vickery, *CFO*
▲ **EMP:** 301
SQ FT: 150,000

SALES (est): 60MM Privately Held
WEB: www.mertzok.com
SIC: 3441 Fabricated structural metal
PA: Mfg Holdings, Inc.
1701 N Waverly St
Ponca City OK 74601

(G-7850)
METAL FAB INC
2200 N Ash St (74601-1107)
PHONE...................580 762-2421
Greg Neisen, *President*
EMP: 2
SQ FT: 1,200
SALES (est): 160K Privately Held
SIC: 3441 7692 3469 3446 Fabricated structural metal; welding repair; metal stampings; architectural metalwork; sheet metalwork; fabricated plate work (boiler shop)

(G-7851)
MICHEAL T ROBINSON
6491 E Tower Rd (74604-6843)
PHONE...................580 767-9414
Michael Robinson, *Owner*
EMP: 1
SALES (est): 70.1K Privately Held
SIC: 1442 Construction sand & gravel

(G-7852)
MID-AMERICA DOOR COMPANY
1001 W Hartford Ave (74601-1131)
PHONE...................580 765-9994
Martin Gendreau, *Co-President*
Maxime Gendreau, *Co-President*
Carl Christensen, *CFO*
Michael Curfman, *Sales Mgr*
▲ **EMP:** 90
SQ FT: 170,000
SALES (est): 18.8MM
SALES (corp-wide): 24.9MM Privately Held
SIC: 3442 5072 Garage doors, overhead: metal; rolling doors for industrial buildings or warehouses, metal; hardware
HQ: Garaga Inc
8500 25e Av
Saint-Georges QC G6A 1
418 227-2828

(G-7853)
MITCHCO FABRICATION INC
2104 N Ash St (74601-1105)
P.O. Box 2626 (74602-2626)
PHONE...................580 762-0256
George M Garrity III, *President*
Deanna Garrity, *Corp Secy*
EMP: 5
SQ FT: 25,000
SALES (est): 600K Privately Held
SIC: 3441 3446 Fabricated structural metal; architectural metalwork

(G-7854)
MOCCASINS OF HOPE SOCIETY
7447 E Coleman Rd (74604-6825)
PHONE...................605 431-3738
J Geraldine Anne Burnett, *Owner*
EMP: 1
SALES (est): 49.1K Privately Held
SIC: 3149 Moccasins

(G-7855)
MOONLIGHT MACHINE LLC
3908 Santa Fe St (74601-1063)
P.O. Box 2516 (74602-2516)
PHONE...................580 718-5111
Cathy Bliss, *Principal*
EMP: 5
SALES (est): 545.7K Privately Held
SIC: 3599 Machine shop, jobbing & repair

(G-7856)
MUSGROVE ENERGY INC
1121 N Prentice Rd (74604-5128)
PHONE...................580 765-7314
EMP: 6
SALES (est): 620K Privately Held
SIC: 1311 Crude Petroleum/Natural Gas Production

GEOGRAPHIC SECTION
Ponca City - Kay County (G-7887)

(G-7857)
NANCY NELSON & ASSOCIATES
Also Called: User Friendly
7879 Lake Rd (74604-7249)
PHONE..................580 765-0115
Nancy Nelson, *Principal*
EMP: 2
SALES (est): 168.7K **Privately Held**
SIC: 5734 7378 2796 2789 Computer & software stores; computer maintenance & repair; platemaking services; bookbinding & related work; commercial printing

(G-7858)
NEISEN FAMILY LLC
2200 N Ash St (74601-1107)
PHONE..................580 762-2421
Greg Neisen,
Debbie Seals,
EMP: 30
SALES (est): 2.3MM **Privately Held**
SIC: 3441 Fabricated structural metal

(G-7859)
NICKLES INDUSTRIES
600 S 1st St (74601-6231)
PHONE..................580 762-9300
Don Johnson, *Principal*
▲ **EMP:** 8
SALES (est): 950.2K **Privately Held**
SIC: 3999 Manufacturing industries

(G-7860)
NORTH CENTRAL PUMP
3912 Santa Fe St (74601-1063)
PHONE..................580 765-9348
Cecil B Sparks Jr, *Owner*
EMP: 1
SALES (est): 126.9K **Privately Held**
SIC: 3599 7699 Machine shop, jobbing & repair; pumps & pumping equipment repair

(G-7861)
OCTOBER GRAPHICS
Also Called: ARA
2300 E Hubbard Rd (74604-1221)
PHONE..................580 765-5089
Thomas Rhodes, *Owner*
Rosanne Rhodes, *Owner*
EMP: 1
SALES (est): 100K **Privately Held**
SIC: 2754 Commercial printing, gravure

(G-7862)
OLD WEST CABINETS INC
122 S Pine St (74601-5218)
PHONE..................580 762-7474
Roger Funkhouser, *Principal*
EMP: 4
SALES (est): 440.2K **Privately Held**
SIC: 2434 Wood kitchen cabinets

(G-7863)
OPPORTUNITY CENTER INC
Also Called: VILLAGE SCREENPRINT EMBROIDERY
3007 N Union St (74601-7400)
PHONE..................580 765-6782
Julie Grigsba, *Exec Dir*
EMP: 120
SALES: 3MM **Privately Held**
SIC: 8331 2759 2396 3585 Vocational training agency; screen printing; automotive & apparel trimmings; compressors for refrigeration & air conditioning equipment

(G-7864)
P C CONCRETE CO INC
3320 Lake Rd (74604-5006)
P.O. Box 30 (74602-0030)
PHONE..................580 762-1302
Lloyd I Evans, *President*
Linda Brown, *Vice Pres*
Katie Goss, *Asst Sec*
EMP: 300
SQ FT: 10,000
SALES (est): 27.5MM
SALES (corp-wide): 100.1MM **Privately Held**
WEB: www.evans-assoc.com
SIC: 3273 Ready-mixed concrete
PA: Evans & Associates Enterprises, Inc.
3320 N 14th St
Ponca City OK 74601
580 765-6693

(G-7865)
PHILLIPS 66 COMPANY
Also Called: Ponca City Refinery
1000 S Pine St (74601-7509)
P.O. Box 1267 (74602-1267)
PHONE..................580 767-3456
Chundi Cao, *Engineer*
Dale Coffin, *Engineer*
George Paczkowski, *Manager*
Lowry Blakeburn, *Supervisor*
EMP: 9
SALES (corp-wide): 109.5B **Publicly Held**
SIC: 2911 Petroleum refining
HQ: Phillips 66 Company
2331 Citywest Blvd
Houston TX 77042
281 293-6600

(G-7866)
PONCA CITY PUBLISHING CO INC
Also Called: Ponca City News, The
300 N 3rd St (74601-4336)
P.O. Box 191 (74602-0191)
PHONE..................580 765-3311
Thomas Muchmore, *President*
Josh Umholtz, *Publisher*
Kristi Hayes, *Editor*
John Muchmore, *Treasurer*
Clyde Muchmore, *Admin Sec*
EMP: 50 **EST:** 1893
SQ FT: 20,000
SALES (est): 2.8MM **Privately Held**
WEB: www.poncacitynews.com
SIC: 2711 2752 Newspapers, publishing & printing; commercial printing, lithographic

(G-7867)
PONCA MACHINE COMPANY
3913 Santa Fe St (74601-1064)
P.O. Box 1383 (74602-1383)
PHONE..................580 762-1031
Greg Lyons, *Partner*
EMP: 12
SQ FT: 6,500
SALES (est): 2.1MM **Privately Held**
SIC: 3599 Machine shop, jobbing & repair

(G-7868)
PRECISION METAL FAB LLC
2200 N Ash St (74601-1107)
P.O. Box 724 (74602-0724)
PHONE..................580 762-2421
Tom Riley, *Opers Mgr*
Bob Hughes, *Sales Mgr*
Gregory J Neisen, *Mng Member*
Debbie Seals,
EMP: 26
SQ FT: 30,000
SALES (est): 5.8MM **Privately Held**
SIC: 3469 Stamping metal for the trade

(G-7869)
PRECISION TOOL & DIE PONCA CY
2200 N Ash St (74601-1107)
PHONE..................580 762-2421
Gregory Neisen, *President*
Debbie Seals, *Corp Secy*
Doug Flink, *Engineer*
Debbie Scles, *Officer*
Mike Neisen, *Shareholder*
EMP: 7 **EST:** 1978
SQ FT: 10,500
SALES (est): 1MM **Privately Held**
SIC: 3544 3469 Die sets for metal stamping (presses); stamping metal for the trade

(G-7870)
SALTFORK SERVICE
8560 S Ranch Dr (74601-7881)
PHONE..................580 716-1022
James Duane Brown, *Administration*
EMP: 2
SALES (est): 150.5K **Privately Held**
SIC: 2899 Salt

(G-7871)
SAMS WELL SERVICE INC
1216 E Hartford Ave 1b (74601-2060)
P.O. Box 391 (74602-0391)
PHONE..................580 762-6355
Robert Suttles, *President*
Welema Greer, *Corp Secy*
EMP: 12
SALES (est): 884.6K **Privately Held**
SIC: 1311 Crude petroleum & natural gas

(G-7872)
SCHLUMBERGER TECHNOLOGY CORP
1405 N Waverly St (74601-2135)
PHONE..................580 762-2481
Doug Ewing, *Branch Mgr*
EMP: 2 **Publicly Held**
SIC: 1389 Oil field services
HQ: Schlumberger Technology Corp
300 Schlumberger Dr
Sugar Land TX 77478
281 285-8500

(G-7873)
SEISMIC SOURCE COMPANY
2391 E Coleman Rd (74604-5705)
PHONE..................580 762-8233
John Giles, *President*
Beverly Edwards, *Sales Staff*
Chris McGaha, *Director*
EMP: 20
SALES (est): 4MM **Privately Held**
SIC: 3829 Measuring & controlling devices

(G-7874)
SEVEN-UP BOTTLING CO INC
Also Called: 7 Up
1200 N Union St (74601-2559)
P.O. Box 1783 (74602-1783)
PHONE..................580 765-6468
Bill Uhlenhop, *President*
Mark Lott, *Manager*
Ann Heat, *Admin Sec*
EMP: 14
SQ FT: 17,000
SALES: 3.5MM **Privately Held**
SIC: 2086 5149 Bottled & canned soft drinks; groceries & related products

(G-7875)
SMITH INTERNATIONAL INC
1405 N Waverly St (74601-2135)
PHONE..................800 654-6461
Pete Davies, *Manager*
EMP: 12 **Publicly Held**
SIC: 1389 Oil field services
HQ: Smith International, Inc.
1310 Rankin Rd
Houston TX 77073
281 443-3370

(G-7876)
SOONER HOT OIL SERVICE
56 Prospect Rd (74604-6116)
P.O. Box 288 (74602-0288)
PHONE..................580 762-2586
Dorothy Sulks, *Owner*
EMP: 3
SALES (est): 473.1K **Privately Held**
SIC: 1389 Oil field services

(G-7877)
SOURCE FABRICATION LLC
2101 Hall Blvd (74601-2116)
PHONE..................580 762-4114
EMP: 2
SALES (est): 151.8K **Privately Held**
SIC: 3441 Fabricated structural metal

(G-7878)
SOUTHWEST BUSINESS PDTS LLC
1032 N Union St (74601-2555)
P.O. Box 70 (74602-0170)
PHONE..................580 765-4401
Darrel Dye, *Mng Member*
Dennis Dye, *Mng Member*
EMP: 8
SQ FT: 9,600
SALES (est): 1.3MM **Privately Held**
SIC: 5943 2752 5712 Office forms & supplies; commercial printing, offset; office furniture

(G-7879)
SUN MANUFACTURING INC
Also Called: Sun Proecision Machine
2401 N Ash St (74601-1120)
PHONE..................580 765-4786
Kathy Sneath, *Manager*
EMP: 5
SALES (corp-wide): 35MM **Privately Held**
SIC: 3599 Machine shop, jobbing & repair
PA: Sun Manufacturing Inc
1898 N Chouteau St
Orange CA 92865
714 283-3842

(G-7880)
SUPERHEAT FGH SERVICES INC
3287 S 7th St (74601)
PHONE..................580 762-8538
Randy Crawford, *Branch Mgr*
EMP: 3
SALES (corp-wide): 74.8MM **Privately Held**
SIC: 3398 Metal heat treating
PA: Superheat Fgh Services, Inc.
313 Garnet Dr
New Lenox IL 60451
708 478-0205

(G-7881)
T ROWE PIPE LLC
900 E Oakland Ave (74601-7683)
PHONE..................580 765-1500
EMP: 40
SQ FT: 15,000
SALES (est): 9MM **Privately Held**
SIC: 3441 7389 Fabricated Structural Metal

(G-7882)
TESSENDERLO KERLEY INC
200 Jupiter Pkwy (74601-7692)
PHONE..................580 762-1130
Dennis Powers, *Manager*
EMP: 17 **Privately Held**
SIC: 2819 2873 2874 Sodium hyposulfite, sodium hydrosulfite; ammonia & ammonium salts; phosphatic fertilizers
HQ: Tessenderlo Kerley, Inc.
2255 N 44th St Ste 300
Phoenix AZ 85008
602 889-8300

(G-7883)
THOMAS DIST SOLUTIONS LLC
Also Called: Arkansas Surgical Supply-State
2015 N Ash St Ste 113 (74601-1142)
PHONE..................580 304-7741
Vida Thomas, *President*
EMP: 5
SALES: 290K **Privately Held**
SIC: 5047 3841 Medical equipment & supplies; surgical & medical instruments; blood pressure apparatus; needles, suture; surgical knife blades & handles

(G-7884)
TIPTON COMPANY
8725 S R St (74601-7508)
PHONE..................580 762-0800
Raymond Tipton, *Owner*
Patricia Tipton, *Co-Owner*
EMP: 2
SALES (est): 50K **Privately Held**
SIC: 5191 3949 3172 Saddlery; sporting & athletic goods; personal leather goods

(G-7885)
UNICORN WOODWORKING
1901 El Camino St (74604-2711)
PHONE..................580 762-0004
Julie Lawrence, *Principal*
EMP: 2
SALES (est): 306.1K **Privately Held**
SIC: 2431 Millwork

(G-7886)
VISION FABRICATIONS LLC
900 Throup Blvd (74601)
P.O. Box 1630 (74602-1630)
PHONE..................580 304-2444
Shane Burdick,
EMP: 6
SQ FT: 6,000
SALES (est): 823.6K **Privately Held**
SIC: 7692 Welding repair

(G-7887)
WE BUY SCRAP LLC
4423 S Union St (74601-7608)
PHONE..................580 401-3083

Jeffrey Gidcumb, *Mng Member*
EMP: 2 **EST:** 2013
SALES: 82.5K **Privately Held**
SIC: 3533 1382 5093 7389 Oil & gas field machinery; oil & gas exploration services; scrap & waste materials;

(G-7888)
WORLD WEIDNER LLC
1001 Knight St (74601-1093)
P.O. Box 66, Blackwell (74631-0066)
PHONE..................580 765-9999
Oliver Weidner, *Mng Member*
EMP: 6
SALES (est): 368K **Privately Held**
SIC: 3552 3999 Embroidery machines; embroidery kits

Pond Creek
Grant County

(G-7889)
COPPERHEAD COATINGS LLC
419 E Ash St (73766-9757)
PHONE..................580 532-6243
Ford Ay Simpson, *Owner*
EMP: 2
SALES (est): 95.8K **Privately Held**
SIC: 3479 Metal coating & allied service

(G-7890)
HEARTLAND LOCATOR
501 W Broadway St (73766-9645)
PHONE..................580 554-0125
Jerry T Wager, *Owner*
EMP: 1
SALES: 10K **Privately Held**
SIC: 3711 Motor vehicles & car bodies

(G-7891)
STEWART DEFENSE LLC
315 N Biloxi (73766-9501)
P.O. Box 151 (73766-0151)
PHONE..................580 532-6426
Scott Stewart, *Administration*
EMP: 3
SALES (est): 164.9K **Privately Held**
SIC: 3812 Defense systems & equipment

Porter
Wagoner County

(G-7892)
DIVISION ORDER BEGINNINGS (PA)
15248 S 337th East Ave (74454-5764)
PHONE..................918 477-4559
Sherry Robinson, *Mng Member*
EMP: 2
SALES (est): 131K **Privately Held**
SIC: 1311 1382 Natural gas production; oil & gas exploration services

(G-7893)
LILITAD BOATS INC
32558 E 241st St S (74454-5758)
PHONE..................918 482-5992
Mark Childress, *President*
Mary Childress, *Admin Sec*
EMP: 5
SALES (est): 315.1K **Privately Held**
SIC: 3732 Boat building & repairing

(G-7894)
MUSKOGEE SAND COMPANY INC
3202 W 50th St N (74454-2630)
P.O. Box 927, Pryor (74362-0927)
PHONE..................918 683-1766
James A Kemp, *CEO*
Melinda Kemp, *Corp Secy*
EMP: 8
SALES: 950K **Privately Held**
SIC: 1422 1442 5032 Crushed & broken limestone; sand mining; sand, construction

Porum
Muskogee County

(G-7895)
DONALD W COX
Also Called: P&D's
4712 E 308th St S (74455)
P.O. Box 444 (74455-0444)
PHONE..................918 471-8967
Don Cox, *Owner*
EMP: 2
SALES: 40K **Privately Held**
SIC: 2842 Specialty cleaning, polishes & sanitation goods

Poteau
Le Flore County

(G-7896)
BELLE POINT BEVERAGES INC
112 Kerr Ave (74953-5270)
PHONE..................918 649-3921
John Anthony, *Manager*
EMP: 7
SALES (corp-wide): 5.1MM **Privately Held**
SIC: 2086 7363 Carbonated beverages, nonalcoholic: bottled & canned; help supply services
PA: Belle Point Beverages, Inc.
    1 Bellepoint Pl
    Fort Smith AR 72901
    479 782-3511

(G-7897)
BOST WELDING AND FABRICATION
36593 Kerr Mansion Rd (74953-8157)
PHONE..................918 649-1289
Phyllis Bradley, *Principal*
EMP: 1
SALES (est): 37.4K **Privately Held**
SIC: 7692 Welding repair

(G-7898)
C 2 SUPPLY LLC
602 N Broadway St (74953-3524)
PHONE..................918 647-0430
Kevin Sharp, *Mng Member*
Teresa Sharp,
EMP: 3
SALES: 400K **Privately Held**
SIC: 1389 5999 Oil field services; farm equipment & supplies

(G-7899)
CAKES & MORE
804 N Broadway St Ste B (74953-3503)
PHONE..................918 649-0451
Ola Milligan, *Owner*
EMP: 5
SALES (est): 247.6K **Privately Held**
SIC: 2051 5812 Cakes, bakery: except frozen; eating places

(G-7900)
CAVANAL WOODWORKS
4883 Witteville Dr (74953-1932)
PHONE..................909 649-4346
Ben Montoya, *Principal*
EMP: 1
SALES (est): 54.1K **Privately Held**
SIC: 2431 Millwork

(G-7901)
CLAY BENNETT
Also Called: Bennett Drilling
212 Georgia Pl (74953-2004)
PHONE..................918 647-9294
Clay Bennett, *Owner*
EMP: 2
SALES (est): 170.9K **Privately Held**
SIC: 1381 Drilling oil & gas wells

(G-7902)
FALCON MX6 MANUFACTURING LLC
110 S Witte St (74953-4208)
PHONE..................918 647-4433
Falcon Manufacturing, *Principal*
EMP: 3
SALES (est): 256.4K **Privately Held**
WEB: www.gatesbyfalcon.com
SIC: 3999 Manufacturing industries

(G-7903)
FAT ALBERTS MOTOR SPORTS
28871 N Side Ln (74953-8762)
PHONE..................918 647-3069
Brent L Albert, *President*
Denise R Albert, *Admin Sec*
EMP: 4 **EST:** 1997
SALES (est): 799.6K **Privately Held**
WEB: www.fatalberts.com
SIC: 3711 7537 5571 Motor vehicles & car bodies; automotive transmission repair shops; motorcycle dealers

(G-7904)
FREEDOM STONE COMPANY LLC
Also Called: Quarry Services
24075 Picturerock Rd (74953-8279)
PHONE..................918 649-0021
Matt Fisher, *Manager*
Janet Robinett, *Manager*
EMP: 8
SQ FT: 2,400
SALES: 1MM
SALES (corp-wide): 14.5MM **Privately Held**
SIC: 3281 Cut stone & stone products
PA: Creative Mines, Llc
    5840 El Camino Real # 106
    Carlsbad CA 92008
    800 453-7040

(G-7905)
G&G LOGGING LLC
15695 Gap Creek Rd (74953-7343)
PHONE..................918 635-5988
Gwendolyn Williams, *Principal*
EMP: 2
SALES (est): 218.4K **Privately Held**
SIC: 2411 Logging camps & contractors

(G-7906)
GREEN CNTRY TROPHY SCREEN PRTG
Also Called: Skate-Reation
201 Hughes Dr (74953-5417)
P.O. Box 352 (74953-0352)
PHONE..................918 647-2923
Toll Free:..................888 -
Nancy Traywick, *President*
EMP: 2
SQ FT: 14,000
SALES (est): 250K **Privately Held**
SIC: 5999 7999 2396 2395 Trophies & plaques; roller skating rink operation; automotive & apparel trimmings; pleating & stitching

(G-7907)
J GRANTHAM DRILLING INC
305 Dees Rd (74953-5618)
PHONE..................918 647-8926
Jimmy Grantham, *President*
Brian Roberts, *Principal*
EMP: 4
SALES (est): 340K **Privately Held**
SIC: 1781 1381 Water well drilling; drilling oil & gas wells

(G-7908)
MID CONTINENT CONCRETE COMPANY
34500 Us Highway 59 S (74953-9113)
PHONE..................918 647-0550
Kesse Kindrick, *Manager*
EMP: 20
SALES (est): 1MM **Privately Held**
SIC: 3273 4212 5211 Ready-mixed concrete; local trucking, without storage; masonry materials & supplies

(G-7909)
PLAS-TECH INC
28718 State Highway 112 (74953-8773)
P.O. Box 566 (74953-0566)
PHONE..................918 649-0065
Roffi Christenberry, *President*
EMP: 1
SQ FT: 12,000

EMP: 3
SALES: 100K **Privately Held**
SIC: 3089 Injection molding of plastics

(G-7910)
POLYDYNE LLC
28718 State Highway 112 (74953-8773)
P.O. Box 566 (74953-0566)
PHONE..................918 649-0065
Dennis Hope, *Mng Member*
EMP: 10 **EST:** 2015
SALES: 800K **Privately Held**
SIC: 3089 Molding primary plastic

(G-7911)
POTEAU DAILY NEWS
Also Called: Proto Daily News
804 N Broadway St Ste C (74953-3503)
P.O. Box 1237 (74953-1237)
PHONE..................918 647-3335
Samantha Hess, *President*
EMP: 4
SQ FT: 500
SALES (est): 406.2K **Privately Held**
SIC: 2741 2711 Guides: publishing only, not printed on site; shopping news: publishing only, not printed on site; newspapers

(G-7912)
POTEAU PANEL SHOP INCORPORATED
505 N Mckenna St (74953-4018)
P.O. Box 1012 (74953-1012)
PHONE..................918 647-4331
Roy E Mahoney, *President*
Roy Mahoney, *President*
EMP: 5
SQ FT: 6,000
SALES: 500K **Privately Held**
WEB: www.poteau.com
SIC: 3613 3625 3469 Control panels, electric; relays & industrial controls; electronic enclosures, stamped or pressed metal

(G-7913)
SIDEWINDER SIGNS
2300 N Broadway St (74953-2009)
P.O. Box 1145 (74953-1145)
PHONE..................918 647-5306
Billy Spearman, *Principal*
EMP: 2
SALES (est): 134.7K **Privately Held**
SIC: 3993 5099 7312 Signs & advertising specialties; signs, except electric; outdoor advertising services

(G-7914)
TAMATHA HOLT OD
Also Called: Poteau Vision Source
1104 Dewey Ave (74953-4412)
PHONE..................918 649-0524
Tamatha Holt, *President*
EMP: 3 **EST:** 1997
SALES (est): 451.3K **Privately Held**
SIC: 3841 5995 Optometers; optical goods stores

(G-7915)
TREEHOUSE PRIVATE BRANDS INC
400 Industrial Blvd (74953-3706)
PHONE..................270 365-5505
Dale Robert, *Branch Mgr*
EMP: 145
SALES (corp-wide): 4.2B **Publicly Held**
SIC: 2052 Crackers, dry; cookies
HQ: Treehouse Private Brands, Inc.
    2021 Spring Rd Ste 600
    Oak Brook IL 60523

(G-7916)
TWIN CITIES READY MIX INC
1710 S Broadway Ave (74953-6803)
P.O. Box J (74953-1509)
PHONE..................918 647-8218
Bob Jobe, *Manager*
EMP: 5
SALES (corp-wide): 15.7MM **Privately Held**
SIC: 3273 Ready-mixed concrete
PA: Twin Cities Ready Mix, Inc.
    102 W Ashland Ave
    Mcalester OK 74501
    918 423-8855

GEOGRAPHIC SECTION

Pryor - Mayes County (G-7944)

(G-7917)
WEAVERS MEAT PROCESSING INC
34842 Us Highway 59 S (74953-5257)
PHONE..................918 647-9832
Wesley Weaver, *Owner*
EMP: 1
SALES (est): 115.1K **Privately Held**
SIC: 2011 Meat packing plants

(G-7918)
WHOLESALE ELECTRIC SUPPLY CO
106 Ben Klutz Blvd (74953-5411)
PHONE..................918 647-2200
Jerald Fox, *Branch Mgr*
EMP: 2
SALES (corp-wide): 161.5MM **Privately Held**
SIC: 5099 5063 3699 Firearms & ammunition, except sporting; electrical apparatus & equipment; electrical equipment & supplies
PA: Wholesale Electric Supply Company, Inc
   803 S Robison Rd
   Texarkana TX 75501
   903 794-3404

(G-7919)
WISE FOAMCO INC
304 Kerr Ave (74953-5246)
PHONE..................918 839-4784
Donnie Wise, *President*
EMP: 4
SALES (est): 278.9K **Privately Held**
SIC: 3086 Plastics foam products

Prague
Lincoln County

(G-7920)
BARTOSH ELECTRIC MOTOR CENTER
Hwy 62 (74864)
P.O. Box G (74864-1035)
PHONE..................405 567-2840
Leeroy Bartosh, *Owner*
EMP: 2
SALES (est): 62.9K **Privately Held**
SIC: 7694 7699 7623 5999 Electric motor repair; pumps & pumping equipment repair; compressor repair; refrigeration service & repair; electronic parts & equipment

(G-7921)
BEACON SIGN COMPANY INC
8102 Nbu (74864-4005)
PHONE..................405 567-4886
Kendra Mc Bride, *CEO*
Kelli Mc Bride, *President*
Marilyn McBride, *Vice Pres*
EMP: 3
SQ FT: 3,750
SALES (est): 300K **Privately Held**
SIC: 2396 3993 2759 7389 Automotive & apparel trimmings; signs & advertising specialties; screen printing; textile printing rolls: engraving; sign painting & lettering shop

(G-7922)
C&C TRUCKING AND EQP SVCS LLC
357494 E 1000 Rd (74864-7821)
PHONE..................405 567-5194
Christopher Coleman, *President*
EMP: 4
SALES (est): 170.8K **Privately Held**
SIC: 3537 Trucks, tractors, loaders, carriers & similar equipment

(G-7923)
COBBLE ROCK AND STONE LLC
11227 Ns 3520 (74864-1174)
PHONE..................405 567-3552
Ronald Jay Rogers, *President*
EMP: 11
SQ FT: 10,200
SALES (est): 1.3MM **Privately Held**
SIC: 1429 3272 Riprap quarrying; silo staves, cast stone or concrete

(G-7924)
DAILY PERK LLC
101731 S Highway 99 (74864-6441)
PHONE..................405 567-5491
Tedda Auld, *Principal*
EMP: 3
SALES (est): 86.9K **Privately Held**
SIC: 2711 Newspapers, publishing & printing

(G-7925)
DIGGER OIL & GAS CO
Also Called: Digger Oil & Gas Producers
815 W 1st St (74864-4568)
P.O. Box 666 (74864-0666)
PHONE..................405 567-2288
Charles Morgan, *President*
Dorothy Morgan, *Bookkeeper*
EMP: 5 EST: 1969
SQ FT: 3,200
SALES (est): 368.7K **Privately Held**
SIC: 1311 Crude petroleum production; natural gas production

(G-7926)
GR TRAILERS LLC
1422 E Main St (74864-7511)
PHONE..................405 567-0567
Abraham Heidi,
▲ EMP: 6
SQ FT: 9,000
SALES (est): 14.4MM **Privately Held**
SIC: 3792 7539 5084 Travel trailers & campers; trailer repair; trailers, industrial

(G-7927)
HOLMAN OIL AND GAS
104447 S 3580 Rd (74864-9230)
PHONE..................405 567-3528
Robert Holman, *Principal*
EMP: 2
SALES (est): 65.5K **Privately Held**
SIC: 1389 Oil & gas field services

(G-7928)
JONES JERSEYS AND TEES LLC
104524 S 3520 Rd (74864-1077)
PHONE..................405 264-6151
Melissa Jones, *Principal*
EMP: 2
SALES (est): 98.8K **Privately Held**
SIC: 2759 Screen printing

(G-7929)
KLABZUBA ROYALTY COMPANY
814 9th St (74864-4582)
P.O. Box 567 (74864-0567)
PHONE..................405 567-3031
Robert R Klabzuba, *President*
Joe Paul Klabzuba, *Vice Pres*
John S Klabzuba, *Admin Sec*
EMP: 6
SQ FT: 1,750
SALES (est): 1.6MM **Privately Held**
SIC: 1382 Oil & gas exploration services

(G-7930)
MORGAN WELL SERVICE INC
815 W 1st St (74864-4568)
P.O. Box 666 (74864-0666)
PHONE..................405 567-2288
Daniel Morgan, *President*
Dottie Morgan, *Corp Secy*
Kenneth Morgan, *Vice Pres*
Terry Perdue, *Safety Dir*
EMP: 50 EST: 1963
SQ FT: 4,500
SALES (est): 5.6MM **Privately Held**
WEB: www.morganwellservice.com
SIC: 1389 Servicing oil & gas wells

(G-7931)
MOSLEY BACKHOE SERVICE
2 1/2 E Centerview (74864)
P.O. Box 11 (74864-0011)
PHONE..................405 567-4710
Terry N Mosley, *Owner*
EMP: 1

SALES (est): 94.8K **Privately Held**
SIC: 3446 1771 1794 1711 Architectural metalwork; concrete work; excavation work; plumbing, heating, air-conditioning contractors

(G-7932)
PRAGUE TIMES HERALD
1123 N Jim Thorpe Blvd (74864-3524)
P.O. Box U (74864-1100)
PHONE..................405 567-3933
Ken Johnson, *Owner*
EMP: 4
SALES (est): 221.1K **Privately Held**
SIC: 2711 Newspapers, publishing & printing

(G-7933)
PRITCHETTS MACHINING LLC
48955 Moccasin Trail Rd (74864-8912)
PHONE..................405 567-0183
Preston Pritchett,
EMP: 7
SQ FT: 2,314
SALES (est): 822K **Privately Held**
SIC: 3542 Machine tools, metal forming type

(G-7934)
REMPELS ROCK & READY MIX INC
Also Called: Rempels Rock & Ready Mix
Hwy 62 W (74864)
PHONE..................405 567-3991
Neil Rempel, *President*
Ed Lee, *Admin Sec*
EMP: 10
SQ FT: 1,300
SALES (est): 970K **Privately Held**
WEB: www.rempelsrock-n-readymix.com
SIC: 3273 Ready-mixed concrete

(G-7935)
SIMEK OIL PROPERTIES INC
619 Jim Phorte Blvd (74864)
P.O. Box 667 (74864-0667)
PHONE..................405 567-4606
Tj Simek, *President*
Tony Simek, *Vice Pres*
Frances C Simek, *Admin Sec*
EMP: 4
SQ FT: 6,000
SALES (est): 360K **Privately Held**
SIC: 1311 Crude petroleum production; natural gas production

(G-7936)
STRATEGIC ARMORY CORPS LLC (PA)
48955 Moccasin Trail Rd (74864-8912)
PHONE..................623 780-1050
Mark Johnson, *CEO*
EMP: 6
SALES (est): 5.6MM **Privately Held**
SIC: 3542 5941 Machine tools, metal forming type; firearms

(G-7937)
SUNRISE SHEDS
1126 E Main St (74864-7512)
PHONE..................405 831-0904
EMP: 2 EST: 2018
SALES (est): 186.8K **Privately Held**
SIC: 2441 Tool chests, wood

(G-7938)
VAN BRUNT LUMBER
Mbu 4002 (74864)
PHONE..................405 567-3776
Gordon Van Brunt, *Partner*
Ronnie Van Brundt, *Partner*
Jack Van Brunt, *Partner*
EMP: 3
SQ FT: 2,400
SALES (est): 415.8K **Privately Held**
SIC: 5031 5211 2449 Lumber: rough, dressed & finished; planing mill products & lumber; wood containers

Proctor
Adair County

(G-7939)
PUNKIN HOLLERWOOD
13870 N Pumpkin Holw (74457-3236)
PHONE..................918 456-9640
Christine Smith, *Owner*
EMP: 2
SALES (est): 119.1K **Privately Held**
SIC: 2511 Bookcases, household: wood

Pryor
Mayes County

(G-7940)
AIR PRODUCTS AND CHEMICALS INC
4078 Hunt St (74361-4401)
P.O. Box 668 (74362-0668)
PHONE..................918 825-4592
Bob Erwin, *Opers-Prdtn-Mfg*
EMP: 63
SALES (corp-wide): 8.9B **Publicly Held**
SIC: 2813 Industrial gases
PA: Air Products And Chemicals, Inc.
   7201 Hamilton Blvd
   Allentown PA 18195
   610 481-4911

(G-7941)
AMERICAN AUTOMATION INC
4592 E 480 (74361-2829)
P.O. Box 37 (74362-0037)
Fax: 918 825-7905
EMP: 2
SQ FT: 3,750
SALES (est): 185.4K **Privately Held**
SIC: 1731 3613 5084 Electrical Contractor Mfg Switchgear/Switchboards Whol Industrial Equipment

(G-7942)
AMERICAN CASTINGS LLC
5265 Hunt St (74361-4421)
P.O. Box 69 (74362-0069)
PHONE..................918 476-4252
Jason Judalet, *Foreman/Supr*
Deloris Cole, *Buyer*
Jerry Mann, *Engineer*
Pam Young, *Human Res Dir*
Lori Nichols, *Human Resources*
▲ EMP: 315
SALES (est): 30.1MM
SALES (corp-wide): 1.4B **Privately Held**
SIC: 7819 3531 3322 3321 Casting bureau, motion picture; construction machinery; malleable iron foundries; gray & ductile iron foundries
PA: American Cast Iron Pipe Company
   1501 31st Ave N
   Birmingham AL 35207
   205 325-7701

(G-7943)
AMERIINFOVETS INC (PA)
33 Woodcreek Ln (74361-6845)
PHONE..................408 446-4343
James Forrest Cavin, *CEO*
Mahesh Kalva, *President*
Mohana Suggula, *CFO*
EMP: 1
SALES: 2.4MM **Privately Held**
SIC: 7372 7373 7379 7371 Application computer software; computer integrated systems design; ; computer software development & applications;

(G-7944)
ASHLEYS ELECTRICAL SERVICES
249 Cottonwood Rd (74361-9559)
P.O. Box 301 (74362-0301)
PHONE..................918 825-0747
Thomas Ashley, *President*
Miriam Ashley, *Vice Pres*
EMP: 4
SALES (est): 644.5K **Privately Held**
SIC: 3679 1731 Transducers, electrical; computer power conditioning

Pryor - Mayes County (G-7945)

(G-7945)
BERRY GLOBAL INC
1 Stretch Film Way (74362)
PHONE..............................918 824-4288
David Johnson, *Branch Mgr*
EMP: 17 **Publicly Held**
SIC: **3089** 3081 Bottle caps, molded plastic; unsupported plastics film & sheet
HQ: Berry Global, Inc.
  101 Oakley St
  Evansville IN 47710

(G-7946)
BERRY GLOBAL INC
3137 Highway 69a (74361-3515)
PHONE..............................918 824-4400
Rolly Cochlin, *Branch Mgr*
EMP: 60 **Publicly Held**
SIC: **3089** 3081 Bottle caps, molded plastic; unsupported plastics film & sheet
HQ: Berry Global, Inc.
  101 Oakley St
  Evansville IN 47710

(G-7947)
BERRY PLASTICS CORPORATION
1 Armin Rd (74361)
PHONE..............................918 824-4400
Rolly Cochlin, *Branch Mgr*
EMP: 120 **Privately Held**
SIC: **3081** 3089 2671 Mfg Unsupported Plastic Film/Sheet Mfg Plastic Products Mfg Packaging Paper/Film

(G-7948)
BUZZI UNICEM USA INC
2430 S 437 (74361-3475)
P.O. Box 68 (74362-0068)
PHONE..............................918 825-1937
Terry Byrne, *Manager*
EMP: 23
SALES (corp-wide): 395.5MM **Privately Held**
WEB: www.buzziunicemusa.com
SIC: **3241** Portland cement
HQ: Buzzi Unicem Usa Inc.
  100 Brodhead Rd Ste 230
  Bethlehem PA 18017
  610 882-5000

(G-7949)
CABOT NORIT AMERICAS INC
1432 6th St Maip (74361-4434)
PHONE..............................918 825-8332
Terry Silkey, *Production*
David Johnson, *Engineer*
Ivan Nguyen, *Plant Engr*
Chris Soap, *Manager*
EMP: 80
SQ FT: 30,000
SALES (corp-wide): 3.3B **Publicly Held**
SIC: **2895** 2819 Carbon black; industrial inorganic chemicals
HQ: Cabot Norit Americas, Inc.
  3200 University Ave
  Marshall TX 75670
  903 938-9211

(G-7950)
CASCADES HOLDING US INC
Cascades Tissue Group - Okla
4826 Hunt St (74361-4512)
PHONE..............................918 825-0616
EMP: 2
SALES (corp-wide): 3.7B **Privately Held**
SIC: **2621** Wrapping & packaging papers; tissue paper
HQ: Cascades Holding Us Inc.
  4001 Packard Rd
  Niagara Falls NY 14303
  716 285-3681

(G-7951)
CHEROKEE NATION AROSPC DEF LLC
2777 Highway 69a (74361-4565)
PHONE..............................918 430-3492
Bertrand Cochelin, *CFO*
Jennylynn Morton,
EMP: 9
SALES (est): 364.7K **Privately Held**
SIC: **3679** Electronic circuits

(G-7952)
CHEROKEE NATION RED WING LLC
2777 Highway 69a (74361-4565)
PHONE..............................918 824-6050
Chris Moody, *Manager*
EMP: 9
SQ FT: 5,000
SALES (est): 2MM **Privately Held**
SIC: **3679** Harness assemblies for electronic use: wire or cable
HQ: Cherokee Nation Red Wing, L.L.C.
  10838 E Marshall St # 20
  Tulsa OK 74116

(G-7953)
CHEVRON PHILLIPS CHEM CO LP
Also Called: Performance Pipe Div
Mid American Indus Park (74361)
PHONE..............................918 825-0364
Janet Belcher, *Treasurer*
Shawn Spears, *Manager*
EMP: 63
SALES (corp-wide): 8.3B **Privately Held**
SIC: **2821** Plastics materials & resins
HQ: Chevron Phillips Chemical Company Lp
  10001 Six Pines Dr
  The Woodlands TX 77380
  832 813-4100

(G-7954)
CNHI LLC
Also Called: Pryor Daily Times
105 S Adair St (74361-3625)
P.O. Box 248, Claremore (74018-0248)
PHONE..............................918 825-3292
Kenneth Jones, *Manager*
EMP: 12 **Privately Held**
SIC: **2711** Newspapers: publishing only, not printed on site
HQ: Cnhi, Llc
  445 Dexter Ave Ste 7000
  Montgomery AL 36104

(G-7955)
COMPASS UNLIMITED INC
1421 W 440 (74361-2997)
PHONE..............................918 824-1644
Jim Petty, *President*
Carol Petty, *Vice Pres*
EMP: 2
SALES: 400K **Privately Held**
SIC: **2048** 5191 Prepared feeds; farm supplies

(G-7956)
CUSTOM METAL WORKS
2333 E 450 (74361-2136)
PHONE..............................918 231-4151
Larry Baumert, *Owner*
Kendall Baumert, *Co-Owner*
EMP: 2 EST: 2010
SALES: 70K **Privately Held**
SIC: **7692** Welding repair

(G-7957)
DAILY TIMES
105 S Adair St (74361-3625)
P.O. Box 248, Claremore (74018-0248)
PHONE..............................918 825-3292
Carolyn Ashford, *President*
Bailey Babney, *President*
EMP: 9
SALES (est): 518K **Privately Held**
SIC: **2711** Newspapers, publishing & printing

(G-7958)
DALE-CO INDUSTRIES LLC
6170 Country Dr (74361-4446)
PHONE..............................918 864-2041
EMP: 2 EST: 2013
SALES (est): 103.7K **Privately Held**
SIC: **3999** Manufacturing industries

(G-7959)
DEAL USA TODAY LLC
Also Called: Profishing Equipment
9646 W 520 (74361-7384)
PHONE..............................918 825-7835
Leland Newton,
EMP: 3

SALES (est): 123.1K **Privately Held**
SIC: **2711** Newspapers, publishing & printing

(G-7960)
DU PONT DELAWARE INC
Also Called: Dupont
5532 Hunt St (74361-4559)
PHONE..............................918 476-5825
EMP: 9
SALES (corp-wide): 21.5B **Publicly Held**
SIC: **2099** Food preparations
HQ: Du Pont Delaware, Inc.
  974 Centre Rd Chestnut
  Wilmington DE 19805

(G-7961)
ELITE FABRICATORS LLC
49 N 435 (74361-3077)
PHONE..............................918 824-4528
Jerry Cowan, *Partner*
Casey Cowan, *General Mgr*
Todd Williams, *Vice Pres*
Calvin Williams, *Mng Member*
EMP: 40
SALES (est): 8MM **Privately Held**
SIC: **3312** 1799 Pipes, iron & steel; insulation of pipes & boilers

(G-7962)
FABRICUT INC
S Of City On Hwy 69 (74361)
P.O. Box 869 (74362-0869)
PHONE..............................918 825-4400
Debbie Chancellor, *Branch Mgr*
EMP: 10
SALES (corp-wide): 178.6MM **Privately Held**
SIC: **2392** 2391 Bedspreads & bed sets: made from purchased materials; draperies, plastic & textile: from purchased materials
PA: Fabricut, Inc.
  9303 E 46th St
  Tulsa OK 74145
  918 622-7700

(G-7963)
G A P ROOFING INC (PA)
4444 Hunt St (74361-4510)
PHONE..............................918 825-5200
Glen Passmore Jr, *President*
George Beard Jr, *Corp Secy*
Mary Passmore, *Vice Pres*
Mick Von, *Vice Pres*
Tim Williams, *Sales Staff*
▼ EMP: 85
SQ FT: 62,500
SALES (est): 15.6MM **Privately Held**
SIC: **2952** Roofing felts, cements or coatings; roofing materials

(G-7964)
GREEN INDUSTRIES
6471 S Highway 69 (74361-4487)
PHONE..............................918 825-1044
Allan Statham, *Principal*
EMP: 2
SALES (est): 171.7K **Privately Held**
SIC: **3999** Manufacturing industries

(G-7965)
HARBISONWALKER INTL INC
6471 S Highway 69 (74361-4487)
PHONE..............................918 825-1044
Victor Oblock, *Branch Mgr*
EMP: 9
SALES (corp-wide): 618.3MM **Privately Held**
SIC: **3255** Clay refractories
HQ: Harbisonwalker International, Inc.
  1305 Cherrington Pkwy # 100
  Moon Township PA 15108

(G-7966)
HEM INC (PA)
Also Called: Hem-Saw
4065 Main St (74361)
P.O. Box 1148 (74362-1148)
PHONE..............................918 825-4821
Douglas Harris, *President*
Randi Adams, *Corp Secy*
Vitaly Michka, *Mfg Staff*
Mike Bunch, *Senior Buyer*
Amanda Medel, *Purch Agent*
◆ EMP: 135 EST: 1966

SALES: 15MM **Privately Held**
WEB: www.hemsaw.com
SIC: **3541** Machine tools, metal cutting type

(G-7967)
HEM INC
4174 Zarrow St (74361-3468)
PHONE..............................888 729-7787
Doug Harris, *President*
EMP: 98
SALES (corp-wide): 15MM **Privately Held**
SIC: **3541** Saws & sawing machines
PA: Hem, Inc.
  4065 Main St
  Pryor OK 74361
  918 825-4821

(G-7968)
HEM INC
Also Called: Hem East
302 S Hunt (74361)
PHONE..............................918 824-0800
Randi Adams, *Branch Mgr*
EMP: 60
SALES (corp-wide): 15MM **Privately Held**
SIC: **3541** Machine tools, metal cutting type
PA: Hem, Inc.
  4065 Main St
  Pryor OK 74361
  918 825-4821

(G-7969)
HONEYCUTT CONTRUCTION INC
Also Called: Honeycutt Construction
2750 W 530 (74361-6802)
PHONE..............................918 825-6070
Alvin Honeycutt, *President*
Karen Honeycutt, *Admin Sec*
Belinda Johnson, *Administration*
EMP: 10
SQ FT: 20,000
SALES: 2.3MM **Privately Held**
SIC: **3448** 3441 3444 3449 Prefabricated metal buildings; fabricated structural metal; sheet metalwork; miscellaneous metalwork

(G-7970)
INDUSTRIAL PPING COMPANIES LLC
1933 S Elliott St (74361-8078)
PHONE..............................918 825-0900
Jim Hollingshead, *Mng Member*
Eddie Peters,
Keith Sanders,
EMP: 53
SQ FT: 6,500
SALES (est): 6.5MM **Privately Held**
SIC: **7692** 7389 Welding repair; inspection & testing services

(G-7971)
INTERPLASTIC CORPORATION
Also Called: Commercial Resin Division
5019 Hunt St (74361-4479)
PHONE..............................918 825-2755
George Hudack, *Branch Mgr*
EMP: 53
SQ FT: 30,000
SALES (corp-wide): 250.9MM **Privately Held**
SIC: **2821** Plastics materials & resins
PA: Interplastic Corporation
  1225 Willow Lake Blvd
  Saint Paul MN 55110
  651 481-6860

(G-7972)
KEMP STONE INC (PA)
Also Called: Kemp Quarries
1050 E 520 (74361-3441)
P.O. Box 968 (74362-0968)
PHONE..............................918 825-3370
James A Kemp, *President*
McCullin Kevin, *Prdtn Mgr*
David James, *Technology*
Melinda Kemp, *Officer*
Shiela Pilant, *Admin Sec*
EMP: 12
SQ FT: 12,800

SALES (est): 10MM **Privately Held**
WEB: www.kempquarries.com
SIC: 1429 Igneous rock, crushed & broken-quarrying

(G-7973)
L & M FABRICATION
Hc 4 Box 111 (74361)
P.O. Box 841 (74362-0841)
PHONE..........................918 825-7145
David Going, *President*
EMP: 4
SQ FT: 5,000
SALES (est): 479.1K **Privately Held**
SIC: 7539 3564 3446 3444 Automotive repair shops; blowers & fans; architectural metalwork; sheet metalwork

(G-7974)
LONE STAR INDUSTRIES INC
2430 N 437 (74361)
P.O. Box 68 (74362-0068)
PHONE..........................918 825-1937
Garry Harris, *Branch Mgr*
EMP: 7
SALES (corp-wide): 395.5MM **Privately Held**
WEB: www.buzziunicemusa.com
SIC: 3241 Portland cement
HQ: Lone Star Industries Inc
  10401 N Meridian St # 120
  Indianapolis IN 46290
  317 706-3314

(G-7975)
M-A SYSTEMS INC
4811 Ne 1st St (74361-2255)
P.O. Box 894 (74362-0894)
PHONE..........................918 824-3705
Bob Ayres, *President*
Michael Ayres, *Principal*
EMP: 12
SALES (est): 1.4MM **Privately Held**
SIC: 3462 Machinery forgings, ferrous

(G-7976)
MID AMERICA MACHINING INC
1141 2nd St Maip (74361-4508)
PHONE..........................918 825-6202
Robert Carlile, *President*
Tina Carlile, *Technology*
EMP: 12 **EST:** 1997
SQ FT: 15,000
SALES (est): 1.5MM **Privately Held**
SIC: 3599 Machine shop, jobbing & repair

(G-7977)
MTM INC
4811 Ne 1st St (74361-2255)
P.O. Box 991 (74362-0991)
PHONE..........................918 824-3700
Robert Ayres, *President*
EMP: 4
SALES (est): 335.5K **Privately Held**
SIC: 3999 Manufacturing industries

(G-7978)
NEW NGC INC
N G C Industries
4189 Hunt St (74361-4475)
PHONE..........................918 825-0142
Tom Nelson, *President*
E N Stephenson, *Principal*
Kay Smith, *Purch Mgr*
EMP: 95
SQ FT: 9,000
SALES (corp-wide): 795.8MM **Privately Held**
SIC: 3275 Gypsum products
HQ: New Ngc, Inc.
  2001 Rexford Rd
  Charlotte NC 28211

(G-7979)
OKLAHOMA NATIVE ELECTRIC LLC
325 S Mill St (74361-5226)
PHONE..........................918 824-7638
EMP: 2
SALES (est): 93K **Privately Held**
SIC: 3699 Mfg Electrical Equipment/Supplies

(G-7980)
OPP LIQUIDATING COMPANY INC (PA)
Also Called: Orchids
4826 Hunt St (74361-4512)
PHONE..........................918 825-0616
Jeffrey S Schoen, *President*
Melinda S Bartel, *CFO*
Elaine Macdonald, *Director*
Mark Ravich, *Director*
Robert Snyder, *Director*
▲ **EMP:** 231
SALES: 186.6MM **Privately Held**
SIC: 2676 2621 Sanitary paper products; towels, napkins & tissue paper products; facial tissue stock; sanitary tissue paper

(G-7981)
PAPER
Also Called: Prior Creek Publishing
3 N Adair St Ste 7 (74361-2480)
PHONE..........................918 825-2860
Paul Lewis, *President*
EMP: 5 **EST:** 1999
SALES (est): 190.2K **Privately Held**
WEB: www.mayescounty.com
SIC: 2711 Newspapers

(G-7982)
POWER SOAK SYSTEMS INC
4650 54th St Maip (74361-4520)
PHONE..........................800 444-9624
Tod Crimmins, *President*
EMP: 2
SALES (est): 180.5K **Privately Held**
SIC: 3589 Commercial cleaning equipment

(G-7983)
PREMIER SIGNS & DESIGN LLC
210 S Mill St (74361-5222)
PHONE..........................918 825-6422
John H Hare, *President*
Justin Hare, *Vice Pres*
EMP: 5 **EST:** 1948
SQ FT: 2,000
SALES: 480K **Privately Held**
WEB: www.premiersignsdesign.com
SIC: 3993 Neon signs

(G-7984)
PRIORITY PRINTWORKS INC
7 N Adair St (74361-2431)
PHONE..........................918 825-6397
George Fisher, *President*
EMP: 3
SALES: 100K **Privately Held**
SIC: 2759 2791 2789 2752 Commercial printing; typesetting; bookbinding & related work; commercial printing, lithographic; coated & laminated paper

(G-7985)
PRYOR CHEMICAL COMPANY
4463 Hunt St (74361-4511)
P.O. Box 429 (74362-0429)
PHONE..........................918 825-3383
Jack Golsen, *CEO*
Barry Golsen, *Principal*
Phil Gough, *Vice Pres*
Ann Rendon, *Vice Pres*
Matthew Weeks, *Engineer*
EMP: 150 **EST:** 1980
SALES: 100MM
SALES (corp-wide): 365MM **Publicly Held**
SIC: 2873 Ammonium nitrate, ammonium sulfate; anhydrous ammonia; fertilizers: natural (organic), except compost; urea
PA: Lsb Industries, Inc.
  3503 Nw 63rd St Ste 500
  Oklahoma City OK 73116
  405 235-4546

(G-7986)
PRYOR PRINTING INC
Also Called: Pryor Prtg Print & Copy Ctr
15 S Vann St (74361-3622)
PHONE..........................918 825-2888
Anthony J Schenck, *President*
Donna B Schenck, *Treasurer*
Kevin Bruce, *Sales Staff*
EMP: 6
SQ FT: 4,000
SALES (est): 480K **Privately Held**
SIC: 2752 2759 2796 2791 Commercial printing, offset; commercial printing; platemaking services; typesetting; bookbinding & related work

(G-7987)
PRYOR STONE INC
1050 E 520 (74361-3441)
P.O. Box 968 (74362-0968)
PHONE..........................918 825-3370
James Kemp, *President*
Melinda Kemp, *Corp Secy*
Jerry Arnold, *Marketing Staff*
Bruce Pritchett, *Marketing Staff*
EMP: 25
SQ FT: 2,200
SALES: 7MM **Privately Held**
SIC: 1422 Crushed & broken limestone

(G-7988)
RAE CORPORATION (PA)
Also Called: Refrigeration Systems Division
4492 Hunt St (74361-4510)
PHONE..........................918 825-7222
Eric Swank, *President*
Bradley Marshall, *Business Mgr*
Jeremy Colvard, *Vice Pres*
Kevin Trowhill, *Vice Pres*
Jerry Salcher, *Plant Mgr*
EMP: 277
SQ FT: 150,000
SALES: 93.6MM **Privately Held**
SIC: 3585 Refrigeration equipment, complete; air conditioning units, complete: domestic or industrial

(G-7989)
RED DEVIL INCORPORATED
4175 Webb St (74361-6741)
PHONE..........................918 825-5744
Robert Duess, *CFO*
Craig Cartwright, *Manager*
Curt True, *Manager*
Jordan Miller, *Info Tech Dir*
Robert Lee, *Director*
EMP: 68
SALES (corp-wide): 19.1MM **Privately Held**
SIC: 2891 3423 Sealants; hand & edge tools
PA: Red Devil, Incorporated
  1437 S Boulder Ave # 750
  Tulsa OK 74119
  918 585-8111

(G-7990)
SATIN SIREN LLC
4215 S 440 (74361-9031)
PHONE..........................918 803-6351
Katrina Dawn Weaver, *Owner*
EMP: 1
SALES (est): 46.5K **Privately Held**
SIC: 2221 Satins

(G-7991)
SOLAE LLC
Also Called: Pryor Protein Plant
5532 Hunt St (74361-4559)
P.O. Box 248 (74362-0248)
PHONE..........................918 476-5825
Jack Parker, *Manager*
EMP: 50
SALES (corp-wide): 21.5B **Publicly Held**
SIC: 2075 Soybean oil mills
HQ: Solae, Llc
  4300 Duncan Ave
  Saint Louis MO 63110
  314 659-3000

(G-7992)
SPORTS VISION INC
109 Ne 1st St (74361-2403)
P.O. Box 952 (74362-0952)
PHONE..........................918 824-7617
Michael McCollough, *President*
Ron Bradley, *Vice Pres*
Ron Sullivan, *Admin Sec*
EMP: 3 **EST:** 1999
SALES (est): 50K **Privately Held**
SIC: 3949 Sporting & athletic goods

(G-7993)
TACK DESIGNS
1355 Horkey St Maip (74361-4548)
PHONE..........................918 825-1211
Todd Fannin, *Owner*
EMP: 2
SALES (est): 53.7K **Privately Held**
WEB: www.tackpromo.com
SIC: 5999 5941 2759 Trophies & plaques; sporting goods & bicycle shops; screen printing

(G-7994)
TALL CHIEF LLC
Also Called: Tall Chief Smoke Shop
23 Cypress Cir (74361-6849)
PHONE..........................918 783-8255
Tara Hargove, *Mng Member*
EMP: 7
SALES (est): 1MM **Privately Held**
SIC: 2131 Chewing & smoking tobacco

(G-7995)
TIM DEES
Also Called: First Place Sports Center
116 E Graham Ave (74361-2439)
PHONE..........................918 825-1211
Tim Dees, *Owner*
EMP: 4
SQ FT: 6,000
SALES (est): 299.5K **Privately Held**
SIC: 5699 5661 5941 2396 Sports apparel; T-shirts, custom printed; footwear, athletic; team sports equipment; automotive & apparel trimmings

(G-7996)
UNIFIED BRANDS INC
4650 54th St (74361)
PHONE..........................888 994-7636
EMP: 8
SALES (corp-wide): 7.1B **Publicly Held**
SIC: 3469 Metal stampings
HQ: Unified Brands, Inc.
  2016 Gees Mill Rd Ne
  Conyers GA 30013
  601 372-3903

(G-7997)
VETERANS ENG GROUP INC
33 Woodcreek Ln (74361-6845)
PHONE..........................918 864-6006
Brian Ledbetter, *CEO*
Tim Lawson, *President*
James Cavin, *COO*
Danny Hauenstein, *Vice Pres*
David Jordan, *CFO*
EMP: 5
SALES (est): 307.7K **Privately Held**
SIC: 5172 3443 2992 5075 Lubricating oils & greases; boiler & boiler shop work; lubricating oils & greases; furnaces, warm air; furnaces, warm air: electric;

(G-7998)
WHITNEY MANUFACTURING INC
Also Called: Whitney Buildings
4304 Ne 1st St (74361-9633)
PHONE..........................918 825-6062
Charlie Emde, *CEO*
James McAnelly, *Vice Pres*
EMP: 25
SQ FT: 27,000
SALES (est): 6.6MM **Privately Held**
SIC: 3448 Buildings, portable: prefabricated metal

(G-7999)
WORK HORSE WELDING LLC
212 S Gaither Rd (74361-9206)
PHONE..........................918 530-5270
Cole McClain, *Owner*
EMP: 1
SALES (est): 25K **Privately Held**
SIC: 7692 Welding repair

(G-8000)
WORLDWIDE STEEL WORKS INC
650 Highway 69a (74361-4581)
P.O. Box 188 (74362-0188)
PHONE..........................918 825-4545
Dennis W Jones, *President*
Darrell Jenkins, *Prdtn Mgr*
Paul Lucas, *Purch Mgr*
Ron Hurlbut, *Manager*
Caroline Douse, *Admin Asst*
▲ **EMP:** 40

Pryor - Mayes County (G-8001)

SALES (est): 9.3MM **Privately Held**
SIC: 3441 Building components, structural steel

(G-8001)
WYATT ENGINEERING LLC
439 S Wood St (74361-6043)
PHONE..............................918 824-2255
Kathleen Moreau, *Accountant*
Shiela Woodruff, *Branch Mgr*
EMP: 8
SALES (corp-wide): 1.6MM **Privately Held**
SIC: 3823 Temperature measurement instruments, industrial
PA: Wyatt Engineering, Llc
6 Blackstone Valley Pl # 401
Lincoln RI 02865
401 334-1170

Purcell
Mcclain County

(G-8002)
CASTER LLC
408 W Madison St (73080-3206)
PHONE..............................800 255-0480
John David Caster, *Mng Member*
EMP: 8
SALES: 1MM **Privately Held**
SIC: 3562 Casters

(G-8003)
COMPLETE WIRELINE SVCS LTD CO
3207 N 9th Ave (73080-2124)
P.O. Box 1448 (73080-1448)
PHONE..............................405 317-0001
Craig Seidenfus, *Principal*
EMP: 1
SALES (est): 143.8K **Privately Held**
SIC: 1389 Removal of condensate gasoline from field (gathering) lines

(G-8004)
D WILAMS PIPE INSPTN POLY LI
947 Blue Bird Ter (73080-3041)
PHONE..............................405 426-7776
David Williams, *President*
Alicia Williams, *Treasurer*
EMP: 4
SALES (est): 918.6K **Privately Held**
SIC: 1389 Oil field services

(G-8005)
DII LLC
132 W Main St (73080-4220)
PHONE..............................405 514-7365
James Grimsley, *Mng Member*
Warren Thomas,
EMP: 2
SALES (est): 86K **Privately Held**
SIC: 3724 Research & development on aircraft engines & parts

(G-8006)
DOUNUT PALACE
Also Called: Doughnut Palace, The
403 S Green Ave (73080-5232)
PHONE..............................405 527-5746
Byung Choi, *Owner*
EMP: 4
SALES (est): 282.6K **Privately Held**
SIC: 2051 Doughnuts, except frozen

(G-8007)
ELLIS ENTERPRISE
3000 S 9th Ave. Trlr 106 (73080-8442)
P.O. Box 632 (73080-0632)
PHONE..............................405 826-3572
Ronald Ellis, *Owner*
Carolyn Ellis, *Owner*
EMP: 2
SALES: 14K **Privately Held**
SIC: 2741 Business service newsletters: publishing & printing

(G-8008)
GARY GREEN CEMENT CONSTRUCTION
301 W Main St (73080-4223)
PHONE..............................405 527-5606
Gary Green, *Principal*
EMP: 4
SALES (est): 359K **Privately Held**
SIC: 3444 1799 Sheet metalwork; welding on site

(G-8009)
GE OIL & GAS ESP INC
1739 Hardcastle Blvd (73080-8230)
P.O. Box 1680 (73080-7680)
PHONE..............................405 527-1566
Don Blankenchip, *Branch Mgr*
EMP: 30
SALES (corp-wide): 95.2B **Publicly Held**
SIC: 1389 7699 7353 3479 Testing, measuring, surveying & analysis services; pumps & pumping equipment repair; oil field equipment, rental or leasing; coating of metals & formed products
HQ: Ge Oil & Gas Esp, Inc.
5500 Se 59th St
Oklahoma City OK 73135
405 670-1431

(G-8010)
HORIZONTAL WELL DRILLERS LLC (PA)
Also Called: Hwd
2915 Highway 74 (73080-6266)
P.O. Box 1626 (73080-7626)
PHONE..............................405 527-1232
Jeremy Klein, *President*
EMP: 1
SALES: 1.6MM **Privately Held**
SIC: 1381 3533 Drilling oil & gas wells; oil & gas drilling rigs & equipment

(G-8011)
LEXINGTON GAS & GO
326 W Broadway (73080)
PHONE..............................405 527-4009
Mohammad Akatar, *Owner*
EMP: 3
SALES (est): 160.3K **Privately Held**
SIC: 1389 Gas field services

(G-8012)
M A C MANUFACTURING INC
23336 State Highway 74 (73080-6959)
PHONE..............................405 527-8270
Scott McGregor, *President*
EMP: 5
SQ FT: 7,000
SALES: 290K **Privately Held**
SIC: 3441 Fabricated structural metal

(G-8013)
MAC MANUFACTURING INC
23336 State Highway 74 (73080-6959)
PHONE..............................405 527-8270
Scott McGregor, *President*
EMP: 3
SALES (est): 240K **Privately Held**
SIC: 3537 Dollies (hand or power trucks), industrial except mining

(G-8014)
MAP EXPLORATION INC
505 N 4th Ave (73080-3415)
P.O. Box 106 (73080-0106)
PHONE..............................405 527-6038
Michael Pollok, *President*
EMP: 3
SALES (est): 640.7K **Privately Held**
SIC: 1382 Oil & gas exploration services

(G-8015)
MARCELLE PUBLISHING LLC
2585 E Redbud Rd (73080-9305)
PHONE..............................405 288-2317
Kenneth Reece, *Principal*
EMP: 1
SALES (est): 37.5K **Privately Held**
SIC: 2741 Miscellaneous publishing

(G-8016)
MC CLAIN COUNTY PUBLISHING CO
Also Called: Purcell Register
225 W Main St (73080-4221)
P.O. Box 191 (73080-0191)
PHONE..............................405 527-2126
John Montgomery, *President*
Grace Montgomery, *Treasurer*
EMP: 20
SQ FT: 12,000
SALES (est): 1.2MM **Privately Held**
SIC: 2711 2791 2759 Commercial printing & newspaper publishing combined; typesetting; commercial printing

(G-8017)
MONDO SOLUTIONS LLC
911 N 4th Ave (73080-2413)
PHONE..............................405 788-0056
Monna Blackmore, *Vice Pres*
EMP: 1
SALES (est): 57.6K **Privately Held**
SIC: 3842 Bulletproof vests

(G-8018)
SANCHEZ CNSTR & RMDLG LLC
101 S 8th Ave (73080-5023)
PHONE..............................405 443-8324
Ricardo Sanchez,
EMP: 1
SALES (est): 25K **Privately Held**
SIC: 1389 Construction, repair & dismantling services

(G-8019)
SHEEHY SIGNS
218 W Main St (73080-4222)
PHONE..............................405 623-7777
EMP: 1
SALES (est): 46K **Privately Held**
SIC: 3993 Signs & advertising specialties

(G-8020)
SOUTHWEST SHUTTER CO
21197 Fir Ln (73080-4464)
PHONE..............................405 344-6406
EMP: 3
SALES (est): 164.8K **Privately Held**
SIC: 3442 Shutters, door or window: metal

(G-8021)
SUPERIOR SPLING ENRGY SVCS LLC
2630 N 9th Ave (73080-1710)
P.O. Box 264 (73080-0264)
PHONE..............................405 613-0329
Zackary Sims, *Mng Member*
EMP: 4
SALES: 3MM **Privately Held**
SIC: 3561 Pumps, oil well & field

(G-8022)
SUPERIOR SPOOLING LLC
508 W Pierce St (73080-2229)
P.O. Box 264 (73080-0264)
PHONE..............................405 613-0329
Zachary Sims,
EMP: 8
SALES (est): 600.8K **Privately Held**
SIC: 1389 Bailing, cleaning, swabbing & treating of wells

(G-8023)
TOUCH UP UNLIMITED
23759 180th St (73080-6721)
P.O. Box 1523 (73080-1523)
PHONE..............................405 527-5609
Selton Mullins, *Owner*
Janet Mullins, *Co-Owner*
EMP: 3
SQ FT: 900
SALES (est): 750K **Privately Held**
SIC: 5198 5231 2851 Colors & pigments; paint; paints & allied products

(G-8024)
TRIM LINE CABINETS INC
910 S 6th Ave (73080-6240)
P.O. Box 789 (73080-0789)
PHONE..............................405 664-1439
Virginia Crook, *President*
Vrian Crook, *Vice Pres*
EMP: 17
SQ FT: 22,000
SALES: 1.1MM **Privately Held**
SIC: 1751 2434 Cabinet building & installation; vanities, bathroom: wood

(G-8025)
TRINITY SHTMTL FABRICATION LLC
23670 240th St (73080-6807)
PHONE..............................918 899-6030
Joseph Uhl, *Principal*
EMP: 1
SALES (est): 54.3K **Privately Held**
SIC: 3499 Fabricated metal products

(G-8026)
WALKUP WELLHEAD
1806 N 4th Ave (73080-1901)
PHONE..............................580 320-5913
Steven Walkup, *Owner*
EMP: 2
SALES (est): 65.5K **Privately Held**
SIC: 1389 Oil & gas field services

Quapaw
Ottawa County

(G-8027)
ADV-TEC SYSTEMS INC
Also Called: A T S
2201 S 700 Rd (74363-2201)
PHONE..............................918 542-4710
Leroy Shockley, *President*
Gary Shockley, *Vice Pres*
Jodie Franklin, *Admin Sec*
EMP: 3
SQ FT: 2,800
SALES: 200K **Privately Held**
SIC: 3613 Control panels, electric

(G-8028)
CARTER FIBERGLASS
Also Called: Carter Custom Fiberglass
100 N Main St (74363)
P.O. Box 623 (74363-0623)
PHONE..............................918 674-2325
Tim McMaster, *President*
EMP: 9
SQ FT: 7,000
SALES: 600K **Privately Held**
SIC: 2221 Fiberglass fabrics

(G-8029)
CERADYNE INC
3250 S 614 Rd (74363-2269)
PHONE..............................918 673-2201
Dave Gunderson, *Officer*
EMP: 90
SALES (corp-wide): 32.1B **Publicly Held**
SIC: 2819 Industrial inorganic chemicals
HQ: Ceradyne, Inc.
1922 Barranca Pkwy
Irvine CA 92606
949 862-9600

(G-8030)
FOOD SVCS AUTH OF QUAPAW TRIBE
Also Called: Quapaw Food Services
5681 S 630 Rd (74363-1998)
P.O. Box 765 (74363-0765)
PHONE..............................918 542-1853
John Berrey, *Ch of Bd*
Tamara Smiley-Reeves, *Corp Secy*
EMP: 10
SALES (est): 311.7K **Privately Held**
SIC: 2011 Beef products from beef slaughtered on site

(G-8031)
GALLIUM COMPOUNDS LLC
3225 S 625 Rd (74363-1802)
P.O. Box 67 (74363-0067)
PHONE..............................918 673-2511
Greg Evans,
Kevin Reading,
EMP: 10
SALES (est): 1.4MM
SALES (corp-wide): 407.4MM **Privately Held**
SIC: 2899 Chemical preparations

GEOGRAPHIC SECTION

Ratliff City - Carter County (G-8061)

HQ: Neo Performance Materials Ulc
121 King St W Suite 1740
Toronto ON M5H 3
416 367-8588

(G-8032)
MOLYCORP RARE METALS
3225 S 625 Rd (74363-1802)
PHONE.................918 673-2511
Greg Evans, *Principal*
EMP: 1
SALES (est): 105.2K **Privately Held**
SIC: 2899 Chemical preparations

(G-8033)
NEO RARE METALS OKLAHOMA LLC
3225 S 625 Rd (74363-1802)
PHONE.................918 673-2511
Kevin Reading, *Mng Member*
EMP: 13
SALES: 2MM
SALES (corp-wide): 407.4MM **Privately Held**
SIC: 2819 7389 Industrial inorganic chemicals;
HQ: Neo Performance Materials Ulc
121 King St W Suite 1740
Toronto ON M5H 3
416 367-8588

(G-8034)
UMICORE OPTICAL MTLS USA INC (DH)
2976 S 614 Rd (74363-1884)
P.O. Box 737 (74363-0737)
PHONE.................918 673-1650
Michel Cauwe, *President*
Richard Laird, *Vice Pres*
◆ **EMP:** 99
SQ FT: 96,210
SALES (est): 20.5MM
SALES (corp-wide): 3.7B **Privately Held**
SIC: 3674 3339 Diodes, solid state (germanium, silicon, etc.); germanium refining (primary)

Quinton
Pittsburg County

(G-8035)
CHOCTAW GAS COMPANY
1118 Main St (74561)
P.O. Box 660 (74561-0660)
PHONE.................918 469-3394
Jeff Miller, *President*
Carolyn Fowler, *Corp Secy*
Marydene Streich, *Vice Pres*
EMP: 7 **EST:** 1927
SQ FT: 2,500
SALES (est): 1MM **Privately Held**
SIC: 1311 Natural gas production

(G-8036)
EAGLE URNS INC
412 Etchison Rd (74561-9727)
PHONE.................918 469-3024
Robert T Cass, *President*
Jeremy Fitzer, *Vice Pres*
Linda Cass, *Admin Sec*
▼ **EMP:** 6
SQ FT: 8,000
SALES: 750K **Privately Held**
SIC: 3281 Urns, cut stone

(G-8037)
J BERNARDONI PATTERN CO LLC
17165 E State Highway 31 (74561-5096)
PHONE.................520 390-0663
EMP: 2
SALES (est): 109.8K **Privately Held**
SIC: 3543 Industrial patterns

(G-8038)
PHOENIX FABWORX LLC
5389 Bascum Rd (74561-5127)
P.O. Box 392 (74561-0392)
PHONE.................918 429-8388
Chris Morris,
EMP: 1 **EST:** 2015
SALES (est): 90.9K **Privately Held**
SIC: 3441 Fabricated structural metal

(G-8039)
PODUNK HUNTING PRODUCTS LLC
30707 S Lone Valley Rd (74561)
PHONE.................918 617-0358
Roy Dugan, *Owner*
EMP: 2 **EST:** 2012
SALES (est): 114.7K **Privately Held**
SIC: 3462 Gears, forged steel

(G-8040)
QUALITY CABINETRY
N Highway 71 (74561)
P.O. Box 782 (74561-0782)
PHONE.................918 469-2119
EMP: 2
SALES (est): 205.8K **Privately Held**
SIC: 2434 Mfg Wood Kitchen Cabinets

(G-8041)
REDBUD E&P INC
100 E Main St (74561)
P.O. Box 250 (74561-0250)
PHONE.................918 469-3600
EMP: 20 **Privately Held**
WEB: www.redbudinc.com
SIC: 1382 Oil & gas exploration services
PA: Redbud E&P Inc.
16000 Stuebner Airline Rd # 320
Spring TX 77379

(G-8042)
SOUTHEASTERN DRILLING
N Of Town (74561)
P.O. Box 817 (74561-0817)
PHONE.................918 469-3489
George Brennan, *Owner*
EMP: 1 **EST:** 1977
SALES (est): 90.9K **Privately Held**
SIC: 1221 1381 Bituminous coal & lignite-surface mining; drilling oil & gas wells

Ramona
Washington County

(G-8043)
AG QUIP INC
400261 W 3400 Rd (74061-3307)
PHONE.................918 536-4325
Bret Chew, *President*
EMP: 2 **EST:** 2000
SALES (est): 239.4K **Privately Held**
SIC: 3533 Oil field machinery & equipment

(G-8044)
APERGY ESP SYSTEMS LLC
401 Wyandotte Ave (74061)
PHONE.................918 536-3038
EMP: 2
SALES (corp-wide): 1.1B **Publicly Held**
SIC: 1389 Construction, repair & dismantling services
HQ: Apergy Esp Systems, Llc
19425 E 54th St S
Broken Arrow OK 74014
918 396-0558

(G-8045)
FIVE STAR EQUIPMENT LLC
404 Wyandotte Ave (74061)
PHONE.................918 637-0200
▲ **EMP:** 18
SALES (est): 194.9K
SALES (corp-wide): 30.6MM **Privately Held**
SIC: 3423 Mfg Hand/Edge Tools
PA: Accelerated Production Systems, Inc.
7227 Wright Rd
Houston TX 77041
713 937-6838

(G-8046)
INTEGRITY SIGNS
399700 W 3100 Rd (74061-3488)
PHONE.................918 520-2802
Kerry Fielding, *Principal*
EMP: 2
SALES (est): 142.5K **Privately Held**
SIC: 3993 Signs & advertising specialties

(G-8047)
WILD LEAF SCREEN PRTG & DESIGN
398408 W 4000 Rd (74061-2555)
PHONE.................918 440-4945
Pepper Pryce, *Principal*
EMP: 2
SALES (est): 83.9K **Privately Held**
SIC: 2752 Commercial printing, lithographic

Ratliff City
Carter County

(G-8048)
AMERICAN PETROLEUM CORPORATION
Also Called: Lewis Oil Properties
25525 Hwy 76 (73481)
P.O. Box 217 (73481-0217)
PHONE.................580 856-3580
James Lewis, *President*
Rhonda Lewis, *Admin Sec*
EMP: 11
SALES: 3MM **Privately Held**
SIC: 1311 Crude petroleum production

(G-8049)
CITATION OIL & GAS CORP
Nw Tatums Fld (73481)
PHONE.................580 856-3014
Curtis Harrell, *Branch Mgr*
EMP: 3
SALES (corp-wide): 283.5MM **Privately Held**
WEB: www.cogc.com
SIC: 1311 Crude petroleum production
PA: Citation Oil & Gas Corp.
14077 Cutten Rd
Houston TX 77069
281 891-1000

(G-8050)
DON-NAN PUMP AND SUPPLY CO INC
1548 Old Highway 7 (73481-8148)
PHONE.................432 682-7742
EMP: 1
SALES (corp-wide): 163.3MM **Privately Held**
SIC: 1389 Oil field services
PA: Don-Nan Pump And Supply Co., Inc.
3427 E Garden Cy Hwy 158
Midland TX 79706
432 682-7742

(G-8051)
EDDIE JOHNSONS WLDG & MCH CO
Also Called: Eddie Johnson's Crane Service
75a Kirkpatrick Curv (73481)
P.O. Box 71 (73481-0071)
PHONE.................580 856-3418
Jay Keith Johnson, *President*
Gladys Johnson, *Corp Secy*
Nina K Johnson, *Vice Pres*
EMP: 16 **EST:** 1951
SQ FT: 25,000
SALES (est): 1.6MM **Privately Held**
SIC: 7389 7692 3599 6512 Crane & aerial lift service; welding repair; machine shop, jobbing & repair; nonresidential building operators; local trucking, without storage

(G-8052)
ELLIS WELDING
Hc 1 (73481)
PHONE.................580 856-3907
EMP: 1
SALES (est): 62K **Privately Held**
SIC: 7692 Miscellaneous Repair Service

(G-8053)
FIVE POINT SERVICES INC
28217 State Highway 76 (73481-8229)
P.O. Box 326 (73481-0326)
PHONE.................580 856-3670
Randall Trachtenberg, *CEO*
Ed Foreman, *President*
James E Tow, *Senior VP*
EMP: 20

SQ FT: 2,500
SALES: 1.8MM
SALES (corp-wide): 15.8MM **Privately Held**
SIC: 1389 Oil field services
PA: M&M Acquisition, Llc
909 W Peach Ave
Duncan OK 73533
580 252-7879

(G-8054)
FLINT ENERGY SERVICES INC
3 Miles S Highway 76 (73481)
PHONE.................580 856-3251
EMP: 5
SALES (corp-wide): 18.2B **Publicly Held**
SIC: 1389 Oil/Gas Field Services
HQ: Flint Energy Services Inc.
6200 S Quebec St Ste 1
Greenwood Village CO 80111
918 294-3030

(G-8055)
HOGGARD WELDING & BACKHOE SVC
1952 Pelton Rd (73481-8052)
PHONE.................580 856-3934
Jim G Hoggard, *Owner*
Fern Kirkpatrick, *Bookkeeper*
EMP: 3
SALES (est): 210K **Privately Held**
SIC: 1389 Construction, repair & dismantling services

(G-8056)
LAMAMCO DRILLING CO
3100 Continental Rd (73481-8300)
PHONE.................580 856-3561
EMP: 2
SALES (est): 97K **Privately Held**
SIC: 1389 1781 Oil And Gas Field Services, Nec, Nsk

(G-8057)
MACK ENERGY CO
3730 Samedan Rd (73481-8103)
PHONE.................580 856-3705
EMP: 4
SALES (est): 290.4K **Privately Held**
SIC: 1311 Crude petroleum production

(G-8058)
NUBS WELL SERVICING INC
25627 State Highway 76 (73481-5011)
P.O. Box 206, Fox (73435-0206)
PHONE.................580 856-3887
Joe D Sullivan, *President*
Judy Sullivan, *Treasurer*
EMP: 15 **EST:** 1974
SQ FT: 2,700
SALES: 1MM **Privately Held**
SIC: 1311 1389 Crude petroleum production; natural gas production; oil field services

(G-8059)
OK PUMP AND SUPPLY
1 Mile Hwy 776 (73481)
P.O. Box 217 (73481-0217)
PHONE.................580 856-4010
James Luis, *Owner*
Bonnie Martin, *Co-Owner*
EMP: 4
SALES (est): 603.5K **Privately Held**
SIC: 3533 Oil & gas drilling rigs & equipment

(G-8060)
ONSITE OIL TOOLS INC
1390 Old Hwy 7 (73481)
P.O. Box 489, Rockwall TX (75087-0489)
PHONE.................580 856-3367
EMP: 15
SQ FT: 6,000
SALES (est): 3.6MM **Privately Held**
SIC: 1389 Oil/Gas Field Services

(G-8061)
P V VALVE
22727 State Highway 76 (73481-8201)
P.O. Box 40 (73481-0040)
PHONE.................580 856-3844
Rosella Pevehouse,
Carl Pevehouse,
EMP: 5

Ratliff City - Carter County (G-8062)

SALES (est): 1.7MM **Privately Held**
SIC: 5085 7699 3533 Valves & fittings; valve repair, industrial; oil & gas field machinery

(G-8062)
PATRIOT CHEMICALS & SVCS LLC
11506 State Highway 7 (73481-8126)
P.O. Box 149 (73481-0149)
PHONE 580 856-3114
Leon Joyce, *CEO*
EMP: 22
SALES (est): 1.9MM **Privately Held**
SIC: 2899 Oil treating compounds
PA: Energy And Environmental Services, Inc.
6300 Boucher Dr
Edmond OK 73034

(G-8063)
RAY CLOUR WELL SERVICE INC
23932 State Highway 76 (73481-8216)
P.O. Box 130 (73481-0130)
PHONE 580 856-3905
Tracy Clour, *President*
Vera Clour, *Vice Pres*
Casey Clour, *Admin Sec*
EMP: 20 EST: 1962
SQ FT: 500
SALES (est): 1.5MM **Privately Held**
SIC: 1389 Oil & gas wells: building, repairing & dismantling

(G-8064)
RC PUMPS LLC
721 Old Hwy 76 (73481)
P.O. Box 416, Velma (73491-0416)
PHONE 580 444-2227
Kevin Oneal, *Mng Member*
EMP: 6
SALES (est): 440K **Privately Held**
SIC: 3561 Pumps & pumping equipment

(G-8065)
RIFLE TOOL COMPANY
W Hwy 7 (73481)
P.O. Box 118 (73481-0118)
PHONE 580 856-3030
Gary Hodge, *Principal*
EMP: 2
SALES (est): 255.5K **Privately Held**
SIC: 1389 Oil field services

(G-8066)
SAMEDAN OIL CORP
3730 Samedan Rd (73481-8103)
PHONE 580 856-3705
EMP: 2
SALES (est): 100.8K **Privately Held**
SIC: 1311 Crude Petroleum/Natural Gas Production

(G-8067)
STALLION OILFIELD SERVICES LTD
Stallion Heavy Haulers
24130 State Highway 76 (73481-8220)
P.O. Box 247 (73481-0247)
PHONE 580 856-3169
EMP: 100
SALES (corp-wide): 1.4B **Privately Held**
SIC: 4212 4213 1794 1771 Local & Long Dist Trucking Dirt Excav Work Sets Portable Cement Pumping Pads Roustabout Oil Field Svc & Repairs Pumping Units
HQ: Stallion Oilfield Services Ltd.
950 Corbindale Rd Ste 300
Houston TX 77024
713 528-5544

(G-8068)
SUMMIT WELL SERVICING LLC
3100 Continental Rd (73481-8300)
PHONE 580 467-0886
Larry Pulis, *Principal*
EMP: 1 EST: 2010
SALES (est): 81K **Privately Held**
SIC: 1389 Oil field services

(G-8069)
SUTHERLAND WELL SERVICE INC
207 W Hwy 7 (73481)
P.O. Box 224 (73481-0224)
PHONE 580 856-3538
EMP: 15
SALES (corp-wide): 7.3MM **Privately Held**
SIC: 1381 8711 Oil/Gas Well Drilling Engineering Services
PA: Sutherland Well Service Inc
S On Hwy 76
Healdton OK 73438
580 229-1338

(G-8070)
TEXOMA PUMPING UNIT SVC INC
119 Doral Rd (73481-8145)
P.O. Box 875, Healdton (73438-0875)
PHONE 580 856-4024
Brian Johnson, *President*
Mark Teal, *Vice Pres*
EMP: 28
SALES (est): 10.4MM **Privately Held**
SIC: 1389 Pumping of oil & gas wells

Rattan
Pushmataha County

(G-8071)
DIAMOND T TRAILER MFG CO
429157 State Highway 3 (74562-7512)
PHONE 580 587-2432
Charles Teague, *President*
Philip Teague, *Vice Pres*
▲ EMP: 28
SALES (est): 12.8MM **Privately Held**
SIC: 5084 3792 Trailers, industrial; travel trailers & campers

Ravia
Johnston County

(G-8072)
WEST TEXAS BY PRODUCTS LP
Also Called: Sugar Trading
108 N Easton (73455)
P.O. Box 350 (73455-0350)
PHONE 580 371-9413
Jeff Earles, *Partner*
Jamie Earles, *Partner*
EMP: 10
SQ FT: 2,500
SALES (est): 593.6K **Privately Held**
SIC: 2048 Feed supplements

Red Oak
Latimer County

(G-8073)
A/C MATTHEWS & REFRIGERATION
1351 Ne 1070th Ave (74563-2213)
PHONE 918 465-6337
EMP: 2
SALES (est): 91.7K **Privately Held**
SIC: 3585 Parts for heating, cooling & refrigerating equipment

(G-8074)
BENDED KNEE CONSTRUCTION LLC
798 Ne 1095th Ave (74563-2413)
P.O. Box 179, Panola (74559-0179)
PHONE 918 465-4700
Jeff Davis, *Mng Member*
EMP: 5
SALES (est): 912.2K **Privately Held**
SIC: 1389 Construction, repair & dismantling services; roustabout service

(G-8075)
BOOTH ENVMTL SLS & SVC LLC
Also Called: Booth Environmental Sls & Svc
7298 Ne Highway 270 (74563-2401)
P.O. Box 728, Wilburton (74578-0728)
PHONE 918 465-0214
James Booth,
EMP: 50
SALES (est): 8.1MM **Privately Held**
SIC: 1629 1389 Pond construction; cutting of right-of-way; earthmoving contractor; building oil & gas well foundations on site; grading oil & gas well foundations

(G-8076)
GREEN VALLEY DISTILLERY LLC
501 Se 1160th Ave (74563-2345)
PHONE 918 413-5199
Calvin Alford,
EMP: 2
SALES (est): 62.3K **Privately Held**
SIC: 2085 Scotch whiskey

(G-8077)
HOT ROD WELDING AND MECH LLC
1597 Se 1108th Ave (74563-2320)
PHONE 918 754-2548
Roy Herren, *Principal*
EMP: 1 EST: 2016
SALES (est): 30.3K **Privately Held**
SIC: 7692 Welding repair

(G-8078)
INNOVATIVE OILFIELD SVCS LLC
5828 Ne Highway 270 (74563-2289)
PHONE 918 521-8317
Kenneth Maroon, *Administration*
EMP: 2 EST: 2014
SALES (est): 140.7K **Privately Held**
SIC: 1389 Oil field services

Red Rock
Noble County

(G-8079)
J & J CUSTOM FIRE INC
22274 Valley (74651-0449)
PHONE 405 747-4442
Jerry Potter, *Principal*
EMP: 5 EST: 2007
SQ FT: 50,000
SALES: 490K **Privately Held**
WEB: www.jandjcustomfire.com
SIC: 3713 Truck & bus bodies

Reydon
Roger Mills County

(G-8080)
STATE LINE SWD LLC
9473 N 1690 Rd (73660)
P.O. Box 86 (73660-0086)
PHONE 580 515-1468
Tim Hartley, *Mng Member*
Derek Hawkins,
EMP: 5 EST: 2009
SALES (est): 200K **Privately Held**
SIC: 3533 Derricks, oil or gas field

Ringling
Jefferson County

(G-8081)
PHELPS MACHINE & FABRICATION
1000 W Pine St (73456-5001)
P.O. Box 423 (73456-0423)
PHONE 580 662-2465
Steve Phelps, *President*
Billy Phelps, *President*
EMP: 10

SALES (est): 690K **Privately Held**
SIC: 3469 7692 3548 3544 Machine parts, stamped or pressed metal; welding repair; welding apparatus; special dies, tools, jigs & fixtures; fabricated plate work (boiler shop)

(G-8082)
RINGLING EAGLE
103 E Main St (73456)
P.O. Box 626 (73456-0626)
PHONE 580 662-2221
Melissa Grace, *Owner*
Jay Grace, *Co-Owner*
EMP: 3
SALES: 89K **Privately Held**
SIC: 2711 Newspapers, publishing & printing

Ringwood
Major County

(G-8083)
AMAZING GRACE FUDGE LLC
263025 E County Road 48 (73768-1222)
PHONE 580 883-4693
EMP: 2
SALES (est): 89.9K **Privately Held**
SIC: 2064 Fudge (candy)

(G-8084)
B & B HYDROSEEDING LLC
42666 S 264 Rd (73768)
PHONE 580 883-5997
Roger Bowling, *Mng Member*
EMP: 17
SALES: 1.9MM **Privately Held**
WEB: www.hydroseeding.yolasite.com
SIC: 2819 Hydrochloric acid

(G-8085)
BERMUDA KING LLC
Also Called: Bermuda King
44501 S County Road 266 (73768-3426)
PHONE 405 375-5000
Brian Henderson,
Brett Henderson,
EMP: 5 EST: 1965
SQ FT: 20,000
SALES (est): 798.8K **Privately Held**
WEB: www.bermudaking.com
SIC: 3523 Farm machinery & equipment

(G-8086)
CONTINENTAL RESOURCES INC
3 S Of Ringwood (73768)
PHONE 580 883-2838
Angelo Corso, *Sales Staff*
Ken Stamball, *Manager*
EMP: 3
SALES (corp-wide): 4.6B **Publicly Held**
SIC: 1381 Drilling oil & gas wells
PA: Continental Resources, Inc.
20 N Broadway
Oklahoma City OK 73102
405 234-9000

(G-8087)
D & B OIL FIELD SERVICES INC
223 W Melrose St (73768)
P.O. Box 234 (73768-0234)
PHONE 580 883-2897
Preston Jones, *President*
Lacey Rains, *Controller*
Penny Watkins, *Controller*
Donna Nightingale, *Admin Sec*
EMP: 65
SALES (est): 2.9MM **Privately Held**
WEB: www.dboilfieldservicesinc.com
SIC: 1389 Oil field services; gas field services

(G-8088)
DOUBLE R SERVICES COMPANY INC
46953 S County Road 267 (73768-2531)
PHONE 580 883-4637
Ronald Robinson, *President*
Ronald L Robinson, *President*
Roger Snodgrass, *Vice Pres*
EMP: 20

GEOGRAPHIC SECTION

Roosevelt - Kiowa County (G-8116)

SALES: 3.5MM **Privately Held**
SIC: 1389 Oil field services

(G-8089)
PHIL LACK
Also Called: Permian Well Service
S Main St (73768)
P.O. Box 177 (73768-0177)
PHONE.................580 883-4945
Phil Lack, *Owner*
EMP: 50
SQ FT: 2,000
SALES (est): 2.4MM **Privately Held**
SIC: 1381 7353 Drilling oil & gas wells; oil well drilling equipment, rental or leasing

(G-8090)
R&R ROUSTABOUT SERVICES LLC
Also Called: R&R Roustabout Rental Services
220 N Main St (73768)
P.O. Box 253 (73768-0253)
PHONE.................580 883-4647
Jorge Rodriguez, *CEO*
Charles Prado, *CFO*
EMP: 44
SALES: 10MM **Privately Held**
SIC: 1389 3441 3533 7389 Construction, repair & dismantling services; fabricated structural metal; oil & gas field machinery; crane & aerial lift service

(G-8091)
REDDING WELDING LLC
42015 S 264 Rd (73768)
PHONE.................580 883-4683
Donn Redding, *Administration*
EMP: 1
SALES (est): 44.4K **Privately Held**
SIC: 7692 Welding repair

(G-8092)
S&S CANVAS & UPHOLSTERY
10510 Highway 58 (73768-5822)
PHONE.................580 231-2587
Shawn Miller, *Principal*
EMP: 1
SALES (est): 46.5K **Privately Held**
SIC: 2211 Canvas

(G-8093)
STRIDE WELL SERVICE
Hwy 60 58 12 Mile St (73768)
PHONE.................580 883-4931
Leo Lucas, *Manager*
EMP: 45 **Privately Held**
SIC: 1389 Construction, repair & dismantling services
PA: Stride Well Service
Kleberg Cnty N
Kingsville TX 78363

(G-8094)
TARGA PPLINE MID-CONTINENT LLC
3196 Highway 58 (73768-9651)
PHONE.................580 883-2273
Tony Aldrich, *Branch Mgr*
EMP: 51 **Publicly Held**
SIC: 1389 Processing service, gas
HQ: Targa Pipeline Mid-Continent Llc
110 W 7th St Ste 2300
Tulsa OK 74119
918 574-3500

(G-8095)
TARGA RESOURCES CORP
3196 Highway 58 (73768-9651)
PHONE.................580 883-2273
Arnie Krush, *Branch Mgr*
Cody Trahan, *Executive*
Blade Rowe, *Technician*
Melissa Winters, *Analyst*
EMP: 100 **Publicly Held**
SIC: 1311 Natural gas production
PA: Targa Resources Corp
811 Louisiana St Ste 2100
Houston TX 77002

(G-8096)
VERNON E FAULCONER INC
7122 Highway 58 (73768-5820)
PHONE.................580 883-2892
Vernon Faulconer, *Branch Mgr*
EMP: 2
SALES (corp-wide): 84.9MM **Privately Held**
WEB: www.vefinc.com
SIC: 1311 Crude petroleum production
PA: Vernon E. Faulconer, Inc.
1001 E Se Loop 323 # 160
Tyler TX 75701
903 581-4382

(G-8097)
WESTERN GAS RESOURCES INC
Also Called: Chaney Dell Plant
3 N Hwy 58 (73768)
PHONE.................580 883-2273
Rex Specht, *Manager*
EMP: 31
SALES (corp-wide): 21.2B **Publicly Held**
SIC: 1311 Crude petroleum production
HQ: Western Gas Resources, Inc.
1099 18th St
Denver CO 80202

(G-8098)
XTO ENERGY INC
501 S Highway 58 (73768)
P.O. Box 197 (73768-0197)
PHONE.................580 883-2253
Scott Griffith, *Superintendent*
EMP: 39
SALES (corp-wide): 264.9B **Publicly Held**
WEB: www.xtoenergy.com
SIC: 1311 Crude petroleum production
HQ: Xto Energy Inc.
110 W 7th St
Fort Worth TX 76102

Ripley
Payne County

(G-8099)
CHER OIL COMPANY INC
7317 S Ripley Rd (74062-6227)
PHONE.................405 454-1575
Rick Nossaman, *President*
EMP: 7
SQ FT: 500
SALES (est): 810K **Privately Held**
SIC: 1311 Crude petroleum production; natural gas production

(G-8100)
DAVID D KUYKENDALL
8414 W Grandstaff (74062-6408)
PHONE.................918 223-5055
David Kuykendall, *Principal*
EMP: 1
SALES (est): 77.7K **Privately Held**
SIC: 7692 Welding repair

(G-8101)
KUYKENDAL WLDG BACKHOE SVC LLC
8414 W Grandstaff (74062-6408)
PHONE.................918 372-4899
Max Myers,
EMP: 1
SALES (est): 13.3K **Privately Held**
SIC: 3531 Backhoes

(G-8102)
MOORE CONTRACT PUMPING
11906 E 68th St (74062-6299)
PHONE.................918 372-4645
EMP: 1 **EST:** 1988
SALES (est): 70K **Privately Held**
SIC: 1389 Oil/Gas Field Services

(G-8103)
NANCYS TRUNK
9211 W Main St (74062-6526)
PHONE.................405 413-5037
Nancy Schlegel, *Principal*
EMP: 7
SALES (est): 752.6K **Privately Held**
WEB: www.nancystrunk.com
SIC: 3161 Trunks

Rocky
Washita County

(G-8104)
L&C METAL BUILDINGS LLC
22380 E 1250 Rd (73661-2006)
PHONE.................580 660-5515
Lance McCuistion,
EMP: 2
SALES (est): 150.2K **Privately Held**
SIC: 3448 Prefabricated metal buildings

(G-8105)
ROCKY FARMERS COOPERATIVE INC (PA)
105 N Main St (73661-4000)
P.O. Box 245 (73661-0245)
PHONE.................580 666-2440
Ron Koper, *President*
Lynn Wood, *Corp Secy*
EMP: 11 **EST:** 1920
SQ FT: 2,400
SALES (est): 4.7MM **Privately Held**
WEB: www.westernproducerscoop.com
SIC: 5153 2048 5191 Grain elevators; grains; prepared feeds; feed; seeds: field, garden & flower; fertilizer & fertilizer materials

(G-8106)
WESTERN WELDING
22444 E 1240 Rd (73661-6157)
PHONE.................580 832-2985
Rebecca Schmidt, *Principal*
EMP: 1 **EST:** 2018
SALES (est): 30K **Privately Held**
SIC: 7692 Welding repair

Roff
Pontotoc County

(G-8107)
COVIA HOLDINGS CORPORATION
3rd & Walling St (74865)
P.O. Box 159 (74865-0159)
PHONE.................580 456-7772
Gary Froemming, *General Mgr*
EMP: 21
SALES (corp-wide): 125.5MM **Publicly Held**
SIC: 1446 1442 Silica mining; construction sand & gravel
HQ: Covia Holdings Corporation
3 Summit Park Dr Ste 700
Independence OH 44131
440 214-3284

(G-8108)
FAIRMOUNT MINERALS
8834 Mayfield Rd (74865)
P.O. Box 368 (74865-0368)
PHONE.................580 456-7791
EMP: 4 **EST:** 2008
SALES (est): 610K **Privately Held**
SIC: 3533 Drilling tools for gas, oil or water wells

(G-8109)
JEFFERY MARIOTT
Also Called: K&K Hardwood
27800 County Road 3500 (74865-9040)
PHONE.................580 320-5474
Jeffery Mariott, *Owner*
EMP: 23 **EST:** 2013
SALES (est): 701.8K **Privately Held**
SIC: 2421 Sawmills & planing mills, general

(G-8110)
ROFF IRON & SALES INC
7010 County Road 1650 (74865-6015)
P.O. Box 146 (74865-0146)
PHONE.................580 456-7850
James Cornell, *President*
Denzil F Lowry Jr, *Principal*
Sherry Cornell, *Admin Sec*
EMP: 30

SALES (est): 4.9MM **Privately Held**
SIC: 1542 4213 7692 Nonresidential construction; trucking, except local; welding repair

(G-8111)
SELF-SUSPENDING PROPPANT LLC
Cr 1650 & 14th St (74865)
PHONE.................580 456-7791
Jenniffer Deckard, *President*
EMP: 20 **EST:** 2013
SALES (est): 1.2MM
SALES (corp-wide): 125.5MM **Publicly Held**
SIC: 2891 Adhesives
HQ: Covia Holdings Corporation
3 Summit Park Dr Ste 700
Independence OH 44131
440 214-3284

(G-8112)
TECHNISAND INC
Also Called: Technisand Plant 2
900 S Hickory (74865)
P.O. Box 368 (74865-0368)
PHONE.................580 456-7791
Robert Bigbee, *Branch Mgr*
EMP: 57
SALES (corp-wide): 125.5MM **Publicly Held**
SIC: 1442 Construction sand & gravel
HQ: Technisand, Inc.
11833 Ravenna Rd
Chardon OH 44024

Roland
Sequoyah County

(G-8113)
S S DESIGN CO
420 W Ray Fine Blvd (74954-5101)
P.O. Box 303 (74954-0303)
PHONE.................918 427-3230
Sarah Watson, *Owner*
EMP: 2 **EST:** 2012
SALES (est): 171.4K **Privately Held**
WEB: www.ssdesigncompany.com
SIC: 7389 3993 Design services; signs & advertising specialties

(G-8114)
STACEY OIL SERVICES
479273 Us Highway 64 (74954)
PHONE.................918 427-3940
David Fletcher, *Manager*
EMP: 2
SALES (est): 124.1K **Privately Held**
SIC: 1389 Oil field services

(G-8115)
WHIMSICAL SIGN AND CRAFTING CO
512 Carson Rd (74954-5169)
PHONE.................918 315-4715
Elizabeth Wiggins, *Principal*
EMP: 1
SALES (est): 46K **Privately Held**
SIC: 3993 Signs & advertising specialties

Roosevelt
Kiowa County

(G-8116)
DOLESE BROS CO
15129 N 2220 Rd (73564-5103)
PHONE.................580 576-9478
EMP: 1
SALES (corp-wide): 8.5MM **Privately Held**
SIC: 3273 Ready-mixed concrete
PA: Dolese Bros. Co.
20 Nw 13th St
Oklahoma City OK 73103
405 235-2311

Rose
Mayes County

(G-8117)
DIAMOND R SADDLE SHOP
8134 S 448 Rd (74364-2142)
PHONE..................918 479-6279
Harold Reed, *Owner*
EMP: 1 **EST:** 1998
SALES (est): 86.4K **Privately Held**
SIC: 3111 Saddlery leather

(G-8118)
KERN VALLEY INDUSTRIES
Also Called: K V I
6248 E 526 Rd (74364-1262)
P.O. Box 126 (74364-0126)
PHONE..................918 868-3911
Donald C Fleming, *Owner*
EMP: 1
SALES (est): 104.4K **Privately Held**
SIC: 3812 3728 3537 7363 Search & navigation equipment; aircraft parts & equipment; industrial trucks & tractors; pilot service, aviation

Rush Springs
Grady County

(G-8119)
BOBBY FOSTER
Also Called: Foster Feed & Produce Company
5 Mi N Of City (73082)
P.O. Box 45 (73082-0045)
PHONE..................580 476-3417
Bobby Foster, *Owner*
EMP: 1
SALES (est): 62.3K **Privately Held**
SIC: 2048 Stock feeds, dry

(G-8120)
DOUBLE J BEEF JERKY
430 County St 2820 (73082)
PHONE..................580 476-2465
Jerry Bewley, *Owner*
Angela Bewley, *Co-Owner*
EMP: 2
SALES: 20K **Privately Held**
SIC: 2013 Snack sticks, including jerky: from purchased meat; spiced meats from purchased meat

(G-8121)
H DIAMOND RESOURCES INC
Also Called: Dhr Manufacturing
S Hwy 81 (73082)
P.O. Box 207 (73082-0207)
PHONE..................580 476-3733
Larry D Hayes, *President*
Debbie K Hayes, *Corp Secy*
EMP: 10
SQ FT: 8,000
SALES (est): 1.6MM **Privately Held**
SIC: 3523 Plows, agricultural: disc, moldboard, chisel, listers, etc.

(G-8122)
J & C MANUFACTURING INC
Hwy 81 S (73082)
P.O. Box 555 (73082-0555)
PHONE..................580 476-3217
Larry Jackson Jr, *President*
Nick Jackson, *Vice Pres*
Ora Jackson, *Vice Pres*
Joan Jackson, *Treasurer*
EMP: 12
SALES (est): 1.8MM **Privately Held**
SIC: 3715 3713 Trailer bodies; truck beds

(G-8123)
LINDSEY PRINTING
207 W Blakely St (73082)
P.O. Box 846 (73082-0846)
PHONE..................580 476-2278
Steve Lindsey, *Owner*
EMP: 1 **EST:** 1977
SALES (est): 100K **Privately Held**
SIC: 3993 2759 2752 Signs, not made in custom sign painting shops; commercial printing; commercial printing, lithographic

(G-8124)
P H D OIL & GAS INC
223 W Blakely St (73082-1709)
PHONE..................580 476-3005
EMP: 2 **EST:** 1980
SQ FT: 3,000
SALES: 60K **Privately Held**
SIC: 1311 Crude Petroleum/Natural Gas Production

(G-8125)
RUSH SPRINGS GAZETTE
220 W Blakely St (73082-1709)
P.O. Box 597 (73082-0597)
PHONE..................580 476-2525
Karen Goodwin, *Owner*
EMP: 2
SALES (est): 75K **Privately Held**
SIC: 2711 Newspapers, publishing & printing

(G-8126)
SUPERIOR WELDING & FABRICATION
4245 County Street 2845 (73082-2438)
PHONE..................580 641-0634
Tony Willeford, *Principal*
EMP: 1
SALES (est): 25K **Privately Held**
SIC: 7692 Welding repair

(G-8127)
TAFF WELDING LLC
24805 Ne Welch Rd (73082-3505)
PHONE..................580 678-8978
EMP: 1
SALES (est): 43K **Privately Held**
SIC: 7692 Welding repair

(G-8128)
TRI RED LLC
4624 Highway 81 (73082-3164)
PHONE..................580 476-2551
David L Graves,
Dusty Graves,
Michael Graves,
EMP: 22
SQ FT: 7,260
SALES (est): 5.6MM **Privately Held**
SIC: 3441 Fabricated structural metal

(G-8129)
TROUTMAN ENTERPRISES LLC
Also Called: Troutman Dragline Service
4401 County Street 2760 (73082-3070)
PHONE..................405 351-0665
Ben Troutman, *Mng Member*
EMP: 2
SALES (est): 60.2K **Privately Held**
SIC: 7692 8748 1799 8711 Welding repair; business consulting; welding on site; consulting engineer

(G-8130)
VON TROUTMAN TIMOTHY
472 County Road 1560 (73082-3031)
PHONE..................580 583-7004
Von Troutman Timothy, *Principal*
EMP: 1 **EST:** 2010
SALES (est): 35.3K **Privately Held**
SIC: 7692 Welding repair

Saint Louis
Pottawatomie County

(G-8131)
BILL LAIRD OIL COMPANY
Also Called: Les Well Service
123 Town Cir (74866)
P.O. Box 120 (74866-0120)
PHONE..................405 289-3346
Bill Laird, *Owner*
EMP: 8
SQ FT: 660
SALES (est): 570K **Privately Held**
SIC: 1389 Oil & gas wells: building, repairing & dismantling

(G-8132)
SAINT LOUIS WELL SERVICE INC
1 Main St (74866)
P.O. Box 51 (74866-0051)
PHONE..................405 289-3314
Michael Goodnight, *President*
Karen Goodnight, *Corp Secy*
John Goodnight, *Vice Pres*
EMP: 20
SALES (est): 1.5MM **Privately Held**
SIC: 1389 1382 Servicing oil & gas wells; oil & gas exploration services

Salina
Mayes County

(G-8133)
BUTCHER & SONS STEEL INDS
155 S 4477 (74365-2079)
PHONE..................918 434-5276
Dolores H Butcher, *President*
William O Butcher, *Vice Pres*
EMP: 5
SALES (est): 413.6K **Privately Held**
SIC: 3441 Fabricated structural metal

(G-8134)
GREG BUTCHER
Also Called: Kenwood Industries
923 County Road 487 (74365-1425)
PHONE..................918 434-6892
Greg Butcher, *Owner*
Jan Butcher, *Co-Owner*
EMP: 2
SQ FT: 7,200
SALES (est): 1MM **Privately Held**
SIC: 4953 3441 Rubbish collection & disposal; fabricated structural metal

(G-8135)
R W D 9 MAYES COUNTY
3134 E 523 (74365-2367)
P.O. Box 916 (74365-0916)
PHONE..................918 434-5000
Brent Bridges, *Manager*
EMP: 3
SALES (est): 366K **Privately Held**
SIC: 5074 2086 Water softeners; pasteurized & mineral waters, bottled & canned

Sallisaw
Sequoyah County

(G-8136)
A-OK PRINTING MILL
1101 E Cherokee Ave (74955-5035)
PHONE..................918 775-6809
Wayne Nicholson, *Owner*
EMP: 2
SALES (est): 110K **Privately Held**
SIC: 2752 2791 2789 Commercial printing, offset; typesetting; bookbinding & related work

(G-8137)
APAC-CENTRAL INC
1000 W Cherokee Ave 683 (74955-4006)
P.O. Box 190 (74955-0190)
PHONE..................918 775-3251
Perry Poindexter, *Manager*
EMP: 6
SALES (corp-wide): 29.7B **Privately Held**
SIC: 3273 Ready-mixed concrete
HQ: Apac-Central, Inc.
  755 E Millsap Rd
  Fayetteville AR 72703

(G-8138)
AUTOMATIC & AUTO MACHINING INC
460 Jenkins Rd (74955-5449)
PHONE..................918 775-9770
EMP: 4
SALES: 100K **Privately Held**
SIC: 3599 Mfg Industrial Machinery

(G-8139)
AUTOMOTIVE MACHINE SHOP
460 Jenkins Rd (74955-5449)
P.O. Box 772 (74955-0772)
PHONE..................918 775-9770
EMP: 3 **EST:** 1996
SALES (est): 270.1K **Privately Held**
SIC: 3519 Mfg Automobile Engines

(G-8140)
C & P MANUFACTURING INC
Rr 2 Box 96 (74955-9057)
P.O. Box 416 (74955-0416)
PHONE..................918 773-5060
EMP: 15 **EST:** 1997
SQ FT: 6,500
SALES: 500K **Privately Held**
SIC: 3599 Mfg Industrial Machinery

(G-8141)
CECILS ELECTRIC MOTOR CO
28 E Interstate Cir (74955-7003)
PHONE..................918 775-3968
Cecil Mantil, *Owner*
EMP: 1
SALES (est): 40.5K **Privately Held**
SIC: 7694 7629 Electric motor repair; electrical repair shops

(G-8142)
CELLOFOAM NORTH AMERICA INC
1330 W Redwood Ave (74955)
P.O. Box 976 (74955-0976)
PHONE..................918 775-7758
Perry Carlson, *Manager*
EMP: 30
SALES (corp-wide): 155.4MM **Privately Held**
SIC: 3089 3086 Extruded finished plastic products; plastics foam products
PA: Cellofoam North America Inc.
  1917 Rockdale Indstrl Blv
  Conyers GA 30012
  770 929-3688

(G-8143)
COOKSON HILLS PUBLISHERS INC
Also Called: Sequoyah County Times
111 N Oak St (74955-4637)
PHONE..................918 775-4433
Jim Mayo, *President*
Jeff Mayo, *Principal*
Smith Regina, *Editor*
Becky Mayo, *Office Mgr*
Delanna Nutter, *Manager*
EMP: 28 **EST:** 1893
SQ FT: 10,000
SALES (est): 1.6MM **Privately Held**
WEB: www.sequoyahcountytimes.com
SIC: 2711 Job printing & newspaper publishing combined

(G-8144)
E & E CONSTRUCTION COMPANY
1700 W Ruth Ave (74955-7243)
PHONE..................918 775-6222
Vernon Edwards, *Partner*
Charles Elam, *Partner*
EMP: 2
SALES (est): 150K **Privately Held**
SIC: 7692 5211 Welding repair; prefabricated buildings

(G-8145)
GUTHRIE DARIN CABINET SHOP
456556 E 1080 Rd (74955-8618)
P.O. Box 92 (74955-0092)
PHONE..................918 773-8444
Darin Guthrie, *Principal*
EMP: 1 **EST:** 2010
SALES (est): 103.6K **Privately Held**
WEB: www.guthriecabinets.com
SIC: 2434 Wood kitchen cabinets

(G-8146)
JOHN SCOGGINS COMPANY INC
Hwy 64 E (74955)
P.O. Box 1388 (74955-1388)
PHONE..................918 775-2748
Dan Scoggins, *President*
EMP: 35
SQ FT: 6,000

GEOGRAPHIC SECTION

Sand Springs - Tulsa County (G-8177)

SALES (est): 8.3MM **Privately Held**
SIC: 5169 2842 5172 Industrial chemicals; sweeping compounds, oil or water absorbent, clay or sawdust; lubricating oils & greases

(G-8147)
LDA INDUSTRIES LLC
1502 W Chickasaw Ave # 3 (74955-7262)
PHONE 918 315-9758
Latisha Adams, *Principal*
EMP: 2
SALES (est): 132K **Privately Held**
SIC: 3999 Manufacturing industries

(G-8148)
MEFFORD 4 WELDING INC
108530 S 4550 Rd (74955-4071)
PHONE 918 773-6326
Christopher Mefford, *Principal*
EMP: 1
SALES (est): 28.1K **Privately Held**
WEB: www.b-bwelding.com
SIC: 7692 Welding repair

(G-8149)
MID CONTINENT CONCRETE CO
Also Called: Midco Ready Mix
1515 W Redwood Ave (74955-2438)
P.O. Box 429 (74955-0429)
PHONE 918 775-6858
Dean Ringgold, *Manager*
EMP: 6 **Privately Held**
SIC: 3531 3273 Concrete plants; ready-mixed concrete
HQ: Mid-Continent Concrete Company, Inc.
 431 W 23rd St
 Tulsa OK 74107

(G-8150)
PAGE TOOL & MACHINE SHOP
3009 N Wheeler Ave (74955-4673)
PHONE 918 775-6766
Carl Paige, *Owner*
EMP: 1
SALES (est): 88.8K **Privately Held**
SIC: 3544 7692 Special dies, tools, jigs & fixtures; welding repair

(G-8151)
SLW AUTOMOTIVE INC
Also Called: Slpt Global Pump Group
1300 S Opdyke St (74955-7035)
PHONE 918 776-3157
Douglas Hunter, *Engineer*
Ron Nelson, *Engineer*
James McCawley, *Senior Engr*
Amy Obryan, *Technology*
Mark Lemp, *Director*
EMP: 29
SALES (corp-wide): 93.8MM **Privately Held**
SIC: 3714 Fuel pipes, motor vehicle
HQ: Slw Automotive, Inc.
 1955 W Hamlin Rd
 Rochester Hills MI 48309

(G-8152)
SOONER STEEL RULE DIES
460538 E 1000 Rd (74955-5344)
PHONE 918 775-2668
Ron Bletso, *Owner*
EMP: 1
SALES (est): 54.8K **Privately Held**
SIC: 3544 Special dies, tools, jigs & fixtures

(G-8153)
STONE SPLITTERS INC
300 E Vine Ave (74955-3644)
P.O. Box 1702 (74955-1702)
PHONE 479 651-8873
Jamie Fargo, *President*
Debbie Fargo, *Treasurer*
EMP: 1
SALES (est): 155.4K **Privately Held**
SIC: 3271 Brick, concrete

(G-8154)
SUPERCUTS INC
1108 W Ruth Ave (74955-7208)
PHONE 918 775-6389
Bobby Miller, *General Mgr*
EMP: 5
SALES (est): 38.3K **Privately Held**
WEB: www.supercuts.com
SIC: 7231 2844 7299 Unisex hair salons; hair coloring preparations; massage parlor

(G-8155)
WNDELLS WOODTURNING
465172 E 1060 Rd (74955-7436)
PHONE 918 775-1124
Wendell Mills, *Principal*
EMP: 1 **EST:** 2017
SALES (est): 54.1K **Privately Held**
SIC: 2431 Millwork

Sand Springs
Tulsa County

(G-8156)
ACCENT MACHINE INC
102 Wellston Park Rd (74063-5513)
P.O. Box 104, Prue (74060-0104)
PHONE 918 246-9695
Robert Myers, *President*
EMP: 2
SQ FT: 2,500
SALES (est): 306.4K **Privately Held**
SIC: 3599 Machine shop, jobbing & repair

(G-8157)
ACTION MACHINE SHOP
403 W 2nd St (74063-6701)
PHONE 918 245-8308
Robert F Telford, *Owner*
EMP: 4
SQ FT: 3,000
SALES (est): 240.1K **Privately Held**
SIC: 3599 7692 Machine shop, jobbing & repair; welding repair

(G-8158)
ALLEM SIGN CO
4608 Redbud Dr (74063-3241)
PHONE 918 241-7206
Jon Allem, *Principal*
EMP: 2
SALES (est): 167.7K **Privately Held**
SIC: 3993 Signs & advertising specialties

(G-8159)
AMERICAN HEATING COMPANY INC
11 E Broadway St Ste 200a (74063-7631)
PHONE 918 246-0700
Danny Devilbiss, *Plant Mgr*
Steve Matney, *Project Mgr*
EMP: 8
SALES (corp-wide): 2.6MM **Privately Held**
SIC: 3433 Heating equipment, except electric
PA: American Heating Company, Inc.
 1200 Route 46
 Clifton NJ
 973 777-0100

(G-8160)
AMI INSTRUMENTS INC
4116 Rustic Rd (74063-3101)
PHONE 918 241-2665
Larry E Hocutt, *Principal*
EMP: 2
SALES (est): 171.2K **Privately Held**
SIC: 3699 Electrical equipment & supplies

(G-8161)
ANDY ANDERSON METAL WORKS INC
1064 1/2 N Willow Rd (74063-5714)
P.O. Box 134 (74063-0134)
PHONE 918 245-2355
Mitchell Anderson, *President*
Rebecca Anderson, *Treasurer*
EMP: 12 **EST:** 1967
SQ FT: 1,380
SALES (est): 2.3MM **Privately Held**
WEB: www.andyandersonmetalworks.com
SIC: 7692 3444 Welding repair; sheet metalwork

(G-8162)
ARMED INC
214 N Main St (74063-7652)
PHONE 918 245-1478
EMP: 3
SALES (est): 320K **Privately Held**
SIC: 3559 Mfg Misc Industry Machinery

(G-8163)
AURORA INNOVATIONS LLC
3334 N State Highway 97 (74063-8381)
PHONE 918 519-5356
Freddie G Smith, *Administration*
EMP: 3
SALES (est): 311.5K **Privately Held**
SIC: 2873 Fertilizers: natural (organic), except compost

(G-8164)
B J PRINTING PRODUCTS INC
305 W 40th Pl (74063-2650)
PHONE 918 245-6385
William Nix, *Owner*
EMP: 1
SALES (est): 9.6K **Privately Held**
SIC: 2752 Commercial printing, lithographic

(G-8165)
BAKER PETROLITE LLC
Also Called: Chemlink
9100 W 21st St (74063-8520)
P.O. Box 370 (74063-0370)
PHONE 918 245-2224
Bob Burks, *Branch Mgr*
EMP: 130 **Privately Held**
SIC: 2899 3533 Chemical preparations; oil & gas field machinery
HQ: Baker Petrolite Llc
 12645 W Airport Blvd
 Sugar Land TX 77478
 281 276-5400

(G-8166)
BERKSHIRE HATHAWAY INC
Also Called: Sand Springs Leader
303 N Mckinley Ave (74063-7612)
P.O. Box 1770, Tulsa (74102-1770)
PHONE 918 245-6634
EMP: 3
SALES (corp-wide): 327.2B **Publicly Held**
SIC: 2711 Newspapers
PA: Berkshire Hathaway Inc.
 3555 Farnam St Ste 1140
 Omaha NE 68131
 402 346-1400

(G-8167)
BILLY J VINEYARD
16601 W 21st St S (74063-4995)
PHONE 918 246-2139
Billy J Vineyard, *Principal*
EMP: 4
SALES (est): 156.2K **Privately Held**
SIC: 2084 Wines

(G-8168)
C & C CABINETS
17502 Coyote Trl (74063)
PHONE 918 241-5249
EMP: 4
SALES (est): 220K **Privately Held**
SIC: 2434 Mfg Wood Kitchen Cabinets

(G-8169)
C AND H PUBLISHING CO
Also Called: Hunter's Horn
117 N Garfield Ave (74063-7214)
P.O. Box 426 (74063-0426)
PHONE 918 245-9571
Fax: 918 245-9571
EMP: 4
SALES (corp-wide): 559K **Privately Held**
SIC: 2721 0742 2759 Periodicals-Publishing/Printing Veterinary Services Commercial Printing
PA: C And H Publishing Co
 114 E Franklin St
 Sesser IL 62884
 618 625-2711

(G-8170)
CHUMBOLLY PRESS LLC
223 N Sunset Ave (74063-7363)
PHONE 918 607-3932
Rhonda Churchill, *Mng Member*
EMP: 1 **EST:** 2012
SALES (est): 48.9K **Privately Held**
SIC: 2741 Miscellaneous publishing

(G-8171)
COBRA SELF DEFENSE TULSA
1108 W Wekiwa Rd (74063-6749)
PHONE 918 691-0054
EMP: 3
SALES (est): 176.7K **Privately Held**
SIC: 3812 Defense systems & equipment

(G-8172)
CORRPRO COMPANIES INC
11616 W 59th St S (74063-3740)
PHONE 918 245-8791
Jack Hale, *Branch Mgr*
EMP: 50
SALES (corp-wide): 1.2B **Publicly Held**
SIC: 3699 8711 3643 3317 Electrical equipment & supplies; engineering services; current-carrying wiring devices; steel pipe & tubes; chemical preparations
HQ: Corrpro Companies, Inc.
 1055 W Smith Rd
 Medina OH 44256
 330 723-5082

(G-8173)
CREATIVE MEDIA
712 N Cleveland Ave (74063-7336)
P.O. Box 1252 (74063-1252)
PHONE 918 245-3779
Donna Perryman, *Owner*
EMP: 1
SALES (est): 108.3K **Privately Held**
SIC: 2791 Typesetting

(G-8174)
CUST-O-FAB LLC (PA)
8888 W 21st St (74063-8538)
PHONE 918 245-6685
Berry Keeler, *President*
Carrie Wood, *CFO*
Peter Sawyer, *Sr Software Eng*
▼ **EMP:** 160
SQ FT: 108,000
SALES (est): 35.2MM **Privately Held**
SIC: 7699 3443 Industrial equipment services; heat exchangers, condensers & components

(G-8175)
CUST-O-FAB SPECIALTY SVCS LLC (HQ)
8888 W 21st St (74063-8538)
PHONE 918 245-6685
Richard McDaniel, *President*
JD Hughes, *Manager*
Danny O Brian,
Tony Phillips,
EMP: 67
SQ FT: 5,000
SALES (est): 20.9MM
SALES (corp-wide): 35.2MM **Privately Held**
SIC: 3443 Heat exchangers, plate type
PA: Cust-O-Fab, Llc
 8888 W 21st St
 Sand Springs OK 74063
 918 245-6685

(G-8176)
D & V MANUFACTURING INC
105 Wellston Park Rd (74063-5514)
P.O. Box 6 (74063-0006)
PHONE 918 245-7858
Larry Van Winkle, *President*
Carla Van Winkle, *Corp Secy*
EMP: 10
SQ FT: 6,500
SALES (est): 1.9MM **Privately Held**
SIC: 3599 Machine shop, jobbing & repair

(G-8177)
D PARKS ENTERPRISES LLC
234 Dotson Dr (74063-7068)
PHONE 405 315-1994
EMP: 2 **EST:** 2010
SALES (est): 95.5K **Privately Held**
SIC: 3533 Mfg Oil/Gas Field Machinery

Sand Springs - Tulsa County (G-8178)

GEOGRAPHIC SECTION

(G-8178)
DIVERSIFIED PLASTICS INDS LLC
1606 W Timber Dr (74063-6321)
P.O. Box 1612 (74063-1612)
PHONE..................918 245-0770
Chris Reiss, *Manager*
Larry Hiner, *Analyst*
Harold Tuttle,
EMP: 8
SQ FT: 18,000
SALES (est): 1.9MM **Privately Held**
SIC: 3089 5162 5211 Plastic hardware & building products; plastics products; insulation material, building

(G-8179)
DRYVIT SYSTEMS INC
5850 S 116th West Ave (74063-3757)
PHONE..................918 245-0216
Alex Winiecke, *Principal*
EMP: 20
SQ FT: 37,732
SALES (corp-wide): 5.5B **Publicly Held**
SIC: 2952 1742 Siding, insulating: impregnated, from purchased materials; drywall
HQ: Dryvit Systems, Inc.
 1 Energy Way
 West Warwick RI 02893
 401 822-4100

(G-8180)
DUNHAMS ASPHALT SERVICES INC
Also Called: Ashphalt Plant
8387 W 21st St (74063-8597)
PHONE..................918 246-9210
Jeff Call, *Branch Mgr*
EMP: 1 **Privately Held**
SIC: 5032 2951 Paving materials; asphalt paving mixtures & blocks
PA: Dunham's Asphalt Services Inc
 6213 S 103rd West Ave
 Sapulpa OK 74066

(G-8181)
ECT SERVICES INC
10475 Lance Ln (74063-5908)
PHONE..................918 691-9320
Ronald W Hale, *President*
Nanci L Hale, *Principal*
EMP: 2
SALES (est): 290.5K **Privately Held**
SIC: 3569 Centrifugal purifiers

(G-8182)
EUBANKSWOODWORKS LLC
1201 E 8th St (74063-8771)
PHONE..................918 245-7835
William Alan Eubanks, *Agent*
EMP: 1
SALES (est): 65.9K **Privately Held**
SIC: 2431 Millwork

(G-8183)
FIBER GLASS SYSTEMS LP
Also Called: Smith Fibercast
25 S Main St (74063-6552)
P.O. Box 968 (74063-0968)
PHONE..................918 245-6651
Ray Breshears, *Vice Pres*
Chuck Farnan, *Mng Member*
James King, *IT/INT Sup*
◆ EMP: 115
SQ FT: 230,000
SALES (est): 21.9MM
SALES (corp-wide): 8.4B **Publicly Held**
WEB: www.nov.com
SIC: 3089 Plastic & fiberglass tanks
PA: National Oilwell Varco, Inc.
 7909 Parkwood Circle Dr
 Houston TX 77036
 713 346-7500

(G-8184)
FINELINE MANUFACTURING LLC
5816 S 116th West Ave A (74063-3731)
PHONE..................918 245-0900
Mitchell Bundy, *CEO*
EMP: 17
SALES (est): 3.2MM **Privately Held**
WEB: www.finelinemanufacturing.com
SIC: 3599 Machine & other job shop work

(G-8185)
FRAHM JOHN
Also Called: Frame Builders & Brokerage
302 W 39th St (74063-2639)
PHONE..................213 500-0741
John Henry Frahm, *Owner*
EMP: 5
SALES: 3MM **Privately Held**
SIC: 7389 2448 Brokers, business: buying & selling business enterprises; cargo containers, wood & metal combination

(G-8186)
FRAZIER MFG CO
200 Wellston Park Rd (74063-5515)
PHONE..................918 241-9110
Leon Frazier, *Owner*
EMP: 16
SQ FT: 15,000
SALES (est): 1.3MM **Privately Held**
SIC: 3599 Machine shop, jobbing & repair

(G-8187)
FULLERTON BUILDING SYSTEMS INC
Also Called: Fullerton Finish Systems
8645 W 21st St (74063-8529)
P.O. Box 609 (74063-0609)
PHONE..................918 246-9995
Ray Buchanan, *Branch Mgr*
EMP: 23
SALES (corp-wide): 41.5MM **Privately Held**
SIC: 2452 2431 Prefabricated buildings, wood; panel work, wood
HQ: Fullerton Building Systems, Inc.
 34620 250th St
 Worthington MN 56187
 507 376-3128

(G-8188)
GERDAU AMERISTEEL US INC
404 S Main St (74063-6565)
P.O. Box 280 (74063-0280)
PHONE..................918 241-7762
Ron Ancevic, *Manager*
EMP: 6 **Privately Held**
WEB: www.gerdau.com
SIC: 3312 Hot-rolled iron & steel products
HQ: Gerdau Ameristeel Us Inc.
 4221 W Boy Scout Blvd # 600
 Tampa FL 33607
 813 286-8383

(G-8189)
HARGROVE INDUSTRIES INC
6211 Merrimack Dr (74063-4327)
PHONE..................918 231-7290
Bryan Hargrove, *Principal*
EMP: 3 EST: 2009
SALES (est): 204.3K **Privately Held**
WEB: www.hargrovegaslogs.com
SIC: 3999 Manufacturing industries

(G-8190)
HARGROVE MANUFACTURING CORP
207 Wellston Park Rd (74063-5516)
PHONE..................918 241-7537
Gary Hargrove, *President*
Cindy Hargrove, *Vice Pres*
Douglas Hargrove, *Vice Pres*
Glenna Hargrove, *Vice Pres*
Cynthia Hargrove, *Treasurer*
▲ EMP: 35
SQ FT: 61,000
SALES (est): 6.5MM **Privately Held**
SIC: 3433 3429 Logs, gas fireplace; manufactured hardware (general)

(G-8191)
HODGES MANUFACTURING
106 Wellston Park Rd (74063-5513)
P.O. Box 464, Glenpool (74033-0464)
PHONE..................918 629-8723
Mavis Hodges, *Principal*
▲ EMP: 8
SALES (est): 784.7K **Privately Held**
WEB: www.downholeplunger.com
SIC: 3999 Manufacturing industries

(G-8192)
INDEPENDENT SCHOOL
Sand Springs Kindergarten Ctr
138 Oak St (74063)
PHONE..................918 245-2622
Thersea Ledbetter, *Principal*
EMP: 50
SALES (corp-wide): 44.5MM **Privately Held**
SIC: 8211 2731 Public elementary & secondary schools; book publishing
PA: Independent School District No 2 Of Tulsa County Oklahoma
 11 W Broadway St
 Sand Springs OK 74063
 918 246-1400

(G-8193)
INTEGRITY PIPING SERVICES CO
4801 Bermuda Cir (74063-2120)
PHONE..................918 850-0206
Jeffrey N Brinkley, *President*
EMP: 1
SALES (est): 143.9K **Privately Held**
SIC: 3498 Coils, pipe: fabricated from purchased pipe

(G-8194)
INTERSTATE ELECTRIC CORP
196 E Morrow Rd (74063-6534)
P.O. Box 668 (74063-0668)
PHONE..................918 245-4508
Polly Mae Nobles, *President*
EMP: 6
SQ FT: 11,340
SALES (est): 1.2MM **Privately Held**
SIC: 7694 3621 5999 Electric motor repair; motors & generators; engine & motor equipment & supplies

(G-8195)
JJ PERODEAU GUNMAKER INC
711 S 263rd West Ave (74063-5059)
PHONE..................580 747-1804
Isabelle Perodeau, *Principal*
Jj Perodeau, *Principal*
EMP: 2
SALES (est): 200.2K **Privately Held**
SIC: 3423 3484 Soldering guns or tools, hand: electric; shotguns or shotgun parts, 30 mm. & below

(G-8196)
K & S CONTROLS LLC
4408 S 209th West Ave (74063-4684)
PHONE..................918 363-7268
Kent Alan Van Arsdol, *Mng Member*
EMP: 6
SALES (est): 237K **Privately Held**
SIC: 3625 Control equipment, electric

(G-8197)
KAISER INVESTMENT
3112 S Nassau Ave (74063-2900)
PHONE..................918 245-4719
EMP: 1 EST: 1987
SALES (est): 100K **Privately Held**
SIC: 1311 Crude Petroleum/Natural Gas Production

(G-8198)
KEYSTONE SAND & GRAVEL
1430 N 209th West Ave (74063-5484)
PHONE..................918 241-0415
Glen Quimby, *Principal*
EMP: 3
SALES (est): 239.3K **Privately Held**
SIC: 1442 Construction sand & gravel

(G-8199)
LEATHER STORE
Also Called: Leather Stone
11 W 41st St (74063-2717)
PHONE..................918 245-8676
Pat Hale, *Owner*
EMP: 1
SQ FT: 700
SALES (est): 72K **Privately Held**
SIC: 5948 2386 Leather goods, except luggage & shoes; leather & sheep-lined clothing

(G-8200)
LEEMARK DENTAL PRODUCTS
10331 Edgewood Dr (74063-5808)
PHONE..................918 241-6683
Kellie Alexander, *Owner*
EMP: 2
SALES: 250K **Privately Held**
SIC: 3843 Dental equipment & supplies

(G-8201)
LLOYD FREEMAN CREATIONS LLC
935 S 177th West Ave (74063-9387)
PHONE..................918 245-4921
Lloyd D Freeman, *President*
EMP: 3
SALES (est): 213.8K **Privately Held**
SIC: 3089 Casting of plastic

(G-8202)
MARK MULLIN CO LLC
Also Called: Mark Mullin Company
201 Wellston Park Rd (74063-5516)
P.O. Box 786 (74063-0786)
PHONE..................918 245-1426
Mark Mullin, *Principal*
EMP: 2
SALES (est): 320.3K **Privately Held**
SIC: 3533 Oil & gas field machinery

(G-8203)
MAYCO RESOURCES LLC
1124 N Woodland Pl (74063-8964)
PHONE..................918 241-3392
Kyra Hamilton,
EMP: 5
SALES (est): 470K **Privately Held**
SIC: 1382 Oil & gas exploration services

(G-8204)
MIDWEST EQUIPMENT COMPANY INC
3208 Rawson Rd (74063-4038)
PHONE..................918 241-3672
Tom Cupps, *President*
Shelly Oliverius, *Regl Sales Mgr*
EMP: 2
SALES (est): 335.8K **Privately Held**
SIC: 3829 Vibration meters, analyzers & calibrators

(G-8205)
MOCK BROTHERS SADDLERY INC
17441 W 9th St S (74063-9725)
PHONE..................918 245-7259
Albert R Mock Jr, *Ch of Bd*
Bret Mock, *President*
Greg Mock, *Vice Pres*
Jason Mock, *Treasurer*
EMP: 8 EST: 1941
SQ FT: 5,000
SALES: 950K **Privately Held**
WEB: www.mockbros.com
SIC: 5699 3199 Western apparel; equestrian related leather articles

(G-8206)
MONITRON CORP
733 Greenview Cir (74063-7004)
PHONE..................918 836-6831
Marvin D Nelson II, *President*
Peggy Nelson, *Corp Secy*
EMP: 12
SALES (est): 1.1MM **Privately Held**
SIC: 3699 3663 Electrical equipment & supplies; radio & TV communications equipment

(G-8207)
MONTROSS TIRITA
Also Called: Mtds
21 W 41st St (74063-2717)
PHONE..................918 241-5637
Tirita Montross, *Owner*
EMP: 1
SALES (est): 26K **Privately Held**
SIC: 7991 3561 8711 1623 Aerobic dance & exercise classes; industrial pumps & parts; construction & civil engineering; water, sewer & utility lines; underground utilities contractor; protective lining installation, underground (sewage, etc.)

GEOGRAPHIC SECTION

Sand Springs - Tulsa County (G-8239)

(G-8208)
MORITZ INC
Also Called: Moritz Machine Shop
877 Creek Rd (74063-7056)
PHONE.................................918 834-1064
Ron Munson, *President*
Sharon Munson, *Corp Secy*
Jeff Robinson, *Opers Staff*
Michael Ford, *Finance Dir*
Rino Joseph, *Finance Dir*
EMP: 10
SQ FT: 4,000
SALES (est): 1.5MM **Privately Held**
SIC: 3599 Machine shop, jobbing & repair

(G-8209)
MOUNTAINTOP TEES LLC
10483 Lance Ln (74063-5908)
PHONE.................................918 508-6208
EMP: 2
SALES (est): 120.8K **Privately Held**
SIC: 2759 Screen printing

(G-8210)
NAUMANN MCHINING SOLUTIONS INC
Also Called: Nmsi
11308 W 57th Pl S (74063-3766)
P.O. Box 1967 (74063-1749)
PHONE.................................918 246-9898
Lee Naumann, *President*
Grisella Naumann, *Principal*
EMP: 11
SQ FT: 15,000
SALES (est): 1.5MM **Privately Held**
SIC: 3599 Machine shop, jobbing & repair

(G-8211)
OEM WELDING LLC
14139 W 31st St S (74063-2529)
PHONE.................................918 645-8483
Grady R Vandiver Jr, *Administration*
EMP: 2
SALES (est): 160.8K **Privately Held**
WEB: www.oemweldingllc.com
SIC: 7692 Welding repair

(G-8212)
OGI PROCESS EQUIPMENT INC
8939 W 21st St (74063-8515)
PHONE.................................918 246-1600
William Weber, *President*
Jim Buenzow, *Engineer*
EMP: 11
SQ FT: 2,900
SALES (est): 4.2MM **Privately Held**
SIC: 3567 Electrical furnaces, ovens & heating devices, exc. induction

(G-8213)
PARKER PLASTICS INC
101 S Woodland Dr (74063-8547)
P.O. Box 729 (74063-0729)
PHONE.................................918 241-0350
Chuck Major, *Manager*
EMP: 64
SALES (corp-wide): 43.5MM **Privately Held**
SIC: 3085 Plastics bottles
PA: Parker Plastics, Inc.
 8201 109th St Ste 200
 Pleasant Prairie WI 53158
 262 947-3344

(G-8214)
PIPING ENTERPRISE COMPANY INC
Also Called: Peco
1520 S 129th West Ave (74063-5537)
P.O. Box 1960 (74063-1960)
PHONE.................................918 246-7326
Charlie Blevins, *President*
Leah Blevins, *Admin Sec*
EMP: 300
SQ FT: 60,000
SALES (est): 23.6MM **Privately Held**
SIC: 7692 Welding repair

(G-8215)
PREFERRED FLEETWASH
16615 W Coyote Trl (74063-4781)
PHONE.................................918 281-9325
Aaron McCaffery, *Principal*
EMP: 2
SALES (est): 247.7K **Privately Held**
WEB: www.preferredfleetwash.net
SIC: 3589 Car washing machinery

(G-8216)
PYRAMID PRINTING
104 W 2nd St (74063-7226)
PHONE.................................918 514-4073
Jeff Mayhugh, *Owner*
EMP: 3
SALES (est): 130K **Privately Held**
WEB: www.pyramidprintingok.com
SIC: 2759 Screen printing

(G-8217)
QUIKWATER INC
Also Called: Quikwater.com
8939 W 21st St (74063-8515)
PHONE.................................918 241-8880
Ed Mansell, *President*
Ashley Weber, *Vice Pres*
EMP: 15
SALES (est): 3.1MM **Privately Held**
SIC: 3433 Heating equipment, except electric

(G-8218)
R & M PACKER INC
31 Sunset Dr (74063-7597)
PHONE.................................580 863-2242
Roger Kerstein, *President*
Marion Kerstein, *Admin Sec*
EMP: 6
SALES (est): 1.2MM **Privately Held**
SIC: 1389 Oil field services

(G-8219)
R A BODENHAME ASSOC INC
604 W 36th St (74063-2860)
PHONE.................................918 855-1964
Arandell Bodenhamer, *President*
EMP: 1
SALES (est): 110K **Privately Held**
SIC: 1389 Oil & gas field services

(G-8220)
RAY MCCLAIN INC
6310 Merrimack Dr (74063-4328)
PHONE.................................918 363-7350
Ray Mc Clain, *President*
Robert Ross, *Vice Pres*
Shannon McClain, *Manager*
EMP: 3
SALES (est): 240K **Privately Held**
SIC: 1389 Construction, repair & dismantling services

(G-8221)
REDLINE GASKETS LLC
124 Shawnee Rd (74063-8587)
PHONE.................................918 845-7700
Lindsay Gardner,
EMP: 2
SALES (est): 209K **Privately Held**
SIC: 3053 Gaskets & sealing devices

(G-8222)
SAMUELS JEWELREY L L C
1138 E Charles Page Blvd (74063-8510)
PHONE.................................918 241-6436
Samuel Newport, *Mng Member*
Amy Newport,
EMP: 2 EST: 1999
SALES (est): 215.5K **Privately Held**
SIC: 5944 3911 Jewelry stores; jewelry, precious metal

(G-8223)
SHIPMAN HOME IMPROVEMENT INC
724 N Willow Rd (74063-5725)
PHONE.................................918 514-0049
Mark Stevens, *Owner*
EMP: 1
SALES (est): 120K **Privately Held**
SIC: 2452 1761 1751 Panels & sections, prefabricated, wood; siding contractor; window & door (prefabricated) installation

(G-8224)
SIGNS & STITCHES
200 N Garfield Ave (74063-7215)
PHONE.................................918 245-3301
EMP: 3
SALES (est): 244.8K **Privately Held**
SIC: 3993 Electric signs

(G-8225)
SILVERSTONE LLC
4931 Redbud Dr (74063-3251)
PHONE.................................918 371-3622
Morgan K Powell, *Principal*
EMP: 1
SALES (est): 100.6K **Privately Held**
SIC: 2752 Commercial printing, lithographic

(G-8226)
SS TAG LLC
414 Plaza Ct (74063-7946)
PHONE.................................918 241-3400
M Elizabeth Frasier, *Mng Member*
Molly Elizabeth Frasier, *Mng Member*
EMP: 4
SALES (est): 288.1K **Privately Held**
SIC: 3469 Automobile license tags, stamped metal

(G-8227)
SUPER CUTS
Also Called: Supercuts
430 W Wekiwa Rd Ste D (74063-6767)
PHONE.................................918 245-3320
Chris Serrano, *Owner*
EMP: 1 EST: 2010
SALES (est): 39K **Privately Held**
WEB: www.supercuts.com
SIC: 7231 2842 Unisex hair salons; wax removers

(G-8228)
SWAIM SERUM COMPANY
13602 W 51st St S (74063-3669)
PHONE.................................918 241-4363
EMP: 3
SALES (est): 133K **Privately Held**
SIC: 2836 Serums

(G-8229)
T D H MFG INC
20520 W Wekiwa Rd (74063-8192)
P.O. Box 957 (74063-0957)
PHONE.................................918 241-8800
John Owens Jr, *President*
EMP: 2
SQ FT: 6,000
SALES (est): 100K **Privately Held**
SIC: 3821 Laboratory apparatus, except heating & measuring

(G-8230)
TMS INTERNATIONAL LLC
Olympic Mill Services Division
2300 S Highway 97 (74063-6554)
PHONE.................................918 241-0129
EMP: 8
SALES (corp-wide): 282.4MM **Privately Held**
SIC: 3449 3341 3312 Mfg Misc Structural Metalwork Secondary Nonferrous Metal Producer Blast Furnace-Steel Works
HQ: Tms International Group Llc
 12 Monongahela Ave
 Glassport PA 15203
 412 678-6141

(G-8231)
TROTTER CUSTOM WOODWORKS LLC
4039 S 177th West Ave (74063-4685)
PHONE.................................918 698-5231
Jason Trotter, *Principal*
EMP: 4
SALES (est): 384.4K **Privately Held**
SIC: 2431 Millwork

(G-8232)
TULSA METAL FINISHERS INC
Hwy 97 (74063)
PHONE.................................918 241-1290
Ralph D Gillean, *President*
Danny Gillean, *Vice Pres*
EMP: 2
SALES: 500K **Privately Held**
SIC: 3471 Finishing, metals or formed products

(G-8233)
TURNAIR
11315 W 57th Pl S (74063-3738)
PHONE.................................918 267-3535
Robert Turner, *Owner*
EMP: 1 EST: 2018
SALES (est): 25K **Privately Held**
SIC: 7692 Welding repair

(G-8234)
TWIST A STITCH
23 E 34th St (74063-4022)
PHONE.................................918 514-0143
EMP: 1 EST: 2018
SALES (est): 48.8K **Privately Held**
SIC: 2395 Embroidery & art needlework

(G-8235)
VITA-SOURCE INC
3963 S State Highway 97 (74063-6670)
P.O. Box 1807 (74063-1807)
PHONE.................................918 407-9525
Priscilla Nortey, *President*
Ruth Nortey, *President*
EMP: 5
SALES (est): 150.4K **Privately Held**
SIC: 2086 Carbonated beverages, nonalcoholic; bottled & canned

(G-8236)
WEBCO INDUSTRIES INC
Also Called: Star Center Tube
13701 W Highway 51 (74063-4494)
PHONE.................................918 581-0900
Dana S Weber, *CEO*
EMP: 1
SALES (corp-wide): 480.7MM **Privately Held**
WEB: www.webcotube.com
SIC: 5051 3312 Tubing, metal; tubes, steel & iron
PA: Webco Industries, Inc.
 9101 W 21st St
 Sand Springs OK 74063
 918 245-2211

(G-8237)
WEBCO INDUSTRIES INC (PA)
Also Called: Southwest Tube Mfg Div
9101 W 21st St (74063-8539)
P.O. Box 100 (74063-0100)
PHONE.................................918 245-2211
Dana S Weber, *Ch of Bd*
David E Boyer, *President*
Matt Bredensteiner, *Business Mgr*
Juston Duerson, *Business Mgr*
Erick Hurt, *Business Mgr*
◆ EMP: 429
SQ FT: 250,000
SALES (est): 480.7MM **Privately Held**
WEB: www.webcotube.com
SIC: 3312 5051 Tubes, steel & iron; tubing, metal

(G-8238)
WEBCO INDUSTRIES INC
Southwest Tube Mfg Div
201 S Woodland Dr (74063-8532)
P.O. Box 100 (74063-0100)
PHONE.................................918 241-1086
Wg Bieber, *General Mgr*
Doug Dewoody, *General Mgr*
Shirley Ritchey, *Buyer*
Nathan Barnes, *Sales Staff*
Randy Watson, *Branch Mgr*
EMP: 200
SALES (corp-wide): 480.7MM **Privately Held**
SIC: 3433 3317 Heating equipment, except electric; steel pipe & tubes
PA: Webco Industries, Inc.
 9101 W 21st St
 Sand Springs OK 74063
 918 245-2211

(G-8239)
WEBCO INDUSTRIES INC
Southwest Tube Products
8911 W 21st St (74063-8515)
P.O. Box 100 (74063-0100)
PHONE.................................918 245-9521
Dave Boyer, *Vice Pres*
EMP: 26
SALES (corp-wide): 480.7MM **Privately Held**
SIC: 3317 Steel pipe & tubes

Sand Springs - Tulsa County (G-8240)

PA: Webco Industries, Inc.
9101 W 21st St
Sand Springs OK 74063
918 245-2211

(G-8240)
WELTON ACQUISITIONS LLC
4006 S Bermuda Ave (74063-2947)
PHONE..................918 850-7981
John Welton,
Tammy Welton,
EMP: 2
SALES (est): 179.8K **Privately Held**
SIC: 2499 Decorative wood & woodwork

(G-8241)
WESTROCK CP LLC
Corrugated Container Division
200 W Morrow Rd (74063-6540)
P.O. Box 38 (74063-0038)
PHONE..................918 245-5102
Douglas Youngdahl, Manager
EMP: 130
SALES (corp-wide): 18.2B **Publicly Held**
WEB: www.westrock.com
SIC: 2653 Boxes, corrugated: made from purchased materials
HQ: Westrock Cp, Llc
1000 Abernathy Rd Ste 125
Atlanta GA 30328

(G-8242)
WHEELERS WELDING LLC
5905 S 170th West Ave (74063-2347)
PHONE..................918 246-3811
Roger Wheeler, Principal
EMP: 1
SALES (est): 72.8K **Privately Held**
SIC: 7692 Welding repair

(G-8243)
WOW METALLIZING & HARD
Also Called: WO&w
100 Wellston Park Rd (74063-5513)
PHONE..................918 245-9922
Harrel Wooten, Partner
Deanna Wooten, Partner
EMP: 7
SQ FT: 6,480
SALES (est): 830.6K **Privately Held**
SIC: 1389 Oil field services

Sapulpa
Creek County

(G-8244)
3 D MANUFACTURING
6800 S Highway 97 (74066-9288)
P.O. Box 1760, Sand Springs (74063-1760)
PHONE..................918 224-7717
David Davis, Manager
EMP: 2
SALES (est): 210.9K **Privately Held**
SIC: 3999 3312 Manufacturing industries; blast furnaces & steel mills

(G-8245)
A M & A TECHNICAL SERVICES
9693 Hickory Hill Rd (74066-1132)
P.O. Box 877 (74067-0877)
PHONE..................918 227-5354
Michael Pulley, Owner
April Pulley, Co-Owner
EMP: 2
SQ FT: 1,600
SALES (est): 327.6K **Privately Held**
SIC: 7699 3565 Industrial equipment services; labeling machines, industrial

(G-8246)
ACCESSORY AND PRFMCE SLS INC
1013 S Moccasin Pl (74066-6054)
PHONE..................918 224-5851
Alan Craig, CEO
EMP: 7
SALES: 600K **Privately Held**
SIC: 3465 7389 Body parts, automobile: stamped metal;

(G-8247)
ALLENS WOODCRAFT
3020 Dogwood Ln (74066-1103)
PHONE..................918 224-8796
Dean Allen, Owner
EMP: 1
SALES (est): 45.8K **Privately Held**
SIC: 5947 5199 2499 Gifts & novelties; wood carvings; carved & turned wood

(G-8248)
AMERICAN CUSTOM WOODWORKS LLC
1024 E Hastain Ave (74066-5721)
PHONE..................918 344-4988
Christopher Larson,
EMP: 1
SALES (est): 50K **Privately Held**
SIC: 2511 7389 Wood household furniture;

(G-8249)
AMRON ENTERPRISES LLC
1205 N Frankoma Rd (74066-2325)
PHONE..................918 224-9222
James E Nichols III, President
James Nichols, President
Norma James,
David Nichols,
EMP: 16
SQ FT: 1,200
SALES (est): 1.3MM **Privately Held**
SIC: 3599 3441 Machine shop, jobbing & repair; fabricated structural metal

(G-8250)
ARDAGH GLASS INC
1000 N Mission St (74066-3149)
PHONE..................918 224-1440
Steven Cedoz, Plant Mgr
Richard Cummings, Manager
EMP: 35
SALES (corp-wide): 242.1K **Privately Held**
SIC: 3221 5039 Food containers, glass; glass construction materials
HQ: Ardagh Glass Inc.
10194 Crosspoint Blvd
Indianapolis IN 46256

(G-8251)
BABY BEE SAFE
518 S Oak St (74066-5331)
PHONE..................918 224-1104
Laurie Boyne, Partner
Terry Boyne, Partner
EMP: 3
SALES (est): 179.5K **Privately Held**
SIC: 3699 Security devices

(G-8252)
BENNETT STEEL INC
2210 Industrial Rd (74066-8391)
PHONE..................918 227-2564
David R Bennett, President
Tom Morris, CFO
Jennifer Neal, Manager
Mollie Bennett, Admin Sec
Eli Daniels, Maintence Staff
EMP: 250
SQ FT: 64,000
SALES (est): 62MM **Privately Held**
SIC: 1791 3441 Structural steel erection; fabricated structural metal

(G-8253)
BENNETT STEEL FABRICATION INC
2210 Industrial Rd (74066-8391)
PHONE..................918 227-2564
Mollie Bennett, CEO
David R Bennett, President
David L Beyer, CFO
EMP: 75
SQ FT: 100,000
SALES (est): 16.3MM **Privately Held**
SIC: 3449 Bars, concrete reinforcing: fabricated steel

(G-8254)
BENTWRENCH STUDIOS
1602 S Main St (74066-6452)
PHONE..................918 406-8070
EMP: 2
SALES (est): 77.5K **Privately Held**
SIC: 2759 Screen printing

(G-8255)
BETTER BILT PORTABLE BUILDINGS
301 N Main St (74066-3405)
PHONE..................918 224-3437
Darin Tolivar, Owner
EMP: 8
SALES (est): 795.4K **Privately Held**
SIC: 3448 Buildings, portable: prefabricated metal

(G-8256)
BETTER BUILT STRUCTURES LLC
301 N Main St (74066-3405)
PHONE..................918 224-3437
Darin Tolivar,
EMP: 4
SALES (est): 605.9K **Privately Held**
SIC: 3448 Buildings, portable: prefabricated metal

(G-8257)
BILLS CATFISH BAIT
418 N 2nd St (74066-3014)
PHONE..................918 224-8470
Bill Bowen, Owner
EMP: 1
SALES (est): 101.1K **Privately Held**
SIC: 3949 Bait, artificial: fishing

(G-8258)
BORDEN COMPANY INC
205 E Line Ave (74066-2859)
P.O. Box 505 (74067-0505)
PHONE..................918 224-0816
J W Hastain, President
Mary Lou Brown, Manager
Louise Borden, Admin Sec
EMP: 40 **EST:** 1960
SQ FT: 25,750
SALES (est): 8.8MM **Privately Held**
SIC: 3533 Oil field machinery & equipment

(G-8259)
BRANCHCOMB INC
9845 S Frankoma Rd Ste B (74066-8499)
PHONE..................918 224-8094
Gerald Branchcomb, President
Joanne Branchcomb, Vice Pres
Michelle Parker, Admin Sec
▲ **EMP:** 20
SQ FT: 25,000
SALES (est): 273.7K **Privately Held**
SIC: 3089 3599 Injection molding of plastics; machine shop, jobbing & repair

(G-8260)
CNHI LLC
Also Called: Sapulpa Daily Herald
16 S Park St (74066-4220)
P.O. Box 1370 (74067-1370)
PHONE..................918 224-5185
Tom Quin, Manager
EMP: 35 **Privately Held**
SIC: 2711 Commercial printing & newspaper publishing combined; newspapers: publishing only, not printed on site
HQ: Cnhi, Llc
445 Dexter Ave Ste 7000
Montgomery AL 36104

(G-8261)
CONLEY MACHINE INC
19553 S 145th West Ave (74066-5075)
PHONE..................918 770-3234
David J Conley, President
EMP: 2
SALES (est): 189.7K **Privately Held**
SIC: 3599 Machine shop, jobbing & repair

(G-8262)
COPY WRITE INCORPORATED
1602 S Main St (74066-6452)
P.O. Box 1049 (74067-1049)
PHONE..................918 224-1148
Claudia M Will, President
EMP: 1
SALES (est): 104.6K **Privately Held**
SIC: 2759 7334 Posters, including billboards: printing; photocopying & duplicating services

(G-8263)
CUSTOM WOODWORK INC
221 E Hobson Ave (74066-2809)
PHONE..................918 224-4276
Don Cummins, President
Joy Cummins, Treasurer
EMP: 10
SQ FT: 5,000
SALES (est): 800K **Privately Held**
SIC: 1751 2434 Cabinet building & installation; wood kitchen cabinets

(G-8264)
D AND N FABRICATION
230 E Jackson Ave N (74066-2854)
PHONE..................918 224-4400
Eic Daniel, Owner
Tanya Walters, Manager
EMP: 8
SALES (est): 1.4MM **Privately Held**
SIC: 3441 Fabricated structural metal

(G-8265)
DAVID GORMLEY
Also Called: G Design
1609 E Thompson Ave (74066-4705)
PHONE..................918 845-0443
David Gormley, Owner
EMP: 1
SALES (est): 64.8K **Privately Held**
SIC: 7373 8748 3089 Computer-aided design (CAD) systems service; business consulting; injection molding of plastics

(G-8266)
DERKSEN PORTABLE BUILDING
14905 W 96th St S (74066-6986)
P.O. Box 736 (74067-0736)
PHONE..................918 636-4129
Dustin W Toliver, Principal
EMP: 2
SALES (est): 126.8K **Privately Held**
SIC: 3448 Buildings, portable: prefabricated metal

(G-8267)
DON BATEMAN SHTMTL FABRICATION
107 E Hobson Ave (74066-2807)
P.O. Box 930 (74067-0930)
PHONE..................918 224-0567
Don Bateman, Owner
EMP: 2
SQ FT: 5,220
SALES (est): 110K **Privately Held**
SIC: 3444 1799 7692 Sheet metal specialties, not stamped; welding on site; welding repair

(G-8268)
DR CANNABIS LLC
6234 S 123rd West Ave (74066-7214)
PHONE..................918 277-1105
Valecia Dirck, Owner
EMP: 3
SALES (est): 194.3K **Privately Held**
SIC: 2836 Extracts

(G-8269)
DUDZ AND THINGS INC
10132 W 161st St S (74066-6373)
PHONE..................918 321-9443
Tereasa Whipple, President
EMP: 3
SALES (est): 226.8K **Privately Held**
SIC: 2759 2395 Screen printing; emblems, embroidered

(G-8270)
ESB SALES INC
408 Pioneer Rd (74066-9346)
PHONE..................918 227-0378
Edward S Bayouth, President
▲ **EMP:** 1
SALES (est): 230.5K **Privately Held**
SIC: 5137 2335 Women's & children's clothing; wedding gowns & dresses

(G-8271)
FABSCO SHELL AND TUBE LLC
2410 Industrial Rd (74066-8962)
P.O. Box 988 (74067-0988)
PHONE..................918 224-7550
Lewis Scott, COO
Tammy Slaymaker, Purchasing

GEOGRAPHIC SECTION

Sapulpa - Creek County (G-8302)

Pulley Jeff, *Sales Staff*
David Lamb,
▼ **EMP:** 76
SALES (est): 16.4MM **Privately Held**
SIC: 3443 Heat exchangers: coolers (after, inter), condensers, etc.

(G-8272)
FABWELL CORPORATION
10611 W Houston St (74066-6386)
PHONE..................................918 224-9060
David Pease, *Project Mgr*
Rick Walker, *Purch Agent*
Stephen Bostick, *Engineer*
Bob Strohmeyer, *Manager*
Norma Travelletti, *Comp Tech*
EMP: 45 **EST:** 1967
SALES (est): 13.4MM **Privately Held**
WEB: www.fabwell.com
SIC: 3443 3533 Vessels, process or storage (from boiler shops): metal plate; oil field machinery & equipment

(G-8273)
FASCO DIRECTIONAL DRILLING LLC
1925 Timberton Rd (74066-6131)
PHONE..................................918 224-2756
Barry Edwards, *Principal*
EMP: 4
SALES (est): 299K **Privately Held**
SIC: 1381 Directional drilling oil & gas wells

(G-8274)
GASTECH ENGINEERING LLC
2110 Industrial Rd (74066-8336)
PHONE..................................918 663-8383
Joe Reeble, *CEO*
Randy Nelson, *COO*
Tracy Carroll, *Senior Buyer*
Tagore Vattipalli, *Engineer*
SAI Nidasanametla, *Project Engr*
EMP: 58
SQ FT: 120,000
SALES: 20MM **Privately Held**
SIC: 3533 3433 Oil & gas field machinery; heating equipment, except electric

(G-8275)
GORILLA SYSTEMS INC
815 E Bryan Ave (74066-4421)
PHONE..................................918 227-0230
Charles L Bass Jr, *President*
Brenda L Bass, *CFO*
EMP: 6
SQ FT: 3,000
SALES (est): 636.5K **Privately Held**
SIC: 3575 5734 5045 4899 Computer terminals, monitors & components; computer & software stores; computers, peripherals & software; data communication services

(G-8276)
GREEN COUNTRY S INC
14177 W Highway 66 (74066-8745)
PHONE..................................918 224-8244
Ricky Beane, *Principal*
EMP: 3 **EST:** 2014
SQ FT: 6,640
SALES (est): 382.8K **Privately Held**
SIC: 3272 Septic tanks, concrete

(G-8277)
H2SZERO LLC
14724 Lone Star Rd (74066-7828)
PHONE..................................918 384-9600
Nick Callaway, *Marketing Staff*
Mike Callaway, *Mng Member*
EMP: 1
SALES (est): 122.5K **Privately Held**
SIC: 2869 High purity grade chemicals, organic

(G-8278)
INLAND OIL CORP
Also Called: Central Oil Supply
14920 W Highway 66 (74066-8703)
PHONE..................................918 227-1180
EMP: 3
SALES: 350K **Privately Held**
SIC: 1311 Crude Petroleum/Natural Gas Production

(G-8279)
IRA E RONGEY
Also Called: Keifer Oil & Gas Co
621 Countrywood Way (74066-9317)
PHONE..................................918 227-0046
Ira E Rongey, *President*
EMP: 7
SALES (est): 278.3K **Privately Held**
SIC: 1389 Construction, repair & dismantling services

(G-8280)
J & G STEEL CORPORATION
2429 Industrial Rd (74066-8335)
P.O. Box 1208 (74067-1208)
PHONE..................................918 227-3131
Gary Gilliam, *President*
James C Pharr, *Principal*
Tracy Upton, *Vice Pres*
▲ **EMP:** 125
SQ FT: 500,000
SALES: 40MM **Privately Held**
SIC: 3441 Fabricated structural metal

(G-8281)
J M WELDING
9887 S Frankoma Rd (74066-8312)
PHONE..................................918 277-4480
EMP: 2
SALES (est): 42.2K **Privately Held**
SIC: 7692 Welding repair

(G-8282)
JANEWAY MACHINE INC
6228 S 161st West Ave (74066-9292)
PHONE..................................918 224-0694
Kenny Janeway, *CEO*
Jennifer Henry, *Office Mgr*
EMP: 20
SQ FT: 10,000
SALES (est): 2.8MM **Privately Held**
WEB: www.janewaymachine.com
SIC: 3599 3949 Machine shop, jobbing & repair; sporting & athletic goods

(G-8283)
JIM GILES SAFE ROOMS
2214 Industrial Rd (74066-8391)
PHONE..................................918 639-8102
Charles Dwyer, *Manager*
EMP: 2
SALES (est): 98.6K **Privately Held**
SIC: 3272 Concrete products

(G-8284)
L DEAN HUDGINS INC
Also Called: Hudgins Co Pipe Testing
12 W Goodykoontz Ave (74066-6464)
P.O. Box 507 (74067-0507)
PHONE..................................918 224-6236
L Dean Hudgins, *President*
EMP: 3
SALES (est): 176.3K **Privately Held**
SIC: 1389 Oil field services

(G-8285)
LAWRENCE COUNTY NEWSPAPERS INC
16 S Park St (74066-4220)
PHONE..................................918 224-5185
Tim Gray, *Principal*
EMP: 7 **EST:** 2008
SALES (est): 420.4K **Privately Held**
SIC: 2711 Newspapers

(G-8286)
MARJO ADVERTISING LLC
6167 W Hilton Rd (74066-1161)
PHONE..................................918 500-3108
Mark Yearout, *Mng Member*
Anita Yearout,
▲ **EMP:** 2
SALES: 320K **Privately Held**
SIC: 5045 2759 Keying equipment; magazines: printing

(G-8287)
MARTIN MANUFACTURING INC (PA)
Also Called: Builders Overhead Crane
6917 S Highway 97 (74066-8391)
PHONE..................................918 583-1191
Lauri Noble, *CEO*
Chuck Noble, *Exec VP*
Charles Noble, *Vice Pres*
Karen Douglas, *Admin Sec*
EMP: 48
SQ FT: 60,000
SALES (est): 6.8MM **Privately Held**
SIC: 3441 1791 Fabricated structural metal; structural steel erection

(G-8288)
MID AMERICA ALLOYS LLC
2210 Industrial Rd (74066-8391)
P.O. Box 1304 (74067-1304)
PHONE..................................918 224-3446
Todd Ray, *General Mgr*
Lyle Bachman, *Treasurer*
EMP: 20 **EST:** 1998
SQ FT: 35,000
SALES (est): 2.6MM **Privately Held**
SIC: 3364 3341 Zinc & zinc-base alloy die-castings; secondary nonferrous metals

(G-8289)
MID AMERICA AUTOMOTIVE PDTS
519 W Dewey Ave (74066-3941)
PHONE..................................918 227-1919
R Truman Blankenship, *Ch of Bd*
Maurice Blankenship, *President*
EMP: 30
SALES (est): 3.2MM **Privately Held**
SIC: 3714 Bumpers & bumperettes, motor vehicle

(G-8290)
MID-CONTINENT CONCRETE CO INC
201 S Walnut St (74066-4359)
PHONE..................................918 224-4122
Buddy Brewer, *Manager*
EMP: 10 **Privately Held**
SIC: 3273 Ready-mixed concrete
HQ: Mid-Continent Concrete Company, Inc.
   431 W 23rd St
   Tulsa OK 74107

(G-8291)
MID-WEST PRINTING & PUBG CO
Also Called: Mid West Printing
1227 N 9th St (74066-2221)
P.O. Box 650 (74067-0650)
PHONE..................................918 224-3666
Betty Seay, *President*
Howard L Seay, *Vice Pres*
Scott Seay, *Treasurer*
EMP: 13 **EST:** 1956
SQ FT: 5,000
SALES (est): 1.9MM **Privately Held**
WEB: www.sapulpachamber.com
SIC: 2761 2791 2789 2759 Manifold business forms; typesetting; bookbinding & related work; commercial printing; commercial printing, lithographic

(G-8292)
MOLD TECH INC
Also Called: Precision Products
22239 W Highway 33 (74066-7577)
PHONE..................................918 247-6275
Robert Wayne McDade, *President*
EMP: 3 **EST:** 1977
SQ FT: 5,200
SALES (est): 190K **Privately Held**
SIC: 3089 3599 3544 3369 Molding primary plastic; machine shop, jobbing & repair; special dies, tools, jigs & fixtures; nonferrous foundries; aluminum die-castings

(G-8293)
OKLAHOMA STAIR CRAFT INC
2214 Industrial Rd (74066-8391)
PHONE..................................918 446-1456
Patrick L Murphy, *President*
Judy Murphy, *Corp Secy*
EMP: 12
SALES (est): 1.9MM **Privately Held**
SIC: 2431 3446 Staircases, stairs & railings; architectural metalwork

(G-8294)
OKLAHOMA WORLD ORGANIZ
1811 Glendale Rd (74066-6111)
PHONE..................................918 224-3063
Susan Owen, *Principal*
Lois Higgins, *Vice Pres*
EMP: 1
SALES (est): 42.2K **Privately Held**
SIC: 3952 Paints for china painting

(G-8295)
OUTDOOR INCORPORATED
Also Called: Mustang Manufacturing
7757 S 145th West Ave (74066-8171)
P.O. Box 2457 (74067-2457)
PHONE..................................918 697-1402
Frank Simon, *Principal*
EMP: 3
SALES (est): 100K **Privately Held**
SIC: 3599 Machine shop, jobbing & repair

(G-8296)
PARAGON INDUSTRIES INC (PA)
3378 W Highway 117 (74066-6987)
PHONE..................................918 291-4459
Derek Wachob, *CEO*
Derrick Wachob, *Vice Pres*
Wade Akamine, *Plant Mgr*
Rod Haro, *Foreman/Supr*
Dean Oglesby, *Purchasing*
EMP: 300 **EST:** 1981
SQ FT: 234,290
SALES (est): 125MM **Privately Held**
SIC: 3317 Steel pipe & tubes

(G-8297)
PAXTON MCMILLIN CHRISANNA
15495 Linda Ln (74066-8004)
P.O. Box 111 (74067-0111)
PHONE..................................918 734-5753
Chrisanna Paxton McMillin, *Principal*
EMP: 2
SALES (est): 59.2K **Privately Held**
SIC: 2741 Miscellaneous publishing

(G-8298)
PIVOT POINT PUBLISHING
Also Called: Silver Lining Creative
3106 N Water St (74066-1771)
PHONE..................................918 347-5415
Devin Butler, *Owner*
Linda Butler, *Owner*
EMP: 2
SALES: 45K **Privately Held**
SIC: 2741 7374 Miscellaneous publishing; computer graphics service

(G-8299)
PLASTIC DESIGNS INC
6809 S 124th West Ave (74066-7221)
PHONE..................................918 224-9187
Richard Johnson, *President*
EMP: 1
SALES (est): 85K **Privately Held**
SIC: 3089 Injection molding of plastics

(G-8300)
PREMIER PLANT SERVICES LLC (PA)
2429 Industrial Rd (74066-8335)
PHONE..................................918 227-3131
EMP: 17
SALES (est): 20.6MM **Privately Held**
SIC: 3441 Fabricated structural metal

(G-8301)
PREMIER PLANT SERVICES LLC
8984 Frankoma Rd (74066)
PHONE..................................918 227-1680
EMP: 2
SALES (est): 86.6K
SALES (corp-wide): 20.6MM **Privately Held**
SIC: 3441 Fabricated structural metal
PA: Premier Plant Services, Llc
   2429 Industrial Rd
   Sapulpa OK 74066
   918 227-3131

(G-8302)
PRISM ENERGY INC
4523 Edgewood (74066-8908)
P.O. Box 190, Glenpool (74033-0190)
PHONE..................................918 248-4177
Brian Rice, *President*
EMP: 2
SALES (est): 167.2K **Privately Held**
SIC: 1389 Oil & gas field services

Sapulpa - Creek County (G-8303)

(G-8303)
PRO-TECH DENTAL LABS
9703 W 66th Pl S
(74066-7210)
P.O. Box 107 (74067-0107)
PHONE..................918 227-6407
Doug Donmeyer, *Owner*
EMP: 2
SALES: 70K **Privately Held**
SIC: 3843 8072 Denture materials; dental laboratories

(G-8304)
QUALITY MACHINING LLC
2400 Industrial Rd (74066-8962)
PHONE..................918 512-8593
Brian Lamb,
Susan Lamb,
EMP: 3 EST: 2006
SQ FT: 25,000
SALES (est): 679.1K **Privately Held**
WEB: www.qualitymachining.net
SIC: 3599 Machine shop, jobbing & repair

(G-8305)
REAL ALLOY RECYCLING LLC
1508 N 8th St (74066-2200)
P.O. Box 1070 (74067-1070)
PHONE..................918 224-4746
Steve Whitehead, *Manager*
EMP: 175
SQ FT: 80,000
SALES (corp-wide): 114.3MM **Privately Held**
SIC: 3341 3353 Aluminum smelting & refining (secondary); magnesium smelting & refining (secondary); aluminum sheet, plate & foil
HQ: Real Alloy Recycling, Llc
3700 Park East Dr Ste 300
Beachwood OH 44122
216 755-8900

(G-8306)
REDBIRD WOODWORKS
1001 Hickory Hill Rd (74066-1120)
PHONE..................918 227-5938
John Necochea, *Principal*
EMP: 2 EST: 2012
SALES (est): 160.7K **Privately Held**
SIC: 2431 Millwork

(G-8307)
RESERVE MANAGEMENT INC
10195 S 49th West Ave (74066-8923)
P.O. Box 150737, Fort Worth TX (76108-0737)
PHONE..................918 227-0894
John Elias, *President*
Bob Simpson, *Vice Pres*
Richard Potts, *Treasurer*
Kerry Elias, *Admin Sec*
EMP: 4
SALES (est): 229.1K **Privately Held**
SIC: 1389 Gas field services; oil field services

(G-8308)
RICHARDSON WELLSITE SERVICES
539 Pioneer Rd (74066-9309)
PHONE..................918 807-7105
Todd Richardson, *President*
EMP: 2 EST: 2017
SALES: 350K **Privately Held**
SIC: 8742 1389 Management consulting services; oil & gas field services

(G-8309)
ROSE INC
Also Called: Ultrasound Solutions
14170 W Line St (74066-7088)
PHONE..................918 693-2461
Bryan C Rose, *President*
Catherine Rose, *Admin Sec*
EMP: 2
SQ FT: 150
SALES: 150K **Privately Held**
SIC: 3826 Magnetic resonance imaging apparatus

(G-8310)
SEQUOYAH TECHNOLOGIES LLC
Also Called: Alivecity
201 E Hobson Ave (74066-2809)
PHONE..................918 808-7270
Samuel Haines, *CEO*
Zachary Dajani, *Software Dev*
Suzanne Haines, *Administration*
Dana Dudley,
EMP: 16
SQ FT: 6,000
SALES: 4.1MM **Privately Held**
SIC: 7379 7371 7372 ; custom computer programming services; computer software systems analysis & design, custom; computer software development & applications; prepackaged software

(G-8311)
SHINE ON DESIGNS
Also Called: Shineon Designs
105 S Water St (74066-4233)
PHONE..................918 224-7439
Fax: 918 224-7439
EMP: 1
SALES (est): 55K **Privately Held**
SIC: 5999 2791 2396 Ret Misc Merchandise Typesetting Services Mfg Auto/Apparel Trimming

(G-8312)
SIGNS OF TIMES ◆
18 E Hobson Ave (74066-2806)
PHONE..................918 512-6747
EMP: 1 EST: 2019
SALES (est): 46K **Privately Held**
SIC: 3993 Signs & advertising specialties

(G-8313)
SKY MOTORS LLC
17 S Spruce St (74066-4451)
PHONE..................918 321-2800
Mateen Elass, *President*
Eddie Darcey, *Officer*
EMP: 17 EST: 2016
SALES (est): 3.2MM **Privately Held**
SIC: 5511 3711 8711 7549 New & used car dealers; wreckers (tow truck); assembly of; mechanical engineering; towing service, automotive; high performance auto repair & service

(G-8314)
TANK TRUCKS INC
14473 S Hwy 75a (74066)
P.O. Box 569 (74067-0569)
PHONE..................918 224-7515
Benny Hufft, *President*
EMP: 8 EST: 1961
SALES (est): 675.4K **Privately Held**
SIC: 1389 Cleaning wells; haulage, oil field

(G-8315)
TIMMY PICKENS
Also Called: T&K Auto
9925 W 91st St S Lot 61 (74066-8413)
PHONE..................918 812-5268
Timmy Pickens, *Owner*
EMP: 1 EST: 2014
SALES (est): 74.5K **Privately Held**
SIC: 3799 5531 All terrain vehicles (ATV); automotive parts

(G-8316)
TRIKNTRUX
408 N Mission St (74066-3663)
PHONE..................918 224-2116
Jimmy Porter, *Owner*
EMP: 1
SALES (est): 78.2K **Privately Held**
SIC: 3714 Motor vehicle parts & accessories

(G-8317)
TRIPLE C GRADING & EXCVTG LLC
19495 W 101st St S (74066-1515)
P.O. Box 143 (74067-0143)
PHONE..................918 605-1848
Clifton C Collins III,
EMP: 3
SALES (est): 432.5K **Privately Held**
SIC: 3531 Construction machinery

(G-8318)
TROJAN OIL AND GAS LLC
6478 Mandy Ct (74066-8095)
PHONE..................918 606-0260
Ashford Dennis,
EMP: 3
SALES (est): 256.3K **Privately Held**
SIC: 1382 Oil & gas exploration services

(G-8319)
TULSA MCH SP & HEAT EXCHANGER ◆
2240 Industrial Rd (74066-8391)
PHONE..................918 224-5040
EMP: 2 EST: 2019
SALES (est): 81.4K **Privately Held**
SIC: 3599 Machine shop, jobbing & repair

(G-8320)
VERALLIA
1000 N Mission St (74066-3149)
PHONE..................918 224-1440
Merete Flage, *President*
EMP: 3
SALES (est): 132.9K **Privately Held**
SIC: 3221 Glass containers

(G-8321)
VOGT POWER INTERNATIONAL INC
2110 Industrial Rd (74066-8336)
PHONE..................502 899-4500
Ron Evans, *Manager*
EMP: 3
SALES (corp-wide): 509MM **Privately Held**
SIC: 3511 Gas turbine generator set units, complete
HQ: Vogt Power International Inc.
13551 Triton Park Blvd # 2000
Louisville KY 40223
502 899-4500

(G-8322)
WACHOB INDUSTRIES INC
2786 E Highway 117 (74066)
PHONE..................918 224-0511
Carrol McGowan, *Principal*
Mary Ellen M Cgowan, *Principal*
Jack Wachobb, *Principal*
EMP: 1 EST: 1975
SALES (est): 100K **Privately Held**
SIC: 3541 Pipe cutting & threading machines

(G-8323)
WARRIOR INDUSTRIES INC
13902 W 171st St S (74066-7189)
PHONE..................918 227-3500
EMP: 2 EST: 2011
SALES (est): 67K **Privately Held**
SIC: 3999 Mfg Misc Products

(G-8324)
WEAMCO INCORPORATED
Also Called: Weamcometric
2350 Industrial Rd (74066-8334)
P.O. Box 9555, Tulsa (74157-0555)
PHONE..................918 445-1141
Joseph E Boyle, *President*
Patrick T Boyle, *President*
Michael R Poston, *President*
Lin Williams, *President*
Douglas N Allert, *Vice Pres*
▼ EMP: 23
SQ FT: 24,750
SALES (est): 7.5MM **Privately Held**
SIC: 3824 3494 Liquid meters; line strainers, for use in piping systems

(G-8325)
WHITEHOUSE ENTERPRISES
12082 S Whitehouse Dr (74066-8737)
PHONE..................918 224-2002
Jimmy R Whitehouse, *President*
David Whitehouse, *Vice Pres*
EMP: 6
SQ FT: 8,000
SALES (est): 600K **Privately Held**
SIC: 3949 3599 Archery equipment, general; machine shop, jobbing & repair

(G-8326)
WILLIAMSON MACHINE COMPANY INC
660 E Lakeview Dr (74066-8403)
PHONE..................918 625-9856
Greg Cupples, *President*
Robert Collard, *QC Mgr*
Roger Stubbings, *Manager*
EMP: 14
SALES: 2.4MM **Privately Held**
WEB: www.williamsonmachine.com
SIC: 3599 Machine shop, jobbing & repair

(G-8327)
WORLD WIDE EXCHANGERS INC
Also Called: World Wide Air Coolers
6917 S Highway 97 (74066-8193)
PHONE..................918 240-3193
Scott Edwards, *Branch Mgr*
EMP: 10 **Privately Held**
SIC: 3443 Air coolers, metal plate
HQ: World Wide Exchangers, Llc
601 W 136th St N
Skiatook OK 74070

(G-8328)
YE OLDE WOODSHOP
7425 S 161st West Ave (74066-2960)
PHONE..................918 224-1603
Craig Waller, *Owner*
EMP: 2
SALES (est): 113.8K **Privately Held**
SIC: 1751 2521 2434 Cabinet building & installation; wood office furniture; wood kitchen cabinets

Sasakwa
Seminole County

(G-8329)
BRADY OIL COMPANY INC
36489 E 1420 (74867-6610)
PHONE..................405 941-3368
Tim Brady, *President*
Rosemary Brady, *Treasurer*
EMP: 1 EST: 1962
SALES (est): 40K **Privately Held**
SIC: 1311 Crude petroleum production

(G-8330)
JOHN L LEWIS
Also Called: Lewis Well Service
Half Mile E Of Hwy 56 (74867)
P.O. Box 67 (74867-0067)
PHONE..................405 941-3224
John L Lewis, *Owner*
EMP: 7
SALES (est): 536.8K **Privately Held**
SIC: 1311 1389 Crude petroleum production; oil field services

(G-8331)
LARKIN ENERGY INC
1 2 Mile Of Hwy 56 (74867)
P.O. Box 67 (74867-0067)
PHONE..................405 941-3224
John L Lewis, *President*
Jay Lewis, *Vice Pres*
EMP: 13
SALES (est): 1.1MM **Privately Held**
SIC: 1311 Crude petroleum & natural gas production

(G-8332)
LUCKY FOUR OIL COMPANY
1721 Rt (74867)
PHONE..................405 941-3307
Lester Reich, *Owner*
Demiah Reich, *Co-Owner*
EMP: 2
SALES (est): 50K **Privately Held**
SIC: 1311 Crude petroleum & natural gas

(G-8333)
NORMAN MOORE
Also Called: Norman's Tank Truck Service
3 Miles W 2 S 1/4 E (74867)
P.O. Box 263 (74867-0263)
PHONE..................405 941-3220
Norman Moore, *Owner*
EMP: 1

GEOGRAPHIC SECTION

SALES (est): 82.6K **Privately Held**
SIC: 1389 Oil field services

Sawyer
Choctaw County

(G-8334)
HEADY TRUCKING
242 N 4290 Rd (74756-6605)
PHONE..................580 326-2739
EMP: 1
SALES (est): 116.1K **Privately Held**
SIC: 4212 1442 Local Trucking Operator Construction Sand/Gravel

(G-8335)
MARTIN MARIETTA MATERIALS INC
Hc 66 Box 1135 (74756-9728)
P.O. Box 250 (74756-0250)
PHONE..................580 326-7709
B J Johnson, *Branch Mgr*
EMP: 33 **Publicly Held**
WEB: www.martinmarietta.com
SIC: 1411 Limestone, dimension-quarrying
PA: Martin Marietta Materials Inc
2710 Wycliff Rd
Raleigh NC 27607

(G-8336)
MARTIN MARIETTA MATERIALS INC
Also Called: Sawyer Plant
3239 E 2000 Rd (74756)
P.O. Box 250 (74756-0250)
PHONE..................580 326-9671
Mike Serrano, *Manager*
EMP: 34 **Publicly Held**
SIC: 1423 Crushed & broken granite
PA: Martin Marietta Materials Inc
2710 Wycliff Rd
Raleigh NC 27607

Sayre
Beckham County

(G-8337)
C&J ENERGY SERVICES INC
301 Venture Rd (73662-6203)
PHONE..................580 928-1300
Josh Comstock, *Branch Mgr*
Sandra Franklin, *Administration*
EMP: 6
SALES (corp-wide): 1.8B **Publicly Held**
SIC: 1389 Oil field services
HQ: King Merger Sub Ii Llc
3990 Rogerdale Rd
Houston TX 77042
713 325-6000

(G-8338)
CARNES OILFIELD SERVICES LLC
19348 E 1180 Rd (73662-6013)
PHONE..................580 309-1249
EMP: 2
SALES (est): 102.2K **Privately Held**
SIC: 1389 Oil field services

(G-8339)
D & W CUPP TRUCKING LLC
317 E Kennemer (73662-8407)
PHONE..................580 821-6844
Wanda Cupp, *President*
EMP: 5
SALES (est): 455.7K **Privately Held**
SIC: 3537 Industrial trucks & tractors

(G-8340)
FARMERS CO-OPERATIVE GIN ASSN
109 S 6th St (73662-3300)
PHONE..................580 928-2664
Justin Woodruss, *Manager*
EMP: 3 **EST:** 1922
SQ FT: 10,000
SALES (est): 2MM **Privately Held**
SIC: 0724 5172 5191 3559 Cotton ginning; petroleum products; feed; seeds: field, garden & flower; cotton ginning machinery

(G-8341)
HENDERSON FEEDS LLC
18332 E 1300 Rd (73662)
PHONE..................580 574-5375
Greg Henderson,
EMP: 2
SALES (est): 62.3K **Privately Held**
SIC: 2048 Stock feeds, dry

(G-8342)
JUST-IN-TIME SIGNS LLC
18767 E 1210 Rd (73662-6405)
PHONE..................580 821-1140
Justin, *Principal*
EMP: 1
SALES (est): 50.6K **Privately Held**
SIC: 3993 Signs & advertising specialties

(G-8343)
POST CONSTRUCTION COMPANY
1802 N 4th St (73662-1154)
P.O. Box 367 (73662-0367)
PHONE..................580 928-5983
Joe Post, *Owner*
EMP: 7
SQ FT: 1,800
SALES (est): 622.3K **Privately Held**
SIC: 1629 1389 Oil refinery construction; pumping of oil & gas wells

(G-8344)
RED HILLS HOT SHOT INC
19023 E 1140 Rd (73662-4418)
P.O. Box 1142, Elk City (73648-1142)
PHONE..................580 225-8686
Mike McDaniel, *Principal*
EMP: 4
SALES (est): 476.9K **Privately Held**
SIC: 1389 Oil field services

(G-8345)
SAYRE RECORD
112 E Main St (73662-2914)
PHONE..................580 928-5540
Brad Spitzer, *Owner*
EMP: 7
SALES (est): 228.7K **Privately Held**
SIC: 2711 Newspapers: publishing only, not printed on site

(G-8346)
SPITZER PRINTING
112 E Main St (73662-2914)
PHONE..................580 928-5540
Robert Spitzer, *Owner*
Connie Ferrero, *Director*
EMP: 3 **EST:** 1982
SALES (est): 173.7K **Privately Held**
SIC: 2752 2791 2759 2711 Commercial printing, offset; typesetting; commercial printing; newspapers

(G-8347)
SPITZER PUBLISHING
Also Called: Erik Democrat
112 E Main St (73662-2914)
PHONE..................580 928-5540
Brad Dayva, *Owner*
EMP: 7 **EST:** 1965
SALES (est): 303.4K **Privately Held**
WEB: www.sayrerecord.com
SIC: 2711 Newspapers: publishing only, not printed on site

(G-8348)
SPRINGDALE FOOD CO INC
209 N 5th St (73662-2827)
P.O. Box 279 (73662-0279)
PHONE..................580 928-2598
Matthew R Dugger II, *President*
Lillie Dugger, *President*
John Ivester, *Corp Secy*
Mathew R Dugger II, *Vice Pres*
EMP: 2
SQ FT: 6,000
SALES (est): 78K **Privately Held**
SIC: 2099 2087 Vinegar; honey, strained & bottled; syrups, flavoring (except drink)

Seiling
Dewey County

(G-8349)
GORE NITROGEN PUMPING SVC LLC
916 N Elm St (73663-6345)
P.O. Box 65 (73663-0065)
PHONE..................580 922-4660
Shannon Carrion, *Financial Analy*
Gary Gore, *Mng Member*
Dustin Redinger, *Director*
EMP: 5
SALES (est): 1.6MM **Privately Held**
SIC: 1389 5169 Haulage, oil field; industrial gases

(G-8350)
KIMBALL READY MIX INC
503 S Main (73663)
P.O. Box 565 (73663-0565)
PHONE..................580 922-4444
Dean Gilchrist, *President*
Artelea Gilchrist, *Corp Secy*
EMP: 5
SQ FT: 2,300
SALES: 300K **Privately Held**
SIC: 3273 Ready-mixed concrete

(G-8351)
SANDER SPORTING GDS & ATVS LLC
610 N Main St (73663)
P.O. Box 716 (73663-0716)
PHONE..................580 922-4930
Billy Sander,
Kristy McCurley,
Joy Sander,
EMP: 7
SQ FT: 3,300
SALES (est): 396K **Privately Held**
SIC: 5941 5561 1389 Sporting goods & bicycle shops; recreational vehicle dealers; pumping of oil & gas wells

(G-8352)
WESTERN X-RAY
409 N Elm St (73663)
P.O. Box 1490, Mustang (73064-8490)
PHONE..................580 922-3166
James Peters, *Owner*
EMP: 29
SQ FT: 1,000
SALES (est): 2.1MM **Privately Held**
SIC: 3844 X-ray apparatus & tubes

Seminole
Seminole County

(G-8353)
AERO-TEC INDUSTRIES INC
11990 N Highway 99 (74868-9404)
P.O. Box 1216 (74818-1216)
PHONE..................405 382-8501
Charles Harbert, *President*
Larry Wright, *Corp Secy*
EMP: 6
SQ FT: 4,000
SALES: 463.4K **Privately Held**
SIC: 3728 3812 3613 Aircraft body & wing assemblies & parts; search & navigation equipment; switchgear & switchboard apparatus

(G-8354)
AMERICAN PETRO MINERAL CO INC
220 Quail Creek Rd (74868-9459)
P.O. Box 1559 (74818-1559)
PHONE..................405 382-1255
Ralph Morrison, *President*
Rugena Morrison, *President*
EMP: 3
SALES (est): 280.4K **Privately Held**
SIC: 1311 Crude petroleum production; natural gas production

(G-8355)
AWS LLC
220 Quail Creek Rd (74868-9459)
PHONE..................405 382-1255
Ralph Morrison, *Mng Member*
Morrison Gina,
EMP: 2 **EST:** 2007
SALES: 836K **Privately Held**
SIC: 1389 Construction, repair & dismantling services

(G-8356)
BAKER HGHES OLFLD OPRTIONS INC
Also Called: Baker Oil Tools
4 N Park St (74868-3324)
P.O. Box 1667 (74818-1667)
PHONE..................405 382-0003
EMP: 5
SALES (corp-wide): 24.5B **Publicly Held**
SIC: 1389 Sales & Gas Services
HQ: Baker Hughes Oilfield Operations, Inc.
2929 Allen Pkwy Ste 2100
Houston TX 77073
713 439-8600

(G-8357)
BAR-S FOODS CO
Also Called: Bar S Foods Co
701 E Goodhope Rd (74868-9410)
PHONE..................405 303-2138
Don Schiltz, *Branch Mgr*
EMP: 2 **Privately Held**
SIC: 2013 Sausages & other prepared meats
HQ: Bar-S Foods Co.
5090 N 40th St Ste 300
Phoenix AZ 85018
602 264-7272

(G-8358)
BILL WEEMS OIL INC
2501 Hwy 9 W (74818)
P.O. Box 1258 (74818-1258)
PHONE..................405 382-1813
Connie Weems, *President*
Rocky Weems, *Vice Pres*
Terry Sweringen, *Admin Sec*
EMP: 5
SQ FT: 5,000
SALES (est): 442.8K **Privately Held**
SIC: 1311 Crude petroleum production; natural gas production

(G-8359)
BISON OILFIELD SERVICES LLC
12534 Old Highway 99 (74868-7606)
PHONE..................405 437-1485
North Whipple, *CEO*
EMP: 21
SALES (corp-wide): 18.3MM **Privately Held**
SIC: 1382 Oil & gas exploration services
PA: Bison Oilfield Services Llc
1008 N Little Ave
Cushing OK 74023
405 529-6577

(G-8360)
BOB D BERRY DBA
Also Called: Associated Services Printing
217 W Broadway (74868-3311)
PHONE..................405 382-3360
Bob D Berry, *Owner*
Pat Berry, *Co-Owner*
EMP: 2 **EST:** 1939
SQ FT: 1,125
SALES: 75K **Privately Held**
SIC: 5699 2752 2759 Western apparel; commercial printing, lithographic; screen printing

(G-8361)
BUTCHS PROCESSING PLANT INC
12566 Ns 360 (74868)
PHONE..................405 382-2833
Rodney Sutterfield, *President*
Belinda Sutterfield, *Admin Sec*
EMP: 3
SALES (est): 864K **Privately Held**
SIC: 5147 2011 Meats, fresh; meat packing plants

Seminole - Seminole County (G-8362)

(G-8362)
C & J TRUCKS LLC
3416 N Highway 99 (74868-5406)
PHONE 405 382-1405
Mark White, *Vice Pres*
Sally White, *Treasurer*
Paul White, *Mng Member*
EMP: 14 **EST:** 1945
SALES (est): 1.1MM **Privately Held**
SIC: 1389 Lease tanks, oil field: erecting, cleaning & repairing

(G-8363)
CHRIS HAMMON OIL PROPERTIES
608 N Main St (74868-3434)
P.O. Box 744 (74818-0744)
PHONE 405 382-0250
EMP: 3
SALES (est): 204.7K **Privately Held**
SIC: 1311 Crude petroleum production

(G-8364)
CLEAN PRODUCTS INC
11682 N Highway 99 (74868-6801)
P.O. Box 592 (74818-0592)
PHONE 405 382-1441
Richard Spears, *President*
Vicki Spears, *Treasurer*
EMP: 8
SQ FT: 25,000
SALES: 1.5MM **Privately Held**
SIC: 3549 3535 Metalworking machinery; conveyors & conveying equipment

(G-8365)
COCHRAN CHEMICAL COMPANY INC
1800 Ray Davis Blvd (74868-3508)
PHONE 405 382-8000
EMP: 20
SALES (est): 1.9MM **Privately Held**
SIC: 1389 Oil/Gas Field Services

(G-8366)
COMFORT X-PRESS LLC
2700 N Highway 99 (74868-9496)
PHONE 405 382-5600
Lenard Mathews, *Managing Prtnr*
EMP: 20
SALES (est): 2.1MM **Privately Held**
SIC: 2741 Miscellaneous publishing

(G-8367)
CUDD PRESSURE CONTROL INC
Also Called: Cudd Pumping Services
1701 Ray Davis Blvd (74868-3555)
P.O. Box 1332 (74818-1332)
PHONE 405 382-2803
Tim Mathews, *Vice Pres*
Abel Lyndsey, *Manager*
EMP: 60
SALES (corp-wide): 1.2B **Publicly Held**
WEB: www.cuddenergyservices.com
SIC: 1389 Oil field services
HQ: Cudd Pressure Control, Inc.
2828 Tech Forest Blvd
The Woodlands TX 77381
832 295-5555

(G-8368)
DIALS RACE SHOP
3504 N Highway 3 (74868)
PHONE 405 382-4843
Dawn Dails, *Owner*
EMP: 1 **EST:** 2001
SALES (est): 81.6K **Privately Held**
SIC: 3711 Automobile assembly, including specialty automobiles

(G-8369)
DISA HOLDING CORP
Also Called: Goff Division
1 Pleasant Grove Rd (74868)
P.O. Box 1607 (74818-1607)
PHONE 405 382-6900
Chuck Prucha, *General Mgr*
EMP: 80 **Privately Held**
SIC: 3569 Blast cleaning equipment, dustless
HQ: Disa Holding Corp.
80 Kendall Point Dr
Oswego IL 60543

(G-8370)
DOLESE BROS CO
1600 Wills Rd (74868-3568)
P.O. Box 3309, Shawnee (74802-3309)
PHONE 405 382-2060
Wanda Conner, *Manager*
EMP: 6
SALES (corp-wide): 8.5MM **Privately Held**
SIC: 3273 Ready-mixed concrete
PA: Dolese Bros. Co.
20 Nw 13th St
Oklahoma City OK 73103
405 235-2311

(G-8371)
ENERFIN RESOURCES I LTD PARTNR
400 N Harvey Rd (74868-4118)
P.O. Box 472 (74818-0472)
PHONE 405 382-3049
Brent Warton, *Plant Mgr*
Mark Hanson, *Safety Mgr*
Ron Lyle, *Branch Mgr*
EMP: 35 **Privately Held**
WEB: www.enerfin.com
SIC: 4922 1311 Natural gas transmission; crude petroleum & natural gas
PA: Enerfin Resources I Limited Partnership
1001 S Dairy Ashford Rd
Houston TX 77077

(G-8372)
F & F TOOL CO (PA)
1819 E Highway 270 (74868-6917)
PHONE 405 382-0009
Bobby Friend, *President*
EMP: 4
SQ FT: 3,000
SALES (est): 3.6MM **Privately Held**
SIC: 1389 Fishing for tools, oil & gas field

(G-8373)
F&D DEFENSE LLC
201 W Oak Ave (74868-3321)
PHONE 512 745-6482
Corby Hall, *President*
EMP: 3
SALES (est): 300.9K **Privately Held**
WEB: www.fd-defense.com
SIC: 3484 Guns (firearms) or gun parts, 30 mm. & below

(G-8374)
GOFF INC
12216 Ns 3520 (74868-5874)
P.O. Box 1607 (74818-1607)
PHONE 405 278-6200
Keith Yerby, *President*
David Zehren, *Principal*
Bob Willson, *Sales Staff*
Steve Walker, *Manager*
Belinda Adams, *Admin Sec*
◆ **EMP:** 15
SALES (est): 4.8MM **Privately Held**
WEB: www.goff-inc.com
SIC: 3531 Construction machinery
HQ: Disa Holding Corp.
80 Kendall Point Dr
Oswego IL 60543

(G-8375)
GRACO FISHING & RENTAL TLS INC
Also Called: Graco Oilfield Services
1819 E Highway 270 (74868-6917)
PHONE 405 382-0009
Bobby Friend, *Manager*
EMP: 19
SALES (corp-wide): 28.1MM **Privately Held**
SIC: 1389 Fishing for tools, oil & gas field
PA: Graco Fishing & Rental Tools, Inc.
5300 Town And Cntry Blvd
Frisco TX 75034
214 618-3930

(G-8376)
INGRAM EXPLORATION INC
2 One Half Mi S On Hwy99 (74868)
P.O. Box 1626 (74818-1626)
PHONE 405 382-2040
Wayne Ingram, *President*
EMP: 3
SQ FT: 1,000
SALES (est): 397.5K **Privately Held**
SIC: 1382 Oil & gas exploration services; crude petroleum production; natural gas production

(G-8377)
J & N SMALL ENGINE REPAIR
Also Called: J&N Small Engines
1905 Boren Blvd (74868-2082)
PHONE 405 382-2792
John J Nichols, *Owner*
EMP: 3
SQ FT: 4,000
SALES (est): 150K **Privately Held**
SIC: 3524 Lawn & garden equipment

(G-8378)
JACKS FLEX PIPE
35585 Ew 1270 (74868-5838)
P.O. Box 71, Konawa (74849-0071)
PHONE 405 382-5740
Jack Charber, *Owner*
EMP: 18
SALES (est): 2.2MM **Privately Held**
SIC: 1382 Oil & gas exploration services

(G-8379)
JERRY SCOTT DRILLING CO INC
Hwy 99 N (74868)
P.O. Box 1488 (74818-1488)
PHONE 405 382-2202
Jerry G Scott, *President*
Fred Gipson, *Partner*
Sarah Cunnigham, *Vice Pres*
Jerry W Scott, *Vice Pres*
EMP: 7
SQ FT: 1,000
SALES (est): 1.1MM **Privately Held**
WEB: www.jerryscottdrilling.com
SIC: 1311 Crude petroleum production; natural gas production

(G-8380)
K & H WELL SERVICE INC
1901 N Harvey Rd (74868-3553)
P.O. Box 1462 (74818-1462)
PHONE 405 382-2762
EMP: 16
SQ FT: 6,500
SALES (est): 1.2MM **Privately Held**
SIC: 1389 1381 Oil/Gas Field Services Oil/Gas Well Drilling

(G-8381)
K OIL COMPANY
S Of City (74868)
P.O. Box 1338 (74818-1338)
PHONE 405 382-0891
Kenneth Harbeston, *Partner*
Barbara Bess, *Partner*
EMP: 5 **EST:** 1970
SQ FT: 1,000
SALES (est): 579.7K **Privately Held**
SIC: 1311 Crude petroleum production

(G-8382)
KAY PRODUCTION SERVICES INC
Also Called: Perkins Production Service
35833 Highway 59 E (74868-5827)
P.O. Box 155, Bowlegs (74830-0155)
PHONE 405 398-3109
Phillip David Perkins, *President*
Nick Kay, *Vice Pres*
Diana Kay, *Admin Sec*
EMP: 10
SALES (est): 500K **Privately Held**
SIC: 1381 Drilling oil & gas wells

(G-8383)
LANDMARK ENERGY LLC
319 N Harvey Rd (74868-4116)
P.O. Box 1332 (74818-1332)
PHONE 405 382-3951
Tim Mathews,
Tim Matthews,
EMP: 1 **EST:** 1999
SALES (est): 175K **Privately Held**
SIC: 1389 Oil field services

(G-8384)
MIDWEST LOGGING & PERFORATING
2220 N Harvey Rd (74868-3564)
P.O. Box 1251 (74818-1251)
PHONE 405 382-4200
Steve Smith, *President*
Wanda Smith, *Corp Secy*
Harmon Smith, *Vice Pres*
EMP: 2
SQ FT: 2,400
SALES (est): 281.5K **Privately Held**
SIC: 2411 1389 Logging; perforating well casings

(G-8385)
MILLS WELL SERVICE INC
12525 Ns 356 (74868)
P.O. Box 871 (74818-0871)
PHONE 405 382-4107
Roger Mills, *President*
Rita Ballew, *Corp Secy*
Brad Shultz, *Vice Pres*
EMP: 80 **EST:** 1946
SQ FT: 4,000
SALES (est): 8.1MM **Privately Held**
WEB: www.millswellservice.net
SIC: 1389 Construction, repair & dismantling services; cleaning wells; swabbing wells

(G-8386)
MORAN OIL ENTERPRISES
Also Called: Moran-K Oil
222 N 2nd St (74868-3406)
P.O. Box 1295 (74818-1295)
PHONE 405 382-6001
Melvin Moran, *Partner*
Gary Kleiman, *Partner*
Sidney Moran, *Partner*
EMP: 8
SQ FT: 3,000
SALES (est): 29.2K **Privately Held**
SIC: 1311 Crude petroleum production

(G-8387)
MORAN-K OIL LLC
Also Called: MORAN OIL ENTERPRISES
222 N 2nd St (74868-3406)
P.O. Box 1295 (74818-1295)
PHONE 405 382-6001
Melvin Moran, *Mng Member*
Gary Kleiman,
David Moran,
Elisa Moran,
Jasmine Moran,
EMP: 13
SQ FT: 2,000
SALES (est): 737.1K **Privately Held**
SIC: 1311 Crude petroleum production; natural gas production

(G-8388)
MORGANS REPAIR SHOP INC
398 Boren Rd (74868-3717)
P.O. Box 1188 (74818-1188)
PHONE 405 382-3114
Joe Morgan, *President*
Jana Morgan, *Vice Pres*
EMP: 1
SALES (est): 50K **Privately Held**
SIC: 5251 3599 7699 Chainsaws; machine shop, jobbing & repair; lawn mower repair shop

(G-8389)
NEW DOMINION LLC
11822 N Highway 99 (74868-7200)
PHONE 405 567-3034
Tony McCaig, *Manager*
Blake Hightower, *Administration*
EMP: 5
SALES (est): 920.9K
SALES (corp-wide): 3.8MM **Privately Held**
SIC: 1382 Oil & gas exploration services
PA: New Dominion, Llc
1307 S Boulder Ave # 400
Tulsa OK 74119
918 587-6242

(G-8390)
OGDENS WELDING SERVICE
12916 S Highway 99 (74868-5813)
PHONE 405 380-7649
William Ogden, *Principal*

EMP: 1
SALES (est): 37.9K **Privately Held**
SIC: 7692 Welding repair

(G-8391)
OKLAHOMA CSTM CATING LTD LBLTY (PA)
1801 Boren Blvd (74868-2080)
PHONE..................405 382-0231
Sam L Adkisson, *Mng Member*
▲ EMP: 41
SQ FT: 40,000
SALES (est): 14.9MM **Privately Held**
SIC: 3479 Coating of metals & formed products

(G-8392)
OKLAHOMA SUB SURFC PUMP & SUP
2536 Hwy 99 S (74868)
P.O. Box 2248 (74818-2248)
PHONE..................405 382-7311
Dean E Anderson, *President*
Tim Darr, *Corp Secy*
EMP: 4
SQ FT: 4,000
SALES (est): 1MM **Privately Held**
SIC: 5084 1389 Oil well machinery, equipment & supplies; oil field services

(G-8393)
PARKS MANUFACTURING INC
Also Called: Blue Wave Boats
711 Boren Blvd (74868-3707)
PHONE..................405 382-0349
Roger E Parks, *President*
Pamela S Parks, *Corp Secy*
Gregory B Parks, *Vice Pres*
Richard Parks, *Vice Pres*
Steven Parks, *Vice Pres*
EMP: 123
SQ FT: 160,500
SALES (est): 28.4MM **Privately Held**
SIC: 3732 Boats, fiberglass: building & repairing

(G-8394)
PHOENIX OIL AND GAS INC
35863 E Highway 270 (74868-6906)
P.O. Box 1859 (74818-1859)
PHONE..................405 382-0935
Dan Hamilton, *President*
EMP: 10
SQ FT: 3,000
SALES (est): 1MM **Privately Held**
SIC: 1311 Crude petroleum production; natural gas production

(G-8395)
PROTECTIVE COATINGS INTL LLC
1801 Boren Blvd (74868-2080)
PHONE..................405 716-4734
Sam Adkisson, *Mng Member*
EMP: 2
SQ FT: 60,000
SALES (est): 78.9K **Privately Held**
SIC: 3479 3471 Painting, coating & hot dipping; electroplating & plating

(G-8396)
REEDS POWER TONGS INC
1901 N Harvey Rd (74868-3553)
P.O. Box 1462 (74818-1462)
PHONE..................405 382-2762
EMP: 30
SALES (est): 2.3MM **Privately Held**
SIC: 1389 Oil And Gas Production

(G-8397)
SAFRAN VNTLTION SYSTEMS OKLA I
12037 N Highway 99 (74868-5432)
PHONE..................405 382-0731
Daniel Wyatt, *CEO*
Jeff Griffin, *Opers Dir*
Jack Henderson, *Facilities Mgr*
Tommy Farrow, *Production*
Laura McCammond, *Buyer*
▲ EMP: 208
SQ FT: 86,000
SALES (est): 49.6MM
SALES (corp-wide): 799.9MM **Privately Held**
SIC: 3728 Aircraft parts & equipment

PA: Safran
2 Bd Du General Martial Valin
Paris 75015
140 608-080

(G-8398)
SEMINOLE COUNTY PUBLISHING
2514 Northwood Dr (74868-2269)
P.O. Box 2008 (74818-2008)
PHONE..................405 382-1125
EMP: 2
SALES (est): 77.1K **Privately Held**
SIC: 2741 Miscellaneous publishing

(G-8399)
SEMINOLE MACHINE CO
1 1/2 Miles South On Old (74868)
P.O. Box 1661 (74818-1661)
PHONE..................405 382-0444
Joel Parsons, *Owner*
EMP: 3 EST: 1945
SQ FT: 1,500
SALES (est): 140K **Privately Held**
SIC: 3599 7692 3714 Machine shop, jobbing & repair; welding repair; motor vehicle parts & accessories

(G-8400)
SOONER PRESS
619 N Milt Phillips Ave (74868-2311)
P.O. Box 1358 (74818-1358)
PHONE..................405 382-8351
Ted Hurt, *Owner*
Tammy Hurt, *Co-Owner*
EMP: 2
SALES (est): 194.8K **Privately Held**
SIC: 2752 7334 2791 2789 Commercial printing, offset; photocopying & duplicating services; typesetting; bookbinding & related work; commercial printing

(G-8401)
STOKES PRODUCTION
Hwy 99 S (74868)
P.O. Box 364, Blanchard (73010-0364)
PHONE..................405 485-2402
Wayne Stokes, *Owner*
EMP: 6 EST: 1975
SQ FT: 5,000
SALES (est): 750K **Privately Held**
SIC: 1311 Crude petroleum production; natural gas production

(G-8402)
T & K OIL INC
11609 Ns 357 (74868)
PHONE..................405 382-5241
Tim Porter, *CEO*
Charles M Porter, *President*
EMP: 1
SALES (est): 120.7K **Privately Held**
SIC: 1311 Crude petroleum & natural gas

(G-8403)
T S & H SHIRT CO INC
130 N Milt Phillips Ave (74868-2303)
PHONE..................405 382-3731
Sue Snodgrass, *President*
Hope Pickering, *Vice Pres*
EMP: 8 EST: 1980
SQ FT: 16,000
SALES (est): 902K **Privately Held**
WEB: www.tshadspecialties.com
SIC: 2759 Screen printing

(G-8404)
TCINA HOLDING COMPANY LTD
Also Called: T C I N A
201 N 2nd St (74868-3402)
P.O. Box 470 (74818-0470)
PHONE..................405 382-0399
Charles Berry Doyal, *President*
EMP: 4
SALES (est): 404.5K **Privately Held**
SIC: 1311 Crude petroleum production

(G-8405)
TX3 LLC
Also Called: American Crtfication Pull Tstg
1501 N Harvey Rd (74868-3535)
PHONE..................405 382-2270
Tammy Topping, *Principal*
EMP: 5
SALES (est): 330.5K **Privately Held**
SIC: 1389 Pipe testing, oil field service

(G-8406)
VERSITILE ENTERTAINMENT
Also Called: Versitile Entertainment Group
35679 Ew 1250 (74868)
P.O. Box 549 (74818-0549)
PHONE..................812 913-2677
Ron Reid, *Owner*
EMP: 2
SALES (est): 55K **Privately Held**
SIC: 3651 7929 7389 4832 Music distribution apparatus; musical entertainers; music & broadcasting services; ; radio broadcasting stations, music format

(G-8407)
WOLFF MACHINE INC
404 Boren Blvd (74868-3716)
P.O. Box 722 (74818-0722)
PHONE..................405 382-3000
James Wolff, *President*
Kelly Kilpatrick, *Treasurer*
EMP: 5
SQ FT: 3,300
SALES (est): 430K **Privately Held**
SIC: 3599 7629 Machine shop, jobbing & repair; electrical repair shops

(G-8408)
XGP LLC
545 W Strothers Ave (74868-3126)
PHONE..................405 584-1444
Levi Campbell, *Opers Mgr*
EMP: 5
SALES (est): 388.1K **Privately Held**
WEB: www.xgpmudlogging.com
SIC: 1389 Oil field services

Sentinel
Washita County

(G-8409)
AG YOUTH MAGAZINE
302 E Main St (73664)
PHONE..................800 599-6884
Larry Peck, *Owner*
EMP: 1
SALES (est): 75.7K **Privately Held**
WEB: www.agyouth.com
SIC: 2721 Magazines: publishing only, not printed on site

(G-8410)
BOBBY L GRAHAM
20651 E 1300 Rd (73664-6408)
PHONE..................580 393-2247
Bobby L Graham, *Principal*
EMP: 1
SALES (est): 78.1K **Privately Held**
SIC: 7692 Welding repair

(G-8411)
MUSICK FARMS INC
Also Called: Musick Farms Cattle Co
12692 N 2090 Rd (73664-5037)
PHONE..................580 393-4826
Jimmy Musick, *President*
Tracy Musick, *Vice Pres*
Judy Musick, *Admin Sec*
EMP: 7
SALES (est): 891.2K **Privately Held**
SIC: 0111 0131 0139 3523 Wheat; cotton; alfalfa farm; balers, farm: hay, straw, cotton, etc.

(G-8412)
SENTINEL LEADER
701 E Main St (73664)
P.O. Box 69 (73664-0069)
PHONE..................580 393-4348
Jolene Wolfenbarger, *President*
EMP: 2 EST: 1984
SALES (est): 102K **Privately Held**
WEB: www.thesentinelleader.com
SIC: 2711 Newspapers, publishing & printing

(G-8413)
SUPERIOR RESOURCES
218 E Main St (73664-9068)
P.O. Box 790 (73664-0790)
PHONE..................580 393-4314
Kelly Smith, *President*
Jerry Williams, *Buyer*

EMP: 10
SALES (est): 583.1K **Privately Held**
SIC: 1382 Oil & gas exploration services

Shady Point
Le Flore County

(G-8414)
KENS PLUMBING & BACKHOE
27087 247th Ave (74956)
P.O. Box 738, Panama (74951-0738)
PHONE..................918 963-4223
Kenneth Richard, *Owner*
EMP: 3 EST: 1980
SALES (est): 220K **Privately Held**
SIC: 1711 3531 Plumbing contractors; backhoes

(G-8415)
ROCK PRODUCERS INC
26496 255th Ave (74956-2011)
PHONE..................918 963-2111
Daryl Jackson, *President*
EMP: 8
SALES (est): 251.9K **Privately Held**
SIC: 1422 Crushed & broken limestone

(G-8416)
SUGAR LOAF QUARRIES INC
Arnall Rd & Highway 59 (74956)
P.O. Box 469 (74956-0469)
PHONE..................918 647-4244
Ed Reeves, *President*
Jane Reeves, *Corp Secy*
EMP: 25
SQ FT: 2,700
SALES (est): 3MM **Privately Held**
SIC: 3281 5211 1411 Building stone products; lumber & other building materials; dimension stone

Sharon
Woodward County

(G-8417)
HORSESHOE EXPLORATION LLC
27583 State Highway 34 (73857-5123)
PHONE..................580 866-3207
Robert Garrett, *Owner*
EMP: 1 EST: 2013
SALES (est): 54.2K **Privately Held**
SIC: 3462 Horseshoes

(G-8418)
RAND TRANS INC
54979 S County Road 205 (73857-5094)
PHONE..................580 866-3355
Rick Randall, *Principal*
EMP: 3
SALES (est): 319.1K **Privately Held**
SIC: 3131 Rands

(G-8419)
SHAWN WREATH
48802 S County Road 210 (73857-5065)
PHONE..................580 571-2598
EMP: 2 EST: 2015
SALES (est): 99.9K **Privately Held**
SIC: 3999 Wreaths, artificial

Shattuck
Ellis County

(G-8420)
CSC INC
Also Called: Northwest Oklahoman
329 S Main St (73858-8804)
P.O. Box 460 (73858-0460)
PHONE..................580 938-2533
Neil Colbert, *Manager*
EMP: 3
SALES (corp-wide): 450K **Privately Held**
SIC: 5112 2522 2711 Office supplies; office furniture, except wood; newspapers

Shattuck - Ellis County (G-8421)

PA: Csc Inc
202 N Main St
Mooreland OK 73852
580 994-6110

(G-8421)
DAVES WELDING LLC
218 S Sylvania St (73858-7426)
PHONE.....................580 938-2707
David Kelln,
EMP: 1 EST: 2012
SALES (est): 76K **Privately Held**
SIC: 7692 Welding repair

(G-8422)
J & L OIL FIELD SERVICES LLC
2100 S Main St (73858-7009)
P.O. Box 848 (73858-0848)
PHONE.....................580 938-2205
Rodney Robertson, *Controller*
Doug Brinkley, *Sales Staff*
Jolisa Swanson, *Office Mgr*
Jason Swanson, *Mng Member*
Lance Schultz,
EMP: 320
SALES (est): 47.5MM **Privately Held**
SIC: 1389 Oil field services

(G-8423)
ROCK CREEK DISTILLERY LLC
1204 S Summer St (73858-9402)
PHONE.....................580 254-1407
EMP: 3
SALES (est): 124.5K **Privately Held**
SIC: 2085 Distilled & blended liquors

(G-8424)
ROD WIEDERSTEIN
Also Called: Rod's Welding Service
212 S Olive St (73858-8907)
P.O. Box 411 (73858-0411)
PHONE.....................580 938-2998
EMP: 1
SALES (est): 33K **Privately Held**
SIC: 7692 Welding Shop

(G-8425)
THOMAS WATER WELL SERVICE
Rr 2 (73858)
PHONE.....................580 938-2224
Homer Thomas, *Owner*
EMP: 1
SALES (est): 92.7K **Privately Held**
SIC: 3561 Pumps, domestic: water or sump

Shawnee
Pottawatomie County

(G-8426)
A CBD HEALTHIER LIFE
32 W Macarthur St (74804-2026)
PHONE.....................405 585-0353
EMP: 2 EST: 2017
SALES (est): 86.1K **Privately Held**
SIC: 3999

(G-8427)
AMERICAN ENTPS WHL DSTRIBUTERS (PA)
Also Called: Firecracker Joe
1905 E Walnut St (74801-8146)
PHONE.....................405 273-4516
Joe Snodgrass, *Owner*
EMP: 3
SALES (est): 199.3K **Privately Held**
SIC: 7299 5999 2899 Costume rental; fireworks; fireworks

(G-8428)
ARCHER TECHNOLOGIES INTL INC (PA)
109 N Broadway Ave Ste 1 (74801-6915)
P.O. Box 3406 (74802-3406)
PHONE.....................405 306-3220
Jeffery J Buttram, *President*
James B Wyont, *Vice Pres*
EMP: 2

SALES (est): 729K **Privately Held**
WEB: www.archertechnologies.net
SIC: 3812 3769 3444 3399 Defense systems & equipment; guided missile & space vehicle parts & aux eqpt, rsch & dev; sheet metalwork; metal fasteners; aircraft & marine hardware, inc. pulleys & similar items;

(G-8429)
AUSTIN ATHLETIC CO INC
10987 N Kickapoo Ave (74804-9666)
PHONE.....................405 273-8681
Orville Austin, *President*
Susan Ansell, *Corp Secy*
Craig Ansell, *Vice Pres*
EMP: 14
SQ FT: 10,000
SALES (est): 770K **Privately Held**
SIC: 3949 Football equipment & supplies, general

(G-8430)
BARRETT DRILLING COMPANY
Also Called: Barrett Land & Cattle Co
1210 Gordon Cooper Dr (74801-8632)
P.O. Box 1345 (74802-1345)
PHONE.....................405 273-6217
John A Barrett Jr, *President*
Joshua Barrett, *Vice Pres*
EMP: 4 EST: 1929
SQ FT: 1,000
SALES (est): 570K **Privately Held**
SIC: 1311 0212 Crude petroleum production; natural gas production; beef cattle except feedlots

(G-8431)
BARRICK PHARMACIES INC
3210 Kethley Rd (74804-9625)
PHONE.....................405 273-9417
Tim Barrick, *President*
EMP: 2
SALES (est): 74.4K **Privately Held**
SIC: 2834 Pharmaceutical preparations

(G-8432)
BIMBO BAKERIES USA INC
1515 N Tucker Ave (74801-5239)
PHONE.....................405 273-5049
Brad Allan, *Manager*
EMP: 7 **Privately Held**
SIC: 2051 Bread, cake & related products
HQ: Bimbo Bakeries Usa, Inc
255 Business Center Dr # 200
Horsham PA 19044
215 347-5500

(G-8433)
BISON METALS TECHNOLOGIES LLC
Also Called: Shawnee Tubing Industries
41600 Wolverine Rd (74804-9159)
PHONE.....................403 395-1405
Jim Burton,
Jim Lash,
EMP: 2
SALES (est): 90.8K **Privately Held**
SIC: 3317 Seamless pipes & tubes

(G-8434)
BOOMERANG
400 W Macarthur St (74804-1910)
PHONE.....................405 250-6597
EMP: 1
SALES (est): 47K **Privately Held**
SIC: 3949 Boomerangs

(G-8435)
BRITT OIL CO LLC
19005 S Rock Creek Rd (74804-9613)
PHONE.....................405 275-2115
Rod Britt, *President*
EMP: 1
SALES (est): 138.6K **Privately Held**
SIC: 1389 Oil consultants

(G-8436)
CANARY LLC
37709 45th St (74804-8807)
PHONE.....................405 275-6116
Russell Tarlton, *Opers Mgr*
Lannie Hanks, *QC Mgr*
Tara Nowell, *Office Mgr*
EMP: 5 **Privately Held**
SIC: 1389 Oil field services

PA: Canary, Llc
410 17th St Ste 310
Denver CO 80202

(G-8437)
CHARLEYS GOLF CARS INC
37605 45th St (74804-8806)
PHONE.....................405 273-6901
David Martin, *Principal*
EMP: 1
SALES (est): 61.9K **Privately Held**
SIC: 3949 5599 5088 Golf carts, hand; golf cart, powered; golf carts

(G-8438)
CLICKS MACHINE & SUPPLY
49 Bristow Ln (74804-9701)
P.O. Box 1913 (74802-1913)
PHONE.....................405 273-2497
EMP: 2
SQ FT: 2,096
SALES (est): 120.2K **Privately Held**
SIC: 3545 3541 1799 Mfg Machine Tool Accessories Mfg Machine Tools-Cutting Trade Contractor

(G-8439)
CODE RED INDUSTRIES LLC
37802 Old Highway 270 (74804-9226)
PHONE.....................405 227-1552
Nicholas Punneo, *Agent*
EMP: 2
SALES (est): 84.2K **Privately Held**
SIC: 3999 Manufacturing industries

(G-8440)
CONNOR-WINFIELD CORP
Also Called: Crystal Works
41001 Wolverine Rd (74804-9026)
PHONE.....................405 273-1257
Fax: 405 273-4697
EMP: 50
SALES (corp-wide): 36.6MM **Privately Held**
SIC: 3625 3679 Manufactures Electronic Devices Such As Time Frequency Units Oscillators And Timers
PA: Connor-Winfield Corp.
2111 Comprehensive Dr
Aurora IL 60505
630 851-4722

(G-8441)
COUNTY DEMOCRAT
226 N Broadway Ave (74801-6918)
PHONE.....................405 273-8888
Ronald Henderson, *President*
EMP: 3 EST: 2013
SALES (est): 116.8K **Privately Held**
SIC: 2711 Newspapers, publishing & printing

(G-8442)
CUESTA PETROLEUM
23 E 9th St Ste 403 (74801-6963)
PHONE.....................405 878-0744
James E Richardson, *President*
EMP: 1
SALES (est): 187.2K **Privately Held**
SIC: 1381 Drilling oil & gas wells

(G-8443)
DAKK MFG LLC
14102 Highway 177 (74804-9252)
PHONE.....................405 395-2139
EMP: 3
SALES (est): 58.5K **Privately Held**
SIC: 3999 Manufacturing industries

(G-8444)
DEMCO PRINTING INC
226 N Broadway Ave (74801-6918)
P.O. Box 367 (74802-0367)
PHONE.....................405 273-8888
Ronald Henderson, *President*
EMP: 10 EST: 1946
SQ FT: 7,000
SALES: 750K **Privately Held**
WEB: www.demcoprintinginc.com
SIC: 2711 2791 2789 2759 Commercial printing & newspaper publishing combined; typesetting; bookbinding & related work; commercial printing; commercial printing, lithographic

(G-8445)
DRAKE MANUFACTURING INC
41101 Wolverine Rd (74804-9153)
PHONE.....................405 760-5336
Bobby Boyd, *President*
EMP: 1 EST: 2017
SALES (est): 39.6K **Privately Held**
SIC: 3999 Manufacturing industries

(G-8446)
DUNCAN OIL & GAS INC (PA)
23 E 9th St Ste 213 (74801-6961)
PHONE.....................405 214-1108
Dale Duncan, *President*
Claudia Duncan, *Admin Sec*
EMP: 5
SQ FT: 2,863
SALES: 2MM **Privately Held**
SIC: 1311 Crude petroleum production; natural gas production

(G-8447)
EATON AEROQUIP LLC
8701 N Harrison (74804-9560)
PHONE.....................405 275-5500
Robert Mutersbaugh, *Manager*
EMP: 100
SALES (corp-wide): 1.1B **Privately Held**
SIC: 3494 3432 5099 Valves & pipe fittings; plumbing fixture fittings & trim; brass goods
PA: Eaton Aeroquip Llc
1000 Eaton Blvd
Cleveland OH 44122
216 523-5000

(G-8448)
EXPRESS HOME HELP
Also Called: Express Personnel Services
3903 N Harrison St (74804-1426)
PHONE.....................405 214-6400
Robert Funk, *Principal*
EMP: 1
SALES (est): 57.6K **Privately Held**
SIC: 2741 Miscellaneous publishing

(G-8449)
FAB SEAL INDUSTRIAL LINERS INC
6121 Highway 177 (74804-8602)
PHONE.....................405 878-0166
Daniel Lewis, *President*
Kenneth Kane, *Plant Mgr*
EMP: 11
SQ FT: 8,000
SALES (est): 1.8MM **Privately Held**
SIC: 3443 Fabricated plate work (boiler shop)

(G-8450)
FAITH CHURCH SHAWNEE
130 S Oklahoma Ave (74801-7932)
P.O. Box 3847 (74802-3847)
PHONE.....................405 948-7100
EMP: 2
SALES (est): 104.2K **Privately Held**
SIC: 3826 Analytical instruments

(G-8451)
GE OIL & GAS PRESSURE CTRL LP
Also Called: Wood Group Pressure Control
14311 Highway 177 (74804-9246)
PHONE.....................405 273-7660
Dave Cermak, *Manager*
EMP: 24
SALES (corp-wide): 95.2B **Publicly Held**
SIC: 5085 3533 3494 Valves & fittings; oil & gas field machinery; valves & pipe fittings
HQ: Ge Oil & Gas Pressure Control Lp
4424 W Sam Houston Pkwy N S
Houston TX 77041
281 398-8901

(G-8452)
GE PACKAGED POWER LLC
14311 Highway 177 (74804-9246)
PHONE.....................405 395-0400
Steve Heinley, *Branch Mgr*
EMP: 9
SALES (corp-wide): 95.2B **Publicly Held**
SIC: 3533 Oil field machinery & equipment

GEOGRAPHIC SECTION

Shawnee - Pottawatomie County (G-8483)

HQ: Ge Packaged Power, Llc
1330 West Loop S Ste 1000
Houston TX 77027
713 803-0900

(G-8453)
GENERAL PLASTICS INC
3500 N Harrison St (74804-2200)
PHONE..............................405 275-3171
John Inda, *President*
Phyllis Inda, *Vice Pres*
EMP: 10
SQ FT: 21,000
SALES: 1.3MM **Privately Held**
SIC: 3089 3444 Injection molded finished plastic products; sheet metalwork

(G-8454)
GLO PRESS
3911 N Chapman Ave (74804-1627)
PHONE..............................405 275-1038
Ronald S Smith, *Owner*
EMP: 3
SQ FT: 2,000
SALES (est): 150K **Privately Held**
SIC: 2752 Commercial printing, offset

(G-8455)
GREAT PLINS GRPHICS SHWNEE LLC
414 W Federal St (74804-3626)
PHONE..............................405 273-4263
Beverly Ledbetter, *Mng Member*
Randel Ledbetter,
EMP: 7
SQ FT: 4,000
SALES (est): 550K **Privately Held**
SIC: 2759 2396 2395 Screen printing; automotive & apparel trimmings; embroidery products, except schiffli machine

(G-8456)
HALE EXPLORATION LLC
130 N Broadway Ave (74801-6910)
P.O. Box 1451 (74802-1451)
PHONE..............................405 273-8000
EMP: 2
SALES (est): 104.7K **Privately Held**
SIC: 1382 Oil & gas exploration services

(G-8457)
HANDLE IT 3D PRINTING LLC
33109 Hardesty Rd (74801-5677)
PHONE..............................405 788-9471
Kevin Logan, *Principal*
EMP: 2 **EST:** 2018
SALES (est): 83.9K **Privately Held**
SIC: 2752 Commercial printing, lithographic

(G-8458)
HARRY H DIAMOND INC
116 N Bell Ave (74801-6902)
P.O. Box 20868, Oklahoma City (73156-0868)
PHONE..............................405 275-5788
Jeffrey Diamond, *President*
Lindsay Peters,
EMP: 6
SQ FT: 5,600
SALES (est): 787.8K **Privately Held**
SIC: 3533 Oil & gas field machinery

(G-8459)
HEMBREE LEWIS A PRODUCTION CO
1501 N Shawnee Ave (74804-4163)
P.O. Box 1725 (74802-1725)
PHONE..............................405 273-6137
Lewis A Hembree, *President*
EMP: 4 **EST:** 1970
SQ FT: 1,200
SALES (est): 385.6K **Privately Held**
SIC: 1311 Crude petroleum production

(G-8460)
HENKE PETROLEUM CORP
1421 E 45th St (74804-1447)
PHONE..............................405 878-0909
M Toole, *Principal*
EMP: 2
SALES (est): 232.9K **Privately Held**
SIC: 2911 5172 Petroleum refining; petroleum products

(G-8461)
HOLIDAY CREEK PRTICIPATION LLC
130 N Broadway Ave # 200 (74801-6910)
PHONE..............................405 275-1045
Sid Clark, *Mng Member*
EMP: 2
SALES (est): 100.6K **Privately Held**
SIC: 1381 Drilling oil & gas wells

(G-8462)
INDACO METALS LLC
3 American Way (74804-9255)
PHONE..............................405 273-9200
Josh Inda, *CEO*
Steve Moore, *COO*
Allen Krausse, *Plant Mgr*
Steve Anthony, *Purch Mgr*
EMP: 60
SQ FT: 24,000
SALES: 10MM **Privately Held**
SIC: 3448 Buildings, portable: prefabricated metal

(G-8463)
INDUSTRIAL AXLE COMPANY LLC
301 N Kennedy Ave (74801-6601)
PHONE..............................405 273-9315
Richard Carpenter, *Manager*
EMP: 90
SQ FT: 102,100
SALES (corp-wide): 2.4B **Privately Held**
SIC: 3714 3792 Motor vehicle transmissions, drive assemblies & parts; travel trailers & campers
HQ: Industrial Axle Company, Llc
21608 Protecta Dr
Elkhart IN 46516
574 295-6077

(G-8464)
JM EAGLE CO
7901 N Kickapoo Ave (74804-9107)
PHONE..............................405 273-0900
EMP: 2
SALES (est): 85.6K **Privately Held**
SIC: 3498 Fabricated pipe & fittings

(G-8465)
KOINONIA ENTERPRISES
237 S Draper Ave (74801-8015)
PHONE..............................405 275-7064
David Draper, *Owner*
EMP: 1
SALES (est): 108.1K **Privately Held**
SIC: 3648 Lighting equipment

(G-8466)
L L WILKINS E AND O CO
23 E 9th St (74801-6943)
P.O. Box 1246 (74802-1246)
PHONE..............................405 273-3008
Mark A Wilkins, *Principal*
EMP: 3
SALES (est): 169.1K **Privately Held**
SIC: 1311 Crude petroleum & natural gas

(G-8467)
LACKEY WILLIAM H OIL GAS OPER
624 W Independence St # 107 (74804-4306)
PHONE..............................405 275-4164
Shawn Lackey, *President*
Mary Ellen Lackey, *Vice Pres*
Pam Lackey, *Admin Sec*
EMP: 5
SQ FT: 1,900
SALES (est): 349.6K **Privately Held**
SIC: 1311 Crude petroleum production; natural gas production

(G-8468)
LARRYS TRANSMISSION SERVICE
Also Called: Larrys Transm Parts & Svc
306 E 7th St (74801-7907)
PHONE..............................405 273-3432
Larry Blackburn, *Owner*
EMP: 4
SQ FT: 6,000
SALES: 550K **Privately Held**
SIC: 3714 5013 5531 Transmissions, motor vehicle; automotive supplies & parts; automotive parts

(G-8469)
LINN ENERGY
624 W Independence St # 102 (74804-4306)
PHONE..............................405 273-1185
Randy Colburn, *Principal*
EMP: 3
SALES (est): 206.7K **Privately Held**
SIC: 1311 Crude petroleum production

(G-8470)
MAGIC CIRCLE ENERGY CORP
601 N Broadway Ave (74804-6201)
PHONE..............................405 275-1666
Fax: 405 275-9986
EMP: 10 **EST:** 1998
SALES (est): 560K **Privately Held**
SIC: 1382 Oil/Gas Exploration Services

(G-8471)
MCGUIRE GATEWAY HOLDINGS LLC
Also Called: Gateway Services Group
42005 Moccasin Trl (74804-9503)
PHONE..............................405 285-5884
Selena McGuire, *Mng Member*
Shane McGuire,
Kristin Paule,
EMP: 4
SALES (est): 301.7K **Privately Held**
SIC: 1382 Oil & gas exploration services

(G-8472)
MCSPADDEN BOOKBINDERY
911 W Benedict St (74801-6030)
PHONE..............................405 275-7788
Corry McSpadden, *President*
Gayle McSpadden, *Vice Pres*
EMP: 2
SALES (est): 239.3K **Privately Held**
SIC: 2789 Binding only: books, pamphlets, magazines, etc.

(G-8473)
MEMORIES IN GLASS INC
Also Called: Memories N Glass Studio
7 Limousin Ln (74804-1027)
PHONE..............................405 878-9688
Bob Pickard, *President*
EMP: 3
SALES (est): 111.4K **Privately Held**
WEB: www.pabblaster.com
SIC: 3231 3589 Decorated glassware: chipped, engraved, etched, etc.; sandblasting equipment

(G-8474)
MICHAEL JOHNSON
Also Called: United Airparts
37600 Old Highway 270 # 5 (74804-9281)
PHONE..............................405 882-3744
Michael Johnson, *Owner*
EMP: 20
SALES (est): 1MM **Privately Held**
SIC: 3728 Aircraft parts & equipment

(G-8475)
MILLS MACHINE CO
201 N Oklahoma Ave (74801-7029)
P.O. Box 1514 (74802-1514)
PHONE..............................405 273-4900
Charles D Mills, *President*
Karen W Mills, *Corp Secy*
Kenny Bennet, *Safety Mgr*
Gary Bruce, *Engineer*
John Harris, *Sales Mgr*
EMP: 20
SQ FT: 13,000
SALES (est): 4.2MM **Privately Held**
WEB: www.millsmachine.com
SIC: 3541 Machine tools, metal cutting type

(G-8476)
MOBILE EXPRESS
4901 N Kickapoo Ave (74804-1303)
PHONE..............................405 395-9378
EMP: 1
SALES (est): 54K **Privately Held**
SIC: 2741 Misc Publishing

(G-8477)
MORRIS COMMUNICATIONS CO LLC
Also Called: Shawnee News Star
215 N Bell Ave (74801-6913)
P.O. Box 1688 (74802-1688)
PHONE..............................405 273-4200
Michael Hengel, *Manager*
EMP: 75 **Privately Held**
SIC: 2721 2711 Periodicals; newspapers
HQ: Morris Communications Company Llc
725 Broad St
Augusta GA 30901
706 724-0851

(G-8478)
MW ENGINEERING CO
23 E 9th St Ste 406 (74801-6963)
PHONE..............................405 273-0370
Lloyd L Wilkins, *Principal*
EMP: 2 **EST:** 2001
SALES (est): 125K **Privately Held**
SIC: 1311 Crude petroleum & natural gas

(G-8479)
NORWESCO INC
201 N Kennedy Ave (74801-6600)
PHONE..............................405 275-2034
Coy Carpenter, *Branch Mgr*
EMP: 15
SALES (corp-wide): 44.1MM **Privately Held**
SIC: 3089 Plastic & fiberglass tanks
PA: Norwesco, Inc.
4365 Steiner St
Saint Bonifacius MN 55375
952 446-1945

(G-8480)
OILFIELD EQUIPMENT & MFG
7801 N Harrison St (74804-9537)
PHONE..............................405 275-4500
Dennis Marshala, *President*
EMP: 15
SQ FT: 27,000
SALES (est): 4.2MM **Privately Held**
SIC: 3533 3599 Oil field machinery & equipment; machine shop, jobbing & repair

(G-8481)
OLDCASTLE BUILDINGENVELOPE INC
Also Called: H G P Industries
10000 N Harrison (74804-7503)
PHONE..............................405 275-5510
Don Clark, *Branch Mgr*
EMP: 73
SALES (corp-wide): 30.6B **Privately Held**
SIC: 3231 3211 5039 Tempered glass: made from purchased glass; flat glass; glass construction materials
HQ: Oldcastle Buildingenvelope, Inc.
5005 Lyndon B Johnson Fwy # 1050
Dallas TX 75244
214 273-3400

(G-8482)
ONEOK INC
Also Called: Oneok Gas Transportation
621 W Independence St (74804-4310)
PHONE..............................405 878-6267
Mike Clark, *Vice Pres*
Brad Renegar, *Manager*
Mary Spears, *Manager*
James Kneale,
EMP: 19
SALES (corp-wide): 10.1B **Publicly Held**
WEB: www.oneok.com
SIC: 4922 4924 1321 Pipelines, natural gas; natural gas distribution; natural gas liquids
PA: Oneok, Inc.
100 W 5th St Ste Ll
Tulsa OK 74103
918 588-7000

(G-8483)
PINECLIFFE PRTRS OF TECUMSEH
1815 N Harrison St Ste 1 (74804-4034)
PHONE..............................405 273-1292
Everett Maylen, *President*
Rebecca Maylen, *Corp Secy*
EMP: 8

Shawnee - Pottawatomie County (G-8484)

SQ FT: 2,400
SALES (est): 1.1MM **Privately Held**
SIC: **2752** 2796 2791 2789 Commercial printing, offset; color separations for printing; typesetting; bookbinding & related work

(G-8484)
PRECISION STONE
17501 Highway 102 (74801-3464)
PHONE 405 214-2224
Garin Carey, *Owner*
EMP: 2
SALES (est): 160.2K **Privately Held**
SIC: **3272** Stone, cast concrete

(G-8485)
PRESTIGE MANUFACTURING CO LLC
Also Called: G-T Engineering
7 American Way (74804-9255)
P.O. Box 3637 (74802-3637)
PHONE 405 395-0500
Austin Wright, *CEO*
Darrell Johnson, *Marketing Staff*
Kyle Rocha, *Administration*
EMP: 20
SALES (est): 5.4MM **Privately Held**
SIC: **5084** 3532 Drilling bits; drills, bits & similar equipment

(G-8486)
RANDYS SIGNS INC
34305 Waco Rd (74801-0811)
PHONE 405 273-2564
Randy Penix, *President*
Kathy Penix, *Vice Pres*
Aaron Penix, *Treasurer*
EMP: 8
SQ FT: 10,000
SALES: 500K **Privately Held**
SIC: **3993** Signs & advertising specialties

(G-8487)
REMPEL ROCK-N-READY MIX INC ⊙
1200 N Leo Ave (74801-4604)
PHONE 405 275-1107
EMP: 2 EST: 2019
SALES (est): 91.3K **Privately Held**
SIC: **3273** Ready-mixed concrete

(G-8488)
RESOURCE OIL AND GAS LLC
1421 E 45th St (74804-1447)
PHONE 405 878-7336
EMP: 3
SALES (est): 407.4K **Privately Held**
SIC: **1382** Oil & gas exploration services

(G-8489)
ROMINE OIL & GAS LTD
23 E 9th St Ste 223 (74801-6961)
P.O. Box 3425 (74802-3425)
PHONE 405 273-1171
Richard Romine, *President*
EMP: 1
SALES (est): 1MM **Privately Held**
SIC: **1381** 1311 Drilling oil & gas wells; crude petroleum & natural gas production

(G-8490)
ROUND HOUSE MANUFACTURING LLC
Also Called: Round House Overalls
1 American Way (74804-9255)
PHONE 405 273-0510
David Antosh, *Vice Pres*
James E Antosh, *Mng Member*
▲ EMP: 70
SQ FT: 30,000
SALES (est): 10.2MM **Privately Held**
WEB: www.round-house.com
SIC: **2326** Overalls & coveralls

(G-8491)
S & S FARM CENTER
302 S Beard Ave (74801-7708)
PHONE 405 273-6907
Bill Mathews, *President*
EMP: 10 EST: 1932

SALES (est): 2.9MM **Privately Held**
WEB: www.shawneefeedcenter.com
SIC: **5153** 5999 5191 2048 Grain elevators; feed & farm supply; feed; seeds: field, garden & flower; fertilizer & fertilizer materials; prepared feeds

(G-8492)
SANDY PETROLEUM INC
19109 Highway 102 (74801-5634)
PHONE 405 273-9289
Stanley Moody, *Principal*
EMP: 3
SALES (est): 241K **Privately Held**
SIC: **1311** Crude petroleum production

(G-8493)
SATURN LAND CO INC
624 W Independence St # 107 (74804-4329)
PHONE 405 275-4406
Mary Ellen Lackey, *President*
Shawn Lackey, *Vice Pres*
Pam Lackey, *Admin Sec*
EMP: 4
SQ FT: 2,000
SALES (est): 420K **Privately Held**
SIC: **6211** 1382 Oil & gas lease brokers; oil & gas exploration services

(G-8494)
SHAWNEE FABRICATORS INC
5 American Way (74804-9255)
P.O. Box 261 (74802-0261)
PHONE 405 275-8264
Warren Shaddox, *President*
Ron Hawkins, *Vice Pres*
EMP: 30
SQ FT: 25,000
SALES (est): 7.7MM **Privately Held**
SIC: **3441** Building components, structural steel

(G-8495)
SHAWNEE NEWS-STAR
215 N Bell Ave (74801-6982)
PHONE 405 273-4200
John Stauffer, *Principal*
Brooke Jones, *Graphic Designe*
EMP: 9
SALES (est): 660K **Privately Held**
SIC: **2711** Newspapers, publishing & printing

(G-8496)
SHAWNEE SAWMILL LLC
511 E Highland St (74801-7155)
PHONE 405 788-6186
Anthony Wall,
EMP: 3
SALES (est): 253.5K **Privately Held**
SIC: **2421** Sawmills & planing mills, general

(G-8497)
SHAWNEE STEEL COMPANY
41508 Hardesty Rd (74801)
P.O. Box 1360, Ennis TX (75120-1360)
PHONE 405 919-8582
W Bryce Anderson, *CEO*
James S Hatch, *President*
EMP: 20
SQ FT: 71,000
SALES (est): 4.1MM **Privately Held**
WEB: www.shawneesteel.com
SIC: **3441** Fabricated structural metal

(G-8498)
SIGN FACTORY LLC ⊙
136 W Macarthur St (74804-2011)
PHONE 405 401-9513
EMP: 1 EST: 2019
SALES (est): 46K **Privately Held**
SIC: **3993** Signs & advertising specialties

(G-8499)
SINCLAIR COMPANIES
301 E Highland St (74801-7059)
PHONE 405 637-8444
EMP: 46
SALES (corp-wide): 3.9B **Privately Held**
SIC: **2911** Petroleum refining
PA: The Sinclair Companies
550 E South Temple
Salt Lake City UT 84102
801 524-2700

(G-8500)
SLEEVE IT HANDLES
33109 Hardesty Rd (74801-5677)
PHONE 405 250-2419
Kevin Logan, *Owner*
EMP: 2
SALES (est): 83.9K **Privately Held**
SIC: **2752** Commercial printing, lithographic

(G-8501)
SOLID STATE CONTROLS INC
35431 Hardesty Rd (74801-5753)
PHONE 405 273-9292
Bill Mann, *President*
Brent Ulrich, *Shareholder*
Callie Watkins, *Shareholder*
EMP: 12
SQ FT: 7,500
SALES (est): 1.4MM **Privately Held**
WEB: www.solidstate-ssc.com
SIC: **7373** 3533 Office computer automation systems integration; oil field machinery & equipment

(G-8502)
SOONER COMPLETIONS INC
810 W Ayre St (74801-4709)
P.O. Box 37 (74802-0037)
PHONE 405 273-4599
W T Rapp Jr, *President*
Jack Davies, *Principal*
L R Maddux, *Principal*
Bill Rapp, *Principal*
EMP: 40 EST: 1946
SQ FT: 2,000
SALES (est): 5.5MM **Privately Held**
WEB: www.soonercompletions.com
SIC: **1389** Oil field services

(G-8503)
SPIRAL WAVES INDUSTRIES LLC
2204 Ellis Dr (74804-2460)
PHONE 405 481-7685
Beverly Edwina Butlerwolfe, *Principal*
EMP: 1
SALES (est): 39.6K **Privately Held**
SIC: **3999** Manufacturing industries

(G-8504)
STINK FREE INC
9 Country Club Rd (74801-6550)
PHONE 405 273-0006
J Michael Adcock, *CEO*
Leonard Taron, *Vice Pres*
▲ EMP: 6
SALES (est): 992.3K **Privately Held**
SIC: **2842** Sanitation preparations, disinfectants & deodorants

(G-8505)
SUGGS OREL
Also Called: S&S Printing
35109 Clearpond Rd (74801-2653)
PHONE 405 275-6159
EMP: 1
SALES (est): 77.2K **Privately Held**
SIC: **2732** Instruction Booklet Printing

(G-8506)
SWAN PLASTICS
6500 N Kickapoo Ave (74804-9113)
PHONE 405 275-4826
Robert Campbell, *Owner*
EMP: 3
SQ FT: 5,000
SALES (est): 231.7K **Privately Held**
SIC: **3089** Injection molding of plastics

(G-8507)
T D G I
41901 Wolverine Rd (74804-9160)
PHONE 405 275-8041
Regina Selfridge, *Director*
EMP: 2
SALES (est): 73.4K **Privately Held**
SIC: **3429** Manufactured hardware (general)

(G-8508)
T S & H EMB & SCREEN PRTG
414 W Chicago St (74804-2816)
PHONE 405 214-7701
Sue Snodgrass, *Owner*

Hope Kinparaing, *Partner*
EMP: 7
SALES (est): 310K **Privately Held**
SIC: **2759** 2396 2395 Screen printing; automotive & apparel trimmings; pleating & stitching

(G-8509)
TDK FERRITES CORPORATION
5900 N Harrison (74804-9124)
PHONE 405 275-2100
Yoshiharu Nanami, *President*
▲ EMP: 200
SALES (est): 31.7MM **Privately Held**
SIC: **3264** Magnets, permanent: ceramic or ferrite
HQ: Tdk U.S.A. Corporation
455 Rxr Plz
Uniondale NY 11556
516 535-2600

(G-8510)
TERRY STUTZMANN
Also Called: Stutzman Consulting Service
9 Magnolia Hills Ln (74801-9313)
PHONE 405 481-3853
Terry Stutzman, *Owner*
EMP: 1
SALES (est): 41K **Privately Held**
SIC: **1389** 8721 Oil field services; auditing services

(G-8511)
TIPTON OIL TOOLS LLC
7575 Highway 177 (74804-0614)
PHONE 405 964-3030
Robert G Tipton Jr, *Principal*
EMP: 5
SALES (est): 292.5K **Privately Held**
SIC: **1389** Oil field services

(G-8512)
TREAT METAL STAMPING INC
37609 Old Highway 270 (74804-9281)
PHONE 405 275-3344
David Treat, *President*
Raymond Treat, *Vice Pres*
EMP: 2
SALES: 100K **Privately Held**
SIC: **3469** 3444 Stamping metal for the trade; sheet metalwork

(G-8513)
TUFF SHED INC
14120 Highway 177 (74804-9252)
PHONE 405 788-4143
EMP: 1
SALES (corp-wide): 292.4MM **Privately Held**
SIC: **2452** Prefabricated wood buildings
PA: Tuff Shed, Inc.
1777 S Harrison St # 600
Denver CO 80210
303 753-8833

(G-8514)
U AND S WIRE ROPE
120 Jade Ln (74801-5002)
PHONE 580 421-1077
EMP: 2
SALES (est): 165.9K **Privately Held**
SIC: **3315** Steel wire & related products

(G-8515)
UFP SHAWNEE LLC
Also Called: Universal Forest Products
8702 N Harrison (74804-9560)
PHONE 405 273-1533
Jeff Crisp, *CEO*
EMP: 6 EST: 2015
SALES (est): 708K
SALES (corp-wide): 4.4B **Publicly Held**
SIC: **2421** Building & structural materials, wood; lumber: rough, sawed or planed
PA: Ufp Industries, Inc.
2801 E Beltline Ave Ne
Grand Rapids MI 49525
616 364-6161

(G-8516)
UNIT LINER COMPANY
Also Called: Pondliner.com
7901 N Kickapoo Ave (74804-9107)
PHONE 405 275-4600
Tom Dyer, *CEO*
Randy Stewart, *Division Mgr*

Alisa Light, *Controller*
Holly West, *Human Res Dir*
Frank McCulley, *Sales Mgr*
▲ **EMP:** 90
SQ FT: 280,000
SALES (est): 39.3MM **Privately Held**
SIC: 3081 Plastic film & sheet

(G-8517)
UNITED DYNAMICS INC
41001 Wolverine Rd (74804-9026)
PHONE.................405 275-8041
John Klaser, *President*
Harmik Dersahakian, *Exec VP*
Jim Waldrop, *Prdtn Mgr*
Chris Reynolds, *Senior Buyer*
Chris G Reynolds, *Buyer*
EMP: 30
SQ FT: 14,000
SALES (est): 7.8MM **Privately Held**
SIC: 3728 3429 Aircraft parts & equipment; manufactured hardware (general)

(G-8518)
VAN EATON READY MIX INC (PA)
8 Timber Pond (74804-8849)
P.O. Box 1058 (74802-1058)
PHONE.................405 214-7450
Mike V Eaton, *President*
Brian Bloyed, *Plant Mgr*
Brandi Gonzalez, *Human Res Dir*
Alan Berg, *Sales Staff*
Meredith Gierhart, *Marketing Staff*
EMP: 67
SALES: 63MM **Privately Held**
SIC: 3273 Ready-mixed concrete

(G-8519)
WESTERN CARTOONS
115 Maggies Pl (74801-8644)
PHONE.................405 275-1054
Daryl Talbot, *Owner*
EMP: 1
SALES (est): 56K **Privately Held**
SIC: 2759 7812 Magazines: printing; cartoon motion picture production

(G-8520)
WILKINS L L E & O COMPANY
23 E 9th St Ste 406 (74801-6963)
PHONE.................405 273-0370
Lloyd L Wilkins, *Owner*
EMP: 6 **EST:** 1967
SQ FT: 2,000
SALES (est): 356.2K **Privately Held**
SIC: 1311 Crude petroleum production; natural gas production

(G-8521)
WOLVERINE TUBE INC
41600 Wolverine Rd (74804-9159)
PHONE.................405 275-4850
Bobby Hatcher, *Maint Spvr*
Carl Squires, *Engineer*
Jon Clark, *Sales Staff*
Greg Goldman, *Branch Mgr*
Randy Gardner, *Supervisor*
EMP: 500 **Privately Held**
SIC: 3351 Tubing, copper & copper alloy
PA: Wolverine Tube, Inc.
2100 Market St Ne
Decatur AL 35601

(G-8522)
WOLVERINE TUBE INC
500 Walverine Rd (74801)
PHONE.................405 275-4850
Alan Pace, *Branch Mgr*
EMP: 600 **Privately Held**
SIC: 3351 3498 Tubing, copper & copper alloy; fabricated pipe & fittings
PA: Wolverine Tube, Inc.
2100 Market St Ne
Decatur AL 35601

(G-8523)
XTREME ENERGY COMPANY
624 W Independence St # 10 (74804-4306)
P.O. Box 2326, Victoria TX (77902-2326)
PHONE.................405 273-1185
Mike Hahn, *President*
EMP: 4

SALES (est): 390.4K **Privately Held**
SIC: 4911 1389 Electric services; oil consultants

Shidler
Osage County

(G-8524)
CENTURY LIVESTOCK FEEDERS INC
306 N Cosben (74652)
P.O. Box 501 (74652-0501)
PHONE.................918 793-3382
Joe Lynn Payne, *President*
Donna Lewma, *Sales Mgr*
EMP: 11
SALES (est): 1.9MM **Privately Held**
SIC: 3523 Farm machinery & equipment

(G-8525)
CHAPARRAL ENERGY INC
373 Phillips Rd Ste A (74652-2010)
PHONE.................918 793-2881
Wayne Porter, *Manager*
EMP: 46 **Publicly Held**
SIC: 1311 Crude petroleum production; natural gas production
PA: Chaparral Energy, Inc.
701 Cedar Lake Blvd
Oklahoma City OK 73114

(G-8526)
CHEYENNE INNOVATIONS INC
201 W Barber St (74652)
P.O. Box 459 (74652-0459)
PHONE.................918 793-7521
Kaycee Salyer, *President*
James Salyer, *Vice Pres*
EMP: 3
SALES (est): 187.1K **Privately Held**
SIC: 3441 Fabricated structural metal

(G-8527)
HAT CREEK CONTRACTORS INC
737 S Cosden Ave (74652-5805)
P.O. Box 324 (74652-0324)
PHONE.................580 761-6154
Jace Gullic, *Vice Pres*
EMP: 5
SALES (est): 243K **Privately Held**
SIC: 3548 Resistance welders, electric

(G-8528)
JASON A BLISS
737 S Cosden Ave (74652-5805)
PHONE.................580 304-9432
Ricky Bliss, *CEO*
EMP: 3
SALES (est): 45.7K **Privately Held**
SIC: 7692 Welding repair

Skiatook
Tulsa County

(G-8529)
3 PS INVESTMENT LLC
902 S John Zink St (74070-1719)
PHONE.................918 604-1363
Jerry Brown, *President*
EMP: 1 **EST:** 2017
SALES (est): 56.4K **Privately Held**
SIC: 3448 Prefabricated metal buildings

(G-8530)
A & T OIL COMPANY
14381 Shady Ln (74070-5546)
PHONE.................918 245-7358
EMP: 1
SALES (est): 120K **Privately Held**
SIC: 1311 Crude Petroleum/Natural Gas Production

(G-8531)
AUSSIE BUILT SUPPLIES LLC
386 Lone Wolf Ln (74070-5008)
PHONE.................918 381-9700
Michael Gower,
EMP: 1

SALES (est): 41K **Privately Held**
SIC: 1389 Construction, repair & dismantling services

(G-8532)
BERKSHIRE HATHAWAY INC
Also Called: Skiatook Journal
500 W Rogers Blvd (74070-1081)
PHONE.................918 396-1616
Todd Smith, *Manager*
EMP: 2
SALES (corp-wide): 327.2B **Publicly Held**
SIC: 2711 Newspapers
PA: Berkshire Hathaway Inc.
3555 Farnam St Ste 1140
Omaha NE 68131
402 346-1400

(G-8533)
BG & S MANUFACTURING
1003 S Lombard Ln (74070-1831)
P.O. Box 532 (74070-0532)
PHONE.................918 396-3525
Gene Bias, *Owner*
Robin Bias, *Sales Mgr*
EMP: 21
SQ FT: 7,500
SALES: 2.5MM **Privately Held**
SIC: 3561 5084 3594 7699 Industrial pumps & parts; pumps & pumping equipment; fluid power pumps & motors; pumps & pumping equipment repair

(G-8534)
BRYON K BARROWS
Also Called: Lb Machine & Mfg.
7954 Rock School Rd (74070-6165)
PHONE.................918 519-9369
Bryon K Barrows, *Owner*
EMP: 1
SQ FT: 2,000
SALES: 250K **Privately Held**
SIC: 3541 Machine tools, metal cutting type

(G-8535)
CARTER AEROSPACE MFG CO LLC
901 S John Zink St (74070-1719)
P.O. Box 8 (74070-0008)
PHONE.................918 229-4026
Charles Carter,
Bonnie Carter,
Mike Carter,
EMP: 5
SQ FT: 6,500
SALES (est): 713K **Privately Held**
SIC: 3324 Aerospace investment castings, ferrous

(G-8536)
CHS OIL & GAS LLC
4308 W Rogers Blvd (74070-3916)
PHONE.................918 280-9368
EMP: 2
SALES (est): 70.5K **Privately Held**
WEB: www.acquenergy.com
SIC: 1389 Oil & gas field services

(G-8537)
CUTTING EDGE WOODWORK LLC
820 W 5th St (74070-1319)
PHONE.................918 706-1143
Titus Boudreaux, *Principal*
EMP: 1 **EST:** 2018
SALES (est): 59.5K **Privately Held**
SIC: 2431 Millwork

(G-8538)
D & L ENCLOSURES
14630 N 56th West Ave (74070-6003)
PHONE.................918 396-7355
Daniel Villanella, *President*
Leah Villanella, *President*
Daniel E Villanella, *Agent*
EMP: 2
SALES (est): 370.4K **Privately Held**
SIC: 3825 3699 3444 Radio frequency measuring equipment; electrical equipment & supplies; sheet metalwork

(G-8539)
DC CUSTOM FRAMING
405 S Broadway St (74070-2007)
PHONE.................918 549-8754
EMP: 1 **EST:** 2018
SALES (est): 55.5K **Privately Held**
SIC: 2499 Picture frame molding, finished

(G-8540)
DIAMOND P MACHINE LLC
3875 W 178th St N (74070-4839)
PHONE.................918 396-7192
Zane P Pointer,
Andrea Pointer,
EMP: 2
SALES (est): 268.4K **Privately Held**
SIC: 3999 Manufacturing industries

(G-8541)
DIEMASTERS
Also Called: Die Block
77777 Superdie Indus Park (74070)
P.O. Box 219 (74070-0219)
PHONE.................800 826-2134
David Porter, *Owner*
EMP: 9
SQ FT: 2,000
SALES (est): 435K **Privately Held**
SIC: 3544 3364 Special dies & tools; magnesium & magnesium-base alloy die-castings

(G-8542)
DONMAR INDUSTRIES LLC
14080 N 44th West Ave (74070-5318)
PHONE.................918 688-7277
Donald Brock,
Mary Hamm,
EMP: 1
SALES (est): 53.9K **Privately Held**
SIC: 2511 Club room furniture: wood

(G-8543)
EVANS CONCRETE CO INC
4000 W 133rd St N (74070)
PHONE.................580 765-6693
Mandy Morris, *Vice Pres*
Sherry Smith, *Manager*
EMP: 9
SALES (est): 696.1K
SALES (corp-wide): 100.1MM **Privately Held**
SIC: 3273 Ready-mixed concrete
PA: Evans & Associates Enterprises, Inc.
3320 N 14th St
Ponca City OK 74601
580 765-6693

(G-8544)
G&E POWER LLC
679 W 136th St N (74070-3503)
PHONE.................918 396-2899
James M McIntosh, *Mng Member*
Jim Easton,
EMP: 50
SALES (est): 6.7MM **Privately Held**
SIC: 3441 Fabricated structural metal

(G-8545)
GLENN HAMIL
18300 N Peoria Ave (74070-3168)
PHONE.................918 396-3659
Glenn Hamil, *Principal*
EMP: 1
SALES (est): 52.8K **Privately Held**
SIC: 7692 Welding repair

(G-8546)
GREEN COUNTRY OUTDOOR EQP
542 E Chestnut St (74070-2406)
PHONE.................918 396-4250
Ronnie Roberts, *Principal*
EMP: 1
SALES (est): 146.4K **Privately Held**
SIC: 3546 5261 Saws & sawing equipment; lawnmowers & tractors

(G-8547)
HEAR MY HEART PUBLISHING LLC
313 E Oak St (74070-2227)
PHONE.................918 510-1483
Beth Wilson, *Principal*
EMP: 1

Skiatook - Tulsa County (G-8548)

SALES (est): 45.4K **Privately Held**
SIC: 2741 Miscellaneous publishing

(G-8548)
HIGHWAY MAN SIGNS
603 W Rogers Blvd (74070-1041)
PHONE.....................918 396-8024
EMP: 1
SALES (est): 50.6K **Privately Held**
SIC: 3993 Signs & advertising specialties

(G-8549)
HITCH N POST LLC
5265 W Rogers Blvd Ste A (74070-5228)
PHONE.....................918 396-9480
Shannon Duziecki, *Mng Member*
EMP: 2
SALES (est): 134.7K **Privately Held**
SIC: 7389 2754 Mailbox rental & related service; business form & card printing, gravure

(G-8550)
HLH INDUSTRIES LLC
5435 W Oak St (74070-9207)
PHONE.....................918 217-0100
Len Humphries, *Marketing Staff*
EMP: 1
SALES (est): 82.9K **Privately Held**
SIC: 3599 Machine shop, jobbing & repair

(G-8551)
HOWARD ENGINEERING
1109 E 176th St N (74070-3104)
P.O. Box 69 (74070-0069)
PHONE.....................918 396-3463
H Boyd Howard, *President*
EMP: 4
SQ FT: 1,000
SALES (est): 352.7K **Privately Held**
SIC: 1311 Crude petroleum production; natural gas production

(G-8552)
J MARRS WELDING
4001 W Munson Rd (74070-4081)
PHONE.....................918 396-2221
Jack Marrs, *Owner*
EMP: 3 EST: 1997
SALES (est): 150K **Privately Held**
SIC: 7692 Welding repair

(G-8553)
K & K WOOD PRODUCTS
17000 N Cincinnati Ave (74070-3196)
P.O. Box 444 (74070-0444)
PHONE.....................918 396-4004
Richard Kriege, *Owner*
Michael Kriege, *Owner*
Sharon Kriege, *Manager*
EMP: 4
SQ FT: 4,000
SALES (est): 261.1K **Privately Held**
SIC: 2499 5999 Trophy bases, wood; trophies & plaques

(G-8554)
KANSAS MB PROJECT LLC
1102 N Lenapah Ave (74070-4018)
PHONE.....................760 212-0606
Ron Clark, *Vice Pres*
Ron Herzfeld, *Vice Pres*
Wanda Sanders, *Treasurer*
Rick Coody, *Mng Member*
EMP: 2 EST: 2014
SALES (est): 154.8K **Privately Held**
SIC: 1382 Oil & gas exploration services

(G-8555)
KELLY L YOUNG
Also Called: Idle Time Creations
509 S Creek St (74070-1899)
PHONE.....................918 859-1046
Kelly L Young, *Owner*
EMP: 1
SALES (est): 54.1K **Privately Held**
SIC: 2431 Millwork

(G-8556)
KENNYS MACHINE SHOP
11027 N Cincinnati Ave (74070-3441)
PHONE.....................918 288-7241
K W Baker, *Owner*
EMP: 2

SALES (est): 118.5K **Privately Held**
SIC: 3541 Machine tools, metal cutting type

(G-8557)
LAMAMCO DRILLING LLC
4444 E 146th St N (74070-3212)
P.O. Box 550 (74070-0550)
PHONE.....................918 396-3020
Rick Dugan, *Finance*
Curtis Biram,
EMP: 4
SALES (est): 213.3K **Privately Held**
SIC: 1311 Crude petroleum production

(G-8558)
M & L OIL LLC
4444 E 146th St N (74070-3212)
P.O. Box 737, Collinsville (74021-0737)
PHONE.....................918 798-4511
Gary Lewis, *Partner*
Stan Miller, *Partner*
EMP: 9
SQ FT: 5,000
SALES (est): 750K **Privately Held**
SIC: 1389 Construction, repair & dismantling services

(G-8559)
MACHINE TECHNIQUES
110 N Choctaw Rd (74070-3607)
PHONE.....................918 396-2181
John Shipley, *Principal*
EMP: 2 EST: 2010
SALES (est): 124K **Privately Held**
SIC: 3599 Machine shop, jobbing & repair

(G-8560)
MAYABB OIL CO INC
1721 S Broadway St (74070-3516)
P.O. Box 467 (74070-0467)
PHONE.....................918 396-2654
EMP: 3
SALES (est): 212K **Privately Held**
SIC: 1311 Crude petroleum & natural gas

(G-8561)
MID STATES TECHNICAL SVC LLC
8560 Battle Creek Ct (74070-5383)
P.O. Box 1088 (74070-5088)
PHONE.....................918 260-6912
Greg Davis, *CFO*
Ken Linthicuth, *Mng Member*
EMP: 20
SALES: 2.4MM **Privately Held**
WEB: www.mstsllc.com
SIC: 1731 7389 3643 Electric power systems contractors; pipeline & power line inspection service; plugs, electric

(G-8562)
O K TANK TRUCKS INC
13801 N Cincinnati Ave (74070-3344)
P.O. Box 398 (74070-0398)
PHONE.....................918 396-3043
Scott Underwood, *Owner*
EMP: 10
SQ FT: 2,800
SALES (est): 950.6K **Privately Held**
SIC: 1389 4212 Oil field services; petroleum haulage, local

(G-8563)
PEAK MACHINING GROUP LLC (PA)
1900 S Osage St (74070-2353)
PHONE.....................307 660-1463
Fayleen Prosenick,
Ronnie Mitchell,
Kevin D Prosenick,
EMP: 3
SQ FT: 14,000
SALES: 750K **Privately Held**
SIC: 3599 Oil filters, internal combustion engine, except automotive

(G-8564)
POST OAK PETROLEUM LLC
14054 Rock School Rd (74070-6462)
PHONE.....................918 245-9919
Chad A Sellers, *Principal*
EMP: 3
SALES (est): 138.3K **Privately Held**
SIC: 1311 Crude petroleum production

(G-8565)
PRODUCING LAMAMCO III L P
4444 E 146th St N (74070-3212)
P.O. Box 550 (74070-0550)
PHONE.....................918 396-3020
Stanley J Miller, *Partner*
Connie Lewis, *Partner*
Gary Lewis, *Partner*
James Miller, *Partner*
Louise Miller, *Partner*
EMP: 120
SQ FT: 20,000
SALES (est): 10.3MM **Privately Held**
WEB: www.lamamco.com
SIC: 1311 Crude petroleum production

(G-8566)
REDBUD CANDLES & CREATIONS
10099 Lakewood Rd (74070-5590)
PHONE.....................210 749-6975
EMP: 2 EST: 2015
SALES (est): 66.8K **Privately Held**
SIC: 3999 Candles

(G-8567)
S&J MANUFACTURING INC
1898 S Osage St (74070-2143)
P.O. Box 507 (74070-0507)
PHONE.....................918 636-1224
Vicky Gibson, *President*
Billy R Gibson, *Vice Pres*
EMP: 5
SALES (est): 199.6K **Privately Held**
SIC: 3724 Aircraft engines & engine parts

(G-8568)
SCOOZIES CONEYS & FRZ CUSTARD
1529 W Rogers Blvd Ste A (74070-1086)
PHONE.....................918 396-1500
EMP: 3
SALES (est): 130K **Privately Held**
SIC: 2024 Mfg Ice Cream/Frozen Desert

(G-8569)
SIOSI OIL CO
Rr 1 Box 310 (74070)
P.O. Box 702163, Tulsa (74170-2163)
PHONE.....................918 492-1400
Charels Hatfield, *Owner*
EMP: 1
SQ FT: 20,000
SALES (est): 750K **Privately Held**
SIC: 1389 Pumping of oil & gas wells

(G-8570)
SKIATOOK STATUARY
Also Called: Sky Tech
100 N Quapaw St (74070-3616)
PHONE.....................918 396-1309
Chester W Reyckert, *Owner*
EMP: 7
SQ FT: 20,000
SALES (est): 250K **Privately Held**
SIC: 3272 3446 Monuments, concrete; fences or posts, ornamental iron or steel

(G-8571)
SM OIL & GAS INC
4444 E 146th St N (74070-3212)
P.O. Box 189 (74070-0189)
PHONE.....................918 629-2151
Stan Miller, *CEO*
EMP: 5
SALES (est): 100K **Privately Held**
SIC: 1389 Oil field services

(G-8572)
TSM INDUSTRIAL WELDING
16363 N 36th West Ave (74070-9340)
PHONE.....................720 290-4431
Troy R Anderson, *Principal*
EMP: 1
SALES (est): 34.1K **Privately Held**
SIC: 7692 Welding repair

(G-8573)
TURNING POINT MCH WORKS LLC
17300 N Cincinnati Ave (74070-3140)
PHONE.....................918 396-2560
Charles L Burgess,
EMP: 3

SALES (est): 315.5K **Privately Held**
SIC: 3599 Machine shop, jobbing & repair

(G-8574)
WILDHORSE EXPLORATION PROD LLC
18744 N Javine Hill Rd (74070-4818)
PHONE.....................918 396-3736
J L Holt, *Principal*
EMP: 3 EST: 2012
SALES (est): 216.8K **Privately Held**
SIC: 1311 Crude petroleum production

(G-8575)
WOODEN SOLUTIONS LLC
5433 W Oak St (74070-9207)
PHONE.....................918 396-0774
Kathy Humphries, *Executive*
Len Humphries,
Dean Lester,
EMP: 20
SQ FT: 6,500
SALES (est): 2.6MM **Privately Held**
SIC: 2434 Wood kitchen cabinets

(G-8576)
WORLD WIDE EXCHANGERS LLC (DH)
601 W 136th St N (74070-3503)
P.O. Box 47 (74070-0047)
PHONE.....................918 234-3700
Bob Giammaruti, *CEO*
Brandon Harbin, *CFO*
EMP: 40
SQ FT: 25,000
SALES (est): 6.6MM **Privately Held**
SIC: 3443 Heat exchangers, condensers & components
HQ: Southern Heat Exchanger Corporation
6100 Old Montgomery Hwy
Tuscaloosa AL 35405
205 345-5335

(G-8577)
WORTHINGTON CYLINDER CORP
679 W 136th St N (74070-3503)
PHONE.....................918 396-2899
EMP: 191
SALES (corp-wide): 3.7B **Publicly Held**
SIC: 3443 Cylinders, pressure: metal plate
HQ: Worthington Cylinder Corporation
200 W Old Wlson Bridge Rd
Worthington OH 43085
614 840-3210

Smithville
Mccurtain County

(G-8578)
HUGHES TRUCKING
24005 State Highway 144 (74957-9689)
PHONE.....................580 244-3731
Larry Hughes, *Owner*
EMP: 5
SALES: 75K **Privately Held**
SIC: 1389 Oil field services

(G-8579)
LOGGING CONTRACTOR INC
Hc 15 (74957)
PHONE.....................580 244-3571
Troy Keiss, *President*
Thericia Keiss, *Corp Secy*
EMP: 16
SALES (est): 670K **Privately Held**
SIC: 2411 Logging camps & contractors

(G-8580)
TERRY BELKNAP & SONS LOGGING
Hwy 259 (74957)
P.O. Box 305 (74957-0305)
PHONE.....................580 244-3303
Terry Belknap, *Owner*
EMP: 1
SALES (est): 143.7K **Privately Held**
SIC: 2411 Logging camps & contractors

Snyder
Kiowa County

(G-8581)
KIOWA COUNTY DEMOCRAT
530 E St (73566-1626)
P.O. Box 305 (73566-0305)
PHONE..................580 569-2684
Dee Richardson, *Owner*
EMP: 2
SQ FT: 3,000
SALES: 50K **Privately Held**
SIC: 2711 Newspapers: publishing only, not printed on site

(G-8582)
LAWTON TRANSIT MIX INC
Also Called: T1 Box 190
16725 County Rd N S 219 (73566)
PHONE..................580 569-4333
Johnny Caldwell, *Manager*
EMP: 5
SALES (corp-wide): 100.1MM **Privately Held**
SIC: 1442 5032 5211 Construction sand & gravel; gravel; sand, construction; stone, crushed or broken; sand & gravel
HQ: Lawton Transit Mix Inc
2208 Sw F Ave
Lawton OK 73501
580 353-6900

(G-8583)
MARTIN MARIETTA MATERIALS INC
Also Called: Snyder Plant
Rr 1 (73566)
PHONE..................580 569-2393
Joey Schulte, *Plant Supt*
Linda Hefner, *Office Mgr*
EMP: 18 **Publicly Held**
SIC: 1422 Crushed & broken limestone
PA: Martin Marietta Materials Inc
2710 Wycliff Rd
Raleigh NC 27607

(G-8584)
SOUTHWESTERN STATE SAND CORP
16725 Ns County Road 219 (73566-5024)
PHONE..................580 569-4333
Lloyd I Evans, *President*
Mattie Boyles,
Bruce Evans,
Steve Rohde,
Dale Zehr,
EMP: 27 **EST:** 1986
SALES (est): 461.1K
SALES (corp-wide): 100.1MM **Privately Held**
WEB: www.evans-assoc.com
SIC: 1442 Construction sand mining; gravel mining
PA: Evans & Associates Enterprises, Inc.
3320 N 14th St
Ponca City OK 74601
580 765-6693

(G-8585)
WILLIS BROS LAND & CATTLE CO
904 G St (73566-2244)
PHONE..................580 569-2698
Jackie Willis, *Owner*
EMP: 1
SALES (est): 125.2K **Privately Held**
SIC: 1311 Crude petroleum production

(G-8586)
WILLISCHILD OIL & GAS CORP
621 E St (73566-1849)
PHONE..................580 569-2598
Jackie D Willis, *President*
Donald Willis, *Vice Pres*
Bennie Mc Daniels, *Treasurer*
EMP: 2
SALES (est): 390.4K **Privately Held**
SIC: 1381 Drilling oil & gas wells

Soper
Choctaw County

(G-8587)
GREG E CONARD
Hc 71 Box 53-2 (74759-9708)
PHONE..................580 372-7982
Greg Conard, *Owner*
EMP: 1
SALES (est): 70.7K **Privately Held**
SIC: 3523 Cattle feeding, handling & watering equipment

Southard
Blaine County

(G-8588)
UNITED STATES GYPSUM COMPANY
Hwy 51a (73770)
PHONE..................580 822-6100
Bill Webber, *Branch Mgr*
EMP: 300
SALES (corp-wide): 8.2B **Privately Held**
WEB: www.usg.com
SIC: 3275 Gypsum products
HQ: United States Gypsum Company
550 W Adams St Ste 1300
Chicago IL 60661
312 606-4000

Sparks
Lincoln County

(G-8589)
SPARKS VINEYARD & WINERY INC
351310 E 970 Rd (74869-9770)
PHONE..................918 866-2529
J L Gilbert, *President*
EMP: 6
SALES (est): 460K **Privately Held**
SIC: 2084 Wines

(G-8590)
YOUNG SOFTWARE
353573 E 980 Rd (74869-9073)
PHONE..................918 290-9876
Billy Young, *Principal*
EMP: 2
SALES (est): 110.8K **Privately Held**
WEB: www.youngsoftware.com
SIC: 7372 Prepackaged software

Spavinaw
Mayes County

(G-8591)
JOHNSON LUMBER COMPANY INC
3174 State Highway 20 (74366-1038)
PHONE..................918 253-8786
William C Johnson, *President*
Sherry L Johnson, *Admin Sec*
EMP: 25
SALES (est): 2.9MM **Privately Held**
SIC: 2426 2448 2421 Lumber, hardwood dimension; pallets, wood; sawmills & planing mills, general

(G-8592)
ROUND SPRINGS WATER CO LLC
41624 S 540 Rd (74366-1277)
PHONE..................918 253-8188
Waldo McIntosh, *Manager*
EMP: 2
SQ FT: 2,000
SALES (est): 91.8K **Privately Held**
SIC: 2086 Water, pasteurized: packaged in cans, bottles, etc.

(G-8593)
VANOVER METAL BUILDING SLS INC
540 State Highway 20 (74366)
PHONE..................918 253-6030
Russell Vanover, *President*
EMP: 14 **EST:** 1995
SALES (est): 4.3MM **Privately Held**
WEB: www.vanovermetal.com
SIC: 5039 5211 3442 Metal buildings; prefabricated buildings; metal doors, sash & trim

Spencer
Oklahoma County

(G-8594)
DUDES WELDING & ETC LLC
8400 Ne 34th St (73084-3110)
PHONE..................405 510-4786
Marcus W Williams, *Principal*
EMP: 1
SALES (est): 31.5K **Privately Held**
SIC: 7692 Welding repair

(G-8595)
ESTEY CABINET DOOR CO
9100 Ne 40th St (73084-2827)
P.O. Box 30077, Midwest City (73140-3077)
PHONE..................405 771-3004
Bill Agee, *Owner*
EMP: 22
SQ FT: 10,000
SALES (est): 2.3MM **Privately Held**
SIC: 2541 2431 5211 Cabinets, except refrigerated: show, display, etc..: wood; millwork; door & window products

(G-8596)
INTEGRITY CUSTOM MILL WORKS
9115 Ne 36th St Trlr 1 (73084-2841)
PHONE..................405 495-9732
Maryann Brown, *President*
Madonna Brown-White, *Vice Pres*
EMP: 9 **EST:** 2010
SALES (est): 993.3K **Privately Held**
SIC: 2431 Millwork

(G-8597)
JUST BREATHE PUBLISHING LLC
9801 Ne 30th St (73084-3429)
PHONE..................405 633-0160
Taylor Beardshear, *Principal*
EMP: 1
SALES (est): 37.5K **Privately Held**
SIC: 2741 Miscellaneous publishing

(G-8598)
LEVEL UP PUBLISHING LLC
8900 Ne 51st St (73084-1421)
PHONE..................405 771-4372
Khrishawne Smith, *Principal*
EMP: 1 **EST:** 2017
SALES (est): 59.4K **Privately Held**
SIC: 2741 Miscellaneous publishing

(G-8599)
PFL INDUSTRIES LTD CO
7021 N Post Rd (73084-4017)
PHONE..................405 388-0321
Paul Lowe, *Manager*
EMP: 2
SALES (est): 88.9K **Privately Held**
SIC: 3999 Manufacturing industries

(G-8600)
RAGSDALE WRECKER SERVICE
3728 Spencer Rd (73084-1920)
PHONE..................405 771-5544
Troy Ragsdale, *Owner*
EMP: 4
SALES (est): 260K **Privately Held**
SIC: 3711 Wreckers (tow truck), assembly of

(G-8601)
SPENCER FAITH CHRISTN CTR INC
5401 N Westminster Rd (73084-6220)
PHONE..................812 876-5575
EMP: 2
SALES (est): 85.2K **Privately Held**
SIC: 3542 Machine tools, metal forming type

(G-8602)
THOMAS MILLWORK INC
2421 N Westminster Rd (73084-6401)
P.O. Box 237, Nicoma Park (73066-0237)
PHONE..................405 769-5618
Miles Thomas, *President*
Beverly Thomas, *Treasurer*
EMP: 15
SQ FT: 15,000
SALES (est): 1.7MM **Privately Held**
SIC: 2431 2521 2434 Millwork; wood office furniture; wood kitchen cabinets

(G-8603)
ZEIGLER PUBLISHING
9401 Ne 45th St (73084-2507)
PHONE..................405 771-8754
Roxanne Zeigler, *Principal*
EMP: 3
SALES (est): 120.5K **Privately Held**
SIC: 2741 Miscellaneous publishing

Sperry
Tulsa County

(G-8604)
BENCHMARK STUCCO
10345 N Sheridan Rd (74073-4196)
PHONE..................918 810-2812
EMP: 1 **EST:** 2010
SALES (est): 67.8K **Privately Held**
SIC: 3299 Stucco

(G-8605)
BLUE RIBBON SHOW SUPPLY
9731 N 20th West Ave (74073-4267)
PHONE..................918 288-7396
Buel Jobe, *Owner*
EMP: 5
SALES (est): 636.4K **Privately Held**
SIC: 5083 3523 Livestock equipment; farm machinery & equipment

(G-8606)
C AND C MANUFACTURING LLC
4225 W 88th St N (74073)
P.O. Box 1166, Skiatook (74070-5166)
PHONE..................918 288-6558
Kenny Crase,
Carl Cambell,
EMP: 6
SALES: 400K **Privately Held**
SIC: 3449 Miscellaneous metalwork

(G-8607)
DPS PRINTING SERVICES OF
3419 E 116th St N (74073-4549)
PHONE..................918 794-7755
EMP: 2 **EST:** 2017
SALES (est): 83.9K **Privately Held**
SIC: 2752 Commercial printing, lithographic

(G-8608)
JOHN CLARK
4215 E 106th St N (74073-4584)
PHONE..................918 853-8286
John Clark, *Principal*
EMP: 2
SALES (est): 114.1K **Privately Held**
SIC: 2741 Miscellaneous publishing

(G-8609)
L&M DUMP TRUCK & BACKHOE SERVI
9571 N 68th West Ave (74073-6704)
PHONE..................918 798-4568
EMP: 1 **EST:** 2017
SALES (est): 60K **Privately Held**
SIC: 3531 Backhoes

Sperry - Tulsa County (G-8610)

(G-8610)
MIKE BEATHE
Also Called: Beathe's Knives
3214 E 106th St N (74073-4330)
PHONE..................918 288-7858
Michael Beathe, *Owner*
EMP: 2
SALES (est): 111.2K **Privately Held**
SIC: 5719 3484 Kitchenware; guns (firearms) or gun parts, 30 mm. & below

(G-8611)
SOONER STATE GENERATOR LLC
9839 N Lewis Ave (74073-4314)
PHONE..................918 927-0543
David Gaulrapp, *Administration*
EMP: 4
SALES (est): 156.5K **Privately Held**
SIC: 3621 Generator sets: gasoline, diesel or dual-fuel

(G-8612)
WILLIAM M PARK
Also Called: Park Oil
211a W 113 St N (74073)
P.O. Box 718, Skiatook (74070-0718)
PHONE..................918 288-7752
William M Park, *Owner*
EMP: 1
SALES (est): 126.6K **Privately Held**
SIC: 1311 Crude petroleum production

Spiro
Le Flore County

(G-8613)
ALLEN RATHOLE INC
19279 Us Highway 271 (74959-4449)
PHONE..................918 626-4026
Mark Allen, *President*
Nikki Allen, *Corp Secy*
EMP: 9
SALES (est): 1.6MM **Privately Held**
SIC: 1381 Drilling oil & gas wells

(G-8614)
COAL CREEK MINERALS LLC
25858 Highline Rd (74959-4591)
P.O. Box 453 (74959-0453)
PHONE..................918 962-5335
Roger Hurst,
EMP: 20
SQ FT: 10,000
SALES (est): 1.9MM **Privately Held**
SIC: 1241 Coal mining services

(G-8615)
GEORGES COLLIERS INC
Also Called: G C I
22279 Us Highway 271 (74959-4815)
P.O. Box 70 (74959-0070)
PHONE..................918 962-2202
Craig Jackson, *President*
EMP: 49
SQ FT: 2,000
SALES: 13MM **Privately Held**
SIC: 1221 Bituminous coal & lignite-surface mining

(G-8616)
SEBO LANILA LYNN
21454 Aes Rd (74959-3730)
PHONE..................479 719-5612
Lanila Lynn Sebo, *Owner*
EMP: 1
SALES (est): 31.3K **Privately Held**
SIC: 2395 7389 Embroidery & art needlework;

(G-8617)
SOUTH CENTRAL COAL COMPANY INC (PA)
904 W Broadway St (74959-2458)
P.O. Box 268 (74959-0268)
PHONE..................918 962-2544
Bobby Meadows, *President*
Timothy Ball, *Vice Pres*
Danny Bell, *Admin Sec*
EMP: 4

SALES (est): 5.2MM **Privately Held**
SIC: 1241 Bituminous coal mining services, contract basis

(G-8618)
SPIRO GRAPHIC
212 S Main St (74959-2506)
P.O. Box 190 (74959-0190)
PHONE..................918 962-2075
James Fienup, *President*
John Clarke, *Manager*
EMP: 5 EST: 1977
SQ FT: 3,000
SALES (est): 379.1K **Privately Held**
SIC: 2711 2791 Newspapers: publishing only, not printed on site; typesetting

(G-8619)
SPIRO MINING LLC
25858 Highline Rd (74959-4591)
P.O. Box 453 (74959-0453)
PHONE..................918 962-5335
T J Huffman, *Principal*
EMP: 3
SALES (est): 387.4K **Privately Held**
SIC: 3648 Miners' lamps

(G-8620)
WARRANT DIVISIONS INC
19346 Us Highway 271 (74959-4450)
PHONE..................918 962-4800
Deana Hensley, *Principal*
EMP: 1
SALES (est): 49.1K **Privately Held**
SIC: 1241 Coal mining services

Springer
Carter County

(G-8621)
DAVCO PRODUCTIONS INC
25980 State Highway 53 (73458-8191)
PHONE..................405 266-9832
Fax: 580 561-2173
EMP: 7
SQ FT: 900
SALES (est): 1.1MM **Privately Held**
SIC: 1311 Oil & Gas Production

(G-8622)
DCP MIDSTREAM
11272 State Highway 53 (73458-8196)
PHONE..................580 653-2641
EMP: 2 EST: 2011
SALES (est): 111K **Privately Held**
SIC: 1389 Servicing oil & gas wells

(G-8623)
DRAGON
10834 State Highway 53 (73458-8227)
PHONE..................580 653-2171
EMP: 3
SALES (est): 159.1K **Privately Held**
SIC: 3443 Fabricated plate work (boiler shop)

(G-8624)
SATTERWHITE MACHINE SHOP
2288 Hereford Rd. (73458-8026)
PHONE..................580 653-2821
Jose Satterwhite, *Owner*
EMP: 1
SALES (est): 147.2K **Privately Held**
SIC: 3599 Machine shop, jobbing & repair

(G-8625)
SELECT ENERGY SOLUTIONS RW LLC
Also Called: Rockwater Energy Solutions
11079 State Highway 53 (73458-8236)
PHONE..................580 653-2167
Cliff Price, *Branch Mgr*
EMP: 2
SALES (corp-wide): 1.2B **Publicly Held**
WEB: www.rockwaterenergy.com
SIC: 1389 Construction, repair & dismantling services
HQ: Rockwater Energy Solutions, Llc
1515 W Sam Houston Pkwy N
Houston TX 77043

(G-8626)
SPADE LEASING INC
Also Called: V E Enterprises
1376 Mount Vica Rd (73458-8235)
P.O. Box 790, Beaumont TX (77704-0790)
PHONE..................580 653-2171
Lonnie B Whatley Jr, *President*
Mark Vahala, *Corp Secy*
EMP: 110
SQ FT: 150,000
SALES (est): 5.3MM **Privately Held**
SIC: 3715 3442 Truck trailers; window & door frames
HQ: V. E. Enterprises, Inc.
10834 State Highway 53
Springer OK 73458

(G-8627)
V E ENTERPRISES INC (DH)
10834 State Highway 53 (73458-8227)
P.O. Box 790, Beaumont TX (77704-0790)
PHONE..................580 653-2171
Lonnie B Whatley Jr, *President*
Lonnie B Whatley III, *Exec VP*
▼EMP: 21
SQ FT: 100,000
SALES (est): 10.2MM **Privately Held**
SIC: 3715 3443 Truck trailers; industrial vessels, tanks & containers; tanks for tank trucks, metal plate
HQ: Modern Ag Products, Llc
1655 Louisiana St
Beaumont TX 77701
409 833-2665

Stigler
Haskell County

(G-8628)
AGAVE ENERGY INC
30039 S County Road 4300 (74462-1684)
PHONE..................918 799-6174
Harvey Lunceford, *President*
Rena Schultz, *Corp Secy*
Aggie Lunceford, *Vice Pres*
EMP: 3
SALES (est): 350K **Privately Held**
SIC: 1381 Drilling oil & gas wells

(G-8629)
BLAYLOCK OIL AND GAS LLC
164 N Bk 700 Rd (74462-2172)
PHONE..................918 799-6153
Tobey L Blaylock, *Owner*
EMP: 2
SALES (est): 73.6K **Privately Held**
SIC: 1389 Oil & gas field services

(G-8630)
BROOKEN BOAT & MOTOR
105 E Bk 1200 Rd (74462-2146)
PHONE..................918 799-5227
Charles Durossette, *Owner*
EMP: 1
SALES (est): 73.6K **Privately Held**
SIC: 7694 Electric motor repair

(G-8631)
CLAYTON MACOM
20336 E Garland Rd (74462-2762)
PHONE..................918 967-3350
Macom Clayton, *Principal*
EMP: 3
SALES (est): 176.4K **Privately Held**
SIC: 3674 Semiconductors & related devices

(G-8632)
DAVIS INSULATED BUILDING INC (PA)
Also Called: Davis Building
300 Sw A St (74462-2314)
PHONE..................918 967-2042
Ray Davis, *President*
EMP: 57 EST: 1962
SQ FT: 11,500
SALES (est): 4MM **Privately Held**
WEB: www.davisbuildings.com
SIC: 4222 0751 3448 Storage, frozen or refrigerated goods; slaughtering: custom livestock services; prefabricated metal buildings

(G-8633)
J T HARRISON CONSTRUCTION CO
20289 N Airport Rd (74462-2632)
P.O. Box 120 (74462-0120)
PHONE..................918 967-2852
Randy Harrison, *Principal*
EMP: 10
SALES: 2.3MM **Privately Held**
SIC: 3532 Drills (portable), rock

(G-8634)
JACO ENERGY COMPANY INC
20292 E Highway 9 (74462-3411)
P.O. Box 59 (74462-0059)
PHONE..................918 967-8889
Bobby Coyle, *President*
EMP: 2
SALES (est): 190K **Privately Held**
SIC: 1389 Pumping of oil & gas wells

(G-8635)
KILGORE MEAT PROCESSING PLANT
908 Se E St (74462-2525)
PHONE..................918 967-2613
Fred Kilgore, *Owner*
Milburne Kilgore, *Owner*
EMP: 6
SALES (est): 385.3K **Privately Held**
SIC: 0751 5147 5421 2013 Slaughtering: custom livestock services; meats & meat products; meat & fish markets; sausages & other prepared meats; meat packing plants; butcher service, processing only

(G-8636)
KIMBERLY A JOHNSON
Also Called: Reconnect Mfg
324 Yellow Rock Rd (74462-5151)
PHONE..................918 370-3666
Kimberly Johnson, *Owner*
EMP: 3
SQ FT: 200
SALES (est): 211.6K **Privately Held**
SIC: 3599 Machine & other job shop work

(G-8637)
PARADISE CONSTRUCTION LLC
110 W Main St (74462-2326)
P.O. Box 658 (74462-0658)
PHONE..................918 967-9991
Robert Taylor,
Kim Taylor,
EMP: 2
SALES: 250K **Privately Held**
WEB: www.paradiseconstruction.com
SIC: 1521 2434 Single-family housing construction; wood kitchen cabinets

(G-8638)
PARK ENERGY SERVICES LLC
1408 N Country Ridge Dr (74462-1526)
PHONE..................918 617-4350
EMP: 6
SALES (corp-wide): 46.6MM **Privately Held**
SIC: 1389 Gas compressing (natural gas) at the fields
PA: Park Energy Services, Llc
1015 N Broadway Ave # 301
Oklahoma City OK 73102
405 896-3169

(G-8639)
PCS FERGUSON INC
1212 E Main St (74462-2801)
PHONE..................918 967-3236
Paul Ferguson, *Branch Mgr*
EMP: 5
SALES (corp-wide): 1.1B **Publicly Held**
WEB: www.pcsferguson.com
SIC: 3533 Oil field machinery & equipment
HQ: Pcs Ferguson, Inc.
3771 Eureka Way
Frederick CO 80516
720 407-3550

(G-8640)
QUALITY PRODUCTION CO STIGLER
20292 E Highway 9 (74462-3411)
P.O. Box 635 (74462-0635)
PHONE..................918 967-4383
Bobby Coyle, *Principal*

GEOGRAPHIC SECTION

Stillwater - Payne County (G-8673)

EMP: 60
SALES (est): 6.1MM Privately Held
WEB: www.qualityproductionrock.com
SIC: 1389 Pumping of oil & gas wells

(G-8641)
QUALITY STONE QUARRIES LLC
108 S Broadway St (74462-2318)
PHONE.................................918 967-5195
Johnan Ratliff, *Principal*
EMP: 9
SALES (est): 1.4MM Privately Held
WEB: www.qualitystonequarries.com
SIC: 1422 Crushed & broken limestone

(G-8642)
RESOURCE SERVICES INC
30039 S County Road 4300 (74462-1684)
PHONE.................................918 799-6174
Harvey Lunceford, *President*
EMP: 8
SALES (est): 967.2K Privately Held
SIC: 1389 Chemically treating wells

(G-8643)
RISING M ENTERPRISES
1308 Ne H St (74462-1974)
PHONE.................................918 766-4235
Randy Martin, *Principal*
EMP: 2 EST: 1989
SALES (est): 132.3K Privately Held
SIC: 3448 Carports: prefabricated metal

(G-8644)
ROYE REALTY & DEVELOPING INC
Also Called: Galaxy Energy
603 W Main St (74462-2335)
PHONE.................................918 967-4888
Charles D Roye, *President*
Deloris Roye, *Admin Sec*
EMP: 2
SQ FT: 3,000
SALES (est): 216.2K Privately Held
SIC: 1311 Crude petroleum production; natural gas production

(G-8645)
SAGA CARD CO INC
1707 N Broadway St (74462-2087)
P.O. Box 10 (74462-0010)
PHONE.................................918 967-0333
EMP: 2
SALES (est): 120K Privately Held
SIC: 5947 2771 Ret Gifts/Novelties Mfg Greeting Cards

(G-8646)
SOMETHING PRINTED
112 N Broadway St (74462-2042)
P.O. Box 661 (74462-0661)
PHONE.................................918 967-9188
Amber Dill, *Principal*
EMP: 2
SALES (est): 180.2K Privately Held
SIC: 2759 Screen printing

(G-8647)
STERLING CABINETRY & TRIM LLC
606 Ne F St (74462-1965)
PHONE.................................918 928-9982
Bradley Hall, *Owner*
EMP: 1
SALES (est): 111K Privately Held
SIC: 2434 Wood kitchen cabinets

(G-8648)
STIGLER DIGITAL
116 E Main St (74462-2471)
P.O. Box 156 (74462-0156)
PHONE.................................918 967-8383
Martin Dathan, *Principal*
EMP: 2 EST: 2016
SALES (est): 130.9K Privately Held
SIC: 2752 Commercial printing, offset

(G-8649)
STIGLER STONE COMPANY INC
910377 W 9 Hwy (74462)
PHONE.................................918 967-3316
Rick Bumpers, *President*
Pam Smith, *Admin Sec*
EMP: 18

SALES: 1.5MM Privately Held
SIC: 5211 3281 Masonry materials & supplies; cut stone & stone products

(G-8650)
TWIN CITIES READY MIX INC
1400 Industrial Rd (74462)
P.O. Box 514 (74462-0514)
PHONE.................................918 967-3391
Tim Grizelak, *QC Mgr*
Donald Jones, *Manager*
EMP: 4
SALES (corp-wide): 15.7MM Privately Held
SIC: 3273 5211 Ready-mixed concrete; lumber & other building materials
PA: Twin Cities Ready Mix, Inc.
   102 W Ashland Ave
   Mcalester OK 74501
   918 423-8855

Stillwater
Payne County

(G-8651)
ADVANTAGE CNSTR PDTS INC
2802 S Black Oak Dr (74074-2222)
PHONE.................................405 372-3562
Greg T Harrison, *President*
▲ EMP: 1
SALES (est): 142.7K Privately Held
SIC: 3317 3312 Steel pipe & tubes; tool & die steel

(G-8652)
AIRGAS USA LLC
2607 E 6th Ave (74074-6576)
PHONE.................................405 372-7720
David Spiva, *Manager*
EMP: 5
SALES (corp-wide): 129.8MM Privately Held
SIC: 5084 2911 2813 5099 Welding machinery & equipment; petroleum refining; industrial gases; safety equipment & supplies
HQ: Airgas Usa, Llc
   259 N Radnor Chester Rd
   Radnor PA 19087
   610 687-5253

(G-8653)
ALA INDUSTRIES
424 S Squires St (74074-1236)
PHONE.................................405 533-3260
EMP: 4
SALES (est): 285.6K Privately Held
SIC: 3999 Manufacturing industries

(G-8654)
ANNABELLA OIL & GAS CO LLC
6610 W Coventry Dr (74074-1025)
PHONE.................................405 377-8030
Peggy Williams, *Administration*
EMP: 2 EST: 2010
SALES (est): 150K Privately Held
SIC: 1382 Oil & gas exploration services

(G-8655)
ASCO AEROSPACE USA LLC
3003 N Perkins Rd (74075-2218)
PHONE.................................405 533-5800
Dusty McCoy, *Principal*
Chad Norton, *Engineer*
Richard Ringwald, *Engineer*
◆ EMP: 167
SALES (est): 35.4MM Privately Held
WEB: www.asco.be
SIC: 3728 Aircraft parts & equipment
HQ: Asco Industries
   Weiveldlaan 2
   Zaventem (Brucargo) 1930
   271 606-11

(G-8656)
ASSOCIATED MATERIAL PROC LLC
810 N Country Club Rd (74075-0917)
PHONE.................................405 707-7301
EMP: 1 EST: 2011
SALES (est): 136.1K Privately Held
SIC: 2819 Mfg Industrial Inorganic Chemicals

(G-8657)
B J PRINTING INC
Also Called: Stillwater Screenprinting
520 W 6th Ave (74074-4555)
PHONE.................................405 372-7600
Toll Free:.................................888 -
John E Reeves Jr, *President*
Aaron Reeves, *Mktg Dir*
Lynn Reeves, *Admin Sec*
EMP: 10
SALES (est): 1.2MM Privately Held
SIC: 2759 2396 Screen printing; automotive & apparel trimmings

(G-8658)
BAKER WELL SERVICE INC
406 N Bethel Rd (74075)
PHONE.................................405 372-6380
Amber Baker, *Manager*
EMP: 1
SALES (est): 145.3K Privately Held
SIC: 1389 Oil field services

(G-8659)
BIG ROCK FOODS LLC
1600 N Brush Creek Rd (74075-1832)
PHONE.................................405 269-8558
Shane Lansdown, *Mng Member*
EMP: 2
SALES (est): 71.3K Privately Held
SIC: 2087 Extracts, flavoring

(G-8660)
BILLY GOAT ICE CREAM CO LLC
1414 S Sangre Rd (74074-1810)
PHONE.................................405 332-5508
Rashaun Robinson, *Mng Member*
Caleb Neil, *Mng Member*
EMP: 2
SALES (est): 228.7K Privately Held
SIC: 2052 Cones, ice cream

(G-8661)
BLUE BRIDGE PUBLISHING LLC
120 S Stallard St (74074-6223)
PHONE.................................405 533-2547
Tommy Robert Thomas, *Owner*
EMP: 1
SALES (est): 52.6K Privately Held
SIC: 2741 Miscellaneous publishing

(G-8662)
BOUNTY TRANSFER LLC
1511 S Sangre Rd (74074-1869)
PHONE.................................405 338-1531
Edward Galegos,
EMP: 10
SALES (est): 259.7K Privately Held
SIC: 1382 Oil & gas exploration services

(G-8663)
BULLSEYE BORING TECHNOLOGY
2311 E 56th St (74074-8563)
P.O. Box 223 (74076-0223)
PHONE.................................405 880-1878
Brad Mills, *Principal*
EMP: 1
SALES (est): 104.2K Privately Held
SIC: 3541 Drilling & boring machines

(G-8664)
C R MANUFACTURING
1101 W Lakeview Rd (74075-2739)
PHONE.................................405 780-7368
EMP: 1
SALES (est): 48.3K Privately Held
SIC: 3999 Manufacturing industries

(G-8665)
CAMBRIDGE SOUNDWORKS INC (HQ)
Also Called: Hifi.com
1630 Cimarron Plz (74075-3467)
PHONE.................................405 742-6704
Michael Sullivan, *President*
Robert Cardin, *CFO*
▲ EMP: 130
SQ FT: 73,000
SALES (est): 12.8MM Privately Held
SIC: 5731 5961 3651 High fidelity stereo equipment; catalog sales; household audio & video equipment

(G-8666)
CAUSLEY PRODUCTIONS INC (PA)
205 W 9th Ave (74074-4406)
PHONE.................................405 372-0940
Mary Causley, *President*
James Causley, *Vice Pres*
EMP: 10
SQ FT: 3,750
SALES (est): 995.8K Privately Held
SIC: 2396 5947 2395 2759 Screen printing on fabric articles; gift shop; novelties; embroidery & art needlework; screen printing

(G-8667)
CHRISTIAN CONNECTIONS OF OKLA
9211 W 2nd Ave (74074-6760)
PHONE.................................405 372-2111
Tom Westbrook, *Principal*
Cindy Willis, *Principal*
EMP: 2
SALES (est): 98.9K Privately Held
SIC: 2759 Publication printing

(G-8668)
COASTERWORKS INC
2100 N Jardot Rd (74075-8530)
PHONE.................................405 624-2756
Steven Rogers, *President*
Patty Rogers, *Corp Secy*
EMP: 7
SQ FT: 5,000
SALES (est): 550K Privately Held
SIC: 3089 Plastic kitchenware, tableware & houseware

(G-8669)
COLLIERS CABINETS
5320 E 32nd Ave (74074-6116)
PHONE.................................405 377-3508
Michael Collier, *Owner*
EMP: 1
SALES (est): 69.2K Privately Held
SIC: 2434 Wood kitchen cabinets

(G-8670)
CORE MANUFACTURING LLC
3623 N Star Dr (74075-2500)
PHONE.................................405 747-1980
EMP: 2
SALES (est): 114.4K Privately Held
SIC: 3999 Manufacturing industries

(G-8671)
COWBOY COPY CENTER (PA)
514 S Washington St (74074-3335)
PHONE.................................405 372-8099
James T Cheek, *President*
EMP: 12
SQ FT: 3,000
SALES: 320K Privately Held
SIC: 7334 2791 2789 Blueprinting service; typesetting; bookbinding & related work

(G-8672)
COWBOY COVERS INC
Also Called: Shading Concepts
5601 W 6th Ave (74074-1101)
P.O. Box 351 (74076-0351)
PHONE.................................405 624-2270
James E Berry, *President*
Ann Berry, *Treasurer*
EMP: 5
SQ FT: 4,000
SALES (est): 506.6K Privately Held
SIC: 2591 5023 Drapery hardware & blinds & shades; draperies

(G-8673)
CUNDIFF CUSTOM FABRICATION LLC
318 E Harned Ave (74075-2520)
PHONE.................................405 372-8204
Cody D Cundiff, *Mng Member*
Renee Cundiff,
EMP: 6
SQ FT: 6,000
SALES: 300K Privately Held
SIC: 3462 3443 3444 Iron & steel forgings; fabricated plate work (boiler shop); sheet metalwork

Stillwater - Payne County (G-8674)

(G-8674)
DAILY OCOLLEGIAN
106 Paul Miller Building (74078-4050)
PHONE..................405 744-7371
Fritz Wertz, *General Mgr*
EMP: 66
SALES (est): 1.3MM **Privately Held**
SIC: 2711 Newspapers

(G-8675)
DEARINGER PRINTING & TROPHY
605 S Lewis St (74074-4028)
PHONE..................405 372-5503
Rick Dearinger, *CEO*
Tom Dearinger, *Corp Secy*
Rocky Brown, *Production*
Brennon Dearinger, *Sales Staff*
Camaron Dearinger, *Sales Staff*
EMP: 17 EST: 1960
SQ FT: 37,000
SALES (est): 1.2MM **Privately Held**
WEB: www.dearingers.com
SIC: 7336 5199 3914 Art design services; advertising specialties; trophies, silver; trophies, pewter

(G-8676)
DIRECT OILFIELD SERVICES LLC
Also Called: Direct Tank Services
633 N Husband St (74075-5244)
P.O. Box 1716 (74076-1716)
PHONE..................405 385-4743
Roger Rudd,
EMP: 1
SALES (est): 45.1K **Privately Held**
SIC: 1389 Oil field services

(G-8677)
DOUG ROBERSON
Also Called: Ewing Electric Company
1023 S Perkins Rd (74074-4737)
P.O. Box 1402 (74076-1402)
PHONE..................405 372-2078
Doug Roberson, *Owner*
EMP: 4 EST: 1936
SQ FT: 4,000
SALES (est): 170K **Privately Held**
SIC: 7694 5999 Electric motor repair; motors, electric

(G-8678)
DUFFY DRY CLEAN CITY LLC
2203 W 6th Ave (74074-4104)
PHONE..................405 743-0730
Duffy Johnny, *Mng Member*
EMP: 6
SALES: 340K **Privately Held**
SIC: 3582 7212 Commercial laundry equipment; pickup station, laundry & drycleaning

(G-8679)
DULANEYS LIQUOR STORE
Also Called: Dulaney's Retail Liquor Store
2012 N Boomer Rd (74075-1534)
PHONE..................405 377-9007
Ruth Pals, *Owner*
EMP: 2
SQ FT: 11,050
SALES (est): 273.5K **Privately Held**
SIC: 5921 2082 Hard liquor; beer (alcoholic beverage)

(G-8680)
DW-NATNAL STNDRD-STLLWATER LLC
3602 N Perkins Rd (74075-2221)
PHONE..................405 377-5050
Chad Effinger, *Mng Member*
Brent Steffen,
▲ EMP: 200
SALES (est): 108.4MM **Privately Held**
SIC: 3315 Steel wire & related products
PA: The Heico Companies L L C
70 W Madison St Ste 5600
Chicago IL 60602

(G-8681)
EASTERN RED CEDAR PRODUCTS LLC
6310 W Devonshire Rd (74074-1019)
PHONE..................405 780-7520
Richard Newton, *Branch Mgr*
EMP: 8
SALES (est): 781.9K **Privately Held**
SIC: 2421 Sawmills & planing mills, general
PA: Eastern Red Cedar Products, Llc
9611 S County Road 425 E
Marengo IN 47140

(G-8682)
EDUCATION OKLAHOMA DEPARTMENT
Also Called: Oklahoma Dep't of Career Tech
1201 N Western Rd (74075-2723)
PHONE..................405 743-5531
Danny Darrow, *Manager*
EMP: 17 **Privately Held**
SIC: 2791 2789 2752 9411 Typesetting; bookbinding & related work; commercial printing, lithographic;
HQ: Oklahoma Department Of Education
2500 N Lincoln Blvd # 112
Oklahoma City OK 73105

(G-8683)
ENDURANCE PUBLISHING LLC
5811 Trenton Ave (74074-1176)
PHONE..................405 332-5273
Matt Waits, *Principal*
EMP: 1
SALES (est): 51.9K **Privately Held**
SIC: 2741 Miscellaneous publishing

(G-8684)
ENGINEERED FOOD PROCESSES LLC
Also Called: Food Mech
1010 W Osage Dr (74075-2137)
PHONE..................405 377-7320
Jodi Bowser,
EMP: 3
SALES (est): 166.2K **Privately Held**
SIC: 2499 Food handling & processing products, wood

(G-8685)
ENGIUS LLC
712 Eastgate St (74074-6409)
PHONE..................405 533-3770
Michael Fox, *President*
EMP: 6
SQ FT: 2,000
SALES (est): 1.5MM
SALES (corp-wide): 1.8B **Publicly Held**
SIC: 3829 Physical property testing equipment; testing equipment: abrasion, shearing strength, etc.
PA: Flir Systems, Inc.
27700 Sw Parkway Ave
Wilsonville OR 97070
503 498-3547

(G-8686)
ENVIRONMENTAL CONCEPTS INC
6911 S Prairie Rd (74074-6127)
PHONE..................405 385-0422
Fonda Plunkett, *President*
Leo Plunkett, *Corp Secy*
EMP: 6 EST: 1999
SQ FT: 3,000
SALES (est): 540K **Privately Held**
SIC: 3589 Water treatment equipment, industrial

(G-8687)
EQUIVAQ SOFTWARE LLC
1414 S Sangre Rd (74074-1810)
PHONE..................405 742-0598
Tim Webb, *CEO*
EMP: 2
SALES (est): 125.5K **Privately Held**
SIC: 7372 Business oriented computer software

(G-8688)
FENTON OFFICE SUPPLY CO
Also Called: Fenton Office Mart
111 W Mcelroy Rd (74075-3531)
P.O. Box 2257 (74076-2257)
PHONE..................405 372-5555
Terry Carpenter, *President*
Pamela Carpenter, *Treasurer*
Jennifer Smith, *Sales Staff*
Patti Webb, *Technology*
Suzanne Carpenter, *Admin Sec*
EMP: 20
SQ FT: 8,500
SALES (est): 5.7MM **Privately Held**
WEB: www.fentonoffice.com
SIC: 5712 5943 7389 2752 Office furniture; stationery stores; office forms & supplies; telephone services; commercial printing, lithographic

(G-8689)
FLIR DETECTION INC
Also Called: Icx Biodefense
1024 S Innovation Way (74074-1508)
PHONE..................405 533-6618
Chelsea Pardue, *Administration*
EMP: 29
SQ FT: 10,900
SALES (est): 191.9K
SALES (corp-wide): 1.8B **Publicly Held**
SIC: 8731 3812 3829 Agricultural research; detection apparatus: electronic/magnetic field, light/heat; anamometers
HQ: Flir Detection, Inc.
1024 S Innovation Way
Stillwater OK 74074

(G-8690)
FLIR DETECTION INC (HQ)
1024 S Innovation Way (74074-1508)
PHONE..................703 678-2111
Dennis J Barket, *President*
Colin Cumming, *President*
Doug Knight, *President*
Deborah Mosier, *CFO*
Wayne Bryden, *Officer*
EMP: 10
SQ FT: 7,692
SALES (est): 166.9MM
SALES (corp-wide): 1.8B **Publicly Held**
SIC: 3826 Analytical optical instruments
PA: Flir Systems, Inc.
27700 Sw Parkway Ave
Wilsonville OR 97070
503 498-3547

(G-8691)
FLIR SYSTEMS INC
1110 S Innovation Way (74074-1541)
PHONE..................407 810-3634
Chelsea Pardue, *General Mgr*
Bruce Cumming, *Principal*
EMP: 7
SALES (corp-wide): 1.8B **Publicly Held**
WEB: www.flir.com
SIC: 3812 Search & navigation equipment
PA: Flir Systems, Inc.
27700 Sw Parkway Ave
Wilsonville OR 97070
503 498-3547

(G-8692)
FLIR SYSTEMS INC
1024 S Innovation Way (74074-1508)
P.O. Box 1542 (74076-1542)
PHONE..................405 372-9535
Jim Albright, *Production*
Sylvia Young, *Production*
Kevin Zacharias, *Engineer*
Cayton Jones, *Electrical Engi*
Ruth Anderton, *Accounting Mgr*
EMP: 17
SALES (corp-wide): 1.8B **Publicly Held**
WEB: www.flir.com
SIC: 7389 3826 Personal service agents, brokers & bureaus; analytical instruments
PA: Flir Systems, Inc.
27700 Sw Parkway Ave
Wilsonville OR 97070
503 498-3547

(G-8693)
FLUID TECHNOLOGIES INC
1016 E Airport Rd (74075-1714)
PHONE..................405 624-0400
Brett Wall, *President*
Dennis Baran, *Vice Pres*
John G Eleftherakis, *Vice Pres*
EMP: 20
SQ FT: 30,000
SALES (est): 3.4MM **Privately Held**
SIC: 3829 8734 8711 Measuring & controlling devices; testing laboratories; electrical or electronic engineering

PA: Filtran Holdings Llc
875 Seegers Rd
Des Plaines IL 60016

(G-8694)
FRONTIER ELCTRNIC SYSTEMS CORP
4500 W 6th Ave (74074-1522)
P.O. Box 1023 (74076-1000)
PHONE..................405 624-7708
Lloyd Salsman, *Principal*
Edward Shreve, *Principal*
Peggy J Shreve, *Chairman*
Kelly Nipp, *Mfg Mgr*
James Lee, *Mfg Staff*
EMP: 150
SQ FT: 86,000
SALES: 24MM **Privately Held**
SIC: 3812 3728 3769 Navigational systems & instruments; radar systems & equipment; aircraft parts & equipment; casings, missiles & missile components: storage; guided missile & space vehicle parts & aux eqpt, rsch & dev

(G-8695)
GARAGE STORAGE CABINETS LLC
Also Called: GSC
2805 E 6th Ave (74074-6513)
PHONE..................405 743-0133
Jim Schlimpert,
Judy Schlimpert,
▲ EMP: 12
SQ FT: 11,500
SALES (est): 1.3MM **Privately Held**
WEB: www.garagestoragecabinets.com
SIC: 2542 Cabinets: show, display or storage: except wood

(G-8696)
GUTHRIE INDUSTRIAL COATING
1905 Birchwood Ct (74075-8255)
P.O. Box 789 (74076-0789)
PHONE..................405 377-6649
Amy Guthrie, *Principal*
EMP: 2
SALES (est): 266.3K **Privately Held**
SIC: 3479 Metal coating & allied service

(G-8697)
HADLEYS INDUSTRIES
3505 S Jardot Rd (74074-7205)
PHONE..................405 743-0337
Kristen Hadley, *Principal*
EMP: 1 EST: 2018
SALES (est): 43.6K **Privately Held**
SIC: 3999 Manufacturing industries

(G-8698)
HAYS AND HAYS COMPANIES INC
Also Called: Signs Now
504 W 6th Ave (74074-4555)
PHONE..................405 624-2999
Carolyn Hays, *President*
Larry D Hays, *Vice Pres*
Mary Cobb, *Treasurer*
EMP: 4
SALES (est): 418.3K **Privately Held**
SIC: 3993 5999 Signs & advertising specialties; banners

(G-8699)
HEARTLAND VACCINES LLC
1201 S Innovation Way (74074-1579)
PHONE..................716 848-9251
Robert C Welliver Sr,
EMP: 1
SALES (est): 47.2K **Privately Held**
SIC: 2836 Vaccines

(G-8700)
HERITAGE PETROLEUM INC
1225 N Perkins Rd Ste C (74075-7100)
P.O. Box 935 (74076-0935)
PHONE..................405 377-2689
Mike D Smith, *President*
Marvin Smith, *Vice Pres*
EMP: 4
SQ FT: 200
SALES: 180K **Privately Held**
SIC: 1311 8711 Crude petroleum & natural gas production; petroleum engineering

GEOGRAPHIC SECTION

Stillwater - Payne County (G-8730)

(G-8701)
HIDDEN PEARLS LLC
4700 Sherman Lake Dr (74074-9500)
PHONE...................405 707-0851
EMP: 1
SALES (est): 46K Privately Held
SIC: 2731 Books-Publishing/Printing

(G-8702)
HORIZON ENERGY SERVICES LLC
115 E 80th St (74074-7265)
PHONE...................405 533-4800
Chris McCutchen, Mng Member
EMP: 350
SALES (est): 56.7MM Privately Held
WEB: www.horizonesl.com
SIC: 1381 Drilling oil & gas wells

(G-8703)
HP FIELD SERVICES LLC
3210 W Lakeview Rd (74075-4129)
PHONE...................580 763-1428
Ty Hendrin, Mng Member
EMP: 2
SALES (est): 111.1K Privately Held
SIC: 1389 5172 Oil field services; gasoline

(G-8704)
IRWIN CUSTOM SIGN COMPANY LLC
415 E 14th Ave (74074-5008)
P.O. Box 316 (74076-0316)
PHONE...................405 372-0657
James L Irwin,
Jacquelyn Irwin,
EMP: 6
SQ FT: 5,000
SALES (est): 600K Privately Held
WEB: www.irwincustomsigns.com
SIC: 3993 2394 Signs & advertising specialties; awnings, fabric: made from purchased materials

(G-8705)
ISSKEN INDUSTRIES INC
205 S Main St (74074-3521)
PHONE...................405 623-2177
EMP: 2 EST: 2010
SALES (est): 84K Privately Held
SIC: 3999 Mfg Misc Products

(G-8706)
JAMEY H VOORHEES
724 S Jefferson St Apt 4 (74074-4363)
PHONE...................479 599-9921
Jamey Voorhees, Agent
EMP: 1
SALES (est): 34.5K Privately Held
SIC: 2741 Micropublishing

(G-8707)
JIM CAMPBELL & ASSOCIATES RLTY
1776 W Lakeview Rd (74075-2746)
PHONE...................405 372-9225
Jim Campbell, President
EMP: 6
SQ FT: 1,600
SALES (est): 413.3K Privately Held
SIC: 6513 8742 1311 6515 Apartment building operators; construction project management consultant; crude petroleum production; natural gas production; mobile home site operators; general warehousing; real estate agents & managers

(G-8708)
JUNIPER RIDGE INC
3805 W Rutledge Dr (74075-5001)
PHONE...................405 762-2555
Jim Rutledge, Principal
EMP: 2
SALES (est): 134.9K Privately Held
SIC: 2841 Soap & other detergents

(G-8709)
KENNEL AND CRATE LLC
9521 Perfect Dr (74074-1199)
PHONE...................405 624-0062
Kim Johnson,
EMP: 1
SALES (est): 36K Privately Held
WEB: www.kennelandcrate.com
SIC: 0752 2511 Boarding services, kennels; bed frames, except water bed frames: wood

(G-8710)
KENNETH PETERMANN
Also Called: Ken's Welding
2812 E 56th St (74074-8561)
PHONE...................405 372-0111
Kenneth Petermann, Owner
EMP: 1 EST: 1973
SALES (est): 100K Privately Held
SIC: 7692 1799 3444 3441 Welding repair; welding on site; sheet metalwork; fabricated structural metal

(G-8711)
KERNS ASPHALT COMPANY INC (PA)
1805 S Perkins Rd (74074-7940)
P.O. Box 1628 (74076-1628)
PHONE...................405 372-2750
Jeffery Kerns, President
Robert O Kerns, President
Jeff Kerns, Vice Pres
EMP: 30
SQ FT: 5,000
SALES (est): 2MM Privately Held
SIC: 2951 Asphalt & asphaltic paving mixtures (not from refineries)

(G-8712)
KERNS CONSTRUCTION INC
1805 S Perkins Rd (74074-7940)
P.O. Box 1628 (74076-1628)
PHONE...................405 372-2750
Jeffrey Kerns, President
EMP: 45
SQ FT: 9,000
SALES (est): 6.6MM Privately Held
WEB: www.kernscompanies.com
SIC: 3273 Ready-mixed concrete

(G-8713)
KERNS READY MIXED CONCRETE INC
1805 S Perkins Rd (74074-7940)
P.O. Box 1628 (74076-1628)
PHONE...................405 372-2750
Robert Kerns, President
Robert O Kerns, President
Jeff O Kerns, Vice Pres
Bobby Flowers, Treasurer
EMP: 14
SQ FT: 5,000
SALES (est): 1.8MM Privately Held
SIC: 3273 Ready-mixed concrete

(G-8714)
KITES IN SKY LLC
1024 S Mcdonald St (74074-5219)
PHONE...................405 624-6231
Catherine Gabrel, Principal
EMP: 1
SALES (est): 108K Privately Held
WEB: www.kitekits.com
SIC: 3944 Kites

(G-8715)
KOPCO INC
818 S Main St (74074-4631)
P.O. Box 699 (74076-0699)
PHONE...................405 743-3290
J B Red, President
Rose Anne Red, Corp Secy
Red Mary H, Vice Pres
Mary Red, Vice Pres
EMP: 5
SALES (est): 750K Privately Held
SIC: 1311 Crude petroleum & natural gas

(G-8716)
LACEBARK INC
2104 N Cottonwood Rd (74075-2098)
P.O. Box 2383 (74076-2383)
PHONE...................405 377-3539
Carl Whitcomb, President
Lajean Whitcomb, Corp Secy
EMP: 3
SQ FT: 300
SALES (est): 140K Privately Held
SIC: 0181 3089 2731 8748 Flowers: grown under cover (e.g. greenhouse production); plastic containers, except foam; books: publishing only; agricultural consultant

(G-8717)
LEW GRAPHICS INC
4724 W Village Ct (74074-1435)
PHONE...................405 743-0890
Jeff McMillian, President
EMP: 2
SALES (est): 120K Privately Held
SIC: 2721 Magazines: publishing only, not printed on site

(G-8718)
LEWIS OIL CORPORATION
1905 Cedardale Ln (74075)
P.O. Box 1033 (74076-1033)
PHONE...................405 377-6556
Richard Lewis, President
Virginia Lewis, Vice Pres
Alice Boydston, Admin Sec
EMP: 6
SALES (est): 525.5K Privately Held
SIC: 1311 Crude petroleum production; natural gas production

(G-8719)
LINE X OF STILLWATER
5703 E 6th Ave (74074-6611)
PHONE...................405 743-0911
EMP: 3
SALES (est): 168.9K Privately Held
SIC: 5013 2821 Truck parts & accessories; plastics materials & resins

(G-8720)
LONGHORN ENERGY SERVICES LLC
616 Macy Ln (74075-1875)
PHONE...................918 302-7610
Jonathan Kifer,
Kent Smith,
EMP: 6
SALES (est): 170.8K Privately Held
SIC: 1382 Oil & gas exploration services

(G-8721)
MARGARITA MAN HQ LLC
601 S Washington St 303 (74074-4539)
PHONE...................830 336-4252
Douglas Henderson,
EMP: 5
SALES (est): 139.9K Privately Held
SIC: 2087 Beverage bases, concentrates, syrups, powders & mixes

(G-8722)
MC IRON BLACKSMITHING & WLDG ✪
2405 W 44th St (74074-2689)
PHONE...................405 613-5215
EMP: 1 EST: 2019
SALES (est): 43.1K Privately Held
WEB: www.mcarteriron.com
SIC: 7692 Welding repair

(G-8723)
MC-ALIPAT LLC
1004 W Connell Ave (74075-4607)
PHONE...................405 370-3321
Ali Beker,
EMP: 2 EST: 2017
SALES (est): 106.8K Privately Held
SIC: 3821 7389 Laboratory apparatus, except heating & measuring;

(G-8724)
MCCORMICK & ASSOCIATES LLC
1212 S Range Rd (74074-1096)
P.O. Box 2317 (74076-2317)
PHONE...................405 747-9991
Joan McCormick,
EMP: 1 Privately Held
SIC: 1389 Oil consultants
PA: Mccormick & Associates Llc
5121 Richardson Dr
Odessa TX 79762

(G-8725)
MITO MATERIAL SOLUTIONS INC
1414 S Sangre Rd 103 (74074-1810)
PHONE...................855 344-6486
Haley Kurtz, CEO
Kevin Keith, COO
EMP: 5
SALES (est): 162.9K Privately Held
SIC: 2655 2891 Cans, composite: foil-fiber & other: from purchased fiber; epoxy adhesives

(G-8726)
MUSTANG HEAVY HAUL LLC
Also Called: Latshaw Drilling
4905 S Perkins Rd (74074-7554)
P.O. Box 691017, Tulsa (74169-1017)
PHONE...................405 743-0085
Mike Brown, COO
Mardi De Zerges,
Ed Jacob III,
EMP: 1100
SALES (est): 57.6MM
SALES (corp-wide): 92MM Privately Held
SIC: 1381 Drilling oil & gas wells
PA: Latshaw Drilling & Exploration Co
4500 S 129th East Ave # 150
Tulsa OK 74134
918 355-4380

(G-8727)
NEW FORUMS PRESS INC
1018 S Lewis St (74074-4622)
P.O. Box 876 (74076-0876)
PHONE...................405 372-6158
Douglas Dollar, President
Gayla Dollar, Treasurer
EMP: 5
SALES (est): 300K Privately Held
SIC: 2731 2741 2721 Books: publishing only; miscellaneous publishing; periodicals: publishing only; magazines: publishing only, not printed on site; trade journals: publishing only, not printed on site

(G-8728)
NEWSPAPER HOLDING INC
Also Called: Stillwater News Press
211 W 9th Ave (74074-4406)
P.O. Box 2288 (74076-2288)
PHONE...................405 372-5000
Fred Fehr, Manager
EMP: 65 Privately Held
SIC: 2711 Commercial printing & newspaper publishing combined; newspapers: publishing only, not printed on site
HQ: Newspaper Holding, Inc.
425 Locust St
Johnstown PA 15901
814 532-5102

(G-8729)
NEWSPRESS INC
Also Called: Stillwater News Press
211 W 9th Ave (74074-4406)
P.O. Box 2288 (74076-2288)
PHONE...................405 372-5000
Mike Kellogg, President
Lawrence F Bellatti, President
James R Bellatti, Vice Pres
Dale Van Deventer, Product Mgr
EMP: 10 EST: 1941
SQ FT: 10,000
SALES (est): 716.3K Privately Held
WEB: www.stwnewspress.com
SIC: 2711 4832 Newspapers, publishing & printing; radio broadcasting stations

(G-8730)
OAKLEY PORTABLE BUILDINGS LLC
2623 E 6th Ave (74074-6576)
PHONE...................405 372-6543
Brad Brown, Owner
EMP: 3
SALES (est): 446.5K Privately Held
WEB: www.oakleyportablebuildings.com
SIC: 3448 Buildings, portable: prefabricated metal

Stillwater - Payne County (G-8731)

(G-8731)
OK QUALITY PRINTING INC
901 N Boomer Rd (74075-3504)
PHONE...................405 624-2925
Kathleen Tedder, *President*
Chad Tedder, *Vice Pres*
EMP: 3 **EST:** 1979
SQ FT: 2,400
SALES (est): 379.2K **Privately Held**
SIC: 2752 2791 2789 Commercial printing, offset; typesetting; bookbinding & related work

(G-8732)
OKLAHOMA HEARTLAND INC
9302 E Leisure Ln (74075-8843)
PHONE...................918 914-3124
EMP: 3
SALES (est): 126.6K **Privately Held**
SIC: 2077 Manufacturing Of Biodiesel

(G-8733)
OKLAHOMA STATE UNIVERSITY
Also Called: Fire Protection Pubs
930 N Willis St (74078-8045)
PHONE...................405 744-5723
Sharon S Toy, *Purch Dir*
Mike Wieder, *Finance Mgr*
Mikyla Cooper, *Sales Staff*
David Eller, *Info Tech Mgr*
Chris Neal, *Director*
EMP: 150
SALES (corp-wide): 904MM **Privately Held**
SIC: 2731 2721 Books: publishing only; periodicals
PA: Oklahoma State University
  401 Whitehurst Hall
  Stillwater OK 74078
  405 744-5000

(G-8734)
ORO WOODWORKS
6814 Walnut Crk (74074-6625)
PHONE...................405 334-7445
EMP: 1
SALES (est): 54.1K **Privately Held**
SIC: 2431 Millwork

(G-8735)
PATRIOT DIRECTIONAL DRLG LLC
2417 N Marine Rd Ste 3 (74075-2232)
P.O. Box 31446, Edmond (73003-0025)
PHONE...................405 831-0085
Jimbo Carnley, *Manager*
EMP: 2
SALES (est): 454K **Privately Held**
WEB: www.patriotok.com
SIC: 1381 Directional drilling oil & gas wells

(G-8736)
PEAK EAGLES LANDING
810 S Jardot Rd Trlr 58 (74074-4911)
PHONE...................918 636-5152
Ty Anderson, *Owner*
Thea Anderson, *Co-Owner*
EMP: 2
SALES (est): 86K **Privately Held**
SIC: 3792 House trailers, except as permanent dwellings

(G-8737)
PIONEER DRECTIONAL DRLG II LLC
4815 S Perkins Rd (74074-7548)
PHONE...................405 533-1552
John Special, *Principal*
EMP: 2
SALES (est): 123K **Privately Held**
SIC: 1381 Directional drilling oil & gas wells

(G-8738)
PLASMA BIONICS LLC
1508 W 15th Ave Unit 2 (74074-5254)
PHONE...................405 564-5333
EMP: 2 **EST:** 2012
SALES (est): 91K **Privately Held**
SIC: 2836 Mfg Biological Products

(G-8739)
PLATINUM ARCH MFG & CNSTR LLC
15 E 80th St (74074)
P.O. Box 998 (74076-0998)
PHONE...................316 573-6814
Doug Campbell, *CEO*
EMP: 15
SQ FT: 7,000
SALES (est): 181.9K **Privately Held**
SIC: 1791 3443 Storage tanks, metal: erection, boiler shop products: boilers, smokestacks, steel tanks

(G-8740)
PPR LLC
205 W Mcelroy Rd Ste 1 (74075-3536)
PHONE...................574 516-1131
EMP: 1
SALES (est): 39.7K **Privately Held**
SIC: 3299 Nonmetallic mineral products

(G-8741)
QG LLC
Worldcolor Stillwater
100 W Airport Rd (74075-1660)
PHONE...................405 742-2222
Mark Pound, *Branch Mgr*
EMP: 290
SQ FT: 200,000
SALES (corp-wide): 3.9B **Publicly Held**
SIC: 2732 Books: printing & binding
HQ: Qg, Llc
  N61w23044 Harrys Way
  Sussex WI 53089

(G-8742)
R R DONNELLEY & SONS COMPANY
3100 N Husband St (74075-2516)
PHONE...................405 743-2124
Anthony J Degeorge, *Principal*
Anthony De George, *Div Sub Head*
EMP: 280
SALES (corp-wide): 6.2B **Publicly Held**
SIC: 2761 Manifold business forms
PA: R. R. Donnelley & Sons Company
  35 W Wacker Dr
  Chicago IL 60601
  312 326-8000

(G-8743)
RAILROAD YARD INC
5915 S Perkins Rd (74074-8245)
P.O. Box 2283 (74076-2283)
PHONE...................405 377-8763
William Anderson IV, *President*
Michael Pollaro, *Exec VP*
EMP: 20 **EST:** 1978
SQ FT: 3,500
SALES (est): 12.9MM **Privately Held**
SIC: 5211 5051 5099 3441 Lumber & other building materials; structural shapes, iron or steel; pipe & tubing, steel; timber products, rough; fabricated structural metal; prefabricated metal buildings

(G-8744)
RAM INTERNET MEDIA
4603 White Oak Dr (74074-8535)
PHONE...................405 614-0641
Rachel Dillin, *Partner*
Matt Couden, *Partner*
EMP: 2
SALES (est): 103.4K **Privately Held**
SIC: 2741 7389 ;

(G-8745)
REN HOLDING CORPORATION (PA)
5900 S Perkins Rd (74074-8245)
PHONE...................405 533-2755
Gary Roberts, *President*
▲ **EMP:** 11
SALES (est): 1.5MM **Privately Held**
SIC: 3593 8711 3829 Fluid power cylinders & actuators; consulting engineer; measuring & controlling devices

(G-8746)
REN TESTING CORPORATION
5900 S Perkins Rd (74074-8245)
PHONE...................405 533-2700
Ryan Ashley, *President*
Travis B Rattan, *Vice Pres*
Carol R Donnahue, *Admin Mgr*
Dr Marion Roberts, *Director*
Nancy Roberts, *Director*
▲ **EMP:** 13 **EST:** 1976
SQ FT: 14,000
SALES (est): 1.5MM **Privately Held**
SIC: 3829 Measuring & controlling devices
PA: Ren Holding Corporation
  5900 S Perkins Rd
  Stillwater OK 74074

(G-8747)
RHINESTONE COWGIRL
223 S Knoblock St (74074-3016)
PHONE...................405 564-0512
Miranda Dickinson, *Principal*
EMP: 1
SALES (est): 91.5K **Privately Held**
WEB: www.likearhinestonecowgirl.com
SIC: 7299 5947 2759 Tanning salon; gift, novelty & souvenir shop; screen printing

(G-8748)
ROCKFORD CORPORATION
Also Called: Audio Innovations
2805 E 6th Ave (74074-6513)
PHONE...................405 624-6722
David Cunningham, *President*
EMP: 150
SALES (corp-wide): 177.3MM **Publicly Held**
WEB: www.rockfordcorp.com
SIC: 3651 Speaker systems
PA: Rockford Corporation
  600 S Rockford Dr
  Tempe AZ 85281
  480 967-3565

(G-8749)
ROLL-2-ROLL TECHNOLOGIES LLC
1110 S Innovation Way (74074-1541)
PHONE...................405 726-0985
Carlo Branca, *Research*
Aravind Seshadri,
EMP: 1 **EST:** 2013
SQ FT: 1,600
SALES (est): 228.8K **Privately Held**
SIC: 3823 Industrial process control instruments

(G-8750)
RUSSELLS MACHINE AND FAB LLC
133 S Stallard St (74074-6224)
PHONE...................405 742-6818
EMP: 1
SALES (est): 92.9K **Privately Held**
SIC: 3569 General Industrial Machinery, Nec, Nsk

(G-8751)
S E & M MONOGRAMMING
906 S Main St (74074-4634)
PHONE...................405 377-9677
William Smith, *Owner*
Mona Smith, *Co-Owner*
EMP: 3
SQ FT: 3,400
SALES (est): 242.6K **Privately Held**
SIC: 7389 5719 2395 Embroidering of advertising on shirts, etc.; towels; embroidery products, except schiffli machine

(G-8752)
SANDERS ELECTRIC
3503 N Park Dr (74074-2513)
PHONE...................405 377-1691
Lee Sanders, *Principal*
EMP: 1
SALES (est): 85K **Privately Held**
SIC: 1731 1389 General electrical contractor; oil field services

(G-8753)
SCARAB WOODWORKING LLC
7213 N Western Rd (74075-1167)
PHONE...................405 612-2111
Daniel Jay Mulder, *Administration*
EMP: 4
SALES (est): 165.1K **Privately Held**
SIC: 2431 Millwork

(G-8754)
SHUTTER MILL INC
Also Called: Kirtz Shutters
8517 S Perkins Rd (74074-8103)
P.O. Box 1453 (74076-1453)
PHONE...................405 377-6455
Chris Tietz, *CEO*
Gregory A Kirby, *Principal*
Christopher B Tietz, *Principal*
Denise A Tietz, *Principal*
Ted Williamson, *Sales Mgr*
EMP: 55
SQ FT: 35,000
SALES (est): 8.6MM **Privately Held**
SIC: 2431 5211 Blinds (shutters), wood; millwork & lumber

(G-8755)
STAN CLARK CO
516 W Elm Ave (74074-3013)
P.O. Box 729 (74076-0729)
PHONE...................405 377-0799
Stan Clark, *President*
EMP: 7
SQ FT: 5,000
SALES (est): 852.6K **Privately Held**
SIC: 8748 2396 Business consulting; automotive & apparel trimmings

(G-8756)
STILLWATER BREWING COMPANY LLC
519 S Husband St (74074-4031)
PHONE...................405 614-2520
Jerod Millirnos, *Manager*
Jerod Millirons, *Manager*
EMP: 6
SALES (est): 381.3K **Privately Held**
SIC: 2082 5181 Malt beverages; beer & ale

(G-8757)
STILLWATER MILLING COMPANY LLC (PA)
512 E 6th Ave (74074-3600)
P.O. Box 2407 (74076-2407)
PHONE...................405 372-2766
David F Fairbanks, *President*
Bob Wood, *COO*
Linda Griffin, *Sales Mgr*
David Smith, *Sales Mgr*
Sydnee Donaho, *Sales Executive*
EMP: 83 **EST:** 1891
SQ FT: 3,500
SALES: 100.7MM **Privately Held**
WEB: www.stillwatermill.com
SIC: 2048 5999 Livestock feeds; feed & farm supply

(G-8758)
STILLWATER SIGNS INCORPORATED
1225 N Perkins Rd (74075-7136)
PHONE...................405 533-2828
EMP: 5
SALES: 250K **Privately Held**
SIC: 3993 Mfg Signs/Advertising Specialties

(G-8759)
STILLWATER TRANSFER & STOR CO
Also Called: North American Van Lines
2005 E 6th Ave (74074-3932)
P.O. Box 1477 (74076-1477)
PHONE...................405 372-0577
Linford R Pitts, *President*
Sally Smith, *Office Mgr*
Cy Buiastra, *Manager*
EMP: 15
SQ FT: 15,000
SALES (est): 1.5MM **Privately Held**
WEB: www.stillwatertransfer.com
SIC: 2511 Storage chests, household: wood

(G-8760)
STRENGTH TECH INC
1512 N Hightower St (74075-8505)
P.O. Box 1381 (74076-1381)
PHONE...................405 377-7100
Gary R Polson, *President*
Gary Polson, *Founder*
Lora Dawn Polson, *Vice Pres*
Colleen M Polson, *Treasurer*

EMP: 2
SALES (est): 231.7K Privately Held
SIC: 3949 Exercise equipment

(G-8761)
STRICTLY HARDWOODS
6711 Lilly Ln (74074-6371)
PHONE.................................405 269-1026
Mark R Adams, Owner
EMP: 1
SALES (est): 72.6K Privately Held
SIC: 2426 Flooring, hardwood

(G-8762)
SURGIOTONICS LLC
1105 S Stoneybrook St (74074-1226)
PHONE.................................405 269-9767
EMP: 2 EST: 2017
SALES (est): 92.6K Privately Held
SIC: 3845 Endoscopic equipment, electromedical

(G-8763)
TAG PETROLEUM INC
6519 W Coventry Dr (74074-1024)
P.O. Box 1389 (74076-1389)
PHONE.................................405 377-6185
Johnny W Griffin, President
▲ EMP: 8
SALES (est): 904.8K Privately Held
SIC: 1311 Crude petroleum production

(G-8764)
TAG STILLWATER AGENCY
702 S Western Rd (74074-4125)
PHONE.................................405 624-0200
Kathleen McBee, Owner
EMP: 7
SALES (est): 240K Privately Held
SIC: 3469 Automobile license tags, stamped metal

(G-8765)
TAYLOR STORM SHELTERS LLC
624 N Shallow Brk (74075-8824)
PHONE.................................405 372-8130
Brenda Taylor, Mng Member
Michael Taylor,
EMP: 8
SALES: 380K Privately Held
SIC: 3442 1771 Storm doors or windows, metal; concrete work

(G-8766)
TERRITORY RESOURCES LLC (PA)
1511 S Sangre Rd (74074-1869)
PHONE.................................405 533-1300
Ed Gallegos, Mng Member
EMP: 8
SALES (est): 2.2MM Privately Held
SIC: 1382 Oil & gas exploration services

(G-8767)
THOMAS N BERRY & COMPANY
S On Hwy 177 (74076)
P.O. Box 1958 (74076-1958)
PHONE.................................405 372-5252
Malinda Berry Fischer, Chairman
Judith Kelly, Corp Secy
Hampton Virginia S, Vice Pres
EMP: 3 EST: 1937
SQ FT: 4,000
SALES (est): 350.2K Privately Held
SIC: 1311 Crude petroleum production; natural gas production

(G-8768)
THOMPSON WOODWORKS
1517 Hanson Cir (74075-8245)
PHONE.................................405 269-6480
Taylor Thompson, Owner
EMP: 2 EST: 2016
SALES (est): 93.8K Privately Held
SIC: 2431 Millwork

(G-8769)
TOKATA OIL RECOVERY INC
1414 S Sangre Rd (74074-1810)
PHONE.................................405 595-0072
Thomas Westbrook, CEO
Bruce Nurse, Vice Pres
EMP: 9
SALES (est): 390K Privately Held
SIC: 1389 3533 Oil field services; oil & gas field machinery

(G-8770)
TUNA SPOT TEES LLC
3116 W Shiloh Creek Ave (74074-1879)
PHONE.................................918 931-9589
Aaron C Reeves, Owner
EMP: 2
SALES (est): 79K Privately Held
SIC: 2759 Screen printing

(G-8771)
UNMANNED COWBOYS LLC
Also Called: Uc
1201 S Innovation Way (74074-1579)
PHONE.................................405 744-4156
Dyan Gibbens, CEO
Chowdhary Girish, Vice Pres
Jacob Jamey, Vice Pres
EMP: 4
SQ FT: 1,000
SALES (est): 258.7K Privately Held
SIC: 3721 Airplanes, fixed or rotary wing

(G-8772)
V M PUBLISHING CO
205 W 7th Ave Ste 201e (74074-4041)
PHONE.................................405 533-1883
Robert Smith, Owner
EMP: 1
SALES (est): 66.6K Privately Held
SIC: 2741 Miscellaneous publishing

(G-8773)
WAYLINK SYSTEMS CORPORATION
1414 S Sangre Rd (74074-1810)
PHONE.................................405 261-9896
Kelvin C Wang, President
EMP: 6
SALES (est): 16.9K Privately Held
SIC: 3861 Aerial cameras

(G-8774)
WAYLOLO LLC
3412 W 29th Ave (74074-6972)
PHONE.................................405 714-2353
Sabit Ekin, Principal
EMP: 1
SALES (est): 57.1K Privately Held
SIC: 3674 Semiconductors & related devices

(G-8775)
WOMBAT LABS LLC
1414 S Sangre Rd (74074-1810)
PHONE.................................405 355-9662
Duane Harding, President
EMP: 2 EST: 2009
SQ FT: 750
SALES: 180K Privately Held
WEB: www.wombatlabs.us
SIC: 3949 8742 8711 Sporting & athletic goods; hunting equipment; management engineering; mechanical engineering

(G-8776)
WOODLAND PARK VINEYARDS
3023 N Jardot Rd (74075-8635)
PHONE.................................405 743-2442
Ivol Hane, Owner
EMP: 2
SALES (est): 116.8K Privately Held
SIC: 2084 Wines

(G-8777)
XPLOSAFE LLC
712 Eastgate St (74074-6409)
PHONE.................................405 334-5720
EMP: 6
SQ FT: 6,200
SALES (est): 615.8K Privately Held
SIC: 3826 Analytical instruments

(G-8778)
ZIP ME UP PLEASE LLC
1602 S Hillside Ct (74074-2315)
PHONE.................................405 614-2778
Jody Harris, Mng Member
EMP: 1 EST: 2014
SALES (est): 69.3K Privately Held
SIC: 2844 Toilet preparations

Stilwell
Adair County

(G-8779)
ADAIR COUNTY COMMISIONERS OFF
220 W Division St Ste 102 (74960-3037)
PHONE.................................918 696-7633
Russel Turner, Chairman
EMP: 50
SALES (est): 4.6MM Privately Held
SIC: 3531 Road construction & maintenance machinery

(G-8780)
APAC-CENTRAL INC
Hwy 59 N (74960)
PHONE.................................918 696-2820
Jim Miller, General Mgr
EMP: 4
SALES (corp-wide): 30.6B Privately Held
WEB: www.contractorsofarkansas.com
SIC: 3273 Ready-mixed concrete
HQ: Apac-Central, Inc.
755 E Millsap Rd
Fayetteville AR 72703

(G-8781)
BACKWOODS TRAILERS LLC
84773 S 4771 Rd (74960-2892)
PHONE.................................864 237-5906
James Smith, Mng Member
EMP: 2
SQ FT: 100
SALES: 150K Privately Held
SIC: 3799 Trailers & trailer equipment

(G-8782)
C & B CONSTRUCTION
82280 S 4745 Rd (74960-2851)
PHONE.................................918 696-4476
David Ogden, Owner
Susan Croley, Office Mgr
EMP: 5
SALES: 500K Privately Held
SIC: 3585 Refrigeration & heating equipment

(G-8783)
CHEROKEE MEDICAL SERVICES LLC
470739 Highway 51 (74960-9194)
PHONE.................................918 696-3151
Gary Warnock,
Bryan Collins,
Dennis McLemore,
EMP: 233 EST: 1999
SQ FT: 1,000
SALES: 42.3K Privately Held
SIC: 3679 Harness assemblies for electronic use: wire or cable
HQ: Cherokee Nation Industries, L.L.C.
470739 Highway 51
Stilwell OK 74960
918 696-3151

(G-8784)
CHEROKEE NATION
Also Called: Tribal Complex Office
217 W Oak St (74960-3104)
P.O. Box 913 (74960-0913)
PHONE.................................918 696-3124
Chad Smith, Branch Mgr
EMP: 11 Privately Held
SIC: 3679 Harness assemblies for electronic use: wire or cable
PA: The Cherokee Nation
17675 S Muskogee Ave
Tahlequah OK 74464
918 453-5000

(G-8785)
CHEROKEE NATION AROSPC DEF LLC (PA)
470739 Highway 51 (74960-9194)
PHONE.................................918 696-3151
Bryan Collins,
EMP: 1
SALES: 3.8MM Privately Held
SIC: 3679 Electronic circuits

(G-8786)
CHEROKEE NATION INDUSTRIES LLC (DH)
470739 Highway 51 (74960-9194)
Rural Route 3 (74960)
PHONE.................................918 696-3151
Chris Moody, President
Jill Burns, Vice Pres
Nathan Moore, IT/INT Sup
Robert Lamar, Director
EMP: 34
SQ FT: 125,000
SALES: 6.6MM Privately Held
SIC: 3679 Harness assemblies for electronic use: wire or cable
HQ: Cherokee Nation Businesses Llc
777 W Cherokee St
Catoosa OK 74015
918 384-7474

(G-8787)
CONNER INDUSTRIES INC
Us Hwy 59 N (74960)
PHONE.................................918 696-5885
Grady Mays, Branch Mgr
EMP: 48
SQ FT: 22,500
SALES (corp-wide): 173.3MM Privately Held
SIC: 2421 2426 Resawing lumber into smaller dimensions; hardwood dimension & flooring mills
PA: Conner Industries, Inc.
3800 Sandshell Dr Ste 235
Fort Worth TX 76137
800 413-8006

(G-8788)
F G SAWMILL LLC
723 Hwy 51 (74960)
PHONE.................................918 905-1132
EMP: 2
SALES (est): 81.7K Privately Held
SIC: 2411 Logging camps & contractors

(G-8789)
FACET (OKLAHOMA) LLC
Also Called: Facet USA
470555 E 868 Rd (74960-9176)
PHONE.................................918 696-3161
Doyle Czapansky, Branch Mgr
EMP: 64
SQ FT: 56,000
SALES (corp-wide): 344.8MM Privately Held
SIC: 3714 3728 3564 Filters: oil, fuel & air, motor vehicle; aircraft parts & equipment; blowers & fans
HQ: Facet (Oklahoma) Llc
11607 E 43rd St N
Tulsa OK 74116
918 272-8700

(G-8790)
FACET (OKLAHOMA) LLC
470555 E 868 Rd (74960-9176)
PHONE.................................918 696-3161
Seth Soltow, Manager
EMP: 125
SALES (corp-wide): 344.8MM Privately Held
SIC: 3569 Filters, general line: industrial
HQ: Facet (Oklahoma) Llc
11607 E 43rd St N
Tulsa OK 74116
918 272-8700

(G-8791)
INDIAN NATIONS COMMUNICATIONS
Also Called: Democrat Journal
118 N 2nd St (74960-3028)
P.O. Box 508 (74960-0508)
PHONE.................................918 696-2228
Keith Neil, Principal
EMP: 7
SALES (est): 235.5K Privately Held
SIC: 2711 Newspapers, publishing & printing

Stilwell - Adair County (G-8792)

(G-8792)
LENORA ELIZABETH BROWN
Also Called: Lightninb Saddlery
475633 E 810 Rd (74960-2293)
P.O. Box 1280 (74960-1280)
PHONE..............................918 797-2034
Lenora Elizath Brown, *Owner*
Craig Brown, *Co-Owner*
EMP: 4
SALES (est): 124.3K **Privately Held**
SIC: **2399** 3111 3199 7389 Horse harnesses & riding crops, etc.: non leather; equestrian leather products; accessory products, leather; equestrian related leather articles; holsters, leather;

(G-8793)
NEWSPAPER HOLDING INC
Also Called: Stillwell Democrat Journal
118 N 2nd St (74960-3028)
PHONE..............................918 696-2228
EMP: 38 **Privately Held**
SIC: **2711** Newspapers: publishing only, not printed on site
HQ: Newspaper Holding, Inc.
425 Locust St
Johnstown PA 15901
814 532-5102

(G-8794)
NIX BODY SHOP LLC
413 W Blackjack St (74960-1653)
PHONE..............................918 797-2484
Nick Fredrick, *Principal*
EMP: 2 EST: 2008
SALES (est): 113K **Privately Held**
SIC: **7532** 3713 Paint shop, automotive; truck & bus bodies

(G-8795)
SFC GLOBAL SUPPLY CHAIN INC
Also Called: Mrs Smiths Bakery of Stillwell
5 E Walnut St (74960-4033)
P.O. Box 432 (74960-0432)
PHONE..............................918 696-8325
Danny Banks, *Branch Mgr*
Richard Lore, *Info Tech Dir*
EMP: 120 **Privately Held**
SIC: **2038** 2051 Frozen specialties; bread, cake & related products
HQ: Sfc Global Supply Chain, Inc.
115 W College Dr
Marshall MN 56258
507 532-3274

(G-8796)
TYSON FOODS INC
N Hwy 59 (74960)
PHONE..............................918 696-4530
Jimmy Shreve, *Manager*
EMP: 35
SALES (corp-wide): 42.4B **Publicly Held**
SIC: **2015** Poultry slaughtering & processing
PA: Tyson Foods, Inc.
2200 W Don Tyson Pkwy
Springdale AR 72762
479 290-4000

Stonewall
Pontotoc County

(G-8797)
B&G MEADERY LLC
36695 Old State Highway 3 (74871-7108)
PHONE..............................580 272-7197
Cassandra Gore, *Principal*
EMP: 2 EST: 2017
SALES (est): 168.9K **Privately Held**
SIC: **2084** Wines

(G-8798)
BYNUM & COMPANY INC
22040 County Road 1690 (74871-1854)
P.O. Box 397 (74871-0397)
PHONE..............................580 265-7747
Fax: 580 265-4373
EMP: 15
SQ FT: 8,400
SALES (est): 3.1MM **Privately Held**
SIC: **3533** 3599 3444 3443 Mfg Oil/Gas Field Mach Mfg Industrial Machinery Mfg Sheet Metalwork Mfg Fabricated Plate Wrk Structural Metal Fabrctn

(G-8799)
CITATION OIL & GAS CORP
22019 County Road 1650 (74871-1813)
PHONE..............................580 265-4534
John Gibson, *Manager*
EMP: 32
SALES (corp-wide): 283.5MM **Privately Held**
SIC: **1311** Crude petroleum production
PA: Citation Oil & Gas Corp.
14077 Cutten Rd
Houston TX 77069
281 891-1000

(G-8800)
ED F DAVIS INC
20987 County Road 1597 (74871)
P.O. Box 118 (74871-0118)
PHONE..............................580 265-4210
EMP: 3
SALES (est): 154K **Privately Held**
SIC: **2082** Mfg Malt Beverages

(G-8801)
J & J SERVICES INC
22527 County Road 3 Dr (74871-2029)
PHONE..............................580 265-9466
Jeff Curtis, *President*
Julie Curtis, *Vice Pres*
EMP: 2
SALES (est): 301K **Privately Held**
SIC: **1389** Oil field services

(G-8802)
PONTOTOC SANDS COMPANY LLC (PA)
18644 County Road 1720 (74871-6419)
PHONE..............................580 777-2735
Joshua Lehde,
Deejay Huckie,
EMP: 50
SALES (est): 4.9MM **Privately Held**
SIC: **1081** Metal mining services

Strang
Mayes County

(G-8803)
OUTWEST WELDING SERVICES LLC
6123 N 4435 (74367-3411)
PHONE..............................918 593-2345
Weston D West, *Principal*
EMP: 2
SALES (est): 43.7K **Privately Held**
SIC: **7692** Welding repair

Stratford
Garvin County

(G-8804)
DOUBLE D SAND AND GRAVEL LLC
106 N Spruce (74872)
P.O. Box 366 (74872-0366)
PHONE..............................405 207-8050
EMP: 3
SALES (est): 132.3K **Privately Held**
SIC: **1442** Construction sand & gravel

(G-8805)
KELLEY PUBLICATIONS LLC
Also Called: Stratford Times, The
321 Jan Dr (74872-4427)
PHONE..............................405 585-7210
Christopher W Kelley,
EMP: 2 EST: 2010
SALES (est): 121.7K **Privately Held**
WEB: www.mystratfordtimes.com
SIC: **2741** Miscellaneous publishing

(G-8806)
PERSONALI TEES LLC
48128 E County Road 1510 (74872-8270)
PHONE..............................580 759-2188
EMP: 2 EST: 2017
SALES (est): 122.2K **Privately Held**
SIC: **2759** Screen printing

(G-8807)
SAFE SHED
12482 Highway 177 (74872-1020)
PHONE..............................580 759-3456
Bradley Cottrell, *Principal*
EMP: 4
SALES (est): 406.4K **Privately Held**
SIC: **3448** Buildings, portable: prefabricated metal

Stroud
Lincoln County

(G-8808)
BOOMER BLINDS & SHUTTERS LLC
718 W Main St (74079-3620)
PHONE..............................918 968-2579
John Teters, *Mng Member*
Karen Teters,
EMP: 6
SALES (est): 558.7K **Privately Held**
SIC: **5719** 3442 Venetian blinds; shutters, door or window: metal

(G-8809)
CAMPBELL FBRCATION TOOLING INC
221 W Elm St (74079-5021)
PHONE..............................918 987-0047
Albert Campbell, *Principal*
Sherry Campbell, *Principal*
▼ EMP: 4
SQ FT: 30,000
SALES (est): 1MM **Privately Held**
SIC: **3537** Industrial trucks & tractors

(G-8810)
GORDON BROS SUPPLY INC
5498 Hwy 66 W (74079)
P.O. Box 355 (74079-0355)
PHONE..............................918 968-2591
Robert Gordon, *President*
Dixie Gordon, *Vice Pres*
EMP: 43
SQ FT: 5,000
SALES (est): 21.1MM **Privately Held**
SIC: **3533** Oil field machinery & equipment

(G-8811)
MELTON RH
401 W Main St (74079-3613)
PHONE..............................918 968-1606
R H Mielton, *Principal*
EMP: 2
SALES (est): 113.6K **Privately Held**
SIC: **3843** Enamels, dentists'

(G-8812)
MIDWAY MACHINE & WELDING LLC
Hwy 66 W (74079)
PHONE..............................918 968-3316
Larry Inman,
Cindy Inman,
EMP: 2
SALES (est): 126.7K **Privately Held**
SIC: **1799** 1389 7699 3599 Welding on site; oil field services; industrial machinery & equipment repair; machine shop, jobbing & repair; welding repair

(G-8813)
MILLER BROS WLDG & ROUSTABOUT
314 W Main St (74079-3612)
P.O. Box 386 (74079-0386)
PHONE..............................918 968-1611
Ron Miller, *CEO*
Anther Miller, *Corp Secy*
Grant Miller, *Vice Pres*
EMP: 7
SQ FT: 2,000
SALES (est): 660K **Privately Held**
SIC: **1389** Oil field services

(G-8814)
MINT TURBINES LLC
2915 N Highway 99 (74079-4756)
P.O. Box 460 (74079-0460)
PHONE..............................918 968-9561
Richard McConn, *CEO*
Robert Timm, *Top Exec*
Kenneth Arnold, *Production*
Mehdi Protzuk, *CFO*
Chris Vandenhende, *CFO*
▲ EMP: 45
SQ FT: 29,100
SALES (est): 20MM
SALES (corp-wide): 44MM **Privately Held**
SIC: **3724** Aircraft engines & engine parts
PA: M International, Inc.
1301 Dolley Madison Blvd
Mc Lean VA 22101
703 448-4400

(G-8815)
PALM OPERATING LLC
509 N 2nd Ave (74079-3406)
PHONE..............................918 968-0574
EMP: 2
SALES (est): 204.1K **Privately Held**
SIC: **1381** Drilling oil & gas wells

(G-8816)
ROD PUMPS INC
817 S 8th Ave (74079-5227)
P.O. Box 972 (74079-0972)
PHONE..............................918 968-4369
Rodney McKnight, *President*
Mary Macknight, *Treasurer*
EMP: 3
SALES (est): 310K **Privately Held**
SIC: **1389** Construction, repair & dismantling services

(G-8817)
RUSTY ROOSTER METAL
2023 Briarwood St (74079-9786)
PHONE..............................918 290-9113
EMP: 2
SALES (est): 150.4K **Privately Held**
SIC: **3993** Signs & advertising specialties

(G-8818)
SCISSORTAIL ENERGY LLC
222 S Allied Rd (74079-4256)
PHONE..............................918 968-0422
Lee Figner, *Branch Mgr*
EMP: 9 **Publicly Held**
SIC: **1311** Crude petroleum & natural gas
HQ: Scissortail Energy, Llc
8811 S Yale Ave Ste 200
Tulsa OK 74137
918 588-5000

(G-8819)
STABLERIDGE LLC
Also Called: Stableridge Vineyards
2016 Rte 66 W (74079)
PHONE..............................918 968-2568
Annetta Neal,
Don Neal,
EMP: 12
SALES (est): 780K **Privately Held**
SIC: **2084** Wines

(G-8820)
STROUD AMERICAN INC
315 W Main St (74079-3611)
P.O. Box 400 (74079-0400)
PHONE..............................918 968-2310
Mike Brown, *President*
EMP: 5 EST: 1898
SQ FT: 5,000
SALES (est): 349.3K **Privately Held**
WEB: www.cityofstroud.com
SIC: **2711** Newspapers: publishing only, not printed on site

(G-8821)
STROUD CORRIDOR LLC
518 W Main St (74079-3616)
P.O. Box 708 (74079-0708)
PHONE..............................405 823-7561
Judy Gooch, *Mng Member*
EMP: 2

GEOGRAPHIC SECTION

Tahlequah - Cherokee County (G-8850)

SALES (est): 174K **Privately Held**
SIC: **2759** 7389 Magazines: printing; design services

(G-8822)
TERRITORY CELLARS LLC
1521 N Highway 99 Apt 1 (74079-4761)
P.O. Box 897 (74079-0897)
PHONE.................................918 987-1800
Judy Walkingstick, *Principal*
EMP: 2
SALES (est): 94.1K **Privately Held**
SIC: **2084** Wines

(G-8823)
TIMCO BLASTING & COATINGS
820 E Highway 66 (74079-5304)
PHONE.................................918 605-1179
A Don Jolley, *CEO*
Tim Farley, *Manager*
EMP: 5
SALES (corp-wide): 6MM **Privately Held**
SIC: **1799** 7532 1446 1794 Paint & wallpaper stripping; truck painting & lettering; industrial sand; excavation work
PA: Timco Blasting & Coatings, Inc
200 N Main St
Bristow OK 74010
918 367-1700

(G-8824)
TIMCO BLASTING & COATINGS
301 S Allied Rd Track 103 (74079)
PHONE.................................918 608-1179
Tim Farley, *Branch Mgr*
EMP: 3
SALES (corp-wide): 6MM **Privately Held**
SIC: **1799** 7532 1446 1794 Paint & wallpaper stripping; truck painting & lettering; industrial sand; excavation work
PA: Timco Blasting & Coatings, Inc
200 N Main St
Bristow OK 74010
918 367-1700

Stuart
Hughes County

(G-8825)
J&K RSTBOUT WEED CTRL SVCS LLC
4071 S Pine Hollow Rd (74570-5101)
PHONE.................................918 429-2392
EMP: 3 EST: 2009
SALES (est): 122.7K **Privately Held**
SIC: **1389** Roustabout service

Sulphur
Murray County

(G-8826)
007 OPERATING LLC
1098 Sheppard Rd (73086)
P.O. Box 898, Davis (73030-0898)
PHONE.................................580 467-2744
April French,
EMP: 1
SALES (est): 107.9K **Privately Held**
SIC: **1389** 1794 1611 1623 Oil field services; excavation & grading, building construction; gravel or dirt road construction; oil & gas pipeline construction; pipe laying construction; pond construction

(G-8827)
A & S GRAPHIX
2770 Standifer Rd (73086-8820)
PHONE.................................918 640-1292
EMP: 2 EST: 2016
SALES (est): 76.8K **Privately Held**
SIC: **3993** Signs & advertising specialties

(G-8828)
AUTO TRIM DESIGN SIGNS SE OKLA
Also Called: Auto-Trim Design SE Oklahoma
1400 W 1st St (73086-2610)
PHONE.................................580 622-3830
Thomas Davila Jr, *Owner*
EMP: 4
SALES (est): 244.3K **Privately Held**
SIC: **7549** 7532 3993 5999 Sun roof installation, automotive; customizing services, non-factory basis; signs & advertising specialties; telephone equipment & systems; truck tires & tubes; glass tinting, architectural or automotive

(G-8829)
BILLY COOK HARN & SADDLE MFG
320 W Muskogee Ave (73086-4812)
P.O. Box 577 (73086-0577)
PHONE.................................580 622-5505
Billy Cook, *President*
Ruth Cook, *Vice Pres*
Mary Rico, *Shareholder*
◆ EMP: 64
SQ FT: 10,000
SALES (est): 6.9MM **Privately Held**
SIC: **3199** 5941 Saddles or parts; harness or harness parts; saddlery & equestrian equipment

(G-8830)
CRAZY SOCKS PRODUCTIONS INC
4374 Gddard Youth Camp Rd (73086-9279)
PHONE.................................580 618-1228
David Magee, *Director*
EMP: 5
SALES (est): 118.2K **Privately Held**
SIC: **2252** Socks

(G-8831)
DAWG POUND
1904 W Broadway Ave (73086-4233)
PHONE.................................580 622-2695
Cody Freeman, *Principal*
EMP: 2
SALES (est): 127.4K **Privately Held**
SIC: **3949** Bowling alleys & accessories

(G-8832)
FLOW VALVE LLC
2214 W 14th St (73086-1107)
P.O. Box 695 (73086-0695)
PHONE.................................580 622-2294
Mark Steerman, *Mng Member*
EMP: 23
SALES (est): 5.4MM **Privately Held**
SIC: **3491** 3317 Industrial valves; steel pipe & tubes

(G-8833)
GONZALES MFG & MCH INC
2410 W Broadway Ave (73086-6500)
PHONE.................................580 622-2025
Justin Gonzales, *Officer*
Rachel Gonzales, *Officer*
EMP: 4
SALES (est): 139.1K **Privately Held**
SIC: **3599** Machine & other job shop work

(G-8834)
H2S SAFETY PLUS INC
1133 Fletcher Rd (73086-9257)
PHONE.................................580 622-4796
Carolynn Johnson, *CEO*
James B Johnson, *President*
Jeremiah B Johnson, *Vice Pres*
EMP: 50
SQ FT: 3,000
SALES (est): 2.1MM **Privately Held**
SIC: **1389** Roustabout service

(G-8835)
JACK EXPLORATION INC (PA)
812 W 11th St (73086-4404)
P.O. Box 1279 (73086-8279)
PHONE.................................580 622-2310
Clayton Jack, *Owner*
James Jack, *Data Proc Dir*
EMP: 2
SQ FT: 3,000
SALES (est): 700.9K **Privately Held**
SIC: **1382** Oil & gas exploration services

(G-8836)
KEMPER VALVE AND FITTINGS
2733 Industrial Dr (73086-1124)
PHONE.................................580 622-2048
Joe Kemper, *President*
Sharon Kemper, *Corp Secy*
Karen Wood, *Corp Secy*
EMP: 8
SQ FT: 5,000
SALES (est): 804.3K
SALES (corp-wide): 53.8B **Publicly Held**
SIC: **1389** 5082 3451 Construction, repair & dismantling services; oil field equipment; screw machine products
HQ: Kemper Valve & Fittings Corp.
3001 Darrell Rd
Island Lake IL 60042
847 526-2166

(G-8837)
KERR MACHINE CO
Also Called: Kerr Pump
2214 W 14th St (73086-1107)
P.O. Box 735 (73086-0735)
PHONE.................................580 622-4207
Eddie L Nowell, *President*
Dianne Nowell, *Corp Secy*
Mark Nowell, *Vice Pres*
Guy Lapointe, *Plant Mgr*
Tyler Bradley, *Project Mgr*
▲ EMP: 30
SQ FT: 40,000
SALES (est): 16MM **Privately Held**
WEB: www.kerrpumps.com
SIC: **3533** Oil & gas field machinery

(G-8838)
MIKE LATHAM
Also Called: Collector Knives
2175 Leveridge Rd (73086-9047)
PHONE.................................580 622-6980
Mike Latham, *Owner*
EMP: 2
SALES: 54K **Privately Held**
SIC: **3421** Knife blades & blanks

(G-8839)
NYES CABINET SHOP
4990 N Us Highway 177 (73086)
PHONE.................................580 622-6323
Carol Nye, *Principal*
EMP: 2
SALES (est): 100K **Privately Held**
SIC: **2434** Wood kitchen cabinets

(G-8840)
OKIE PLUMBING AND BACKHOE
1501 W Broadway Ave (73086-4217)
PHONE.................................580 302-5018
EMP: 1
SALES (est): 74.5K **Privately Held**
WEB: www.okieplumbingandbackhoe.com
SIC: **3531** Backhoes

(G-8841)
REDLINE INSTRUMENTS INC (PA)
1091 Fletcher Rd (73086-7718)
PHONE.................................580 622-4745
James B Johnson, *President*
Gary Keating, *President*
Jeremiah Johnson, *Vice Pres*
EMP: 12
SALES (est): 1.6MM **Privately Held**
SIC: **3829** 5065 7389 Gauges, motor vehicle: oil pressure, water temperature; communication equipment;

(G-8842)
RUSTY NAIL WINERY
218 W Muskogee Ave (73086-4817)
PHONE.................................580 622-8466
Debbie Alexander, *Principal*
Melissa Lee, *Marketing Mgr*
EMP: 4 EST: 2010
SALES (est): 284.1K **Privately Held**
WEB: www.rustynailwinery.com
SIC: **2084** Wines

(G-8843)
SAFETY PLUS USA LLC
1091 Fletcher Rd (73086-7718)
PHONE.................................580 622-4796
Amanda Clayburn, *Office Mgr*
EMP: 30
SALES (est): 1.3MM **Privately Held**
SIC: **1389** Oil field services

(G-8844)
TIMES-DEMOCRAT COMPANY INC
Also Called: Sulphur Times Democrat
115 W Muskogee Ave (73086-4809)
P.O. Box 131 (73086-0131)
PHONE.................................580 622-2102
James C John, *President*
Kathy John, *Corp Secy*
Lorine John, *Vice Pres*
EMP: 7 EST: 1929
SQ FT: 3,000
SALES (est): 544.1K **Privately Held**
WEB: www.sulphurtimes.com
SIC: **2711** Newspapers, publishing & printing

(G-8845)
TRIPLE H INDUSTRIES LLC
4685 Highway 177 N (73086-9129)
PHONE.................................405 201-8820
Cody Hallmark, *Manager*
EMP: 3
SALES (est): 178.6K **Privately Held**
SIC: **3999** Manufacturing industries

(G-8846)
W R MEAT CO
2354 Highway 7 E (73086-9190)
PHONE.................................580 622-2494
Jean Williams, *Owner*
EMP: 4
SQ FT: 1,200
SALES (est): 330.5K **Privately Held**
SIC: **2011** Meat packing plants

Sweetwater
Roger Mills County

(G-8847)
ELK CITY WIND LLC
17265 E 1070 Rd (73666-6529)
PHONE.................................580 772-2080
EMP: 3
SALES (est): 325.7K **Privately Held**
SIC: **3629** Electrochemical generators (fuel cells)

Tahlequah
Cherokee County

(G-8848)
262 LLC
Also Called: Tahlequah Printing
618 E Downing St (74464-3212)
P.O. Box 2007 (74465-2007)
PHONE.................................918 458-5511
Angela Rhea, *President*
EMP: 11 EST: 1958
SQ FT: 4,600
SALES (est): 140K **Privately Held**
WEB: www.tpok.com
SIC: **2752** 2759 5943 2761 Commercial printing, offset; promotional printing, lithographic; letterpress printing; office forms & supplies; continuous forms, office & business; photocopying & duplicating services; direct mail advertising services

(G-8849)
A&K MANUFACTURING SERVICES LLC
24688 Ok 51 (74464)
PHONE.................................918 986-1637
Kelsi McCraoi, *Mng Member*
Aaron McCraoi,
EMP: 2
SALES (est): 173.3K **Privately Held**
SIC: **1799** 3548 5084 Welding on site; welding & cutting apparatus & accessories; electrodes, electric welding; arc welding generators, alternating current & direct current; welding machinery & equipment

(G-8850)
ARKHOLA SAND & GRAVEL CO
14199 W 834 Rd (74464-1514)
P.O. Box 1401 (74465-1401)
PHONE.................................918 456-2683

Tahlequah - Cherokee County (G-8851)

Darwin Tackett, *Principal*
EMP: 3
SALES (est): 152.1K **Privately Held**
SIC: 1442 Construction sand & gravel

(G-8851)
BACKWOODS FOOD MFG INC
Also Called: Backwoods Foods
591 Main Pkwy (74464-2430)
PHONE 918 458-9300
Danielle Coursey, *President*
EMP: 12
SALES (est): 2.2MM **Privately Held**
SIC: 2035 Pickles, sauces & salad dressings

(G-8852)
BECKYS EMBROIDERY DESIGN
16254 E Red Fuller Rd (74464-0224)
PHONE 918 456-1235
Becky Lamons, *Owner*
EMP: 1
SALES (est): 95.1K **Privately Held**
SIC: 3552 Embroidery machines

(G-8853)
BEDSIDE GUNLOCK PRODUCTS
8195 Highway 82a (74464-8627)
PHONE 713 443-8172
Fermin Trevino III, *Principal*
EMP: 2
SALES: 11K **Privately Held**
SIC: 3949 Cases, gun & rod (sporting equipment)

(G-8854)
CANYON CRAFT
119 N Muskogee Ave (74464-3621)
PHONE 918 456-3552
James Mahaney, *President*
EMP: 3 **EST:** 1999
SALES (est): 144K **Privately Held**
SIC: 3732 Motorized boat, building & repairing

(G-8855)
CAPES CUSTOM WELDING & FABRICA
1005 E Lowe Dr (74464-2139)
PHONE 918 453-0594
Andrea Capes, *Principal*
EMP: 2
SALES (est): 151.5K **Privately Held**
SIC: 1799 3444 7692 Welding on site; sheet metalwork; welding repair

(G-8856)
CHEROKEE PIPING SERVICES LLC
24688 Highway 51 (74464-1966)
PHONE 918 931-8593
Melvin D Thomas,
EMP: 8
SALES: 2.5MM **Privately Held**
SIC: 3317 3449 Welded pipe & tubes; bars, concrete reinforcing: fabricated steel

(G-8857)
CITY ELECTRIC SUPPLY COMPANY
1598 S Park Hill Rd (74464-5676)
PHONE 918 871-2640
EMP: 3
SALES (corp-wide): 1.3B **Privately Held**
WEB: www.cityelectricsupply.com
SIC: 5063 4911 3699 1731 Electrical apparatus & equipment; electric services; electrical equipment & supplies; electrical work
PA: City Electric Supply Company
400 S Record St Ste 1250
Dallas TX 75202
214 865-6801

(G-8858)
CITY OF TAHLEQUAH
Also Called: Tahlequah Solid Waste Services
1851 N Douglas Ave (74464-5194)
PHONE 918 456-8332
Mitchell Dodd, *Director*
EMP: 25 **Privately Held**
SIC: 2842 Sanitation preparations

PA: City Of Tahlequah
111 S Cherokee Ave
Tahlequah OK 74464
918 456-0651

(G-8859)
COUNTY OF OKLAHOMA
Also Called: State of Oklahoma
5102 S Muskogee Ave (74464-5473)
PHONE 918 456-3622
Jeff Perry, *Manager*
EMP: 9 **Privately Held**
SIC: 9111 3711 City & town managers' offices; fire department vehicles (motor vehicles), assembly of
PA: County Of Oklahoma
320 Robert S Kerr Ave # 505
Oklahoma City OK 73102
405 713-1540

(G-8860)
CRAWFORD CABINETRY & CNSTR INC
17877 W Murrel Rd (74464-8036)
PHONE 918 453-0164
Chuck Crawford, *Owner*
EMP: 3
SALES (est): 272.8K **Privately Held**
WEB: www.crawfordcabinetry.com
SIC: 2434 Wood kitchen cabinets

(G-8861)
CURRENT ALTERNATIVE NEWS ADVG
328 E Downing St (74464-3014)
PHONE 918 431-0392
EMP: 5
SALES (est): 298.9K **Privately Held**
SIC: 2789 Bookbinding/Related Work

(G-8862)
DAVID BATES
Also Called: Viper Products
721 E Ward St (74464-3129)
PHONE 918 457-6169
David Bates, *Owner*
EMP: 2 **EST:** 2017
SALES (est): 88.3K **Privately Held**
SIC: 3699 Security control equipment & systems

(G-8863)
ELDON VALLEY CHOPPERS
25976 Highway 62 (74464-1928)
PHONE 918 931-2925
EMP: 1
SALES (est): 56.5K **Privately Held**
SIC: 3751 Motorcycles & related parts

(G-8864)
FARMERS CO OP (PA)
1501 S Parkhill Rd (74464)
P.O. Box 1157 (74465-1157)
PHONE 918 456-0557
Morgan Whittmore, *President*
Tommie L Heaton, *Admin Sec*
Tommie Heaton, *Admin Sec*
EMP: 12 **EST:** 1951
SQ FT: 10,000
SALES (est): 1.3MM **Privately Held**
WEB: www.farmerscoop.biz
SIC: 5999 5261 2048 2047 Feed & farm supply; fertilizer; prepared feeds; dog & cat food

(G-8865)
FITZGERALD &SONS STEEL LLC
13435 Highway 62 (74464-1407)
PHONE 918 453-3369
Michael Fitzgerald, *Mng Member*
EMP: 12
SQ FT: 1,800
SALES: 2.5MM **Privately Held**
WEB: www.fitzgeraldandsonssteelllc.com
SIC: 3441 Building components, structural steel

(G-8866)
HAWKEYE SIGNS & PRINTING
3865 Suthridge Cir Apt 12 (74464)
PHONE 918 864-2035
Teresa Young, *Owner*
Kevin Rogers, *Director*
EMP: 2

SALES (est): 83.9K **Privately Held**
SIC: 2752 Commercial printing, lithographic

(G-8867)
HAYS PUBLISHING
21922 Sequoyah Club Dr (74464-0644)
P.O. Box 777, Park Hill (74451-0777)
PHONE 918 456-7717
Louis Hays, *Owner*
EMP: 1 **EST:** 1991
SALES (est): 35.2K **Privately Held**
SIC: 2731 Book publishing

(G-8868)
JIM DUNN
119 N Muskogee Ave (74464-3621)
PHONE 918 456-3552
James G Mahaney Od, *Principal*
EMP: 2
SALES (est): 107.7K **Privately Held**
SIC: 3699 Laser systems & equipment

(G-8869)
JUSTUS FABRICATION
1841 W Choctaw St (74464-3483)
PHONE 918 207-5192
Kevin Justus, *Principal*
EMP: 2 **EST:** 2018
SALES (est): 105.7K **Privately Held**
SIC: 3499 Fabricated metal products

(G-8870)
KELLEY REPAIR LLC
1111 E Allen Rd (74464-2119)
PHONE 918 456-6514
Tim Kelley, *Partner*
Gerald Kelley, *Partner*
EMP: 4
SALES (est): 230K **Privately Held**
SIC: 3714 7699 Motor vehicle engines & parts; professional instrument repair services

(G-8871)
LACY LOCKWOOD
15198 W 850 Rd (74464-1331)
PHONE 918 456-6837
Lacy Lockwood, *Owner*
EMP: 4
SALES (est): 200K **Privately Held**
SIC: 3523 Planting, haying, harvesting & processing machinery

(G-8872)
LISA SNELL
Also Called: Native American Times
14113 Ranch Acres Dr (74464-0383)
P.O. Box 411 (74465-0411)
PHONE 918 708-5838
Lisa Snell, *Owner*
EMP: 1
SALES (est): 126K **Privately Held**
SIC: 2711 7389 Newspapers, publishing & printing;

(G-8873)
METALFAB LLC
14553 Highway 62 (74464-1538)
PHONE 918 718-4040
Luis Uribe, *Principal*
EMP: 2
SALES (est): 122K **Privately Held**
SIC: 3441 Fabricated structural metal

(G-8874)
MIDWEST WELDERS
5971 N 510 Rd (74464-8750)
PHONE 918 456-5981
Gerald W Hammond, *Owner*
EMP: 2
SALES (est): 72.9K **Privately Held**
SIC: 7692 Welding repair

(G-8875)
MORGANS BAKERY
131 N Muskogee Ave (74464-3621)
PHONE 918 456-3731
Linda Shoun, *Owner*
EMP: 8 **EST:** 1944
SQ FT: 1,700
SALES (est): 493.8K **Privately Held**
SIC: 2051 5461 Bread, all types (white, wheat, rye, etc): fresh or frozen; bakeries

(G-8876)
NEWSPAPER HOLDING INC
Also Called: Tahlequah Daily Press
106 W 2nd St (74464-4724)
P.O. Box 888 (74465-0888)
PHONE 918 456-8833
Donna Barrett, *CEO*
Barbara Fritts, *Business Mgr*
Kevin Blevins, *Exec VP*
Pam Hudson, *Sales Staff*
Denise Butler, *Mktg Dir*
EMP: 35
SQ FT: 2,100 **Privately Held**
WEB: www.tribdem.com
SIC: 2711 2752 Newspapers: publishing only, not printed on site; commercial printing, lithographic
HQ: Newspaper Holding, Inc.
425 Locust St
Johnstown PA 15901
814 532-5102

(G-8877)
OAKLEY DEFENSE LLC
508 Talley St (74464-6336)
PHONE 918 457-8089
Thomas O Salmon, *Owner*
EMP: 3
SALES (est): 153.8K **Privately Held**
SIC: 3812 Defense systems & equipment

(G-8878)
OZMO DESIGN AND PRINT LLC
919 Mike Ave (74464-7035)
PHONE 417 655-5615
Frankie Cope, *Principal*
EMP: 2
SALES (est): 83.9K **Privately Held**
SIC: 2752 Commercial printing, lithographic

(G-8879)
QMI INC
1195 E Allen Rd (74464-2119)
PHONE 918 456-6777
Kenny Stilwell, *Owner*
EMP: 2
SALES (est): 157.5K **Privately Held**
SIC: 3599 Machine shop, jobbing & repair

(G-8880)
RHODES PRINTING INC
1106 S Muskogee Ave (74464-3660)
PHONE 918 457-7801
EMP: 2 **EST:** 2016
SALES (est): 81.2K **Privately Held**
SIC: 2759 Screen printing

(G-8881)
ROBBINS SALVAGE & AUTO SALES
23591 Highway 51 (74464-2019)
PHONE 918 431-1000
Monty Robbins, *Owner*
EMP: 1
SALES (est): 81K **Privately Held**
SIC: 3713 Automobile wrecker truck bodies

(G-8882)
SAND TECH SCREENING AND EMB
120 N Water Ave (74464-2824)
PHONE 918 458-0312
Sandy Fisher, *Partner*
Brandi Donatelli, *Partner*
EMP: 2
SQ FT: 3,000
SALES (est): 258.8K **Privately Held**
SIC: 2759 2395 2396 Screen printing; embroidery & art needlework; automotive & apparel trimmings

(G-8883)
SANDSTAR CUSTOM CABINETS LLC
419 E Fuller St (74464-4107)
PHONE 918 456-2964
Thomas Retherford, *Principal*
EMP: 2 **EST:** 2016
SALES (est): 111.5K **Privately Held**
SIC: 2434 Wood kitchen cabinets

GEOGRAPHIC SECTION
Tecumseh - Pottawatomie County (G-8913)

(G-8884)
SMITH SEPTIC TANK INC
18050 S Muskogee Ave (74464-8085)
PHONE................918 456-8741
Rick Prewitt, *President*
Janet Prewitt, *Treasurer*
EMP: 9
SQ FT: 2,600
SALES (est): 1.5MM **Privately Held**
SIC: 3272 Septic tanks, concrete

(G-8885)
SYNERGY PETROLEUM LLC
104 S Muskogee Ave (74464-3834)
PHONE................918 456-9991
Clayton Alan Chapman, *Owner*
EMP: 2
SALES (est): 150.6K **Privately Held**
SIC: 1389 Construction, repair & dismantling services

(G-8886)
TAHLEQUAH PUBLIC WORKS AUTH
Also Called: Publics Water Company
1410 E Powell Rd (74464-5685)
PHONE................918 456-9251
Stanley Day, *General Mgr*
EMP: 10 **Privately Held**
SIC: 2899 Water treating compounds
PA: Tahlequah Public Works Authority
710 W Choctaw St
Tahlequah OK 74464

(G-8887)
TAMMY BROWN
Also Called: O Klahoma Sign Co
17954 S Muskogee Ave (74464-5494)
PHONE................918 456-1959
Tammy Brown, *Owner*
Michael Brown, *Co-Owner*
EMP: 7
SALES: 500K **Privately Held**
SIC: 3993 Signs & advertising specialties

(G-8888)
TIMS SHEDS
14490 U S 62 (74464)
PHONE................918 506-7741
Roger Henriquez, *Owner*
EMP: 1
SALES (est): 54.3K **Privately Held**
SIC: 3496 3448 Cages, wire; prefabricated metal buildings

(G-8889)
TRICKED OUT PONY
17587 N Baker Rd (74464-1170)
PHONE................918 931-2646
Lori Carlile, *Principal*
EMP: 2
SALES (est): 131.1K **Privately Held**
SIC: 3111 Accessory products, leather

(G-8890)
TWIN CITIES READY MIX INC
4612 S Muskogee Ave (74464)
P.O. Box 300 (74465-0300)
PHONE................918 458-0323
Rusty Bennett, *Manager*
EMP: 8
SALES (corp-wide): 15.7MM **Privately Held**
SIC: 3273 Ready-mixed concrete
PA: Twin Cities Ready Mix, Inc.
102 W Ashland Ave
Mcalester OK 74501
918 423-8855

(G-8891)
WADES CABINET DOOR SHOP
18403 E 626 Rd (74464-8761)
PHONE................918 868-2516
Don Wade, *Owner*
EMP: 2
SALES: 40K **Privately Held**
SIC: 2431 2434 5712 5031 Doors & door parts & trim, wood; wood kitchen cabinets; cabinet work, custom; kitchen cabinets

(G-8892)
WEEKLY LEADER
1596 S Muskogee Ave (74464-5284)
P.O. Box 825 (74465-0825)
PHONE................918 458-8001
Mike Malone, *Principal*
EMP: 4
SALES (est): 210.6K **Privately Held**
SIC: 2711 Newspapers: publishing only, not printed on site

(G-8893)
YOUNG CONSTRUCTION SUPPLY LLC
1506 W Choctaw St (74464-3467)
PHONE................918 456-3250
Jay Young,
Aaron Young,
EMP: 4
SQ FT: 5,000
SALES (est): 350K **Privately Held**
SIC: 2431 5211 2521 2511 Millwork; millwork & lumber; lumber products; wood office furniture; wood household furniture; wood kitchen cabinets

(G-8894)
ZON INC
Also Called: Zon Graphics
618 E Downing St (74464-3212)
PHONE................918 458-5511
Dirk Van Veen, *President*
EMP: 12
SALES (est): 731.6K **Privately Held**
SIC: 7299 7334 2759 Tanning salon; photocopying & duplicating services; commercial printing

Talala
Rogers County

(G-8895)
AIROFAB LTD CO
7801 S 4060 Rd (74080-3048)
PHONE................918 693-1230
Darrell Wilson,
EMP: 4
SALES: 50K **Privately Held**
SIC: 3728 Aircraft parts & equipment

(G-8896)
BOBS BACKHOE SEVICE
11531 S 4050 Rd (74080-3447)
PHONE................918 391-0901
Bobby Joe Sligar, *Principal*
EMP: 2
SALES (est): 141.6K **Privately Held**
SIC: 3531 Backhoes

(G-8897)
BUTCHER WELL SERVICE
5021 E 320 Rd (74080-3548)
PHONE................918 275-4439
Coeta Butcher, *Owner*
EMP: 5
SALES (est): 413.5K **Privately Held**
SIC: 1389 Cementing oil & gas well casings

(G-8898)
CALICHE RESOURCES INC
9700 E 340 Rd (74080-9684)
PHONE................918 492-5170
Alan W Meeks, *Principal*
EMP: 1 **EST:** 1997
SALES (est): 216.1K **Privately Held**
SIC: 1382 Geological exploration, oil & gas field

(G-8899)
COE PRODUCTION
6552 E 310 Rd (74080-3065)
P.O. Box 264 (74080-0264)
PHONE................918 275-4529
Cletis Coe, *Owner*
Diana Coe,
EMP: 15
SALES (est): 1.1MM **Privately Held**
SIC: 1389 Servicing oil & gas wells

(G-8900)
MID AMERICA FARM & RANCH
308 S Elm St (74080-9688)
PHONE................918 275-4984
Allen Long, *President*
EMP: 6
SALES (est): 491.3K
SALES (corp-wide): 40MM **Privately Held**
SIC: 2048 5154 Livestock feeds; livestock
PA: Mid-America Feeds, Inc.
101 E Sequoyah St
Talala OK 74080
918 275-4292

(G-8901)
MISS PRISS MONOGRAMS & EMB
4888 E 360 Rd (74080-3125)
PHONE................918 697-9468
Jill Hoisington, *Principal*
EMP: 1 **EST:** 2013
SALES (est): 42.6K **Privately Held**
SIC: 2395 Embroidery & art needlework

(G-8902)
PRIMARILY PUZZLES
7915 S Country Ln (74080-3090)
PHONE................918 275-8270
Christine Newton, *Principal*
EMP: 2
SALES (est): 86.8K **Privately Held**
SIC: 3944 Puzzles

(G-8903)
TEXOMA TRACTOR LLC
10780 S 4050 Rd (74080-3586)
P.O. Box 1054, Oologah (74053-1054)
PHONE................918 640-7949
Matt Penner,
EMP: 2 **EST:** 2011
SALES (est): 209.3K **Privately Held**
WEB: www.texomatractor.com
SIC: 0721 0711 1389 0782 Planting services; soil preparation services; construction, repair & dismantling services; highway lawn & garden maintenance services; bermuda sprigging services; seeding services, lawn; mowing services, lawn; sandblasting of building exteriors; herbicides

(G-8904)
TITAN OVERHEAD DOOR LLC
5175 S 4110 Rd (74080-9479)
PHONE................918 606-0094
EMP: 2
SALES (est): 88.9K **Privately Held**
SIC: 3442 Metal doors, sash & trim

Talihina
Latimer County

(G-8905)
CHEROKEE HART RANCH
164342 Indian Hwy (74571-1206)
PHONE................918 563-4244
EMP: 2
SALES (est): 91K **Privately Held**
SIC: 3523 Cattle Ranch

(G-8906)
COLLINS CNSTR FABRICATIONS LLC
13191 Se 1060th Ave (74571-5826)
PHONE................918 522-4855
Delbert Collins,
EMP: 2
SALES (est): 276.7K **Privately Held**
SIC: 1442 Construction sand & gravel

Taloga
Dewey County

(G-8907)
ONE MOORE EMBROIDERY PLACE
66205 N 2170 Rd (73667-1027)
PHONE................580 328-5755
Denise Moore, *Principal*
EMP: 1
SALES (est): 57K **Privately Held**
WEB: www.onemooreembroidery.com
SIC: 2395 Embroidery & art needlework

(G-8908)
TALOGA TIMES ADVOCATE
Broadway (73667)
P.O. Box 191 (73667-0191)
PHONE................580 328-5619
Dutch Miller, *Principal*
EMP: 1
SALES (est): 111.8K **Privately Held**
SIC: 2711 Newspapers, publishing & printing

Tecumseh
Pottawatomie County

(G-8909)
COMPLETE SIGN SERVICE LLC
133 Betty Dr (74873-9588)
PHONE................405 273-7567
Mike Grain, *Owner*
Sheila Green, *Principal*
EMP: 1
SALES (est): 130.8K **Privately Held**
SIC: 3993 Signs & advertising specialties

(G-8910)
COUNTYWIDE NEWS INC
Also Called: Tecumseh County Wide News
108 E Washington St (74873-3242)
P.O. Box 38 (74873-0038)
PHONE................405 598-3793
Wayne Trotter, *President*
Gloria Trotter, *Vice Pres*
Aaron McDonald, *Accounts Exec*
EMP: 16
SQ FT: 2,000
SALES (est): 760K **Privately Held**
SIC: 2711 2796 2791 2741 Newspapers: publishing only, not printed on site; platemaking services; typesetting; miscellaneous publishing

(G-8911)
DAYLIGHT DONUTS
421 E Walnut St (74873-2239)
PHONE................405 598-8707
Terry Busley, *Owner*
Bridget Tooman, *Partner*
EMP: 6
SALES (est): 216K **Privately Held**
SIC: 5461 2051 Doughnuts; doughnuts, except frozen

(G-8912)
DICKSON INDUSTRIES INC
Rr 1 Box 234 (74873-9801)
P.O. Box 684 (74873-0684)
PHONE................405 598-6547
Wayne Dickson, *President*
Terri Dickson, *Corp Secy*
Chris Dickson, *Vice Pres*
Nathan Dickson, *Vice Pres*
EMP: 40
SQ FT: 60,000
SALES (est): 8.7MM **Privately Held**
WEB: www.roadproonline.com
SIC: 3589 3715 3531 3541 Sandblasting equipment; truck trailers; road construction & maintenance machinery; saws & sawing machines; industrial trucks & tractors

(G-8913)
EDDIES SUBMERSIBLE SERVICE INC
1019 N Broadway St (74873-1422)
PHONE................405 273-9292
Bryan Newell, *Branch Mgr*
EMP: 15
SALES (corp-wide): 12.4MM **Privately Held**
SIC: 3561 1389 Pumps & pumping equipment; oil field services
PA: Eddie"s Submersible Service, Inc.
35431 Hardesty Rd
Shawnee OK

Tecumseh - Pottawatomie County (G-8914)

(G-8914)
FARLEY REDFIELD
Also Called: Redfield Refrigeration
20874 Rock Creek Rd (74873-7108)
PHONE.................................405 275-2266
Farley Redfield, *Owner*
EMP: 3 **EST:** 1973
SALES: 157K **Privately Held**
SIC: 1711 2721 Refrigeration contractor; warm air heating & air conditioning contractor; television schedules: publishing only, not printed on site

(G-8915)
G HIGHFILL
Also Called: Highfill Welding & Fabrication
36492 Rattlesnake Hill Rd (74873-7488)
PHONE.................................405 598-5576
G M Highfill, *Owner*
EMP: 1
SALES (est): 98.4K **Privately Held**
SIC: 3441 1799 Fabricated structural metal; welding on site

(G-8916)
GATOR RIGS LLC
26541 Old Highway 18 (74873-7392)
P.O. Box 267 (74873-0267)
PHONE.................................405 598-3266
Jr Amos, *CEO*
Lori Amos, *CFO*
◆ **EMP:** 2 **EST:** 2008
SQ FT: 11,326
SALES (est): 327.8K **Privately Held**
WEB: www.gatorrigs.com
SIC: 3533 Oil & gas drilling rigs & equipment

(G-8917)
HIGGINS & SONS TRUSS COMPANY
20923 Rock Creek Rd (74873-7179)
PHONE.................................405 997-5455
Maxine Higgins, *Partner*
EMP: 34
SALES (corp-wide): 5.7MM **Privately Held**
WEB: www.higginsandsons.com
SIC: 2439 Trusses, wooden roof
PA: Higgins & Sons Truss Company Inc
E On Hwy 9
Tecumseh OK 74873
405 997-5455

(G-8918)
HIGGINS & SONS TRUSS COMPANY (PA)
Also Called: Higgins & Sons Roof, Truss
E On Hwy 9 (74873)
PHONE.................................405 997-5455
Willie E Higgins, *President*
Maxine Higgins, *Corp Secy*
Mike Higgins, *Vice Pres*
Wesley Higgins, *Vice Pres*
EMP: 16
SQ FT: 3,000
SALES (est): 5.7MM **Privately Held**
SIC: 5211 2439 Lumber & other building materials; trusses, wooden roof

(G-8919)
HUDSON BROS RMANUFACTURED ENGS
38434 Highway 9 (74873-5135)
PHONE.................................405 598-2260
Hershel Hudson, *Partner*
Rick Hudson, *Partner*
EMP: 2
SQ FT: 2,500
SALES (est): 168.8K **Privately Held**
SIC: 3519 5531 3714 Gas engine rebuilding; automotive & home supply stores; motor vehicle parts & accessories

(G-8920)
JG WELDING LLC
505 Mark St (74873-1803)
PHONE.................................405 301-3126
John Goodall, *Principal*
EMP: 1
SALES (est): 34.8K **Privately Held**
SIC: 7692 Welding repair

(G-8921)
JOHN A LITTLEAXE
29223 Sunshine Dr (74873-6615)
PHONE.................................405 365-5117
John A Littleaxe, *Principal*
EMP: 2 **EST:** 2011
SALES (est): 165.9K **Privately Held**
SIC: 3531 Log splitters

(G-8922)
LONGREACH STEEL INC
38174 Hwy 9 (74873)
P.O. Box 195 (74873-0195)
PHONE.................................405 598-5691
Don Southwell, *President*
EMP: 15
SQ FT: 30,000
SALES (est): 2.7MM **Privately Held**
SIC: 3441 3444 Fabricated structural metal; siding, sheet metal

(G-8923)
MJS CRAFTS
38763 New Hope Rd (74873-5107)
PHONE.................................405 598-8105
EMP: 2 **EST:** 2001
SALES (est): 65K **Privately Held**
SIC: 2499 Mfg Wood Products

(G-8924)
PATRIOT SMALL ARMS LLC
19208 Patterson Rd (74873-5557)
PHONE.................................405 567-7890
Michael Fesler, *Principal*
EMP: 2 **EST:** 2017
SALES (est): 73.4K **Privately Held**
SIC: 3484 Small arms

(G-8925)
R & P MACHINE SHOP
19705 Gordon Cooper Dr (74873-9126)
PHONE.................................405 275-1321
Rex Vandyke, *Owner*
EMP: 1
SALES (est): 78K **Privately Held**
SIC: 7538 3599 General automotive repair shops; machine shop, jobbing & repair

(G-8926)
SANDERS LABORATORIES INC
402 W Highland St (74873-4029)
P.O. Box 863 (74873-0863)
PHONE.................................405 598-2131
Lawanah Sanders Leba, *President*
Paula Pettit, *Admin Sec*
EMP: 1
SQ FT: 2,000
SALES (est): 200K **Privately Held**
SIC: 2023 Dietary supplements, dairy & non-dairy based

(G-8927)
SCORPION PUMP AND INDUS LLC
37515 New Hope Rd (74873-5125)
PHONE.................................785 285-1421
Amber Broxterman,
EMP: 3
SALES (est): 217.6K **Privately Held**
SIC: 3561 5072 5084 5085 Industrial pumps & parts; hand tools; machine tools & accessories; metalworking tools (such as drills, taps, dies, files); industrial tools

(G-8928)
SFM INCORPORATED
37515 New Hope Rd (74873-5125)
PHONE.................................405 788-9453
John Carter, *Principal*
EMP: 3
SALES (est): 140.6K **Privately Held**
SIC: 5084 1761 3599 3589 Machine tools & metalworking machinery; metalworking tools (such as drills, taps, dies, files); sheet metalwork; crankshafts & camshafts, machining; service industry machinery;

(G-8929)
SIGMAN WELDING
43360 Hickory Dr (74873-7153)
PHONE.................................405 596-3035
Billydon Sigman, *Principal*
EMP: 1

SALES (est): 39.2K **Privately Held**
SIC: 7692 Welding repair

(G-8930)
UNITED SLINGS INC
110 E Washington St (74873-3242)
P.O. Box 1161, Shawnee (74802-1161)
PHONE.................................405 598-2616
Charles Gray, *President*
Pete Dailey, *Corp Secy*
Wanda C Hixson, *Vice Pres*
EMP: 3
SQ FT: 4,500
SALES (est): 422K **Privately Held**
SIC: 3496 3536 5063 Slings, lifting: made from purchased wire; hoists; wire & cable

(G-8931)
YORK METAL FABRICATION
311 Debbie Ln (74873-3603)
PHONE.................................405 598-6239
John York, *Owner*
Carla York, *Co-Owner*
EMP: 2
SALES: 60K **Privately Held**
SIC: 3499 Fire- or burglary-resistive products

Temple
Cotton County

(G-8932)
BURROW TOOL
112 N Commercial St (73568)
P.O. Box 662 (73568-0662)
PHONE.................................580 240-1045
Fritz Burrow, *Owner*
EMP: 2
SALES: 90K **Privately Held**
SIC: 3599 Machine shop, jobbing & repair

(G-8933)
KFM INC
201 E Main St (73568)
P.O. Box 10 (73568-0010)
PHONE.................................580 342-6293
Teresa Keaton, *President*
▲ **EMP:** 10
SALES (est): 829.8K **Privately Held**
SIC: 2048 Prepared feeds

(G-8934)
RJC WELDING LLC
186119 N 2700 Rd (73568-6069)
PHONE.................................580 281-0516
EMP: 1
SALES (est): 32.3K **Privately Held**
SIC: 7692 Welding repair

(G-8935)
SMITH & SONS SALVAGE
Rr 1 (73568)
P.O. Box 176 (73568-0176)
PHONE.................................580 342-6218
Leonard Smith, *Owner*
EMP: 6
SALES (est): 551.5K **Privately Held**
SIC: 1389 Oil field services

(G-8936)
TEMPLE CUSTOM SLAUGHTER & PROC
Also Called: Temple Meat Processing
521 W Central St (73568)
PHONE.................................580 342-5031
Donald Adams, *Owner*
Joyce Adams, *Co-Owner*
EMP: 3
SALES (est): 118.5K **Privately Held**
SIC: 0751 2013 2011 Slaughtering: custom livestock services; sausages & other prepared meats; meat packing plants

Terlton
Pawnee County

(G-8937)
AMYS CANDLES AND GIFTS LLC
370340 E 5605 Rd (74081-3470)
PHONE.................................918 865-2827
Amelia Young, *Principal*
EMP: 2 **EST:** 2016
SALES (est): 72.5K **Privately Held**
SIC: 3999 Candles

(G-8938)
WEINS MACHINE CO INC
3 One Half Mi N On Hwy 48 (74081)
PHONE.................................918 865-2187
Henry Weins, *President*
Patty Weins, *Corp Secy*
EMP: 18
SQ FT: 10,000
SALES (est): 2.2MM **Privately Held**
SIC: 3599 7692 Machine shop, jobbing & repair; welding repair

Texhoma
Texas County

(G-8939)
SEWELLS MACHINE & WELDING
122 S 2nd St (73949)
P.O. Box 393 (73949-0393)
PHONE.................................580 423-7004
Gene Sewell, *Owner*
EMP: 1
SALES (est): 154.8K **Privately Held**
SIC: 5084 7692 Welding machinery & equipment; welding repair

Thomas
Custer County

(G-8940)
BUSY BEE
100 W South Rd (73669-7613)
PHONE.................................580 661-2946
EMP: 1
SALES (est): 44.1K **Privately Held**
SIC: 5949 2759 Sewing, needlework & piece goods; screen printing

(G-8941)
CRAVENS BACKHOE SERVICE LLC
844 N 15th St (73669-8111)
PHONE.................................580 661-3652
Sherri Lee Cravens, *Principal*
EMP: 1
SALES (est): 60K **Privately Held**
SIC: 3531 Backhoes

(G-8942)
DRC SERVICE CO
401 N 1st St (73669)
P.O. Box 578 (73669-0578)
PHONE.................................580 661-3300
EMP: 5
SALES (est): 584.5K **Privately Held**
SIC: 1389 Oil field services

(G-8943)
ENABLE OKLAHOMA INT TRANSM LLC
Also Called: Thomas Processing Plant
23584 E 880 Rd (73669-8299)
PHONE.................................580 661-2266
Bryan Fairns, *General Mgr*
EMP: 8
SALES (corp-wide): 12.3B **Publicly Held**
SIC: 1311 Crude petroleum & natural gas
HQ: Enable Oklahoma Intrastate Transmission, Llc
499 W Sheridan Ave # 1500
Oklahoma City OK 73102
405 525-7788

(G-8944)
J & C ENTERPRISES AVIATION
721 N Missouri St (73669-8134)
PHONE.................................580 661-3591
Cecilia Buster, *President*
Grant Kohout, *Vice Pres*
Denise Sprinkle, *Treasurer*
EMP: 9
SALES (est): 1.9MM **Privately Held**
SIC: 5088 3724 Aircraft & parts; aircraft equipment & supplies; aircraft engines & engine parts

GEOGRAPHIC SECTION

(G-8945)
KAUTZS PUMPING INC
121 N 11th St (73669-8035)
P.O. Box 280 (73669-0280)
PHONE.................................580 661-3397
Gary Kautz, *President*
Janet Kautz, *Vice Pres*
EMP: 2
SALES (est): 181.7K **Privately Held**
SIC: 1389 Oil field services

(G-8946)
KING DESIGN & PRINTING LLC
623 E Hughes St (73669-7405)
PHONE.................................580 661-3061
EMP: 2
SALES (est): 134.8K **Privately Held**
SIC: 2752 Commercial printing, lithographic

(G-8947)
PAYNE FARMS
8890 N 2445 Rd (73669-6900)
PHONE.................................580 661-2351
Rex Payne, *Owner*
Karen Miller, *Co-Owner*
Betty Payne, *Co-Owner*
Rick Payne, *Co-Owner*
EMP: 3
SALES (est): 373.4K **Privately Held**
SIC: 1311 Crude petroleum production; natural gas production

(G-8948)
T AND A SAWMILL LLC
235171 E 815 Rd (73669-6003)
PHONE.................................580 309-3100
Troy Fisher, *Owner*
EMP: 3
SALES (est): 270.9K **Privately Held**
WEB: www.tandasawmill.com
SIC: 2421 Sawmills & planing mills, general

(G-8949)
THOMAS TRIBUTE INC
Also Called: Tribune
115 W Orient St (73669)
P.O. Box 10 (73669-0010)
PHONE.................................580 661-3524
Mr Harold Gleason, *President*
Donna Gleason, *Manager*
EMP: 4
SALES (est): 78K **Privately Held**
SIC: 2711 2741 Newspapers: publishing only, not printed on site; miscellaneous publishing

(G-8950)
VENTURA LLC
24322 E 910 Rd (73669-8292)
P.O. Box 621 (73669-0621)
PHONE.................................580 661-2924
Dee Christopher, *Principal*
EMP: 23 **Privately Held**
SIC: 2911 Gasoline
PA: Ventura, Llc
6100 N Western Ave
Oklahoma City OK 73118

(G-8951)
W-W MANUFACTURING CO INC (HQ)
Also Called: Ww Livestock Systems
8832 State Highway 54 (73669-5101)
PHONE.................................580 661-3720
Steve Zamzow, *President*
Ted Webster, *Vice Pres*
Greg Overton, *Mfg Staff*
▼ **EMP:** 60 **EST:** 1953
SQ FT: 80,000
SALES (est): 12.1MM
SALES (corp-wide): 27.2MM **Privately Held**
WEB: www.wwmanufacturing.com
SIC: 3523 Cattle feeding, handling & watering equipment
PA: W-W Capital Corporation
235 Welch Ave 2
Berthoud CO 80513
970 532-2506

(G-8952)
W-W MANUFACTURING CO INC
108 S Main St (73669)
PHONE.................................580 661-3720
Greg Overton, *Manager*
EMP: 65
SALES (corp-wide): 27.2MM **Privately Held**
SIC: 3523 Cattle feeding, handling & watering equipment
HQ: W-W Manufacturing Co., Inc.
8832 State Highway 54
Thomas OK 73669
580 661-3720

Tinker Afb
Oklahoma County

(G-8953)
DLA DOCUMENT SERVICES
3420 D Ave Ste 105 (73145-9112)
PHONE.................................405 734-2177
Patrick Cobain, *Director*
EMP: 25 **Publicly Held**
WEB: www.documentservices.dla.mil
SIC: 2752 9711 Commercial printing, lithographic; national security;
HQ: Dla Document Services
5450 Carlisle Pike Bldg 9
Mechanicsburg PA 17050
717 605-2362

(G-8954)
L3 TECHNOLOGIES INC
7641 Mercury Rd 830l62 (73145-8707)
PHONE.................................405 739-3700
Ted Alexander, *Manager*
EMP: 50
SALES (corp-wide): 6.8B **Publicly Held**
SIC: 3699 Flight simulators (training aids), electronic
HQ: L3 Technologies, Inc.
600 3rd Ave Fl 34
New York NY 10016
212 697-1111

(G-8955)
TINKER AFB
3301 F Ave Dr 22 (73145)
PHONE.................................405 739-2349
EMP: 2
SALES (est): 86K **Privately Held**
SIC: 3728 Military aircraft equipment & armament

(G-8956)
U T C PRATT & WHITNEY OKLA CY
3001 Staff Dr (73145-3303)
PHONE.................................405 455-2001
Luis Zubillaga, *Manager*
EMP: 30
SALES (est): 3.1MM **Privately Held**
SIC: 3724 Aircraft engines & engine parts

Tipton
Tillman County

(G-8957)
ALLPRO MFG LLC
16775 County Road Ns 220 (73570-9208)
PHONE.................................580 512-7248
EMP: 1 **EST:** 2015
SALES (est): 49.2K **Privately Held**
SIC: 3999 Manufacturing industries

(G-8958)
DERRICK HOPPES
Also Called: Hoppes Oil Field Svc
310 E Main St (73570-5034)
P.O. Box 351 (73570-0351)
PHONE.................................580 667-4373
Derrick Hoppes, *Owner*
EMP: 1
SALES (est): 123.2K **Privately Held**
SIC: 1389 Oil field services

(G-8959)
DOSHER KENNON
423 Nw 2nd St (73570-9606)
PHONE.................................580 667-5708
Dosher Kennon, *Principal*
EMP: 1
SALES (est): 56.4K **Privately Held**
SIC: 7692 Welding repair

(G-8960)
TREEHOUSE EMBROIDERY
17419 County Road Ns 212 (73570-9539)
PHONE.................................580 667-4322
Linda J Boyd, *Owner*
EMP: 2 **EST:** 1998
SALES (est): 85K **Privately Held**
SIC: 2759 Commercial printing

Tishomingo
Johnston County

(G-8961)
ALLURE SALON AND SPA LLC
103 N Broadway St (73460-1709)
PHONE.................................580 371-9333
Robin Ferris, *Mng Member*
EMP: 4 **EST:** 2012
SALES (est): 68.4K **Privately Held**
SIC: 7231 2844 Beauty shops; manicure preparations

(G-8962)
BLESSING GRAVEL LLC
1415 E Harbert Rd (73460)
PHONE.................................580 513-4009
Joyce Stowers,
EMP: 5
SALES (est): 594.6K **Privately Held**
SIC: 1423 3299 Crushed & broken granite; blocks & brick, sand lime

(G-8963)
BUILT RIGHT COMPRESSOR
309 E 18th St (73460-2605)
PHONE.................................580 371-2007
Ronald Coppedge, *Owner*
EMP: 3
SQ FT: 2,000
SALES (est): 120.7K **Privately Held**
SIC: 7699 7694 3563 Compressor repair; electric motor repair; air & gas compressors

(G-8964)
CANYON WELDING SERVICE INC
11443 S Canyon Ln (73460-3747)
PHONE.................................580 371-8805
Rebecca Reid, *Principal*
EMP: 1
SALES (est): 313.6K **Privately Held**
SIC: 7692 Welding repair

(G-8965)
GOOD SPRINGS ENERGY LLC
1234 N Kemp Ave (73460-4402)
PHONE.................................580 257-9762
Bobby Berna,
EMP: 1
SALES: 100K **Privately Held**
SIC: 1382 7389 Oil & gas exploration services;

(G-8966)
INDUSTRIAL EQUIPMENT REPAIR
1509 Industrial Ln (73460-4901)
PHONE.................................580 371-3361
Vance McDaniel, *Co-Owner*
Shari McDaniel, *Co-Owner*
EMP: 2
SQ FT: 2,100
SALES (est): 145.1K **Privately Held**
SIC: 3541 Machine tool replacement & repair parts, metal cutting types

(G-8967)
LOG CUTTERS
1455 N Elks Rd (73460-4805)
PHONE.................................580 371-8349
Butch Smith, *Owner*
EMP: 2
SALES (est): 89.1K **Privately Held**
SIC: 2421 Sawmills & planing mills, general

(G-8968)
STANSBURY NOBLE JR INC
Also Called: Noble Signs
10650 Canada Ln (73460-4933)
PHONE.................................209 847-8408
Noble Stansbury Jr, *President*
Mary Stansbury, *Vice Pres*
EMP: 2
SALES (est): 275.2K **Privately Held**
SIC: 3993 Neon signs

(G-8969)
TAPE-MATICS INC
1539 Industrial Ln (73460-4901)
P.O. Box 789 (73460-0789)
PHONE.................................580 371-2510
Robin Smith, *President*
Marvin Smith, *Vice Pres*
Tate Streater, *Vice Pres*
Debrah E White, *Admin Sec*
EMP: 20
SQ FT: 12,000
SALES (est): 1.5MM **Privately Held**
WEB: www.tapematics.com
SIC: 7699 3451 Industrial machinery & equipment repair; screw machine products

Tonkawa
Kay County

(G-8970)
A-LINE TDS INC
1500 N Main St (74653-1011)
PHONE.................................580 628-5371
Ben Stroh, *President*
Glenn Scott, *Controller*
Frank Martuscelli, *Accounts Exec*
EMP: 45
SALES (est): 7.6MM **Privately Held**
SIC: 3677 Electronic coils, transformers & other inductors

(G-8971)
AMERICAN IRON SPORTS
108 W Grand Ave (74653-3018)
PHONE.................................580 716-5662
Matt Bixler, *Owner*
EMP: 1
SALES (est): 47K **Privately Held**
SIC: 3949 Sporting & athletic goods

(G-8972)
ASBURY MACHINE CORPORATION
Also Called: Throop Rock Bits
1995 N Public St (74653-4720)
P.O. Box 416 (74653-0416)
PHONE.................................580 628-3416
Gary Hayes, *President*
Steve Warren, *Principal*
Holly A Harpster, *Vice Pres*
Paul Brown, *Plant Mgr*
Lana Cleave, *CFO*
EMP: 18 **EST:** 1960
SQ FT: 22,000
SALES (est): 4.1MM **Privately Held**
WEB: www.throoprockbit.com
SIC: 3532 3533 Drills, bits & similar equipment; oil & gas drilling rigs & equipment

(G-8973)
DANIEL GARAGE DOOR SALES & SVC
1011 E Oklahoma Ave (74653-6025)
P.O. Box 177 (74653-0177)
PHONE.................................580 628-3769
Tom Daniel, *Owner*
EMP: 2
SALES: 90K **Privately Held**
SIC: 5211 3699 Garage doors, sale & installation; door opening & closing devices, electrical

(G-8974)
DIEMER CONSTRUCTION CO LLC
14211 S 13th St (74653-4210)
PHONE.................................580 628-3052

Tonkawa - Kay County (G-8975)

Robert Q Diemer, *Mng Member*
Robert Diemer, *Mng Member*
Christy Desjarlais,
Carol Diemer,
Misty Truley,
EMP: 25
SQ FT: 1,500
SALES: 2MM **Privately Held**
SIC: 1389 1741 Grading oil & gas well foundations; foundation building

(G-8975)
HURST CNSTR & FABRICATION LLC
207 S 7th St (74653-5016)
PHONE................580 628-2388
Drew Hurst, *Mng Member*
EMP: 32
SQ FT: 40,000
SALES (est): 6.4MM **Privately Held**
SIC: 3449 Bars, concrete reinforcing: fabricated steel

(G-8976)
K & S ALUMINUM BOOMS
9825 S 44th St (74653-4760)
PHONE................580 761-3238
Bryan Kugel, *Principal*
EMP: 6 **EST:** 2009
SALES (est): 723.6K **Privately Held**
WEB: www.ksbooms.com
SIC: 3494 Sprinkler systems, field

(G-8977)
KAY HOLDING CO
Also Called: Holiday Lighting Specialist
100 Holiday Ln (74653-5540)
PHONE................580 628-4146
Eric Martin, *President*
Gaylord Martin, *Vice Pres*
Margaret C Martin, *Vice Pres*
Neil Martin, *Vice Pres*
▲ **EMP:** 20 **EST:** 1974
SQ FT: 21,000
SALES (est): 1.4MM **Privately Held**
SIC: 1799 3993 Welding on site; electric signs

(G-8978)
LINTON JIM & JOHN
Also Called: J L'S Retipping
307 Thunderbird Rd (74653-1042)
PHONE................580 628-3093
Jim Linton, *Partner*
EMP: 2
SALES (est): 138.6K **Privately Held**
SIC: 3545 Drill bits, metalworking

(G-8979)
PRELESNICKS REPAIR SERVICE
117 N Public St (74653-3564)
P.O. Box 398 (74653-0398)
PHONE................580 628-3179
Terry Prelesnick, *Owner*
EMP: 1
SALES (est): 65K **Privately Held**
SIC: 3545 Drill bits, metalworking

(G-8980)
RANGE PRODUCTION COMPANY
303 Thunderbird Rd (74653-1042)
PHONE................580 628-3700
Harold Platt, *Manager*
Nelly Marler, *Receptionist*
EMP: 1 **EST:** 2008
SALES (est): 110.1K
SALES (corp-wide): 2.8B **Publicly Held**
SIC: 1382 Oil & gas exploration services
PA: Range Resources Corporation
100 Throckmorton St # 1200
Fort Worth TX 76102
817 870-2601

(G-8981)
SAMHILL LLC
312 S 3rd St (74653-5533)
PHONE................580 761-1255
Joel V Roth, *Mng Member*
James Roth,
EMP: 4
SALES: 150K **Privately Held**
SIC: 1389 Oil field services

(G-8982)
TONKAWA FOUNDRY INC
510 S 7th St (74653-5004)
P.O. Box 504 (74653-0504)
PHONE................580 628-2575
Sandy Linton, *CEO*
Jim Salisbury, *COO*
Don Reimer, *Vice Pres*
Sandy Salisbury Linton, *CFO*
EMP: 34 **EST:** 1951
SQ FT: 25,800
SALES (est): 3MM **Privately Held**
WEB: www.tonkawafoundry.com
SIC: 3366 Copper foundries

(G-8983)
TONKAWA MEAT PROCESSING
707 S Public St (74653-4444)
P.O. Box 116 (74653-0116)
PHONE................580 628-4550
Betty Bradford, *Owner*
EMP: 7
SALES (est): 240K **Privately Held**
SIC: 2011 5421 2013 Meat packing plants; meat markets, including freezer provisioners; sausages & other prepared meats

(G-8984)
TONKAWA NEWS
108 N 7th St (74653-3578)
P.O. Box 250 (74653-0250)
PHONE................580 628-2532
Lyle Becker, *Owner*
EMP: 5 **EST:** 1951
SQ FT: 3,125
SALES (est): 227.4K **Privately Held**
WEB: www.tonkawanews.com
SIC: 2711 2752 Newspapers: publishing only, not printed on site; lithographing on metal

---

Tulsa
Creek County

(G-8985)
ABITL FINISHING INC
6755 State Highway 66 (74131-6632)
PHONE................918 446-5363
Rob Bartlett, *President*
Luis Acevedo, *President*
Gail Runnels, *Shareholder*
EMP: 25
SQ FT: 50,000
SALES (est): 3.9MM **Privately Held**
WEB: www.abitl.com
SIC: 3479 Coating of metals & formed products

(G-8986)
ACCURATE BY DESIGN
5800 W 68th St (74131-2427)
PHONE................918 445-0292
EMP: 1 **EST:** 1995
SQ FT: 750
SALES: 100K **Privately Held**
SIC: 7389 3674 Commercial And Industrial Product Design And Mfg Specialized Computer Related Oil Field Equipment

(G-8987)
ACTION MACHINE INC
8335 S 89th West Ave (74131-3614)
P.O. Box 700120 (74170-0120)
PHONE................918 248-6847
James C Muir, *President*
Mary Muir, *Corp Secy*
◆ **EMP:** 31
SQ FT: 41,000
SALES (est): 4MM **Privately Held**
SIC: 3599 Machine shop, jobbing & repair

(G-8988)
AETHER DBS LLC (PA)
Also Called: Hard Hat Services
8101 State Highway 66 (74131-6607)
P.O. Box 4738, Naperville IL (60567-4738)
PHONE................918 317-2375
Jack Kelley, *Project Engr*
Thomas A Blair, *Mng Member*
John McDonough,
Stuart Russell,
EMP: 5
SALES: 15MM **Privately Held**
SIC: 3533 Oil & gas field machinery

(G-8989)
B & W MANUFACTURING CO LTD
8700 S Regency Dr (74131-3609)
PHONE................918 248-5201
Tom J Weathers, *President*
EMP: 12 **EST:** 1964
SQ FT: 6,500
SALES (est): 2.4MM **Privately Held**
SIC: 3441 3446 Fabricated structural metal; architectural metalwork

(G-8990)
BERRY GLOBAL FILMS LLC
Also Called: Plant 4
6940 W 76th St S (74131-3243)
PHONE................918 227-1616
Mark Carraway, *Area Mgr*
Sharon Sanders, *Area Mgr*
Michelle Harris, *Purchasing*
Kelly Lamastus, *Cust Mgr*
William Lee, *Sales Staff*
EMP: 64
SQ FT: 100,000 **Publicly Held**
SIC: 3081 2671 Polyethylene film; packaging paper & plastics film, coated & laminated
HQ: Berry Global Films, Llc
95 Chestnut Ridge Rd
Montvale NJ 07645
201 641-6600

(G-8991)
BERRY GLOBAL FILMS LLC
Also Called: Plant 1
6940 W 76th St S (74131-3243)
PHONE................918 446-1651
Joe Piccione, *Branch Mgr*
Dale McQueen, *Manager*
EMP: 100 **Publicly Held**
SIC: 3081 Polyethylene film
HQ: Berry Global Films, Llc
95 Chestnut Ridge Rd
Montvale NJ 07645
201 641-6600

(G-8992)
BROOX CREATIVE INDUSTRIES LLC
9999 W 81st St (74131-2812)
PHONE................918 691-8834
EMP: 2
SALES (est): 80.5K **Privately Held**
SIC: 3999 Manufacturing industries

(G-8993)
BROWN MINNEAPOLIS TANK
7274 W 81st St (74131-3244)
PHONE................918 224-2358
EMP: 5
SALES (est): 387.1K **Privately Held**
SIC: 3443 Mfg Fabricated Plate Work

(G-8994)
CARLS CHILI COMPANY INC
8622 S Regency Dr (74131-3625)
PHONE................918 227-1623
Carl Kennedy, *President*
EMP: 3
SQ FT: 3,000
SALES: 200K **Privately Held**
SIC: 2032 Chili with or without meat: packaged in cans, jars, etc.

(G-8995)
CASTING COATING CORP
5700 W 68th St (74131-2425)
PHONE................918 445-4141
Carl Coman, *President*
Doug Coman, *Vice Pres*
Clyde Coman, *Treasurer*
David Coman, *Shareholder*
EMP: 10
SQ FT: 4,000
SALES (est): 1.1MM **Privately Held**
SIC: 3479 3398 Coating of metals & formed products; metal heat treating

(G-8996)
CENTRAL BURIAL VAULTS INC
Also Called: Doric Vaults
8500 W 81st St (74131-2805)
PHONE................918 224-5701
Jean Cooper, *Manager*
EMP: 25
SALES (corp-wide): 3.9MM **Privately Held**
SIC: 5087 3272 Concrete burial vaults & boxes; concrete products
PA: Central Burial Vaults Inc
9700 Nw 4th St
Oklahoma City OK
405 495-7075

(G-8997)
CONSIDILATED FABRICATIONS
7963 S Regency Dr (74131-3628)
PHONE................918 224-3563
Mark Ekaitekiaitis, *Principal*
EMP: 2
SALES (est): 88.9K **Privately Held**
SIC: 3443 Fabricated plate work (boiler shop)

(G-8998)
CONSOLDTED FABRICATION CONSTRS
7963 S Regency Dr (74131-3628)
PHONE................918 224-3500
Tor Larson, *Branch Mgr*
EMP: 1
SALES (est): 82.1K
SALES (corp-wide): 148MM **Privately Held**
SIC: 3325 Steel foundries
PA: Consolidated Fabrication And Constructors Inc
3851 Ellsworth St
Gary IN 46408
219 884-6150

(G-8999)
CONSOLDTED FBRCTION CNSTRUCTOR
7963 S Regency Dr (74131-3628)
PHONE................918 224-3500
Dean Hughes, *President*
Matthew Thompson, *Engineer*
EMP: 1
SALES (est): 315.5K **Privately Held**
SIC: 3441 Fabricated structural metal

(G-9000)
CREMATORY MANUFACTURING & SVC
6802 S 65th West Ave (74131-2423)
P.O. Box 371 (74101-0371)
PHONE................918 446-1475
Lawrence Stuart Sr, *President*
Frank Byrant, *Vice Pres*
EMP: 35
SQ FT: 25,000
SALES (est): 2MM **Privately Held**
SIC: 7699 3569 Industrial equipment services; cremating ovens

(G-9001)
DOWNING MANUFACTURING INC (PA)
Also Called: Dmi
8504 S Regency Dr (74131-3623)
PHONE................918 224-1116
Dan Downing, *President*
Deanie Downing, *President*
Dennis Downing, *Vice Pres*
Danny Downing, *Treasurer*
EMP: 12 **EST:** 1959
SQ FT: 10,600
SALES (est): 1MM **Privately Held**
WEB: www.downinginc.com
SIC: 3674 1781 1381 3993 Solid state electronic devices; water well drilling; directional drilling oil & gas wells; signs & advertising specialties

(G-9002)
ELECTROTECH INC
7221 S 81st West Pl (74131-2819)
PHONE................918 224-5869
Floyd Prestridge, *President*
David Hunter, *Corp Secy*
Bruce Johnson, *Vice Pres*
EMP: 3

GEOGRAPHIC SECTION
Tulsa - Creek County (G-9031)

SALES (est): 675K **Privately Held**
SIC: 3533 3699 Oil & gas field machinery; electrical equipment & supplies

(G-9003)
ERNST VALVE & FITTINGS
6503 S 57th West Ave (74131-2408)
PHONE.................................918 446-0313
David Ernst, *Owner*
EMP: 2
SQ FT: 3,500
SALES (est): 150K **Privately Held**
SIC: 3599 3494 Machine shop, jobbing & repair; valves & pipe fittings

(G-9004)
FABRICATION DYNAMICS
6611 State Highway 66 (74131-6625)
P.O. Box 9714 (74157-0714)
PHONE.................................918 445-6100
Kenneth Gruse, *President*
Robert Bruse, *Vice Pres*
EMP: 70
SQ FT: 50,000
SALES: 354.4K **Privately Held**
SIC: 3444 Sheet metal specialties, not stamped

(G-9005)
FASCAST INC
7835 State Highway 66 (74131-6611)
PHONE.................................918 445-7405
Bill Travis, *President*
EMP: 32
SALES (est): 6.9MM **Privately Held**
SIC: 3321 Gray iron castings

(G-9006)
FIN FAB INCORPORATED
8315 S 89th West Ave (74131-3614)
P.O. Box 9651 (74157-0651)
PHONE.................................918 227-1866
Donald W Williams, *President*
Lori Prince, *Corp Secy*
Jeff Williams, *Vice Pres*
EMP: 4 **EST:** 1980
SQ FT: 14,000
SALES (est): 500K **Privately Held**
SIC: 3443 Finned tubes, for heat transfer

(G-9007)
FLOWELL CORPORATION
8308 S Regency Dr (74131-3684)
P.O. Box 1800, Oakhurst (74050-1800)
PHONE.................................918 224-6969
Stan Bridgeford, *President*
Rick Walker, *Vice Pres*
EMP: 10
SQ FT: 8,000
SALES: 2MM **Privately Held**
SIC: 3545 3494 Machine tool accessories; valves & pipe fittings

(G-9008)
GREEN BAY PACKAGING INC
Green Bay Packaging Tulsa Div
6106 W 68th St (74131-2429)
PHONE.................................918 446-3341
Ryan Boega, *General Mgr*
EMP: 101
SQ FT: 161,930
SALES (corp-wide): 1.3B **Privately Held**
SIC: 2653 Boxes, corrugated: made from purchased materials
PA: Green Bay Packaging Inc.
1700 N Webster Ave
Green Bay WI 54302
920 433-5111

(G-9009)
HANLOCK-CAUSEWAY COMPANY LLC
6802 S 65th West Ave (74131-2423)
P.O. Box 371 (74101-0371)
PHONE.................................918 446-1450
Jay Bryant, *President*
EMP: 15
SALES (est): 5.2MM
SALES (corp-wide): 13.4MM **Privately Held**
SIC: 3315 Wire & fabricated wire products
PA: Bryant Refractory Company
6802 S 65th West Ave
Tulsa OK
918 446-1481

(G-9010)
HAPPY CAMPER SIGNS
9400 W 61st St (74131-2005)
PHONE.................................918 856-4279
EMP: 1
SALES (est): 46K **Privately Held**
SIC: 3993 Signs & advertising specialties

(G-9011)
HARRIS PATTERN & MFG INC
8200 S 89th West Ave (74131-3611)
P.O. Box 883, Sand Springs (74063-0883)
PHONE.................................918 227-3228
Kim A Harris, *President*
EMP: 6
SQ FT: 6,000
SALES (est): 440K **Privately Held**
SIC: 3543 Foundry patternmaking

(G-9012)
HELMERICH & PAYNE INC
6105 W 68th St (74131-2430)
PHONE.................................918 447-2630
Wh Helmerich, *Branch Mgr*
EMP: 10
SQ FT: 127,871
SALES (corp-wide): 2.8B **Publicly Held**
WEB: www.hpinc.com
SIC: 1381 Directional drilling oil & gas wells
PA: Helmerich & Payne, Inc.
1437 S Boulder Ave # 1400
Tulsa OK 74119
918 742-5531

(G-9013)
HIPOWER SYSTEMS OKLAHOMA LLC
7249 State Highway 66 (74131-6629)
PHONE.................................918 512-6321
John Larson,
EMP: 6
SALES (est): 334.7K **Privately Held**
SIC: 3621 3569 7539 Power generators; electric motor & generator auxillary parts; gas generators; alternators & generators, rebuilding & repair

(G-9014)
HYDRANT REPAIR PARTS INC
7835 State Highway 66 (74131-6611)
PHONE.................................918 224-8713
Bill Travis, *President*
Debbie Golden, *Vice Pres*
Jon Massaro, *Purchasing*
EMP: 27
SQ FT: 36,000
SALES (est): 6.7MM **Privately Held**
SIC: 3829 Measuring & controlling devices

(G-9015)
J & M WELDING
7862 S Regency Dr (74131-3620)
PHONE.................................918 216-2090
Jim Miller, *CEO*
EMP: 45 **EST:** 2010
SALES (est): 1MM **Privately Held**
SIC: 7692 Welding repair

(G-9016)
LASER SPECIALITIES INC
Also Called: LSI
6611 State Highway 66 (74131-6625)
P.O. Box 570975 (74157-0975)
PHONE.................................918 760-5690
James Clark, *CEO*
Jim Clark, *President*
Chris Jouppi, *President*
Merle Margindale, *Vice Pres*
Charlie Hough, *Purch Mgr*
▲ **EMP:** 50
SQ FT: 125,000
SALES (est): 13.7MM **Privately Held**
SIC: 3444 Sheet metalwork

(G-9017)
MADISON INC OF OKLAHOMA ✪
8301 State Highway 66 (74131-6608)
PHONE.................................918 587-4501
Karla Crabtree, *Executive*
EMP: 2 **EST:** 2019
SALES (est): 88.9K **Privately Held**
SIC: 3448 Prefabricated metal buildings

(G-9018)
MAGNESIUM PRODUCTS INC
5105 W 66th Pl (74131-2673)
PHONE.................................918 587-9930
Lawrence Wheeler, *President*
Brad D Fuller, *Principal*
Marjorie Matthews, *Vice Pres*
▲ **EMP:** 12
SQ FT: 21,000
SALES (est): 3.6MM **Privately Held**
SIC: 2819 2834 2899 3339 Magnesium compounds or salts, inorganic; pharmaceutical preparations; chemical preparations; primary nonferrous metals

(G-9019)
MAGPRO CHLOR-ALKALI LLC
5105 W 66th Pl (74131-2673)
PHONE.................................918 587-9930
Gregory O'Donnell,
Larry Wheeler,
EMP: 4
SALES (est): 156.7K **Privately Held**
SIC: 2869 Industrial organic chemicals

(G-9020)
MERE SOFTWARE INC
8538 Gary Dr (74131-3817)
PHONE.................................918 740-5018
Dale Stewart, *Principal*
EMP: 2
SALES (est): 153.5K **Privately Held**
WEB: www.meresoftware.com
SIC: 7372 Prepackaged software

(G-9021)
MFG SPECIALISTS INC
5770 W 68th St (74131-2425)
PHONE.................................918 445-9040
Ray Neicke, *Principal*
EMP: 8
SALES (est): 1MM **Privately Held**
SIC: 3599 Machine shop, jobbing & repair

(G-9022)
NATIONAL OILWELL VARCO INC
Nov Completion Prod Solutions
6750 S 57th West Ave (74131-2411)
P.O. Box 2069 (74101-2069)
PHONE.................................918 447-4600
Manuel Moeller, *Engineer*
Dana Buxton, *Cust Mgr*
Dana Matlock, *Marketing Staff*
Carlos Rein, *Branch Mgr*
John Beu, *Manager*
EMP: 25
SALES (corp-wide): 8.4B **Publicly Held**
SIC: 3533 Oil field machinery & equipment
PA: National Oilwell Varco, Inc.
7909 Parkwood Circle Dr
Houston TX 77036
713 346-7500

(G-9023)
OK FABRICATORS LLC
Also Called: OK Fab and Machining
8630 S Regency Dr (74131-3625)
PHONE.................................918 224-3977
Greg Arrington, *Managing Prtnr*
Susan Arrington, *Principal*
James S Arrington, *Mng Member*
Paula Hutchinson, *Manager*
Michael Arrington,
EMP: 35
SQ FT: 27,500
SALES (est): 5.3MM **Privately Held**
SIC: 3441 Fabricated structural metal

(G-9024)
PIPELINE EQUIPMENT INC
8403 S 89th West Ave (74131-3616)
PHONE.................................918 224-4144
Jack D Lollis, *President*
Jack Lollis, *President*
Susan Lollis, *Vice Pres*
EMP: 24
SQ FT: 27,500
SALES (est): 9.7MM **Privately Held**
SIC: 3498 3533 Fabricated pipe & fittings; oil & gas field machinery

(G-9025)
PRECISION HEAT TREATING
6300 S 57th West Ave (74131-2403)
P.O. Box 9676 (74157-0676)
PHONE.................................918 445-7424
Jim Moss, *Principal*
Kyle Corriveau, *Engineer*
Anna Williams, *CFO*
Brent Lollis, *VP Sales*
EMP: 7
SQ FT: 13,832
SALES (est): 1.1MM **Privately Held**
SIC: 3398 Metal heat treating

(G-9026)
PRECISON PARTS INC
7207 W 81st St (74131-3245)
PHONE.................................918 261-6962
Cecilio Munoz, *Owner*
EMP: 2 **EST:** 1997
SALES: 200K **Privately Held**
SIC: 3599 Machine shop, jobbing & repair

(G-9027)
PRESCOR LLC (PA)
8601 State Highway 66 (74131-6604)
P.O. Box 9856 (74157-0856)
PHONE.................................918 224-6626
Wally Trepp, *President*
Tom Trepp, *Vice Pres*
Robert Trepp, *Treasurer*
EMP: 45
SQ FT: 38,000
SALES (est): 9.7MM **Privately Held**
WEB: www.prescor.com
SIC: 3443 Process vessels, industrial: metal plate

(G-9028)
PRESTON-EASTIN INC
9490 N Ridgeway St (74131-6200)
P.O. Box 582288 (74158-2288)
PHONE.................................918 834-5591
Dennis George, *President*
Tiffany Burns, *Prdtn Mgr*
Charles Dennis, *Senior Buyer*
Spencer Jones, *Regl Sales Mgr*
Rose Marie Cannon, *Admin Sec*
EMP: 31
SQ FT: 40,000
SALES (est): 9.4MM **Privately Held**
SIC: 3599 Machine shop, jobbing & repair

(G-9029)
PROCESS MANUFACTURING CO INC
Also Called: Process Service & Mfg
5800 W 68th St (74131-2415)
PHONE.................................918 445-0909
Christopher Schutte, *Principal*
Robert Chrisco, *Principal*
Julie Schutte, *Controller*
Terry Fallis, *Executive*
EMP: 110
SQ FT: 125,000
SALES: 25MM **Privately Held**
SIC: 3533 3599 Oil field machinery & equipment; machine shop, jobbing & repair

(G-9030)
PYROTEK INCORPORATED
8521 S Regency Dr (74131-3624)
PHONE.................................918 224-1937
David Bridgewater, *Branch Mgr*
EMP: 32
SALES (corp-wide): 502.7MM **Privately Held**
SIC: 3559 Glass making machinery: blowing, molding, forming, etc.
PA: Pyrotek Incorporated
705 W 1st Ave
Spokane WA 99201
509 926-6212

(G-9031)
ROLLED ALLOYS INC
6555 S 57th West Ave (74131-2408)
PHONE.................................918 594-2600
John Sappington, *Branch Mgr*
Molly Johnson, *Representative*
EMP: 32
SALES (corp-wide): 217.4MM **Privately Held**
SIC: 3341 3317 Secondary nonferrous metals; steel pipe & tubes

Tulsa - Creek County (G-9032) GEOGRAPHIC SECTION

PA: Rolled Alloys, Inc.
125 W Sterns Rd
Temperance MI 48182
734 847-0561

(G-9032)
S&S FABRICATION
9635 W 71st St (74131-2826)
PHONE..................................918 447-0447
Steve Case, *Owner*
Sharon Case, *Co-Owner*
EMP: 4
SALES: 180K **Privately Held**
SIC: 3441 Fabricated structural metal

(G-9033)
SAFECO FILTER PRODUCTS INC
6440 S 57th West Ave (74131-2405)
PHONE..................................918 455-0100
Cynthia Williams, *President*
EMP: 17
SALES (est): 683.4K **Privately Held**
SIC: 3498 Fabricated pipe & fittings

(G-9034)
SAWYER MANUFACTURING COMPANY
7799 S Regency Dr (74131-3629)
PHONE..................................918 834-2550
Thomas G Sawyer, *President*
Dave Hembree, *Vice Pres*
Deborah Jordan, *Accountant*
Warrick Howard, *Sales Dir*
Sara Jordan, *Sales Staff*
▲ **EMP:** 47
SQ FT: 45,000
SALES: 2.5MM **Privately Held**
WEB: www.sawyermfg.com
SIC: 3541 3429 3531 3443 Pipe cutting & threading machines; clamps, metal; construction machinery; tanks, standard or custom fabricated: metal plate; fabricated structural metal

(G-9035)
SEAN JOSEPHSON LLC
Also Called: Stryker Service
7885 W 75th St (74131-3004)
PHONE..................................918 606-9677
Sean Josephson,
EMP: 1 EST: 2010
SALES (est): 49.6K **Privately Held**
SIC: 1389 7389 Oil field services;

(G-9036)
SI PRECAST CONCRETE PRODUCTS
6505 S 57th West Ave (74131-2408)
PHONE..................................918 446-2131
Matt Beal, *Branch Mgr*
EMP: 32
SALES (corp-wide): 2.1MM **Privately Held**
SIC: 3995 Burial caskets
PA: Si Precast Concrete Products
11919 Cartwright Ln
Grandview MO 64030
816 966-9000

(G-9037)
SISCO SPECIALTY PRODUCTS INC
8403 S 89th West Ave (74131-3616)
PHONE..................................918 266-2304
Jack Lollis, *President*
Susan Lollis, *Vice Pres*
EMP: 8 EST: 1995
SQ FT: 20,000
SALES (est): 608.1K **Privately Held**
SIC: 3599 Machine shop, jobbing & repair

(G-9038)
SOUND INK 2 PUBLISHING LLC
8220 Gary Dr (74131-3811)
PHONE..................................918 605-6026
Sally Harris, *Principal*
EMP: 1 EST: 2016
SALES (est): 37.5K **Privately Held**
SIC: 2741 Miscellaneous publishing

(G-9039)
SUN HEAT TREATING INC
Also Called: Sun Materials Testing
8500 S 89th West Ave (74131-3617)
P.O. Box 9921 (74157-0921)
PHONE..................................918 227-2188
Paul R Secrest, *President*
Carole Secrest, *Corp Secy*
EMP: 3
SQ FT: 1,200
SALES (est): 246.5K **Privately Held**
SIC: 3479 Coating, rust preventive

(G-9040)
TDW (US) INC
6645 S 61st West Ave (74131-2413)
PHONE..................................918 447-5519
David James, *Principal*
EMP: 3
SALES (est): 94.2K **Privately Held**
SIC: 3494 Valves & pipe fittings

(G-9041)
TDW SERVICES INC (HQ)
6801 S 65th West Ave (74131-2424)
P.O. Box 2217 (74101-2217)
PHONE..................................918 447-5000
D Bruce Binkley, *President*
Richard B Williamson, *Chairman*
Robert Johnson, *Vice Pres*
Bruce A Thames, *Vice Pres*
Matthew Hendricks, *Opers Staff*
▲ **EMP:** 25 EST: 1969
SQ FT: 125,000
SALES (est): 25.7MM
SALES (corp-wide): 306.7MM **Privately Held**
SIC: 7389 1382 Pipeline & power line inspection service; oil & gas exploration services
PA: T. D. Williamson, Inc.
6120 S Yale Ave Ste 1700
Tulsa OK 74136
918 493-9494

(G-9042)
TECHNOTHERM CORPORATION
5505 W 66th Pl (74131-2675)
PHONE..................................918 446-1533
Albert Presslauer, *President*
Siegfried Presslauer, *Vice Pres*
Teresa Gambill, *Buyer*
▼ **EMP:** 48
SQ FT: 4,500
SALES (est): 9.7MM **Privately Held**
SIC: 3443 Boiler & boiler shop work; economizers (boilers)

(G-9043)
TEK FINS INC
Also Called: Rainey Oil
8301 State Highway 66 (74131-6608)
PHONE..................................918 747-7447
Jim Rainey, *President*
Elizabeth Rainey, *Vice Pres*
EMP: 12
SALES (est): 3.4MM **Privately Held**
SIC: 3443 Heat exchangers: coolers (after, inter), condensers, etc.

(G-9044)
THERMAL SPECIALTIES LLC
Also Called: Tsi Heat Treating
8181 S 88th West Ave (74131-2813)
PHONE..................................918 227-4800
Dan Odell, *General Mgr*
EMP: 12
SQ FT: 36,050
SALES (corp-wide): 29.1MM **Privately Held**
SIC: 3398 5085 Metal heat treating: refractory material
PA: Thermal Specialties, Llc
6314 E 15th St
Tulsa OK 74112
918 836-4800

(G-9045)
TULSA PRESSURE VESSELS LLC
7861 S Regency Dr (74131)
PHONE..................................918 512-8346
Anthony James,
Micheal Brown,
EMP: 12

SALES (est): 522K **Privately Held**
SIC: 3443 Industrial vessels, tanks & containers

(G-9046)
TULSA STEEL MFG COMPANY INC
7600 New Sapulpa Rd (74131-3235)
PHONE..................................918 227-0110
Fax: 918 227-0113
EMP: 46
SQ FT: 44,000
SALES (est): 5.8MM **Privately Held**
SIC: 3441 Structural Metal Fabrication

(G-9047)
USA ENERGY FABRICATION LLC
6444 S 57th West Ave (74131-2405)
PHONE..................................918 445-4792
EMP: 4 EST: 2012
SALES (est): 84.1K **Privately Held**
SIC: 7692 Welding Repair

(G-9048)
VERNON MANUFACTURING COMPANY
8403 S 89th West Ave (74131-3616)
PHONE..................................918 224-4068
Vernon Bindel, *President*
Brenda Bindel, *Vice Pres*
EMP: 4
SQ FT: 6,500
SALES (est): 230K **Privately Held**
SIC: 3441 3443 Fabricated structural metal; fabricated plate work (boiler shop)

(G-9049)
VORTEX FLUID SYSTEMS INC
Also Called: Vortex Manufacturing
7108 W 76th St S (74131-3267)
PHONE..................................918 810-7798
Grant Young, *President*
EMP: 2
SALES (est): 396.6K **Privately Held**
SIC: 1389 Oil consultants

(G-9050)
WAR METALS INC
5375 W Canyon Rd (74131-4440)
PHONE..................................918 224-2155
Kim Richards, *President*
Wayne Richards, *Vice Pres*
EMP: 3
SALES (est): 574.3K **Privately Held**
SIC: 3449 Miscellaneous metalwork

(G-9051)
WILBERT FUNERAL SERVICES INC
Also Called: Tulsa Wilbert Vault Co
6505 S 57th West Ave (74131-2408)
PHONE..................................918 446-2131
Gary Mosier, *Sales Mgr*
Rick Pilgrim, *Manager*
Matt Beal, *Manager*
EMP: 25
SQ FT: 21,087
SALES (corp-wide): 9B **Publicly Held**
WEB: www.greensborowilbert.com
SIC: 3272 Burial vaults, concrete or precast terrazzo
HQ: Wilbert Funeral Services, Inc.
10965 Granada Ln Ste 300
Overland Park KS 66211
913 345-2120

(G-9052)
WILSON PRODUCTS INC
8250 S 89th West Ave (74131-3611)
PHONE..................................918 224-1327
Donald Wilson, *President*
EMP: 10
SQ FT: 7,500
SALES (est): 1.2MM **Privately Held**
SIC: 3534 3599 Elevators & moving stairways; machine shop, jobbing & repair

(G-9053)
WIN HY FOODS INC
Also Called: Bil-Jac Pet Foods
8620 S Regency Dr (74131-3625)
PHONE..................................918 227-0004
R J Bingham, *President*
Ray Kelly, *Corp Secy*

William Kelly, *Vice Pres*
EMP: 17
SQ FT: 9,000
SALES (est): 2MM **Privately Held**
SIC: 2047 5191 Dog food; farm supplies

Tulsa
Tulsa County

(G-9054)
2 VICTORY GRAPHICS MEDIA ◆
3207 S Norwood Ave (74135-5409)
PHONE..................................918 394-2665
EMP: 1 EST: 2019
SALES (est): 37.5K **Privately Held**
SIC: 2741 Miscellaneous publishing

(G-9055)
2011 USSA LIMITED PARTNERSHIP
Also Called: US Shooting Academy
6500 E 66th St N (74117-1825)
PHONE..................................918 948-7856
Steven Dixon, *Managing Prtnr*
Charles Peters, *COO*
Patrick Oglesbee, *Opers Staff*
EMP: 11
SQ FT: 8,000
SALES (est): 956K **Privately Held**
SIC: 3949 8211 Shooting equipment & supplies, general; academy

(G-9056)
2012 H & H MANUFACTURING INC (PA)
1711 N Sheridan Rd (74115-4623)
PHONE..................................918 838-0744
Harold Haley, *Owner*
EMP: 6
SQ FT: 3,000
SALES (est): 1.1MM **Privately Held**
WEB: www.hh-mfg.com
SIC: 3599 Machine shop, jobbing & repair

(G-9057)
2012 H & H MANUFACTURING INC
1249 E 29th Pl (74114-5206)
PHONE..................................918 747-7563
William E Foote, *Principal*
EMP: 2 EST: 2012
SALES (est): 96K **Privately Held**
SIC: 3999 Manufacturing industries

(G-9058)
209 LLC
209 N Boulder Ave (74103-1803)
PHONE..................................918 584-9944
Greg Gray, *Owner*
EMP: 4
SALES (est): 214.8K **Privately Held**
SIC: 2741 Miscellaneous publishing

(G-9059)
7B CUSTOM WELDING FABRICATION
4748 S 27th West Ave (74107-7628)
PHONE..................................918 850-1066
EMP: 1 EST: 2014
SALES (est): 51.7K **Privately Held**
SIC: 7692 Welding repair

(G-9060)
918 SCREEN PRINTERS
4155 S Rockford Pl (74105-4045)
PHONE..................................918 850-9542
Jed Krout, *Principal*
EMP: 2
SALES (est): 83.9K **Privately Held**
SIC: 2752 Commercial printing, lithographic

(G-9061)
A & B ENGRAVING INC
Also Called: A&B Identity
2020 E 3rd St (74104-1816)
PHONE..................................918 663-7446
Ann Bogie, *Principal*
Charles Bogie, *Principal*
Mary Scribner, *Accounts Exec*
EMP: 9

▲ = Import ▼ = Export
◆ = Import/Export

SALES (est): 997.1K **Privately Held**
SIC: **5699** 2396 2759 3479 Customized clothing & apparel; screen printing on fabric articles; poster & decal printing & engraving; etching & engraving; advertising, promotional & trade show services; engraving service

(G-9062)
A & M MANUFACTURING CO
1421 S 70th East Ave (74112-6611)
PHONE..................................918 835-2272
Alvin Moss, *Owner*
EMP: 1
SQ FT: 6,752
SALES (est): 107.3K **Privately Held**
SIC: **3599** Machine shop, jobbing & repair

(G-9063)
A & S OPERATING INC
233 S Detroit Ave Ste 200 (74120-2420)
PHONE..................................918 582-7205
Barbara Blackwell, *Principal*
EMP: 3
SALES (est): 246.3K **Privately Held**
SIC: **1382** Geological exploration, oil & gas field

(G-9064)
A & T RESOURCES LLC
5416 S Yale Ave Ste 615 (74135-6249)
PHONE..................................918 582-7894
W H Thompson, *Principal*
EMP: 5
SALES (est): 233.8K **Privately Held**
SIC: **1382** Oil & gas exploration services

(G-9065)
A AND E MANUFACTURING CO
6468 N Yale Ave (74117-2411)
P.O. Box 9457 (74157-0457)
PHONE..................................918 583-7184
Sabra Steele, *General Mgr*
EMP: 12
SALES (est): 1.8MM **Privately Held**
SIC: **3599** Machine shop, jobbing & repair

(G-9066)
A B PRINTING
4109 E 11th St (74112-4117)
PHONE..................................918 834-2054
Anthony R Conwell, *Owner*
EMP: 2 EST: 1975
SQ FT: 1,600
SALES (est): 125K **Privately Held**
SIC: **2752** 2796 2791 2789 Commercial printing, offset; platemaking services; typesetting; bookbinding & related work; commercial printing

(G-9067)
A MAIL CALL SERVICE INC
6915 E 38th St (74145-3202)
PHONE..................................918 610-8533
Joyce Sparks, *President*
EMP: 15
SALES (est): 1.4MM **Privately Held**
SIC: **2542** Postal lock boxes, mail racks & related products

(G-9068)
A PLUS PRINTING INC
1211 S Memorial Dr (74112-6004)
PHONE..................................918 836-8659
John Miller, *President*
Terry Miller, *President*
Annette Miller, *Admin Sec*
EMP: 1
SQ FT: 1,200
SALES (est): 169.7K **Privately Held**
SIC: **2752** 2789 Commercial printing, offset; bookbinding & related work

(G-9069)
A PLUS SCRUBS TO YOU
12012 E 20th Pl (74128-6422)
PHONE..................................918 691-0556
EMP: 2
SALES (est): 137.1K **Privately Held**
SIC: **2844** Toilet preparations

(G-9070)
A Q PRINTING
Also Called: A/Q Printing
7039 E 40th St (74145-4511)
PHONE..................................918 438-1161

Thomas R McHenry, *President*
EMP: 3
SQ FT: 1,200
SALES (est): 250K **Privately Held**
SIC: **2752** 2796 2791 2789 Commercial printing, offset; platemaking services; typesetting; bookbinding & related work

(G-9071)
A X-CEPTIONAL QUALITY DNTL LAB
6333 S Memorial Dr Ste D (74133-1947)
PHONE..................................918 406-1835
Tracy Davis, *Owner*
Brent Davis, *Owner*
EMP: 3
SQ FT: 1,100
SALES (est): 160K **Privately Held**
SIC: **3842** Prosthetic appliances

(G-9072)
A-1 MACHINE SHOP INC
Also Called: The Machine Shop
10312 E 52nd St (74146-5809)
PHONE..................................918 665-0706
Debra Shaw, *President*
Steve Shaw, *Vice Pres*
EMP: 5
SQ FT: 4,000
SALES (est): 717.3K **Privately Held**
SIC: **3599** Machine shop, jobbing & repair

(G-9073)
A-1 SHEET METAL INC
5909 E 15th St (74112-6403)
PHONE..................................918 835-6200
Mike Juliano, *President*
Steve Lemaster, *Clerk*
EMP: 15
SQ FT: 19,000
SALES (est): 3.4MM **Privately Held**
SIC: **3444** Sheet metalwork

(G-9074)
A-ACCURATE WELDING INC
1136 S Hudson Ave (74112-5422)
PHONE..................................918 838-1111
Bill Cleary, *President*
Nathalie Cleary, *Manager*
EMP: 8
SQ FT: 2,700
SALES (est): 300K **Privately Held**
SIC: **7692** 1799 5039 Welding repair; welding on site; prefabricated structures

(G-9075)
A-MAX SIGNS CO
9520 E 55th Pl (74145-8108)
PHONE..................................918 622-0651
Catherine Westbrook, *President*
Marceline M Rorax, *Principal*
Max J Westbrook, *Principal*
Debbie Beatt, *Corp Secy*
Chris Krohn, *Technology*
EMP: 30
SQ FT: 19,000
SALES (est): 6MM **Privately Held**
SIC: **1799** 3993 Sign installation & maintenance; signs & advertising specialties

(G-9076)
A1 VINYL SIGNS LLC
5590 S Garnett Rd (74146-6834)
PHONE..................................918 392-9905
Mike Heaps, *President*
EMP: 6
SQ FT: 2,060
SALES (est): 611.2K **Privately Held**
SIC: **3993** Signs & advertising specialties

(G-9077)
AAA CRIMSTONE OPERATING CO LP
4422 W 49th St (74107-7314)
PHONE..................................918 445-5500
Stephanie Raifsnider, *Principal*
EMP: 4
SALES (est): 286.8K **Privately Held**
SIC: **2448** Pallets, wood

(G-9078)
AAA SIGN & SUPPLY CO
9946 E 21st St (74129-1620)
P.O. Box 9798 (74157-0798)
PHONE..................................918 622-7883

Paul Hachem, *Owner*
EMP: 2
SALES (est): 120K **Privately Held**
SIC: **7311** 3993 Advertising agencies; signs & advertising specialties

(G-9079)
AAON INC (PA)
Also Called: AAON HEATING AND COOLING PRODU
2425 S Yukon Ave (74107-2728)
PHONE..................................918 583-2266
Norman H Asbjornson, *CEO*
Mikel D Crews, *Vice Pres*
Scott M Asbjornson, *CFO*
Rebecca A Thompson, *Treasurer*
Michael Straub, *Prgrmr*
◆ EMP: 7
SQ FT: 15,000
SALES: 469.3MM **Publicly Held**
SIC: **3585** Air conditioning units, complete: domestic or industrial

(G-9080)
AARS
Also Called: Aars Notary and Tax
3171 S 129th East Ave (74134-3205)
PHONE..................................918 313-4512
Millage House, *Owner*
EMP: 5
SALES (est): 54.9K **Privately Held**
SIC: **7291** 7389 5943 3953 Tax return preparation services; notary publics; notary & corporate seals; seal presses, notary & hand; tax refund discounting; billing & bookkeeping service

(G-9081)
ABERDEEN DYNAMICS LLC
Valteccnc
17751 E Admiral Pl (74158)
PHONE..................................918 794-0042
Linda Davis, *Opers Mgr*
EMP: 3
SALES (corp-wide): 3.3MM **Privately Held**
SIC: **3599** Machine shop, jobbing & repair
PA: Aberdeen Dynamics, L.L.C.
17717 E Admiral Pl
Tulsa OK 74158
918 794-0042

(G-9082)
ABLE ENGINEERING SERVICES
227 S 72nd East Ave (74112-1915)
PHONE..................................918 835-3161
EMP: 2
SALES (est): 73.1K **Privately Held**
SIC: **2721** Periodicals

(G-9083)
ABSOLUTE MARKINGS INC
8710 E 41st St (74145-3310)
PHONE..................................918 660-0600
Mark Wiltshire, *Principal*
EMP: 17
SALES (est): 2.5MM **Privately Held**
SIC: **3993** Signs & advertising specialties

(G-9084)
AC SYSTEMS INTEGRATION INC
Also Called: Applied Cntrls Sys Integration
10325 E 58th St (74146-6504)
P.O. Box 471736 (74147-1736)
PHONE..................................918 259-0020
Tim Leger, *President*
Robert Vanskike, *President*
◆ EMP: 20
SQ FT: 26,000
SALES (est): 9.4MM **Privately Held**
SIC: **3823** 8711 5075 5084 Industrial flow & liquid measuring instruments; control engineering; air pollution control equipment & supplies; pollution control equipment, air (environmental); pollution control equipment installation; industrial equipment services

(G-9085)
AC WOODWORKS INC
11223 S Quebec Ave (74137-7506)
PHONE..................................918 298-6948
EMP: 4
SALES (est): 432.2K **Privately Held**
SIC: **2431** Millwork

(G-9086)
AC WOODWORKS INC DBA WOOD
6341 E 41st St (74135-6103)
PHONE..................................918 384-0111
EMP: 1
SALES (est): 54.1K **Privately Held**
SIC: **2431** Millwork

(G-9087)
ACCENT DISPLAYS & GRAPHICS
112 S 109th East Pl (74128-1646)
P.O. Box 801, Salem OH (44460-0801)
PHONE..................................918 437-4338
Irene Barns, *President*
EMP: 2
SALES (est): 193.3K **Privately Held**
SIC: **3993** Signs & advertising specialties

(G-9088)
ACCU CAST
3806 Charles Page Blvd (74127-8033)
PHONE..................................918 582-3466
Thomas Frey, *Owner*
Terry Cisco, *Technician*
EMP: 2
SQ FT: 1,725
SALES: 200K **Privately Held**
WEB: www.accu-cast.com
SIC: **5051** 3365 Steel; aluminum foundries

(G-9089)
ACCURATE MACHINE & MAINTENANCE
1228 S Detroit Ave (74120-4260)
PHONE..................................918 585-1125
Jack Pierce, *President*
Beverly Pierce, *Vice Pres*
EMP: 5
SQ FT: 13,000
SALES (est): 450K **Privately Held**
SIC: **3599** Machine shop, jobbing & repair

(G-9090)
ACCURATE MANUFACTURING INC
2765 Dawson Rd (74110-5035)
PHONE..................................918 582-2585
Tom Hancock, *President*
Don Moore, *Vice Pres*
Rocky Teel, *Vice Pres*
EMP: 32
SQ FT: 70,000
SALES: 8MM **Privately Held**
SIC: **3441** Building components, structural steel

(G-9091)
ACCURUS AEROSPACE CORPORATION (PA)
12716 E Pine St (74116-2033)
PHONE..................................918 438-3121
Jim Gibson, *CEO*
Robert A Kirkpatrick, *President*
Steve Pulliam, *President*
James Garrison, *Purchasing*
Bobby Gravison, *Engineer*
EMP: 5
SALES (est): 149.4MM **Privately Held**
SIC: **3728** Aircraft parts & equipment

(G-9092)
ACCURUS AEROSPACE TULSA LLC
12716 E Pine St (74116-2033)
PHONE..................................918 438-3121
Steve Mosher, *Mng Member*
EMP: 210
SQ FT: 90,000
SALES (est): 61.6MM
SALES (corp-wide): 149.4MM **Privately Held**
SIC: **3728** Aircraft assemblies, subassemblies & parts
PA: Accurus Aerospace Corporation
12716 E Pine St
Tulsa OK 74116
918 438-3121

(G-9093)
ACCUTEC-IHS INC
1408 S Denver Ave (74119-3423)
PHONE..................................918 984-9838

Eric Daley, *President*
William Hill, *Principal*
Minoru Kano, *Principal*
Bruce Levitt, *Principal*
John Tisch, *Principal*
EMP: 3
SQ FT: 1,000
SALES (est): 140.9K **Privately Held**
SIC: 3829 8748 Humidity instruments, except industrial process type; stress, strain & flaw detecting/measuring equipment; gas detectors; environmental consultant; safety training service

(G-9094)
ACE GRINDING
12515 E 11th St (74128-4422)
PHONE.................................918 439-4113
EMP: 2
SALES (est): 94.1K **Privately Held**
SIC: 3999 Custom pulverizing & grinding of plastic materials

(G-9095)
ACE SIGN COMPANY INC
5823 S 65th West Ave (74107-8607)
PHONE.................................918 446-3030
Marilyn Williams, *President*
Ryan Williams, *Vice Pres*
Spike Williams, *Treasurer*
Rickey Gerken, *Admin Sec*
EMP: 2
SALES (est): 409.2K **Privately Held**
SIC: 7532 3993 Truck painting & lettering; signs, not made in custom sign painting shops

(G-9096)
ACME BRICK COMPANY
Also Called: Acme Brick Tile & More
4103 Dawson Rd (74115-4101)
P.O. Box 582590 (74158-2590)
PHONE.................................918 834-3384
Pete Trumbull, *Manager*
EMP: 60
SALES (corp-wide): 327.2B **Publicly Held**
WEB: www.brick.com
SIC: 5211 3251 Brick; tile, ceramic; brick & structural clay tile
HQ: Acme Brick Company
3024 Acme Brick Plz
Fort Worth TX 76109

(G-9097)
ACTION SPRING COMPANY
3003 E Apache St (74110-2232)
P.O. Box 50307 (74150-0307)
PHONE.................................918 836-9000
Rhonda Miller, *CEO*
Gregory Miller, *President*
Norma Jackson, *Corp Secy*
Karen Prickett, *Exec VP*
Debbie Read, *Sales Staff*
EMP: 45
SQ FT: 72,000
SALES (est): 8.3MM **Privately Held**
WEB: www.actionspringco.com
SIC: 3469 3493 5085 3496 Stamping metal for the trade; steel springs, except wire; springs; miscellaneous fabricated wire products; wire springs

(G-9098)
ACTIVE VIOLINIST LLC
2101 S Boston Ave Apt 3 (74114-1155)
PHONE.................................612 532-1829
Hannah Murray, *Principal*
EMP: 2
SALES (est): 83.3K **Privately Held**
SIC: 3931 Violins & parts

(G-9099)
ACTUALIZING APPS LLC
8282 E 33rd Pl (74145-1461)
PHONE.................................918 627-7450
Keith Smith, *Principal*
EMP: 2 **EST:** 2016
SALES (est): 56.5K **Privately Held**
SIC: 7372 Prepackaged software

(G-9100)
ACUREN INSPECTION INC
5208 N Lawton St (74110-9405)
PHONE.................................405 452-3337
Gerald Northcutt, *President*
EMP: 51
SALES (corp-wide): 1.7B **Privately Held**
SIC: 1389 Testing, measuring, surveying & analysis services
HQ: Acuren Inspection, Inc.
30 Main St Ste 402
Danbury CT 06810
203 702-8740

(G-9101)
ADAMS AFFILIATES INC (PA)
1437 S Boulder Ave (74119-3609)
P.O. Box 21470 (74121-1470)
PHONE.................................918 582-7713
Gary C Adams, *President*
K G Adams, *Principal*
W A Hensley, *Principal*
J D Stotts, *Principal*
EMP: 10 **EST:** 1976
SQ FT: 15,000
SALES (est): 8.1MM **Privately Held**
SIC: 6512 1311 5082 7353 Commercial & industrial building operation; crude petroleum production; natural gas production; oil field equipment; oil field equipment, rental or leasing; investment counselors; short-term business credit

(G-9102)
ADAMS ELECTRONICS INC (PA)
1611 S Utica Ave Pmb 408 (74104-4909)
PHONE.................................918 622-5000
Robert E Adams, *President*
Gina Adams, *Vice Pres*
EMP: 4
SQ FT: 3,000
SALES (est): 384.7K **Privately Held**
WEB: www.adamsinc.com
SIC: 3699 3829 Security control equipment & systems; measuring & controlling devices

(G-9103)
ADAPTIVE CORPORATION
4150 S 100th East Ave # 301 (74146-3650)
PHONE.................................440 257-7460
EMP: 2
SALES (est): 88.3K **Privately Held**
SIC: 3621 Motors & generators; electric motor & generator parts

(G-9104)
ADEMCO INC
Also Called: ADI Global Distribution
4731 S Memorial Dr (74145-6904)
PHONE.................................918 663-2822
Marshall Smith, *Sales Staff*
Elizabeth Brady, *Branch Mgr*
EMP: 3
SALES (corp-wide): 4.9B **Publicly Held**
SIC: 5063 3669 3822 Electrical apparatus & equipment; emergency alarms; auto controls regulating residntl & coml environmt & applncs
HQ: Ademco Inc.
1985 Douglas Dr N
Golden Valley MN 55422
800 468-1502

(G-9105)
ADL GROUP LLC
Also Called: Oklahoma Led
10302 E 55th Pl Ste A (74146-6507)
PHONE.................................918 960-0388
Josef Schrader,
Sean Orourke, *Analyst*
EMP: 8
SALES (est): 146.4K **Privately Held**
SIC: 3674 Light emitting diodes

(G-9106)
ADVANCE EQP & CONTRLS LLC
9428 S 68th East Ave (74133-5344)
PHONE.................................918 496-2606
Kenneth Morrow,
EMP: 1
SALES: 40K **Privately Held**
SIC: 3563 Air & gas compressors

(G-9107)
ADVANCED EMC TECHNOLOGIES LLC
5903 S 107th East Ave # 108 (74146-6740)
PHONE.................................918 994-7776
William Vardeman,
EMP: 4
SALES (est): 216K **Privately Held**
SIC: 3053 Gaskets, packing & sealing devices

(G-9108)
ADVANCED GRAPHIC DESIGN
6605 E 19th St Apt A (74112-7317)
PHONE.................................918 960-0407
Rafael Powell, *Owner*
EMP: 2
SALES (est): 73.2K **Privately Held**
SIC: 2759 Commercial printing

(G-9109)
ADVANCED HYDRCRBON STRTIGRAPHY
Also Called: Air and Water
2931 W 21st St (74107-3467)
PHONE.................................918 583-2474
Mike Smith, *CEO*
Janet Haggerty, *Treasurer*
Debra Lee, *Manager*
EMP: 1
SQ FT: 10,000
SALES: 679K **Privately Held**
SIC: 1389 Detection & analysis service, gas

(G-9110)
ADVANCED INDUS DVCS CO LLC (PA)
4323 S Elwood Ave (74107-5833)
PHONE.................................918 445-1254
Russell Claybrook, *CEO*
Mike Nuggett, *Ch of Bd*
Greg Harper, *Vice Pres*
Keith Walker, *Vice Pres*
Christopher Fletcher, *Engineer*
▲ **EMP:** 75
SQ FT: 65,000
SALES (est): 24.7MM **Privately Held**
WEB: www.voyagerspecialtyproducts.com
SIC: 3613 3621 Switchgear & switchboard apparatus; electric motor & generator parts

(G-9111)
ADVANCED RACING COMPOSITES LLC
Also Called: ARC
2720 N Sheridan Rd (74115-2313)
PHONE.................................918 760-9990
Brian Vermillion, *Owner*
Todd Chapman, *Vice Pres*
▲ **EMP:** 2
SALES (est): 168.3K **Privately Held**
SIC: 3714 Motor vehicle body components & frame

(G-9112)
ADVENT AIRCRAFT SYSTEMS INC
8712 S Peoria Ave (74132-2829)
PHONE.................................918 388-5940
Ronald Roberts, *President*
Kennard Goldsmith Jr, *Director*
EMP: 10
SQ FT: 4,500
SALES (est): 820.8K **Privately Held**
SIC: 3492 Control valves, fluid power: hydraulic & pneumatic

(G-9113)
ADVENTURE PUBLISHING LLC
Also Called: Cooper Marketing Solutions
4941 S 78th East Ave (74145-6410)
PHONE.................................918 270-7100
Cheryl Cooper, *Partner*
EMP: 4
SALES (est): 342.2K **Privately Held**
WEB: www.coopermktg.com
SIC: 2741 Miscellaneous publishing

(G-9114)
ADVENTURES IN STITCHING LLC
2821 E 102nd Pl (74137-5650)
PHONE.................................918 995-7445
Audrey Mae Holland, *Principal*
EMP: 1 **EST:** 2011
SALES (est): 54.9K **Privately Held**
SIC: 2395 Embroidery & art needlework

(G-9115)
AERO TECH WELDING
3 S 109th East Pl (74128-1624)
PHONE.................................918 764-9675
EMP: 1
SALES (est): 25K **Privately Held**
SIC: 7692 Welding repair

(G-9116)
AGC MANUFACTORING INC
5853 S Garnett Rd (74146-6812)
PHONE.................................918 258-2506
EMP: 3
SALES (est): 217.2K **Privately Held**
SIC: 3724 Aircraft engines & engine parts

(G-9117)
AGILIS GROUP LLC
7029 E Reading Pl (74115-4670)
P.O. Box 580337 (74158-0337)
PHONE.................................918 584-3553
Donna M Dutton, *Mng Member*
EMP: 28
SALES (est): 4.8MM **Privately Held**
SIC: 3444 Sheet metalwork

(G-9118)
AHMADYS IMPORT LLC
Also Called: Ahmadys Persian Rugs
8027 S Sheridan Rd (74133-8946)
PHONE.................................918 254-4094
Siamak Ahmady, *President*
▲ **EMP:** 6
SQ FT: 5,000
SALES (est): 1MM **Privately Held**
SIC: 2273 Carpets & rugs

(G-9119)
AIR DUCT INC
4434 S Jackson Ave (74107-7041)
PHONE.................................918 445-1196
Gary Tyler, *President*
Scott Tyler, *Vice Pres*
Shirley Ewton, *Admin Sec*
EMP: 15
SQ FT: 13,500
SALES (est): 2.7MM **Privately Held**
SIC: 3441 3444 Fabricated structural metal; ducts, sheet metal

(G-9120)
AIR ELECTRIC INC
7034 S 59th St (74145-8214)
PHONE.................................918 406-3974
EMP: 6 **EST:** 2008
SALES (est): 360K **Privately Held**
SIC: 3585 Mfg Refrigeration/Heating Equipment

(G-9121)
AIR POWER SYSTEMS CO LLC
Also Called: Apsco
8178 E 44th St (74145-4831)
P.O. Box 470948 (74147-0948)
PHONE.................................918 622-5600
Vince Williams, *President*
Ken Thompson, *Vice Pres*
Mark Haney, *Natl Sales Mgr*
Steve Campbell, *Sales Staff*
Robert Sumter, *Manager*
▲ **EMP:** 40 **EST:** 1964
SQ FT: 10,000
SALES (est): 9.9MM **Privately Held**
WEB: www.apscopower.com
SIC: 3443 3494 Cylinders, pressure: metal plate; valves & pipe fittings

(G-9122)
AIR SYSTEMS PUMP SOLUTIONS LLC
1119 N 105th East Pl (74116)
PHONE.................................405 512-5100
Randal C Davis, *Branch Mgr*
EMP: 7
SALES (est): 855.4K **Privately Held**
SIC: 3563 Air & gas compressors
PA: Air Systems And Pump Solutions, Llc
14908 Snta Fe Crssings Dr
Edmond OK 73013

(G-9123)
AIR-X-HEMPHILL LLC
2230 E 49th St Ste D (74105-8780)
PHONE.................................918 712-8268
Ken Jones,

GEOGRAPHIC SECTION

Tulsa - Tulsa County (G-9151)

Nick Breese,
EMP: 8
SALES (est): 842.5K **Privately Held**
SIC: 3443 Heat exchangers, condensers & components

(G-9124)
AIRCRAFT CYLINDERS AMER IINC
1006 E Independence St (74106-5310)
PHONE..................918 582-1785
Rama Palepu, *President*
Karen Soto, *Office Mgr*
EMP: 20
SQ FT: 50,000
SALES (est): 3.3MM **Privately Held**
SIC: 3599 2816 Machine shop, jobbing & repair; chrome pigments: chrome green, chrome yellow, zinc yellow

(G-9125)
AIRCRAFT SPECIALTIES SVC INC
2860 N Sheridan Rd (74115-2304)
P.O. Box 582553 (74158-2553)
PHONE..................918 836-6872
Greg Merrell, *President*
Rick Romans, *Principal*
Velma Sweetapple, *Principal*
Bob Merrell, *Corp Secy*
Vicki Rowland, *Accountant*
▲ **EMP:** 37
SQ FT: 30,000
SALES (est): 8MM **Privately Held**
SIC: 3724 Aircraft engines & engine parts

(G-9126)
AIRCRAFT SYSTEMS
8664 S Peoria Ave Bldg B (74132-2827)
PHONE..................918 388-5943
Ron Roberts, *Vice Pres*
Ron N Roberts, *Manager*
EMP: 7
SALES (est): 1MM **Privately Held**
SIC: 3728 Aircraft parts & equipment

(G-9127)
AIRELECTRIC INC
8815 Airport Way Unit 5 (74132-4014)
P.O. Box 7034 E 59th St (74145)
PHONE..................918 291-7531
David Momquist, *President*
EMP: 3
SQ FT: 3,000
SALES: 450K **Privately Held**
SIC: 4581 3699 Hangar operation; sound signaling devices, electrical

(G-9128)
AIRFLO COOLING TECH LLC
728 S Wheeling Ave (74104-3216)
PHONE..................918 585-5638
Greg Vogt, *Mng Member*
EMP: 35
SQ FT: 50,000
SALES (est): 11.2MM **Privately Held**
SIC: 3564 Blowing fans: industrial or commercial

(G-9129)
AIRFLOW SOLUTIONS LLC
11541 E Pine St (74116-2022)
PHONE..................918 574-2748
Edward Clark,
EMP: 27
SALES (est): 5.8MM **Privately Held**
SIC: 3444 7997 3724 Sheet metalwork; aviation club, membership; air scoops, aircraft

(G-9130)
AIRICO INC
6530 E Independence St (74115-7861)
PHONE..................918 836-2675
Lowell M Tucker, *President*
Roger Tucker, *Vice Pres*
EMP: 3 **EST:** 1965
SQ FT: 1,500
SALES (est): 220K **Privately Held**
SIC: 3599 7699 Grinding castings for the trade; precision instrument repair

(G-9131)
AIRSORCE LLC
1343 N 108th East Ave (74116-5666)
PHONE..................918 519-7520
EMP: 3
SALES (est): 173.6K **Privately Held**
WEB: www.airsorce.com
SIC: 3563 Air & gas compressors

(G-9132)
AIRTECH PRODUCTS INC
1550 S 81st West Ave (74127-7152)
P.O. Box 790, Sand Springs (74063-0790)
PHONE..................918 241-0264
Larry G Miller, *President*
Lea S Miller,
EMP: 37
SQ FT: 23,000
SALES (est): 8.4MM **Privately Held**
SIC: 3446 Louvers, ventilating

(G-9133)
AJT ENTERPRISES INC
Also Called: Premiere Press & Graphics
2727 S Memorial Dr (74129-2610)
PHONE..................918 665-7083
Dirk Hume, *President*
Angie Field, *President*
EMP: 13
SQ FT: 10,500
SALES (est): 2.6MM **Privately Held**
SIC: 2752 2791 7334 2796 Commercial printing, offset; typesetting; photocopying & duplicating services; platemaking services; bookbinding & related work; commercial printing

(G-9134)
ALBERT J GEIGER REVOCABLE TR
3701 S 57th West Ave (74107-4845)
PHONE..................918 446-6388
Albert J Geiger, *Owner*
EMP: 1
SALES (est): 91.5K **Privately Held**
SIC: 1311 Crude petroleum production

(G-9135)
ALL AMERICAN BOTTLING COR
2759 N Garnett Rd (74116-1609)
PHONE..................918 831-3800
Jeff Gunter, *Principal*
EMP: 4
SALES (est): 270.5K **Privately Held**
SIC: 2086 Bottled & canned soft drinks

(G-9136)
ALL AMERICAN BUILDING
11915 E 51st St Ste 25 (74146-6014)
PHONE..................918 249-0515
Jerry Merrill, *Principal*
EMP: 4
SALES (est): 427.8K **Privately Held**
WEB: www.aabpinc.com
SIC: 3448 Prefabricated metal buildings

(G-9137)
ALL SIGNS
16401 E Admiral Pl (74116-3910)
P.O. Box 1887, Catoosa (74015-1887)
PHONE..................918 739-3660
Jeremy Warren, *Mng Member*
EMP: 1
SALES (est): 93.2K **Privately Held**
WEB: www.allsignsok.com
SIC: 3993 Signs, not made in custom sign painting shops

(G-9138)
ALL WOOD PRODUCTS CO INC
538 S Victor Ave (74104-2615)
P.O. Box 4450 (74159-0450)
PHONE..................918 585-9739
Robert Wann, *President*
Cathy Evans, *Vice Pres*
EMP: 20
SQ FT: 20,000
SALES (est): 2.4MM **Privately Held**
SIC: 2541 2431 Cabinets, except refrigerated: show, display, etc.: wood; millwork

(G-9139)
ALLAN EDWARDS INCORPORATED (PA)
6468 N Yale Ave (74117-2411)
PHONE..................918 583-7184
Scotty Edwards, *President*
Allan Edwards III, *President*
John Disher, *Vice Pres*
Allan Edwards Jr, *Treasurer*
◆ **EMP:** 3
SALES (est): 5MM **Privately Held**
SIC: 3272 Concrete products, precast

(G-9140)
ALLEGRA MARKETING PRINT MAIL
7497 E 46th Pl Ste 1 (74145-6305)
PHONE..................539 302-2229
EMP: 2 **EST:** 2018
SALES (est): 118.8K **Privately Held**
SIC: 2752 Commercial printing, offset

(G-9141)
ALLEN SHEET METAL INC
8724 E 11th St (74112-7952)
PHONE..................918 834-2279
Bret Allen, *President*
Bryan Allen, *Vice Pres*
EMP: 6
SQ FT: 3,200
SALES (est): 500K **Privately Held**
SIC: 3444 Sheet metal specialties, not stamped

(G-9142)
ALLIANCE COAL LLC (DH)
1717 S Boulder Ave # 400 (74119-4833)
P.O. Box 22027 (74121-2027)
PHONE..................918 295-7600
Robert G Sachse, *Exec VP*
Brian L Cantrell, *Senior VP*
R Eberley Davis, *Senior VP*
Thomas M Wynne, *Senior VP*
Kevin J Larkin, *Vice Pres*
▼ **EMP:** 88 **EST:** 1999
SQ FT: 25,000
SALES (est): 1.7B **Publicly Held**
SIC: 1221 1222 Bituminous coal surface mining; coal preparation plant, bituminous or lignite; bituminous coal-underground mining

(G-9143)
ALLIANCE HOLDINGS GP LP (PA)
1717 S Boulder Ave # 400 (74119-4805)
P.O. Box 22027 (74121-2027)
PHONE..................918 295-1415
Joseph W Craft III, *Ch of Bd*
David Gilbert, *President*
Alliance GP, *General Ptnr*
Brian L Cantrell, *CFO*
EMP: 190
SALES: 1.8B **Publicly Held**
SIC: 1221 1222 Bituminous coal & lignite-surface mining; bituminous coal-underground mining

(G-9144)
ALLIANCE MACHINE SERVICE INC
1151 N Delaware Pl (74110-5100)
P.O. Box 4825 (74159-0825)
PHONE..................918 836-5588
Jeff Parks, *President*
EMP: 6
SALES (est): 727.8K **Privately Held**
WEB: www.alliancemachineservice.com
SIC: 3599 Machine shop, jobbing & repair

(G-9145)
ALLIANCE RESOURCE FINANCE CORP
1717 S Boulder Ave # 400 (74119-4805)
PHONE..................918 295-1415
EMP: 2
SALES (est): 66K **Privately Held**
SIC: 1221 Bituminous coal & lignite-surface mining

(G-9146)
ALLIANCE RESOURCE HOLDINGS INC (PA)
1717 S Boulder Ave Fl 6 (74119-4805)
P.O. Box 22027 (74121-2027)
PHONE..................918 295-7600
Joseph W Craft III, *Mng Member*
EMP: 3
SQ FT: 25,000
SALES (est): 159MM **Privately Held**
SIC: 1221 1222 Bituminous coal surface mining; coal preparation plant, bituminous or lignite; bituminous coal-underground mining

(G-9147)
ALLIANCE RESOURCE PARTNERS LP (HQ)
1717 S Boulder Ave # 400 (74119-4805)
PHONE..................918 295-7600
Joseph W Craft III, *Ch of Bd*
Kendall Barret, *Vice Pres*
Brian L Cantrell, *CFO*
Brian Cantrell, *CFO*
Robert J Fouch, *Officer*
EMP: 179
SALES: 1.9B **Publicly Held**
SIC: 1221 1222 1241 Coal preparation plant, bituminous or lignite; bituminous coal-underground mining; coal mining services

(G-9148)
ALLIANCE RSRCE OPER PRTNERS LP (DH)
1717 S Boulder Ave # 600 (74119-4805)
PHONE..................918 295-7600
Joseph W Craft III, *Principal*
EMP: 1
SALES (est): 1.2B **Publicly Held**
SIC: 1221 Bituminous coal & lignite-surface mining
HQ: Alliance Resource Partners Lp
1717 S Boulder Ave # 400
Tulsa OK 74119
918 295-7600

(G-9149)
ALLIANCE WOR PROPERTIES LLC
1717 S Boulder Ave # 400 (74119-4805)
PHONE..................918 295-7600
EMP: 46 **EST:** 2017
SALES (est): 1.5MM **Publicly Held**
SIC: 1221 Bituminous coal & lignite-surface mining
HQ: Alliance Resource Partners Lp
1717 S Boulder Ave # 400
Tulsa OK 74119
918 295-7600

(G-9150)
ALLIED MANUFACTURING TECH
1424 S Knoxville Ave (74112-5808)
PHONE..................918 899-9504
Harley Smith, *President*
EMP: 1
SALES (est): 69.7K **Privately Held**
SIC: 3339 Primary nonferrous metals

(G-9151)
ALLIED MOTION TECHNOLOGIES INC
10002 E 43rd St (74146-3657)
P.O. Box 470009 (74147-0009)
PHONE..................918 627-1845
Brad Jones, *Opers Mgr*
Derek Ward, *Opers Mgr*
David Hawes, *Engineer*
Rick Sakalys, *Regl Sales Mgr*
Richard S Warzala, *Branch Mgr*
EMP: 15
SALES (corp-wide): 371MM **Publicly Held**
WEB: www.alliedmotion.com
SIC: 3621 Motors, electric
PA: Allied Motion Technologies Inc.
495 Commerce Dr Ste 3
Amherst NY 14228
716 242-8634

Tulsa - Tulsa County (G-9152) — GEOGRAPHIC SECTION

(G-9152)
ALPHA COMBUSTION LLC
2206 E 24th St (74114-2912)
PHONE...................918 851-1751
Pawel Mosiewicz,
◆ EMP: 1
SQ FT: 1,000
SALES: 100K Privately Held
SIC: 3433 Gas burners, industrial

(G-9153)
ALPHA INVESTMENT CASTING CORP (PA)
6160 S New Haven Ave (74136-1508)
PHONE...................918 834-4686
Dell Frazier, President
EMP: 21
SQ FT: 20,000
SALES (est): 5.3MM Privately Held
SIC: 3324 3364 3325 Steel investment foundries; copper & copper alloy die-castings; steel foundries

(G-9154)
ALPHA INVESTMENT CASTING LLC
6160 S New Haven Ave (74136-1508)
PHONE...................918 834-4686
EMP: 28
SALES (corp-wide): 5.3MM Privately Held
SIC: 3364 Copper & copper alloy die-castings
PA: Alpha Investment Casting Corporation
6160 S New Haven Ave
Tulsa OK 74136
918 834-4686

(G-9155)
ALPHA MACHINING & MFG INC
Also Called: Lou Ann Amstutz
1604 N 161st East Ave (74116-4823)
PHONE...................918 438-2755
Andy Amstutz, President
Lou Ann Amstutz, Vice Pres
EMP: 15
SQ FT: 8,500
SALES (est): 2.8MM Privately Held
WEB: www.alphamachining.net
SIC: 3599 Machine shop, jobbing & repair

(G-9156)
ALRO STEEL CORPORATION
4321 N Garnett Rd (74116-5202)
PHONE...................918 439-1000
John Rumler, Principal
Greg Clanton, Sales Mgr
EMP: 11
SALES (corp-wide): 2.2B Privately Held
SIC: 5051 3541 Steel; machine tool replacement & repair parts, metal cutting types
PA: Alro Steel Corporation
3100 E High St
Jackson MI 49203
517 787-5500

(G-9157)
ALTMAN ENERGY INC
15 W 6th St Ste 2301 (74119-5401)
PHONE...................918 584-4781
Ronny G Altman, President
Sheila Butler, Treasurer
EMP: 3
SQ FT: 2,000
SALES (est): 500K Privately Held
SIC: 1311 Crude petroleum production; natural gas production

(G-9158)
ALVIN STONE
2404 W 41st St (74107-6532)
PHONE...................918 447-4455
Wesley Nelson, Owner
EMP: 2
SALES (est): 169.3K Privately Held
SIC: 3299 Architectural sculptures: gypsum, clay, papier mache, etc.

(G-9159)
ALWAYS BLESSED
552 N 28th West Pl (74127)
PHONE...................918 592-2200
Janice Kelley, Principal
EMP: 3

SALES (est): 207.2K Privately Held
SIC: 3999 Hair curlers, designed for beauty parlors

(G-9160)
AMARILLO CHITTOM AIRSLO
728 S Wheeling Ave (74104-3216)
PHONE...................918 585-5638
Bill Emil, Principal
William Immell, Research
Mike Rush, Controller
Rick Lopez, Sales Mgr
EMP: 50 EST: 1957
SALES: 3.1MM
SALES (corp-wide): 327.2B Publicly Held
SIC: 3443 3089 3564 3442 Heat exchangers: coolers (after, inter), condensers, etc.; plastic hardware & building products; blowers & fans; metal doors, sash & trim
HQ: Amarillo Gear Company Llc
2401 W Sundown Ln
Amarillo TX 79118
806 622-1273

(G-9161)
AMERACRANE AND HOIST LLC
16645 Eastpark St (74116)
P.O. Box 1467, Owasso (74055-1467)
PHONE...................918 437-4775
Steve Miller,
Bill Evans,
David Miller,
EMP: 21
SQ FT: 12,000
SALES (est): 3.8MM Privately Held
SIC: 8742 3536 Materials mgmt. (purchasing, handling, inventory) consultant; cranes & monorail systems; cranes, industrial plant; cranes, overhead traveling

(G-9162)
AMERCOOL MANUFACTURING CO INC (PA)
Also Called: AMI
6312 S 39th West Ave (74132-1237)
P.O. Box 571330 (74157-1330)
PHONE...................918 445-5366
Judith A Smith, Ch of Bd
Wayne Pyle, President
Susan Lawrence, Corp Secy
EMP: 65
SQ FT: 20,000
SALES (est): 6.3MM Privately Held
SIC: 3443 Heat exchangers: coolers (after, inter), condensers, etc.

(G-9163)
AMERICAN AIRLINES INC
3900 N Mingo Rd (74116-5000)
PHONE...................918 292-2698
Erik Olund, Managing Dir
EMP: 5200
SALES (corp-wide): 45.7B Publicly Held
SIC: 4581 3724 Airport terminal services; aircraft engines & engine parts
HQ: American Airlines, Inc.
1 Skyview Dr
Fort Worth TX 76155
817 963-1234

(G-9164)
AMERICAN ASSN PETRO GEOLOGISTS (PA)
Also Called: Aapg
1444 S Boulder Ave (74119-3604)
P.O. Box 979 (74101-0979)
PHONE...................918 584-2555
Lee Krystinic, President
Joetta Cox, General Mgr
Sandra K Paskvan, COO
John Kaldi, Vice Pres
Deborah K Sacrey, Treasurer
EMP: 64
SQ FT: 8,890
SALES: 12.9MM Privately Held
SIC: 8731 8621 2721 Commercial physical research; professional membership organizations; periodicals

(G-9165)
AMERICAN BEAUTY MANUFACTURING
1623 E Apache St (74106-4006)
PHONE...................918 671-0351
Larry H Cardwell Jr, President
EMP: 8
SALES (est): 1.1MM Privately Held
SIC: 2844 Toilet preparations

(G-9166)
AMERICAN CRATING COMPANY
11343 E Tecumseh St (74116-1602)
PHONE...................918 425-8787
Jeff Park, President
Jim Cooper, General Mgr
Carol Park, Corp Secy
▼ EMP: 30 EST: 1975
SQ FT: 35,000
SALES (est): 6.2MM Privately Held
SIC: 2441 Shipping cases, wood: nailed or lock corner

(G-9167)
AMERICAN INDUSTRIAL INC
1218 W 41st St Ste B (74107-7031)
PHONE...................918 445-0627
EMP: 2
SQ FT: 5,000
SALES (est): 210K Privately Held
SIC: 2851 Mfg Paints/Allied Products

(G-9168)
AMERICAN LASER INC
5138 S 94th East Ave (74145-8172)
PHONE...................918 234-9700
Bernie Susman, Principal
EMP: 5
SALES (est): 443.2K Privately Held
SIC: 3577 Computer peripheral equipment

(G-9169)
AMERICAN MARBLE
3815 Charles Page Blvd (74127-8032)
PHONE...................918 812-7940
Eloy Lopez, Partner
EMP: 2
SALES (est): 160K Privately Held
SIC: 3281 Marble, building: cut & shaped

(G-9170)
AMERICAN MFG CO OF OKLA
1025 W 41st St (74107-7026)
PHONE...................918 446-1968
Robert M Hunter, President
Linda Hunter, Admin Sec
EMP: 20
SQ FT: 6,000
SALES (est): 1.7MM Privately Held
SIC: 3599 Machine shop, jobbing & repair

(G-9171)
AMERICAN PIPE BENDING INC
Also Called: American Pipe Bending Company
3207 Dawson Rd (74110-5111)
PHONE...................918 749-2363
Larry Houston, President
▲ EMP: 29
SQ FT: 30,000
SALES (est): 8.6MM Privately Held
SIC: 3498 Tube fabricating (contract bending & shaping)

(G-9172)
AMERICAN SPORTSWEAR INC
7636 E 46th St (74145-6304)
P.O. Box 35157 (74153-0157)
PHONE...................918 665-7636
James Maness, President
Judy Maness, Corp Secy
EMP: 6 EST: 1977
SQ FT: 12,000
SALES (est): 402.5K Privately Held
SIC: 2396 5136 Screen printing on fabric articles; sportswear, men's & boys'

(G-9173)
AMERICAN TANK & CNSTR CO
1451 N Fulton Ave (74115-5319)
P.O. Box 580994 (74158-0994)
PHONE...................918 254-6292
John Michael Hess, President
Patrick M Hess, Corp Secy
Matt Hess, Manager

EMP: 8
SQ FT: 13,000
SALES (est): 1.3MM Privately Held
SIC: 3443 3441 Tanks, lined: metal plate; fabricated structural metal

(G-9174)
AMERICAN TRADITION
5834 S 129th East Ave (74134-6705)
PHONE...................918 688-7725
Dwain Boren, Principal
EMP: 3
SALES (est): 239.9K Privately Held
SIC: 2759 5199 7319 Screen printing; nondurable goods; advertising

(G-9175)
AMERICAN TRADITIONS CLOTHING
Also Called: Brennan Properties
10306 E 52nd St (74146-5809)
PHONE...................918 622-8337
Mary Ellen Brennan, President
Peter Brennan, Vice Pres
EMP: 5
SQ FT: 4,440
SALES (est): 479.5K Privately Held
SIC: 2759 Screen printing

(G-9176)
AMERIFLEX HOSE AND ACC LLC
12940 E Admiral Pl (74116-2119)
P.O. Box 690595 (74169-0595)
PHONE...................918 437-7002
Corvan Robison,
EMP: 9
SALES (est): 1.4MM Privately Held
SIC: 3492 Hose & tube fittings & assemblies, hydraulic/pneumatic

(G-9177)
AMERIGLOBE LLC
1887 E 71st St (74136-3922)
PHONE...................918 496-7711
Randy Girouard, CFO
EMP: 49 Privately Held
SIC: 3089 Plastic containers, except foam
PA: Ameriglobe, Llc
153 S Long St
Lafayette LA 70506

(G-9178)
AMERIPUMP MFG LLC
13759 E Apache St (74116-1408)
PHONE...................918 438-2953
Tyrrell Brooks, Mng Member
EMP: 4
SQ FT: 10,000
SALES (est): 580.8K Privately Held
SIC: 3443 7699 5013 5084 Tanks for tank trucks, metal plate; pumps & pumping equipment repair; pumps, oil & gas; industrial machinery & equipment

(G-9179)
AMERISTAR PRIMETER SEC USA INC (HQ)
Also Called: Assa Abloy Group Company
1555 N Mingo Rd (74116-1506)
P.O. Box 581000 (74158-1000)
PHONE...................918 835-0898
Mark Meek, President
Barry Willingham, Vice Pres
Dembie Moss, Opers Staff
John Stacy, Opers Staff
Eric Phillips, Engineer
EMP: 26
SQ FT: 850,000
SALES (est): 122.4MM
SALES (corp-wide): 9.3B Privately Held
SIC: 3089 3446 1799 Fences, gates & accessories: plastic; fences, gates, posts & flagpoles; fence construction
PA: Assa Abloy Ab
Klarabergsviadukten 90
Stockholm 111 6
850 648-500

(G-9180)
AMERON INTERNATIONAL CORP
4903 E 66th St N (74117-1817)
PHONE...................918 858-3973
Greg Baird, Manager

▲ = Import ▼ = Export
◆ = Import/Export

GEOGRAPHIC SECTION

Tulsa - Tulsa County (G-9209)

EMP: 104
SALES (corp-wide): 8.4B **Publicly Held**
SIC: 3272 Cylinder pipe, prestressed or pretensioned concrete
HQ: Ameron International Corporation
7909 Parkwood Circle Dr
Houston TX 77036
713 375-3700

(G-9181)
AMERON POLE PRODUCTS LLC
2333 S Yukon Ave (74107-2760)
PHONE...............................918 585-5611
Wayne Liechti, *Mng Member*
EMP: 21
SALES (est): 4MM
SALES (corp-wide): 8.4B **Publicly Held**
SIC: 3272 Poles & posts, concrete
PA: National Oilwell Varco, Inc.
7909 Parkwood Circle Dr
Houston TX 77036
713 346-7500

(G-9182)
AMS MACHINING SPECIALISTS LLC
7400 E 42nd Pl (74145-4702)
PHONE...............................918 610-2570
Britt Radford, *CEO*
EMP: 3
SALES (est): 325.9K **Privately Held**
SIC: 3599 Machine shop, jobbing & repair

(G-9183)
ANADARKO DOZER AND TRCKG LLC
1869 E 71st St (74136-3922)
PHONE...............................918 496-4777
EMP: 1
SALES (corp-wide): 7.3MM **Privately Held**
SIC: 1389 Oil field services
PA: Anadarko Dozer And Trucking, L.L.C.
1121 S Main St
Elk City OK 73644
580 243-0466

(G-9184)
ANCHOR GASOLINE CORPORATION (PA)
2847 E 36th Pl (74105-3607)
PHONE...............................918 584-5291
Betty Ann Mockley, *President*
Michael E Mockley, *COO*
C Cooke Newman, *VP Finance*
Wanda McCreedy, *Admin Sec*
EMP: 90
SQ FT: 17,000
SALES (est): 6MM **Privately Held**
SIC: 5411 2911 Convenience stores; petroleum refining

(G-9185)
ANCHOR PAINT MFG CO (PA)
6707 E 14th St (74112-6615)
P.O. Box 1305 (74101-1305)
PHONE...............................918 836-4626
Roy Blair Meade, *CEO*
Charles Taylor, *President*
Carter Beuttel, *Vice Pres*
Toby Wood, *Opers Mgr*
Gary Lollis, *Mfg Staff*
▲ **EMP:** 65 **EST:** 1962
SQ FT: 60,000
SALES (est): 25MM **Privately Held**
WEB: www.anchorpaint.com
SIC: 2851 2842 Paints & allied products; specialty cleaning, polishes & sanitation goods

(G-9186)
ANCHOR STONE CO (PA)
4124 S Rockford Ave # 201 (74105-4248)
PHONE...............................918 599-7255
Joseph L Parker Jr, *Ch of Bd*
Joseph L Parker Sr, *Vice Ch Bd*
Scott Hughes, *Vice Pres*
Kevin McKean, *Vice Pres*
David Delozier, *Plant Mgr*
EMP: 14 **EST:** 1959
SQ FT: 5,000
SALES (est): 81.4MM **Privately Held**
WEB: www.anchor-stone.com
SIC: 1422 Limestones, ground

(G-9187)
ANCHOR STONE CO
11302 S Delaware Ave (74137)
PHONE...............................918 299-6384
Tom Snyder, *President*
EMP: 1
SALES (corp-wide): 81.4MM **Privately Held**
SIC: 1422 Limestones, ground
PA: Anchor Stone Co.
4124 S Rockford Ave # 201
Tulsa OK 74105
918 599-7255

(G-9188)
ANCHOR STONE CO
66 St N North (74137)
PHONE...............................918 438-1060
Tom Snyder, *Branch Mgr*
EMP: 75
SALES (corp-wide): 81.4MM **Privately Held**
SIC: 1422 Crushed & broken limestone
PA: Anchor Stone Co.
4124 S Rockford Ave # 201
Tulsa OK 74105
918 599-7255

(G-9189)
ANDREA KOENIG
2892 E 51st St Apt D (74105-1730)
PHONE...............................918 745-0828
Andrea Koenig, *Partner*
EMP: 2
SALES (est): 52.5K **Privately Held**
SIC: 2731 Book publishing

(G-9190)
ANDREWS WOODWORKING
14217 E 33rd St (74134-4430)
PHONE...............................918 664-6722
Andrew Ziegler, *Principal*
EMP: 1 **EST:** 2017
SALES (est): 54.1K **Privately Held**
WEB: www.andrewswoodworking.com
SIC: 2431 Millwork

(G-9191)
ANGEL ORNAMENTAL IRON WORKS
1407 E 6th St (74120-4023)
PHONE...............................918 584-8726
Ernie Martin, *Owner*
EMP: 6
SQ FT: 6,700
SALES (est): 586.1K **Privately Held**
SIC: 3446 3496 3442 2514 Architectural metalwork; miscellaneous fabricated wire products; metal doors, sash & trim; metal household furniture

(G-9192)
ANGUS NATURAL RESOURCES LLC
2 W 2nd St Ste 1700 (74103-3100)
PHONE...............................918 712-8487
Charles Stephenson,
EMP: 4
SALES (est): 340.1K **Privately Held**
SIC: 1381 Directional drilling oil & gas wells

(G-9193)
ANTOINETTE BAKING CO LLC
207 N Main St (74103-2005)
PHONE...............................918 808-0875
Antoinette Llempicki, *Principal*
EMP: 5
SALES (est): 346K **Privately Held**
SIC: 2051 Bread, cake & related products

(G-9194)
ANYWHERE INFLTABLE SCREENS LLC
6908 E 64th Pl (74133-4001)
PHONE...............................918 260-4146
Mark Smith, *Owner*
EMP: 2
SALES (est): 141.1K **Privately Held**
SIC: 3069 Life jackets, inflatable: rubberized fabric

(G-9195)
APAC-CENTRAL INC
4608 S Garnett Rd Ste 600 (74146-5226)
PHONE...............................918 921-6491
EMP: 2
SALES (corp-wide): 30.6B **Privately Held**
WEB: www.contractorsofarkansas.com
SIC: 3273 Ready-mixed concrete
HQ: Apac-Central, Inc.
755 E Millsap Rd
Fayetteville AR 72703

(G-9196)
APACHE MACHINE CO INC
4316 E Pine Pl (74115-4148)
PHONE...............................918 834-0022
Owen Campbell, *President*
Mark Giddens, *Vice Pres*
EMP: 7
SQ FT: 4,000
SALES: 700K **Privately Held**
SIC: 3599 3541 Machine shop, jobbing & repair; machine tools, metal cutting type

(G-9197)
APC LLC
1307 S Boulder Ave # 400 (74119-9700)
PHONE...............................918 587-6242
Thomas P Schroedter,
EMP: 6 **EST:** 2003
SALES (est): 416.6K **Privately Held**
SIC: 1311 Crude petroleum production

(G-9198)
APERGY ARTFL LIFT INTL LLC
Also Called: Norris Rods
4801 W 49th St (74107-7321)
P.O. Box 1496 (74101-1496)
PHONE...............................432 561-8101
Todd Crandell, *Branch Mgr*
EMP: 250
SALES (corp-wide): 1.1B **Publicly Held**
SIC: 3533 Oil field machinery & equipment
HQ: Apergy Artificial Lift International, Llc
2445 Tech Frest Blvd Ste
Spring TX 77381
281 403-5742

(G-9199)
APPLETON GRP LLC
Nelson Firestop Products
9810 E 42nd St Ste 102 (74146-3675)
P.O. Box 726 (74101-0708)
PHONE...............................918 627-5530
Dusty Brown, *General Mgr*
EMP: 10
SALES (corp-wide): 18.3B **Publicly Held**
WEB: www.emerson.com
SIC: 3823 Industrial instrmnts msrmnt display/control process variable
HQ: Appleton Grp Llc
9377 W Higgins Rd
Rosemont IL 60018
847 268-6000

(G-9200)
APPLIED LASER SYSTEMS
Also Called: Cartridge Smart
7110 S Mingo Rd Ste 105 (74133-3273)
PHONE...............................918 249-9025
Josh O'Leary, *Principal*
EMP: 4 **EST:** 1997
SALES (est): 371.1K **Privately Held**
WEB: www.cartridge-smart.com
SIC: 2893 Printing ink

(G-9201)
APSCO INC
8178 E 44th St (74145-4831)
P.O. Box 470948 (74147-0948)
PHONE...............................918 622-5600
William W Cole, *Principal*
Chris Wunsch, *Vice Pres*
Tim Stewart, *Production*
Frank Horn, *Engineer*
Melissa Lockhart, *Human Res Dir*
EMP: 2
SALES (est): 156K **Privately Held**
SIC: 3593 Fluid power cylinders & actuators

(G-9202)
ARC DOCUMENT SOLUTIONS LLC
7022 E 41st St (74145-4515)
PHONE...............................918 663-8100
Darin Garner, *Branch Mgr*
EMP: 20
SALES (corp-wide): 382.4MM **Publicly Held**
WEB: www.riotcolor.com
SIC: 7334 2759 Blueprinting service; commercial printing
HQ: Arc Document Solutions, Llc
6300 Gulfton St
Houston TX 77081
713 988-9200

(G-9203)
ARC-ANGEL WELDING
5961 E 12th St (74112-5479)
PHONE...............................918 838-0047
Alfred J Karleskint, *Owner*
EMP: 1 **EST:** 1962
SQ FT: 5,200
SALES: 25K **Privately Held**
SIC: 7692 Welding repair

(G-9204)
ARCHITECTURAL PAV SYSTEMS LLC
3220 E 27th Pl (74114-5712)
PHONE...............................918 747-9302
David C De Angelis, *Principal*
EMP: 4
SALES (est): 508.4K **Privately Held**
SIC: 3272 Concrete products

(G-9205)
ARCHROCK INC
5727 S Lewis Ave Ste 610 (74105-7147)
PHONE...............................918 900-4200
Mike Redding, *Vice Pres*
EMP: 1 **Publicly Held**
SIC: 1389 5084 Gas compressing (natural gas) at the fields; petroleum industry machinery
PA: Archrock, Inc.
9807 Katy Fwy Ste 100
Houston TX 77024

(G-9206)
ARCOSA WIND TOWERS INC
15300 Tiger Switch Rd (74116-2700)
PHONE...............................918 560-4911
Kerry Cole, *President*
EMP: 3
SALES (corp-wide): 1.7B **Publicly Held**
SIC: 3441 Fabricated structural metal
HQ: Arcosa Wind Towers, Inc.
500 N Akard St
Dallas TX 75201
972 942-6500

(G-9207)
ARENA RESOURCES INC
6555 S Lewis Ave (74136-1010)
P.O. Box 108827, Oklahoma City (73101-8827)
PHONE...............................918 747-6060
Fax: 918 747-7620
EMP: 71
SALES (est): 6.9MM
SALES (corp-wide): 768.7MM **Privately Held**
SIC: 1311 1382 Crude Petroleum And Natural Gas Production And Exploration
PA: Sandridge Energy, Inc.
123 Robert S Kerr Ave
Oklahoma City OK 73102
405 429-5500

(G-9208)
ARKANSAS RIVER PRESS
223 E 25th St (74114-2611)
PHONE...............................918 744-1730
Philip Bruns, *Principal*
EMP: 2
SALES (est): 44.3K **Privately Held**
SIC: 2741 Miscellaneous publishing

(G-9209)
ARMOR ENERGY LLC
4500 S Garnett Rd Ste 250 (74146-5203)
PHONE...............................918 986-9459
Justin Allison, *Engineer*

Tulsa - Tulsa County (G-9210) GEOGRAPHIC SECTION

Stephen Gressett,
Jim Wilson,
EMP: 9
SQ FT: 5,500
SALES (est): 1MM **Privately Held**
SIC: 1382 Oil & gas exploration services

(G-9210)
ARP SEBREE SOUTH LLC
1717 S Boulder Ave # 400 (74119-4805)
PHONE..................918 295-1415
EMP: 35 **EST:** 2017
SALES (est): 72.6K **Publicly Held**
SIC: 1221 Bituminous coal & lignite-surface mining
PA: Alliance Holdings Gp, L.P.
1717 S Boulder Ave # 400
Tulsa OK 74119

(G-9211)
ARROW ENGINE COMPANY (HQ)
2301 E Independence St (74110-4937)
PHONE..................918 583-5711
Len Turner, *President*
Cathy Covington, *Materials Mgr*
Jeff Rusiewicz, *CFO*
Jarrell Delk, *Manager*
▲ **EMP:** 80 **EST:** 1955
SQ FT: 130,000
SALES (est): 25.9MM
SALES (corp-wide): 723.5MM **Publicly Held**
WEB: www.arrowengine.com
SIC: 3563 3443 3519 Air & gas compressors; industrial vessels, tanks & containers; parts & accessories, internal combustion engines
PA: Trimas Corporation
38505 Woodward Ave # 200
Bloomfield Hills MI 48304
248 631-5450

(G-9212)
ARROW TOOL & GAGE CO INC
14323 E Marshall St (74116-2136)
PHONE..................918 438-3600
Mary Chesser, *President*
Wayne Chesser, *Vice Pres*
EMP: 16 **EST:** 1976
SQ FT: 19,000
SALES (est): 4MM **Privately Held**
SIC: 3544 3469 Special dies & tools; metal stampings

(G-9213)
ARROWHEAD SOFTWARE
4624 E 24th St (74114-3612)
P.O. Box 14222 (74159-1222)
PHONE..................918 744-7239
Rick Rada, *Principal*
EMP: 2
SALES (est): 160.2K **Privately Held**
SIC: 7372 Business oriented computer software

(G-9214)
ART OF MANLINESS LLC
4115 E 86th St (74137-2615)
PHONE..................405 613-3340
Brett McKay, *Owner*
Jeremy Anderberg, *Manager*
EMP: 1
SALES (est): 61.6K **Privately Held**
WEB: www.artofmanliness.com
SIC: 2741 Miscellaneous publishing

(G-9215)
ASC INC
Also Called: Advanced Steel & Crane, Inc.
6420 S 39th West Ave (74132-1245)
P.O. Box 9187 (74157-0187)
PHONE..................918 445-0260
Shyamal Ganguly, *President*
EMP: 44
SQ FT: 20,000
SALES: 8MM **Privately Held**
SIC: 3612 3441 Voltage regulators, transmission & distribution; fabricated structural metal; tower sections, radio & television transmission

(G-9216)
ASPECT OILFIELD SERVICES LLC
1803 E 17th St (74104-5304)
PHONE..................504 812-5330
Douglas Swift Jr, *Principal*
EMP: 3 **EST:** 2016
SALES (est): 631K **Privately Held**
SIC: 1382 Oil & gas exploration services

(G-9217)
ASSOCIATED LITHOGRAPHING CO
6580 E Skelly Dr (74145-1324)
PHONE..................918 663-9091
Kendall Minnix, *President*
Carol Minnix, *Corp Secy*
Herb Kelley, *Purchasing*
EMP: 21 **EST:** 1967
SQ FT: 13,000
SALES (est): 219.7K **Privately Held**
SIC: 2752 2791 2759 Commercial printing, offset; typesetting; commercial printing

(G-9218)
ASSOCIATED RESOURCES INC
15 E 5th St Ste 200 (74103-4323)
PHONE..................918 584-2111
Jeff Myers, *President*
Bill Harwell, *Vice Pres*
Charlie Hancock, *CFO*
EMP: 45 **EST:** 1993
SQ FT: 8,000
SALES (est): 3.9MM **Privately Held**
SIC: 1382 8742 Oil & gas exploration services; management consulting services

(G-9219)
ASSOCTED WIRE ROPE FABRICATORS
1369 S Garnett Rd (74128-1826)
PHONE..................918 234-7450
Buck Willis, *President*
EMP: 2
SALES (est): 168K **Privately Held**
SIC: 5051 3496 Rope, wire (not insulated); miscellaneous fabricated wire products

(G-9220)
AT&L RESOURCES LLC
2900 E Apache St (74110-2253)
PHONE..................918 925-0154
Allen Cameron, *President*
EMP: 15
SALES (corp-wide): 105MM **Privately Held**
SIC: 2759 Labels & seals: printing
HQ: At&L Resources, Llc
444 W Interstate Rd
Addison IL 60101
918 925-0154

(G-9221)
ATALAYA RESOURCES
15 E 5th St (74103-4346)
PHONE..................918 949-4551
EMP: 2
SALES (est): 92.5K **Privately Held**
SIC: 1389 Building oil & gas well foundations on site

(G-9222)
ATLAS PIPELINE MID-CONTINENT W
110 W 7th St Ste 2300 (74119-1017)
PHONE..................918 574-3500
Eugene N Dubay, *President*
Robert Firth,
Atlas Pipeline Mid-Continent L,
EMP: 350
SALES (est): 11.8MM **Publicly Held**
SIC: 1389 Processing service, gas
HQ: Targa Pipeline Partners Lp
1000 Commerce Dr Ste 400
Pittsburgh PA 15275
877 950-7473

(G-9223)
AURYN CREATIVE
1315 E 6th St (74120-4021)
PHONE..................918 876-0974
Carlos Moreno, *Owner*
EMP: 1
SALES: 12K **Privately Held**
SIC: 2731 Book publishing

(G-9224)
AUSTIN POWDER CO
3122 N Mingo Valley Expy (74116-1209)
P.O. Box 240, Owasso (74055-0240)
PHONE..................918 835-9244
Randy Brook, *Principal*
EMP: 2
SALES (est): 238.9K **Privately Held**
SIC: 2892 Explosives

(G-9225)
AUSTINN INDUSTRIES INC NCS LLC
1566 E 22nd St (74114-1306)
PHONE..................918 408-2058
Nicollette Smith, *Principal*
EMP: 2
SALES (est): 70.3K **Privately Held**
SIC: 3999 Manufacturing industries

(G-9226)
AUTO CRANE COMPANY
4707 N Mingo Rd (74117-5927)
P.O. Box 580697 (74158-0697)
PHONE..................918 438-2760
John Celoni Jr, *President*
Robert Heffron, *President*
Bruce Barron, *Exec VP*
Sam Dallas, *Design Engr*
Roddy Mears, *Sales Staff*
◆ **EMP:** 110
SQ FT: 120,000
SALES (est): 38.4MM
SALES (corp-wide): 253.4MM **Privately Held**
SIC: 3713 3537 3563 3536 Truck bodies (motor vehicles); cranes, industrial truck; air & gas compressors; hoists, cranes & monorails
HQ: Ramsey Industries Inc
4707 N Mingo Rd
Tulsa OK 74117
918 438-2760

(G-9227)
AVALON EXPLORATION INC
15 W 6th St Ste 2300 (74119-5401)
PHONE..................918 523-0600
John Wieczorek, *President*
Randall Sullivan, *Vice Pres*
EMP: 18
SQ FT: 8,400
SALES (est): 5.7MM **Privately Held**
SIC: 1311 1321 4922 Crude petroleum production; natural gas production; natural gas liquids production; pipelines, natural gas

(G-9228)
AVALON OPERATING LLC
15 W 6th St Ste 2300 (74119-5401)
PHONE..................918 523-0600
EMP: 2
SALES (est): 184K **Privately Held**
SIC: 1311 Crude petroleum & natural gas

(G-9229)
AVERY BARRON INDUSTIRES LLC
2102 W Skelly Dr (74107-9048)
PHONE..................918 779-6903
Bruce Barron, *President*
Michael Barber, *President*
Don Helms, *CFO*
Phil Halt, *Manager*
EMP: 39
SALES: 9.7MM **Privately Held**
WEB: www.abi-us.com
SIC: 3441 Fabricated structural metal

(G-9230)
AVERY BARRON INDUSTRIES
1044 N Columbia Pl (74110-5027)
PHONE..................918 834-6647
Bruce Barron, *Mng Member*
Donald Helms,
EMP: 2
SALES (est): 353.5K **Privately Held**
SIC: 3469 Stamping metal for the trade

(G-9231)
AVITROL CORP
7644 E 46th St (74145-6370)
PHONE..................918 622-7763
Kelly Swindle, *President*

EMP: 4
SALES (est): 298.6K
SALES (corp-wide): 1.1MM **Privately Held**
SIC: 2879 Agricultural chemicals
PA: Tulsa Investments Inc
7644 E 46th St
Tulsa OK 74145
918 622-7763

(G-9232)
AWNINGS OF TULSA INC
1428 E 1st St (74120-2204)
PHONE..................918 747-2050
Steven Caldwell, *Principal*
Paula Caldwell, *Principal*
EMP: 8
SQ FT: 6,000
SALES (est): 290.2K **Privately Held**
SIC: 2394 Awnings, fabric: made from purchased materials; liners & covers, fabric: made from purchased materials

(G-9233)
AXEL ROYAL LLC (DH)
516 S 25th West Ave (74127-8406)
P.O. Box 3308 (74101-3308)
PHONE..................918 584-2671
William R Mallory Jr, *President*
Brad Julian, *Business Mgr*
Kari Mallory, *Corp Secy*
EMP: 23
SALES (est): 9MM
SALES (corp-wide): 295.7K **Privately Held**
SIC: 2992 2911 Lubricating oils & greases; petroleum refining
HQ: Axel Americas, Llc
1440 Erie St
Kansas City MO 64116
816 471-4590

(G-9234)
AXELS TRANSMISSIONS TRANSFERS
Also Called: Axle Transmission & Transfers
3244 N Lewis Ave (74110-1534)
PHONE..................918 425-7725
Jerry Springer, *President*
EMP: 3
SQ FT: 8,860
SALES (est): 233.9K **Privately Held**
SIC: 7539 7537 3462 Automotive repair shops; automotive transmission repair shops; iron & steel forgings

(G-9235)
AXON INDUSTRIES LLC
4115 S 33rd West Ave (74107-5902)
PHONE..................918 313-8955
EMP: 2
SALES (est): 92.1K **Privately Held**
SIC: 3999 Manufacturing industries

(G-9236)
AZURE ENERGY LTD
3737 E 59th Pl (74135-7825)
PHONE..................918 712-2727
Robert Morse, *President*
Diana Hale, *Admin Sec*
EMP: 3
SALES (est): 300K **Privately Held**
SIC: 1311 Crude petroleum production; natural gas production

(G-9237)
AZZ INCORPORATED
2506 E 26th St (74114)
PHONE..................918 584-6668
David Brade, *Manager*
EMP: 38
SALES (corp-wide): 1B **Publicly Held**
WEB: www.azz.com
SIC: 3479 3312 Galvanizing of iron, steel or end-formed products; blast furnaces & steel mills
PA: Azz Inc.
3100 W 7th St Ste 500
Fort Worth TX 76107
817 810-0095

(G-9238)
AZZ INCORPORATED
1800 W 21st St (74107-2712)
PHONE..................918 295-8702
Nick Miller, *Branch Mgr*

GEOGRAPHIC SECTION

Tulsa - Tulsa County (G-9268)

EMP: 33
SALES (corp-wide): 1B **Publicly Held**
WEB: www.azz.com
SIC: 3699 Electrical equipment & supplies
PA: Azz Inc.
3100 W 7th St Ste 500
Fort Worth TX 76107
817 810-0095

(G-9239)
B & B ELECTRIC CO
501 N Trenton Ave (74120-1236)
PHONE 918 583-6274
Dan Thomson, *President*
EMP: 8 **EST:** 1950
SQ FT: 5,500
SALES (est): 2.6MM **Privately Held**
WEB: www.bbelectricco.com
SIC: 5063 7694 Motors, electric; rewinding stators

(G-9240)
B & B RESOURCES
3637 E 67th St (74136-2655)
PHONE 918 495-1128
Charles Barrow, *Owner*
EMP: 1
SALES (est): 500K **Privately Held**
SIC: 1311 Crude petroleum & natural gas

(G-9241)
B & C CUSTOM WOODWORKS
7739 E 38th St Ste B (74145-3222)
PHONE 918 830-2416
EMP: 1
SALES (est): 54.1K **Privately Held**
SIC: 2431 Millwork

(G-9242)
B & P INDUSTRIAL INC
Also Called: Remwood Products
4649 S 83rd East Ave (74145-6901)
P.O. Box 35305 (74153-0305)
PHONE 918 665-3301
Bill Robertson, *President*
Sue Robertson, *Corp Secy*
EMP: 12
SQ FT: 5,220
SALES (est): 2.2MM **Privately Held**
SIC: 2841 Soap & other detergents

(G-9243)
B G SPECIALTIES INC
Also Called: Brown & Hartman Engraving Co
552 S Quincy Ave (74120-4033)
P.O. Box 327 (74101-0327)
PHONE 918 582-1165
Connie Bryant, *President*
Wes Hines, *Treasurer*
Dennis Shelton, *Admin Sec*
EMP: 7
SQ FT: 5,000
SALES (est): 732K **Privately Held**
WEB: www.bhengraving.com
SIC: 2796 3479 3993 Photoengraving plates, linecuts or halftones; lithographic plates, positives or negatives; engraving jewelry silverware, or metal; signs & advertising specialties

(G-9244)
B J M CONSULTING INC
10906 E 2nd St (74128-1642)
P.O. Box 692083 (74169-2083)
PHONE 918 665-8737
Jerry Gustin, *President*
Philip R Gustin, *Corp Secy*
EMP: 9
SALES (est): 1MM **Privately Held**
SIC: 8748 1799 1623 3663 Communications consulting; antenna installation; communication line & transmission tower construction; antennas, transmitting & communications

(G-9245)
B S & B SAFETY SYSTEMS INC (PA)
7422 E 46th Pl (74145-6306)
PHONE 918 622-5950
A Huse, *Principal*
EMP: 4
SALES: 900.3K **Privately Held**
SIC: 3491 0782 Industrial valves; garden services

(G-9246)
B T MACHINE INC
16210 E Marshall St (74116-4019)
PHONE 918 834-3340
Brian Thomas, *President*
Kristi Thomas, *Principal*
EMP: 22
SQ FT: 25,000
SALES (est): 4.3MM **Privately Held**
SIC: 3599 Machine shop, jobbing & repair

(G-9247)
B&C CUSTOM WOODWORKS LLC
2551 E 22nd Pl (74114-3137)
PHONE 918 639-2416
Matthew Blair, *Principal*
EMP: 2
SALES (est): 72K **Privately Held**
SIC: 2431 Millwork

(G-9248)
B&M DIGITAL GARMENT PRINTING
1553 S 74th East Ave (74112-7732)
PHONE 918 954-6994
Brenda Lara, *Principal*
EMP: 2
SALES (est): 83.9K **Privately Held**
SIC: 2752 Commercial printing, lithographic

(G-9249)
B&M MACHINE WORKS LLC
620 N Rockford Ave (74106-5434)
PHONE 918 583-4067
Kenneth Bays,
EMP: 2
SQ FT: 11,000
SALES (est): 209.1K **Privately Held**
SIC: 3599 Machine shop, jobbing & repair

(G-9250)
BABE NAIL SPA
8102 S Lewis Ave Ste D (74137-1226)
PHONE 918 298-2200
EMP: 4
SALES (est): 294.5K **Privately Held**
SIC: 2844 Manicure preparations

(G-9251)
BACK ROAD OIL & GAS LLC
205 E 29th St (74114-3902)
PHONE 918 932-8452
David Spitz, *Owner*
EMP: 2
SALES (est): 76.5K **Privately Held**
SIC: 1389 Oil & gas field services

(G-9252)
BACKBONE MOUNTAIN LLC
1717 S Boulder Ave # 400 (74119-4805)
PHONE 918 295-7600
EMP: 128 **EST:** 2017
SALES (est): 2.5MM **Publicly Held**
SIC: 1222 Bituminous coal-underground mining
HQ: Alliance Resource Partners Lp
1717 S Boulder Ave # 400
Tulsa OK 74119
918 295-7600

(G-9253)
BADGER METER INC
6116 E 15th St (74112-6400)
PHONE 918 836-8411
Rod Cumber, *Branch Mgr*
EMP: 161
SQ FT: 60,000
SALES (corp-wide): 424.6MM **Publicly Held**
SIC: 3824 Fluid meters & counting devices
PA: Badger Meter, Inc.
4545 W Brown Deer Rd
Milwaukee WI 53223
414 355-0400

(G-9254)
BADGER METER INC
Badger Meter Industrial Div
7420 E 46th Pl (74145-6306)
PHONE 918 628-7403
Rick Phillips, *Manager*
EMP: 6
SALES (corp-wide): 424.6MM **Publicly Held**
SIC: 3824 Fluid meters & counting devices
PA: Badger Meter, Inc.
4545 W Brown Deer Rd
Milwaukee WI 53223
414 355-0400

(G-9255)
BAKER HUGHES A GE COMPANY LLC
Also Called: Centrilift Division
7655 E 46th St (74145-6303)
PHONE 918 828-1600
Kellie Grayson, *Branch Mgr*
EMP: 200
SALES (corp-wide): 23.8B **Publicly Held**
SIC: 2865 3561 3533 Cyclic organic crudes; cyclic organic intermediates; pumps, oil well & field; bits, oil & gas field tools: rock
HQ: Baker Hughes Holdings Llc
17021 Aldine Westfield Rd
Houston TX 77073
713 439-8600

(G-9256)
BAKER PETROLITE LLC
1818 W 21st St (74107-2712)
PHONE 918 599-8886
Todd Ost, *Manager*
EMP: 4
SQ FT: 7,500 **Privately Held**
SIC: 1389 Oil field services
HQ: Baker Petrolite Llc
12645 W Airport Blvd
Sugar Land TX 77478
281 276-5400

(G-9257)
BAKER SURVEYING LLC
4677 S 83rd East Ave (74145-6901)
PHONE 918 271-5793
Gerald Baker, *Mng Member*
Sam Daniel, *Mng Member*
Clayton Eager, *Mng Member*
EMP: 9
SALES (est): 60.1K **Privately Held**
SIC: 1389 7389 Testing, measuring, surveying & analysis services;

(G-9258)
BAMA COMPANIES INC (PA)
Also Called: Bama Pie
2745 E 11th St (74104-3913)
P.O. Box 4829 (74159-0829)
PHONE 918 592-0778
Lilah B Marshall, *Ch of Bd*
Paula Marshall, *President*
Eduardo Von Simson, *Partner*
Donnie Stelling, *General Mgr*
Jim Youngblood, *General Mgr*
▲ **EMP:** 1150 **EST:** 1937
SALES (est): 228.8MM **Privately Held**
WEB: www.bama.com
SIC: 2041 2051 2053 Pizza dough, prepared; biscuits, baked: baking powder & raised; pies, bakery: frozen

(G-9259)
BAMA COS INC
2435 N Lewis Ave (74110-2121)
P.O. Box 4829 (74159-0829)
PHONE 918 732-2640
Russ Wells, *Director*
EMP: 2
SALES (est): 68.6K **Privately Held**
SIC: 2045 Prepared flour mixes & doughs

(G-9260)
BAMA FOODS LIMITED PARTNERSHIP
5377 E 66th St N (74117-1813)
PHONE 918 732-2399
J Corp, *General Ptnr*
Matt Brooner, *Branch Mgr*
Amy St Clair, *Manager*
Jeff Richardson, *Admin Asst*
Richard Zoromski, *Maintence Staff*
EMP: 160
SQ FT: 135,000
SALES (est): 42.1MM **Privately Held**
SIC: 2051 5411 Bread, cake & related products; grocery stores

(G-9261)
BAMA PIE LTD
2745 E 11th St (74104-3949)
PHONE 918 592-0778
Paula Marshall-Chapman, *General Ptnr*
EMP: 800
SQ FT: 60,000
SALES (est): 30.5MM **Privately Held**
SIC: 2053 Pies, bakery: frozen

(G-9262)
BANDERA INC
Also Called: Bandera Petroleum
7134 S Yale Ave Ste 510 (74136-6387)
PHONE 918 747-7771
M G Whitmyre, *CEO*
Flo Whitmyre, *President*
Matt Pride, *Vice Pres*
Mary Robles, *Vice Pres*
EMP: 4
SALES (est): 75K **Privately Held**
SIC: 1382 Oil & gas exploration services

(G-9263)
BANNER OIL & GAS LLC
907 S Detroit Ave # 1035 (74120-4317)
PHONE 405 642-4382
Jeff Peles, *Bd of Directors*
EMP: 5
SALES (est): 438.9K **Privately Held**
SIC: 1311 Crude petroleum production

(G-9264)
BARBARA J LANDRETH SEWING
10427 S 67th East Ave (74133-6712)
PHONE 918 298-8141
Barbara Landreth, *Owner*
EMP: 1 **EST:** 1998
SALES (est): 22K **Privately Held**
SIC: 5999 2399 Art, picture frames & decorations; emblems, badges & insignia

(G-9265)
BARLOW-HUNT INC
10322 E 58th St (74146-6503)
PHONE 918 250-0828
Rex Hunt, *President*
EMP: 100
SQ FT: 60,000
SALES (est): 11.5MM
SALES (corp-wide): 1B **Publicly Held**
SIC: 3061 3083 3494 2821 Mechanical rubber goods; thermosetting laminates: rods, tubes, plates & sheet; valves & pipe fittings; plastics materials & resins
HQ: Oil States Industries, Inc.
7701 S Cooper St
Arlington TX 76001

(G-9266)
BARRETT PERFORMANCE AIRCRAFT
2870b N Sheridan Rd (74115-2304)
PHONE 918 835-1089
Burton M Barrett, *President*
Betty Barrett, *Corp Secy*
Monty Lynn Barrett, *Vice Pres*
▲ **EMP:** 8
SALES (est): 815.9K **Privately Held**
SIC: 3724 7692 3829 3812 Aircraft engines & engine parts; welding repair; measuring & controlling devices; search & navigation equipment

(G-9267)
BARRETT PRECISION ENGINES INC
2870b N Sheridan Rd (74115-2304)
PHONE 918 835-1089
Burton Barrett, *President*
EMP: 1 **EST:** 2015
SALES (est): 185.6K **Privately Held**
SIC: 3724 Aircraft engines & engine parts

(G-9268)
BARRON AND STEVENSON EMC LLC
1117 S Birmingham Ave (74104-3924)
PHONE 918 804-8440
Carole Stevenson, *Owner*
EMP: 2
SALES (est): 85.9K **Privately Held**
SIC: 3572 Computer storage devices

Tulsa - Tulsa County (G-9269)

(G-9269)
BARTEC DISPENSING TECH INC
Also Called: Bdtronic
11130 E 56th St (74146-6713)
PHONE..................918 250-6496
Michael Yarnall, *President*
◆ EMP: 9
SQ FT: 12,000
SALES (est): 2.3MM
SALES (corp-wide): 470.7MM **Privately Held**
SIC: 3559 3586 Plastics working machinery; measuring & dispensing pumps
PA: Max Automation Se
Breite Str. 29-31
Dusseldorf 40213
211 909-910

(G-9270)
BASE SCALE COMPANY
6825 S Delaware Ave (74136-4502)
PHONE..................918 523-9559
Roger Marshall, *Owner*
EMP: 7
SALES (est): 420.5K **Privately Held**
SIC: 3596 Truck (motor vehicle) scales

(G-9271)
BAXTER HEALTHCARE CORPORATION
Also Called: Baxter Health Care
11333 E Pine St (74116-2023)
PHONE..................918 513-8980
EMP: 28
SALES (corp-wide): 11.3B **Publicly Held**
SIC: 3841 Surgical & medical instruments
HQ: Baxter Healthcare Corporation
1 Baxter Pkwy
Deerfield IL 60015
224 948-2000

(G-9272)
BAYOU OIL FIELD SERVICE & SUP
1550 N 105th East Ave (74116-1516)
PHONE..................918 398-2166
Brad Bryant, *Partner*
EMP: 3
SALES (est): 163.9K **Privately Held**
SIC: 1389 Oil field services

(G-9273)
BAYTIDE PETROLEUM INC (HQ)
7105 E Admiral Pl Ste 200 (74115-8712)
P.O. Box 580220 (74158-0220)
PHONE..................918 585-8150
Warren Young, *President*
Warren F Young,
EMP: 15
SQ FT: 1,000
SALES (est): 4.7MM
SALES (corp-wide): 1MM **Privately Held**
SIC: 1311 6211 Crude petroleum production; natural gas production; dealers, security
PA: Gomaco Inc
415 S Boston Ave Ste 500
Tulsa OK 74103
918 585-8077

(G-9274)
BB2 LLC
Also Called: Bricktown Brewery
3301 S Peoria Ave (74105-2028)
PHONE..................918 895-7878
EMP: 2 **Privately Held**
SIC: 2082 Malt beverages
PA: Bb2 Llc
1 N Oklahoma Ave
Oklahoma City OK 73104

(G-9275)
BE-HIVE INTERIOR DRAPERY FCTRY
Also Called: Beehive Interiors
1343 S Harvard Ave (74112-5817)
PHONE..................918 599-0292
Pat Warnock, *Owner*
EMP: 6
SALES (est): 270K **Privately Held**
SIC: 2391 7389 Curtains & draperies; interior design services

(G-9276)
BEACON STAMP & SEAL CO
2521 S Sheridan Rd (74129-1007)
PHONE..................918 834-2322
Larry Sims, *President*
Sams Larry, *Manager*
EMP: 4
SQ FT: 3,000
SALES (est): 415.1K **Privately Held**
WEB: www.beaconstamp.com
SIC: 3953 5085 3993 2671 Embossing seals & hand stamps; cancelling stamps, hand: rubber or metal; seal presses, notary & hand; stencil machines (marking devices); rope, cord & thread; signs & advertising specialties; packaging paper & plastics film, coated & laminated

(G-9277)
BEARWOOD CONCEPTS INC
6202 E 30th St N (74115-2916)
PHONE..................918 933-6600
G Duane Walker, *CEO*
Ken Hird, *Exec VP*
Jeff Cronin, *Vice Pres*
Travis Ogle, *Vice Pres*
James Sellers, *Vice Pres*
▲ EMP: 72
SQ FT: 45,000
SALES (est): 11.9MM **Privately Held**
SIC: 2521 Cabinets, office: wood

(G-9278)
BECKY WELCH VACUUM FORMING
260 S 104th East Ave (74128-1242)
PHONE..................918 836-7301
Becky Welch, *Principal*
EMP: 2 EST: 1998
SALES (est): 155.1K **Privately Held**
SIC: 3843 3086 Dental equipment & supplies; plastics foam products

(G-9279)
BELPORT OIL INC
1719 S Boston Ave (74119-4809)
PHONE..................918 637-5476
George L Davenport, *President*
John W Campbell IV, *Vice Pres*
Tracy Davenport, *Admin Sec*
EMP: 20
SALES (est): 2.5MM **Privately Held**
SIC: 1382 Geological exploration, oil & gas field

(G-9280)
BENCHMARK MONUMENT
1735 E 11th St (74104-3632)
PHONE..................918 582-8600
Michael Rives, *President*
EMP: 5
SALES (est): 429K **Privately Held**
SIC: 3281 Cut stone & stone products

(G-9281)
BENDCO CORP
Also Called: Bendco Pipe & Tube Bending
1625 E Easton St (74120-1216)
PHONE..................918 583-1566
Fax: 918 587-0738
EMP: 15 EST: 1960
SQ FT: 25,000
SALES (est): 1.6MM **Privately Held**
SIC: 3498 3441 Pipe & Tube Bending

(G-9282)
BENDMASTERS INC
7100 Charles Page Blvd (74127-7315)
PHONE..................918 585-3755
Kenneth Lord, *President*
Summer Janison, *Administration*
EMP: 3
SALES (est): 543.6K **Privately Held**
SIC: 3498 7542 Tube fabricating (contract bending & shaping); washing & polishing, automotive

(G-9283)
BENT TEES SCREEN PRINTING
1819 S Irvington Ave (74112-7119)
PHONE..................918 734-3996
EMP: 2
SALES (est): 83.9K **Privately Held**
SIC: 2752 Commercial printing, lithographic

(G-9284)
BEQUETTES GOURMET FOODS INC
4515 E 39th St (74135-2530)
PHONE..................918 946-4212
Dave Bequette, *President*
EMP: 2
SALES (est): 89.7K **Privately Held**
SIC: 2033 Barbecue sauce: packaged in cans, jars, etc.

(G-9285)
BERRY HOLDINGS LP
Also Called: Bay
6218 S Lewis Ave Ste 100 (74136-1030)
PHONE..................918 582-3461
Jim Fretz, *Manager*
EMP: 3
SALES (corp-wide): 432.6MM **Privately Held**
SIC: 3443 7692 Fabricated plate work (boiler shop); welding repair
PA: Berry Holdings, Lp
1414 Corn Product Rd
Corpus Christi TX 78409
361 693-2100

(G-9286)
BERT PARSONS 2ND GEN LCKSMTH L
8132 E 9th St (74112-4818)
PHONE..................918 794-7131
Bert Parsons,
Andrea Parsons,
EMP: 2
SQ FT: 3,000
SALES (est): 205.5K **Privately Held**
SIC: 3429 Locks or lock sets

(G-9287)
BEST PRINTING SOLUTION LLC
1414 N 163rd East Ave (74116-4445)
PHONE..................918 794-1771
EMP: 2
SALES (est): 83.9K **Privately Held**
SIC: 2752 Lithographic Commercial Printing

(G-9288)
BIG CREEK CUSTOM EMBROIDERY
3735 S 63rd West Ave (74107-4831)
PHONE..................918 446-6054
Elizabeth Cox, *Principal*
EMP: 1
SALES: 50K **Privately Held**
SIC: 2397 Schiffli machine embroideries

(G-9289)
BIG EASY
6533 S Peoria Ave (74136-2208)
PHONE..................918 493-6280
Tressie Loper, *Principal*
EMP: 7
SALES (est): 491.7K **Privately Held**
SIC: 2064 Candy bars, including chocolate covered bars

(G-9290)
BIG ELK ENERGY SYSTEMS LLC
4140 S Galveston Ave (74107-7035)
PHONE..................918 947-6800
Geoffrey Hager, *General Mgr*
Steven Doughman, *Prdtn Mgr*
Doug Pruitt, *QC Mgr*
Jeff Wilkie, *Human Res Mgr*
Susan Hainzinger, *Human Resources*
EMP: 20
SALES: 25MM **Privately Held**
SIC: 3494 Valves & pipe fittings

(G-9291)
BIG G PRECISION WELDING
1632 S 69th East Ave (74112-7439)
PHONE..................918 406-2876
EMP: 1
SALES (est): 37.2K **Privately Held**
SIC: 7692 Welding repair

(G-9292)
BIG HOUSE SPECIALTY PRTG INC
1147 S Owasso Ave (74120-5011)
PHONE..................918 271-1414
Jennifer Grant, *President*
Pam Harris, *Vice Pres*
EMP: 4
SALES: 100K **Privately Held**
SIC: 2759 Commercial printing

(G-9293)
BIG SHOT LLC
2526 E 71st St Ste G (74136-5576)
PHONE..................918 712-7110
Mark Skaggf, *Branch Mgr*
EMP: 2
SALES (corp-wide): 124.2K **Privately Held**
SIC: 3949 Sporting & athletic goods
PA: Big Shot, Llc
7107 S Yale Ave 312
Tulsa OK 74136
918 712-7110

(G-9294)
BIG SHOT LLC (PA)
7107 S Yale Ave 312 (74136-6308)
PHONE..................918 712-7110
Mark Skaggf,
EMP: 2
SALES (est): 124.2K **Privately Held**
SIC: 3949 Sporting & athletic goods

(G-9295)
BIGGS COMMUNICATIONS INC
Also Called: Tulsa Beacon
6784 S 67th East Ave (74133-1723)
P.O. Box 35099 (74153-0099)
PHONE..................918 523-4425
Charles R Biggs, *President*
Susan Biggs, *Vice Pres*
EMP: 4
SALES (est): 203.6K **Privately Held**
SIC: 2711 Newspapers, publishing & printing

(G-9296)
BILLIARDS OF TULSA INC (PA)
Also Called: Galaxy Distributing
7813 E Admiral Pl (74115-7914)
PHONE..................918 835-1166
Ronac Shah, *President*
Michael A Gill, *Principal*
Varsha Shah, *Corp Secy*
▲ EMP: 25 EST: 1975
SQ FT: 42,000
SALES (est): 3.5MM **Privately Held**
WEB: www.galaxyhomerecreation.com
SIC: 5941 5099 3949 3645 Pool & billiard tables; coin-operated machines & mechanisms; playground equipment; garden, patio, walkway & yard lighting fixtures: electric; spas & hot tubs

(G-9297)
BIRD CREEK RESOURCES INC
1437 S Boulder Ave # 930 (74119-3618)
PHONE..................918 582-7713
Gary C Adams, *Ch of Bd*
EMP: 5
SQ FT: 5,400
SALES (est): 717.5K **Privately Held**
SIC: 1381 Drilling oil & gas wells

(G-9298)
BK EXPLORATION CORPORATION
10159 E 11th St Ste 401 (74128-3028)
PHONE..................918 582-3855
Bob Kimmel, *Principal*
Bill M Burks, *Principal*
EMP: 4
SQ FT: 1,000
SALES (est): 510K **Privately Held**
SIC: 1382 Oil & gas exploration services

(G-9299)
BKW INC (PA)
2469 E King St (74110-5043)
P.O. Box 581611 (74158-1611)
PHONE..................918 836-6767
Brian Webb, *President*
Corene Webb, *Corp Secy*
EMP: 7

GEOGRAPHIC SECTION

Tulsa - Tulsa County (G-9328)

SALES (est): 800K **Privately Held**
SIC: 3499 3317 Fire- or burglary-resistive products; seamless pipes & tubes

(G-9300)
BLACK & DECKER (US) INC
11414 E 51st St Ste C (74146-5800)
PHONE 918 249-8641
Jim Rieder, *Manager*
EMP: 7
SALES (corp-wide): 14.4B **Publicly Held**
SIC: 3546 Power-driven handtools
HQ: Black & Decker (U.S.) Inc.
1000 Stanley Dr
New Britain CT 06053
860 225-5111

(G-9301)
BLACK BOX NETWORK SERVICES ✪
8023 E 63rd Pl Ste 225 (74133-1232)
PHONE 800 949-4039
Linda Godinez, *Info Tech Dir*
EMP: 2 **EST:** 2019
SALES (est): 85.9K **Privately Held**
SIC: 3577 Computer peripheral equipment

(G-9302)
BLANKENSHIP BROTHERS INC
Also Called: Fastsigns
4735 S Memorial Dr Ste A (74145-6925)
PHONE 918 627-3278
Alda Blankenship, *Owner*
EMP: 4
SALES (corp-wide): 4.1MM **Privately Held**
SIC: 3993 Signs & advertising specialties
PA: Blankenship Brothers Inc
1401 S Meridian Ave A
Oklahoma City OK 73108
405 943-3278

(G-9303)
BLESSETTIS INC
Also Called: Blessttis Grmet Itln Psta Sces
9918 S 106th East Ave (74133-5113)
PHONE 918 830-5481
Judy Scovil, *President*
Jim Scovil, *Vice Pres*
EMP: 4
SALES (est): 404.6K **Privately Held**
SIC: 2033 Spaghetti & other pasta sauce: packaged in cans, jars, etc.

(G-9304)
BLIND DOCTOR
4204 Southwest Blvd (74107-6523)
P.O. Box 377, Oakhurst (74050-0377)
PHONE 918 638-1487
Marvin Pike, *Owner*
EMP: 1
SALES (est): 118.7K **Privately Held**
SIC: 2591 Window blinds

(G-9305)
BLUE RIBBON FORMS INC
1208 S Hudson Ave Ste D (74112-5408)
P.O. Box 52041 (74152-0041)
PHONE 918 834-8838
Sharron Doris, *President*
Pam Norberg, *Corp Secy*
Pic Dorris, *Vice Pres*
EMP: 5
SQ FT: 1,500
SALES (est): 495.3K **Privately Held**
SIC: 2759 2761 Commercial printing; manifold business forms

(G-9306)
BLUE SPEED LLC
7803 S Urbana Ave (74136-8112)
PHONE 918 856-3547
Ryan Sullivan, *Principal*
EMP: 3
SALES (est): 180K **Privately Held**
WEB: www.bluespeedav.com
SIC: 3639 Household appliances

(G-9307)
BLUE STONE OPERATING LLC
Also Called: Bluestone Natural Resources
2 W 2nd St Ste 1700 (74103-3100)
PHONE 918 392-9209
John Redmond, *CEO*
EMP: 62
SQ FT: 1,100

SALES (est): 4.9MM **Privately Held**
SIC: 1382 Oil & gas exploration services

(G-9308)
BLUEGRASS ENERGY INC
4637 E 91st St (74137-2852)
PHONE 918 743-8060
Phil Wade, *President*
John Heinsius, *Vice Pres*
EMP: 6
SQ FT: 4,000
SALES (est): 905.7K **Privately Held**
SIC: 1311 Crude petroleum production

(G-9309)
BLUESTEM INTEGRATED LLC
5301 S 125th East Ave (74146-6223)
PHONE 918 660-0492
Blake Hendrickson, *COO*
Lori Graflund, *CFO*
Hal Salisbury, *Mng Member*
EMP: 38 **EST:** 2012
SQ FT: 33,000
SALES (est): 4.8MM **Privately Held**
SIC: 2752 Commercial printing, lithographic

(G-9310)
BLUESTONE NATURAL RESOURCES HL
2 W 2nd St Ste 1700 (74103-3100)
PHONE 918 392-9200
John M Redmond, *Mng Member*
EMP: 2
SALES (est): 140.5K **Privately Held**
SIC: 1382 Oil & gas exploration services

(G-9311)
BLUESTONE NTRAL RSURCES II LLC
2 W 2nd St Ste 1700 (74103-3100)
PHONE 918 392-9200
John Redmond, *President*
EMP: 2
SALES (est): 459.4K **Privately Held**
SIC: 1382 Oil & gas exploration services

(G-9312)
BLUESTONE NTURAL RESOURCES LLC (PA)
2 W 2nd St Ste 1700 (74103-3100)
PHONE 918 392-9200
Ken Gibson, *Vice Pres*
Doug Redmond, *Vice Pres*
John M Redmond, *Mng Member*
EMP: 16
SQ FT: 7,000
SALES (est): 15.8MM **Privately Held**
SIC: 1382 Oil & gas exploration services

(G-9313)
BOARDWALK DISTRIBUTION CO
5402 S 129th East Ave (74134-6706)
PHONE 918 551-6275
Andrew Gray, *Partner*
Bryan Hendershot, *Partner*
Bill Dekanich, *Manager*
EMP: 19
SALES (est): 4.5MM **Privately Held**
SIC: 2084 5182 Wines; wine & distilled beverages; wine

(G-9314)
BODYCOTE THERMAL PROC INC
1520 N 170th East Ave (74116-4907)
PHONE 214 904-2420
Steve Cargill, *Manager*
EMP: 5
SQ FT: 1,119
SALES (corp-wide): 929.6MM **Privately Held**
SIC: 3398 Metal heat treating
HQ: Bodycote Thermal Processing, Inc.
12750 Merit Dr Ste 1400
Dallas TX 75251
214 904-2420

(G-9315)
BOEING COMPANY
3330 N Mingo Rd (74116-1211)
P.O. Box 582808 (74158-2808)
PHONE 918 835-3111
D L Laughlin, *Purch Dir*
Dave Rowley, *Human Res Dir*

Jeanie Dodd, *Pub Rel Dir*
Don Carlisle, *Marketing Staff*
EMP: 900
SQ FT: 769,000
SALES (corp-wide): 76.5B **Publicly Held**
WEB: www.boeing.com
SIC: 3812 3721 3728 Missile guidance systems & equipment; space vehicle guidance systems & equipment; aircraft control systems, electronic; airplanes, fixed or rotary wing; aircraft parts & equipment
PA: The Boeing Company
100 N Riverside Plz
Chicago IL 60606
312 544-2000

(G-9316)
BOEING COMPANY
3800 N Mingo Rd (74116-5003)
PHONE 918 292-2707
Joe Rosco, *Manager*
EMP: 5
SALES (corp-wide): 76.5B **Publicly Held**
SIC: 3721 Aircraft
PA: The Boeing Company
100 N Riverside Plz
Chicago IL 60606
312 544-2000

(G-9317)
BOG RESOURCES LLC
525 S Main St Ste 1120 (74103-4512)
PHONE 918 592-1010
EMP: 2
SALES (est): 81.9K **Privately Held**
SIC: 1311 Crude petroleum & natural gas

(G-9318)
BONAVISTA TECHNOLOGIES INC
6004 S 118th East Ave (74146-6820)
PHONE 918 250-3435
Gary Ferrell, *President*
Beverly Ferrell, *Admin Sec*
▼ **EMP:** 8
SQ FT: 4,400
SALES (est): 1.6MM **Privately Held**
SIC: 3441 7363 3825 8711 Fabricated structural metal; engineering help service; instruments to measure electricity; professional engineer

(G-9319)
BOOMERANG PRINTING LLC
3615 S Harvard Ave (74135-2227)
PHONE 918 747-1844
Tom Wilson, *President*
EMP: 8
SALES (est): 707.8K **Privately Held**
SIC: 2752 Commercial printing, offset

(G-9320)
BORETS US INC (DH)
1600 N Garnett Rd (74116-1633)
PHONE 918 439-7000
Keith Russell, *CEO*
Michael Parks, *Engineer*
Eric Wickham, *Accountant*
Mike Hendrix, *Sales Mgr*
◆ **EMP:** 252
SALES (est): 142.7MM **Privately Held**
SIC: 3533 Oil & gas field machinery
HQ: Pk Borets, Ooo Proizvodstvennaya Kompaniya Borets, Ooo
5 Ul. Moldavskaya
Moscow 12146
821 442-0287

(G-9321)
BORG COMPRESSED STEEL CORP
1032 N Lewis Ave (74110-4768)
PHONE 918 587-2437
Jeff Ray, *President*
EMP: 100
SQ FT: 4,000
SALES (est): 39.1MM
SALES (corp-wide): 88.6MM **Privately Held**
WEB: www.yaffeco.net
SIC: 5093 3341 Ferrous metal scrap & waste; secondary nonferrous metals

PA: The Yaffe Companies Incorporated
1200 S G St
Muskogee OK 74403
918 687-7543

(G-9322)
BORN INC
5400 S 49th West Ave (74107-8813)
P.O. Box 102 (74101-0102)
PHONE 918 582-2186
Sidney L Born, *CEO*
Binaya Thapa, *President*
Dhananjay Dhane, *Engineer*
Gloria Meyers, *Admin Sec*
EMP: 20 **EST:** 1917
SQ FT: 6,400
SALES (est): 4.6MM **Privately Held**
WEB: www.borninc.com
SIC: 8711 3567 Mechanical engineering; industrial furnaces & ovens

(G-9323)
BOSS SEALS & PARTS LLC
8687 E 105th Ct (74133-7088)
PHONE 918 237-6991
Alan Dick, *Mng Member*
▲ **EMP:** 9
SQ FT: 16,000
SALES (est): 1MM **Privately Held**
SIC: 3713 5013 Truck bodies & parts; truck parts & accessories

(G-9324)
BOTTOMLINE LLC
9721 S 70th East Ave (74133-5903)
PHONE 918 261-2354
Lisa Decarlo, *Principal*
EMP: 2
SALES (est): 98.6K **Privately Held**
WEB: www.bottomline.com
SIC: 7372 Business oriented computer software

(G-9325)
BPC INDUSTRIES INC
624 N Rockford Ave (74106-5434)
PHONE 918 584-4848
Joanne G Beckmann, *Ch of Bd*
Thomas Beckmann Jr, *President*
Rolanda S Beckmann, *Treasurer*
EMP: 22
SQ FT: 28,000
SALES (est): 2.5MM **Privately Held**
SIC: 5072 3053 Bolts; nuts (hardware); gaskets, packing & sealing devices; gaskets, all materials

(G-9326)
BRADEN FILTRATION LLC
5199 N Mingo Rd Unit B (74117-4902)
PHONE 918 283-4818
McLeod Stephens,
EMP: 3
SALES (est): 142.6K **Privately Held**
SIC: 3569 Filters

(G-9327)
BRADEN SHIELDING SYSTEMS CONST
9260 Broken Arrow Expy (74145-3339)
PHONE 918 624-2888
Steve Pittman, *Principal*
Tom Foyil, *Principal*
EMP: 40 **EST:** 1999
SQ FT: 52,000
SALES (est): 5.6MM **Privately Held**
SIC: 2599 3469 3444 Hospital furniture, except beds; metal stampings; sheet metalwork

(G-9328)
BRADEN SHIELDING SYSTEMS LLC
9260 Broken Arrow Expy (74145-3339)
PHONE 918 624-2888
Tom Foyil, *President*
Steve Pittman, *Vice Pres*
Katie Daniel, *Purchasing*
◆ **EMP:** 20
SALES (est): 4.8MM **Privately Held**
SIC: 3448 3469 Buildings, portable: prefabricated metal; metal stampings

Tulsa - Tulsa County (G-9329)   GEOGRAPHIC SECTION

(G-9329)
BRADSHAW HOME LLC
15 E 5th St (74103-4346)
PHONE..................................918 582-5404
Kristin Bradshaw, *Principal*
EMP: 3
SALES (est): 242.9K **Privately Held**
SIC: 3533 Oil & gas field machinery

(G-9330)
BRAINERD CHEMICAL MIDWEST LLC (HQ)
427 S Boston Ave (74103-4141)
PHONE..................................918 622-1214
Erika Coates, *CFO*
Zachary Taylor, *Marketing Mgr*
EMP: 3
SALES (est): 494.6K
SALES (corp-wide): 78.9MM **Privately Held**
SIC: 2819 Hydrochloric acid
PA: Brainerd Holdings Company
   427 S Boston Ave
   Tulsa OK 74103
   918 622-1214

(G-9331)
BRAKE REBUILDERS INC
Also Called: Brake & Clutch Service
7605 E 11th St (74112-5719)
PHONE..................................918 834-0200
EMP: 12 EST: 1962
SQ FT: 120,000
SALES (est): 93.8K **Privately Held**
SIC: 3714 7538 Mfg Motor Vehicle Parts/Accessories General Auto Repair

(G-9332)
BRASS BUFF
9828 E 7th St (74128-2604)
PHONE..................................918 592-1717
Bob Bolton, *Owner*
Joyce Bolton, *Co-Owner*
EMP: 2
SALES: 66K **Privately Held**
SIC: 7699 5932 3471 General household repair services; used merchandise stores; plating & polishing

(G-9333)
BRAVO NATURAL GAS LLC
1323 E 71st St Ste 200 (74136-5065)
PHONE..................................918 712-7008
Peggy Gwartney, *Principal*
EMP: 4
SALES (est): 986.6K **Privately Held**
SIC: 1321 1389 Propane (natural) production; construction, repair & dismantling services

(G-9334)
BREEZE INVESTMENTS LLC
7170 S Braden Ave Ste 200 (74136-6316)
PHONE..................................918 492-5090
Jim Bush, *President*
Mary Bush, *Vice Pres*
EMP: 1
SQ FT: 2,800
SALES: 8.9K **Privately Held**
SIC: 1311 Crude petroleum production; natural gas production

(G-9335)
BRENDA K TOUPIN
Also Called: Bk Products
5103 S Sheridan Rd (74145-7627)
PHONE..................................918 527-6948
Brenda Toupin, *Principal*
Paul Toupin, *Principal*
EMP: 1
SALES (est): 117.3K **Privately Held**
SIC: 3599 Machine shop, jobbing & repair

(G-9336)
BRG ENERGY INC
7134 S Yale Ave Ste 600 (74136-6353)
PHONE..................................918 496-2626
James L Burkhart, *Chairman*
Kenneth Whitson, *Production*
EMP: 3
SALES (est): 131.5K **Privately Held**
SIC: 1382 Oil & gas exploration services

(G-9337)
BRG PRODUCTION COMPANY (PA)
7134 S Yale Ave Ste 600 (74136-6353)
PHONE..................................918 496-2626
B Reid, *President*
J L Burkhart, *Chairman*
Mike W Burkhart, *Exec VP*
Brian Flynn, *Vice Pres*
Steven Williams, *Treasurer*
EMP: 24 EST: 1979
SQ FT: 12,000
SALES (est): 8.5MM **Privately Held**
WEB: www.brgcorp.com
SIC: 1311 Crude petroleum production; natural gas production

(G-9338)
BRIX INC
Also Called: Brix Office Products
4657 S 83rd East Ave K (74145-6927)
PHONE..................................918 584-6484
Neil A Pittman, *President*
EMP: 6
SQ FT: 33,000
SALES (est): 500K **Privately Held**
SIC: 5943 5021 2752 2791 Office forms & supplies; office & public building furniture; commercial printing, lithographic; typesetting; commercial printing

(G-9339)
BROADLAND STUMP REMOVAL
6208 S Victor Ave (74136-0809)
PHONE..................................918 743-7014
Richard Broadland, *Owner*
EMP: 1
SALES (est): 74.8K **Privately Held**
SIC: 2411 0782 Stumps, wood; landscape contractors

(G-9340)
BRONCO MANUFACTURING LLC (PA)
4953 S 48th West Ave (74107-7202)
PHONE..................................918 446-7196
Max Mantooth, *CEO*
Seth Brady, *General Mgr*
Aaron Guthrie, *Opers Mgr*
Rico Garza, *Mfg Mgr*
Melanie Foltz, *Production*
◆ EMP: 23
SQ FT: 20,000
SALES: 35MM **Privately Held**
SIC: 5084 3533 Oil well machinery, equipment & supplies; oil field machinery & equipment

(G-9341)
BROOKS CUSTOM FABRICATION
10604 E Ute St (74116-1521)
PHONE..................................918 836-2556
Gary Brooks, *Principal*
EMP: 7
SALES (est): 828.7K **Privately Held**
SIC: 3441 Fabricated structural metal

(G-9342)
BROOKSIDE POTTERY
3710 S Peoria Ave (74105)
PHONE..................................918 697-6364
Linda Coward, *Owner*
EMP: 1
SALES (est): 71.6K **Privately Held**
SIC: 3269 5719 Art & ornamental ware, pottery; pottery

(G-9343)
BS & W SOLUTIONS LLC (DH)
6655 S Lewis Ave Ste 200 (74136-1031)
PHONE..................................918 392-9356
Timothy Purcell, *Mng Member*
EMP: 5
SALES (est): 772.9K
SALES (corp-wide): 88.2MM **Privately Held**
SIC: 7699 1382 2911 4953 Tank & boiler cleaning service; oil & gas exploration services; oils, partly refined: sold for re-running; recycling, waste materials

(G-9344)
BS&B PRESSURE SAFETY MGT LLC
7422 E 46th Pl (74145-6306)
P.O. Box 470590 (74147-0590)
PHONE..................................918 664-3725
EMP: 3
SALES (est): 323.4K **Privately Held**
SIC: 3491 Industrial valves

(G-9345)
BS&B SAFETY SYSTEMS LLC (HQ)
7455 E 46th St (74145-6379)
P.O. Box 470590 (74147-0590)
PHONE..................................918 622-5950
AR Huse, *President*
Arod Huse, *Vice Pres*
Anthony Simon, *Sales Staff*
Jim Hull, *Marketing Staff*
Arnold Mundt, *Manager*
◆ EMP: 6
SQ FT: 7,000
SALES: 41.8MM
SALES (corp-wide): 43.4MM **Privately Held**
WEB: www.bsbsystems.com
SIC: 3491 Pressure valves & regulators, industrial
PA: International Systems & Controls Corporation
   2950 North Loop W Ste 500
   Houston TX 77092
   713 526-5461

(G-9346)
BS&B SAFETY SYSTEMS LLC
7455 E 46th St (74145-6379)
P.O. Box 470590 (74147-0590)
PHONE..................................918 622-5950
John Smallwood, *Manager*
EMP: 133
SALES (corp-wide): 43.4MM **Privately Held**
SIC: 3494 8711 Valves & pipe fittings; engineering services
HQ: Bs&B Safety Systems, L.L.C.
   7455 E 46th St
   Tulsa OK 74145
   918 622-5950

(G-9347)
BUBBLE BEE BAKERY AND SUPPLIES
Also Called: Bubble Bee Bakery
4712 S 74th East Pl Apt 5 (74145-6338)
PHONE..................................918 209-8658
Amy Beverley, *Partner*
Amy Berverley, *Partner*
Steven Beverley, *Partner*
EMP: 3
SALES (est): 146.8K **Privately Held**
SIC: 2051 Cakes, bakery: except frozen; pies, bakery: except frozen

(G-9348)
BURNS MANUFACTURING INC
1855 N 105th East Ave (74116-1513)
PHONE..................................918 622-3305
Kevin Burns, *President*
EMP: 3
SQ FT: 8,000
SALES: 300K **Privately Held**
SIC: 3714 Motor vehicle parts & accessories

(G-9349)
BUSH PUBLISHING & ASSOC LLC
321 S Boston Ave (74103-3302)
PHONE..................................251 424-7298
Margo Bush, *Administration*
EMP: 1
SALES (est): 70K **Privately Held**
WEB: www.bushpublishing.com
SIC: 2741 Miscellaneous publishing

(G-9350)
BUSINESS CARDS UNLIMITED
9723 E 33rd St Apt 712 (74146-1313)
PHONE..................................918 810-6265
Gary Slaughter, *Principal*
EMP: 2

SALES (est): 187K **Privately Held**
SIC: 2752 Commercial printing, lithographic

(G-9351)
BUSINESS PRINTING INC 1
5315 E 77th St (74136-8232)
PHONE..................................918 481-6078
John Bensinger, *Principal*
EMP: 2
SALES (est): 182.1K **Privately Held**
SIC: 2752 Commercial printing, lithographic

(G-9352)
BUSINET
4608 S Garnett Rd Ste 300 (74146-5223)
PHONE..................................918 858-4440
Rick Arrington, *Principal*
Jason Baney, *Administration*
EMP: 15
SALES (est): 1.3MM **Privately Held**
SIC: 7372 Business oriented computer software

(G-9353)
BUSTER DORSCH
Also Called: Polisher, The
3231 E 19th St (74104-6104)
PHONE..................................918 743-4509
Buster Dorsch, *Owner*
EMP: 1
SALES (est): 73.6K **Privately Held**
SIC: 7641 5099 3471 Antique furniture repair & restoration; brass goods; plating & polishing

(G-9354)
BUSTER PAR CORP
1209 E 3rd St (74120-2605)
PHONE..................................918 585-8542
Catherine Nickels, *President*
Marcus Makar, *Principal*
EMP: 10 EST: 1962
SQ FT: 12,000
SALES (est): 680K **Privately Held**
WEB: www.parbuster.com
SIC: 3949 3523 Nets: badminton, volleyball, tennis, etc.; golf equipment; turf & grounds equipment

(G-9355)
BUYERS TRADING DESIGNS
1130 S Oxford Ave (74112-5402)
PHONE..................................918 592-5477
David Bynum, *Owner*
EMP: 2
SALES: 500K **Privately Held**
WEB: www.buyerstrading.com
SIC: 2759 Screen printing

(G-9356)
C & F CUSTOM CHROME
1312 N Utica Ave (74110-4637)
PHONE..................................918 587-1110
Charlie Strong, *Owner*
Freddie Phillip, *Partner*
EMP: 5
SALES (est): 274.5K **Privately Held**
SIC: 3471 Electroplating of metals or formed products

(G-9357)
C & P CATALYST INC
4224 S Pittsburg Ave (74135-2856)
P.O. Box 520984 (74152-0984)
PHONE..................................918 747-8379
Ted Cowan, *President*
Pete Nicklau, *Treasurer*
Pat Cowan, *Admin Sec*
EMP: 4
SALES (est): 514.2K **Privately Held**
SIC: 2819 8734 3821 3621 Catalysts, chemical; testing laboratories; laboratory apparatus & furniture; motors & generators; chemical preparations; industrial organic chemicals

(G-9358)
C & S TECHNICAL SERVICES LLC
1336 N 143rd East Ave (74116-2122)
P.O. Box 989, Catoosa (74015-0989)
PHONE..................................918 258-8324
Tim Callis, *Vice Pres*
Rickie O Dean, *Mng Member*

▲ = Import ▼=Export
◆ =Import/Export

GEOGRAPHIC SECTION
Tulsa - Tulsa County (G-9390)

David Franklin, *Mng Member*
EMP: 20
SALES (est): 3.7MM **Privately Held**
WEB: www.cstechservices.com
SIC: 3713 3714 Truck bodies & parts; motor vehicle parts & accessories

(G-9359)
C E HARMON OIL INC (PA)
5555 E 71st St Ste 9300 (74136-6559)
PHONE...................918 663-8515
Charles E Harmon, *President*
Evelyn Harmon, *Vice Pres*
EMP: 12 **EST:** 1980
SQ FT: 3,100
SALES (est): 2.6MM **Privately Held**
SIC: 1311 Crude petroleum production

(G-9360)
C EASLEYS TOUCH
18503 E 31st St (74134-5306)
P.O. Box 423, Foyil (74031-0423)
PHONE...................918 284-9384
Carol Easley, *Principal*
EMP: 1
SALES (est): 207.6K **Privately Held**
SIC: 3553 Cabinet makers' machinery

(G-9361)
C TRIPLE INC
1015 E 2nd St (74120-2005)
PHONE...................918 664-2144
EMP: 1
SALES (est): 56K **Privately Held**
SIC: 3641 Mfg Electric Lamps

(G-9362)
C&A INTERNATIONAL LLC
Also Called: Hide-Away Ironing Boards
5861c S Garnett Rd (74146-6812)
P.O. Box 471009 (74147-1009)
PHONE...................918 872-1645
Jerry Murphy,
Loretta Murphy,
▲ **EMP:** 41
SQ FT: 20,000
SALES (est): 7.6MM **Privately Held**
SIC: 3499 5046 Ironing boards, metal; commercial equipment

(G-9363)
CABINET SOLUTIONS LLC
Also Called: Cabinet Solutions Innovations
1513 E Haskell St Ste A (74106-5471)
PHONE...................918 592-4497
Mark Yates,
EMP: 8
SALES (est): 66.3K **Privately Held**
SIC: 2434 Wood kitchen cabinets

(G-9364)
CALLIDUS TECHNOLOGIES LLC (HQ)
Also Called: Honeywell Ecc Callidus
7130 S Lewis Ave Ste 500 (74136-5417)
PHONE...................918 496-7599
Bob Rose, *President*
Brian Duck, *Vice Pres*
Mitch Bernhard, *Admin Sec*
◆ **EMP:** 250
SQ FT: 40,000
SALES (est): 67.8MM
SALES (corp-wide): 36.7B **Publicly Held**
SIC: 2899 3567 Flares, fireworks & similar preparations; incinerators, metal: domestic or commercial; kilns
PA: Honeywell International Inc.
300 S Tryon St
Charlotte NC 28202
704 627-6200

(G-9365)
CALYX ENERGY III LLC
6120 S Yale Ave Ste 1480 (74136-4226)
PHONE...................918 949-4224
Calvin D Cahill, *CEO*
John Podowski, *COO*
Jim Stephenson, *CFO*
Kari Williams, *Accountant*
Patrick Fincannon, *Technology*
EMP: 17 **EST:** 2014
SALES (est): 7MM **Privately Held**
SIC: 1311 Crude petroleum & natural gas

PA: Calyx Energy Iii Holdings, Llc
6120 S Yale Ave Ste 1480
Tulsa OK 74136
918 949-4224

(G-9366)
CALYX ENERGY III HOLDINGS LLC (PA)
6120 S Yale Ave Ste 1480 (74136-4226)
PHONE...................918 949-4224
Calvin Cahill, *CEO*
John Podowski, *COO*
Jim Stephenson, *CFO*
EMP: 3 **EST:** 2016
SALES (est): 7MM **Privately Held**
SIC: 1382 Oil & gas exploration services

(G-9367)
CAMP CHIPPEWA FOR BOYS INC
15 E 5th St Ste 4022 (74103-4347)
PHONE...................218 335-8807
Dr Robert K Endres, *President*
Richard O Endres, *Corp Secy*
John Endres, *Vice Pres*
Mike Thompson, *Director*
Helen Endres, *Director*
EMP: 20
SALES (est): 200K **Privately Held**
SIC: 7032 2731 Boys' camp; book publishing

(G-9368)
CAMPO ALEGRE FOODS
7633 E 63rd Pl Ste 300 (74133-1202)
PHONE...................918 271-6775
Carlos Ochoa, *Manager*
EMP: 2
SALES (est): 62.3K **Privately Held**
SIC: 2099 Food preparations

(G-9369)
CANDLE ELECTRIC
6902 W 34th St (74107-4012)
PHONE...................918 232-0558
EMP: 1
SALES (est): 39.6K **Privately Held**
SIC: 3999 Candles

(G-9370)
CANO PETROLEUM INC (PA)
Also Called: Huron Ventures
823 S Detroit Ave Ste 300 (74120-4281)
PHONE...................918 398-2728
James R Latimer III, *CEO*
Donald Niemiec, *Ch of Bd*
John H Homier, *CFO*
EMP: 11
SQ FT: 9,163
SALES (est): 26.1MM **Privately Held**
SIC: 1382 Oil & gas exploration services

(G-9371)
CAPITALIST PUBLISHING CO
3216 E 28th St (74114-5720)
PHONE...................918 808-5665
EMP: 1
SALES (est): 37.5K **Privately Held**
SIC: 2741 Miscellaneous publishing

(G-9372)
CAPTIVE IMAGING LLC
5541 S Norfolk Ave (74105-6813)
PHONE...................918 340-3053
EMP: 1
SALES (est): 60K **Privately Held**
SIC: 2335 Wedding gowns & dresses

(G-9373)
CAPTIVE-AIRE SYSTEMS INC
12101 E 51st St Ste 101a (74146-6018)
PHONE...................918 258-0291
EMP: 13
SALES (corp-wide): 389.2MM **Privately Held**
SIC: 3444 Restaurant sheet metalwork
PA: Captive-Aire Systems, Inc.
4641 Paragon Park Rd # 104
Raleigh NC 27616
919 882-2410

(G-9374)
CARBOLINE COMPANY
S 72nd East Ave (74145)
PHONE...................918 622-3028

John Byrd, *Branch Mgr*
EMP: 20
SALES (corp-wide): 5.5B **Publicly Held**
SIC: 2851 Lacquers, varnishes, enamels & other coatings
HQ: Carboline Company
2150 Schuetz Rd Fl 1
Saint Louis MO 63146
314 644-1000

(G-9375)
CARDINAL INDUSTRIES LLC
2850 E 101st St (74137-5601)
P.O. Box 35218 (74153-0218)
PHONE...................918 299-0396
Robert Lemons,
EMP: 1
SALES (est): 225K **Privately Held**
SIC: 1446 Industrial sand

(G-9376)
CARLSON COMPANY
4333 S 86th East Ave (74145-4837)
P.O. Box 470075 (74147-0075)
PHONE...................918 627-4334
James Carlson, *President*
Venny Sneed, *Opers Mgr*
Mike Barnes, *Mfg Staff*
Joyce Carlson, *CFO*
Brian Allen, *Sales Staff*
▲ **EMP:** 40
SQ FT: 5,000
SALES (est): 9.8MM **Privately Held**
WEB: www.carlson-company.com
SIC: 3316 3312 3494 Cold finishing of steel shapes; forgings, iron & steel; valves & pipe fittings

(G-9377)
CARLSON DESIGN CORPORATION
539 S Trenton Ave (74120-4017)
PHONE...................918 438-8344
Greg Carlson, *President*
Thomas Carlson, *Sales Staff*
EMP: 5
SQ FT: 5,500
SALES (est): 989.5K **Privately Held**
SIC: 3829 3545 Map plotting instruments; machine tool accessories

(G-9378)
CARPENTREE INC
4946 E 66th St N (74117-1801)
P.O. Box 472206 (74147-2206)
PHONE...................918 582-3600
Daniel L Hobson, *President*
Natasha Voss, *Graphic Designe*
◆ **EMP:** 45 **EST:** 1976
SALES (est): 7.5MM **Privately Held**
SIC: 3952 5947 Frames for artists' canvases; gifts & novelties

(G-9379)
CARR GRAPHICS INC
8199 E 46th St (74145-4801)
PHONE...................918 835-0605
Brigham Carr, *Owner*
EMP: 1
SQ FT: 1,400
SALES (est): 118K **Privately Held**
SIC: 2752 2791 2789 Lithographing on metal; typesetting; bookbinding & related work

(G-9380)
CARRERA GAS COMPANIES LLC (PA)
6120 S Yale Ave Ste 1640 (74136-4240)
PHONE...................918 359-0980
Robert Jackson, *CEO*
Robert W Mitchell III, *Principal*
EMP: 4
SQ FT: 5,000
SALES (est): 5.5MM **Privately Held**
SIC: 1389 Processing service, gas

(G-9381)
CARTER & HIGGINS ORTHODONTICS
3232 E 31st St (74105-2442)
PHONE...................918 986-9986
Shana Ritz, *Regional Mgr*
EMP: 9 **EST:** 2015

SALES (est): 108.9K **Privately Held**
WEB: www.carterandhigginsortho.com
SIC: 8021 2834 Orthodontist; intravenous solutions

(G-9382)
CARTER DAVIS MACHINE SHOP INC
102 S 111th East Ave C (74128-1614)
PHONE...................918 437-2939
Burt Davis, *President*
EMP: 1 **EST:** 1971
SQ FT: 4,700
SALES (est): 150K **Privately Held**
SIC: 3559 Automotive related machinery

(G-9383)
CARTER PRODUCTION CO
2526 E 71st St Ste I (74136-5576)
P.O. Box 33129 (74153-1129)
PHONE...................918 493-7064
Bill Carter, *President*
Gina Parsons, *Manager*
EMP: 2
SALES (est): 218K **Privately Held**
SIC: 1382 Oil & gas exploration services

(G-9384)
CARTERS MANUFACTURING
10835 E Admiral Pl (74116-3023)
P.O. Box 581118 (74158-1118)
PHONE...................918 437-5428
EMP: 1
SALES (est): 39.6K **Privately Held**
SIC: 3999 Manufacturing industries

(G-9385)
CASEWORK SPECIALTIES INC LLC
1323 E 5th St (74120-3405)
PHONE...................918 382-0037
EMP: 1
SALES (est): 65.5K **Privately Held**
SIC: 2434 Wood kitchen cabinets

(G-9386)
CASILLAS OPERATING LLC
401 S Boston Ave Ste 2400 (74103-4060)
P.O. Box 3411 (74101-3411)
PHONE...................918 582-5310
Greg Casillas, *CEO*
EMP: 21 **EST:** 2016
SALES (est): 712.2K **Privately Held**
SIC: 1381 Drilling oil & gas wells

(G-9387)
CASILLAS PETROLEUM CORP (PA)
401 S Boston Ave Ste 2400 (74103-4060)
P.O. Box 3411 (74101-3411)
PHONE...................918 582-5310
Greg Casillas, *President*
Darrel Reneau, *Superintendent*
Tom Allen, *Foreman/Supr*
Wade Loeppke, *Foreman/Supr*
Victor Jordan, *Engineer*
EMP: 5
SALES (est): 8.8MM **Privately Held**
SIC: 1382 Oil & gas exploration services

(G-9388)
CAT-EYES DRONE IMAGERY SVC LLC
7224 S Elwood Ave Apt 420 (74132-2401)
PHONE...................918 344-8324
Matt E Reinke, *Principal*
EMP: 3
SALES (est): 151.8K **Privately Held**
SIC: 3728 Aircraft parts & equipment

(G-9389)
CATOOSA 2 WAY
850 N 163rd East Ave (74116-4016)
PHONE...................918 234-0055
Dave Burham, *Owner*
EMP: 2
SALES (est): 99K **Privately Held**
SIC: 3661 Fiber optics communications equipment

(G-9390)
CAVEMAN SCREEN PRINTING
3702 W 61st St (74132-1219)
PHONE...................918 446-6440
Chris Townsend, *Owner*

Tulsa - Tulsa County (G-9391) — GEOGRAPHIC SECTION

EMP: 4
SALES (est): 521.4K **Privately Held**
SIC: **2893** 5699 2396 Printing ink; miscellaneous apparel & accessories; automotive & apparel trimmings

(G-9391)
CBL RESOURCES
4138 S Harvard Ave Ste C1 (74135-2653)
PHONE....................................918 551-6760
Dick Clark, *Principal*
EMP: 3
SALES (est): 445.6K **Privately Held**
SIC: **1382** Oil & gas exploration services

(G-9392)
CECILIAS SALSAS
8661 E 61st St (74133-1339)
PHONE....................................918 984-1491
EMP: 2
SALES (est): 78.4K **Privately Held**
SIC: **2099** Food preparations

(G-9393)
CEI PETROLEUM INC
427 S Boston Ave Ste 409 (74103-4109)
PHONE....................................918 582-4284
Lee Francis, *President*
EMP: 1
SALES (est): 200K **Privately Held**
SIC: **1311** Crude petroleum production

(G-9394)
CEJA CORPORATION (PA)
1437 S Boulder Ave # 1250 (74119-3620)
PHONE....................................918 496-0770
Donald P Carpenter, *President*
James Horne, *Buyer*
Sam Sheehan, *Engineer*
Kim Kraemaer, *Accountant*
Barbara Youngblood, *Accountant*
EMP: 25
SQ FT: 14,000
SALES (est): 25MM **Privately Held**
SIC: **1311** Crude petroleum production; natural gas production

(G-9395)
CEMENT TEST EQUIPMENT INC
4001 W Edison St (74127-5017)
PHONE....................................918 835-4454
Wc Jones, *President*
Chris Duke, *Vice Pres*
Ben Kraft, *Opers Mgr*
Mark Andrews, *Treasurer*
Cory Davis, *Director*
EMP: 10
SQ FT: 6,000
SALES (est): 930K **Privately Held**
SIC: **3829** Gauging instruments, thickness ultrasonic

(G-9396)
CENTENNIAL GAS LIQUIDS ULC
6120 S Yale Ave Ste 805 (74136-4217)
PHONE....................................918 481-1119
Michael Krimbill, *CEO*
EMP: 2
SALES (est): 84.5K **Privately Held**
SIC: **1321** Natural gas liquids

(G-9397)
CENTREX OPERATING CO INC
5550 S Lewis Ave Ste 304 (74105-7178)
P.O. Box 1000, Jenks (74037-1000)
PHONE....................................918 747-9997
Dusty Smith, *President*
Greg Owen, *Vice Pres*
Darren Laptad, *Treasurer*
EMP: 3
SALES (est): 376.4K **Privately Held**
SIC: **1311** Crude petroleum production; natural gas production

(G-9398)
CENTURION RESOURCES LLC
7404 S Yale Ave (74136-7029)
PHONE....................................918 493-1110
Bruce Randall,
EMP: 6
SQ FT: 2,000
SALES (est): 803.5K **Privately Held**
SIC: **1311** Natural gas production

(G-9399)
CENTURY GEOPHYSICAL CORP (PA)
1223 S 71st East Ave (74112-5609)
PHONE....................................918 838-9811
John McCormick, *President*
Chuck Gillis, *Mfg Staff*
Miguel Barahona, *Engineer*
Linda McGrath, *CFO*
John M McGrath, *Treasurer*
EMP: 25
SQ FT: 50,000
SALES (est): 10MM **Privately Held**
SIC: **1382** 3532 Geophysical exploration, oil & gas field; mining machinery

(G-9400)
CENTURY PLATING INC
8831 E 38th St (74145-1522)
PHONE....................................918 835-1482
Bobbie Attebury, *President*
EMP: 3
SALES (est): 264.4K **Privately Held**
SIC: **3471** Anodizing (plating) of metals or formed products; electroplating of metals or formed products

(G-9401)
CEP MID-CONTINENT LLC
1560 E 21st St Ste 215 (74114-1345)
P.O. Box 970, Skiatook (74070-0970)
PHONE....................................918 270-9927
EMP: 5
SALES (est): 209.6K **Privately Held**
SIC: **1382** Oil & gas exploration services

(G-9402)
CFMI LLC (PA)
Also Called: Wallace Energy
3845 S 103rd East Ave # 101 (74146-2452)
PHONE....................................918 877-5000
Cameron Long,
Edwin Morris,
Robert Phillips,
EMP: 2
SQ FT: 1,900
SALES (est): 716.6K **Privately Held**
SIC: **1382** Oil & gas exploration services

(G-9403)
CHANDLER MATERIALS COMPANY
5519 E 15th St (74112)
PHONE....................................918 836-9151
Claude W Chandler, *Principal*
Kellie Russell, *Accounts Mgr*
EMP: 40
SQ FT: 10,000
SALES (est): 4MM
SALES (corp-wide): 7.3MM **Privately Held**
SIC: **3271** 3272 2899 Blocks, concrete or cinder: standard; pipe, concrete or lined with concrete; concrete curing & hardening compounds
PA: Midwest Block & Brick
1001 Estelle St
Paducah KY 42001
270 442-3585

(G-9404)
CHANNEL ONE LIGHTING SYSTEMS
Also Called: Channel One Lightning Systems
1522 E 6th St (74120-4026)
PHONE....................................918 587-2663
W Blair Powell, *President*
Tammy Powell, *Vice Pres*
EMP: 8
SQ FT: 8,000
SALES (est): 954.2K **Privately Held**
SIC: **3648** 3663 Lighting equipment; radio & TV communications equipment

(G-9405)
CHART COOLER SERVICE CO INC (DH)
5615 S 129th East Ave (74134-6708)
PHONE....................................918 834-0002
Wayne Pyle, *President*
▼ EMP: 84
SALES (est): 31.1MM **Publicly Held**
SIC: **3443** Heat exchangers, condensers & components
HQ: Chart Inc.
407 7th St Nw
New Prague MN 56071
952 758-4484

(G-9406)
CHART INDUSTRIES INC
5615 S 129th East Ave (74134-6708)
PHONE....................................918 621-5246
EMP: 9 EST: 1992
SALES (est): 1.4MM **Privately Held**
SIC: **3443** Fabricated plate work (boiler shop)

(G-9407)
CHASTAIN ENTERPRISES LLC
Also Called: Relay Creative Group
16410 E 50th St (74134-7183)
PHONE....................................918 615-9355
Shawn Sturm, *Mng Member*
EMP: 5 EST: 2015
SALES: 500K **Privately Held**
SIC: **7336** 2721 2731 Commercial art & graphic design; periodicals; magazines: publishing only, not printed on site; statistical reports (periodicals): publishing only; trade journals: publishing only, not printed on site; books: publishing only

(G-9408)
CHECOTAH PARTNERS LLC
2512 E 71st St (74136-5533)
PHONE....................................918 935-2795
EMP: 2
SALES (est): 146.1K **Privately Held**
SIC: **1311** Sand & shale oil mining

(G-9409)
CHEMCO
8242 S Sandusky Ave (74137-1833)
PHONE....................................918 481-0537
Charles Alcott, *President*
EMP: 3
SQ FT: 2,500
SALES (est): 321K **Privately Held**
SIC: **3559** 3829 3821 3612 Refinery, chemical processing & similar machinery; measuring & controlling devices; laboratory apparatus & furniture; transformers, except electric

(G-9410)
CHEMPROOF POLYMERS INC
2750 Charles Page Blvd (74127-8315)
PHONE....................................918 584-0364
Jeff Glass, *President*
Marty Testa, *Vice Pres*
EMP: 4
SQ FT: 13,000
SALES (est): 671.6K **Privately Held**
SIC: **3479** Coating of metals & formed products

(G-9411)
CHEMTRADE REFINERY SVCS INC
5201 W 21st St (74107-2232)
PHONE....................................918 587-7613
Terry Reinshagen, *Purchasing*
Corky Botts, *Maintence Staff*
EMP: 18
SALES (corp-wide): 1.1B **Privately Held**
SIC: **2819** Industrial inorganic chemicals
HQ: Chemtrade Refinery Services Inc.
440 N 9th St
Lawrence KS 66044
785 843-2290

(G-9412)
CHERNICO EXPLORATION INC
1307 S Boulder Ave # 400 (74119-9700)
PHONE....................................918 587-6242
David Cherincky, *President*
Pat Cherincky, *Corp Secy*
Susan Keary, *CFO*
John Cavert, *IT/INT Sup*
EMP: 3
SALES (est): 251.4K **Privately Held**
SIC: **1382** Oil & gas exploration services

(G-9413)
CHEROKEE INSIGHTS LLC
10838 E Marshall St # 22 (74116-5682)
PHONE....................................918 430-3409
Doug Zwiselsberger, *Principal*
Janice Dearman, *Administration*

EMP: 1
SQ FT: 200
SALES (est): 74.4K **Privately Held**
SIC: **3724** Research & development on aircraft engines & parts

(G-9414)
CHEROKEE NATION RED WING LLC (DH)
10838 E Marshall St # 20 (74116-5682)
PHONE....................................918 430-3437
Chris Moody, *President*
Janice Dearman, *Exec Dir*
Amy Barnett, *Director*
▲ EMP: 28
SQ FT: 2,900
SALES: 29.7MM **Privately Held**
SIC: **3444** 3679 3728 Sheet metalwork; harness assemblies for electronic use: wire or cable; military aircraft equipment & armament; wing assemblies & parts, aircraft
HQ: Cherokee Nation Businesses Llc
777 W Cherokee St
Catoosa OK 74015
918 384-7474

(G-9415)
CHEROKEE NTION ARMRED SLTONS L
10838 E Marshall St # 22 (74116-5682)
PHONE....................................918 696-3151
Chris Moody, *CEO*
Bryan Collins,
EMP: 37
SALES (est): 138.8K **Privately Held**
SIC: **3599** Machine & other job shop work

(G-9416)
CHEROKEE WOODWORK INC
2746 E King St (74110-5036)
PHONE....................................918 798-5037
Albert E Grant, *Principal*
EMP: 2
SALES (est): 221.7K **Privately Held**
SIC: **2431** Millwork

(G-9417)
CHERRY STREET PRINT SHOP INC
608 E 3rd St Ste 7 (74120-2408)
P.O. Box 14578 (74159-1578)
PHONE....................................918 584-0022
Michael L Robertson, *President*
EMP: 4
SALES (est): 493.8K **Privately Held**
SIC: **2752** 2791 2789 Commercial printing, offset; typesetting; bookbinding & related work

(G-9418)
CHEYENNE WOODWORKS INC
402 Heavy Traffic Way (74127-8906)
PHONE....................................918 587-3533
David Hollingsworth, *Administration*
EMP: 4
SALES (est): 313.7K **Privately Held**
SIC: **2431** Woodwork, interior & ornamental

(G-9419)
CHISELED IN STONE
401 S Memorial Dr (74112-2203)
PHONE....................................918 813-5409
Kevin Parquette, *Owner*
EMP: 1
SALES (est): 55.7K **Privately Held**
SIC: **3423** Carpenters' hand tools, except saws: levels, chisels, etc.

(G-9420)
CHISHOLM OIL AND GAS OPER LLC
6100 S Yale Ave Ste 1700 (74136-1921)
PHONE....................................918 488-6400
EMP: 3
SALES (est): 205.2K **Privately Held**
SIC: **1389** Oil field services

(G-9421)
CHROME RIVER WHOLESALE LLC
5412 S Mingo Rd Ste I (74146-5739)
P.O. Box 471107 (74147-1107)
PHONE....................................918 610-0810

GEOGRAPHIC SECTION

Tulsa - Tulsa County (G-9449)

Marian Henderson, *Manager*
Tim Spencer,
EMP: 3 **EST:** 1996
SALES (est): 290K **Privately Held**
SIC: 2759 2752 Commercial printing; commercial printing, lithographic

(G-9422)
CHROMIUM PLATING COMPANY (PA)
Also Called: Norco-Northeastern Okla Roll
412 N Cheyenne Ave (74103-1418)
PHONE..................................918 583-4118
William W Tabler Jr, *President*
Debra Tabler, *Vice Pres*
EMP: 30 **EST:** 1929
SQ FT: 55,000
SALES: 4.5MM **Privately Held**
SIC: 3471 3599 Chromium plating of metals or formed products; grinding castings for the trade

(G-9423)
CHRYSALIS SOFTWARE INC
1 W 3rd St Ste 1115 (74103-3515)
PHONE..................................831 761-1307
Debbie Diersch, *President*
MO Pierce, *CFO*
Bill Eckert, *CTO*
EMP: 20
SQ FT: 1,000
SALES (est): 1.4MM
SALES (corp-wide): 7.5MM **Privately Held**
WEB: www.chrysalis.net
SIC: 7372 7371 Prepackaged software; computer software development & applications
PA: Waterfield Technologies, Inc.
 1 W 3rd St Ste 1115
 Tulsa OK 74103
 918 858-6400

(G-9424)
CIENA CORPORATION
100 W 5th St Ste 520 (74103-4288)
PHONE..................................918 925-5000
Colin Tucker, *Principal*
EMP: 10 **Publicly Held**
SIC: 3661 Fiber optics communications equipment
PA: Ciena Corporation
 7035 Ridge Rd
 Hanover MD 21076

(G-9425)
CIMAREX ENERGY CO
202 S Cheyenne Ave # 1000 (74103-3000)
PHONE..................................918 585-1100
Gerald Nagel, *Vice Pres*
Philip Johnson, *Engineer*
Michael Wiley, *Engineer*
Mike Glisson, *Senior Engr*
Ken McBride, *Accountant*
EMP: 250
SALES (corp-wide): 2.3B **Publicly Held**
SIC: 1382 Oil & gas exploration services
PA: Cimarex Energy Co.
 1700 N Lincoln St # 3700
 Denver CO 80203
 303 295-3995

(G-9426)
CIMAREX ENERGY CO
1000 S Denver Ave # 5102 (74119-9800)
PHONE..................................918 295-1638
David Cook, *Principal*
Julia Kirby, *IT/INT Sup*
EMP: 76
SALES (corp-wide): 2.3B **Publicly Held**
SIC: 1382 Oil & gas exploration services
PA: Cimarex Energy Co.
 1700 N Lincoln St # 3700
 Denver CO 80203
 303 295-3995

(G-9427)
CIMARRON EQUIPMENT COMPANY
7828 S Granite Ave (74136-8456)
PHONE..................................918 625-1647
William Bunting, *Principal*
▲ **EMP:** 1
SQ FT: 1,200
SALES (est): 2MM **Privately Held**
SIC: 1389 Oil field services

(G-9428)
CIMARRON MACHINE SERVICES INC
Also Called: Advance Flo Systems
7734 E 11th St (74112-5718)
PHONE..................................918 835-3333
Scott Wilkinson, *President*
Carrie Wilkison, *Corp Secy*
Marcia K Robb, *Vice Pres*
EMP: 20
SQ FT: 11,500
SALES (est): 2.8MM **Privately Held**
SIC: 3599 Machine shop, jobbing & repair

(G-9429)
CIRCLE B MSRMENT FBRCATION LLC (PA)
14034 E Marshall St (74116-2138)
P.O. Box 1, Beaver (73932-0001)
PHONE..................................918 445-4488
Steven Bell, *CEO*
Will Rotert, *Vice Pres*
Tim Howard, *Prdtn Mgr*
Bart Vanvickle, *Purch Mgr*
Roy Murray, *QC Mgr*
EMP: 1
SALES (est): 1MM **Privately Held**
SIC: 3533 Oil & gas field machinery

(G-9430)
CISCO CONTAINERS LLC
17515 E Admiral Pl (74116-3932)
PHONE..................................918 439-9244
James Hensley, *Opers Staff*
Kimberly Cisco,
EMP: 2
SALES (est): 445.6K **Privately Held**
SIC: 2448 Cargo containers, wood & metal combination

(G-9431)
CISCO SYSTEMS INC
1 Memorial Pl (74133)
PHONE..................................999 505-5901
EMP: 691
SALES (corp-wide): 49.1B **Publicly Held**
SIC: 3577 Mfg Computer Equipment
PA: Cisco Systems, Inc.
 170 W Tasman Dr
 San Jose CA 95134
 408 526-4000

(G-9432)
CISKOEAGLE INC
10015 E 51st St (74146-5730)
PHONE..................................918 622-9010
Steve Strifler, *President*
William Cupps, *Vice Pres*
◆ **EMP:** 17
SQ FT: 2,000
SALES (est): 2.2MM **Privately Held**
SIC: 1311 Crude petroleum production; natural gas production

(G-9433)
CITIZEN ENERGY II LLC
320 S Boston Ave Ste 1300 (74103-4702)
PHONE..................................918 949-4680
Greg Augsburger,
Robbie Woodard,
James Woods,
EMP: 15
SALES (est): 208.6K **Privately Held**
SIC: 1382 Geological exploration, oil & gas field

(G-9434)
CITIZEN ENERGY III LLC
320 S Boston Ave Ste 900 (74103-3729)
PHONE..................................918 949-4680
Stephen R McAnamara,
EMP: 2
SALES (est): 81.9K **Privately Held**
SIC: 1382 Oil & gas exploration services

(G-9435)
CITIZEN ENERGY OPERATING LLC (PA)
320 S Boston Ave Ste 900 (74103-3729)
PHONE..................................918 949-4680
Gregory A Augsburger, *CEO*
EMP: 3
SALES (est): 517.8MM **Privately Held**
SIC: 1382 Oil & gas exploration services

(G-9436)
CITIZEN ENRGY INTERMEDIATE LLC
320 S Boston Ave Ste 900 (74103-3729)
PHONE..................................918 949-4680
EMP: 2
SALES (est): 81.9K **Privately Held**
SIC: 1382 Geological exploration, oil & gas field

(G-9437)
CITY TENT & AWNING CO INC
Also Called: City Awning Company
12234 E 60th St (74146-6901)
PHONE..................................918 583-5003
Jack Leon Kelley, *President*
Elaina Kelly, *Admin Sec*
EMP: 6
SQ FT: 7,000
SALES (est): 550.2K **Privately Held**
SIC: 2394 Canopies, fabric: made from purchased materials; awnings, fabric: made from purchased materials

(G-9438)
CLARION EVENTS INC (DH)
Also Called: Pennwell Corporation
110 S Hartford Ave # 200 (74120-1820)
PHONE..................................918 835-3161
Mark C Wilmoth, *President*
Jeff Postelwait, *Editor*
Jayne Gilsinger, *Exec VP*
Paul Andrews, *Vice Pres*
Benjamin Hofmann, *Research*
EMP: 125
SQ FT: 120,000
SALES (est): 127.5MM **Privately Held**
WEB: www.pennwell.com
SIC: 7389 2721 ; magazines: publishing & printing
HQ: Clarion Events Limited
 Bedford House
 London SW6 3
 207 384-7700

(G-9439)
CLARIOS
Also Called: Johnson Controls
6533 E 46th St (74145-5812)
PHONE..................................918 641-0660
EMP: 2 **Privately Held**
SIC: 2531 Seats, automobile
HQ: Johnson Controls, Inc.
 5757 N Green Bay Ave
 Milwaukee WI 53209
 414 524-1200

(G-9440)
CLARK SEALS LLC
3824 S 79th East Ave (74145-3232)
PHONE..................................918 664-0587
Henry Zahn, *Mng Member*
Tina Zahn, *Executive*
▲ **EMP:** 50
SQ FT: 35,500
SALES (est): 8.5MM **Privately Held**
WEB: www.clarkseals.com
SIC: 3053 5085 Oil seals, rubber; seals, industrial

(G-9441)
CLARK SEALS LTD
7704 E 38th St (74145-3211)
PHONE..................................918 610-1006
Veronica Shanahan, *Administration*
EMP: 1
SALES (est): 39.6K **Privately Held**
SIC: 3999 Manufacturing industries

(G-9442)
CLASSIC SHUTTERS
10914 E 2nd St (74128-1642)
PHONE..................................918 234-0657
Georgia Stevens, *Co-Owner*
David Stevens, *Co-Owner*
EMP: 2
SALES (est): 140.8K **Privately Held**
WEB: www.classicshuttersok.com
SIC: 3442 Shutters, door or window: metal

(G-9443)
CLAUDE NEON FEDERAL
533 S Rockford Ave (74120-4097)
PHONE..................................918 585-9010
Fax: 918 587-7176
EMP: 3 **EST:** 2013
SALES (est): 170K **Privately Held**
SIC: 2813 Mfg Industrial Gases

(G-9444)
CLAUDE NEON FEDERAL SIGNS INC
1225 N Lansing Ave (74106-5943)
PHONE..................................918 587-7171
Scott Sanford, *President*
John Sanford, *Principal*
Richard Sanford, *Principal*
Daniel Sanford, *Vice Pres*
Patrick Sanford, *Vice Pres*
▲ **EMP:** 54
SQ FT: 28,000
SALES (est): 7.7MM **Privately Held**
WEB: www.cnfsigns.com
SIC: 3993 Neon signs; scoreboards, electric

(G-9445)
CLAY SERIGRAPHICS INC
Also Called: U.s Safety Sign and Decal
1433 E 6th St (74120-4023)
PHONE..................................918 592-2529
Randal A Clay, *President*
Melanie Clay, *Corp Secy*
Ivan Matthiesen, *Vice Pres*
Jackie Matthiesen, *Vice Pres*
EMP: 12
SQ FT: 3,000
SALES (est): 1.5MM **Privately Held**
SIC: 3993 2396 Signs, not made in custom sign painting shops; screen printing on fabric articles

(G-9446)
CLEANNG LLC
Also Called: Infinite Composites Tech
10738 E 55th Pl (74146-6701)
PHONE..................................918 409-0384
Robert Villarreal, *CEO*
Michael Tate, *COO*
Lance Adams,
EMP: 7
SALES (est): 499K **Privately Held**
SIC: 3085 Plastics bottles

(G-9447)
CLEAR EDGE FILTRATION INC (HQ)
Also Called: Madison Filter
11607 E 43rd St N (74116-2103)
PHONE..................................918 984-6000
Rick V Drehle, *President*
Christopher Roth, *Plant Mgr*
Paul McClellan, *Mfg Mgr*
Joshua Rowell, *Buyer*
Randall Schmitz, *CFO*
▲ **EMP:** 85
SQ FT: 120,000
SALES (est): 57.7MM
SALES (corp-wide): 320.9MM **Privately Held**
WEB: www.clear-edge.com
SIC: 2295 3569 Coated fabrics, not rubberized; filters, general line: industrial
PA: Filtration Group Llc
 912 E Washington St Ste 1
 Joliet IL 60433
 815 726-4600

(G-9448)
CLEAR EDGE FILTRATION INC
11607 E 43rd St N (74116-2103)
PHONE..................................800 637-6206
Michael Kriever, *Branch Mgr*
EMP: 85
SALES (corp-wide): 320.9MM **Privately Held**
SIC: 3569 2295 Filters, general line: industrial; coated fabrics, not rubberized
HQ: Clear Edge Filtration, Inc.
 11607 E 43rd St N
 Tulsa OK 74116
 918 984-6000

(G-9449)
CLEAR TONE HEARING CENTER INC
2323 S Sheridan Rd (74129-1043)
PHONE..................................918 838-1000
Jim Feeley, *President*
Mike Feeley, *Chief Mktg Ofcr*

Tulsa - Tulsa County (G-9450) GEOGRAPHIC SECTION

EMP: 34
SQ FT: 12,000
SALES (est): 4.9MM **Privately Held**
SIC: 3842 5999 3651 Hearing aids; hearing aids; household audio & video equipment

(G-9450)
CLEARITY LLC
8408 S Delaware Ave (74137-1403)
PHONE 918 388-9000
Roland Minnis, *CFO*
EMP: 8
SALES (est): 1MM **Privately Held**
SIC: 3842 Hearing aids

(G-9451)
CLEARWATER ENTERPRISES
6315 E 102nd St (74137-7052)
PHONE 918 296-7007
EMP: 2
SALES (est): 88.9K **Privately Held**
SIC: 1382 Oil & gas exploration services

(G-9452)
CLEOPTRAZ SCRETZ HNDMADE SOAPS
9401 E Admiral Pl (74115-8121)
PHONE 918 272-3319
EMP: 2
SALES (est): 80.3K **Privately Held**
SIC: 2844 Toilet preparations

(G-9453)
CLINE MACHINE INC
1552 N 168th East Ave (74116-4903)
P.O. Box 581563 (74158-1563)
PHONE 918 587-0126
Robin Pfeiffer, *President*
Anthony Pfeiffer, *Vice Pres*
Deborah Davis, *Office Mgr*
Tony Pfeiffer, *Manager*
EMP: 29 EST: 1955
SQ FT: 37,000
SALES: 8.3MM **Privately Held**
WEB: www.clinemachine.com
SIC: 3599 Machine shop, jobbing & repair

(G-9454)
CLINK INDUSTRIES
6528 E 101st St (74133-6724)
PHONE 918 970-6537
EMP: 3
SALES (est): 153.9K **Privately Held**
SIC: 3999 Manufacturing industries

(G-9455)
CLOCK SHOP INC
Also Called: TCS Systems
1236 S Peoria Ave (74120-5020)
PHONE 918 583-5835
Ted Bullinger, *President*
EMP: 3 EST: 1926
SQ FT: 2,000
SALES: 150K **Privately Held**
SIC: 3579 7631 Time clocks & time recording devices; clock repair

(G-9456)
CLOSEBEND INC
4812 W 52nd St (74107-8939)
PHONE 918 445-1131
Paul Secrest, *Vice Pres*
EMP: 18 EST: 1973
SQ FT: 6,000
SALES (est): 4MM **Privately Held**
SIC: 3321 3494 Pressure pipe & fittings, cast iron; valves & pipe fittings

(G-9457)
CLR ENTERPRISES LLC
5423 E 109th Pl (74137-7280)
PHONE 918 298-1943
Charles L Rufo,
EMP: 1
SALES (est): 154.3K **Privately Held**
SIC: 3565 5199 Packaging machinery; packaging materials

(G-9458)
CLYDES GOOD GRUEL LLC
917 N Knoxville Ave (74115-6222)
PHONE 918 323-6143
Clyde Griffith Jr,
EMP: 1

SALES (est): 113.8K **Privately Held**
SIC: 3531 Construction machinery

(G-9459)
CMARK RESOURCES LLC
7170 S Braden Ave (74136-6329)
PHONE 918 492-5170
EMP: 5
SALES (est): 241.1K **Privately Held**
SIC: 1389 Oil & gas field services

(G-9460)
CMT WELL COMPLETIONS INC
110 W 7th St Ste 2700 (74119-1199)
PHONE 918 523-0600
Alan Michael, *Principal*
EMP: 5
SALES (est): 305.8K **Privately Held**
SIC: 1389 Oil & gas wells: building, repairing & dismantling

(G-9461)
CNC PATTERNS & TOOLING
4310 E Pine Pl (74115-4148)
PHONE 918 835-2344
EMP: 4
SALES (est): 220K **Privately Held**
SIC: 3542 3543 3544 Mfg Machine Tools-Forming Mfg Industrial Patterns Mfg Dies/Tools/Jigs/Fixtures

(G-9462)
COAST TO COAST POWER SPT LLC
6100 S Yale Ave Ste 900 (74136-1935)
PHONE 918 712-8487
Todd Pals, *CFO*
L Williams,
EMP: 1
SALES (est): 99.4K **Privately Held**
SIC: 2721 Magazines: publishing & printing

(G-9463)
COBO INDUSTRIES LLC
7302 E 38th St (74145-3224)
PHONE 918 574-2123
Bill Gregorovic, *Principal*
EMP: 2
SALES (est): 76.2K **Privately Held**
SIC: 3999 Manufacturing industries

(G-9464)
COCA-COLA ENTERPRISES INC
14002 E 21st St Ste 800 (74134-1401)
PHONE 918 619-8200
EMP: 5 **Privately Held**
SIC: 2086 Carb Sft Drnkbtlcn
PA: Coca-Cola Enterprises, Inc.
2500 Windy Ridge Pkwy Se # 700
Atlanta GA 30339

(G-9465)
COEN CO INC
11920 E Apache St (74116-1309)
PHONE 918 234-1800
Ken Siu, *Engineer*
Bob Wakelee, *Manager*
EMP: 2
SALES (est): 127.1K **Privately Held**
SIC: 3433 Heating equipment, except electric

(G-9466)
COILED TUBING SPECIALTIES LLC
7404 S Yale Ave (74136-7029)
PHONE 918 878-7460
EMP: 2
SALES (est): 88.1K **Privately Held**
SIC: 1389 Oil field services

(G-9467)
COLEMAN PRESS
13737 E 31st Pl (74134-4213)
PHONE 918 437-0000
David L Coleman, *Owner*
EMP: 2
SALES (est): 182.5K **Privately Held**
SIC: 2752 Commercial printing, offset

(G-9468)
COLLINS QUALITY PRINTING
3236 E 15th St (74104-5248)
PHONE 918 744-0077
Wanda Duffy, *Owner*

EMP: 4
SQ FT: 2,500
SALES (est): 416.7K **Privately Held**
SIC: 2752 2791 2789 2759 Lithographing on metal; typesetting; bookbinding & related work; commercial printing

(G-9469)
COLORADO FUEL MANUFACTURERS
3845 S 103rd East Ave # 101 (74146-2456)
PHONE 918 877-5102
EMP: 4 EST: 2010
SALES (est): 380.7K **Privately Held**
SIC: 2869 Fuels

(G-9470)
COLORCOMM
4134 E 49th St (74135-3218)
PHONE 918 398-7777
Dustin Elliott, *Owner*
EMP: 5
SALES (est): 540K **Privately Held**
SIC: 3577 Printers, computer

(G-9471)
COLT EXPRESS
4110 S 100th East Ave (74146-3628)
PHONE 918 455-2658
Jack Brassfield, *Principal*
EMP: 2
SALES (est): 121.3K **Privately Held**
WEB: www.coltexpressdelivery.com
SIC: 2741 Miscellaneous publishing

(G-9472)
COLUMBIA DEVELOPMENT CORP
15 E 5th St Ste 3530 (74103-4342)
PHONE 918 587-5521
Lee A Keeling, *President*
Nancy Grayson, *Admin Sec*
EMP: 3
SQ FT: 2,000
SALES (est): 320K **Privately Held**
SIC: 1311 Crude petroleum & natural gas

(G-9473)
COMAN PATTERN WORKS
3806 S Granite Ave (74135-5556)
PHONE 918 270-1775
David P Coman, *Owner*
EMP: 70 EST: 1929
SQ FT: 20,000
SALES (est): 5.4MM **Privately Held**
SIC: 3469 3543 Patterns on metal; industrial patterns

(G-9474)
COMMERCIAL METALS COMPANY
Also Called: CMC Recycling
3105 E Skelly Dr (74105-6358)
P.O. Box 1768, Catoosa (74015-1768)
PHONE 918 437-5377
Steven Noack, *Branch Mgr*
EMP: 10
SALES (corp-wide): 5.8B **Publicly Held**
SIC: 3312 Bars & bar shapes, steel, hot-rolled
PA: Commercial Metals Company
6565 N Macarthur Blvd # 800
Irving TX 75039
214 689-4300

(G-9475)
COMMERCIAL PRINTING MARKETING
608 E 3rd St Ste 5 (74120-2408)
PHONE 918 494-7072
James C Elliott, *Principal*
EMP: 4
SALES (est): 367.4K **Privately Held**
SIC: 2752 Commercial printing, offset

(G-9476)
COMMERCIAL PROPERTY RESEARCH
Also Called: Research America
8301 E 74th Pl (74133-2971)
P.O. Box 33074 (74153-1074)
PHONE 918 481-8882
Richard Sudduth, *President*
Melanie Richards, *Vice Pres*

EMP: 3
SALES (est): 270K **Privately Held**
SIC: 8742 8732 2721 Real estate consultant; commercial nonphysical research; periodicals

(G-9477)
CONFED OIL INCORPORATED (PA)
Also Called: Kimbrel Oil
2121 S Columbia Ave # 200 (74114-3516)
P.O. Box 14064 (74159-1064)
PHONE 918 582-0018
Mike Kimbrel, *President*
Dante Vitulano, *Technology*
Marion Kincer, *Admin Sec*
EMP: 4
SQ FT: 1,300
SALES (est): 812.8K **Privately Held**
SIC: 1311 Crude petroleum production; natural gas production

(G-9478)
CONTINENTAL INDUSTRIES
2416 S Joplin Ave (74114-3826)
PHONE 918 284-9013
EMP: 2 EST: 2018
SALES (est): 66.1K **Privately Held**
SIC: 3999 Manufacturing industries

(G-9479)
CONTINENTAL STONEWORKS INC
10026a S Mingo Rd Ste 168 (74133-5700)
P.O. Box 330229 (74133-0229)
PHONE 918 835-6725
Phillip D Ruble, *President*
EMP: 10 EST: 1997
SQ FT: 3,000
SALES (est): 960.9K **Privately Held**
WEB: www.cstoneworks.com
SIC: 8611 2541 1799 Contractors' association; counter & sink tops; counter top installation

(G-9480)
COOK COMPRESSION
5411 S 125th East Ave (74146-6227)
PHONE 918 254-0660
Marc Edmonson, *Regional Mgr*
Mike Holt, *Manager*
EMP: 3
SALES (est): 342.1K **Privately Held**
SIC: 3563 Air & gas compressors

(G-9481)
COOL HARD HAT INC
2511 S Cincinnati Ave (74114-2619)
PHONE 918 812-7636
James Welsh, *President*
EMP: 4
SALES: 80K **Privately Held**
WEB: www.coolhardhat.net
SIC: 2353 7389 Uniform hats & caps;

(G-9482)
COOLEY CREEK PRINTING
6825 E 15th St (74112-6607)
PHONE 918 835-8200
Nell Cooley, *Owner*
EMP: 2
SALES (est): 88.6K **Privately Held**
SIC: 2759 Publication printing

(G-9483)
COOLEY ENTERPRISES INC
Also Called: Kwik Kopy Printing
10755 E Admiral Pl (74116-3012)
PHONE 918 437-6900
Rolla Nell Cooley, *President*
Shirley Cossey, *Corp Secy*
EMP: 4
SQ FT: 4,000
SALES (est): 310.9K **Privately Held**
WEB: www.homewatchcaregivers.com
SIC: 2752 7334 2791 2789 Commercial printing, offset; photocopying & duplicating services; typesetting; bookbinding & related work

(G-9484)
COPES WOODWORKING
9928 S 107th East Ave (74133-5117)
PHONE 918 698-2104
Chris Cope, *Administration*

GEOGRAPHIC SECTION
Tulsa - Tulsa County (G-9512)

EMP: 1 EST: 2014
SALES (est): 54.1K **Privately Held**
SIC: 2431 Millwork

(G-9485)
COPPERHEAD INDUSTRIES
2651 E 21st St Ste 405 (74114-1731)
PHONE....................918 712-9927
Ralph Stone, *Principal*
EMP: 2
SALES (est): 111.8K **Privately Held**
SIC: 3999 Manufacturing industries

(G-9486)
CORE LABORATORIES LP
4616 N Mingo Rd (74117-5901)
PHONE....................918 834-2337
Paul R Brauer, *Branch Mgr*
EMP: 16
SALES (corp-wide): 700.8MM **Privately Held**
SIC: 1389 Oil field services
HQ: Core Laboratories Lp
  6316 Windfern Rd
  Houston TX 77040

(G-9487)
CORESLAB STRUCTURES TULSA INC
3206 N 129th East Ave (74116-1431)
PHONE....................918 438-0230
Mario Franciosa, *President*
Mark Davis, *Production*
EMP: 35
SALES (est): 5.4MM
SALES (corp-wide): 27.3MM **Privately Held**
SIC: 3272 Concrete products, precast
HQ: Coreslab Structures (Ont) Inc
  205 Coreslab Dr
  Dundas ON L9H 0
  905 689-3993

(G-9488)
CORETEC GROUP INC (PA)
6804 S Canton Ave Ste 150 (74136-3419)
PHONE....................918 494-0505
Michael A Kraft, *CEO*
Simon Calton, *Ch of Bd*
Victor F Keen, *Ch of Bd*
Ronald Robinson, *CFO*
EMP: 4
SALES (est): 564.8K **Publicly Held**
SIC: 3823 Digital displays of process variables

(G-9489)
CORNERSTONE PETROLEUM OPER LLC
20 E 5th St Ste 1300 (74103-4462)
PHONE....................817 730-5200
H Lee Matthews, *President*
Brian Benge, *President*
Don Pearce, *President*
Jim Holcomb, *Vice Pres*
EMP: 1
SALES: 2MM **Privately Held**
SIC: 1311 Crude petroleum & natural gas
PA: Cornerstone Petroleum Resources, Llc
  20 E 5th St Ste 1300
  Tulsa OK

(G-9490)
CORONA TECHNICAL SERVICES LLC
6914 S Yorktown Ave # 115 (74136-3931)
PHONE....................918 398-8052
Danny George, *Mng Member*
Brett Organ, *Technology*
EMP: 8
SQ FT: 2,000
SALES: 2.2MM **Privately Held**
SIC: 7372 Educational computer software

(G-9491)
CORONADO RESOURCES MGT LLC
4745 E 91st St Ste 200 (74137-2832)
PHONE....................918 591-3500
Mark D Wilson, *Mng Member*
John Mark Coates,
EMP: 8
SQ FT: 2,400
SALES (est): 756.2K **Privately Held**
SIC: 1382 Oil & gas exploration services

(G-9492)
CORSER GROUP INC
Also Called: Advertising Specialties
2849 E 35th St (74105-2921)
PHONE....................918 749-6456
Bob Pritchard, *President*
Leslie Pritchard, *Vice Pres*
EMP: 2
SALES: 1MM **Privately Held**
SIC: 5199 2395 Advertising specialties; embroidery products, except schiffli machine

(G-9493)
COUNCIL OAK RESOURCES LLC
1 W 3rd St Ste 1000 (74103-3500)
PHONE....................918 513-0900
Rick Fritz,
EMP: 19
SALES (est): 498K
SALES (corp-wide): 4.9MM **Privately Held**
SIC: 1382 Oil & gas exploration services
PA: Cor Operating, Llc
  1 W 3rd St Ste 1000
  Tulsa OK 74103
  918 513-0900

(G-9494)
COVE PETROLEUM CORPORATION
114 E 5th St Ste 300 (74103-4621)
PHONE....................918 584-5291
Michael E Mockley, *President*
C Cooke Newman, *Vice Pres*
Betty Ann Mockley, *Treasurer*
Wanda McCreedy, *Admin Sec*
EMP: 2
SQ FT: 17,000
SALES (est): 292K
SALES (corp-wide): 6MM **Privately Held**
SIC: 1311 Crude petroleum production; natural gas production
PA: Anchor Gasoline Corporation
  2847 E 36th Pl
  Tulsa OK 74105
  918 584-5291

(G-9495)
CP SOLUTIONS INC
2757 S Memorial Dr (74129-2603)
PHONE....................918 664-6642
Mike Vaughan, *President*
Roger Cox, *President*
Paul Nichols, *General Mgr*
Tom Tirrell, *Purchasing*
Tom Hille, *Controller*
EMP: 60 EST: 1935
SQ FT: 90,000
SALES (est): 27.2MM
SALES (corp-wide): 6.2B **Publicly Held**
WEB: www.cpsolutions.biz
SIC: 2752 2789 2759 2396 Commercial printing, lithographic; bookbinding & related work; commercial printing; automotive & apparel trimmings
PA: R. R. Donnelley & Sons Company
  35 W Wacker Dr
  Chicago IL 60601
  312 326-8000

(G-9496)
CR SERVICES LLC
1717 S Boulder Ave # 400 (74119-4805)
PHONE....................918 295-7600
EMP: 46
SALES (est): 1.4MM **Publicly Held**
SIC: 1221 Coal preparation plant, bituminous or lignite
HQ: Alliance Resource Partners Lp
  1717 S Boulder Ave # 400
  Tulsa OK 74119
  918 295-7600

(G-9497)
CRACKSHOT CORPORATION
3616 N Columbia Ave (74110-1231)
PHONE....................918 838-1272
Tom Hargrove, *President*
EMP: 8
SQ FT: 7,500
SALES (est): 830K **Privately Held**
SIC: 3021 Protective footwear, rubber or plastic

(G-9498)
CRAFT PRINTED ENVELOPES INC
5663 N Mingo Rd (74117)
PHONE....................918 249-8887
Dayna York, *President*
Danna Mackenie, *President*
EMP: 3
SALES (est): 293.8K **Privately Held**
SIC: 2752 Commercial printing, offset

(G-9499)
CRAIN DISPLAYS & EXHIBITS INC
1510 S Memorial Dr (74112-7039)
PHONE....................918 585-9797
Steve Milam, *President*
EMP: 10
SQ FT: 30,000
SALES (est): 989.2K **Privately Held**
SIC: 7389 7359 3993 Exhibit construction by industrial contractors; equipment rental & leasing; signs & advertising specialties

(G-9500)
CRANE CARRIER CO
1925 N Sheridan Rd (74115-3602)
PHONE....................918 836-1651
Butch Butler, *Sales Staff*
EMP: 2
SALES (est): 87.2K **Privately Held**
SIC: 3713 Truck & bus bodies

(G-9501)
CRANE CARRIER COMPANY
5874 S Mingo Rd (74146-6425)
PHONE....................918 286-2300
EMP: 1 EST: 2018
SALES (est): 60K **Privately Held**
SIC: 3531 Crane carriers

(G-9502)
CRANE MANUFACTURING INC
5531 E Admiral Pl (74115-8411)
PHONE....................918 838-8800
EMP: 20
SQ FT: 58,000
SALES (est): 3.5MM **Privately Held**
SIC: 3823 3829 Mfg Process Control Instruments Mfg Measuring/Controlling Devices

(G-9503)
CRC EVANS WEIGHTING SYSTEMS
10700 E Independence St (74116-5601)
P.O. Box 50038 (74150-0038)
PHONE....................918 438-2100
Fred Lysak, *President*
▲ EMP: 5
SALES (est): 616.7K
SALES (corp-wide): 14.4B **Publicly Held**
WEB: www.crc-evans.com
SIC: 1771 3272 2891 Concrete work; concrete products; adhesives & sealants
HQ: Crc-Evans International Holdings, Inc.
  7011 High Life Dr
  Houston TX 77066
  832 249-3100

(G-9504)
CRC-EVANS PIPELINE INTL INC
10700 E Independence St (74116-5601)
P.O. Box 50368 (74150-0368)
PHONE....................918 438-2100
M Timothy Carey, *Branch Mgr*
EMP: 108
SALES (corp-wide): 14.4B **Publicly Held**
SIC: 3531 5082 3548 3547 Construction machinery; excavating machinery & equipment; cranes, construction; welding apparatus; rolling mill machinery; machine tools, metal cutting type
HQ: Crc-Evans Pipeline International, Inc.
  7011 High Life Dr
  Houston TX 77066
  800 664-9224

(G-9505)
CREATIVE PACKAGING INC
2837 Charles Page Blvd (74127-8316)
PHONE....................918 587-0347
Michael Bell, *President*
EMP: 8
SQ FT: 20,000
SALES (est): 1MM **Privately Held**
SIC: 7389 2653 Design services; boxes, corrugated: made from purchased materials

(G-9506)
CREDITPOINT SOFTWARE LLC
Also Called: Creditmaster Software
20 E 5th St Ste 900 (74103-4448)
PHONE....................918 376-9440
John Powers, *CEO*
George Garner, *COO*
Kevin Murray, *CFO*
EMP: 25
SALES (est): 4.6MM **Privately Held**
SIC: 7372 Business oriented computer software

(G-9507)
CREEK INTERNATIONAL RIG CORP
8 E 3rd St (74103-3610)
PHONE....................918 585-8221
John E Menger, *Principal*
EMP: 2
SALES (est): 100.6K
SALES (corp-wide): 571.1MM **Publicly Held**
SIC: 1381 Drilling oil & gas wells
PA: Parker Drilling Company
  5 Greenway Plz Ste 100
  Houston TX 77046
  281 406-2000

(G-9508)
CREST RESOURCES INC
Also Called: Crest Energy
15 E 5th St Ste 3650 (74103-4310)
PHONE....................918 585-2900
Glenn H Hudgens, *President*
EMP: 9
SQ FT: 4,000
SALES (est): 2.9MM **Privately Held**
SIC: 1382 Oil & gas exploration services

(G-9509)
CROSBY GROUP LLC
2857 Dawson Rd (74110-5042)
P.O. Box 3128 (74101-3128)
PHONE....................918 834-4611
Ron Vander Slice, *Marketing Mgr*
Earl Wilson, *Manager*
EMP: 265
SALES (corp-wide): 307.9MM **Privately Held**
SIC: 3429 3462 Manufactured hardware (general); iron & steel forgings
PA: The Crosby Group Llc
  2801 Dawson Rd
  Tulsa OK 74110
  918 834-4611

(G-9510)
CROSBY GROUP LLC (PA)
Also Called: National Swage
2801 Dawson Rd (74110-5040)
P.O. Box 3128 (74101-3128)
PHONE....................918 834-4611
Robert Desel, *CEO*
Bob Coleman, *Controller*
Steve Heifner, *Manager*
Cindy Gruver, *Supervisor*
Brian Lavarnway, *Officer*
◆ EMP: 19
SQ FT: 15,000
SALES (est): 307.9MM **Privately Held**
SIC: 3429 Manufactured hardware (general)

(G-9511)
CROSBY US ACQUISITION CORP (HQ)
2801 Dawson Rd (74110-5042)
PHONE....................918 834-4611
Jason Struthers, *President*
EMP: 9
SALES (est): 2.3B **Publicly Held**
SIC: 3629 Current collector wheels, for trolley rigging

(G-9512)
CROSBY WORLDWIDE LIMITED
2801 Dawson Rd (74110-5042)
PHONE....................918 834-4611
Jason Struthers, *President*
David Dixon, *CFO*

Tulsa - Tulsa County (G-9513)

Samuel Hale, *Asst Sec*
EMP: 10
SALES (est): 1MM **Privately Held**
SIC: 3429 3462 6719 Manufactured hardware (general); iron & steel forgings; investment holding companies, except banks

(G-9513)
CROW CREEK ENERGY LLC
11920 S Erie Ave (74137-8432)
PHONE...................918 970-6706
Patrick Hall,
EMP: 7
SALES (est): 717.4K **Privately Held**
SIC: 1382 Oil & gas exploration services

(G-9514)
CROWLEY OIL & MFG
5312 E 26th St (74114-4902)
PHONE...................918 744-8129
Pat Crowley, *Owner*
EMP: 3
SALES (est): 341.3K **Privately Held**
SIC: 3533 Oil & gas field machinery

(G-9515)
CROWN GEOCHEMISTRY INC
427 S Boston Ave (74103-4141)
PHONE...................918 392-0334
EMP: 2 **EST:** 2011
SALES (est): 110K **Privately Held**
SIC: 1381 Oil/Gas Well Drilling

(G-9516)
CROWN NEON SIGNS INC
5676 S 107th East Ave (74146-6715)
PHONE...................918 437-7446
Justin Moydell, *Incorporator*
EMP: 5
SALES (est): 503.4K **Privately Held**
SIC: 3993 Signs & advertising specialties

(G-9517)
CROWN PRODUCTS INC (PA)
912 W Skelly Dr (74107-9411)
P.O. Box 9157 (74157-0157)
PHONE...................918 446-4591
Fred Dilibero, *President*
Diane Dilibero, *Corp Secy*
Tracy Smith, *Accounts Mgr*
EMP: 28
SQ FT: 18,400
SALES (est): 6.4MM **Privately Held**
WEB: www.crownproductsinc.com
SIC: 3492 5085 8711 Valves, hydraulic, aircraft; gaskets; aviation &/or aeronautical engineering

(G-9518)
CSI COMPRESSCO SUB INC
6140 S 104th East Ave (74133-1523)
PHONE...................918 250-9471
Brent Chadwick, *Production*
Rick Jacoby, *Branch Mgr*
EMP: 1
SALES (corp-wide): 1B **Publicly Held**
SIC: 7359 7699 3563 Propane equipment rental; industrial equipment services; air & gas compressors
HQ: Csi Compressco Sub Inc.
  24955 I 45 N
  The Woodlands TX 77380
  832 482-1399

(G-9519)
CTI SERVICES LLC (HQ)
Also Called: Citadel Technologies
1261 E 25th St (74114-2600)
PHONE...................918 584-2220
Roger Walker, *President*
EMP: 6
SALES (est): 1.4MM **Privately Held**
SIC: 2851 Epoxy coatings

(G-9520)
CULBREATH OIL & GAS CO INC
3501 S Yale Ave (74135-8014)
PHONE...................918 749-3508
Charles Culbreath, *President*
Chance Culbreath, *Vice Pres*
EMP: 2
SALES (est): 9.1MM **Privately Held**
SIC: 1382 Oil & gas exploration services

(G-9521)
CUMBERLAND PIPELINE CO LLC
6100 S Yale Ave Ste 2050 (74136-1934)
PHONE...................918 359-0980
Robert Jackson, *President*
Robert Mitchell, *Vice Pres*
EMP: 2
SALES (est): 96K **Privately Held**
SIC: 1389 Gas field services

(G-9522)
CUMMINS SOUTHERN PLAINS LLC
Also Called: Southern Plains Power
16525 E Skelly Dr (74116-4045)
PHONE...................918 234-3240
Jake Linnabery, *Opers Mgr*
Brian Fowler, *Manager*
EMP: 35
SALES (corp-wide): 23.5B **Publicly Held**
WEB: www.cummins-sp.com
SIC: 7538 5084 3519 Diesel engine repair: automotive; engines & parts, diesel; internal combustion engines
HQ: Cummins Southern Plains Llc
  600 N Watson Rd
  Arlington TX 76011
  817 640-6801

(G-9523)
CURA TELEHEALTH WELLNESS LLC
4920 E 113th St (74137-7606)
PHONE...................918 513-1062
Clinton Baird, *Mng Member*
EMP: 12
SALES (est): 74.5K **Privately Held**
SIC: 8099 7372 7389 Health & allied services; application computer software;

(G-9524)
CURRY SHADES LLC
3116 E 45th St (74105-5233)
PHONE...................918 779-3902
Leon Curry, *Principal*
EMP: 1
SALES (est): 76.3K **Privately Held**
SIC: 2391 2431 2591 Curtains & draperies; awnings, blinds & shutters, wood; window blinds

(G-9525)
CUST O BEND
1350 S 74th West Ave (74127-7308)
PHONE...................918 241-0514
Jerry Herrington, *President*
Ryan Herrington, *Opers Staff*
EMP: 4
SALES (est): 406.4K **Privately Held**
SIC: 3498 Tube fabricating (contract bending & shaping)

(G-9526)
CUST-O-BEND INC
7512 Charles Page Blvd (74127-7157)
P.O. Box 548, Sand Springs (74063-0548)
PHONE...................918 241-0514
Jerry Herrington, *President*
EMP: 25
SQ FT: 13,000
SALES (est): 5.9MM **Privately Held**
SIC: 3498 3494 3316 3312 Tube fabricating (contract bending & shaping); pipe fittings, fabricated from purchased pipe; valves & pipe fittings; cold finishing of steel shapes; blast furnaces & steel mills

(G-9527)
CUSTOM CABINET SERVICES
5328 E Admiral Pl (74115-8410)
PHONE...................918 340-9015
Lynn Aimie, *Principal*
EMP: 1
SALES (est): 142.5K **Privately Held**
SIC: 2434 Wood kitchen cabinets

(G-9528)
CUSTOM DESIGN BY ROBERTS
9756 E 55th Pl (74146-6453)
PHONE...................918 664-0466
Fax: 918 664-1305
EMP: 3 **EST:** 1977
SQ FT: 3,500
SALES: 250K **Privately Held**
SIC: 1799 3496 3446 3366 Special Trade Contractor Mfg Misc Fab Wire Prdts Mfg Architectural Mtlwrk Copper Foundry Mfg Alumnm Extrded Prdts

(G-9529)
CUSTOM METAL WORKS INC
1830 N 106th East Ave (74116-1511)
PHONE...................918 388-1881
Jeff Clifton, *Principal*
EMP: 7
SALES (est): 714K **Privately Held**
SIC: 3444 Roof deck, sheet metal

(G-9530)
CUTTING EDGE INDUSTRIES CORP
6931 S 66th St East Ave (74133)
PHONE...................918 523-7373
Paula Umscheid, *CEO*
Virginia White, *Business Mgr*
EMP: 2
SALES (est): 97.6K **Privately Held**
SIC: 2841 Soap & other detergents

(G-9531)
CYANOSTAR ENERGY INC
616 S Boston Ave Ste 402 (74119-1216)
PHONE...................918 582-2069
Stuart Garmaker, *President*
EMP: 1
SQ FT: 1,000
SALES (est): 202.2K **Privately Held**
SIC: 1311 1382 Crude petroleum & natural gas; oil & gas exploration services

(G-9532)
CYMSTAR LLC
12214 E 55th St (74146-6919)
PHONE...................918 251-8100
Garret Cook, *Info Tech Mgr*
Roger Anderson, *Instructor*
EMP: 7
SALES (est): 531.5K
SALES (corp-wide): 96.8MM **Privately Held**
SIC: 3699 Flight simulators (training aids), electronic
PA: Cymstar Llc
  1700 W Albany St Ste 500
  Broken Arrow OK 74012
  918 251-8100

(G-9533)
CYPRESS ENERGY HOLDINGS LLC (PA)
5727 S Lewis Ave Ste 300 (74105-7144)
PHONE...................918 748-3900
Peter C Boylan III, *Ch of Bd*
EMP: 10
SALES (est): 2.5MM **Privately Held**
WEB: www.cypressenergy.com
SIC: 1389 7389 Impounding & storing salt water, oil & gas field; pipeline & power line inspection service

(G-9534)
CYPRESS ENERGY HOLDINGS II LLC (HQ)
5727 S Lewis Ave Ste 500 (74105-7145)
PHONE...................918 748-3900
Peter C Boylan III, *Ch of Bd*
EMP: 3
SALES (est): 539.4K
SALES (corp-wide): 2.5MM **Privately Held**
SIC: 1389 7389 Impounding & storing salt water, oil & gas field; pipeline & power line inspection service
PA: Cypress Energy Holdings, Llc
  5727 S Lewis Ave Ste 300
  Tulsa OK 74105
  918 748-3900

(G-9535)
CYPRESS ENERGY PARTNERS LP (PA)
5727 S Lewis Ave Ste 300 (74105-7144)
PHONE...................918 748-3900
Peter C Boylan III, *Ch of Bd*
Cypress E GP, *General Ptnr*
G Les Austin, *CFO*
EMP: 6
SALES: 401.6MM **Publicly Held**
SIC: 7389 1389 Pipeline & power line inspection service; impounding & storing salt water, oil & gas field

(G-9536)
D & J ENTERPRISES
10902 S 77th East Ave (74133-7174)
PHONE...................918 906-3951
Gail L Phillipo, *Owner*
Dennis Phillipo, *Principal*
EMP: 3
SALES (est): 250K **Privately Held**
SIC: 3612 Transformers, except electric

(G-9537)
D E ZIEGLER ART CRAFT SUPPLY
6 N Lewis Ave (74110-5342)
P.O. Box 50037 (74150-0037)
PHONE...................918 584-2217
Allan Morrow, *President*
Timothy Ziegler, *Vice Pres*
Daniel Ziegler Jr, *Admin Sec*
EMP: 20
SQ FT: 20,000
SALES (est): 2.8MM **Privately Held**
SIC: 5999 2499 Artists' supplies & materials; picture frame molding, finished

(G-9538)
D I V C O INC
Also Called: Divco Supply
2806 N Sheridan Rd (74115-2332)
PHONE...................918 836-9101
Sandy Jarvis, *President*
Charles Jarvis, *Vice Pres*
▲ **EMP:** 25
SQ FT: 22,400
SALES (est): 5.9MM **Privately Held**
SIC: 5084 7692 3599 Machine tools & accessories; welding repair; machine shop, jobbing & repair

(G-9539)
D LLOYD HOLLINGSWORTH
Also Called: Wood Working
5 N Cheyenne Ave (74103-2213)
PHONE...................918 587-3533
Lloyd Hollingsworth, *Owner*
EMP: 4
SALES (est): 168K **Privately Held**
SIC: 2499 2521 Woodenware, kitchen & household; wood office furniture

(G-9540)
D VONTZ LLC
7208 E 38th St (74145-3230)
PHONE...................918 622-3600
Amy Bell, *CFO*
Juan Alcala, *Finance Mgr*
Greg Hoff,
John Kellerstrass,
▲ **EMP:** 12
SQ FT: 12,000
SALES (est): 4MM **Privately Held**
SIC: 5074 3432 Plumbing fittings & supplies; plumbing fixture fittings & trim

(G-9541)
D&L MANUFACTURING INC
1924 S 49th West Ave (74107-2204)
PHONE...................918 587-3504
EMP: 2
SALES (est): 126.6K **Privately Held**
SIC: 1389 Oil field services

(G-9542)
D&L MANUFACTURING INC
Also Called: D&L Oil Tools
1915 S 49th West Ave (74107-2200)
P.O. Box 52220 (74152-0220)
PHONE...................918 587-3504
Lee Eslicker, *President*
Pamela Eslicker, *Vice Pres*
David Roberson, *Purch Mgr*
Bingham Casey, *CFO*
Sheri White, *Accounting Mgr*
EMP: 33
SQ FT: 10,000
SALES (est): 21.6MM **Privately Held**
SIC: 3533 Oil & gas field machinery

GEOGRAPHIC SECTION
Tulsa - Tulsa County (G-9573)

(G-9543)
DA BOMB CUPCAKES
6722 S 110th East Ave (74133-2609)
PHONE..........................918 261-3595
Courtney Bycroft, *Principal*
EMP: 2
SALES (est): 77.2K **Privately Held**
WEB: www.dabombcupcakes.com
SIC: 2051 Bread, cake & related products

(G-9544)
DA/PRO RUBBER INC
6712 N Canton Ave (74117-1800)
PHONE..........................918 272-7799
EMP: 50
SALES (corp-wide): 69.1MM **Privately Held**
SIC: 3069 Mfg Fabricated Rubber Products Mfg Synthetic Rubber
PA: Da/Pro Rubber, Inc.
601 N Poplar Ave
Broken Arrow OK 74012
918 258-9386

(G-9545)
DA/PRO RUBBER INC
4505 E 100th St (74137-5308)
PHONE..........................918 299-5480
Gretchen A Brauninger, *Principal*
EMP: 4
SALES (corp-wide): 69.2MM **Privately Held**
WEB: www.daprorubber.com
SIC: 3069 Molded rubber products
PA: Da/Pro Rubber, Inc.
601 N Poplar Ave
Broken Arrow OK 74012
918 258-9386

(G-9546)
DAGWOOD ENERGY INC
427 S Boston Ave Ste 604 (74103-4111)
PHONE..........................918 582-6604
EMP: 3
SALES (est): 271.8K **Privately Held**
SIC: 1382 Oil/Gas Exploration Services

(G-9547)
DAKOTA EXPLORATION LLC
110 W 7th St 210 (74119-1031)
PHONE..........................918 806-8687
Paul Collins, *Mng Member*
Brian Hurst,
EMP: 6 EST: 2010
SALES (est): 678.7K **Privately Held**
SIC: 1381 Drilling oil & gas wells

(G-9548)
DALE E DYER
3530 S 39th West Ave (74107)
PHONE..........................918 519-0189
Dale E Dyer, *Owner*
EMP: 3
SALES (est): 192.4K **Privately Held**
SIC: 1389 Oil & gas field services

(G-9549)
DAMAR MANUFACTURING CO INC
3332 W 45th Pl (74107-6457)
PHONE..........................918 445-2445
Damon E Horton, *President*
Charlotte Horton, *Corp Secy*
EMP: 20
SQ FT: 20,000
SALES (est): 3.5MM **Privately Held**
SIC: 3599 3356 7692 Machine shop, jobbing & repair; welding rods; welding repair

(G-9550)
DANIEL E AND MARL NEWPORT
1103 W 49th St (74107-8011)
PHONE..........................918 445-9129
Daniel Newport, *Principal*
EMP: 2
SALES (est): 135.4K **Privately Held**
SIC: 2741 Miscellaneous publishing

(G-9551)
DANIEL H FINNEFROCK
427 S Boston Ave Ste 614 (74103-4111)
PHONE..........................918 585-3350
Daniel Finnefrock, *Owner*
EMP: 1
SALES (est): 86.5K **Privately Held**
SIC: 1382 Oil & gas exploration services

(G-9552)
DARBY EQUIPMENT CO (PA)
2940 N Toledo Ave (74115-2707)
PHONE..........................918 582-2340
Edward Darby, *CEO*
Robert Darby, *President*
Ryan Darby, *Vice Pres*
Bonnie Darby, *CFO*
Nick Minden, *CFO*
◆ EMP: 32
SQ FT: 67,000
SALES (est): 8.2MM **Privately Held**
SIC: 3531 3533 3542 7353 Construction machinery; oil & gas field machinery; bending machines; heavy construction equipment rental

(G-9553)
DARTMOUTH JOURNAL SERVICE
6606 S 77th East Ave (74133-1837)
PHONE..........................918 286-3513
Bernie Stukenborg, *Principal*
EMP: 3
SALES (est): 164.7K **Privately Held**
SIC: 2711 Newspapers, publishing & printing

(G-9554)
DATALOG SYSTEMS
Also Called: 1450 Ne 2nd Ave M
410 W 7th St Apt 1428 (74119-1054)
PHONE..........................918 245-3939
Bill Hart, *Owner*
EMP: 5
SQ FT: 3,000
SALES (est): 591.9K **Privately Held**
SIC: 3625 8711 8731 Relays & industrial controls; engineering services; electronic research

(G-9555)
DATAPAGES INC
1444 S Boulder Ave (74119-3604)
P.O. Box 979 (74101-0979)
PHONE..........................918 584-2555
James Blankenship, *President*
David E Lange, *Corp Secy*
Ann Hutchison, *Admin Asst*
EMP: 4
SALES (est): 473K
SALES (corp-wide): 12.9MM **Privately Held**
SIC: 2721 Magazines: publishing & printing
PA: American Association Of Petroleum Geologists
1444 S Boulder Ave
Tulsa OK 74119
918 584-2555

(G-9556)
DAVENPORT CLOAKS INC
716 S Troost Ave (74120-4834)
PHONE..........................918 932-8600
Kathryn Hall Shackelford, *President*
EMP: 1
SALES (est): 126.6K **Privately Held**
SIC: 2512 Upholstered household furniture

(G-9557)
DAVID DENHAM INTERIORS
1540 S Peoria Ave (74120-6202)
PHONE..........................918 585-3161
David D Denham, *Owner*
EMP: 2
SQ FT: 3,000
SALES (est): 116K **Privately Held**
SIC: 7389 1311 Interior decorating; crude petroleum & natural gas

(G-9558)
DAVID STEVENS CABINETS & TRIM
Also Called: David Stevens Cabinetmaker
10914 E 2nd St (74128-1642)
PHONE..........................918 234-0656
David Stevens, *President*
EMP: 3
SQ FT: 9,000
SALES (est): 282.4K **Privately Held**
SIC: 2434 Wood kitchen cabinets

(G-9559)
DAVIS BROS OIL PRODUCERS INC (PA)
110 W 7th St Ste 1000 (74119-1109)
PHONE..........................918 584-3581
Lee Davis, *President*
Barry Davis, *Vice Pres*
H Lee Frost, *Treasurer*
Elmer C Wilkening, *Admin Sec*
EMP: 8
SQ FT: 11,000
SALES (est): 618.3K **Privately Held**
SIC: 1311 Crude petroleum production; natural gas production

(G-9560)
DAVIS GULF COAST INC
401 S Boston Ave Ste 2800 (74103-4064)
PHONE..........................918 587-7782
William H Davis, *President*
EMP: 3
SALES (est): 267.5K **Privately Held**
SIC: 1311 Crude petroleum production; natural gas production

(G-9561)
DAVIS OPERATING COMPANY
1924 S Utica Ave Ste 1218 (74104-6530)
PHONE..........................918 587-7782
William H Davis, *President*
Tony Benavibes, *Vice Pres*
EMP: 9
SALES (est): 1.3MM **Privately Held**
WEB: www.davisnet.com
SIC: 1382 Oil & gas exploration services

(G-9562)
DAYTONS TRAILER HITCH INC
2920 S Yale Ave (74114-6252)
PHONE..........................918 744-0341
Dayton Girdner, *President*
EMP: 5 EST: 1975
SQ FT: 6,000
SALES (est): 575K **Privately Held**
SIC: 5531 5013 7692 Automotive accessories; trailer hitches, automotive; trailer parts & accessories; welding repair

(G-9563)
DB UNLIMITED LLC
2876 E 49th St (74105-6218)
PHONE..........................855 437-7766
Denese Brewer, *CEO*
EMP: 1
SALES (est): 25K **Privately Held**
SIC: 5999 3915 8999 3999 Perfumes & colognes; alcoholic beverage making equipment & supplies; jewelers' materials & lapidary work; artists & artists' studios; hair & hair-based products

(G-9564)
DEAN FOODS COMPANY
215 N Denver Ave (74103-1821)
P.O. Box 3047 (74101-3047)
PHONE..........................918 587-2471
Mark A Mobbs, *Manager*
EMP: 1 **Publicly Held**
SIC: 2026 Fluid milk
PA: Dean Foods Company
2711 N Haskell Ave # 340
Dallas TX 75204

(G-9565)
DEANS GRINDING SERVICE
9201 E Admiral Ct (74115-8114)
P.O. Box 580026 (74158-0026)
PHONE..........................918 838-0756
Dean Cooper Sr, *Owner*
EMP: 2
SQ FT: 4,000
SALES (est): 80K **Privately Held**
SIC: 7699 3541 Knife, saw & tool sharpening & repair; grinding machines, metalworking

(G-9566)
DECO DEVELOPMENT COMPANY INC
2809 E 29th St (74114-5801)
PHONE..........................918 747-6366
Charles O Meyers Jr, *President*
Charles Meyer Sr, *Corp Secy*
C O Meyers Sr, *Vice Pres*
EMP: 2
SALES: 225K **Privately Held**
SIC: 1311 3533 Crude petroleum production; natural gas production; oil field machinery & equipment; gas field machinery & equipment

(G-9567)
DEISENROTH GAS PRODUCTS INC
1924 S Utica Ave Ste 540 (74104-6511)
PHONE..........................918 742-4769
Craig Deisenroth, *President*
Patricia Deisenroth, *Corp Secy*
Malcolm Deisenroth, *Vice Pres*
EMP: 5
SQ FT: 1,200
SALES (est): 5MM **Privately Held**
SIC: 2911 5172 Gases & liquefied petroleum gases; petroleum products

(G-9568)
DELPHI INTERNATIONAL INC
1924 S Utica Ave Ste 1201 (74104-6527)
PHONE..........................918 749-9401
William C Athens, *President*
Mary M Athens, *Corp Secy*
John Stephen Athens II, *Vice Pres*
EMP: 4 EST: 1974
SQ FT: 2,000
SALES (est): 365.8K **Privately Held**
SIC: 1382 1311 Oil & gas exploration services; crude petroleum production; natural gas production

(G-9569)
DELTA OIL AND GAS LLC
601 S Boulder Ave # 1310 (74119-1300)
PHONE..........................918 599-9800
David Harber, *Principal*
EMP: 2
SALES (est): 286.7K **Privately Held**
SIC: 1382 Oil & gas exploration services

(G-9570)
DELTA PLATING INC
1923 W 48th St (74107-7811)
PHONE..........................918 664-6880
EMP: 3
SALES: 120K **Privately Held**
SIC: 3471 Plating/Polishing Service

(G-9571)
DENALI INCORPORATED (HQ)
9910 E 56th St N (74117-4011)
PHONE..........................713 627-0933
Richard W Volk, *Ch of Bd*
Robert B Bennett, *President*
Lee W Orr, *Vice Pres*
Cathy L Smith, *Vice Pres*
Timothy D Maynard, *CFO*
EMP: 4
SALES (est): 6.6B
SALES (corp-wide): 8.4B **Publicly Held**
SIC: 3089 Plastic & fiberglass tanks
PA: National Oilwell Varco, Inc.
7909 Parkwood Circle Dr
Houston TX 77036
713 346-7500

(G-9572)
DENHAM OPERATING CO
Also Called: Denham, David Design
1540 S Peoria Ave (74120-6202)
P.O. Box 3627 (74101-3627)
PHONE..........................918 585-3161
David Denham, *Owner*
EMP: 2
SQ FT: 192
SALES (est): 162.5K **Privately Held**
SIC: 1311 Crude petroleum production; natural gas production

(G-9573)
DENTSPLY SIRONA INC
Also Called: Dentsply International
5100 E Skelly Dr Ste 300 (74135-6560)
PHONE..........................918 878-0189
Wilkinson Kevin, *Research*
Kevin Wilkinson, *Research*
Heather Ward, *Finance*
Gregg Gavin, *VP Human Res*
Stacy Charais, *Sales Staff*
EMP: 13
SALES (corp-wide): 4B **Publicly Held**
WEB: www.sirona.es
SIC: 3843 Dental equipment & supplies

PA: Dentsply Sirona Inc.
13320 Bllntyne Crprtate P
Charlotte NC 28277
844 848-0137

(G-9574)
DENTSPLY SIRONA INC
2131 S Lewis Ave (74114-1455)
P.O. Box 700874 (74170-0874)
PHONE..................................918 878-0001
EMP: 2
SALES (corp-wide): 4B Publicly Held
SIC: 3843 Dental equipment & supplies
PA: Dentsply Sirona Inc.
13320 Bllntyne Crprtate P
Charlotte NC 28277
844 848-0137

(G-9575)
DESIGN & MFG INC
1174 N 169th East Ave (74116-4209)
PHONE..................................918 576-6659
EMP: 2 EST: 2018
SALES (est): 194K Privately Held
SIC: 3599 Machine shop, jobbing & repair

(G-9576)
DEVAULT ENTERPRISES INC
7440 E 46th Pl (74145-6306)
PHONE..................................918 249-1595
Mike Devault, President
Tammy J Devault, Vice Pres
▲ EMP: 5 EST: 1995
SQ FT: 8,000
SALES (est): 752.2K Privately Held
SIC: 3089 Injection molded finished plastic products

(G-9577)
DEVCO PROCESS HEATERS LLC
2504 E 71st St Ste A (74136-5504)
PHONE..................................918 221-9629
Jeff Hutsell, President
EMP: 6
SALES (est): 320.6K Privately Held
SIC: 3567 Industrial furnaces & ovens

(G-9578)
DIAMOND ENERGY SERVICES LP (PA)
406 S Boulder Ave Ste 708 (74103-3862)
PHONE..................................918 764-4000
Brice Bogle, Partner
EMP: 14 EST: 2004
SALES: 11.2MM Privately Held
WEB: www.diamondenergyservices.com
SIC: 1389 Oil field services

(G-9579)
DIAMOND TEES
8335 E 51st St Ste J (74145-9029)
PHONE..................................918 665-0815
Paul Buser, Owner
EMP: 1
SALES: 50K Privately Held
SIC: 2396 Screen printing on fabric articles

(G-9580)
DIAMONDBACK OPERATING LP
6660 S Sheridan Rd # 250 (74133-1730)
PHONE..................................918 477-7755
EMP: 13
SALES (est): 1.7MM Privately Held
SIC: 1382 Oil/Gas Exploration Services

(G-9581)
DIECO MANUFACTURING INC
15715 E Pine St (74116-2442)
PHONE..................................918 438-2193
Robert Buchanan, President
Jim Dixon, Vice Pres
Darrin C Hanby, Vice Pres
Helen Buchanan, Treasurer
Myron V Meter, Manager
EMP: 60
SQ FT: 35,000
SALES (est): 11.3MM Privately Held
SIC: 3544 7692 Special dies & tools; welding repair

(G-9582)
DIGI SECURITY SYSTEMS LLC (PA)
11333 E 51st Pl (74146-5910)
P.O. Box 470708 (74147-0708)
PHONE..................................918 824-2520
Eric Swank, Mng Member
Dan Crofford,
Joshua Herron,
EMP: 10
SALES (est): 1.9MM Privately Held
SIC: 3699 7382 Security devices; security systems services

(G-9583)
DIGITAL RESOURCES INC
12626 E 60th St (74146-6905)
PHONE..................................866 823-6328
Timothy M Bock, President
Kenneth G Ostmo, Principal
EMP: 1
SALES (est): 110.8K Privately Held
SIC: 3651 Household audio & video equipment

(G-9584)
DILBECK MFG INC
1871 N 106th East Ave (74116-1510)
P.O. Box 690332 (74169-0332)
PHONE..................................918 836-1555
Gary L Dilbeck, President
Gary Dilbeck, President
Sherry Dilbeck, Vice Pres
EMP: 35
SALES (est): 5MM Privately Held
SIC: 3444 Sheet metal specialties, not stamped

(G-9585)
DIRECT COMMUNICATIONS INC
11063 S Memorial Dr Ste D (74133-7366)
PHONE..................................918 291-0092
Steven W Vandervort, President
EMP: 25 EST: 2001
SALES (est): 4.2MM Privately Held
WEB: www.directok.com
SIC: 3699 Security control equipment & systems

(G-9586)
DIVERSIFIED PRINTING INC
10021 E 44th Pl (74146-4707)
PHONE..................................918 665-2275
Glatha Agee, President
Roger Agee, Treasurer
EMP: 10
SQ FT: 11,000
SALES (est): 1.1MM Privately Held
SIC: 2759 2796 2791 2789 Commercial printing; platemaking services; typesetting; bookbinding & related work; commercial printing, lithographic

(G-9587)
DIVERSIFIED RUBBER PDTS INC
7650 Charles Page Blvd (74127-7158)
PHONE..................................918 241-0193
Dell Frazier, President
EMP: 25
SQ FT: 40,000
SALES (est): 4.2MM Privately Held
SIC: 3061 5031 Oil & gas field machinery rubber goods (mechanical); molding, all materials

(G-9588)
DIVINE CULTURED MARBLE
1831 N 105th East Ave (74116-1513)
PHONE..................................918 836-2121
EMP: 3 EST: 2010
SALES (est): 140K Privately Held
SIC: 3281 Mfg Cut Stone/Products

(G-9589)
DMI INTERNATIONAL INC
15615 E Pine St (74116-2430)
PHONE..................................918 438-2213
EMP: 2
SALES (est): 86.6K Privately Held
SIC: 3441 Fabricated structural metal

(G-9590)
DOG DISH LLC
1778 Utica Sq (74114-1400)
PHONE..................................918 624-2600
Bill Handy,
Shelli Holland-Handy,
EMP: 5
SALES (est): 397.3K Privately Held
SIC: 2047 Dog food

(G-9591)
DOLESE BROS CO
13521 E 11th St (74108-2701)
PHONE..................................918 437-6535
Max Robertson, Branch Mgr
EMP: 16
SALES (corp-wide): 8.5MM Privately Held
SIC: 3273 Ready-mixed concrete
PA: Dolese Bros. Co.
20 Nw 13th St
Oklahoma City OK 73103
405 235-2311

(G-9592)
DOME BLUE OPERATING LLC
15 E 5th St Ste 3300 (74103-4340)
PHONE..................................918 583-3333
James F Adelson, President
EMP: 4
SALES (est): 344.2K Privately Held
SIC: 1311 Crude petroleum & natural gas

(G-9593)
DOMECK INDUSTRIES INC
3031 W 101st St (74132-3846)
PHONE..................................260 833-0917
EMP: 1
SALES (est): 46.2K Privately Held
SIC: 3999 Manufacturing industries

(G-9594)
DOMINION CORP
4444 S Lewis Ave (74105-4305)
PHONE..................................918 270-1722
Mary Sokolosky, Principal
EMP: 3
SALES (est): 264.8K Privately Held
SIC: 1382 Oil & gas exploration services

(G-9595)
DOMINION REFUSE INC
4444 S Lewis Ave (74105-4305)
P.O. Box 641, Owasso (74055-0641)
PHONE..................................918 743-8860
Noble Fokolosky, President
EMP: 2
SALES (est): 187.7K Privately Held
SIC: 3713 4953 Garbage, refuse truck bodies; garbage: collecting, destroying & processing

(G-9596)
DONALD L STAFFORD CO
Also Called: J-Tech
7824 S Evanston Ave (74136-8703)
PHONE..................................918 492-0324
Donald Stafford, President
Judy Stafford, Corp Secy
Sherrie Roland, Treasurer
EMP: 2
SALES (est): 104.8K Privately Held
SIC: 1389 Oil consultants

(G-9597)
DORADO E&P PARTNERS LLC (PA)
1 W 3rd St Ste 1000 (74103-3500)
PHONE..................................720 402-3700
E Murphy Markham IV, Principal
EMP: 15
SALES (est): 11MM Privately Held
SIC: 1389 Oil & gas field services

(G-9598)
DORIS WINFORD
Also Called: Creative Quilting
4905 W 7th St (74127-7453)
PHONE..................................918 599-8931
Doris Winford, Owner
James Winford, Co-Owner
EMP: 2
SALES: 30K Privately Held
SIC: 2395 7299 2392 Quilting & quilting supplies; quilting for individuals; household furnishings

(G-9599)
DOUG BUTLER ENTERPRISES INC
Also Called: Pallet Supply Co
1111 E 32nd St N (74105)
P.O. Box 6461 (74148-0461)
PHONE..................................918 425-3565
Doug Butler, President
EMP: 10
SQ FT: 9,000
SALES: 1.3MM Privately Held
SIC: 2448 7699 5211 Pallets, wood; pallet repair; lumber products

(G-9600)
DOVER ARTIFICIAL LIFT
4801 W 49th St (74107-7321)
PHONE..................................918 796-1000
EMP: 6
SALES (est): 545K Privately Held
SIC: 3446 Scaffolds, mobile or stationary: metal

(G-9601)
DOYLE DRYERS INC
1404 S Quaker Ave (74120-5806)
PHONE..................................918 224-4002
E Clyde Doyle, President
Judy Doyle, Corp Secy
EMP: 3 EST: 1980
SQ FT: 1,400
SALES (est): 599.5K Privately Held
WEB: www.doyledryers.com
SIC: 3567 3559 3556 Driers & redriers, industrial process; refinery, chemical processing & similar machinery; food products machinery

(G-9602)
DRAEGER INTERLOCK
4125 S 68th East Ave P (74145-4622)
PHONE..................................918 270-1600
EMP: 2
SALES (est): 88.3K Privately Held
SIC: 3694 Engine electrical equipment

(G-9603)
DRAGONSLAYER GAMES LLC
3929 S Granite Ave (74135-5557)
PHONE..................................918 665-1472
Daniel Irving Parham, Owner
EMP: 2 EST: 2015
SALES (est): 127.9K Privately Held
WEB: www.dragonslayer-games.com
SIC: 3944 Games, toys & children's vehicles

(G-9604)
DREAM BUILDINGS OF TULSA
11212 E Admiral Pl (74116-3026)
PHONE..................................918 437-9233
EMP: 2
SALES (est): 122.9K Privately Held
SIC: 3448 1542 Mfg Prefabricated Metal Buildings Nonresidential Construction

(G-9605)
DRESSER-RAND COMPANY
Also Called: Dresser-Rand Repair Center
1354 S Sheridan Rd (74112-5416)
PHONE..................................918 835-8437
C D Shepherd, Manager
EMP: 33
SALES (corp-wide): 96.9B Privately Held
SIC: 3563 Air & gas compressors
HQ: Dresser-Rand Company
500 Paul Clark Dr
Olean NY 14760
716 375-3000

(G-9606)
DRESSER-RAND GROUP INC
1354 S Sheridan Rd (74112-5416)
PHONE..................................918 695-2368
Robert K Kennedy, Branch Mgr
EMP: 3
SALES (corp-wide): 96.9B Privately Held
SIC: 3563 Air & gas compressors
HQ: Dresser-Rand Group Inc.
15375 Memorial Dr Ste 600
Houston TX 77079

GEOGRAPHIC SECTION

Tulsa - Tulsa County (G-9637)

(G-9607)
DRESSER-RAND LLC
Also Called: Gas Field Compressor Sales
1354 S Sheridan Rd (74112-5416)
PHONE..................918 254-4099
Ralph Nugent, *Manager*
EMP: 11
SALES (corp-wide): 96.9B **Privately Held**
SIC: 3563 Air & gas compressors
HQ: Dresser-Rand Llc
    1200 W Sam Houston Pkwy N
    Houston TX 77043

(G-9608)
DRIVE SHAFTS INC
6960 E 11th St (74112-4610)
PHONE..................918 836-0111
Rick Whitehead, *President*
Rita Whitehead, *Corp Secy*
EMP: 7 **EST:** 1977
SQ FT: 6,700
SALES: 1.2MM **Privately Held**
SIC: 7539 5531 5013 3714 Automotive repair shops; automotive parts; automotive supplies & parts; motor vehicle parts & accessories; power transmission equipment

(G-9609)
DRONE VIU LLC
6120 S Yale Ave Ste 500 (74136-4251)
PHONE..................405 867-4690
EMP: 2 **EST:** 2015
SALES (est): 91.2K **Privately Held**
SIC: 3721 Mfg Aircraft

(G-9610)
DRUG WAREHOUSE
1437 S Boulder Ave # 1050 (74119-3609)
PHONE..................918 592-4545
Paul McDaniel, *Owner*
EMP: 2 **EST:** 2018
SALES (est): 81.9K **Privately Held**
SIC: 1382 Oil & gas exploration services

(G-9611)
DUCOMMUN LABARGE TECH INC
Also Called: Labarge Inc Electronics Div
11616 E 51st St (74146-5911)
PHONE..................918 459-2200
Anthony Reardon, *President*
Joyce O'Neal, *Human Res Dir*
Jodi Hawkins, *Executive*
Traci Patton, *Executive*
EMP: 170
SALES (corp-wide): 721MM **Publicly Held**
SIC: 3663 3643 3489 3679 Radio & TV communications equipment; current-carrying wiring devices; ordnance & accessories; electronic circuits; emergency alarms; guided missile & space vehicle parts & auxiliary equipment
HQ: Ducommun Labarge Technologies, Inc.
    689 Craig Rd 200
    Saint Louis MO 63141
    314 997-0800

(G-9612)
DUNLAP MANUFACTURING CO INC
3250 N Sheridan Rd (74115-2310)
PHONE..................918 838-1383
Robert Reed Moore, *CEO*
Rudy Heaton, *President*
Jamie Jansson, *Corp Secy*
EMP: 28
SQ FT: 49,500
SALES (est): 2.1MM
SALES (corp-wide): 2.4MM **Privately Held**
SIC: 3442 3354 Metal doors; aluminum extruded products
PA: Maro International Corp
    3250 N Sheridan Rd
    Tulsa OK 74115
    918 836-7749

(G-9613)
DUSTY TRUNK
8515 S 33rd West Ave (74132-3503)
PHONE..................918 446-4203
Paula Osburn, *Principal*
EMP: 3 **EST:** 2010
SALES (est): 168.8K **Privately Held**
SIC: 3161 Trunks

(G-9614)
DVORAK INSTRUMENTS
6818 E 96th Pl (74133-5908)
P.O. Box 701716 (74170-1716)
PHONE..................918 299-2223
Albert Dvorak, *President*
EMP: 1
SALES: 400K **Privately Held**
SIC: 3826 Analytical instruments

(G-9615)
DVORAK INSTRUMENTS INC
9402 E 55th St (74145-8111)
PHONE..................918 447-0022
Albert Dvorak, *President*
▲ **EMP:** 14
SALES: 200K **Privately Held**
SIC: 3823 Industrial instrmnts msrmnt display/control process variable

(G-9616)
DYCO PETROLEUM CORPORATION
2 W 2nd St Ste 1500 (74103-3135)
PHONE..................918 591-1917
C Phil Tholen, *President*
Dennis Neill, *Senior VP*
EMP: 15 **EST:** 1971
SQ FT: 1,500
SALES (est): 1.9MM **Privately Held**
SIC: 1311 Crude petroleum production; natural gas production

(G-9617)
DYNAMIC MAPPING SOLUTIONS INC
3021 W 68th Pl (74132-1755)
PHONE..................918 446-7803
Jon A Ferris, *Principal*
EMP: 1
SALES (est): 67.9K **Privately Held**
SIC: 2741 Maps: publishing & printing

(G-9618)
DYNE EXPLORATION COMPANY
Also Called: Dynex
5100 E Skelly Dr Ste 650 (74135-6559)
PHONE..................405 245-0624
Carol Starbuck, *President*
Janice Blaylock, *Admin Sec*
EMP: 2 **EST:** 1980
SALES (est): 210K **Privately Held**
SIC: 1311 Crude petroleum production; natural gas production

(G-9619)
E AND H SALES
3539 S Fulton Ave (74135-5247)
PHONE..................918 742-1091
Harvey Brown, *Partner*
Eloise Brown, *Partner*
EMP: 2
SALES (est): 66.1K **Privately Held**
SIC: 5945 3944 Dolls & accessories; dollhouses & furniture

(G-9620)
E C CARMAN CASING GAUGE CO
9220 E 77th St (74133-4919)
PHONE..................918 605-5093
EMP: 2
SALES (est): 85.3K **Privately Held**
SIC: 1389 Oil field services

(G-9621)
E F L INC
Also Called: Laser Ennovation and Engrg
9401 E 54th St (74145-8101)
P.O. Box 470284 (74147-0284)
PHONE..................918 665-7799
George Juanitis, *President*
Troy Kuske, *Vice Pres*
Steve Hash, *Manager*
Rodney Smith, *Manager*
Aimee Lapelle, *Info Tech Mgr*
EMP: 60
SQ FT: 15,550
SALES (est): 16.1MM **Privately Held**
SIC: 3444 7692 Sheet metal specialties, not stamped; welding repair

(G-9622)
E&M SOLUTIONS LLC
12317 E 13th Pl (74128-5227)
PHONE..................918 551-9515
EMP: 2
SALES (est): 163.9K **Privately Held**
SIC: 2434 Wood kitchen cabinets

(G-9623)
EAGLE ENERGY COMPANY LLC
2488 E 81st St Ste 2000 (74137-4224)
PHONE..................918 746-1350
Steve Antry, *CEO*
Michael Okelley, *President*
EMP: 9
SALES (est): 1.2MM **Privately Held**
WEB: www.eagleenergyexploration.com
SIC: 1382 Oil & gas exploration services

(G-9624)
EAGLE EXPLORATION PROD LLC
2488 E 81st St Ste 2000 (74137-4224)
PHONE..................918 746-1350
Steve Antry, *CEO*
Randy Nerger, *Controller*
EMP: 4
SALES (est): 369K **Privately Held**
SIC: 1081 Exploration, metal mining

(G-9625)
EAGLE EXPLRTION OPRTING GP LLC
6100 S Yale Ave Ste 700 (74136-1935)
PHONE..................918 746-1350
Steve Antry, *Principal*
EMP: 2 **EST:** 2014
SALES (est): 171.8K **Privately Held**
SIC: 1081 Exploration, metal mining

(G-9626)
EAGLE PUMP & MFG LLC
1013 N Columbia Ave (74110-5021)
PHONE..................918 906-1080
Robert Easley,
EMP: 1
SALES (est): 105.7K **Privately Held**
SIC: 3999 Manufacturing industries

(G-9627)
EAGLE REDI-MIX CONCRETE LLC
2761 E Skelly Dr Ste 300 (74105-6214)
PHONE..................918 355-5700
Angela Holt, *Manager*
Michael Schultz, *Technical Staff*
EMP: 2 **EST:** 2008
SALES (est): 866.8K **Privately Held**
WEB: www.eagleredimix.com
SIC: 3273 Ready-mixed concrete

(G-9628)
EAGLE ROAD OIL LLC
321 S Boston Ave Ste 700 (74103-3312)
PHONE..................844 211-2961
EMP: 4
SALES (est): 646.2K **Privately Held**
SIC: 1389 Pumping of oil & gas wells

(G-9629)
EAGLE ROCK ENERGY PARTNERS LP
1717 S Boulder Ave # 100 (74119-4833)
PHONE..................281 408-1467
EMP: 5
SALES (corp-wide): 788MM **Publicly Held**
SIC: 1311 1321 Crude Petroleum/Natural Gas Production Natural Gas Liquids Production
HQ: Eagle Rock Energy Partners, L.P.
    1415 La St Ste 2700
    Houston TX 77057
    281 408-1200

(G-9630)
EAGLECLAW FABRICATION
11818 S Oswego Ave (74137-6719)
P.O. Box 9615 (74157-0615)
PHONE..................918 691-2519
Thomas Word, *Principal*
EMP: 99
SALES (est): 5.8MM **Privately Held**
SIC: 3441 Fabricated structural metal

(G-9631)
EAST 74TH STREET HOLDINGS INC
Also Called: Thermoweld
1140 N 129th East Ave (74116-1724)
P.O. Box 994 (74101-0994)
PHONE..................918 437-3037
Rick Ceass, *Business Mgr*
Robert Brooks, *Exec VP*
Tim Hoagland, *Vice Pres*
Todd Lehmann, *Vice Pres*
Kurt Campbell, *Prdtn Mgr*
◆ **EMP:** 175
SQ FT: 54,000
SALES (est): 54.3MM
SALES (corp-wide): 1.5B **Publicly Held**
SIC: 3089 3494 3399 Fittings for pipe, plastic; pipe fittings; thermite
HQ: Handy & Harman
    C/O Steel Partners
    New York NY 10022
    212 520-2300

(G-9632)
EASTECH BADGER ✪
4250 S 76th East Ave (74145-4712)
PHONE..................918 664-1212
EMP: 2 **EST:** 2019
SALES (est): 147.2K **Privately Held**
SIC: 3829 Measuring & controlling devices

(G-9633)
EASTECH FLOW CONTROLS INC
4250 S 76th East Ave (74145-4712)
PHONE..................918 664-1212
Franklin Sinclair, *President*
Duane Dunlap, *Purch Mgr*
EMP: 11
SALES (est): 2.4MM **Privately Held**
SIC: 3823 Industrial instrmnts msrmnt display/control process variable

(G-9634)
EASY CAR WASH SYSTEMS INC
2302 Charles Page Blvd (74127-8421)
P.O. Box 1212 (74101-1212)
PHONE..................918 582-4355
Edwin A Lloyd, *President*
Dan Lloyd, *Vice Pres*
EMP: 5
SQ FT: 2,000
SALES (est): 480.1K **Privately Held**
SIC: 3589 2841 Car washing machinery; soap & other detergents

(G-9635)
EBENEZER TRUCK TRAILER LL ✪
45 S Fulton Ave (74112-1414)
PHONE..................918 289-6669
EMP: 2 **EST:** 2019
SALES (est): 87.2K **Privately Held**
SIC: 3715 Truck trailers

(G-9636)
EBSCO SPRING CO INC
4949 S 83rd East Ave (74145-6919)
P.O. Box 472265 (74147-2265)
PHONE..................918 628-1680
Cheryl Dooley, *President*
John Chappell, *COO*
Larry Dunagan, *Exec VP*
Liz Jeter, *Vice Pres*
Todd Pfeifer, *Vice Pres*
EMP: 80
SQ FT: 56,000
SALES (est): 17.5MM **Privately Held**
WEB: www.ebscospring.com
SIC: 3495 Wire springs

(G-9637)
ECHOTA DEFENSE SERVICES
10838 E Marshall St Ste 2 (74116-5682)
PHONE..................918 384-7409
Russell Claybrook, *Principal*
EMP: 1
SALES (est): 66.9K **Privately Held**
SIC: 3711 3795 Motor vehicles & car bodies; cars, armored, assembly of; specialized tank components, military

Tulsa - Tulsa County (G-9638)   GEOGRAPHIC SECTION

(G-9638)
ECO-BRIGHT INDUSTRIES LLC
3835 E 56th Pl (74135-4140)
PHONE.................................918 728-1644
Dustin Dowd, *Principal*
EMP: 2
SALES (est): 155K **Privately Held**
WEB: www.ecobrightindustries.com
SIC: 3999 Manufacturing industries

(G-9639)
ECOHAWK ADVNCED WTR RSRCES LLC
1620 S Lewis Ave (74104-4922)
PHONE.................................918 694-6011
Joan K Crager,
James Dallke,
EMP: 2
SALES (est): 125.6K **Privately Held**
SIC: 3589 Water treatment equipment, industrial

(G-9640)
ECONOMASTERS LLC
3209 W 21st St (74107-3463)
PHONE.................................918 241-8244
Virgil Howard,
Paul Hildebrand,
EMP: 18
SALES (est): 4.3MM **Privately Held**
SIC: 3441 Building components, structural steel

(G-9641)
ECONOMY LUMBER COMPANY INC
4221 E Pine St (74115-5100)
PHONE.................................918 835-4933
Harry H Poarch Jr, *President*
Michael Manley, *Sales Associate*
EMP: 8
SQ FT: 10,000
SALES (est): 3.2MM **Privately Held**
WEB: www.economylumbercompany.com
SIC: 5211 2449 0811 5031 Home centers; planing mill products & lumber; shipping cases & drums, wood: wirebound & plywood; timber tracts, hardwood; lumber, plywood & millwork

(G-9642)
ECONTROLS LLC
4646 S Harvard Ave #100 (74135-2952)
PHONE.................................918 957-1000
EMP: 14
SALES (corp-wide): 1.6MM **Privately Held**
SIC: 3714 Motor vehicle engines & parts
HQ: Econtrols, Llc
5757 Farinon Dr
San Antonio TX 78249
210 495-9772

(G-9643)
EDITORIAL GRAMA INC
Also Called: Imagen Latino Americana Mag
100 W 5th St Ste 701 (74103-4290)
PHONE.................................918 744-9502
Guillermo Rojas, *President*
Alex Delgado, *Manager*
Carlos Moreno, *Manager*
EMP: 10
SALES (est): 694.3K **Privately Held**
WEB: www.editorialgrama.com
SIC: 2721 2711 Magazines: publishing & printing; newspapers, publishing & printing

(G-9644)
EDUCATIONAL CONCEPTS LLC
Also Called: Brief Media
2021 S Lewis Ave Ste 760 (74104-5713)
PHONE.................................918 749-0118
Dawn McCluskey, *Editor*
Jackie Yoken, *Human Res Mgr*
Jeanine Nicosia, *Accounts Mgr*
Holly Williams, *Accounts Mgr*
Shelbi Ford, *Sales Staff*
EMP: 15
SALES (est): 7.4MM **Privately Held**
SIC: 2741 Technical papers: publishing only, not printed on site

(G-9645)
EDWARD C LAWSON PROPERTIES
401 S Boston Ave Ste 2100 (74103-4057)
PHONE.................................918 584-5155
Edward C Lawson, *Partner*
Kimberly Park, *Partner*
Alice K Willard, *Partner*
Kimberly Parks, *Vice Pres*
EMP: 5 EST: 1931
SQ FT: 1,000
SALES (est): 253.5K **Privately Held**
SIC: 1311 Crude petroleum production; natural gas production

(G-9646)
EDWARDS PIPELINE SERVICES LLC
7647b E 46th Pl (74145-6307)
PHONE.................................918 627-8288
Don Edwards, *President*
Bradley Beasley,
EMP: 150
SALES (est): 1.5MM **Privately Held**
SIC: 1389 Pipe testing, oil field service

(G-9647)
EFDYN INCORPORATED
7734 E 11th St (74112-5718)
PHONE.................................918 838-1170
R Chris Robb, *President*
Carrie Wilkinson, *Corp Secy*
Marcia K Robb, *Vice Pres*
EMP: 7
SQ FT: 15,000
SALES (est): 1.4MM **Privately Held**
SIC: 3569 Jacks, hydraulic

(G-9648)
EHRLES CARNIVAL & PARTY SUPS
Also Called: Ehrle's Party Supply
5150 S Sheridan Rd (74145-7626)
PHONE.................................918 622-5266
Floyd Hannah, *President*
Lynn Hannah, *Vice Pres*
EMP: 6
SQ FT: 8,000
SALES (est): 613.3K **Privately Held**
WEB: www.costumespartyandevents.com
SIC: 5947 2396 Gift shop; greeting cards; novelties; party favors; automotive & apparel trimmings

(G-9649)
EL JAY ENTERPRISES INC
Also Called: El-Jayvideoaudio.com
5905 E 26th St (74114-5121)
PHONE.................................918 836-8273
Leon Whitman, *President*
Jeff Whitman, *Corp Secy*
Jean Whitman, *Vice Pres*
EMP: 3
SQ FT: 1,000
SALES: 100K **Privately Held**
WEB: www.el-jayvideoaudio.com
SIC: 7819 3652 Video tape or disk reproduction; pre-recorded records & tapes

(G-9650)
EL MOJADO
6827 S Peoria Ave (74136-3620)
PHONE.................................918 492-1138
Elias Rodriguez, *Owner*
EMP: 1
SALES (est): 67.4K **Privately Held**
SIC: 2032 Mexican foods: packaged in cans, jars, etc.

(G-9651)
ELCO TECH ENGINEERING
Also Called: Custom Jewelry By Robert Ellis
5256 S Irvyngton Pl (74135-7516)
PHONE.................................918 664-4646
Robert Ellis, *Principal*
EMP: 3
SQ FT: 680
SALES (est): 340.2K **Privately Held**
SIC: 8711 3911 Consulting engineer; jewelry, precious metal

(G-9652)
ELECTRANETICS INC
1811 S Baltimore Ave (74119-5215)
PHONE.................................918 960-0818
Bryan Noland, *Director*
EMP: 8
SALES (est): 780.4K **Privately Held**
SIC: 3679 Electronic circuits

(G-9653)
ELECTRONIC ASSEMBLY CORP
Also Called: EAC
8120 E 12th St Ste A (74112-7966)
PHONE.................................918 286-2816
Ronald E Sanders, *President*
Rus Sanders, *Vice Pres*
Sheila V Sanders, *Vice Pres*
EMP: 9
SQ FT: 3,500
SALES (est): 760K **Privately Held**
SIC: 3679 3823 Electronic circuits; computer interface equipment for industrial process control

(G-9654)
ELENS
4138 S 88th East Ave (74145-3331)
PHONE.................................918 627-5395
EMP: 2 EST: 2012
SALES (est): 161.6K **Privately Held**
SIC: 3827 Optical instruments & lenses

(G-9655)
ELI LILLY AND COMPANY
Also Called: Elanco Animal Health
7633 E 63rd Pl Ste 300 (74133-1202)
PHONE.................................918 459-4540
Bob Dempsey, *Manager*
EMP: 30
SALES (corp-wide): 22.3B **Publicly Held**
SIC: 2834 Pharmaceutical preparations
PA: Eli Lilly And Company
1 Lilly Corporate Ctr
Indianapolis IN 46285
317 276-2000

(G-9656)
ELITE CABINETS
11320 E 20th St (74128-6402)
PHONE.................................918 794-0757
EMP: 4 EST: 2014
SALES (est): 493.4K **Privately Held**
SIC: 2434 Wood kitchen cabinets

(G-9657)
ELKHORN OPERATING COMPANY (PA)
Also Called: Elkhorn Energy
4613 E 91st St (74137-2852)
PHONE.................................918 492-4418
Tom Rinehart, *CEO*
Mack Baughn, *President*
Jack Bentley, *Corp Secy*
EMP: 8
SQ FT: 7,000
SALES (est): 46.8MM **Privately Held**
SIC: 1311 Natural gas production

(G-9658)
ELLEN BROACH CPA
8123 E 48th St (74145-6906)
P.O. Box 284, Broken Arrow (74013-0284)
PHONE.................................918 665-7773
Ellen Broach, *Owner*
EMP: 1
SALES (est): 29K **Privately Held**
SIC: 3443 Fabricated plate work (boiler shop)

(G-9659)
ELLIOT ENTERPRISES
Also Called: Elliott, Lloyd S
2761 E Skelly Dr Ste 700e (74105-6232)
PHONE.................................918 742-9916
Lloyd S Elliot, *Owner*
EMP: 1
SALES (est): 72K **Privately Held**
SIC: 1389 Oil consultants

(G-9660)
ELLIOTT DIVERSIFIED INDS LLC
4171 E 47th St (74135-4736)
PHONE.................................918 293-2218
Patrick Elliot, *Principal*
EMP: 2
SALES (est): 120.9K **Privately Held**
SIC: 3999 Manufacturing industries

(G-9661)
ELLIOTT PRECISION PRODUCTS INC
16309 E Latimer St (74116-4014)
PHONE.................................918 234-4001
Steve Elliott, *President*
EMP: 22 EST: 1975
SQ FT: 20,000
SALES (est): 3.8MM **Privately Held**
SIC: 3599 7692 Machine shop, jobbing & repair; welding repair

(G-9662)
ELLIS BRIDAL LLC
8931 S Yale Ave (74137-3526)
PHONE.................................501 247-8698
EMP: 1
SALES (est): 42.5K **Privately Held**
SIC: 2335 Bridal & formal gowns

(G-9663)
ELSON OIL CO
20 E 5th St Ste 1404 (74103-4429)
PHONE.................................918 584-5225
William Elson Jr, *Partner*
EMP: 2 EST: 1920
SQ FT: 1,450
SALES (est): 208K **Privately Held**
SIC: 1311 Crude petroleum production

(G-9664)
ELYNX TECHNOLOGIES LLC (PA)
2431 E 6th St (74104-2810)
PHONE.................................877 643-5969
Stephen E Jackson, *President*
James Bygland, *COO*
Matt Cook, *Foreman/Supr*
Jeff Rusiewicz, *CFO*
Dan Van Wormer, *CFO*
EMP: 25
SALES (est): 31.5MM **Privately Held**
SIC: 1389 Testing, measuring, surveying & analysis services

(G-9665)
EMBROIDME OF TULSA
7115 S Mingo Rd (74133-3242)
PHONE.................................918 459-6699
Peter Brennan, *Principal*
EMP: 3
SALES (est): 234.6K **Privately Held**
SIC: 2395 Embroidery & art needlework

(G-9666)
EMC
1437 S Boulder Ave #940 (74119-3618)
P.O. Box 1125, Jenks (74037-1125)
PHONE.................................918 583-6363
Fax: 918 583-7530
EMP: 8
SALES (est): 840.1K **Privately Held**
SIC: 3572 Mfg Computer Storage Devices

(G-9667)
EMC LAW PLLC
1132 E 21st St (74114-1210)
PHONE.................................832 560-6280
Buford Pollett, *Principal*
EMP: 2 EST: 2017
SALES (est): 85.9K **Privately Held**
WEB: www.emclaw.us
SIC: 3572 Computer storage devices

(G-9668)
EMERGENCY ALERT RESPONSE
6725 E 102nd St (74133-6744)
PHONE.................................918 298-0500
Julie Ann Shiever, *Principal*
EMP: 2
SALES (est): 178.5K **Privately Held**
SIC: 3669 Emergency alarms

(G-9669)
EMERGING FUELS TECHNOLOGY LLC
6024 S 116th East Ave (74146-6821)
PHONE.................................918 286-6802
Mark Agee, *Vice Pres*
Kym Arcuri, *Vice Pres*
James Engman, *VP Opers*
Ed Holcomb, *CFO*
Kenneth Agee, *Mng Member*
EMP: 11 EST: 2008
SQ FT: 4,500

GEOGRAPHIC SECTION

Tulsa - Tulsa County (G-9698)

SALES (est): 2.2MM **Privately Held**
WEB: www.emfuelstech.com
SIC: 2869 Fuels

(G-9670)
EMERSON PROCESS MANAGEMENT
Also Called: Enardo
9932 E 58th St (74146-6411)
PHONE...................................918 622-6161
Jimmy Holman, *Principal*
Peter Barry, *Manager*
▼ EMP: 140
SQ FT: 37,000
SALES (est): 35.1MM
SALES (corp-wide): 18.3B **Publicly Held**
WEB: www.enardo.com
SIC: 3822 Vapor heating controls
HQ: Emerson Process Management Regulator Technologies, Inc.
3200 Emerson Way
Mckinney TX 75069

(G-9671)
EMERY BAY CORPORATION (PA)
Also Called: Bayville
4938 E 73rd St (74136-7007)
PHONE...................................918 494-2988
Norman Briscoe, *President*
EMP: 5 EST: 2016
SALES (est): 535K **Privately Held**
SIC: 2321 5023 2337 5137 Men's & boys' furnishings; decorative home furnishings & supplies; women's & misses' suits & coats; women's & children's clothing; men's & boys' clothing

(G-9672)
EMG GRAPHIC SYSTEMS INC
1110 N Iroquois Ave (74106-5901)
PHONE...................................918 835-5300
James Millspaugh, *President*
Diana H Millspaugh, *Vice Pres*
Sean Grubb, *Mfg Mgr*
Andrew Millspaugh, *Sales Associate*
▼ EMP: 15 EST: 1975
SQ FT: 14,000
SALES: 1.4MM **Privately Held**
SIC: 3993 Signs, not made in custom sign painting shops; advertising artwork

(G-9673)
EMMAUS GROUP LLC
2202 N 170th East Ave (74116-4921)
PHONE...................................918 834-8787
Dan Ford, *Mng Member*
Steve Coder, *Mng Member*
EMP: 6
SALES (est): 424.5K **Privately Held**
SIC: 3549 Metalworking machinery

(G-9674)
EMOTEQ CORPORATION (HQ)
10002 E 43rd St (74146-3657)
P.O. Box 470009 (74147-0009)
PHONE...................................918 627-1845
Richard Smith, *President*
Pat Obrien, *Purch Agent*
Craig Cosgrove, *Controller*
▲ EMP: 115
SALES (est): 18.8MM
SALES (corp-wide): 371MM **Publicly Held**
WEB: www.emoteq.com
SIC: 3621 Motors & generators
PA: Allied Motion Technologies Inc.
495 Commerce Dr Ste 3
Amherst NY 14228
716 242-8634

(G-9675)
EMPIRE LOUISIANA LLC
Also Called: Empire Louisiana LLC Delaware
1203 E 33rd St Ste 250 (74105-2048)
PHONE...................................539 444-8002
Michael R Morrisett, *President*
EMP: 1
SALES (est): 61K
SALES (corp-wide): 5.8MM **Publicly Held**
SIC: 1382 Oil & gas exploration services
PA: Empire Petroleum Corporation
1203 E 33rd St Ste 250
Tulsa OK 74105
539 444-8002

(G-9676)
EMPIRE OPTICAL INC
3220 E 21st St (74114-1857)
P.O. Box 4568 (74159-0568)
PHONE...................................918 744-8005
Charles M Hargrove, *President*
Mary Ann Hargrove, *Corp Secy*
Christian Hargrove, *Vice Pres*
EMP: 20 EST: 1964
SALES (est): 3.2MM **Privately Held**
WEB: www.empireoptical.com
SIC: 3851 5995 Lenses, ophthalmic; optical goods stores; opticians

(G-9677)
EMPIRE PETROLEUM CORPORATION (PA)
1203 E 33rd St Ste 250 (74105-2048)
PHONE...................................539 444-8002
Thomas Pritchard, *CEO*
Anthony N Kamin, *Ch of Bd*
Michael R Morrisett, *President*
Sultan Poonawala, *Vice Pres*
EMP: 3
SALES: 5.8MM **Publicly Held**
SIC: 1382 Oil & gas exploration services

(G-9678)
EMPOWERED LIFE STORES LLC
7498 E 46th Pl (74145-6306)
PHONE...................................918 523-5700
Troy William Wormell,
EMP: 1
SALES (est): 33.3K **Privately Held**
SIC: 2731 Book publishing

(G-9679)
ENARDO INC
4470 S 70th East Ave (74145-4607)
PHONE...................................918 622-6161
EMP: 2
SALES (est): 117.6K **Privately Held**
SIC: 3823 Industrial instrmnts msrmnt display/control process variable

(G-9680)
ENARDO MANUFACTURING CO
9932 E 58th St (74146-6411)
PHONE...................................918 622-6161
Mark J Tomer, *Principal*
EMP: 2
SALES (est): 183.8K **Privately Held**
SIC: 3999 Manufacturing industries

(G-9681)
ENCINOS 3D CUSTOM PRODUCTS LLC
9810 E 58th St (74146-6409)
PHONE...................................918 286-8535
Jesus Ortiz, *Mng Member*
EMP: 14
SQ FT: 11,000
SALES: 900K **Privately Held**
WEB: www.encinos3d.com
SIC: 3993 1799 Signs & advertising specialties; sign installation & maintenance

(G-9682)
ENERFIN RESOURCES COMPANY
2250 E 73rd St Ste 410 (74136-6833)
PHONE...................................918 492-8686
Art Webb, *Manager*
EMP: 6 **Privately Held**
SIC: 1382 Oil & gas exploration services
PA: Enerfin Resources Company
1001 S Dairy Ashford Rd # 220
Houston TX 77077

(G-9683)
ENERGY CONTROL SYSTEM INC
1787 N 71st St (74136-5108)
PHONE...................................918 481-3244
Bruce Walker, *President*
EMP: 4
SQ FT: 953
SALES (est): 353.3K **Privately Held**
SIC: 1382 Oil & gas exploration services

(G-9684)
ENERGYVEST INC
8211 E Regal Pl Ste 103 (74133-7181)
PHONE...................................918 549-1838
Lee Jenkins, *President*
Jalal Alghani, *CFO*
Carl Pomeroy, *Officer*
EMP: 15
SQ FT: 3,000
SALES: 4MM **Privately Held**
SIC: 1311 Crude petroleum & natural gas

(G-9685)
ENERSOURCE PETROLEUM INC
4550 W 57th St (74107-9135)
P.O. Box 1000, Bixby (74008-1000)
PHONE...................................918 446-8028
Loren D Frederick, *President*
Muriel B Frederick, *Corp Secy*
Vicki Frederick, *Vice Pres*
Gerald Frederick, *Controller*
EMP: 6
SQ FT: 7,500
SALES (est): 844.4K **Privately Held**
SIC: 1311 Crude petroleum production; natural gas production

(G-9686)
ENGATECH INC (PA)
Also Called: Engineering Automation Tech
233 S Detroit Ave Ste 300 (74120-2425)
PHONE...................................918 599-7500
Clay Slaton, *President*
EMP: 10 EST: 1999
SQ FT: 2,000
SALES (est): 1.1MM **Privately Held**
WEB: www.engatech.com
SIC: 8711 2759 Consulting engineer; commercial printing

(G-9687)
ENGINEERING TECHNOLOGY INC
11920 E Apache St (74116-1309)
PHONE...................................918 492-0508
Jackie L Earls, *President*
Larry Walker, *Vice Pres*
Stephen Rehm, *Research*
Dwight Rhodes, *Project Engr*
Kim Little, *Sales Staff*
◆ EMP: 25
SQ FT: 4,100
SALES (est): 6.5MM **Privately Held**
SIC: 3533 8748 Oil & gas drilling rigs & equipment; business consulting

(G-9688)
ENHANCED PRINTING PRODUCTS INC
Also Called: Phoenix Products
6315 E 12th St (74112-5419)
PHONE...................................918 585-1991
Greg Mosley, *President*
EMP: 5
SQ FT: 2,000
SALES (est): 430K **Privately Held**
SIC: 3579 Envelope stuffing, sealing & addressing machines

(G-9689)
ENOVATION CONTROLS LLC (HQ)
5311 S 122nd East Ave (74146-6006)
P.O. Box 470248 (74147-0248)
PHONE...................................918 317-4100
Gene Bazemore, *President*
Lisa Clevenger, *Materials Mgr*
Brenda Kresta, *Buyer*
Robert Mastin, *Engineer*
Jake Pratt, *Engineer*
▲ EMP: 327
SALES (est): 134.5MM
SALES (corp-wide): 554.6MM **Publicly Held**
SIC: 3625 3714 3694 8711 Motor starters & controllers, electric; motor vehicle steering systems & parts; ignition apparatus, internal combustion engines; mechanical engineering
PA: Helios Technologies, Inc.
1500 W University Pkwy
Sarasota FL 34243
941 362-1200

(G-9690)
ENTERPRISE EXPLORATION INC
Also Called: Enterprise Energy Production
6528 D 1 Ste 392 (74133)
PHONE...................................918 481-2125
EMP: 3

SALES (est): 304.6K **Privately Held**
SIC: 1382 Oil Field Drilling & Exploration

(G-9691)
ENTERPRISE MANUFACTURING LLC
16309 E Latimer St (74116-4014)
P.O. Box 582200 (74158-2200)
PHONE...................................918 438-4455
Steven Elliott, *Mng Member*
Bryan Collins,
Mark Mitchell,
EMP: 6
SQ FT: 20,000
SALES (est): 968K **Privately Held**
WEB: www.enterprise-mfg.com
SIC: 3441 Fabricated structural metal

(G-9692)
ENTERPRISE MANUFACTURING LLC
1720 N 161st East Ave (74116-4825)
PHONE...................................918 438-4455
Mark Mitchell, *Principal*
EMP: 1
SALES (est): 46.2K **Privately Held**
SIC: 3999 Manufacturing industries

(G-9693)
ENXNET INC
7450 S Winston Ave (74136-6118)
PHONE...................................918 494-6663
Ryan Corley, *Ch of Bd*
Michael Jackson, *Exec VP*
Stephen Hoelscher, *CFO*
EMP: 3
SALES (est): 401.8K **Privately Held**
SIC: 1311 Gas & hydrocarbon liquefaction from coal

(G-9694)
EQUAL ENERGY US INC
15 W 6th St Ste 1201 (74119-5406)
PHONE...................................405 242-6000
Tom Lough, *CFO*
EMP: 52
SQ FT: 12,100
SALES (est): 8.5MM
SALES (corp-wide): 58.9MM **Privately Held**
SIC: 1311 Crude petroleum & natural gas production
PA: Equal Energy Ltd
500 4 Ave Sw Suite 2700
Calgary AB

(G-9695)
EQUUS METALCRAFT LLC
303 S 123rd East Pl (74128-2427)
PHONE...................................918 832-0956
Ann Morris,
EMP: 1
SALES (est): 62.4K **Privately Held**
SIC: 1799 2431 Ornamental metal work; staircases, stairs & railings

(G-9696)
EQUUS METALS INC
303 S 123rd East Pl (74128-2427)
PHONE...................................918 834-9872
Tim Morris, *President*
Bill Joe Slaughter, *Vice Pres*
Nancy Slaughter, *Asst Treas*
Jeff Beames, *Sales Mgr*
EMP: 40 EST: 1997
SQ FT: 7,000
SALES (est): 9.9MM **Privately Held**
WEB: www.equusmetals.com
SIC: 3441 Fabricated structural metal

(G-9697)
ERIN TURNER CUSTOM EMB LLC
5426 E 110th Pl (74137-7253)
PHONE...................................918 869-6481
EMP: 1
SALES (est): 45.6K **Privately Held**
SIC: 2395 Embroidery & art needlework

(G-9698)
ERNEST WIEMANN IRON WORKS
Also Called: Wiemann Ironworks
639 W 41st St (74107-7018)
PHONE...................................918 592-1700

Doug Bracken, *President*
Gary M Martin, *Division Mgr*
Gary Bracken, *Chairman*
Dave Bracken, *Treasurer*
Lori Combs, *Human Resources*
◆ **EMP:** 20
SQ FT: 48,000
SALES (corp-wide): 5.5MM **Privately Held**
WEB: www.wmcraft.com
SIC: 3446 3441 Architectural metalwork; fabricated structural metal

(G-9699)
ERSHIGS INC
9910 E 56th St N (74117-4011)
PHONE 918 477-9371
EMP: 24
SALES (corp-wide): 8.4B **Publicly Held**
WEB: www.ershigs.com
SIC: 3083 Laminated plastics plate & sheet
HQ: Ershigs, Inc.
   742 Marine Dr
   Bellingham WA 98225
   360 733-2620

(G-9700)
ESKRIDGE PRODUCTION CO INC
412 S Allegheny Ave (74112-1428)
PHONE 918 836-3058
John Eskridge, *President*
Jan Eskridge, *Vice Pres*
Buster Eskridge, *Treasurer*
Bruce Alsup, *Admin Sec*
EMP: 1
SALES (est): 150K **Privately Held**
SIC: 1311 Crude petroleum production

(G-9701)
ESPERANZA RESOURCES CORP
7170 S Braden Ave Ste 200 (74136-6316)
P.O. Box 702784 (74170-2784)
PHONE 918 497-1231
John R Brower, *President*
EMP: 2 **EST:** 1996
SQ FT: 800
SALES (est): 800K **Privately Held**
SIC: 1382 Oil & gas exploration services

(G-9702)
ESSILOR LABORATORIES AMER INC
Also Called: Duffens Optical
7633 E 63rd Pl Ste 300 (74133-1202)
PHONE 800 568-5367
Renee Durkee, *Manager*
EMP: 25
SALES (corp-wide): 1.7MM **Privately Held**
SIC: 5048 3851 3229 Ophthalmic goods; ophthalmic goods; pressed & blown glass
HQ: Essilor Laboratories Of America, Inc.
   13515 N Stemmons Fwy
   Dallas TX 75234
   972 241-4141

(G-9703)
ETX ENERGY LLC (PA)
6100 S Yale Ave Ste 500 (74136-1906)
PHONE 918 728-3020
Ralph Hill, *CEO*
Mark Castell, *Vice Pres*
EMP: 55
SALES (est): 51.8MM **Privately Held**
SIC: 1311 1382 Natural gas production; geological exploration, oil & gas field

(G-9704)
EUFRATES COM LLC
9810 E 42nd St Ste 102 (74146-3675)
PHONE 918 280-9270
EMP: 2
SALES (est): 170K **Privately Held**
SIC: 7372 Prepackaged Software Services

(G-9705)
EVANS ENTERPRISES
2020 Southwest Blvd (74107-1718)
P.O. Box 1316 (74101-1316)
PHONE 918 587-1566
Evan Thrash, *Plant Mgr*
EMP: 11
SALES (est): 1.4MM **Privately Held**
SIC: 7694 Electric motor repair

(G-9706)
EVANS ENTERPRISES INC
2002 Southwest Blvd (74107-1718)
PHONE 918 587-1566
Rusty Thrash, *Branch Mgr*
EMP: 49
SQ FT: 1,500
SALES (corp-wide): 148.9MM **Privately Held**
SIC: 7694 5063 5084 Electric motor repair; motors, electric; industrial machinery & equipment
PA: Evans Enterprises, Inc.
   6707 N Interstate Dr
   Norman OK 73069
   405 631-1344

(G-9707)
EVANS ENTERPRISES INC
Also Called: Evans Electric Motors
2002 Southwest Blvd (74107-1718)
P.O. Box 1063, Pryor (74362-1063)
PHONE 918 825-2200
Benny Beneux, *Manager*
EMP: 8
SALES (corp-wide): 148.9MM **Privately Held**
SIC: 7694 5999 Electric motor repair; engine & motor equipment & supplies
PA: Evans Enterprises, Inc.
   6707 N Interstate Dr
   Norman OK 73069
   405 631-1344

(G-9708)
EVELYN CO INC
7401 E 46th Pl (74145-6305)
P.O. Box 35265 (74153-0265)
PHONE 918 665-3952
Ralph Mays, *President*
EMP: 2
SALES (est): 302.5K **Privately Held**
SIC: 5047 3843 3842 Dental equipment & supplies; dental equipment & supplies; surgical appliances & supplies

(G-9709)
EVEREST ACQSITION HOLDINGS INC
7737 E 42nd Pl Ste H (74145-4719)
PHONE 918 770-7190
David Voeller, *President*
EMP: 15
SALES (est): 1.2MM **Privately Held**
WEB: www.everestsciences.com
SIC: 3585 Air conditioning units, complete: domestic or industrial

(G-9710)
EVEREST SCIENCES AN S T CO LLC
17411 E Pine St (74116-4928)
PHONE 918 770-7190
Bill Tolbert, *President*
EMP: 15
SALES (est): 615K
SALES (corp-wide): 19MM **Privately Held**
SIC: 3585 Refrigeration & heating equipment
PA: S & T Mfg. Co.
   17411 E Pine St
   Tulsa OK 74116
   918 234-4151

(G-9711)
EVERSHARP TOOL INC
11350 E 60th Pl (74146-6817)
PHONE 918 250-9400
Douglas Turner, *President*
Jeffery Turner, *Vice Pres*
EMP: 13
SQ FT: 6,900
SALES (est): 1.2MM **Privately Held**
WEB: www.eversharptool.com
SIC: 3599 5084 Custom machinery; machine tools & metalworking machinery

(G-9712)
EVOQUA WATER TECHNOLOGIES LLC
9410 E 51st St (74145-9032)
PHONE 978 614-7233
Ron Deschwing, *Branch Mgr*
EMP: 146
SALES (corp-wide): 1.4B **Publicly Held**
SIC: 3589 3569 3823 3826 Water treatment equipment, industrial; filters, general line: industrial; water quality monitoring & control systems; magnetic resonance imaging apparatus; water supply
HQ: Evoqua Water Technologies Llc
   210 6th Ave Ste 3300
   Pittsburgh PA 15222
   724 772-0044

(G-9713)
EXCEL MINING LLC (DH)
Also Called: Pontiki Coal
1717 S Boulder Ave (74119-4805)
P.O. Box 645 (74101-0645)
PHONE 918 295-7600
Joseph W Craft III, *President*
William D Jaggers Jr, *General Mgr*
Mitzi Shcumacker, *Business Mgr*
Gordon E Schaechterle, *Vice Pres*
Donald R Wellendorf, *Vice Pres*
EMP: 240
SALES (est): 40.6MM **Publicly Held**
SIC: 1221 Bituminous coal & lignite-surface mining
HQ: Alliance Coal, Llc
   1717 S Boulder Ave # 400
   Tulsa OK 74119
   918 295-7600

(G-9714)
EXCELLENCE LOGGING
7136 S Yale Ave Ste 420 (74136-6357)
PHONE 815 272-7622
Sandra Dylka, *Principal*
EMP: 2
SALES (est): 81.7K **Privately Held**
SIC: 2411 Logging

(G-9715)
EXCO RESOURCES INC
Also Called: Exco Mid Continent Division
2100 One Williams Ctr (74172-0121)
PHONE 918 592-7300
Charles Evans, *Exec VP*
EMP: 70
SALES (est): 3.9MM **Privately Held**
SIC: 1311 Crude petroleum production

(G-9716)
EXPONENT ENERGY LLC
1560 E 21st St Ste 215 (74114-1345)
PHONE 918 906-6045
Chris Bird, *Mng Member*
EMP: 7
SALES (est): 1MM **Privately Held**
SIC: 2813 Industrial gases

(G-9717)
EXPRESS BUS INC
6333 E Apache St (74115-3405)
PHONE 918 835-2040
Ron Hall, *Manager*
EMP: 1
SALES (corp-wide): 1.2MM **Privately Held**
SIC: 2741 Miscellaneous publishing
PA: Express Bus Inc
   1465 Highway 365 S
   Conway AR 72032
   501 329-6634

(G-9718)
EXTRACT PRODUCTION SVCS LLC
1336 N 143rd East Ave (74116-2122)
PHONE 918 938-6828
Matt Gibson, *Mng Member*
EMP: 150 **EST:** 2017
SALES (est): 72K **Privately Held**
SIC: 1389 1799 Pumping of oil & gas wells; petroleum storage tanks, pumping & draining

(G-9719)
EXTRACT SURFACE SYSTEMS LLC
1336 N 143rd East Ave (74116-2122)
PHONE 918 938-6828
EMP: 3
SALES (est): 81.8K **Privately Held**
SIC: 2836 Extracts

(G-9720)
EZEKIEL CHRLES PBLICATIONS LLC
8709 S 70th East Ave (74133-5058)
PHONE 918 747-8841
Charles Duhon, *Principal*
EMP: 1 **EST:** 2010
SALES (est): 75.8K **Privately Held**
SIC: 2741 Miscellaneous publishing

(G-9721)
F C ZIEGLER CO (PA)
Also Called: Catholic Art & Gifts
2111 E 11th St Ste A-B (74104-3625)
PHONE 918 587-7639
Dennis J Ziegler, *President*
Terrence Ziegler, *Vice Pres*
William Zitter, *Vice Pres*
Troy Bates, *Warehouse Mgr*
Sarah Pennington, *Purchasing*
▲ **EMP:** 48
SQ FT: 55,000
SALES (est): 31.6MM **Privately Held**
WEB: www.zieglers.com
SIC: 5199 3299 5947 5942 Art goods & supplies; ecclesiastical statuary: gypsum, clay or papier mache; gift shop; books, religious; jewelry, precious metal; fabricated plate work (boiler shop)

(G-9722)
FABRICATION DYNAMICS INC ○
2102 W Skelly Dr (74107-9048)
PHONE 918 446-1638
EMP: 2 **EST:** 2019
SALES (est): 148.8K **Privately Held**
SIC: 3444 Sheet metalwork

(G-9723)
FABRICATION SOLUTIONS LLC
109 S 122nd East Ave (74128-2405)
PHONE 918 398-7162
Michael Owings Sr, *General Mgr*
Bobby Milliser, *Prdtn Mgr*
EMP: 12 **EST:** 2007
SALES (est): 2.4MM **Privately Held**
WEB: www.fabsol.com
SIC: 3599 Machine shop, jobbing & repair

(G-9724)
FABRICUT INC
Universal Convertors Importers
9303 E 46th St (74145-4895)
PHONE 918 622-7700
EMP: 19
SALES (corp-wide): 178.6MM **Privately Held**
SIC: 2261 Finishing plants, cotton
PA: Fabricut, Inc.
   9303 E 46th St
   Tulsa OK 74145
   918 622-7700

(G-9725)
FACET (OKLAHOMA) LLC (HQ)
11607 E 43rd St N (74116-2103)
PHONE 918 272-8700
George C Nolen, *CEO*
Trevor Marois, *Project Mgr*
◆ **EMP:** 27 **EST:** 1979
SQ FT: 111,000
SALES (est): 48.3MM
SALES (corp-wide): 344.8MM **Privately Held**
WEB: www.pecofacet.com
SIC: 3569 Filters, general line: industrial
PA: Filtration Group Corporation
   600 W 22nd St Ste 300
   Oak Brook IL 60523
   512 593-7999

(G-9726)
FADCO OF ARKANSAS LLC
5531 E Admiral Pl (74115-8411)
PHONE 918 832-1641
Larry Vincent, *Mng Member*
EMP: 3
SALES: 184.5K **Privately Held**
SIC: 2431 Millwork

(G-9727)
FAMMCO MFG CO INC
17309 E Pine St (74116-4923)
PHONE 918 437-0456

GEOGRAPHIC SECTION

Tulsa - Tulsa County (G-9755)

Jonathan Tolbert, *CEO*
Onita Johnson, *Principal*
Gary Tolbert, *Principal*
Larry Tolbert, *Principal*
Ronnie Tolbert, *Principal*
EMP: 5
SALES (est): 945.3K **Privately Held**
SIC: 3441 3533 3444 Fabricated structural metal; oil & gas field machinery; sheet metalwork

(G-9728)
FARMER BROS CO
Also Called: Farmers Brothers Coffee
11529 E Pine St (74116-2022)
PHONE 918 439-9262
Bob King, *Vice Pres*
Dave Petty, *Supervisor*
EMP: 5
SALES (corp-wide): 595.9MM **Publicly Held**
SIC: 2095 Coffee roasting (except by wholesale grocers)
PA: Farmer Bros. Co.
1912 Farmer Brothers Dr
Northlake TX 76262
888 998-2468

(G-9729)
FARMERS ENERGY CORP
Also Called: Silvan Oil
1 W 3rd St Ste 918 (74103-3517)
PHONE 918 587-6756
David R Sylvan, *President*
EMP: 6 **EST:** 1974
SALES (est): 659.4K **Privately Held**
SIC: 1311 Crude petroleum production; natural gas production

(G-9730)
FDND OIL AND GAS LLC
124 E 4th St (74103-5027)
PHONE 918 583-9960
Frederic Dorwart, *Principal*
EMP: 2
SALES (est): 87.6K **Privately Held**
SIC: 1389 Oil & gas field services

(G-9731)
FEDERAL METALS INC
2107 E 48th St (74105-8702)
PHONE 918 838-1725
EMP: 12
SALES (est): 1.6MM **Privately Held**
SIC: 3441 3423 Whol Metals Service Center

(G-9732)
FEDEX OFFICE & PRINT SVCS INC
Also Called: Fedex Office Print & Ship
1324 E 71st St (74136-5034)
PHONE 918 492-6701
EMP: 13
SALES (corp-wide): 69.6B **Publicly Held**
SIC: 7334 2789 Photocopying & duplicating services; bookbinding & related work
HQ: Fedex Office And Print Services, Inc.
7900 Legacy Dr
Plano TX 75024
800 463-3339

(G-9733)
FEDEX OFFICE & PRINT SVCS INC
8228 E 61st St Ste 105 (74133-1905)
PHONE 918 252-3757
EMP: 25
SALES (corp-wide): 69.6B **Publicly Held**
SIC: 7334 2791 2789 Photocopying & duplicating services; typesetting; bookbinding & related work
HQ: Fedex Office And Print Services, Inc.
7900 Legacy Dr
Plano TX 75024
800 463-3339

(G-9734)
FELINIS COOKIES INC (PA)
Also Called: Felini's Cookies & Deli
3533 S Harvard Ave (74135-1840)
PHONE 918 742-3638
Vickie Martinus, *President*
James Martinus, *Vice Pres*
EMP: 7
SQ FT: 1,200
SALES: 500K **Privately Held**
SIC: 5149 5963 5812 2052 Crackers, cookies & bakery products; food services, direct sales; delicatessen (eating places); cookies & crackers; bread, cake & related products

(G-9735)
FELLERS INC
7101 E 38th St Unit 7184 (74145-3235)
PHONE 918 621-4412
Kevin Copeland, *Manager*
EMP: 10
SALES (corp-wide): 69.9MM **Privately Held**
SIC: 3993 Signs & advertising specialties
PA: Fellers Inc
6566 E Skelly Dr
Tulsa OK 74145
918 621-4400

(G-9736)
FELLERS INC (PA)
6566 E Skelly Dr (74145-1324)
PHONE 918 621-4400
Frank Fellers, *CEO*
Doug Smith, *Vice Pres*
Jan Rohlman, *Asst Controller*
Lynne Weaver, *Credit Mgr*
Vicki Hancock, *Financial Exec*
▲ **EMP:** 125
SQ FT: 50,000
SALES (est): 69.9MM **Privately Held**
SIC: 3993 5099 Signs & advertising specialties; signs, except electric

(G-9737)
FENNER INC
Also Called: Specialty Prosthetic
10338 E 21st St (74129-1606)
PHONE 918 832-7768
Michael O Fenner, *CEO*
Terry Fenner, *Corp Secy*
EMP: 6
SQ FT: 3,200
SALES (est): 664.2K **Privately Held**
SIC: 3842 Prosthetic appliances

(G-9738)
FERGUSON
231 S Memorial Dr (74112-2201)
PHONE 918 835-4813
EMP: 2
SALES (est): 88.8K **Privately Held**
SIC: 3432 Plumbing fixture fittings & trim

(G-9739)
FIBER PAD INC (PA)
17260 Tiger Switch Rd (74116-4915)
P.O. Box 690660 (74169-0660)
PHONE 918 438-7430
Donald W Law II, *CEO*
Grace E Law, *President*
Rene Ploch, *Corp Secy*
EMP: 65 **EST:** 1977
SQ FT: 30,000
SALES (est): 10.5MM **Privately Held**
SIC: 3089 Injection molding of plastics; plastic processing

(G-9740)
FIBER PAD INC
2201 N 170th East Ave (74116-4922)
P.O. Box 690660 (74169-0660)
PHONE 918 438-7430
Grace E Law II, *President*
Teresa Lovelace, *Human Res Mgr*
EMP: 50
SQ FT: 33,000
SALES (est): 6.1MM
SALES (corp-wide): 10.5MM **Privately Held**
SIC: 3089 Plastic containers, except foam; injection molding of plastics
PA: Fiber Pad, Inc.
17260 Tiger Switch Rd
Tulsa OK 74116
918 438-7430

(G-9741)
FIELDPOINT ENERGY SERVICES LLC
7030 S Yale Ave Ste 100 (74136-5709)
PHONE 918 691-3427
EMP: 5
SALES (est): 689.1K **Privately Held**
SIC: 1389 Construction, repair & dismantling services

(G-9742)
FILTER SUPPLY AND RECYCLING
4214 S 76th East Ave (74145-4712)
PHONE 918 663-3143
EMP: 7
SALES (est): 957.9K
SALES (corp-wide): 311.2K **Privately Held**
SIC: 3564 3569 Filters, air: furnaces, air conditioning equipment, etc.; filters
PA: Filter Supply And Recycling
3511 S Sheridan Rd
Tulsa OK

(G-9743)
FINE ARTS ENGRAVING CO INC
6716 E 12th St (74112-5620)
PHONE 918 835-6400
Masood Khaleeli, *Manager*
EMP: 7
SALES (corp-wide): 4MM **Privately Held**
SIC: 2759 Publication printing
PA: Fine Arts Engraving Co, Inc
4401 Sw 23rd St
Oklahoma City OK
405 947-6730

(G-9744)
FINISH LINE POWDER COATING
191 S 122nd East Ave (74128-2405)
PHONE 918 938-6292
Terry Easum, *Principal*
EMP: 3
SALES (est): 56.7K **Privately Held**
SIC: 1799 3479 Coating of metal structures at construction site; coating of metals & formed products

(G-9745)
FINISHED SEAM
3611 S Atlanta Pl (74105-3511)
PHONE 918 742-4727
Anna Jordan, *Owner*
EMP: 1
SALES (est): 55.8K **Privately Held**
SIC: 2391 Curtains & draperies

(G-9746)
FINISHING TECHNOLOGY INC
11384 E Tecumseh St (74116-1603)
PHONE 918 437-3820
Webb Kane, *President*
EMP: 8
SALES (est): 418.2K **Privately Held**
WEB: www.finishingtechnologies.com
SIC: 3471 Finishing, metals or formed products

(G-9747)
FIRST STUART CORPORATION
2431 E 61st St Ste 600 (74136-1244)
PHONE 918 744-5222
Jon R Stuart, *President*
Harold C Stuart, *Chairman*
John B Turner, *Vice Pres*
EMP: 5 **EST:** 1924
SQ FT: 20,000
SALES (est): 490K **Privately Held**
SIC: 6799 1311 Real estate investors, except property operators; crude petroleum production; natural gas production

(G-9748)
FIRSTLINE FILTERS LLC
2201 S Jackson Ave (74107-3011)
PHONE 918 660-8772
Mylum Ache,
EMP: 7
SALES (est): 1.2MM **Privately Held**
SIC: 3569 Filters, general line: industrial; filters

(G-9749)
FIS OPERATIONS LLC
Also Called: Frontier Integrity Solutions
2100 S Utica Ave Ste 200 (74114-1437)
PHONE 918 246-7100
Keyth Pengal, *CEO*
Zyrius Niklu, *President*
Keith Tengal, *COO*
Stanley Huang, *CFO*
Tracey Toops, *Controller*
EMP: 250 **EST:** 2016
SALES (est): 3.8MM **Privately Held**
SIC: 1389 Pipe testing, oil field service

(G-9750)
FISHER PRODUCTS LLC
1320 W 22nd Pl (74107-2750)
PHONE 918 582-2204
Dick Gregory, *VP Opers*
Christopher White, *Purch Mgr*
Pamela Fisher, *Human Res Mgr*
Roy Hilton, *Sales Mgr*
Michael E Short, *Mng Member*
EMP: 56
SQ FT: 45,000
SALES (est): 11.1MM **Privately Held**
WEB: www.fisherproductsllc.com
SIC: 3599 3563 Machine shop, jobbing & repair; spraying & dusting equipment

(G-9751)
FIXTURES & DRYWALL CO OKLA INC
Also Called: Fadco
5531 E Admiral Pl (74115-8411)
PHONE 918 832-1641
Robert Vincent, *President*
Larry Vincent, *Vice Pres*
EMP: 19
SQ FT: 25,000
SALES (est): 4.2MM **Privately Held**
WEB: www.fadco.com
SIC: 2522 2541 Office furniture, except wood; store fixtures, wood

(G-9752)
FKI INDUSTRIES INC (DH)
Also Called: Acco Chain & Lifting Products
2801 Dawson Rd (74110-5042)
PHONE 918 834-4611
James Slattery, *Ch of Bd*
Robert G Beeston, *Ch of Bd*
Robert Miller, *Vice Pres*
Matt Nozemack, *Vice Pres*
Robert Sook, *Vice Pres*
◆ **EMP:** 4 **EST:** 1912
SQ FT: 8,000
SALES (est): 387.2MM **Publicly Held**
SIC: 3429 3536 3535 3496 Furniture hardware; hoists, cranes & monorails; hoists; cranes & monorail systems; belt conveyor systems, general industrial use; chain, welded; baling machines, for scrap metal, paper or similar material; industrial process control instruments; industrial process measurement equipment; digital displays of process variables
HQ: Crosby Us Acquisition Corp.
2801 Dawson Rd
Tulsa OK 74110
918 834-4611

(G-9753)
FLAMECO INDUSTRIES INC
5943 E 13th St (74112-5407)
P.O. Box 4303 (74159-0303)
PHONE 918 832-1100
Douglas A Lee, *President*
David Ray, *Corp Secy*
Robert Archuleta, *Safety Mgr*
John Danne, *Purchasing*
Dave Ray, *Treasurer*
EMP: 20 **EST:** 1979
SQ FT: 20,000
SALES (est): 4.5MM **Privately Held**
WEB: www.flameco.com
SIC: 3433 Gas burners, domestic

(G-9754)
FLASH FLOOD PRINT STUDIOS LLC
2421 E Admiral Blvd (74110-5322)
PHONE 918 794-3527
May Yang, *Principal*
EMP: 2
SALES (est): 183.5K **Privately Held**
SIC: 2752 7336 Commercial printing, lithographic; commercial art & graphic design

(G-9755)
FLASHLIGHTZ
7122 S Sheridan Rd 2-546 (74133-2748)
PHONE 918 260-5882
Sean Wyatt, *Principal*
EMP: 2

SALES (est): 218.7K **Privately Held**
SIC: 3648 Lighting equipment

(G-9756)
FLINT INDUSTRIES
322 E Archer St (74120-1404)
PHONE..................................918 599-7162
EMP: 1
SALES (est): 53K **Privately Held**
SIC: 3999 Mfg Misc Products

(G-9757)
FLOW MEASUREMENT COMPANY INC
1214 S Joplin Ave (74112-5428)
PHONE..................................918 493-3443
George Sly Jr, *Ch of Bd*
Charles McNamara, *President*
EMP: 7
SQ FT: 1,800
SALES (est): 426.3K **Privately Held**
SIC: 1389 5085 Measurement of well flow rates, oil & gas; gas equipment, parts & supplies

(G-9758)
FLOW-QUIP INC
4433 W 49th St Ste D (74107-7307)
PHONE..................................918 663-3313
Robert H Arnold, *President*
Jarod Carmichael, *Engineer*
Dustin Rhodes, *Engineer*
▲ EMP: 25
SALES (est): 5MM **Privately Held**
SIC: 3491 Industrial valves

(G-9759)
FLOWERS BKG CO LYNCHBURG LLC
12787 E 41st St (74146-3502)
PHONE..................................918 270-1182
EMP: 2
SALES (corp-wide): 4.1B **Publicly Held**
SIC: 2051 Bread, cake & related products
HQ: Flowers Baking Co. Of Lynchburg, Llc
    1905 Hollins Mill Rd
    Lynchburg VA 24503
    434 528-0441

(G-9760)
FLOWSERVE CORPORATION
4501 S 86th East Ave (74145-4808)
P.O. Box 472250 (74147-2250)
PHONE..................................918 627-8400
Joe Marenghi, *Manager*
EMP: 280
SALES (corp-wide): 3.9B **Publicly Held**
WEB: www.flowserve.com
SIC: 3561 Pumps & pumping equipment
PA: Flowserve Corporation
    5215 N Ocnnor Blvd Ste 23 Connor
    Irving TX 75039
    972 443-6500

(G-9761)
FLOWSERVE US INC
724 W 41st St (74107-7032)
PHONE..................................918 599-6000
Doug Richison, *District Mgr*
Daryl Garrison, *Sales Engr*
Lew Kling, *Branch Mgr*
EMP: 118
SALES (corp-wide): 3.9B **Publicly Held**
SIC: 3561 Pumps & pumping equipment
HQ: Flowserve Us Inc.
    5215 N Ocnnor Blvd Ste Connor
    Irving TX 75039
    972 443-6500

(G-9762)
FLUID CONTROLS INC
10050 S 33rd West Ave (74132-3733)
P.O. Box 307, Jenks (74037-0307)
PHONE..................................918 299-0442
Henry T Haynes, *President*
Joanne Haynes, *Vice Pres*
Leta Whitetree, *Admin Sec*
EMP: 20
SQ FT: 10,000
SALES (est): 3.3MM **Privately Held**
SIC: 3823 3612 3494 3491 Fluidic devices, circuits & systems for process control; transformers, except electric; valves & pipe fittings; industrial valves

(G-9763)
FLUID TREATMENT SYSTEMS INC
5123 S 103rd East Ave (74146-5814)
PHONE..................................918 933-5678
EMP: 2
SALES (est): 79.9K **Privately Held**
SIC: 3589 Service industry machinery

(G-9764)
FOR HIS GLORY CUTTING BOARDS
6539 E 46th St (74145-5812)
PHONE..................................918 633-7233
EMP: 2
SALES (est): 118.7K **Privately Held**
SIC: 2431 Millwork

(G-9765)
FORESTER LLC
Also Called: Forester Machine & Mfg
6929 E 15th St (74112-6621)
PHONE..................................918 835-6533
Russell Forester, *General Mgr*
Jeremy Forester, *Plant Mgr*
EMP: 9
SQ FT: 6,000
SALES (est): 1.3MM **Privately Held**
WEB: www.foresterllc.com
SIC: 3599 Machine shop, jobbing & repair

(G-9766)
FOSTER MACHINE SHOP
15856 E Pine St (74116-2464)
PHONE..................................918 438-4001
Jack W Foster, *Owner*
EMP: 3
SQ FT: 2,824
SALES (est): 60K **Privately Held**
SIC: 3599 Machine shop, jobbing & repair

(G-9767)
FOUNDATION ENERGY COMPANY LLC
15 E 5th St Ste 1200 (74103-4328)
PHONE..................................918 585-1650
Richard Payne, *Vice Pres*
EMP: 15
SALES (est): 3.8MM **Privately Held**
WEB: www.foundationenergy.com
SIC: 4911 1382 Electric services; oil & gas exploration services

(G-9768)
FOUNDATION ENERGY MGT LLC
15 E 5th St Ste 1200 (74103-4328)
PHONE..................................918 526-5521
EMP: 1 **Privately Held**
SIC: 1382 Oil & gas exploration services
PA: Foundation Energy Management, L.L.C.
    5057 Keller Springs Rd # 650
    Addison TX 75001

(G-9769)
FOUR STAR CRATING CO
9911 E 54th St Ste D (74146-5743)
PHONE..................................918 663-6689
Dwight Newton, *Owner*
EMP: 2
SALES (est): 143.2K **Privately Held**
SIC: 2449 Rectangular boxes & crates, wood

(G-9770)
FOXHEAD OIL & GAS COMPANY
320 S Boston Ave Ste 1104 (74103-4700)
PHONE..................................918 582-2124
EMP: 3 EST: 1992
SALES (est): 300K **Privately Held**
SIC: 1382 Oil/Gas Exploration Services

(G-9771)
FRANCIS OIL & GAS INC
6733 S Yale Ave Ste 202 (74136-3302)
P.O. Box 21468 (74121-1468)
PHONE..................................918 491-4253
Joel Jankowsky, *President*
Brenda R Magoon, *Senior VP*
Phyllis Rossier, *Vice Pres*
EMP: 2 EST: 1932
SALES (est): 210K **Privately Held**
WEB: www.kfoc.net
SIC: 1311 Crude petroleum production; natural gas production

(G-9772)
FRANK G LOVE ENVELOPES INC (PA)
10733 E Ute St (74116-1518)
PHONE..................................214 637-5900
Michael Edward Love, *Ch of Bd*
Ron Wilson, *President*
Jim Ballard, *COO*
Daniel Love, *Vice Pres*
Michael J Love, *Vice Pres*
EMP: 100 EST: 1958
SQ FT: 50,000
SALES (est): 33.9MM **Privately Held**
WEB: www.loveenvelopes.com
SIC: 2677 Envelopes

(G-9773)
FREDERICK SOMMERS WSTN SIGN CO
Also Called: Frederick Sommers & Wstn Sign
10017 E 46th Pl (74146-4717)
PHONE..................................918 587-2300
Randy Frederick, *Partner*
Deborah Frederick, *Partner*
EMP: 12
SQ FT: 5,000
SALES (est): 1MM **Privately Held**
SIC: 7389 3993 Lettering service; sign painting & lettering shop; signs & advertising specialties

(G-9774)
FREEDOM BELL INC
Also Called: Freedom Bell Wireless
2607 N Quincy Ave (74106-2603)
P.O. Box 48584 (74148-0584)
PHONE..................................918 671-1089
Marion Avance, *President*
EMP: 4
SALES (est): 193.9K **Privately Held**
SIC: 8748 2731 Telecommunications consultant; book publishing

(G-9775)
FREEDOM HOMES
9516 E Admiral Pl (74115-8132)
PHONE..................................918 728-2277
EMP: 2
SALES (est): 86.7K **Privately Held**
SIC: 2451 Mobile homes

(G-9776)
FREEDOM MIDSTREAM SERVICES LLC
20 E 5th St Ste 1403 (74103-4463)
PHONE..................................918 582-5313
EMP: 6 EST: 2008
SALES (est): 950K **Privately Held**
SIC: 1389 Oil/Gas Field Services

(G-9777)
FRENCHES QUARTER
10622 E 17th Pl (74128-6202)
PHONE..................................918 691-2553
Bradley C French, *Owner*
EMP: 1
SALES (est): 150K **Privately Held**
SIC: 3161 Clothing & apparel carrying cases

(G-9778)
FRICTION SOLUTIONS LLC
7427 E 46th Pl (74145-6305)
PHONE..................................918 622-8989
EMP: 6
SALES (est): 380K **Privately Held**
SIC: 3471 Plating/Polishing Service

(G-9779)
FRISCO ENERGY LLC
4124 S Rockford Ave # 102 (74105-4248)
PHONE..................................918 742-5200
Philip J Wilner,
C E Butch Smith,
EMP: 4 EST: 1996
SQ FT: 2,700
SALES (est): 350K **Privately Held**
WEB: www.friscoenergy.com
SIC: 1311 Crude petroleum production

(G-9780)
FRONTIER ENERGY SERVICES LLC
4200 E Skelly Dr Ste 700 (74135-3256)
PHONE..................................918 754-2226
Dave Presley, *Branch Mgr*
EMP: 9
SALES (corp-wide): 6.9MM **Privately Held**
WEB: www.frontierenergyllc.com
SIC: 1321 Natural gas liquids production
PA: Frontier Energy Services, Llc
    4200 E Skelly Dr Ste 400
    Tulsa OK 74135
    918 388-8438

(G-9781)
FRONTIER ENERGY SERVICES LLC (PA)
4200 E Skelly Dr Ste 400 (74135-3243)
PHONE..................................918 388-8438
Lee Williams, *Opers Staff*
Dave Presley,
Ken Snyder,
Mindy Stephens,
Lew Ward,
EMP: 15
SQ FT: 4,000
SALES (est): 6.9MM **Privately Held**
SIC: 1321 Natural gas liquids production

(G-9782)
FRONTIER GAS SERVICES LLC
4200 E Skelly Dr Ste 400 (74135-3243)
PHONE..................................918 388-8438
Timothy Young, *Exec VP*
Kelly Wood, *CFO*
Dave Presley, *Mng Member*
EMP: 3
SQ FT: 9,000
SALES (est): 66.2MM **Privately Held**
SIC: 1311 Natural gas production

(G-9783)
FRONTIER LAND CO INC
Also Called: Frontier Energy Leasing Svc
601 S Boulder Ave Ste 810 (74119-1308)
PHONE..................................918 584-2050
Bruce Belvins, *President*
EMP: 3
SALES (est): 286.6K **Privately Held**
SIC: 6541 1311 Title search companies; crude petroleum production; natural gas production

(G-9784)
FRONTIER MIDSTREAM LLC
4200 E Skelly Dr Ste 400 (74135-3243)
PHONE..................................918 388-8438
Kelly Wood, *CFO*
Frontier Energy Services,
EMP: 6
SALES (est): 66.2MM **Privately Held**
SIC: 1321 Natural gas liquids

(G-9785)
FRONTIER PLASTIC FABRICATORS
4518 W 56th St (74107-9127)
P.O. Box 9666 (74157-0666)
PHONE..................................918 445-5208
Dennis Bilyeu, *President*
EMP: 15
SQ FT: 8,000
SALES (est): 2.4MM **Privately Held**
SIC: 3089 Injection molding of plastics

(G-9786)
FS & J MUSIC PUBLISHING LLC
8805 E 106th St (74133-7344)
PHONE..................................918 369-6010
John Fannell, *Owner*
EMP: 2
SALES (est): 59.2K **Privately Held**
SIC: 2741 Miscellaneous publishing

(G-9787)
FW MURPHY PROD CONTRLS LLC
4646 S Harvard Ave # 100 (74135-2951)
PHONE..................................918 317-4280
EMP: 3
SALES: 82.1K **Privately Held**
SIC: 3625 7389 Relays & industrial controls;

GEOGRAPHIC SECTION

Tulsa - Tulsa County (G-9818)

(G-9788)
G B E SERVICES CORPORATION
6011 N Yorktown Ave (74130-1575)
PHONE..................918 428-8665
Rick Foster, *President*
Michael Reiss, *Manager*
Manfred Uekermann, *Manager*
▼ **EMP:** 5
SALES: 800K **Privately Held**
SIC: 3599 3533 Machine shop, jobbing & repair; oil & gas field machinery

(G-9789)
G B K HOLDINGS INC (PA)
6733 S Yale Ave (74136-3302)
PHONE..................918 494-0000
George Kaiser, *President*
Fred Dorwart, *Treasurer*
EMP: 4
SALES (est): 743.7K **Privately Held**
SIC: 1381 1382 Drilling oil & gas wells; oil & gas exploration services

(G-9790)
G C BROACH COMPANY (PA)
7667 E 46th Pl (74145-6307)
PHONE..................918 627-9632
Clayton Broach, *Ch of Bd*
Roger C Broach, *President*
Brain R Broach, *Vice Pres*
Jerry Parchman, *Mfg Staff*
Dan Dyer, *Engineer*
▼ **EMP:** 55 **EST:** 1960
SQ FT: 11,000
SALES: 6.4MM **Privately Held**
WEB: www.broach.com
SIC: 3443 3567 Fabricated plate work (boiler shop); radiant heating systems, industrial process

(G-9791)
G C BROACH COMPANY
8199 E 44th St (74145-4830)
PHONE..................918 627-9632
Jerry Parchman, *Manager*
EMP: 55
SALES (corp-wide): 6.4MM **Privately Held**
SIC: 3443 Fabricated plate work (boiler shop)
PA: The G C Broach Company
7667 E 46th Pl
Tulsa OK 74145
918 627-9632

(G-9792)
G P D INC
16719 E Admiral Pl (74116-3916)
P.O. Box 1159, Broken Arrow (74013-1159)
PHONE..................918 234-4404
Elizabeth Taylor, *President*
Jay Taylor, *Vice Pres*
EMP: 7
SQ FT: 20,000
SALES (est): 1.1MM **Privately Held**
SIC: 3599 Machine shop, jobbing & repair

(G-9793)
G PC INC (PA)
Also Called: Kimbel Oil
2121 S Columbia Ave # 200 (74114-3505)
PHONE..................918 582-0018
Michael W Kimbrel, *President*
EMP: 1
SALES (est): 281.8K **Privately Held**
SIC: 1311 Crude petroleum production; natural gas production

(G-9794)
G T BYNUM COMPANY
Also Called: Gtbco LLC
1116 N Peoria Ave (74106-4946)
P.O. Box 52429 (74152-0429)
PHONE..................918 587-9118
Ted Bynum, *President*
Joann S Bynum, *Corp Secy*
Iven Bell,
EMP: 5 **EST:** 1932
SQ FT: 7,500
SALES: 390K **Privately Held**
SIC: 7699 3569 3531 7692 Hydraulic equipment repair; jacks, hydraulic; bituminous, cement & concrete related products & equipment; welding repair; rolling mill machinery

(G-9795)
G T R NEWSPAPERS INC
7116 S Mingo Rd Ste 103 (74133-3268)
PHONE..................918 254-1515
Sharon Cambrin, *Owner*
EMP: 3 **EST:** 2013
SALES (est): 126K **Privately Held**
SIC: 2711 Newspapers, publishing & printing

(G-9796)
GAIL EVANS EMBROIDERY
5757 E 97th Pl (74137-5005)
PHONE..................918 605-1013
James Evans, *Principal*
EMP: 1
SALES (est): 71.9K **Privately Held**
WEB: www.expertembroidery.com
SIC: 2395 Embroidery products, except schiffli machine; embroidery & art needlework

(G-9797)
GALAXY DISTRIBUTING
7813 E Admiral Pl (74115-7914)
PHONE..................918 835-1186
Mukesh Shah, *Principal*
EMP: 2
SALES (est): 63.4K **Privately Held**
SIC: 5087 3556 Vending machines & supplies; food products machinery

(G-9798)
GANOA IMPORTS
2121 S Garnett Rd (74129-5105)
PHONE..................918 622-3788
Betty Ganoa, *Owner*
EMP: 1
SALES (est): 89.3K **Privately Held**
SIC: 2386 Leather & sheep-lined clothing

(G-9799)
GARDEN INTERLOCK SYSTEMS TULS
5130 S 94th East Ave (74145-8172)
PHONE..................918 369-9935
Les Freeman, *President*
EMP: 2
SALES (est): 308K **Privately Held**
SIC: 3829 Breathalyzers

(G-9800)
GARDNER DENVER INC
4747 S 83rd East Ave (74145-6921)
P.O. Box 470486 (74147-0486)
PHONE..................918 664-1151
Adam Avey, *Research*
Greg Bridgewater, *Engineer*
Greg Hash, *Engineer*
Jacob Rupp, *Engineer*
Jim Yanus, *Engineer*
EMP: 52
SALES (corp-wide): 2.4B **Publicly Held**
SIC: 3563 3533 3561 Air & gas compressors; oil & gas field machinery; industrial pumps & parts
HQ: Gardner Denver, Inc.
222 E Erie St Ste 500
Milwaukee WI 53202

(G-9801)
GARDNER INDUSTRIES INC
Also Called: Gardner Spring
1115 N Utica Ave (74110-4632)
PHONE..................918 583-0171
Katherine McGrini, *President*
Mike Esche, *Sales Mgr*
Bill Wynn, *Mktg Dir*
▼ **EMP:** 15 **EST:** 1907
SALES (est): 5.7MM **Privately Held**
SIC: 5085 3496 3495 3493 Springs; miscellaneous fabricated wire products; wire springs; steel springs, except wire; metal stampings; bolts, nuts, rivets & washers

(G-9802)
GARNETT CORPORATION
7070 S Garnett Rd (74133)
P.O. Box 470076 (74147-0076)
PHONE..................918 252-2515
Robert W Frederick, *President*
David Frederick, *Corp Secy*
EMP: 14
SQ FT: 8,000
SALES (est): 1.9MM **Privately Held**
SIC: 3599 Machine shop, jobbing & repair

(G-9803)
GARRETT PETROLEUM INC (PA)
8801 S Yale Ave Ste 240 (74137-3535)
PHONE..................918 492-3239
John P Garrett, *President*
Linda Warwick, *Corp Secy*
Garrett K W, *Vice Pres*
Noel Swinney, *Admin Sec*
EMP: 1
SALES (est): 2.2MM **Privately Held**
SIC: 1382 Oil & gas exploration services

(G-9804)
GAS PRODUCTS INC
Also Called: Russell Sales
4530 S Sheridan Rd # 219 (74145-1141)
P.O. Box 33182 (74153-1182)
PHONE..................918 664-5679
Jim L Russell, *President*
Debbie Russel, *Vice Pres*
EMP: 3
SQ FT: 1,500
SALES (est): 330K **Privately Held**
SIC: 3491 3494 Industrial valves; valves & pipe fittings

(G-9805)
GASOLEC AMERICA INC
5818 S 129th East Ave (74134-6705)
PHONE..................918 286-8700
Rex Jones, *President*
▲ **EMP:** 4
SALES (est): 458.5K **Privately Held**
SIC: 3433 Gas infrared heating units

(G-9806)
GASTAR EXPLORATION INC
6100 S Yale Ave Ste 1700 (74136-1921)
PHONE..................405 772-1500
EMP: 31 **Privately Held**
SIC: 1382 Oil & gas exploration services
PA: Gastar Exploration Inc.
1331 Lamar St Ste 650
Houston TX 77010

(G-9807)
GATEWAY INTERNATIONAL INC
6506 S Lewis Ave Ste 112 (74136-1020)
PHONE..................918 747-8393
Cliff Richards, *President*
EMP: 5
SALES (est): 360K **Privately Held**
SIC: 2731 Book publishing

(G-9808)
GAUGE METAL FAB LLC
1004 N Victor Ave (74110-4901)
PHONE..................918 794-1700
Michael Carper, *President*
EMP: 2
SALES (est): 232.8K **Privately Held**
SIC: 3444 Ducts, sheet metal

(G-9809)
GBK CORPORATION (PA)
Also Called: Kaiser-Francis Oil Company
6733 S Yale Ave (74136-3302)
PHONE..................918 494-0000
George B Kaiser, *President*
Anil Khatod, *Managing Dir*
James A Willis, *Exec VP*
Joey Wignarajah, *Vice Pres*
Josh Simons, *VP Opers*
▲ **EMP:** 12
SQ FT: 55,000
SALES (est): 678.5MM **Privately Held**
WEB: www.kfoc.net
SIC: 1311 Crude petroleum production; natural gas production

(G-9810)
GC&I GLOBAL INC
Also Called: Innovation Controls
3511 122nd E Ave (74146)
P.O. Box 470248 (74147-0248)
PHONE..................918 317-4244
Dave Prowl, *Vice Pres*
EMP: 2 **EST:** 2009
SALES (est): 127.3K **Privately Held**
SIC: 3694 Engine electrical equipment

(G-9811)
GCC READY MIX LLC
431 W 23rd St (74107-3005)
PHONE..................918 582-8111
Carlos Lopez, *Mng Member*
EMP: 8
SALES (est): 2.1MM **Privately Held**
SIC: 3273 Ready-mixed concrete

(G-9812)
GEIGER PRINTING & PROMOTION
4512 E 51st St (74135-3700)
PHONE..................918 810-2833
EMP: 2 **EST:** 2014
SALES (est): 97.1K **Privately Held**
SIC: 2752 Lithographic Commercial Printing

(G-9813)
GEM DIRT LLC
2526 W 101st St (74132-3837)
P.O. Box 9751 (74157-0751)
PHONE..................918 298-0299
Jayne Propst, *Principal*
EMP: 1
SALES (est): 267.5K **Privately Held**
SIC: 3714 Dump truck lifting mechanism

(G-9814)
GEMINI OIL CO INC
427 S Boston Ave Ste 320 (74103-4108)
PHONE..................918 582-3935
Thomas E Matson Sr, *President*
Steve A Geddie, *Corp Secy*
Thomas E Matson Jr, *Vice Pres*
EMP: 6
SQ FT: 1,600
SALES (est): 750K **Privately Held**
SIC: 1311 Crude petroleum production; natural gas production

(G-9815)
GEN X MACHINE TECHNOLOGIES
4470 S 70th East Ave (74145-4607)
PHONE..................918 836-4200
Larry Battaglia, *President*
Kathryn A Herwig, *Principal*
EMP: 2 **EST:** 2008
SALES (est): 258.2K **Privately Held**
WEB: www.genxmachine.com
SIC: 3599 Machine shop, jobbing & repair

(G-9816)
GEN X MACHINE TECHNOLOGIES
4470 S 70th East Ave (74145-4607)
PHONE..................918 836-4200
Pete Moss, *President*
Kathryn A Herwig, *Principal*
Peter Moss, *Vice Pres*
Mark Adams, *CFO*
Art Bennett, *Sales Staff*
EMP: 42
SQ FT: 35,000
SALES (est): 1.2MM **Privately Held**
SIC: 3599 Machine shop, jobbing & repair

(G-9817)
GENERAL WIRE & SUPPLY CO INC (PA)
1800 S 81st West Ave (74127-4837)
PHONE..................918 245-5961
Gerald J Estep, *President*
Raymond H Estep, *Vice Pres*
Roger Estep, *Vice Pres*
Raymond E Estep, *Purch Mgr*
EMP: 26 **EST:** 1963
SQ FT: 23,000
SALES (est): 2.2MM **Privately Held**
WEB: www.generalwireco.com
SIC: 3315 3496 Steel wire & related products; fencing, made from purchased wire

(G-9818)
GENESIS TECHNOLOGIES INC
5812 S 129th East Ave (74134-6705)
PHONE..................918 307-0098
Donald Carrington, *President*
EMP: 8
SQ FT: 1,200
SALES: 870K **Privately Held**
SIC: 7372 Business oriented computer software

Tulsa - Tulsa County (G-9819)

(G-9819)
GENIE OIL & GAS CORPORATION
2424 E 21st St Ste 500 (74114-1723)
P.O. Box 3783, Broken Arrow (74013-3783)
PHONE..................918 747-3675
Michael Stovall, *President*
Corbett Stovall, *Treasurer*
EMP: 4
SALES (est): 352.4K **Privately Held**
WEB: www.geniewell.com
SIC: 1311 Crude petroleum production

(G-9820)
GEO SHACK
5125 S Garnett Rd Ste A (74146-5908)
PHONE..................918 665-1880
EMP: 2
SALES (est): 154K **Privately Held**
SIC: 3829 Measuring & controlling devices

(G-9821)
GEOAMERICAN RESOURCES INC
6011 N Yorktown Ave (74130-1575)
PHONE..................918 428-8665
David M Whitney, *President*
EMP: 5 EST: 1981
SALES (est): 287.3K **Privately Held**
SIC: 1311 Crude petroleum production; natural gas production

(G-9822)
GEODYNE PRODUCTION COMPANY
2 W 2nd St (74103-3123)
PHONE..................918 583-1791
Philip Tholen, *President*
Judy F Hughes, *Treasurer*
Pat Hall, *Office Mgr*
Annabel M Jones, *Admin Sec*
EMP: 4
SQ FT: 13,000
SALES (est): 410K **Privately Held**
SIC: 1311 Crude petroleum production; natural gas production

(G-9823)
GET THREADED LLC
10846 S Memorial Dr # 112 (74133-7392)
PHONE..................918 943-6156
EMP: 3
SALES (est): 198.1K **Privately Held**
SIC: 3724 Aircraft engines & engine parts

(G-9824)
GH CO
6033 S 66th East Ave (74145-9228)
PHONE..................918 488-0014
Doug Dickson, *Principal*
EMP: 2
SALES (est): 128.1K **Privately Held**
SIC: 1382 Oil & gas exploration services

(G-9825)
GILES PRINTING CO INC
Also Called: Commercial Printing
520a S Peoria Ave (74120)
PHONE..................918 584-1583
Earl Giles, *President*
Judy Giles, *Admin Sec*
EMP: 1
SALES (est): 142.2K **Privately Held**
SIC: 2752 2791 2789 Commercial printing, offset; typesetting; bookbinding & related work

(G-9826)
GILL X-STREAM INVESTMENTS LLC
4972 S Detroit Ave (74105-4610)
PHONE..................918 743-8379
Robert Gilliam, *Principal*
EMP: 1
SALES (est): 83K **Privately Held**
SIC: 1311 Oil sand mining

(G-9827)
GILMORES SPORTS CONCEPTS INC
5949 S Garnett Rd (74146-6825)
PHONE..................918 250-3910
W Riley Gilmore III, *President*
EMP: 1
SQ FT: 1,000
SALES (est): 128.4K **Privately Held**
SIC: 3827 5049 2387 Gun sights, optical; optical goods; apparel belts

(G-9828)
GIRLPOWER DEFENSE LLC
7017 E 63rd St (74133-4050)
PHONE..................918 494 9072
Michael Scott Marney, *Owner*
EMP: 2
SALES (est): 151.7K **Privately Held**
SIC: 3812 Defense systems & equipment

(G-9829)
GLOBAL BEARINGS INC
3818 S 79th East Ave (74145-3219)
PHONE..................918 664-8902
Henry Zahn, *President*
Tina Zahn, *Treasurer*
▲ **EMP:** 46
SQ FT: 33,000
SALES (est): 7.5MM **Privately Held**
SIC: 5085 3053 Bearings; oil seals, rubber

(G-9830)
GLOBAL FILTER LLC (PA)
11607 E 43rd St N (74116-2103)
PHONE..................319 743-0110
Todd Younggreen,
▲ **EMP:** 16
SQ FT: 2,500
SALES (est): 4.7MM **Privately Held**
SIC: 3569 Filters, general line: industrial; filters

(G-9831)
GLOBAL INDUSTRIAL INC
19801 E 6th St (74108-7961)
PHONE..................918 266-5656
Clayton Rash, *President*
Rebecca Dobbins, *Safety Mgr*
Toni Rash, *Admin Sec*
EMP: 60
SALES (est): 16.1MM **Privately Held**
SIC: 5999 3567 3443 Welding supplies; industrial furnaces & ovens; industrial vessels, tanks & containers

(G-9832)
GLOBAL INTERFACE SOLUTIONS INC
Also Called: Secure Agent Software
2448 E 81st St Ste 2000 (74137-4271)
PHONE..................918 971-1600
Brent Johnson, *CEO*
Brenda Melancon, *Marketing Mgr*
EMP: 8
SQ FT: 15,000
SALES (est): 1.5MM **Privately Held**
SIC: 7372 Prepackaged software

(G-9833)
GLOBAL OIL GAS FIELDS OKLA LLC
9726 E 42nd St Ste 230 (74146-3645)
PHONE..................918 392-3345
Bill Dement, *Manager*
Jan M Herbst, *Manager*
EMP: 3 EST: 2008
SALES (est): 252.8K **Privately Held**
SIC: 1382 Oil & gas exploration services

(G-9834)
GLOBAL WIRE CLOTH LLC
1550 N 105th East Ave (74116-1516)
P.O. Box 312, Stilwell (74960-0312)
PHONE..................918 836-7211
Leon Martinez, *President*
Jim Carson, *Mng Member*
Drew Carson,
EMP: 25
SQ FT: 43,000
SALES (est): 3.8MM **Privately Held**
SIC: 3496 3564 Wire cloth & woven wire products; blowers & fans

(G-9835)
GMS LALOS CUSTOM WHEELS LTD CO
3927 E 123rd East Pl (74146-3326)
PHONE..................918 622-3616
EMP: 2 EST: 2008
SALES (est): 140K **Privately Held**
SIC: 3312 Blast Furnace-Steel Works

(G-9836)
GNC CONCRETE PRODUCTS INC
2100 N 161st East Ave (74116-4833)
P.O. Box 2010, Catoosa (74015-2909)
PHONE..................918 438-1182
Robbe Grider, *President*
Robbie Grider, *President*
Donald Carr, *Vice Pres*
EMP: 55
SQ FT: 50,000
SALES (est): 14.3MM **Privately Held**
SIC: 3272 Manhole covers or frames, concrete; pipe, concrete or lined with concrete

(G-9837)
GODIVA CHOCOLATIER INC
7021 S Memorial Dr 235a (74123-2025)
PHONE..................918 459-2635
EMP: 7 **Privately Held**
SIC: 2066 Mfg Chocolate/Cocoa Products
HQ: Godiva Chocolatier, Inc.
333 W 34th St Fl 6
New York NY 10001
212 984-5900

(G-9838)
GOLDEN GAS SERVICE CO
2502 E 21st St Ste B (74114-1757)
PHONE..................918 582-0139
Alan Staab, *President*
EMP: 6
SALES (est): 1.1MM **Privately Held**
SIC: 1382 Oil & gas exploration services

(G-9839)
GOLF ADVISORS
3701 S Harvard Ave Ste A (74135-2282)
PHONE..................918 645-6179
Golf Advisors, *Principal*
EMP: 2 EST: 2016
SALES (est): 74.4K **Privately Held**
SIC: 2834 Pharmaceutical preparations

(G-9840)
GOMACO INC (PA)
415 S Boston Ave Ste 500 (74103-5021)
PHONE..................918 585-8077
Warren F Young, *President*
Beverly A Young, *Treasurer*
EMP: 5
SQ FT: 3,000
SALES (est): 1MM **Privately Held**
SIC: 1311 Crude petroleum production; natural gas production

(G-9841)
GORFAM MARKETING INC
5666 S 122nd East Ave (74146-6924)
PHONE..................918 252-3733
David W Gordon, *President*
EMP: 7
SALES (est): 500K **Privately Held**
SIC: 3552 2281 Silk screens for textile industry; embroidery yarn, spun

(G-9842)
GORFAM MARKETING INC
Also Called: G M I
9495 E 55th St (74145-8191)
PHONE..................918 388-9935
David Gordon, *President*
EMP: 14
SALES (est): 3.2MM **Privately Held**
SIC: 5136 2759 5941 2253 Men's & boys' robes, nightwear & undergarments; screen printing; exercise equipment; T-shirts & tops, knit

(G-9843)
GOTHIC PRODUCTION LLC
6120 S Yale Ave Ste 1200 (74136-4241)
P.O. Box 18496, Oklahoma City (73154-0496)
PHONE..................918 749-5666
John J Flemming, *Ch of Bd*
Michael Paulk, *President*
Steven P Ensz, *Vice Pres*
EMP: 30
SALES (est): 874.8K **Publicly Held**
SIC: 1311 Crude petroleum production
PA: Chesapeake Energy Corporation
6100 N Western Ave
Oklahoma City OK 73118

(G-9844)
GRAND JUNCTION CUSTOM TRUCKS
8100 Charles Page Blvd (74127-7107)
PHONE..................918 245-6362
Jimmie W Burdge, *Owner*
EMP: 2
SQ FT: 4,500
SALES (est): 170.3K **Privately Held**
SIC: 3716 Recreational van conversion (self-propelled), factory basis

(G-9845)
GRAND RESOURCES INC
2448 E 81st St Ste 4040 (74137-4201)
PHONE..................918 492-2366
Marvin J Robinowitz, *President*
Scott Robinowitz, *Vice Pres*
EMP: 38
SQ FT: 3,100
SALES (est): 6MM **Privately Held**
SIC: 1311 Crude petroleum production; natural gas production

(G-9846)
GRANOLA SHIRTS
1130 S Oxford Ave Ste B (74112-5402)
PHONE..................918 592-5477
EMP: 1 EST: 2017
SALES (est): 46.1K **Privately Held**
SIC: 2043 Granola & muesli, except bars & clusters

(G-9847)
GRAPHICS UNIVERSAL INC
Also Called: Calvert Co
12437 E 60th St (74146-6906)
PHONE..................918 461-0609
A Leon Calvert, *CEO*
Cynthia Calvert, *Vice Pres*
EMP: 3
SQ FT: 24,630
SALES (est): 324.3K **Privately Held**
SIC: 7335 2796 Color separation, photographic & movie film; platemaking services

(G-9848)
GRATING COMPANY LLC
2443 Dawson Rd (74110-5028)
P.O. Box 581415 (74158-1415)
PHONE..................918 834-8100
Jim Dorough, *Principal*
Ronald Nick,
EMP: 5 EST: 1999
SALES (est): 470.6K **Privately Held**
SIC: 3449 3446 3441 Bars, concrete reinforcing: fabricated steel; gratings, tread: fabricated metal; fabricated structural metal

(G-9849)
GRAVES COS MICHAEL L
4880 S Lewis Ave (74105-5181)
PHONE..................918 293-1500
Michael L Graves, *Principal*
EMP: 5
SALES: 685.6K **Privately Held**
SIC: 1382 Oil & gas exploration services

(G-9850)
GRAVLEY COMPANIES INC
Also Called: Store 1500
1919 S Harvard Ave (74112-6827)
PHONE..................918 743-6619
Chris Masterson, *Manager*
EMP: 3 **Privately Held**
SIC: 2752 2791 2789 2759 Commercial printing, offset; typesetting; bookbinding & related work; commercial printing
PA: Gravley Companies Inc
3401 Nw Expressway
Oklahoma City OK 73112

(G-9851)
GRAYHORSE ENERGY LLC
Also Called: Grayhorse Operating
20 E 5th St Ste 320 (74103-4435)
PHONE..................918 382-9201
Charles A Ellis, *President*
Charles Ellis, *Partner*
Gary Johnson, *Exec VP*
EMP: 9 EST: 2000
SQ FT: 4,367

GEOGRAPHIC SECTION

Tulsa - Tulsa County (G-9879)

SALES (est): 1.3MM **Privately Held**
SIC: **1382** Oil & gas exploration services

(G-9852)
GRB RESOURCES INC
1789 E 71st St (74136-5108)
PHONE..................................918 587-0036
R Garvin Berry Jr, *President*
Robert O Berry, *Vice Pres*
Robert Berry, *Vice Pres*
Margitta C Grona, *Admin Sec*
EMP: 3
SALES (est): 277.7K **Privately Held**
SIC: **1311** Crude petroleum production; natural gas production

(G-9853)
GREAT PLAINS COCA-COLA BTLG CO
1224 N Lewis Ave (74110-4701)
PHONE..................................918 439-3013
Steve McKenzie, *Branch Mgr*
EMP: 100 **Privately Held**
SIC: **2086** Bottled & canned soft drinks
HQ: Great Plains Coca-Cola Bottling Company
600 N May Ave
Oklahoma City OK 73107
405 280-2000

(G-9854)
GREAT PLAINS COCA-COLA BTLG CO
11333 E Pine St Ste 141 (74116-2030)
PHONE..................................800 753-2653
EMP: 147 **Privately Held**
SIC: **2086** Carb Sft Drnkbtlcn
HQ: Great Plains Coca-Cola Bottling Company
600 N May Ave
Oklahoma City OK 73107
405 280-2000

(G-9855)
GREATER TLSA RPRTER NEWSPAPERS
5341 S Yorktown Ave (74105-6447)
PHONE..................................918 743-3458
Carol Y Kealiher, *Principal*
EMP: 3
SALES (est): 120K **Privately Held**
WEB: www.gtrnews.com
SIC: **2711** Newspapers, publishing & printing

(G-9856)
GREATER TLSA RPRTER NEWSPAPERS
Also Called: Union Bndary Grter Tlsa Rprter
5401 S Sheridan Rd # 302 (74145-7531)
P.O. Box 470645 (74147-0645)
PHONE..................................918 254-1515
Forrest Cameron, *President*
Sharon Cameron, *Treasurer*
EMP: 2
SQ FT: 1,500
SALES (est): 181.4K **Privately Held**
SIC: **2711 2741** Newspapers, publishing & printing; miscellaneous publishing

(G-9857)
GREEN CNTRY ARCFT EXHAUST INC
Also Called: G C A
1876 N 106th East Ave (74116-1511)
P.O. Box 150259 (74115-0259)
PHONE..................................918 832-1769
Mike Teague, *President*
Mike Pentedemos, *Business Mgr*
Tony Dietz, *Director*
EMP: 33
SQ FT: 18,000
SALES (est): 6.7MM **Privately Held**
SIC: **3724** Aircraft engines & engine parts

(G-9858)
GREEN CNTRY CSTM WOODWORKS LLC
2323 S 49th West Ave (74107-2217)
P.O. Box 991, Sand Springs (74063-0991)
PHONE..................................918 585-1040
EMP: 1
SALES (est): 81.3K **Privately Held**
SIC: **2431** Millwork

(G-9859)
GREEN CO CORPORATION
Also Called: Wsnusa
7424 E 46th St (74145-6302)
PHONE..................................918 221-3997
Yasir Jahangir, *President*
EMP: 4
SQ FT: 6,000
SALES (est): 300K **Privately Held**
SIC: **3089 5159 5947 3674** Holders: paper towel, grocery bag, etc.: plastic; tobacco distributors & products; gifts & novelties; light emitting diodes; closed circuit television services

(G-9860)
GREEN COUNTRY AIRCRAFT LLC
1876 N 106th East Ave (74116-1511)
P.O. Box 150259 (74115-0259)
PHONE..................................918 832-1769
Mike Pentedemos, *President*
EMP: 1 EST: 2007
SALES (est): 97.2K **Privately Held**
SIC: **3724** Aircraft engines & engine parts

(G-9861)
GREEN COUNTRY FILTER MFG LLC
1415 S 70th East Ave (74112-6611)
PHONE..................................918 455-0100
Carla Bray, *Owner*
David Williams, *Engineer*
Carla R Bray,
EMP: 10
SALES (est): 1.8MM **Privately Held**
SIC: **3599** Gasoline filters, internal combustion engine, except auto

(G-9862)
GREEN OPERATING COMPANY INC
2222 S Utica Pl Ste 200 (74114-7013)
PHONE..................................918 746-1700
Curtis S Green, *President*
EMP: 20 EST: 1955
SQ FT: 2,000
SALES (est): 1.1MM **Privately Held**
SIC: **1311** Crude petroleum production; natural gas production

(G-9863)
GREYSTONE LOGISTICS INC (PA)
1613 E 15th St (74120-6007)
PHONE..................................918 583-7441
Warren F Kruger, *Ch of Bd*
William W Rahhal, *CFO*
EMP: 19
SALES: 71MM **Publicly Held**
SIC: **3089** Pallets, plastic

(G-9864)
GRIP JAR OPENER LLC
36 E Cameron St (74103-1405)
P.O. Box 3586, Broken Arrow (74013-3586)
PHONE..................................918 766-2711
EMP: 2
SALES (est): 162K **Privately Held**
SIC: **3069** Grips or handles, rubber

(G-9865)
GRIZZLY GRIN PRINTING LLC
8280 S Yorktown Ct Apt B (74137-1513)
PHONE..................................918 351-9066
Bobby Ross, *Principal*
EMP: 2 EST: 2016
SALES (est): 90.4K **Privately Held**
SIC: **2752** Commercial printing, lithographic

(G-9866)
GS RESTORATION SERVICES INC
8815 Airport Way Unit 6 (74132-4014)
PHONE..................................918 408-2848
EMP: 3
SALES: 50K **Privately Held**
SIC: **3721** Mfg Aircraft

(G-9867)
GUNNEBO CORPORATION U S A
Also Called: Gunnebo Johnson
1240 N Harvard Ave (74115-6103)
PHONE..................................918 832-8933
William Shenloogian, *President*
Sylvia Walton, *Vice Pres*
Bryan Shahan, *Regl Sales Mgr*
Sandy Hindman,
▲ EMP: 45
SALES (est): 8.7MM
SALES (corp-wide): 307.9MM **Privately Held**
WEB: www.gunnebojohnson.com
SIC: **3536** Hoists, cranes & monorails
HQ: Gunnebo Industrier Ab
Vasagatan 20a
Vasteras 722 1
218 382-00

(G-9868)
GUNNEBO INDUSTRIES INC (DH)
Also Called: Gunnebo Johnson Corporation
1240 N Harvard Ave (74115-6103)
PHONE..................................918 832-8933
Maurice Boukelif, *CEO*
Nicke Astermo, *CEO*
Sylvia Walton, *Vice Pres*
Darla Brandon, *Senior Buyer*
Kay Ozmun, *Engineer*
◆ EMP: 182
SQ FT: 120,000
SALES (est): 31.9MM
SALES (corp-wide): 307.9MM **Privately Held**
SIC: **3536** Hoists, cranes & monorails
HQ: Gunnebo Industrier Ab
Vasagatan 20a
Vasteras 722 1
218 382-00

(G-9869)
GUY W LOGSDON
4645 S Columbia Ave (74105-5129)
PHONE..................................918 743-2171
Guy W Logsdon, *Principal*
EMP: 2
SALES (est): 116.4K **Privately Held**
SIC: **2731** Book publishing

(G-9870)
GWACS DEFENSE INC
7130 S Lewis Ave Ste 300 (74136-5429)
PHONE..................................918 794-5670
Judson Gudgel, *President*
EMP: 15
SALES (est): 2.4MM **Privately Held**
SIC: **3812** Warfare counter-measure equipment

(G-9871)
H & H PROTECTIVE COATING CO
4849 W 21st St (74107-2210)
P.O. Box 9336 (74157-0336)
PHONE..................................918 582-9187
Matthew Val Halloran Jr, *President*
Della Halloran, *Admin Sec*
EMP: 7
SQ FT: 12,000
SALES (est): 979.3K **Privately Held**
WEB: www.handhpro.com
SIC: **3479 3471** Coating of metals & formed products; plating & polishing

(G-9872)
H & L TOOTH COMPANY
Also Called: H & L Forge
10055 E 56th St N (74117-4016)
P.O. Box 48, Owasso (74055-0048)
PHONE..................................918 272-0951
Brian Launder, *Vice Pres*
Chuck Clendenning, *Engineer*
Cindy Kline, *MIS Dir*
EMP: 75
SQ FT: 160,300
SALES (corp-wide): 13.2MM **Privately Held**
SIC: **3531** Backhoes, tractors, cranes, plows & similar equipment
PA: H & L Tooth Company
1540 S Greenwood Ave
Montebello CA 90640
323 721-5146

(G-9873)
H & M PIPE BEVELING MCH CO INC
311 E 3rd St (74120-2401)
PHONE..................................918 582-9984
Margaret J Stallard, *President*
▲ EMP: 7 EST: 1934
SQ FT: 3,500
SALES (est): 1.4MM **Privately Held**
WEB: www.hmpipe.com
SIC: **3541** Pipe cutting & threading machines

(G-9874)
H & P FINCO
1437 S Bulgar (74119)
PHONE..................................918 742-5531
Hans Helmerich, *CEO*
EMP: 100
SALES (est): 3.6MM
SALES (corp-wide): 2.8B **Publicly Held**
SIC: **1381** Drilling oil & gas wells
HQ: Helmerich & Payne International Drilling Co Inc
1437 S Boulder Ave # 1400
Tulsa OK 74119
918 742-5531

(G-9875)
H & S DRILLING CO
320 S Boston Ave Ste 1910 (74103-4734)
PHONE..................................918 794-9944
Bill Snow, *President*
Philip Snow, *Vice Pres*
Katherine Wood, *Admin Sec*
EMP: 3 EST: 1947
SQ FT: 1,940
SALES (est): 220K **Privately Held**
SIC: **1311** Crude petroleum production

(G-9876)
H S BOYD COMPANY INC
6915 E 14th St (74112-6617)
PHONE..................................918 835-9359
Richard A Booth, *President*
▲ EMP: 12
SQ FT: 9,000
SALES (est): 2.1MM **Privately Held**
WEB: www.hsboyd.com
SIC: **3555 3542 3425** Printing trades machinery; machine tools, metal forming type; saw blades & handsaws

(G-9877)
H W ALLEN CO LLC
Also Called: Venture Properties
4835 S Peoria Ave Ste 20 (74105-4561)
PHONE..................................918 747-8700
Philip Allen, *President*
Robert Allen, *Chairman*
Andrew Allen, *Vice Pres*
EMP: 24
SQ FT: 10,000
SALES: 2MM **Privately Held**
WEB: www.ventureproperties.com
SIC: **6531 1311** Real estate leasing & rentals; crude petroleum production; natural gas production

(G-9878)
H&R LIFTING & BUCKET SERVICE
7411 S Jackson Ave (74132-2308)
PHONE..................................918 446-5549
Harry S Walker, *President*
EMP: 2
SALES (est): 300K **Privately Held**
SIC: **7353 3993** Cranes & aerial lift equipment, rental or leasing; signs & advertising specialties

(G-9879)
H3 CUSTOM WOOD MOLDINGS LLC
12933 E Apache St (74116-1438)
PHONE..................................918 250-8746
Charles Chelsell, *President*
EMP: 5
SALES: 1.5MM **Privately Held**
SIC: **2431** Moldings, wood: unfinished & prefinished

Tulsa - Tulsa County (G-9880)

(G-9880)
HALCON OPERATING CO INC
5100 E Skelly Dr Ste 650 (74135-6559)
PHONE..................832 649-4015
Mark Mize, *Exec VP*
EMP: 1
SALES (est): 111.4K **Privately Held**
SIC: 1311 Crude petroleum production
PA: Battalion Oil Corporation
1000 La St Ste 6700
Houston TX 77002

(G-9881)
HALLIBURTON COMPANY
Also Called: Halliburton Energy Services
1 W 3rd St Ste 1400 (74103-3519)
PHONE..................918 587-3117
Shean Brown, *Manager*
EMP: 20 **Publicly Held**
SIC: 1389 Oil field services
PA: Halliburton Company
3000 N Sam Houston Pkwy E
Houston TX 77032

(G-9882)
HALO INDUCTION LOOPING LLC
4564 S Harvard Ave Ste A (74135-2918)
PHONE..................918 638-1599
EMP: 3
SALES (est): 246.4K **Privately Held**
SIC: 3812 Detection apparatus: electronic/magnetic field, light/heat

(G-9883)
HAM VENTURES LLC
8119 E 48th St (74145-6906)
PHONE..................918 277-9500
Victor Ham, *President*
EMP: 5
SALES (est): 235K **Privately Held**
SIC: 2396 Automotive & apparel trimmings

(G-9884)
HANCOCK INDUSTRIES INC
6533 E Independence St (74115-7861)
PHONE..................918 835-5441
Charles Hancock, *CEO*
Lynn Hancock, *President*
Jason Hancock, *Vice Pres*
EMP: 15
SQ FT: 7,200
SALES: 700K **Privately Held**
SIC: 3599 Machine shop, jobbing & repair

(G-9885)
HANGER INC
2116 E 15th St (74104-4614)
PHONE..................918 742-6464
Mike Harrington, *Manager*
Barbara Miller, *Executive*
EMP: 11
SALES (corp-wide): 1.1B **Publicly Held**
SIC: 3842 Surgical appliances & supplies
PA: Hanger, Inc.
10910 Domain Dr Ste 300
Austin TX 78758
512 777-3800

(G-9886)
HANGER PRSTHETCS & ORTHO INC
6052 S Sheridan Rd (74145-9212)
PHONE..................918 488-0400
Larry E Kindle, *Manager*
EMP: 5
SALES (corp-wide): 1.1B **Publicly Held**
SIC: 3842 Surgical appliances & supplies
HQ: Hanger Prosthetics & Orthotics, Inc.
10910 Domain Dr Ste 300
Austin TX 78758
512 777-3800

(G-9887)
HANNAH INDUSTRIES INC
6525 N 57th West Ave (74126-4119)
PHONE..................918 430-0743
Curtis Carter, *Principal*
EMP: 3
SALES (est): 142.6K **Privately Held**
SIC: 3999 Manufacturing industries

(G-9888)
HANSON INC
209 N Main St (74103-2005)
PHONE..................918 447-0777
Walker Hanson, *President*
Clare Mayo, *Human Res Dir*
EMP: 3
SALES (est): 397.1K **Privately Held**
SIC: 3931 Guitars & parts, electric & non-electric

(G-9889)
HAPPY TOOTH DENTAL
7104 S Sheridan Rd Ste 8 (74133-2765)
PHONE..................918 492-8793
Sean Costello, *Principal*
EMP: 2
SALES (est): 196.9K **Privately Held**
SIC: 3843 Enamels, dentists'

(G-9890)
HARDESTY COMPANY INC (DH)
Also Called: United States Aviation
4141 N Memorial Dr (74115-1400)
PHONE..................918 585-3100
Floyd R Hardesty, *President*
Thomas L Parkinson, *Corp Secy*
J Michael Hays, *Exec VP*
Randall Edgar, *Vice Pres*
EMP: 20 **EST:** 1974
SQ FT: 13,735
SALES (est): 101.3MM **Privately Held**
SIC: 3273 6799 1542 1522 Ready-mixed concrete; investors; commercial & office building, new construction; apartment building construction

(G-9891)
HARDESTY PRESS INC
1317 E 11th St (74120-4605)
PHONE..................918 582-5306
Samuel G Hardesty, *President*
EMP: 10 **EST:** 1970
SQ FT: 10,000
SALES (est): 1.5MM **Privately Held**
SIC: 2752 2759 2791 2789 Commercial printing, offset; letterpress printing; typesetting; bookbinding & related work

(G-9892)
HARLEY INDUSTRIES INC (HQ)
Also Called: Harley Valve & Instrument
4530 S Sheridan Rd # 218 (74145)
PHONE..................918 451-2323
Joe Cheatham, *President*
EMP: 8
SQ FT: 4,500
SALES (est): 23MM
SALES (corp-wide): 3.9B **Publicly Held**
SIC: 3561 Pumps & pumping equipment
PA: Flowserve Corporation
5215 N Ocnnor Blvd Ste 23 Connor
Irving TX 75039
972 443-6500

(G-9893)
HARRELL ENERGY CO
15 W 6th St Ste 2510 (74119-5433)
PHONE..................918 587-2750
Kent J Harrell, *Owner*
Deidra Alderson, *Manager*
EMP: 6
SALES (est): 439.6K **Privately Held**
SIC: 1311 Crude petroleum production

(G-9894)
HARRELL EXPLORATION CORP
15 W 6th St Ste 2510 (74119-5419)
PHONE..................918 587-2750
Kent J Harrell, *President*
EMP: 5
SALES (est): 520.9K **Privately Held**
SIC: 1311 Crude petroleum production

(G-9895)
HARRIK COMPANY LLC
5317 E 5th Pl (74112-2817)
PHONE..................918 691-6417
Rick Nahkala, *Owner*
EMP: 1
SALES (est): 100K **Privately Held**
SIC: 3599 Air intake filters, internal combustion engine, except auto

(G-9896)
HARRISON HOUSE INC
1029 N Utica Ave (74110-4910)
PHONE..................918 582-2126
EMP: 1
SALES (est): 37.5K **Privately Held**
SIC: 2741 Miscellaneous publishing

(G-9897)
HARRISON MANUFACTURING CO INC
6130 E 13th St (74112-5410)
P.O. Box 581655 (74158-1655)
PHONE..................918 838-9961
Tom Schick, *President*
Ann Schick, *Vice Pres*
Annaruth Schick, *Vice Pres*
EMP: 10
SQ FT: 18,600
SALES (est): 1.7MM **Privately Held**
WEB: www.harrisongasket.com
SIC: 3053 5085 Gaskets, all materials; fasteners, industrial: nuts, bolts, screws, etc.

(G-9898)
HARSCO CORPORATION
Also Called: Harsco Indus Air-X-Changers
5555 S 129th East Ave (74134-6714)
P.O. Box 1804 (74101-1804)
PHONE..................918 619-8000
Ron Kuegler, *Opers Staff*
EMP: 23
SALES (corp-wide): 1.5B **Publicly Held**
SIC: 3443 Fabricated plate work (boiler shop)
PA: Harsco Corporation
350 Poplar Church Rd
Camp Hill PA 17011
717 763-7064

(G-9899)
HARSCO CORPORATION
Also Called: Harsco Indus Air-X-Changers
5615 S 129th East Ave (74134-6708)
PHONE..................918 619-8000
EMP: 20
SALES (corp-wide): 1.5B **Publicly Held**
SIC: 7359 7353 5082 3443 Equipment rental & leasing; heavy construction equipment rental; construction & mining machinery; scaffolding; fuel tanks (oil, gas, etc.): metal plate; cryogenic tanks, for liquids & gases; cylinders, pressure: metal plate; heat exchangers: coolers (after, inter), condensers, etc.; evaporative condensers, heat transfer equipment; railroad maintenance & repair services
PA: Harsco Corporation
350 Poplar Church Rd
Camp Hill PA 17011
717 763-7064

(G-9900)
HARSCO INDUSTRIAL HAMMCO LLC
5615 S 129th East Ave (74134-6708)
P.O. Box 1804 (74101-1804)
PHONE..................918 619-8000
Kari Hendrix, *Treasurer*
EMP: 70
SALES (est): 13.3MM
SALES (corp-wide): 1.5B **Publicly Held**
SIC: 3443 Air coolers, metal plate
PA: Harsco Corporation
350 Poplar Church Rd
Camp Hill PA 17011
717 763-7064

(G-9901)
HASTY-BAKE INC
Also Called: Hasty Bake Charcoal Ovens
1313 S Lewis Ave (74104-4215)
P.O. Box 4609 (74159-0609)
PHONE..................918 665-8220
Richard Alexander, *President*
Rick Nacke, *Mfg Staff*
Jennifer Caudle, *Mktg Dir*
▼ **EMP:** 18
SQ FT: 60,000
SALES (est): 9.9MM **Privately Held**
SIC: 5046 3631 5722 Cooking equipment, commercial; barbecues, grills & braziers (outdoor cooking); household appliance stores

(G-9902)
HAWKEYE PRINTING CO
2707 E 15th St (74104-4713)
PHONE..................918 744-0158
James Larry Skelton, *Owner*
EMP: 3
SQ FT: 2,800
SALES (est): 500K **Privately Held**
SIC: 2752 Lithographing on metal

(G-9903)
HAWKINS INTERNATIONAL INC
427 S Boston Ave Ste 210 (74103-4107)
PHONE..................918 592-4422
James F Hawkins Jr, *Ch of Bd*
John B Hawkins, *President*
Clifford S Lewis, *CFO*
EMP: 7 **EST:** 1977
SQ FT: 16,000
SALES (est): 850K **Privately Held**
SIC: 1311 Crude petroleum production; natural gas production

(G-9904)
HAWKINS OIL CO LLC
427 S Boston Ave Ste 915 (74103-4114)
PHONE..................918 382-7743
James Hawkins,
EMP: 2
SALES (est): 309.8K **Privately Held**
SIC: 1311 Crude petroleum production

(G-9905)
HAWLEY & CO
Also Called: Hawley Design Furnishings
702 S Utica Ave (74104-3213)
PHONE..................918 587-0510
Mark Hawley, *President*
▲ **EMP:** 2
SQ FT: 8,000
SALES (est): 288.8K **Privately Held**
SIC: 2511 2434 Wood household furniture; wood kitchen cabinets

(G-9906)
HCF WELDING SERVICES
2305 S 96th East Ave B (74129-4029)
PHONE..................918 907-4274
Cindy Franco, *Principal*
EMP: 2 **EST:** 2018
SALES (est): 45.1K **Privately Held**
SIC: 7692 Welding repair

(G-9907)
HEAT TRANSFER EQUIPMENT CO
Also Called: Hte
1515 N 93rd East Ave (74115-4701)
PHONE..................918 836-8721
Fred Gibson, *Ch of Bd*
Timothy Gibson, *President*
Jason Carrison, *Exec VP*
Daniel Gaddis, *Exec VP*
David Woods, *Vice Pres*
▼ **EMP:** 140
SQ FT: 70,000
SALES (est): 21.1MM **Privately Held**
SIC: 3443 Heat exchangers: coolers (after, inter), condensers, etc.

(G-9908)
HEATER FABRICATORS TULSA LLC
5426 S 49th West Ave (74107-8813)
PHONE..................918 430-1127
David Ridgeway, *Mng Member*
Erin Brown,
▲ **EMP:** 48
SALES (est): 8.1MM **Privately Held**
SIC: 2911 Petroleum refining

(G-9909)
HEATER SPECIALISTS LLC (HQ)
Also Called: H S I
3171 N Toledo Ave (74115-1804)
P.O. Box 582707 (74158-2707)
PHONE..................918 835-3126
Don Mellott,
W Alan Jackson,
◆ **EMP:** 80
SQ FT: 6,000

GEOGRAPHIC SECTION

Tulsa - Tulsa County (G-9932)

SALES (est): 62.5MM
SALES (corp-wide): 66.5MM **Privately Held**
SIC: **3255** 3443 Cement, clay refractory; industrial vessels, tanks & containers
PA: Energy Process Technologies, Inc.
3172 N Toledo Ave
Tulsa OK 74115
918 835-1011

(G-9910)
HEATER SPECIALISTS LLC
5500 E Independence St (74115-7621)
PHONE.....................918 835-3126
Don Mellott, *President*
EMP: 35
SALES (corp-wide): 66.5MM **Privately Held**
SIC: **3443** Industrial vessels, tanks & containers
HQ: Heater Specialists, L.L.C.
3171 N Toledo Ave
Tulsa OK 74115
918 835-3126

(G-9911)
HELICOMB INTERNATIONAL INC
1402 S 69th East Ave (74112-6603)
PHONE.....................918 835-3999
John A Philbin, *Principal*
Howard H Hendrick, *Principal*
Donald R Philbin, *Principal*
EMP: 100
SQ FT: 78,000
SALES (est): 15.6MM
SALES (corp-wide): 327.2B **Publicly Held**
WEB: www.helicomb.com
SIC: **7699** 3728 3721 Aircraft & heavy equipment repair services; aircraft parts & equipment; aircraft
HQ: Precision Castparts Corp.
4650 Sw Mcdam Ave Ste 300
Portland OR 97239
503 946-4800

(G-9912)
HELMERICH & PAYNE INC (PA)
1437 S Boulder Ave # 1400 (74119-3623)
PHONE.....................918 742-5531
Hans Helmerich, *Ch of Bd*
John W Lindsay, *President*
Mike Fletcher, *Superintendent*
James Bishop, *Vice Pres*
Ronald Fullerton, *Vice Pres*
▼ EMP: 840
SALES: 2.8B **Publicly Held**
WEB: www.hpinc.com
SIC: **1381** 1389 6512 Drilling oil & gas wells; gas field services; nonresidential building operators; commercial & industrial building operation; shopping center, property operation only

(G-9913)
HELMERICH & PAYNE INC
5416 S 49th West Ave (74107-8813)
PHONE.....................918 447-8692
EMP: 4
SALES (corp-wide): 2.8B **Publicly Held**
WEB: www.hpinc.com
SIC: **1381** Drilling oil & gas wells
PA: Helmerich & Payne, Inc.
1437 S Boulder Ave # 1400
Tulsa OK 74119
918 742-5531

(G-9914)
HELMERICH & PAYNE INC
3003 N Sheridan Rd (74115-2345)
PHONE.....................918 835-6071
Alan Heginbotham, *Branch Mgr*
EMP: 4
SALES (corp-wide): 2.8B **Publicly Held**
WEB: www.hpinc.com
SIC: **1381** Drilling oil & gas wells
PA: Helmerich & Payne, Inc.
1437 S Boulder Ave # 1400
Tulsa OK 74119
918 742-5531

(G-9915)
HELMERICH & PAYNE DE VENEZUELA
1437 S Boulder Ave # 1400 (74119-3623)
PHONE.....................918 742-5531
Hans Helmerich, *CEO*
Walter H Helmerich III, *Ch of Bd*
Steve R Mackey, *Admin Sec*
EMP: 150
SALES (est): 5.5MM
SALES (corp-wide): 2.8B **Publicly Held**
WEB: www.hpinc.com
SIC: **1381** Drilling oil & gas wells
HQ: Helmerich & Payne International Drilling Co Inc
1437 S Boulder Ave # 1400
Tulsa OK 74119
918 742-5531

(G-9916)
HELMERICH & PAYNE INTL DRLG CO (HQ)
1437 S Boulder Ave # 1400 (74119-3623)
PHONE.....................918 742-5531
Hans Helmerich, *CEO*
John Lindsay, *Exec VP*
Rob Stauder, *Vice Pres*
Dustin Hornok, *Opers Mgr*
Will Proctor, *Foreman/Supr*
◆ EMP: 400 EST: 1967
SQ FT: 30,447
SALES (est): 2.2B
SALES (corp-wide): 2.8B **Publicly Held**
WEB: www.hpinc.com
SIC: **1381** Directional drilling oil & gas wells
PA: Helmerich & Payne, Inc.
1437 S Boulder Ave # 1400
Tulsa OK 74119
918 742-5531

(G-9917)
HELMERICH & PAYNE RASCO INC (DH)
1437 S Boulder Ave # 1400 (74119-3623)
PHONE.....................918 742-5531
Hans Helmerich, *President*
EMP: 6
SQ FT: 6,000
SALES (est): 36.9MM
SALES (corp-wide): 2.8B **Publicly Held**
WEB: www.hpinc.com
SIC: **1381** Drilling oil & gas wells
HQ: Helmerich & Payne International Drilling Co Inc
1437 S Boulder Ave # 1400
Tulsa OK 74119
918 742-5531

(G-9918)
HELMERICH & PAYNE TECH LLC
Also Called: H&P Technologies
1437 S Boulder Ave # 1400 (74119-3623)
PHONE.....................918 742-5531
John Lindsay, *President*
EMP: 2
SALES (est): 687.3K
SALES (corp-wide): 2.8B **Publicly Held**
SIC: **1381** Drilling oil & gas wells
PA: Helmerich & Payne, Inc.
1437 S Boulder Ave # 1400
Tulsa OK 74119
918 742-5531

(G-9919)
HELMERICH PAYNE ARGENTINA DRLG
1437 S Boulder Ave # 1400 (74119-3623)
PHONE.....................918 742-5531
George S Dotson, *President*
Walter H Helmerich III, *Chairman*
Hans Helmerich, *COO*
Steve R Mackey, *Admin Sec*
EMP: 400
SQ FT: 6,000
SALES (est): 12.1MM
SALES (corp-wide): 2.8B **Publicly Held**
WEB: www.hpinc.com
SIC: **1381** Drilling oil & gas wells
HQ: Helmerich & Payne International Drilling Co Inc
1437 S Boulder Ave # 1400
Tulsa OK 74119
918 742-5531

(G-9920)
HELMERICH PAYNE BOULDER DRLG (DH)
1437 S Boulder Ave # 1400 (74119-3623)
PHONE.....................918 742-5531
Hans Helmerich, *President*
George Dotson, *COO*
Steve Macky, *Vice Pres*
Marilyn Hyatt, *Admin Sec*
◆ EMP: 6
SALES (est): 12.6MM
SALES (corp-wide): 2.8B **Publicly Held**
SIC: **1381** Drilling oil & gas wells
HQ: Helmerich & Payne International Drilling Co Inc
1437 S Boulder Ave # 1400
Tulsa OK 74119
918 742-5531

(G-9921)
HELMERICH PAYNE COLUMBIA DRLG
1437 S Boulder Ave # 1400 (74119-3623)
PHONE.....................918 742-5531
Walter H Helmerich III, *Ch of Bd*
George S Dotson, *President*
Hans Helmerich, *President*
James W Bishop Jr, *Vice Pres*
Steve R Mackey, *Vice Pres*
EMP: 275
SQ FT: 6,000
SALES (est): 7.8MM
SALES (corp-wide): 2.8B **Publicly Held**
SIC: **1381** Drilling oil & gas wells
HQ: Helmerich & Payne International Drilling Co Inc
1437 S Boulder Ave # 1400
Tulsa OK 74119
918 742-5531

(G-9922)
HELMERICH PAYNE TRINIDAD DRLG
Also Called: Helmerich/Payne Intrntnl Drll
1437 S Boulder Ave # 1400 (74119-3623)
PHONE.....................918 742-5531
Walter H Helmerich III, *Ch of Bd*
Hans Helmerich, *President*
George S Dotson, *President*
Robert G Gambrell, *Treasurer*
Michael Jeffcoat, *Manager*
EMP: 260
SQ FT: 6,000
SALES (est): 15.6MM
SALES (corp-wide): 2.8B **Publicly Held**
SIC: **1381** Drilling oil & gas wells
HQ: Helmerich & Payne International Drilling Co Inc
1437 S Boulder Ave # 1400
Tulsa OK 74119
918 742-5531

(G-9923)
HERALD JAMES M AND TERESA
15326 E 13th St (74108-4709)
PHONE.....................918 437-7016
James Herald, *Principal*
EMP: 2
SALES (est): 84.3K **Privately Held**
SIC: **2711** Newspapers, publishing & printing

(G-9924)
HERFF JONES LLC
Also Called: Graduate Services
1640 S Boston Ave (74119-4416)
PHONE.....................918 664-2544
W R Lierman, *Partner*
EMP: 4
SALES (corp-wide): 1.1B **Privately Held**
WEB: www.yearbookdiscoveries.com
SIC: **3911** Rings, finger; precious metal
HQ: Herff Jones, Llc
4501 W 62nd St
Indianapolis IN 46268
800 419-5462

(G-9925)
HERMANS CHILI MIX INC
1251 E 31st Pl (74105-2009)
PHONE.....................918 743-1832
Herman Berg, *Owner*
EMP: 2

SALES (est): 106.6K **Privately Held**
SIC: **2035** 2099 Pickles, sauces & salad dressings; food preparations

(G-9926)
HEWLETT-PACKARD ENTP SVCS
11618 S Hudson Pl (74137-8533)
PHONE.....................918 939-4072
EMP: 2
SALES (est): 62.6K **Privately Held**
SIC: **3296** Mineral wool

(G-9927)
HIGGS-PALMER TECHNOLOGIES LLC (PA)
3206 S Darlington Ave (74135-5238)
PHONE.....................918 585-3775
Nigel G Higgs, *Mng Member*
Ian Palmer,
EMP: 1
SQ FT: 300
SALES (est): 173.8K **Privately Held**
SIC: **1389** Oil consultants

(G-9928)
HIGH COUNTRY TEK INC
5311 S 122nd East Ave (74146-6006)
PHONE.....................530 265-3236
Lennard Hjord, *President*
John Scott, *Chairman*
Gary Gotting, *Vice Pres*
Sandra Hackala, *Controller*
EMP: 35
SQ FT: 6,400
SALES (est): 6.2MM
SALES (corp-wide): 554.6MM **Publicly Held**
SIC: **3625** 3559 Control equipment, electric; screening equipment, electric
PA: Helios Technologies, Inc.
1500 W University Pkwy
Sarasota FL 34243
941 362-1200

(G-9929)
HIGH TIMES TULSA
7030 S Lewis Ave Ste C (74136-3915)
PHONE.....................918 600-2110
EMP: 2
SALES (est): 71K **Privately Held**
SIC: **2711** Newspapers, publishing & printing

(G-9930)
HILLSBORO CO
8016 S Joplin Ave (74136-9103)
PHONE.....................918 481-0484
Giles A Penick III, *President*
EMP: 1 EST: 1968
SQ FT: 1,200
SALES (est): 135.1K **Privately Held**
WEB: www.sportingdogsolutions.com
SIC: **2833** Animal based products

(G-9931)
HILTI INC
Also Called: Diagnostic Center
10660 E 31st St (74146-1601)
PHONE.....................918 252-6000
Gil Morris, *President*
Nathan Gressle, *Regional Mgr*
James Barton, *Accounts Mgr*
Alexander Garcia, *Accounts Mgr*
Joel Petersen, *Accounts Mgr*
EMP: 6
SALES (corp-wide): 242.1K **Privately Held**
SIC: **3399** 3545 Metal fasteners; tools & accessories for machine tools; drill bits, metalworking; drills (machine tool accessories)
HQ: Hilti, Inc.
7250 Dallas Pkwy Ste 1000
Plano TX 75024
800 879-8000

(G-9932)
HILTI NORTH AMERICA LTD (DH)
5400 S 122nd East Ave (74146-6099)
P.O. Box 21148 (74121-1148)
PHONE.....................918 252-6000
Cary Evert, *President*
Lillian Martindale, *Principal*
John W Shearing, *Vice Pres*
Samuel Polk, *Sales Staff*

Tulsa - Tulsa County (G-9933)

Zachary Swalley, *Sales Staff*
◆ **EMP:** 6
SQ FT: 100,000
SALES (est): 56.1MM
SALES (corp-wide): 242.1K **Privately Held**
WEB: www.hilti.com
SIC: 3546 5072 2821 7699 Power-driven handtools; hand tools; plastics materials & resins; industrial equipment services
HQ: Hilti Of America Inc.
7250 Dallas Pkwy Ste 1000
Plano TX 75024
800 879-8000

(G-9933)
HILTI OF AMERICA INC
5400 S 122nd East Ave (74146-6099)
PHONE 800 879-8000
EMP: 12
SALES (corp-wide): 242.1K **Privately Held**
SIC: 3545 3825 Precision measuring tools; standards & calibration equipment for electrical measuring
HQ: Hilti Of America Inc.
7250 Dallas Pkwy Ste 1000
Plano TX 75024
800 879-8000

(G-9934)
HKS ENERGY SOLUTIONS INC
Also Called: Es2-Tulsa
10404 E 55th Pl Ste E (74146-6509)
P.O. Box 470010 (74147-0010)
PHONE 918 279-6450
Justin Stonehocker, *President*
Claire Farr, *Opers Staff*
EMP: 10 **EST:** 2012
SALES (est): 282.7K **Privately Held**
SIC: 1711 1731 3822 Heating systems repair & maintenance; energy management controls; temperature controls, automatic

(G-9935)
HL WIRICK JR LLP
907 S Detroit Ave (74120-4205)
PHONE 918 587-4548
Harry L Wirick, *Partner*
EMP: 3 **EST:** 1952
SQ FT: 500
SALES (est): 270K **Privately Held**
SIC: 1311 Crude petroleum production; natural gas production

(G-9936)
HOFFMAN FIXTURES COMPANY (PA)
Also Called: Hoffman Fixture Company
6031 S 129th East Ave B (74134-6702)
PHONE 918 252-0451
Joseph A Hoffman Sr, *CEO*
Jerrod Roark, *General Mgr*
Jamie Myers, *COO*
Joseph A Hoffman Jr, *CFO*
Angela Scott, *Sales Executive*
EMP: 50
SQ FT: 9,200
SALES (est): 9.7MM **Privately Held**
WEB: www.hfcountertops.com
SIC: 2499 1743 2541 Kitchen, bathroom & household ware: wood; marble installation, interior; counters or counter display cases, wood

(G-9937)
HOGAN ASSESSMENT SYSTEMS INC (PA)
11 S Greenwood Ave (74120-1400)
PHONE 918 293-2300
Robert Hogan, *President*
Mark Stewart, *Vice Pres*
Rodney Warrenfeltz, *Vice Pres*
Sarah Phelps, *Human Res Dir*
Christopher Duffy, *Sales Staff*
EMP: 56
SQ FT: 10,000
SALES (est): 18.8MM **Privately Held**
SIC: 8742 2741 Business consultant; miscellaneous publishing

(G-9938)
HOLBROOK PRINTING
6351 E Newton St (74115-6619)
PHONE 918 835-5950
Lonnie Holbrook, *Owner*

Debbie Campbell, *Office Mgr*
EMP: 4
SALES (est): 270.8K **Privately Held**
SIC: 2752 2791 2789 Commercial printing, offset; typesetting; bookbinding & related work

(G-9939)
HOLLOWAY WIRE ROPE SVCS INC
14620 E Pine St (74116-2205)
P.O. Box 2670, Catoosa (74015-2670)
PHONE 918 582-1807
Derrick Deakins, *President*
EMP: 18
SQ FT: 18,500
SALES (est): 1.4MM
SALES (corp-wide): 3.3B **Privately Held**
SIC: 3496 Miscellaneous fabricated wire products
HQ: Delta Rigging & Tools, Inc.
125 Mccarty St
Houston TX 77029

(G-9940)
HOLLY REF & MKTG - TULSA LLC
1307 W 35th St (74107-3811)
PHONE 918 445-0056
Merle Fritz,
EMP: 13
SALES (corp-wide): 17.4B **Publicly Held**
SIC: 2911 Petroleum refining
HQ: Holly Refining & Marketing - Tulsa Llc
902 W 25th St
Tulsa OK 74107

(G-9941)
HOLLY REF & MKTG - TULSA LLC (HQ)
902 W 25th St (74107)
PHONE 918 594-6000
George J Damiris, *Principal*
David L Lamp, *COO*
Denise C McWatters, *Senior VP*
P Dean Ridenour, *Vice Pres*
Doug S Aron, *CFO*
▲ **EMP:** 39
SALES (est): 11.2MM
SALES (corp-wide): 17.4B **Publicly Held**
SIC: 4612 2911 Crude petroleum pipelines; gasoline
PA: Hollyfrontier Corporation
2828 N Harwood St # 1300
Dallas TX 75201
214 871-3555

(G-9942)
HOLLYFRONTIER CORPORATION
1700 S Union Ave (74107-1707)
PHONE 918 581-1800
Dustin Simmonds, *Superintendent*
Ryan Summers, *Opers Mgr*
Leslie Carrasco, *Accountant*
Brad Payne, *Credit Staff*
Larry Lee, *Financial Analy*
EMP: 375
SALES (corp-wide): 17.4B **Publicly Held**
SIC: 2911 3559 Petroleum refining; petroleum refinery equipment
PA: Hollyfrontier Corporation
2828 N Harwood St # 1300
Dallas TX 75201
214 871-3555

(G-9943)
HOLLYFRONTIER CORPORATION
907 S Detroit Ave (74120-4205)
PHONE 918 594-6000
Michael C Jennings, *Branch Mgr*
EMP: 3
SALES (corp-wide): 17.4B **Publicly Held**
SIC: 4612 2911 Crude petroleum pipelines; gasoline
PA: Hollyfrontier Corporation
2828 N Harwood St # 1300
Dallas TX 75201
214 871-3555

(G-9944)
HOLLYFRONTIER REF & MKTG LLC
1700 S Union Ave (74107-1707)
PHONE 918 588-1142
Nancy Riggs, *Marketing Staff*
Larry Quinn, *Branch Mgr*
EMP: 800
SALES (corp-wide): 17.4B **Publicly Held**
SIC: 2911 Gasoline
HQ: Hollyfrontier Refining & Marketing Llc
2828 N Harwood St # 1300
Dallas TX 75201

(G-9945)
HONEYWELL AEROSPACE TULSA/LORI
6930 N Lakewood Ave (74117-1807)
P.O. Box 3629 (74101-3629)
PHONE 918 272-4574
Greg Gomez-Cornejo, *Mayor*
EMP: 64
SQ FT: 137,000
SALES (est): 13.9MM
SALES (corp-wide): 36.7B **Publicly Held**
SIC: 7699 3724 5084 3728 Aircraft & heavy equipment repair services; aircraft engines & engine parts; engine heaters, aircraft; cooling systems, aircraft engine; industrial machinery & equipment; aircraft parts & equipment
PA: Honeywell International Inc.
300 S Tryon St
Charlotte NC 28202
704 627-6200

(G-9946)
HOOT OF LOOT
1322 S Guthrie Ave (74119-3020)
PHONE 918 743-9802
EMP: 1
SALES (est): 48.9K **Privately Held**
SIC: 2741 Miscellaneous publishing

(G-9947)
HOPKINS COUNTY COAL LLC
1717 S Boulder Ave # 400 (74119-4805)
PHONE 918 295-7600
EMP: 69 **EST:** 2017
SALES (est): 72.6K **Publicly Held**
SIC: 1221 Coal preparation plant, bituminous or lignite
HQ: Alliance Resource Partners Lp
1717 S Boulder Ave # 400
Tulsa OK 74119
918 295-7600

(G-9948)
HORIZON ENERGY SERVICES LLC
5727 S Lewis Ave Ste 550 (74105-7197)
P.O. Box 637, Perkins (74059-0637)
PHONE 918 392-9351
EMP: 10
SALES (corp-wide): 201.4MM **Privately Held**
SIC: 1381 Oil/Gas Well Drilling
PA: Horizon Energy Services, Llc
203 E 80th St
Stillwater OK 74074
405 533-4800

(G-9949)
HORIZON NATURAL RESOURCES INC
2131 W 73rd St (74132-2221)
PHONE 918 494-0790
Dale Rich, *President*
Mike Wilson, *Admin Sec*
EMP: 10
SQ FT: 3,000
SALES (est): 1.1MM **Privately Held**
SIC: 1311 Crude petroleum & natural gas production

(G-9950)
HORTON INDUSTRIES INC
Also Called: Horton Mfg
2001 N 69th East Ave (74115-3600)
PHONE 918 836-3971
Louis S Horton Jr, *President*
Paulette Horton, *Corp Secy*
EMP: 23
SQ FT: 8,200

SALES (est): 5.3MM **Privately Held**
SIC: 3492 Control valves, fluid power: hydraulic & pneumatic

(G-9951)
HOSPITAL PRODUCTS OKLAHOMA LLC
1323 E 53rd Pl Ste A (74105-6900)
PHONE 918 271-7169
Thomas Fitzgerald,
Glen R Platner,
EMP: 3 **EST:** 2010
SQ FT: 5,000
SALES (est): 350K **Privately Held**
SIC: 2591 Curtain & drapery rods, poles & fixtures

(G-9952)
HOSS LLC
4405 S 74th East Ave (74145-4710)
PHONE 918 660-7220
Phillip Ginn, *CEO*
Thomas Cole, *VP Sales*
Stasia Gardner, *Office Mgr*
EMP: 11
SALES (est): 1.3MM **Privately Held**
SIC: 3533 Oil & gas field machinery

(G-9953)
HOT OFF PRESS
6047 S Sheridan Rd (74145-9211)
PHONE 918 492-2313
Sharon Gardner, *Managing Prtnr*
Dennis Gardner, *Partner*
EMP: 2
SALES (est): 175.2K **Privately Held**
SIC: 2741 Miscellaneous publishing

(G-9954)
HOT STUFF AIRBRUSH INC
7021 S Memorial Dr (74133-2025)
PHONE 918 249-0458
EMP: 4 **EST:** 2000
SALES (est): 260K **Privately Held**
SIC: 3469 Mfg Metal Stampings

(G-9955)
HOWARDS PRECISION MFG INC
2730 Charles Page Blvd (74127-8315)
PHONE 918 599-7588
Jimmy Howard, *President*
EMP: 2
SALES (est): 336.5K **Privately Held**
SIC: 3599 Machine shop, jobbing & repair

(G-9956)
HOWMEDICA OSTEONICS CORP
11811 E 51st St (74146-6000)
PHONE 918 461-0152
EMP: 2
SALES (corp-wide): 14.8B **Publicly Held**
SIC: 3842 Surgical appliances & supplies
HQ: Howmedica Osteonics Corp.
325 Corporate Dr
Mahwah NJ 07430
201 831-5000

(G-9957)
HUGHES-ANDERSON HEAT EXCHANGER
1001 N Fulton Ave (74115-6445)
P.O. Box 582710 (74158-2710)
PHONE 918 836-1681
Jeff Gilbert, *President*
Kevin Gordon, *Exec VP*
Jim Harrison, *Vice Pres*
Kelly Bock, *Mfg Staff*
Michael Longo, *CFO*
◆ **EMP:** 126
SQ FT: 72,250
SALES: 33.9MM **Privately Held**
SIC: 3443 Heat exchangers: coolers (after, inter), condensers, etc.

(G-9958)
HUNTERS LASER CARTRIDGES
1126 S Evanston Ave (74104-4132)
PHONE 918 740-8164
Edward Bathanti, *Partner*
Saundra Bathanti, *Partner*
EMP: 2
SALES (est): 120K **Privately Held**
SIC: 2759 Laser printing

GEOGRAPHIC SECTION
Tulsa - Tulsa County (G-9989)

(G-9959)
HURRICANE GAS PROCESS PLANT
4613 E 91st St (74137-2852)
PHONE..................918 492-4418
Jack L Bentley, *Manager*
EMP: 3
SALES (est): 323.2K **Privately Held**
SIC: 2911 Gases & liquefied petroleum gases

(G-9960)
HYDRA SERVICE INC
12332 E 1st St (74128-2419)
PHONE..................918 438-3700
Rick Bentley, *President*
John D Fisher, *Corp Secy*
Jimmy Doyle, *Executive*
▲ **EMP:** 22
SQ FT: 20,000
SALES: 5MM **Privately Held**
WEB: www.hydraservice.com
SIC: 7699 5084 3594 Industrial machinery & equipment repair; industrial machinery & equipment; fluid power pumps & motors

(G-9961)
HYDRO CHART
7709 E 42nd Pl Ste 104 (74145-4724)
PHONE..................918 932-8586
EMP: 2 **EST:** 2015
SALES (est): 121.4K **Privately Held**
SIC: 3829 Measuring & controlling devices

(G-9962)
I & GN RESOURCES INC
6585 S Yale Ave Ste 900 (74136-8322)
PHONE..................918 481-7927
Paul Woodel, *President*
EMP: 2
SALES (est): 89.4K **Privately Held**
SIC: 1389 Oil & gas field services

(G-9963)
I-MAC PETROLEUM SERVICE INC
11726 S Sandusky Ave (74137-1855)
PHONE..................918 348-9400
Rick McQueen, *President*
EMP: 2
SQ FT: 4,000
SALES: 1.2MM **Privately Held**
SIC: 1382 Oil & gas exploration services

(G-9964)
IC BUS OF OKLAHOMA LLC
2322 N Mingo Rd (74116-1218)
PHONE..................918 833-4000
Grant Tick, *President*
Michael Cancelliere, *Vice Pres*
Dragos Vintila, *Engineer*
David Romig, *Electrical Engi*
EMP: 1000 **EST:** 2000
SQ FT: 980,000
SALES (est): 214.1MM
SALES (corp-wide): 11.2B **Publicly Held**
WEB: www.navistar.com
SIC: 3711 3713 Motor vehicles & car bodies; truck & bus bodies
HQ: Ic Bus, Llc
600 Bayford Dr
Conway AR 72034
501 327-7761

(G-9965)
ICEE COMPANY
2642 Mohawk Blvd (74110-1229)
PHONE..................800 423-3872
EMP: 2
SALES (corp-wide): 1.1B **Publicly Held**
SIC: 2038 Frozen specialties
HQ: The Icee Company
265 Mason Rd
La Vergne TN 37086
800 426-4233

(G-9966)
IDEAL CRANE CORPORATION
4632 S Lakewood Ave (74135-6879)
PHONE..................800 622-6163
Manfred Uekermann, *Mng Member*
EMP: 14
SQ FT: 15,000
SALES: 2.5MM **Privately Held**
WEB: www.idealcrane.com
SIC: 3531 Construction machinery

(G-9967)
IDEAL SPECIALTY INC
2531 E Independence St (74110-5056)
PHONE..................918 834-1657
Cynthia Buckingham, *CEO*
Robert Buckingham, *President*
Jon Parris, *Vice Pres*
Jennifer Sharber, *Accountant*
Dan Buckingham, *VP Sales*
◆ **EMP:** 16
SQ FT: 12,000
SALES (est): 1.8MM **Privately Held**
WEB: www.tagsandsigns.com
SIC: 3479 3599 3825 7692 Etching & engraving; machine shop, jobbing & repair; standards & calibration equipment for electrical measuring; welding repair

(G-9968)
II L W BARRETT
3727 E 56th St (74135-3822)
PHONE..................918 496-8309
EMP: 1 **EST:** 1923
SALES (est): 75K **Privately Held**
SIC: 1389 Oil/Gas Field Services

(G-9969)
IKG INDUSTRIES
1514 Sheldon Rd (74120)
PHONE..................918 599-8417
EMP: 2
SALES (est): 75K **Privately Held**
SIC: 3999 Mfg Misc Products

(G-9970)
ILLBIRD PRESS
4426 E 14th St (74112-6106)
PHONE..................918 859-7789
David Jurkiewicz, *Principal*
EMP: 1
SALES (est): 37.5K **Privately Held**
SIC: 2741 Miscellaneous publishing

(G-9971)
IMOCO LLC
6404 S 110th East Ave (74133-1623)
PHONE..................918 459-8366
Paul Brodsky, *Principal*
EMP: 2
SALES (est): 104K **Privately Held**
SIC: 2741 Miscellaneous publishing

(G-9972)
IMPERIAL LLC (PA)
2020 N Mingo Rd (74116-1220)
PHONE..................918 437-1300
Lance Whorton, *President*
Kevin Hinds, *Vice Pres*
Ron Morrow, *Opers Mgr*
Keith Duty, *Controller*
Nancy McDuffie, *Accountant*
EMP: 300 **EST:** 1979
SQ FT: 92,000
SALES (est): 78.3MM **Privately Held**
SIC: 2095 5962 5812 Roasted coffee; sandwich & hot food vending machines; beverage vending machines; candy & snack food vending machines; cigarettes vending machines; eating places

(G-9973)
IMPERIAL PRINTING INC
4153 S 87th East Ave (74145-3320)
PHONE..................918 663-1302
Donald R Dale, *President*
Glenda Dale, *Treasurer*
EMP: 5
SQ FT: 10,000
SALES (est): 450K **Privately Held**
SIC: 2752 2791 2789 Lithographing on metal; typesetting; bookbinding & related work

(G-9974)
IMPRESSIONS IN STONE LLC
1415 S Joplin Ave (74112-6414)
PHONE..................918 828-9745
Dax Davison, *Vice Pres*
Dagan Heaps, *Mng Member*
Mike Howell, *Executive*
▼ **EMP:** 9
SQ FT: 6,000
SALES (est): 1.4MM **Privately Held**
SIC: 3272 5032 Concrete products, pre-cast; building stone

(G-9975)
IMS ERP SOFTWARE LLC
401 S Boston Ave Ste 500 (74103-4023)
PHONE..................918 508-9544
EMP: 5
SALES (est): 348.6K **Privately Held**
SIC: 7372 Prepackaged software

(G-9976)
INDEL-DAVIS INC (PA)
4401 S Jackson Ave (74107-7040)
PHONE..................918 587-2151
Robert W Langholz, *CEO*
Calvin O Vogt, *President*
G R Runnels, *Treasurer*
▲ **EMP:** 11
SQ FT: 88,000
SALES (est): 10.5MM **Privately Held**
SIC: 5084 3861 3695 Oil well machinery, equipment & supplies; photographic equipment & supplies; magnetic & optical recording media

(G-9977)
INDIAN CREEK GAS PROCESSING LP
6100 S Yale Ave Ste 2050 (74136-1934)
PHONE..................918 359-0980
Donne Pitman, *Principal*
EMP: 5
SALES (est): 460K **Privately Held**
SIC: 1389 Processing service, gas

(G-9978)
INDIGO STREAMS PUBLISHING LLC
5138 E 30th Pl (74114-6312)
PHONE..................918 293-0247
Abir Wood, *Principal*
EMP: 1
SALES (est): 37.5K **Privately Held**
SIC: 2741 Miscellaneous publishing

(G-9979)
INDUSTRIAL DIST RESOURCES LLC
7255 E 46th St (74145-5901)
PHONE..................239 591-3777
Steven Moellers,
EMP: 8
SQ FT: 2,000
SALES (est): 1.4MM **Privately Held**
SIC: 3561 5085 5084 3563 Pumps & pumping equipment; industrial supplies; industrial machinery & equipment; air & gas compressors; blowers & fans
PA: Mecca Resources, Inc
6609 Willow Park Dr # 101
Naples FL 34109

(G-9980)
INDUSTRIAL MARKING CO
Also Called: McCullough Sales Co
6216 S Lewis Ave Ste 136 (74136-1017)
PHONE..................918 749-8851
Janine Bodson, *President*
EMP: 3 **EST:** 1960
SQ FT: 600
SALES (est): 482.9K **Privately Held**
SIC: 5113 3999 Pressure sensitive tape; identification tags, except paper

(G-9981)
INDUSTRIAL SPLICING SLING LLC (PA)
1842 N 109th East Ave (74116-1519)
PHONE..................918 835-4452
Dennis Mabry, *General Mgr*
Woodrow Rial, *Vice Pres*
Mike Parham, *Sales Mgr*
Jason Cox, *Sales Staff*
Curtis Rutherford, *Sales Staff*
EMP: 16 **EST:** 1976
SQ FT: 6,000
SALES: 8.6MM **Privately Held**
WEB: www.industrialsplicing.com
SIC: 3496 5084 Slings, lifting: made from purchased wire; industrial machinery & equipment

(G-9982)
INDUSTRIAL STRUCTURES INC
Also Called: ISI
1931 N 170th East Ave (74116-4925)
PHONE..................918 341-0300
Jeff Simpson, *President*
Dan Hutchison, *Vice Pres*
James Redfearn, *Vice Pres*
EMP: 26
SQ FT: 50,000
SALES (est): 4.9MM **Privately Held**
SIC: 3743 1541 Railroad equipment; industrial buildings & warehouses

(G-9983)
INDUSTRIAL VEHICLES INTL INC (PA)
6737 E 12th St (74112-5684)
PHONE..................918 836-6516
James M Bird Jr, *President*
Villard Martin Jr, *Principal*
Ronald G Raynolds, *Principal*
Elmo Christensen, *Vice Pres*
Brian Perkins, *Prdtn Mgr*
▲ **EMP:** 26
SQ FT: 30,000
SALES (est): 6.9MM **Privately Held**
WEB: www.indvehicles.com
SIC: 3533 3537 Oil field machinery & equipment; industrial trucks & tractors

(G-9984)
INGEVITY
1540 N 107th East Ave (74116-1512)
PHONE..................918 704-6423
EMP: 4 **EST:** 2018.
SALES (est): 276.7K **Privately Held**
SIC: 2819 Industrial inorganic chemicals

(G-9985)
INGREDION INCORPORATED
810 S Cincinnati Ave (74119-1635)
PHONE..................539 292-4369
EMP: 4
SALES (corp-wide): 6.2B **Publicly Held**
SIC: 2046 Starch
PA: Ingredion Incorporated
5 Westbrook Corporate Ctr # 500
Westchester IL 60154
708 551-2600

(G-9986)
INITIALLY YOURS INC
1539 N 105th East Ave (74116-1515)
PHONE..................918 832-9889
Ewald Kempa, *President*
Ashley Turner, *Admin Sec*
EMP: 9
SQ FT: 12,000
SALES (est): 838.1K **Privately Held**
SIC: 2395 2396 5199 7389 Embroidery products, except schiffli machine; screen printing on fabric articles; stamping fabric articles; advertising specialties; engraving service; commercial printing; commercial printing, lithographic

(G-9987)
INK IMAGES INC
4305 S Mingo Rd Ste C (74146-4746)
PHONE..................918 828-0300
Patrick Thresher, *President*
EMP: 6
SALES (est): 680K **Privately Held**
WEB: www.inkimagestulsa.com
SIC: 2752 2791 2789 2759 Advertising posters, lithographed; typesetting; bookbinding & related work; commercial printing

(G-9988)
INKWELL PRINTING
4195 S 69th West Ave (74107-8283)
PHONE..................918 508-3634
EMP: 2
SALES (est): 83.9K **Privately Held**
SIC: 2752 Commercial printing, lithographic

(G-9989)
INNOVATIVE PRODUCTION INC
4602 W 51st St (74107-7338)
PHONE..................918 729-9312
Darin Austin, *Director*
Robert Hicks, *Director*

Tulsa - Tulsa County (G-9990)

EMP: 3
SQ FT: 6,000
SALES: 1MM **Privately Held**
SIC: 1382 Oil & gas exploration services

(G-9990)
INSIGHT PUBLISHING GROUP
4739 E 91st St Ste 210 (74137-2808)
PHONE.................................918 493-1718
John Mason, *Principal*
EMP: 2 EST: 2010
SALES (est): 114.3K **Privately Held**
SIC: 2741 Miscellaneous publishing

(G-9991)
INSTITUTE OPTICAL INC
1717 S Utica Ave Ste 105 (74104-5345)
PHONE.................................918 747-3937
Gerard Hunter, *President*
Todd Brockman, *Shareholder*
Joseph Flemming, *Shareholder*
Robert Gragg, *Shareholder*
Kenneth Mc Coy, *Shareholder*
EMP: 4
SQ FT: 2,500
SALES (est): 277.7K **Privately Held**
SIC: 3851 8042 5995 Frames, lenses & parts, eyeglass & spectacle; offices & clinics of optometrists; optical goods stores

(G-9992)
INSUL-VEST INC (PA)
6417 S 39th West Ave (74132-1244)
PHONE.................................918 445-2279
Gordon Pendergraft, *Chairman*
Jason Pendergraft, *Vice Pres*
John Pendergraft, *Vice Pres*
▲ EMP: 6
SALES (est): 1.3MM **Privately Held**
SIC: 2221 3299 Fiberglass fabrics; ceramic fiber

(G-9993)
INTEGRATED CONTROLS INC
1537 S Harvard Ave (74112-5821)
PHONE.................................918 747-5811
EMP: 2
SALES (est): 170.2K **Privately Held**
WEB: www.intcontrols.com
SIC: 3829 Measuring & controlling devices

(G-9994)
INTEGRATED CONTROLS INC
5236 S Zunis Ave (74105-6429)
PHONE.................................918 747-7820
Allen Forman, *President*
Amanda Forman, *VP Bus Dvlpt*
Jason Forman, *Sales Engr*
EMP: 4
SALES (est): 416.5K **Privately Held**
SIC: 3823 Industrial instrmnts msrmnt display/control process variable

(G-9995)
INTEGRATED PAYMENT SVCS LLC
1703 E Skelly Dr Ste 105 (74105-5948)
PHONE.................................918 492-7094
Dave Miley, *Mng Member*
EMP: 1
SALES (est): 110K **Privately Held**
SIC: 3578 Banking machines

(G-9996)
INTEGRATED SERVICE CO MFG LLC
1900 N 161st East Ave (74116-4829)
PHONE.................................918 234-4150
EMP: 2
SALES (est): 104.2K **Privately Held**
SIC: 3823 Industrial process control instruments

(G-9997)
INTEGRATED SERVICE COMPANY LLC
Also Called: Inserv's
4300 E 36th St N (74115-1715)
PHONE.................................918 556-3600
Troy Jones, *Principal*
EMP: 3
SALES (est): 331.1K **Privately Held**
SIC: 3795 Tanks & tank components

(G-9998)
INTEGRATED TOWER SYSTEMS INC
2703 Dawson Rd (74110-5033)
PHONE.................................918 749-8535
Brad Harwood, *President*
▼ EMP: 25
SALES (est): 950K **Privately Held**
SIC: 3441 Fabricated structural metal

(G-9999)
INTEGRITY SCREEN WORKS INC
Also Called: Integriteezv
6580 E Skelly Dr (74145-1324)
PHONE.................................918 663-8339
Jess Kennon, *President*
Jesse Channon, *President*
Jesse Kennon, *Principal*
EMP: 40
SQ FT: 3,000
SALES (est): 1.1MM **Privately Held**
SIC: 2395 2759 Embroidery products, except schiffli machine; screen printing

(G-10000)
INTEGRITY WOODCRAFTERS LLC
8809 E 34th St (74145-3408)
PHONE.................................918 664-1041
Michael Coursey, *Principal*
EMP: 1 EST: 2016
SALES (est): 42.3K **Privately Held**
SIC: 2499 Wood products

(G-10001)
INTELLEVUE LTD
11102 E 75th Pl (74133-2518)
PHONE.................................918 250-5561
Jeff Davis, *CEO*
EMP: 4
SALES (est): 349.3K **Privately Held**
SIC: 7372 Prepackaged software

(G-10002)
INTENSITY MIDSTREAM LLC (PA)
320 S Boston Ave Ste 705 (74103-3757)
PHONE.................................918 949-9098
Joseph L Griffin, *CEO*
Derek G Gipson, *President*
Roger A Farrell, *Chairman*
Matthew Briscoe, *Vice Pres*
J Michael Cockrell, *Vice Pres*
EMP: 9
SALES (est): 291.4K **Privately Held**
SIC: 1311 Natural gas production

(G-10003)
INTERFACEFLOR LLC
Also Called: Iffia
4207 S Wheeling Ave (74105-4233)
PHONE.................................918 746-0501
Jim Sedlacek, *General Mgr*
EMP: 1
SALES (corp-wide): 1.3B **Publicly Held**
SIC: 2273 Finishers of tufted carpets & rugs
HQ: Interfaceflor, Llc
1503 Orchard Hill Rd
Lagrange GA 30240

(G-10004)
INTERNATIONAL ENERGY CORP
1801 E 71st St (74136-3922)
PHONE.................................918 743-7300
Peter Power PHD, *Ch of Bd*
Richard A Adrey, *President*
Daniel J Lanskey, *Managing Dir*
EMP: 15
SALES (est): 3.8MM **Privately Held**
WEB: www.ienergycorp.com
SIC: 1382 Oil & gas exploration services
HQ: International Energy Holding Company, Llc
1801 E 71st St
Tulsa OK

(G-10005)
INTERNTNAL MKTG RESOURCES CORP
Also Called: I M R
1200 N Peoria Ave (74106-4952)
P.O. Box 690175 (74169-0175)
PHONE.................................918 270-1200
Dan Ward, *President*
EMP: 4
SALES: 600K **Privately Held**
SIC: 2899 Water treating compounds

(G-10006)
INTERPLASTIC CORPORATION
Also Called: Interplastic Dist Group
1012 E Oklahoma St (74106-5917)
PHONE.................................918 592-0205
Gary Killingsworth, *Sales Staff*
Morris Brandt, *Branch Mgr*
EMP: 13
SALES (corp-wide): 250.9MM **Privately Held**
SIC: 2821 Plastics materials & resins
PA: Interplastic Corporation
1225 Willow Lake Blvd
Saint Paul MN 55110
651 481-6860

(G-10007)
INTERSTATE SUPPLY COMPANY
11915 E 51st St Ste 57 (74146-6014)
PHONE.................................918 461-0177
EMP: 2
SALES (corp-wide): 42.9MM **Privately Held**
WEB: www.iscsurfaces.com
SIC: 3996 Hard surface floor coverings
PA: Interstate Supply Company
9245 Dielman Indus Dr
Saint Louis MO 63132
314 994-7100

(G-10008)
INTERSTATE TOOL & MFG CO
1044 N Columbia Pl (74110-5027)
P.O. Box 50326 (74150-0326)
PHONE.................................918 834-6647
Douglas Edwards, *President*
EMP: 35
SQ FT: 75,000
SALES (est): 5.9MM **Privately Held**
WEB: www.abi-us.com
SIC: 3469 3544 Stamping metal for the trade; special dies & tools

(G-10009)
INVIA PAVEMENT TECH LLC
1540 N 107th East Ave (74116-1512)
PHONE.................................918 878-7890
Brain Majeska, *President*
David Reynolds, *Vice Pres*
Timothy O'Connell,
EMP: 15
SALES (est): 3.2MM
SALES (corp-wide): 1.2B **Publicly Held**
WEB: www.thunderheadtesting.com
SIC: 2819 Industrial inorganic chemicals
PA: Ingevity Corporation
5255 Virginia Ave
North Charleston SC 29406
843 740-2300

(G-10010)
INVITING PLACE
3525 S Harvard Ave (74135-1840)
PHONE.................................918 488-0525
Sara Younger, *Principal*
EMP: 2
SALES (est): 171.5K **Privately Held**
SIC: 2759 5943 Invitation & stationery printing & engraving; stationery stores

(G-10011)
IQ SURGICAL LLC
22 S Lewis Ave (74104-1615)
PHONE.................................918 932-2734
Ryan Jude Tanner, *CEO*
Jay Krottinger, *COO*
EMP: 10
SALES (est): 1.4MM **Privately Held**
WEB: www.iqsurgical.com
SIC: 3842 Implants, surgical

(G-10012)
IRON BEAR JEWELRY & LEA CO LLC
6527 N Trenton Ave (74126-1712)
PHONE.................................918 289-1420
Michelle Heath, *Mng Member*
EMP: 1
SALES: 25K **Privately Held**
WEB: www.ironbearjewelry.com
SIC: 5944 3111 Jewelry, precious stones & precious metals; accessory products, leather

(G-10013)
ISABELS CANDLES
1746 W Young St (74127-2513)
PHONE.................................918 595-5358
Jayson Summers, *Principal*
EMP: 1
SALES (est): 39.6K **Privately Held**
SIC: 3999 Candles

(G-10014)
ITS IN PRINT
6131 S Joplin Ave (74136-2107)
PHONE.................................918 493-4141
EMP: 2 EST: 2009
SALES (est): 130K **Privately Held**
SIC: 2752 Lithographic Commercial Printing

(G-10015)
IZOOM INC
Also Called: Izoom Graphics
9015 S 48th West Ave (74132-3412)
PHONE.................................918 836-9666
Sean Grubb, *President*
EMP: 1
SQ FT: 800
SALES: 90K **Privately Held**
SIC: 3993 Signs & advertising specialties

(G-10016)
J & B DEEP DISCOUNT
6525 E 51st St (74145-7604)
PHONE.................................918 622-7600
Bob Rusley, *Owner*
EMP: 4
SALES (est): 267.2K **Privately Held**
SIC: 2084 Wines

(G-10017)
J & D MACHINE INC
2700 N Erie Ave (74115-2807)
PHONE.................................918 425-5704
Jack Evans, *President*
Suzanne Evans, *Admin Sec*
EMP: 8 EST: 1962
SQ FT: 3,000
SALES (est): 980.2K **Privately Held**
WEB: www.jdmachinetulsa.com
SIC: 3599 Machine shop, jobbing & repair

(G-10018)
J & L TOOL CO INC
63 N Yale Ave (74115-8400)
PHONE.................................918 835-8484
John Austin, *President*
EMP: 8
SALES (est): 960.3K **Privately Held**
SIC: 7699 3312 Industrial tool grinding; tool & die steel

(G-10019)
J E & L E MABEE FOUNDATION (PA)
401 S Boston Ave Ste 3001 (74103-4066)
PHONE.................................918 584-4286
Joe Mabee, *Chairman*
EMP: 14 EST: 1948
SQ FT: 5,500
SALES: 68.1MM **Privately Held**
WEB: www.mabeefoundation.com
SIC: 8699 1311 Charitable organization; crude petroleum production

(G-10020)
J FRANKLIN PUBLISHERS INC
4926 S Boston Pl (74105-4606)
P.O. Box 14057 (74159-1057)
PHONE.................................628 400-3382
EMP: 1
SALES (est): 33.3K **Privately Held**
SIC: 2731 Book publishing

GEOGRAPHIC SECTION

Tulsa - Tulsa County (G-10050)

(G-10021)
J MOTTOS LLC
Also Called: J Mottos Italian Ice Sorbet
8759 S Lewis Ave Ste A (74137-3208)
PHONE..................918 760-3866
Greg Jeffries, *Principal*
Kelly Jeffries,
EMP: 2
SQ FT: 2,000
SALES (est): 50K **Privately Held**
SIC: 2024 5143 5999 Ices, flavored (frozen dessert); sorbets, non-dairy based; ice cream & ices; ice

(G-10022)
J SPENCER JEWELRY & GIFTS (PA)
8303 S Memorial Dr (74133-4304)
PHONE..................918 250-5587
Julie Spencer, *Owner*
Chris Spencer, *Vice Pres*
EMP: 7
SALES (est): 1MM **Privately Held**
SIC: 3915 5947 5944 Jewelers' findings & materials; gift, novelty & souvenir shop; jewelry stores

(G-10023)
J STEPHENS LLC
5415 E 109th Pl (74137-7280)
PHONE..................918 299-2900
Jeff Stephens, *Principal*
EMP: 2 **EST:** 2010
SALES (est): 199.3K **Privately Held**
SIC: 3721 Aircraft

(G-10024)
J&J POWDER COATING & FABR
6410 E Archer St (74115-8635)
PHONE..................918 836-9700
Jamie McDonald, *Principal*
EMP: 2
SALES (est): 203.3K **Privately Held**
SIC: 3479 Coating of metals & formed products

(G-10025)
J-M MANUFACTURING COMPANY INC
Also Called: J M Eagle
4501 W 49th St (74107-7315)
PHONE..................918 446-4471
Robert Kirchmer, *Branch Mgr*
EMP: 83
SALES (corp-wide): 1B **Privately Held**
SIC: 2821 3085 Polyvinyl chloride resins (PVC); plastics bottles
PA: J-M Manufacturing Company, Inc.
5200 W Century Blvd
Los Angeles CA 90045
800 621-4404

(G-10026)
JAMES R BIDDICK
Also Called: Unit Energy Company
427 S Boston Ave Ste 1036 (74103-4115)
P.O. Box 52476 (74152-0476)
PHONE..................918 587-1551
James R Biddick, *Owner*
EMP: 2
SQ FT: 300
SALES (est): 175K **Privately Held**
SIC: 1382 1311 Geological exploration, oil & gas field; crude petroleum & natural gas production

(G-10027)
JANIMALS
7803 S 28th West Ave (74132-2673)
PHONE..................918 587-4799
Jan Eckardt Butler, *Owner*
EMP: 1
SALES (est): 60.1K **Privately Held**
SIC: 3269 Figures: pottery, china, earthenware & stoneware

(G-10028)
JARRT HOLDINGS INC
Also Called: Tulsa Plastics
6112 E 32nd Pl (74135-5406)
PHONE..................918 664-0931
James R Blakemore, *CEO*
Abraham Abuali, *Vice Pres*
Tom Blakemore, *Vice Pres*
David Bridges, *CTO*
EMP: 18
SQ FT: 12,000
SALES (est): 5.5MM **Privately Held**
WEB: www.tulsaplastics.com
SIC: 3089 Injection molding of plastics; plastic processing

(G-10029)
JARVIS INC
8321 E 61st St Ste 201 (74133-1911)
PHONE..................918 437-1100
Ray Jarvis, *President*
Cindy Jarvis, *Vice Pres*
Mark Jarvis, *Vice Pres*
Christopher Morris, *Supervisor*
Kalissa Stimson, *Executive Asst*
EMP: 45
SQ FT: 2,200
SALES (est): 7.8MM **Privately Held**
SIC: 3699 8249 7382 Security control equipment & systems; vocational schools; confinement surveillance systems maintenance & monitoring

(G-10030)
JAY RAMBO CO HAHN SHOWROOM
6710 S 105th East Ave (74133-5833)
PHONE..................918 615-3370
Jay Rambo, *Principal*
EMP: 1
SALES (est): 86.7K **Privately Held**
SIC: 2434 Wood kitchen cabinets

(G-10031)
JB BOOKS UNLIMITED LLC
4823 S Sheridan Rd 305a (74145-5755)
PHONE..................918 954-8308
Julia Buckner,
EMP: 1 **EST:** 2017
SALES (est): 33.3K **Privately Held**
SIC: 2731 5942 5192 Books: publishing only; book stores; books

(G-10032)
JB MACHINING INC
6227 N Peoria Ave (74126-1748)
PHONE..................918 425-3337
Willie Bewley, *President*
Barbara Bewley, *Corp Secy*
EMP: 20
SALES (est): 2.5MM **Privately Held**
SIC: 3599 Machine shop, jobbing & repair; custom machinery

(G-10033)
JDW HOTSHOT SERVICES
5206 S Harvard Ave # 308 (74135-3565)
P.O. Box 405 (74101-0405)
PHONE..................918 407-8787
Jeffrey Leon Willison, *Owner*
EMP: 5
SALES (est): 395.6K **Privately Held**
SIC: 1389 Hot shot service

(G-10034)
JENCO FABRICATORS INC
1850 N 170th East Ave (74116-4913)
PHONE..................918 234-3364
Gary A Jennings, *President*
Janice Jennings, *Corp Secy*
EMP: 30
SQ FT: 20,000
SALES (est): 5.7MM **Privately Held**
SIC: 3441 Building components, structural steel

(G-10035)
JENSEN MIXERS INTL INC
5354 S Garnett Rd (74146-5905)
P.O. Box 470368 (74147-0368)
PHONE..................918 627-5770
Louis C Jensen, *President*
Peyton Nielsen, *Sales Staff*
▼ **EMP:** 45
SQ FT: 64,000
SALES (est): 12.4MM **Privately Held**
SIC: 3531 Mixers: ore, plaster, slag, sand, mortar, etc.

(G-10036)
JERICHO OIL (OKLAHOMA) CORP
321 S Boston Ave Ste 300 (74103-3311)
PHONE..................215 383-2433
Allen Wilson, *President*
Tony Blancato, *Director*
EMP: 5
SALES (est): 192.6K **Privately Held**
SIC: 1389 Servicing oil & gas wells

(G-10037)
JERO MANUFACTURING INC
5117 S 100th East Ave (74146-5728)
P.O. Box 472033 (74147-2033)
PHONE..................918 628-0230
John Pingleton, *President*
Gary Richardson, *Vice Pres*
EMP: 30
SQ FT: 20,000
SALES (est): 7.3MM **Privately Held**
SIC: 3589 Dirt sweeping units, industrial

(G-10038)
JERRY SWANSON SALES CO INC
Also Called: Signs Now
3229 S Harvard Ave (74135-4447)
PHONE..................918 712-7446
Jerry Swanson, *President*
Ann Swanson, *Corp Secy*
EMP: 9
SQ FT: 3,600
SALES (est): 764.1K **Privately Held**
SIC: 3993 Signs & advertising specialties

(G-10039)
JESSE HARBIN
Also Called: Unique Wireless
9346 S 94th East Ave (74133-5615)
PHONE..................918 734-3980
Jesse Harbin, *Owner*
EMP: 3
SALES (est): 185.9K **Privately Held**
SIC: 3661 Switching equipment, telephone

(G-10040)
JESSIE SHAW
Also Called: Mat Assembly, The
1041 N Madison Ave (74106-5360)
PHONE..................918 587-6329
Jessie Shaw, *Owner*
EMP: 1
SALES (est): 59K **Privately Held**
SIC: 5999 2394 3069 Foam & foam products; air cushions & mattresses, canvas; foam rubber

(G-10041)
JETT OIL AND GAS LLC
10319 S 67th East Ave (74133-6710)
PHONE..................918 995-7430
Shawn McCarthy, *Principal*
EMP: 2
SALES (est): 84.5K **Privately Held**
SIC: 1389 Oil & gas field services

(G-10042)
JETTA CORPORATION
Also Called: Jetta of Tulsa
9515 E 51st St Ste E (74145-9053)
PHONE..................918 574-2151
EMP: 1
SALES (corp-wide): 12.8MM **Privately Held**
WEB: www.jettacorporation.com
SIC: 3088 Tubs (bath, shower & laundry), plastic
PA: Jetta Corporation
425 Centennial Blvd
Edmond OK 73013
405 340-6661

(G-10043)
JETTA PRODUCTION COMPANY INC
Also Called: Marketing Office
10949 S Urbana Ave (74137-7128)
PHONE..................918 299-0107
Teresa Angel, *Manager*
EMP: 2 **Privately Held**
SIC: 1311 1382 Crude petroleum production; oil & gas exploration services
PA: Jetta Production Company Inc
777 Taylor St Ph P1d
Fort Worth TX 76102

(G-10044)
JEWEL TECH MFG INC
Also Called: Creative Jewelry Designers
8223 S Marion Ave (74137-1624)
P.O. Box 703054 (74170-3054)
PHONE..................918 828-9700
Michael Letney, *President*
EMP: 10
SALES (est): 4MM **Privately Held**
SIC: 5944 3911 5094 Jewelry, precious stones & precious metals; jewelry, precious metal; jewelry

(G-10045)
JEWELS BY JAMES INC
Also Called: Jewels By James.com
3329 E 31st St (74135-1502)
PHONE..................918 745-2004
James Williams, *President*
Sherry Williams, *Corp Secy*
Kenneth Williams, *Vice Pres*
EMP: 2
SQ FT: 1,000
SALES (est): 78K **Privately Held**
SIC: 3911 3915 Jewelry apparel; jewelers' materials & lapidary work

(G-10046)
JO ROSE FINE CABINETS INC
1810 N 75th East Ave (74115-4613)
P.O. Box 470818 (74147-0818)
PHONE..................918 832-1500
Michael R Webb, *President*
Robert Hughes, *Vice Pres*
EMP: 24
SQ FT: 27,000
SALES (est): 3.3MM **Privately Held**
SIC: 2434 Wood kitchen cabinets

(G-10047)
JOANS PRINT SHOP INC
5505 S Mingo Rd Ste A (74146-6419)
P.O. Box 1632, Broken Arrow (74013-1632)
PHONE..................918 624-5858
EMP: 3
SALES (est): 336.2K **Privately Held**
SIC: 2752 2789 Lithographic Commercial Printing Bookbinding/Related Work

(G-10048)
JOCO ASSEMBLY LLC
1575 N 93rd East Ave (74115-4701)
PHONE..................918 622-5111
Joseph Kurek, *Mng Member*
EMP: 37
SALES (est): 7.3MM
SALES (corp-wide): 39.4B **Privately Held**
SIC: 3312 Blast furnaces & steel mills
HQ: Magna Mirrors Of America, Inc.
5085 Kraft Ave Se
Grand Rapids MI 49512
616 786-5120

(G-10049)
JOHN CRANE INC
Also Called: John Crane Lemco
2931 E Apache St (74110-2245)
PHONE..................918 664-5156
Gary Jones, *Opers Mgr*
Mike Bates, *Production*
Joe Haas, *VP Engrg*
Israel Cruz, *QC Mgr*
Troy Grissen, *Engineer*
EMP: 58
SALES (corp-wide): 3.1B **Privately Held**
WEB: www.johncrane.com
SIC: 3561 3625 3443 3053 Pumps & pumping equipment; relays & industrial controls; fabricated plate work (boiler shop); gaskets & sealing devices
HQ: John Crane Inc.
227 W Monroe St Ste 1800
Chicago IL 60606
312 605-7800

(G-10050)
JOHN CRANE LEMCO INC
2931 E Apache St (74110-2245)
PHONE..................918 835-7325
William L Strang, *CEO*
Linda Mullis, *Principal*
Morgan K Powell, *Principal*
Bryan Burcham, *Executive*
▲ **EMP:** 45

Tulsa - Tulsa County (G-10051)

SALES (est): 11.8MM
SALES (corp-wide): 3.1B **Privately Held**
SIC: **3561** 3053 Pumps & pumping equipment; gaskets & sealing devices
HQ: John Crane Inc.
227 W Monroe St Ste 1800
Chicago IL 60606
312 605-7800

(G-10051)
JOHN E ROUGEOT OIL & GAS
8187 S Harvard Ave (74137-1612)
PHONE 918 494-9978
John E Rougeot, *President*
EMP: 5
SALES (est): 238.7K **Privately Held**
SIC: **1311** Crude petroleum production; natural gas production

(G-10052)
JOHN H BOOTH INC
1787 E 71st St (74136-5108)
PHONE 918 481-0383
John H Booth, *President*
Amy R Booth, *Corp Secy*
James Blurton, *Vice Pres*
EMP: 3
SALES: 250K **Privately Held**
SIC: **1311** Crude petroleum production; natural gas production

(G-10053)
JOHN W STONE OIL DISTRIBUTING
2825 E Skelly Dr (74105-6235)
PHONE 918 744-8168
EMP: 1
SALES (est): 67K **Privately Held**
SIC: **1389** Oil/Gas Field Services

(G-10054)
JOHN ZINK CO LLC
3914 E 51st Pl (74135-3831)
PHONE 918 749-9345
Zachary Kodesh, *Principal*
EMP: 3 EST: 2011
SALES (est): 263.4K **Privately Held**
WEB: www.johnzink.com
SIC: **3823** Industrial instrmnts msrmnt display/control process variable

(G-10055)
JOHN ZINK COMPANY LLC (DH)
Also Called: John Zink Hamworthy Combustion
11920 E Apache St (74116-1300)
P.O. Box 21220 (74121-1220)
PHONE 918 234-1800
Casey Chambers, *President*
Alan Gerber, *Vice Pres*
Gary Goodnight, *Plant Mgr*
Scott Reid, *Project Mgr*
Christian Tello, *Production*
◆ EMP: 800
SQ FT: 150,000
SALES (est): 276MM
SALES (corp-wide): 48.9B **Privately Held**
SIC: **3823** Combustion control instruments
HQ: Koch Engineered Solutions, Llc
4111 E 37th St N
Wichita KS 67220
316 828-8515

(G-10056)
JOHNNY BEARD CO
14308 E 11th St (74108-2716)
PHONE 918 438-4901
Johnny Beard, *Owner*
EMP: 1
SALES (est): 78.6K **Privately Held**
SIC: **5719** 3599 3429 3199 Fireplace equipment & accessories; industrial machinery; manufactured hardware (general); leather goods

(G-10057)
JOHNSONWOODWORKS
8525 E 41st St 1017 (74145-3305)
PHONE 918 407-7747
Dedrick Johnson, *Principal*
EMP: 2
SALES (est): 113.5K **Privately Held**
SIC: **2431** Millwork

(G-10058)
JORAME INC
Also Called: Superior Honing and Grinding
1605 N 168th East Ave (74116-4929)
PHONE 918 582-5663
Robert Elliott, *President*
Linda Elliott, *Corp Secy*
EMP: 15
SQ FT: 27,351
SALES (est): 2.2MM **Privately Held**
SIC: **3599** Machine shop, jobbing & repair

(G-10059)
JOSHI TECHNOLOGIES INTL INC (PA)
Also Called: Jti
5801 E 41st St Ste 603 (74135-5628)
PHONE 918 665-6419
Sada D Joshi, *President*
Chirag Patel, *Business Mgr*
Claudette Joshi, *Admin Sec*
Lillian Goelz, *Admin Asst*
EMP: 12
SQ FT: 5,000
SALES (est): 1.9MM **Privately Held**
SIC: **1389** 7371 1311 Oil consultants; computer software development; crude petroleum production; natural gas production

(G-10060)
JOYEAUX INC
Also Called: Seahawk Manufacturing
9802 E 58th St (74146-6409)
P.O. Box 470648 (74147-0648)
PHONE 918 252-7660
Greg Lamoreaux, *President*
Derek Davis,
EMP: 10
SQ FT: 11,000
SALES (est): 1.8MM **Privately Held**
SIC: **3061** Automotive rubber goods (mechanical)

(G-10061)
JOYS UNIFORMS BOUTIQUE LTD (PA)
Also Called: Spirit Spot
1518 S Harvard Ave (74112-5822)
PHONE 918 747-4114
Nancy Maselli, *President*
Harry Maselli, *Corp Secy*
Tani Maselli, *Vice Pres*
EMP: 9
SQ FT: 3,000
SALES (est): 1.5MM **Privately Held**
SIC: **7336** 5651 5947 5199 Silk screen design; unisex clothing stores; gift shop; novelties; souvenirs; gifts & novelties; automotive & apparel trimmings

(G-10062)
JPM PRECISION MACHINE INC
19715 E 6th St (74108-7948)
PHONE 918 739-4777
Jake Mosley, *Owner*
EMP: 6
SALES (est): 654.5K **Privately Held**
SIC: **3599** Machine shop, jobbing & repair

(G-10063)
JS METAL FABRICATION LLC
4686 N Boston Pl (74126-3142)
PHONE 918 428-2242
Jeffrey L Willis, *Principal*
EMP: 2
SALES (est): 95K **Privately Held**
SIC: **3499** Fabricated metal products

(G-10064)
JU JU JAMS
2440 E 29th St (74114-5619)
PHONE 918 230-6650
Julie Christner, *Prgrmr*
EMP: 3
SALES (est): 186K **Privately Held**
WEB: www.jujujams.com
SIC: **2033** Jams, jellies & preserves: packaged in cans, jars, etc.

(G-10065)
JUMPING BONE LLC
2825 S 124th East Ave (74129-8239)
PHONE 918 853-2836
Johnny Thao,
Barry Barker,
EMP: 2
SALES (est): 119K **Privately Held**
SIC: **3999** 7371 7389 Pet supplies; computer software development;

(G-10066)
JUNIPER NETWORKS INC
1831 E 71st St (74136-3922)
PHONE 918 877-2642
Tommy Drolinger, *Branch Mgr*
EMP: 72 **Publicly Held**
SIC: **7373** 7372 Local area network (LAN) systems integrator; prepackaged software
PA: Juniper Networks, Inc.
1133 Innovation Way
Sunnyvale CA 94089

(G-10067)
JUNO COMPANIES INCORPORATED
Also Called: Accurate Juno Engraving Co.
8702 E 41st St (74145-3310)
PHONE 918 627-8868
Donald Dickson, *President*
Jean Dickson, *Co-Owner*
EMP: 4 EST: 1958
SQ FT: 1,850
SALES (est): 382.3K **Privately Held**
SIC: **3479** 5044 Engraving jewelry silverware, or metal; cash registers

(G-10068)
JV INDUSTRIAL COMPANIES LTD
2642 E 21st St Ste 170 (74114-1743)
PHONE 918 591-5450
Robert Fudge, *Branch Mgr*
EMP: 8 **Privately Held**
SIC: **7692** 7699 Welding repair; boiler repair shop
HQ: J.V. Industrial Companies, Ltd.
527 Logwood Ave
San Antonio TX 78221
713 568-2600

(G-10069)
K W B INC (PA)
20 E 5th St Ste 1100 (74103-4416)
PHONE 918 583-8300
C Arnold Brown, *President*
William J Burk, *Treasurer*
EMP: 20
SALES (est): 3.9MM **Privately Held**
SIC: **1311** 6531 Crude petroleum production; natural gas production; real estate agents & managers

(G-10070)
K W B OIL PROPERTY MANAGEMENT (HQ)
20 E 5th St Ste 1100 (74103-4420)
PHONE 918 583-8300
C Arnold Brown, *President*
Arnold Brown, *President*
Michael H Vaughn, *VP Finance*
Michael Vaughn, *VP Finance*
EMP: 10 EST: 1963
SALES (est): 2MM
SALES (corp-wide): 3.9MM **Privately Held**
SIC: **1389** Oil field services; gas field services
PA: K W B Inc
20 E 5th St Ste 1100
Tulsa OK 74103
918 583-8300

(G-10071)
KAISER ENERGY LTD
Also Called: Kaiser Francis Oil Co
6733 S Yale Ave (74136-3302)
PHONE 918 494-0000
George Kaiser, *President*
EMP: 5
SALES (est): 408K
SALES (corp-wide): 743.7K **Privately Held**
WEB: www.kfoc.net
SIC: **1381** 1382 Drilling oil & gas wells; oil & gas exploration services
PA: G B K Holdings Inc
6733 S Yale Ave
Tulsa OK 74136
918 494-0000

(G-10072)
KAISER FRANCIS GULF COAST LLC
5001 E 68th St (74136-3315)
PHONE 918 491-4490
Don P Millican, *Principal*
EMP: 2
SALES (est): 274.9K **Privately Held**
SIC: **1381** Drilling oil & gas wells

(G-10073)
KAISER MARKETING NORTHEAST LLC
6733 S Yale Ave (74136-3302)
PHONE 918 494-0000
John Boone, *Vice Pres*
EMP: 2 EST: 2014
SALES (est): 199K **Privately Held**
SIC: **3569** Gas producers, generators & other gas related equipment

(G-10074)
KAISER-FRANCIS OIL COMPANY (HQ)
Also Called: Pilgrim Drilling Co
6733 S Yale Ave (74136-3330)
P.O. Box 21468 (74121-1468)
PHONE 918 494-0000
George B Kaiser, *President*
Brian Jobe, *General Mgr*
Wayne Fields, *Managing Dir*
Jim Willis, *COO*
Angela Swift, *Exec VP*
▲ EMP: 180
SQ FT: 55,000
SALES: 8.1MM
SALES (corp-wide): 678.5MM **Privately Held**
SIC: **1382** 1311 Oil & gas exploration services; crude petroleum & natural gas
PA: Gbk Corporation
6733 S Yale Ave
Tulsa OK 74136
918 494-0000

(G-10075)
KANE/MILLER BOOK PUBLISHERS
10302 E 55th Pl (74146-6507)
PHONE 918 346-6118
Keith Provance, *Principal*
▲ EMP: 2
SALES (est): 87.3K **Privately Held**
SIC: **2741** Miscellaneous publishing

(G-10076)
KARACON SOLUTIONS LLC
3123 E 48th St (74105-5312)
P.O. Box 7, Ketchum (74349-0007)
PHONE 918 231-1001
Kara Shilling,
EMP: 1
SALES: 100K **Privately Held**
SIC: **1521** 3444 2394 Single-family housing construction; awnings & canopies; canvas awnings & canopies

(G-10077)
KASM PUBLISHING LLC
5200 S Yale Ave (74135-7451)
PHONE 918 798-8908
EMP: 1
SALES (est): 37.5K **Privately Held**
SIC: **2741** Miscellaneous publishing

(G-10078)
KC WOODWORK & FIXTURE INC
1131 E Easton St (74120-1210)
PHONE 918 582-5300
Phil King, *President*
Cheryl King, *Admin Sec*
EMP: 2
SQ FT: 7,000
SALES (est): 275K **Privately Held**
SIC: **2434** 2521 2511 2431 Wood kitchen cabinets; wood office furniture; wood household furniture; millwork

(G-10079)
KEENER OIL & GAS COMPANY
1648 S Boston Ave Ste 200 (74119-4434)
PHONE 918 587-4154
Dewey F Bartlett Jr, *President*
Robert Fisher, *Admin Sec*
EMP: 6

▲ = Import ▼ = Export
◆ = Import/Export

GEOGRAPHIC SECTION

Tulsa - Tulsa County (G-10110)

SQ FT: 4,829
SALES (est): 983.9K **Privately Held**
SIC: **1311** Crude petroleum production; natural gas production

(G-10080)
KEL-CRETE INDUSTRIES INC
1257 E 29th St (74114-3906)
P.O. Box 52217 (74152-0217)
PHONE.................................918 744-0800
Charles Green, *President*
Jane Green, *Vice Pres*
EMP: 2
SALES (est): 1MM **Privately Held**
WEB: www.kelcrete.com
SIC: **3272** Concrete products; chemical preparations

(G-10081)
KELIX HEAT TRANSF SYSTEMS LLC
4725b S Memorial Dr (74145-6904)
PHONE.................................918 200-0996
Eric Wiklendt, *Mng Member*
EMP: 4
SALES (est): 364.5K **Privately Held**
SIC: **3826** Thermal analysis instruments, laboratory type

(G-10082)
KENNETH A WEIKEL
233 S Detroit Ave Ste 200 (74120-2420)
PHONE.................................918 582-7205
Kenneth A Weikel, *Owner*
Barbara Blackwell, *Co-Owner*
EMP: 2
SALES (est): 146.7K **Privately Held**
SIC: **1382** Oil & gas exploration services

(G-10083)
KENNETH H KNEPPER
Also Called: Knepper Kenneth H Mfg Co
1001 N Wheeling Ave (74110-4918)
PHONE.................................918 582-1954
K A Knepper, *Owner*
EMP: 2
SQ FT: 5,544
SALES (est): 150K **Privately Held**
SIC: **3599** Industrial machinery

(G-10084)
KENTON KNORPP
13142 E 44th St (74134-5807)
PHONE.................................918 629-0968
Kenton Knorpp, *Principal*
EMP: 2
SALES (est): 131.5K **Privately Held**
SIC: **1382** Geological exploration, oil & gas field

(G-10085)
KERR SALESMAKERS & MARINE INC
Also Called: Kerr Sail Makers
11429 E 20th St (74128-6403)
PHONE.................................918 437-0544
Roger Kerr, *President*
EMP: 2 EST: 1980
SQ FT: 3,000
SALES (est): 150K **Privately Held**
WEB: www.kerrsails.com
SIC: **2394** Sails: made from purchased materials

(G-10086)
KEY GENERAL CONTRACTORS LLC
8166 S Memorial Dr (74133-4309)
PHONE.................................918 280-8539
Christopher S Key, *Principal*
EMP: 7
SALES (est): 958.8K **Privately Held**
WEB: www.keyoklahoma.com
SIC: **3429** Keys, locks & related hardware

(G-10087)
KEYSTONE TEST FACILITY LLC
2111 S Atlanta Pl (74114-1709)
PHONE.................................405 213-5965
Craig Brown, *Partner*
Ann Copple, *Partner*
EMP: 2 EST: 2015
SALES (est): 174.3K **Privately Held**
SIC: **1382** Oil & gas exploration services

(G-10088)
KEYSTONE TOOL & FABRICATION
6033 E Tecumseh St (74115-4354)
PHONE.................................918 933-6100
Jerry Horton, *Regional Mgr*
EMP: 2
SALES (est): 177.1K **Privately Held**
SIC: **3599** Machine shop, jobbing & repair

(G-10089)
KIMS INTERNATIONAL OKLA INC
11516 E 58th St (74146-6829)
PHONE.................................918 250-9441
John Firstone, *President*
EMP: 7
SQ FT: 10,000
SALES (est): 1.2MM **Privately Held**
SIC: **3492** **5085** Hose & tube fittings & assemblies, hydraulic/pneumatic; hose, belting & packing; valves & fittings

(G-10090)
KINDA WILSON LLC
2950 E 76th Pl (74136-8721)
PHONE.................................405 880-5308
Kinda June Wilson, *Owner*
EMP: 2
SALES (est): 57.2K **Privately Held**
SIC: **2731** Book publishing

(G-10091)
KINGDOM ALARMS INC
1044 E Pine St (74106-4903)
P.O. Box 1503 (74101-1503)
PHONE.................................918 627-5454
Kevin Dorsey, *President*
Harvey Jones, *Vice Pres*
EMP: 10
SALES (est): 1.4MM **Privately Held**
SIC: **3699** Security control equipment & systems

(G-10092)
KISKA OIL COMPANY
6 E 5th St Ste 300 (74103-4430)
P.O. Box 35532 (74153-0532)
PHONE.................................918 584-4251
Don Bradshaw, *President*
Sally F Reid, *Corp Secy*
P E Tapp, *Vice Pres*
EMP: 1
SQ FT: 800
SALES (est): 201.3K **Privately Held**
SIC: **1311** Crude petroleum production; natural gas production

(G-10093)
KITCHEN KORNER INC
1408 S Peoria Ave (74120)
PHONE.................................918 582-9951
Troy Mansfield Jr, *President*
EMP: 3
SQ FT: 7,000
SALES (est): 250K **Privately Held**
SIC: **3469** **5722** Kitchen fixtures & equipment, porcelain enameled; household appliance stores

(G-10094)
KITE VIRGINIA
3429 E 56th Pl (74135-4136)
PHONE.................................918 747-9803
Virginia Kite, *Principal*
EMP: 3
SALES (est): 251.3K **Privately Held**
SIC: **3944** Kites

(G-10095)
KLA INDUSTRIES LLC
9802 E 45th Pl (74146-4708)
PHONE.................................918 994-2123
Scott Levy, *Administration*
EMP: 2
SALES (est): 202.6K **Privately Held**
SIC: **3825** Instruments to measure electricity

(G-10096)
KLINE OILFIELD EQUIPMENT INC
8531 E 44th St (74145-4826)
PHONE.................................918 445-0588
A Edward Kline, *President*

Sheryl Kline, *Corp Secy*
Curtis Kline, *Vice Pres*
Rick Hackathorn, *Mfg Mgr*
Bobby Caine, *Supervisor*
EMP: 30
SQ FT: 8,000
SALES (est): 7.4MM
SALES (corp-wide): 215.2MM **Privately Held**
WEB: www.klinetools.com
SIC: **3533** Bits, oil & gas field tools: rock
PA: Logan Oil Tools, Inc.
   11006 Lucerne St
   Houston TX 77016
   281 219-6613

(G-10097)
KNIGHT AUTOMATICS CO INC
6527 E Independence St (74115-7861)
PHONE.................................918 836-6122
Chuck Knight, *President*
EMP: 5
SQ FT: 4,000
SALES (est): 634.1K **Privately Held**
SIC: **3599** **3533** Machine shop, jobbing & repair; oil & gas field machinery

(G-10098)
KNOWCANDO LTD
5918 E 31st St (74135-5114)
PHONE.................................918 599-8600
EMP: 1
SALES (est): 54.3K **Privately Held**
SIC: **1311** Crude Petroleum/Natural Gas Production

(G-10099)
KOKO-BEST INC
2030 N Mingo Rd (74116-1220)
PHONE.................................918 836-2400
Joe Moore, *President*
Joseph W Martin, *Vice Pres*
EMP: 4
SALES (est): 950K **Privately Held**
SIC: **2075** Soybean oil mills

(G-10100)
KRAUSE PLASTICS (PA)
7412 E 11th St (74112-5706)
PHONE.................................918 835-4202
Arthur A Krause, *Owner*
Karl Arthur Krause, *Manager*
EMP: 5 EST: 1953
SQ FT: 1,000
SALES (est): 570.3K **Privately Held**
WEB: www.krauseplastics.com
SIC: **3089** **3993** **2789** **2672** Engraving of plastic; molding primary plastic; signs & advertising specialties; bookbinding & related work; coated & laminated paper

(G-10101)
KREBS BREWING CO INC
3733 S Wheeling Ave (74105-8133)
PHONE.................................918 740-9293
EMP: 18 **Privately Held**
WEB: www.chocbeer.com
SIC: **2082** Malt beverages
PA: Krebs Brewing Co., Inc.
   120 S 8th
   Krebs OK 74554

(G-10102)
KREBS BREWING CO INC
9435 S Hudson Ave (74137-4412)
PHONE.................................918 488-8910
Colin Healey, *Principal*
EMP: 13 **Privately Held**
SIC: **2082** Malt beverages
PA: Krebs Brewing Co., Inc.
   120 S 8th
   Krebs OK 74554

(G-10103)
KRISPY KREME
10128 E 71st St (74133-3205)
PHONE.................................918 294-5293
Aaron Suntken, *Principal*
EMP: 6
SALES (est): 181.4K **Privately Held**
WEB: www.krispykreme.com
SIC: **5461** **2051** Doughnuts; doughnuts, except frozen

(G-10104)
KSQUARED WOODWORKS LLC
6119 S Joplin Ave (74136-2107)
PHONE.................................918 496-3681
EMP: 1 EST: 2018
SALES (est): 59.5K **Privately Held**
SIC: **2431** Millwork

(G-10105)
KTAK CORPORATION
2019 E 81st St (74137-4232)
PHONE.................................918 492-0505
EMP: 1
SALES (est): 61.1K **Privately Held**
SIC: **3421** Table & food cutlery, including butchers'

(G-10106)
KZB STUDIOS LLC
5724 E 30th St (74114-6410)
PHONE.................................918 734-4399
Kyndra Z Baker, *Principal*
EMP: 1
SALES (est): 75K **Privately Held**
SIC: **3999** Hair, dressing of, for the trade

(G-10107)
L & M PATTERN MFG CO INC
10031 E 52nd St (74146-5714)
P.O. Box 470569 (74147-0569)
PHONE.................................918 663-2977
Scott Neff, *President*
Tracy Neff, *Vice Pres*
David Durand, *Treasurer*
Mark Chandler, *Controller*
Nathaniel Hale, *Sales Staff*
EMP: 8 EST: 1964
SQ FT: 9,000
SALES (est): 1.1MM **Privately Held**
WEB: www.sunengineeringinc.com
SIC: **3543** Industrial patterns

(G-10108)
L3 WESTWOOD CORPORATION
Also Called: Mc II Electric Division
12402 E 60th St (74146-6920)
PHONE.................................918 250-4444
Ernest H McKee, *President*
EMP: 175
SALES (corp-wide): 6.8B **Publicly Held**
SIC: **3621** **3661** Motors & generators; switching equipment, telephone
HQ: L3 Westwood Corporation
   12402 E 60th St
   Tulsa OK 74146
   918 252-0481

(G-10109)
L3 WESTWOOD CORPORATION
Also Called: Nmp Division
12402 E 60th St (74146-6920)
PHONE.................................918 250-4444
Ernest H McKee, *Branch Mgr*
EMP: 100
SALES (corp-wide): 6.8B **Publicly Held**
SIC: **3621** **3613** Motors & generators; switchgear & switchboard apparatus
HQ: L3 Westwood Corporation
   12402 E 60th St
   Tulsa OK 74146
   918 252-0481

(G-10110)
L3 WESTWOOD CORPORATION (DH)
Also Called: L-3 Cmmnications Westwood Corp
12402 E 60th St (74146-6920)
P.O. Box 35493 (74153-0493)
PHONE.................................918 252-0481
Clayton McClain, *President*
Ahmad Zahedi, *Vice Pres*
Lynn McGowan, *CFO*
Larry Jensen, *Director*
EMP: 165
SQ FT: 132,000
SALES (est): 49.4MM
SALES (corp-wide): 6.8B **Publicly Held**
SIC: **3621** **3613** Motors & generators; switchgear & switchboard apparatus
HQ: L3 Technologies, Inc.
   600 3rd Ave Fl 34
   New York NY 10016
   212 697-1111

(G-10111)
LA MAISON INC
1736 E 11th St (74104-3602)
PHONE..................................918 592-1222
Dick Bendel, *President*
Christopher Barry Bendel, *Vice Pres*
▲ EMP: 2
SQ FT: 5,000
SALES (est): 92.4K **Privately Held**
SIC: 3645 Boudoir lamps

(G-10112)
LAHMEYER PATTERN SHOP
2715 N Madison Ave (74106-2510)
P.O. Box 6116 (74148-0116)
PHONE..................................918 425-6008
T J Lahmeyer, *Owner*
EMP: 6 EST: 1953
SQ FT: 25,000
SALES (est): 100K **Privately Held**
SIC: 3365 5261 3543 5599 Aluminum foundries; lawnmowers & tractors; foundry patternmaking; go-carts; refrigeration service & repair

(G-10113)
LAHMEYER WELDING
65 N Madison Ave (74120-1218)
PHONE..................................918 588-2450
EMP: 2 EST: 2016
SALES (est): 81.4K **Privately Held**
SIC: 3599 Mfg Industrial Machinery

(G-10114)
LAKEWOOD DISPOSAL LLC
Also Called: West OK Disposal
6655 S Lewis Ave Ste 200 (74136-1031)
PHONE..................................918 392-9356
Timothy E Purcell, *Mng Member*
EMP: 25
SALES (est): 587.5K
SALES (corp-wide): 88.2MM **Privately Held**
SIC: 1389 Impounding & storing salt water, oil & gas field
HQ: Lakewood Midstream Llc
6655 S Lewis Ave Ste 200
Tulsa OK 74136

(G-10115)
LAKEWOOD ENERGY SOLUTIONS LLC (DH)
Also Called: Itero Energy, Inc.
6655 S Lewis Ave Ste 200 (74136-1031)
PHONE..................................918 392-9356
Michael Gruener,
Scott Schroeder,
EMP: 10 EST: 2011
SALES (est): 3MM
SALES (corp-wide): 88.2MM **Privately Held**
SIC: 1311 Crude petroleum & natural gas

(G-10116)
LAKEY PRINTING CO
2707 E 15th St (74104-4713)
PHONE..................................918 744-0158
EMP: 2
SALES (est): 83.9K **Privately Held**
SIC: 2752 Commercial printing, offset

(G-10117)
LAM RESEARCH CORPORATION
521 S Boston Ave (74103-4602)
P.O. Box 3643 (74101-3643)
PHONE..................................866 323-1834
Garnetta Glissman, *Principal*
EMP: 86
SALES (corp-wide): 9.6B **Publicly Held**
SIC: 3559 Semiconductor manufacturing machinery
PA: Lam Research Corporation
4650 Cushing Pkwy
Fremont CA 94538
510 572-0200

(G-10118)
LAMAR SYSTEMS LLC
1224 S 141st East Ave (74108-4322)
PHONE..................................918 770-0941
Jarett Boss, *Vice Pres*
Chad Boss,
EMP: 4

SALES (est): 533K **Privately Held**
SIC: 3663 Radio & TV communications equipment

(G-10119)
LAMIMA CORP
2940 E 76th St (74136-8719)
PHONE..................................918 491-6846
EMP: 2 EST: 1972
SALES (est): 200K **Privately Held**
SIC: 1311 Produces Crude Petroleum & Natural Gas

(G-10120)
LANDA MOBILE SYSTEMS LLC (PA)
2239 S Jackson Ave (74107-3011)
P.O. Box 9492 (74157-0492)
PHONE..................................360 474-8991
Michael Landa, *Mng Member*
▼ EMP: 11
SQ FT: 65,000
SALES: 4MM **Privately Held**
SIC: 3663 Antennas, transmitting & communications; mobile communication equipment

(G-10121)
LANDA MOBILE SYSTEMS LLC
2211 S Jackson Ave (74107-3011)
PHONE..................................571 272-3350
Michael Landa, *President*
EMP: 1
SALES (corp-wide): 4MM **Privately Held**
SIC: 3441 Tower sections, radio & television transmission
PA: Landa Mobile Systems, Llc
2239 S Jackson Ave
Tulsa OK 74107
360 474-8991

(G-10122)
LANDERS & MUSGROVES OIL & GAS (PA)
3884 Old Bridge Ln (74132-2171)
PHONE..................................918 623-2740
Phillip E Landers, *Partner*
EMP: 5
SALES: 31.4K **Privately Held**
SIC: 1311 Crude petroleum production; natural gas production

(G-10123)
LANGDON PUBLISHING CO INC
1603 S Boulder Ave (74119-4407)
PHONE..................................918 585-9924
Jim Langdon, *Ch of Bd*
EMP: 15
SALES (est): 1.7MM **Privately Held**
SIC: 2721 Magazines: publishing only, not printed on site

(G-10124)
LANGUAGE LINKS LLC
2459 E 23rd St (74114-3114)
PHONE..................................918 749-7350
Kathleen Plumb,
EMP: 2
SALES (est): 79.6K **Privately Held**
SIC: 3999 Education aids, devices & supplies

(G-10125)
LAREDO MIDSTREAM SERVICES LLC
15 W 6th St Ste 1800 (74119-5412)
PHONE..................................918 513-4570
Randy A Foutch, *CEO*
Hillary Rankin, *Associate*
EMP: 340
SALES (est): 10.2MM
SALES (corp-wide): 837.2MM **Publicly Held**
SIC: 1311 Crude petroleum & natural gas production
PA: Laredo Petroleum, Inc.
15 W 6th St Ste 900
Tulsa OK 74119
918 513-4570

(G-10126)
LAREDO PETROLEUM INC (PA)
15 W 6th St Ste 900 (74119-5422)
PHONE..................................918 513-4570
Randy A Foutch, *Ch of Bd*

Mark D Denny, *Senior VP*
Kenneth E Dornblaser, *Senior VP*
Daniel C Schooley, *Senior VP*
Michael T Beyer, *Vice Pres*
EMP: 43
SALES: 837.2MM **Publicly Held**
SIC: 1311 Crude petroleum & natural gas production

(G-10127)
LAREDO PETROLEUM LLC (PA)
15 W 6th St Ste 1800 (74119-5412)
PHONE..................................918 513-4570
Randy A Foutch, *CEO*
Jay P Still, *President*
Jerry R Schuyler, *President*
Peter R Kagan,
James R Levy,
EMP: 35
SALES (est): 7.2MM **Privately Held**
SIC: 1311 Crude petroleum & natural gas

(G-10128)
LAREDO PETROLEUM-DALLAS INC
15 W 6th St Ste 1800 (74119-5412)
PHONE..................................469 522-7800
David B Braddock, *CEO*
Randy A Foutch, *CEO*
John M Coss, *President*
Jay P Still, *President*
Richard C Buterbaugh, *Exec VP*
EMP: 35
SQ FT: 12,000
SALES (est): 4.7MM **Privately Held**
SIC: 1311 Crude petroleum production
PA: Laredo Petroleum, Llc
15 W 6th St Ste 1800
Tulsa OK 74119

(G-10129)
LARKIN PRODUCTS LLC (PA)
3105 Charles Page Blvd (74127-8319)
P.O. Box 3644 (74101-3644)
PHONE..................................918 584-3475
Wallace R Tipsword, *President*
Nancy T Trainor, *Treasurer*
EMP: 8
SALES (est): 4.6MM **Privately Held**
SIC: 3561 3533 Pumps, oil well & field; oil & gas field machinery

(G-10130)
LARRY MUSTIN CONSTRUCTION
2926 E 93rd Pl Apt 2101 (74137-3682)
PHONE..................................918 995-7055
Larry Mustin, *Co-Owner*
EMP: 2
SALES (est): 110K **Privately Held**
SIC: 1389 1542 7389 Construction, repair & dismantling services; commercial & office building, new construction;

(G-10131)
LASH AMOR
5840 S Memorial Dr # 203 (74145-9023)
PHONE..................................918 893-2424
Carol Singleton, *Owner*
EMP: 3 EST: 2011
SALES (est): 94.2K **Privately Held**
SIC: 3999 7231 Eyelashes, artificial; facial salons

(G-10132)
LAST STITCH STUDIO
5309 S Irvington Ave (74135-7524)
PHONE..................................918 200-5859
Kathryn Meyers, *Principal*
EMP: 1
SALES (est): 43.5K **Privately Held**
SIC: 2395 Embroidery & art needlework

(G-10133)
LASTER/CASTOR CORPORATION (PA)
1101 N 161st East Ave (74116-4000)
PHONE..................................918 234-7777
Jim Castor, *President*
Ben Laster, *Vice Pres*
EMP: 6
SQ FT: 8,000
SALES (est): 904.7K **Privately Held**
SIC: 2851 5999 5169 Paints & allied products; alcoholic beverage making equipment & supplies; chemicals & allied products

(G-10134)
LATIMERS BARBEQUE
1533 N Frankfort Pl (74106-4305)
P.O. Box 6061 (74148-0061)
PHONE..................................918 425-1242
Cecil Latimer, *Owner*
Caesar Latimer, *Co-Owner*
EMP: 2
SQ FT: 3,000
SALES (est): 90K **Privately Held**
SIC: 5812 2035 Barbecue restaurant; pickles, sauces & salad dressings

(G-10135)
LATSHAW DRILLING COMPANY LLC
4500 S 129th East Ave (74134-5801)
PHONE..................................918 355-4380
Trent Latshaw, *President*
Bill Cobb, *Exec VP*
Joseph Hudson, *Vice Pres*
Steve J McCoy, *Vice Pres*
Leroy Peterson, *Vice Pres*
EMP: 2
SALES (est): 578K **Privately Held**
SIC: 1381 Drilling oil & gas wells

(G-10136)
LAUGHING WATER ENTERPRISES LLC
Also Called: Iron Decor
1131 E Archer St (74120-1204)
PHONE..................................918 584-2080
Jason Axtell, *Manager*
Lawana Axtell, *Co-Mgr*
EMP: 7
SALES (est): 690K **Privately Held**
SIC: 3441 Fabricated structural metal for bridges

(G-10137)
LAWYER GRAPHIC SCREEN PROCESS
11332a E 19th St Ste A (74128-6400)
PHONE..................................918 438-2725
Charles Lawyer, *President*
Paul E Burris Jr, *Owner*
Wilma N Lawyer, *Corp Secy*
EMP: 3
SQ FT: 2,500
SALES (est): 220K **Privately Held**
SIC: 2759 3545 2752 2396 Screen printing; machine tool accessories; commercial printing, lithographic; automotive & apparel trimmings

(G-10138)
LAXSON INDUSTRIES LLC
6750 S Lewis Ave (74136-4032)
PHONE..................................918 494-6677
Glen Montgomery, *Principal*
EMP: 2
SALES (est): 128.9K **Privately Held**
SIC: 3999 Manufacturing industries

(G-10139)
LAYTON & SMALLWOOD
3730 S 63rd West Ave (74107-4832)
PHONE..................................918 446-6945
C R Layton, *Partner*
M Smallwood, *Partner*
EMP: 2
SALES (est): 180K **Privately Held**
SIC: 1381 Drilling oil & gas wells

(G-10140)
LAZARUS MEDICAL LLC
10805 S Marion Ave (74137-6415)
PHONE..................................918 232-6915
Brian Worley, *CEO*
EMP: 2
SALES (est): 184.4K **Privately Held**
SIC: 3841 Surgical & medical instruments

(G-10141)
LD CONSULTANTS LLC
2 W 2nd St Ste 1205 (74103-3120)
PHONE..................................432 230-1098
Rick Vanee,
EMP: 1
SALES: 150K **Privately Held**
SIC: 1389 Oil consultants

GEOGRAPHIC SECTION

Tulsa - Tulsa County (G-10174)

(G-10142)
LE GRAVIS LLC
8270 E 41st St (74145-3322)
PHONE..................................918 346-6313
Leah Gravis, *Principal*
EMP: 2 **EST:** 2015
SQ FT: 2,160
SALES (est): 156.3K **Privately Held**
SIC: 3993 Signs & advertising specialties

(G-10143)
LEAM DRILLING SYSTEMS
7136 S Yale Ave Ste 206 (74136-6356)
PHONE..................................918 794-3457
EMP: 2
SALES (est): 142.5K **Privately Held**
SIC: 1381 Oil/Gas Well Drilling

(G-10144)
LECHE LOUNGE LLC
Also Called: Leche Express
125 W 3rd St Fl 1 (74103-3427)
PHONE..................................918 409-5426
Stephanie Conduff, *CEO*
Elena Conduff, *President*
EMP: 2
SALES (est): 130.5K **Privately Held**
SIC: 3089 Prefabricated plastic buildings

(G-10145)
LECHHNER WALLCOVERING
2536 E 55th Pl (74105-7211)
PHONE..................................918 744-1742
Linus R Lechner, *Owner*
EMP: 1
SALES (est): 110K **Privately Held**
SIC: 2621 Wallpaper (hanging paper)

(G-10146)
LED SIGNS OF OKLAHOMA
10101 E 46th Pl (74146-4804)
PHONE..................................918 619-9798
EMP: 1
SALES (est): 46K **Privately Held**
SIC: 3993 Signs & advertising specialties

(G-10147)
LEDIGITAL SIGNS LLC
8922 E 88th St (74133-4400)
PHONE..................................918 504-8506
Robert M Honea,
Kelly Honea,
▲ **EMP:** 5
SALES (est): 342.6K **Privately Held**
WEB: www.ledigital.net
SIC: 3993 Electric signs

(G-10148)
LEGACY ADVNCED INTLLCTUALS LLC
7433 E 3rd St (74112-2109)
PHONE..................................707 358-0332
Eric Williams,
EMP: 4
SALES (est): 231.9K **Privately Held**
SIC: 3674 Microprocessors

(G-10149)
LEGACY SIGNS
3023 S Harvard Ave Ste G (74114-6123)
PHONE..................................918 409-0835
EMP: 1
SALES (est): 46K **Privately Held**
SIC: 3993 Signs & advertising specialties

(G-10150)
LEGAL NEWS
315 S Boulder Ave (74103-3401)
PHONE..................................918 259-7500
Jamey Honeycutt, *General Mgr*
EMP: 3
SALES (est): 111.3K **Privately Held**
SIC: 2711 Newspapers, publishing & printing

(G-10151)
LEGION ENERGY LLC
8801 S Yale Ave Ste 100 (74137-3513)
P.O. Box 382, Davenport (74026-0382)
PHONE..................................918 895-8785
EMP: 4
SALES (est): 561.1K **Privately Held**
SIC: 1311 Crude Petroleum/Natural Gas Production

(G-10152)
LEKTRON INC
Also Called: Lektron Led Technology
4111 S 74th East Ave (74136-4706)
PHONE..................................918 622-4978
Johnny Hillenberg, *Opers Mgr*
Gordon Gray, *Engineer*
Kevin Rubottom, *Accounts Mgr*
◆ **EMP:** 20
SALES (est): 5.3MM **Privately Held**
SIC: 3674 Light emitting diodes

(G-10153)
LEONARD MOUNTAIN INC
4401 S 72nd East Ave (74145-4626)
P.O. Box 67, Leonard (74043-0067)
PHONE..................................800 822-7700
Fred Berckefeldt, *CEO*
Deborah Berckefeldt, *President*
▲ **EMP:** 30
SQ FT: 23,000
SALES (est): 948.8K **Privately Held**
SIC: 2033 2034 5149 Vegetables: packaged in cans, jars, etc.; soup mixes; dried or canned foods

(G-10154)
LETTERCRAFTS
Also Called: Sport Signs
4148 S 70th East Ave (74145-4605)
PHONE..................................918 584-2400
Mike Hendrickson, *President*
EMP: 6
SALES (est): 400K **Privately Held**
SIC: 3993 Signs, not made in custom sign painting shops

(G-10155)
LEXSO T SHIRT PRINTING
10863 E 15th St (74128-4873)
PHONE..................................918 861-0772
EMP: 2
SALES (est): 83.9K **Privately Held**
SIC: 2752 Commercial printing, lithographic

(G-10156)
LIBERTY FENCE CO INC (PA)
6901 E 11th St (74112-4621)
PHONE..................................918 834-6553
Dewayne C Thetford, *President*
Paula Thetford, *Corp Secy*
EMP: 4
SQ FT: 7,000
SALES (est): 741K **Privately Held**
SIC: 1799 3446 3496 Fence construction; architectural metalwork; miscellaneous fabricated wire products

(G-10157)
LIBERTY SIGNS
3109 S Jamestown Ave (74135-4407)
PHONE..................................918 409-4470
Joe Btesh, *Principal*
EMP: 1
SALES (est): 82.4K **Privately Held**
SIC: 3993 Signs & advertising specialties

(G-10158)
LIFE IMPACT PUBLISHING LLC
9916 S 107th East Ave (74133-5117)
PHONE..................................918 407-9938
Jacob Andrew Provance, *Principal*
EMP: 1 **EST:** 2018
SALES (est): 37.5K **Privately Held**
SIC: 2741 Miscellaneous publishing

(G-10159)
LIFT TECHNOLOGIES INC
5162 S 24th West Ave (74107-9045)
P.O. Box 471676 (74147-1676)
PHONE..................................918 794-8088
David Black, *President*
Jennifer Black, *Corp Secy*
▲ **EMP:** 9 **EST:** 2005
SALES (est): 1.6MM **Privately Held**
WEB: www.lifttechnologiesinc.com
SIC: 3537 Lift trucks, industrial: fork, platform, straddle, etc.

(G-10160)
LIGHTBE CORPORATION
2713 S 79th East Ave (74129-2702)
PHONE..................................918 760-6968
Pamela Cook, *CEO*
Bernard Dreyer, *Exec VP*
EMP: 2
SALES (est): 159.8K **Privately Held**
SIC: 7372 8742 8748 7371 Application computer software; business oriented computer software; educational computer software; management consulting services; systems engineering consultant, ex. computer or professional; computer software writing services; computer software writers, freelance; computer software development & applications

(G-10161)
LIMCO AIREPAIR INC (DH)
5304 S Lawton Ave (74107-9428)
PHONE..................................918 445-4300
Yair Raz, *President*
Sheila Shaikho, *Senior Buyer*
Fallon Salazar, *Buyer*
Christopher Dintelmann, *Engineer*
Mary Dowdy, *CFO*
▲ **EMP:** 93
SQ FT: 70,000
SALES (est): 29.8MM **Privately Held**
WEB: www.limcoairepair.com
SIC: 3728 3724 Aircraft parts & equipment; aircraft engines & engine parts

(G-10162)
LIMCO-PIEDMONT INC (HQ)
5304 S Lawton Ave (74107-9428)
PHONE..................................918 445-4300
Shmuel Fledel, *Ch of Bd*
Yair Raz, *President*
EMP: 19
SQ FT: 55,000
SALES (est): 29.8MM **Privately Held**
SIC: 4581 3728 Aircraft maintenance & repair services; aircraft parts & equipment

(G-10163)
LINDA L HARGRAVES
Also Called: Computer Xpressions
828 S Wheeling Ave # 207 (74104-3635)
PHONE..................................918 584-3442
Linda Hargraves, *Owner*
EMP: 1
SALES (est): 44.2K **Privately Held**
SIC: 3944 Craft & hobby kits & sets

(G-10164)
LINDE ENGINEERING N AMER LLC (DH)
6100 S Yale Ave Ste 1200 (74136-1905)
PHONE..................................918 477-1424
Jason Uthe, *CEO*
Carlos Conerly, *President*
William Gibson, *Principal*
John Martin, *Principal*
Tamara Volmer, *Principal*
◆ **EMP:** 105
SALES (est): 97.5MM **Privately Held**
SIC: 3443 8711 Fabricated plate work (boiler shop); engineering services
HQ: Linde Holdings, Llc
6100 S Yale Ave Ste 1200
Tulsa OK 74136
918 477-1424

(G-10165)
LINDE ENGINEERING N AMER LLC
6100 S Yale Ave Ste 1200 (74136-1905)
PHONE..................................281 717-9090
Grant McCool, *Plant Engr*
EMP: 1 **Privately Held**
SIC: 3567 8711 Incinerators, metal: domestic or commercial; industrial engineers
HQ: Linde Engineering North America Llc
6100 S Yale Ave Ste 1200
Tulsa OK 74136
918 477-1424

(G-10166)
LINK OIL COMPANY
427 S Boston Ave Ste 1000 (74103-4115)
PHONE..................................918 585-8343
Robert B Lyon Sr, *President*
Barbara Crussell, *Corp Secy*
EMP: 5 **EST:** 1907
SALES (est): 640K **Privately Held**
SIC: 1311 Crude petroleum production; natural gas production

(G-10167)
LITGISTIX LLC
Also Called: Copyshop Printing Downtown
5 E 5th St (74103-4401)
PHONE..................................918 585-5875
Brian Grossman,
Chris Sloan,
EMP: 20 **EST:** 1980
SQ FT: 7,000
SALES (est): 3MM **Privately Held**
SIC: 2789 Bookbinding & related work

(G-10168)
LITHAPRINT INC
802 W 1st St (74127-8714)
PHONE..................................918 587-7746
Billy Thresher, *President*
Ron Thresher, *Vice Pres*
Judy Wyers, *Admin Sec*
EMP: 11
SQ FT: 5,000
SALES (est): 1.6MM **Privately Held**
WEB: www.lithaprint.com
SIC: 2752 2791 2789 Commercial printing, offset; typesetting; bookbinding & related work

(G-10169)
LIVELY PRINTING
6365 E 41st St (74135-6110)
P.O. Box 471881 (74147-1881)
PHONE..................................918 582-3668
V J Lively, *Owner*
EMP: 2
SQ FT: 3,600
SALES (est): 140K **Privately Held**
SIC: 2752 Commercial printing, offset

(G-10170)
LIVERPOOL PRODUCTION COMPANY
Also Called: Priam Oil
2642 E 21st St Ste 288 (74114-1789)
P.O. Box 35979 (74153-0979)
PHONE..................................918 523-9595
Robert Mase, *President*
EMP: 2
SALES (est): 208.5K **Privately Held**
SIC: 1311 Crude petroleum & natural gas production

(G-10171)
LKQ CORPORATION
Also Called: Lkq Self Service
7600 Charles Page Blvd (74127-7158)
PHONE..................................918 428-3835
Jeff Maice, *General Mgr*
EMP: 15
SALES (corp-wide): 12.5B **Publicly Held**
SIC: 5531 3531 5399 Automotive parts; automobile wrecker hoists; surplus & salvage goods
PA: Lkq Corporation
500 W Madison St Ste 2800
Chicago IL 60661
312 621-1950

(G-10172)
LLOYD WORDS LLC
Also Called: Rebel Press
5906 S Knoxville Ave (74135-7805)
PHONE..................................918 457-6852
Grant Lloyd,
Karen Lloyd,
EMP: 2
SALES (est): 90.9K **Privately Held**
SIC: 2731 Book publishing

(G-10173)
LMI AEROSPACE INC
16900 Tiger Switch Rd (74116-4819)
PHONE..................................918 281-0124
Billy Sapp, *Branch Mgr*
EMP: 22 **Privately Held**
SIC: 3369 Aerospace castings, nonferrous: except aluminum
HQ: Lmi Aerospace, Inc.
411 Fountain Lakes Blvd
Saint Charles MO 63301
636 946-6525

(G-10174)
LMI FINISHING INC
2104 N 170th East Ave (74116-4919)
PHONE..................................918 438-1012

Ronald Saks, *President*
▲ **EMP:** 80
SQ FT: 75,000
SALES (est): 12MM **Privately Held**
SIC: 3728 3471 Aircraft parts & equipment; plating & polishing
HQ: Lmi Aerospace, Inc.
411 Fountain Lakes Blvd
Saint Charles MO 63301
636 946-6525

(G-10175)
LOBITO TECHNOLOGY GROUP INC
11605 E 27th St N Ste B (74116-3606)
PHONE..........................918 619-9885
Jaime Ballesteros, *President*
Marcelo Rinaldis, *Vice Pres*
EMP: 12
SALES (est): 1.4MM **Privately Held**
SIC: 3569 Assembly machines, non-metalworking

(G-10176)
LOGO MARKETING COMPANY INC
3730 E 82nd St (74137-1633)
PHONE..........................918 496-2989
Robert T Montgomery, *President*
Elizabeth Montgomery, *Vice Pres*
Lorin H Smith, *Vice Pres*
EMP: 6
SQ FT: 4,000
SALES: 1.7MM **Privately Held**
SIC: 3663 Cellular radio telephone

(G-10177)
LONE STAR INDUSTRIES INC
8242 S Harvard Ave Ste D (74137-1648)
PHONE..........................918 492-2121
Gerry McBride, *Manager*
EMP: 4
SALES (corp-wide): 395.5MM **Privately Held**
SIC: 3241 Portland cement
HQ: Lone Star Industries Inc
10401 N Meridian St # 120
Indianapolis IN 46290
317 706-3314

(G-10178)
LONEWLF WELDING
13005 E 30th St (74134-2435)
PHONE..........................918 625-9128
EMP: 1
SALES (est): 43.2K **Privately Held**
SIC: 7692 Welding repair

(G-10179)
LOVE LETTERS MONOGRAMMING LLC
5507 E 109th St (74137-7245)
PHONE..........................918 231-6691
EMP: 1 **EST:** 2015
SALES (est): 40.8K **Privately Held**
SIC: 2395 Embroidery & art needlework

(G-10180)
LOWERY WELL HEADS INC
5908 E Tecumseh St (74115-4322)
P.O. Box 582565 (74158-2565)
PHONE..........................918 836-1760
Donald W Walford, *President*
Paula R Lowery, *Treasurer*
EMP: 9
SQ FT: 20,000
SALES (est): 1.7MM **Privately Held**
SIC: 3533 Oil field machinery & equipment

(G-10181)
LOWRY EXPLORATION INC
616 S Boston Ave Ste 402 (74119-1216)
PHONE..........................918 587-5094
R G Lowry, *President*
EMP: 2
SQ FT: 750
SALES: 450K **Privately Held**
SIC: 1382 Oil & gas exploration services

(G-10182)
LUCKY 13 MOTORCYCLE SHOP
Also Called: Lucky 13 Salvage
636 W 14th St (74127-9168)
PHONE..........................816 808-0985
EMP: 10

SALES: 49K **Privately Held**
SIC: 2411 Logging

(G-10183)
LUMEN ENERGY CORPORATION (DH)
Also Called: Lumen Midstream Partnership
4200 E Skelly Dr Ste 760 (74135-3214)
PHONE..........................918 584-0052
Mike Hicks, *President*
Brian J Briscoe, *President*
Barbara Eickman, *Principal*
Raymond C Kane, *Exec VP*
Thomas B Williams, *Exec VP*
EMP: 11
SQ FT: 7,000
SALES (est): 4.8MM **Privately Held**
SIC: 1389 Gas compressing (natural gas) at the fields
HQ: Aka Energy Group, Llc
65 Mercado St Ste 250
Durango CO 81301
970 764-6650

(G-10184)
LUX GROOMING QUARTERS LLC
1821 W Queen St (74127-2543)
PHONE..........................918 259-9910
EMP: 1
SALES (est): 49.1K **Privately Held**
SIC: 3131 Mfg Footwear Cut Stock

(G-10185)
LYNXSYSTEMS LLC
11415 E 19th St Ste B (74128-6412)
PHONE..........................918 728-6000
Bill Morgan,
Shon Logsdon,
EMP: 2 **EST:** 2007
SALES (est): 1.6MM **Privately Held**
WEB: www.lynxsystemsusa.com
SIC: 2298 4813 7382 Cable, fiber; telephone cable service, land or submarine; protective devices, security

(G-10186)
LYONS & LYONS INC
1519 S Baltimore Ave (74119-4005)
P.O. Box 14148 (74159-1148)
PHONE..........................918 587-2497
Trevor Lyons, *President*
EMP: 3
SQ FT: 2,700
SALES (est): 572K **Privately Held**
SIC: 6792 1311 1389 Oil royalty traders; crude petroleum & natural gas; oil consultants

(G-10187)
M & M MATTRESS COMPANY
717 N Sheridan Rd (74115-7830)
PHONE..........................918 834-2033
Ken Madewell Jr, *Partner*
EMP: 3
SQ FT: 12,000
SALES (est): 373.7K **Privately Held**
WEB: www.mandmmattress.com
SIC: 2515 Mattresses, innerspring or box spring; mattresses, containing felt, foam rubber, urethane, etc.

(G-10188)
M CRAIG DEISENROTH OIL & GAS
1924 S Utica Ave Ste 540 (74104-6511)
PHONE..........................918 742-4769
Craig Deisenroth,
EMP: 5 **EST:** 2012
SQ FT: 1,500
SALES (est): 349.4K **Privately Held**
SIC: 1311 Crude petroleum & natural gas production

(G-10189)
M T H INC
2526 W 68th Pl (74132-1749)
PHONE..........................918 445-9235
Sheila Trompler, *Principal*
Lenee Condray, *Principal*
Charles Trompler, *Principal*
EMP: 3
SALES (est): 263K **Privately Held**
SIC: 2353 Hats & caps

(G-10190)
M W BEVINS CO
Also Called: Bevins Co
9903 E 54th St (74146-5718)
PHONE..........................918 627-1273
Richard Bevins Jr, *President*
Mike Cotner, *Vice Pres*
Denver Kimberlin, *VP Engrg*
Heather Bevins, *Office Mgr*
Cameron Beckfield, *Info Tech Mgr*
▲ **EMP:** 23
SQ FT: 12,800
SALES: 608.2K **Privately Held**
WEB: www.bevinsco.com
SIC: 3423 3825 Hand & edge tools; instruments to measure electricity

(G-10191)
M&M PRECISION COMPONENTS LLC
13914 E Admiral Pl Ste A (74116-2107)
PHONE..........................918 933-6500
Al Altieri, *CEO*
Rocky Payton, *General Mgr*
EMP: 86 **EST:** 2015
SQ FT: 43,733
SALES (est): 13MM
SALES (corp-wide): 16.9MM **Privately Held**
SIC: 3545 Precision tools, machinists'
PA: Whi Global, Llc
90 New Dutch Ln
Fairfield NJ 07004
855 944-4562

(G-10192)
M&T PRODUCTION CO
4412 W 91st St (74132-3742)
PHONE..........................918 227-1528
Thomas Mac Laskey, *President*
EMP: 2
SALES (est): 144.7K **Privately Held**
SIC: 1311 Crude petroleum & natural gas

(G-10193)
MACCOR INC
4322 S 49th West Ave (74107-6100)
PHONE..........................918 445-1874
Andrew Mackay, *President*
Deonn Odell, *Human Res Dir*
EMP: 72
SQ FT: 70,000
SALES (est): 25.3MM **Privately Held**
SIC: 3825 Battery testers, electrical

(G-10194)
MACHINE WORKS LLC
220 N Boston Ave (74103-2018)
PHONE..........................918 584-6496
EMP: 2 **EST:** 2010
SALES (est): 71.8K **Privately Held**
WEB: www.machineworksllc.com
SIC: 3599 Machine shop, jobbing & repair

(G-10195)
MACHINE WORKS LLC
6767 E Virgin St (74115-3647)
P.O. Box 380 (74101-0380)
PHONE..........................405 205-4206
Brian Wernimont, *Owner*
EMP: 2 **EST:** 2008
SALES (est): 107.4K **Privately Held**
SIC: 3566 Speed changers, drives & gears

(G-10196)
MACS ELECTRIC SUPPLY COMPANY (PA)
1624 E 3rd St (74120-2808)
PHONE..........................918 583-3101
Jack McGlumphy, *President*
Joe Goeser, *Sales Staff*
EMP: 10 **EST:** 1965
SQ FT: 77,000
SALES (est): 3MM **Privately Held**
WEB: www.macselectricsupply.com
SIC: 5063 3471 5812 Electrical supplies; electroplating & plating; eating places

(G-10197)
MADISON AVENUE FIREARMS LLC
3111 S Madison Ave (74105-2019)
PHONE..........................918 629-6910
Masaru Iwata, *President*
Kathryn Iwata, *Vice Pres*

EMP: 3
SALES (est): 146.6K **Privately Held**
SIC: 8711 3484 Mechanical engineering; guns (firearms) or gun parts, 30 mm. & below

(G-10198)
MADISON FILTER INCORPORATED
11607 E 43rd St N (74116-2103)
PHONE..........................315 685-3466
Mark Angus, *Manager*
EMP: 5
SALES (est): 416.3K **Privately Held**
WEB: www.clear-edge.com
SIC: 2393 Textile bags

(G-10199)
MADISON MACHINE COMPANIES INC
Also Called: M.M.C. I.
65 N Madison Ave (74120-1218)
P.O. Box 14464 (74159-1464)
PHONE..........................918 584-6496
Richard Caudle, *President*
Brian Wernimont, *Vice Pres*
EMP: 10
SALES (est): 1.2MM **Privately Held**
SIC: 3599 Machine shop, jobbing & repair

(G-10200)
MAGGIE COMPANY INC
5109 W 31st St N (74127)
PHONE..........................918 438-7800
Ron Hall, *Manager*
EMP: 20
SALES (corp-wide): 187MM **Privately Held**
SIC: 3621 Motors & generators
HQ: Maggie Company, Inc.
206 E Reynolds Dr Ste E2
Ruston LA
318 255-7400

(G-10201)
MAGNUM RACING COMPONENTS INC
Also Called: Magnum Racing Componets
4632 S 102nd East Ave (74146-4827)
PHONE..........................918 627-0204
Michael Greene, *President*
Michael Mickey Greene, *President*
Stacy England, *Manager*
EMP: 1
SQ FT: 4,784
SALES (est): 123.2K **Privately Held**
SIC: 3089 3714 Automotive parts, plastic; motor vehicle parts & accessories

(G-10202)
MAGNUM SCREEN PRINT INC
Also Called: Magnum Screen Printing
7636 E 46th St (74145-6304)
P.O. Box 35157 (74153-0157)
PHONE..........................918 665-7636
James H Maness, *President*
Michael Maness, *Exec VP*
Michelle Maness, *Treasurer*
EMP: 6
SQ FT: 12,500
SALES (est): 866.5K **Privately Held**
SIC: 2759 2396 Screen printing; automotive & apparel trimmings

(G-10203)
MAINSTREAM MANUFACTURING LLC
8170 S 40th West Ave (74132-3005)
PHONE..........................918 447-1008
Melissa Ray, *Principal*
EMP: 2
SALES (est): 48K **Privately Held**
SIC: 3999 Manufacturing industries

(G-10204)
MAJESKA & ASSOCIATES LLC
1540 N 107th East Ave (74116-1512)
PHONE..........................918 576-6878
Brian Majeska, *Mng Member*
Buddy Clark,
David M Reynolds,
EMP: 13

GEOGRAPHIC SECTION

Tulsa - Tulsa County (G-10232)

SALES (est): 895.3K **Privately Held**
SIC: **8742** 8732 2951 Marketing consulting services; market analysis or research; market analysis, business & economic research; asphalt paving mixtures & blocks

(G-10205)
MAKEFIELD OIL CO
7170 S Braden Ave (74136-6329)
PHONE..................................918 492-1463
Doug Farquharson, *President*
EMP: 1
SALES (est): 94K **Privately Held**
WEB: www.makefieldoil.com
SIC: **1382** Oil & gas exploration services

(G-10206)
MALCO INCORPORATED
1120 E 1st St (74120-2001)
PHONE..................................918 876-1934
Earl F Malherbe Jr, *Principal*
Mike Alexander, *Principal*
Dianne Malherbe, *Principal*
Jesse Poe, *Manager*
◆ EMP: 24
SALES (est): 5MM **Privately Held**
SIC: **3462** Anchors, forged

(G-10207)
MARATHON OIL COMPANY
15 E 5th St Ste 1100 (74103-4361)
P.O. Box 147, Houston TX (77001-0147)
PHONE..................................866 323-1836
Mike Lawson, *Principal*
EMP: 1
SALES (corp-wide): 5.1B **Publicly Held**
WEB: www.marathonoil.com
SIC: **5541** 1382 Gasoline service stations; oil & gas exploration services
HQ: Marathon Oil Company
5555 San Felipe St B1
Houston TX 77056
713 629-6600

(G-10208)
MARCO INDUSTRIES INC (PA)
4150 S 100th East Ave # 301 (74146-3662)
P.O. Box 54640 (74155-4640)
PHONE..................................918 622-4535
Mark Polumbus, *President*
David Piersol, *Opers Staff*
George Allaster Jr, *Sales Staff*
Jose Castro, *Sales Staff*
Gary Demarco, *Sales Staff*
▲ EMP: 97
SALES: 31.2MM **Privately Held**
SIC: **3448** Prefabricated metal buildings

(G-10209)
MARIS HEALTH LLC
6936 E 13th St (74112-5616)
PHONE..................................888 429-1117
Amanda Holcomb, *Mng Member*
James R Holcomb, *Mng Member*
▼ EMP: 2 EST: 2016
SALES (est): 286.1K **Privately Held**
SIC: **8082** 3842 5999 Home health care services; braces, orthopedic; medical apparatus & supplies

(G-10210)
MARJO OIL COMPANY INC
427 S Boston Ave (74103-4141)
P.O. Box 729 (74101-0729)
PHONE..................................918 583-0241
Joseph F Mueller, *President*
Marie Mueller, *Treasurer*
EMP: 8
SQ FT: 10,000
SALES (est): 717.2K **Privately Held**
SIC: **1311** Crude petroleum production; natural gas production

(G-10211)
MARJO OPERATING CO INC
427 S Boston Ave Ste 240 (74103-4100)
P.O. Box 729 (74101-0729)
PHONE..................................918 583-0241
Mark Meador, *President*
EMP: 7
SQ FT: 900
SALES (est): 1.2MM **Privately Held**
SIC: **8711** 1311 Petroleum engineering; crude petroleum production

(G-10212)
MARK WEST HYDROCARBON INC
2448 E 81st St Ste 5400 (74137-4324)
PHONE..................................800 730-8388
EMP: 3 EST: 2015
SALES (est): 233.9K **Privately Held**
SIC: **1321** Natural gas liquids

(G-10213)
MARKWEST ENRGY E TEXAS GAS LP (DH)
2448 E 81st St Ste 5400 (74137-4324)
PHONE..................................918 477-8000
Frank M Semple, *CEO*
Randy S Nickerson, *President*
John C Mollenkopf, *COO*
C Corwin Bromley, *Exec VP*
Nancy K Buese, *CFO*
EMP: 17
SALES (est): 6.3MM
SALES (corp-wide): 9B **Publicly Held**
SIC: **1382** Oil & gas exploration services
HQ: Markwest Energy Partners, L.P.
1515 Arapahoe St
Denver CO 80202
303 925-9200

(G-10214)
MARKWEST PIONEER LLC
2448 E 81st St Ste 5400 (74137-4324)
PHONE..................................918 477-8000
Kevin Kubat, *Manager*
EMP: 8
SALES: 13.1MM
SALES (corp-wide): 9B **Publicly Held**
SIC: **1321** Natural gas liquids
HQ: Markwest Energy Partners, L.P.
1515 Arapahoe St
Denver CO 80202
303 925-9200

(G-10215)
MARO INTERNATIONAL CORP (PA)
3250 N Sheridan Rd (74115-2310)
PHONE..................................918 836-7749
Robert Reed Moore, *CEO*
Rudy Heaton, *President*
Elizabeth V Moore, *Corp Secy*
EMP: 3 EST: 1960
SQ FT: 49,500
SALES (est): 2.4MM **Privately Held**
WEB: www.marointernationalcorp.com
SIC: **3442** 3648 Louver doors, metal; airport lighting fixtures: runway approach, taxi or ramp

(G-10216)
MARRARA GROUP INC
Also Called: Oakwood Graphics
5150 S 94th East Ave (74145-8172)
PHONE..................................918 379-0993
Michael Marrara, *President*
Michelle Boudreaux, *Vice Pres*
EMP: 7
SQ FT: 3,000
SALES: 650K **Privately Held**
SIC: **2499** 3993 Signboards, wood; signs & advertising specialties

(G-10217)
MART TROPHY CO INC
2901 E 73rd St (74136-5631)
PHONE..................................918 481-3388
Albert F Cuite, *President*
EMP: 2
SQ FT: 2,500
SALES: 175K **Privately Held**
SIC: **3999** 3499 3993 Plaques, picture, laminated; trophies, metal, except silver; signs & advertising specialties

(G-10218)
MARVEL PHOTO INC (PA)
Also Called: Databadge
1720 N Sheridan Rd (74115-4624)
PHONE..................................918 836-0741
Anthony Perrault, *President*
EMP: 7
SQ FT: 14,000
SALES (est): 984.8K **Privately Held**
WEB: www.databadgeid.com
SIC: **3861** 7221 7359 3577 Cameras, still & motion picture (all types); passport photographer; photographic equipment rental; computer peripheral equipment; paper industries machinery; coated & laminated paper

(G-10219)
MASSOUDS FINE JWLY & ARTSPACE
Also Called: Massouds A Fine Jwly Dsgn Std
6540 E 51st St (74145-7603)
PHONE..................................918 663-4884
Massoud Moheb, *President*
Kathy Moheb, *Vice Pres*
EMP: 5 EST: 1982
SQ FT: 800
SALES (est): 478K **Privately Held**
SIC: **5944** 7631 3911 Jewelry, precious stones & precious metals; watches; jewelry repair services; jewelry, precious metal

(G-10220)
MASTER KRAFT TOOLING CORP
425 S 122nd East Ave (74128-2425)
PHONE..................................918 437-2366
Milton Whitmarsh, *President*
T Ray Abernathie, *Vice Pres*
Marketta Abernathie, *Treasurer*
Claudia Whitmarsh, *Admin Sec*
▲ EMP: 20
SQ FT: 26,000
SALES (est): 3.4MM **Privately Held**
WEB: www.mktooling.com
SIC: **3599** 3544 Machine shop, jobbing & repair; special dies, tools, jigs & fixtures

(G-10221)
MASTERS TECHNICAL ADVISORS INC
12002 S Pittsburg Ave (74137-1651)
PHONE..................................918 949-1641
Christopher Masters, *Principal*
EMP: 5
SALES (est): 117.7K **Privately Held**
SIC: **7375** 7372 7371 On-line data base information retrieval; application computer software; computer software systems analysis & design, custom

(G-10222)
MATHEY DEARMAN INC
10541 E Ute St (74116-1522)
PHONE..................................918 447-1288
Doug Hughes, *CEO*
John D Hughes, *President*
Larry Ashmore, *Vice Pres*
Kevin Dooley, *Vice Pres*
Frank McCauley, *Vice Pres*
▲ EMP: 32
SQ FT: 24,000
SALES (est): 9.6MM **Privately Held**
SIC: **3533** 5084 3549 Oil & gas field machinery; welding machinery & equipment; metalworking machinery

(G-10223)
MATHEY DEARMAN INC
1851 N 106th East Ave (74116-1510)
PHONE..................................918 447-1288
EMP: 4
SALES (est): 505.1K **Privately Held**
SIC: **3533** Oil & gas field machinery

(G-10224)
MAUVAISTERRE PUBLISHING LLC
5727 E 62nd St (74136-2713)
PHONE..................................918 492-3846
Robert Miller, *Principal*
EMP: 1
SALES (est): 37.5K **Privately Held**
SIC: **2741** Miscellaneous publishing

(G-10225)
MAVERICK ENERGY GROUP LTD (PA)
406 S Boulder Ave Ste 708 (74103-3862)
P.O. Box 14018 (74159-1018)
PHONE..................................918 764-4081
James McCabe, *CEO*
Richard Bednar, *President*
Brice Bogle, *CFO*
EMP: 25
SQ FT: 3,500
SALES (est): 3.4MM **Privately Held**
SIC: **1382** Oil & gas exploration services

(G-10226)
MAYCO FIXTURE CO INC
2400 N Lewis Ave (74110-2122)
PHONE..................................918 428-5305
Mark Yates, *President*
Ron Bonner, *Project Mgr*
Renee Juby, *Admin Asst*
EMP: 10
SQ FT: 25,000
SALES (est): 1.5MM **Privately Held**
WEB: www.maycofixture.com
SIC: **2542** Partitions & fixtures, except wood

(G-10227)
MBC GRAPHICS
316 S Rockford Ave (74120-2821)
P.O. Box 4608 (74159-0608)
PHONE..................................918 585-2321
Marjorie Conley, *President*
Claudia Hamilton, *Vice Pres*
EMP: 7
SQ FT: 2,000
SALES (est): 551.8K **Privately Held**
SIC: **2752** 2796 2759 2396 Commercial printing, offset; platemaking services; commercial printing; automotive & apparel trimmings

(G-10228)
MCCABE INDUSTRIAL MINERALS (PA)
7225 S 85th East Ave # 400 (74133-3157)
PHONE..................................918 252-5090
Henry F McCabe, *Ch of Bd*
Verne L McCabe, *President*
Joann McCabe, *Corp Secy*
EMP: 6 EST: 1976
SQ FT: 1,400
SALES (est): 4.3MM **Privately Held**
SIC: **3295** 2952 Minerals, ground or treated; asphalt felts & coatings

(G-10229)
MCCABE INDUSTRIAL MNRL CORP
7225 S 85th East Ave # 400 (74133-3157)
PHONE..................................918 252-5090
Henry F McCabe, *CEO*
Vern McCabe, *President*
EMP: 19
SQ FT: 500
SALES (est): 1MM **Privately Held**
SIC: **3295** Minerals, ground or treated

(G-10230)
MCCLURE FURNITURE REFINISHING
4107 S 72nd East Ave (74145-4608)
PHONE..................................918 587-7779
Fax: 918 587-7779
EMP: 2
SQ FT: 5,700
SALES (est): 125K **Privately Held**
SIC: **3429** Furniture Builders And Other Household Hardware

(G-10231)
MCCUTCHEN ENTERPRISES INC
Also Called: McCutchen Welding
17408 E Pine St (74116-4927)
P.O. Box 692, Catoosa (74015-0692)
PHONE..................................918 234-7406
William Robert Mc Cutchen, *President*
EMP: 2
SQ FT: 2,000
SALES: 100K **Privately Held**
SIC: **3444** 7692 1799 Sheet metalwork; welding repair; welding on site

(G-10232)
MCELROY MANUFACTURING INC (PA)
833 N Fulton Ave (74115-6408)
P.O. Box 580550 (74158-0550)
PHONE..................................918 836-8611
Arthur H McElroy II, *President*
William A Goffe, *Principal*

Jack H Santee, *Principal*
Peggy M Tanner, *Exec VP*
Curtis Mora, *Plant Mgr*
◆ **EMP:** 560
SQ FT: 230,000
SALES (est): 144MM **Privately Held**
WEB: www.mcelroy.com
SIC: 3599 Machine shop, jobbing & repair

(G-10233)
MCF SERVICES INC
8177 S Harvard Ave (74137-1612)
PHONE..................918 481-1620
Ivan J McFarland, *Director*
EMP: 3
SALES (est): 195.4K **Privately Held**
SIC: 3272 Concrete products

(G-10234)
MCNALLY AND ASSOCIATES INC
Also Called: McNally Printing
505 S Quaker Ave (74120-4011)
P.O. Box 1570, Sand Springs (74063-1570)
PHONE..................918 587-7068
Mike McNally, *President*
Gail Mc Nally, *Corp Secy*
EMP: 9
SQ FT: 4,400
SALES: 1MM **Privately Held**
SIC: 7389 2752 Personal investigation service; commercial printing, lithographic

(G-10235)
MEAGHER ENERGY ADVISORS INC
1731 E 71st St (74136-5108)
PHONE..................918 481-5900
Matthew E Meagher, *Branch Mgr*
EMP: 10 **Privately Held**
SIC: 1389 Oil consultants
PA: Meagher Energy Advisors Inc
6040 Greenwood Plaza Blvd
Greenwood Village CO 80111

(G-10236)
MECCO EDGEMONT CLUTCH CO INC
308 S Lansing Ave (74120-2433)
P.O. Box 52373 (74152-0373)
PHONE..................918 583-3060
Harry R Aschan, *President*
EMP: 1
SQ FT: 6,000
SALES (est): 190K **Privately Held**
SIC: 3568 Clutches, except vehicular

(G-10237)
MEDALLION PETROLEUM INC
2021 S Lewis Ave (74104-5733)
PHONE..................918 582-1320
John A Brock, *CEO*
William E Warnock Jr, *President*
Christopher Girouard, *Vice Pres*
▲ **EMP:** 4
SALES (est): 273.8K **Privately Held**
SIC: 1311 Crude petroleum production; natural gas production

(G-10238)
MEDIA SPECIALISTS INC
5333 S Mingo Rd Ste E (74146-5744)
PHONE..................918 622-0077
Corinne Dalby, *President*
EMP: 6
SQ FT: 2,000
SALES (est): 300K **Privately Held**
SIC: 3651 5065 Television receiving sets; electronic parts & equipment

(G-10239)
MEEKS LITHOGRAPHING COMPANY
Also Called: Meeks Group, Prepress Division
6913 E 13th St (74112-5615)
PHONE..................918 838-9900
Brian Procknow, *Manager*
EMP: 3
SALES (corp-wide): 6.6MM **Privately Held**
WEB: www.meeksgroup.com
SIC: 2752 2791 2789 Commercial printing, lithographic; typesetting; bookbinding & related work
PA: Meeks Lithographing Company
6913 E 13th St
Tulsa OK 74112
918 836-0900

(G-10240)
MEEKS LITHOGRAPHING COMPANY (PA)
Also Called: Meeks Group
6913 E 13th St (74112-5615)
PHONE..................918 836-0900
Mike Wilbins, *COO*
Frank Crockett, *Vice Pres*
Candy Ogden, *Treasurer*
Diane Hixson, *Admin Sec*
EMP: 23
SQ FT: 60,000
SALES (est): 6.6MM **Privately Held**
WEB: www.meeksgroup.com
SIC: 2752 Commercial printing, offset

(G-10241)
MEEKS LITHOGRAPHING COMPANY
Also Called: Meeks Group
6913 E 13th St (74112-5615)
PHONE..................918 836-0900
Desiree Beeman, *Branch Mgr*
EMP: 2
SALES (corp-wide): 6.6MM **Privately Held**
SIC: 2752 2791 2789 Commercial printing, lithographic; typesetting; bookbinding & related work
PA: Meeks Lithographing Company
6913 E 13th St
Tulsa OK 74112
918 836-0900

(G-10242)
MENA MANUFACTURING
1735 S Gary Ave (74104-6113)
PHONE..................918 955-0518
Kyle Martin, *Principal*
EMP: 2
SALES (est): 131.8K **Privately Held**
SIC: 3999 Manufacturing industries

(G-10243)
MESA BLACK PRODUCTION LLC
401 S Boston Ave Ste 450 (74103-4045)
PHONE..................918 933-4454
Bill Warnock, *Ch of Bd*
Chris Girouard, *President*
John Schumer, *Vice Pres*
Lee Francis, *VP Opers*
EMP: 1
SALES (est): 98.3K **Privately Held**
SIC: 1382 Oil & gas exploration services

(G-10244)
METAL DYNAMICS CORP
1145 N Iroquois Ave (74106-5904)
PHONE..................918 582-0124
Donald Doss, *President*
Steve Pinix, *COO*
EMP: 27
SQ FT: 28,000
SALES (est): 6.4MM **Privately Held**
WEB: www.metaldynamics.com
SIC: 3324 3369 Steel investment foundries; machinery castings, nonferrous: ex. alum., copper, die, etc.

(G-10245)
METAL GOODS MANUFACTURING
1732 S Yorktown Ave (74104-5339)
PHONE..................918 633-9069
Chris McAbery, *Principal*
EMP: 1
SALES (est): 39.6K **Privately Held**
SIC: 3999 Manufacturing industries

(G-10246)
METAL PANELS INC
131 S 147th East Ave (74116-2564)
PHONE..................918 641-0641
Mitchell Hentkowski, *President*
Michael Harner, *Sales Staff*
Susan Sowerby, *Sales Staff*
EMP: 6
SQ FT: 38,000
SALES (est): 1.4MM **Privately Held**
SIC: 3444 3448 Roof deck, sheet metal; panels for prefabricated metal buildings

(G-10247)
METALFORM INC
1346 E Haskell St (74106-5449)
PHONE..................918 585-8300
Robert Beesley, *President*
Robert Fairchild, *Corp Secy*
EMP: 10
SQ FT: 60,000
SALES (est): 1.4MM **Privately Held**
SIC: 3444 Sheet metalwork

(G-10248)
METALLIC WORKS INC
1228 S Erie Ave (74112-5341)
PHONE..................918 527-6477
Kristofer Hanselman, *Principal*
EMP: 1
SALES (est): 91.1K **Privately Held**
SIC: 3444 3443 3446 Metal housings, enclosures, casings & other containers; pipe, sheet metal; weldments; architectural metalwork

(G-10249)
METRO GRAPHIC SYSTEMS
1545 S Harvard Ave A (74112-5821)
PHONE..................918 744-0308
Robert Alexander, *Owner*
EMP: 3
SQ FT: 2,200
SALES (est): 434.2K **Privately Held**
SIC: 5112 2791 Business forms; office supplies; typesetting

(G-10250)
METRO MACHINE WORKS INC
5204 S 49th West Ave (74107-8809)
PHONE..................918 446-2705
Charles Elliott, *President*
Billy Elliot, *Vice Pres*
EMP: 13
SQ FT: 25,000
SALES (est): 2MM **Privately Held**
WEB: www.metromachine.com
SIC: 3599 Machine shop, jobbing & repair

(G-10251)
METRO MECHANICAL SUPPLY INC
9900 E 47th Pl (74146-4730)
PHONE..................918 622-2288
Everett Ives, *President*
Darlene Ives, *Treasurer*
Sandy White, *Admin Sec*
EMP: 15 **EST:** 1978
SQ FT: 16,000
SALES (est): 3.5MM **Privately Held**
SIC: 3441 3444 3443 Fabricated structural metal; sheet metalwork; fabricated plate work (boiler shop)

(G-10252)
METRO MECHANICAL SUPPLY LLC
9900 E 47th Pl (74146-4730)
PHONE..................918 622-2288
Yvonne Beecham, *Mng Member*
EMP: 26
SALES (est): 1MM **Privately Held**
SIC: 3441 Fabricated structural metal

(G-10253)
METRO OUTDOOR LIVING
6235 S Mingo Rd (74133-6318)
PHONE..................918 893-2960
EMP: 1
SALES (est): 98K **Privately Held**
SIC: 3631 3567 Mfg Household Cooking Equipment Mfg Industrial Furnaces/Ovens

(G-10254)
MICHAEL J SIMMONS AND DIE
315 N Santa Fe Ave (74127-6922)
PHONE..................918 295-0057
Michael Simmons, *Principal*
EMP: 2
SALES (est): 110K **Privately Held**
SIC: 3544 Special dies & tools

(G-10255)
MICRO MACHINE INC
5937 E 12th St (74112-5418)
PHONE..................918 836-1646
Rose Lowe, *President*
Rick Moore, *Corp Secy*
EMP: 9
SQ FT: 8,900
SALES (est): 1.1MM **Privately Held**
SIC: 3599 Machine shop, jobbing & repair

(G-10256)
MICROSOFT CORPORATION
7633 E 63rd Pl (74133-1273)
PHONE..................469 775-6864
Orlando Villarreal, *Manager*
Robert Stewart, *Technical Staff*
Jack Tang, *Director*
Julie Larson-Green, *Officer*
EMP: 100
SALES (corp-wide): 125.8B **Publicly Held**
SIC: 7372 Application computer software
PA: Microsoft Corporation
1 Microsoft Way
Redmond WA 98052
425 882-8080

(G-10257)
MID-CON ENERGY GP LLC
2431 E 61st St Ste 850 (74136-1261)
PHONE..................972 479-5980
Jeffery R Olmstead, *CEO*
Chad B Roller, *Vice Pres*
Charles L McLawhorn III, *Vice Pres*
Philip Houchin, *CFO*
EMP: 75 **EST:** 2011
SQ FT: 5,400
SALES (est): 2.2MM **Privately Held**
SIC: 1311 Crude petroleum & natural gas

(G-10258)
MID-CON ENERGY II LLC
2431 E 61st St Ste 850 (74136-1261)
PHONE..................918 743-7575
Randy Olmstead, *President*
EMP: 3
SALES (est): 269K **Privately Held**
SIC: 1311 Natural gas production

(G-10259)
MID-CON ENERGY OPERATING LLC (PA)
Also Called: Midcon Energy
2431 E 61st St Ste 850 (74136-1261)
PHONE..................918 743-7575
Charles R Olmstead, *CEO*
Jeffrey R Olmstead, *President*
Karen Jones, *Principal*
Craig S George, *Chairman*
David A Culbertson, *Vice Pres*
EMP: 11 **EST:** 1986
SQ FT: 2,200
SALES (est): 6.2MM **Privately Held**
SIC: 1311 Crude petroleum production; natural gas production

(G-10260)
MID-CON ENERGY PARTNERS LP (PA)
2431 E 61st St Ste 850 (74136-1261)
PHONE..................918 743-7575
Jeffrey R Olmstead, *President*
Larry Morphew, *Superintendent*
Chad B Roller, *General Ptnr*
Chad Roller, *COO*
Philip R Houchin, *CFO*
EMP: 90
SALES: 55.5MM **Publicly Held**
SIC: 1311 Crude petroleum production

(G-10261)
MID-CON ENERGY PROPERTIES LLC
2431 E 61st St Ste 850 (74136-1261)
PHONE..................918 743-7575
Charles R Olmstead, *CEO*
EMP: 5
SALES: 699K **Publicly Held**
SIC: 1311 Crude petroleum production
PA: Mid-Con Energy Partners, Lp
2431 E 61st St Ste 850
Tulsa OK 74136

GEOGRAPHIC SECTION

Tulsa - Tulsa County (G-10290)

(G-10262)
MID-SOUTH METALS LLC
1031 N Columbia Pl (74110-5026)
PHONE..................................918 835-8055
Dwayne Defatta, *Administration*
EMP: 1 Privately Held
WEB: www.midsouthmetals.com
SIC: 3322 Malleable iron foundries
PA: Mid-South Metals, Llc
3849 Southern Ave
Shreveport LA 71106

(G-10263)
MIDLAND STAMPING AND FABG CORP
1010 W 37th Pl (74107-5716)
PHONE..................................918 446-1458
Jim Henry, *Branch Mgr*
EMP: 17 Privately Held
WEB: www.midlandstamping.com
SIC: 3469 Stamping metal for the trade
PA: Midland Stamping And Fabricating Corporation
9521 Ainslie St
Schiller Park IL 60176

(G-10264)
MIDTOWN PRINTING INC
Also Called: Midtown Printing Services
5110 S 95th East Ave (74145-8115)
PHONE..................................918 295-0090
Russell Goleman, *President*
EMP: 6
SQ FT: 3,100
SALES (est): 781.9K Privately Held
SIC: 2752 2791 2789 Commercial printing, offset; typesetting; bookbinding & related work

(G-10265)
MIDTOWN VENTURES LLC
3311 S Peoria Ave (74105-2028)
PHONE..................................918 728-3102
R Scott Vaughn, *Mng Member*
EMP: 5
SALES (est): 506.6K Privately Held
SIC: 2449 Baskets: fruit & vegetable, round stave, till, etc.

(G-10266)
MIDWESCO INDUSTRIES INC
Also Called: Midwestern Pipe Line Pdts Co
2119 S Union Ave (74107-2703)
PHONE..................................918 858-4200
Angela Judkins, *Branch Mgr*
EMP: 5
SALES (corp-wide): 43.8MM Privately Held
SIC: 3569 1623 Filters & strainers, pipeline; pipeline construction
PA: Midwesco Industries, Inc.
2119 S Union Ave
Tulsa OK 74107
918 446-6144

(G-10267)
MIDWEST EXPDTION OTFITTERS LLC
5508 E 11th St (74112-2917)
PHONE..................................918 260-1771
EMP: 2
SALES (est): 233.4K Privately Held
WEB: www.meooffroad.com
SIC: 3714 Motor vehicle parts & accessories

(G-10268)
MIDWEST MARBLE CO
510 S Quincy Ave (74120-4014)
PHONE..................................918 587-8193
Richard W McMahon Jr, *President*
William Carl McMahon, *Vice Pres*
Steve Ferguson, *Admin Sec*
EMP: 23
SQ FT: 10,000
SALES (est): 3MM Privately Held
SIC: 3281 1743 Granite, cut & shaped; marble, building: cut & shaped; terrazzo, tile, marble, mosaic work

(G-10269)
MIDWEST PORTABLE BUILDING
Also Called: Midwest Pole Barns & Buildings
6800 Charles Page Blvd (74127-7343)
PHONE..................................918 245-9335
Carl Morris, *Owner*
EMP: 7
SQ FT: 1,800
SALES (est): 742.7K Privately Held
SIC: 5211 3448 2452 Prefabricated buildings; prefabricated metal buildings; prefabricated wood buildings

(G-10270)
MIDWEST PRECISION INC
9725 E Admiral Pl (74116-2527)
PHONE..................................918 835-8900
Ron Miller, *President*
Brian Miller, *Vice Pres*
Laurie Hinkle, *Manager*
EMP: 80
SQ FT: 40,000
SALES (est): 20.4MM Privately Held
SIC: 3444 3599 Sheet metal specialties, not stamped; machine shop, jobbing & repair

(G-10271)
MIDWEST PUBLISHING CO INC
2230 E 49th St Ste E (74105-8771)
P.O. Box 4468 (74159-0468)
PHONE..................................918 582-2000
Will Hammack, *President*
Todd Maxey, *Research*
Charley Chamberlain, *Director*
EMP: 6
SALES (est): 569.5K Privately Held
WEB: www.midwestpublishing.com
SIC: 2741 Directories: publishing only, not printed on site

(G-10272)
MIDWEST URETHANE INC
6417 S 39th West Ave (74132-1244)
PHONE..................................918 445-2277
Gordon Pendergrast, *President*
EMP: 12
SALES (est): 1.9MM Privately Held
SIC: 3081 Plastics materials & resins

(G-10273)
MIDWEST WRAPS
6417 E 53rd St (74135-7722)
PHONE..................................918 624-2111
Travis Haremza, *Owner*
EMP: 2
SALES (est): 166K Privately Held
SIC: 3993 Signs & advertising specialties

(G-10274)
MIDWESTERN MANUFACTURING CO
2119 S Union Ave (74107-2703)
PHONE..................................918 446-1587
Jim Bost, *Ch of Bd*
▲ EMP: 2
SALES (est): 1.8MM Privately Held
SIC: 5084 3531 Hydraulic systems equipment & supplies; tractors, crawler

(G-10275)
MIGHTY CLEAN CORPORATION
Also Called: Mighty Clean, The
10050 S 33rd West Ave (74132-3733)
P.O. Box 307, Jenks (74037-0307)
PHONE..................................918 299-7970
Henry Haynes, *President*
Jo Ann Haynes, *Vice Pres*
Leda Whitetree, *Admin Sec*
EMP: 5
SQ FT: 10,000
SALES (est): 441.4K Privately Held
SIC: 3589 High pressure cleaning equipment

(G-10276)
MIKE ALEXANDER COMPANY INC
Also Called: Malco
1120 E 1st St (74120-2001)
PHONE..................................580 765-8085
Mike Alexander, *President*
Marvin L Wilkinson, *Vice Pres*
Shawn Alexander, *Admin Sec*
◆ EMP: 30
SALES (est): 7.2MM Privately Held
SIC: 3462 3317 3297 Anchors, forged; tubes, seamless steel; nonclay refractories

(G-10277)
MIKE CLINE INC
4704 Charles Page Blvd (74127-8027)
PHONE..................................918 592-3712
Mike Cline, *President*
Joy Cline, *Vice Pres*
EMP: 12
SQ FT: 20,000
SALES (est): 2.9MM Privately Held
SIC: 3599 3498 Machine shop, jobbing & repair; fabricated pipe & fittings

(G-10278)
MIKE S WELDING
6930 E Newton St (74115-5630)
PHONE..................................918 381-0273
EMP: 1
SALES (est): 34.2K Privately Held
SIC: 7692 Welding repair

(G-10279)
MILL CREEK LUMBER & SUPPLY CO (PA)
6974 E 38th St (74145-3203)
PHONE..................................918 794-3600
Jeffrey T Dunn, *President*
Jim Cavanaugh, *Vice Pres*
James D Dunn, *Vice Pres*
Wade Lennon, *CFO*
Emily Avants, *Human Res Dir*
▲ EMP: 60
SQ FT: 170,000
SALES (est): 163.4MM Privately Held
WEB: www.millcreeklumber.com
SIC: 3442 1771 5031 5211 Casements, aluminum; flooring contractor; lumber, plywood & millwork; building materials, exterior; building materials, interior; lumber: rough, dressed & finished; lumber & other building materials; millwork & lumber; doors, wood or metal, except storm; windows, storm: wood or metal

(G-10280)
MILL WORK SPECIALTIES LLC
712 N 95th East Pl # 293 (74115-7112)
PHONE..................................918 639-8385
Nigel Fuentes, *Principal*
EMP: 1
SALES (est): 54.1K Privately Held
SIC: 2431 Millwork

(G-10281)
MILLER PRINTING COMPANY INC
4932 S Peoria Ave (74105-4623)
PHONE..................................918 749-0981
Wayne Elliott, *President*
EMP: 17
SQ FT: 10,813
SALES (est): 2MM Privately Held
SIC: 2752 Commercial printing, offset

(G-10282)
MILLER SALES WHOLESALE DISTR
6224 S Victor Ave (74136-0809)
PHONE..................................918 629-4064
C Dianne McLaughlin, *Owner*
EMP: 1 EST: 2013
SALES (est): 95.1K Privately Held
SIC: 5199 3229 3269 Baskets; vases, glass; vases, pottery

(G-10283)
MILLERS SUPERIOR ELECTRIC LLC
8 S 109th East Pl (74128-1623)
PHONE..................................918 933-4006
Matthew Miller, *Mng Member*
EMP: 3 EST: 2017
SALES (est): 106.9K Privately Held
SIC: 3699 1731 Electrical equipment & supplies; electrical work

(G-10284)
MINKO DESIGN LLC (PA)
Also Called: Minko Design-Millwork
1131 E Easton Pl (74120-1210)
PHONE..................................918 895-6498
Ryan King, *President*
Matt King, *Vice Pres*
Kyle King, *Treasurer*
EMP: 1
SALES (est): 372.8K Privately Held
SIC: 7389 8712 1751 2541 Design services; architectural services; finish & trim carpentry; store & office display cases & fixtures; office fixtures, wood

(G-10285)
MINKO DESIGN LLC
Also Called: Minko Design Architecture
108 N Greenwood Ave (74120-1409)
PHONE..................................918 895-6498
Ryan King, *President*
Kyle King, *Treasurer*
EMP: 2
SQ FT: 1,000
SALES (corp-wide): 203.3K Privately Held
SIC: 7389 8712 1751 2541 Design services; architectural services; finish & trim carpentry; store & office display cases & fixtures; office fixtures, wood
PA: Minko Design Llc
1131 E Easton St
Tulsa OK 74120
918 895-6498

(G-10286)
MIRATECH CORPORATION
420 S 145th East Ave A (74108-1305)
PHONE..................................918 622-7077
Mike Owings, *Principal*
Brady Carter, *Plant Mgr*
Lance Price, *Prdtn Mgr*
Scott Worstell, *Production*
George Snitz, *Engineer*
EMP: 4 EST: 2014
SALES (est): 236.7K Privately Held
WEB: www.miratechcorp.com
SIC: 3563 Air & gas compressors

(G-10287)
MIRATECH GROUP LLC (PA)
420 S 145th East Ave (74108-1303)
PHONE..................................918 622-7077
Dean Glover, *President*
David Zenthoefer, *Exec VP*
◆ EMP: 35
SALES (est): 27.4MM Privately Held
SIC: 3563 Air & gas compressors

(G-10288)
MOBILE MINI INC
12044 E Pine St (74116-2027)
PHONE..................................918 582-5857
Dave Walton, *Manager*
EMP: 13
SALES (corp-wide): 612.6MM Publicly Held
SIC: 3448 3441 3412 7359 Buildings, portable: prefabricated metal; fabricated structural metal; drums, shipping: metal; shipping container leasing; general warehousing & storage
PA: Mobile Mini, Inc.
4646 E Van Buren St # 400
Phoenix AZ 85008
480 894-6311

(G-10289)
MOBILITY ONE TRANSPORTATION
17520 E Pine St Unit C (74116-4926)
PHONE..................................918 437-4488
William Ward, *President*
Todd Collier, *Principal*
Michael Collier, *Principal*
EMP: 3 EST: 2015
SALES: 450K Privately Held
SIC: 3842 7352 Wheelchairs; invalid supplies rental

(G-10290)
MODERN BINDERY INC
5408 S 103rd East Ave (74146-5815)
PHONE..................................918 250-9486
James A Talley, *President*
Brad Sauders, *Vice Pres*
Mack Talley, *Vice Pres*
Jim Talley, *Executive*
EMP: 21
SQ FT: 40,000
SALES (est): 2.2MM Privately Held
WEB: www.modernbindery.com
SIC: 2789 Binding only: books, pamphlets, magazines, etc.

Tulsa - Tulsa County (G-10291) GEOGRAPHIC SECTION

(G-10291)
MODERN PLATING CO INC (PA)
1125 S Norwood Ave (74112-5429)
PHONE..................................918 836-5081
Terrence W Lazar, *President*
Lesley Ault, *Admin Sec*
EMP: 14 EST: 1964
SQ FT: 8,000
SALES (est): 1.7MM **Privately Held**
WEB: www.modernplatingok.com
SIC: **3471** 3479 Electroplating of metals or formed products; finishing, metals or formed products; painting of metal products

(G-10292)
MODERNBLOX LLC
1305 N Louisville Ave (74115-5111)
PHONE..................................405 673-6215
Lee Easton, *Vice Pres*
Swapneel Deshpande,
Ben Loh,
Chad Magruder,
EMP: 4
SALES (est): 162.4K **Privately Held**
SIC: **2451** Mobile homes, personal or private use; mobile home frames; mobile buildings: for commercial use

(G-10293)
MODULAR SQUAD LLC
2864 S Gary Ave (74114-5812)
PHONE..................................918 695-0114
Kimberly A Norman, *President*
EMP: 1
SALES (est): 171.3K **Privately Held**
SIC: **2542** Partitions & fixtures, except wood

(G-10294)
MOGAR INDUSTRIES
6440 S 39th West Ave (74132-1245)
PHONE..................................918 445-3747
Roy L Moss, *Partner*
Richard E Garner, *Partner*
EMP: 4 EST: 1981
SQ FT: 6,000
SALES: 400K **Privately Held**
SIC: **3443** 3599 3545 Heat exchangers, condensers & components; machine shop, jobbing & repair; machine tool accessories

(G-10295)
MOHAWK MATERIALS CO INC (PA)
2521 Charles Page Blvd (74127-8312)
P.O. Box 640, Sand Springs (74063-0640)
PHONE..................................918 584-2707
Scott A Waller, *President*
Scott Waller, *General Mgr*
Matthew Waller, *Vice Pres*
Chris Brennan, *Materials Mgr*
Cathy Waller, *Treasurer*
EMP: 7
SQ FT: 7,500
SALES (est): 10.9MM **Privately Held**
SIC: **7389** 1446 5085 1442 Packaging & labeling services; blast sand mining; industrial supplies; construction sand & gravel

(G-10296)
MOLDMAN KANSAS CITY
3315 E 39th St (74135-4631)
PHONE..................................918 921-6823
Mitchell Renberg, *Branch Mgr*
EMP: 1
SALES (corp-wide): 161.9K **Privately Held**
SIC: **3442** Molding, trim & stripping
PA: Moldman Kansas City
  8513 Ward Pkwy
  Kansas City MO 64114
  816 256-2499

(G-10297)
MOMENTUM COMPLETION
4302 E 116th Pl (74137-6121)
PHONE..................................918 364-9444
Teala McKenzie, *Principal*
EMP: 2 EST: 2018
SALES (est): 121.2K **Privately Held**
SIC: **1389** Oil field services

(G-10298)
MONGOOSE ENERGY LLC
1 W 3rd St Ste 1700 (74103-3522)
PHONE..................................918 884-3508
Stephen Ferguson, *CEO*
Steve Widner, *President*
Kirk Harlton, *Vice Pres*
Kale Wallace, *Vice Pres*
EMP: 4
SALES (est): 498.2K **Privately Held**
SIC: **1382** Oil & gas exploration services

(G-10299)
MONOD BLOC INC
5556 S Mingo Rd (74146-6456)
P.O. Box 470384 (74147-0384)
PHONE..................................918 622-8132
John Coleman, *Principal*
EMP: 2
SALES (est): 155.2K **Privately Held**
SIC: **2759** Screen printing

(G-10300)
MONSON ASSOCIATES INC
6014 E 101st St (74137-7016)
PHONE..................................918 298-0037
William Monson, *President*
Susan Monson, *Vice Pres*
EMP: 2
SQ FT: 1,000
SALES (est): 680.3K **Privately Held**
SIC: **5051** 3446 Steel; open flooring & grating for construction

(G-10301)
MONTELLO INC
6106 E 32nd Pl Ste 100 (74135-5495)
PHONE..................................918 665-1170
Allen Johnson, *President*
Leo Wooldridge, *Vice Pres*
Anita Mitchell, *Office Mgr*
▼ EMP: 5 EST: 1957
SQ FT: 3,700
SALES: 6MM **Privately Held**
WEB: www.montelloinc.com
SIC: **2899** 2869 Drilling mud; perfumes, flavorings & food additives

(G-10302)
MOODYS JEWELRY INCORPORATED (PA)
1137 S Harvard Ave (74112-4913)
PHONE..................................918 834-3371
Ernest L Moody III, *President*
Kevin G Moody, *Treasurer*
Emily M Boyd, *Admin Sec*
EMP: 15
SQ FT: 3,700
SALES (est): 7.5MM **Privately Held**
WEB: www.moodysjewelry.com
SIC: **3911** 5944 Jewelry, precious metal; clocks

(G-10303)
MOODYS JEWELRY INCORPORATED
Also Called: Store 6
1812 Utica Sq (74114-1408)
PHONE..................................918 747-5599
Mike Guillory, *Manager*
EMP: 6
SALES (corp-wide): 7.5MM **Privately Held**
SIC: **3911** 7631 5944 Jewelry, precious metal; jewelry repair services; jewelry stores
PA: Moody's Jewelry Incorporated
  1137 S Harvard Ave
  Tulsa OK 74112
  918 834-3371

(G-10304)
MORRILL & ASSOC INC
6011 S Sheridan Rd (74145-9211)
PHONE..................................918 481-1055
David L Morrill, *President*
EMP: 2
SALES (est): 121.5K **Privately Held**
SIC: **1389** Oil consultants

(G-10305)
MORTON MANUFACTURING CO INC
839 N Wheeling Ave (74110-4916)
P.O. Box 140992, Broken Arrow (74014-0009)
PHONE..................................918 584-0333
Eugene Morton, *President*
Diana Neal, *Vice Pres*
EMP: 5
SALES (est): 820K **Privately Held**
SIC: **3533** 3549 3433 Oil field machinery & equipment; metalworking machinery; radiators, except electric

(G-10306)
MOSS SEAT COVER MFG & SLS CO
Also Called: Moss Seat Covers
4954 S Peoria Ave (74105-4623)
PHONE..................................918 742-3326
David Winkle, *President*
Jody Winkle, *Corp Secy*
EMP: 10 EST: 1945
SQ FT: 25,000
SALES (est): 400K **Privately Held**
SIC: **2399** 7641 3714 2531 Seat covers, automobile; reupholstery & furniture repair; motor vehicle parts & accessories; public building & related furniture; carpets & rugs

(G-10307)
MPF INDUSTRIES LLC
2448 E 81st St Ste 4550 (74137-4201)
PHONE..................................918 492-0809
J Patrick Carter, *Mng Member*
EMP: 2
SALES (est): 184.1K **Privately Held**
SIC: **3545** Machine tool accessories

(G-10308)
MS ENTERPRISES
3823 S 99th East Ave (74146-2430)
PHONE..................................918 627-1824
Marvin De Vries, *Owner*
EMP: 1 EST: 1999
SALES (est): 58.5K **Privately Held**
SIC: **3581** Automatic vending machines

(G-10309)
MSC INC
Also Called: Martin Service Company
3123 N Lewis Ave (74110-1527)
P.O. Box 581944 (74158-1944)
PHONE..................................918 425-4996
Michael Lageose, *President*
EMP: 1
SQ FT: 6,000
SALES (est): 500K **Privately Held**
SIC: **3443** Fabricated plate work (boiler shop)

(G-10310)
MT PERCUSSION DRILLING LLC
Also Called: M T P Drilling
6237 S Indianapolis Pl (74136-1418)
PHONE..................................918 232-5472
James Coffman, *Mng Member*
EMP: 1
SALES (est): 75.4K **Privately Held**
SIC: **1389** Oil field services

(G-10311)
MT VERNON COAL TRANSFER CO (DH)
1717 S Boulder Ave (74119-4805)
P.O. Box 22027 (74121-2027)
PHONE..................................918 295-7600
Joseph W Craft III, *President*
EMP: 14
SALES (est): 2.3MM **Publicly Held**
SIC: **1221** 4491 Bituminous coal surface mining; loading vessels
HQ: Alliance Coal, Llc
  1717 S Boulder Ave # 400
  Tulsa OK 74119
  918 295-7600

(G-10312)
MUIRFIELD PRODUCTION CO INC
Also Called: Muirfield Resources
2627 E 21st St (74114-1714)
P.O. Box 3166 (74101-3166)
PHONE..................................918 744-5604
John W Pilkington Jr, *President*
Roger B Collins, *Chairman*
Luann P Lyman, *Treasurer*
EMP: 12
SALES (est): 790.6K
SALES (corp-wide): 1.5MM **Privately Held**
SIC: **1311** Crude petroleum production
PA: Muirfield Resources Company Inc
  2642 E 21st St Ste 285
  Tulsa OK 74114
  918 744-5604

(G-10313)
MUIRFIELD RESOURCES COMPANY (PA)
2642 E 21st St Ste 285 (74114-1789)
P.O. Box 3166 (74101-3166)
PHONE..................................918 744-5604
Roger B Collins, *Ch of Bd*
John Pilkington, *President*
Pattie Jarolim, *Partner*
Luanne Hale, *Controller*
EMP: 12
SQ FT: 2,000
SALES (est): 1.5MM **Privately Held**
SIC: **1311** Crude petroleum production; natural gas production

(G-10314)
MULTIPLES INC
110 S Norfolk Ave (74120-2012)
PHONE..................................918 584-7982
Stuart Hawley, *President*
EMP: 2
SQ FT: 5,300
SALES (est): 83K **Privately Held**
SIC: **2499** Knobs, wood

(G-10315)
MULTIPRINT CORP
Also Called: Five Star Technologies
6915 E 38th St (74145-3202)
PHONE..................................918 832-0300
Dean Martin, *President*
Tracy Johnson, *Vice Pres*
EMP: 4
SQ FT: 4,000
SALES: 700K **Privately Held**
SIC: **2752** 2791 2789 2759 Commercial printing, offset; typesetting; bookbinding & related work; commercial printing

(G-10316)
MUNCIE POWER PRODUCTS INC
Manufacturing Div & Dist Ctr
7217 E Pine St (74115-5649)
PHONE..................................918 838-0900
Doug Sullivent, *Plant Mgr*
Dale Wilson, *QC Mgr*
Roger Merritt, *Senior Engr*
Joe Harris, *Administration*
EMP: 150
SQ FT: 131,000
SALES (corp-wide): 109.4MM **Privately Held**
SIC: **3714** Drive shafts, motor vehicle
HQ: Muncie Power Products, Inc.
  201 E Jackson St Ste 500
  Muncie IN 47305
  765 284-7721

(G-10317)
MURPHY WALLBED USA LLC
1835 N 105th East Ave (74116-1513)
PHONE..................................918 836-5833
Aleksandr Diky Jr, *Principal*
EMP: 4
SALES (est): 426.6K **Privately Held**
WEB: www.murphywallbedusa.com
SIC: **5712** 2519 Furniture stores; household furniture

(G-10318)
MUSIC GAMES N THINGS INC
1556 E 37th St (74105-3224)
PHONE..................................918 742-4349

GEOGRAPHIC SECTION

Tulsa - Tulsa County (G-10348)

Karen Harrington, *President*
John Harrington, *Vice Pres*
EMP: 1
SALES (est): 81K **Privately Held**
SIC: 3944 Board games, children's & adults'

(G-10319)
MW PIPING FABRICATION LLC
Also Called: Word Inds Piping Fabrication
5001 W 21st St (74107-2227)
PHONE.................................918 836-4200
Mark Adams, *CFO*
EMP: 13
SALES (est): 1MM **Privately Held**
SIC: 3498 Pipe fittings, fabricated from purchased pipe

(G-10320)
MWH ENTERPRISES INC
Also Called: Allegra Print & Imaging
7707 E 38th St (74145-3210)
PHONE.................................918 665-0944
Martin Hanna, *President*
Kevin Hill, *President*
Donna R Hanna, *Admin Sec*
EMP: 14
SQ FT: 11,000
SALES (est): 2.4MM **Privately Held**
SIC: 2752 7374 Commercial printing, offset; data processing service

(G-10321)
MYTHIC PRESS
2015 E 3rd St (74104-1815)
PHONE.................................918 516-8255
EMP: 2 **EST:** 2017
SALES (est): 62.7K **Privately Held**
SIC: 2741 Miscellaneous publishing

(G-10322)
N M & O OPERATING COMPANY
15 E 5th St Ste 3000 (74103-4337)
PHONE.................................918 584-3802
Larry Sweet, *President*
Sandy McAllister, *Admin Sec*
EMP: 2
SALES (est): 257.5K **Privately Held**
SIC: 1311 Crude petroleum production; natural gas production

(G-10323)
NADEL AND GUSSMAN LLC (PA)
Also Called: Nadel & Gussman Anadarko
15 E 5th St Ste 3300 (74103-4340)
PHONE.................................918 583-3333
James F Adelson, *President*
Kevin Delay, *COO*
Jim Bucci, *Vice Pres*
Dave Yaeger, *Engineer*
Shelley Nichols, *CFO*
EMP: 45
SQ FT: 20,000
SALES (est): 206.2MM **Privately Held**
WEB: www.nadelgussman.com
SIC: 1311 Crude petroleum production; natural gas production

(G-10324)
NAMEPLATES INC (PA)
325 S Quincy Ave (74120-2814)
P.O. Box 4608 (74159-0608)
PHONE.................................918 584-2651
Claudia Hamilton, *President*
Donald D Angove, *Principal*
Candace Conley, *Vice Pres*
▲ **EMP:** 86
SQ FT: 48,000
SALES (est): 13.4MM **Privately Held**
SIC: 3479 2759 Name plates: engraved, etched, etc.; decals: printing

(G-10325)
NAMEPLATES INC
Also Called: Images Ink
325 S Quincy Ave (74120-2814)
P.O. Box 4608 (74159-0608)
PHONE.................................918 561-8372
Candace Trombka, *Manager*
EMP: 5
SALES (corp-wide): 13.4MM **Privately Held**
SIC: 2759 Poster & decal printing & engraving

PA: Nameplates, Inc.
325 S Quincy Ave
Tulsa OK 74120
918 584-2651

(G-10326)
NATIONAL CLIMATE SOLUTIONS
1418 E 71st St (74136-5076)
PHONE.................................844 682-4247
Christopher Blount, *President*
EMP: 10
SALES (est): 5MM **Privately Held**
SIC: 3585 Refrigeration & heating equipment

(G-10327)
NATIONS CRANE SALES INC
3101 N Toledo Ave (74115-1804)
PHONE.................................918 836-2000
EMP: 3
SALES (est): 294.3K **Privately Held**
SIC: 3625 Crane & hoist controls, including metal mill

(G-10328)
NAVICO INC (PA)
Also Called: Lowrance Smrad B G Gfree Brnds
4500 S 129th East Ave # 200 (74134-5885)
PHONE.................................918 437-6881
Knut Frostad, *President*
Jamie Elgie, *COO*
Lucinda Abood, *Exec VP*
Jim Brailey, *Exec VP*
Jonathan Cathey, *Exec VP*
▲ **EMP:** 267
SQ FT: 116,000
SALES (est): 411.2MM **Privately Held**
WEB: www.navico.com
SIC: 3812 Navigational systems & instruments

(G-10329)
NAVICO INC
Also Called: Eagle Electronics
4500 S 129th East Ave # 200 (74134-5885)
PHONE.................................918 437-6881
EMP: 13
SALES (corp-wide): 411.2MM **Privately Held**
SIC: 3812 Search & navigation equipment
PA: Navico, Inc.
4500 S 129th East Ave # 200
Tulsa OK 74134
918 437-6881

(G-10330)
NAVISTAR INC
2322 N Mingo Rd (74116-1218)
PHONE.................................918 833-4065
Candy Hackworth, *Mfg Staff*
Michelle Shay, *Accountant*
Kyle Howard, *Sales Dir*
Larry Goodall, *Manager*
Brian Powell, *Data Proc Dir*
EMP: 70
SALES (corp-wide): 11.2B **Publicly Held**
SIC: 3711 Motor vehicles & car bodies
HQ: Navistar, Inc.
2701 Navistar Dr
Lisle IL 60532
331 332-5000

(G-10331)
NEILSON MANUFACTURING INC (PA)
3517 Charles Page Blvd (74127-8206)
PHONE.................................918 587-5548
R L Walker, *President*
James Brazeal, *Vice Pres*
EMP: 15
SQ FT: 26,800
SALES (est): 2.4MM **Privately Held**
SIC: 3441 Fabricated structural metal

(G-10332)
NELSON INCORPORATED
209 E 19th St (74119-5211)
P.O. Box 52783 (74152-0783)
PHONE.................................918 812-5876
Mike Nelson, *President*
Alicia Nelson, *President*
EMP: 2
SALES: 250K **Privately Held**
SIC: 7629 2759 Electrical repair shops; commercial printing

(G-10333)
NEMINIS INC
1350 S Boulder Ave # 400 (74119-3224)
PHONE.................................918 582-8083
Ruth Nelson, *President*
EMP: 5 **EST:** 1982
SALES (est): 482K **Privately Held**
WEB: www.okganesha.com
SIC: 1381 Drilling oil & gas wells

(G-10334)
NEOSOURCE INC
9422 E 55th Pl (74145-8154)
PHONE.................................918 622-4493
Bill Graif, *President*
EMP: 8
SQ FT: 15,000
SALES (est): 1.6MM **Privately Held**
SIC: 3728 Airframe assemblies, except for guided missiles

(G-10335)
NEW DOMINION LLC (PA)
1307 S Boulder Ave # 400 (74119-3220)
PHONE.................................918 587-6242
Fred Buxton, *Counsel*
Tommy Boullt, *Exec VP*
Jim Beckert Jim BEC, *Exec VP*
Virginia Albert, *Vice Pres*
Virginia Albert Bullock, *Vice Pres*
EMP: 25
SQ FT: 16,000
SALES (est): 3.8MM **Privately Held**
SIC: 1311 Crude petroleum production; natural gas production

(G-10336)
NEW GENERATION DRONES
18579 E 3rd St (74108-2329)
PHONE.................................918 553-8703
EMP: 2
SALES (est): 86K **Privately Held**
SIC: 3721 Motorized aircraft

(G-10337)
NEW X DRIVE TECH INC
Also Called: Natural Fusion Energy
613 E Young Pl (74106-3838)
PHONE.................................918 850-4463
Deanna Secrest, *CEO*
Deanna Nixon, *President*
EMP: 5
SALES (est): 236.4K **Privately Held**
SIC: 4812 7371 8731 7373 Cellular telephone services; custom computer programming services; computer software systems analysis & design, custom; computer (hardware) development; computer systems analysis & design; photoconductive cells; solar cells

(G-10338)
NEW X DRIVES INC
613 E Young Pl (74106-3838)
PHONE.................................918 850-4463
EMP: 10 **EST:** 2012
SQ FT: 5,000
SALES (est): 300K **Privately Held**
SIC: 3571 7372 8733 8732 Mfg Electronic Computers Prepackaged Software Svc Coml Physical Research Noncoml Research Orgnztn Coml Nonphysical Rsrch

(G-10339)
NEWFIELD EXPLORATION 2003 INC
Also Called: Newfield Explrtion Md-Cntinent
7134 S Yale Ave Ste 430 (74136-6351)
PHONE.................................918 495-0598
G R Talley, *President*
Lanny A Woods, *Vice Pres*
David W House, *CFO*
EMP: 35
SQ FT: 6,000
SALES (est): 1.5MM
SALES (corp-wide): 8.5MM **Publicly Held**
SIC: 1382 Oil & gas exploration services
HQ: Ovintiv Mid-Continent Inc,
101 E 2nd St
Tulsa OK 74103
918 582-2690

(G-10340)
NEWSTAR NETRONICS LLC
3926 E 3rd St (74112-1220)
PHONE.................................918 932-8343
Chris Debon, *General Mgr*
EMP: 7
SALES (est): 963.2K **Privately Held**
WEB: www.newstarnetronics.com
SIC: 3672 3669 7389 Printed circuit boards; signaling apparatus, electric; intercommunication systems, electric;

(G-10341)
NICK & PAULS QUALITY CAR CORNR
Also Called: Nick and Paul's
7658 E 46th Pl (74145-6308)
PHONE.................................918 933-4000
Nick Jacewitz, *Owner*
Joseph McLaughlin, *Manager*
EMP: 3
SALES (est): 172K **Privately Held**
SIC: 5521 3465 Automobiles, used cars only; body parts, automobile: stamped metal

(G-10342)
NICKEL & COMPANY LLC
5807 S Garnett Rd Ste J (74146-6824)
P.O. Box 35547 (74153-0547)
PHONE.................................918 744-6384
Dennis Nickel, *Principal*
EMP: 21 **EST:** 2011
SALES (est): 2.6MM **Privately Held**
SIC: 3356 Nickel

(G-10343)
NICKEL CREEK PHOTOGRAPHY
7370 S 26th West Ave (74132-2218)
PHONE.................................918 447-2688
Sara Carter, *Principal*
EMP: 3
SALES (est): 253.7K **Privately Held**
SIC: 3356 Nickel

(G-10344)
NICKOLAS MANUFACTURING INC
11311 E 4th St (74128-2006)
P.O. Box 690203 (74169-0203)
PHONE.................................918 698-7109
Phillip N Jackson Sr, *President*
Shirley Jackson, *President*
Tammy Shatwellmullis, *Corp Secy*
Kerry Jackson, *Vice Pres*
Phillip Jackson Jr, *Vice Pres*
EMP: 9
SALES (est): 926K **Privately Held**
SIC: 3799 3544 Trailers & trailer equipment; special dies, tools, jigs & fixtures

(G-10345)
NIKE EXPLORATION LLC
7404 S Yale Ave (74136-7029)
PHONE.................................918 878-7410
John Nikkel, *President*
EMP: 2
SALES (est): 177.4K **Privately Held**
SIC: 1382 Oil & gas exploration services

(G-10346)
NOCO INVESTMENT CO INC
16 E 16th St Ste 300 (74119-4400)
P.O. Box 4470 (74159-0470)
PHONE.................................918 582-0090
Richard J Nichols, *President*
EMP: 6
SQ FT: 1,176
SALES (est): 750.4K **Privately Held**
SIC: 1311 Crude petroleum & natural gas

(G-10347)
NOLAN CUSTOM WOODWORK
4132 E Admiral Pl (74115-7444)
PHONE.................................918 576-1158
EMP: 1 **EST:** 2016
SALES (est): 54.1K **Privately Held**
SIC: 2431 Millwork

(G-10348)
NONNIS FOODS LLC (PA)
Also Called: Nonni's
3920 E Pine St (74115-5126)
PHONE.................................918 621-1200
Dave Bere, *Mng Member*

Tulsa - Tulsa County (G-10349)　　　GEOGRAPHIC SECTION

EMP: 68
SALES (est): 84.7MM **Privately Held**
SIC: 2052 2053 Bakery products, dry; frozen bakery products, except bread

(G-10349)
NORBERG INDUSTRIES INC
4237 S 74th East Ave (74145-4708)
PHONE..................918 665-6888
William Drotar, *President*
▲ **EMP:** 35
SQ FT: 10,000
SALES (est): 14MM **Privately Held**
SIC: 3613 Fuses, electric

(G-10350)
NORDAM
11153 E Newton St (74116-5624)
PHONE..................918 878-4325
EMP: 3
SALES (est): 322.9K **Privately Held**
SIC: 3728 Aircraft parts & equipment

(G-10351)
NORDAM GROUP INC
11200 E Pine St (74116-1613)
PHONE..................918 878-8962
Raegen Siegfried, *Vice Pres*
Duane Helling, *Mfg Staff*
Matt Fritz, *Engrg Dir*
Terry Walker, *Design Engr Mgr*
Mark Baker, *Engineer*
EMP: 36
SALES (corp-wide): 868.2MM **Privately Held**
SIC: 3728 3724 Aircraft parts & equipment; aircraft engines & engine parts
PA: The Nordam Group Llc
  6910 Whirlpool Dr
  Tulsa OK 74117
  918 878-4000

(G-10352)
NORDAM GROUP LLC
Also Called: Nordam Intriors Structures Div
6910 Whirlpool Dr (74117-1305)
P.O. Box 3365 (74101-3365)
PHONE..................918 401-5000
Kate Kennedy, *Engineer*
Kirby McCoy, *Engineer*
Justin Patterson, *Engineer*
Rebecca Johnson, *Business Anlyst*
Gary Ball, *Branch Mgr*
EMP: 675
SALES (corp-wide): 868.2MM **Privately Held**
WEB: www.nordam.com
SIC: 3728 Aircraft parts & equipment
PA: The Nordam Group Llc
  6910 Whirlpool Dr
  Tulsa OK 74117
  918 878-4000

(G-10353)
NORDAM GROUP LLC
Also Called: W A A
11200 E Pine St (74116-1613)
P.O. Box 3365 (74101-3365)
PHONE..................918 878-6682
Meredith Siegfried, *Branch Mgr*
Mike Boydstun, *Manager*
Steven Morin, *Manager*
James J Lane, *Director*
EMP: 800
SALES (corp-wide): 868.2MM **Privately Held**
WEB: www.nordam.com
SIC: 3728 Aircraft parts & equipment
PA: The Nordam Group Llc
  6910 Whirlpool Dr
  Tulsa OK 74117
  918 878-4000

(G-10354)
NORDAM GROUP LLC (PA)
Also Called: Nordam Repair Division
6910 Whirlpool Dr (74117-1305)
P.O. Box 3365 (74101-3365)
PHONE..................918 878-4000
Peter Greig, *General Mgr*
Paul Kenneth Lackey Jr, *Chairman*
Basil Barimo, *Exec VP*
Terry Gray, *Vice Pres*
Jamie Lane, *Vice Pres*
◆ **EMP:** 1543 **EST:** 1969
SQ FT: 200,000
SALES (est): 868.2MM **Privately Held**
SIC: 3724 3728 Aircraft engines & engine parts; bodies, aircraft

(G-10355)
NORDAM GROUP LLC
Also Called: Nordam Repair Division
11200 E Pine St (74116-1613)
P.O. Box 3365 (74101-3365)
PHONE..................918 234-5155
Tom Wilson, *Branch Mgr*
EMP: 900
SALES (corp-wide): 868.2MM **Privately Held**
SIC: 3728 Aircraft parts & equipment
PA: The Nordam Group Llc
  6910 Whirlpool Dr
  Tulsa OK 74117
  918 878-4000

(G-10356)
NORDAM GROUP LLC
Also Called: Nordam Transparency Division
1050 E Archer St (74120-1203)
P.O. Box 3365 (74101-3365)
PHONE..................918 274-2742
David Vance, *Branch Mgr*
EMP: 130
SALES (corp-wide): 868.2MM **Privately Held**
SIC: 3369 2821 3728 3721 Castings, except die-castings, precision; plastics materials & resins; aircraft parts & equipment; aircraft; power transmission equipment
PA: The Nordam Group Llc
  6910 Whirlpool Dr
  Tulsa OK 74117
  918 878-4000

(G-10357)
NORDAM GROUP LLC
Nordam Transparency Division
7018 N Lakewood Ave (74117-1814)
P.O. Box 3365 (74101-3365)
PHONE..................918 274-2700
Dee Littlefield, *Purch Agent*
Emma Roberts, *Accountant*
Martin Wilding, *Accountant*
Hastings Siegfried, *Branch Mgr*
EMP: 140
SALES (corp-wide): 868.2MM **Privately Held**
SIC: 3728 8742 Aircraft parts & equipment; management consulting services
PA: The Nordam Group Llc
  6910 Whirlpool Dr
  Tulsa OK 74117
  918 878-4000

(G-10358)
NORDAM GROUP LLC
Also Called: Nordam Nacelle & Thrust Revers
6911 Whirlpool Dr (74117-1306)
P.O. Box 3365 (74101-3365)
PHONE..................918 476-8338
Wade Phares, *Engineer*
Steve Pack, *Branch Mgr*
EMP: 394
SALES (corp-wide): 868.2MM **Privately Held**
SIC: 3724 3728 Jet assisted takeoff devices (JATO); aircraft parts & equipment
PA: The Nordam Group Llc
  6910 Whirlpool Dr
  Tulsa OK 74117
  918 878-4000

(G-10359)
NORDIC PURE INC
14602 Clean Air Dr (74116-2645)
PHONE..................918 234-2355
EMP: 1
SALES (corp-wide): 300K **Privately Held**
WEB: www.nordicpure.com
SIC: 3564 Blower filter units (furnace blowers)
PA: Nordic Pure, Inc
  2500 N Louisiana Dr
  Celina TX 75009
  972 382-2355

(G-10360)
NORTH AMERICAN COS
2400 N Lewis Ave (74110-2122)
PHONE..................918 592-2000
Ric Shust, *President*
Linda B Shust, *Treasurer*
EMP: 14
SQ FT: 65,000
SALES (est): 1.8MM **Privately Held**
SIC: 1542 7389 3993 2542 Custom builders, non-residential; exhibit construction by industrial contractors; trade show arrangement; signs & advertising specialties; partitions & fixtures, except wood; wood partitions & fixtures

(G-10361)
NORTHEAST OKLAHOMA MFG
10730 E 55th Pl (74146-6701)
P.O. Box 471616 (74147-1616)
PHONE..................918 663-8805
David Bartmier, *President*
Steve Bartmier, *Vice Pres*
EMP: 7
SQ FT: 6,000
SALES (est): 1.3MM **Privately Held**
SIC: 3599 Custom machinery

(G-10362)
NORTHSTAR ENERGY LLC
3211 S Lakewood Ave (74135-4903)
PHONE..................231 941-0073
Mark D Willson, *Mng Member*
John Coates,
EMP: 63
SQ FT: 14,645
SALES (est): 6.7MM **Privately Held**
SIC: 1311 Gas & hydrocarbon liquefaction from coal

(G-10363)
NOVARTIS CORPORATION
3737 E 37th Pl (74135-2225)
PHONE..................918 845-0906
EMP: 4
SALES (corp-wide): 47.5B **Privately Held**
WEB: www.us.novartis.com
SIC: 2834 Pharmaceutical preparations
HQ: Novartis Corporation
  1 S Ridgedale Ave Ste 1 # 1
  East Hanover NJ 07936
  212 307-1122

(G-10364)
NSI FRACTURING LLC
7030 S Yale Ave Ste 502 (74136-5746)
PHONE..................918 496-2072
EMP: 1
SALES (est): 84K **Privately Held**
SIC: 1389 Oil/Gas Field Services

(G-10365)
NTU PIPELINE LLC
2 W 2nd St Ste 1700 (74103-3100)
PHONE..................918 392-9255
Charles Rowan, *President*
EMP: 10
SALES (est): 259.7K **Privately Held**
SIC: 1311 Natural gas production

(G-10366)
NU-TIER BRANDS INC
8282 S Memorial Dr # 302 (74133-4351)
PHONE..................918 550-8026
Lou Polsinell II, *Ch of Bd*
Vincent Rudolph, *President*
Patrick Boss, *Vice Pres*
Vince Huschle, *Vice Pres*
Stephen Martin, *Finance*
▼ **EMP:** 8
SALES: 38MM **Privately Held**
WEB: www.nu-tierbrands.com
SIC: 2992 Lubricating oils

(G-10367)
NUCKOLLS DISTRIBUTING INC
9513 E 55th St Ste B (74145-8119)
PHONE..................918 663-0555
Wayne Hutchison, *Owner*
EMP: 2
SALES (est): 178.8K **Privately Held**
SIC: 3631 Gas ranges, domestic

(G-10368)
NYIKOS INC
4815 S Harvard Ave # 360 (74135-3077)
PHONE..................918 299-3190
Michael Nyikos, *President*
EMP: 7
SQ FT: 4,000

SALES (est): 250K **Privately Held**
SIC: 7629 3672 Electronic equipment repair; printed circuit boards

(G-10369)
O E N T INSTRUMENTS INC
9021 S Gary Ave (74137-3335)
PHONE..................918 299-4343
Harry French, *President*
Patti French, *Vice Pres*
EMP: 2
SALES (est): 180K **Privately Held**
SIC: 3841 Medical instruments & equipment, blood & bone work

(G-10370)
O FIZZ INC
Also Called: Fizz-O-Water Co
809 N Lewis Ave (74110-5365)
PHONE..................918 834-3691
Harry Doerner Jr, *President*
Harry Doerner Sr, *Vice Pres*
Kim Doerner, *Executive*
W D Phillips, *Admin Sec*
Ricky Mulkey, *Administration*
EMP: 18 **EST:** 1933
SQ FT: 12,000
SALES (est): 4MM **Privately Held**
WEB: www.fizzowater.com
SIC: 2899 5499 8742 5149 Distilled water; distilled mineral or spring; distribution channels consultant; mineral or spring water bottling

(G-10371)
O K COUNTRY DONUT SHOPPE
8048 S Yale Ave (74136-9003)
PHONE..................918 493-6455
Bill Francisco, *President*
EMP: 2
SALES (est): 170K **Privately Held**
SIC: 2051 5461 Doughnuts, except frozen; bakeries

(G-10372)
OAI ELECTRONICS LLC
6960 E 12th St (74112-5619)
PHONE..................918 836-9077
Roger Evoniuk, *President*
Kathleen Rooney, *Director*
▲ **EMP:** 59
SQ FT: 55,000
SALES (est): 14.3MM **Privately Held**
SIC: 3672 Circuit boards, television & radio printed

(G-10373)
OAKLAND PETROLEUM OPERATING CO
7318 S Yale Ave Ste A (74136-7000)
PHONE..................918 496-3027
William D Heldmar, *President*
William Blake Heldmar, *Vice Pres*
Debbie Harrod, *Admin Sec*
EMP: 7
SALES (est): 814K **Privately Held**
SIC: 1311 Crude petroleum production; natural gas production

(G-10374)
OCCIDENTAL PETROLEUM CORP
110 W 7th St Ste 1600 (74119-1065)
PHONE..................918 610-1990
J Niehaus, *Branch Mgr*
Shayne Buchanan, *Manager*
Monica Goins, *Manager*
Robert M Mahaffey, *Director*
Shannon Davis, *Advisor*
EMP: 11
SALES (corp-wide): 21.2B **Publicly Held**
SIC: 1311 Crude petroleum production; natural gas production
PA: Occidental Petroleum Corporation
  5 Greenway Plz Ste 110
  Houston TX 77046
  713 215-7000

(G-10375)
OCCUSCREEN ASSOCIATES LLC
1044 N Sheridan Rd (74115-6870)
PHONE..................918 292-8865
Russell J Green Ms, *Principal*
EMP: 5

GEOGRAPHIC SECTION

Tulsa - Tulsa County (G-10404)

SALES (est): 228.1K **Privately Held**
SIC: **1389** Testing, measuring, surveying & analysis services

(G-10376)
OCV CONTROL VALVES LLC
Also Called: Oil Capital Valve Company
7400 E 42nd Pl (74145-4744)
PHONE..................918 627-1942
Britt Radford, *CEO*
Janis Radford, *Corp Secy*
Craig Cox, *Plant Mgr*
Melissa Kessler, *Buyer*
Lori Devries, *Purchasing*
▲ EMP: 48
SQ FT: 50,000
SALES (est): 10.5MM **Privately Held**
WEB: www.controlvalves.com
SIC: **3491** 3599 Industrial valves; machine shop, jobbing & repair

(G-10377)
ODUM MACHINE & TOOL INC
9933 E 44th Pl (74146-4706)
PHONE..................918 663-6966
Roger P Odum, *President*
Pat Odum, *Corp Secy*
Russell Odum, *Vice Pres*
EMP: 5
SQ FT: 7,000
SALES (est): 568.2K **Privately Held**
SIC: **3599** 3561 Machine shop, jobbing & repair; pumps & pumping equipment

(G-10378)
OEX-1 LLC
4870 S Lewis Ave Ste 240 (74105-5153)
PHONE..................918 492-0254
Steve Miller,
John Brown,
Daniel Honeyman,
David Tschopp,
EMP: 5
SQ FT: 1,200
SALES (est): 411.1K **Privately Held**
SIC: **1382** Oil & gas exploration services

(G-10379)
OGCI BUILDING FUND LLC
2930 S Yale Ave (74114-6252)
PHONE..................918 828-2500
EMP: 2
SALES (est): 141.5K **Privately Held**
SIC: **1389** Measurement of well flow rates, oil & gas

(G-10380)
OHGOODYGOODYCOM
1616 S Peoria Ave Apt 3 (74120-6206)
PHONE..................315 727-5960
Linda Erb, *Principal*
EMP: 2
SALES (est): 139K **Privately Held**
WEB: www.ohgoodygoody.com
SIC: **2759** Commercial printing

(G-10381)
OIL & GAS CONSULTANTS INTL INC (PA)
Also Called: Ogci
2930 S Yale Ave (74114-6252)
P.O. Box 35448 (74153-0448)
PHONE..................918 828-2500
James Ford Brett, *President*
Kevin Lacy, *Exec VP*
Mason Gomez, *Vice Pres*
Dennis Wing, *Treasurer*
Weston Shepherd, *Marketing Staff*
EMP: 49
SQ FT: 18,000
SALES (est): 6.5MM **Privately Held**
SIC: **7371** 7375 8299 1389 Computer software development; information retrieval services; educational service, non-degree granting: continuing educ.; detection & analysis service, gas; oil & gas exploration services

(G-10382)
OIL & GAS DIVISION
440 S Houston Ave Ste 114 (74127-8917)
PHONE..................918 581-2296
Curtis M Johnson, *Principal*
EMP: 2

SALES (est): 117.7K **Privately Held**
WEB: www.occeweb.com
SIC: **1382** Oil & gas exploration services

(G-10383)
OIL & GAS OPTIMIZATION SPECIAL
2601 E 74th Pl (74136-5555)
PHONE..................432 685-0029
EMP: 2
SALES (est): 75.9K **Privately Held**
SIC: **1389** Oil & gas field services

(G-10384)
OIL CAPITAL LAND EXPLORATION
Also Called: Oil Capital Land Exploration
320 S Boston Ave Ste 807 (74103-3728)
PHONE..................918 582-2603
Nancy Yeager, *Vice Pres*
Carol Muntford, *Treasurer*
EMP: 4
SQ FT: 1,500
SALES (est): 449.8K **Privately Held**
SIC: **2813** 6799 Industrial gases; investors

(G-10385)
OIL CAPITAL VALVE COMPANY
7400 E 42nd Pl (74145-4702)
PHONE..................918 627-2474
Britt Radford, *CEO*
James Gibson, *Regl Sales Mgr*
Mike Woods, *Info Tech Mgr*
EMP: 75
SQ FT: 53,603
SALES (est): 8.1MM **Privately Held**
WEB: www.controlvalves.com
SIC: **3599** 3494 Machine shop, jobbing & repair; valves & pipe fittings

(G-10386)
OIL CAPITOL NEON INC
4419 W 55th Pl (74107-9110)
PHONE..................918 582-9031
EMP: 6
SQ FT: 5,000
SALES (est): 500K **Privately Held**
SIC: **3993** Mfg Signs/Advertising Specialties

(G-10387)
OIL STATES INDUSTRIES INC
5563 S 104th East Ave (74146-6506)
PHONE..................918 250-0828
EMP: 2
SALES (corp-wide): 1B **Publicly Held**
SIC: **1389** 3061 3561 3533 Oil & gas wells: building, repairing & dismantling; oil field services; oil & gas field machinery rubber goods (mechanical); pumps & pumping equipment; drilling tools for gas, oil or water wells
HQ: Oil States Industries, Inc.
7701 S Cooper St
Arlington TX 76001

(G-10388)
OIL STATES INDUSTRIES INC
Also Called: Barlow Hunt
10322 E 58th St (74146-6503)
PHONE..................918 250-0828
Jim Barlow, *Branch Mgr*
EMP: 36
SALES (corp-wide): 1B **Publicly Held**
SIC: **3061** Mechanical rubber goods
HQ: Oil States Industries, Inc.
7701 S Cooper St
Arlington TX 76001

(G-10389)
OILS UNLIMITED LLC (PA)
Also Called: Industrial Oils Unlimited
3621 W 5th St (74127-8228)
P.O. Box 3066 (74101-3066)
PHONE..................918 583-1155
Charles Stinson, *CEO*
▼ EMP: 90
SQ FT: 14,000
SALES (est): 18.7MM **Privately Held**
SIC: **2992** 5172 Lubricating oils & greases; lubricating oils & greases

(G-10390)
OK MACHINE AND MFG CO INC
2522 N Columbia Pl (74110-2212)
PHONE..................918 838-1300
Glenn A Strobel, *CEO*
Joan Strobel, *Corp Secy*
EMP: 35
SQ FT: 43,000
SALES (est): 5.8MM **Privately Held**
SIC: **3599** 7692 3441 Machine shop, jobbing & repair; welding repair; fabricated structural metal

(G-10391)
OK PRODUCTS OF TULSA INC
4925 W 50th St (74107-7227)
PHONE..................918 445-2471
Jimmie L Belcher, *President*
Janet Belcher, *Corp Secy*
Jimmie Belcher, *Vice Pres*
Mike Belcher, *Vice Pres*
EMP: 9
SQ FT: 13,000
SALES (est): 979.3K **Privately Held**
SIC: **3599** 3471 Machine shop, jobbing & repair; chromium plating of metals or formed products

(G-10392)
OK RAIL SIGNALS INC
1515 W 36th Pl (74107-5639)
PHONE..................918 378-9520
Marlene Bootenhoff, *President*
EMP: 5
SQ FT: 5,000
SALES: 800K **Privately Held**
SIC: **3669** Railroad signaling devices, electric

(G-10393)
OKIE OPERATING CO LTD
Also Called: Okie Crude Company
401 S Boston Ave Ste 715 (74103-4040)
PHONE..................918 582-2594
Thomas M Atkinson, *President*
Jack Meek, *Vice Pres*
EMP: 3
SQ FT: 5,000
SALES (est): 400K **Privately Held**
SIC: **1311** Crude petroleum production; natural gas production

(G-10394)
OKLAHOMA AEROSPACE ALLIANCE
1800 S Baltimore Ave # 830 (74119-5216)
PHONE..................918 527-0980
Jim Rice, *Chairman*
EMP: 2
SALES: 183.9K **Privately Held**
SIC: **3812** Aircraft/aerospace flight instruments & guidance systems

(G-10395)
OKLAHOMA CUSTOM CANVAS PDTS
2 S 109th East Pl (74128-1623)
PHONE..................918 438-4040
Dan Hayes Sr, *President*
Cyndi Hayes, *Treasurer*
EMP: 13
SQ FT: 6,000
SALES: 630K **Privately Held**
SIC: **5999** 2394 Canvas products; awnings, fabric: made from purchased materials

(G-10396)
OKLAHOMA DEPARTMENT OF MINES
Also Called: Wagoner Field Office
4845 S Sheridan Rd # 514 (74145-5719)
PHONE..................918 485-3999
Rhonda Dossett, *Manager*
EMP: 7 **Privately Held**
SIC: **1241** 9511 Coal mining exploration & test boring;
HQ: Department Of Mines Oklahoma
2915 N Clken Blvd Ste 213
Oklahoma City OK 73106

(G-10397)
OKLAHOMA DISTILLING COMPANY
1724 E 7th St (74104-3202)
PHONE..................918 505-4861
Hunter Gambill, *Principal*
EMP: 7
SALES (est): 537.1K **Privately Held**
SIC: **2085** Distilled & blended liquors

(G-10398)
OKLAHOMA EAGLE LLC
Also Called: Oklahoma Eagle, The
624 E Archer St (74120-1002)
P.O. Box 3267 (74101-3267)
PHONE..................918 582-7124
James G Goodwin, *Chairman*
EMP: 5
SALES (est): 229.8K **Privately Held**
SIC: **2711** 8999 7313 Newspapers; editorial service; electronic media advertising representatives

(G-10399)
OKLAHOMA EAGLE PUBLISHING CO
624 E Archer St (74120-1002)
P.O. Box 3267 (74101-3267)
PHONE..................918 582-7124
James O Goodwin, *Ch of Bd*
Joseph Goodwin, *COO*
EMP: 8
SQ FT: 7,000
SALES (est): 414.2K **Privately Held**
SIC: **2711** Newspapers: publishing only, not printed on site

(G-10400)
OKLAHOMA ENERGY SOURCE LLC
7136 S Yale Ave Ste 210 (74136-6356)
PHONE..................918 307-8142
Bill G Crow,
EMP: 3
SALES (est): 178.1K **Privately Held**
SIC: **1389** Gas field services

(G-10401)
OKLAHOMA FORGE INC
5259 S 49th West Ave (74107-8808)
P.O. Box 701500 (74170-1500)
PHONE..................918 446-4486
Stephen R Duenner, *President*
Jessica Phillips, *Sales Staff*
Kim Yocham, *Sales Staff*
▲ EMP: 44
SQ FT: 120,000
SALES (est): 10.1MM **Privately Held**
WEB: www.oklahomaforge.com
SIC: **3462** Iron & steel forgings

(G-10402)
OKLAHOMA MAGAZINE
1609 S Boston Ave (74119-4439)
P.O. Box 14204 (74159-1204)
PHONE..................918 744-6205
Daniel Schuman, *Owner*
Vida Schuman, *Co-Owner*
EMP: 10
SALES (est): 410K **Privately Held**
WEB: www.okmag.com
SIC: **2711** 7313 2721 Newspapers; magazine advertising representative; periodicals

(G-10403)
OKLAHOMA MOBIL CONCRETE INC
10313 E 48th St (74146-5004)
PHONE..................918 622-3930
Linda Crowl, *President*
Darryl Crowl, *Corp Secy*
EMP: 3
SQ FT: 5,000
SALES (est): 280K **Privately Held**
WEB: www.oklahomamobileconcrete.com
SIC: **3273** Ready-mixed concrete

(G-10404)
OKLAHOMA OFFSET VEBA INC
1415 S Quincy Ave (74120-5838)
P.O. Box 1770 (74102-1770)
PHONE..................918 582-0921
EMP: 2

SALES (est): 120K **Privately Held**
SIC: 2752 Lithographic Commercial Printing

(G-10405)
OKLAHOMA POST TENSION INC
4119 S 88th East Ave (74145-3330)
P.O. Box 700702 (74170-0702)
PHONE..................................918 627-6013
E C C Williamson, *President*
EMP: 10
SQ FT: 10,000
SALES (est): 2.4MM **Privately Held**
SIC: 5051 3496 3441 Reinforcement mesh, wire; rods, wire (not insulated); miscellaneous fabricated wire products; fabricated structural metal

(G-10406)
OKLAHOMA RBR & GASKET CO INC
3216 Charles Page Blvd (74127-8321)
P.O. Box 3284 (74101-3284)
PHONE..................................918 585-3484
Jackie Garrett, *President*
Tony Holt, *Corp Secy*
EMP: 15
SQ FT: 18,500
SALES (est): 6.7MM **Privately Held**
SIC: 5085 3599 3053 Rubber goods, mechanical; hose, flexible metallic; gaskets & sealing devices

(G-10407)
OKLAHOMA SCREEN MFG LLC
10838 E Marshall St 102 (74116-5682)
PHONE..................................918 443-6500
Tommy Mitchell,
EMP: 4 **Privately Held**
WEB: www.psm-mfg.com
SIC: 3496 Miscellaneous fabricated wire products
PA: Oklahoma Screen Manufacturing, Llc
7287 E Highway 88
Oologah OK 74053

(G-10408)
OKLAHOMA SIGN ASSOCIATION
533 S Rockford Ave (74120-4015)
PHONE..................................918 587-7171
Melissa Mirsaeidi, *Administration*
EMP: 2
SALES (est): 72.6K **Privately Held**
SIC: 3993 Signs & advertising specialties

(G-10409)
OKLAHOMANS FOR VACCINE
6011 E 115th St (74137-7750)
PHONE..................................918 606-9213
Crystal Mackey, *Principal*
EMP: 2
SALES (est): 74.4K **Privately Held**
SIC: 2836 Vaccines

(G-10410)
OLAM PUBLISHING LLC
8525 E 75th St (74133-2938)
PHONE..................................918 200-9770
Jose Aizpiri, *Mng Member*
EMP: 1
SALES (est): 33.3K **Privately Held**
SIC: 2731 7389 Books: publishing only;

(G-10411)
OLD WORLD IRON INC
4718 S 25th West Ave (74107-7642)
PHONE..................................918 445-3063
Harlan Wayland, *President*
EMP: 4
SQ FT: 7,500
SALES (est): 399.3K **Privately Held**
SIC: 1799 3446 5211 3444 Fence construction; architectural metalwork; fencing; sheet metalwork; fabricated plate work (boiler shop); fabricated structural metal

(G-10412)
OLD WRLD MSTERS DIV BLDG PDTS
2651 E 21st St (74114-1715)
PHONE..................................918 230-0340
EMP: 2 **EST:** 2015
SALES (est): 123.4K **Privately Held**
SIC: 2434 Wood kitchen cabinets

(G-10413)
OLDCASTLE MATERIALS INC
4150 S 100th East Ave # 300 (74146-3650)
PHONE..................................918 978-0459
EMP: 154
SALES (corp-wide): 30.6B **Privately Held**
SIC: 2951 1611 1622 Asphalt paving mixtures & blocks; general contractor, highway & street construction; bridge construction
HQ: Oldcastle Materials, Inc.
900 Ashwood Pkwy Ste 700
Atlanta GA 30338

(G-10414)
OLIFANT ENERGY LLC
15 W 6th St Ste 2200 (74119-5416)
PHONE..................................918 984-9074
Donald G Burdick, *CEO*
EMP: 4
SALES (est): 869.1K **Privately Held**
SIC: 1382 Oil & gas exploration services

(G-10415)
OLMSTEAD OIL COMPANY
Also Called: Midcon Energy
2431 E 61st St Ste 850 (74136-1236)
PHONE..................................918 743-2360
Randy Olmstead, *President*
EMP: 27
SALES (est): 5.1MM **Privately Held**
WEB: www.midconenergypartners.com
SIC: 1311 Crude petroleum production

(G-10416)
OMNI DESIGN
6131 S Oswego Ave (74136-1511)
PHONE..................................918 495-0841
Coyote Johnson, *President*
EMP: 1
SALES (est): 111.9K **Privately Held**
SIC: 3699 Electrical equipment & supplies

(G-10417)
OMNI LIGHTING
212 N Main St (74103-2006)
PHONE..................................918 633-7245
Brent Johnson, *Owner*
EMP: 2
SALES (est): 56.5K **Privately Held**
SIC: 7372 Prepackaged software

(G-10418)
ONE GAS INC (PA)
15 E 5th St (74103-4346)
P.O. Box 21049 (74121-1049)
PHONE..................................918 947-7000
John W Gibson, *Ch of Bd*
Pierce H Norton II, *President*
Mark A Bender, *Senior VP*
Caron A Lawhorn, *Senior VP*
Robert S McAnnally, *Senior VP*
EMP: 100
SALES: 1.6B **Publicly Held**
SIC: 1311 4924 Natural gas production; natural gas distribution

(G-10419)
ONE GAS INC
5848 E 15th St (74112-6402)
PHONE..................................918 831-8218
EMP: 3
SALES (est): 161.5K **Privately Held**
SIC: 1311 Natural gas production

(G-10420)
ONEGAS
100 W 5th St (74103-4279)
PHONE..................................918 947-7000
Terry K Spencer, *President*
EMP: 5 **EST:** 2014
SALES (est): 985.9K **Privately Held**
WEB: www.onegas.com
SIC: 1382 Oil & gas exploration services

(G-10421)
ONEOK INC (PA)
100 W 5th St Ste LI (74103-4298)
P.O. Box 871 (74102-0871)
PHONE..................................918 588-7000
John W Gibson, *Ch of Bd*
Terry K Spencer, *President*
Kevin Oakes, *Area Mgr*
Kevin L Burdick, *COO*
Stephen B Allen, *Senior VP*
EMP: 1000

SALES: 10.1B **Publicly Held**
WEB: www.oneok.com
SIC: 4922 1311 1321 5172 Natural gas distribution; crude petroleum & natural gas; crude petroleum production; natural gas production; natural gas liquids; gases; pipelines, natural gas

(G-10422)
ONEOK INC
Also Called: Oklahoma Natural Gas
205 E Pine St Ste 2 (74106-4855)
PHONE..................................918 588-7000
Warren Grubb, *Manager*
EMP: 40
SALES (corp-wide): 10.1B **Publicly Held**
SIC: 4922 4924 1321 5172 Pipelines, natural gas; storage, natural gas; natural gas distribution; natural gas liquids; gases; crude petroleum production; natural gas production; drilling oil & gas wells
PA: Oneok, Inc.
100 W 5th St Ste LI
Tulsa OK 74103
918 588-7000

(G-10423)
ONEOK FIELD SERVICES CO LLC (DH)
100 W 5th St Ste LI (74103-4298)
P.O. Box 871 (74102-0871)
PHONE..................................918 588-7000
John W Gibson, *CEO*
Terry K Spencer, *President*
Robert F Martinovich, *Exec VP*
Pierce H Norton, *Exec VP*
Stephen W Lake, *Senior VP*
EMP: 500
SALES (est): 398.9MM
SALES (corp-wide): 10.1B **Publicly Held**
SIC: 1321 Natural gas liquids

(G-10424)
ONEOK GAS PROCESSING LLC
100 W 5th St Ste LI (74103-4298)
PHONE..................................918 588-7000
EMP: 2
SALES (est): 81.9K **Privately Held**
SIC: 1311 Crude petroleum & natural gas

(G-10425)
ONEOK GAS TRANSPORTATION LLC
100 W 5th St Md14-5 (74103-4279)
PHONE..................................918 588-7000
Kent Shortridge, *Manager*
EMP: 142
SALES (est): 6.5MM
SALES (corp-wide): 10.1B **Publicly Held**
SIC: 1311 Crude petroleum & natural gas
HQ: Oneok Partners, L.P.
100 W 5th St Ste LI
Tulsa OK 74103

(G-10426)
ONEOK MIDSTREAM GAS SUPPLY LLC
100 W 5th St Ste 450 (74103-4254)
PHONE..................................918 588-7000
John Gibbson, *President*
Curtis Dinan, *Vice Pres*
James Kneale, *CFO*
Julie Edwards, *Bd of Directors*
EMP: 13
SALES (est): 762.5K
SALES (corp-wide): 10.1B **Publicly Held**
SIC: 1321 Natural gas liquids production
PA: Oneok, Inc.
100 W 5th St Ste LI
Tulsa OK 74103
918 588-7000

(G-10427)
ONEOK PARTNERS LP (HQ)
100 W 5th St Ste LI (74103-4298)
PHONE..................................918 588-7000
Terry K Spencer, *President*
Michael A Fitzgibbons, *Senior VP*
Walter S Hulse III, *CFO*
EMP: 50

SALES: 8.9B
SALES (corp-wide): 10.1B **Publicly Held**
SIC: 4922 1321 1381 4925 Natural gas transmission; natural gas liquids; drilling oil & gas wells; gas production and/or distribution
PA: Oneok, Inc.
100 W 5th St Ste LI
Tulsa OK 74103
918 588-7000

(G-10428)
ONEOK PRODUCER SERVICES CO
100 W 5th St Ste LI (74103-4298)
P.O. Box 871 (74102-0871)
PHONE..................................918 588-7000
David Kyle, *President*
Don Jacobson, *Vice Pres*
EMP: 3
SALES (est): 207.7K
SALES (corp-wide): 10.1B **Publicly Held**
SIC: 1311 Crude petroleum production; natural gas production
HQ: Oneok Resources Company
100 W 5th St Ste 450
Tulsa OK 74103
918 588-7000

(G-10429)
ONEOK RESOURCES COMPANY (HQ)
100 W 5th St Ste 450 (74103-4254)
P.O. Box 871 (74102-0871)
PHONE..................................918 588-7000
David Kyle, *President*
Curtis Dinan, *Vice Pres*
EMP: 51
SQ FT: 8,000
SALES (est): 7.1MM
SALES (corp-wide): 10.1B **Publicly Held**
SIC: 1311 Crude petroleum production; natural gas production
PA: Oneok, Inc.
100 W 5th St Ste LI
Tulsa OK 74103
918 588-7000

(G-10430)
ONEOK TEXAS FIELD SERVICES LP (PA)
100 W 5th St Ste LI (74103-4298)
PHONE..................................918 588-7000
Oneok Field Services Holdings, *Partner*
John Manning, *Principal*
EMP: 80
SQ FT: 45,000
SALES (est): 90.6MM **Privately Held**
SIC: 1321 Natural gas liquids production

(G-10431)
ONYX IMAGING CORPORATION
7446 E 46th Pl (74145-6306)
PHONE..................................918 627-6611
Jean Nicklas, *President*
Lee W Nicklas, *Vice Pres*
Stephen Nicklas, *Vice Pres*
EMP: 8
SQ FT: 5,000
SALES (est): 1MM **Privately Held**
SIC: 3577 Computer peripheral equipment

(G-10432)
OPB PIPE BENDING
1625 E Easton St (74120-1216)
PHONE..................................918 583-1566
Darrel Smith, *Owner*
EMP: 2
SALES (est): 134.1K **Privately Held**
SIC: 3599 Industrial machinery

(G-10433)
OPENLINK FINANCIAL LLC
320 S Boston Ave Ste 600 (74103-3713)
PHONE..................................918 594-7320
Diane Summers, *Branch Mgr*
EMP: 75
SALES (corp-wide): 177.9K **Privately Held**
SIC: 7372 Business oriented computer software
HQ: Openlink Financial Llc
800 Rxr Plz Fl 8
Uniondale NY 11556

GEOGRAPHIC SECTION
Tulsa - Tulsa County (G-10464)

(G-10434)
ORACLE AMERICA INC
Also Called: Sun Microsystems
321 S Boston Ave Ste 600 (74103-3310)
PHONE 918 587-9016
EMP: 3
SALES (corp-wide): 38.2B **Publicly Held**
SIC: 3571 Mfg Electronic Computers
HQ: Oracle America, Inc.
500 Oracle Pkwy
Redwood City CA 94065
650 506-7000

(G-10435)
ORAL HEALTH PRODUCTS INC
Also Called: P O H
6855 E 40th St (74145)
PHONE 918 622-9412
Stanton Jones, *Finance*
Robert G Jones II, *Branch Mgr*
Bob Jones, *CTO*
EMP: 10
SALES (corp-wide): 5.5MM **Privately Held**
SIC: 3991 3843 Toothbrushes, except electric; dental materials
PA: Oral Health Products, Inc.
6863 E 40th St
Tulsa OK
918 622-9412

(G-10436)
ORAL RBRTS EVNGLISTIC ASSN INC (PA)
6201 E 43rd St (74135-6562)
P.O. Box 2187 (74102-2187)
PHONE 918 591-2000
Jeff Ogle, *Dean*
Lindsey Roberts, *Exec VP*
Coleen Barker, *Vice Pres*
D Michael Bernard, *Vice Pres*
David Ellsworth, *CFO*
EMP: 70
SALES: 7.9MM **Privately Held**
WEB: www.oralroberts.com
SIC: 8661 2721 8299 6311 Religious organizations; periodicals: publishing only; educational services; life insurance

(G-10437)
ORCA OPERATING COMPANY LLC
427 S Boston Ave Ste 400 (74103-4122)
PHONE 918 587-1312
Jeff Kennedy, *Principal*
EMP: 3 EST: 2008
SALES (est): 211.3K **Privately Held**
SIC: 1389 Construction, repair & dismantling services

(G-10438)
ORCUTT MACHINE
3129 Charles Page Blvd (74127)
PHONE 918 629-7930
Roger Orcutt, *Owner*
EMP: 4
SALES: 100K **Privately Held**
SIC: 3999 Manufacturing industries

(G-10439)
ORICA USA INC
12502 E 36th St N (74116-1313)
PHONE 918 437-1644
Bill Brown, *Branch Mgr*
EMP: 6 **Privately Held**
SIC: 2892 Explosives
HQ: Orica Usa Inc.
33101 E Quincy Ave
Watkins CO 80137

(G-10440)
ORION EXPLORATION LLC
4870 S Lewis Ave Ste 240 (74105-5153)
PHONE 918 492-0254
Steve Miller, *President*
Vicki Kruse, *Vice Pres*
Regina Weeks, *Production*
EMP: 3
SALES (est): 399.3K **Privately Held**
WEB: www.orionexploration.com
SIC: 1382 Oil & gas exploration services

(G-10441)
ORMCA
2526 E 71st St Ste H (74136-5576)
PHONE 918 296-7711
John Petreikis, *Principal*
EMP: 3
SALES (est): 222.6K **Privately Held**
WEB: www.ormca.com
SIC: 3273 Ready-mixed concrete

(G-10442)
OSAGE LEATHER INC
3220 S Peoria Ave Ste 202 (74105-2003)
PHONE 918 745-0772
George Coen, *President*
▲ EMP: 4
SQ FT: 1,800
SALES (est): 2MM **Privately Held**
SIC: 3111 5199 Leather tanning & finishing; leather & cut stock

(G-10443)
OSAGE NEON
915 N 33rd West Ave (74127-5003)
PHONE 918 583-4430
Harold Hawkins, *Owner*
EMP: 1
SALES (est): 81.9K **Privately Held**
SIC: 3993 7629 Neon signs; electrical repair shops

(G-10444)
OSBORNE DESIGN CO
4524 W 21st St (74107-3453)
PHONE 918 585-3212
Chuck Osborne, *Owner*
EMP: 1
SALES (est): 90K **Privately Held**
SIC: 3993 7312 2759 Signs & advertising specialties; outdoor advertising services; commercial printing

(G-10445)
OUT ON LIMB PUBLISHING
Also Called: Out On A Limb Publishing
1810 E 51st St Ste C (74105)
PHONE 918 743-4408
Susan Coman, *Partner*
John Coman, *Partner*
EMP: 5
SALES (est): 264.5K **Privately Held**
SIC: 2731 Book publishing

(G-10446)
OUTSOURCE GROUP LLC
15 E 5th St Ste 2221 (74103-4300)
PHONE 918 307-0110
Matthew D Lamb,
Stacey Lamb,
EMP: 6
SALES (est): 540K **Privately Held**
SIC: 1389 Oil field services

(G-10447)
OVINTIV EXPLORATION INC
110 W 7th St (74119-1031)
PHONE 918 740-1400
Lee Boothby, *Branch Mgr*
EMP: 2
SALES (corp-wide): 8.5MM **Publicly Held**
WEB: www.theinnatrsf.com
SIC: 1382 Oil & gas exploration services
HQ: Ovintiv Exploration Inc.
4 Waterway Square Pl # 100
The Woodlands TX 77380
281 210-5100

(G-10448)
OVINTIV MID-CONTINENT INC (DH)
101 E 2nd St (74103)
PHONE 918 582-2690
Lee K Boothby, *CEO*
Larry S Massaro, *Exec VP*
Gary D Packer, *Exec VP*
Terry W Rathert, *Exec VP*
George T Dunn, *Senior VP*
EMP: 225 EST: 2001
SQ FT: 105,000
SALES: 196.2MM
SALES (corp-wide): 8.5MM **Publicly Held**
SIC: 1311 Crude petroleum production; natural gas production
HQ: Ovintiv Exploration Inc.
4 Waterway Square Pl # 100
The Woodlands TX 77380
281 210-5100

(G-10449)
OWNER VALUE NEWS
5800 E Skelly Dr Ste 708 (74135-6444)
P.O. Box 35525 (74153-0525)
PHONE 918 828-9600
EMP: 6 EST: 2017
SALES (est): 321K **Privately Held**
WEB: www.valuenews.com
SIC: 2711 Newspapers

(G-10450)
OZARK STEEL LLC
908 W 41st St (74107-7025)
PHONE 918 438-4330
Jim Welch, *General Mgr*
Jimmy Downey, *Prdtn Mgr*
Gary Sample, *Prdtn Mgr*
Johnie Cowles, *Purch Mgr*
Landon Walker, *Controller*
EMP: 27
SQ FT: 19,500
SALES (est): 14.4MM **Privately Held**
SIC: 3441 Fabricated structural metal

(G-10451)
P & M INDUSTRIES INC
4450 S Mingo Rd (74146-4703)
P.O. Box 471069 (74147-1069)
PHONE 918 660-0055
James E Parker, *President*
Mark A Parker, *President*
Betty Reininger, *Vice Pres*
Betty R Reininger, *Purch Mgr*
▲ EMP: 26 EST: 1978
SALES (est): 6MM **Privately Held**
SIC: 3441 Fabricated structural metal

(G-10452)
P H C EXPLORATIONS INC
11111 S Fulton Ave (74137-7615)
PHONE 918 298-2008
Patrick H Clare, *President*
EMP: 1
SALES (est): 117.1K **Privately Held**
SIC: 1382 Oil & gas exploration services

(G-10453)
P I SPEAKERS
10608 E 18th St (74128-6206)
PHONE 918 663-2131
Wayne Parham, *Owner*
EMP: 7 EST: 1979
SALES (est): 390.8K **Privately Held**
WEB: www.pispeakers.com
SIC: 2517 Wood television & radio cabinets

(G-10454)
PACE PRINTING INC
611 E 4th St (74120-3017)
PHONE 918 585-5664
Frankie Lantz, *President*
Jack Lantz, *Vice Pres*
Desiree Spencer, *Manager*
EMP: 7
SALES (est): 467.4K **Privately Held**
SIC: 2752 2789 Commercial printing, offset; bookbinding & related work

(G-10455)
PADGETT MACHINE SHOP INC
1226 N 143rd East Ave (74116-2120)
PHONE 918 438-3444
Edward Padgett Jr, *President*
Randy Padgett, *General Mgr*
Randy W Padgett, *Vice Pres*
David Schell, *Opers Staff*
Debby C Lampkins, *Administration*
▼ EMP: 18
SQ FT: 10,250
SALES (est): 3.1MM **Privately Held**
SIC: 3599 Machine shop, jobbing & repair

(G-10456)
PADGETT MACHINE SHOP LLC
1226 N 143rd East Ave (74116-2120)
PHONE 918 636-9334
Edward Padgett, *Principal*
Randy Padgett, *Principal*
EMP: 2

(G-10457)
PALADIN LAND GROUP LLC
15 E 5th St Ste 1602 (74103-4362)
P.O. Box 52400 (74152-0400)
PHONE 918 582-5404
Jayme Willis, *Manager*
EMP: 2
SALES (est): 159K **Privately Held**
WEB: www.paladinlandgroup.com
SIC: 1382 Oil & gas exploration services

(G-10458)
PANDA SCREEN PRINTING ENTPS
3927 E Admiral Pl (74115-8305)
PHONE 918 622-3601
Alfonzo Salazar, *Partner*
EMP: 2
SALES (est): 164.1K **Privately Held**
WEB: www.pandaapparel.com
SIC: 2759 Screen printing

(G-10459)
PANDERIA LA GUADALUPANA
1126 E 61st St (74136-0523)
PHONE 918 764-9000
Artemis Solis, *Owner*
EMP: 8
SALES (est): 617.5K **Privately Held**
SIC: 2051 Cakes, bakery: except frozen

(G-10460)
PANOAK OIL & GAS CORPORATION (PA)
403 S Cheyenne Ave # 1000 (74103-3852)
PHONE 918 857-4929
David M Harl, *President*
EMP: 8
SQ FT: 2,000
SALES (est): 1.2MM **Privately Held**
SIC: 1311 Crude petroleum production; natural gas production

(G-10461)
PANTHER ENERGY COMPANY LLC
Also Called: Holmes Exparation
6100 S Yale Ave Ste 600 (74136-1922)
PHONE 918 583-1396
James R Stone, *Exec VP*
Roy Grossman, *Senior VP*
Don Burdick, *Vice Pres*
Jeff L Nevins, *Vice Pres*
David Sims, *Controller*
EMP: 53
SQ FT: 20,000
SALES (est): 23.6MM **Privately Held**
SIC: 1382 Oil & gas exploration services

(G-10462)
PANTHER ENERGY COMPANY II LLC
6100 S Yale Ave Ste 600 (74136-1922)
PHONE 918 583-1396
Berry J Mullennix, *CEO*
Roy H Grossman, *Exec VP*
James R Stone, *Exec VP*
Don Burdick, *Vice Pres*
Jeff L Nevins, *CFO*
EMP: 10
SALES (est): 1.1MM **Privately Held**
SIC: 1382 Oil & gas exploration services

(G-10463)
PAPER HOUSE PRODUCTIONS LLC
Also Called: Hero Printworks
6103 E Admiral Blvd (74115-8634)
PHONE 918 835-0172
Charles Taylor, *Mng Member*
EMP: 5
SALES: 750K **Privately Held**
SIC: 2752 Commercial printing, lithographic

(G-10464)
PAPPAN AND SPEARS LLC
11108 E Admiral Pl (74116-3024)
P.O. Box 609, Pawnee (74058-0609)
PHONE 405 742-6900
William Pappan,
Richard Spears,

EMP: 1
SQ FT: 2,000
SALES (est): 113K **Privately Held**
SIC: **3589** Car washing machinery

(G-10465)
PARADISE POOLS & HOT TUBS
6353 E 41st St (74135-6103)
PHONE..................................918 938-7727
EMP: 1
SALES (est): 39.6K **Privately Held**
SIC: **3999** Hot tubs

(G-10466)
PARALLEL ENERGY LP
1323 E 71st St Ste 200 (74136-5065)
P.O. Box 691500 (74169-1500)
PHONE..................................918 712-7008
Tony Swindell, *Vice Pres*
EMP: 23 **EST:** 2011
SALES (est): 3.2MM **Privately Held**
SIC: **1389** Testing, measuring, surveying & analysis services

(G-10467)
PARCO MASTS & SUBSTRUCTURES
8 E 3rd St (74103-3610)
PHONE..................................918 585-8221
John E Menger, *Principal*
EMP: 2
SALES (est): 126K
SALES (corp-wide): 571.1MM **Publicly Held**
SIC: **3533** Oil field machinery & equipment; gas field machinery & equipment
PA: Parker Drilling Company
    5 Greenway Plz Ste 100
    Houston TX 77046
    281 406-2000

(G-10468)
PARKER DRILLING COMPANY
2021 S Lewis Ave Ste 410 (74104-5722)
PHONE..................................918 281-2708
EMP: 6
SALES (corp-wide): 442.5MM **Publicly Held**
SIC: **1381** Drilling Contractor
PA: Parker Drilling Company
    5 Greenway Plz Ste 100
    Houston TX 77046
    281 406-2000

(G-10469)
PARKING DRILLING COMPANY INTL
8 E 3rd St (74103-3610)
PHONE..................................281 406-2000
David Parker, *President*
Steven Noid, *Corp Secy*
◆ EMP: 120
SALES (est): 3.3MM
SALES (corp-wide): 571.1MM **Publicly Held**
SIC: **1381** Drilling oil & gas wells
PA: Parker Drilling Company
    5 Greenway Plz Ste 100
    Houston TX 77046
    281 406-2000

(G-10470)
PARRA WORLD CREATIONS LLC
8001 S Mingo Rd Apt 1901 (74133-0833)
PHONE..................................918 938-2278
Diego Parra, *Principal*
EMP: 1
SALES (est): 55K **Privately Held**
SIC: **3842** Personal safety equipment; gloves, safety

(G-10471)
PARSAGE OIL COMPANY LLC
1821 E 71st St (74136-3922)
P.O. Box 700037 (74170-0037)
PHONE..................................918 846-2358
Jerry T Parker,
Erik Block,
Tom Parker,
EMP: 4
SALES (est): 156.1K **Privately Held**
SIC: **1311** Crude petroleum production

(G-10472)
PATRICK A MCGINLEY
1105 E 21st Pl (74114-1213)
P.O. Box 3126 (74101-3126)
PHONE..................................918 583-3267
Patrick A McGinley, *Owner*
EMP: 3 **EST:** 1960
SALES (est): 242.2K **Privately Held**
SIC: **1311** Crude petroleum production

(G-10473)
PATRICK ENERGY GROUP
Also Called: Patrick Petroleum
7380 S Olympia Ave (74132-1849)
PHONE..................................918 477-7755
EMP: 4 **EST:** 1999
SQ FT: 4,000
SALES (est): 550K **Privately Held**
SIC: **1382** 8741 Oil/Gas Exploration Services Management Services

(G-10474)
PATRICK MICHAEL PALAZZO
577 E 32nd St N Apt C (74106-1829)
PHONE..................................918 344-3724
Patrick Palazzo, *Owner*
EMP: 1
SALES (est): 55.3K **Privately Held**
SIC: **3711** Automobile assembly, including specialty automobiles

(G-10475)
PAUL KING COMPANY
1030 N Owasso Ave (74106-5337)
P.O. Box 580817 (74158-0817)
PHONE..................................918 592-5464
Larry Wagner, *President*
Sally Payton, *Purchasing*
E McClain, *CFO*
EMP: 4
SQ FT: 5,500
SALES (est): 1.3MM **Privately Held**
WEB: www.paulkingco.com
SIC: **5084** 3613 Indicating instruments & accessories; control panels, electric

(G-10476)
PAUL PRECISION MACHINE INC
5908 E 12th St (74112-5418)
PHONE..................................918 835-6175
John C Paul Jr, *President*
T Lou Paul, *Vice Pres*
EMP: 13
SQ FT: 16,000
SALES (est): 2MM **Privately Held**
SIC: **3599** Machine shop, jobbing & repair

(G-10477)
PAYSMITH PROCESSING LLC
4500 S 129th East Ave # 175 (74134-5870)
PHONE..................................918 858-5599
EMP: 2
SALES (est): 90.1K **Privately Held**
SIC: **3471** Plating & polishing

(G-10478)
PEABODY & KENT DESIGNS INC
6935 E 13th St (74112-5615)
PHONE..................................918 439-4300
Preston Reynolds, *President*
EMP: 4
SQ FT: 3,000
SALES: 250K **Privately Held**
SIC: **2395** Embroidery products, except schiffli machine

(G-10479)
PEAK INDUSTRIES
9955 E 55th Pl (74146-6404)
P.O. Box 471373 (74147-1373)
PHONE..................................918 289-0424
EMP: 1 **EST:** 2012
SALES (est): 51K **Privately Held**
SIC: **3999** Mfg Misc Products

(G-10480)
PEAK SULFUR INC
5201 W 21st St (74107-2232)
PHONE..................................918 587-7613
Paul Ferrall, *President*
EMP: 163
SQ FT: 50,000
SALES: 39.5MM **Privately Held**
SIC: **2819** Sulfuric acid, oleum

(G-10481)
PEARL DISTRICT EMBROIDERY LLC
716 S Troost Ave (74120-4834)
PHONE..................................918 269-3347
Mary D Hill, *President*
EMP: 1
SALES (est): 31.2K **Privately Held**
SIC: **2395** Pleating & stitching

(G-10482)
PECOS PIPELINE LLC
110 W 7th St Ste 2300 (74119-1017)
PHONE..................................918 574-3500
EMP: 1 **EST:** 2013
SALES (est): 344.7K **Publicly Held**
SIC: **1389** Gas field services
HQ: Targa Midstream Services Llc
    811 Louisiana St Ste 2100
    Houston TX 77002

(G-10483)
PENDLETON WOOLEN MILLS INC
1828 Utica Sq (74114-1408)
PHONE..................................918 712-8545
Angel Anderson, *Branch Mgr*
EMP: 51
SALES (corp-wide): 137.5MM **Privately Held**
SIC: **2231** Wool broadwoven fabrics
PA: Pendleton Woolen Mills, Inc.
    220 Nw Broadway
    Portland OR 97209
    503 226-4801

(G-10484)
PENLOYD LLC
2900 E Apache St (74110-2253)
P.O. Box 701648 (74170-1648)
PHONE..................................918 836-3794
Tim Nagle, *Chairman*
EMP: 4 **EST:** 2011
SALES (est): 514.3K **Privately Held**
SIC: **2521** Wood office furniture

(G-10485)
PENNANT OIL & GAS LLC
Also Called: Banner Oil & Gas
907 S Detroit Ave # 1035 (74120-4317)
PHONE..................................405 642-4382
Jeff Peles, *Mng Member*
EMP: 4
SALES: 6MM **Privately Held**
SIC: **1311** Crude petroleum production

(G-10486)
PENNINGTON ALLEN CPITL PRTNERS
5100 E Skelly Dr (74135-6565)
PHONE..................................918 749-6811
Sow Kam Ng, *General Mgr*
W Lane Pennington, *Founder*
Mark H Allen,
EMP: 25
SALES: 68.7K
SALES (corp-wide): 17MM **Privately Held**
SIC: **3531** Hammer mills (rock & ore crushing machines), portable
PA: Bliss Industries, Llc
    900 E Oakland Ave
    Ponca City OK 74601
    580 765-7787

(G-10487)
PENNSYLVANIA CHERNICKY LLC
1307 S Boulder Ave # 400 (74119-9700)
PHONE..................................918 587-6242
Thomas P Schroedter, *Principal*
EMP: 2
SALES (est): 127.7K **Privately Held**
SIC: **1382** Oil & gas exploration services

(G-10488)
PEPPER LAND INC
4645 S 189th East Ave (74134-7245)
PHONE..................................918 691-7241
Juan Carlos Barajas, *President*
▲ EMP: 2
SALES (est): 165.8K **Privately Held**
SIC: **2099** Chili pepper or powder

(G-10489)
PEPSI COLA COMPANY
Also Called: Pepsico
510 W Skelly Dr (74107-9453)
PHONE..................................918 446-6601
Indra K Nooyi, *CEO*
Zein Abdalla, *President*
Umran Beba, *Senior VP*
Jon Banner, *Vice Pres*
Chris Boyett, *Sales Staff*
EMP: 425
SALES (est): 59.3MM
SALES (corp-wide): 67.1B **Publicly Held**
SIC: **2086** Carbonated soft drinks, bottled & canned
PA: Pepsico, Inc.
    700 Anderson Hill Rd
    Purchase NY 10577
    914 253-2000

(G-10490)
PEPSI-COLA BTLG MCALESTER INC
Also Called: Pepsico
510 W Skelly Dr (74107-9453)
PHONE..................................918 446-6601
Connie Bohnefield, *Principal*
Curt Clark, *Manager*
EMP: 9
SALES (est): 846.8K
SALES (corp-wide): 5.5MM **Privately Held**
SIC: **2086** Carbonated soft drinks, bottled & canned
PA: Pepsi-Cola Bottling Co. Of Mcalester, Inc.
    1528 E Electric Ave
    Mcalester OK 74501
    918 423-2360

(G-10491)
PEREGRINE PRODUCTS LLC
5510 S Lewis Ave Ste 201 (74105-7105)
PHONE..................................918 361-4304
Kaitlyn Nagle, *Principal*
Diana Nagle, *Finance*
EMP: 2
SALES (est): 156.6K **Privately Held**
SIC: **1382** Oil & gas exploration services

(G-10492)
PERFECT CIRCLE PUBLISHING INC
10026a S Mingo Rd Ste 440 (74133-5700)
PHONE..................................918 629-0061
Elizabeth T Sherman, *President*
EMP: 1
SALES: 4K **Privately Held**
SIC: **2741** 7389 Miscellaneous publishing;

(G-10493)
PERFECTING SOFTWARE LLC
10707 E 76th St (74133-2515)
PHONE..................................918 250-7610
Paul Krueger, *Principal*
EMP: 2
SALES (est): 38.1K **Privately Held**
WEB: www.perfectingsoftware.com
SIC: **7372** Prepackaged software

(G-10494)
PERFORMANCE PLASTICS INC
4747 S 102nd East Ave (74146-4818)
PHONE..................................918 627-9621
Don Stephens, *President*
Charlotte Stephens, *Treasurer*
EMP: 1
SQ FT: 18,000
SALES (est): 204.5K **Privately Held**
SIC: **3711** 3713 Trucks, pickup, assembly of; truck & bus bodies

(G-10495)
PERKINS DEVELOPMENT CORP
Also Called: Linsay Perkins Development
2223 E Skelly Dr 10 (74105-5913)
PHONE..................................918 749-2152
D Lindsay Perkins, *President*
Brandon Perkins, *Vice Pres*
Patricia Diane Perkins, *Treasurer*
EMP: 2
SQ FT: 1,000

GEOGRAPHIC SECTION

Tulsa - Tulsa County (G-10525)

SALES (est): 210K **Privately Held**
WEB: www.newlots.com
SIC: 6531 1311 Real estate agent, residential; crude petroleum & natural gas

(G-10496)
PERMAC INC (HQ)
1717 S Boulder Ave (74119-4805)
PHONE..................................918 295-7600
Joseph W Craft III, *President*
R E Perkinson Jr, *VP Opers*
Brenda T Acken, *Treasurer*
EMP: 2
SQ FT: 10,000
SALES (est): 234.3K **Privately Held**
SIC: 1221 Bituminous coal surface mining

(G-10497)
PERMIAN BASIN BANDING
3166 S 57th West Ave (74107-4102)
PHONE..................................432 238-1483
Isaac Goodman, *Principal*
EMP: 5
SALES (est): 213.3K **Privately Held**
SIC: 1389 Oil field services

(G-10498)
PERSONAL EXPRESSIONS INC
4107 S Yale Ave Ste 120 (74135-6012)
PHONE..................................918 660-0494
Jaime Mueller, *Principal*
EMP: 2
SALES (est): 123.1K **Privately Held**
WEB: www.personal-expressions.com
SIC: 2395 Embroidery products, except schiffli machine

(G-10499)
PERSONAL EXPRESSIONS INC
8009 S Sheridan Rd Unit D (74133-8960)
PHONE..................................918 660-0494
Linda Palkowski, *Owner*
EMP: 1
SALES (est): 84K **Privately Held**
WEB: www.personal-expressions.com
SIC: 2395 Embroidery products, except schiffli machine

(G-10500)
PETRO MAC CORPORATION
20 E 5th St Ste 710 (74103-4449)
P.O. Box 3405 (74101-3405)
PHONE..................................918 585-5853
J McGinley, *Principal*
EMP: 2
SQ FT: 62,776
SALES (est): 166.5K **Privately Held**
SIC: 1382 Oil & gas exploration services

(G-10501)
PETROCORP INCORPORATED
6733 S Yale Ave (74136-3302)
P.O. Box 702500 (74170-2500)
PHONE..................................918 491-4500
John G Nikkel, *CEO*
EMP: 1
SALES (est): 95.3K
SALES (corp-wide): 674.6MM **Privately Held**
SIC: 1311 1382 Crude petroleum production; oil & gas exploration services
PA: Unit Corporation
8200 S Unit Dr
Tulsa OK 74132
918 493-7700

(G-10502)
PETROFLOW ENERGY CORPORATION (PA)
114 E 5th St Ste 300 (74103-4621)
PHONE..................................918 592-1010
Richard Menchaca, *President*
Dennis Baggett, *COO*
Louis Schott, *General Counsel*
EMP: 13
SALES (est): 3.2MM **Privately Held**
SIC: 1311 Crude petroleum production

(G-10503)
PETROFLOW ENERGY LTD
Also Called: Napcus
114 E 5th St Ste 300 (74103-4621)
PHONE..................................918 592-1010
Richard Menchaca, *CEO*
Jamie Wilson, *Production*
EMP: 20 **EST:** 2005

SALES (est): 1.4MM
SALES (corp-wide): 5.1MM **Privately Held**
WEB: www.petroflowenergy.com
SIC: 1381 Drilling oil & gas wells
PA: Petroflow Energy Ltd
717 7 Ave Sw Suite 970
Calgary AB

(G-10504)
PETROLEUM ARTIFACTS LTD
32 E 25th St (74114-2410)
P.O. Box 821 (74101-0821)
PHONE..................................918 949-6101
Joel A Shadday, *Owner*
Elaine Shadday, *Co-Owner*
EMP: 2
SALES (est): 140K **Privately Held**
SIC: 3873 3646 3645 3429 Clocks, assembly of; commercial indusl & institutional electric lighting fixtures; residential lighting fixtures; manufactured hardware (general); pressed & blown glass

(G-10505)
PETROLEUM DEVELOPMENT COMPANY
Also Called: PDC
401 S Boston Ave Ste 1850 (74103-4005)
PHONE..................................918 583-7434
Wm Dennis Ingram, *President*
EMP: 4
SQ FT: 1,500
SALES (est): 2MM **Privately Held**
SIC: 1381 1382 Drilling oil & gas wells; oil & gas exploration services

(G-10506)
PETROLEUM INTERNATIONAL INC
Also Called: Mc Mahon Operating Company
1818 E 42nd St (74105-4208)
PHONE..................................918 712-1840
Mary McMahon, *President*
John McMahon, *Vice Pres*
Susan Stearns, *Treasurer*
EMP: 8 **EST:** 1962
SALES (est): 838.3K **Privately Held**
SIC: 1311 Crude petroleum production; natural gas production

(G-10507)
PETROSKILLS LLC (PA)
2930 S Yale Ave (74114-6252)
PHONE..................................918 828-2500
J Ford Brett, *CEO*
Ron Hinn, *Vice Pres*
Buck Titsworth, *Project Mgr*
Bob Lippincott, *Engineer*
Cindi Newman, *Accounting Mgr*
EMP: 29
SALES (est): 22.1MM **Privately Held**
SIC: 1389 Detection & analysis service, gas

(G-10508)
PHELPS RA EQUIPMENT CO INC (PA)
3220 S 85th East Ave (74145-1415)
PHONE..................................918 622-2724
Robert A Phelps, *President*
Sharlene Phelps, *Corp Secy*
EMP: 4
SALES (est): 269.1K **Privately Held**
SIC: 3589 Sewage treatment equipment

(G-10509)
PHILIP LEWIS
3508 E 70th St (74136-2649)
PHONE..................................918 850-6195
Philip Lewis, *Owner*
EMP: 2
SALES (est): 107.4K **Privately Held**
SIC: 3561 Pumps & pumping equipment

(G-10510)
PHOENIX SOFTWARE INTL INC
Also Called: Viking Software Solutions
6660 S Sheridan Rd # 202 (74133-1730)
PHONE..................................918 491-6144
Eric Chevalier, *Branch Mgr*
EMP: 5

SALES (corp-wide): 8.7MM **Privately Held**
SIC: 7372 7371 Operating systems computer software; computer software development
PA: Phoenix Software International, Inc.
831 N Park View Dr
El Segundo CA 90245
310 338-0400

(G-10511)
PHX & CO LLC
2121 S Yorktown Ave # 904 (74114-1426)
PHONE..................................918 747-9770
James T Phoenix, *Principal*
EMP: 3 **EST:** 2011
SALES (est): 227.5K **Privately Held**
SIC: 3577 Computer peripheral equipment

(G-10512)
PICKERING METAL CASTING LLC
2729 Charles Page Blvd (74127-8314)
P.O. Box 287, Lubbock TX (79408-0287)
PHONE..................................806 747-3411
Clay Pickering, *Purch Mgr*
David R Pickering, *Mng Member*
Don A Pickering,
EMP: 50 **EST:** 2013
SALES (est): 7.4MM **Privately Held**
SIC: 3365 Aluminum & aluminum-based alloy castings

(G-10513)
PIE IN SKY TULSA LLC
7912 E 27th Pl (74129-2420)
PHONE..................................918 527-5855
Shelley D Faught, *Mng Member*
EMP: 2
SALES (est): 5K **Privately Held**
SIC: 2099 Food preparations

(G-10514)
PIERPONT LAMONT LLC
320 S Boston Ave Ste 2200 (74103-3726)
P.O. Box 701378 (74170-1378)
PHONE..................................918 592-1705
Steve Cobb, *CEO*
EMP: 2
SALES (est): 131.4K **Privately Held**
SIC: 1389 Oil & gas field services

(G-10515)
PINBALL DOCTOR
2831 E 1st St (74104-1701)
PHONE..................................918 582-3130
Wes Johnson, *Owner*
EMP: 1
SALES (est): 60K **Privately Held**
SIC: 3599 5962 7993 Carnival machines & equipment, amusement park; merchandising machine operators; juke boxes

(G-10516)
PINION MANUFACTURING & SUPPLY
1319 N Mingo Rd (74116-5620)
P.O. Box 581118 (74158-1118)
PHONE..................................918 437-5428
Leon Dean Carter, *President*
EMP: 10
SQ FT: 10,000
SALES (est): 1.7MM **Privately Held**
SIC: 3561 3599 Pumps & pumping equipment; machine shop, jobbing & repair

(G-10517)
PIPEGLOVE LLC
2915 E 74th St (74136-5637)
PHONE..................................918 629-7116
Dewey Brett Bond, *Principal*
EMP: 10
SALES (est): 1.8MM **Privately Held**
SIC: 3842 Gloves, safety

(G-10518)
PIPELINE COATING SERVICES LLC
Also Called: P C S
2940 N Toledo Ave (74115-2707)
PHONE..................................936 494-2919
Andre Decastro, *Sales Staff*
Ferrell Lake, *Sales Staff*
Cathy Watson, *Sales Staff*
Troy Young, *Sales Staff*

Dennis Roberson,
EMP: 5
SALES (est): 205.2K **Privately Held**
SIC: 3621 5074 Motors & generators; heating equipment (hydronic)
PA: Darby Equipment Co.
2940 N Toledo Ave
Tulsa OK 74115

(G-10519)
PISTOL WEAR LLC (PA)
11063 S Memorial Dr 337d (74133-7347)
PHONE..................................918 364-5617
Richard Tuggle,
Amie Tuggle,
EMP: 2
SALES (est): 236.2K **Privately Held**
SIC: 3949 Sporting & athletic goods

(G-10520)
PITEZELS INK & PRINT INC
Also Called: Pitezel's Screen Printing
8943 E 76th St (74133-4407)
PHONE..................................918 663-2393
Dee Pitezel, *President*
EMP: 2
SALES (est): 200K **Privately Held**
SIC: 2759 2396 Screen printing; automotive & apparel trimmings

(G-10521)
PITNEY BOWES INC
5115 S 122nd East Ave # 20 (74146-6017)
PHONE..................................918 779-7552
EMP: 2
SALES (est): 109.5K **Privately Held**
SIC: 3579 Office machines

(G-10522)
PLAN BIBLE
10026 S Mingo Rd Ste A (74133-5717)
PHONE..................................918 254-6983
Jeff Swanson, *CEO*
EMP: 1
SALES (est): 33.9K **Privately Held**
SIC: 2731 Book publishing

(G-10523)
PLASTIC ENGRG CO TULSA INC
6801 E 44th St (74145-4641)
P.O. Box 470532 (74147-0532)
PHONE..................................918 622-9660
Dennis M Byrne, *President*
Mary Byrne, *COO*
Matthew Byrne, *Vice Pres*
Virginia Gleason, *CFO*
Henry Spencer, *Manager*
EMP: 20 **EST:** 1945
SQ FT: 25,000
SALES (est): 7.5MM **Privately Held**
WEB: www.pecot.com
SIC: 5162 3444 Plastics products; skylights, sheet metal

(G-10524)
PLASTIC FABRICATORS INC
8822 E Admiral Pl (74115-8137)
PHONE..................................918 836-6611
Jack McCall, *President*
Lenny McCall, *Corp Secy*
Judy McCall, *Vice Pres*
Tom McCall, *Vice Pres*
EMP: 6 **EST:** 1977
SQ FT: 20,000
SALES: 300K **Privately Held**
SIC: 3083 Window sheeting, plastic; thermoplastic laminates: rods, tubes, plates & sheet

(G-10525)
PLASTIC RESEARCH AND DEV CORP
Also Called: Gene Larew
10702 E 11th St (74128-3204)
P.O. Box 141287, Broken Arrow (74014-0013)
PHONE..................................918 949-6291
Bruce Stanton, *Vice Pres*
EMP: 15
SALES (corp-wide): 2.8B **Privately Held**
SIC: 3949 Lures, fishing: artificial
HQ: Plastic Research And Development Corporation
5724 Highway 280 E
Birmingham AL 35242
205 995-4500

Tulsa - Tulsa County (G-10526)

GEOGRAPHIC SECTION

(G-10526)
PLASTIC SUP & FABRICATION CO
7328 E 38th St (74145-3224)
PHONE..................918 622-8430
Charles Lawrence, *President*
Gwen Rowe, *Corp Secy*
Jane Lawrence, *Vice Pres*
EMP: 7
SQ FT: 5,800
SALES: 750K **Privately Held**
WEB: www.plasticsupplyandfab.com
SIC: 3089 Injection molding of plastics

(G-10527)
PLASTICON FLUID SYSTEMS INC
7134 S Yale Ave Ste 560 (74136-6352)
PHONE..................918 477-9371
Lee W Orr, *President*
Melford Carter, *Vice Pres*
Timothy D Maynard, *Treasurer*
Cathy Smith, *Admin Sec*
EMP: 250
SALES (est): 21.5MM
SALES (corp-wide): 8.4B **Publicly Held**
SIC: 3083 Laminated plastics plate & sheet
HQ: Denali Incorporated
9910 E 56th St N
Tulsa OK 74117

(G-10528)
PLX INC
7030 S Yale Ave Ste 402 (74136-5729)
PHONE..................918 551-6722
Phillip Lakin, *Principal*
EMP: 3
SALES (est): 337K **Privately Held**
SIC: 3827 Optical instruments & apparatus

(G-10529)
PLYMOUTH RESOURCES INC (PA)
2200 S Utica Pl Ste 430 (74114-7101)
PHONE..................918 599-1880
Edwin Kronfeld, *President*
James Flaherty, *Vice Pres*
Drew Phillips, *Vice Pres*
Renee Kallenberger, *Accountant*
Sara Bolch, *Legal Staff*
EMP: 5
SQ FT: 4,500
SALES (est): 5.8MM **Privately Held**
SIC: 1311 1381 Crude petroleum production; natural gas production; drilling oil & gas wells

(G-10530)
POLK APPLIANCES CO
1511 E Admiral Blvd (74120-1611)
PHONE..................918 592-6858
Nancy M Polk, *Owner*
EMP: 1
SQ FT: 2,400
SALES (est): 79.2K **Privately Held**
SIC: 2599 Factory furniture & fixtures; cabinets, factory

(G-10531)
PONTOTOC GATHERING LLC
1345 E 29th St (74114-5301)
PHONE..................918 742-5835
Jim Jurek, *CEO*
EMP: 1
SALES (est): 138K **Privately Held**
SIC: 1311 Natural gas production

(G-10532)
POPEFASTENERS INC
8159 S 39th West Ave (74132-3050)
PHONE..................918 740-4801
Larry Pope, *President*
EMP: 3
SALES (est): 162K **Privately Held**
SIC: 3452 Bolts, nuts, rivets & washers

(G-10533)
POQUITA CIRCLE LLC
5825 E 78th Pl (74136-8439)
PHONE..................918 794-0750
Megan Brown, *Principal*
EMP: 3
SALES (est): 135.5K **Privately Held**
SIC: 3577 Computer peripheral equipment

(G-10534)
PORCELAIN TREASURE
1127 S Quebec Ave (74112-5207)
PHONE..................918 230-9618
Treasure Doty, *Owner*
EMP: 1
SALES (est): 83.4K **Privately Held**
SIC: 3469 Porcelain enameled products & utensils

(G-10535)
POST SOFTWARE INTERNATIONAL
11722 S Erie Ave (74137-8430)
PHONE..................918 299-2158
Robert M Bodily Jr, *Principal*
EMP: 2
SALES (est): 116K **Privately Held**
SIC: 7372 Prepackaged software

(G-10536)
POWDER BLUE
7203 E Reading Pl (74115-4638)
PHONE..................918 835-2629
Bud Slusher, *Vice Pres*
EMP: 14
SALES (est): 2.9MM **Privately Held**
SIC: 2851 Coating, air curing

(G-10537)
POWDER COATINGS INCORPORATED (PA)
9832 E 58th St (74146-6428)
PHONE..................918 627-6225
David Blackburn, *President*
Linda Blackburn, *Corp Secy*
EMP: 9
SQ FT: 6,000
SALES (est): 833.3K **Privately Held**
SIC: 3479 Coating of metals & formed products

(G-10538)
POWER DYNE INC
3628 S Elwood Ave (74107-5805)
P.O. Box 639, Sand Springs (74063-0639)
PHONE..................918 587-1272
Dan W Hilsheimer, *President*
Dan Hilsheimer, *President*
Mark Hilsheimer, *Vice Pres*
EMP: 6 EST: 1977
SALES (est): 963.7K **Privately Held**
SIC: 3599 Machine shop, jobbing & repair

(G-10539)
POWER READY LLC
4121 S Sheridan Rd (74145-1117)
P.O. Box 35327 (74153-0327)
PHONE..................918 289-0088
Gabriel Schlaf, *Director*
Ginette Overall,
EMP: 10 EST: 2008
SALES (est): 1.7MM **Privately Held**
WEB: www.powerready.net
SIC: 3699 Electrical equipment & supplies

(G-10540)
PRACTICAL SALES AND SVC INC
4411 S Elwood Ave (74107-8105)
PHONE..................918 446-5515
Johnny Davis, *President*
▲ EMP: 6
SQ FT: 20,000
SALES (est): 1MM **Privately Held**
SIC: 5085 3561 7699 3699 Industrial supplies; pumps & pumping equipment; industrial equipment services; electrical equipment & supplies; air & gas compressors

(G-10541)
PRE-PRESS GRAPHICS INC
1307 E 11th St (74120-4605)
PHONE..................918 582-2775
Ken Robinson, *President*
Rick Hardesty, *Principal*
Dorothy Anderson, *Corp Secy*
EMP: 6
SQ FT: 1,400
SALES (est): 400K **Privately Held**
SIC: 2752 2796 2791 Photolithographic printing; platemaking services; typesetting

(G-10542)
PRECISION ALLOY
5436 S Mingo Rd Ste K (74146-5740)
PHONE..................918 665-3952
Barbara Mays, *Owner*
EMP: 1
SALES (est): 120K **Privately Held**
SIC: 5047 3843 Dental equipment & supplies; dental equipment & supplies

(G-10543)
PRECISION COATINGS LLC
7448 E 42nd Pl (74145-4702)
PHONE..................918 622-1876
Ronald D Hamby, *President*
George Underwood, *Corp Secy*
Phyllis Hamby, *Vice Pres*
EMP: 7
SQ FT: 18,500
SALES (est): 500K **Privately Held**
SIC: 3479 3471 Coating of metals & formed products; sand blasting of metal parts

(G-10544)
PRECISION FABRICATORS INC
Also Called: Pfi
3928 N Osage Dr (74127-1594)
PHONE..................918 428-7600
Charles M Bretanus, *President*
Chuck Bretanus, *Principal*
EMP: 18
SQ FT: 60,000
SALES (est): 743.4K **Privately Held**
SIC: 3441 Fabricated structural metal

(G-10545)
PRECISION HOSE TECHNOLOGY INC
2702 N Sheridan Rd Bldg D (74115-2321)
PHONE..................918 835-3660
Robert Williams, *President*
EMP: 6
SQ FT: 5,000
SALES: 800K **Privately Held**
SIC: 3728 3052 Aircraft parts & equipment; rubber & plastics hose & beltings

(G-10546)
PRECISION IMAGE CNVERSIONS LLC
195 S 122nd East Ave (74128-2405)
PHONE..................918 430-1102
Steve Ballard,
EMP: 10
SALES (est): 1MM **Privately Held**
SIC: 3993 Signs, not made in custom sign painting shops

(G-10547)
PRECISION INDUSTRIES IC T
2322 N Mingo Rd D (74116-1218)
PHONE..................918 833-6072
Tom Scism, *Principal*
Coleman Randy, *Auditor*
EMP: 5 EST: 2010
SALES (est): 1.3MM **Privately Held**
SIC: 3999 Manufacturing industries

(G-10548)
PRECISION METALS LLC
19504 E 6th St (74108-7958)
PHONE..................918 266-2202
Christian Quick, *President*
EMP: 5
SALES (est): 213.6K **Privately Held**
SIC: 3312 Blast furnaces & steel mills

(G-10549)
PRECISION SIGN & DESIGN
195 S 122nd East Ave (74128-2405)
PHONE..................918 430-1102
EMP: 2
SALES (est): 157.2K **Privately Held**
WEB: www.precisionsigntulsa.com
SIC: 3993 Signs & advertising specialties

(G-10550)
PRECISION SINTERED PARTS L L C
9902 E 46th Pl (74146-4714)
PHONE..................918 663-7511
Jim Barnes, *Prdtn Mgr*
William Martinson,
Joseph M Ball,
EMP: 12
SQ FT: 15,000
SALES: 1.5MM **Privately Held**
WEB: www.precisionsinteredparts.com
SIC: 3599 Machine shop, jobbing & repair

(G-10551)
PREFERRED UTILITIES MFG CORP
10001 E 44th Pl Ste A (74146-4764)
PHONE..................203 743-6741
EMP: 5 **Privately Held**
SIC: 3829 3433 8711 Measuring & controlling devices; gas burners, industrial; designing: ship, boat, machine & product
HQ: Preferred Utilities Manufacturing Corporation
31-35 South St
Danbury CT 06810
203 743-6741

(G-10552)
PREGIS LLC
10838 E Marshall St # 14 (74116-5682)
PHONE..................918 439-9916
Amanda Maledon, *Branch Mgr*
EMP: 65 **Privately Held**
WEB: www.pregis.com
SIC: 2671 Paper coated or laminated for packaging
HQ: Pregis Llc
1650 Lake Cook Rd Ste 400
Deerfield IL 60015

(G-10553)
PREMIERE LOCK CO LLC
Also Called: Weslock
10203 E 61st St Ste A (74133-1514)
PHONE..................918 294-8179
Mike Driggers,
Clint Brumble,
▲ EMP: 22 EST: 2001
SQ FT: 15,000
SALES (est): 4.2MM **Privately Held**
WEB: www.weslock.com
SIC: 3429 Manufactured hardware (general)

(G-10554)
PREMIERFLOW LLC
2716 E Apache St (74110-2242)
P.O. Box 472084 (74147-2084)
PHONE..................918 346-6312
Marvin Yoder, *Mng Member*
EMP: 25
SQ FT: 30,000
SALES (est): 6.4MM **Privately Held**
SIC: 3561 Industrial pumps & parts

(G-10555)
PRESSURE POINT LLC
4127 S 185th East Ave (74134-6013)
PHONE..................918 695-8799
Gerald Richardson, *President*
EMP: 1
SALES (est): 130.5K **Privately Held**
WEB: www.pressurepointok.com
SIC: 3589 High pressure cleaning equipment

(G-10556)
PREVIEW OF GREEN COUNTRY INC
Also Called: Preview Magazine
4150 S 100th East Ave # 200 (74146-3650)
PHONE..................918 745-1190
Randy Dietzel, *President*
Stephen Hurt, *Opers Mgr*
Karen Kirby, *Admin Sec*
EMP: 5
SQ FT: 600
SALES: 450K **Privately Held**
SIC: 2721 Magazines: publishing only, not printed on site

(G-10557)
PRIDE ENERGY COMPANY
4641 E 91st St (74137-2852)
P.O. Box 701950 (74170-1950)
PHONE..................918 524-9200
Matthew L Pride, *Partner*
John W Pride, *Partner*
John Pride, *Partner*
Matt Pride, *Partner*
EMP: 25 EST: 1981

GEOGRAPHIC SECTION — Tulsa - Tulsa County (G-10587)

SALES (est): 7.2MM **Privately Held**
WEB: www.pride-energy.com
SIC: **1382** Oil & gas exploration services

(G-10558)
PRIMARY NTRAL RSOURCES III LLC
7134 S Yale Ave Ste 430 (74136-6351)
PHONE.....................918 495-0598
G R Rich Talley, *CEO*
Mark Sheehan, *President*
Jack Fritts, *COO*
EMP: 5
SALES (est): 1.4MM **Privately Held**
SIC: **1382** Oil & gas exploration services

(G-10559)
PRIME SIGNS OF OKLAHOMA INC
5840 S Memorial Dr (74145-9023)
PHONE.....................918 500-2213
EMP: 1
SALES (est): 46K **Privately Held**
SIC: **3993** Signs & advertising specialties

(G-10560)
PRIMUS INTERNATIONAL INC
3030 N Erie Ave (74115-2804)
PHONE.....................918 836-6317
Rick Thomas, *Principal*
EMP: 123
SALES (corp-wide): 327.2B **Publicly Held**
SIC: **3728** Aircraft body & wing assemblies & parts
HQ: Primus International Inc
610 Bllvue Way Ne Ste 200
Auburn WA 98001
425 688-0444

(G-10561)
PRINTED PRODUCTS INC
1144 E Haskell St (74106-5308)
PHONE.....................918 295-9950
Michael Chamberlain, *President*
Vickie Chamberlain, *Vice Pres*
EMP: 10
SQ FT: 7,400
SALES (est): 1.4MM **Privately Held**
WEB: www.ppi-tulsa.com
SIC: **2761** 2752 2796 2791 Computer forms, manifold or continuous; commercial printing, lithographic; platemaking services; typesetting

(G-10562)
PRISM ELECTRIC INC
6558 E 40th St (74145-4517)
PHONE.....................918 425-2000
EMP: 1 **Privately Held**
SIC: **3699** 1731 Electrical equipment & supplies; electrical work
PA: Prism Electric, Inc.
2985 Market St
Garland TX 75041

(G-10563)
PRL MANUFACTURING INC
4946 E 66th St N (74117-1801)
PHONE.....................918 280-1090
Ricky Don Page, *President*
Gail Runnels, *Vice Pres*
Jeannell Rimas, *Treasurer*
EMP: 3
SALES (est): 627.4K **Privately Held**
SIC: **3356** Silver & silver alloy bars, rods, sheets, etc.

(G-10564)
PRO BATTERY INC
1731 N 168th East Ave (74116-4931)
PHONE.....................918 437-1920
Bob Koch, *President*
EMP: 2
SALES: 400K **Privately Held**
SIC: **3625** 5999 Truck controls, industrial battery; batteries, non-automotive

(G-10565)
PRO PIPING & FABRICATION LLC
1925 S 33rd West Ave (74107-3427)
PHONE.....................918 599-8218
Brandon Foote, *Mng Member*
Clinton Saxton,

EMP: 117
SQ FT: 20,000
SALES: 3MM **Privately Held**
SIC: **3449** Bars, concrete reinforcing; fabricated steel

(G-10566)
PRODUCERS OIL COMPANY INC
427 S Boston Ave Ste 711 (74103-4112)
PHONE.....................918 582-1188
Bessie Goodall, *President*
EMP: 20
SQ FT: 6,000
SALES (est): 1.1MM **Privately Held**
SIC: **1311** Crude petroleum production; natural gas production

(G-10567)
PROFESSIONAL DATASOLUTIONS INC
Also Called: Pdi
5147 S Garnett Rd Ste D (74146-5915)
PHONE.....................512 218-0463
Scott Tedford, *Branch Mgr*
EMP: 24
SALES (corp-wide): 68.1MM **Privately Held**
SIC: **7372** Business oriented computer software
HQ: Professional Datasolutions, Inc.
11675 Rainwater Dr # 350
Alpharetta GA 30009

(G-10568)
PROFESSIONAL FABRICATORS INC
Also Called: Pfi
2765 Dawson Rd (74110-5035)
PHONE.....................918 388-1090
Don Moore, *President*
Tom Hancock, *Principal*
EMP: 35
SQ FT: 7,500
SALES: 8MM **Privately Held**
WEB: www.professionalfabinc.com
SIC: **3441** Fabricated structural metal

(G-10569)
PROFESSIONAL IMAGE INC
12437 E 60th St (74146-6906)
PHONE.....................918 461-0609
Cynthia Calvert, *President*
Bobby Grimes, *Corp Secy*
Tracy Auen, *Vice Pres*
Beverly Calvert, *Vice Pres*
Michelle Glass, *Project Mgr*
▲ EMP: 48
SQ FT: 15,000
SALES (est): 12.6MM **Privately Held**
SIC: **2752** 2652 Commercial printing, offset; setup paperboard boxes

(G-10570)
PROGRESSIVE ORTHOTIC
Also Called: Progressive O & P Services
9511 E 46th St Ste 1 (74145-7222)
PHONE.....................918 786-7701
Jeff Arnett, *Branch Mgr*
EMP: 3
SALES (est): 215.6K **Privately Held**
SIC: **3842** Orthopedic appliances
PA: Progressive Orthotic And Prosthetic Services, Inc.
9511 E 46th St Ste 4
Tulsa OK 74145

(G-10571)
PROGRESSIVE ORTHOTIC & PR
9511 E 46th St Ste 1 (74145-7222)
PHONE.....................918 681-2346
Matt Conrad, *Principal*
EMP: 2
SALES (est): 179.1K **Privately Held**
SIC: **3842** Orthopedic appliances

(G-10572)
PROGRESSIVE TOOLING INC
Also Called: Progressive Tooling & Mfg
7739 E 38th St Ste C (74145-3222)
PHONE.....................918 622-0506
Bob Roth, *President*
EMP: 1
SQ FT: 1,000
SALES (est): 174.1K **Privately Held**
SIC: **3544** Special dies & tools

(G-10573)
PROMOTIONS - FORMS UNLIMITED
Also Called: P-F Unlimited
8644 S Peoria Ave (74132-2827)
P.O. Box 470145 (74147-0145)
PHONE.....................918 627-8800
Laura L Ransbottom, *CEO*
James Ransbottom, *President*
Jason Staurovsky, *Sales Staff*
EMP: 8 EST: 2009
SALES (est): 900K **Privately Held**
WEB: www.p-funlimited.com
SIC: **2759** 2761 Commercial printing; manifold business forms

(G-10574)
PROMOZ SCREEN PRINTING INC
1345 N 108th East Ave (74116-5666)
PHONE.....................918 439-4030
Jim Moseby, *President*
Joe Moseby, *Vice Pres*
EMP: 5
SALES: 525K **Privately Held**
SIC: **2396** Screen printing on fabric articles

(G-10575)
PROTEGE ENERGY III LLC (PA)
2200 S Utica Pl Ste 400 (74114-7040)
PHONE.....................918 728-3092
Martin Thalken, *Ch of Bd*
David Boncaldo, *President*
Morris Hall, *Vice Pres*
Jason Pugh, *Opers Staff*
Jose Martinez, *Production*
EMP: 15
SQ FT: 11,000
SALES: 500K **Privately Held**
SIC: **1382** Oil & gas exploration services

(G-10576)
PROTYPE INC
Also Called: Coman & Associates
2208 E 14th St (74104-4412)
PHONE.....................918 743-4408
Susan Coman, *President*
John Coman, *Corp Secy*
EMP: 4
SALES (est): 383.6K **Privately Held**
SIC: **2752** 2796 2791 Commercial printing, lithographic; platemaking services; typesetting

(G-10577)
PROVIDENCE ENERGY CORP
2424 E 21st St Ste 500 (74114-1723)
P.O. Box 3783, Broken Arrow (74013-3783)
PHONE.....................918 747-3675
Corbett Stovall, *President*
EMP: 3 EST: 1972
SQ FT: 2,800
SALES (est): 206.4K **Privately Held**
SIC: **1311** Crude petroleum production; natural gas production

(G-10578)
PRYER AEROSPACE LLC
2230 N Sheridan Rd (74115-3634)
PHONE.....................918 835-8885
EMP: 99
SQ FT: 120,000
SALES (est): 7.3MM **Privately Held**
SIC: **3599** Machine shop, jobbing & repair

(G-10579)
PRYER MACHINE & TOOL CO INC
2230 N Sheridan Rd (74115-3634)
PHONE.....................918 341-4900
Brenton Pryer, *Principal*
▲ EMP: 2
SALES (est): 193.3K **Privately Held**
SIC: **3599** Machine shop, jobbing & repair

(G-10580)
PRYER MACHINE & TOOL COMPANY
2230 N Sheridan Rd (74115-3634)
PHONE.....................918 835-8885
Scott Pryer, *President*
Brent Pryer, *Vice Pres*
Cayla Brumble, *Director*
Doug Smith, *Director*
Ed Unger, *Director*

▲ EMP: 155 EST: 1966
SQ FT: 130,000
SALES (est): 31.7MM **Privately Held**
WEB: www.pryer.aero
SIC: **3812** 3599 3728 Search & navigation equipment; machine & other job shop work; aircraft parts & equipment

(G-10581)
PRYER TECHNOLOGY GROUP LLC
2230 N Sheridan Rd (74115-3634)
PHONE.....................918 835-8885
Scott Pryer, *President*
Bob Blood, *Technical Staff*
◆ EMP: 5
SALES (est): 319.6K **Privately Held**
SIC: **3728** Aircraft parts & equipment

(G-10582)
PUMP & SEAL IMPROVEMENTS
Also Called: P S Improvements
3336 E 32nd St Ste 220 (74135-4442)
PHONE.....................918 747-7742
Anthony Perez, *President*
Lise Carter, *Office Mgr*
EMP: 2
SALES (est): 410.3K **Privately Held**
WEB: www.psimprovements.com
SIC: **3561** Pumps, oil well & field

(G-10583)
PUMP SHOP
802 N Lewis Pl (74110-5051)
PHONE.....................918 834-8829
Carl Dean Dewberry, *Owner*
EMP: 3
SQ FT: 2,500
SALES: 450K **Privately Held**
SIC: **5172** 5084 3594 3561 Service station supplies, petroleum; industrial machinery & equipment; fluid power pumps & motors; pumps & pumping equipment

(G-10584)
PURE DIGITAL PRINT
5301 S 125th East Ave (74146-6223)
PHONE.....................918 899-2000
Adam Stewart, *General Mgr*
EMP: 6
SALES (est): 267.9K **Privately Held**
WEB: www.pdpscodix.com
SIC: **2752** Commercial printing, offset

(G-10585)
PUZZLE APPS INC
1432 S Trenton Ave (74120-6050)
PHONE.....................918 815-6444
EMP: 1
SALES (est): 41K **Privately Held**
SIC: **3944** Puzzles

(G-10586)
PYR ENERGY CORPORATION (HQ)
2 W 2nd St Ste 1500 (74103-3135)
PHONE.....................918 591-1791
C Philip Tholen, *President*
Scott Rowland, *Vice Pres*
Alisa Moore Copeland, *Controller*
Annabel Jones, *Admin Sec*
EMP: 5
SQ FT: 3,800
SALES (est): 3MM
SALES (corp-wide): 1.4B **Privately Held**
SIC: **1382** Oil & gas exploration services
PA: Samson Resources Corporation
15 E 5th St Ste 1000
Tulsa OK 74103
918 591-1791

(G-10587)
Q7 INC
Also Called: Q7 Services
2940 E 26th St (74114-4422)
PHONE.....................918 609-3251
Jeremy Bjorlie, *CEO*
EMP: 4
SALES (est): 330K **Privately Held**
SIC: **3823** 7699 Industrial process measurement equipment; laboratory instrument repair

Tulsa - Tulsa County (G-10588)

(G-10588)
QUAIL TOOLS LP
11811 E 51st St (74146-6000)
PHONE..................918 994-4695
EMP: 3
SALES (corp-wide): 571.1MM **Publicly Held**
SIC: 1389 Oil field services
HQ: Quail Tools, L.P.
3713 Highway 14
New Iberia LA 70560
337 365-8154

(G-10589)
QUAL-TRON INC
9409 E 55th Pl (74145-8157)
PHONE..................918 622-7052
Robert H Kane, *President*
Thomas Kotch, *Vice Pres*
Teresa McGuire, *Purchasing*
Bob Johnston, *Director*
Robert M Kane, *Admin Sec*
EMP: 40
SQ FT: 18,000
SALES: 5.5MM **Privately Held**
SIC: 3679 3812 Electronic circuits; detection apparatus: electronic/magnetic field, light/heat

(G-10590)
QUALITY BAKERY PRODUCTS LLC
20 East St Ste 620 (74103)
PHONE..................609 871-7393
Gaile Withenburg, *Branch Mgr*
EMP: 18 **Privately Held**
SIC: 5149 2099 2051 Groceries & related products; food preparations; bread, cake & related products
HQ: Quality Bakery Products, Llc
888 E Las Olas Blvd # 700
Fort Lauderdale FL 33301

(G-10591)
QUALITY EQUIPMENT DESIGN INC
4246 S 74th East Ave (74145-4709)
PHONE..................918 492-4019
Laverle Morrow, *President*
Shane Morrow, *Vice Pres*
Judy Arent-Morency, *Mktg Dir*
Judy Morrow, *Admin Sec*
EMP: 10
SALES (est): 1.3MM **Privately Held**
WEB: www.qed-corp.com
SIC: 3559 8711 Electroplating machinery & equipment; engineering services

(G-10592)
QUALITY PARTS MFG CO INC
10218 E 47th Pl (74146-4809)
PHONE..................918 627-3307
Mike Landers, *President*
Christy Pinsart, *Office Mgr*
EMP: 4
SQ FT: 4,000
SALES: 150K **Privately Held**
WEB: www.qualitypartsmfg.com
SIC: 3599 3053 1389 Machine shop, jobbing & repair; gaskets, packing & sealing devices; oil field services

(G-10593)
QUALITY PLATING CO OF TULSA
2665 N Darlington Ave (74115-2809)
PHONE..................918 835-2278
Reginald Collins, *President*
Patricia Collins, *Vice Pres*
JD Key, *Prdtn Mgr*
EMP: 40
SQ FT: 30,000
SALES (est): 5.4MM **Privately Held**
SIC: 3471 Electroplating of metals or formed products; anodizing (plating) of metals or formed products

(G-10594)
QUIK PRINT OF TULSA INC
6111 S Mingo Rd Ste A (74133-6305)
PHONE..................918 250-5466
Bill Wilkerson, *Branch Mgr*
EMP: 8 **Privately Held**
SIC: 2752 2791 2789 Commercial printing, offset; typesetting; bookbinding & related work
PA: Quik Print Of Tulsa, Inc.
3711 S Sheridan Rd
Tulsa OK 74145

(G-10595)
QUIK PRINT OF TULSA INC (PA)
Also Called: Quick Print
3711 S Sheridan Rd (74145-1127)
PHONE..................918 665-6246
Gary F Gravely, *President*
Brenda Price, *Sales Mgr*
Brian Barton, *Manager*
EMP: 40
SQ FT: 4,000
SALES (est): 7.7MM **Privately Held**
SIC: 2752 2791 2789 2759 Commercial printing, offset; typesetting; bookbinding & related work; commercial printing

(G-10596)
QUIK PRINT OF TULSA INC
402 S Main St (74103-5033)
PHONE..................918 582-1825
Mark Piersall, *Manager*
EMP: 5 **Privately Held**
SIC: 2752 2796 2789 2759 Commercial printing, offset; platemaking services; bookbinding & related work; commercial printing
PA: Quik Print Of Tulsa, Inc.
3711 S Sheridan Rd
Tulsa OK 74145

(G-10597)
QUIK PRINT OF TULSA INC
6620 S Lewis Ave (74136-1011)
PHONE..................918 491-9292
Gary Gravley, *Principal*
EMP: 2 **Privately Held**
SIC: 2752 Commercial printing, offset
PA: Quik Print Of Tulsa, Inc.
3711 S Sheridan Rd
Tulsa OK 74145

(G-10598)
QUIKRETE COMPANIES LLC
6204 E 11th St (74112-3122)
PHONE..................918 835-4441
Shane Scoggins, *Plant Mgr*
Randy Fowble, *Executive*
EMP: 45 **Privately Held**
SIC: 3272 Concrete products
HQ: The Quikrete Companies Llc
5 Concourse Pkwy Ste 1900
Atlanta GA 30328
404 634-9100

(G-10599)
QUIKTRIP CORPORATION (PA)
4705 S 129th East Ave (74134-7008)
P.O. Box 3475 (74101-3475)
PHONE..................918 615-7700
Chet Cadieux, *President*
Steve Wilson, *Division Mgr*
Mike Stanford, *COO*
Sarah B Bryan, *Counsel*
Truesdell Chris, *Vice Pres*
EMP: 350
SQ FT: 160,000
SALES (est): 897.5MM **Privately Held**
WEB: www.quiktrip.com
SIC: 5411 5541 5172 2099 Convenience stores; gasoline service stations; petroleum products; gasoline; diesel fuel; ready-to-eat meals, salads & sandwiches; box lunches, for sale off premises; sandwiches, assembled & packaged: for wholesale market; groceries, general line; commercial & industrial building operation

(G-10600)
R & J FOOD TULSA LLC
1232 E 2nd St (74120-2010)
PHONE..................918 520-0484
Rolando Perez,
Antonio Perez,
EMP: 1
SALES (est): 47.9K **Privately Held**
SIC: 2099 Food preparations

(G-10601)
R & R MEDIA SYSTEMS LLC
5332 E 21st Pl (74114-2222)
PHONE..................918 978-0578
Roger Owings, *Mng Member*
Rhonda Owings,
EMP: 6
SQ FT: 2,000
SALES (est): 841.5K **Privately Held**
SIC: 3651 Home entertainment equipment, electronic

(G-10602)
R C RAMSEY CO
2916 E 21st St (74114-1808)
P.O. Box 14262 (74159-1262)
PHONE..................918 746-4300
EMP: 11
SQ FT: 1,200
SALES (est): 1.3MM **Privately Held**
SIC: 5063 3825 3812 Whol Electrical Equipment Mfg Electrical Measuring Instruments Mfg Search/Navigation Equipment

(G-10603)
R F LINDGREN ENCLOSURES INC
8751 S College Pl (74137-2515)
PHONE..................918 299-7572
John Clark, *Manager*
EMP: 1
SALES (est): 179.7K **Privately Held**
SIC: 5047 3444 Hospital equipment & furniture; sheet metalwork

(G-10604)
R G BERRY CO
1789 E 71st St (74136-5108)
PHONE..................918 587-0036
R Garvin Berry Jr, *Partner*
Beverly Disney, *Partner*
EMP: 3
SQ FT: 2,000
SALES (est): 287.1K **Privately Held**
SIC: 1311 Crude petroleum production; natural gas production

(G-10605)
R P SMALL CORP
1585 E 22nd St (74114-1305)
PHONE..................918 712-2226
Richard Small, *President*
EMP: 2
SALES (est): 250K **Privately Held**
SIC: 1382 Aerial geophysical exploration oil & gas

(G-10606)
R R DONNELLEY & SONS COMPANY
Also Called: R R Donnelley
2757 S Memorial Dr (74129-2603)
PHONE..................918 749-6496
Ralph A Androde, *Manager*
EMP: 3
SALES (corp-wide): 6.2B **Publicly Held**
SIC: 2752 Commercial printing, lithographic
PA: R. R. Donnelley & Sons Company
35 W Wacker Dr
Chicago IL 60601
312 326-8000

(G-10607)
R SQUARED CHEMICALS LLC
1350 N Louisville Ave # 1 (74115-5137)
PHONE..................918 520-2384
Kurt Lampi, *Principal*
EMP: 2
SALES (est): 135K **Privately Held**
SIC: 2899 Chemical preparations

(G-10608)
RABER RENOVATIONS INC
5605 E 109th St (74137-7267)
PHONE..................918 499-3030
EMP: 1 EST: 2018
SALES (est): 53.7K **Privately Held**
SIC: 2434 Wood kitchen cabinets

(G-10609)
RAF MIDSOUTH TECHNOLOGIES LLC
2728 Charles Page Blvd (74127-8315)
PHONE..................918 352-8300
Joe Carter, *Mng Member*
EMP: 12
SALES (est): 1.7MM **Privately Held**
SIC: 3579 Mailing machines
PA: Raf Technology, Inc.
15400 Ne 90th St Ste 300
Redmond WA

(G-10610)
RAINBOW AWNINGS & SIGNS
6422 S 112th East Ave (74133-2674)
PHONE..................918 249-0003
John Jaberi, *Owner*
EMP: 2
SALES (est): 101.3K **Privately Held**
SIC: 3993 Signs & advertising specialties

(G-10611)
RAINBOW CONCRETE COMPANY
13521 E 11th St (74108-2701)
PHONE..................918 234-9044
Waylan McLain, *Ch of Bd*
Arlen W Halvorson, *President*
Bill Autry, *Principal*
Connie Hall, *Corp Secy*
Tommy Thompson, *Vice Pres*
EMP: 55
SQ FT: 3,500
SALES (est): 4.5MM **Privately Held**
SIC: 3273 Ready-mixed concrete

(G-10612)
RAM ENERGY LLC
2100 S Utica Ave Ste 165 (74114-1440)
PHONE..................918 947-6300
Jason T Meek, *Vice Pres*
Matt Patterson, *Opers Mgr*
Sabrina Gicaletto, *Treasurer*
Larry E Lee,
EMP: 13
SALES (est): 2.2MM **Privately Held**
SIC: 1382 Oil & gas exploration services

(G-10613)
RAM MACHINE INC
9312 S 46th West Ave (74132-3727)
PHONE..................918 224-8028
Ron J Shelton, *President*
Jack Patty, *Vice Pres*
EMP: 6
SALES (est): 660K **Privately Held**
SIC: 3599 7692 Machine shop, jobbing & repair; welding repair

(G-10614)
RAM OILFIELD SERVICES LLC
5858 S 129th East Ave (74134-6705)
PHONE..................918 639-2827
EMP: 2
SALES (est): 80.9K **Privately Held**
SIC: 1389 Oil field services

(G-10615)
RAMBO ACQUISITION COMPANY (PA)
Also Called: Rambo, Jay Company
8401 E 41st St (74145-3324)
PHONE..................918 627-6222
Ralph Lackner, *President*
Jonathan Faylor, *Prgrmr*
EMP: 81
SQ FT: 60,000
SALES (est): 8.7MM **Privately Held**
WEB: www.jayrambo.com
SIC: 2599 3821 2522 2521 Cabinets, factory; laboratory apparatus & furniture; office furniture, except wood; wood office furniture; wood television & radio cabinets; wood kitchen cabinets

(G-10616)
RAMCCO CONCRETE CNSTR LLC
Also Called: Ramcco Trucking
19548 E 6th St (74108-7958)
PHONE..................918 266-3838
Janet Meiza,
Jose Ramirez,
EMP: 17 EST: 2011

GEOGRAPHIC SECTION

Tulsa - Tulsa County (G-10645)

SQ FT: 5,000
SALES: 2MM Privately Held
SIC: 3271 5012 Architectural concrete: block, split, fluted, screen, etc.; trucks, commercial

(G-10617)
RAMSEY INDUSTRIES INC (HQ)
4707 N Mingo Rd (74117-5904)
P.O. Box 581510 (74158-1510)
PHONE.................918 438-2760
John R Celoni Jr, *President*
Michael A Barber, *COO*
Don Helms, *CFO*
Bruce Barron, *Executive*
Steve Luther,
▲ EMP: 101
SQ FT: 132,000
SALES (est): 129.7MM
SALES (corp-wide): 253.4MM Privately Held
WEB: www.ramseyindustries.com
SIC: 3531 3536 Winches; cranes, industrial plant
PA: Gridiron Capital, Llc
220 Elm St Fl 2
New Canaan CT 06840
203 972-1100

(G-10618)
RAMSEY WINCH COMPANY
4707 N Mingo Rd (74117-5904)
P.O. Box 581510 (74158-1510)
PHONE.................918 438-2760
Robert Heffron, *CEO*
Bruce Barron, *Exec VP*
Mark Cramer, *Manager*
◆ EMP: 250
SQ FT: 132,000
SALES (est): 63MM
SALES (corp-wide): 253.4MM Privately Held
WEB: www.ramsey.com
SIC: 3531 Winches
HQ: Ramsey Industries Inc
4707 N Mingo Rd
Tulsa OK 74117
918 438-2760

(G-10619)
RANCH ACRES CAR CARE
Also Called: Ranch Acres Texaco
3003 S Harvard Ave (74114-6121)
PHONE.................918 742-3902
Paul D Clayton, *Owner*
EMP: 4 EST: 1962
SQ FT: 3,762
SALES (est): 348.6K Privately Held
SIC: 3061 Automotive rubber goods (mechanical)

(G-10620)
RAPID WIRELESS LLC
8221 S 69th East Ave (74133-4172)
PHONE.................918 605-9717
Williams J Barnes,
Hazem Refai,
EMP: 4
SALES (est): 241.6K Privately Held
SIC: 3669 Communications equipment

(G-10621)
RAW ELEMENTS LLC
2510 E 15th St Ste 102 (74104-4643)
PHONE.................918 392-4957
EMP: 4
SALES (est): 386.1K Privately Held
WEB: www.rawelementssalon.com
SIC: 2819 Industrial inorganic chemicals

(G-10622)
RAYMONDS DONUT SHOP
4955 S Memorial Dr Ste H (74145-6923)
PHONE.................918 660-0644
Raymond Pascarella, *Principal*
EMP: 2
SALES (est): 74K Privately Held
SIC: 2051 5461 Doughnuts, except frozen; bakeries

(G-10623)
RBC EXPLORATION COMPANY (PA)
2627 E 21st St Ste 200 (74114-1728)
P.O. Box 2070 (74101-2070)
PHONE.................918 744-5607
Roger B Collins, *President*
Anthony D Allen, *CFO*
Frances Collins, *Assistant*
EMP: 1
SQ FT: 12,000
SALES (est): 1.2MM Privately Held
SIC: 1311 6531 Crude petroleum production; natural gas production; real estate agents & managers

(G-10624)
RBI ADVERTISING
Also Called: Rbi Company
1637 S Boston Ave 310 (74119-4415)
PHONE.................918 592-1836
James V Smith, *Principal*
▲ EMP: 2
SQ FT: 600
SALES (est): 277.1K Privately Held
SIC: 3993 7319 Signs & advertising specialties; media buying service

(G-10625)
RCS CORPORATION
9231 S 36th West Ave (74132-3748)
P.O. Box 417, Jenks (74037-0417)
PHONE.................918 227-7497
Don Gabbard, *President*
Sheri Gabbard, *Corp Secy*
EMP: 3
SALES (est): 125.6K Privately Held
SIC: 7372 Prepackaged software

(G-10626)
REAUX CORPORATION
Also Called: Reaux Medical Molding
9802 E 58th St (74146-6409)
P.O. Box 470648 (74147-0648)
PHONE.................918 252-7660
Robert Lamoreaux, *President*
Carolyn Herndon, *Vice Pres*
EMP: 10 EST: 2012
SQ FT: 20,000
SALES (est): 791.8K Privately Held
SIC: 3843 Dental equipment & supplies

(G-10627)
REBELLION ENERGY LLC
5416 S Yale Ave Ste 300 (74135-6241)
PHONE.................918 779-3163
Staci Taruscio, *President*
Danny Daniels, *Vice Pres*
Stephanie Orr, *Vice Pres*
Tom Walton, *Vice Pres*
Eric Sundstrom, *Senior Engr*
EMP: 6
SALES (est): 145.1K Privately Held
SIC: 1382 Oil & gas exploration services

(G-10628)
REBELLION ENERGY II LLC
5416 S Yale Ave Ste 300 (74135-6241)
PHONE.................918 779-3163
Staci Taruscio, *CEO*
Chris Weatherl, *COO*
Jim Qualls, *Vice Pres*
Melanie Warren, *CFO*
EMP: 2
SALES (est): 81.9K Privately Held
SIC: 1382 Oil & gas exploration services

(G-10629)
RED DEVIL INCORPORATED (PA)
Also Called: RPI
1437 S Boulder Ave # 750 (74119-3644)
PHONE.................918 585-8111
William Lee, *CEO*
Jane Lee, *Chairman*
Craig Cartwright, *Senior VP*
Kolin Kimura, *Vice Pres*
George Lee, *Vice Pres*
◆ EMP: 10 EST: 1872
SQ FT: 8,000
SALES (est): 19.1MM Privately Held
WEB: www.reddevil.com
SIC: 2891 3423 Sealants; caulking compounds; hand & edge tools

(G-10630)
RED FORK MOTOR CO
5015 W 27th St (74107-3339)
PHONE.................918 587-2778
Lessie Hill, *Owner*
EMP: 3

SALES (est): 218.1K Privately Held
SIC: 1311 Crude petroleum & natural gas

(G-10631)
RED FORK USA INVESTMENTS INC
Also Called: Redfork Energy
1437 S Boulder Ave # 700 (74119-3609)
PHONE.................918 270-2941
Michael Fry, *Ch of Bd*
Eugene I Davis, *President*
Perry Gilstrat, *President*
Chris Girouard, *President*
Jeffrey Steinke, *Principal*
EMP: 8
SALES (est): 1.5MM Privately Held
SIC: 1382 Oil & gas exploration services

(G-10632)
REDBONE TOOL AND MACHINE INC
10837 E Marshall St # 10 (74116-5674)
P.O. Box 581688 (74158-1688)
PHONE.................918 625-1617
Raymond Chronister, *President*
Ann Shelly, *Principal*
EMP: 2
SALES (est): 195K Privately Held
WEB: www.redbonetool.com
SIC: 3599 Machine & other job shop work

(G-10633)
REDDY ICE CORPORATION
8904 E Admiral Pl (74115-8128)
PHONE.................918 836-8223
Tammy Anthony, *Principal*
EMP: 20 Privately Held
SIC: 2097 Manufactured ice
HQ: Reddy Ice Corporation
5720 Lyndon B Johnson Fwy # 200
Dallas TX 75240
214 526-6740

(G-10634)
REECE SUPPLY COMPANY HOUSTON
3148 S 108th East Ave # 130 (74146-1638)
PHONE.................918 556-5000
Aaron Wieburg, *Branch Mgr*
EMP: 12
SALES (corp-wide): 64.3MM Privately Held
SIC: 3993 Signs & advertising specialties
HQ: Reece Supply Company Of Houston
2606 Bell St
Houston TX 77003

(G-10635)
REFINERY SUPPLY CO INC
Also Called: RSC Scientific Lab Products
1104 N 105th East Ave (74116-1527)
PHONE.................918 621-1700
Charles A Monsalve, *President*
Jason Smith, *Vice Pres*
Darlynn Monsalve, *Admin Sec*
EMP: 5
SQ FT: 12,000
SALES (est): 1.1MM Privately Held
SIC: 3826 5049 3829 3821 Liquid testing apparatus; petroleum product analyzing apparatus; gas testing apparatus; gas analyzing apparatus; scientific & engineering equipment & supplies; measuring & controlling devices; laboratory apparatus & furniture

(G-10636)
REFUGE LIFESTYLE
4221 S 68th East Ave (74145-4617)
PHONE.................918 366-6650
Clinton Taylor, *Principal*
Clinton Wayne Taylor Jr,
EMP: 10
SALES (est): 1.1MM Privately Held
SIC: 2511 Wood household furniture

(G-10637)
RELIANCE OFS
2 W 2nd St (74103-3123)
PHONE.................303 317-6565
EMP: 2
SALES (est): 156.1K Privately Held
SIC: 1389 Oil field services

(G-10638)
RELIANCE OILFIELD SERVICES LLC (PA)
2 W 2nd St Fl 15 (74103-3114)
PHONE.................918 392-9000
Austin Roberts, *CEO*
Tom Aucario, *COO*
Fred Nicholson, *Manager*
Tiffany Cruce, *Office Admin*
Zacheriah Hare, *IT/INT Sup*
EMP: 31
SALES: 19MM Privately Held
WEB: www.relianceofs.com
SIC: 1389 Oil field services

(G-10639)
REMOTE CONNECTIONS INC
1809 E 11th St (74104-3603)
P.O. Box 52066 (74152-0066)
PHONE.................918 743-3355
Joyce Randolph, *President*
Jep Randolph, *Exec VP*
Nicole Randolph, *Business Dir*
▲ EMP: 10
SQ FT: 4,000
SALES (est): 1.7MM Privately Held
SIC: 5063 3694 3643 3625 Switches, except electronic; engine electrical equipment; current-carrying wiring devices; relays & industrial controls

(G-10640)
RENAVOTIO INFRATECH INC
601 S Boulder Ave Ste 600 (74119-1306)
PHONE.................504 722-7402
William Robinson, *Principal*
EMP: 5
SALES (est): 186.2K Privately Held
SIC: 2389 Apparel & accessories

(G-10641)
RENTAL READY
1217 E Admiral Blvd (74120-1605)
PHONE.................918 500-6922
Luis Freyre, *Principal*
James Handy, *Principal*
EMP: 2
SALES (est): 87.4K Privately Held
SIC: 3273 Ready-mixed concrete

(G-10642)
RENTPATH LLC
Also Called: Primedia
5125 S Garnett Rd Ste A (74146-5908)
PHONE.................918 307-8980
EMP: 15 Privately Held
WEB: www.rentpath.com
SIC: 2731 Books: publishing only
PA: Rentpath, Llc
950 E Paces Ferry Rd Ne # 26
Atlanta GA 30326

(G-10643)
REPUTATION SERVICES & MFG LLC
Also Called: Fleet Service of Tulsa
15855 E Pine St (74116-2434)
PHONE.................918 437-2077
Steve Walter, *CEO*
▼ EMP: 35
SQ FT: 30,000
SALES: 21.5MM Privately Held
SIC: 7538 1389 3524 3531 General truck repair; construction, repair & dismantling services; lawn & garden tractors & equipment; forestry related equipment; oil & gas drilling rigs & equipment; automotive related machinery

(G-10644)
RESOLUTE WYOMING INC
Also Called: Primary Natural Resources III
7134 S Yale Ave Ste 430 (74136-6351)
PHONE.................918 495-0598
David House, *President*
EMP: 30
SALES (est): 2.2MM Privately Held
SIC: 1382 Oil & gas exploration services

(G-10645)
RESOURCE DEVELOPMENT CO LLC (HQ)
2930 S Yale Ave (74114-6252)
PHONE.................248 646-2300
Thomas J Connaughton,

Fe Stuart,
EMP: 20
SQ FT: 15,000
SALES (est): 4.6MM Privately Held
WEB: www.resourcedev.com
SIC: 5999 7371 7372 Educational aids & electronic training materials; computer software development & applications; educational computer software

(G-10646)
RESOURCEONE COMMUNICATIONS INC
2900 E Apache St (74110-2253)
PHONE................................918 295-0112
Jess Pelcher, *President*
Jeff Sellers, *Info Tech Mgr*
EMP: 2
SALES (est): 280.8K Privately Held
SIC: 2759 Commercial printing

(G-10647)
RESPONSE SOLUTIONS INC
5800 E Skelly Dr Ste 830 (74135-6445)
PHONE................................918 508-7022
Frank Daniel Stroud, *President*
Jayson Charles Stroud, *Vice Pres*
EMP: 7
SQ FT: 1,000
SALES (est): 1.9MM Privately Held
SIC: 2677 Envelopes

(G-10648)
RESTAURANT EQUIPMENT & SUP LLC
9070 E 31st St (74145-1704)
PHONE................................918 664-1778
Michael O Stuart,
EMP: 8
SQ FT: 10,175
SALES (est): 1.2MM Privately Held
WEB: www.restaurantequipmentsupplyoftulsa.com
SIC: 2599 5712 Carts, restaurant equipment; bar fixtures, equipment & supplies

(G-10649)
REX LABORATORIES INC
1320 S Wheeling Ave (74104-4428)
PHONE................................918 742-9545
E Donald Souders, *President*
Sheryl Plemons, *Corp Secy*
EMP: 1
SALES (est): 140.7K Privately Held
SIC: 8042 3851 Contact lense specialist optometrist; contact lenses

(G-10650)
RICHARD BROWN
7115 S Yale Ave (74136-6308)
PHONE................................918 492-1991
Richard Brown, *Principal*
EMP: 2
SALES (est): 138.9K Privately Held
SIC: 3843 Enamels, dentists'

(G-10651)
RICO WOODWORKING LLC
171 E 57th St (74105-7714)
PHONE................................918 743-0741
Enrique Maldonado, *Principal*
EMP: 1
SALES (est): 69.7K Privately Held
SIC: 2431 Millwork

(G-10652)
RIGGS HEINRICH MEDIA INC
Also Called: Imirus
7715 E 111th St Ste 111 (74133-2572)
PHONE................................918 492-0660
Chris Riggs, *President*
EMP: 32
SALES (est): 700K Privately Held
SIC: 5192 7372 Magazines; business oriented computer software

(G-10653)
RIM MOLDED PRODUCTS CO
1222 N Garnett Rd (74116-2005)
PHONE................................918 438-7070
Hyun Cho, *President*
EMP: 10
SQ FT: 5,000

SALES (est): 1.7MM Privately Held
SIC: 3089 Injection molded finished plastic products

(G-10654)
RING ENERGY INC
6555 S Lewis Ave Ste 200 (74136-1010)
PHONE................................918 499-3880
William Broaddrick, *Branch Mgr*
EMP: 2
SALES (corp-wide): 195.7MM Publicly Held
SIC: 1382 1389 Oil & gas exploration services; oil field services
PA: Ring Energy Inc.
    901 W Wall St Fl 3
    Midland TX 79701
    432 682-7464

(G-10655)
RINGSIDE PRODUCTIONS
2222 S 85th East Ave (74129-3015)
PHONE................................818 974-2673
Gary Sievers, *Principal*
EMP: 1
SALES (est): 67.5K Privately Held
SIC: 3511 Turbines & turbine generator sets

(G-10656)
RIVERS EDGE PUBLICATIONS
4636 W 43rd St (74107-6220)
PHONE................................918 855-9469
EMP: 2 EST: 2013
SALES (est): 119.1K Privately Held
SIC: 2741 Misc Publishing

(G-10657)
RIVERSIDE LABORATORIES INC
516 S 25th West Ave (74127-8406)
PHONE................................918 585-3064
Bill Mallory, *President*
EMP: 5
SALES (est): 256.3K
SALES (corp-wide): 98MM Privately Held
SIC: 1389 Oil sampling service for oil companies
HQ: Troco Oil Co
    516 S 25th West Ave
    Tulsa OK 74127

(G-10658)
RIVERSIDE MACHINE INC
Also Called: Riverside Machine Works
2313 W 41st St (74107-6707)
PHONE................................918 445-5141
Fax: 918 445-4178
EMP: 15
SQ FT: 5,644
SALES (est): 1MM Privately Held
SIC: 3599 Machine Shop

(G-10659)
RIVERSIDE MDSTREAM PRTNERS LLC
6120 S Yale Ave Ste 1480 (74136-4226)
PHONE................................918 949-4224
Calvin D Cahill,
EMP: 16 EST: 2017
SALES (est): 109.8K
SALES (corp-wide): 15.6MM Privately Held
SIC: 1382 Oil & gas exploration services
PA: Calyx Energy, Llc
    6120 S Yale Ave Ste 1480
    Tulsa OK 74136

(G-10660)
RIVES ENTERPRISES INC
1735 E 11th St (74104-3632)
P.O. Box 1089, Skiatook (74070-5089)
PHONE................................918 671-4099
D M Rives, *President*
EMP: 6
SQ FT: 3,238
SALES (est): 442.9K Privately Held
SIC: 3281 Granite, cut & shaped

(G-10661)
ROAD SCIENCE LLC (HQ)
6502 S Yale Ave (74136-8329)
PHONE................................918 960-3800
Frank Panzer, *Mng Member*
▲ EMP: 65
SQ FT: 3,000

SALES (est): 11.9MM Privately Held
SALES (corp-wide): 189MM Privately Held
SIC: 2951 Asphalt paving mixtures & blocks
PA: Arr-Maz Custom Chemicals, Inc.
    4800 State Road 60 E
    Mulberry FL 33860
    863 578-1206

(G-10662)
ROBERT M BEIRUTE
Also Called: Beirute Consulting
10104 S Urbana Ave (74137-5921)
PHONE................................918 299-4259
Robert M Beirute, *Owner*
EMP: 1
SALES (est): 87.2K Privately Held
SIC: 1389 Oil consultants

(G-10663)
ROBERT W BERRY INC (PA)
Also Called: Berry, Robt W
2200 S Utica Pl Ste 410 (74114-7012)
PHONE................................918 492-1140
Robert W Berry, *President*
EMP: 3 EST: 1975
SALES (est): 562.3K Privately Held
SIC: 1311 Crude petroleum production; natural gas production

(G-10664)
ROBINHOOD STAMP & SEAL CO INC
2323 E 71st St (74136-5414)
PHONE................................918 493-6506
Scott Robinett, *President*
Hazel Robinett, *Treasurer*
Thomas Robinett, *Admin Sec*
Cindy Robinett,
EMP: 2
SALES (est): 130K Privately Held
SIC: 3953 Time stamps, hand: rubber or metal

(G-10665)
ROBS MAGNETO SERVICE
144 E 1st St (74103)
PHONE................................918 367-5735
Robert Carmon, *Owner*
EMP: 1
SALES (est): 75K Privately Held
SIC: 7629 3599 Electrical repair shops; industrial machinery

(G-10666)
ROCKFORD ENERGY PARTNER
15 E 5th St Ste 2800 (74103-4335)
PHONE................................918 592-0679
EMP: 2
SALES (est): 115.4K Privately Held
SIC: 1382 Oil & gas exploration services

(G-10667)
ROCKFORD EXPLORATION INC
2021 S Lewis Ave (74104-5733)
PHONE................................918 582-1320
John Brock, *President*
Donnie Brock, *Vice Pres*
Christine Fletcher, *Admin Sec*
EMP: 2 EST: 1981
SALES (est): 2MM Privately Held
SIC: 1382 Geophysical exploration, oil & gas field

(G-10668)
ROCKY MTN MDSTREAM HLDINGS LLC
1 Williams Ctr (74172-0140)
PHONE................................918 573-2000
Stephen W Bergstrom, *Principal*
EMP: 6
SALES (corp-wide): 8.2B Publicly Held
SIC: 6719 1389 Investment holding companies, except banks; gas field services; oil field services
PA: The Williams Companies Inc
    1 Williams Ctr
    Tulsa OK 74172
    918 573-2000

(G-10669)
ROOKS FABRICATION LLC
6500 S 39th West Ave (74132-1242)
PHONE................................918 447-1990

Mark Rooks,
EMP: 16
SQ FT: 4,000
SALES (est): 1MM Privately Held
SIC: 3441 Fabricated structural metal

(G-10670)
ROSA & UNIS LLC
4141 S Galveston Ave (74107-7044)
PHONE................................918 445-4204
Jacinto Rosa, *CEO*
Joseph Unis, *CFO*
EMP: 100
SQ FT: 250,000
SALES (est): 25MM Privately Held
SIC: 3317 Boiler tubes (wrought)

(G-10671)
ROSE ROCK MIDSTREAM CORP
6120 S Yale Ave Ste 700 (74136-4216)
PHONE................................918 524-8100
David Minielly, *Vice Pres*
Alisa Perkins, *Officer*
EMP: 6
SALES (est): 1.6MM Privately Held
SIC: 1311 Crude petroleum & natural gas

(G-10672)
ROSE ROCK MIDSTREAM FIELD SVCS
2 Warren Pl 6120 S Yal (74136)
PHONE................................918 524-7700
EMP: 2
SALES (est): 70.5K Publicly Held
SIC: 1389 4612 5171 2951 Oil field services; crude petroleum pipelines; petroleum bulk stations & terminals; asphalt paving mixtures & blocks
HQ: Semgroup Corporation
    6120 S Yale Ave Ste 1500
    Tulsa OK 74136
    918 524-8100

(G-10673)
ROSE ROCK MIDSTREAM OPER LLC
6120 S Yale Ave Ste 700 (74136-4216)
PHONE................................918 524-7700
Carlin G Conner, *President*
Robert N Fitzgerald, *CFO*
Cheryl Janicek, *Manager*
EMP: 4
SALES (est): 265.1K Publicly Held
SIC: 1311 Crude petroleum & natural gas
HQ: Semgroup Corporation
    6120 S Yale Ave Ste 1500
    Tulsa OK 74136
    918 524-8100

(G-10674)
ROTERT WELD & FAB LLC
1565 N 166th East Ave (74116-4941)
PHONE................................918 671-2170
Justin Rotert, *Principal*
EMP: 1
SALES (est): 76.3K Privately Held
SIC: 7692 Welding repair

(G-10675)
ROTH MANUFACTURING CO INC (PA)
1379 E 45th St (74105-4105)
P.O. Box 2965 (74101-2965)
PHONE................................918 743-4477
Alan Stuart, *President*
Iris C Stuart, *Corp Secy*
EMP: 1
SALES (est): 804.7K Privately Held
SIC: 5084 3564 Oil well machinery, equipment & supplies; heat exchange equipment, industrial; blowing fans: industrial or commercial

(G-10676)
ROTOCOLOR INC
7221 S Gary Pl (74136-5925)
PHONE................................510 785-7686
Paul Close, *Ch of Bd*
EMP: 18
SQ FT: 17,000
SALES (est): 2.1MM Privately Held
SIC: 2679 Labels, paper: made from purchased material

GEOGRAPHIC SECTION

Tulsa - Tulsa County (G-10702)

(G-10677)
ROTORK VALVEKITS INC
Also Called: Rotork Valvekits USA
4433 W 49th St Ste D (74107-7307)
PHONE..................918 259-8100
Michael J Renfro, *Principal*
Gerald L Kinion Jr, *Principal*
N J Renfro, *Principal*
Shari Hargrove, *Corp Secy*
Pat Renfro, *Vice Pres*
EMP: 16
SQ FT: 17,000
SALES (est): 7.1MM
SALES (corp-wide): 864.5MM **Privately Held**
SIC: 5084 3599 3494 Industrial machinery & equipment; machine shop, jobbing & repair; valves & pipe fittings
PA: Rotork P.L.C.
Rotork House
Bath BA1 3
122 573-3200

(G-10678)
ROUGEOT OIL & GAS CORP
8177 S Harvard Ave # 734 (74137-1612)
PHONE..................918 288-2022
John E Rougeot, *President*
EMP: 2
SALES: 300K **Privately Held**
SIC: 1311 Crude petroleum production; natural gas production

(G-10679)
ROXTEC INC (DH)
10127 E Admiral Pl (74116-2529)
P.O. Box 690177 (74169-0177)
PHONE..................918 254-9872
Mark Nygren, *President*
Graham Ohare, *Managing Dir*
Gerald Golightly, *Business Mgr*
Rich Story, *Business Mgr*
Christian Briggs, *QC Mgr*
▲ **EMP:** 17
SQ FT: 15,000
SALES (est): 4.3MM **Privately Held**
WEB: www.roxtec.com
SIC: 3053 Gaskets, packing & sealing devices
HQ: Roxtec International Ab
Lyckeby 371 2
455 366-700

(G-10680)
RP POWER LLC
1111 N 105th East Ave (74116-1527)
PHONE..................918 960-6000
John Ronza, *Branch Mgr*
EMP: 6
SALES (corp-wide): 18MM **Privately Held**
WEB: www.rp-corp.com
SIC: 3621 Generators & sets, electric
PA: Rp Power, Llc
7777 Northshore Pl
North Little Rock AR 72118
501 568-3000

(G-10681)
RSGA INCORPORATED
Also Called: Innovasia
10496 S 86th East Ave (74133-7084)
PHONE..................918 978-6800
Jon Darin Long, *Principal*
EMP: 1
SALES (est): 46.5K **Privately Held**
SIC: 2221 Apparel & outerwear fabric, manmade fiber or silk

(G-10682)
RUSSELLS WELDING INC
7756 Charles Page Blvd (74127-7159)
PHONE..................918 245-7395
Gene Russell, *President*
Wade Russell, *Vice Pres*
Tami Sisemore, *Treasurer*
Vicki Longoria, *Admin Sec*
EMP: 8
SQ FT: 4,800
SALES (est): 1.3MM **Privately Held**
SIC: 7692 1799 Welding repair; welding on site

(G-10683)
S & S TIME CORPORATION
Also Called: S & S Watches & Clocks
8909 E 21st St (74129-1417)
PHONE..................918 437-3572
Vl Smith Schulmeier, *President*
Charles Hines, *Corp Secy*
Floyd Schulmeier, *Exec VP*
EMP: 36
SQ FT: 9,500
SALES (est): 7.3MM **Privately Held**
SIC: 5094 2759 3873 Watches & parts; clocks; imprinting; screen printing; watches, clocks, watchcases & parts

(G-10684)
S & T MFG CO (PA)
17411 E Pine St (74116-4928)
P.O. Box 1179, Catoosa (74015-1179)
PHONE..................918 234-4151
Bill Tolbert, *President*
Ronnie Tolbert, *Vice Pres*
Brad Turner, *Purchasing*
Misha Tolbert, *CFO*
Gary Tolbert, *Treasurer*
▲ **EMP:** 40 **EST:** 1973
SQ FT: 12,000
SALES (est): 19MM **Privately Held**
SIC: 3441 7692 Fabricated structural metal; cracked casting repair

(G-10685)
S K WARREN RESOURSES LLC
6585 S Yale Ave Ste 900 (74136-8322)
P.O. Box 470372 (74147-0372)
PHONE..................918 491-5900
Stephen K Warren,
EMP: 1 **EST:** 1992
SALES (est): 119K **Privately Held**
SIC: 1382 Oil & gas exploration services

(G-10686)
S M SADLER INC
1423 E 41st St (74105-4033)
P.O. Box 520946 (74152-0946)
PHONE..................918 743-1048
Susan Sadler, *Owner*
EMP: 2
SQ FT: 1,600
SALES (est): 675K **Privately Held**
SIC: 3911 Jewelry, precious metal

(G-10687)
SAFETAC PUBLISHING LLC
1209 S Frankfort Ave 200a (74120-4247)
PHONE..................559 640-7233
Travis Yates, *Principal*
EMP: 1
SALES (est): 41.3K **Privately Held**
WEB: www.safetac.org
SIC: 2741 Miscellaneous publishing

(G-10688)
SAFETY TRAINING SYSTEMS INC
Also Called: S T S
7373 E 38th St (74145-3209)
P.O. Box 471350 (74147-1350)
PHONE..................918 665-0125
Bruce Bartovick, *CEO*
Miike Wilson, *President*
Kenneth C Ellison, *Principal*
Mark A Hacker, *Principal*
Lisa Hendricks, *Purch Mgr*
▲ **EMP:** 50
SQ FT: 60,000
SALES (est): 10.3MM **Privately Held**
WEB: www.ststulsa.com
SIC: 3699 Flight simulators (training aids), electronic

(G-10689)
SAGE NATURAL RESOURCES LLC
6100 S Yale Ave Ste 900 (74136-1935)
PHONE..................940 539-2225
EMP: 3
SALES (est): 72K **Privately Held**
SIC: 1389 Gas compressing (natural gas) at the fields; gas field services

(G-10690)
SALTUS TECHNOLOGIES LLC
907 S Detroit Ave Ste 820 (74120-4207)
PHONE..................918 392-3900
Eric Fultz, *CEO*
EMP: 11 **EST:** 2010
SQ FT: 6,500
SALES (est): 1.3MM **Privately Held**
SIC: 7372 Application computer software

(G-10691)
SAM W MAYS JR
427 S Boston Ave Ste 1207 (74103-4141)
P.O. Box 391, Eureka KS (67045-0391)
PHONE..................918 382-9170
Sam W Mays Jr, *Principal*
EMP: 4
SALES (est): 425.5K **Privately Held**
SIC: 1311 Crude petroleum production

(G-10692)
SAMSON ENERGY COMPANY LLC (PA)
110 W 7th St Ste 2000 (74119-1076)
PHONE..................918 879-0279
Keith Stgemme, *Vice Pres*
Matt Stewart, *Engineer*
Scott Rowland, *VP Bus Dvlpt*
Sharon Fuller, *Accountant*
Shoba Rosario, *Accountant*
EMP: 17 **EST:** 2011
SALES (est): 57.6MM **Privately Held**
SIC: 1389 1741 Building oil & gas well foundations on site; chimney construction & maintenance

(G-10693)
SAMSON EXPLORATION LLC
110 W 7th St Ste 2000 (74119-1076)
P.O. Box 629 (74101-0629)
PHONE..................918 879-0279
Mark Lauer, *Legal Staff*
EMP: 10 **EST:** 2007
SALES (est): 50.6MM
SALES (corp-wide): 57.6MM **Privately Held**
SIC: 1389 1382 Cementing oil & gas well casings; aerial geophysical exploration oil & gas
PA: Samson Energy Company, Llc
110 W 7th St Ste 2000
Tulsa OK 74119
918 879-0279

(G-10694)
SAMSON INVESTMENT COMPANY (HQ)
2 W 2nd St Ste 1500 (74103-3135)
PHONE..................918 583-1791
Randy Limbacher, *President*
Philip Cook, *Exec VP*
Richard Fraley, *Exec VP*
Louis Jones, *Exec VP*
John McCready, *Treasurer*
EMP: 400
SQ FT: 90,000
SALES (est): 1.1B
SALES (corp-wide): 1.4B **Privately Held**
SIC: 1311 7353 5082 Crude petroleum production; natural gas production; oil field equipment, rental or leasing; oil field equipment
PA: Samson Resources Corporation
15 E 5th St Ste 1000
Tulsa OK 74103
918 591-1791

(G-10695)
SAMSON NATURAL GAS COMPANY
Also Called: Samson Production Services
2 W 2nd St Ste 1500 (74103-3135)
PHONE..................918 583-1791
C Philip Tholen, *President*
Bill McLaughlin, *Vice Pres*
Judy Hughes, *Treasurer*
Jay Wayne Tate, *VP Sales*
Annabel M Jones, *Admin Sec*
EMP: 270
SQ FT: 80,000
SALES (est): 20.8MM
SALES (corp-wide): 1.4B **Privately Held**
WEB: www.samson.com
SIC: 4924 7353 1311 1381 Natural gas distribution; oil field equipment, rental or leasing; crude petroleum production; natural gas production; drilling oil & gas wells
HQ: Samson Investment Company
2 W 2nd St Ste 1500
Tulsa OK 74103
918 583-1791

(G-10696)
SAMSON RESOURCES COMPANY (DH)
Also Called: Samson Contour
2 W 2nd St Ste 1500 (74103-3103)
P.O. Box 21022 (74121-1022)
PHONE..................918 583-1791
Randy Limbacher, *CEO*
Paul Smolarchuk, *President*
Matthew Phillips, *General Mgr*
Erik Evans, *Superintendent*
Thomas R Dimelow, *Co-President*
EMP: 70 **EST:** 1971
SQ FT: 90,000
SALES (est): 130.6MM
SALES (corp-wide): 1.4B **Privately Held**
SIC: 1311 2911 Crude petroleum production; natural gas production; petroleum refining
HQ: Samson Investment Company
2 W 2nd St Ste 1500
Tulsa OK 74103
918 583-1791

(G-10697)
SAMSON RESOURCES CORPORATION (PA)
15 E 5th St Ste 1000 (74103-4311)
PHONE..................918 591-1791
Randy L Limbacher, *CEO*
Joseph A Mills, *President*
Louis Jones, *COO*
Richard Fraley, *Exec VP*
Sharolyn C Whiting-Ralston, *Admin Sec*
EMP: 10
SALES (est): 1.4B **Privately Held**
SIC: 1311 Crude petroleum production

(G-10698)
SAMSON RESOURCES II LLC
15 E 5th St Ste 1000 (74103-4311)
PHONE..................918 591-1791
EMP: 2
SALES (est): 90.1K **Privately Held**
SIC: 1311 Crude petroleum & natural gas

(G-10699)
SAMSON RESOURCES II OPCO LLC
15 E 5th St Ste 1000 (74103-4311)
PHONE..................918 591-1791
EMP: 2 **EST:** 2017
SALES (est): 99.1K **Privately Held**
SIC: 1311 Crude petroleum & natural gas

(G-10700)
SAMSON-INTERNATIONAL LTD (DH)
2 W 2nd St Ste 1800 (74103-3107)
PHONE..................918 583-1791
C Philip Tholen, *President*
Jack Cannon, *Vice Pres*
EMP: 26
SALES (est): 10.3MM
SALES (corp-wide): 1.4B **Privately Held**
SIC: 1382 Oil & gas exploration services
HQ: Samson Investment Company
2 W 2nd St Ste 1500
Tulsa OK 74103
918 583-1791

(G-10701)
SAMURAI EQUIPMENT LLC
15627 E Pine St (74116-2430)
PHONE..................918 878-7715
Raymond Forsythe,
EMP: 12
SALES (est): 592.4K **Privately Held**
SIC: 3569 Filters & strainers, pipeline

(G-10702)
SAN JUAN POOLS OF OKLAHOMA
1518 E 5th Ct (74120-4052)
PHONE..................918 582-8169
Charles H King Jr, *President*
Caroline Molesworth, *Admin Sec*
EMP: 6
SQ FT: 3,400

Tulsa - Tulsa County (G-10703) GEOGRAPHIC SECTION

SALES (est): 700K **Privately Held**
SIC: 3949 Swimming pools, plastic

(G-10703)
SAND RUN LLC
3328 E 99th St (74137-5207)
PHONE..........................918 296-3205
Edgar Wilkinson, *Principal*
EMP: 2
SALES (est): 109.3K **Privately Held**
SIC: 1442 Construction sand & gravel

(G-10704)
SANDERSON CUSTOM WOODWORKS
112 N 46th West Ave (74127-6309)
PHONE..........................918 361-1921
EMP: 1 EST: 2017
SALES (est): 54.1K **Privately Held**
SIC: 2431 Millwork

(G-10705)
SANDS WELD AND FAB INC (PA)
7905 W 18th St (74127-4830)
PHONE..........................918 419-2222
Glen Sands, *President*
Linda Patterson, *Vice Pres*
EMP: 2
SQ FT: 2,400
SALES (est): 285.2K **Privately Held**
SIC: 7692 1522 Welding repair; residential construction

(G-10706)
SANFORD BROTHERS CO INC
Also Called: Signs Today
3801 S 79th East Ave (74145-3218)
PHONE..........................918 665-7358
Ted Lacina, *Owner*
EMP: 10
SQ FT: 20,000
SALES (est): 1.1MM **Privately Held**
SIC: 3993 1793 Signs, not made in custom sign painting shops; glass & glazing work

(G-10707)
SANGUINE LTD
110 W 7th St Ste 2700 (74119-1199)
PHONE..........................918 494-6070
Andrew McGuire, *Controller*
EMP: 3
SALES (est): 175.2K **Privately Held**
SIC: 1382 Oil & gas exploration services

(G-10708)
SARDUCCIS METAL WORKS INC
8820 S 33rd West Ave (74132-3460)
PHONE..........................918 694-3466
Brian R Marion, *President*
Trisha Marion, *Treasurer*
EMP: 2
SALES: 60K **Privately Held**
SIC: 3423 7389 Tools or equipment for use with sporting arms;

(G-10709)
SARIEL INC
Also Called: Avinash Paul
7723 S Yale Ave Apt 206 (74136-8222)
PHONE..........................918 855-1400
Avinash Paul, *President*
Benjamin Murphy, *Admin Sec*
EMP: 2
SALES (est): 268.6K **Privately Held**
SIC: 5044 5052 5172 1311 Office equipment; coal & other minerals & ores; petroleum products; crude petroleum & natural gas; television & radio time sales

(G-10710)
SASHAY CORPORATE SERVICES LLC
Also Called: Automated Mail Service
6915 E 38th St (74145-3202)
PHONE..........................918 664-2507
Carla Covey, *Mng Member*
Michael Covey,
EMP: 45
SALES (est): 7.6MM **Privately Held**
SIC: 2759 Advertising literature: printing

(G-10711)
SBS INDUSTRIES
191 S 122nd East Ave (74128-2405)
PHONE..........................918 749-8221
Jeff Myers, *Owner*
EMP: 2
SALES (est): 81.4K **Privately Held**
SIC: 3599 Industrial machinery

(G-10712)
SBS INDUSTRIES LLC (HQ)
10541 E Ute St (74116-1522)
PHONE..........................918 836-7756
Jeff Greer, *CEO*
Ron Garrett, *Vice Pres*
Matt Stewart, *Purchasing*
Mindi Fuser, *CFO*
▲ EMP: 102
SQ FT: 82,000
SALES (est): 46.4MM **Publicly Held**
SIC: 5072 3452 3451 Nuts (hardware); bolts; screws; bolts, nuts, rivets & washers; screw machine products

(G-10713)
SCFM INC
3701 S Maybelle Ave (74107-5708)
PHONE..........................918 663-1309
Jay Stephens, *CEO*
Stephen Miller, *President*
Jose Cosa, *Exec VP*
Andrew Connor, *Vice Pres*
▲ EMP: 35
SQ FT: 5,000
SALES (est): 19.1MM **Privately Held**
SIC: 3533 Oil & gas field machinery

(G-10714)
SCHLUMBERGER TECHNOLOGY CORP
525 S Main St Ste 1000 (74103-4504)
PHONE..........................918 584-6651
EMP: 6 **Publicly Held**
SIC: 1389 Oil field services
HQ: Schlumberger Technology Corp
   300 Schlumberger Dr
   Sugar Land TX 77478
   281 285-8500

(G-10715)
SCHUMAN PUBLISHING COMPANY
1609 S Boston Ave (74119-4439)
P.O. Box 14204 (74159-1204)
PHONE..........................918 744-6205
Daniel Schuman, *Principal*
EMP: 9 EST: 2008
SALES (est): 869.1K **Privately Held**
WEB: www.okmag.com
SIC: 2721 Magazines: publishing only, not printed on site

(G-10716)
SCISSORTAIL ENERGY LLC (HQ)
8811 S Yale Ave Ste 200 (74137-3650)
PHONE..........................918 588-5000
Jay Precourt, *Mng Member*
Jack Elgin,
Lee Fiegner,
EMP: 12 EST: 2000
SALES (est): 87.5MM **Publicly Held**
SIC: 1311 Crude petroleum & natural gas

(G-10717)
SCOUT GUIDE TULSA LLC
3701 S Harvard Ave (74135-2290)
PHONE..........................918 693-1198
EMP: 2
SALES (est): 83.1K **Privately Held**
SIC: 2741 Miscellaneous publishing

(G-10718)
SCRATCHOUT LLC
6216 S Lewis Ave Ste 200 (74136-1065)
PHONE..........................918 740-8665
Chris Shell, *Principal*
EMP: 1
SALES (est): 93.3K **Privately Held**
SIC: 3651 Household video equipment

(G-10719)
SDS INDUSTRIES LLC
2705 S 117th East Ave (74129-8057)
PHONE..........................918 863-3740
Stanley Scarborough, *President*
EMP: 1
SALES (est): 51.6K **Privately Held**
SIC: 3999 Manufacturing industries

(G-10720)
SEAMLESS LLC
Also Called: Seamless Ehr
2250 E 73rd St (74136-6844)
PHONE..........................918 743-7935
Steven Hays,
EMP: 4
SALES (est): 172.5K **Privately Held**
SIC: 7372 Application computer software

(G-10721)
SECRET GARDEN CANDLE COMPANY
9999 S Mingo Rd Ste Q (74133-5170)
PHONE..........................918 497-8699
EMP: 1
SALES (est): 43.6K **Privately Held**
SIC: 3999 Candles

(G-10722)
SECUREAGENT SOFTWARE INC
Also Called: Global Interface Solutions
2448 E 81st St Ste 2000 (74137-4271)
PHONE..........................918 971-1600
Brent Johnson, *President*
Brenda Melancon, *Vice Pres*
John Sawyer, *Vice Pres*
Kindel Carpenter, *Manager*
Steve Soodsma, *Prgrmr*
EMP: 20
SALES (est): 1.6MM **Privately Held**
SIC: 7372 7371 3577 Prepackaged software; custom computer programming services; computer peripheral equipment

(G-10723)
SEISMIC DRILLING SERVICES LLC
1437 S Boulder Ave # 930 (74119-3609)
P.O. Box 21470 (74121-1470)
PHONE..........................918 587-2225
William Pritchard,
Wade Alexander,
EMP: 65 EST: 1997
SQ FT: 8,000
SALES (est): 3.6MM **Privately Held**
SIC: 1381 Service well drilling

(G-10724)
SEISMIC EXCHANGE INC
2021 S Lewis Ave Ste 580 (74104-5733)
PHONE..........................918 712-7186
EMP: 20
SALES (corp-wide): 29MM **Privately Held**
SIC: 1382 Seismograph surveys
PA: Seismic Exchange, Inc.
   4805 Westway Park Blvd
   Houston TX 77041
   832 590-5100

(G-10725)
SELCO LLC
8909 E 21st St (74129-1417)
PHONE..........................918 622-6100
Craig Naumann, *Opers Staff*
Martha Arrowood, *Credit Mgr*
Jackie Smith, *Sales Staff*
Mark Abels, *Mng Member*
Theresa Brauer, *Manager*
▲ EMP: 30
SQ FT: 18,000
SALES (est): 13.1MM **Privately Held**
WEB: www.selcotime.com
SIC: 5094 3873 Watches & parts; clocks; watches, clocks, watchcases & parts

(G-10726)
SELF PRINTING INC
10021 E 44th Pl (74146-4707)
PHONE..........................918 838-2113
Barbara Self, *CEO*
Roy Self, *President*
EMP: 6
SQ FT: 13,000
SALES (est): 454K **Privately Held**
SIC: 2752 2791 2789 Commercial printing, offset; typesetting; bookbinding & related work

(G-10727)
SEMCRUDE LP (DH)
6120 S Yale Ave Ste 700 (74136-4216)
PHONE..........................918 524-8100
Norman J Szydlowski, *CEO*
Peter Schwiering, *President*
Robert N Fitzgerald, *CFO*
EMP: 10
SALES (est): 4.7MM **Publicly Held**
SIC: 4612 5171 2951 Crude petroleum pipelines; petroleum bulk stations & terminals; asphalt paving mixtures & blocks
HQ: Semgroup Corporation
   6120 S Yale Ave Ste 1500
   Tulsa OK 74136
   918 524-8100

(G-10728)
SEMGROUP CORPORATION (HQ)
6120 S Yale Ave Ste 1500 (74136-4231)
PHONE..........................918 524-8100
Kelcy L Warren, *CEO*
Tyler Ricke, *Purchasing*
Thomas E Long, *CFO*
Mark Magers, *Controller*
Marty Coats, *Accountant*
▲ EMP: 369 EST: 2000
SALES: 2.5B **Publicly Held**
WEB: www.semgroupcorp.com
SIC: 1389 4612 5171 2951 Oil field services; crude petroleum pipelines; petroleum bulk stations & terminals; asphalt paving mixtures & blocks

(G-10729)
SEMMATERIALS LP (DH)
6520 S Yale Ave Ste 700 (74136)
PHONE..........................918 524-8100
Parker Strickland, *CFO*
EMP: 100
SALES (est): 102.7MM **Publicly Held**
SIC: 2951 Asphalt paving mixtures & blocks
HQ: Semgroup Corporation
   6120 S Yale Ave Ste 1500
   Tulsa OK 74136
   918 524-8100

(G-10730)
SEMMEXICO LLC
6120 S Yale Ave (74136-4234)
PHONE..........................918 524-8100
EMP: 3
SALES (est): 182.1K **Publicly Held**
SIC: 1389 Oil & gas field services
HQ: Semgroup Corporation
   6120 S Yale Ave Ste 1500
   Tulsa OK 74136
   918 524-8100

(G-10731)
SENAX INC
1844 E 31st Pl (74105-2206)
PHONE..........................918 494-0681
Michael Wise, *President*
John Powell, *Opers Staff*
EMP: 6
SALES (est): 764.6K **Privately Held**
WEB: www.senaxinc.com
SIC: 1311 Crude petroleum production

(G-10732)
SEQUOIA CUSTOM CABINETS LLC
12135 E 11th St Ste E (74128-4404)
PHONE..........................801 830-2741
Cesar Rodriguez Almazan, *Owner*
EMP: 1 EST: 2016
SALES (est): 58K **Privately Held**
SIC: 2434 Wood kitchen cabinets

(G-10733)
SERCEL-GRC CORP
13914 E Admiral Pl Ste B (74116-2107)
P.O. Box 581570 (74158-1570)
PHONE..........................918 834-9600
Richard Kriege, *General Mgr*
Jeffrey C Rambach, *Principal*
Dustin Manry, *Engineer*
Martin Walter, *CFO*
Robin Bond, *Human Res Mgr*
▲ EMP: 130

GEOGRAPHIC SECTIONTulsa - Tulsa County (G-10764)

SALES (est): 38.2MM
SALES (corp-wide): 29.2MM **Privately Held**
WEB: www.sercel-grc.com
SIC: 3561 Pumps & pumping equipment
HQ: Sercel
Zone Industrielle
Carquefou 44470

(G-10734)
SERVICIOS PETROLEROS FLINT CA
1625 W 21st St (74107-2707)
P.O. Box 490 (74101-0490)
PHONE.................................918 587-7131
Gary Whipple, *President*
EMP: 25 **Privately Held**
SIC: 1311 Crude petroleum production; natural gas production
PA: Servicios Petroleros Flint, C.A.
Edif. Flint, Ave. Espana C/Ave. Penalver
El Tigre

(G-10735)
SETH W HERNDON JR
6440 S Lewis Ave Ste 2200 (74136-1060)
P.O. Box 702158 (74170-2158)
PHONE.................................918 744-4072
EMP: 2
SQ FT: 500
SALES (est): 160K **Privately Held**
SIC: 1311 Crude Petroleum/Natural Gas Production

(G-10736)
SEW TULSA
Also Called: Sidekick Embroidery Works
5412 S Mingo Rd Ste G (74146-5739)
P.O. Box 472193 (74147-2193)
PHONE.................................918 627-1577
Rick Kuerston, *President*
EMP: 4
SQ FT: 2,800
SALES: 250K **Privately Held**
SIC: 2395 Emblems, embroidered

(G-10737)
SEXTANT MINERAL GROUP LLC
5308 E 102nd St (74137-6037)
PHONE.................................918 299-5115
Fred Emmer, *Principal*
EMP: 3 EST: 2014
SALES (est): 262.7K **Privately Held**
SIC: 3812 Sextants

(G-10738)
SHAFER KLINE & WARREN INC
7615 E 63rd Pl Ste 210 (74133-1244)
PHONE.................................918 499-6000
Daniel Coltrane, *Branch Mgr*
Danny Coltrane, *Branch Mgr*
EMP: 20
SALES (corp-wide): 38MM **Privately Held**
SIC: 8713 1389 Surveying services; pipe testing, oil field service
PA: Shafer, Kline & Warren, Inc.
11250 Corporate Ave
Lenexa KS 66219
913 888-7800

(G-10739)
SHAW GROUP INC
Also Called: CHICAGO BRIDGE & IRON
626 W 41st St (74107-7019)
PHONE.................................918 445-7744
EMP: 502
SALES (corp-wide): 10.6B **Privately Held**
SIC: 8734 8711 1629 3498 Testing Laboratory Engineering Services Heavy Construction Mfg Fabrctd Pipe/Fitting
HQ: The Shaw Group Inc
4171 Essen Ln
Baton Rouge LA 70809

(G-10740)
SHAWNS SMALL ENG EQP REPR LLC
Also Called: Tulsa Gas Oil
101 N Garnett Rd Apt 331 (74116-6002)
PHONE.................................918 734-1565
Alfred Johnson, *Mng Member*
EMP: 7
SQ FT: 400

SALES (est): 178.8K **Privately Held**
SIC: 7694 Motor repair services

(G-10741)
SHELBY STEEL SERVICE
16850 E Pine St (74116-4815)
P.O. Box 567, Catoosa (74015-0567)
PHONE.................................918 234-3098
Jeff Shelby, *Owner*
EMP: 1
SALES (est): 92K **Privately Held**
SIC: 1799 3441 Welding on site; fabricated structural metal

(G-10742)
SHEN TE ENTERPRISES INC
5888 W 55th St (74107-9140)
PHONE.................................918 505-7711
Bonnie Berney, *President*
Kaye Sawyer, *Prdtn Mgr*
Chris Morgan, *Electrical Engi*
Helga Camp, *VP Finance*
Anna Dale, *Manager*
EMP: 28
SALES (est): 2MM **Privately Held**
SIC: 8711 3578 Electrical or electronic engineering; calculating & accounting equipment

(G-10743)
SHERRIF
12629 E 31st Ct (74146-2302)
PHONE.................................918 663-3705
Jim Rice, *Principal*
EMP: 2
SALES (est): 69.2K **Privately Held**
SIC: 2711 Newspapers

(G-10744)
SHERYLS PRINT SERVICES
13225 E 32nd Ct (74134-4005)
PHONE.................................918 724-2452
Sheryl Calupitan, *Principal*
EMP: 1 EST: 2010
SALES (est): 86.5K **Privately Held**
SIC: 2752 Commercial printing, lithographic

(G-10745)
SHI INTERNATIONAL CORP
307 W Young St (74106-3653)
PHONE.................................918 583-4182
Steve Wiliey, *Principal*
Travis Harbour, *Executive*
Jonathan Schanke, *Executive*
Symeja Seji, *Executive*
EMP: 1 **Privately Held**
SIC: 7372 Prepackaged software
PA: Shi International Corp.
290 Davidson Ave
Somerset NJ 08873

(G-10746)
SHIELDING RESOURCES GROUP
Also Called: S R G
9512 E 55th St (74145-8106)
PHONE.................................918 663-1985
Michael John Lahita, *President*
Theresa Mary Lahita, *Corp Secy*
Terri Loud, *Vice Pres*
Theresa Lahita, *CFO*
EMP: 18
SQ FT: 18,000
SALES (est): 4.8MM **Privately Held**
SIC: 1542 8711 3444 Custom builders, non-residential; consulting engineer; sheet metalwork

(G-10747)
SHIPROCK MIDSTREAM LLC (PA)
Also Called: Whiptail Midstream
15 W 6th St Ste 2901 (74119-5423)
PHONE.................................918 289-2949
Josh Lamberton, *CEO*
Bob O'Neal, *Vice Pres*
EMP: 8
SALES: 31MM **Privately Held**
SIC: 1382 Oil & gas exploration services

(G-10748)
SHIPZEN INC
36 E Cameron St (74103-1405)
PHONE.................................949 357-2127

Wassim Metallaoui, *Manager*
EMP: 1
SALES (corp-wide): 274.7K **Privately Held**
SIC: 7371 7372 Computer software development & applications; application computer software
PA: Shipzen Inc.
2107 Canyon Cir
Costa Mesa CA 92627
949 357-2125

(G-10749)
SHIRTS & STUFF
4222 S 73rd West Ave (74107-8295)
PHONE.................................918 445-0323
Carl Westfall, *Owner*
Nancy Westfall, *Partner*
EMP: 2
SQ FT: 800
SALES (est): 132K **Privately Held**
SIC: 2396 5699 2395 Screen printing on fabric articles; shirts, custom made; embroidery & art needlework

(G-10750)
SHORT OIL CO
2536 E 51st St (74105-6041)
PHONE.................................918 747-8200
Short Mark, *Partner*
Carl Short, *Partner*
EMP: 25
SQ FT: 2,904
SALES (est): 2.2MM **Privately Held**
SIC: 1311 Crude petroleum production

(G-10751)
SHOULDERS INTERNATIONAL
4714 S 176th East Pl (74134-7110)
PHONE.................................918 728-2999
EMP: 9 EST: 2017
SALES (est): 1.2MM **Privately Held**
SIC: 3724 Aircraft engines & engine parts

(G-10752)
SIEGFRIED COMPANIES INC
1924 S Utica Ave Ste 1120 (74104-6527)
PHONE.................................918 747-3411
Phil Frohlich, *President*
Sibyl Curtis, *Treasurer*
Kay Hill, *Admin Sec*
EMP: 6
SQ FT: 3,000
SALES (est): 901.7K **Privately Held**
SIC: 6799 1311 Venture capital companies; crude petroleum production; natural gas production

(G-10753)
SIEMENS INDUSTRY SOFTWARE INC
7645 E 63rd St Ste 105 (74133-1249)
PHONE.................................918 505-4220
EMP: 3
SALES (corp-wide): 96.9B **Privately Held**
SIC: 7372 Business oriented computer software
HQ: Siemens Industry Software Inc.
5800 Granite Pkwy Ste 600
Plano TX 75024
997 397-3000

(G-10754)
SIERRA TECHNOLOGIES INC
5124 E Archer St (74115-8427)
PHONE.................................918 445-1090
Randy Drake, *President*
John Drake, *Vice Pres*
EMP: 13
SQ FT: 5,500
SALES (est): 1.2MM **Privately Held**
SIC: 3443 3585 Heat exchangers, condensers & components; refrigeration & heating equipment

(G-10755)
SIGMA EXTRUDING CORP
Also Called: Sigma Stretch Film
4035 W 49th St (74107-7305)
PHONE.................................918 446-6265
Rick Haskins, *Plant Mgr*
Rick Haskine, *Manager*
EMP: 16 **Privately Held**

SIC: 2673 3081 2671 Garment bags (plastic film); made from purchased materials; unsupported plastics film & sheet; packaging paper & plastics film, coated & laminated
HQ: Sigma Extruding Corp.
Page & Schuyler Ave
Lyndhurst NJ 07071
201 933-5353

(G-10756)
SIGN & SEND IT LLC
8033 S Mingo Rd (74133-0900)
PHONE.................................918 730-9309
George Barnett, *Manager*
EMP: 17 EST: 2017
SALES (est): 1.4MM **Privately Held**
SIC: 3993 Signs & advertising specialties

(G-10757)
SIGN MAKER LLC
10926 E 55th Pl (74146-6705)
PHONE.................................918 728-6060
Bill Rodgers, *Principal*
EMP: 3
SALES (est): 309.1K **Privately Held**
SIC: 3993 Signs, not made in custom sign painting shops

(G-10758)
SIGNALTEK INC
1502 W 37th Pl (74107-5634)
PHONE.................................918 583-4335
Derryl Willis, *President*
EMP: 2
SALES (est): 153.2K **Privately Held**
SIC: 3669 Transportation signaling devices

(G-10759)
SIGNATURE CABINETS LLC
8196 E 46th St (74145-4807)
PHONE.................................918 636-3433
EMP: 1 EST: 2017
SALES (est): 64.3K **Privately Held**
SIC: 2434 Wood kitchen cabinets

(G-10760)
SIGNS ETC
8274 E 71st St (74133)
PHONE.................................918 447-1065
David Gillespie, *Principal*
EMP: 2
SALES (est): 109.7K **Privately Held**
SIC: 3993 Signs & advertising specialties

(G-10761)
SILEX INTERIORS INC (PA)
10011 E 51st St (74146-5730)
PHONE.................................918 836-5454
Mike Baxter, *Production*
Tammy Trotter, *Manager*
EMP: 3
SALES (est): 2.4MM **Privately Held**
SIC: 7389 3281 5211 1743 Interior design services; granite, cut & shaped; table tops, marble; tile, ceramic; tile installation, ceramic

(G-10762)
SILVERADO OIL & GAS LLP
320 S Boston Ave Ste 1504 (74103-4704)
P.O. Box 52308 (74152-0308)
PHONE.................................918 592-3060
Greg Dukes, *Owner*
EMP: 2
SALES (est): 232.2K **Privately Held**
SIC: 1382 Oil & gas exploration services

(G-10763)
SIMPSON ENTERPRISES LLC
7108 S Sleepy Hollow Dr (74136-5913)
PHONE.................................918 495-1819
Robert Simpson, *Principal*
EMP: 2
SALES (est): 168.5K **Privately Held**
WEB: www.simpsonenterprises.net
SIC: 1382 Oil & gas exploration services

(G-10764)
SIMPSON PHOTOGRAPHICS TULSA
7335 S Lewis Ave (74136-6845)
P.O. Box 700216 (74170-0216)
PHONE.................................918 630-1134
Robert Simpson, *Principal*

Tulsa - Tulsa County (G-10765)   GEOGRAPHIC SECTION

EMP: 2
SALES (est): 141.4K **Privately Held**
SIC: 1382 Oil & gas exploration services

(G-10765)
SIMULATOR SYSTEMS INTL INC
11130 E 56th St (74146-6713)
PHONE 800 843-4764
Todd Roberts, *Branch Mgr*
EMP: 2
SALES (corp-wide): 355.8K **Privately Held**
WEB: www.simulatorsystems.com
SIC: 3699 Teaching machines & aids, electronic
HQ: Simulator Systems International, Inc.
5358 S 125th East Ave D
Tulsa OK 74146

(G-10766)
SIMULATOR SYSTEMS INTL INC (DH)
5358 S 125th East Ave D (74146-6235)
PHONE 918 250-4500
John M Patrick, *President*
Larry B Lipe, *Principal*
Todd Roberts, *Sales Staff*
James Bonds, *Prgrmr*
EMP: 6
SQ FT: 11,500
SALES (est): 1.2MM
SALES (corp-wide): 355.8K **Privately Held**
SIC: 3699 Teaching machines & aids, electronic

(G-10767)
SINGER BROS (PA)
4124 S Rockford Ave # 101 (74105-4248)
P.O. Box 755 (74101-0755)
PHONE 918 582-6237
George A Singer, *Partner*
Alex S Singer, *Partner*
EMP: 6 **EST:** 1962
SQ FT: 3,600
SALES (est): 835.2K **Privately Held**
SIC: 1311 6792 Crude petroleum production; oil royalty traders

(G-10768)
SINTIES CORPORATION
5151 S 110th East Ave (74146-5840)
PHONE 918 359-2000
Larry Born, *CEO*
Denton Smith, *President*
William Counts, *Corp Secy*
James C McGill, *Vice Pres*
Tracy Barrett, *Mktg Coord*
EMP: 48
SQ FT: 24,500
SALES (corp-wide): 355.8K **Privately Held**
SIC: 6719 3949 3841 Investment holding companies, except banks; exercise equipment; diagnostic apparatus, medical
HQ: Life Fitness, Llc
9525 Bryn Mawr Ave # 500
Rosemont IL 60018
847 288-3300

(G-10769)
SITE DISTRIBUTION LLC (PA)
Also Called: Site Solar
5314 S Yale Ave Ste 510 (74135-6272)
PHONE 918 625-7980
Randy Heckenkemper,
EMP: 4
SALES (est): 520.8K **Privately Held**
SIC: 7353 3648 3433 5211 Heavy construction equipment rental; floodlights; solar heaters & collectors; solar heating equipment

(G-10770)
SITRIN PETROLEUM CORP
5910 S Delaware Ave (74105-7332)
PHONE 918 747-1111
Thomas V Sitrin, *President*
EMP: 5
SALES (est): 380K **Privately Held**
SIC: 6512 1311 Commercial & industrial building operation; crude petroleum production

(G-10771)
SKINNER BROTHERS COMPANY INC
Also Called: S.B.c
1317 E 5th Pl (74120-4008)
P.O. Box 3063 (74101-3063)
PHONE 918 585-5708
Robert Langholz, *Ch of Bd*
Calvin O Vogt, *Vice Pres*
Gail R Runnels, *Treasurer*
▲ **EMP:** 17
SQ FT: 12,000
SALES (est): 4.1MM **Privately Held**
SIC: 3533 3069 Oil field machinery & equipment; molded rubber products

(G-10772)
SLIM HANEY INC
5615 N Mingo Rd (74117-4002)
PHONE 918 274-1082
Newton Box, *President*
Dennis Brock, *Vice Pres*
Brian Bakelaar, *Opers Mgr*
EMP: 25 **EST:** 1967
SQ FT: 9,000
SALES (est): 4.1MM **Privately Held**
WEB: www.slimhaney.com
SIC: 3599 3451 Machine shop, jobbing & repair; screw machine products

(G-10773)
SLIM HANEY MACHINING INC
5615 N Mingo Rd (74117-4002)
PHONE 918 274-1082
Newton Box II, *President*
EMP: 62
SQ FT: 20,000
SALES (est): 9.4MM **Privately Held**
SIC: 3599 Machine shop, jobbing & repair

(G-10774)
SLONE CENTERLESS GRINDING
5434 S 99th East Ave (74146-5725)
PHONE 918 497-0654
Anthony W Slone, *Principal*
EMP: 2
SALES (est): 132.4K **Privately Held**
SIC: 3599 Grinding castings for the trade

(G-10775)
SLOW N LOW SMOKED MEATS
11451 E 37th Pl (74146-2810)
PHONE 918 946-6894
Kevin Lockridge, *Principal*
EMP: 2 **EST:** 2017
SALES (est): 62.3K **Privately Held**
SIC: 2013 Smoked meats from purchased meat

(G-10776)
SMART OFFICE STORES LLC
Also Called: Ink & Toner Outlet
7107 S Memorial Dr (74133-2934)
P.O. Box 471527 (74147-1527)
PHONE 918 994-5300
Michael L Morris,
EMP: 3
SQ FT: 1,800
SALES: 600K **Privately Held**
WEB: www.inktoneroutlet.com
SIC: 3861 Toners, prepared photographic (not made in chemical plants)

(G-10777)
SMARTMAX SOFTWARE INC
8801 S Yale Ave Ste 460 (74137-3503)
PHONE 918 388-5900
Eric Weber, *President*
Ron Turnage, *Manager*
EMP: 25
SALES (est): 2.2MM **Privately Held**
WEB: www.chatbeacon.io
SIC: 7372 Prepackaged software

(G-10778)
SMITH LIGHTING SALES INC
1221 E 33rd St (74105-2043)
PHONE 918 794-2525
EMP: 6
SALES (corp-wide): 4.1MM **Privately Held**
WEB: www.smithlighting.com
SIC: 3648 Lighting fixtures, except electric: residential

PA: Smith Lighting Sales Inc
4101 N Walnut Ave
Oklahoma City OK 73105
405 521-0093

(G-10779)
SMITH WELDING FABG & REPR
Also Called: Smiths Welding & Fabg Repr
5301 S Union Ave (74107-9056)
PHONE 918 446-2293
David L Smith, *President*
Renee Ridener, *Corp Secy*
Avalon Smith, *Vice Pres*
EMP: 3
SALES: 250K **Privately Held**
SIC: 7692 3444 3398 Welding repair; sheet metalwork; metal heat treating

(G-10780)
SMITHCO ENGINEERING INC (HQ)
5615 S 129th East Ave (74134-6708)
PHONE 918 446-4406
Grady Walker, *President*
Judith A Smith, *Principal*
Brett Jones, *Project Mgr*
▼ **EMP:** 30
SALES (est): 17.9MM **Privately Held**
WEB: www.smithco-eng.com
SIC: 3443 Heat exchangers, condensers & components

(G-10781)
SMITTYS BACKHOE SERVICE LLC
6204 E Latimer Pl (74115-6730)
P.O. Box 582215 (74158-2215)
PHONE 918 630-1090
William Smith, *Mng Member*
EMP: 1
SALES (est): 127.3K **Privately Held**
SIC: 3531 Backhoes

(G-10782)
SMYTH LAND SERVICES
3829 E 51st Pl (74135-3843)
PHONE 918 745-9210
Sally Smyth, *Owner*
EMP: 1
SALES (est): 119.2K **Privately Held**
SIC: 1382 Oil & gas exploration services

(G-10783)
SOLAR EXPLORATION OK LLC
7867 S 95th East Ave (74133-4947)
PHONE 918 252-2203
Larry Burroughs, *Manager*
EMP: 3
SALES (est): 206.8K **Privately Held**
SIC: 1311 Crude petroleum production

(G-10784)
SOLID PATH SERVICES
10838 E Marshall St 200f (74116-5682)
PHONE 918 384-7409
Russell Claybrook, *Partner*
EMP: 1
SALES (est): 80.4K **Privately Held**
SIC: 3721 Aircraft

(G-10785)
SOLIDROOTS LLC
1119 N Main St (74106-4650)
PHONE 918 770-3549
Janet Armstrong, *Principal*
Justin Slaton, *Principal*
EMP: 5
SALES (est): 126.7K **Privately Held**
SIC: 7389 3944 5092 ; board games, puzzles & models, except electronic; board games

(G-10786)
SONOCO PRODUCTS COMPANY
Also Called: Sonoco Industrial Products
10008 E 52nd St (74146-5756)
PHONE 918 622-3370
Danny Cook, *Manager*
EMP: 34
SQ FT: 36,000
SALES (corp-wide): 5.3B **Publicly Held**
WEB: www.sonoco.com
SIC: 2655 Tubes, fiber or paper: made from purchased material; cores, fiber: made from purchased material

PA: Sonoco Products Company
1 N 2nd St
Hartsville SC 29550
843 383-7000

(G-10787)
SOONER CNC LLC
6912 E 66th St (74133-1707)
PHONE 918 261-5231
Vacilio Terronez,
Krystofer Allen,
EMP: 2
SALES (est): 174.4K **Privately Held**
SIC: 2431 Millwork

(G-10788)
SOONER HOLDINGS INC (DH)
Also Called: Syntroleum
5416 S Yale Ave Ste 400 (74135-6267)
PHONE 918 592-7900
Robert B Rosene Jr, *Ch of Bd*
Robert W Karlovich III, *Controller*
Vanessa V Tharp, *Accountant*
▲ **EMP:** 12
SALES (est): 2.2MM
SALES (corp-wide): 2.6B **Publicly Held**
SIC: 1311 1321 Natural gas production; natural gas liquids production
HQ: Reg Synthetic Fuels, Llc
416 S Bell Ave
Ames IA 50010
515 239-8000

(G-10789)
SOONER MANUFACTURING CO INC (PA)
1529 N 168th East Ave (74116-4912)
P.O. Box 581231 (74158-1231)
PHONE 918 835-5019
Darin Maddox, *General Mgr*
Ray Turner, *Principal*
EMP: 3
SALES (est): 694.9K **Privately Held**
SIC: 3599 Machine shop, jobbing & repair

(G-10790)
SOONER MANUFACTURING CO INC
Also Called: Center Mfg
1019 N Columbia Ave (74110-5021)
PHONE 918 835-5019
Evan Hudson, *President*
Ray Turner, *Corp Secy*
Rhonda Turner, *Corp Secy*
Lee Naumann, *Vice Pres*
EMP: 10
SQ FT: 5,000
SALES (est): 1.1MM **Privately Held**
SIC: 3599 Machine shop, jobbing & repair

(G-10791)
SOONER REPAIR
1146 E 61st St (74136-0523)
PHONE 918 742-4653
David Bringaze, *Principal*
EMP: 3 **EST:** 2008
SALES (est): 285.5K **Privately Held**
SIC: 5094 3961 3911 Jewelry; costume jewelry; jewelry, precious metal

(G-10792)
SOONER RUBBER PRODUCTS COMPANY
5833 S Garnett Rd (74146-6849)
PHONE 918 461-1391
Don Shelley, *Principal*
EMP: 1
SALES (corp-wide): 9.8MM **Privately Held**
WEB: www.soonerrubber.com
SIC: 2399 Belting & belt products
PA: Sooner Rubber Products Company
1312 Se Grand Blvd
Oklahoma City OK 73129
405 672-7861

(G-10793)
SOUND IQ
3105 S Harvard Ave (74135-4402)
PHONE 918 442-2588
EMP: 1 **EST:** 2017
SALES (est): 64.3K **Privately Held**
SIC: 3651 Audio electronic systems

GEOGRAPHIC SECTION

Tulsa - Tulsa County (G-10820)

(G-10794)
SOUNO LLC
6737 S 85th East Ave (74133-2057)
PHONE..................918 495-1771
Lynn Mitchell, *Mng Member*
EMP: 20
SALES (est): 1.6MM **Privately Held**
SIC: 2741 2721 Directories, telephone: publishing & printing; magazines: publishing & printing

(G-10795)
SOURCE ROCK ENRGY PARTNERS LLC
1714 S Boston Ave (74119-4810)
PHONE..................918 728-3116
Brian D Weatherl, *Mng Member*
EMP: 3
SALES (est): 818.5K **Privately Held**
SIC: 1382 Oil & gas exploration services

(G-10796)
SOUTH CENTRAL GOLF INC
Also Called: South Central Publications
6218 S Lewis Ave Ste 102 (74136-1030)
PHONE..................918 280-0787
Landon Jones, *President*
Ken Macleod, *Publisher*
Ken McCloud, *Vice Pres*
EMP: 4 **EST:** 1999
SALES (est): 416.6K **Privately Held**
WEB: www.golfoklahoma.org
SIC: 2759 Commercial printing

(G-10797)
SOUTHERN AERO PARTNERS INC
4085 Southwest Blvd (74107-6503)
PHONE..................918 437-7676
Brian A Hoffman, *President*
Phillip Naegele, *Project Engr*
Dean Dorris, *Director*
EMP: 40
SALES (est): 5.2MM
SALES (corp-wide): 5.1B **Publicly Held**
SIC: 3728 Aircraft parts & equipment
PA: Ametek, Inc.
  1100 Cassatt Rd
  Berwyn PA 19312
  610 647-2121

(G-10798)
SOUTHERN BREEZE CANDLE CO LLC
4606 W 90th St (74132-3404)
PHONE..................918 402-4040
EMP: 2
SALES (est): 68.7K **Privately Held**
SIC: 3999 Candles

(G-10799)
SOUTHERN FOODS GROUP LLC
Also Called: Bordens-Meadow Gold Division
215 N Denver Ave (74103-1821)
P.O. Box 3047 (74101-3047)
PHONE..................918 587-2471
Bill Witt, *Manager*
EMP: 130 **Publicly Held**
WEB: www.oakfarmsdairy.com
SIC: 2026 Fluid milk
HQ: Southern Foods Group, Llc
  3114 S Haskell Ave
  Dallas TX 75223
  214 824-8163

(G-10800)
SOUTHERN MILLWORK INC
525 S Troost Ave (74120-4054)
PHONE..................918 585-8125
William Vogle, *President*
Dean Stephenson, *Vice Pres*
EMP: 25
SQ FT: 40,000
SALES (est): 1.4MM **Privately Held**
SIC: 2431 Doors, wood

(G-10801)
SOUTHERN RUBBER STAMP CO INC
2637 E Marshall St (74110-4757)
PHONE..................918 587-3818
Mike Forehand, *President*
David Purnell, *Vice Pres*
▲ **EMP:** 4
SQ FT: 3,000
SALES (est): 570.7K **Privately Held**
WEB: www.southernmark.com
SIC: 3953 3053 Date stamps, hand: rubber or metal; gaskets, packing & sealing devices

(G-10802)
SOUTHERN SHEET METAL WORKS INC
1225 E 2nd St (74120-2009)
P.O. Box 50008 (74150-0008)
PHONE..................918 584-3371
Michael L Tidwell, *President*
Ron McGill, *Vice Pres*
Tony Barton, *Project Mgr*
EMP: 50 **EST:** 1904
SQ FT: 37,000
SALES (est): 12.2MM **Privately Held**
WEB: www.southernsheetmetal.com
SIC: 3444 Ducts, sheet metal

(G-10803)
SOUTHERN SPECIALTIES CORP
1828 N 105th East Ave (74116-1514)
P.O. Box 580550 (74158-0550)
PHONE..................918 584-3553
Hayden Davis, *General Mgr*
EMP: 32
SALES (est): 6.4MM **Privately Held**
SIC: 3444 3824 3599 Sheet metalwork; parking meters; machine shop, jobbing & repair

(G-10804)
SOUTHWEST CNSTR NEWS SVC
7170 S Braden Ave Ste 180 (74136-6324)
PHONE..................918 493-5066
Ed Minks, *President*
EMP: 7
SALES (est): 347.9K
SALES (corp-wide): 508.8K **Privately Held**
SIC: 2711 Newspapers: publishing only, not printed on site
PA: Southwest Construction News Service Inc
  3616 Nw 58th St
  Oklahoma City OK 73112
  405 948-7474

(G-10805)
SOUTHWEST ELECTRIC CO
1304 N 143rd East Ave (74116-2130)
PHONE..................918 437-9494
Darren Womack, *Manager*
EMP: 13
SALES (corp-wide): 68MM **Privately Held**
SIC: 7694 3625 3621 3613 Electric motor repair; relays & industrial controls; motors & generators; switchgear & switchboard apparatus
PA: Southwest Electric Co.
  6503 Se 74th St
  Oklahoma City OK 73135
  800 364-4445

(G-10806)
SOUTHWEST ENERGY LP
1869 E 71st St (74136-3922)
PHONE..................918 779-0699
EMP: 2
SALES (corp-wide): 15.5B **Privately Held**
SIC: 1311 Crude petroleum production
HQ: Southwest Energy, L.P.
  3900 Essex Ln Ste 610
  Houston TX 77027
  713 235-7500

(G-10807)
SOUTHWEST FILTER COMPANY (PA)
7435 E Reading St (74115-4634)
P.O. Box 580608 (74158-0608)
PHONE..................918 835-1179
Doug Thompson, *President*
Max W Thompson, *Vice Pres*
Nathan Moyer, *Project Mgr*
Mike Fugett, *Purchasing*
Jim R Brewer, *Treasurer*
▲ **EMP:** 7
SQ FT: 1,900
SALES (est): 1.9MM **Privately Held**
WEB: www.southwestfilter.com
SIC: 3443 Vessels, process or storage (from boiler shops): metal plate

(G-10808)
SOUTHWEST FILTER COMPANY
1534 N 75th East Ave (74115-4628)
P.O. Box 580608 (74158-0608)
PHONE..................918 835-1179
Doug Thompson, *President*
EMP: 3
SALES (corp-wide): 1.9MM **Privately Held**
SIC: 3443 Fabricated plate work (boiler shop)
PA: Southwest Filter Company
  7435 E Reading St
  Tulsa OK 74115
  918 835-1179

(G-10809)
SOUTHWEST PETROLEUM CORP
4815 S Harvard Ave # 460 (74135-3055)
PHONE..................918 352-2700
Richard A Seller III, *Ch of Bd*
Mary Beth Sellers, *Admin Sec*
EMP: 25
SQ FT: 22,000
SALES (est): 3.8MM **Privately Held**
SIC: 1311 Crude petroleum production

(G-10810)
SOUTHWEST UNITED INDS INC (DH)
422 S Saint Louis Ave (74120-3418)
PHONE..................918 587-4161
W A Emery, *President*
James M Emery, *Vice Pres*
Rick B Holder, *CFO*
▲ **EMP:** 175
SQ FT: 150,000
SALES (est): 38.3MM
SALES (corp-wide): 327.2B **Publicly Held**
WEB: www.swunited.com
SIC: 3728 Aircraft parts & equipment
HQ: Precision Castparts Corp.
  4650 Sw Mcdam Ave Ste 300
  Portland OR 97239
  503 946-4800

(G-10811)
SOUTHWESTERN MOTOR REBUILDERS
2201 E 3rd St (74104-1829)
PHONE..................918 585-1519
Harley Martin, *President*
Trevin Martin, *Corp Secy*
EMP: 7
SQ FT: 17,000
SALES (est): 738K **Privately Held**
SIC: 7538 3519 Engine rebuilding: automotive; internal combustion engines

(G-10812)
SOUTHWESTERN PROCESS SUPPLY CO (PA)
325 S Quincy Ave (74120-2815)
P.O. Box 1033 (74101-1033)
PHONE..................918 582-8211
Claudia Hamilton, *President*
Candace Conley, *Vice Pres*
EMP: 23
SQ FT: 8,500
SALES (est): 3.9MM **Privately Held**
SIC: 2893 5085 3555 Screen process ink; ink, printers'; printing trades machinery

(G-10813)
SPACE CON SYSTEMS INC
6567 E 21st Pl Ste A (74129-2014)
PHONE..................918 835-6580
Gene Lazzelle, *President*
Irene Lazzelle, *Principal*
EMP: 4 **EST:** 1977
SQ FT: 3,750
SALES (est): 402.2K **Privately Held**
SIC: 3599 Machine shop, jobbing & repair

(G-10814)
SPACE TECH INC
1535 E Marshall St (74106-5001)
P.O. Box 50459 (74150-0459)
PHONE..................918 582-2616
Paul Suhomske, *President*
EMP: 10
SQ FT: 10,000
SALES (est): 1.1MM **Privately Held**
SIC: 3599 Machine shop, jobbing & repair

(G-10815)
SPEAKER WORLD LLC
2032 E 12th St (74104-3805)
PHONE..................918 973-1700
James Jones,
EMP: 4
SALES (est): 120K **Privately Held**
SIC: 3651 Loudspeakers, electrodynamic or magnetic

(G-10816)
SPECIAL SERVICE SYSTEMS INC
4627 E 56th Pl (74135-4311)
PHONE..................918 582-7777
Gary Drummond, *President*
Margaret Drummond, *Corp Secy*
Denise Armiger, *Finance*
Gary Flatt, *Supervisor*
EMP: 20
SALES (est): 600K **Privately Held**
SIC: 7389 7377 3643 3578 Credit card service; computer rental & leasing; current-carrying wiring devices; calculating & accounting equipment; computer peripheral equipment

(G-10817)
SPECIFIC SYSTEMS LTD (PA)
439 W 41st St (74107-7037)
PHONE..................918 663-9321
Michael Bolick Jr, *President*
Michael Bolick, *President*
Jason Brazeal, *Project Mgr*
Colby Pierce, *Prdtn Mgr*
Camry Collins, *Buyer*
▲ **EMP:** 189 **EST:** 1974
SALES (est): 61.3MM **Privately Held**
SIC: 1711 3585 Mechanical contractor; refrigeration & heating equipment

(G-10818)
SPECTRUM LNG LLC (PA)
8605 S Elwood Ave Ste B12 (74132-3628)
PHONE..................918 298-6660
Raymond Latchem, *President*
Tom Steeper, *Opers Dir*
Shannon Latchem, *Analyst*
EMP: 10
SALES (est): 2.3MM **Privately Held**
SIC: 1321 Natural gas liquids

(G-10819)
SPECTRUM TRACER SERVICES LLC (HQ)
9111 E Pine St Ste 104 (74115-5912)
PHONE..................405 470-5566
Steve Faurot, *President*
Michael Porter, *Division Mgr*
Jon Larue, *Exec VP*
Dan Schlosser, *Engineer*
Ryan Hummer, *CFO*
EMP: 55 **EST:** 2010
SALES: 15MM
SALES (corp-wide): 205.4MM **Publicly Held**
WEB: www.spectrumtracer.com
SIC: 1389 Oil field services
PA: Ncs Multistage Holdings, Inc.
  19350 State Highway 249 # 6
  Houston TX 77070
  281 453-2222

(G-10820)
SPECTRUMFX INC
9733 E 54th St (74146-5716)
PHONE..................918 392-9799
Kent Faith, *CEO*
Ross Faith, *Vice Pres*
EMP: 2 **EST:** 2012
SQ FT: 300
SALES (est): 150K **Privately Held**
SIC: 5099 2899 Fire extinguishers; fire retardant chemicals

Tulsa - Tulsa County (G-10821)

(G-10821)
SPIRIT AEROSYSTEMS INC
11333 E Pine St (74116-2023)
PHONE..................918 832-3424
EMP: 13 Publicly Held
WEB: www.spiritaero.com
SIC: 3728 Aircraft parts & equipment
HQ: Spirit Aerosystems, Inc.
3801 S Oliver St
Wichita KS 67210
316 526-9000

(G-10822)
SPIRIT AROSYSTEMS HOLDINGS INC
1541 N Garnett Rd (74116-1632)
PHONE..................918 832-2891
EMP: 3 Publicly Held
SIC: 3724 Engine mount parts, aircraft
PA: Spirit Aerosystems Holdings, Inc.
3801 S Oliver St
Wichita KS 67210

(G-10823)
SPIRIT AROSYSTEMS HOLDINGS INC
2035 N 85th East Ave (74115-3801)
PHONE..................918 832-2131
EMP: 11 Publicly Held
SIC: 3724 Engine mount parts, aircraft
PA: Spirit Aerosystems Holdings, Inc.
3801 S Oliver St
Wichita KS 67210

(G-10824)
SPORTS FITNES PUBLICATIONS LLC
2448 E 81st St Ste 2051 (74137-4281)
PHONE..................918 587-7223
EMP: 2
SALES (est): 59.2K Privately Held
SIC: 2741 Miscellaneous publishing

(G-10825)
SPORTSTECH QUALITY CARDIO LLC
10909c E 56th St (74146-6710)
PHONE..................918 461-9177
Dan Mc Intosh,
Dan McIntosh,
EMP: 11
SALES (est): 1.8MM Privately Held
SIC: 3949 Exercise equipment

(G-10826)
SPOT MY BAG LLC
1722 E King Pl (74110-4903)
PHONE..................918 895-8810
Rod Coulter,
EMP: 2
SALES (est): 140K Privately Held
SIC: 3161 Luggage

(G-10827)
SPX HEAT TRANSFER LLC (HQ)
2121 N 161st East Ave (74116-4834)
P.O. Box 3158 (74101-3158)
PHONE..................918 234-6000
Tom Brown, Principal
Upendra Gupta, Manager
Pradeep Pottumuthu, Manager
Rob Gorman, Director
Bryan Brown, Analyst
◆ EMP: 151
SQ FT: 28,000
SALES (est): 70.8MM
SALES (corp-wide): 1.5B Publicly Held
SIC: 3443 3444 Condensers, steam; sheet metalwork
PA: Spx Corporation
13320a Balntyn Corp Pl
Charlotte NC 28277
980 474-3700

(G-10828)
SPYGLASS ENERGY GROUP LLC
15 E 5th St Ste 4000 (74103-4347)
PHONE..................918 582-9900
Charles Wickstrom,
EMP: 4
SALES (est): 410.2K
SALES (corp-wide): 1.6MM Publicly Held
SIC: 1311 Crude petroleum & natural gas

PA: Petro River Oil Corp.
205 E 42nd St Fl 14
New York NY 10017
469 828-3900

(G-10829)
ST BONAVENTURE PRESS LTD
2232 E 45th Pl (74105-4218)
PHONE..................918 770-8546
Bob Healey, Principal
EMP: 1 EST: 2008
SALES: 10K Privately Held
SIC: 2741 Miscellaneous publishing

(G-10830)
STADIA ENERGY PARTNERS LLC
10804 S 93rd East Ave (74133-6181)
PHONE..................918 812-6169
Gregory Delaune, Principal
EMP: 4
SALES (est): 242.7K Privately Held
SIC: 1311 Crude petroleum production

(G-10831)
STAGHORN ENERGY LLC
1 W 3rd St Ste 1000 (74103-3500)
PHONE..................918 584-2558
Frank EBY,
Karen Reid,
EMP: 4
SALES (est): 777.3K Privately Held
SIC: 1382 Oil & gas exploration services

(G-10832)
STAGHORN PETROLEUM LLC
1 W 3rd St Ste 1000 (74103-3500)
PHONE..................918 584-2558
Frank EBY, CEO
EMP: 1
SALES (est): 316.1K Privately Held
SIC: 1382 Oil & gas exploration services

(G-10833)
STAGHORN PETROLEUM II LLC
1 W 3rd St Ste 1000 (74103-3500)
PHONE..................918 584-2558
Frank EBY, CEO
Charles Hancock, Controller
EMP: 2 EST: 2017
SALES (est): 138.1K Privately Held
SIC: 1382 Oil & gas exploration services

(G-10834)
STAND BY PERSONNEL
1530 E 1st St (74120-2206)
PHONE..................918 582-0522
Mark Morris, Owner
Bryan Davis, Sales Staff
Janice Wine, Manager
Larry Wine, Director
EMP: 8 Privately Held
WEB: www.standbypersonnel.com
SIC: 7363 7692 Temporary help service; welding repair
PA: Stand By Personnel
1531 E 2nd St
Tulsa OK 74120

(G-10835)
STANDARD MATERIALS GROUP
4608 S Garnett Rd Ste 600 (74146-5226)
PHONE..................479 587-3300
EMP: 12
SALES (est): 4.4MM Privately Held
SIC: 3273 Ready-mixed concrete

(G-10836)
STANDARD MATERIALS GROUP INC
4608 S Garnett Rd Ste 600 (74146-5226)
PHONE..................918 582-8111
EMP: 2
SALES (corp-wide): 30.6B Privately Held
SIC: 3273 Ready-mixed concrete
HQ: Standard Materials Group, Inc.
755 E Millsap Rd
Fayetteville AR 72703
479 587-3300

(G-10837)
STANDARD PANEL LLC
1355 N Louisville Ave (74115)
PHONE..................918 984-1717
EMP: 9

SALES (est): 1.3MM Privately Held
SIC: 2452 Prefabricated wood buildings

(G-10838)
STANLEY FILTER COMPANY LLC
8189 E 44th St (74145-4830)
PHONE..................800 545-9926
John Morton,
E Kay Morton,
▲ EMP: 5
SALES (est): 864.2K Privately Held
SIC: 3561 Pumps & pumping equipment

(G-10839)
STATELINE PROCESSING LLC
3500 One Williams Ctr (74172-0135)
PHONE..................855 979-2012
Clay M Gaspar, Manager
EMP: 20
SALES (est): 1MM Publicly Held
SIC: 1311 Crude petroleum & natural gas
PA: Wpx Energy, Inc.
3500 One Williams Ctr
Tulsa OK 74172

(G-10840)
STATELINE WATER LLC
3500 One Williams Ctr (74172-0135)
PHONE..................855 979-2012
Clay M Gaspar, President
EMP: 21 EST: 2016
SALES (est): 771.4K Publicly Held
SIC: 1311 Crude petroleum & natural gas
PA: Wpx Energy, Inc.
3500 One Williams Ctr
Tulsa OK 74172

(G-10841)
STEAMPORT LLC
1717 S Boulder Ave # 400 (74119-4805)
PHONE..................918 295-7600
EMP: 46
SALES (est): 1.4MM Publicly Held
SIC: 1221 Bituminous coal & lignite-surface mining
HQ: Alliance Resource Partners Lp
1717 S Boulder Ave # 400
Tulsa OK 74119
918 295-7600

(G-10842)
STEAMPUNK BNICS INNVATIONS LLC
28 S Lakewood Ave (74112-1712)
PHONE..................866 795-6645
Ricky Sevier,
Ian Sevier,
Yolanda Sevier,
EMP: 3
SALES (est): 152K Privately Held
SIC: 3842 Surgical appliances & supplies

(G-10843)
STEEL CREEK MANUFACTURING LLC
2972 E 76th St (74136-8719)
PHONE..................918 698-3318
Allen Hall,
EMP: 1
SALES (est): 68.3K Privately Held
SIC: 3443 7389 Weldments;

(G-10844)
STEELTEK INC
4141 S Jackson Ave (74107-7017)
PHONE..................918 446-4001
Steve Smith, CEO
Stan Kitchen, President
Annette Hathcoat, Corp Secy
Linsay Carter, Vice Pres
Tony Osborn, Vice Pres
▼ EMP: 100
SQ FT: 132,000
SALES: 22MM Privately Held
SIC: 3443 Heat exchangers, condensers & components

(G-10845)
STEP ENERGY SVCS HOLDINGS LTD
12607 E 60th St (74146-6910)
PHONE..................918 252-5416
EMP: 2

SALES (corp-wide): 501.9MM Privately Held
SIC: 1389 3533 Oil consultants; well logging equipment
HQ: Step Energy Services Holdings Ltd.
480 Wildwood Forest Dr
Spring TX 77380

(G-10846)
STEPHEN J HEYMAN
Also Called: Heyman Stephen J Operating Co
15 E 5th St Ste 3300 (74103-4340)
PHONE..................918 583-3333
Stephen J Heyman, Owner
EMP: 1
SALES (est): 111.7K Privately Held
SIC: 1311 Crude petroleum production; natural gas production

(G-10847)
STEPHENS SCHEDULING SVCS INC
Also Called: Pro-Tech Mobile Solutions
11063 S Memorial Dr Ste D (74133-7366)
PHONE..................918 630-1614
EMP: 2
SALES: 100K Privately Held
SIC: 3571 Mfg Electronic Computers

(G-10848)
STERLING CRANE LLC
5104 W 21st St (74107-2229)
PHONE..................918 728-8613
EMP: 3
SALES (est): 249.7K Privately Held
SIC: 3531 Cranes

(G-10849)
STEVE HARRISON GAME CALLS
3714 Silver Oak Ct (74107-4050)
PHONE..................918 688-0807
Steven Harrison, Principal
EMP: 4
SALES (est): 203K Privately Held
SIC: 3949 Game calls

(G-10850)
STEVEN JACKSON
Also Called: Ice Global
9759 E 4th St (74128-1211)
PHONE..................918 813-7184
Steven Jackson, Principal
EMP: 1
SALES (est): 62.3K Privately Held
SIC: 3672 Circuit boards, television & radio printed

(G-10851)
STILES SERVICES LLC
15 E 5th St Ste 3650 (74103-4310)
PHONE..................918 582-7894
Wh Thompson, Mng Member
EMP: 3
SALES (est): 181.2K Privately Held
SIC: 3731 Drilling & production platforms, floating (oil & gas)

(G-10852)
STOKELY OUTDOOR ADVERTISING
10111 E 45th Pl (74146-4802)
PHONE..................918 664-4724
Bill R Stokely, President
Sarah Stokely, Vice Pres
EMP: 20
SQ FT: 8,000
SALES (est): 2.2MM Privately Held
SIC: 7312 3993 Billboard advertising; signs & advertising specialties

(G-10853)
STONEBRIDGE ACQUISITION INC (PA)
4200 E Skelly Dr Ste 1000 (74135-3241)
PHONE..................918 663-8000
James Ivy, President
Amy Moore, Business Mgr
Adam Hutchinson, Vice Pres
Mike Keys, Vice Pres
Samir Kumar, Vice Pres
EMP: 70
SQ FT: 7,000

GEOGRAPHIC SECTION

Tulsa - Tulsa County (G-10886)

SALES (est): 17.9MM **Privately Held**
SIC: 7373 7371 7372 Computer integrated systems design; custom computer programming services; prepackaged software

(G-10854)
STONEBRIDGE PARTNERSHIP 1 LP
4815 S Harvard Ave # 450 (74135-3055)
PHONE.....................................918 747-7594
William M Wiles, *Principal*
EMP: 2
SALES (est): 107.7K **Privately Held**
SIC: 1311 Crude petroleum & natural gas

(G-10855)
STONECOAT OF TULSA LLC
5423 S 101st East Ave (74146-5732)
PHONE.....................................918 551-6868
EMP: 3
SALES (est): 258.6K **Privately Held**
SIC: 3272 Concrete products, precast

(G-10856)
STONEMEN GRANITE & MARBLE
4702 S 103rd East Ave (74146-4821)
PHONE.....................................918 851-3400
EMP: 3 EST: 2014
SALES (est): 212.8K **Privately Held**
SIC: 1411 5032 Granite dimension stone; marble building stone

(G-10857)
STOREHOUSE PRINTING
5666 S 122nd East Ave B-5 (74146-6931)
PHONE.....................................918 286-7222
EMP: 6
SALES (est): 424.4K **Privately Held**
SIC: 2752 Commercial printing, lithographic

(G-10858)
STRAITS STEEL AND WIRE LLC
5525 E 13th St (74112)
PHONE.....................................231 843-3416
EMP: 2
SALES (est): 90.8K **Privately Held**
SIC: 3312 Wire products, steel or iron

(G-10859)
STRAT LAND EXPLORATION CO (PA)
15 E 5th St Ste 2020 (74103-4318)
PHONE.....................................918 584-3844
Larry B Darden, *President*
Rick Spellman, *Vice Pres*
Russell McGhee, *Treasurer*
Doris Darden, *Admin Sec*
Annette Boyd, *Analyst*
EMP: 15
SQ FT: 5,000
SALES (est): 6.8MM **Privately Held**
WEB: www.stratland.com
SIC: 1311 Crude petroleum production; natural gas production

(G-10860)
STROHEIM ROMANN UPHOLSTERY
9303 E 46th St (74145-4829)
PHONE.....................................918 622-7700
EMP: 1
SALES (est): 46.5K **Privately Held**
SIC: 2211 Broadwoven fabric mills, cotton

(G-10861)
STROPE MANUFACTURING INC
1240 S Joplin Ave (74112-5483)
PHONE.....................................918 835-8729
Jack L Strope, *President*
Sherry Strope, *Vice Pres*
Jack Strope, *Manager*
EMP: 6
SQ FT: 10,000
SALES (est): 1MM **Privately Held**
SIC: 3599 3545 3494 Machine shop, jobbing & repair; machine tool accessories; valves & pipe fittings

(G-10862)
STS LOGGING SERVICES LLC
9111 E Pine St (74115-5912)
PHONE.....................................918 933-5653
Andrew Knott, *Parts Mgr*
Jeff Lower, *Finance*
Mike Silow, *Sales Mgr*
EMP: 2 EST: 2012
SALES (est): 150K **Privately Held**
SIC: 2411 Logging

(G-10863)
STUCCO 2 STONE
2623 E 1st St (74104-1605)
PHONE.....................................918 770-2944
EMP: 1
SALES (est): 49.3K **Privately Held**
SIC: 3299 Stucco

(G-10864)
SULLIVAN AND COMPANY LLC
1437 S Boulder Ave # 700 (74119-3609)
PHONE.....................................918 584-4288
R J Sullivan Jr,
EMP: 14
SQ FT: 4,700
SALES (est): 2.3MM **Privately Held**
SIC: 1311 Crude petroleum production; natural gas production

(G-10865)
SULLIVANS CUSTOM CABINETRY
5235 S 43rd West Ave (74107-8969)
PHONE.....................................918 445-9191
Bobby E Sullivan Jr, *President*
Jack Martin, *Manager*
Lisa Sullivan, *Admin Sec*
EMP: 50
SQ FT: 18,000
SALES (est): 4.6MM **Privately Held**
SIC: 2434 Wood kitchen cabinets

(G-10866)
SUMMIT ESP LLC (HQ)
835 W 41st St (74107-7022)
P.O. Box 9616 (74157-0616)
PHONE.....................................918 392-7820
John Kenner, *President*
Greg Davis, *Engineer*
Michael Owen, *Engineer*
Rianne McIntosh, *Credit Staff*
Jill Henderson, *Human Res Mgr*
▲ EMP: 277
SALES (est): 990.1MM **Publicly Held**
SIC: 3561 7699 Pumps & pumping equipment; pumps & pumping equipment repair

(G-10867)
SUMMIT EXPLORATION LLC
2530 E 71st St Ste K (74136-5577)
P.O. Box 14068 (74159-1068)
PHONE.....................................918 583-0933
Judy Gorrell, *Administration*
Patric R McConn,
Clark Millspaugh,
Bob Rosene,
Paul Sims,
EMP: 5
SQ FT: 3,000
SALES (est): 404.1K **Privately Held**
SIC: 1382 Oil & gas exploration services

(G-10868)
SUMMIT LABELS INC
5420 E 9th St (74112-4315)
PHONE.....................................918 936-4950
Melissa Butterfield, *President*
Nathan Butterfield, *Vice Pres*
EMP: 2
SALES (est): 315.2K **Privately Held**
SIC: 2672 2679 2759 Adhesive papers, labels or tapes: from purchased material; tags & labels, paper; flexographic printing

(G-10869)
SUN DIRECT POWER INC
6730 W Archer St (74127-5615)
PHONE.....................................918 612-4090
Joshua Daniels, *President*
EMP: 2
SALES (est): 139.1K **Privately Held**
SIC: 3674 Solar cells

(G-10870)
SUN ENGINEERING INC
Also Called: Winter Hawk Pipe Line Services
10031 E 52nd St (74146-5714)
P.O. Box 470569 (74147-0569)
PHONE.....................................918 627-0426
Scott Neff, *President*
Shane Stevens, *Exec VP*
Tracy Neff, *Shareholder*
EMP: 12
SQ FT: 11,000
SALES (est): 3MM **Privately Held**
SIC: 3089 7513 3498 Hardware, plastic; truck rental & leasing, no drivers; fabricated pipe & fittings

(G-10871)
SUN OF A BEACH
6848 S 32nd West Ave (74132-1729)
PHONE.....................................918 938-6219
EMP: 2
SALES (est): 94.4K **Privately Held**
SIC: 2711 Newspapers, publishing & printing

(G-10872)
SUNDANCE WELDING INC
5410 S 108th East Ave (74146-5817)
PHONE.....................................918 627-4065
Owen Johnston, *President*
EMP: 2
SQ FT: 2,500
SALES (est): 193.6K **Privately Held**
SIC: 7692 Welding repair

(G-10873)
SUNOCO (R&M) LLC
907 S Detroit Ave # 1025 (74120-4205)
P.O. Box 1559 (74101-1559)
PHONE.....................................918 586-6246
Paul S Broker, *Manager*
EMP: 14 **Publicly Held**
SIC: 5541 2865 2869 2911 Filling stations, gasoline; benzene; toluene; xylene; ethylene glycols; petroleum refining; convenience stores, chain; petroleum products
HQ: Sunoco (R&M), Llc
3801 West Chester Pike
Newtown Square PA 19073
215 977-3000

(G-10874)
SUNSHINE PRINTING
4523 N Hartford Ave (74106-1241)
PHONE.....................................918 951-6349
EMP: 2
SALES (est): 100K **Privately Held**
SIC: 2752 Lithographic Commercial Printing

(G-10875)
SUNTIME PRODUCTS INC
5566 S 79th East Pl (74145-7844)
PHONE.....................................918 664-8330
EMP: 1 EST: 1994
SALES (est): 100K **Privately Held**
SIC: 2392 Mfr Attachable Beach Towels

(G-10876)
SUPER SAVER DRY CLEANING
Also Called: Silver Star Cleaners
2036 E 81st St Ste 110 (74137-4347)
PHONE.....................................918 296-7168
EMP: 2 EST: 2010
SALES (est): 164.2K **Privately Held**
SIC: 2842 Laundry cleaning preparations

(G-10877)
SUPERIOR PELLET FUELS LLC
2131 W 73rd St (74132-2221)
PHONE.....................................918 494-0790
EMP: 3
SALES (est): 202.9K **Privately Held**
SIC: 2869 Fuels

(G-10878)
SUPERIOR PIPELINE TEXAS LLC
8200 S Unit Dr (74132-5300)
P.O. Box 702500 (74170-2500)
PHONE.....................................918 382-7200
Bob Parks, *President*
Ed Alexander, *Senior VP*
Mike Hicks, *Senior VP*
Bill Ward, *Senior VP*
Kevin Koerner, *Vice Pres*
EMP: 45
SALES (est): 197,000
SALES (est): 2MM
SALES (corp-wide): 674.6MM **Privately Held**
SIC: 1382 Oil & gas exploration services
PA: Unit Corporation
8200 S Unit Dr
Tulsa OK 74132
918 493-7700

(G-10879)
SUPERIOR WELDING
1606 N 168th East Ave (74116-4930)
PHONE.....................................918 439-9332
EMP: 1
SALES (est): 32.3K **Privately Held**
SIC: 7692 Welding Repair

(G-10880)
SUPPLY COMPANY INC
Also Called: Nature's Choice
6924 E 38th St (74145-3203)
PHONE.....................................918 585-2863
John Hess, *President*
EMP: 8
SALES (est): 1MM **Privately Held**
SIC: 2842 Specialty cleaning preparations; sanitation preparations, disinfectants & deodorants

(G-10881)
SUPPLYONE OKLAHOMA CITY INC
10590 E Pine St (74116-1543)
PHONE.....................................918 446-4428
J R Clonts, *Manager*
EMP: 25
SALES (corp-wide): 327.1MM **Privately Held**
SIC: 5113 2653 Corrugated & solid fiber boxes; corrugated & solid fiber boxes
HQ: Supplyone Oklahoma City, Inc.
3801 Nw 3rd St
Oklahoma City OK 73107
405 947-7373

(G-10882)
SUSAN C WILLARD LLC
6009 S Atlanta Ct (74105-7524)
PHONE.....................................918 740-4630
Susan Willard, *Principal*
EMP: 2 EST: 2015
SALES (est): 61.3K **Privately Held**
WEB: www.fhawamerica.com
SIC: 3993 Signs & advertising specialties

(G-10883)
SWANDERLAND ASSOCIATES LLC
5153 E 51st St Ste 110 (74135-7430)
PHONE.....................................918 621-6533
Connie Swan, *Principal*
EMP: 2
SALES (est): 126.5K **Privately Held**
SIC: 1389 1382 Oil & gas field services; oil & gas exploration services

(G-10884)
SWEET SCRUBS LLC
7455 S Yale Ave Apt 137 (74136-7023)
PHONE.....................................918 513-1176
Leanne Alyias, *Principal*
EMP: 1 EST: 2012
SALES (est): 74K **Privately Held**
SIC: 2844 Toilet preparations

(G-10885)
SYLVAN OIL OPERATING COMPANY
1 W 3rd St Ste 918 (74103-3517)
PHONE.....................................918 267-3764
David R Sylvan, *President*
Janan Martin, *Admin Sec*
EMP: 1
SALES (est): 143.4K **Privately Held**
SIC: 1311 Crude petroleum production; natural gas production

(G-10886)
SYNERGY SOURCING SOLUTIONS LLC
1529 N 168th East Ave (74116-4912)
P.O. Box 581231 (74158-1231)
PHONE.....................................918 835-5019
Eric Gonseth,
Darrin Maddox,

EMP: 2
SQ FT: 25,000
SALES (est): 81.4K **Privately Held**
SIC: 3599 Crankshafts & camshafts, machining

(G-10887)
T & A GASKET CO INC
Also Called: Turben & Associates Affiliate
3148 S 108th East Ave # 100 (74146-1638)
PHONE..................................918 664-7600
Frosty Turpen, *President*
Gayla Turpen, *Vice Pres*
▲ EMP: 6
SALES (est): 69.6K **Privately Held**
WEB: www.turpen.com
SIC: 3053 Gaskets, packing & sealing devices

(G-10888)
T D WILLIAMSON INC
Picking Products Division
10727 E 55th Pl (74146-6702)
PHONE..................................918 447-5400
Jack Rankin, *Manager*
EMP: 30
SALES (corp-wide): 306.7MM **Privately Held**
SIC: 3533 2821 Gas field machinery & equipment; oil field machinery & equipment; plastics materials & resins
PA: T. D. Williamson, Inc.
    6120 S Yale Ave Ste 1700
    Tulsa OK 74136
    918 493-9494

(G-10889)
T F T INC
Also Called: Tulsa Fin Tube
2991 N Osage Dr (74127-1529)
P.O. Box 445 (74101-0445)
PHONE..................................918 834-2366
Donald Hoose, *CEO*
Justin Hoose, *President*
Todd Richmond, *Production*
John Freeny, *Purch Mgr*
Karla Hoose, *Treasurer*
▲ EMP: 45
SQ FT: 60,000
SALES (est): 10MM **Privately Held**
SIC: 3469 Tube fins, stamped metal

(G-10890)
T K DRILLING CORP
8131 E 49th St (74145-6908)
PHONE..................................918 270-1084
Teerakun Karnchanakphan, *President*
Nat Karnchanakphan, *Corp Secy*
EMP: 4
SQ FT: 2,000
SALES (est): 784.8K **Privately Held**
SIC: 1311 Crude petroleum production; natural gas production

(G-10891)
T K PUBLISHING INC
Also Called: Tulsa Kids Magazine
1622 S Denver Ave (74119-4233)
PHONE..................................918 582-8504
Charles Foshee, *President*
EMP: 6
SALES (est): 558.5K **Privately Held**
WEB: www.tulsakids.com
SIC: 2721 Magazines: publishing only, not printed on site

(G-10892)
T TOWN LIGHTING
6918 E 19th St (74112-7610)
PHONE..................................918 693-2063
EMP: 3
SALES (est): 408.5K **Privately Held**
SIC: 3648 Lighting equipment

(G-10893)
T TOWN SHEET METAL
1920 S 129th East Ave A (74108-6710)
PHONE..................................918 437-4756
Ken Stallard,
Kathleen Stallard,
EMP: 7
SALES (est): 811.6K **Privately Held**
SIC: 3444 Sheet metalwork

(G-10894)
T-BIRDS CUSTOM SCREENPRINTING
5206 S Harvard Ave # 333 (74135-3565)
PHONE..................................918 521-3996
Susan Mullen, *Principal*
EMP: 2
SALES (est): 119.1K **Privately Held**
SIC: 2759 Screen printing

(G-10895)
T-SHIRTS & HOODIES PRINT SHOP
10318 E 21st St (74129-1606)
PHONE..................................918 861-0772
EMP: 2
SALES (est): 83.9K **Privately Held**
SIC: 2752 Commercial printing, lithographic

(G-10896)
T-SHIRTS & HOODIES PRINT SHOP
10318 E 21st St (74129-1606)
PHONE..................................918 861-0772
EMP: 2
SALES (est): 83.9K **Privately Held**
SIC: 2752 Lithographic Commercial Printing

(G-10897)
TANGIER EXPLORATIONS
427 S Boston Ave (74103-4141)
PHONE..................................918 585-3350
Laura Daniel, *Owner*
EMP: 2
SALES (est): 178.8K **Privately Held**
SIC: 1382 Oil & gas exploration services

(G-10898)
TANK SPECIALTIES INC
Also Called: T S I
3319 N Lewis Ave (74110-1515)
PHONE..................................918 599-8111
Michael Ross, *President*
EMP: 10
SQ FT: 16,000
SALES (est): 1.3MM **Privately Held**
SIC: 3443 Fabricated plate work (boiler shop)

(G-10899)
TARGA PIPELINE MID-CONTINENT W
110 W 7th St Ste 2300 (74119-1017)
PHONE..................................918 574-3500
Eugene N Dubay, *President*
EMP: 10
SALES (est): 1.1MM **Publicly Held**
SIC: 1389 Processing service, gas
HQ: Targa Pipeline Mid-Continent Llc
    110 W 7th St Ste 2300
    Tulsa OK 74119
    918 574-3500

(G-10900)
TARGA PPLINE MID-CONTINENT LLC (DH)
Also Called: Atlas Pipeline
110 W 7th St Ste 2300 (74119-1017)
PHONE..................................918 574-3500
Eugene N Dubay, *President*
Daniel C Herz, *President*
Patrick McDonie, *COO*
Robert Karlovich III, *CFO*
Trent Partain, *Analyst*
EMP: 114
SQ FT: 8,000
SALES (est): 398.1MM **Publicly Held**
SIC: 1389 Processing service, gas
HQ: Targa Pipeline Mid-Continent Holdings, Llc
    110 W 7th St Ste 2300
    Tulsa OK 74119
    918 574-3500

(G-10901)
TATERMASH OILCLOTH LLC
3101 S Jamestown Ave (74135-4407)
PHONE..................................918 743-3888
Lori Alison,
EMP: 5 EST: 2009
SALES (est): 486.3K **Privately Held**
WEB: www.tatermash.com
SIC: 2295 Oilcloth

(G-10902)
TATUR
13839 E 28th St (74134-3022)
PHONE..................................918 244-6918
Brian Hoover, *Principal*
EMP: 2
SALES (est): 164.1K **Privately Held**
WEB: www.tatur.org
SIC: 3949 Sporting & athletic goods

(G-10903)
TAYLOR ENERGY LLC
7170 S Braden Ave Ste 200 (74136-6316)
PHONE..................................918 481-1241
Bob Key, *Owner*
EMP: 3
SALES (est): 206.2K **Privately Held**
SIC: 1382 Oil & gas exploration services

(G-10904)
TAYLOR FORGE ENGINEERED
6333 N Erie Ave (74117-2410)
PHONE..................................918 280-1183
Tony Osborne, *Branch Mgr*
EMP: 30
SALES (corp-wide): 54.1MM **Privately Held**
SIC: 3351 Tubing, copper & copper alloy
PA: Taylor Forge Engineered Systems, Inc.
    208 N Iron St
    Paola KS 66071
    785 867-2590

(G-10905)
TAYLOR INDUSTRIES LLC
6015 N Xanthus Ave (74130-1509)
PHONE..................................918 266-7301
Cheryl Bergrin, *Vice Pres*
Cheryl Majors, *Vice Pres*
David Wood, *Prdtn Mgr*
Jerry Sutter, *Engineer*
Joseph Welk, *Engineer*
EMP: 1
SALES (corp-wide): 567.2MM **Publicly Held**
SIC: 3533 Oil & gas drilling rigs & equipment
HQ: Taylor Industries, Llc
    801 Cherry St Unit 2
    Fort Worth TX 76102

(G-10906)
TAYLOR RIG LLC
6015 N Xanthus Ave (74130-1509)
PHONE..................................918 266-7301
Oscar Taylor, *CEO*
Brett Taylor, *President*
David Wood, *Prdtn Mgr*
Douglas Brownell, *Project Engr*
Terry Lewis, *Cust Mgr*
EMP: 90
SQ FT: 67,000
SALES (est): 1.4MM **Privately Held**
WEB: www.taylorindustries.net
SIC: 1389 Oil field services

(G-10907)
TC MACHINE & MANUFACTURING INC
7657 E 46th Pl (74145-6307)
PHONE..................................918 986-7920
Jeff Copeland, *President*
Mark Turney, *Vice Pres*
Stephanie Turney, *Treasurer*
Michelle Copeland, *Admin Sec*
EMP: 4
SQ FT: 4,000
SALES: 450K **Privately Held**
SIC: 3599 Machine & other job shop work

(G-10908)
TCAE ENTERPRISES INC
Also Called: Sunglow
3801 S 79th East Ave (74145-3218)
PHONE..................................918 664-5977
Ted Lacina, *President*
EMP: 9
SALES: 650K **Privately Held**
SIC: 7539 7549 3993 Automotive repair shops; glass tinting, automotive; signs & advertising specialties

(G-10909)
TEAM INC
12204 E Admiral Pl (74116-3813)
PHONE..................................918 234-9600
Chris Bickett, *Opers Staff*
Bryan Rice, *Manager*
Chad Ryals, *Officer*
EMP: 20
SALES (corp-wide): 1.1B **Publicly Held**
SIC: 3398 3567 Metal heat treating; heating units & devices, industrial: electric; fuel-fired furnaces & ovens
HQ: Team, Inc.
    5095 Paris St
    Denver CO 80239

(G-10910)
TECH PACK INC
6947 E 13th St (74112-5615)
PHONE..................................918 836-8493
Paul Jenkins, *President*
EMP: 3
SALES (est): 166.8K **Privately Held**
SIC: 2673 Plastic bags: made from purchased materials

(G-10911)
TECH-AID PRODUCTS
2708 N Sheridan Rd (74115-2313)
PHONE..................................918 838-8711
Kim Wiolland, *Owner*
EMP: 1
SQ FT: 3,000
SALES: 27K **Privately Held**
SIC: 3829 3812 Aircraft & motor vehicle measurement equipment; search & navigation equipment

(G-10912)
TECH-MESH APPAREL LLC
7494 S Sleepy Hollow Dr (74136-5919)
P.O. Box 702357 (74170-2357)
PHONE..................................918 492-1193
Jean Barrett, *Principal*
▲ EMP: 3
SQ FT: 1,000
SALES (est): 305.1K **Privately Held**
SIC: 2329 Athletic (warmup, sweat & jogging) suits: men's & boys'

(G-10913)
TECHSICO ENTP SOLUTIONS INC
910 S Hudson Ave (74112-2945)
PHONE..................................918 585-2347
Todd Blackburn, *President*
Brett Kozlowski, *President*
Jessica Lundy, *Principal*
Daniel Schneider, *Principal*
Marty Seat, *Vice Pres*
EMP: 60 EST: 2008
SALES (est): 21MM **Privately Held**
WEB: www.techsico.com
SIC: 5099 3357 7382 Video & audio equipment; fiber optic cable (insulated); security systems services
PA: Techsico, Llc
    910 S Hudson Ave
    Tulsa OK 74112

(G-10914)
TECHSPEEDY LLC
6368 S 80th East Ave C (74133-4615)
PHONE..................................918 406-0008
Virgil Jones, *Principal*
EMP: 2
SALES (est): 107.6K **Privately Held**
SIC: 3861 Photographic equipment & supplies

(G-10915)
TECOLOTE ENERGY LLC
2 W 2nd St Ste 1700 (74103-3100)
PHONE..................................918 513-4100
Allen Brewster, *Prdtn Mgr*
EMP: 6 EST: 2015
SALES (est): 388.1K **Privately Held**
SIC: 1382 Oil & gas exploration services

(G-10916)
TECOLOTE ENERGY OPERATING LLC
Also Called: Tecolote Operating
2 W 2nd St Ste 1700 (74103-3100)
PHONE..................................918 513-4121

GEOGRAPHIC SECTION

Tulsa - Tulsa County (G-10948)

Patrick M Hall,
EMP: 8
SALES (est): 1MM Privately Held
SIC: 1382 Oil & gas exploration services

(G-10917)
TEFI TEK INDUSTRIES LLC
2222 W Newton St (74127-3016)
PHONE..................918 728-7381
Thomas A Boxley, *Owner*
EMP: 1 EST: 2018
SALES (est): 29.2K Privately Held
SIC: 3999 Manufacturing industries

(G-10918)
TEKTRONIX INC
9902 E 43rd St Ste D (74146-4756)
PHONE..................918 627-1500
Don Crain, *Manager*
EMP: 11
SQ FT: 2,700
SALES (corp-wide): 7.3B Publicly Held
WEB: www.tektronix.com
SIC: 3829 Measuring & controlling devices
HQ: Tektronix, Inc.
    14150 Sw Karl Braun Dr
    Beaverton OR 97005
    800 833-9200

(G-10919)
TELLICO ENGINEERING SERVICES
10838 E Marshall St (74116-5682)
PHONE..................918 384-7409
Russell Claybrook, *Partner*
EMP: 2 EST: 2014
SALES (est): 125.5K Privately Held
SIC: 3721 3728 Aircraft; aircraft parts & equipment; aircraft body & wing assemblies & parts

(G-10920)
TERRY COMPANY INC
2433 E 31st St (74105-2305)
PHONE..................918 629-0926
Tim Monkres, *President*
Terry Monkres, *Owner*
EMP: 4
SALES (est): 437.3K Privately Held
SIC: 3823 Industrial instrmnts msrmnt display/control process variable

(G-10921)
TEXOAK PETRO HOLDINGS LLC
114 E 5th St Ste 300 (74103-4621)
PHONE..................918 592-1010
Richard Menchaca, *CEO*
Dennis Baggett, *Vice Pres*
EMP: 2 EST: 2013
SALES (est): 109.8K Privately Held
SIC: 2911 5171 Petroleum refining; petroleum bulk stations

(G-10922)
TEXRE INC
Also Called: Fo Mac
2621 N Iroquois Ave (74106-2431)
P.O. Box 6217 (74148-0217)
PHONE..................918 425-5524
Tom Kupke, *President*
Matt Kupke, *QC Mgr*
EMP: 100
SQ FT: 150,000
SALES (est): 17.8MM Privately Held
SIC: 3069 3089 Molded rubber products; injection molding of plastics

(G-10923)
TFG IN-STORE DISPLAY LLC
1507 E 7th St (74120-4805)
PHONE..................918 592-2834
Gary Geppelt, *Mng Member*
EMP: 15
SQ FT: 15,000
SALES (est): 1.5MM Privately Held
SIC: 3993 Displays & cutouts, window & lobby

(G-10924)
TGI ENTERPRISES INC
Also Called: Tracy's Graphics
1219 S Hudson Ave (74112-5423)
PHONE..................918 835-4330
Tracy Copeland, *President*
Susie Cross, *Vice Pres*
TGI Greek, *Sales Staff*

Sandy Caldwell, *Creative Dir*
EMP: 20
SQ FT: 15,000
SALES (est): 1.4MM Privately Held
SIC: 2759 5199 Screen printing; advertising specialties

(G-10925)
TGS PLASTICS INC
12528 E 60th St (74146-6907)
P.O. Box 470651 (74147-0651)
PHONE..................918 252-3636
Wesley Lawson, *President*
Patricia Lawson, *Office Mgr*
▲ EMP: 30
SQ FT: 30,000
SALES (est): 3.1MM Privately Held
SIC: 3089 Injection molding of plastics

(G-10926)
THERMAL SPECIALTIES LLC (PA)
6314 E 15th St (74112-6411)
P.O. Box 3623 (74101-3623)
PHONE..................918 836-4800
Mitch Myers, *Owner*
Kent Charles, *COO*
Jeff Bates, *Plant Mgr*
Keith Mueller, *Plant Mgr*
Billy Muskrat, *Warehouse Mgr*
EMP: 15
SQ FT: 32,000
SALES (est): 29.1MM Privately Held
WEB: www.tsi-aic.com
SIC: 1741 2895 7389 Refractory or acid brick masonry; furnace black; finishing services

(G-10927)
THERMTECH INDUSTRIES LLC
8526 S Elwood Ave (74132-3617)
PHONE..................918 299-5473
Craig Rosencutter,
EMP: 2
SALES (est): 168.8K Privately Held
SIC: 3999 Atomizers, toiletry

(G-10928)
THINK HEALTHY SYSTEMS
5321 S Sheridan Rd (74145-7532)
PHONE..................918 384-0555
Patricia Stuart, *Owner*
EMP: 2
SALES (est): 140K Privately Held
SIC: 2899 Water treating compounds

(G-10929)
THOMAS DIGITAL LLC
6817 E 65th Pl (74133-4010)
PHONE..................918 836-1540
Warren L Thomas, *Principal*
EMP: 4
SALES (est): 345.1K Privately Held
SIC: 2754 Commercial printing, gravure

(G-10930)
THOMAS ENERGY SYSTEMS INC (PA)
8525 E 46th St (74145-4803)
P.O. Box 471453 (74147-1453)
PHONE..................918 665-0031
Vince Thomas, *President*
D J Parker, *Vice Pres*
Dj Thomas, *Vice Pres*
Linda Thomas, *Vice Pres*
EMP: 24
SQ FT: 18,500
SALES (est): 5.8MM Privately Held
SIC: 3563 8711 3999 Air & gas compressors including vacuum pumps; sanitary engineers; barber & beauty shop equipment

(G-10931)
THOMAS ENGINEERING CO INC
Also Called: Topog-E Gasket Company
1224 N Utica Ave (74110-4635)
PHONE..................918 587-6649
Roger Thomas, *President*
Roger M Thomas, *Vice Pres*
Walter L Thomas, *Vice Pres*
Edwin Thomas, *CFO*
Gayla Thomas, *Treasurer*
EMP: 20
SQ FT: 8,000

SALES (est): 3.5MM Privately Held
WEB: www.topog-e.com
SIC: 3053 3061 Gaskets, all materials; mechanical rubber goods

(G-10932)
THOMAS EXPLORATION COMPANY
7159 S Braden Ave (74136-6302)
PHONE..................918 496-1414
E Laroque Thomas, *President*
Roger L Thomas, *Vice Pres*
EMP: 3
SALES (est): 430K Privately Held
SIC: 1311 Crude petroleum production

(G-10933)
THOMAS P HARRIS JR
1503 E 19th St (74120-7612)
PHONE..................918 742-6414
Thomas P Harris Jr, *Owner*
EMP: 1
SALES (est): 83.1K Privately Held
SIC: 1389 Pumping of oil & gas wells

(G-10934)
THOMAS P SHAW
Also Called: Thomas Pv Shell
5721 S Delaware Ave (74105-7327)
PHONE..................918 742-4673
Thomas P Shaw, *Owner*
EMP: 1
SALES (est): 102.1K Privately Held
SIC: 1311 Crude petroleum production

(G-10935)
THOMPSON MANUFACTURING COMPANY
Also Called: Enhanced Printing Products
6315 E 12th St (74112-5419)
PHONE..................918 585-1991
Greg Mosley, *Officer*
EMP: 5
SQ FT: 18,200
SALES (est): 916.5K Privately Held
SIC: 2752 3554 3535 3555 Commercial printing, lithographic; paper industries machinery; conveyors & conveying equipment; rules, printers'

(G-10936)
THOMSONS TRENCHING INC (PA)
Also Called: Aggregate Materials
4124 S Rockford Ave # 201 (74105-4247)
PHONE..................918 745-1030
Robert C Thomson, *President*
Carolyn Guthery, *Treasurer*
▼ EMP: 4
SALES (est): 4.1MM Privately Held
SIC: 1423 Crushed & broken granite

(G-10937)
THORPE PLANT SERVICES INC
5125 S Garnett Rd Ste E (74146-5908)
PHONE..................918 455-8928
EMP: 7
SALES (est): 536.8K Privately Held
SIC: 3441 Building components, structural steel

(G-10938)
THREE RIVERS CORP
8801 S Yale Ave Ste 240 (74137-3535)
PHONE..................918 492-3239
Pat Garrett, *President*
EMP: 2
SALES (est): 110K Privately Held
SIC: 1389 Oil field services

(G-10939)
THUNDERBIRD ENERGY RESOURCES
4786 S Irvington Ave (74135-6852)
PHONE..................918 627-5433
Harrill Rockett Jr, *President*
Peggy Rockett, *Corp Secy*
Jack Rockett, *Vice Pres*
EMP: 4
SALES (est): 301.7K Privately Held
SIC: 1381 1311 Drilling oil & gas wells; crude petroleum production

(G-10940)
TIGHT LINE PRODUCTS LLC
Also Called: Tight Line Enterprises
9014 S Gary Ave (74137-3313)
PHONE..................918 231-0934
Wayne L Weatherly,
Patrick Dougal,
EMP: 2
SALES (est): 175.1K Privately Held
SIC: 3949 Rods & rod parts, fishing

(G-10941)
TIM E HUTCHESON
Also Called: United Pallet
1135 S Fulton Ave (74112-5309)
PHONE..................918 313-5710
Tim E Hutcheson, *Principal*
EMP: 4
SALES (est): 249.9K Privately Held
SIC: 2448 Pallets, wood & wood with metal

(G-10942)
TIME MARK INC
11440 E Pine St (74116-2098)
PHONE..................918 438-1220
Stan Allina, *CEO*
Brian Williams, *Vice Pres*
Ron Andoe, *Engineer*
Charles Witt, *Natl Sales Mgr*
EMP: 54
SALES (est): 7.8MM Privately Held
SIC: 3671 Electronic tube parts, except glass blanks

(G-10943)
TIMOTHY J AND SHARO FLICK
6407 S 73rd East Ave (74133-7530)
PHONE..................918 250-2456
Flick Timothy, *Owner*
EMP: 2
SALES (est): 213.6K Privately Held
SIC: 3555 Bronzing or dusting machines for the printing trade

(G-10944)
TIN ROOF QUILTING LLC
3106 E 26th Pl (74114-4314)
PHONE..................918 551-7282
Susan L Gartman,
EMP: 1
SALES (est): 36.4K Privately Held
SIC: 2395 Quilting & quilting supplies

(G-10945)
TITAN MACHINE SERVICES INC
124 S 147th East Ave (74116-2566)
P.O. Box 1484, Inola (74036-1484)
PHONE..................918 437-2411
Lyle Johnson, *President*
Jan Johnson, *Vice Pres*
EMP: 6
SALES (est): 1MM Privately Held
SIC: 3545 7699 Machine tool accessories; industrial machinery & equipment repair

(G-10946)
TITAN PROPANE LLC
Also Called: Synergy Gas Bartlesville 1141
3602 N Mingo Valley Expy (74116-5016)
PHONE..................918 838-8804
Randi Morrison, *Manager*
EMP: 5
SALES (corp-wide): 7.3B Publicly Held
SIC: 1321 Propane (natural) production
HQ: Titan Propane Llc
    460 N Gulph Rd Ste 100
    King Of Prussia PA 19406
    610 337-7000

(G-10947)
TITAN RESOURCES LIMITED
11114 S Yale Ave Ste B (74137-7620)
PHONE..................918 298-1811
Kevin Creedon, *President*
EMP: 2
SQ FT: 919
SALES (est): 269.1K Privately Held
SIC: 1381 1382 Drilling oil & gas wells; oil & gas exploration services

(G-10948)
TOGETHER TULSA PUBLICATIONS
2631 S Boston Pl (74114-2437)
PHONE..................918 269-1085

(PA)=Parent Co (HQ)=Headquarters (DH)=Div Headquarters
✪ = New Business established in last 2 years

2020 Oklahoma Directory
of Manufacturers & Processors

367

Brooke Myers, *Principal*
EMP: 2
SALES (est): 83.7K **Privately Held**
SIC: 2741 Miscellaneous publishing

(G-10949)
TOKLAN OIL AND GAS CORPORATION
7404 S Yale Ave (74136-7029)
PHONE..............................918 582-5400
Robert E Nikkel, *President*
Dwayne Allen, *Manager*
EMP: 14
SQ FT: 10,000
SALES (est): 2.2MM **Privately Held**
SIC: 1311 Crude petroleum production

(G-10950)
TOM MEASON OIL VENTURES
427 S Boston Ave Lbby (74103-4140)
PHONE..............................918 587-3492
EMP: 1
SALES (est): 150K **Privately Held**
SIC: 1311 Oil Producer

(G-10951)
TONY OIL COMPANY
6821 S Richmond Pl (74136-4641)
PHONE..............................918 493-1882
Arthur M Alloway, *President*
Tom Harris, *Principal*
Annette Alloway, *Admin Sec*
EMP: 1
SALES (est): 86.9K **Privately Held**
SIC: 1311 Crude petroleum production

(G-10952)
TONY SMALLWOOD
Also Called: Tony's
2016 W Ute St (74127-2204)
PHONE..............................918 402-9267
Tony Smallwood, *Owner*
EMP: 1
SALES (est): 66.5K **Privately Held**
SIC: 2844 Bath salts

(G-10953)
TOOL CENTER
1447 N Yale Ave (74115-5362)
P.O. Box 580981 (74158-0981)
PHONE..............................918 838-7411
Bill Bowles, *Owner*
Robin Chaisson, *Corp Secy*
Tracy Hester, *Sales Staff*
Dwayne Holland, *Sales Associate*
EMP: 10
SQ FT: 8,000
SALES (est): 1.7MM **Privately Held**
SIC: 3599 Machine shop, jobbing & repair

(G-10954)
TOOMEY OIL COMPANY INC
1126 S Frankfort Ave # 200 (74120-4288)
P.O. Box 1090 (74101-1090)
PHONE..............................918 583-1166
D Burdette Blue III, *President*
Charles T Blue, *Vice Pres*
EMP: 4 **EST:** 1918
SQ FT: 18,000
SALES (est): 448K **Privately Held**
SIC: 1311 6512 Crude petroleum production; natural gas production; commercial & industrial building operation

(G-10955)
TORNADO ALLEY ARMOR LLC
9300 Broken Arrow Expy B (74145-3319)
PHONE..............................918 856-3569
Leslie A McGee, *Partner*
Monty McGee, *Partner*
EMP: 6
SALES (est): 892K **Privately Held**
SIC: 3448 Prefabricated metal buildings

(G-10956)
TORTILLERIA MILAGRO
6314 S Peoria Ave (74136-0517)
PHONE..............................918 895-8225
Juan Oropeza, *President*
EMP: 6 **EST:** 2009
SALES (est): 370.4K **Privately Held**
SIC: 2099 Tortillas, fresh or refrigerated

(G-10957)
TORTILLERIA MILARGO
2128 S Garnett Rd (74129-5106)
PHONE..............................918 439-9977
Juan Oroperza, *President*
EMP: 6
SALES (est): 696.7K **Privately Held**
WEB: www.tortilleriamilarcos.com
SIC: 2099 Tortillas, fresh or refrigerated

(G-10958)
TORTILLERIA PUEBLA INC
3118 S Mingo Rd (74146-1257)
PHONE..............................918 610-8816
Alfonso Medrano, *President*
EMP: 6
SALES (est): 555.4K **Privately Held**
SIC: 2099 Tortillas, fresh or refrigerated

(G-10959)
TOTAL CARE ORTHTICS PRSTHTICS
6565 S Yale Ave Ste 909 (74136-8310)
PHONE..............................918 502-5975
Theresa Boyd, *Office Admin*
John Brest,
EMP: 7
SALES (est): 1.1MM **Privately Held**
WEB: www.totalcareop.com
SIC: 3842 Limbs, artificial; orthopedic appliances

(G-10960)
TOTAL SYSTEMS AND CONTROLS INC
5122 E 84th Pl (74137-2017)
PHONE..............................918 481-9215
Garrett Lalli, *President*
EMP: 1
SALES (est): 182.6K **Privately Held**
SIC: 3829 Aircraft & motor vehicle measurement equipment

(G-10961)
TOTAL WELL SOLUTIONS LLC
5727 S Lewis Ave Ste 550 (74105-7197)
PHONE..............................918 392-9352
EMP: 5
SALES (est): 312.6K **Privately Held**
SIC: 1311 Crude Petroleum/Natural Gas Production

(G-10962)
TPL ARKOMA MIDSTREAM LLC (DH)
110 W 7th St Ste 2300 (74119-1017)
PHONE..............................918 574-3500
Eugene Dubay, *President*
EMP: 8
SALES (est): 1.1MM **Publicly Held**
SIC: 2022 Whey, raw or liquid

(G-10963)
TPL SOUTHTEX GAS UTILITY CO LP
Also Called: Target Pipe Line
110 W 7th St Ste 2300 (74119-1017)
PHONE..............................918 574-3500
EMP: 28
SALES (est): 113.7K **Publicly Held**
SIC: 1389 3561 Oil field services; pumps, oil well & field
HQ: Targa Resources Partners Lp
811 Louisiana St Ste 2100
Houston TX 77002

(G-10964)
TRACE LLC
7101 S Yale Ave Ste 348 (74136)
PHONE..............................918 510-0210
Jimmy Dixon,
EMP: 15
SALES: 2MM **Privately Held**
SIC: 3559 Fiber optics strand coating machinery

(G-10965)
TRACEYS WINDOW BOUTIQUE INC
4206 E 80th Pl (74136-8139)
PHONE..............................918 495-1806
Tracey Stimson, *President*
EMP: 1

SALES (est): 94.1K **Privately Held**
SIC: 2391 Curtains & draperies

(G-10966)
TRACYS WOOD SHOP INC
Also Called: Tracy Wood Shop
1338 E 2nd St (74120-2201)
PHONE..............................918 587-4860
Ralph Klumpp, *President*
EMP: 6 **EST:** 1950
SQ FT: 2,500
SALES (est): 1MM **Privately Held**
SIC: 5712 2431 Cabinet work, custom; millwork

(G-10967)
TRADESHOWSTUFF LLC
112 S 109th East Pl (74128-1646)
PHONE..............................918 437-4338
EMP: 1
SALES (est): 52K **Privately Held**
SIC: 3993 Signs & advertising specialties

(G-10968)
TRANAM SYSTEMS INTL INC
6131 E 32nd Pl (74135-5405)
PHONE..............................918 488-0007
S Fred Isaacs, *Ch of Bd*
R H Ladd, *President*
Richard C Letourneau, *President*
William E Shouse Jr, *Vice Pres*
Brook Iwata, *Engineer*
EMP: 6
SALES (est): 1.6MM **Privately Held**
SIC: 3613 Switchgear & switchboard apparatus

(G-10969)
TRANSFUND
1 Williams Ctr Bsmt 1 # 1 (74172-0172)
PHONE..............................918 588-6707
Jeff Geren, *Assistant VP*
Deena Barr, *Vice Pres*
Tim Brown, *Vice Pres*
Shannon Devlin, *Vice Pres*
Pam Elder, *Vice Pres*
EMP: 5
SALES (est): 751.8K **Privately Held**
WEB: www.transfund.com
SIC: 3578 Automatic teller machines (ATM)

(G-10970)
TRANSTRADE LLC
4404 S Maybelle Ave (74107-7011)
PHONE..............................918 521-7271
Nick Stephen Mason, *Administration*
EMP: 5 **EST:** 2006
SALES (est): 202.5K **Privately Held**
SIC: 3356 Nickel

(G-10971)
TRANSWESTERN PIPELINE CO LLC
8801 S Yale Ave Ste 310 (74137-3536)
PHONE..............................918 492-7272
EMP: 4 **Publicly Held**
SIC: 1321 Natural gas liquids
HQ: Transwestern Pipeline Company, Llc
711 Louisiana St Ste 900
Houston TX 77002
281 714-2000

(G-10972)
TRAVERTINE INC (PA)
Also Called: Travertine Elevator Interiors
1325 E 35th Pl (74105-2614)
PHONE..............................918 583-5210
Christine Lamber, *President*
Scott Lambert, *Corp Secy*
Dave McCabe, *COO*
Randy Richenberger, *Senior VP*
Norman Oklahoma, *Marketing Staff*
EMP: 9
SALES (est): 4.7MM **Privately Held**
SIC: 3534 Elevators & equipment

(G-10973)
TRI-STATE INDUSTRIES INC
8620 E 46th St (74145-4805)
PHONE..............................918 938-6004
Rich Kerby, *Branch Mgr*
EMP: 10
SALES (corp-wide): 9.9MM **Privately Held**
SIC: 1389 Oil field services

PA: Tri-State Industries, Inc.
510 Limestone Ave
Gillette WY 82716
307 682-9730

(G-10974)
TRIAD PRECISION PRODUCTS INC
888 E Marshall St (74106-5900)
P.O. Box 3265 (74101-3265)
PHONE..............................918 584-3543
Jack Adkisson, *President*
Nancy Adkisson, *Corp Secy*
Thomas D Gable,
EMP: 35
SQ FT: 33,000
SALES (est): 5.7MM **Privately Held**
SIC: 3053 Gaskets, all materials

(G-10975)
TRIPLE CROWN ENERGY-BH LLC
2201 S Utica Pl Ste 100 (74114-7099)
PHONE..............................918 518-5422
Doyle Williams,
Chase Williams,
EMP: 2
SALES (est): 230K **Privately Held**
SIC: 1382 1389 Oil & gas exploration services; cementing oil & gas well casings

(G-10976)
TRIPLE M ROUSTABOUTS LLC
15 E 5th St Ste 3000 (74103-4337)
PHONE..............................918 619-7610
Maria Sweet, *Principal*
EMP: 2
SALES (est): 100K **Privately Held**
SIC: 1389 Roustabout service

(G-10977)
TRISMS INC
Also Called: Trism's Home School
1203 S Delaware Pl (74104-4129)
PHONE..............................918 585-2778
EMP: 1
SALES: 50K **Privately Held**
SIC: 5999 2731 Ret Misc Merchandise Books-Publishing/Printing

(G-10978)
TRIUMPH ARSTRCTRES - TULSA LLC
3330 N Mingo Rd (74116-1211)
P.O. Box 150010 (74115-0010)
PHONE..............................615 361-2061
Steve Blackwell, *President*
▲ **EMP:** 800
SQ FT: 2,500
SALES (est): 156.3MM **Publicly Held**
SIC: 3728 3724 2273 Aircraft body & wing assemblies & parts; aircraft engines & engine parts; aircraft & automobile floor coverings
PA: Triumph Group, Inc.
899 Cassatt Rd Ste 210
Berwyn PA 19312

(G-10979)
TRIUMPH ENERGY PARTNERS LLC
8908 S Yale Ave Ste 2 (74137-3557)
PHONE..............................918 986-8283
John Kueser, *CEO*
Joel Blake, *Executive*
Sarah Harris, *Technician*
David Ledoux, *Analyst*
EMP: 7
SALES (est): 510K **Privately Held**
SIC: 1382 Oil & gas exploration services

(G-10980)
TRUE TURN OF TULSA LLC
423 N Boulder Ave (74103-1403)
P.O. Box 1265, Sapulpa (74067-1265)
PHONE..............................918 224-5040
Paul Hempton, *Director*
Leon James,
Sherry Gabbard,
Jim Hampton,
Paul Hampton,
EMP: 10

GEOGRAPHIC SECTION

Tulsa - Tulsa County (G-11008)

SALES (est): 1.2MM **Privately Held**
SIC: 3599 3443 3053 Machine shop, jobbing & repair; fabricated plate work (boiler shop); gaskets, packing & sealing devices

(G-10981)
TRUEX LLC
Also Called: Truex Lighting
11108 E 56th St (74146-6713)
PHONE..................918 250-7641
Alan Simpson, *General Mgr*
Dennis K Andersen,
▼ EMP: 5
SQ FT: 45,000
SALES: 4.5MM **Privately Held**
SIC: 3646 Commercial indusl & institutional electric lighting fixtures

(G-10982)
TRULITE GL ALUM SOLUTIONS LLC
4363 S 86th East Ave (74145-4837)
PHONE..................918 665-6655
Ayanna McCloud, *Accounting Mgr*
Kevin Orlando, *Sales Staff*
Lanny Dickmann, *Branch Mgr*
Patty Decamp, *Manager*
Mark Cooper,
EMP: 6 **Privately Held**
SIC: 3354 Aluminum extruded products
PA: Trulite Glass & Aluminum Solutions, Llc
403 Westpark Ct Ste 201
Peachtree City GA 30269

(G-10983)
TSI-ENQUIP INC
3319 N Lewis Ave (74110-1515)
PHONE..................918 599-8111
Michael Ross, *President*
EMP: 30
SQ FT: 6,000
SALES (est): 6.8MM **Privately Held**
SIC: 3823 3443 Industrial instrmnts msrmnt display/control process variable; fabricated plate work (boiler shop)

(G-10984)
TUCKER ENERGY SERVICES INC
12607 E 60th St (74146-6910)
PHONE..................918 806-5647
Randy Nitz, *President*
Chandika Mannah, *Supervisor*
EMP: 15
SALES (est): 2.6MM
SALES (corp-wide): 501.9MM **Privately Held**
SIC: 1389 Oil field services
HQ: Step Energy Services Holdings Ltd.
480 Wildwood Forest Dr
Spring TX 77380

(G-10985)
TULSA AMERICAN SHAMAN
5455 S Mingo Rd (74146-5757)
PHONE..................918 938-0718
EMP: 2
SALES (est): 117.4K **Privately Held**
SIC: 2833 Medicinals & botanicals

(G-10986)
TULSA AUTO CORE
Also Called: T A C
1130 N Lewis Ave (74110-4766)
PHONE..................918 584-5899
Bill Painter, *Owner*
EMP: 5
SALES (est): 850K **Privately Held**
SIC: 1499 5015 Precious stones mining; engines, used

(G-10987)
TULSA AUTO SPRING CO
6545 E 21st Pl (74129-2001)
PHONE..................918 835-6926
William C Baughman, *President*
Alan Baughman, *Vice Pres*
Dan Oxford, *Treasurer*
John Oxford, *Admin Sec*
EMP: 45
SQ FT: 35,000
SALES (est): 4.6MM **Privately Held**
WEB: www.tulsaautospring.com
SIC: 7538 5531 3493 General automotive repair shops; automotive & home supply stores; steel springs, except wire

(G-10988)
TULSA BAKING INC
3202 E 15th St (74104-5221)
PHONE..................918 712-2918
Larry Merritt, *President*
EMP: 80 **Privately Held**
SIC: 5461 2052 2051 Cakes; cookies & crackers; bread, cake & related products
PA: Tulsa Baking, Inc.
7712 E 11th St
Tulsa OK 74112

(G-10989)
TULSA BAKING INC (PA)
Also Called: Merritt's Bakery
7712 E 11th St (74112-5718)
PHONE..................918 747-2301
Larry Merritt, *President*
EMP: 30
SALES (est): 9.8MM **Privately Held**
SIC: 5461 2052 2051 Bread; cookies & crackers, bread, cake & related products

(G-10990)
TULSA BRAKE & CLUTCH CO LLC
Also Called: Brake & Clutch of Tulsa
129 N Lewis Ave (74110-5346)
PHONE..................918 582-2165
Jerry Springer,
EMP: 5 EST: 1964
SQ FT: 10,600
SALES (est): 670K **Privately Held**
SIC: 5013 3714 3625 Automotive brakes; motor vehicle brake systems & parts; brakes, electromagnetic

(G-10991)
TULSA CEMENT LLC
Also Called: Central Plains Cement Company
2609 N 145th East Ave (74116-2217)
PHONE..................918 437-3902
Leslie Clark, *Controller*
David Challacomb, *Mng Member*
Craig Kesler,
▲ EMP: 300 EST: 2012
SQ FT: 252,000
SALES (est): 64.4MM
SALES (corp-wide): 1.3B **Publicly Held**
SIC: 3241 Masonry cement; natural cement; portland cement
PA: Eagle Materials Inc.
5960 Berkshire Ln Ste 900
Dallas TX 75225
214 432-2000

(G-10992)
TULSA CENTERLESS BAR PROC INC
1605 N 168th East Ave (74116-4929)
PHONE..................918 438-0000
Evan Hudson, *President*
JD Mallow, *Opers Staff*
Kari Lacount, *Controller*
Shari Blankenship, *Sales Staff*
EMP: 50
SQ FT: 35,000
SALES (est): 6.9MM **Privately Held**
SIC: 3999 Custom pulverizing & grinding of plastic materials

(G-10993)
TULSA COFFEE SERVICE INC (PA)
Also Called: Java Daves Executive Cof Svc
6239 E 15th St (74112-6407)
P.O. Box 581238 (74158-1238)
PHONE..................918 836-5570
David Neighbors, *President*
EMP: 38
SQ FT: 25,000
SALES (est): 8.6MM **Privately Held**
SIC: 5149 5113 2095 5499 Coffee, green or roasted; towels, paper; cups, disposable plastic & paper; roasted coffee; coffee

(G-10994)
TULSA COPPER SPECIALTIES
5910 S 107th East Ave (74146-6721)
PHONE..................918 249-4809
EMP: 5
SALES (est): 317.8K **Privately Held**
SIC: 3444 Mfg Sheet Metalwork

(G-10995)
TULSA COUNTY MEDICAL SOCIETY
5315 S Lewis Ave (74105-6539)
PHONE..................918 743-6184
Paul Patton, *Director*
EMP: 4
SALES (est): 491.1K **Privately Held**
SIC: 8621 2721 Medical field-related associations; periodicals

(G-10996)
TULSA DYNASPAN INC
Also Called: Arrow Concrete Division
1241 E 29th Pl (74114-5206)
PHONE..................918 258-8693
Phil G Rush, *President*
David G Markle, *Principal*
James D Markle, *Principal*
Paul K MAI, *Principal*
Jerry Duncan, *Vice Pres*
▲ EMP: 125
SQ FT: 7,000
SALES (est): 13.8MM
SALES (corp-wide): 143.7MM **Publicly Held**
WEB: www.dynaspan.com
SIC: 3272 3273 1796 Prestressed concrete products; ready-mixed concrete; installing building equipment
PA: The Monarch Cement Company
449 1200th St
Humboldt KS 66748
620 473-2222

(G-10997)
TULSA GAMMA RAY INC
3487 N Osage Dr (74127-1573)
PHONE..................918 425-3112
Pete Moss, *Branch Mgr*
EMP: 4
SALES (corp-wide): 46.6MM **Privately Held**
SIC: 8734 3398 X-ray inspection service, industrial; metal heat treating
HQ: Tulsa Gamma Ray, Inc.
1023 N Victor Ave
Tulsa OK 74110
918 585-3228

(G-10998)
TULSA GLASS BLOWING STUDIO INC
7440 E 7th St (74112-4716)
P.O. Box 3325 (74101-3325)
PHONE..................918 582-4527
Linda Clark, *President*
Susan Teeters, *Program Dir*
EMP: 3
SALES: 480.1K **Privately Held**
SIC: 3229 Pressed & blown glass

(G-10999)
TULSA HEATERS INC
Also Called: T H I
1215 S Boulder Ave # 1200 (74119-2843)
PHONE..................918 582-9918
Mat Loveless, *President*
Robert Debes, *Engineer*
Jennifer Loveless, *Treasurer*
◆ EMP: 46
SQ FT: 18,000
SALES (est): 21MM **Privately Held**
SIC: 3433 Heating equipment, except electric

(G-11000)
TULSA INSTANT PRINTING
6380 E 31st St Ste D (74135-5456)
PHONE..................918 627-0730
Gary Wilfong, *Owner*
EMP: 3
SQ FT: 1,300
SALES (est): 400K **Privately Held**
SIC: 2752 2791 2789 Lithographing on metal; typesetting; bookbinding & related work

(G-11001)
TULSA LITHO CO CONSOLIDAT
2757 S Memorial Dr (74129-2603)
PHONE..................918 582-8185
EMP: 2

SALES (est): 83.9K **Privately Held**
SIC: 2752 Commercial printing, lithographic

(G-11002)
TULSA METAL FINISHING COMPANY
1705 N 166th East Ave (74116-4938)
P.O. Box 279, Catoosa (74015-0279)
PHONE..................918 609-5410
Mark Kennedy, *President*
EMP: 12
SALES (est): 1.9MM **Privately Held**
SIC: 3471 Finishing, metals or formed products

(G-11003)
TULSA PACKING SPECIALIST INC
4245 S Jackson Ave (74107-7005)
P.O. Box 470166 (74147-0166)
PHONE..................918 459-8991
Todd Dearman, *President*
Debbie Dearman, *Corp Secy*
Jeff Wilson, *Vice Pres*
EMP: 18
SQ FT: 1,800
SALES (est): 4.3MM **Privately Held**
SIC: 2631 2441 Container, packaging & boxboard; nailed wood boxes & shook

(G-11004)
TULSA POWDER COATING INC
1815 N 75th East Ave (74115-4612)
PHONE..................918 832-1741
Ken Bayer, *President*
Ron Ross, *Vice Pres*
EMP: 5
SALES (est): 574.5K **Privately Held**
SIC: 3479 Coating of metals & formed products

(G-11005)
TULSA PRO TURN INC
16803 E Pine St (74116-4805)
P.O. Box 581232 (74158-1232)
PHONE..................918 439-9232
Eric Gonseth, *Owner*
EMP: 14
SQ FT: 9,000
SALES (est): 2.1MM **Privately Held**
WEB: www.tulsaproturn.com
SIC: 3469 Machine parts, stamped or pressed metal

(G-11006)
TULSA RUBBER CO
401 S Boston Ave Ste 2200 (74103-4058)
P.O. Box 470692 (74147-0692)
PHONE..................918 627-1371
EMP: 14
SQ FT: 22,500
SALES: 1MM **Privately Held**
SIC: 3069 3561 3061 3053 Mfg Fabrcatd Rubber Prdt Mfg Pumps/Pumping Equip Mfg Mechanical Rubber Gd Mfg Gasket/Packing/Seals

(G-11007)
TULSA SHEET METAL INC
42 N Quincy Ave (74120-1610)
PHONE..................918 587-3141
Tom H Brown, *Chairman*
Mike Brown, *Chairman*
Daryl Keiser, *Vice Pres*
R Keiser, *Opers Dir*
EMP: 18
SQ FT: 18,000
SALES: 2MM **Privately Held**
WEB: www.tulsasheetmetal.com
SIC: 3444 7623 Sheet metal specialties, not stamped; refrigeration service & repair

(G-11008)
TULSA SIGN COMPANY
12121 E 51st St Ste 106 (74146-6019)
PHONE..................918 215-7131
EMP: 1
SALES (est): 46K **Privately Held**
WEB: www.tulsasigncompany.com
SIC: 3993 Signs & advertising specialties

Tulsa - Tulsa County (G-11009) GEOGRAPHIC SECTION

(G-11009)
TULSA TONER TECHNOLOGY
2122 S 67th East Ave C (74129-2025)
PHONE.....................................918 838-0323
Beverly Pflieger, *Owner*
EMP: 5
SQ FT: 4,182
SALES (est): 200K **Privately Held**
SIC: 3577 7378 3861 Computer peripheral equipment; computer maintenance & repair; photographic equipment & supplies

(G-11010)
TULSA TRAILER LLC
4231 S Elwood Ave (74107-5800)
PHONE.....................................918 447-2100
EMP: 5
SALES (est): 127.7K **Privately Held**
SIC: 3715 Truck trailers

(G-11011)
TULSA TUBE BENDING CO INC
4192 S Galveston Ave (74107-7035)
PHONE.....................................888 882-3637
Brad Frank, *Principal*
Page Isley, *Project Dir*
Sam Schaffler, *Mfg Staff*
Eller Aaron, *Engineer*
Jonathan Franks, *Engineer*
▲ **EMP:** 48
SQ FT: 70,000
SALES (est): 18.8MM **Privately Held**
WEB: www.ttb.com
SIC: 3498 Coils, pipe: fabricated from purchased pipe; tube fabricating (contract bending & shaping)

(G-11012)
TULSA WOOD ARTS LLC
1108 S Atlanta Ave (74104-3921)
PHONE.....................................918 576-6142
K Benfield, *Office Mgr*
Kathleen Benfield, *Manager*
Steven Walter,
EMP: 3
SALES (est): 280.3K **Privately Held**
SIC: 2499 Decorative wood & woodwork

(G-11013)
TULSA WORLD
5915 E 28th St (74114-6401)
PHONE.....................................918 664-8683
Heather J Weathers, *Principal*
EMP: 2
SALES (est): 118.8K **Privately Held**
SIC: 2711 Newspapers, publishing & printing

(G-11014)
TULSA WORLD
214 W Oklahoma St (74106-4666)
PHONE.....................................918 582-5921
Jesse Aycock, *Principal*
EMP: 3 EST: 2011
SALES (est): 130.7K **Privately Held**
SIC: 2711 Newspapers, publishing & printing

(G-11015)
TULSAPETS MAGAZINE
1439 S Marion Ave (74112-5922)
PHONE.....................................918 834-1252
Marilyn King, *Principal*
Steve Kirkpatrick, *Advt Staff*
EMP: 3 EST: 2009
SALES (est): 244.4K **Privately Held**
WEB: www.tulsapetsmagazine.com
SIC: 2721 Magazines: publishing only, not printed on site

(G-11016)
TULSAT INC
1513 S Boston Ave (74119-4049)
PHONE.....................................918 587-4729
Jonathan D Helmerich, *Principal*
EMP: 2
SALES (est): 148.2K **Privately Held**
SIC: 3663 Cable television equipment

(G-11017)
TURN QUICK MANUFACTURING LLC
5302 W 21st St (74107-2223)
PHONE.....................................918 599-0011
William Garrison, *President*
EMP: 4
SQ FT: 2,100
SALES (est): 775K **Privately Held**
SIC: 3599 Machine shop, jobbing & repair

(G-11018)
TURNBOW-KIKER LTD
5504 E 89th Ct (74137-3581)
PHONE.....................................918 481-8871
John R Turnbow, *Principal*
EMP: 3
SALES (est): 199.9K **Privately Held**
SIC: 1382 Oil & gas exploration services

(G-11019)
TURNER MACHINE CO INC
5311 Southwest Blvd (74107-8968)
PHONE.....................................918 446-3581
Joe Ridener, *President*
Geraldine Ridener, *Admin Sec*
EMP: 20
SQ FT: 8,500
SALES (est): 3.3MM **Privately Held**
SIC: 3599 Machine shop, jobbing & repair

(G-11020)
TUUN LEH ZUA PRINTING SERVICES
7702 S Victor Ave (74136-7704)
PHONE.....................................918 809-7925
Kham Lian, *Principal*
EMP: 2
SALES (est): 83.9K **Privately Held**
SIC: 2752 Commercial printing, lithographic

(G-11021)
TWELVE STATES OIL & GAS CO LLC
5714 E 108th St (74137-7296)
PHONE.....................................918 296-7625
Adam Peterson, *Owner*
EMP: 2
SALES (est): 65.5K **Privately Held**
SIC: 1389 Oil & gas field services

(G-11022)
TWI INDUSTRIES INC
Also Called: Press Group, The
8605 S Elwood Ave B108 (74132-3637)
PHONE.....................................918 663-6655
Troy Wormell, *President*
Joyce Wormell, *Vice Pres*
EMP: 45
SALES (est): 4.8MM **Privately Held**
SIC: 2759 Screen printing

(G-11023)
TWIN CITIES READY MIX INC
1818 N 127th East Ave (74116-1711)
PHONE.....................................918 438-8888
John Schwarz, *Plant Mgr*
John Swartz, *Manager*
EMP: 30
SALES (corp-wide): 15.7MM **Privately Held**
SIC: 3273 Ready-mixed concrete
PA: Twin Cities Ready Mix, Inc.
102 W Ashland Ave
Mcalester OK 74501
918 423-8855

(G-11024)
TWIN EAGLE MIDSTREAM LLC
7633 E 63rd Pl Ste 316 (74133-1273)
PHONE.....................................918 459-4548
EMP: 4
SALES (est): 288.3K **Privately Held**
SIC: 1311 Crude Petroleum/Natural Gas Production
PA: Twin Eagle Resource Management, Llc
8847 W Sam Houston Pkwy N
Houston TX 77040

(G-11025)
TWO CANDLE GUYS LLC
9402 E 55th Pl Ste B (74145-8173)
PHONE.....................................918 271-5244
EMP: 1 EST: 2018
SALES (est): 39.6K **Privately Held**
SIC: 3999 Candles

(G-11026)
TWO GUYS BOWTIE COMPANY LLC
623 S Peoria Ave Ste B (74120-4411)
PHONE.....................................405 612-0116
▲ **EMP:** 7 EST: 2015
SALES (est): 656.3K **Privately Held**
SIC: 2323 5611 Bow ties, men's & boys': made from purchased materials; tie shops

(G-11027)
TWO LEES INC
Also Called: Print Shoppe Etc
6915 E 38th St (74145-3202)
PHONE.....................................918 663-2390
Billy L Lee, *President*
Christina F Lee, *Vice Pres*
EMP: 3
SALES: 300K **Privately Held**
SIC: 2752 7334 Commercial printing, offset; photocopying & duplicating services

(G-11028)
TYPE HOUSE INC
3224 E 69th St (74136-4500)
PHONE.....................................918 492-8513
Carolotta Perry, *President*
EMP: 2
SQ FT: 2,800
SALES (est): 140K **Privately Held**
SIC: 2791 Typesetting

(G-11029)
U S POLY COMPANY (DH)
4501 W 49th St (74107-7315)
P.O. Box 9616 (74157-0616)
PHONE.....................................918 446-4471
Frank Bailor, *President*
Herb Fry, *CFO*
EMP: 150
SQ FT: 98,000
SALES (est): 20.9MM
SALES (corp-wide): 1B **Privately Held**
SIC: 3084 Plastics pipe
HQ: Uspoly Company, Llc
1933 W 2nd St
Hastings NE 68901
402 462-6006

(G-11030)
U SAVE MACHINE SHOP
510 S Sheridan Rd (74112-3144)
PHONE.....................................918 836-7163
Wayne Gibson, *Principal*
EMP: 2 EST: 2010
SALES (est): 220.1K **Privately Held**
SIC: 3599 Machine shop, jobbing & repair

(G-11031)
UC OIL & GAS LLC
4634 S Norwood Ave (74135-6827)
PHONE.....................................918 270-2383
Umer M Chaudhry, *Principal*
EMP: 2
SALES (est): 94.7K **Privately Held**
SIC: 1389 Oil & gas field services

(G-11032)
ULTIMATE MACHINE INC
1238 W 41st St Ste E (74107-7014)
PHONE.....................................918 232-6676
EMP: 2
SALES (est): 161.3K **Privately Held**
SIC: 3599 Mfg Industrial Machinery

(G-11033)
ULTRA FAST SIGNS
1808 E 66th Pl Unit D301 (74136-2465)
PHONE.....................................405 269-9468
Mike Edmondson, *Principal*
Cynthia Hughes, *Education*
EMP: 2
SALES (est): 104K **Privately Held**
SIC: 3993 Signs & advertising specialties

(G-11034)
UNICORP SYSTEMS INC
2625 W 40th Pl (74107-5417)
PHONE.....................................918 446-1874
Andrew D Mackay, *President*
Kasey Baumann, *Principal*
Sharon D Meier, *Principal*
Jerry L Zimmerman, *Principal*
Jim Schonefeld, *Vice Pres*
EMP: 46

SQ FT: 25,000
SALES (est): 7.3MM **Privately Held**
SIC: 7629 8711 3613 Aircraft electrical equipment repair; electrical or electronic engineering; control panels, electric

(G-11035)
UNIQUE STITCHES INC
9435 E 51st St Ste B (74145-9047)
PHONE.....................................918 794-5494
Marilyn J Funk, *President*
Bill Funk, *Vice Pres*
EMP: 8
SALES (est): 504.7K **Privately Held**
SIC: 5949 2395 Sewing supplies; embroidery & art needlework

(G-11036)
UNIT CORPORATION
8200 S U Dr 74132 (74132)
PHONE.....................................918 493-7700
EMP: 2
SALES (corp-wide): 674.6MM **Privately Held**
SIC: 1381 Drilling oil & gas wells
PA: Unit Corporation
8200 S Unit Dr
Tulsa OK 74132
918 493-7700

(G-11037)
UNIT CORPORATION (PA)
8200 S Unit Dr (74132-5300)
PHONE.....................................918 493-7700
Larry D Pinkston, *President*
Mark E Schell, *Senior VP*
David Dunham, *Vice Pres*
Michael Earl, *Vice Pres*
Jack Womack, *Safety Mgr*
EMP: 81
SALES: 674.6MM **Privately Held**
SIC: 1381 1382 1311 Drilling oil & gas wells; oil & gas exploration services; crude petroleum production; natural gas production

(G-11038)
UNIT DRILLING COMPANY (HQ)
8200 S U Dr (74132)
P.O. Box 702500 (74170-2500)
PHONE.....................................918 493-7700
Larry Pinkston, *President*
Don Goodson, *Business Mgr*
Mark Schell, *Vice Pres*
Joe Hermisillo, *Safety Mgr*
Art Adkison, *Purch Mgr*
EMP: 200
SQ FT: 15,000
SALES (est): 130.3MM
SALES (corp-wide): 674.6MM **Privately Held**
SIC: 1381 Redrilling oil & gas wells
PA: Unit Corporation
8200 S Unit Dr
Tulsa OK 74132
918 493-7700

(G-11039)
UNIT PETROLEUM COMPANY (HQ)
8200 S U Dr (74132)
P.O. Box 702500 (74170-2500)
PHONE.....................................918 493-7700
John G Nikkel, *Ch of Bd*
Larry D Pinkston, *President*
Mark E Shell, *Senior VP*
Jason McGregor, *Production*
Glen Starling, *Production*
EMP: 102
SQ FT: 10,000
SALES (est): 127.3MM
SALES (corp-wide): 674.6MM **Privately Held**
SIC: 1311 Crude petroleum production; natural gas production
PA: Unit Corporation
8200 S Unit Dr
Tulsa OK 74132
918 493-7700

(G-11040)
UNITED CONTRACTING SVCS INC
5114 W 46th St (74107-5028)
P.O. Box 1674, Broken Arrow (74013-1674)
PHONE.....................................918 551-7659

GEOGRAPHIC SECTION   Tulsa - Tulsa County (G-11068)

Hector Estrada, *President*
Jose Estrada, *General Mgr*
Yesenia Estrada, *Corp Secy*
EMP: 150 **EST:** 2007
SQ FT: 6,000
SALES (est): 11MM **Privately Held**
WEB: www.unitedcontractingservices.com
SIC: 3441 1623 Fabricated structural metal; oil & gas pipeline construction

(G-11041)
UNITED ENERGY TRADING LLC
7645 E 63rd St Ste 103 (74133-1249)
PHONE................................918 392-8444
Kevin Kirk, *Branch Mgr*
EMP: 1 **Privately Held**
SIC: 1311 Natural gas production
HQ: United Energy Trading Llc
   919 S 7th St Ste 405
   Bismarck ND 58504
   701 250-9367

(G-11042)
UNITED PLATING WORKS INC
4118 N Mingo Rd (74116-5026)
PHONE................................918 835-4683
Fred Block, *President*
Heather Dodgin, *Vice Pres*
Jackie Dodgin, *Vice Pres*
Ellen Block, *CFO*
EMP: 25
SQ FT: 16,800
SALES (est): 4.2MM **Privately Held**
SIC: 3471 3728 Plating of metals or formed products; aircraft parts & equipment

(G-11043)
UNITED VIDEO LLC
7140 S Lewis Ave (74136-5401)
PHONE................................918 488-4000
Jeff Shell, *CEO*
EMP: 60
SALES (est): 155.7K
SALES (corp-wide): 3.6B **Privately Held**
SIC: 3651 Household audio & video equipment
HQ: Tv Guide, Inc.
   7140 S Lewis Ave Fl 2nd
   Tulsa OK 74136
   918 488-4000

(G-11044)
UNITED WE STAND INC
205 E Pine St Ste 16 (74106-4855)
PHONE................................918 382-1766
Bert Philip, *CEO*
EMP: 2
SQ FT: 1,000
SALES (est): 85.2K **Privately Held**
WEB: www.unitedwestandok.com
SIC: 7219 2341 2399 Tailor shop, except custom or merchant tailor; nightgowns & negligees: women's & children's; saddle cloth

(G-11045)
UNITY PRESS INC
10733 E Ute St (74116-1518)
PHONE................................405 232-8910
Guy St Denis, *President*
EMP: 30
SQ FT: 30,000
SALES (est): 2.5MM **Privately Held**
SIC: 2677 2752 Envelopes; commercial printing, offset

(G-11046)
UNIVERSAL COMBUSTION CORP
8312 S 75th East Ave (74133-4215)
PHONE................................918 254-1828
Lee Massey, *President*
Sandra Massey, *Admin Sec*
EMP: 2 **EST:** 1995
SQ FT: 2,500
SALES: 400K **Privately Held**
SIC: 8711 3823 Consulting engineer; combustion control instruments

(G-11047)
UNIVERSAL COMPRESSION INC
5727 S Lewis Ave Ste 610 (74105-7147)
PHONE................................918 742-1801
Jim Slaymaker, *CTO*
EMP: 2

SALES (est): 79.9K **Privately Held**
SIC: 3585 Refrigeration & heating equipment

(G-11048)
UNIVERSAL JINT SPECIALISTS INC
6960 E 11th St (74112-4622)
PHONE................................918 836-0111
EMP: 2
SQ FT: 3,000
SALES (est): 230K **Privately Held**
SIC: 3714 Mfg Motor Vehicle Parts/Accessories

(G-11049)
UNIVERSAL LAND SERVICES LLC
1323 E 71st St Ste 400 (74136-5067)
PHONE................................918 712-9038
EMP: 2
SALES (est): 150K **Privately Held**
SIC: 1389 Oil/Gas Field Services

(G-11050)
UNIVERSAL RIG SERVICE CORP
8 E 3rd St (74103-3610)
PHONE................................918 585-8221
John E Menger, *Principal*
EMP: 2
SALES (est): 99.9K
SALES (corp-wide): 571.1MM **Publicly Held**
SIC: 1381 Drilling oil & gas wells
PA: Parker Drilling Company
   5 Greenway Plz Ste 100
   Houston TX 77046
   281 406-2000

(G-11051)
UNIVISION DISPLAY USA LLC
10203 E 61st St Ste B (74133-1514)
PHONE................................918 289-6611
Yil P Kim, *Mng Member*
Yipyo Kim,
EMP: 4
SQ FT: 3,000
SALES: 1MM **Privately Held**
SIC: 3679 Liquid crystal displays (LCD)

(G-11052)
UPCO INC
4801 W 49th St (74107-7321)
P.O. Box 725, Claremore (74018-0725)
PHONE................................918 342-1270
Bill Ridenour, *President*
Victor Felix, *General Mgr*
Darla Bugg, *Vice Pres*
Erik T Pe, *Vice Pres*
Donald Williamson, *Buyer*
▼ **EMP:** 100
SALES (est): 34.2MM
SALES (corp-wide): 1.1B **Publicly Held**
SIC: 3533 Oil field machinery & equipment
PA: Championx Corporation
   2445 Tech Frest Blvd Bldg
   The Woodlands TX 77381
   281 403-5772

(G-11053)
UPLANDS RESOURCES INC
427 S Boston Ave Ste 800 (74103-4113)
PHONE................................918 592-0305
Herbert C Oven Jr, *President*
J Bingman, *Manager*
EMP: 7
SQ FT: 3,500
SALES (est): 781.3K **Privately Held**
SIC: 1311 Crude petroleum production; natural gas production

(G-11054)
UPONOR ALDYL CO INC
4501 W 49th St (74107-7315)
P.O. Box 9616 (74157-0616)
PHONE................................918 446-4771
Frank Bailor, *Principal*
EMP: 6
SALES (est): 715.9K **Privately Held**
SIC: 3085 Plastics bottles

(G-11055)
US PIONEER LLC
4450 S 70th East Ave (74145-4607)
P.O. Box 472065 (74147-2065)
PHONE................................918 359-5200
Seth Lapidus, *Vice Pres*
Phillip Paul, *Vice Pres*
Tony Steelman, *Plant Mgr*
Cliff Schramm, *Engineer*
Charles Thompson, *CFO*
▲ **EMP:** 45
SQ FT: 30,000
SALES (est): 13.8MM **Privately Held**
SIC: 3357 3646 Shipboard cable, nonferrous; commercial indusl & institutional electric lighting fixtures

(G-11056)
US PIONEER LED SPECIALISTS LLC
4450 S 70th East Ave (74145-4607)
P.O. Box 472065 (74147-2065)
PHONE................................918 359-5200
Lester Lapidus, *Manager*
EMP: 2
SALES (est): 123.9K **Privately Held**
SIC: 3613 Switchgear & switchboard apparatus

(G-11057)
US SAFETYSIGN & DECAL LLC
1433 E 6th St (74120-4023)
PHONE................................800 678-2529
Chris Kern, *Production*
Joy Goldesberry, *Sales Mgr*
Vonda Zimmerman, *Sales Staff*
Cody Clark,
EMP: 10
SALES (est): 702.5K **Privately Held**
SIC: 3993 Signs & advertising specialties

(G-11058)
USA COMPRESSION PARTNERS LLC
5801 E 41st St Ste 505 (74135-5619)
PHONE................................918 742-6548
Dennis Moody, *Manager*
Eddie Burns, *Manager*
EMP: 5
SALES (corp-wide): 698.3MM **Publicly Held**
SIC: 1389 Gas compressing (natural gas) at the fields
HQ: Usa Compression Partners, Llc
   111 Congress Ave Ste 2400
   Austin TX 78701
   512 369-1380

(G-11059)
USA SIGNS INC
9242 S Sheridan Rd Ste D (74133-5435)
PHONE................................918 392-5544
Donnie Faulkner, *Principal*
EMP: 4
SALES (est): 304.1K **Privately Held**
SIC: 3993 Signs & advertising specialties

(G-11060)
USER FRIENDLY PHONE BOOK LLC
4150 S 100th East Ave # 106 (74146-3650)
PHONE................................918 384-0224
Justin Armstong, *General Mgr*
EMP: 10
SALES (corp-wide): 94.5MM **Privately Held**
SIC: 2741 Telephone & other directory publishing
PA: User Friendly Phone Book, Llc
   10200 Grogans Mill Rd # 440
   The Woodlands TX 77380
   281 465-5400

(G-11061)
USUT LABS INC
12505 E 55th St Ste A (74146-6209)
PHONE................................918 459-3844
Dennis Wulf, *President*
Lawrence Busse, *Vice Pres*
EMP: 4
SALES (est): 408.3K **Privately Held**
SIC: 3845 5047 Ultrasonic medical equipment, except cleaning; medical & hospital equipment

(G-11062)
UTOWN LLC
36 E Cameron St (74103-1405)
PHONE................................918 261-3402
Nick Salis, *CEO*
EMP: 2
SALES (est): 82.7K **Privately Held**
SIC: 7372 Application computer software

(G-11063)
VACULIFT INCORPORATED (PA)
Also Called: Vacuworx International
10105 E 55th Pl (74146-6406)
PHONE................................918 438-9875
Bill Solomon, *President*
Anne Rojas, *CFO*
Cory Capps, *Info Tech Dir*
Steve Smith, *Director*
Ed R Crockett, *Incorporator*
▲ **EMP:** 53
SQ FT: 32,000
SALES (est): 10.5MM **Privately Held**
SIC: 3569 3537 Filters & strainers, pipeline; lift trucks, industrial: fork, platform, straddle, etc.

(G-11064)
VALHOMA CORPORATION
1617 N 93rd East Ave (74115-4702)
P.O. Box 580698 (74158-0698)
PHONE................................918 836-7135
Tony Foster, *President*
Gail Foster, *Vice Pres*
◆ **EMP:** 27
SALES (est): 4.7MM **Privately Held**
SIC: 2844 5191 2399 Toilet preparations; farm supplies; horse harnesses & riding crops, etc.: non-leather

(G-11065)
VALMONT INDUSTRIES INC
Also Called: Valmont/Tulsa
801 N Xanthus Ave (74110-4928)
P.O. Box 2620 (74101-2620)
PHONE................................918 583-5881
Kevin Halstead, *Vice Pres*
Robert Chada, *Engineer*
Ryan Wragge, *Controller*
Bob Nichols, *Branch Mgr*
Timothy Bible, *Analyst*
EMP: 260
SALES (corp-wide): 2.7B **Publicly Held**
SIC: 3441 Fabricated structural metal
PA: Valmont Industries, Inc.
   1 Valmont Plz Ste 500
   Omaha NE 68154
   402 963-1000

(G-11066)
VALUE COMPONENTS CORP
308 S Lansing Ave (74120-2433)
P.O. Box 52306 (74152-0306)
PHONE................................918 749-1689
Harry Aschan, *President*
EMP: 5
SQ FT: 10,000
SALES (est): 677.6K **Privately Held**
SIC: 3568 3545 3462 Clutches, except vehicular; machine tool accessories; iron & steel forgings

(G-11067)
VAXART INC
Also Called: Nabi Biomedical Center
824 S Cheyenne Ave (74119-1408)
PHONE................................918 582-4346
Barbara Wagner, *Manager*
EMP: 1
SALES (corp-wide): 9.8MM **Publicly Held**
SIC: 8099 2836 Plasmapherous center; blood derivatives
PA: Vaxart, Inc.
   290 Utah Ave Ste 200
   South San Francisco CA 94080
   650 550-3500

(G-11068)
VB WELDING LLC
11718 E Admiral Pl (74116-3807)
PHONE................................918 695-0258
Victor Becerra, *Principal*
EMP: 1 **EST:** 2016
SALES (est): 35.5K **Privately Held**
SIC: 7692 Welding repair

Tulsa - Tulsa County (G-11069)

(G-11069)
VEEM JADE OIL & GAS LLC
11417 S Granite Ave (74137-8110)
PHONE 918 298-1555
Jim Harrington, *Administration*
EMP: 2 EST: 2001
SALES (est): 124.5K **Privately Held**
SIC: 1389 Oil & gas field services

(G-11070)
VENTAIRE LLC
Also Called: Sagebrush Building Systems
909 N Wheeling Ave (74110-4917)
PHONE 918 622-1191
Jeff Weaver, *Sales Executive*
Judy Lasiter, *Executive*
EMP: 40
SQ FT: 66,450
SALES (est): 10.6MM **Privately Held**
SIC: 3444 3448 Sheet metalwork; prefabricated metal buildings

(G-11071)
VENTAIRE CORPORATION
909 N Wheeling Ave (74110-4917)
PHONE 918 622-1191
Jeff Weaver, *President*
EMP: 1
SALES (est): 428.1K **Privately Held**
WEB: www.ventairecorp.com
SIC: 3444 Sheet metalwork

(G-11072)
VERACITY TECH SOLUTIONS LLC (PA)
11331 E 20th St Ste A (74128-6401)
PHONE 208 821-8888
EMP: 4
SALES (est): 553.2K **Privately Held**
SIC: 3829 8734 8331 Measuring & controlling devices; testing laboratories; job training services

(G-11073)
VERTICAL LIMIT LLC
1660 E 71st St Ste O (74136-5191)
PHONE 918 409-1633
Doug Decker, *Owner*
EMP: 4
SALES (est): 216.3K **Privately Held**
SIC: 2591 Blinds vertical

(G-11074)
VESTA MIDSTREAM PARTNERS LLC
2431 E 61st St Ste 310 (74136-1231)
PHONE 918 986-9520
Debbie Branch, *Owner*
EMP: 5
SALES (est): 620.6K **Privately Held**
SIC: 1382 Oil & gas exploration services

(G-11075)
VICTORY HOUSE INC (PA)
6506 S Lewis Ave Ste 114 (74136-1020)
P.O. Box 700238 (74170-0238)
PHONE 918 747-5009
Clift Richards, *President*
EMP: 6
SQ FT: 1,800
SALES (est): 673.6K **Privately Held**
SIC: 2731 8661 Books: publishing only; religious organizations

(G-11076)
VIERSEN OIL & GAS CO
7130 S Lewis Ave Ste 200 (74136-5484)
P.O. Box 702708 (74170-2708)
PHONE 918 742-1979
Marylin Sant, *President*
Leo Sant, *CFO*
Luana Dickerson, *Admin Sec*
EMP: 10 EST: 1921
SALES (est): 1.8MM **Privately Held**
WEB: www.viersenoilandgas.com
SIC: 1382 Oil & gas exploration services

(G-11077)
VIKING SALES LLC
Also Called: Ledusa
1849 N 105th East Ave (74116-1513)
P.O. Box 52067 (74152-0067)
PHONE 918 742-7796
Kevin Hannah, *Mng Member*
EMP: 2
SALES (est): 306K **Privately Held**
SIC: 3648 5063 Strobe lighting systems; lighting fixtures

(G-11078)
VINTAGE PLASTICS LLC
1305 N 143rd East Ave (74116-2123)
P.O. Box 582001 (74158-2001)
PHONE 918 439-1016
Lee Johnson,
EMP: 13
SALES (est): 2.4MM **Privately Held**
SIC: 3559 Recycling machinery

(G-11079)
VINTAGE VAULT
1134 S Harvard Ave (74112-4914)
PHONE 918 619-9954
Sheila Alley, *Principal*
EMP: 2
SALES (est): 224.6K **Privately Held**
SIC: 3272 Burial vaults, concrete or precast terrazzo

(G-11080)
VIRTUOSO SOFTWARE LLC
6415 S 110th East Ave (74133-1624)
PHONE 918 813-4941
Jonathan Torkelson, *CEO*
EMP: 9
SALES (est): 204.2K **Privately Held**
SIC: 7372 Prepackaged software

(G-11081)
VISION MOTORSPORTS
6863 E 40th St (74145-4509)
PHONE 918 260-4981
Bourget Christopher, *Principal*
EMP: 4 EST: 2011
SALES (est): 189.2K **Privately Held**
WEB: www.visionmotorsportsonline.com
SIC: 3999 Pet supplies

(G-11082)
VISION TYPE & DESIGN INC
Also Called: Womack, Dana Typesetting
6329 S 109th East Ave (74133-1616)
PHONE 918 252-3817
Dana Womack, *President*
EMP: 1
SALES (est): 88.1K **Privately Held**
SIC: 2791 Typesetting

(G-11083)
VISTA DISPOSAL SOLUTIONS LLC
4124 St (74105)
PHONE 918 623-0333
EMP: 2
SALES (est): 90.4K
SALES (corp-wide): 186K **Privately Held**
SIC: 2542 Postal lock boxes, mail racks & related products
PA: Vista Disposal Solutions, Llc
104188 State Hwy 56
Okemah OK 74859
918 623-0333

(G-11084)
VORTEX PARTS WASHER
427 S Boston Ave Ste 353 (74103-4129)
PHONE 918 582-4445
EMP: 3 EST: 2011
SALES (est): 210K **Privately Held**
SIC: 3452 Mfg Bolts/Screws/Rivets

(G-11085)
VYPE HIGH SCHOOL SPT MAG LLC
8282 S Memorial Dr # 300 (74133-4351)
PHONE 918 495-1771
Charles Scott, *Mng Member*
Kevin Hern,
EMP: 15
SQ FT: 9,900
SALES (est): 1.3MM **Privately Held**
SIC: 2721 Magazines: publishing only, not printed on site

(G-11086)
W C BRADLEY CO
Also Called: Zebco
6101 E Apache St (74115-3370)
P.O. Box 270 (74101-0270)
PHONE 918 836-5581
Jeff Pontius, *Principal*
EMP: 95
SALES (corp-wide): 230.3MM **Privately Held**
SIC: 3949 Fishing equipment
PA: W. C. Bradley Co.
1017 Front Ave
Columbus GA 31901
706 571-7000

(G-11087)
W C BRDLY/ZEBCO HOLDINGS INC (HQ)
6105 E Apache St (74115-3370)
PHONE 706 571-6080
Marc R Olivie, *President*
James G Hillenbrand, *President*
▲ EMP: 18
SALES (est): 13MM
SALES (corp-wide): 230.3MM **Privately Held**
SIC: 3631 Barbecues, grills & braziers (outdoor cooking)
PA: W. C. Bradley Co.
1017 Front Ave
Columbus GA 31901
706 571-7000

(G-11088)
W J L S INC
Also Called: Royal Vista Plastics
12528 E 60th St (74146-6907)
P.O. Box 470651 (74147-0651)
PHONE 918 252-3636
Wesley Leon Lawson, *President*
Patricia Lawson, *Admin Sec*
EMP: 36
SALES (est): 3MM **Privately Held**
SIC: 3089 Injection molding of plastics

(G-11089)
W L WALKER CO INC (PA)
330 N Boulder Ave (74103-1402)
PHONE 918 583-3109
Anne W Bracket, *President*
Dallas Graye, *Purchasing*
Lyric Wright, *Manager*
Curtis Reed, *Supervisor*
EMP: 25 EST: 1926
SQ FT: 20,000
SALES (est): 11.2MM **Privately Held**
WEB: www.wlwalker.com
SIC: 5084 3829 3821 3444 Oil well machinery, equipment & supplies; measuring & controlling devices; laboratory apparatus & furniture; sheet metalwork; luggage

(G-11090)
WAGNER PLATE WORKS LLC
4142 W 49th St (74107-7311)
P.O. Box 9756 (74157-0756)
PHONE 918 447-4488
Eric Wagner, *Branch Mgr*
EMP: 6
SALES (corp-wide): 14.4MM **Privately Held**
WEB: www.wagnerplateworks.com
SIC: 3444 3443 Sheet metalwork; fabricated plate work (boiler shop)
PA: Wagner Plate Works Llc
6250 N Rosslyn Rd
Houston TX 77091
713 462-1946

(G-11091)
WALDEN ENERGY LLC
5115 E 84th Pl (74137-2016)
PHONE 918 488-8663
Tamara Walden, *President*
Larry David, *Vice Pres*
EMP: 1
SQ FT: 2,200
SALES (est): 238.8K **Privately Held**
SIC: 1311 Crude petroleum production

(G-11092)
WALDENS MACHINE LLC
Also Called: Wmi
3030 N Erie Ave (74115-2803)
PHONE 918 794-0289
Randy Baskins, *President*
Robert Kirkpatrick, *Vice Pres*
◆ EMP: 285
SQ FT: 135,000
SALES (est): 62.2MM
SALES (corp-wide): 327.2B **Publicly Held**
SIC: 3728 Aircraft parts & equipment
HQ: Primus International Inc
610 Bllvue Way Ne Ste 200
Auburn WA 98001
425 688-0444

(G-11093)
WALKER FORKLIFT SERVICE LLC
5944 W 43rd St (74107-6035)
PHONE 918 671-0317
Randy Walker, *Administration*
EMP: 4 EST: 2012
SALES (est): 396.2K **Privately Held**
WEB: www.walkerforkliftservice.com
SIC: 3537 Forklift trucks

(G-11094)
WANDERLUST PEN COMPANY
1254 E 29th Pl (74114-5207)
PHONE 918 551-6809
Lauren Houston, *Principal*
EMP: 3
SALES (est): 76.2K **Privately Held**
SIC: 2711 Newspapers

(G-11095)
WAR METALS INC
6306 S 40th West Ave (74132-1224)
PHONE 918 629-8057
EMP: 1
SALES (est): 83.9K **Privately Held**
SIC: 3449 Miscellaneous metalwork

(G-11096)
WARREN AMERICAN OIL COMPANY (PA)
6585 S Yale Ave Ste 800 (74136-8321)
PHONE 918 481-7990
W K Warren Jr, *President*
Valorie J Henry, *Vice Pres*
David B Whitehill, *Admin Sec*
EMP: 20 EST: 1938
SQ FT: 1,500
SALES (est): 4.3MM **Privately Held**
SIC: 1311 Crude petroleum production; natural gas production

(G-11097)
WASSCO CORPORATION
Also Called: Wassco Bottling Company
515 S 25th West Ave (74127-8405)
PHONE 918 834-4444
Britt Wasson, *President*
Micheal Ryan, *Vice Pres*
▲ EMP: 16
SQ FT: 42,000
SALES (est): 1.5MM **Privately Held**
SIC: 5499 5092 3446 Coffee; toy novelties & amusements; ornamental metalwork

(G-11098)
WATER BIONICS INC
4207 S 33rd West Ave (74107-5904)
P.O. Box 14061 (74159-1061)
PHONE 918 446-1988
Tom H Deck, *President*
Blake Adkins, *Admin Sec*
EMP: 3
SQ FT: 2,000
SALES (est): 550.3K **Privately Held**
SIC: 5074 3589 Water purification equipment; sewage & water treatment equipment

(G-11099)
WEAR-TECH
6945 E 38th St Ste C (74145-3228)
PHONE 918 663-2009
John Haspell, *Owner*
EMP: 3
SALES (est): 165.2K **Privately Held**
SIC: 5699 2396 T-shirts, custom printed; automotive & apparel trimmings

(G-11100)
WEBCO INDUSTRIES INC
Also Called: Distribution Div
3116 E 31st St N (74110-1908)
PHONE 918 836-1188
Wg Bieber, *General Mgr*

▲ = Import ▼=Export
◆ =Import/Export

GEOGRAPHIC SECTION

Tulsa - Tulsa County (G-11128)

EMP: 1
SALES (corp-wide): 480.7MM Privately Held
SIC: 5051 3312 Tubing, metal; tubes, steel & iron
PA: Webco Industries, Inc.
9101 W 21st St
Sand Springs OK 74063
918 245-2211

(G-11101)
WEBERS SUPERIOR ROOT BEER INC
Also Called: Weber Root Beer
3817 S Peoria Ave (74105-3152)
PHONE..................918 742-1082
Rick Bilby, *Principal*
EMP: 1
SALES (corp-wide): 282.2K Privately Held
SIC: 5812 2087 Soft drink stand; flavoring extracts & syrups
PA: Webers Superior Root Beer Inc
3228 W 71st St
Tulsa OK 74132
918 446-8534

(G-11102)
WEBSTER COUNTY COAL LLC
1717 S Boulder Ave # 400 (74119-4805)
PHONE..................918 295-7600
Joe Kraft,
EMP: 350
SALES (est): 8.8MM Publicly Held
SIC: 1241 Coal mining services
PA: Alliance Holdings Gp, L.P.
1717 S Boulder Ave # 400
Tulsa OK 74119

(G-11103)
WEDLAKE FABRICATING INC
3989 N Osage Dr (74127-1519)
PHONE..................918 428-1641
Brian Wedlake Jr, *President*
Richard Blevins, *Principal*
Danny Foster, *Principal*
Greg Pylant, *Principal*
Joe Krause, *Engineer*
EMP: 30
SQ FT: 30,000
SALES (est): 9.2MM Privately Held
SIC: 3441 Fabricated structural metal

(G-11104)
WEINKAUF EXPLORATION
6540 S Lewis Ave (74136-1009)
PHONE..................918 749-8383
Donald Weinkauf, *Owner*
EMP: 11 EST: 1974
SQ FT: 5,200
SALES (est): 730K Privately Held
SIC: 1382 Oil & gas exploration services

(G-11105)
WEINKAUF PETROLEUM INC (PA)
6540 S Lewis Ave (74136-1009)
PHONE..................918 749-8383
Douglas Kirk Weinkauf, *President*
EMP: 12
SQ FT: 5,200
SALES (est): 2.5MM Privately Held
WEB: www.wpitulsa.com
SIC: 1311 1382 Crude petroleum production; natural gas production; oil & gas exploration services

(G-11106)
WELDPRO MANUFACTURING LLC
5306 W 31st St (74107-4219)
PHONE..................918 724-3862
Kyle Ray Johnson, *Owner*
EMP: 2
SALES (est): 85.2K Privately Held
SIC: 3999 Manufacturing industries

(G-11107)
WELLTEC INC
320 S Boston Ave (74103-3706)
PHONE..................918 585-6122
Jorgen Hallundb K, *Branch Mgr*
EMP: 3

SALES (corp-wide): 249MM Privately Held
WEB: www.welltec.com
SIC: 1389 Oil field services
HQ: Welltec, Inc.
22440 Merchants Way
Katy TX 77449
281 371-1200

(G-11108)
WENCO ENERGY CORPORATION
11102 E 56th St Ste D (74146-6727)
P.O. Box 35444 (74153-0444)
PHONE..................918 252-4511
Martin Booth, *President*
Virginia Booth, *Principal*
Sabrina Row, *Opers Mgr*
EMP: 15
SQ FT: 5,000
SALES (est): 4.2MM Privately Held
WEB: www.wencoenergy.com
SIC: 3533 Oil field machinery & equipment

(G-11109)
WESTERN PRNTING COMPANY INC
5129 S 95th East Ave (74145-8112)
PHONE..................918 665-2874
Patrick Coughlin, *President*
Jack Douglas Talley, *Vice Pres*
Barbara Coughlin, *Treasurer*
EMP: 23
SQ FT: 18,000
SALES (est): 3.8MM Privately Held
SIC: 2752 Commercial printing, offset

(G-11110)
WESTERN TECHNOLOGIES INC (PA)
Also Called: Westech
4404 S Maybelle Ave (74107-7011)
PHONE..................918 712-2406
Russell W Patterson, *President*
Christopher Mason, *Vice Pres*
Tim Mason, *Project Mgr*
Kandace Hancock, *Purchasing*
Michael Patterson, *Project Engr*
▲ EMP: 12 EST: 1971
SQ FT: 6,000
SALES (est): 4MM Privately Held
WEB: www.westechgalv.com
SIC: 3547 Galvanizing lines (rolling mill equipment)

(G-11111)
WESTFALL PRODUCING COMPANY
2610 S Birmingham Pl (74114-4321)
PHONE..................918 743-1192
Jim Westfall, *Principal*
EMP: 3
SALES (est): 217.2K Privately Held
SIC: 1311 Crude petroleum production

(G-11112)
WESTWIND SHEET METAL
152 S 122nd East Ave (74128-2406)
PHONE..................918 437-9976
Robert Hale, *Owner*
EMP: 2
SALES (est): 159.4K Privately Held
SIC: 3444 Sheet metal specialties, not stamped

(G-11113)
WESTWOOD FURNITURE INC
Also Called: Westwood Cabinets & Furniture
5744 E 30th Pl (74114-6416)
PHONE..................918 508-7657
Ross Felice, *President*
EMP: 1
SALES (est): 110K Privately Held
SIC: 2511 Wood household furniture

(G-11114)
WHEELER ENERGY CORPORATION
4835 S Peoria Ave Ste 4 (74105-4561)
P.O. Box 1439 (74101-1439)
PHONE..................918 587-7474
Roger Wheeler Jr, *President*
Johanna Smart, *Admin Sec*
EMP: 3 EST: 1981

SALES (est): 489.1K Privately Held
SIC: 1382 1311 Oil & gas exploration services; crude petroleum production

(G-11115)
WHIRLPOOL CORPORATION
7301 Whirlpool Dr (74117-1303)
PHONE..................918 274-6000
Gabriel Hernandez, *Engineer*
Timothy Moriarty, *Engineer*
Wes Reynolds, *Engineer*
Steve Stocking, *Engineer*
Jim Gifford, *Branch Mgr*
EMP: 300
SQ FT: 470,000
SALES (corp-wide): 20.4B Publicly Held
SIC: 3631 5064 Gas ranges, domestic; electric ranges, domestic; electrical appliances, major
PA: Whirlpool Corporation
2000 N M 63
Benton Harbor MI 49022
269 923-5000

(G-11116)
WHISPERING VINES VINYRD WINERY
7374 W 51st St (74107-8664)
PHONE..................918 447-0808
Doreen Riesen, *Owner*
EMP: 3
SALES (est): 263.5K Privately Held
WEB: www.whisperingvines.net
SIC: 5921 2084 Wine; wines

(G-11117)
WHISTLER MEDIA GROUP
6304 E 102nd St (74137-7061)
PHONE..................918 605-7446
EMP: 1
SALES (est): 46K Privately Held
WEB: www.whistleradvantage.com
SIC: 3993 Signs & advertising specialties

(G-11118)
WHISTLER SIGN CO LLC
11063 S Memorial Dr Ste D (74133-7366)
PHONE..................918 491-7446
Shawn Whistler, *Principal*
EMP: 10 EST: 2010
SALES (est): 1.2MM Privately Held
WEB: www.whistlerworks.com
SIC: 3993 Signs & advertising specialties

(G-11119)
WHITACRE GLASS WORKS LLC
8177 E 44th St (74145-4830)
P.O. Box 471127 (74147-1127)
PHONE..................918 366-6646
John Whitacre, *Mng Member*
EMP: 1
SALES (est): 206.6K Privately Held
SIC: 3231 1793 3211 Mirrored glass; glass & glazing work; building glass, flat

(G-11120)
WHITE COUNTY COAL LLC
1717 S Boulder Ave # 400 (74119-4805)
PHONE..................918 295-7600
EMP: 1
SALES (est): 42.6K Publicly Held
SIC: 1221 Coal preparation plant, bituminous or lignite
HQ: Alliance Coal, Llc
1717 S Boulder Ave # 400
Tulsa OK 74119
918 295-7600

(G-11121)
WILJACKAL LLC
5910 E 87th St (74137-3013)
PHONE..................918 252-2663
Paul Ramsey,
EMP: 15
SQ FT: 2,200
SALES (est): 1.5MM Privately Held
SIC: 2024 5812 Ice cream & frozen desserts; custard, frozen; snack bar

(G-11122)
WILLIAM C JACKSON
1762 S Utica Ave (74104-5336)
P.O. Box 4990 (74159-0990)
PHONE..................918 742-0602
William C Jackson, *Owner*
EMP: 2

SQ FT: 1,400
SALES (est): 215.7K Privately Held
SIC: 1311 8111 7389 Crude petroleum production; general practice attorney, lawyer; fund raising organizations

(G-11123)
WILLIAM DERREVERE DESIGNS
1347 E 19th St (74120-7620)
PHONE..................918 260-5607
William Derrevere, *Owner*
EMP: 1
SALES (est): 66K Privately Held
SIC: 3911 Jewelry, precious metal

(G-11124)
WILLIAM H DAVIS
1924 S Utica Ave Ste 1218 (74104-6530)
PHONE..................918 587-7782
William H Davis, *Owner*
EMP: 7 EST: 1969
SALES (est): 667.4K Privately Held
SIC: 1311 Crude petroleum production; natural gas production

(G-11125)
WILLIAM L RIGGS COMPANY INC
Also Called: Tulsa Masurement Gauge Lab Div
600 S 129th East Ave (74108-2514)
PHONE..................918 437-3245
Ruth Riggs, *President*
Tim Riggs, *Vice Pres*
Elizabeth Riggs, *Treasurer*
EMP: 6
SQ FT: 1,300
SALES (est): 640K Privately Held
SIC: 3823 3423 7699 3544 Industrial instrmnts msrmnt display/control process variable; hand & edge tools; precision instrument repair; special dies, tools, jigs & fixtures; construction machinery; valves & pipe fittings

(G-11126)
WILLIAM W MCCLURE JR
427 S Boston Ave Ste 952 (74103-4114)
PHONE..................918 747-6094
William W McClure Jr, *Owner*
EMP: 1
SALES (est): 116.8K Privately Held
SIC: 1311 Crude petroleum & natural gas production

(G-11127)
WILLIAMS COMPANIES INC (PA)
1 Williams Ctr (74172-0140)
PHONE..................918 573-2000
Stephen W Bergstrom, *Ch of Bd*
Alan S Armstrong, *President*
Micheal G Dunn, *COO*
Walter J Bennett, *Senior VP*
Debbie Cowan, *Senior VP*
▲ EMP: 1819 EST: 1908
SALES: 8.2B Publicly Held
WEB: www.co.williams.com
SIC: 4922 4924 1311 1321 Pipelines, natural gas; natural gas distribution; natural gas production; natural gas liquids

(G-11128)
WILLIAMS ENERGY RESOURCES LLC
Also Called: Williams Companies, The
1 Williams Ctr Bsmt 2 (74172-0172)
P.O. Box 2400 (74102-2400)
PHONE..................918 573-2000
Alan Armstrong, *President*
Frank E Billings, *Senior VP*
Allison G Bridges, *Senior VP*
Donald R Chappel, *Senior VP*
Mark Gauldin, *Opers Spvr*
EMP: 36
SALES (est): 11.4MM
SALES (corp-wide): 8.2B Publicly Held
SIC: 1321 Natural gas liquids
PA: The Williams Companies Inc
1 Williams Ctr
Tulsa OK 74172
918 573-2000

Tulsa - Tulsa County (G-11129) GEOGRAPHIC SECTION

(G-11129)
WILLIAMS FIELD SERVICES CO LLC (HQ)
1 Williams Ctr (74172-0140)
PHONE...........................918 573-2000
Alan S Armstrong, *President*
EMP: 104
SALES (est): 17.9MM
SALES (corp-wide): 8.2B **Publicly Held**
SIC: 1311 Crude petroleum & natural gas
PA: The Williams Companies Inc
  1 Williams Ctr
  Tulsa OK 74172
  918 573-2000

(G-11130)
WILLIAMS GAS PIPELINE CO LLC (HQ)
1 Williams Ctr Bsmt 2 (74172-0172)
P.O. Box 1396, Houston TX (77251-1396)
PHONE...........................918 573-2000
Neal Sorensen, *Engineer*
Randy Bernard,
Frank E Billings,
John R Dearborn Jr,
Travis Bonine, *Representative*
EMP: 2 **EST:** 1997
SALES (est): 994.4K
SALES (corp-wide): 8.2B **Publicly Held**
WEB: www.williams.com
SIC: 1311 4922 Natural gas production; natural gas transmission
PA: The Williams Companies Inc
  1 Williams Ctr
  Tulsa OK 74172
  918 573-2000

(G-11131)
WILLIAMS MBL BAY PROD SVCS LLC
1 Williams Ctr (74172-0140)
PHONE...........................918 573-2000
Steven J Malcolm, *CEO*
Frank E Billings, *Vice Pres*
Frank Billings, *VP Bus Dvlpt*
Joseph Williams,
EMP: 1
SALES (est): 663.7K
SALES (corp-wide): 8.2B **Publicly Held**
SIC: 1311 Crude petroleum & natural gas
PA: The Williams Companies Inc
  1 Williams Ctr
  Tulsa OK 74172
  918 573-2000

(G-11132)
WILLIAMS PARTNERS LP (HQ)
1 Williams Ctr (74172-0140)
PHONE...........................918 573-2000
Alan Armstrong, *President*
Chad J Zamarin, *Senior VP*
Dave Kcylor, *Vice Pres*
John Poarch, *Vice Pres*
Jasen Davis, *Foreman/Supr*
EMP: 102
SALES: 8B
SALES (corp-wide): 8.2B **Publicly Held**
SIC: 1311 4922 Natural gas production; natural gas transmission
PA: The Williams Companies Inc
  1 Williams Ctr
  Tulsa OK 74172
  918 573-2000

(G-11133)
WILLIAMS PROD APPALACHIA LLC
1 One Williams Ctr (74172-0140)
PHONE...........................918 573-2000
Ralph Hill, *President*
Gary Belitz, *Vice Pres*
Neo Buck, *Vice Pres*
EMP: 100
SALES (est): 2.5MM
SALES (corp-wide): 8.2B **Publicly Held**
SIC: 1382 Oil & gas exploration services
PA: The Williams Companies Inc
  1 Williams Ctr
  Tulsa OK 74172
  918 573-2000

(G-11134)
WILLIFORD ENERGY COMPANY (PA)
6060 S American Plz (74135-4335)
PHONE...........................918 495-2700
Mollie Williford, *Ch of Bd*
David Foster, *President*
Frederic Dorwart, *Corp Secy*
Douglas P Storts, *Senior VP*
EMP: 15 **EST:** 1979
SQ FT: 8,000
SALES (est): 3.1MM **Privately Held**
SIC: 1311 Crude petroleum production; natural gas production

(G-11135)
WILLIFORD RESOURCES LLC
6506 S Lewis Ave Ste 102 (74136-1020)
PHONE...........................918 712-8828
A Hearne Williford,
EMP: 6
SQ FT: 1,500
SALES (est): 981K **Privately Held**
SIC: 1382 Oil & gas exploration services

(G-11136)
WINARR GOLF TECH LLC
6912 E 12th St (74112-5619)
P.O. Box 470508 (74147-0508)
PHONE...........................918 994-2191
Richard Butefish,
EMP: 1
SQ FT: 300
SALES (est): 71.5K **Privately Held**
SIC: 3949 Golf equipment

(G-11137)
WINDOR SUPPLY & MFG INC
6537 E 46th St (74145-5812)
PHONE...........................918 664-4017
Dan Brambl, *Owner*
Todd Edmonds, *General Mgr*
Larry Evans, *Principal*
Jim Stevens, *Purch Agent*
Henry Haney, *Controller*
EMP: 25
SQ FT: 66,000
SALES: 8.3MM **Privately Held**
SIC: 5031 5211 2431 Doors; windows; door & window products; doors, wood; window frames, wood

(G-11138)
WINDSOR QUALITY FOOD CO LTD
9016 E 46th St (74145-4822)
PHONE...........................918 628-0277
EMP: 2
SALES (est): 62.3K **Privately Held**
SIC: 2038 Frozen specialties

(G-11139)
WINK EYELASH SALON
3807 S Peoria Ave (74105-3145)
PHONE...........................918 949-6299
Stacy Lamb, *Owner*
EMP: 7
SALES (est): 108.1K **Privately Held**
WEB: www.winkeyelashsalon.com
SIC: 7231 3999 Facial salons; eyelashes, artificial

(G-11140)
WINSTON COMPANY INC
3824 S 79th East Ave (74145-3219)
PHONE...........................800 331-9099
Henry W Zahn, *CEO*
Neal Zahn, *President*
Brenda Armstrong, *Principal*
Robert D Avery, *Principal*
Kim Kaase, *Principal*
▲ **EMP:** 23 **EST:** 1983
SQ FT: 20,000
SALES (est): 5.9MM **Privately Held**
SIC: 2869 Enzymes

(G-11141)
WIRE CLOTH MANUFACTURERS INC
7136 S Yale Ave Ste 300 (74136-6381)
PHONE...........................918 493-9400
Joel Hudson, *Principal*
EMP: 1

SALES (est): 90.7K
SALES (corp-wide): 4.9MM **Privately Held**
SIC: 3496 Miscellaneous fabricated wire products
PA: Wire Cloth Manufacturers, Inc.
  110 Iron Mountain Rd
  Mine Hill NJ 07803
  973 328-1000

(G-11142)
WITHERS MANUFACTURING INC
5811 S Mingo Rd (74146-6426)
PHONE...........................918 994-7787
West Withers, *President*
Tammy Skaggs, *Office Mgr*
EMP: 15
SALES (est): 1MM **Privately Held**
SIC: 3999 Manufacturing industries

(G-11143)
WIZARD INDUSTRIES
10150 E 47th Pl (74146-4807)
PHONE...........................918 622-5234
Kyle McCraray, *Owner*
Doreena Hoss, *Manager*
EMP: 2
SALES (est): 190K **Privately Held**
SIC: 3599 3496 Machine shop, jobbing & repair; miscellaneous fabricated wire products

(G-11144)
WM HEITGRAS COMPANY
1316 N Osage Dr 18 (74106-6917)
P.O. Box 2044 (74101-2044)
PHONE...........................918 583-3131
Charles L Shadday, *President*
Charles A Shadday, *President*
Josephine H Shadday, *Corp Secy*
David M Shadday, *Vice Pres*
Joel A Shadday, *Vice Pres*
EMP: 30
SQ FT: 40,000
SALES (est): 8MM **Privately Held**
WEB: www.wmheitgras.com
SIC: 3965 5085 Fasteners; industrial supplies; fasteners, industrial: nuts, bolts, screws, etc.

(G-11145)
WOLF PUBLISHING
5946 E 26th Pl (74114-5124)
PHONE...........................918 500-9921
EMP: 1
SALES (est): 41.2K **Privately Held**
SIC: 2741 Miscellaneous publishing

(G-11146)
WOLFE HEAVY HAUL AND HOTSHOT
9133 E Newton St (74115-5939)
PHONE...........................918 695-7836
Christopher Wolfe, *Owner*
EMP: 3
SALES: 120K **Privately Held**
SIC: 3537 Trucks: freight, baggage, etc.: industrial, except mining

(G-11147)
WOOD CONCEPTS INC
Also Called: Art Crved Signs By WD Concepts
2640 N Darlington Ave (74115-2808)
P.O. Box 150007 (74115-0007)
PHONE...........................918 836-9481
Kenneth C Van Treese, *President*
EMP: 5 **EST:** 1976
SQ FT: 10,000
SALES (est): 568.7K **Privately Held**
SIC: 3993 Signs, not made in custom sign painting shops

(G-11148)
WOOD SYSTEMS INC
Also Called: Mill Creek Granite & Stone
4706 W 46th St (74107-5038)
P.O. Box 4770 (74159-0770)
PHONE...........................918 388-0900
Jim Dunn, *CEO*
Jeffrey T Dunn, *President*
EMP: 80
SQ FT: 127,000

SALES (est): 11.4MM
SALES (corp-wide): 163.4MM **Privately Held**
SIC: 2434 2431 Wood kitchen cabinets; moldings, wood: unfinished & prefinished
PA: Mill Creek Lumber & Supply Company Inc
  6974 E 38th St
  Tulsa OK 74145
  918 794-3600

(G-11149)
WOODBINE FINANCIAL CORPORATION
427 S Boston Ave Ste 303 (74103-4108)
P.O. Box 52296 (74152-0296)
PHONE...........................918 584-5309
Alan Ratliff, *President*
Jo Ratliff, *Vice Pres*
EMP: 3
SQ FT: 500
SALES (est): 305.5K **Privately Held**
SIC: 8742 1311 Marketing consulting services; crude petroleum production; natural gas production

(G-11150)
WOODSTOCK CABINET LLC
4129 S 72nd East Ave (74145-4608)
PHONE...........................918 834-4840
Scott Cottongim, *Mng Member*
EMP: 18
SALES: 1.5MM **Privately Held**
SIC: 2521 5712 2434 Cabinets, office: wood; cabinets, except custom made: kitchen; wood kitchen cabinets

(G-11151)
WORD AMONG US
7521 S 69th East Pl (74133-3014)
PHONE...........................918 812-5254
Gail Knox, *Principal*
EMP: 2
SALES (est): 86.6K **Privately Held**
SIC: 2731 Book publishing

(G-11152)
WORD INDS FABRICATION LLC
1150a N Peoria Ave (74106-4901)
PHONE...........................918 382-7704
Tom Word,
EMP: 30
SALES (est): 5.4MM **Privately Held**
SIC: 3498 Fabricated pipe & fittings

(G-11153)
WORLD PUBLISHING COMPANY VEBA
1415 S Quincy Ave (74120-5838)
P.O. Box 1770 (74102-1770)
PHONE...........................918 582-0921
EMP: 2
SALES (est): 94K **Privately Held**
SIC: 2741 Miscellaneous publishing

(G-11154)
WORLDWIDE PRINTING & DIST INC (HQ)
Also Called: Resource One
2900 E Apache St (74110-2253)
PHONE...........................918 295-0112
James R Moore, *CEO*
Twila Flynn, *President*
Bill Maddox, *President*
Rick Rodgers, *Business Mgr*
Bryan Lank, *Exec VP*
◆ **EMP:** 152 **EST:** 1995
SQ FT: 82,000
SALES (est): 92.1MM
SALES (corp-wide): 105MM **Privately Held**
WEB: www.resource-one.us
SIC: 2759 7331 Commercial printing; direct mail advertising services
PA: Dm Moore Group Llc
  2900 E Apache St
  Tulsa OK 74110
  800 566-0062

(G-11155)
WPX ENERGY INC (PA)
3500 One Williams Ctr (74172-0151)
P.O. Box 21218 (74121-1218)
PHONE...........................855 979-2012
Richard E Muncrief, *President*

Clay M Gaspar, *President*
John Ridenour, *Superintendent*
Tim Smiley, *Superintendent*
Dennis C Cameron, *Senior VP*
EMP: 99
SALES: 2.2B **Publicly Held**
SIC: 1311 Crude petroleum & natural gas

(G-11156)
WPX ENERGY APPALACHIA LLC
1 Williams Ctr Ste 4700 (74172-0140)
P.O. Box 3102 (74101-3102)
PHONE..................866 326-3190
EMP: 16 **EST:** 2016
SALES (est): 459.9K **Publicly Held**
SIC: 1382 Oil & gas exploration services
PA: Wpx Energy, Inc.
  3500 One Williams Ctr
  Tulsa OK 74172

(G-11157)
WPX ENERGY KEYSTONE LLC
1 Williams Ctr (74172-0140)
PHONE..................918 573-2000
Ralph A Hill, *CEO*
Robert Goodwin, *Engineer*
Desiree Miller, *Manager*
Randy Vandenberg, *Manager*
EMP: 10 **EST:** 2017
SALES (est): 99.1K **Publicly Held**
SIC: 1311 Crude petroleum & natural gas
PA: Wpx Energy, Inc.
  3500 One Williams Ctr
  Tulsa OK 74172

(G-11158)
WPX ENERGY MARKETING LLC
11005 S Granite Ave (74137-7272)
PHONE..................918 573-0068
Michael Gettel, *Principal*
EMP: 4 **Publicly Held**
SIC: 1321 Natural gasoline production
HQ: Wpx Energy Marketing, Llc
  1 One Williams Ctr
  Tulsa OK 74172

(G-11159)
WPX ENERGY MARKETING LLC (HQ)
1 One Williams Ctr (74172-0140)
P.O. Box 2400 (74102-2400)
PHONE..................918 573-2000
Alan S Armstrong, *President*
Frank E Billings, *Senior VP*
Allison G Bridges, *Senior VP*
Don R Chappel, *Senior VP*
Ralph A Hill, *Senior VP*
EMP: 29
SQ FT: 4,000
SALES (est): 29.4MM **Publicly Held**
SIC: 1321 Natural gasoline production

(G-11160)
WPX ENERGY PERMIAN LLC
3500 One Williams Ctr (74172-0151)
P.O. Box 3102 (74101-3102)
PHONE..................855 979-2102
Ronnie K Irani, *President*
Jack Rawdon, *President*
Jeffrey A Bonney, *CFO*
Wanzalle Beck,
EMP: 38
SQ FT: 15,000
SALES (est): 41.6MM **Publicly Held**
SIC: 1382 Oil & gas exploration services
PA: Wpx Energy, Inc.
  3500 One Williams Ctr
  Tulsa OK 74172

(G-11161)
WPX ENERGY RM COMPANY
1 Williams Ctr (74172-0140)
PHONE..................918 573-2000
Brad Goodman, *Accounts Mgr*
EMP: 16
SALES (est): 139.1K **Publicly Held**
SIC: 1311 Crude petroleum & natural gas
PA: Wpx Energy, Inc.
  3500 One Williams Ctr
  Tulsa OK 74172

(G-11162)
WR MACHINE SHOP INC
6514 E Independence St (74115-7861)
PHONE..................918 834-7682

Phil Lucas, *President*
Margi Lucas, *Corp Secy*
Jodi Jordon, *Vice Pres*
EMP: 5 **EST:** 1980
SQ FT: 3,000
SALES (est): 518.4K **Privately Held**
SIC: 3599 Machine shop, jobbing & repair

(G-11163)
WYNDHAM TULSA
10918 E 41st St (74146-2711)
PHONE..................918 627-5000
EMP: 8 **EST:** 2011
SALES (est): 600K **Privately Held**
SIC: 3421 Mfg Cutlery

(G-11164)
XANADU EXPLORATION COMPANY
320 S Boston Ave (74103-3706)
PHONE..................918 584-3802
Larry Sweet, *President*
EMP: 6
SALES (est): 1MM **Privately Held**
SIC: 1311 Crude petroleum production; natural gas production

(G-11165)
XPOSURE INC
20 E 5th St Ste 400 (74103-4443)
PHONE..................918 581-8900
Risha Brent, *President*
EMP: 6
SALES (est): 496.9K **Privately Held**
SIC: 2759 Magazines: printing

(G-11166)
YANKEE PACIFIC AEROSPACE
8664 S Peoria Ave (74132-2827)
PHONE..................918 894-8586
EMP: 3
SALES (est): 136.8K **Privately Held**
SIC: 3728 Aircraft parts & equipment

(G-11167)
YANKEE PACIFIC AEROSPACE INC
4325 E 51st St Ste 116 (74135-3646)
PHONE..................918 388-5940
Hue Tran, *Owner*
EMP: 2
SALES (est): 209.6K **Privately Held**
SIC: 3721 Aircraft

(G-11168)
YESCO
4312 S Mingo Rd (74146-4734)
PHONE..................918 524-9914
EMP: 1
SALES (est): 78K **Privately Held**
SIC: 3993 Signs & advertising specialties

(G-11169)
YOLANDA OLMOS
514 S 78th East Ave (74112-3312)
PHONE..................918 850-8334
Yolanda Olmos, *Principal*
EMP: 1
SALES (est): 83.8K **Privately Held**
SIC: 3299 Stucco

(G-11170)
YORKSHIRE PUBLISHING LLC
3207 S Norwood Ave (74135-5409)
PHONE..................918 394-2665
Ryan Sheehan, *Manager*
Roger Chasteen,
EMP: 50
SQ FT: 5,500
SALES (est): 300K **Privately Held**
SIC: 2731 Book publishing

(G-11171)
YP LLC
Also Called: AT&T
10159 E 11th St Ste 600 (74128-3038)
PHONE..................918 835-8600
Jackie Payne, *Branch Mgr*
EMP: 65
SALES (corp-wide): 1.1B **Privately Held**
SIC: 2741 Directories: publishing only, not printed on site

HQ: Yp Llc
  2247 Northlake Pkwy Fl 4
  Tucker GA 30084
  866 570-8863

(G-11172)
ZEBCO CORPORATION
6101 E Apache St (74115-3300)
P.O. Box 270 (74101-0270)
PHONE..................918 836-5581
Jeff Pontius, *President*
David Kern, *Senior VP*
EMP: 615
SQ FT: 160,000
SALES (est): 28.9K
SALES (corp-wide): 230.3MM **Privately Held**
SIC: 3949 3699 Rods & rod parts, fishing; reels, fishing; outboard motors, electric
PA: W. C. Bradley Co.
  1017 Front Ave
  Columbus GA 31901
  706 571-7000

(G-11173)
ZEBCO SALES COMPANY LLC
6101 E Apache St (74115-3300)
PHONE..................800 588-9030
▼ **EMP:** 9
SALES (est): 1.1MM
SALES (corp-wide): 230.3MM **Privately Held**
SIC: 3949 Fishing equipment
PA: W. C. Bradley Co.
  1017 Front Ave
  Columbus GA 31901
  706 571-7000

(G-11174)
ZEDCO LLC
2121 S Columbia Ave # 210 (74114-3505)
PHONE..................918 521-7587
Russell Cunningham,
EMP: 1
SALES (est): 39.6K **Privately Held**
SIC: 3999 Manufacturing industries

(G-11175)
ZENTECH
3744 S Jackson Ave (74107-5703)
PHONE..................918 445-1881
EMP: 2
SALES (est): 88.3K **Privately Held**
SIC: 3629 Electrical industrial apparatus

(G-11176)
ZENTECH LLC
1030 N Iroquois Ave (74106-5944)
P.O. Box 14093 (74159-1093)
PHONE..................918 585-8200
Emine Nese Sanders,
EMP: 10
SQ FT: 15,000
SALES (est): 1MM **Privately Held**
SIC: 3398 Metal heat treating

(G-11177)
ZEPHYRUS ELECTRONICS LTD
Also Called: Zephyrus Manufacturing
168 S 122nd East Ave (74128-2406)
PHONE..................918 437-3333
Robert Hale, *President*
Pete Ward, *Vice Pres*
George Owens, *Admin Sec*
EMP: 15
SQ FT: 13,000
SALES (est): 3.9MM **Privately Held**
SIC: 3663 Satellites, communications

(G-11178)
ZINKE & TRUMBO INC
6100 S Yale Ave Ste 1700 (74136-1921)
PHONE..................918 488-6400
David B Trumbo, *President*
C L Carter, *Vice Pres*
EMP: 14
SQ FT: 11,000
SALES (est): 1.5MM **Privately Held**
SIC: 1382 1311 Oil & gas exploration services; crude petroleum production; natural gas production

(G-11179)
ZOMM LLC
8620 S Peoria Ave (74132-2827)
P.O. Box 701320 (74170-1320)
PHONE..................918 995-2233
Henry A Penix, *Mng Member*
▲ **EMP:** 8
SALES (est): 964.2K **Privately Held**
SIC: 3661 Telephone & telegraph apparatus

(G-11180)
ZULU 4 TACTICAL LLC
4108 E 47th St (74135-4735)
PHONE..................918 978-6810
Justin K Zell, *Mng Member*
EMP: 1
SALES (est): 50.9K **Privately Held**
SIC: 3484 Guns (firearms) or gun parts, 30 mm. & below

Turpin
Beaver County

(G-11181)
BRIANS HOT OIL SERVICE LLC
Rr 2 (73950)
PHONE..................580 778-3549
Brian Riddle, *President*
EMP: 5 **EST:** 1998
SALES (est): 420K **Privately Held**
SIC: 1389 Oil field services

(G-11182)
JV ENERGY SERVICES INC
240 Quail Cir (73950)
PHONE..................620 482-0244
Jose Vasquez, *Director*
EMP: 12
SALES (est): 1MM **Privately Held**
SIC: 3533 Oil & gas drilling rigs & equipment

Tuskahoma
Pushmataha County

(G-11183)
W 2 ENTERPRISES LLC
13618 Sw Highway 2 (74574)
PHONE..................918 429-8793
Scotty Warren, *President*
EMP: 2
SALES (est): 36K **Privately Held**
SIC: 0212 0219 1389 1623 Beef cattle except feedlots; general livestock; oil consultants; oil & gas pipeline construction; local trucking, without storage;

Tuttle
Grady County

(G-11184)
5 STONES DEFENSE LLC
874 County Street 2922 (73089-3712)
PHONE..................405 313-9729
Eric Canaday, *Principal*
EMP: 3
SALES (est): 158.9K **Privately Held**
SIC: 3812 Defense systems & equipment

(G-11185)
ATLAS TUCK CONCRETE INC
Also Called: ATLAS TUCK CONCRETE INC
620 N Cimarron St (73089)
PHONE..................405 381-2393
Steve Boren, *Manager*
EMP: 6
SALES (corp-wide): 1.4B **Publicly Held**
SIC: 3273 Ready-mixed concrete
HQ: Atlas-Tuck Concrete, Inc.
  2112 W Bois D Arc Ave
  Duncan OK 73533
  580 255-1716

(G-11186)
BILL JONES MFG
877 Squirrel Ct (73089-7520)
PHONE..................405 392-4525

Tuttle - Grady County (G-11187)

Bill Jones, *Principal*
EMP: 2
SALES (est): 157.1K **Privately Held**
SIC: 3999 Manufacturing industries

(G-11187)
BRENTLY PUBLISHING INTL LLC
4706 Lake Ridge Ct (73089-5505)
PHONE..............................405 381-9069
EMP: 2
SALES (est): 68.9K **Privately Held**
SIC: 2711 Newspapers-Publishing/Printing

(G-11188)
BRITTER CREEK HUNTING BLI
2178 Fox Ln (73089-4410)
PHONE..............................405 392-3588
Forrest Shifflett, *President*
EMP: 10 EST: 2010
SALES (est): 694.3K **Privately Held**
SIC: 3949 Hunting equipment

(G-11189)
CHEMICAL DYNAMICS CORPORATION
7516 E Highway 37 (73089-8301)
P.O. Box 246 (73089-0246)
PHONE..............................405 392-3505
J P Clingman, *President*
EMP: 4
SQ FT: 5,000
SALES (est): 1.4MM **Privately Held**
SIC: 5169 1389 Chemicals, industrial & heavy; oil field services

(G-11190)
CORTER ENTERPRISES LLC
1472 County Road 1190 (73089-2202)
PHONE..............................405 326-7001
Eric Corter, *CEO*
EMP: 4
SALES (est): 125.8K **Privately Held**
SIC: 3993 Signs & advertising specialties

(G-11191)
COWAN PRINTING & LITHO INC
803 Schumann Ct (73089-8987)
PHONE..............................405 789-1961
Boyd D Cable, *President*
Shelley Downs, *Vice Pres*
Kenna Green, *Receptionist*
EMP: 10
SALES: 1.3MM **Privately Held**
WEB: www.cowanprinting.com
SIC: 2752 2791 2789 Commercial printing, offset; typesetting; bookbinding & related work

(G-11192)
CROSSTIMBERS HOT SHOT SVCS LLC
4200 E Highway 37 (73089)
P.O. Box 68, Newcastle (73065-0068)
PHONE..............................405 740-2900
Steve Johnson, *Mng Member*
Shelley Johnson, *Mng Member*
EMP: 2 EST: 2011
SALES (est): 129K **Privately Held**
SIC: 1389 Hot shot service

(G-11193)
CURING SYSTEM COMPONENTS INC
2916 E Highway 37 (73089-9519)
P.O. Box 1078 (73089-1078)
PHONE..............................405 381-9794
Tim Thomas, *President*
EMP: 10
SQ FT: 9,000
SALES: 1MM **Privately Held**
SIC: 3599 5084 Machine shop, jobbing & repair; industrial machinery & equipment

(G-11194)
DCP MIDSTREAM LLC
2609 E Tyler Dr (73089-8458)
PHONE..............................405 362-2200
Steve Thompson, *Branch Mgr*
EMP: 11
SALES (corp-wide): 2B **Privately Held**
SIC: 5172 2911 Gases, liquefied petroleum (propane); gases & liquefied petroleum gases

PA: Dcp Midstream, Llc
370 17th St Ste 2500
Denver CO 80202
303 633-2900

(G-11195)
DELTA WELL LOGGING SVC
Rr Rt (73089)
P.O. Box 985 (73089-0985)
PHONE..............................405 381-2954
Howard W Hall, *Owner*
EMP: 1
SALES (est): 72K **Privately Held**
SIC: 1389 Oil field services

(G-11196)
DENNIS L DICKERSON
Also Called: Central Handpiece Repair
1709 Riviera Dr (73089-8107)
PHONE..............................405 626-8630
Dennis Dickerson, *Owner*
Dennis L Dickerson, *Principal*
EMP: 1
SQ FT: 250
SALES (est): 24.8K **Privately Held**
SIC: 7699 3843 Dental instrument repair; dental hand instruments; dental tools

(G-11197)
ENGINEERING TOOLING SVC LLC
5911 Aero Dr (73089-8640)
PHONE..............................405 381-9322
Karen Baker, *Mng Member*
Steve Baker,
EMP: 2
SALES: 150K **Privately Held**
SIC: 3544 Special dies & tools

(G-11198)
EVCO SERVICE CO INC
1317 County St Ste 2910 (73089)
P.O. Box 907 (73089-0907)
PHONE..............................405 381-2172
Mark Evans, *President*
Brad Dibert, *Vice Pres*
Jack Gibson, *Treasurer*
EMP: 30
SQ FT: 20,000
SALES (est): 7MM **Privately Held**
WEB: www.evcoservice.com
SIC: 3594 7699 5084 Pumps, hydraulic power transfer; hydraulic equipment repair; hydraulic systems equipment & supplies

(G-11199)
FERGUSON WELDING LLC
2178 Fox Ln (73089-4410)
PHONE..............................405 534-1517
EMP: 5
SALES (est): 54.7K **Privately Held**
SIC: 7692 Welding repair

(G-11200)
FRENCH PRINTING INC
408 E Main St (73089-9140)
P.O. Box 612 (73089-0612)
PHONE..............................405 381-4057
Rodney French, *President*
Phil French, *Vice Pres*
Sammy Day, *Treasurer*
Mark French, *Admin Sec*
EMP: 1
SALES (est): 118.4K **Privately Held**
SIC: 2752 2791 2789 Commercial printing, offset; typesetting; bookbinding & related work

(G-11201)
GORE NITROGEN
1202 Prairie Hills Dr (73089-1047)
PHONE..............................405 381-4928
Tony Gore, *Principal*
EMP: 5
SALES (est): 474.6K **Privately Held**
SIC: 1389 Oil field services

(G-11202)
GRACE MACHINE INC
213 S Mustang Rd (73089-7948)
PHONE..............................405 381-4640
Chris Andrews, *President*
EMP: 4
SALES (est): 549.7K **Privately Held**
SIC: 3599 Machine shop, jobbing & repair

(G-11203)
GRS HOT SHOT TRUCKING LLC
2005 County Road 1199 (73089-3203)
PHONE..............................580 353-9449
Grant Byrns, *Partner*
Robert Dodrill, *Partner*
EMP: 2
SALES (est): 115.8K **Privately Held**
SIC: 1389 4212 Hot shot service; moving services

(G-11204)
IDENTITY & TANNING SALON
Also Called: Identity Hair & Tanning Salon
1301 Antler Rdg (73089-1803)
PHONE..............................412 269-7879
Shirly Semich, *Owner*
EMP: 2
SALES (est): 77.3K **Privately Held**
SIC: 7231 3341 Unisex hair salons; babbitt metal smelting & refining (secondary)

(G-11205)
JOHNSON WLDG & FABRICATION LLC
206 Sw 3rd St (73089-8925)
PHONE..............................405 474-3541
Joe C Johnson,
EMP: 3
SALES: 25K **Privately Held**
SIC: 3443 7389 Fabricated plate work (boiler shop);

(G-11206)
MBI INDUSTRIAL INC
323 W Main St (73089-9061)
PHONE..............................405 387-4003
John B Davis, *CEO*
EMP: 14
SALES (est): 2.7MM **Privately Held**
SIC: 3444 Sheet metalwork

(G-11207)
POWER CABLE SOLUTIONS LLC
832 County Street 2920 (73089-3022)
PHONE..............................405 818-1993
Daniel Franks, *President*
EMP: 2
SALES (est): 88.3K **Privately Held**
SIC: 3629 3052 Rectifiers (electrical apparatus); rubber hose

(G-11208)
PRESSURE SOLUTIONS LLC
12 Nw 4th St (73089)
P.O. Box 1077 (73089-1077)
PHONE..............................405 370-1830
Angela Bumgarner,
Mark Bumgarner,
EMP: 3
SALES (est): 150K **Privately Held**
SIC: 3563 Air & gas compressors

(G-11209)
R K MANUFACTURING LLC
1884 County Road 1250 (73089-3701)
P.O. Box 1174 (73089-1174)
PHONE..............................405 626-8922
EMP: 2
SALES (est): 105.7K **Privately Held**
SIC: 3999 Manufacturing industries

(G-11210)
R M MACHINE SHOP INC
1227 County Street 2960 (73089-3824)
PHONE..............................405 209-7242
Ronnie Bartmess, *Principal*
EMP: 3
SALES (est): 266K **Privately Held**
SIC: 3599 Machine shop, jobbing & repair

(G-11211)
RIVERS EDGE COUNTERTOPS INC
632 Wildwood Dr (73089-8568)
PHONE..............................405 532-3180
Jeremiah Rivers, *CEO*
EMP: 2
SALES (est): 371.4K **Privately Held**
SIC: 2541 Counter & sink tops

(G-11212)
SUMMERSIDE VINEYARDS & WINERY
1611 N Morgan Rd (73089-8680)
PHONE..............................918 256-3000
Gary Butler, *CEO*
EMP: 17
SALES (est): 1.8MM **Privately Held**
SIC: 2084 0172 Wines; grapes

(G-11213)
SUMMERSIDE WINERY & MEADERY
1611 N Morgan Rd (73089-8680)
PHONE..............................405 514-6360
EMP: 2 EST: 2013
SALES (est): 105K **Privately Held**
WEB: www.summersidevineyards.com
SIC: 2084 Wines

(G-11214)
T JOHN CO INC
2705 E Highway 37 (73089-8411)
PHONE..............................405 761-3460
John Ross, *President*
EMP: 2
SALES (est): 250K **Privately Held**
SIC: 2759 4813 Screen printing; telephone cable service, land or submarine

(G-11215)
TEN MFG LLC
414 Case (73089-8875)
PHONE..............................405 381-3752
James D Tennison, *Owner*
EMP: 1 EST: 2018
SALES (est): 48.3K **Privately Held**
SIC: 3999 Manufacturing industries

(G-11216)
TINHORNS ARE US (PA)
1884 County Rd Ste 1250 (73089)
PHONE..............................405 381-4044
Ricky Sowers, *Owner*
EMP: 7
SQ FT: 30,000
SALES: 2.2MM **Privately Held**
SIC: 3444 Culverts, sheet metal

(G-11217)
TWJ INC
Also Called: Pathkiller
2413 County Road 1196 (73089-2436)
PHONE..............................405 392-4366
Tom W Johnson, *President*
Melody Johnson, *Corp Secy*
EMP: 1
SALES (est): 107.9K **Privately Held**
SIC: 5712 5943 3993 3479 Office furniture; office forms & supplies; signs & advertising specialties; etching & engraving

Tyrone
Texas County

(G-11218)
ARCHER-DANIELS-MIDLAND COMPANY
Also Called: ADM
204 W Oklahoma St (73951)
P.O. Box 208 (73951-0208)
PHONE..............................580 854-6285
Stephen Lake, *Manager*
EMP: 6
SALES (corp-wide): 64.6B **Publicly Held**
SIC: 2041 Flour & other grain mill products
PA: Archer-Daniels-Midland Company
77 W Wacker Dr Ste 4600
Chicago IL 60601
312 634-8100

(G-11219)
KERR WELL SERVICE INC (PA)
704 N Florence (73951)
P.O. Box 184 (73951-0184)
PHONE..............................620 629-0400
Ronald Kerr, *President*
Sheryl Kerr, *Corp Secy*
EMP: 2
SALES (est): 1.4MM **Privately Held**
SIC: 1382 Oil & gas exploration services

GEOGRAPHIC SECTION

Union City
Canadian County

(G-11220)
QES PRESSURE PUMPING LLC
701 Main St (73090)
PHONE..................405 483-8000
EMP: 2
SALES (corp-wide): 1.1B **Privately Held**
SIC: **1389** Oil field services
HQ: Qes Pressure Pumping Llc
1322 S Grant Ave
Chanute KS 66720
620 431-9210

(G-11221)
STRAIGHT EDGE SAWMILL
12200 S Country Club Rd (73090-7056)
PHONE..................405 401-7798
EMP: 1
SALES (est): 41.5K **Privately Held**
SIC: **2499** Mfg Wood Products

Valliant
Mccurtain County

(G-11222)
CHIPS VALIANT INC
Hwy 70 Byp (74764)
PHONE..................580 933-5323
Dick Carmical, *President*
▲ EMP: 13
SALES: 1.7MM
SALES (corp-wide): 101.5MM **Privately Held**
SIC: **2421** Wood chips, produced at mill
PA: The Price Companies Inc
218 Midway Rte
Monticello AR 71655
870 367-9751

(G-11223)
F & F AUTOMOTIVE INC
Also Called: Seo Bio
1 And A Half Mi E On Hwy (74764)
PHONE..................580 933-4262
Martha Francis, *President*
W Dwight Francis, *Vice Pres*
EMP: 6 EST: 1973
SQ FT: 30,000
SALES (est): 508.9K **Privately Held**
SIC: **7699** 3715 Industrial machinery & equipment repair; truck trailers

(G-11224)
GARY MOSS
Also Called: Gary Moss Trucking
969 Cotton Moss Rd (74764-5310)
PHONE..................580 286-1359
Gary Moss, *Owner*
EMP: 1 EST: 2012
SALES (est): 92.6K **Privately Held**
SIC: **2411** Timber, cut at logging camp

(G-11225)
GARYS INDUSTRIAL MACHINE LLC
202 Roady Rd (74764-5379)
PHONE..................580 933-4514
Gary Milner, *Mng Member*
Darren Milner, *Manager*
Patria Milner,
EMP: 10
SALES (est): 1.7MM **Privately Held**
SIC: **3599** Machine shop, jobbing & repair

(G-11226)
INSIGHT TECHNOLOGIES INC
52 E Wilson St (74764)
P.O. Box 1183 (74764-1183)
PHONE..................580 933-4109
Mike Manning, *President*
EMP: 14 EST: 2000
SALES (est): 1.5MM **Privately Held**
WEB: www.in-sighttech.biz
SIC: **7382** 1731 5051 3441 Protective devices, security; general electrical contractor; steel; building components, structural steel

(G-11227)
INTERNATIONAL PAPER COMPANY
890 International Ppr Ln (74764-8018)
PHONE..................580 933-7211
Harris Logan, *Opers Mgr*
Brandy Campbell, *Buyer*
Bill Chivers, *Branch Mgr*
Brad Burris, *Manager*
Glen Luna, *Info Tech Mgr*
EMP: 73
SALES (corp-wide): 22.3B **Publicly Held**
SIC: **2421** 2671 2657 2621 Sawmills & planing mills, general; packaging paper & plastics film, coated & laminated; folding paperboard boxes; paper mills
PA: International Paper Company
6400 Poplar Ave
Memphis TN 38197
901 419-9000

(G-11228)
J&J LOGGING LLC
1356 Pine Creek Rd (74764-5129)
PHONE..................580 933-7218
EMP: 3 EST: 2008
SALES (est): 120K **Privately Held**
SIC: **2411** Logging

(G-11229)
JOHNNIE & LONNIE SMITH
Also Called: Smith Brothers Logging
1970 Rufe Rd (74764-5019)
PHONE..................580 933-4323
Johnnie R Smith, *Principal*
EMP: 3
SALES (est): 211K **Privately Held**
SIC: **2411** Logging

(G-11230)
LUNA LOGGING
156 Wading Bird Ln (74764-5263)
Rural Route 1 (74764-9801)
PHONE..................580 933-7517
Alvin Luna, *Owner*
EMP: 6
SALES (est): 440.7K **Privately Held**
SIC: **2411** Logging

(G-11231)
PINE CREEK SAW SHOP INC
267 Gray Jay Rd (74764-5231)
PHONE..................580 933-7376
Robert L Tally, *President*
Barbra Talley, *Vice Pres*
Tom Hunter, *Manager*
EMP: 6
SALES (est): 400K **Privately Held**
SIC: **3553** 7699 Bandsaws, woodworking; power tool repair

(G-11232)
TERRY HALL
Also Called: Terry's Acoustics
760 Chickadee Ln (74764-5487)
PHONE..................817 271-4838
Terry Hall, *Owner*
EMP: 35
SALES (est): 1.3MM **Privately Held**
SIC: **1742** 2452 Drywall; acoustical & ceiling work; panels & sections, prefabricated, wood

(G-11233)
VALLIANT LEADER INC
Also Called: Valliant Leader, The
119 N Dalton St (74764)
PHONE..................580 933-4570
Naomi Wilson, *President*
EMP: 4
SQ FT: 1,800
SALES (est): 280K **Privately Held**
SIC: **5994** 2711 Newsstand; commercial printing & newspaper publishing combined

(G-11234)
WILSON-MONROE PUBLISHING CO
Also Called: Valliant Leader
119 N Dalton St (74764)
P.O. Box 89 (74764-0089)
PHONE..................580 933-4579
Peter A Wilson, *President*
EMP: 4
SQ FT: 5,000
SALES (est): 87K **Privately Held**
SIC: **2711** 2752 5943 2791 Newspapers: publishing only, not printed on site; commercial printing, lithographic; office forms & supplies; typesetting; bookbinding & related work

Velma
Stephens County

(G-11235)
LELAND CHAPMAN
Also Called: Chapman Oil Co
Old Hwy 7 Industrial Park (73491)
P.O. Box 537 (73491-0537)
PHONE..................580 444-2511
Leland Chapman, *Owner*
EMP: 2
SQ FT: 10,000
SALES (est): 292.3K **Privately Held**
SIC: **1311** Oil shale mining

(G-11236)
PIXLEY COATING INC
Velma Industrial Park Dr (73491)
P.O. Box 536 (73491-0536)
PHONE..................580 444-2140
Charles Jenkins, *President*
EMP: 2 EST: 1970
SALES (est): 190.1K **Privately Held**
SIC: **3479** 2851 Coating of metals with plastic or resins; paints & allied products

Verden
Grady County

(G-11237)
LAKEWOOD ENERGY SOLUTIONS LLC
216 County Road 1290 (73092-8302)
PHONE..................918 392-9356
EMP: 4
SALES (corp-wide): 88.2MM **Privately Held**
SIC: **1311** Crude petroleum & natural gas
HQ: Lakewood Energy Solutions Llc
6655 S Lewis Ave Ste 200
Tulsa OK 74136
918 392-9356

Vian
Sequoyah County

(G-11238)
CUSTOM DESIGN FABRICATION LLC
450122 Highway 64 (74962-6046)
PHONE..................918 773-5691
John Ford,
EMP: 3
SALES: 100K **Privately Held**
SIC: **3441** Fabricated structural metal

(G-11239)
DAVES WELDING & DOCK SVC LLC
97113 S 4536 Rd (74962-5182)
PHONE..................918 773-5179
David E Nelson, *Owner*
EMP: 1
SALES (est): 33.2K **Privately Held**
SIC: **7692** Welding repair

Vici
Dewey County

(G-11240)
CLASSIC DESIGN & PRINT LLC
107 E Broadway (73859)
P.O. Box 573 (73859-0573)
PHONE..................580 216-0653
Alma Miramontes, *Principal*
EMP: 2 EST: 2014
SALES (est): 131.2K **Privately Held**
SIC: **2752** Commercial printing, lithographic

(G-11241)
DEWEY COUNTY
Also Called: Dewey County District 3
Hwy 60 E (73859)
PHONE..................580 995-3444
Melvin Salisbury, *Manager*
EMP: 14 **Privately Held**
WEB: www.deweycountyconservation.com
SIC: **3531** 9199 Road construction & maintenance machinery;
PA: Dewey County
Corner Of Broadway Rubel
Taloga OK 73667
580 328-5361

(G-11242)
EVERETTS WELDING & REPAIR
412 E Broadway (73859)
P.O. Box 143 (73859-0143)
PHONE..................580 995-4942
Leslie Hutchins, *President*
Buddy Hutchens, *Vice Pres*
EMP: 7
SALES (est): 401.6K **Privately Held**
SIC: **7692** Welding repair

(G-11243)
IOCHEM CORPORATION
3 Miles East Hwy 60 (73859)
P.O. Box 550 (73859-0550)
PHONE..................580 995-3198
Bruce Vaverka, *Systems Mgr*
EMP: 25
SALES (corp-wide): 11.2MM **Privately Held**
SIC: **2819** 2869 2833 Iodine, elemental; industrial organic chemicals; medicinals & botanicals
PA: Iochem Corporation
5801 Broadway Ext Ste 305
Oklahoma City OK 73118
405 848-8611

(G-11244)
KEY WELDING INC
608 N Wells St (73859)
P.O. Box 453 (73859-0453)
PHONE..................580 995-4278
Bill Key, *President*
EMP: 1
SALES (est): 230.3K **Privately Held**
SIC: **7692** Welding repair

(G-11245)
LAIRD WELDING LLC
61606 N 2070 Rd (73859-5260)
PHONE..................580 995-4495
Gary Laird,
Kameen Liard,
EMP: 1
SALES (est): 72.3K **Privately Held**
SIC: **7692** Welding repair

(G-11246)
MOSS WELDING LLC
204225 E County Road 57 (73859-5002)
PHONE..................580 216-1605
Charles Moss, *Principal*
EMP: 1
SALES (est): 33.4K **Privately Held**
SIC: **7692** Welding repair

Vinita
Craig County

(G-11247)
APAC OKLAHOMA INC
Also Called: APAC Central
26457 S 4460 Rd (74301)
P.O. Box 358 (74301-0358)
PHONE..................918 256-8397
Kris McClanahan, *President*
Jerry Kreymer, *President*
EMP: 20
SALES (est): 296.4K **Privately Held**
WEB: www.apaccentralinc.com
SIC: **2951** Asphalt paving mixtures & blocks

Vinita - Craig County (G-11248)

GEOGRAPHIC SECTION

(G-11248)
APAC-CENTRAL INC
26457 S 4460 Rd (74301)
P.O. Box 358 (74301-0358)
PHONE.................................918 256-7853
Jerry Kreymer, *President*
Robyn Lewis, *Sales Mgr*
EMP: 30
SALES (corp-wide): 30.6B Privately Held
WEB: www.contractorsofarkansas.com
SIC: 1411 2951 1422 Limestone, dimension-quarrying; asphalt paving mixtures & blocks; crushed & broken limestone
HQ: Apac-Central, Inc.
    755 E Millsap Rd
    Fayetteville AR 72703

(G-11249)
BOATRIGHT ENTERPRISES INC
665 Lori Ln (74301-5117)
PHONE.................................405 612-2473
EMP: 1
SALES (est): 25K Privately Held
SIC: 7692 Welding repair

(G-11250)
C AND D FASHION FLOORS LLC
423 S Wilson St (74301-4200)
PHONE.................................918 256-8018
Chris Hopwood,
Donni Hopwood,
EMP: 2
SALES (est): 110K Privately Held
SIC: 3069 Flooring, rubber: tile or sheet

(G-11251)
CP & C SERVICES
443954 E 340 Rd (74301-7790)
PHONE.................................918 497-6606
Clay Armstrong, *President*
EMP: 2
SALES (est): 237.9K Privately Held
SIC: 1389 Oil field services

(G-11252)
DAYLIGHT DONUTS
425 S Wilson St (74301-4245)
PHONE.................................918 256-6236
Sherry Cornwell, *Partner*
Rusty Cornwell, *Partner*
EMP: 3
SALES (est): 130K Privately Held
SIC: 5461 2051 Doughnuts; doughnuts, except frozen

(G-11253)
DIXON & SONS INC
441469 E 270 Rd (74301-6556)
PHONE.................................918 256-7455
E Ben Dixon, *President*
Ben L Dixon, *Vice Pres*
Steven B Dixon, *Vice Pres*
Marilyen Dixon, *Treasurer*
EMP: 5
SQ FT: 9,000
SALES (est): 290K Privately Held
SIC: 3599 7692 Machine & other job shop work; welding repair

(G-11254)
DIXON AUTO ENGINE MACHINE SHOP
27155 S 4380 Rd (74301-7916)
PHONE.................................918 256-6780
Terry Dixon, *Owner*
Debbie Dixon, *Analyst*
EMP: 1
SALES (est): 105.4K Privately Held
SIC: 7538 7699 7692 General automotive repair services; aircraft & heavy equipment repair services; welding repair

(G-11255)
DOCTORS OPTICAL SUPPLY INC (PA)
613 N Wilson St (74301-2223)
P.O. Box 926 (74301-0926)
PHONE.................................918 256-6416
James K Butner, *President*
Verna K Butner, *Corp Secy*
EMP: 8
SQ FT: 1,500
SALES (est): 1.3MM Privately Held
SIC: 5048 3211 Lenses, ophthalmic; frames, ophthalmic; contact lenses; spectacle glass

(G-11256)
EXCEL MANUFACTURING LLC
435426 E 300 Rd (74301-7979)
PHONE.................................918 418-9589
Adam Lima, *Principal*
EMP: 3
SALES (est): 179.6K Privately Held
SIC: 3999 Manufacturing industries

(G-11257)
FD PRODUCTS LLC
36154 S Highway 82 (74301-7974)
P.O. Box 960, Ketchum (74349-0960)
PHONE.................................918 698-1644
Peter Seitz, *President*
EMP: 1
SALES (est): 131.4K Privately Held
WEB: www.floatingdoor.us
SIC: 5084 3999 5199 Industrial machine parts; manufacturing industries; general merchandise, non-durable

(G-11258)
FLOYDS MACHINE SHOP
Also Called: Floyd's Automotive Machine
415 S Wilson St (74301-4245)
PHONE.................................918 256-8440
Gerald Floyd, *Owner*
EMP: 1
SALES: 150K Privately Held
SIC: 7538 3714 3561 3519 Engine rebuilding: automotive; motor vehicle parts & accessories; pumps & pumping equipment; internal combustion engines; machine shop, jobbing & repair

(G-11259)
HIGHNOON TACTICAL LLC
232 N Thompson St (74301-3128)
PHONE.................................918 801-8737
Kevin Barton, *Principal*
EMP: 3
SALES: 50K Privately Held
SIC: 3949 Cases, gun & rod (sporting equipment)

(G-11260)
HYPRO INC
1100 Industrial Ave (74301-4801)
PHONE.................................918 549-3600
Derek Giles, *Prdtn Mgr*
EMP: 45
SALES (corp-wide): 326.2MM Privately Held
SIC: 3599 Machine shop, jobbing & repair
PA: Hypro, Inc.
    600 S Jefferson St
    Waterford WI 53185
    262 534-5141

(G-11261)
IM STITCHED & STONED
431224 E 273 Rd (74301-7996)
PHONE.................................918 418-9107
EMP: 1
SALES (est): 40.3K Privately Held
SIC: 2395 Embroidery & art needlework

(G-11262)
INMAN WELDING SERVICE
23580 S 4430 Rd (74301-5520)
PHONE.................................918 323-0022
David Inman, *Principal*
EMP: 1
SALES (est): 31.2K Privately Held
SIC: 7692 Welding repair

(G-11263)
J DUKE LOGAN FAMILY TRUST
101 S Wilson St (74301-3729)
P.O. Box 558 (74301-0558)
PHONE.................................918 256-7511
Leonard Logan, *Trustee*
EMP: 1 EST: 2000
SALES (est): 35.1K Privately Held
SIC: 0971 2411 0212 0179 Animal hunting & trapping, commercial; timber, cut at logging camp; beef cattle except feedlots; fruits & tree nuts

(G-11264)
MICHAEL R WILLIAMS
Also Called: Williams 3g Ranch
33784 S 4440 Rd (74301-7042)
PHONE.................................918 418-9344
Michael Williams, *Owner*
Lisa Williams, *Bookkeeper*
EMP: 1
SALES (est): 60K Privately Held
SIC: 3523 Harvesters, fruit, vegetable, tobacco, etc.

(G-11265)
OKLAHOMA DEPT PUBLIC SAFETY
Also Called: Oklahoma Highway Patrol
441276 E Highway 60 (74301-6558)
PHONE.................................918 256-3388
Jack McCoy, *Principal*
EMP: 27 Privately Held
WEB: www.dps.state.ok.us
SIC: 3711 9229 Patrol wagons (motor vehicles), assembly of; buses, all types, assembly of;
HQ: Oklahoma Dept Of Public Safety
    3600 N Martin Luther Knl
    Oklahoma City OK 73111

(G-11266)
OMNI WATER CONSULTANTS INC
1580 Industrial Ave (74301-4803)
P.O. Box 891 (74301-0891)
PHONE.................................918 323-0001
Ed Delozer, *President*
Cale Delozier, *Prdtn Mgr*
EMP: 10
SALES (est): 1.9MM Privately Held
SIC: 3589 Water treatment equipment, industrial

(G-11267)
PHOENIX MINING COMPANY
310 S Scraper St (74301-4248)
P.O. Box 384 (74301-0384)
PHONE.................................918 256-7873
Robert Hartley, *President*
Jim Brakefield, *Vice Pres*
EMP: 60
SQ FT: 100
SALES (est): 8.8MM Privately Held
SIC: 1221 Bituminous coal & lignite-surface mining

(G-11268)
PROMETHEUS PUBLICATIONS LLC
125 E Euclid (74301-4643)
P.O. Box 972 (74301-0972)
PHONE.................................717 460-4881
Brian L Jackson, *Principal*
EMP: 1
SALES (est): 37.5K Privately Held
SIC: 2741 Miscellaneous publishing

(G-11269)
RED BUD GLASS INC
733 Maple Brook Ln (74301-6726)
PHONE.................................405 685-3331
Jan Voskamp, *President*
▲ EMP: 50
SQ FT: 60,000
SALES (est): 7.9MM Privately Held
SIC: 3231 Insulating glass: made from purchased glass

(G-11270)
RMH SURVEY LLC
41755 E Highway 60 (74301)
PHONE.................................918 927-8868
Ralph Herman, *Principal*
EMP: 3
SALES (est): 144.6K Privately Held
SIC: 8713 1389 8711 9651 Photogrammetric engineering; testing, measuring, surveying & analysis services; construction & civil engineering; licensing & permits for professional occupations, government; systems analysis & engineering consulting services

(G-11271)
VINITA PRINTING CO INC
Also Called: Vinita Daily Journal
140 S Wilson St (74301-3730)
P.O. Box 328 (74301-0328)
PHONE.................................918 256-6422
John Link, *President*
David Burgess, *Manager*
EMP: 44
SALES (est): 2.3MM
SALES (corp-wide): 4.5MM Privately Held
WEB: www.vdjonline.com
SIC: 2711 2759 2752 2791 Newspapers, publishing & printing; letterpress printing; commercial printing, offset; typesetting
PA: Weatherford News, Inc.
    118 S Broadway St
    Weatherford OK 73096
    580 772-3301

(G-11272)
WOODSHED
111 N 1st St (74301-3205)
PHONE.................................918 256-9868
Rick Wood, *Principal*
EMP: 20
SALES (corp-wide): 3.5MM Privately Held
WEB: www.vinita.com
SIC: 2499 Applicators, wood
PA: The Woodshed
    998 4000 Rd
    Edna KS 67342
    620 922-7200

(G-11273)
ZARA GROUP INC
32244 S 4470 Rd (74301-7019)
P.O. Box 987, Ketchum (74349-0987)
PHONE.................................918 782-4473
Harold Maxwell, *President*
EMP: 10
SQ FT: 35,000
SALES: 477K Privately Held
SIC: 2439 2426 2431 Structural wood members; hardwood dimension & flooring mills; moldings, wood: unfinished & prefinished

Wagoner
Wagoner County

(G-11274)
AUTOMTIVE CTING SPECIALIST INC
22493 State Highway 51 (74467-9119)
PHONE.................................918 698-1560
April Parnell, *President*
Mark Parnell, *Principal*
EMP: 3
SALES (est): 202.4K Privately Held
SIC: 3499 Fabricated metal products

(G-11275)
BEAR PAW MANUFACTURING
72149 S 322 Way (74467-7361)
PHONE.................................918 637-4775
Louis Twist, *CEO*
EMP: 8
SALES (est): 321.5K Privately Held
SIC: 3999 3569 Manufacturing industries; general industrial machinery

(G-11276)
BERKSHIRE HATHAWAY INC
Also Called: Coweta American
221 E Cherokee St (74467-4703)
PHONE.................................918 486-4444
Christy Wheilan, *Manager*
EMP: 3
SALES (corp-wide): 327.2B Publicly Held
SIC: 2752 2711 Commercial printing, lithographic; newspapers
PA: Berkshire Hathaway Inc.
    3555 Farnam St Ste 1140
    Omaha NE 68131
    402 346-1400

GEOGRAPHIC SECTION

(G-11277)
BERKSHIRE HATHAWAY INC
Also Called: Wagner Tribune
221 E Cherokee St (74467-4703)
PHONE.................................918 485-5505
Bill Retherford, *President*
EMP: 2
SALES (corp-wide): 327.2B **Publicly Held**
SIC: 2711 Newspapers
PA: Berkshire Hathaway Inc.
3555 Farnam St Ste 1140
Omaha NE 68131
402 346-1400

(G-11278)
BOYD WELDING INC
605 Sw 15th St (74467-7813)
PHONE.................................918 485-3534
Russell Boyd, *President*
Caroline Boyd, *Corp Secy*
Evan Boyd, *Vice Pres*
EMP: 4
SQ FT: 2,000
SALES (est): 302.2K **Privately Held**
SIC: 7692 1799 Welding repair; welding on site

(G-11279)
DUCT MATE INDUSTRIES
301 Se 15th St (74467-7917)
PHONE.................................918 340-5122
EMP: 3
SALES (est): 227.4K **Privately Held**
SIC: 3999 Manufacturing industries

(G-11280)
ELASTOMER SPECIALTIES INC
25981 State Highway 51 (74467-8676)
PHONE.................................800 786-4244
Orlin W Emmons, *Branch Mgr*
EMP: 15
SALES (est): 3.3MM
SALES (corp-wide): 2.9MM **Privately Held**
WEB: www.elastomer.com
SIC: 3089 Injection molding of plastics
PA: Elastomer Specialties, Inc.
2210 S Highway 69
Wagoner OK 74467
918 485-0276

(G-11281)
ELASTOMER SPECIALTIES INC (PA)
2210 S Highway 69 (74467-9357)
P.O. Box 323, Broken Arrow (74013-0323)
PHONE.................................918 485-0276
Orlin W Emmons, *President*
Glenda M Emmons, *Principal*
Richard A Willis, *Principal*
Darrin Emmons, *Vice Pres*
Kerrie Montgomery, *Treasurer*
EMP: 15 EST: 1979
SQ FT: 31,000
SALES (est): 2.9MM **Privately Held**
SIC: 3089 3599 1799 Injection molding of plastics; machine shop, jobbing & repair; coating, caulking & weather, water & fireproofing

(G-11282)
ELASTOMER SPECIALTIES INC
Also Called: Gator Hyde Bedliners
902 S Adams Ave (74467-7514)
PHONE.................................918 485-0276
Darin Emmons, *VP Opers*
Orlin Emmons, *Branch Mgr*
EMP: 4
SALES (est): 561.5K
SALES (corp-wide): 2.9MM **Privately Held**
SIC: 3711 Trucks, pickup, assembly of
PA: Elastomer Specialties, Inc.
2210 S Highway 69
Wagoner OK 74467
918 485-0276

(G-11283)
ET INDUSTRIES LLC
603 W Cherokee St (74467-4611)
PHONE.................................918 485-3374
EMP: 2 EST: 2010
SALES (est): 72K **Privately Held**
SIC: 3999 Mfg Misc Products

(G-11284)
HOFFMAN ESSENTIALS
71559 S 230 Rd (74467-6936)
P.O. Box 1126 (74477-1126)
PHONE.................................918 485-4679
Teri Hoffman, *Principal*
EMP: 2
SALES (est): 123.4K **Privately Held**
WEB: www.hoffmanessentials.com
SIC: 2844 Toilet preparations

(G-11285)
LAKESIDE POLARIS INC
33508 State Highway 51 (74467-3707)
PHONE.................................918 485-2887
Arthur Brown, *President*
EMP: 3
SALES (est): 231.1K **Privately Held**
SIC: 7549 3826 Automotive services; polariscopes

(G-11286)
LEGACY METALCRAFT LLC
1209 Sw 9th St (74467-6821)
PHONE.................................918 612-0001
Matthew Enlow,
Miscy Enlow,
EMP: 8
SALES (est): 50.9K **Privately Held**
SIC: 2511 2514 Wood household furniture; metal household furniture

(G-11287)
MRC GLOBAL (US) INC
Also Called: Labarge Rolled & Welded Plant
1300 N Labarge Ave (74467)
PHONE.................................918 485-9511
Pat Condry, *Manager*
EMP: 7 **Publicly Held**
SIC: 3317 3498 3312 Steel pipe & tubes; fabricated pipe & fittings; blast furnaces & steel mills
HQ: Mrc Global (Us) Inc.
1301 Mckinney St Ste 2300
Houston TX 77010
877 294-7574

(G-11288)
MUELLER SUPPLY COMPANY INC
2110 S Highway 69 (74467-9311)
PHONE.................................918 485-2034
Mark Richards, *Branch Mgr*
EMP: 8
SALES (corp-wide): 189.5MM **Privately Held**
SIC: 3444 Sheet metalwork
PA: Mueller Supply Company, Inc.
1913 Hutchins Ave
Ballinger TX 76821
325 365-3555

(G-11289)
RICHARDS PERFORMANCE MACHINE
126 N Main St (74467-4426)
PHONE.................................918 485-6393
Richard Hartsell, *Owner*
EMP: 1
SALES (est): 87.8K **Privately Held**
SIC: 3599 7539 Machine shop, jobbing & repair; machine shop, automotive

(G-11290)
SOCK MONKEY BIZZ LLC
70076 S 336 Ct (74467-8293)
PHONE.................................918 462-7392
Laura Haddock, *Principal*
EMP: 3
SALES (est): 84K **Privately Held**
SIC: 2252 Socks

(G-11291)
SUPER DAVES POWER SPORTS
25981 State Highway 51 (74467-8676)
PHONE.................................918 485-9205
Dave Wilmer, *Owner*
EMP: 1
SALES (est): 93.5K **Privately Held**
SIC: 3799 All terrain vehicles (ATV)

(G-11292)
TECHNICAL MANUFACTURING INC
305 Se 11th St (74467-7513)
PHONE.................................918 485-0380
J R Marks, *President*
▲ EMP: 17
SQ FT: 12,000
SALES (est): 4MM **Privately Held**
WEB: www.millenniumwireline.com
SIC: 3713 3532 Truck bodies & parts; drills & drilling equipment, mining (except oil & gas)

(G-11293)
TOMMY BIFFLE LAKESIDE POLARIS
33508 State Highway 51 (74467-3707)
PHONE.................................918 485-2887
Tommy Biffle, *Principal*
Sharon Biffle, *Principal*
EMP: 6
SALES (est): 950K **Privately Held**
SIC: 3799 All terrain vehicles (ATV)

(G-11294)
TULSA HOSE & FITTINGS INC
305 Se 11th St (74467-7513)
PHONE.................................918 485-0348
Charlie Harder, *General Mgr*
EMP: 3
SALES (est): 348.7K **Privately Held**
SIC: 3052 Plastic hose

(G-11295)
UNARCO INDUSTRIES LLC (DH)
400 Se 15th St (74467-7900)
PHONE.................................918 485-9531
Kenneth Bush, *President*
Robert Musslewhite, *CFO*
Robert Webb, *Admin Sec*
◆ EMP: 163
SQ FT: 560,000
SALES (est): 80.2MM
SALES (corp-wide): 327.2B **Publicly Held**
SIC: 3496 Woven wire products

(G-11296)
UNITED PROCESS SYSTEMS CORP
Also Called: Unipro
68912 S 313 Ct (74467-8226)
PHONE.................................918 462-1143
Carol Hixon, *Principal*
▲ EMP: 6
SQ FT: 1,200
SALES (est): 866.3K **Privately Held**
SIC: 5084 3533 Oil well machinery, equipment & supplies; oil & gas field machinery

Wakita
Grant County

(G-11297)
BROCKUS CREAT HANDCRAFTED JWLY
78262 Jefferson Rd (73771-5035)
PHONE.................................580 594-2215
CJ Brockus-Rapp, *Principal*
EMP: 3
SALES (est): 160.7K **Privately Held**
SIC: 3961 Costume jewelry

(G-11298)
HERALD WAKITA
104 W Main St (73771)
PHONE.................................580 594-2440
Ken Kiser, *Owner*
EMP: 2
SQ FT: 2,700
SALES (est): 83.8K **Privately Held**
SIC: 2711 Newspapers: publishing only, not printed on site

Walters
Cotton County

(G-11299)
ALFRED N SMITH
Also Called: Al-S Pump & Supply
176976 Highway 65 (73572-3899)
P.O. Box 3 (73572-0003)
PHONE.................................580 875-3317
Alfred N Smith, *Owner*
EMP: 1
SALES: 100K **Privately Held**
SIC: 1389 Oil field services

(G-11300)
FLANAGAN ENERGY
217 N Broadway St (73572-1225)
P.O. Box 5 (73572-0005)
PHONE.................................580 357-1227
EMP: 1
SALES (est): 110K **Privately Held**
SIC: 1382 Oil & Gas Exploration & Production

(G-11301)
HATHAWAY & SIMPSON
528 W Missouri St (73572-1022)
PHONE.................................580 875-3177
Gary Hathaway, *Partner*
Kent Simpson, *Partner*
EMP: 4
SQ FT: 14,000
SALES (est): 271.3K **Privately Held**
SIC: 1799 6552 7692 Welding on site; subdividers & developers; welding repair

(G-11302)
HERALD PUBLISHING CO (PA)
Also Called: Walters Herald
112 S Broadway St (73572-2033)
P.O. Box 247 (73572-0247)
PHONE.................................580 875-3326
Brett Wesner, *President*
Blaine Wesner, *Principal*
Ken Wesner, *Principal*
Scott Wesner, *Principal*
EMP: 3
SQ FT: 2,500
SALES (est): 280.3K **Privately Held**
WEB: www.waltersherald.com
SIC: 2711 2791 2752 Newspapers: publishing only, not printed on site; typesetting; commercial printing, lithographic

(G-11303)
TONGS
129 W Missouri St (73572-1243)
PHONE.................................580 875-2053
James Kim, *Owner*
EMP: 2
SALES (est): 141.3K **Privately Held**
SIC: 1389 Construction, repair & dismantling services

(G-11304)
WALTERS OILWELL SERVICE INC
623 N 3rd St (73572-1451)
P.O. Box 342 (73572-0342)
PHONE.................................580 875-2601
Donald Ray Smith, *President*
Connie Smith, *Corp Secy*
Richard Smith, *Vice Pres*
EMP: 5
SALES (est): 554.3K **Privately Held**
SIC: 1389 Servicing oil & gas wells

Wanette
Pottawatomie County

(G-11305)
HIX INDUSTRIES
Rr 2 Box 303a (74878)
PHONE.................................405 640-6980
Nicholas Hicks, *Owner*
EMP: 1
SALES: 100K **Privately Held**
SIC: 3999 Manufacturing industries

Wardville
Pittsburg County

(G-11306)
CLARK RHYNE
Also Called: Rhyneco
726 E 131 West Hwy (74576-5000)
PHONE..................................918 874-3563
Clark Rhyne, *Partner*
James Rhyne, *Partner*
Samuel Rhyne, *Partner*
Tod Rhyne, *Partner*
EMP: 5
SALES (est): 688.2K **Privately Held**
SIC: 3537 Trucks, tractors, loaders, carriers & similar equipment

Warner
Muskogee County

(G-11307)
DC EXTERIORS & MORE LLC
Also Called: DC Metal Fab
101 Warmac St (74469)
P.O. Box 648 (74469-0648)
PHONE..................................918 231-7303
Brandon Drake, *Mng Member*
Jason Cantwell,
EMP: 1
SALES: 75K **Privately Held**
SIC: 3441 Fabricated structural metal

(G-11308)
PATTERSON MACHINE SHOP
3805 E 153rd St S (74469-2604)
PHONE..................................918 463-3600
Kendall Patterson, *Owner*
EMP: 2
SALES (est): 81.4K **Privately Held**
SIC: 3599 Machine shop, jobbing & repair

Warr Acres
Oklahoma County

(G-11309)
4 B HUNTING INDUSTRIES LLC
6508 N Grove Ave (73132-7719)
PHONE..................................405 823-9100
Daniel Banta Mason, *Administration*
EMP: 1
SALES (est): 42.8K **Privately Held**
SIC: 3999 Manufacturing industries

(G-11310)
50TH XPRESS MART
5025 N Meridian Ave (73112-2222)
PHONE..................................405 491-7381
Eric Mack, *Principal*
EMP: 1
SALES (est): 60.9K **Privately Held**
SIC: 2741 5411 Miscellaneous publishing; convenience stores

(G-11311)
ACCUTECH LABORATORIES
5565 Nw Expressway (73132-5230)
PHONE..................................405 603-2956
Larry Demaio, *Principal*
EMP: 2
SALES (est): 90.6K **Privately Held**
SIC: 8734 5048 3827 Testing laboratories; optometric equipment & supplies; optical instruments & lenses

(G-11312)
ACCUTECH LABORATORIES INC
5565 Nw Expressway (73132-5230)
P.O. Box 271505, Oklahoma City (73137-1505)
PHONE..................................405 946-6446
Larry Demaio, *President*
Regina Demaio, *Corp Secy*
Steve Hopper, *Vice Pres*
EMP: 15
SALES (est): 1.9MM **Privately Held**
SIC: 5048 3229 Lenses, ophthalmic; frames, ophthalmic; pressed & blown glass

(G-11313)
BIG RED SHOP INC (PA)
5104 N Macarthur Blvd (73122-6124)
PHONE..................................405 495-5551
David Smith, *President*
EMP: 6 **EST:** 1967
SQ FT: 1,800
SALES (est): 562.8K **Privately Held**
SIC: 5699 5947 2396 2395 Sports apparel; novelties; automotive & apparel trimmings; pleating & stitching

(G-11314)
BOATMAN MARINE CANVAS
5924 Seminole Rd (73132-5705)
PHONE..................................405 628-7844
Michael Boatman, *Principal*
EMP: 1
SALES (est): 46.5K **Privately Held**
WEB: www.boatmanmarinecanvas.com
SIC: 2211 Canvas

(G-11315)
CLEMENTS EXPLORATION CO
5601 Nw 72nd St Ste 354 (73132-5922)
PHONE..................................405 722-3100
Paul Clements, *President*
Fredda Cohn, *Corp Secy*
EMP: 3 **EST:** 1972
SQ FT: 1,000
SALES (est): 410K **Privately Held**
SIC: 1311 Crude petroleum production; natural gas production

(G-11316)
COLLINS METAL COMPANY INC
4710 N Grove Ave (73122-5115)
PHONE..................................405 373-3309
Lynn D Collins, *President*
Janice Collins, *Vice Pres*
Tim Bricker,
Jeff Cavaness,
EMP: 3
SQ FT: 525
SALES (est): 650K **Privately Held**
SIC: 5051 3471 Steel; copper products; copper; aluminum bars, rods, ingots, sheets, pipes, plates, etc.; plating & polishing

(G-11317)
CYNERGY SOFTWARE CORP LLC
5770 Nw Expressway (73132-5241)
PHONE..................................405 603-2953
EMP: 2
SALES (est): 190K **Privately Held**
SIC: 7372 Prepackaged software

(G-11318)
DEALERS MARKET
4409 N State St (73122-4314)
PHONE..................................405 789-6455
EMP: 2
SALES (est): 11.3K **Privately Held**
SIC: 2721 Magazines: publishing only, not printed on site

(G-11319)
FRANK G LOVE ENVELOPES INC
5601 Nw 72nd St Ste 342 (73132-5922)
PHONE..................................405 720-9177
Randy Ritchie, *Branch Mgr*
EMP: 2
SALES (corp-wide): 33.9MM **Privately Held**
SIC: 2677 Envelopes
PA: Frank G. Love Envelopes, Inc.
  10733 E Ute St
  Tulsa OK 74116
  214 637-5900

(G-11320)
GOLD STRIKE CHILI
5901 Nw 41st St (73122-3004)
PHONE..................................405 606-1819
Ken Brown, *Manager*
EMP: 2
SALES (est): 62.3K **Privately Held**
SIC: 2099 Food preparations

(G-11321)
H GELLAR
5830 Nw Expressway (73132-5239)
PHONE..................................617 834-0602
H Gellar, *Owner*
EMP: 1
SALES (est): 43.1K **Privately Held**
SIC: 2099 Food preparations

(G-11322)
HEMISPHERES (PA)
5561 Nw Expressway (73132-5230)
PHONE..................................405 773-8410
Steve Green, *President*
EMP: 2
SALES (est): 480.6K **Privately Held**
SIC: 7389 5713 2519 Interior designer; carpets; household furniture, except wood or metal: upholstered

(G-11323)
J THOMPSON CUSTOM JEWELERS
5770 Nw Expressway # 101 (73132-5241)
PHONE..................................405 495-6610
Jeff Thomson, *President*
EMP: 6
SQ FT: 1,250
SALES (est): 638K **Privately Held**
SIC: 3911 5094 Jewelry, precious metal; precious stones & metals

(G-11324)
JEWELERS BENCH
4716 N Macarthur Blvd (73122-5012)
PHONE..................................405 495-1800
Valerie Monday, *Owner*
EMP: 2
SQ FT: 870
SALES (est): 152.9K **Privately Held**
SIC: 5944 3911 Jewelry, precious stones & precious metals; jewelry, precious metal

(G-11325)
NORTHWEST WELDING INC
5717 Nw 64th St (73132-7754)
PHONE..................................405 621-0201
Timothy Benner, *President*
EMP: 1
SALES (est): 124.4K **Privately Held**
SIC: 7692 Welding repair

(G-11326)
PRINTER STORE LLC
Also Called: Oklahoma Document Solutions
5107 N Macarthur Blvd (73122-6116)
PHONE..................................405 782-0755
EMP: 3
SQ FT: 1,700
SALES: 250K **Privately Held**
SIC: 2759 Commercial Printing

(G-11327)
RED RIVER IMAGING LP
5601 Nw 72nd St Ste 232 (73132-5932)
PHONE..................................405 308-4545
Scott McKenzie, *Managing Prtnr*
EMP: 2
SALES (est): 2MM **Privately Held**
SIC: 1382 Oil & gas exploration services

(G-11328)
ROHLMAN WELDING SERVICE INC
5713 Nw 46th St (73122-5101)
PHONE..................................405 420-4033
Samuel Rohlman, *President*
EMP: 5
SALES (est): 227.9K **Privately Held**
WEB: www.rohlmanwelding.com
SIC: 7692 Welding repair

(G-11329)
SIGNS 405 LLC
4307 N Meridian Ave (73112-2458)
PHONE..................................405 470-1616
Robel Arreaga, *Owner*
EMP: 1
SALES (est): 46K **Privately Held**
SIC: 3993 Signs & advertising specialties

(G-11330)
WHITE GORDON LBR CO OF LINDSAY
Also Called: Gordon White Lumber
5801 Nw 36th St (73122-2102)
P.O. Box 75698, Oklahoma City (73147-0698)
PHONE..................................405 946-9032
Henry Bockus, *Manager*
EMP: 7
SALES (est): 1.1MM
SALES (corp-wide): 2.7MM **Privately Held**
SIC: 2421 2426 Lumber: rough, sawed or planed; hardwood dimension & flooring mills
PA: White Gordon Lumber Co Of Lindsay Inc
  302 E Cherokee St
  Lindsay OK 73052
  405 756-2035

(G-11331)
WOLF SOFTWARE GROUP CO
6117 Covington Ln (73132-6402)
P.O. Box 32635, Oklahoma City (73123-0835)
PHONE..................................405 721-0577
Timothy Wolf, *Principal*
EMP: 2
SALES (est): 142.9K **Privately Held**
SIC: 7372 Prepackaged software

Washington
Mcclain County

(G-11332)
ACME CUSTOM WELDING
27567 State Highway 74 (73093-4731)
P.O. Box 722433, Norman (73070-8844)
PHONE..................................405 288-0187
Victor Sobrado, *Owner*
EMP: 1
SALES: 200K **Privately Held**
SIC: 7692 Welding repair

(G-11333)
BELLER BORING BACKHOE L
22901 Canary Ln (73093-4450)
PHONE..................................405 288-6638
Rayford E Beller, *Principal*
EMP: 2
SALES (est): 225K **Privately Held**
SIC: 3531 Backhoes

(G-11334)
COIL CHEM LLC (PA)
2103 E Ladd Rd (73093-9188)
PHONE..................................405 445-5545
Jerry Noles, *CEO*
Troy Bishop, *Principal*
Sheri Vickery, *Vice Pres*
Jason Watts, *Vice Pres*
EMP: 14
SQ FT: 5,000
SALES: 30.2MM **Privately Held**
SIC: 5169 5999 2899 Industrial chemicals; cleaning equipment & supplies; water treating compounds

(G-11335)
MORTON BUILDINGS INC
527 E Center Rd (73093-9021)
P.O. Box 720730, Norman (73070-4562)
PHONE..................................405 288-1031
Steve Meek, *Sales/Mktg Mgr*
EMP: 20
SALES (corp-wide): 462.5MM **Privately Held**
SIC: 3448 Prefabricated metal buildings
PA: Morton Buildings, Inc.
  252 W Adams St
  Morton IL 61550
  800 447-7436

(G-11336)
SANDY CREEK MILLWORKS INC
5475 Se 12th Ave (73093-4765)
PHONE..................................405 288-0670
John David Price, *President*
EMP: 1
SALES (est): 110K **Privately Held**
SIC: 2431 Millwork

GEOGRAPHIC SECTION

Waurika - Jefferson County (G-11363)

(G-11337)
STEEL THINKING INC
27699 Western Ave (73093-4531)
PHONE.................405 485-2204
Heather Queen, *President*
Ron Queen, *Vice Pres*
EMP: 10
SQ FT: 10,000
SALES: 1.6MM **Privately Held**
SIC: 3441 Fabricated structural metal

(G-11338)
SWH CONSTRUCTION LLC
468 Sw 24th Ave (73093-4493)
PHONE.................405 317-0663
Brett Adkins, *Mng Member*
EMP: 12
SALES (est): 82.7K **Privately Held**
SIC: 1521 3531 Single-family housing construction; road construction & maintenance machinery

Watonga
Blaine County

(G-11339)
AT & L ENERGY LLC
505 W Main St (73772-4235)
P.O. Box 29 (73772-0029)
PHONE.................580 623-7265
Mike Mahoney, *Mng Member*
Rick Cowan,
EMP: 1
SALES (est): 54.4K **Privately Held**
SIC: 1381 Drilling oil & gas wells

(G-11340)
B & W READY MIX LLC
Hwy 33 E (73772)
P.O. Box 26 (73772-0026)
PHONE.................580 623-5059
Larry Bernhardt, *Co-Owner*
Alan Bernhardt, *Mng Member*
EMP: 5
SQ FT: 500
SALES (est): 606.6K **Privately Held**
SIC: 3273 1521 Ready-mixed concrete; new construction, single-family houses

(G-11341)
BARNES WELDING LLC
79317 N 2560 Rd (73772-5165)
PHONE.................580 774-5491
Vince Barnes, *Principal*
EMP: 1
SALES (est): 25K **Privately Held**
SIC: 7692 Welding repair

(G-11342)
BLANKENSHIP ROUSTABOUT
1710 W Russworm Dr (73772-4851)
P.O. Box 674 (73772-0674)
PHONE.................580 791-0237
Rowdy Blankenship, *Owner*
EMP: 2
SALES (est): 67.5K **Privately Held**
SIC: 1389 Roustabout service

(G-11343)
CASS HOLDINGS LLC
500 E Russworm Dr (73772-5026)
PHONE.................405 359-5053
Christopher Nighbor, *Principal*
EMP: 9
SALES (corp-wide): 2.4MM **Privately Held**
SIC: 2851 2821 5162 Lacquers, varnishes, enamels & other coatings; plastics materials & resins; epoxy resins; polyesters; plastics materials & basic shapes
PA: Cass Holdings, L.L.C.
311 Nw 122nd St Ste 100
Oklahoma City OK 73114
405 755-8448

(G-11344)
DAVID ADKINSON
Also Called: Dave's Welding
Rr 1 (73772)
PHONE.................580 623-7301
David Adkinson, *Owner*
EMP: 1

SALES (est): 66.8K **Privately Held**
SIC: 7692 Welding repair

(G-11345)
DIAMOND GYPSUM LLC
E0790 Rd (73772)
PHONE.................580 623-2868
Clay Hufnagel, *President*
EMP: 6
SQ FT: 500
SALES (est): 1MM
SALES (corp-wide): 1.7B **Publicly Held**
SIC: 1499 3275 Gypsum mining; gypsum products
HQ: Harrison Gypsum, Llc
1550 Double C Dr
Norman OK 73069
405 366-9500

(G-11346)
E J R ENTERPISES LLC
802 N Noble Ave (73772-2228)
P.O. Box 411 (73772-0411)
PHONE.................580 623-0051
Ed Roberson,
Sha Stephens,
EMP: 6
SALES: 15MM **Privately Held**
SIC: 1389 Oil field services; mud service, oil field drilling

(G-11347)
HG SCREEN PRINTING
201 Rice Dr (73772-1215)
PHONE.................580 623-3638
Karen Kathleen Harris, *Principal*
EMP: 2
SALES (est): 108.9K **Privately Held**
SIC: 2752 Commercial printing, lithographic

(G-11348)
JOHN THOMPSON ENTERPRISES INC (PA)
Also Called: J & M Pipe & Supply
W Highway 33 (73772)
Rural Route 1 Box 193 (73772-9796)
PHONE.................580 623-5820
John Thompson, *President*
Miranda Thompson, *Corp Secy*
EMP: 19
SQ FT: 12,000
SALES (est): 6.9MM **Privately Held**
SIC: 5084 1389 Oil well machinery, equipment & supplies; roustabout service

(G-11349)
S & J MACHINE INC
E On Hwy 33 (73772)
PHONE.................580 623-8130
Brenda Bailey, *President*
EMP: 3
SQ FT: 3,300
SALES (est): 370.3K **Privately Held**
SIC: 3599 1799 Machine shop, jobbing & repair; welding on site

(G-11350)
TESTCO INC
1 Half Mile W On Hwy 33 (73772)
P.O. Box 589 (73772-0589)
PHONE.................580 623-4900
Patricia Rother, *President*
Matt Crum, *General Mgr*
Steven Rother, *Opers Mgr*
Tara Cowan, *Office Mgr*
Joe Compton, *Manager*
EMP: 13
SQ FT: 4,000
SALES (est): 1.5MM **Privately Held**
SIC: 1389 Oil field services

(G-11351)
W FLYING INC
Also Called: Flying W Livestock Equipment
922 W Russworm Rd (73772-4829)
P.O. Box 565 (73772-0565)
PHONE.................580 623-5566
Kyle Widney, *President*
Darlene Widney, *President*
Laura Widney, *Corp Secy*
EMP: 10
SQ FT: 2,000
SALES: 1MM **Privately Held**
SIC: 3523 Barn, silo, poultry, dairy & livestock machinery

(G-11352)
WATONGA MACHINE & STEEL WORKS
Also Called: Keen Development Co
12855 Us Highway 270 (73772-5808)
PHONE.................580 623-5830
Barbara Keen, *Owner*
▲ **EMP:** 6 **EST:** 1962
SQ FT: 6,000
SALES (est): 849K **Privately Held**
SIC: 3599 6512 7692 Machine shop, jobbing & repair; nonresidential building operators; welding repair

(G-11353)
WATONGA PRINTING & OFFICE SUPS
108 E Main St (73772-3831)
PHONE.................580 623-4989
Curtis White, *President*
Maudie White, *Treasurer*
Rita White, *Admin Sec*
EMP: 3
SQ FT: 2,000
SALES (est): 301.5K **Privately Held**
SIC: 2752 5943 5942 2759 Commercial printing, offset; office forms & supplies; books, religious; commercial printing

(G-11354)
WATONGA REPUBLICAN INC
Also Called: Hinton Record
104 E Main St (73772-3831)
P.O. Box 30 (73772-0030)
PHONE.................580 623-4922
Chester Tim Curtin, *President*
Norita Curtin, *Treasurer*
Darrel Rice, *Admin Sec*
EMP: 8 **EST:** 1892
SQ FT: 12,250
SALES: 375K **Privately Held**
WEB: www.thewatongarepublican.com
SIC: 2711 2791 Newspapers: publishing only, not printed on site; typesetting

Watson
Mccurtain County

(G-11355)
KENNETH D JEWELL
Also Called: Kenneth D Jewell Logging
1948 Plunketville Rd (74963)
P.O. Box 120 (74963-0120)
PHONE.................580 244-7450
Kenneth D Jewell, *Owner*
EMP: 5
SALES (est): 453.6K **Privately Held**
SIC: 2411 Logging

Watts
Adair County

(G-11356)
GRAPHIC EXCURSIONS
1576 S Highway 59 (74964-5039)
PHONE.................918 422-5318
Mike Adkins, *Owner*
EMP: 2
SALES (est): 83K **Privately Held**
SIC: 3993 Signs & advertising specialties

(G-11357)
GRIFFIN INDUSTRIES LLC
Also Called: Bakery Feeds
Hwy 59 (74964)
P.O. Box 209 (74964-0209)
PHONE.................918 422-4790
Ron Winter, *Manager*
Carroll Nelson, *Manager*
EMP: 25
SALES (corp-wide): 3.3B **Publicly Held**
SIC: 2077 2048 Animal & marine fats & oils; prepared feeds
HQ: Griffin Industries Llc
4221 Alexandria Pike
Cold Spring KY 41076
859 781-2010

(G-11358)
TIGHT WIRE FENCE LLC
59168 S 4720 Rd (74964-6862)
PHONE.................479 220-1171
Phillip Vandyke, *Principal*
EMP: 2
SALES (est): 150.3K **Privately Held**
SIC: 3496 Fencing, made from purchased wire

Waukomis
Garfield County

(G-11359)
BASIC ENERGY SERVICES INC
10830 S Oakwood Rd (73773-0630)
P.O. Box 175 (73773-0175)
PHONE.................580 758-1234
Johnny McConnell, *Manager*
EMP: 12
SALES (corp-wide): 567.2MM **Publicly Held**
SIC: 1389 Oil field services
PA: Basic Energy Services, Inc.
801 Cherry St Unit 2
Fort Worth TX 76102
817 334-4100

(G-11360)
TRI RESOURCES INC
Also Called: Dynegy
Rr 1 Box 112 (73773-9726)
PHONE.................580 493-2249
Danny Bull, *Manager*
EMP: 43 **Publicly Held**
SIC: 1311 Crude petroleum & natural gas
HQ: Tri Resources Inc.
811 Louisiana St Ste 2100
Houston TX 77002
713 584-1000

(G-11361)
WELDING INDUSTRY SERVICES LLC
307 Highland Dr (73773-9518)
PHONE.................580 479-7068
Douglas Castleberry Jr, *Principal*
EMP: 1
SALES (est): 30K **Privately Held**
SIC: 7692 Welding repair

Waurika
Jefferson County

(G-11362)
D-K METAL FORM COMPANY INC
122 W D Ave (73573-2226)
P.O. Box 266 (73573-0266)
PHONE.................580 228-3516
Thomas Ruddy, *President*
Donnie Watkins, *Vice Pres*
Keith Watkins, *Admin Sec*
EMP: 5
SQ FT: 1,500
SALES: 500K **Privately Held**
SIC: 3441 3443 Fabricated structural metal; fabricated plate work (boiler shop)

(G-11363)
METALSPAND INC
Also Called: Metalspand By Niles
1000 E G Ave (73573-5147)
P.O. Box 119 (73573-0119)
PHONE.................580 228-2393
Gary Gerken, *President*
Carter Waid, *Corp Secy*
EMP: 11
SQ FT: 46,000
SALES (est): 1.2MM
SALES (corp-wide): 13.8MM **Privately Held**
SIC: 3444 Sheet metalwork
PA: Nmc Metals Inc.
310 N Pleasant Ave
Niles OH 44446
330 652-2501

Waurika - Jefferson County (G-11364)

(G-11364)
SIMMONS TOOL LLC
804 E Florida Ave (73573-1408)
P.O. Box 1 (73573-0001)
PHONE.................................580 228-2799
◆ EMP: 1
SALES: 250K **Privately Held**
SIC: 3531 Mfg Construction Machinery

Wayne
McClain County

(G-11365)
AMERICAN DIRECTIONAL TECH
Also Called: Adtech
26426 120th St (73095-3030)
P.O. Box F (73095-0150)
PHONE.................................405 449-3362
Robert Rankin III, *President*
Buck Millsap, *Representative*
◆ EMP: 6
SALES (est): 1.3MM **Privately Held**
WEB: www.adtechmotors.com
SIC: 3491 3533 Industrial valves; oil & gas field machinery

(G-11366)
DAN ABNEY
25507 State Highway 59 (73095-3400)
PHONE.................................405 527-0675
Dan Abney, *Owner*
EMP: 2
SALES (est): 115.3K **Privately Held**
SIC: 1389 Oil consultants

(G-11367)
NICHOLS MACHINE AND MFG LLC
31058 State Highway 59 (73095-3326)
PHONE.................................405 637-7175
Joshua Nichols,
EMP: 1
SALES (est): 85.5K **Privately Held**
SIC: 3599 Machine shop, jobbing & repair

(G-11368)
PALIN WELDING SERVICE LLC
15243 Hopping Ave (73095-3178)
PHONE.................................405 449-3541
EMP: 1 EST: 2009
SALES (est): 46.1K **Privately Held**
SIC: 7692 Welding Repair

(G-11369)
PERMA-STRONG WOOD PRODUCTS INC
Rr 1 (73095)
P.O. Box 36 (73095-0036)
PHONE.................................405 449-3376
Goldie Ann Posey, *President*
▲ EMP: 20
SQ FT: 28,000
SALES (est): 1.6MM **Privately Held**
SIC: 2431 Millwork

Waynoka
Woods County

(G-11370)
ALLIED CUSTOM GYPSUM
17 Miles E Of Mreland Hwy (73860)
PHONE.................................580 337-6371
Rusty Harrison, *Owner*
EMP: 12
SALES (est): 673.6K **Privately Held**
SIC: 1499 Gypsum mining

(G-11371)
ARCHROCK INC
32728 State Highway 45 (73860-5001)
PHONE.................................580 824-0102
EMP: 1 **Publicly Held**
SIC: 1389 Gas compressing (natural gas) at the fields
PA: Archrock, Inc.
9807 Katy Fwy Ste 100
Houston TX 77024

(G-11372)
B BAR INC (PA)
1723 E Broadway St (73860-1256)
P.O. Box 157 (73860-0157)
PHONE.................................580 824-8338
Bill Bixler, *President*
Charlene Bixler, *Admin Sec*
EMP: 2
SQ FT: 10,000
SALES: 100K **Privately Held**
SIC: 5947 3993 7011 Gifts & novelties; signs & advertising specialties; motels

(G-11373)
BCE-MACH LLC
103 N Missouri St (73860)
PHONE.................................580 824-7251
Kevin White, *CFO*
EMP: 183
SALES (corp-wide): 135MM **Privately Held**
SIC: 1382 Oil & gas exploration services
PA: Bce-Mach Llc
14201 Wireless Way # 300
Oklahoma City OK 73134
405 252-8100

(G-11374)
BLUFF SERVICE DISPOSAL
Cheyenne Vly (73860)
PHONE.................................580 438-2262
EMP: 1
SALES (est): 89K **Privately Held**
SIC: 1389 Oil/Gas Field Services

(G-11375)
BURTON CONTROLS INC
2164 Faurot Dr (73860-4022)
PHONE.................................405 692-7278
Kyle Stevens, *Manager*
EMP: 4
SALES (corp-wide): 2.6MM **Privately Held**
WEB: www.burtoncontrols.com
SIC: 1389 Haulage, oil field
PA: Burton Controls, Inc.
11600 S Meridian Ave
Oklahoma City OK 73173
405 692-7278

(G-11376)
HULL CONTRACT PUMPING
1646 Santa Fe St (73860-3946)
PHONE.................................580 824-0440
Dwight Hull, *Owner*
EMP: 2
SALES (est): 147.7K **Privately Held**
SIC: 1389 Pumping of oil & gas wells

(G-11377)
KLX ENERGY SERVICES
942 Main St (73860-6871)
PHONE.................................580 824-0955
EMP: 2
SALES (est): 80.5K **Privately Held**
SIC: 1389 Oil & gas field services

(G-11378)
LITTLE SAHARA SANDSPORTS LLC
Also Called: Little Sahara Powers Store
137 Main St (73860-6834)
PHONE.................................580 824-0569
EMP: 7
SALES (est): 958.9K **Privately Held**
WEB: www.lspsonline.com
SIC: 2389 Apparel for handicapped
PA: Sahara Little Sandsports Llc
189 Main St
Waynoka OK 73860

(G-11379)
LITZENBERGER EXPLORATION INC
515 Main St (73860-6869)
P.O. Box 217 (73860-0217)
PHONE.................................580 824-9351
David Litzenberger, *President*
Coette Litzenberger, *Corp Secy*
EMP: 1 EST: 1980
SALES (est): 163.5K **Privately Held**
SIC: 1311 Crude petroleum production

(G-11380)
MILLER GRAPHICS
1111 Church St (73860-1382)
PHONE.................................580 824-2698
Donnie Millers, *Owner*
EMP: 2
SALES (est): 127.9K **Privately Held**
SIC: 2759 Screen printing

(G-11381)
WAYNOKA PUBG CO WOODS CNTY
Also Called: Woods County Enterprise
1643 Main St (73860)
PHONE.................................580 824-2171
Mark Carson, *Partner*
Karen Carson, *Partner*
EMP: 3
SALES (est): 112.1K **Privately Held**
WEB: www.woodscountyenterprise.com
SIC: 2711 Newspapers: publishing only, not printed on site

(G-11382)
WAYNOKA SIGN SHOP
1511 Missouri St (73860-1244)
PHONE.................................580 824-1717
Wayne Lamunyon, *Owner*
EMP: 3
SALES (est): 120K **Privately Held**
SIC: 3993 Signs & advertising specialties

(G-11383)
WHITE STONE LLC
15639 State Highway 14 (73860-4801)
PHONE.................................580 824-3271
Chris Olson,
Marilynn Olson,
EMP: 2
SALES (est): 172.5K **Privately Held**
SIC: 1381 Drilling oil & gas wells

(G-11384)
WOODS COUNTY ENTERPRISE
1543 Main St (73860-2008)
PHONE.................................580 824-2171
Mark Carson, *Owner*
Karen Carson, *Admin Sec*
EMP: 2
SQ FT: 3,000
SALES (est): 135.5K **Privately Held**
WEB: www.woodscountyenterprise.com
SIC: 2711 2752 Job printing & newspaper publishing combined; commercial printing, lithographic

Weatherford
Custer County

(G-11385)
24 HR INC
2811 E Main St (73096-2607)
PHONE.................................844 370-1726
John Millspaugh, *President*
EMP: 2
SALES (est): 62.3K **Privately Held**
SIC: 2023 Dietary supplements, dairy & non-dairy based

(G-11386)
3D FARMS & MACHINE L L C
1600 E Loomis Rd (73096-3316)
PHONE.................................580 772-5543
Kenneth R Dobrinski, *Mng Member*
Kenneth Dobrinski, *Executive*
John W Dobrinski,
Michael Dobrinski,
EMP: 6 EST: 2000
SQ FT: 6,000
SALES: 300K **Privately Held**
WEB: www.3dfarms.com
SIC: 3625 3545 3599 Relays & industrial controls; tools & accessories for machine tools; custom machinery

(G-11387)
ADVANCED POWER INC
Also Called: Robison Solar Systems
1520 E Eagle Rd (73096-9206)
P.O. Box 1937 (73096-1937)
PHONE.................................580 774-2220
Merlin Robison Jr, *President*
Mark Fuqua, *Admin Sec*
▼ EMP: 10
SQ FT: 4,000
SALES: 876K **Privately Held**
SIC: 5211 5074 3674 Solar heating equipment; heating equipment & panels, solar; integrated circuits, semiconductor networks, etc.

(G-11388)
AGT MACHINING CO INC
4701 Engineering Way (73096-4249)
PHONE.................................580 774-8359
Terry Iafrate, *President*
EMP: 8
SQ FT: 6,000
SALES (est): 1.1MM **Privately Held**
SIC: 3599 3544 Machine shop, jobbing & repair; special dies, tools, jigs & fixtures

(G-11389)
ALBERTS AUTO & TRUCK REPR INC
Also Called: Alberts Truck Service and Sup
4900 S Frontage Rd (73096-6124)
P.O. Box 228 (73096-0228)
PHONE.................................866 772-6065
Albert Seibold Jr, *President*
EMP: 40 EST: 1973
SQ FT: 4,000
SALES (est): 99.8K **Privately Held**
SIC: 7538 5531 7549 3713 Engine repair, except diesel: automotive; general truck repair; automotive parts; towing service, automotive; truck bodies & parts; professional instrument repair services

(G-11390)
ALPHA OILFIELD SERVICES LLC
704 Highland Dr (73096-6103)
PHONE.................................580 330-1285
Scott Scanlan, *Principal*
EMP: 2
SALES (est): 178.8K **Privately Held**
SIC: 1389 Oil & gas field services

(G-11391)
ASPECT OIL FIELD SERVVICES LLC
23851 Route 66 N (73096-3090)
PHONE.................................580 774-5006
EMP: 2 EST: 2018
SALES (est): 126K **Privately Held**
SIC: 1389 Oil field services

(G-11392)
BALDERAS LLC
2512 Harvest Dr (73096-3184)
PHONE.................................580 821-4134
Michael Balderas, *Owner*
EMP: 2
SALES (est): 120.8K **Privately Held**
SIC: 1389 Oil field services

(G-11393)
BONANZA LAND LLC
2811 E Main St (73096-2607)
P.O. Box 131 (73096-0131)
PHONE.................................580 772-2680
John Millspaugh, *Principal*
EMP: 2
SALES (est): 124.6K **Privately Held**
WEB: www.bonanzaland.com
SIC: 1389 Oil & gas field services

(G-11394)
BOP RAM-BLOCK IR RENTALS INC
Also Called: Bop Ram & Iron Rental
717 S Custer St (73096-9714)
P.O. Box 872 (73096-0872)
PHONE.................................580 772-0250
Dan Villines, *President*
EMP: 90
SALES: 1.1MM **Privately Held**
SIC: 1389 7353 7359 Oil field services; oil equipment rental services; equipment rental & leasing

(G-11395)
BRUCE BURDICK WELDING
604 N Loomis Rd (73096-3302)
PHONE.................................580 774-2906
Bruce Burdick,
EMP: 5

GEOGRAPHIC SECTION

Weatherford - Custer County (G-11427)

SALES (est): 1MM **Privately Held**
SIC: 7692 1389 Welding repair; roustabout service

(G-11396)
CADDO ELECTRIC CORP
3701 E Main St (73096-3309)
PHONE 580 774-5280
EMP: 2
SALES (est): 110K **Privately Held**
SIC: 3699 Mfg Electrical Equipment/Supplies

(G-11397)
CANOPY UPSTREAM LLC
2208 Valley View Rd (73096-6108)
PHONE 620 717-3263
David Girllot,
EMP: 1 **EST:** 2017
SALES: 67K **Privately Held**
SIC: 1389 7371 Oil & gas field services; software programming applications

(G-11398)
CATTLEAC CATTLE EQUIPMENT INC
3 4 Mile S Of I On Hwy 54 (73096)
P.O. Box 1678 (73096-1678)
PHONE 580 774-1010
Mitchell Haynes, *President*
Jackie Haynes, *Vice Pres*
EMP: 8
SALES (est): 740K **Privately Held**
SIC: 5083 2741 Livestock equipment; miscellaneous publishing

(G-11399)
CHESAPEAKE OPERATING LLC
310 N State St Ste 4 (73096-5157)
P.O. Box 2058 (73096-8058)
PHONE 580 772-7255
Ted Campbell, *Manager*
EMP: 25 **Publicly Held**
WEB: www.chk.com
SIC: 1311 Crude petroleum production
HQ: Chesapeake Operating, L.L.C.
6100 N Western Ave
Oklahoma City OK 73118

(G-11400)
CHIEF DRLG & FOUNDATION SVCS
Also Called: Chief Drilling Services
24250 E 990 Rd (73096-3133)
PHONE 580 302-0124
David Heath, *President*
EMP: 4 **EST:** 2007
SALES (est): 319.7K **Privately Held**
WEB: www.chiefdrilling.com
SIC: 1794 1629 1389 Excavation & grading, building construction; caisson drilling; pier construction; blasting contractor, except building demolition; oil field services

(G-11401)
CIRCLE A WELDING LLC
10398 N 2385 Rd (73096-4661)
PHONE 580 890-9617
Larry Alexander,
EMP: 2 **EST:** 2012
SALES (est): 84.5K **Privately Held**
SIC: 7692 Welding repair

(G-11402)
CITY OF WEATHERFORD
Also Called: Weatherford Sewage Plant
700 S Access Rd (73096-9740)
PHONE 580 772-5315
Jack Olson, *Superintendent*
EMP: 6 **Privately Held**
SIC: 3589 Water treatment equipment, industrial
PA: City Of Weatherford
522 W Rainey Ave
Weatherford OK 73096
580 772-1206

(G-11403)
CWG WELDING SERVICES LLC
23983 E 1013 Rd (73096-3500)
PHONE 580 819-1045
Chadley Wayne Glassey, *Principal*
EMP: 2
SALES (est): 43.7K **Privately Held**
SIC: 7692 Welding repair

(G-11404)
DOLESE BROS CO
315 S Broadway St (73096-4950)
P.O. Box 148 (73096-0148)
PHONE 405 235-2311
Joe Sheldon, *Manager*
EMP: 9
SALES (corp-wide): 8.5MM **Privately Held**
SIC: 3273 Ready-mixed concrete
PA: Dolese Bros. Co.
20 Nw 13th St
Oklahoma City OK 73103
405 235-2311

(G-11405)
DON REGIER
Also Called: Market 54
10152 Highway 54 (73096-3019)
PHONE 580 772-3510
Don Regier, *Owner*
EMP: 8
SALES (est): 370K **Privately Held**
SIC: 0751 5421 2013 2011 Slaughtering: custom livestock services; meat & fish markets; sausages & other prepared meats; meat packing plants

(G-11406)
DOWNHOLE HINTON SERVICES LLC
315 W Tom Stafford St (73096-4846)
PHONE 580 302-4129
Erin Hin, *President*
EMP: 2
SALES (est): 151.7K **Privately Held**
SIC: 1389 7389 Construction, repair & dismantling services;

(G-11407)
E-SAW WLDG & FABRICATION LLC
1200 E Loomis Rd (73096-3308)
PHONE 580 772-2448
Earl Sawatzky, *Mng Member*
Tami Sawatzky,
EMP: 15 **EST:** 2012
SALES (est): 1.5MM **Privately Held**
SIC: 7692 Welding repair

(G-11408)
EAGLE OILFIELD SERVICE LLC
300 S Access Rd (73096-9731)
P.O. Box 80129, Lafayette LA (70598-0129)
PHONE 580 774-2240
Vernon Hamar, *Principal*
EMP: 2 **EST:** 2001
SALES (est): 295.7K **Privately Held**
SIC: 1389 Oil field services

(G-11409)
ECO OIL FILL SERVICES
1200 E Loomis Rd (73096-3308)
P.O. Box 887 (73096-0887)
PHONE 580 774-2240
Bob Viliyus, *President*
EMP: 22 **EST:** 1999
SALES (est): 3MM **Privately Held**
SIC: 3533 Oil & gas drilling rigs & equipment

(G-11410)
ECO-LIFT ENERGY SERVICES INC
1450 E Loomis Rd (73096-3348)
PHONE 580 772-5157
Henry Eugene Burdick, *President*
EMP: 5
SALES (est): 2.3MM **Privately Held**
SIC: 1389 Oil field services

(G-11411)
ENVIRNMNTAL TCHNCIANS OKLA LLC
720 N Wilson Rd (73096-3303)
PHONE 580 772-7805
Larry Heger, *Branch Mgr*
EMP: 1
SALES (corp-wide): 496.1K **Privately Held**
SIC: 1389 Oil field services
PA: Environmental Technicians Of Oklahoma Llc
302 N Independence St # 11
Enid OK 73701
580 242-1876

(G-11412)
EXCALIBUR WELDING SERVICE LLC
1800 Pleasant Ln (73096-2677)
PHONE 580 302-2570
Joe Shelton, *Principal*
EMP: 1 **EST:** 2016
SALES (est): 49.5K **Privately Held**
SIC: 7692 Welding repair

(G-11413)
FARMERS COOP (PA)
300 E Clark Ave (73096-5204)
P.O. Box 188 (73096-0188)
PHONE 580 772-3334
Vincent Smith, *General Mgr*
EMP: 10 **EST:** 1948
SQ FT: 2,000
SALES (est): 23.7MM **Privately Held**
WEB: www.weatherfordcoop.com
SIC: 5191 5153 2048 Feed; seeds: field, garden & flower; fertilizer & fertilizer materials; grain elevators; grains; prepared feeds

(G-11414)
FLEX CHEM CORPORATION (PA)
700 N Wilson Rd (73096-3303)
P.O. Box 1647 (73096-1647)
PHONE 580 772-2386
Bryce Conway, *CEO*
EMP: 8
SALES (est): 3MM **Privately Held**
SIC: 1389 Oil field services

(G-11415)
FLEX-CHEM SERVICES CORPORATION
700 N Wilson Rd (73096-3303)
PHONE 580 772-2386
Bryce Conway, *CEO*
Jeramey McClure, *Principal*
Tami Special, *Principal*
EMP: 41
SALES (est): 547.8K **Privately Held**
SIC: 1389 Oil & gas field services

(G-11416)
FOSSIL FLUIDS LLC
9742 N 2350 Rd (73096-4120)
P.O. Box 151 (73096-0151)
PHONE 580 515-5402
Martin Kelley, *Mng Member*
EMP: 8
SALES: 10MM **Privately Held**
SIC: 3824 Fluid meters & counting devices

(G-11417)
H & C SERVICES INC
Also Called: H & C Service & Supply
400 S Access Rd (73096-9758)
P.O. Box 594 (73096-0594)
PHONE 580 772-2521
Greg Butler, *CEO*
Dale Butler, *President*
EMP: 14
SQ FT: 7,500
SALES (est): 5.5MM **Privately Held**
SIC: 5251 3492 5085 5039 Hardware; hose & tube fittings & assemblies, hydraulic/pneumatic; hose, belting & packing; fasteners & fastening equipment; metal buildings; safety equipment & supplies

(G-11418)
HUERECAS WOODWORKING LLC
515 N 8th St (73096-4815)
PHONE 580 302-2687
EMP: 1
SALES (est): 54.1K **Privately Held**
SIC: 2431 Millwork

(G-11419)
HUNTINGTON ENERGY USA INC
23900 E 1020 Rd (73096-3018)
PHONE 580 772-3644
EMP: 2

SALES (est): 107.8K **Privately Held**
SIC: 1382 1389 Oil/Gas Exploration Services Oil/Gas Field Services

(G-11420)
IMPAC EXPLORATION SERVICES INC (PA)
1501 Lera Ste 3 (73096-2670)
PHONE 580 772-3117
Chris Craighead, *President*
Paige Craighead, *Vice Pres*
Boone Price, *CFO*
EMP: 6
SQ FT: 2,600
SALES: 15MM **Privately Held**
SIC: 2411 Logging camps & contractors

(G-11421)
JEREMYS RUSTABOUTS BACKHOE INC
23986 E 1013 Rd (73096-3500)
PHONE 580 772-5157
Jeremy Motsch, *President*
EMP: 10 **EST:** 2007
SALES (est): 1.4MM **Privately Held**
SIC: 1623 1389 Oil & gas pipeline construction; oil field services

(G-11422)
JOHNSON MINFORD
128 Jackson Ave (73096-5808)
PHONE 580 772-0430
EMP: 1
SALES (est): 61K **Privately Held**
SIC: 2869 Mfg Industrial Organic Chemicals

(G-11423)
KAISER SIGN & GRAPHICS CO INC
Also Called: Kaiser Outdoor Advertising
820 W Main St (73096-4422)
PHONE 580 772-3880
Mary Lou Kaiser, *President*
Marylou Kaiser, *President*
Cindy Broadbent, *Vice Pres*
EMP: 6 **EST:** 1965
SQ FT: 4,000
SALES (est): 440K **Privately Held**
SIC: 7312 7336 3993 Billboard advertising; commercial art & graphic design; signs & advertising specialties

(G-11424)
LARRY L WILLIAMS
Also Called: Cedar Tree Cutter
10125 N 2350 Rd (73096-4114)
PHONE 580 772-3303
Larry L Williams, *Owner*
Cara Williams, *Co-Owner*
EMP: 1
SALES (est): 69.2K **Privately Held**
SIC: 0783 2411 Removal services, bush & tree; logging

(G-11425)
LINE X OF WESTERN OKLAHOMA
2200 S Frontage Rd (73096-6106)
PHONE 580 774-5000
Keith Head, *Owner*
EMP: 3
SALES (est): 341.4K **Privately Held**
SIC: 3714 Pickup truck bed liners

(G-11426)
MCCRARY WELDING INC
1424 Plains Ave (73096-2511)
PHONE 620 200-4733
Joshua McCrary, *Owner*
EMP: 1
SALES (est): 56.3K **Privately Held**
SIC: 7692 Welding repair

(G-11427)
MID-STATES MINERALS LLC
1014 Camelot St (73096-3404)
PHONE 405 298-7043
Kyle Gotcher, *Principal*
EMP: 2
SALES (est): 103.1K **Privately Held**
SIC: 1382 Oil & gas exploration services

Weatherford - Custer County (G-11428)

(G-11428)
MIRACLON CORPORATION (PA)
2720 S Frontage Rd (73096-6105)
PHONE.................................580 772-5502
Chris Payne, *CEO*
EMP: 14
SALES (est): 4.8MM **Privately Held**
SIC: **3861** 7384 Photographic equipment & supplies; film developing & printing

(G-11429)
MOONEY OILFIELD SERVICES LLC
2109 Ez Go Dr (73096-1055)
PHONE.................................580 660-5203
Perry Mooney, *Administration*
EMP: 2
SALES (est): 99K **Privately Held**
SIC: **1389** Oil field services

(G-11430)
NEXTIER CMPLTION SOLUTIONS INC
Also Called: Casedhole Solutions
1720 N Airport Rd (73096-3321)
PHONE.................................580 772-3100
Paula Tharp, *Manager*
EMP: 27
SALES (corp-wide): 1.8B **Publicly Held**
SIC: **1389** Oil field services
HQ: Nextier Completion Solutions Inc.
3990 Rogerdale Rd
Houston TX 77042
713 325-6000

(G-11431)
ONE OAKS FIELD SERVICE
605 N Loomis Rd (73096-3302)
PHONE.................................580 816-4500
Kevin Oaks, *Manager*
EMP: 65
SALES (est): 1.4MM **Privately Held**
SIC: **1389** Oil field services

(G-11432)
PARTY KING GRILLS COMPANY LLC
400 E Main St Ste B (73096-5352)
P.O. Box 2084 (73096-8084)
PHONE.................................580 774-2828
Charles G Frantz, *Mng Member*
Cindy Bruce, *Manager*
Ron Shotts,
▲ EMP: 7
SQ FT: 1,000
SALES: 700K **Privately Held**
SIC: **3631** Barbecues, grills & braziers (outdoor cooking)

(G-11433)
POWERS DRILLING INC
11163 Highway 54 (73096-3199)
PHONE.................................580 343-2444
Norma Powers, *President*
Michael Powers, *Admin Sec*
EMP: 4 EST: 1969
SALES (est): 760.4K **Privately Held**
SIC: **1381** Drilling oil & gas wells

(G-11434)
PRO JECT CHEMICALS
900 Sw 4th St (73096-4611)
PHONE.................................580 445-4345
EMP: 5
SALES (est): 310.2K **Privately Held**
SIC: **1389** Oil field services

(G-11435)
R T C RESOURCES LLP
316 W Kee St (73096-3856)
P.O. Box 2117 (73096-2117)
PHONE.................................580 774-2313
Chip Anderson, *Managing Prtnr*
Randy Malson, *Partner*
Tim Malson, *Partner*
EMP: 5 EST: 2001
SALES (est): 509.9K **Privately Held**
SIC: **1311** Crude petroleum & natural gas production

(G-11436)
RAWHIDE N RUSTICS
115 W Main St (73096-4939)
PHONE.................................580 307-9941
EMP: 1
SALES (est): 49.1K **Privately Held**
SIC: **3111** Rawhide

(G-11437)
RON WILLIAMS
24086 E 990 Rd (73096-3050)
PHONE.................................580 772-3513
Ron Williams, *Owner*
EMP: 1
SALES (est): 62.8K **Privately Held**
SIC: **3714** Wipers, windshield, motor vehicle

(G-11438)
SASKAS SWEETS
501 E Main St (73096-5347)
PHONE.................................580 772-3476
Bean Koch, *Owner*
Saska Koch, *Co-Owner*
EMP: 2
SALES (est): 63K **Privately Held**
SIC: **2051** Doughnuts, except frozen

(G-11439)
SCHLUMBERGER TECHNOLOGY CORP
1620 N Airport Rd (73096-3323)
PHONE.................................580 774-7557
EMP: 2 **Publicly Held**
SIC: **1389** Oil field services
HQ: Schlumberger Technology Corp
300 Schlumberger Dr
Sugar Land TX 77478
281 285-8500

(G-11440)
SELMAN WLDG & FABRICATION LLC
4701 Engineering Way (73096-4249)
PHONE.................................580 330-0887
Kory Selman, *Principal*
EMP: 1
SQ FT: 4,800
SALES (est): 54.9K **Privately Held**
SIC: **3441** Fabricated structural metal

(G-11441)
SHORT WORK INDUSTRIES INC
1404 E Quail Ave (73096-2536)
PHONE.................................580 774-8563
Edward Jeffrey, *Principal*
EMP: 1 EST: 2011
SALES (est): 52.6K **Privately Held**
WEB: www.shortworkindustries.com
SIC: **3999** Manufacturing industries

(G-11442)
SIOUX LEASING COMPANY LLC
23807 Route 66 N (73096-3090)
P.O. Box 486 (73096-0486)
PHONE.................................580 772-7100
Allison Biscoe, *President*
EMP: 2
SQ FT: 3,000
SALES: 349K **Privately Held**
SIC: **3715** Truck trailers

(G-11443)
SKYBIRD SALES INC
10289 N 2422 Cir (73096-7505)
PHONE.................................580 772-5100
Jerry Meier, *President*
EMP: 2
SALES (est): 218.4K **Privately Held**
SIC: **3721** Aircraft

(G-11444)
SOUTHWEST OILFIELD SERVICE
115 Bluestem St (73096-9222)
P.O. Box 230 (73096-0230)
PHONE.................................580 302-4069
James Opitz, *Owner*
EMP: 1
SALES (est): 99K **Privately Held**
SIC: **1389** Oil field services

(G-11445)
TAP WOODWORKS LLC
23982 E 1047 Rd (73096-6302)
PHONE.................................580 819-0455
Paul Staggs, *Principal*
EMP: 2
SALES (est): 72K **Privately Held**
SIC: **2431** Millwork

(G-11446)
THURMOND-MCGLOTHLIN LLC
3301 E Main St (73096-3312)
PHONE.................................580 774-2659
Jack Chisum, *President*
EMP: 1
SALES (corp-wide): 38.4MM **Privately Held**
WEB: www.tm-ems.com
SIC: **8733** 8731 1389 Noncommercial research organizations; commercial research laboratory; oil field services
PA: Thurmond-Mcglothlin, Llc
1428 N Banks St
Pampa TX 79065
806 665-5700

(G-11447)
TOMMY LUETKEMEYER
Also Called: T-N-T Machine
24069 E 1040 Rd (73096-3111)
PHONE.................................580 772-1517
Tommy Luetkemeyer, *Owner*
EMP: 1
SALES (est): 138.1K **Privately Held**
SIC: **3599** Machine shop, jobbing & repair

(G-11448)
TORCSILL FOUNDATIONS LLC
404 N Wilson Rd (73096-3349)
PHONE.................................281 825-5200
Greg Roper, *Regional Mgr*
Brandon Irvin, *District Mgr*
Gary Johnson, *District Mgr*
BJ McCurdy, *District Mgr*
Renee Ardoin, *Business Mgr*
EMP: 60
SALES (corp-wide): 216.8MM **Privately Held**
WEB: www.torcsill.com
SIC: **3451** 1796 Screw machine products; machinery installation
PA: Torcsill Foundations, Llc
12000 Aerospace Ave # 115
Houston TX 77034
281 825-5200

(G-11449)
TRACEY GREGORY
24219 E 1040 Rd (73096-7502)
PHONE.................................580 819-0057
Tracey Gregory, *Principal*
EMP: 2
SALES (est): 138.9K **Privately Held**
SIC: **1382** Oil & gas exploration services

(G-11450)
TRI-CO TESTING
114 Clover Ln (73096-9357)
P.O. Box 798 (73096-0798)
PHONE.................................580 772-8829
Marty Declined, *Principal*
EMP: 1
SALES (est): 74K **Privately Held**
SIC: **1389** Oil field services

(G-11451)
TROJAN LIVESTOCK EQUIPMENT
24169 Lawter Rd (73096)
P.O. Box 453 (73096-0453)
PHONE.................................580 772-1849
Bob Lanier, *President*
Patty Lanier, *Vice Pres*
EMP: 2
SALES: 750K **Privately Held**
SIC: **5083** 3594 3523 3444 Livestock equipment; fluid power pumps & motors; farm machinery & equipment; sheet metalwork

(G-11452)
TRPR OILFIELD SERVICES LLC
2221 Berry Ave (73096-2987)
PHONE.................................405 853-1988
Patrick Reyburn, *Principal*
EMP: 2
SALES (est): 121.7K **Privately Held**
SIC: **1389** Oil field services

(G-11453)
UNIT CORPORATION
1635 E Loomis Rd (73096-3316)
PHONE.................................580 774-5200
EMP: 109
SALES (corp-wide): 674.6MM **Privately Held**
SIC: **1381** Drilling oil & gas wells
PA: Unit Corporation
8200 S Unit Dr
Tulsa OK 74132
918 493-7700

(G-11454)
US CASING SERVICE OK INC
1710 N Airport Rd (73096-3321)
PHONE.................................701 713-0047
EMP: 2
SALES (est): 126.4K **Privately Held**
SIC: **1389** Cementing oil & gas well casings; oil field services

(G-11455)
WATSON WELL SOLUTIONS
9851 N 2430 Rd (73096-3068)
PHONE.................................580 772-3059
EMP: 2
SALES (est): 140K **Privately Held**
SIC: **1382** Oil/Gas Exploration Services

(G-11456)
WEATHERFORD CABINETS
201 S Custer St (73096-4933)
PHONE.................................580 772-7511
Randy Skinner, *Owner*
EMP: 1 EST: 1976
SQ FT: 2,500
SALES (est): 146.6K **Privately Held**
SIC: **2434** 5712 2541 2517 Wood kitchen cabinets; furniture stores; wood partitions & fixtures; wood television & radio cabinets; wood household furniture

(G-11457)
WEATHERFORD MACHINE WORKS
110 N Custer St (73096-4928)
PHONE.................................580 772-5287
Kevin Fischer, *President*
Anita Fischer, *Admin Sec*
EMP: 3
SQ FT: 2,000
SALES (est): 423.9K **Privately Held**
SIC: **3599** 7692 3714 Machine shop, jobbing & repair; welding repair; motor vehicle parts & accessories

(G-11458)
WEATHERFORD NEWS INC (PA)
Also Called: Weatherford Daily News, The
118 S Broadway St (73096-4924)
P.O. Box 191 (73096-0191)
PHONE.................................580 772-3301
Phillip Reid, *President*
Jeanne Ann Reid, *Corp Secy*
EMP: 25
SQ FT: 12,500
SALES (est): 4.5MM **Privately Held**
SIC: **2711** 8661 2752 Commercial printing & newspaper publishing combined; religious organizations; commercial printing, lithographic

(G-11459)
WEATHERFORD PRESS INC
Also Called: Commercial Printing
114 S Broadway St (73096-4924)
PHONE.................................580 772-5300
Deloris Reed, *President*
EMP: 12 EST: 1972
SQ FT: 7,000
SALES (est): 1.6MM **Privately Held**
SIC: **2752** 2791 Commercial printing, offset; typesetting

(G-11460)
WILLOUGHBY PHARMACY SVCS LLC
600 W Arlington Ave # 18 (73096-2872)
PHONE.................................580 214-1043
EMP: 1
SALES (est): 40K **Privately Held**
SIC: **2834** Mfg Pharmaceutical Preparations

(G-11461)
WOODEN CONCEPTS LLC
Also Called: Hidden Whiteboard, The
11142 N 2370 Rd (73096-4127)
PHONE.................................405 459-0411

Erick Marshall,
EMP: 2 **EST:** 2011
SALES (est): 110K **Privately Held**
SIC: 2499 5999 Laundry products, wood; picture frames, ready made

Welch
Craig County

(G-11462)
BATIES CUSTOM SADDLE TREE
346 S Commercial St (74369)
P.O. Box 327 (74369-0327)
PHONE 918 788-3686
Randy Batie, *Owner*
EMP: 12
SQ FT: 2,100
SALES (est): 1.1MM **Privately Held**
SIC: 2499 Saddle trees, wood

Weleetka
Okfuskee County

(G-11463)
BAKER WIRELINE
212 E Jack Johnson Ave (74880)
P.O. Box 791 (74880-0791)
PHONE 405 786-3283
Terry Baker, *Partner*
Gary Baker, *Partner*
EMP: 4
SALES: 190K **Privately Held**
SIC: 1389 Oil field services

(G-11464)
EMBROIDERY PLUS
116025 Highway 124 (74880-8037)
PHONE 918 652-2117
Patricia Humphrey, *Owner*
EMP: 1
SALES (est): 74.8K **Privately Held**
SIC: 2395 Embroidery & art needlework

(G-11465)
SAVOY LEATHER LLC
110027 Us Highway 75 S (74880-8097)
P.O. Box 336 (74880-0336)
PHONE 405 786-2296
Jeremiah Savoy,
Jerri Savoy,
EMP: 2
SALES (est): 273.9K **Privately Held**
WEB: www.savoyleather.com
SIC: 3172 Personal leather goods

Welling
Cherokee County

(G-11466)
D & Z METAL FABRICATION
19334 S Welling Rd (74471-2017)
PHONE 918 456-3841
Don Halsey, *Owner*
EMP: 1
SALES (est): 102.3K **Privately Held**
SIC: 1799 3441 Welding on site; fabricated structural metal

(G-11467)
KINGS REMNANT MINISTRY INC
18767 S Welling Rd (74471-2020)
P.O. Box 174 (74471-0174)
PHONE 918 207-0866
Marie Sears, *President*
Ray Sears, *Vice Pres*
EMP: 2
SALES (est): 92.4K **Privately Held**
SIC: 2731 8322 Book publishing; general counseling services

Wellston
Lincoln County

(G-11468)
CUSTOM EMBROIDERY & GIFTS LLC
950852 S 3360 Rd (74881-8837)
P.O. Box 677 (74881-0677)
PHONE 405 240-7950
EMP: 1
SALES (est): 35.3K **Privately Held**
SIC: 2395 Embroidery & art needlework

(G-11469)
ENABLE OKLAHOMA INT TRANSM LLC
Also Called: Wellston Plant
500 Ash St (74881)
PHONE 405 356-4060
EMP: 2
SALES (corp-wide): 3.6B **Publicly Held**
SIC: 1321 Natural Gas Liquids Production
HQ: Enable Oklahoma Intrastate Transmission, Llc
211 N Robinson Ave N950
Oklahoma City OK 73102
405 558-4652

(G-11470)
FILTER WINGS CORPORATION
930554 S 3390 Rd (74881-8915)
PHONE 405 258-3183
Clarkson Binkley, *President*
EMP: 3
SALES (est): 240K **Privately Held**
SIC: 3569 Filters

(G-11471)
GREGS PRESS
990221 S Highway 102 (74881-8137)
PHONE 405 356-4156
Greg Nedrow, *Principal*
EMP: 1
SALES (est): 81.4K **Privately Held**
SIC: 2741 Miscellaneous publishing

(G-11472)
IMEL WOODWORKS INC
910480 S 3340 Rd (74881-8932)
PHONE 405 356-2505
Ben Imel, *President*
EMP: 1
SALES (est): 98K **Privately Held**
SIC: 2434 2511 Wood kitchen cabinets; wood household furniture

(G-11473)
J & D FABRICATORS INC
334760 E Highway 66 (74881-4409)
PHONE 405 356-2243
John O'Day Jr, *President*
Jerry Bailey, *Vice Pres*
EMP: 12
SQ FT: 16,000
SALES (est): 2.3MM **Privately Held**
SIC: 3441 Fabricated structural metal

(G-11474)
M & P MANUFACTURING
960205 S Highway 102 (74881-8194)
PHONE 405 356-2805
Jim Piercey, *President*
EMP: 5
SALES (est): 337.7K **Privately Held**
SIC: 3599 Machine shop, jobbing & repair

(G-11475)
RANDY MULKEY
Also Called: Batesfield GPU
930335 S Pilot Dr (74881-9242)
PHONE 405 258-2600
Randy Mulkey, *Owner*
▼ **EMP:** 5
SQ FT: 6,000
SALES (est): 574.6K **Privately Held**
SIC: 3724 External power units, for hand inertia starters, aircraft

(G-11476)
REYNARD PROMOTIONS LLC
940163 S Highway 177 (74881-8342)
PHONE 405 793-1049
EMP: 5 **EST:** 2012
SALES (est): 229.9K **Privately Held**
SIC: 3644 Raceways

(G-11477)
RIFLE SHOPPE INC
Also Called: T R S
870740 S Highway 177 (74881-8058)
PHONE 405 356-2583
Jane Melot, *President*
Jesse Melot, *Vice Pres*
EMP: 4
SALES: 185K **Privately Held**
SIC: 3484 Revolvers or revolver parts, 30 mm. & below; rifles or rifle parts, 30 mm. & below

(G-11478)
ROSS FABRICATION & DETAILING
98053 S Hwy 177 (74881)
PHONE 405 356-9955
Paul Ross, *President*
EMP: 10
SALES (est): 1.6MM **Privately Held**
SIC: 3449 Bars, concrete reinforcing: fabricated steel

(G-11479)
SYDNIS SHAG SOCKS
930319 S 3330 Rd (74881-7018)
PHONE 405 664-5333
Sabrina Case, *Principal*
EMP: 2
SALES (est): 72.2K **Privately Held**
SIC: 2252 Socks

Westville
Adair County

(G-11480)
AUTOMATED MACHINING CO INC
107 E Main St (74965-2001)
P.O. Box 326 (74965-0326)
PHONE 918 723-3503
Wl Bill Skipper, *President*
EMP: 17 **EST:** 1978
SQ FT: 20,000
SALES (est): 3MM **Privately Held**
SIC: 3599 Machine shop, jobbing & repair

(G-11481)
CNHI COMMUNICATIONS
Also Called: Westville Reporter The
122 S Williams St (74965)
PHONE 918 723-5445
EMP: 5
SALES (est): 360K **Privately Held**
SIC: 2711 2752 Newspaper Publishing & Commercial Offset Printing

(G-11482)
CONBRACO INDUSTRIES INC
300 N Industrial Pkwy (74965-9412)
PHONE 704 841-6000
EMP: 2
SALES (est): 78.5K **Privately Held**
SIC: 3999 Manufacturing industries

(G-11483)
FLAMING HCKSAW FABRICATION LLC
476086 E 740 Rd (74965-5328)
PHONE 479 228-0809
Daniel S Atchison, *President*
Daniel Atchison, *President*
EMP: 4 **EST:** 2009
SQ FT: 5,000
SALES: 600K **Privately Held**
SIC: 3799 Trailers & trailer equipment

(G-11484)
LASCO FITTINGS INC
300 Industrial Park Rd (74965)
PHONE 800 776-2756
EMP: 4
SALES (est): 256.4K **Privately Held**
SIC: 3494 Valves & pipe fittings

(G-11485)
TAJOUR SPECIALTY PRODUCTS LLC
65294 S 4710 Rd (74965-5189)
PHONE 479 684-7445
Terry Lamb, *Mng Member*
EMP: 2
SALES (est): 62.3K **Privately Held**
SIC: 2099 7389 Seasonings & spices;

(G-11486)
TYSON FOODS INC
Hwy 59 N (74965)
PHONE 918 723-5494
Ron Rice, *Manager*
EMP: 33
SALES (corp-wide): 42.4B **Publicly Held**
SIC: 2015 Poultry slaughtering & processing
PA: Tyson Foods, Inc.
2200 W Don Tyson Pkwy
Springdale AR 72762
479 290-4000

(G-11487)
TYSON FOODS INC
67378 S 4744 Rd (74965-5375)
PHONE 918 723-5091
Doug McCloud, *Manager*
EMP: 6
SALES (corp-wide): 42.4B **Publicly Held**
SIC: 2011 Meat packing plants
PA: Tyson Foods, Inc.
2200 W Don Tyson Pkwy
Springdale AR 72762
479 290-4000

(G-11488)
WOODS SADDLERY
70246 S 4760 Rd (74965-5113)
PHONE 918 723-5503
Vol Woods, *Owner*
EMP: 1
SALES (est): 74.8K **Privately Held**
SIC: 3199 Saddles or parts

Wetumka
Hughes County

(G-11489)
A T S WELDING SERVICE
8164 E 127 (74883-6248)
P.O. Box 246 (74883-0246)
PHONE 405 452-5979
Nancy Cillery, *Owner*
EMP: 1
SALES (est): 62.6K **Privately Held**
SIC: 7692 Welding repair

(G-11490)
CHESTER OIL COMPANY
8163 E 131 (74883-6227)
PHONE 405 379-2600
Carol W Byrd, *President*
Rogers Toni A, *Vice Pres*
EMP: 3
SALES (est): 390K **Privately Held**
SIC: 1311 Crude petroleum production; natural gas production

(G-11491)
HOPE MINERALS INTERNATIONAL
7333 E 119 (74883-6136)
PHONE 405 452-3529
EMP: 6
SQ FT: 2,500
SALES (est): 510K **Privately Held**
SIC: 2879 2621 Mfg Soil Conditioners & Absorbents

(G-11492)
HOUSE OF TROPHIES
115 N Main St (74883-3028)
PHONE 405 452-3524
Tony Dean, *Owner*
Monica Dean, *Owner*
EMP: 2
SQ FT: 2,000

Wetumka - Hughes County (G-11493)

SALES (est): 159.2K **Privately Held**
SIC: **5999** 2752 3993 2396 Trophies & plaques; commercial printing, lithographic; signs & advertising specialties; automotive & apparel trimmings

(G-11493)
HUGHES COUNTY PUBLISHING CO
Also Called: Hughes County Times
501 E Highway 9 (74883-6048)
PHONE.............................405 452-3294
William C Morgan, *President*
EMP: 4
SALES (est): 179.6K **Privately Held**
WEB: www.hughescountytimes.com
SIC: **2711** Newspapers: publishing only, not printed on site

(G-11494)
HUGHES GAS MEASUREMENT INC (PA)
2919 Highway 75 (74883-6222)
PHONE.............................405 227-0904
Steve Hughes, *President*
Ronda Hughes, *Vice Pres*
EMP: 5
SQ FT: 800
SALES (est): 582.4K **Privately Held**
SIC: **1389** 7371 5999 Measurement of well flow rates, oil & gas; computer software development; alarm & safety equipment stores

(G-11495)
MIKE MCCALIP
515 S Washita St (74883-6025)
PHONE.............................405 452-5730
Mike McCalip, *Principal*
EMP: 2
SALES (est): 142.3K **Privately Held**
SIC: **3531** Backhoes

(G-11496)
XAE CORP
915 N Alex Noon St (74883-1051)
P.O. Box 39 (74883-0039)
PHONE.............................405 452-5735
Randy Brown, *Manager*
EMP: 7
SALES (est): 380.6K
SALES (corp-wide): 500K **Privately Held**
SIC: **1311** Crude petroleum & natural gas
PA: Xae Corp
  100 N Broadway Ave # 3280
  Oklahoma City OK

Wewoka
Seminole County

(G-11497)
AMERICAN MACHINE & TOOL CO
36690 State Highway 270 (74884-6104)
P.O. Box 1559, Delta Junction AK (99737-1559)
PHONE.............................405 794-9820
Hugh W Knowles Jr, *President*
James Knowles, *Vice Pres*
EMP: 8
SQ FT: 6,500
SALES (est): 1.1MM **Privately Held**
SIC: **3599** 3463 3533 3494 Machine shop, jobbing & repair; flange, valve or pipe fitting forgings, nonferrous; oil & gas field machinery; valves & pipe fittings

(G-11498)
COMMERCIAL BRICK CORPORATION
Old Hwy 270 (74884)
P.O. Box 1382 (74884-1382)
PHONE.............................405 257-6613
Dick Liddell, *Ch of Bd*
Aurva Brown, *Plant Mgr*
Dale Wolf, *Engineer*
Bryce Aleman, *Sales Mgr*
EMP: 155
SQ FT: 100,000
SALES (est): 24.6MM **Privately Held**
SIC: **3255** 4213 3251 Brick, clay refractory; building materials transport; brick & structural clay tile

(G-11499)
D & M DIRECTIONAL DRILLING LLC
1722 Seran Dr (74884-4133)
PHONE.............................405 221-2959
Mike Venable, *Administration*
EMP: 2
SALES (est): 180.5K **Privately Held**
SIC: **1381** Directional drilling oil & gas wells

(G-11500)
DOYLE COOK
Also Called: Cook Oil Company
120 W 2nd St (74884-2502)
P.O. Box 875 (74884-0875)
PHONE.............................405 257-3301
Doyle Cook, *Owner*
EMP: 13
SALES (est): 3MM **Privately Held**
SIC: **1311** Crude petroleum production; natural gas production

(G-11501)
EXPANDED SOLUTIONS LLC
300 N Wewoka Ave (74884-2224)
PHONE.............................405 946-6791
Rick Bahner,
EMP: 37
SALES (corp-wide): 17.6MM **Privately Held**
WEB: www.expandedsolutions.com
SIC: **3469** 3542 3444 Metal stampings; machine tools, metal forming type; sheet metalwork
PA: Expanded Solutions, L.L.C.
  5300 Nw 5th St
  Oklahoma City OK 73127
  405 946-6791

(G-11502)
FRANKS GARAGE AUTO SLS & SALV
12297 Ns 3650 (74884-6011)
PHONE.............................405 257-6198
Frank Moore, *Owner*
EMP: 1
SALES (est): 106.5K **Privately Held**
SIC: **3711** Automobile assembly, including specialty automobiles

(G-11503)
MADRON WELDING SERVICE
423 S Okfuskee St (74884-2547)
P.O. Box 1253 (74884-1253)
PHONE.............................405 257-6161
EMP: 1
SALES (est): 60.8K **Privately Held**
SIC: **7692** Welding Repair

(G-11504)
MEKUSUKEY OIL CO INC
201 S Wewoka Ave (74884-2639)
P.O. Box 816 (74884-0816)
PHONE.............................405 257-5431
Duke Ligon, *President*
Joan R Ligon, *Vice Pres*
Carolyn Yerby, *Treasurer*
EMP: 2
SALES (est): 460.8K **Privately Held**
WEB: www.mekusukey.com
SIC: **1382** Oil & gas exploration services

(G-11505)
MICHAEL S AZLIN
Also Called: Azlin Trackhoe and Dozer Svc
12725 Ns 3665 (74884-6024)
PHONE.............................405 257-3581
Shane Azlin, *Owner*
EMP: 5
SALES (est): 400K **Privately Held**
SIC: **1389** 1794 Oil field services; excavation work

(G-11506)
P & H CONSTRUCTION INC
125 W Park St (74884-2132)
P.O. Box 598 (74884-0598)
PHONE.............................405 257-3307
Don Powell, *President*
Stephen Powell, *Corp Secy*
Shirley Roberts, *Office Mgr*
EMP: 9 EST: 1978
SQ FT: 3,000
SALES (est): 1.5MM **Privately Held**
SIC: **1389** 1623 Building oil & gas well foundations on site; oil & gas pipeline construction

(G-11507)
PATTERSON OIL COMPANY INC
201 S Wewoka Ave (74884-2639)
P.O. Box 1262 (74884-1262)
PHONE.............................405 257-3241
Robert S Patterson, *President*
Jacklyn Patterson, *Vice Pres*
Paige Sheffield, *Admin Sec*
EMP: 6
SQ FT: 2,000
SALES (est): 42.3K **Privately Held**
SIC: **1311** Crude petroleum production; natural gas production

(G-11508)
R & R RADIATOR CO
207 E 2nd St (74884-2603)
P.O. Box 995 (74884-0995)
PHONE.............................405 257-3557
EMP: 2
SQ FT: 6,000
SALES (est): 130K **Privately Held**
SIC: **7539** 3433 Automotive Repair Mfg Heating Equipment-Nonelectric

(G-11509)
REDLINE CONSTRUCTN SAND DIRT
36416 Us Highway 270b (74884-5000)
PHONE.............................405 380-6994
EMP: 2
SALES (est): 66K **Privately Held**
SIC: **1442** Construction sand & gravel

(G-11510)
ROYALTY FABRICATION LLC
12828 Ns 3650 (74884-5438)
PHONE.............................405 257-6654
Troy Eckard,
EMP: 6
SALES (est): 250K **Privately Held**
SIC: **3443** Fuel tanks (oil, gas, etc.): metal plate

(G-11511)
SNIDER PRINTING & OFFICE SUP
210 S Wewoka Ave (74884-2640)
P.O. Box 456 (74884-0456)
PHONE.............................405 257-3402
Floyd Snider, *Partner*
Carrinna Snider, *Partner*
EMP: 2
SQ FT: 2,400
SALES (est): 274.9K **Privately Held**
SIC: **2752** 5943 2791 2789 Commercial printing, offset; office forms & supplies; typesetting; bookbinding & related work

(G-11512)
TMCO INC
108 W Cedar St (74884-2110)
P.O. Box 40, Simonton TX (77476-0040)
PHONE.............................405 257-9373
Mike Kuepker, *Branch Mgr*
EMP: 41
SQ FT: 50,000
SALES (est): 436.6K **Privately Held**
SIC: **3494** Valves & pipe fittings

(G-11513)
WEWOKA TIMES
210 S Wewoka Ave (74884-2640)
P.O. Box 601 (74884-0601)
PHONE.............................405 257-3341
Stu Philips, *Owner*
EMP: 1
SALES (est): 73K **Privately Held**
SIC: **2711** Newspapers, publishing & printing

(G-11514)
WEWOKA WINDOW WORKS LLC
1024 S Eufaula Ave (74884-3426)
PHONE.............................405 257-3109
Dennis Myers, *Mng Member*
EMP: 10
SALES (est): 1MM **Privately Held**
SIC: **2431** Millwork

Wheatland
Oklahoma County

(G-11515)
QUEST PROPERTY INC
11117 Folkstone (73097)
P.O. Box 42238, Oklahoma City (73123-3238)
PHONE.............................405 722-7530
Preston G Wheeler, *President*
EMP: 3
SQ FT: 1,200
SALES (est): 354.4K **Privately Held**
SIC: **1311** 1382 Crude petroleum production; natural gas production; oil & gas exploration services

Whitefield
Haskell County

(G-11516)
BKG INDUSTRIES LLC
10861 W Highway 9 (74472-3003)
PHONE.............................918 694-3390
Kaleb Boren, *Principal*
Barry Hamlin, *Principal*
EMP: 2 EST: 2014
SALES (est): 187.3K **Privately Held**
SIC: **3999** Atomizers, toiletry

(G-11517)
PRYOR SAND & REDI-MIX INC
Highway 2 (74472)
P.O. Box 117 (74472-0117)
PHONE.............................918 484-2150
Thomas Pryor Jr, *President*
EMP: 5
SALES (est): 500K **Privately Held**
SIC: **1442** 1771 Construction sand & gravel; concrete work

Wilburton
Latimer County

(G-11518)
BP AMERICA PRODUCTION COMPANY
1455 Nw Highway 2 (74578-6845)
PHONE.............................918 465-2343
Jason Green, *Vice Pres*
Jordan Haverly, *Internal Med*
EMP: 16
SALES (corp-wide): 278.4B **Privately Held**
SIC: **1311** 1321 Crude petroleum production; natural gas production; natural gas liquids
HQ: Bp America Production Company
  501 Westlake Park Blvd
  Houston TX 77079
  281 366-2000

(G-11519)
CIRCLE 7 SIGNS AND WONDERS
5918 Se 1030th Ave (74578-7517)
PHONE.............................918 448-7744
Malissa Evans, *Principal*
EMP: 1
SALES (est): 46K **Privately Held**
SIC: **3993** Signs & advertising specialties

(G-11520)
FRANKLIN ELECTRIC CO INC
1301 W Stovall Rd (74578-5137)
PHONE.............................918 465-2348
R Trumbull, *CEO*
Eddie Mayo, *Production*
Clay McAlester, *Engineer*
Greg Emshwiller, *Manager*
Beth Bunton, *CTO*
EMP: 400

GEOGRAPHIC SECTION

SALES (corp-wide): 1.3B Publicly Held
WEB: www.franklinwater.com
SIC: 3621 3822 3561 Motors, electric; auto controls regulating residntl & coml environmt & applncs; pumps & pumping equipment
PA: Franklin Electric Co., Inc.
    9255 Coverdale Rd
    Fort Wayne IN 46809
    260 824-2900

(G-11521)
JW MEASUREMENT CO
1210 W Main St (74578-5014)
PHONE..................918 465-5605
EMP: 2
SALES (est): 160.3K Privately Held
SIC: 3499 7389 Mfg Misc Fabricated Metal Products Business Services

(G-11522)
LATIMER COUNTY NEWS TRIBUNE
111 W Ada Ave (74578-2416)
P.O. Box 10 (74578-0010)
PHONE..................918 465-2321
Mitch Mullen, Owner
Patricia Winslett, Principal
EMP: 5
SALES (est): 190K Privately Held
SIC: 2759 5994 2711 Commercial printing; newsstand; newspapers

(G-11523)
LUKE MITCHELL
Also Called: L & L Hot Shot Service
1314 Nw Highway 2 (74578-6914)
PHONE..................918 429-0373
EMP: 2 EST: 2012
SALES (est): 81K Privately Held
SIC: 1389 Oil/Gas Field Services

(G-11524)
SOUTHEASTERN ICE
Also Called: Harbour AC & Refrigeration
1202 W Stovall Rd 1 (74578-5141)
PHONE..................918 465-2500
Destry Harber, President
EMP: 20 EST: 1996
SALES (est): 2MM Privately Held
WEB: www.southeasternice.com
SIC: 5999 2097 Ice; manufactured ice

(G-11525)
STITCH N STUFF EMBROIDERY SHOP
114 E Main St (74578-4230)
PHONE..................918 465-3036
Toni Hall, Owner
EMP: 4
SALES (est): 198.7K Privately Held
SIC: 2395 Embroidery products, except schiffli machine

(G-11526)
TRI COUNTY PUBLICATIONS INC (PA)
Also Called: Latimer County Today
134 E Main St (74578-4230)
P.O. Box 606 (74578-0606)
PHONE..................918 465-3851
Mitch Mullin, President
EMP: 7
SQ FT: 5,000
SALES (est): 782.3K Privately Held
SIC: 2711 Newspapers: publishing only, not printed on site

(G-11527)
TWIN CITIES READY MIX INC
1004 W Stovall Rd (74578-5164)
P.O. Box 542 (74578-0542)
PHONE..................918 465-2555
Gordan Schwarz, Partner
EMP: 7
SALES (corp-wide): 15.7MM Privately Held
SIC: 5032 3273 3272 Brick, stone & related material; ready-mixed concrete; concrete products
PA: Twin Cities Ready Mix, Inc.
    102 W Ashland Ave
    Mcalester OK 74501
    918 423-8855

(G-11528)
WARD BROTHERS PRINTING
102 W Main St (74578-4044)
PHONE..................918 465-5551
Bobbi Ward, Owner
EMP: 2
SALES (est): 123.1K Privately Held
SIC: 2752 Commercial printing, lithographic

(G-11529)
WOOLDRIDGE OIL CO INC
250 Nw 1014th Ave (74578)
PHONE..................918 465-3073
Cathy Wooldridge, President
Carl Wooldridge, President
EMP: 9
SALES (est): 7.6MM Privately Held
SIC: 5172 1389 Diesel fuel; oil field services

Willow
Greer County

(G-11530)
HAYS WELDING & BLACKSMITH
201 S Stepp Ave (73673-8071)
P.O. Box 206 (73673-0206)
PHONE..................580 287-3458
Charles Hays, Owner
EMP: 2
SQ FT: 2,400
SALES (est): 70.3K Privately Held
SIC: 7692 7699 Welding repair; blacksmith shop

Wilson
Carter County

(G-11531)
ARKOMA TANKS LLC
6988 Reck Rd (73463-7268)
P.O. Box 199 (73463-0199)
PHONE..................580 622-4794
David Hull,
EMP: 30
SALES (est): 7.5MM Privately Held
WEB: www.arkomatanks.com
SIC: 1389 Oil field services

(G-11532)
DONNIE GAINES WLDG FABRICATION
Hwy 70 & 76 N (73463)
P.O. Box 164 (73463-0164)
PHONE..................580 668-3249
Donnie Gaines, Owner
EMP: 1
SALES (est): 96.2K Privately Held
SIC: 1389 Oil field services

(G-11533)
FORSYTHE OILFIELD SERVICE INC
7183 Dillard Rd (73463-7104)
P.O. Box 438 (73463-0438)
PHONE..................580 668-3371
Lawrence B Forsythe, President
Lawana K Forsythe, Principal
Benny C Forsythe, Treasurer
EMP: 28 EST: 1969
SALES (est): 497.5K Privately Held
SIC: 1389 Oil field services; roustabout service

(G-11534)
GO ROWDY GIRL SCREEN PRINT EMB
204 Mulberry Ln (73463-6268)
PHONE..................580 668-2545
EMP: 2 EST: 2016
SALES (est): 111.6K Privately Held
SIC: 2752 Commercial printing, lithographic

(G-11535)
HEIRSTON WELDING & CNSTR
6309 Oil City Rd (73463-6521)
PHONE..................580 657-2518
Forrest Heirston, Owner
EMP: 1
SALES (est): 150K Privately Held
SIC: 1629 7692 Trenching contractor; welding repair

(G-11536)
HULLS OILFIELD LLC
3001 State Highway 76 (73463-6604)
P.O. Box 130 (73463-0130)
PHONE..................580 668-2619
Daniel Hull, Principal
EMP: 11
SALES (est): 1.7MM Privately Held
SIC: 1389 Oil field services

(G-11537)
KAISER-FRANCIS OIL COMPANY
11832 Memorial Rd (73463-7161)
P.O. Box 197 (73463-0197)
PHONE..................580 668-2335
Bill Wilkinson, Principal
Bill Wilkson, Facilities Mgr
EMP: 15
SALES (corp-wide): 678.5MM Privately Held
SIC: 1311 Crude petroleum production
HQ: Kaiser-Francis Oil Company
    6733 S Yale Ave
    Tulsa OK 74136
    918 494-0000

(G-11538)
MINNETTE COMPANY LTD
Also Called: Jolliff Coffee Company
1161 Us Highway 70a (73463-1481)
P.O. Box 10 (73463-0010)
PHONE..................580 226-2929
Greg Jolliff, President
Greg Joliff, President
Kyle Joliff, Vice Pres
EMP: 8
SQ FT: 20,000
SALES: 1MM Privately Held
SIC: 2095 2086 5149 5499 Coffee roasting (except by wholesale grocers); water, pasteurized: packaged in cans, bottles, etc.; coffee & tea; coffee

(G-11539)
MS 3 OIL & GAS LLC
374 Santa Fe Rd (73463-6556)
PHONE..................580 465-7354
Stacy Shores, Owner
EMP: 2
SALES (est): 73.6K Privately Held
SIC: 1389 Oil & gas field services

(G-11540)
NEXSTREEM RECLAIM PLANT
10472 Dillard Rd (73463-6610)
PHONE..................580 657-4580
EMP: 2 EST: 2014
SALES (est): 109.8K Privately Held
SIC: 1389 Oil field services

(G-11541)
NIPPS WELDING
8863 Buck Skin Rd (73463-6235)
PHONE..................580 668-2915
Donald Nipp, Owner
EMP: 1
SALES (est): 75.4K Privately Held
SIC: 7692 Welding repair

(G-11542)
SOUTH CENTRAL OILFLD SVCS INC
251 Locust Rd (73463-7235)
P.O. Box 730 (73463-0730)
PHONE..................580 465-4498
Daniel J Brooks, President
EMP: 7
SALES (est): 1.3MM Privately Held
SIC: 3531 Construction machinery

(G-11543)
STEPHEN BURNS
1421 Woodland Rd (73463-6660)
PHONE..................580 657-3237
Stephen Burns, Principal
EMP: 2
SALES (est): 100.3K Privately Held
SIC: 7692 Welding repair

(G-11544)
TED S CABINET
366 Tabor Rd (73463-6617)
PHONE..................580 668-5207
Ted S Cabinet, Principal
EMP: 2
SALES (est): 181.1K Privately Held
SIC: 2434 Wood kitchen cabinets

(G-11545)
WEATHERFORD INTERNATIONAL LLC
Us Hwy 70 E (73463)
PHONE..................580 490-1476
Brian Johnson, Branch Mgr
EMP: 25 Privately Held
SIC: 3498 Fabricated pipe & fittings
HQ: Weatherford International, Llc
    2000 Saint James Pl
    Houston TX 77056
    713 693-4000

(G-11546)
XTO ENERGY INC
8871 Dillard Rd (73463-7117)
PHONE..................580 668-2332
Ernest Franklin, President
EMP: 2 EST: 1990
SALES (est): 132.8K
SALES (corp-wide): 264.9B Publicly Held
SIC: 4925 1311 Gas production and/or distribution; crude petroleum & natural gas production
PA: Exxon Mobil Corporation
    5959 Las Colinas Blvd
    Irving TX 75039
    972 940-6000

Wister
Le Flore County

(G-11547)
A AND L WELDING SERVICES LLC
35210 Horse Ranch Rd (74966-2681)
PHONE..................918 649-7538
Adam Langley, Principal
EMP: 1
SALES (est): 25K Privately Held
SIC: 7692 Welding repair

(G-11548)
DUSTIN HOLBIRD
46145 Bengal Rd (74966-2867)
PHONE..................918 448-7687
Dustin Holbird, Principal
EMP: 2
SALES (est): 148.3K Privately Held
SIC: 2411 Logging

(G-11549)
JAMES BETHELL
48521 Us Highway 271 (74966-2391)
PHONE..................918 677-2328
James Bethell, Owner
EMP: 2
SALES (est): 81K Privately Held
SIC: 2421 Custom sawmill

(G-11550)
L&E HOT SHOT LLC
25758 370th St (74966-2647)
PHONE..................918 839-2419
Eric Bryan Essman, Owner
EMP: 2 EST: 2017
SALES (est): 99.2K Privately Held
SIC: 1389 Hot shot service

(G-11551)
WOOTEN WELDING
29032 Pocohontas Rd (74966-9146)
PHONE..................918 655-6981
Katie Wooten, Principal
EMP: 1
SALES (est): 50.7K Privately Held
SIC: 7692 Welding repair

Woodward
Woodward County

(G-11552)
4D DOZER SERVICE INC
202683 E County Road 35 (73801-5474)
PHONE.....................................580 256-2076
Steven Dewesse, *President*
Donald Dewesse, *Vice Pres*
EMP: 4
SQ FT: 3,200
SALES (est): 197.2K **Privately Held**
SIC: 1389 Excavating slush pits & cellars

(G-11553)
ADVANCED AERIAL SERVICES LLC (PA)
9818 State Highway 34 # 28 (73801-6170)
PHONE.....................................580 571-1980
Don Whitten, *Mng Member*
◆ **EMP:** 5
SQ FT: 8,000
SALES: 500K **Privately Held**
SIC: 3728 7389 Bodies, aircraft; inspection & testing services; safety inspection service

(G-11554)
APOLLO OILFIELD SUPPLY LLC
1416 46th St (73801-3847)
P.O. Box 155 (73802-0155)
PHONE.....................................580 254-0164
EMP: 2
SALES (est): 95.5K **Privately Held**
SIC: 3533 Drill rigs

(G-11555)
ARCRITE MANUFACTURING LLC
6745 State Highway 15 (73801-6102)
P.O. Box 95 (73802-0095)
PHONE.....................................580 216-1050
Tyler Grunewald, *Mng Member*
EMP: 21
SQ FT: 1,500
SALES: 3.5MM **Privately Held**
SIC: 3443 Industrial vessels, tanks & containers; process vessels, industrial: metal plate; tank towers, metal plate

(G-11556)
B & G PRODUCTION INC
1010 Oklahoma Ave (73801-4662)
PHONE.....................................580 256-5100
C H Gabrel, *Mng Member*
Helen B Gabrel, *Mng Member*
Ronald D Kirkpatrick, *Mng Member*
EMP: 6
SALES (est): 944.9K **Privately Held**
SIC: 1389 Gas field services

(G-11557)
B & R CONSTRUCTION OF WOODWARD
102 E Madison Ave (73801-3615)
P.O. Box 2092 (73802-2092)
PHONE.....................................580 256-5522
Bill Owens, *Owner*
EMP: 2
SALES (est): 327.7K **Privately Held**
SIC: 1389 Oil & gas field services

(G-11558)
BADGER PRESSURE CONTROL LLC
1310 Airport Pkwy Rd (73802)
P.O. Box 1246 (73802-1246)
PHONE.....................................580 256-9555
Michael White, *Chairman*
EMP: 1 **Privately Held**
SIC: 1389 Oil sampling service for oil companies
PA: Badger Pressure Control Llc
1197 Magnolia Rd Ste B
Waskom TX 75692

(G-11559)
BAKER HGHES OLFLD OPRTIONS LLC
Also Called: Baker Oil Tools
910 Jimar Way (73801-1510)
PHONE.....................................580 256-7471
Mark Firnsworth, *Sales/Mktg Mgr*
EMP: 5 **Privately Held**
SIC: 1389 Oil field services
PA: Baker Hughes Oilfield Operations Llc
2001 Rankin Rd
Houston TX 77073

(G-11560)
BASIC ENERGY SERVICES INC
500 Oklahoma Ave (73801)
PHONE.....................................580 254-3600
EMP: 1
SALES (corp-wide): 567.2MM **Publicly Held**
SIC: 1389 Oil field services
PA: Basic Energy Services, Inc.
801 Cherry St Unit 2
Fort Worth TX 76102
817 334-4100

(G-11561)
BENDERS
120 Pen Mar Dr (73801-1709)
P.O. Box 365 (73802-0365)
PHONE.....................................580 256-5656
Bob Bender, *Owner*
EMP: 1
SALES (est): 123.9K **Privately Held**
SIC: 2752 5712 Commercial printing, offset; office furniture

(G-11562)
BO-MAX INDUSTRIES INC
Also Called: Woodward Concrete
4215 Oklahoma Ave (73801-3838)
P.O. Box 1828 (73802-1828)
PHONE.....................................580 256-4555
Maxine Schmitz, *Principal*
Robert L Schmitz, *Principal*
EMP: 10
SALES (est): 1.4MM **Privately Held**
SIC: 3273 Ready-mixed concrete

(G-11563)
BOC GASES
1002 Terra Dr (73801-9596)
PHONE.....................................580 254-2259
Ron Matthews, *Principal*
EMP: 2 **EST:** 2008
SALES (est): 165.2K **Privately Held**
SIC: 5169 2813 Industrial gases; industrial gases

(G-11564)
BUDDIES BARS
620 Main St (73801-3233)
PHONE.....................................580 254-5778
Duana Adams, *Principal*
EMP: 2
SALES (est): 134.6K **Privately Held**
SIC: 2599 Bar, restaurant & cafeteria furniture

(G-11565)
BUTCHERS METAL SHOP
1206 4th St (73801-3342)
PHONE.....................................580 256-7660
Donald Westenhaver, *Owner*
Don Westenhaver, *Owner*
EMP: 1 **EST:** 1940
SQ FT: 2,400
SALES (est): 96.3K **Privately Held**
SIC: 1711 3444 Warm air heating & air conditioning contractor; ventilation & duct work contractor; sheet metalwork

(G-11566)
C & C NITROGEN LLC
203081 E County Road 35 (73801-5782)
PHONE.....................................580 216-4871
Brandon O'Neal, *Owner*
EMP: 2
SALES (est): 74.4K **Privately Held**
SIC: 2813 Nitrogen

(G-11567)
CASE WIRELINE SERVICES INC
105 48th St (73801-2524)
P.O. Box 646 (73802-0646)
PHONE.....................................580 254-3036
Guy Clark, *President*
EMP: 22
SALES (est): 4.3MM **Privately Held**
SIC: 1389 Oil field services

(G-11568)
CIRCLE K SERVICES INC
4915 Western Ave (73801-9463)
P.O. Box 1987 (73802-1987)
PHONE.....................................580 254-3568
Wesley A Kerby, *President*
Rita Kerby, *Vice Pres*
EMP: 10
SALES (est): 1.4MM **Privately Held**
SIC: 1389 Pumping of oil & gas wells; servicing oil & gas wells

(G-11569)
COBRA OIL & GAS CORPORATION
1211 34th St Ste 3 (73801-1861)
PHONE.....................................580 254-2027
EMP: 2
SALES (corp-wide): 30.4MM **Privately Held**
SIC: 1311 1382 Crude Petroleum/Natural Gas Production Oil/Gas Exploration Services
PA: Cobra Oil & Gas Corporation
2201 Kell Blvd
Wichita Falls TX 76308
940 723-4331

(G-11570)
COCA COLA BOTTLING CO
Also Called: Coca-Cola
3003 Lakeview Dr (73801-6615)
PHONE.....................................580 256-2350
Ralph Pedersen, *Principal*
EMP: 7
SALES (est): 382.5K **Privately Held**
SIC: 2086 Bottled & canned soft drinks

(G-11571)
COMBS OILFIELD SERVICES INC
405 W Hanks Trl (73801-7319)
PHONE.....................................580 571-2315
Charles Combs, *President*
Tammy Combs, *Treasurer*
EMP: 8
SALES (est): 200K **Privately Held**
SIC: 1381 Drilling oil & gas wells

(G-11572)
COOL BILLET CUSTOMS
2133 3rd St (73801-5927)
PHONE.....................................580 216-0104
Brian Laverentz, *Owner*
EMP: 1
SALES: 42K **Privately Held**
SIC: 3541 Machine tools, metal cutting type

(G-11573)
CPV KEENAN RENEWABLE ENRGY LLC
Also Called: Keenan II
197352 E County Road 51 (73801-5555)
PHONE.....................................580 698-2278
Gary Lambert, *CEO*
EMP: 7 **EST:** 2007
SALES (est): 619.8K **Privately Held**
SIC: 3621 Windmills, electric generating

(G-11574)
CROSSFIRE PRODUCTION SVCS LLC
46005 S County Road 202 (73801-5172)
P.O. Box 1761 (73802-1761)
PHONE.....................................580 254-3766
Kandice Baker, *Admin Sec*
EMP: 5
SALES (est): 494.2K **Privately Held**
SIC: 1389 Cementing oil & gas well casings

(G-11575)
CUDD PUMPING SERVICES
2627 3rd St (73801-6061)
PHONE.....................................580 256-7000
Bruce Radden, *Principal*
EMP: 1
SALES (est): 65.7K **Privately Held**
SIC: 1389 Oil field services

(G-11576)
DANS BACKHOE & DOZER SERVICE
20145 E 29 Rd (73801-4773)
PHONE.....................................580 256-0865
Dan B Deloise, *Owner*
EMP: 2
SALES (est): 168.9K **Privately Held**
SIC: 3531 Backhoes

(G-11577)
DEEPWATER CHEMICALS INC
196122 E County Road 40 (73801-5656)
PHONE.....................................580 256-0500
Masahiro Akiba, *President*
K Mushika, *Treasurer*
J Maraia, *Admin Sec*
◆ **EMP:** 24
SQ FT: 40,000
SALES (est): 7.2MM **Privately Held**
SIC: 2819 2899 2879 Iodine, elemental; iodides; chemical preparations; agricultural chemicals
PA: Toyota Tsusho Corporation
4-9-8, Meieki, Nakamura-Ku
Nagoya AIC 450-0

(G-11578)
DIAMOND CNSTR CO SHATTUCK INC (PA)
Also Called: Diamond Services
4220 Oklahoma Ave (73801-3839)
P.O. Box 1025 (73802-1025)
PHONE.....................................580 256-3385
Kerry Martin, *President*
Mark Campbell, *Exec VP*
Joshua Richardson, *Project Mgr*
Joy Martin, *Treasurer*
Laura Ferguson, *Office Mgr*
EMP: 110
SQ FT: 2,000
SALES (est): 32.8MM **Privately Held**
WEB: www.diamond-services.com
SIC: 1389 1623 Grading oil & gas well foundations; roustabout service; haulage, oil field; cleaning wells; pipeline construction

(G-11579)
DOWNHOLE WIRELINE SPECIAL
43718 S County Road 206 (73801-5140)
PHONE.....................................580 254-3842
EMP: 2 **EST:** 2007
SALES (est): 96K **Privately Held**
SIC: 1389 Oil/Gas Field Services

(G-11580)
DR PEPPER BOTTLING CO
3003 Lakeview Dr (73801-6615)
PHONE.....................................580 256-2350
EMP: 3
SALES (est): 109K **Privately Held**
SIC: 2086 Soft drinks: packaged in cans, bottles, etc.

(G-11581)
EDGE SERVICES INC
4420 Anderson Rd (73801-2509)
P.O. Box 609 (73802-0609)
PHONE.....................................580 254-3216
Tommy Weder Jr, *President*
Terry Conn, *Sales Staff*
Alan Rickers, *Manager*
EMP: 20
SALES (est): 11.8MM **Privately Held**
WEB: www.edgedrillservices.com
SIC: 1381 Drilling oil & gas wells

(G-11582)
EXCEL PRODUCTS
202573 E County Road 43 # 13 (73801-5599)
P.O. Box 856 (73802-0856)
PHONE.....................................580 216-0784
Brad Smith, *Owner*
EMP: 8
SALES: 4MM **Privately Held**
WEB: www.excelproductsusa.com
SIC: 3561 Pumps & pumping equipment

(G-11583)
FIELD SERVICES
N Of City (73801)
PHONE.....................................580 256-3338
Greg Balch, *Owner*

GEOGRAPHIC SECTION

Woodward - Woodward County (G-11613)

Lynette Balch, *Co-Owner*
EMP: 1
SALES: 46K **Privately Held**
SIC: 1389 Oil field services

(G-11584)
FOAMTECH INC
Also Called: IBP
4515 Western Ave (73801-9410)
P.O. Box 925 (73802-0925)
PHONE.................580 256-3979
Monte Waggoner, *CEO*
Richard Waggoner, *President*
Claudia Waggoner, *Corp Secy*
Mike Brown, *COO*
Courtney Kidd, *Vice Pres*
EMP: 27
SQ FT: 21,000
SALES (est): 3.2MM
SALES (corp-wide): 1.5B **Publicly Held**
SIC: 1389 Oil field services
PA: Installed Building Products, Inc.
495 S High St Ste 50
Columbus OH 43215
614 221-3399

(G-11585)
FROM HEART CANDLES AND MORE
122 Oklahoma Ave (73801-4813)
PHONE.................580 334-4104
EMP: 1
SALES (est): 39.6K **Privately Held**
SIC: 3999 Candles

(G-11586)
FUEL
4856 Berryhill Dr (73801-3703)
PHONE.................903 948-3125
Holly Daniels, *Principal*
EMP: 3
SALES (est): 188.6K **Privately Held**
SIC: 2869 Fuels

(G-11587)
GENE COOK INC
4325 Oil Patch Dr (73801-1513)
P.O. Box 689 (73802-0689)
PHONE.................580 256-5335
Gene Cook, *President*
EMP: 1 **EST:** 1992
SALES (est): 106.5K **Privately Held**
SIC: 1311 Natural gas production

(G-11588)
GRAY WIRELINE
4100 Oklahoma Ave (73801-3940)
P.O. Box 709 (73802-0709)
PHONE.................580 256-3775
Fax: 580 254-3653
EMP: 2
SALES (est): 130K **Privately Held**
SIC: 1389 Oil/Gas Field Services

(G-11589)
GRUNEWALD WELDING LLC
4921 Pleasant View St (73801-3716)
PHONE.................580 256-2674
Tyler Grunewald, *Principal*
EMP: 1 **EST:** 2009
SALES (est): 76.6K **Privately Held**
SIC: 7692 Welding repair

(G-11590)
HAMM AND PHILLIPS SERVICES CO
1010 E Hanks Trl (73801-6636)
PHONE.................580 256-8686
Niel Cooper, *Principal*
EMP: 1
SALES (est): 69.6K **Privately Held**
SIC: 1389 Oil field services

(G-11591)
HANDY MART INC
1201 Oklahoma Ave (73801-4673)
PHONE.................580 254-5889
EMP: 1
SALES (corp-wide): 7.8MM **Privately Held**
SIC: 2131 Smoking tobacco
PA: Handy Mart Inc
1751 E Us Highway 377
Granbury TX 76049
817 573-4265

(G-11592)
HOT OIL UNITS INC
Also Called: J & R Transport
4616 Oil Patch Dr (73801-1504)
P.O. Box 781 (73802-0781)
PHONE.................580 256-6461
Kevin Halley, *President*
David Christian, *Vice Pres*
Donna Murphy, *Treasurer*
EMP: 7
SQ FT: 2,400
SALES: 1MM **Privately Held**
SIC: 1389 Oil field services

(G-11593)
IMPACT CASING SERVICES LLC
1419 Ctr Dr (73802)
P.O. Box 2781 (73802-2781)
PHONE.................580 216-1159
EMP: 10 **EST:** 2008
SALES (est): 590K **Privately Held**
SIC: 1389 Oil/Gas Field Services

(G-11594)
J & R SERVICE INC
4230 Oklahoma Ave (73801-3839)
P.O. Box 781 (73802-0781)
PHONE.................580 256-6461
Susanne Christian, *Principal*
EMP: 6
SQ FT: 4,000
SALES (est): 482.8K **Privately Held**
SIC: 1389 Oil field services

(G-11595)
J AND S TRUCKING COMPANY
1023 Oak Ave (73801-4653)
PHONE.................580 216-7213
Jason Richey, *Principal*
Sonja Russell, *General Ptnr*
EMP: 3
SALES (est): 90K **Privately Held**
SIC: 4212 2611 Local trucking, without storage; pulp mills, mechanical & recycling processing

(G-11596)
J-W POWER COMPANY
1307 46th St (73801-3848)
PHONE.................580 254-5663
Mike Carter, *Principal*
EMP: 8 **Privately Held**
SIC: 1311 1321 Crude petroleum & natural gas production; natural gas liquids production
HQ: J-W Power Company
15505 Wright Brothers Dr
Addison TX 75001
972 233-8191

(G-11597)
JUDY AIRSON
Also Called: Judies Custom Creations
2727 Oklahoma Ave (73801-4011)
PHONE.................580 254-9076
Judy Airson, *Owner*
EMP: 1 **EST:** 1998
SALES (est): 44.4K **Privately Held**
SIC: 2395 Embroidery & art needlework

(G-11598)
KAY ELECTRIC MOTORS INC
810 48th St (73801-1526)
P.O. Box 1778 (73802-1778)
PHONE.................580 256-3254
Curtis Hensley, *President*
Judy Hensley, *Corp Secy*
EMP: 7 **EST:** 1977
SQ FT: 7,500
SALES (est): 1.7MM **Privately Held**
SIC: 7694 5063 5084 5072 Electric motor repair; motors, electric; industrial machinery & equipment; hardware

(G-11599)
KETCHERSIDE CUSTOM CABINETS
1404 19th St (73801-4216)
PHONE.................580 254-2672
John Ketcherside, *Owner*
EMP: 2

SALES (est): 160K **Privately Held**
SIC: 2599 2541 2521 2517 Cabinets, factory; wood partitions & fixtures; wood office furniture; wood television & radio cabinets; wood kitchen cabinets

(G-11600)
KEY ENERGY SERVICES INC
4009 Oklahoma Ave (73801-3937)
P.O. Box 907 (73802-0907)
PHONE.................405 262-1231
Dean Wheeler, *Manager*
EMP: 125
SALES (corp-wide): 413.8MM **Publicly Held**
WEB: www.keyenergy.com
SIC: 1389 Oil field services
PA: Key Energy Services, Inc.
1301 Mckinney St Ste 1800
Houston TX 77010
713 651-4300

(G-11601)
KEY ENERGY SERVICES INC
206 48th St (73801-2508)
PHONE.................580 256-7413
EMP: 2
SALES (est): 65.5K
SALES (corp-wide): 436.1MM **Publicly Held**
SIC: 1389 Oil And Gas Field Services, Nec, Nsk
PA: Key Energy Services, Inc.
1301 Mckinney St Ste 1800
Houston TX 77010
713 651-4300

(G-11602)
KEY ENERGY SERVICES INC
4009 Oklahoma Ave (73801-3937)
P.O. Box 1286, Perryton TX (79070-1286)
PHONE.................806 435-5583
EMP: 12
SALES (corp-wide): 521.7MM **Publicly Held**
SIC: 1389 7353 Oil And Gas Field Services, Nec, Nsk
PA: Key Energy Services, Inc.
1301 Mckinney St Ste 1800
Houston TX 77010
713 651-4300

(G-11603)
KLINE MATERIALS INC
Ne Of City (73802)
P.O. Box 215 (73802-0215)
PHONE.................580 256-2062
Dwight Kline, *President*
Karen Arnold, *Corp Secy*
David Kline, *Vice Pres*
John Kline, *Vice Pres*
EMP: 13
SQ FT: 5,000
SALES: 500K **Privately Held**
SIC: 5032 3273 2951 1442 Sand, construction; ready-mixed concrete; asphalt paving mixtures & blocks; construction sand & gravel

(G-11604)
KLINES SIGNS & CRANE
626 E Oklahoma Ave (73801-5000)
P.O. Box 1066 (73802-1066)
PHONE.................580 256-2374
Jimmie E Kline, *Partner*
Jeffrey Kline, *Partner*
Linda Kline, *Partner*
EMP: 4
SALES (est): 140K **Privately Held**
SIC: 7389 1799 7359 3993 Sign painting & lettering shop; sign installation & maintenance; equipment rental & leasing; signs & advertising specialties

(G-11605)
LATIGO OIL & GAS INC
5815 Oklahoma Ave (73801-9006)
P.O. Box 1206 (73802-1206)
PHONE.................580 256-1416
Brad Barby, *President*
EMP: 14 **EST:** 1979
SQ FT: 800
SALES (est): 2.7MM **Privately Held**
SIC: 1311 Crude petroleum production; natural gas production

(G-11606)
MESSER LLC
1002 Terra Dr (73801-9596)
PHONE.................580 254-2259
Ron Matthews, *Branch Mgr*
John Hamilton, *Manager*
EMP: 15
SALES (corp-wide): 1.1B **Privately Held**
SIC: 2813 2911 Carbon dioxide; petroleum refining
HQ: Messer Llc
200 Somerset Corp Blvd # 7000
Bridgewater NJ 08807
908 464-8100

(G-11607)
MESSER LLC
802 Jimar Way (73801-1500)
PHONE.................580 254-2929
Vown Epperson, *Manager*
EMP: 15
SALES (corp-wide): 1.1B **Privately Held**
SIC: 2813 Industrial gases
HQ: Messer Llc
200 Somerset Corp Blvd # 7000
Bridgewater NJ 08807
908 464-8100

(G-11608)
MESSER NORTH AMERICA INC
Also Called: Boc
802 Jimar Way (73801-1500)
PHONE.................580 254-2929
Brian Crowley, *Manager*
EMP: 8
SALES (corp-wide): 1.1B **Privately Held**
SIC: 2813 Industrial gases
HQ: Messer North America, Inc.
200 Somerset Corporate Bl
Bridgewater NJ 08807
908 464-8100

(G-11609)
MEWBOURNE OIL COMPANY
6535 State Highway 15 (73801-6130)
P.O. Box 1233 (73802-1233)
PHONE.................903 561-2900
Ronnie Howell, *Opers-Prdtn-Mfg*
EMP: 14
SQ FT: 1,500
SALES (corp-wide): 458.1MM **Privately Held**
SIC: 1382 Oil & gas exploration services
HQ: Mewbourne Oil Company
3620 Old Bullard Rd
Tyler TX 75701
903 561-2900

(G-11610)
MID-CON EXPLORATION LLC
2816 Oak Hollow Rd (73801-7126)
P.O. Box 2576 (73802-2576)
PHONE.................580 571-7929
Ryan Guy Barby, *Principal*
EMP: 2 **EST:** 2008
SALES (est): 249.4K **Privately Held**
SIC: 1382 Oil & gas exploration services

(G-11611)
MID-CONTINENT CONDUCTOR LLC
199584 E County Road 39 (73801-5876)
P.O. Box 1570 (73802-1570)
PHONE.................580 254-3232
Bobby Alexander, *Mng Member*
EMP: 5
SALES (est): 1MM **Privately Held**
SIC: 1382 Oil & gas exploration services

(G-11612)
MIKES TRUCKING CO
5015 Western Ave (73801-9431)
P.O. Box 621 (73802-0621)
PHONE.................580 256-5063
Mike Hensel, *Owner*
EMP: 20
SALES (est): 151.1K **Privately Held**
SIC: 1389 Haulage, oil field

(G-11613)
NBC CHEMICAL CO INC
1603 9th St (73801-4609)
P.O. Box 37 (73802-0037)
PHONE.................580 256-2627
Loren Ansley, *President*

Woodward - Woodward County (G-11614)   GEOGRAPHIC SECTION

Ansley Sherry, *Treasurer*
EMP: 1
SALES (est): 75K **Privately Held**
SIC: 2841 Soap & other detergents

(G-11614)
NEWSPAPER HOLDING INC
Also Called: Woodward News
904 Oklahoma Ave (73801-4660)
P.O. Box 1046 (73802-1046)
PHONE.................................580 256-2200
Pam Nelson, *Principal*
EMP: 38 **Privately Held**
SIC: 2711 Commercial printing & newspaper publishing combined
HQ: Newspaper Holding, Inc.
 425 Locust St
 Johnstown PA 15901
 814 532-5102

(G-11615)
NORTH STAR WELL SERVICES INC
502 48th St (73801-2504)
P.O. Box 2167 (73802-2167)
PHONE.................................580 256-5644
Greg Jeter, *President*
Larry Pangry, *President*
EMP: 60
SQ FT: 45,000
SALES (est): 8.1MM **Privately Held**
WEB: www.nswsi.com
SIC: 1389 Oil field services

(G-11616)
PAT MCVICKER OILFIELD SERVICES
131 Spruce Dr (73801-5931)
PHONE.................................580 256-1577
EMP: 2
SALES (est): 227.5K **Privately Held**
SIC: 1389 Oil/Gas Field Services

(G-11617)
PATRICK MCVICKER
2728 Williams Ave (73801-5841)
PHONE.................................580 256-1577
Patrick McVicker, *Owner*
EMP: 2
SALES (est): 139.8K **Privately Held**
SIC: 1389 Oil field services

(G-11618)
PATTEN EQUIPMENT & WELDING LLC
41791 S County Road 200 # 9 (73801-5604)
PHONE.................................580 334-7035
EMP: 2
SALES (est): 58.9K **Privately Held**
SIC: 7692 Welding repair

(G-11619)
PCS FERGUSON INC
3510 Williams Ave (73801-7405)
PHONE.................................580 256-1317
Will Buie, *Sales Staff*
Pete Ramirez, *Branch Mgr*
EMP: 5
SALES (corp-wide): 1.1B **Publicly Held**
WEB: www.pcsferguson.com
SIC: 1389 Oil field services
HQ: Pcs Ferguson, Inc.
 3771 Eureka Way
 Frederick CO 80516
 720 407-3550

(G-11620)
PERRYTON IRON AND METAL LLC
1002 5th St (73801-3344)
PHONE.................................580 256-5536
EMP: 3
SALES (est): 327.3K **Privately Held**
SIC: 3446 Architectural metalwork

(G-11621)
PISTOL DRILLING LLC
4420 Anderson Rd (73801-2509)
P.O. Box 1067 (73802-1067)
PHONE.................................580 256-9371
Tommy W Weder Sr, *President*
Pamela S Weder, *CFO*
EMP: 4
SALES (est): 420K **Privately Held**
SIC: 1381 Drilling oil & gas wells

(G-11622)
POWER RIG LLC
199584 E County Road 39 (73801-5876)
P.O. Box 1570 (73802-1570)
PHONE.................................580 254-3232
Bobby Alexander, *Principal*
Casey Vinson, *Sales Staff*
Jeff Owen, *Manager*
EMP: 15
SALES (est): 2MM **Privately Held**
SIC: 1389 Oil field services

(G-11623)
PRECISION MACHINE & TOOL LLC
819 48th St (73801-1525)
P.O. Box 787 (73802-0787)
PHONE.................................580 256-2219
EMP: 3
SQ FT: 10,000
SALES (est): 190K **Privately Held**
SIC: 3541 Machine & Tools

(G-11624)
PURCELL JACK OIL GAS CNSULTING
3319 Hidden Ridge Rd (73801-6213)
PHONE.................................580 256-2040
Jack Purcell, *President*
EMP: 1
SALES (est): 150K **Privately Held**
SIC: 1389 Oil consultants

(G-11625)
R & R WELL SERVICE INC
507 48th St (73801-2505)
P.O. Box 1805 (73802-1805)
PHONE.................................580 254-3068
Michael Reasner, *Manager*
EMP: 6
SALES (corp-wide): 1MM **Privately Held**
SIC: 1389 Servicing oil & gas wells
PA: R & R Well Service Inc
 2 Prinz Cir
 Saint Charles MO 63303
 636 240-3347

(G-11626)
R-5 CAPS & TEES
43151 S County Road 203 (73801-5578)
PHONE.................................580 256-3579
Kathleen Roach, *Partner*
Faith Roach, *Partner*
EMP: 2 **EST:** 1994
SALES (est): 120K **Privately Held**
SIC: 2395 2396 Embroidery & art needlework; automotive & apparel trimmings

(G-11627)
RAY MEAT MARKET
3605 Williams Ave (73801-7418)
PHONE.................................580 256-6031
Chad O' Blander, *Owner*
Chad O'Blander, *Owner*
Gerry O' Blander, *Co-Owner*
EMP: 3
SALES (est): 172.1K **Privately Held**
SIC: 2011 5421 2013 Meat packing plants; meat markets, including freezer provisioners; sausages & other prepared meats

(G-11628)
RENEGADE SERVICES
22154 Us Highway 270 (73801-7730)
PHONE.................................580 254-2828
Charles Green, *Manager*
EMP: 4
SALES (est): 299K **Privately Held**
WEB: www.renegadewls.com
SIC: 1389 Oil field services

(G-11629)
RIDDLE CONSTRUCTION CO INC
3110 Robin Ridge Rd (73801-6365)
PHONE.................................580 256-8109
Rick Riddle, *President*
Berylene Riddle, *Admin Sec*
EMP: 2
SALES (est): 150K **Privately Held**
SIC: 1389 Construction, repair & dismantling services

(G-11630)
RIG CHASERS LLC
202672 E County Road 44 # 2 (73801-5964)
P.O. Box 127 (73802-0127)
PHONE.................................580 254-3830
Bryan Combs, *Mng Member*
Rose Combs,
EMP: 20
SALES (est): 1MM **Privately Held**
SIC: 1389 7353 Oil field services; cranes & aerial lift equipment, rental or leasing

(G-11631)
SIEMENS ENERGY
1123 Airpark Rd (73801)
PHONE.................................580 254-7824
EMP: 2
SALES (est): 198.2K **Privately Held**
SIC: 3511 Turbines & turbine generator sets

(G-11632)
SLAVIN WELDING SERVICES LLC
206493 E County Road 46 (73801-5054)
PHONE.................................806 217-0429
EMP: 1 **EST:** 2015
SALES (est): 32.6K **Privately Held**
SIC: 7692 Welding repair

(G-11633)
SOONER PRODUCTION SERVICES INC
3921 Oklahoma Ave (73801-3935)
P.O. Box 1659 (73802-1659)
PHONE.................................580 256-1155
Michael Reinhart, *President*
EMP: 10
SQ FT: 5,000
SALES (est): 522.2K **Privately Held**
SIC: 1389 Oil field services

(G-11634)
STOUT WELDING LLC
4832 Berryhill Dr (73801-3703)
P.O. Box 776 (73802-0776)
PHONE.................................580 254-2139
Bruce Stout, *Principal*
EMP: 1
SALES (est): 70.2K **Privately Held**
SIC: 7692 Welding repair

(G-11635)
STRIDE WELL SERVICE INC
1010 E Hanks Trl (73801-6636)
PHONE.................................580 254-2353
Ron Boyd, *President*
EMP: 28
SALES (est): 783.1K **Privately Held**
SIC: 1389 Oil field services

(G-11636)
SUMMIT LAYDOWN SERVICES INC
Also Called: Summit Casing Services
207694 E County Road 40 (73801-5794)
P.O. Box 872 (73802-0872)
PHONE.................................580 256-5700
Mitchel Hansen, *President*
EMP: 22 **EST:** 2005
SALES (est): 500K **Privately Held**
SIC: 3533 Oil field machinery & equipment

(G-11637)
SUN WEST MUD COMPANY INC
1107 Lakeview Dr (73801)
PHONE.................................580 256-2865
Frank James, *Branch Mgr*
EMP: 3
SALES (corp-wide): 40.8MM **Privately Held**
WEB: www.sunwestfluids.com
SIC: 1389 Mud service, oil field drilling
PA: Sun West Mud Company, Inc
 3002 W Front St
 Midland TX 79701
 432 689-0777

(G-11638)
SURESHOT CANS INC
194234 E County Road 50 (73801-5323)
PHONE.................................580 698-2800
John Bowser, *President*
EMP: 3 **EST:** 1976
SALES (est): 280.7K **Privately Held**
SIC: 2655 Cans, fiber: made from purchased material

(G-11639)
TACTICAL BALLISTIC SYSTEM
1703 8th St (73801-4737)
PHONE.................................580 254-5468
Dustin Ketron, *President*
Ann Ketron, *Vice Pres*
EMP: 5
SALES (est): 267.7K **Privately Held**
SIC: 3812 8731 Defense systems & equipment; commercial physical research

(G-11640)
TAZZ TOO EMBROIDERY
1120 6th St (73801-3366)
PHONE.................................580 334-7373
EMP: 1
SALES (est): 31.2K **Privately Held**
SIC: 2395 Embroidery & art needlework

(G-11641)
TERRA NITROGEN
1000 Terra Dr (73801-9596)
PHONE.................................580 256-8651
EMP: 4
SALES (est): 293.2K **Privately Held**
SIC: 2813 Nitrogen

(G-11642)
THOMPSON SERVICES
202201 E County Road 434 (73801-5588)
PHONE.................................580 256-5005
Paul Thompson, *Owner*
EMP: 50
SALES (est): 2.1MM **Privately Held**
SIC: 7692 Welding repair

(G-11643)
TORO WELDING INC
321 E Oklahoma Ave (73801-5005)
PHONE.................................580 334-8221
Mayte Rosales, *Administration*
EMP: 2
SALES (est): 156.8K **Privately Held**
SIC: 7692 Welding repair

(G-11644)
TRI STATE MACHINE & SUPPLY LLC
220 48th St (73801-2508)
P.O. Box 967 (73802-0967)
PHONE.................................580 256-6265
Fax: 580 256-1565
EMP: 9
SALES: 50K **Privately Held**
SIC: 3599 3533 Machine Shop/Mfg Oil Field Equipment

(G-11645)
TRONOX INCORPORATED
1222 10th St Ste 115 (73801-3156)
PHONE.................................580 921-5411
Tommie Deese, *Branch Mgr*
EMP: 5
SALES (corp-wide): 2.9MM **Privately Held**
SIC: 1321 Natural gas liquids
HQ: Tronox Incorporated
 1 Stamford Plz
 Stamford CT 06901
 203 705-3800

(G-11646)
UNIBRIDGE SCALE SYSTEMS
4902 Oklahoma Ave (73801-3713)
PHONE.................................580 254-3131
Joe Hamilton, *Owner*
EMP: 3
SQ FT: 2,000
SALES (est): 432.8K **Privately Held**
SIC: 5046 7699 3596 Scales, except laboratory; scale repair service; scales & balances, except laboratory

(G-11647)
UNIT DRILLING COMPANY
Woodward Division
1623 Downs Ave (73801-5437)
P.O. Box 38 (73802-0038)
PHONE.................................580 256-8688
EMP: 144

SALES (corp-wide): 1.5B **Publicly Held**
SIC: 1381 Oil/Gas Well Drilling
HQ: Unit Drilling Company
7130 S Lewis Ave Ste 1000
Tulsa OK 74132
918 493-7700

(G-11648)
UNITED SERVICES LIMITED
4325 Oil Patch Dr (73801-1513)
P.O. Box 689 (73802-0689)
PHONE..................580 256-5335
Mike Cook, *President*
EMP: 15
SALES (est): 3.3MM **Privately Held**
SIC: 1389 Oil field services

(G-11649)
US OIL TOOLS INC
6699 S 8th St (73801)
P.O. Box 567 (73802-0567)
PHONE..................580 256-6874
Mike Upchurch, *President*
EMP: 3
SALES (est): 232.3K **Privately Held**
SIC: 1389 Oil field services

(G-11650)
WESTERN METALSMITH DESIGN LLC
199416 E County Road 39 (73801-5958)
PHONE..................580 938-2153
Terry Daniel, *Mng Member*
Debi Daniel, *Mng Member*
EMP: 2
SALES (est): 128.1K **Privately Held**
SIC: 3911 Jewelry, precious metal

(G-11651)
WESTOAK PRODUCTION SVCS INC
4915 Western Ave (73801-9463)
P.O. Box 1975 (73802-1975)
PHONE..................580 254-3568
Wesley Kerby, *President*
Rita Kerby, *Corp Secy*
Shayne Castor, *Sales Staff*
EMP: 36
SALES (est): 6.4MM **Privately Held**
SIC: 1389 Lease tanks, oil field: erecting, cleaning & repairing

(G-11652)
WHITES WELDING LLC
46005 S County Road 202 (73801-5172)
P.O. Box 1761 (73802-1761)
PHONE..................580 254-3766
Calvin White, *CEO*
Kyle Bertholf, *CFO*
Jk Meadors, *Director*
EMP: 110
SQ FT: 30,000
SALES: 19MM
SALES (corp-wide): 79MM **Privately Held**
SIC: 1799 3561 Welding on site; pumps, oil well & field
PA: White's Energy Services, Llc
46005 S County Road 202
Woodward OK 73801
580 254-3766

(G-11653)
WILDCAT MINERALS
110 22nd St (73801-1016)
PHONE..................580 254-0141
EMP: 2
SALES (est): 124K **Privately Held**
SIC: 3295 Mfg Minerals-Ground/Treated

(G-11654)
WILDCATE DRILLING SERVICES INC
605 Martin Rd (73801-1517)
P.O. Box 905 (73802-0905)
PHONE..................580 254-3306
Martin Kirkley, *President*
Herman Crockett, *Vice Pres*
Donald C Gaston, *Admin Sec*
EMP: 20
SALES (est): 4.5MM **Privately Held**
SIC: 1381 Drilling oil & gas wells

(G-11655)
WOLF CREEK ENTERPRISES INC
1222 10th St Ste 109n (73801-3161)
PHONE..................580 254-3361
Bill Smithton, *President*
Linda Smithton, *Vice Pres*
Michell Wilson, *Admin Sec*
EMP: 4
SALES: 1MM **Privately Held**
SIC: 1311 Crude petroleum production

(G-11656)
WOODWARD IND SCHL DST I-1
Also Called: Woodward Prffsion Developement
1023 10th St (73801-3133)
PHONE..................580 256-5910
Wilmetta Dowell, *Manager*
Brian Wallace, *Director*
EMP: 2
SALES (corp-wide): 23.2MM **Privately Held**
SIC: 3554 Die cutting & stamping machinery, paper converting
PA: Woodward Independent School District I-1
1023 10th St
Woodward OK 73801
580 256-6063

(G-11657)
WOODWARD IODINE CORPORATION
205865 E County Rd 54 (73801)
P.O. Box 1245 (73802-1245)
PHONE..................580 254-3311
Leroy Goodman, *President*
Terry Davis, *Vice Pres*
Jack Woodard, *VP Engrg*
▲ **EMP:** 27
SALES (est): 6.6MM **Privately Held**
SIC: 2819 Iodine, elemental
HQ: Ise Chemicals Corporation
1-3-1, Kyobashi
Chuo-Ku TKY 104-0

(G-11658)
WOODWARD NEWS
904 Oklahoma Ave (73801-4660)
P.O. Box 1046 (73802-1046)
PHONE..................580 256-2200
Rich Macke, *Principal*
EMP: 45
SQ FT: 22,000
SALES (est): 1.8MM **Privately Held**
SIC: 2711 Newspapers: publishing only, not printed on site

(G-11659)
WYOMING CASING SERVICE INC
1020 Energy Rd (73801-5441)
PHONE..................580 256-1222
Tom Farrar, *Manager*
EMP: 20
SALES (corp-wide): 182.2MM **Privately Held**
SIC: 1389 Oil field services
PA: Wyoming Casing Service, Inc.
198 40th St E
Dickinson ND 58601
701 225-8521

Wyandotte
Ottawa County

(G-11660)
LUX ORTHOTICS & PROSTHETICS
9100 S 680 Rd (74370-1720)
PHONE..................417 624-2332
EMP: 4
SQ FT: 1,200
SALES (est): 498.6K **Privately Held**
SIC: 3842 Mfg Custom Braces

(G-11661)
OTTAWA OAK MFG
15604 S Highway 10 (74370-2342)
PHONE..................918 541-8996
EMP: 1 **EST:** 2016
SALES (est): 55.4K **Privately Held**
WEB: www.ottawaoak.com
SIC: 3999 Manufacturing industries

(G-11662)
RD LOGGING
69998 E 152 Rd (74370-2224)
PHONE..................918 666-2556
Rick Prater, *Owner*
EMP: 10
SALES (est): 457.7K **Privately Held**
SIC: 2411 2426 Logging camps & contractors; hardwood dimension & flooring mills

(G-11663)
WOOD TECH STRUCTURES
66301 E Highway 60 (74370-2093)
PHONE..................918 678-2108
John Zimmerman, *Owner*
EMP: 1
SALES (est): 106.5K **Privately Held**
SIC: 2452 Prefabricated wood buildings

Wynnewood
Garvin County

(G-11664)
CARDINAL ENERGY INC
207 S Dean A Mcgee Ave (73098-7809)
P.O. Box 2329, Ada (74821-2329)
PHONE..................405 331-9206
EMP: 3 **EST:** 2017
SALES (est): 228.7K **Privately Held**
SIC: 1382 Oil & gas exploration services

(G-11665)
CISPER WELDING
906 S Powell Ave (73098-7023)
PHONE..................405 665-2599
EMP: 1 **EST:** 2012
SALES (est): 43K **Privately Held**
SIC: 7692 Welding Repair

(G-11666)
CVR ENERGY INC
113 E Robert S Kerr Blvd (73098-6620)
P.O. Box 305 (73098-0305)
PHONE..................913 982-0500
Steve Lafferty, *Safety Mgr*
Jody Tinnin, *Manager*
Jack Parsons, *Technology*
EMP: 10 **EST:** 2013
SALES (est): 933.5K **Privately Held**
WEB: www.cvrenergy.com
SIC: 2911 Petroleum refining

(G-11667)
DDB UNLIMITED INCORPORATED (PA)
8445 Highway 77 N (73098-8915)
P.O. Box 669 (73098-0669)
PHONE..................405 665-2876
Dustin Mahorney, *President*
Mike Mahorney, *General Mgr*
Lester Mahorney, *Senior VP*
Howard Kirtley, *Warehouse Mgr*
Marvin Saucer, *Engineer*
EMP: 57
SQ FT: 28,500
SALES: 14MM **Privately Held**
SIC: 3354 Shapes, extruded aluminum

(G-11668)
DDB UNLIMITED INCORPORATED
Rr 1 Box 14 (73098-9801)
P.O. Box 669 (73098-0669)
PHONE..................800 753-8459
EMP: 10
SALES (corp-wide): 14MM **Privately Held**
SIC: 3354 Shapes, extruded aluminum
PA: Ddb Unlimited Incorporated
8445 Highway 77 N
Wynnewood OK 73098
405 665-2876

(G-11669)
DDB UNLIMITED INCORPORATED
8580 Highway 77 N (73098-8922)
P.O. Box 669 (73098-0669)
PHONE..................800 753-8459
Dustin Mahorney, *Branch Mgr*
EMP: 25
SALES (corp-wide): 14MM **Privately Held**
SIC: 3354 Shapes, extruded aluminum
PA: Ddb Unlimited Incorporated
8445 Highway 77 N
Wynnewood OK 73098
405 665-2876

(G-11670)
DIXON CONSTRUCTION CO
110 N Dean A Mcgee Ave (73098-7609)
P.O. Box 631 (73098-0631)
PHONE..................405 665-5515
Clifton R Dixon Jr, *President*
Sonya Dixon, *Corp Secy*
EMP: 25
SQ FT: 2,000
SALES (est): 5.7MM **Privately Held**
SIC: 1389 1794 1623 Oil field services; excavation work; water main construction; sewer line construction

(G-11671)
NATIONAL COATING
25679 Highway 77 N (73098-8968)
PHONE..................405 251-5065
EMP: 2
SALES (est): 84.6K **Privately Held**
SIC: 3479 Coating of metals & formed products

(G-11672)
RUSSELL PUBLISHING COMPANY
Also Called: Wynnewood Gazette
40752 Highway 29 (73098-9108)
P.O. Box 309 (73098-0309)
PHONE..................405 665-4333
Larry G Russell, *President*
Shannon Sharp, *Vice Pres*
Robin K Jolly, *Treasurer*
Shelly Lindsey, *Admin Sec*
EMP: 4 **EST:** 1994
SQ FT: 3,300
SALES (est): 175.6K **Privately Held**
WEB: www.thewynnewoodgazette.com
SIC: 2711 2791 Newspapers: publishing only, not printed on site; typesetting

(G-11673)
SPENCERS CONTRACT PUMPING LLC
42607 E County Road 1570 (73098-9060)
PHONE..................405 238-6363
Keith Spencer, *Mng Member*
Debbie Spencer, *Mng Member*
EMP: 2 **EST:** 2015
SALES (est): 79.2K **Privately Held**
SIC: 1389 7389 Pumping of oil & gas wells;

(G-11674)
TESSENDERLO KERLEY INC
307 W South St (73098)
P.O. Box 667 (73098-0667)
PHONE..................405 665-2544
Ed Golden, *Branch Mgr*
EMP: 20 **Privately Held**
SIC: 2819 2873 2874 Sodium hyposulfite, sodium hydrosulfite; ammonia & ammonium salts; phosphatic fertilizers
HQ: Tessenderlo Kerley, Inc.
2255 N 44th St Ste 300
Phoenix AZ 85008
602 889-8300

(G-11675)
WYNNEWOOD 1500 LLC
1500 E Kerr Blvd (73098-1007)
PHONE..................248 268-3289
Kirk Bruce, *Principal*
EMP: 1
SALES (est): 41.5K **Privately Held**
SIC: 2499 Wood products

Wynnewood - Garvin County

(G-11676)
WYNNEWOOD LLC
1500 E Kerr Blvd (73098-1007)
PHONE..............................248 268-3289
Kirk Bruce, *Principal*
EMP: 1
SALES (est): 41.5K **Privately Held**
SIC: 2499 Wood products

(G-11677)
WYNNEWOOD REFINING COMPANY LLC
906 S Powell Ave (73098-7023)
P.O. Box 305 (73098-0305)
PHONE..............................405 665-6565
Dan Looney, *Safety Dir*
Susan Ball, *Manager*
EMP: 41 **Publicly Held**
SIC: 2911 Petroleum refining
HQ: Wynnewood Refining Company, Llc
2277 Plaza Dr Ste 500
Sugar Land TX 77479

Wynona
Osage County

(G-11678)
GOOBERS DRILLING LLC
415 W 7th St (74084-5008)
P.O. Box 152 (74084-0152)
PHONE..............................918 846-2732
Chris McCutchen, *Mng Member*
EMP: 3
SALES (est): 297.2K **Privately Held**
SIC: 1381 Drilling oil & gas wells

(G-11679)
HOWELLS WELL SERVICE INC
203 E 6th St (74084)
P.O. Box 516 (74084-0516)
PHONE..............................918 846-2531
Barbara Howell-Taylor, *President*
Barbara Howell Taylor, *President*
James Howell, *Vice Pres*
EMP: 5
SQ FT: 2,000
SALES (est): 472.6K **Privately Held**
SIC: 1389 Running, cutting & pulling casings, tubes & rods

(G-11680)
HURD OIL INC
2 Mi North Of City (74084)
P.O. Box 28 (74084-0028)
PHONE..............................918 846-2725
Billy G Hurd Sr, *President*
Patricia Hurd, *Corp Secy*
Billy G Hurd Jr, *Vice Pres*
EMP: 4 **EST:** 1982
SALES (est): 335K **Privately Held**
SIC: 1311 Crude petroleum production

Yale
Payne County

(G-11681)
CORNERSTONE WELDING
1609 S Underwood (74085-2667)
PHONE..............................918 387-2538
EMP: 1 **EST:** 2010
SALES (est): 50K **Privately Held**
SIC: 7692 Welding Repair

(G-11682)
CTM WELDING & FABRICATION LLC
824 W Beaumont Ave (74085-4504)
PHONE..............................405 408-4628
Josh Garnett, *Mng Member*
EMP: 1
SALES (est): 30.3K **Privately Held**
SIC: 7692 Welding repair

(G-11683)
CUSHING TRUSS MANUFACTURING
1010 N Highway 18 (74085-6698)
PHONE..............................918 387-2080
Harry Sneed III, *President*
Scott Skidmore, *Vice Pres*
Joyce Sneed, *Vice Pres*
EMP: 15
SQ FT: 40,000
SALES (est): 1MM **Privately Held**
WEB: www.cushingtruss.com
SIC: 2439 3448 3441 Trusses, wooden roof; trusses & framing; prefabricated metal; fabricated structural metal

(G-11684)
DH WELDING LLC
26810 E 19th St (74085-6410)
PHONE..............................918 906-6534
Dalton Raydean Hendrix, *Owner*
EMP: 1 **EST:** 2017
SALES (est): 38.2K **Privately Held**
SIC: 7692 Welding repair

(G-11685)
LVM OIL PRODUCTION LLC
16010 E Mcelroy (74085-6688)
PHONE..............................918 387-2822
Tammi Truitt, *Principal*
EMP: 3
SALES (est): 186.5K **Privately Held**
SIC: 1311 Crude petroleum production

(G-11686)
MOORE IRON & STEEL CORP
Also Called: Misco
201 W Charleston Ave (74085-6001)
PHONE..............................918 387-2639
David Moore, *President*
Matthew Moore, *Vice Pres*
Mike McCull, *CFO*
Tyler Scheller, *Manager*
EMP: 90
SQ FT: 9,300
SALES (est): 36.4MM **Privately Held**
SIC: 3441 Fabricated structural metal

(G-11687)
SUPREME MCH & STL FABRICATION
305 S Main St (74085-6007)
PHONE..............................918 387-2036
Michael Prince, *President*
Tammy Prince, *Vice Pres*
Linda Prince, *Admin Sec*
EMP: 16
SQ FT: 4,000
SALES (est): 3.2MM **Privately Held**
SIC: 3533 3441 Oil & gas field machinery; fabricated structural metal

Yukon
Canadian County

(G-11688)
A ROYAL FLUSH LLC
213 Kingsgate Rd (73099-4435)
P.O. Box 851164 (73085-1164)
PHONE..............................405 422-2077
Hillis James, *Mng Member*
EMP: 4 **EST:** 2010
SALES (est): 453.5K **Privately Held**
WEB: www.aroyalflushok.com
SIC: 3089 1711 Toilets, portable chemical: plastic; plumbing contractors

(G-11689)
ACQUIRE CCTV INC
Also Called: Acquire Video Security
13101 Sw 10th St (73099-6383)
PHONE..............................405 324-1300
Travis Ray, *President*
EMP: 3
SALES (est): 337.3K **Privately Held**
SIC: 3699 Security devices

(G-11690)
ALPHAGRAFFIX INC
302 W Main St (73099-1216)
PHONE..............................405 354-3000
Janet Fish, *President*
Jennifer Krieger, *Vice Pres*
EMP: 1
SALES (est): 150K **Privately Held**
SIC: 3993 Signs & advertising specialties

(G-11691)
APT INC
Also Called: Aniti Pollution Tank
1135 Industrial Dr (73099-2827)
PHONE..............................405 354-8438
Jerry Bird, *President*
Annette Bird, *Corp Secy*
EMP: 2
SQ FT: 5,000
SALES: 100K **Privately Held**
SIC: 3533 5082 Oil field machinery & equipment; oil field equipment

(G-11692)
ARCHITECTURAL SIGN & GRAPHICS
839 Industrial Dr (73099-2834)
PHONE..............................405 354-8829
John Abrell, *President*
Debbie Abrell, *Corp Secy*
EMP: 4
SQ FT: 3,200
SALES (est): 533.7K **Privately Held**
SIC: 3993 1799 Signs & advertising specialties; sign installation & maintenance

(G-11693)
ARMACELL LLC
524 N Sara Rd (73099-5112)
PHONE..............................405 494-2800
Tom Anen, *Director*
EMP: 2 **Privately Held**
WEB: www.armacell.com
SIC: 3086 Plastics foam products
HQ: Armacell, Llc
55 Vilcom Center Dr # 200
Chapel Hill NC 27514

(G-11694)
BACKUP FORTRESS LLC
11221 Nw 97th St (73099-4000)
PHONE..............................405 314-2436
Gardner Wendy,
EMP: 1
SALES: 4K **Privately Held**
SIC: 3579 Office machines

(G-11695)
BAKER HUGHES A GE COMPANY LLC
11041 Nw 10th St (73099-5125)
PHONE..............................806 435-4096
Peggy Dunn, *Admin Sec*
EMP: 45
SALES (corp-wide): 23.8B **Publicly Held**
SIC: 1389 Oil field services
HQ: Baker Hughes Holdings Llc
17021 Aldine Westfield Rd
Houston TX 77073
713 439-8600

(G-11696)
BASIC ENERGY SERVICES INC
Also Called: G & L Tool
804 S Mustang Rd (73099-6767)
PHONE..............................405 324-0848
William Jones, *Human Res Mgr*
EMP: 8
SALES (corp-wide): 567.2MM **Publicly Held**
SIC: 1389 Oil field services
PA: Basic Energy Services, Inc.
801 Cherry St Unit 2
Fort Worth TX 76102
817 334-4100

(G-11697)
BATH BOMB DYES
733 S Mustang Rd (73099-6778)
PHONE..............................405 406-1823
Lacey Ogden, *Principal*
EMP: 2
SALES (est): 80.3K **Privately Held**
SIC: 2844 Bath salts

(G-11698)
BJH SERVICES INC
2805 Melina Dr (73099-6978)
PHONE..............................281 686-3408
Harry Crossley, *Director*
EMP: 2
SALES (est): 76.4K **Privately Held**
SIC: 1389 Oil field services

(G-11699)
BLAIRS OIL FIELD SERVICES LLC
7675 N Gregory Rd (73099-9063)
PHONE..............................405 698-9987
Eric Blair,
EMP: 2
SALES (est): 65.5K **Privately Held**
SIC: 1389 Haulage, oil field

(G-11700)
BR ELECTRIC
1112 S 2nd St (73099-4624)
PHONE..............................405 354-8994
John C Robert, *Owner*
EMP: 1
SALES (est): 40.7K **Privately Held**
SIC: 1731 3643 General electrical contractor; lightning protection equipment

(G-11701)
BRUINS OIL & GAS LLC
2201 Waterford Ln (73099-4672)
PHONE..............................806 323-8353
EMP: 2
SALES (est): 76.5K **Privately Held**
SIC: 1389 Oil & gas field services

(G-11702)
CAROLYNS MOUSE HOUSE
7700 N Cimarron Rd (73099-9037)
PHONE..............................405 354-2858
EMP: 2
SALES (est): 79K **Privately Held**
SIC: 2395 Pleating/Stitching Services

(G-11703)
CAS MONOGRAMMING INC
Also Called: Cas Monogramming and Team Spt
200 S Ranchwood Blvd # 10 (73099-2740)
PHONE..............................405 350-6556
Susan Roesch, *President*
Hank Roesch, *Corp Secy*
EMP: 3
SQ FT: 1,800
SALES (est): 190K **Privately Held**
SIC: 5651 5699 7336 2395 Unisex clothing stores; uniforms; silk screen design; pleating & stitching

(G-11704)
CERDAFIED WELDING LLC
10701 Sw 31st Ct (73099-3334)
PHONE..............................405 578-8035
Juan Cerda, *Principal*
EMP: 1 **EST:** 2017
SALES (est): 25K **Privately Held**
SIC: 7692 Welding repair

(G-11705)
CIMARRON EQUINE STATION
11630 N Cimarron Rd (73099-9219)
PHONE..............................405 373-0358
Daniel Fine, *Principal*
EMP: 2 **EST:** 2009
SALES (est): 113.9K **Privately Held**
WEB: www.cimarronequine.com
SIC: 2399 Horse harnesses & riding crops, etc.: non-leather

(G-11706)
CLASSIC IRON WORKS INC
Also Called: American Iron Works
201 Arlington Dr (73099-2832)
PHONE..............................405 577-2877
Steve Beeson, *President*
Jana Beeson, *CFO*
▼ **EMP:** 12
SQ FT: 42,000
SALES: 10MM **Privately Held**
SIC: 3084 Plastics pipe

(G-11707)
COASTLINE OIL & GAS LLC
705 Kingston Dr (73099-3820)
PHONE..............................405 354-6507
Alan Berry White, *Principal*
EMP: 2 **EST:** 2016
SALES (est): 110.1K **Privately Held**
SIC: 1389 Oil & gas field services

GEOGRAPHIC SECTION

Yukon - Canadian County (G-11741)

(G-11708)
COLOR-RITE INC
600 S Ranchwood Blvd (73099-2730)
PHONE..................................405 354-3644
Floyd Meinke, *President*
Jeff Hopper, *General Mgr*
Pat Meinke, *Corp Secy*
Adam Meinke, *Vice Pres*
Wendy Billey, *Marketing Staff*
EMP: 14
SQ FT: 15,000
SALES (est): 3.4MM **Privately Held**
SIC: 2891 Caulking compounds

(G-11709)
COMMUNITY RACKS LLC
9325 Nw 75th St (73099-9665)
P.O. Box 42776, Oklahoma City (73123-3776)
PHONE..................................405 210-7950
John Ray, *Mng Member*
EMP: 15
SQ FT: 200
SALES (est): 750K **Privately Held**
SIC: 2741 7319 Racing forms & programs: publishing only, not printing; distribution of advertising material or sample services

(G-11710)
COMPLETE ENERGY LLC
Also Called: Fluid Management
220 N Sara Rd (73099-5182)
PHONE..................................405 748-2200
EMP: 5 **Publicly Held**
SIC: 1389 Oil field services
HQ: Complete Energy, Llc
 1001 La St Ste 2900
 Houston TX 77002

(G-11711)
COMPLETE ENERGY SERVICES INC
220 N Sara Rd (73099-5182)
PHONE..................................405 748-2211
Kelly Gray, *Vice Pres*
EMP: 99 **Publicly Held**
SIC: 1389 Oil field services
HQ: Complete Energy Services, Inc.
 1001 La St Ste 2900
 Houston TX 77002
 713 654-2200

(G-11712)
COMPTON INDUSTRIES LLC
720 Greenfield Dr (73099-7135)
PHONE..................................405 496-6269
EMP: 3
SALES (est): 176.2K **Privately Held**
SIC: 3999 Manufacturing industries

(G-11713)
CORK AND BOTTLE WINE AND
9621 High Noon Rd (73099-9299)
PHONE..................................405 318-6842
EMP: 1
SALES (est): 41.5K **Privately Held**
SIC: 2499 Corks, bottle

(G-11714)
D B W INC
201 Oak Ave (73099-2635)
P.O. Box 850678 (73085-0678)
PHONE..................................405 354-6211
Barry West, *President*
EMP: 9
SQ FT: 6,500
SALES (est): 1.2MM **Privately Held**
SIC: 3544 3089 Special dies, tools, jigs & fixtures; injection molded finished plastic products

(G-11715)
DATHNEY INC
717 Vickery Ave (73099-5958)
P.O. Box 851385 (73085-1385)
PHONE..................................405 354-0381
Mike Kennemer, *President*
Dana Kennemer, *Vice Pres*
EMP: 3
SALES (est): 180K **Privately Held**
SIC: 3559 8999 Chemical machinery & equipment; chemical consultant

(G-11716)
DEFENSE ANGEL LLC
4013 Chase Cir (73099-7212)
P.O. Box 175, Dibble (73031-0175)
PHONE..................................405 476-4222
EMP: 3
SALES (est): 181.8K **Privately Held**
SIC: 3812 Defense systems & equipment

(G-11717)
DEVINE INDUSTRIAL SYSTEMS INC
10108 Thompson Ave (73099-7961)
PHONE..................................405 627-3448
Andrew Devine, *Principal*
EMP: 7 **EST:** 2009
SALES (est): 1.2MM **Privately Held**
WEB: www.devineindustrialsystems.com
SIC: 3492 Control valves, fluid power: hydraulic & pneumatic

(G-11718)
DIAMOND OIL FIELD SERVICES INC
6521 Lois Ln (73099-7278)
P.O. Box 850689 (73085-0689)
PHONE..................................405 863-1052
Marga Miller, *President*
EMP: 1
SALES (est): 244.7K **Privately Held**
SIC: 1389 Oil field services

(G-11719)
DIAMOND OILFIELD SERVICES INC
7941 N Richland Rd (73099-9128)
P.O. Box 850689 (73085-0689)
PHONE..................................405 243-7113
Lee W Spence III, *Principal*
EMP: 6
SALES (est): 726.6K **Privately Held**
SIC: 1311 Oil sand mining

(G-11720)
DOLESE BROS CO
Also Called: Yukon Stone Yard
10700 Nw 10th St (73099-5118)
PHONE..................................405 324-2944
Jim Clymer, *Manager*
EMP: 2
SALES (corp-wide): 8.5MM **Privately Held**
SIC: 3273 Ready-mixed concrete
PA: Dolese Bros. Co.
 20 Nw 13th St
 Oklahoma City OK 73103
 405 235-2311

(G-11721)
DOODLE AND PECK PUBLISHING
413 Cedarburg Ct (73099-5764)
PHONE..................................405 354-7422
EMP: 2
SALES (est): 59.2K **Privately Held**
SIC: 2741 Miscellaneous publishing

(G-11722)
ESSEX ENERGY INC
11141 Nw 10th St (73099-5126)
PHONE..................................405 350-1351
Jim Niles, *President*
Jason Niles, *Admin Sec*
EMP: 3
SQ FT: 3,200
SALES (est): 260K **Privately Held**
SIC: 1382 Oil & gas exploration services

(G-11723)
FHE USA LLC
12451 Nw 10th St (73099-5839)
PHONE..................................405 350-2544
EMP: 1
SALES (corp-wide): 125.5MM **Privately Held**
SIC: 3533 Oil & gas field machinery
PA: Fhe Usa Llc
 1597 Cipolla Rd
 Fruita CO 81521
 970 243-0727

(G-11724)
FIFTEEN FIVE GTTER SLTIONS LLC
3601 Mustang Creek Cir (73099-7630)
PHONE..................................405 219-6741
Randel Scott Taylor, *Owner*
EMP: 2 **EST:** 2013
SQ FT: 1,500
SALES (est): 139.8K **Privately Held**
SIC: 8748 3444 1761 Business consulting; gutters, sheet metal; gutter & downspout contractor

(G-11725)
FLORES WELDING SERVICES LLC
11857 Sw 4th St (73099-7142)
PHONE..................................405 473-5534
EMP: 1 **EST:** 2015
SALES (est): 35.6K **Privately Held**
SIC: 7692 Welding repair

(G-11726)
GO PRINT USA
719 Garden Grv (73099-4213)
PHONE..................................405 708-7000
EMP: 2 **EST:** 2014
SALES (est): 83.9K **Privately Held**
SIC: 2752 Commercial printing, lithographic

(G-11727)
GONZO LLC
15750 Nw Expressway (73099-9245)
PHONE..................................405 373-1715
EMP: 5
SALES (est): 264.5K **Privately Held**
SIC: 1389 Oil field services

(G-11728)
GRAYFOX VINEYARDS LLC
6745 N Gregory Rd (73099-9261)
PHONE..................................918 378-2214
Oscar Cremer,
EMP: 2 **EST:** 2017
SALES (est): 62.3K **Privately Held**
SIC: 2084 Wines

(G-11729)
H/H MOBILE WELDING LLC
14525 W Frisco Dr (73099-9087)
PHONE..................................405 830-5525
Kathy Harris, *Administration*
EMP: 1
SALES (est): 48.3K **Privately Held**
SIC: 7692 Welding repair

(G-11730)
HOLLYWOOD EXPRESS OKLAHOMA INC
14700 Nw 10th St (73099-4149)
P.O. Box 850278 (73085-0278)
PHONE..................................405 324-8111
Terri Pettigrew, *Principal*
EMP: 3
SALES (est): 338.4K **Privately Held**
SIC: 2329 Knickers, dress (separate): men's & boys'

(G-11731)
HOUSE INDUSTRIES LLC
16100 W Britton Rd (73099-8546)
PHONE..................................405 761-5574
Jennie House,
EMP: 2 **EST:** 2009
SALES (est): 145.4K **Privately Held**
SIC: 3999 Manufacturing industries

(G-11732)
IFE NDT LLC
14698 Clair Ct W (73099-8534)
PHONE..................................405 642-4899
EMP: 2
SALES (est): 253.6K **Privately Held**
SIC: 1389 Testing, measuring, surveying & analysis services

(G-11733)
J H B & COMPANY INC
809 Lancaster Dr (73099-4931)
PHONE..................................405 354-6709
James H Blurton, *President*
EMP: 2
SALES (est): 80K **Privately Held**
SIC: 1381 Drilling oil & gas wells

(G-11734)
J ROSE PRINTING LLC
301 Pointe Parkway Blvd # 1402 (73099-0618)
PHONE..................................210 875-0947
Kiara Dean, *Owner*
EMP: 2
SALES (est): 83.9K **Privately Held**
SIC: 2752 Commercial printing, lithographic

(G-11735)
JAN FARHA
Also Called: Jan Farha Interiors
400 Poplar Ave (73099-2659)
PHONE..................................405 848-1388
Jan Farha, *Owner*
EMP: 1
SQ FT: 1,300
SALES (est): 109.4K **Privately Held**
SIC: 7389 2339 Interior designer; women's & misses' athletic clothing & sportswear

(G-11736)
JKJ PROCESSING INC
12204 W Reno Ave Ste B (73099-7738)
PHONE..................................405 606-9711
Ioannis Gregory Koumbis Jr, *CEO*
EMP: 1
SALES (est): 39.5K **Privately Held**
SIC: 2099 Dessert mixes & fillings

(G-11737)
JOB PAPER LLC
Also Called: Calico Dragon
113 W Olympic Dr (73099-5809)
PHONE..................................405 242-4804
Candace Brown,
EMP: 5
SQ FT: 5,800
SALES: 550K **Privately Held**
SIC: 2711 3171 Newspapers, publishing & printing; handbags, women's

(G-11738)
JOHNS PROFESSIONAL SHARPENING
316 Partridge Run Rd (73099-9512)
P.O. Box 851024 (73085-1024)
PHONE..................................405 313-7027
John Ryan, *Owner*
EMP: 1
SALES (est): 84.6K **Privately Held**
SIC: 3421 7389 Scissors, shears, clippers, snips & similar tools;

(G-11739)
KELLY-MOORE PAINT COMPANY INC
1224 Garth Brooks Blvd (73099-4107)
PHONE..................................405 350-2375
EMP: 1
SALES (corp-wide): 696.6MM **Privately Held**
WEB: www.kellymoore.com
SIC: 2851 5198 Paints & allied products; paints, varnishes & supplies
PA: Kelly-Moore Paint Company Northwest, Inc.
 987 Commercial St
 San Carlos CA 94070
 650 592-8337

(G-11740)
KODIAK PRODUCTION COMPANY
505 W Main St (73099-1219)
PHONE..................................405 350-6465
Charles R Hensley, *President*
Debbie Stewart, *Admin Sec*
EMP: 5
SQ FT: 3,887
SALES (est): 596K **Privately Held**
SIC: 1382 Oil & gas exploration services

(G-11741)
KOMMUNITEES LLC
4825 Elk Run (73099-3111)
PHONE..................................405 203-2491
EMP: 3
SALES (est): 265.1K **Privately Held**
SIC: 2759 Screen printing

Yukon - Canadian County (G-11742)

(G-11742)
LKQ REMANUFACTURING YUKON
600 N Sara Rd (73099-5117)
PHONE...................405 494-4908
EMP: 1
SALES (est): 52.6K Privately Held
SIC: 3999 Manufacturing industries

(G-11743)
M P READY MIX INC (PA)
Also Called: Schwarz Ready Mix
1400 Holly Ave (73099-5322)
P.O. Box 850450 (73085-0450)
PHONE...................405 354-8824
Philip Schwarz, *President*
Gene Schwarz, *Vice Pres*
Mark Schwarz, *Vice Pres*
James Schwarz, *Treasurer*
EMP: 32
SALES (est): 3.7MM Privately Held
SIC: 3273 5032 Ready-mixed concrete; brick, stone & related material

(G-11744)
M2PRINT LLC
2248 Timber Xing (73099-5037)
PHONE...................505 263-7999
EMP: 2
SALES (est): 83.9K Privately Held
SIC: 2752 Commercial printing, lithographic

(G-11745)
MAKEBA DESIGN & PRINTS LLC
13908 Teagen Ln (73099-1045)
PHONE...................405 719-0104
EMP: 2
SALES (est): 83.9K Privately Held
SIC: 2752 Commercial printing, lithographic

(G-11746)
MAR WELDING LLC
3209 Canton Trl (73099-4174)
PHONE...................580 747-9967
Michelle Rutz, *Administration*
EMP: 1
SALES (est): 44.4K Privately Held
SIC: 7692 Welding repair

(G-11747)
MARSHALL PRINTING
11120 Nw 111th St (73099-8031)
PHONE...................405 883-6122
Mark Marshall, *Principal*
EMP: 2
SALES (est): 83.9K Privately Held
SIC: 2752 Commercial printing, lithographic

(G-11748)
MARTIN-DECKER TOTCO INC
888 17th St (73099)
PHONE...................405 350-7408
Danny Van Demeter, *Branch Mgr*
EMP: 10
SALES (corp-wide): 8.4B Publicly Held
SIC: 3533 Oil & gas field machinery
HQ: Martin-Decker Totco, Inc.
  1200 Cypress Creek Rd
  Cedar Park TX 78613

(G-11749)
MARY K ROSE INC
632 Westridge Dr (73099-6728)
PHONE...................405 324-5612
Mary Rose, *President*
EMP: 1
SALES (est): 84.7K Privately Held
SIC: 1389 Oil consultants

(G-11750)
MCALISTER DRUG CORPORATION
948 S Yukon Pkwy (73099-4589)
PHONE...................405 354-2582
Craig McAlister, *Vice Pres*
EMP: 3
SALES (est): 167.4K Privately Held
SIC: 3841 8099 Muscle exercise apparatus, ophthalmic; blood bank

(G-11751)
MCELROYS WELDING SERVICES LLC
13008 Nw 91st St (73099-8461)
PHONE...................405 354-2019
Joshua McElroy, *Owner*
EMP: 1 EST: 2018
SALES (est): 30K Privately Held
SIC: 7692 Welding repair

(G-11752)
MELMARK SERVICES INC
12228 Sw 26th St (73099-7086)
PHONE...................405 324-6999
Mark Lowe, *President*
EMP: 2
SALES (est): 190K Privately Held
SIC: 1382 Oil & gas exploration services

(G-11753)
METRO PUBLISHING LLC
916 Preston Park Dr (73099-2152)
PHONE...................405 593-1335
Elizabeth Smith,
EMP: 1
SALES (est): 66.4K Privately Held
SIC: 2741 Miscellaneous publishing

(G-11754)
MIKE MACDOWELL WELDING
14540 W Wilshire Blvd (73099-8464)
PHONE...................405 354-1221
EMP: 1 EST: 2010
SALES (est): 49K Privately Held
SIC: 7692 Welding Repair

(G-11755)
MILITARY PARTS MFG LLC
420 Winding Creek Rd (73099-4472)
PHONE...................405 301-2990
Matt Poursaba, *Mng Member*
Corby Poursaba,
EMP: 1
SALES (est): 62K Privately Held
SIC: 3999 Manufacturing industries

(G-11756)
MITCH BASKETT
Also Called: 3b Backhoe Services
11704 Sw 4th St (73099-6758)
PHONE...................405 324-7810
Mitch Baskett, *Owner*
EMP: 1
SALES (est): 109.6K Privately Held
SIC: 3531 Backhoes

(G-11757)
MOORE SCENTS LLC
10637 Sw 36th St (73099-0447)
PHONE...................405 642-5472
Ashley Dixon, *Administration*
EMP: 2
SALES (est): 116.3K Privately Held
SIC: 2844 Toilet preparations

(G-11758)
NEW U CBD OIL
7605 Harold Dr (73099-9744)
PHONE...................405 568-8750
Anita Walker, *Principal*
EMP: 1
SALES (est): 44.7K Privately Held
SIC: 3999

(G-11759)
NOMACO INC
524 N Sara Rd (73099-5112)
PHONE...................405 494-2800
Michael Beavers, *Branch Mgr*
EMP: 100
SALES (corp-wide): 108.1MM Privately Held
SIC: 3086 Plastics foam products
HQ: Nomaco Inc.
  501 Innovative Way
  Zebulon NC 27597
  919 269-6500

(G-11760)
NOMAD DEFENSE LLC
101 E Mesa Verde St (73099-5932)
P.O. Box 851957 (73085-1957)
PHONE...................405 808-4325
Erick Westfahl,
EMP: 1
SALES (est): 57.6K Privately Held
SIC: 3315 7389 Steel wire & related products;

(G-11761)
OKLAHOMA STONE
9311 Nw Expressway (73099-8346)
PHONE...................405 721-6775
Mitch Short, *Principal*
▼ EMP: 16
SALES (est): 2.5MM Privately Held
SIC: 1411 Dimension stone

(G-11762)
OUT N BACK HOT SHOT LLC
4608 Deer Creek Ct (73099-3101)
PHONE...................405 201-3576
Jimmy Keith Milhoan, *Owner*
EMP: 2 EST: 2017
SALES (est): 101.3K Privately Held
SIC: 1389 Hot shot service

(G-11763)
PACIFIC OIL & GAS LLC
16300 W Highway 66 (73099-9075)
PHONE...................405 835-2790
EMP: 2 EST: 2016
SALES (est): 81.9K Privately Held
SIC: 1382 Oil & gas exploration services

(G-11764)
PATRIOT PRSTHTICS ORTHTICS INC
1804 Commons Cir Ste A (73099-9525)
PHONE...................405 577-6778
Michael Huggins, *CEO*
EMP: 3 EST: 2014
SALES (est): 326.5K Privately Held
SIC: 3842 Limbs, artificial; prosthetic appliances

(G-11765)
PENN ALUMINUM INC
4121 Lake Dr (73099-3252)
PHONE...................405 476-5222
EMP: 2
SALES (est): 158.5K Privately Held
SIC: 3444 Sheet metalwork

(G-11766)
PLANE NAKED LLC
Also Called: Akmfd
950 E Wagner Rd (73099-2128)
PHONE...................405 317-7661
Karly Levi,
EMP: 1
SALES (est): 54K Privately Held
SIC: 2842 Cleaning or polishing preparations

(G-11767)
PRECAST SOLUTIONS LLC
1809 Grainer St (73099-3537)
PHONE...................580 819-2455
Tina Barnhill, *Principal*
EMP: 5 EST: 2011
SALES (est): 486.9K Privately Held
SIC: 3272 Precast terrazo or concrete products

(G-11768)
PRIORITY ARTIFICIAL LIFT
1509 Commerce (73099-2236)
PHONE...................405 265-1696
EMP: 2
SALES (est): 128.9K Privately Held
SIC: 1389 Oil field services

(G-11769)
PROTRAC INDUSTRIES LLC
10020 Leeds Dr (73099-7903)
PHONE...................405 312-5122
Brett Shelton, *Principal*
EMP: 2
SALES (est): 92.6K Privately Held
SIC: 3999 Manufacturing industries

(G-11770)
QUIKRETE HOLDINGS INC
1400 Holly Ave Ste 100 (73099-5322)
PHONE...................405 354-8824
EMP: 1 Privately Held
WEB: www.quikrete.com
SIC: 3272 Concrete products
PA: Quikrete Holdings, Inc.
  5 Concourse Pkwy Ste 1900
  Atlanta GA 30328

(G-11771)
REVIEW NEWS CO
Also Called: Yukon Review
335 S Mustang Rd Ste F (73099-7440)
P.O. Box 851400 (73085-1400)
PHONE...................405 354-5264
Randel Grigsby, *President*
Karen Grigsby, *Corp Secy*
EMP: 15
SALES (est): 983.5K Privately Held
SIC: 2711 Newspapers: publishing only, not printed on site

(G-11772)
ROBS WELDING LLC
10304 Nw 39th St (73099-3227)
PHONE...................405 596-4906
Rob Horn, *Principal*
EMP: 8
SALES (est): 88.7K Privately Held
SIC: 7692 Welding repair

(G-11773)
ROCKING C WELDING LLC
316 Yuhoma Dr (73099-3941)
PHONE...................405 589-8903
Coby Grimes, *Principal*
EMP: 1 EST: 2017
SALES (est): 25K Privately Held
SIC: 7692 Welding repair

(G-11774)
SALAMANDER GAMES INC
10805 Nw 118th Pl (73099-8154)
P.O. Box 720685, Oklahoma City (73172-0685)
PHONE...................405 633-2725
Joshua Ryan Fry, *President*
Chad Scott, *Vice Pres*
EMP: 2
SALES (est): 152.1K Privately Held
SIC: 3944 Electronic games & toys

(G-11775)
SANDRIDGE ENERGY INC
410 Maple St (73099-2600)
PHONE...................405 354-2727
Dennis Miller, *Branch Mgr*
EMP: 542
SALES (corp-wide): 266.8MM Publicly Held
WEB: www.sandridgeenergy.com
SIC: 1311 Crude petroleum production
PA: Sandridge Energy, Inc.
  123 Robert S Kerr Ave
  Oklahoma City OK 73102
  405 429-5500

(G-11776)
SCAN TO
353 E Main St (73099-2240)
PHONE...................405 413-8015
EMP: 2 EST: 2016
SALES (est): 85.9K Privately Held
SIC: 3577 Computer peripheral equipment

(G-11777)
SCHLUMBERGER TECHNOLOGY CORP
10546 Nw 10th St (73099-5193)
PHONE...................405 682-2284
James Leshikar, *Branch Mgr*
EMP: 2 Publicly Held
SIC: 1389 Oil field services
HQ: Schlumberger Technology Corp
  300 Schlumberger Dr
  Sugar Land TX 77478
  281 285-8500

(G-11778)
SCHWARZ READY MIX OF OKC
1400 Holly Ave (73099-5322)
P.O. Box 850450 (73085-0450)
PHONE...................405 354-6671
EMP: 5
SALES (est): 1.3MM Privately Held
SIC: 3273 Ready-mixed concrete

GEOGRAPHIC SECTION

Yukon - Canadian County (G-11809)

(G-11779)
SCIENTIFIC DRILLING INTL
11220 Nw 10th St (73099-5947)
PHONE..................405 787-3663
Larry Nobles, *Manager*
Benjamin Bluhm, *Supervisor*
EMP: 6
SALES (est): 300.9K **Privately Held**
SIC: 1381 Drilling oil & gas wells

(G-11780)
SCIENTIFIC DRILLING INTL INC
11220 Nw 10th St (73099-5947)
PHONE..................405 787-3663
EMP: 100
SALES (corp-wide): 20.8MM **Privately Held**
SIC: 1381 8713 1382 1389 Directional drilling oil & gas wells; surveying services; oil & gas exploration services; oil field services
PA: Scientific Drilling International, Inc.
16071 Grnspint Pk Dr Ste
Houston TX 77060
281 443-3300

(G-11781)
SHELL CREEK VINEYARDS LLC
15400 Kyles Cir (73099-6209)
PHONE..................214 415-4741
EMP: 2 **EST:** 2013
SALES (est): 76.8K **Privately Held**
SIC: 2084 Wines

(G-11782)
SIGNCO INC
810 Lancaster Dr (73099-4932)
PHONE..................405 615-7572
EMP: 1
SALES (est): 46K **Privately Held**
SIC: 3993 Signs & advertising specialties

(G-11783)
SILVERTREE SOLUTIONS LLC
424 Sage Brush Rd (73099-6892)
PHONE..................405 922-7281
EMP: 2
SALES (est): 122.2K **Privately Held**
SIC: 7372 Application computer software

(G-11784)
SOUTHERN LACE STITCHERY
8712 Ally Way (73099-9646)
PHONE..................405 414-3550
Jennifer Wathor, *Principal*
EMP: 1
SALES (est): 50.8K **Privately Held**
SIC: 2395 Embroidery & art needlework

(G-11785)
SPANGENHELM PUBLISHING
1000 Cornwell Dr Apt 307 (73099-4509)
PHONE..................405 430-6464
James Kane, *Principal*
EMP: 2
SALES (est): 59.2K **Privately Held**
SIC: 2741 Miscellaneous publishing

(G-11786)
SPRAYCAN CREATIVE LLC
420 W Main St (73099-1218)
PHONE..................405 494-0321
Patrick McClung, *Administration*
EMP: 2 **EST:** 2016
SALES (est): 142.9K **Privately Held**
SIC: 3993 Signs & advertising specialties

(G-11787)
SRM INC (PA)
Also Called: Schwarz Ready Mix
1400 S Holly St (73099)
P.O. Box 850450 (73085-0450)
PHONE..................405 354-8824
Philip Schwarz, *President*
Bill Anderson, *Area Mgr*
James Schwarz, *Corp Secy*
Gene Schwarz, *Vice Pres*
Marvin Cobb, *Sales Staff*
EMP: 10 **EST:** 1976
SQ FT: 10,000
SALES (est): 50.6MM **Privately Held**
WEB: www.srmokc.com
SIC: 3273 Ready-mixed concrete

(G-11788)
STAHLE TOOL COMPANY LLC
825 Preston Park Dr (73099-2143)
PHONE..................405 265-4360
Shawn Stahle, *Principal*
EMP: 2
SALES (est): 108.4K **Privately Held**
SIC: 3599 Machine shop, jobbing & repair

(G-11789)
STITCH DESIGN
300 S Ranchwood Blvd # 4 (73099-2741)
PHONE..................405 350-0126
EMP: 2
SALES (est): 104.3K **Privately Held**
SIC: 2395 Pleating And Stitching, Nsk

(G-11790)
SWEETANDSASSYTINYTEES LLC
9825 Nw 100th St (73099-8586)
PHONE..................405 470-1170
Lindsay McRae Zody, *Principal*
EMP: 2
SALES (est): 79K **Privately Held**
SIC: 2759 Screen printing

(G-11791)
TESPRINTING LLC
719 Garden Grv (73099-4213)
PHONE..................405 708-7000
Trudi Sargent, *Administration*
EMP: 2
SALES (est): 129.7K **Privately Held**
SIC: 2759 Commercial printing

(G-11792)
TIES OILFIELD SERVICE INC
4225 Bridle Path (73099-7237)
P.O. Box 850368 (73085-0368)
PHONE..................405 306-2655
Tom Eudey, *President*
EMP: 1
SALES (est): 111.1K **Privately Held**
SIC: 1389 Pumping of oil & gas wells

(G-11793)
TREPCO INC
9320 Nw Expressway (73099-8790)
PHONE..................405 722-1400
Harold J Trepagnier Jr, *President*
Dorothy Trepagnier, *Treasurer*
EMP: 9
SALES (est): 687.2K **Privately Held**
SIC: 1382 Oil & gas exploration services

(G-11794)
TREPCO PRODUCTION CO INC
9320 Nw Expressway (73099-8790)
PHONE..................405 722-1400
Dennis Trepagnier, *President*
EMP: 5
SALES (est): 634K **Privately Held**
SIC: 1311 Crude petroleum production; natural gas production

(G-11795)
TRS CABINETS & TRIM LLC
110 Asbill Ave (73099-4626)
PHONE..................405 234-7276
Sheldon Thompson, *Principal*
EMP: 1
SALES (est): 86.2K **Privately Held**
SIC: 2434 Wood kitchen cabinets

(G-11796)
TWIGGS COMPANY
Also Called: Machine Shop
633 W Vandament Ave # 164 (73099-3846)
PHONE..................405 882-0308
Andrew Hutchison, *Principal*
EMP: 2
SALES (est): 114.8K **Privately Held**
SIC: 3599 Industrial machinery

(G-11797)
TWO BROTHERS SAND GRAVE
11200 Sundance Dr (73099-9132)
PHONE..................405 923-6752
Michael Henson, *Principal*
EMP: 3 **EST:** 2010
SALES (est): 208.7K **Privately Held**
SIC: 1442 Construction sand & gravel

(G-11798)
UNIVERSAL MACHINE INC
15511 Hwy 3 & Cimarron Rd (73099)
P.O. Box 399, Piedmont (73078-0399)
PHONE..................405 373-2248
Greg Smith, *Owner*
Diane Smith, *Co-Owner*
EMP: 5
SQ FT: 2,400
SALES (est): 466K **Privately Held**
SIC: 3599 Machine shop, jobbing & repair

(G-11799)
US SIGNS & LED LLC
912 Justin Dr (73099-2150)
PHONE..................405 819-3086
EMP: 1
SALES (est): 46K **Privately Held**
SIC: 3993 Signs & advertising specialties

(G-11800)
VAN HORN JAMES
Also Called: Jvh Marketing
10124 Thompson Ave (73099-7961)
PHONE..................405 324-2456
James Van Horn, *Owner*
EMP: 1
SALES (est): 500K **Privately Held**
SIC: 3993 Advertising novelties

(G-11801)
VANDE LUNE PACKAGING LLC
12009 Somerville Dr (73099-8136)
PHONE..................405 517-0098
Steve Vande Lune, *Owner*
EMP: 1 **EST:** 2013
SALES (est): 300K **Privately Held**
SIC: 2653 Corrugated & solid fiber boxes

(G-11802)
VEOLIA WATER NORTH AMERICA OPE
501 W Wagner Rd (73099-1053)
PHONE..................405 354-6245
EMP: 4
SALES (corp-wide): 559.3MM **Privately Held**
SIC: 3589 Water treatment equipment, industrial
HQ: Veolia Water North America Operating Services, Llc
53 State St Ste 14
Boston MA 02109
617 849-6600

(G-11803)
WEATHERFORD DISTRICT OFFICE
3500 N Cimarron Rd (73099-3012)
PHONE..................405 354-7711
Mark Vincent, *Principal*
EMP: 5
SALES (est): 681.8K **Privately Held**
SIC: 3533 Gas field machinery & equipment

(G-11804)
WEATHERFORD INTERNATIONAL LLC
11133 Nw 10th St (73099-5126)
PHONE..................405 350-3357
Ernie Moore, *Branch Mgr*
EMP: 7 **Privately Held**
SIC: 3533 Oil & gas field machinery
HQ: Weatherford International, Llc
2000 Saint James Pl
Houston TX 77056
713 693-4000

(G-11805)
WRITE GREEN LIGHT
9109 Nw 101st St (73099-8333)
PHONE..................405 722-7823
Nancy Kamp, *Owner*
EMP: 3
SALES (est): 121K **Privately Held**
SIC: 2741 Miscellaneous publishing

(G-11806)
YDF INC
9500 Sw 15th (73085)
PHONE..................405 324-2216
Harold Puage, *President*
EMP: 1
SALES: 1MM **Privately Held**
SIC: 1389 Oil & gas wells: building, repairing & dismantling

(G-11807)
YUKON DOOR AND PLYWOOD INC
900 S 17th St (73099-4424)
P.O. Box 850440 (73085-0440)
PHONE..................405 354-4861
Freddie D Baker, *President*
Hawana L Baker, *Corp Secy*
Walter G Baker, *Vice Pres*
EMP: 30 **EST:** 1974
SQ FT: 20,000
SALES (est): 6.2MM **Privately Held**
SIC: 5031 2431 5211 Lumber: rough, dressed & finished; millwork; lumber & other building materials

(G-11808)
YUKON TROPHY & AWARDS INC
1007 W Main St (73099-1043)
PHONE..................405 354-5184
Bernice Johnson, *President*
Al Johnson, *Corp Secy*
Todd Johnson, *Vice Pres*
EMP: 7
SALES: 90K **Privately Held**
SIC: 3914 5999 Trophies; trophies & plaques

(G-11809)
ZZW GLOBAL INC (PA)
13109 Nw 7th St (73099-9721)
PHONE..................405 388-8720
Zane Z Woods, *Principal*
EMP: 5
SALES (est): 1.6MM **Privately Held**
WEB: www.zanezwoods.wordpress.com
SIC: 1389 Haulage, oil field

SIC INDEX

Standard Industrial Classification Alphabetical Index

SIC NO	PRODUCT

A

3291 Abrasive Prdts
2891 Adhesives & Sealants
3563 Air & Gas Compressors
3585 Air Conditioning & Heating Eqpt
3721 Aircraft
3724 Aircraft Engines & Engine Parts
3728 Aircraft Parts & Eqpt, NEC
2812 Alkalies & Chlorine
3363 Aluminum Die Castings
3354 Aluminum Extruded Prdts
3365 Aluminum Foundries
3355 Aluminum Rolling & Drawing, NEC
3353 Aluminum Sheet, Plate & Foil
3826 Analytical Instruments
2077 Animal, Marine Fats & Oils
1231 Anthracite Mining
2389 Apparel & Accessories, NEC
2387 Apparel Belts
3446 Architectural & Ornamental Metal Work
7694 Armature Rewinding Shops
2952 Asphalt Felts & Coatings
3822 Automatic Temperature Controls
3581 Automatic Vending Machines
3465 Automotive Stampings
2396 Automotive Trimmings, Apparel Findings, Related Prdts

B

2673 Bags: Plastics, Laminated & Coated
3562 Ball & Roller Bearings
2836 Biological Prdts, Exc Diagnostic Substances
1221 Bituminous Coal & Lignite: Surface Mining
1222 Bituminous Coal: Underground Mining
2782 Blankbooks & Looseleaf Binders
3312 Blast Furnaces, Coke Ovens, Steel & Rolling Mills
3564 Blowers & Fans
3732 Boat Building & Repairing
3452 Bolts, Nuts, Screws, Rivets & Washers
2732 Book Printing, Not Publishing
2789 Bookbinding
2731 Books: Publishing & Printing
3131 Boot & Shoe Cut Stock & Findings
2342 Brassieres, Girdles & Garments
2051 Bread, Bakery Prdts Exc Cookies & Crackers
3251 Brick & Structural Clay Tile
3991 Brooms & Brushes
3995 Burial Caskets

C

3578 Calculating & Accounting Eqpt
2064 Candy & Confectionery Prdts
2033 Canned Fruits, Vegetables & Preserves
2032 Canned Specialties
2394 Canvas Prdts
3624 Carbon & Graphite Prdts
2895 Carbon Black
3955 Carbon Paper & Inked Ribbons
3592 Carburetors, Pistons, Rings & Valves
2273 Carpets & Rugs
2823 Cellulosic Man-Made Fibers
3241 Cement, Hydraulic
3253 Ceramic Tile
2043 Cereal Breakfast Foods
2022 Cheese
1479 Chemical & Fertilizer Mining
2899 Chemical Preparations, NEC
2361 Children's & Infants' Dresses & Blouses
3261 China Plumbing Fixtures & Fittings
2066 Chocolate & Cocoa Prdts
3255 Clay Refractories
1241 Coal Mining Svcs
3479 Coating & Engraving, NEC
2095 Coffee
3316 Cold Rolled Steel Sheet, Strip & Bars
3582 Commercial Laundry, Dry Clean & Pressing Mchs
2759 Commercial Printing
2754 Commercial Printing: Gravure
2752 Commercial Printing: Lithographic
3646 Commercial, Indl & Institutional Lighting Fixtures
3669 Communications Eqpt, NEC
3577 Computer Peripheral Eqpt, NEC
3572 Computer Storage Devices
3575 Computer Terminals
3271 Concrete Block & Brick
3272 Concrete Prdts
3531 Construction Machinery & Eqpt
1442 Construction Sand & Gravel
2679 Converted Paper Prdts, NEC
3535 Conveyors & Eqpt
2052 Cookies & Crackers
3366 Copper Foundries
2298 Cordage & Twine
2653 Corrugated & Solid Fiber Boxes
3961 Costume Jewelry & Novelties
2261 Cotton Fabric Finishers
2211 Cotton, Woven Fabric
2074 Cottonseed Oil Mills
1311 Crude Petroleum & Natural Gas
1423 Crushed & Broken Granite
1422 Crushed & Broken Limestone
1429 Crushed & Broken Stone, NEC
3643 Current-Carrying Wiring Devices
2391 Curtains & Draperies
3087 Custom Compounding Of Purchased Plastic Resins
3281 Cut Stone Prdts
3421 Cutlery
2865 Cyclic-Crudes, Intermediates, Dyes & Org Pigments

D

3843 Dental Eqpt & Splys
2835 Diagnostic Substances
2675 Die-Cut Paper & Board
3544 Dies, Tools, Jigs, Fixtures & Indl Molds
1411 Dimension Stone
2047 Dog & Cat Food
3942 Dolls & Stuffed Toys
2591 Drapery Hardware, Window Blinds & Shades
2034 Dried Fruits, Vegetables & Soup
1381 Drilling Oil & Gas Wells

E

3634 Electric Household Appliances
3641 Electric Lamps
3694 Electrical Eqpt For Internal Combustion Engines
3629 Electrical Indl Apparatus, NEC
3699 Electrical Machinery, Eqpt & Splys, NEC
3845 Electromedical & Electrotherapeutic Apparatus
3313 Electrometallurgical Prdts
3677 Electronic Coils & Transformers
3679 Electronic Components, NEC
3571 Electronic Computers
3678 Electronic Connectors
3676 Electronic Resistors
3471 Electroplating, Plating, Polishing, Anodizing & Coloring
3534 Elevators & Moving Stairways
3431 Enameled Iron & Metal Sanitary Ware
2677 Envelopes
2892 Explosives

F

2241 Fabric Mills, Cotton, Wool, Silk & Man-Made
3499 Fabricated Metal Prdts, NEC
3498 Fabricated Pipe & Pipe Fittings
3443 Fabricated Plate Work
3069 Fabricated Rubber Prdts, NEC
3441 Fabricated Structural Steel
2399 Fabricated Textile Prdts, NEC
2295 Fabrics Coated Not Rubberized
2297 Fabrics, Nonwoven
3523 Farm Machinery & Eqpt
3965 Fasteners, Buttons, Needles & Pins
2875 Fertilizers, Mixing Only
2655 Fiber Cans, Tubes & Drums
3211 Flat Glass
2087 Flavoring Extracts & Syrups
2045 Flour, Blended & Prepared
2041 Flour, Grain Milling
3824 Fluid Meters & Counters
3593 Fluid Power Cylinders & Actuators
3594 Fluid Power Pumps & Motors
3492 Fluid Power Valves & Hose Fittings
2657 Folding Paperboard Boxes
3556 Food Prdts Machinery
2099 Food Preparations, NEC
3149 Footwear, NEC
2053 Frozen Bakery Prdts
2037 Frozen Fruits, Juices & Vegetables
2038 Frozen Specialties
2599 Furniture & Fixtures, NEC

G

3944 Games, Toys & Children's Vehicles
3524 Garden, Lawn Tractors & Eqpt
3053 Gaskets, Packing & Sealing Devices
3221 Glass Containers
3231 Glass Prdts Made Of Purchased Glass
3321 Gray Iron Foundries
2771 Greeting Card Publishing
3769 Guided Missile/Space Vehicle Parts & Eqpt, NEC
3761 Guided Missiles & Space Vehicles
3275 Gypsum Prdts

H

3423 Hand & Edge Tools
3425 Hand Saws & Saw Blades
3171 Handbags & Purses
3429 Hardware, NEC
2426 Hardwood Dimension & Flooring Mills
2435 Hardwood Veneer & Plywood
2353 Hats, Caps & Millinery
3433 Heating Eqpt
3536 Hoists, Cranes & Monorails
2252 Hosiery, Except Women's
2392 House furnishings: Textile
3639 Household Appliances, NEC
3651 Household Audio & Video Eqpt
3631 Household Cooking Eqpt
2519 Household Furniture, NEC
3635 Household Vacuum Cleaners

I

2097 Ice
2024 Ice Cream
2819 Indl Inorganic Chemicals, NEC
3823 Indl Instruments For Meas, Display & Control
3569 Indl Machinery & Eqpt, NEC
3567 Indl Process Furnaces & Ovens
3537 Indl Trucks, Tractors, Trailers & Stackers
2813 Industrial Gases
2869 Industrial Organic Chemicals, NEC
3543 Industrial Patterns
1446 Industrial Sand
3491 Industrial Valves
2816 Inorganic Pigments
3825 Instrs For Measuring & Testing Electricity
3519 Internal Combustion Engines, NEC
3462 Iron & Steel Forgings

J

3915 Jewelers Findings & Lapidary Work
3911 Jewelry: Precious Metal

K

1455 Kaolin & Ball Clay
2253 Knit Outerwear Mills
2254 Knit Underwear Mills
2259 Knitting Mills, NEC

L

3821 Laboratory Apparatus & Furniture
1031 Lead & Zinc Ores
3952 Lead Pencils, Crayons & Artist's Mtrls
2386 Leather & Sheep Lined Clothing
3199 Leather Goods, NEC
3111 Leather Tanning & Finishing
3648 Lighting Eqpt, NEC
3274 Lime
3996 Linoleum & Hard Surface Floor Coverings, NEC
2085 Liquors, Distilled, Rectified & Blended
2411 Logging
2992 Lubricating Oils & Greases
3161 Luggage

M

2098 Macaroni, Spaghetti & Noodles
3545 Machine Tool Access
3541 Machine Tools: Cutting
3542 Machine Tools: Forming
3599 Machinery & Eqpt, Indl & Commercial, NEC
3322 Malleable Iron Foundries
2082 Malt Beverages
2761 Manifold Business Forms

SIC INDEX

SIC NO	PRODUCT
3999	Manufacturing Industries, NEC
3953	Marking Devices
2515	Mattresses & Bedsprings
3829	Measuring & Controlling Devices, NEC
3586	Measuring & Dispensing Pumps
2011	Meat Packing Plants
3568	Mechanical Power Transmission Eqpt, NEC
2833	Medicinal Chemicals & Botanical Prdts
2329	Men's & Boys' Clothing, NEC
2323	Men's & Boys' Neckwear
2325	Men's & Boys' Separate Trousers & Casual Slacks
2321	Men's & Boys' Shirts
2311	Men's & Boys' Suits, Coats & Overcoats
2322	Men's & Boys' Underwear & Nightwear
2326	Men's & Boys' Work Clothing
3412	Metal Barrels, Drums, Kegs & Pails
3411	Metal Cans
3442	Metal Doors, Sash, Frames, Molding & Trim
3398	Metal Heat Treating
2514	Metal Household Furniture
1081	Metal Mining Svcs
3469	Metal Stampings, NEC
3549	Metalworking Machinery, NEC
2026	Milk
2023	Milk, Condensed & Evaporated
2431	Millwork
3296	Mineral Wool
3295	Minerals & Earths: Ground Or Treated
3532	Mining Machinery & Eqpt
3496	Misc Fabricated Wire Prdts
2741	Misc Publishing
3449	Misc Structural Metal Work
1499	Miscellaneous Nonmetallic Mining
2451	Mobile Homes
3061	Molded, Extruded & Lathe-Cut Rubber Mechanical Goods
3716	Motor Homes
3714	Motor Vehicle Parts & Access
3711	Motor Vehicles & Car Bodies
3751	Motorcycles, Bicycles & Parts
3621	Motors & Generators
3931	Musical Instruments

N

SIC NO	PRODUCT
1321	Natural Gas Liquids
2711	Newspapers: Publishing & Printing
2873	Nitrogenous Fertilizers
3297	Nonclay Refractories
3644	Noncurrent-Carrying Wiring Devices
3364	Nonferrous Die Castings, Exc Aluminum
3463	Nonferrous Forgings
3369	Nonferrous Foundries: Castings, NEC
3357	Nonferrous Wire Drawing
3299	Nonmetallic Mineral Prdts, NEC
1481	Nonmetallic Minerals Svcs, Except Fuels

O

SIC NO	PRODUCT
2522	Office Furniture, Except Wood
3579	Office Machines, NEC
1382	Oil & Gas Field Exploration Svcs
1389	Oil & Gas Field Svcs, NEC
3533	Oil Field Machinery & Eqpt
3851	Ophthalmic Goods
3827	Optical Instruments
3489	Ordnance & Access, NEC
3842	Orthopedic, Prosthetic & Surgical Appliances/Splys

P

SIC NO	PRODUCT
3565	Packaging Machinery
2851	Paints, Varnishes, Lacquers, Enamels
2671	Paper Coating & Laminating for Packaging
2672	Paper Coating & Laminating, Exc for Packaging
3554	Paper Inds Machinery
2621	Paper Mills
2631	Paperboard Mills
2542	Partitions & Fixtures, Except Wood
2951	Paving Mixtures & Blocks
3951	Pens & Mechanical Pencils
2844	Perfumes, Cosmetics & Toilet Preparations
2721	Periodicals: Publishing & Printing

SIC NO	PRODUCT
3172	Personal Leather Goods
2879	Pesticides & Agricultural Chemicals, NEC
2911	Petroleum Refining
2834	Pharmaceuticals
3652	Phonograph Records & Magnetic Tape
1475	Phosphate Rock
2874	Phosphatic Fertilizers
3861	Photographic Eqpt & Splys
2035	Pickled Fruits, Vegetables, Sauces & Dressings
3085	Plastic Bottles
3086	Plastic Foam Prdts
3083	Plastic Laminated Plate & Sheet
3084	Plastic Pipe
3088	Plastic Plumbing Fixtures
3089	Plastic Prdts
3082	Plastic Unsupported Profile Shapes
3081	Plastic Unsupported Sheet & Film
2821	Plastics, Mtrls & Nonvulcanizable Elastomers
2796	Platemaking & Related Svcs
2395	Pleating & Stitching For The Trade
3432	Plumbing Fixture Fittings & Trim, Brass
3264	Porcelain Electrical Splys
2096	Potato Chips & Similar Prdts
3269	Pottery Prdts, NEC
2015	Poultry Slaughtering, Dressing & Processing
3546	Power Hand Tools
3612	Power, Distribution & Specialty Transformers
3448	Prefabricated Metal Buildings & Cmpnts
2452	Prefabricated Wood Buildings & Cmpnts
7372	Prepackaged Software
2048	Prepared Feeds For Animals & Fowls
3229	Pressed & Blown Glassware, NEC
3399	Primary Metal Prdts, NEC
3339	Primary Nonferrous Metals, NEC
3334	Primary Production Of Aluminum
3672	Printed Circuit Boards
2893	Printing Ink
3555	Printing Trades Machinery & Eqpt
2999	Products Of Petroleum & Coal, NEC
2531	Public Building & Related Furniture
2611	Pulp Mills
3561	Pumps & Pumping Eqpt

R

SIC NO	PRODUCT
3663	Radio & T V Communications, Systs & Eqpt, Broadcast/Studio
3671	Radio & T V Receiving Electron Tubes
3743	Railroad Eqpt
3273	Ready-Mixed Concrete
2493	Reconstituted Wood Prdts
3695	Recording Media
3625	Relays & Indl Controls
3645	Residential Lighting Fixtures
2384	Robes & Dressing Gowns
3547	Rolling Mill Machinery & Eqpt
3351	Rolling, Drawing & Extruding Of Copper
3356	Rolling, Drawing-Extruding Of Nonferrous Metals
3021	Rubber & Plastic Footwear
3052	Rubber & Plastic Hose & Belting

S

SIC NO	PRODUCT
2068	Salted & Roasted Nuts & Seeds
2656	Sanitary Food Containers
2676	Sanitary Paper Prdts
2013	Sausages & Meat Prdts
2421	Saw & Planing Mills
3596	Scales & Balances, Exc Laboratory
2397	Schiffli Machine Embroideries
3451	Screw Machine Prdts
3812	Search, Detection, Navigation & Guidance Systs & Instrs
3341	Secondary Smelting & Refining Of Nonferrous Metals
3674	Semiconductors
3589	Service Ind Machines, NEC
2652	Set-Up Paperboard Boxes
3444	Sheet Metal Work
3731	Shipbuilding & Repairing
2079	Shortening, Oils & Margarine
3993	Signs & Advertising Displays
2262	Silk & Man-Made Fabric Finishers
2221	Silk & Man-Made Fiber

SIC NO	PRODUCT
1044	Silver Ores
3914	Silverware, Plated & Stainless Steel Ware
3484	Small Arms
3482	Small Arms Ammunition
2841	Soap & Detergents
2086	Soft Drinks
2075	Soybean Oil Mills
2842	Spec Cleaning, Polishing & Sanitation Preparations
3559	Special Ind Machinery, NEC
2429	Special Prdt Sawmills, NEC
3566	Speed Changers, Drives & Gears
3949	Sporting & Athletic Goods, NEC
2678	Stationery Prdts
3511	Steam, Gas & Hydraulic Turbines & Engines
3325	Steel Foundries, NEC
3324	Steel Investment Foundries
3317	Steel Pipe & Tubes
3493	Steel Springs, Except Wire
3315	Steel Wire Drawing & Nails & Spikes
3691	Storage Batteries
3259	Structural Clay Prdts, NEC
2439	Structural Wood Members, NEC
2843	Surface Active & Finishing Agents, Sulfonated Oils
3841	Surgical & Medical Instrs & Apparatus
3613	Switchgear & Switchboard Apparatus
2824	Synthetic Organic Fibers, Exc Cellulosic
2822	Synthetic Rubber (Vulcanizable Elastomers)

T

SIC NO	PRODUCT
3795	Tanks & Tank Components
3661	Telephone & Telegraph Apparatus
2393	Textile Bags
2299	Textile Goods, NEC
3552	Textile Machinery
2284	Thread Mills
3011	Tires & Inner Tubes
2131	Tobacco, Chewing & Snuff
3799	Transportation Eqpt, NEC
3792	Travel Trailers & Campers
3713	Truck & Bus Bodies
3715	Truck Trailers
2791	Typesetting

V

SIC NO	PRODUCT
3494	Valves & Pipe Fittings, NEC
3647	Vehicular Lighting Eqpt

W

SIC NO	PRODUCT
3873	Watch & Clock Devices & Parts
2385	Waterproof Outerwear
3548	Welding Apparatus
7692	Welding Repair
2046	Wet Corn Milling
2084	Wine & Brandy
3495	Wire Springs
2331	Women's & Misses' Blouses
2335	Women's & Misses' Dresses
2339	Women's & Misses' Outerwear, NEC
2337	Women's & Misses' Suits, Coats & Skirts
3144	Women's Footwear, Exc Athletic
2341	Women's, Misses' & Children's Underwear & Nightwear
2441	Wood Boxes
2449	Wood Containers, NEC
2511	Wood Household Furniture
2512	Wood Household Furniture, Upholstered
2434	Wood Kitchen Cabinets
2521	Wood Office Furniture
2448	Wood Pallets & Skids
2499	Wood Prdts, NEC
2491	Wood Preserving
2517	Wood T V, Radio, Phono & Sewing Cabinets
2541	Wood, Office & Store Fixtures
3553	Woodworking Machinery
2231	Wool, Woven Fabric

X

SIC NO	PRODUCT
3844	X-ray Apparatus & Tubes

Y

SIC NO	PRODUCT
2281	Yarn Spinning Mills

SIC INDEX

Standard Industrial Classification Numerical Index

SIC NO	PRODUCT

10 metal mining
1031 Lead & Zinc Ores
1044 Silver Ores
1081 Metal Mining Svcs

12 coal mining
1221 Bituminous Coal & Lignite: Surface Mining
1222 Bituminous Coal: Underground Mining
1231 Anthracite Mining
1241 Coal Mining Svcs

13 oil and gas extraction
1311 Crude Petroleum & Natural Gas
1321 Natural Gas Liquids
1381 Drilling Oil & Gas Wells
1382 Oil & Gas Field Exploration Svcs
1389 Oil & Gas Field Svcs, NEC

14 mining and quarrying of nonmetallic minerals, except fuels
1411 Dimension Stone
1422 Crushed & Broken Limestone
1423 Crushed & Broken Granite
1429 Crushed & Broken Stone, NEC
1442 Construction Sand & Gravel
1446 Industrial Sand
1455 Kaolin & Ball Clay
1475 Phosphate Rock
1479 Chemical & Fertilizer Mining
1481 Nonmetallic Minerals Svcs, Except Fuels
1499 Miscellaneous Nonmetallic Mining

20 food and kindred products
2011 Meat Packing Plants
2013 Sausages & Meat Prdts
2015 Poultry Slaughtering, Dressing & Processing
2022 Cheese
2023 Milk, Condensed & Evaporated
2024 Ice Cream
2026 Milk
2032 Canned Specialties
2033 Canned Fruits, Vegetables & Preserves
2034 Dried Fruits, Vegetables & Soup
2035 Pickled Fruits, Vegetables, Sauces & Dressings
2037 Frozen Fruits, Juices & Vegetables
2038 Frozen Specialties
2041 Flour, Grain Milling
2043 Cereal Breakfast Foods
2045 Flour, Blended & Prepared
2046 Wet Corn Milling
2047 Dog & Cat Food
2048 Prepared Feeds For Animals & Fowls
2051 Bread, Bakery Prdts Exc Cookies & Crackers
2052 Cookies & Crackers
2053 Frozen Bakery Prdts
2064 Candy & Confectionery Prdts
2066 Chocolate & Cocoa Prdts
2068 Salted & Roasted Nuts & Seeds
2074 Cottonseed Oil Mills
2075 Soybean Oil Mills
2077 Animal, Marine Fats & Oils
2079 Shortening, Oils & Margarine
2082 Malt Beverages
2084 Wine & Brandy
2085 Liquors, Distilled, Rectified & Blended
2086 Soft Drinks
2087 Flavoring Extracts & Syrups
2095 Coffee
2096 Potato Chips & Similar Prdts
2097 Ice
2098 Macaroni, Spaghetti & Noodles
2099 Food Preparations, NEC

21 tobacco products
2131 Tobacco, Chewing & Snuff

22 textile mill products
2211 Cotton, Woven Fabric
2221 Silk & Man-Made Fiber
2231 Wool, Woven Fabric
2241 Fabric Mills, Cotton, Wool, Silk & Man-Made
2252 Hosiery, Except Women's
2253 Knit Outerwear Mills
2254 Knit Underwear Mills
2259 Knitting Mills, NEC
2261 Cotton Fabric Finishers
2262 Silk & Man-Made Fabric Finishers
2273 Carpets & Rugs
2281 Yarn Spinning Mills
2284 Thread Mills
2295 Fabrics Coated Not Rubberized
2297 Fabrics, Nonwoven
2298 Cordage & Twine
2299 Textile Goods, NEC

23 apparel and other finished products made from fabrics and similar material
2311 Men's & Boys' Suits, Coats & Overcoats
2321 Men's & Boys' Shirts
2322 Men's & Boys' Underwear & Nightwear
2323 Men's & Boys' Neckwear
2325 Men's & Boys' Separate Trousers & Casual Slacks
2326 Men's & Boys' Work Clothing
2329 Men's & Boys' Clothing, NEC
2331 Women's & Misses' Blouses
2335 Women's & Misses' Dresses
2337 Women's & Misses' Suits, Coats & Skirts
2339 Women's & Misses' Outerwear, NEC
2341 Women's, Misses' & Children's Underwear & Nightwear
2342 Brassieres, Girdles & Garments
2353 Hats, Caps & Millinery
2361 Children's & Infants' Dresses & Blouses
2384 Robes & Dressing Gowns
2385 Waterproof Outerwear
2386 Leather & Sheep Lined Clothing
2387 Apparel Belts
2389 Apparel & Accessories, NEC
2391 Curtains & Draperies
2392 House furnishings: Textile
2393 Textile Bags
2394 Canvas Prdts
2395 Pleating & Stitching For The Trade
2396 Automotive Trimmings, Apparel Findings, Related Prdts
2397 Schiffli Machine Embroideries
2399 Fabricated Textile Prdts, NEC

24 lumber and wood products, except furniture
2411 Logging
2421 Saw & Planing Mills
2426 Hardwood Dimension & Flooring Mills
2429 Special Prdt Sawmills, NEC
2431 Millwork
2434 Wood Kitchen Cabinets
2435 Hardwood Veneer & Plywood
2439 Structural Wood Members, NEC
2441 Wood Boxes
2448 Wood Pallets & Skids
2449 Wood Containers, NEC
2451 Mobile Homes
2452 Prefabricated Wood Buildings & Cmpnts
2491 Wood Preserving
2493 Reconstituted Wood Prdts
2499 Wood Prdts, NEC

25 furniture and fixtures
2511 Wood Household Furniture
2512 Wood Household Furniture, Upholstered
2514 Metal Household Furniture
2515 Mattresses & Bedsprings
2517 Wood TV, Radio, Phono & Sewing Cabinets
2519 Household Furniture, NEC
2521 Wood Office Furniture
2522 Office Furniture, Except Wood
2531 Public Building & Related Furniture
2541 Wood, Office & Store Fixtures
2542 Partitions & Fixtures, Except Wood
2591 Drapery Hardware, Window Blinds & Shades
2599 Furniture & Fixtures, NEC

26 paper and allied products
2611 Pulp Mills
2621 Paper Mills
2631 Paperboard Mills
2652 Set-Up Paperboard Boxes
2653 Corrugated & Solid Fiber Boxes
2655 Fiber Cans, Tubes & Drums
2656 Sanitary Food Containers
2657 Folding Paperboard Boxes
2671 Paper Coating & Laminating for Packaging
2672 Paper Coating & Laminating, Exc for Packaging
2673 Bags: Plastics, Laminated & Coated
2675 Die-Cut Paper & Board
2676 Sanitary Paper Prdts
2677 Envelopes
2678 Stationery Prdts
2679 Converted Paper Prdts, NEC

27 printing, publishing, and allied industries
2711 Newspapers: Publishing & Printing
2721 Periodicals: Publishing & Printing
2731 Books: Publishing & Printing
2732 Book Printing, Not Publishing
2741 Misc Publishing
2752 Commercial Printing: Lithographic
2754 Commercial Printing: Gravure
2759 Commercial Printing
2761 Manifold Business Forms
2771 Greeting Card Publishing
2782 Blankbooks & Looseleaf Binders
2789 Bookbinding
2791 Typesetting
2796 Platemaking & Related Svcs

28 chemicals and allied products
2812 Alkalies & Chlorine
2813 Industrial Gases
2816 Inorganic Pigments
2819 Indl Inorganic Chemicals, NEC
2821 Plastics, Mtrls & Nonvulcanizable Elastomers
2822 Synthetic Rubber (Vulcanizable Elastomers)
2823 Cellulosic Man-Made Fibers
2824 Synthetic Organic Fibers, Exc Cellulosic
2833 Medicinal Chemicals & Botanical Prdts
2834 Pharmaceuticals
2835 Diagnostic Substances
2836 Biological Prdts, Exc Diagnostic Substances
2841 Soap & Detergents
2842 Spec Cleaning, Polishing & Sanitation Preparations
2843 Surface Active & Finishing Agents, Sulfonated Oils
2844 Perfumes, Cosmetics & Toilet Preparations
2851 Paints, Varnishes, Lacquers, Enamels
2865 Cyclic-Crudes, Intermediates, Dyes & Org Pigments
2869 Industrial Organic Chemicals, NEC
2873 Nitrogenous Fertilizers
2874 Phosphatic Fertilizers
2875 Fertilizers, Mixing Only
2879 Pesticides & Agricultural Chemicals, NEC
2891 Adhesives & Sealants
2892 Explosives
2893 Printing Ink
2895 Carbon Black
2899 Chemical Preparations, NEC

29 petroleum refining and related industries
2911 Petroleum Refining
2951 Paving Mixtures & Blocks
2952 Asphalt Felts & Coatings
2992 Lubricating Oils & Greases
2999 Products Of Petroleum & Coal, NEC

30 rubber and miscellaneous plastics products
3011 Tires & Inner Tubes
3021 Rubber & Plastic Footwear
3052 Rubber & Plastic Hose & Belting
3053 Gaskets, Packing & Sealing Devices
3061 Molded, Extruded & Lathe-Cut Rubber Mechanical Goods
3069 Fabricated Rubber Prdts, NEC
3081 Plastic Unsupported Sheet & Film
3082 Plastic Unsupported Profile Shapes
3083 Plastic Laminated Plate & Sheet
3084 Plastic Pipe
3085 Plastic Bottles
3086 Plastic Foam Prdts
3087 Custom Compounding Of Purchased Plastic Resins
3088 Plastic Plumbing Fixtures
3089 Plastic Prdts

31 leather and leather products
3111 Leather Tanning & Finishing
3131 Boot & Shoe Cut Stock & Findings

SIC INDEX

SIC NO	PRODUCT
3144	Women's Footwear, Exc Athletic
3149	Footwear, NEC
3161	Luggage
3171	Handbags & Purses
3172	Personal Leather Goods
3199	Leather Goods, NEC

32 stone, clay, glass, and concrete products

- 3211 Flat Glass
- 3221 Glass Containers
- 3229 Pressed & Blown Glassware, NEC
- 3231 Glass Prdts Made Of Purchased Glass
- 3241 Cement, Hydraulic
- 3251 Brick & Structural Clay Tile
- 3253 Ceramic Tile
- 3255 Clay Refractories
- 3259 Structural Clay Prdts, NEC
- 3261 China Plumbing Fixtures & Fittings
- 3264 Porcelain Electrical Splys
- 3269 Pottery Prdts, NEC
- 3271 Concrete Block & Brick
- 3272 Concrete Prdts
- 3273 Ready-Mixed Concrete
- 3274 Lime
- 3275 Gypsum Prdts
- 3281 Cut Stone Prdts
- 3291 Abrasive Prdts
- 3295 Minerals & Earths: Ground Or Treated
- 3296 Mineral Wool
- 3297 Nonclay Refractories
- 3299 Nonmetallic Mineral Prdts, NEC

33 primary metal industries

- 3312 Blast Furnaces, Coke Ovens, Steel & Rolling Mills
- 3313 Electrometallurgical Prdts
- 3315 Steel Wire Drawing & Nails & Spikes
- 3316 Cold Rolled Steel Sheet, Strip & Bars
- 3317 Steel Pipe & Tubes
- 3321 Gray Iron Foundries
- 3322 Malleable Iron Foundries
- 3324 Steel Investment Foundries
- 3325 Steel Foundries, NEC
- 3334 Primary Production Of Aluminum
- 3339 Primary Nonferrous Metals, NEC
- 3341 Secondary Smelting & Refining Of Nonferrous Metals
- 3351 Rolling, Drawing & Extruding Of Copper
- 3353 Aluminum Sheet, Plate & Foil
- 3354 Aluminum Extruded Prdts
- 3355 Aluminum Rolling & Drawing, NEC
- 3356 Rolling, Drawing-Extruding Of Nonferrous Metals
- 3357 Nonferrous Wire Drawing
- 3363 Aluminum Die Castings
- 3364 Nonferrous Die Castings, Exc Aluminum
- 3365 Aluminum Foundries
- 3366 Copper Foundries
- 3369 Nonferrous Foundries: Castings, NEC
- 3398 Metal Heat Treating
- 3399 Primary Metal Prdts, NEC

34 fabricated metal products, except machinery and transportation equipment

- 3411 Metal Cans
- 3412 Metal Barrels, Drums, Kegs & Pails
- 3421 Cutlery
- 3423 Hand & Edge Tools
- 3425 Hand Saws & Saw Blades
- 3429 Hardware, NEC
- 3431 Enameled Iron & Metal Sanitary Ware
- 3432 Plumbing Fixture Fittings & Trim, Brass
- 3433 Heating Eqpt
- 3441 Fabricated Structural Steel
- 3442 Metal Doors, Sash, Frames, Molding & Trim
- 3443 Fabricated Plate Work
- 3444 Sheet Metal Work
- 3446 Architectural & Ornamental Metal Work
- 3448 Prefabricated Metal Buildings & Cmpnts
- 3449 Misc Structural Metal Work
- 3451 Screw Machine Prdts
- 3452 Bolts, Nuts, Screws, Rivets & Washers
- 3462 Iron & Steel Forgings
- 3463 Nonferrous Forgings
- 3465 Automotive Stampings
- 3469 Metal Stampings, NEC
- 3471 Electroplating, Plating, Polishing, Anodizing & Coloring
- 3479 Coating & Engraving, NEC
- 3482 Small Arms Ammunition
- 3484 Small Arms
- 3489 Ordnance & Access, NEC
- 3491 Industrial Valves
- 3492 Fluid Power Valves & Hose Fittings
- 3493 Steel Springs, Except Wire
- 3494 Valves & Pipe Fittings, NEC
- 3495 Wire Springs
- 3496 Misc Fabricated Wire Prdts
- 3498 Fabricated Pipe & Pipe Fittings
- 3499 Fabricated Metal Prdts, NEC

35 industrial and commercial machinery and computer equipment

- 3511 Steam, Gas & Hydraulic Turbines & Engines
- 3519 Internal Combustion Engines, NEC
- 3523 Farm Machinery & Eqpt
- 3524 Garden, Lawn Tractors & Eqpt
- 3531 Construction Machinery & Eqpt
- 3532 Mining Machinery & Eqpt
- 3533 Oil Field Machinery & Eqpt
- 3534 Elevators & Moving Stairways
- 3535 Conveyors & Eqpt
- 3536 Hoists, Cranes & Monorails
- 3537 Indl Trucks, Tractors, Trailers & Stackers
- 3541 Machine Tools: Cutting
- 3542 Machine Tools: Forming
- 3543 Industrial Patterns
- 3544 Dies, Tools, Jigs, Fixtures & Indl Molds
- 3545 Machine Tool Access
- 3546 Power Hand Tools
- 3547 Rolling Mill Machinery & Eqpt
- 3548 Welding Apparatus
- 3549 Metalworking Machinery, NEC
- 3552 Textile Machinery
- 3553 Woodworking Machinery
- 3554 Paper Inds Machinery
- 3555 Printing Trades Machinery & Eqpt
- 3556 Food Prdts Machinery
- 3559 Special Ind Machinery, NEC
- 3561 Pumps & Pumping Eqpt
- 3562 Ball & Roller Bearings
- 3563 Air & Gas Compressors
- 3564 Blowers & Fans
- 3565 Packaging Machinery
- 3566 Speed Changers, Drives & Gears
- 3567 Indl Process Furnaces & Ovens
- 3568 Mechanical Power Transmission Eqpt, NEC
- 3569 Indl Machinery & Eqpt, NEC
- 3571 Electronic Computers
- 3572 Computer Storage Devices
- 3575 Computer Terminals
- 3577 Computer Peripheral Eqpt, NEC
- 3578 Calculating & Accounting Eqpt
- 3579 Office Machines, NEC
- 3581 Automatic Vending Machines
- 3582 Commercial Laundry, Dry Clean & Pressing Mchs
- 3585 Air Conditioning & Heating Eqpt
- 3586 Measuring & Dispensing Pumps
- 3589 Service Ind Machines, NEC
- 3592 Carburetors, Pistons, Rings & Valves
- 3593 Fluid Power Cylinders & Actuators
- 3594 Fluid Power Pumps & Motors
- 3596 Scales & Balances, Exc Laboratory
- 3599 Machinery & Eqpt, Indl & Commercial, NEC

36 electronic and other electrical equipment and components, except computer

- 3612 Power, Distribution & Specialty Transformers
- 3613 Switchgear & Switchboard Apparatus
- 3621 Motors & Generators
- 3624 Carbon & Graphite Prdts
- 3625 Relays & Indl Controls
- 3629 Electrical Indl Apparatus, NEC
- 3631 Household Cooking Eqpt
- 3634 Electric Household Appliances
- 3635 Household Vacuum Cleaners
- 3639 Household Appliances, NEC
- 3641 Electric Lamps
- 3643 Current-Carrying Wiring Devices
- 3644 Noncurrent-Carrying Wiring Devices
- 3645 Residential Lighting Fixtures
- 3646 Commercial, Indl & Institutional Lighting Fixtures
- 3647 Vehicular Lighting Eqpt
- 3648 Lighting Eqpt, NEC
- 3651 Household Audio & Video Eqpt
- 3652 Phonograph Records & Magnetic Tape
- 3661 Telephone & Telegraph Apparatus
- 3663 Radio & T V Communications, Systs & Eqpt, Broadcast/Studio
- 3669 Communications Eqpt, NEC
- 3671 Radio & T V Receiving Electron Tubes
- 3672 Printed Circuit Boards
- 3674 Semiconductors
- 3676 Electronic Resistors
- 3677 Electronic Coils & Transformers
- 3678 Electronic Connectors
- 3679 Electronic Components, NEC
- 3691 Storage Batteries
- 3694 Electrical Eqpt For Internal Combustion Engines
- 3695 Recording Media
- 3699 Electrical Machinery, Eqpt & Splys, NEC

37 transportation equipment

- 3711 Motor Vehicles & Car Bodies
- 3713 Truck & Bus Bodies
- 3714 Motor Vehicle Parts & Access
- 3715 Truck Trailers
- 3716 Motor Homes
- 3721 Aircraft
- 3724 Aircraft Engines & Engine Parts
- 3728 Aircraft Parts & Eqpt, NEC
- 3731 Shipbuilding & Repairing
- 3732 Boat Building & Repairing
- 3743 Railroad Eqpt
- 3751 Motorcycles, Bicycles & Parts
- 3761 Guided Missiles & Space Vehicles
- 3769 Guided Missile/Space Vehicle Parts & Eqpt, NEC
- 3792 Travel Trailers & Campers
- 3795 Tanks & Tank Components
- 3799 Transportation Eqpt, NEC

38 measuring, analyzing and controlling instruments; photographic, medical an

- 3812 Search, Detection, Navigation & Guidance Systs & Instrs
- 3821 Laboratory Apparatus & Furniture
- 3822 Automatic Temperature Controls
- 3823 Indl Instruments For Meas, Display & Control
- 3824 Fluid Meters & Counters
- 3825 Instrs For Measuring & Testing Electricity
- 3826 Analytical Instruments
- 3827 Optical Instruments
- 3829 Measuring & Controlling Devices, NEC
- 3841 Surgical & Medical Instrs & Apparatus
- 3842 Orthopedic, Prosthetic & Surgical Appliances/Splys
- 3843 Dental Eqpt & Splys
- 3844 X-ray Apparatus & Tubes
- 3845 Electromedical & Electrotherapeutic Apparatus
- 3851 Ophthalmic Goods
- 3861 Photographic Eqpt & Splys
- 3873 Watch & Clock Devices & Parts

39 miscellaneous manufacturing industries

- 3911 Jewelry: Precious Metal
- 3914 Silverware, Plated & Stainless Steel Ware
- 3915 Jewelers Findings & Lapidary Work
- 3931 Musical Instruments
- 3942 Dolls & Stuffed Toys
- 3944 Games, Toys & Children's Vehicles
- 3949 Sporting & Athletic Goods, NEC
- 3951 Pens & Mechanical Pencils
- 3952 Lead Pencils, Crayons & Artist's Mtrls
- 3953 Marking Devices
- 3955 Carbon Paper & Inked Ribbons
- 3961 Costume Jewelry & Novelties
- 3965 Fasteners, Buttons, Needles & Pins
- 3991 Brooms & Brushes
- 3993 Signs & Advertising Displays
- 3995 Burial Caskets
- 3996 Linoleum & Hard Surface Floor Coverings, NEC
- 3999 Manufacturing Industries, NEC

73 business services

- 7372 Prepackaged Software

76 miscellaneous repair services

- 7692 Welding Repair
- 7694 Armature Rewinding Shops

SIC SECTION

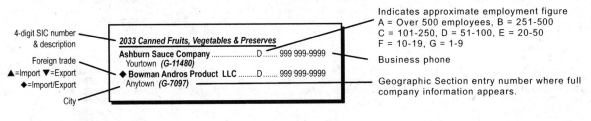

4-digit SIC number & description
Foreign trade
▲=Import ▼=Export
◆=Import/Export
City

2033 Canned Fruits, Vegetables & Preserves
Ashburn Sauce Company ....D 999 999-9999
Yourtown *(G-11480)*
◆ Bowman Andros Product LLC ....D 999 999-9999
Anytown *(G-7097)*

Indicates approximate employment figure
A = Over 500 employees, B = 251-500
C = 101-250, D = 51-100, E = 20-50
F = 10-19, G = 1-9
Business phone
Geographic Section entry number where full company information appears.

See footnotes for symbols and codes identification.

- The SIC codes in this section are from the latest Standard Industrial Classification manual published by the U.S. Government's Office of Management and Budget. For more information regarding SICs, see the Explanatory Notes.
- Companies may be listed under multiple classifications.

10 METAL MINING

1031 Lead & Zinc Ores
American Zinc Recycling Corp..............D....... 918 336-7100
Bartlesville *(G-447)*

1044 Silver Ores
Inglesrud Corp ....G....... 405 429-7928
Oklahoma City *(G-6304)*

1081 Metal Mining Svcs
Buckley Powder Company................F....... 580 384-5547
Mill Creek *(G-4467)*
Eagle Exploration Prod LLC ....G....... 918 746-1350
Tulsa *(G-9624)*
Eagle Explrtion Oprting GP LLC...........G....... 918 746-1350
Tulsa *(G-9625)*
Pontotoc Sands Company LLC ....E....... 580 777-2735
Stonewall *(G-8802)*

12 COAL MINING

1221 Bituminous Coal & Lignite: Surface Mining
▼ Alliance Coal LLC..........................D....... 918 295-7600
Tulsa *(G-9142)*
Alliance Holdings Gp LP ....C....... 918 295-1415
Tulsa *(G-9143)*
Alliance Resource Finance Corp.........G....... 918 295-1415
Tulsa *(G-9145)*
Alliance Resource Holdings Inc ....G....... 918 295-7600
Tulsa *(G-9146)*
Alliance Resource Partners LP............C....... 918 295-7600
Tulsa *(G-9147)*
Alliance Rsrce Oper Prtners LP..........G....... 918 295-7600
Tulsa *(G-9148)*
Alliance Wor Properties LLC ....E....... 918 295-7600
Tulsa *(G-9149)*
Arp Sebree South LLC.....................C....... 918 295-1415
Tulsa *(G-9210)*
Cr Services LLC ....E....... 918 295-7600
Tulsa *(G-9496)*
Excel Mining LLC ....C....... 918 295-7600
Tulsa *(G-9713)*
Georges Colliers Inc........................E....... 918 962-2202
Spiro *(G-8615)*
Hopkins County Coal LLC ....D....... 918 295-7600
Tulsa *(G-9947)*
Joshua Coal Company ....G....... 918 652-3023
Henryetta *(G-3511)*
Mt Vernon Coal Transfer Co............F....... 918 295-7600
Tulsa *(G-10311)*
Permac Inc.....................................G....... 918 295-7600
Tulsa *(G-10496)*
Phoenix Mining Company ....D....... 918 256-7873
Vinita *(G-11267)*
Southeastern Drilling........................G....... 918 469-3489
Quinton *(G-8042)*
Steamport LLC ....E....... 918 295-7600
Tulsa *(G-10841)*
White County Coal LLC ....G....... 918 295-7600
Tulsa *(G-11120)*

1222 Bituminous Coal: Underground Mining
▼ Alliance Coal LLC..........................D....... 918 295-7600
Tulsa *(G-9142)*

Alliance Holdings Gp LP ....C....... 918 295-1415
Tulsa *(G-9143)*
Alliance Resource Holdings Inc ....G....... 918 295-7600
Tulsa *(G-9146)*
Alliance Resource Partners LP............G....... 918 295-7600
Tulsa *(G-9147)*
Backbone Mountain LLC..................C....... 918 295-7600
Tulsa *(G-9252)*
Dig It Rocks LLC.............................G....... 580 362-6211
Ponca City *(G-7820)*

1231 Anthracite Mining
Walter Baker ....G....... 580 233-7820
Enid *(G-3073)*

1241 Coal Mining Svcs
Alliance Resource Partners LP............C....... 918 295-7600
Tulsa *(G-9147)*
Coal Creek Minerals LLC..................E....... 918 962-5335
Spiro *(G-8614)*
Evans Coal Company ....G....... 405 202-3239
Oklahoma City *(G-6055)*
James D Pate Jr ....G....... 405 942-3647
Oklahoma City *(G-6347)*
Oklahoma Department of Mines ....G....... 918 485-3999
Tulsa *(G-10396)*
South Central Coal Company Inc........G....... 918 962-2544
Spiro *(G-8617)*
Warrant Divisions Inc ....G....... 918 962-4800
Spiro *(G-8620)*
Webster County Coal LLC ....B....... 918 295-7600
Tulsa *(G-11102)*

13 OIL AND GAS EXTRACTION

1311 Crude Petroleum & Natural Gas
A & T Oil Company ....G....... 918 245-7358
Skiatook *(G-8530)*
A B N G Inc ....F....... 405 222-0024
Chickasha *(G-1426)*
Access Midstream Ventures LLC ....E....... 405 935-3500
Oklahoma City *(G-5361)*
Access Mlp Operating LLc................C....... 405 935-8000
Oklahoma City *(G-5362)*
Acott Oil Operations ....G....... 918 885-2736
Hominy *(G-3573)*
Adams Affiliates Inc........................F....... 918 582-7713
Tulsa *(G-9101)*
Aegeos Oilfield Technology LLC.........G....... 918 906-4328
Owasso *(G-7542)*
Agape Inc......................................G....... 918 455-9516
Broken Arrow *(G-820)*
Alan L Lamb ....G....... 405 755-2233
Oklahoma City *(G-5409)*
Albert J Geiger Revocable Tr.............G....... 918 446-6388
Tulsa *(G-9134)*
Altman Energy Inc ....G....... 918 584-4781
Tulsa *(G-9157)*
American Petro Mineral Co Inc...........G....... 405 382-1255
Seminole *(G-8354)*
American Petroleum Corporation........F....... 580 856-3580
Ratliff City *(G-8048)*
Americana Energy Company Inc........G....... 580 310-0084
Ada *(G-7)*
Angel Exploration ....G....... 405 848-8360
Oklahoma City *(G-5445)*
Anstine-Musgrove...........................G....... 580 762-6355
Ponca City *(G-7796)*

Apache Corporation ....E....... 405 222-5040
Chickasha *(G-1431)*
Apc LLC ....G....... 918 587-6242
Tulsa *(G-9197)*
Arbuckle Enterprises Inc..................E....... 405 359-2815
Edmond *(G-2307)*
Ardmore Prod & Exploration ....G....... 580 223-2292
Ardmore *(G-249)*
Arena Resources Inc ....D....... 918 747-6060
Tulsa *(G-9207)*
Arnold Oil Properties LLC.................F....... 405 842-1488
Oklahoma City *(G-5468)*
Arrow Oil & Gas Inc ....G....... 405 364-2601
Norman *(G-4918)*
Atlas Resource Partners LP..............F....... 918 654-3702
Cameron *(G-1254)*
Avalon Exploration Inc ....F....... 918 523-0600
Tulsa *(G-9227)*
Avalon Operating LLC ....G....... 918 523-0600
Tulsa *(G-9228)*
Azure Energy Ltd............................G....... 918 712-2727
Tulsa *(G-9236)*
B & B Resources............................G....... 918 495-1128
Tulsa *(G-9240)*
B B Royalty Company ....G....... 405 672-3381
Oklahoma City *(G-5504)*
B R Polk Inc ....G....... 405 286-9666
Oklahoma City *(G-5505)*
Bale Corporation.............................G....... 405 848-8797
Oklahoma City *(G-5520)*
Bandon Oil & Gas GP LLC ....G....... 405 429-5500
Oklahoma City *(G-5524)*
Banner Oil & Gas LLC ....G....... 405 642-4382
Tulsa *(G-9263)*
Banner Pipeline Company LLC ....G....... 580 233-8955
Enid *(G-2913)*
Barbour Energy Corporation ....G....... 405 848-7671
Oklahoma City *(G-5527)*
Barnes Oil Co ....G....... 918 352-2308
Drumright *(G-2051)*
Baron Exploration Co Inc ....F....... 405 341-1779
Edmond *(G-2317)*
Barrett Drilling Company ....G....... 405 273-6217
Shawnee *(G-8430)*
Barrett Oil Company ....G....... 580 436-1896
Ada *(G-11)*
Bays Enterprises Inc ....G....... 405 235-2297
Oklahoma City *(G-5532)*
Baytide Petroleum Inc ....F....... 405 585-8150
Tulsa *(G-9273)*
Bbr Oil Corp...................................G....... 580 223-2887
Ardmore *(G-254)*
Bce - Mach III LLC ....D....... 405 252-8100
Oklahoma City *(G-5536)*
Bce-Mach II LLC.............................D....... 405 252-8100
Oklahoma City *(G-5537)*
Bear Productions Inc ....F....... 918 768-3364
Kinta *(G-3833)*
Beck Resources Incorporated ....E....... 405 853-2736
Hennessey *(G-3446)*
Beckham and Butler ....G....... 918 885-4406
Hominy *(G-3576)*
Becks Farm Equipment Inc..............G....... 405 282-1196
Guthrie *(G-3299)*
Bell & Kinley Company ....G....... 405 373-5356
Piedmont *(G-7756)*
Benson Mineral Group Inc ....G....... 918 762-3651
Pawnee *(G-7700)*
Berexco LLC..................................F....... 918 352-2588
Drumright *(G-2052)*

Beta Oil Company .... G 405 601-3389
Oklahoma City *(G-5559)*
Bill Weems Oil Inc .... G 405 382-1813
Seminole *(G-8358)*
Billy Carroll .... G 918 352-9228
Drumright *(G-2053)*
Binger Operations LLC .... G 405 232-0201
Oklahoma City *(G-5570)*
Bkep Crude LLC .... B 405 278-6452
Oklahoma City *(G-5578)*
Black Bayou Exploration LLC .... G 405 753-5500
Oklahoma City *(G-5579)*
Blackburn Oil & Gas Inc .... G 918 688-1067
Pawnee *(G-7701)*
Blair Oil Co Inc .... G 405 263-4445
Kingfisher *(G-3785)*
Blake Production Company Inc .... G 405 286-9800
Oklahoma City *(G-5584)*
Blue Mountain Midstream LLC .... G 281 377-8770
Oklahoma City *(G-5593)*
Bluegrass Energy Inc .... G 918 743-8060
Tulsa *(G-9308)*
Bo Mc Resources Corporation .... G 580 237-2324
Enid *(G-2920)*
Bob & Son Oil Co Inc .... G 405 853-6261
Hennessey *(G-3447)*
Bob Clemishire Oil Co .... G 918 885-4755
Hominy *(G-3577)*
Bob Gene Moore .... G 918 371-4381
Collinsville *(G-1804)*
Bobby J Darnell .... G 405 524-8891
Oklahoma City *(G-5603)*
Bog Resources LLC .... G 918 592-1010
Tulsa *(G-9317)*
Bogo Energy Corporation .... G 405 840-1067
Oklahoma City *(G-5615)*
Bogo Energy Corporation .... G 580 237-3756
Enid *(G-2921)*
Boje Oil Co .... G 918 885-2456
Hominy *(G-3579)*
Boyles & Associates Inc .... G 580 353-7056
Lawton *(G-3899)*
BP America Production Company .... F 918 465-2343
Wilburton *(G-11518)*
Brady Oil Company Inc .... G 405 941-3368
Sasakwa *(G-8329)*
Bratco Operating Company .... F 918 534-2322
Dewey *(G-2018)*
Breeze Investments LLC .... G 918 492-5090
Tulsa *(G-9334)*
Brg Production Company .... E 918 496-2626
Tulsa *(G-9337)*
Brg Production Company .... G 580 233-9302
Enid *(G-2922)*
Brians Hot Oil Service .... G 580 431-2070
Cherokee *(G-1414)*
Briscoe Oil Co .... G 405 375-3700
Kingfisher *(G-3786)*
Bromide Inc .... G 405 360-2999
Norman *(G-4945)*
Brower Oil & Gas Co Inc .... G 918 298-7200
Jenks *(G-3695)*
Brown & Borelli Inc .... G 405 375-5788
Kingfisher *(G-3787)*
Bud Oil Inc .... G 580 251-1378
Duncan *(G-2092)*
Bullseye Operating LLC .... G 918 336-7898
Bartlesville *(G-458)*
Butkin Oil Co LLC .... F 580 444-2561
Duncan *(G-2093)*
C & L Oil and Gas Corporation .... G 405 364-1950
Norman *(G-4950)*
C C McMillin & Company Inc .... G 405 282-3637
Guthrie *(G-3304)*
C E Harmon Oil Inc .... F 918 663-8515
Tulsa *(G-9359)*
C&Y Caseing Pulling Co Inc .... G 580 255-4453
Duncan *(G-2096)*
Calumet Oil Co .... G 405 478-8770
Oklahoma City *(G-5674)*
Calvert Company .... G 405 848-2222
Oklahoma City *(G-5675)*
Calyx Energy III LLC .... F 918 949-4224
Tulsa *(G-9365)*
▼ Canaan Natural Gas Corp .... F 405 604-9300
Oklahoma City *(G-5685)*
Capital Risk Management Corp .... G 405 848-5420
Oklahoma City *(G-5692)*
Caprock Inc .... G 580 255-0831
Duncan *(G-2098)*

Carl A Nilsen .... G 405 236-4554
Oklahoma City *(G-5701)*
Carl E Gungoll Exploration LLC .... F 405 848-7898
Oklahoma City *(G-5702)*
Carnes Petroleum Corporation .... G 918 358-2541
Cleveland *(G-1718)*
Cascade Oil LLC .... G 405 236-4554
Edmond *(G-2338)*
Castlerock Resources Inc .... G 405 842-4249
Oklahoma City *(G-5710)*
Cbhc Resources Inc .... G 405 905-9791
Oklahoma City *(G-5716)*
Cei Petroleum Inc .... G 918 582-4284
Tulsa *(G-9393)*
Ceja Corporation .... E 918 496-0770
Tulsa *(G-9394)*
Ceja Corporation .... E 918 648-5215
Burbank *(G-1214)*
Centaur Resources Inc .... G 405 603-8800
Oklahoma City *(G-5723)*
Centerpint Enrgy Rsources Corp .... G 580 512-5903
McAlester *(G-4279)*
Centrex Operating Co Inc .... G 918 747-9997
Tulsa *(G-9397)*
Centurion Pipeline LP .... G 405 262-4750
El Reno *(G-2705)*
Centurion Resources LLC .... G 918 493-1110
Tulsa *(G-9398)*
Champlin Exploration Inc .... G 580 233-1155
Enid *(G-2928)*
Chaparral Energy Inc .... E 918 793-2881
Shidler *(G-8525)*
Chaparral Energy Inc .... F 918 287-2977
Pawhuska *(G-7682)*
Chaparral Energy Inc .... E 580 673-2815
Healdton *(G-3410)*
Chaparral Energy Inc .... D 405 478-8770
Oklahoma City *(G-5739)*
Chaparral Energy LLC .... C 405 478-8770
Oklahoma City *(G-5740)*
Chaparral Exploration LLC .... G 405 426-4449
Oklahoma City *(G-5741)*
Charles F Doornbos Revocable T .... G 918 336-0611
Bartlesville *(G-461)*
Charles H Colpitt .... G 918 371-2455
Collinsville *(G-1805)*
Checotah Partners LLC .... G 918 935-2795
Tulsa *(G-9408)*
Cher Oil Company Inc .... G 405 454-1575
Ripley *(G-8099)*
Chermac Energy Corporation .... F 405 341-3506
Edmond *(G-2348)*
Chesapeake Energy Corporation .... E 877 245-1427
Elk City *(G-2794)*
Chesapeake Energy Corporation .... A 405 848-8000
Oklahoma City *(G-5751)*
Chesapeake Exploration LLC .... B 405 848-8000
Oklahoma City *(G-5754)*
Chesapeake Louisiana LP .... B 405 848-8000
Oklahoma City *(G-5755)*
Chesapeake Midstream Dev LP .... G 405 935-8000
Oklahoma City *(G-5756)*
Chesapeake Operating LLC .... E 580 772-7255
Weatherford *(G-11399)*
Chesapeake Operating LLC .... F 405 375-6755
Kingfisher *(G-3789)*
Chesapeake Operating LLC .... F 405 375-6755
Kingfisher *(G-3790)*
Chesapeake Operating LLC .... A 405 848-8000
Oklahoma City *(G-5757)*
Chesapeake Operating LLC .... E 405 756-8700
Lindsay *(G-4056)*
Chester Oil Company .... G 405 379-2600
Wetumka *(G-11490)*
Chew Coast & Sons .... G 918 333-3318
Bartlesville *(G-464)*
Cheyenne Petro Co Ltd Partnr .... E 405 936-6220
Oklahoma City *(G-5758)*
Chk Cleveland Tonkawa LLC .... G 405 848-8000
Oklahoma City *(G-5761)*
Chk Louisiana LLC .... G 405 935-7871
Oklahoma City *(G-5762)*
Choctaw Gas Company .... G 918 469-3394
Quinton *(G-8035)*
Choctaw Travel Plaza .... G 580 920-2186
Durant *(G-2214)*
Chris Hammon Oil Properties .... G 405 382-0250
Seminole *(G-8363)*
Christian Martin Lavery .... G 405 810-0900
Nichols Hills *(G-4857)*

Cimarex Energy Co .... G 580 330-0188
Clinton *(G-1743)*
Cimarron River Operation Corp .... G 918 633-2911
Mannford *(G-4179)*
Cirrus Production Company .... G 580 237-0002
Enid *(G-2930)*
◆ Ciskoeagle Inc .... F 918 622-9010
Tulsa *(G-9432)*
Citation Oil & Gas Corp .... G 580 856-3014
Ratliff City *(G-8049)*
Citation Oil & Gas Corp .... E 580 229-1756
Healdton *(G-3411)*
Citation Oil & Gas Corp .... E 580 265-4534
Stonewall *(G-8799)*
Clark Ellison .... G 405 525-3583
Oklahoma City *(G-5775)*
Clearwter Entps LLC Ntural Gas .... G 918 296-7007
Jenks *(G-3699)*
Clements Exploration Co .... G 405 722-3100
Warr Acres *(G-11315)*
Coal Oil & Gas Company .... G 580 332-6170
Ada *(G-26)*
Cobra Oil & Gas Corporation .... G 580 254-2027
Woodward *(G-11569)*
Colston Corporation .... G 580 223-1309
Ardmore *(G-269)*
Columbia Development Corp .... G 918 587-5521
Tulsa *(G-9472)*
Combined Resources Corporation .... G 405 341-7700
Edmond *(G-2361)*
Compass Energy Operating LLC .... D 405 594-4141
Oklahoma City *(G-5808)*
Concorde Resource Corporation .... G 918 689-9510
Eufaula *(G-3099)*
Confed Oil Incorporated .... G 918 582-0018
Tulsa *(G-9477)*
Conocophillips Company .... F 580 243-6000
Elk City *(G-2795)*
Continental Oil & Refining Co .... G 918 266-4420
Catoosa *(G-1313)*
Continental Resources Inc .... C 405 234-9000
Oklahoma City *(G-5823)*
Cornelius Oil Inc .... G 918 247-6743
Kellyville *(G-3762)*
Cornerstone Petroleum Oper LLC .... G 817 730-5200
Tulsa *(G-9489)*
Coronado Petroleum Corporation .... E 405 232-9700
Oklahoma City *(G-5837)*
Cove Petroleum Corporation .... G 918 584-5291
Tulsa *(G-9494)*
Covington Oil Co Inc .... G 405 842-8727
Oklahoma City *(G-5847)*
▼ Crawley Petroleum Corporation .... C 405 232-9700
Oklahoma City *(G-5852)*
Crm Energy Inc .... G 405 848-5420
Oklahoma City *(G-5858)*
Cross Timbers Operating Co .... E 405 232-4011
Oklahoma City *(G-5859)*
CSC Oil Co .... G 918 287-1138
Pawhuska *(G-7684)*
Cummings Oil Company .... G 405 948-1818
Oklahoma City *(G-5866)*
Curzon Operating Company Ltd .... G 405 235-8180
Oklahoma City *(G-5871)*
Cyanostar Energy Inc .... G 918 582-2069
Tulsa *(G-9531)*
D E M Operations Inc .... G 580 388-4315
Lamont *(G-3865)*
Darling Oil Corporation .... G 580 388-6681
Lamont *(G-3867)*
Darnell Drilling Inc .... G 405 524-8816
Oklahoma City *(G-5898)*
Daube Company .... F 580 223-7403
Ardmore *(G-274)*
Davco Productions Inc .... G 405 266-9832
Springer *(G-8621)*
Dave Bolton .... G 205 637-1402
Oklahoma City *(G-5902)*
David Denham Interiors .... G 918 585-3161
Tulsa *(G-9557)*
David L Greene Inc .... G 918 335-3855
Bartlesville *(G-474)*
Davis Bros Oil Producers Inc .... G 918 584-3581
Tulsa *(G-9559)*
Davis Gulf Coast Inc .... G 918 587-7782
Tulsa *(G-9560)*
Davis Oil Co .... G 918 333-5871
Bartlesville *(G-475)*
Dawson-Markwell Exploration Co .... G 405 232-0418
Oklahoma City *(G-5907)*

13 OIL AND GAS EXTRACTION

Deco Development Company Inc .... G 918 747-6366
  Tulsa *(G-9566)*
Deeprock Oil Operating LLC .... G 918 225-7100
  Cushing *(G-1930)*
Dehart Company .... G 580 223-7792
  Ardmore *(G-278)*
Delphi International Inc .... G 918 749-9401
  Tulsa *(G-9568)*
Demco Oil & Gas Company .... G 580 363-4223
  Blackwell *(G-681)*
Denham Operating Co .... G 918 585-3161
  Tulsa *(G-9572)*
Destin Corporation .... G 580 242-6627
  Enid *(G-2940)*
Devon Energy Corporation .... F 405 235-7798
  Oklahoma City *(G-5928)*
◆ Devon Energy Corporation .... C 405 235-3611
  Oklahoma City *(G-5929)*
Devon Energy Corporation .... F 405 235-3611
  Oklahoma City *(G-5930)*
▲ Devon Energy Production Co LP .... A 405 235-3611
  Oklahoma City *(G-5932)*
Devon Gas Services LP .... G 405 228-7543
  Oklahoma City *(G-5934)*
◆ Devon Oei Operating Inc .... A 405 235-3611
  Oklahoma City *(G-5936)*
Diamond Oilfield Services Inc .... G 405 243-7113
  Yukon *(G-11719)*
Diamondback E&P LLC .... E 432 221-7400
  Oklahoma City *(G-5939)*
Digger Oil & Gas Co .... G 405 567-2288
  Prague *(G-7925)*
Division Order Beginnings .... G 918 477-4559
  Porter *(G-7892)*
Djf Services Inc .... G 405 380-7273
  Holdenville *(G-3553)*
Doco Development Corp .... G 405 321-7493
  Norman *(G-4982)*
Dome Blue Operating LLC .... G 918 583-3333
  Tulsa *(G-9592)*
Don Dennis .... G 580 662-3163
  Grady *(G-3255)*
Doyle Cook .... F 405 257-3301
  Wewoka *(G-11500)*
Dublin Petroleum Corp .... G 580 234-7718
  Enid *(G-2945)*
Duncan Inc Walter .... E 405 272-1800
  Oklahoma City *(G-5987)*
Duncan Oil & Gas Inc .... G 405 214-1108
  Shawnee *(G-8446)*
Duncan Oil Properties Inc .... E 405 272-1800
  Oklahoma City *(G-5988)*
Dunlap & Company .... G 580 223-8181
  Ardmore *(G-281)*
Dyco Petroleum Corporation .... F 918 591-1917
  Tulsa *(G-9616)*
Dyne Exploration Company .... G 405 245-0624
  Tulsa *(G-9618)*
E Lyle Johnson Inc .... G 405 470-2047
  Bethany *(G-577)*
Eagle Resources Inc .... G 918 342-5733
  Claremore *(G-1615)*
Eagle River Energy Corporation .... G 918 494-8928
  Broken Arrow *(G-892)*
Eagle Rock Energy Partners LP .... G 281 408-1467
  Tulsa *(G-9629)*
Earlsboro Energies Corporation .... G 405 848-2829
  Oklahoma City *(G-5999)*
Ed Prentice .... G 580 857-2713
  Allen *(G-134)*
Edinger Engineering Inc .... G 405 232-6315
  Oklahoma City *(G-6010)*
Edward C Lawson Properties .... G 918 584-5155
  Tulsa *(G-9645)*
Elkhorn Operating Company .... G 918 492-4418
  Tulsa *(G-9657)*
Elson Oil Co .... G 918 584-5225
  Tulsa *(G-9663)*
Enable Midstream Partners LP .... G 580 225-7190
  Elk City *(G-2811)*
Enable Okla Intrstate Trnsm LL .... F 405 969-3906
  Crescent *(G-1914)*
Enable Oklahoma Int Transm LLC .... G 580 661-2266
  Thomas *(G-8943)*
Enerfin Resources I Ltd Partnr .... E 405 382-3049
  Seminole *(G-8371)*
Energas Corp .... E 405 879-1752
  Oklahoma City *(G-6037)*
Energy Financial and Physcl LP .... G 405 702-4700
  Oklahoma City *(G-6039)*

Energyvest Inc .... F 918 549-1838
  Tulsa *(G-9684)*
Enerlabs Inc .... G 405 879-1752
  Oklahoma City *(G-6040)*
Enersource Petroleum Inc .... G 918 446-8028
  Tulsa *(G-9685)*
Enxnet Inc .... G 918 494-6663
  Tulsa *(G-9693)*
Eog Resources Inc .... E 405 246-3100
  Oklahoma City *(G-6048)*
Equal Energy US Inc .... D 405 242-6000
  Tulsa *(G-9694)*
Escher Corp .... G 405 751-2893
  Oklahoma City *(G-6050)*
Eskridge Production Co Inc .... G 918 836-3058
  Tulsa *(G-9700)*
Etx Energy LLC .... D 918 728-3020
  Tulsa *(G-9703)*
Evans & Associates Entps Inc .... E 580 765-6693
  Ponca City *(G-7828)*
Exco Resources Inc .... D 918 592-7300
  Tulsa *(G-9715)*
Exok Inc .... G 405 840-9196
  Oklahoma City *(G-6062)*
Fairway E&P LLC .... G 918 284-5322
  Bixby *(G-622)*
Falcon Oil Properties .... G 918 367-5596
  Bristow *(G-777)*
Farmers Energy Corp .... G 918 587-6756
  Tulsa *(G-9729)*
Farmers Royalty Company .... G 405 521-9685
  Oklahoma City *(G-6075)*
First Stuart Corporation .... G 918 744-5222
  Tulsa *(G-9747)*
Flywheel Energy LLC .... G 405 702-6991
  Oklahoma City *(G-6095)*
Flywheel Energy Operating LLC .... G 405 702-6991
  Oklahoma City *(G-6097)*
Ford Energy Corporation .... G 405 224-3620
  Chickasha *(G-1458)*
Forward Oil and Gas Inc .... G 405 607-2247
  Oklahoma City *(G-6106)*
Fossil Creek Energy Corp .... G 405 949-0880
  Oklahoma City *(G-6107)*
Four-O-One Corporation .... G 405 848-0425
  Edmond *(G-2419)*
Fox Northeastern Oil Gas Corp .... G 918 331-7791
  Bartlesville *(G-484)*
Francis Oil & Gas Inc .... G 918 491-4253
  Tulsa *(G-9771)*
Frank K Young Oil Properties .... G 405 340-2500
  Edmond *(G-2421)*
Frank Priegel Co .... G 918 756-3161
  Okmulgee *(G-7502)*
Frank T Fleet Inc .... G 580 332-1422
  Ada *(G-37)*
Fred M Buxton .... G 405 840-4331
  Oklahoma City *(G-6115)*
Fredrick F Drummond .... G 918 287-4400
  Pawhuska *(G-7685)*
French Oil .... G 580 248-3131
  Lawton *(G-3930)*
Frisco Energy LLC .... G 918 742-5200
  Tulsa *(G-9779)*
Frontier Gas Services LLC .... G 918 388-6438
  Tulsa *(G-9782)*
Frontier Land Co Inc .... G 918 584-2050
  Tulsa *(G-9783)*
Furseth G N Oil & Gas Producer .... G 405 848-1232
  Oklahoma City *(G-6127)*
G PC Inc .... G 918 582-0018
  Tulsa *(G-9793)*
Gary L Deaton Corporation .... G 405 521-8811
  Oklahoma City *(G-6136)*
Gary M Lake & Company .... G 405 340-6138
  Edmond *(G-2429)*
▲ Gbk Corporation .... F 918 494-0000
  Tulsa *(G-9809)*
Gemini Oil Co Inc .... G 918 582-3935
  Tulsa *(G-9814)*
Gene Cook Inc .... G 580 256-5335
  Woodward *(G-11587)*
Genie Oil & Gas Corporation .... G 918 747-3675
  Tulsa *(G-9819)*
Geoamerican Resources Inc .... G 918 428-8665
  Tulsa *(G-9821)*
Geodyne Production Company .... G 918 583-1791
  Tulsa *(G-9822)*
Gerald W Davidson LLC .... G 580 336-9303
  Perry *(G-7734)*

Gh Land Co .... G 405 947-5500
  Oklahoma City *(G-6150)*
▲ Ghk Company LLC .... E 405 858-9800
  Oklahoma City *(G-6151)*
Gill Operating Company .... G 918 756-1873
  Okmulgee *(G-7505)*
Gill X-Stream Investments LLC .... G 918 743-8379
  Tulsa *(G-9826)*
Gilliland Oil & Gas Inc .... F 405 853-7116
  Hennessey *(G-3463)*
Glacier Petroleum Co of Okla .... G 405 840-2625
  Edmond *(G-2436)*
Gloria Corp Inc .... G 580 332-4050
  Ada *(G-44)*
Godfrey Oil Properties .... F 580 795-3087
  Madill *(G-4148)*
Golsen Petroleum Corp .... G 405 232-7033
  Oklahoma City *(G-6170)*
Gomaco Inc .... G 918 585-8077
  Tulsa *(G-9840)*
Good Oil Company .... F 580 233-3899
  Enid *(G-2963)*
Gothic Production LLC .... E 918 749-5666
  Tulsa *(G-9843)*
Grand Resources Inc .... E 918 492-2366
  Tulsa *(G-9845)*
GRB Resources Inc .... G 918 587-0036
  Tulsa *(G-9852)*
Green Operating Company Inc .... G 918 746-1700
  Tulsa *(G-9862)*
Greer Oil Company .... G 580 762-6355
  Ponca City *(G-7833)*
Griffin Oil Properties LLC .... G 580 226-0461
  Ardmore *(G-298)*
Griffin Resources .... G 405 853-4688
  Hennessey *(G-3464)*
Guest Petroleum Incorporated .... F 405 341-8698
  Edmond *(G-2448)*
Gulfport Energy Corporation .... G 405 756-0060
  Lindsay *(G-4065)*
H & S Drilling Co .... G 918 794-9944
  Tulsa *(G-9875)*
H S Milam .... G 918 789-2666
  Chelsea *(G-1405)*
H W Allen Co LLC .... E 918 747-8700
  Tulsa *(G-9877)*
Halcon Operating Co Inc .... G 832 649-4015
  Tulsa *(G-9880)*
Harding & Shelton Inc .... F 405 236-0080
  Oklahoma City *(G-6218)*
Harrell Energy Co .... G 918 587-2750
  Tulsa *(G-9893)*
Harrell Exploration Corp .... G 918 587-2750
  Tulsa *(G-9894)*
Harrell Verlan W Oil & Gas Co .... G 405 272-9345
  Oklahoma City *(G-6220)*
Haub Oil and Gas LLC .... G 580 765-3585
  Ponca City *(G-7834)*
Hawkins International Inc .... G 918 592-4422
  Tulsa *(G-9903)*
Hawkins Oil Co LLc .... G 918 382-7743
  Tulsa *(G-9904)*
Hazelwood Inc .... G 405 848-6884
  Oklahoma City *(G-6228)*
Hazelwood Prod Exploration LLC .... G 405 848-6884
  Oklahoma City *(G-6229)*
Hazlewood Oil & Gas Co Inc .... G 405 631-3532
  Oklahoma City *(G-6230)*
Helen Murphy Colpitt Trust .... G 918 371-9930
  Collinsville *(G-1813)*
Hembree Lewis A Production Co .... G 405 273-6137
  Shawnee *(G-8459)*
Hendrie Resources Ltd .... G 918 948-4459
  Oklahoma City *(G-6239)*
Henry Gungoll Operating Inc .... G 580 234-2302
  Enid *(G-2970)*
Heritage Petroleum Inc .... G 405 377-2689
  Stillwater *(G-8700)*
Hillenburg Oil Co LLC .... G 918 455-4444
  Broken Arrow *(G-928)*
Hinkle Oil and Gas .... F 405 848-0924
  Oklahoma City *(G-6251)*
HI Wirick Jr LLP .... G 918 587-4548
  Tulsa *(G-9935)*
Hodgden Operating Company Inc .... G 580 233-2870
  Enid *(G-2973)*
Hoke James T Jr Oil Producer .... G 405 341-1779
  Edmond *(G-2457)*
Holden Energy Corp .... E 580 226-3960
  Ardmore *(G-306)*

Employee Codes: A=Over 500 employees, B=251-500
C=101-250, D=51-100, E=20-50, F=10-19, G=1-9

Hollrah Exploration Company ....G....... 405 773-5440
Oklahoma City (G-6258)
Horizon Natural Resources Inc............F....... 918 494-0790
Tulsa (G-9949)
Howard Engineering............G....... 918 396-3463
Skiatook (G-8551)
Hunton Oil and Gas Corp............G....... 405 848-5545
Oklahoma City (G-6275)
Hurd Oil Inc............G....... 918 846-2725
Wynona (G-11680)
Huston Energy Corporation............G....... 580 233-6030
Enid (G-2975)
Illinois Refining Co............G....... 918 367-5562
Bristow (G-779)
Infinity Resources LLC............G....... 405 767-3519
Oklahoma City (G-6303)
Ingram Exploration Inc............G....... 405 382-2040
Seminole (G-8376)
Inland Oil Corp............G....... 918 227-1180
Sapulpa (G-8278)
Intensity Midstream LLC............G....... 918 949-9098
Tulsa (G-10002)
Ips............G....... 405 722-0896
Oklahoma City (G-6326)
J & F Oil Co............G....... 918 652-7957
Henryetta (G-3509)
J & M Investment............G....... 405 848-3755
Oklahoma City (G-6332)
J C N Petroleum Corp............G....... 405 341-8179
Edmond (G-2465)
J C Petroleum Inc............G....... 405 222-1412
Chickasha (G-1473)
J E & L E Mabee Foundation............F....... 918 584-4286
Tulsa (G-10019)
J M A Resources Inc............G....... 405 947-4322
Oklahoma City (G-6336)
J Walter Duncan Jr Oil Inc............E....... 405 272-1800
Oklahoma City (G-6339)
J-W Power Company............G....... 580 254-5663
Woodward (G-11596)
Jack Oil Company............G....... 580 255-2310
Duncan (G-2132)
Jacmac Energy Corp............G....... 405 224-1284
Chickasha (G-1474)
Jacmor Inc............G....... 405 843-0203
Oklahoma City (G-6344)
James B Read Operating Inc............G....... 580 226-0055
Ardmore (G-311)
James H Milligan Enterprises............G....... 405 525-8331
Oklahoma City (G-6348)
James K Anderson Inc............G....... 405 329-7414
Norman (G-5041)
James R Biddick............G....... 918 587-1551
Tulsa (G-10026)
Jath Oil Co............C....... 580 252-5580
Duncan (G-2133)
Jerry Bendorf Trustee............G....... 405 840-9900
Oklahoma City (G-6357)
Jerry Sanner Oil Properties............G....... 580 233-2442
Enid (G-2985)
Jerry Scott Drilling Co Inc............G....... 405 382-2202
Seminole (G-8379)
Jess Harris Inc............G....... 405 840-3271
Oklahoma City (G-6359)
Jetta Production Company Inc............G....... 918 299-0107
Tulsa (G-10043)
Jim Campbell & Associates Rlty............G....... 405 372-9225
Stillwater (G-8707)
Jim Haynes............G....... 918 733-2517
Haskell (G-3399)
John E Rougeot Oil & Gas............G....... 918 494-9978
Tulsa (G-10051)
John H Booth Inc............G....... 918 481-0383
Tulsa (G-10052)
John L Lewis............G....... 405 941-3224
Sasakwa (G-8330)
John M Beard............G....... 405 751-2727
Oklahoma City (G-6368)
John R Warren............G....... 405 843-9402
Oklahoma City (G-6370)
Johnson Exploration Company............G....... 405 235-4454
Oklahoma City (G-6375)
Johnson Marcum Oil and Gas LLC............F....... 918 949-8901
Muskogee (G-4701)
Jolen Operating Company............F....... 405 235-8444
Oklahoma City (G-6379)
Jolen Production Company............G....... 405 235-8444
Oklahoma City (G-6380)
Jones Energy Inc............G....... 405 832-5100
Oklahoma City (G-6381)
Jones Energy Inc............E....... 512 328-2953
Oklahoma City (G-6382)
Jones Energy Finance Corp............G....... 512 328-2953
Oklahoma City (G-6383)
Jones Energy Holdings LLC............E....... 512 328-2953
Oklahoma City (G-6384)
Jones Oil Co LLC............F....... 580 255-9400
Duncan (G-2139)
Jones-Kalkman Mineral Co............G....... 580 223-3101
Ardmore (G-319)
Joshi Technologies Intl Inc............F....... 918 665-6419
Tulsa (G-10059)
K Oil Company............G....... 405 382-0891
Seminole (G-8381)
K S Oil Company Inc............G....... 405 634-5115
Norman (G-5047)
K W B Inc............E....... 918 583-8300
Tulsa (G-10069)
Kaiser Investment............G....... 918 245-4719
Sand Springs (G-8197)
Kaiser-Francis Oil Company............F....... 580 668-2335
Wilson (G-11537)
Kaiser-Francis Oil Company............G....... 405 262-5511
El Reno (G-2730)
Kaiser-Francis Oil Company............F....... 405 577-5347
Oklahoma City (G-6395)
▲ Kaiser-Francis Oil Company............C....... 918 494-0000
Tulsa (G-10074)
Kay Production Co Inc............G....... 405 398-4254
Bowlegs (G-759)
Kechi Energy LLC............G....... 405 222-1412
Chickasha (G-1477)
Keener Oil & Gas Company............G....... 918 587-4154
Tulsa (G-10079)
Keith F Walker Oil Gas Co LLC............G....... 580 223-1575
Ardmore (G-321)
Kencan Flowback LLC............G....... 580 429-8913
Cache (G-1228)
Kiamichi Resources Inc............G....... 405 364-8176
Norman (G-5050)
King Properties Inc............G....... 918 366-6868
Bixby (G-641)
Kingery Drilling Company Inc............G....... 580 223-6823
Ardmore (G-322)
Kingery Drilling Company Inc............G....... 580 229-0716
Healdton (G-3418)
Kingfisher Resources Inc............G....... 580 323-6097
Clinton (G-1755)
Kirkpatrick Oil Company Inc............F....... 405 840-2882
Oklahoma City (G-6426)
Kirkpatrick Oil Company Inc............G....... 405 853-2922
Hennessey (G-3471)
Kiska Oil Company............G....... 918 584-4251
Tulsa (G-10092)
Knowcando Ltd............G....... 918 599-8600
Tulsa (G-10098)
Kopco Inc............G....... 405 743-3290
Stillwater (G-8715)
Krumme Oil Company LLP............F....... 918 367-5562
Bristow (G-787)
L & R Properties Inc............G....... 405 263-7404
Okarche (G-5245)
L C B Resources............G....... 405 375-3718
Kingfisher (G-3807)
▲ L E Jones Production Co............G....... 580 255-1191
Duncan (G-2144)
L I B Ventures Company Inc............G....... 405 659-8800
Oklahoma City (G-6439)
L L Wilkins E and O Co............G....... 405 273-3008
Shawnee (G-8466)
Lackey William H Oil Gas Oper............G....... 405 275-4164
Shawnee (G-8467)
Lake Oil Company Inc............G....... 580 332-1737
Ada (G-57)
Lakewood Energy Solutions LLC............F....... 918 392-9356
Tulsa (G-10115)
Lakewood Energy Solutions LLC............G....... 918 392-9356
Verden (G-11237)
Lamamco Drilling Company............G....... 580 336-3524
Perry (G-7740)
Lamamco Drilling LLC............G....... 918 396-3020
Skiatook (G-8557)
Lamima Corp............G....... 918 491-6846
Tulsa (G-10119)
Landers & Musgroves Oil & Gas............G....... 918 623-2740
Tulsa (G-10122)
Laredo Midstream Services LLC............B....... 918 513-4570
Tulsa (G-10125)
Laredo Petroleum Inc............E....... 918 513-4570
Tulsa (G-10126)
Laredo Petroleum LLC............E....... 918 513-4570
Tulsa (G-10127)
Laredo Petroleum-Dallas Inc............E....... 469 522-7800
Tulsa (G-10128)
Lario Oil & Gas Company............G....... 405 238-5609
Pauls Valley (G-7665)
Larkin Energy Inc............F....... 405 941-3224
Sasakwa (G-8331)
Larry Chinn Oil............G....... 918 336-4269
Pawhuska (G-7688)
Larry Sherman Oil LLC............G....... 405 258-0816
Chandler (G-1384)
Latigo Oil & Gas Inc............F....... 580 256-1416
Woodward (G-11605)
Leasehold Management Corp............G....... 405 670-5535
Oklahoma City (G-6462)
Legion Energy LLC............G....... 918 895-8785
Tulsa (G-10151)
Leland Chapman............G....... 580 444-2511
Velma (G-11235)
Lema Petroleum Inc............G....... 405 379-6678
Holdenville (G-3556)
Lewis Oil Corporation............G....... 405 377-6556
Stillwater (G-8718)
Liberty Operating Inc............G....... 405 329-6200
Norman (G-5058)
Link Oil Company............G....... 918 585-8343
Tulsa (G-10166)
Linn Energy............G....... 405 273-1185
Shawnee (G-8469)
Linn Energy Inc............D....... 405 241-2100
Oklahoma City (G-6481)
Litzenberger Exploration Inc............G....... 580 824-9351
Waynoka (G-11379)
Liverpool Production Company............G....... 918 523-9595
Tulsa (G-10170)
Lobar Oil Co............G....... 405 330-7938
Edmond (G-2491)
Lorraine Oil Co Inc............G....... 405 853-2715
Hennessey (G-3474)
Lucky Four Oil Company............G....... 405 941-3307
Sasakwa (G-8332)
Lvm Oil Production LLC............G....... 918 387-2822
Yale (G-11685)
Lyons & Lyons Inc............G....... 918 587-2497
Tulsa (G-10186)
M and V Resources Inc............G....... 405 969-2338
Crescent (G-1918)
M Craig Deisenroth Oil & Gas............G....... 918 742-4769
Tulsa (G-10188)
M&T Production Co............G....... 918 227-1528
Tulsa (G-10192)
Mack Energy Co............G....... 580 856-3705
Ratliff City (G-8057)
Mack Energy Co............C....... 580 252-5580
Duncan (G-2150)
Madill Gas Processing Co LLC............F....... 580 795-7396
Madill (G-4154)
Maggard Supply and Oil Co Inc............G....... 918 865-4333
Mannford (G-4186)
Marjo Oil Company Inc............G....... 918 583-0241
Tulsa (G-10210)
Marjo Operating Co Inc............G....... 918 583-0241
Tulsa (G-10211)
Mark Holloway Inc............G....... 405 833-7947
Oklahoma City (G-6527)
Markwest Energy Partners LP............G....... 580 225-5400
Elk City (G-2845)
Markwest Oklahoma Gas Co LLC............E....... 580 225-5400
Elk City (G-2846)
Marlin Oil Corporation............E....... 405 478-1900
Oklahoma City (G-6529)
Marsh Oil & Gas Co............G....... 405 238-9660
Pauls Valley (G-7667)
Maxim Energy Corp............G....... 405 348-9669
Edmond (G-2507)
Mayabb Oil Co Inc............G....... 918 396-2654
Skiatook (G-8560)
McCasland Mercantile LLC............G....... 580 252-5580
Duncan (G-2153)
McGonigal Ted Oil and Well Svc............G....... 918 299-5250
Jenks (G-3716)
Meadowbrook Oil Corp of Okla............G....... 405 672-0240
Del City (G-2001)
▲ Medallion Petroleum Inc............G....... 918 582-1320
Tulsa (G-10237)
Mercer Petroleum Management............G....... 405 341-1110
Edmond (G-2513)
Metzger Oil Tools Inc............G....... 918 885-2456
Hominy (G-3592)

13 OIL AND GAS EXTRACTION

Mexco Energy Corporation .... G 405 330-4042
  Edmond *(G-2516)*
Mfp Petroleum Ltd Partnership .... G 405 728-5588
  Oklahoma City *(G-6584)*
Mid-America Midstream Gas .... G 405 935-8000
  Oklahoma City *(G-6589)*
Mid-American Oil Co Inc .... G 405 848-7551
  Oklahoma City *(G-6590)*
Mid-Con Energy Gp LLC .... D 972 479-5980
  Tulsa *(G-10257)*
Mid-Con Energy II LLC .... G 918 743-7575
  Tulsa *(G-10258)*
Mid-Con Energy Operating LLC .... F 918 743-7575
  Tulsa *(G-10259)*
Mid-Con Energy Partners LP .... D 918 743-7575
  Tulsa *(G-10260)*
Mid-Con Energy Properties LLC .... G 918 743-7575
  Tulsa *(G-10261)*
Midcon Midstream LP .... G 405 429-5500
  Oklahoma City *(G-6596)*
Midwest Enterprises Inc .... G 405 433-2419
  Cashion *(G-1290)*
Mineral Resources Company .... G 405 234-9000
  Oklahoma City *(G-6615)*
Miracle Production Inc .... F 405 324-2216
  Oklahoma City *(G-6618)*
MJM Resources Inc .... G 405 579-4455
  Norman *(G-5076)*
Montgomery Exploration Company .... G 405 232-1169
  Norman *(G-5080)*
Monty L Hott Production Corp .... G 405 495-3311
  Oklahoma City *(G-6628)*
Moran Oil Enterprises .... G 405 382-6001
  Seminole *(G-8386)*
Moran-K Oil LLC .... F 405 382-6001
  Seminole *(G-8387)*
MRC Global (us) Inc .... F 405 491-7392
  El Reno *(G-2740)*
Muirfield Production Co Inc .... F 918 744-5604
  Tulsa *(G-10312)*
Muirfield Resources Company .... F 918 744-5604
  Tulsa *(G-10313)*
Musgrove Energy Inc .... G 580 765-7314
  Ponca City *(G-7856)*
▲ Mustang Fuel Corporation .... D 405 884-2092
  Oklahoma City *(G-6641)*
Mw Engineering Co .... G 405 273-0370
  Shawnee *(G-8478)*
N M & O Operating Company .... G 918 584-3802
  Tulsa *(G-10322)*
Nadel and Gussman LLC .... E 918 583-3333
  Tulsa *(G-10323)*
Nelson Exploration Corp .... G 405 853-6933
  Cleveland *(G-1729)*
New Dominion LLC .... E 918 587-6242
  Tulsa *(G-10335)*
Noco Investment Co Inc .... G 918 582-0090
  Tulsa *(G-10346)*
Northport Production Co Inc .... G 405 848-1212
  Edmond *(G-2541)*
Northstar Energy LLC .... D 231 941-0073
  Tulsa *(G-10362)*
Norville Oil Co LLC .... G 405 286-9100
  Oklahoma City *(G-6696)*
Nosley Scoop LLC .... G 512 328-2953
  Oklahoma City *(G-6697)*
Ntu Pipeline LLC .... F 918 392-9255
  Tulsa *(G-10365)*
Nubs Well Servicing Inc .... F 580 856-3887
  Ratliff City *(G-8058)*
Nye Oil Co .... G 405 843-6609
  Oklahoma City *(G-6705)*
Oak Hill Petroleum Corporation .... G 405 842-1568
  Nichols Hills *(G-4861)*
Oakland Petroleum Operating Co .... G 918 496-3027
  Tulsa *(G-10373)*
Occidental Petroleum Corp .... F 918 610-1990
  Tulsa *(G-10374)*
▼ Octagon Resources Inc .... F 405 366-8885
  Norman *(G-5097)*
Ogp Energy L P .... G 405 235-9571
  Oklahoma City *(G-6715)*
Oilfield R T .... G 405 238-2026
  Pauls Valley *(G-7669)*
OK Swabbing Inc .... G 405 853-6953
  Hennessey *(G-3478)*
Okc Energy Corporation .... G 405 330-5586
  Oklahoma City *(G-6728)*
Okie Operating Co Ltd .... G 918 582-2594
  Tulsa *(G-10393)*

Oklahoma Basic Economy Corp .... F 580 332-4710
  Ada *(G-73)*
Okland Oil Company .... E 405 236-3046
  Oklahoma City *(G-6766)*
Oky Investments Inc .... G 405 850-4533
  Edmond *(G-2555)*
Olmstead Oil Company .... E 918 743-2360
  Tulsa *(G-10415)*
Olympia Oil Inc .... G 405 726-8400
  Oklahoma City *(G-6773)*
One Gas Inc .... D 918 947-7000
  Tulsa *(G-10418)*
One Gas Inc .... G 918 831-8218
  Tulsa *(G-10419)*
Oneok Inc .... A 918 588-7000
  Tulsa *(G-10421)*
Oneok Inc .... E 918 588-7000
  Tulsa *(G-10422)*
Oneok Gas Processing LLC .... G 918 588-7000
  Tulsa *(G-10424)*
Oneok Gas Transportation LLC .... C 918 588-7000
  Tulsa *(G-10425)*
Oneok Producer Services Co .... G 918 588-7000
  Tulsa *(G-10428)*
Oneok Resources Company .... D 918 588-7000
  Tulsa *(G-10429)*
Osage Surveying Service .... G 918 287-4029
  Pawhuska *(G-7692)*
Otc Petroleum Corporation .... G 405 840-2255
  Oklahoma City *(G-6788)*
Ouachita Exploration Inc .... G 405 222-0024
  Chickasha *(G-1496)*
Ovintiv Exploration Inc .... G 580 927-9064
  McAlester *(G-4327)*
Ovintiv Exploration Inc .... G 918 420-5086
  Mc Alester *(G-4265)*
Ovintiv Mid-Continent Inc .... C 918 582-2690
  Tulsa *(G-10448)*
OXY Inc .... G 580 338-6593
  Guymon *(G-3358)*
P D I Inc .... E 405 232-9700
  Oklahoma City *(G-6791)*
P F Beeler LLC .... G 405 364-0799
  Norman *(G-5107)*
P H D Oil & Gas Inc .... G 580 476-3005
  Rush Springs *(G-8124)*
Paleo Inc .... G 405 942-1546
  Oklahoma City *(G-6795)*
Paloma Partners IV .... G 405 295-6755
  El Reno *(G-2745)*
Panhandle Royalty Co .... G 405 945-6100
  Oklahoma City *(G-6800)*
Panoak Oil & Gas Corporation .... G 918 857-4929
  Tulsa *(G-10460)*
Pappe Court Jr Office .... G 405 375-5450
  Kingfisher *(G-3810)*
Paragon Production Co .... G 405 348-1116
  Edmond *(G-2562)*
Parsage Oil Company LLC .... G 918 846-2358
  Tulsa *(G-10471)*
Patrick A McGinley .... G 918 583-3267
  Tulsa *(G-10472)*
Patterson Oil Company Inc .... G 918 257-3241
  Wewoka *(G-11507)*
Paul E Kloberdanz .... G 405 947-5570
  Oklahoma City *(G-6812)*
Paulaura Cattle Co .... G 918 682-6030
  Muskogee *(G-4732)*
Pauline Oil and Gas Co .... G 405 842-4213
  Nichols Hills *(G-4862)*
Payne Farms .... G 580 661-2351
  Thomas *(G-8947)*
Peake Fuel Solutions LLC .... G 405 935-8000
  Oklahoma City *(G-6817)*
Pedestal Oil Company Inc .... F 405 236-8596
  Oklahoma City *(G-6819)*
Pelican Energy LLC .... G 405 418-8000
  Oklahoma City *(G-6823)*
Pennant Oil & Gas LLC .... G 405 642-4382
  Tulsa *(G-10485)*
Penner Energy Inc .... G 405 751-7504
  Oklahoma City *(G-6826)*
Performance Operating Co LLC .... F 918 847-3830
  Barnsdall *(G-439)*
Performance Petroleum Co .... E 918 847-2531
  Barnsdall *(G-440)*
Perkins Development Corp .... G 918 749-2152
  Tulsa *(G-10495)*
Perkins Energy Co .... G 580 255-5400
  Duncan *(G-2164)*

Petro Speed Inc .... G 405 364-6785
  Norman *(G-5114)*
Petrocorp Incorporated .... G 918 491-4500
  Tulsa *(G-10501)*
Petroflow Energy Corporation .... F 918 592-1010
  Tulsa *(G-10502)*
Petroleum International Inc .... G 918 712-1840
  Tulsa *(G-10506)*
Phoenix Oil and Gas Inc .... F 405 382-0935
  Seminole *(G-8394)*
Platt Energy Corporation .... G 405 840-5081
  Oklahoma City *(G-6856)*
Pletcher Oil Company .... F 580 657-4221
  Ardmore *(G-346)*
Plymouth Resources Inc .... G 918 599-1880
  Tulsa *(G-10529)*
Pontotoc Gathering LLC .... G 918 742-5835
  Tulsa *(G-10531)*
Portman Minerals LLC .... G 405 843-4063
  Oklahoma City *(G-6864)*
Post Oak Oil Co .... G 405 621-1300
  Oklahoma City *(G-6865)*
Post Oak Petroleum LLC .... G 918 245-9919
  Skiatook *(G-8564)*
Pre Mc Inc .... G 580 857-2408
  Allen *(G-137)*
Prentice Napier & Green Inc .... F 405 752-7680
  Oklahoma City *(G-6888)*
Pressburg LLC .... G 405 896-8050
  Oklahoma City *(G-6891)*
Primeenergy Corporation .... F 405 942-2897
  Oklahoma City *(G-6894)*
Primeenergy Corporation .... E 405 375-5203
  Oklahoma City *(G-6895)*
Producers Oil Company Inc .... E 918 582-1188
  Tulsa *(G-10566)*
Producing Lamamco III L P .... C 918 396-3020
  Skiatook *(G-8565)*
Providence Energy Corp .... G 918 747-3675
  Tulsa *(G-10577)*
Qep Energy Company .... E 405 263-4831
  Okarche *(G-5250)*
Quail Creek Oil Corporation .... E 405 755-7419
  Oklahoma City *(G-6934)*
Quail Creek Production Company .... G 405 755-7419
  Oklahoma City *(G-6935)*
Quest Property Inc .... G 405 722-7530
  Wheatland *(G-11515)*
Quintin Little Company Inc .... E 580 226-7600
  Ardmore *(G-348)*
R C Taylor Companies Inc .... G 405 840-2700
  Oklahoma City *(G-6961)*
R E Blaik Inc .... G 405 285-8000
  Edmond *(G-2582)*
R E G Energy .... G 405 842-4249
  Oklahoma City *(G-6963)*
R G Berry Co .... G 918 587-0036
  Tulsa *(G-10604)*
R T C Resources LLP .... G 580 774-2313
  Weatherford *(G-11435)*
Rainbow Oil & Gas Inc .... G 918 335-2188
  Bartlesville *(G-521)*
Ramsey Property Management LLC .... G 405 302-6200
  Oklahoma City *(G-6971)*
Range Energy Services Company .... F 580 227-3762
  Fairview *(G-3148)*
Raven Resources LLC .... G 405 773-7340
  Edmond *(G-2586)*
Ray Lu Petroleum LLC .... G 405 424-4006
  Oklahoma City *(G-6974)*
Raydon Exploration Inc .... G 405 478-8585
  Oklahoma City *(G-6975)*
Rbc Exploration Company .... G 918 744-5607
  Tulsa *(G-10623)*
Rebel Oil Company .... G 405 848-2208
  Oklahoma City *(G-6981)*
Reclaimed Oil & Gas Prpts LLC .... G 580 234-8085
  Enid *(G-3045)*
Red Fork Motor Co .... G 918 587-2778
  Tulsa *(G-10630)*
Red Plains Oil & Gas LLC .... G 405 375-3377
  Kingfisher *(G-3812)*
Redland Resources Inc .... G 405 789-7104
  Oklahoma City *(G-6996)*
Reserve Petroleum Company .... G 405 848-7551
  Oklahoma City *(G-7009)*
Resources Operating Company .... G 580 237-7744
  Enid *(G-3047)*
Rexbo Energy Co .... G 405 359-0458
  Edmond *(G-2598)*

Richard Exploration Co Inc....G....405 840-0101
Oklahoma City (G-7017)
Richland Resources Corporation....F....405 732-0045
Oklahoma City (G-7019)
Rick Davis....G....918 733-4760
Morris (G-4602)
Riviera Operating LLC....E....405 375-6065
Kingfisher (G-3813)
Rkk Production Company....G....405 376-2223
Mustang (G-4790)
Roberson Oil Co Inc....G....580 332-6170
Ada (G-83)
Robert W Berry Inc....G....918 492-1140
Tulsa (G-10663)
Rockland Oil Co....G....580 223-0960
Ardmore (G-350)
Rocky Mountain Prod Co LLC....G....405 720-2000
Oklahoma City (G-7046)
Rogers Resources Inc....G....580 237-7744
Enid (G-3050)
Romayne - Baker Oil & Gas Ltd....G....580 237-1626
Enid (G-3051)
Romine Oil & Gas Ltd....G....405 273-1171
Shawnee (G-8489)
Rose Rock Midstream Corp....G....918 524-8100
Tulsa (G-10671)
Rose Rock Midstream Oper LLC....G....918 524-7700
Tulsa (G-10673)
Rougeot Oil & Gas Corp....G....918 288-2022
Tulsa (G-10678)
Rox Exploration Inc....G....405 329-0009
Norman (G-5136)
Royalok Royalty LLC....G....405 721-9771
Oklahoma City (G-7055)
Roye Realty & Developing Inc....G....918 967-4888
Stigler (G-8644)
Ruffel Lance Oil & Gas Corp....F....405 239-7036
Oklahoma City (G-7060)
Sagebrush Pipeline LLC....G....405 753-5500
Oklahoma City (G-7073)
Sallee Oil Corp....G....918 371-2290
Collinsville (G-1824)
Sam W Mays Jr....G....918 382-9170
Tulsa (G-10691)
Samedan Oil Corp....G....580 856-3705
Ratliff City (G-8066)
Sams Well Service Inc....F....580 762-6355
Ponca City (G-7871)
Samson Investment Company....B....918 583-1791
Tulsa (G-10694)
Samson Natural Gas Company....B....918 583-1791
Tulsa (G-10695)
Samson Resources Company....D....918 583-1791
Tulsa (G-10696)
Samson Resources Corporation....F....918 591-1791
Tulsa (G-10697)
Samson Resources II LLC....G....918 591-1791
Tulsa (G-10698)
Samson Resources II Opco LLC....G....918 591-1791
Tulsa (G-10699)
Sandridge Co2 LLC....G....405 429-5500
Oklahoma City (G-7078)
Sandridge Energy Inc....G....580 430-4500
Alva (G-191)
Sandridge Energy Inc....A....405 354-2727
Yukon (G-11775)
Sandridge Energy Inc....C....405 429-5500
Oklahoma City (G-7079)
Sandridge Exploration Prod LLC....G....405 429-5734
Oklahoma City (G-7080)
Sandridge Offshore LLC....G....405 429-5500
Oklahoma City (G-7081)
Sandridge Operating Company....C....405 753-5500
Oklahoma City (G-7082)
Sandstone Enrgy Acqstions Corp....G....405 239-2150
Oklahoma City (G-7083)
Sandy Petroleum Inc....G....405 273-9289
Shawnee (G-8492)
Sariel Inc....G....918 855-1400
Tulsa (G-10709)
Scissortail Energy LLC....F....918 588-5000
Tulsa (G-10716)
Scissortail Energy LLC....G....918 968-0422
Stroud (G-8818)
Seaboard Gas Company....G....405 341-1779
Edmond (G-2614)
SEC Production Inc....G....405 715-0088
Edmond (G-2615)
Sell Well Servicing Company....G....918 287-1711
Pawhuska (G-7695)
Semgroup Corporation....G....918 225-7758
Cushing (G-1958)
Semgroup Corporation....E....405 945-6300
Oklahoma City (G-7108)
Senax Inc....G....918 494-0681
Tulsa (G-10731)
Servicios Petroleros Flint CA....E....918 587-7131
Tulsa (G-10734)
Seth W Herndon Jr....G....918 744-4072
Tulsa (G-10735)
Shelburne Oil Company....G....405 843-1352
Oklahoma City (G-7120)
Sherman Oil and Gas Company....G....405 258-5932
Chandler (G-1386)
Shields Operating Inc....G....405 341-7607
Edmond (G-2620)
Short Oil Co....E....918 747-8200
Tulsa (G-10750)
Short Oil Co Yard....G....918 287-2925
Pawhuska (G-7696)
Siegfried Companies Inc....G....918 747-3411
Tulsa (G-10752)
Sierra Madera Co2 Pipeline LLC....G....405 753-5500
Oklahoma City (G-7129)
Simek Oil Properties Inc....G....405 567-4606
Prague (G-7935)
Singer Bros....G....405 236-8596
Oklahoma City (G-7143)
Singer Bros....G....918 582-6237
Tulsa (G-10767)
Singer Oil Company LLC....G....405 853-6807
Hennessey (G-3486)
Sitrin Petroleum Corp....G....918 747-1111
Tulsa (G-10770)
Solar Exploration OK LLC....G....918 252-2203
Tulsa (G-10783)
▲ Sooner Holdings Inc....F....918 592-7900
Tulsa (G-10788)
Sooner Tool Company....G....918 352-4440
Drumright (G-2071)
Sooner Trend Exploration Inc....G....405 375-3405
Kingfisher (G-3816)
Southern Resources Inc....G....405 601-1322
Oklahoma City (G-7172)
Southwest Energy LP....G....918 779-0699
Tulsa (G-10806)
Southwest Petroleum Corp....E....918 352-2700
Tulsa (G-10809)
Speller Oil Corporation....F....405 942-7869
Oklahoma City (G-7182)
Speller Petroleum Corporation....G....405 942-7869
Oklahoma City (G-7183)
Spess Drilling Company....F....918 358-5831
Cleveland (G-1734)
Spiral Exploration LLC....G....330 936-4689
Oklahoma City (G-7186)
Spring Harry A Geological Engr....G....580 226-1910
Ardmore (G-361)
Spyglass Energy Group LLC....G....918 582-9900
Tulsa (G-10828)
Ssb Production LLC....G....580 226-7000
Ardmore (G-362)
Stadia Energy Partners LLC....G....918 812-6169
Tulsa (G-10830)
Stagestand Ranch....G....580 255-1161
Duncan (G-2184)
Stars Restaurants LLC....E....405 947-1396
Edmond (G-2631)
Stateline Processing LLC....E....855 979-2012
Tulsa (G-10839)
Stateline Water LLC....E....855 979-2012
Tulsa (G-10840)
Stephen J Heyman....G....918 583-3333
Tulsa (G-10846)
Stokes Production....G....405 485-2402
Seminole (G-8401)
Stonebridge Partnership 1 LP....G....918 747-7594
Tulsa (G-10854)
Strat Land Exploration Co....F....918 584-3844
Tulsa (G-10859)
Strata Minerals Inc....G....405 722-3227
Oklahoma City (G-7214)
Stream Energy Inc....F....405 272-1080
Oklahoma City (G-7216)
Stream Line....G....405 756-4422
Lindsay (G-4087)
Sullivan and Company LLC....F....918 584-4288
Tulsa (G-10864)
Summit Oil Company Inc....G....405 842-7896
Oklahoma City (G-7224)
Sunoco Logistics Partners LP....G....918 352-9442
Drumright (G-2072)
Sutherland Well Service Inc....D....580 229-1338
Healdton (G-3422)
Sweetwater Exploration LLC....G....405 329-1967
Norman (G-5166)
Sylvan Oil Operating Company....G....918 267-3764
Tulsa (G-10885)
Synergex Inc....E....405 748-5050
Oklahoma City (G-7239)
T & K Oil Inc....G....405 382-5241
Seminole (G-8402)
T A T Inc....G....405 942-0489
Oklahoma City (G-7242)
T C Craighead & Company....F....580 223-7470
Ardmore (G-365)
T K Drilling Corp....G....918 270-1084
Tulsa (G-10890)
▲ Tag Petroleum Inc....G....405 377-6185
Stillwater (G-8763)
Targa Resources Corp....D....580 883-2273
Ringwood (G-8095)
Taylor International Inc....G....918 352-9511
Cushing (G-1964)
Tcina Holding Company Ltd....G....405 382-0399
Seminole (G-8404)
Technical Energy Services Inc....G....405 329-8196
Norman (G-5171)
Templar Operating LLC....F....405 548-1200
Oklahoma City (G-7267)
Thomas Exploration Company....G....918 496-1414
Tulsa (G-10932)
Thomas N Berry & Company....G....405 372-5252
Stillwater (G-8767)
Thomas P Shaw....G....918 742-4673
Tulsa (G-10934)
Three B Land & Cattle Company....G....580 332-9480
Ada (G-94)
Three Sands Oil Inc....G....580 336-2410
Perry (G-7749)
Thunderbird Energy Resources....G....918 627-5433
Tulsa (G-10939)
Thundrbird Rsources Equity Inc....F....405 600-0711
Edmond (G-2642)
Tilley Oil & Gas Inc....G....405 608-4970
Oklahoma City (G-7289)
Toklan Oil and Gas Corporation....F....918 582-5400
Tulsa (G-10949)
Toland & Johnston Inc....G....405 330-2006
Edmond (G-2646)
Tom Meason Oil Ventures....G....918 587-3492
Tulsa (G-10950)
Tony Oil Company....G....918 493-1882
Tulsa (G-10951)
Toomey Oil Company Inc....G....918 583-1166
Tulsa (G-10954)
Total Well Solutions LLC....G....918 392-9352
Tulsa (G-10961)
Tpi Petroleum Inc....C....580 221-6288
Ardmore (G-373)
Trace Oil....G....405 222-4449
Chickasha (G-1518)
Trees Oil Co....G....918 257-5050
Afton (G-123)
Trepco Production Co Inc....G....405 722-1400
Yukon (G-11794)
Tri Production Inc....G....580 229-1280
Healdton (G-3423)
Tri Resources Inc....E....580 493-2249
Waukomis (G-11360)
Triad Operating Corporation....F....405 842-4312
Oklahoma City (G-7326)
Tridon Oil Inc....G....918 682-6801
Muskogee (G-4754)
Trinity Gas Corporation....G....580 233-1155
Enid (G-3067)
Tripledee Drilling Co Inc....G....580 223-8181
Ardmore (G-374)
Tripower Resources LLC....F....580 226-6700
Ardmore (G-375)
Truman F Logsdon....G....405 348-4504
Edmond (G-2655)
Tsalta Corporation....G....405 607-4141
Oklahoma City (G-7345)
Turner Resources Inc....G....405 853-6275
Hennessey (G-3494)
Twenty-Twenty Oil & Gas Co....G....405 853-4607
Hennessey (G-3495)
Twin Eagle Midstream LLC....G....918 459-4548
Tulsa (G-11024)

Union Valley Petroleum Corp.....G..... 580 237-3959
Enid *(G-3069)*
Unit Corporation.....D..... 918 493-7700
Tulsa *(G-11037)*
Unit Petroleum Company.....C..... 918 493-7700
Tulsa *(G-11039)*
United Energy Trading LLC.....G..... 918 392-8444
Tulsa *(G-11041)*
United Production Co L L C.....G..... 405 728-8900
Edmond *(G-2657)*
Uplands Resources Inc.....G..... 918 592-0305
Tulsa *(G-11053)*
Valiant Midstream LLC.....G..... 405 286-5580
Edmond *(G-2665)*
Van Eaton C W.....G..... 580 223-4374
Ardmore *(G-378)*
Vernon E Faulconer Inc.....G..... 580 883-2892
Ringwood *(G-8096)*
Vm Arkoma Stack LLC.....G..... 405 286-5580
Oklahoma City *(G-7404)*
W F D Oil Corporation.....G..... 405 715-3130
Edmond *(G-2677)*
Wachtman-Schroeder.....G..... 918 287-3122
Pawhuska *(G-7697)*
Wadley Bill & Son Drilling Co.....G..... 918 756-4650
Okmulgee *(G-7529)*
Walden Energy LLC.....G..... 918 488-8663
Tulsa *(G-11091)*
Walker Resources Inc.....G..... 405 751-5357
Oklahoma City *(G-7414)*
Warren American Oil Company.....E..... 918 481-7990
Tulsa *(G-11096)*
Warren American Oil Company.....G..... 918 846-2294
Barnsdall *(G-442)*
Warwick Energy Group LLC.....F..... 405 607-3400
Oklahoma City *(G-7423)*
Warwick Energy Group LLC.....E..... 972 351-2740
Oklahoma City *(G-7424)*
Warwick Energy Inv Group LLC.....E..... 405 607-3400
Oklahoma City *(G-7425)*
Weaver Energy Corporation.....G..... 405 853-6068
Hennessey *(G-3498)*
Wehlu Producers Inc.....G..... 405 844-9487
Edmond *(G-2683)*
Weinkauf Petroleum Inc.....F..... 918 749-8383
Tulsa *(G-11105)*
West Valbel Corporation.....G..... 580 223-3494
Ardmore *(G-381)*
Western Gas Resources Inc.....E..... 580 883-2273
Ringwood *(G-8097)*
Western Oil and Gas Dev Corp.....F..... 405 235-4590
Oklahoma City *(G-7440)*
Westfall Producing Company.....G..... 918 743-1192
Tulsa *(G-11111)*
Wetzel Producing Company.....G..... 580 255-2929
Duncan *(G-2198)*
Wheeler & Sons Oil and Gas.....G..... 405 375-4613
Kingfisher *(G-3821)*
Wheeler Energy Corporation.....G..... 918 587-7474
Tulsa *(G-11114)*
White Operating Company.....G..... 405 735-8419
Oklahoma City *(G-7445)*
Whiteman Industries Inc.....G..... 405 879-0077
Oklahoma City *(G-7446)*
Whiting Petroleum Corporation.....C..... 580 234-5554
Enid *(G-3079)*
Wildhorse Exploration Prod LLC.....G..... 918 396-3736
Skiatook *(G-8574)*
Wildhorse Oil & Gas Corp.....G..... 580 223-0936
Ardmore *(G-382)*
Wilkins L L E & O Company.....G..... 405 273-0370
Shawnee *(G-8520)*
William C Jackson.....G..... 918 742-0602
Tulsa *(G-11122)*
William Cloud Oil.....G..... 405 751-8422
Oklahoma City *(G-7455)*
William H Davis.....G..... 918 587-7782
Tulsa *(G-11124)*
William M Park.....G..... 918 288-7752
Sperry *(G-8612)*
William Pettit.....F..... 918 297-2564
Hartshorne *(G-3396)*
William W McClure Jr.....G..... 918 747-6094
Tulsa *(G-11126)*
▲ **Williams Companies Inc**.....A..... 918 573-2000
Tulsa *(G-11127)*
Williams Field Services Co LLC.....C..... 918 573-2000
Tulsa *(G-11129)*
Williams Gas Pipeline Co LLC.....G..... 918 573-2000
Tulsa *(G-11130)*
Williams MBL Bay Prod Svcs LLC.....G..... 918 573-2000
Tulsa *(G-11131)*
Williams Partners LP.....C..... 918 573-2000
Tulsa *(G-11132)*
Williford Energy Company.....F..... 918 495-2700
Tulsa *(G-11134)*
Willis Bros Land & Cattle Co.....G..... 580 569-2698
Snyder *(G-8585)*
Wolf Creek Enterprises Inc.....G..... 580 254-3361
Woodward *(G-11655)*
Wood Oil Company.....F..... 405 948-1560
Oklahoma City *(G-7463)*
Woodbine Financial Corporation.....G..... 918 584-5309
Tulsa *(G-11149)*
Worstell Oil.....G..... 918 371-5425
Collinsville *(G-1831)*
Wpx Energy Inc.....D..... 855 979-2012
Tulsa *(G-11155)*
Wpx Energy Keystone LLC.....F..... 918 573-2000
Tulsa *(G-11157)*
Wpx Energy Rm Company.....F..... 918 573-2000
Tulsa *(G-11161)*
Xae Corp.....G..... 405 452-5735
Wetumka *(G-11496)*
Xanadu Exploration Company.....G..... 918 584-3802
Tulsa *(G-11164)*
Xplorer Midstream LLC.....F..... 918 237-5885
Oklahoma City *(G-7478)*
Xto Energy Inc.....E..... 580 883-2253
Ringwood *(G-8098)*
Xto Energy Inc.....D..... 580 653-3200
Ardmore *(G-383)*
Xto Energy Inc.....G..... 580 668-2332
Wilson *(G-11546)*
Yukon Drilling Fluid Inc.....G..... 405 324-8876
Oklahoma City *(G-7483)*
Zephyr Operating Co LLC.....G..... 405 286-4771
Oklahoma City *(G-7486)*
Zinke & Trumbo Inc.....F..... 918 488-6400
Tulsa *(G-11178)*

1321 Natural Gas Liquids

Avalon Exploration Inc.....F..... 918 523-0600
Tulsa *(G-9227)*
Bluehawk Energy Inc.....G..... 405 406-1580
Edmond *(G-2327)*
BP America Production Company.....F..... 918 465-2343
Wilburton *(G-11518)*
Bravo Natural Gas LLC.....G..... 918 712-7008
Tulsa *(G-9333)*
C & R Olfld Pntg Rustabout Svc.....G..... 620 272-6699
Ponca City *(G-7804)*
Centennial Gas Liquids Ulc.....G..... 918 481-1119
Tulsa *(G-9396)*
Dcp Midstream LLC.....F..... 405 705-7400
Edmond *(G-2385)*
Deeprock Tank Oper Colo LLC.....E..... 918 225-7100
Cushing *(G-1931)*
Eagle Rock Energy Partners LP.....G..... 281 408-1467
Tulsa *(G-9629)*
Enable Okla Intrstate Trnsm LL.....C..... 405 525-7788
Oklahoma City *(G-6033)*
Enable Oklahoma Int Transm LLC.....G..... 405 356-4060
Wellston *(G-11469)*
Enable Oklahoma Int Transm LLC.....G..... 580 323-7450
Clinton *(G-1750)*
Enogex Services Corporation.....G..... 405 525-7788
Oklahoma City *(G-6042)*
Enogex Services Corporation.....E..... 405 893-2267
Calumet *(G-1246)*
Frontier Energy Services LLC.....G..... 918 754-2226
Tulsa *(G-9780)*
Frontier Energy Services LLC.....F..... 918 388-8438
Tulsa *(G-9781)*
Frontier Midstream LLC.....G..... 918 388-8438
Tulsa *(G-9784)*
G&J Measurement Inc.....G..... 580 560-3190
Duncan *(G-2119)*
Hiland Lp LLC.....F..... 713 369-9000
Enid *(G-2972)*
J-W Power Company.....G..... 580 254-5663
Woodward *(G-11596)*
Mark West Hydrocarbon Inc.....G..... 800 730-8388
Tulsa *(G-10212)*
Markwest Hydrocarbon Inc.....E..... 580 664-5282
Butler *(G-1221)*
Markwest Pioneer LLC.....G..... 918 477-8000
Tulsa *(G-10214)*
Oklahoma Propane Gas Assn.....G..... 405 424-1775
Oklahoma City *(G-6758)*
Oneok Inc.....F..... 405 878-6267
Shawnee *(G-8482)*
Oneok Inc.....A..... 918 588-7000
Tulsa *(G-10421)*
Oneok Inc.....E..... 918 588-7000
Tulsa *(G-10422)*
Oneok Field Services Co LLC.....B..... 918 588-7000
Tulsa *(G-10423)*
Oneok Midstream Gas Supply LLC.....F..... 918 588-7000
Tulsa *(G-10426)*
Oneok Partners LP.....E..... 918 588-7000
Tulsa *(G-10427)*
Oneok Texas Field Services LP.....D..... 918 588-7000
Tulsa *(G-10430)*
PTL Prop Solutions LLC.....G..... 405 848-8000
Oklahoma City *(G-6920)*
Pvr Midstream LLC.....F..... 580 837-5265
Beaver *(G-545)*
Range Rsurces-Midcontinent LLC.....C..... 405 810-7359
Oklahoma City *(G-6972)*
Red Mountain Energy LLC.....F..... 405 842-4500
Oklahoma City *(G-6986)*
Red Mountain Operating LLC.....G..... 405 842-9200
Oklahoma City *(G-6987)*
Riley Explration - Permian LLC.....G..... 405 415-8699
Oklahoma City *(G-7026)*
▲ **Sooner Holdings Inc**.....F..... 918 592-7900
Tulsa *(G-10788)*
Spectrum Lng LLC.....F..... 918 298-6660
Tulsa *(G-10818)*
Templar Operating LLC.....F..... 405 548-1200
Oklahoma City *(G-7267)*
Titan Propane LLC.....G..... 918 838-8804
Tulsa *(G-10946)*
Tom-Stack LLC.....F..... 405 888-5585
Edmond *(G-2647)*
Transwestern Pipeline Co LLC.....G..... 918 492-7272
Tulsa *(G-10971)*
Tri Resources Inc.....G..... 580 363-0243
Blackwell *(G-694)*
Tronox Incorporated.....G..... 580 921-5411
Woodward *(G-11645)*
▲ **Williams Companies Inc**.....A..... 918 573-2000
Tulsa *(G-11127)*
Williams Energy Resources LLC.....E..... 918 573-2000
Tulsa *(G-11128)*
Woodford Express LLC.....F..... 405 437-0857
Oklahoma City *(G-7465)*
Wpx Energy Marketing LLC.....G..... 918 573-0068
Tulsa *(G-11158)*
Wpx Energy Marketing LLC.....E..... 918 573-2000
Tulsa *(G-11159)*

1381 Drilling Oil & Gas Wells

Agave Energy Inc.....G..... 918 799-6174
Stigler *(G-8628)*
Akerman Drilling Inc.....E..... 580 925-3938
Konawa *(G-3842)*
Allen Rathole Inc.....G..... 918 626-4026
Spiro *(G-8613)*
Angus Natural Resources LLC.....G..... 918 712-8487
Tulsa *(G-9192)*
Ardmore Prod & Exploration.....G..... 580 223-2292
Ardmore *(G-249)*
Arrow Drilling LLC.....E..... 405 749-7860
Edmond *(G-2310)*
At & L Energy LLC.....G..... 580 623-7265
Watonga *(G-11339)*
Atchley Resources Inc.....G..... 405 848-3331
Oklahoma City *(G-5484)*
Badlands Petroleum LLC.....G..... 303 921-2854
Oklahoma City *(G-5508)*
Bailey Production Company.....G..... 405 932-5293
Paden *(G-7633)*
Baker Energy Solutions LLC.....G..... 405 691-1202
Oklahoma City *(G-5510)*
Baker Hghes Olfld Oprtions LLC.....G..... 918 341-9600
Claremore *(G-1589)*
Bays Enterprises Inc.....G..... 405 235-2297
Oklahoma City *(G-5532)*
Bays Exploration Inc.....G..... 405 235-2297
Oklahoma City *(G-5533)*
Big Buckets Rathole Drilling.....G..... 580 233-9850
Enid *(G-2917)*
Bill Sneed Oilfield.....G..... 918 358-3487
Cleveland *(G-1717)*
Bird Creek Resources Inc.....G..... 918 582-7713
Tulsa *(G-9297)*
Bison Energy Services LLC.....F..... 405 529-6577
Oklahoma City *(G-5577)*

S I C

Employee Codes: A=Over 500 employees, B=251-500
C=101-250, D=51-100, E=20-50, F=10-19, G=1-9
2020 Oklahoma Directory
of Manufacturers & Processors
407

Black Gold Stone Ranch LLC ....G....... 405 590-0700
Norman *(G-4936)*
Blazer Oilfield Services LLC ....E....... 405 756-4800
Lindsay *(G-4049)*
Bob Pound Drilling Inc ....F....... 918 367-6262
Bristow *(G-767)*
Boone Operating Inc..............................G....... 405 879-2332
Oklahoma City *(G-5618)*
Brexco Inc...G....... 405 348-8124
Edmond *(G-2332)*
Bucks Directional Drilling ....G....... 580 276-2238
Marietta *(G-4201)*
Can Global Usa Inc ....F....... 405 261-0417
Oklahoma City *(G-5683)*
Canfield Ranch Energy LLC...................G....... 405 272-1080
Oklahoma City *(G-5687)*
Cardinal River Energy Co.......................G....... 405 606-7481
Oklahoma City *(G-5697)*
Carel Pumping..G....... 405 485-3495
Blanchard *(G-705)*
Casillas Operating LLC ....E....... 918 582-5310
Tulsa *(G-9386)*
Cathedral Energy Services Inc ....D....... 405 261-6011
Oklahoma City *(G-5713)*
Chesapeake Energy La Corp ....G....... 405 848-8000
Oklahoma City *(G-5752)*
Circle V Energy Services LLC...............G....... 405 614-0891
Glencoe *(G-3219)*
Clay Bennett...G....... 918 647-9294
Poteau *(G-7901)*
Cleary Petroleum Corporation..............F....... 405 672-4544
Edmond *(G-2357)*
Combs Oilfield Services Inc..................G....... 580 571-2315
Woodward *(G-11571)*
Continental Resources Inc....................G....... 580 883-2838
Ringwood *(G-8086)*
Creek International Rig Corp ....G....... 918 585-8221
Tulsa *(G-9507)*
Crown Energy Company ....E....... 405 526-0111
Oklahoma City *(G-5861)*
Crown Geochemistry Inc........................G....... 918 392-0334
Tulsa *(G-9515)*
Cuesta Petroleum ....G....... 405 878-0744
Shawnee *(G-8442)*
D & M Directional Drilling LLC.............G....... 405 221-2959
Wewoka *(G-11499)*
D and R Directional Drilling ....G....... 405 208-1399
Crescent *(G-1912)*
Dakota Exploration LLC ....G....... 918 806-8687
Tulsa *(G-9547)*
Darling Oil Corp ....G....... 580 388-4567
Lamont *(G-3866)*
Darrells Drilling Inc...............................G....... 580 925-3854
Konawa *(G-3844)*
David Dodd Inc..G....... 405 216-5412
Edmond *(G-2381)*
Destiny Petroleum LLC ....F....... 281 362-2833
Moore *(G-4515)*
Diamondback Energy Inc ....G....... 405 600-0711
Oklahoma City *(G-5940)*
Directional Boring Inc.............................G....... 405 842-8850
Oklahoma City *(G-5949)*
Directional Fluid Disposals....................G....... 405 626-3261
Oklahoma City *(G-5950)*
Downing Manufacturing Inc...................F....... 918 224-1116
Tulsa *(G-9001)*
Drillworx Directional Drlg LLC..............G....... 405 386-3380
Choctaw *(G-1540)*
Dunlap Drilling Producing Inc ....G....... 918 237-0015
Glenpool *(G-3233)*
Eagle Drilling LLC..................................G....... 405 447-8181
Norman *(G-4986)*
Edge Services Inc ....E....... 580 254-3216
Woodward *(G-11581)*
Farallon Petroleum LLC ....G....... 405 225-1009
Oklahoma City *(G-6073)*
Fasco Directional Drilling LLC..............G....... 918 224-2756
Sapulpa *(G-8273)*
Foam Unit Inc ....G....... 580 921-3366
Laverne *(G-3877)*
Foti Directional LLC...............................G....... 352 848-5281
Edmond *(G-2418)*
Frontier Drilling LLC..............................C....... 405 745-7700
Oklahoma City *(G-6120)*
Frontier Drilling LLC..............................D....... 405 745-7700
Oklahoma City *(G-6121)*
G B K Holdings Inc ....G....... 918 494-0000
Tulsa *(G-9789)*
Gateway Directional Drilling ....G....... 405 752-4230
Edmond *(G-2433)*
George B Hughes....................................G....... 405 784-5575
Asher *(G-389)*
Gillham Oil & Gas Inc ....G....... 405 997-8549
Maud *(G-4252)*
Goobers Drilling LLC..............................G....... 918 846-2732
Wynona *(G-11678)*
Great Plains Oilfld Rentl LLC................A....... 405 422-2873
El Reno *(G-2720)*
H & P Finco...D....... 918 742-5531
Tulsa *(G-9874)*
H Rockn Inc ....G....... 405 323-6593
Chickasha *(G-1467)*
Halliburton Company.............................C....... 580 251-2847
Duncan *(G-2124)*
▼ **Helmerich & Payne Inc** ....A....... 918 742-5531
Tulsa *(G-9912)*
Helmerich & Payne Inc ....F....... 918 447-2630
Tulsa *(G-9012)*
Helmerich & Payne Inc ....G....... 918 447-8692
Tulsa *(G-9913)*
Helmerich & Payne Inc ....G....... 918 835-6071
Tulsa *(G-9914)*
Helmerich & Payne De Venezuela ....C....... 918 742-5531
Tulsa *(G-9915)*
◆ **Helmerich & Payne Intl Drlg Co** ....B....... 918 742-5531
Tulsa *(G-9916)*
Helmerich & Payne Intl Drlg Co.............B....... 918 742-5531
Oklahoma City *(G-6236)*
Helmerich & Payne Rasco Inc ....G....... 918 742-5531
Tulsa *(G-9917)*
Helmerich & Payne Tech LLC ....G....... 918 742-5531
Tulsa *(G-9918)*
Helmerich Payne Argentina Drlg ....B....... 918 742-5531
Tulsa *(G-9919)*
◆ **Helmerich Payne Boulder Drlg**..........G....... 918 742-5531
Tulsa *(G-9920)*
Helmerich Payne Columbia Drlg ....B....... 918 742-5531
Tulsa *(G-9921)*
Helmerich Payne Trinidad Drlg.............B....... 918 742-5531
Tulsa *(G-9922)*
▲ **Hendershot Tool Company** ....E....... 405 677-3386
Oklahoma City *(G-6238)*
Hewitt Mineral Corp ....G....... 580 223-3619
Ardmore *(G-303)*
Holiday Creek Prticipation LLC ....G....... 405 275-1045
Shawnee *(G-8461)*
Horizon Energy Services LLC...............B....... 405 533-4800
Stillwater *(G-8702)*
Horizon Energy Services LLC...............F....... 918 392-9351
Tulsa *(G-9948)*
Horizontal Well Drillers LLC..................G....... 405 527-1232
Purcell *(G-8010)*
Hoss Directional Service Inc..................G....... 405 822-0551
Norman *(G-5027)*
Hulen Operating Company.....................G....... 405 848-5252
Oklahoma City *(G-6271)*
Huntington Energy LLC.........................F....... 405 840-9876
Oklahoma City *(G-6274)*
Hybrid Tool Solutions LLC.....................G....... 405 756-1408
Lindsay *(G-4069)*
Inglesrud Corp ....G....... 405 429-7928
Oklahoma City *(G-6304)*
Integrity Directional Svcs LLC ....F....... 817 731-8881
Oklahoma City *(G-6315)*
Intrepid Directional Drilling...................G....... 405 607-0422
Oklahoma City *(G-6324)*
J Grantham Drilling Inc ....G....... 918 647-8926
Poteau *(G-7907)*
J H B & Company Inc............................G....... 405 354-6709
Yukon *(G-11733)*
Ja Marrs Oil Co Inc ....G....... 918 352-2798
Drumright *(G-2064)*
Jack Exploration Inc................................G....... 580 621-3679
Cherokee *(G-1417)*
Jbk Well Service LLC..............................F....... 918 695-6062
Barnsdall *(G-437)*
Jeffries Pumping Service Inc..................F....... 580 628-2769
Guthrie *(G-3320)*
JMJ Petroleum Inc ....G....... 918 209-5913
Jenks *(G-3711)*
Jordan Services Inc.................................G....... 405 748-3997
Oklahoma City *(G-6385)*
K & H Well Service Inc............................F....... 405 382-2762
Seminole *(G-8380)*
Kaiser Energy Ltd ....G....... 918 494-0000
Tulsa *(G-10071)*
Kaiser Francis Gulf Coast LLC..............G....... 918 491-4490
Tulsa *(G-10072)*
Kay Production Services Inc ....F....... 405 398-3109
Seminole *(G-8382)*
Key Energy Services Inc ....E....... 405 843-6854
Oklahoma City *(G-6406)*
Koby Oil Company LLC..........................G....... 405 236-3551
Oklahoma City *(G-6432)*
L and A Filtration LLC............................G....... 580 380-2976
Durant *(G-2242)*
L E Jones Drilling LLC...........................G....... 580 255-3532
Duncan *(G-2143)*
Latigo Drilling Corporation ....G....... 580 255-1674
Duncan *(G-2145)*
Latshaw Drilling Company LLC............G....... 918 355-4380
Tulsa *(G-10135)*
Layton & Smallwood...............................G....... 918 446-6945
Tulsa *(G-10139)*
Leam Drilling Systems ....G....... 918 794-3457
Tulsa *(G-10143)*
Leam Drilling Systems LLC ....F....... 405 440-9436
Oklahoma City *(G-6461)*
Lejones Operating Inc ....F....... 580 255-3532
Duncan *(G-2147)*
▲ **Liberty Bit Co** ....G....... 580 255-6400
Duncan *(G-2148)*
Liberty Minerals LLC ....G....... 405 317-8107
Ardmore *(G-325)*
Mammoth Energy Partners LLC............F....... 405 265-4600
Oklahoma City *(G-6518)*
Marmac Resources Company.................G....... 918 846-2293
Barnsdall *(G-438)*
Mason Enterprises Group LLC..............G....... 918 230-5782
Coweta *(G-1890)*
Millbrae Energy LLC ....G....... 405 286-1941
Oklahoma City *(G-6610)*
Mitchell Oil Company ....G....... 918 652-9175
Broken Arrow *(G-979)*
Mustang Heavy Haul LLC ....A....... 405 743-0085
Stillwater *(G-8726)*
Nabors Drilling Tech USA Inc ....E....... 405 324-8081
Oklahoma City *(G-6646)*
Nabors Drilling Tech USA Inc ....E....... 405 745-3457
Oklahoma City *(G-6647)*
Nabors Drilling Usa LP..........................G....... 580 225-0072
Elk City *(G-2854)*
Natural Gas Commpression Corp ....G....... 918 243-7500
Cleveland *(G-1728)*
Neminis Inc..G....... 918 582-8083
Tulsa *(G-10333)*
Noble Resources Inc ....G....... 918 865-3301
Mannford *(G-4188)*
Nomac Drilling...G....... 405 242-4444
Edmond *(G-2539)*
Nomac Drilling LLC................................G....... 405 422-2754
El Reno *(G-2743)*
Oneok Inc...E....... 918 588-7000
Tulsa *(G-10422)*
Oneok Partners LP..................................E....... 918 588-7000
Tulsa *(G-10427)*
Osage Land Company.............................F....... 405 946-8402
Oklahoma City *(G-6784)*
Ouachita Exploration Inc........................G....... 405 222-0024
Chickasha *(G-1496)*
Palm Operating LLC ....G....... 918 968-0574
Stroud *(G-8815)*
Panther Drilling Systems LLC ....E....... 405 896-9300
Oklahoma City *(G-6801)*
Parker Drilling Company.........................G....... 918 281-2708
Tulsa *(G-10468)*
◆ **Parking Drilling Company Intl** ....C....... 281 406-2000
Tulsa *(G-10469)*
Patriot Directional Drlg LLC...................G....... 405 831-0085
Stillwater *(G-8735)*
Pearl Petroleum Inc ....G....... 580 355-6477
Lawton *(G-3981)*
Petroflow Energy Ltd...............................E....... 918 592-1010
Tulsa *(G-10503)*
Petroleum Development Company ....G....... 918 583-7434
Tulsa *(G-10505)*
Phil Lack ....E....... 580 883-4945
Ringwood *(G-8089)*
Pioneer Drectional Drlg II LLC...............G....... 405 533-1552
Stillwater *(G-8737)*
Pistol Drilling LLC...................................G....... 580 256-9371
Woodward *(G-11621)*
Plymouth Resources Inc ....G....... 918 599-1880
Tulsa *(G-10529)*
Png Operation ....G....... 405 470-4333
Oklahoma City *(G-6859)*
Poteet Oil Co Inc......................................G....... 405 756-4530
Lindsay *(G-4077)*
Powers Drilling Inc...................................G....... 580 343-2444
Weatherford *(G-11433)*

SIC SECTION
13 OIL AND GAS EXTRACTION

Prairie Exploration Co ....G...... 405 360-7077
  Norman (G-5119)
Qes Pressure Control LLC ....E...... 580 885-7885
  Arnett (G-388)
Qes Pressure Control LLC ....D...... 580 243-6622
  Elk City (G-2863)
Quest Cherokee LLC ....G...... 405 371-1653
  Oklahoma City (G-6941)
Ra Jac Inc ....G...... 405 701-5222
  Norman (G-5128)
Ricks Rig Service ....G...... 405 619-9193
  Oklahoma City (G-7021)
Robert C Beard ....G...... 918 534-2020
  Dewey (G-2031)
Robert R Cantrell ....F...... 580 332-9495
  Ada (G-84)
Romine Oil & Gas Ltd ....G...... 405 273-1171
  Shawnee (G-8489)
Rose Rock Petroleum LLC ....G...... 405 212-6987
  Edmond (G-2603)
Rowe Wireline Services LLC ....G...... 580 541-5086
  Enid (G-3052)
Rupp Drilling Inc ....G...... 580 336-4717
  Perry (G-7744)
Samson Natural Gas Company ....B...... 918 583-1791
  Tulsa (G-10695)
Sb Consulting LLC ....F...... 405 926-7177
  Oklahoma City (G-7088)
Scientific Drilling Intl ....G...... 405 787-3663
  Yukon (G-11779)
Scientific Drilling Intl Inc ....D...... 405 787-3663
  Yukon (G-11780)
Seismic Drilling Services LLC ....D...... 918 587-2225
  Tulsa (G-10723)
Southeastern Drilling ....G...... 918 469-3489
  Quinton (G-8042)
Spring Drilling Corp ....G...... 580 226-3800
  Ardmore (G-360)
Sutherland Well Service Inc ....F...... 580 856-3538
  Ratliff City (G-8069)
Talon/Lpe Ltd ....G...... 806 467-0607
  Oklahoma City (G-7249)
Taylor Resources ....G...... 405 850-2283
  Oklahoma City (G-7260)
Thunderbird Energy Resources ....G...... 918 627-5433
  Tulsa (G-10939)
Titan Resources Limited ....G...... 918 298-1811
  Tulsa (G-10947)
Topco Oilsite Products USA Inc ....F...... 405 491-8521
  Oklahoma City (G-7304)
Troy Hulett ....G...... 580 922-5298
  Cleo Springs (G-1713)
Unit Corporation ....C...... 580 774-5200
  Weatherford (G-11453)
Unit Corporation ....G...... 918 493-7700
  Tulsa (G-11036)
Unit Corporation ....D...... 918 493-7700
  Tulsa (G-11037)
Unit Drilling Co ....E...... 281 446-6889
  Oklahoma City (G-7362)
Unit Drilling Company ....G...... 580 256-8688
  Woodward (G-11647)
Unit Drilling Company ....C...... 405 745-4948
  Oklahoma City (G-7363)
Unit Drilling Company ....C...... 918 493-7700
  Tulsa (G-11038)
Unit Drilling Company ....F...... 405 745-4948
  Oklahoma City (G-7364)
Unit Texas Drilling LLC ....G...... 281 446-6889
  Oklahoma City (G-7365)
Universal Rig Service Corp ....G...... 918 585-8221
  Tulsa (G-11050)
Vassal Well Services LLC ....F...... 580 279-1579
  Ada (G-101)
Vernon L Smith & Assoc Inc ....G...... 405 360-3374
  Norman (G-5194)
W F D Oil Corporation ....G...... 405 715-3130
  Edmond (G-2677)
Wagon Wheel Production Co ....G...... 580 983-2371
  Crawford (G-1906)
White Stone LLC ....G...... 580 824-3271
  Waynoka (G-11383)
Wildcate Drilling Services Inc ....E...... 580 254-3306
  Woodward (G-11654)
Willischild Oil & Gas Corp ....G...... 580 569-2598
  Snyder (G-8586)
Winter Creek Drilling LLC ....G...... 405 321-1200
  Norman (G-5201)
Woody Creek Ranch ....G...... 580 658-5448
  Marlow (G-4249)

▼ Woolslayer Companies Inc ....C...... 918 523-9191
  Catoosa (G-1368)

1382 Oil & Gas Field Exploration Svcs

89 Energy LLC ....F...... 405 600-6040
  Oklahoma City (G-5338)
89 Energy II LLC ....F...... 405 600-6040
  Oklahoma City (G-5339)
9800 North Oklahoma LLC ....G...... 405 748-9400
  Oklahoma City (G-5341)
A & S Operating Inc ....G...... 918 582-7205
  Tulsa (G-9063)
A & T Resources LLC ....G...... 918 582-7894
  Tulsa (G-9064)
Ada Energy Service LLC ....D...... 580 436-5228
  Ada (G-5)
Aexco Petroleum Inc ....G...... 405 844-1991
  Edmond (G-2292)
Alpine Inc ....G...... 405 507-1111
  Edmond (G-2299)
Amazing Graze LLC ....G...... 405 447-4893
  Norman (G-4905)
Amcon Resources ....G...... 405 236-4100
  Oklahoma City (G-5430)
Amerex Corp ....G...... 405 216-5548
  Edmond (G-2301)
American Manifold ....G...... 580 225-1116
  Elk City (G-2783)
American Petroleum & Envrnmntl ....G...... 405 513-6055
  Edmond (G-2302)
Amerril Energy LLC ....G...... 770 856-2662
  Oklahoma City (G-5443)
Anadarko Petroleum Corporation ....E...... 405 756-4347
  Lindsay (G-4043)
Anchor Exploration of Oklahoma ....G...... 918 605-1005
  Claremore (G-1582)
Annabella Oil & Gas Co LLC ....G...... 405 377-8030
  Stillwater (G-8654)
Antioch Operating LLC ....G...... 405 236-0080
  Oklahoma City (G-5449)
Apollo Exploration LLC ....G...... 405 286-0600
  Oklahoma City (G-5453)
Apss Inc ....G...... 405 324-2071
  Oklahoma City (G-5459)
Arcadia Resources LP ....D...... 405 608-5453
  Oklahoma City (G-5461)
Arena Resources Inc ....D...... 918 747-6060
  Tulsa (G-9207)
Arkos Field Services LP ....G...... 405 262-1548
  El Reno (G-2699)
Armor Energy LLC ....G...... 918 986-9459
  Tulsa (G-9209)
Arnold Oil Properties LLC ....F...... 405 842-1488
  Oklahoma City (G-5468)
Arrowood Companies ....G...... 405 701-3673
  Norman (G-4919)
Ascent Resources - Utica LLC ....D...... 405 608-5544
  Oklahoma City (G-5470)
Ascent Resources Operating LLC ....F...... 405 608-5544
  Oklahoma City (G-5471)
Ascent Rsrces Utica Hldngs LLC ....G...... 405 608-5544
  Oklahoma City (G-5472)
Aspect Oilfield Services LLC ....G...... 504 812-5330
  Tulsa (G-9216)
Associated Resources Inc ....E...... 918 584-2111
  Tulsa (G-9218)
B & W Exploration Inc ....G...... 405 236-1807
  Oklahoma City (G-5503)
B R Polk Inc ....G...... 405 286-9666
  Oklahoma City (G-5505)
B Raye Oil Environmental ....G...... 405 818-6996
  Mustang (G-4763)
B&W Operating LLC ....G...... 405 236-1807
  Oklahoma City (G-5506)
Babb Land & Development ....G...... 405 340-1178
  Oklahoma City (G-2315)
Bailey Production Company ....G...... 405 932-5293
  Paden (G-7633)
Baker Hghes Olfld Oprtions LLC ....E...... 580 256-3333
  Oklahoma City (G-5512)
Baker Hghes Olfld Oprtions LLC ....C...... 405 670-3354
  Oklahoma City (G-5513)
Bakken Hbt LP ....G...... 405 516-8241
  Oklahoma City (G-5518)
Bandera Inc ....G...... 918 747-7771
  Tulsa (G-9262)
Barbour Energy Corporation ....G...... 405 848-7671
  Oklahoma City (G-5527)
Bbr Oil Corp ....G...... 405 366-8019
  Norman (G-4926)

Bce-Mach II LLC ....D...... 405 252-8100
  Oklahoma City (G-5537)
Bce-Mach LLC ....D...... 405 252-8100
  Oklahoma City (G-5538)
Bce-Mach LLC ....C...... 580 824-7251
  Waynoka (G-11373)
Bean Chris Oil & Gas Service ....G...... 918 298-1569
  Jenks (G-3690)
Becsul Energy Incorporated ....G...... 405 789-1061
  Oklahoma City (G-5541)
Bedford Energy Inc ....G...... 405 820-2711
  Oklahoma City (G-5542)
Bellwood Petroleum ....G...... 405 254-3113
  Oklahoma City (G-5547)
Belport Oil Inc ....E...... 918 637-5476
  Tulsa (G-9279)
Benchmark 77 Energy ....G...... 405 239-3291
  Oklahoma City (G-5549)
Beredco Inc ....C...... 405 858-2326
  Oklahoma City (G-5554)
Berexco LLC ....G...... 405 848-1165
  Oklahoma City (G-5555)
Beta Oil Company ....G...... 405 601-3389
  Oklahoma City (G-5559)
Billy Jack Sharber Oper LLC ....G...... 405 382-5740
  Konawa (G-3843)
Bint Exploration & Development ....G...... 405 848-2113
  Oklahoma City (G-5571)
Bison Oilfield Services LLC ....E...... 405 437-1485
  Seminole (G-8359)
Bk Exploration Corporation ....G...... 918 582-3855
  Tulsa (G-9298)
Black Swan Oil & Gas ....G...... 405 285-1996
  Edmond (G-2325)
Blaine Exploration Ltd ....G...... 918 333-2115
  Bartlesville (G-456)
Blue Star Gas Corp ....G...... 405 321-1397
  Norman (G-4937)
Blue Stone Operating LLC ....D...... 918 392-9209
  Tulsa (G-9307)
Blue Valley Energy Corp ....G...... 918 298-1032
  Jenks (G-3692)
Bluestone Natural Resources HI ....G...... 918 392-9200
  Tulsa (G-9310)
Bluestone Ntral Rsurces II LLC ....G...... 918 392-9200
  Tulsa (G-9311)
Bluestone Ntrual Resources LLC ....F...... 918 392-9200
  Tulsa (G-9312)
Bob Pound Drilling Inc ....F...... 918 367-6262
  Bristow (G-767)
Boelte Explorations LLC ....G...... 405 285-0063
  Edmond (G-2328)
Boone Operating Inc ....G...... 405 879-2332
  Oklahoma City (G-5618)
Bosendorfer Oil Company ....G...... 405 604-9025
  Oklahoma City (G-5622)
Bounty Transfer LLC ....F...... 405 338-1531
  Stillwater (G-8662)
Brett Exploration ....G...... 405 842-2322
  Oklahoma City (G-5625)
Brg Energy Inc ....G...... 918 496-2626
  Tulsa (G-9336)
Brigham Company LLC ....G...... 405 843-2660
  Oklahoma City (G-5628)
Brookline Minerals LLC ....G...... 405 359-0900
  Edmond (G-2333)
Bs & W Solutions LLC ....G...... 918 392-9356
  Tulsa (G-9343)
Buckeye Exploration Company ....G...... 405 258-5428
  Chandler (G-1377)
C & J Minerals LLC ....G...... 580 504-4048
  Ardmore (G-262)
Cadence Energy Partners LLC ....E...... 405 485-8200
  Oklahoma City (G-5668)
Caerus Operating LLC ....G...... 580 468-3527
  Guymon (G-3345)
Cagan Land Services LLC ....G...... 405 757-4046
  Edmond (G-2336)
Calebs Resources LLC ....G...... 405 330-8252
  Edmond (G-2337)
Caliber Completion Svcs LLC ....G...... 405 385-3761
  Moore (G-4502)
Caliche Resources Inc ....G...... 918 492-5170
  Talala (G-8898)
Callie Oil Company LLC ....G...... 918 521-9292
  Agra (G-124)
Calyx Energy III Holdings LLC ....G...... 918 949-4224
  Tulsa (G-9366)
Canaan Energy Corp ....G...... 405 604-9200
  Oklahoma City (G-5684)

Employee Codes: A=Over 500 employees, B=251-500
C=101-250, D=51-100, E=20-50, F=10-19, G=1-9

2020 Oklahoma Directory
of Manufacturers & Processors

Cano Petroleum Inc ....F 918 398-2728
Tulsa *(G-9370)*
Cantrell Energy Corporation ....G 580 332-4710
Ada *(G-19)*
Capstone Oil & Gas Inc ....G 405 853-7170
Hennessey *(G-3448)*
Cardinal Energy Inc ....G 405 331-9206
Wynnewood *(G-11664)*
Cardinal Midstream ....G 405 706-4161
Mustang *(G-4766)*
Cardinal Midstream LLC ....G 580 927-2799
Coalgate *(G-1777)*
Cardinal River Energy Co ....G 405 606-7481
Oklahoma City *(G-5697)*
Carter Production Co ....G 918 493-7064
Tulsa *(G-9383)*
Casillas Petroleum Corp ....G 918 582-5310
Tulsa *(G-9387)*
Cbl Resources ....G 918 551-6760
Tulsa *(G-9391)*
CBS Energy LLC ....G 405 470-4644
Oklahoma City *(G-5717)*
Century Geophysical Corp ....E 918 838-9811
Tulsa *(G-9399)*
Cep Mid-Continent LLC ....G 918 270-9927
Tulsa *(G-9401)*
Cfmi LLC ....G 918 877-5000
Tulsa *(G-9402)*
Chaparral Energy Inc ....D 405 478-8770
Oklahoma City *(G-5739)*
Chaparral Energy LLC ....C 405 478-8770
Oklahoma City *(G-5740)*
Charles D Mayhue ....G 580 436-6500
Ada *(G-20)*
Charter Oak Production Co LLC ....F 405 286-0361
Oklahoma City *(G-5744)*
Chaston Oil & Gas LLC ....G 580 226-2640
Ardmore *(G-266)*
Cheftain Royalty Company ....G 405 767-1251
Edmond *(G-2347)*
Chernico Exploration Inc ....G 918 587-6242
Tulsa *(G-9412)*
Chesapeake Energy Corporation ....E 877 245-1427
Elk City *(G-2794)*
Cheyenne Petro Co Ltd Partnr ....E 405 936-6220
Oklahoma City *(G-5758)*
Cimarex Energy Co ....C 918 585-1100
Tulsa *(G-9425)*
Cimarex Energy Co ....F 405 262-2966
El Reno *(G-2706)*
Cimarex Energy Co ....D 918 295-1638
Tulsa *(G-9426)*
Cimarex Energy Co ....G 580 330-0188
Clinton *(G-1743)*
Circle 9 Resources LLC ....F 972 528-6773
Oklahoma City *(G-5767)*
Citation Oil & Gas Corp ....F 405 681-9400
Oklahoma City *(G-5769)*
Citizen Energy II LLC ....F 918 949-4680
Tulsa *(G-9433)*
Citizen Energy III LLC ....G 918 949-4680
Tulsa *(G-9434)*
Citizen Energy Operating LLC ....G 918 949-4680
Tulsa *(G-9435)*
Citizen Enrgy Intermediate LLC ....G 918 949-4680
Tulsa *(G-9436)*
Clearwater Enterprises ....G 918 296-7007
Tulsa *(G-9451)*
Cobra Oil & Gas Corporation ....G 580 254-2027
Woodward *(G-11569)*
Cockerell Energy ....G 405 463-7118
Oklahoma City *(G-5799)*
Colter Bay LLC ....G 405 842-7622
Nichols Hills *(G-4858)*
Comanche Exploration Co LLC ....E 405 755-5900
Oklahoma City *(G-5804)*
Concorde Resource Corporation ....G 918 689-9510
Eufaula *(G-3099)*
Conocophillips Company ....E 281 293-1000
Bartlesville *(G-468)*
Coronado Resources MGT LLC ....G 918 591-3500
Tulsa *(G-9491)*
Corp Comm Oil & Gas Div ....G 405 375-5570
Kingfisher *(G-3793)*
Council Oak Resources LLC ....F 918 513-0900
Tulsa *(G-9493)*
CP Energy LLC ....F 405 513-6006
Edmond *(G-2370)*
Craig Elder Oil and Gas LLC ....G 405 917-7860
Edmond *(G-2371)*
Crest Resources Inc ....G 918 585-2900
Tulsa *(G-9508)*
Crow Creek Energy LLC ....G 918 970-6706
Tulsa *(G-9513)*
Crystal River Operating Co LLC ....G 405 510-0440
Oklahoma City *(G-5864)*
Cudd Pressure Control Inc ....E 405 756-4337
Lindsay *(G-4058)*
Cudd Pressure Control Inc ....E 580 225-6922
Elk City *(G-2798)*
Culbreath Oil & Gas Co Inc ....G 918 749-3508
Tulsa *(G-9520)*
Cummings Oil Company ....G 405 948-1818
Oklahoma City *(G-5866)*
Cyanostar Energy Inc ....G 918 582-2069
Tulsa *(G-9531)*
Dagwood Energy Inc ....G 918 582-6604
Tulsa *(G-9546)*
Daniel H Finnefrock ....G 918 585-3350
Tulsa *(G-9551)*
Daniel R Willits Offices ....G 580 227-2592
Fairview *(G-3134)*
Danlin Industries Corp ....G 405 853-2559
Hennessey *(G-3457)*
Dannys Bop LLC ....D 405 815-4041
Oklahoma City *(G-5895)*
David Greens Office ....G 918 335-3855
Bartlesville *(G-473)*
David W Potts Land Exploration ....G 580 226-3633
Ardmore *(G-276)*
Davis Operating Company ....G 918 587-7782
Tulsa *(G-9561)*
Dawson Geophysical Company ....F 405 848-7512
Oklahoma City *(G-5906)*
Dee-Jay Exploration ....G 405 773-8500
Oklahoma City *(G-5918)*
Delphi International Inc ....G 918 749-9401
Tulsa *(G-9568)*
Delta Oil and Gas LLC ....G 918 599-9800
Tulsa *(G-9569)*
◆ Devon Energy Corporation ....C 405 235-3611
Oklahoma City *(G-5929)*
Devon Gas Services LP ....G 405 235-3611
Oklahoma City *(G-5933)*
Diamondback Operating LP ....F 918 477-7755
Tulsa *(G-9580)*
Diversified Energy Svcs LLC ....G 405 775-0414
Oklahoma City *(G-5951)*
Division Order Beginnings ....G 918 477-4559
Porter *(G-7892)*
Djf Services Inc ....G 405 380-7273
Holdenville *(G-3553)*
Dolphin Blue Production LLC ....G 405 285-5388
Oklahoma City *(G-5965)*
Dominion Corp ....G 918 270-1722
Tulsa *(G-9594)*
Donray Petroleum LLC ....E 405 418-4348
Oklahoma City *(G-5967)*
Double J Production LLC ....G 918 691-4060
Broken Arrow *(G-891)*
Drug Warehouse ....G 918 592-4545
Tulsa *(G-9610)*
Duncan Inc Walter ....E 405 272-1800
Oklahoma City *(G-5987)*
Duncan Oil & Gas Inc ....G 405 360-2183
Norman *(G-4984)*
Duncan Oil Properties Inc ....E 405 272-1800
Oklahoma City *(G-5988)*
Eagle Chief Midstream LLC ....E 405 888-5585
Edmond *(G-2398)*
Eagle Energy Company LLC ....G 918 746-1350
Tulsa *(G-9623)*
Earlsboro Energies Corp ....G 405 282-5007
Guthrie *(G-3312)*
East Texas Exploration LLC ....G 405 245-6568
Edmond *(G-2399)*
Easton Land Services ....G 405 842-1930
Oklahoma City *(G-6001)*
Echo Energy LLC ....D 405 753-4232
Oklahoma City *(G-6005)*
Edinger Engineering Inc ....G 405 232-6315
Oklahoma City *(G-6010)*
Edrio Oil Co ....G 405 621-1300
Oklahoma City *(G-6011)*
Egret Operating Company Inc ....G 918 687-8665
Muskogee *(G-4672)*
Ek Exploration LLC ....G 405 285-1220
Edmond *(G-2408)*
El Toro Resources LLC ....E 405 242-2777
Oklahoma City *(G-6019)*
Eland Energy Inc ....F 405 840-9885
Oklahoma City *(G-6020)*
Empire Louisiana LLC ....G 539 444-8002
Tulsa *(G-9675)*
Empire Petroleum Corporation ....G 539 444-8002
Tulsa *(G-9677)*
Encompass Media LLC ....G 405 823-8081
Oklahoma City *(G-6035)*
Endico Inc ....G 405 340-8009
Edmond *(G-2411)*
Enerfin Resources Company ....G 918 492-8686
Tulsa *(G-9682)*
Energy Annastin ....G 405 810-5460
Oklahoma City *(G-6038)*
Energy Control System Inc ....G 918 481-3244
Tulsa *(G-9683)*
Energy Partners ....G 405 573-9064
Norman *(G-4992)*
Enerlabs Inc ....G 405 879-1752
Oklahoma City *(G-6040)*
Enerquest Oil & Gas LLC ....F 405 478-3300
Oklahoma City *(G-6041)*
Enterprise Exploration Inc ....G 918 481-2125
Tulsa *(G-9690)*
Entransco Inc ....G 916 628-6835
Dewey *(G-2021)*
Eog Resources Inc ....F 580 225-8314
Elk City *(G-2813)*
Eog Resources Inc ....E 405 246-3100
Oklahoma City *(G-6048)*
Esperanza Resources Corp ....G 918 497-1231
Tulsa *(G-9701)*
Essex Energy Inc ....G 405 350-1351
Yukon *(G-11722)*
Etx Energy LLC ....D 918 728-3020
Tulsa *(G-9703)*
Exco Resources Inc ....G 405 756-4347
Lindsay *(G-4062)*
Exok Inc ....G 405 840-9196
Oklahoma City *(G-6062)*
F & F Production Eqp Svcs LLC ....G 479 414-2772
Bokoshe *(G-753)*
Fairway Energy LLC ....G 405 286-9796
Oklahoma City *(G-6069)*
Flanagan Energy ....G 580 357-1227
Walters *(G-11300)*
Flatrock Energy Advisers ....G 405 341-9993
Edmond *(G-2416)*
Flexx Wireline Services LLC ....G 405 990-1593
El Reno *(G-2717)*
Ford Exploration Inc ....G 405 341-7502
Edmond *(G-2417)*
Forum Us Inc ....G 405 260-7800
Guthrie *(G-3314)*
Forward Oil and Gas Inc ....G 405 607-2247
Oklahoma City *(G-6106)*
Fossil Creek Energy Corp ....G 405 949-0880
Oklahoma City *(G-6107)*
Foundation Energy Company LLC ....F 918 585-1650
Tulsa *(G-9767)*
Foundation Energy MGT LLC ....G 918 526-5521
Tulsa *(G-9768)*
Fourpoint Energy LLC ....G 580 225-8556
Elk City *(G-2815)*
Foxborough Energy Company LLC ....G 405 286-3526
Oklahoma City *(G-6109)*
Foxhead Oil & Gas Company ....G 918 582-2124
Tulsa *(G-9770)*
Freedom Energy Ltd ....G 405 285-2682
Edmond *(G-2422)*
Friedel Petroleum Corporation ....G 405 359-1285
Edmond *(G-2424)*
Funk ....G 405 329-7571
Norman *(G-5005)*
G B K Holdings Inc ....G 918 494-0000
Tulsa *(G-9789)*
G L B Exploration Inc ....G 405 787-0049
Oklahoma City *(G-6132)*
G M C Oil & Gas ....G 405 701-5515
Norman *(G-5006)*
Garrett Petroleum Inc ....G 918 492-3239
Tulsa *(G-9803)*
Gary D Adams Geologist ....G 405 691-5380
Oklahoma City *(G-5292)*
Gary L Deaton Corporation ....G 405 521-8811
Oklahoma City *(G-6136)*
Gary Land Services Inc ....G 580 226-9808
Ardmore *(G-295)*
Gary Rumsey ....G 405 330-5732
Edmond *(G-2430)*

SIC SECTION

13 OIL AND GAS EXTRACTION

Company	Code	Phone
Gary Underwood	G	405 341-0935
Edmond (G-2431)		
Gas Development Corporation	G	918 523-9090
Broken Arrow (G-917)		
Gastar Exploration Inc	E	405 772-1500
Tulsa (G-9806)		
Gaston H L III Oil Properties	G	918 758-0008
Okmulgee (G-7503)		
Gateway Resources USA Inc	G	918 333-2115
Bartlesville (G-486)		
Gaylan Adams Inc	G	405 751-9668
Oklahoma City (G-6137)		
Gb Energy Inc	G	405 224-8634
Chickasha (G-1461)		
Gh Co	G	918 488-0014
Tulsa (G-9824)		
Glenna F Kirk	G	580 497-3435
Cheyenne (G-1424)		
Glm Energy Inc	G	405 470-2873
Oklahoma City (G-6160)		
Global Oil Gas Fields Okla LLC	G	918 392-3345
Tulsa (G-9833)		
Gmg Oil & Gas Corporation	G	918 756-5308
Morris (G-4596)		
Golden Gas Service Co	G	918 582-0139
Tulsa (G-9838)		
Golden Trend Gas Gathering LLC	G	405 749-7860
Edmond (G-2438)		
Good Springs Energy LLC	G	580 257-9762
Tishomingo (G-8965)		
Gore Exploration LLC	G	580 922-4673
Edmond (G-2440)		
Gourley Royalty Company LLC	G	580 223-8783
Ardmore (G-297)		
Grande Oil & Gas Inc	G	405 348-8135
Edmond (G-2442)		
Graves Cos Michael L	G	918 293-1500
Tulsa (G-9849)		
Grayhorse Energy LLC	G	918 382-9201
Tulsa (G-9851)		
Great Salt Plains Midstream	G	405 608-8569
Oklahoma City (G-6184)		
Greenleaf Energy Corporation	G	405 239-7763
Oklahoma City (G-6188)		
Greenstar Energy LLC	G	205 349-2852
Oklahoma City (G-6189)		
Greenstar Energy LLC	G	405 604-0781
Oklahoma City (G-6190)		
Greg Hall Oil & Gas LLC	G	405 330-6238
Edmond (G-2445)		
Greg Riepl	G	405 232-6818
Oklahoma City (G-6191)		
Groves Oil Investments	G	405 341-8828
Edmond (G-2447)		
Guard Exploration Partnership	G	580 234-3229
Enid (G-2965)		
Gulf Exploration LLC	F	405 840-3381
Oklahoma City (G-6193)		
Gulfport Energy Corporation	D	405 252-4600
Oklahoma City (G-6194)		
Hale Exploration LLC	G	405 273-8000
Shawnee (G-8456)		
Halliburton Company	C	405 231-1800
Oklahoma City (G-6207)		
Harrell Exploration	G	580 226-8887
Ardmore (G-302)		
Hawthorne Resources	G	405 840-1928
Oklahoma City (G-6227)		
Hazelwood Prod Exploration LLC	G	405 848-6884
Oklahoma City (G-6229)		
Hefner Co Inc	G	405 236-4404
Oklahoma City (G-6235)		
Holden Energy Corp	E	580 226-3960
Ardmore (G-306)		
Hollrah Exploration Company	G	405 773-5440
Oklahoma City (G-6258)		
Hornbeek and Wadley	G	405 604-2874
Oklahoma City (G-6263)		
Hub Oil & Gas Inc	G	405 236-3354
Oklahoma City (G-6269)		
Hughes Exploration Consulting	G	918 486-3188
Coweta (G-1886)		
Hungerford Oil & Gas Inc	G	580 852-3288
Helena (G-3434)		
Huntington Energy USA Inc	G	580 772-3644
Weatherford (G-11419)		
Hunton Oil and Gas Corp	G	405 848-5545
Oklahoma City (G-6275)		
Husky Ventures Inc	G	405 600-9393
Oklahoma City (G-6276)		
I-Mac Petroleum Service Inc	G	918 348-9400
Tulsa (G-9963)		
Indian Exploration Company LLC	G	405 231-2476
Oklahoma City (G-6295)		
Infinity Resources Company	G	405 701-3229
Norman (G-5032)		
Ingram Exploration Inc	G	405 382-2040
Seminole (G-8376)		
Innovative Production Inc	G	918 729-9312
Tulsa (G-9989)		
Integral Geophysics Inc	G	405 848-4573
Oklahoma City (G-6313)		
International Energy Corp	F	918 743-7300
Tulsa (G-10004)		
J & L Exploration LLC	G	405 842-6876
Oklahoma City (G-6331)		
J & S of Enid Inc	G	580 237-6152
Enid (G-2978)		
J Walter Duncan Jr Oil Inc	E	405 272-1800
Oklahoma City (G-6339)		
Jack Exploration Inc	G	580 622-2310
Sulphur (G-8835)		
Jacks Flex Pipe	F	405 382-5740
Seminole (G-8378)		
Jalex LLC	G	405 627-7856
Bixby (G-637)		
James R Biddick	G	918 587-1551
Tulsa (G-10026)		
James S Jim Vanway	G	580 223-8962
Ardmore (G-312)		
Jath Oil Co	C	580 252-5580
Duncan (G-2133)		
Jcl & Jfl Oil & Gas	G	405 360-1620
Norman (G-5042)		
Jcr Exploration Inc	G	918 682-8200
Muskogee (G-4699)		
Jeroco Inc	G	405 222-1179
Chickasha (G-1476)		
Jetta Production Company Inc	G	918 299-0107
Tulsa (G-10043)		
Jma Energy Company LLC	E	405 418-2853
Oklahoma City (G-6366)		
Jmd Properties	G	405 848-5722
Oklahoma City (G-6367)		
Jo Sco Environmental	G	405 340-5499
Edmond (G-2472)		
John C Parks II Energy LLC	G	918 885-6197
Hominy (G-3590)		
Jones Energy Holdings LLC	E	512 328-2953
Oklahoma City (G-6384)		
Kaiser Energy Ltd	G	918 494-0000
Tulsa (G-10071)		
Kaiser-Francis Oil Company	F	405 577-5347
Oklahoma City (G-6395)		
▲ Kaiser-Francis Oil Company	C	918 494-0000
Tulsa (G-10074)		
Kansas MB Project LLC	G	760 212-0606
Skiatook (G-8554)		
Keepa LLC	G	405 235-4968
Oklahoma City (G-6404)		
Kelmar Oil Co	G	405 222-2364
Chickasha (G-1478)		
Kendol Resources LLC	G	405 627-3523
Oklahoma City (G-6405)		
Kenneth A Weikel	G	918 582-7205
Tulsa (G-10082)		
Kenneth Valliquette Inc	G	405 969-3317
Crescent (G-1917)		
Kenton Knorpp	G	918 629-0968
Tulsa (G-10084)		
Kerr Well Service Inc	G	620 629-0400
Tyrone (G-11219)		
Key Energy Services Inc	D	580 338-0664
Guymon (G-3354)		
Keystone Gas Corporation	E	918 352-2443
Drumright (G-2065)		
Keystone Gas Corporation	E	918 352-2443
Drumright (G-2066)		
Keystone Production Co	G	580 255-2162
Duncan (G-2141)		
Keystone Test Facility LLC	G	405 213-5965
Tulsa (G-10087)		
Khody Land & Minerals Company	G	405 949-2221
Oklahoma City (G-6416)		
King Energy LLC	G	405 463-0909
Oklahoma City (G-6419)		
Klabzuba Royalty Company	G	405 567-3031
Prague (G-7929)		
Kodiak Corp	G	405 478-1900
Oklahoma City (G-6433)		
Kodiak Production Company	G	405 350-6465
Yukon (G-11740)		
L & M Exploration	G	405 359-6060
Edmond (G-2482)		
L Z Williams Energy Inc	G	918 296-3555
Jenks (G-3714)		
Ladder Energy Co	G	918 467-3323
Delaware (G-2008)		
Lamamco Drilling Company	G	580 336-3524
Perry (G-7740)		
▲ Lariat Services Inc	E	405 753-5500
Oklahoma City (G-6449)		
Lariat Services Inc	G	580 977-5050
Alva (G-184)		
Lasser Inc	G	405 842-4010
Oklahoma City (G-6452)		
Lasso Oil & Gas LLC	G	405 753-5300
Oklahoma City (G-6453)		
Lata Group	F	918 535-2147
Ochelata (G-5236)		
Levelops Inc	E	405 602-8040
Bethany (G-586)		
Linn Energy LLC	G	281 605-4100
Collinsville (G-1816)		
Linn Operating LLC	G	918 642-1265
Fairfax (G-3120)		
London Montin Harbert Inc	G	405 879-1900
Oklahoma City (G-6491)		
Lonestar Gphysical Surveys LLC	D	405 726-8626
Edmond (G-2493)		
Longhorn Energy Services LLC	G	918 302-7610
Stillwater (G-8720)		
Lortz R Michael Office	G	405 236-3230
Oklahoma City (G-6496)		
Lowry Exploration Inc	G	918 587-5094
Tulsa (G-10181)		
M E Klein & Associates Inc	G	405 288-2804
Goldsby (G-3245)		
M L S Oil Properties	G	405 720-8867
Oklahoma City (G-6507)		
Mach Resources LLC	E	405 252-8100
Oklahoma City (G-6514)		
Mack Energy Co	C	580 252-5580
Duncan (G-2150)		
Maf Seismic LLC	G	405 285-6444
Edmond (G-2500)		
Magic Circle Energy Corp	F	405 275-1666
Shawnee (G-8470)		
Makefield Oil Co	G	918 492-1463
Tulsa (G-10205)		
Map Exploration Inc	G	405 527-6038
Purcell (G-8014)		
Marathon Oil Company	G	866 323-1836
Tulsa (G-10207)		
Marexco Inc	G	405 286-5657
Oklahoma City (G-6523)		
Mark Cromwell Inc	G	580 233-7992
Enid (G-3006)		
Markwest Enrgy E Texas Gas LP	G	918 389-5100
McAlester (G-4315)		
Markwest Enrgy E Texas Gas LP	F	918 477-8000
Tulsa (G-10213)		
Markwest Oklahoma Gas Co LLC	E	580 225-5400
Elk City (G-2846)		
Maverick Bros Resources LLC	G	580 233-4701
Enid (G-3010)		
Maverick Energy Group Ltd	E	918 764-4081
Tulsa (G-10225)		
Maxim Energy Corp	G	405 348-9669
Edmond (G-2507)		
Maximus Exploration LLC	G	405 239-2829
Oklahoma City (G-6541)		
Mayco Resources LLC	G	918 241-3392
Sand Springs (G-8203)		
McGuire Gateway Holdings LLC	G	405 285-5884
Shawnee (G-8471)		
McMur Oil and Gas LLC	G	405 834-2221
Edmond (G-2509)		
Meadows Oil Gas Corp	F	405 285-8500
Edmond (G-2510)		
Medina Exploration Inc	G	405 579-4200
Norman (G-5069)		
Mekusukey Oil Co Inc	G	405 257-5431
Wewoka (G-11504)		
Melmark Services Inc	G	405 324-6999
Yukon (G-11752)		
Mesa Black Production LLC	G	918 933-4454
Tulsa (G-10243)		
Mewbourne Oil Company	F	405 235-6374
Oklahoma City (G-6582)		

Employee Codes: A=Over 500 employees, B=251-500
C=101-250, D=51-100, E=20-50, F=10-19, G=1-9

13 OIL AND GAS EXTRACTION

Mewbourne Oil Company ....F...... 903 561-2900
  Woodward *(G-11609)*
Micaehl A Sleem ....G...... 405 947-6288
  Oklahoma City *(G-6585)*
Michael Feezel ....G...... 580 332-5544
  Ada *(G-65)*
Michael Nelson ....G...... 580 922-5074
  Chester *(G-1420)*
Mid Continent Minerals Inc ....G...... 405 272-0204
  Oklahoma City *(G-6588)*
Mid-Con Data Services Inc ....E...... 405 478-1234
  Oklahoma City *(G-6592)*
Mid-Con Exploration LLC ....G...... 580 571-7929
  Woodward *(G-11610)*
Mid-Continent Conductor LLC ....G...... 580 254-3232
  Woodward *(G-11611)*
Mid-States Minerals LLC ....G...... 405 298-7043
  Weatherford *(G-11427)*
Millennium Prod Explrtion Corp .....G...... 405 495-3311
  Oklahoma City *(G-6612)*
Milton Nichols Inc ....G...... 405 769-2216
  Oklahoma City *(G-6614)*
Moeder Oil & Gas LLC ....G...... 405 286-9192
  Oklahoma City *(G-6625)*
Moi Oil & Gas Inc ....G...... 580 753-4266
  Ames *(G-198)*
Mongoose Energy LLC ....G...... 918 884-3508
  Tulsa *(G-10298)*
Montgomery Exploration Company ..G...... 405 232-1169
  Norman *(G-5080)*
Morgan Drilling Co ....G...... 580 657-3659
  Ardmore *(G-336)*
Mustang Gas Products LLC ....E...... 405 748-9400
  Oklahoma City *(G-6642)*
Mustang Ventures Company ....G...... 405 748-9400
  Oklahoma City *(G-6644)*
Myers & Myers Inc ....G...... 405 341-5861
  Edmond *(G-2524)*
National Oilwell Varco Inc ....E...... 580 225-4136
  Elk City *(G-2855)*
Native American Capital LLC ....G...... 918 289-7489
  Broken Arrow *(G-985)*
Native Exploration Mnrl LLC ....G...... 405 603-5520
  Oklahoma City *(G-6661)*
Native Explration Holdings LLC .....G...... 405 603-5520
  Oklahoma City *(G-6662)*
Native Explrtion Operating LLC ......G...... 405 603-5520
  Oklahoma City *(G-6663)*
▼ Natural Resources Oper LLC ......F...... 405 997-3869
  Norman *(G-5088)*
Needham Royalty Company LLC ...G...... 405 297-0177
  Oklahoma City *(G-6668)*
Nelson Exploration Corp ....G...... 405 853-6933
  Cleveland *(G-1729)*
Neok Production Company ....G...... 918 273-5662
  Nowata *(G-5222)*
Ness Energy International ....G...... 405 285-1140
  Edmond *(G-2534)*
New Dominion LLC ....G...... 405 567-3034
  Seminole *(G-8389)*
Newfield Exploration 2003 Inc ....E...... 918 495-0598
  Tulsa *(G-10339)*
Ng Discovery LLC ....G...... 405 945-0940
  Oklahoma City *(G-6676)*
Nichols Land Services Inc ....G...... 405 840-1344
  Oklahoma City *(G-6679)*
Nike Exploration LLC ....G...... 918 878-7410
  Tulsa *(G-10345)*
Northshore Corp ....G...... 405 329-8026
  Norman *(G-5095)*
Northwest Oil Gas Explrtn ....G...... 405 974-0165
  Oklahoma City *(G-6692)*
Northwest Royalty LLC ....G...... 405 241-9707
  Oklahoma City *(G-6693)*
Novo Oil & Gas ....G...... 405 286-4391
  Oklahoma City *(G-6701)*
Novo Oil & Gas LLC ....F...... 405 609-1625
  Oklahoma City *(G-6702)*
Nye Investment Co LLC ....G...... 405 923-7155
  Oklahoma City *(G-6704)*
Oak Tree Natural Resources LLC ..C...... 405 775-0987
  Oklahoma City *(G-6707)*
OBrien Oil Corporation ....G...... 405 282-6500
  Guthrie *(G-3327)*
Oex-1 LLC ....G...... 918 492-0254
  Tulsa *(G-10378)*
Oil & Gas Consultants Intl Inc ....E...... 918 828-2500
  Tulsa *(G-10381)*
Oil & Gas Division ....G...... 918 581-2296
  Tulsa *(G-10382)*

Oil-Law Records Corporation ....E...... 405 840-1631
  Oklahoma City *(G-6722)*
Oilwell Tech & Enhancement ....G...... 405 202-9720
  Oklahoma City *(G-6725)*
OK Contract Services LLC ....G...... 918 352-5369
  Braman *(G-761)*
Okki Industries LLC ....G...... 405 204-6357
  Oklahoma City *(G-6733)*
Oklahoma Comm On Consmr Cr ....F...... 918 367-3396
  Bristow *(G-791)*
Oklahoma Oil Gas Management ....G...... 405 341-1856
  Edmond *(G-2553)*
Oklahoma Territory Land Co LLC ...G...... 405 329-1142
  Norman *(G-5101)*
Okland Oil Company ....E...... 405 236-3046
  Oklahoma City *(G-6766)*
Okt Resources LLC ....G...... 405 285-1140
  Edmond *(G-2554)*
Old Inc ....G...... 405 840-3017
  Oklahoma City *(G-6770)*
Olifant Energy LLC ....G...... 918 984-9074
  Tulsa *(G-10414)*
One Grand Center ....G...... 580 234-6600
  Enid *(G-3026)*
Onegas ....G...... 918 947-7000
  Tulsa *(G-10420)*
Orion Exploration LLC ....G...... 918 492-0254
  Tulsa *(G-10440)*
Orr Oil & Gas E & P Inc ....G...... 580 224-9290
  Ardmore *(G-340)*
Orthwein Petroleum ....G...... 405 478-7663
  Oklahoma City *(G-6783)*
Osage Oil and Gas Property ....G...... 405 841-7600
  Oklahoma City *(G-6785)*
Otc Petroleum Corporation ....G...... 405 840-2255
  Oklahoma City *(G-6788)*
Ovintiv Exploration Inc ....G...... 918 740-1400
  Tulsa *(G-10447)*
Ovintiv Mid-Continent Inc ....E...... 580 243-4101
  Elk City *(G-2858)*
P H C Explorations Inc ....G...... 918 298-2008
  Tulsa *(G-10452)*
Pacific Oil & Gas LLC ....G...... 405 835-2790
  Yukon *(G-11763)*
Paladin Land Group LLC ....G...... 918 582-5404
  Tulsa *(G-10457)*
Paluca Petroleum Inc ....G...... 405 379-5656
  Holdenville *(G-3558)*
Panhandle Oil and Gas Inc ....F...... 405 948-1560
  Oklahoma City *(G-6798)*
Panther Energy Company LLC ......D...... 918 583-1396
  Tulsa *(G-10461)*
Panther Energy Company II LLC ....F...... 918 583-1396
  Tulsa *(G-10462)*
Parker & Parsley Petroleum ....G...... 405 756-1912
  Lindsay *(G-4076)*
Parwest Land Exploration Inc ....G...... 405 843-1917
  Oklahoma City *(G-6805)*
Patrick Energy Group ....G...... 918 477-7755
  Tulsa *(G-10473)*
Peak Operating LLC ....G...... 405 343-7590
  Oklahoma City *(G-6816)*
Penn-OK Gathering Systems Inc ...E...... 405 843-1544
  Oklahoma City *(G-6825)*
Pennmark Energy LLC ....G...... 405 840-9885
  Oklahoma City *(G-6827)*
Pennsylvania Chernicky LLC ....G...... 918 587-6242
  Tulsa *(G-10644)*
Peregrine Products LLC ....G...... 918 361-4304
  Tulsa *(G-10491)*
Permian Resources Holdings LLC ..G...... 405 418-8000
  Oklahoma City *(G-6833)*
Petro Mac Corporation ....G...... 918 585-5853
  Tulsa *(G-10500)*
Petrocorp Incorporated ....G...... 918 491-4500
  Tulsa *(G-10501)*
Petroleum Development Company ..G...... 918 583-7434
  Tulsa *(G-10505)*
Petroleum Strategies Unlimited .....F...... 405 720-0200
  Oklahoma City *(G-6838)*
Pierco Petroleum Inc ....G...... 405 379-0038
  Holdenville *(G-3559)*
Piranha Proppant LLC ....G...... 715 642-4192
  Oklahoma City *(G-6854)*
Plow Technologies LLC ....E...... 405 265-6072
  Oklahoma City *(G-6857)*
Potoco LLC ....G...... 405 600-3065
  Oklahoma City *(G-6867)*
Powerco Seismic Services LLC .....G...... 918 424-3745
  McAlester *(G-4330)*

Prairie Oil & Gas ....G...... 405 464-6060
  Norman *(G-5120)*
Premier Energy LLC ....G...... 405 286-0615
  Oklahoma City *(G-6884)*
Prentice Napier & Green Inc ....F...... 405 752-7680
  Oklahoma City *(G-6888)*
Pride Energy Company ....E...... 918 524-9200
  Tulsa *(G-10557)*
Primary Ntral Rsources III LLC ......G...... 918 495-0598
  Tulsa *(G-10575)*
Primeenergy Corporation ....F...... 405 942-2897
  Oklahoma City *(G-6894)*
Protege Energy III LLC ....G...... 918 286-2457
  Broken Arrow *(G-1013)*
Protege Energy III LLC ....F...... 918 728-3092
  Tulsa *(G-10575)*
Pyr Energy Corporation ....G...... 918 591-1791
  Tulsa *(G-10586)*
Qep Energy Company ....E...... 405 263-4831
  Okarche *(G-5250)*
Quest Cherokee LLC ....G...... 405 371-1653
  Oklahoma City *(G-6941)*
Quest Energy Partners LP ....G...... 405 600-7704
  Oklahoma City *(G-6942)*
Quest Midstream Partners LP ....D...... 405 702-7410
  Oklahoma City *(G-6943)*
Quest Property Inc ....G...... 405 722-7530
  Wheatland *(G-11515)*
R D Davis & Associates Inc ....G...... 405 720-2882
  Oklahoma City *(G-6962)*
R P Small Corp ....G...... 918 712-2226
  Tulsa *(G-10605)*
Ram Energy LLC ....F...... 918 947-6300
  Tulsa *(G-10612)*
Rambler Energy Services Inc ....E...... 580 242-7447
  Enid *(G-3042)*
Range Production Company ....G...... 580 628-3700
  Tonkawa *(G-8980)*
Reagan Resources Inc ....G...... 405 848-2707
  Oklahoma City *(G-6980)*
Rebellion Energy LLC ....G...... 918 779-3163
  Tulsa *(G-10627)*
Rebellion Energy II LLC ....G...... 918 779-3163
  Tulsa *(G-10628)*
Red Bluff Resources Oper LLC ......G...... 405 605-8360
  Oklahoma City *(G-6983)*
Red Fork USA Investments Inc ......G...... 918 270-2941
  Tulsa *(G-10631)*
Red Land Energy LLC ....G...... 405 520-1205
  Edmond *(G-2589)*
Red River Imaging LP ....G...... 405 308-4545
  Warr Acres *(G-11327)*
Red Rocks Resources LLC ....F...... 405 600-3065
  Oklahoma City *(G-6990)*
Redback Coil Tubing LLC ....E...... 405 265-4600
  Oklahoma City *(G-6991)*
Redbud E&P Inc ....E...... 918 469-3600
  Quinton *(G-8041)*
Redhawk Pressure Control LLC .....F...... 405 605-1958
  Oklahoma City *(G-6995)*
Redsky Land LLC ....D...... 405 470-2015
  Edmond *(G-2592)*
Regency Gas ....G...... 580 487-3862
  Beaver *(G-547)*
Resco Enterprises Inc ....G...... 918 298-0052
  Jenks *(G-3726)*
Resolute Wyoming Inc ....E...... 918 495-0598
  Tulsa *(G-10644)*
Resource Oil and Gas LLC ....G...... 405 878-7336
  Shawnee *(G-8488)*
◆ Reveille Energy Innovation LLC ..E...... 405 577-6438
  Oklahoma City *(G-7012)*
Rhino Oil & Gas Inc ....G...... 405 657-2999
  Edmond *(G-2599)*
Riddle Corporation ....G...... 405 728-7504
  Oklahoma City *(G-7023)*
Riley Exploration LLC ....D...... 405 485-8200
  Oklahoma City *(G-7024)*
Riley Exploration Group LLC ....F...... 405 485-8200
  Oklahoma City *(G-7025)*
Riley Explration - Permian LLC .....G...... 405 415-8699
  Oklahoma City *(G-7026)*
Riley Permian Operating Co LLC ...E...... 405 415-8699
  Oklahoma City *(G-7027)*
Ring Energy Inc ....G...... 918 499-3880
  Tulsa *(G-10654)*
Rio Vista Operating LLC ....D...... 918 689-5600
  Eufaula *(G-3110)*
River Rock Energy LLC ....D...... 405 606-7481
  Oklahoma City *(G-7029)*

Riverside Mdstream Prtners LLC..........F....... 918 949-4224
Tulsa *(G-10659)*
Roan Resources LLC........................E....... 405 241-2271
Oklahoma City *(G-7032)*
Robert L Scott Co..................................G....... 405 235-5345
Oklahoma City *(G-7034)*
Robinowitz Oil Company.........................G....... 918 557-1544
Bixby *(G-654)*
Rock Creek Land and Energy................G....... 405 358-6090
Oklahoma City *(G-5313)*
Rock Island Exploration LLC.................G....... 405 232-7077
Oklahoma City *(G-7042)*
Rockford Energy Partner.......................G....... 918 592-0679
Tulsa *(G-10666)*
Rockford Exploration Inc.......................G....... 918 582-1320
Tulsa *(G-10667)*
Rogue Industrial LLC..............................G....... 580 832-7060
Cordell *(G-1863)*
Rose Rock Resources Inc.......................G....... 918 752-0511
Beggs *(G-559)*
Rox Exploration Inc................................G....... 405 329-0009
Norman *(G-5136)*
Royce Dublin Inc....................................G....... 219 324-7995
Oklahoma City *(G-7056)*
RTS Energy Services LLC.......................F....... 432 617-2243
Oklahoma City *(G-7058)*
Russell Oil Inc..G....... 405 752-7600
Edmond *(G-2608)*
S K Warren Resourses LLC....................G....... 918 491-5900
Tulsa *(G-10685)*
S S & L Oil and Gas Properties.............G....... 405 603-6996
Oklahoma City *(G-7066)*
Saint Louis Well Service Inc..................E....... 405 289-3314
Saint Louis *(G-8132)*
Samson Exploration LLC........................F....... 918 879-0279
Tulsa *(G-10693)*
Samson Resources Company................E....... 580 225-4272
Elk City *(G-2872)*
Samson-International Ltd.......................E....... 918 583-1791
Tulsa *(G-10700)*
Sand Point LLC..G....... 405 728-2111
Oklahoma City *(G-7077)*
Sandollar Exploration Co LLC................G....... 405 513-7715
Edmond *(G-2611)*
Sanguine Gas Exploration LLC..............G....... 405 285-1904
Edmond *(G-2613)*
Sanguine Ltd..G....... 918 494-6070
Tulsa *(G-10707)*
Sara Oil & Gas Inc...................................G....... 405 721-2117
Oklahoma City *(G-7084)*
Saturn Land Co Inc..................................G....... 405 275-4406
Shawnee *(G-8493)*
Schlumberger Technology Corp............C....... 405 422-8700
El Reno *(G-2753)*
Scientific Drilling Intl Inc.......................D....... 405 787-3663
Yukon *(G-11780)*
Seal Seismic Service LLC.......................G....... 405 603-2121
Oklahoma City *(G-7105)*
SEC Production Inc.................................G....... 405 715-0088
Edmond *(G-2615)*
Sedona Energy LLC.................................G....... 405 973-7366
Norman *(G-5140)*
Seismic Exchange Inc.............................E....... 918 712-7186
Tulsa *(G-10724)*
Sequoia Natural Resources LLC............G....... 405 463-0355
Oklahoma City *(G-7111)*
Sheridan Production Co LLC..................D....... 405 756-4347
Lindsay *(G-4083)*
Sheridan Production Co LLC..................G....... 405 453-7860
Chickasha *(G-1509)*
Shields Operating Inc..............................G....... 479 785-1222
Oklahoma City *(G-7123)*
Shiprock Midstream LLC..........................G....... 918 289-2949
Tulsa *(G-10747)*
Sierra Hamilton LLC................................G....... 405 843-5566
Oklahoma City *(G-7128)*
Sierra Resources Inc...............................E....... 405 946-2242
Oklahoma City *(G-7130)*
Silverado Oil & Gas LLP..........................G....... 918 592-3060
Tulsa *(G-10762)*
Simpson Enterprises LLC.........................G....... 918 495-1819
Tulsa *(G-10763)*
Simpson Photographics Tulsa................G....... 918 630-1134
Tulsa *(G-10764)*
Six S Energy Group LLC..........................G....... 405 819-8053
Oklahoma City *(G-7144)*
Smart Oilfield Solutions LLC..................G....... 580 243-9571
Elk City *(G-2873)*
Smyth Land Services...............................G....... 918 745-9210
Tulsa *(G-10782)*
Snuffys Oilfield Services..........................G....... 405 368-9333
Hennessey *(G-3490)*
Sothwestern Exploration Cons...............G....... 405 767-0041
Oklahoma City *(G-7170)*
Source Rock Enrgy Partners LLC.........G....... 918 728-3116
Tulsa *(G-10795)*
Southern Resources Inc..........................G....... 405 601-1322
Oklahoma City *(G-7172)*
Spanish Lady Oil Co................................G....... 405 659-3515
Edmond *(G-2626)*
Sparks Greg Operating Co......................F....... 918 633-8807
Bixby *(G-663)*
Spartan Resources LLC..........................G....... 405 843-0420
Oklahoma City *(G-7179)*
Spartan Resources LLC..........................G....... 580 226-2400
Ardmore *(G-358)*
Spring Energy Co.....................................G....... 405 340-6811
Edmond *(G-2628)*
Staghorn Energy LLC..............................G....... 918 584-2558
Tulsa *(G-10831)*
Staghorn Petroleum LLC.........................G....... 918 584-2558
Tulsa *(G-10832)*
Staghorn Petroleum II LLC......................G....... 918 584-2558
Tulsa *(G-10833)*
Star Royalty Co..G....... 405 748-5070
Oklahoma City *(G-7195)*
Steden Oil Corp..G....... 405 364-7611
Norman *(G-5157)*
Stingray Cmnting Acidizing LLC............G....... 432 617-2243
Oklahoma City *(G-7207)*
Stingray Pressure Pumping LLC............C....... 405 242-4998
Oklahoma City *(G-7208)*
Stone Creek Operating LLC....................G....... 405 395-4313
Oklahoma City *(G-7211)*
Stone Oak Operating LLC.......................G....... 888 606-4744
Oklahoma City *(G-7212)*
Stream Energy...G....... 405 272-1080
Oklahoma City *(G-7215)*
Sturgeon Acquisitions LLC......................G....... 405 608-6007
Oklahoma City *(G-7219)*
Summit Energy Explorations LLC..........G....... 918 396-3020
Owasso *(G-7622)*
Summit Exploration LLC..........................G....... 918 583-0933
Tulsa *(G-10867)*
Superior Oil and Gas Co..........................G....... 405 884-2069
Calumet *(G-1250)*
Superior Pipeline Texas LLC..................E....... 918 382-7200
Tulsa *(G-10878)*
Superior Resources..................................F....... 580 393-4314
Sentinel *(G-8413)*
Swanderland Associates LLC.................G....... 918 621-6533
Tulsa *(G-10883)*
Swc Production Inc...................................G....... 405 948-1559
Oklahoma City *(G-7234)*
Sweetwater Exploration LLC...................G....... 405 329-1967
Norman *(G-5166)*
T A T Inc...G....... 405 942-0489
Oklahoma City *(G-7242)*
T K Exploration Co.....................................G....... 405 239-7006
Oklahoma City *(G-7245)*
Tangier Explorations.................................G....... 918 585-3350
Tulsa *(G-10897)*
Taos Exploration..G....... 405 840-5398
Oklahoma City *(G-7252)*
Tapstone Energy LLC...............................E....... 405 702-1600
Oklahoma City *(G-7253)*
Tates Flow Back LLC................................G....... 405 663-2179
Hydro *(G-3635)*
Taylor Energy LLC.....................................G....... 918 481-1241
Tulsa *(G-10903)*
Tdp Energy Company LLC.......................F....... 580 226-6700
Ardmore *(G-366)*
▲ **Tdw Services Inc**...................................E....... 918 447-5000
Tulsa *(G-9041)*
Te-Ray Energy Inc.....................................G....... 405 232-4121
Oklahoma City *(G-7261)*
Te-Ray Resources Inc...............................G....... 405 792-7486
Oklahoma City *(G-7262)*
Tecolote Energy LLC.................................G....... 918 513-4100
Tulsa *(G-10915)*
Tecolote Energy Operating LLC..............G....... 918 513-4121
Tulsa *(G-10916)*
Templar Energy LLC..................................G....... 405 548-1200
Oklahoma City *(G-7266)*
Templar Operating LLC..............................F....... 405 548-1200
Oklahoma City *(G-7267)*
Terraquest Corporation.............................E....... 405 359-0773
Edmond *(G-2638)*
Territory Resources LLC...........................G....... 405 533-1300
Stillwater *(G-8766)*
Testers Inc..G....... 580 243-0148
Elk City *(G-2881)*
Thomas Oil Tools LLC...............................G....... 580 252-4672
Duncan *(G-2188)*
Thunder Oil & Gas LLC..............................G....... 580 226-3800
Ardmore *(G-368)*
Tilford Pinson Exploration LLC..................F....... 405 348-7201
Edmond *(G-2643)*
Titan Resources Limited............................G....... 918 298-1811
Tulsa *(G-10947)*
Tlp Energy LLC...G....... 405 241-1800
Oklahoma City *(G-7296)*
Tompc LLC..E....... 405 888-5585
Edmond *(G-2649)*
Tracey Gregory...G....... 580 819-0057
Weatherford *(G-11449)*
Trepco Inc...G....... 405 722-1400
Yukon *(G-11793)*
Triad Energy Inc..F....... 405 842-4312
Oklahoma City *(G-7325)*
Triple Crown Energy-Bh LLC....................G....... 918 518-5422
Tulsa *(G-10975)*
Triumph Energy Partners LLC..................G....... 918 986-8283
Tulsa *(G-10979)*
Triumph Resources Inc..............................G....... 405 478-8770
Oklahoma City *(G-7338)*
Trojan Oil and Gas LLC..............................G....... 918 606-0260
Sapulpa *(G-8318)*
Tropical Minerals Inc..................................G....... 405 236-2700
Oklahoma City *(G-7344)*
True Energy Services LLC.........................G....... 580 421-9808
Ada *(G-97)*
Turnbow-Kiker Ltd......................................G....... 918 481-8871
Tulsa *(G-11018)*
Turner Oil & Gas Properties......................G....... 405 752-8000
Oklahoma City *(G-7352)*
Unit Corp...G....... 405 222-6441
Chickasha *(G-1520)*
Unit Corporation...D....... 918 493-7700
Tulsa *(G-11037)*
United Land Co LLC...................................G....... 405 840-2666
Oklahoma City *(G-7370)*
Valiant Midstream LLC...............................G....... 405 286-5580
Edmond *(G-2665)*
Vector Exploration Inc.................................G....... 405 340-5373
Edmond *(G-2668)*
Ventana Exploration & Prod LLC...............F....... 405 754-5000
Oklahoma City *(G-7396)*
Verexco Inc..G....... 405 341-4302
Edmond *(G-2670)*
Vesta Midstream Partners LLC..................G....... 918 986-9520
Tulsa *(G-11074)*
Viersen Oil & Gas Co..................................F....... 918 742-1979
Tulsa *(G-11076)*
Vision Energy Group LLC...........................G....... 405 848-3933
Oklahoma City *(G-7401)*
Vitol Inc...G....... 405 228-8100
Oklahoma City *(G-7403)*
Vitruvian II Woodford LLC..........................G....... 405 428-2491
Lindsay *(G-4098)*
Waggoner Oil & Gas...................................G....... 580 234-0030
Enid *(G-3071)*
Waller Exploration LLC...............................G....... 405 359-2050
Edmond *(G-2679)*
Ward Petroleum Corporation......................D....... 580 234-3229
Enid *(G-3074)*
Ward Petroleum Corporation......................G....... 405 242-4188
Oklahoma City *(G-7419)*
Watson Well Solutions................................G....... 580 772-3059
Weatherford *(G-11455)*
We Buy Scrap LLC......................................G....... 580 401-3083
Ponca City *(G-7887)*
Weinkauf Exploration..................................F....... 918 749-8383
Tulsa *(G-11104)*
Weinkauf Petroleum Inc..............................F....... 918 749-8383
Tulsa *(G-11105)*
Weir Oil Gas...G....... 580 225-2381
El Reno *(G-2769)*
Wentworth Operating Co.............................F....... 405 341-6122
Oklahoma City *(G-7435)*
Westenergy..G....... 405 607-6604
Oklahoma City *(G-7438)*
Westport Oil Company Inc..........................G....... 405 239-2829
Oklahoma City *(G-7443)*
Weststar Oil and Gas Inc............................G....... 405 341-2338
Edmond *(G-2685)*
Wheeler Energy Corporation......................G....... 918 587-7474
Tulsa *(G-11114)*
White Sail Energy LLC................................G....... 405 255-4669
Edmond *(G-2687)*

Employee Codes: A=Over 500 employees, B=251-500
C=101-250, D=51-100, E=20-50, F=10-19, G=1-9
2020 Oklahoma Directory
of Manufacturers & Processors
413

William B Hugos........G....... 405 810-0909
Oklahoma City *(G-7454)*
Williams Prod Appalachia LLC........D....... 918 573-2000
Tulsa *(G-11133)*
Williford Resources LLC........G....... 918 712-8828
Tulsa *(G-11135)*
Winzeler Family LLC........G....... 405 218-2829
Edmond *(G-2690)*
Word Exploration LP........D....... 580 234-3229
Enid *(G-3083)*
World Energy Resources Inc........G....... 405 375-6484
Kingfisher *(G-3823)*
Wpx Energy Appalachia LLC........F....... 866 326-3190
Tulsa *(G-11156)*
Wpx Energy Permian LLC........E....... 855 979-2102
Tulsa *(G-11160)*
Xpect Energy Services LLC........F....... 405 641-7537
Edmond *(G-2693)*
Zinke & Trumbo Inc........F....... 918 488-6400
Tulsa *(G-11178)*

1389 Oil & Gas Field Svcs, NEC

007 Operating LLC........G....... 580 467-2744
Sulphur *(G-8826)*
300 PSI Inc........G....... 918 358-5713
Cleveland *(G-1714)*
3t Oil & Gas LLC........G....... 918 758-3269
Okmulgee *(G-7491)*
4d Dozer Service Inc........G....... 580 256-2076
Woodward *(G-11552)*
4k Spooling Banding Sales & SE........F....... 918 766-0001
Bartlesville *(G-443)*
66 Oilfield Services LLC........G....... 405 735-6666
Oklahoma City *(G-5337)*
A & M Blaylock Cnstr & Parts........G....... 918 945-7081
Mc Curtain *(G-4267)*
A P & R Industries Inc........F....... 405 702-7661
Oklahoma City *(G-5347)*
A T Roustabouts........G....... 405 788-0735
Meeker *(G-4374)*
A-1 Sure Shot........F....... 405 677-9800
Oklahoma City *(G-5353)*
AB Swabbing Incorporated........G....... 219 765-3239
El Reno *(G-2695)*
ABC Services LLC........G....... 580 242-1015
Enid *(G-2903)*
AC Oil & Gas LLC........G....... 405 919-8088
Hennessey *(G-3442)*
Accelerated Production Svcs........G....... 405 603-7492
Oklahoma City *(G-5360)*
Ace Completions OK........G....... 580 547-4088
Clinton *(G-1736)*
Ace NDT LLC........G....... 580 323-8601
Clinton *(G-1737)*
Acid Inc........E....... 580 363-5413
Blackwell *(G-673)*
Acidizing & Cementing Service........F....... 405 969-3093
Crescent *(G-1907)*
Action Petroleum Services Corp........G....... 580 223-6544
Ardmore *(G-237)*
Action Pipe and Supply Inc........G....... 405 853-7170
Hennessey *(G-3443)*
Acuren Inspection Inc........D....... 405 452-3337
Tulsa *(G-9100)*
Ada Energy Cementing LLC........G....... 580 436-5228
Ada *(G-4)*
Advance Roustabout Svcs LLC........G....... 405 612-0781
Guthrie *(G-3296)*
Advanced Hydrcrbon Strtigraphy........G....... 918 583-2474
Tulsa *(G-9109)*
Advanced Pressure Incorporated........E....... 405 324-5600
Oklahoma City *(G-5385)*
Advanced Pumping Unit Service........G....... 580 658-2050
Marlow *(G-4220)*
Advanced Welding & Excav LLC........G....... 918 306-2061
Bristow *(G-763)*
AES Drilling Fluids........G....... 580 225-3450
Elk City *(G-2782)*
Akita Compression Services LLC........G....... 405 201-2677
Edmond *(G-2294)*
Akl Services........E....... 918 225-5533
Cushing *(G-1922)*
Alan L Buck........G....... 405 401-9372
Chandler *(G-1374)*
Alfred N Smith........G....... 580 875-3317
Walters *(G-11299)*
Allan Bghs Wldg Roustabout Svc........G....... 918 625-1712
Drumright *(G-2050)*
Allegiant Energy Production &........F....... 405 550-2331
Oklahoma City *(G-5417)*
Allied Wireline Services LLC........E....... 405 445-7135
Moore *(G-4485)*
Alpha Oilfield Services LLC........G....... 580 330-1285
Weatherford *(G-11390)*
Altman Engineering Inc........G....... 405 368-7889
Kingfisher *(G-3784)*
American Tank Gauge Inc........F....... 405 224-7881
Chickasha *(G-1428)*
Anadarko Consultants Ltd........G....... 405 354-7788
Mustang *(G-4761)*
Anadarko Dozer and Trckg LLC........G....... 918 496-4777
Tulsa *(G-9183)*
Anadarko Dozer and Trckg LLC........G....... 405 542-3297
Hinton *(G-3521)*
Andy Cross Roustabout Svc LLC........G....... 918 906-1240
Mannford *(G-4174)*
Angel Exploration........G....... 405 848-8360
Oklahoma City *(G-5445)*
Apergy Artfl Lift Intl LLC........E....... 405 677-3153
Oklahoma City *(G-5451)*
Apergy Artfl Lift Systems LLC........G....... 918 396-0558
Broken Arrow *(G-1109)*
▲ **Apergy ESP Systems LLC**........D....... 918 396-0558
Broken Arrow *(G-1110)*
Apergy ESP Systems LLC........G....... 918 536-3038
Ramona *(G-8044)*
Appli-Fab Custom Coating........G....... 405 235-7039
Chandler *(G-1375)*
April Oilfield Services........G....... 405 756-5688
Lindsay *(G-4044)*
Arbuckle Wireline........G....... 405 620-6739
Edmond *(G-2308)*
Arbuckle Wireline LLC........G....... 580 226-4001
Ardmore *(G-244)*
Arcadia Oil Corp........G....... 405 409-2013
Edmond *(G-2309)*
Archrock Inc........G....... 580 824-0102
Waynoka *(G-11371)*
Archrock Inc........F....... 580 225-2091
Elk City *(G-2784)*
Archrock Inc........G....... 918 558-2216
Alderson *(G-127)*
Archrock Inc........G....... 918 900-4200
Tulsa *(G-9205)*
Arkhoma Transports Inc........G....... 580 651-2682
Beaver *(G-538)*
Arkoma Tanks LLC........E....... 580 622-4794
Wilson *(G-11531)*
Armada Land LC........G....... 405 210-7554
Norman *(G-4916)*
Armer & Quillen LLC........F....... 405 842-3222
Oklahoma City *(G-5466)*
Asher Oilfield Specialty Inc........G....... 405 677-7868
Oklahoma City *(G-5475)*
Asher Oilfield Specialty Inc........G....... 405 568-3433
Oklahoma City *(G-5476)*
Ashton Gas Gathering LLC........G....... 918 291-3200
Jenks *(G-3689)*
Aspect Oil Field Servvices LLC........G....... 580 774-5006
Weatherford *(G-11391)*
Associated Wire Line Svcs Inc........F....... 580 229-0731
Healdton *(G-3407)*
Atalaya Resources........G....... 918 949-4551
Tulsa *(G-9221)*
Atlas Pipeline Mid-Continent W........B....... 918 574-3500
Tulsa *(G-9222)*
Aussie Built Supplies LLC........G....... 918 381-9700
Skiatook *(G-8531)*
Austin Gas Properties LLC........G....... 405 229-2391
Oklahoma City *(G-5490)*
Aws LLC........G....... 405 382-1255
Seminole *(G-8355)*
B & A Producing LLC........G....... 405 664-3628
Arcadia *(G-228)*
B & B Tool Co Inc........G....... 405 756-4530
Lindsay *(G-4045)*
B & G Production Inc........G....... 580 256-5100
Woodward *(G-11556)*
B & R Construction of Woodward........G....... 580 256-5522
Woodward *(G-11557)*
B & R Pump & Equipment Inc........G....... 405 632-3051
Oklahoma City *(G-5502)*
B & S Roustabouts LLC........G....... 405 779-0842
Chickasha *(G-1434)*
Bacas Oilfield Services LLC........G....... 580 461-8458
Beaver *(G-539)*
Back Road Oil & Gas LLC........G....... 918 932-8452
Tulsa *(G-9251)*
Badger Pressure Control LLC........G....... 580 256-9555
Woodward *(G-11558)*
▲ **Baker Centrilift Cable Inc**........F....... 713 439-8600
Claremore *(G-1588)*
Baker Hghes Olfld Oprtions Inc........G....... 405 382-0003
Seminole *(G-8356)*
Baker Hghes Olfld Oprtions Inc........G....... 405 681-2175
Oklahoma City *(G-5511)*
Baker Hghes Olfld Oprtions LLC........E....... 580 256-3333
Oklahoma City *(G-5512)*
Baker Hghes Olfld Oprtions LLC........C....... 405 670-3354
Oklahoma City *(G-5513)*
Baker Hghes Olfld Oprtions LLC........G....... 918 847-3296
Barnsdall *(G-434)*
Baker Hghes Olfld Oprtions LLC........B....... 918 455-3000
Broken Arrow *(G-843)*
Baker Hghes Olfld Oprtions LLC........G....... 580 243-3424
Elk City *(G-2785)*
Baker Hghes Olfld Oprtions LLC........G....... 918 283-7911
Claremore *(G-1590)*
Baker Hghes Olfld Oprtions LLC........G....... 580 256-7471
Woodward *(G-11559)*
Baker Hghes Olfld Oprtions LLC........B....... 918 341-9600
Claremore *(G-1591)*
Baker Hghes Olfld Oprtions LLC........G....... 405 756-3384
Lindsay *(G-4046)*
Baker Hughes A GE Company LLC........D....... 580 327-2162
Alva *(G-176)*
Baker Hughes A GE Company LLC........E....... 806 435-4096
Yukon *(G-11695)*
Baker Hughes A GE Company LLC........G....... 580 323-4541
Clinton *(G-1738)*
Baker Hughes A GE Company LLC........G....... 918 302-0490
Mcalester *(G-4271)*
Baker Hughes A GE Company LLC........E....... 918 283-1957
Claremore *(G-1592)*
Baker Petrolite Inc........G....... 918 302-0490
Bache *(G-429)*
Baker Petrolite LLC........G....... 918 599-8886
Tulsa *(G-9256)*
Baker Petrolite LLC........D....... 580 323-4541
Clinton *(G-1739)*
Baker Surveying LLC........G....... 918 271-5793
Tulsa *(G-9257)*
Baker Well Service Inc........G....... 405 372-6380
Stillwater *(G-8658)*
Baker Wireline........G....... 405 786-3283
Weleetka *(G-11463)*
Balderas LLC........G....... 580 821-4134
Weatherford *(G-11392)*
Barclay Contract Pumping........G....... 580 541-7439
Enid *(G-2914)*
Baroid Drilling Fluids........G....... 405 459-6611
Pocasset *(G-7774)*
Barrichem Inc........G....... 580 276-3125
Marietta *(G-4199)*
Barry Fennel LLC........G....... 405 745-7645
Mustang *(G-4765)*
Basic Energy Services Inc........E....... 580 227-3144
Fairview *(G-3132)*
Basic Energy Services Inc........G....... 580 252-6200
Duncan *(G-2088)*
Basic Energy Services Inc........G....... 580 254-3600
Woodward *(G-11560)*
Basic Energy Services Inc........G....... 918 225-0161
Cushing *(G-1923)*
Basic Energy Services Inc........G....... 918 287-3388
Pawhuska *(G-7677)*
Basic Energy Services Inc........E....... 405 756-1820
Lindsay *(G-4047)*
Basic Energy Services Inc........G....... 405 324-0848
Yukon *(G-11696)*
Basic Energy Services Inc........F....... 580 758-1234
Waukomis *(G-11359)*
Bayou Oil Field Service & Sup........G....... 918 398-2166
Tulsa *(G-9272)*
Bc Field Services Inc........G....... 918 839-0490
Heavener *(G-3425)*
Bcej Company........G....... 405 470-3790
Oklahoma City *(G-5539)*
Bcrk Limited Partnership........G....... 405 321-0089
Norman *(G-4927)*
Beck Resources Incorporated........E....... 405 853-2736
Hennessey *(G-3446)*
Bended Knee Construction LLC........G....... 918 465-4700
Red Oak *(G-8074)*
Bennett Construction........G....... 405 756-1918
Lindsay *(G-4048)*
Best Oil Field Service Inc........E....... 405 262-5060
El Reno *(G-2701)*
Big Dipper Hot Oil Service........G....... 580 363-0168
Blackwell *(G-674)*

13 OIL AND GAS EXTRACTION

Big Gas Oil LLC ....G........ 405 763-9844
　Oklahoma City (G-5564)
Big League Oil and Gas LLC ....G........ 405 433-9908
　Cashion (G-1285)
Bill Laird Oil Company ....G........ 405 289-3346
　Saint Louis (G-8131)
Biodynamics Corp ....G........ 405 201-1289
　Norman (G-4933)
BJH Services Inc ....G........ 281 686-3408
　Yukon (G-11698)
Bjs Oilfield Cnstr Inc ....E........ 405 485-3390
　Blanchard (G-701)
Blackhawk Safety LLC ....G........ 580 574-1271
　Lawton (G-3898)
Blackhawk Wireline Services ....G........ 405 238-2929
　Pauls Valley (G-7651)
Blackrock Services LLC ....G........ 405 254-3939
　Oklahoma City (G-5583)
Blairs Oil Field Services LLC ....G........ 405 698-9987
　Yukon (G-11699)
Blankenship Roustabout ....G........ 580 791-0237
　Watonga (G-11342)
Blaylock Oil and Gas LLC ....G........ 918 799-6153
　Stigler (G-8629)
Blazer Oilfield Services LLC ....E........ 405 756-4800
　Lindsay (G-4049)
Blevins Oil Field ....G........ 405 619-9909
　Oklahoma City (G-5591)
Bleything Oil & Gas LLC ....G........ 405 535-0253
　Edmond (G-2326)
Blue Rock Oil & Gas LLC ....G........ 580 229-5697
　Ardmore (G-258)
Blue Sky Oil Field Svcs LLC ....G........ 580 491-2349
　Kaw City (G-3756)
Blue Star Acid Service Inc ....G........ 918 324-5350
　Depew (G-2010)
Bluestem Gas Services LLC ....F........ 580 658-6530
　Lindsay (G-4050)
Bluff Service Disposal ....G........ 580 438-2262
　Waynoka (G-11374)
BMC Enterprise LLC ....G........ 918 336-4431
　Bartlesville (G-457)
BMC Petroleum Inc ....G........ 580 234-3725
　Enid (G-2919)
Bob Gene Moore ....G........ 918 371-4381
　Collinsville (G-1804)
BOB Lumber & Grain LLC ....F........ 580 927-3168
　Coalgate (G-1775)
Bobby Joe Cudd Company ....G........ 580 515-3131
　Elk City (G-2787)
Bobby Prater ....G........ 918 885-4864
　Hominy (G-3578)
Bonanza Land LLC ....G........ 580 772-2680
　Weatherford (G-11393)
Boomer Sooie LLC ....E........ 501 827-0269
　Norman (G-4939)
Booth Envmtl Sls & Svc LLC ....E........ 918 465-0214
　Red Oak (G-8075)
BOp Ram-Block Ir Rentals Inc ....D........ 580 772-0250
　Weatherford (G-11394)
Bostick Service Corporation ....G........ 405 969-2198
　Crescent (G-1908)
Bostick Services Corporation ....F........ 405 260-0306
　Guthrie (G-3301)
Brady Welding & Machine Shop ....D........ 580 229-1168
　Healdton (G-3408)
Bravo Natural Gas LLC ....G........ 918 712-7008
　Tulsa (G-9333)
Brg Production Company ....G........ 580 233-9302
　Enid (G-2922)
Brians Hot Oil Service LLC ....G........ 580 778-3549
　Turpin (G-11181)
Brickman Fast Line ....G........ 405 756-1665
　Lindsay (G-4051)
Bristow Hot Oil & Steam Svc ....G........ 918 367-2121
　Bristow (G-769)
Britt Oil Co LLC ....G........ 405 275-2115
　Shawnee (G-8435)
Brothers Construction and Rous ....G........ 405 602-3275
　Oklahoma City (G-5633)
Brown Oil Tools Inc ....G........ 580 436-0002
　Ada (G-14)
Bruce Burdick Welding ....G........ 580 774-2906
　Weatherford (G-11395)
Bruffett Electric ....G........ 918 426-1875
　McAlester (G-4278)
Bruins Oil & Gas LLC ....G........ 806 323-8353
　Yukon (G-11701)
Bs Oil Company ....G........ 405 756-8357
　Lindsay (G-4052)

Bull Dog Welding ....G........ 405 412-8199
　Oklahoma City (G-5644)
Bulldog Energy Services LLC ....G........ 405 919-9950
　Guthrie (G-3302)
Burton Controls Inc ....G........ 405 692-7278
　Waynoka (G-11375)
Burton Controls Inc ....E........ 405 692-7278
　Oklahoma City (G-5647)
Butcher Well Service ....G........ 918 275-4439
　Talala (G-8897)
Buy Rite Services LLC ....F........ 580 984-1008
　Enid (G-2924)
C & J Trucks LLC ....F........ 405 382-1405
　Seminole (G-8362)
C & R Olfld Pntg Rustabout Svc ....G........ 620 272-6699
　Ponca City (G-7804)
C & W Construction Inc ....F........ 580 625-4520
　Beaver (G-540)
C 2 Supply Llc ....G........ 918 647-0430
　Poteau (G-7898)
C C & R Construction Inc ....G........ 405 756-4710
　Lindsay (G-4053)
C D Adkerson Consultant Inc ....G........ 580 225-7860
　Elk City (G-2790)
C&J Energy Services Inc ....E........ 405 222-8304
　Oklahoma City (G-5664)
C&J Energy Services Inc ....G........ 580 928-1300
　Sayre (G-8337)
C&J Well Services Inc ....E........ 405 234-9800
　El Reno (G-2704)
Cactus Wellhead LLC ....G........ 405 708-7200
　Oklahoma City (G-5667)
Calvin Mays Oilfield Svcs Inc ....F........ 405 282-6664
　Guthrie (G-3306)
Camargo Jacks Backhoe Service ....G........ 580 926-3378
　Camargo (G-1251)
Cameron Solutions Inc ....F........ 405 677-8827
　Oklahoma City (G-5680)
Cameron Solutions Inc ....G........ 580 821-0494
　Elk City (G-2791)
Cameron Technologies Inc ....E........ 405 703-8632
　Moore (G-4504)
Can-OK Oil Field Services Inc ....E........ 405 222-2474
　Chickasha (G-1446)
Canadian Global Mfg Ltd ....G........ 405 250-1785
　Oklahoma City (G-5686)
Canadian Pipe & Supply Co ....G........ 405 794-6825
　Moore (G-4505)
Canary LLC ....G........ 405 275-6116
　Shawnee (G-8436)
Cannon Oilfield Services ....G........ 405 387-2644
　Newcastle (G-4820)
Canopy Upstream LLC ....G........ 620 717-3263
　Weatherford (G-11397)
Canyon Oilfield Services LLC ....E........ 580 225-7100
　Elk City (G-2792)
Caprock Plungers LLC ....F........ 580 799-1387
　Cordell (G-1855)
Capstone Oil & Gas Inc ....G........ 405 853-7168
　Hennessey (G-3449)
Carbon Economy LLC ....G........ 405 222-9399
　Chickasha (G-1448)
Carls Backhoe & Roustabout ......G........ 405 893-7212
　Calumet (G-1245)
Carmen Natural Gas Measurement ....G........ 580 987-2778
　Carmen (G-1272)
Carnes Oilfield Services LLC ......G........ 580 309-1249
　Sayre (G-2934)
Carrera Gas Companies LLC .....G........ 918 359-0980
　Tulsa (G-9380)
Case Wireline Services Inc ....E........ 580 254-3036
　Woodward (G-11567)
Caseing Crews Inc ....G........ 405 867-1500
　Maysville (G-4256)
Casing Crews Incorporated ......D........ 580 388-4567
　Lamont (G-3864)
Casing Point LLC ....G........ 405 245-9855
　Midwest City (G-4438)
Cassiday Pumping Service Inc ....G........ 405 969-3374
　Crescent (G-1909)
Caves Hot Shot Services LLC ....G........ 405 397-2569
　Mustang (G-4767)
Cdl Construction LLC ....E........ 580 323-2847
　Clinton (G-1741)
Cei Pipeline LLC ....G........ 405 478-8770
　Oklahoma City (G-5719)
Cement Specialists LLC ....G........ 432 617-2243
　Oklahoma City (G-5722)
Central Chemical Company ...G........ 580 234-8245
　Enid (G-2926)

Challenger Downhole Tools Inc ....G........ 405 604-0096
　Oklahoma City (G-5736)
▲ Champion Drilling Fluids Inc ....G........ 580 323-0044
　Clinton (G-1742)
Chandler Well Services LLC ....G........ 817 673-8140
　Edmond (G-2344)
Chemical Dynamics Corporation ....G........ 405 392-3505
　Tuttle (G-11189)
Chemoil Energy Inc ....B........ 405 605-5436
　Oklahoma City (G-5749)
Chesapeake Energy Mktg LLC .....C........ 877 245-1427
　Oklahoma City (G-5753)
Chesapeake Operating LLC ....A........ 405 848-8000
　Oklahoma City (G-5757)
Chesser Contract Pumping LLC ...G........ 405 820-7240
　Meeker (G-4376)
Chief Drlg & Foundation Svcs ......G........ 580 302-0124
　Weatherford (G-11400)
Chisholm Oil and Gas Oper LLC ..G........ 918 488-6400
　Tulsa (G-9420)
Christ Centered Carriers LLC .....E........ 417 850-8137
　Canute (G-1267)
CHS Oil & Gas LLC ....G........ 918 280-9368
　Skiatook (G-8536)
Cimarron Energy Holding Co LLC .....D........ 405 928-7373
　Norman (G-4957)
Cimarron Energy Inc ....G........ 405 928-2940
　Newcastle (G-4822)
▲ Cimarron Equipment Company ...G........ 918 625-1647
　Tulsa (G-9427)
Cimarron Pipeline LLC ....G........ 405 286-9797
　Oklahoma City (G-5766)
Circle K Services Inc ....F........ 580 254-3568
　Woodward (G-11568)
Circle V Energy Services LLC ...G........ 405 614-0891
　Glencoe (G-3219)
Clearpoint Chemicals LLC ......G........ 405 320-1719
　Pocasset (G-7775)
Clearview International ....G........ 580 332-2384
　Ada (G-24)
Cleveland Lease Service Inc ...F........ 918 358-2791
　Cleveland (G-1720)
Cmark Resources LLC ....G........ 918 492-5170
　Tulsa (G-9459)
Cmt Well Completions Inc ....G........ 918 523-0600
　Tulsa (G-9460)
Coastline Oil & Gas LLC ......G........ 405 354-6507
　Yukon (G-11707)
Cochran Chemical Company Inc ....E........ 405 382-8000
　Seminole (G-8366)
Cody Mud Company Inc .....G........ 580 237-5347
　Enid (G-2932)
Coe Production ....F........ 918 275-4459
　Talala (G-8899)
Coiled Tubing Specialties LLC ...G........ 918 878-7460
　Tulsa (G-9466)
Compass Production Partners LP ..D........ 405 594-4141
　Oklahoma City (G-5810)
Complete Energy LLC ....G........ 405 748-2200
　Yukon (G-11710)
Complete Energy Services Inc ...G........ 405 748-2211
　Yukon (G-11711)
Complete Energy Services Inc ...G........ 580 249-3200
　Enid (G-2933)
Complete Wireline Svcs Ltd Co ...G........ 405 317-0001
　Purcell (G-8003)
Completion Oil Tools LLC ...G........ 580 478-6263
　Enid (G-2934)
Compressco Partners Sub Inc ...C........ 405 677-0221
　Oklahoma City (G-5816)
Computalog Wireline Inc ...G........ 918 225-1187
　Cushing (G-1926)
Concorde Resources Corporation ...G........ 918 291-3200
　Jenks (G-3700)
Constien and Associates Inc ...G........ 918 272-9099
　Owasso (G-7554)
Continntal Oil Gas Enrgy Ntwrk ...G........ 214 636-2401
　Oklahoma City (G-5825)
Control Devices Intl Inc ...G........ 918 258-6068
　Broken Arrow (G-876)
Cook Roustabout LLC ...G........ 405 410-7951
　Guthrie (G-3310)
Cooper Contract Pumping Svc ...G........ 580 487-3552
　Forgan (G-3169)
Cooper Machinery Services Inc ...C........ 713 354-4068
　Oklahoma City (G-5830)
Copeland Hot Oil Service LLC ...G........ 405 853-2179
　Hennessey (G-3452)
Core Laboratories LP ...F........ 918 834-2337
　Tulsa (G-9486)

Employee Codes: A=Over 500 employees, B=251-500
C=101-250, D=51-100, E=20-50, F=10-19, G=1-9

13 OIL AND GAS EXTRACTION

Corpo Commission OK ....F 580 332-3441
  Ada *(G-27)*
Corpo Commission OK ....F 405 521-4683
  Oklahoma City *(G-5838)*
Coulter Oil Field Services LLC ....G 580 504-0813
  Ardmore *(G-270)*
Coupling Specialties Inc ....F 281 457-2000
  Oklahoma City *(G-5845)*
Cowboy Pmpg Unit Sls Repr LLC .....G 405 853-7170
  Hennessey *(G-3454)*
CP & C Services ....G 918 497-6606
  Vinita *(G-11251)*
Crd Oil Corp ....G 918 885-4527
  Hominy *(G-3581)*
Crescent Companies LLC ....G 405 721-5511
  Oklahoma City *(G-5855)*
Crescent Services LLC ....D 405 603-1200
  Oklahoma City *(G-5856)*
Crescent Services LLC ....D 580 225-4346
  Elk City *(G-2796)*
Crimson Hot Shot Service LLC ....G 469 358-2005
  Norman *(G-4969)*
Critical Components Inc ....G 405 212-9166
  Oklahoma City *(G-5857)*
Cross Roll Inc ....G 405 348-9663
  Edmond *(G-2375)*
Crossfire Production Svcs LLC ....G 580 254-3766
  Woodward *(G-11574)*
Crosstimbers Hot Shot Svcs LLC ......G 405 740-2900
  Tuttle *(G-11192)*
Crown Oil Field Services LLC ....G 580 363-0269
  Blackwell *(G-679)*
Cryogas Services LLC ....F 580 252-6200
  Duncan *(G-2100)*
Csi Measurement LLC ....G 580 234-4979
  Enid *(G-2936)*
Cudd Energy Services ....G 405 756-4344
  Lindsay *(G-4057)*
Cudd Operating Corp ....G 405 841-1144
  Oklahoma City *(G-5865)*
Cudd Pressure Control Inc ....E 580 243-5890
  Elk City *(G-2797)*
Cudd Pressure Control Inc ....E 405 756-4337
  Lindsay *(G-4058)*
Cudd Pressure Control Inc ....E 580 225-6922
  Elk City *(G-2798)*
Cudd Pressure Control Inc ....D 405 382-2803
  Seminole *(G-8367)*
Cudd Pressure Control Inc ....E 918 423-0160
  Krebs *(G-3849)*
Cudd Pumping Services ....G 580 256-7000
  Woodward *(G-11575)*
Cumberland Pipeline Co LLC ....G 918 359-0980
  Tulsa *(G-9521)*
Custom Manufacturing Inc ....E 405 692-6311
  Oklahoma City *(G-5874)*
Custom Manufacturing & Maint ....G 405 872-1000
  Noble *(G-4877)*
Cvr Energy ....G 405 286-0341
  Oklahoma City *(G-5882)*
Cws Wireline LLC ....E 405 828-4225
  Dover *(G-2039)*
Cypress Energy Holdings LLC ....F 918 748-3900
  Tulsa *(G-9533)*
Cypress Energy Holdings II LLC ....G 918 748-3900
  Tulsa *(G-9534)*
Cypress Energy Partners LP ....G 918 748-3900
  Tulsa *(G-9535)*
D & B Oil Field Services Inc ....D 580 883-2897
  Ringwood *(G-8087)*
D & M Oil Flds Svc Csing Crews ....G 918 623-0492
  Okemah *(G-5267)*
D & P Tank Service Inc ....E 580 762-4526
  Ponca City *(G-7817)*
D & P Tank Service Inc ....G 580 762-4526
  Ponca City *(G-7816)*
D & T Swabbing & Well Service ....G 405 853-7045
  Hennessey *(G-3456)*
D Willams Pipe Insptn Poly Ll ....G 405 426-7776
  Purcell *(G-8004)*
D&L Manufacturing Inc ....G 918 587-3504
  Tulsa *(G-9541)*
Dale E Dyer ....G 918 519-0189
  Tulsa *(G-9548)*
Dan Abney ....G 405 527-0675
  Wayne *(G-11366)*
Danco Inspection Service Inc ....G 405 691-5752
  Oklahoma City *(G-5284)*
Dannys Oilfield Services Inc ....G 918 645-1651
  Bristow *(G-775)*

Dark Horse Oil Field Svcs LLC ....G 580 229-0626
  Healdton *(G-3412)*
Dasa Investments Inc ....G 405 820-7703
  Edmond *(G-2380)*
Datalog Lwt Inc ....G 405 286-0418
  Oklahoma City *(G-5900)*
Davenport Oilfield Services ....G 580 465-0314
  Ardmore *(G-275)*
Davenport Roustabout Service ....G 918 377-2987
  Chandler *(G-1378)*
David Lacy ....G 918 519-1873
  Broken Arrow *(G-889)*
David Smith ....G 580 229-1195
  Healdton *(G-3413)*
Davis Cnstr Rcvery Sltions LLC ....F 580 500-7527
  Oklahoma City *(G-5905)*
Davis Pipe Testing Company ....F 918 358-5272
  Cleveland *(G-1722)*
Db Wireline Services Inc ....G 918 389-5038
  McAlester *(G-4292)*
Dbk Contract Pumping ....G 580 225-2009
  Elk City *(G-2802)*
Dbr Construction Services Inc ....G 580 327-4335
  Alva *(G-181)*
DC Consulting Inc ....G 405 833-4856
  Oklahoma City *(G-5909)*
Dcp Midstream ....G 580 653-2641
  Springer *(G-8622)*
Deans Casing Service ....F 405 379-3495
  Holdenville *(G-3552)*
Deep Well Tubular Services Inc ....F 405 850-5826
  Oklahoma City *(G-5919)*
Degges Oil Field Service ....G 918 623-1373
  Okemah *(G-5268)*
Dejay Oil & Gas Inc ....G 405 390-0906
  Choctaw *(G-1538)*
Delta Well Logging Svc ....G 405 381-2954
  Tuttle *(G-11195)*
Denneny Oil and Gas LLC ....G 405 229-4885
  Edmond *(G-2389)*
Derrick Hoppes ....G 580 667-4373
  Tipton *(G-8958)*
Devilbiss Coring Service Inc ....G 405 392-2515
  Blanchard *(G-711)*
Deviney Contract Pumping LLC ....G 405 428-2192
  Maysville *(G-4258)*
Deviney Paraffin Scraping ....G 405 867-5945
  Maysville *(G-4259)*
Dewitt Trucking & Excavation ....G 580 669-2534
  Glencoe *(G-3221)*
Dexxon Inc ....G 918 321-9331
  Kiefer *(G-3778)*
Diamond Cnstr Co Shattuck Inc ....G 580 256-3385
  Woodward *(G-11578)*
Diamond Energy Services LP ....F 918 764-4000
  Tulsa *(G-9578)*
Diamond Oil Field Services Inc ....G 405 863-1052
  Yukon *(G-11718)*
Diamond R Wireline LLC ....G 405 361-7933
  Pauls Valley *(G-7657)*
Diamondback Energy Services ....G 405 242-4080
  Oklahoma City *(G-5941)*
Diamondback Energy Svcs LLC ....F 405 789-3499
  Oklahoma City *(G-5942)*
Diane Oil Co ....G 405 528-5100
  Oklahoma City *(G-5943)*
Diemer Construction Co LLC ....E 580 628-3052
  Tonkawa *(G-8974)*
Direct Downhole Rentals LLC ....G 281 531-8881
  Oklahoma City *(G-5948)*
Direct Oilfield Services LLC ....G 405 385-4743
  Stillwater *(G-8676)*
Diversified Geosynthetics Inc ....G 580 395-0041
  Earlsboro *(G-2280)*
Dixie Wireline ....G 405 853-5402
  Hennessey *(G-3458)*
Dixon Construction Co ....E 405 665-5515
  Wynnewood *(G-11670)*
DK&k Energy LLC ....G 540 395-2400
  Okmulgee *(G-7499)*
Don Betchan ....G 580 336-5954
  Perry *(G-7730)*
Don Scott ....G 405 969-3649
  Crescent *(G-1913)*
Don-Nan Pump and Supply Co Inc ....G 432 682-7742
  Ratliff City *(G-8050)*
Donald L Stafford Co ....G 918 492-0324
  Tulsa *(G-9596)*
Donnie Gaines Wldg Fabrication ......G 580 668-3249
  Wilson *(G-11532)*

Dorado E&P Partners LLC ....F 720 402-3700
  Tulsa *(G-9597)*
Double C Oil and Gas LLC ....G 918 518-5047
  Jenks *(G-3703)*
Double R Oilfield Services LLC ....G 580 388-4567
  Lamont *(G-3868)*
Double R Services Company Inc ......E 580 883-4637
  Ringwood *(G-8088)*
Double S Tank Truck Service ....G 580 863-5231
  Garber *(G-3212)*
Douglas Group LLC ....G 405 946-6853
  Oklahoma City *(G-5972)*
Downhole Hinton Services LLC ....G 580 302-4129
  Weatherford *(G-11406)*
Downhole Wireline Special ....G 580 254-3842
  Woodward *(G-11579)*
Drc Service Co ....G 580 661-3300
  Thomas *(G-8942)*
Dresser-Rand Services LLC ....G 918 321-3690
  Kiefer *(G-3779)*
Drilling Fluids Technology ....G 580 225-1009
  Elk City *(G-2805)*
Drilling Tools Intl Inc ....F 405 604-2763
  Oklahoma City *(G-5981)*
Drovers Trail Land Company LLC ......G 405 702-6300
  Oklahoma City *(G-5985)*
Drumright Oil Well Servic ....G 918 704-0252
  Henryetta *(G-3505)*
Drumright Oilwell Services LLC ....D 918 352-9646
  Drumright *(G-2057)*
Duane Durkee Pumping Svc ....G 405 820-3256
  Perry *(G-7731)*
Duane Waugh ....G 580 596-2485
  Cherokee *(G-1416)*
Dunlap Oil Tools ....G 918 885-6353
  Hominy *(G-3582)*
Dunlap Well Service Inc ....G 918 367-2660
  Bristow *(G-776)*
Dunns Tank Service Inc ....E 580 465-1687
  Foster *(G-3185)*
Dywy Spooling LLC ....G 405 469-4148
  Byars *(G-1222)*
E & K Oilfield Services Inc ....G 580 994-2442
  Mooreland *(G-4589)*
E C Carman Casing Gauge Co ....G 918 605-5093
  Tulsa *(G-9620)*
E J R Enterpises LLC ....G 580 623-0051
  Watonga *(G-11346)*
Eagle Oilfield Service LLC ....G 580 774-2240
  Weatherford *(G-11408)*
Eagle Road Oil LLC ....G 844 211-2961
  Tulsa *(G-9628)*
Earl-Le Dozer Service LLC ....D 918 352-2072
  Drumright *(G-2059)*
Eastern Oil Well Services ....G 405 947-1091
  Oklahoma City *(G-6000)*
Echo E&P LLC ....D 405 753-4232
  Oklahoma City *(G-6004)*
Eco-Lift Energy Services Inc ....G 580 772-5157
  Weatherford *(G-11410)*
Eco-Tech Inc ....F 405 542-6483
  Hinton *(G-3524)*
Eddies Submersible Service Inc ....F 405 273-9292
  Tecumseh *(G-8913)*
Edwards Pipeline Services LLC ....C 918 627-8288
  Tulsa *(G-9646)*
El Paso Prod Oil Gas Texas LP ....E 580 994-2171
  Mooreland *(G-4590)*
Elk City Forklift Service Inc ....G 580 225-0855
  Elk City *(G-2809)*
Elkouri Land Services LLC ....G 405 604-5580
  Moore *(G-4519)*
Elliot Enterprises ....G 918 742-9916
  Tulsa *(G-9659)*
Elvis S Seshie ....G 405 887-3050
  Mustang *(G-4770)*
Elynx Technologies LLC ....E 877 643-5969
  Tulsa *(G-9664)*
Emjo Operations Inc ....G 580 658-6457
  Marlow *(G-4232)*
Encore Cnstr Solutions LLC ....F 405 542-3311
  Hinton *(G-3525)*
Ener-Corr Solutions LLC ....G 405 509-9291
  Oklahoma City *(G-6036)*
Energes ....G 580 339-8044
  Elk City *(G-2812)*
Enos Kauk ....G 580 488-3375
  Leedey *(G-4028)*
Entz Ground Sterilant Inc ....G 405 542-3174
  Hinton *(G-3526)*

Entz Oilfield Chemicals Inc....F....405 542-3174
Hinton (G-3527)
Envirnmntal Tchncians Okla LLC....G....580 772-7805
Weatherford (G-11411)
Envirnmntal Tchncians Okla LLC....G....580 227-2521
Fairview (G-3135)
Enviro Log Operating LLC....G....405 834-1417
Piedmont (G-7761)
Enviro-Clean Services L L C....E....405 373-4545
Oklahoma City (G-6045)
Evan & Sons Inc....G....405 756-2704
Lindsay (G-4061)
Express Energy Svcs Oper LP....E....405 763-5850
Oklahoma City (G-6063)
Expro Americas LLC....E....405 378-6762
Oklahoma City (G-6065)
Extract Production Svcs LLC....C....918 938-6828
Tulsa (G-9718)
F & F Tool Co....G....405 382-0009
Seminole (G-8372)
F W Grubb Oilfield Service....G....580 863-2395
Garber (G-3213)
Falcon Field Service Inc....E....918 885-2244
Hominy (G-3583)
Falcon Flowback Services LLC....B....405 563-0163
Oklahoma City (G-6071)
Family Tree Corporation....G....307 850-4147
McAlester (G-4297)
Far West Development LLC....G....405 557-1384
Oklahoma City (G-6072)
Fdnd Oil and Gas LLC....G....918 583-9960
Tulsa (G-9730)
Fhl Hot Shot Trucking Services....G....405 615-6658
El Reno (G-2716)
Fidgets Oilfield Services LLC....G....918 473-2765
Checotah (G-1393)
Field Services....G....580 256-3338
Woodward (G-11583)
Fieldpoint Energy Services LLC....G....918 691-3427
Tulsa (G-9741)
Fis Operations LLC....C....918 246-7100
Tulsa (G-9749)
Fisher Wireline Services Inc....G....918 885-6564
Hominy (G-3584)
Five Point Services Inc....E....580 856-3670
Ratliff City (G-8053)
Fletcher Lewis Engineering....G....405 840-5675
Oklahoma City (G-6090)
Flex Chem Corporation....F....580 772-2386
Weatherford (G-11414)
Flex-Chem Services Corporation....E....580 772-2386
Weatherford (G-11415)
Flint Energy Services Inc....G....580 856-3251
Ratliff City (G-8054)
Flow Measurement Company Inc....G....918 493-3443
Tulsa (G-9757)
Flow Testing Inc....E....918 423-0017
Krebs (G-3850)
Flowco Energy Service LLC....G....405 385-1062
Perkins (G-7717)
Fluid Lift Inc....G....405 853-6876
Hennessey (G-3461)
Flywheel Energy Management LLC....D....405 702-6991
Oklahoma City (G-6096)
Foamtech Inc....E....580 256-3979
Woodward (G-11584)
Forsythe Oilfield Service Inc....E....580 668-3371
Wilson (G-11533)
▲ Frac Specialists LLC....F....432 617-3722
Oklahoma City (G-6110)
Fracdogs....G....918 786-9797
Grove (G-3271)
Fractalsoft LLC....G....405 330-3555
Edmond (G-2420)
Fraser Oilfield Service LLC....G....918 716-0665
Okemah (G-5269)
Freds Rat Hole Service Inc....F....405 756-4300
Lindsay (G-4063)
Freedom Midstream Services LLC....G....918 582-5313
Tulsa (G-9776)
Freepoint Pipe & Supply Inc....G....405 341-1913
Edmond (G-2423)
Frenchs Blue River Cnstr....F....580 274-3444
Longdale (G-4123)
Frontier Land Surveying LLC....F....405 285-0433
Edmond (G-2426)
Frontier Logging Corporation....G....405 787-3952
Oklahoma City (G-6122)
G & G Steam Service Inc....C....580 225-4254
Elk City (G-2816)

G&J Enterprises....G....580 237-2029
Enid (G-2960)
Galmors Inc....G....580 225-4254
Elk City (G-2817)
Gambill Oilfield Services LLC....G....580 471-1451
Mangum (G-4171)
Gaston Services Inc....G....580 328-5647
Camargo (G-1252)
Gb Energy Inc....G....405 224-8634
Chickasha (G-1461)
Gbg Earthmovers LLC....G....580 243-5662
Elk City (G-2819)
GE Oil & Gas Esp Inc....E....405 527-1566
Purcell (G-8009)
◆ GE Oil & Gas Esp Inc....C....405 670-1431
Oklahoma City (G-6140)
General Inc....E....580 921-3365
Laverne (G-3878)
Genesis Oil Tool International....G....403 298-2430
Oklahoma City (G-6143)
Genie Well Service Inc....E....405 969-2141
Crescent (G-1916)
Geolog LLC....G....405 745-2197
Oklahoma City (G-6144)
Gilchrist Construction Inc....G....580 886-2540
Canton (G-1265)
Gilliland Fluid Corporation....G....405 853-7188
Hennessey (G-3462)
Glenn Brents Sales Inc....G....405 733-4960
Oklahoma City (G-6156)
Glimp Oil Company LLC....G....918 352-2978
Drumright (G-2060)
Glm Energy Inc....G....405 470-2873
Oklahoma City (G-6160)
Gonzo LLC....G....405 373-1715
Yukon (G-11727)
Gore Nitrogen....G....405 381-4928
Tuttle (G-11201)
Gore Nitrogen Pumping Svc LLC....G....580 922-4660
Seiling (G-8349)
Gourdin Consulting LLC....G....918 207-9825
McAlester (G-4302)
Graco Fishing & Rental Tls Inc....F....405 382-0009
Seminole (G-8375)
Gray Mud Disposal....G....580 635-2225
Kremlin (G-3852)
Gray Wireline....G....580 256-3775
Woodward (G-11588)
Green Country Wireline Inc....G....918 534-2107
Dewey (G-2022)
Green River Operating Co....G....405 872-9616
Noble (G-4881)
Greenbriar Resources Corp....G....405 348-7114
Edmond (G-2444)
Greg Tucker Construction....E....405 756-3958
Lindsay (G-4064)
▲ Grisham Services Incorporated....F....918 307-7635
Broken Arrow (G-924)
▲ Griswold Trucking Randy....G....580 476-3590
Ninnekah (G-4872)
Grs Hot Shot Trucking LLC....G....580 353-9449
Tuttle (G-11203)
Gryphon Oilfield Solutions....G....405 446-8065
Chickasha (G-1465)
Guardian Tubular Services Inc....G....405 262-3800
El Reno (G-2721)
Gyrodata Incorporated....D....405 677-0200
Oklahoma City (G-6195)
H & J Services....F....580 237-4613
Enid (G-2966)
H & M Energy Services LLC....G....405 428-0740
Blanchard (G-715)
H 5 C Pumping Inc....G....580 487-3869
Forgan (G-3170)
H2 Services LLC....E....405 388-9049
Guthrie (G-3317)
H2s Safety Plus Inc....E....580 622-4796
Sulphur (G-8834)
Haken Dozer Service....G....580 669-2211
Glencoe (G-3223)
Hall & Anderson Services Inc....E....580 319-5624
Ardmore (G-300)
Hall Energy....G....405 231-2490
Oklahoma City (G-6205)
Halliburton Company....C....580 251-3002
Duncan (G-2122)
Halliburton Company....E....580 251-3379
Duncan (G-2123)
Halliburton Company....G....580 251-3420
Oklahoma City (G-6206)

Halliburton Company....C....580 251-2847
Duncan (G-2124)
Halliburton Company....E....918 587-3117
Tulsa (G-9881)
Halliburton Company....E....405 278-9685
Duncan (G-2125)
Halliburton Company....G....580 251-4421
Duncan (G-2126)
Halliburton Company....C....405 231-1800
Oklahoma City (G-6207)
Halliburton Company....C....806 665-0005
Duncan (G-2127)
Halliburton Company....E....580 251-3406
Duncan (G-2128)
Halliburton Company....G....405 459-6611
Pocasset (G-7777)
Halliburton Company....E....405 552-8520
Oklahoma City (G-6208)
Halliburton Company....E....405 805-2200
Oklahoma City (G-6209)
Halliburton Company....D....580 251-3760
Duncan (G-2129)
Halliburton Company....E....405 231-1800
Moore (G-4527)
Halliburton Company....G....405 459-6611
Pocasset (G-7776)
Hamil Service LLC....F....405 375-3815
Kingfisher (G-3800)
Hamm and Phillips Services Co....G....580 256-8686
Woodward (G-11590)
Hammer Construction Inc....C....405 310-3160
Norman (G-5014)
Harbison-Fischer Inc....G....405 677-3393
Oklahoma City (G-6215)
Harbor Light Hospice LLC....F....405 949-1200
Oklahoma City (G-6216)
Harvey Kates....G....918 225-2567
Cushing (G-1934)
Hassler Hot Oil Service LLC....G....405 756-0448
Lindsay (G-4066)
Hawley Hot Oil LLC....G....580 839-2416
Nash (G-4803)
Heartland Oil & Gas LLC....G....405 848-8099
Oklahoma City (G-6233)
▼ Helmerich & Payne Inc....A....918 742-5531
Tulsa (G-9912)
Henry & Son Roustabouts LLC....G....580 747-8400
Hennessey (G-3468)
Herriman Oilfield Services....G....580 925-2144
Konawa (G-3846)
Hext Trucking LLC....G....580 821-6150
Erick (G-3087)
Higgs-Palmer Technologies LLC....G....918 585-3775
Tulsa (G-9927)
High Plains Services Inc....D....580 225-7388
Elk City (G-2822)
Hoggard Welding & Backhoe Svc....G....580 856-3934
Ratliff City (G-8055)
Holasek Oil & Gas Co LLC....G....405 321-6663
Norman (G-5025)
Holden Energy Corp....E....580 226-3960
Ardmore (G-306)
Holland Services LLC....G....405 842-9393
Oklahoma City (G-6257)
Holman Oil and Gas....G....405 567-3528
Prague (G-7927)
Homer Rinehart Company....D....405 756-2785
Lindsay (G-4067)
Homer Rinehart Company....E....405 756-2785
Lindsay (G-4068)
Horizon Well Servicing LLC....G....580 482-7500
Altus (G-158)
Horizon Welltesting LLC....G....918 429-1200
Mcalester (G-4304)
Horton Tool Company....F....918 885-6941
Hominy (G-3588)
Horton Tool Corporation....F....918 885-6941
Hominy (G-3589)
Hoskins Wireline LLC....F....580 303-9101
Elk City (G-2824)
Hoss Consulting Serv....G....405 324-5543
Mustang (G-4776)
Hot Oil Units Inc....G....580 256-6461
Woodward (G-11592)
Hot Rod Hot Shot Service Inc....G....405 834-5591
Edmond (G-2458)
Hough Oilfield Service Inc....E....918 225-1851
Cushing (G-1936)
Howells Well Service Inc....G....918 846-2531
Wynona (G-11679)

Employee Codes: A=Over 500 employees, B=251-500
C=101-250, D=51-100, E=20-50, F=10-19, G=1-9
2020 Oklahoma Directory
of Manufacturers & Processors
417

13 OIL AND GAS EXTRACTION

HP Field Services LLC ....G....... 580 763-1428
  Stillwater *(G-8703)*
HS Field Services Inc ....E...... 918 534-9121
  Dewey *(G-2025)*
Hughes Gas Measurement Inc............G...... 405 227-0904
  Wetumka *(G-11494)*
Hughes Trucking ....G...... 580 244-3731
  Smithville *(G-8578)*
Hull Contract Pumping ....G...... 580 824-0440
  Waynoka *(G-11376)*
Hulls Oilfield LLC ....F...... 580 668-2619
  Wilson *(G-11536)*
Huntington Energy USA Inc ....G...... 580 772-3644
  Weatherford *(G-11419)*
Hutton Inc ....F...... 580 225-0225
  Elk City *(G-2825)*
Hydrostatic Engineers Inc ....G...... 405 677-7169
  Oklahoma City *(G-6280)*
Hyperion Energy LP ....G...... 918 321-3350
  Kiefer *(G-3780)*
I & Gn Resources Inc ....G...... 918 481-7927
  Tulsa *(G-9962)*
I Enrg ....G...... 405 360-4600
  Norman *(G-5028)*
IFE Ndt LLC ....G...... 405 642-4899
  Yukon *(G-11732)*
II L W Barrett ....G...... 918 496-8309
  Tulsa *(G-9968)*
Impact Casing Services LLC ....F...... 580 216-1159
  Woodward *(G-11593)*
Independent Trucking Co Inc ....F...... 918 352-2539
  Drumright *(G-2063)*
Indian Creek Gas Processing LP ....G...... 918 359-0980
  Tulsa *(G-9977)*
Industrial Equipment Services ....G...... 580 765-5544
  Ponca City *(G-7837)*
Inman Well Service ....G...... 918 440-3151
  Bartlesville *(G-497)*
Innovative Oilfield Svcs LLC ....G...... 918 521-8317
  Red Oak *(G-8078)*
Integrated Fluid Systems ....G...... 405 418-2897
  Chickasha *(G-1471)*
Integrated Fluid Systems LLC ....G...... 580 323-8431
  Clinton *(G-1753)*
Integrated Production Services ....G...... 580 225-5667
  Elk City *(G-2828)*
Integrity Rmdlg Cnstr Svcs LLC ....G...... 405 754-9836
  Oklahoma City *(G-6316)*
Integrity Trckg Cnstr Svcs Inc ....E...... 580 361-2387
  Balko *(G-432)*
Ira E Rongey ....G...... 918 227-0046
  Sapulpa *(G-8279)*
Iron Gate Tubular Services ....G...... 580 303-9046
  Elk City *(G-2829)*
Iron Horse Roustabout Svcs LLC ....G...... 918 352-8586
  Bristow *(G-780)*
J & A Hot Oilers Inc ....G...... 405 341-7600
  Edmond *(G-2464)*
J & D Potter Oil LLC ....G...... 405 375-6303
  Kingfisher *(G-3802)*
J & J Oil Tools LLC ....G...... 580 523-1995
  Guymon *(G-3352)*
J & J Services Inc ....G...... 580 265-9466
  Stonewall *(G-8801)*
▲ J & J Solutions LLC ....D...... 580 336-3050
  Perry *(G-7737)*
J & L Oil Field Services LLC ....B...... 580 938-2205
  Shattuck *(G-8422)*
J & R Service Inc ....G...... 580 256-6461
  Woodward *(G-11594)*
J & S of Enid Inc ....G...... 580 237-6152
  Enid *(G-2978)*
J B Hot Oil and Steam Co Inc ....G...... 918 366-3872
  Bixby *(G-636)*
J Price Energy Services LLC ....F...... 580 795-6106
  Madill *(G-4151)*
J Scott Inc ....F...... 405 262-5900
  El Reno *(G-2727)*
J&K Rstbout Weed Ctrl Svcs LLC .....G...... 918 429-2392
  Stuart *(G-8825)*
J-B Oilfield Services LLC ....F...... 580 388-4484
  Lamont *(G-3869)*
Jacks Backhoe Service ....G...... 580 926-3378
  Camargo *(G-1253)*
Jaco Energy Company Inc ....G...... 918 967-8889
  Stigler *(G-8634)*
Jaguar Meter Service Inc ....G...... 405 670-2327
  Oklahoma City *(G-6346)*
James A Taylor ....G...... 918 724-3121
  Pawhuska *(G-7687)*

James K Anderson Inc ....G...... 405 329-7414
  Norman *(G-5041)*
JB Oil Field Services ....G...... 580 363-3030
  Blackwell *(G-684)*
JC Hot Shot Services Inc ....G...... 918 782-7922
  Glenpool *(G-3236)*
Jdw Hotshot Services ....G...... 918 407-8787
  Tulsa *(G-10033)*
Jec Operating LLC ....G...... 405 235-4454
  Oklahoma City *(G-6352)*
Jeffrey C James ....G...... 405 728-8145
  Oklahoma City *(G-6355)*
Jeremys Rustabouts Backhoe Inc ....F...... 580 772-5157
  Weatherford *(G-11421)*
Jericho Oil (oklahoma) Corp ....G...... 215 383-2433
  Tulsa *(G-10036)*
Jerry Dunkin Well Services ....G...... 580 237-6152
  Enid *(G-2984)*
Jett Oil and Gas LLC ....G...... 918 995-7430
  Tulsa *(G-10041)*
Jim Haynes ....G...... 918 733-2517
  Haskell *(G-3399)*
JM Oilfield Services Inc ....E...... 501 589-4044
  Enid *(G-2986)*
John L Lewis ....G...... 405 941-3224
  Sasakwa *(G-8330)*
John Thompson Enterprises Inc ....F...... 580 623-5820
  Watonga *(G-11348)*
John W Stone Oil Distributing ....B...... 918 744-8168
  Tulsa *(G-10053)*
Johnson Otey Properties Inc ....G...... 580 226-8425
  Ardmore *(G-318)*
Johnson Well Logging Inc ....G...... 405 721-5989
  Oklahoma City *(G-6377)*
Joshi Technologies Intl Inc ....F...... 918 665-6419
  Tulsa *(G-10059)*
Joshua Oil & Gas LLC ....G...... 620 672-5505
  Cache *(G-1227)*
JS Oilfield Services LLC ....G...... 580 542-7822
  Enid *(G-2989)*
K & H Well Service Inc ....F...... 405 382-2762
  Seminole *(G-8380)*
K & S Hotshot Services LLC ....G...... 918 899-2649
  Cleveland *(G-1726)*
K & W Well Service Inc ....E...... 918 225-7855
  Cushing *(G-1940)*
K W B Oil Property Management ....F...... 918 583-8300
  Tulsa *(G-10070)*
K3 LLC ....G...... 580 231-2040
  Enid *(G-2992)*
Kalamar Inc ....F...... 580 242-5121
  Enid *(G-2993)*
Kathy Tim Lowery ....G...... 580 925-2171
  Konawa *(G-3847)*
Kautzs Pumping Inc ....G...... 580 661-3397
  Thomas *(G-8945)*
Keck Oil & Gas LLC ....G...... 918 756-6688
  Okmulgee *(G-7511)*
Kemah Oil & Gas Co LLC ....G...... 405 364-3899
  Norman *(G-5048)*
Kemper Valve and Fittings ....G...... 580 622-2048
  Sulphur *(G-8836)*
Kenmar Energy Services LLC ....F...... 405 844-2500
  Edmond *(G-2485)*
Kens Hot Oil & Steam Service ....G...... 405 382-3052
  Earlsboro *(G-2281)*
Kent Engineering Inc ....G...... 405 364-2207
  Norman *(G-5049)*
Keta Oil Rural ....G...... 580 537-2443
  Loco *(G-4102)*
Key Energy Services Inc ....C...... 405 262-1231
  Woodward *(G-11600)*
Key Energy Services Inc ....D...... 405 853-4327
  Hennessey *(G-3470)*
Key Energy Services Inc ....F...... 405 262-1190
  El Reno *(G-2731)*
Key Energy Services Inc ....G...... 713 651-4300
  Oklahoma City *(G-6407)*
Key Energy Services Inc ....G...... 580 256-7413
  Woodward *(G-11601)*
Key Energy Services Inc ....G...... 918 302-0372
  McAlester *(G-4310)*
Key Energy Services Inc ....G...... 580 338-0664
  Guymon *(G-3354)*
Key Energy Services Inc ....F...... 806 435-5583
  Woodward *(G-11602)*
Key Energy Services Inc ....G...... 806 323-8361
  Elk City *(G-2835)*
Key Energy Services Inc ....E...... 405 262-1231
  El Reno *(G-2732)*

Key Energy Services Inc ....F...... 405 756-3347
  Lindsay *(G-4071)*
Kiester Operating Company ....G...... 580 255-4020
  Duncan *(G-2142)*
Kingfisher Midstream LLC ....G...... 281 655-3200
  Oklahoma City *(G-6422)*
Kings Well Service ....F...... 580 363-3912
  Blackwell *(G-686)*
Kirk Tank Trucks Inc ....G...... 918 733-4503
  Morris *(G-4598)*
Kirks Contract Pumping ....G...... 580 541-6405
  Lahoma *(G-3857)*
Kleen Oilfield Services Co ....F...... 580 657-3967
  Lone Grove *(G-4117)*
Klx Energy Services ....G...... 580 824-0955
  Waynoka *(G-11377)*
Klx Energy Services LLC ....G...... 405 838-1230
  Oklahoma City *(G-6429)*
Kodiak Corp ....G...... 405 478-1900
  Oklahoma City *(G-6433)*
Kog Production LLC ....G...... 580 621-3510
  Freedom *(G-3207)*
L & B Pipe & Fabrication Inc ....G...... 580 234-0712
  Enid *(G-2998)*
L & O Pump and Supply Inc ....G...... 405 756-3877
  Lindsay *(G-4072)*
L Dean Hudgins Inc ....G...... 918 224-6236
  Sapulpa *(G-8284)*
L&E Hot Shot LLC ....G...... 918 839-2419
  Wister *(G-11550)*
Lakewood Disposal LLC ....E...... 918 392-9356
  Tulsa *(G-10014)*
Lamamco Drilling Co ....G...... 580 856-3561
  Ratliff City *(G-8056)*
Lamamco Drilling Company ....G...... 580 336-3524
  Perry *(G-7740)*
Landmark Energy LLC ....G...... 405 382-3951
  Seminole *(G-8383)*
Larry Mustin Construction ....G...... 918 995-7055
  Tulsa *(G-10130)*
Ld Consultants LLC ....G...... 432 230-1098
  Tulsa *(G-10141)*
Ledford Oil & Gas LLC ....G...... 580 467-0593
  Duncan *(G-2146)*
Legacy Resources LLC ....G...... 405 359-1080
  Edmond *(G-2485)*
Legend Energy Services LLC ....E...... 580 225-4500
  Elk City *(G-2837)*
Legend Energy Services LLC ....E...... 405 600-1264
  Oklahoma City *(G-6464)*
Lewis Oil & Gas Inc ....G...... 918 272-1278
  Owasso *(G-7585)*
Lexington Gas & Go ....G...... 405 527-4009
  Purcell *(G-8011)*
Liberty Swabbing Inc ....G...... 405 828-4427
  Dover *(G-2041)*
Liberty Transportation LLC ....G...... 580 225-2784
  Elk City *(G-2838)*
Lightning Services Inc ....G...... 405 853-6669
  Hennessey *(G-3472)*
Linda Sullivan ....G...... 918 629-7223
  Owasso *(G-7587)*
Litta Solutions LLC ....G...... 918 845-4854
  Bixby *(G-642)*
Logic Energy Solutions LLC ....G...... 405 601-9037
  Oklahoma City *(G-6489)*
Longhorn Service Company LLC ....E...... 405 853-7170
  Hennessey *(G-3473)*
Lost River Oilfield Services L ....G...... 208 670-5787
  Edmond *(G-2496)*
Lubri Flange LLC ....G...... 580 303-9139
  Elk City *(G-2840)*
Lucas Oil & Gas Service Inc ....G...... 580 225-3006
  Elk City *(G-2841)*
Luke Mitchell ....G...... 918 429-0373
  Wilburton *(G-11523)*
Lumen Energy Corporation ....F...... 918 584-0052
  Tulsa *(G-10183)*
Lyons & Lyons Inc ....G...... 918 587-2497
  Tulsa *(G-10186)*
M & D Oilfield Services ....G...... 405 677-5720
  Oklahoma City *(G-6505)*
M & L Oil LLC ....G...... 918 798-4511
  Skiatook *(G-8558)*
M & M Electric ....G...... 580 233-8999
  Enid *(G-3002)*
M & W Oilfield Service LLC ....G...... 580 927-2200
  Coalgate *(G-1782)*
M M Energy Inc ....G...... 405 463-3355
  Oklahoma City *(G-6508)*

M&M Hot Oil Service LLC ....G 580 651-1746
Guymon (G-3355)
M-I LLC ....G 580 225-2482
Elk City (G-2844)
M-I LLC ....E 405 224-4170
Chickasha (G-1482)
Mac Oil & Gas ....G 405 375-5619
Kingfisher (G-3808)
Mackellar Inc ....F 405 433-2658
Cashion (G-1289)
Mackellar Services Inc ....G 405 848-2877
Oklahoma City (G-6515)
Mackellar Services Inc ....G 580 237-9383
Enid (G-3004)
Magnum Diversified Services ....F 405 391-9653
Newalla (G-4813)
Magnum Energy Inc ....G 405 360-2784
Norman (G-5063)
Malone Contract Pumping Inc ....G 918 767-2450
Pawnee (G-7706)
Mammoth Energy Partners LLC ....F 405 265-4600
Oklahoma City (G-6518)
Mammoth Energy Services Inc ....F 405 608-6007
Oklahoma City (G-6519)
Manford Oilfield Services LLC ....G 918 424-3280
McAlester (G-4314)
Mark A Holkum LLC ....G 405 735-3463
Oklahoma City (G-5305)
Marsau ....G 580 432-5000
Foster (G-3186)
Marsau Enterprises Inc ....A 580 233-3910
Enid (G-3007)
Martin Tank Trck Csing Pulling ....F 918 225-2388
Cushing (G-1944)
Martin-Decker Totco Inc ....G 580 225-8980
Elk City (G-2847)
Martindale Consultants Inc ....E 405 728-3003
Oklahoma City (G-6534)
Martinez Fencing Construction ....F 580 309-2046
Clinton (G-1758)
Mary K Rose Inc ....G 405 324-5612
Yukon (G-11749)
Mason Pipe & Supply Company ....G 405 942-6926
Oklahoma City (G-6536)
Master Movers Incorporated ....G 918 408-1490
Owasso (G-7590)
McAdams Energy LLC ....G 918 758-0308
Okmulgee (G-7515)
McCabe Roustabout Service ....G 918 534-3131
Dewey (G-2028)
McCormick & Associates LLC ....G 405 747-9991
Stillwater (G-8724)
McDonald Safety Anchor Inc ....G 405 574-4151
Chickasha (G-1483)
McIntyre Transports Inc ....E 580 526-3121
Erick (G-3089)
McWI Inc ....G 405 360-2277
Norman (G-5068)
ME Oil Co ....G 405 232-9541
Oklahoma City (G-6552)
Meagher Energy Advisors Inc ....F 918 481-5900
Tulsa (G-10235)
Mels Construction Inc ....G 405 853-4621
Hennessey (G-3477)
Metco Inc ....G 580 233-6717
Enid (G-3012)
Metzger Oil Tools Inc ....G 918 885-2456
Hominy (G-3592)
Michael S Azlin ....G 405 257-3581
Wewoka (G-11505)
Mid Continent Well Log Svcs ....G 405 360-7333
Norman (G-5075)
Mid-Central Energy Svcs LLC ....D 405 815-4041
Oklahoma City (G-6591)
Mid-States Oilfield Mch LLC ....E 405 605-5656
Oklahoma City (G-6593)
Midcentral Completion Services ....G 405 445-5979
El Reno (G-2738)
Midway Machine & Welding LLC ....G 918 968-3316
Stroud (G-8812)
Midway Services LLC ....G 405 820-8850
Edmond (G-2518)
Midwest Logging & Perforating ....G 405 382-4200
Seminole (G-8384)
Mikes Trucking Co ....E 580 256-5063
Woodward (G-11612)
Miller Bros Wldg & Roustabout ....G 918 968-1611
Stroud (G-8813)
Miller Pump Systems Inc ....G 918 455-4556
Broken Arrow (G-977)
Mills Well Service Inc ....D 405 382-4107
Seminole (G-8385)
Misson Fluid King Oil Field ....G 405 670-8771
Oklahoma City (G-6619)
Mitchells Tank Truck Service ....G 580 229-1880
Healdton (G-3419)
Mlb Consulting LLC ....G 405 285-8559
Edmond (G-2520)
Mlb Consulting LLC ....G 580 225-2717
Elk City (G-2849)
Mlb Consulting LLC ....D 580 504-8810
Ardmore (G-333)
Moes Portable Steam Co Inc ....G 580 432-5467
Foster (G-3187)
Momentum Completion ....G 918 364-9444
Tulsa (G-10297)
Monroe Natural Gas Inc ....G 405 321-5647
Norman (G-5079)
Mooney Oilfield Services LLC ....G 580 660-5203
Weatherford (G-11429)
Moore Contract Pumping ....G 918 372-4645
Ripley (G-8102)
Moran Equipment ....G 405 262-1422
El Reno (G-2739)
Moran Equipment LLC ....E 580 225-2575
Elk City (G-2850)
Morgan Well Service Inc ....E 405 567-2288
Prague (G-7930)
Morrill & Assoc Inc ....G 918 481-1055
Tulsa (G-10304)
Morris Richardson ....G 918 427-7323
Muldrow (G-4634)
Morton Leases Inc ....G 918 733-2331
Morris (G-4601)
MRW Technologies Inc ....E 918 827-6030
Glenpool (G-3239)
Ms 3 Oil & Gas LLC ....G 580 465-7354
Wilson (G-11539)
MSI Inspection Service LLC ....G 405 265-2121
Oklahoma City (G-6632)
Mt Percussion Drilling LLC ....G 918 232-5472
Tulsa (G-10310)
Mud Haulers LLC ....G 580 338-3830
Guymon (G-3357)
Mud Mixers LLC ....F 580 243-7826
Elk City (G-2851)
Mueggs Hot Shot Service LLC ....G 405 368-8362
Okarche (G-5246)
Munoz Oilfield Services LLC ....G 580 799-5857
Elk City (G-2852)
Muras Energy Inc ....F 405 751-0442
Edmond (G-2523)
Mustang Extreme Environmental ....F 405 681-1800
Oklahoma City (G-6639)
Mustang Fuel Corporation ....G 580 446-5552
Enid (G-3017)
Mv Pipeline Company ....G 918 689-5600
Eufaula (G-3105)
Mwd Services LLC ....G 918 698-6109
Owasso (G-7595)
Nabors Completion Prod Svcs Co ....E 580 323-0058
Clinton (G-1760)
Nabors Drilling Tech USA Inc ....C 580 243-4000
Elk City (G-2853)
Nabors Well Services Ltd ....E 405 262-6262
El Reno (G-2742)
Nafta Mud Inc ....G 405 751-6261
Oklahoma City (G-6648)
Nafta Mud LLC ....G 405 751-6261
Oklahoma City (G-6649)
Nance Solutions Inc ....G 918 804-9301
Mustang (G-4785)
National Oilwell Varco Inc ....D 580 251-6900
Duncan (G-2158)
National Oilwell Varco Inc ....E 580 225-4136
Elk City (G-2855)
New Tongs ....G 580 335-3030
Frederick (G-3197)
Newpark Drilling Fluids LLC ....C 580 323-1612
Clinton (G-1761)
Nexstreem Reclaim Plant ....G 580 657-4580
Wilson (G-11540)
Nextier Cmpltion Solutions Inc ....E 580 772-3100
Weatherford (G-11430)
Nine Energy Service ....G 405 601-5336
Oklahoma City (G-6682)
Nitro Lift Holdings LLC ....D 405 620-3274
Mill Creek (G-4470)
Norman Moore ....G 405 941-3220
Sasakwa (G-8333)
North Star Well Services Inc ....D 580 256-5644
Woodward (G-11615)
Northwest Measurement ....G 580 822-3528
Okeene (G-5260)
Nov Downhole ....G 405 688-5000
Oklahoma City (G-6698)
Nov Tuboscope Inc ....G 405 677-8889
Oklahoma City (G-6699)
NRG Wireline LLC ....F 918 768-3210
Kinta (G-3835)
Nsi Fracturing LLC ....G 918 496-2072
Tulsa (G-10364)
Nubs Well Servicing Inc ....F 580 856-3887
Ratliff City (G-8058)
Nutech Energy Alliance Ltd ....G 405 388-4236
Oklahoma City (G-5309)
O K Plunger Service ....G 918 352-4269
Drumright (G-2068)
O K Tank Trucks Inc ....F 918 396-3043
Skiatook (G-8562)
Occuscreen Associates LLC ....G 918 292-8865
Tulsa (G-10375)
Ogci Building Fund LLC ....G 918 828-2500
Tulsa (G-10379)
Ohana Oil & Gas LLC ....G 405 341-8822
Edmond (G-2545)
Oil & Gas Consultants Intl Inc ....E 918 828-2500
Tulsa (G-10381)
Oil & Gas Optimization Special ....G 432 685-0029
Tulsa (G-10383)
Oil States Industries Inc ....D 405 671-2000
Oklahoma City (G-6721)
Oil States Industries Inc ....G 918 250-0828
Tulsa (G-10387)
Oil Tools Rentals Inc ....F 580 242-1140
Enid (G-3024)
Oil Well Cementers Inc ....F 580 229-1776
Healdton (G-3420)
Oilab Inc ....G 405 528-8378
Oklahoma City (G-6723)
Oilfield Dstrbtons Spclsts LLC ....G 580 237-1237
Enid (G-3025)
Oilfield Lease Maintenance ....G 405 348-1562
Edmond (G-2546)
Oilfield Technical Svcs LLC ....G 405 603-4288
Oklahoma City (G-6724)
OK Contract Services LLC ....G 918 352-5369
Braman (G-761)
Okla Casing Co ....G 580 432-5311
Foster (G-3188)
Oklahoma Cellulose Inc ....G 918 706-5279
Cleveland (G-1730)
Oklahoma Cementing Cushing LLC ....G 918 225-0688
Cushing (G-1949)
Oklahoma Energy Source LLC ....G 918 307-8142
Tulsa (G-10400)
Oklahoma Hot Shot Service ....G 405 605-0464
Oklahoma City (G-6752)
Oklahoma Prime Energy LLC ....G 580 226-2373
Ardmore (G-338)
Oklahoma Sub Surfc Pump & Sup ....G 405 382-7311
Seminole (G-8392)
On The Go Hot Shot Svcs LLC ....G 405 471-2055
Edmond (G-2557)
One Oaks Field Service ....D 580 816-4500
Weatherford (G-11431)
Onsite Oil Tools Inc ....F 580 856-3367
Ratliff City (G-8060)
Orca Operating Company LLC ....G 918 587-1312
Tulsa (G-10437)
Osage Land Company ....F 405 946-8402
Oklahoma City (G-6784)
Osage Wireline Service Inc ....G 918 358-5155
Cleveland (G-1731)
Out N Back Hot Shot LLC ....G 405 201-3576
Yukon (G-11762)
Outlaw Oilfield Supply LLC ....E 580 526-3792
Erick (G-3091)
Outsource Group LLC ....G 918 307-0110
Tulsa (G-10446)
Owen Oil Tools LP ....G 405 495-4441
Oklahoma City (G-6789)
P & H Construction Inc ....G 405 257-3307
Wewoka (G-11506)
P /Masters C Inc ....E 405 293-9777
Guthrie (G-3332)
PAK Oilfield Services LLC ....G 580 504-7049
Ardmore (G-343)
Panhandle Construction Svcs ....F 580 338-7667
Guymon (G-3359)

SIC

Employee Codes: A=Over 500 employees, B=251-500
C=101-250, D=51-100, E=20-50, F=10-19, G=1-9
2020 Oklahoma Directory
of Manufacturers & Processors
419

13 OIL AND GAS EXTRACTION

Panhandle Corrosion LLC .... G 580 651-3208
  Goodwell (G-3249)
Panhandle Oilfield Service Com .... D 405 608-5330
  Oklahoma City (G-6799)
Panthera Roustabout Svcs LLC .... G 405 826-8466
  Jones (G-3751)
Parallel Energy LP .... E 918 712-7008
  Tulsa (G-10466)
Park Energy Services LLC .... G 918 617-4350
  Stigler (G-8638)
Parker Energy Services Co .... G 918 626-4982
  Pocola (G-7784)
Parks Oil Tools LLC .... G 405 485-9515
  Blanchard (G-725)
Partners Oilfield Services LLC .... F 580 625-2239
  Beaver (G-543)
Paschall Land Management .... G 405 842-1391
  Oklahoma City (G-6806)
Pat McVicker Oilfield Services .... G 580 256-1577
  Woodward (G-11616)
Patrick McVicker .... G 580 256-1577
  Woodward (G-11617)
Paul Philp Gchmical Conslt LLC .... G 405 325-4469
  Norman (G-5111)
Payrock II LLC .... G 405 608-8077
  Oklahoma City (G-6814)
Payzone Completion Svcs LLC .... D 405 772-7184
  Oklahoma City (G-6815)
Pcs Ferguson Inc .... G 580 256-1317
  Woodward (G-11619)
Peak Oilfield Services .... G 405 884-2379
  Geary (G-3217)
Pearl Energy Group LLC .... G 281 799-7459
  Oklahoma City (G-6818)
Pearson Pumping Inc .... G 918 486-2386
  Coweta (G-1893)
Pecos Pipeline LLC .... G 918 574-3500
  Tulsa (G-10482)
Penterra Services LLC .... G 405 726-2762
  Edmond (G-2566)
Performance Technologies LLC .... D 405 262-2441
  El Reno (G-2746)
Permian Basin Banding .... G 432 238-1483
  Tulsa (G-10497)
Peters Oil & Gas .... G 405 315-6378
  Bristow (G-793)
Petra Solutions LLC .... G 316 554-6586
  Edmond (G-2567)
Petro Source Consultants .... G 405 751-0474
  Oklahoma City (G-6835)
Petroleum Elastomers .... G 405 672-0900
  Oklahoma City (G-6836)
Petroskills LLC .... E 918 828-2500
  Tulsa (G-10507)
Pettitt Wireline Service LLC .... G 580 234-0550
  Enid (G-3035)
Pierpont Lamont LLC .... G 918 592-1705
  Tulsa (G-10514)
Pinnacle Energy Services LLC .... G 405 810-9151
  Oklahoma City (G-6849)
Pinson Well Logging .... G 405 604-5036
  Oklahoma City (G-6851)
Pioneer Oilfield Services Inc .... E 580 243-4000
  Elk City (G-2859)
Pioneer Wireline Services .... G 405 601-8755
  Oklahoma City (G-6852)
Plains Nitrogen LLC .... G 405 418-8426
  Oklahoma City (G-6855)
Plains Nitrogen LLC .... G 918 429-0041
  McAlester (G-4329)
Pml Exploration Services LLC .... E 405 606-2701
  Oklahoma City (G-6858)
Post Construction Company .... G 580 928-5983
  Sayre (G-8343)
Powell Services Inc .... G 580 225-9017
  Elk City (G-2861)
Power Rig LLC .... F 580 254-3232
  Woodward (G-11622)
Precision Wireline LLC .... F 580 233-0033
  Enid (G-3037)
Premiere Inc .... F 405 262-1554
  El Reno (G-2748)
Presley Operating LLC .... G 405 526-3000
  Oklahoma City (G-6889)
Prime Operating Company .... G 405 947-1091
  Oklahoma City (G-6893)
Primeenergy Corporation .... E 405 375-5203
  Oklahoma City (G-6895)
Priority Artificial Lift .... G 405 265-1696
  Yukon (G-11768)

Prism Energy Inc .... G 918 248-4177
  Sapulpa (G-8302)
Pro Directional .... G 405 200-1450
  Oklahoma City (G-6903)
Pro Ject Chemicals .... G 580 445-4345
  Weatherford (G-11434)
Pro Oilfield Services LLC .... G 405 778-8844
  Oklahoma City (G-6904)
Pro Technics International .... G 405 680-5560
  Oklahoma City (G-6907)
Prochem Energy Services Inc .... F 580 465-1737
  Healdton (G-3421)
Production String Services .... G 580 747-4017
  Enid (G-3039)
Protechnics Okc Chemical Off .... G 405 601-3078
  Oklahoma City (G-6918)
Proven Torque LLC .... G 780 982-7597
  Mooreland (G-4593)
Purcell Jack Oil Gas Cnsulting .... G 580 256-2040
  Woodward (G-11624)
Qes Pressure Control LLC .... D 405 605-2700
  Oklahoma City (G-6930)
Qes Pressure Pumping LLC .... E 918 338-0808
  Bartlesville (G-519)
Qes Pressure Pumping LLC .... G 405 483-8000
  Union City (G-11220)
Quail Tools LP .... G 918 994-4695
  Tulsa (G-10588)
Quality Parts Mfg Co Inc .... G 918 627-3307
  Tulsa (G-10592)
Quality Production Co Stigler .... D 918 967-4383
  Stigler (G-8640)
Quality Tank Manufacturing .... G 580 756-1188
  Lindsay (G-4078)
Quinque Operating Company .... G 405 840-9876
  Oklahoma City (G-6954)
R & J Oil and Gas Royalty LLC .... G 405 562-3334
  Edmond (G-2581)
R & M Packer Inc .... G 580 863-2242
  Sand Springs (G-8218)
R & R Well Service Inc .... G 580 254-3068
  Woodward (G-11625)
R & S Swabbing Inc .... G 405 853-5445
  Hennessey (G-3480)
R A Bodenhame Assoc Inc .... G 918 855-1964
  Sand Springs (G-8219)
R M Swabbing LLC .... G 405 828-7213
  Dover (G-2043)
R&R Roustabout Services LLC .... E 580 883-4647
  Ringwood (G-8090)
R360 Oklahoma LLC .... E 405 262-5900
  El Reno (G-2750)
Rafter H Operating LLC .... G 405 295-2100
  El Reno (G-2751)
Rainbo Service Co .... G 405 677-5353
  Oklahoma City (G-6966)
Ram Oilfield Services LLC .... G 918 639-2827
  Tulsa (G-10614)
Rambler Energy Services Inc .... E 580 242-7447
  Enid (G-3042)
Ramco Packers .... G 405 485-8804
  Blanchard (G-729)
Rameys Welding & Roustabout .... G 918 321-3156
  Kiefer (G-3781)
Ramon & Bennett Roustabout .... E 580 625-4092
  Beaver (G-546)
Ranger Oilfield Services Corp .... E 405 853-7279
  Hennessey (G-3481)
Ranger Rentals LLC .... G 580 541-4242
  Enid (G-3043)
Rauh Oilfield Services Co .... G 580 796-2128
  Lahoma (G-3860)
Ray Clour Well Service Inc .... G 580 856-3905
  Ratliff City (G-8063)
Ray McClain Inc .... G 918 363-7350
  Sand Springs (G-8220)
Rayco Paraffin Service Inc .... G 405 853-2055
  Hennessey (G-3482)
Razor Oilfield Services LLC .... F 405 661-0008
  Hinton (G-3535)
Reach Wireline .... G 405 872-8828
  Noble (G-4889)
Recoil Energy Rental LLC .... G 405 650-1373
  Blanchard (G-731)
Recoil Oilfield Services LLC .... C 405 227-4198
  Blanchard (G-732)
▲ Red Bone Services LLC .... F 580 225-1200
  Elk City (G-2865)
Red Bud Resources .... G 580 227-2592
  Fairview (G-3149)

Red Dirt Msurement Contrls LLC .... E 405 422-5085
  El Reno (G-2752)
Red Hills Hot Shot Inc .... G 580 225-8686
  Sayre (G-8344)
Red River Oilfield Svcs LLC .... G 405 802-4280
  Edmond (G-2590)
Reddirt Oilfield Services .... G 580 665-9321
  Elk City (G-2866)
Redzone Coil Tubing LLC .... G 580 237-3663
  Enid (G-3046)
Reeds Power Tongs Inc .... E 405 382-2762
  Seminole (G-8396)
Reliance Ofs .... G 303 317-6565
  Tulsa (G-10637)
Reliance Oilfield Services LLC .... E 918 392-9000
  Tulsa (G-10638)
Reliance Pressure Control .... G 405 320-5074
  Norman (G-5131)
Renegade Services .... G 580 254-2828
  Woodward (G-11628)
▼ Reputation Services & Mfg LLC .... E 918 437-2077
  Tulsa (G-10643)
Reserve Management Inc .... G 918 227-0894
  Sapulpa (G-8307)
Resource Services Inc .... G 918 799-6174
  Stigler (G-8642)
Rex B Benway .... G 918 366-3626
  Bixby (G-653)
Rice Welding Inc .... G 580 776-2584
  Meno (G-4387)
Richardson Wellsite Services .... G 918 807-7105
  Sapulpa (G-8308)
Riddle Construction Co Inc .... G 580 256-8109
  Woodward (G-11629)
Rifle Tool Company .... G 580 856-3030
  Ratliff City (G-8065)
Rig Chasers LLC .... E 580 254-3830
  Woodward (G-11630)
Riley Explration - Permian LLC .... G 405 415-8699
  Oklahoma City (G-7026)
Ring Energy Inc .... G 918 499-3880
  Tulsa (G-10654)
Riverside Laboratories Inc .... G 918 585-3064
  Tulsa (G-10657)
RMH Survey LLC .... G 918 927-8868
  Vinita (G-11270)
Robert C Brooks Inc .... G 405 478-0260
  Edmond (G-2602)
Robert M Beirute .... G 918 299-4259
  Tulsa (G-10662)
Robert M Cobb Oilfield Eqp Sls .... G 405 840-2902
  Oklahoma City (G-7035)
Robert S Cargile .... G 405 732-7915
  Oklahoma City (G-7036)
Rocking P Sales & Services LLC .... G 580 530-0028
  Hobart (G-3544)
Rocky Mtn Mdstream Hldings LLC ..... G 918 573-2000
  Tulsa (G-10668)
Rocky Top Energy LLC .... G 918 273-7444
  Nowata (G-5228)
Rod Pumps Inc .... G 918 968-4369
  Stroud (G-8816)
Rolco Energy Services LLC .... G 580 657-2602
  Ardmore (G-351)
Rolling Thunder Oilfield .... G 580 303-4587
  Elk City (G-2869)
Rose Rock Midstream Field Svcs .... G 918 524-7700
  Tulsa (G-10672)
Rpc Inc .... E 580 225-0843
  Elk City (G-2871)
Rufnex Oilfield Services LLC .... G 405 741-8322
  Oklahoma City (G-7061)
Rugged Roustabout LLC .... F 918 225-0700
  Cushing (G-1957)
Russell W Mackey .... G 580 571-7595
  Gage (G-3211)
S & H Tank Service Inc .... E 405 756-3121
  Lindsay (G-4081)
S & H Tank Service of Oklahoma .... F 405 756-3121
  Lindsay (G-4082)
S & T Rose Inc .... G 580 657-4906
  Lone Grove (G-4120)
S&S Star Operating LLC .... G 817 676-1638
  Oklahoma City (G-7068)
Safety Plus USA LLC .... E 580 622-4796
  Sulphur (G-8843)
Sage Natural Resources LLC .... G 940 539-2225
  Tulsa (G-10689)
Saint Louis Well Service Inc .... E 405 289-3314
  Saint Louis (G-8132)

Samco Anchors........G....... 806 435-6870
Clinton *(G-1767)*
Samhill LLC........G....... 580 761-1255
Tonkawa *(G-8981)*
Sampson Brothers Inc........G....... 580 994-2464
Mooreland *(G-4594)*
Samson Energy Company LLC........F....... 918 879-0279
Tulsa *(G-10692)*
Samson Exploration LLC........F....... 918 879-0279
Tulsa *(G-10693)*
Sanchez Cnstr & Rmdlg LLC........G....... 405 443-8324
Purcell *(G-8018)*
Sand Resources LLC........G....... 405 573-0242
Norman *(G-5137)*
Sander Sporting Gds & Atvs LLC........G....... 580 922-4930
Seiling *(G-8351)*
Sanders Electric........G....... 405 377-1691
Stillwater *(G-8752)*
Santana Inc........G....... 405 826-8817
Oklahoma City *(G-5315)*
Saxet Energy........G....... 405 752-9544
Oklahoma City *(G-7087)*
Schlumberger Technology Corp........C....... 405 789-1515
Oklahoma City *(G-7089)*
Schlumberger Technology Corp........C....... 405 422-8700
El Reno *(G-2753)*
Schlumberger Technology Corp........G....... 580 762-2481
Ponca City *(G-7872)*
Schlumberger Technology Corp........E....... 405 942-0002
Oklahoma City *(G-7090)*
Schlumberger Technology Corp........D....... 918 661-2000
Bartlesville *(G-525)*
Schlumberger Technology Corp........G....... 918 584-6651
Tulsa *(G-10714)*
Schlumberger Technology Corp........G....... 405 306-8244
Moore *(G-4564)*
Schlumberger Technology Corp........G....... 580 252-3355
Duncan *(G-2173)*
Schlumberger Technology Corp........G....... 580 774-7557
Weatherford *(G-11439)*
Schlumberger Technology Corp........C....... 580 225-0730
El Reno *(G-2754)*
Schlumberger Technology Corp........E....... 918 247-1300
Kellyville *(G-3767)*
Schlumberger Technology Corp........G....... 405 682-2284
Yukon *(G-11777)*
Scientific Drilling Intl Inc........D....... 405 787-3663
Yukon *(G-11780)*
Scott Craig Consulting LLC........G....... 580 571-4199
Leedey *(G-4031)*
Scott Greer Sales Inc........G....... 405 670-4654
Oklahoma City *(G-7095)*
Sean Josephson LLC........G....... 918 606-9677
Tulsa *(G-9035)*
Secure Operations Group LLC........G....... 918 642-3444
Fairfax *(G-3121)*
Select Energy Services LLC........G....... 405 295-2566
El Reno *(G-2756)*
Select Energy Services LLC........D....... 918 302-0069
Alderson *(G-128)*
Select Energy Solutions Rw LLC........G....... 580 653-2167
Springer *(G-8625)*
▲ **Semgroup Corporation**........B....... 918 524-8100
Tulsa *(G-10728)*
Seminole Oilfield Supply........G....... 918 623-9900
Okemah *(G-5275)*
Semmexico LLC........G....... 918 524-8100
Tulsa *(G-10730)*
Sequoia Natural Resources LLC........G....... 405 463-0355
Oklahoma City *(G-7111)*
Seventy Seven Energy LLC........D....... 405 608-7777
Oklahoma City *(G-7112)*
Seventy Seven Operating LLC........D....... 405 608-7777
Oklahoma City *(G-7113)*
Shafer Kline & Warren Inc........E....... 918 499-6000
Tulsa *(G-10738)*
Sharpshooters Inc........G....... 580 332-3109
Ada *(G-85)*
Shaw Wireline LLC........G....... 405 853-2168
Hennessey *(G-3485)*
Shebester Bechtel Inc........E....... 405 577-2700
Oklahoma City *(G-7117)*
Shebester Bechtel Inc........D....... 405 513-8580
Edmond *(G-2619)*
Shebester Bechtel Inc........D....... 580 363-4124
Blackwell *(G-691)*
Shebester Bechtel Inc........E....... 580 242-4876
Enid *(G-3055)*
Silver City Excavating LLC........G....... 405 673-3062
Newcastle *(G-4840)*

Silver Cliff Resourse........G....... 405 842-8698
Oklahoma City *(G-7140)*
Sims Electric of Oklahoma Inc........F....... 580 338-8932
Guymon *(G-3366)*
Siosi Oil Co........G....... 918 492-1400
Skiatook *(G-8569)*
Sirrah Investments........G....... 405 853-4909
Hennessey *(G-3487)*
Sisk Construction Co........G....... 405 375-5318
Kingfisher *(G-3815)*
Sjl Oil and Gas Inc........E....... 405 853-2044
Hennessey *(G-3488)*
Sjl Well Service LLC........G....... 405 853-2044
Hennessey *(G-3489)*
Skyline Drctonal Drilling LLC........E....... 405 429-4050
Moore *(G-4570)*
SM Oil & Gas Inc........G....... 918 629-2151
Skiatook *(G-8571)*
Smeac Group International LLC........G....... 580 574-4092
Lawton *(G-3999)*
Smith & Sons Salvage........G....... 580 342-6218
Temple *(G-8935)*
Smith Construction Inc........E....... 580 226-2159
Ardmore *(G-355)*
Smith Energy Services........G....... 580 596-2104
Cherokee *(G-1419)*
Smith International Inc........E....... 405 670-7200
Oklahoma City *(G-7155)*
Smith International Inc........F....... 800 654-6461
Ponca City *(G-7875)*
Smith International Inc........G....... 580 252-3355
Duncan *(G-2178)*
Smith Petroleum LLC........G....... 918 638-1301
Barnsdall *(G-441)*
Smith Pump Supply........G....... 405 258-0834
Chandler *(G-1387)*
Snwellservice Llc........G....... 580 430-9346
Dacoma *(G-1977)*
SOO & Associates........G....... 405 397-5072
Norman *(G-5149)*
Sooner Completions Inc........E....... 405 273-4599
Shawnee *(G-8502)*
Sooner Hot Oil Service........G....... 580 762-2586
Ponca City *(G-7876)*
Sooner Production Services Inc........F....... 580 256-1155
Woodward *(G-11633)*
Sooner Swabbing Services Inc........G....... 580 233-4347
Enid *(G-3059)*
South Tulsa Hot Shot Svcs LLC........G....... 918 299-7373
Jenks *(G-3728)*
Southern International Inc........F....... 405 943-5288
Oklahoma City *(G-7171)*
Southern Plains Enrgy Svcs LLC........G....... 918 225-3570
Cushing *(G-1960)*
Southern Plains Enrgy Svcs LLC........F....... 580 336-7444
Perry *(G-7745)*
Southstar Energy Corp........G....... 580 223-1553
Ardmore *(G-356)*
Southwest Oilfield Service........G....... 580 302-4069
Weatherford *(G-11444)*
Sparlin Hot Oil Service Inc........G....... 580 795-2513
Madill *(G-4163)*
Spearhead Services........G....... 405 756-8615
Lindsay *(G-4086)*
Spectrum Tracer Services LLC........D....... 405 470-5566
Tulsa *(G-10819)*
Spencer Machine Works LLC........G....... 580 332-1551
Ada *(G-91)*
Spencers Contract Pumping LLC........G....... 405 238-6363
Wynnewood *(G-11673)*
Spinnaker Oil Company LLC........E....... 405 345-9556
El Reno *(G-2759)*
Spread Tech LLC........E....... 580 994-2506
Mooreland *(G-4595)*
Spurlock Co Satellite Mapping........G....... 405 495-8628
Oklahoma City *(G-7189)*
Ss Roustabout Services........G....... 405 320-2183
Ninnekah *(G-4874)*
Stacey Oil Services........G....... 918 427-3940
Roland *(G-8114)*
Stallion Oilfield Services Ltd........E....... 580 225-5800
Elk City *(G-2876)*
Stallion Oilfield Services Ltd........E....... 580 225-8990
Elk City *(G-2877)*
Stallion Oilfield Services Ltd........D....... 580 856-3169
Ratliff City *(G-8067)*
Star Industries........G....... 580 977-4576
Enid *(G-3062)*
Star Pipe Service Inc........F....... 405 672-6688
Oklahoma City *(G-7194)*

Star Well Services Inc........F....... 405 222-4606
Chickasha *(G-1513)*
Stars Stripes Construction........G....... 405 387-4847
Newcastle *(G-4842)*
Statewide Roustabouts Inc........G....... 405 262-5934
El Reno *(G-2760)*
Step Energy Svcs Holdings Ltd........E....... 918 423-4300
McAlester *(G-4339)*
Step Energy Svcs Holdings Ltd........G....... 918 252-5416
Tulsa *(G-10845)*
Stephens & Johnson Oper Co........G....... 405 619-1866
Oklahoma City *(G-7202)*
Stephens Oil & Gas Exploration........G....... 214 773-5898
Oklahoma City *(G-7203)*
Steves Construction Company........G....... 580 432-5398
Elmore City *(G-2897)*
▼ **Stinger Wllhead Protection Inc**........F....... 405 702-6575
Oklahoma City *(G-7205)*
Stinger Wllhead Protection Inc........E....... 405 684-2940
Oklahoma City *(G-7206)*
Stockton Transports Inc........G....... 580 227-3793
Fairview *(G-3152)*
Strata View Operating LLC........G....... 405 364-1613
Norman *(G-5161)*
Stride Well Service........E....... 580 883-4931
Ringwood *(G-8093)*
Stride Well Service Inc........E....... 580 254-2353
Woodward *(G-11635)*
Stride Well Service Inc........F....... 580 242-7300
Lindsay *(G-4088)*
Stride Well Service Inc........G....... 405 375-4129
Enid *(G-3063)*
Strong Service LP........G....... 405 756-1716
Lindsay *(G-4089)*
Sum Professionals Inc........F....... 580 983-2379
Durham *(G-2273)*
Summit Energy Services Inc........G....... 405 366-9999
Norman *(G-5164)*
Summit Well Servicing LLC........G....... 580 467-0886
Ratliff City *(G-8068)*
Sun West Mud Company Inc........G....... 580 256-2865
Woodward *(G-11637)*
Sunwest Mud........G....... 405 631-2101
Oklahoma City *(G-7226)*
Super Flow Testers Inc........E....... 405 756-8795
Lindsay *(G-4090)*
Super Heaters LLC........F....... 580 225-3196
Elk City *(G-2880)*
Superior Energy Services LLC........E....... 405 722-0896
Oklahoma City *(G-7228)*
Superior Spooling LLC........G....... 405 613-0329
Purcell *(G-8022)*
Superior Tool Services Inc........G....... 918 640-5503
Bristow *(G-797)*
Sutherland Well Service Inc........D....... 580 229-1338
Healdton *(G-3422)*
Sutherland Well Service Inc........G....... 580 795-5525
Madill *(G-4165)*
Swabbing Johns LLC........F....... 405 756-8141
Lindsay *(G-4091)*
Swabbing Johns Inc........F....... 405 756-8141
Lindsay *(G-4092)*
Swanderland Associates LLC........G....... 918 621-6533
Tulsa *(G-10883)*
Swiftwater Energy Services LLC........G....... 405 820-7612
Oklahoma City *(G-7238)*
Synergy Petroleum LLC........G....... 918 456-9991
Tahlequah *(G-8885)*
T & C Construction........G....... 580 432-5413
Foster *(G-3189)*
T D Craighead........G....... 405 329-2229
Norman *(G-5169)*
T K Stanley Inc........G....... 405 745-3479
Oklahoma City *(G-7246)*
T&M Roustabout Services LLC........G....... 580 796-2478
Lahoma *(G-3861)*
T&T Forklift Service Inc........G....... 405 756-3451
Lindsay *(G-4093)*
T3 Energy LLC........G....... 405 677-8051
Oklahoma City *(G-7247)*
Tall Oak Woodford LLC........G....... 405 888-5585
Edmond *(G-2636)*
Tamco Plunger & Lift Inc........G....... 405 853-6195
Hennessey *(G-3491)*
Tami Wheeler LLC........G....... 405 759-2239
Oklahoma City *(G-7251)*
Tank Masters........G....... 580 332-3325
Ada *(G-92)*
Tank Trucks Inc........G....... 918 224-7515
Sapulpa *(G-8314)*

SIC

13 OIL AND GAS EXTRACTION SIC SECTION

Tapoil Inc G 580 788-4576
Elmore City *(G-2898)*

Targa Pipeline Mid-Continent W F 918 574-3500
Tulsa *(G-10899)*

Targa Ppline Mid-Continent LLC E 580 435-2267
Alva *(G-194)*

Targa Ppline Mid-Continent LLC C 918 574-3500
Tulsa *(G-10900)*

Targa Ppline Mid-Continent LLC D 580 883-2273
Ringwood *(G-8094)*

Target Completions LLC G 918 872-6115
Broken Arrow *(G-1071)*

Tarhay LLC G 940 655-4210
Hollis *(G-3569)*

Tarheel Oil & Gas LLC G 405 823-9965
Oklahoma City *(G-7254)*

Taylor Rig LLC D 918 266-7301
Tulsa *(G-10906)*

Tcj Oilfield Services LLC G 580 687-4454
Elmer *(G-2892)*

Ted Smith G 405 677-8402
Oklahoma City *(G-7264)*

Teg Solutions LLC F 405 354-1951
El Reno *(G-2761)*

Terra Pilot Mwd Tools LLC F 405 603-2200
Oklahoma City *(G-7271)*

Terra Star Inc E 405 200-1336
Kingfisher *(G-3817)*

Terraco Production Leasing LLC G 580 658-3000
Marlow *(G-4245)*

Terry Stutzmann G 405 481-3853
Shawnee *(G-8510)*

Terrys Contract Pumping G 580 554-2387
Covington *(G-1868)*

Terrys Pump & Supply Inc G 405 853-6550
Hennessey *(G-3492)*

Testco Inc F 580 623-4900
Watonga *(G-11350)*

Testers Inc G 580 243-0148
Elk City *(G-2881)*

Testers Inc E 405 235-9911
Oklahoma City *(G-7273)*

Tetra Technologies Inc G 405 542-5461
Hinton *(G-3538)*

Texas Transco Inc G 903 857-9136
Marietta *(G-4214)*

Texoma Pumping Unit Svc Inc E 580 856-4024
Ratliff City *(G-8070)*

Texoma Tractor LLC G 918 640-7949
Talala *(G-8903)*

Thomas P Harris Jr G 918 742-6414
Tulsa *(G-10933)*

Three Rivers Corp G 918 492-3239
Tulsa *(G-10938)*

Thru Tubing Solutions G 405 692-1900
Newcastle *(G-4844)*

Thru Tubing Solutions Inc G 918 429-7700
McAlester *(G-4341)*

Thru Tubing Solutions Inc C 405 692-1900
Oklahoma City *(G-5320)*

Thru Tubing Solutions Inc F 580 225-6977
Elk City *(G-2882)*

Thurmond-Mcglothlin LLC G 405 853-2248
Hennessey *(G-3493)*

Thurmond-Mcglothlin LLC G 580 223-9632
Ardmore *(G-369)*

Thurmond-Mcglothlin LLC G 580 774-2659
Weatherford *(G-11446)*

Ties Oilfield Service Inc G 405 306-2655
Yukon *(G-11792)*

Tiger Mountain Gas & Oil G 405 605-1181
Oklahoma City *(G-7287)*

Tim Scoggins G 580 438-2476
Cleo Springs *(G-1712)*

Tipton Oil Tools LLC G 405 964-3030
Shawnee *(G-8511)*

Tiptop Energy Prod US LLC G 405 821-0796
Oklahoma City *(G-7293)*

Tking Energy Solutions LLC G 740 827-4599
Lawton *(G-4013)*

Tlr Well Services Inc E 580 225-4096
Elk City *(G-2883)*

Tmg Service Company LLC E 405 213-4317
Oklahoma City *(G-7297)*

Tokata Oil Recovery Inc G 405 595-0072
Stillwater *(G-8769)*

Toms Hot Shot Service F 580 243-4300
Elk City *(G-2884)*

Tongs G 580 875-2053
Walters *(G-11303)*

Toolbox Oil Gas Consulting Inc G 432 234-2067
Duncan *(G-2189)*

Top O Texas Oilfield Services G 806 662-5206
Atoka *(G-425)*

Total Rod Concepts Inc G 405 677-0585
Oklahoma City *(G-7311)*

Town & Country Hardware G 918 865-2888
Mannford *(G-4192)*

Tpl Southtex Gas Utility Co LP E 918 574-3500
Tulsa *(G-10963)*

Tracy Tarrent G 405 969-2343
Crescent *(G-1920)*

Trade Trucking LLC G 405 443-5375
Oklahoma City *(G-7314)*

TRC Rod Services of Oklahoma F 405 677-0585
Oklahoma City *(G-7320)*

Tri State Industrial F 918 286-8110
Broken Arrow *(G-1084)*

Tri-Co Testing G 580 772-8829
Weatherford *(G-11450)*

Tri-State Industries Inc F 918 938-6004
Tulsa *(G-10973)*

Triple Crown Energy-Bh LLC G 918 518-5422
Tulsa *(G-10975)*

Triple M G 580 488-3468
Leedey *(G-4032)*

Triple M Roustabouts LLC G 918 619-7610
Tulsa *(G-10976)*

Triple T Hotshot G 405 745-6698
Mustang *(G-4798)*

Troglin Tank Gauge Svcs LLC G 806 275-0010
Blanchard *(G-739)*

Trpr Oilfield Services LLC G 405 853-1988
Weatherford *(G-11452)*

Truevine Operating LLC G 580 427-7919
Ada *(G-99)*

Tuboscope Pipeline Svcs Inc F 405 478-2441
Edmond *(G-2656)*

Tucker Energy Services Inc F 918 806-5647
Tulsa *(G-10984)*

Turney Bros Oilfld Svcs & Pp E 918 470-6937
McAlester *(G-4345)*

Twelve States Oil & Gas Co LLC G 918 296-7625
Tulsa *(G-11021)*

Two K Enterprises LLC G 918 964-7004
Grove *(G-3290)*

Tx3 LLC G 405 382-2270
Seminole *(G-8405)*

U S Weatherford L P F 405 756-4389
Lindsay *(G-4096)*

U S Weatherford L P E 918 465-2311
Oklahoma City *(G-7357)*

UC Oil & Gas LLC G 918 270-2383
Tulsa *(G-11031)*

Ulterra Drilling Tech LP G 405 751-6212
Oklahoma City *(G-7358)*

United Services Limited F 580 256-5335
Woodward *(G-11648)*

Universal Land Services LLC G 918 712-9038
Tulsa *(G-11049)*

Universal Pressure Pumping Inc G 405 608-7346
Oklahoma City *(G-7372)*

US Casing Service OK Inc G 701 713-0047
Weatherford *(G-11454)*

US Oil Tools Inc G 580 256-6874
Woodward *(G-11649)*

USA Compression G 405 790-0300
Oklahoma City *(G-7377)*

USA Compression Partners LLC G 918 742-6548
Tulsa *(G-11058)*

USA Compression Partners LLC G 405 234-3850
Oklahoma City *(G-7378)*

Valor Energy Services LLC G 405 513-5043
Edmond *(G-2666)*

Valor Energy Services LLC E 405 209-6081
Elk City *(G-2887)*

Varco LP G 405 677-8889
Oklahoma City *(G-7393)*

Varco LP E 405 478-3400
Oklahoma City *(G-7394)*

Veem Jade Oil & Gas LLC G 918 298-1555
Tulsa *(G-11069)*

Vickers Construction Inc D 405 756-4386
Lindsay *(G-4097)*

Victory Oil Field Services Co G 405 694-0468
Noble *(G-4893)*

Viking Pipe and Supply LLC G 405 262-9337
El Reno *(G-2767)*

Vincent Enterprises Inc G 580 252-1322
Duncan *(G-2194)*

Vinces Lease Service F 405 542-3908
Hinton *(G-3539)*

Vortex Fluid Systems Inc G 918 810-7798
Tulsa *(G-9049)*

W 2 Enterprises LLC G 918 429-8793
Tuskahoma *(G-11183)*

W A Waterman and Co Inc G 405 632-5631
Oklahoma City *(G-7409)*

W E O C Inc G 918 367-5918
Bristow *(G-804)*

W K Linduff Inc G 918 225-6000
Cushing *(G-1968)*

Wagon Wheel Exploration LLC G 918 746-7477
Jenks *(G-3738)*

Waid Group Inc G 817 980-8985
Medicine Park *(G-4373)*

Wajo Chemical Inc G 580 255-1191
Duncan *(G-2197)*

Walkup Wellhead G 580 320-5913
Purcell *(G-8026)*

Walters Oil G 580 432-5294
Elmore City *(G-2899)*

Walters Oilwell Service Inc G 580 875-2601
Walters *(G-11304)*

Waltman Oil & Gas G 405 374-2694
Maud *(G-4253)*

Wapco Inc G 405 489-3212
Cement *(G-1370)*

Washita Flow Testers Inc D 405 756-3397
Lindsay *(G-4099)*

Washita Valley Enterprises G 405 568-4525
Oklahoma City *(G-7426)*

Washita Valley Enterprises Inc G 580 540-9277
Enid *(G-3075)*

Washita Valley Enterprises Inc D 918 429-0186
McAlester *(G-4349)*

Washita Valley Enterprises Inc D 405 670-5338
Oklahoma City *(G-7427)*

We-Go Perforators Inc G 580 332-1346
Ada *(G-105)*

We-Go Perforators Inc G 405 364-3618
Norman *(G-5197)*

Weatherford Artificia F 405 853-7181
Hennessey *(G-3496)*

Weatherford Artificia G 405 677-2410
Oklahoma City *(G-7429)*

Weatherford International LLC F 580 225-1237
Elk City *(G-2888)*

Weatherford International LLC E 405 773-1100
Oklahoma City *(G-7431)*

Webster Drilling Services LLC G 405 517-5585
Lindsay *(G-4100)*

Well Completions Inc E 918 654-3030
Cameron *(G-1259)*

Well Solutions Inc G 580 775-2373
Marietta *(G-4218)*

Wellstar Downhole Services LLC G 580 542-6982
Enid *(G-3078)*

Welltec Inc G 918 585-6122
Tulsa *(G-11107)*

Westoak Production Svcs Inc E 580 254-3568
Woodward *(G-11651)*

Whiterock Oil & Gas LLC G 580 307-5565
Perry *(G-7750)*

Whites Roustabout Service Inc G 405 489-7126
Cement *(G-1371)*

Whitetail Well Testing LLC F 580 225-4200
Lone Wolf *(G-4122)*

Wild Horse Distrubuting LLC G 405 691-0755
Oklahoma City *(G-5323)*

Wild Well Control Inc G 405 686-0330
Oklahoma City *(G-7452)*

Wildcat Field Services LLC G 918 606-6217
Collinsville *(G-1829)*

Williams Water Well Co G 405 250-8531
Enid *(G-3080)*

Wilson & Wilson G 405 375-5194
Kingfisher *(G-3822)*

Wilson Pinstar Co G 580 255-5899
Marlow *(G-4248)*

Woods Pumping Service Inc G 405 449-3485
Maysville *(G-4263)*

Wooldridge Oil Co Inc G 918 465-3073
Wilburton *(G-11529)*

Wooten Pumping Service G 918 642-5312
Fairfax *(G-3122)*

WOW Metallizing & Hard G 918 245-9922
Sand Springs *(G-8243)*

Wright Lease Services G 806 857-9116
Enid *(G-3084)*

Wtl Oil LLC .... D 405 608-6007
  Oklahoma City (G-7475)
Wyoming Casing Service Inc .... E 580 256-1222
  Woodward (G-11659)
Wyoming Casing Service In .... G 701 456-0136
  Chickasha (G-1526)
Xgp LLC .... G 405 584-1444
  Seminole (G-8408)
Xtra Oil Field & Cnstr Co .... G 918 352-3722
  Drumright (G-2077)
Xtreme Energy Company .... G 405 273-1185
  Shawnee (G-8523)
Yandells Well Service .... G 405 756-3407
  Lindsay (G-4101)
Ydf Inc .... G 405 324-2216
  Yukon (G-11806)
Young Tool Company LLC .... G 918 352-2213
  Drumright (G-2078)
Zzw Global Inc .... G 405 388-8720
  Yukon (G-11809)
Zzw Global Inc .... G 405 985-8759
  Oklahoma City (G-7490)

14 MINING AND QUARRYING OF NONMETALLIC MINERALS, EXCEPT FUELS

1411 Dimension Stone

Apac-Central Inc .... E 918 256-7853
  Vinita (G-11248)
Bison Materials LLC .... G 918 333-2266
  Bartlesville (G-455)
Cornerstone Quarries Inc .... G 918 647-2117
  Cameron (G-1256)
Dream Green International LLC .... G 814 616-7800
  Norman (G-4983)
Eaves Stones Products .... F 580 889-7858
  Atoka (G-410)
Grecian Marble & Granite LLC ..... F 405 632-3802
  Oklahoma City (G-6185)
Hansons Stone & Landscape .... G 580 310-0071
  Ada (G-47)
Keystone Rock & Excavation LLC .. G 405 608-7777
  Oklahoma City (G-6414)
Majestic Marble & Granite .... E 918 266-1121
  Catoosa (G-1337)
Martin Marietta Materials Inc .... E 580 326-7709
  Sawyer (G-8335)
▼ Oklahoma Stone .... F 405 721-6775
  Yukon (G-11761)
Polycor Oklahoma Inc .... G 770 735-2611
  Marble City (G-4197)
Quapaw Company Inc .... E 918 767-2985
  Pawnee (G-7710)
Stonemen Granite & Marble .... G 918 851-3400
  Tulsa (G-10856)
Sugar Loaf Quarries Inc .... E 918 647-4244
  Shady Point (G-8416)
Texhoma Limestone .... F 580 889-8808
  Caney (G-1263)
Whm Granite Products Inc .... F 580 535-2184
  Granite (G-3257)

1422 Crushed & Broken Limestone

Anchor Stone Co .... F 918 599-7255
  Tulsa (G-9186)
Anchor Stone Co .... G 918 872-8449
  Broken Arrow (G-827)
Anchor Stone Co .... G 918 299-6384
  Tulsa (G-9187)
Anchor Stone Co .... D 918 438-1060
  Tulsa (G-9188)
Apac-Central Inc .... E 918 256-7853
  Vinita (G-11248)
Apac-Central Inc .... F 918 683-1362
  Okay (G-5256)
▲ Dolese Bros Co .... C 405 235-2311
  Oklahoma City (G-5957)
Dolese Bros Co .... D 580 492-4771
  Elgin (G-2775)
Dolese Bros Co .... E 405 670-9626
  Oklahoma City (G-5962)
Dolese Bros Co .... E 580 226-8737
  Ardmore (G-280)
Dolese Bros Co .... F 580 937-4889
  Coleman (G-1794)
Dream Green International LLC .... G 814 616-7800
  Norman (G-4983)
Jenkins Quary .... G 580 588-3020
  Apache (G-219)
Jennings Stone Company Inc .... E 580 777-2880
  Fittstown (G-3159)
Kemp Stone Inc .... F 918 772-3366
  Hulbert (G-3624)
Martin Marietta Materials Inc .... G 405 799-7799
  Oklahoma City (G-6533)
Martin Marietta Materials Inc .... E 580 369-2706
  Davis (G-1989)
Martin Marietta Materials Inc .... G 580 286-3290
  Idabel (G-3640)
Martin Marietta Materials Inc .... F 580 569-2393
  Snyder (G-8583)
Martin Marietta Materials Inc .... G 580 835-7311
  Broken Bow (G-1198)
Muskogee Sand Company Inc ..... G 918 683-1766
  Porter (G-7894)
Pryor Stone Inc .... E 918 825-3370
  Pryor (G-7987)
Quality Stone Quarries LLC .... G 918 967-5195
  Stigler (G-8641)
Quapaw Company Inc .... E 918 767-2985
  Pawnee (G-7710)
Rock Producers Inc .... G 918 963-2111
  Shady Point (G-8415)
Schweitzer Gypsum & Lime .... G 405 263-7967
  Okarche (G-5251)
Souter Limestone and Mnrl LLC ... F 918 489-5589
  Gore (G-3252)
Stewart Stone Inc .... F 918 225-2704
  Cushing (G-1962)
US Lime Company - St Clair .... D 918 775-4466
  Marble City (G-4198)

1423 Crushed & Broken Granite

Blessing Gravel LLC .... G 580 513-4009
  Tishomingo (G-8962)
Martin Marietta Materials Inc .... E 580 384-5246
  Mill Creek (G-4469)
Martin Marietta Materials Inc .... E 580 326-9671
  Sawyer (G-8336)
▼ Thomsons Trenching Inc .... F 918 745-1030
  Tulsa (G-10936)
Youngman Rock Inc .... F 918 682-7070
  Muskogee (G-4759)

1429 Crushed & Broken Stone, NEC

Apac-Central .... G 918 534-1741
  Dewey (G-2016)
Cobble Rock and Stone LLC .... F 405 567-3552
  Prague (G-7923)
Hanson Aggregates Wrp Inc .... E 580 369-3773
  Davis (G-1985)
Hoskins Gypsum Company LLC ... F 580 274-3446
  Longdale (G-4124)
Kemp Stone Inc .... F 918 825-3370
  Pryor (G-7972)
Rock Producers Inc .... E 918 969-2100
  Bokoshe (G-754)
Souter Limestone and Mnrl LLC ... F 918 489-5589
  Gore (G-3252)
Texoma Materials .... G 580 367-2339
  Caddo (G-1237)
Third Rock Construction LLC .... G 918 429-2011
  McAlester (G-4340)

1442 Construction Sand & Gravel

Anna Lightle .... G 405 853-4530
  Hennessey (G-3445)
Arkhola Sand & Gravel Co .... G 918 687-4771
  Muskogee (G-4650)
Arkhola Sand & Gravel Co .... G 918 456-2683
  Tahlequah (G-8850)
Arkhola Sand & Gravel Co Tahle .. G 918 456-6121
  Park Hill (G-7640)
B B Sand and Gravel .... G 405 944-1163
  Paden (G-7632)
Bosendorfer Oil Company .... G 405 604-9025
  Oklahoma City (G-5622)
Brandon Hyde .... G 405 919-4520
  Goldsby (G-3244)
Cardinal Fg Minerals LLC .... E 580 367-2123
  Coleman (G-1793)
Clements Sand Gravel & Excavat .. G 580 465-4191
  Ardmore (G-268)
Collins Cnstr Fabrications LLC ..... G 918 522-4855
  Talihina (G-8906)
Covia Holdings Corporation .... E 580 456-7772
  Roff (G-8107)
Dereks Pit LLC .... G 405 485-2562
  Blanchard (G-710)
▲ Dolese Bros Co .... C 405 235-2311
  Oklahoma City (G-5957)
Dolese Bros Co .... E 405 670-9626
  Oklahoma City (G-5962)
Double D Sand and Gravel LLC ... G 405 207-8050
  Stratford (G-8804)
Doug Troxell .... G 405 387-3574
  Newcastle (G-4824)
Elm Creek Gravel LLC .... G 405 360-7300
  Norman (G-4990)
Evans & Associates Entps Inc ..... E 580 765-6693
  Ponca City (G-7828)
Gravel Group LLC .... G 405 359-4932
  Edmond (G-2443)
Gravel Road LLC .... G 918 766-6368
  Bartlesville (G-488)
Heady Trucking .... G 580 326-2739
  Sawyer (G-8334)
Holliday Sand & Gravel Co .... G 918 486-1413
  Coweta (G-1885)
Holliday Sand Gravel Co LLC .... G 918 369-8850
  Bixby (G-632)
Jr Sand & Gravel Inc .... G 405 474-8730
  Edmond (G-2474)
K and G Sand & Gravel LLC .... G 580 369-2244
  Davis (G-1987)
Keystone Sand & Gravel .... G 918 241-0415
  Sand Springs (G-8198)
Kline Materials Inc .... F 580 256-2062
  Woodward (G-11603)
Lattimore Materials Company LP .. F 580 276-4631
  Marietta (G-4208)
Lawton Transit Mix Inc .... G 580 569-4333
  Snyder (G-8582)
Lightfoot Ready Mix LLC .... G 405 714-5539
  Perkins (G-7720)
Mark C Blakley .... G 405 245-3606
  Oklahoma City (G-6526)
Meridian Contracting Inc .... D 405 928-5959
  Norman (G-5072)
Micheal T Robinson .... G 580 767-9414
  Ponca City (G-7851)
▲ Minick Materials Company .... E 405 789-2068
  Oklahoma City (G-6616)
Mohawk Materials Co Inc .... G 918 584-2707
  Tulsa (G-10295)
Muskie Proppant LLC .... G 405 233-3558
  Oklahoma City (G-6638)
Muskogee Sand Company Inc ..... G 918 683-1766
  Porter (G-7894)
Nancy W Gravel .... G 405 348-4409
  Edmond (G-2528)
Oklahoma Aztec Co Inc .... G 405 784-2475
  Asher (G-393)
Perkins Sand LLC .... G 405 240-7870
  Carney (G-1279)
Pryor Sand & Redi-Mix Inc .... G 918 484-2150
  Whitefield (G-11517)
Rcr Construction .... G 918 682-9033
  Muskogee (G-4742)
Redline Constructn Sand Dirt .... G 405 380-6994
  Wewoka (G-11509)
Sand Run LLC .... G 918 296-3205
  Tulsa (G-10703)
Southern Boys Clay Gravel LLC ... G 580 584-6711
  Broken Bow (G-1208)
Southwestern State Sand Corp .... E 580 569-4333
  Snyder (G-8584)
Stanton Sand & Gravel Inc .... G 580 229-3353
  Ardmore (G-363)
Summit Sand & Gravel LLC .... G 405 256-6029
  Mustang (G-4797)
Technisand Inc .... D 580 456-7791
  Roff (G-8112)
TNT Sand & Gravel LLC .... G 580 277-0640
  Ardmore (G-372)
Two Brothers Sand Grave .... G 405 923-6762
  Yukon (G-11797)
V5 Contracting LLC .... G 918 720-4675
  Claremore (G-1699)
Vickers Sand and Gravel .... G 405 573-1989
  Norman (G-5195)
Watkins Sand Co .... E 918 369-5238
  Bixby (G-671)

1446 Industrial Sand

Badger Mining Corporation .... G 608 864-1157
  Erick (G-3085)

14 MINING AND QUARRYING OF NONMETALLIC MINERALS, EXCEPT FUELS

Cardinal Industries LLC .... G 918 299-0396
  Tulsa *(G-9375)*
Covia Holdings Corporation .... E 580 456-7772
  Roff *(G-8107)*
Fairmount Minerals .... G 580 303-9160
  Elk City *(G-2814)*
Mohawk Materials Co Inc .... G 918 584-2707
  Tulsa *(G-10295)*
Taylor Frac LLC .... E 405 293-4208
  Oklahoma City *(G-7259)*
Timco Blasting & Coatings .... E 918 367-1700
  Bristow *(G-799)*
Timco Blasting & Coatings .... F 918 605-1179
  Bristow *(G-800)*
Timco Blasting & Coatings .... G 918 605-1179
  Stroud *(G-8823)*
Timco Blasting & Coatings .... G 918 605-1179
  Bristow *(G-801)*
Timco Blasting & Coatings .... F 918 608-1179
  Stroud *(G-8824)*

1455 Kaolin & Ball Clay

JM Huber Corporation .... C 580 584-7002
  Broken Bow *(G-1194)*

1475 Phosphate Rock

D and M Resources Inc .... G 405 375-4602
  Kingfisher *(G-3795)*

1479 Chemical & Fertilizer Mining

Ovintiv Exploration Inc .... G 580 243-4101
  Elk City *(G-2857)*

1481 Nonmetallic Minerals Svcs, Except Fuels

Kully Chaha Native Stone LLC .... G 918 654-3005
  Cameron *(G-1258)*
Myers & Myers Inc .... G 405 341-5861
  Edmond *(G-2524)*
Pats Phase II Hair & Nail Sln .... G 405 232-4746
  Oklahoma City *(G-6811)*
Stoney Point Mine .... G 580 362-3916
  Newkirk *(G-4853)*
▼ Trans-Tel Central Inc .... C 405 447-5025
  Norman *(G-5180)*

1499 Miscellaneous Nonmetallic Mining

Allied Custom Gypsum .... F 580 337-6371
  Waynoka *(G-11370)*
Diamond Gypsum LLC .... G 580 623-2868
  Watonga *(G-11345)*
Greenhill Materials LLC .... F 918 274-6560
  Owasso *(G-7572)*
▲ Harrison Gypsum LLC .... F 405 366-9500
  Norman *(G-5018)*
Harrison Gypsum LLC .... E 580 994-6048
  Mooreland *(G-4591)*
Harrison Gypsum LLC .... F 580 994-6050
  Mooreland *(G-4592)*
Harrison Gypsum Holdings LLC ...... C 405 366-9500
  Norman *(G-5019)*
Noble Acquisition LLC .... G 405 872-5660
  Noble *(G-4887)*
Schweitzer Gypsum & Lime .... G 405 263-7967
  Okarche *(G-5251)*
Tulsa Auto Core .... G 918 584-5899
  Tulsa *(G-10986)*

20 FOOD AND KINDRED PRODUCTS

2011 Meat Packing Plants

Alex Rogers .... G 405 677-2306
  Oklahoma City *(G-5412)*
B & B Butlers Custom Process .... G 580 795-2667
  Madill *(G-4144)*
Barnsdall Meat Processors Inc .... G 918 847-2814
  Barnsdall *(G-436)*
Bob Mc Kinney & Sons .... G 918 387-2401
  Cushing *(G-1924)*
Browns Meat Processing .... G 405 379-2979
  Holdenville *(G-3550)*
Butchs Processing Plant Inc .... G 405 382-2833
  Seminole *(G-8361)*
Cable Meat Center Inc .... F 580 658-6646
  Marlow *(G-4224)*
Circle D Meat .... G 580 921-5500
  Laverne *(G-3876)*

Cook Processing .... G 918 542-5796
  Miami *(G-4392)*
Country Home Meat Company .... G 405 341-0267
  Edmond *(G-2368)*
Cuts Custom Butchering LLC .... G 918 534-1382
  Dewey *(G-2019)*
Don Regier .... G 580 772-3510
  Weatherford *(G-11405)*
Double D Foods Inc .... F 405 245-8909
  Oklahoma City *(G-5970)*
Food Svcs Auth of Quapaw Tribe .... F 918 542-1853
  Quapaw *(G-8030)*
Fort Cobb Locker Plant .... G 405 643-2355
  Fort Cobb *(G-3171)*
Four State Meat Processing LLC .... F 918 783-5556
  Big Cabin *(G-604)*
Gage Locker Service .... G 580 923-7661
  Gage *(G-3210)*
Hilltop Custom Processing .... G 405 527-7048
  Lexington *(G-4035)*
Janice Sue Daniel .... G 580 237-2695
  Enid *(G-2981)*
Janice Sue Daniel .... G 580 233-8666
  Enid *(G-2982)*
Kilgore Meat Processing Plant .... G 918 967-2613
  Stigler *(G-8635)*
Lawton Meat Processing .... G 580 353-6448
  Lawton *(G-3957)*
Lopez Foods Inc .... E 405 789-7500
  Oklahoma City *(G-6494)*
M & M Custom Butchering .... G 918 542-6421
  Miami *(G-4410)*
Mc Ferrons Quality Meats Inc .... F 918 273-2892
  Nowata *(G-5220)*
O H S N Inc .... G 580 248-1299
  Lawton *(G-3977)*
Okeen Motel .... G 580 822-4491
  Okeene *(G-5261)*
Prairie Rose Processing Inc .... G 405 224-6429
  Chickasha *(G-1500)*
Ralphs Packing Company .... E 405 547-2464
  Perkins *(G-7721)*
Ray Meat Market .... G 580 256-6031
  Woodward *(G-11627)*
Robertsons Hams Inc .... F 580 276-3395
  Marietta *(G-4211)*
Rowlands Proc & Cattle Co .... F 580 924-2560
  Durant *(G-2253)*
Sallee Meat Processing Inc .... G 405 282-1241
  Guthrie *(G-3336)*
Schones Butcher Shop & Market ..... G 580 472-3300
  Canute *(G-1270)*
Seaboard Corporation .... G 580 468-3790
  Guymon *(G-3362)*
Seaboard Farms Inc .... E 580 338-4900
  Guymon *(G-3363)*
Seaboard Foods LLC .... G 580 338-4900
  Guymon *(G-3365)*
Sooner Food Group LLC .... G 703 791-9069
  Newalla *(G-4816)*
Stinebrings Custom Processing ...... G 405 828-4247
  Dover *(G-2045)*
Temple Custom Slaughter & Proc ... G 580 342-5031
  Temple *(G-8936)*
Tenderette Steak Co Inc .... F 405 634-5655
  Oklahoma City *(G-7268)*
Thompsons Custom Butcher Barn ... G 918 476-5508
  Chouteau *(G-1572)*
Tonkawa Meat Processing .... G 580 628-4550
  Tonkawa *(G-8983)*
Tyson Foods Inc .... G 918 723-5091
  Westville *(G-11487)*
Tyson Foods Inc .... E 405 379-7241
  Holdenville *(G-3561)*
Unrau Meat Co Inc .... G 918 543-8245
  Inola *(G-3676)*
Victory Garden Homestead LLC ...... G 405 306-0308
  Blanchard *(G-744)*
W R Meat Co .... G 580 622-2494
  Sulphur *(G-8846)*
Walke Brothers Meats Inc .... G 918 341-3236
  Claremore *(G-1704)*
Weavers Meat Processing Inc .... G 918 647-9832
  Poteau *(G-7917)*

2013 Sausages & Meat Prdts

▲ Advance Food Company Inc .... C 800 969-2747
  Enid *(G-2905)*
Advance Food Company Inc .... A 580 237-6656
  Enid *(G-2906)*

Alex Rogers .... G 405 677-2306
  Oklahoma City *(G-5412)*
B & B Butlers Custom Process .... G 580 795-2667
  Madill *(G-4144)*
B&L Smoked Meats .... G 580 641-1677
  Marlow *(G-4222)*
Bar-S Foods Co .... A 580 331-1628
  Clinton *(G-1740)*
Bar-S Foods Co .... G 405 303-2138
  Seminole *(G-8357)*
Bar-S Foods Co .... C 580 821-5700
  Altus *(G-144)*
Bar-S Foods Co .... B 580 510-3300
  Lawton *(G-3896)*
Barnsdall Meat Processors Inc .... G 918 847-2814
  Barnsdall *(G-436)*
Big Ricks Jerky LLC .... G 405 414-9096
  Oklahoma City *(G-5565)*
Blue & Gold Sausage Inc .... G 405 399-2954
  Jones *(G-3742)*
Bob Mc Kinney & Sons .... G 918 387-2401
  Cushing *(G-1924)*
Bruce Packing Company Inc .... G 503 874-3000
  Durant *(G-2210)*
Bulldog Jerky Co .... G 580 479-5542
  Grandfield *(G-3256)*
Cable Meat Center Inc .... F 580 658-6646
  Marlow *(G-4224)*
Circle D Meat .... G 580 921-5500
  Laverne *(G-3876)*
Country Home Meat Company .... G 405 341-0267
  Edmond *(G-2368)*
Cuts Custom Butchering LLC .... G 918 534-1382
  Dewey *(G-2019)*
Davis Morgan International .... G 405 598-2380
  Macomb *(G-4141)*
Don Regier .... G 580 772-3510
  Weatherford *(G-11405)*
Double J Beef Jerky .... G 580 476-2465
  Rush Springs *(G-8120)*
Dustys Jerky LLC .... G 405 702-8016
  Oklahoma City *(G-5991)*
GOAT Beef Jerky Co LLC .... G 405 627-5096
  Oklahoma City *(G-6164)*
Goodtimes Beef Jerky .... G 405 387-5448
  Newcastle *(G-4829)*
Hardtimes Real Beef Jerky Inc .... E 580 497-7695
  El Reno *(G-2723)*
Hilltop Custom Processing .... G 405 527-7048
  Lexington *(G-4035)*
Janice Sue Daniel .... G 580 233-8666
  Enid *(G-2982)*
Jiggs Smokehouse .... G 580 323-5641
  Clinton *(G-1754)*
Kilgore Meat Processing Plant .... G 918 967-2613
  Stigler *(G-8635)*
Kormondy Enterprises Inc .... B 918 274-8787
  Owasso *(G-7584)*
Lopez Foods Inc .... B 405 499-0131
  Oklahoma City *(G-6493)*
Lopez Foods Inc .... E 405 789-7500
  Oklahoma City *(G-6494)*
Lopez Foods Inc .... B 405 789-7500
  Oklahoma City *(G-6495)*
M & M Custom Butchering .... G 918 542-6421
  Miami *(G-4410)*
Mc Ferrons Quality Meats Inc .... F 918 273-2892
  Nowata *(G-5220)*
McLane Foodservice Dist Inc .... C 405 632-0118
  Oklahoma City *(G-6549)*
Mikes Famous Beef Jerky .... G 405 414-7501
  Chickasha *(G-1489)*
National Steak Processors LLC ...... D 918 274-8787
  Owasso *(G-7596)*
No Mans Land Foods LLC .... D 580 297-5142
  Boise City *(G-748)*
OSteen Meat Specialties Inc .... D 405 236-1952
  Oklahoma City *(G-6787)*
Pine Cove Jerky LLC .... G 918 872-1138
  Broken Arrow *(G-1007)*
Prairie Rose Processing Inc .... G 405 224-6429
  Chickasha *(G-1500)*
Ray Meat Market .... G 580 256-6031
  Woodward *(G-11627)*
Ridleys Butcher Shop Inc .... G 580 255-9330
  Duncan *(G-2169)*
Robertsons Hams Inc .... F 580 276-3395
  Marietta *(G-4211)*
Rowlands Proc & Cattle Co .... F 580 924-2560
  Durant *(G-2253)*

Sallee Meat Processing Inc....G.... 405 282-1241
Guthrie *(G-3336)*
Seaboard Farms Inc....F.... 580 338-3311
Guymon *(G-3364)*
Slow N Low Smoked Meats....G.... 918 946-6894
Tulsa *(G-10775)*
Temple Custom Slaughter & Proc....G.... 580 342-5031
Temple *(G-8936)*
Thompsons Custom Butcher Barn....G.... 918 476-5508
Chouteau *(G-1572)*
Tonkawa Meat Processing....G.... 580 628-4550
Tonkawa *(G-8983)*
Unrau Meat Co Inc....G.... 918 543-8245
Inola *(G-3676)*
Walke Brothers Meats Inc....G.... 918 341-3236
Claremore *(G-1704)*

2015 Poultry Slaughtering, Dressing & Processing

▲ **Advance Food Company Inc**....C.... 800 969-2747
Enid *(G-2905)*
Advance Food Company Inc....A.... 580 237-6656
Enid *(G-2906)*
Bar-S Foods Co....A.... 580 331-1628
Clinton *(G-1740)*
Bar-S Foods Co....C.... 580 821-5700
Altus *(G-144)*
Dorada Poultry LLC....E.... 580 718-4700
Ponca City *(G-7822)*
Free Ranger LLC....C.... 918 253-4223
Jay *(G-3681)*
Kormondy Enterprises Inc....B.... 918 274-8787
Owasso *(G-7584)*
Liberty Free Range Poultry LLC....C.... 319 627-6000
Jay *(G-3682)*
O K Foods Inc....A.... 918 653-2819
Heavener *(G-3432)*
O K Foods Inc....B.... 918 427-7000
Muldrow *(G-4635)*
OSteen Meat Specialties Inc....D.... 405 236-1952
Oklahoma City *(G-6787)*
Rath Inc....F.... 580 588-3064
Apache *(G-221)*
Simmons Foods Inc....F.... 918 676-3285
Fairland *(G-3130)*
Simmons Foods Inc....G.... 918 791-0010
Grove *(G-3288)*
Tyson Foods Inc....E.... 918 723-5494
Westville *(G-11486)*
Tyson Foods Inc....A.... 580 584-9191
Broken Bow *(G-1211)*
Tyson Foods Inc....E.... 918 696-4530
Stilwell *(G-8796)*

2022 Cheese

Cheese Factory LLC....G.... 405 375-4004
Kingfisher *(G-3788)*
George E Christian....G.... 405 375-6711
Kingfisher *(G-3798)*
Los Quesitos De Mama LLC....G.... 312 276-2638
Edmond *(G-2495)*
Swan Brothers Dairy Inc....G.... 918 341-2069
Claremore *(G-1690)*
Tpl Arkoma Midstream LLC....G.... 918 574-3500
Tulsa *(G-10962)*
Watonga Cheese Plant....G.... 580 623-5915
Balko *(G-433)*

2023 Milk, Condensed & Evaporated

24 Hr Inc....G.... 844 370-1726
Weatherford *(G-11385)*
All Things Bugs LLC....G.... 352 281-3643
Oklahoma City *(G-5415)*
Biorite Acquisition Co LLC....G.... 405 701-1515
Norman *(G-4935)*
Juice Blendz Cafe....G.... 405 285-0133
Edmond *(G-2475)*
JW Nutritional LLC....G.... 214 221-0404
Broken Arrow *(G-953)*
Native Distributing LLC....D.... 405 316-9223
Norman *(G-5086)*
▲ **Natures Rx Inc**....G.... 405 484-7302
Paoli *(G-7638)*
Nucleic Products LLC....G.... 818 419-9176
Grove *(G-3283)*
Sanders Laboratories Inc....G.... 405 598-2131
Tecumseh *(G-8926)*
Ultra Botanica LLC....G.... 405 694-4175
Oklahoma City *(G-7359)*

2024 Ice Cream

Blue Bell Creameries LP....B.... 918 258-5100
Broken Arrow *(G-1113)*
C&K Inc....G.... 918 299-6307
Jenks *(G-3697)*
Hiland Dairy Foods Company LLC....B.... 405 258-3100
Chandler *(G-1380)*
J Mottos LLC....G.... 918 760-3866
Tulsa *(G-10021)*
M-O Masonry LLC....G.... 405 219-4220
Oklahoma City *(G-6512)*
Olh Moore LLC....G.... 405 703-0250
Moore *(G-4549)*
Scoozies Coneys & Frz Custard....G.... 918 396-1500
Skiatook *(G-8568)*
W H Braum Inc....E.... 405 340-9288
Edmond *(G-2678)*
Wiljackal LLC....F.... 918 252-2663
Tulsa *(G-11121)*

2026 Milk

Borden Dairy Company Texas LLC....G.... 405 232-7955
Oklahoma City *(G-5620)*
Dean Foods Company....G.... 918 587-2471
Tulsa *(G-9564)*
Hiland Dairy Foods Company LLC....B.... 405 258-3100
Chandler *(G-1380)*
Hiland Dairy Foods Company LLC....D.... 405 321-3191
Norman *(G-5023)*
James Porter Shorty....G.... 580 326-0592
Hugo *(G-3615)*
McAllister Farms....G.... 580 512-9009
Hollis *(G-3567)*
Passion Berri....G.... 405 310-6669
Norman *(G-5109)*
Southern Foods Group LLC....C.... 918 587-2471
Tulsa *(G-10799)*
Swan Brothers Dairy Inc....G.... 918 341-2069
Claremore *(G-1690)*

2032 Canned Specialties

Cable Meat Center Inc....F.... 580 658-6646
Marlow *(G-4224)*
Carls Chili Company Inc....G.... 918 227-1623
Tulsa *(G-8994)*
El Mojado....G.... 918 492-1138
Tulsa *(G-9650)*
Grannas LLC....F.... 580 337-6360
Bessie *(G-568)*
Head Country Inc....F.... 580 762-1227
Ponca City *(G-7835)*
Manila Foods....G.... 580 262-9900
Blackwell *(G-689)*
Polish Kitchen LLC....G.... 580 583-5970
Lawton *(G-3984)*
Rockin L-H Asparagus Farms....G.... 918 689-5086
Eufaula *(G-3111)*
S & S Foods Inc....F.... 405 256-6557
Mustang *(G-4792)*
Silas Salsa Company LLC....G.... 469 556-9762
Oklahoma City *(G-7139)*

2033 Canned Fruits, Vegetables & Preserves

Bequettes Gourmet Foods Inc....G.... 918 946-4212
Tulsa *(G-9284)*
Billy Sims Barbeque LLC....E.... 918 258-1978
Broken Arrow *(G-852)*
Blessettis Inc....G.... 918 830-5481
Tulsa *(G-9303)*
Claras Kitchen LLC....G.... 229 669-1493
Oklahoma City *(G-5772)*
Dewaynes Bbq Sauce Catering....G.... 580 363-3394
Newkirk *(G-4847)*
Dorians Foods Inc....G.... 580 658-3022
Marlow *(G-4229)*
Griffin Food Company....D.... 918 687-6311
Muskogee *(G-4683)*
Ju Ju Jams....G.... 918 230-6650
Tulsa *(G-10064)*
▲ **Leonard Mountain Inc**....E.... 800 822-7700
Tulsa *(G-10153)*
Maria Raes Inc....G.... 580 242-3342
Enid *(G-3005)*
Okie Ferments....G.... 405 310-9724
Oklahoma City *(G-6731)*
▲ **Pepper Creek Farms Inc**....G.... 580 536-1300
Lawton *(G-3982)*
Prairie Gypsies Inc....G.... 405 525-3013
Oklahoma City *(G-6873)*

Southern Okie LLC....G.... 405 657-7765
Edmond *(G-2625)*
Suans Inc....G.... 405 413-1751
Oklahoma City *(G-7220)*
Two Territories Trading Co LLC....G.... 580 679-4701
Duke *(G-2081)*

2034 Dried Fruits, Vegetables & Soup

Alfalfa Dehydrating Plant Inc....G.... 918 482-3267
Coweta *(G-1871)*
▲ **Leonard Mountain Inc**....E.... 800 822-7700
Tulsa *(G-10153)*

2035 Pickled Fruits, Vegetables, Sauces & Dressings

Backwoods Food Mfg Inc....F.... 918 458-9300
Tahlequah *(G-8851)*
Clements Foods Co....C.... 405 842-3308
Oklahoma City *(G-5783)*
Daddy Hinkles Inc....G.... 918 358-2129
Cleveland *(G-1721)*
Dorians Foods Inc....G.... 580 658-3022
Marlow *(G-4229)*
Griffin Food Company....D.... 918 687-6311
Muskogee *(G-4683)*
Hermans Chili Mix Inc....G.... 918 743-1832
Tulsa *(G-9925)*
Latimers Barbeque....G.... 918 425-1242
Tulsa *(G-10134)*
Maria Raes Inc....G.... 580 242-3342
Enid *(G-3005)*
▲ **Pepper Creek Farms Inc**....G.... 580 536-1300
Lawton *(G-3982)*
Pickles of Edmond Inc....G.... 405 285-4342
Edmond *(G-2568)*
Plainview Winery....G.... 580 796-2902
Lahoma *(G-3859)*

2037 Frozen Fruits, Juices & Vegetables

ICEE Company....G.... 405 685-7739
Oklahoma City *(G-6285)*

2038 Frozen Specialties

Guymon Extracts Inc....E.... 580 338-2624
Guymon *(G-3349)*
ICEE Company....G.... 800 423-3872
Tulsa *(G-9965)*
Sfc Global Supply Chain Inc....C.... 918 696-8325
Stilwell *(G-8795)*
Windsor Quality Food Co Ltd....G.... 918 628-0277
Tulsa *(G-11138)*

2041 Flour, Grain Milling

ADM Milling Co....D.... 580 237-8000
Enid *(G-2904)*
Archer-Daniels-Midland Company....D.... 580 237-8000
Enid *(G-2910)*
Archer-Daniels-Midland Company....G.... 580 652-3761
Hooker *(G-3595)*
Archer-Daniels-Midland Company....G.... 580 233-3800
Enid *(G-2911)*
Archer-Daniels-Midland Company....G.... 580 652-2623
Hooker *(G-3596)*
Archer-Daniels-Midland Company....G.... 580 854-6285
Tyrone *(G-11218)*
Archer-Daniels-Midland Company....G.... 580 233-5100
Enid *(G-2912)*
Archer-Daniels-Midland Company....G.... 580 482-7100
Altus *(G-143)*
▲ **Bama Companies Inc**....A.... 918 592-0778
Tulsa *(G-9258)*
▲ **Big v Feeds Inc**....D.... 918 423-1565
McAlester *(G-4276)*
Lanie Farms....G.... 580 694-2259
Manchester *(G-4168)*
Shawnee Milling Company....E.... 580 822-4415
Okeene *(G-5262)*
Shawnee Milling Company....G.... 405 263-4566
Okarche *(G-5252)*
Shawnee Milling Company....G.... 405 352-4336
Minco *(G-4481)*
Stockmans Mill & Grain Inc....G.... 918 762-3459
Pawnee *(G-7711)*
Value Added Products....D.... 580 327-0400
Alva *(G-195)*

SIC

20 FOOD AND KINDRED PRODUCTS SIC SECTION

2043 Cereal Breakfast Foods

Alan Ware .... G 918 658-5267
Paoli *(G-7637)*
Granola Shirts .... G 918 592-5477
Tulsa *(G-9846)*
Oatskc Granola Company LLC .... G 405 834-6159
Oklahoma City *(G-6709)*

2045 Flour, Blended & Prepared

Bama Cos Inc .... G 918 732-2640
Tulsa *(G-9259)*
Okie Dough LLC .... G 580 606-0142
Owasso *(G-7597)*

2046 Wet Corn Milling

Ingredion Incorporated .... G 539 292-4369
Tulsa *(G-9985)*

2047 Dog & Cat Food

▲ **Big v Feeds Inc** .... D 918 423-1565
McAlester *(G-4276)*
Blue Bonnet Feeds LP .... D 580 223-3010
Ardmore *(G-257)*
Dog Dish LLC .... G 918 624-2600
Tulsa *(G-9590)*
Farmers Co Op .... F 918 456-0557
Tahlequah *(G-8864)*
House Dog Industries LLC .... G 405 761-5576
El Reno *(G-2724)*
Mars Petcare Us Inc .... E 918 540-0045
Miami *(G-4412)*
Midwestern Pet Foods Inc .... F 405 224-2691
Chickasha *(G-1487)*
Mountain Country Foods LLC .... E 580 822-4130
Okeene *(G-5259)*
Nestle Purina Petcare Company .... D 405 751-4550
Edmond *(G-2535)*
Ralston Purina .... G 405 751-4550
Edmond *(G-2585)*
Rbs Pet Products .... G 405 373-0235
Piedmont *(G-7769)*
Red Collar Pet Foods Inc .... D 580 323-3359
Clinton *(G-1765)*
Win Hy Foods Inc .... F 918 227-0004
Tulsa *(G-9053)*

2048 Prepared Feeds For Animals & Fowls

AC Nutrition LP .... F 580 223-3900
Ardmore *(G-236)*
Advantage Supplements LLC .... G 866 226-9613
Hennessey *(G-3444)*
Alfalfa Dehydrating Plant Inc .... G 918 482-3267
Coweta *(G-1871)*
Allen Brothers Feed .... G 918 287-4379
Pawhuska *(G-7676)*
▲ **Big v Feeds Inc** .... D 918 423-1565
McAlester *(G-4276)*
Blue Bonnet Feeds LP .... D 580 223-3010
Ardmore *(G-257)*
Bobby Foster .... G 580 476-3417
Rush Springs *(G-8119)*
C & H Ranch .... G 918 479-8460
Locust Grove *(G-4105)*
Cargill Incorporated .... D 405 270-7011
Oklahoma City *(G-5698)*
Cargill Incorporated .... E 405 236-0525
Oklahoma City *(G-5699)*
Choska Alfalfa Mills LLC .... G 918 687-5805
Muskogee *(G-4660)*
Compass Unlimited Inc .... G 918 824-1644
Pryor *(G-7955)*
Custer Enterprises Inc .... F 580 371-9588
Mannsville *(G-4195)*
Custom Mser Lvstk Pre Mix Whse .... G 580 336-2053
Perry *(G-7729)*
Darling Ingredients Inc .... E 918 371-2528
Collinsville *(G-1808)*
Diane Barcheers .... G 918 649-0440
McAlester *(G-4293)*
Douglas A Pharr .... G 405 200-4983
Ninnekah *(G-4870)*
Dvm Nutrion Pets Corp Inc .... F 918 686-6111
Muskogee *(G-4668)*
Espiritu Miki .... G 405 213-5167
Oklahoma City *(G-6051)*
Eve Breathe .... G 918 454-2866
Pawnee *(G-7704)*
Farmers Co Op .... F 918 456-0557
Tahlequah *(G-8864)*
Farmers Coop .... F 580 772-3334
Weatherford *(G-11413)*
Fisher AG Enterprises Inc .... F 918 367-6382
Bristow *(G-778)*
Frontier Elevator Inc .... G 888 421-9400
Ada *(G-38)*
Griffin Industries LLC .... E 918 422-4790
Watts *(G-11357)*
Hanor Company of Wisconsin LLC .... E 580 237-3255
Enid *(G-2969)*
Hart Feeds Inc .... G 405 224-0102
Chickasha *(G-1468)*
Henderson Feeds LLC .... G 580 574-5375
Sayre *(G-8341)*
Hl Pro Feeds Inc .... F 580 497-2219
Cheyenne *(G-1425)*
Hitch Enterprises Inc .... G 580 338-6510
Hooker *(G-3597)*
Hollis Cotton Oil Mill Inc .... F 580 688-3394
Hollis *(G-3565)*
Hubbard .... G 918 785-2000
Adair *(G-110)*
▲ **Kfm Inc** .... F 580 342-6293
Temple *(G-8933)*
Luther Mill and Farm Supply .... G 405 277-3221
Luther *(G-4135)*
Marshall Minerals LLC .... G 405 848-5715
Oklahoma City *(G-6531)*
Mid America Farm & Ranch .... G 918 275-4984
Talala *(G-8900)*
Midwestern Pet Foods Inc .... F 405 224-2691
Chickasha *(G-1487)*
Mountain Country Foods LLC .... E 580 822-4130
Okeene *(G-5259)*
Nestle Purina Petcare Company .... D 405 751-4550
Edmond *(G-2535)*
O K Foods Inc .... A 918 653-1640
Heavener *(G-3431)*
Oklahoma Tool & Machine .... G 405 262-2624
El Reno *(G-2744)*
Purina Animal Nutrition LLC .... E 405 232-6171
Oklahoma City *(G-6925)*
Purina Mills LLC .... E 405 232-6171
Oklahoma City *(G-6926)*
Quality Liquid Feeds Inc .... G 918 683-7215
Muskogee *(G-4740)*
Red Seal Feeds LLC .... G 918 423-3710
McAlester *(G-4332)*
Rocky Farmers Cooperative Inc .... F 580 666-2440
Rocky *(G-8105)*
Rocky Farmers Cooperative Inc .... G 580 674-3356
Dill City *(G-2037)*
S & S Farm Center .... F 405 273-6907
Shawnee *(G-8491)*
Shawnee Milling Company .... G 405 352-4336
Minco *(G-4481)*
Spring Hollow Feed Mill Inc .... G 918 453-9933
Hulbert *(G-3628)*
Stillwater Milling Company LLC .... D 405 372-2766
Stillwater *(G-8757)*
Stockmans Mill & Grain Inc .... G 918 762-3459
Pawnee *(G-7711)*
Ultra Botanica LLC .... G 405 694-4175
Oklahoma City *(G-7359)*
W C Bradley Co .... G 918 379-6238
Claremore *(G-1703)*
West Texas By Products LP .... F 580 371-9413
Ravia *(G-8072)*
Westway Feed Products LLC .... G 918 266-5911
Catoosa *(G-1366)*
Winfield Solutions LLC .... G 580 237-2456
Enid *(G-3082)*
Wister Lake Feed Inc .... G 918 655-7954
Howe *(G-3601)*

2051 Bread, Bakery Prdts Exc Cookies & Crackers

Ambrosia Sweet Inc .... G 405 816-2887
Oklahoma City *(G-5429)*
Angela Lyn Sarabia .... G 405 808-8576
Oklahoma City *(G-5446)*
Antoinette Baking Co LLC .... G 918 808-0875
Tulsa *(G-9193)*
▲ **Bama Companies Inc** .... A 918 592-0778
Tulsa *(G-9258)*
Bama Foods Limited Partnership .... C 918 732-2399
Tulsa *(G-9260)*
Berryfields Cinnamon Roll LLC .... G 405 248-0777
Oklahoma City *(G-5558)*
Bimbo Bakeries Usa Inc .... G 580 234-1213
Enid *(G-2918)*
Bimbo Bakeries Usa Inc .... G 405 273-5049
Shawnee *(G-8432)*
Bimbo Bakeries Usa Inc .... B 405 556-2135
Oklahoma City *(G-5569)*
Browns Bakery Inc .... E 405 232-0363
Oklahoma City *(G-5637)*
Bubble Bee Bakery and Supplies .... G 918 209-8658
Tulsa *(G-9347)*
Cakes & More .... G 918 649-0451
Poteau *(G-7899)*
Cloverleaf Baking Co .... G 612 708-8196
Bartlesville *(G-466)*
Cupcakes & Sweets Galore .... G 405 641-7760
Oklahoma City *(G-5870)*
Cupcakes By Lu .... G 918 671-0599
Bixby *(G-619)*
Da Bomb Cupcakes .... G 918 261-3595
Tulsa *(G-9543)*
Dandee Donuts .... G 580 332-7700
Ada *(G-30)*
Dandy Donuts .... G 580 924-7872
Durant *(G-2220)*
Daylight Donuts .... G 918 256-6236
Vinita *(G-11252)*
Daylight Donuts .... G 405 598-8707
Tecumseh *(G-8911)*
Daylight Donuts .... G 580 279-6560
Ada *(G-31)*
Daylight Donuts Inc .... G 405 359-9016
Edmond *(G-2384)*
Dizzy Lizzy Cupcakery LLC .... G 405 263-7667
Okarche *(G-5242)*
Donut Shop .... G 580 276-3910
Marietta *(G-4206)*
Dounut Palace .... G 405 527-5746
Purcell *(G-8006)*
Felinis Cookies Inc .... G 918 742-3638
Tulsa *(G-9734)*
Flowers Baking Co Denton LLC .... G 405 366-2175
Norman *(G-5002)*
Flowers Bkg Co Lynchburg LLC .... G 918 270-1182
Tulsa *(G-9759)*
Flowers Foods Inc .... G 405 270-7880
Oklahoma City *(G-6093)*
Franklin Baking Company LLC .... G 918 423-2888
McAlester *(G-4300)*
Grahams Bakery & Cafe .... G 918 543-4244
Inola *(G-3659)*
J BS Donuts .... G 918 486-4022
Coweta *(G-1887)*
Jemison Denna .... G 405 922-7830
Oklahoma City *(G-6356)*
Key To Natures Blessings LLC .... G 405 603-8200
Bethany *(G-585)*
Krispy Kreme .... G 918 294-5293
Tulsa *(G-10103)*
Legend Enterprises Inc .... G 405 340-0410
Edmond *(G-2486)*
Mc Alester Food Warehouse .... D 580 436-4302
Ada *(G-64)*
Mitchells Sausage Rolls .... G 918 342-5852
Claremore *(G-1657)*
Morgans Bakery .... G 918 456-3731
Tahlequah *(G-8875)*
Nut House .... G 918 266-1604
Claremore *(G-1664)*
O K Country Donut Shoppe .... G 918 493-6455
Tulsa *(G-10371)*
Order Here Tulsa LLC .... G 888 633-9905
Muskogee *(G-4728)*
Panderia La Guadalupana .... G 918 764-9000
Tulsa *(G-10459)*
Paradise Doughnuts .... G 405 224-2907
Chickasha *(G-1499)*
Precious Memories By M L .... G 405 427-7007
Oklahoma City *(G-6878)*
Quality Bakery Products LLC .... F 609 871-7393
Tulsa *(G-10590)*
Raymonds Donut Shop .... G 918 660-0644
Tulsa *(G-10622)*
Saskas Sweets .... G 580 772-3476
Weatherford *(G-11438)*
Sfc Global Supply Chain Inc .... C 918 696-8325
Stilwell *(G-8795)*
Sophisticated Sweets Inc .... G 580 704-8038
Cache *(G-1231)*
Sweet Memories By Heather LLC .... G 360 608-1600
Cushing *(G-1963)*

SIC SECTION 20 FOOD AND KINDRED PRODUCTS

Sweetiesrite Baking....G....405 400-6581
Oklahoma City (G-7236)
Tower Cafe Inc....F....405 263-4853
Okarche (G-5255)
Tulsa Baking Inc....D....918 712-2918
Tulsa (G-10988)
Tulsa Baking Inc....E....918 747-2301
Tulsa (G-10989)

2052 Cookies & Crackers

Billy Goat Ice Cream Co LLC....G....405 332-5508
Stillwater (G-8660)
Dandee Donuts....G....580 332-7700
Ada (G-30)
Fehr Foods Inc....E....580 276-4100
Marietta (G-4207)
Felinis Cookies Inc....G....918 742-3638
Tulsa (G-9734)
Masons Pecans & Peanuts Inc....G....405 329-7828
Norman (G-5065)
Nonnis Foods LLC....D....918 621-1200
Tulsa (G-10348)
Pure Creativity LLC....G....918 272-3152
Owasso (G-7605)
Treehouse Private Brands Inc....C....270 365-5505
Poteau (G-7915)
Tulsa Baking Inc....D....918 712-2918
Tulsa (G-10988)
Tulsa Baking Inc....E....918 747-2301
Tulsa (G-10989)

2053 Frozen Bakery Prdts

▲ Bama Companies Inc....A....918 592-0778
Tulsa (G-9258)
Bama Pie Ltd....A....918 592-0778
Tulsa (G-9261)
Enchanted Delights LLC....G....405 202-5782
Oklahoma City (G-6034)
Fields Inc....E....405 238-7381
Pauls Valley (G-7659)
Nonnis Foods LLC....D....918 621-1200
Tulsa (G-10348)

2064 Candy & Confectionery Prdts

Amazing Grace Fudge LLC....G....580 883-4693
Ringwood (G-8083)
Aucora Breakfast Bar Backyard....G....405 609-8854
Oklahoma City (G-5488)
Big Easy....G....918 493-6280
Tulsa (G-9289)
Castle Rock Kitchens....G....405 751-1822
Oklahoma City (G-5709)
Cotton Candi Creations LLC....G....580 471-6550
Altus (G-151)
Fudgenomics 101 LLC....G....405 401-3832
Norman (G-5004)
Jackson Holdings LLC....G....405 842-8903
Oklahoma City (G-6343)
Ladybugs and Lollipops LLC....G....405 919-8555
Guthrie (G-3322)
Masons Pecans & Peanuts Inc....G....405 329-7828
Norman (G-5065)
Mollycoddled Hash Slinger LLC....G....918 236-1196
Fort Gibson (G-3176)
Nutopia Nuts & More....G....405 663-2330
Hydro (G-3633)
Peanut Products Co Inc....F....580 296-4888
Calera (G-1243)
Woody Candy Company Inc....G....405 842-8903
Oklahoma City (G-7468)
Zoo Too....G....580 250-1088
Lawton (G-4026)

2066 Chocolate & Cocoa Prdts

Castle Rock Kitchens....G....405 751-1822
Oklahoma City (G-5709)
Chickasaw Nation....G....405 331-2300
Davis (G-1980)
▲ Executive Coffee Service Co....D....405 236-3932
Oklahoma City (G-6059)
Godiva Chocolatier Inc....G....918 459-2635
Tulsa (G-9837)
Nut House....G....918 266-1604
Claremore (G-1664)

2068 Salted & Roasted Nuts & Seeds

Gunter Peanut Co....E....405 656-2398
Binger (G-606)
Joa Inc....G....580 367-2616
Caddo (G-1236)
Masons Pecans & Peanuts Inc....G....405 329-7828
Norman (G-5065)
Nutopia Nuts & More....G....405 663-2330
Hydro (G-3633)
Peanut Products Co Inc....F....580 296-4888
Calera (G-1243)
Red River Cold Storage LLC....G....580 795-9948
Madill (G-4161)

2074 Cottonseed Oil Mills

Producers Cooperative Oil Mill....G....405 232-7555
Oklahoma City (G-6909)

2075 Soybean Oil Mills

Koko-Best Inc....G....918 836-2400
Tulsa (G-10099)
Solae LLC....E....918 476-5825
Pryor (G-7991)

2077 Animal, Marine Fats & Oils

Darling Ingredients Inc....E....918 371-2528
Collinsville (G-1808)
Griffin Industries LLC....E....918 422-4790
Watts (G-11357)
Oklahoma Heartland Inc....G....918 914-3124
Stillwater (G-8732)

2079 Shortening, Oils & Margarine

Davis Hudson Inc....G....405 203-0604
Edmond (G-2383)
Rock Oil Co....G....918 357-1188
Broken Arrow (G-1157)

2082 Malt Beverages

Azimuth Spirits LLC....G....317 468-3931
Norman (G-4922)
Back Alley Brewers & More LLC....G....580 716-2571
Ponca City (G-7799)
Bb2 LLC....G....918 895-7878
Tulsa (G-9274)
Bb2 LLC....G....405 726-8300
Edmond (G-2319)
Bb2 LLC....E....405 232-2739
Oklahoma City (G-5534)
Brewer Media LLC....G....405 236-4143
Oklahoma City (G-5626)
Choc Brewing Company Inc....G....918 302-3002
McAlester (G-4282)
Dulaneys Liquor Store....G....405 377-9007
Stillwater (G-8679)
Ed F Davis Inc....G....580 265-4210
Stonewall (G-8800)
Krebs Brewing Co Inc....F....918 740-9293
Tulsa (G-10101)
Krebs Brewing Co Inc....F....918 488-8910
Tulsa (G-10102)
Stillwater Brewing Company LLC....G....405 614-2520
Stillwater (G-8756)
Union Brewers....G....405 604-8989
Oklahoma City (G-7360)

2084 Wine & Brandy

Allen Vineyards LLC....G....405 240-7147
Bethany (G-572)
B&G Meadery LLC....G....580 272-7197
Stonewall (G-8797)
Billy J Vineyard....G....918 246-2139
Sand Springs (G-8167)
Blue Coyote Winery....G....918 785-4727
Adair (G-107)
Boardwalk Distribution Co....F....918 551-6275
Tulsa (G-9313)
Broken Bone Vnyards Winery LLC....G....405 585-8319
McLoud (G-4354)
Canadian Rver Vnyrds Wnery LLC....G....405 872-5565
Lexington (G-4034)
Canyon Lakes Winery LLC....G....405 367-7291
Oklahoma City (G-5690)
Coyote Run Vineyard LLC....G....918 785-4727
Adair (G-108)
Deangel Farms & Winery LLC....G....405 996-0914
Blanchard (G-709)
Deep Branch Winery LLC....G....918 519-5490
Cookson (G-1850)
Diane E Dean....G....580 775-4203
Caddo (G-1233)
Dynamic Brands Inc....G....918 630-7083
Broken Arrow (G-1123)
Entwined Vines Winery LLC....G....405 320-0452
Anadarko (G-203)
Fish Tale Winery....G....580 494-6115
Broken Bow (G-1190)
Frozen Mesa Winery LLC....G....405 281-5962
Choctaw (G-1543)
Girls Gone Wine....E....580 494-6243
Broken Bow (G-1191)
Grayfox Vineyards LLC....G....918 378-2214
Yukon (G-11728)
Ingels Vineyard LLC....G....405 321-1008
Norman (G-5034)
Iron Post Winery LLC....G....918 479-3600
Locust Grove (G-4111)
Island Palm LLC....G....405 321-1056
Norman (G-5038)
J & B Deep Discount....G....918 622-7600
Tulsa (G-10016)
Joullian Vineyards Ltd....E....405 848-4585
Oklahoma City (G-6386)
Judy Tomlinson....G....580 252-2559
Duncan (G-2140)
Knotted Rope Winery LLC....G....918 839-1464
Broken Bow (G-1197)
Legends Vineyard & Winery....G....405 823-8265
Lindsay (G-4073)
Native Spirits Winery LLC....G....405 329-9942
Norman (G-5087)
Nellis Vineyards LLC....G....405 826-5279
Edmond (G-2532)
New Moon Vineyard....G....405 364-8655
Norman (G-5090)
Nuyaka Creek Winery LLC....G....918 756-8485
Bristow (G-790)
Pecan Creek Winery LLC....G....918 683-1087
Muskogee (G-4733)
Plainview Winery....G....580 796-2902
Lahoma (G-3859)
Plymouth Valley Cellars Inc....G....580 227-0348
Fairview (G-3146)
Ramiiisol Vineyards LLC....G....405 858-9800
Oklahoma City (G-6969)
Rocky Top Winery LLC....G....580 857-2869
Allen (G-138)
Rusty Nail Winery....G....580 622-8466
Sulphur (G-8842)
Sailing Horse Enterprises LLC....G....918 618-4824
Eufaula (G-3112)
Sand Hill Vineyards LLC....G....405 760-1268
Calumet (G-1248)
Shell Creek Vineyards LLC....G....214 415-4741
Yukon (G-11781)
Sine Qua Non LLC....G....405 478-2539
Oklahoma City (G-7142)
Sparks Vineyard & Winery Inc....G....918 866-2529
Sparks (G-8589)
Stableridge LLC....F....918 968-2568
Stroud (G-8819)
Strebel Creek Vineyard....G....405 720-7779
Oklahoma City (G-7217)
Summerside Vineyards & Winery....F....918 256-3000
Tuttle (G-11212)
Summerside Winery & Meadery....G....405 514-6360
Tuttle (G-11213)
Territory Cellars LLC....G....918 987-1800
Stroud (G-8822)
Tidal School Winery....G....918 352-4900
Drumright (G-2076)
Trio Di Vino LLC....F....405 494-1954
Oklahoma City (G-7336)
Twiss Sueons Winery Inc....E....405 277-7089
Luther (G-4140)
Waddell Vineyards LLC....G....580 421-6933
Ada (G-103)
Waters Edge Winery On Rose....G....918 286-0086
Broken Arrow (G-1092)
Whispering Vines Vinyrd Winery....G....918 447-0808
Tulsa (G-11116)
Whispring Mdows Vnyards Winery....G....918 423-9463
McAlester (G-4351)
Woodland Park Vineyards....G....405 743-2442
Stillwater (G-8776)
Woods and Waters Holdings LLC....F....405 347-3000
Anadarko (G-210)
Woods Wters Wnery Vneyards LLC....G....405 247-3000
Anadarko (G-211)
Yippee Ay-O-K Winery....G....580 515-8214
Clinton (G-1773)

SIC

Employee Codes: A=Over 500 employees, B=251-500
C=101-250, D=51-100, E=20-50, F=10-19, G=1-9
2020 Oklahoma Directory
of Manufacturers & Processors
427

20 FOOD AND KINDRED PRODUCTS SIC SECTION

2085 Liquors, Distilled, Rectified & Blended

19th Hole ....G....... 405 424-0520
Oklahoma City *(G-5328)*
Green Valley Distillery LLC ....G....... 918 413-5199
Red Oak *(G-8076)*
Oklahoma Distilling Company ....G....... 918 505-4861
Tulsa *(G-10397)*
Rock Creek Distillery LLC ....G....... 580 254-1407
Shattuck *(G-8423)*
Scissortail Distillery LLC ....G....... 405 326-5466
Moore *(G-4565)*
Twisters Distillery ....G....... 405 237-3499
Moore *(G-4580)*

2086 Soft Drinks

7 Up Bottle ....G....... 918 426-0310
McAlester *(G-4268)*
Ada Coca Cola Bottling Company ....D....... 580 427-2000
Ada *(G-3)*
All American Bottling Cor ....G....... 918 831-3800
Tulsa *(G-9135)*
American Bottling Company ....D....... 405 680-5150
Oklahoma City *(G-5433)*
Belle Point Beverages Inc ....G....... 918 649-3921
Poteau *(G-7896)*
Browne Bottling Co Inc ....F....... 405 232-1158
Oklahoma City *(G-5636)*
Coca Cola Bottling Co ....G....... 580 256-2350
Woodward *(G-11570)*
Coca-Cola Enterprises Inc ....G....... 918 619-8200
Tulsa *(G-9464)*
Dr Pepper Bottling Co ....G....... 580 256-2350
Woodward *(G-11580)*
Dr Pepper Bottling Co Elk City ....F....... 580 225-3186
Elk City *(G-2804)*
Dr Pepper Co ....G....... 580 765-6468
Ponca City *(G-7823)*
Dr Pepper Snapple Group ....G....... 405 680-5150
Oklahoma City *(G-5978)*
Dr Pepper-Royal Crown Btlg Co ....F....... 405 224-1260
Chickasha *(G-1453)*
Dust Cutter ....E....... 405 615-7788
Norman *(G-4985)*
Fresh Promise Foods Inc ....G....... 561 703-4659
Midwest City *(G-4441)*
Great Plains Coca Cola Btlg Co ....G....... 405 503-9328
Oklahoma City *(G-6178)*
Great Plains Coca Cola Btlg Co ....B....... 405 280-2000
Oklahoma City *(G-6179)*
Great Plains Coca-Cola Btlg Co ....D....... 918 439-3013
Tulsa *(G-9853)*
Great Plains Coca-Cola Btlg Co ....D....... 405 280-2000
Oklahoma City *(G-6180)*
Great Plains Coca-Cola Btlg Co ....C....... 405 280-2700
Oklahoma City *(G-6181)*
Great Plains Coca-Cola Btlg Co ....C....... 800 753-2653
Tulsa *(G-9854)*
Great Plains Design ....G....... 405 943-9018
Oklahoma City *(G-6182)*
Hometown Bottled Water LLC ....G....... 918 786-4426
Grove *(G-3274)*
Ice-T King LLC ....G....... 405 206-1185
Oklahoma City *(G-6284)*
Lake Country Beverage Inc ....G....... 918 426-0310
McAlester *(G-4313)*
Minnette Company Ltd ....G....... 580 226-2929
Wilson *(G-11538)*
Niagara Bottling LLC ....G....... 909 230-5000
Oklahoma City *(G-6677)*
P-Americas LLC ....G....... 580 326-8333
Hugo *(G-3617)*
Pepsi Cola Btlg Clinton Okla ....E....... 580 323-1666
Clinton *(G-1763)*
Pepsi Cola Company ....B....... 918 446-6601
Tulsa *(G-10489)*
Pepsi-Cola Btlg McAlester Inc ....E....... 918 423-2360
McAlester *(G-4328)*
Pepsi-Cola Btlg McAlester Inc ....G....... 918 446-6601
Tulsa *(G-10490)*
Pepsi-Cola Metro Btlg Co Inc ....C....... 580 326-8333
Hugo *(G-3618)*
Pepsi-Cola Metro Btlg Co Inc ....E....... 580 585-6281
Lawton *(G-3983)*
Pure Mountain ....G....... 918 254-2225
Broken Arrow *(G-1014)*
R W D 9 Mayes County ....G....... 918 434-5000
Salina *(G-8135)*
Round Springs Water Co LLC ....G....... 918 253-8188
Spavinaw *(G-8592)*
Seven-Up Bottling Co Inc ....F....... 580 765-6468
Ponca City *(G-7874)*
Sooner Coca-Cola Bottling Co ....G....... 918 423-0911
Mc Alester *(G-4266)*
Total Beverage Services LLC ....G....... 405 366-1344
Norman *(G-5177)*
Vita-Source Inc ....G....... 918 407-9525
Sand Springs *(G-8235)*

2087 Flavoring Extracts & Syrups

Arctic Blends Corporation ....G....... 918 455-2079
Broken Arrow *(G-832)*
Big Rock Foods LLC ....G....... 405 269-8558
Stillwater *(G-8659)*
◆ Cesi Chemical Inc ....B....... 580 658-6608
Marlow *(G-4225)*
Griffin Food Company ....D....... 918 687-6311
Muskogee *(G-4683)*
Margarita Man Hq LLC ....G....... 830 336-4252
Stillwater *(G-8721)*
Midwest Bakers Supply Co Inc ....G....... 405 942-3489
Oklahoma City *(G-6599)*
▲ Pepper Creek Farms Inc ....G....... 580 536-1300
Lawton *(G-3982)*
Springdale Food Co Inc ....G....... 580 928-2598
Sayre *(G-8348)*
Webers Superior Root Beer Inc ....G....... 918 742-1082
Tulsa *(G-11101)*

2095 Coffee

Charlie Bean Coffee LLC ....F....... 405 376-4815
Oklahoma City *(G-5743)*
Compadres Trading Co ....G....... 405 816-9911
Oklahoma City *(G-5807)*
▲ Executive Coffee Service Co ....D....... 405 236-3932
Oklahoma City *(G-6059)*
Farmer Bros Co ....G....... 918 439-9262
Tulsa *(G-9728)*
Farmer Bros Co ....G....... 405 751-7222
Oklahoma City *(G-6074)*
Henderson Coffee Corp ....E....... 918 682-8751
Muskogee *(G-4690)*
Hillshire Brands Company ....C....... 405 751-7222
Oklahoma City *(G-6249)*
Imperial Inc ....F....... 580 357-8300
Lawton *(G-3940)*
Imperial LLC ....B....... 918 437-1300
Tulsa *(G-9972)*
Minnette Company Ltd ....G....... 580 226-2929
Wilson *(G-11538)*
Okie Roasters LLC ....G....... 405 699-2007
Guthrie *(G-3328)*
Royal Cup Inc ....G....... 405 943-6088
Oklahoma City *(G-7052)*
Tulsa Coffee Service Inc ....E....... 918 836-5570
Tulsa *(G-10993)*
Viridian Coffee LLC ....G....... 405 795-0773
Duncan *(G-2195)*

2096 Potato Chips & Similar Prdts

Tortilleria Lupita Inc ....G....... 405 232-2760
Oklahoma City *(G-7306)*

2097 Ice

Clinton Ice LLC ....F....... 580 331-6060
Clinton *(G-1746)*
Enterprise Ice Inc ....G....... 580 237-4015
Enid *(G-2955)*
Freeman Ice LLC ....G....... 580 263-0021
Madill *(G-4147)*
K-Dub LLC ....G....... 580 353-6899
Lawton *(G-3948)*
Reddy Ice Corporation ....F....... 918 682-2471
Muskogee *(G-4744)*
Reddy Ice Corporation ....E....... 405 681-2892
Oklahoma City *(G-6994)*
Reddy Ice Corporation ....E....... 580 323-3080
Clinton *(G-1766)*
Reddy Ice Corporation ....E....... 918 836-8223
Tulsa *(G-10633)*
Southeastern Ice ....E....... 918 465-2500
Wilburton *(G-11524)*
Sub Zero Ice Services LLC ....G....... 405 387-2224
Newcastle *(G-4843)*

2098 Macaroni, Spaghetti & Noodles

Pasta Pizzaz Inc ....G....... 405 848-9966
Oklahoma City *(G-6808)*

2099 Food Preparations, NEC

▲ Advance Food Company Inc ....C....... 800 969-2747
Enid *(G-2905)*
Advancepierre Foods Inc ....F....... 800 969-2747
Enid *(G-2907)*
Amigos Salsa ....G....... 580 224-0667
Ardmore *(G-239)*
Amigos Salsa ....G....... 580 224-1424
Ardmore *(G-240)*
Big Productions LLC ....G....... 405 513-6545
Edmond *(G-2321)*
Bishop Brothers ....G....... 918 367-2270
Bristow *(G-766)*
Campo Alegre Foods ....G....... 918 271-6775
Tulsa *(G-9368)*
Cecilias Salsas ....G....... 918 984-1491
Tulsa *(G-9392)*
Chelinos Tortilla Factory ....F....... 405 631-3188
Oklahoma City *(G-5747)*
Cimarron Docs Bar-B-Que Chili ....G....... 918 787-7881
Grove *(G-3261)*
Clements Foods Co ....G....... 405 842-3308
Oklahoma City *(G-5784)*
Designs By Lex LLC ....G....... 580 280-2557
Lawton *(G-3919)*
Du Pont Delaware Inc ....G....... 918 476-5825
Pryor *(G-7960)*
El Capora Tortilleria ....G....... 405 662-0427
Oklahoma City *(G-6014)*
Everyday Foods LLC ....G....... 918 299-7939
Jenks *(G-3705)*
▲ Executive Coffee Service Co ....D....... 405 236-3932
Oklahoma City *(G-6059)*
Gold Strike Chili ....G....... 405 606-1819
Warr Acres *(G-11320)*
Griffin Food Company ....D....... 918 687-6311
Muskogee *(G-4683)*
▲ Griffin Holdings Inc ....D....... 918 687-6311
Muskogee *(G-4684)*
H Gellar ....G....... 617 834-0602
Warr Acres *(G-11321)*
Hermans Chili Mix Inc ....G....... 918 743-1832
Tulsa *(G-9925)*
Hillshire Brands Company ....C....... 405 751-7222
Oklahoma City *(G-6249)*
Hollis Home Made Salsa LLC ....G....... 405 464-6249
Midwest City *(G-4442)*
J-M Farms Inc ....B....... 918 540-1567
Miami *(G-4409)*
JKJ Processing Inc ....G....... 405 606-9711
Yukon *(G-11736)*
Kize Concepts Inc ....F....... 405 226-0701
Oklahoma City *(G-6427)*
Maria Raes Inc ....G....... 580 242-3342
Enid *(G-3005)*
Markenia Foods LLC ....G....... 405 751-8616
Edmond *(G-2505)*
Matador Processing LLC ....E....... 405 485-3567
Blanchard *(G-722)*
Midwest Bakers Supply Co Inc ....G....... 405 942-3489
Oklahoma City *(G-6599)*
Nut House ....G....... 918 266-1604
Claremore *(G-1664)*
O K Foods Inc ....B....... 918 427-7000
Muldrow *(G-4635)*
Peanut Products Co Inc ....F....... 580 296-4888
Calera *(G-1243)*
▲ Pepper Creek Farms Inc ....G....... 580 536-1300
Lawton *(G-3982)*
▲ Pepper Land Inc ....G....... 918 691-7241
Tulsa *(G-10488)*
Pie In Sky Tulsa LLc ....G....... 918 527-5855
Tulsa *(G-10513)*
Premeir Companies Inc ....F....... 405 895-7100
Moore *(G-4555)*
Quality Bakery Products LLC ....F....... 609 871-7393
Tulsa *(G-10590)*
Quiktrip Corporation ....B....... 918 615-7700
Tulsa *(G-10599)*
R & J Food Tulsa LLC ....G....... 918 520-0484
Tulsa *(G-10600)*
Ross Honey Co ....G....... 405 352-4125
Minco *(G-4480)*
Royal Cup Inc ....G....... 405 943-6088
Oklahoma City *(G-7052)*
S and J Foods LLC ....E....... 580 337-6360
Bessie *(G-570)*
Sneaky Ts Salsa LLC ....G....... 405 323-7244
Piedmont *(G-7771)*

22 TEXTILE MILL PRODUCTS

Snider Farms Peanut Barn LLC .... G 580 471-3470
　Hollis *(G-3568)*
Springdale Food Co Inc .... G 580 928-2598
　Sayre *(G-8348)*
Tajour Specialty Products LLC .... G 479 684-7445
　Westville *(G-11485)*
Tortilla Velasquez .... G 580 468-6753
　Guymon *(G-3368)*
Tortilleria Azteca Inc .... G 405 632-5382
　Oklahoma City *(G-7305)*
Tortilleria Milagro .... G 918 895-8225
　Tulsa *(G-10956)*
Tortilleria Milargo .... G 918 439-9977
　Tulsa *(G-10957)*
Tortilleria Puebla Inc .... G 918 610-8816
　Tulsa *(G-10958)*
Twisted Oak Foods LLC .... G 405 720-7059
　Oklahoma City *(G-7353)*

21 TOBACCO PRODUCTS

2131 Tobacco, Chewing & Snuff

Handy Mart Inc .... G 580 254-5889
　Woodward *(G-11591)*
Osage Trading Co Inc .... G 918 287-4544
　Pawhuska *(G-7693)*
Tall Chief LLC .... G 918 783-8255
　Pryor *(G-7994)*
Treehouse Vapor Co LLC .... G 405 601-6867
　Oklahoma City *(G-7322)*

22 TEXTILE MILL PRODUCTS

2211 Cotton, Woven Fabric

8bit Canvas LLC .... G 405 924-3298
　Oklahoma City *(G-5340)*
Allys Discount Scrubs .... G 918 935-1359
　Broken Arrow *(G-826)*
Anything Canvas LLC .... G 580 658-9330
　Marlow *(G-4221)*
Awesome Acres Pacas Pyrs .... G 405 990-8205
　Oklahoma City *(G-5279)*
Bills Marine Canvas Upholstery .... G 405 306-2936
　Norman *(G-4931)*
Blue Canvas LLC .... G 580 327-3406
　Alva *(G-179)*
Boatman Marine Canvas .... G 405 628-7844
　Warr Acres *(G-11314)*
Burns & McDonnell Inc .... G 405 200-0300
　Oklahoma City *(G-5646)*
Canvas Sky Studios LLC .... G 917 514-9632
　Broken Arrow *(G-864)*
Clean Canvas Laser Tattoo Remo .... G 580 919-5466
　Lawton *(G-3906)*
Cliftton Wallcovering .... G 918 638-4454
　Broken Arrow *(G-870)*
Custom 4 X 4 Fabrication .... G 405 799-7599
　Oklahoma City *(G-5282)*
Dans Custom Canvas .... G 405 525-2419
　Oklahoma City *(G-5897)*
Dear John Denim Inc .... G 580 334-6637
　Oklahoma City *(G-5913)*
▲ Duncan Ticking Inc .... F 405 528-5480
　Oklahoma City *(G-5989)*
Faded Canvas Barber Studio .... G 405 735-7105
　Moore *(G-4521)*
Michael Sherry Alpert .... G 405 912-0062
　Oklahoma City *(G-5306)*
Paint On Canvas .... G 405 574-6689
　Chickasha *(G-1498)*
Rockin Dolls Denim .... G 918 402-6151
　Collinsville *(G-1822)*
S&S Canvas & Upholstery .... G 580 231-2587
　Ringwood *(G-8092)*
Sage Premium Denim Bar .... G 405 288-1503
　Goldsby *(G-3246)*
Salt Soothers LLC .... G 405 201-2020
　Edmond *(G-2610)*
Sooner Denim Inc .... G 405 641-4720
　Oklahoma City *(G-7161)*
Stroheim Romann Upholstery .... G 918 622-7700
　Tulsa *(G-10860)*
▲ Wohali Outdoors LLC .... F 918 343-3500
　Broken Arrow *(G-1100)*

2221 Silk & Man-Made Fiber

B B Fiberglass LLC .... G 405 755-5895
　Guthrie *(G-3298)*

Carter Fiberglass .... G 918 674-2325
　Quapaw *(G-8028)*
▲ Insul-Vest Inc .... G 918 445-2279
　Tulsa *(G-9992)*
Jacob Manufacturing Inc .... F 918 787-6606
　Grove *(G-3276)*
Jerry Beagley Braiding Company .... G 580 924-4995
　Calera *(G-1240)*
Okc Fabric Market .... G 405 531-0546
　Oklahoma City *(G-6729)*
Ray Harrington Draperies .... G 405 789-6710
　Bethany *(G-593)*
Rsga Incorporated .... G 918 978-6800
　Tulsa *(G-10681)*
Satin Siren LLC .... G 918 803-6351
　Pryor *(G-7990)*
Wing-It Concepts .... G 405 691-8053
　Oklahoma City *(G-5325)*

2231 Wool, Woven Fabric

Hooty Creek Alpacas .... G 918 284-5025
　Claremore *(G-1635)*
Icandee Refinishings LLC .... G 405 923-4956
　Oklahoma City *(G-6283)*
Jr Alpacas LLC .... G 405 771-2636
　Jones *(G-3749)*
Land Run Alpacas .... G 405 226-9005
　Agra *(G-126)*
Northwest Alpacas Ltd .... G 903 450-1999
　Edmond *(G-2542)*
Pendleton Woolen Mills Inc .... D 918 712-8545
　Tulsa *(G-10483)*
Storm Haven Alpaca LLC .... G 405 391-2767
　Choctaw *(G-1555)*

2241 Fabric Mills, Cotton, Wool, Silk & Man-Made

Central Texas Ex Metalwork LLC .... G 765 492-9058
　Oklahoma City *(G-5727)*
Dill City Embroidery .... G 580 674-3989
　Dill City *(G-2035)*
Jerry Beagley Braiding Company .... G 580 924-4995
　Calera *(G-1240)*
Mammoth Manufacturing Inc .... G 405 820-8301
　Bethany *(G-587)*

2252 Hosiery, Except Women's

Advanced Foot & Ankle .... G 405 692-7114
　Oklahoma City *(G-5382)*
Crazy Socks Productions Inc .... G 580 618-1228
　Sulphur *(G-8830)*
Sock Monkey Bizz LLC .... G 918 462-7392
　Wagoner *(G-11290)*
Sydnis Shag Socks .... G 405 664-5333
　Wellston *(G-11479)*
Two Socks LLC .... G 405 535-4753
　Norman *(G-5184)*

2253 Knit Outerwear Mills

Calamity Janes Funk & Junk Inc .... G 405 759-3383
　Oklahoma City *(G-5671)*
Gorfam Marketing Inc .... F 918 388-9935
　Tulsa *(G-9842)*
Kelly Loyd .... G 405 740-2345
　Ada *(G-55)*

2254 Knit Underwear Mills

House of Bedlam LLC .... G 405 946-3100
　Oklahoma City *(G-6266)*
Hyatt Ladona .... G 580 889-0199
　Atoka *(G-414)*
Uniquely Yours LLC .... G 918 283-2228
　Claremore *(G-1696)*

2259 Knitting Mills, NEC

E E Sewing Inc .... E 918 789-5881
　Chelsea *(G-1404)*

2261 Cotton Fabric Finishers

Body Billboards .... G 405 282-9922
　Guthrie *(G-3300)*
Fabricut Inc .... F 918 622-7700
　Tulsa *(G-9724)*
Hard Edge Design Inc .... F 405 360-9714
　Norman *(G-5016)*
Massive Graphic Screen Prtg .... F 405 364-3594
　Norman *(G-5066)*

Misaco Sign and Screen Prtg .... G 918 542-4188
　Miami *(G-4420)*

2262 Silk & Man-Made Fabric Finishers

Monograms Elite Inc .... G 580 353-1635
　Lawton *(G-3973)*
Promo Print 4 U LLC .... G 405 259-6721
　Oklahoma City *(G-6915)*
Semasys Inc .... E 405 525-2335
　Oklahoma City *(G-7107)*

2273 Carpets & Rugs

▲ Ahmadys Import LLC .... G 918 254-4094
　Tulsa *(G-9118)*
Aladdin Manufacturing Corp .... F 405 943-3037
　Oklahoma City *(G-5407)*
Brow Art 23 .... G 405 848-3346
　Oklahoma City *(G-5634)*
Burtco Enterprises LLC .... G 918 857-1293
　Catoosa *(G-1307)*
Classic Carpets Lawton Inc .... G 580 713-0653
　Lawton *(G-3904)*
Interfaceflor .... G 918 746-0501
　Tulsa *(G-10003)*
Kingston Flooring LLC .... G 405 470-3494
　Oklahoma City *(G-6423)*
Kinrich .... G 405 842-4307
　Oklahoma City *(G-6424)*
Mike McGills Carpet Inc .... G 405 222-0899
　Chickasha *(G-1488)*
Mohawk Industries .... G 214 309-4652
　Enid *(G-3015)*
Moss Seat Cover Mfg & Sls Co .... F 918 742-3326
　Tulsa *(G-10306)*
Oklahoma Interpak Inc .... E 918 687-1681
　Muskogee *(G-4724)*
▲ Triumph Arstrctres - Tulsa LLC .... A 615 361-2061
　Tulsa *(G-10978)*

2281 Yarn Spinning Mills

Gorfam Marketing Inc .... G 918 252-3733
　Tulsa *(G-9841)*

2284 Thread Mills

Boley One .... G 405 301-7692
　Oklahoma City *(G-5616)*

2295 Fabrics Coated Not Rubberized

▲ Clear Edge Filtration Inc .... D 918 984-6000
　Tulsa *(G-9447)*
Clear Edge Filtration Inc .... D 800 637-6206
　Tulsa *(G-9448)*
Cytec Industrial Mtls OK Inc .... G 918 252-3922
　Broken Arrow *(G-885)*
Leather Guns & Etc .... F 580 296-2616
　Colbert *(G-1785)*
Tatermash Oilcloth LLC .... G 918 743-3888
　Tulsa *(G-10901)*

2297 Fabrics, Nonwoven

Nxtnano LLC .... E 918 923-4824
　Claremore *(G-1665)*

2298 Cordage & Twine

Lynxsystems LLC .... S 918 728-6000
　Tulsa *(G-10185)*
Surface Mount Depot Inc .... D 405 948-8763
　Oklahoma City *(G-7232)*
Texhoma Fiber LLC .... G 918 747-7000
　Medicine Park *(G-4371)*

2299 Textile Goods, NEC

Mabels Fashion Alteration .... G 405 605-4558
　Oklahoma City *(G-6513)*
◆ Sooner Wiping Rags LLC .... F 405 670-3100
　Oklahoma City *(G-7168)*
▲ World Trading Company Inc .... A 405 787-1982
　Oklahoma City *(G-7471)*

23 APPAREL AND OTHER FINISHED PRODUCTS MADE FROM FABRICS AND SIMILAR MATERIAL

2311 Men's & Boys' Suits, Coats & Overcoats

Douglas Rose Custom Tailoring............G........ 918 366-6002
  Bixby *(G-620)*
Globe Mfg Company-OK LLC ....E........ 580 272-9400
  Ada *(G-43)*
Mobetta..G........ 580 588-9222
  Apache *(G-220)*
Sage Brush Junction ....G........ 580 227-3434
  Fairview *(G-3150)*
Synergy Maintenance LLC ....G........ 580 574-7355
  Lawton *(G-4009)*

2321 Men's & Boys' Shirts

Apex405 ....G........ 405 313-5145
  Norman *(G-4911)*
Emery Bay Corporation ....G........ 918 494-2988
  Tulsa *(G-9671)*
▲ Finish Line of Oklahoma Inc ....G........ 918 341-8291
  Claremore *(G-1621)*
Mobetta..G........ 580 588-9222
  Apache *(G-220)*
Slapsok LLC ....G........ 405 845-2299
  Edmond *(G-2622)*
Synergy Maintenance LLC ....G........ 580 574-7355
  Lawton *(G-4009)*

2322 Men's & Boys' Underwear & Nightwear

Synergy Maintenance LLC ....G........ 580 574-7355
  Lawton *(G-4009)*

2323 Men's & Boys' Neckwear

▲ Two Guys Bowtie Company LLC.............G........ 405 612-0116
  Tulsa *(G-11026)*

2325 Men's & Boys' Separate Trousers & Casual Slacks

Synergy Maintenance LLC ....G........ 580 574-7355
  Lawton *(G-4009)*

2326 Men's & Boys' Work Clothing

Barbara J McGinnis ....G........ 580 226-7675
  Ardmore *(G-253)*
Beane Development Corp ....G........ 580 222-1150
  Ardmore *(G-255)*
Corporate Image Inc ....G........ 918 516-8376
  Owasso *(G-7556)*
▲ Round House Manufacturing LLC..........D........ 405 273-0510
  Shawnee *(G-8490)*
Synergy Maintenance LLC ....G........ 580 574-7355
  Lawton *(G-4009)*

2329 Men's & Boys' Clothing, NEC

Anvil Land and Properties Inc ....G........ 580 336-4402
  Perry *(G-7726)*
Creative Apparel and More Inc ....G........ 918 682-1283
  Muskogee *(G-4664)*
Hollywood Express Oklahoma Inc ....G........ 405 324-8111
  Yukon *(G-11730)*
Mule Hunting Clothes Inc ....G........ 601 856-5169
  Collinsville *(G-1817)*
Synergy Maintenance LLC ....G........ 580 574-7355
  Lawton *(G-4009)*
▲ Tech-Mesh Apparel LLC ....G........ 918 492-1193
  Tulsa *(G-10912)*

2331 Women's & Misses' Blouses

▲ Relevant Products LLC ....E........ 405 524-5250
  Oklahoma City *(G-7005)*
U Big TS Designs Inc ....G........ 405 401-4327
  Oklahoma City *(G-7356)*

2335 Women's & Misses' Dresses

Bricktown Real Estate & Develo ....G........ 405 236-4143
  Oklahoma City *(G-5627)*
Captive Imaging LLC ....G........ 918 340-3053
  Tulsa *(G-9372)*
Ellis Bridal LLC ....G........ 501 247-8698
  Tulsa *(G-9662)*
▲ Esb Sales Inc..G........ 918 227-0378
  Sapulpa *(G-8270)*

Fancy Cakes ....G........ 405 701-3434
  Norman *(G-4996)*
▲ Glitter Gear LLC ....F........ 405 321-4327
  Oklahoma City *(G-6159)*
Mobetta..G........ 580 588-9222
  Apache *(G-220)*
Pixel Park LLC...G........ 405 613-0924
  Mustang *(G-4789)*
Sandy Childress Inc ....G........ 405 748-4949
  Edmond *(G-2612)*

2337 Women's & Misses' Suits, Coats & Skirts

Emery Bay Corporation ....G........ 918 494-2988
  Tulsa *(G-9671)*
Nine West Holdings Inc ....G........ 405 810-8568
  Oklahoma City *(G-6683)*

2339 Women's & Misses' Outerwear, NEC

Ajs Tees Inc ....G........ 918 455-6751
  Broken Arrow *(G-821)*
Bellylove Maternity Gifts ....G........ 405 818-3339
  Oklahoma City *(G-5548)*
Charles Komar & Sons Inc ....B........ 918 423-3535
  McAlester *(G-4280)*
First Class Outlet ....G........ 918 808-3405
  McAlester *(G-4299)*
Flaming Hope LLC ....G........ 405 924-4380
  Noble *(G-4880)*
Jan Farha ....G........ 405 848-1388
  Yukon *(G-11735)*
Jps Creations ....G........ 580 892-3455
  Allen *(G-135)*
Mule Hunting Clothes Inc ....G........ 601 856-5169
  Collinsville *(G-1817)*
Ndn Enterprises LLC ....G........ 703 772-6635
  Pawhuska *(G-7690)*
Rustic Rehab ....G........ 918 314-6647
  Grove *(G-3287)*
St John ....G........ 405 364-1917
  Norman *(G-5155)*
Team Spirit Sales ....G........ 918 296-5620
  Jenks *(G-3734)*
Titanium Phoenix Inc ....G........ 405 305-1304
  Oklahoma City *(G-7294)*

2341 Women's, Misses' & Children's Underwear & Nightwear

Charles Komar & Sons Inc ....B........ 918 423-3535
  McAlester *(G-4280)*
Charles Komar & Sons Inc ....G........ 918 423-1227
  Mcalester *(G-4281)*
Southwest Corset Corporation ....C........ 580 363-1935
  Blackwell *(G-693)*
United We Stand Inc ....G........ 918 382-1766
  Tulsa *(G-11044)*

2342 Brassieres, Girdles & Garments

Cupid Foundations Inc ....C........ 580 363-1935
  Blackwell *(G-680)*

2353 Hats, Caps & Millinery

Anvil Land and Properties Inc ....G........ 580 336-4402
  Perry *(G-7726)*
Cool Hard Hat Inc ....G........ 918 812-7636
  Tulsa *(G-9481)*
M T H Inc ....G........ 918 445-9235
  Tulsa *(G-10189)*
Shortys Hattery ....G........ 405 232-4287
  Oklahoma City *(G-7125)*

2361 Children's & Infants' Dresses & Blouses

Closet Consignments LLC ....G........ 405 387-3100
  Newcastle *(G-4823)*
Justice ....G........ 405 842-7180
  Oklahoma City *(G-6392)*
Slapsok LLC ....G........ 405 845-2299
  Edmond *(G-2622)*

2384 Robes & Dressing Gowns

Charles Komar & Sons Inc ....B........ 918 423-3535
  McAlester *(G-4280)*

2385 Waterproof Outerwear

▲ Wohali Outdoors LLC ....F........ 918 343-3800
  Broken Arrow *(G-1100)*

2386 Leather & Sheep Lined Clothing

Ganoa Imports..G........ 918 622-3788
  Tulsa *(G-9798)*
Leather Store ....G........ 918 245-8676
  Sand Springs *(G-8199)*

2387 Apparel Belts

Gilmores Sports Concepts Inc ....G........ 918 250-3910
  Tulsa *(G-9827)*

2389 Apparel & Accessories, NEC

Apex Inc...E........ 405 247-7377
  Anadarko *(G-200)*
Apothem ....G........ 405 447-2345
  Norman *(G-4912)*
Applause Apparel...G........ 580 762-1349
  Ponca City *(G-7797)*
Blush Boutique Inc ....G........ 405 701-8600
  Norman *(G-4938)*
Brims & Accessories ....G........ 580 357-2746
  Lawton *(G-3901)*
Easleys Performance Wear Inc.................G........ 918 357-2400
  Broken Arrow *(G-1125)*
Flaming Hope LLC ....G........ 405 924-4380
  Noble *(G-4880)*
Little Sahara Sandsports LLC....................G........ 580 824-0569
  Waynoka *(G-11378)*
Mascots Etc Inc ....G........ 405 722-3406
  Oklahoma City *(G-6535)*
Mrsdish LLC ....G........ 405 447-3813
  Norman *(G-5083)*
▲ Mtm Recognition Corporation ....B........ 405 609-6900
  Oklahoma City *(G-6634)*
Rainbow Creations ....G........ 405 942-6207
  Oklahoma City *(G-6967)*
Rainbow Spreme Assmbly I O R G........G........ 918 423-1328
  McAlester *(G-4331)*
Renavotio Infratech Inc ....G........ 504 722-7402
  Tulsa *(G-10640)*
Sherri Burch ....G........ 405 720-9021
  Oklahoma City *(G-7121)*
Witter Marketing Inc....................................G........ 918 369-8639
  Broken Arrow *(G-1099)*

2391 Curtains & Draperies

Be-Hive Interior Drapery Fctry ....G........ 918 599-0292
  Tulsa *(G-9275)*
Clearco Window Cleaning LLC ....G........ 580 248-9547
  Lawton *(G-3907)*
Cord & Pleat Design Inc ....G........ 918 622-7676
  Broken Arrow *(G-1117)*
Curry Shades LLC ....G........ 918 779-3902
  Tulsa *(G-9524)*
Decorator Drapery Mfg Inc ....E........ 405 942-5613
  Oklahoma City *(G-5917)*
Fabricut Inc..F........ 918 825-4400
  Pryor *(G-7962)*
Finished Seam ....G........ 918 742-4727
  Tulsa *(G-9745)*
▲ Hoppis Interiors ....G........ 405 390-2963
  Choctaw *(G-1545)*
Interior Designers Supply Inc ....F........ 405 521-1551
  Oklahoma City *(G-6318)*
Johnsons Spring Crest Drpery C ....G........ 405 238-7341
  Pauls Valley *(G-7662)*
Patricia McKay ....G........ 580 355-2739
  Cache *(G-1230)*
Pats Custom Draperies ....G........ 405 794-1019
  Moore *(G-4551)*
Ray Harrington Draperies ....G........ 405 789-6710
  Bethany *(G-593)*
Sam Dee Custom Draperies ....G........ 405 631-6128
  Oklahoma City *(G-7074)*
Springcrest Drapery Center ....G........ 918 258-5644
  Broken Arrow *(G-1058)*
Traceys Window Boutique Inc ....G........ 918 495-1806
  Tulsa *(G-10965)*
Vus Fabrics LLC ....G........ 405 330-9050
  Edmond *(G-2676)*

2392 House furnishings: Textile

Adairs Sleep World Inc ....F........ 405 341-9468
  Edmond *(G-2289)*
Cozy Cub Products LLP ....G........ 405 386-2879
  Newalla *(G-4807)*
Decorator Drapery Mfg Inc ....E........ 405 942-5613
  Oklahoma City *(G-5917)*
Doris Winford ....G........ 918 599-8931
  Tulsa *(G-9598)*

23 APPAREL AND OTHER FINISHED PRODUCTS MADE FROM FABRICS AND SIMILAR MATERIAL

E E Sewing Inc .... E 918 789-5881
  Chelsea (G-1404)
Fabricut Inc .... F 918 825-4400
  Pryor (G-7962)
Gilded Gate .... G 405 590-3139
  Oklahoma City (G-6155)
▲ Hoppis Interiors .... G 405 390-2963
  Choctaw (G-1545)
Interior Designers Supply Inc .... F 405 521-1551
  Oklahoma City (G-6318)
◆ Jobri LLC .... F 580 925-3500
  Ada (G-54)
▲ Leachco Inc .... E 580 436-1142
  Ada (G-59)
Life Lift Systems Inc .... F 904 635-8231
  Oklahoma City (G-6474)
Patricia McKay .... G 580 355-2739
  Cache (G-1230)
Quilts Unlimited .... G 580 746-2770
  Millerton (G-4474)
Ray Harrington Draperies .... G 405 789-6710
  Bethany (G-593)
Suntime Products Inc .... G 918 664-8330
  Tulsa (G-10875)
Tuffroots LLC .... G 580 728-0000
  Idabel (G-3650)
Whistle Stop Bedding & More .... G 405 620-5749
  Edmond (G-2686)

2393 Textile Bags

Beths Bags and More LLC .... G 918 451-7346
  Broken Arrow (G-848)
Fashionable Medical Covers .... G 405 414-1147
  Norman (G-4998)
Madison Filter Incorporated .... G 315 685-3466
  Tulsa (G-10198)
Pestco Inc .... G 405 485-8060
  Blanchard (G-727)
Speer Cushion Co .... G 970 854-2911
  Bixby (G-664)

2394 Canvas Prdts

Awnings of Tulsa Inc .... G 918 747-2050
  Tulsa (G-9232)
Awnings Unique .... G 405 249-2488
  Moore (G-4496)
City Tent & Awning Co Inc .... G 918 583-5003
  Tulsa (G-9437)
◆ Covercraft Industries LLC .... C 405 238-9651
  Pauls Valley (G-7655)
Covers Plus Inc .... G 405 670-2221
  Oklahoma City (G-5846)
Dans Custom Awnings LLC .... G 405 601-2703
  Oklahoma City (G-5896)
Dobbs & Crowder Inc .... G 918 452-3211
  Eufaula (G-3100)
Edwards Canvas Inc .... E 405 238-7551
  Pauls Valley (G-7658)
Hays Tent & Awning .... G 918 534-1663
  Dewey (G-2023)
Irwin Custom Sign Company LLC .... G 405 372-0657
  Stillwater (G-8704)
Jessie Shaw .... G 918 587-6329
  Tulsa (G-10040)
Karacon Solutions LLC .... G 918 231-1001
  Tulsa (G-10076)
Kerr Salesmakers & Marine Inc .... G 918 437-0544
  Tulsa (G-10085)
Oklahoma Custom Canvas Pdts .... F 918 438-4040
  Tulsa (G-10395)
Roper Product .... G 580 795-2293
  Lebanon (G-4027)
Shur-Co LLC .... G 405 262-7600
  El Reno (G-2757)

2395 Pleating & Stitching For The Trade

4524 LLC .... G 405 620-3711
  Edmond (G-2285)
A Stitch of Art .... G 918 638-2511
  Owasso (G-7540)
Adairs Sleep World Inc .... F 405 341-9468
  Edmond (G-2289)
Adventures In Stitching LLC .... G 918 995-7445
  (G-9114)
Alico Embroidery Etc .... G 405 321-2998
  Norman (G-4903)
American TS .... G 918 288-6682
  Glenpool (G-3230)
Apothem .... G 405 447-2345
  Norman (G-4912)

Baywest Embroidery .... G 580 626-4728
  Jet (G-3741)
Big Red Shop Inc .... G 405 495-5551
  Warr Acres (G-11313)
Bordeauxs Embroidery .... G 405 227-0958
  Oklahoma City (G-5619)
Carolyns Mouse House .... G 405 354-2858
  Yukon (G-11702)
Cas Monogramming Inc .... G 405 350-6556
  Yukon (G-11703)
Causley Productions Inc .... F 405 372-0940
  Stillwater (G-8666)
Cejco Inc .... F 405 366-8256
  Norman (G-4954)
Christys Quilts .... G 405 853-2155
  Hennessey (G-3450)
Cindys Stitching .... G 405 735-7126
  Oklahoma City (G-5281)
Complete Graphics Inc .... G 405 232-8882
  Oklahoma City (G-5812)
Corporate Image Inc .... G 918 516-8376
  Owasso (G-7556)
Corporate Image Apparel LLC .... G 405 659-8264
  Oklahoma City (G-5839)
Corser Group Inc .... G 918 749-6456
  Tulsa (G-9492)
Cr Stripes Ltd Co .... G 405 946-8577
  Oklahoma City (G-5850)
Creative Apparel and More Inc .... G 918 682-1283
  Muskogee (G-4664)
Creative Stitches By C S .... G 918 418-9049
  Afton (G-116)
Creativestitch LLC .... G 405 664-1144
  Edmond (G-2373)
Custom Embroidery & Gifts LLC .... G 405 240-7950
  Wellston (G-11468)
Debbie Do EMB & Screen Prtg .... G 580 353-2606
  Lawton (G-3918)
Design It .... G 405 756-3635
  Lindsay (G-4060)
Dinks Monogramming & EMB LLC ..... G 580 541-4371
  Enid (G-2941)
Doris Winford .... G 918 599-8931
  Tulsa (G-9598)
Dudz and Things Inc .... G 918 321-9443
  Sapulpa (G-8269)
Embrodred Mnograms Designs LLC ... G 918 335-5055
  Bartlesville (G-481)
Embroidery By Stacie .... G 580 656-5232
  Ardmore (G-285)
Embroidery Creations .... G 405 728-1355
  Oklahoma City (G-6029)
Embroidery Plus .... G 918 652-2117
  Weleetka (G-11464)
Embroidme of Tulsa .... G 918 459-6699
  Tulsa (G-9665)
Erin Turner Custom EMB LLC .... G 918 869-6481
  Tulsa (G-9697)
Fancy Stitch .... G 580 699-2112
  Lawton (G-3926)
Fashion Sports By Sia Inc .... F 405 524-9990
  Oklahoma City (G-6077)
First Impression Custom EMB .... G 918 787-4182
  Grove (G-3270)
Free Spirit Embroidery .... G 918 429-4552
  McAlester (G-4301)
Freedom Embroidery LLC .... G 580 540-8504
  Enid (G-2959)
Freestyle Embroidery .... G 405 802-5838
  Oklahoma City (G-6116)
Ft Sill Tees & Embroidery .... G 580 248-8484
  Lawton (G-3932)
Gail Evans Embroidery .... G 918 605-1013
  Tulsa (G-9796)
Genes Customized Tags & EMB .... G 580 225-8247
  Elk City (G-2820)
Gold Star Graphics Inc .... F 405 677-1529
  Oklahoma City (G-6168)
Great Plins Grphics Shwnee LLC ...... G 405 273-4263
  Shawnee (G-8455)
Green Cntry Trophy Screen Prtg .... G 918 647-2923
  Poteau (G-7906)
Heart 2 Heart Embroidery .... G 405 401-7408
  Oklahoma City (G-6232)
Im Stitched & Stoned .... G 918 418-9107
  Vinita (G-11261)
Initially Yours Inc .... G 918 832-9889
  Tulsa (G-9986)
Inspiration Logos Inc .... G 405 741-5646
  Oklahoma City (G-6310)

Integrity Screen Works Inc .... E 918 663-8339
  Tulsa (G-9999)
Jans Digitizing & EMB LLC .... G 970 587-2834
  Choctaw (G-1547)
Jlm2 LLC .... G 918 258-0239
  Broken Arrow (G-946)
Judy Airson .... G 580 254-9076
  Woodward (G-11597)
K A G U Inc .... G 405 364-4637
  Norman (G-5045)
L C D Embroidery .... G 405 379-6083
  Holdenville (G-3555)
Label Stable Inc .... G 580 223-2037
  Ardmore (G-323)
Lane Victory Screen Printing .... G 580 924-3556
  Durant (G-2243)
Last Stitch Studio .... G 918 200-5859
  Tulsa (G-10132)
Lightstitching .... G 405 210-7645
  Norman (G-5059)
Love Letters Monogramming LLC ...... G 918 231-6691
  Tulsa (G-10179)
Marketing & Embroidery Magic .... G 405 340-9677
  Edmond (G-2506)
McSmith Creations LLC .... G 405 596-2301
  Bethany (G-588)
Melbre Southern Stitches LLC .... G 918 399-4966
  Cushing (G-1945)
Merritts Monograms LLC .... G 918 346-2757
  Oklahoma City (G-6569)
Miss Priss Monograms & EMB .... G 918 697-9468
  Talala (G-8901)
Mobile PC Manager LLC .... G 574 551-4521
  Jenks (G-3717)
Monogram Hut .... G 214 707-4196
  Jenks (G-3718)
Monograms Elite Inc .... G 580 353-1635
  Lawton (G-3973)
Mulberry Tree Graphics .... G 580 248-3194
  Lawton (G-3974)
Munger and Krout Inc .... F 580 237-7060
  Enid (G-3016)
Mzmouze Embroidery Creat LLP .... G 405 696-6545
  Guthrie (G-3326)
▲ Oklahoma EMB Sup & Design ...... G 405 359-2741
  Edmond (G-2549)
One Moore Embroidery Place .... G 580 328-5755
  Taloga (G-8907)
Parkerville USA EMB & More .... G 918 636-0048
  Owasso (G-7601)
Peabody & Kent Designs Inc .... G 918 439-4300
  Tulsa (G-10478)
Pearl District Embroidery LLC .... G 918 269-3347
  Tulsa (G-10481)
Personal Expressions .... G 918 406-4581
  Broken Arrow (G-1003)
Personal Expressions Inc .... G 918 660-0494
  Tulsa (G-10498)
Personal Expressions Inc .... G 918 660-0494
  Tulsa (G-10499)
Pinpoint Monograms Inc .... F 405 228-0600
  Oklahoma City (G-6850)
Play 2 Win Athletics .... G 918 341-9500
  Claremore (G-1671)
Precision Punch .... G 405 340-7546
  Edmond (G-2574)
Productive Clutter Inc .... G 405 447-3839
  Norman (G-5124)
R-5 Caps & Tees .... G 580 256-3579
  Woodward (G-11626)
S & S Textile Inc .... F 405 632-9928
  Oklahoma City (G-7065)
S and W Embroidery .... G 580 654-2929
  Carnegie (G-1278)
S E & M Monogramming .... G 405 377-9677
  Stillwater (G-8751)
Sand Tech Screening and EMB .... G 918 458-0312
  Tahlequah (G-8882)
Sebo Lanila Lynn .... G 479 719-5612
  Spiro (G-8616)
Sew Glam Monogram LLC .... G 918 606-2644
  Broken Arrow (G-1049)
Sew Graphics Plus Inc .... G 405 364-1707
  Norman (G-5141)
Sew Much Fun .... G 405 359-1544
  Edmond (G-2616)
Sew Stylish Embroidery LLC .... G 580 238-8797
  Marietta (G-4212)
Sew Tulsa .... G 918 627-1577
  Tulsa (G-10736)

23 APPAREL AND OTHER FINISHED PRODUCTS MADE FROM FABRICS AND SIMILAR MATERIAL SIC SECTION

Sewcool Embroidery LLC ....G.... 405 326-2854
Edmond (G-2617)
Sewfly Embroidery ....G.... 580 477-1957
Altus (G-168)
Shirts & Stuff ....G.... 918 445-0323
Tulsa (G-10749)
Shops of Standing Rock Inc ....G.... 580 364-0834
Atoka (G-423)
Showstring USA Inc ....G.... 580 335-7171
Frederick (G-3200)
Southern Lace Stitchery ....G.... 405 414-3550
Yukon (G-11784)
Spinning Star Design ....G.... 405 359-3965
Edmond (G-2627)
Star Corral ....G.... 918 251-9795
Broken Arrow (G-1060)
Stitch Boom Ba LLC ....G.... 918 518-5859
Jenks (G-3729)
Stitch Design ....G.... 405 350-0126
Yukon (G-11789)
Stitch N Sew Embroidery ....G.... 432 741-0433
Ochelata (G-5239)
Stitch N Stuff Embroidery Shop ....G.... 918 465-3036
Wilburton (G-11525)
Stitch Witch ....G.... 918 371-3568
Collinsville (G-1825)
Stitch Wizard ....G.... 405 816-6356
Mustang (G-4796)
Stitchabella LLC ....G.... 405 562-3316
Edmond (G-2633)
Stitched By Shayna ....G.... 405 708-8614
Oklahoma City (G-7210)
Stitchin Acres ....G.... 405 740-6035
Kremlin (G-3855)
Stitchin Stitches ....G.... 918 251-9696
Broken Arrow (G-1063)
Stitchsumm LLC ....G.... 918 201-2148
Jenks (G-3730)
Sues Monogramming ....G.... 918 455-1011
Broken Arrow (G-1066)
Sunflower Embroidery LLC ....G.... 918 869-9646
Fort Gibson (G-3179)
T and L Embroidery ....G.... 580 493-2239
Drummond (G-2048)
T S & H EMB & Screen Prtg ....G.... 405 214-7701
Shawnee (G-8508)
Tazz Too Embroidery ....G.... 580 334-7373
Woodward (G-11640)
Tin Roof Quilting LLC ....G.... 918 551-7282
Tulsa (G-10944)
Tonis Stitches-N-Stuff Inc ....G.... 580 688-2697
Hollis (G-3570)
Tony Newcomb Sportswear Inc ....G.... 405 232-0022
Oklahoma City (G-7303)
Tts Embroiderys Plus ....G.... 918 770-3515
Glenpool (G-3243)
Tumbleweed Embroidery and Scre ....G.... 580 371-9742
Mannsville (G-4196)
Twist A Stitch ....G.... 918 514-0143
Sand Springs (G-8234)
Unique Stitches Inc ....G.... 918 794-5494
Tulsa (G-11035)
USA Industries Oklahoma Inc ....G.... 405 840-5577
Edmond (G-2661)
USA Screen Prtg & EMB Co Inc ....E.... 405 946-3100
Oklahoma City (G-7380)
Webber Kathryn ....G.... 405 379-3872
Holdenville (G-3562)

2396 Automotive Trimmings, Apparel Findings, Related Prdts

4524 LLC ....G.... 405 620-3711
Edmond (G-2285)
A & B Engraving Inc ....G.... 918 663-7446
Tulsa (G-9061)
All-Star Trophies & Ribbon Mfg ....G.... 918 283-2200
Claremore (G-1581)
American Sportswear Inc ....G.... 918 665-7636
Tulsa (G-9172)
B J Printing Inc ....F.... 405 372-7600
Stillwater (G-8657)
Bartlesville Print Shop ....G.... 918 336-6070
Bartlesville (G-452)
Beacon Sign Company Inc ....G.... 405 567-4886
Prague (G-7921)
Big Red Shop Inc ....G.... 405 495-5551
Warr Acres (G-11313)
Causley Productions Inc ....F.... 405 372-0940
Stillwater (G-8666)
Caveman Screen Printing ....G.... 918 446-6440
Tulsa (G-9390)
Cimarron Screen Printing ....G.... 405 755-8337
Edmond (G-2352)
Clay Serigraphics Inc ....F.... 918 592-2529
Tulsa (G-9445)
Complete Graphics Inc ....G.... 405 232-8882
Oklahoma City (G-5812)
Corner Copy & Printing LLC ....G.... 405 801-2020
Norman (G-4966)
CP Solutions Inc ....D.... 918 664-6642
Tulsa (G-9495)
Cr Stripes Ltd Co ....G.... 405 946-8577
Oklahoma City (G-5850)
Creative Apparel and More Inc ....G.... 918 682-1283
Muskogee (G-4664)
Cunningham Graphics Inc ....G.... 918 337-9100
Bartlesville (G-470)
Custom Monograms & Lettering ....G.... 405 495-8586
Bethany (G-574)
Custom Screen Printers ....G.... 918 423-3696
McAlester (G-4290)
Customized Fctry Interiors LLC ....G.... 405 848-9999
Oklahoma City (G-5880)
D & B Printing Inc ....G.... 405 632-0055
Oklahoma City (G-5884)
Dean Printing ....G.... 580 782-3777
Mangum (G-4170)
Design It ....G.... 405 756-3635
Lindsay (G-4060)
Diamond Tees ....G.... 918 665-0815
Tulsa (G-9579)
Ehrles Carnival & Party Sups ....G.... 918 622-5266
Tulsa (G-9648)
Emert Enterprises LLC ....G.... 580 495-5511
Bennington (G-563)
First Impression Prtg Co Inc ....G.... 918 749-5446
Beggs (G-553)
Gold Star Graphics Inc ....F.... 405 677-1529
Oklahoma City (G-6168)
Graphix Xpress ....G.... 580 765-7324
Ponca City (G-7831)
Great Plins Grphics Shwnee LLC ....G.... 405 273-4263
Shawnee (G-8455)
Green Cntry Trophy Screen Prtg ....G.... 918 647-2923
Poteau (G-7906)
Ham Ventures LLC ....G.... 918 277-9500
Tulsa (G-9883)
Holloways Bluprt & Copy Sp Inc ....G.... 918 682-0280
Muskogee (G-4692)
House of Trophies ....G.... 405 452-3524
Wetumka (G-11492)
House of Trophies ....G.... 918 341-2111
Claremore (G-1637)
House T Shirt & Silk Screening ....G.... 405 457-6321
Lookeba (G-4129)
Imaging Concepts ....G.... 918 534-1761
Dewey (G-2026)
Impact Screen Printing ....G.... 918 258-8337
Broken Arrow (G-934)
Initially Yours Inc ....G.... 918 832-9889
Tulsa (G-9986)
Inkling Design ....G.... 405 495-5575
Bethany (G-583)
Jan L Jobe ....G.... 918 683-0404
Muskogee (G-4698)
Jeff Mc Kenzie & Co Inc ....G.... 405 236-5848
Oklahoma City (G-6354)
Joys Uniforms Boutique Ltd ....G.... 918 747-4114
Tulsa (G-10061)
King Screen Co ....G.... 405 258-0416
Chandler (G-1383)
Knl Screenprinting ....G.... 580 654-5394
Carnegie (G-1277)
Label Stable Inc ....G.... 580 223-2037
Ardmore (G-323)
Lawyer Graphic Screen Process ....G.... 918 438-2725
Tulsa (G-10137)
Leda Grimm ....G.... 918 225-0507
Cushing (G-1942)
Magic TS ....G.... 580 332-6675
Ada (G-62)
Magnum Screen Print Inc ....G.... 918 665-7636
Tulsa (G-10202)
Massive Graphic Screen Prtg ....F.... 405 364-3594
Norman (G-5066)
MBC Graphics ....G.... 918 585-2321
Tulsa (G-10227)
Midwest Decals LLC ....G.... 405 787-8747
Oklahoma City (G-6602)
Midwest Publishing Co ....G.... 405 282-1890
Guthrie (G-3325)
Misaco Sign & Screen Printing ....G.... 918 542-4188
Miami (G-4419)
Mobonoto Automotive LLC ....G.... 580 480-0410
Altus (G-163)
Munger and Krout Inc ....F.... 580 237-7060
Enid (G-3016)
Opportunity Center Inc ....C.... 580 765-6782
Ponca City (G-7863)
Options Inc ....F.... 918 473-2614
Checotah (G-1398)
Peabodys Printing & A Brush Sp ....G.... 580 248-8317
Lawton (G-3980)
Performance Screen Printing ....G.... 405 247-9891
Anadarko (G-205)
Pinpoint Monograms Inc ....F.... 405 228-0600
Oklahoma City (G-6850)
Pitezels Ink & Print Inc ....G.... 918 663-2393
Tulsa (G-10520)
Prairie Graphics & Sportswear ....G.... 405 789-0028
Bethany (G-592)
Print Imaging Group LLC ....E.... 405 235-4888
Oklahoma City (G-6898)
Promo Print 4 U LLC ....G.... 405 259-6721
Oklahoma City (G-6915)
Promoz Screen Printing Inc ....G.... 918 439-4030
Tulsa (G-10574)
Quantum Forms Corporation ....F.... 918 665-1320
Oklahoma City (G-6940)
R-5 Caps & Tees ....G.... 580 256-3579
Woodward (G-11626)
Reflective Edge Screenprinting ....G.... 405 917-7837
Oklahoma City (G-7001)
▲ Relevant Products LLC ....E.... 405 524-5250
Oklahoma City (G-7005)
S & S Textile Inc ....F.... 405 632-9928
Oklahoma City (G-7065)
Sand Tech Screening and EMB ....G.... 918 458-0312
Tahlequah (G-8882)
Semasys Inc ....E.... 405 525-2335
Oklahoma City (G-7107)
Shine On Designs ....G.... 918 224-7439
Sapulpa (G-8311)
Shirts & Stuff ....G.... 918 445-0323
Tulsa (G-10749)
Shops of Standing Rock Inc ....G.... 580 364-0834
Atoka (G-423)
Sides Screenprinting More LLC ....G.... 580 772-8888
Oklahoma City (G-7127)
Speedys TS & More LLC ....G.... 580 748-0067
Alva (G-192)
Stan Clark Co ....G.... 405 377-0799
Stillwater (G-8755)
T S & H EMB & Screen Prtg ....G.... 405 214-7701
Shawnee (G-8508)
T-Shirts Unlimited ....G.... 580 286-5223
Idabel (G-3649)
Tigers Den By Dreamcatcher ....G.... 918 478-4873
Fort Gibson (G-3180)
Tim Dees ....G.... 918 825-1211
Pryor (G-7995)
Tom Bennett Manufacturing ....F.... 405 528-5671
Oklahoma City (G-7302)
Tony Newcomb Sportswear Inc ....G.... 405 232-0022
Oklahoma City (G-7303)
Townsend Marketing Inc ....G.... 918 496-9222
Bixby (G-666)
U Big TS Designs Inc ....G.... 405 401-4327
Oklahoma City (G-7356)
▲ Ultra Thin Inc ....E.... 405 794-7892
Moore (G-4582)
USA Screen Prtg & EMB Co Inc ....E.... 405 946-3100
Oklahoma City (G-7380)
Wallis Printing Inc ....G.... 580 223-7473
Ardmore (G-379)
Way-Wear LLC ....G.... 405 410-8367
Kingfisher (G-3820)
Wear-Tech ....G.... 918 663-2009
Tulsa (G-11099)
Wet Willies Screen Print & CU ....G.... 405 262-6076
El Reno (G-2770)
Witty Ideas Inc ....G.... 918 367-9528
Bristow (G-806)

2397 Schiffli Machine Embroideries

Baywest Embroidery ....G.... 580 626-4728
Jet (G-3741)
Big Creek Custom Embroidery ....G.... 918 446-6054
Tulsa (G-9288)

C&S Design ....G.... 918 455-8137
Broken Arrow *(G-1116)*

2399 Fabricated Textile Prdts, NEC

Barbara J Landreth Sewing ....G.... 918 298-8141
Tulsa *(G-9264)*
Casa Dosa ....G.... 918 243-7277
Cleveland *(G-1719)*
Chris Johnson ....G.... 405 364-3879
Norman *(G-4956)*
Cimarron Equine Station ....G.... 405 373-0358
Yukon *(G-11705)*
Crochetangel ....G.... 918 282-3056
Broken Arrow *(G-879)*
DSA Designs LLC ....G.... 580 493-2723
Drummond *(G-2047)*
▲ **Elqui International Ltd Co** ....G.... 918 335-5002
Bartlesville *(G-480)*
Inspiration Logos Inc ....G.... 405 741-5646
Oklahoma City *(G-6310)*
Lenora Elizabeth Brown ....G.... 918 797-2034
Stilwell *(G-8792)*
Moss Seat Cover Mfg & Sls Co ....F.... 918 742-3326
Tulsa *(G-10306)*
Rainbow Pennant Inc ....E.... 405 524-1577
Oklahoma City *(G-6968)*
Red Earth Farm Store Inc ....F.... 405 478-3424
Oklahoma City *(G-6985)*
Sooner Rubber Products Company ....G.... 918 461-1391
Tulsa *(G-10792)*
South Central Machine ....G.... 580 775-1623
Durant *(G-2258)*
Speer Cushion Co ....G.... 970 854-2911
Bixby *(G-664)*
Tr Tack Supply ....G.... 918 543-4095
Inola *(G-3674)*
▲ **Ultra Thin Inc** ....E.... 405 794-7892
Moore *(G-4582)*
United We Stand Inc ....G.... 918 382-1766
Tulsa *(G-11044)*
◆ **Valhoma Corporation** ....E.... 918 836-7135
Tulsa *(G-11064)*
Wave On Flags and Banners LLC ....G.... 918 782-3330
Langley *(G-3875)*

24 LUMBER AND WOOD PRODUCTS, EXCEPT FURNITURE

2411 Logging

Anderson Logging LLC ....G.... 580 584-9898
Broken Bow *(G-1183)*
Arthur Crews Logging ....G.... 580 889-7757
Lane *(G-3870)*
▲ **B & B Log & Lumber Co Inc** ....F.... 580 889-2438
Atoka *(G-399)*
B & P Logging LLC ....G.... 580 584-6718
Broken Bow *(G-1184)*
Bloods Logging & Land Svcs LLC ....G.... 405 314-4275
Lamar *(G-3863)*
Broadland Stump Removal ....G.... 918 743-7014
Tulsa *(G-9339)*
Bruce Hopson Logging Inc ....G.... 580 835-7145
Eagletown *(G-2274)*
Bucky McGee Logging ....G.... 918 635-0909
Heavener *(G-3426)*
Donald Standridge ....G.... 580 298-3760
Mounds *(G-4613)*
Dustin Holbird ....G.... 918 448-7687
Wister *(G-11548)*
Erik Robins ....G.... 580 371-1470
Ardmore *(G-287)*
Excellence Logging ....G.... 815 272-7622
Tulsa *(G-9714)*
F G Sawmill LLC ....G.... 918 905-1132
Stilwell *(G-8788)*
Fortress Whitetails ....G.... 405 401-5533
Guthrie *(G-3313)*
G&G Logging LLC ....G.... 918 635-5988
Poteau *(G-7905)*
Gary Moss ....G.... 580 286-1359
Valliant *(G-11224)*
Hadley-Keeney Chipping Inc ....E.... 580 835-2645
Eagletown *(G-2275)*
Harrison Logging Lc ....G.... 580 245-2179
Haworth *(G-3404)*
Impac Exploration Services Inc ....G.... 580 772-3117
Weatherford *(G-11420)*
J Duke Logan Family Trust ....G.... 918 256-7511
Vinita *(G-11263)*
J&J Logging LLC ....G.... 580 933-7218
Valliant *(G-11228)*
James Jeremy Burcham ....G.... 580 420-3243
Broken Bow *(G-1193)*
James Roy Hopson ....G.... 580 835-2288
Eagletown *(G-2276)*
Johnnie & Lonnie Smith ....G.... 580 933-4323
Valliant *(G-11229)*
Karen E Hopson ....G.... 580 584-7221
Broken Bow *(G-1195)*
Kenneth D Jewell ....G.... 580 244-7450
Watson *(G-11355)*
Larry L Williams ....G.... 580 772-3303
Weatherford *(G-11424)*
Lloyd Provence Logging ....G.... 580 245-1170
Haworth *(G-3405)*
Logging Contractor Inc ....F.... 580 244-3571
Smithville *(G-8579)*
Lucky 13 Motorcycle Shop ....F.... 816 808-0985
Tulsa *(G-10182)*
Luna Logging ....G.... 580 933-7517
Valliant *(G-11230)*
Midwest Logging & Perforating ....G.... 405 382-4200
Seminole *(G-8384)*
Mixon Brothers Wood Prsv Co ....F.... 580 286-9494
Idabel *(G-3643)*
Nancy Dalrymple ....G.... 405 525-7544
Oklahoma City *(G-6650)*
Paladin Geological Svcs LLC ....F.... 405 463-3270
Edmond *(G-2560)*
R & D Mud Logging Services LLP ....G.... 405 969-2587
Crescent *(G-1919)*
Rd Logging ....F.... 918 666-2556
Wyandotte *(G-11662)*
Rex Ross ....G.... 580 835-7244
Eagletown *(G-2277)*
River Ridge Logging LLC ....G.... 580 380-2948
Durant *(G-2252)*
Shawn Gibson ....E.... 580 584-5537
Broken Bow *(G-1205)*
Silver Creek Logging ....G.... 580 241-7717
Broken Bow *(G-1206)*
SMA Surface Logging LLC ....G.... 405 301-3375
Oklahoma City *(G-7150)*
STS Logging Services LLC ....G.... 918 933-5653
Tulsa *(G-10862)*
Terry Belknap & Sons Logging ....G.... 580 244-3303
Smithville *(G-8580)*
Tunnell Chance ....G.... 580 245-2422
Haworth *(G-3406)*
Wacky Logging LLC ....G.... 918 457-9393
Hulbert *(G-3630)*
Walker Woods Inc ....G.... 208 266-1601
Oklahoma City *(G-7416)*
Will Robinson Logging LLC ....G.... 918 569-4248
Clayton *(G-1711)*

2421 Saw & Planing Mills

Browns Sawmill ....G.... 918 617-7935
Atwood *(G-428)*
▲ **Chips Valiant Inc** ....F.... 580 933-5323
Valliant *(G-11222)*
Conner Industries Inc ....E.... 918 696-5885
Stilwell *(G-8787)*
Diamond P Forrest Products Co ....F.... 918 266-2478
Catoosa *(G-1316)*
Eastern Red Cedar Products LLC ....G.... 405 780-7520
Stillwater *(G-8681)*
Gray & Sons Sawmill & Sup LLC ....G.... 580 924-2941
Durant *(G-2231)*
Grays Sawmill Inc ....F.... 580 924-2941
Durant *(G-2232)*
Hugo Wyrick Lumber ....E.... 580 326-5569
Hugo *(G-3614)*
International Paper Company ....D.... 580 933-7211
Valliant *(G-11227)*
James Bethell ....G.... 918 677-2328
Wister *(G-11549)*
Jeffery Mariott ....E.... 580 320-5474
Roff *(G-8109)*
John R Little Jr ....G.... 405 751-5227
Oklahoma City *(G-6369)*
Johnson Lumber Company Inc ....E.... 918 253-8786
Spavinaw *(G-8591)*
Limbsaw Company ....G.... 580 272-3194
Noble *(G-4885)*
Log Cutters ....G.... 580 371-8349
Tishomingo *(G-8967)*
Newview Oklahoma Inc ....D.... 405 232-4644
Oklahoma City *(G-6672)*
Og Sawmill ....G.... 918 598-3464
Hulbert *(G-3627)*
Oklahoma Home Centers Inc ....E.... 405 260-7625
Guthrie *(G-3329)*
Sanders Sawmill & Forest Pdts ....G.... 405 799-0899
Moore *(G-4562)*
Shawnee Sawmill LLC ....G.... 405 788-6186
Shawnee *(G-8496)*
Shelley Benefield ....G.... 580 436-0296
Ada *(G-86)*
Singing Wire Cedar ....G.... 918 607-8643
Beggs *(G-561)*
T and A Sawmill LLC ....G.... 580 309-3100
Thomas *(G-8948)*
Ufp Shawnee LLC ....G.... 405 273-1533
Shawnee *(G-8515)*
White Gordon Lbr Co of Lindsay ....G.... 405 946-9032
Warr Acres *(G-11330)*
Whitlock Saw Mill ....G.... 918 652-4410
Henryetta *(G-3518)*
Woodstock Sawmill & Timbers Co ....G.... 405 673-7966
Oklahoma City *(G-7467)*

2426 Hardwood Dimension & Flooring Mills

▲ **B & B Log & Lumber Co Inc** ....F.... 580 889-2438
Atoka *(G-399)*
Conner Industries Inc ....E.... 918 696-5885
Stilwell *(G-8787)*
Diamond P Forrest Products Co ....F.... 918 266-2478
Catoosa *(G-1316)*
Egr Construction Inc ....E.... 405 943-0900
Oklahoma City *(G-6013)*
Flooring Outfitters ....G.... 580 286-3030
Idabel *(G-3637)*
Grays Sawmill Inc ....F.... 580 924-2941
Durant *(G-2232)*
Hugo Wyrick Lumber ....E.... 580 326-5569
Hugo *(G-3614)*
Johnson Lumber Company Inc ....E.... 918 253-8786
Spavinaw *(G-8591)*
Juan Manzo Custom Refinishing ....G.... 405 848-3843
Oklahoma City *(G-6390)*
Moores Hardware and Home Ctr ....G.... 918 287-4458
Pawhuska *(G-7689)*
Pioneer Sport Floors LLC ....G.... 214 460-6921
Calera *(G-1244)*
Ram Design Inc ....G.... 918 342-4051
Claremore *(G-1678)*
Rd Logging ....F.... 918 666-2556
Wyandotte *(G-11662)*
Strictly Hardwoods ....G.... 405 269-1026
Stillwater *(G-8761)*
White Gordon Lbr Co of Lindsay ....G.... 405 946-9032
Warr Acres *(G-11330)*
Zara Group Inc ....F.... 918 782-4473
Vinita *(G-11273)*

2429 Special Prdt Sawmills, NEC

Farmers Coop Gin of Martha ....G.... 580 266-3222
Martha *(G-4251)*

2431 Millwork

12 Acre Woodwork LLC ....G.... 405 328-0655
Chandler *(G-1372)*
A R T T Corp ....G.... 405 681-0749
Oklahoma City *(G-5348)*
Aaron Custom Creations ....G.... 580 603-0467
Enid *(G-2902)*
AC Woodworks Inc ....G.... 918 298-6948
Tulsa *(G-9085)*
AC Woodworks Inc DBA Wood ....G.... 918 384-0111
Tulsa *(G-9086)*
Accurate Blinds ....G.... 405 396-8583
Arcadia *(G-226)*
Ace Hardware ....G.... 580 225-0100
Elk City *(G-2781)*
All Wood Products Co Inc ....E.... 918 585-9739
Tulsa *(G-9138)*
American Millwork Company Inc ....E.... 405 681-5347
Oklahoma City *(G-5440)*
Andrews Woodworking ....G.... 918 664-6722
Tulsa *(G-9190)*
Ardmore Construction Sup Inc ....G.... 580 223-2322
Ardmore *(G-245)*
B & C Custom Woodworks ....G.... 918 830-2416
Tulsa *(G-9241)*
B&C Custom Woodworks LLC ....G.... 918 639-2416
Tulsa *(G-9247)*
Bales Custom Woodwork Inc ....G.... 918 277-6612
Beggs *(G-549)*

S I C

Bobs Wood Working....G....405 632-4894
Oklahoma City (G-5604)
Cabinet Doors Unlimited....F....918 257-5765
Afton (G-114)
Caston Architectural Mllwk Inc....E....405 843-6652
Oklahoma City (G-5711)
Cavanal Woodworks....G....909 649-4346
Poteau (G-7900)
Centerpiece Custom Wdwkg LLC....G....405 387-9312
Blanchard (G-706)
Cherokee Architectural Mtls LLC....F....918 258-5700
Broken Arrow (G-868)
Cherokee Woodwork Inc....G....918 798-5037
Tulsa (G-9416)
Cheyenne Woodworks Inc....G....918 587-3533
Tulsa (G-9418)
Classic Overhead Doo....G....580 931-0340
Durant (G-2215)
Contemporary Cabinets Inc....D....405 330-4592
Edmond (G-2365)
Copes Woodworking....G....918 698-2104
Tulsa (G-9484)
Crawson Corporation....F....918 427-8400
Muldrow (G-4633)
Creekside Woodworks....G....405 528-5432
Oklahoma City (G-5854)
Croan Custom Woodworks LLC....G....405 227-2067
Edmond (G-2374)
Crosby Custom Woodwork....G....405 802-9615
Moore (G-4512)
Curry Shades LLC....G....918 779-3902
Tulsa (G-9524)
Custom Cutting Millwork Inc....F....405 942-3196
Oklahoma City (G-5872)
▲ Custom Seating Incorporated....C....918 682-4400
Muskogee (G-4666)
Custom Wood Creations....G....580 512-6994
Lawton (G-3915)
Custom Wood Creations LLC....G....405 517-8689
Crescent (G-1911)
Custom Wood Works....G....918 279-1333
Coweta (G-1877)
Cutting Edge Woodwork LLC....G....918 706-1143
Skiatook (G-8537)
Dale P Jackson....F....580 332-1988
Ada (G-29)
Die Tech Tool Machine....G....918 683-3422
Okay (G-5257)
Display With Honor Wdwkg LLC....G....405 659-9894
Oklahoma City (G-5286)
Egr Construction Inc....E....405 943-0900
Oklahoma City (G-6013)
Elite Wood Creations LLC....G....580 220-1153
Ardmore (G-284)
Elk Valley Woodworking Inc....G....580 486-3337
Carter (G-1281)
Equus Metalcraft Llc....G....918 832-0956
Tulsa (G-9695)
Estey Cabinet Door Co....E....405 771-3004
Spencer (G-8595)
Eubankswoodworks LLC....G....918 245-7835
Sand Springs (G-8182)
Extraordinary Woodworks....G....801 995-0906
Enid (G-2956)
Fadco of Arkansas LLC....G....918 832-1641
Tulsa (G-9726)
For His Glory Cutting Boards....G....918 633-7233
Tulsa (G-9764)
Forrest Valentine....G....580 309-2190
Custer City (G-1974)
Fullerton Building Systems Inc....E....918 246-9995
Sand Springs (G-8187)
Furrs Custom Woodwork....G....918 406-7021
Bixby (G-624)
Gemini Woodworks....G....405 630-8586
Jones (G-3746)
Gps Woodworks LLC....G....405 399-2369
Jones (G-3747)
Grain and Grit Woodworks LLC....G....405 250-6824
Oklahoma City (G-6175)
Green Cntry Cstm Woodworks LLC....G....918 585-1040
Tulsa (G-9858)
Gurley Custom Woodwork....G....580 235-3350
Ada (G-46)
H3 Custom Wood Moldings LLC....G....918 250-8746
Tulsa (G-9879)
Hansen Millwork & Trim Inc....E....405 239-2564
Oklahoma City (G-6214)
Hardwood Innovations Inc....F....405 722-5588
Oklahoma City (G-6219)
Huerecas Woodworking LLC....G....580 302-2687
Weatherford (G-11418)
Hughes Lumber Company....G....918 266-9100
Catoosa (G-1322)
Hugo Sash & Door Inc....F....580 326-5569
Hugo (G-3613)
Hugo Wyrick Lumber....E....580 326-5569
Hugo (G-3614)
Hutchinson Products Company....E....405 946-4403
Oklahoma City (G-6277)
Integrity Custom Mill Works....G....405 495-9732
Spencer (G-8596)
J & Js Wdwrk HM Decor & Gifts....G....918 420-9411
McAlester (G-4307)
J & S Woodworking Inc....G....405 619-9910
Oklahoma City (G-6333)
J B Woodworking....G....918 760-2399
Bristow (G-781)
J&Js Woodwork and More....G....918 429-9704
McAlester (G-4308)
Japa Corp....G....918 893-6763
Broken Arrow (G-943)
Johnsonwoodworks....G....918 407-7747
Tulsa (G-10057)
Jts Woodworks LLC....G....918 640-1791
Broken Arrow (G-951)
Kaonohi Woodworks....G....918 893-4661
Broken Arrow (G-954)
Kc Woodwork & Fixture Inc....G....918 582-5300
Tulsa (G-10078)
Kelly L Young....G....918 859-1046
Skiatook (G-8555)
Knock On Wood Custom....G....918 261-6948
Claremore (G-1650)
Kohns Doors & Woodworking LLC....G....405 596-8245
Piedmont (G-7766)
Ksquared Woodworks LLC....G....918 496-3681
Tulsa (G-10104)
Lakewood Cabinetry Inc....F....918 782-2203
Langley (G-3871)
LDS Building Specialties LLC....G....405 917-9901
Oklahoma City (G-6460)
Leon Kinder....G....580 323-0365
Clinton (G-1756)
Lindsay Woodworks....G....405 370-9712
Choctaw (G-1550)
M1 Woodworks....G....405 923-4144
Edmond (G-2499)
Mastercraft Millwork Inc....G....405 895-6050
Moore (G-4537)
McElyea Custom Woodworking LLC....G....918 332-7651
Bartlesville (G-510)
McMurtry Cabinet Shop....G....405 627-3275
Oklahoma City (G-6550)
Mez Woodworks LLC....G....405 589-5408
Edmond (G-2517)
Mh Woodworking LLC....G....405 799-2661
Moore (G-4540)
Mike Pung....G....405 736-6282
Oklahoma City (G-6607)
Mill Work Specialties LLC....G....918 639-8385
Tulsa (G-10280)
Mystik River Woodworks....G....580 606-0071
Comanche (G-1843)
Naked Wood Works....G....918 864-0229
Broken Arrow (G-984)
Nicnik Woodworks....G....703 474-7994
Choctaw (G-1552)
Nolan Custom Woodwork....G....918 576-1158
Tulsa (G-10347)
Note-Able Workshop LLC....G....918 801-2725
Grove (G-3281)
Note-Able Workshop LLC....G....918 801-2725
Grove (G-3282)
Novalco Inc....F....405 528-2711
Oklahoma City (G-6700)
Nxt Lvl Woodworking LLC....G....405 613-6637
Norman (G-5096)
Oconnell Woodworks LLC....G....918 805-7233
Broken Arrow (G-992)
Oklahoma City Shutter Co Inc....F....405 787-1234
Oklahoma City (G-6742)
Oklahoma Stair Craft Inc....F....918 446-1456
Sapulpa (G-8293)
Okrusticwoodworks....G....405 562-0371
Guthrie (G-3331)
Oro Woodworks....G....405 334-7445
Stillwater (G-8734)
Osage Door Co Inc....G....918 542-7281
Miami (G-4426)
Paramount Building Pdts LLC....G....405 470-5073
Oklahoma City (G-6804)
Parker Kustom Woodworking....G....405 414-2820
Del City (G-2005)
Pawnee Millworks LLC....G....918 767-2565
Pawnee (G-7707)
▲ Perma-Strong Wood Products Inc....E....405 449-3376
Wayne (G-11369)
▲ Quality Wholesale Millwork Inc....G....405 681-6575
Oklahoma City (G-6938)
Quality Woodworks Inc....G....918 944-3314
Muskogee (G-4741)
R and P Cabinetry LLC....G....405 230-0495
Oklahoma City (G-6959)
Rar Wood Works LLC....G....205 233-2920
Broken Arrow (G-1022)
RC Custom Woodwork....G....405 414-1162
Norman (G-5130)
Rccs Woodworking LLC....G....405 694-9680
Edmond (G-2587)
Red Dirt Wood Works LLC....G....918 640-5917
Edmond (G-2588)
Redbird Woodworks....G....918 227-5938
Sapulpa (G-8306)
Redbud Woodworks....G....316 765-4079
Midwest City (G-4451)
Rescue Lumber & Wdwkg LLC....G....405 650-4637
Edmond (G-2597)
Reynolds Custom Woodworks....G....918 595-5988
Claremore (G-1681)
Rico Woodworking LLC....G....918 743-0741
Tulsa (G-10651)
Rkb Woodworks....G....405 919-4149
Oklahoma City (G-7030)
Rockin Wood LLC....G....405 673-5171
Oklahoma City (G-7045)
S & S Woodworks Inc....G....405 627-8195
Edmond (G-2609)
S Coker Custom Woodworks....G....918 638-3443
Broken Arrow (G-1042)
▲ S&S Custom Wood Moldings LLC....F....214 995-8710
Bixby (G-657)
Sanderson Custom Woodworks....G....918 361-1921
Tulsa (G-10704)
Sandy Creek Millworks Inc....G....405 288-0670
Washington (G-11336)
Scarab Woodworking LLC....G....405 612-2111
Stillwater (G-8753)
Secure Screen LLC....G....918 294-4444
Broken Arrow (G-1048)
Shellback Woodworks....G....918 851-3992
Bristow (G-796)
Shofner Custom Wood....G....405 787-5768
Bethany (G-594)
Shutter Mill Inc....D....405 377-6455
Stillwater (G-8754)
Shutters Unlimited Ltd....F....405 843-7762
Oklahoma City (G-7126)
Skykae Kreations....G....405 250-4055
Piedmont (G-7770)
Sooner Cabinet & Trim Inc....E....405 820-2920
Moore (G-4571)
Sooner Cnc LLC....G....918 261-5231
Tulsa (G-10787)
Southern Millwork Inc....E....918 585-8125
Tulsa (G-10800)
Stephens Custom Woodworks....G....405 938-7065
Edmond (G-2632)
Steveos Custom Wood-Work LLC....G....405 532-1863
Bethany (G-597)
Sylvan Croft Woodworks....G....405 329-6668
Norman (G-5168)
Tap Woodworks LLC....G....580 819-0455
Weatherford (G-11445)
Thomas Millwork Inc....F....405 769-5618
Spencer (G-8602)
Thompson Woodworks....G....405 269-6480
Stillwater (G-8768)
Tilman Woodworks LLC....G....405 441-3324
Oklahoma City (G-7290)
Tracys Wood Shop Inc....G....918 587-4860
Tulsa (G-10966)
Trim Rite Moldings Inc....G....918 423-2525
McAlester (G-4344)
Trinity Wood Works....G....918 619-3959
Muskogee (G-4755)
Trotter Custom Woodworks LLC....G....918 698-5231
Sand Springs (G-8231)
Unicorn Woodworking....G....580 762-0004
Ponca City (G-7885)

SIC SECTION
24 LUMBER AND WOOD PRODUCTS, EXCEPT FURNITURE

Company	Code	Phone
Unique Wood Works Inc — Maysville (G-4262)	G	405 249-6615
Urban Okie Custom Woodwork — Edmond (G-2658)	G	405 420-1176
Urban Okie Custom Woodwork LLC — Edmond (G-2659)	G	405 635-7800
Urbane Commercial Contrs LLC — Midwest City (G-4460)	G	405 534-1677
Vanhoose Wood Creations — Blanchard (G-742)	G	405 443-0454
Wades Cabinet Door Shop — Tahlequah (G-8891)	G	918 868-2516
Wayland Woodworks LLC — Bristow (G-805)	G	918 799-6196
Wendell Hicks Construction — Nowata (G-5232)	G	918 520-9128
Wewoka Window Works LLC — Wewoka (G-11514)	F	405 257-3109
Wfwoodworks LLC — Norman (G-5200)	G	405 740-8920
White Bffalo Cstm Wdwrk Rnvtio — Blanchard (G-745)	G	405 387-3278
Wild West Creations — Hinton (G-3540)	G	405 542-6507
Windor Supply & Mfg Inc — Tulsa (G-11137)	E	918 664-4017
Winkles Woodworks Ltd — Coweta (G-1902)	F	918 486-5022
Wndells Woodturning — Sallisaw (G-8155)	G	918 775-1124
Wood Creations By Rod LLC — Oklahoma City (G-7462)	G	405 235-2222
Wood Creations By Rod LLC — Moore (G-4583)	G	405 912-8099
Wood Systems Inc — Tulsa (G-11148)	D	918 388-0900
Woodwright Woodworking LLC — Broken Arrow (G-1102)	G	918 254-6577
Young Construction Supply LLC — Tahlequah (G-8893)	G	918 456-3250
Yukon Door and Plywood Inc — Yukon (G-11807)	E	405 354-4861
Zara Group Inc — Vinita (G-11273)	F	918 782-4473

2434 Wood Kitchen Cabinets

Company	Code	Phone
3d Cabinetry LLC — Lindsay (G-4042)	G	405 488-5604
Aaron Son Custom Cabinets — Muskogee (G-4640)	G	918 537-2129
Alleman Trim & Cabinets — Oklahoma City (G-5418)	G	405 942-7876
Artisan Custom Cabinetry Inc — Broken Arrow (G-834)	G	918 645-3874
Bartlesville Custom Cabinets — Bartlesville (G-451)	G	918 440-5981
Beauchamp Cabinets Cstm Homes — Chouteau (G-1558)	G	918 476-5532
Becca Vermelis — Norman (G-4929)	G	405 701-1638
Boxco Trim Cabinets — Catoosa (G-1305)	G	918 266-4030
Boyds Cstm Trim Cabinetry LLC — Glenpool (G-3231)	G	918 724-7033
Brays Cabinet Shop — Broken Bow (G-1186)	G	580 584-6771
Broken Arrow Woodworks — Broken Arrow (G-859)	F	918 893-6763
C & C Cabinets — Sand Springs (G-8168)	G	918 241-5249
Cabinet Cures Oklahoma LLC — Edmond (G-2335)	G	405 285-5700
Cabinet Doors Unlimited — Afton (G-114)	F	918 257-5765
Cabinet Solutions LLC — Tulsa (G-9363)	G	918 592-4497
Cabinetworks Inc — Oklahoma City (G-5666)	G	405 286-1053
Casework Specialties Inc LLC — Tulsa (G-9385)	G	918 382-0037
Charles Dale Keller — Ardmore (G-265)	G	940 597-1763
Classic Marble Design Inc — Clinton (G-1744)	G	580 323-4917
Close Custom Cabinets Inc — Oklahoma City (G-5790)	E	405 840-8226
Colliers Cabinets — Stillwater (G-8669)	G	405 377-3508
Contemporary Cabinets Inc — Edmond (G-2365)	D	405 330-4592
Cooper Cabinet Systems Inc — Oklahoma City (G-5828)	D	405 528-7220
Cooper Cabinets Inc — Oklahoma City (G-5829)	E	405 528-7220
Crawford Cabinetry & Cnstr Inc — Tahlequah (G-8860)	G	918 453-0164
Creative Cabinets — Ponca City (G-7811)	G	580 762-9500
Creative Spaces — Edmond (G-2372)	G	405 341-8710
Custom Cabinet Services — Tulsa (G-9527)	G	918 340-9015
Custom Wood Craft Construction — El Reno (G-2708)	G	405 262-5228
Custom Woodwork Inc — Sapulpa (G-8263)	F	918 224-4276
Dale P Jackson — Ada (G-29)	F	580 332-1988
David Stevens Cabinets & Trim — Tulsa (G-9558)	G	918 234-0656
Davis Cabinet Shop — Newalla (G-4808)	G	405 391-5527
DH Cabinet and Trim Inc — Mustang (G-4769)	G	405 376-1709
Dynosaw Inc — Oklahoma City (G-5992)	G	405 418-6060
E&M Solutions LLC — Tulsa (G-9622)	G	918 551-9515
Elite Cabinets — Tulsa (G-9656)	G	918 794-0757
Enviro Clean — Park Hill (G-7642)	G	918 207-9779
Guthrie Darin Cabinet Shop — Sallisaw (G-8145)	G	918 773-8444
▲ Hawley & Co — Tulsa (G-9905)	G	918 587-0510
Heister Custom Cabinets Inc — Norman (G-5021)	G	405 329-6318
Hugo Wyrick Lumber — Hugo (G-3614)	E	580 326-5569
Imel Woodworks Inc — Wellston (G-11472)	G	405 356-2505
Jay Rambo Co Hahn Showroom — Tulsa (G-10030)	G	918 615-3370
Jo Rose Fine Cabinets Inc — Tulsa (G-10046)	E	918 832-1500
John Henley Cstm Cabinets LLC — Edmond (G-2473)	G	405 535-9143
Johnson Kendall Cnstr Co — Ardmore (G-317)	G	580 223-5954
Jon A Belonoik — Chandler (G-1382)	G	405 258-4131
Jones & Jackson Cabinets — Atoka (G-416)	G	580 889-8978
Kc Woodwork & Fixture Inc — Tulsa (G-10078)	G	918 582-5300
Ketcherside Custom Cabinets — Woodward (G-11599)	G	580 254-2672
Lakewood Cabinetry Inc — Langley (G-3871)	F	918 782-2203
Majestic Marble & Granite — Catoosa (G-1337)	E	918 266-1121
Mass Brothers Inc — Hartshorne (G-3393)	G	918 527-3753
Mastercraft Millwork Inc — Moore (G-4537)	G	405 895-6050
McCollum Custom Cabinets — Helena (G-3435)	G	580 548-5851
Monticello Cabinets Doors Inc — Oklahoma City (G-6627)	G	405 228-4900
Morrow Wood Products Inc — Norman (G-5081)	G	405 579-5200
Nash Custom Cabinets — Oklahoma City (G-6654)	G	405 919-7711
Norwood Custom Cabinets — Hulbert (G-3626)	G	918 478-2462
Nyes Cabinet Shop — Sulphur (G-8839)	G	580 622-6323
Oak Tree Sales — Chickasha (G-1493)	G	405 224-9332
Oklahoma Millworks Inc — Guthrie (G-3330)	D	405 282-4887
Old West Cabinets Inc — Ponca City (G-7862)	G	580 762-7474
Old Wrld Msters Div Bldg Pdts — Tulsa (G-10412)	G	405 230-0340
Paradise Construction LLC — Stigler (G-8637)	G	918 967-9991
Parks Custom Cabinets LLC — Chelsea (G-1409)	G	918 789-2694
Pedros Cstm Cabinets Trim LLC — Duncan (G-2163)	G	580 656-3982
Perkins Cabinet Trim — Chouteau (G-1569)	G	918 476-6567
Pruett Cabinet and Trim LLC — Oklahoma City (G-5312)	G	405 692-1552
Quality Cabinet Company — Jenks (G-3724)	G	918 299-2721
Quality Cabinetry — Quinton (G-8040)	G	918 469-2119
Quarry — Dewey (G-2030)	G	918 534-2120
R and P Cabinetry LLC — Oklahoma City (G-6959)	G	405 230-0495
Raber Renovations Inc — Tulsa (G-10608)	G	918 499-3030
Rambo Acquisition Company — Tulsa (G-10615)	D	918 627-6222
Real Cabinets — Bartlesville (G-522)	G	918 336-0255
Reid Manufacturing LLC — Oklahoma City (G-7004)	G	405 606-7006
Richard Douglas Co — Oklahoma City (G-7016)	G	405 577-6626
Sand Creek Custom Cabinets LLC — Fairview (G-3151)	G	580 822-1269
Sandstar Custom Cabinets LLC — Tahlequah (G-8883)	G	918 456-2964
Sequoia Custom Cabinets LLC — Tulsa (G-10732)	G	801 830-2741
Sharp Cuts Custom Cabinets — Guthrie (G-3338)	G	405 282-3657
Signature Cabinets LLC — Tulsa (G-10759)	G	918 636-3433
Sooner Cabinet & Trim Inc — Moore (G-4571)	E	405 820-2920
Spencers Custom Cabinets — Peggs (G-7713)	G	918 598-3208
Sterling Cabinetry & Trim LLC — Stigler (G-8647)	G	918 928-9982
Suburban Cabinet Shop — Oklahoma City (G-7221)	E	405 231-3110
Sullivans Custom Cabinetry — Tulsa (G-10865)	E	918 445-9191
Taylormade Cbntry Cntrtops LLC — Jones (G-3753)	G	405 227-4063
Ted S Cabinet — Wilson (G-11544)	G	580 668-5207
Thomas Cabinet Company — Apache (G-223)	G	580 588-9231
Thomas Millwork Inc — Spencer (G-8602)	F	405 769-5618
Thomco Cabinet Co — Oklahoma City (G-7284)	G	405 627-1445
Three Rivers Custom Cabinets — Muskogee (G-4752)	G	918 537-2311
Tillison Cabinet Company LLC — Moore (G-4577)	E	405 793-2940
Trim Line Cabinets Inc — Purcell (G-8024)	F	405 664-1439
Trs Cabinets & Trim LLC — Yukon (G-11795)	G	405 234-7276
United Millwork — Oklahoma City (G-7371)	G	405 670-3999
Vanderbilt Cabinet & Trim — Mustang (G-4800)	G	405 376-3876
W & W Custom Cabinets — Chickasha (G-1521)	G	405 222-1410
Wades Cabinet Door Shop — Tahlequah (G-8891)	G	918 868-2516
Ward Wood Products Inc — Oklahoma City (G-7420)	D	405 681-5522
Watkins Cabinet Doors LLC — Ada (G-104)	G	580 320-6301
WD Sales Inc — Enid (G-3076)	F	580 237-1220
Weatherford Cabinets — Weatherford (G-11456)	G	580 772-7511
Wildwood Fine Cabinet Doors — Bartlesville (G-535)	G	918 331-0007
Wilshire Cabinet & Company LLC — Oklahoma City (G-7457)	G	405 286-6282
Wolher Company — Guthrie (G-3341)	G	405 282-6210
Wood Systems Inc — Tulsa (G-11148)	D	918 388-0900
Wooden Solutions LLC — Skiatook (G-8575)	E	918 396-0774
Woodshop Cstm Cbinets Trim LLC — Oklahoma City (G-7466)	G	405 673-7139

Employee Codes: A=Over 500 employees, B=251-500, C=101-250, D=51-100, E=20-50, F=10-19, G=1-9

24 LUMBER AND WOOD PRODUCTS, EXCEPT FURNITURE

Woodstock Cabinet LLC ....F 918 834-4840
  Tulsa *(G-11150)*
Woodwork Productions LLC ....G 918 639-3167
  Catoosa *(G-1367)*
Ye Olde Woodshop ....G 918 224-1603
  Sapulpa *(G-8328)*
Young Construction Supply LLC ....G 918 456-3250
  Tahlequah *(G-8893)*

2435 Hardwood Veneer & Plywood

Hugo Wyrick Lumber ....E 580 326-5569
  Hugo *(G-3614)*
Morton Buildings Inc ....E 918 683-6668
  Muskogee *(G-4715)*

2439 Structural Wood Members, NEC

Antlers Roof-Truss & Bldrs Sup ....G 580 298-3560
  Antlers *(G-213)*
Ardmore Construction Sup Inc ....G 580 223-2322
  Ardmore *(G-245)*
Builders Firstsource Inc ....D 918 459-6872
  Broken Arrow *(G-860)*
Builders Firstsource Inc ....E 405 321-2255
  Oklahoma City *(G-5641)*
▲ Burrow Construction LLC ....E 800 766-5793
  Fort Gibson *(G-3174)*
Coreslab Structures Okla Inc ....C 405 632-4944
  Oklahoma City *(G-5835)*
Craco Truss Post Frame Sup LLC ....G 918 457-1111
  Park Hill *(G-7641)*
Cushing Truss Manufacturing ....F 918 387-2080
  Yale *(G-11683)*
David Kempe ....F 580 924-6798
  Durant *(G-2221)*
Do It Best Hardware ....G 580 482-8898
  Altus *(G-154)*
En-Fab Corp ....F 918 251-9647
  Broken Arrow *(G-1126)*
Harrison Roof Truss Co ....G 580 937-4900
  Coleman *(G-1795)*
Henderson Truss Incorporated ....F 918 473-5573
  Checotah *(G-1394)*
Higgins & Sons Truss Company ....E 405 997-5455
  Tecumseh *(G-8917)*
Higgins & Sons Truss Company ....E 405 997-5455
  Tecumseh *(G-8918)*
McFarland Cascade ....G 580 584-3511
  Broken Bow *(G-1200)*
Mills Enterprises Inc ....G 405 236-4470
  Oklahoma City *(G-6613)*
Newell Wood Products ....F 918 686-8060
  Muskogee *(G-4721)*
Northwest Truss ....G 580 496-2420
  Goltry *(G-3248)*
Overstreet Building & Supply ....G 580 234-5666
  Enid *(G-3028)*
Quality Line Truss Inc ....G 918 783-5227
  Adair *(G-111)*
Quality Truss Co Inc ....G 918 543-2077
  Claremore *(G-1677)*
Sawdust Ltd ....G 918 809-3456
  Broken Arrow *(G-1044)*
Schultz Roof Truss Inc ....G 405 364-6530
  Norman *(G-5138)*
Timberlake Trussworks LLC ....G 580 852-3660
  Helena *(G-3437)*
Zara Group Inc ....F 918 782-4473
  Vinita *(G-11273)*

2441 Wood Boxes

▼ American Crating Company ....E 918 425-8787
  Tulsa *(G-9166)*
Johnson Crating Services LLC ....G 405 672-7964
  Oklahoma City *(G-6374)*
Pratt Industries USA Inc ....B 405 787-3500
  Oklahoma City *(G-6874)*
Sunrise Sheds ....G 405 831-0904
  Prague *(G-7937)*
Tulsa Packing Specialist Inc ....F 918 459-8991
  Tulsa *(G-11003)*

2448 Wood Pallets & Skids

AAA Crimstone Operating Co LP ....G 918 445-5500
  Tulsa *(G-9077)*
Alex Pallets ....G 405 414-2710
  Oklahoma City *(G-5411)*
Betty E Jester ....G 580 564-9396
  Kingston *(G-3824)*

Burgess Manufacturing Okla Inc ....E 405 282-1913
  Guthrie *(G-3303)*
Choctaw Mfg Def Contrs Inc ....F 580 326-8365
  Hugo *(G-3608)*
Choctaw Mfg Def Contrs Inc ....G 580 298-2203
  Antlers *(G-215)*
Choctaw Mfg Def Contrs Inc ....G 918 426-2871
  McAlester *(G-4286)*
Chouteau Pallet ....G 918 476-6098
  Chouteau *(G-1561)*
Cimarron Pallet Mfg Co 405 228-0288
  Oklahoma City *(G-5765)*
Cisco Containers LLC ....G 918 439-9244
  Tulsa *(G-9430)*
Doug Butler Enterprises Inc ....F 918 425-3565
  Tulsa *(G-9599)*
Duncan Wood Works LLC ....G 580 641-1190
  Duncan *(G-2113)*
Fat & Happy Services Inc ....G 405 834-5782
  Oklahoma City *(G-6078)*
Frahm John ....G 213 500-0741
  Sand Springs *(G-8185)*
Frontier Resource Development ....G 918 682-6571
  Muskogee *(G-4676)*
Henryetta Pallet Company ....E 918 652-9897
  Henryetta *(G-3508)*
Hernandez Pallets 405 636-0503
  Oklahoma City *(G-6243)*
Ifco Systems ....G 405 491-9300
  Oklahoma City *(G-6289)*
▲ Ifco Systems Us LLC ....G 405 681-8090
  Oklahoma City *(G-6290)*
Johnson Lumber Company Inc ....E 918 253-8786
  Spavinaw *(G-8591)*
Oklahoma AAA Pallet Company ....E 405 670-1414
  Oklahoma City *(G-6734)*
Pal-Serv Oklahoma City LLC ....E 405 672-1155
  Oklahoma City *(G-6794)*
Pallet Liquidations Okc LLC ....G 405 843-0402
  Oklahoma City *(G-6796)*
Pallet Logistics of America ....G 405 670-1414
  Oklahoma City *(G-6797)*
Pallets Plus LLC 580 513-4090
  Davis *(G-1992)*
Pauls Pallet Co ....G 918 435-4321
  Eucha *(G-3095)*
Prime Pallet LLC ....G 918 683-0907
  Muskogee *(G-4737)*
Pro Pallets 405 679-8076
  Oklahoma City *(G-6905)*
Propak Logistics Inc ....D 405 694-4441
  Oklahoma City *(G-6916)*
Simer Pallet Recycling Inc ....F 405 224-8583
  Chickasha *(G-1511)*
Sooner Pallet Services Inc 918 342-9663
  Claremore *(G-1686)*
Tasler Pallet Inc ....F 580 276-9800
  Marietta *(G-4213)*
Tim E Hutcheson ....G 918 313-5710
  Tulsa *(G-10941)*

2449 Wood Containers, NEC

Burgess Manufacturing Okla Inc ....E 405 282-1913
  Guthrie *(G-3303)*
Choctaw Mfg Def Contrs Inc 580 326-8365
  Hugo *(G-3609)*
Economy Lumber Company Inc ....G 918 835-4933
  Tulsa *(G-9641)*
Four Star Crating Co ....G 918 663-6689
  Tulsa *(G-9769)*
Johnson Crating Services LLC ....G 405 672-7964
  Oklahoma City *(G-6374)*
Midtown Ventures LLC ....G 918 728-3102
  Tulsa *(G-10265)*
Van Brunt Lumber 405 567-3776
  Prague *(G-7938)*
▲ Weilert Enterprises Inc ....E 918 252-5515
  Catoosa *(G-1365)*
▲ Western Industries Corporation ....C 405 419-3100
  Oklahoma City *(G-7439)*

2451 Mobile Homes

Bill Durbins Mobile Home Tra ....G 405 799-3557
  Oklahoma City *(G-5280)*
Clayton Homes Inc ....E 918 686-0584
  Muskogee *(G-4661)*
Clayton Homes Inc ....G 405 341-4479
  Edmond *(G-2356)*
Clayton Homes Inc ....G 580 237-7094
  Enid *(G-2931)*

Freedom Homes ....G 918 728-2277
  Tulsa *(G-9775)*
Hollands Mobile Homes ....G 918 476-5663
  Chouteau *(G-1565)*
Housing USA ....G 405 631-3653
  Oklahoma City *(G-6267)*
Modernblox LLC ....G 405 673-6215
  Tulsa *(G-10292)*

2452 Prefabricated Wood Buildings & Cmpnts

Better Built Barns 405 547-2066
  Perkins *(G-7715)*
▲ Burrow Construction LLC ....E 800 766-5793
  Fort Gibson *(G-3174)*
Cedar Built USA Inc ....G 405 794-0811
  Moore *(G-4508)*
David Davis ....G 405 354-6974
  El Reno *(G-2710)*
Flex-Ability Concepts LLC 405 996-5343
  Oklahoma City *(G-6091)*
Fullerton Building Systems Inc ....E 918 246-9995
  Sand Springs *(G-8187)*
Icon Construction Inc ....F 580 931-3806
  Durant *(G-2236)*
Katahdin Cedar Log Homes OK 918 473-7020
  Checotah *(G-1396)*
◆ Midwest Cooling Towers Inc ....C 405 224-4622
  Chickasha *(G-1486)*
Midwest Portable Building ....G 918 245-9335
  Tulsa *(G-10269)*
Molitor Design & Cnstr LLC ....G 405 802-8302
  Moore *(G-4542)*
Morton Buildings Inc ....G 580 323-1172
  Clinton *(G-1759)*
Morton Buildings Inc ....E 918 683-6668
  Muskogee *(G-4715)*
Roadrunner Portable Buildings 918 272-7788
  Owasso *(G-7608)*
Rons Discount Lumber Inc ....D 918 658-3857
  Howe *(G-3599)*
Shipman Home Improvement Inc 918 514-0049
  Sand Springs *(G-8223)*
Solitaire Holdings LLC 580 252-6060
  Duncan *(G-2179)*
Solitaire Homes Inc ....E 580 252-6060
  Duncan *(G-2180)*
Standard Panel LLC ....G 918 984-1717
  Tulsa *(G-10837)*
Terry Hall ....E 817 271-4838
  Valliant *(G-11232)*
Tuff Shed Inc ....G 405 272-1011
  Oklahoma City *(G-7348)*
Tuff Shed Inc 405 788-4143
  Shawnee *(G-8513)*
Victory Garden Homestead LLC 405 306-0308
  Blanchard *(G-744)*
Wood Tech Structures 918 678-2108
  Wyandotte *(G-11663)*

2491 Wood Preserving

▲ Cowans Millwork Inc ....G 918 357-3725
  Broken Arrow *(G-1118)*
McFarland Cascade Holdings Inc 580 584-2272
  Broken Bow *(G-1201)*
Mixon Brothers Wood Prsv Co ....F 580 286-9494
  Idabel *(G-3643)*

2493 Reconstituted Wood Prdts

Black Thunder Roofing LLC ....G 405 473-8028
  Oklahoma City *(G-5582)*
▲ Dominance Industries Inc ....C 580 584-7000
  Broken Bow *(G-1189)*
Heintzelman Cons & Rofing 405 409-8954
  Oklahoma City *(G-5294)*
Huber Engineered Woods LLC ....E 580 584-7000
  Broken Bow *(G-1192)*
Icon Roofing and Cnstr LLC ....G 405 403-6615
  Mustang *(G-4777)*
Riverside Ranch LLC ....F 405 360-7300
  Norman *(G-5132)*

2499 Wood Prdts, NEC

Allens Woodcraft ....G 918 224-8796
  Sapulpa *(G-8247)*
American International Ltd ....G 405 364-1776
  Norman *(G-4907)*
Artisan Design Inc ....G 918 251-9795
  Broken Arrow *(G-835)*

AS Designs LLC .... G 918 381-2390
  Owasso (G-7546)
Baties Custom Saddle Tree .... F 918 788-3686
  Welch (G-11462)
Bell Timber Inc .... G 580 584-6902
  Broken Bow (G-1185)
Bristow 800 Kelly LLC .... G 248 268-3289
  Bristow (G-768)
Clubbs Wood Art .... G 918 569-4401
  Clayton (G-1708)
Cork and Bottle Wine and .... G 405 318-6842
  Yukon (G-11713)
Country Crafts .... G 918 247-6144
  Kellyville (G-3763)
Custom WD Fbers Cdar Mulch LLC .... G 405 745-2270
  Oklahoma City (G-5879)
D & S Refinishing .... G 580 233-4351
  Enid (G-2938)
D E Ziegler Art Craft Supply .... E 918 584-2217
  Tulsa (G-9537)
D Lloyd Hollingsworth .... G 918 587-3533
  Tulsa (G-9539)
DC Custom Framing .... G 918 549-8754
  Skiatook (G-8539)
Desert Moon Enterprises .... G 918 540-0333
  Miami (G-4395)
Dovetail Enterprises LLC .... G 405 476-3953
  Bethany (G-576)
Edmond Trophy Co .... G 405 341-4631
  Edmond (G-2405)
Engineered Food Processes LLC .... G 405 377-7320
  Stillwater (G-8684)
Eric Adams Trim .... G 405 570-5931
  Jones (G-3745)
From Heart .... G 405 348-3009
  Edmond (G-2425)
Handle LLC .... G 405 822-9312
  Oklahoma City (G-6211)
Hardwood Innovations Inc .... F 405 722-5588
  Oklahoma City (G-6219)
Hoffman Fixtures Company .... E 918 252-0451
  Tulsa (G-9936)
Integrity Woodcrafters LLC .... G 918 664-1041
  Tulsa (G-10000)
K & K Wood Products .... G 918 396-4004
  Skiatook (G-8553)
Kactus Rose LLC .... G 405 830-7551
  El Reno (G-2729)
Marrara Group Inc .... G 918 379-0993
  Tulsa (G-10216)
Midwest Cooling Towers Inc .... G 580 389-5421
  Ardmore (G-332)
◆ Midwest Cooling Towers Inc .... C 405 224-4622
  Chickasha (G-1486)
Mitre Box Frame Shop .... G 580 338-2319
  Guymon (G-3356)
Mjs Crafts .... G 405 598-8105
  Tecumseh (G-8923)
▲ Mtm Recognition Corporation .... B 405 609-6900
  Oklahoma City (G-6634)
Multiples Inc .... G 918 584-7982
  Tulsa (G-10314)
Okiewood LLC .... G 405 245-5257
  Oklahoma City (G-6732)
Patternwork Veneering Inc .... G 405 447-1800
  Norman (G-5110)
PEL Company LLC .... G 405 816-6553
  Oklahoma City (G-6821)
Progressive Industries Inc .... G 405 843-0597
  Oklahoma City (G-6912)
Rabid .... G 580 234-3632
  Enid (G-3041)
Red Cedar Creations .... G 580 227-3198
  Longdale (G-4127)
Rick Woodten .... G 580 786-5050
  Duncan (G-2167)
Safe Harbor Docks Inc .... G 918 376-2756
  Owasso (G-7610)
Safe Harbor Products LLC .... G 918 376-2756
  Owasso (G-7611)
Smallwood Building LLC .... G 918 424-9378
  McAlester (G-4336)
Southwest Interiors Inc .... G 580 323-3050
  Clinton (G-1769)
Straight Edge Sawmill .... G 405 401-7798
  Union City (G-11221)
Tulsa Wood Arts LLC .... G 918 576-6142
  Tulsa (G-11012)
Waterwood Parkway LLC .... G 405 341-5077
  Edmond (G-2682)
Welton Acquisitions LLC .... G 918 850-7981
  Sand Springs (G-8240)
Wooden Concepts LLC .... G 405 459-0411
  Weatherford (G-11461)
Woodshed .... E 918 256-9868
  Vinita (G-11272)
Wynnewood 1500 LLC .... G 248 268-3289
  Wynnewood (G-11675)
Wynnewood LLC .... G 248 268-3289
  Wynnewood (G-11676)
Yester Year Carousel .... G 405 427-5863
  Oklahoma City (G-7479)

25 FURNITURE AND FIXTURES

2511 Wood Household Furniture

American Custom Woodworks LLC ..... G 918 344-4988
  Sapulpa (G-8248)
Billiards & Bar Stools Inc .... F 405 722-2400
  Oklahoma City (G-5566)
Breshears Enterprises Inc .... F 405 236-4523
  Oklahoma City (G-5624)
Cedar Chest .... G 918 287-9129
  Pawhuska (G-7681)
Close Custom Cabinets Inc .... E 405 840-8226
  Oklahoma City (G-5790)
Creative Spaces .... G 405 341-8710
  Edmond (G-2372)
Days Wood Products Inc .... F 405 238-6477
  Pauls Valley (G-7656)
Desert Moon Enterprises .... G 918 540-0333
  Miami (G-4395)
Donmar Industries LLC .... G 918 688-7277
  Skiatook (G-8542)
▲ Fabric Factory .... F 405 521-1694
  Oklahoma City (G-6067)
▲ Hawley & Co .... G 918 587-0510
  Tulsa (G-9905)
Imel Woodworks Inc .... G 405 356-2505
  Wellston (G-11472)
Johnson Woodcraft .... G 918 693-2388
  Claremore (G-1645)
Jos Lamerton Woodworking LLC .... G 580 336-8448
  Enid (G-2988)
Juan Manzo Custom Refinishing .... G 405 848-3843
  Oklahoma City (G-6390)
Kc Woodwork & Fixture Inc .... G 918 582-5300
  Tulsa (G-10078)
Kennel and Crate LLC .... G 405 624-0062
  Stillwater (G-8709)
Legacy Metalcraft LLC .... G 918 612-0001
  Wagoner (G-11286)
Mass Brothers Inc .... G 918 527-3753
  Hartshorne (G-3393)
Milot James Residence Cnstr .... G 405 433-2661
  Cashion (G-1291)
Punkin Hollerwood .... G 918 456-9640
  Proctor (G-7939)
Refuge Lifestyle .... F 918 366-6650
  Tulsa (G-10636)
Stillwater Transfer & Stor Co .... F 405 372-0577
  Stillwater (G-8759)
▼ Troy Wesnidge Inc .... F 405 387-4720
  Newcastle (G-4845)
United Millwork Inc .... G 405 670-3999
  Oklahoma City (G-7371)
Weatherford Cabinets .... G 580 772-7511
  Weatherford (G-11456)
Westwood Furniture Inc .... G 918 508-7657
  Tulsa (G-11113)
Winkles Woodworks Ltd .... F 918 486-5022
  Coweta (G-1902)
Woodshop Ltd .... G 405 922-3789
  Edmond (G-2692)
Young Construction Supply LLC .... G 918 456-3250
  Tahlequah (G-8893)

2512 Wood Household Furniture, Upholstered

Custom Lea Sad & Cowboy Decor .... G 918 335-2277
  Bartlesville (G-471)
Custom Upholstery Contracting .... F 405 236-3505
  Oklahoma City (G-5878)
Davenport Cloaks Inc .... G 918 932-8600
  Tulsa (G-9556)
James D Johnson .... G 580 464-3299
  Cyril (G-1975)
La-Z-Boy Incorporated .... G 405 417-5704
  Oklahoma City (G-6443)
La-Z-Boy Incorporated .... G 405 951-1437
  Oklahoma City (G-6444)
Patricia McKay .... G 580 355-2739
  Cache (G-1230)
Relf Upholstery .... G 405 454-3295
  Luther (G-4137)
Sendee Sales Inc .... E 918 427-3318
  Muldrow (G-4636)
Warren Ramsey Inc .... G 405 528-2828
  Oklahoma City (G-7422)

2514 Metal Household Furniture

Angel Ornamental Iron Works .... G 918 584-8726
  Tulsa (G-9191)
Billiards & Bar Stools Inc .... F 405 722-2400
  Oklahoma City (G-5566)
Chris Green Greens Construct .... G 405 207-0690
  Pauls Valley (G-7653)
Glenn Schlarb Welding .... G 580 327-3832
  Alva (G-182)
Ironcraft Urban Products LLC .... G 855 601-1647
  Oklahoma City (G-6327)
J&M Stainless Fabricators Ltd .... G 405 517-0875
  Oklahoma City (G-6340)
Legacy Metalcraft LLC .... G 918 612-0001
  Wagoner (G-11286)
Life Lift Systems Inc .... F 904 635-8231
  Oklahoma City (G-6474)
Melton Co Inc .... G 405 524-2281
  Oklahoma City (G-6563)
Pro Stainless & Shtmtl LLC .... G 405 787-4400
  Oklahoma City (G-6906)
▲ Webcoat Inc .... C 918 426-5100
  McAlester (G-4350)

2515 Mattresses & Bedsprings

Adairs Sleep World Inc .... F 405 341-9468
  Edmond (G-2289)
B & B Haybeds .... G 580 357-5083
  Lawton (G-3894)
Leggett & Platt Incorporated .... G 405 787-1212
  Oklahoma City (G-6465)
M & M Mattress Company .... G 918 834-2033
  Tulsa (G-10187)
Melton Co Inc .... G 405 524-2281
  Oklahoma City (G-6563)
Montgomery Mattress .... G 580 255-8979
  Duncan (G-2156)
Tote4me .... G 405 664-1144
  Edmond (G-2651)
Treble Services LLC .... G 405 401-1217
  Oklahoma City (G-7321)

2517 Wood T V, Radio, Phono & Sewing Cabinets

Beauchamp Cabinets Cstm Homes ..... G 918 476-5532
  Chouteau (G-1558)
Contemporary Cabinets Inc .... D 405 330-4592
  Edmond (G-2365)
Creative Spaces .... G 405 341-8710
  Edmond (G-2372)
Ketcherside Custom Cabinets .... G 580 254-2672
  Woodward (G-11599)
P I Speakers .... G 918 663-2131
  Tulsa (G-10453)
Parkers Custom Hardwoods Inc .... G 405 341-9663
  Edmond (G-2563)
Rambo Acquisition Company .... D 918 627-6222
  Tulsa (G-10615)
United Millwork Inc .... G 405 670-3999
  Oklahoma City (G-7371)
Weatherford Cabinets .... G 580 772-7511
  Weatherford (G-11456)

2519 Household Furniture, NEC

Hemispheres .... G 405 773-8410
  Warr Acres (G-11322)
Murphy Wallbed USA LLC .... G 918 836-5833
  Tulsa (G-10317)
World Imports At Wholesale Inc .... G 405 947-7710
  Oklahoma City (G-7469)

2521 Wood Office Furniture

▲ Bearwood Concepts Inc .... D 918 933-6600
  Tulsa (G-9277)
Beauchamp Cabinets Cstm Homes ..... G 918 476-5532
  Chouteau (G-1558)
D Lloyd Hollingsworth .... G 918 587-3533
  Tulsa (G-9539)

27 PRINTING, PUBLISHING, AND ALLIED INDUSTRIES

Green Ox Pallet Technology LLC .... G 720 276-8013
  Oklahoma City *(G-6187)*
International Paper Company .... D 405 745-5800
  Oklahoma City *(G-6320)*
Oklahoma Interpak Inc .... E 918 687-1681
  Muskogee *(G-4724)*
Olson Packaging Service .... G 405 224-5577
  Chickasha *(G-1494)*
▲ Republic Paperboard Co LLC .... C 580 510-2200
  Lawton *(G-3993)*
Tulsa Packing Specialist Inc .... F 918 459-8991
  Tulsa *(G-11003)*

2652 Set-Up Paperboard Boxes

▲ Professional Image Inc .... E 918 461-0609
  Tulsa *(G-10569)*

2653 Corrugated & Solid Fiber Boxes

Corrugated Services LP .... G 405 672-1695
  Oklahoma City *(G-5840)*
Creative Packaging Inc .... G 918 587-0347
  Tulsa *(G-9505)*
Georgia-Pacific LLC .... C 580 549-7100
  Fletcher *(G-3162)*
Green Bay Packaging Inc .... E 405 222-2306
  Chickasha *(G-1463)*
Green Bay Packaging Inc .... C 918 446-3341
  Tulsa *(G-9008)*
International Paper Company .... D 405 745-5800
  Oklahoma City *(G-6320)*
Oklahoma Interpak Inc .... E 918 687-1681
  Muskogee *(G-4724)*
Pratt Industries USA Inc .... B 405 787-3500
  Oklahoma City *(G-6874)*
▼ Professional Packaging Inc .... E 918 682-9531
  Muskogee *(G-4738)*
Smurfit Kappa .... G 405 672-1695
  Oklahoma City *(G-7156)*
Smurfit Kappa North Amer LLC .... B 405 672-1695
  Oklahoma City *(G-7157)*
Southern Box Company .... G 580 255-7969
  Duncan *(G-2181)*
Stan-Mel Industries Inc .... E 918 436-0056
  Pocola *(G-7787)*
Supplyone Oklahoma City Inc .... C 405 947-7373
  Oklahoma City *(G-7230)*
Supplyone Oklahoma City Inc .... E 918 446-4428
  Tulsa *(G-10881)*
Vande Lune Packaging LLC .... G 405 517-0098
  Yukon *(G-11801)*
Westrock Cp LLC .... C 918 245-5102
  Sand Springs *(G-8241)*

2655 Fiber Cans, Tubes & Drums

Capitol Tube Co Inc .... G 405 632-9901
  Oklahoma City *(G-5696)*
EZ Mail Express .... G 918 542-2057
  Miami *(G-4403)*
▲ High Caliper Growing Inc .... D 405 842-7700
  Oklahoma City *(G-6246)*
Mito Material Solutions Inc .... G 855 344-6486
  Stillwater *(G-8725)*
Sonoco Products Company .... E 918 622-3370
  Tulsa *(G-10786)*
Sureshot Cans Inc .... G 580 698-2800
  Woodward *(G-11638)*

2656 Sanitary Food Containers

Hobby Supermarket Inc .... E 405 239-6864
  Oklahoma City *(G-6256)*
Solo Cup Operating Corporation .... C 580 436-1500
  Ada *(G-90)*

2657 Folding Paperboard Boxes

Artur Bookbinding Intl .... G 918 478-4888
  Fort Gibson *(G-3173)*
International Paper Company .... D 580 933-7211
  Valliant *(G-11227)*
▼ Media Resources Inc .... E 405 682-4400
  Oklahoma City *(G-6555)*
▲ Warner Jwly Box Display Co LLC .... D 580 536-8885
  Lawton *(G-4021)*

2671 Paper Coating & Laminating for Packaging

Beacon Stamp & Seal Co .... G 918 834-2322
  Tulsa *(G-9276)*
Bemis Company Inc .... C 405 207-2200
  Pauls Valley *(G-7650)*
Berry Global Films LLC .... D 918 227-1616
  Tulsa *(G-8990)*
Berry Plastics Corporation .... C 918 824-4400
  Pryor *(G-7947)*
International Paper Company .... D 580 933-7211
  Valliant *(G-11227)*
Pregis LLC .... D 918 439-9916
  Tulsa *(G-10552)*
Regency Labels Inc .... E 405 682-3460
  Oklahoma City *(G-7002)*
Sigma Extruding Corp .... F 918 446-6265
  Tulsa *(G-10755)*
Tom Bennett Manufacturing .... F 405 528-5671
  Oklahoma City *(G-7302)*

2672 Paper Coating & Laminating, Exc for Packaging

A-1 Specialties .... G 405 942-1341
  Oklahoma City *(G-5352)*
Giesecke & Devrient Amer Inc .... D 405 270-8400
  Oklahoma City *(G-6154)*
Keystone Tape & Label Inc .... G 405 631-2341
  Oklahoma City *(G-6415)*
Krause Plastics .... G 918 835-4202
  Tulsa *(G-10100)*
Marpro Label Inc .... G 405 672-3344
  Oklahoma City *(G-6530)*
Martin Thomas Enterprises Inc .... D 918 739-4015
  Catoosa *(G-1338)*
Marvel Photo Inc .... G 918 836-0741
  Tulsa *(G-10218)*
Priority Printworks Inc .... G 918 825-6397
  Pryor *(G-7984)*
Regency Labels Inc .... E 405 682-3460
  Oklahoma City *(G-7002)*
▲ Stonehouse Marketing Svcs LLC .... D 405 360-5674
  Norman *(G-5160)*
Summit Labels Inc .... G 918 936-4950
  Tulsa *(G-10868)*

2673 Bags: Plastics, Laminated & Coated

Advance Polybag Inc .... G 405 677-8383
  Oklahoma City *(G-5377)*
▲ API Enterprises Inc .... C 713 580-4800
  Oklahoma City *(G-5452)*
▼ Bags Inc .... E 405 427-5473
  Oklahoma City *(G-5509)*
Richard Bolusky .... G 918 381-5694
  Broken Arrow *(G-1031)*
Sigma Extruding Corp .... F 918 446-6265
  Tulsa *(G-10755)*
Tech Pack Inc .... G 918 836-8493
  Tulsa *(G-10910)*
Transcontinental Holding Corp .... F 918 739-4907
  Catoosa *(G-1358)*
Transcontinental US LLC .... D 918 739-4906
  Catoosa *(G-1359)*

2675 Die-Cut Paper & Board

Quik-Print of Oklahoma City .... G 405 840-3275
  Oklahoma City *(G-6950)*

2676 Sanitary Paper Prdts

Cool Baby Inc .... G 405 755-1100
  Edmond *(G-2367)*
Fatutyi Adeshola .... G 785 424-4208
  Lawton *(G-3928)*
Kimberly-Clark Corporation .... B 918 366-5000
  Jenks *(G-3713)*
▲ Opp Liquidating Company Inc .... C 918 825-0616
  Pryor *(G-7980)*

2677 Envelopes

Frank G Love Envelopes Inc .... D 214 637-5900
  Tulsa *(G-9772)*
Frank G Love Envelopes Inc .... G 405 720-9177
  Warr Acres *(G-11319)*
Response Solutions Inc .... G 918 508-7022
  Tulsa *(G-10647)*
Unity Press Inc .... E 405 232-8910
  Tulsa *(G-11045)*
Western Web Envelope Co Inc .... F 405 682-0207
  Oklahoma City *(G-7442)*

2678 Stationery Prdts

R&D Labs LLC .... G 405 875-9937
  Edmond *(G-2583)*

2679 Converted Paper Prdts, NEC

Brenda Riggs .... G 918 543-3530
  Inola *(G-3652)*
County of Comanche .... G 580 355-3810
  Lawton *(G-3911)*
▼ Media Resources Inc .... E 405 682-4400
  Oklahoma City *(G-6555)*
Metcel LLC .... G 405 334-7846
  Edmond *(G-2514)*
Paper Concierge .... G 405 286-3322
  Edmond *(G-2561)*
Pink Petals Flowers Gifts LLC .... G 580 317-8200
  Hugo *(G-3619)*
Regency Labels Inc .... E 405 682-3460
  Oklahoma City *(G-7002)*
Rotocolor Inc .... F 510 785-7686
  Tulsa *(G-10676)*
Summit Labels Inc .... G 918 936-4950
  Tulsa *(G-10868)*

27 PRINTING, PUBLISHING, AND ALLIED INDUSTRIES

2711 Newspapers: Publishing & Printing

Aaron Lance Butler .... G 580 220-7715
  Ardmore *(G-235)*
Adams Investment Company .... D 918 661-2100
  Dewey *(G-2013)*
Allen Advocate .... G 580 857-2687
  Allen *(G-132)*
American-Chief Co .... G 918 358-2553
  Cleveland *(G-1715)*
American-Chief Co .... G 918 762-2552
  Pawnee *(G-7699)*
American-Chief Co .... G 918 885-2101
  Hominy *(G-3575)*
Anadarko Publishing Co .... E 405 247-3331
  Anadarko *(G-199)*
Apache News .... G 580 588-3862
  Apache *(G-217)*
Ardmore Inc .... G 405 201-1288
  Ardmore *(G-247)*
Bam Journal LLC .... G 405 307-8220
  Norman *(G-4925)*
Bargain Journal .... G 918 426-5500
  McAlester *(G-4273)*
Beacon Publishing Co Inc .... G 405 232-4151
  Oklahoma City *(G-5540)*
Berkshire Hathaway Inc .... G 918 245-6634
  Sand Springs *(G-8166)*
Berkshire Hathaway Inc .... G 918 272-1155
  Owasso *(G-7548)*
Berkshire Hathaway Inc .... G 918 396-1616
  Skiatook *(G-8532)*
Berkshire Hathaway Inc .... G 918 485-5505
  Wagoner *(G-11277)*
Berkshire Hathaway Inc .... G 918 486-4444
  Wagoner *(G-11276)*
Beths Baubles and Bits .... G 405 659-3841
  Luther *(G-4134)*
Biggs Communications Inc .... G 918 523-4425
  Tulsa *(G-9295)*
Black Chronicle Inc .... F 405 424-4695
  Oklahoma City *(G-5581)*
Blackwell Wind .... G 580 363-0553
  Blackwell *(G-675)*
Blanchard News Publishing .... G 405 485-2311
  Blanchard *(G-702)*
Brently Publishing Intl LLC .... G 405 381-9069
  Tuttle *(G-11187)*
Buffalo Examiner .... G 580 326-3926
  Hugo *(G-3604)*
Cable Printing Co Inc .... F 405 756-4045
  Lindsay *(G-4055)*
Cache Times .... G 580 429-8200
  Cache *(G-1225)*
Carnegie Herald .... G 580 654-1443
  Carnegie *(G-1274)*
Chadwick Paper Inc .... G 580 369-2807
  Davis *(G-1979)*
Cheyenne Star .... G 580 497-3324
  Cheyenne *(G-1423)*
Choate Publishing Inc .... F 580 276-3255
  Marietta *(G-4204)*

Employee Codes: A=Over 500 employees, B=251-500
C=101-250, D=51-100, E=20-50, F=10-19, G=1-9

2020 Oklahoma Directory of Manufacturers & Processors

SIC SECTION
27 PRINTING, PUBLISHING, AND ALLIED INDUSTRIES

Nichols Hills Publishing Co.....F..... 405 755-3311
Oklahoma City *(G-6678)*
Northern Arizona Newspaper.....F..... 928 524-6203
Edmond *(G-2540)*
Nuestra Comunidad.....G..... 405 685-3822
Oklahoma City *(G-6703)*
Okemah Leader.....G..... 918 623-0123
Okemah *(G-5271)*
Oklahoma Assn of Elc Coop.....E..... 405 478-1455
Oklahoma City *(G-6735)*
Oklahoma Bankers.....E..... 405 424-5252
Oklahoma City *(G-6736)*
Oklahoma City Herald.....G..... 405 842-7827
Oklahoma City *(G-6741)*
Oklahoma Eagle LLC.....G..... 918 582-7124
Tulsa *(G-10398)*
Oklahoma Eagle Publishing Co.....G..... 918 582-7124
Tulsa *(G-10399)*
Oklahoma Magazine.....F..... 918 744-6205
Tulsa *(G-10402)*
Oklahoma Newspaper.....F..... 405 475-3989
Oklahoma City *(G-6755)*
Oklahoma Newspaper Foundation.....E..... 405 499-0020
Oklahoma City *(G-6756)*
Oklahoma Publishing Co of Okla.....E..... 405 475-3585
Oklahoma City *(G-6759)*
Oklahoman Media Company.....F..... 405 475-3311
Oklahoma City *(G-6765)*
Omni LLC.....G..... 405 246-9252
Oklahoma City *(G-6777)*
Opubco Development Co.....E..... 405 475-3311
Oklahoma City *(G-6780)*
Owner Value News.....G..... 918 828-9600
Tulsa *(G-10449)*
Paper.....G..... 918 825-2860
Pryor *(G-7981)*
Paxton Publishing Co.....G..... 580 782-3321
Mangum *(G-4173)*
Perry Broadcasting Company.....F..... 405 427-5877
Oklahoma City *(G-6834)*
Perry Dailey Journal Inc.....G..... 580 336-2222
Perry *(G-7741)*
Ponca City Publishing Co Inc.....E..... 580 765-3311
Ponca City *(G-7866)*
Poteau Daily News.....G..... 918 647-3335
Poteau *(G-7911)*
Prague Times Herald.....G..... 405 567-3933
Prague *(G-7932)*
Premier Printing.....G..... 405 632-1132
Oklahoma City *(G-6886)*
Randy Wyrick.....G..... 918 848-0117
Fairland *(G-3128)*
Reid Communications LLC.....G..... 918 285-5555
Cushing *(G-1955)*
Reporter Publishing Co Inc.....G..... 918 789-2331
Chelsea *(G-1411)*
Review News Co.....F..... 405 354-5264
Yukon *(G-11771)*
Review Printing Company Inc.....F..... 580 658-6657
Marlow *(G-4241)*
Ringling Eagle.....G..... 580 662-2221
Ringling *(G-8082)*
Rosemon Martin LLC.....G..... 918 272-7145
Owasso *(G-7609)*
Rush Springs Gazette.....G..... 580 476-2525
Rush Springs *(G-8125)*
Russell Publishing Company.....G..... 405 665-4333
Wynnewood *(G-11672)*
Salina Journal.....G..... 785 822-1470
Collinsville *(G-1823)*
Sayre Record.....G..... 580 928-5540
Sayre *(G-8345)*
Sentinel Leader.....G..... 580 393-4348
Sentinel *(G-8412)*
Shawnee News-Star.....G..... 405 273-4200
Shawnee *(G-8495)*
Sherrif.....G..... 918 663-3705
Tulsa *(G-10743)*
Southeast Times.....G..... 580 286-2628
Idabel *(G-3646)*
Southwest Cnstr News Svc.....G..... 405 948-7474
Oklahoma City *(G-7173)*
Southwest Cnstr News Svc.....G..... 918 493-5066
Tulsa *(G-10804)*
Spiro Graphic.....G..... 918 962-2075
Spiro *(G-8618)*
Spitzer Printing.....G..... 580 928-5540
Sayre *(G-8346)*
Spitzer Publishing.....G..... 580 928-5540
Sayre *(G-8347)*

Star Nowata.....G..... 918 273-2446
Nowata *(G-5230)*
Stroud American Inc.....G..... 918 968-2310
Stroud *(G-8820)*
Sun of A Beach.....G..... 918 938-6219
Tulsa *(G-10871)*
Taloga Times Advocate.....G..... 580 328-5619
Taloga *(G-8908)*
Thomas Tribute Inc.....G..... 580 661-3524
Thomas *(G-8949)*
Times Star.....G..... 918 710-5740
Collinsville *(G-1827)*
Times-Democrat Company Inc.....G..... 580 622-2102
Sulphur *(G-8844)*
Tonkawa News.....G..... 580 628-2532
Tonkawa *(G-8984)*
Tri County Publications Inc.....G..... 918 465-3851
Wilburton *(G-11526)*
Tribune Corp.....E..... 405 262-5180
El Reno *(G-2764)*
Triple B Media LLC.....G..... 405 732-7577
Midwest City *(G-4459)*
Tulsa World.....G..... 918 664-8683
Tulsa *(G-11013)*
Tulsa World.....G..... 918 582-5921
Tulsa *(G-11014)*
Tulsa World Capitol Bureau.....G..... 405 528-2465
Oklahoma City *(G-7350)*
University of Oklahoma.....C..... 405 325-3666
Norman *(G-5188)*
Valliant Leader Inc.....G..... 580 933-4570
Valliant *(G-11233)*
Vinita Printing Co Inc.....E..... 918 256-6422
Vinita *(G-11271)*
Wanderlust Pen Company.....G..... 918 551-6809
Tulsa *(G-11094)*
Washita Valley Weekly.....G..... 405 224-7467
Chickasha *(G-1522)*
Watonga Republican Inc.....G..... 580 623-4922
Watonga *(G-11354)*
Waynoka Pubg Co Woods Cnty.....G..... 580 824-2171
Waynoka *(G-11381)*
Weatherford News Inc.....E..... 580 772-3301
Weatherford *(G-11458)*
Weekly Leader.....G..... 918 458-8001
Tahlequah *(G-8892)*
Wesner Publications Company.....F..... 405 789-1962
Bethany *(G-600)*
Wesner Publications Company.....E..... 580 832-3333
Cordell *(G-1865)*
Wewoka Times.....G..... 405 257-3341
Wewoka *(G-11513)*
Wilson-Monroe Publishing Co.....G..... 580 933-4579
Valliant *(G-11234)*
Woods County Enterprise.....G..... 580 824-2171
Waynoka *(G-11384)*
Woodward News.....E..... 580 256-2200
Woodward *(G-11658)*

2721 Periodicals: Publishing & Printing

Able Engineering Services.....G..... 918 835-3161
Tulsa *(G-9082)*
AG Youth Magazine.....G..... 800 599-6884
Sentinel *(G-8409)*
AGC Inc.....G..... 913 451-8900
Oklahoma City *(G-5398)*
American Assn Petro Geologists.....D..... 918 584-2555
Tulsa *(G-9164)*
American Choral Directors Assn.....F..... 405 232-8161
Oklahoma City *(G-5434)*
Black Belt Magazine 1000 LLC.....G..... 405 732-5111
Oklahoma City *(G-5580)*
C and H Publishing Co.....G..... 918 245-9571
Sand Springs *(G-8169)*
Chastain Enterprises LLC.....G..... 918 615-9355
Tulsa *(G-9407)*
Clarion Events Inc.....C..... 918 835-3161
Tulsa *(G-9438)*
Coast To Coast Power Spt LLC.....G..... 918 712-8487
Tulsa *(G-9462)*
Commercial Property Research.....G..... 918 481-8882
Tulsa *(G-9476)*
Datapages Inc.....G..... 918 584-2555
Tulsa *(G-9555)*
Dealers Market.....G..... 405 789-6455
Warr Acres *(G-11318)*
Dharma Inc.....G..... 405 366-1336
Norman *(G-4978)*
DPM Group LLC.....F..... 405 682-3468
Oklahoma City *(G-5976)*

Editorial Grama Inc.....F..... 918 744-9502
Tulsa *(G-9643)*
Farley Redfield.....G..... 405 275-2266
Tecumseh *(G-8914)*
Hoffman Printing LLC.....F..... 918 682-8341
Muskogee *(G-4691)*
International Gymnast Magazine.....G..... 405 447-9988
Norman *(G-5035)*
International Journal of Ph.....F..... 405 330-0094
Edmond *(G-2463)*
International Pro Rodeo Assn.....G..... 405 235-6540
Oklahoma City *(G-6321)*
Journal Record Publishing Co.....D..... 405 278-2848
Oklahoma City *(G-6388)*
Just Two Publishing Inc.....G..... 405 607-2902
Edmond *(G-2476)*
K9 Media.....E..... 504 233-2576
Del City *(G-1998)*
Key Magazine.....G..... 405 602-3300
Oklahoma City *(G-6408)*
Langdon Publishing Co Inc.....F..... 918 585-9924
Tulsa *(G-10123)*
Lew Graphics Inc.....G..... 405 743-0890
Stillwater *(G-8717)*
Lost Treasure Inc.....G..... 918 786-2182
Grove *(G-3279)*
Loud Graphic Studios LLC.....G..... 405 520-5349
Edmond *(G-2497)*
Mastermind Comics.....G..... 315 308-0593
Del City *(G-2000)*
Meridian Press Publications.....G..... 405 751-2342
Oklahoma City *(G-6568)*
Metro Family Magazine.....G..... 405 601-2081
Oklahoma City *(G-6579)*
Morning Fax.....G..... 918 357-5245
Broken Arrow *(G-1145)*
Morris Communications Co LLC.....D..... 405 273-4200
Shawnee *(G-8477)*
New Forums Press Inc.....G..... 405 372-6158
Stillwater *(G-8727)*
Nightowl Publications Main Off.....G..... 405 603-8130
Oklahoma City *(G-6681)*
Oklahoma Bar Foundation Inc.....E..... 405 416-7000
Oklahoma City *(G-6737)*
Oklahoma Electric Cooperative.....D..... 405 321-2024
Norman *(G-5100)*
Oklahoma Grocers Association.....F..... 405 525-9419
Oklahoma City *(G-6750)*
Oklahoma Magazine.....F..... 918 744-6205
Tulsa *(G-10402)*
Oklahoma Propane Gas Assn.....G..... 405 424-1775
Oklahoma City *(G-6758)*
Oklahoma Restaurant Assn.....F..... 405 942-8181
Oklahoma City *(G-6761)*
Oklahoma Soc Prof Engineers.....G..... 405 528-1435
Oklahoma City *(G-6763)*
Oklahoma State University.....F..... 918 253-4332
Jay *(G-3684)*
Oklahoma State University.....C..... 405 744-5723
Stillwater *(G-8733)*
Oral Rbrts Evnglistic Assn Inc.....D..... 918 591-2000
Tulsa *(G-10436)*
Paul Ziert & Associates Inc.....D..... 405 364-5344
Norman *(G-5112)*
Pdqlipprints LLC.....G..... 580 233-3241
Enid *(G-3033)*
Phoenix Trade Publication.....G..... 405 948-6555
Oklahoma City *(G-6846)*
Pigeon Debut.....G..... 405 686-0412
Oklahoma City *(G-6848)*
Preview of Green Country Inc.....G..... 918 745-1190
Tulsa *(G-10556)*
Schuman Publishing Company.....G..... 918 744-6205
Tulsa *(G-10715)*
Sheet Metal Contractors Assn.....G..... 405 848-3683
Oklahoma City *(G-7119)*
Souno LLC.....E..... 918 495-1771
Tulsa *(G-10794)*
T K Publishing Inc.....G..... 918 582-8504
Tulsa *(G-10891)*
Thunder Road Magazine Oklahoma.....G..... 405 612-3844
Oklahoma City *(G-7285)*
Tulsa County Medical Society.....G..... 918 743-6184
Tulsa *(G-10995)*
Tulsapets Magazine.....G..... 918 834-1252
Tulsa *(G-11015)*
University of Oklahoma.....G..... 405 325-4531
Norman *(G-5185)*
Vype High School Spt Mag LLC.....F..... 918 495-1771
Tulsa *(G-11085)*

S I C

Employee Codes: A=Over 500 employees, B=251-500
C=101-250, D=51-100, E=20-50, F=10-19, G=1-9
2020 Oklahoma Directory
of Manufacturers & Processors
441

Dynamic Mapping Solutions Inc............G....... 918 446-7803
Tulsa *(G-9617)*
E H Publishing Inc ....G....... 405 258-0877
Chandler *(G-1379)*
Earlywine Press LLC ....G....... 405 820-8208
Oklahoma City *(G-5289)*
Editorial Annex.......................................G....... 405 474-2114
Edmond *(G-2400)*
Educational Concepts LLC ....F........ 918 749-0118
Tulsa *(G-9644)*
Ellis Enterprise.......................................G....... 405 826-3572
Purcell *(G-8007)*
Ellis Enterprises Inc..............................G....... 405 917-5336
Oklahoma City *(G-6027)*
Emerald Quest...G....... 580 920-5917
Durant *(G-2229)*
Endurance Publishing LLC ....G....... 405 332-5273
Stillwater *(G-8683)*
Everhart Publishing LLC ....G....... 405 370-4850
Oklahoma City *(G-6056)*
Ex-Press Vac LLC ....G....... 580 606-0799
Duncan *(G-2117)*
Express Bus Inc......................................G....... 918 835-2040
Tulsa *(G-9717)*
Express Home Help ....G....... 405 214-6400
Shawnee *(G-8448)*
Ezekiel Chrles Pblications LLC ....G....... 918 747-8841
Tulsa *(G-9720)*
Featherston Publishing LLC ....G....... 918 289-7877
Owasso *(G-7567)*
Finity Enterprises Inc ....G....... 580 699-2640
Lawton *(G-3929)*
Five F Publishing ....G....... 405 732-1050
Oklahoma City *(G-6085)*
Flamingo Media Inc................................G....... 405 620-5889
Oklahoma City *(G-5291)*
Fronttoback Studio LLC ....G....... 405 788-4400
Oklahoma City *(G-6124)*
Fs & J Music Publishing LLC.................G....... 918 369-6010
Tulsa *(G-9786)*
Ghost Town Press..................................G....... 405 396-2166
Arcadia *(G-229)*
Greater Tlsa Rprter Newspapers ....G....... 918 254-1515
Tulsa *(G-9856)*
Gregs Press..G....... 405 356-4156
Wellston *(G-11471)*
Gust Media LLC......................................G....... 641 715-3900
Edmond *(G-2449)*
Gypsy Twang Publishing ....G....... 918 398-3116
Bixby *(G-630)*
Hale Publications....................................G....... 405 632-2450
Oklahoma City *(G-6204)*
Harrison House Inc.................................G....... 918 582-2126
Tulsa *(G-9896)*
Hear My Heart Publishing LLC ....G....... 918 510-1483
Skiatook *(G-8547)*
Highlands Publishing LLC ....G....... 405 596-8391
Norman *(G-5022)*
His Publishing LLC.................................G....... 405 390-0518
Choctaw *(G-1544)*
Hmh Publishing.......................................G....... 405 788-5589
Elk City *(G-2823)*
Hogan Assessment Systems Inc...........D....... 918 293-2300
Tulsa *(G-9937)*
Hoot of Loot..G....... 918 743-9802
Tulsa *(G-9946)*
Hot Off Press..G....... 918 492-2313
Tulsa *(G-9953)*
Illbird Press ....G....... 918 859-7789
Tulsa *(G-9970)*
Imoco LLC ....G....... 918 459-8366
Tulsa *(G-9971)*
Indigo Streams Publishing LLC.............G....... 918 293-0247
Tulsa *(G-9978)*
Industrial City Press ....G....... 918 299-2767
Jenks *(G-3707)*
Infinitee By Mars LLC ....G....... 405 474-6505
Oklahoma City *(G-6302)*
Inkana Publishing ....G....... 937 760-8446
Ada *(G-51)*
Inkana Publishing LLC ....G....... 937 725-1296
Moore *(G-4528)*
Insight Publishing Group........................G....... 918 493-1718
Tulsa *(G-9990)*
Interstate Trucker Ltd ....E....... 405 948-6576
Oklahoma City *(G-6323)*
Jamey H Voorhees..................................G....... 479 599-9921
Stillwater *(G-8706)*
Janet D Redd..G....... 580 243-0595
Elk City *(G-2830)*
Jeremy Hart Music Inc............................G....... 918 687-3605
Muskogee *(G-4700)*
Jewell Jordan Publishing LLC...............G....... 405 496-2672
Oklahoma City *(G-6362)*
JM Publications LLC...............................G....... 405 639-9472
Oklahoma City *(G-6365)*
JM Publishing LLC..................................G....... 405 684-0450
Edmond *(G-2471)*
John Clark ....G....... 918 853-8286
Sperry *(G-8608)*
Just Breathe Publishing LLC..................G....... 405 633-0160
Spencer *(G-8597)*
▲ Kane/Miller Book Publishers ....G....... 918 346-6118
Tulsa *(G-10075)*
Kasm Publishing LLC..............................G....... 918 798-8908
Tulsa *(G-10077)*
Kelley Publications LLC ....G....... 405 585-7210
Stratford *(G-8805)*
Kh Publishing LLC...................................G....... 405 378-7539
Oklahoma City *(G-5301)*
Kobe Express LLC ....G....... 580 889-2420
Atoka *(G-418)*
Kp Designs LLC ....G....... 865 776-7769
Lawton *(G-3951)*
L S Marann Publishing ....G....... 405 751-9369
Oklahoma City *(G-6441)*
Level Up Publishing LLC.........................G....... 405 771-4372
Spencer *(G-8598)*
Life Impact Publishing LLC.....................G....... 918 407-9938
Tulsa *(G-10158)*
Lindsey Webb Press...............................G....... 405 756-9551
Lindsay *(G-4074)*
Local Hometown Publishing Inc.............G....... 405 273-3838
McLoud *(G-4359)*
Local Telephone Directory.......................G....... 580 762-9359
Ponca City *(G-7846)*
Lw Publications.......................................G....... 405 203-6740
Norman *(G-5061)*
Mac Publishing Company LLC ....G....... 405 964-3576
McLoud *(G-4360)*
Marcelle Publishing LLC ....G....... 405 288-2317
Purcell *(G-8015)*
Marie Thierrey Lucinda............................G....... 405 623-9431
Oklahoma City *(G-6525)*
Mauvaisterre Publishing LLC ....G....... 918 492-3846
Tulsa *(G-10224)*
McCurtain County News Inc ....F....... 580 286-3321
Idabel *(G-3642)*
Meeker Football Press Box.....................G....... 405 279-1075
Meeker *(G-4381)*
Mental Note LLC......................................G....... 405 301-4182
Edmond *(G-2512)*
Metro Publishing LLC..............................G....... 405 593-1335
Yukon *(G-11753)*
Midwest Publication ....G....... 405 948-6506
Oklahoma City *(G-6606)*
Midwest Publishing Co Inc ....G....... 918 582-2000
Tulsa *(G-10271)*
MO Publishing LLC..................................G....... 580 284-3719
Lawton *(G-3972)*
Mobile Express..G....... 405 395-9378
Shawnee *(G-8476)*
Mongrel Empire Press LLC ....G....... 405 459-0042
Norman *(G-5078)*
Morning Fax...G....... 918 357-5245
Broken Arrow *(G-1145)*
Mpress Cards ....G....... 405 590-5393
Norman *(G-5082)*
Musicware Press......................................G....... 405 627-1894
Oklahoma City *(G-6637)*
Mythic Press..G....... 918 516-8255
Tulsa *(G-10321)*
N2r Media LLC...G....... 405 301-0188
Edmond *(G-2527)*
New Forums Press Inc ....G....... 405 372-6158
Stillwater *(G-8727)*
New Plains Review...................................G....... 405 974-5613
Edmond *(G-2536)*
Nonovels Press LLC ....G....... 325 721-2577
Oklahoma City *(G-6684)*
Northwood Publishing LLC......................G....... 918 451-9388
Broken Arrow *(G-989)*
Oklahoma Ntry Svc A Div of M- ....G....... 405 948-8900
Oklahoma City *(G-6757)*
Oklahoma Publishing Company.............G....... 405 475-4040
Oklahoma City *(G-6760)*
Okstyle Publishing LLC...........................G....... 405 816-3338
Oklahoma City *(G-6768)*
Old Farm Publishing LLC ....G....... 405 237-1153
Moore *(G-4548)*
Oremus Press & Publishing....................G....... 405 368-4645
Dover *(G-2042)*
Original Productions Pubg LLC ....G....... 405 420-9559
Norman *(G-5104)*
Osage County Treasurer ....G....... 918 287-3101
Pawhuska *(G-7691)*
Paige Publishing......................................G....... 405 527-3245
Lexington *(G-4039)*
Patricia Lyons ....G....... 850 445-4782
Jenks *(G-3722)*
Paxton McMillin Chrisanna ....G....... 918 734-5753
Sapulpa *(G-8297)*
Pegleg Publishing LLC............................G....... 405 618-7740
Oklahoma City *(G-6820)*
Perfect Circle Publishing Inc ....G....... 918 629-0061
Tulsa *(G-10492)*
Philip H Brewer ....G....... 580 657-8029
Ardmore *(G-345)*
Pie In Sky Publishing Co LLC..................G....... 918 762-3310
Pawnee *(G-7709)*
Pivot Point Publishing..............................G....... 918 347-5415
Sapulpa *(G-8298)*
Poteau Daily News ....G....... 918 647-3335
Poteau *(G-7911)*
Press ....G....... 405 464-6181
Oklahoma City *(G-6890)*
Press Go ....G....... 580 889-2399
Atoka *(G-421)*
▲ Princo Press Corp...............................G....... 405 760-6064
Edmond *(G-2575)*
Pringle Publications Corp ....G....... 405 848-4859
Oklahoma City *(G-6896)*
Professional Communications ....G....... 580 745-9838
Durant *(G-2249)*
Prometheus Publications LLC..................G....... 717 460-4881
Vinita *(G-11268)*
Purpose Publishing ....G....... 405 808-1332
Oklahoma City *(G-6927)*
Pv Publishing Inc......................................G....... 405 409-1799
Oklahoma City *(G-6928)*
Ram Internet Media...................................G....... 405 614-0641
Stillwater *(G-8744)*
Raymond L Weil Pblications LLC.............G....... 580 323-4594
Clinton *(G-1764)*
Red Dog Press LLC ....G....... 405 703-2896
Moore *(G-4560)*
Rigyard Publications LLC ....G....... 405 330-1456
Edmond *(G-2600)*
Rivers Edge Publications..........................G....... 918 855-9469
Tulsa *(G-10656)*
Roadrunner Press......................................G....... 405 524-6205
Oklahoma City *(G-7031)*
▼ Rocking Chair Enterprises LLC...........G....... 918 455-3744
Broken Arrow *(G-1037)*
Rwdesign Publishing.................................G....... 918 924-8865
Broken Arrow *(G-1041)*
Safetac Publishing LLC.............................G....... 559 640-7233
Tulsa *(G-10687)*
Samson Publishing Company LLC ....G....... 918 344-7416
Beggs *(G-560)*
Schatz Publishing Group LLC ....F....... 580 628-4607
Blackwell *(G-690)*
Scout Guide Tulsa LLC.............................G....... 918 693-1198
Tulsa *(G-10717)*
Scriptorium..G....... 405 203-5943
Moore *(G-4566)*
Seminole County Publishing ....G....... 405 382-1125
Seminole *(G-8398)*
Shepherds Heart Music Inc......................G....... 918 781-1200
Muskogee *(G-4749)*
Shopper News Note..................................F....... 405 756-3169
Lindsay *(G-4084)*
Show and Tell Times Inc ....G....... 918 225-4111
Cushing *(G-1959)*
Sooner Publishing Inc...............................G....... 580 233-8400
Enid *(G-3058)*
Sound Ink 2 Publishing LLC ....G....... 918 605-6026
Tulsa *(G-9038)*
Souno LLC...E....... 918 495-1771
Tulsa *(G-10794)*
Spacebar Publishing LLC ....G....... 918 852-6311
Claremore *(G-1687)*
Spangenhelm Publishing...........................G....... 405 430-6464
Yukon *(G-11785)*
Sports Fitnes Publications LLC.................G....... 918 587-7223
Tulsa *(G-10824)*
St Bonaventure Press Ltd ....G....... 918 770-8546
Tulsa *(G-10829)*
Starfall Press LLC ....G....... 405 343-2369
Edmond *(G-2630)*

SIC

SIC SECTION | 27 PRINTING, PUBLISHING, AND ALLIED INDUSTRIES

Digital Prints Plus Inc ... G ... 918 520-7630
Collinsville *(G-1810)*

Diversified Printing Inc ... F ... 918 665-2275
Tulsa *(G-9586)*

Dla Document Services ... E ... 405 734-2177
Tinker Afb *(G-8953)*

Document Centre Inc ... G ... 405 879-1101
Oklahoma City *(G-5955)*

Dps Printing Services of ... G ... 918 794-7755
Sperry *(G-8607)*

Dreamers Screen Print and More ... G ... 580 761-4376
Blackwell *(G-682)*

Drivin Printing By Aaron ... G ... 405 609-9608
Oklahoma City *(G-5983)*

Durant Printing ... G ... 580 924-2271
Durant *(G-2228)*

Edmond Printings ... G ... 405 341-4330
Edmond *(G-2404)*

Education Oklahoma Department ... F ... 405 743-5531
Stillwater *(G-8682)*

Ellis County Capital ... G ... 580 885-7788
Arnett *(G-387)*

Felkins Enterprises LLC ... G ... 918 272-3456
Owasso *(G-7568)*

Fenton Office Supply Co ... E ... 405 372-5555
Stillwater *(G-8688)*

Fifth Quarter Printing LLC ... G ... 918 471-9390
McAlester *(G-4298)*

First Impression Prtg Co Inc ... G ... 918 749-5446
Beggs *(G-553)*

First Impression Prtg Co Inc ... G ... 918 749-5446
Beggs *(G-554)*

Flash Flood Print Studios LLC ... G ... 918 794-3527
Tulsa *(G-9754)*

Franklin Graphics Inc ... F ... 918 687-6149
Muskogee *(G-4675)*

French Printing Inc ... G ... 405 381-4057
Tuttle *(G-11200)*

G & S Printing Inc ... G ... 405 789-6813
Oklahoma City *(G-6129)*

Gameday Screen Printing ... G ... 405 570-0176
Oklahoma City *(G-6135)*

Geary Star ... G ... 405 884-2424
Geary *(G-3216)*

Geiger Printing & Promotion ... G ... 918 810-2833
Tulsa *(G-9812)*

Genral Enquries ... G ... 918 749-1301
Broken Arrow *(G-918)*

Gh Printing Solutions Inc ... G ... 405 630-0609
Edmond *(G-2435)*

Giles Printing Co Inc ... G ... 918 584-1583
Tulsa *(G-9825)*

Glo Press ... G ... 405 275-1038
Shawnee *(G-8454)*

Globe Marketing Services Inc ... B ... 800 742-6787
Oklahoma City *(G-6162)*

Go Print USA ... G ... 405 708-7000
Yukon *(G-11726)*

Go Rowdy Girl Screen Print EMB ... G ... 580 668-2545
Wilson *(G-11534)*

Good Printing Co Inc ... G ... 405 235-9593
Oklahoma City *(G-6171)*

Graphics Etc ... G ... 918 274-4744
Owasso *(G-7571)*

Gravley Companies Inc ... G ... 405 842-1404
Oklahoma City *(G-6176)*

Gravley Companies Inc ... G ... 918 743-6619
Tulsa *(G-9850)*

Grizzly Grin Printing LLC ... G ... 918 351-9066
Tulsa *(G-9865)*

Hammer Hoby ... G ... 580 227-2100
Fairview *(G-3137)*

Handle It 3d Printing LLC ... G ... 405 788-9471
Shawnee *(G-8457)*

Hardesty Press Inc ... F ... 918 582-5306
Tulsa *(G-9891)*

Hawkeye Printing Co ... G ... 918 744-0158
Tulsa *(G-9902)*

Hawkeye Signs & Printing ... G ... 918 864-2035
Tahlequah *(G-8866)*

Heavener Ledger ... G ... 918 653-2425
Heavener *(G-3429)*

Hendryx Printing Brokerage LLC ... G ... 405 532-1255
Edmond *(G-2455)*

Hennessey Clipper ... G ... 405 853-4888
Hennessey *(G-3466)*

Herald Publishing Co ... G ... 580 875-3326
Walters *(G-11302)*

Hg Screen Printing ... G ... 580 623-3638
Watonga *(G-11347)*

Hilton Herald Corp Oklahama ... G ... 580 229-0132
Healdton *(G-3414)*

Hinkle Printing & Office Sup ... G ... 405 238-9308
Pauls Valley *(G-7660)*

Hipsleys Litho & Prtg Co LLC ... G ... 405 528-2686
Oklahoma City *(G-6252)*

Hoffman Printing LLC ... F ... 918 682-8341
Muskogee *(G-4691)*

Holbrook Printing ... G ... 918 835-5950
Tulsa *(G-9938)*

Holloways Bluprt & Copy Sp Inc ... G ... 918 682-0280
Muskogee *(G-4692)*

Hooker Advance & Office Supply ... G ... 580 652-2476
Hooker *(G-3598)*

Hooper Printing Company Inc ... F ... 405 321-4288
Norman *(G-5026)*

Horsepower Printing Inc ... G ... 405 631-3800
Oklahoma City *(G-6264)*

House of Trophies ... G ... 405 452-3524
Wetumka *(G-11492)*

Hugo Publishing Company ... G ... 580 326-3311
Hugo *(G-3612)*

Image Print & Promo LLC ... G ... 405 408-6763
Edmond *(G-2459)*

Imperial Printing Inc ... G ... 918 663-1302
Tulsa *(G-9973)*

Impressions Printing A ... E ... 405 722-2442
Oklahoma City *(G-6293)*

Infocus Print Co LLC ... G ... 918 465-5572
McAlester *(G-4306)*

Initially Yours Inc ... G ... 918 832-9889
Tulsa *(G-9986)*

Ink Images Inc ... G ... 918 828-0300
Tulsa *(G-9987)*

Ink Masters Screen Printing ... G ... 918 399-5220
Cushing *(G-1938)*

Ink Spot Tttoo Bdy Percing LLC ... G ... 918 637-2897
Broken Arrow *(G-1135)*

Inked Custom Printing ... G ... 918 872-6544
Broken Arrow *(G-937)*

Inkwell Printing ... G ... 918 508-3634
Tulsa *(G-9988)*

Inspired Gifts & Graphics LLC ... G ... 405 295-1669
El Reno *(G-2725)*

Its In Print ... G ... 918 493-4141
Tulsa *(G-10014)*

J Rose Printing LLC ... G ... 210 875-0947
Yukon *(G-11734)*

Jet Printing Co Inc ... G ... 405 732-1262
Oklahoma City *(G-6361)*

Jet Set Screen Printing I ... G ... 918 294-1053
Broken Arrow *(G-944)*

Joans Print Shop Inc ... G ... 918 624-5858
Tulsa *(G-10047)*

Joe Brent Lansden ... G ... 580 625-3241
Beaver *(G-541)*

Johnny L Ruth ... G ... 580 223-3061
Ardmore *(G-316)*

JPS LLC ... G ... 405 535-5136
Oklahoma City *(G-6389)*

Kdl Print Production Svcs LLC ... G ... 918 254-8150
Broken Arrow *(G-955)*

Kelley Printing ... G ... 405 238-4848
Pauls Valley *(G-7663)*

Kimberling City Publishing Co ... G ... 918 367-2282
Bristow *(G-786)*

Kindrick Co Prtg & Copying Svc ... G ... 580 332-1022
Ada *(G-56)*

King Design & Printing LLC ... G ... 580 661-3061
Thomas *(G-8946)*

King Graphics Inc ... G ... 405 232-2369
Oklahoma City *(G-6420)*

Kingdom Printing ... G ... 580 512-3789
Lawton *(G-3950)*

Kingfisher Office Supply Inc ... G ... 405 375-3404
Kingfisher *(G-3806)*

Kobe Express LLC ... G ... 580 920-0444
Durant *(G-2241)*

L W Duncan Printing Inc ... G ... 580 355-6229
Lawton *(G-3953)*

Lakey Printing Co ... G ... 918 744-0158
Tulsa *(G-10116)*

Larry D Hammer ... F ... 580 227-2100
Fairview *(G-3140)*

Larry D Hammer ... G ... 580 596-3344
Cherokee *(G-1418)*

Lawyer Graphic Screen Process ... G ... 918 438-2725
Tulsa *(G-10137)*

Lbz Prints ... G ... 405 905-1607
Oklahoma City *(G-6459)*

Leda Grimm ... G ... 918 225-0507
Cushing *(G-1942)*

Lettering Express ... G ... 405 260-9022
Oklahoma City *(G-6468)*

Lewis Printing & Office Supply ... F ... 405 379-5124
Holdenville *(G-3557)*

Lexso T Shirt Printing ... G ... 918 861-0772
Tulsa *(G-10155)*

Linderer Printing Co Inc ... F ... 580 323-2102
Clinton *(G-1757)*

Lindsey Printing ... G ... 580 476-2278
Rush Springs *(G-8123)*

Lithaprint Inc ... F ... 918 587-7746
Tulsa *(G-10168)*

Lively Printing ... G ... 918 582-3668
Tulsa *(G-10169)*

M2print LLC ... G ... 505 263-7999
Yukon *(G-11744)*

Makeba Design & Prints LLC ... G ... 405 719-0104
Yukon *(G-11745)*

Marshall County Publishing Co ... F ... 580 795-3355
Madill *(G-4155)*

Marshall Printing ... G ... 405 883-6122
Yukon *(G-11747)*

Mathis Printing Inc ... G ... 918 682-2999
Muskogee *(G-4708)*

Matrix Print & Promo LLC ... G ... 918 994-1943
Bartlesville *(G-509)*

Mattocks Printing Co LLC ... G ... 405 794-2307
Moore *(G-4538)*

MBC Graphics ... G ... 918 585-2321
Tulsa *(G-10227)*

McCullough Printing ... G ... 580 286-7681
Idabel *(G-3641)*

McNally and Associates Inc ... G ... 918 587-7068
Tulsa *(G-10234)*

Meeks Lithographing Company ... G ... 918 838-9900
Tulsa *(G-10239)*

Meeks Lithographing Company ... E ... 918 836-0900
Tulsa *(G-10240)*

Meeks Lithographing Company ... G ... 918 836-0900
Tulsa *(G-10241)*

Menz Printing Service LLC ... G ... 405 620-3673
Harrah *(G-3381)*

Merrick Printing ... G ... 918 876-6264
Bartlesville *(G-511)*

Mesa Black Publishing LLC ... G ... 580 544-2222
Boise City *(G-747)*

Mid-West Printing & Pubg Co ... F ... 918 224-3666
Sapulpa *(G-8291)*

Midtown Printing Inc ... G ... 918 295-0090
Tulsa *(G-10264)*

Midwest Copy and Printing ... G ... 405 737-8311
Oklahoma City *(G-6601)*

Midwest Decals LLC ... G ... 405 787-8747
Oklahoma City *(G-6602)*

Midwest Publishing Co ... G ... 405 282-1890
Guthrie *(G-3325)*

Miller Printing Company Inc ... F ... 918 749-0981
Tulsa *(G-10281)*

Minor Printing Company ... G ... 580 795-3745
Madill *(G-4158)*

Minuteman Press ... G ... 405 942-5595
Oklahoma City *(G-6617)*

Moe Mark of Excellence LLC ... G ... 405 650-9898
Oklahoma City *(G-6624)*

Moore Printing Co Inc ... E ... 417 866-6696
Moore *(G-4543)*

Mounds Printing ... G ... 918 827-6573
Mounds *(G-4621)*

Mudd Print & Promo LLC ... G ... 405 501-6107
Edmond *(G-2522)*

Multiprint Corp ... G ... 918 832-0300
Tulsa *(G-10315)*

MWH Enterprises Inc ... F ... 918 665-0944
Tulsa *(G-10320)*

Newkirk Herald Journal ... G ... 580 362-2140
Newkirk *(G-4850)*

Newspaper Holding Inc ... E ... 918 456-8833
Tahlequah *(G-8876)*

Newspaper Holding Inc ... D ... 580 233-6600
Enid *(G-3018)*

Newspaper Holding Inc ... E ... 580 332-4433
Ada *(G-72)*

Nextstep Custom Printing ... G ... 580 678-4331
Duncan *(G-2160)*

Nice Printing Co ... G ... 405 673-9437
Midwest City *(G-4449)*

North Star Publishing LLC ... D ... 405 415-2400
Oklahoma City *(G-6688)*

SIC SECTION — 27 PRINTING, PUBLISHING, AND ALLIED INDUSTRIES

Company	Code	Phone
Vox Printing Incorporated — Oklahoma City (G-7406)	D	800 654-8437
Wallace Printing Company — Hugo (G-3622)	G	580 326-6323
Wallis Printing Inc — Ardmore (G-379)	G	580 223-7473
Ward Brothers Printing — Wilburton (G-11528)	G	918 465-5551
Warren Products Inc — Oklahoma City (G-7421)	F	405 947-5676
Warrens Screen Prtg EMB L L C — El Reno (G-2768)	G	405 422-3900
Watonga Printing & Office Sups — Watonga (G-11353)	G	580 623-4989
Weatherford News Inc — Weatherford (G-11458)	E	580 772-3301
Weatherford Press Inc — Weatherford (G-11459)	F	580 772-5300
Western Prnting Company Inc — Tulsa (G-11109)	E	918 665-2874
Westwood Printing Center — Norman (G-5199)	G	405 366-8961
What Print Now — Altus (G-172)	G	580 649-7996
Wild Leaf Screen Prtg & Design — Ramona (G-8047)	G	918 440-4945
Wilson-Monroe Publishing Co — Valliant (G-11234)	G	580 933-4579
Woodcrest Litho Inc — Broken Arrow (G-1178)	F	918 357-1676
Woods County Enterprise — Waynoka (G-11384)	G	580 824-2171

2754 Commercial Printing: Gravure

Company	Code	Phone
American-Chief Co — Pawnee (G-7699)	G	918 762-2552
Deans Typesetting Service — Oklahoma City (G-5912)	G	405 842-7247
Franklin Digital Inc — Muskogee (G-4674)	F	918 687-6149
Hitch N Post LLC — Skiatook (G-8549)	G	918 396-9480
Mojo Sports LLC — Midwest City (G-4447)	F	405 390-8935
October Graphics — Ponca City (G-7861)	G	580 765-5089
Thomas Digital LLC — Tulsa (G-10929)	G	918 836-1540
Wallace Printing Company — Hugo (G-3622)	G	580 326-6323

2759 Commercial Printing

Company	Code	Phone
262 LLC — Tahlequah (G-8848)	F	918 458-5511
3 Cs Tees LLC — Ada (G-2)	G	405 208-1320
A & B Engraving Inc — Tulsa (G-9061)	G	918 663-7446
A B Printing — Tulsa (G-9066)	G	918 834-2054
A Plus Printing — Ponca City (G-7791)	G	580 765-7752
A1 Screen Printing — Norman (G-4895)	G	405 701-6735
AAA Kopy — Oklahoma City (G-5354)	G	405 741-5679
Abco Printing & Office Supply — Idabel (G-3636)	G	580 286-7575
Adams Printing — Cordell (G-1853)	G	580 832-2123
Advance Graphics & Printing — Chandler (G-1373)	G	405 258-0794
Advanced Graphic Design — Tulsa (G-9108)	G	918 960-0407
Affinitee Graphics — Lawton (G-3885)	G	580 861-2253
Ajt Enterprises Inc — Tulsa (G-9133)	F	918 665-7083
All-Star Trophies & Ribbon Mfg — Claremore (G-1581)	G	918 283-2200
American Angler Publications — Catoosa (G-1297)	G	918 364-4210
American Signworx — Pocola (G-7780)		479 650-4562
American Tradition — Tulsa (G-9174)	G	918 688-7725
American Traditions Clothing — Tulsa (G-9175)	G	918 622-8337
American TS — Mounds (G-4609)	G	918 284-7685
Anns Quick Print Co Inc — Chickasha (G-1429)	G	405 222-1871
Apache News — Apache (G-217)	G	580 588-3862
ARC Document Solutions LLC — Tulsa (G-9202)	E	918 663-8100
Ardellas Flowers Inc — Norman (G-4915)	F	405 321-6850
Artistic Apparel — Bartlesville (G-449)	G	918 338-0038
Associated Lithographing Co — Tulsa (G-9217)	E	918 663-9091
AT&I Resources LLC — Tulsa (G-9220)	F	918 925-0154
B J Printing — Stillwater (G-8657)	F	405 372-7600
Bad Boy Signs Graphic — Chickasha (G-1436)	D	405 224-2059
Bakers Printing Co Inc — Oklahoma City (G-5517)	G	405 842-6944
Bargain Journal — McAlester (G-4273)	G	918 426-5500
Beacon Sign Company Inc — Prague (G-7921)	G	405 567-4886
Bees Knees Tees — Choctaw (G-1530)	G	405 370-2132
Bentwrench Studios — Sapulpa (G-8254)	G	918 406-8070
Big House Specialty Prtg Inc — Tulsa (G-9292)	G	918 271-1414
Bill Rathbone — Coweta (G-1872)	G	918 486-3028
Black Cat Screen Printing LLC — Moore (G-4498)	G	405 895-6635
Black Gold — Jay (G-3679)	G	918 253-3344
Blankenship Brothers Inc — Oklahoma City (G-5587)	G	405 943-3278
Blue Ribbon Forms Inc — Tulsa (G-9305)	G	918 834-8838
Board of Trustees of The Teach — Oklahoma City (G-5597)	E	405 521-2387
Bob D Berry DBA — Seminole (G-8360)	G	405 382-3360
Boley One — Oklahoma City (G-5616)	G	405 301-7692
Breast & Bdy Thermography Ctr — Nichols Hills (G-4855)	G	405 596-8099
Britton Printing — Oklahoma City (G-5630)	G	405 840-3291
Brix Inc — Tulsa (G-9338)	G	918 584-6484
▲ Broken Arrow Productions Inc — Norman (G-4944)	E	405 360-8702
Brown Printing Co Inc — Henryetta (G-3500)	G	918 652-9611
Burch Printing Co — Elk City (G-2788)	G	580 225-3270
Business Cards & More — Oklahoma City (G-5648)	G	405 235-9621
Busy Bee — Thomas (G-8940)	G	580 661-2946
Buyers Trading Designs — Tulsa (G-9355)	G	918 592-5477
C & H Safety Pin Inc — Newalla (G-4806)	G	405 949-5843
C & J Printing Co — Lawton (G-3902)	G	580 355-3099
C & R Print Shop Inc — Duncan (G-2095)	G	580 255-5656
C & R Print Shop Inc — Chickasha (G-1445)	G	405 224-7921
C and H Publishing Co — Sand Springs (G-8169)	G	918 245-9571
Cable Printing Co Inc — Lindsay (G-4055)	F	405 756-4045
Campus Ragz — Norman (G-4952)	G	405 329-3300
Cane Advertising LLC — Broken Arrow (G-863)	G	918 806-6817
Capital Business Forms Inc — Oklahoma City (G-5691)	F	405 524-2010
Capitol Hill Graffix LLC — Oklahoma City (G-5694)	G	405 616-3050
Causley Productions Inc — Stillwater (G-8666)	F	405 372-0940
Charles E Morrison Co — Oklahoma City (G-5742)	G	405 840-1604
Cheaper TS Inc — Broken Arrow (G-867)	G	918 615-6262
Christian Connections of Okla — Stillwater (G-8667)	G	405 372-2111
Chrome River Wholesale LLC — Tulsa (G-9421)	G	918 610-0810
Cimarron Screen Printing — Edmond (G-2352)	G	405 755-8337
Civitas Media LLC — Altus (G-149)	F	580 482-1221
Cjs Custom Apparel — Edmond (G-2355)	G	405 340-9677
Clark Printing Inc — Oklahoma City (G-5776)	G	405 528-5396
Collins Quality Printing — Tulsa (G-9468)	G	918 744-0077
▲ Communication Graphics Inc — Broken Arrow (G-871)	D	918 258-6502
Cooley Creek Printing — Tulsa (G-9482)	G	918 835-8200
Copper Cup Images — Bartlesville (G-469)	G	918 337-2781
Copy Write Incorporated — Sapulpa (G-8262)	G	918 224-1148
Corporate Image Inc — Owasso (G-7556)	G	918 516-8376
Corporate To Causal Screen — Muskogee (G-4662)	G	918 686-6688
Corporate To Csual Screen Prtg — Muskogee (G-4663)	G	918 686-6688
CP Solutions Inc — Tulsa (G-9495)	D	918 664-6642
Cplp LLC — Lawton (G-3913)	G	580 355-5515
Cr Stripes Ltd Co — Oklahoma City (G-5850)	G	405 946-8577
Crafty Manatees LLC — Blanchard (G-708)	G	405 630-5415
Cromwells Inc — Enid (G-2935)	G	580 234-6561
CSC Inc — Mooreland (G-4587)	G	580 994-6110
Custom Graphics — Altus (G-152)	G	580 477-4597
D & B Printing Inc — Oklahoma City (G-5884)	G	405 632-0055
Daniel P Wollaston — Ardmore (G-272)	G	580 768-4694
Davis Printing Company Inc — Elk City (G-2800)	G	580 225-2902
Daybreak Screen Printing LLC — Oklahoma City (G-5908)	G	405 919-6386
Dbmac 50 Inc — Claremore (G-1613)	G	918 342-5590
Dbr Publishing Co LLC — Owasso (G-7560)	E	918 250-1984
Decal Shop — Big Cabin (G-602)	G	918 783-5206
Delson Properties Ltd — El Reno (G-2711)	D	405 262-5005
Demco Printing Inc — Shawnee (G-8444)	F	405 273-8888
Design It — Lindsay (G-4060)	G	405 756-3635
Dhs Tees — Edmond (G-2391)	G	405 397-0274
Diversified Printing Inc — Tulsa (G-9586)	F	918 665-2275
Dos Tees LLC — Edmond (G-2392)	G	405 323-2382
Dps Printing Services Inc — Edmond (G-2394)	G	405 285-4614
Dudz and Things Inc — Sapulpa (G-8269)	G	918 321-9443
E C Beights — Miami (G-4400)	G	918 674-2773
Eagle Imaging Management — Oklahoma City (G-5995)	G	405 286-4114
Edmond Printings — Edmond (G-2404)	G	405 341-4330
Elite Creative Solutions LLC — Broken Arrow (G-897)	E	918 994-5435
Ellis County Capital — Arnett (G-387)	G	580 885-7788
Engatech Inc — Tulsa (G-9686)	F	918 599-7500
Engraving Designs LLC — Ponca City (G-7826)	G	580 763-4228
Executive Forms & Supplies — Oklahoma City (G-6060)	G	817 423-9088
Felkins Enterprises LLC — Owasso (G-7568)	G	918 272-3456

Employee Codes: A=Over 500 employees, B=251-500, C=101-250, D=51-100, E=20-50, F=10-19, G=1-9

2020 Oklahoma Directory of Manufacturers & Processors

Quik Print of Tulsa Inc .... G 918 582-1825
Tulsa *(G-10596)*
Quik-Print of Oklahoma City .... G 405 943-3222
Oklahoma City *(G-6949)*
Quik-Print of Oklahoma City .... G 405 528-7976
Oklahoma City *(G-6951)*
Quik-Print of Oklahoma City .... G 405 842-1404
Oklahoma City *(G-6946)*
Quik-Print of Oklahoma City .... G 405 840-3275
Oklahoma City *(G-6950)*
Ragtops Athletics Inc .... G 918 274-3575
Owasso *(G-7606)*
Reflection Foil and Ltr Press .... G 405 341-8660
Edmond *(G-2593)*
Reflective Edge Screenprinting .... G 405 917-7837
Oklahoma City *(G-7001)*
Regency Labels Inc .... E 405 682-3460
Oklahoma City *(G-7002)*
Resourceone Communications Inc .... G 918 295-0112
Tulsa *(G-10646)*
Rhinestone Cowgirl .... F 405 387-3111
Newcastle *(G-4838)*
Rhinestone Cowgirl .... G 405 564-0512
Stillwater *(G-8747)*
Rhodes Printing .... G 918 445-7444
Coweta *(G-1896)*
Rhodes Printing .... G 918 965-1005
Claremore *(G-1682)*
Rhodes Printing Inc .... G 918 457-7801
Tahlequah *(G-8880)*
Robyn Holdings LLC .... E 405 722-4600
Oklahoma City *(G-7041)*
Royal Printing Co Inc .... F 405 235-8581
Oklahoma City *(G-7054)*
Royal Sign & Graphic Inc .... G 918 682-6151
Muskogee *(G-4746)*
S & S Promotions Inc .... E 405 631-6516
Oklahoma City *(G-7064)*
S & S Time Corporation .... E 918 437-3572
Tulsa *(G-10683)*
Saan World LLC .... G 405 494-1282
Oklahoma City *(G-7070)*
Safetyco LLC .... G 405 603-3306
Oklahoma City *(G-7072)*
Sand Tech Screening and EMB .... G 918 458-0312
Tahlequah *(G-8882)*
Sashay Corporate Services LLC .... E 918 664-2507
Tulsa *(G-10710)*
Scissortail Tees .... G 405 706-6371
Oklahoma City *(G-7094)*
Semasys Inc .... E 405 525-2335
Oklahoma City *(G-7107)*
Shirt Nutz LLC .... G 918 900-2362
Owasso *(G-7617)*
Sign Depot .... F 580 931-9363
Durant *(G-2257)*
Silsby Media LLC .... G 405 733-9727
Midwest City *(G-4454)*
Simply Vintage Tees LLC .... G 405 239-0444
Norman *(G-5146)*
Skyy Screen Printing .... G 405 412-4646
Norman *(G-5147)*
Small Potato Tees LLC .... G 405 264-6330
Chickasha *(G-1512)*
Something Printed .... G 918 967-9188
Stigler *(G-8646)*
Sooner Industries Inc .... G 918 540-2422
Miami *(G-4431)*
Sooner Press .... G 405 382-8351
Seminole *(G-8400)*
South Central Golf Inc .... G 918 280-0787
Tulsa *(G-10796)*
Southwstern Group of Companies .... D 405 525-9411
Oklahoma City *(G-7178)*
Specialty Advertising Co Inc .... G 405 495-3838
Oklahoma City *(G-7180)*
Spitzer Printing .... G 580 928-5540
Sayre *(G-8346)*
Sportees .... G 918 618-6201
Eufaula *(G-3115)*
Sprekelmeyer Printing Company .... G 580 223-5100
Ardmore *(G-359)*
Stantons Apparel Inc .... G 580 353-1777
Lawton *(G-4004)*
Stitch N Print .... F 405 789-8862
Oklahoma City *(G-7209)*
Stroud Corridor LLC .... G 405 823-7561
Stroud *(G-8821)*
Stuart Beverly & .... G 580 286-5586
Idabel *(G-3648)*
Summit Labels Inc .... G 918 936-4950
Tulsa *(G-10868)*
Sweetandsassytinytees LLC .... G 405 470-1170
Yukon *(G-11790)*
T John Co Inc .... G 405 761-3460
Tuttle *(G-11214)*
T S & H EMB & Screen Prtg .... G 405 214-7701
Shawnee *(G-8508)*
T S & H Shirt Co Inc .... G 405 382-3731
Seminole *(G-8403)*
T-Birds Custom Screenprinting .... G 918 521-3996
Tulsa *(G-10894)*
Tack Designs .... G 918 825-1211
Pryor *(G-7993)*
Tee For Soul .... G 405 237-3186
Moore *(G-4576)*
Teeds Up Printing .... G 918 279-1018
Coweta *(G-1899)*
Tees For Soul .... G 405 844-7685
Edmond *(G-2637)*
Tees Q Usbs Llc .... G 405 414-3264
Oklahoma City *(G-7265)*
Tesprinting LLC .... G 405 708-7000
Yukon *(G-11791)*
Texoma Engraving LLC .... G 580 775-7333
Durant *(G-2264)*
TGI Enterprises Inc .... E 918 835-4330
Tulsa *(G-10924)*
Think Ability Inc .... C 580 252-8000
Duncan *(G-2187)*
Tier Lvel Thrads Stuff Screen .... G 918 808-7290
Broken Arrow *(G-1074)*
Tiger Town Tees .... G 918 409-4282
Broken Arrow *(G-1075)*
TO Digital Media LLC .... G 405 639-8219
Oklahoma City *(G-7299)*
Toner Express .... G 405 517-8817
Norman *(G-5175)*
Tony Newcomb Sportswear Inc .... G 405 232-0022
Oklahoma City *(G-7303)*
Torbett Printing Co & Off Sup .... G 918 756-5789
Okmulgee *(G-7528)*
Tornados Screen Printing .... G 405 964-5339
McLoud *(G-4363)*
Tourkick LLC .... G 918 409-2543
Owasso *(G-7626)*
Treehouse Embroidery .... G 580 667-4322
Tipton *(G-8960)*
Trendy Tees .... G 405 620-3673
McLoud *(G-4364)*
Triple Elite LLC .... G 405 610-5200
Oklahoma City *(G-7337)*
Tuna Spot Tees LLC .... G 918 931-9586
Stillwater *(G-8770)*
TWI Industries Inc .... E 918 663-6655
Tulsa *(G-11022)*
U Big TS Designs Inc .... G 405 401-4327
Oklahoma City *(G-7356)*
Unique Designs Studio More LLC .... G 580 237-0034
Enid *(G-3070)*
UPS Store 6206 .... G 580 248-7800
Fort Sill *(G-3182)*
Usher Corporation .... G 405 495-2125
Oklahoma City *(G-7382)*
Victortees LLC .... G 405 889-7763
Norman *(G-5196)*
Vinita Printing Co Inc .... E 918 256-6422
Vinita *(G-11271)*
Wallace Printing Company .... G 580 326-6323
Hugo *(G-3622)*
Wallis Printing Inc .... G 580 223-7473
Ardmore *(G-379)*
Watonga Printing & Office Sups .... G 580 623-4989
Watonga *(G-11353)*
Wecktees .... G 580 747-5363
Glencoe *(G-3227)*
Western Cartoons .... G 405 275-1054
Shawnee *(G-8519)*
Western Web Envelope Co Inc .... F 405 682-0207
Oklahoma City *(G-7442)*
Witty Ideas Inc .... G 918 367-9528
Bristow *(G-806)*
◆ Worldwide Printing & Dist Inc .... C 918 295-0112
Tulsa *(G-11154)*
Wright Way Screen Printing .... G 918 787-7898
Grove *(G-3294)*
Xposure Inc .... G 918 581-8900
Tulsa *(G-11165)*
Xzube Tees .... G 405 249-9506
Norman *(G-5203)*
Zon Inc .... F 918 458-5511
Tahlequah *(G-8894)*

2761 Manifold Business Forms

262 LLC .... F 918 458-5511
Tahlequah *(G-8848)*
▲ Adams Investment Company .... D 918 335-1234
Dewey *(G-2012)*
Blue Ribbon Forms Inc .... G 918 834-8838
Tulsa *(G-9305)*
Media Technology Incorporated .... E 405 682-4400
Oklahoma City *(G-6556)*
Mid-West Printing & Pubg Co .... F 918 224-3666
Sapulpa *(G-8291)*
Printed Products Inc .... F 918 295-9950
Tulsa *(G-10561)*
Promotions - Forms Unlimited .... G 918 627-8800
Tulsa *(G-10573)*
R R Donnelley & Sons Company .... B 405 743-2124
Stillwater *(G-8742)*

2771 Greeting Card Publishing

Saga Card Co Inc .... G 918 967-0333
Stigler *(G-8645)*

2782 Blankbooks & Looseleaf Binders

Scrapworx .... G 918 259-9547
Broken Arrow *(G-1045)*
Tumbleweed Creek Cottage .... G 580 242-2767
Enid *(G-3068)*

2789 Bookbinding

A 1 Master Print Inc .... G 405 787-0505
Bethany *(G-571)*
A B Printing .... G 918 834-2054
Tulsa *(G-9066)*
A Plus Printing .... G 580 765-7752
Ponca City *(G-7791)*
A Plus Printing Inc .... G 918 836-8659
Tulsa *(G-9068)*
A Q Printing .... G 918 438-1161
Tulsa *(G-9070)*
A-OK Printing Mill .... G 918 775-6809
Sallisaw *(G-8136)*
AAA Kopy .... G 405 741-5679
Oklahoma City *(G-5354)*
Abco Printing & Office Supply .... G 580 286-7575
Idabel *(G-3636)*
Adams Printing .... G 580 832-2123
Cordell *(G-1853)*
Advance Graphics & Printing .... G 405 258-0796
Chandler *(G-1373)*
Ajt Enterprises Inc .... F 918 665-7083
Tulsa *(G-9133)*
Altus Printing Co Inc .... G 580 482-2020
Altus *(G-141)*
Anns Quick Print Co Inc .... G 405 222-1871
Chickasha *(G-1429)*
Artur Bookbinding Intl .... G 918 478-4888
Fort Gibson *(G-3173)*
B & L Printing Inc .... G 918 258-6655
Broken Arrow *(G-839)*
Bartlesville Print Shop .... G 918 336-6070
Bartlesville *(G-452)*
Bell Printing and Advertising .... G 405 769-6445
Nicoma Park *(G-4866)*
Bill Rathbone .... G 918 486-3028
Coweta *(G-1872)*
Britton Printing .... G 405 840-3291
Oklahoma City *(G-5630)*
Brown Printing Co Inc .... G 918 652-9611
Henryetta *(G-3500)*
Burch Printing Co .... G 580 225-3270
Elk City *(G-2788)*
C & J Printing Co .... G 580 355-3099
Lawton *(G-3902)*
C & R Print Shop Inc .... G 405 224-7921
Chickasha *(G-1445)*
Carr Graphics Inc .... G 918 835-0605
Tulsa *(G-9379)*
Cherry Street Print Shop Inc .... G 918 584-0022
Tulsa *(G-9417)*
Choate Publishing Inc .... F 580 276-3255
Marietta *(G-4204)*
Clark Printing Inc .... G 405 528-5396
Oklahoma City *(G-5776)*
Collins Quality Printing .... G 918 744-0077
Tulsa *(G-9468)*

SIC

Employee Codes: A=Over 500 employees, B=251-500
C=101-250, D=51-100, E=20-50, F=10-19, G=1-9
2020 Oklahoma Directory
of Manufacturers & Processors
449

Brown Printing Co Inc............................G....... 918 652-9611
Henryetta ***(G-3500)***
Burch Printing Co...................................G....... 580 225-3270
Elk City ***(G-2788)***
C & J Printing Co...................................G....... 580 355-3099
Lawton ***(G-3902)***
C & R Print Shop Inc...............................G....... 405 224-7921
Chickasha ***(G-1445)***
Cable Printing Co Inc.............................F....... 405 756-4045
Lindsay ***(G-4055)***
Carnegie Herald......................................G....... 580 654-1443
Carnegie ***(G-1274)***
Carr Graphics Inc....................................G....... 918 835-0605
Tulsa ***(G-9379)***
Cherry Street Print Shop Inc.................G....... 918 584-0022
Tulsa ***(G-9417)***
CJ Graphics...G....... 405 636-0400
Oklahoma City ***(G-5771)***
Clark Printing Inc....................................G....... 405 528-5396
Oklahoma City ***(G-5776)***
Cnhi LLC...G....... 918 652-3311
Henryetta ***(G-3501)***
Cnhi LLC...F....... 580 338-3355
Guymon ***(G-3346)***
Collins Quality Printing..........................G....... 918 744-0077
Tulsa ***(G-9468)***
Cooley Enterprises Inc............................G....... 918 437-6900
Tulsa ***(G-9483)***
Copy Fast Printing Inc............................F....... 405 947-7468
Oklahoma City ***(G-5834)***
Countywide News Inc.............................F....... 405 598-3793
Tecumseh ***(G-8910)***
Cowan Printing & Litho Inc....................F....... 405 789-1961
Tuttle ***(G-11191)***
Cowboy Copy Center...............................F....... 405 372-8099
Stillwater ***(G-8671)***
Creative Media...G....... 918 245-3779
Sand Springs ***(G-8173)***
Cromwells Inc...G....... 580 234-6561
Enid ***(G-2935)***
CSC Inc...G....... 580 994-6110
Mooreland ***(G-4587)***
Davis Printing Company Inc...................G....... 580 225-2902
Elk City ***(G-2800)***
Dbmac 50 Inc...G....... 918 342-5590
Claremore ***(G-1613)***
Dean Printing...G....... 580 782-3777
Mangum ***(G-4170)***
Deans Typesetting Service.....................G....... 405 842-7247
Oklahoma City ***(G-5912)***
Demco Printing Inc.................................F....... 405 273-8888
Shawnee ***(G-8444)***
Digi Print LLC...G....... 405 947-0099
Oklahoma City ***(G-5945)***
Diversified Printing Inc..........................F....... 918 665-2275
Tulsa ***(G-9586)***
Edmond Printings....................................G....... 405 341-4330
Edmond ***(G-2404)***
Education Oklahoma Department........F....... 405 743-5531
Stillwater ***(G-8682)***
Ellis County Capital................................G....... 580 885-7788
Arnett ***(G-387)***
Fedex Office & Print Svcs Inc................E....... 918 252-3757
Tulsa ***(G-9733)***
Felkins Enterprises LLC.........................G....... 918 272-3456
Owasso ***(G-7568)***
First Impression Prtg Co Inc..................G....... 918 749-5446
Beggs ***(G-553)***
Franklin Graphics Inc.............................F....... 918 687-6149
Muskogee ***(G-4675)***
French Printing Inc..................................G....... 405 381-4057
Tuttle ***(G-11200)***
G & S Printing Inc...................................G....... 405 789-6813
Oklahoma City ***(G-6129)***
Geary Star...G....... 405 884-2424
Geary ***(G-3216)***
Giles Printing Co Inc...............................G....... 918 584-1583
Tulsa ***(G-9825)***
Good Printing Co Inc..............................G....... 405 235-9593
Oklahoma City ***(G-6171)***
Graphics Etc..G....... 918 274-4744
Owasso ***(G-7571)***
Gravley Companies Inc...........................G....... 918 743-6619
Tulsa ***(G-9850)***
Gregath Publishing Company................G....... 918 542-4148
Miami ***(G-4407)***
Hammer Hoby...G....... 580 227-2100
Fairview ***(G-3137)***
Hardesty Press Inc...................................F....... 918 582-5306
Tulsa ***(G-9891)***
Heavener Ledger.......................................G....... 918 653-2425
Heavener ***(G-3429)***
Herald Publishing Co..............................G....... 580 875-3326
Walters ***(G-11302)***
Hinkle Printing & Office Sup..................G....... 405 238-9308
Pauls Valley ***(G-7660)***
Hipsleys Litho & Prtg Co LLC................G....... 405 528-2686
Oklahoma City ***(G-6252)***
Hoffman Printing LLC.............................F....... 918 682-8341
Muskogee ***(G-4691)***
Holbrook Printing....................................G....... 918 835-5950
Tulsa ***(G-9938)***
Hooper Printing Company Inc...............F....... 405 321-4288
Norman ***(G-5026)***
Imperial Printing Inc..............................G....... 918 663-1302
Tulsa ***(G-9973)***
Ink Images Inc..G....... 918 828-0300
Tulsa ***(G-9987)***
K D Typesetting..G....... 405 302-0799
Edmond ***(G-2477)***
Kelley Printing..G....... 405 238-4848
Pauls Valley ***(G-7663)***
Kindrick Co Prtg & Copying Svc............G....... 580 332-1022
Ada ***(G-56)***
King Graphics Inc.....................................G....... 405 232-2369
Oklahoma City ***(G-6420)***
Kingfisher Office Supply Inc..................G....... 405 375-3404
Kingfisher ***(G-3806)***
Kolb Type Service Incorporated............G....... 405 341-0984
Agra ***(G-125)***
L W Duncan Printing Inc.........................G....... 580 355-6229
Lawton ***(G-3953)***
Larry D Hammer.......................................F....... 580 227-2100
Fairview ***(G-3140)***
Leda Grimm...G....... 918 225-0507
Cushing ***(G-1942)***
Lincoln County Publishing Co...............F....... 405 258-1818
Chandler ***(G-1385)***
Linderer Printing Co Inc..........................F....... 580 323-2102
Clinton ***(G-1757)***
Lithaprint Inc...F....... 918 587-7746
Tulsa ***(G-10168)***
Liv3design LLC...G....... 432 296-1968
Norman ***(G-5060)***
Mattocks Printing Co LLC......................G....... 405 794-2307
Moore ***(G-4538)***
Mc Clain County Publishing Co............E....... 405 527-2126
Purcell ***(G-8016)***
McCullough Printing................................G....... 580 286-7681
Idabel ***(G-3641)***
Meeks Lithographing Company............G....... 918 838-9900
Tulsa ***(G-10239)***
Meeks Lithographing Company............G....... 918 836-0900
Tulsa ***(G-10241)***
Mesa Black Publishing LLC....................G....... 580 544-2222
Boise City ***(G-747)***
Metro Graphic Systems...........................G....... 918 744-0308
Tulsa ***(G-10249)***
Mid-West Printing & Pubg Co...............F....... 918 224-3666
Sapulpa ***(G-8291)***
Midtown Printing Inc...............................G....... 918 295-0090
Tulsa ***(G-10264)***
Midwest Publishing Co...........................G....... 405 282-1890
Guthrie ***(G-3325)***
Minor Printing Company........................G....... 580 795-3745
Madill ***(G-4158)***
Minuteman Press.......................................G....... 405 942-5595
Oklahoma City ***(G-6617)***
▲ **Mtm Recognition Corporation**............B....... 405 609-6900
Oklahoma City ***(G-6634)***
Multiprint Corp..G....... 918 832-0300
Tulsa ***(G-10315)***
Newcastle Pacer Inc.................................G....... 405 387-5277
Newcastle ***(G-4833)***
Northwest Printing Inc............................G....... 580 234-0953
Enid ***(G-3022)***
OK Quality Printing Inc............................G....... 405 624-2925
Stillwater ***(G-8731)***
Oklahoma Assn of Elc Coop...................E....... 405 478-1455
Oklahoma City ***(G-6735)***
Oklahoma Executive Printing................G....... 405 948-8136
Oklahoma City ***(G-6748)***
Peabodys Printing & A Brush Sp...........G....... 580 248-8317
Lawton ***(G-3980)***
Pinecliffe Prtrs of Tecumseh.................G....... 405 273-1292
Shawnee ***(G-8483)***
Pony Express Printing LLC.....................G....... 405 375-5064
Kingfisher ***(G-3811)***
Pre-Press Graphics Inc............................G....... 918 582-2775
Tulsa ***(G-10541)***
Premier Printing.......................................G....... 405 632-1132
Oklahoma City ***(G-6886)***
Prices Quality Printing Inc....................G....... 580 924-2271
Durant ***(G-2248)***
Print N Copy Inc.......................................G....... 918 258-8200
Broken Arrow ***(G-1011)***
Print Shop...G....... 918 342-3993
Claremore ***(G-1674)***
Printed Products Inc................................F....... 918 295-9950
Tulsa ***(G-10561)***
Printing Center..G....... 405 681-5303
Oklahoma City ***(G-6901)***
Priority Printworks Inc............................G....... 918 825-6397
Pryor ***(G-7984)***
Pronto Print Inc...G....... 580 223-1612
Ardmore ***(G-347)***
Protype Inc...G....... 918 743-4408
Tulsa ***(G-10576)***
Pryor Printing Inc......................................G....... 918 825-2888
Pryor ***(G-7986)***
Quik Print of Tulsa Inc............................G....... 918 250-5466
Tulsa ***(G-10594)***
Quik Print of Tulsa Inc............................E....... 918 665-6246
Tulsa ***(G-10595)***
Quik-Print of Oklahoma City..................G....... 405 943-3222
Oklahoma City ***(G-6949)***
Quik-Print of Oklahoma City..................G....... 405 842-1404
Oklahoma City ***(G-6946)***
Review Printing Company Inc................F....... 580 658-6657
Marlow ***(G-4241)***
Russell Publishing Company.................G....... 405 665-4333
Wynnewood ***(G-11672)***
Self Printing Inc...G....... 918 838-2113
Tulsa ***(G-10726)***
Shine On Designs......................................G....... 918 224-7439
Sapulpa ***(G-8311)***
Shopper News Note..................................F....... 405 756-3169
Lindsay ***(G-4084)***
Signature Graphics Corp.........................G....... 918 294-3485
Bixby ***(G-658)***
Snider Printing & Office Sup..................G....... 405 257-3402
Wewoka ***(G-11511)***
Snyder Printing Inc...................................F....... 405 682-8880
Oklahoma City ***(G-5317)***
Sooner Industries Inc...............................G....... 918 540-2422
Miami ***(G-4431)***
Sooner Press...G....... 405 382-8351
Seminole ***(G-8400)***
Spiro Graphic..G....... 918 962-2075
Spiro ***(G-8618)***
Spitzer Printing..G....... 580 928-5540
Sayre ***(G-8346)***
Sprekelmeyer Printing Company...........G....... 580 223-5100
Ardmore ***(G-359)***
Standard Printing Co Inc..........................G....... 405 840-0001
Oklahoma City ***(G-7192)***
Star Nowata...G....... 918 273-2446
Nowata ***(G-5230)***
Tom Bennett Manufacturing....................F....... 405 528-5671
Oklahoma City ***(G-7302)***
▲ **Tommy Higle Publishers**......................G....... 580 276-5136
Marietta ***(G-4215)***
Torbett Printing Co & Off Sup................G....... 918 756-5789
Okmulgee ***(G-7528)***
Transcript Press Inc..................................E....... 405 360-7999
Norman ***(G-5181)***
Tulsa Instant Printing...............................G....... 918 627-0730
Tulsa ***(G-11000)***
Type House Inc...G....... 918 492-8513
Tulsa ***(G-11028)***
Unique Printing Inc....................................G....... 405 842-3966
Oklahoma City ***(G-7361)***
Usher Corporation.....................................G....... 405 495-2125
Oklahoma City ***(G-7382)***
Vans Printing Service................................G....... 918 786-9496
Grove ***(G-3291)***
Vinita Printing Co Inc................................E....... 918 256-6422
Vinita ***(G-11271)***
Vision Type & Design Inc..........................G....... 918 252-3817
Tulsa ***(G-11082)***
Wallace Printing Company........................G....... 580 326-6323
Hugo ***(G-3622)***
Wallis Printing Inc.......................................G....... 580 223-7473
Ardmore ***(G-379)***
Watonga Republican Inc...........................G....... 580 623-4922
Watonga ***(G-11354)***
Weatherford Press Inc...............................F....... 580 772-5300
Weatherford ***(G-11459)***
Westwood Printing Center........................G....... 405 366-8961
Norman ***(G-5199)***

Employee Codes: A=Over 500 employees, B=251-500
C=101-250, D=51-100, E=20-50, F=10-19, G=1-9

2020 Oklahoma Directory
of Manufacturers & Processors

451

SIC SECTION

28 CHEMICALS AND ALLIED PRODUCTS

◆ Tronox LLC ....A 405 775-5000
  Oklahoma City *(G-7340)*
Tronox Pigments LLC ....G 405 775-5000
  Oklahoma City *(G-7341)*
◆ Tronox US Holdings Inc ....E 405 775-5000
  Oklahoma City *(G-7342)*
▼ Tronox Worldwide LLC ....F 405 775-5000
  Oklahoma City *(G-7343)*
U S Silica Company ....D 580 384-5241
  Mill Creek *(G-4472)*
Ultimate Chemicals LLC ....G 405 703-2771
  Moore *(G-4581)*
Umicore Autocat USA Inc ....D 918 266-8923
  Catoosa *(G-1361)*
▲ Woodward Iodine Corporation ....E 580 254-3311
  Woodward *(G-11657)*

2821 Plastics, Mtrls & Nonvulcanizable Elastomers

AO Inc ....G 918 623-1711
  Okemah *(G-5263)*
Baker Petrolite LLC ....C 918 847-2522
  Barnsdall *(G-435)*
Barlow-Hunt Inc ....D 918 250-0828
  Tulsa *(G-9265)*
Bluehawk Energy Inc ....G 405 406-1580
  Edmond *(G-2327)*
Cass Holdings LLC ....E 405 755-8448
  Oklahoma City *(G-5707)*
Cass Holdings LLC ....G 405 359-5053
  Watonga *(G-11343)*
Chevron Phillips Chem Co LP ....D 918 825-0364
  Pryor *(G-7953)*
Chevron Phillips Chem Co LP ....G 918 977-6846
  Bartlesville *(G-462)*
Chevron Phillips Chem Co LP ....C 918 661-3317
  Bartlesville *(G-463)*
Elastech Technologies LLC ....G 405 470-1539
  Oklahoma City *(G-6021)*
Grace Fibrgls & Composites LLC ......G 405 233-3203
  Harrah *(G-3378)*
◆ Hilti North America Ltd ....G 918 252-6000
  Tulsa *(G-9932)*
Hobby Supermarket Inc ....E 405 239-6864
  Oklahoma City *(G-6256)*
Interplastic Corporation ....D 918 825-2755
  Pryor *(G-7971)*
Interplastic Corporation ....F 918 592-0205
  Tulsa *(G-10006)*
J-M Manufacturing Company Inc ......D 918 446-4471
  Tulsa *(G-10025)*
Line X of Stillwater ....G 405 743-0911
  Stillwater *(G-8719)*
Nordam Group LLC ....C 918 274-2742
  Tulsa *(G-10356)*
Prime Conduit Inc ....E 405 670-6132
  Oklahoma City *(G-6892)*
Rapid Application Group LLC ....G 918 760-1242
  Broken Arrow *(G-1021)*
T D Williamson Inc ....E 918 447-5400
  Tulsa *(G-10888)*
Tetrachem Seal Company Inc ....F 580 924-1717
  Durant *(G-2263)*

2822 Synthetic Rubber (Vulcanizable Elastomers)

Henley Sealants Inc ....G 405 235-7325
  Oklahoma City *(G-6240)*
Neoinsulation LLC ....G 405 605-6518
  Oklahoma City *(G-6669)*
Southwest Latex LLC ....G 405 420-0018
  Marlow *(G-4243)*

2823 Cellulosic Man-Made Fibers

▲ Western Hull Sacking Inc ....G 580 335-2144
  Frederick *(G-3204)*

2824 Synthetic Organic Fibers, Exc Cellulosic

Midland Vinyl Products Inc ....G 405 755-4972
  Oklahoma City *(G-6597)*
Progressive Windows Inc ....G 580 227-9915
  Fairview *(G-3147)*

2833 Medicinal Chemicals & Botanical Prdts

Environmate Inc ....G 817 707-5282
  Catoosa *(G-1318)*

Environmental Remediation ....G 405 235-9999
  Oklahoma City *(G-6047)*
▲ Haus Bioceuticals Inc ....G 405 295-5257
  Oklahoma City *(G-6225)*
Hillsboro Co ....G 918 481-0484
  Tulsa *(G-9930)*
Iochem Corporation ....E 580 995-3198
  Vici *(G-11243)*
Ocubrite LLC ....G 405 250-2084
  Edmond *(G-2544)*
Potions By Pier LLC ....G 580 658-2900
  Marlow *(G-4237)*
Rtpr LLC ....G 877 787-7180
  Edmond *(G-2607)*
Tulsa American Shaman ....G 918 938-0718
  Tulsa *(G-10985)*

2834 Pharmaceuticals

Abbott Laboratories ....A 405 329-5513
  Norman *(G-4896)*
Al Pharma Inc ....G 405 848-3299
  Oklahoma City *(G-5406)*
▲ Avara Pharmaceutical Tech Inc ......C 405 217-7670
  Norman *(G-4921)*
Barrick Pharmacies Inc ....G 405 273-9417
  Shawnee *(G-8431)*
Btg Inc ....G 405 604-9145
  Oklahoma City *(G-5638)*
Carter & Higgins Orthodontics ....G 918 986-9986
  Tulsa *(G-9381)*
Cytovance Biologics Inc ....G 405 319-8310
  Oklahoma City *(G-5883)*
David W and Abbe Belcher ....G 918 376-9816
  Owasso *(G-7559)*
▲ Dermamedics LLC ....G 405 319-8130
  Oklahoma City *(G-5925)*
Eden Pharmaceuticals ....G 405 455-7200
  Midwest City *(G-4439)*
Eli Lilly and Company ....G 918 250-6848
  Broken Arrow *(G-896)*
Eli Lilly and Company ....E 918 459-4540
  Tulsa *(G-9655)*
Golf Advisors ....G 918 645-6179
  Tulsa *(G-9839)*
Hospice Pharmacy Providers LLC ....G 918 633-6229
  Owasso *(G-7574)*
Kmh Enterprises Inc ....G 405 722-4600
  Oklahoma City *(G-6430)*
Loud City Pharmaceutical ....G 405 259-9014
  Oklahoma City *(G-6497)*
▲ Magnesium Products Inc ....F 918 587-9930
  Tulsa *(G-9018)*
Marie Anastasia Labs Inc ....G 405 840-0123
  Oklahoma City *(G-6524)*
Medcraft LLC ....G 918 938-0642
  Mounds *(G-4620)*
Midwest Med Istpes Nclear Phrm ....G 405 604-4438
  Oklahoma City *(G-6605)*
Natural Care Solution LLC ....G 405 919-1982
  Mustang *(G-4786)*
Naturalock Solutions LLC ....G 405 812-9058
  Norman *(G-5089)*
North Amrcn Brine Rsources LLC ....G 405 828-7123
  Enid *(G-3021)*
Novartis Corporation ....G 918 845-0906
  Tulsa *(G-10363)*
Okc Allergy Supplies Inc ....D 405 235-1451
  Oklahoma City *(G-6726)*
Onesource LLC ....G 580 434-6250
  Calera *(G-1242)*
Optionone LLC ....E 405 548-4848
  Oklahoma City *(G-6779)*
Phillips & Company ....G 714 663-6324
  Millerton *(G-4473)*
Prescription Care LLC ....G 405 310-9230
  Norman *(G-5121)*
Pure Transplant Solutions LLC ....G 512 697-8144
  Oklahoma City *(G-6924)*
Qualgen LLC ....E 405 551-8216
  Edmond *(G-2578)*
Qualgen LLC ....E 405 551-8216
  Edmond *(G-2579)*
Rta Systems Incorporated ....G 405 388-6802
  Choctaw *(G-1554)*
Sports & Stress Marketing ....G 580 327-3463
  Alva *(G-193)*
Takeda Phrmceuticals N Amer In ....G 405 317-7495
  Norman *(G-5170)*
Tcaacp LLC ....G 918 251-6655
  Broken Arrow *(G-1072)*

Tetherex Pharmaceuticals Corp ....G 405 206-1843
  Oklahoma City *(G-7274)*
Trimark Labs ....G 405 942-3289
  Oklahoma City *(G-7333)*
Ultra Botanica LLC ....G 405 694-4175
  Oklahoma City *(G-7359)*
Willoughby Pharmacy Svcs LLC ......G 580 214-1043
  Weatherford *(G-11460)*
Winds of Heartland ....G 405 947-8558
  Oklahoma City *(G-7460)*

2835 Diagnostic Substances

Bounce Diagnostics Inc ....G 405 740-5889
  Edmond *(G-2331)*
Eden Clinic Inc ....G 405 579-4673
  Norman *(G-4988)*
Immuno-Mycologics Inc ....F 405 360-4669
  Norman *(G-5030)*
Petnet Solutions Inc ....G 918 259-0899
  Broken Arrow *(G-1004)*
Sarvam Solutions Corporation ....G 918 346-9502
  Bartlesville *(G-524)*

2836 Biological Prdts, Exc Diagnostic Substances

Coare Biotechnology Inc ....G 405 227-0406
  Oklahoma City *(G-5797)*
Dr Cannabis LLC ....G 918 277-1105
  Sapulpa *(G-8268)*
Envirnmental Toxin Removal LLC .....G 405 757-4099
  Oklahoma City *(G-6044)*
Extract Surface Systems LLC ....G 918 938-6828
  Tulsa *(G-9719)*
Extract Touch-Up LLC ....G 918 639-4011
  Broken Arrow *(G-903)*
Heartland Vaccines LLC ....G 716 848-9251
  Stillwater *(G-8699)*
Jimmy Fuchs ....G 580 225-7784
  Elk City *(G-2833)*
Leonard Skodak Distributors ....G 405 787-8044
  Oklahoma City *(G-6466)*
M Shawn Anderson Rph PC ....G 580 595-9500
  Lawton *(G-3967)*
Octapharma Plasma ....G 405 686-9226
  Oklahoma City *(G-6711)*
Oklahomans For Vaccine ....G 918 606-9213
  Tulsa *(G-10409)*
Plasma Bionics LLC ....G 405 564-5333
  Stillwater *(G-8738)*
Plasma Solutions 1 ....G 918 543-2178
  Inola *(G-3673)*
Pure Protein LLC ....G 405 271-3838
  Oklahoma City *(G-6923)*
Solidtech Animal Health Inc ....F 405 387-3300
  Newcastle *(G-4841)*
Swaim Serum Company ....G 918 241-4363
  Sand Springs *(G-8228)*
Sweet Sap Extracts Inc ....G 405 205-8706
  Harrah *(G-3386)*
Vaxart Inc ....G 918 582-4346
  Tulsa *(G-11067)*
Zlb Behring ....G 405 521-9204
  Oklahoma City *(G-7487)*
Zlb Bio Services ....G 580 248-4851
  Lawton *(G-4025)*

2841 Soap & Detergents

B & P Industrial Inc ....F 918 665-3301
  Tulsa *(G-9242)*
Berkshire Corporation ....G 405 677-3391
  Oklahoma City *(G-5556)*
Brenntag Southwest Inc ....E 918 266-2951
  Catoosa *(G-1306)*
Cutting Edge Industries Corp ....G 918 523-7373
  Tulsa *(G-9530)*
▲ Dermamedics LLC ....G 405 319-8130
  Oklahoma City *(G-5925)*
E Environmental LLC ....G 405 604-0000
  Oklahoma City *(G-5993)*
Easy Car Wash Systems Inc ....G 918 582-4355
  Tulsa *(G-9634)*
Juniper Ridge Inc ....G 405 762-2555
  Stillwater *(G-8708)*
Kleen Products Inc ....G 405 495-1168
  Oklahoma City *(G-6428)*
Laughing Rabbit Soap ....G 405 737-7413
  Choctaw *(G-1549)*
Melanie Margaret Dennis ....G 405 760-1978
  Mustang *(G-4782)*

Employee Codes: A=Over 500 employees, B=251-500
C=101-250, D=51-100, E=20-50, F=10-19, G=1-9

SIC SECTION

28 CHEMICALS AND ALLIED PRODUCTS

Emerging Fuels Technology LLC ....F 918 286-6802
  Tulsa *(G-9669)*
Excel Paralubes LLC ....G..... 800 527-3236
  Bartlesville *(G-482)*
Fairwind LLC ....E 580 492-5209
  Lawton *(G-3925)*
Fast Fuel LLC ....G..... 405 375-6666
  Kingfisher *(G-3797)*
Fuel...G..... 903 948-3125
  Woodward *(G-11586)*
Fuel Haulers LLC ....G..... 405 830-3385
  Guthrie *(G-3315)*
Fuel Inc ....G..... 580 583-5202
  Lawton *(G-3933)*
Fuels Marketing Inc ....G..... 405 433-9935
  Cashion *(G-1288)*
▲ Galaxy Chemicals LLC ....F 918 379-0820
  Claremore *(G-1625)*
Grayson Investments LLC ....G..... 580 421-9770
  Ada *(G-45)*
H2szero LLC ....G..... 918 384-9600
  Sapulpa *(G-8277)*
Iochem Corporation ....E 580 995-3198
  Vici *(G-11243)*
Jag Fuels Company Inc ....G..... 580 465-3256
  Ardmore *(G-310)*
Johnson Minford ....G..... 580 772-0430
  Weatherford *(G-11422)*
L&S Fuels LLC ....G..... 580 227-0999
  Fairview *(G-3139)*
Magpro Chlor-Alkali LLC ....G..... 918 587-9930
  Tulsa *(G-9019)*
Melton Dental Lab ....G..... 580 369-2448
  Davis *(G-1991)*
Mid-Continent Fuel Co Inc ....G..... 918 266-1923
  Catoosa *(G-1341)*
▼ Montello Inc ....G..... 918 665-1170
  Tulsa *(G-10301)*
Oklahoma Biorefining Corp ....G..... 405 201-1824
  Norman *(G-5098)*
Oklahoma Fuel Athletics LLC ....G..... 405 286-3144
  Edmond *(G-2550)*
Plainsman Technology Inc ....F 580 658-6608
  Marlow *(G-4236)*
Premier Chem & Oilfld Sup LLC ....F 405 893-2321
  Enid *(G-3038)*
Pruitt Oil Company LLc ....G..... 580 889-2413
  Atoka *(G-422)*
Rovill Biodiesel Solution LLC ....G..... 580 339-6815
  Elk City *(G-2870)*
Rs Fuel LLC ....G..... 405 748-4277
  Oklahoma City *(G-7057)*
Station 7 ....G..... 405 470-4317
  Oklahoma City *(G-7196)*
Sunoco (R&m) LLC ....F 918 586-6246
  Tulsa *(G-10873)*
Superior Pellet Fuels LLC ....G..... 918 494-0790
  Tulsa *(G-10877)*
Titan Chemical ....G..... 918 420-5990
  McAlester *(G-4342)*
Trusty Willow LLC ....G..... 253 241-0520
  Bokoshe *(G-755)*
United Fuels & Energy ....G..... 405 945-7400
  Oklahoma City *(G-7368)*
United Fuels Energy ....G..... 580 332-5222
  Ada *(G-100)*
▲ Winston Company Inc ....E 800 331-9099
  Tulsa *(G-11140)*

2873 Nitrogenous Fertilizers

Agrium Advanced Tech US Inc ....F 405 948-1084
  Oklahoma City *(G-5399)*
Aurora Innovations LLC ....G....... 918 519-5356
  Sand Springs *(G-8163)*
I Chemex Corporation ....G..... 405 947-0764
  Oklahoma City *(G-6281)*
▲ Koch Fertilizer Enid LLC ....A 580 249-4870
  Enid *(G-2996)*
Koch Industries Inc ....D..... 580 233-3900
  Enid *(G-2997)*
◆ LSB Chemical LLC ....F 405 235-4546
  Oklahoma City *(G-6498)*
LSB Industries Inc ....E 405 235-4546
  Oklahoma City *(G-6499)*
Pryor Chemical Company ....C 918 825-3383
  Pryor *(G-7985)*
Tessenderlo Kerley Inc ....E 405 665-2544
  Wynnewood *(G-11674)*
Tessenderlo Kerley Inc ....F 580 762-1130
  Ponca City *(G-7882)*

2874 Phosphatic Fertilizers

Dib 718 LLC ....G........ 405 525-2151
  Oklahoma City *(G-5944)*
Tessenderlo Kerley Inc ....E 405 665-2544
  Wynnewood *(G-11674)*
Tessenderlo Kerley Inc ....F 580 762-1130
  Ponca City *(G-7882)*

2875 Fertilizers, Mixing Only

Bloomin Crazy Ldscp Flral Dsig ....G........ 405 238-3416
  Pauls Valley *(G-7652)*
Cowboy Compost ....G..... 405 853-0462
  Hennessey *(G-3453)*
Eckroat Seed Co ....F 405 427-2484
  Oklahoma City *(G-6006)*
Edc AG Products Company LLC ....D..... 405 235-4546
  Oklahoma City *(G-6008)*
El Dorado Chemical Company ....G..... 405 235-4546
  Oklahoma City *(G-6015)*
Farmers Union Co-Operative Gin ....G..... 580 482-5136
  Altus *(G-156)*
Garbage To Garden Compost Inc ....G..... 918 260-4463
  Bixby *(G-628)*
Stillwater Milling Company LLC ....F 580 369-2354
  Perry *(G-7747)*
Stockmans Mill & Grain Inc ....G..... 918 762-3459
  Pawnee *(G-7711)*
Traci Rae Woolman ....G..... 580 544-2521
  Boise City *(G-749)*
Urban Worm Compost LLC ....G..... 918 557-9255
  Broken Arrow *(G-1089)*

2879 Pesticides & Agricultural Chemicals, NEC

Armour Pest Control LLC ....G..... 918 489-5734
  Hendrix *(G-3439)*
Avitrol Corp ....G..... 918 622-7763
  Tulsa *(G-9231)*
Bug Right ....G..... 918 367-9792
  Bristow *(G-771)*
Christina Stokes ....G..... 405 551-1017
  Edmond *(G-2350)*
Chromatech Scientific Corp ....G..... 405 370-4466
  Edmond *(G-2351)*
Darren McIninch ....G..... 405 912-8403
  Oklahoma City *(G-5285)*
◆ Deepwater Chemicals Inc ....E 580 256-0500
  Woodward *(G-11577)*
Goff Associates Inc ....G..... 615 750-2900
  Oklahoma City *(G-6167)*
Green Horizons LLC ....G..... 405 364-9921
  Norman *(G-5010)*
Helena Agri-Enterprises LLC ....F 580 477-0986
  Altus *(G-157)*
Hope Minerals International ....G..... 405 452-3529
  Wetumka *(G-11491)*
Houston Brothers Inc ....G..... 918 449-1175
  Broken Arrow *(G-1134)*
Integrity Tech & Svcs LLC ....G..... 405 482-9206
  Edmond *(G-2462)*
Red River Specialties LLC ....G..... 580 436-0883
  Ada *(G-81)*
Redbud Soil Company LLC ....G..... 405 476-0429
  Oklahoma City *(G-6993)*
Shawn Schaeffer ....G..... 918 689-6781
  Eufaula *(G-3113)*
Tex Star AG LLC ....G..... 580 579-9877
  Coalgate *(G-1784)*

2891 Adhesives & Sealants

Alliance Sealants & Waterproof ....G........ 405 627-9474
  Oklahoma City *(G-5419)*
Appli-Fab Custom Coating ....G..... 405 235-7039
  Chandler *(G-1375)*
Color-Rite Inc ....F 405 354-3644
  Yukon *(G-11708)*
▲ CRC Evans Weighting Systems ....G..... 918 438-2100
  Tulsa *(G-9503)*
▼ Flanco Gasket and Mfg Inc ....E 405 672-7893
  Oklahoma City *(G-6088)*
Havard Industries LLC ....G..... 405 888-0961
  Edmond *(G-2453)*
Henley Sealants Inc ....G..... 405 235-7325
  Tulsa *(G-6240)*
Line X Prtctive Ctngs Okla LLC ....F 405 232-4994
  Oklahoma City *(G-6479)*
Mito Material Solutions Inc ....G..... 855 344-6486
  Stillwater *(G-8725)*
National Coating Mfg Inc ....F 580 332-8751
  Ada *(G-70)*
◆ Red Devil Incorporated ....F 918 585-8111
  Tulsa *(G-10629)*
Red Devil Incorporated ....D..... 918 825-5744
  Pryor *(G-7989)*
Seal Support Systems Inc ....F 918 258-6484
  Broken Arrow *(G-1046)*
Self-Suspending Proppant LLC ....E 580 456-7791
  Roff *(G-8111)*
Tile Shop LLC ....F 580 920-1570
  Durant *(G-2269)*
Tower Sealants LLC ....G..... 405 528-4411
  Oklahoma City *(G-7312)*
Versum Materials Us LLC ....E 918 379-7101
  Catoosa *(G-1363)*

2892 Explosives

All Decked Out ....G..... 918 313-9691
  Claremore *(G-1580)*
Austin Powder Co ....G..... 918 835-9244
  Tulsa *(G-9224)*
El Dorado Chemical Company ....G..... 405 235-4546
  Oklahoma City *(G-6015)*
Hman Global Solutions LLC ....G..... 405 338-5348
  Morrison *(G-4603)*
◆ LSB Chemical LLC ....F 405 235-4546
  Oklahoma City *(G-6498)*
Orica USA Inc ....G..... 918 437-1644
  Tulsa *(G-10439)*
Utec Corporation LLC ....G..... 405 928-7061
  Norman *(G-5190)*

2893 Printing Ink

Applied Laser Systems ....G..... 918 249-9025
  Tulsa *(G-9200)*
Caveman Screen Printing ....G..... 918 446-6440
  Tulsa *(G-9390)*
H&H Retail Services LLC ....F 918 369-4055
  Bixby *(G-631)*
Southwestern Process Supply Co ....E 918 582-8211
  Tulsa *(G-10812)*

2895 Carbon Black

Cabot Norit Americas Inc ....D..... 918 825-8332
  Pryor *(G-7949)*
Continental Carbon Company ....C 580 763-8100
  Ponca City *(G-7809)*
Thermal Specialties LLC ....C 918 836-4800
  Tulsa *(G-10926)*

2899 Chemical Preparations, NEC

Adko Inc ....G..... 405 677-6507
  Oklahoma City *(G-5375)*
Advanced Chemical Tech Inc ....G..... 405 843-2585
  Oklahoma City *(G-5379)*
American Entps Whl Dstributers ....G..... 405 273-4516
  Shawnee *(G-8427)*
▲ Bachman Services Inc ....E 405 677-8296
  Oklahoma City *(G-5507)*
Baker Petrolite LLC ....G..... 918 245-2224
  Sand Springs *(G-8165)*
Best Building Materials Inc ....G..... 405 755-0554
  Edmond *(G-2320)*
Bici LLC ....G..... 918 625-8811
  Broken Arrow *(G-849)*
Biotech Products Inc ....G..... 405 235-7575
  Oklahoma City *(G-5574)*
Blue ARC Metal Specialties ....G..... 918 341-3903
  Claremore *(G-1597)*
Brenntag Southwest Inc ....E 918 273-2265
  Nowata *(G-5209)*
C & P Catalyst Inc ....G..... 918 747-8379
  Tulsa *(G-9357)*
◆ Callidus Technologies LLC ....C 918 496-7599
  Tulsa *(G-9364)*
Callidus Technologies LLC ....D..... 918 267-4920
  Beggs *(G-550)*
Cargill Incorporated ....E 580 621-3246
  Freedom *(G-3205)*
▲ Ceralusa LLC ....G..... 405 455-7720
  Oklahoma City *(G-5730)*
Chandler Materials Company ....E 918 836-9151
  Tulsa *(G-9403)*
▲ Chemical Products Inds Inc ....G..... 405 745-2070
  Oklahoma City *(G-5748)*
Coil Chem LLC ....F 405 445-5545
  Washington *(G-11334)*

Oldcastle Materials Inc ....C....... 918 978-0459
Tulsa *(G-10413)*
Overland Federal LLC ....F....... 469 269-2303
Ardmore *(G-341)*
Overland Materials and Mfg Inc ....E....... 580 223-8432
Ardmore *(G-342)*
Paving Materials Inc ....G....... 405 799-9880
Moore *(G-4552)*
Quapaw Company ....F....... 918 225-0580
Cushing *(G-1951)*
Quapaw Company Inc ....E....... 918 352-2533
Drumright *(G-2070)*
Rdnj LLC ....G....... 405 418-4741
Oklahoma City *(G-6978)*
RLC Holding Co Inc ....D....... 580 233-6000
Enid *(G-3048)*
RLC Holding Co Inc ....E....... 580 332-3080
Ada *(G-82)*
▲ Road Science LLC ....D....... 918 960-3800
Tulsa *(G-10661)*
Rose Rock Midstream Field Svcs ....G....... 918 524-7700
Tulsa *(G-10672)*
Seal Masters Inc ....E....... 580 369-2393
Davis *(G-1993)*
Semcrude LP ....F....... 918 524-8100
Tulsa *(G-10727)*
▲ Semgroup Corporation ....B....... 918 524-8100
Tulsa *(G-10728)*
Semmaterials LP ....G....... 918 683-1732
Muskogee *(G-4747)*
Semmaterials LP ....G....... 580 223-8010
Ardmore *(G-353)*
Semmaterials LP ....G....... 580 536-0098
Lawton *(G-3996)*
Semmaterials LP ....G....... 918 266-1606
Catoosa *(G-1352)*
Semmaterials LP ....D....... 918 524-8100
Tulsa *(G-10729)*
T & G Construction Inc ....C....... 580 355-6655
Lawton *(G-4010)*
T J Campbell Construction Co ....C....... 405 672-6800
Oklahoma City *(G-7244)*
Teeters Asphalt & Materials ....G....... 918 673-1243
Picher *(G-7751)*
Vance Brothers Inc ....G....... 405 427-1389
Oklahoma City *(G-7390)*

2952 Asphalt Felts & Coatings

Acme Manufacturing Corporation ....E....... 918 266-3097
Claremore *(G-1575)*
Atlas Roofing Corporation ....C....... 580 226-3283
Ardmore *(G-251)*
Black Thunder Roofing LLC ....G....... 405 473-8028
Oklahoma City *(G-5582)*
Butaphalt Products LLC ....G....... 918 740-7290
Claremore *(G-1600)*
Dryvit Systems Inc ....E....... 918 245-0216
Sand Springs *(G-8179)*
▼ G A P Roofing Inc ....D....... 918 825-5200
Pryor *(G-7963)*
Global Sealcoating Inc ....G....... 918 283-2040
Claremore *(G-1626)*
McCabe Industrial Minerals ....G....... 918 252-5090
Tulsa *(G-10228)*
McCabe Industrial Minerals ....F....... 580 369-3660
Davis *(G-1990)*
Schwarz Asphalt LLC ....E....... 405 789-7203
Oklahoma City *(G-7092)*
Vance Brothers Inc ....G....... 405 427-1389
Oklahoma City *(G-7390)*

2992 Lubricating Oils & Greases

Axel Royal LLC ....E....... 918 584-2671
Tulsa *(G-9233)*
Broken Arrow Quality Lube ....G....... 918 258-5823
Broken Arrow *(G-858)*
Legendary Lube and Oil LLC ....G....... 918 351-5312
Muskogee *(G-4706)*
▼ Nu-Tier Brands Inc ....G....... 918 550-8026
Tulsa *(G-10366)*
▼ Oils Unlimited LLC ....D....... 918 583-1155
Tulsa *(G-10389)*
Phillips 66 Spectrum Corp ....F....... 918 977-7909
Bartlesville *(G-516)*
Sterling Properties ....G....... 580 357-6095
Lawton *(G-4005)*
Veterans Eng Group Inc ....G....... 918 864-6006
Pryor *(G-7997)*

2999 Products Of Petroleum & Coal, NEC

Trillium Trnsp Fuels LLC ....F....... 800 920-1166
Oklahoma City *(G-7330)*
Trillium Trnsp Fuels LLC ....G....... 405 302-6500
Oklahoma City *(G-7331)*

30 RUBBER AND MISCELLANEOUS PLASTICS PRODUCTS

3011 Tires & Inner Tubes

Airgo Systems ....G....... 877 550-6111
Oklahoma City *(G-5403)*
Carter BF ....G....... 918 486-7208
Coweta *(G-1874)*
Charles Service Station LLC ....G....... 918 297-3308
Hartshorne *(G-3390)*
Michelin North America Inc ....D....... 580 226-1200
Ardmore *(G-331)*
Nutting Custom Trikes ....G....... 918 257-8795
Afton *(G-119)*
Setco Inc ....D....... 580 286-6531
Idabel *(G-3645)*
▲ Southeast Tire Inc ....D....... 580 286-6531
Idabel *(G-3647)*
West Worldwide Services Inc ....G....... 405 601-9877
Oklahoma City *(G-7437)*

3021 Rubber & Plastic Footwear

Crackshot Corporation ....G....... 918 838-1272
Tulsa *(G-9497)*
Vans Inc ....F....... 405 843-5286
Oklahoma City *(G-7391)*
Vans Inc ....F....... 405 787-9992
Oklahoma City *(G-7392)*

3052 Rubber & Plastic Hose & Belting

▲ Miami Industrial Supply & Mfg ....E....... 918 542-6317
Miami *(G-4415)*
Power Cable Solutions LLC ....G....... 405 818-1993
Tuttle *(G-11207)*
Precision Hose Technology Inc ....G....... 918 835-3660
Tulsa *(G-10545)*
Tulsa Hose & Fittings Inc ....G....... 918 485-0348
Wagoner *(G-11294)*

3053 Gaskets, Packing & Sealing Devices

Advanced EMC Technologies LLC ....G....... 918 994-7776
Tulsa *(G-9107)*
Automated Gasket Company LLc ....F....... 405 951-5301
Oklahoma City *(G-5494)*
Bpc Industries Inc ....E....... 918 584-4848
Tulsa *(G-9325)*
▲ Clark Seals LLC ....E....... 918 664-0587
Tulsa *(G-9440)*
▼ Flanco Gasket and Mfg Inc ....E....... 405 672-7893
Oklahoma City *(G-6088)*
Freedom Rubber LLC ....G....... 918 250-4673
Broken Arrow *(G-914)*
G & D Industries Inc ....G....... 918 369-2648
Bixby *(G-625)*
▲ Global Bearings Inc ....E....... 918 664-8902
Tulsa *(G-9829)*
Harrison Manufacturing Co Inc ....F....... 918 838-9961
Tulsa *(G-9897)*
Hunt Jim Sales & Mfg ....G....... 405 670-5663
Oklahoma City *(G-6272)*
▲ Industrial Gasket Inc ....E....... 405 376-9393
Mustang *(G-4778)*
John Crane Inc ....D....... 918 664-5156
Tulsa *(G-10049)*
▲ John Crane Lemco Inc ....E....... 918 835-7325
Tulsa *(G-10050)*
▲ Kt Plastics Inc ....E....... 580 434-5655
Calera *(G-1241)*
Oklahoma Metal Creations LLC ....G....... 580 917-5434
Fletcher *(G-3165)*
Oklahoma Rbr & Gasket Co Inc ....F....... 918 585-3484
Tulsa *(G-10406)*
Quality Parts Mfg Co Inc ....G....... 918 627-3307
Tulsa *(G-10592)*
Redline Gaskets LLC ....G....... 918 845-7700
Sand Springs *(G-8221)*
▲ Roxtec Inc ....F....... 918 254-9872
Tulsa *(G-10679)*
Seal Company Enterprises Inc ....G....... 405 947-3307
Oklahoma City *(G-7104)*
▲ Southern Rubber Stamp Co Inc ....G....... 918 587-3818
Tulsa *(G-10801)*
▲ T & A Gasket Co Inc ....G....... 918 664-7600
Tulsa *(G-10887)*
Tetrachem Seal Company Inc ....F....... 580 924-1717
Durant *(G-2263)*
Thomas Engineering Co Inc ....E....... 918 587-6649
Tulsa *(G-10931)*
Triad Precision Products Inc ....E....... 918 584-3543
Tulsa *(G-10974)*
True Turn of Tulsa LLC ....F....... 918 224-5040
Tulsa *(G-10980)*
Tulsa Rubber Co ....F....... 918 627-1371
Tulsa *(G-11006)*

3061 Molded, Extruded & Lathe-Cut Rubber Mechanical Goods

▲ Baker Hughes Elasto Systems ....F....... 405 670-3354
Oklahoma City *(G-5516)*
Barlow-Hunt Inc ....D....... 918 250-0828
Tulsa *(G-9265)*
Diversified Rubber Pdts Inc ....E....... 918 241-0193
Tulsa *(G-9587)*
Joyeaux Inc ....F....... 918 252-7660
Tulsa *(G-10060)*
Oil States Industries Inc ....E....... 918 250-0828
Tulsa *(G-10388)*
Oil States Industries Inc ....D....... 405 671-2000
Oklahoma City *(G-6721)*
Oil States Industries Inc ....G....... 918 250-0828
Tulsa *(G-10387)*
Oklahoma Custom Rubber Co ....G....... 405 634-3943
Moore *(G-4545)*
Ranch Acres Car Care ....G....... 918 742-3902
Tulsa *(G-10619)*
Seal Company Enterprises Inc ....G....... 405 947-3307
Oklahoma City *(G-7104)*
Thomas Engineering Co Inc ....E....... 918 587-6649
Tulsa *(G-10931)*
Tjk Molded Products LLC ....F....... 409 200-1007
Ardmore *(G-370)*
Tjk Molded Products LLC ....G....... 409 200-1007
Ardmore *(G-371)*
Tulsa Rubber Co ....F....... 918 627-1371
Tulsa *(G-11006)*

3069 Fabricated Rubber Prdts, NEC

American Phoenix Inc ....C....... 580 248-1488
Lawton *(G-3887)*
Anywhere Infltable Screens LLC ....G....... 918 260-4146
Tulsa *(G-9194)*
C and D Fashion Floors LLC ....G....... 918 256-8018
Vinita *(G-11250)*
▼ Custom Identification Products ....G....... 405 745-1010
Oklahoma City *(G-5873)*
▲ Da/Pro Rubber Inc ....C....... 918 258-9386
Broken Arrow *(G-886)*
Da/Pro Rubber Inc ....E....... 918 272-7799
Tulsa *(G-9544)*
Da/Pro Rubber Inc ....G....... 918 299-5480
Tulsa *(G-9545)*
Grip Jar Opener LLC ....G....... 918 766-2711
Tulsa *(G-9864)*
Jessie Shaw ....G....... 918 587-6329
Tulsa *(G-10040)*
Molded Products Incorporated ....E....... 918 254-9061
Broken Arrow *(G-1144)*
▲ Northwest Rubber ....G....... 405 681-2667
Oklahoma City *(G-6694)*
▼ Rubber Mold Company ....F....... 405 673-7177
Oklahoma City *(G-7059)*
Shelby Trailer Service LLC ....G....... 580 252-2922
Comanche *(G-1846)*
▲ Skinner Brothers Company Inc ....F....... 918 585-5708
Tulsa *(G-10771)*
Texre Inc ....D....... 918 425-5524
Tulsa *(G-10922)*
Tulsa Rubber Co ....F....... 918 627-1371
Tulsa *(G-11006)*

3081 Plastic Unsupported Sheet & Film

▼ Bags Inc ....E....... 405 427-5473
Oklahoma City *(G-5509)*
Berry Global Inc ....F....... 918 824-4288
Pryor *(G-7945)*
Berry Global Inc ....D....... 918 824-4400
Pryor *(G-7946)*
Berry Global Inc ....C....... 918 426-4800
McAlester *(G-4275)*
Berry Global Films LLC ....D....... 918 227-1616
Tulsa *(G-8990)*

SIC SECTION

31 LEATHER AND LEATHER PRODUCTS

Hackney Ladish Inc ....D...... 580 237-4212
  Enid *(G-2967)*
Hopkins Manufacturing Corp ....F...... 918 961-8722
  Miami *(G-4408)*
House of Trophies ....G...... 918 341-2111
  Claremore *(G-1637)*
Imperial Molding LLC ....F...... 580 362-3412
  Newkirk *(G-4848)*
Imperial Plastics Inc ....F...... 580 362-3412
  Newkirk *(G-4849)*
J & S Fittings Inc ....G...... 918 324-5777
  Depew *(G-2011)*
Jarrt Holdings Inc ....F...... 918 664-0931
  Tulsa *(G-10028)*
K & C Manufacturing Inc ....G...... 580 362-2979
  Ponca City *(G-7842)*
Kratos Unmnned Arial Systems I ....G...... 405 248-9545
  Oklahoma City *(G-6435)*
Krause Plastics ....G...... 918 835-4202
  Tulsa *(G-10100)*
Lacebark Inc ....G...... 405 377-3539
  Stillwater *(G-8716)*
Lansing Building Products Inc ....G...... 405 943-2493
  Oklahoma City *(G-6448)*
Laska LLC ....G...... 405 820-7617
  Edmond *(G-2483)*
Layle Company Corporation ....G...... 405 329-5143
  Norman *(G-5056)*
Leche Lounge Llc ....G...... 918 409-5426
  Tulsa *(G-10144)*
Letica Corporation ....C...... 405 745-2781
  Oklahoma City *(G-6467)*
Lloyd Freeman Creations LLC ....G...... 918 245-4921
  Sand Springs *(G-8201)*
M-D Plastics Group ....G...... 503 981-3726
  Oklahoma City *(G-6511)*
Mac Industries Inc ....G...... 405 631-8553
  Moore *(G-4535)*
Magnum Racing Components Inc ....G...... 918 627-0204
  Tulsa *(G-10201)*
Mark Stevens Industries Inc ....D...... 405 948-1077
  Edmond *(G-2504)*
McClarin Plastics Llc ....E...... 877 912-6297
  Oklahoma City *(G-6545)*
Mold Tech Inc ....G...... 918 247-6275
  Sapulpa *(G-8292)*
New Day Creations LLC ....G...... 918 576-9619
  Bixby *(G-648)*
Norwesco Inc ....F...... 405 275-2034
  Shawnee *(G-8479)*
O C & Associates Inc ....G...... 918 251-0971
  Broken Arrow *(G-991)*
Oklahoma Hand Pours ....F...... 580 669-2520
  Glencoe *(G-3225)*
▲ Phil-Good Products Inc ....E...... 405 942-5527
  Oklahoma City *(G-6842)*
Plas-Tech Inc ....G...... 918 649-0065
  Poteau *(G-7909)*
Plastic Designs Inc ....G...... 918 224-9187
  Sapulpa *(G-8299)*
Plastic Sup & Fabrication Co ....G...... 918 622-8430
  Tulsa *(G-10526)*
Polydyne LLC ....F...... 918 649-0065
  Poteau *(G-7910)*
Precision Rotational Molding ....G...... 580 362-3262
  Newkirk *(G-4851)*
Quarry ....G...... 918 534-2120
  Dewey *(G-2030)*
Reasor Enterprises ....G...... 918 633-1746
  Broken Arrow *(G-1029)*
Rim Molded Products Co ....F...... 918 438-7070
  Tulsa *(G-10653)*
◆ RL Hudson & Company ....C...... 918 259-6600
  Broken Arrow *(G-1035)*
Rotational Technologies Inc ....F...... 918 343-1450
  Claremore *(G-1684)*
Rusco Plastics ....G...... 580 234-1596
  Enid *(G-3053)*
Samco Polishing Inc ....F...... 918 789-5541
  Chelsea *(G-1412)*
Sanco Enterprises Inc ....E...... 405 634-2120
  Oklahoma City *(G-7075)*
▲ Sanco Products Inc ....G...... 405 634-2120
  Oklahoma City *(G-7076)*
Scepter Manufacturing LLC ....D...... 918 544-2222
  Miami *(G-4430)*
Solo Cup Operating Corporation ....C...... 580 436-1500
  Ada *(G-90)*
Southern Plastics LLC ....G...... 918 274-6767
  Owasso *(G-7618)*

Specialty Plastics Inc ....F...... 580 237-1018
  Enid *(G-3061)*
▲ Stonehouse Marketing Svcs LLC ....D...... 405 360-5674
  Norman *(G-5160)*
SUN Engineering Inc ....F...... 918 627-0426
  Tulsa *(G-10870)*
Surface Mount Depot Inc ....G...... 405 789-0670
  Oklahoma City *(G-7231)*
Swan Plastics ....G...... 405 275-4826
  Shawnee *(G-8506)*
Tech Inc ....F...... 405 547-8324
  Perkins *(G-7724)*
Texre Inc ....D...... 918 425-5524
  Tulsa *(G-10922)*
▲ Tgs Plastics Inc ....E...... 918 252-3636
  Tulsa *(G-10925)*
Viking Rain Covers ....F...... 405 359-1850
  Edmond *(G-2671)*
W J L S Inc ....E...... 918 252-3636
  Tulsa *(G-11088)*
▼ Western Plastics LLC ....F...... 405 235-7272
  Oklahoma City *(G-7441)*
Wilson II Geary Wayne ....G...... 405 330-4888
  Edmond *(G-2689)*
Wing-It Concepts ....G...... 405 691-8053
  Oklahoma City *(G-5325)*

31 LEATHER AND LEATHER PRODUCTS

3111 Leather Tanning & Finishing

Blinkers & Silks Unlimited Inc ....G...... 405 463-0391
  Lamar *(G-3862)*
Diamond R Saddle Shop ....G...... 918 479-6279
  Rose *(G-8117)*
Iron Bear Jewelry & Lea Co LLC ....G...... 918 289-1420
  Tulsa *(G-10012)*
Lenora Elizabeth Brown ....G...... 918 797-2034
  Stilwell *(G-8792)*
Oklahoma Leather Products Inc ....D...... 918 542-6651
  Miami *(G-4424)*
▲ Osage Leather Inc ....G...... 918 745-0772
  Tulsa *(G-10442)*
Rawhide Custom Leather ....G...... 918 273-0511
  Nowata *(G-5227)*
Rawhide Dirt Works ....G...... 580 367-5242
  Coalgate *(G-1783)*
Rawhide N Rustics ....G...... 580 307-9941
  Weatherford *(G-11436)*
Stockmans Supply Company ....G...... 580 255-7762
  Duncan *(G-2186)*
Tricked Out Pony ....G...... 918 931-2646
  Tahlequah *(G-8889)*

3131 Boot & Shoe Cut Stock & Findings

Bean Counter Inc ....G...... 918 925-9667
  Claremore *(G-1594)*
Counter Canter Inc ....G...... 405 321-8326
  Norman *(G-4967)*
Countrstrike Lghtning Prtction ....G...... 405 863-8480
  Oklahoma City *(G-5844)*
Ingersoll-Rand Air Solutio ....G...... 918 451-9747
  Broken Arrow *(G-936)*
Lux Grooming Quarters LLC ....G...... 918 259-9910
  Tulsa *(G-10184)*
Quality In Counters Inc ....G...... 405 664-2744
  Guthrie *(G-3333)*
Quarter Midgets of America ....G...... 918 371-9410
  Collinsville *(G-1820)*
Rand Trans Inc ....G...... 580 866-3355
  Sharon *(G-8418)*
Upper Room ....G......
  Oklahoma City *(G-7374)*

3144 Women's Footwear, Exc Athletic

C & W Shoes of Georgia Inc ....F...... 405 755-7112
  Oklahoma City *(G-5658)*

3149 Footwear, NEC

Island Disc Golf Course ....G...... 541 337-8668
  Pawhuska *(G-7686)*
Moccasin Trail Company ....G...... 405 380-8221
  Paden *(G-7636)*
Moccasins of Hope Society ....G...... 605 431-3738
  Ponca City *(G-7854)*

3161 Luggage

Briefcase Solutions Ltd LLC ....G...... 405 788-9250
  McLoud *(G-4353)*
D Gala ....G...... 580 468-4980
  Guymon *(G-3347)*
Dusty Trunk ....G...... 918 446-4203
  Tulsa *(G-9613)*
Floyd Craig Company ....G...... 580 832-2597
  Cordell *(G-1859)*
Frenches Quarter ....G...... 918 691-2553
  Tulsa *(G-9777)*
Gra Enterprises Inc ....G...... 405 848-1300
  Oklahoma City *(G-6173)*
Junk N Leslies Trunk LLC ....G...... 405 748-6702
  Oklahoma City *(G-6391)*
Nancys Trunk ....G...... 405 413-5037
  Ripley *(G-8103)*
Spot My Bag LLC ....G...... 918 895-8810
  Tulsa *(G-10826)*
Titanium Phoenix Inc ....G...... 405 305-1304
  Oklahoma City *(G-7294)*
W L Walker Co Inc ....E...... 918 583-3109
  Tulsa *(G-11089)*

3171 Handbags & Purses

Accessories-To-Go ....G...... 580 467-7408
  Comanche *(G-1833)*
Job Paper LLC ....G...... 405 242-4804
  Yukon *(G-11737)*
Sew N Saw ....G...... 405 282-2241
  Guthrie *(G-3337)*

3172 Personal Leather Goods

Harry A Lippert Jr ....G...... 512 705-1248
  Lawton *(G-3939)*
Leather Our Way ....G...... 918 214-2036
  Bartlesville *(G-506)*
Nupocket LLC ....F...... 918 850-1903
  Broken Arrow *(G-990)*
Savoy Leather LLC ....G...... 405 786-2296
  Weleetka *(G-11465)*
Tipton Company ....G...... 580 762-0800
  Ponca City *(G-7884)*
▲ Warner Jwly Box Display Co LLC ....D...... 580 536-8885
  Lawton *(G-4021)*

3199 Leather Goods, NEC

◆ Billy Cook Harn & Saddle Mfg ....D...... 580 622-5505
  Sulphur *(G-8829)*
Comanche Leather Works Inc ....G...... 580 439-6276
  Comanche *(G-1837)*
Cornerstone Leather ....G...... 817 598-0367
  Comanche *(G-1840)*
Crossroad Holsters LLC ....G...... 405 317-7405
  Oklahoma City *(G-5860)*
Custom Lea Sad & Cowboy Decor ....G...... 918 335-2277
  Bartlesville *(G-471)*
D R Topping Saddlery ....G...... 918 273-2812
  Nowata *(G-5212)*
Don Hume Company LLC ....E...... 918 542-6604
  Miami *(G-4397)*
Don Hume Leathergoods Inc ....D...... 918 542-6604
  Miami *(G-4398)*
▲ Finish Line of Oklahoma Inc ....G...... 918 341-8291
  Claremore *(G-1621)*
Geronimo Manufacturing Inc ....G...... 580 336-5707
  Perry *(G-7735)*
Gj Leather LLC ....G...... 405 795-2998
  Newcastle *(G-4828)*
Jerry Beagley Braiding Company ....G...... 580 924-4995
  Calera *(G-1240)*
Johnny Beard Co ....G...... 918 438-4901
  Tulsa *(G-10056)*
Kens Handcrafted Leather Gds ....G...... 918 616-5804
  Muskogee *(G-4702)*
Leather Doctor ....G...... 918 271-4600
  Broken Arrow *(G-965)*
Lenora Elizabeth Brown ....G...... 918 797-2034
  Stilwell *(G-8792)*
Lewis Manufacturing Co LLC ....E...... 405 279-2553
  Meeker *(G-4378)*
▲ Lewis Manufacturing Co LLC ....G...... 405 634-5401
  Oklahoma City *(G-6471)*
Mock Brothers Saddlery Inc ....G...... 918 245-7259
  Sand Springs *(G-8205)*
Okc Boys of Leather ....G...... 318 564-0312
  Oklahoma City *(G-6727)*
Scissor Tail Custom Holster ....G...... 405 595-6315
  Norman *(G-5139)*

Employee Codes: A=Over 500 employees, B=251-500
C=101-250, D=51-100, E=20-50, F=10-19, G=1-9

Arrowhead Precast LLC ....D 918 995-2227
Broken Arrow (G-833)
Baray Enterprises Inc ....E 405 373-1800
Piedmont (G-7755)
Blackstone Capital Partners SE ....G 424 355-5050
El Reno (G-2702)
Bmi Management Inc ....G 580 762-5659
Ponca City (G-7801)
Carnegie Precast Inc ....F 580 654-1718
Carnegie (G-1275)
Cellfill LLC ....G 918 787-2355
Grove (G-3260)
Central Burial Vaults Inc ....E 918 224-5701
Tulsa (G-8996)
Champion Designs & Systems LLC ....G 405 888-8370
Oklahoma City (G-5737)
Chandler Materials Company ....E 918 836-9151
Tulsa (G-9403)
Cobble Rock and Stone LLC ....F 405 567-3552
Prague (G-7923)
Concrete Products Inc ....E 405 427-8686
Oklahoma City (G-5819)
▲ Construction Supply House Inc ....G 405 214-9366
Norman (G-4964)
Coppedge Septic Tank ....G 918 371-4549
Collinsville (G-1806)
Coreslab Structures Okla Inc ....C 405 632-4944
Oklahoma City (G-5835)
Coreslab Structures Oklahoma ....F 405 672-2325
Oklahoma City (G-5836)
Coreslab Structures Tulsa Inc ....E 918 438-0230
Tulsa (G-9487)
▲ CRC Evans Weighting Systems ....G 918 438-2100
Tulsa (G-9503)
Decorative Rock & Stone ....G 405 341-8900
Edmond (G-2388)
Dolese Bros Co ....F 580 225-1247
Elk City (G-2803)
Dolese Bros Co ....E 405 670-9626
Oklahoma City (G-5962)
Dover Products Inc ....G 918 476-5688
Chouteau (G-1562)
Downtown Pub ....F 918 274-8202
Owasso (G-7563)
Eastside Septic Tank ....G 918 486-2290
Coweta (G-1881)
Eaves Stones Products ....F 580 889-7858
Atoka (G-410)
Excalibur Cast Stone LLC ....E 405 702-4314
Oklahoma City (G-6057)
Excalibur Stoneworks LLC ....D 405 702-4314
Oklahoma City (G-6058)
Foresee Ready-Mix Concrete Inc ....F 918 689-3951
Eufaula (G-3101)
Forterra Pipe & Precast LLC ....G 405 677-8811
Oklahoma City (G-6104)
▲ Gifford Monument Works Inc ....F 580 332-1271
Ada (G-42)
GNC Concrete Products Inc ....D 918 438-1182
Tulsa (G-9836)
Green Country S Inc ....G 918 224-8244
Sapulpa (G-8276)
Handi-Sak Inc ....E 405 789-3001
Oklahoma City (G-6210)
Haskell Lemon Construction Co ....C 405 947-6069
Oklahoma City (G-6223)
Hausners Limited ....F 580 924-6988
Mead (G-4366)
Hausners Precast Con Pdts Inc ....E 918 352-3479
Drumright (G-2061)
Heritage Burial Park ....G 405 692-5503
Oklahoma City (G-6242)
▼ Impressions In Stone LLC ....G 918 828-9745
Tulsa (G-9974)
Improved Cnstr Methods Inc ....G 405 235-2609
Oklahoma City (G-6294)
Jim Giles Safe Rooms ....G 918 639-8102
Sapulpa (G-8283)
Keith Lyons ....F 580 584-3360
Broken Bow (G-1196)
Kel-Crete Industries Inc ....G 918 744-0800
Tulsa (G-10080)
McF Services Inc ....G 918 481-1620
Tulsa (G-10233)
McLemore Monument Services ....G 405 788-0164
El Reno (G-2737)
Monumental Rocks ....G 918 240-8398
Broken Arrow (G-981)
Palm Vault Co Inc ....G 580 332-7565
Ada (G-74)
Precast Solutions LLC ....G 580 819-2455
Yukon (G-11767)
Precast Trtmnt Solutions LLC ....G 405 455-5303
Oklahoma City (G-6877)
Precision Stone ....G 405 214-2224
Shawnee (G-8484)
Quikrete Companies LLC ....E 918 835-4441
Tulsa (G-10598)
Quikrete Holdings Inc ....G 405 354-8824
Yukon (G-11770)
Rinker Materials Concrete Pipe ....G 405 745-3404
Oklahoma City (G-7028)
Rn Concrete Products ....G 405 564-3020
Perry (G-7743)
Schwarz Sand ....G 405 789-7914
Oklahoma City (G-7093)
Scurlock Industries Miami Inc ....F 918 542-1884
North Miami (G-5208)
Skiatook Statuary ....G 918 396-1309
Skiatook (G-8570)
Smith Septic Tank Inc ....G 918 456-8741
Tahlequah (G-8884)
Spencer L Rosson ....G 918 682-4291
Muskogee (G-4750)
Stone Mill Inc ....F 918 812-4438
Kansas (G-3755)
Stone Warehouse ....F 918 250-0800
Broken Arrow (G-1064)
Stonecoat of Tulsa LLC ....G 918 551-6868
Tulsa (G-10855)
Tricon Unlmited Cnstr Svcs LLC ....G 405 473-9186
Oklahoma City (G-7329)
Triguard of Oklahoma ....G 580 243-8015
Elk City (G-2885)
Tulsa Casting Inc ....G 918 366-1272
Bixby (G-667)
▲ Tulsa Dynaspan Inc ....C 918 258-8693
Tulsa (G-10996)
Twin Cities Ready Mix Inc ....G 918 465-2555
Wilburton (G-11527)
V&H Coatings Co ....G 405 819-4163
Oklahoma City (G-7384)
Vintage Vault ....G 918 619-9954
Tulsa (G-11079)
Wilbert Funeral Services Inc ....E 918 446-2131
Tulsa (G-9051)
Wilbert Funeral Services Inc ....E 405 752-9033
Oklahoma City (G-7451)
Williams Monuments ....G 918 225-1344
Cushing (G-1971)

3273 Ready-Mixed Concrete

Altus Ready-Mix Inc ....F 580 482-3418
Altus (G-142)
Alva Concrete Inc ....B 580 327-2281
Alva (G-173)
Apac-Central Inc ....G 918 696-2820
Stilwell (G-8780)
Apac-Central Inc ....G 918 921-6491
Tulsa (G-9195)
Apac-Central Inc ....G 918 775-3251
Sallisaw (G-8137)
Atlas Concrete Inc ....G 580 255-7280
Duncan (G-2083)
Atlas Tuck Concrete Inc ....F 580 355-8241
Lawton (G-3892)
Atlas Tuck Concrete Inc ....G 405 224-5005
Chickasha (G-1433)
Atlas Tuck Concrete Inc ....G 405 381-2393
Tuttle (G-11185)
Atlas-Tuck Concrete Inc ....G 580 255-1716
Duncan (G-2084)
B & W Ready Mix LLC ....G 580 623-5059
Watonga (G-11340)
Bartlesville Redi-Mix Inc ....F 580 765-6693
Bartlesville (G-453)
Block Sand Co Inc ....E 405 391-2919
McLoud (G-4352)
Bo-Max Industries Inc ....F 580 256-4555
Woodward (G-11562)
Carnegie Concrete Company ....G 580 654-1208
Carnegie (G-1273)
Caswell Construction Co Inc ....D 580 225-6833
Elk City (G-2793)
Connelly Ready-Mix Con LLC ....D 405 943-8388
Oklahoma City (G-5820)
Crescent Ready Mix Inc ....G 405 853-1599
Crescent (G-1910)
Day Concrete Block Company ....F 580 223-3317
Ardmore (G-277)
▲ Dolese Bros Co ....C 405 235-2311
Oklahoma City (G-5957)
Dolese Bros Co ....F 580 795-3549
Madill (G-4146)
Dolese Bros Co ....G 405 947-7085
Oklahoma City (G-5958)
Dolese Bros Co ....G 580 924-4944
Durant (G-2224)
Dolese Bros Co ....G 580 237-2650
Enid (G-2942)
Dolese Bros Co ....G 405 454-2478
Harrah (G-3377)
Dolese Bros Co ....E 580 639-2237
Mountain View (G-4627)
Dolese Bros Co ....F 918 437-6535
Tulsa (G-9591)
Dolese Bros Co ....F 580 332-0820
Ada (G-32)
Dolese Bros Co ....G 405 382-2060
Seminole (G-8370)
Dolese Bros Co ....G 405 795-9757
Oklahoma City (G-5959)
Dolese Bros Co ....E 580 369-2834
Davis (G-1982)
Dolese Bros Co ....G 580 576-9478
Roosevelt (G-8116)
Dolese Bros Co ....G 580 761-0022
Ponca City (G-7821)
Dolese Bros Co ....G 918 423-1061
McAlester (G-4294)
Dolese Bros Co ....G 580 323-1202
Clinton (G-1748)
Dolese Bros Co ....G 580 889-6033
Atoka (G-408)
Dolese Bros Co ....G 405 247-2564
Anadarko (G-202)
Dolese Bros Co ....G 405 262-0226
El Reno (G-2713)
Dolese Bros Co ....G 918 297-2376
Hartshorne (G-3391)
Dolese Bros Co ....G 405 235-2311
Weatherford (G-11404)
Dolese Bros Co ....F 405 235-1515
Chickasha (G-1452)
Dolese Bros Co ....E 405 794-0546
Moore (G-4518)
Dolese Bros Co ....E 580 832-2720
Cordell (G-1858)
Dolese Bros Co ....G 405 282-2153
Guthrie (G-3311)
Dolese Bros Co ....G 405 672-4577
Oklahoma City (G-5960)
Dolese Bros Co ....G 405 732-0909
Oklahoma City (G-5961)
Dolese Bros Co ....E 405 670-9626
Oklahoma City (G-5962)
Dolese Bros Co ....G 405 373-2102
Piedmont (G-7760)
Dolese Bros Co ....F 405 232-1228
Oklahoma City (G-5963)
Dolese Bros Co ....G 405 324-2944
Yukon (G-11720)
Dolese Bros Co ....F 580 223-2243
Ardmore (G-279)
Dolese Bros Co ....E 405 949-2278
Oklahoma City (G-5964)
Dolese Bros Co ....F 580 225-1247
Elk City (G-2803)
Dolese Bros Co ....F 580 255-3046
Duncan (G-2107)
Eagle Redi-Mix Concrete LLC ....G 918 355-5700
Tulsa (G-9627)
Enid Concrete Co Inc ....B 580 237-7766
Enid (G-2950)
Evans & Associates Entps Inc ....F 580 482-3418
Altus (G-155)
Evans & Associates Entps Inc ....E 580 765-6693
Ponca City (G-7828)
Evans Asphalt Co Inc ....G 580 765-6693
Ponca City (G-7829)
Evans Concrete Co Inc ....G 580 765-6693
Skiatook (G-8543)
Foresee Ready-Mix Concrete Inc ....F 918 689-3951
Eufaula (G-3101)
Gcc Ready Mix LLC ....G 918 582-8111
Tulsa (G-9811)
Goddards Ready Mix Con Inc ....F 405 424-4383
Oklahoma City (G-6165)
Goddards Ready Mix Concrete ....G 405 424-4383
Oklahoma City (G-6166)

S I C

Employee Codes: A=Over 500 employees, B=251-500
C=101-250, D=51-100, E=20-50, F=10-19, G=1-9
2020 Oklahoma Directory
of Manufacturers & Processors
461

SIC SECTION

McCabe Industrial Minerals ....G....... 918 252-5090
Tulsa *(G-10228)*
McCabe Industrial Minerals ....F....... 580 369-3660
Davis *(G-1990)*
McCabe Industrial Mnrl Corp ....F....... 918 252-5090
Tulsa *(G-10229)*
Mesquite Minerals Inc.................G....... 405 848-7551
Oklahoma City *(G-6571)*
Wildcat Minerals.................G....... 580 254-0141
Woodward *(G-11653)*

3296 Mineral Wool

Ets-Lindgren Inc.................E....... 580 434-7490
Durant *(G-2230)*
Hewlett-Packard Entp Svcs.................G....... 918 939-4072
Tulsa *(G-9926)*
Johns Manville Corporation.................E....... 405 552-4115
Oklahoma City *(G-6372)*
Owens Corning Sales LLC.................F....... 405 235-2491
Oklahoma City *(G-6790)*
Scott Manufacturing LLC.................E....... 405 949-2728
Oklahoma City *(G-7096)*
Scott Manufacturing of Ky.................E....... 405 949-2728
Oklahoma City *(G-7097)*
Western Fibers Inc.................E....... 509 679-4786
Hollis *(G-3571)*

3297 Nonclay Refractories

Acid Specialists LLC.................G....... 432 617-2243
Oklahoma City *(G-5366)*
Bpi Inc.................G....... 918 682-5044
Muskogee *(G-4654)*
◆ Mike Alexander Company Inc.................E....... 580 765-8085
Tulsa *(G-10276)*
Quikrete Companies LLC.................E....... 405 787-2050
Oklahoma City *(G-6953)*
◆ Refractory Anchors Inc.................E....... 918 455-8485
Broken Arrow *(G-1154)*

3299 Nonmetallic Mineral Prdts, NEC

Alvin Stone.................G....... 918 447-4455
Tulsa *(G-9158)*
Architectural Models.................G....... 405 360-2828
Norman *(G-4913)*
Benchmark Stucco.................G....... 918 810-2812
Sperry *(G-8604)*
Blessing Gravel LLC.................G....... 580 513-4009
Tishomingo *(G-8962)*
CD Industrys Corporation.................G....... 580 317-8448
Hugo *(G-3605)*
▲ F C Ziegler Co.................E....... 918 587-7639
Tulsa *(G-9721)*
▲ Insul-Vest Inc.................G....... 918 445-2279
Tulsa *(G-9992)*
Phelps Sculpture Studio.................G....... 405 752-9512
Oklahoma City *(G-6841)*
Ppr LLC.................G....... 574 516-1131
Stillwater *(G-8740)*
Snyders Stucco and Stone.................G....... 580 421-9747
Ada *(G-89)*
Stucco 2 Stone.................G....... 918 770-2944
Tulsa *(G-10863)*
▲ To Market LLC.................G....... 405 236-2878
Oklahoma City *(G-7300)*
Yolanda Olmos.................G....... 918 850-8334
Tulsa *(G-11169)*

33 PRIMARY METAL INDUSTRIES

3312 Blast Furnaces, Coke Ovens, Steel & Rolling Mills

3 D Manufacturing.................G....... 918 224-7717
Sapulpa *(G-8244)*
Abco Steel Inc.................F....... 918 322-3435
Glenpool *(G-3228)*
▲ Advantage Cnstr Pdts Inc.................G....... 405 372-3562
Stillwater *(G-8651)*
Albright Steel and Wire Co.................F....... 405 232-7526
Oklahoma City *(G-5410)*
Azz Incorporated.................E....... 918 584-6668
Tulsa *(G-9237)*
Balero.................G....... 580 221-6202
Ardmore *(G-252)*
Bucke-Tee LLC.................G....... 580 747-9288
Enid *(G-2923)*
Bullet Fence Systems LLC.................G....... 918 777-3973
Okmulgee *(G-7496)*
C & B Fabricators Inc.................G....... 918 760-6508
Bokoshe *(G-752)*

▲ Carlson Company.................E....... 918 627-4334
Tulsa *(G-9376)*
Chickasaw Defense Services Inc.................G....... 405 203-0144
Oklahoma City *(G-5759)*
CMC Steel Oklahoma LLC.................G....... 580 634-5092
Durant *(G-2217)*
Commercial Metals Company.................G....... 580 634-5046
Durant *(G-2218)*
Commercial Metals Company.................F....... 918 437-5377
Tulsa *(G-9474)*
Cust-O-Bend Inc.................E....... 918 241-0514
Tulsa *(G-9526)*
Cyber Stitchery.................G....... 405 329-6018
Norman *(G-4975)*
Danlin Industries LLC.................C....... 580 661-3248
Clinton *(G-1747)*
Elite Fabricators LLC.................E....... 918 824-4528
Pryor *(G-7961)*
Gerdau Ameristeel US Inc.................G....... 918 241-7762
Sand Springs *(G-8188)*
Gms Lalos Custom Wheels Ltd Co.................G....... 918 622-3616
Tulsa *(G-9835)*
Hartco Metal Products Inc.................G....... 405 471-2784
Edmond *(G-2452)*
Ipsco Tubulars Inc.................C....... 918 384-6400
Catoosa *(G-1323)*
J & L Tool Co Inc.................G....... 918 835-8484
Tulsa *(G-10018)*
Joco Assembly LLC.................E....... 918 622-5111
Tulsa *(G-10048)*
Karchmer Pipe & Supply Co Inc.................G....... 405 236-3568
Oklahoma City *(G-6398)*
Kingfisher Pipe Sales and Svc.................G....... 405 262-4422
El Reno *(G-2733)*
Kloeckner Metals Corporation.................E....... 918 266-1666
Catoosa *(G-1328)*
Lawton Window Co Inc.................G....... 580 353-4655
Lawton *(G-3962)*
Metals USA Plates and Shap.................E....... 918 682-7833
Muskogee *(G-4713)*
Mobile Hightech.................G....... 405 942-4600
Oklahoma City *(G-6620)*
MRC Global (us) Inc.................G....... 918 485-9511
Wagoner *(G-11287)*
National Oilwell Varco Inc.................C....... 918 781-4436
Muskogee *(G-4719)*
Precision Metals LLC.................G....... 918 266-2202
Tulsa *(G-10548)*
◆ Refractory Anchors Inc.................E....... 918 455-8485
Broken Arrow *(G-1154)*
Ross Dub Company Inc.................E....... 405 495-3611
Oklahoma City *(G-7049)*
S E A Y Manufacturing LLC.................G....... 405 454-2328
Harrah *(G-3385)*
Sherrell Steel LLC.................F....... 580 436-4322
Ada *(G-87)*
Straits Steel and Wire LLC.................G....... 231 843-3416
Tulsa *(G-10858)*
Tms International LLC.................G....... 918 241-0129
Sand Springs *(G-8230)*
TRC Rod Services of Oklahoma.................F....... 405 677-0585
Oklahoma City *(G-7320)*
Tubacex Durant Inc.................G....... 724 646-4301
Durant *(G-2270)*
United Axle.................G....... 918 344-1157
Claremore *(G-1697)*
Vam Usa LLC.................G....... 405 720-2200
Oklahoma City *(G-7388)*
◆ Webco Industries Inc.................B....... 918 245-2211
Sand Springs *(G-8237)*
Webco Industries Inc.................G....... 865 388-5001
Catoosa *(G-1364)*
Webco Industries Inc.................G....... 918 581-0900
Sand Springs *(G-8236)*
Webco Industries Inc.................G....... 918 836-1188
Tulsa *(G-11100)*
Wire Twisters Inc.................G....... 405 376-0052
Mustang *(G-4802)*

3313 Electrometallurgical Prdts

Cutting Edge Machine Inc.................G....... 580 658-5036
Marlow *(G-4226)*

3315 Steel Wire Drawing & Nails & Spikes

Albright Steel and Wire Co.................G....... 580 357-3596
Lawton *(G-3886)*
American Fence Company Inc.................E....... 405 685-4800
Oklahoma City *(G-5435)*
Automatic Gate Systems of Okla.................G....... 580 920-8752
Durant *(G-2203)*

▲ Dw-Natnal Stndrd-Stllwater LLC.................C....... 405 377-5050
Stillwater *(G-8680)*
General Wire & Supply Co Inc.................E....... 918 245-5961
Tulsa *(G-9817)*
Givens Manufacturing Inc.................G....... 888 302-2774
Mounds *(G-4616)*
Hanlock-Causeway Company LLC.................F....... 918 446-1450
Tulsa *(G-9009)*
Jackson Clip Co Inc.................C....... 918 476-8331
Mazie *(G-4264)*
Kaydawn Manufacturing Co Inc.................G....... 918 321-5017
Glenpool *(G-3237)*
▲ Lewis Manufacturing Co LLC.................G....... 405 634-5401
Oklahoma City *(G-6471)*
M & R Wire Works Inc.................G....... 580 795-4290
Madill *(G-4153)*
Nomad Defense LLC.................G....... 405 808-4325
Yukon *(G-11760)*
Pinpoint Wire Technologies LLC.................G....... 405 447-6900
Norman *(G-5116)*
Screen Tech Intl Ltd Co.................F....... 918 234-0010
Broken Arrow *(G-1161)*
U and S Wire Rope.................G....... 580 421-1077
Shawnee *(G-8514)*
William B Finley.................G....... 580 512-7573
Lawton *(G-4023)*

3316 Cold Rolled Steel Sheet, Strip & Bars

Albright Steel and Wire Co.................G....... 405 232-7526
Oklahoma City *(G-5410)*
Carefusion Corporation.................G....... 918 865-4727
Mannford *(G-4178)*
▲ Carlson Company.................E....... 918 627-4334
Tulsa *(G-9376)*
Cust-O-Bend Inc.................E....... 918 241-0514
Tulsa *(G-9526)*
Tmk Ipsco International LLC.................G....... 918 384-6400
Catoosa *(G-1356)*
Worthington Industries Inc.................G....... 614 438-3048
Catoosa *(G-1369)*

3317 Steel Pipe & Tubes

▲ Advantage Cnstr Pdts Inc.................G....... 405 372-3562
Stillwater *(G-8651)*
Albright Steel and Wire Co.................F....... 405 232-7526
Oklahoma City *(G-5410)*
▲ Baker Hughes Elasto Systems.................F....... 405 670-3354
Oklahoma City *(G-5516)*
Bison Metals Technologies LLC.................G....... 403 395-1405
Shawnee *(G-8433)*
Bkw Inc.................G....... 918 836-6767
Tulsa *(G-9299)*
Cherokee Piping Services LLC.................G....... 918 931-8593
Tahlequah *(G-8856)*
Corrpro Companies Inc.................E....... 918 245-8791
Sand Springs *(G-8172)*
Cutting Edge Machine Inc.................G....... 580 658-5036
Marlow *(G-4226)*
Flow Valve LLC.................E....... 580 622-2294
Sulphur *(G-8832)*
Hunter Steel LLC.................G....... 918 684-9600
Muskogee *(G-4693)*
Innovex Downhole Solutions Inc.................G....... 405 491-2658
Oklahoma City *(G-6308)*
▲ Lps Specialty Products Inc.................G....... 918 893-5486
Catoosa *(G-1334)*
▲ Mid American Stl & Wire Co LLC.................E....... 580 795-2559
Madill *(G-4157)*
◆ Mike Alexander Company Inc.................E....... 580 765-8085
Tulsa *(G-10276)*
MRC Global (us) Inc.................G....... 918 485-9511
Wagoner *(G-11287)*
Oilfield Equipment Company.................G....... 405 850-1406
Duncan *(G-2161)*
Ops Sales Company.................G....... 918 534-3760
Dewey *(G-2029)*
Paragon Industries Inc.................E....... 918 781-1430
Muskogee *(G-4731)*
Paragon Industries Inc.................B....... 918 291-4459
Sapulpa *(G-8296)*
Rolled Alloys Inc.................E....... 918 594-2600
Tulsa *(G-9031)*
Rosa & Unis LLC.................D....... 918 445-4204
Tulsa *(G-10670)*
Ross Dub Company Inc.................E....... 405 495-3611
Oklahoma City *(G-7049)*
Taylor & Sons Pipe and Stl Inc.................F....... 405 222-0751
Chickasha *(G-1516)*
Webco Industries Inc.................C....... 918 865-6215
Mannford *(G-4194)*

34 FABRICATED METAL PRODUCTS, EXCEPT MACHINERY AND TRANSPORTATION EQUIPMENT

3369 Nonferrous Foundries: Castings, NEC

Camcast Corp .... C 918 371-9966
　Owasso *(G-7551)*
Crucible LLC .... F 405 579-2700
　Norman *(G-4971)*
LMI Aerospace Inc .... E 918 281-0124
　Tulsa *(G-10173)*
Metal Dynamics Corp .... E 918 582-0124
　Tulsa *(G-10244)*
Mold Tech Inc .... G 918 247-6275
　Sapulpa *(G-8292)*
Nordam Group LLC .... C 918 274-2742
　Tulsa *(G-10356)*
Tatco Metals Inc .... G 918 853-4663
　Jenks *(G-3733)*

3398 Metal Heat Treating

Bodycote Thermal Proc Inc .... F 405 670-5710
　Oklahoma City *(G-5605)*
Bodycote Thermal Proc Inc .... G 214 904-2420
　Tulsa *(G-9314)*
Cargill Heat Treat LLC .... G 405 510-3404
　Oklahoma City *(G-5700)*
Casting Coating Corp .... F 918 445-4141
　Tulsa *(G-8995)*
Hinderliter Heat Treating Inc .... G 405 670-5710
　Oklahoma City *(G-6250)*
National Oilwell Varco Inc .... C 918 781-4436
　Muskogee *(G-4719)*
O S R Inc .... G 281 422-7206
　Inola *(G-3668)*
Onsite Stress Relieving Svc .... E 918 234-1222
　Inola *(G-3669)*
Osr Services LP .... F 918 234-1222
　Inola *(G-3670)*
Precision Heat Treating .... G 918 445-7424
　Tulsa *(G-9025)*
▼ Q B Johnson Mfg Inc .... D 405 677-6676
　Moore *(G-4558)*
Smith Welding Fabg & Repr .... G 918 446-2293
　Tulsa *(G-10779)*
Superheat Fgh Services Inc .... G 580 762-8538
　Ponca City *(G-7880)*
Team Inc .... E 918 234-9600
　Tulsa *(G-10909)*
Thermal Specialties LLC .... G 970 532-3796
　Owasso *(G-7623)*
Thermal Specialties LLC .... F 918 227-4800
　Tulsa *(G-9044)*
Thermal Specialties LLC .... G 405 681-4400
　Oklahoma City *(G-7282)*
Tulsa Gamma Ray Inc .... G 918 425-3112
　Tulsa *(G-10997)*
▲ V M Star .... C 918 781-4400
　Muskogee *(G-4757)*
Zentech LLC .... F 918 585-8200
　Tulsa *(G-11176)*

3399 Primary Metal Prdts, NEC

Archer Technologies Intl Inc .... G 405 306-3220
　Shawnee *(G-8428)*
E E Sewing Inc .... G 918 214-5343
　Bartlesville *(G-476)*
◆ East 74th Street Holdings Inc ..... C 918 437-3037
　Tulsa *(G-9631)*
Hilti Inc .... G 918 252-6000
　Tulsa *(G-9931)*
Walkers Powder Coating LLC .... G 580 355-5000
　Lawton *(G-4018)*
Weldco Mfg .... G 580 296-1585
　Colbert *(G-1788)*

34 FABRICATED METAL PRODUCTS, EXCEPT MACHINERY AND TRANSPORTATION EQUIPMENT

3411 Metal Cans

▲ Blitz USA Inc .... B 918 676-3620
　Miami *(G-4391)*
Herbert Malarkey Roofing Co .... C 405 261-6900
　Oklahoma City *(G-6241)*
Keymiaee Aero-Tech Inc .... F 405 235-5010
　Oklahoma City *(G-6409)*
Metal Container Corporation .... C 405 680-3140
　Oklahoma City *(G-6574)*
Mullins Salvage Inc .... G 918 352-9612
　Cushing *(G-1946)*

3412 Metal Barrels, Drums, Kegs & Pails

B A Stevens .... G 918 695-4362
　Ochelata *(G-5233)*
Custom Manufacturing Inc .... E 405 692-6311
　Oklahoma City *(G-5874)*
Davco Manufacturing .... F 918 535-2360
　Ochelata *(G-5234)*
Keymiaee Aero-Tech Inc .... F 405 235-5010
　Oklahoma City *(G-6409)*
Mobile Mini Inc .... F 918 582-5857
　Tulsa *(G-10288)*
Pratt Industries USA Inc .... B 405 787-3500
　Oklahoma City *(G-6874)*

3421 Cutlery

Cmg Operations LLC .... G 580 477-0880
　Altus *(G-150)*
Cmg Operations LLC .... G 580 353-2835
　Lawton *(G-3908)*
EDS Inc .... G 405 416-6700
　Oklahoma City *(G-6012)*
Eppingers .... G 580 248-1442
　Lawton *(G-3922)*
Every Nook & Cranny .... G 580 332-3899
　Ada *(G-34)*
Johns Professional Sharpening ... G 405 313-7027
　Yukon *(G-11738)*
Ktak Corporation .... G 918 492-0505
　Tulsa *(G-10105)*
Mike Latham .... G 580 622-6980
　Sulphur *(G-8838)*
Solo Cup Operating Corporation .. C 580 436-1500
　Ada *(G-90)*
Wyndham Tulsa .... G 918 627-5000
　Tulsa *(G-11163)*

3423 Hand & Edge Tools

Chiseled In Stone .... G 918 813-5409
　Tulsa *(G-9419)*
Evans Tool Co Inc .... G 580 889-5770
　Atoka *(G-412)*
Federal Metals Inc .... F 918 838-1725
　Tulsa *(G-9731)*
▲ Five Star Equipment LLC .... G 918 637-0200
　Ramona *(G-8045)*
Helton Custom Knives LLC .... G 918 230-1773
　Claremore *(G-1633)*
▲ Hisco Inc .... F 405 524-2700
　Oklahoma City *(G-6254)*
J R Lukeman & Associates Inc .... G 405 842-6548
　Oklahoma City *(G-6338)*
JJ Perodeau Gunmaker Inc .... G 580 747-1804
　Sand Springs *(G-8195)*
▲ M W Bevins Co .... E 918 627-1273
　Tulsa *(G-10190)*
Rd Roofing and Carpentry .... G 580 341-0607
　Ada *(G-80)*
◆ Red Devil Incorporated .... F 918 585-8111
　Tulsa *(G-10629)*
Red Devil Incorporated .... D 918 825-5744
　Pryor *(G-7989)*
Sarduccis Metal Works Inc .... G 918 694-3466
　Tulsa *(G-10708)*
William L Riggs Company Inc ...... G 918 437-3245
　Tulsa *(G-11125)*
William Reed .... G 405 912-8153
　Oklahoma City *(G-5324)*
Zoop-Corp .... G 405 239-8184
　Oklahoma City *(G-7489)*

3425 Hand Saws & Saw Blades

▲ H S Boyd Company Inc .... F 918 835-9359
　Tulsa *(G-9876)*
Saw Swan Service Inc .... G 918 249-3821
　Broken Arrow *(G-1043)*

3429 Hardware, NEC

Archer Technologies Intl Inc .... G 405 306-3220
　Shawnee *(G-8428)*
Beekmann Enterprises .... G 918 272-7197
　Owasso *(G-7547)*
Bert Parsons 2nd Gen Lcksmth L G 918 794-7131
　Tulsa *(G-9286)*
▼ Campbell Specialty Co Inc .... F 918 756-3640
　Okmulgee *(G-7497)*
Cole Industrial Services Inc .... G 580 775-0949
　Caddo *(G-1232)*
Cook Machine Company .... E 580 252-1699
　Duncan *(G-2099)*
Crosby Group LLC .... B 918 834-4611
　Tulsa *(G-9509)*
◆ Crosby Group LLC .... G 918 834-4611
　Tulsa *(G-9510)*
Crosby Worldwide Limited .... F 918 834-4611
　Tulsa *(G-9512)*
D R Topping Saddlery .... G 918 273-2812
　Nowata *(G-5212)*
Dynamic Machine .... G 918 791-1114
　Grove *(G-3266)*
◆ Fki Industries Inc .... G 918 834-4611
　Tulsa *(G-9752)*
Genes Customized Tags & EMB ... G 580 225-8247
　Elk City *(G-2820)*
Get A Grip Inc .... G 405 286-4778
　Oklahoma City *(G-6148)*
H-V Manufacturing Company .... G 918 756-9620
　Okmulgee *(G-7509)*
Hansen Research LLC .... G 405 659-5079
　Norman *(G-5015)*
Hardin Ignition Inc .... G 405 853-4324
　Hennessey *(G-3465)*
▲ Hargrove Manufacturing Corp .. E 918 241-7537
　Sand Springs *(G-8190)*
Integrted Lock SEC Systems LLC G 918 232-3436
　Jenks *(G-3708)*
Johnny Beard Co .... G 918 438-4901
　Tulsa *(G-10056)*
KB Enterprise LLC .... G 580 789-0119
　Ponca City *(G-7843)*
Key Cut Express .... G 405 353-3026
　Mustang *(G-4780)*
Key General Contractors LLC ...... G 918 280-8539
　Tulsa *(G-10086)*
Keys N More .... G 405 415-1797
　Oklahoma City *(G-6410)*
Keys N More .... G 405 415-2105
　Oklahoma City *(G-6411)*
Luxe Kitchen & Bath .... G 405 471-5557
　Oklahoma City *(G-6504)*
McClure Furniture Refinishing ..... G 918 587-7779
　Tulsa *(G-10230)*
OH Keys .... G 405 529-5202
　Oklahoma City *(G-6716)*
OH Keys .... G 405 378-5674
　Oklahoma City *(G-6717)*
P W Manufacturing Company Inc G 918 652-4981
　Henryetta *(G-3514)*
◆ P-T Coupling Company .... E 580 237-4033
　Enid *(G-3029)*
▲ Parrish Enterprises .... D 580 233-4757
　Enid *(G-3030)*
▲ Parrish Enterprises Ltd .... C 580 237-4033
　Enid *(G-3031)*
▲ Pelco Products Inc .... C 405 340-3434
　Edmond *(G-2565)*
Pelco Products Inc .... G 405 842-6978
　Oklahoma City *(G-6822)*
Petroleum Artifacts Ltd .... G 918 949-6101
　Tulsa *(G-10504)*
Pickard Projects Inc .... G 405 321-7072
　Norman *(G-5115)*
▲ Premiere Lock Co LLC .... G 918 294-8179
　Tulsa *(G-10553)*
Punch-Lok Co .... E 580 233-4757
　Enid *(G-3040)*
▲ Sawyer Manufacturing Company E 918 834-2550
　Tulsa *(G-9034)*
Shur-Co LLC .... G 405 262-7600
　El Reno *(G-2757)*
Straitline Inc .... F 405 263-4604
　Lone Grove *(G-4121)*
Straitline Inc .... G 405 263-4604
　Okarche *(G-5253)*
Superior Companies Inc .... D 918 534-0755
　Dewey *(G-2033)*
T D G I .... G 405 275-8041
　Shawnee *(G-8507)*
Taylor & Sons Farms Inc .... G 405 222-0751
　Chickasha *(G-1515)*
Transponder Key .... G 405 757-3199
　Edmond *(G-2652)*
U-Change Lock Industries Inc ..... E 405 376-1600
　Mustang *(G-4799)*
United Dynamics Inc .... E 405 275-8041
　Shawnee *(G-8517)*
Wayne Burt Machine .... G 918 786-4415
　Grove *(G-3293)*

H K & S Iron Co .... E 405 745-2761
Oklahoma City *(G-6198)*
Hackney Ladish Inc .... D 580 237-4212
Enid *(G-2967)*
High Pointe Construction .... G 405 685-8303
Oklahoma City *(G-6247)*
Honeycutt Contruction Inc .... F 918 825-6070
Pryor *(G-7969)*
Insight Technologies Inc .... F 580 933-4109
Valliant *(G-11226)*
▼ **Integrated Tower Systems Inc** .... E 918 749-8535
Tulsa *(G-9998)*
J & D Fabricators Inc .... F 405 356-2243
Wellston *(G-11473)*
▲ **J & G Steel Corporation** .... C 918 227-3131
Sapulpa *(G-8280)*
J R Lukeman & Associates Inc .... G 405 842-6548
Oklahoma City *(G-6338)*
JB Metal Fabrication .... G 918 266-3228
Catoosa *(G-1324)*
Jeffery W Matlock .... G 918 367-9828
Bristow *(G-782)*
Jenco Fabricators Inc .... E 918 234-3364
Tulsa *(G-10034)*
Jerrys Dock Construction Inc .... F 918 256-3390
Bernice *(G-567)*
Johnston Test Cell Group LLC .... G 405 604-2804
Oklahoma City *(G-6378)*
Kenneth Petermann .... G 405 372-0111
Stillwater *(G-8710)*
Keymiaee Aero-Tech Inc .... F 405 235-5010
Oklahoma City *(G-6409)*
Landa Mobile Systems LLC .... G 571 272-3350
Tulsa *(G-10121)*
Laughing Water Enterprises LLC .... G 918 584-2080
Tulsa *(G-10136)*
Lbr Smith LLC .... G 405 601-7051
Oklahoma City *(G-6458)*
Lofland Co .... G 405 631-9555
Oklahoma City *(G-6488)*
Longreach Steel Inc .... F 405 598-5691
Tecumseh *(G-8922)*
M A C Manufacturing Inc .... G 405 527-8270
Purcell *(G-8012)*
Maddens Portable Buildings .... E 405 799-4989
Norman *(G-5062)*
Manufacturing Jack LLC Ram .... D 580 332-6694
Ada *(G-63)*
Martin Manufacturing Inc .... E 918 583-1191
Sapulpa *(G-8287)*
▲ **Mertz Manufacturing Inc** .... B 580 762-5646
Ponca City *(G-7849)*
Metal Building Services .... G 580 657-3339
Ardmore *(G-330)*
Metal Fab Inc .... G 580 762-2421
Ponca City *(G-7850)*
Metalfab LLC .... G 918 718-4040
Tahlequah *(G-8873)*
Metro Mechanical Supply Inc .... F 918 622-2288
Tulsa *(G-10251)*
Metro Mechanical Supply LLC .... E 918 622-2288
Tulsa *(G-10252)*
Midstate Mfg & Mktg Inc .... E 405 751-6227
Oklahoma City *(G-6598)*
Miller Welding & Supply .... G 580 492-5464
Lawton *(G-3970)*
Mitchco Fabrication Inc .... G 580 762-0256
Ponca City *(G-7853)*
Mobile Mini Inc .... F 918 582-5857
Tulsa *(G-10288)*
Moore Iron & Steel Corp .... D 918 387-2639
Yale *(G-11686)*
Morton Buildings Inc .... E 918 683-6668
Muskogee *(G-4715)*
Neilson Manufacturing Inc .... F 918 587-5548
Tulsa *(G-10331)*
Neisen Fabricators LLC .... E 580 762-2421
Ponca City *(G-7858)*
OK Fabricators LLC .... E 918 224-3977
Tulsa *(G-9023)*
OK Machine and Mfg Co Inc .... E 918 838-1300
Tulsa *(G-10390)*
Oklahoma City Steel LLC .... G 405 235-2300
Oklahoma City *(G-6743)*
Oklahoma Post Tension Inc .... F 918 627-6013
Tulsa *(G-10405)*
Old World Iron Inc .... G 918 445-3063
Tulsa *(G-10411)*
▲ **Orizon Arstrctures - Grove Inc** .... D 918 786-9094
Grove *(G-3284)*

Ozark Steel LLC .... E 918 438-4330
Tulsa *(G-10450)*
▲ **P & M Industries Inc** .... E 918 660-0055
Tulsa *(G-10451)*
Pattison Metal Fab Inc .... E 918 251-9967
Broken Arrow *(G-1000)*
Pelco Structural LLC .... D 918 283-4004
Claremore *(G-1668)*
Phoenix Fabworx LLC .... G 918 429-8388
Quinton *(G-8038)*
Powder Coating of Muskogee .... G 918 681-4494
Muskogee *(G-4736)*
Power Lift Fndtn RPR OK Inc .... E 580 332-8282
Ada *(G-75)*
Precision Fabricators Inc .... F 918 428-7600
Tulsa *(G-10544)*
Premier Fabricators LLC .... G 580 251-9525
Duncan *(G-2165)*
Premier Plant Services LLC .... F 918 227-3131
Sapulpa *(G-8300)*
Premier Plant Services LLC .... G 918 227-1680
Sapulpa *(G-8301)*
Premier Steel Services LLC .... E 918 227-0110
Glenpool *(G-3241)*
Professional Fabricators Inc .... E 918 388-1090
Tulsa *(G-10568)*
Professional Metal Works Inc .... G 580 584-7890
Idabel *(G-3644)*
Pruitt Company of Ada Inc .... E 580 332-3523
Ada *(G-78)*
R&R Roustabout Services LLC .... E 580 883-4647
Ringwood *(G-8090)*
Railroad Sgnling Solutions Inc .... G 918 973-1888
Broken Arrow *(G-1020)*
Railroad Yard Inc .... E 405 377-8763
Stillwater *(G-8743)*
Rise Manufacturing LLC .... E 918 994-6240
Broken Arrow *(G-1032)*
River Bend Industries LLC .... C 405 703-2758
Blanchard *(G-734)*
Robert Mrrson Autocad Svcs LLC .... G 918 257-4622
Afton *(G-120)*
Rooks Fabrication LLC .... F 918 447-1990
Tulsa *(G-10669)*
Rt Manufacturing LLC .... F 405 222-7180
Chickasha *(G-1504)*
▲ **S & T Mfg Co** .... E 918 234-4151
Tulsa *(G-10684)*
S&S Fabrication .... G 918 447-0447
Tulsa *(G-9032)*
Safeco Manufacturing Inc .... F 918 455-0100
Broken Arrow *(G-1160)*
▲ **Sawyer Manufacturing Company** .... E 918 834-2550
Tulsa *(G-9034)*
Selman Wldg & Fabrication LLC .... G 580 330-0887
Weatherford *(G-11440)*
Shawnee Fabricators Inc .... E 405 275-8264
Shawnee *(G-8494)*
Shawnee Steel Company .... E 405 919-8582
Shawnee *(G-8497)*
Shelby Steel Service .... G 918 234-3098
Tulsa *(G-10741)*
Sooner Steel and Truss LLC .... G 405 232-5542
Oklahoma City *(G-7167)*
Source Fabrication LLC .... G 580 762-4114
Ponca City *(G-7877)*
Southwest Fabricators Inc .... F 580 326-3589
Hugo *(G-3621)*
Specialty Sales Associates .... G 405 495-1136
Chandler *(G-1388)*
Steel Thinking Inc .... F 405 485-2204
Washington *(G-11337)*
Steelfab Texas Inc .... E 972 562-7720
Durant *(G-2262)*
Storm SF Ngrnd Trnd Shltrs NC .... D 405 606-2563
Oklahoma City *(G-7213)*
Studs Unlimited LLC .... G 214 683-8012
Oklahoma City *(G-7218)*
Sufrank Corporation .... E 580 353-4600
Lawton *(G-4006)*
Supreme Mch & Stl Fabrication .... F 918 387-2036
Yale *(G-11687)*
Sweeper Metal Fabricators Corp .... E 918 352-9180
Drumright *(G-2073)*
T & D Fabrication Inc .... E 918 352-8031
Drumright *(G-2074)*
T Rowe Pipe LLC .... E 580 765-1500
Ponca City *(G-7881)*
Thorpe Plant Services Inc .... G 918 455-8928
Tulsa *(G-10937)*

Tj Services LLC .... G 405 596-5124
Oklahoma City *(G-7295)*
Tower Components Inc .... E 918 379-0769
Catoosa *(G-1357)*
Tri Red LLC .... E 580 476-2551
Rush Springs *(G-8128)*
Tulsa Metal Fab Inc .... F 918 451-7150
Broken Arrow *(G-1175)*
Tulsa Steel Mfg Company Inc .... E 918 227-0110
Tulsa *(G-9046)*
United Contracting Svcs Inc .... C 918 551-7659
Tulsa *(G-11040)*
United Holdings LLC .... G 405 947-3321
Oklahoma City *(G-7369)*
V&S Schuler Tubular Pdts LLC .... B 918 687-7701
Muskogee *(G-4758)*
Valmont Industries Inc .... D 918 266-2800
Claremore *(G-1700)*
Valmont Industries Inc .... B 918 583-5881
Tulsa *(G-11065)*
Vann Metal Products Inc .... G 918 341-0469
Claremore *(G-1701)*
Vernon Manufacturing Company .... G 918 224-4068
Tulsa *(G-9048)*
W & W Asco Steel LLC .... G 405 235-3621
Oklahoma City *(G-7407)*
W&W Steel Erectors LLC .... G 405 235-3621
Oklahoma City *(G-7412)*
W&W-Afco Steel LLC .... B 405 235-3621
Oklahoma City *(G-7413)*
Wayne Burt Machine .... G 918 786-4415
Grove *(G-3293)*
Wayne Winkler .... G 918 689-9745
Eufaula *(G-3117)*
Wedlake Fabricating Inc .... E 918 428-1641
Tulsa *(G-11103)*
Weibee Steel Inc .... F 405 360-7055
Norman *(G-5198)*
Weldco Mfg .... G 580 296-1585
Colbert *(G-1788)*
Werco Aviation Inc .... G 918 251-6880
Broken Arrow *(G-1094)*
Werco Manufacturing Inc .... E 918 251-6880
Broken Arrow *(G-1095)*
Western Frontier LLC .... E 918 760-4977
Locust Grove *(G-4113)*
Willie Dewayne Brown .... F 918 482-1115
Haskell *(G-3403)*
▲ **Worldwide Steel Works Inc** .... E 918 825-4545
Pryor *(G-8000)*
Wwsc Holdings LLC .... F 405 235-3621
Oklahoma City *(G-7476)*
York Metal Fabricators Inc .... E 405 528-7495
Oklahoma City *(G-7481)*
Zkc Welding .... F 580 220-7685
Ardmore *(G-384)*

3442 Metal Doors, Sash, Frames, Molding & Trim

Amarillo Chittom Airslo .... E 918 585-5638
Tulsa *(G-9160)*
Angel Ornamental Iron Works .... G 918 584-8726
Tulsa *(G-9191)*
Boomer Blinds & Shutters LLC .... G 918 968-2579
Stroud *(G-8808)*
Charles ODell .... G 405 745-3353
Mustang *(G-4768)*
Classic Shutters .... G 918 234-0657
Tulsa *(G-9442)*
Consolidated Builders Supply .... E 405 631-3033
Oklahoma City *(G-5821)*
Custom Shutters Inc .... G 918 924-3489
Broken Arrow *(G-882)*
D & M Steel Manufacturing .... G 405 631-5027
Oklahoma City *(G-5887)*
Don Young Company Incorporated .... G 405 947-2000
Oklahoma City *(G-5966)*
Dormakaba USA Inc .... G 405 232-6761
Oklahoma City *(G-5969)*
Dunlap Manufacturing Co Inc .... E 918 838-1383
Tulsa *(G-9612)*
Dynomite Custom Screens LLC .... G 844 396-6648
Lawton *(G-3921)*
Enid Insulation & Siding Inc .... G 580 237-5317
Enid *(G-2953)*
Eseco-Speedmaster .... D 918 225-1266
Cushing *(G-1933)*
Ets-Lindgren Inc .... E 580 434-7490
Durant *(G-2230)*

S I C

Employee Codes: A=Over 500 employees, B=251-500
C=101-250, D=51-100, E=20-50, F=10-19, G=1-9
2020 Oklahoma Directory
of Manufacturers & Processors
467

34 FABRICATED METAL PRODUCTS, EXCEPT MACHINERY AND TRANSPORTATION EQUIPMENT

Reading Equipment & Dist LLC............E....... 918 283-2999
  Claremore *(G-1679)*
Reece-Ats Holding LLC......................E....... 918 225-1010
  Cushing *(G-1954)*
Rise Manufacturing LLC.....................E....... 918 994-6240
  Broken Arrow *(G-1032)*
Royalty Fabrication LLC......................G....... 405 257-6654
  Wewoka *(G-11510)*
Ruby Industrial Tech LLC...................G....... 580 223-9301
  Ardmore *(G-352)*
Safeco Manufacturing Inc..................F....... 918 455-0100
  Broken Arrow *(G-1160)*
▲ Sawyer Manufacturing Company.....E....... 918 834-2550
  Tulsa *(G-9034)*
Scrap Management Oklahoma Inc........F....... 405 677-7000
  Oklahoma City *(G-7100)*
Seal Support Systems Inc...................F....... 918 258-6484
  Broken Arrow *(G-1046)*
Service Tech Coolg Towers LLC..........F....... 405 222-0722
  Chickasha *(G-1508)*
Sharp Metal Fabricators Inc................F....... 405 899-4849
  Noble *(G-4891)*
Shelton Sanitation..............................G....... 918 469-3498
  Kinta *(G-3836)*
Sierra Technologies Inc.......................F....... 918 445-1090
  Tulsa *(G-10754)*
▼ Smithco Engineering Inc..................E....... 918 446-4406
  Tulsa *(G-10780)*
▲ Southwest Filter Company................G....... 918 835-1179
  Tulsa *(G-10807)*
Southwest Filter Company...................G....... 918 835-1179
  Tulsa *(G-10808)*
◆ SPX Heat Transfer LLC.....................C....... 918 234-6000
  Tulsa *(G-10827)*
Steel Creek Manufacturing LLC..........G....... 918 698-3318
  Tulsa *(G-10843)*
▼ Steeltek Inc...D....... 918 446-4001
  Tulsa *(G-10844)*
Sufrank Corporation............................E....... 580 353-4600
  Lawton *(G-4006)*
Susan L Chung Chirprtr......................G....... 405 773-8225
  Oklahoma City *(G-7233)*
Tank Specialties Inc............................F....... 918 599-8111
  Tulsa *(G-10898)*
▼ Technotherm Corporation.................E....... 918 446-1533
  Tulsa *(G-9042)*
Tek Fins Inc...F....... 918 747-7447
  Tulsa *(G-9043)*
Titan Fuel Systems LLC......................G....... 405 788-2412
  Norman *(G-5174)*
True Turn of Tulsa LLC........................F....... 918 224-5040
  Tulsa *(G-10980)*
Tsi-Enquip Inc......................................E....... 918 599-8111
  Tulsa *(G-10983)*
Tulsa Pressure Vessels LLC................F....... 918 512-8346
  Tulsa *(G-9045)*
▼ V E Enterprises Inc.............................E....... 580 653-2171
  Springer *(G-8627)*
Vernon Manufacturing Company.........G....... 918 224-4068
  Tulsa *(G-9048)*
Veterans Eng Group Inc......................G....... 918 864-6006
  Pryor *(G-7997)*
Wagner Plate Works LLC....................G....... 918 447-4488
  Tulsa *(G-11090)*
Wastequip Manufacturing Co LLC........E....... 580 924-1575
  Durant *(G-2272)*
Water Tank Service.............................G....... 918 786-7850
  Grove *(G-3292)*
World Wide Exchangers LLC...............E....... 918 234-3700
  Skiatook *(G-8576)*
World Wide Exchangers Inc................F....... 918 240-3193
  Sapulpa *(G-8327)*
Worthington Cylinder Corp..................C....... 918 396-2899
  Skiatook *(G-8577)*

3444 Sheet Metal Work

4-Star Trailers Inc...............................C....... 405 324-7827
  Oklahoma City *(G-5331)*
A B Curbs Inc......................................G....... 405 427-1222
  Oklahoma City *(G-5344)*
A-1 Sheet Metal Inc............................F....... 918 835-6200
  Tulsa *(G-9073)*
Acme Manufacturing Corporation........E....... 918 266-3097
  Claremore *(G-1575)*
Acme Manufacturing Corporation........G....... 800 647-8671
  Claremore *(G-1576)*
Advanced Fabrication Svcs LLC..........G....... 405 339-4867
  Oklahoma City *(G-5381)*
Adventure Manufacturing Inc..............G....... 405 682-3833
  Oklahoma City *(G-5387)*

Aeron Group LLC................................F....... 918 294-1167
  Broken Arrow *(G-819)*
Agilis Group LLC.................................E....... 918 584-3553
  Tulsa *(G-9117)*
Air Duct Inc..F....... 918 445-1196
  Tulsa *(G-9119)*
Airflow Solutions LLC..........................E....... 918 574-2748
  Tulsa *(G-9129)*
All Sheet Metal Co...............................G....... 405 733-0039
  Del City *(G-1996)*
Allen Sheet Metal Inc..........................G....... 918 834-2279
  Tulsa *(G-9141)*
Allstate Sheet Metal Inc......................F....... 405 636-1914
  Oklahoma City *(G-5422)*
Always Done Right LLC......................G....... 405 615-5955
  Edmond *(G-2300)*
Andy Anderson Metal Works Inc.........F....... 918 245-2355
  Sand Springs *(G-8161)*
Apollo Metal Specialties Inc................F....... 918 341-7650
  Claremore *(G-1583)*
Archer Technologies Intl Inc...............F....... 405 306-3220
  Shawnee *(G-8428)*
Architectural Fabricators Inc...............E....... 918 331-0393
  Bartlesville *(G-448)*
Awnique..F....... 405 818-8032
  Oklahoma City *(G-5497)*
Axiom Metal Solutions LLC.................G....... 918 361-5982
  Okmulgee *(G-7494)*
B & B Sheet Metal Heat & A Inc.........G....... 918 371-1335
  Collinsville *(G-1801)*
Ba Manufacturing LLC.........................G....... 239 246-3606
  Broken Arrow *(G-842)*
Bacco Inc..G....... 918 344-3670
  Claremore *(G-1587)*
Balco Inc...E....... 316 945-9328
  Oklahoma City *(G-5519)*
Big River Sales Inc..............................G....... 580 657-4950
  Lone Grove *(G-4115)*
Boxel LLC...G....... 580 239-0819
  Atoka *(G-400)*
Braden Shielding Systems Const........E....... 918 624-2888
  Tulsa *(G-9327)*
Breshears Enterprises Inc...................F....... 405 236-4523
  Oklahoma City *(G-5624)*
Briggs Rainbow Buildings Inc.............C....... 918 683-3695
  Muskogee *(G-4655)*
Butchers Metal Shop...........................G....... 580 256-7660
  Woodward *(G-11565)*
Bynum & Company Inc.......................F....... 580 265-7747
  Stonewall *(G-8798)*
Canopies Plus Inc................................G....... 918 689-7077
  Eufaula *(G-3098)*
Capes Custom Welding & Fabrica......G....... 918 453-0594
  Tahlequah *(G-8855)*
Captive-Aire Systems Inc....................F....... 918 258-0291
  Tulsa *(G-9373)*
Captive-Aire Systems Inc....................D....... 918 686-6717
  Muskogee *(G-4658)*
Carlsons Rural Mailbox Co..................G....... 405 632-7338
  Oklahoma City *(G-5704)*
CCL Acquisition LLC............................D....... 918 739-4400
  Catoosa *(G-1309)*
▲ Cherokee Nation Red Wing LLC.......E....... 918 430-3437
  Tulsa *(G-9414)*
Choctaw Mfg & Dev Corp....................D....... 580 326-8365
  Hugo *(G-3607)*
Choctaw Nation of Oklahoma..............D....... 580 326-8365
  Hugo *(G-3610)*
Clinco Mfg LLC.....................................G....... 580 759-3434
  Ada *(G-25)*
◆ CMI Terex Corporation.......................A....... 405 787-6020
  Oklahoma City *(G-5792)*
▼ Contech Enterprises LLC...................F....... 918 341-6232
  Claremore *(G-1609)*
Contech Mfg Inc..................................G....... 918 341-6232
  Claremore *(G-1610)*
Cool Green Roofing Supply LLC.........G....... 918 860-7525
  Broken Arrow *(G-1623)*
Copper Accents By Jerry....................G....... 918 724-8473
  Bixby *(G-618)*
Council Stainless & Shtmtl..................G....... 405 787-4400
  Oklahoma City *(G-5842)*
Cundiff Custom Fabrication LLC.........G....... 405 372-8204
  Stillwater *(G-8673)*
Custom Metal Works Inc.....................G....... 918 388-1881
  Tulsa *(G-9529)*
Custom Storm Shelters LLC................G....... 405 209-5525
  Oklahoma City *(G-5876)*
D & D Design & Mfg Inc......................F....... 405 745-2126
  Oklahoma City *(G-5885)*

D & L Enclosures.................................G....... 918 396-7355
  Skiatook *(G-8538)*
Darrell Monroe.....................................F....... 405 793-2976
  Moore *(G-4513)*
David Muzny..G....... 405 681-7593
  Oklahoma City *(G-5904)*
Del Nero Manufacturing Co.................G....... 405 364-4800
  Norman *(G-4976)*
Dilbeck Mfg Inc....................................F....... 918 836-1555
  Tulsa *(G-9584)*
Diw Engneering Fabrication LLC.........E....... 918 534-0001
  Dewey *(G-2020)*
Don Bateman Shtmtl Fabrication........G....... 918 224-0567
  Sapulpa *(G-8267)*
E F L Inc..D....... 918 665-7799
  Tulsa *(G-9621)*
Earl Bannon..F....... 405 236-8829
  Oklahoma City *(G-5998)*
Eastern Sheet Metal Co Inc................F....... 918 687-6231
  Muskogee *(G-4669)*
Elk City Sheet Metal Inc.....................G....... 580 225-5844
  Elk City *(G-2810)*
▲ Ellis Construction Spc LLC................E....... 405 848-4676
  Oklahoma City *(G-6026)*
Empire Laser & Metal Work LLC........F....... 918 584-6232
  Broken Arrow *(G-898)*
Eric Turner...G....... 918 423-7330
  McAlester *(G-4295)*
Ets-Lindgren Inc..................................E....... 580 434-7490
  Durant *(G-2230)*
Expanded Solutions LLC......................E....... 405 946-6791
  Wewoka *(G-11501)*
Fabricating Specialists Inc..................F....... 405 476-1959
  Oklahoma City *(G-6068)*
Fabrication Dynamics..........................D....... 918 445-6100
  Tulsa *(G-9004)*
Fabrication Dynamics Inc...................G....... 918 446-1638
  Tulsa *(G-9722)*
Fammco Mfg Co Inc............................G....... 918 437-0456
  Tulsa *(G-9727)*
Fifteen Five Gtter Sltions LLC.............G....... 405 219-6741
  Yukon *(G-11724)*
Gary Green Cement Construction.......G....... 405 527-5606
  Purcell *(G-8008)*
Gauge Metal Fab LLC..........................F....... 918 794-1700
  Tulsa *(G-9808)*
General Plastics Inc............................F....... 405 275-3171
  Shawnee *(G-8453)*
Glover Sheet Metal Inc.......................E....... 405 619-7117
  Edmond *(G-2437)*
Hill Metal Inc..G....... 405 375-6284
  Kingfisher *(G-3801)*
Hindman Metal Fabricators................G....... 918 251-3949
  Broken Arrow *(G-930)*
Holman Manufacturing........................F....... 918 479-5861
  Locust Grove *(G-4109)*
Honeycutt Contruction Inc..................F....... 918 825-6070
  Pryor *(G-7969)*
Hu Don Manufacturing Co Inc............F....... 580 223-7333
  Ardmore *(G-307)*
Ideas Manufacturing Inc......................G....... 405 691-5525
  Oklahoma City *(G-5296)*
J C Sheet Metal Fabrication................G....... 405 787-1902
  Oklahoma City *(G-6335)*
▲ JC Fab LLC..F....... 580 920-0878
  Durant *(G-2240)*
Johnson Welding..................................G....... 580 569-2231
  Mountain Park *(G-4626)*
K and E Fabrication.............................G....... 405 635-8552
  Oklahoma City *(G-6393)*
Karacon Solutions LLC........................G....... 918 231-1001
  Tulsa *(G-10076)*
Kenneth Petermann.............................G....... 405 372-0111
  Stillwater *(G-8710)*
Keymiaee Aero-Tech Inc.....................F....... 405 235-5010
  Oklahoma City *(G-6409)*
Kice Industries Inc..............................E....... 580 363-2850
  Blackwell *(G-685)*
L & M Fabrication................................G....... 918 825-7145
  Pryor *(G-7973)*
L & S Seamless Guttering Inc............G....... 405 392-4487
  Blanchard *(G-719)*
▲ Laser Specialities Inc........................E....... 918 760-5690
  Tulsa *(G-9016)*
Linde Engineering N Amer LLC..........G....... 918 266-5700
  Catoosa *(G-1331)*
Lockdown Ltd Co.................................F....... 405 605-6161
  Oklahoma City *(G-6485)*
Longreach Steel Inc............................F....... 405 598-5691
  Tecumseh *(G-8922)*

34 FABRICATED METAL PRODUCTS, EXCEPT MACHINERY AND TRANSPORTATION EQUIPMENT

All Steel Carports LLC..................G...... 918 683-1717
  Muskogee *(G-4646)*
▲ Alliance Steel Inc.....................C...... 405 745-7500
  Oklahoma City *(G-5420)*
Architectural Metal Panels LLC........G...... 405 672-7407
  Oklahoma City *(G-5462)*
Aztec Building Systems Inc............E...... 405 329-0255
  Norman *(G-4923)*
Bc Steel Buildings Inc..................D...... 405 324-5100
  Oklahoma City *(G-5535)*
Better Bilt Portable Buildings.........G...... 918 224-3437
  Sapulpa *(G-8255)*
Better Built Structures LLC...........G...... 918 224-3437
  Sapulpa *(G-8256)*
◆ Braden Shielding Systems LLC......E...... 918 624-2888
  Tulsa *(G-9328)*
Buildings By Madden LLC..............G...... 405 677-0466
  Oklahoma City *(G-5643)*
▲ Byers Products Group Inc...........G...... 405 491-8550
  Oklahoma City *(G-5652)*
Circle K Steel Bldg Cnstr LLC.........F...... 405 932-4664
  Paden *(G-7634)*
Cojac Portable Buildings Inc..........E...... 405 232-1229
  Oklahoma City *(G-5800)*
Cojac Portable Buildings Inc..........G...... 405 232-1229
  Oklahoma City *(G-5801)*
Cushing Truss Manufacturing........F...... 918 387-2080
  Yale *(G-11683)*
Davco Manufacturing...................F...... 918 535-2360
  Ochelata *(G-5234)*
David Davis...............................G...... 405 354-6974
  El Reno *(G-2710)*
Davis Insulated Building Inc..........G...... 918 423-2636
  McAlester *(G-4291)*
Davis Insulated Building Inc..........D...... 918 967-2042
  Stigler *(G-8632)*
Derksen Portable Building............G...... 918 636-4129
  Sapulpa *(G-8266)*
Dream Buildings of Tulsa..............G...... 918 437-9233
  Tulsa *(G-9604)*
Durnal Construction LLC..............G...... 405 413-5458
  Perkins *(G-7716)*
Fincher & Son Pipe & Steel............G...... 580 889-6778
  Caddo *(G-1235)*
G & L Metal Buildings..................G...... 918 687-1867
  Muskogee *(G-4677)*
Gideon Steel Panel Company LLC....F...... 405 942-7878
  Oklahoma City *(G-6153)*
Honeycutt Contruction Inc...........F...... 918 825-6070
  Pryor *(G-7969)*
Indaco Metals LLC......................D...... 405 273-9200
  Shawnee *(G-8462)*
James Case...............................G...... 918 846-2884
  Fairfax *(G-3119)*
L&C Metal Buildings LLC...............G...... 580 660-5515
  Rocky *(G-8104)*
Lafes...G...... 918 423-5311
  McAlester *(G-4312)*
Leddy Construction.....................G...... 580 332-3056
  Ada *(G-60)*
Madden Steel Buildings Lawton......G...... 580 357-1699
  Lawton *(G-3968)*
Maddens Portable Buildings..........E...... 405 799-4989
  Norman *(G-5062)*
Madison Inc of Oklahoma.............G...... 918 587-4501
  Tulsa *(G-9017)*
▲ Marco Industries Inc.................D...... 918 622-4535
  Tulsa *(G-10208)*
Martinez Metal Buildings..............G...... 580 821-2780
  Elk City *(G-2848)*
McCawley Service........................G...... 918 484-2189
  Muskogee *(G-4709)*
Meeco Sullivan LLC.....................F...... 918 423-6833
  McAlester *(G-4320)*
Metal Buildings Inc......................E...... 405 672-6766
  Oklahoma City *(G-6572)*
Metal Panels Inc..........................G...... 918 641-0641
  Tulsa *(G-10246)*
Metro Portable Buildings..............G...... 405 921-5688
  Oklahoma City *(G-6580)*
Midwest Portable Building............G...... 918 245-9335
  Tulsa *(G-10269)*
Mobile Mini Inc............................F...... 918 582-5857
  Tulsa *(G-10288)*
Mobile Mini Inc............................E...... 405 682-9333
  Oklahoma City *(G-6622)*
Morton Buildings Inc....................G...... 918 683-6668
  Muskogee *(G-4715)*
Morton Buildings Inc....................E...... 405 288-1031
  Washington *(G-11335)*

Morton Buildings Inc....................G...... 580 323-1172
  Clinton *(G-1759)*
Nci Group Inc.............................E...... 405 672-7676
  Oklahoma City *(G-6665)*
Oakley Portable Buildings LLC.......G...... 405 372-6543
  Stillwater *(G-8730)*
Petzold Buildings LLC..................F...... 580 563-2818
  Blair *(G-697)*
Plumb Square Construction..........G...... 405 619-9898
  Del City *(G-2006)*
Polar Insulated Sheds Oklah.........G...... 580 799-2265
  Elk City *(G-2860)*
Quality Buildings Inc....................G...... 888 430-7721
  Norman *(G-5126)*
Quality Buildings Inc....................E...... 405 364-0516
  Norman *(G-5127)*
Railroad Yard Inc........................E...... 405 377-8763
  Stillwater *(G-8743)*
Redibuilt Metal Pdts & Cnstr..........G...... 580 225-2829
  Elk City *(G-2867)*
Rising M Enterprises....................G...... 918 766-4235
  Stigler *(G-8643)*
Roadrunner Portable Buildings......G...... 918 272-7788
  Owasso *(G-7608)*
Robertson-Ceco II Corporation......C...... 405 636-2010
  Oklahoma City *(G-7039)*
Robertson-Ceco II Corporation......C...... 405 636-2010
  Oklahoma City *(G-7040)*
Ronnie Nevitt............................G...... 918 687-5284
  Muskogee *(G-4745)*
Rons Discount Lumber Inc............D...... 918 658-3857
  Howe *(G-3599)*
Safe Shed..................................G...... 580 759-3456
  Stratford *(G-8807)*
▼ Star Building Systems Inc..........E...... 405 636-2010
  Oklahoma City *(G-7193)*
TDS Portable Buildings LLC..........G...... 918 422-4009
  Colcord *(G-1791)*
Terry Building Co Inc...................F...... 405 634-5777
  Oklahoma City *(G-7272)*
Terry Tylor Wldg Fbrcation LLC......G...... 405 205-2964
  Chickasha *(G-1517)*
Texoma Sheds...........................G...... 580 223-0000
  Ardmore *(G-367)*
Tims Sheds................................G...... 918 506-7741
  Tahlequah *(G-8888)*
Tornado Alley Armor LLC..............G...... 918 856-3569
  Tulsa *(G-10955)*
Tornado Alley OK Storm Shlters.....G...... 918 706-1341
  Coweta *(G-1901)*
Ventaire LLC..............................E...... 918 622-1191
  Tulsa *(G-11070)*
Whitney Manufacturing Inc...........E...... 918 825-6062
  Pryor *(G-7998)*
Zieglers Bob Portable Bldg Sls.......G...... 918 486-4462
  Broken Arrow *(G-1181)*

3449 Misc Structural Metal Work

Aerostar International Inc............G...... 918 789-3000
  Chelsea *(G-1401)*
Bennett Steel Fabrication Inc........D...... 918 227-2564
  Sapulpa *(G-8253)*
Bison Welding LLC......................G...... 580 758-3359
  Bison *(G-607)*
C and C Manufacturing LLC..........G...... 918 288-6558
  Sperry *(G-8606)*
C Johnstone Welding Fabricat......G...... 580 362-2400
  Newkirk *(G-4846)*
Cherokee Piping Services LLC.......G...... 918 931-8593
  Tahlequah *(G-8856)*
Forbes Enterprises Inc.................G...... 580 564-2599
  Kingston *(G-3828)*
Grating Company LLC..................G...... 918 834-8100
  Tulsa *(G-9848)*
Honeycutt Contruction Inc............F...... 918 825-6070
  Pryor *(G-7969)*
Hurst Cnstr & Fabrication LLC.......E...... 580 628-2388
  Tonkawa *(G-8975)*
J&K Machining Inc......................G...... 918 243-7936
  Cleveland *(G-1725)*
J&M Stainless Fabricators Ltd.......G...... 405 517-0875
  Oklahoma City *(G-6340)*
Ketchum Group LLC....................G...... 918 407-2228
  Jenks *(G-3712)*
Mayhem Cstm Fbrcation Wldg LLC..G...... 405 406-5160
  Newalla *(G-4814)*
Phillips Prcsion Machining LLC......F...... 918 914-2131
  Bartlesville *(G-517)*
Post-Tension Services of Okla.......F...... 405 751-1582
  Oklahoma City *(G-6866)*

Premier Business Solutions LLC....G...... 405 650-3131
  Meeker *(G-4385)*
Premiercraft Incorporated............F...... 405 600-9339
  Oklahoma City *(G-6887)*
Pro Piping & Fabrication LLC........C...... 918 599-8218
  Tulsa *(G-10565)*
Reinforcing Services Inc...............F...... 918 379-0090
  Catoosa *(G-1350)*
Ross Fabrication & Detailing.........F...... 405 356-9955
  Wellston *(G-11478)*
Tms International LLC.................G...... 918 241-0129
  Sand Springs *(G-8230)*
War Metals Inc...........................G...... 918 224-2155
  Tulsa *(G-9050)*
War Metals Inc...........................G...... 918 629-8057
  Tulsa *(G-11095)*

3451 Screw Machine Prdts

▲ Badgett Corporation..................D...... 405 224-4138
  Chickasha *(G-1437)*
Freedom Manufacturing LLC.........G...... 918 283-1520
  Claremore *(G-1623)*
Hem Industries...........................G...... 918 534-0579
  Dewey *(G-2024)*
Kemper Valve and Fittings............G...... 580 622-2048
  Sulphur *(G-8836)*
Kenneth Pace.............................E...... 405 222-1426
  Chickasha *(G-1479)*
Madewell Machine Works Company..G...... 918 543-2904
  Inola *(G-3666)*
Psf Services LLC.........................G...... 707 386-8805
  Marlow *(G-4239)*
Rightway Mfg Solutions LLC..........E...... 580 252-2284
  Duncan *(G-2170)*
▲ SBS Industries LLC..................C...... 918 836-7756
  Tulsa *(G-10712)*
Slim Haney Inc...........................E...... 918 274-1082
  Tulsa *(G-10772)*
Tape-Matics Inc..........................E...... 580 371-2510
  Tishomingo *(G-8969)*
Torcsill Foundations LLC..............D...... 281 825-5200
  Weatherford *(G-11448)*

3452 Bolts, Nuts, Screws, Rivets & Washers

▼ Gardner Industries Inc..............F...... 918 583-0171
  Tulsa *(G-9801)*
Integrity Machine Source LLC........G...... 918 230-9657
  Owasso *(G-7575)*
Jasars Enterprises Inc..................G...... 405 808-6460
  Edmond *(G-2468)*
Kennedy Restorations Llc.............G...... 405 761-5303
  Oklahoma City *(G-5300)*
Manufacturing Solutions Inc..........G...... 918 951-0750
  Broken Arrow *(G-1141)*
Pin Efx LLC................................G...... 405 341-9956
  Edmond *(G-2570)*
Popefasteners Inc.......................G...... 918 740-4801
  Tulsa *(G-10532)*
Psf Services LLC.........................G...... 707 386-8805
  Marlow *(G-4239)*
◆ Refractory Anchors Inc.............E...... 918 455-8485
  Broken Arrow *(G-1154)*
▲ SBS Industries LLC..................C...... 918 836-7756
  Tulsa *(G-10712)*
Smith Precision Products LLC.......G...... 918 691-5797
  Broken Arrow *(G-1165)*
Vortex Parts Washer....................G...... 918 582-4445
  Tulsa *(G-11084)*
Witten Company Inc....................E...... 918 272-9567
  Owasso *(G-7630)*

3462 Iron & Steel Forgings

Axels Transmissions Transfers.......G...... 918 425-7725
  Tulsa *(G-9234)*
Crosby Group LLC.......................B...... 918 834-4611
  Tulsa *(G-9509)*
Crosby Worldwide Limited............F...... 918 834-4611
  Tulsa *(G-9512)*
Cundiff Custom Fabrication LLC....G...... 405 372-8204
  Stillwater *(G-8673)*
Ftdm Investments Llc..................D...... 918 598-3430
  Locust Grove *(G-4107)*
Horseshoe Exploration LLC...........G...... 580 866-3207
  Sharon *(G-8417)*
J & D Gearing & Machining Inc......G...... 405 677-7667
  Oklahoma City *(G-6329)*
Kloefkorn Entps Ltd Partnr...........G...... 580 694-2292
  Manchester *(G-4167)*
Lufkin Industries LLC...................F...... 405 677-0567
  Oklahoma City *(G-6501)*

34 FABRICATED METAL PRODUCTS, EXCEPT MACHINERY AND TRANSPORTATION EQUIPMENT

Be Custom Coatings ....G....... 405 205-9347
  Harrah *(G-3374)*
Broken Arrow Powdr Coating Inc ....E....... 918 251-2192
  Broken Arrow *(G-856)*
Broken Arrow Powdr Coating Inc ....E....... 918 258-1017
  Broken Arrow *(G-857)*
Casting Coating Corp ....F....... 918 445-4141
  Tulsa *(G-8995)*
Chemproof Polymers Inc ....G....... 918 584-0364
  Tulsa *(G-9410)*
Coat Pro LLC ....G....... 405 672-0705
  Oklahoma City *(G-5798)*
Coating Solution ....G....... 580 276-5432
  Leon *(G-4033)*
Commercial Coatings Okla LLC ....G....... 405 226-8739
  Oklahoma City *(G-5805)*
Copperhead Coatings LLC ....G....... 580 532-6243
  Pond Creek *(G-7889)*
Custom Catings of Broken Arrow ....G....... 918 258-0996
  Coweta *(G-1876)*
Custom Powder Coating & Dustle ....G....... 580 382-8000
  Ponca City *(G-7815)*
Eagle Rock Coatings Inc ....G....... 405 948-8900
  Oklahoma City *(G-5996)*
▲ Energy and Envmtl Svcs Inc ....G....... 405 843-8996
  Edmond *(G-2413)*
Energy and Envmtl Svcs Inc ....G....... 405 285-8767
  Edmond *(G-2412)*
▲ Etched In Stone ....G....... 918 369-0500
  Bixby *(G-621)*
Finish Line Powder Coating ....G....... 918 938-6292
  Tulsa *(G-9744)*
GE Oil & Gas Esp Inc ....E....... 405 527-1566
  Purcell *(G-8009)*
Gerdau Ameristeel US Inc ....F....... 918 682-2600
  Muskogee *(G-4679)*
Guthrie Industrial Coating ....G....... 405 377-6649
  Stillwater *(G-8696)*
H & H Protective Coating Co ....G....... 918 582-9187
  Tulsa *(G-9871)*
H-V Manufacturing Company ....G....... 918 756-9620
  Okmulgee *(G-7509)*
House of Trophies ....G....... 918 341-2111
  Claremore *(G-1637)*
◆ Ideal Specialty Inc ....F....... 918 834-1657
  Tulsa *(G-9967)*
Industrial Coatings Oklahoma ....G....... 918 638-5606
  Claremore *(G-1640)*
J&J Powder Coating & Fabr ....G....... 918 836-9700
  Tulsa *(G-10024)*
Juno Companies Incorporated ....G....... 918 627-8868
  Tulsa *(G-10067)*
Kuykendall Welding LLC ....G....... 405 905-0389
  Chickasha *(G-1480)*
Mid-America Indus Coatings LLC ....G....... 580 239-9003
  Atoka *(G-419)*
Milamar Coatings LLC ....F....... 405 755-8448
  Oklahoma City *(G-6608)*
Modern Coatings LLC ....G....... 405 795-2633
  Oklahoma City *(G-5307)*
Modern Plating Co Inc ....F....... 918 836-5081
  Tulsa *(G-10291)*
Mtw Powder Coating ....G....... 918 638-4795
  Coweta *(G-1892)*
Nacols Jewelry ....G....... 580 355-4280
  Lawton *(G-3975)*
Nafcoat Inc ....G....... 918 367-9606
  Bristow *(G-789)*
▲ Nameplates Inc ....D....... 918 584-2651
  Tulsa *(G-10324)*
National Coating ....G....... 405 251-5065
  Wynnewood *(G-11671)*
Oerlikon Blzers Cating USA Inc ....G....... 405 745-1026
  Oklahoma City *(G-6713)*
Oklahoma Coating Specialists ....G....... 405 447-0448
  Norman *(G-5099)*
▲ Oklahoma Cstm Cating Ltd Lblty .....E....... 405 382-0231
  Seminole *(G-8391)*
Performance Coatings Inc ....G....... 405 525-9790
  Oklahoma City *(G-6829)*
Pixley Coating Inc ....G....... 580 444-2140
  Velma *(G-11236)*
Powder Coatings Incorporated ....G....... 918 627-6225
  Tulsa *(G-10537)*
Powder Coatings Plus LLC ....F....... 405 232-5707
  Oklahoma City *(G-6868)*
Precision Coatings LLC ....G....... 918 622-1876
  Tulsa *(G-10543)*
Precision Metal Forming LLC ....E....... 405 677-3777
  Oklahoma City *(G-6882)*

Premier Metal Finishing Inc ....G....... 405 947-0200
  Oklahoma City *(G-6885)*
Protective Coatings Intl LLC ....G....... 405 716-4734
  Seminole *(G-8395)*
Quality Galvanizing ....G....... 918 789-9333
  Chelsea *(G-1410)*
Quality Steel Coatings Inc ....G....... 918 269-9104
  Broken Arrow *(G-1151)*
Southside Powder Coating ....G....... 405 623-8557
  Noble *(G-4892)*
▲ Spray-Rite Inc ....E....... 479 648-3351
  Pocola *(G-7786)*
Sprayfoam Banks & Coatings ....G....... 580 490-6308
  Overbrook *(G-7539)*
Sun Heat Treating Inc ....G....... 918 227-2188
  Tulsa *(G-9039)*
Texoma Engraving LLC ....G....... 580 775-7333
  Durant *(G-2264)*
Thompsons Metal Coating ....G....... 918 272-5711
  Owasso *(G-7624)*
Topps Powder Coating ....G....... 405 794-2900
  Moore *(G-4578)*
Trophies n Things ....G....... 405 247-9771
  Anadarko *(G-207)*
Tulsa Powder Coating Inc ....G....... 918 832-1741
  Tulsa *(G-11004)*
Twj Inc ....G....... 405 392-4366
  Tuttle *(G-11217)*
Walkers Powder Coating LLC ....G....... 580 355-5000
  Lawton *(G-4018)*

3482 Small Arms Ammunition

Choctaw Defense Munitions LLC ....G....... 918 426-7871
  Mcalester *(G-4284)*
Hailey Ordnance Company ....G....... 405 813-0700
  Oklahoma City *(G-6203)*
Johnny L Windsor ....G....... 405 691-3083
  Oklahoma City *(G-6371)*
Nash Tactical LLC ....G....... 405 589-6425
  Norman *(G-5085)*
Robertson Arms & Munitions Co ....G....... 405 376-2360
  Mustang *(G-4791)*
Sandman Sports ....G....... 918 272-0862
  Owasso *(G-7612)*
United States Dept of Army ....A....... 918 420-6642
  McAlester *(G-4348)*

3484 Small Arms

Alex Arms and Instruction LLC ....G....... 405 351-0806
  Alex *(G-129)*
Champlin Firearms Inc ....G....... 580 237-7388
  Enid *(G-2929)*
Dark Ops Designs ....G....... 918 269-0049
  Claremore *(G-1612)*
Duncan Machine Products Inc ....E....... 580 467-6784
  Duncan *(G-2110)*
F&D Defense LLC ....G....... 512 745-6482
  Seminole *(G-8373)*
Garys Guns ....G....... 405 789-6896
  Bethany *(G-579)*
Gun World Inc ....G....... 405 670-5885
  Del City *(G-1997)*
Hailey Ordnance Company ....G....... 405 813-0700
  Oklahoma City *(G-6203)*
Jean Jacques Perodeau Gunmaker ......G....... 580 237-7388
  Enid *(G-2983)*
JJ Perodeau Gunmaker Inc ....G....... 580 747-1804
  Sand Springs *(G-8195)*
Leather Guns & Etc ....F....... 580 296-2616
  Colbert *(G-1785)*
Madison Avenue Firearms LLC ....G....... 918 629-6910
  Tulsa *(G-10197)*
Mike Beathe ....G....... 918 288-7858
  Sperry *(G-8610)*
Newman Precision ....G....... 580 339-0097
  Elk City *(G-2856)*
Oklahoma Machine Guns LLC ....G....... 405 418-4867
  Oklahoma City *(G-6754)*
Old Sarges Armory LLC ....G....... 270 945-8324
  Miami *(G-4425)*
Patriot Small Arms LLC ....G....... 405 567-7890
  Tecumseh *(G-8924)*
Redneck Firearms Inc ....G....... 405 650-6605
  Harrah *(G-3384)*
Reliance Mfg Solutions LLC ....G....... 405 640-9660
  Oklahoma City *(G-7006)*
Rifle Shoppe Inc ....G....... 405 356-2583
  Wellston *(G-11477)*
Rise Manufacturing LLC ....E....... 918 994-6240
  Broken Arrow *(G-1032)*

Stevens & Sons LLC ....G....... 580 482-4142
  Altus *(G-169)*
Three Prcent Frrms Catings LLC ....G....... 580 931-9908
  Mead *(G-4368)*
Zulu 4 Tactical LLC ....G....... 918 978-6810
  Tulsa *(G-11180)*

3489 Ordnance & Access, NEC

Artillery Nation LLC ....G....... 405 606-5080
  Moore *(G-4495)*
Cutting Edge Arms LLC ....G....... 405 603-6723
  Oklahoma City *(G-5881)*
Ducommun Labarge Tech Inc ....C....... 918 459-2200
  Tulsa *(G-9611)*
Etched Ordnance LLC ....G....... 918 855-8779
  Coweta *(G-1882)*
Gun World Inc ....G....... 405 670-5885
  Del City *(G-1997)*
Hailey Ordnance Company ....G....... 405 813-0700
  Oklahoma City *(G-6203)*
Red River Gunsmithing LLC ....G....... 580 770-1911
  Frederick *(G-3198)*
Redrhino LLC ....G....... 405 740-5132
  Blanchard *(G-733)*

3491 Industrial Valves

Alfa Laval Inc ....G....... 918 251-7477
  Broken Arrow *(G-824)*
Alfa Lval A Cled Exchngers Inc ....G....... 918 251-7477
  Broken Arrow *(G-825)*
◆ American Directional Tech ....G....... 405 449-3362
  Wayne *(G-11365)*
B P S Inc ....G....... 918 258-7554
  Broken Arrow *(G-841)*
B S & B Safety Systems Inc ....G....... 918 622-5950
  Tulsa *(G-9245)*
▲ Balon Corporation ....A....... 405 677-3321
  Oklahoma City *(G-5522)*
Balon Valves ....G....... 405 670-8300
  Oklahoma City *(G-5523)*
Bellofram ....E....... 405 677-7222
  Oklahoma City *(G-5545)*
Bgr LLC ....E....... 405 671-2000
  Oklahoma City *(G-5562)*
BS&b Pressure Safety MGT LLC ....G....... 918 664-3725
  Tulsa *(G-9344)*
◆ BS&b Safety Systems LLC ....G....... 918 622-5950
  Tulsa *(G-9345)*
Cameron International Corp ....B....... 405 631-1321
  Oklahoma City *(G-5676)*
Cameron International Corp ....C....... 405 745-2715
  Oklahoma City *(G-5677)*
Curtiss-Wright Corporation ....G....... 405 515-8235
  Norman *(G-4973)*
▲ Cyclonic Valve Company ....E....... 918 317-8200
  Broken Arrow *(G-883)*
Eichler Valve ....G....... 405 370-6891
  Edmond *(G-2407)*
Enviro Valve (us) Inc ....G....... 918 251-6103
  Broken Arrow *(G-902)*
Flow Valve LLC ....E....... 580 622-2294
  Sulphur *(G-8832)*
▲ Flow-Quip Inc ....E....... 918 663-3313
  Tulsa *(G-9758)*
Fluid Controls Inc ....E....... 918 299-0442
  Tulsa *(G-9762)*
Gas Products Inc ....G....... 918 664-5679
  Tulsa *(G-9804)*
Kimray Inc ....C....... 405 525-6601
  Oklahoma City *(G-6417)*
King Valve Inc ....F....... 405 672-0046
  Oklahoma City *(G-6421)*
▲ L6 Inc ....E....... 918 251-5791
  Broken Arrow *(G-963)*
▼ Mercer Valve Co Inc ....G....... 405 470-5213
  Oklahoma City *(G-6566)*
▲ Ocv Control Valves LLC ....E....... 918 627-1942
  Tulsa *(G-10376)*
Oklahoma Safety Eqp Co Inc ....C....... 918 258-5626
  Broken Arrow *(G-994)*
▲ Omni Valve Company LLC ....E....... 918 687-6100
  Muskogee *(G-4725)*
Ops Valves LLC ....G....... 918 273-3300
  Nowata *(G-5224)*
Premier Valve Group ....G....... 918 519-4309
  Broken Arrow *(G-1009)*
▼ Rupture Pin Technology ....E....... 405 789-1884
  Oklahoma City *(G-7062)*
Turbulator Company LLC ....F....... 405 820-3026
  Oklahoma City *(G-7351)*

SIC SECTION

35 INDUSTRIAL AND COMMERCIAL MACHINERY AND COMPUTER EQUIPMENT

National Oilwell Varco Inc ....C...... 918 781-4436
   Muskogee *(G-4719)*
Nortek Air Solutions LLC ....B...... 405 263-7286
   Okarche *(G-5247)*
Oilfield Equipment Company ....G...... 405 850-1406
   Duncan *(G-2161)*
Oilfield Improvements Inc ....G...... 918 250-5584
   Broken Arrow *(G-993)*
Pipeline Equipment Inc ....E...... 918 224-4144
   Tulsa *(G-9024)*
Pro-Fab Industries Inc ....E...... 918 865-7590
   Mannford *(G-4190)*
Rise Manufacturing LLC ....E...... 918 994-6240
   Broken Arrow *(G-1032)*
Safeco Filter Products Inc ....F...... 918 455-0100
   Tulsa *(G-9033)*
Safeco Manufacturing Inc ....F...... 918 455-0100
   Broken Arrow *(G-1160)*
Sharp Metal Fabricators Inc ....F...... 405 899-4849
   Noble *(G-4891)*
Shaw Group Inc ....A...... 918 445-7744
   Tulsa *(G-10739)*
Sooner Swage & Coating Co Inc ....G...... 918 689-7142
   Eufaula *(G-3114)*
SUN Engineering Inc ....F...... 918 627-0426
   Tulsa *(G-10870)*
Superior Dynmics Fbrcation LLC ....G...... 918 698-9846
   Bartlesville *(G-531)*
▲ Tulsa Tube Bending Co Inc ....E...... 888 882-3637
   Tulsa *(G-11011)*
U S Weatherford L P ....C...... 580 276-5362
   Marietta *(G-4216)*
Weatherford International LLC ....E...... 405 773-1100
   Oklahoma City *(G-7430)*
Weatherford International LLC ....E...... 580 490-1476
   Wilson *(G-11545)*
Wolverine Tube Inc ....A...... 405 275-4850
   Shawnee *(G-8522)*
Wood Pipe Service Inc ....G...... 405 672-6097
   Oklahoma City *(G-7464)*
Word Inds Fabrication LLC ....E...... 918 382-7704
   Tulsa *(G-11152)*

3499 Fabricated Metal Prdts, NEC

Aerostar International Inc ....G...... 918 789-3000
   Chelsea *(G-1401)*
All-Star Trophies & Ribbon Mfg ....G...... 918 283-2200
   Claremore *(G-1581)*
American Intellectual LLC ....G...... 405 605-2378
   Oklahoma City *(G-5436)*
Automtive Cting Specialist Inc ....G...... 918 698-1560
   Wagoner *(G-11274)*
B Rowdy Rnch Met Fbrcation LLC ...G...... 405 973-5976
   Luther *(G-4132)*
Bkw Inc ....G...... 918 836-6767
   Tulsa *(G-9299)*
Built Better Enterprises LLC ....G...... 580 492-5227
   Fletcher *(G-3161)*
▲ C&A International LLC ....E...... 918 872-1645
   Tulsa *(G-9362)*
C&M Enterprises ....G...... 918 683-4456
   Muskogee *(G-4657)*
Cheyenne Products LLC ....G...... 918 639-8583
   Owasso *(G-7553)*
Clark Mtal Bldngs Fbrcation LL ....G...... 580 695-4915
   Guthrie *(G-3309)*
Cni Manufacturing LLC ....G...... 580 276-3306
   Marietta *(G-4205)*
Del Nero Manufacturing Co ....G...... 405 364-4800
   Norman *(G-4976)*
Frog Printing & Awards Ctr LLC ....G...... 580 678-1114
   Lawton *(G-3931)*
Gary Mace ....G...... 580 654-2660
   Carnegie *(G-1276)*
Gloria Rae Travel Accessories ....G...... 405 848-1300
   Oklahoma City *(G-6163)*
House of Trophies ....G...... 918 341-2111
   Claremore *(G-1637)*
Js Metal Fabrication LLC ....G...... 918 428-2242
   Tulsa *(G-10063)*
Justus Fabrication ....G...... 918 207-5192
   Tahlequah *(G-8869)*
JW Measurement Co ....G...... 918 465-5605
   Wilburton *(G-11521)*
Lothrop Technologies Inc ....G...... 405 390-3499
   Choctaw *(G-1551)*
Mart Trophy Co Inc ....G...... 918 481-3388
   Tulsa *(G-10217)*
Midwest Industries Inc ....G...... 405 279-3595
   Meeker *(G-4382)*

▲ Mtm Recognition Corporation ....B...... 405 609-6900
   Oklahoma City *(G-6634)*
Oklahoma Safety Eqp Co Inc ....C...... 918 258-5626
   Broken Arrow *(G-994)*
RB Cnstr Met Fabrication LLC ....G...... 580 367-5039
   Caney *(G-1262)*
Ricks Rod Reel Svc-High ....G...... 405 823-7581
   Oklahoma City *(G-7022)*
River Industries LLC ....G...... 918 406-8991
   Collinsville *(G-1821)*
Southwest Engineering ....G...... 405 634-2841
   Oklahoma City *(G-7176)*
Sparks Mtal Dsign Fbrction LLC ....G...... 918 676-5112
   Fairland *(G-3131)*
Taraco Enterprises LLC ....G...... 580 679-3956
   Duke *(G-2080)*
Trinity Shtmtl Fabrication LLC ....G...... 918 899-6030
   Purcell *(G-8025)*
USA Metal Fabrication LLC ....G...... 918 845-6500
   Oklahoma City *(G-7379)*
W E Industries Inc ....G...... 405 949-0222
   Oklahoma City *(G-7410)*
Western Iron Works LLC ....G...... 405 779-1961
   Chickasha *(G-1524)*
York Metal Fabrication ....G...... 405 598-6239
   Tecumseh *(G-8931)*

35 INDUSTRIAL AND COMMERCIAL MACHINERY AND COMPUTER EQUIPMENT

3511 Steam, Gas & Hydraulic Turbines & Engines

◆ Bergey Windpower Company Inc ...E...... 405 364-4212
   Norman *(G-4930)*
Caprock Country Entps Inc ....F...... 580 924-1647
   Calera *(G-1239)*
Dewind Co ....G...... 580 338-3271
   Guymon *(G-3348)*
Integrity Power Solutions LLC ....G...... 918 925-9693
   Edmond *(G-2461)*
Next-Gen Wind LLC ....G...... 405 948-1556
   Oklahoma City *(G-6674)*
Ringside Productions ....G...... 818 974-2673
   Tulsa *(G-10655)*
Schock Manufacturing LLC ....E...... 918 609-3600
   Owasso *(G-7615)*
Siemens Energy ....G...... 580 254-7824
   Woodward *(G-11631)*
Solar Turbines Incorporated ....G...... 918 459-5100
   Broken Arrow *(G-1054)*
Suzlon Wind Energy Corporation ......G...... 580 468-2641
   Guymon *(G-3367)*
Universal Pressure Pumping Inc ....B...... 405 262-2441
   El Reno *(G-2765)*
Vogt Power International Inc ....G...... 502 899-4500
   Sapulpa *(G-8321)*

3519 Internal Combustion Engines, NEC

▲ Arrow Engine Company ....D...... 918 583-5711
   Tulsa *(G-9211)*
Automotive Machine Shop ....G...... 918 775-9770
   Sallisaw *(G-8139)*
Bach Welding & Diesel Service ....G...... 580 593-2599
   Custer City *(G-1973)*
Cummins - Allison Corp ....F...... 405 321-1411
   Norman *(G-4972)*
Cummins Enterprises Inc ....G...... 405 232-9022
   Oklahoma City *(G-5867)*
Cummins Inc ....B...... 405 946-4481
   Oklahoma City *(G-5868)*
Cummins Southern Plains LLC ....G...... 918 234-3240
   Tulsa *(G-9522)*
Cummins Southern Plains LLC ....E...... 405 946-4481
   Oklahoma City *(G-5869)*
Engines Alive ....G...... 918 406-8149
   Broken Arrow *(G-901)*
Floyds Machine Shop ....G...... 918 256-8440
   Vinita *(G-11258)*
Hoss Marine Propulsion Inc ....G...... 918 479-5167
   Locust Grove *(G-4110)*
Hudson Bros Rmanufactured Engs ...G...... 405 598-2260
   Tecumseh *(G-8919)*
Independent Diesel Service ....F...... 580 234-0435
   Enid *(G-2977)*
Memorial Auto Supply Inc ....F...... 405 324-5400
   Oklahoma City *(G-6564)*

Pacific Power Group LLC ....G...... 405 685-4630
   Oklahoma City *(G-6793)*
Production Engine & Pump Inc ....F...... 405 672-3644
   Oklahoma City *(G-6910)*
Russell Baker Racing Engines ....G...... 918 533-3825
   Miami *(G-4429)*
Southwestern Motor Rebuilders ....G...... 918 585-1519
   Tulsa *(G-10811)*
Thomas H Scott Western LLC ....G...... 405 632-6860
   Oklahoma City *(G-7283)*
United Engines Manufacture ....G...... 405 601-9861
   Oklahoma City *(G-7366)*
White Dove Small Engines ....G...... 580 857-2201
   Allen *(G-139)*
Woltjer Engines ....G...... 918 258-0598
   Broken Arrow *(G-1101)*

3523 Farm Machinery & Eqpt

3 C Cattle Feeders Inc ....F...... 580 384-3943
   Mill Creek *(G-4465)*
Allied H2o Inc ....G...... 405 550-3085
   Edmond *(G-2296)*
Audio Link Inc ....G...... 405 359-0017
   Edmond *(G-2311)*
Baker Manufacturing Inc ....F...... 580 327-0234
   Alva *(G-177)*
Bermuda King LLC ....G...... 405 375-5000
   Ringwood *(G-8085)*
Blue Ribbon Show Supply ....G...... 918 288-7396
   Sperry *(G-8605)*
Blue River Ventures Inc ....G...... 580 920-0111
   Durant *(G-2206)*
Blue River Ventures Inc ....G...... 580 798-4810
   Overbrook *(G-7538)*
Blue River Ventures Inc ....G...... 580 920-0111
   Calera *(G-1238)*
Bramco Inc ....F...... 580 227-2345
   Fairview *(G-3133)*
Built Better Enterprises LLC ....G...... 580 492-5227
   Fletcher *(G-3161)*
Buster Par Corp ....F...... 918 585-8542
   Tulsa *(G-9354)*
Cammond Industries LLC ....F...... 580 332-9300
   Ada *(G-18)*
Cardon Trailers ....G...... 580 327-0701
   Alva *(G-180)*
Century Livestock Feeders Inc ....F...... 918 793-3382
   Shidler *(G-8524)*
Century Products LLC ....G...... 908 793-3382
   Kaw City *(G-3757)*
Cherokee Hart Ranch ....G...... 918 563-4244
   Talihina *(G-8905)*
Craigs Oklahoma Pride LLC ....G...... 405 224-6410
   Chickasha *(G-1451)*
Dale Case Homes Inc ....G...... 405 755-5055
   Oklahoma City *(G-5890)*
Davids Trading Yard ....G...... 918 432-5671
   Kiowa *(G-3837)*
Deans Machine & Welding Inc ....G...... 580 688-3374
   Hollis *(G-3564)*
Dover Products Inc ....G...... 918 476-5688
   Chouteau *(G-1562)*
Enterprise Grain Company LLC ....G...... 580 874-2286
   Kremlin *(G-3851)*
Five Star Cub Cadet ....G...... 918 542-4070
   Miami *(G-4404)*
Forster & Son Inc ....G...... 580 332-6020
   Ada *(G-36)*
▼ Garfield Inc ....E...... 580 242-6411
   Enid *(G-2961)*
Gilliman Cattle ....G...... 405 392-4204
   Newcastle *(G-4827)*
Greg E Conard ....G...... 580 372-7982
   Soper *(G-8587)*
Gregory Dee Spahn Trust ....G...... 405 826-6777
   Broken Arrow *(G-922)*
H Diamond Resources Inc ....F...... 580 476-3733
   Rush Springs *(G-8121)*
Heather Harjochee ....G...... 405 615-3273
   Oklahoma City *(G-5293)*
Heavybilt Mfg Inc ....D...... 580 927-3003
   Coalgate *(G-1781)*
Hidden Valley Manufacturing ....G...... 580 343-2303
   Corn *(G-1867)*
Johnson Welding ....G...... 580 569-2231
   Mountain Park *(G-4626)*
Just Plant It LLC ....G...... 405 226-3111
   Macomb *(G-4142)*
Kelly Labs ....G...... 682 367-8743
   Longdale *(G-4125)*

Employee Codes: A=Over 500 employees, B=251-500
C=101-250, D=51-100, E=20-50, F=10-19, G=1-9

SIC SECTION
35 INDUSTRIAL AND COMMERCIAL MACHINERY AND COMPUTER EQUIPMENT

Ron Griggs Backhoe & Dump...........G...... 918 440-1334
  Dewey *(G-2032)*
▲ Sawyer Manufacturing Company....E...... 918 834-2550
  Tulsa *(G-9034)*
◆ Simmons Tool LLC..........................G...... 580 228-2799
  Waurika *(G-11364)*
Sjh Welding & Backhoe LLC..............G...... 405 833-8353
  Calumet *(G-1249)*
Smiths Backhoe and Utility.................G...... 405 202-7056
  Perkins *(G-7722)*
Smittys Backhoe Service LLC............G...... 918 630-1090
  Tulsa *(G-10781)*
South Central Oilfld Svcs Inc..............G...... 580 465-4498
  Wilson *(G-11542)*
Spragues Backhoe LLC.....................G...... 405 600-4905
  Oklahoma City *(G-7188)*
Sterling Crane LLC.............................G...... 918 728-8613
  Tulsa *(G-10848)*
Swh Construction LLC........................F...... 405 317-0663
  Washington *(G-11338)*
T2t Storm Shelters.............................G...... 580 512-4890
  Lawton *(G-4011)*
Terex Cranes......................................G...... 405 491-2006
  Oklahoma City *(G-7269)*
Terex Mining......................................G...... 918 296-0530
  Jenks *(G-3735)*
Terex USA LLC...................................F...... 405 787-6020
  Oklahoma City *(G-7270)*
Thomas Appraisal Service.................G...... 918 341-5860
  Claremore *(G-1692)*
Toms Tree Svc & Backhoe.................G...... 918 865-4861
  Jennings *(G-3740)*
Tribal Consortium Inc.........................G...... 580 332-1134
  Ada *(G-96)*
Triple C Grading & Excvtg LLC...........G...... 918 605-1848
  Sapulpa *(G-8317)*
▲ Tulsa Winch Inc...............................C...... 918 298-8300
  Jenks *(G-3736)*
▼ V M I Inc..F...... 918 225-7000
  Cushing *(G-1965)*
Varners Eqp Sls & Svc LLC................G...... 918 367-3800
  Bristow *(G-803)*
▲ Waldon Equipment LLC...................F...... 580 227-3711
  Fairview *(G-3155)*
Western Fibers Inc............................E...... 509 679-4786
  Hollis *(G-3571)*
William L Riggs Company Inc.............G...... 918 437-3245
  Tulsa *(G-11125)*

3532 Mining Machinery & Eqpt

Asbury Machine Corporation..............F...... 580 628-3416
  Tonkawa *(G-8972)*
Audio Link Inc....................................G...... 405 359-0017
  Edmond *(G-2311)*
Century Geophysical Corp..................E...... 918 838-9811
  Tulsa *(G-9399)*
Cutting Edge Technologies LLC.........G...... 918 284-6069
  Owasso *(G-7558)*
Dorssers Usa Inc................................G...... 918 422-5881
  Colcord *(G-1789)*
Enid Drill Systems Inc........................G...... 580 234-5971
  Enid *(G-2951)*
Flotek Industries Inc..........................G...... 580 252-5111
  Duncan *(G-2118)*
Helvey International Usa Inc..............E...... 405 203-0251
  Oklahoma City *(G-6237)*
J T Harrison Construction Co.............F...... 918 967-2852
  Stigler *(G-8633)*
Prestige Manufacturing Co LLC..........E...... 405 395-0500
  Shawnee *(G-8485)*
Riverside Operations Group LLC........E...... 918 908-9480
  Broken Arrow *(G-1034)*
South Central Machine......................G...... 580 775-1623
  Durant *(G-2258)*
▲ Technical Manufacturing Inc...........F...... 918 485-0380
  Wagoner *(G-11292)*

3533 Oil Field Machinery & Eqpt

Aceco Valve Inc.................................E...... 918 827-3669
  Mounds *(G-4608)*
Adko Inc...G...... 405 677-6507
  Oklahoma City *(G-5375)*
Aether Dbs LLC..................................G...... 918 317-2375
  Tulsa *(G-8988)*
AG Quip Inc..G...... 918 536-4325
  Ramona *(G-8043)*
All States Production Eqp Co.............G...... 405 672-2323
  Oklahoma City *(G-5414)*
◆ American Directional Tech..............G...... 405 449-3362
  Wayne *(G-11365)*

American Machine & Tool Co.............G...... 405 794-9820
  Wewoka *(G-11497)*
Apergy Artfl Lift Intl LLC.....................C...... 432 561-8101
  Tulsa *(G-9198)*
Apollo Engineering Company.............G...... 918 251-6780
  Broken Arrow *(G-830)*
Apollo Oilfield Supply LLC..................G...... 580 254-0164
  Woodward *(G-11554)*
Appli-Fab Custom Coating.................G...... 405 235-7039
  Chandler *(G-1375)*
APT Inc...G...... 405 354-8438
  Yukon *(G-11691)*
Asbury Machine Corporation..............F...... 580 628-3416
  Tonkawa *(G-8972)*
Atlas Instrument & Mfg Co.................G...... 918 371-1976
  Collinsville *(G-1800)*
▲ Atlas Rock Bit Service Inc...............F...... 405 691-4848
  Oklahoma City *(G-5486)*
Axis Technologies LLC......................G...... 580 467-4257
  Duncan *(G-2085)*
Baker Hughes A GE Company LLC...G...... 405 227-8471
  Oklahoma City *(G-5515)*
Baker Hughes A GE Company LLC...C...... 918 828-1600
  Tulsa *(G-9255)*
▲ Baker Hughes Elasto Systems.........F...... 405 670-3354
  Oklahoma City *(G-5516)*
Baker Hughes Incorporated...............D...... 918 426-6585
  McAlester *(G-4272)*
Baker Petrolite LLC............................C...... 918 245-2224
  Sand Springs *(G-8165)*
Bauman Machine Inc..........................E...... 918 745-3484
  Oklahoma City *(G-5531)*
BF Machines Shop Inc.......................F...... 580 255-5899
  Duncan *(G-2091)*
Bico Drilling Tools Inc.........................G...... 918 872-9983
  Broken Arrow *(G-850)*
Big Iron Oilfield Services...................G...... 580 788-2247
  Elmore City *(G-2894)*
Borden Company Inc..........................E...... 918 224-0816
  Sapulpa *(G-8258)*
◆ Borets US Inc..................................B...... 918 439-7000
  Tulsa *(G-9320)*
Borets US Inc.....................................E...... 405 949-0031
  Oklahoma City *(G-5621)*
Bradshaw Home LLC.........................G...... 918 582-5404
  Tulsa *(G-9329)*
Bri-Chem Supply Corp LLC................G...... 405 200-5466
  Chickasha *(G-1444)*
◆ Bronco Manufacturing LLC..............E...... 918 446-7196
  Tulsa *(G-9340)*
Bynum & Company Inc.......................F...... 580 265-7747
  Stonewall *(G-8798)*
C & C Equipment Specialist Inc.........G...... 405 677-3110
  Oklahoma City *(G-5655)*
C & H Safety Pin Inc...........................G...... 405 949-5843
  Newalla *(G-4806)*
C & H Tool & Machine Inc..................G...... 580 332-1929
  Ada *(G-16)*
▲ C & H Tool & Machine Inc..............F...... 580 332-1929
  Ada *(G-17)*
C&H Safety Pin Inc............................G...... 405 386-3942
  McLoud *(G-4356)*
C-Star Mfg Inc....................................G...... 405 756-1530
  Lindsay *(G-4054)*
Callaway Equipment & Mfg................F...... 405 632-1870
  Oklahoma City *(G-5672)*
Cameron International Corp...............C...... 405 745-2715
  Oklahoma City *(G-5677)*
Cameron International Corp...............E...... 405 843-5578
  Oklahoma City *(G-5678)*
Cameron International Corp...............E...... 405 789-8065
  Oklahoma City *(G-5679)*
Cameron Technologies Inc................G...... 405 682-1661
  Moore *(G-4503)*
Cameron Technologies Inc................E...... 580 470-9600
  Duncan *(G-2097)*
Carl Bright Inc....................................G...... 405 761-7129
  McLoud *(G-4357)*
▲ Centek Inc.......................................E...... 405 219-3200
  Oklahoma City *(G-5724)*
Circle B Msrment Fbrcation LLC........G...... 918 445-4488
  Tulsa *(G-9429)*
Cnc Metal Shape Cnstr LLC..............F...... 405 605-5500
  Oklahoma City *(G-5794)*
◆ Comanche Bit Service Inc..............G...... 580 439-6424
  Comanche *(G-1836)*
Compass Manufacturing LLC.............G...... 405 735-3518
  Oklahoma City *(G-5809)*
▲ Compressco Inc..............................D...... 405 677-0221
  Oklahoma City *(G-5814)*

Compressco Partners Sub Inc...........C...... 405 677-0221
  Oklahoma City *(G-5816)*
Cougar Drilling Solutions USA...........E...... 405 789-4945
  Oklahoma City *(G-5841)*
CP Energy Holdings LLC...................F...... 405 513-6006
  Edmond *(G-2369)*
Crowley Oil & Mfg...............................G...... 918 744-8129
  Tulsa *(G-9514)*
Crown Energy Technology Okla.........E...... 405 348-9954
  Edmond *(G-2376)*
▲ Crystaltech Inc................................G...... 580 252-8893
  Duncan *(G-2101)*
▲ Cyclonic Valve Company................E...... 918 317-8200
  Broken Arrow *(G-883)*
D C Jones Machine Co.......................G...... 918 786-6855
  Grove *(G-3265)*
D Parks Enterprises LLC....................G...... 405 315-1994
  Sand Springs *(G-8177)*
D&L Manufacturing Inc......................G...... 918 587-3504
  Tulsa *(G-9542)*
◆ Darby Equipment Co......................G...... 918 582-2340
  Tulsa *(G-9552)*
Davco Fab Inc....................................G...... 918 757-2504
  Jennings *(G-3739)*
Davis Machine Shop Inc....................G...... 918 756-3055
  Lindsay *(G-4059)*
Deco Development Company Inc......G...... 918 747-6366
  Oklahoma City *(G-9566)*
◆ Den-Con Tool Co.............................F...... 405 670-5942
  Oklahoma City *(G-5921)*
◆ Double Life Corporation..................F...... 405 789-7867
  Oklahoma City *(G-5971)*
▲ Downing Wellhead Equipment LLC.E...... 405 486-7858
  Oklahoma City *(G-5973)*
Downing Wellhead Equipment LLC...G...... 405 789-8182
  Oklahoma City *(G-5974)*
Drillers Service Center Inc................G...... 405 631-3728
  Oklahoma City *(G-5980)*
Eco Oil Fill Services...........................E...... 580 774-2240
  Weatherford *(G-11409)*
Electrotech Inc...................................G...... 918 224-5869
  Tulsa *(G-9002)*
Energy Meter Systems LLC...............E...... 405 853-4976
  Hennessey *(G-3460)*
◆ Engineering Technology Inc...........G...... 918 492-0508
  Tulsa *(G-9687)*
Enid Mack Sales Inc..........................D...... 580 234-0043
  Enid *(G-2954)*
Fabricating Specialists Inc................F...... 405 476-1959
  Oklahoma City *(G-6068)*
Fabwell Corporation..........................E...... 918 224-9060
  Sapulpa *(G-8272)*
Fairmount Minerals............................G...... 580 456-7791
  Roff *(G-8108)*
Fammco Mfg Co Inc..........................G...... 918 437-0456
  Tulsa *(G-9727)*
Fhe USA LLC.....................................G...... 405 350-2544
  Yukon *(G-11723)*
▲ Fibre Reduction Inc........................G...... 580 223-3401
  Ardmore *(G-289)*
FMC Technologies Inc.......................F...... 405 787-6301
  Oklahoma City *(G-6098)*
FMC Technologies Inc.......................G...... 405 972-1305
  Oklahoma City *(G-6099)*
FMC Technologies Inc.......................G...... 405 415-9532
  Oklahoma City *(G-6100)*
Forum Energy Technologies Inc........D...... 405 603-7198
  Oklahoma City *(G-6105)*
Forum Energy Technologies Inc........D...... 405 224-5779
  Chickasha *(G-1459)*
Forum Energy Technologies Inc........G...... 580 622-5058
  Davis *(G-1983)*
Forum Production Equipment............D...... 580 622-5058
  Davis *(G-1984)*
Forum Us Inc.....................................D...... 580 788-2333
  Elmore City *(G-2896)*
Ftdm Investments Llc.........................D...... 918 598-3430
  Locust Grove *(G-4107)*
G & G Quality Services LLC..............G...... 918 961-0288
  Miami *(G-4406)*
▼ G B E Services Corporation............G...... 918 428-8665
  Tulsa *(G-9788)*
Gardner Denver Inc...........................D...... 918 664-1151
  Tulsa *(G-9800)*
Gastech Engineering LLC..................D...... 918 663-8274
  Sapulpa *(G-8274)*
◆ Gator Rigs LLC................................G...... 405 598-3266
  Tecumseh *(G-8916)*
GE Oil & Gas Pressure Ctrl LP..........E...... 405 273-7660
  Shawnee *(G-8451)*

Employee Codes: A=Over 500 employees, B=251-500
C=101-250, D=51-100, E=20-50, F=10-19, G=1-9

2020 Oklahoma Directory of Manufacturers & Processors

SIC SECTION
35 INDUSTRIAL AND COMMERCIAL MACHINERY AND COMPUTER EQUIPMENT

Weatherford District Office ....G...... 405 354-7711
  Yukon *(G-11803)*
Weatherford International LLC ....E...... 405 577-5590
  Oklahoma City *(G-7432)*
Weatherford International LLC ....E...... 940 683-8393
  Oklahoma City *(G-7433)*
Weatherford International LLC ....G...... 405 350-3357
  Yukon *(G-11804)*
Weatherford International LLC ....G...... 405 853-7127
  Hennessey *(G-3497)*
Weatherford International LLC ....F...... 405 619-7238
  Oklahoma City *(G-7434)*
Weatherford International LLC ....E...... 405 773-1100
  Oklahoma City *(G-7430)*
Wenco Energy Corporation ....F...... 918 252-4511
  Tulsa *(G-11108)*
Wenzel Downhole Tools Us Inc ....G...... 405 787-4145
  Oklahoma City *(G-7436)*
Wilco Machine & Fab Inc ....B...... 580 658-6993
  Marlow *(G-4247)*
Wildman Manufacturing Inc ....F...... 405 235-1264
  Oklahoma City *(G-7453)*
▼ Woolslayer Companies Inc ....C...... 918 523-9191
  Catoosa *(G-1368)*

3534 Elevators & Moving Stairways

American Accessibility Eqp Svc ....G...... 405 631-4142
  Oklahoma City *(G-5431)*
▼ Hy-H Manufacturing Co Inc ....E...... 918 341-6811
  Claremore *(G-1638)*
Travertine Inc ....G...... 918 583-5210
  Tulsa *(G-10972)*
Vasser Machine ....G...... 918 225-2677
  Cushing *(G-1966)*
Wilson Products Inc ....F...... 918 224-1527
  Tulsa *(G-9052)*

3535 Conveyors & Eqpt

Chickasaw Nation Inds Inc ....D...... 580 276-3305
  Marietta *(G-4203)*
Clean Products Inc ....G...... 405 382-1441
  Seminole *(G-8364)*
◆ Fki Industries Inc ....G...... 918 834-4611
  Tulsa *(G-9752)*
Marietta Filtra Systems ....G...... 580 276-3306
  Marietta *(G-4209)*
Overhead Door Solutions LLC ....G...... 918 686-8847
  Muskogee *(G-4729)*
Redback Energy Services LLC ....E...... 405 265-4608
  Oklahoma City *(G-6992)*
Thompson Manufacturing Company ....G...... 918 585-1991
  Tulsa *(G-10935)*

3536 Hoists, Cranes & Monorails

Ameracrane and Hoist LLC ....E...... 918 437-4775
  Tulsa *(G-9161)*
◆ Auto Crane Company ....C...... 918 438-2760
  Tulsa *(G-9226)*
Boat Floaters Ind LLC ....F...... 918 256-3330
  Afton *(G-113)*
▲ Bridge Crane Specialists LLC ....E...... 918 321-3953
  Kiefer *(G-3776)*
Campbell Crane and Service LLC ....G...... 405 245-8983
  Oklahoma City *(G-5682)*
Central States Crane Hoist LLC ....F...... 918 341-2320
  Claremore *(G-1603)*
Central States Crane Hoist LLC ....G...... 918 341-2320
  Claremore *(G-1604)*
◆ Fki Industries Inc ....G...... 918 834-4611
  Tulsa *(G-9752)*
▲ Gunnebo Corporation U S A ....E...... 918 832-8933
  Tulsa *(G-9867)*
◆ Gunnebo Industries Inc ....C...... 918 832-8933
  Tulsa *(G-9868)*
▼ Hy-H Manufacturing Co Inc ....E...... 918 341-6811
  Claremore *(G-1638)*
Hydrohoist Boat Lifts ....G...... 918 256-8125
  Bernice *(G-565)*
Hydrohoist Marine Group Inc ....G...... 918 256-8775
  Bernice *(G-566)*
Kevin Davis Company ....G...... 918 280-0717
  Bixby *(G-639)*
Konecranes Inc ....G...... 405 208-8808
  Oklahoma City *(G-6434)*
▲ Ramsey Industries Inc ....C...... 918 438-2760
  Tulsa *(G-10617)*
United Slings Inc ....G...... 405 598-2616
  Tecumseh *(G-8930)*

3537 Indl Trucks, Tractors, Trailers & Stackers

4-Star Trailers Inc ....C...... 405 324-7827
  Oklahoma City *(G-5331)*
◆ Auto Crane Company ....C...... 918 438-2760
  Tulsa *(G-9226)*
Becks Forklift Svc LLC ....G...... 580 303-8038
  Elk City *(G-2786)*
C&C Trucking and Eqp Svcs LLC ....G...... 405 567-5194
  Prague *(G-7922)*
▼ Campbell Fbrcation Tooling Inc ....G...... 918 987-0047
  Stroud *(G-8809)*
Clark Rhyne ....G...... 918 874-3563
  Wardville *(G-11306)*
Crandell Salvage Incorporated ....F...... 918 429-0001
  Mcalester *(G-4287)*
D & W Cupp Trucking LLC ....G...... 580 821-6844
  Sayre *(G-8339)*
Darr Lift Main Line ....G...... 580 657-6337
  Ardmore *(G-273)*
Ddieci Midwest LLC ....G...... 816 591-1350
  Edmond *(G-2386)*
Dickson Industries Inc ....E...... 405 598-6547
  Tecumseh *(G-8912)*
Forklift Parts and Service LLC ....G...... 918 251-5119
  Broken Arrow *(G-913)*
Green Edward DBA Ed Green Trck .....G...... 405 672-4522
  Oklahoma City *(G-6186)*
Gurley Troy Mattingly ....G...... 580 924-3042
  Durant *(G-2234)*
Hawkeye Fleet Services ....E...... 405 495-9939
  Oklahoma City *(G-6226)*
Hejin Waldran ....G...... 918 408-3500
  Claremore *(G-1632)*
▲ Industrial Vehicles Intl Inc ....E...... 918 836-6516
  Tulsa *(G-9983)*
Karl Amanns Trucking ....G...... 580 226-2082
  Ardmore *(G-320)*
Kern Valley Industries ....G...... 918 868-3911
  Rose *(G-8118)*
Kirkland Express LLC ....G...... 405 312-3061
  El Reno *(G-2734)*
Kremlin Welding & Fabrication ....G...... 580 874-2522
  Kremlin *(G-3853)*
▲ Lift Technologies Inc ....G...... 918 794-8088
  Tulsa *(G-10159)*
Mac Manufacturing Inc ....G...... 405 527-8270
  Purcell *(G-8013)*
Mid Continent Lift and Eqp LLC ....F...... 580 255-3867
  Duncan *(G-2155)*
Mobile Mini Inc ....E...... 405 682-9333
  Oklahoma City *(G-6622)*
◆ Mobile Products Inc ....G...... 580 227-3711
  Fairview *(G-3143)*
Moblie Products Inc ....C...... 580 227-3711
  Fairview *(G-3144)*
OEM Systems LLC ....G...... 405 263-7529
  Okarche *(G-5248)*
Shelley Benefield ....G...... 580 436-0296
  Ada *(G-86)*
▲ Vaculift Incorporated ....D...... 918 438-9875
  Tulsa *(G-11063)*
▲ W - W Trailer Mfrs Inc ....C...... 580 795-5571
  Madill *(G-4166)*
Walker Forklift Service LLC ....G...... 918 671-0317
  Tulsa *(G-11093)*
Wkd Associates ....G...... 918 336-9865
  Bartlesville *(G-536)*
Wolfe Heavy Haul and Hotshot ....G...... 918 695-7836
  Tulsa *(G-11146)*

3541 Machine Tools: Cutting

Accu-Turn Machine LLC ....G...... 580 704-8876
  Lawton *(G-3883)*
Alro Steel Corporation ....F...... 918 439-1000
  Tulsa *(G-9156)*
American Swat Solutions LLC ....G...... 405 568-1413
  Fort Gibson *(G-3172)*
Apache Machine Co Inc ....G...... 918 834-0022
  Tulsa *(G-9196)*
Bliss Industries LLC ....D...... 580 765-7787
  Ponca City *(G-7800)*
Bryon K Barrows ....G...... 918 519-9369
  Skiatook *(G-8534)*
Bullseye Boring Technology ....G...... 405 880-1878
  Stillwater *(G-8663)*
C&D Machine Tool Svc & Parts ....G...... 405 943-6033
  Oklahoma City *(G-5662)*
▼ Charles Machine Works Inc ....A...... 580 572-2693
  Perry *(G-7728)*
Clicks Machine & Supply ....G...... 405 273-2497
  Shawnee *(G-8438)*
◆ CMI Terex Corporation ....A...... 405 787-6020
  Oklahoma City *(G-5792)*
Cool Billet Customs ....G...... 580 216-0104
  Woodward *(G-11572)*
Crankshaft Service Company ....G...... 405 685-7553
  Oklahoma City *(G-5851)*
CRC-Evans Pipeline Intl Inc ....G...... 918 438-2100
  Tulsa *(G-9504)*
Cutting Edge Robotic Tech LLC ....G...... 918 247-6012
  Kellyville *(G-3764)*
D & B Processing LLC ....F...... 918 619-6452
  Broken Arrow *(G-1119)*
Deans Grinding Service ....G...... 918 838-0756
  Tulsa *(G-9565)*
Dickson Industries Inc ....E...... 405 598-6547
  Tecumseh *(G-8912)*
Duracoatings Holdings LLC ....D...... 405 692-2249
  Oklahoma City *(G-5990)*
Forster & Son Inc ....G...... 580 332-6020
  Ada *(G-36)*
G C Broach Co ....G...... 918 369-4320
  Bixby *(G-626)*
▲ H & M Pipe Beveling Mch Co Inc ....G...... 918 582-9984
  Tulsa *(G-9873)*
Helmco Manufacturing Inc ....G...... 918 336-4757
  Bartlesville *(G-492)*
◆ Hem Inc ....C...... 918 825-4821
  Pryor *(G-7966)*
Hem Inc ....D...... 888 729-7787
  Pryor *(G-7967)*
Hem Inc ....D...... 918 824-0800
  Pryor *(G-7968)*
I AM Drilling LLC ....G...... 580 234-2277
  Enid *(G-2976)*
Industrial Equipment Repair ....G...... 580 371-3361
  Tishomingo *(G-8966)*
J & D Gearing & Machining Inc ....G...... 405 677-7667
  Oklahoma City *(G-6329)*
J&K Machining Inc ....G...... 918 243-7936
  Cleveland *(G-1725)*
Kennys Machine Shop ....G...... 918 288-7241
  Skiatook *(G-8556)*
Mfg Solutions LLC ....G...... 918 232-3503
  Broken Arrow *(G-1143)*
Mills Machine Co ....E...... 405 273-4900
  Shawnee *(G-8475)*
Precision Machine & Tool LLC ....G...... 580 256-2219
  Woodward *(G-11623)*
Rent-A-Crane Inc ....G...... 405 745-2318
  Oklahoma City *(G-7007)*
Rent-A-Crane of Okla Inc ....F...... 405 745-2318
  Oklahoma City *(G-7008)*
▲ Sawyer Manufacturing Company ....E...... 918 834-2550
  Tulsa *(G-9034)*
Steven Campbell ....G...... 580 764-3469
  Chester *(G-1421)*
Triangular Silt Dike Co Inc ....G...... 405 277-7015
  Luther *(G-4139)*
Tulsa Trenchless Inc ....G...... 918 321-3330
  Kiefer *(G-3782)*
Wachob Industries Inc ....G...... 918 224-0511
  Sapulpa *(G-8322)*
Wayne Burt Machine ....G...... 918 786-4415
  Grove *(G-3293)*
Wesok Drilling Corp ....G...... 580 226-2450
  Ardmore *(G-380)*

3542 Machine Tools: Forming

Cnc Patterns & Tooling ....G...... 918 835-2344
  Tulsa *(G-9461)*
◆ Darby Equipment Co ....E...... 918 582-2340
  Tulsa *(G-9552)*
Delco LLC ....G...... 918 527-8058
  Broken Arrow *(G-1122)*
Dentcraft Tools ....F...... 405 495-0533
  Oklahoma City *(G-5924)*
Expanded Solutions LLC ....E...... 405 946-6791
  Wewoka *(G-11501)*
▲ H S Boyd Company Inc ....F...... 918 835-9359
  Tulsa *(G-9876)*
McCaskill Machining & Repair ....G...... 918 266-5186
  Catoosa *(G-1340)*
Pritchetts Machining LLC ....G...... 405 567-0183
  Tulsa *(G-7933)*
Spencer Faith Christn Ctr Inc ....G...... 812 876-5575
  Spencer *(G-8601)*
Strategic Armory Corps LLC ....G...... 623 780-1050
  Prague *(G-7936)*

Employee Codes: A=Over 500 employees, B=251-500
C=101-250, D=51-100, E=20-50, F=10-19, G=1-9

SIC SECTION 35 INDUSTRIAL AND COMMERCIAL MACHINERY AND COMPUTER EQUIPMENT

Rick Leaming Construction LLC .... G....... 580 362-2262
Newkirk *(G-4852)*
Rollett Mfg Inc .... G....... 405 427-9707
Oklahoma City *(G-7048)*
Safeco Manufacturing Inc .... F....... 918 455-0100
Broken Arrow *(G-1160)*
Starlite Welding Supplies .... G....... 580 252-8320
Duncan *(G-2185)*

3552 Textile Machinery

B Sew Inn LLC .... G....... 918 687-5762
Muskogee *(G-4652)*
Beckys Embroidery Design .... G....... 918 456-1235
Tahlequah *(G-8852)*
Creative Monogramming EMB .... G....... 580 762-6694
Ponca City *(G-7812)*
Gorfam Marketing Inc .... G....... 918 252-3733
Tulsa *(G-9841)*
House T Shirt & Silk Screening .... G....... 405 457-6321
Lookeba *(G-4129)*
Roses Custom .... G....... 580 252-9633
Duncan *(G-2172)*
United Axle .... G....... 918 344-1157
Claremore *(G-1697)*
World Weidner LLC .... G....... 580 765-9999
Ponca City *(G-7888)*

3553 Woodworking Machinery

C Easleys Touch .... G....... 918 284-9384
Tulsa *(G-9360)*
Classic Chisel Cabinet Shop .... G....... 405 387-2216
Blanchard *(G-707)*
Custom Drawers and Cabinetry .... G....... 918 322-9819
Glenpool *(G-3232)*
Marcy A Sharp .... G....... 405 615-9879
Asher *(G-391)*
Michael Allan Sharp .... G....... 405 615-3771
Asher *(G-392)*
Pine Creek Saw Shop Inc .... G....... 580 933-7376
Valliant *(G-11231)*
Tsdr LLC .... G....... 405 823-1518
Oklahoma City *(G-7346)*

3554 Paper Inds Machinery

Magnat-Fairview LLC .... F....... 413 593-5742
Oklahoma City *(G-6517)*
Marvel Photo Inc .... G....... 918 836-0741
Tulsa *(G-10218)*
▲ Maxcess Americas Inc .... G....... 405 755-1600
Oklahoma City *(G-6538)*
◆ Maxcess International Corp .... G....... 405 755-1600
Oklahoma City *(G-6539)*
Maxcess Intl Holdg Corp .... G....... 405 755-1600
Oklahoma City *(G-6540)*
Thompson Manufacturing Company .... G....... 918 585-1991
Tulsa *(G-10935)*
Woodward Ind Schl Dst I-1 .... G....... 580 256-5910
Woodward *(G-11656)*

3555 Printing Trades Machinery & Eqpt

Eagle Marketing .... G....... 580 548-8186
Enid *(G-2948)*
Fenimore Manufacturing Inc .... F....... 405 224-2637
Chickasha *(G-1457)*
▲ H S Boyd Company Inc .... F....... 918 835-9359
Tulsa *(G-9876)*
▲ Print Finishing Systems Inc .... G....... 405 232-1750
Oklahoma City *(G-6897)*
Rowmark LLC .... E....... 405 787-4542
Oklahoma City *(G-7051)*
Southwestern Process Supply Co .... E....... 918 582-8211
Tulsa *(G-10812)*
Thompson Manufacturing Company .... G....... 918 585-1991
Tulsa *(G-10935)*
Timothy J and Sharo Flick .... G....... 918 250-2456
Tulsa *(G-10943)*

3556 Food Prdts Machinery

Bar-S Foods Co .... B....... 580 510-3300
Lawton *(G-3896)*
Breshears Enterprises Inc .... F....... 405 236-4523
Oklahoma City *(G-5624)*
◆ Burford Corp .... D....... 405 867-4467
Maysville *(G-4255)*
Contact Process Piping .... G....... 405 948-9125
Oklahoma City *(G-5822)*
▼ Cookshack Inc .... E....... 580 765-3669
Ponca City *(G-7810)*
Doyle Dryers Inc .... G....... 918 224-4002
Tulsa *(G-9601)*
Forster & Son Inc .... G....... 580 332-6020
Ada *(G-36)*
Galaxy Distributing .... G....... 918 835-1186
Tulsa *(G-9797)*
Midwest Performance Pack Inc .... E....... 405 485-3567
Blanchard *(G-723)*
O K Restaurant Supply .... G....... 405 330-9932
Edmond *(G-2543)*
Rick Leaming Construction LLC .... G....... 580 362-2262
Newkirk *(G-4852)*
Schones Butcher Shop & Market .... G....... 580 472-3300
Canute *(G-1270)*
Sophisticated Sweets Inc .... G....... 580 704-8038
Cache *(G-1231)*
Swift Eckrich Inc .... G....... 918 258-4565
Broken Arrow *(G-1069)*
▲ Unitherm Food Systems LLC .... E....... 918 367-0197
Bristow *(G-802)*

3559 Special Ind Machinery, NEC

Armed Inc .... G....... 918 245-1478
Sand Springs *(G-8162)*
◆ Bartec Dispensing Tech Inc .... G....... 918 250-6496
Tulsa *(G-9269)*
Bolt It Hydraulic Solutions .... F....... 918 296-0202
Jenks *(G-3693)*
Carter Davis Machine Shop Inc .... G....... 918 437-2939
Tulsa *(G-9382)*
Central Sttes Shrdding Systems .... G....... 405 752-8300
Oklahoma City *(G-5726)*
Centrifugal Casting Mch Co Inc .... G....... 918 835-7323
Owasso *(G-7552)*
Chemco .... G....... 918 481-0537
Tulsa *(G-9409)*
Copper Kiln LLC .... G....... 918 272-5200
Owasso *(G-7555)*
Dathney Inc .... G....... 405 354-0481
Yukon *(G-11715)*
Doyle Dryers Inc .... G....... 918 224-4002
Tulsa *(G-9601)*
Energy Equip Sales Co .... G....... 580 276-5900
Burneyville *(G-1216)*
Farmers Co-Operative Gin Assn .... G....... 580 928-2664
Sayre *(G-8340)*
Formulated Materials LLC .... G....... 405 310-1650
Oklahoma City *(G-6102)*
▲ Health Engineering System .... G....... 405 329-6810
Norman *(G-5020)*
High Country Tek Inc .... E....... 530 265-3236
Tulsa *(G-9928)*
Hollyfrontier Corporation .... B....... 918 581-1800
Tulsa *(G-9942)*
J&K Machining Inc .... G....... 918 243-7936
Cleveland *(G-1725)*
Janes Machine Shop LLC .... G....... 580 237-4434
Enid *(G-2980)*
Kice Industries Inc .... E....... 580 363-2850
Blackwell *(G-685)*
Lam Research Corporation .... D....... 866 323-1834
Tulsa *(G-10117)*
Martin Bionics Innovations LLC .... G....... 405 850-2069
Oklahoma City *(G-6532)*
▲ Optical Works Corporation .... F....... 918 682-1806
Muskogee *(G-4726)*
◆ Parfab Field Services LLC .... G....... 918 543-6310
Inola *(G-3671)*
Powerhouse Resources Intl Inc .... D....... 405 232-7474
Oklahoma City *(G-6870)*
Pyrotek Incorporated .... E....... 918 224-1937
Tulsa *(G-9030)*
Quality Equipment Design Inc .... F....... 918 492-4019
Tulsa *(G-10591)*
▼ Reputation Services & Mfg LLC .... E....... 918 437-2077
Tulsa *(G-10643)*
Texas Refinery Corp .... G....... 918 455-6881
Broken Arrow *(G-1073)*
Tip Top Prop Shop .... G....... 580 564-3712
Kingston *(G-3831)*
Trace LLC .... F....... 918 510-0210
Tulsa *(G-10964)*
US Ferroics LLC .... G....... 601 763-1058
Ardmore *(G-376)*
US Shotblast Parts & Svc Corp .... G....... 405 842-6766
Oklahoma City *(G-7376)*
Vintage Plastics Llc .... F....... 918 439-1016
Tulsa *(G-11078)*
Young & New Century LLC .... G....... 281 968-0718
Norman *(G-5205)*

3561 Pumps & Pumping Eqpt

Accelated Artfl List Systems .... F....... 405 207-9449
Pauls Valley *(G-7649)*
Additive Systems Inc .... F....... 918 357-3433
Broken Arrow *(G-814)*
Baker Hughes A GE Company LLC .... C....... 918 828-1600
Tulsa *(G-9255)*
Bartling Pumps & Supplies LLC .... G....... 580 444-2227
Duncan *(G-2087)*
Bg & S Manufacturing .... E....... 918 396-3525
Skiatook *(G-8533)*
◆ Blackhawk Industrial Dist Inc .... C....... 918 610-4700
Broken Arrow *(G-853)*
Blm Equipment & Mfg Co Inc .... F....... 918 266-5282
Catoosa *(G-1304)*
Burleson Pump Company .... G....... 405 677-6881
Oklahoma City *(G-5645)*
C & B Pump Rebuilders .... G....... 405 789-4808
Oklahoma City *(G-5654)*
Climate Control Group Inc .... E....... 405 745-6858
Oklahoma City *(G-5786)*
Design Ready Controls Inc .... F....... 405 605-8234
Oklahoma City *(G-5926)*
Eddies Submersible Service Inc .... F....... 405 273-9292
Tecumseh *(G-8913)*
Excel Products .... G....... 580 216-0784
Woodward *(G-11582)*
Fabricating Specialists Inc .... F....... 405 476-1959
Oklahoma City *(G-6068)*
Flowserve Corporation .... B....... 918 627-8400
Tulsa *(G-9760)*
Flowserve US Inc .... C....... 918 599-6000
Tulsa *(G-9761)*
Floyds Machine Shop .... G....... 918 256-8440
Vinita *(G-11258)*
Franklin Electric Co Inc .... G....... 405 947-2511
Oklahoma City *(G-6112)*
Franklin Electric Co Inc .... B....... 501 455-1234
Oklahoma City *(G-6113)*
Franklin Electric Co Inc .... B....... 918 465-2348
Wilburton *(G-11520)*
Fts International Services LLC .... F....... 405 574-3900
Chickasha *(G-1460)*
Gardner Denver Inc .... D....... 918 664-1151
Tulsa *(G-9800)*
Global Oilfield Services Inc .... F....... 918 885-4024
Hominy *(G-3585)*
▲ Global Oilfield Services LLC .... E....... 405 741-0163
Oklahoma City *(G-6161)*
Harley Industries Inc .... G....... 918 451-2323
Tulsa *(G-9892)*
HEanderson Company .... F....... 918 687-4426
Muskogee *(G-4688)*
Hfe Process Inc .... G....... 918 663-9083
Inola *(G-3661)*
Ideas Manufacturing Inc .... G....... 405 691-5525
Oklahoma City *(G-5296)*
Idex Corporation .... D....... 405 609-1116
Oklahoma City *(G-6288)*
Industrial Dist Resources LLC .... G....... 239 591-3777
Tulsa *(G-9979)*
John Crane Inc .... D....... 918 664-5156
Tulsa *(G-10049)*
▲ John Crane Lemco Inc .... E....... 918 835-7325
Tulsa *(G-10050)*
K & S Pumping Unit Repair Inc .... F....... 580 237-7343
Enid *(G-2991)*
Kimray Inc .... C....... 405 525-6601
Oklahoma City *(G-6417)*
Larkin Products LLC .... G....... 918 584-3475
Tulsa *(G-10129)*
◆ Little Giant Pump Company LLC .... B....... 405 947-2511
Oklahoma City *(G-6483)*
Lloyd Edge .... G....... 580 726-2905
Hobart *(G-3543)*
Montross Tirita .... G....... 918 241-5637
Sand Springs *(G-8207)*
National Oilwell Varco Inc .... G....... 918 423-8000
McAlester *(G-4323)*
O K Plunger Service .... G....... 918 352-4269
Drumright *(G-2068)*
Odum Machine & Tool Inc .... G....... 918 663-6966
Tulsa *(G-10377)*
Oil States Industries Inc .... D....... 405 671-2000
Oklahoma City *(G-6721)*
Oil States Industries Inc .... G....... 918 250-0828
Tulsa *(G-10387)*
Perkins South Plains Inc .... E....... 405 685-4630
Oklahoma City *(G-6832)*

S I C

Employee Codes: A=Over 500 employees, B=251-500
C=101-250, D=51-100, E=20-50, F=10-19, G=1-9
2020 Oklahoma Directory
of Manufacturers & Processors
481

SIC SECTION
35 INDUSTRIAL AND COMMERCIAL MACHINERY AND COMPUTER EQUIPMENT

3569 Indl Machinery & Eqpt, NEC

24 7 Machinery LLC ....G....... 580 762-8965
  Ponca City *(G-7789)*
Advance Oil Corporation ....G....... 918 321-9034
  Kiefer *(G-3775)*
Alfa Laval Inc ....G....... 918 251-7477
  Broken Arrow *(G-824)*
All American Fire Systems Inc ....F....... 918 341-6977
  Claremore *(G-1579)*
Bear Paw Manufacturing ....G....... 918 637-4775
  Wagoner *(G-11275)*
Bechtels Heavy Metal Works LLC ....G....... 580 251-1412
  Duncan *(G-2089)*
Blastpro Manufacturing Inc ....G....... 877 495-6464
  Oklahoma City *(G-5589)*
▲ Blastpro Manufacturing Inc ....E....... 405 491-6464
  Oklahoma City *(G-5590)*
Braden Filtration LLC ....G....... 918 283-4818
  Tulsa *(G-9326)*
Clear Edge Filtration Inc ....D....... 800 637-6206
  Tulsa *(G-9448)*
▲ Clear Edge Filtration Inc ....D....... 918 984-6000
  Tulsa *(G-9447)*
▲ Coyote Enterprises Inc ....F....... 918 486-8411
  Coweta *(G-1875)*
Crematory Manufacturing & Svc ....E....... 918 446-1475
  Tulsa *(G-9000)*
Crown Midstream LLC ....G....... 405 753-1955
  Oklahoma City *(G-5862)*
D & J Filter Ltd Liability Co ....G....... 405 376-5343
  Oklahoma City *(G-5886)*
Disa Holding Corp ....D....... 405 382-6900
  Seminole *(G-8369)*
Ect Services Inc ....G....... 918 691-9320
  Sand Springs *(G-8181)*
Efdyn Incorporated ....G....... 918 838-1170
  Tulsa *(G-9647)*
Evoqua Water Technologies LLC ....C....... 978 614-7233
  Tulsa *(G-9712)*
◆ Facet (oklahoma) LLC ....E....... 918 272-8700
  Tulsa *(G-9725)*
Facet (oklahoma) LLC ....C....... 918 696-3161
  Stilwell *(G-8790)*
Filter Supply and Recycling ....G....... 918 663-3143
  Tulsa *(G-9742)*
Filter Wings Corporation ....G....... 405 258-3183
  Wellston *(G-11470)*
Firetech Automatic Sprinklers ....G....... 918 633-3773
  Henryetta *(G-3506)*
Firstline Filters LLC ....G....... 918 660-8772
  Tulsa *(G-9748)*
◆ Fki Industries Inc ....G....... 918 834-4611
  Tulsa *(G-9752)*
Flanders Corporation ....G....... 580 223-1853
  Ardmore *(G-290)*
Fluid Art Technology LLC ....G....... 405 843-2009
  Oklahoma City *(G-6094)*
G T Bynum Company ....G....... 918 587-9118
  Tulsa *(G-9794)*
▲ Global Filter LLC ....F....... 319 743-0110
  Tulsa *(G-9830)*
Hipower Systems Oklahoma LLC ....G....... 918 512-6321
  Tulsa *(G-9013)*
▲ Husky Portable Containment Co ......E....... 918 333-2000
  Bartlesville *(G-496)*
Invictus Engrg Cnstr Svcs ....G....... 405 701-5622
  Norman *(G-5037)*
J&K Machining Inc ....G....... 918 243-7936
  Cleveland *(G-1725)*
Kaiser Marketing Northeast LLC ....G....... 918 494-0000
  Tulsa *(G-10073)*
Knowles Performance Engines ....G....... 580 821-4825
  Dill City *(G-2036)*
Lake Ice LLC ....G....... 405 882-7227
  Jones *(G-3750)*
Lobito Technology Group Inc ....F....... 918 619-9885
  Tulsa *(G-10175)*
Midwesco Industries Inc ....G....... 918 858-4200
  Tulsa *(G-10266)*
Mosley ....G....... 918 407-6519
  Broken Arrow *(G-982)*
▲ N A Blastrac Inc ....D....... 405 478-3440
  Oklahoma City *(G-6645)*
◆ Nmw Inc ....G....... 918 273-2204
  Nowata *(G-5223)*
OK Fire LLC ....G....... 918 424-1808
  McAlester *(G-4325)*
Penn Machine Inc ....F....... 405 789-0084
  Oklahoma City *(G-6824)*

Robinson Manufacturing Co ....G....... 918 251-0353
  Broken Arrow *(G-1036)*
Royal Filter Manufacturing Co ....E....... 405 224-0229
  Chickasha *(G-1503)*
Russells Machine and Fab LLC ....G....... 405 742-6818
  Stillwater *(G-8750)*
Samurai Equipment LLC ....F....... 918 878-7715
  Tulsa *(G-10701)*
Smico Manufacturing Co Inc ....E....... 405 946-1461
  Oklahoma City *(G-7153)*
Travis Quality Pdts & Sls Inc ....G....... 918 251-0115
  Broken Arrow *(G-1082)*
Turnair Fab LLC ....G....... 918 379-0796
  Catoosa *(G-1360)*
Usfilter ....G....... 405 359-7441
  Edmond *(G-2663)*
▲ Vaculift Incorporated ....D....... 918 438-9875
  Tulsa *(G-11063)*
Versum Materials Us LLC ....E....... 918 379-7101
  Catoosa *(G-1363)*
Wyatts Oil Corp ....G....... 918 287-4285
  Pawhuska *(G-7698)*

3571 Electronic Computers

ABB Inc ....C....... 918 338-4888
  Bartlesville *(G-444)*
Alpha Research & Tech Inc ....G....... 405 733-1919
  Oklahoma City *(G-5425)*
Apple Street Inc ....G....... 918 367-9898
  Bristow *(G-764)*
CIS Investors LLC ....G....... 405 370-5812
  Oklahoma City *(G-5768)*
◆ Computer Dlers Rcyclers Globl ....E....... 405 749-7989
  Oklahoma City *(G-5818)*
Eves Apple ....G....... 512 970-9016
  Norman *(G-4995)*
Innovative Technology Ltd ....F....... 580 243-1559
  Elk City *(G-2827)*
Johnny Apple Seed Store ....G....... 918 304-2055
  Okmulgee *(G-7510)*
Mc Connells Systems ....G....... 918 322-5426
  Glenpool *(G-3238)*
New X Drives Inc ....F....... 918 850-4463
  Tulsa *(G-10338)*
Oracle America Inc ....G....... 918 587-9016
  Tulsa *(G-10434)*
Stephens Scheduling Svcs Inc ....G....... 918 630-1614
  Tulsa *(G-10847)*
Visuals Tech Solutions LLC ....G....... 913 526-1775
  Edmond *(G-2674)*

3572 Computer Storage Devices

Barron and Stevenson EMC LLC ....G....... 918 804-8440
  Tulsa *(G-9268)*
Business Records Storage LLC ....E....... 405 232-7867
  Oklahoma City *(G-5649)*
EMC ....G....... 918 583-6363
  Tulsa *(G-9666)*
EMC ....G....... 405 320-5675
  Chickasha *(G-1456)*
EMC Beauty LLC ....G....... 316 655-8839
  Oklahoma City *(G-6030)*
EMC Law Pllc ....G....... 832 560-6280
  Tulsa *(G-9667)*
EMC Services LLC ....G....... 405 596-0050
  Oklahoma City *(G-6031)*
▲ Hitachi Computer Pdts Amer Inc .....B....... 405 360-5500
  Norman *(G-5024)*
Quantum Builds Company ....G....... 727 504-1628
  Oklahoma City *(G-6939)*
Seagate Technology LLC ....B....... 405 324-3000
  Oklahoma City *(G-7102)*
Seagate Technology LLC ....A....... 800 732-4283
  Oklahoma City *(G-7103)*
Vault Management Inc ....G....... 918 258-7782
  Broken Arrow *(G-1090)*

3575 Computer Terminals

Gorilla Systems Inc ....G....... 918 227-0230
  Sapulpa *(G-8275)*

3577 Computer Peripheral Eqpt, NEC

American Laser Inc ....G....... 918 234-9700
  Tulsa *(G-9168)*
Aventura Technologies Inc ....F....... 631 300-4000
  Oklahoma City *(G-5495)*
Black Box Network Services ....G....... 800 949-4039
  Tulsa *(G-9301)*

Cisco Systems Inc ....A....... 999 505-5901
  Tulsa *(G-9431)*
Colorcomm ....G....... 918 398-7777
  Tulsa *(G-9470)*
▲ Hitachi Computer Pdts Amer Inc .....B....... 405 360-5500
  Norman *(G-5024)*
Kirklind Global Inc ....G....... 580 618-2527
  El Reno *(G-2735)*
Marvel Photo Inc ....G....... 918 836-0741
  Tulsa *(G-10218)*
News OK LLC ....F....... 405 475-4000
  Oklahoma City *(G-6671)*
Onyx Imaging Corporation ....G....... 918 627-6611
  Tulsa *(G-10431)*
Order-Matic Electronics Corp ....C....... 405 672-1487
  Oklahoma City *(G-6781)*
Phx & Co LLC ....G....... 918 747-9770
  Tulsa *(G-10511)*
Poquita Circle LLC ....G....... 918 794-0750
  Tulsa *(G-10533)*
Radiotronix Inc ....E....... 405 794-7730
  Edmond *(G-2584)*
Scan To ....G....... 405 413-8015
  Yukon *(G-11776)*
Secureagent Software Inc ....E....... 918 971-1600
  Tulsa *(G-10722)*
Special Service Systems Inc ....E....... 918 582-7777
  Tulsa *(G-10816)*
Spor Enterprises Inc ....G....... 918 745-9888
  Oklahoma City *(G-7187)*
Tulsa Toner Technology ....G....... 918 838-0323
  Tulsa *(G-11009)*

3578 Calculating & Accounting Eqpt

Campaign Technologies Professi ....G....... 405 286-2686
  Oklahoma City *(G-5681)*
Cummins - Allison Corp ....F....... 405 321-1411
  Norman *(G-4972)*
Gibsons Treasures ....G....... 405 835-1109
  Oklahoma City *(G-6152)*
Integrated Payment Svcs LLC ....G....... 918 492-7094
  Tulsa *(G-9995)*
Metavante Holdings LLC ....G....... 800 554-8095
  Oklahoma City *(G-6576)*
Order-Matic Electronics Corp ....C....... 405 672-1487
  Oklahoma City *(G-6781)*
Shen Te Enterprises Inc ....E....... 918 505-7711
  Tulsa *(G-10742)*
Special Service Systems Inc ....E....... 918 582-7777
  Tulsa *(G-10816)*
Superior Federal Bank ....G....... 405 224-1021
  Chickasha *(G-1514)*
Transfund ....G....... 918 588-6707
  Tulsa *(G-10969)*

3579 Office Machines, NEC

Backup Fortress LLC ....G....... 405 314-2436
  Yukon *(G-11694)*
Clock Shop Inc ....G....... 918 583-5835
  Tulsa *(G-9455)*
Enhanced Printing Products Inc ....G....... 918 585-1991
  Tulsa *(G-9688)*
Pitney Bowes Inc ....G....... 918 779-7552
  Tulsa *(G-10521)*
Pitney Bowes Inc ....G....... 405 341-3279
  Edmond *(G-2572)*
Raf Midsouth Technologies LLC ....F....... 918 352-8300
  Tulsa *(G-10609)*

3581 Automatic Vending Machines

Anytime Propane LLC ....F....... 405 417-0222
  Chickasha *(G-1430)*
Crankshaft Service Company ....G....... 405 685-7553
  Oklahoma City *(G-5851)*
Ms Enterprises ....G....... 918 627-1824
  Tulsa *(G-10308)*

3582 Commercial Laundry, Dry Clean & Pressing Mchs

Duffy Dry Clean City LLC ....G....... 405 743-0730
  Stillwater *(G-8678)*
Hospital Linen Services LLC ....G....... 405 473-0422
  Oklahoma City *(G-6265)*

3585 Air Conditioning & Heating Eqpt

A/C Matthews & Refrigeration ....G....... 918 465-6337
  Red Oak *(G-8073)*
A1 Heat and Air ....G....... 580 832-2605
  Cordell *(G-1852)*

*Employee Codes: A=Over 500 employees, B=251-500
C=101-250, D=51-100, E=20-50, F=10-19, G=1-9*

SIC SECTION | 35 INDUSTRIAL AND COMMERCIAL MACHINERY AND COMPUTER EQUIPMENT

3599 Machinery & Eqpt, Indl & Commercial, NEC

2012 H & H Manufacturing Inc G 918 838-0744
Tulsa *(G-9056)*
3d Farms & Machine L L C G 580 772-5543
Weatherford *(G-11386)*
A & E Frame Mfg Inc G 918 251-3343
Broken Arrow *(G-808)*
A & M Manufacturing Co G 918 835-2272
Tulsa *(G-9062)*
A and E Manufacturing Co F 918 583-7184
Tulsa *(G-9065)*
A W Brueggemann Company Inc F 580 237-3857
Enid *(G-2900)*
A W Pool Inc G 580 323-3454
Clinton *(G-1735)*
A-1 Machine Shop Inc G 918 665-0706
Tulsa *(G-9072)*
A-1 Machine Works Inc G 918 367-2788
Bristow *(G-762)*
Aaron Willis President G 405 219-9411
Edmond *(G-2287)*
Aberdeen Dynamics LLC G 918 794-0042
Tulsa *(G-9081)*
Accent Machine Inc G 918 246-9695
Sand Springs *(G-8156)*
Accu-Turn Machine LLC G 580 704-8876
Lawton *(G-3883)*
Accurate Machine & Maintenance G 918 585-1125
Tulsa *(G-9089)*
Aceco Valve Inc E 918 827-3669
Mounds *(G-4608)*
◆ **Action Machine Inc** E 918 248-6847
Tulsa *(G-8987)*
Action Machine Shop G 918 245-8308
Sand Springs *(G-8157)*
Advanced Machining & Fabg E 918 664-5410
Owasso *(G-7541)*
Advanced McHning Solutions LLC G 405 208-8737
Oklahoma City *(G-5384)*
Aero Components Inc E 405 631-6644
Oklahoma City *(G-5390)*
Aero Dynamics F 918 258-0290
Broken Arrow *(G-818)*
Affordable Leak Detection G 405 594-2341
Oklahoma City *(G-5396)*
Agt Machining Co Inc G 580 774-8359
Weatherford *(G-11388)*
Aircraft Cylinders Amer Iinc E 918 582-1785
Tulsa *(G-9124)*
Airico Inc G 918 836-2675
Tulsa *(G-9130)*
Alliance Machine Service Inc G 918 836-5588
Tulsa *(G-9144)*
Alpha Machining & Mfg Inc F 918 438-2755
Tulsa *(G-9155)*
American Machine & Tool Co G 405 794-9820
Wewoka *(G-11497)*
American Machining Company LLC G 918 885-6194
Hominy *(G-3574)*
American McHning Solutions LLC G 405 606-7038
Oklahoma City *(G-5439)*
American Mfg Co of Okla E 918 446-1968
Tulsa *(G-9170)*
Amron Enterprises LLC F 918 224-9222
Sapulpa *(G-8249)*
AMS Machining Specialists LLC G 918 610-2570
Tulsa *(G-9182)*
Anson Desimone G 610 433-1299
Hinton *(G-3522)*
Apache Machine Co Inc G 918 834-0022
Tulsa *(G-9196)*
Apollo Engineering Company G 918 251-6780
Broken Arrow *(G-830)*
Applied Indus Machining Inc D 405 672-2222
Oklahoma City *(G-5456)*
Applied Indus Machining LLC C 405 672-2222
Oklahoma City *(G-5457)*
Atlas Instrument & Mfg Co G 918 371-1976
Collinsville *(G-1800)*
Auto-Turn Manufacturing Inc E 918 451-4511
Broken Arrow *(G-1111)*
Automated Machining Co Inc F 918 723-3503
Westville *(G-11480)*
Automatic & Auto Machining Inc G 918 775-9770
Sallisaw *(G-8138)*
Automted McHning Solutions LLC G 405 697-6234
Mustang *(G-4762)*
B & B Machine G 918 686-9900
Muskogee *(G-4651)*
B & B Machine of Norman Inc F 405 799-9878
Norman *(G-4924)*
B & C Machine Company Inc F 405 787-8862
Oklahoma City *(G-5500)*
B & D Eagle Machine Shop F 405 787-3232
Oklahoma City *(G-5501)*
B T Machine Inc E 918 834-3340
Tulsa *(G-9246)*
B&M Machine Works LLC G 918 583-4067
Tulsa *(G-9249)*
Baity Screw Products Inc E 405 222-1520
Chickasha *(G-1439)*
Barker Machine Shop G 405 828-4683
Dover *(G-2038)*
Barnetts G 405 390-3026
Choctaw *(G-1529)*
Baskins Machined Products LLC G 918 284-4298
Collinsville *(G-1802)*
Bauman Machine Inc E 405 745-3484
Oklahoma City *(G-5531)*
Bb Machine & Supply Inc G 580 237-8686
Enid *(G-2915)*
Benchmark Completions LLC F 405 691-5659
Oklahoma City *(G-5550)*
Berry Machine & Tool Company G 580 536-4382
Lawton *(G-3897)*
Best Mold Technology LLC G 405 659-1991
Cache *(G-1224)*
BF Machine Shop Inc G 580 255-6119
Duncan *(G-2090)*
BF Machines Shop Inc F 580 255-5899
Duncan *(G-2091)*
Bobby K Birdwell G 580 799-2357
Burns Flat *(G-1218)*
Boyds Auto Parts & Machine F 405 329-3855
Norman *(G-4940)*
Bradley Machine & Design L L C F 405 224-2223
Chickasha *(G-1443)*
Bradley Welding & Machine G 580 223-2250
Ardmore *(G-260)*
Brady Welding & Machine Shop G 405 262-3665
El Reno *(G-2703)*
Brady Welding & Machine Shop D 580 229-1168
Healdton *(G-3408)*
▲ **Branchcomb Inc** E 918 224-8094
Sapulpa *(G-8259)*
Brenda K Toupin G 918 527-6948
Tulsa *(G-9335)*
Burgess Tool & Cutter Grinding G 580 765-0954
Ponca City *(G-7803)*
Burrow Tool G 580 240-1045
Temple *(G-8932)*
Bynum & Company Inc F 580 265-7747
Stonewall *(G-8798)*
C & C Machine Inc G 918 342-1950
Claremore *(G-1601)*
C & D Manufacturing Co Inc G 918 251-8535
Broken Arrow *(G-861)*
C & M Precision Inc F 405 691-0984
Oklahoma City *(G-5657)*
C & P Manufacturing Inc F 918 773-5060
Sallisaw *(G-8140)*
Canfield Machine Inc G 580 673-2185
Fox *(G-3190)*
Casady N Company LLC G 405 528-4299
Oklahoma City *(G-5706)*
▼ **Centerline Inc** E 580 762-5451
Ponca City *(G-7805)*
Central Machine & Tool Company B 580 237-4033
Enid *(G-2927)*
Central Parts & Machine Inc G 405 631-5460
Oklahoma City *(G-5725)*
Certified Machine & Design Inc G 405 672-9607
Oklahoma City *(G-5731)*
Chase Industries Inc G 816 850-5323
Okemah *(G-5266)*
Checos Machine Shop & General G 405 680-0900
Oklahoma City *(G-5746)*
Cherokee Ntion Armred Sltons L E 918 696-3151
Tulsa *(G-9415)*
Chickasha Manufacturing Co Inc E 405 224-0229
Chickasha *(G-1449)*
Choctaw Nation of Oklahoma D 580 326-8365
Hugo *(G-3610)*
Chromium Plating Company E 918 583-4118
Tulsa *(G-9422)*
Cimarron Aerospace LLC G 405 260-0990
Guthrie *(G-3308)*
Cimarron Machine Inc G 972 658-7051
Bokchito *(G-750)*
Cimarron Machine Services Inc E 918 835-3333
Tulsa *(G-9428)*
▼ **Cimarron Machine Works Inc** G 405 375-6452
Kingfisher *(G-3791)*
City Machine Shop G 580 795-2282
Madill *(G-4145)*
CJ Hill Inc E 918 251-1164
Broken Arrow *(G-869)*
Claco Enterprises G 918 343-0276
Claremore *(G-1607)*
Cline Machine Inc E 918 587-0126
Tulsa *(G-9453)*
Clint Dodson Enterprises LLC G 580 931-9410
Durant *(G-2216)*
Cmd Inc G 405 672-9607
Oklahoma City *(G-5791)*
Conley Machine Inc G 918 770-3234
Sapulpa *(G-8261)*
Contech Mfg Inc G 918 341-6232
Claremore *(G-1610)*
Cox Machine and Tool G 405 681-1445
Oklahoma City *(G-5848)*
Curing System Components Inc F 405 381-9794
Tuttle *(G-11193)*
D & G Machine G 918 486-3501
Coweta *(G-1878)*
D & V Manufacturing Inc F 918 245-7858
Sand Springs *(G-8176)*
▲ **D I V C O Inc** E 918 836-9101
Tulsa *(G-9538)*
Dads Machine & Custom Welding G 580 470-8334
Duncan *(G-2103)*
Damar Manufacturing Co Inc E 918 445-2445
Tulsa *(G-9549)*
Design & Mfg Inc G 918 576-6659
Tulsa *(G-9575)*
Dixon & Sons Inc G 918 256-7455
Vinita *(G-11253)*
DK Machine Inc G 918 251-1034
Broken Arrow *(G-890)*
Duncan Machine Products Inc E 580 467-6784
Duncan *(G-2110)*
Dunsworth Machine G 580 233-5812
Enid *(G-2947)*
Dww Inc G 580 255-7886
Duncan *(G-2114)*
Dyna-Turn of Oklahoma Inc F 580 243-1291
Elk City *(G-2806)*
▼ **Eastpointe Industries Inc** E 918 683-2169
Muskogee *(G-4670)*
Eddie Johnsons Wldg & Mch Co F 580 856-3418
Ratliff City *(G-8051)*
Elastomer Specialties Inc F 918 485-0276
Wagoner *(G-11281)*
Element Design & Fabrication G 720 372-1940
Edmond *(G-2410)*
Elite Polishing Co G 405 371-5780
Blanchard *(G-714)*
Elliott Precision Products Inc E 918 234-4001
Tulsa *(G-9661)*
Elroy Machine Inc G 580 658-6725
Marlow *(G-4231)*
Emp Incorporated G 918 756-5767
Okmulgee *(G-7501)*
EMR Machine G 405 361-7991
Noble *(G-4879)*
Ernst Valve & Fittings G 918 446-0313
Tulsa *(G-9003)*
Eversharp Tool Inc F 918 250-9400
Tulsa *(G-9711)*
F & F Machine Shop Inc G 405 680-0900
Oklahoma City *(G-6066)*
Fabrication Solutions LLC F 918 398-7162
Tulsa *(G-9723)*
Fineline Manufacturing LLC F 918 245-0900
Sand Springs *(G-8184)*
Finish Line Machining LLC G 918 258-2944
Broken Arrow *(G-908)*
Fisher Products LLC D 918 582-2204
Tulsa *(G-9750)*
Floyds Machine Shop G 918 256-8440
Vinita *(G-11258)*
Forester LLC G 918 835-6533
Tulsa *(G-9765)*
Foster Machine Shop G 918 438-4001
Tulsa *(G-9766)*
Frazier Mfg Co F 918 241-9110
Sand Springs *(G-8186)*
Freedom Manufacturing LLC G 918 283-1520
Claremore *(G-1623)*

S I C

Employee Codes: A=Over 500 employees, B=251-500
C=101-250, D=51-100, E=20-50, F=10-19, G=1-9

2020 Oklahoma Directory
of Manufacturers & Processors

485

SIC SECTION
13 OIL AND GAS EXTRACTION

M&M Hot Oil Service LLC ....G..... 580 651-1746
  Guymon *(G-3355)*
M-I LLC ....G..... 580 225-2482
  Elk City *(G-2844)*
M-I LLC ....E..... 405 224-4170
  Chickasha *(G-1482)*
Mac Oil & Gas ....G..... 405 375-5619
  Kingfisher *(G-3808)*
Mackellar Inc ....F..... 405 433-2658
  Cashion *(G-1289)*
Mackellar Services Inc ....G..... 405 848-2877
  Oklahoma City *(G-6515)*
Mackellar Services Inc ....G..... 580 237-9383
  Enid *(G-3004)*
Magnum Diversified Services ......F..... 405 391-9653
  Newalla *(G-4813)*
Magnum Energy Inc ....G..... 405 360-2784
  Norman *(G-5063)*
Malone Contract Pumping Inc .....G..... 918 767-2450
  Pawnee *(G-7706)*
Mammoth Energy Partners LLC ...F..... 405 265-4600
  Oklahoma City *(G-6518)*
Mammoth Energy Services Inc ....F..... 405 608-6007
  Oklahoma City *(G-6519)*
Manford Oilfield Services LLC .....G..... 918 424-3280
  McAlester *(G-4314)*
Mark A Holkum LLC ....G..... 405 735-3463
  Oklahoma City *(G-5305)*
Marsau ....G..... 580 432-5000
  Foster *(G-3186)*
Marsau Enterprises Inc ....A..... 580 233-3910
  Enid *(G-3007)*
Martin Tank Trck Csing Pulling ....F..... 918 225-2388
  Cushing *(G-1944)*
Martin-Decker Totco Inc ....G..... 580 225-8980
  Elk City *(G-2847)*
Martindale Consultants Inc ....E..... 405 728-3003
  Oklahoma City *(G-6534)*
Martinez Fencing Construction ...F..... 580 309-2046
  Clinton *(G-1758)*
Mary K Rose Inc ....G..... 405 324-5612
  Yukon *(G-11749)*
Mason Pipe & Supply Company ....G..... 405 942-6926
  Oklahoma City *(G-6536)*
Master Movers Incorporated ....G..... 918 408-1490
  Owasso *(G-7590)*
McAdams Energy LLC ....G..... 918 758-0308
  Okmulgee *(G-7515)*
McCabe Roustabout Service ....G..... 918 534-3131
  Dewey *(G-2028)*
McCormick & Associates LLC .....G..... 405 747-9991
  Stillwater *(G-8724)*
McDonald Safety Anchor Inc ....G..... 405 574-4151
  Chickasha *(G-1483)*
McIntyre Transports Inc ....E..... 580 526-3121
  Erick *(G-3089)*
McWI Inc ....G..... 405 360-2277
  Norman *(G-5068)*
ME Oil Co ....G..... 405 232-9541
  Oklahoma City *(G-6552)*
Meagher Energy Advisors Inc .....F..... 918 481-5900
  Tulsa *(G-10235)*
Mels Construction Inc ....G..... 405 853-4621
  Hennessey *(G-3477)*
Metco Inc ....G..... 580 233-6717
  Enid *(G-3012)*
Metzger Oil Tools Inc ....G..... 918 885-2456
  Hominy *(G-3592)*
Michael S Azlin ....G..... 405 257-3581
  Wewoka *(G-11505)*
Mid Continent Well Log Svcs ......G..... 405 360-7333
  Norman *(G-5075)*
Mid-Central Energy Svcs LLC .....D..... 405 815-4041
  Oklahoma City *(G-6591)*
Mid-States Oilfield Mch LLC ....E..... 405 605-5656
  Oklahoma City *(G-6593)*
Midcentral Completion Services ..G..... 405 445-5979
  El Reno *(G-2738)*
Midway Machine & Welding LLC ...G..... 918 968-3316
  Stroud *(G-8812)*
Midway Services LLC ....G..... 405 820-8850
  Edmond *(G-2518)*
Midwest Logging & Perforating ...G..... 405 382-4200
  Seminole *(G-8384)*
Mikes Trucking Co ....E..... 580 256-5063
  Woodward *(G-11612)*
Miller Bros Wldg & Roustabout ...G..... 918 968-1611
  Stroud *(G-8813)*
Miller Pump Systems Inc ....G..... 918 455-4556
  Broken Arrow *(G-977)*

Mills Well Service Inc ....D..... 405 382-4107
  Seminole *(G-8385)*
Misson Fluid King Oil Field ....G..... 405 670-8771
  Oklahoma City *(G-6619)*
Mitchells Tank Truck Service ......G..... 580 229-1880
  Healdton *(G-3419)*
Mlb Consulting LLC ....G..... 405 285-8559
  Edmond *(G-2520)*
Mlb Consulting LLC ....G..... 580 225-2717
  Elk City *(G-2849)*
Mlb Consulting LLC ....D..... 580 504-8810
  Ardmore *(G-333)*
Moes Portable Steam Co Inc ......G..... 580 432-5467
  Foster *(G-3187)*
Momentum Completion ....G..... 918 364-9444
  Tulsa *(G-10297)*
Monroe Natural Gas Inc ....G..... 405 321-5647
  Norman *(G-5079)*
Mooney Oilfield Services LLC ......G..... 580 660-5203
  Weatherford *(G-11429)*
Moore Contract Pumping ....G..... 918 372-4645
  Ripley *(G-8102)*
Moran Equipment ....G..... 405 262-1422
  El Reno *(G-2739)*
Moran Equipment LLC ....E..... 580 225-2575
  Elk City *(G-2850)*
Morgan Well Service Inc ....E..... 405 567-2288
  Prague *(G-7930)*
Morrill & Assoc Inc ....G..... 918 481-1055
  Tulsa *(G-10304)*
Morris Richardson ....G..... 918 427-7323
  Muldrow *(G-4634)*
Morton Leases Inc ....G..... 918 733-2331
  Morris *(G-4601)*
MRW Technologies Inc ....E..... 918 827-6030
  Glenpool *(G-3239)*
Ms 3 Oil & Gas LLC ....G..... 580 465-7354
  Wilson *(G-11539)*
MSI Inspection Service LLC ....G..... 405 265-2121
  Oklahoma City *(G-6632)*
Mt Percussion Drilling LLC ....G..... 918 232-5472
  Tulsa *(G-10310)*
Mud Haulers LLC ....G..... 580 338-3830
  Guymon *(G-3357)*
Mud Mixers LLC ....F..... 580 243-7826
  Elk City *(G-2851)*
Mueggs Hot Shot Service LLC ....G..... 405 368-8362
  Okarche *(G-5246)*
Munoz Oilfield Services LLC ....G..... 580 799-5857
  Elk City *(G-2852)*
Muras Energy Inc ....F..... 405 751-0442
  Edmond *(G-2523)*
Mustang Extreme Environmental ..F..... 405 681-1800
  Oklahoma City *(G-6639)*
Mustang Fuel Corporation ....G..... 580 446-5552
  Enid *(G-3017)*
Mv Pipeline Company ....G..... 918 689-5600
  Eufaula *(G-3105)*
Mwd Services LLC ....G..... 918 698-6109
  Owasso *(G-7595)*
Nabors Completion Prod Svcs Co ..E..... 580 323-0058
  Clinton *(G-1760)*
Nabors Drilling Tech USA Inc .....C..... 580 243-4000
  Elk City *(G-2853)*
Nabors Well Services Ltd ....E..... 405 262-6262
  El Reno *(G-2742)*
Nafta Mud Inc ....G..... 405 751-6261
  Oklahoma City *(G-6648)*
Nafta Mud LLC ....G..... 405 751-6261
  Oklahoma City *(G-6649)*
Nance Solutions Inc ....G..... 918 804-9301
  Mustang *(G-4785)*
National Oilwell Varco Inc ....D..... 580 251-6900
  Duncan *(G-2158)*
National Oilwell Varco Inc ....E..... 580 225-4136
  Elk City *(G-2855)*
New Tongs ....G..... 580 335-3030
  Frederick *(G-3197)*
Newpark Drilling Fluids LLC ....C..... 580 323-1612
  Clinton *(G-1761)*
Nexstreem Reclaim Plant ....G..... 580 657-4580
  Wilson *(G-11540)*
Nextier Cmpltion Solutions Inc ....E..... 580 772-3100
  Weatherford *(G-11430)*
Nine Energy Service ....G..... 405 601-5336
  Oklahoma City *(G-6682)*
Nitro Lift Holdings LLC ....D..... 405 620-3274
  Mill Creek *(G-4470)*
Norman Moore ....G..... 405 941-3220
  Sasakwa *(G-8333)*

North Star Well Services Inc ......D..... 580 256-5644
  Woodward *(G-11615)*
Northwest Measurement ....G..... 580 822-3528
  Okeene *(G-5260)*
Nov Downhole ....G..... 405 688-5000
  Oklahoma City *(G-6698)*
Nov Tuboscope Inc ....G..... 405 677-8889
  Oklahoma City *(G-6699)*
NRG Wireline LLC ....F..... 918 768-3210
  Kinta *(G-3835)*
Nsi Fracturing LLC ....G..... 918 496-2072
  Tulsa *(G-10364)*
Nubs Well Servicing Inc ....F..... 580 856-3887
  Ratliff City *(G-8058)*
Nutech Energy Alliance Ltd ....G..... 405 388-4236
  Oklahoma City *(G-5309)*
O K Plunger Service ....G..... 918 352-4269
  Drumright *(G-2068)*
O K Tank Trucks Inc ....F..... 918 396-3043
  Skiatook *(G-8562)*
Occuscreen Associates LLC ....G..... 918 292-8865
  Tulsa *(G-10375)*
Ogci Building Fund LLC ....G..... 918 828-2500
  Tulsa *(G-10381)*
Ohana Oil & Gas LLC ....G..... 405 341-8822
  Edmond *(G-2545)*
Oil & Gas Consultants Intl Inc ....E..... 918 828-2500
  Tulsa *(G-10381)*
Oil & Gas Optimization Special ...G..... 432 685-0029
  Tulsa *(G-10383)*
Oil States Industries Inc ....D..... 405 671-2000
  Oklahoma City *(G-6721)*
Oil States Industries Inc ....G..... 918 250-0828
  Tulsa *(G-10387)*
Oil Tools Rentals ....F..... 580 242-1140
  Enid *(G-3024)*
Oil Well Cementers Inc ....F..... 580 229-1776
  Healdton *(G-3420)*
Oilab Inc ....G..... 405 528-8378
  Oklahoma City *(G-6723)*
Oilfield Dstrbtons Spclsts LLC ....G..... 580 237-1237
  Enid *(G-3025)*
Oilfield Lease Maintenance ....G..... 405 348-1562
  Edmond *(G-2546)*
Oilfield Technical Svcs LLC ....G..... 405 603-4288
  Oklahoma City *(G-6724)*
OK Contract Services LLC ....G..... 918 352-5369
  Braman *(G-761)*
Okla Casing Co ....G..... 580 432-5311
  Foster *(G-3188)*
Oklahoma Cellulose Inc ....G..... 918 706-5279
  Cleveland *(G-1730)*
Oklahoma Cementing Cushing LLC ..G..... 918 225-0688
  Cushing *(G-1949)*
Oklahoma Energy Source LLC ....G..... 918 307-8142
  Tulsa *(G-10400)*
Oklahoma Hot Shot Service ....G..... 405 605-0464
  Oklahoma City *(G-6752)*
Oklahoma Prime Energy LLC .....G..... 580 226-2373
  Oklahoma City *(G-338)*
Oklahoma Sub Surfc Pump & Sup ..G..... 405 382-7311
  Seminole *(G-8392)*
On The Go Hot Shot Svcs LLC ....G..... 405 471-2055
  Edmond *(G-2557)*
One Oaks Field Service ....D..... 580 816-4500
  Weatherford *(G-11431)*
Onsite Oil Tools Inc ....G..... 580 856-3367
  Ratliff City *(G-8060)*
Orca Operating Company LLC ...G..... 918 587-1312
  Tulsa *(G-10437)*
Osage Land Company ....F..... 405 946-8402
  Oklahoma City *(G-6784)*
Osage Wireline Service Inc ....G..... 918 358-5155
  Cleveland *(G-1731)*
Out N Back Hot Shot LLC ....G..... 405 201-3576
  Yukon *(G-11762)*
Outlaw Oilfield Supply LLC ....E..... 580 526-3792
  Erick *(G-3091)*
Outsource Group LLC ....G..... 918 307-0110
  Tulsa *(G-10446)*
Owen Oil Tools LP ....G..... 405 495-4441
  Oklahoma City *(G-6789)*
P & H Construction Inc ....G..... 405 257-3307
  Wewoka *(G-11506)*
P /Masters C Inc ....E..... 405 293-9777
  Guthrie *(G-3332)*
PAK Oilfield Services LLC ....G..... 580 504-7049
  Ardmore *(G-343)*
Panhandle Construction Svcs .....F..... 580 338-7667
  Guymon *(G-3359)*

Panhandle Corrosion LLC G 580 651-3208
Goodwell *(G-3249)*
Panhandle Oilfield Service Com D 405 608-5330
Oklahoma City *(G-6799)*
Panthera Roustabout Svcs LLC G 405 826-8466
Jones *(G-3751)*
Parallel Energy LP E 918 712-7008
Tulsa *(G-10466)*
Park Energy Services LLC G 918 617-4350
Stigler *(G-8638)*
Parker Energy Services Co G 918 626-4982
Pocola *(G-7784)*
Parks Oil Tools LLC G 405 485-9515
Blanchard *(G-725)*
Partners Oilfield Services LLC F 580 625-2239
Beaver *(G-543)*
Paschall Land Management G 405 842-1391
Oklahoma City *(G-6806)*
Pat McVicker Oilfield Services G 580 256-1577
Woodward *(G-11616)*
Patrick McVicker G 580 256-1577
Woodward *(G-11617)*
Paul Philp Gchmical Conslt LLC G 405 325-4469
Norman *(G-5111)*
Payrock II LLC G 405 608-8077
Oklahoma City *(G-6814)*
Payzone Completion Svcs LLC D 405 772-7184
Oklahoma City *(G-6815)*
Pcs Ferguson Inc G 580 256-1317
Woodward *(G-11619)*
Peak Oilfield Services G 405 884-2379
Geary *(G-3217)*
Pearl Energy Group LLC G 281 799-7459
Oklahoma City *(G-6818)*
Pearson Pumping Inc G 918 486-2386
Coweta *(G-1893)*
Pecos Pipeline LLC G 918 574-3500
Tulsa *(G-10482)*
Penterra Services LLC G 405 726-2762
Edmond *(G-2566)*
Performance Technologies LLC D 405 262-2441
El Reno *(G-2746)*
Permian Basin Banding G 432 238-1483
Tulsa *(G-10497)*
Peters Oil & Gas G 405 315-6378
Bristow *(G-793)*
Petra Solutions LLC G 316 554-6586
Edmond *(G-2567)*
Petro Source Consultants G 405 751-0474
Oklahoma City *(G-6835)*
Petroleum Elastomers G 405 672-0900
Oklahoma City *(G-6836)*
Petroskills LLC E 918 828-2500
Tulsa *(G-10507)*
Pettitt Wireline Service LLC G 580 234-0550
Enid *(G-3035)*
Pierpont Lamont LLC G 918 592-1705
Tulsa *(G-10514)*
Pinnacle Energy Services LLC G 405 810-9151
Oklahoma City *(G-6849)*
Pinson Well Logging G 405 604-5036
Oklahoma City *(G-6851)*
Pioneer Oilfield Services Inc E 580 243-4000
Elk City *(G-2859)*
Pioneer Wireline Services G 405 601-8755
Oklahoma City *(G-6852)*
Plains Nitrogen LLC G 405 418-8426
Oklahoma City *(G-6855)*
Plains Nitrogen LLC G 918 429-0041
McAlester *(G-4329)*
Pml Exploration Services LLC E 405 606-2701
Oklahoma City *(G-6858)*
Post Construction Company G 580 928-5983
Sayre *(G-8343)*
Powell Services Inc G 580 225-9017
Elk City *(G-2861)*
Power Rig LLC F 580 254-3232
Woodward *(G-11622)*
Precision Wireline LLC F 580 233-0033
Enid *(G-3037)*
Premiere Inc F 405 262-1554
El Reno *(G-2748)*
Presley Operating LLC G 405 526-3000
Oklahoma City *(G-6889)*
Prime Operating Company G 405 947-1091
Oklahoma City *(G-6893)*
Primeenergy Corporation E 405 375-5203
Oklahoma City *(G-6895)*
Priority Artificial Lift G 405 265-1696
Yukon *(G-11768)*
Prism Energy Inc G 918 248-4177
Sapulpa *(G-8302)*
Pro Directional G 405 200-1450
Oklahoma City *(G-6903)*
Pro Ject Chemicals G 580 445-4345
Weatherford *(G-11434)*
Pro Oilfield Services LLC G 405 778-8844
Oklahoma City *(G-6904)*
Pro Technics International G 405 680-5560
Oklahoma City *(G-6907)*
Prochem Energy Services Inc F 580 465-1737
Healdton *(G-3421)*
Production String Services G 580 747-4017
Enid *(G-3039)*
Protechnics Okc Chemical Off G 405 601-3078
Oklahoma City *(G-6918)*
Proven Torque LLC G 780 982-7597
Mooreland *(G-4593)*
Purcell Jack Oil Gas Cnsulting G 580 256-2040
Woodward *(G-11624)*
Qes Pressure Control LLC D 405 605-2700
Oklahoma City *(G-6930)*
Qes Pressure Pumping LLC E 918 338-0808
Bartlesville *(G-519)*
Qes Pressure Pumping LLC G 405 483-8000
Union City *(G-11220)*
Quail Tools LP G 918 994-4695
Tulsa *(G-10588)*
Quality Parts Mfg Co Inc G 918 627-3307
Tulsa *(G-10592)*
Quality Production Co Stigler D 918 967-4383
Stigler *(G-8640)*
Quality Tank Manufacturing G 405 756-1188
Lindsay *(G-4078)*
Quinque Operating Company G 405 840-9876
Oklahoma City *(G-6954)*
R & J Oil and Gas Royalty LLC G 405 562-3334
Edmond *(G-2581)*
R & M Packer Inc G 580 863-2242
Sand Springs *(G-8218)*
R & R Well Service Inc G 580 254-3068
Woodward *(G-11625)*
R & S Swabbing Inc G 405 853-5445
Hennessey *(G-3480)*
R A Bodenhame Assoc Inc G 918 855-1964
Sand Springs *(G-8219)*
R M Swabbing LLC G 405 828-7213
Dover *(G-2043)*
R&R Roustabout Services LLC E 580 883-4647
Ringwood *(G-8090)*
R360 Oklahoma LLC E 405 262-5900
El Reno *(G-2750)*
Rafter H Operating LLC G 405 295-2100
El Reno *(G-2751)*
Rainbo Service Co G 405 677-5353
Oklahoma City *(G-6966)*
Ram Oilfield Services LLC G 918 639-2827
Tulsa *(G-10614)*
Rambler Energy Services Inc E 580 242-7447
Enid *(G-3042)*
Ramco Packers G 405 485-8804
Blanchard *(G-729)*
Rameys Welding & Roustabout G 918 321-3156
Kiefer *(G-3781)*
Ramon & Bennett Roustabout E 580 625-4092
Beaver *(G-546)*
Ranger Oilfield Services Corp E 405 853-7279
Hennessey *(G-3481)*
Ranger Rentals LLC G 580 541-4242
Enid *(G-3043)*
Rauh Oilfield Services Co G 580 796-2128
Lahoma *(G-3860)*
Ray Clour Well Service Inc E 580 856-3905
Ratliff City *(G-8063)*
Ray McClain Inc G 918 363-7350
Sand Springs *(G-8220)*
Rayco Paraffin Service Inc G 405 853-2055
Hennessey *(G-3482)*
Razor Oilfield Services LLC F 405 661-0008
Hinton *(G-3535)*
Reach Wireline G 405 872-8828
Noble *(G-4889)*
Recoil Energy Rental LLC G 405 650-1373
Blanchard *(G-731)*
Recoil Oilfield Services LLC C 405 227-4198
Blanchard *(G-732)*
▲ **Red Bone Services LLC** F 580 225-1200
Elk City *(G-2865)*
Red Bud Resources G 580 227-2592
Fairview *(G-3149)*
Red Dirt Msurement Contrls LLC E 405 422-5085
El Reno *(G-2752)*
Red Hills Hot Shot Inc G 580 225-8686
Sayre *(G-8344)*
Red River Oilfield Svcs LLC G 405 802-4280
Edmond *(G-2590)*
Reddirt Oilfield Services G 580 665-9321
Elk City *(G-2866)*
Redzone Coil Tubing LLC G 580 237-3663
Enid *(G-3046)*
Reeds Power Tongs Inc E 405 382-2762
Seminole *(G-8396)*
Reliance Ofs G 303 317-6565
Tulsa *(G-10637)*
Reliance Oilfield Services LLC E 918 392-9000
Tulsa *(G-10638)*
Reliance Pressure Control G 405 320-5074
Norman *(G-5131)*
Renegade Services G 580 254-2828
Woodward *(G-11628)*
▼ **Reputation Services & Mfg LLC** E 918 437-2077
Tulsa *(G-10643)*
Reserve Management Inc G 918 227-0894
Sapulpa *(G-8307)*
Resource Services Inc G 918 799-6174
Stigler *(G-8642)*
Rex B Benway G 918 366-3626
Bixby *(G-653)*
Rice Welding Inc G 580 776-2584
Meno *(G-4387)*
Richardson Wellsite Services G 918 807-7105
Sapulpa *(G-8308)*
Riddle Construction Co Inc G 580 256-8109
Woodward *(G-11629)*
Rifle Tool Company G 580 856-3030
Ratliff City *(G-8065)*
Rig Chasers LLC E 580 254-3830
Woodward *(G-11630)*
Riley Explration - Permian LLC G 405 415-8699
Oklahoma City *(G-7026)*
Ring Energy Inc G 918 499-3880
Tulsa *(G-10654)*
Riverside Laboratories Inc G 918 585-3064
Tulsa *(G-10657)*
RMH Survey LLC G 918 927-8868
Vinita *(G-11270)*
Robert C Brooks Inc G 405 478-0260
Edmond *(G-2602)*
Robert M Beirute G 918 299-4259
Tulsa *(G-10662)*
Robert M Cobb Oilfield Eqp Sls G 405 840-2902
Oklahoma City *(G-7035)*
Robert S Cargile G 405 732-7915
Oklahoma City *(G-7036)*
Rocking P Sales & Services LLC G 580 530-0028
Hobart *(G-3544)*
Rocky Mtn Mdstream Hldings LLC G 918 573-2000
Tulsa *(G-10668)*
Rocky Top Energy LLC G 918 273-7444
Nowata *(G-5228)*
Rod Pumps Inc G 918 968-4369
Stroud *(G-8816)*
Rolco Energy Services LLC G 580 657-2602
Ardmore *(G-351)*
Rolling Thunder Oilfield G 580 303-4587
Elk City *(G-2869)*
Rose Rock Midstream Field Svcs G 918 524-7700
Tulsa *(G-10672)*
Rpc Inc E 580 225-0843
Elk City *(G-2871)*
Rufnex Oilfield Services LLC G 405 741-8322
Oklahoma City *(G-7061)*
Rugged Roustabout LLC F 918 225-0700
Cushing *(G-1957)*
Russell W Mackey G 580 571-7595
Gage *(G-3211)*
S & H Tank Service Inc E 405 756-3121
Lindsay *(G-4081)*
S & H Tank Service of Oklahoma F 405 756-3121
Lindsay *(G-4082)*
S & T Rose Inc G 580 657-4906
Lone Grove *(G-4120)*
S&S Star Operating LLC G 817 676-1638
Oklahoma City *(G-7068)*
Safety Plus USA LLC E 580 622-4796
Sulphur *(G-8843)*
Sage Natural Resources LLC G 940 539-2225
Tulsa *(G-10689)*
Saint Louis Well Service Inc E 405 289-3314
Saint Louis *(G-8132)*

13 OIL AND GAS EXTRACTION

Samco Anchors .... G 806 435-6870
  Clinton *(G-1767)*
Samhill LLC .... G 580 761-1255
  Tonkawa *(G-8981)*
Sampson Brothers Inc .... G 580 994-2464
  Mooreland *(G-4594)*
Samson Energy Company LLC .... F 918 879-0279
  Tulsa *(G-10692)*
Samson Exploration LLC .... F 918 879-0279
  Tulsa *(G-10693)*
Sanchez Cnstr & Rmdlg LLC .... G 405 443-8324
  Purcell *(G-8018)*
Sand Resources LLC .... G 405 573-0242
  Norman *(G-5137)*
Sander Sporting Gds & Atvs LLC .... G 580 922-4930
  Seiling *(G-8351)*
Sanders Electric .... G 405 377-1691
  Stillwater *(G-8752)*
Santana Inc .... G 405 826-8817
  Oklahoma City *(G-5315)*
Saxet Energy .... G 405 752-9544
  Oklahoma City *(G-7087)*
Schlumberger Technology Corp ..... C 405 789-1515
  Oklahoma City *(G-7089)*
Schlumberger Technology Corp ..... C 405 422-8700
  El Reno *(G-2753)*
Schlumberger Technology Corp ..... G 580 762-2481
  Ponca City *(G-7872)*
Schlumberger Technology Corp ..... E 405 942-0002
  Oklahoma City *(G-7090)*
Schlumberger Technology Corp ..... D 918 661-2000
  Bartlesville *(G-525)*
Schlumberger Technology Corp ..... G 918 584-6651
  Tulsa *(G-10714)*
Schlumberger Technology Corp ..... G 405 306-8244
  Moore *(G-4564)*
Schlumberger Technology Corp ..... G 580 252-3355
  Duncan *(G-2173)*
Schlumberger Technology Corp ..... G 580 774-7557
  Weatherford *(G-11439)*
Schlumberger Technology Corp ..... C 580 225-0730
  El Reno *(G-2754)*
Schlumberger Technology Corp ..... E 918 247-1300
  Kellyville *(G-3767)*
Schlumberger Technology Corp ..... G 405 682-2284
  Yukon *(G-11777)*
Scientific Drilling Intl Inc .... D 405 787-3663
  Yukon *(G-11780)*
Scott Craig Consulting LLC .... G 580 571-4199
  Leedey *(G-4031)*
Scott Greer Sales Inc .... G 405 670-4654
  Oklahoma City *(G-7095)*
Sean Josephson LLC .... G 918 606-9677
  Tulsa *(G-9035)*
Secure Operations Group LLC .... G 918 642-3444
  Fairfax *(G-3121)*
Select Energy Services LLC .... G 405 295-2566
  El Reno *(G-2756)*
Select Energy Services LLC .... D 918 302-0069
  Alderson *(G-128)*
Select Energy Solutions Rw LLC .... G 580 653-2167
  Springer *(G-8625)*
▲ Semgroup Corporation .... B 918 524-8100
  Tulsa *(G-10728)*
Seminole Oilfield Supply .... G 918 623-9900
  Okemah *(G-5275)*
Semmexico LLC .... G 918 524-8100
  Tulsa *(G-10730)*
Sequoia Natural Resources LLC ..... G 405 463-0355
  Oklahoma City *(G-7111)*
Seventy Seven Energy LLC .... D 405 608-7777
  Oklahoma City *(G-7112)*
Seventy Seven Operating LLC .... D 405 608-7777
  Oklahoma City *(G-7113)*
Shafer Kline & Warren Inc .... E 918 499-6000
  Tulsa *(G-10738)*
Sharpshooters Inc .... G 580 332-3109
  Ada *(G-85)*
Shaw Wireline LLC .... G 405 853-2168
  Hennessey *(G-3485)*
Shebester Bechtel Inc .... E 405 577-2700
  Oklahoma City *(G-7117)*
Shebester Bechtel Inc .... D 405 513-4580
  Edmond *(G-2619)*
Shebester Bechtel Inc .... D 580 363-4124
  Blackwell *(G-691)*
Shebester Bechtel Inc .... E 580 242-4876
  Enid *(G-3055)*
Silver City Excavating LLC .... G 405 673-3062
  Newcastle *(G-4840)*

Silver Cliff Resourse .... G 405 842-8698
  Oklahoma City *(G-7140)*
Sims Electric of Oklahoma Inc .... F 580 338-8932
  Guymon *(G-3366)*
Siosi Oil Co .... G 918 492-1400
  Skiatook *(G-8569)*
Sirrah Investments .... G 405 853-4909
  Hennessey *(G-3487)*
Sisk Construction Co .... G 405 375-5318
  Kingfisher *(G-3815)*
Sjl Oil and Gas Inc .... E 405 853-2044
  Hennessey *(G-3488)*
Sjl Well Service LLC .... G 405 853-2044
  Hennessey *(G-3489)*
Skyline Drctonal Drillling LLC .... E 405 429-4050
  Moore *(G-4570)*
SM Oil & Gas Inc .... G 918 629-2151
  Skiatook *(G-8571)*
Smeac Group International LLC ..... G 580 574-4092
  Lawton *(G-3999)*
Smith & Sons Salvage .... G 580 342-6218
  Temple *(G-8935)*
Smith Construction Inc .... E 580 226-2159
  Ardmore *(G-355)*
Smith Energy Services .... G 580 596-2104
  Cherokee *(G-1419)*
Smith International Inc .... E 405 670-7200
  Oklahoma City *(G-7155)*
Smith International Inc .... F 800 654-6461
  Ponca City *(G-7875)*
Smith International Inc .... G 580 252-3355
  Duncan *(G-2178)*
Smith Petroleum LLC .... G 918 638-1301
  Barnsdall *(G-441)*
Smith Pump Supply .... G 405 258-0834
  Chandler *(G-1387)*
Snwellservice Llc .... G 580 430-9346
  Dacoma *(G-1977)*
SOO & Associates .... G 405 397-5072
  Norman *(G-5149)*
Sooner Completions Inc .... E 405 273-4599
  Shawnee *(G-8502)*
Sooner Hot Oil Service .... G 580 762-2586
  Ponca City *(G-7876)*
Sooner Production Services Inc ..... F 580 256-1155
  Woodward *(G-11633)*
Sooner Swabbing Services Inc .... G 580 233-4347
  Enid *(G-3059)*
South Tulsa Hot Shot Svcs LLC ..... G 918 299-7373
  Jenks *(G-3728)*
Southern International Inc .... F 405 943-5288
  Oklahoma City *(G-7171)*
Southern Plains Enrgy Svcs LLC .... G 918 225-3570
  Cushing *(G-1960)*
Southern Plains Enrgy Svcs LLC .... F 580 336-7444
  Perry *(G-7745)*
Southstar Energy Corp .... G 580 223-1553
  Ardmore *(G-356)*
Southwest Oilfield Service .... G 580 302-4069
  Weatherford *(G-11444)*
Sparlin Hot Oil Service Inc .... G 580 795-2513
  Madill *(G-4163)*
Spearhead Services .... G 405 756-8615
  Lindsay *(G-4086)*
Spectrum Tracer Services LLC ...... D 405 470-5566
  Tulsa *(G-10819)*
Spencer Machine Works LLC .... G 580 332-1551
  Ada *(G-91)*
Spencers Contract Pumping LLC ... G 405 238-6363
  Wynnewood *(G-11673)*
Spinnaker Oil Company LLC .... E 405 345-9556
  El Reno *(G-2759)*
Spread Tech LLC .... E 580 994-2506
  Mooreland *(G-4595)*
Spurlock Co Satellite Mapping ...... G 405 495-8628
  Oklahoma City *(G-7189)*
Ss Roustabout Services .... G 405 320-2183
  Ninnekah *(G-4874)*
Stacey Oil Services .... G 918 427-3940
  Roland *(G-8114)*
Stallion Oilfield Services Ltd .... E 580 225-5800
  Elk City *(G-2876)*
Stallion Oilfield Services Ltd .... E 580 225-8990
  Elk City *(G-2877)*
Stallion Oilfield Services Ltd .... D 580 856-3169
  Ratliff City *(G-8067)*
Star Industries .... G 580 977-4576
  Enid *(G-3062)*
Star Pipe Service Inc .... F 405 672-6688
  Oklahoma City *(G-7194)*

Star Well Services Inc .... F 405 222-4606
  Chickasha *(G-1513)*
Stars Stripes Construction .... G 405 387-4847
  Newcastle *(G-4842)*
Statewide Roustabouts Inc .... G 405 262-5934
  El Reno *(G-2760)*
Step Energy Svcs Holdings Ltd ...... E 918 423-4300
  McAlester *(G-4339)*
Step Energy Svcs Holdings Ltd ...... G 918 252-5416
  Tulsa *(G-10845)*
Stephens & Johnson Oper Co .... G 405 619-1866
  Oklahoma City *(G-7202)*
Stephens Oil & Gas Exploration ..... G 214 773-5898
  Oklahoma City *(G-7203)*
Steves Construction Company .... G 580 432-5398
  Elmore City *(G-2897)*
▼ Stinger Wllhead Protection Inc .. F 405 702-6575
  Oklahoma City *(G-7205)*
Stinger Wllhead Protection Inc ...... E 405 684-2940
  Oklahoma City *(G-7206)*
Stockton Transports Inc .... G 580 227-3793
  Fairview *(G-3152)*
Strata View Operating LLC .... G 405 364-1613
  Norman *(G-5161)*
Stride Well Service .... E 580 883-4931
  Ringwood *(G-8093)*
Stride Well Service Inc .... E 580 254-2353
  Woodward *(G-11635)*
Stride Well Service Inc .... F 580 242-7300
  Lindsay *(G-4088)*
Stride Well Service Inc .... G 405 375-4129
  Enid *(G-3063)*
Strong Service LP .... G 405 756-1716
  Lindsay *(G-4089)*
Sum Professionals Inc .... F 580 983-2379
  Durham *(G-2273)*
Summit Energy Services Inc .... G 405 366-9999
  Norman *(G-5164)*
Summit Well Servicing LLC .... G 580 467-0886
  Ratliff City *(G-8068)*
Sun West Mud Company Inc .... G 580 256-2865
  Woodward *(G-11637)*
Sunwest Mud .... G 405 631-2101
  Oklahoma City *(G-7226)*
Super Flow Testers Inc .... E 405 756-8795
  Lindsay *(G-4090)*
Super Heaters LLC .... F 580 225-3196
  Elk City *(G-2880)*
Superior Energy Services LLC .... E 405 722-0896
  Oklahoma City *(G-7228)*
Superior Spooling LLC .... G 405 613-0329
  Purcell *(G-8022)*
Superior Tool Services Inc .... G 918 640-5503
  Bristow *(G-797)*
Sutherland Well Service Inc .... D 580 229-1338
  Healdton *(G-3422)*
Sutherland Well Service Inc .... G 580 795-5525
  Madill *(G-4165)*
Swabbing Johns LLC .... F 405 756-8141
  Lindsay *(G-4091)*
Swabbing Johns Inc .... F 405 756-8141
  Lindsay *(G-4092)*
Swanderland Associates LLC .... G 918 621-6533
  Tulsa *(G-10883)*
Swiftwater Energy Services LLC .... G 405 820-7612
  Oklahoma City *(G-7238)*
Synergy Petroleum LLC .... G 918 456-9991
  Tahlequah *(G-8885)*
T & C Construction .... G 580 432-5413
  Foster *(G-3189)*
T D Craighead .... G 405 329-2229
  Norman *(G-5169)*
T K Stanley Inc .... G 405 745-3479
  Oklahoma City *(G-7246)*
T&M Roustabout Services LLC .... G 580 796-2478
  Lahoma *(G-3861)*
T&T Forklift Service Inc .... G 405 756-3451
  Lindsay *(G-4093)*
T3 Energy LLC .... G 405 677-8051
  Oklahoma City *(G-7247)*
Tall Oak Woodford LLC .... G 405 888-5585
  Edmond *(G-2636)*
Tamco Plunger & Lift Inc .... G 405 853-6195
  Hennessey *(G-3491)*
Tami Wheeler LLC .... G 405 759-2239
  Oklahoma City *(G-7251)*
Tank Masters .... G 580 332-3325
  Ada *(G-92)*
Tank Trucks Inc .... G 918 224-7515
  Sapulpa *(G-8314)*

13 OIL AND GAS EXTRACTION

Company	Code	Phone
Tapoil Inc — Elmore City (G-2898)	G	580 788-4576
Targa Pipeline Mid-Continent W — Tulsa (G-10899)	F	918 574-3500
Targa Ppline Mid-Continent LLC — Alva (G-194)	E	580 435-2267
Targa Ppline Mid-Continent LLC — Tulsa (G-10900)	C	918 574-3500
Targa Ppline Mid-Continent LLC — Ringwood (G-8094)	D	580 883-2273
Target Completions LLC — Broken Arrow (G-1071)	G	918 872-6115
Tarhay LLC — Hollis (G-3569)	G	940 655-4210
Tarheel Oil & Gas LLC — Oklahoma City (G-7254)	G	405 823-9965
Taylor Rig LLC — Tulsa (G-10906)	D	918 266-7301
Tcj Oilfield Services LLC — Elmer (G-2892)	G	580 687-4454
Ted Smith — Oklahoma City (G-7264)	G	405 677-8402
Teg Solutions LLC — El Reno (G-2761)	F	405 354-1951
Terra Pilot Mwd Tools LLC — Oklahoma City (G-7271)	F	405 603-2200
Terra Star Inc — Kingfisher (G-3817)	E	405 200-1336
Terraco Production Leasing LLC — Marlow (G-4245)	G	580 658-3000
Terry Stutzmann — Shawnee (G-8510)	G	405 481-3853
Terrys Contract Pumping — Covington (G-1868)	G	580 554-2387
Terrys Pump & Supply Inc — Hennessey (G-3492)	G	405 853-6550
Testco Inc — Watonga (G-11350)	F	580 623-4900
Testers Inc — Elk City (G-2881)	G	580 243-0148
Testers Inc — Oklahoma City (G-7273)	E	405 235-9911
Tetra Technologies Inc — Hinton (G-3538)	G	405 542-5461
Texas Transco Inc — Marietta (G-4214)	G	903 857-9136
Texoma Pumping Unit Svc Inc — Ratliff City (G-8070)	E	580 856-4024
Texoma Tractor LLC — Talala (G-8903)	G	918 640-7949
Thomas P Harris Jr — Tulsa (G-10933)	G	918 742-6414
Three Rivers Corp — Tulsa (G-10938)	G	918 492-3239
Thru Tubing Solutions — Newcastle (G-4844)	G	405 692-1900
Thru Tubing Solutions Inc — McAlester (G-4341)	G	918 429-7700
Thru Tubing Solutions Inc — Oklahoma City (G-5320)	C	405 692-1900
Thru Tubing Solutions Inc — Elk City (G-2882)	F	580 225-6977
Thurmond-Mcglothlin LLC — Hennessey (G-3493)	G	405 853-2248
Thurmond-Mcglothlin LLC — Ardmore (G-369)	G	580 223-9632
Thurmond-Mcglothlin LLC — Weatherford (G-11446)	G	580 774-2659
Ties Oilfield Service Inc — Yukon (G-11792)	G	405 306-2655
Tiger Mountain Gas & Oil — Oklahoma City (G-7287)	G	405 605-1181
Tim Scoggins — Cleo Springs (G-1712)	G	580 438-2476
Tipton Oil Tools LLC — Shawnee (G-8511)	G	405 964-3030
Tiptop Energy Prod US LLC — Oklahoma City (G-7293)	G	405 821-0796
Tking Energy Solutions LLC — Lawton (G-4013)	G	740 827-4599
Tlr Well Services Inc — Elk City (G-2883)	E	580 225-4096
Tmg Service Company LLC — Oklahoma City (G-7297)	E	405 213-4317
Tokata Oil Recovery Inc — Stillwater (G-8769)	G	405 595-0072
Toms Hot Shot Service — Elk City (G-2884)	F	580 243-4300
Tongs — Walters (G-11303)	G	580 875-2053
Toolbox Oil Gas Consulting Inc — Duncan (G-2189)	G	432 234-2067
Top O Texas Oilfield Services — Atoka (G-425)	G	806 662-5206
Total Rod Concepts Inc — Oklahoma City (G-7311)	G	405 677-0585
Town & Country Hardware — Mannford (G-4192)	G	918 865-2888
Tpl Southtex Gas Utility Co LP — Tulsa (G-10963)	E	918 574-3500
Tracy Tarrent — Crescent (G-1920)	G	405 969-2343
Trade Trucking LLC — Oklahoma City (G-7314)	G	405 443-5375
TRC Rod Services of Oklahoma — Oklahoma City (G-7320)	F	405 677-0585
Tri State Industrial — Broken Arrow (G-1084)	F	918 286-8110
Tri-Co Testing — Weatherford (G-11450)	G	580 772-8829
Tri-State Industries Inc — Tulsa (G-10973)	F	918 938-6004
Triple Crown Energy-Bh LLC — Tulsa (G-10975)	G	918 518-5422
Triple M — Leedey (G-4032)	G	580 488-3468
Triple M Roustabouts LLC — Tulsa (G-10976)	G	918 619-7610
Triple T Hotshot — Mustang (G-4798)	G	405 745-6698
Troglin Tank Gauge Svcs LLC — Blanchard (G-739)	G	806 275-0010
Trpr Oilfield Services LLC — Weatherford (G-11452)	G	405 853-1988
Truevine Operating LLC — Ada (G-99)	G	580 427-7919
Tuboscope Pipeline Svcs Inc — Edmond (G-2656)	F	405 478-2441
Tucker Energy Services Inc — Tulsa (G-10984)	F	918 806-5647
Turney Bros Oilfld Svcs & Pp — McAlester (G-4345)	E	918 470-6937
Twelve States Oil & Gas Co LLC — Tulsa (G-11021)	G	918 296-7625
Two K Enterprises LLC — Grove (G-3290)	F	918 964-7004
Tx3 LLC — Seminole (G-8405)	G	405 382-2270
U S Weatherford L P — Lindsay (G-4096)	F	405 756-4389
U S Weatherford L P — Oklahoma City (G-7357)	E	918 465-2311
UC Oil & Gas LLC — Tulsa (G-11031)	G	918 270-2383
Ulterra Drilling Tech LP — Oklahoma City (G-7358)	G	405 751-6212
United Services Limited — Woodward (G-11648)	F	580 256-5335
Universal Land Services LLC — Tulsa (G-11049)	G	918 712-9038
Universal Pressure Pumping Inc — Oklahoma City (G-7372)	G	405 608-7346
US Casing Service OK Inc — Weatherford (G-11454)	G	701 713-0047
US Oil Tools Inc — Woodward (G-11649)	G	580 256-6874
USA Compression — Oklahoma City (G-7377)	G	405 790-0300
USA Compression Partners LLC — Tulsa (G-11058)	G	918 742-6548
USA Compression Partners LLC — Oklahoma City (G-7378)	G	405 234-3850
Valor Energy Services LLC — Edmond (G-2666)	G	405 513-5043
Valor Energy Services LLC — Elk City (G-2887)	E	405 209-6081
Varco LP — Oklahoma City (G-7393)	G	405 677-8889
Varco LP — Oklahoma City (G-7394)	E	405 478-3400
Veem Jade Oil & Gas LLC — Tulsa (G-11069)	G	918 298-1555
Vickers Construction Inc — Lindsay (G-4097)	D	405 756-4386
Victory Oil Field Services Co — Noble (G-4893)	G	405 694-0468
Viking Pipe and Supply LLC — El Reno (G-2767)	G	405 262-9337
Vincent Enterprises Inc — Duncan (G-2194)	G	580 252-1322
Vinces Lease Service — Hinton (G-3539)	F	405 542-3908
Vortex Fluid Systems Inc — Tulsa (G-9049)	G	918 810-7798
W 2 Enterprises LLC — Tuskahoma (G-11183)	G	918 429-8793
W A Waterman and Co Inc — Oklahoma City (G-7409)	G	405 632-5631
W E O C Inc — Bristow (G-804)	G	918 367-5918
W K Linduff Inc — Cushing (G-1968)	G	918 225-6000
Wagon Wheel Exploration LLC — Jenks (G-3738)	G	918 746-7477
Waid Group Inc — Medicine Park (G-4373)	G	817 980-8985
Wajo Chemical Inc — Duncan (G-2197)	G	580 255-1191
Walkup Wellhead — Purcell (G-8026)	G	580 320-5913
Walters Oil — Elmore City (G-2899)	G	580 432-5294
Walters Oilwell Service Inc — Walters (G-11304)	G	580 875-2601
Waltman Oil & Gas — Maud (G-4253)	G	405 374-2694
Wapco Inc — Cement (G-1370)	G	405 489-3212
Washita Flow Testers Inc — Lindsay (G-4099)	D	405 756-3397
Washita Valley Enterprises — Oklahoma City (G-7426)	G	405 568-4525
Washita Valley Enterprises Inc — Enid (G-3075)	G	580 540-9277
Washita Valley Enterprises Inc — McAlester (G-4349)	D	918 429-0186
Washita Valley Enterprises Inc — Oklahoma City (G-7427)	D	405 670-5338
We-Go Perforators Inc — Ada (G-105)	G	580 332-1346
We-Go Perforators Inc — Norman (G-5197)	G	405 364-3618
Weatherford Artificia — Hennessey (G-3496)	F	405 853-7181
Weatherford Artificia — Oklahoma City (G-7429)	G	405 677-2410
Weatherford International LLC — Elk City (G-2888)	F	580 225-1237
Weatherford International LLC — Oklahoma City (G-7431)	E	405 773-1100
Webster Drilling Services LLC — Lindsay (G-4100)	G	405 517-5585
Well Completions Inc — Cameron (G-1259)	E	918 654-3030
Well Solutions Inc — Marietta (G-4218)	G	580 775-2373
Wellstar Downhole Services LLC — Enid (G-3078)	G	580 542-6982
Welltec Inc — Tulsa (G-11107)	G	918 585-6122
Westoak Production Svcs Inc — Woodward (G-11651)	E	580 254-3568
Whiterock Oil & Gas LLC — Perry (G-7750)	G	580 307-5565
Whites Roustabout Service Inc — Cement (G-1371)	G	405 489-7126
Whitetail Well Testing LLC — Lone Wolf (G-4122)	F	580 225-4200
Wild Horse Distrubuting LLC — Oklahoma City (G-5323)	G	405 691-0755
Wild Well Control Inc — Oklahoma City (G-7452)	G	405 686-0330
Wildcat Field Services LLC — Collinsville (G-1829)	G	918 606-6217
Williams Water Well Co — Enid (G-3080)	G	405 250-8531
Wilson & Wilson — Kingfisher (G-3822)	G	405 375-5194
Wilson Pinstar Co — Marlow (G-4248)	G	580 255-5899
Woods Pumping Service Inc — Maysville (G-4263)	G	405 449-3485
Wooldridge Oil Co Inc — Wilburton (G-11529)	G	918 465-3073
Wooten Pumping Service — Fairfax (G-3122)	G	918 642-5312
WOW Metallizing & Hard — Sand Springs (G-8243)	G	918 245-9922
Wright Lease Services — Enid (G-3084)	G	806 857-9116

Wtl Oil LLC....D.... 405 608-6007
Oklahoma City *(G-7475)*
Wyoming Casing Service Inc....E.... 580 256-1222
Woodward *(G-11659)*
Wyoming Casing Service In....G.... 701 456-0136
Chickasha *(G-1526)*
Xgp LLC....G.... 405 584-1444
Seminole *(G-8408)*
Xtra Oil Field & Cnstr Co....G.... 918 352-3722
Drumright *(G-2077)*
Xtreme Energy Company....G.... 405 273-1185
Shawnee *(G-8523)*
Yandells Well Service....G.... 405 756-3407
Lindsay *(G-4101)*
Ydf Inc....G.... 405 324-2216
Yukon *(G-11806)*
Young Tool Company LLC....G.... 918 352-2213
Drumright *(G-2078)*
Zzw Global Inc....G.... 405 388-8720
Yukon *(G-11809)*
Zzw Global Inc....G.... 405 985-8759
Oklahoma City *(G-7490)*

14 MINING AND QUARRYING OF NONMETALLIC MINERALS, EXCEPT FUELS

1411 Dimension Stone

Apac-Central Inc....E.... 918 256-7853
Vinita *(G-11248)*
Bison Materials LLC....G.... 918 333-2266
Bartlesville *(G-455)*
Cornerstone Quarries Inc....G.... 918 647-2117
Cameron *(G-1256)*
Dream Green International LLC....G.... 814 616-7800
Norman *(G-4983)*
Eaves Stones Products....F.... 580 889-7858
Atoka *(G-410)*
Grecian Marble & Granite LLC....F.... 405 632-3802
Oklahoma City *(G-6185)*
Hansons Stone & Landscape....G.... 580 310-0071
Ada *(G-47)*
Keystone Rock & Excavation LLC....G.... 405 608-7777
Oklahoma City *(G-6414)*
Majestic Marble & Granite....E.... 918 266-1121
Catoosa *(G-1337)*
Martin Marietta Materials Inc....E.... 580 326-7709
Sawyer *(G-8335)*
▼ Oklahoma Stone....F.... 405 721-6775
Yukon *(G-11761)*
Polycor Oklahoma Inc....G.... 770 735-2611
Marble City *(G-4197)*
Quapaw Company Inc....E.... 918 767-2985
Pawnee *(G-7710)*
Stonemen Granite & Marble....G.... 918 851-3400
Tulsa *(G-10856)*
Sugar Loaf Quarries Inc....E.... 918 647-4244
Shady Point *(G-8416)*
Texhoma Limestone....G.... 580 889-8808
Caney *(G-1263)*
Whm Granite Products Inc....F.... 580 535-2184
Granite *(G-3257)*

1422 Crushed & Broken Limestone

Anchor Stone Co....F.... 918 599-7255
Tulsa *(G-9186)*
Anchor Stone Co....G.... 918 872-8449
Broken Arrow *(G-827)*
Anchor Stone Co....G.... 918 299-6384
Tulsa *(G-9187)*
Anchor Stone Co....D.... 918 438-1060
Tulsa *(G-9188)*
Apac-Central Inc....E.... 918 256-7853
Vinita *(G-11248)*
Apac-Central Inc....F.... 918 683-1362
Okay *(G-5256)*
▲ Dolese Bros Co....C.... 405 235-2311
Oklahoma City *(G-5957)*
Dolese Bros Co....D.... 580 492-4771
Elgin *(G-2775)*
Dolese Bros Co....E.... 405 670-9626
Oklahoma City *(G-5962)*
Dolese Bros Co....E.... 580 226-8737
Ardmore *(G-280)*
Dolese Bros Co....F.... 580 937-4889
Coleman *(G-1794)*
Dream Green International LLC....G.... 814 616-7800
Norman *(G-4983)*
Jenkins Quary....G.... 580 588-3020
Apache *(G-219)*
Jennings Stone Company Inc....E.... 580 777-2880
Fittstown *(G-3159)*
Kemp Stone Inc....F.... 918 772-3366
Hulbert *(G-3624)*
Martin Marietta Materials Inc....G.... 405 799-7799
Oklahoma City *(G-6533)*
Martin Marietta Materials Inc....E.... 580 369-2706
Davis *(G-1989)*
Martin Marietta Materials Inc....G.... 580 286-3290
Idabel *(G-3640)*
Martin Marietta Materials Inc....F.... 580 569-2393
Snyder *(G-8583)*
Martin Marietta Materials Inc....G.... 580 835-7311
Broken Bow *(G-1198)*
Muskogee Sand Company Inc....G.... 918 683-1766
Porter *(G-7894)*
Pryor Stone Inc....E.... 918 825-3370
Pryor *(G-7987)*
Quality Stone Quarries LLC....G.... 918 967-5195
Stigler *(G-8641)*
Quapaw Company Inc....E.... 918 767-2985
Pawnee *(G-7710)*
Rock Producers Inc....G.... 918 963-2111
Shady Point *(G-8415)*
Schweitzer Gypsum & Lime....G.... 405 263-7967
Okarche *(G-5251)*
Souter Limestone and Mnrl LLC....F.... 918 489-5589
Gore *(G-3252)*
Stewart Stone Inc....F.... 918 225-2704
Cushing *(G-1962)*
US Lime Company - St Clair....D.... 918 775-4466
Marble City *(G-4198)*

1423 Crushed & Broken Granite

Blessing Gravel LLC....G.... 580 513-4009
Tishomingo *(G-8962)*
Martin Marietta Materials Inc....E.... 580 384-5246
Mill Creek *(G-4469)*
Martin Marietta Materials Inc....E.... 580 326-9671
Sawyer *(G-8336)*
▼ Thomsons Trenching Inc....G.... 918 745-1030
Tulsa *(G-10936)*
Youngman Rock Inc....F.... 918 682-7070
Muskogee *(G-4759)*

1429 Crushed & Broken Stone, NEC

Apac-Central....G.... 918 534-1741
Dewey *(G-2016)*
Cobble Rock and Stone LLC....F.... 405 567-3552
Prague *(G-7923)*
Hanson Aggregates Wrp Inc....E.... 580 369-3773
Davis *(G-1985)*
Hoskins Gypsum Company LLC....F.... 580 274-3446
Longdale *(G-4124)*
Kemp Stone Inc....F.... 918 825-3370
Pryor *(G-7972)*
Rock Producers Inc....E.... 918 969-2100
Bokoshe *(G-754)*
Souter Limestone and Mnrl LLC....F.... 918 489-5589
Gore *(G-3252)*
Texoma Materials....G.... 580 367-2339
Caddo *(G-1237)*
Third Rock Construction LLC....G.... 918 429-2011
McAlester *(G-4340)*

1442 Construction Sand & Gravel

Anna Lightle....G.... 405 853-4530
Hennessey *(G-3445)*
Arkhola Sand & Gravel Co....G.... 918 687-4771
Muskogee *(G-4650)*
Arkhola Sand & Gravel Co....G.... 918 456-2683
Tahlequah *(G-8850)*
Arkhola Sand & Gravel Co Tahle....G.... 918 456-6121
Park Hill *(G-7640)*
B B Sand and Gravel....G.... 405 944-1163
Paden *(G-7632)*
Bosendorfer Oil Company....G.... 405 604-9025
Oklahoma City *(G-5622)*
Brandon Hyde....G.... 405 919-4520
Goldsby *(G-3244)*
Cardinal Fg Minerals LLC....E.... 580 367-2123
Coleman *(G-1793)*
Clements Sand Gravel & Excavat....G.... 580 465-4191
Ardmore *(G-268)*
Collins Cnstr Fabrications LLC....G.... 918 522-4855
Talihina *(G-8906)*
Covia Holdings Corporation....E.... 580 456-7772
Roff *(G-8107)*
Dereks Pit LLC....G.... 405 485-2562
Blanchard *(G-710)*
▲ Dolese Bros Co....C.... 405 235-2311
Oklahoma City *(G-5957)*
Dolese Bros Co....E.... 405 670-9626
Oklahoma City *(G-5962)*
Double D Sand and Gravel LLC....G.... 405 207-8050
Stratford *(G-8804)*
Doug Troxell....G.... 405 387-3574
Newcastle *(G-4824)*
Elm Creek Gravel LLC....E.... 405 360-7300
Norman *(G-4990)*
Evans & Associates Entps Inc....E.... 580 765-6693
Ponca City *(G-7828)*
Gravel Group LLC....G.... 405 359-4932
Edmond *(G-2443)*
Gravel Road LLC....G.... 918 766-6368
Bartlesville *(G-488)*
Heady Trucking....G.... 580 326-2739
Sawyer *(G-8334)*
Holliday Sand & Gravel Co....G.... 918 486-1413
Coweta *(G-1885)*
Holliday Sand Gravel Co LLC....G.... 918 369-8850
Bixby *(G-632)*
Jr Sand & Gravel Inc....G.... 405 474-8730
Edmond *(G-2474)*
K and G Sand & Gravel LLC....G.... 580 369-2244
Davis *(G-1987)*
Keystone Sand & Gravel....G.... 918 241-0415
Sand Springs *(G-8198)*
Kline Materials Inc....F.... 580 256-2062
Woodward *(G-11603)*
Lattimore Materials Company LP....F.... 580 276-4631
Marietta *(G-4208)*
Lawton Transit Mix Inc....G.... 580 569-4333
Snyder *(G-8582)*
Lightfoot Ready Mix LLC....G.... 405 714-5539
Perkins *(G-7720)*
Mark C Blakley....G.... 405 245-3606
Oklahoma City *(G-6526)*
Meridian Contracting Inc....D.... 405 928-5959
Norman *(G-5072)*
Micheal T Robinson....G.... 580 767-9414
Ponca City *(G-7851)*
▲ Minick Materials Company....E.... 405 789-2068
Oklahoma City *(G-6616)*
Mohawk Materials Co Inc....G.... 918 584-2707
Tulsa *(G-10295)*
Muskie Proppant LLC....G.... 405 233-3558
Oklahoma City *(G-6638)*
Muskogee Sand Company Inc....G.... 918 683-1766
Porter *(G-7894)*
Nancy W Gravel....G.... 405 348-4409
Edmond *(G-2528)*
Oklahoma Aztec Co Inc....G.... 405 784-2475
Asher *(G-393)*
Perkins Sand LLC....G.... 405 240-7870
Carney *(G-1279)*
Pryor Sand & Redi-Mix Inc....G.... 918 484-2150
Whitefield *(G-11517)*
Rcr Construction....G.... 918 682-9033
Muskogee *(G-4742)*
Redline Constructn Sand Dirt....G.... 405 380-6994
Wewoka *(G-11509)*
Sand Run LLC....G.... 918 296-3205
Tulsa *(G-10703)*
Southern Boys Clay Gravel LLC....G.... 580 584-6711
Broken Bow *(G-1208)*
Southwestern State Sand Corp....E.... 580 569-4333
Snyder *(G-8584)*
Stanton Sand & Gravel Inc....G.... 580 229-3353
Ardmore *(G-363)*
Summit Sand & Gravel LLC....G.... 405 256-6029
Mustang *(G-4797)*
Technisand Inc....D.... 580 456-7791
Roff *(G-8112)*
TNT Sand & Gravel LLC....G.... 580 277-0640
Ardmore *(G-372)*
Two Brothers Sand Grave....G.... 405 923-6762
Yukon *(G-11797)*
V5 Contracting LLC....G.... 918 720-4675
Claremore *(G-1699)*
Vickers Sand and Gravel....G.... 405 573-1989
Norman *(G-5195)*
Watkins Sand Co....E.... 918 369-5238
Bixby *(G-671)*

1446 Industrial Sand

Badger Mining Corporation....G.... 608 864-1157
Erick *(G-3085)*

S I C

14 MINING AND QUARRYING OF NONMETALLIC MINERALS, EXCEPT FUELS

Cardinal Industries LLC .... G 918 299-0396
 Tulsa (G-9375)
Covia Holdings Corporation .... E 580 456-7772
 Roff (G-8107)
Fairmount Minerals .... G 580 303-9160
 Elk City (G-2814)
Mohawk Materials Co Inc .... G 918 584-2707
 Tulsa (G-10295)
Taylor Frac LLC .... E 405 293-4208
 Oklahoma City (G-7259)
Timco Blasting & Coatings .... E 918 367-1700
 Bristow (G-799)
Timco Blasting & Coatings .... F 918 605-1179
 Bristow (G-800)
Timco Blasting & Coatings .... G 918 605-1179
 Stroud (G-8823)
Timco Blasting & Coatings .... G 918 605-1179
 Bristow (G-801)
Timco Blasting & Coatings .... G 918 608-1179
 Stroud (G-8824)

1455 Kaolin & Ball Clay

JM Huber Corporation .... C 580 584-7002
 Broken Bow (G-1194)

1475 Phosphate Rock

D and M Resources Inc .... G 405 375-4602
 Kingfisher (G-3795)

1479 Chemical & Fertilizer Mining

Ovintiv Exploration Inc .... G 580 243-4101
 Elk City (G-2857)

1481 Nonmetallic Minerals Svcs, Except Fuels

Kully Chaha Native Stone LLC .... G 918 654-3005
 Cameron (G-1258)
Myers & Myers Inc .... G 405 341-5861
 Edmond (G-2524)
Pats Phase II Hair & Nail Sln .... G 405 232-4746
 Oklahoma City (G-6811)
Stoney Point Mine .... G 580 362-3916
 Newkirk (G-4853)
▼ Trans-Tel Central Inc .... C 405 447-5025
 Norman (G-5180)

1499 Miscellaneous Nonmetallic Mining

Allied Custom Gypsum .... F 580 337-6371
 Waynoka (G-11370)
Diamond Gypsum LLC .... G 580 623-2868
 Watonga (G-11345)
Greenhill Materials LLC .... F 918 274-6560
 Owasso (G-7572)
▲ Harrison Gypsum LLC .... F 405 366-9500
 Norman (G-5018)
Harrison Gypsum LLC .... E 580 994-6048
 Mooreland (G-4591)
Harrison Gypsum LLC .... F 580 994-6050
 Mooreland (G-4592)
Harrison Gypsum Holdings LLC ..... C 405 366-9500
 Norman (G-5019)
Noble Acquisition LLC .... G 405 872-5660
 Noble (G-4887)
Schweitzer Gypsum & Lime .... G 405 263-7967
 Okarche (G-5251)
Tulsa Auto Core .... G 918 584-5899
 Tulsa (G-10986)

20 FOOD AND KINDRED PRODUCTS

2011 Meat Packing Plants

Alex Rogers .... G 405 677-2306
 Oklahoma City (G-5412)
B & B Butlers Custom Process .... G 580 795-2667
 Madill (G-4144)
Barnsdall Meat Processors Inc .... G 918 847-2814
 Barnsdall (G-436)
Bob Mc Kinney & Sons .... G 918 387-2401
 Cushing (G-1924)
Browns Meat Processing .... G 405 379-2979
 Holdenville (G-3550)
Butchs Processing Plant Inc .... G 405 382-2833
 Seminole (G-8361)
Cable Meat Center Inc .... F 580 658-6646
 Marlow (G-4224)
Circle D Meat .... G 580 921-5500
 Laverne (G-3876)

Cook Processing .... G 918 542-5796
 Miami (G-4392)
Country Home Meat Company .... G 405 341-0267
 Edmond (G-2368)
Cuts Custom Butchering LLC .... G 918 534-1382
 Dewey (G-2019)
Don Regier .... G 580 772-3510
 Weatherford (G-11405)
Double D Foods Inc .... F 405 245-8909
 Oklahoma City (G-5970)
Food Svcs Auth of Quapaw Tribe .... F 918 542-1853
 Quapaw (G-8030)
Fort Cobb Locker Plant .... G 405 643-2355
 Fort Cobb (G-3171)
Four State Meat Processing LLC .... F 918 783-5556
 Big Cabin (G-604)
Gage Locker Service .... G 580 923-7661
 Gage (G-3210)
Hilltop Custom Processing .... G 405 527-7048
 Lexington (G-4035)
Janice Sue Daniel .... G 580 237-2695
 Enid (G-2981)
Janice Sue Daniel .... G 580 233-8666
 Enid (G-2982)
Kilgore Meat Processing Plant .... G 918 967-2613
 Stigler (G-8635)
Lawton Meat Processing .... G 580 353-6448
 Lawton (G-3957)
Lopez Foods Inc .... E 405 789-7500
 Oklahoma City (G-6494)
M & M Custom Butchering .... G 918 542-6421
 Miami (G-4410)
Mc Ferrons Quality Meats Inc .... F 918 273-2892
 Nowata (G-5220)
O H S N Inc .... E 580 248-1299
 Lawton (G-3977)
Okeen Motel .... G 580 822-4491
 Okeene (G-5261)
Prairie Rose Processing Inc .... G 405 224-6429
 Chickasha (G-1500)
Ralphs Packing Company .... E 405 547-2464
 Perkins (G-7721)
Ray Meat Market .... G 580 256-6031
 Woodward (G-11627)
Robertsons Hams Inc .... F 580 276-3395
 Marietta (G-4211)
Rowlands Proc & Cattle Co .... F 580 924-2560
 Durant (G-2253)
Sallee Meat Processing Inc .... G 405 282-1241
 Guthrie (G-3336)
Schones Butcher Shop & Market ... G 580 472-3300
 Canute (G-1270)
Seaboard Corporation .... G 580 468-3790
 Guymon (G-3362)
Seaboard Farms Inc .... E 580 338-4900
 Guymon (G-3363)
Seaboard Foods LLC .... G 580 338-4900
 Guymon (G-3365)
Sooner Food Group LLC .... G 703 791-9069
 Newalla (G-4816)
Stinebrings Custom Processing ..... G 405 828-4247
 Dover (G-2045)
Temple Custom Slaughter & Proc ... G 580 342-5031
 Temple (G-8936)
Tenderette Steak Co Inc .... F 405 634-5655
 Oklahoma City (G-7268)
Thompsons Custom Butcher Barn .. G 918 476-5508
 Chouteau (G-1572)
Tonkawa Meat Processing .... G 580 628-4550
 Tonkawa (G-8983)
Tyson Foods Inc .... G 918 723-5091
 Westville (G-11487)
Tyson Foods Inc .... E 405 379-7241
 Holdenville (G-3561)
Unrau Meat Co Inc .... G 918 543-8245
 Inola (G-3676)
Victory Garden Homestead LLC ..... G 405 306-0308
 Blanchard (G-744)
W R Meat Co .... G 580 622-2494
 Sulphur (G-8846)
Walke Brothers Meats Inc .... G 918 341-3236
 Claremore (G-1704)
Weavers Meat Processing Inc .... G 918 647-9832
 Poteau (G-7917)

2013 Sausages & Meat Prdts

▲ Advance Food Company Inc ...... C 800 969-2747
 Enid (G-2905)
Advance Food Company Inc .... A 580 237-6656
 Enid (G-2906)

Alex Rogers .... G 405 677-2306
 Oklahoma City (G-5412)
B & B Butlers Custom Process .... G 580 795-2667
 Madill (G-4144)
B&L Smoked Meats .... G 580 641-1677
 Marlow (G-4222)
Bar-S Foods Co .... A 580 331-1628
 Clinton (G-1740)
Bar-S Foods Co .... G 405 303-2138
 Seminole (G-8357)
Bar-S Foods Co .... C 580 821-5700
 Altus (G-144)
Bar-S Foods Co .... B 580 510-3300
 Lawton (G-3896)
Barnsdall Meat Processors Inc ...... G 918 847-2814
 Barnsdall (G-436)
Big Ricks Jerky LLC .... G 405 414-9096
 Oklahoma City (G-5565)
Blue & Gold Sausage Inc .... G 405 399-2954
 Jones (G-3742)
Bob Mc Kinney & Sons .... G 918 387-2401
 Cushing (G-1924)
Bruce Packing Company Inc .... G 503 874-3000
 Durant (G-2210)
Bulldog Jerky Co .... G 580 479-5542
 Grandfield (G-3256)
Cable Meat Center Inc .... F 580 658-6646
 Marlow (G-4224)
Circle D Meat .... G 580 921-5500
 Laverne (G-3876)
Country Home Meat Company .... G 405 341-0267
 Edmond (G-2368)
Cuts Custom Butchering LLC .... G 918 534-1382
 Dewey (G-2019)
Davis Morgan International .... G 405 598-2380
 Macomb (G-4141)
Don Regier .... G 580 772-3510
 Weatherford (G-11405)
Double J Beef Jerky .... G 580 476-2465
 Rush Springs (G-8120)
Dustys Jerky LLC .... G 405 702-8016
 Oklahoma City (G-5991)
GOAT Beef Jerky Co LLC .... G 405 627-5096
 Oklahoma City (G-6164)
Goodtimes Beef Jerky .... G 405 387-5448
 Newcastle (G-4829)
Hardtimes Real Beef Jerky Inc ...... E 580 497-7695
 El Reno (G-2723)
Hilltop Custom Processing .... G 405 527-7048
 Lexington (G-4035)
Janice Sue Daniel .... G 580 233-8666
 Enid (G-2982)
Jiggs Smokehouse .... G 580 323-5641
 Clinton (G-1754)
Kilgore Meat Processing Plant .... G 918 967-2613
 Stigler (G-8635)
Kormondy Enterprises Inc .... B 918 274-8787
 Owasso (G-7584)
Lopez Foods Inc .... B 405 499-0131
 Oklahoma City (G-6493)
Lopez Foods Inc .... E 405 789-7500
 Oklahoma City (G-6494)
Lopez Foods Inc .... B 405 789-7500
 Oklahoma City (G-6495)
M & M Custom Butchering .... G 918 542-6421
 Miami (G-4410)
Mc Ferrons Quality Meats Inc .... F 918 273-2892
 Nowata (G-5220)
McLane Foodservice Dist Inc .... C 405 632-0118
 Oklahoma City (G-6549)
Mikes Famous Beef Jerky .... G 405 414-7501
 Chickasha (G-1489)
National Steak Processors LLC .... D 918 274-8787
 Owasso (G-7596)
No Mans Land Foods LLC .... D 580 297-5142
 Boise City (G-748)
OSteen Meat Specialties Inc .... D 405 236-1952
 Oklahoma City (G-6787)
Pine Cove Jerky LLC .... G 918 872-1138
 Broken Arrow (G-1007)
Prairie Rose Processing Inc .... G 405 224-6429
 Chickasha (G-1500)
Ray Meat Market .... G 580 256-6031
 Woodward (G-11627)
Ridleys Butcher Shop Inc .... G 580 255-9330
 Duncan (G-2169)
Robertsons Hams Inc .... F 580 276-3395
 Marietta (G-4211)
Rowlands Proc & Cattle Co .... F 580 924-2560
 Durant (G-2253)

SIC SECTION

20 FOOD AND KINDRED PRODUCTS

Sallee Meat Processing Inc .... G 405 282-1241
  Guthrie *(G-3336)*
Seaboard Farms Inc .... F 580 338-3311
  Guymon *(G-3364)*
Slow N Low Smoked Meats .... G 918 946-6894
  Tulsa *(G-10775)*
Temple Custom Slaughter & Proc .... G 580 342-5031
  Temple *(G-8936)*
Thompsons Custom Butcher Barn .... G 918 476-5508
  Chouteau *(G-1572)*
Tonkawa Meat Processing .... G 580 628-4550
  Tonkawa *(G-8983)*
Unrau Meat Co Inc .... G 918 543-8245
  Inola *(G-3676)*
Walke Brothers Meats Inc .... G 918 341-3236
  Claremore *(G-1704)*

2015 Poultry Slaughtering, Dressing & Processing

▲ Advance Food Company Inc .... C 800 969-2747
  Enid *(G-2905)*
Advance Food Company Inc .... A 580 237-6656
  Enid *(G-2906)*
Bar-S Foods Co .... A 580 331-1628
  Clinton *(G-1740)*
Bar-S Foods Co .... C 580 821-5700
  Altus *(G-144)*
Dorada Poultry LLC .... E 580 718-4700
  Ponca City *(G-7822)*
Free Ranger LLC .... C 918 253-4223
  Jay *(G-3681)*
Kormondy Enterprises Inc .... B 918 274-8787
  Owasso *(G-7584)*
Liberty Free Range Poultry LLC .... C 319 627-6000
  Jay *(G-3682)*
O K Foods Inc .... A 918 653-2819
  Heavener *(G-3432)*
O K Foods Inc .... B 918 427-7000
  Muldrow *(G-4635)*
OSteen Meat Specialties Inc .... D 405 236-1952
  Oklahoma City *(G-6787)*
Rath Inc .... F 580 588-3064
  Apache *(G-221)*
Simmons Foods Inc .... F 918 676-3285
  Fairland *(G-3130)*
Simmons Foods Inc .... G 918 791-0010
  Grove *(G-3288)*
Tyson Foods Inc .... E 918 723-5494
  Westville *(G-11486)*
Tyson Foods Inc .... A 580 584-9191
  Broken Bow *(G-1211)*
Tyson Foods Inc .... E 918 696-4530
  Stilwell *(G-8796)*

2022 Cheese

Cheese Factory LLC .... G 405 375-4004
  Kingfisher *(G-3788)*
George E Christian .... G 405 375-6711
  Kingfisher *(G-3798)*
Los Quesitos De Mama LLC .... G 312 276-2638
  Edmond *(G-2495)*
Swan Brothers Dairy Inc .... G 918 341-2069
  Claremore *(G-1690)*
Tpl Arkoma Midstream LLC .... G 918 574-3500
  Tulsa *(G-10962)*
Watonga Cheese Plant .... G 580 623-5915
  Balko *(G-433)*

2023 Milk, Condensed & Evaporated

24 Hr Inc .... G 844 370-1726
  Weatherford *(G-11385)*
All Things Bugs LLC .... G 352 281-3643
  Oklahoma City *(G-5415)*
Biorite Acquisition Co LLC .... G 405 701-1515
  Norman *(G-4935)*
Juice Blendz Cafe .... G 405 285-0133
  Edmond *(G-2475)*
JW Nutritional LLC .... G 214 221-0404
  Broken Arrow *(G-953)*
Native Distributing LLC .... D 405 316-9223
  Norman *(G-5086)*
▲ Natures Rx Inc .... G 405 484-7302
  Paoli *(G-7638)*
Nucleic Products LLC .... G 818 419-9176
  Grove *(G-3283)*
Sanders Laboratories Inc .... G 405 598-2131
  Tecumseh *(G-8926)*
Ultra Botanica LLC .... G 405 694-4175
  Oklahoma City *(G-7359)*

2024 Ice Cream

Blue Bell Creameries LP .... B 918 258-5100
  Broken Arrow *(G-1113)*
C&K Inc .... G 918 299-6307
  Jenks *(G-3697)*
Hiland Dairy Foods Company LLC .... B 405 258-3100
  Chandler *(G-1380)*
J Mottos LLC .... G 918 760-3866
  Tulsa *(G-10021)*
M-O Masonry LLC .... G 405 219-4220
  Oklahoma City *(G-6512)*
Olh Moore LLC .... G 405 703-0250
  Moore *(G-4549)*
Scoozies Coneys & Frz Custard .... G 918 396-1500
  Skiatook *(G-8568)*
W H Braum Inc .... E 405 340-9288
  Edmond *(G-2678)*
Wiljackal LLC .... F 918 252-2663
  Tulsa *(G-11121)*

2026 Milk

Borden Dairy Company Texas LLC .... G 405 232-7955
  Oklahoma City *(G-5620)*
Dean Foods Company .... G 918 587-2471
  Tulsa *(G-9564)*
Hiland Dairy Foods Company LLC .... B 405 258-3100
  Chandler *(G-1380)*
Hiland Dairy Foods Company LLC .... D 405 321-3191
  Norman *(G-5023)*
James Porter Shorty .... G 580 326-0592
  Hugo *(G-3615)*
McAllister Farms .... G 580 512-9009
  Hollis *(G-3567)*
Passion Berri .... G 405 310-6669
  Norman *(G-5109)*
Southern Foods Group LLC .... C 918 587-2471
  Tulsa *(G-10799)*
Swan Brothers Dairy Inc .... G 918 341-2069
  Claremore *(G-1690)*

2032 Canned Specialties

Cable Meat Center Inc .... F 580 658-6646
  Marlow *(G-4224)*
Carls Chili Company Inc .... G 918 227-1623
  Tulsa *(G-8994)*
El Mojado .... G 918 492-1138
  Tulsa *(G-9650)*
Grannas LLC .... F 580 337-6360
  Bessie *(G-568)*
Head Country Inc .... F 580 762-1227
  Ponca City *(G-7835)*
Manila Foods .... G 580 262-9900
  Blackwell *(G-689)*
Polish Kitchen LLC .... G 580 583-5970
  Lawton *(G-3984)*
Rockin L-H Asparagus Farms .... G 918 689-5086
  Eufaula *(G-3111)*
S & S Foods Inc .... F 405 256-6557
  Mustang *(G-4792)*
Silas Salsa Company LLC .... G 469 556-9762
  Oklahoma City *(G-7139)*

2033 Canned Fruits, Vegetables & Preserves

Bequettes Gourmet Foods Inc .... G 918 946-4212
  Tulsa *(G-9284)*
Billy Sims Barbeque LLC .... E 918 258-1978
  Broken Arrow *(G-852)*
Blessettis Inc .... G 918 830-5481
  Tulsa *(G-9303)*
Claras Kitchen LLC .... G 229 669-1493
  Oklahoma City *(G-5772)*
Dewaynes Bbq Sauce Catering .... G 580 363-3394
  Newkirk *(G-4847)*
Dorians Foods Inc .... G 580 658-3022
  Marlow *(G-4229)*
Griffin Food Company .... D 918 687-6311
  Muskogee *(G-4683)*
Ju Ju Jams .... G 918 230-6650
  Tulsa *(G-10064)*
▲ Leonard Mountain Inc .... E 800 822-7700
  Tulsa *(G-10153)*
Maria Raes Inc .... G 580 242-3342
  Enid *(G-3005)*
Okie Ferments .... G 405 310-9274
  Oklahoma City *(G-6731)*
▲ Pepper Creek Farms Inc .... G 580 536-1300
  Lawton *(G-3982)*
Prairie Gypsies Inc .... G 405 525-3013
  Oklahoma City *(G-6873)*

Southern Okie LLC .... G 405 657-7765
  Edmond *(G-2625)*
Suans Inc .... G 405 413-1751
  Oklahoma City *(G-7220)*
Two Territories Trading Co LLC .... G 580 679-4701
  Duke *(G-2081)*

2034 Dried Fruits, Vegetables & Soup

Alfalfa Dehydrating Plant Inc .... G 918 482-3267
  Coweta *(G-1871)*
▲ Leonard Mountain Inc .... E 800 822-7700
  Tulsa *(G-10153)*

2035 Pickled Fruits, Vegetables, Sauces & Dressings

Backwoods Food Mfg Inc .... F 918 458-9300
  Tahlequah *(G-8851)*
Clements Foods Co .... C 405 842-3308
  Oklahoma City *(G-5783)*
Daddy Hinkles Inc .... G 918 358-2129
  Cleveland *(G-1721)*
Dorians Foods Inc .... G 580 658-3022
  Marlow *(G-4229)*
Griffin Food Company .... D 918 687-6311
  Muskogee *(G-4683)*
Hermans Chili Mix Inc .... G 918 743-1832
  Tulsa *(G-9925)*
Latimers Barbeque .... G 918 425-1242
  Tulsa *(G-10134)*
Maria Raes Inc .... G 580 242-3342
  Enid *(G-3005)*
▲ Pepper Creek Farms Inc .... G 580 536-1300
  Lawton *(G-3982)*
Pickles of Edmond Inc .... G 405 285-4342
  Edmond *(G-2568)*
Plainview Winery .... G 580 796-2902
  Lahoma *(G-3859)*

2037 Frozen Fruits, Juices & Vegetables

ICEE Company .... G 405 685-7739
  Oklahoma City *(G-6285)*

2038 Frozen Specialties

Guymon Extracts Inc .... E 580 338-2624
  Guymon *(G-3349)*
ICEE Company .... G 800 423-3872
  Tulsa *(G-9965)*
Sfc Global Supply Chain Inc .... C 918 696-8325
  Stilwell *(G-8795)*
Windsor Quality Food Co Ltd .... G 918 628-0277
  Tulsa *(G-11138)*

2041 Flour, Grain Milling

ADM Milling Co .... D 580 237-8000
  Enid *(G-2904)*
Archer-Daniels-Midland Company .... D 580 237-8000
  Enid *(G-2910)*
Archer-Daniels-Midland Company .... G 580 652-3761
  Hooker *(G-3595)*
Archer-Daniels-Midland Company .... G 580 233-3800
  Enid *(G-2911)*
Archer-Daniels-Midland Company .... G 580 652-2623
  Hooker *(G-3596)*
Archer-Daniels-Midland Company .... G 580 854-6285
  Tyrone *(G-11218)*
Archer-Daniels-Midland Company .... G 580 233-5100
  Enid *(G-2912)*
Archer-Daniels-Midland Company .... G 580 482-7100
  Altus *(G-143)*
▲ Bama Companies Inc .... A 918 592-0778
  Tulsa *(G-9258)*
▲ Big v Feeds Inc .... D 918 423-1565
  McAlester *(G-4276)*
Lanie Farms .... G 580 694-2259
  Manchester *(G-4168)*
Shawnee Milling Company .... E 580 822-4415
  Okeene *(G-5262)*
Shawnee Milling Company .... G 405 263-4566
  Okarche *(G-5252)*
Shawnee Milling Company .... G 405 352-4336
  Minco *(G-4481)*
Stockmans Mill & Grain Inc .... G 918 762-3459
  Pawnee *(G-7711)*
Value Added Products .... D 580 327-0400
  Alva *(G-195)*

20 FOOD AND KINDRED PRODUCTS SIC SECTION

2043 Cereal Breakfast Foods

Alan Ware ....G.... 918 658-5267
Paoli *(G-7637)*
Granola Shirts ....G.... 918 592-5477
Tulsa *(G-9846)*
Oatskc Granola Company LLC ....G.... 405 834-6159
Oklahoma City *(G-6709)*

2045 Flour, Blended & Prepared

Bama Cos Inc ....G.... 918 732-2640
Tulsa *(G-9259)*
Okie Dough LLC ....G.... 580 606-0142
Owasso *(G-7597)*

2046 Wet Corn Milling

Ingredion Incorporated ....G.... 539 292-4369
Tulsa *(G-9985)*

2047 Dog & Cat Food

▲ **Big v Feeds Inc** ....D.... 918 423-1565
McAlester *(G-4276)*
Blue Bonnet Feeds LP ....D.... 580 223-3010
Ardmore *(G-257)*
Dog Dish LLC ....G.... 918 624-2600
Tulsa *(G-9590)*
Farmers Co Op ....F.... 918 456-0557
Tahlequah *(G-8864)*
House Dog Industries LLC ....G.... 405 761-5576
El Reno *(G-2724)*
Mars Petcare Us Inc ....E.... 918 540-0045
Miami *(G-4412)*
Midwestern Pet Foods Inc ....F.... 405 224-2691
Chickasha *(G-1487)*
Mountain Country Foods LLC ....E.... 580 822-4130
Okeene *(G-5259)*
Nestle Purina Petcare Company ....D.... 405 751-4550
Edmond *(G-2535)*
Ralston Purina ....G.... 405 751-4550
Edmond *(G-2585)*
Rbs Pet Products ....G.... 405 373-0235
Piedmont *(G-7769)*
Red Collar Pet Foods Inc ....D.... 580 323-3359
Clinton *(G-1765)*
Win Hy Foods Inc ....F.... 918 227-0004
Tulsa *(G-9053)*

2048 Prepared Feeds For Animals & Fowls

AC Nutrition LP ....F.... 580 223-3900
Ardmore *(G-236)*
Advantage Supplements LLC ....G.... 866 226-9613
Hennessey *(G-3444)*
Alfalfa Dehydrating Plant Inc ....G.... 918 482-3267
Coweta *(G-1871)*
Allen Brothers Feed ....G.... 918 287-4379
Pawhuska *(G-7676)*
▲ **Big v Feeds Inc** ....D.... 918 423-1565
McAlester *(G-4276)*
Blue Bonnet Feeds LP ....D.... 580 223-3010
Ardmore *(G-257)*
Bobby Foster ....G.... 580 476-3417
Rush Springs *(G-8119)*
C & H Ranch ....G.... 918 479-8460
Locust Grove *(G-4105)*
Cargill Incorporated ....D.... 405 270-7011
Oklahoma City *(G-5698)*
Cargill Incorporated ....E.... 405 236-0525
Oklahoma City *(G-5699)*
Choska Alfalfa Mills LLC ....G.... 918 687-5805
Muskogee *(G-4660)*
Compass Unlimited Inc ....G.... 918 824-1644
Pryor *(G-7955)*
Custer Enterprises Inc ....F.... 580 371-9588
Mannsville *(G-4195)*
Custom Mser Lvstk Pre Mix Whse ....G.... 580 336-2053
Perry *(G-7729)*
Darling Ingredients Inc ....E.... 918 371-2528
Collinsville *(G-1808)*
Diane Barcheers ....G.... 918 649-0440
McAlester *(G-4293)*
Douglas A Pharr ....G.... 405 200-4983
Ninnekah *(G-4870)*
Dvm Nutrion Pets Corp Inc ....F.... 918 686-6111
Muskogee *(G-4668)*
Espiritu Miki ....G.... 405 213-5167
Oklahoma City *(G-6051)*
Eve Breathe ....G.... 918 454-2866
Pawnee *(G-7704)*
Farmers Co Op ....F.... 918 456-0557
Tahlequah *(G-8864)*
Farmers Coop ....F.... 580 772-3334
Weatherford *(G-11413)*
Fisher AG Enterprises Inc ....F.... 918 367-6382
Bristow *(G-778)*
Frontier Elevator Inc ....G.... 888 421-9400
Ada *(G-38)*
Griffin Industries LLC ....E.... 918 422-4790
Watts *(G-11357)*
Hanor Company of Wisconsin LLC ....E.... 580 237-3255
Enid *(G-2969)*
Hart Feeds Inc ....G.... 405 224-0102
Chickasha *(G-1468)*
Henderson Feeds LLC ....G.... 580 574-5375
Sayre *(G-8341)*
Hl Pro Feeds Inc ....F.... 580 497-2219
Cheyenne *(G-1425)*
Hitch Enterprises Inc ....G.... 580 338-6510
Hooker *(G-3597)*
Hollis Cotton Oil Mill Inc ....F.... 580 688-3394
Hollis *(G-3565)*
Hubbard ....G.... 918 785-2000
Adair *(G-110)*
▲ **Kfm Inc** ....F.... 580 342-6293
Temple *(G-8933)*
Luther Mill and Farm Supply ....G.... 405 277-3221
Luther *(G-4135)*
Marshall Minerals LLC ....G.... 405 848-5715
Oklahoma City *(G-6531)*
Mid America Farm & Ranch ....G.... 918 275-4984
Talala *(G-8900)*
Midwestern Pet Foods Inc ....F.... 405 224-2691
Chickasha *(G-1487)*
Mountain Country Foods LLC ....E.... 580 822-4130
Okeene *(G-5259)*
Nestle Purina Petcare Company ....D.... 405 751-4550
Edmond *(G-2535)*
O K Foods Inc ....A.... 918 653-1640
Heavener *(G-3431)*
Oklahoma Tool & Machine ....G.... 405 262-2624
El Reno *(G-2744)*
Purina Animal Nutrition LLC ....E.... 405 232-6171
Oklahoma City *(G-6925)*
Purina Mills LLC ....E.... 405 232-6171
Oklahoma City *(G-6926)*
Quality Liquid Feeds Inc ....G.... 918 683-7215
Muskogee *(G-4740)*
Red Seal Feeds LLC ....G.... 918 423-3710
McAlester *(G-4332)*
Rocky Farmers Cooperative Inc ....F.... 580 666-2440
Rocky *(G-8105)*
Rocky Farmers Cooperative Inc ....G.... 580 674-3356
Dill City *(G-2037)*
S & S Farm Center ....F.... 405 273-6907
Shawnee *(G-8491)*
Shawnee Milling Company ....G.... 405 352-4336
Minco *(G-4481)*
Spring Hollow Feed Mill Inc ....G.... 918 453-9933
Hulbert *(G-3628)*
Stillwater Milling Company LLC ....D.... 405 372-2766
Stillwater *(G-8757)*
Stockmans Mill & Grain Inc ....G.... 918 762-3459
Pawnee *(G-7711)*
Ultra Botanica LLC ....G.... 405 694-4175
Oklahoma City *(G-7359)*
W C Bradley Co ....G.... 918 379-6238
Claremore *(G-1703)*
West Texas By Products LP ....F.... 580 371-9413
Ravia *(G-8072)*
Westway Feed Products LLC ....G.... 918 266-5911
Catoosa *(G-1366)*
Winfield Solutions LLC ....G.... 580 237-2456
Enid *(G-3082)*
Wister Lake Feed Inc ....G.... 918 655-7954
Howe *(G-3601)*

2051 Bread, Bakery Prdts Exc Cookies & Crackers

Ambrosia Sweet Inc ....G.... 405 816-2887
Oklahoma City *(G-5429)*
Angela Lyn Sarabia ....G.... 405 808-8576
Oklahoma City *(G-5446)*
Antoinette Baking Co LLC ....G.... 918 808-0875
Tulsa *(G-9193)*
▲ **Bama Companies Inc** ....A.... 918 592-0778
Tulsa *(G-9258)*
Bama Foods Limited Partnership ....C.... 918 732-2399
Tulsa *(G-9260)*
Berryfields Cinnamon Roll LLC ....G.... 405 248-0777
Oklahoma City *(G-5558)*
Bimbo Bakeries Usa Inc ....G.... 580 234-1213
Enid *(G-2918)*
Bimbo Bakeries Usa Inc ....G.... 405 273-5049
Shawnee *(G-8432)*
Bimbo Bakeries Usa Inc ....B.... 405 556-2135
Oklahoma City *(G-5569)*
Browns Bakery Inc ....E.... 405 232-0363
Oklahoma City *(G-5637)*
Bubble Bee Bakery and Supplies ....G.... 918 209-8658
Tulsa *(G-9347)*
Cakes & More ....G.... 918 649-0451
Poteau *(G-7899)*
Cloverleaf Baking Co ....G.... 612 708-8196
Bartlesville *(G-466)*
Cupcakes & Sweets Galore ....G.... 405 641-7760
Oklahoma City *(G-5870)*
Cupcakes By Lu ....G.... 918 671-0599
Bixby *(G-619)*
Da Bomb Cupcakes ....G.... 918 261-3595
Tulsa *(G-9543)*
Dandee Donuts ....G.... 580 332-7700
Ada *(G-30)*
Dandy Donuts ....G.... 580 924-7872
Durant *(G-2220)*
Daylight Donuts ....G.... 918 256-6236
Vinita *(G-11252)*
Daylight Donuts ....G.... 405 598-8707
Tecumseh *(G-8911)*
Daylight Donuts ....G.... 580 279-6560
Ada *(G-31)*
Daylight Donuts Inc ....G.... 405 359-9016
Edmond *(G-2384)*
Dizzy Lizzy Cupcakery LLC ....G.... 405 263-7667
Okarche *(G-5242)*
Donut Shop ....G.... 580 276-3910
Marietta *(G-4206)*
Dounut Palace ....G.... 405 527-5746
Purcell *(G-8006)*
Felinis Cookies Inc ....G.... 918 742-3638
Tulsa *(G-9734)*
Flowers Baking Co Denton LLC ....G.... 405 366-2175
Norman *(G-5002)*
Flowers Bkg Co Lynchburg LLC ....G.... 918 270-1182
Tulsa *(G-9759)*
Flowers Foods Inc ....G.... 405 270-7880
Oklahoma City *(G-6093)*
Franklin Baking Company LLC ....G.... 918 423-2888
McAlester *(G-4300)*
Grahams Bakery & Cafe ....G.... 918 543-4244
Inola *(G-3659)*
J BS Donuts ....G.... 918 486-4022
Coweta *(G-1887)*
Jemison Denna ....G.... 405 922-7830
Oklahoma City *(G-6356)*
Key To Natures Blessings LLC ....G.... 405 603-8200
Bethany *(G-585)*
Krispy Kreme ....G.... 918 294-5293
Tulsa *(G-10103)*
Legend Enterprises Inc ....G.... 405 340-0410
Edmond *(G-2486)*
Mc Alester Food Warehouse ....D.... 580 436-4302
Ada *(G-64)*
Mitchells Sausage Rolls ....G.... 918 342-5852
Claremore *(G-1657)*
Morgans Bakery ....G.... 918 456-3731
Tahlequah *(G-8875)*
Nut House ....G.... 918 266-1604
Claremore *(G-1664)*
O K Country Donut Shoppe ....G.... 918 493-6455
Tulsa *(G-10371)*
Order Here Tulsa LLC ....G.... 888 633-9905
Muskogee *(G-4728)*
Panderia La Guadalupana ....G.... 918 764-9000
Tulsa *(G-10459)*
Paradise Doughnuts ....G.... 405 224-2907
Chickasha *(G-1499)*
Precious Memories By M L ....G.... 405 427-7007
Oklahoma City *(G-6878)*
Quality Bakery Products LLC ....F.... 609 871-7393
Tulsa *(G-10590)*
Raymonds Donut Shop ....G.... 918 660-0644
Tulsa *(G-10622)*
Saskas Sweets ....G.... 580 772-3476
Weatherford *(G-11438)*
Sfc Global Supply Chain Inc ....C.... 918 696-8325
Stilwell *(G-8795)*
Sophisticated Sweets Inc ....G.... 580 704-8038
Cache *(G-1231)*
Sweet Memories By Heather LLC ....G.... 360 608-1600
Cushing *(G-1963)*

20 FOOD AND KINDRED PRODUCTS

Sweetiesrite Baking ....G...... 405 400-6581
  Oklahoma City *(G-7236)*
Tower Cafe Inc ....F 405 263-4853
  Okarche *(G-5255)*
Tulsa Baking Inc ....D...... 918 712-2918
  Tulsa *(G-10988)*
Tulsa Baking Inc ....E 918 747-2301
  Tulsa *(G-10989)*

2052 Cookies & Crackers

Billy Goat Ice Cream Co LLC ....G...... 405 332-5508
  Stillwater *(G-8660)*
Dandee Donuts.......................................G...... 580 332-7700
  Ada *(G-30)*
Fehr Foods Inc ....E 580 276-4100
  Marietta *(G-4207)*
Felinis Cookies Inc ....G...... 918 742-3638
  Tulsa *(G-9734)*
Masons Pecans & Peanuts Inc ....G...... 405 329-7828
  Norman *(G-5065)*
Nonnis Foods LLC ....D...... 918 621-1200
  Tulsa *(G-10348)*
Pure Creativity LLC ....G...... 918 272-3152
  Owasso *(G-7605)*
Treehouse Private Brands Inc ....C 270 365-5505
  Poteau *(G-7915)*
Tulsa Baking Inc ....D...... 918 712-2918
  Tulsa *(G-10988)*
Tulsa Baking Inc ....E 918 747-2301
  Tulsa *(G-10989)*

2053 Frozen Bakery Prdts

▲ Bama Companies Inc ....A...... 918 592-0778
  Tulsa *(G-9258)*
Bama Pie Ltd ....A...... 918 592-0778
  Tulsa *(G-9261)*
Enchanted Delights LLC ....G...... 405 202-5782
  Oklahoma City *(G-6034)*
Fields Inc ....E 405 238-7381
  Pauls Valley *(G-7659)*
Nonnis Foods LLC ....D...... 918 621-1200
  Tulsa *(G-10348)*

2064 Candy & Confectionery Prdts

Amazing Grace Fudge LLC ....G...... 580 883-4693
  Ringwood *(G-8083)*
Aucora Breakfast Bar Backyard ....G...... 405 609-8854
  Oklahoma City *(G-5488)*
Big Easy ....G...... 918 493-6280
  Tulsa *(G-9289)*
Castle Rock Kitchens ....G...... 405 751-1822
  Oklahoma City *(G-5709)*
Cotton Candi Creations LLC ....G...... 580 471-6550
  Altus *(G-151)*
Fudgenomics 101 LLC ....G...... 405 401-3832
  Norman *(G-5004)*
Jackson Holdings LLC ....G...... 405 842-8903
  Oklahoma City *(G-6343)*
Ladybugs and Lollipops LLC ....G...... 405 919-8555
  Guthrie *(G-3322)*
Masons Pecans & Peanuts Inc ....G...... 405 329-7828
  Norman *(G-5065)*
Mollycoddled Hash Slinger LLC ....G...... 918 236-1196
  Fort Gibson *(G-3176)*
Nutopia Nuts & More ....G...... 405 663-2330
  Hydro *(G-3633)*
Peanut Products Co Inc ....F 580 296-4888
  Calera *(G-1243)*
Woody Candy Company Inc ....G...... 405 842-4900
  Oklahoma City *(G-7468)*
Zoo Too ....G...... 580 250-1088
  Lawton *(G-4026)*

2066 Chocolate & Cocoa Prdts

Castle Rock Kitchens ....G...... 405 751-1822
  Oklahoma City *(G-5709)*
Chickasaw Nation ....G...... 405 331-2300
  Davis *(G-1980)*
▲ Executive Coffee Service Co ....D...... 405 236-3932
  Oklahoma City *(G-6059)*
Godiva Chocolatier Inc ....G...... 918 459-2635
  Tulsa *(G-9837)*
Nut House ....G...... 918 266-1604
  Claremore *(G-1664)*

2068 Salted & Roasted Nuts & Seeds

Gunter Peanut Co ....E 405 656-2398
  Binger *(G-606)*

Joa Inc ....G...... 580 367-2616
  Caddo *(G-1236)*
Masons Pecans & Peanuts Inc ....G...... 405 329-7828
  Norman *(G-5065)*
Nutopia Nuts & More ....G...... 405 663-2330
  Hydro *(G-3633)*
Peanut Products Co Inc ....F 580 296-4888
  Calera *(G-1243)*
Red River Cold Storage LLC ....G...... 580 795-9948
  Madill *(G-4161)*

2074 Cottonseed Oil Mills

Producers Cooperative Oil Mill..............G...... 405 232-7555
  Oklahoma City *(G-6909)*

2075 Soybean Oil Mills

Koko-Best Inc ....G...... 918 836-2400
  Tulsa *(G-10099)*
Solae LLC ....E 918 476-5825
  Pryor *(G-7991)*

2077 Animal, Marine Fats & Oils

Darling Ingredients Inc ....E 918 371-2528
  Collinsville *(G-1808)*
Griffin Industries LLC ....E 918 422-4790
  Watts *(G-11357)*
Oklahoma Heartland Inc ....G...... 918 914-3124
  Stillwater *(G-8732)*

2079 Shortening, Oils & Margarine

Davis Hudson Inc ....G...... 405 203-0604
  Edmond *(G-2383)*
Rock Oil Co ....G...... 918 357-1188
  Broken Arrow *(G-1157)*

2082 Malt Beverages

Azimuth Spirits LLC ....G...... 317 468-3931
  Norman *(G-4922)*
Back Alley Brewers & More LLC ....G...... 580 716-2571
  Ponca City *(G-7799)*
Bb2 LLC ....G...... 918 895-7878
  Tulsa *(G-9274)*
Bb2 LLC ....G...... 405 726-8300
  Edmond *(G-2319)*
Bb2 LLC ....E 405 232-2739
  Oklahoma City *(G-5534)*
Brewer Media LLC ....G...... 405 236-4143
  Oklahoma City *(G-5626)*
Choc Brewing Company Inc ....G...... 918 302-3002
  McAlester *(G-4282)*
Dulaneys Liquor Store ....G...... 405 377-9007
  Stillwater *(G-8679)*
Ed F Davis Inc ....G...... 580 265-4210
  Stonewall *(G-8800)*
Krebs Brewing Co Inc ....F 918 740-9293
  Tulsa *(G-10101)*
Krebs Brewing Co Inc ....F 918 488-8910
  Tulsa *(G-10102)*
Stillwater Brewing Company LLC ....G...... 405 614-2520
  Stillwater *(G-8756)*
Union Brewers ....G...... 405 604-8989
  Oklahoma City *(G-7360)*

2084 Wine & Brandy

Allen Vineyards LLC ....G...... 405 240-7147
  Bethany *(G-572)*
B&G Meadery LLC ....G...... 580 272-7197
  Stonewall *(G-8797)*
Billy J Vineyard ....G...... 918 246-2139
  Sand Springs *(G-8167)*
Blue Coyote Winery ....G...... 918 785-4727
  Adair *(G-107)*
Boardwalk Distribution Co ....F 918 551-6275
  Tulsa *(G-9313)*
Broken Bone Vnyards Winery LLC ....G...... 405 585-8319
  McLoud *(G-4354)*
Canadian Rver Vnyrds Wnery LLC ....G...... 405 872-5565
  Lexington *(G-4034)*
Canyon Lakes Winery LLC ....G...... 405 367-7291
  Oklahoma City *(G-5690)*
Coyote Run Vineyard LLC ....G...... 918 785-4727
  Adair *(G-108)*
Deangel Farms & Winery LLC ....G...... 405 996-0914
  Blanchard *(G-709)*
Deep Branch Winery LLC ....G...... 918 519-5490
  Cookson *(G-1850)*
Diane E Dean ....G...... 580 775-4203
  Caddo *(G-1233)*

Dynamic Brands Inc ....G...... 918 630-7083
  Broken Arrow *(G-1123)*
Entwined Vines Winery LLC ....G...... 405 320-0452
  Anadarko *(G-203)*
Fish Tale Winery ....G...... 580 494-6115
  Broken Bow *(G-1190)*
Frozen Mesa Winery LLC ....G...... 405 281-5962
  Choctaw *(G-1543)*
Girls Gone Wine ....E 580 494-6243
  Broken Bow *(G-1191)*
Grayfox Vineyards LLC ....G...... 918 378-2214
  Yukon *(G-11728)*
Ingels Vineyard LLC ....G...... 405 321-1008
  Norman *(G-5034)*
Iron Post Winery LLC ....G...... 918 479-3600
  Locust Grove *(G-4111)*
Island Palm LLC ....G...... 405 321-1056
  Norman *(G-5038)*
J & B Deep Discount ....G...... 918 622-7600
  Tulsa *(G-10016)*
Joullian Vineyards Ltd ....E 405 848-4585
  Oklahoma City *(G-6386)*
Judy Tomlinson ....G...... 580 252-2559
  Duncan *(G-2140)*
Knotted Rope Winery LLC ....G...... 918 839-1464
  Broken Bow *(G-1197)*
Legends Vineyard & Winery ....G...... 405 823-8265
  Lindsay *(G-4073)*
Native Spirits Winery LLC ....G...... 405 329-9942
  Norman *(G-5087)*
Nellis Vineyards LLC ....G...... 405 826-5279
  Edmond *(G-2532)*
New Moon Vineyard ....G...... 405 364-8655
  Norman *(G-5090)*
Nuyaka Creek Winery LLC ....G...... 918 756-8485
  Bristow *(G-790)*
Pecan Creek Winery LLC ....G...... 918 683-1087
  Muskogee *(G-4733)*
Plainview Winery ....G...... 580 796-2902
  Lahoma *(G-3859)*
Plymouth Valley Cellars Inc ....G...... 580 227-0348
  Fairview *(G-3146)*
Ramiiisol Vineyards LLC ....G...... 405 858-9800
  Oklahoma City *(G-6969)*
Rocky Top Winery LLC ....G...... 580 857-2869
  Allen *(G-138)*
Rusty Nail Winery ....G...... 580 622-8466
  Sulphur *(G-8842)*
Sailing Horse Enterprises LLC ....G...... 918 618-4824
  Eufaula *(G-3112)*
Sand Hill Vineyards LLC ....G...... 405 760-1268
  Calumet *(G-1248)*
Shell Creek Vineyards LLC ....G...... 214 415-4741
  Yukon *(G-11781)*
Sine Qua Non LLC ....G...... 405 478-2539
  Oklahoma City *(G-7142)*
Sparks Vineyard & Winery Inc ....G...... 918 866-2529
  Sparks *(G-8589)*
Stableridge LLC ....F 918 968-2568
  Stroud *(G-8819)*
Strebel Creek Vineyard ....G...... 405 720-7779
  Oklahoma City *(G-7217)*
Summerside Vineyards & Winery ....F 918 256-3000
  Tuttle *(G-11212)*
Summerside Winery & Meadery ....G...... 405 514-6360
  Tuttle *(G-11213)*
Territory Cellars LLC ....G...... 918 987-1800
  Stroud *(G-8822)*
Tidal School Winery ....G...... 918 352-4900
  Drumright *(G-2076)*
Trio Di Vino LLC ....F 405 494-1954
  Oklahoma City *(G-7336)*
Twiss Sueons Winery Inc ....E 405 277-7089
  Luther *(G-4140)*
Waddell Vineyards LLC ....G...... 580 421-6933
  Ada *(G-103)*
Waters Edge Winery On Rose ....G...... 918 286-0086
  Broken Arrow *(G-1092)*
Whispering Vines Vinyrd Winery ....G...... 918 447-0808
  Tulsa *(G-11116)*
Whispring Mdows Vnyards Winery ....G...... 918 423-9463
  McAlester *(G-4351)*
Woodland Park Vineyards ....G...... 405 743-2442
  Stillwater *(G-8776)*
Woods and Waters Holdings LLC ....F 405 347-3000
  Anadarko *(G-210)*
Woods Wters Wnry Vneyards LLC ....G...... 405 247-3000
  Anadarko *(G-211)*
Yippee Ay-O-K Winery ....G...... 580 515-8214
  Clinton *(G-1773)*

Employee Codes: A=Over 500 employees, B=251-500
C=101-250, D=51-100, E=20-50, F=10-19, G=1-9

20 FOOD AND KINDRED PRODUCTS
SIC SECTION

2085 Liquors, Distilled, Rectified & Blended

19th Hole..........G....... 405 424-0520
Oklahoma City *(G-5328)*
Green Valley Distillery LLC..........G....... 918 413-5199
Red Oak *(G-8076)*
Oklahoma Distilling Company..........G....... 918 505-4861
Tulsa *(G-10397)*
Rock Creek Distillery LLC..........G....... 580 254-1407
Shattuck *(G-8423)*
Scissortail Distillery LLC..........G....... 405 326-5466
Moore *(G-4565)*
Twisters Distillery..........G....... 405 237-3499
Moore *(G-4580)*

2086 Soft Drinks

7 Up Bottle..........G....... 918 426-0310
McAlester *(G-4268)*
Ada Coca Cola Bottling Company..........D....... 580 427-2000
Ada *(G-3)*
All American Bottling Cor..........G....... 918 831-3800
Tulsa *(G-9135)*
American Bottling Company..........D....... 405 680-5150
Oklahoma City *(G-5433)*
Belle Point Beverages Inc..........G....... 918 649-3921
Poteau *(G-7896)*
Browne Bottling Co Inc..........F....... 405 232-1158
Oklahoma City *(G-5636)*
Coca Cola Bottling Co..........G....... 580 256-2350
Woodward *(G-11570)*
Coca-Cola Enterprises Inc..........G....... 918 619-8200
Tulsa *(G-9464)*
Dr Pepper Bottling Co..........G....... 580 256-2350
Woodward *(G-11580)*
Dr Pepper Bottling Co Elk City..........F....... 580 225-3186
Elk City *(G-2804)*
Dr Pepper Co..........G....... 580 765-6468
Ponca City *(G-7823)*
Dr Pepper Snapple Group..........G....... 405 680-5150
Oklahoma City *(G-5978)*
Dr Pepper-Royal Crown Btlg Co..........F....... 405 224-1260
Chickasha *(G-1453)*
Dust Cutter..........E....... 405 615-7788
Norman *(G-4985)*
Fresh Promise Foods Inc..........G....... 561 703-4659
Midwest City *(G-4441)*
Great Plains Coca Cola Btlg Co..........G....... 405 503-9328
Oklahoma City *(G-6178)*
Great Plains Coca Cola Btlg Co..........B....... 405 280-2000
Oklahoma City *(G-6179)*
Great Plains Coca-Cola Btlg Co..........D....... 918 439-3013
Tulsa *(G-9853)*
Great Plains Coca-Cola Btlg Co..........D....... 405 280-2000
Oklahoma City *(G-6180)*
Great Plains Coca-Cola Btlg Co..........C....... 405 280-2700
Oklahoma City *(G-6181)*
Great Plains Coca-Cola Btlg Co..........C....... 800 753-2653
Tulsa *(G-9854)*
Great Plains Design..........G....... 405 943-9018
Oklahoma City *(G-6182)*
Hometown Bottled Water LLC..........G....... 918 786-4426
Grove *(G-3274)*
Ice-T King LLC..........G....... 405 206-1185
Oklahoma City *(G-6284)*
Lake Country Beverage Inc..........G....... 918 426-0310
McAlester *(G-4313)*
Minnette Company Ltd..........G....... 580 226-2929
Wilson *(G-11538)*
Niagara Bottling LLC..........G....... 909 230-5000
Oklahoma City *(G-6677)*
P-Americas LLC..........G....... 580 326-8333
Hugo *(G-3617)*
Pepsi Cola Btlg Clinton Okla..........E....... 580 323-1666
Clinton *(G-1763)*
Pepsi Cola Company..........B....... 918 446-6601
Tulsa *(G-10489)*
Pepsi-Cola Btlg McAlester Inc..........E....... 918 423-2360
McAlester *(G-4328)*
Pepsi-Cola Btlg McAlester Inc..........G....... 918 446-6601
Tulsa *(G-10490)*
Pepsi-Cola Metro Btlg Co Inc..........C....... 580 326-8333
Hugo *(G-3618)*
Pepsi-Cola Metro Btlg Co Inc..........E....... 580 585-6281
Lawton *(G-3983)*
Pure Mountain..........G....... 918 254-2225
Broken Arrow *(G-1014)*
R W D 9 Mayes County..........G....... 918 434-5000
Salina *(G-8135)*
Round Springs Water Co LLC..........G....... 918 253-8188
Spavinaw *(G-8592)*
Seven-Up Bottling Co Inc..........F....... 580 765-6468
Ponca City *(G-7874)*
Sooner Coca-Cola Bottling Co..........G....... 918 423-0911
Mc Alester *(G-4266)*
Total Beverage Services LLC..........G....... 405 366-1344
Norman *(G-5177)*
Vita-Source Inc..........G....... 918 407-9525
Sand Springs *(G-8235)*

2087 Flavoring Extracts & Syrups

Arctic Blends Corporation..........G....... 918 455-2079
Broken Arrow *(G-832)*
Big Rock Foods LLC..........G....... 405 269-8558
Stillwater *(G-8659)*
◆ **Cesi Chemical Inc**..........B....... 580 658-6608
Marlow *(G-4225)*
Griffin Food Company..........D....... 918 687-6311
Muskogee *(G-4683)*
Margarita Man Hq LLC..........G....... 830 336-4252
Stillwater *(G-8721)*
Midwest Bakers Supply Co Inc..........G....... 405 942-3489
Oklahoma City *(G-6599)*
▲ **Pepper Creek Farms Inc**..........G....... 580 536-1300
Lawton *(G-3982)*
Springdale Food Co Inc..........G....... 580 928-2598
Sayre *(G-8348)*
Webers Superior Root Beer Inc..........G....... 918 742-1082
Tulsa *(G-11101)*

2095 Coffee

Charlie Bean Coffee LLC..........F....... 405 376-4815
Oklahoma City *(G-5743)*
Compadres Trading Co..........G....... 405 816-9911
Oklahoma City *(G-5807)*
▲ **Executive Coffee Service Co**..........D....... 405 236-3932
Oklahoma City *(G-6059)*
Farmer Bros Co..........G....... 918 439-9262
Tulsa *(G-9728)*
Farmer Bros Co..........G....... 405 751-7222
Oklahoma City *(G-6074)*
Henderson Coffee Corp..........E....... 918 682-8751
Muskogee *(G-4690)*
Hillshire Brands Company..........C....... 405 751-7222
Oklahoma City *(G-6249)*
Imperial Inc..........F....... 580 357-8300
Lawton *(G-3940)*
Imperial LLC..........B....... 918 437-1300
Tulsa *(G-9972)*
Minnette Company Ltd..........G....... 580 226-2929
Wilson *(G-11538)*
Okie Roasters LLC..........G....... 405 699-2007
Guthrie *(G-3328)*
Royal Cup Inc..........G....... 405 943-6088
Oklahoma City *(G-7052)*
Tulsa Coffee Service Inc..........E....... 918 836-5570
Tulsa *(G-10993)*
Viridian Coffee LLC..........G....... 405 795-0773
Duncan *(G-2195)*

2096 Potato Chips & Similar Prdts

Tortilleria Lupita Inc..........G....... 405 232-2760
Oklahoma City *(G-7306)*

2097 Ice

Clinton Ice LLC..........F....... 580 331-6060
Clinton *(G-1746)*
Enterprise Ice Inc..........G....... 580 237-4015
Enid *(G-2955)*
Freeman Ice LLC..........G....... 580 263-0021
Madill *(G-4147)*
K-Dub LLC..........G....... 580 353-6899
Lawton *(G-3948)*
Reddy Ice Corporation..........F....... 918 682-2471
Muskogee *(G-4744)*
Reddy Ice Corporation..........E....... 405 681-2892
Oklahoma City *(G-6994)*
Reddy Ice Corporation..........E....... 580 323-3080
Clinton *(G-1766)*
Reddy Ice Corporation..........E....... 918 836-8223
Tulsa *(G-10633)*
Southeastern Ice..........E....... 918 465-2500
Wilburton *(G-11524)*
Sub Zero Ice Services LLC..........G....... 405 387-2224
Newcastle *(G-4843)*

2098 Macaroni, Spaghetti & Noodles

Pasta Pizzaz Inc..........G....... 405 848-9966
Oklahoma City *(G-6808)*

2099 Food Preparations, NEC

▲ **Advance Food Company Inc**..........C....... 800 969-2747
Enid *(G-2905)*
Advancepierre Foods Inc..........F....... 800 969-2747
Enid *(G-2907)*
Amigos Salsa..........G....... 580 224-0667
Ardmore *(G-239)*
Amigos Salsa..........G....... 580 224-1424
Ardmore *(G-240)*
Big Productions LLC..........G....... 405 513-6545
Edmond *(G-2321)*
Bishop Brothers..........G....... 918 367-2270
Bristow *(G-766)*
Campo Alegre Foods..........G....... 918 271-6775
Tulsa *(G-9368)*
Cecilias Salsas..........G....... 918 984-1491
Tulsa *(G-9392)*
Chelinos Tortilla Factory..........F....... 405 631-3188
Oklahoma City *(G-5747)*
Cimarron Docs Bar-B-Que Chili..........G....... 918 787-7881
Grove *(G-3261)*
Clements Foods Co..........G....... 405 842-3308
Oklahoma City *(G-5784)*
Designs By Lex LLC..........G....... 580 280-2557
Lawton *(G-3919)*
Du Pont Delaware Inc..........G....... 918 476-5825
Pryor *(G-7960)*
El Capora Tortilleria..........G....... 405 662-0427
Oklahoma City *(G-6014)*
Everyday Foods LLC..........G....... 918 299-7939
Jenks *(G-3705)*
▲ **Executive Coffee Service Co**..........D....... 405 236-3932
Oklahoma City *(G-6059)*
Gold Strike Chili..........G....... 405 606-1819
Warr Acres *(G-11320)*
Griffin Food Company..........D....... 918 687-6311
Muskogee *(G-4683)*
▲ **Griffin Holdings Inc**..........D....... 918 687-6311
Muskogee *(G-4684)*
H Gellar..........G....... 617 834-0602
Warr Acres *(G-11321)*
Hermans Chili Mix Inc..........G....... 918 743-1832
Tulsa *(G-9925)*
Hillshire Brands Company..........C....... 405 751-7222
Oklahoma City *(G-6249)*
Hollis Home Made Salsa LLC..........G....... 405 464-6249
Midwest City *(G-4442)*
J-M Farms Inc..........B....... 918 540-1567
Miami *(G-4409)*
JKJ Processing Inc..........G....... 405 606-9711
Yukon *(G-11736)*
Kize Concepts Inc..........F....... 405 226-0701
Oklahoma City *(G-6427)*
Maria Raes Inc..........G....... 580 242-3342
Enid *(G-3005)*
Markenia Foods LLC..........G....... 405 751-8616
Edmond *(G-2505)*
Matador Processing LLC..........E....... 405 485-3567
Blanchard *(G-722)*
Midwest Bakers Supply Co Inc..........G....... 405 942-3489
Oklahoma City *(G-6599)*
Nut House..........G....... 918 266-1604
Claremore *(G-1664)*
O K Foods Inc..........B....... 918 427-7000
Muldrow *(G-4635)*
Peanut Products Co Inc..........F....... 580 296-4888
Calera *(G-1243)*
▲ **Pepper Creek Farms Inc**..........G....... 580 536-1300
Lawton *(G-3982)*
▲ **Pepper Land Inc**..........G....... 918 691-7241
Tulsa *(G-10488)*
Pie In Sky Tulsa LLc..........G....... 918 527-5855
Tulsa *(G-10513)*
Premeir Companies Inc..........F....... 405 895-7100
Moore *(G-4555)*
Quality Bakery Products LLC..........F....... 609 871-7393
Tulsa *(G-10590)*
Quiktrip Corporation..........B....... 918 615-7700
Tulsa *(G-10599)*
R & J Food Tulsa LLC..........G....... 918 520-0484
Tulsa *(G-10600)*
Ross Honey Co..........G....... 405 352-4125
Minco *(G-4480)*
Royal Cup Inc..........G....... 405 943-6088
Oklahoma City *(G-7052)*
S and J Foods LLC..........E....... 580 337-6360
Bessie *(G-570)*
Sneaky Ts Salsa LLC..........G....... 405 323-7244
Piedmont *(G-7771)*

SIC SECTION

22 TEXTILE MILL PRODUCTS

Snider Farms Peanut Barn LLC..............G....... 580 471-3470
  Hollis *(G-3568)*
Springdale Food Co Inc..............G....... 580 928-2598
  Sayre *(G-8348)*
Tajour Specialty Products LLC..............G....... 479 684-7445
  Westville *(G-11485)*
Tortilla Velasquez..............G....... 580 468-6753
  Guymon *(G-3368)*
Tortilleria Azteca Inc..............G....... 405 632-5382
  Oklahoma City *(G-7305)*
Tortilleria Milagro..............G....... 918 895-8225
  Tulsa *(G-10956)*
Tortilleria Milargo..............G....... 918 439-9977
  Tulsa *(G-10957)*
Tortilleria Puebla Inc..............G....... 918 610-8816
  Tulsa *(G-10958)*
Twisted Oak Foods LLC..............G....... 405 720-7059
  Oklahoma City *(G-7353)*

21 TOBACCO PRODUCTS

2131 Tobacco, Chewing & Snuff

Handy Mart Inc..............G....... 580 254-5889
  Woodward *(G-11591)*
Osage Trading Co Inc..............G....... 918 287-4544
  Pawhuska *(G-7693)*
Tall Chief LLC..............G....... 918 783-8255
  Pryor *(G-7994)*
Treehouse Vapor Co LLC..............G....... 405 601-6867
  Oklahoma City *(G-7322)*

22 TEXTILE MILL PRODUCTS

2211 Cotton, Woven Fabric

8bit Canvas LLC..............G....... 405 924-3298
  Oklahoma City *(G-5340)*
Allys Discount Scrubs..............G....... 918 935-1359
  Broken Arrow *(G-826)*
Anything Canvas LLC..............G....... 580 658-9330
  Marlow *(G-4221)*
Awesome Acres Pacas Pyrs..............G....... 405 990-8205
  Oklahoma City *(G-5279)*
Bills Marine Canvas Upholstery..............G....... 405 306-2936
  Norman *(G-4931)*
Blue Canvas LLC..............G....... 580 327-3406
  Alva *(G-179)*
Boatman Marine Canvas..............G....... 405 628-7844
  Warr Acres *(G-11314)*
Burns & McDonnell Inc..............G....... 405 200-0300
  Oklahoma City *(G-5646)*
Canvas Sky Studios LLC..............G....... 917 514-9632
  Broken Arrow *(G-864)*
Clean Canvas Laser Tattoo Remo..............G....... 580 919-5466
  Lawton *(G-3906)*
Cliftton Wallcovering..............G....... 918 638-4454
  Broken Arrow *(G-870)*
Custom 4 X 4 Fabrication..............G....... 405 799-7599
  Oklahoma City *(G-5282)*
Dans Custom Canvas..............G....... 405 525-2419
  Oklahoma City *(G-5897)*
Dear John Denim Inc..............G....... 580 334-6637
  Oklahoma City *(G-5913)*
▲ Duncan Ticking Inc..............F....... 405 528-5480
  Oklahoma City *(G-5989)*
Faded Canvas Barber Studio..............G....... 405 735-7105
  Moore *(G-4521)*
Michael Sherry Alpert..............G....... 405 912-0062
  Oklahoma City *(G-5306)*
Paint On Canvas..............G....... 405 574-6689
  Chickasha *(G-1498)*
Rockin Dolls Denim..............G....... 918 402-6151
  Collinsville *(G-1822)*
S&S Canvas & Upholstery..............G....... 580 231-2587
  Ringwood *(G-8092)*
Sage Premium Denim Bar..............G....... 405 288-1503
  Goldsby *(G-3246)*
Salt Soothers LLC..............G....... 405 201-2020
  Edmond *(G-2610)*
Sooner Denim Inc..............G....... 405 641-4720
  Oklahoma City *(G-7161)*
Stroheim Romann Upholstery..............G....... 918 622-7700
  Tulsa *(G-10860)*
▲ Wohali Outdoors LLC..............F....... 918 343-3800
  Broken Arrow *(G-1100)*

2221 Silk & Man-Made Fiber

B B Fiberglass LLC..............G....... 405 755-5895
  Guthrie *(G-3298)*

Carter Fiberglass..............G....... 918 674-2325
  Quapaw *(G-8028)*
▲ Insul-Vest Inc..............G....... 918 445-2279
  Tulsa *(G-9992)*
Jacob Manufacturing Inc..............F....... 918 787-6606
  Grove *(G-3276)*
Jerry Beagley Braiding Company..............G....... 580 924-4995
  Calera *(G-1240)*
Okc Fabric Market..............G....... 405 531-0546
  Oklahoma City *(G-6729)*
Ray Harrington Draperies..............G....... 405 789-6710
  Bethany *(G-593)*
Rsga Incorporated..............G....... 918 978-6800
  Tulsa *(G-10681)*
Satin Siren LLC..............G....... 918 803-6351
  Pryor *(G-7990)*
Wing-It Concepts..............G....... 405 691-8053
  Oklahoma City *(G-5325)*

2231 Wool, Woven Fabric

Hooty Creek Alpacas..............G....... 918 284-5025
  Claremore *(G-1635)*
Icandee Refinishings LLC..............G....... 405 923-4956
  Oklahoma City *(G-6283)*
Jr Alpacas LLC..............G....... 405 771-2636
  Jones *(G-3749)*
Land Run Alpacas..............G....... 405 226-9005
  Agra *(G-126)*
Northwest Alpacas Ltd..............G....... 903 450-1999
  Edmond *(G-2542)*
Pendleton Woolen Mills Inc..............D....... 918 712-8545
  Tulsa *(G-10483)*
Storm Haven Alpaca LLC..............G....... 405 391-2767
  Choctaw *(G-1555)*

2241 Fabric Mills, Cotton, Wool, Silk & Man-Made

Central Texas Ex Metalwork LLC..............G....... 765 492-9058
  Oklahoma City *(G-5727)*
Dill City Embroidery..............G....... 580 674-3989
  Dill City *(G-2035)*
Jerry Beagley Braiding Company..............G....... 580 924-4995
  Calera *(G-1240)*
Mammoth Manufacturing Inc..............G....... 405 820-8301
  Bethany *(G-587)*

2252 Hosiery, Except Women's

Advanced Foot & Ankle..............G....... 405 692-7114
  Oklahoma City *(G-5382)*
Crazy Socks Productions Inc..............G....... 580 618-1228
  Sulphur *(G-8830)*
Sock Monkey Bizz LLC..............G....... 918 462-7392
  Wagoner *(G-11290)*
Sydnis Shag Socks..............G....... 405 664-5333
  Wellston *(G-11479)*
Two Socks LLC..............G....... 405 535-4753
  Norman *(G-5184)*

2253 Knit Outerwear Mills

Calamity Janes Funk & Junk Inc..............G....... 405 759-3383
  Oklahoma City *(G-5671)*
Gorfam Marketing Inc..............F....... 918 388-9935
  Tulsa *(G-9842)*
Kelly Loyd..............G....... 405 740-2345
  Ada *(G-55)*

2254 Knit Underwear Mills

House of Bedlam LLC..............G....... 405 946-3100
  Oklahoma City *(G-6266)*
Hyatt Ladona..............G....... 580 889-0199
  Atoka *(G-414)*
Uniquely Yours LLC..............G....... 918 283-2228
  Claremore *(G-1696)*

2259 Knitting Mills, NEC

E E Sewing Inc..............E....... 918 789-5881
  Chelsea *(G-1404)*

2261 Cotton Fabric Finishers

Body Billboards..............G....... 405 282-9922
  Guthrie *(G-3300)*
Fabricut Inc..............F....... 918 622-7700
  Tulsa *(G-9724)*
Hard Edge Design Inc..............G....... 405 360-9714
  Norman *(G-5016)*
Massive Graphic Screen Prtg..............F....... 405 364-3594
  Norman *(G-5066)*

Misaco Sign and Screen Prtg..............G....... 918 542-4188
  Miami *(G-4420)*

2262 Silk & Man-Made Fabric Finishers

Monograms Elite Inc..............G....... 580 353-1635
  Lawton *(G-3973)*
Promo Print 4 U LLC..............G....... 405 259-6721
  Oklahoma City *(G-6915)*
Semasys Inc..............E....... 405 525-2335
  Oklahoma City *(G-7107)*

2273 Carpets & Rugs

▲ Ahmadys Import LLC..............G....... 918 254-4094
  Tulsa *(G-9118)*
Aladdin Manufacturing Corp..............F....... 405 943-3037
  Oklahoma City *(G-5407)*
Brow Art 23..............G....... 405 848-3346
  Oklahoma City *(G-5634)*
Burtco Enterprises LLC..............G....... 918 857-1293
  Catoosa *(G-1307)*
Classic Carpets Lawton Inc..............G....... 580 713-0653
  Lawton *(G-3904)*
Interfaceflor LLC..............G....... 918 746-0501
  Tulsa *(G-10003)*
Kingston Flooring LLC..............G....... 405 470-3494
  Oklahoma City *(G-6423)*
Kinrich..............G....... 405 842-4307
  Oklahoma City *(G-6424)*
Mike McGills Carpet Inc..............G....... 405 222-0899
  Chickasha *(G-1488)*
Mohawk Industries..............G....... 214 309-4652
  Enid *(G-3015)*
Moss Seat Cover Mfg & Sls Co..............F....... 918 742-3326
  Tulsa *(G-10306)*
Oklahoma Interpak Inc..............E....... 918 687-1681
  Muskogee *(G-4724)*
▲ Triumph Arstrctres - Tulsa LLC..............A....... 615 361-2061
  Tulsa *(G-10978)*

2281 Yarn Spinning Mills

Gorfam Marketing Inc..............G....... 918 252-3733
  Tulsa *(G-9841)*

2284 Thread Mills

Boley One..............G....... 405 301-7692
  Oklahoma City *(G-5616)*

2295 Fabrics Coated Not Rubberized

▲ Clear Edge Filtration Inc..............D....... 918 984-6000
  Tulsa *(G-9447)*
Clear Edge Filtration Inc..............D....... 800 637-6206
  Tulsa *(G-9448)*
Cytec Industrial Mtls OK Inc..............G....... 918 252-3922
  Broken Arrow *(G-885)*
Leather Guns & Etc..............F....... 580 296-2616
  Colbert *(G-1785)*
Tatermash Oilcloth LLC..............G....... 918 743-3888
  Tulsa *(G-10901)*

2297 Fabrics, Nonwoven

Nxtnano LLC..............E....... 918 923-4824
  Claremore *(G-1665)*

2298 Cordage & Twine

Lynxsystems LLC..............G....... 918 728-6000
  Tulsa *(G-10185)*
Surface Mount Depot Inc..............D....... 405 948-8763
  Oklahoma City *(G-7232)*
Texhoma Fiber LLC..............G....... 918 747-7000
  Medicine Park *(G-4371)*

2299 Textile Goods, NEC

Mabels Fashion Alteration..............G....... 405 605-4558
  Oklahoma City *(G-6513)*
◆ Sooner Wiping Rags LLC..............F....... 405 670-3100
  Oklahoma City *(G-7168)*
▲ World Trading Company Inc..............A....... 405 787-1982
  Oklahoma City *(G-7471)*

Employee Codes: A=Over 500 employees, B=251-500
C=101-250, D=51-100, E=20-50, F=10-19, G=1-9

23 APPAREL AND OTHER FINISHED PRODUCTS MADE FROM FABRICS AND SIMILAR MATERIAL

2311 Men's & Boys' Suits, Coats & Overcoats

Douglas Rose Custom Tailoring............G....... 918 366-6002
  Bixby *(G-620)*
Globe Mfg Company-OK LLC ....E....... 580 272-9400
  Ada *(G-43)*
Mobetta ....G....... 580 588-9222
  Apache *(G-220)*
Sage Brush Junction ....G....... 580 227-3434
  Fairview *(G-3150)*
Synergy Maintenance LLC ....G....... 580 574-7355
  Lawton *(G-4009)*

2321 Men's & Boys' Shirts

Apex405 ....G....... 405 313-5145
  Norman *(G-4911)*
Emery Bay Corporation ....G....... 918 494-2988
  Tulsa *(G-9671)*
▲ Finish Line of Oklahoma Inc ....G....... 918 341-8291
  Claremore *(G-1621)*
Mobetta ....G....... 580 588-9222
  Apache *(G-220)*
Slapsok LLC ....G....... 405 845-2299
  Edmond *(G-2622)*
Synergy Maintenance LLC ....G....... 580 574-7355
  Lawton *(G-4009)*

2322 Men's & Boys' Underwear & Nightwear

Synergy Maintenance LLC ....G....... 580 574-7355
  Lawton *(G-4009)*

2323 Men's & Boys' Neckwear

▲ Two Guys Bowtie Company LLC ......G....... 405 612-0116
  Tulsa *(G-11026)*

2325 Men's & Boys' Separate Trousers & Casual Slacks

Synergy Maintenance LLC ....G....... 580 574-7355
  Lawton *(G-4009)*

2326 Men's & Boys' Work Clothing

Barbara J McGinnis ....G....... 580 226-7675
  Ardmore *(G-253)*
Beane Development Corp ....G....... 580 222-1150
  Ardmore *(G-255)*
Corporate Image Inc ....G....... 918 516-8376
  Owasso *(G-7556)*
▲ Round House Manufacturing LLC ....D....... 405 273-0510
  Shawnee *(G-8490)*
Synergy Maintenance LLC ....G....... 580 574-7355
  Lawton *(G-4009)*

2329 Men's & Boys' Clothing, NEC

Anvil Land and Properties Inc ....G....... 580 336-4402
  Perry *(G-7726)*
Creative Apparel and More Inc ....G....... 918 682-1283
  Muskogee *(G-4664)*
Hollywood Express Oklahoma Inc ....G....... 405 324-8111
  Yukon *(G-11730)*
Mule Hunting Clothes Inc ....G....... 601 856-5169
  Collinsville *(G-1817)*
Synergy Maintenance LLC ....G....... 580 574-7355
  Lawton *(G-4009)*
▲ Tech-Mesh Apparel LLC ....G....... 918 492-1193
  Tulsa *(G-10912)*

2331 Women's & Misses' Blouses

▲ Relevant Products LLC ....E....... 405 524-5250
  Oklahoma City *(G-7005)*
U Big TS Designs Inc ....G....... 405 401-4327
  Oklahoma City *(G-7356)*

2335 Women's & Misses' Dresses

Bricktown Real Estate & Develo ....G....... 405 236-4143
  Oklahoma City *(G-5627)*
Captive Imaging LLC ....G....... 918 340-3053
  Tulsa *(G-9372)*
Ellis Bridal LLC ....G....... 501 247-8698
  Tulsa *(G-9662)*
▲ Esb Sales Inc ....G....... 918 227-0378
  Sapulpa *(G-8270)*

Fancy Cakes ....G....... 405 701-3434
  Norman *(G-4996)*
▲ Glitter Gear LLC ....F....... 405 321-4327
  Oklahoma City *(G-6159)*
Mobetta ....G....... 580 588-9222
  Apache *(G-220)*
Pixel Park LLC ....G....... 405 613-0924
  Mustang *(G-4789)*
Sandy Childress Inc ....G....... 405 748-4949
  Edmond *(G-2612)*

2337 Women's & Misses' Suits, Coats & Skirts

Emery Bay Corporation ....G....... 918 494-2988
  Tulsa *(G-9671)*
Nine West Holdings Inc ....G....... 405 810-8568
  Oklahoma City *(G-6683)*

2339 Women's & Misses' Outerwear, NEC

Ajs Tees Inc ....G....... 918 455-6751
  Broken Arrow *(G-821)*
Bellylove Maternity Gifts ....G....... 405 818-3339
  Oklahoma City *(G-5548)*
Charles Komar & Sons Inc ....B....... 918 423-3535
  McAlester *(G-4280)*
First Class Outlet ....G....... 918 808-3405
  McAlester *(G-4299)*
Flaming Hope LLC ....G....... 405 924-4380
  Noble *(G-4880)*
Jan Farha ....G....... 405 848-1388
  Yukon *(G-11735)*
Jps Creations ....G....... 580 892-3455
  Allen *(G-135)*
Mule Hunting Clothes Inc ....G....... 601 856-5169
  Collinsville *(G-1817)*
Ndn Enterprises LLC ....G....... 703 772-6635
  Pawhuska *(G-7690)*
Rustic Rehab ....G....... 918 314-6647
  Grove *(G-3287)*
St John ....G....... 405 364-1917
  Norman *(G-5155)*
Team Spirit Sales ....G....... 918 296-5620
  Jenks *(G-3734)*
Titanium Phoenix Inc ....G....... 405 305-1304
  Oklahoma City *(G-7294)*

2341 Women's, Misses' & Children's Underwear & Nightwear

Charles Komar & Sons Inc ....B....... 918 423-3535
  McAlester *(G-4280)*
Charles Komar & Sons Inc ....G....... 918 423-1227
  Mcalester *(G-4281)*
Southwest Corset Corporation ....C....... 580 363-1935
  Blackwell *(G-693)*
United We Stand Inc ....G....... 918 382-1766
  Tulsa *(G-11044)*

2342 Brassieres, Girdles & Garments

Cupid Foundations Inc ....C....... 580 363-1935
  Blackwell *(G-680)*

2353 Hats, Caps & Millinery

Anvil Land and Properties Inc ....G....... 580 336-4402
  Perry *(G-7726)*
Cool Hard Hat Inc ....G....... 918 812-7636
  Tulsa *(G-9481)*
M T H Inc ....G....... 918 445-9235
  Tulsa *(G-10189)*
Shortys Hattery ....G....... 405 232-4287
  Oklahoma City *(G-7125)*

2361 Children's & Infants' Dresses & Blouses

Closet Consignments LLC ....G....... 405 387-3100
  Newcastle *(G-4823)*
Justice ....G....... 405 842-7180
  Oklahoma City *(G-6392)*
Slapsok LLC ....G....... 405 845-2299
  Edmond *(G-2622)*

2384 Robes & Dressing Gowns

Charles Komar & Sons Inc ....B....... 918 423-3535
  McAlester *(G-4280)*

2385 Waterproof Outerwear

▲ Wohali Outdoors LLC ....F....... 918 343-3800
  Broken Arrow *(G-1100)*

2386 Leather & Sheep Lined Clothing

Ganoa Imports ....G....... 918 622-3788
  Tulsa *(G-9798)*
Leather Store ....G....... 918 245-8676
  Sand Springs *(G-8199)*

2387 Apparel Belts

Gilmores Sports Concepts Inc ....G....... 918 250-3910
  Tulsa *(G-9827)*

2389 Apparel & Accessories, NEC

Apex Inc ....E....... 405 247-7377
  Anadarko *(G-200)*
Apothem ....G....... 405 447-2345
  Norman *(G-4912)*
Applause Apparel ....G....... 580 762-1349
  Ponca City *(G-7797)*
Blush Boutique Inc ....G....... 405 701-8600
  Norman *(G-4938)*
Brims & Accessories ....G....... 580 357-2746
  Lawton *(G-3901)*
Easleys Performance Wear Inc ....G....... 918 357-2400
  Broken Arrow *(G-1125)*
Flaming Hope LLC ....G....... 405 924-4380
  Noble *(G-4880)*
Little Sahara Sandsports LLC ....G....... 580 824-0569
  Waynoka *(G-11378)*
Mascots Etc Inc ....G....... 405 722-3406
  Oklahoma City *(G-6535)*
Mrsdish LLC ....G....... 405 447-3813
  Norman *(G-5083)*
▲ Mtm Recognition Corporation ....B....... 405 609-6900
  Oklahoma City *(G-6634)*
Rainbow Creations ....G....... 405 942-6207
  Oklahoma City *(G-6967)*
Rainbow Spreme Assmbly I O R G ....G....... 918 423-1328
  McAlester *(G-4331)*
Renavotio Infratech Inc ....G....... 504 722-7402
  Tulsa *(G-10640)*
Sherri Burch ....G....... 405 720-9021
  Oklahoma City *(G-7121)*
Witter Marketing Inc ....G....... 918 369-8639
  Broken Arrow *(G-1099)*

2391 Curtains & Draperies

Be-Hive Interior Drapery Fctry ....G....... 918 599-0292
  Tulsa *(G-9275)*
Clearco Window Cleaning LLC ....G....... 580 248-9547
  Lawton *(G-3907)*
Cord & Pleat Design Inc ....G....... 918 622-7676
  Broken Arrow *(G-1117)*
Curry Shades LLC ....G....... 918 779-3902
  Tulsa *(G-9524)*
Decorator Drapery Mfg Inc ....E....... 405 942-5613
  Oklahoma City *(G-5917)*
Fabricut Inc ....F....... 918 825-4400
  Pryor *(G-7962)*
Finished Seam ....G....... 918 742-4727
  Tulsa *(G-9745)*
▲ Hoppis Interiors ....G....... 405 390-2963
  Choctaw *(G-1545)*
Interior Designers Supply Inc ....F....... 405 521-1551
  Oklahoma City *(G-6318)*
Johnsons Spring Crest Drpery C ....G....... 405 238-7341
  Pauls Valley *(G-7662)*
Patricia McKay ....G....... 580 355-2739
  Cache *(G-1230)*
Pats Custom Draperies ....G....... 405 794-1019
  Moore *(G-4551)*
Ray Harrington Draperies ....G....... 405 789-6710
  Bethany *(G-593)*
Sam Dee Custom Draperies ....G....... 405 631-6128
  Oklahoma City *(G-7074)*
Springcrest Drapery Center ....G....... 918 258-5644
  Broken Arrow *(G-1058)*
Traceys Window Boutique Inc ....G....... 918 495-1806
  Tulsa *(G-10965)*
Vus Fabrics LLC ....G....... 405 330-9050
  Edmond *(G-2676)*

2392 House furnishings: Textile

Adairs Sleep World Inc ....F....... 405 341-9468
  Edmond *(G-2289)*
Cozy Cub Products LLP ....G....... 405 386-2879
  Newalla *(G-4807)*
Decorator Drapery Mfg Inc ....E....... 405 942-5613
  Oklahoma City *(G-5917)*
Doris Winford ....G....... 918 599-8931
  Tulsa *(G-9598)*

SIC SECTION 23 APPAREL AND OTHER FINISHED PRODUCTS MADE FROM FABRICS AND SIMILAR MATERIAL

E E Sewing Inc........E....... 918 789-5881
Chelsea *(G-1404)*
Fabricut Inc........F....... 918 825-4400
Pryor *(G-7962)*
Gilded Gate........G....... 405 590-3139
Oklahoma City *(G-6155)*
▲ **Hoppis Interiors**........G....... 405 390-2963
Choctaw *(G-1545)*
Interior Designers Supply Inc........F....... 405 521-1551
Oklahoma City *(G-6318)*
◆ **Jobri LLC**........F....... 580 925-3500
Ada *(G-54)*
▲ **Leachco Inc**........E....... 580 436-1142
Ada *(G-59)*
Life Lift Systems Inc........F....... 904 635-8231
Oklahoma City *(G-6474)*
Patricia McKay........G....... 580 355-2739
Cache *(G-1230)*
Quilts Unlimited........G....... 580 746-2770
Millerton *(G-4474)*
Ray Harrington Draperies........G....... 405 789-6710
Bethany *(G-593)*
Suntime Products Inc........G....... 918 664-8330
Tulsa *(G-10875)*
Tuffroots LLC........G....... 580 728-0000
Idabel *(G-3650)*
Whistle Stop Bedding & More........G....... 405 620-5749
Edmond *(G-2686)*

2393 Textile Bags

Beths Bags and More LLC........G....... 918 451-7346
Broken Arrow *(G-848)*
Fashionable Medical Covers........G....... 405 414-1147
Norman *(G-4998)*
Madison Filter Incorporated........G....... 315 685-3466
Tulsa *(G-10198)*
Pestco Inc........G....... 405 485-8060
Blanchard *(G-727)*
Speer Cushion Co........G....... 970 854-2911
Bixby *(G-664)*

2394 Canvas Prdts

Awnings of Tulsa Inc........G....... 918 747-2050
Tulsa *(G-9232)*
Awnings Unique........G....... 405 249-2488
Moore *(G-4496)*
City Tent & Awning Co Inc........G....... 918 583-5003
Tulsa *(G-9437)*
◆ **Covercraft Industries LLC**........C....... 405 238-9651
Pauls Valley *(G-7655)*
Covers Plus Inc........G....... 405 670-2221
Oklahoma City *(G-5846)*
Dans Custom Awnings LLC........G....... 405 601-2703
Oklahoma City *(G-5896)*
Dobbs & Crowder Inc........G....... 918 452-3211
Eufaula *(G-3100)*
Edwards Canvas Inc........E....... 405 238-7551
Pauls Valley *(G-7658)*
Hays Tent & Awning........G....... 918 534-1663
Dewey *(G-2023)*
Irwin Custom Sign Company LLC........G....... 405 372-0657
Stillwater *(G-8704)*
Jessie Shaw........G....... 918 587-6329
Tulsa *(G-10040)*
Karacon Solutions LLC........G....... 918 231-1001
Tulsa *(G-10076)*
Kerr Salesmakers & Marine Inc........G....... 918 437-0544
Tulsa *(G-10085)*
Oklahoma Custom Canvas Pdts........F....... 918 438-4040
Tulsa *(G-10395)*
Roper Product........G....... 580 795-2293
Lebanon *(G-4027)*
Shur-Co LLC........G....... 405 262-7600
El Reno *(G-2757)*

2395 Pleating & Stitching For The Trade

4524 LLC........G....... 405 620-3711
Edmond *(G-2285)*
A Stitch of Art........G....... 918 638-2511
Owasso *(G-7540)*
Adairs Sleep World Inc........F....... 405 341-9468
Edmond *(G-2289)*
Adventures In Stitching LLC........G....... 918 995-7445
Tulsa *(G-9114)*
Alico Embroidery Etc........G....... 405 321-2998
Norman *(G-4903)*
American TS........G....... 918 288-6682
Glenpool *(G-3230)*
Apothem........G....... 405 447-2345
Norman *(G-4912)*
Baywest Embroidery........G....... 580 626-4728
Jet *(G-3741)*
Big Red Shop Inc........G....... 405 495-5551
Warr Acres *(G-11313)*
Bordeauxs Embroidery........G....... 405 227-0958
Oklahoma City *(G-5619)*
Carolyns Mouse House........G....... 405 354-2858
Yukon *(G-11702)*
Cas Monogramming Inc........G....... 405 350-6556
Yukon *(G-11703)*
Causley Productions Inc........F....... 405 372-0940
Stillwater *(G-8666)*
Cejco Inc........F....... 405 366-8256
Norman *(G-4954)*
Christys Quilts........G....... 405 853-2155
Hennessey *(G-3450)*
Cindys Stitching........G....... 405 735-7126
Oklahoma City *(G-5281)*
Complete Graphics Inc........G....... 405 232-8882
Oklahoma City *(G-5812)*
Corporate Image Inc........G....... 918 516-8376
Owasso *(G-7556)*
Corporate Image Apparel LLC........G....... 405 659-8264
Oklahoma City *(G-5839)*
Corser Group Inc........G....... 918 749-6456
Tulsa *(G-9492)*
Cr Stripes Ltd Co........G....... 405 946-8577
Oklahoma City *(G-5850)*
Creative Apparel and More Inc........G....... 918 682-1283
Muskogee *(G-4664)*
Creative Stitches By C S........G....... 918 418-9049
Afton *(G-116)*
Creativestitch LLC........G....... 405 664-1144
Edmond *(G-2373)*
Custom Embroidery & Gifts LLC........G....... 405 240-7950
Wellston *(G-11468)*
Debbie Do EMB & Screen Prtg........G....... 580 353-2606
Lawton *(G-3918)*
Design It........G....... 405 756-3635
Lindsay *(G-4060)*
Dinks Monogramming & EMB LLC........G....... 580 541-4371
Enid *(G-2941)*
Doris Winford........G....... 918 599-8931
Tulsa *(G-9598)*
Dudz and Things Inc........G....... 918 321-9443
Sapulpa *(G-8269)*
Embrodred Mnograms Designs LLC........G....... 918 335-5055
Bartlesville *(G-481)*
Embroidery By Stacie........G....... 580 656-5232
Ardmore *(G-285)*
Embroidery Creations........G....... 405 728-1355
Oklahoma City *(G-6029)*
Embroidery Plus........G....... 918 652-2117
Weleetka *(G-11464)*
Embroidme of Tulsa........G....... 918 459-6699
Tulsa *(G-9665)*
Erin Turner Custom EMB LLC........G....... 918 869-6481
Tulsa *(G-9697)*
Fancy Stitch........G....... 580 699-2112
Lawton *(G-3926)*
Fashion Sports By Sia Inc........F....... 405 524-9990
Oklahoma City *(G-6077)*
First Impression Custom EMB........G....... 918 787-4182
Grove *(G-3270)*
Free Spirit Embroidery........G....... 918 429-4552
McAlester *(G-4301)*
Freedom Embroidery LLC........G....... 580 540-8504
Enid *(G-2959)*
Freestyle Embroidery........G....... 405 802-5838
Oklahoma City *(G-6116)*
Ft Sill Tees & Embroidery........G....... 580 248-8484
Lawton *(G-3932)*
Gail Evans Embroidery........G....... 918 605-1013
Tulsa *(G-9796)*
Genes Customized Tags & EMB........G....... 580 225-8247
Elk City *(G-2820)*
Gold Star Graphics Inc........F....... 405 677-1529
Oklahoma City *(G-6168)*
Great Plins Grphics Shwnee LLC........G....... 405 273-4263
Shawnee *(G-8455)*
Green Cntry Trophy Screen Prtg........G....... 918 647-2923
Poteau *(G-7906)*
Heart 2 Heart Embroidery........G....... 405 401-7408
Oklahoma City *(G-6232)*
Im Stitched & Stoned........G....... 918 418-9107
Vinita *(G-11261)*
Initially Yours Inc........G....... 918 832-9889
Tulsa *(G-9986)*
Inspiration Logos Inc........G....... 405 741-5646
Oklahoma City *(G-6310)*
Integrity Screen Works Inc........E....... 918 663-8339
Tulsa *(G-9999)*
Jans Digitzing & EMB LLC........G....... 970 587-2834
Choctaw *(G-1547)*
Jlm2 LLC........G....... 918 258-0239
Broken Arrow *(G-946)*
Judy Airson........G....... 580 254-9076
Woodward *(G-11597)*
K A G U Inc........G....... 405 364-4637
Norman *(G-5045)*
L C D Embroidery........G....... 405 379-6083
Holdenville *(G-3555)*
Label Stable Inc........G....... 580 223-2037
Ardmore *(G-323)*
Lane Victory Screen Printing........G....... 580 924-3556
Durant *(G-2243)*
Last Stitch Studio........G....... 918 200-5859
Tulsa *(G-10132)*
Lightstitching........G....... 405 210-7645
Norman *(G-5059)*
Love Letters Monogramming LLC........G....... 918 231-6691
Tulsa *(G-10179)*
Marketing & Embroidery Magic........G....... 405 340-9677
Edmond *(G-2506)*
McSmith Creations LLC........G....... 405 596-2301
Bethany *(G-588)*
Melbre Southern Stitches LLC........G....... 918 399-4966
Cushing *(G-1945)*
Merritts Monograms LLC........G....... 918 346-2757
Oklahoma City *(G-6569)*
Miss Priss Monograms & EMB........G....... 918 697-9468
Talala *(G-8901)*
Mobile PC Manager LLC........G....... 574 551-4521
Jenks *(G-3717)*
Monogram Hut........G....... 214 707-4196
Jenks *(G-3718)*
Monograms Elite Inc........G....... 580 353-1635
Lawton *(G-3973)*
Mulberry Tree Graphics........G....... 580 248-3194
Lawton *(G-3974)*
Munger and Krout Inc........F....... 580 237-7060
Enid *(G-3016)*
Mzmouze Embroidery Creat LLP........G....... 405 696-6545
Guthrie *(G-3326)*
▲ **Oklahoma EMB Sup & Design**........G....... 405 359-2741
Edmond *(G-2549)*
One Moore Embroidery Place........G....... 580 328-5755
Taloga *(G-8907)*
Parkerville USA EMB & More........G....... 918 636-0048
Owasso *(G-7601)*
Peabody & Kent Designs Inc........G....... 918 439-4300
Tulsa *(G-10478)*
Pearl District Embroidery LLC........G....... 918 269-3347
Tulsa *(G-10481)*
Personal Expressions........G....... 918 406-4581
Broken Arrow *(G-1003)*
Personal Expressions Inc........G....... 918 660-0494
Tulsa *(G-10498)*
Personal Expressions Inc........G....... 918 660-0494
Tulsa *(G-10499)*
Pinpoint Monograms Inc........F....... 405 228-0600
Oklahoma City *(G-6850)*
Play 2 Win Athletics........G....... 918 341-9500
Claremore *(G-1671)*
Precision Punch........G....... 405 340-7546
Edmond *(G-2574)*
Productive Clutter Inc........G....... 405 447-3839
Norman *(G-5124)*
R-5 Caps & Tees........G....... 580 256-3579
Woodward *(G-11626)*
S & S Textile Inc........F....... 405 632-9928
Oklahoma City *(G-7065)*
S and W Embroidery........G....... 580 654-2929
Carnegie *(G-1278)*
S E & M Monogramming........G....... 405 377-9677
Stillwater *(G-8751)*
Sand Tech Screening and EMB........G....... 918 458-0312
Tahlequah *(G-8882)*
Sebo Lanila Lynn........G....... 479 719-5612
Spiro *(G-8616)*
Sew Glam Monogram LLC........G....... 918 606-2644
Broken Arrow *(G-1049)*
Sew Graphics Plus Inc........G....... 405 364-1707
Norman *(G-5141)*
Sew Much Fun........G....... 405 359-1544
Edmond *(G-2616)*
Sew Stylish Embroidery LLC........G....... 580 238-8797
Marietta *(G-4212)*
Sew Tulsa........G....... 918 627-1577
Tulsa *(G-10736)*

S
I
C

Employee Codes: A=Over 500 employees, B=251-500
C=101-250, D=51-100, E=20-50, F=10-19, G=1-9
2020 Oklahoma Directory
of Manufacturers & Processors
431

23 APPAREL AND OTHER FINISHED PRODUCTS MADE FROM FABRICS AND SIMILAR MATERIAL

Sewcool Embroidery LLC ....G....... 405 326-2854
Edmond *(G-2617)*
Sewfly Embroidery ....G....... 580 477-1957
Altus *(G-168)*
Shirts & Stuff ....G....... 918 445-0323
Tulsa *(G-10749)*
Shops of Standing Rock Inc ....G....... 580 364-0834
Atoka *(G-423)*
Showstring USA Inc ....G....... 580 335-7171
Frederick *(G-3200)*
Southern Lace Stitchery ....G....... 405 414-3550
Yukon *(G-11784)*
Spinning Star Design ....G....... 405 359-3965
Edmond *(G-2627)*
Star Corral ....G....... 918 251-9795
Broken Arrow *(G-1060)*
Stitch Boom Ba LLC ....G....... 918 518-5859
Jenks *(G-3729)*
Stitch Design ....G....... 405 350-0126
Yukon *(G-11789)*
Stitch N Sew Embroidery ....G....... 432 741-0433
Ochelata *(G-5239)*
Stitch N Stuff Embroidery Shop ....G....... 918 465-3036
Wilburton *(G-11525)*
Stitch Witch ....G....... 918 371-3568
Collinsville *(G-1825)*
Stitch Wizard ....G....... 405 816-6356
Mustang *(G-4796)*
Stitchabella LLC ....G....... 405 562-3316
Edmond *(G-2633)*
Stitched By Shayna ....G....... 405 708-8614
Oklahoma City *(G-7210)*
Stitchin Acres ....G....... 405 740-6035
Kremlin *(G-3855)*
Stitchin Stitches ....G....... 918 251-9696
Broken Arrow *(G-1063)*
Stitchsumm LLC ....G....... 918 201-2148
Jenks *(G-3730)*
Sues Monogramming ....G....... 918 455-1011
Broken Arrow *(G-1066)*
Sunflower Embroidery LLC ....G....... 918 869-9646
Fort Gibson *(G-3179)*
T and L Embroidery ....G....... 580 493-2239
Drummond *(G-2048)*
T S & H EMB & Screen Prtg ....G....... 405 214-7701
Shawnee *(G-8508)*
Tazz Too Embroidery ....G....... 580 334-7373
Woodward *(G-11640)*
Tin Roof Quilting LLC ....G....... 918 551-7282
Tulsa *(G-10944)*
Tonis Stitches-N-Stuff Inc ....G....... 580 688-2697
Hollis *(G-3570)*
Tony Newcomb Sportswear Inc ....G....... 405 232-0022
Oklahoma City *(G-7303)*
Tts Embroiderys Plus ....G....... 918 770-3515
Glenpool *(G-3243)*
Tumbleweed Embroidery and Scre ....G....... 580 371-9742
Mannsville *(G-4196)*
Twist A Stitch ....G....... 918 514-0143
Sand Springs *(G-8234)*
Unique Stitches Inc ....G....... 918 794-5494
Tulsa *(G-11035)*
USA Industries Oklahoma Inc ....G....... 405 840-5577
Edmond *(G-2661)*
USA Screen Prtg & EMB Co Inc ....E....... 405 946-3100
Oklahoma City *(G-7380)*
Webber Kathryn ....G....... 405 379-3872
Holdenville *(G-3562)*

2396 Automotive Trimmings, Apparel Findings, Related Prdts

4524 LLC ....G....... 405 620-3711
Edmond *(G-2285)*
A & B Engraving Inc ....G....... 918 663-7446
Tulsa *(G-9061)*
All-Star Trophies & Ribbon Mfg ....G....... 918 283-2200
Claremore *(G-1581)*
American Sportswear Inc ....G....... 918 665-7636
Tulsa *(G-9172)*
B J Printing Inc ....F....... 405 372-7600
Stillwater *(G-8657)*
Bartlesville Print Shop ....G....... 918 336-6070
Bartlesville *(G-452)*
Beacon Sign Company Inc ....G....... 405 567-4886
Prague *(G-7921)*
Big Red Shop Inc ....G....... 405 495-5551
Warr Acres *(G-11313)*
Causley Productions Inc ....F....... 405 372-0940
Stillwater *(G-8666)*
Caveman Screen Printing ....G....... 918 446-6440
Tulsa *(G-9390)*
Cimarron Screen Printing ....G....... 405 755-8337
Edmond *(G-2352)*
Clay Serigraphics Inc ....F....... 918 592-2529
Tulsa *(G-9445)*
Complete Graphics Inc ....G....... 405 232-8882
Oklahoma City *(G-5812)*
Corner Copy & Printing LLC ....G....... 405 801-2020
Norman *(G-4966)*
CP Solutions Inc ....D....... 918 664-6642
Tulsa *(G-9495)*
Cr Stripes Ltd Co ....G....... 405 946-8577
Oklahoma City *(G-5850)*
Creative Apparel and More Inc ....G....... 918 682-1283
Muskogee *(G-4664)*
Cunningham Graphics Inc ....G....... 918 337-9100
Bartlesville *(G-470)*
Custom Monograms & Lettering ....G....... 405 495-8586
Bethany *(G-574)*
Custom Screen Printers ....G....... 918 423-3696
McAlester *(G-4290)*
Customized Fctry Interiors LLC ....G....... 405 848-9999
Oklahoma City *(G-5880)*
D & B Printing Inc ....G....... 405 632-0055
Oklahoma City *(G-5884)*
Dean Printing ....G....... 580 782-3777
Mangum *(G-4170)*
Design It ....G....... 405 756-3635
Lindsay *(G-4060)*
Diamond Tees ....G....... 918 665-0815
Tulsa *(G-9579)*
Ehrles Carnival & Party Sups ....G....... 918 622-5266
Tulsa *(G-9648)*
Emert Enterprises LLC ....G....... 580 495-5511
Bennington *(G-563)*
First Impression Prtg Co Inc ....G....... 918 749-5446
Beggs *(G-553)*
Gold Star Graphics Inc ....F....... 405 677-1529
Oklahoma City *(G-6168)*
Graphix Xpress ....G....... 580 765-7324
Ponca City *(G-7831)*
Great Plins Grphics Shwnee LLC ....G....... 405 273-4263
Shawnee *(G-8455)*
Green Cntry Trophy Screen Prtg ....G....... 918 647-2923
Poteau *(G-7906)*
Ham Ventures LLC ....G....... 918 277-9500
Tulsa *(G-9883)*
Holloways Bluprt & Copy Sp Inc ....G....... 918 682-0280
Muskogee *(G-4692)*
House of Trophies ....G....... 405 452-3524
Wetumka *(G-11492)*
House of Trophies ....G....... 918 341-2111
Claremore *(G-1398)*
House T Shirt & Silk Screening ....G....... 405 457-6321
Lookeba *(G-4129)*
Imaging Concepts ....G....... 918 534-1761
Dewey *(G-2026)*
Impact Screen Printing ....G....... 918 258-8337
Broken Arrow *(G-934)*
Initially Yours Inc ....G....... 918 832-9889
Tulsa *(G-9986)*
Inkling Design ....G....... 405 495-5575
Bethany *(G-583)*
Jan L Jobe ....G....... 918 683-0404
Muskogee *(G-4698)*
Jeff Mc Kenzie & Co Inc ....G....... 405 236-5848
Oklahoma City *(G-6354)*
Joys Uniforms Boutique Ltd ....G....... 918 747-4114
Tulsa *(G-10061)*
King Screen Co ....G....... 405 258-0416
Chandler *(G-1383)*
Knl Screenprinting ....G....... 580 654-5394
Carnegie *(G-1277)*
Label Stable Inc ....G....... 580 223-2037
Ardmore *(G-323)*
Lawyer Graphic Screen Process ....G....... 918 438-2725
Tulsa *(G-10137)*
Leda Grimm ....G....... 918 225-0507
Cushing *(G-1942)*
Magic TS ....G....... 580 332-6675
Ada *(G-62)*
Magnum Screen Print Inc ....G....... 918 665-9636
Tulsa *(G-10202)*
Massive Graphic Screen Prtg ....F....... 405 364-3594
Norman *(G-5066)*
MBC Graphics ....G....... 918 585-2321
Tulsa *(G-10227)*
Midwest Decals LLC ....G....... 405 787-8747
Oklahoma City *(G-6602)*
Midwest Publishing Co ....G....... 405 282-1890
Guthrie *(G-3325)*
Misaco Sign & Screen Printing ....G....... 918 542-4188
Miami *(G-4419)*
Mobonoto Automotive LLC ....G....... 580 480-0410
Altus *(G-163)*
Munger and Krout Inc ....F....... 580 237-7060
Enid *(G-3016)*
Opportunity Center Inc ....C....... 580 765-6782
Ponca City *(G-7863)*
Options Inc ....F....... 918 473-2614
Checotah *(G-1398)*
Peabodys Printing & A Brush Sp ....G....... 580 248-8317
Lawton *(G-3980)*
Performance Screen Printing ....G....... 405 247-9891
Anadarko *(G-205)*
Pinpoint Monograms Inc ....F....... 405 228-0600
Oklahoma City *(G-6850)*
Pitezels Ink & Print Inc ....G....... 918 663-2393
Tulsa *(G-10520)*
Prairie Graphics & Sportswear ....G....... 405 789-0028
Bethany *(G-592)*
Print Imaging Group LLC ....E....... 405 235-4888
Oklahoma City *(G-6898)*
Promo Print 4 U LLC ....G....... 405 259-6721
Oklahoma City *(G-6915)*
Promoz Screen Printing Inc ....G....... 918 439-4030
Tulsa *(G-10574)*
Quantum Forms Corporation ....F....... 918 665-1320
Oklahoma City *(G-6940)*
R-5 Caps & Tees ....G....... 580 256-3579
Woodward *(G-11626)*
Reflective Edge Screenprinting ....G....... 405 917-7837
Oklahoma City *(G-7001)*
▲ Relevant Products LLC ....E....... 405 524-5250
Oklahoma City *(G-7005)*
S & S Textile Inc ....F....... 405 632-9928
Oklahoma City *(G-7065)*
Sand Tech Screening and EMB ....G....... 918 458-0312
Tahlequah *(G-8882)*
Semasys Inc ....E....... 405 525-2335
Oklahoma City *(G-7107)*
Shine On Designs ....G....... 918 224-7439
Sapulpa *(G-8311)*
Shirts & Stuff ....G....... 918 445-0323
Tulsa *(G-10749)*
Shops of Standing Rock Inc ....G....... 580 364-0834
Atoka *(G-423)*
Sides Screenprinting More LLC ....G....... 580 772-8888
Oklahoma City *(G-7127)*
Speedys TS & More LLC ....G....... 580 748-0067
Alva *(G-192)*
Stan Clark Co ....G....... 405 377-0799
Stillwater *(G-8755)*
T S & H EMB & Screen Prtg ....G....... 405 214-7701
Shawnee *(G-8508)*
T-Shirts Unlimited ....G....... 580 286-5223
Idabel *(G-3649)*
Tigers Den By Dreamcatcher ....G....... 918 478-4873
Fort Gibson *(G-3180)*
Tim Dees ....G....... 918 825-1211
Pryor *(G-7995)*
Tom Bennett Manufacturing ....F....... 405 528-5671
Oklahoma City *(G-7302)*
Tony Newcomb Sportswear Inc ....G....... 405 232-0022
Oklahoma City *(G-7303)*
Townsend Marketing Inc ....G....... 918 496-9222
Bixby *(G-666)*
U Big TS Designs Inc ....G....... 405 401-4327
Oklahoma City *(G-7356)*
▲ Ultra Thin Inc ....E....... 405 794-7892
Moore *(G-4582)*
USA Screen Prtg & EMB Co Inc ....E....... 405 946-3100
Oklahoma City *(G-7380)*
Wallis Printing Inc ....G....... 580 223-7473
Ardmore *(G-379)*
Way-Wear LLC ....G....... 405 410-8367
Kingfisher *(G-3820)*
Wear-Tech ....G....... 918 663-2009
Tulsa *(G-11099)*
Wet Willies Screen Print & CU ....G....... 405 262-6076
El Reno *(G-2770)*
Witty Ideas Inc ....G....... 918 367-9528
Bristow *(G-806)*

2397 Schiffli Machine Embroideries

Baywest Embroidery ....G....... 580 626-4728
Jet *(G-3741)*
Big Creek Custom Embroidery ....G....... 918 446-6054
Tulsa *(G-9288)*

SIC SECTION

24 LUMBER AND WOOD PRODUCTS, EXCEPT FURNITURE

C&S Design .... G 918 455-8137
  Broken Arrow *(G-1116)*

2399 Fabricated Textile Prdts, NEC

Barbara J Landreth Sewing .... G 918 298-8141
  Tulsa *(G-9264)*
Casa Dosa .... G 918 243-7277
  Cleveland *(G-1719)*
Chris Johnson .... G 405 364-3879
  Norman *(G-4956)*
Cimarron Equine Station .... G 405 373-0358
  Yukon *(G-11705)*
Crochetangel .... G 918 282-3056
  Broken Arrow *(G-879)*
DSA Designs LLC .... G 580 493-2723
  Drummond *(G-2047)*
▲ Elqui International Ltd Co .... G 918 335-5002
  Bartlesville *(G-480)*
Inspiration Logos Inc .... G 405 741-5646
  Oklahoma City *(G-6310)*
Lenora Elizabeth Brown .... G 918 797-2034
  Stilwell *(G-8792)*
Moss Seat Cover Mfg & Sls Co ...... F 918 742-3326
  Tulsa *(G-10306)*
Rainbow Pennant Inc .... E 405 524-1577
  Oklahoma City *(G-6968)*
Red Earth Farm Store Inc .... F 405 478-3424
  Oklahoma City *(G-6985)*
Sooner Rubber Products Company G 918 461-1391
  Tulsa *(G-10792)*
South Central Machine .... G 580 775-1623
  Durant *(G-2258)*
Speer Cushion Co .... G 970 854-2911
  Bixby *(G-664)*
Tr Tack Supply .... G 918 543-4095
  Inola *(G-3674)*
▲ Ultra Thin Inc .... E 405 794-7892
  Moore *(G-4582)*
United We Stand Inc .... G 918 382-1766
  Tulsa *(G-11044)*
◆ Valhoma Corporation .... E 918 836-7135
  Tulsa *(G-11064)*
Wave On Flags and Banners LLC . G 918 782-3330
  Langley *(G-3875)*

24 LUMBER AND WOOD PRODUCTS, EXCEPT FURNITURE

2411 Logging

Anderson Logging LLC .... G 580 584-9898
  Broken Bow *(G-1183)*
Arthur Crews Logging .... G 580 889-7757
  Lane *(G-3870)*
▲ B & B Log & Lumber Co Inc .... F 580 889-2438
  Atoka *(G-399)*
B & P Logging LLC .... G 580 584-6718
  Broken Bow *(G-1184)*
Bloods Logging & Land Svcs LLC . G 405 314-4275
  Lamar *(G-3863)*
Broadland Stump Removal .... G 918 743-7014
  Tulsa *(G-9339)*
Bruce Hopson Logging Inc .... G 580 835-7145
  Eagletown *(G-2274)*
Bucky McGee Logging .... G 918 635-0909
  Heavener *(G-3426)*
Donald Standridge .... G 580 298-3760
  Mounds *(G-4613)*
Dustin Holbird .... G 918 448-7687
  Wister *(G-11548)*
Erik Robins .... G 580 371-1470
  Ardmore *(G-287)*
Excellence Logging .... G 815 272-5422
  Tulsa *(G-9714)*
F G Sawmill LLC .... G 918 905-1132
  Stilwell *(G-8788)*
Fortress Whitetails .... G 405 401-5533
  Guthrie *(G-3313)*
G&G Logging LLC .... G 918 635-5988
  Poteau *(G-7905)*
Gary Moss .... G 580 286-1359
  Valliant *(G-11224)*
Hadley-Keeney Chipping Inc .... E 580 835-2645
  Eagletown *(G-2275)*
Harrison Logging Lc .... G 580 245-2179
  Haworth *(G-3404)*
Impac Exploration Services Inc .... G 580 772-3117
  Weatherford *(G-11420)*
J Duke Logan Family Trust .... G 918 256-7511
  Vinita *(G-11263)*
J&J Logging LLC .... G 580 933-7218
  Valliant *(G-11228)*
James Jeremy Burcham .... G 580 420-3243
  Broken Bow *(G-1193)*
James Roy Hopson .... G 580 835-2288
  Eagletown *(G-2276)*
Johnnie & Lonnie Smith .... G 580 933-4323
  Valliant *(G-11229)*
Karen E Hopson .... G 580 584-7221
  Broken Bow *(G-1195)*
Kenneth D Jewell .... G 580 244-7450
  Watson *(G-11355)*
Larry L Williams .... G 580 772-3303
  Weatherford *(G-11424)*
Lloyd Provence Logging .... G 580 245-1170
  Haworth *(G-3405)*
Logging Contractor Inc .... F 580 244-3571
  Smithville *(G-8579)*
Lucky 13 Motorcycle Shop .... F 816 808-0985
  Tulsa *(G-10182)*
Luna Logging .... G 580 933-7517
  Valliant *(G-11230)*
Midwest Logging & Perforating ..... G 405 382-4200
  Seminole *(G-8384)*
Mixon Brothers Wood Prsv Co ...... F 580 286-9494
  Idabel *(G-3643)*
Nancy Dalrymple .... G 580 525-7544
  Oklahoma City *(G-6650)*
Paladin Geological Svcs LLC .... F 405 463-3270
  Edmond *(G-2560)*
R & D Mud Logging Services LLP G 405 969-2587
  Crescent *(G-1919)*
Rd Logging .... F 918 666-2556
  Wyandotte *(G-11662)*
Rex Ross .... G 580 835-7244
  Eagletown *(G-2277)*
River Ridge Logging LLC .... G 580 380-2948
  Durant *(G-2252)*
Shawn Gibson .... E 580 584-5537
  Broken Bow *(G-1205)*
Silver Creek Logging .... G 580 241-7717
  Broken Bow *(G-1206)*
SMA Surface Logging LLC .... G 405 301-3375
  Oklahoma City *(G-7150)*
STS Logging Services LLC .... G 918 933-5653
  Tulsa *(G-10862)*
Terry Belknap & Sons Logging ..... G 580 244-7336
  Smithville *(G-8580)*
Tunnell Chance .... G 580 245-2422
  Haworth *(G-3406)*
Wacky Logging LLC .... G 918 457-9393
  Hulbert *(G-3630)*
Walker Woods Inc .... G 208 266-1601
  Oklahoma City *(G-7416)*
Will Robinson Logging LLC .... G 918 569-4248
  Clayton *(G-1711)*

2421 Saw & Planing Mills

Browns Sawmill .... G 918 617-7935
  Atwood *(G-428)*
▲ Chips Valiant Inc .... F 580 933-5323
  Valliant *(G-11222)*
Conner Industries Inc .... E 918 696-5885
  Stilwell *(G-8787)*
Diamond P Forrest Products Co ... F 918 266-2478
  Catoosa *(G-1316)*
Eastern Red Cedar Products LLC . G 405 780-7520
  Stillwater *(G-8681)*
Gray & Sons Sawmill & Sup LLC .. G 580 924-2941
  Durant *(G-2231)*
Grays Sawmill Inc .... F 580 924-2941
  Durant *(G-2232)*
Hugo Wyrick Lumber .... E 580 326-5569
  Hugo *(G-3614)*
International Paper Company .... D 580 933-7211
  Valliant *(G-11227)*
James Bethell .... G 918 677-2328
  Wister *(G-11549)*
Jeffery Mariott .... E 580 320-5474
  Roff *(G-8109)*
John R Little Jr .... G 405 751-5227
  Oklahoma City *(G-6369)*
Johnson Lumber Company Inc ..... E 918 253-8786
  Spavinaw *(G-8591)*
Limbsaw Company .... G 580 272-3194
  Noble *(G-4885)*
Log Cutters .... G 580 371-8349
  Tishomingo *(G-8967)*
Newview Oklahoma Inc .... D 405 232-4644
  Oklahoma City *(G-6672)*
Og Sawmill .... G 918 598-3464
  Hulbert *(G-3627)*
Oklahoma Home Centers Inc .... E 405 260-7625
  Guthrie *(G-3329)*
Sanders Sawmill & Forest Pdts .... G 405 799-0899
  Moore *(G-4562)*
Shawnee Sawmill LLC .... G 405 788-6186
  Shawnee *(G-8496)*
Shelley Benefield .... G 580 436-0296
  Ada *(G-86)*
Singing Wire Cedar .... G 918 607-8643
  Beggs *(G-561)*
T and A Sawmill LLC .... G 580 309-3100
  Thomas *(G-8948)*
Ufp Shawnee LLC .... G 405 273-1533
  Shawnee *(G-8515)*
White Gordon Lbr Co of Lindsay .. G 405 946-9032
  Warr Acres *(G-11330)*
Whitlock Saw Mill .... G 918 652-4410
  Henryetta *(G-3518)*
Woodstock Sawmill & Timbers Co G 405 673-7966
  Oklahoma City *(G-7467)*

2426 Hardwood Dimension & Flooring Mills

▲ B & B Log & Lumber Co Inc .... F 580 889-2438
  Atoka *(G-399)*
Conner Industries Inc .... E 918 696-5885
  Stilwell *(G-8787)*
Diamond P Forrest Products Co ... F 918 266-2478
  Catoosa *(G-1316)*
Egr Construction Inc .... E 405 943-0900
  Oklahoma City *(G-6013)*
Flooring Outfitters .... G 580 286-3030
  Idabel *(G-3637)*
Grays Sawmill Inc .... F 580 924-2941
  Durant *(G-2232)*
Hugo Wyrick Lumber .... E 580 326-5569
  Hugo *(G-3614)*
Johnson Lumber Company Inc ..... E 918 253-8786
  Spavinaw *(G-8591)*
Juan Manzo Custom Refinishing .. G 405 848-3843
  Oklahoma City *(G-6390)*
Moores Hardware and Home Ctr .. G 918 287-4458
  Pawhuska *(G-7689)*
Pioneer Sport Floors LLC .... G 214 460-6921
  Calera *(G-1244)*
Ram Design Inc .... G 918 342-4051
  Claremore *(G-1678)*
Rd Logging .... F 918 666-2556
  Wyandotte *(G-11662)*
Strictly Hardwoods .... G 405 269-1026
  Stillwater *(G-8761)*
White Gordon Lbr Co of Lindsay .. G 405 946-9032
  Warr Acres *(G-11330)*
Zara Group Inc .... F 918 782-4473
  Vinita *(G-11273)*

2429 Special Prdt Sawmills, NEC

Farmers Coop Gin of Martha .... G 580 266-3222
  Martha *(G-4251)*

2431 Millwork

12 Acre Woodwork LLC .... G 405 328-0655
  Chandler *(G-1372)*
A R T T Corp .... G 405 681-0749
  Oklahoma City *(G-5348)*
Aaron Custom Creations .... G 580 603-0467
  Enid *(G-2902)*
AC Woodworks Inc .... G 918 298-6948
  Tulsa *(G-9085)*
AC Woodworks Inc DBA Wood ...... G 918 384-0111
  Tulsa *(G-9086)*
Accurate Blinds .... G 405 396-8583
  Arcadia *(G-226)*
Ace Hardware .... G 580 225-0100
  Elk City *(G-2781)*
All Wood Products Co Inc .... E 918 585-9739
  Tulsa *(G-9138)*
American Millwork Company Inc .. E 405 681-5347
  Oklahoma City *(G-5440)*
Andrews Woodworking .... G 918 664-6722
  Tulsa *(G-9190)*
Ardmore Construction Sup Inc ..... G 580 223-2322
  Ardmore *(G-245)*
B & C Custom Woodworks .... G 918 830-2416
  Tulsa *(G-9241)*
B&C Custom Woodworks LLC .... G 918 639-2416
  Tulsa *(G-9247)*
Bales Custom Woodwork Inc .... G 918 277-6612
  Beggs *(G-549)*

Employee Codes: A=Over 500 employees, B=251-500
C=101-250, D=51-100, E=20-50, F=10-19, G=1-9

Bobs Wood Working..............................G....... 405 632-4894
Oklahoma City *(G-5604)*
Cabinet Doors Unlimited........................F....... 918 257-5765
Afton *(G-114)*
Caston Architectural Mllwk Inc..............E....... 405 843-6652
Oklahoma City *(G-5711)*
Cavanal Woodworks..............................G....... 909 649-4346
Poteau *(G-7900)*
Centerpiece Custom Wdwkg LLC.........G....... 405 387-9312
Blanchard *(G-706)*
Cherokee Archtectural Mtls LLC...........F....... 918 258-5700
Broken Arrow *(G-868)*
Cherokee Woodwork Inc........................G....... 918 798-5037
Tulsa *(G-9416)*
Cheyenne Woodworks Inc......................G....... 918 587-3533
Tulsa *(G-9418)*
Classic Overhead Doo...........................G....... 580 931-0340
Durant *(G-2215)*
Contemporary Cabinets Inc...................D....... 405 330-4592
Edmond *(G-2365)*
Copes Woodworking..............................G....... 918 698-2104
Tulsa *(G-9484)*
Crawson Corporation.............................F....... 918 427-8400
Muldrow *(G-4633)*
Creekside Woodworks...........................G....... 405 528-5432
Oklahoma City *(G-5854)*
Croan Custom Woodworks LLC..............G....... 405 227-2067
Edmond *(G-2374)*
Crosby Custom Woodwork.....................G....... 405 802-9615
Moore *(G-4512)*
Curry Shades LLC..................................G....... 918 779-3902
Tulsa *(G-9524)*
Custom Cutting Millwork Inc.................F....... 405 942-3196
Oklahoma City *(G-5872)*
▲ Custom Seating Incorporated..........C....... 918 682-4400
Muskogee *(G-4666)*
Custom Wood Creations........................G....... 580 512-6994
Lawton *(G-3915)*
Custom Wood Creations LLC.................G....... 405 517-8689
Crescent *(G-1911)*
Custom Wood Works.............................G....... 918 279-1333
Coweta *(G-1877)*
Cutting Edge Woodwork LLC.................G....... 918 706-1143
Skiatook *(G-8537)*
Dale P Jackson......................................F....... 580 332-1988
Ada *(G-29)*
Die Tech Tool Machine..........................G....... 918 683-3422
Okay *(G-5257)*
Display With Honor Wdwkg LLC............G....... 405 659-9894
Oklahoma City *(G-5286)*
Egr Construction Inc.............................E....... 405 943-0900
Oklahoma City *(G-6013)*
Elite Wood Creations LLC......................G....... 580 220-1153
Ardmore *(G-284)*
Elk Valley Woodworking Inc...................G....... 580 486-3337
Carter *(G-1281)*
Equus Metalcraft Llc.............................G....... 918 832-0956
Tulsa *(G-9695)*
Estey Cabinet Door Co...........................E....... 405 771-3004
Spencer *(G-8595)*
Eubankswoodworks LLC.........................G....... 918 245-7835
Sand Springs *(G-8182)*
Extraordinary Woodworks.....................G....... 801 995-0906
Enid *(G-2956)*
Fadco of Arkansas LLC..........................G....... 918 832-1641
Tulsa *(G-9726)*
For His Glory Cutting Boards.................G....... 918 633-7233
Tulsa *(G-9764)*
Forrest Valentine....................................G....... 580 309-2190
Custer City *(G-1974)*
Fullerton Building Systems Inc..............E....... 918 246-9995
Sand Springs *(G-8187)*
Furrs Custom Woodwork........................G....... 918 406-7021
Bixby *(G-624)*
Gemini Woodworks................................G....... 405 630-8586
Jones *(G-3746)*
Gps Woodworks LLC..............................G....... 405 399-2369
Jones *(G-3747)*
Grain and Grit Woodworks LLC..............G....... 405 250-6824
Oklahoma City *(G-6175)*
Green Cntry Cstm Woodworks LLC.......G....... 918 585-1040
Tulsa *(G-9858)*
Gurley Custom Woodwork......................G....... 580 235-3350
Ada *(G-46)*
H3 Custom Wood Moldings LLC.............G....... 918 250-8746
Tulsa *(G-9879)*
Hansen Millwork & Trim Inc..................E....... 405 239-2564
Oklahoma City *(G-6214)*
Hardwood Innovations Inc.....................F....... 405 722-5588
Oklahoma City *(G-6219)*
Huerecas Woodworking LLC..................G....... 580 302-2687
Weatherford *(G-11418)*
Hughes Lumber Company.......................G....... 918 266-9100
Catoosa *(G-1322)*
Hugo Sash & Door Inc...........................F....... 580 326-5569
Hugo *(G-3613)*
Hugo Wyrick Lumber..............................E....... 580 326-5569
Hugo *(G-3614)*
Hutchinson Products Company.............E....... 405 946-4403
Oklahoma City *(G-6277)*
Integrity Custom Mill Works..................G....... 405 495-9732
Spencer *(G-8596)*
J & Js Wdwrk HM Decor & Gifts.............G....... 918 420-9411
McAlester *(G-4307)*
J & S Woodworking Inc..........................G....... 405 619-9910
Oklahoma City *(G-6333)*
J B Woodworking...................................G....... 918 760-2399
Bristow *(G-781)*
J&Js Woodwork and More......................G....... 918 429-9704
McAlester *(G-4308)*
Japa Corp..G....... 918 893-6763
Broken Arrow *(G-943)*
Johnsonwoodworks................................G....... 918 407-7747
Tulsa *(G-10057)*
Jts Woodworks LLC................................G....... 918 640-1791
Broken Arrow *(G-951)*
Kaonohi Woodworks...............................G....... 918 893-4661
Broken Arrow *(G-954)*
Kc Woodwork & Fixture Inc....................G....... 918 582-5300
Tulsa *(G-10078)*
Kelly L Young..G....... 918 859-1046
Skiatook *(G-8555)*
Knock On Wood Custom.........................G....... 918 261-6948
Claremore *(G-1650)*
Kohns Doors & Woodworking LLC.........G....... 405 596-8245
Piedmont *(G-7766)*
Ksquared Woodworks LLC.....................G....... 918 496-3681
Tulsa *(G-10104)*
Lakewood Cabinetry Inc.........................F....... 918 782-2203
Langley *(G-3871)*
LDS Building Specialties LLC.................G....... 405 917-9901
Oklahoma City *(G-6460)*
Leon Kinder..G....... 580 323-0365
Clinton *(G-1756)*
Lindsay Woodworks................................G....... 405 370-9712
Choctaw *(G-1550)*
M1 Woodworks..G....... 405 923-4144
Edmond *(G-2499)*
Mastercraft Millwork Inc........................G....... 405 895-6050
Moore *(G-4537)*
McElyea Custom Woodworking LLC......G....... 918 332-7651
Bartlesville *(G-510)*
McMurtry Cabinet Shop..........................G....... 405 627-3275
Oklahoma City *(G-6550)*
Mez Woodworks LLC...............................G....... 405 589-5408
Edmond *(G-2517)*
Mh Woodworking LLC.............................G....... 405 799-2661
Moore *(G-4540)*
Mike Pung...G....... 405 736-6282
Oklahoma City *(G-6607)*
Mill Work Specialties LLC.......................G....... 918 639-8385
Tulsa *(G-10280)*
Mystik River Woodworks.........................G....... 580 606-0071
Comanche *(G-1843)*
Naked Wood Works.................................G....... 918 864-0229
Broken Arrow *(G-984)*
Nicnik Woodworks...................................G....... 703 474-7994
Choctaw *(G-1552)*
Nolan Custom Woodwork........................G....... 918 576-1158
Tulsa *(G-10347)*
Note-Able Workshop LLC........................G....... 918 801-2725
Grove *(G-3281)*
Note-Able Workshop LLC........................G....... 918 801-2725
Grove *(G-3282)*
Novalco Inc..F....... 405 528-2711
Oklahoma City *(G-6700)*
Nxt Lvl Woodworking LLC......................G....... 405 613-6637
Norman *(G-5096)*
Oconnell Woodworks LLC.......................G....... 918 805-7233
Broken Arrow *(G-992)*
Oklahoma City Shutter Co Inc................F....... 405 787-1234
Oklahoma City *(G-6742)*
Oklahoma Stair Craft Inc.......................F....... 918 446-1456
Sapulpa *(G-8293)*
Okrusticwoodworks................................G....... 405 562-0371
Guthrie *(G-3331)*
Oro Woodworks.......................................G....... 405 334-7445
Stillwater *(G-8734)*
Osage Door Co Inc..................................G....... 918 542-7281
Miami *(G-4426)*
Paramount Building Pdts LLC................G....... 405 470-5073
Oklahoma City *(G-6804)*
Parker Kustom Woodworking.................G....... 405 414-2820
Del City *(G-2005)*
Pawnee Millworks LLC...........................G....... 918 767-2565
Pawnee *(G-7707)*
▲ Perma-Strong Wood Products Inc....E....... 405 449-3376
Wayne *(G-11369)*
▲ Quality Wholesale Millwork Inc........G....... 405 681-6575
Oklahoma City *(G-6938)*
Quality Woodworks Inc...........................G....... 918 944-3314
Muskogee *(G-4741)*
R and P Cabinetry LLC...........................G....... 405 230-0495
Oklahoma City *(G-6959)*
Rar Wood Works LLC..............................G....... 205 233-2920
Broken Arrow *(G-1022)*
RC Custom Woodwork.............................G....... 405 414-1162
Norman *(G-5130)*
Rccs Woodworking LLC...........................G....... 405 694-9680
Edmond *(G-2587)*
Red Dirt Wood Works LLC......................G....... 918 640-5917
Edmond *(G-2588)*
Redbird Woodworks................................G....... 918 227-5938
Sapulpa *(G-8306)*
Redbud Woodworks.................................G....... 316 765-4079
Midwest City *(G-4451)*
Rescue Lumber & Wdwkg LLC................G....... 405 650-4637
Edmond *(G-2597)*
Reynolds Custom Woodworks................G....... 918 595-5988
Claremore *(G-1681)*
Rico Woodworking LLC...........................G....... 918 743-0741
Tulsa *(G-10651)*
Rkb Woodworks.......................................G....... 405 919-4149
Oklahoma City *(G-7030)*
Rockin Wood LLC....................................G....... 405 673-5171
Oklahoma City *(G-7045)*
S & S Woodworks Inc..............................G....... 405 627-8195
Edmond *(G-2609)*
S Coker Custom Woodworks..................G....... 918 638-3443
Broken Arrow *(G-1042)*
▲ S&S Custom Wood Moldings LLC......F....... 214 995-8710
Bixby *(G-657)*
Sanderson Custom Woodworks..............G....... 918 361-1921
Tulsa *(G-10704)*
Sandy Creek Millworks Inc.....................G....... 405 288-0670
Washington *(G-11336)*
Scarab Woodworking LLC.......................G....... 405 612-2111
Stillwater *(G-8753)*
Secure Screen LLC..................................G....... 918 294-4444
Broken Arrow *(G-1048)*
Shellback Woodworks.............................G....... 918 851-3992
Bristow *(G-796)*
Shofner Custom Wood............................G....... 405 787-5768
Bethany *(G-594)*
Shutter Mill Inc......................................D....... 405 377-6455
Stillwater *(G-8754)*
Shutters Unlimited Ltd...........................F....... 405 843-7762
Oklahoma City *(G-7126)*
Skykae Kreations....................................G....... 405 250-4055
Piedmont *(G-7770)*
Sooner Cabinet & Trim Inc.....................E....... 405 820-2920
Moore *(G-4571)*
Sooner Cnc LLC......................................G....... 918 261-5231
Tulsa *(G-10787)*
Southern Millwork Inc.............................E....... 918 585-8125
Tulsa *(G-10800)*
Stephens Custom Woodworks................G....... 405 938-7065
Edmond *(G-2632)*
Steveos Custom Wood-Work LLC...........G....... 405 532-1863
Bethany *(G-597)*
Sylvan Croft Woodworks.........................G....... 405 329-6668
Norman *(G-5168)*
Tap Woodworks LLC................................G....... 580 819-0455
Weatherford *(G-11445)*
Thomas Millwork Inc...............................F....... 405 769-5618
Spencer *(G-8602)*
Thompson Woodworks.............................G....... 405 269-6480
Stillwater *(G-8768)*
Tilman Woodworks LLC...........................G....... 405 441-3324
Oklahoma City *(G-7290)*
Tracys Wood Shop Inc.............................G....... 918 587-4860
Tulsa *(G-10966)*
Trim Rite Moldings Inc............................G....... 918 423-2525
McAlester *(G-4344)*
Trinity Wood Works.................................G....... 918 619-3959
Muskogee *(G-4755)*
Trotter Custom Woodworks LLC............G....... 918 698-5231
Sand Springs *(G-8231)*
Unicorn Woodworking.............................G....... 580 762-0004
Ponca City *(G-7885)*

Unique Wood Works Inc........................G....... 405 249-6615
Maysville *(G-4262)*
Urban Okie Custom Woodwork.............G....... 405 420-1176
Edmond *(G-2658)*
Urban Okie Custom Woodwork LLC.....G....... 405 635-7800
Edmond *(G-2659)*
Urbane Commercial Contrs LLC...........G....... 405 534-1677
Midwest City *(G-4460)*
Vanhoose Wood Creations....................G....... 405 443-0454
Blanchard *(G-742)*
Wades Cabinet Door Shop.....................G....... 918 868-2516
Tahlequah *(G-8891)*
Wayland Woodworks LLC......................G....... 918 799-6196
Bristow *(G-805)*
Wendell Hicks Construction..................G....... 918 520-9128
Nowata *(G-5232)*
Wewoka Window Works LLC.................F....... 405 257-3109
Wewoka *(G-11514)*
Wfwoodworks LLC.................................G....... 405 740-8920
Norman *(G-5200)*
White Bffalo Cstm Wdwrk Rnvtio..........G....... 405 387-3278
Blanchard *(G-745)*
Wild West Creations..............................G....... 405 542-6507
Hinton *(G-3540)*
Windor Supply & Mfg Inc......................E....... 918 664-4017
Tulsa *(G-11137)*
Winkles Woodworks Ltd........................F....... 918 486-5022
Coweta *(G-1902)*
Wndells Woodturning.............................G....... 918 775-1124
Sallisaw *(G-8155)*
Wood Creations By Rod LLC................G....... 405 235-2222
Oklahoma City *(G-7462)*
Wood Creations By Rod LLC................G....... 405 912-8099
Moore *(G-4583)*
Wood Systems Inc.................................D....... 918 388-0900
Tulsa *(G-11148)*
Woodwright Woodworking LLC.............G....... 918 254-6577
Broken Arrow *(G-1102)*
Young Construction Supply LLC...........G....... 918 456-3250
Tahlequah *(G-8893)*
Yukon Door and Plywood Inc...............E....... 405 354-4861
Yukon *(G-11807)*
Zara Group Inc......................................F....... 918 782-4473
Vinita *(G-11273)*

2434 Wood Kitchen Cabinets

3d Cabinetry LLC..................................G....... 405 488-5604
Lindsay *(G-4042)*
Aaron Son Custom Cabinets..................G....... 918 537-2129
Muskogee *(G-4640)*
Alleman Trim & Cabinets......................G....... 405 942-7876
Oklahoma City *(G-5418)*
Artisan Custom Cabinetry Inc...............G....... 918 645-3874
Broken Arrow *(G-834)*
Bartlesville Custom Cabinets................G....... 918 440-5981
Bartlesville *(G-451)*
Beauchamp Cabinets Cstm Homes......G....... 918 476-5532
Chouteau *(G-1558)*
Becca Vermelis.......................................G....... 405 701-1638
Norman *(G-4929)*
Boxco Trim Cabinets..............................G....... 918 266-4030
Catoosa *(G-1305)*
Boyds Cstm Trim Cabinetry LLC...........G....... 918 724-7033
Glenpool *(G-3231)*
Brays Cabinet Shop................................G....... 580 584-6771
Broken Bow *(G-1186)*
Broken Arrow Woodworks.....................F....... 918 893-6763
Broken Arrow *(G-859)*
C & C Cabinets.......................................G....... 918 241-5249
Sand Springs *(G-8168)*
Cabinet Cures Oklahoma LLC..............G....... 405 285-5700
Edmond *(G-2335)*
Cabinet Doors Unlimited........................F....... 918 257-5765
Afton *(G-114)*
Cabinet Solutions LLC...........................G....... 918 592-4497
Tulsa *(G-9363)*
Cabinetworks Inc...................................G....... 405 286-1053
Oklahoma City *(G-5666)*
Casework Specialties Inc LLC...............G....... 918 382-0037
Tulsa *(G-9385)*
Charles Dale Keller.................................G....... 940 597-1763
Ardmore *(G-265)*
Classic Marble Design Inc.....................G....... 580 323-4917
Clinton *(G-1744)*
Close Custom Cabinets Inc...................E....... 405 840-8226
Oklahoma City *(G-5790)*
Colliers Cabinets....................................G....... 405 377-3508
Stillwater *(G-8669)*
Contemporary Cabinets Inc...................D....... 405 330-4592
Edmond *(G-2365)*
Cooper Cabinet Systems Inc.................D....... 405 528-7220
Oklahoma City *(G-5828)*
Cooper Cabinets Inc..............................E....... 405 528-7220
Oklahoma City *(G-5829)*
Crawford Cabinetry & Cnstr Inc............G....... 918 453-0164
Tahlequah *(G-8860)*
Creative Cabinets...................................G....... 580 762-9500
Ponca City *(G-7811)*
Creative Spaces.....................................G....... 405 341-8710
Edmond *(G-2372)*
Custom Cabinet Services.......................G....... 918 340-9015
Tulsa *(G-9527)*
Custom Wood Craft Construction.........G....... 405 262-5228
El Reno *(G-2708)*
Custom Woodwork Inc...........................F....... 918 224-4276
Sapulpa *(G-8263)*
Dale P Jackson.......................................F....... 580 332-1988
Ada *(G-29)*
David Stevens Cabinets & Trim............G....... 918 234-0656
Tulsa *(G-9558)*
Davis Cabinet Shop................................G....... 405 391-5527
Newalla *(G-4808)*
DH Cabinet and Trim Inc.......................G....... 405 376-1709
Mustang *(G-4769)*
Dynosaw Inc...G....... 405 418-6060
Oklahoma City *(G-5992)*
E&M Solutions LLC................................G....... 918 551-9515
Tulsa *(G-9622)*
Elite Cabinets...G....... 918 794-0757
Tulsa *(G-9656)*
Enviro Clean...G....... 918 207-9779
Park Hill *(G-7642)*
Guthrie Darin Cabinet Shop..................G....... 918 773-8444
Sallisaw *(G-8145)*
▲ Hawley & Co.......................................G....... 918 587-0510
Tulsa *(G-9905)*
Heister Custom Cabinets Inc.................G....... 405 329-6318
Norman *(G-5021)*
Hugo Wyrick Lumber..............................E....... 580 326-5569
Hugo *(G-3614)*
Imel Woodworks Inc..............................G....... 405 356-2505
Wellston *(G-11472)*
Jay Rambo Co Hahn Showroom...........G....... 918 615-3370
Tulsa *(G-10030)*
Jo Rose Fine Cabinets Inc.....................E....... 918 832-1500
Tulsa *(G-10046)*
John Henley Cstm Cabinets LLC...........G....... 405 535-9143
Edmond *(G-2473)*
Johnson Kendall Cnstr Co.....................G....... 580 223-5954
Ardmore *(G-317)*
Jon A Belonoik..G....... 405 258-4131
Chandler *(G-1382)*
Jones & Jackson Cabinets.....................G....... 580 889-8978
Atoka *(G-416)*
Kc Woodwork & Fixture Inc...................G....... 918 582-5300
Tulsa *(G-10078)*
Ketcherside Custom Cabinets...............G....... 580 254-2672
Woodward *(G-11599)*
Lakewood Cabinetry Inc........................F....... 918 782-2203
Langley *(G-3871)*
Majestic Marble & Granite.....................E....... 918 266-1121
Catoosa *(G-1337)*
Mass Brothers Inc..................................G....... 918 527-3753
Hartshorne *(G-3393)*
Mastercraft Millwork Inc........................G....... 405 895-6050
Moore *(G-4537)*
McCollum Custom Cabinets..................G....... 580 548-5851
Helena *(G-3435)*
Monticello Cabinets Doors Inc..............G....... 405 228-4900
Oklahoma City *(G-6627)*
Morrow Wood Products Inc...................G....... 405 579-5200
Norman *(G-5081)*
Nash Custom Cabinets..........................G....... 405 919-7711
Oklahoma City *(G-6654)*
Norwood Custom Cabinets....................G....... 918 478-2462
Hulbert *(G-3626)*
Nyes Cabinet Shop.................................G....... 580 622-6323
Sulphur *(G-8839)*
Oak Tree Sales.......................................G....... 405 224-9332
Chickasha *(G-1493)*
Oklahoma Millworks Inc........................D....... 405 282-4887
Guthrie *(G-3330)*
Old West Cabinets Inc...........................G....... 580 762-7474
Ponca City *(G-7862)*
Old Wrld Msters Div Bldg Pdts.............G....... 918 230-0340
Tulsa *(G-10412)*
Paradise Construction LLC...................G....... 918 967-9991
Stigler *(G-8637)*
Parks Custom Cabinets LLC.................G....... 918 789-2694
Chelsea *(G-1409)*
Pedros Cstm Cabinets Trim LLC...........G....... 580 656-3982
Duncan *(G-2163)*
Perkins Cabinet Trim.............................G....... 918 476-6567
Chouteau *(G-1569)*
Pruett Cabinet and Trim LLC................G....... 405 692-1552
Oklahoma City *(G-5312)*
Quality Cabinet Company.......................G....... 918 299-2721
Jenks *(G-3724)*
Quality Cabinetry...................................G....... 918 469-2119
Quinton *(G-8040)*
Quarry...G....... 918 534-2120
Dewey *(G-2030)*
R and P Cabinetry LLC.........................G....... 405 230-0495
Oklahoma City *(G-6959)*
Raber Renovations Inc..........................G....... 918 499-3030
Tulsa *(G-10608)*
Rambo Acquisition Company.................D....... 918 627-6222
Tulsa *(G-10615)*
Real Cabinets...G....... 918 336-0255
Bartlesville *(G-522)*
Reid Manufacturing LLC.......................G....... 405 606-7006
Oklahoma City *(G-7004)*
Richard Douglas Co...............................G....... 405 577-6626
Oklahoma City *(G-7016)*
Sand Creek Custom Cabinets LLC........G....... 580 822-1269
Fairview *(G-3151)*
Sandstar Custom Cabinets LLC............G....... 918 456-2964
Tahlequah *(G-8883)*
Sequoia Custom Cabinets LLC.............G....... 801 830-2741
Tulsa *(G-10732)*
Sharp Cuts Custom Cabinets................G....... 405 282-3657
Guthrie *(G-3338)*
Signature Cabinets LLC........................G....... 918 636-3433
Tulsa *(G-10759)*
Sooner Cabinet & Trim Inc....................E....... 405 820-2920
Moore *(G-4571)*
Spencers Custom Cabinets...................G....... 918 598-3208
Peggs *(G-7713)*
Sterling Cabinetry & Trim LLC..............G....... 918 928-9982
Stigler *(G-8647)*
Suburban Cabinet Shop.........................E....... 405 231-3110
Oklahoma City *(G-7221)*
Sullivans Custom Cabinetry..................E....... 918 445-9191
Tulsa *(G-10865)*
Taylormade Cbntry Cntrtops LLC.........G....... 405 227-4063
Jones *(G-3753)*
Ted S Cabinet..G....... 580 668-5207
Wilson *(G-11544)*
Thomas Cabinet Company......................G....... 580 588-9231
Apache *(G-223)*
Thomas Millwork Inc..............................F....... 405 769-5618
Spencer *(G-8602)*
Thomco Cabinet Co...............................G....... 405 627-1445
Oklahoma City *(G-7284)*
Three Rivers Custom Cabinets..............G....... 918 537-2311
Muskogee *(G-4752)*
Tillison Cabinet Company LLC..............E....... 405 793-2940
Moore *(G-4577)*
Trim Line Cabinets Inc..........................F....... 405 664-1439
Purcell *(G-8024)*
Trs Cabinets & Trim LLC.......................G....... 405 234-7276
Yukon *(G-11795)*
United Millwork Inc................................G....... 405 670-3999
Oklahoma City *(G-7371)*
Vanderbilt Cabinet & Trim.....................G....... 405 376-3876
Mustang *(G-4800)*
W & W Custom Cabinets........................G....... 405 222-1410
Chickasha *(G-1521)*
Wades Cabinet Door Shop.....................G....... 918 868-2516
Tahlequah *(G-8891)*
Ward Wood Products Inc.......................D....... 405 681-5522
Oklahoma City *(G-7420)*
Watkins Cabinet Doors LLC..................G....... 580 320-6301
Ada *(G-104)*
WD Sales Inc..F....... 580 237-1220
Enid *(G-3076)*
Weatherford Cabinets............................G....... 580 772-7511
Weatherford *(G-11456)*
Wildwood Fine Cabinet Doors...............G....... 918 331-0007
Bartlesville *(G-535)*
Wilshire Cabinet & Company LLC.........G....... 405 286-6282
Oklahoma City *(G-7457)*
Wolher Company....................................G....... 405 282-6210
Guthrie *(G-3341)*
Wood Systems Inc.................................D....... 918 388-0900
Tulsa *(G-11148)*
Wooden Solutions LLC..........................E....... 918 396-0774
Skiatook *(G-8575)*
Woodshop Cstm Cbinets Trim LLC.......G....... 405 673-7139
Oklahoma City *(G-7466)*

Employee Codes: A=Over 500 employees, B=251-500
C=101-250, D=51-100, E=20-50, F=10-19, G=1-9
2020 Oklahoma Directory
of Manufacturers & Processors
435

24 LUMBER AND WOOD PRODUCTS, EXCEPT FURNITURE

Woodstock Cabinet LLC ....F...... 918 834-4840
  Tulsa (G-11150)
Woodwork Productions LLC ....G...... 918 639-3167
  Catoosa (G-1367)
Ye Olde Woodshop ....G...... 918 224-1603
  Sapulpa (G-8328)
Young Construction Supply LLC ....G...... 918 456-3250
  Tahlequah (G-8893)

2435 Hardwood Veneer & Plywood

Hugo Wyrick Lumber ....E...... 580 326-5569
  Hugo (G-3614)
Morton Buildings Inc ....E...... 918 683-6668
  Muskogee (G-4715)

2439 Structural Wood Members, NEC

Antlers Roof-Truss & Bldrs Sup ....G...... 580 298-3560
  Antlers (G-213)
Ardmore Construction Sup Inc ....G...... 580 223-2322
  Ardmore (G-245)
Builders Firstsource Inc ....D...... 918 459-6872
  Broken Arrow (G-860)
Builders Firstsource Inc ....E...... 405 321-2255
  Oklahoma City (G-5641)
▲ Burrow Construction LLC ....E...... 800 766-5793
  Fort Gibson (G-3174)
Coreslab Structures Okla Inc ....C...... 405 632-4944
  Oklahoma City (G-5835)
Craco Truss Post Frame Sup LLC .....G...... 918 457-1111
  Park Hill (G-7641)
Cushing Truss Manufacturing ....F...... 918 387-2080
  Yale (G-11683)
David Kempe ....F...... 580 924-6798
  Durant (G-2221)
Do It Best Hardware ....G...... 580 482-8898
  Altus (G-154)
En-Fab Corp ....F...... 918 251-9647
  Broken Arrow (G-1126)
Harrison Roof Truss Co ....G...... 580 937-4900
  Coleman (G-1795)
Henderson Truss Incorporated ....F...... 918 473-5573
  Checotah (G-1394)
Higgins & Sons Truss Company ....E...... 405 997-5455
  Tecumseh (G-8917)
Higgins & Sons Truss Company ....F...... 405 997-5455
  Tecumseh (G-8918)
McFarland Cascade ....G...... 580 584-3511
  Broken Bow (G-1200)
Mills Enterprises Inc ....G...... 405 236-4470
  Oklahoma City (G-6613)
Newell Wood Products ....F...... 918 686-8060
  Muskogee (G-4721)
Northwest Truss ....G...... 580 496-2420
  Goltry (G-3248)
Overstreet Building & Supply ....G...... 580 234-5666
  Enid (G-3028)
Quality Line Truss Inc ....G...... 918 783-5227
  Adair (G-111)
Quality Truss Co Inc ....G...... 918 543-2077
  Claremore (G-1677)
Sawdust Ltd ....G...... 918 809-3456
  Broken Arrow (G-1044)
Schultz Roof Truss Inc ....G...... 405 364-6530
  Norman (G-5138)
Timberlake Trussworks LLC ....G...... 580 852-3660
  Helena (G-3437)
Zara Group Inc ....F...... 918 782-4473
  Vinita (G-11273)

2441 Wood Boxes

▼ American Crating Company ....E...... 918 425-8787
  Tulsa (G-9166)
Johnson Crating Services LLC ....G...... 405 672-7964
  Oklahoma City (G-6374)
Pratt Industries USA Inc ....B...... 405 787-3500
  Oklahoma City (G-6874)
Sunrise Sheds ....G...... 405 831-0904
  Prague (G-7937)
Tulsa Packing Specialist Inc ....F...... 918 459-8991
  Tulsa (G-11003)

2448 Wood Pallets & Skids

AAA Crimstone Operating Co LP ......G...... 918 445-5500
  Tulsa (G-9077)
Alex Pallets ....G...... 405 414-2710
  Oklahoma City (G-5411)
Betty E Jester ....G...... 580 564-9396
  Kingston (G-3824)

Burgess Manufacturing Okla Inc ....E...... 405 282-1913
  Guthrie (G-3303)
Choctaw Mfg Def Contrs Inc ....F...... 580 326-8365
  Hugo (G-3608)
Choctaw Mfg Def Contrs Inc ....G...... 580 298-2203
  Antlers (G-215)
Choctaw Mfg Def Contrs Inc ....G...... 918 426-2871
  McAlester (G-4286)
Chouteau Pallet ....G...... 918 476-6098
  Chouteau (G-1561)
Cimarron Pallet Mfg Co ....G...... 405 228-0288
  Oklahoma City (G-5765)
Cisco Containers LLC ....G...... 918 439-9244
  Tulsa (G-9430)
Doug Butler Enterprises Inc ....F...... 918 425-3565
  Tulsa (G-9599)
Duncan Wood Works LLC ....G...... 580 641-1190
  Duncan (G-2113)
Fat & Happy Services Inc ....G...... 405 834-5782
  Oklahoma City (G-6078)
Frahm John ....G...... 213 500-0741
  Sand Springs (G-8185)
Frontier Resource Development ....G...... 918 682-6571
  Muskogee (G-4676)
Henryetta Pallet Company ....E...... 918 652-9897
  Henryetta (G-3508)
Hernandez Pallets ....G...... 405 636-0503
  Oklahoma City (G-6243)
Ifco Systems ....G...... 405 491-9300
  Oklahoma City (G-6289)
▲ Ifco Systems Us LLC ....G...... 405 681-8090
  Oklahoma City (G-6290)
Johnson Lumber Company Inc ....E...... 918 253-8786
  Spavinaw (G-8591)
Oklahoma AAA Pallet Company ....E...... 405 670-1414
  Oklahoma City (G-6734)
Pal-Serv Oklahoma City LLC ....E...... 405 672-1155
  Oklahoma City (G-6794)
Pallet Liquidations Okc LLC ....G...... 405 843-0402
  Oklahoma City (G-6796)
Pallet Logistics of America ....G...... 405 670-1414
  Oklahoma City (G-6797)
Pallets Plus LLC ....G...... 580 513-4090
  Davis (G-1992)
Pauls Pallet Co ....G...... 918 435-4321
  Eucha (G-3095)
Prime Pallet LLC ....G...... 918 683-0907
  Muskogee (G-4737)
Pro Pallets ....G...... 405 679-8076
  Oklahoma City (G-6905)
Propak Logistics Inc ....D...... 405 694-4441
  Oklahoma City (G-6916)
Simer Pallet Recycling Inc ....F...... 405 224-8583
  Chickasha (G-1511)
Sooner Pallet Services Inc ....G...... 918 342-9663
  Claremore (G-1686)
Tasler Pallet Inc ....F...... 580 276-9800
  Marietta (G-4213)
Tim E Hutcheson ....G...... 918 313-5710
  Tulsa (G-10941)

2449 Wood Containers, NEC

Burgess Manufacturing Okla Inc ....E...... 405 282-1913
  Guthrie (G-3303)
Choctaw Mfg Def Contrs Inc ....G...... 580 326-8365
  Hugo (G-3609)
Economy Lumber Company Inc ....G...... 918 835-4933
  Tulsa (G-9641)
Four Star Crating Co ....G...... 918 663-6689
  Tulsa (G-9769)
Johnson Crating Services LLC ....G...... 405 672-7964
  Oklahoma City (G-6374)
Midtown Ventures LLC ....G...... 918 728-3102
  Tulsa (G-10265)
Van Brunt Lumber ....G...... 405 567-3776
  Prague (G-7938)
▲ Weilert Enterprises Inc ....E...... 918 252-5515
  Catoosa (G-1365)
▲ Western Industries Corporation ....C...... 405 419-3100
  Oklahoma City (G-7439)

2451 Mobile Homes

Bill Durbins Mobile Home Tra ....G...... 405 799-3557
  Oklahoma City (G-5280)
Clayton Homes Inc ....E...... 918 686-0584
  Muskogee (G-4661)
Clayton Homes Inc ....G...... 405 341-4479
  Edmond (G-2356)
Clayton Homes Inc ....G...... 580 237-7094
  Enid (G-2931)

Freedom Homes ....G...... 918 728-2277
  Tulsa (G-9775)
Hollands Mobile Homes ....G...... 918 476-5663
  Chouteau (G-1565)
Housing USA ....G...... 405 631-3653
  Oklahoma City (G-6267)
Modernblox LLC ....G...... 405 673-6215
  Tulsa (G-10292)

2452 Prefabricated Wood Buildings & Cmpnts

Better Built Barns ....G...... 405 547-2066
  Perkins (G-7715)
▲ Burrow Construction LLC ....E...... 800 766-5793
  Fort Gibson (G-3174)
Cedar Built USA Inc ....G...... 405 794-0811
  Moore (G-4508)
David Davis ....G...... 405 354-6974
  El Reno (G-2710)
Flex-Ability Concepts LLC ....G...... 405 996-5343
  Oklahoma City (G-6091)
Fullerton Building Systems Inc ....E...... 918 246-9995
  Sand Springs (G-8187)
Icon Construction Inc ....F...... 580 931-3806
  Durant (G-2236)
Katahdin Cedar Log Homes OK ....G...... 918 473-7020
  Checotah (G-1396)
◆ Midwest Cooling Towers Inc ....C...... 405 224-4622
  Chickasha (G-1486)
Midwest Portable Building ....G...... 918 245-9335
  Tulsa (G-10269)
Molitor Design & Cnstr LLC ....G...... 405 802-8302
  Moore (G-4542)
Morton Buildings Inc ....G...... 580 323-1172
  Clinton (G-1759)
Morton Buildings Inc ....E...... 918 683-6668
  Muskogee (G-4715)
Roadrunner Portable Buildings ....G...... 918 272-7788
  Owasso (G-7608)
Rons Discount Lumber Inc ....D...... 918 658-3857
  Howe (G-3599)
Shipman Home Improvement Inc ......G...... 918 514-0049
  Sand Springs (G-8223)
Solitaire Holdings LLC ....G...... 580 252-6060
  Duncan (G-2179)
Solitaire Homes Inc ....E...... 580 252-6060
  Duncan (G-2180)
Standard Panel LLC ....G...... 918 984-1717
  Tulsa (G-10837)
Terry Hall ....E...... 817 271-4838
  Valliant (G-11232)
Tuff Shed Inc ....G...... 405 272-1011
  Oklahoma City (G-7348)
Tuff Shed Inc ....G...... 405 788-4143
  Shawnee (G-8513)
Victory Garden Homestead LLC ....G...... 405 306-0308
  Blanchard (G-744)
Wood Tech Structures ....G...... 918 678-2108
  Wyandotte (G-11663)

2491 Wood Preserving

▲ Cowans Millwork Inc ....G...... 918 357-3725
  Broken Arrow (G-1118)
McFarland Cascade Holdings Inc ......G...... 580 584-2272
  Broken Bow (G-1201)
Mixon Brothers Wood Prsv Co ....F...... 580 286-9494
  Idabel (G-3643)

2493 Reconstituted Wood Prdts

Black Thunder Roofing LLC ....G...... 405 473-8028
  Oklahoma City (G-5582)
▲ Dominance Industries Inc ....C...... 580 584-6247
  Broken Bow (G-1189)
Heintzelman Cons & Rofing ....G...... 405 409-8954
  Oklahoma City (G-5294)
Huber Engineered Woods LLC ....E...... 580 584-7000
  Broken Bow (G-1192)
Icon Roofing and Cnstr LLC ....G...... 405 403-6615
  Mustang (G-4777)
Riverside Ranch LLC ....F...... 405 360-7300
  Norman (G-5132)

2499 Wood Prdts, NEC

Allens Woodcraft ....G...... 918 224-8796
  Sapulpa (G-8247)
American International Ltd ....G...... 405 364-1776
  Norman (G-4907)
Artisan Design Inc ....G...... 918 251-9795
  Broken Arrow (G-835)

SIC SECTION

25 FURNITURE AND FIXTURES

AS Designs LLC ....G..... 918 381-2390
  Owasso (G-7546)
Baties Custom Saddle Tree................F..... 918 788-3686
  Welch (G-11462)
Bell Timber Inc ....G..... 580 584-6902
  Broken Bow (G-1185)
Bristow 800 Kelly LLC ....G..... 248 268-3289
  Bristow (G-768)
Clubbs Wood Art ....G..... 918 569-4401
  Clayton (G-1708)
Cork and Bottle Wine and ....G..... 405 318-6842
  Yukon (G-11713)
Country Crafts ....G..... 918 247-6144
  Kellyville (G-3763)
Custom WD Fbers Cdar Mulch LLC ...G..... 405 745-2270
  Oklahoma City (G-5879)
D & S Refinishing ....G..... 580 233-4351
  Enid (G-2938)
D E Ziegler Art Craft Supply ....E..... 918 584-2217
  Tulsa (G-9537)
D Lloyd Hollingsworth ....G..... 918 587-3533
  Tulsa (G-9539)
DC Custom Framing ....G..... 918 549-8754
  Skiatook (G-8539)
Desert Moon Enterprises ....G..... 918 540-0333
  Miami (G-4395)
Dovetail Enterprises LLC ....G..... 405 476-3953
  Bethany (G-576)
Edmond Trophy Co ....G..... 405 341-4631
  Edmond (G-2405)
Engineered Food Processes LLC......G..... 405 377-7320
  Stillwater (G-8684)
Eric Adams Trim ....G..... 405 570-5931
  Jones (G-3745)
From Heart ....G..... 405 348-3009
  Edmond (G-2425)
Handle LLC ....G..... 405 822-9312
  Oklahoma City (G-6211)
Hardwood Innovations Inc ....F..... 405 722-5588
  Oklahoma City (G-6219)
Hoffman Fixtures Company ....E..... 918 252-0451
  Tulsa (G-9936)
Integrity Woodcrafters LLC ....G..... 918 664-1041
  Tulsa (G-10000)
K & K Wood Products ....G..... 918 396-4004
  Skiatook (G-8553)
Kactus Rose LLC ....G..... 405 830-7551
  El Reno (G-2729)
Marrara Group Inc ....G..... 918 379-0993
  Tulsa (G-10216)
Midwest Cooling Towers Inc ....G..... 580 389-5421
  Ardmore (G-332)
◆ Midwest Cooling Towers Inc ....C..... 405 224-4622
  Chickasha (G-1486)
Mitre Box Frame Shop ....G..... 580 338-2319
  Guymon (G-3356)
Mjs Crafts ....G..... 405 598-8105
  Tecumseh (G-8923)
▲ Mtm Recognition Corporation ....B..... 405 609-6900
  Oklahoma City (G-6634)
Multiples Inc ....G..... 918 584-7982
  Tulsa (G-10314)
Okiewood LLC ....G..... 405 245-5257
  Oklahoma City (G-6732)
Patternwork Veneering Inc ....G..... 405 447-1800
  Norman (G-5110)
PEL Company LLC ....G..... 405 816-6553
  Oklahoma City (G-6821)
Progressive Industries Inc ....G..... 405 843-0597
  Oklahoma City (G-6912)
Rabid ....G..... 580 234-3632
  Enid (G-3041)
Red Cedar Creations ....G..... 580 227-3198
  Longdale (G-4127)
Rick Woodten ....G..... 580 786-5050
  Duncan (G-2167)
Safe Harbor Docks Inc ....G..... 918 376-2756
  Owasso (G-7610)
Safe Harbor Products LLC ....G..... 918 376-2756
  Owasso (G-7611)
Smallwood Building LLC ....G..... 918 424-9378
  McAlester (G-4336)
Southwest Interiors Inc ....G..... 580 323-3050
  Clinton (G-1769)
Straight Edge Sawmill ....G..... 405 401-7798
  Union City (G-11221)
Tulsa Wood Arts LLC..........................G..... 918 576-6142
  Tulsa (G-11012)
Waterwood Parkway LLC ....G..... 405 341-5077
  Edmond (G-2682)

Welton Acquisitions LLC....................G..... 918 850-7981
  Sand Springs (G-8240)
Wooden Concepts LLC ....G..... 405 459-0411
  Weatherford (G-11461)
Woodshed ....E..... 918 256-9868
  Vinita (G-11272)
Wynnewood 1500 LLC ....G..... 248 268-3289
  Wynnewood (G-11675)
Wynnewood LLC ....G..... 248 268-3289
  Wynnewood (G-11676)
Yester Year Carousel ....G..... 405 427-5863
  Oklahoma City (G-7479)

25 FURNITURE AND FIXTURES

2511 Wood Household Furniture

American Custom Woodworks LLC ....G..... 918 344-4988
  Sapulpa (G-8248)
Billiards & Bar Stools Inc ....F..... 405 722-2400
  Oklahoma City (G-5566)
Breshears Enterprises Inc ....F..... 405 236-4523
  Oklahoma City (G-5624)
Cedar Chest ....G..... 918 287-9129
  Pawhuska (G-7681)
Close Custom Cabinets Inc ....E..... 405 840-8226
  Oklahoma City (G-5790)
Creative Spaces ....G..... 405 341-8710
  Edmond (G-2372)
Days Wood Products Inc ....F..... 405 238-6477
  Pauls Valley (G-7656)
Desert Moon Enterprises ....G..... 918 540-0333
  Miami (G-4395)
Donmar Industries LLC ....G..... 918 688-7277
  Skiatook (G-8542)
▲ Fabric Factory ....F..... 405 521-1694
  Oklahoma City (G-6067)
▲ Hawley & Co ....G..... 918 587-0510
  Tulsa (G-9905)
Imel Woodworks Inc ....G..... 405 356-2505
  Wellston (G-11472)
Johnson Woodcraft ....G..... 918 693-2388
  Claremore (G-1645)
Jos Lamerton Woodworking LLC.......G..... 580 336-8448
  Enid (G-2988)
Juan Manzo Custom Refinishing ....G..... 405 848-3843
  Oklahoma City (G-6390)
Kc Woodwork & Fixture Inc ....G..... 918 582-5300
  Tulsa (G-10078)
Kennel and Crate LLC ....G..... 405 624-0062
  Stillwater (G-8709)
Legacy Metalcraft LLC ....G..... 918 612-0001
  Wagoner (G-11286)
Mass Brothers Inc ....G..... 918 527-3753
  Hartshorne (G-3393)
Milot James Residence Cnstr ....G..... 405 433-2661
  Cashion (G-1291)
Punkin Hollerwood ....G..... 918 456-9640
  Proctor (G-7939)
Refuge Lifestyle ....F..... 918 366-6650
  Tulsa (G-10636)
Stillwater Transfer & Stor Co ....F..... 405 372-0577
  Stillwater (G-8759)
▼ Troy Wesnidge Inc ....E..... 405 387-4720
  Newcastle (G-4845)
United Millwork Inc ....G..... 405 670-3999
  Oklahoma City (G-7371)
Weatherford Cabinets ....G..... 580 772-7511
  Weatherford (G-11456)
Westwood Furniture Inc ....G..... 918 508-7657
  Tulsa (G-11113)
Winkles Woodworks Ltd ....F..... 918 486-5022
  Coweta (G-1902)
Woodshop Ltd ....G..... 405 922-3789
  Edmond (G-2692)
Young Construction Supply LLC ....G..... 918 456-3250
  Tahlequah (G-8893)

2512 Wood Household Furniture, Upholstered

Custom Lea Sad & Cowboy Decor .....G..... 918 335-2277
  Bartlesville (G-471)
Custom Upholstery Contracting ....F..... 405 236-3505
  Oklahoma City (G-5878)
Davenport Cloaks Inc ....G..... 918 932-8600
  Tulsa (G-9556)
James D Johnson ....G..... 580 464-3299
  Cyril (G-1975)
La-Z-Boy Incorporated ....G..... 405 417-5704
  Oklahoma City (G-6443)

La-Z-Boy Incorporated ....G..... 405 951-1437
  Oklahoma City (G-6444)
Patricia McKay ....G..... 580 355-2739
  Cache (G-1230)
Relf Upholstery ....G..... 405 454-3295
  Luther (G-4137)
Sendee Sales Inc ....E..... 918 427-3318
  Muldrow (G-4636)
Warren Ramsey Inc ....G..... 405 528-2828
  Oklahoma City (G-7422)

2514 Metal Household Furniture

Angel Ornamental Iron Works ....G..... 918 584-8726
  Tulsa (G-9191)
Billiards & Bar Stools Inc ....F..... 405 722-2400
  Oklahoma City (G-5566)
Chris Green Greens Construct ....G..... 405 207-0690
  Pauls Valley (G-7653)
Glenn Schlarb Welding ....G..... 580 327-3832
  Alva (G-182)
Ironcraft Urban Products LLC ....G..... 855 601-1647
  Oklahoma City (G-6327)
J&M Stainless Fabricators Ltd ....G..... 405 517-0875
  Oklahoma City (G-6340)
Legacy Metalcraft LLC ....G..... 918 612-0001
  Wagoner (G-11286)
Life Lift Systems Inc ....F..... 904 635-8231
  Oklahoma City (G-6474)
Melton Co Inc ....G..... 405 524-2281
  Oklahoma City (G-6563)
Pro Stainless & Shtmtl LLC ....G..... 405 787-4400
  Oklahoma City (G-6906)
▲ Webcoat Inc ....C..... 918 426-5100
  McAlester (G-4350)

2515 Mattresses & Bedsprings

Adairs Sleep World Inc ....F..... 405 341-9468
  Edmond (G-2289)
B & B Haybeds ....G..... 580 357-5083
  Lawton (G-3894)
Leggett & Platt Incorporated ....G..... 405 787-1212
  Oklahoma City (G-6465)
M & M Mattress Company ....G..... 918 834-2033
  Tulsa (G-10187)
Melton Co Inc ....G..... 405 524-2281
  Oklahoma City (G-6563)
Montgomery Mattress ....G..... 580 255-8979
  Duncan (G-2156)
Tote4me ....G..... 405 664-1144
  Edmond (G-2651)
Treble Services LLC ....G..... 405 401-1217
  Oklahoma City (G-7321)

2517 Wood T V, Radio, Phono & Sewing Cabinets

Beauchamp Cabinets Cstm Homes ...G..... 918 476-5532
  Chouteau (G-1558)
Contemporary Cabinets Inc ....D..... 405 330-4592
  Edmond (G-2365)
Creative Spaces ....G..... 405 341-8710
  Edmond (G-2372)
Ketcherside Custom Cabinets ....G..... 580 254-2672
  Woodward (G-11599)
P I Speakers ....G..... 918 663-2131
  Tulsa (G-10453)
Parkers Custom Hardwoods Inc ....G..... 405 341-9663
  Edmond (G-2563)
Rambo Acquisition Company ....D..... 918 627-6222
  Tulsa (G-10615)
United Millwork Inc ....G..... 405 670-3999
  Oklahoma City (G-7371)
Weatherford Cabinets ....G..... 580 772-7511
  Weatherford (G-11456)

2519 Household Furniture, NEC

Hemispheres ....G..... 405 773-8410
  Warr Acres (G-11322)
Murphy Wallbed USA LLC ....G..... 918 836-5833
  Tulsa (G-10317)
World Imports At Wholesale Inc ....G..... 405 947-7710
  Oklahoma City (G-7469)

2521 Wood Office Furniture

▲ Bearwood Concepts Inc ....D..... 918 933-6600
  Tulsa (G-9277)
Beauchamp Cabinets Cstm Homes ...G..... 918 476-5532
  Chouteau (G-1558)
D Lloyd Hollingsworth ....G..... 918 587-3533
  Tulsa (G-9539)

Employee Codes: A=Over 500 employees, B=251-500
C=101-250, D=51-100, E=20-50, F=10-19, G=1-9

25 FURNITURE AND FIXTURES

Dale P Jackson .... F 580 332-1988
  Ada *(G-29)*
Days Wood Products Inc .... F 405 238-6477
  Pauls Valley *(G-7656)*
Kc Woodwork & Fixture Inc .... G 918 582-5300
  Tulsa *(G-10078)*
Ketcherside Custom Cabinets .... G 580 254-2672
  Woodward *(G-11599)*
Narcomey LLC .... G 405 473-1350
  Oklahoma City *(G-6653)*
Penloyd LLC .... G 918 836-3794
  Tulsa *(G-10484)*
Polyvision Corporation .... F 918 756-7392
  Okmulgee *(G-7522)*
Rambo Acquisition Company .... D 918 627-6222
  Tulsa *(G-10615)*
Thomas Millwork Inc .... F 405 769-5618
  Spencer *(G-8602)*
Winkles Woodworks Ltd .... F 918 486-5022
  Coweta *(G-1902)*
Wolher Company .... G 405 282-6210
  Guthrie *(G-3341)*
Woodstock Cabinet LLC .... F 918 834-4840
  Tulsa *(G-11150)*
Ye Olde Woodshop .... G 918 224-1603
  Sapulpa *(G-8328)*
Young Construction Supply LLC ..... G 918 456-3250
  Tahlequah *(G-8893)*

2522 Office Furniture, Except Wood

Close Custom Cabinets Inc .... E 405 840-8226
  Oklahoma City *(G-5790)*
CSC Inc .... G 580 938-2533
  Shattuck *(G-8420)*
Fixtures & Drywall Co Okla Inc .... F 918 832-1641
  Tulsa *(G-9751)*
Melton Co Inc .... G 405 524-2281
  Oklahoma City *(G-6563)*
Michael Gipson LLC .... G 405 819-6349
  Oklahoma City *(G-6587)*
Rambo Acquisition Company .... D 918 627-6222
  Tulsa *(G-10615)*
Sweeper Metal Fabricators Corp ..... E 918 352-9180
  Drumright *(G-2073)*

2531 Public Building & Related Furniture

Aviation Training Devices Inc .... F 918 366-6680
  Bixby *(G-613)*
Born Again Pews .... F 918 868-7613
  Kansas *(G-3754)*
City of Davis .... E 580 369-2988
  Davis *(G-1981)*
Clarios .... G 405 688-3730
  Oklahoma City *(G-5773)*
Clarios .... G 918 641-0660
  Tulsa *(G-9439)*
Kingsview Freewill Baptist Ch .... G 405 692-1554
  Oklahoma City *(G-5302)*
Moss Seat Cover Mfg & Sls Co ...... F 918 742-3326
  Tulsa *(G-10306)*
Sweeper Metal Fabricators Corp ..... E 918 352-9180
  Drumright *(G-2073)*

2541 Wood, Office & Store Fixtures

All Wood Products Co Inc .... E 918 585-9739
  Tulsa *(G-9138)*
Brays Cabinet Shop .... G 580 584-6771
  Broken Bow *(G-1186)*
Breshears Enterprises Inc .... F 405 236-4523
  Oklahoma City *(G-5624)*
Cals Plastics Designs & Fabg .... G 405 670-1690
  Oklahoma City *(G-5673)*
Cmg International LLC .... G 918 493-5888
  Bixby *(G-617)*
Contemporary Cabinets Inc .... D 405 330-4592
  Edmond *(G-2365)*
Continental Stoneworks Inc .... F 918 835-6725
  Tulsa *(G-9479)*
Countertop Werks Inc .... G 405 943-1988
  Oklahoma City *(G-5843)*
Dale P Jackson .... F 580 332-1988
  Ada *(G-29)*
Days Wood Products Inc .... F 405 238-6477
  Pauls Valley *(G-7656)*
E J Higgins Interior Design .... G 405 387-3434
  Newcastle *(G-4825)*
Estey Cabinet Door Co .... E 405 771-3004
  Spencer *(G-8595)*
▲ Eurocraft Ltd .... E 918 322-5500
  Glenpool *(G-3234)*
Fixtures & Drywall Co Okla Inc .... F 918 832-1641
  Tulsa *(G-9751)*
Hoffman Fixtures Company .... E 918 252-0451
  Tulsa *(G-9936)*
Holick Family LLC .... G 580 765-3209
  Ponca City *(G-7836)*
Kelley Retha .... G 580 317-7483
  Grant *(G-3258)*
Ketcherside Custom Cabinets .... G 580 254-2672
  Woodward *(G-11599)*
Majestic Marble & Granite .... E 918 266-1121
  Catoosa *(G-1337)*
Mastercraft Millwork Inc .... G 405 895-6050
  Moore *(G-4537)*
Minko Design LLC .... G 918 895-6498
  Tulsa *(G-10284)*
Minko Design LLC .... G 918 895-6498
  Tulsa *(G-10285)*
North American Cos .... F 918 592-2000
  Tulsa *(G-10360)*
Perceptions .... G 405 964-7000
  McLoud *(G-4362)*
Red Rock Fabrication .... G 405 602-4602
  Edmond *(G-2591)*
Rivers Edge Countertops Inc .... G 405 532-3180
  Tuttle *(G-11211)*
▼ Troy Wesnidge Inc .... E 405 387-4720
  Newcastle *(G-4845)*
Weatherford Cabinets .... G 580 772-7511
  Weatherford *(G-11456)*
Zimmermans Custom Design Inc ... G 918 486-4179
  Coweta *(G-1903)*

2542 Partitions & Fixtures, Except Wood

A Mail Call Service Inc .... F 918 610-8533
  Tulsa *(G-9067)*
Amarillo Cstm Fixs Co Inc Okla ..... F 918 266-7752
  Catoosa *(G-1296)*
Compusign Vinyl Graphics .... G 580 762-4930
  Ponca City *(G-7807)*
Devon Industries Inc .... E 405 943-3881
  Oklahoma City *(G-5935)*
E J Higgins Interior Design .... G 405 387-3434
  Newcastle *(G-4825)*
▲ Garage Storage Cabinets LLC ... F 405 743-0133
  Stillwater *(G-8695)*
Mayco Fixture Co Inc .... F 918 428-5305
  Tulsa *(G-10226)*
Modular Squad LLC .... G 918 695-0114
  Tulsa *(G-10293)*
North American Cos .... F 918 592-2000
  Tulsa *(G-10360)*
Perceptions .... G 405 964-7000
  McLoud *(G-4362)*
Semasys Inc .... E 405 525-2335
  Oklahoma City *(G-7107)*
Service Pipe & Supply Company .... E 918 336-8433
  Bartlesville *(G-527)*
Sweeper Metal Fabricators Corp ..... E 918 352-9180
  Drumright *(G-2073)*
Vista Disposal Solutions LLC .... G 918 623-0333
  Tulsa *(G-11083)*

2591 Drapery Hardware, Window Blinds & Shades

Beyond Blinds LLC .... G 918 935-6317
  Bixby *(G-614)*
Blind Doctor .... G 918 638-1487
  Tulsa *(G-9304)*
Carolyns Cheesecake House .... G 918 839-5757
  Cameron *(G-1255)*
Classic Collectn Interiors Inc .... G 580 351-0024
  Lawton *(G-3905)*
Cowboy Covers Inc .... G 405 624-2270
  Stillwater *(G-8672)*
Curry Shades LLC .... G 918 779-3902
  Tulsa *(G-9524)*
Grace Allen Design - Custom .... G 405 509-5164
  Edmond *(G-2441)*
Hospital Products Oklahoma LLC .. G 918 271-7169
  Tulsa *(G-9951)*
Howes Ltg & Win Blinds LLC .... G 918 791-4101
  Bartlesville *(G-495)*
Johnsons Spring Crest Drpery C ... G 405 238-7341
  Pauls Valley *(G-7662)*
Lawton Council of The Blind .... G 580 536-1650
  Lawton *(G-3955)*
Patricia McKay .... G 580 355-2739
  Cache *(G-1230)*
Vertical Limit LLC .... G 918 409-1633
  Tulsa *(G-11073)*

2599 Furniture & Fixtures, NEC

Accord Upholstery & Fabric .... G 405 634-4070
  Oklahoma City *(G-5363)*
Affordable Restorations LLC .... G 918 609-5399
  Owasso *(G-7543)*
Beefys Beastro Food Svc LLC .... G 580 491-0325
  Broken Arrow *(G-844)*
Braden Shielding Systems Const ... E 918 624-2888
  Tulsa *(G-9327)*
Buddies Bars .... G 580 254-5778
  Woodward *(G-11564)*
Creative Spaces .... G 405 341-8710
  Edmond *(G-2372)*
Eat It Up LLC .... G 405 853-2313
  Hennessey *(G-3459)*
J&M Stainless Fabricators Ltd .... G 405 517-0875
  Oklahoma City *(G-6340)*
Ketcherside Custom Cabinets .... G 580 254-2672
  Woodward *(G-11599)*
Ki Inc .... G 918 289-0200
  Broken Arrow *(G-956)*
Kimbro Furniture LLC .... G 580 351-7304
  Lawton *(G-3949)*
Md-Advantages LLC .... G 405 996-6125
  Oklahoma City *(G-6551)*
Milot James Residence Cnstr .... G 405 433-2661
  Cashion *(G-1291)*
Modular Services Company .... G 405 521-9923
  Arcadia *(G-231)*
Polk Appliances Co .... G 918 592-6858
  Tulsa *(G-10530)*
Rambo Acquisition Company .... D 918 627-6222
  Tulsa *(G-10615)*
Restaurant Equipment & Sup LLC .. G 918 664-1778
  Tulsa *(G-10648)*
South Edge .... G 918 286-4936
  Broken Arrow *(G-1055)*
Total Restaurant Interiors .... G 405 535-6348
  Oklahoma City *(G-7310)*

26 PAPER AND ALLIED PRODUCTS

2611 Pulp Mills

Custom Yarmuck Scrap Proc LLC .. G 580 354-9134
  Lawton *(G-3916)*
J and S Trucking Company .... G 580 216-7213
  Woodward *(G-11595)*
Okc Soda Co LLC .... G 405 628-9543
  Oklahoma City *(G-6730)*
Paper Plus .... G 405 948-1120
  Oklahoma City *(G-6802)*
S Kat Embroidery & Quilting .... G 405 200-6283
  Chickasha *(G-1505)*

2621 Paper Mills

American Tissue Industries LLC ..... G 562 207-6814
  Oklahoma City *(G-5441)*
Audrey Parks & Associates Llc ...... G 405 328-3186
  Oklahoma City *(G-5489)*
Black Thunder Roofing LLC .... G 405 473-8028
  Oklahoma City *(G-5582)*
Cascades Holding US Inc .... G 918 825-0616
  Pryor *(G-7950)*
Hope Minerals International .... G 405 452-3529
  Wetumka *(G-11491)*
International Paper Company .... D 580 933-7211
  Valliant *(G-11227)*
Kimberly-Clark Corporation .... B 918 366-5000
  Jenks *(G-3713)*
Lechhner Wallcovering .... G 918 744-1742
  Tulsa *(G-10145)*
Midwest City Pub Schools I-52 ...... G 405 739-1665
  Oklahoma City *(G-6600)*
Oklahoma Interpak Inc .... E 918 687-1681
  Muskogee *(G-4724)*
Online Packaging .... G 580 389-5373
  Ardmore *(G-339)*
▲ Opp Liquidating Company Inc ... C 918 825-0616
  Pryor *(G-7980)*
Pechiney Plastic Packaging .... G 918 739-4900
  Catoosa *(G-1346)*

2631 Paperboard Mills

Cardboard Junkeez LLC .... G 405 990-9443
  Norman *(G-4953)*

SIC SECTION

27 PRINTING, PUBLISHING, AND ALLIED INDUSTRIES

Green Ox Pallet Technology LLC ....G....... 720 276-8013
  Oklahoma City (G-6187)
International Paper Company ....D....... 405 745-5800
  Oklahoma City (G-6320)
Oklahoma Interpak Inc ....E....... 918 687-1681
  Muskogee (G-4724)
Olson Packaging Service ....G....... 405 224-5577
  Chickasha (G-1494)
▲ Republic Paperboard Co LLC ....C....... 580 510-2200
  Lawton (G-3993)
Tulsa Packing Specialist Inc ....F....... 918 459-8991
  Tulsa (G-11003)

2652 Set-Up Paperboard Boxes

▲ Professional Image Inc ....E....... 918 461-0609
  Tulsa (G-10569)

2653 Corrugated & Solid Fiber Boxes

Corrugated Services LP ....G....... 405 672-1695
  Oklahoma City (G-5840)
Creative Packaging Inc ....G....... 918 587-0347
  Tulsa (G-9505)
Georgia-Pacific LLC ....C....... 580 549-7100
  Fletcher (G-3162)
Green Bay Packaging Inc ....G....... 405 222-2306
  Chickasha (G-1463)
Green Bay Packaging Inc ....C....... 918 446-3341
  Tulsa (G-9008)
International Paper Company ....D....... 405 745-5800
  Oklahoma City (G-6320)
Oklahoma Interpak Inc ....E....... 918 687-1681
  Muskogee (G-4724)
Pratt Industries USA Inc ....B....... 405 787-3500
  Oklahoma City (G-6874)
▼ Professional Packaging Inc ....E....... 918 682-9531
  Muskogee (G-4738)
Smurfit Kappa ....G....... 405 672-1695
  Oklahoma City (G-7156)
Smurfit Kappa North Amer LLC ....B....... 405 672-1695
  Oklahoma City (G-7157)
Southern Box Company ....G....... 580 255-7969
  Duncan (G-2181)
Stan-Mel Industries Inc ....G....... 918 436-0056
  Pocola (G-7787)
Supplyone Oklahoma City Inc ....C....... 405 947-7373
  Oklahoma City (G-7230)
Supplyone Oklahoma City Inc ....G....... 918 446-4428
  Tulsa (G-10881)
Vande Lune Packaging LLC ....G....... 405 517-0098
  Yukon (G-11801)
Westrock Cp LLC ....G....... 918 245-5102
  Sand Springs (G-8241)

2655 Fiber Cans, Tubes & Drums

Capitol Tube Co Inc ....G....... 405 632-9901
  Oklahoma City (G-5696)
EZ Mail Express ....G....... 918 542-2057
  Miami (G-4403)
▲ High Caliper Growing Inc ....D....... 405 842-7700
  Oklahoma City (G-6246)
Mito Material Solutions Inc ....G....... 855 344-6486
  Stillwater (G-8725)
Sonoco Products Company ....E....... 918 622-3370
  Tulsa (G-10786)
Sureshot Cans Inc ....G....... 580 698-2800
  Woodward (G-11638)

2656 Sanitary Food Containers

Hobby Supermarket Inc ....E....... 405 239-6864
  Oklahoma City (G-6256)
Solo Cup Operating Corporation ....C....... 580 436-1500
  Ada (G-90)

2657 Folding Paperboard Boxes

Artur Bookbinding Intl ....G....... 918 478-4888
  Fort Gibson (G-3173)
International Paper Company ....D....... 580 933-7211
  Valliant (G-11227)
▼ Media Resources Inc ....E....... 405 682-4400
  Oklahoma City (G-6555)
▲ Warner Jwly Box Display Co LLC ....D....... 580 536-8885
  Lawton (G-4021)

2671 Paper Coating & Laminating for Packaging

Beacon Stamp & Seal Co ....G....... 918 834-2322
  Tulsa (G-9276)

Bemis Company Inc ....C....... 405 207-2200
  Pauls Valley (G-7650)
Berry Global Films LLC ....D....... 918 227-1616
  Tulsa (G-8990)
Berry Plastics Corporation ....C....... 918 824-4400
  Pryor (G-7947)
International Paper Company ....D....... 580 933-7211
  Valliant (G-11227)
Pregis LLC ....D....... 918 439-9916
  Tulsa (G-10552)
Regency Labels Inc ....E....... 405 682-3460
  Oklahoma City (G-7002)
Sigma Extruding Corp ....F....... 918 446-6265
  Tulsa (G-10755)
Tom Bennett Manufacturing ....F....... 405 528-5671
  Oklahoma City (G-7302)

2672 Paper Coating & Laminating, Exc for Packaging

A-1 Specialties ....G....... 405 942-1341
  Oklahoma City (G-5352)
Giesecke & Devrient Amer Inc ....D....... 405 270-8400
  Oklahoma City (G-6154)
Keystone Tape & Label Inc ....G....... 405 631-2341
  Oklahoma City (G-6415)
Krause Plastics ....G....... 918 835-4202
  Tulsa (G-10100)
Marpro Label Inc ....G....... 405 672-3344
  Oklahoma City (G-6530)
Martin Thomas Enterprises Inc ....D....... 918 739-4015
  Catoosa (G-1338)
Marvel Photo Inc ....G....... 918 836-0741
  Tulsa (G-10218)
Priority Printworks Inc ....G....... 918 825-6397
  Pryor (G-7984)
Regency Labels Inc ....E....... 405 682-3460
  Oklahoma City (G-7002)
▲ Stonehouse Marketing Svcs LLC ....D....... 405 360-5674
  Norman (G-5160)
Summit Labels Inc ....G....... 918 936-4950
  Tulsa (G-10868)

2673 Bags: Plastics, Laminated & Coated

Advance Polybag Inc ....G....... 405 677-8383
  Oklahoma City (G-5377)
▲ API Enterprises Inc ....C....... 713 580-4800
  Oklahoma City (G-5452)
▼ Bags Inc ....E....... 405 427-5473
  Oklahoma City (G-5509)
Richard Bolusky ....G....... 918 381-5694
  Broken Arrow (G-1031)
Sigma Extruding Corp ....F....... 918 446-6265
  Tulsa (G-10755)
Tech Pack Inc ....G....... 918 836-8493
  Tulsa (G-10910)
Transcontinental Holding Corp ....F....... 918 739-4907
  Catoosa (G-1358)
Transcontinental US LLC ....D....... 918 739-4906
  Catoosa (G-1359)

2675 Die-Cut Paper & Board

Quik-Print of Oklahoma City ....G....... 405 840-3275
  Oklahoma City (G-6950)

2676 Sanitary Paper Prdts

Cool Baby Inc ....G....... 405 755-1100
  Edmond (G-2367)
Fatutyi Adeshola ....G....... 785 424-4208
  Lawton (G-3928)
Kimberly-Clark Corporation ....B....... 918 366-5000
  Jenks (G-3713)
▲ Opp Liquidating Company Inc ....C....... 918 825-0616
  Pryor (G-7980)

2677 Envelopes

Frank G Love Envelopes Inc ....D....... 214 637-5900
  Tulsa (G-9772)
Frank G Love Envelopes Inc ....G....... 405 720-9177
  Warr Acres (G-11319)
Response Solutions Inc ....G....... 918 508-7022
  Tulsa (G-10647)
Unity Press Inc ....E....... 405 232-8910
  Tulsa (G-11045)
Western Web Envelope Co Inc ....G....... 405 682-0207
  Oklahoma City (G-7442)

2678 Stationery Prdts

R&D Labs LLC ....G....... 405 875-9937
  Edmond (G-2583)

2679 Converted Paper Prdts, NEC

Brenda Riggs ....G....... 918 543-3530
  Inola (G-3652)
County of Comanche ....G....... 580 355-3810
  Lawton (G-3911)
▼ Media Resources Inc ....E....... 405 682-4400
  Oklahoma City (G-6555)
Metcel LLC ....G....... 405 334-7846
  Edmond (G-2514)
Paper Concierge ....G....... 405 286-3322
  Edmond (G-2561)
Pink Petals Flowers Gifts LLC ....G....... 580 317-8200
  Hugo (G-3619)
Regency Labels Inc ....E....... 405 682-3460
  Oklahoma City (G-7002)
Rotocolor Inc ....F....... 510 785-7686
  Tulsa (G-10676)
Summit Labels Inc ....G....... 918 936-4950
  Tulsa (G-10868)

27 PRINTING, PUBLISHING, AND ALLIED INDUSTRIES

2711 Newspapers: Publishing & Printing

Aaron Lance Butler ....G....... 580 220-7715
  Ardmore (G-235)
Adams Investment Company ....D....... 918 661-2100
  Dewey (G-2013)
Allen Advocate ....G....... 580 857-2687
  Allen (G-132)
American-Chief Co ....G....... 918 358-2553
  Cleveland (G-1715)
American-Chief Co ....G....... 918 762-2552
  Pawnee (G-7699)
American-Chief Co ....G....... 918 885-2101
  Hominy (G-3575)
Anadarko Publishing Co ....E....... 405 247-3331
  Anadarko (G-199)
Apache News ....G....... 580 588-3862
  Apache (G-217)
Ardmore Inc ....G....... 405 201-1288
  Ardmore (G-247)
Bam Journal LLC ....G....... 405 307-8220
  Norman (G-4925)
Bargain Journal ....G....... 918 426-5500
  McAlester (G-4273)
Beacon Publishing Co Inc ....G....... 405 232-4151
  Oklahoma City (G-5540)
Berkshire Hathaway Inc ....G....... 918 245-6634
  Sand Springs (G-8166)
Berkshire Hathaway Inc ....G....... 918 272-1155
  Owasso (G-7548)
Berkshire Hathaway Inc ....G....... 918 396-1616
  Skiatook (G-8532)
Berkshire Hathaway Inc ....G....... 918 485-5505
  Wagoner (G-11277)
Berkshire Hathaway Inc ....G....... 918 486-4444
  Wagoner (G-11276)
Beths Baubles and Bits ....G....... 405 659-3841
  Luther (G-4134)
Biggs Communications Inc ....G....... 918 523-4425
  Tulsa (G-9295)
Black Chronicle Inc ....F....... 405 424-4695
  Oklahoma City (G-5581)
Blackwell Wind ....G....... 580 363-0553
  Blackwell (G-675)
Blanchard News Publishing ....G....... 405 485-2311
  Blanchard (G-702)
Brently Publishing Intl LLC ....G....... 405 381-9069
  Tuttle (G-11187)
Buffalo Examiner ....G....... 580 326-3926
  Hugo (G-3604)
Cable Printing Co Inc ....F....... 405 756-4045
  Lindsay (G-4055)
Cache Times ....G....... 580 429-8200
  Cache (G-1225)
Carnegie Herald ....G....... 580 654-1443
  Carnegie (G-1274)
Chadwick Paper Inc ....G....... 580 369-2807
  Davis (G-1979)
Cheyenne Star ....G....... 580 497-3324
  Cheyenne (G-1423)
Choate Publishing Inc ....F....... 580 276-3255
  Marietta (G-4204)

27 PRINTING, PUBLISHING, AND ALLIED INDUSTRIES

Company	Class	Phone
Christian Chronicle Inc — Edmond (G-2349)	G	405 425-5070
Civitas Media LLC — Altus (G-149)	F	580 482-1221
Clarence & Lois Parker — Ponca City (G-7806)	G	580 765-8188
Clinton Daily News Company — Clinton (G-1745)	F	580 323-5151
Cnhi LLC — Guymon (G-3346)	F	580 338-3355
Cnhi LLC — Pauls Valley (G-7654)	F	405 238-6464
Cnhi LLC — Henryetta (G-3501)	G	918 652-3311
Cnhi LLC — Edmond (G-2359)	G	405 341-2121
Cnhi LLC — Sapulpa (G-8260)	E	918 224-5185
Cnhi LLC — Pryor (G-7954)	F	918 825-3292
Cnhi Communications — Westville (G-11481)	G	918 723-5445
Coalgate Record Register — Coalgate (G-1778)	G	580 927-2355
Comanche Nation Pub Info Off — Lawton (G-3909)	G	580 492-3381
Comanche Sports Group LLC — Comanche (G-1838)	G	580 439-5230
Comanche Times — Comanche (G-1839)	G	580 439-6500
Cookson Hills Publishers Inc — Sallisaw (G-8143)	E	918 775-4433
Country Connection News Inc — Eakly (G-2278)	G	405 797-3648
County Democrat — Shawnee (G-8441)	G	405 273-8888
Countywide News Inc — Tecumseh (G-8910)	F	405 598-3793
Cromwells Inc — Enid (G-2935)	G	580 234-6561
CSC Inc — Mooreland (G-4587)	G	580 994-6110
CSC Inc — Shattuck (G-8420)	G	580 938-2533
Daily Dental Solutions Inc — Piedmont (G-7759)	G	405 373-3299
Daily OCollegian — Stillwater (G-8674)	D	405 744-7371
Daily Perk LLC — Prague (G-7924)	G	405 567-5491
Daily Stop — Oklahoma City (G-5889)	G	405 495-5556
Daily Times — Pryor (G-7957)	G	918 825-3292
Dan Quyen Newspaper — Oklahoma City (G-5283)	G	405 691-2522
Dartmouth Journal Service — Tulsa (G-9553)	G	918 286-3513
Deal USA Today LLC — Pryor (G-7959)	G	918 825-7835
Delaware County Journal Inc — Jay (G-3680)	G	918 253-4322
Demco Printing Inc — Shawnee (G-8444)	F	405 273-8888
Democrat Chief Publishing Co — Hobart (G-3541)	G	580 726-3333
Dmn Inc — Oklahoma City (G-5954)	G	405 848-9401
Driver Examiner Div — Ponca City (G-7824)	G	580 762-1728
Drumright Gusher Inc — Drumright (G-2056)	G	918 352-2284
Editorial Grama Inc — Tulsa (G-9643)	F	918 744-9502
Edmond Life & Leisure — Edmond (G-2403)	F	405 340-3311
El Latino American Inc — Oklahoma City (G-6016)	G	405 632-1934
El Nacional — Oklahoma City (G-6017)	F	405 632-4531
▲ El Nacional News Inc — Oklahoma City (G-6018)	G	405 632-4531
El Reno Tribune — El Reno (G-2715)	G	405 262-7231
Elk Citian — Elk City (G-2807)	G	580 799-0925
Elk City Daily News Inc — Elk City (G-2808)	F	580 225-3000
Ellis County Capital — Arnett (G-387)	G	580 885-7788
Fairfax Chief — Fairfax (G-3118)	G	918 642-3814
Ferguson & Ferguson — Cleveland (G-1723)	G	918 358-2553
Fire Song Publishing — Moore (G-4524)	G	405 799-2799
Freedom Call LLC — Freedom (G-3206)	G	580 621-3578
Frost Entertainment — Oklahoma City (G-6125)	G	405 834-8484
Fungo Designs — Edmond (G-2427)	G	405 348-9922
G T R Newspapers Inc — Tulsa (G-9795)	G	918 254-1515
Gatehuse Mdia Okla Hldings Inc — Ardmore (G-296)	G	585 598-0030
Gayly — Oklahoma City (G-6138)	G	405 496-0011
Gazette Media Inc — Oklahoma City (G-6139)	E	405 528-6000
Geary Star — Geary (G-3216)	G	405 884-2424
Grand River Chronicle-Grove — Grove (G-3272)	G	918 786-8722
Greater Tlsa Rprter Newspapers — Tulsa (G-9855)	G	918 743-3458
Greater Tlsa Rprter Newspapers — Tulsa (G-9856)	G	918 254-1515
Harper County Journal — Buffalo (G-1213)	G	580 735-2526
Haskell News — Haskell (G-3398)	G	918 482-5619
Heavener Ledger — Heavener (G-3429)	G	918 653-2425
Hennessey Clipper — Hennessey (G-3466)	G	405 853-4888
Herald James M and Teresa — Tulsa (G-9923)	G	918 437-7016
Herald Publishing Co — Walters (G-11302)	G	580 875-3326
Herald Wakita — Wakita (G-11298)	G	580 594-2440
High Times Tulsa — Tulsa (G-9929)	G	918 600-2110
Hilton Herald Corp Oklahoma — Healdton (G-3414)	G	580 229-0132
Holdenville News — Holdenville (G-3554)	G	405 379-5411
Hooker Advance & Office Supply — Hooker (G-3598)	G	580 652-2476
Hughes County Publishing Co — Wetumka (G-11493)	G	405 452-3294
Hugo Publishing Company — Hugo (G-3612)	G	580 326-3311
Humps N Horns Bull Riding News — Broken Arrow (G-932)	G	918 872-9713
Humps N Hrns Bull Rdng Nws LLC — Chouteau (G-1566)	G	918 476-8213
Imagine Durant Inc — Durant (G-2238)	G	580 380-0743
Indian Nations Communications — Stilwell (G-8791)	G	918 696-2228
Jim Roth — Oklahoma City (G-6363)	G	405 235-4100
Job Paper LLC — Yukon (G-11737)	G	405 242-4804
Joe Brent Lansden — Beaver (G-541)	G	580 625-3241
Journal Record — Oklahoma City (G-6387)	G	405 524-7777
Journal Record Publishing Co — Oklahoma City (G-6388)	D	405 278-2848
Kimberling City Publishing Co — Okmulgee (G-7512)	E	918 756-3600
Kimberling City Publishing Co — Bristow (G-786)	G	918 367-2282
Kingfisher Newspaper Inc — Kingfisher (G-3805)	G	405 375-3220
Kiowa County Democrat — Snyder (G-8581)	G	580 569-2684
Lake Oologah Leader LLC — Oologah (G-7534)	G	918 443-2428
Larry D Hammer — Fairview (G-3140)	F	580 227-2100
Larry D Hammer — Cherokee (G-1418)	G	580 596-3344
Latimer County News Tribune — Wilburton (G-11522)	G	918 465-2321
Lawrence County Newspapers Inc — Sapulpa (G-8285)	G	918 224-5185
Lawton Media Inc — Lawton (G-3958)	C	580 355-8920
Lawton Newspapers LLC — Lawton (G-3959)	D	580 585-5115
Leader Tribune — Laverne (G-3879)	G	580 921-3391
Legal News — Tulsa (G-10150)	G	918 259-7500
Lewis County Press LLC — Blackwell (G-687)	G	580 363-3370
Lifes Adult Day Services — Broken Arrow (G-967)	G	918 664-9000
Lincoln County Publishing Co — Chandler (G-1385)	F	405 258-1818
Lisa Snell — Tahlequah (G-8872)	G	918 708-5838
Lone Grove Ledger — Lone Grove (G-4118)	G	580 657-6492
Marshall County Publishing Co — Madill (G-4155)	F	580 795-3355
Martin Broadcasting Corp — Alva (G-186)	E	580 327-1510
Maysville Publishing Co — Maysville (G-4261)	G	405 867-4457
Mc Clain County Publishing Co — Purcell (G-8016)	G	405 527-2126
McAlester Democrat Inc — McAlester (G-4316)	G	918 423-1700
McCurtain County News Inc — Idabel (G-3642)	F	580 286-3321
McCurtain County News Inc — Broken Bow (G-1199)	F	580 584-6210
McIntosh County Democrat — Checotah (G-1397)	G	918 473-2313
Mesa Black Publishing LLC — Boise City (G-747)	G	580 544-2222
Metro Publishing LLC — Oklahoma City (G-6581)	G	405 631-5100
Miami Newspapers Inc — Miami (G-4417)	E	918 542-5533
Morris Communications Co LLC — Shawnee (G-8477)	D	405 273-4200
Morris News — Morris (G-4600)	G	918 733-4898
Mountain View Printing Company — Mountain View (G-4628)	G	580 347-2231
Mustang Times — Oklahoma City (G-6643)	G	405 606-1023
Navajo County Publishers Inc — Edmond (G-2531)	F	928 524-6203
Nayfa Publications Inc — Piedmont (G-7767)	G	405 373-1616
New ERA — Davenport (G-1978)	G	918 377-2259
Newcastle Pacer Inc — Newcastle (G-4833)	G	405 387-5277
Newkirk Herald Journal — Newkirk (G-4850)	G	580 362-2140
News Enterprises Inc — Mustang (G-4787)	G	405 376-4571
Newspaper Holding Inc — Tahlequah (G-8876)	E	918 456-8833
Newspaper Holding Inc — Enid (G-3018)	D	580 233-6600
Newspaper Holding Inc — Duncan (G-2159)	G	580 255-5354
Newspaper Holding Inc — Woodward (G-11614)	E	580 256-2200
Newspaper Holding Inc — Ada (G-72)	E	580 332-4433
Newspaper Holding Inc — Stillwater (G-8728)	D	405 372-5000
Newspaper Holding Inc — McAlester (G-4324)	D	918 423-1700
Newspaper Holding Inc — Norman (G-5091)	D	405 321-1800
Newspaper Holding Inc — Claremore (G-1661)	E	918 341-1101
Newspaper Holding Inc — Hartshorne (G-3394)	E	918 297-2544
Newspaper Holding Inc — Muskogee (G-4722)	F	918 684-2922
Newspaper Holding Inc — Stilwell (G-8793)	E	918 696-2228
Newspaper Sales LLC — Broken Arrow (G-1146)	G	918 357-5070
Newspaper Services — Claremore (G-1662)	G	918 283-1564
Newspress Inc — Stillwater (G-8729)	F	405 372-5000

SIC SECTION 27 PRINTING, PUBLISHING, AND ALLIED INDUSTRIES

Nichols Hills Publishing Co ... F ... 405 755-3311
Oklahoma City (G-6678)
Northern Arizona Newspaper ... F ... 928 524-6203
Edmond (G-2540)
Nuestra Comunidad ... G ... 405 685-3822
Oklahoma City (G-6703)
Okemah Leader ... G ... 918 623-0123
Okemah (G-5271)
Oklahoma Assn of Elc Coop ... E ... 405 478-1455
Oklahoma City (G-6735)
Oklahoma Bankers ... E ... 405 424-5252
Oklahoma City (G-6736)
Oklahoma City Herald ... G ... 405 842-7827
Oklahoma City (G-6741)
Oklahoma Eagle LLC ... G ... 918 582-7124
Tulsa (G-10398)
Oklahoma Eagle Publishing Co ... G ... 918 582-7124
Tulsa (G-10399)
Oklahoma Magazine ... F ... 918 744-6205
Tulsa (G-10402)
Oklahoma Newspaper ... F ... 405 475-3989
Oklahoma City (G-6755)
Oklahoma Newspaper Foundation ... E ... 405 499-0020
Oklahoma City (G-6756)
Oklahoma Publishing Co of Okla ... E ... 405 475-3585
Oklahoma City (G-6759)
Oklahoman Media Company ... F ... 405 475-3311
Oklahoma City (G-6765)
Omni LLC ... G ... 405 246-9252
Oklahoma City (G-6777)
Opubco Development Co ... E ... 405 475-3311
Oklahoma City (G-6780)
Owner Value News ... G ... 918 828-9600
Tulsa (G-10449)
Paper ... G ... 918 825-2860
Pryor (G-7981)
Paxton Publishing Co ... G ... 580 782-3321
Mangum (G-4173)
Perry Broadcasting Company ... F ... 405 427-5877
Oklahoma City (G-6834)
Perry Daily Journal Inc ... G ... 580 336-2222
Perry (G-7741)
Ponca City Publishing Co Inc ... E ... 580 765-3311
Ponca City (G-7866)
Poteau Daily News ... G ... 918 647-3335
Poteau (G-7911)
Prague Times Herald ... G ... 405 567-3933
Prague (G-7932)
Premier Printing ... G ... 405 632-1132
Oklahoma City (G-6886)
Randy Wyrick ... G ... 918 848-0117
Fairland (G-3128)
Reid Communications LLC ... G ... 918 285-5555
Cushing (G-1955)
Reporter Publishing Co Inc ... G ... 918 789-2331
Chelsea (G-1411)
Review News Co ... F ... 405 354-5264
Yukon (G-11771)
Review Printing Company Inc ... F ... 580 658-6657
Marlow (G-4241)
Ringling Eagle ... G ... 580 662-2221
Ringling (G-8082)
Rosemon Martin LLC ... G ... 918 272-7145
Owasso (G-7609)
Rush Springs Gazette ... G ... 580 476-2525
Rush Springs (G-8125)
Russell Publishing Company ... G ... 405 665-4333
Wynnewood (G-11672)
Salina Journal ... G ... 785 822-1470
Collinsville (G-1823)
Sayre Record ... G ... 580 928-5540
Sayre (G-8345)
Sentinel Leader ... G ... 580 393-4348
Sentinel (G-8412)
Shawnee News-Star ... G ... 405 273-4200
Shawnee (G-8495)
Sherrif ... G ... 918 663-3705
Tulsa (G-10743)
Southeast Times ... G ... 580 286-2628
Idabel (G-3646)
Southwest Cnstr News Svc ... G ... 405 948-7474
Oklahoma City (G-7173)
Southwest Cnstr News Svc ... G ... 918 493-5066
Tulsa (G-10804)
Spiro Graphic ... G ... 918 962-2075
Spiro (G-8618)
Spitzer Printing ... G ... 580 928-5540
Sayre (G-8346)
Spitzer Publishing ... G ... 580 928-5540
Sayre (G-8347)

Star Nowata ... G ... 918 273-2446
Nowata (G-5230)
Stroud American Inc ... G ... 918 968-2310
Stroud (G-8820)
Sun of A Beach ... G ... 918 938-6219
Tulsa (G-10871)
Taloga Times Advocate ... G ... 580 328-5619
Taloga (G-8908)
Thomas Tribute Inc ... G ... 580 661-3524
Thomas (G-8949)
Times Star ... G ... 918 710-5740
Collinsville (G-1827)
Times-Democrat Company Inc ... G ... 580 622-2102
Sulphur (G-8844)
Tonkawa News ... G ... 580 628-2532
Tonkawa (G-8984)
Tri County Publications Inc ... G ... 918 465-3851
Wilburton (G-11526)
Tribune Corp ... E ... 405 262-5180
El Reno (G-2764)
Triple B Media LLC ... G ... 405 732-7577
Midwest City (G-4459)
Tulsa World ... G ... 918 664-8683
Tulsa (G-11013)
Tulsa World ... G ... 918 582-5921
Tulsa (G-11014)
Tulsa World Capitol Bureau ... G ... 405 528-2465
Oklahoma City (G-7350)
University of Oklahoma ... C ... 405 325-3666
Norman (G-5188)
Valliant Leader Inc ... G ... 580 933-4570
Valliant (G-11233)
Vinita Printing Co Inc ... E ... 918 256-6422
Vinita (G-11271)
Wanderlust Pen Company ... G ... 918 551-6809
Tulsa (G-11094)
Washita Valley Weekly ... G ... 405 224-7467
Chickasha (G-1522)
Watonga Republican Inc ... G ... 580 623-4922
Watonga (G-11354)
Waynoka Pubg Co Woods Cnty ... G ... 580 824-2171
Waynoka (G-11381)
Weatherford News Inc ... E ... 580 772-3301
Weatherford (G-11458)
Weekly Leader ... G ... 918 458-8001
Tahlequah (G-8892)
Wesner Publications Company ... F ... 405 789-1962
Bethany (G-600)
Wesner Publications Company ... E ... 580 832-3333
Cordell (G-1865)
Wewoka Times ... G ... 405 257-3341
Wewoka (G-11513)
Wilson-Monroe Publishing Co ... G ... 580 933-4579
Valliant (G-11234)
Woods County Enterprise ... G ... 580 824-2171
Waynoka (G-11384)
Woodward News ... E ... 580 256-2200
Woodward (G-11658)

2721 Periodicals: Publishing & Printing

Able Engineering Services ... G ... 918 835-3161
Tulsa (G-9082)
AG Youth Magazine ... G ... 800 599-6884
Sentinel (G-8409)
AGC Inc ... G ... 913 451-8900
Oklahoma City (G-5398)
American Assn Petro Geologists ... D ... 918 584-2555
Tulsa (G-9164)
American Choral Directors Assn ... F ... 405 232-8161
Oklahoma City (G-5434)
Black Belt Magazine 1000 LLC ... G ... 405 732-5111
Oklahoma City (G-5580)
C and H Publishing Co ... G ... 918 245-9571
Sand Springs (G-8169)
Chastain Enterprises LLC ... G ... 918 615-9355
Tulsa (G-9407)
Clarion Events Inc ... C ... 918 835-3161
Tulsa (G-9438)
Coast To Coast Power Spt LLC ... G ... 918 712-8487
Tulsa (G-9462)
Commercial Property Research ... G ... 918 481-8882
Tulsa (G-9476)
Datapages Inc ... G ... 918 584-2555
Tulsa (G-9555)
Dealers Market ... G ... 405 789-6455
Warr Acres (G-11318)
Dharma Inc ... G ... 405 366-1336
Norman (G-4978)
DPM Group LLC ... F ... 405 682-3468
Oklahoma City (G-5976)

Editorial Grama Inc ... F ... 918 744-9502
Tulsa (G-9643)
Farley Redfield ... G ... 405 275-2266
Tecumseh (G-8914)
Hoffman Printing LLC ... F ... 918 682-8341
Muskogee (G-4691)
International Gymnast Magazine ... G ... 405 447-9988
Norman (G-5035)
International Journal of Ph ... F ... 405 330-0094
Edmond (G-2463)
International Pro Rodeo Assn ... G ... 405 235-6540
Oklahoma City (G-6321)
Journal Record Publishing Co ... D ... 405 278-2848
Oklahoma City (G-6388)
Just Two Publishing Inc ... G ... 405 607-2902
Edmond (G-2476)
K9 Media ... E ... 504 233-2576
Del City (G-1998)
Key Magazine ... G ... 405 602-3300
Oklahoma City (G-6408)
Langdon Publishing Co Inc ... F ... 918 585-9924
Tulsa (G-10123)
Lew Graphics Inc ... G ... 405 743-0890
Stillwater (G-8717)
Lost Treasure Inc ... G ... 918 786-2182
Grove (G-3279)
Loud Graphic Studios LLC ... G ... 405 520-5349
Edmond (G-2497)
Mastermind Comics ... G ... 315 308-0593
Del City (G-2000)
Meridian Press Publications ... G ... 405 751-2342
Oklahoma City (G-6568)
Metro Family Magazine ... G ... 405 601-2081
Oklahoma City (G-6579)
Morning Fax ... G ... 918 357-5245
Broken Arrow (G-1145)
Morris Communications Co LLC ... D ... 405 273-4200
Shawnee (G-8477)
New Forums Press Inc ... G ... 405 372-6158
Stillwater (G-8727)
Nightowl Publications Main Off ... G ... 405 603-8130
Oklahoma City (G-6681)
Oklahoma Bar Foundation Inc ... E ... 405 416-7000
Oklahoma City (G-6737)
Oklahoma Electric Cooperative ... D ... 405 321-2024
Norman (G-5100)
Oklahoma Grocers Association ... F ... 405 525-9419
Oklahoma City (G-6750)
Oklahoma Magazine ... F ... 918 744-6205
Tulsa (G-10402)
Oklahoma Propane Gas Assn ... G ... 405 424-1775
Oklahoma City (G-6758)
Oklahoma Restaurant Assn ... F ... 405 942-8181
Oklahoma City (G-6761)
Oklahoma Soc Prof Engineers ... G ... 405 528-1435
Oklahoma City (G-6763)
Oklahoma State University ... F ... 918 253-4332
Jay (G-3684)
Oklahoma State University ... C ... 405 744-5723
Stillwater (G-8733)
Oral Rbrts Evnglistic Assn Inc ... D ... 918 591-2000
Tulsa (G-10436)
Paul Ziert & Associates Inc ... D ... 405 364-5344
Norman (G-5112)
Pdqlipprints LLC ... G ... 580 233-3241
Enid (G-3033)
Phoenix Trade Publication ... G ... 405 948-6555
Oklahoma City (G-6846)
Pigeon Debut ... G ... 405 686-0412
Oklahoma City (G-6848)
Preview of Green Country Inc ... G ... 918 745-1190
Tulsa (G-10556)
Schuman Publishing Company ... G ... 918 744-6205
Tulsa (G-10715)
Sheet Metal Contractors Assn ... G ... 405 848-3683
Oklahoma City (G-7119)
Souno LLC ... E ... 918 495-1771
Tulsa (G-10794)
T K Publishing Inc ... G ... 918 582-8504
Tulsa (G-10891)
Thunder Road Magazine Oklahoma ... G ... 405 612-3844
Oklahoma City (G-7285)
Tulsa County Medical Society ... G ... 918 743-6184
Tulsa (G-10995)
Tulsapets Magazine ... G ... 918 834-1252
Tulsa (G-11015)
University of Oklahoma ... G ... 405 325-4531
Norman (G-5185)
Vype High School Spt Mag LLC ... F ... 918 495-1771
Tulsa (G-11085)

SIC

Employee Codes: A=Over 500 employees, B=251-500
C=101-250, D=51-100, E=20-50, F=10-19, G=1-9
2020 Oklahoma Directory
of Manufacturers & Processors
441

27 PRINTING, PUBLISHING, AND ALLIED INDUSTRIES

West Mattison Publishing Inc ....F 405 842-2266
　Edmond *(G-2684)*
World Organization China Pntrs ....E 405 521-1484
　Oklahoma City *(G-7470)*
Xzeno Productions ....G 405 974-4016
　Edmond *(G-2694)*

2731 Books: Publishing & Printing

412 Comics LLC ....G 479 414-0891
　Pocola *(G-7779)*
A Fuller Measure ....G 405 755-5036
　Oklahoma City *(G-5346)*
Acp Inc ....G 405 249-8835
　Oklahoma City *(G-5369)*
Andrea Koenig ....G 918 745-0828
　Tulsa *(G-9189)*
Anvil House Publishers LLC ....G 918 760-8991
　Owasso *(G-7545)*
Arista ....G 405 948-1500
　Oklahoma City *(G-5464)*
Auryn Creative ....G 918 876-0974
　Tulsa *(G-9223)*
Bordon David & Associates LLC ....G 918 495-3508
　Broken Arrow *(G-855)*
Camp Chippewa For Boys Inc ....E 218 335-8807
　Tulsa *(G-9367)*
Catch 21 ....G 617 227-0730
　Oklahoma City *(G-5712)*
Chastain Enterprises LLC ....G 918 615-9355
　Tulsa *(G-9407)*
▲ Child Heroes LLC ....G 757 286-8181
　Oklahoma City *(G-5760)*
▲ Cross Shadows Inc ....G 405 262-9777
　El Reno *(G-2707)*
Dragonfly Publishing Inc ....G 405 359-6952
　Edmond *(G-2395)*
Empowered Life Stores LLC ....G 918 523-5700
　Tulsa *(G-9678)*
Freedom Bell Inc ....G 918 671-1089
　Tulsa *(G-9774)*
Garrett Educational Corp ....E 580 332-6884
　Ada *(G-39)*
Gateway International Inc ....G 918 747-8393
　Tulsa *(G-9807)*
Gregath Publishing Company ....G 918 542-4148
　Miami *(G-4407)*
Gregory Prizzell P & R M Inc ....G 405 752-0782
　Oklahoma City *(G-6192)*
Gretchen Cagle Publications ....G 918 342-1080
　Claremore *(G-1629)*
Guy W Logsdon ....G 918 743-2171
　Tulsa *(G-9869)*
Hale Publications ....G 405 632-2450
　Oklahoma City *(G-6204)*
Hays Publishing ....G 918 456-7717
　Tahlequah *(G-8867)*
Hidden Pearls LLC ....G 405 707-0851
　Stillwater *(G-8701)*
Hoffman Printing LLC ....F 918 682-8341
　Muskogee *(G-4691)*
Independent School ....E 918 245-2622
　Sand Springs *(G-8192)*
J Franklin Publishers Inc ....G 628 400-3382
　Tulsa *(G-10020)*
JB Books Unlimited LLC ....G 918 954-8308
　Tulsa *(G-10031)*
Jomaga House ....G 918 455-0794
　Broken Arrow *(G-950)*
Kinda Wilson LLC ....G 405 880-5308
　Tulsa *(G-10090)*
Kings Remnant Ministry Inc ....G 918 207-0866
　Welling *(G-11467)*
Lacebark Inc ....G 405 377-3539
　Stillwater *(G-8716)*
Lloyd Words LLC ....G 918 457-6852
　Tulsa *(G-10172)*
Mentorhope LLC ....G 405 752-0940
　Oklahoma City *(G-6565)*
Meridian Press Publications ....G 405 751-2342
　Oklahoma City *(G-6568)*
Michelangelo Properties LLC ....G 918 341-4771
　Claremore *(G-1654)*
Midwest Publishing Co ....G 405 282-1890
　Guthrie *(G-3325)*
Nedley Publishing Co ....F 580 223-5980
　Ardmore *(G-337)*
New Forums Press Inc ....G 405 372-6158
　Stillwater *(G-8727)*
Oklahoma Academy Publishing ....G 405 454-6211
　Harrah *(G-3383)*

Oklahoma State University ....C 405 744-5723
　Stillwater *(G-8733)*
Olam Publishing LLC ....G 918 200-9770
　Tulsa *(G-10410)*
Out On Limb Publishing ....G 918 743-4408
　Tulsa *(G-10445)*
Paige 1 Publishing ....G 918 706-4359
　Broken Arrow *(G-997)*
Paige Publishing ....G 405 527-3245
　Lexington *(G-4039)*
Penielite Ggg Press ....G 405 850-5795
　McLoud *(G-4361)*
Plan Bible ....G 918 254-6983
　Tulsa *(G-10522)*
Rentpath LLC ....F 918 307-8980
　Tulsa *(G-10642)*
Rutherford Lterary Group L L C ....G 405 623-9031
　Midwest City *(G-4452)*
▲ Tommy Higle Publishers ....G 580 276-5136
　Marietta *(G-4215)*
Trisms Inc ....G 918 585-2778
　Tulsa *(G-10977)*
University of Oklahoma ....E 405 325-3189
　Norman *(G-5186)*
University of Oklahoma ....E 405 325-3276
　Norman *(G-5187)*
Victory House Inc ....G 918 747-5009
　Tulsa *(G-11075)*
Vmebus Intl Trade Assn ....E 480 577-1916
　Oklahoma City *(G-7405)*
West Mattison Publishing Inc ....F 405 842-2266
　Edmond *(G-2684)*
Word Among US ....G 918 812-5254
　Tulsa *(G-11151)*
World Energy Resources Inc ....G 405 375-6484
　Kingfisher *(G-3823)*
Wynn Wynn Media ....G 918 283-1834
　Claremore *(G-1705)*
Yellow Bird Communication ....G 405 238-6260
　Pauls Valley *(G-7675)*
Yorkshire Publishing LLC ....E 918 394-2665
　Tulsa *(G-11170)*

2732 Book Printing, Not Publishing

Corner Copy & Printing LLC ....G 405 801-2020
　Norman *(G-4966)*
Qg LLC ....B 405 742-2222
　Stillwater *(G-8741)*
Silver Quill LLC ....G 405 735-9191
　Moore *(G-4569)*
Sugar Pills Apparel ....G 580 277-0231
　Ardmore *(G-364)*
Suggs Orel ....G 405 275-6159
　Shawnee *(G-8505)*

2741 Misc Publishing

12th Gate Publishing LLC ....G 405 735-7611
　Oklahoma City *(G-5327)*
1tr3 Publishing LLC ....G 580 350-9280
　Lawton *(G-3880)*
2 Victory Graphics Media ....G 918 394-2665
　Tulsa *(G-9054)*
209 LLC ....G 918 584-9944
　Tulsa *(G-9058)*
2b Publishing LLC ....G 405 209-8465
　Edmond *(G-2282)*
405 Magazine Inc ....G 405 604-2623
　Oklahoma City *(G-5332)*
4rv Publishing LLC ....G 405 225-7298
　Edmond *(G-2286)*
50th Xpress Mart ....G 405 491-7381
　Warr Acres *(G-11310)*
5a Enterprises Inc ....G 918 260-8909
　Drumright *(G-2049)*
A Prior Publishing ....G 903 882-5019
　Lawton *(G-3881)*
Abundant Grace Companies LLC ....F 405 682-2589
　Oklahoma City *(G-5359)*
Adventure Publishing LLC ....G 918 270-7100
　Tulsa *(G-9113)*
Agion Press ....G 405 341-7477
　Edmond *(G-2293)*
Aj Publishers LLC ....G 580 234-0064
　Enid *(G-2909)*
Allsbury Marketing & Pubg LLC ....G 405 412-0809
　Edmond *(G-2297)*
Anatole Publishing LLC ....G 405 609-0763
　Norman *(G-4909)*
Anvil House Publishers LLC ....G 918 760-8991
　Owasso *(G-7545)*

Arkansas River Press ....G 918 744-1730
　Tulsa *(G-9208)*
Art of Manliness LLC ....G 405 613-3340
　Tulsa *(G-9214)*
Attorney and Legal Publica ....G 405 728-0392
　Oklahoma City *(G-5487)*
Bankers Online ....G 888 229-8872
　Edmond *(G-2316)*
Bennie Publications LLC ....G 918 873-0250
　Oklahoma City *(G-5552)*
Blackjack Express LLC ....G 405 462-7410
　Bradley *(G-760)*
Blue Bridge Publishing LLC ....G 405 533-2547
　Stillwater *(G-8661)*
Blue Sail Publishing Inc ....G 630 851-4731
　Ardmore *(G-259)*
Bobay Nutrition LLC ....G 405 708-0407
　Oklahoma City *(G-5602)*
Book Villages LLC ....G 719 339-8048
　Edmond *(G-2329)*
Books In Sight Inc ....G 405 810-9501
　Oklahoma City *(G-5617)*
Bridge Creek Publishing Co ....G 405 519-6982
　Mulhall *(G-4637)*
Brown Publishing Inc ....G 405 842-5089
　Nichols Hills *(G-4856)*
Buffalo Nickel Press ....G 918 287-3899
　Pawhuska *(G-7680)*
Bush Publishing ....G 901 468-8388
　Broken Arrow *(G-1114)*
Bush Publishing & Assoc LLC ....G 251 424-7298
　Tulsa *(G-9349)*
Capitalist Publishing Co ....G 918 808-5665
　Tulsa *(G-9371)*
Cattleac Cattle Equipment Inc ....G 580 774-1010
　Weatherford *(G-11398)*
CCS Publishing LLC ....G 405 359-0656
　Edmond *(G-2340)*
CD Services ....G 918 341-1032
　Claremore *(G-1602)*
Cedar Gate LLC ....G 405 640-3235
　Edmond *(G-2341)*
Chic Galleria Publications ....G 918 671-2379
　Bartlesville *(G-465)*
Chickasaw Press ....G 580 436-7282
　Ada *(G-22)*
Choctaw Manufacturing & Dev Co .....G 580 310-6021
　Ada *(G-23)*
Chumbolly Press LLC ....G 918 607-3932
　Sand Springs *(G-8170)*
Colt Express ....G 918 455-2658
　Tulsa *(G-9471)*
Comfort X-Press LLC ....E 405 382-5600
　Seminole *(G-8366)*
Community Publishers ....E 918 273-1040
　Nowata *(G-5211)*
Community Publishers Inc ....G 918 259-7500
　Broken Arrow *(G-872)*
Community Racks LLC ....F 405 210-7950
　Yukon *(G-11709)*
Comptech Computer Tech Inc ....E 937 228-2667
　Oklahoma City *(G-5817)*
Copypasta Publishing ....G 580 236-4071
　Broken Bow *(G-1188)*
Counterbattery Press LLC ....G 405 794-2885
　Moore *(G-4510)*
Countywide News Inc ....F 405 598-3793
　Tecumseh *(G-8910)*
Ctsa LLC ....G 405 478-3501
　Edmond *(G-2377)*
Dancey-Meador Publishing Co ....G 580 762-9359
　Ponca City *(G-7819)*
Daniel E and Marl Newport ....G 918 445-9129
　Tulsa *(G-9550)*
Danny Bowen ....G 405 618-3377
　Meeker *(G-4377)*
Datebox Inc Okc ....G 253 678-1173
　Oklahoma City *(G-5901)*
Dbr Publishing Co LLC ....E 918 250-1984
　Owasso *(G-7560)*
Delphia Publishing LLC ....G 918 232-8709
　Drumright *(G-2055)*
Document Imging Ntwrk Slutions ......G 405 818-3888
　Oklahoma City *(G-5956)*
Don Wilmut ....G 405 785-9192
　Alex *(G-130)*
Doodle and Peck Publishing ....G 405 354-7422
　Yukon *(G-11721)*
Draft2digital LLC ....G 405 708-7894
　Oklahoma City *(G-5979)*

27 PRINTING, PUBLISHING, AND ALLIED INDUSTRIES

Dynamic Mapping Solutions Inc ....G....... 918 446-7803
 Tulsa *(G-9617)*
E H Publishing Inc ....G....... 405 258-0877
 Chandler *(G-1379)*
Earlywine Press LLC ....G....... 405 820-8208
 Oklahoma City *(G-5289)*
Editorial Annex ....G....... 405 474-2114
 Edmond *(G-2400)*
Educational Concepts LLC ....F....... 918 749-0118
 Tulsa *(G-9644)*
Ellis Enterprise ....G....... 405 826-3572
 Purcell *(G-8007)*
Ellis Enterprises Inc ....G....... 405 917-5336
 Oklahoma City *(G-6027)*
Emerald Quest ....G....... 580 920-5917
 Durant *(G-2229)*
Endurance Publishing LLC ....G....... 405 332-5273
 Stillwater *(G-8683)*
Everhart Publishing LLC ....G....... 405 370-4850
 Oklahoma City *(G-6056)*
Ex-Press Vac LLC ....G....... 580 606-0799
 Duncan *(G-2117)*
Express Bus Inc ....G....... 918 835-2040
 Tulsa *(G-9717)*
Express Home Help ....G....... 405 214-6400
 Shawnee *(G-8448)*
Ezekiel Chrles Pblications LLC ....G....... 918 747-8841
 Tulsa *(G-9720)*
Featherston Publishing LLC ....G....... 918 289-7877
 Owasso *(G-7567)*
Finity Enterprises Inc ....G....... 580 699-2640
 Lawton *(G-3929)*
Five F Publishing ....G....... 405 732-1050
 Oklahoma City *(G-6085)*
Flamingo Media Inc ....G....... 405 620-5889
 Oklahoma City *(G-5291)*
Fronttoback Studio LLC ....G....... 405 788-4400
 Oklahoma City *(G-6124)*
Fs & J Music Publishing LLC ....G....... 918 369-6010
 Tulsa *(G-9786)*
Ghost Town Press ....G....... 405 396-2166
 Arcadia *(G-229)*
Greater Tlsa Rprter Newspapers ....G....... 918 254-1515
 Tulsa *(G-9856)*
Gregs Press ....G....... 405 356-4156
 Wellston *(G-11471)*
Gust Media LLC ....G....... 641 715-3900
 Edmond *(G-2449)*
Gypsy Twang Publishing ....G....... 918 398-3116
 Bixby *(G-630)*
Hale Publications ....G....... 405 632-2450
 Oklahoma City *(G-6204)*
Harrison House Inc ....G....... 918 582-2126
 Tulsa *(G-9896)*
Hear My Heart Publishing LLC ....G....... 918 510-1483
 Skiatook *(G-8547)*
Highlands Publishing LLC ....G....... 405 596-8391
 Norman *(G-5022)*
His Publishing LLC ....G....... 405 390-0518
 Choctaw *(G-1544)*
Hmh Publishing ....G....... 405 788-5589
 Elk City *(G-2823)*
Hogan Assessment Systems Inc ....D....... 918 293-2300
 Tulsa *(G-9937)*
Hoot of Loot ....G....... 918 743-9802
 Tulsa *(G-9946)*
Hot Off Press ....G....... 918 492-2313
 Tulsa *(G-9953)*
Illbird Press ....G....... 918 859-7789
 Tulsa *(G-9970)*
Imoco LLC ....G....... 918 459-8366
 Tulsa *(G-9971)*
Indigo Streams Publishing LLC ....G....... 918 293-0247
 Tulsa *(G-9978)*
Industrial City Press ....G....... 918 299-2767
 Jenks *(G-3707)*
Infinitee By Mars LLC ....G....... 405 474-4505
 Oklahoma City *(G-6302)*
Inkana Publishing ....G....... 937 760-8446
 Ada *(G-51)*
Inkana Publishing LLC ....G....... 937 725-1296
 Moore *(G-4528)*
Insight Publishing Group ....G....... 918 493-1718
 Tulsa *(G-9990)*
Interstate Trucker Ltd ....E....... 405 948-6576
 Oklahoma City *(G-6323)*
Jamey H Voorhees ....G....... 479 599-9921
 Stillwater *(G-8706)*
Janet D Redd ....G....... 580 243-0595
 Elk City *(G-2830)*

Jeremy Hart Music Inc ....G....... 918 687-3605
 Muskogee *(G-4700)*
Jewell Jordan Publishing LLC ....G....... 405 496-2672
 Oklahoma City *(G-6362)*
JM Publications LLC ....G....... 918 639-9472
 Oklahoma City *(G-6365)*
JM Publishing LLC ....G....... 405 684-0450
 Edmond *(G-2471)*
John Clark ....G....... 918 853-8286
 Sperry *(G-8608)*
Just Breathe Publishing LLC ....G....... 405 633-0160
 Spencer *(G-8597)*
▲ Kane/Miller Book Publishers ....G....... 918 346-6118
 Tulsa *(G-10075)*
Kasm Publishing LLC ....G....... 918 798-8908
 Tulsa *(G-10077)*
Kelley Publications LLC ....G....... 405 585-7210
 Stratford *(G-8805)*
Kh Publishing LLC ....G....... 405 378-7539
 Oklahoma City *(G-5301)*
Kobe Express LLC ....G....... 580 889-2420
 Atoka *(G-418)*
Kp Designs LLC ....G....... 865 776-7769
 Lawton *(G-3951)*
L S Marann Publishing ....G....... 405 751-9369
 Oklahoma City *(G-6441)*
Level Up Publishing LLC ....G....... 405 771-4372
 Spencer *(G-8598)*
Life Impact Publishing LLC ....G....... 918 407-9938
 Tulsa *(G-10158)*
Lindsey Webb Press ....G....... 405 756-9551
 Lindsay *(G-4074)*
Local Hometown Publishing Inc ....G....... 405 273-3838
 McLoud *(G-4359)*
Local Telephone Directory ....G....... 580 762-9359
 Ponca City *(G-7846)*
Lw Publications ....G....... 405 203-6740
 Norman *(G-5061)*
Mac Publishing Company LLC ....G....... 405 964-3576
 McLoud *(G-4360)*
Marcelle Publishing LLC ....G....... 405 288-2317
 Purcell *(G-8015)*
Marie Thierrey Lucinda ....G....... 405 623-9431
 Oklahoma City *(G-6525)*
Mauvaisterre Publishing LLC ....G....... 918 492-3846
 Tulsa *(G-10224)*
McCurtain County News Inc ....F....... 580 286-3321
 Idabel *(G-3642)*
Meeker Football Press Box ....G....... 405 279-1075
 Meeker *(G-4381)*
Mental Note LLC ....G....... 405 301-4182
 Edmond *(G-2512)*
Metro Publishing LLC ....G....... 405 593-1335
 Yukon *(G-11753)*
Midwest Publication ....G....... 405 948-6506
 Oklahoma City *(G-6606)*
Midwest Publishing Co Inc ....G....... 918 582-2000
 Tulsa *(G-10271)*
MO Publishing LLC ....G....... 580 284-3719
 Lawton *(G-3972)*
Mobile Express ....G....... 405 395-9378
 Shawnee *(G-8476)*
Mongrel Empire Press LLC ....G....... 405 459-0042
 Norman *(G-5078)*
Morning Fax ....G....... 918 357-5245
 Broken Arrow *(G-1145)*
Mpress Cards ....G....... 405 590-5393
 Norman *(G-5082)*
Musicware Press ....G....... 405 627-1894
 Oklahoma City *(G-6637)*
Mythic Press ....G....... 918 516-8255
 Tulsa *(G-10321)*
N2r Media LLC ....G....... 405 301-0188
 Edmond *(G-2527)*
New Forums Press Inc ....G....... 405 372-6158
 Stillwater *(G-8727)*
New Plains Review ....G....... 405 974-5613
 Edmond *(G-2536)*
Nonovels Press LLC ....G....... 325 721-2577
 Oklahoma City *(G-6684)*
Northwood Publishing LLC ....G....... 918 451-9388
 Broken Arrow *(G-989)*
Oklahoma Ntry Svc A Div of M- ....G....... 405 948-8900
 Oklahoma City *(G-6757)*
Oklahoma Publishing Company ....G....... 405 475-4040
 Oklahoma City *(G-6760)*
Okstyle Publishing LLC ....G....... 405 816-3338
 Oklahoma City *(G-6768)*
Old Farm Publishing LLC ....G....... 405 237-1153
 Moore *(G-4548)*

Oremus Press & Publishing ....G....... 405 368-4645
 Dover *(G-2042)*
Original Productions Pubg LLC ....G....... 405 420-9559
 Norman *(G-5104)*
Osage County Treasurer ....G....... 918 287-3101
 Pawhuska *(G-7691)*
Paige Publishing ....G....... 405 527-3245
 Lexington *(G-4039)*
Patricia Lyons ....G....... 850 445-4782
 Jenks *(G-3722)*
Paxton McMillin Chrisanna ....G....... 918 734-5753
 Sapulpa *(G-8297)*
Pegleg Publishing LLC ....G....... 405 618-7740
 Oklahoma City *(G-6820)*
Perfect Circle Publishing Inc ....G....... 918 629-0061
 Tulsa *(G-10492)*
Philip H Brewer ....G....... 580 657-8029
 Ardmore *(G-345)*
Pie In Sky Publishing Co LLC ....G....... 918 762-3310
 Pawnee *(G-7709)*
Pivot Point Publishing ....G....... 918 347-5415
 Sapulpa *(G-8298)*
Poteau Daily News ....G....... 918 647-3335
 Poteau *(G-7911)*
Press ....G....... 405 464-6181
 Oklahoma City *(G-6890)*
Press Go ....G....... 580 889-2399
 Atoka *(G-421)*
▲ Princo Press Corp ....G....... 405 760-6064
 Edmond *(G-2575)*
Pringle Publications Corp ....G....... 405 848-4859
 Oklahoma City *(G-6896)*
Professional Communications ....G....... 580 745-9838
 Durant *(G-2249)*
Prometheus Publications LLC ....G....... 717 460-4881
 Vinita *(G-11268)*
Purpose Publishing ....G....... 405 808-1332
 Oklahoma City *(G-6927)*
Pv Publishing Inc ....G....... 405 409-1799
 Oklahoma City *(G-6928)*
Ram Internet Media ....G....... 405 614-0641
 Stillwater *(G-8744)*
Raymond L Weil Pblications LLC ....G....... 580 323-4594
 Clinton *(G-1764)*
Red Dog Press LLC ....G....... 405 703-2896
 Moore *(G-4560)*
Rigyard Publications LLC ....G....... 405 330-1456
 Edmond *(G-2600)*
Rivers Edge Publications ....G....... 918 855-9469
 Tulsa *(G-10656)*
Roadrunner Press ....G....... 405 524-6205
 Oklahoma City *(G-7031)*
▼ Rocking Chair Enterprises LLC ....G....... 918 455-3744
 Broken Arrow *(G-1037)*
Rwdesign Publishing ....G....... 918 924-8865
 Broken Arrow *(G-1041)*
Safetac Publishing LLC ....G....... 559 640-7233
 Tulsa *(G-10687)*
Samson Publishing Company LLC ....G....... 918 344-7416
 Beggs *(G-560)*
Schatz Publishing Group LLC ....F....... 580 628-4607
 Blackwell *(G-690)*
Scout Guide Tulsa LLC ....G....... 918 693-1198
 Tulsa *(G-10717)*
Scriptorium ....G....... 405 203-5943
 Moore *(G-4566)*
Seminole County Publishing ....G....... 405 382-1125
 Seminole *(G-8398)*
Shepherds Heart Music Inc ....G....... 918 781-1200
 Muskogee *(G-4749)*
Shopper News Note ....F....... 405 756-3169
 Lindsay *(G-4084)*
Show and Tell Times Inc ....G....... 918 225-4111
 Cushing *(G-1959)*
Sooner Publishing Inc ....G....... 580 233-8400
 Enid *(G-3058)*
Sound Ink 2 Publishing LLC ....G....... 918 605-6026
 Tulsa *(G-9038)*
Souno LLC ....E....... 918 495-1771
 Tulsa *(G-10794)*
Spacebar Publishing LLC ....G....... 918 852-6311
 Claremore *(G-1687)*
Spangenhelm Publishing ....G....... 405 430-6464
 Yukon *(G-11785)*
Sports Fitnes Publications LLC ....G....... 918 587-7223
 Tulsa *(G-10824)*
St Bonaventure Press Ltd ....G....... 918 770-8546
 Tulsa *(G-10829)*
Starfall Press LLC ....G....... 405 343-2369
 Edmond *(G-2630)*

Employee Codes: A=Over 500 employees, B=251-500
C=101-250, D=51-100, E=20-50, F=10-19, G=1-9

2020 Oklahoma Directory
of Manufacturers & Processors

Steeley D Upshaw Pubg LLC ....G....... 405 948-7802
Oklahoma City (G-7201)
Stellar Art Publishing Inc ....G....... 918 277-3325
Bixby (G-665)
Strawberry Valley Press LLC ....G....... 405 237-1893
Oklahoma City (G-5318)
Subtledemon Publishing LLC..............G....... 405 670-3471
Oklahoma City (G-5319)
Thomas Tribute Inc...............................G....... 580 661-3524
Thomas (G-8949)
Tigers Express.......................................G....... 918 251-0118
Broken Arrow (G-1076)
Timothy Publishing Services................G....... 918 924-6246
Broken Arrow (G-1077)
Together Tulsa Publications ....G....... 918 269-1085
Tulsa (G-10948)
Towne Publishing LLC ....G....... 405 473-7436
Norman (G-5178)
Trenary Publishing LLC.........................G....... 918 607-3280
Broken Arrow (G-1083)
University of Oklahoma Press..............G....... 405 325-2000
Norman (G-5189)
User Friendly Phone Book LLC...........F 918 384-0224
Tulsa (G-11060)
V M Publishing Co ....G....... 405 533-1883
Stillwater (G-8772)
Verdavia Press LLC ....G....... 405 254-5030
Edmond (G-2669)
Vinson James R Linda F Co..................G....... 405 478-1330
Edmond (G-2672)
Vmebus Intl Trade Assn ....G....... 480 577-1916
Oklahoma City (G-7405)
Western Web Envelope Co Inc ....F 405 682-0207
Oklahoma City (G-7442)
Wine Press...G....... 580 540-8913
Enid (G-3081)
Wolf Publishing......................................G....... 918 500-9921
Tulsa (G-11145)
World Arts Press LLC............................G....... 405 314-2578
Nichols Hills (G-4865)
World Publishing Company Veba.........G....... 918 582-0921
Tulsa (G-11153)
Write Green Light...................................G....... 405 722-7823
Yukon (G-11805)
Writers Research Group LLC...............F 405 682-2589
Oklahoma City (G-7474)
You Are Here Curriculum ....G....... 918 650-8586
Henryetta (G-3519)
Yp LLC..D....... 918 835-8600
Tulsa (G-11171)
Zeigler Publishing..................................G....... 405 771-8754
Spencer (G-8603)

2752 Commercial Printing: Lithographic

262 LLC...F....... 918 458-5511
Tahlequah (G-8848)
30 Cent Print LLC ....G....... 469 408-8968
Blanchard (G-698)
3g Printing ....G....... 918 284-9433
Coweta (G-1869)
3g Printing ....G....... 918 346-0035
Broken Arrow (G-1107)
918 Screen Printers ....G....... 918 850-9542
Tulsa (G-9060)
A & B Printing & Office Supply.............G....... 580 889-5103
Atoka (G-395)
A 1 Master Print Inc ....G....... 405 787-0505
Bethany (G-571)
A B Printing ....G....... 918 834-2054
Tulsa (G-9066)
A Plus Printing ....G....... 580 765-7752
Ponca City (G-7791)
A Plus Printing Inc.................................G....... 918 836-8659
Tulsa (G-9068)
A Plus Printing LLC ....G....... 580 765-7752
Ponca City (G-7792)
A Q Printing..G....... 918 438-1161
Tulsa (G-9070)
A-1 Mster Prnta/Hooper Prtg Si ....G....... 518 427-0282
Oklahoma City (G-5351)
A-OK Printing Mill..................................G....... 918 775-6809
Sallisaw (G-8136)
Abco Printing & Office Supply..............G....... 580 286-7575
Idabel (G-3636)
Ace Information Co................................G....... 405 677-6747
Oklahoma City (G-5364)
Action Graphics Printing Inc ....G....... 918 540-3336
Miami (G-4388)
Action Graphics Prtg & Design ....G....... 918 540-3336
Miami (G-4389)
Action Printing Norman Inc ....E....... 405 364-3615
Norman (G-4897)
Adams Printing ....G....... 580 832-2123
Cordell (G-1853)
Advance Graphics & Printing................G....... 405 258-0796
Chandler (G-1373)
Affordable Signs & Decals Inc..............G....... 405 942-7059
Oklahoma City (G-5397)
Ajt Enterprises Inc ....F....... 918 665-7083
Tulsa (G-9133)
Allegra Marketing Print Mail.................G....... 539 302-2229
Tulsa (G-9140)
Altus Print Ship......................................G....... 580 482-6855
Altus (G-140)
Altus Printing Co Inc ....G....... 580 482-2020
Altus (G-141)
American Bank Systems Inc.................E....... 405 607-7000
Oklahoma City (G-5432)
American-Chief Co.................................G....... 918 358-2553
Cleveland (G-1715)
Annie Printer ....G....... 405 670-9640
Oklahoma City (G-5447)
Anns Quick Print Co Inc.........................G....... 405 222-1871
Chickasha (G-1429)
Apache News..G....... 580 588-3862
Apache (G-217)
ARC Document Solutions LLC ....F....... 405 943-0378
Oklahoma City (G-5460)
Arcadia Printing of Tulsa Inc ....G....... 918 622-1875
Bixby (G-611)
Archer Printing Inc.................................G....... 405 236-1607
Moore (G-4493)
Associated Lithographing Co................E....... 918 663-9091
Tulsa (G-9217)
Avalanche Print Company ....G....... 405 808-4229
Edmond (G-2313)
Awesome Apparel Printing ....G....... 918 402-3672
Broken Arrow (G-838)
B & L Printing Inc...................................G....... 918 258-6655
Broken Arrow (G-839)
B J Printing Products Inc.......................G....... 918 245-6385
Sand Springs (G-8164)
B&M Digital Garment Printing ....G....... 918 954-6994
Tulsa (G-9248)
Bakers Printing Co Inc ....G....... 405 842-6944
Oklahoma City (G-5517)
Bartlesville Print Shop...........................G....... 918 336-6070
Bartlesville (G-452)
Baywest Embroidery ....G....... 580 626-4728
Jet (G-3741)
Beavers Independent Printe ....G....... 405 205-5300
Moore (G-4497)
Bell Printing and Advertising................G....... 405 769-6445
Nicoma Park (G-4866)
Benders..G....... 580 256-5656
Woodward (G-11561)
Bent Tees Screen Printing ....G....... 918 734-3996
Tulsa (G-9283)
Berkshire Hathaway Inc ....G....... 918 486-4444
Wagoner (G-11276)
Berry Custom Printing LLC...................G....... 918 266-3732
Catoosa (G-1302)
Best Printing Solution LLC ....G....... 918 794-1771
Tulsa (G-9287)
Big Time Designs Screen Prtg..............G....... 580 658-5000
Marlow (G-4223)
Bigfoot Prints LLC ....G....... 918 805-0543
Collinsville (G-1803)
Bill Rathbone..G....... 918 486-3028
Coweta (G-1872)
Biz Networks LLC ....G....... 405 348-6090
Edmond (G-2323)
Bluestem Integrated LLC ....E....... 918 660-0492
Tulsa (G-9309)
Bob D Berry DBA ....G....... 405 382-3360
Seminole (G-8360)
Boomerang Printing LLC ....G....... 918 747-1844
Tulsa (G-9319)
Boxing Bear LLC....................................G....... 918 606-9991
Jenks (G-3694)
Boxing Bear LLC....................................G....... 918 606-9991
Claremore (G-1599)
Braudrick Printery..................................G....... 405 762-2054
Ponca City (G-7802)
Britton Printing.......................................G....... 405 840-3291
Oklahoma City (G-5630)
Brix Inc...G....... 918 584-6484
Tulsa (G-9338)
Brown Printing Co Inc ....G....... 918 652-9611
Henryetta (G-3500)
Burch Printing Co ....G....... 580 225-3270
Elk City (G-2788)
Business Cards Unlimited ....G....... 918 810-6265
Tulsa (G-9350)
Business Printing Inc 1 ....G....... 918 481-6078
Tulsa (G-9351)
C & J Printing Co ....G....... 580 355-3099
Lawton (G-3902)
C & R Print Shop Inc..............................G....... 580 255-5656
Duncan (G-2095)
C & R Print Shop Inc..............................G....... 405 224-7921
Chickasha (G-1445)
Cable Printing Co Inc.............................F....... 405 756-4045
Lindsay (G-4055)
Capital Business Forms Inc..................F....... 405 524-2010
Oklahoma City (G-5691)
Carnegie Herald ....G....... 580 654-1443
Carnegie (G-1274)
Carr Graphics Inc...................................G....... 918 835-0605
Tulsa (G-9379)
CB Printing and More LLC ....G....... 405 488-7107
Jenks (G-3698)
Century Printing Inc...............................G....... 405 942-7171
Oklahoma City (G-5729)
Cg Printing...G....... 405 818-4371
Oklahoma City (G-5735)
Charles E Morrison Co ....G....... 405 840-1604
Oklahoma City (G-5742)
Cherry Street Print Shop Inc.................G....... 918 584-0022
Tulsa (G-9417)
Choate Publishing Inc ....F....... 580 276-3255
Marietta (G-4204)
Chrome River Wholesale LLC..............G....... 918 610-0810
Tulsa (G-9421)
Cimarron Screen Printing ....G....... 405 755-8337
Edmond (G-2352)
CJ Graphics..G....... 405 636-0400
Oklahoma City (G-5771)
Clark Printing Inc ....G....... 405 528-5396
Oklahoma City (G-5776)
Classic Design & Print LLC...................G....... 580 216-0653
Vici (G-11240)
Classic Printing Inc................................F....... 405 524-6889
Oklahoma City (G-5778)
Cnhi Communications............................G....... 918 723-5445
Westville (G-11481)
Coleman Press ....G....... 918 437-0000
Tulsa (G-9467)
Collins Quality Printing ....G....... 918 744-0077
Tulsa (G-9468)
Color Express...G....... 214 384-0887
Mead (G-4365)
Commercial Printing Marketing............G....... 918 494-7072
Tulsa (G-9475)
Cooley Enterprises Inc...........................G....... 918 437-6900
Tulsa (G-9483)
Copy Box Inc...F....... 918 257-8000
Afton (G-115)
Copy Fast Printing Inc...........................F....... 405 947-7468
Oklahoma City (G-5834)
Cowan Printing & Litho Inc...................F....... 405 789-1961
Tuttle (G-11191)
CP Solutions Inc ....D....... 918 664-6642
Tulsa (G-9495)
Craft Printed Envelopes Inc ....G....... 918 249-8887
Tulsa (G-9498)
Cromwells Inc...G....... 580 234-6561
Enid (G-2935)
CSC Inc ....G....... 580 256-2409
Mooreland (G-4588)
CSC Inc ....G....... 580 994-6110
Mooreland (G-4587)
Cushing Screen Printing LLC ....G....... 646 267-3513
Cushing (G-1927)
Custom Monograms & Lettering...........G....... 405 495-8586
Bethany (G-574)
Dancey-Meador Publishing Co.............G....... 580 762-9359
Ponca City (G-7819)
Davis Printing Company Inc ....G....... 580 225-2902
Elk City (G-2800)
Dbmac 50 Inc...G....... 918 342-5590
Claremore (G-1613)
Dbr Publishing Co LLC..........................E....... 918 250-1984
Owasso (G-7560)
Dean Printing..G....... 580 782-3777
Mangum (G-4170)
Demco Printing Inc ....F....... 405 273-8888
Shawnee (G-8444)
Digi Print LLC ....G....... 405 947-0099
Oklahoma City (G-5945)

SIC SECTION 27 PRINTING, PUBLISHING, AND ALLIED INDUSTRIES

Digital Prints Plus Inc.....G..... 918 520-7630
Collinsville *(G-1810)*
Diversified Printing Inc.....F..... 918 665-2275
Tulsa *(G-9586)*
Dla Document Services.....E..... 405 734-2177
Tinker Afb *(G-8953)*
Document Centre Inc.....G..... 405 879-1101
Oklahoma City *(G-5955)*
Dps Printing Services of.....G..... 918 794-7755
Sperry *(G-8607)*
Dreamers Screen Print and More.....G..... 580 761-4376
Blackwell *(G-682)*
Drivin Printing By Aaron.....G..... 405 609-9608
Oklahoma City *(G-5983)*
Durant Printing.....G..... 580 924-2271
Durant *(G-2228)*
Edmond Printings.....G..... 405 341-4330
Edmond *(G-2404)*
Education Oklahoma Department.....F..... 405 743-5531
Stillwater *(G-8682)*
Ellis County Capital.....G..... 580 885-7788
Arnett *(G-387)*
Felkins Enterprises LLC.....G..... 918 272-3456
Owasso *(G-7568)*
Fenton Office Supply Co.....E..... 405 372-5555
Stillwater *(G-8688)*
Fifth Quarter Printing LLC.....G..... 918 471-9390
McAlester *(G-4298)*
First Impression Prtg Co Inc.....G..... 918 749-5446
Beggs *(G-553)*
First Impression Prtg Co Inc.....G..... 918 749-5446
Beggs *(G-554)*
Flash Flood Print Studios LLC.....G..... 918 794-3527
Tulsa *(G-9754)*
Franklin Graphics Inc.....F..... 918 687-6149
Muskogee *(G-4675)*
French Printing Inc.....G..... 405 381-4057
Tuttle *(G-11200)*
G & S Printing Inc.....G..... 405 789-6813
Oklahoma City *(G-6129)*
Gameday Screen Printing.....G..... 405 570-0176
Oklahoma City *(G-6135)*
Geary Star.....G..... 405 884-2424
Geary *(G-3216)*
Geiger Printing & Promotion.....G..... 918 810-2833
Tulsa *(G-9812)*
Genral Enquries.....G..... 918 749-1301
Broken Arrow *(G-918)*
Gh Printing Solutions Inc.....G..... 405 630-0609
Edmond *(G-2435)*
Giles Printing Co Inc.....G..... 918 584-1583
Tulsa *(G-9825)*
Glo Press.....G..... 405 275-1038
Shawnee *(G-8454)*
Globe Marketing Services Inc.....B..... 800 742-6787
Oklahoma City *(G-6162)*
Go Print USA.....G..... 405 708-7000
Yukon *(G-11726)*
Go Rowdy Girl Screen Print EMB.....G..... 580 668-2545
Wilson *(G-11534)*
Good Printing Co Inc.....G..... 405 235-9593
Oklahoma City *(G-6171)*
Graphics Etc.....G..... 918 274-4744
Owasso *(G-7571)*
Gravley Companies Inc.....G..... 405 842-1404
Oklahoma City *(G-6176)*
Gravley Companies Inc.....G..... 918 743-6619
Tulsa *(G-9850)*
Grizzly Grin Printing LLC.....G..... 918 351-9066
Tulsa *(G-9865)*
Hammer Hoby.....G..... 580 227-2100
Fairview *(G-3137)*
Handle It 3d Printing LLC.....G..... 405 788-9471
Shawnee *(G-8457)*
Hardesty Press Inc.....F..... 918 582-5306
Tulsa *(G-9891)*
Hawkeye Printing Co.....G..... 918 744-0158
Tulsa *(G-9902)*
Hawkeye Signs & Printing.....G..... 918 864-2035
Tahlequah *(G-8866)*
Heavener Ledger.....G..... 918 653-2425
Heavener *(G-3429)*
Hendryx Printing Brokerage LLC.....G..... 405 532-1255
Edmond *(G-2455)*
Hennessey Clipper.....G..... 405 853-4888
Hennessey *(G-3466)*
Herald Publishing Co.....G..... 580 875-3326
Walters *(G-11302)*
Hg Screen Printing.....G..... 580 623-3638
Watonga *(G-11347)*
Hilton Herald Corp Oklahama.....G..... 580 229-0132
Healdton *(G-3414)*
Hinkle Printing & Office Sup.....G..... 405 238-9308
Pauls Valley *(G-7660)*
Hipsleys Litho & Prtg Co LLC.....G..... 405 528-2686
Oklahoma City *(G-6252)*
Hoffman Printing LLC.....F..... 918 682-8341
Muskogee *(G-4691)*
Holbrook Printing.....G..... 918 835-5950
Tulsa *(G-9938)*
Holloways Bluprt & Copy Sp Inc.....G..... 918 682-0280
Muskogee *(G-4692)*
Hooker Advance & Office Supply.....G..... 580 652-2476
Hooker *(G-3598)*
Hooper Printing Company Inc.....F..... 405 321-4288
Norman *(G-5026)*
Horsepower Printing Inc.....G..... 405 631-3800
Oklahoma City *(G-6264)*
House of Trophies.....G..... 405 452-3524
Wetumka *(G-11492)*
Hugo Publishing Company.....G..... 580 326-3311
Hugo *(G-3612)*
Image Print & Promo LLC.....G..... 405 408-6763
Edmond *(G-2459)*
Imperial Printing Inc.....G..... 918 663-1302
Tulsa *(G-9973)*
Impressions Printing A.....E..... 405 722-2442
Oklahoma City *(G-6293)*
Infocus Print Co LLC.....G..... 918 465-5572
McAlester *(G-4306)*
Initially Yours Inc.....G..... 918 832-9889
Tulsa *(G-9986)*
Ink Images Inc.....G..... 918 828-0300
Tulsa *(G-9987)*
Ink Masters Screen Printing.....G..... 918 399-5220
Cushing *(G-1938)*
Ink Spot Tttoo Bdy Percing LLC.....G..... 918 637-2897
Broken Arrow *(G-1135)*
Inked Custom Printing.....G..... 918 872-6544
Broken Arrow *(G-937)*
Inkwell Printing.....G..... 918 508-3634
Tulsa *(G-9988)*
Inspired Gifts & Graphics LLC.....G..... 405 295-1669
El Reno *(G-2725)*
Its In Print.....G..... 918 493-4141
Tulsa *(G-10014)*
J Rose Printing LLC.....G..... 210 875-0947
Yukon *(G-11734)*
Jet Printing Co Inc.....G..... 405 732-1262
Oklahoma City *(G-6361)*
Jet Set Screen Printing I.....G..... 918 294-1053
Broken Arrow *(G-944)*
Joans Print Shop Inc.....G..... 918 624-5858
Tulsa *(G-10047)*
Joe Brent Lansden.....G..... 580 625-3241
Beaver *(G-541)*
Johnny L Ruth.....G..... 580 223-3061
Ardmore *(G-316)*
JPS LLC.....G..... 405 535-5136
Oklahoma City *(G-6389)*
Kdl Print Production Svcs LLC.....G..... 918 254-8150
Broken Arrow *(G-955)*
Kelley Printing.....G..... 405 238-4848
Pauls Valley *(G-7663)*
Kimberling City Publishing Co.....G..... 918 367-2282
Bristow *(G-786)*
Kindrick Co Prtg & Copying Svc.....G..... 580 332-1022
Ada *(G-56)*
King Design & Printing LLC.....G..... 580 661-3061
Thomas *(G-8946)*
King Graphics Inc.....G..... 405 232-2369
Oklahoma City *(G-6420)*
Kingdom Printing.....G..... 580 512-3789
Lawton *(G-3950)*
Kingfisher Office Supply Inc.....G..... 405 375-3404
Kingfisher *(G-3806)*
Kobe Express LLC.....G..... 580 920-0444
Durant *(G-2241)*
L W Duncan Printing Inc.....G..... 580 355-6229
Lawton *(G-3953)*
Lakey Printing Co.....G..... 918 744-0158
Tulsa *(G-10116)*
Larry D Hammer.....F..... 580 227-2100
Fairview *(G-3140)*
Larry D Hammer.....G..... 580 596-3344
Cherokee *(G-1418)*
Lawyer Graphic Screen Process.....G..... 918 438-2725
Tulsa *(G-10137)*
Lbz Prints.....G..... 405 905-1607
Oklahoma City *(G-6459)*
Leda Grimm.....G..... 918 225-0507
Cushing *(G-1942)*
Lettering Express.....G..... 405 260-9022
Oklahoma City *(G-6468)*
Lewis Printing & Office Supply.....F..... 405 379-5124
Holdenville *(G-3557)*
Lexso T Shirt Printing.....G..... 918 861-0772
Tulsa *(G-10155)*
Linderer Printing Co Inc.....F..... 580 323-2102
Clinton *(G-1757)*
Lindsey Printing.....G..... 580 476-2278
Rush Springs *(G-8123)*
Lithaprint Inc.....F..... 918 587-7746
Tulsa *(G-10168)*
Lively Printing.....G..... 918 582-3668
Tulsa *(G-10169)*
M2print LLC.....G..... 505 263-7999
Yukon *(G-11744)*
Makeba Design & Prints LLC.....G..... 405 719-0104
Yukon *(G-11745)*
Marshall County Publishing Co.....F..... 580 795-3355
Madill *(G-4155)*
Marshall Printing.....G..... 405 883-6122
Yukon *(G-11747)*
Mathis Printing Inc.....G..... 918 682-2999
Muskogee *(G-4708)*
Matrix Print & Promo LLC.....G..... 918 994-1943
Bartlesville *(G-509)*
Mattocks Printing Co LLC.....G..... 405 794-2307
Moore *(G-4538)*
MBC Graphics.....G..... 918 585-2321
Tulsa *(G-10227)*
McCullough Printing.....G..... 580 286-7681
Idabel *(G-3641)*
McNally and Associates Inc.....G..... 918 587-7068
Tulsa *(G-10234)*
Meeks Lithographing Company.....G..... 918 838-9900
Tulsa *(G-10239)*
Meeks Lithographing Company.....E..... 918 836-0900
Tulsa *(G-10240)*
Meeks Lithographing Company.....G..... 918 836-0900
Tulsa *(G-10241)*
Menz Printing Service LLC.....G..... 405 620-3673
Harrah *(G-3381)*
Merrick Printing.....G..... 918 876-6264
Bartlesville *(G-511)*
Mesa Black Publishing LLC.....G..... 580 544-2222
Boise City *(G-747)*
Mid-West Printing & Pubg Co.....F..... 918 224-3666
Sapulpa *(G-8291)*
Midtown Printing Inc.....G..... 918 295-0090
Tulsa *(G-10264)*
Midwest Copy and Printing.....G..... 405 737-8311
Oklahoma City *(G-6601)*
Midwest Decals LLC.....G..... 405 787-8747
Oklahoma City *(G-6602)*
Midwest Publishing Co.....G..... 405 282-1890
Guthrie *(G-3325)*
Miller Printing Company Inc.....F..... 918 749-0981
Tulsa *(G-10281)*
Minor Printing Company.....G..... 580 795-3745
Madill *(G-4158)*
Minuteman Press.....G..... 405 942-5595
Oklahoma City *(G-6617)*
Moe Mark of Excellence LLC.....G..... 405 650-9898
Oklahoma City *(G-6624)*
Moore Printing Co Inc.....E..... 417 866-6696
Moore *(G-4543)*
Mounds Printing.....G..... 918 827-6573
Mounds *(G-4621)*
Mudd Print & Promo LLC.....G..... 405 501-6107
Edmond *(G-2522)*
Multiprint Corp.....G..... 918 832-0300
Tulsa *(G-10315)*
MWH Enterprises Inc.....F..... 918 665-0944
Tulsa *(G-10320)*
Newkirk Herald Journal.....G..... 580 362-2140
Newkirk *(G-4850)*
Newspaper Holding Inc.....E..... 918 456-8833
Tahlequah *(G-8876)*
Newspaper Holding Inc.....D..... 580 233-6600
Enid *(G-3018)*
Newspaper Holding Inc.....E..... 580 332-4433
Ada *(G-72)*
Nextstep Custom Printing.....G..... 580 678-4331
Duncan *(G-2160)*
Nice Printing Co.....G..... 405 673-9437
Midwest City *(G-4449)*
North Star Publishing LLC.....D..... 405 415-2400
Oklahoma City *(G-6688)*

S
I
C

Northwest Printing Inc G 580 234-0953
Enid *(G-3022)*
OK Quality Printing Inc G 405 624-2925
Stillwater *(G-8731)*
Okay See Ltd Co G 405 562-3154
Edmond *(G-2547)*
Oklahoma City Blazers G 405 543-2922
Oklahoma City *(G-6739)*
Oklahoma Executive Printing G 405 948-8136
Oklahoma City *(G-6748)*
Oklahoma Offset Veba Inc G 918 582-0921
Tulsa *(G-10404)*
Ozmo Design and Print LLC G 417 655-5615
Tahlequah *(G-8878)*
Pace Printing Inc G 918 585-5664
Tulsa *(G-10454)*
Panhandle Printing G 580 338-1633
Guymon *(G-3360)*
Paper House Productions LLC G 918 835-0172
Tulsa *(G-10463)*
Paperwork Company F 918 369-1014
Bixby *(G-652)*
Paragon Press Inc G 405 681-5757
Oklahoma City *(G-6803)*
Paula Gallaher G 580 439-6484
Comanche *(G-1844)*
PDQ Printing LLC G 580 233-3241
Enid *(G-3032)*
Phillips Printing Co G 918 266-3373
Claremore *(G-1670)*
Pinecliffe Prtrs of Tecumseh G 405 273-1292
Shawnee *(G-8483)*
Pioneer Printing Inc G 918 542-5521
Miami *(G-4428)*
Ponca City Publishing Co Inc E 580 765-3311
Ponca City *(G-7866)*
Pony Express Printing LLC G 405 375-5064
Kingfisher *(G-3811)*
Pre-Press Graphics Inc G 918 582-2775
Tulsa *(G-10541)*
Precision Printing Corporation G 405 794-2500
Moore *(G-4554)*
Premier Printing G 405 632-1132
Oklahoma City *(G-6886)*
Prices Quality Printing Inc G 580 924-2271
Durant *(G-2248)*
Print Happy Fundraising G 918 355-4368
Broken Arrow *(G-1149)*
Print Happy LLC G 918 270-1300
Broken Arrow *(G-1010)*
Print Imaging Group LLC E 405 235-4888
Oklahoma City *(G-6898)*
Print Master General LLC G 580 442-2474
Elgin *(G-2778)*
Print Monkey LLC G 405 735-8999
Moore *(G-4556)*
Print Monkey LLC G 405 249-6926
Oklahoma City *(G-6899)*
Print N Copy Inc G 918 258-8200
Broken Arrow *(G-1011)*
Print Party G 405 206-2191
Edmond *(G-2576)*
Print People USA G 918 346-2560
Owasso *(G-7604)*
Print Plus OK LLC G 405 371-5365
Blanchard *(G-728)*
Print Shop G 918 342-3993
Claremore *(G-1674)*
Print This G 918 693-5581
Okmulgee *(G-7523)*
Printed Products Inc F 918 295-9950
Tulsa *(G-10561)*
Printers of Oklahoma LLC G 405 943-8855
Oklahoma City *(G-6900)*
Printing Center G 405 681-5303
Oklahoma City *(G-6901)*
Priority Printworks Inc G 918 825-6397
Pryor *(G-7984)*
▲ **Professional Image Inc** E 918 461-0609
Tulsa *(G-10569)*
Professional Prtg Norman LLC G 405 823-3383
Norman *(G-5125)*
Pronto Print Inc G 580 223-1612
Ardmore *(G-347)*
Protype Inc G 918 743-4408
Tulsa *(G-10576)*
Pryor Printing Inc G 918 825-2888
Pryor *(G-7986)*
Pure Digital Print G 918 899-2000
Tulsa *(G-10584)*
Qp Broadway EXT G 405 843-9820
Oklahoma City *(G-6931)*
Quad/Graphics Inc E 405 264-4341
Oklahoma City *(G-6932)*
Quad/Graphics Inc B 405 264-4000
Oklahoma City *(G-6933)*
Quantum Forms Corporation F 918 665-1320
Oklahoma City *(G-6940)*
Quik Print of Tulsa Inc G 918 250-5466
Tulsa *(G-10594)*
Quik Print of Tulsa Inc E 918 665-6246
Tulsa *(G-10595)*
Quik Print of Tulsa Inc G 918 582-1825
Tulsa *(G-10596)*
Quik Print of Tulsa Inc G 918 491-9292
Tulsa *(G-10597)*
Quik Print Oklahoma City Inc E 405 840-3275
Oklahoma City *(G-6945)*
Quik-Print of Oklahoma City G 405 842-1404
Oklahoma City *(G-6946)*
Quik-Print of Oklahoma City G 405 843-9820
Oklahoma City *(G-6947)*
Quik-Print of Oklahoma City G 405 232-7579
Oklahoma City *(G-6948)*
Quik-Print of Oklahoma City G 405 840-3275
Oklahoma City *(G-6950)*
Quik-Print of Oklahoma City G 405 528-7976
Oklahoma City *(G-6951)*
Quik-Print of Oklahoma City G 405 751-5315
Oklahoma City *(G-6952)*
Quik-Print of Oklahoma City G 405 943-3222
Oklahoma City *(G-6949)*
Quintella Printing Company Inc G 405 631-6566
Oklahoma City *(G-6955)*
R R Donnelley & Sons Company G 918 749-6496
Tulsa *(G-10606)*
Ra Graphix G 405 703-3599
Moore *(G-4559)*
RCP Print Solutions G 918 341-1950
Broken Arrow *(G-1024)*
RCP Printing G 918 341-1950
Broken Arrow *(G-1025)*
Red River Custom Camo & Hydro G 580 745-5262
Durant *(G-2251)*
Red River Printing Corp F 405 685-1794
Oklahoma City *(G-6988)*
Reid Printing Inc G 405 348-0066
Edmond *(G-2596)*
Review Printing Company Inc F 580 658-6657
Marlow *(G-4241)*
Richards Printing Co G 405 224-8640
Chickasha *(G-1501)*
Robyn Holdings LLC E 405 722-4600
Oklahoma City *(G-7041)*
Rocket Color Inc G 405 842-6001
Oklahoma City *(G-7043)*
Ross Printing LLC G 405 947-0099
Oklahoma City *(G-7050)*
Royal Printing Co Inc F 405 235-8581
Oklahoma City *(G-7054)*
Scissortail Graphics Inc G 580 255-2914
Duncan *(G-2174)*
Scotts Printing & Copying Inc F 405 236-0821
Oklahoma City *(G-7099)*
Self Printing Inc G 918 838-2113
Tulsa *(G-10726)*
Sew Graphics Plus Inc G 405 364-1707
Norman *(G-5141)*
Shadowkast Screen Printing LLC G 405 808-5148
Edmond *(G-2618)*
Sheryls Print Services G 918 724-2452
Tulsa *(G-10744)*
▲ **Sign Innovations LLC** G 405 840-1151
Oklahoma City *(G-7132)*
Signature Graphics Corp G 918 294-3485
Bixby *(G-658)*
Silsby Media LLC G 405 733-9727
Midwest City *(G-4454)*
Silverstone LLC G 918 371-3622
Sand Springs *(G-8225)*
Silverstone LLC G 918 373-2437
Broken Arrow *(G-1051)*
Sleeve It Handles G 405 250-2419
Shawnee *(G-8500)*
Snider Printing & Office Sup G 405 257-3402
Wewoka *(G-11511)*
Snyder Printing Inc F 405 682-8880
Oklahoma City *(G-5317)*
Soltow Business Supply G 918 786-4465
Grove *(G-3289)*
Sooner Industries Inc G 918 540-2422
Miami *(G-4431)*
Sooner Press G 405 382-8351
Seminole *(G-8400)*
Sooner Print Imaging G 405 272-0600
Oklahoma City *(G-7162)*
Sorrels Ventures LLC G 903 556-2941
Broken Bow *(G-1207)*
Southwest Business Pdts LLC G 580 765-4401
Ponca City *(G-7878)*
Southwest Cnstr News Svc G 405 948-7474
Oklahoma City *(G-7173)*
Southwestern Sty & Bnk Sup Inc D 405 525-9411
Oklahoma City *(G-7177)*
Spitzer Printing G 580 928-5540
Sayre *(G-8346)*
Sprekelmeyer Printing Company G 580 223-5100
Ardmore *(G-359)*
Ssi Technologies Inc G 918 451-6160
Broken Arrow *(G-1059)*
Standard Printing Co Inc G 405 840-0001
Oklahoma City *(G-7192)*
Steves Bindery Service Inc G 405 946-2183
Oklahoma City *(G-7204)*
Stich This and More G 405 207-9922
Pauls Valley *(G-7672)*
Stigler Digital G 918 967-8383
Stigler *(G-8648)*
Storehouse Printing G 918 286-7222
Tulsa *(G-10857)*
Sugarwood Digital Printing G 918 378-5771
Jenks *(G-3731)*
Sunshine Printing G 918 951-6349
Tulsa *(G-10874)*
Super Signs & Printing LLC G 405 842-7070
Oklahoma City *(G-7227)*
T-Shirts & Hoodies Print Shop G 918 861-0772
Tulsa *(G-10895)*
T-Shirts & Hoodies Print Shop G 918 861-0772
Tulsa *(G-10896)*
Taxes Print Shop G 405 521-3165
Oklahoma City *(G-7255)*
Texoma Printing Inc G 580 924-1120
Durant *(G-2267)*
Think Screenprinting LLC G 405 590-5131
Edmond *(G-2640)*
Thompson Manufacturing Company G 918 585-1991
Tulsa *(G-10935)*
Tom Bennett Manufacturing F 405 528-5671
Oklahoma City *(G-7302)*
▲ **Tommy Higle Publishers** G 580 276-5136
Marietta *(G-4215)*
Tonkawa News G 580 628-2532
Tonkawa *(G-8984)*
Torbett Printing Co & Off Sup G 918 756-5789
Okmulgee *(G-7528)*
Transcript Press Inc E 405 360-7999
Norman *(G-5181)*
Trinity Scrnprntng/Dmond Awrds G 580 364-3752
Atoka *(G-426)*
Triple T Printing G 405 912-1212
Moore *(G-4579)*
Tulsa Instant Printing G 918 627-0730
Tulsa *(G-11000)*
Tulsa Litho Co Consolidat G 918 582-8185
Tulsa *(G-11001)*
Tulsa Screen Printing G 918 488-1331
Broken Arrow *(G-1085)*
Tuun Leh Zua Printing Services G 918 809-7925
Tulsa *(G-11020)*
Two Lees Inc G 918 663-2390
Tulsa *(G-11027)*
U Big TS Designs Inc G 405 401-4327
Oklahoma City *(G-7356)*
Unique Printing Inc G 405 842-3966
Oklahoma City *(G-7361)*
Unity Press Inc E 405 232-8910
Tulsa *(G-11045)*
Usher Corporation G 405 495-2125
Oklahoma City *(G-7382)*
V O Inc G 405 659-0654
Edmond *(G-2664)*
Vans Printing Service G 918 786-9496
Grove *(G-3291)*
Vinita Printing Co Inc E 918 256-6422
Vinita *(G-11271)*
Vision Print PPG G 405 519-4047
Oklahoma City *(G-7402)*
VITs Screen Printing G 405 531-6012
Edmond *(G-2675)*

27 PRINTING, PUBLISHING, AND ALLIED INDUSTRIES

Vox Printing Incorporated .... D 800 654-8437
  Oklahoma City (G-7406)
Wallace Printing Company .... G 580 326-6323
  Hugo (G-3622)
Wallis Printing Inc .... G 580 223-7473
  Ardmore (G-379)
Ward Brothers Printing .... G 918 465-5551
  Wilburton (G-11528)
Warren Products Inc .... F 405 947-5676
  Oklahoma City (G-7421)
Warrens Screen Prtg EMB L L C .... G 405 422-3900
  El Reno (G-2768)
Watonga Printing & Office Sups .... G 580 623-4989
  Watonga (G-11353)
Weatherford News Inc .... E 580 772-3301
  Weatherford (G-11458)
Weatherford Press Inc .... F 580 772-5300
  Weatherford (G-11459)
Western Prnting Company Inc .... E 918 665-2874
  Tulsa (G-11109)
Westwood Printing Center .... G 405 366-8961
  Norman (G-5199)
What Print Now .... G 580 649-7996
  Altus (G-172)
Wild Leaf Screen Prtg & Design .... G 918 440-4945
  Ramona (G-8047)
Wilson-Monroe Publishing Co .... G 580 933-4579
  Valliant (G-11234)
Woodcrest Litho Inc .... F 918 357-1676
  Broken Arrow (G-1178)
Woods County Enterprise .... G 580 824-2171
  Waynoka (G-11384)

2754 Commercial Printing: Gravure

American-Chief Co .... G 918 762-2552
  Pawnee (G-7699)
Deans Typesetting Service .... G 405 842-7247
  Oklahoma City (G-5912)
Franklin Digital Inc .... F 918 687-6149
  Muskogee (G-4674)
Hitch N Post LLC .... G 918 396-9480
  Skiatook (G-8549)
Mojo Sports LLC .... F 405 390-8935
  Midwest City (G-4447)
October Graphics .... G 580 765-5089
  Ponca City (G-7861)
Thomas Digital LLC .... G 918 836-1540
  Tulsa (G-10929)
Wallace Printing Company .... G 580 326-6323
  Hugo (G-3622)

2759 Commercial Printing

262 LLC .... F 918 458-5511
  Tahlequah (G-8848)
3 Cs Tees LLC .... G 405 208-1320
  Ada (G-2)
A & B Engraving Inc .... G 918 663-7446
  Tulsa (G-9061)
A B Printing .... G 918 834-2054
  Tulsa (G-9066)
A Plus Printing .... G 580 765-7752
  Ponca City (G-7791)
A1 Screen Printing .... G 405 701-6735
  Norman (G-4895)
AAA Kopy .... G 405 741-5679
  Oklahoma City (G-5354)
Abco Printing & Office Supply .... G 580 286-7575
  Idabel (G-3636)
Adams Printing .... G 580 832-2123
  Cordell (G-1853)
Advance Graphics & Printing .... G 405 258-0796
  Chandler (G-1373)
Advanced Graphic Design .... G 918 960-0407
  Tulsa (G-9108)
Affinitee Graphics .... G 580 861-2253
  Lawton (G-3885)
Ajt Enterprises Inc .... F 918 665-7083
  Tulsa (G-9133)
All-Star Trophies & Ribbon Mfg .... G 918 283-2200
  Claremore (G-1581)
American Angler Publications .... G 918 364-4210
  Catoosa (G-1297)
American Signworx .... G 479 650-4562
  Pocola (G-7780)
American Tradition .... G 918 688-7725
  Tulsa (G-9174)
American Traditions Clothing .... G 918 622-8337
  Tulsa (G-9175)
American TS .... G 918 284-7685
  Mounds (G-4609)

Anns Quick Print Co Inc .... G 405 222-1871
  Chickasha (G-1429)
Apache News .... G 580 588-3862
  Apache (G-217)
ARC Document Solutions LLC .... E 918 663-8100
  Tulsa (G-9202)
Ardelias Flowers Inc .... F 405 321-6850
  Norman (G-4915)
Artistic Apparel .... G 918 338-0038
  Bartlesville (G-449)
Associated Lithographing Co .... E 918 663-9091
  Tulsa (G-9217)
AT&I Resources LLC .... F 918 925-0154
  Tulsa (G-9220)
B J Printing Inc .... F 405 372-7600
  Stillwater (G-8657)
Bad Boy Signs Graphic .... D 405 224-2059
  Chickasha (G-1436)
Bakers Printing Co Inc .... G 405 842-6944
  Oklahoma City (G-5517)
Bargain Journal .... G 918 426-5500
  McAlester (G-4273)
Beacon Sign Company Inc .... G 405 567-4886
  Prague (G-7921)
Bees Knees Tees .... G 405 370-2132
  Choctaw (G-1530)
Bentwrench Studios .... G 918 406-8070
  Sapulpa (G-8254)
Big House Specialty Prtg Inc .... G 918 271-1414
  Tulsa (G-9292)
Bill Rathbone .... G 918 486-3028
  Coweta (G-1872)
Black Cat Screen Printing LLC .... G 405 895-6635
  Moore (G-4498)
Black Gold .... G 918 253-3344
  Jay (G-3679)
Blankenship Brothers Inc .... G 918 943-3278
  Oklahoma City (G-5587)
Blue Ribbon Forms Inc .... G 918 834-8838
  Tulsa (G-9305)
Board of Trustees of The Teach .... E 405 521-2387
  Oklahoma City (G-5597)
Bob D Berry DBA .... G 405 382-3360
  Seminole (G-8360)
Boley One .... G 405 301-7692
  Oklahoma City (G-5616)
Breast & Bdy Thermography Ctr .... G 405 596-8099
  Nichols Hills (G-4855)
Britton Printing .... G 405 840-3291
  Oklahoma City (G-5630)
Brix Inc .... G 918 584-6484
  Tulsa (G-9338)
▲ Broken Arrow Productions Inc .... E 405 360-8702
  Norman (G-4944)
Brown Printing Co Inc .... G 918 652-9611
  Henryetta (G-3500)
Burch Printing Co .... G 580 225-3270
  Elk City (G-2788)
Business Cards & More .... G 405 235-9621
  Oklahoma City (G-5648)
Busy Bee .... G 580 661-2946
  Thomas (G-8940)
Buyers Trading Designs .... G 918 592-5477
  Tulsa (G-9355)
C & H Safety Pin Inc .... G 405 949-5843
  Newalla (G-4806)
C & J Printing Co .... G 580 355-3099
  Lawton (G-3902)
C & R Print Shop Inc .... G 580 255-5656
  Duncan (G-2095)
C & R Print Shop Inc .... G 405 224-7921
  Chickasha (G-1445)
C and H Publishing Co .... G 918 245-9571
  Sand Springs (G-8169)
Cable Printing Co Inc .... F 405 756-4045
  Lindsay (G-4055)
Campus Ragz .... G 405 329-3300
  Norman (G-4952)
Cane Advertising LLC .... G 918 806-6817
  Broken Arrow (G-863)
Capital Business Forms Inc .... F 405 524-2010
  Oklahoma City (G-5691)
Capitol Hill Graffix LLC .... G 405 616-3050
  Oklahoma City (G-5694)
Causley Productions Inc .... F 405 372-0940
  Stillwater (G-8666)
Charles E Morrison Co .... G 405 840-1604
  Oklahoma City (G-5742)
Cheaper TS Inc .... G 918 615-6262
  Broken Arrow (G-867)

Christian Connections of Okla .... G 405 372-2111
  Stillwater (G-8667)
Chrome River Wholesale LLC .... G 918 610-0810
  Tulsa (G-9421)
Cimarron Screen Printing .... G 405 755-8337
  Edmond (G-2352)
Civitas Media LLC .... F 580 482-1221
  Altus (G-149)
Cjs Custom Apparel .... G 405 340-9677
  Edmond (G-2355)
Clark Printing Inc .... G 405 528-5396
  Oklahoma City (G-5776)
Collins Quality Printing .... G 918 744-0077
  Tulsa (G-9468)
▲ Communication Graphics Inc .... D 918 258-6502
  Broken Arrow (G-871)
Cooley Creek Printing .... G 918 835-8200
  Tulsa (G-9482)
Copper Cup Images .... G 918 337-2781
  Bartlesville (G-469)
Copy Write Incorporated .... G 918 224-1148
  Sapulpa (G-8262)
Corporate Image Inc .... G 918 516-8376
  Owasso (G-7556)
Corporate To Causal Screen .... G 918 686-6688
  Muskogee (G-4662)
Corporate To Csual Screen Prtg .... G 918 686-6688
  Muskogee (G-4663)
CP Solutions Inc .... D 918 664-6642
  Tulsa (G-9495)
Cplp LLC .... G 580 355-5515
  Lawton (G-3913)
Cr Stripes Ltd Co .... G 405 946-8577
  Oklahoma City (G-5850)
Crafty Manatees LLC .... G 405 630-5415
  Blanchard (G-708)
Cromwells Inc .... G 580 234-6561
  Enid (G-2935)
CSC Inc .... G 580 994-6110
  Mooreland (G-4587)
Custom Graphics .... G 580 477-4597
  Altus (G-152)
D & B Printing Inc .... G 405 632-0055
  Oklahoma City (G-5884)
Daniel P Wollaston .... G 580 768-4694
  Ardmore (G-272)
Davis Printing Company Inc .... G 580 225-2902
  Elk City (G-2800)
Daybreak Screen Printing LLC .... G 405 919-6386
  Oklahoma City (G-5908)
Dbmac 50 Inc .... G 918 342-5590
  Claremore (G-1613)
Dbr Publishing Co LLC .... E 918 250-1984
  Owasso (G-7560)
Decal Shop .... G 918 783-5206
  Big Cabin (G-602)
Delson Properties Ltd .... D 405 262-5005
  El Reno (G-2711)
Demco Printing Inc .... F 405 273-8888
  Shawnee (G-8444)
Design It .... G 405 756-3635
  Lindsay (G-4060)
Dhs Tees .... G 405 397-0274
  Edmond (G-2391)
Diversified Printing Inc .... F 918 665-2275
  Tulsa (G-9586)
Dos Tees LLC .... G 405 323-2382
  Edmond (G-2392)
Dps Printing Services Inc .... G 405 285-4614
  Edmond (G-2394)
Dudz and Things Inc .... G 918 321-9443
  Sapulpa (G-8269)
E C Beights .... G 918 674-2773
  Miami (G-4400)
Eagle Imaging Management .... G 405 286-4114
  Oklahoma City (G-5995)
Edmond Printings .... G 405 341-4330
  Edmond (G-2404)
Elite Creative Solutions LLC .... E 918 994-5435
  Broken Arrow (G-897)
Ellis County Capital .... G 580 885-7788
  Arnett (G-387)
Engatech Inc .... F 918 599-7500
  Tulsa (G-9686)
Engraving Designs LLC .... G 580 763-4228
  Ponca City (G-7826)
Executive Forms & Supplies .... G 817 423-9088
  Oklahoma City (G-6060)
Felkins Enterprises LLC .... G 918 272-3456
  Owasso (G-7568)

Employee Codes: A=Over 500 employees, B=251-500
C=101-250, D=51-100, E=20-50, F=10-19, G=1-9

Fine Arts Engraving Co Inc....................G....... 918 835-6400
Tulsa *(G-9743)*
Firefly Custom Laser Engrv LLC...........G....... 405 664-4145
Norman *(G-5000)*
First Impression Prtg Co Inc.................G....... 918 749-5446
Beggs *(G-553)*
Fortis Solutions Group..........................G....... 918 258-8321
Catoosa *(G-1320)*
Frog Printing & Awards Ctr LLC...........G....... 580 678-1114
Lawton *(G-3931)*
Game Time Designs LLC.........................G....... 405 702-1318
Oklahoma City *(G-6134)*
Gameday Screen Prtg Promotions........G....... 405 637-8577
Bethany *(G-578)*
Girlinghouse Unlimited LLC.................G....... 405 265-3330
Mustang *(G-4773)*
Good Printing Co Inc..............................G....... 405 235-9593
Oklahoma City *(G-6171)*
Goprints..G....... 918 798-0643
Okmulgee *(G-7506)*
Gorfam Marketing Inc.............................F....... 918 388-9935
Tulsa *(G-9842)*
Graf-X LLC..G....... 405 542-6631
Hinton *(G-3529)*
Gravley Companies Inc..........................G....... 918 743-6619
Tulsa *(G-9850)*
Great Plins Grphics Shwnee LLC..........G....... 405 273-4263
Shawnee *(G-8455)*
H&A Shirt Cafe Cstm Screen Prt...........G....... 918 357-1115
Broken Arrow *(G-1129)*
Hammer Hoby..G....... 580 227-2100
Fairview *(G-3137)*
Hardesty Press Inc..................................F....... 918 582-5306
Tulsa *(G-9891)*
Heartbeat Designs LLC..........................G....... 918 333-0833
Bartlesville *(G-490)*
Heavener Ledger.....................................G....... 918 653-2425
Heavener *(G-3429)*
Hermann Jermey.....................................G....... 918 200-2604
Catoosa *(G-1321)*
High Five Graphics..................................G....... 918 636-3312
Mannford *(G-4182)*
Hipsleys Litho & Prtg Co LLC................G....... 405 528-2686
Oklahoma City *(G-6252)*
Hoffman Printing LLC............................F....... 918 682-8341
Muskogee *(G-4691)*
Hooper Printing Company Inc...............F....... 405 321-4288
Norman *(G-5026)*
Hot Rod Shirts & Stuff...........................G....... 580 669-2531
Glencoe *(G-3224)*
Hunters Laser Cartridges.......................G....... 918 740-8164
Tulsa *(G-9958)*
ID Solutions LLC.....................................F....... 405 677-8833
Oklahoma City *(G-6287)*
Imaging Concepts...................................G....... 918 534-1761
Dewey *(G-2026)*
In His Name Screenprinting LLC...........G....... 405 756-8911
Maysville *(G-4260)*
Infinity Screenprinting LLC...................G....... 405 485-3203
Blanchard *(G-716)*
Initially Yours Inc..................................G....... 918 832-9889
Tulsa *(G-9986)*
Ink Images Inc...G....... 918 828-0300
Tulsa *(G-9987)*
Inklahoma Screen Prtg & EMB..............G....... 405 206-0500
Mustang *(G-4779)*
Inkspot..G....... 405 793-7200
Moore *(G-4529)*
Inspired Gifts & Graphics LLC..............G....... 405 295-1669
El Reno *(G-2725)*
Integrity Screen Works Inc....................E....... 918 663-8339
Tulsa *(G-9999)*
Inviting Place...G....... 918 488-0525
Tulsa *(G-10010)*
J W Companies...G....... 405 789-2460
Bethany *(G-584)*
Jak D Up Tees Inc....................................F....... 405 260-0007
Edmond *(G-2467)*
Jbs Graphic Repair..................................G....... 918 272-3522
Owasso *(G-7579)*
Jeff Mc Kenzie & Co Inc...........................G....... 405 236-5848
Oklahoma City *(G-6354)*
Jet Printing Co Inc...................................G....... 405 732-1262
Oklahoma City *(G-6361)*
Jones Jerseys and Tees LLC...................G....... 405 264-6151
Prague *(G-7928)*
Joshua Promotions...................................G....... 405 590-8894
Harrah *(G-3379)*
Kelley Printing..G....... 405 238-4848
Pauls Valley *(G-7663)*
Kens Advertising......................................G....... 405 527-6030
Lexington *(G-4036)*
Keystone Labels LLC..............................G....... 405 631-2341
Oklahoma City *(G-6413)*
Kindrick Co Prtg & Copying Svc...........G....... 580 332-1022
Ada *(G-56)*
King Kopy LLC..G....... 405 321-0202
Norman *(G-5052)*
King Screens...G....... 918 845-0004
Broken Arrow *(G-957)*
Kinkos Inc..G....... 303 449-9247
Broken Arrow *(G-959)*
Klassen Enterprises Inc..........................G....... 918 342-1850
Claremore *(G-1649)*
Kolb Type Service Incorporated............G....... 405 341-0984
Agra *(G-125)*
Kommunitees LLC....................................G....... 405 203-2491
Yukon *(G-11741)*
Lane Victory Screen Printing.................G....... 580 924-3556
Durant *(G-2243)*
Larry D Hammer.......................................G....... 580 596-3344
Cherokee *(G-1418)*
Larry D Hammer.......................................F....... 580 227-2100
Fairview *(G-3140)*
Lateesha D Hunter PC.............................G....... 405 534-2200
Oklahoma City *(G-6456)*
Latimer County News Tribune...............G....... 918 465-2321
Wilburton *(G-11522)*
Lawyer Graphic Screen Process............G....... 918 438-2725
Tulsa *(G-10137)*
Leda Grimm...G....... 918 225-0507
Cushing *(G-1942)*
Lighthouse Graphics................................G....... 405 635-0022
Oklahoma City *(G-6476)*
Linder Screen Printing.............................G....... 405 558-1275
Moore *(G-4533)*
Lindsey Printing..G....... 580 476-2278
Rush Springs *(G-8123)*
Liv3design LLC...G....... 432 296-1968
Norman *(G-5060)*
Lodestone Letterpress LLC.....................G....... 405 269-9111
Edmond *(G-2492)*
Loporchio Silk Screen.............................G....... 323 258-6459
Ada *(G-61)*
Magic TS..G....... 580 332-6675
Ada *(G-62)*
Magnum Screen Print Inc.......................G....... 918 665-7636
Tulsa *(G-10202)*
▲ **Marjo Advertising LLC**........................G....... 918 500-3108
Sapulpa *(G-8286)*
Mark W McGuffee Inc...............................G....... 405 603-8113
Oklahoma City *(G-6528)*
Marpro Label Inc......................................G....... 405 672-3344
Oklahoma City *(G-6530)*
Martin Thomas Enterprises Inc..............D....... 918 739-4015
Catoosa *(G-1338)*
Mattocks Printing Co LLC........................G....... 405 794-2307
Moore *(G-4538)*
MBC Graphics...G....... 918 585-2321
Tulsa *(G-10227)*
Mc Clain County Publishing Co..............E....... 405 527-2126
Purcell *(G-8016)*
Merrick Printing.......................................G....... 918 876-6264
Bartlesville *(G-511)*
Mesa Black Publishing LLC....................G....... 580 544-2222
Boise City *(G-747)*
Miami Designs..G....... 918 542-9553
Miami *(G-4414)*
Mid-West Printing & Pubg Co.................F....... 918 224-3666
Sapulpa *(G-8291)*
Midwest Publishing Co.............................G....... 405 282-1890
Guthrie *(G-3325)*
Miller Graphics..G....... 580 824-2698
Waynoka *(G-11380)*
Minor Printing Company..........................G....... 580 795-3745
Madill *(G-4158)*
Misaco Sign & Screen Printing...............G....... 918 542-4188
Miami *(G-4419)*
Mom Hustle Tee Co...................................G....... 417 658-6450
Broken Arrow *(G-980)*
Monod Bloc Inc..G....... 918 622-8132
Tulsa *(G-10299)*
Mountaintop Tees LLC.............................G....... 918 508-6208
Sand Springs *(G-8209)*
Multiprint Corp..G....... 918 832-0300
Tulsa *(G-10315)*
Mustard Seed Screen Printing................G....... 918 687-6290
Muskogee *(G-4718)*
My Man Tees LLC......................................G....... 580 695-9474
Fletcher *(G-3164)*
Nameplates Inc..G....... 918 561-8732
Tulsa *(G-10325)*
▲ **Nameplates Inc**......................................D....... 918 584-2651
Tulsa *(G-10324)*
Nancy Nelson & Associates.....................G....... 580 765-0115
Ponca City *(G-7857)*
Nelson Incorporated..................................G....... 918 812-5876
Tulsa *(G-10332)*
Neo Sign Company....................................G....... 918 456-1959
Fort Gibson *(G-3177)*
Offices Etc...G....... 918 342-1501
Claremore *(G-1666)*
Ohgoodygoodycom.....................................G....... 315 727-5960
Tulsa *(G-10380)*
Okie Ink Screenprinting LLC....................G....... 918 681-0736
Muskogee *(G-4723)*
Oklahoma Envelope Company LLC.........F....... 405 946-2169
Oklahoma City *(G-6746)*
Oklahoma Flding Crton Prtg Inc..............F....... 405 352-9920
Minco *(G-4478)*
Oklahoma Promo LLC...............................G....... 918 248-8145
Jenks *(G-3719)*
Oliver & Olivia Apparel.............................E....... 405 300-8906
Edmond *(G-2556)*
Onedoc Managed Print Svcs LLC............G....... 405 633-3050
Oklahoma City *(G-6778)*
Opportunity Center Inc.............................C....... 580 765-6782
Ponca City *(G-7863)*
Options Inc..F....... 918 473-2614
Checotah *(G-1398)*
Osborne Design Co....................................G....... 918 585-3212
Tulsa *(G-10444)*
Over 60 LLC..G....... 405 224-0711
Chickasha *(G-1497)*
P M Graphics...G....... 405 525-8789
Oklahoma City *(G-5310)*
Panda Screen Printing Entps...................G....... 918 622-3601
Tulsa *(G-10458)*
Paul Clinton Hughes...................................G....... 918 273-1888
Nowata *(G-5225)*
Peabodys Printing & A Brush Sp.............G....... 580 248-8317
Lawton *(G-3980)*
Performance Screen Printing...................G....... 405 247-9891
Anadarko *(G-205)*
Personali Tees LLC.....................................G....... 580 759-2188
Stratford *(G-8806)*
Pioneer Printing Inc...................................G....... 918 542-5521
Miami *(G-4428)*
Pitezels Ink & Print Inc..............................G....... 918 663-2393
Tulsa *(G-10520)*
Play 2 Win Athletics...................................G....... 918 341-9500
Claremore *(G-1671)*
Pony Express Printing LLC.......................G....... 405 375-5064
Kingfisher *(G-3811)*
Premier Printing..G....... 405 632-1132
Oklahoma City *(G-6886)*
Pressley Press N Prod Fcilty....................G....... 405 752-5700
Oklahoma City *(G-5311)*
Price Prints Inc..F....... 580 832-2492
Cordell *(G-1862)*
Print Imaging Group LLC...........................E....... 405 235-4888
Oklahoma City *(G-6898)*
Print Shop...G....... 918 342-3993
Claremore *(G-1674)*
Printer Store LLC...G....... 405 782-0755
Warr Acres *(G-11326)*
Printing and Design....................................G....... 580 871-2396
Dacoma *(G-1976)*
Printing Solutions Inc.................................G....... 580 421-6446
Ada *(G-76)*
Priority Printworks Inc...............................G....... 918 825-6397
Pryor *(G-7984)*
Productive Clutter Inc.................................G....... 405 447-3839
Norman *(G-5124)*
Promos Advertising Pdts Inc.....................G....... 918 343-9675
Claremore *(G-1676)*
Promotions - Forms Unlimited..................G....... 918 627-8800
Tulsa *(G-10573)*
Pryor Printing Inc..G....... 918 825-2888
Pryor *(G-7986)*
Ps Tees LLC...G....... 405 694-7979
Oklahoma City *(G-6919)*
Pueblo Motors Inc.......................................G....... 520 297-3244
Edmond *(G-2577)*
Put On Your Armor Inc................................G....... 918 259-5000
Broken Arrow *(G-1015)*
Pyramid Printing..G....... 918 514-4073
Sand Springs *(G-8216)*
Quik Print of Tulsa Inc.................................E....... 918 665-6246
Tulsa *(G-10595)*

Quik Print of Tulsa Inc .... G 918 582-1825
Tulsa *(G-10596)*
Quik-Print of Oklahoma City .... G 405 943-3222
Oklahoma City *(G-6949)*
Quik-Print of Oklahoma City .... G 405 528-7976
Oklahoma City *(G-6951)*
Quik-Print of Oklahoma City .... G 405 842-1404
Oklahoma City *(G-6946)*
Quik-Print of Oklahoma City .... G 405 840-3275
Oklahoma City *(G-6950)*
Ragtops Athletics Inc .... G 918 274-3575
Owasso *(G-7606)*
Reflection Foil and Ltr Press .... G 405 341-8660
Edmond *(G-2593)*
Reflective Edge Screenprinting .... G 405 917-7837
Oklahoma City *(G-7001)*
Regency Labels Inc .... E 405 682-3460
Oklahoma City *(G-7002)*
Resourceone Communications Inc .... G 918 295-0112
Tulsa *(G-10646)*
Rhinestone Cowgirl .... F 405 387-3111
Newcastle *(G-4838)*
Rhinestone Cowgirl .... G 405 564-0512
Stillwater *(G-8747)*
Rhodes Printing .... G 918 445-7444
Coweta *(G-1896)*
Rhodes Printing .... G 918 965-1005
Claremore *(G-1682)*
Rhodes Printing Inc .... G 918 457-7801
Tahlequah *(G-8880)*
Robyn Holdings LLC .... E 405 722-4600
Oklahoma City *(G-7041)*
Royal Printing Co Inc .... F 405 235-8581
Oklahoma City *(G-7054)*
Royal Sign & Graphic Inc .... G 918 682-6151
Muskogee *(G-4746)*
S & S Promotions Inc .... E 405 631-6516
Oklahoma City *(G-7064)*
S & S Time Corporation .... E 918 437-3572
Tulsa *(G-10683)*
Saan World LLC .... G 405 494-1282
Oklahoma City *(G-7070)*
Safetyco LLC .... G 405 603-3306
Oklahoma City *(G-7072)*
Sand Tech Screening and EMB .... G 918 458-0312
Tahlequah *(G-8882)*
Sashay Corporate Services LLC .... E 918 664-2507
Tulsa *(G-10710)*
Scissortail Tees .... G 405 706-6371
Oklahoma City *(G-7094)*
Semasys Inc .... E 405 525-2335
Oklahoma City *(G-7107)*
Shirt Nutz LLC .... G 918 900-2362
Owasso *(G-7617)*
Sign Depot .... F 580 931-9363
Durant *(G-2257)*
Silsby Media LLC .... G 405 733-9727
Midwest City *(G-4454)*
Simply Vintage Tees LLC .... G 405 239-0444
Norman *(G-5146)*
Skyy Screen Printing .... G 405 412-4646
Norman *(G-5147)*
Small Potato Tees LLC .... G 405 264-6330
Chickasha *(G-1512)*
Something Printed .... G 918 967-9188
Stigler *(G-8646)*
Sooner Industries Inc .... G 918 540-2422
Miami *(G-4431)*
Sooner Press .... G 405 382-8351
Seminole *(G-8400)*
South Central Golf Inc .... G 918 280-0787
Tulsa *(G-10796)*
Southwstern Group of Companies .... D 405 525-9411
Oklahoma City *(G-7178)*
Specialty Advertising Co Inc .... G 405 495-3838
Oklahoma City *(G-7180)*
Spitzer Printing .... G 580 928-5540
Sayre *(G-8346)*
Sportees .... G 918 618-6201
Eufaula *(G-3115)*
Sprekelmeyer Printing Company .... G 580 223-5100
Ardmore *(G-359)*
Stantons Apparel Inc .... G 580 353-1777
Lawton *(G-4004)*
Stitch N Print .... F 405 789-8862
Oklahoma City *(G-7209)*
Stroud Corridor LLC .... G 405 823-7561
Stroud *(G-8821)*
Stuart Beverly & .... G 580 286-5586
Idabel *(G-3648)*
Summit Labels Inc .... G 918 936-4950
Tulsa *(G-10868)*
Sweetandsassytinytees LLC .... G 405 470-1170
Yukon *(G-11790)*
T John Co Inc .... G 405 761-3460
Tuttle *(G-11214)*
T S & H EMB & Screen Prtg .... G 405 214-7701
Shawnee *(G-8508)*
T S & H Shirt Co Inc .... G 405 382-3731
Seminole *(G-8403)*
T-Birds Custom Screenprinting .... G 918 521-3996
Tulsa *(G-10894)*
Tack Designs .... G 918 825-1211
Pryor *(G-7993)*
Tee For Soul .... G 405 237-3186
Moore *(G-4576)*
Teeds Up Printing .... G 918 279-1018
Coweta *(G-1899)*
Tees For Soul .... G 405 844-7685
Edmond *(G-2637)*
Tees Q Usbs Llc .... G 405 414-3264
Oklahoma City *(G-7265)*
Tesprinting LLC .... G 405 708-7000
Yukon *(G-11791)*
Texoma Engraving LLC .... G 580 775-7333
Durant *(G-2264)*
TGI Enterprises Inc .... E 918 835-4330
Tulsa *(G-10924)*
Think Ability Inc .... C 580 252-8000
Duncan *(G-2187)*
Tier Lvel Thrads Stuff Screen .... G 918 808-7290
Broken Arrow *(G-1074)*
Tiger Town Tees .... G 918 409-4282
Broken Arrow *(G-1075)*
TO Digital Media LLC .... G 405 639-8219
Oklahoma City *(G-7299)*
Toner Express .... G 405 517-8817
Norman *(G-5175)*
Tony Newcomb Sportswear Inc .... G 405 232-0022
Oklahoma City *(G-7303)*
Torbett Printing Co & Off Sup .... G 918 756-5789
Okmulgee *(G-7528)*
Tornados Screen Printing .... G 405 964-5339
McLoud *(G-4363)*
Tourkick LLC .... G 918 409-2543
Owasso *(G-7626)*
Treehouse Embroidery .... G 580 667-4322
Tipton *(G-8960)*
Trendy Tees .... G 405 620-3673
McLoud *(G-4364)*
Triple Elite LLC .... G 405 610-5200
Oklahoma City *(G-7337)*
Tuna Spot Tees LLC .... G 918 931-9586
Stillwater *(G-8770)*
TWI Industries Inc .... E 918 663-6655
Tulsa *(G-11022)*
U Big TS Designs Inc .... G 405 401-4327
Oklahoma City *(G-7356)*
Unique Designs Studio More LLC .... G 580 237-0034
Enid *(G-3070)*
UPS Store 6206 .... G 580 248-7800
Fort Sill *(G-3182)*
Usher Corporation .... G 405 495-2125
Oklahoma City *(G-7382)*
Victortees LLC .... G 405 889-7763
Norman *(G-5196)*
Vinita Printing Co Inc .... E 918 256-6422
Vinita *(G-11271)*
Wallace Printing Company .... G 580 326-6323
Hugo *(G-3622)*
Wallis Printing Inc .... G 580 223-7473
Ardmore *(G-379)*
Watonga Printing & Office Sups .... G 580 623-4989
Watonga *(G-11353)*
Wecktees .... G 580 747-5363
Glencoe *(G-3227)*
Western Cartoons .... G 405 275-1054
Shawnee *(G-8519)*
Western Web Envelope Co Inc .... F 405 682-0207
Oklahoma City *(G-7442)*
Witty Ideas Inc .... G 918 367-9528
Bristow *(G-806)*
◆ Worldwide Printing & Dist Inc .... C 918 295-0112
Tulsa *(G-11154)*
Wright Way Screen Printing .... G 918 787-7898
Grove *(G-3294)*
Xposure Inc .... G 918 581-8900
Tulsa *(G-11165)*
Xzube Tees .... G 405 249-9506
Norman *(G-5203)*
Zon Inc .... F 918 458-5511
Tahlequah *(G-8894)*

2761 Manifold Business Forms

262 LLC .... F 918 458-5511
Tahlequah *(G-8848)*
▲ Adams Investment Company .... D 918 335-1234
Dewey *(G-2012)*
Blue Ribbon Forms Inc .... G 918 834-8838
Tulsa *(G-9305)*
Media Technology Incorporated .... E 405 682-4400
Oklahoma City *(G-6556)*
Mid-West Printing & Pubg Co .... F 918 224-3666
Sapulpa *(G-8291)*
Printed Products Inc .... F 918 295-9950
Tulsa *(G-10561)*
Promotions - Forms Unlimited .... G 918 627-8800
Tulsa *(G-10573)*
R R Donnelley & Sons Company .... B 405 743-2124
Stillwater *(G-8742)*

2771 Greeting Card Publishing

Saga Card Co Inc .... G 918 967-0333
Stigler *(G-8645)*

2782 Blankbooks & Looseleaf Binders

Scrapworx .... G 918 259-9547
Broken Arrow *(G-1045)*
Tumbleweed Creek Cottage .... G 580 242-2767
Enid *(G-3068)*

2789 Bookbinding

A 1 Master Print Inc .... G 405 787-0505
Bethany *(G-571)*
A B Printing .... G 918 834-2054
Tulsa *(G-9066)*
A Plus Printing .... G 580 765-7752
Ponca City *(G-7791)*
A Plus Printing Inc .... G 918 836-8659
Tulsa *(G-9068)*
A Q Printing .... G 918 438-1161
Tulsa *(G-9070)*
A-OK Printing Mill .... G 918 775-6809
Sallisaw *(G-8136)*
AAA Kopy .... G 405 741-5679
Oklahoma City *(G-5354)*
Abco Printing & Office Supply .... G 580 286-7575
Idabel *(G-3636)*
Adams Printing .... G 580 832-2123
Cordell *(G-1853)*
Advance Graphics & Printing .... G 405 258-0796
Chandler *(G-1373)*
Ajt Enterprises Inc .... F 918 665-7083
Tulsa *(G-9133)*
Altus Printing Co Inc .... G 580 482-2020
Altus *(G-141)*
Anns Quick Print Co Inc .... G 405 222-1871
Chickasha *(G-1429)*
Artur Bookbinding Intl .... G 918 478-4888
Fort Gibson *(G-3173)*
B & L Printing Inc .... G 918 258-6655
Broken Arrow *(G-839)*
Bartlesville Print Shop .... G 918 336-6070
Bartlesville *(G-452)*
Bell Printing and Advertising .... G 405 769-6445
Nicoma Park *(G-4866)*
Bill Rathbone .... G 918 486-3028
Coweta *(G-1872)*
Britton Printing .... G 405 840-3291
Oklahoma City *(G-5630)*
Brown Printing Co Inc .... G 918 652-9611
Henryetta *(G-3500)*
Burch Printing Co .... G 580 225-3270
Elk City *(G-2788)*
C & J Printing Co .... G 580 355-3099
Lawton *(G-3902)*
C & R Print Shop Inc .... G 405 224-7921
Chickasha *(G-1445)*
Carr Graphics Inc .... G 918 835-0605
Tulsa *(G-9379)*
Cherry Street Print Shop Inc .... G 918 584-0022
Tulsa *(G-9417)*
Choate Publishing Inc .... F 580 276-3255
Marietta *(G-4204)*
Clark Printing Inc .... G 405 528-5396
Oklahoma City *(G-5776)*
Collins Quality Printing .... G 918 744-0077
Tulsa *(G-9468)*

SIC

Cooley Enterprises Inc ... G ... 918 437-6900
Tulsa *(G-9483)*

Copy Fast Printing Inc ... F ... 405 947-7468
Oklahoma City *(G-5834)*

Cowan Printing & Litho Inc ... F ... 405 789-1961
Tuttle *(G-11191)*

Cowboy Copy Center ... F ... 405 372-8099
Stillwater *(G-8671)*

CP Solutions Inc ... D ... 918 664-6642
Tulsa *(G-9495)*

Cromwells Inc ... G ... 580 234-6561
Enid *(G-2935)*

CSC Inc ... G ... 580 994-6110
Mooreland *(G-4587)*

Current Alternative News Advg ... G ... 918 431-0392
Tahlequah *(G-8861)*

Davis Printing Company Inc ... G ... 580 225-2902
Elk City *(G-2800)*

Dbmac 50 Inc ... G ... 918 342-5590
Claremore *(G-1613)*

Demco Printing Inc ... F ... 405 273-8888
Shawnee *(G-8444)*

Digi Print LLC ... G ... 405 947-0099
Oklahoma City *(G-5945)*

Diversified Printing Inc ... F ... 918 665-2275
Tulsa *(G-9586)*

Edmond Printings ... G ... 405 341-4330
Edmond *(G-2404)*

Education Oklahoma Department ... F ... 405 743-5531
Stillwater *(G-8682)*

Ellis County Capital ... G ... 580 885-7788
Arnett *(G-387)*

Fedex Office & Print Svcs Inc ... F ... 918 492-6701
Tulsa *(G-9732)*

Fedex Office & Print Svcs Inc ... E ... 918 252-3757
Tulsa *(G-9733)*

Felkins Enterprises LLC ... G ... 918 272-3456
Owasso *(G-7568)*

First Impression Prtg Co Inc ... G ... 918 749-5446
Beggs *(G-553)*

Franklin Graphics Inc ... F ... 918 687-6149
Muskogee *(G-4675)*

French Printing Inc ... G ... 405 381-4057
Tuttle *(G-11200)*

G & S Printing Inc ... G ... 405 789-6813
Oklahoma City *(G-6129)*

Giles Printing Co Inc ... G ... 918 584-1583
Tulsa *(G-9825)*

Gravley Companies Inc ... G ... 918 743-6619
Tulsa *(G-9850)*

Gregath Publishing Company ... G ... 918 542-4148
Miami *(G-4407)*

Hammer Hoby ... G ... 580 227-2100
Fairview *(G-3137)*

Hardesty Press Inc ... F ... 918 582-5306
Tulsa *(G-9891)*

Heavener Ledger ... G ... 918 653-2425
Heavener *(G-3429)*

Hinkle Printing & Office Sup ... G ... 405 238-9308
Pauls Valley *(G-7660)*

Hipsleys Litho & Prtg Co LLC ... G ... 405 528-2686
Oklahoma City *(G-6252)*

Hoffman Printing LLC ... F ... 918 682-8341
Muskogee *(G-4691)*

Holbrook Printing ... G ... 918 835-5950
Tulsa *(G-9938)*

Hooper Printing Company Inc ... F ... 405 321-4288
Norman *(G-5026)*

Imperial Printing Inc ... G ... 918 663-1302
Tulsa *(G-9973)*

Ink Images Inc ... G ... 918 828-0300
Tulsa *(G-9987)*

Jet Printing Co Inc ... G ... 405 732-1262
Oklahoma City *(G-6361)*

Joans Print Shop Inc ... G ... 918 624-5858
Tulsa *(G-10047)*

Kelley Printing ... G ... 405 238-4848
Pauls Valley *(G-7663)*

Kindrick Co Prtg & Copying Svc ... G ... 580 332-1022
Ada *(G-56)*

King Kopy LLC ... G ... 405 321-0202
Norman *(G-5052)*

Kingfisher Office Supply Inc ... G ... 405 375-3404
Kingfisher *(G-3806)*

Krause Plastics ... G ... 918 835-4202
Tulsa *(G-10100)*

L W Duncan Printing Inc ... G ... 580 355-6229
Lawton *(G-3953)*

Larry D Hammer ... F ... 580 227-2100
Fairview *(G-3140)*

Leda Grimm ... G ... 918 225-0507
Cushing *(G-1942)*

Linderer Printing Co Inc ... F ... 580 323-2102
Clinton *(G-1757)*

Litgistix LLC ... E ... 918 585-5875
Tulsa *(G-10167)*

Lithaprint Inc ... F ... 918 587-7746
Tulsa *(G-10168)*

Mattocks Printing Co LLC ... G ... 405 794-2307
Moore *(G-4538)*

McCullough Printing ... G ... 580 286-7681
Idabel *(G-3641)*

McSpadden Bookbindery ... G ... 405 275-7788
Shawnee *(G-8472)*

Meeks Lithographing Company ... G ... 918 838-9900
Tulsa *(G-10239)*

Meeks Lithographing Company ... G ... 918 836-0900
Tulsa *(G-10241)*

Mesa Black Publishing LLC ... G ... 580 544-2222
Boise City *(G-747)*

Mid-West Printing & Pubg Co ... F ... 918 224-3666
Sapulpa *(G-8291)*

Midtown Printing Inc ... G ... 918 295-0090
Tulsa *(G-10264)*

Midwest Publishing Co ... G ... 405 282-1890
Guthrie *(G-3325)*

Minor Printing Company ... G ... 580 795-3745
Madill *(G-4158)*

Minuteman Press ... G ... 405 942-5595
Oklahoma City *(G-6617)*

Modern Bindery Inc ... E ... 918 250-9486
Tulsa *(G-10290)*

Multiprint Corp ... G ... 918 832-0300
Tulsa *(G-10315)*

Nancy Nelson & Associates ... G ... 580 765-0115
Ponca City *(G-7857)*

North Star Publishing LLC ... D ... 405 415-2400
Oklahoma City *(G-6688)*

Northwest Printing Inc ... G ... 580 234-0953
Enid *(G-3022)*

OK Quality Printing Inc ... G ... 405 624-2925
Stillwater *(G-8731)*

Oklahoma Bindery Inc ... G ... 405 235-4802
Oklahoma City *(G-6738)*

Pace Printing Inc ... G ... 918 585-5664
Tulsa *(G-10454)*

Peabodys Printing & A Brush Sp ... G ... 580 248-8317
Lawton *(G-3980)*

Pinecliffe Prtrs of Tecumseh ... G ... 405 273-1292
Shawnee *(G-8483)*

Pioneer Printing Inc ... G ... 918 542-5521
Miami *(G-4428)*

Pony Express Printing LLC ... G ... 405 375-5064
Kingfisher *(G-3811)*

Premier Printing ... G ... 405 632-1132
Oklahoma City *(G-6886)*

Prices Quality Printing Inc ... G ... 580 924-2271
Durant *(G-2248)*

Print N Copy Inc ... G ... 918 258-8200
Broken Arrow *(G-1011)*

Print Shop ... G ... 918 342-3993
Claremore *(G-1674)*

Printers Bindery Inc ... E ... 405 236-8423
Norman *(G-5122)*

Printers of Oklahoma LLC ... G ... 405 943-8855
Oklahoma City *(G-6900)*

Printing Center ... G ... 405 681-5303
Oklahoma City *(G-6901)*

Priority Printworks Inc ... G ... 918 825-6397
Pryor *(G-7984)*

Pronto Print Inc ... G ... 580 223-1612
Ardmore *(G-347)*

Pryor Printing Inc ... G ... 918 825-2888
Pryor *(G-7986)*

Quantum Forms Corporation ... F ... 918 665-1320
Oklahoma City *(G-6940)*

Quik Print of Tulsa Inc ... G ... 918 250-5466
Tulsa *(G-10594)*

Quik Print of Tulsa Inc ... E ... 918 665-6246
Tulsa *(G-10595)*

Quik Print of Tulsa Inc ... G ... 918 582-1825
Tulsa *(G-10596)*

Quik-Print of Oklahoma City ... G ... 405 843-9820
Oklahoma City *(G-6947)*

Quik-Print of Oklahoma City ... G ... 405 528-7976
Oklahoma City *(G-6951)*

Quik-Print of Oklahoma City ... G ... 405 842-1404
Oklahoma City *(G-6946)*

Quik-Print of Oklahoma City ... G ... 405 840-3275
Oklahoma City *(G-6950)*

Reid Printing Inc ... G ... 405 348-0066
Edmond *(G-2596)*

Review Printing Company Inc ... F ... 580 658-6657
Marlow *(G-4241)*

Self Printing Inc ... G ... 918 838-2113
Tulsa *(G-10726)*

Signature Graphics Corp ... G ... 918 294-3485
Bixby *(G-658)*

Silver Quill LLC ... G ... 405 735-9191
Moore *(G-4569)*

Snider Printing & Office Sup ... G ... 405 257-3402
Wewoka *(G-11511)*

Snyder Printing Inc ... F ... 405 682-8880
Oklahoma City *(G-5317)*

Sooner Bindery Inc ... G ... 405 232-4764
Del City *(G-2007)*

Sooner Industries Inc ... G ... 918 540-2422
Miami *(G-4431)*

Sooner Press ... G ... 405 382-8351
Seminole *(G-8400)*

Sprekelmeyer Printing Company ... G ... 580 223-5100
Ardmore *(G-359)*

Standard Printing Co Inc ... G ... 405 840-0001
Oklahoma City *(G-7192)*

Torbett Printing Co & Off Sup ... G ... 918 756-5789
Okmulgee *(G-7528)*

Transcript Press Inc ... E ... 405 360-7999
Norman *(G-5181)*

Tulsa Instant Printing ... G ... 918 627-0730
Tulsa *(G-11000)*

Unique Printing Inc ... G ... 405 842-3966
Oklahoma City *(G-7361)*

Usher Corporation ... G ... 405 495-2125
Oklahoma City *(G-7382)*

Wallace Printing Company ... G ... 580 326-6323
Hugo *(G-3622)*

Wallis Printing Inc ... G ... 580 223-7473
Ardmore *(G-379)*

Wilson-Monroe Publishing Co ... G ... 580 933-4579
Valliant *(G-11234)*

Work Activity Center Inc ... E ... 405 799-6911
Moore *(G-4584)*

2791 Typesetting

A & B Printing & Office Supply ... G ... 580 889-5103
Atoka *(G-395)*

A 1 Master Print Inc ... G ... 405 787-0505
Bethany *(G-571)*

A B Printing ... G ... 918 834-2054
Tulsa *(G-9066)*

A Plus Printing ... G ... 580 765-7752
Ponca City *(G-7791)*

A Q Printing ... G ... 918 438-1161
Tulsa *(G-9070)*

A-OK Printing Mill ... G ... 918 775-6809
Sallisaw *(G-8136)*

Abco Printing & Office Supply ... G ... 580 286-7575
Idabel *(G-3636)*

Ad Type Inc ... G ... 405 942-7951
Oklahoma City *(G-5371)*

Adams Printing ... G ... 580 832-2123
Cordell *(G-1853)*

Advance Graphics & Printing ... G ... 405 258-0796
Chandler *(G-1373)*

Ajt Enterprises Inc ... F ... 918 665-7083
Tulsa *(G-9133)*

Altus Printing Co Inc ... G ... 580 482-2020
Altus *(G-141)*

American-Chief Co ... G ... 918 885-2101
Hominy *(G-3575)*

Anns Quick Print Co Inc ... G ... 405 222-1871
Chickasha *(G-1429)*

Associated Lithographing Co ... E ... 918 663-9091
Tulsa *(G-9217)*

B & L Printing Inc ... G ... 918 258-6655
Broken Arrow *(G-839)*

Bakers Printing Co Inc ... G ... 405 842-6944
Oklahoma City *(G-5517)*

Bartlesville Print Shop ... G ... 918 336-6070
Bartlesville *(G-452)*

Bell Printing and Advertising ... G ... 405 769-6445
Nicoma Park *(G-4866)*

Bill Rathbone ... G ... 918 486-3028
Coweta *(G-1872)*

Blanchard News Publishing ... G ... 405 485-2311
Blanchard *(G-702)*

Britton Printing ... G ... 405 840-3291
Oklahoma City *(G-5630)*

Brix Inc ... G ... 918 584-6484
Tulsa *(G-9338)*

Brown Printing Co Inc .... G 918 652-9611
Henryetta *(G-3500)*
Burch Printing Co .... G 580 225-3270
Elk City *(G-2788)*
C & J Printing Co .... G 580 355-3099
Lawton *(G-3902)*
C & R Print Shop Inc .... G 405 224-7921
Chickasha *(G-1445)*
Cable Printing Co Inc .... F 405 756-4045
Lindsay *(G-4055)*
Carnegie Herald .... G 580 654-1443
Carnegie *(G-1274)*
Carr Graphics Inc .... G 918 835-0605
Tulsa *(G-9379)*
Cherry Street Print Shop Inc .... G 918 584-0022
Tulsa *(G-9417)*
CJ Graphics .... G 405 636-0400
Oklahoma City *(G-5771)*
Clark Printing Inc .... G 405 528-5396
Oklahoma City *(G-5776)*
Cnhi LLC .... G 918 652-3311
Henryetta *(G-3501)*
Cnhi LLC .... F 580 338-3355
Guymon *(G-3346)*
Collins Quality Printing .... G 918 744-0077
Tulsa *(G-9468)*
Cooley Enterprises Inc .... G 918 437-6900
Tulsa *(G-9483)*
Copy Fast Printing Inc .... F 405 947-7468
Oklahoma City *(G-5834)*
Countywide News Inc .... F 405 598-3793
Tecumseh *(G-8910)*
Cowan Printing & Litho Inc .... F 405 789-1961
Tuttle *(G-11191)*
Cowboy Copy Center .... F 405 372-8099
Stillwater *(G-8671)*
Creative Media .... G 918 245-3779
Sand Springs *(G-8173)*
Cromwells Inc .... G 580 234-6561
Enid *(G-2935)*
CSC Inc .... G 580 994-6110
Mooreland *(G-4587)*
Davis Printing Company Inc .... G 580 225-2902
Elk City *(G-2800)*
Dbmac 50 Inc .... G 918 342-5590
Claremore *(G-1613)*
Dean Printing .... G 580 782-3777
Mangum *(G-4170)*
Deans Typesetting Service .... G 405 842-7247
Oklahoma City *(G-5912)*
Demco Printing Inc .... F 405 273-8888
Shawnee *(G-8444)*
Digi Print LLC .... G 405 947-0099
Oklahoma City *(G-5945)*
Diversified Printing Inc .... F 918 665-2275
Tulsa *(G-9586)*
Edmond Printings .... G 405 341-4330
Edmond *(G-2404)*
Education Oklahoma Department .... F 405 743-5531
Stillwater *(G-8682)*
Ellis County Capital .... G 580 885-7788
Arnett *(G-387)*
Fedex Office & Print Svcs Inc .... E 918 252-3757
Tulsa *(G-9733)*
Felkins Enterprises LLC .... G 918 272-3456
Owasso *(G-7568)*
First Impression Prtg Co Inc .... G 918 749-5446
Beggs *(G-553)*
Franklin Graphics Inc .... F 918 687-6149
Muskogee *(G-4675)*
French Printing Inc .... G 405 381-4057
Tuttle *(G-11200)*
G & S Printing Inc .... G 405 789-6813
Oklahoma City *(G-6129)*
Geary Star .... G 405 884-2424
Geary *(G-3216)*
Giles Printing Co Inc .... G 918 584-1583
Tulsa *(G-9825)*
Good Printing Co Inc .... G 405 235-9593
Oklahoma City *(G-6171)*
Graphics Etc .... G 918 274-4744
Owasso *(G-7571)*
Gravley Companies Inc .... G 918 743-6619
Tulsa *(G-9850)*
Gregath Publishing Company .... G 918 542-4148
Miami *(G-4407)*
Hammer Hoby .... G 580 227-2100
Fairview *(G-3137)*
Hardesty Press Inc .... F 918 582-5306
Tulsa *(G-9891)*
Heavener Ledger .... G 918 653-2425
Heavener *(G-3429)*
Herald Publishing Co .... G 580 875-3326
Walters *(G-11302)*
Hinkle Printing & Office Sup .... G 405 238-9308
Pauls Valley *(G-7660)*
Hipsleys Litho & Prtg Co LLC .... G 405 528-2686
Oklahoma City *(G-6252)*
Hoffman Printing LLC .... F 918 682-8341
Muskogee *(G-4691)*
Holbrook Printing .... G 918 835-5950
Tulsa *(G-9938)*
Hooper Printing Company Inc .... F 405 321-4288
Norman *(G-5026)*
Imperial Printing Inc .... G 918 663-1302
Tulsa *(G-9973)*
Ink Images Inc .... G 918 828-0300
Tulsa *(G-9987)*
K D Typesetting .... G 405 302-0799
Edmond *(G-2477)*
Kelley Printing .... G 405 238-4848
Pauls Valley *(G-7663)*
Kindrick Co Prtg & Copying Svc .... G 580 332-1022
Ada *(G-56)*
King Graphics Inc .... G 405 232-2369
Oklahoma City *(G-6420)*
Kingfisher Office Supply Inc .... G 405 375-3404
Kingfisher *(G-3806)*
Kolb Type Service Incorporated .... G 405 341-0984
Agra *(G-125)*
L W Duncan Printing Inc .... G 580 355-6229
Lawton *(G-3953)*
Larry D Hammer .... F 580 227-2100
Fairview *(G-3140)*
Leda Grimm .... G 918 225-0507
Cushing *(G-1942)*
Lincoln County Publishing Co .... F 405 258-1818
Chandler *(G-1385)*
Linderer Printing Co Inc .... F 580 323-2102
Clinton *(G-1757)*
Lithaprint Inc .... F 918 587-7746
Tulsa *(G-10168)*
Liv3design LLC .... G 432 296-1968
Norman *(G-5060)*
Mattocks Printing Co LLC .... G 405 794-2307
Moore *(G-4538)*
Mc Clain County Publishing Co .... E 405 527-2126
Purcell *(G-8016)*
McCullough Printing .... G 580 286-7681
Idabel *(G-3641)*
Meeks Lithographing Company .... G 918 838-9900
Tulsa *(G-10239)*
Meeks Lithographing Company .... G 918 836-0900
Tulsa *(G-10241)*
Mesa Black Publishing LLC .... G 580 544-2222
Boise City *(G-747)*
Metro Graphic Systems .... G 918 744-0308
Tulsa *(G-10249)*
Mid-West Printing & Pubg Co .... F 918 224-3666
Sapulpa *(G-8291)*
Midtown Printing Inc .... G 918 295-0090
Tulsa *(G-10264)*
Midwest Publishing Co .... G 405 282-1890
Guthrie *(G-3325)*
Minor Printing Company .... G 580 795-3745
Madill *(G-4158)*
Minuteman Press .... G 405 942-5595
Oklahoma City *(G-6617)*
▲ **Mtm Recognition Corporation** .... B 405 609-6900
Oklahoma City *(G-6634)*
Multiprint Corp .... G 918 832-0300
Tulsa *(G-10315)*
Newcastle Pacer Inc .... G 405 387-5277
Newcastle *(G-4833)*
Northwest Printing Inc .... G 580 234-0953
Enid *(G-3022)*
OK Quality Printing Inc .... G 405 624-2925
Stillwater *(G-8731)*
Oklahoma Assn of Elc Coop .... E 405 478-1455
Oklahoma City *(G-6735)*
Oklahoma Executive Printing .... G 405 948-8136
Oklahoma City *(G-6748)*
Peabodys Printing & A Brush Sp .... G 580 248-8317
Lawton *(G-3980)*
Pinecliffe Prtrs of Tecumseh .... G 405 273-1292
Shawnee *(G-8483)*
Pony Express Printing LLC .... G 405 375-5064
Kingfisher *(G-3811)*
Pre-Press Graphics Inc .... G 918 582-2775
Tulsa *(G-10541)*
Premier Printing .... G 405 632-1132
Oklahoma City *(G-6886)*
Prices Quality Printing Inc .... G 580 924-2271
Durant *(G-2248)*
Print N Copy Inc .... G 918 258-8200
Broken Arrow *(G-1011)*
Print Shop .... G 918 342-3993
Claremore *(G-1674)*
Printed Products Inc .... F 918 295-9950
Tulsa *(G-10561)*
Printing Center .... G 405 681-5303
Oklahoma City *(G-6901)*
Priority Printworks Inc .... G 918 825-6397
Pryor *(G-7984)*
Pronto Print Inc .... G 580 223-1612
Ardmore *(G-347)*
Protype Inc .... G 918 743-4408
Tulsa *(G-10576)*
Pryor Printing Inc .... G 918 825-2888
Pryor *(G-7986)*
Quik Print of Tulsa Inc .... G 918 250-5466
Tulsa *(G-10594)*
Quik Print of Tulsa Inc .... E 918 665-6246
Tulsa *(G-10595)*
Quik-Print of Oklahoma City .... G 405 943-3222
Oklahoma City *(G-6949)*
Quik-Print of Oklahoma City .... G 405 842-1404
Oklahoma City *(G-6946)*
Review Printing Company Inc .... F 580 658-6657
Marlow *(G-4241)*
Russell Publishing Company .... G 405 665-4333
Wynnewood *(G-11672)*
Self Printing Inc .... G 918 838-2113
Tulsa *(G-10726)*
Shine On Designs .... G 918 224-7439
Sapulpa *(G-8311)*
Shopper News Note .... F 405 756-3169
Lindsay *(G-4084)*
Signature Graphics Corp .... G 918 294-3485
Bixby *(G-658)*
Snider Printing & Office Sup .... G 405 257-3402
Wewoka *(G-11511)*
Snyder Printing Inc .... F 405 682-8880
Oklahoma City *(G-5317)*
Sooner Industries Inc .... G 918 540-2422
Miami *(G-4431)*
Sooner Press .... G 405 382-8351
Seminole *(G-8400)*
Spiro Graphic .... G 918 962-2075
Spiro *(G-8618)*
Spitzer Printing .... G 580 928-5540
Sayre *(G-8346)*
Sprekelmeyer Printing Company .... G 580 223-5100
Ardmore *(G-359)*
Standard Printing Co Inc .... G 405 840-0001
Oklahoma City *(G-7192)*
Star Nowata .... G 918 273-2446
Nowata *(G-5230)*
Tom Bennett Manufacturing .... F 405 528-5671
Oklahoma City *(G-7302)*
▲ **Tommy Higle Publishers** .... G 580 276-5136
Marietta *(G-4215)*
Torbett Printing Co & Off Sup .... G 918 756-5789
Okmulgee *(G-7528)*
Transcript Press Inc .... E 405 360-7999
Norman *(G-5181)*
Tulsa Instant Printing .... G 918 627-0730
Tulsa *(G-11000)*
Type House Inc .... G 918 492-8513
Tulsa *(G-11028)*
Unique Printing Inc .... G 405 842-3966
Oklahoma City *(G-7361)*
Usher Corporation .... G 405 495-2125
Oklahoma City *(G-7382)*
Vans Printing Service .... G 918 786-9496
Grove *(G-3291)*
Vinita Printing Co Inc .... E 918 256-6422
Vinita *(G-11271)*
Vision Type & Design Inc .... G 918 252-3817
Tulsa *(G-11082)*
Wallace Printing Company .... G 580 326-6323
Hugo *(G-3622)*
Wallis Printing Inc .... G 580 223-7473
Ardmore *(G-379)*
Watonga Republican Inc .... G 580 623-4922
Watonga *(G-11354)*
Weatherford Press Inc .... F 580 772-5300
Weatherford *(G-11459)*
Westwood Printing Center .... G 405 366-8961
Norman *(G-5199)*

Employee Codes: A=Over 500 employees, B=251-500
C=101-250, D=51-100, E=20-50, F=10-19, G=1-9

2020 Oklahoma Directory
of Manufacturers & Processors

451

Wilson-Monroe Publishing Co..............G....... 580 933-4579
Valliant (G-11234)

2796 Platemaking & Related Svcs

A B Printing..............G....... 918 834-2054
Tulsa (G-9066)
A Q Printing..............G....... 918 438-1161
Tulsa (G-9070)
Advance Graphics & Printing..............G....... 405 258-0796
Chandler (G-1373)
Ajt Enterprises Inc..............F....... 918 665-7083
Tulsa (G-9133)
B G Specialties Inc..............G....... 918 582-1165
Tulsa (G-9243)
C & J Printing Co..............G....... 580 355-3099
Lawton (G-3902)
C & R Print Shop Inc..............G....... 405 224-7921
Chickasha (G-1445)
Carnegie Herald..............G....... 580 654-1443
Carnegie (G-1274)
Cnhi LLC..............F....... 580 338-3355
Guymon (G-3346)
Copy Fast Printing Inc..............F....... 405 947-7468
Oklahoma City (G-5834)
Countywide News Inc..............F....... 405 598-3793
Tecumseh (G-8910)
CSC Inc..............G....... 580 994-6110
Mooreland (G-4587)
Diversified Printing Inc..............F....... 918 665-2275
Tulsa (G-9586)
First Impression Prtg Co Inc..............G....... 918 749-5446
Beggs (G-553)
Franklin Graphics Inc..............F....... 918 687-6149
Muskogee (G-4675)
G & S Printing Inc..............G....... 405 789-6813
Oklahoma City (G-6129)
Graphics Universal Inc..............G....... 918 461-0609
Tulsa (G-9847)
Inspired Gifts & Graphics LLC..............G....... 405 295-1669
El Reno (G-2725)
Mattocks Printing Co LLC..............G....... 405 794-2307
Moore (G-4538)
MBC Graphics..............G....... 918 585-2321
Tulsa (G-10227)
Mesa Black Publishing LLC..............G....... 580 544-2222
Boise City (G-747)
Nancy Nelson & Associates..............G....... 580 765-0115
Ponca City (G-7857)
North Star Publishing LLC..............D....... 405 415-2400
Oklahoma City (G-6688)
Oklahoma Assn of Elc Coop..............E....... 405 478-1455
Oklahoma City (G-6735)
Oklahoma Executive Printing..............G....... 405 948-8136
Oklahoma City (G-6748)
Paperwork Company..............F....... 918 369-1014
Bixby (G-652)
Peabodys Printing & A Brush Sp..............G....... 580 248-8317
Lawton (G-3980)
Pinecliffe Prtrs of Tecumseh..............G....... 405 273-1292
Shawnee (G-8483)
Pre-Press Graphics Inc..............G....... 918 582-2775
Tulsa (G-10541)
Prices Quality Printing Inc..............G....... 580 924-2271
Durant (G-2248)
Print Shop..............G....... 918 342-3993
Claremore (G-1674)
Printed Products Inc..............F....... 918 295-9950
Tulsa (G-10561)
Protype Inc..............G....... 918 743-4408
Tulsa (G-10576)
Pryor Printing Inc..............G....... 918 825-2888
Pryor (G-7986)
Quik Print of Tulsa Inc..............G....... 918 582-1825
Tulsa (G-10596)
Quintella Printing Company Inc..............G....... 405 631-6566
Oklahoma City (G-6955)
Reflection Foil and Ltr Press..............G....... 405 341-8660
Edmond (G-2593)
Signs To Go LLC..............G....... 405 348-8646
Edmond (G-2621)
Torbett Printing Co & Off Sup..............G....... 918 756-5789
Okmulgee (G-7528)
Transcript Press Inc..............E....... 405 360-7999
Norman (G-5181)
Usher Corporation..............G....... 405 495-2125
Oklahoma City (G-7382)
Wallis Printing Inc..............G....... 580 223-7473
Ardmore (G-379)
Westwood Printing Center..............G....... 405 366-8961
Norman (G-5199)

28 CHEMICALS AND ALLIED PRODUCTS

2812 Alkalies & Chlorine

Brenntag Southwest Inc..............E....... 918 273-2265
Nowata (G-5209)

2813 Industrial Gases

Air Products and Chemicals Inc..............D....... 918 825-4592
Pryor (G-7940)
Air Products and Chemicals Inc..............F....... 580 994-2732
Mooreland (G-4585)
Air Products and Chemicals Inc..............E....... 918 266-8800
Catoosa (G-1295)
Airgas Usa LLC..............G....... 405 745-2732
Oklahoma City (G-5401)
Airgas Usa LLC..............F....... 580 767-1313
Ponca City (G-7795)
Airgas Usa LLC..............G....... 405 372-7720
Stillwater (G-8652)
Airgas Usa LLC..............G....... 405 235-0009
Oklahoma City (G-5402)
Boc Gases..............G....... 580 254-2259
Woodward (G-11563)
C & C Nitrogen LLC..............G....... 580 216-4871
Woodward (G-11566)
City Carbonic LLC..............G....... 405 239-2068
Oklahoma City (G-5770)
Claude Neon Federal..............G....... 918 585-9010
Tulsa (G-9443)
Exponent Energy LLC..............G....... 918 906-6045
Tulsa (G-9716)
Hydrogen On Demand..............G....... 405 618-6644
Oklahoma City (G-6279)
Lincoln Electric Holdings Inc..............G....... 405 681-0183
Oklahoma City (G-6478)
Matheson Tri-Gas Inc..............F....... 580 536-2965
Lawton (G-3969)
Messer LLC..............F....... 580 254-2259
Woodward (G-11606)
Messer LLC..............F....... 580 254-2929
Woodward (G-11607)
Messer North America Inc..............G....... 580 254-2929
Woodward (G-11608)
Neon Creative LLC..............G....... 405 837-0178
Edmond (G-2533)
Nextstream Heavy Oil LLC..............G....... 405 808-5435
Oklahoma City (G-6675)
Nitro Lift Technologies LLC..............D....... 580 371-3700
Mill Creek (G-4471)
Nitro Lift Technologies LLC..............G....... 405 618-3026
Norman (G-5093)
▲ O2 Concepts LLC..............E....... 877 867-4008
Oklahoma City (G-6706)
Oil Capital Land Exploration..............G....... 918 582-2603
Tulsa (G-10384)
Praxair Distribution Inc..............E....... 918 266-3210
Claremore (G-1673)
Sooner Neon..............G....... 918 269-5250
Catoosa (G-1354)
Terra Nitrogen..............G....... 580 256-8651
Woodward (G-11641)

2816 Inorganic Pigments

Aircraft Cylinders Amer Iinc..............E....... 918 582-1785
Tulsa (G-9124)
Performance Coatings Inc..............G....... 405 525-9790
Oklahoma City (G-6829)
◆ Tronox LLC..............A....... 405 775-5000
Oklahoma City (G-7340)
◆ Tronox US Holdings Inc..............E....... 405 775-5000
Oklahoma City (G-7342)
▼ Tronox Worldwide LLC..............F....... 405 775-5000
Oklahoma City (G-7343)

2819 Indl Inorganic Chemicals, NEC

Acid Specialists LLC..............G....... 432 617-2243
Oklahoma City (G-5366)
▲ Advance RES Chem & Mfg LLC..............G....... 918 266-6789
Catoosa (G-1293)
◆ Advance Research Chemicals Inc..............D....... 918 266-6789
Catoosa (G-1294)
Air Products and Chemicals Inc..............E....... 918 266-8800
Catoosa (G-1295)
Airgas Usa LLC..............G....... 405 235-0009
Oklahoma City (G-5402)
American Zinc Recycling Corp..............D....... 918 336-7100
Bartlesville (G-447)

Associated Material Proc LLC..............G....... 405 707-7301
Stillwater (G-8656)
B & B Hydroseeding LLC..............F....... 580 883-5997
Ringwood (G-8084)
Bilco Construction Inc..............G....... 405 386-5591
Newalla (G-4804)
Bpi Inc..............G....... 918 682-5044
Muskogee (G-4654)
Brainerd Chemical Midwest LLC..............G....... 918 622-1214
Tulsa (G-9330)
Brenntag Southwest Inc..............E....... 918 273-2265
Nowata (G-5209)
C & P Catalyst Inc..............G....... 918 747-8379
Tulsa (G-9357)
Cabot Norit Americas Inc..............D....... 918 825-8332
Pryor (G-7949)
Cardinal Fg Minerals LLC..............E....... 580 367-2123
Coleman (G-1793)
Ceradyne Inc..............D....... 918 673-2201
Quapaw (G-8029)
Chemplex Advanced Mtls LLC..............G....... 580 832-5288
Cordell (G-1856)
Chemtrade Refinery Svcs Inc..............F....... 918 587-7613
Tulsa (G-9411)
Custom Carbide Application LLC..............G....... 580 799-5575
Elk City (G-2799)
◆ Deepwater Chemicals Inc..............E....... 580 256-0500
Woodward (G-11577)
Dewey Chemical Inc..............G....... 405 848-8611
Oklahoma City (G-5937)
Edc AG Products Company LLC..............D....... 405 235-4546
Oklahoma City (G-6008)
El Dorado Chemical Company..............G....... 405 235-4546
Oklahoma City (G-6015)
Eurecat U S Incorporated..............G....... 918 423-5800
McAlester (G-4296)
Fake Bake LLC..............E....... 405 843-9660
Oklahoma City (G-6070)
Flotek Chemistry LLC..............G....... 713 849-9911
Marlow (G-4233)
▲ Galaxy Chemicals LLC..............F....... 918 379-0820
Claremore (G-1625)
Ingevity..............G....... 918 704-6423
Tulsa (G-9984)
Invia Pavement Tech LLC..............F....... 918 878-7890
Tulsa (G-10009)
Invisible Element LLC..............G....... 918 296-7562
Jenks (G-3709)
◆ Iochem Corporation..............E....... 405 848-8611
Oklahoma City (G-6325)
Iochem Corporation..............E....... 580 995-3198
Vici (G-11243)
Jupiter Sulphur LLC..............G....... 580 762-1130
Ponca City (G-7841)
Kesc Enterprises LLC..............G....... 918 297-2501
Hartshorne (G-3392)
◆ LSB Chemical LLC..............F....... 405 235-4546
Oklahoma City (G-6498)
▲ Magnesium Products Inc..............F....... 918 587-9930
Tulsa (G-9018)
Neo Rare Metals Oklahoma LLC..............F....... 918 673-2511
Quapaw (G-8033)
Peak Sulfur Inc..............C....... 918 587-7613
Tulsa (G-10480)
Peroxychem LLC..............F....... 918 626-8020
Pocola (G-7785)
Raw Elements LLC..............G....... 918 392-4957
Tulsa (G-10621)
Reagent Chemical & RES Inc..............G....... 580 233-1024
Enid (G-3044)
Reagent Chemical & RES Inc..............F....... 580 436-4100
Francis (G-3191)
Sequoyah Fuels Corporation..............G....... 918 489-5511
Gore (G-3251)
▲ Sooner Energy Services Inc..............G....... 405 579-3200
Marlow (G-4242)
▲ Sunbelt Industries Inc..............G....... 405 843-1275
Oklahoma City (G-7225)
Tessenderlo Kerley Inc..............E....... 405 665-2544
Wynnewood (G-11674)
Tessenderlo Kerley Inc..............F....... 580 762-1130
Ponca City (G-7882)
Tetra Technologies Inc..............G....... 405 606-8600
Oklahoma City (G-7275)
Thermaclime LLC..............E....... 405 235-4546
Oklahoma City (G-7279)
Tricat Inc..............E....... 918 423-5800
McAlester (G-4343)
Tronox Incorporated..............D....... 405 775-5000
Oklahoma City (G-7339)

SIC SECTION

28 CHEMICALS AND ALLIED PRODUCTS

◆ Tronox LLC .... A 405 775-5000
  Oklahoma City (G-7340)
Tronox Pigments LLC .... G 405 775-5000
  Oklahoma City (G-7341)
◆ Tronox US Holdings Inc .... E 405 775-5000
  Oklahoma City (G-7342)
▼ Tronox Worldwide LLC .... F 405 775-5000
  Oklahoma City (G-7343)
U S Silica Company .... D 580 384-5241
  Mill Creek (G-4472)
Ultimate Chemicals LLC .... G 405 703-2771
  Moore (G-4581)
Umicore Autocat USA Inc .... D 918 266-8923
  Catoosa (G-1361)
▲ Woodward Iodine Corporation .... E 580 254-3311
  Woodward (G-11657)

2821 Plastics, Mtrls & Nonvulcanizable Elastomers

AO Inc .... G 918 623-1711
  Okemah (G-5263)
Baker Petrolite LLC .... C 918 847-2522
  Barnsdall (G-435)
Barlow-Hunt Inc .... D 918 250-0828
  Tulsa (G-9265)
Bluehawk Energy Inc .... G 405 406-1580
  Edmond (G-2327)
Cass Holdings LLC .... E 405 755-8448
  Oklahoma City (G-5707)
Cass Holdings LLC .... G 405 359-5053
  Watonga (G-11343)
Chevron Phillips Chem Co LP .... D 918 825-0364
  Pryor (G-7953)
Chevron Phillips Chem Co LP .... C 918 977-6846
  Bartlesville (G-462)
Chevron Phillips Chem Co LP .... C 918 661-3317
  Bartlesville (G-463)
Elastech Technologies LLC .... G 405 470-1539
  Oklahoma City (G-6021)
Grace Fibrgls & Composites LLC .... G 405 233-3203
  Harrah (G-3378)
◆ Hilti North America Ltd .... G 918 252-6000
  Tulsa (G-9932)
Hobby Supermarket Inc .... E 405 239-6864
  Oklahoma City (G-6256)
Interplastic Corporation .... D 918 825-2755
  Pryor (G-7971)
Interplastic Corporation .... F 918 592-0205
  Tulsa (G-10006)
J-M Manufacturing Company Inc .... D 918 446-4471
  Tulsa (G-10025)
Line X of Stillwater .... G 405 743-0911
  Stillwater (G-8719)
Nordam Group LLC .... C 918 274-2742
  Tulsa (G-10356)
Prime Conduit Inc .... E 405 670-6132
  Oklahoma City (G-6892)
Rapid Application Group LLC .... G 918 760-1242
  Broken Arrow (G-1021)
T D Williamson Inc .... E 918 447-5400
  Tulsa (G-10888)
Tetrachem Seal Company Inc .... F 580 924-1717
  Durant (G-2263)

2822 Synthetic Rubber (Vulcanizable Elastomers)

Henley Sealants Inc .... G 405 235-7325
  Oklahoma City (G-6240)
Neoinsulation LLC .... G 405 605-6518
  Oklahoma City (G-6669)
Southwest Latex LLC .... G 405 420-0018
  Marlow (G-4243)

2823 Cellulosic Man-Made Fibers

▲ Western Hull Sacking Inc .... G 580 335-2144
  Frederick (G-3204)

2824 Synthetic Organic Fibers, Exc Cellulosic

Midland Vinyl Products Inc .... G 405 755-4972
  Oklahoma City (G-6597)
Progressive Windows Inc .... G 580 227-9915
  Fairview (G-3147)

2833 Medicinal Chemicals & Botanical Prdts

Environmate Inc .... G 817 707-5282
  Catoosa (G-1318)

Environmental Remediation .... G 405 235-9999
  Oklahoma City (G-6047)
▲ Haus Bioceuticals Inc .... G 405 295-5257
  Oklahoma City (G-6225)
Hillsboro Co .... G 918 481-0484
  Tulsa (G-9930)
Iochem Corporation .... E 580 995-3198
  Vici (G-11243)
Ocubrite LLC .... G 405 250-2084
  Edmond (G-2544)
Potions By Pier LLC .... G 580 658-2900
  Marlow (G-4237)
Rtpr LLC .... G 877 787-7180
  Edmond (G-2607)
Tulsa American Shaman .... G 918 938-0718
  Tulsa (G-10985)

2834 Pharmaceuticals

Abbott Laboratories .... A 405 329-5513
  Norman (G-4896)
AI Pharma Inc .... G 405 848-3299
  Oklahoma City (G-5406)
▲ Avara Pharmaceutical Tech Inc .... C 405 217-7670
  Norman (G-4921)
Barrick Pharmacies Inc .... G 405 273-9417
  Shawnee (G-8431)
Btg Inc .... G 405 604-9145
  Oklahoma City (G-5638)
Carter & Higgins Orthodontics .... G 918 986-9986
  Tulsa (G-9381)
Cytovance Biologics Inc .... G 405 319-8210
  Oklahoma City (G-5883)
David W and Abbe Belcher .... G 918 376-9816
  Owasso (G-7559)
▲ Dermamedics LLC .... G 405 319-8130
  Oklahoma City (G-5925)
Eden Pharmaceuticals .... G 405 455-7200
  Midwest City (G-4439)
Eli Lilly and Company .... G 918 250-6848
  Broken Arrow (G-896)
Eli Lilly and Company .... E 918 459-4540
  Tulsa (G-9655)
Golf Advisors .... G 918 645-6179
  Tulsa (G-9839)
Hospice Pharmacy Providers LLC .... G 918 633-6229
  Owasso (G-7574)
Kmh Enterprises Inc .... G 405 722-4600
  Oklahoma City (G-6430)
Loud City Pharmaceutical .... G 405 259-9014
  Oklahoma City (G-6497)
▲ Magnesium Products Inc .... F 918 587-9930
  Tulsa (G-9018)
Marie Anastasia Labs Inc .... G 405 840-0123
  Oklahoma City (G-6524)
Medcraft LLC .... G 918 938-0642
  Mounds (G-4620)
Midwest Med Istpes Nclear Phrm .... G 405 604-4438
  Oklahoma City (G-6605)
Natural Care Solution LLC .... G 405 919-1982
  Mustang (G-4786)
Naturalock Solutions LLC .... G 405 812-9058
  Norman (G-5089)
North Amrcn Brine Rsources LLC .... G 405 828-7123
  Enid (G-3021)
Novartis Corporation .... G 918 845-0906
  Tulsa (G-10363)
Okc Allergy Supplies Inc .... D 405 235-1451
  Oklahoma City (G-6726)
Onesource LLC .... G 580 434-6250
  Calera (G-1242)
Optionone LLC .... E 405 548-4848
  Oklahoma City (G-6779)
Phillips & Company .... G 714 663-6324
  Millerton (G-4473)
Prescription Care LLC .... G 405 310-9230
  Norman (G-5121)
Pure Transplant Solutions LLC .... G 512 697-8144
  Oklahoma City (G-6924)
Qualgen LLC .... E 405 551-8216
  Edmond (G-2578)
Qualgen LLC .... E 405 551-8216
  Edmond (G-2579)
Rta Systems Incorporated .... G 405 388-6802
  Choctaw (G-1554)
Sports & Stress Marketing .... G 580 327-3463
  Alva (G-193)
Takeda Phrmceuticals N Amer In .... G 405 317-7495
  Norman (G-5170)
Tcaacp LLC .... G 918 251-6655
  Broken Arrow (G-1072)

Tetherex Pharmaceuticals Corp .... G 405 206-7843
  Oklahoma City (G-7274)
Trimark Labs .... G 405 942-3289
  Oklahoma City (G-7333)
Ultra Botanica LLC .... G 405 694-4175
  Oklahoma City (G-7359)
Willoughby Pharmacy Svcs LLC .... G 580 214-1043
  Weatherford (G-11460)
Winds of Heartland .... G 405 947-8558
  Oklahoma City (G-7460)

2835 Diagnostic Substances

Bounce Diagnostics Inc .... G 405 740-5889
  Edmond (G-2331)
Eden Clinic Inc .... G 405 579-4673
  Norman (G-4988)
Immuno-Mycologics Inc .... F 405 360-4669
  Norman (G-5030)
Petnet Solutions Inc .... G 918 259-0899
  Broken Arrow (G-1004)
Sarvam Solutions Corporation .... G 918 346-9502
  Bartlesville (G-524)

2836 Biological Prdts, Exc Diagnostic Substances

Coare Biotechnology Inc .... G 405 227-0406
  Oklahoma City (G-5797)
Dr Cannabis LLC .... G 918 277-1105
  Sapulpa (G-8268)
Envirnmental Toxin Removal LLC .... G 405 757-4099
  Oklahoma City (G-6044)
Extract Surface Systems LLC .... G 918 938-6828
  Tulsa (G-9719)
Extract Touch-Up LLC .... G 918 639-4011
  Broken Arrow (G-903)
Heartland Vaccines LLC .... G 716 848-9251
  Stillwater (G-8699)
Jimmy Fuchs .... G 580 225-7784
  Elk City (G-2833)
Leonard Skodak Distributors .... G 405 787-8044
  Oklahoma City (G-6466)
M Shawn Anderson Rph PC .... G 580 595-9500
  Lawton (G-3967)
Octapharma Plasma .... G 405 686-9226
  Oklahoma City (G-6711)
Oklahomans For Vaccine .... G 918 606-9213
  Tulsa (G-10409)
Plasma Bionics LLC .... G 405 564-5333
  Stillwater (G-8738)
Plasma Solutions 1 .... G 918 543-2178
  Inola (G-3673)
Pure Protein LLC .... G 405 271-3838
  Oklahoma City (G-6923)
Solidtech Animal Health Inc .... F 405 387-3300
  Newcastle (G-4841)
Swaim Serum Company .... G 918 241-4363
  Sand Springs (G-8228)
Sweet Sap Extracts Inc .... G 405 205-8706
  Harrah (G-3386)
Vaxart Inc .... G 918 582-4346
  Tulsa (G-11067)
Zlb Behring .... G 405 521-9204
  Oklahoma City (G-7487)
Zlb Bio Services .... G 580 248-4851
  Lawton (G-4025)

2841 Soap & Detergents

B & P Industrial Inc .... F 918 665-3301
  Tulsa (G-9242)
Berkshire Corporation .... G 405 677-3391
  Oklahoma City (G-5556)
Brenntag Southwest Inc .... E 918 266-2951
  Catoosa (G-1306)
Cutting Edge Industries Corp .... G 918 523-7373
  Tulsa (G-9530)
▲ Dermamedics LLC .... G 405 319-8130
  Oklahoma City (G-5925)
E Environmental LLC .... G 405 604-0000
  Oklahoma City (G-5993)
Easy Car Wash Systems Inc .... G 918 582-4355
  Tulsa (G-9634)
Juniper Ridge Inc .... G 405 762-2555
  Stillwater (G-8708)
Kleen Products Inc .... F 405 495-1168
  Oklahoma City (G-6428)
Laughing Rabbit Soap .... G 405 737-7413
  Choctaw (G-1549)
Melanie Margaret Dennis .... G 405 760-1978
  Mustang (G-4782)

Employee Codes: A=Over 500 employees, B=251-500
C=101-250, D=51-100, E=20-50, F=10-19, G=1-9

2020 Oklahoma Directory
of Manufacturers & Processors

453

28 CHEMICALS AND ALLIED PRODUCTS

NBC Chemical Co Inc .... G 580 256-2627
　Woodward (G-11613)
Remwood Products Co .... G 918 251-8399
　Broken Arrow (G-1030)
Schmidt Farms At String Ridge .... G 580 919-2111
　Fletcher (G-3167)
Shabby Chicks Smart Clean LLC .... G 405 414-8938
　Duncan (G-2176)
SMC Technologies Inc .... F 405 737-3740
　Midwest City (G-4455)
Strop Shoppe LLc .... G 775 557-8767
　Norman (G-5162)

2842 Spec Cleaning, Polishing & Sanitation Preparations

▲ Anchor Paint Mfg Co .... D 918 836-4626
　Tulsa (G-9185)
Baker Petrolite LLC .... C 918 847-2522
　Barnsdall (G-435)
▲ Big D Industries Inc .... E 405 682-2541
　Oklahoma City (G-5563)
Bio-Cide International Inc .... G 405 364-1940
　Norman (G-4932)
Brenntag Southwest Inc .... E 918 266-2951
　Catoosa (G-1306)
Brenntag Southwest Inc .... E 918 273-2265
　Nowata (G-5209)
Carlisle Sanitary Maintenance .... G 405 475-5600
　Oklahoma City (G-5703)
▲ Chemical Products Inds Inc .... G 405 745-2070
　Oklahoma City (G-5748)
City of Tahlequah .... E 918 456-8332
　Tahlequah (G-8858)
Donald W Cox .... G 918 471-8967
　Porum (G-7895)
Empire Plumbing Contrs LLC .... G 918 320-1427
　Grove (G-3267)
Integrity Tech & Svcs LLC .... G 405 482-9206
　Edmond (G-2462)
John Scoggins Company Inc .... E 918 775-2748
　Sallisaw (G-8146)
Johnsonm3 LLC .... G 580 353-5550
　Lawton (G-3946)
Kar Glo Tuffy .... G 405 631-4091
　Oklahoma City (G-6397)
Km Metal Polishing .... G 918 397-2221
　Bartlesville (G-503)
Mother Earth Eco Entps LLC .... G 785 250-8706
　Ada (G-68)
Plane Naked LLC .... G 405 317-7661
　Yukon (G-11766)
Rp Window Washing .... G 405 341-0065
　Edmond (G-2606)
Shabby Chicks Smart Clean LLC .... G 405 414-8938
　Duncan (G-2176)
SMC Technologies Inc .... F 405 737-3740
　Midwest City (G-4455)
▲ Sooner Energy Services Inc .... G 405 579-3200
　Marlow (G-4242)
▲ Stink Free Inc .... G 405 273-0006
　Shawnee (G-8504)
Super Cuts .... G 918 245-3320
　Sand Springs (G-8227)
Super Saver Dry Cleaning .... G 918 296-7168
　Tulsa (G-10876)
Supply Company Inc .... G 918 585-2863
　Tulsa (G-10880)
Todd J Nightengale .... G 580 227-2646
　Fairview (G-3154)
Versum Materials Us LLC .... E 918 379-7101
　Catoosa (G-1363)
Vvc Dry Cleaning & Laundry .... G 580 255-2121
　Duncan (G-2196)

2843 Surface Active & Finishing Agents, Sulfonated Oils

▼ Wood Finishers Supply Inc .... C 405 422-1025
　El Reno (G-2772)

2844 Perfumes, Cosmetics & Toilet Preparations

A Plus Scrubs To You .... G 918 691-0556
　Tulsa (G-9069)
Allure Salon and Spa LLC .... G 580 371-9333
　Tishomingo (G-8961)
American Beauty Manufacturing .... G 918 671-0351
　Tulsa (G-9165)
Babe Nail Spa .... G 918 298-2200
　Tulsa (G-9250)
Bath & Body Works LLC .... E 405 748-3197
　Oklahoma City (G-5529)
Bath Bomb Dyes .... G 405 406-1823
　Yukon (G-11697)
Cleoptraz Scretz Hndmade Soaps .... G 918 272-3319
　Tulsa (G-9452)
Coalton Road Enterprises LLC .... G 918 652-0474
　Henryetta (G-3502)
Coolbodispa .... G 405 420-9785
　Norman (G-4965)
Cypress Scents .... G 918 629-8610
　Inola (G-3657)
Estee Lauder Companies Inc .... G 405 949-9757
　Oklahoma City (G-6053)
French Nail Spa LLC .... G 405 843-2080
　Oklahoma City (G-6117)
Hoffman Essentials .... G 918 485-4679
　Wagoner (G-11284)
K2 Bath Salts Online .... G 405 445-4295
　Oklahoma City (G-6394)
Lavishea LLC .... G 303 805-0805
　Broken Arrow (G-1138)
Legends Hair Studio .... G 580 237-5524
　Enid (G-2999)
Lipstick Chica .... G 405 432-6399
　Edmond (G-2488)
Mah Industries LLC .... G 918 540-0656
　Miami (G-4411)
Mere Minerals .... G 918 902-3156
　Broken Arrow (G-970)
Moore Scents LLC .... G 405 642-5472
　Yukon (G-11757)
Natures Light LLC .... G 925 209-1766
　Broken Arrow (G-986)
Op Nail .... G 405 222-1829
　Chickasha (G-1495)
Outback Laboratories .... G 405 527-6355
　Lexington (G-4038)
Pham Thuy .... G 918 623-0700
　Okemah (G-5273)
Pointer Waddell & Associates .... G 405 942-5600
　Oklahoma City (G-6862)
Raymac Corp .... G 918 752-0002
　Okmulgee (G-7524)
Salt Soothers LLC .... G 405 201-2020
　Edmond (G-2610)
Scents In Soy Naturals .... G 918 269-8322
　Jenks (G-3727)
Simply Scentsational .... G 918 691-8027
　Broken Arrow (G-1052)
Snuffy Scents LLC .... G 405 850-6889
　Mustang (G-4795)
Strop Shoppe LLc .... G 775 557-8767
　Norman (G-5162)
Sugar Sisters LLC .... G 405 722-9266
　Nichols Hills (G-4863)
Supercuts Inc .... G 918 775-6389
　Sallisaw (G-8154)
Sweet Organic Scrubs & More .... G 203 465-2683
　Oklahoma City (G-7235)
Sweet Scrubs LLC .... G 918 513-1176
　Tulsa (G-10884)
Tony Smallwood .... G 918 402-9267
　Tulsa (G-10952)
Useful Products Inc .... G 918 715-2639
　Edmond (G-2662)
◆ Valhoma Corporation .... E 918 836-7135
　Tulsa (G-11064)
Whitetail Bath Bombs .... G 405 474-8017
　El Reno (G-2771)
Zip ME Up Please LLC .... G 405 614-2778
　Stillwater (G-8778)

2851 Paints, Varnishes, Lacquers, Enamels

405 Coatings LLC .... G 405 822-5095
　Edmond (G-2284)
Advanced Aircraft Coatings .... G 405 495-7545
　Oklahoma City (G-5378)
Aerochem Inc .... G 405 440-0380
　Oklahoma City (G-5391)
American Industrial Inc .... G 918 445-0627
　Tulsa (G-9167)
▲ Anchor Paint Mfg Co .... D 918 836-4626
　Tulsa (G-9185)
Anchor Paint Mfg Co .... G 918 272-0880
　Owasso (G-7544)
Appli-Fab Custom Coating .... G 405 235-7039
　Chandler (G-1375)
Black & Puryear Paint Mfg Co .... G 405 348-0447
　Edmond (G-2324)
Capitol Paint Manufacturing .... G 405 634-3383
　Oklahoma City (G-5695)
Carboline Company .... E 918 622-3028
　Tulsa (G-9374)
Cass Holdings LLC .... E 405 755-8448
　Oklahoma City (G-5707)
Cass Holdings LLC .... G 405 359-5053
　Watonga (G-11343)
Cass Polymers Inc .... E 405 755-8448
　Oklahoma City (G-5708)
Cooper Consulting LLC .... G 918 427-7171
　Muldrow (G-4632)
▼ Crown Paint Company .... E 405 232-8580
　Oklahoma City (G-5863)
CTI Services LLC .... G 918 584-2220
　Tulsa (G-9519)
Dale P Jackson .... F 580 332-1988
　Ada (G-29)
Del Technical Coatings Inc .... E 405 672-1431
　Oklahoma City (G-5920)
Frog Printing & Awards Ctr LLC .... G 580 678-1114
　Lawton (G-3931)
▲ Gemini Coatings Inc .... C 405 262-5710
　El Reno (G-2718)
▲ Gemini Industries Inc .... D 405 262-5710
　El Reno (G-2719)
Gra Services International LP .... G 405 672-8885
　Oklahoma City (G-6174)
H-I-S Paint Mfg Co Inc .... G 405 232-2077
　Oklahoma City (G-6201)
Kelly-Moore Paint Company Inc .... G 405 350-2375
　Yukon (G-11739)
L M R General Contracting LLC .... G 405 605-6547
　Oklahoma City (G-6440)
Laster/Castor Corporation .... G 918 234-7777
　Tulsa (G-10133)
Mann Solvents Inc .... G 918 626-3733
　Arkoma (G-386)
National Coating Mfg Inc .... F 580 332-8751
　Ada (G-70)
Paint Handy LLC .... G 918 734-3422
　Bixby (G-651)
Paint Pros Inc .... G 405 226-8898
　Norman (G-5108)
Pixley Coating Inc .... G 580 444-2140
　Velma (G-11236)
Powder Blue .... F 918 835-2629
　Tulsa (G-10536)
Schmoldt Engineering Services .... F 918 336-1221
　Bartlesville (G-526)
Select Coatings Inc .... F 405 745-9011
　Oklahoma City (G-7106)
Spectrum Paint Company Inc .... G 405 525-6519
　Oklahoma City (G-7181)
Touch Up Unlimited .... G 405 527-5609
　Purcell (G-8023)
Ultimate Chemicals LLC .... G 405 703-2771
　Moore (G-4581)
▼ Wood Finishers Supply Inc .... G 405 422-1025
　El Reno (G-2772)

2865 Cyclic-Crudes, Intermediates, Dyes & Org Pigments

Baker Hughes A GE Company LLC ..... C 918 828-1600
　Tulsa (G-9255)
Brenntag Southwest Inc .... E 918 273-2265
　Nowata (G-5209)
Drumright Tar .... G 918 352-4000
　Drumright (G-2058)
Sunoco (R&m) LLC .... F 918 586-6246
　Tulsa (G-10873)

2869 Industrial Organic Chemicals, NEC

Bio-Cide International Inc .... G 405 364-1940
　Norman (G-4932)
▲ Biosphere Fuels LLC .... G 713 332-5726
　Oklahoma City (G-5573)
Bluehawk Energy Inc .... G 405 406-1580
　Edmond (G-2327)
Brenntag Southwest Inc .... E 918 266-2951
　Catoosa (G-1306)
C & P Catalyst Inc .... G 918 747-8379
　Tulsa (G-9357)
Chouteau Fuels Company .... G 405 249-8273
　Chouteau (G-1560)
Colorado Fuel Manufacturers .... G 918 877-5102
　Tulsa (G-9469)
Efficient Fuel Solutions Llc .... G 713 466-1400
　Caddo (G-1234)

SIC SECTION 28 CHEMICALS AND ALLIED PRODUCTS

Emerging Fuels Technology LLC ....F 918 286-6802
Tulsa *(G-9669)*
Excel Paralubes LLC ....G 800 527-3236
Bartlesville *(G-482)*
Fairwind LLC ....E 580 492-5209
Lawton *(G-3925)*
Fast Fuel LLC ....G 405 375-6666
Kingfisher *(G-3797)*
Fuel ....G 903 948-3125
Woodward *(G-11586)*
Fuel Haulers LLC ....G 405 830-3385
Guthrie *(G-3315)*
Fuel Inc ....G 580 583-5202
Lawton *(G-3933)*
Fuels Marketing Inc ....G 405 433-9935
Cashion *(G-1288)*
▲ **Galaxy Chemicals LLC** ....F 918 379-0820
Claremore *(G-1625)*
Grayson Investments LLC ....G 580 421-9770
Ada *(G-45)*
H2szero LLC ....G 918 384-9600
Sapulpa *(G-8277)*
Iochem Corporation ....E 580 995-3198
Vici *(G-11243)*
Jag Fuels Company Inc ....G 580 465-3256
Ardmore *(G-310)*
Johnson Minford ....G 580 772-0430
Weatherford *(G-11422)*
L&S Fuels LLC ....G 580 227-0999
Fairview *(G-3139)*
Magpro Chlor-Alkali LLC ....G 918 587-9930
Tulsa *(G-9019)*
Melton Dental Lab ....G 580 369-2448
Davis *(G-1991)*
Mid-Continent Fuel Co Inc ....G 918 266-1923
Catoosa *(G-1341)*
▼ **Montello Inc** ....G 918 665-1170
Tulsa *(G-10301)*
Oklahoma Biorefining Corp ....G 405 201-1824
Norman *(G-5098)*
Oklahoma Fuel Athletics LLC ....G 405 286-3144
Edmond *(G-2550)*
Plainsman Technology Inc ....F 580 658-6608
Marlow *(G-4236)*
Premier Chem & Oilfld Sup LLC ....F 405 893-2321
Enid *(G-3038)*
Pruitt Oil Company LLc ....G 580 889-2413
Atoka *(G-422)*
Rovill Biodiesel Solution LLC ....G 580 339-6815
Elk City *(G-2870)*
Rs Fuel LLC ....G 405 748-4277
Oklahoma City *(G-7057)*
Station 7 ....G 405 470-4317
Oklahoma City *(G-7196)*
Sunoco (R&m) LLC ....F 918 586-6246
Tulsa *(G-10873)*
Superior Pellet Fuels LLC ....G 918 494-0790
Tulsa *(G-10877)*
Titan Chemical ....G 918 420-5990
McAlester *(G-4342)*
Trusty Willow LLC ....G 253 241-0520
Bokoshe *(G-755)*
United Fuels & Energy ....G 405 945-7400
Oklahoma City *(G-7368)*
United Fuels Energy ....G 580 332-5222
Ada *(G-100)*
▲ **Winston Company Inc** ....E 800 331-9099
Tulsa *(G-11140)*

2873 Nitrogenous Fertilizers

Agrium Advanced Tech US Inc ....F 405 948-1084
Oklahoma City *(G-5399)*
Aurora Innovations LLC ....G 918 519-5356
Sand Springs *(G-8163)*
I Chemex Corporation ....G 405 947-0764
Oklahoma City *(G-6281)*
▲ **Koch Fertilizer Enid LLC** ....A 580 249-4870
Enid *(G-2996)*
Koch Industries Inc ....D 580 233-3900
Enid *(G-2997)*
◆ **LSB Chemical LLC** ....F 405 235-4546
Oklahoma City *(G-6498)*
LSB Industries Inc ....E 405 235-4546
Oklahoma City *(G-6499)*
Pryor Chemical Company ....C 918 825-3383
Pryor *(G-7985)*
Tessenderlo Kerley Inc ....E 405 665-2544
Wynnewood *(G-11674)*
Tessenderlo Kerley Inc ....F 580 762-1130
Ponca City *(G-7882)*

2874 Phosphatic Fertilizers

Dib 718 LLC ....G 405 525-2151
Oklahoma City *(G-5944)*
Tessenderlo Kerley Inc ....E 405 665-2544
Wynnewood *(G-11674)*
Tessenderlo Kerley Inc ....F 580 762-1130
Ponca City *(G-7882)*

2875 Fertilizers, Mixing Only

Bloomin Crazy Ldscp Flral Dsig ....G 405 238-3416
Pauls Valley *(G-7652)*
Cowboy Compost ....G 405 853-0462
Hennessey *(G-3453)*
Eckroat Seed Co ....F 405 427-2484
Oklahoma City *(G-6006)*
Edc AG Products Company LLC ....D 405 235-4546
Oklahoma City *(G-6008)*
El Dorado Chemical Company ....G 405 235-4546
Oklahoma City *(G-6015)*
Farmers Union Co-Operative Gin ....G 580 482-5136
Altus *(G-156)*
Garbage To Garden Compost Inc ....G 918 260-4463
Bixby *(G-628)*
Stillwater Milling Company LLC ....F 580 369-2354
Perry *(G-7747)*
Stockmans Mill & Grain Inc ....G 918 762-3459
Pawnee *(G-7711)*
Traci Rae Woolman ....G 580 544-2521
Boise City *(G-749)*
Urban Worm Compost LLC ....G 918 557-9255
Broken Arrow *(G-1089)*

2879 Pesticides & Agricultural Chemicals, NEC

Armour Pest Control LLC ....G 918 489-5734
Hendrix *(G-3439)*
Avitrol Corp ....G 918 622-7763
Tulsa *(G-9231)*
Bug Right ....G 918 367-9792
Bristow *(G-771)*
Christina Stokes ....G 405 551-1017
Edmond *(G-2350)*
Chromatech Scientific Corp ....G 405 370-4466
Edmond *(G-2351)*
Darren McInnich ....G 405 912-8403
Oklahoma City *(G-5285)*
◆ **Deepwater Chemicals Inc** ....E 580 256-0500
Woodward *(G-11577)*
Goff Associates Inc ....G 615 750-2900
Oklahoma City *(G-6167)*
Green Horizons LLC ....G 405 364-9921
Norman *(G-5010)*
Helena Agri-Enterprises LLC ....F 580 477-0986
Altus *(G-157)*
Hope Minerals International ....G 405 452-3529
Wetumka *(G-11491)*
Houston Brothers Inc ....G 918 449-1175
Broken Arrow *(G-1134)*
Integrity Tech & Svcs LLC ....G 405 482-9206
Edmond *(G-2462)*
Red River Specialties LLC ....G 580 436-0883
Ada *(G-81)*
Redbud Soil Company LLC ....G 405 476-0429
Oklahoma City *(G-6993)*
Shawn Schaeffer ....G 918 689-6781
Eufaula *(G-3113)*
Tex Star AG LLC ....G 580 579-9877
Coalgate *(G-1784)*

2891 Adhesives & Sealants

Alliance Sealants & Waterproof ....G 405 627-9474
Oklahoma City *(G-5419)*
Appli-Fab Custom Coating ....G 405 235-7039
Chandler *(G-1375)*
Color-Rite Inc ....F 405 354-3644
Yukon *(G-11708)*
▲ **CRC Evans Weighting Systems** ....G 918 438-2100
Tulsa *(G-9503)*
▼ **Flanco Gasket and Mfg Inc** ....E 405 672-7893
Oklahoma City *(G-6088)*
Havard Industries LLC ....G 405 888-0961
Edmond *(G-2453)*
Henley Sealants Inc ....G 405 235-7325
Oklahoma City *(G-6240)*
Line X Prtctive Ctngs Okla LLC ....F 405 232-4994
Oklahoma City *(G-6479)*
Mito Material Solutions Inc ....G 855 344-6486
Stillwater *(G-8725)*
National Coating Mfg Inc ....F 580 332-8751
Ada *(G-70)*
◆ **Red Devil Incorporated** ....F 918 585-8111
Tulsa *(G-10629)*
Red Devil Incorporated ....D 918 825-5744
Pryor *(G-7989)*
Seal Support Systems Inc ....F 918 258-6484
Broken Arrow *(G-1046)*
Self-Suspending Proppant LLC ....E 580 456-7791
Roff *(G-8111)*
Tile Shop LLC ....F 580 920-1570
Durant *(G-2269)*
Tower Sealants LLC ....F 405 528-4411
Oklahoma City *(G-7312)*
Versum Materials Us LLC ....E 918 379-7101
Catoosa *(G-1363)*

2892 Explosives

All Decked Out ....G 918 313-9691
Claremore *(G-1580)*
Austin Powder Co ....G 918 835-9244
Tulsa *(G-9224)*
El Dorado Chemical Company ....G 405 235-4546
Oklahoma City *(G-6015)*
Hman Global Solutions LLC ....G 405 338-5348
Morrison *(G-4603)*
◆ **LSB Chemical LLC** ....F 405 235-4546
Oklahoma City *(G-6498)*
Orica USA Inc ....G 918 437-1644
Tulsa *(G-10439)*
Utec Corporation LLC ....G 405 928-7061
Norman *(G-5190)*

2893 Printing Ink

Applied Laser Systems ....G 918 249-9025
Tulsa *(G-9200)*
Caveman Screen Printing ....G 918 446-6440
Tulsa *(G-9390)*
H&H Retail Services LLC ....F 918 369-4055
Bixby *(G-631)*
Southwestern Process Supply Co ....E 918 582-8211
Tulsa *(G-10812)*

2895 Carbon Black

Cabot Norit Americas Inc ....D 918 825-8332
Pryor *(G-7949)*
Continental Carbon Company ....C 580 763-8100
Ponca City *(G-7809)*
Thermal Specialties LLC ....F 918 836-4800
Tulsa *(G-10926)*

2899 Chemical Preparations, NEC

Adko Inc ....G 405 677-6507
Oklahoma City *(G-5375)*
Advanced Chemical Tech Inc ....G 405 843-2585
Oklahoma City *(G-5379)*
American Entps Whl Dstributers ....G 405 273-4516
Shawnee *(G-8427)*
▲ **Bachman Services Inc** ....E 405 677-8296
Oklahoma City *(G-5507)*
Baker Petrolite LLC ....C 918 245-2224
Sand Springs *(G-8165)*
Best Building Materials Inc ....G 405 755-0554
Edmond *(G-2320)*
Bici LLC ....G 918 625-8811
Broken Arrow *(G-849)*
Biotech Products Inc ....G 405 235-7575
Oklahoma City *(G-5574)*
Blue ARC Metal Specialties ....G 918 341-3903
Claremore *(G-1597)*
Brenntag Southwest Inc ....E 918 273-2265
Nowata *(G-5209)*
C & P Catalyst Inc ....G 918 747-8379
Tulsa *(G-9357)*
◆ **Callidus Technologies LLC** ....C 918 496-7599
Tulsa *(G-9364)*
Callidus Technologies LLC ....D 918 267-4920
Beggs *(G-550)*
Cargill Incorporated ....E 580 621-3246
Freedom *(G-3205)*
▲ **Ceralusa LLC** ....G 405 455-7720
Oklahoma City *(G-5730)*
Chandler Materials Company ....E 918 836-9151
Tulsa *(G-9403)*
▲ **Chemical Products Inds Inc** ....G 405 745-2070
Oklahoma City *(G-5748)*
Coil Chem LLC ....F 405 445-5545
Washington *(G-11334)*

SIC

Employee Codes: A=Over 500 employees, B=251-500
C=101-250, D=51-100, E=20-50, F=10-19, G=1-9

2020 Oklahoma Directory
of Manufacturers & Processors

455

28 CHEMICALS AND ALLIED PRODUCTS

Corrpro Companies Inc ....E 918 245-8791
 Sand Springs *(G-8172)*
CP Kelco US Inc ....E 918 758-2600
 Okmulgee *(G-7498)*
Custer Enterprises Inc ....F 580 371-9588
 Mannsville *(G-4195)*
◆ Deepwater Chemicals Inc ....E 580 256-0500
 Woodward *(G-11577)*
Dennis Grothe Water Svc ....G 405 651-5353
 Oklahoma City *(G-5922)*
Desired Size.................................G 405 314-3704
 Oklahoma City *(G-5927)*
Farrier Livingston Technology ....G 580 657-3469
 Ardmore *(G-288)*
Flare Industries ....G 918 376-7811
 Owasso *(G-7570)*
▲ Galaxy Chemicals LLC ....F 918 379-0820
 Claremore *(G-1625)*
Gallium Compounds LLC ....F 918 673-2511
 Quapaw *(G-8031)*
Glencoe Manufacturing Co ....F 580 669-2555
 Glencoe *(G-3222)*
Hero Flare LLC ....E 512 772-5744
 Kellyville *(G-3765)*
Interntnal Mktg Resources Corp ......G 918 270-1200
 Tulsa *(G-10005)*
Jack Warner Fireworks ....G 580 234-3827
 Enid *(G-2979)*
Kel-Crete Industries Inc ....G 918 744-0800
 Tulsa *(G-10080)*
Knox Laboratory Services Inc ....G 918 331-9982
 Bartlesville *(G-504)*
Kopps On Run LLC ....G 580 326-9400
 Hugo *(G-3616)*
Leadership Training Academy ....G 405 551-8059
 Edmond *(G-2484)*
▲ Magnesium Products Inc ....F 918 587-9930
 Tulsa *(G-9018)*
Mid-Continent Packaging Inc ....D 580 234-5200
 Enid *(G-3013)*
Midamerica Water Technologies ......G 405 613-0250
 Oklahoma City *(G-6594)*
Molycorp Rare Metals ....G 918 673-2511
 Quapaw *(G-8032)*
▼ Montello Inc ....G 918 665-1170
 Tulsa *(G-10301)*
Moon Chemical Products Co ....G 405 602-6678
 Oklahoma City *(G-6629)*
MRW Technologies Inc ....E 918 827-6030
 Glenpool *(G-3239)*
Ndn Ink Works LLC ....G 918 708-9250
 Hulbert *(G-3625)*
O Fizz Inc ....F 918 834-3691
 Tulsa *(G-10370)*
Ofs Inc ....F 405 424-1101
 Oklahoma City *(G-6714)*
OK Fire LLC ....G 918 424-1808
 McAlester *(G-4325)*
Orange Oil LLC ....G 405 701-3505
 Norman *(G-5103)*
Patriot Chemicals & Svcs LLC ....E 580 856-3114
 Ratliff City *(G-8062)*
Plainsman Technology Inc ....F 580 658-6608
 Marlow *(G-4236)*
Quikrete Companies LLC ....G 405 787-2050
 Oklahoma City *(G-6953)*
R Squared Chemicals LLC ....G 918 520-2384
 Tulsa *(G-10607)*
Rector Fire Works ....G 918 681-0513
 Muskogee *(G-4743)*
Rocket Science Labs Inc ....G 972 454-0412
 Oklahoma City *(G-7044)*
Roy Slagel Keno ....G 580 585-0283
 Elgin *(G-2779)*
Russell Chemical Sales & Svc ....G 580 234-2100
 Enid *(G-3054)*
Saltfork Service ....G 580 716-1022
 Ponca City *(G-7870)*
Schmoldt Engineering Services ....F 918 336-1221
 Bartlesville *(G-526)*
Silex LLC ....G 844 239-4056
 Moore *(G-4568)*
SMC Technologies Inc ....E 405 737-3740
 Midwest City *(G-4455)*
▲ Sooner Energy Services Inc ....G 405 579-3200
 Marlow *(G-4242)*
Spectrumfx Inc ....G 918 392-9799
 Tulsa *(G-10820)*
Superior Solutions Welding & F ....G 405 623-0104
 Piedmont *(G-7772)*

Tahlequah Public Works Auth ....F 918 456-9251
 Tahlequah *(G-8886)*
Technology Management Inc ....F 580 332-8615
 Ada *(G-93)*
Think Healthy Systems ....G 918 384-0555
 Tulsa *(G-10928)*
Town of Goldsby ....G 405 288-6675
 Goldsby *(G-3247)*
◆ Umicore Precious Metals ....E 918 266-1400
 Catoosa *(G-1362)*
▲ Western Hull Sacking Inc ....G 580 335-2144
 Frederick *(G-3204)*

29 PETROLEUM REFINING AND RELATED INDUSTRIES

2911 Petroleum Refining

Aaron Oil Inc ....G 405 899-4138
 Noble *(G-4875)*
Airgas Usa LLC ....G 405 372-7720
 Stillwater *(G-8652)*
Alice Kidd LLC ....G 405 401-4391
 Hinton *(G-3520)*
Anchor Gasoline Corporation ....D 918 584-5291
 Tulsa *(G-9184)*
Axel Royal LLC ....E 918 584-2671
 Tulsa *(G-9233)*
Baker Petrolite LLC ....C 918 847-2522
 Barnsdall *(G-435)*
Bs & W Solutions LLC ....G 918 392-9356
 Tulsa *(G-9343)*
Caulumet Ore Co ....G 580 673-2815
 Healdton *(G-3409)*
Conoco Inc ....G 580 767-3456
 Ponca City *(G-7808)*
Conocophillips ....B 918 977-6002
 Bartlesville *(G-467)*
Cvr Energy Inc ....F 913 982-0500
 Wynnewood *(G-11666)*
Dcp Midstream LLC ....F 405 362-2200
 Tuttle *(G-11194)*
Deisenroth Gas Products Inc ....G 918 742-4769
 Tulsa *(G-9567)*
Devon Energy International Co ....A 405 235-3611
 Oklahoma City *(G-5931)*
Earnheart Crescent LLC ....G 888 536-8703
 Marshall *(G-4250)*
Econo Biogasoline Corporation ....G 918 347-5408
 Bartlesville *(G-479)*
Enable Okla Intrstate Trnsm LL ....C 405 525-7788
 Oklahoma City *(G-6033)*
Envia Energy Oklahoma City LLC ....G 405 427-0790
 Oklahoma City *(G-6043)*
Ergon Inc ....F 918 266-7070
 Catoosa *(G-1319)*
Frontier Logistical Svcs LLC ....G 405 232-4401
 Oklahoma City *(G-6123)*
H Petro R Inc ....G 405 242-4400
 Oklahoma City *(G-6199)*
▲ Heater Fabricators Tulsa LLC ......E 918 430-1127
 Tulsa *(G-9908)*
Henke Petroleum Corp ....G 405 878-0909
 Shawnee *(G-8460)*
Holly Ref & Mktg - Tulsa LLC ....F 918 445-0056
 Tulsa *(G-9940)*
▲ Holly Ref & Mktg - Tulsa LLC .....E 918 594-6000
 Tulsa *(G-9941)*
Hollyfrontier Corporation ....B 918 581-1800
 Tulsa *(G-9942)*
Hollyfrontier Corporation ....G 918 594-6000
 Tulsa *(G-9943)*
Hollyfrontier Ref & Mktg LLC ....A 918 588-1142
 Tulsa *(G-9944)*
Hurricane Gas Process Plant ....G 918 492-4418
 Tulsa *(G-9959)*
James Land Residual Assets LLC ....G 405 842-2828
 Oklahoma City *(G-6349)*
Jec Production LLC ....G 405 235-4454
 Oklahoma City *(G-6353)*
July Gas Ltd Liability Co ....G 918 367-2831
 Bristow *(G-784)*
Liquefied Petro Gas Bd Okla ....F 918 521-2458
 Oklahoma City *(G-6482)*
Marathon Oil Company ....E 318 624-0874
 Oklahoma City *(G-6521)*
Messer LLC ....F 580 254-2259
 Woodward *(G-11606)*
Mustang Fuel Corporation ....E 405 748-9400
 Oklahoma City *(G-6640)*

Nextstream Heavy Oil LLC ....G 405 808-5435
 Oklahoma City *(G-6675)*
NMB Manufacturing LLC ....F 918 943-6633
 Bixby *(G-649)*
Octagon Resources Inc ....G 405 842-3322
 Oklahoma City *(G-6710)*
▼ Octagon Resources Inc ....F 405 366-8885
 Norman *(G-5097)*
Oxbow Calcining LLC ....F 580 874-2201
 Kremlin *(G-3854)*
Phillips 66 Company ....G 580 767-3456
 Ponca City *(G-7865)*
Phillips 66 Spectrum Corp ....F 918 977-7909
 Bartlesville *(G-516)*
Pinnacle Fuel Additives LLC ....G 405 658-3744
 Mustang *(G-4788)*
Plummer Energy Inc ....G 405 238-9132
 Pauls Valley *(G-7671)*
Pruitt Oil Company LLc ....G 580 889-2413
 Atoka *(G-422)*
Roy Putnam ....G 918 333-5642
 Bartlesville *(G-523)*
Samson Resources Company ....D 918 583-1791
 Tulsa *(G-10696)*
Sinclair Companies ....E 405 637-8444
 Shawnee *(G-8499)*
Sunoco (R&m) LLC ....F 918 586-6246
 Tulsa *(G-10873)*
Tank & Fuel Solutions LLC ....G 918 960-4361
 Claremore *(G-1691)*
Texoak Petro Holdings LLC ....G 918 592-1010
 Tulsa *(G-10921)*
Tpi Petroleum Inc ....C 580 221-6288
 Ardmore *(G-373)*
Tulsa Asphalt LLC ....F 918 445-2684
 Owasso *(G-7627)*
Valero Refining-Texas LP ....C 580 223-0534
 Ardmore *(G-377)*
Ventura LLC ....G 405 418-0300
 Oklahoma City *(G-7397)*
Ventura LLC ....E 580 661-2924
 Thomas *(G-8950)*
Western Gas Resources Inc ....G 580 764-3397
 Chester *(G-1422)*
WRB Refining LP ....E 918 977-6600
 Bartlesville *(G-537)*
Wynnewood Refining Company LLC ..E 405 665-6565
 Wynnewood *(G-11677)*

2951 Paving Mixtures & Blocks

APAC Oklahoma Inc ....E 918 256-8397
 Vinita *(G-11247)*
Apac-Central Inc ....F 918 683-1362
 Okay *(G-5256)*
Apac-Central Inc ....E 918 256-7853
 Vinita *(G-11248)*
Caswell Construction Co Inc ....D 580 225-6833
 Elk City *(G-2793)*
◆ CMI Terex Corporation ....A 405 787-6020
 Oklahoma City *(G-5792)*
Cummins Construction Co Inc ....E 580 233-6000
 Enid *(G-2937)*
Dunhams Asphalt Services Inc ....G 918 246-9210
 Sand Springs *(G-8180)*
Ergon A E Lawton ....G 580 536-0098
 Lawton *(G-3923)*
Ergon Ardmore ....G 580 223-8010
 Ardmore *(G-286)*
Ergon Asphalt & Emulsions Inc ....F 918 683-1732
 Muskogee *(G-4673)*
Evans & Associates Cnstr Co ....D 580 765-6693
 Ponca City *(G-7827)*
Evans & Associates Entps Inc ....E 580 765-6693
 Ponca City *(G-7828)*
Gem Asset Acquisition LLC ....E 405 200-1992
 Oklahoma City *(G-6142)*
Haskell Lemon Construction Co ......G 405 236-2701
 Oklahoma City *(G-6224)*
Haskell Lemon Construction Co ......C 405 947-6069
 Oklahoma City *(G-6223)*
Kerns Asphalt Company Inc ....E 405 372-2750
 Stillwater *(G-8711)*
Kline Materials Inc ....F 580 256-2062
 Woodward *(G-11603)*
Koch Industries Inc ....G 918 266-7070
 Catoosa *(G-1330)*
Logan County Asphalt Co ....E 405 282-3711
 Guthrie *(G-3323)*
Majeska & Associates LLC ....F 918 576-6878
 Tulsa *(G-10204)*

SIC SECTION

30 RUBBER AND MISCELLANEOUS PLASTICS PRODUCTS

Oldcastle Materials Inc..................C...... 918 978-0459
Tulsa *(G-10413)*
Overland Federal LLC....................F...... 469 269-2303
Ardmore *(G-341)*
Overland Materials and Mfg Inc.......E...... 580 223-8432
Ardmore *(G-342)*
Paving Materials Inc.......................G...... 405 799-9880
Moore *(G-4552)*
Quapaw Company............................F...... 918 225-0580
Cushing *(G-1951)*
Quapaw Company Inc......................E...... 918 352-2533
Drumright *(G-2070)*
Rdnj LLC...G...... 405 418-4741
Oklahoma City *(G-6978)*
RLC Holding Co Inc..........................D...... 580 233-6000
Enid *(G-3048)*
RLC Holding Co Inc..........................E...... 580 332-3080
Ada *(G-82)*
▲ Road Science LLC.........................D...... 918 960-3800
Tulsa *(G-10661)*
Rose Rock Midstream Field Svcs.....G...... 918 524-7700
Tulsa *(G-10672)*
Seal Masters Inc..............................E...... 580 369-2393
Davis *(G-1993)*
Semcrude LP...................................F...... 918 524-8100
Tulsa *(G-10727)*
▲ Semgroup Corporation..................B...... 918 524-8100
Tulsa *(G-10728)*
Semmaterials LP.............................G...... 918 683-1732
Muskogee *(G-4747)*
Semmaterials LP.............................G...... 580 223-8010
Ardmore *(G-353)*
Semmaterials LP.............................G...... 580 536-0098
Lawton *(G-3996)*
Semmaterials LP.............................G...... 918 266-1606
Catoosa *(G-1352)*
Semmaterials LP.............................D...... 918 524-8100
Tulsa *(G-10729)*
T & G Construction Inc.....................C...... 580 355-6655
Lawton *(G-4010)*
T J Campbell Construction Co..........C...... 405 672-6800
Oklahoma City *(G-7244)*
Teeters Asphalt & Materials.............G...... 918 673-1243
Picher *(G-7751)*
Vance Brothers Inc..........................G...... 405 427-1389
Oklahoma City *(G-7390)*

2952 Asphalt Felts & Coatings

Acme Manufacturing Corporation.....E...... 918 266-3097
Claremore *(G-1575)*
Atlas Roofing Corporation................C...... 580 226-3283
Ardmore *(G-251)*
Black Thunder Roofing LLC..............G...... 405 473-8028
Oklahoma City *(G-5582)*
Butaphalt Products LLC...................G...... 918 740-7290
Claremore *(G-1600)*
Dryvit Systems Inc..........................E...... 918 245-0216
Sand Springs *(G-8179)*
▼ G A P Roofing Inc.........................D...... 918 825-5200
Pryor *(G-7963)*
Global Sealcoating Inc.....................G...... 918 283-2040
Claremore *(G-1626)*
McCabe Industrial Minerals..............G...... 918 252-5090
Tulsa *(G-10228)*
McCabe Industrial Minerals..............F...... 580 369-3660
Davis *(G-1990)*
Schwarz Asphalt LLC.......................E...... 405 789-7203
Oklahoma City *(G-7092)*
Vance Brothers Inc..........................G...... 405 427-1389
Oklahoma City *(G-7390)*

2992 Lubricating Oils & Greases

Axel Royal LLC................................E...... 918 584-2671
Tulsa *(G-9233)*
Broken Arrow Quality Lube...............G...... 918 258-5823
Broken Arrow *(G-858)*
Legendary Lube and Oil LLC............G...... 918 351-5312
Muskogee *(G-4706)*
▼ Nu-Tier Brands Inc.......................G...... 918 550-8026
Tulsa *(G-10366)*
▼ Oils Unlimited LLC.......................D...... 918 583-1155
Tulsa *(G-10389)*
Phillips 66 Spectrum Corp...............F...... 918 977-7909
Bartlesville *(G-516)*
Sterling Properties..........................G...... 580 357-6095
Lawton *(G-4005)*
Veterans Eng Group Inc..................G...... 918 864-6006
Pryor *(G-7997)*

2999 Products Of Petroleum & Coal, NEC

Trillium Trnsp Fuels LLC..................F...... 800 920-1166
Oklahoma City *(G-7330)*
Trillium Trnsp Fuels LLC..................G...... 405 302-6500
Oklahoma City *(G-7331)*

30 RUBBER AND MISCELLANEOUS PLASTICS PRODUCTS

3011 Tires & Inner Tubes

Airgo Systems.................................G...... 877 550-6111
Oklahoma City *(G-5403)*
Carter BF..G...... 918 486-7208
Coweta *(G-1874)*
Charles Service Station LLC.............G...... 918 297-3308
Hartshorne *(G-3390)*
Michelin North America Inc..............D...... 580 226-1200
Ardmore *(G-331)*
Nutting Custom Trikes.....................G...... 918 257-8795
Afton *(G-119)*
Setco Inc..D...... 580 286-6531
Idabel *(G-3645)*
▲ Southeast Tire Inc.......................D...... 580 286-6531
Idabel *(G-3647)*
West Worldwide Services Inc..........G...... 405 601-9877
Oklahoma City *(G-7437)*

3021 Rubber & Plastic Footwear

Crackshot Corporation.....................G...... 918 838-1272
Tulsa *(G-9497)*
Vans Inc...F...... 405 843-5286
Oklahoma City *(G-7391)*
Vans Inc...F...... 405 787-9992
Oklahoma City *(G-7392)*

3052 Rubber & Plastic Hose & Belting

▲ Miami Industrial Supply & Mfg......E...... 918 542-6317
Miami *(G-4415)*
Power Cable Solutions LLC..............G...... 405 818-1993
Tuttle *(G-11207)*
Precision Hose Technology Inc.........G...... 918 835-3660
Tulsa *(G-10545)*
Tulsa Hose & Fittings Inc................G...... 918 485-0348
Wagoner *(G-11294)*

3053 Gaskets, Packing & Sealing Devices

Advanced EMC Technologies LLC.....G...... 918 994-7776
Tulsa *(G-9107)*
Automated Gasket Company LLc.....F...... 405 951-5301
Oklahoma City *(G-5494)*
Bpc Industries Inc...........................E...... 918 584-4848
Tulsa *(G-9325)*
▲ Clark Seals LLC............................E...... 918 664-0587
Tulsa *(G-9440)*
▼ Flanco Gasket and Mfg Inc..........E...... 405 672-7893
Oklahoma City *(G-6088)*
Freedom Rubber LLC.......................G...... 918 250-4673
Broken Arrow *(G-914)*
G & D Industries Inc........................G...... 918 369-2648
Bixby *(G-625)*
▲ Global Bearings Inc.....................E...... 918 664-8902
Tulsa *(G-9829)*
Harrison Manufacturing Co Inc.........F...... 918 838-9961
Tulsa *(G-9897)*
Hunt Jim Sales & Mfg......................G...... 405 670-5663
Oklahoma City *(G-6272)*
▲ Industrial Gasket Inc...................E...... 405 376-9393
Mustang *(G-4778)*
John Crane Inc................................D...... 918 664-5156
Tulsa *(G-10049)*
▲ John Crane Lemco Inc................E...... 918 835-7325
Tulsa *(G-10050)*
▲ Kt Plastics Inc.............................E...... 580 434-5655
Calera *(G-1241)*
Oklahoma Metal Creations LLC........G...... 580 917-5434
Fletcher *(G-3165)*
Oklahoma Rbr & Gasket Co Inc........F...... 918 585-3484
Tulsa *(G-10406)*
Quality Parts Mfg Co Inc..................G...... 918 627-3307
Tulsa *(G-10592)*
Redline Gaskets LLC........................G...... 918 845-7700
Sand Springs *(G-8221)*
▲ Roxtec Inc...................................F...... 918 254-9872
Tulsa *(G-10679)*
Seal Company Enterprises Inc........G...... 405 947-3307
Oklahoma City *(G-7104)*
▲ Southern Rubber Stamp Co Inc...G...... 918 587-3818
Tulsa *(G-10801)*

▲ T & A Gasket Co Inc....................G...... 918 664-7600
Tulsa *(G-10887)*
Tetrachem Seal Company Inc..........F...... 580 924-1717
Durant *(G-2223)*
Thomas Engineering Co Inc.............E...... 918 587-6649
Tulsa *(G-10931)*
Triad Precision Products Inc............E...... 918 584-3543
Tulsa *(G-10974)*
True Turn of Tulsa LLC....................F...... 918 224-5040
Tulsa *(G-10980)*
Tulsa Rubber Co.............................F...... 918 627-1371
Tulsa *(G-11006)*

3061 Molded, Extruded & Lathe-Cut Rubber Mechanical Goods

▲ Baker Hughes Elasto Systems......F...... 405 670-3354
Oklahoma City *(G-5516)*
Barlow-Hunt Inc..............................D...... 918 250-0828
Tulsa *(G-9265)*
Diversified Rubber Pdts Inc.............G...... 918 241-0193
Tulsa *(G-9587)*
Joyeaux Inc....................................F...... 918 252-7660
Tulsa *(G-10060)*
Oil States Industries Inc..................E...... 918 250-0828
Tulsa *(G-10388)*
Oil States Industries Inc..................D...... 405 671-2000
Oklahoma City *(G-6721)*
Oil States Industries Inc..................G...... 918 250-0828
Tulsa *(G-10387)*
Oklahoma Custom Rubber Co..........G...... 405 634-3943
Moore *(G-4545)*
Ranch Acres Car Care.....................G...... 918 742-3902
Tulsa *(G-10619)*
Seal Company Enterprises Inc........G...... 405 947-3307
Oklahoma City *(G-7104)*
Thomas Engineering Co Inc.............E...... 918 587-6649
Tulsa *(G-10931)*
Tjk Molded Products LLC................F...... 409 200-1007
Ardmore *(G-370)*
Tjk Molded Products LLC................G...... 409 200-1007
Ardmore *(G-371)*
Tulsa Rubber Co.............................F...... 918 627-1371
Tulsa *(G-11006)*

3069 Fabricated Rubber Prdts, NEC

American Phoenix Inc......................C...... 580 248-1488
Lawton *(G-3887)*
Anywhere Inflatable Screens LLC....G...... 918 260-4146
Tulsa *(G-9194)*
C and D Fashion Floors LLC............G...... 918 256-8018
Vinita *(G-11250)*
▼ Custom Identification Products....G...... 405 745-1010
Oklahoma City *(G-5873)*
▲ Da/Pro Rubber Inc......................C...... 918 258-9386
Broken Arrow *(G-886)*
Da/Pro Rubber Inc..........................F...... 918 272-7799
Tulsa *(G-9544)*
Da/Pro Rubber Inc..........................G...... 918 299-5480
Tulsa *(G-9545)*
Grip Jar Opener LLC........................G...... 918 766-2711
Tulsa *(G-9864)*
Jessie Shaw...................................G...... 918 587-6329
Tulsa *(G-10040)*
Molded Products Incorporated........E...... 918 254-9061
Broken Arrow *(G-1144)*
▲ Northwest Rubber.......................G...... 405 681-2667
Oklahoma City *(G-6694)*
▼ Rubber Mold Company................F...... 405 673-7177
Oklahoma City *(G-7059)*
Shelby Trailer Service LLC..............G...... 580 252-2922
Comanche *(G-1846)*
▲ Skinner Brothers Company Inc....F...... 918 585-5708
Tulsa *(G-10771)*
Texre Inc..D...... 918 425-5524
Tulsa *(G-10922)*
Tulsa Rubber Co.............................F...... 918 627-1371
Tulsa *(G-11006)*

3081 Plastic Unsupported Sheet & Film

▼ Bags Inc......................................E...... 405 427-5473
Oklahoma City *(G-5509)*
Berry Global Inc..............................F...... 918 824-4288
Pryor *(G-7945)*
Berry Global Inc..............................D...... 918 824-4400
Pryor *(G-7946)*
Berry Global Inc..............................C...... 918 426-4800
McAlester *(G-4275)*
Berry Global Films LLC....................D...... 918 227-1616
Tulsa *(G-8990)*

Employee Codes: A=Over 500 employees, B=251-500
C=101-250, D=51-100, E=20-50, F=10-19, G=1-9

30 RUBBER AND MISCELLANEOUS PLASTICS PRODUCTS

Berry Global Films LLC .... D 918 446-1651
  Tulsa (G-8991)
Berry Plastics Corporation .... C 918 824-4400
  Pryor (G-7947)
Emerald Manufacturing Corp .... G 405 235-3704
  Oklahoma City (G-6032)
F C Witt Associates Ltd .... F 918 342-0083
  Claremore (G-1618)
Georgia-Pacific LLC .... E 918 687-9800
  Muskogee (G-4678)
Gooden Studios .... G 405 375-3432
  Kingfisher (G-3799)
Hall Painting and Wall Cvg .... G 405 373-2724
  Piedmont (G-7762)
▲ High Caliper Growing Inc .... G 405 842-7700
  Oklahoma City (G-6246)
Midwest Urethane Inc .... F 918 445-2277
  Tulsa (G-10272)
◆ Paragon Films Inc .... C 918 250-3456
  Broken Arrow (G-998)
Sigma Extruding Corp .... F 918 446-6265
  Tulsa (G-10755)
Taylor Foam Inc .... G 405 787-5811
  Oklahoma City (G-7258)
▲ Unit Liner Company .... D 405 275-4600
  Shawnee (G-8516)
▼ Vineyard Plating & Sup Co Tx .... F 918 342-0083
  Claremore (G-1702)

3082 Plastic Unsupported Profile Shapes

▲ Kt Plastics Inc .... E 580 434-5655
  Calera (G-1241)

3083 Plastic Laminated Plate & Sheet

Barlow-Hunt Inc .... D 918 250-0828
  Tulsa (G-9265)
Bostd America LLC .... E 580 670-0594
  Blackwell (G-676)
Ershigs Inc .... E 918 477-9371
  Tulsa (G-9699)
Old Epp Inc .... G 866 408-2837
  Oklahoma City (G-6769)
Patternwork Veneering Inc .... G 405 447-1800
  Norman (G-5110)
Plastic Fabricators Inc .... G 918 836-6611
  Tulsa (G-10524)
Plasticon Fluid Systems Inc .... C 918 477-9371
  Tulsa (G-10527)

3084 Plastic Pipe

Advanced Drainage Systems .... G 405 272-1541
  Oklahoma City (G-5380)
Beetle Plastics LLC .... E 580 389-5421
  Ardmore (G-256)
▼ Classic Iron Works Inc .... F 405 577-2877
  Yukon (G-11706)
Dura-Line Corporation .... E 918 302-0330
  Bache (G-430)
Dylans Precision Stainless LLC .... G 918 207-9149
  Hulbert (G-3623)
Prime Conduit Inc .... E 405 670-6132
  Oklahoma City (G-6892)
Silver-Line Plastics Corp .... E 828 252-8755
  Lawton (G-3998)
U S Poly Company .... C 918 446-4471
  Tulsa (G-11029)

3085 Plastic Bottles

405 Plastics & Distribution .... G 405 562-8800
  Oklahoma City (G-5333)
Ansa Company Inc .... F 918 687-1664
  Muskogee (G-4648)
▲ Blitz USA Inc .... B 918 676-3620
  Miami (G-4391)
Cleanng LLC .... G 918 409-0384
  Tulsa (G-9446)
J-M Manufacturing Company Inc ..... D 918 446-4471
  Tulsa (G-10025)
Parker Plastics Inc .... D 918 241-0350
  Sand Springs (G-8213)
Relyassist LLC .... G 918 260-6517
  Broken Arrow (G-1156)
Uponor Aldyl Co Inc .... G 918 446-4471
  Tulsa (G-11054)

3086 Plastic Foam Prdts

Allied Foam Fabricators Inc .... G 405 946-0384
  Oklahoma City (G-5421)

Armacell LLC .... G 405 494-2800
  Yukon (G-11693)
Atlas Roofing Corporation .... C 580 226-3283
  Ardmore (G-251)
Becky Welch Vacuum Forming .... G 918 836-7301
  Tulsa (G-9278)
Bemis Company Inc .... E 918 739-4907
  Catoosa (G-1301)
Carpenter Co .... F 405 634-8124
  Moore (G-4506)
Cellofoam North America Inc .... E 918 775-7758
  Sallisaw (G-8142)
Emerald Isle of Midwest Inc .... G 405 802-0092
  Choctaw (G-1541)
Environmental Compliance LLC ...... F 405 949-0103
  Oklahoma City (G-6046)
Future Foam Inc .... G 405 948-0001
  Oklahoma City (G-6128)
Nomaco Inc .... D 405 494-2800
  Yukon (G-11759)
Scott Manufacturing LLC .... E 405 949-2728
  Oklahoma City (G-7096)
Taylor Foam Inc .... G 405 787-5811
  Oklahoma City (G-7258)
Tbk Industries LLC .... E 405 789-6940
  Bethany (G-598)
Tech Inc .... F 405 547-8324
  Perkins (G-7724)
Timber Ridge Spray Foam .... G 405 608-5995
  Oklahoma City (G-7292)
▲ Warner Jwly Box Display Co LLC ... D 580 536-8885
  Lawton (G-4021)
▲ Western Industries Corporation .... E 405 419-3100
  Oklahoma City (G-7439)
Wise Foamco Inc .... G 918 839-4784
  Poteau (G-7919)

3087 Custom Compounding Of Purchased Plastic Resins

Hite Plastics Inc .... E 405 297-9818
  Oklahoma City (G-6255)
Quikrete Companies LLC .... E 405 787-2050
  Oklahoma City (G-6953)

3088 Plastic Plumbing Fixtures

Cimarron Tank Service .... G 405 853-6523
  Hennessey (G-3451)
Country Leisure Inc .... E 405 799-7745
  Moore (G-4511)
G & D Industries Inc .... G 918 369-2648
  Bixby (G-625)
Jetta Corporation .... G 918 574-2151
  Tulsa (G-10042)
Jetta Corporation .... E 405 340-6661
  Edmond (G-2469)
Majestic Marble & Granite .... G 918 266-1121
  Catoosa (G-1337)
Pipes Plus LLC .... G 405 942-7473
  Oklahoma City (G-6853)

3089 Plastic Prdts

▲ 2by2 Industries LLC .... G 877 234-6558
  Edmond (G-2283)
A Royal Flush LLC .... G 405 422-2077
  Yukon (G-11688)
A&B Home Improvement .... G 918 341-7410
  Claremore (G-1574)
Abmi Inc .... G 405 485-9608
  Blanchard (G-699)
Aco Inc .... G 405 239-6863
  Oklahoma City (G-5368)
Amarillo Chittom Airslo .... E 918 585-5638
  Tulsa (G-9160)
American Fence Company Inc .... E 405 685-4800
  Oklahoma City (G-5435)
Ameriglobe LLC .... E 918 496-7711
  Tulsa (G-9177)
Ameristar Primeter SEC USA Inc .... E 918 835-0898
  Tulsa (G-9179)
Ashley Cameron Building Prods ...... G 405 236-0617
  Oklahoma City (G-5477)
Associated Plastics LLC .... G 405 390-0406
  Choctaw (G-1527)
Aztec Manufacturing Corp .... G 405 330-4888
  Edmond (G-2314)
Banks Motor Co .... G 580 924-8883
  Durant (G-2204)
Beetle Plastics LLC .... E 580 389-5421
  Ardmore (G-256)

Berry Global Inc .... F 812 424-2904
  McAlester (G-4274)
Berry Global Inc .... F 918 824-4288
  Pryor (G-7945)
Berry Global Inc .... D 918 824-4400
  Pryor (G-7946)
Berry Global Inc .... C 918 426-4800
  McAlester (G-4275)
Berry Plastics Corporation .... C 918 824-4400
  Pryor (G-7947)
▲ Branchcomb Inc .... E 918 224-8094
  Sapulpa (G-8259)
Cals Plastics Designs & Fabg .... G 405 670-1690
  Oklahoma City (G-5673)
Carlsons Rural Mailbox Co .... G 405 632-7338
  Oklahoma City (G-5704)
Cellofoam North America Inc .... E 918 775-7758
  Sallisaw (G-8142)
CFS Brands LLC .... F 405 397-0103
  Oklahoma City (G-5733)
◆ CFS Brands LLC .... B 405 475-5600
  Oklahoma City (G-5732)
Cfsp Acquisition Corp .... G 405 475-5600
  Oklahoma City (G-5734)
Champion Opco LLC .... G 405 708-6858
  Oklahoma City (G-5738)
Coasterworks Inc .... G 405 624-2756
  Stillwater (G-8668)
Commerce Plastics Inc .... F 918 675-4506
  North Miami (G-5206)
Cope Plastics Inc .... G 405 528-5697
  Oklahoma City (G-5833)
Cpk Manufacturing LLC .... E 405 290-7788
  Oklahoma City (G-5849)
Creative Pultrusions Inc .... G 405 979-2141
  Oklahoma City (G-5853)
Custom Molding Services Inc .... G 918 333-4872
  Bartlesville (G-472)
D B W Inc .... G 405 354-6211
  Yukon (G-11714)
Dale Kreimeyer Co .... E 405 789-9499
  Bethany (G-575)
David Gormley .... G 918 845-0443
  Sapulpa (G-8265)
David Logan .... G 918 739-4231
  Catoosa (G-1315)
Denali Incorporated .... G 713 627-0933
  Tulsa (G-9571)
▲ Devault Enterprises Inc .... G 918 249-1595
  Tulsa (G-9576)
▲ Discovery Plastics LLC .... D 918 540-2822
  Miami (G-4396)
Diversified Plastics Inds LLC .... G 918 245-0770
  Sand Springs (G-8178)
Durant Plastics & Mfg .... G 580 745-9430
  Durant (G-2227)
◆ East 74th Street Holdings Inc ...... C 918 437-3037
  Tulsa (G-9631)
Eaton-Quade Company .... F 405 236-4475
  Oklahoma City (G-6002)
Elastomer Specialties Inc .... F 800 786-4244
  Wagoner (G-11280)
Elastomer Specialties Inc .... F 918 485-0276
  Wagoner (G-11281)
◆ Fiber Glass Systems LP .... G 918 245-6651
  Sand Springs (G-8183)
Fiber Pad Inc .... D 918 438-7430
  Tulsa (G-9739)
Fiber Pad Inc .... F 918 438-7430
  Tulsa (G-9740)
▲ Fibre Reduction Inc .... G 580 223-3401
  Ardmore (G-289)
Frontier Plastic Fabricators .... F 918 445-5208
  Tulsa (G-9785)
G & H Decoy Inc .... D 918 652-3314
  Henryetta (G-3507)
General Plastics Inc .... F 405 275-3171
  Shawnee (G-8453)
Georgia-Pacific LLC .... E 918 687-9800
  Muskogee (G-4678)
Gooden Studios .... G 405 375-3432
  Kingfisher (G-3799)
Graham Packaging Company LP ..... G 918 680-7900
  Muskogee (G-4682)
Green Co Corporation .... G 918 221-3997
  Tulsa (G-9859)
Greystone Logistics Inc .... F 918 583-7441
  Tulsa (G-9863)
▲ H C E Inc .... E 405 745-2145
  Oklahoma City (G-6197)

Hackney Ladish Inc .... D 580 237-4212
  Enid *(G-2967)*
Hopkins Manufacturing Corp .... F 918 961-8722
  Miami *(G-4408)*
House of Trophies .... G 918 341-2111
  Claremore *(G-1637)*
Imperial Molding LLC .... F 580 362-3412
  Newkirk *(G-4848)*
Imperial Plastics Inc .... F 580 362-3412
  Newkirk *(G-4849)*
J & S Fittings Inc .... G 918 324-5777
  Depew *(G-2011)*
Jarrt Holdings Inc .... F 918 664-0931
  Tulsa *(G-10028)*
K & C Manufacturing Inc .... G 580 362-2979
  Ponca City *(G-7842)*
Kratos Unmnned Arial Systems I .... G 405 248-9545
  Oklahoma City *(G-6435)*
Krause Plastics .... G 918 835-4202
  Tulsa *(G-10100)*
Lacebark Inc .... G 405 377-3539
  Stillwater *(G-8716)*
Lansing Building Products Inc .... G 405 943-2493
  Oklahoma City *(G-6448)*
Laska LLC .... G 405 820-7617
  Edmond *(G-2483)*
Layle Company Corporation .... G 405 329-5143
  Norman *(G-5056)*
Leche Lounge Llc .... G 918 409-5426
  Tulsa *(G-10144)*
Letica Corporation .... C 405 745-2781
  Oklahoma City *(G-6467)*
Lloyd Freeman Creations LLC .... G 918 245-4921
  Sand Springs *(G-8201)*
M-D Plastics Group .... G 503 981-3726
  Oklahoma City *(G-6511)*
Mac Industries Inc .... G 405 631-8553
  Moore *(G-4535)*
Magnum Racing Components Inc .... G 918 627-0204
  Tulsa *(G-10201)*
Mark Stevens Industries Inc .... D 405 948-1077
  Edmond *(G-2504)*
McClarin Plastics Llc .... E 877 912-6297
  Oklahoma City *(G-6545)*
Mold Tech Inc .... G 918 247-6275
  Sapulpa *(G-8292)*
New Day Creations LLC .... G 918 576-9619
  Bixby *(G-648)*
Norwesco Inc .... F 405 275-2034
  Shawnee *(G-8479)*
O C & Associates Inc .... G 918 251-0971
  Broken Arrow *(G-991)*
Oklahoma Hand Pours .... F 580 669-2520
  Glencoe *(G-3225)*
▲ Phil-Good Products Inc .... E 405 942-5527
  Oklahoma City *(G-6842)*
Plas-Tech Inc .... G 918 649-0065
  Poteau *(G-7909)*
Plastic Designs Inc .... G 918 224-9187
  Sapulpa *(G-8299)*
Plastic Sup & Fabrication Co .... G 918 622-8430
  Tulsa *(G-10526)*
Polydyne LLC .... F 918 649-0065
  Poteau *(G-7910)*
Precision Rotational Molding .... G 580 362-3262
  Newkirk *(G-4851)*
Quarry .... G 918 534-2120
  Dewey *(G-2030)*
Reasor Enterprises .... G 918 633-1746
  Broken Arrow *(G-1029)*
Rim Molded Products Co .... F 918 438-7070
  Tulsa *(G-10653)*
◆ RL Hudson & Company .... G 918 259-6600
  Broken Arrow *(G-1035)*
Rotational Technologies Inc .... F 918 343-1350
  Claremore *(G-1684)*
Rusco Plastics .... G 580 234-1596
  Enid *(G-3053)*
Samco Polishing Inc .... F 918 789-5541
  Chelsea *(G-1412)*
Sanco Enterprises Inc .... E 405 634-2120
  Oklahoma City *(G-7075)*
▲ Sanco Products Inc .... G 405 634-2120
  Oklahoma City *(G-7076)*
Scepter Manufacturing LLC .... D 918 544-2222
  Miami *(G-4430)*
Solo Cup Operating Corporation .... C 580 436-1500
  Ada *(G-90)*
Southern Plastics LLC .... G 918 274-6767
  Owasso *(G-7618)*

Specialty Plastics Inc .... F 580 237-1018
  Enid *(G-3061)*
▲ Stonehouse Marketing Svcs LLC ..... D 405 360-5674
  Norman *(G-5160)*
SUN Engineering Inc .... F 918 627-0426
  Tulsa *(G-10870)*
Surface Mount Depot Inc .... G 405 789-0670
  Oklahoma City *(G-7231)*
Swan Plastics .... G 405 275-4826
  Shawnee *(G-8506)*
Tech Inc .... F 405 547-8324
  Perkins *(G-7724)*
Texre Inc .... D 918 425-5524
  Tulsa *(G-10922)*
▲ Tgs Plastics Inc .... F 918 252-3636
  Tulsa *(G-10925)*
Viking Rain Covers .... G 405 359-1850
  Edmond *(G-2671)*
W J L S Inc .... E 918 252-3636
  Tulsa *(G-11088)*
▼ Western Plastics LLC .... F 405 235-7272
  Oklahoma City *(G-7441)*
Wilson II Geary Wayne .... G 405 330-4888
  Edmond *(G-2689)*
Wing-It Concepts .... G 405 691-8053
  Oklahoma City *(G-5325)*

31 LEATHER AND LEATHER PRODUCTS

3111 Leather Tanning & Finishing

Blinkers & Silks Unlimited Inc .... G 405 463-0391
  Lamar *(G-3862)*
Diamond R Saddle Shop .... G 918 479-6279
  Rose *(G-8117)*
Iron Bear Jewelry & Lea Co LLC .... G 918 289-1420
  Tulsa *(G-10012)*
Lenora Elizabeth Brown .... G 918 797-2034
  Stilwell *(G-8792)*
Oklahoma Leather Products Inc .... D 918 542-6651
  Miami *(G-4424)*
▲ Osage Leather Inc .... G 918 745-0772
  Tulsa *(G-10442)*
Rawhide Custom Leather .... G 918 273-0511
  Nowata *(G-5227)*
Rawhide Dirt Works .... G 580 367-5242
  Coalgate *(G-1783)*
Rawhide N Rustics .... G 580 307-9941
  Weatherford *(G-11436)*
Stockmans Supply Company .... G 580 255-7762
  Duncan *(G-2186)*
Tricked Out Pony .... G 918 931-2646
  Tahlequah *(G-8889)*

3131 Boot & Shoe Cut Stock & Findings

Bean Counter Inc .... G 918 925-9667
  Claremore *(G-1594)*
Counter Canter Inc .... G 405 321-8326
  Norman *(G-4967)*
Countrstrike Lghtning Prtction .... G 405 863-8480
  Oklahoma City *(G-5844)*
Ingersoll-Rand Air Solutio .... G 918 451-9747
  Broken Arrow *(G-936)*
Lux Grooming Quarters LLC .... G 918 259-9910
  Tulsa *(G-10184)*
Quality In Counters Inc .... G 405 664-2744
  Guthrie *(G-3333)*
Quarter Midgets of America .... G 918 371-9410
  Collinsville *(G-1820)*
Rand Trans Inc .... G 580 866-3355
  Sharon *(G-8418)*
Upper Room .... G ......
  Oklahoma City *(G-7374)*

3144 Women's Footwear, Exc Athletic

C & W Shoes of Georgia Inc .... F 405 755-7112
  Oklahoma City *(G-5658)*

3149 Footwear, NEC

Island Disc Golf Course .... G 541 337-8668
  Pawhuska *(G-7686)*
Moccasin Trail Company .... G 405 380-8221
  Paden *(G-7636)*
Moccasins of Hope Society .... G 605 431-3738
  Ponca City *(G-7854)*

3161 Luggage

Briefcase Solutions Ltd LLC .... G 405 788-9250
  McLoud *(G-4353)*
D Gala .... G 580 468-4980
  Guymon *(G-3347)*
Dusty Trunk .... G 918 446-4203
  Tulsa *(G-9613)*
Floyd Craig Company .... G 580 832-2597
  Cordell *(G-1859)*
Frenches Quarter .... G 918 691-2553
  Tulsa *(G-9777)*
Gra Enterprises Inc .... G 405 848-1300
  Oklahoma City *(G-6173)*
Junk N Leslies Trunk LLC .... G 405 748-6702
  Oklahoma City *(G-6391)*
Nancys Trunk .... G 405 413-5037
  Ripley *(G-8103)*
Spot My Bag LLC .... G 918 895-8810
  Tulsa *(G-10826)*
Titanium Phoenix Inc .... G 405 305-1304
  Oklahoma City *(G-7294)*
W L Walker Co Inc .... E 918 583-3109
  Tulsa *(G-11089)*

3171 Handbags & Purses

Accessories-To-Go .... G 580 467-7408
  Comanche *(G-1833)*
Job Paper LLC .... G 405 242-4804
  Yukon *(G-11737)*
Sew N Saw .... G 405 282-2241
  Guthrie *(G-3337)*

3172 Personal Leather Goods

Harry A Lippert Jr .... G 512 705-1248
  Lawton *(G-3939)*
Leather Our Way .... G 918 214-2036
  Bartlesville *(G-506)*
Nupocket LLC .... F 918 850-1903
  Broken Arrow *(G-990)*
Savoy Leather LLC .... G 405 786-2296
  Weleetka *(G-11465)*
Tipton Company .... G 580 762-0800
  Ponca City *(G-7884)*
▲ Warner Jwly Box Display Co LLC .... D 580 536-8885
  Lawton *(G-4021)*

3199 Leather Goods, NEC

◆ Billy Cook Harn & Saddle Mfg .... D 580 622-5505
  Sulphur *(G-8829)*
Comanche Leather Works Inc .... G 580 439-6276
  Comanche *(G-1837)*
Cornerstone Leather .... G 817 598-0367
  Comanche *(G-1840)*
Crossroad Holsters LLC .... G 405 317-7405
  Oklahoma City *(G-5860)*
Custom Lea Sad & Cowboy Decor .... G 918 335-2277
  Bartlesville *(G-471)*
D R Topping Saddlery .... G 918 273-2812
  Nowata *(G-5212)*
Don Hume Company LLC .... E 918 542-6604
  Miami *(G-4397)*
Don Hume Leathergoods Inc .... D 918 542-6604
  Miami *(G-4398)*
▲ Finish Line of Oklahoma Inc .... G 918 341-8291
  Claremore *(G-1621)*
Geronimo Manufacturing Inc .... G 580 336-5707
  Perry *(G-7735)*
Gj Leather LLC .... G 405 795-2998
  Newcastle *(G-4828)*
Jerry Beagley Braiding Company .... G 580 924-4995
  Calera *(G-1240)*
Johnny Beard Co .... G 918 438-4901
  Tulsa *(G-10056)*
Kens Handcrafted Leather Gds .... G 918 616-5804
  Muskogee *(G-4702)*
Leather Doctor .... G 918 271-4600
  Broken Arrow *(G-965)*
Lenora Elizabeth Brown .... G 918 797-2034
  Stilwell *(G-8792)*
Lewis Manufacturing Co LLC .... E 405 279-2553
  Meeker *(G-4378)*
▲ Lewis Manufacturing Co LLC .... G 405 634-5401
  Oklahoma City *(G-6471)*
Mock Brothers Saddlery Inc .... G 918 245-7259
  Sand Springs *(G-8205)*
Okc Boys of Leather .... G 318 560-0312
  Oklahoma City *(G-6727)*
Scissor Tail Custom Holster .... G 405 595-6315
  Norman *(G-5139)*

T R Tack Supply ... G ... 918 299-5880
Jenks *(G-3732)*

▲ **US Whip Inc** ... E ... 918 542-6453
Miami *(G-4435)*

W R Western Company Inc ... G ... 405 605-5586
Oklahoma City *(G-7411)*

Wicho Leather Creations LLC ... G ... 405 885-8644
Oklahoma City *(G-7450)*

Woods Saddlery ... G ... 918 723-5503
Westville *(G-11488)*

32 STONE, CLAY, GLASS, AND CONCRETE PRODUCTS

3211 Flat Glass

Doctors Optical Supply Inc ... G ... 918 256-6416
Vinita *(G-11255)*

Edmond Glass ... G ... 405 751-5900
Edmond *(G-2402)*

Guys Wise ... G ... 405 801-3339
Norman *(G-5012)*

Oldcastle Buildingenvelope Inc ... D ... 405 275-5510
Shawnee *(G-8481)*

Skyview Products Inc ... G ... 405 745-6064
Mustang *(G-4794)*

Striper Tinting ... G ... 918 636-4043
Claremore *(G-1689)*

Tietsort LLC ... G ... 405 664-7353
Oklahoma City *(G-7286)*

Whitacre Glass Works LLC ... G ... 918 366-6646
Tulsa *(G-11119)*

3221 Glass Containers

Anchor Glass Container Corp ... B ... 918 652-9631
Henryetta *(G-3499)*

Ardagh Glass Inc ... E ... 918 224-1440
Sapulpa *(G-8250)*

Owens-Brockway Glass Cont Inc ... C ... 918 684-4526
Muskogee *(G-4730)*

Verallia ... G ... 918 224-1440
Sapulpa *(G-8320)*

3229 Pressed & Blown Glassware, NEC

Accutech Laboratories Inc ... F ... 405 946-6446
Warr Acres *(G-11312)*

Bella Forte Glass Studio LLC ... G ... 405 659-6169
Oklahoma City *(G-5544)*

Blue Sage Studios ... G ... 405 601-2583
Oklahoma City *(G-5594)*

Chickasaw Nation ... G ... 580 332-2796
Ada *(G-21)*

Distinctive Decor LLC ... F ... 580 252-9494
Duncan *(G-2105)*

Dlubak Glass Company ... F ... 918 752-0226
Okmulgee *(G-7500)*

Dunlaw Optical Labs Inc ... F ... 580 355-8410
Lawton *(G-3920)*

Essilor Laboratories Amer Inc ... E ... 800 568-5367
Tulsa *(G-9702)*

Help Housing ... G ... 918 258-7252
Broken Arrow *(G-927)*

Miller Sales Wholesale Distr ... G ... 918 629-4064
Tulsa *(G-10282)*

Petroleum Artifacts Ltd ... G ... 918 949-6101
Tulsa *(G-10504)*

Tulsa Glass Blowing Studio Inc ... G ... 918 582-4527
Tulsa *(G-10998)*

3231 Glass Prdts Made Of Purchased Glass

▲ **Cameron Glass Inc** ... D ... 918 254-6000
Broken Arrow *(G-862)*

Cardinal Glass Industries Inc ... C ... 580 924-2142
Durant *(G-2211)*

Cardinal Glass Industries Inc ... C ... 580 924-2142
Durant *(G-2212)*

Central Glass Products Inc ... F ... 918 436-2401
Pocola *(G-7782)*

Cimarron Glass LLC ... G ... 918 225-6600
Cushing *(G-1925)*

Dlubak Glass Company ... F ... 918 752-0226
Okmulgee *(G-7500)*

Hourglass Transport LLC ... G ... 580 937-4569
Coleman *(G-1796)*

Mel Robinson ... G ... 405 843-7529
Oklahoma City *(G-6561)*

Memories In Glass Inc ... G ... 405 878-9688
Shawnee *(G-8473)*

Michael and Mary Seever ... G ... 405 808-2494
Bethany *(G-590)*

Oklahoma Metal Creations LLC ... G ... 580 917-5434
Fletcher *(G-3165)*

Oldcastle Buildingenvelope Inc ... D ... 405 275-5510
Shawnee *(G-8481)*

Owasso Glass ... G ... 918 272-4490
Owasso *(G-7600)*

▼ **Professional Packaging Inc** ... E ... 918 682-9531
Muskogee *(G-4738)*

▲ **Red Bud Glass Inc** ... E ... 405 685-3331
Vinita *(G-11269)*

Shack Little Glass ... G ... 405 364-2649
Norman *(G-5143)*

Victory Glass Co Inc ... G ... 405 232-5114
Oklahoma City *(G-7400)*

Whitacre Glass Works LLC ... G ... 918 366-6646
Tulsa *(G-11119)*

Zephyr Southwest Orna LLC ... E ... 918 251-4133
Broken Arrow *(G-1104)*

3241 Cement, Hydraulic

Buzzi Unicem USA Inc ... E ... 918 825-1937
Pryor *(G-7948)*

Buzzi Unicem USA Inc P ... G ... 405 670-0677
Oklahoma City *(G-5650)*

Holcim (us) Inc ... C ... 580 332-1512
Ada *(G-48)*

Holcim (us) Inc ... C ... 573 242-3571
Ada *(G-49)*

Lone Star Industries Inc ... G ... 405 670-0677
Oklahoma City *(G-6492)*

Lone Star Industries Inc ... G ... 918 825-1937
Pryor *(G-7974)*

Lone Star Industries Inc ... G ... 918 492-2121
Tulsa *(G-10177)*

Peak Cement Piedmont ... G ... 405 373-2086
Piedmont *(G-7768)*

▲ **Tulsa Cement LLC** ... B ... 918 437-3902
Tulsa *(G-10991)*

3251 Brick & Structural Clay Tile

Acme Brick Company ... D ... 405 755-5010
Oklahoma City *(G-5367)*

Acme Brick Company ... D ... 918 834-3384
Tulsa *(G-9096)*

Commercial Brick Corporation ... C ... 405 257-6613
Wewoka *(G-11498)*

Mangum Brick ... G ... 405 410-4478
Edmond *(G-2503)*

MB Holdings LLC ... D ... 580 782-2324
Mangum *(G-4172)*

Meridian Brick LLC ... E ... 918 687-6734
Muskogee *(G-4712)*

Meridian Brick LLC ... G ... 918 258-7533
Broken Arrow *(G-971)*

Meridian Brick LLC ... G ... 405 749-9900
Oklahoma City *(G-6567)*

3253 Ceramic Tile

Classic Carpets Lawton Inc ... G ... 580 713-0653
Lawton *(G-3904)*

▲ **Classic Tile Stone & MBL LLC** ... F ... 405 858-8453
Oklahoma City *(G-5779)*

3255 Clay Refractories

▲ **Central Mortar and Grout LLC** ... E ... 918 683-3003
Muskogee *(G-4659)*

Commercial Brick Corporation ... C ... 405 257-6613
Wewoka *(G-11498)*

Harbisonwalker Intl Inc ... G ... 918 825-1044
Pryor *(G-7965)*

◆ **Heater Specialists LLC** ... D ... 918 835-3126
Tulsa *(G-9909)*

Meridian Brick LLC ... G ... 918 258-7533
Broken Arrow *(G-971)*

Meridian Brick LLC ... G ... 405 749-9900
Oklahoma City *(G-6567)*

Quikrete Companies LLC ... E ... 405 787-2050
Oklahoma City *(G-6953)*

3259 Structural Clay Prdts, NEC

Heintzelman Cons & Rofing ... G ... 405 409-8954
Oklahoma City *(G-5294)*

MO Money Minerals LLC ... G ... 405 262-2457
Calumet *(G-1247)*

Ops Sales Company ... G ... 918 534-3760
Dewey *(G-2029)*

3261 China Plumbing Fixtures & Fittings

Bobrick Washroom Equipment Inc ... F ... 580 924-8066
Durant *(G-2207)*

Professional Marble Company ... G ... 918 225-5364
Cushing *(G-1950)*

3264 Porcelain Electrical Splys

Coorstek Inc ... B ... 405 601-4371
Oklahoma City *(G-5832)*

Midwest Industries Inc ... F ... 405 279-2706
Meeker *(G-4383)*

▲ **Tdk Ferrites Corporation** ... C ... 405 275-2100
Shawnee *(G-8509)*

3269 Pottery Prdts, NEC

All American Wrought Iron ... G ... 918 213-9949
Bartlesville *(G-445)*

Brookside Pottery ... G ... 918 697-6364
Tulsa *(G-9342)*

◆ **CFS Brands LLC** ... B ... 405 475-5600
Oklahoma City *(G-5732)*

CFS Brands LLC ... F ... 405 397-0103
Oklahoma City *(G-5733)*

Cfsp Acquisition Corp ... G ... 405 475-5600
Oklahoma City *(G-5734)*

Janimals ... G ... 918 587-4799
Tulsa *(G-10027)*

Miller Sales Wholesale Distr ... G ... 918 629-4064
Tulsa *(G-10282)*

Nell Gavin LLC ... G ... 972 935-6692
Bartlesville *(G-513)*

Paseo Pottery ... G ... 405 525-3017
Oklahoma City *(G-6807)*

Phelps Sculpture Studio ... G ... 405 752-9512
Oklahoma City *(G-6841)*

Roserock Creations Inc ... G ... 405 209-6005
Edmond *(G-2604)*

3271 Concrete Block & Brick

Alpha Concrete Products Inc ... F ... 405 769-7777
Oklahoma City *(G-5424)*

Arrowhead Precast LLC ... D ... 918 995-2227
Broken Arrow *(G-833)*

Baray Enterprises Inc ... E ... 405 373-1800
Piedmont *(G-7755)*

Best Companies ... G ... 918 280-8066
Broken Arrow *(G-847)*

Boomer Foundations & Piers ... G ... 405 799-6811
Moore *(G-4500)*

◆ **Buildblock Bldg Systems LLC** ... G ... 405 840-3386
Oklahoma City *(G-5640)*

Chandler Materials Company ... E ... 918 836-9151
Tulsa *(G-9403)*

Day Concrete Block Company ... F ... 580 223-3317
Ardmore *(G-277)*

Dolese Bros Co ... E ... 405 670-9626
Oklahoma City *(G-5962)*

Meridian Brick LLC ... E ... 918 687-6734
Muskogee *(G-4712)*

Ramcco Concrete Cnstr LLC ... F ... 918 266-3838
Tulsa *(G-10616)*

Rdnj LLC ... G ... 405 418-4741
Oklahoma City *(G-6978)*

Stone Splitters Inc ... G ... 479 651-8873
Sallisaw *(G-8153)*

Tri-State Con Foundations LLC ... E ... 405 341-3043
Oklahoma City *(G-7323)*

3272 Concrete Prdts

52 Stone ... G ... 918 798-9952
Claremore *(G-1573)*

Accurate Fence Contruction LLC ... G ... 580 591-3717
Lawton *(G-3884)*

Advanced Comfort & Energy ... F ... 405 329-2237
Norman *(G-4900)*

Age Stone Manufacturing ... G ... 918 366-3270
Bixby *(G-609)*

◆ **Allan Edwards Incorporated** ... G ... 918 583-7184
Tulsa *(G-9139)*

Allegiant Precast LLC ... F ... 918 486-6227
Broken Arrow *(G-1108)*

Alpha Concrete Products Inc ... F ... 405 769-7777
Oklahoma City *(G-5424)*

Ameron International Corp ... C ... 918 858-3973
Tulsa *(G-9180)*

Ameron Pole Products LLC ... E ... 918 585-5611
Tulsa *(G-9181)*

Architectural Pav Systems LLC ... G ... 918 747-9302
Tulsa *(G-9204)*

32 STONE, CLAY, GLASS, AND CONCRETE PRODUCTS

Arrowhead Precast LLC .... D 918 995-2227
  Broken Arrow *(G-833)*
Baray Enterprises Inc .... E 405 373-1800
  Piedmont *(G-7755)*
Blackstone Capital Partners SE .... G 424 355-5050
  El Reno *(G-2702)*
Bmi Management Inc .... G 580 762-5659
  Ponca City *(G-7801)*
Carnegie Precast Inc .... F 580 654-1718
  Carnegie *(G-1275)*
Cellfill LLC .... G 918 787-2355
  Grove *(G-3260)*
Central Burial Vaults Inc .... E 918 224-5701
  Tulsa *(G-8996)*
Champion Designs & Systems LLC ..... G 405 888-8370
  Oklahoma City *(G-5737)*
Chandler Materials Company .... E 918 836-9151
  Tulsa *(G-9403)*
Cobble Rock and Stone LLC .... F 405 567-3552
  Prague *(G-7923)*
Concrete Products Inc .... E 405 427-8686
  Oklahoma City *(G-5819)*
▲ Construction Supply House Inc ..... G 405 214-9366
  Norman *(G-4964)*
Coppedge Septic Tank .... G 918 371-4549
  Collinsville *(G-1806)*
Coreslab Structures Okla Inc .... C 405 632-4944
  Oklahoma City *(G-5835)*
Coreslab Structures Oklahoma .... F 405 672-2325
  Oklahoma City *(G-5836)*
Coreslab Structures Tulsa Inc .... E 918 438-0230
  Tulsa *(G-9487)*
▲ CRC Evans Weighting Systems ..... G 918 438-2100
  Tulsa *(G-9503)*
Decorative Rock & Stone .... G 405 341-8900
  Edmond *(G-2388)*
Dolese Bros Co .... F 580 225-1247
  Elk City *(G-2803)*
Dolese Bros Co .... E 405 670-9626
  Oklahoma City *(G-5962)*
Dover Products Inc .... G 918 476-5688
  Chouteau *(G-1562)*
Downtown Pub .... F 918 274-8202
  Owasso *(G-7563)*
Eastside Septic Tank .... G 918 486-2290
  Coweta *(G-1881)*
Eaves Stones Products .... F 580 889-7858
  Atoka *(G-410)*
Excalibur Cast Stone LLC .... E 405 702-4314
  Oklahoma City *(G-6057)*
Excalibur Stoneworks LLC .... D 405 702-4314
  Oklahoma City *(G-6058)*
Foresee Ready-Mix Concrete Inc ..... F 918 689-3951
  Eufaula *(G-3101)*
Forterra Pipe & Precast LLC .... G 405 677-8811
  Oklahoma City *(G-6104)*
▲ Gifford Monument Works Inc .... F 580 332-1271
  Ada *(G-42)*
GNC Concrete Products Inc .... D 918 438-1182
  Tulsa *(G-9836)*
Green Country S Inc .... G 918 224-8244
  Sapulpa *(G-8276)*
Handi-Sak Inc .... E 405 789-3001
  Oklahoma City *(G-6210)*
Haskell Lemon Construction Co .... C 405 947-6069
  Oklahoma City *(G-6223)*
Hausners Limited .... F 580 924-6988
  Mead *(G-4366)*
Hausners Precast Con Pdts Inc .... E 918 352-3479
  Drumright *(G-2061)*
Heritage Burial Park .... G 405 692-5503
  Oklahoma City *(G-6242)*
▼ Impressions In Stone LLC .... G 918 828-9745
  Tulsa *(G-9974)*
Improved Cnstr Methods Inc .... G 405 235-2609
  Oklahoma City *(G-6294)*
Jim Giles Safe Rooms .... G 918 639-8102
  Sapulpa *(G-8283)*
Keith Lyons .... F 580 584-3360
  Broken Bow *(G-1196)*
Kel-Crete Industries Inc .... G 918 744-0800
  Tulsa *(G-10080)*
McF Services Inc .... G 918 481-1620
  Tulsa *(G-10233)*
McLemore Monument Services .... G 405 788-0164
  El Reno *(G-2737)*
Monumental Rocks .... G 918 240-8398
  Broken Arrow *(G-981)*
Palm Vault Co Inc .... G 580 332-7565
  Ada *(G-74)*

Precast Solutions LLC .... G 580 819-2455
  Yukon *(G-11767)*
Precast Trtmnt Solutions LLC .... G 405 455-5303
  Oklahoma City *(G-6877)*
Precision Stone .... G 405 214-2224
  Shawnee *(G-8484)*
Quikrete Companies LLC .... E 918 835-4441
  Tulsa *(G-10598)*
Quikrete Holdings Inc .... G 405 354-8824
  Yukon *(G-11770)*
Rinker Materials Concrete Pipe .... G 405 745-3404
  Oklahoma City *(G-7028)*
Rn Concrete Products .... G 405 564-3020
  Perry *(G-7743)*
Schwarz Sand .... G 405 789-7914
  Oklahoma City *(G-7093)*
Scurlock Industries Miami Inc .... F 918 542-1884
  North Miami *(G-5208)*
Skiatook Statuary .... G 918 396-1309
  Skiatook *(G-8570)*
Smith Septic Tank Inc .... G 918 456-8741
  Tahlequah *(G-8884)*
Spencer L Rosson .... G 918 682-4291
  Muskogee *(G-4750)*
Stone Mill Inc .... F 918 812-4438
  Kansas *(G-3755)*
Stone Warehouse .... F 918 250-0800
  Broken Arrow *(G-1064)*
Stonecoat of Tulsa LLC .... G 918 551-6868
  Tulsa *(G-10855)*
Tricon Unlmted Cnstr Svcs LLC .... G 405 473-9186
  Oklahoma City *(G-7329)*
Triguard of Oklahoma .... G 580 243-8015
  Elk City *(G-2885)*
Tulsa Casting Inc .... G 918 366-1272
  Bixby *(G-667)*
▲ Tulsa Dynaspan Inc .... C 918 258-8693
  Tulsa *(G-10996)*
Twin Cities Ready Mix Inc .... G 918 465-2555
  Wilburton *(G-11527)*
V&H Coatings Co .... G 405 819-4163
  Oklahoma City *(G-7384)*
Vintage Vault .... G 918 619-9954
  Tulsa *(G-11079)*
Wilbert Funeral Services Inc .... E 918 446-2131
  Tulsa *(G-9051)*
Wilbert Funeral Services Inc .... E 405 752-9033
  Oklahoma City *(G-7451)*
Williams Monuments .... G 918 225-1344
  Cushing *(G-1971)*

3273 Ready-Mixed Concrete

Altus Ready-Mix Inc .... F 580 482-3418
  Altus *(G-142)*
Alva Concrete Inc .... B 580 327-2281
  Alva *(G-173)*
Apac-Central Inc .... G 918 696-2820
  Stilwell *(G-8780)*
Apac-Central Inc .... G 918 921-6491
  Tulsa *(G-9195)*
Apac-Central Inc .... G 918 775-3251
  Sallisaw *(G-8137)*
Atlas Concrete Inc .... G 580 255-7280
  Duncan *(G-2083)*
Atlas Tuck Concrete Inc .... F 580 355-8241
  Lawton *(G-3892)*
Atlas Tuck Concrete Inc .... G 405 224-5005
  Chickasha *(G-1433)*
Atlas Tuck Concrete Inc .... G 405 381-2393
  Tuttle *(G-11185)*
Atlas-Tuck Concrete Inc .... G 580 255-1716
  Duncan *(G-2084)*
B & W Ready Mix LLC .... G 580 623-5059
  Watonga *(G-11340)*
Bartlesville Redi-Mix Inc .... F 580 765-6693
  Bartlesville *(G-453)*
Block Sand Co Inc .... G 405 391-2919
  McLoud *(G-4352)*
Bo-Max Industries Inc .... F 580 256-4555
  Woodward *(G-11562)*
Carnegie Concrete Company .... G 580 654-1208
  Carnegie *(G-1273)*
Caswell Construction Co Inc .... D 580 225-6833
  Elk City *(G-2793)*
Connelly Ready-Mix Con LLC .... D 405 943-8388
  Oklahoma City *(G-5820)*
Crescent Ready Mix Inc .... G 405 853-1599
  Crescent *(G-1910)*
Day Concrete Block Company .... F 580 223-3317
  Ardmore *(G-277)*

▲ Dolese Bros Co .... C 405 235-2311
  Oklahoma City *(G-5957)*
Dolese Bros Co .... F 580 795-3549
  Madill *(G-4146)*
Dolese Bros Co .... G 405 947-7085
  Oklahoma City *(G-5958)*
Dolese Bros Co .... G 580 924-4944
  Durant *(G-2224)*
Dolese Bros Co .... G 580 237-2650
  Enid *(G-2942)*
Dolese Bros Co .... G 405 454-2478
  Harrah *(G-3377)*
Dolese Bros Co .... E 580 639-2237
  Mountain View *(G-4627)*
Dolese Bros Co .... F 918 437-6535
  Tulsa *(G-9591)*
Dolese Bros Co .... F 580 332-0820
  Ada *(G-32)*
Dolese Bros Co .... G 405 382-2060
  Seminole *(G-8370)*
Dolese Bros Co .... G 405 795-9757
  Oklahoma City *(G-5959)*
Dolese Bros Co .... E 580 369-2834
  Davis *(G-1982)*
Dolese Bros Co .... G 580 576-9478
  Roosevelt *(G-8116)*
Dolese Bros Co .... G 580 761-0022
  Ponca City *(G-7821)*
Dolese Bros Co .... G 918 423-1061
  McAlester *(G-4294)*
Dolese Bros Co .... G 580 323-1202
  Clinton *(G-1748)*
Dolese Bros Co .... G 580 889-6033
  Atoka *(G-408)*
Dolese Bros Co .... G 405 247-2564
  Anadarko *(G-202)*
Dolese Bros Co .... G 405 262-0226
  El Reno *(G-2713)*
Dolese Bros Co .... G 918 297-2376
  Hartshorne *(G-3391)*
Dolese Bros Co .... G 405 235-2311
  Weatherford *(G-11404)*
Dolese Bros Co .... F 405 235-1515
  Chickasha *(G-1452)*
Dolese Bros Co .... E 405 794-0546
  Moore *(G-4518)*
Dolese Bros Co .... G 580 832-2720
  Cordell *(G-1858)*
Dolese Bros Co .... G 405 282-2153
  Guthrie *(G-3311)*
Dolese Bros Co .... G 405 672-4577
  Oklahoma City *(G-5960)*
Dolese Bros Co .... G 405 732-0909
  Oklahoma City *(G-5961)*
Dolese Bros Co .... E 405 670-9626
  Oklahoma City *(G-5962)*
Dolese Bros Co .... G 405 373-2102
  Piedmont *(G-7760)*
Dolese Bros Co .... F 405 232-1228
  Oklahoma City *(G-5963)*
Dolese Bros Co .... G 405 324-2944
  Yukon *(G-11720)*
Dolese Bros Co .... F 580 223-2243
  Ardmore *(G-279)*
Dolese Bros Co .... G 405 949-2278
  Oklahoma City *(G-5964)*
Dolese Bros Co .... F 580 225-1247
  Elk City *(G-2803)*
Dolese Bros Co .... F 580 255-3046
  Duncan *(G-2107)*
Eagle Redi-Mix Concrete LLC .... G 918 355-5700
  Tulsa *(G-9627)*
Enid Concrete Co Inc .... B 580 237-7766
  Enid *(G-2950)*
Evans & Associates Entps Inc .... F 580 482-3418
  Altus *(G-155)*
Evans & Associates Entps Inc .... E 580 765-6693
  Ponca City *(G-7828)*
Evans Asphalt Co Inc .... F 580 765-6693
  Ponca City *(G-7829)*
Evans Concrete Co Inc .... F 580 765-6693
  Skiatook *(G-8543)*
Foresee Ready-Mix Concrete Inc ..... F 918 689-3951
  Eufaula *(G-3101)*
Gcc Ready Mix LLC .... G 918 582-8111
  Tulsa *(G-9811)*
Goddards Ready Mix Con Inc .... F 405 424-4383
  Oklahoma City *(G-6165)*
Goddards Ready Mix Concrete .... G 405 424-4383
  Oklahoma City *(G-6166)*

Employee Codes: A=Over 500 employees, B=251-500
C=101-250, D=51-100, E=20-50, F=10-19, G=1-9

Green Valley Enterprises Inc ....G....... 580 227-4938
Fairview *(G-3136)*
H C Rustin Corporation ....E....... 580 924-3260
Durant *(G-2235)*
H C Rustin Corporation ....G....... 580 224-2672
Ardmore *(G-299)*
Hardesty Company Inc ....E....... 918 585-3100
Tulsa *(G-9890)*
Hennessey Ready Mix Concrete ....G....... 405 853-4473
Hennessey *(G-3467)*
Hodges Materials Inc ....E....... 580 223-3317
Ardmore *(G-305)*
J-A-G Construction Company ....G....... 580 338-3188
Guymon *(G-3353)*
Joe Martin ....G....... 918 850-2776
Broken Arrow *(G-1136)*
Karlin Company ....G....... 405 542-6991
Hydro *(G-3631)*
Keith Lyons ....F....... 580 584-3360
Broken Bow *(G-1196)*
Kerns Construction Inc ....E....... 405 372-2750
Stillwater *(G-8712)*
Kerns Ready Mixed Concrete Inc ....F....... 405 372-2750
Stillwater *(G-8713)*
Kimball Ready Mix Inc ....G....... 580 922-4444
Seiling *(G-8350)*
Kline Materials Inc ....F....... 580 256-2062
Woodward *(G-11603)*
L A Jacobson Inc ....E....... 405 238-9313
Pauls Valley *(G-7664)*
Lafarge North America Inc ....G....... 405 686-0320
Oklahoma City *(G-6445)*
Larry Campbell Ofc ....G....... 918 682-1209
Muskogee *(G-4705)*
Lawton Transit Mix Inc ....E....... 580 353-6900
Lawton *(G-3961)*
M P Ready Mix Inc ....G....... 405 631-6814
Oklahoma City *(G-6509)*
M P Ready Mix Inc ....E....... 405 354-8824
Yukon *(G-11743)*
Metheny Concrete Products Inc ....E....... 405 947-5566
Oklahoma City *(G-6577)*
Metheny Concrete Products Inc ....D....... 405 947-5566
Oklahoma City *(G-6578)*
Mid Continent Concrete Co ....G....... 918 775-6858
Sallisaw *(G-8149)*
Mid Continent Concrete Company ....E....... 918 647-0550
Poteau *(G-7908)*
Mid-Continent Concrete Co Inc ....G....... 918 758-0200
Okmulgee *(G-7516)*
Mid-Continent Concrete Co Inc ....F....... 918 224-4122
Sapulpa *(G-8290)*
Midwest Ready Mix ....G....... 580 625-4477
Beaver *(G-542)*
Mineral Resource Tech Inc ....G....... 918 683-7671
Muskogee *(G-4714)*
Muskogee Ready Mix Inc ....F....... 918 682-3403
Muskogee *(G-4717)*
Neo Concrete & Materials Inc ....E....... 918 542-4456
Miami *(G-4423)*
Nixon Materials Company ....G....... 580 621-3297
Freedom *(G-3208)*
Oklahoma Mobil Concrete Inc ....G....... 918 622-3930
Tulsa *(G-10403)*
Okmulgee Ready Mix Concrete Co ....F....... 918 756-6005
Okmulgee *(G-7520)*
Ormca ....G....... 918 296-7711
Tulsa *(G-10441)*
P C Concrete Co Inc ....B....... 580 762-1302
Ponca City *(G-7864)*
Pawnee Ready Mix Inc ....G....... 918 762-3437
Pawnee *(G-7708)*
Perry Ready Mix Inc ....B....... 580 336-5575
Perry *(G-7742)*
Primo Redimix LLC ....F....... 580 494-7649
Broken Bow *(G-1203)*
Quikrete Companies LLC ....E....... 405 787-2050
Oklahoma City *(G-6953)*
Rainbow Concrete Company ....D....... 918 234-9044
Tulsa *(G-10611)*
Randys Construction ....G....... 405 387-3568
Newcastle *(G-4836)*
Rempel Rock-N-Ready Mix Inc ....G....... 405 275-1107
Shawnee *(G-8487)*
Rempels Rock & Ready Mix Inc ....F....... 405 567-3991
Prague *(G-7934)*
Rental Ready ....G....... 918 500-6922
Tulsa *(G-10641)*
Right Mix ....G....... 580 704-8904
Lawton *(G-3994)*

Schwarz Ready Mix of Okc ....G....... 405 354-6671
Yukon *(G-11778)*
Sooner Ready Mix ....G....... 405 670-3300
Oklahoma City *(G-7163)*
Sooner Ready Mix LLC ....E....... 405 692-5595
Oklahoma City *(G-7164)*
Southwest Ready Mix ....F....... 580 248-4709
Lawton *(G-4001)*
Southwest Ready Mix ....E....... 580 355-2093
Lawton *(G-4002)*
Srm Inc ....F....... 405 354-8824
Yukon *(G-11787)*
Srm Inc ....B....... 405 475-1746
Edmond *(G-2629)*
Standard Materials Group ....F....... 479 587-3300
Tulsa *(G-10835)*
Standard Materials Group Inc ....G....... 918 582-8111
Tulsa *(G-10836)*
▲ Tulsa Dynaspan Inc ....C....... 918 258-8693
Tulsa *(G-10996)*
Twin Cities Ready Mix Inc ....E....... 918 423-8855
McAlester *(G-4346)*
Twin Cities Ready Mix Inc ....G....... 918 647-8218
Poteau *(G-7916)*
Twin Cities Ready Mix Inc ....G....... 918 967-3391
Stigler *(G-8650)*
Twin Cities Ready Mix Inc ....G....... 918 465-2555
Wilburton *(G-11527)*
Twin Cities Ready Mix Inc ....E....... 918 682-8181
Muskogee *(G-4756)*
Twin Cities Ready Mix Inc ....G....... 918 458-0323
Tahlequah *(G-8890)*
Twin Cities Ready Mix Inc ....E....... 918 438-8888
Tulsa *(G-11023)*
Van Eaton Ready Mix Inc ....E....... 405 912-4825
Norman *(G-5192)*
Van Eaton Ready Mix Inc ....G....... 405 364-2028
Norman *(G-5193)*
Van Eaton Ready Mix Inc ....E....... 405 844-2900
Edmond *(G-2667)*
Van Eaton Ready Mix Inc ....E....... 405 789-1795
Oklahoma City *(G-7389)*
Van Eaton Ready Mix Inc ....D....... 405 214-7450
Shawnee *(G-8518)*
Withers Trucking Co ....G....... 580 668-2320
Healdton *(G-3424)*

3274 Lime

Schweitzer Gypsum & Lime ....G....... 405 263-7967
Okarche *(G-5251)*

3275 Gypsum Prdts

▲ American Gypsum Company LLC ....C....... 580 679-3391
Duke *(G-2079)*
Diamond Gypsum LLC ....G....... 580 623-2868
Watonga *(G-11345)*
▲ Freeman Products Inc ....E....... 918 258-8861
Broken Arrow *(G-915)*
Georgia-Pacific LLC ....G....... 405 536-0070
Oklahoma City *(G-6146)*
Harrison Gypsum LLC ....E....... 580 337-6371
Bessie *(G-569)*
New Ngc Inc ....D....... 918 825-0142
Pryor *(G-7978)*
United States Gypsum Company ....B....... 580 822-6100
Southard *(G-8588)*

3281 Cut Stone Prdts

Allied Stone Inc ....E....... 580 931-3388
Durant *(G-2201)*
Alva Monument Works Inc ....G....... 580 327-0626
Alva *(G-174)*
American Marble ....G....... 918 812-7940
Tulsa *(G-9169)*
Anson Memorial Co ....G....... 918 358-2504
Cleveland *(G-1716)*
Benchmark Monument ....G....... 918 582-8600
Tulsa *(G-9280)*
▲ Boadie L Anderson Quarries Inc ......E....... 580 436-2100
Ada *(G-12)*
Buck Creek Homes Cnstr Inc ....F....... 580 272-0102
Ada *(G-15)*
Classic Marble Design Inc ....G....... 580 323-4917
Clinton *(G-1744)*
▲ Classic Tile Stone & MBL LLC ....F....... 405 858-8453
Oklahoma City *(G-5779)*
Conway Custom Marble Co ....G....... 580 357-3757
Lawton *(G-3910)*
Crawford Granite Works ....G....... 918 423-3020
McAlester *(G-4288)*

Custom Tile & Marble Inc ....F....... 405 810-8515
Oklahoma City *(G-5877)*
▲ Decorative Rock & Stone Inc ....G....... 405 672-2564
Oklahoma City *(G-5916)*
Divine Cultured Marble ....G....... 918 836-2121
Tulsa *(G-9588)*
Dolese Bros Co ....D....... 580 492-4771
Elgin *(G-2775)*
▼ Eagle Urns Inc ....G....... 918 469-3024
Quinton *(G-8036)*
Eaves Stones Products ....F....... 580 889-7858
Atoka *(G-410)*
▲ Eurocraft Ltd ....E....... 918 322-5500
Glenpool *(G-3234)*
Fittstone Inc ....E....... 580 777-2808
Fittstown *(G-3158)*
Forged By Creation LLC ....G....... 918 798-0051
Broken Arrow *(G-912)*
Freedom Stone Company LLC ....G....... 918 649-0021
Poteau *(G-7904)*
Grecian Marble & Granite LLC ....F....... 405 632-3802
Oklahoma City *(G-6185)*
How To Build A Flagstone Patio ....G....... 405 478-1200
Bixby *(G-633)*
J B Granite Countertops ....G....... 580 771-6894
Lawton *(G-3944)*
Jones Monuments Co ....G....... 580 255-2276
Duncan *(G-2138)*
Majestic Marble & Granite ....E....... 918 266-1121
Catoosa *(G-1337)*
McAlester Monument Co Inc ....G....... 918 423-1647
McAlester *(G-4317)*
Midwest Marble Co ....E....... 918 587-8193
Tulsa *(G-10268)*
Millers Marble and Granite ....G....... 580 357-1348
Lawton *(G-3971)*
Morris Monuments ....G....... 580 924-1323
Durant *(G-2244)*
Muskogee Marble & Granite LLC ....E....... 918 682-0064
Muskogee *(G-4716)*
Natural Stone Interiors ....F....... 918 851-3451
Bixby *(G-647)*
Nicholson Monument Co ....G....... 580 323-7513
Clinton *(G-1762)*
Okmulgee Monuments Inc ....G....... 918 756-6619
Okmulgee *(G-7519)*
Professional Marble Company ....G....... 918 225-5364
Cushing *(G-1950)*
Rivers Edge Countertops Inc ....F....... 405 387-2930
Newcastle *(G-4839)*
Rives Enterprises Inc ....G....... 918 671-4099
Tulsa *(G-10660)*
Silex Interiors Inc ....G....... 918 836-5454
Tulsa *(G-10761)*
Stigler Stone Company Inc ....F....... 918 967-3316
Stigler *(G-8649)*
Sugar Loaf Quarries Inc ....E....... 918 647-4244
Shady Point *(G-8416)*
▲ Tile & Design Concepts Inc ....E....... 405 842-8551
Oklahoma City *(G-7288)*
V J Stone LLC ....G....... 405 840-2255
Oklahoma City *(G-7383)*
Valley Stone Inc ....F....... 918 647-2388
Howe *(G-3600)*
Warhall Designs LLC ....F....... 405 330-0907
Edmond *(G-2680)*
Whm Granite Products Inc ....F....... 580 535-2184
Granite *(G-3257)*
Young Brothers Inc ....E....... 405 272-0821
Oklahoma City *(G-7482)*

3291 Abrasive Prdts

Albright Steel and Wire Co ....G....... 580 357-3596
Lawton *(G-3886)*
Jesco Products Inc ....G....... 405 943-1721
Oklahoma City *(G-6358)*
▲ Sunbelt Industries Inc ....G....... 405 843-1275
Oklahoma City *(G-7225)*

3295 Minerals & Earths: Ground Or Treated

Arcosa Acg Inc ....G....... 405 366-9500
Norman *(G-4914)*
Arysta Life Science Technology ....G....... 580 871-2316
Alva *(G-175)*
Hewitt Mineral Corporation ....G....... 580 223-6565
Ardmore *(G-304)*
Iofina Natural Gas ....G....... 580 871-2316
Alva *(G-183)*
Martin Marietta Materials Inc ....G....... 580 384-3574
Mill Creek *(G-4468)*

SIC SECTION

McCabe Industrial Minerals ....G....... 918 252-5090
  Tulsa (G-10228)
McCabe Industrial Minerals ....F........ 580 369-3660
  Davis (G-1990)
McCabe Industrial Mnrl Corp ....F........ 918 252-5090
  Tulsa (G-10229)
Mesquite Minerals Inc......................G....... 405 848-7551
  Oklahoma City (G-6571)
Wildcat Minerals..............................G....... 580 254-0141
  Woodward (G-11653)

3296 Mineral Wool

Ets-Lindgren Inc................................E....... 580 434-7490
  Durant (G-2230)
Hewlett-Packard Entp Svcs................G....... 918 939-4072
  Tulsa (G-9926)
Johns Manville Corporation................E....... 405 552-4115
  Oklahoma City (G-6372)
Owens Corning Sales LLC..................F....... 405 235-2491
  Oklahoma City (G-6790)
Scott Manufacturing LLC....................E....... 405 949-2728
  Oklahoma City (G-7096)
Scott Manufacturing of Ky..................E....... 405 949-2728
  Oklahoma City (G-7097)
Western Fibers Inc.............................E....... 509 679-4786
  Hollis (G-3571)

3297 Nonclay Refractories

Acid Specialists LLC..........................G....... 432 617-2243
  Oklahoma City (G-5366)
Bpi Inc..G....... 918 682-5044
  Muskogee (G-4654)
◆ Mike Alexander Company Inc..........E....... 580 765-8085
  Tulsa (G-10276)
Quikrete Companies LLC...................E....... 405 787-2050
  Oklahoma City (G-6953)
◆ Refractory Anchors Inc..................E....... 918 455-8485
  Broken Arrow (G-1154)

3299 Nonmetallic Mineral Prdts, NEC

Alvin Stone......................................G....... 918 447-4455
  Tulsa (G-9158)
Architectural Models........................G....... 405 360-2828
  Norman (G-4913)
Benchmark Stucco.............................G....... 918 810-2812
  Sperry (G-8604)
Blessing Gravel LLC..........................G....... 580 513-4009
  Tishomingo (G-8962)
CD Industrys Corporation.................G....... 580 317-8448
  Hugo (G-3605)
▲ F C Ziegler Co...............................E....... 918 587-7639
  Tulsa (G-9721)
▲ Insul-Vest Inc................................G....... 918 445-2279
  Tulsa (G-9992)
Phelps Sculpture Studio...................G....... 405 752-9512
  Oklahoma City (G-6841)
Ppr LLC..G....... 574 516-1131
  Stillwater (G-8740)
Snyders Stucco and Stone................G....... 580 421-9747
  Ada (G-89)
Stucco 2 Stone...................................G....... 918 770-2944
  Tulsa (G-10863)
▲ To Market LLC................................G....... 405 236-2878
  Oklahoma City (G-7300)
Yolanda Olmos.................................G....... 918 850-8334
  Tulsa (G-11169)

33 PRIMARY METAL INDUSTRIES

3312 Blast Furnaces, Coke Ovens, Steel & Rolling Mills

3 D Manufacturing............................G....... 918 224-7717
  Sapulpa (G-8244)
Abco Steel Inc...................................F........ 918 322-3435
  Glenpool (G-3228)
▲ Advantage Cnstr Pdts Inc................G....... 405 372-3562
  Stillwater (G-8651)
Albright Steel and Wire Co.................F........ 405 232-7526
  Oklahoma City (G-5410)
Azz Incorporated...............................G....... 918 584-6668
  Tulsa (G-9237)
Balero...G....... 580 221-6202
  Ardmore (G-252)
Bucke-Tee LLC...................................G....... 580 747-9288
  Enid (G-2923)
Bullet Fence Systems LLC.................G....... 918 777-3973
  Okmulgee (G-7496)
C & B Fabricators Inc.........................G....... 918 760-6508
  Bokoshe (G-752)

▲ Carlson Company............................E....... 918 627-4334
  Tulsa (G-9376)
Chickasaw Defense Services Inc........G....... 405 203-0144
  Oklahoma City (G-5759)
CMC Steel Oklahoma LLC..................G....... 580 634-5092
  Durant (G-2217)
Commercial Metals Company............G....... 580 634-5046
  Durant (G-2218)
Commercial Metals Company............F........ 918 437-5377
  Tulsa (G-9474)
Cust-O-Bend Inc................................E....... 918 241-0514
  Tulsa (G-9526)
Cyber Stitchery................................G....... 405 329-6018
  Norman (G-4975)
Danlin Industries LLC.......................C....... 580 661-3248
  Clinton (G-1747)
Elite Fabricators LLC.......................E....... 918 824-4528
  Pryor (G-7961)
Gerdau Ameristeel US Inc.................G....... 918 241-7762
  Sand Springs (G-8188)
Gms Lalos Custom Wheels Ltd Co......G....... 918 622-3616
  Tulsa (G-9835)
Hartco Metal Products Inc.................G....... 405 471-2784
  Edmond (G-2452)
Ipsco Tubulars Inc.............................C....... 918 384-6400
  Catoosa (G-1323)
J & L Tool Co Inc................................G....... 918 835-8484
  Tulsa (G-10018)
Joco Assembly LLC............................E....... 918 622-5111
  Tulsa (G-10048)
Karchmer Pipe & Supply Co Inc..........G....... 405 236-3568
  Oklahoma City (G-6398)
Kingfisher Pipe Sales and Svc............G....... 405 262-4422
  El Reno (G-2733)
Kloeckner Metals Corporation...........E....... 918 266-1666
  Catoosa (G-1328)
Lawton Window Co Inc......................G....... 580 353-4655
  Lawton (G-3962)
Metals USA Plates and Shap..............E....... 918 682-7833
  Muskogee (G-4713)
Mobile Hightech.................................G....... 405 942-4600
  Oklahoma City (G-6620)
MRC Global (us) Inc...........................G....... 918 485-9511
  Wagoner (G-11287)
National Oilwell Varco Inc..................C....... 918 781-4436
  Muskogee (G-4719)
Precision Metals LLC.........................G....... 918 266-2202
  Tulsa (G-10548)
◆ Refractory Anchors Inc....................E....... 918 455-8485
  Broken Arrow (G-1154)
Ross Dub Company Inc......................E....... 405 495-3611
  Oklahoma City (G-7049)
S E A Y Manufacturing LLC................G....... 405 454-2328
  Harrah (G-3385)
Sherrell Steel LLC..............................F........ 580 436-4322
  Ada (G-87)
Straits Steel and Wire LLC..................G....... 231 843-3416
  Tulsa (G-10858)
Tms International LLC.......................G....... 918 241-0129
  Sand Springs (G-8230)
TRC Rod Services of Oklahoma..........F........ 405 677-0585
  Oklahoma City (G-7320)
Tubacex Durant Inc............................G....... 724 646-4301
  Durant (G-2270)
United Axle.......................................G....... 918 344-1157
  Claremore (G-1697)
Vam Usa LLC.....................................G....... 405 720-2200
  Oklahoma City (G-7388)
◆ Webco Industries Inc......................B....... 918 245-2211
  Sand Springs (G-8237)
Webco Industries Inc..........................G....... 865 388-5001
  Catoosa (G-1364)
Webco Industries Inc..........................G....... 918 581-0900
  Sand Springs (G-8236)
Webco Industries Inc..........................G....... 918 836-1188
  Tulsa (G-11100)
Wire Twisters Inc...............................G....... 405 376-0052
  Mustang (G-4802)

3313 Electrometallurgical Prdts

Cutting Edge Machine Inc..................G....... 580 658-5036
  Marlow (G-4226)

3315 Steel Wire Drawing & Nails & Spikes

Albright Steel and Wire Co.................G....... 580 357-3596
  Lawton (G-3886)
American Fence Company Inc............E....... 405 685-4800
  Oklahoma City (G-5435)
Automatic Gate Systems of Okla........G....... 580 920-8752
  Durant (G-2203)

33 PRIMARY METAL INDUSTRIES

▲ Dw-Natnal Stndrd-Stllwater LLC......C....... 405 377-5050
  Stillwater (G-8680)
General Wire & Supply Co Inc............E....... 918 245-5961
  Tulsa (G-9817)
Givens Manufacturing Inc..................G....... 888 302-2774
  Mounds (G-4616)
Hanlock-Causeway Company LLC......F........ 918 446-1450
  Tulsa (G-9009)
Jackson Clip Co Inc...........................C....... 918 476-8331
  Mazie (G-4264)
Kaydawn Manufacturing Co Inc..........G....... 918 321-5017
  Glenpool (G-3237)
▲ Lewis Manufacturing Co LLC............G....... 405 634-5401
  Oklahoma City (G-6471)
M & R Wire Works Inc........................G....... 580 795-4290
  Madill (G-4153)
Nomad Defense LLC...........................G....... 405 808-4325
  Yukon (G-11760)
Pinpoint Wire Technologies LLC........G....... 405 447-6900
  Norman (G-5116)
Screen Tech Intl Ltd Co......................F........ 918 234-0010
  Broken Arrow (G-1161)
U and S Wire Rope.............................G....... 580 421-1077
  Shawnee (G-8514)
William B Finley................................G....... 580 512-7573
  Lawton (G-4023)

3316 Cold Rolled Steel Sheet, Strip & Bars

Albright Steel and Wire Co.................F........ 405 232-7526
  Oklahoma City (G-5410)
Carefusion Corporation......................C....... 918 865-4727
  Mannford (G-4178)
▲ Carlson Company............................E....... 918 627-4334
  Tulsa (G-9376)
Cust-O-Bend Inc................................E....... 918 241-0514
  Tulsa (G-9526)
Tmk Ipsco International LLC..............G....... 918 384-6400
  Catoosa (G-1356)
Worthington Industries Inc................G....... 614 438-3048
  Catoosa (G-1369)

3317 Steel Pipe & Tubes

▲ Advantage Cnstr Pdts Inc................G....... 405 372-3562
  Stillwater (G-8651)
Albright Steel and Wire Co.................F........ 405 232-7526
  Oklahoma City (G-5410)
▲ Baker Hughes Elasto Systems.........F........ 405 670-3354
  Oklahoma City (G-5516)
Bison Metals Technologies LLC..........G....... 403 395-1405
  Shawnee (G-8433)
Bkw Inc...G....... 918 836-6767
  Tulsa (G-9299)
Cherokee Piping Services LLC...........G....... 918 931-8593
  Tahlequah (G-8856)
Corrpro Companies Inc......................G....... 918 245-8791
  Sand Springs (G-8172)
Cutting Edge Machine Inc..................G....... 580 658-5036
  Marlow (G-4226)
Flow Valve LLC..................................E....... 580 622-2294
  Sulphur (G-8832)
Hunter Steel LLC................................G....... 918 684-9600
  Muskogee (G-4693)
Innovex Downhole Solutions Inc.......G....... 405 491-2658
  Oklahoma City (G-6308)
▲ Lps Specialty Products Inc..............G....... 918 893-5486
  Catoosa (G-1334)
▲ Mid American Stl & Wire Co LLC......E....... 580 795-2559
  Madill (G-4157)
◆ Mike Alexander Company Inc..........E....... 580 765-8085
  Tulsa (G-10276)
MRC Global (us) Inc...........................G....... 918 485-9511
  Wagoner (G-11287)
Oilfield Equipment Company.............G....... 405 850-1406
  Duncan (G-2161)
Ops Sales Company..........................G....... 918 534-3760
  Dewey (G-2029)
Paragon Industries Inc......................E....... 918 781-1430
  Muskogee (G-4731)
Paragon Industries Inc......................B....... 918 291-4459
  Sapulpa (G-8296)
Rolled Alloys Inc...............................E....... 918 594-2600
  Tulsa (G-9031)
Rosa & Unis LLC................................D....... 918 445-4204
  Tulsa (G-10670)
Ross Dub Company Inc......................E....... 405 495-3611
  Oklahoma City (G-7049)
Taylor & Sons Pipe and Stl Inc...........F........ 405 222-0751
  Chickasha (G-1516)
Webco Industries Inc.........................C....... 918 865-6215
  Mannford (G-4194)

Employee Codes: A=Over 500 employees, B=251-500
C=101-250, D=51-100, E=20-50, F=10-19, G=1-9

2020 Oklahoma Directory
of Manufacturers & Processors

33 PRIMARY METAL INDUSTRIES

Webco Industries Inc .... E 918 245-9521
　Sand Springs *(G-8239)*
Webco Industries Inc .... G 918 865-6215
　Kellyville *(G-3769)*
Webco Industries Inc .... C 918 241-1086
　Sand Springs *(G-8238)*

3321 Gray Iron Foundries

▲ American Castings LLC .... B 918 476-4252
　Pryor *(G-7942)*
Camcast Corp .... C 918 371-9966
　Owasso *(G-7551)*
CFM Corporation .... F 580 363-2850
　Blackwell *(G-678)*
Closebend Inc .... F 918 445-1131
　Tulsa *(G-9456)*
Concessions Mfg Co LLC .... G 918 786-5100
　Grove *(G-3262)*
Ej Usa Inc .... C 231 536-2261
　Ardmore *(G-282)*
Fascast Inc .... E 918 445-7405
　Tulsa *(G-9005)*
Mayco Inc .... E 405 677-5969
　Oklahoma City *(G-6543)*
Supco Inc .... C 918 336-5075
　Bartlesville *(G-529)*
Superior Companies Inc .... C 918 336-5075
　Bartlesville *(G-530)*
United Utlties Specialists LLC .... E 918 342-0840
　Claremore *(G-1698)*
Wh International Casting LLC .... G 562 521-0727
　Haskell *(G-3402)*

3322 Malleable Iron Foundries

▲ American Castings LLC .... B 918 476-4252
　Pryor *(G-7942)*
Ej Usa Inc .... C 231 536-2261
　Ardmore *(G-282)*
Mid-South Metals LLC .... G 918 835-8055
　Tulsa *(G-10262)*
R & L Endeavors LLC .... G 405 826-8226
　Oklahoma City *(G-6957)*

3324 Steel Investment Foundries

Afg Acquisition Group LLC .... B 918 366-4401
　Bixby *(G-608)*
Alpha Investment Casting Corp .... E 918 834-4686
　Tulsa *(G-9153)*
Camcast Corp .... C 918 371-9966
　Owasso *(G-7551)*
Carter Aerospace Mfg Co LLC .... G 918 229-4026
　Skiatook *(G-8535)*
Metal Dynamics Corp .... E 918 582-0124
　Tulsa *(G-10244)*
Mingo Aerospace LLC .... F 918 272-7371
　Owasso *(G-7591)*
Mingo Aerospace LLC .... G 918 272-7371
　Owasso *(G-7592)*
North Amercn Precision Cast Co .... D 580 237-4033
　Enid *(G-3019)*
▲ Parrish Enterprises Ltd .... C 580 237-4033
　Enid *(G-3031)*

3325 Steel Foundries, NEC

Alpha Investment Casting Corp .... E 918 834-4686
　Tulsa *(G-9153)*
▲ Burrow Construction LLC .... E 800 766-5793
　Fort Gibson *(G-3174)*
Consoldted Fabrication Constrs .... G 918 224-3500
　Tulsa *(G-8998)*
Southwest Pickling Inc .... G 580 924-6996
　Durant *(G-2259)*

3334 Primary Production Of Aluminum

◆ Fortiflex Inc .... F 918 540-3131
　Miami *(G-4405)*

3339 Primary Nonferrous Metals, NEC

Allied Manufacturing Tech .... G 918 899-9504
　Tulsa *(G-9150)*
American Zinc Recycling Corp .... D 918 336-7100
　Bartlesville *(G-447)*
Elemetal .... G 405 605-2402
　Oklahoma City *(G-6023)*
Heartland Precious Metals .... G 405 254-6870
　Edmond *(G-2454)*
▲ Magnesium Products Inc .... F 918 587-9930
　Tulsa *(G-9018)*

Oklahoma Industrial Silver .... G 405 341-6021
　Edmond *(G-2551)*
Probuilt Spincasting LLC .... G 918 617-9053
　Eufaula *(G-3109)*
◆ Umicore Optical Mtls USA Inc .... D 918 673-1650
　Quapaw *(G-8034)*

3341 Secondary Smelting & Refining Of Nonferrous Metals

Borg Compressed Steel Corp .... D 918 587-2437
　Tulsa *(G-9321)*
Brown Metals .... G 405 321-6866
　Norman *(G-4946)*
Dastar Inc .... G 580 786-8833
　Duncan *(G-2104)*
Durant Iron & Metal Inc .... E 580 924-0595
　Durant *(G-2226)*
Identity & Tanning Salon .... G 412 269-7879
　Tuttle *(G-11204)*
Metal Check Inc .... F 405 636-1916
　Oklahoma City *(G-6573)*
Mid America Alloys LLC .... E 918 224-3446
　Sapulpa *(G-8288)*
Oklahoma Industrial Silver .... G 405 341-6021
　Edmond *(G-2551)*
Real Alloy Recycling LLC .... C 918 224-4746
　Sapulpa *(G-8305)*
Rolled Alloys Inc .... E 918 594-2600
　Tulsa *(G-9031)*
Tms International LLC .... G 918 241-0129
　Sand Springs *(G-8230)*

3351 Rolling, Drawing & Extruding Of Copper

Albright Steel and Wire Co .... F 405 232-7526
　Oklahoma City *(G-5410)*
Taylor Forge Engineered .... E 918 280-1183
　Tulsa *(G-10904)*
Wolverine Tube Inc .... B 405 275-4850
　Shawnee *(G-8521)*
Wolverine Tube Inc .... A 405 275-4850
　Shawnee *(G-8522)*

3353 Aluminum Sheet, Plate & Foil

Clinco Mfg LLC .... G 580 759-3434
　Ada *(G-25)*
Real Alloy Recycling LLC .... G 918 224-4746
　Sapulpa *(G-8305)*
Reel Power International Corp .... F 405 609-3326
　Oklahoma City *(G-6999)*

3354 Aluminum Extruded Prdts

Acme Manufacturing Corporation .... E 918 266-3097
　Claremore *(G-1575)*
Armstrong Products Inc .... G 405 282-7584
　Guthrie *(G-3297)*
Ballews Aluminum Products Inc .... G 405 917-2225
　Oklahoma City *(G-5521)*
Custom Design By Roberts .... G 918 664-0466
　Tulsa *(G-9528)*
DDB Unlimited Incorporated .... D 405 665-2876
　Wynnewood *(G-11667)*
DDB Unlimited Incorporated .... F 800 753-8459
　Wynnewood *(G-11668)*
DDB Unlimited Incorporated .... E 800 753-8459
　Wynnewood *(G-11669)*
Dunlap Manufacturing Co Inc .... E 918 838-1383
　Tulsa *(G-9612)*
Herbert Malarkey Roofing Co .... C 405 261-6900
　Oklahoma City *(G-6241)*
Trulite GL Alum Solutions LLC .... G 918 665-6655
　Tulsa *(G-10982)*

3355 Aluminum Rolling & Drawing, NEC

Nixon Materials Company .... G 580 621-3297
　Freedom *(G-3208)*

3356 Rolling, Drawing-Extruding Of Nonferrous Metals

Buffalo Nickel Industries LLC .... G 918 287-3899
　Pawhuska *(G-7679)*
Cindy Nickel Aesthetics .... G 405 513-6690
　Edmond *(G-2353)*
Cindy Nickel Inc .... G 405 209-1444
　Edmond *(G-2354)*
Damar Manufacturing Co Inc .... G 918 445-2445
　Tulsa *(G-9549)*
Lonnie B Nickels Jr .... G 918 756-3426
　Okmulgee *(G-7514)*

Nickel & Company LLC .... E 918 744-6384
　Tulsa *(G-10342)*
Nickel 8 LLC .... G 405 721-7945
　Oklahoma City *(G-6680)*
Nickel Creek Photography .... G 918 447-2688
　Tulsa *(G-10343)*
Prl Manufacturing Inc .... G 918 280-1090
　Tulsa *(G-10563)*
Titanium Nutrition LLC .... G 918 697-1012
　Broken Arrow *(G-1078)*
Transtrade LLC .... G 918 521-7271
　Tulsa *(G-10970)*

3357 Nonferrous Wire Drawing

Grw Inc .... F 918 681-3282
　Muskogee *(G-4685)*
Holloway Technical Svcs LLC .... G 405 223-9352
　Duncan *(G-2130)*
▲ Reel Power Industrial Inc .... D 405 609-3326
　Oklahoma City *(G-6998)*
Reel Power Wire & Cable Inc .... E 918 584-1000
　Oklahoma City *(G-7000)*
Techsico Entp Solutions Inc .... D 918 585-2347
　Tulsa *(G-10913)*
▲ US Pioneer LLC .... E 918 359-5200
　Tulsa *(G-11055)*

3363 Aluminum Die Castings

Mold Tech Inc .... G 918 247-6275
　Sapulpa *(G-8292)*
Transtate Castings Inc .... G 405 232-3936
　Oklahoma City *(G-7319)*

3364 Nonferrous Die Castings, Exc Aluminum

Alpha Investment Casting Corp .... E 918 834-4686
　Tulsa *(G-9153)*
Alpha Investment Casting LLC .... E 918 834-4686
　Tulsa *(G-9154)*
Cutting Edge Machine Inc .... G 580 658-5036
　Marlow *(G-4226)*
Diemasters 800 826-2134
　Skiatook *(G-8541)*
Mid America Alloys LLC .... E 918 224-3446
　Sapulpa *(G-8288)*

3365 Aluminum Foundries

Accu Cast .... G 918 582-3466
　Tulsa *(G-9088)*
Camcast Corp .... C 918 371-9966
　Owasso *(G-7551)*
CP Industries Inc .... G 918 468-2230
　Grove *(G-3264)*
Hurst Aerospace Inc .... G 918 543-6527
　Inola *(G-3663)*
Jag Machine Inc .... F 918 791-0004
　Grove *(G-3277)*
Lahmeyer Pattern Shop .... G 918 425-6008
　Tulsa *(G-10112)*
Neco Industries Inc .... E 405 682-3003
　Oklahoma City *(G-6667)*
Permocast Inc .... G 918 652-8812
　Henryetta *(G-3516)*
Pickering Metal Casting LLC .... E 806 747-3411
　Tulsa *(G-10512)*
Transtate Castings Inc .... G 405 232-3936
　Oklahoma City *(G-7319)*

3366 Copper Foundries

ARk -Ramos Fndry Mfg Co Inc .... D 405 235-5505
　Oklahoma City *(G-5465)*
Bronze Horse Inc .... G 918 287-4433
　Pawhuska *(G-7678)*
Custom Design By Roberts .... G 918 664-0466
　Tulsa *(G-9528)*
Fancy Dancer Leather Designs .... G 405 247-7030
　Anadarko *(G-204)*
Maverick Machinery LLC .... G 918 584-2504
　Broken Arrow *(G-968)*
T & L Foundry Inc .... D 918 322-3310
　Glenpool *(G-3242)*
Tonkawa Foundry Inc .... E 580 628-2575
　Tonkawa *(G-8982)*
Transtate Castings Inc .... G 405 232-3936
　Oklahoma City *(G-7319)*

SIC SECTION
34 FABRICATED METAL PRODUCTS, EXCEPT MACHINERY AND TRANSPORTATION EQUIPMENT

3369 Nonferrous Foundries: Castings, NEC

Camcast Corp .... C 918 371-9966
  Owasso *(G-7551)*
Crucible LLC .... F 405 579-2700
  Norman *(G-4971)*
LMI Aerospace Inc .... E 918 281-0124
  Tulsa *(G-10173)*
Metal Dynamics Corp .... E 918 582-0124
  Tulsa *(G-10244)*
Mold Tech Inc .... G 918 247-6275
  Sapulpa *(G-8292)*
Nordam Group LLC .... C 918 274-2742
  Tulsa *(G-10356)*
Tatco Metals Inc .... G 918 853-4663
  Jenks *(G-3733)*

3398 Metal Heat Treating

Bodycote Thermal Proc Inc .... F 405 670-5710
  Oklahoma City *(G-5605)*
Bodycote Thermal Proc Inc .... G 214 904-2420
  Tulsa *(G-9314)*
Cargill Heat Treat LLC .... G 405 510-3404
  Oklahoma City *(G-5700)*
Casting Coating Corp .... F 918 445-4141
  Tulsa *(G-8995)*
Hinderliter Heat Treating Inc .... G 405 670-5710
  Oklahoma City *(G-6250)*
National Oilwell Varco Inc .... C 918 781-4436
  Muskogee *(G-4719)*
O S R Inc .... G 281 422-7206
  Inola *(G-3668)*
Onsite Stress Relieving Svc .... E 918 234-1222
  Inola *(G-3669)*
Osr Services LP .... F 918 234-1222
  Inola *(G-3670)*
Precision Heat Treating .... G 918 445-7424
  Tulsa *(G-9025)*
▼ Q B Johnson Mfg Inc .... D 405 677-6676
  Moore *(G-4558)*
Smith Welding Fabg & Repr .... G 918 446-2293
  Tulsa *(G-10779)*
Superheat Fgh Services Inc .... G 580 762-8538
  Ponca City *(G-7880)*
Team Inc .... E 918 234-9600
  Tulsa *(G-10909)*
Thermal Specialties LLC .... G 970 532-3796
  Owasso *(G-7623)*
Thermal Specialties LLC .... F 918 227-4800
  Tulsa *(G-9044)*
Thermal Specialties LLC .... G 405 681-4400
  Oklahoma City *(G-7282)*
Tulsa Gamma Ray Inc .... G 918 425-3112
  Tulsa *(G-10997)*
▲ V M Star .... C 918 781-4400
  Muskogee *(G-4757)*
Zentech LLC .... F 918 585-8200
  Tulsa *(G-11176)*

3399 Primary Metal Prdts, NEC

Archer Technologies Intl Inc .... G 405 306-3220
  Shawnee *(G-8428)*
E E Sewing Inc .... G 918 214-5343
  Bartlesville *(G-476)*
◆ East 74th Street Holdings Inc .... C 918 437-3037
  Tulsa *(G-9631)*
Hilti Inc .... G 918 252-6000
  Tulsa *(G-9931)*
Walkers Powder Coating LLC .... G 580 355-5000
  Lawton *(G-4018)*
Weldco Mfg .... G 580 296-1485
  Colbert *(G-1788)*

34 FABRICATED METAL PRODUCTS, EXCEPT MACHINERY AND TRANSPORTATION EQUIPMENT

3411 Metal Cans

▲ Blitz USA Inc .... B 918 676-3620
  Miami *(G-4391)*
Herbert Malarkey Roofing Co .... C 405 261-6900
  Oklahoma City *(G-6241)*
Keymiaee Aero-Tech Inc .... F 405 235-5010
  Oklahoma City *(G-6409)*
Metal Container Corporation .... C 405 680-3140
  Oklahoma City *(G-6574)*
Mullins Salvage Inc .... G 918 352-9612
  Cushing *(G-1946)*

3412 Metal Barrels, Drums, Kegs & Pails

B A Stevens .... G 918 695-4362
  Ochelata *(G-5233)*
Custom Manufacturing Inc .... E 405 692-6311
  Oklahoma City *(G-5874)*
Davco Manufacturing .... F 918 535-2360
  Ochelata *(G-5234)*
Keymiaee Aero-Tech Inc .... F 405 235-5010
  Oklahoma City *(G-6409)*
Mobile Mini Inc .... F 918 582-5857
  Tulsa *(G-10288)*
Pratt Industries USA Inc .... B 405 787-3500
  Oklahoma City *(G-6874)*

3421 Cutlery

Cmg Operations LLC .... G 580 477-0880
  Altus *(G-150)*
Cmg Operations LLC .... G 580 353-2835
  Lawton *(G-3908)*
EDS Inc .... G 405 416-6700
  Oklahoma City *(G-6012)*
Eppingers .... G 580 248-1442
  Lawton *(G-3922)*
Every Nook & Cranny .... G 580 332-3899
  Ada *(G-34)*
Johns Professional Sharpening .... G 405 313-7027
  Yukon *(G-11738)*
Ktak Corporation .... G 918 492-0505
  Tulsa *(G-10105)*
Mike Latham .... G 580 622-6980
  Sulphur *(G-8838)*
Solo Cup Operating Corporation .... C 580 436-1500
  Ada *(G-90)*
Wyndham Tulsa .... G 918 627-5000
  Tulsa *(G-11163)*

3423 Hand & Edge Tools

Chiseled In Stone .... Q 918 813-5409
  Tulsa *(G-9419)*
Evans Tool Co Inc .... G 580 889-5770
  Atoka *(G-412)*
Federal Metals Inc .... F 918 838-1725
  Tulsa *(G-9731)*
▲ Five Star Equipment LLC .... F 918 637-0200
  Ramona *(G-8045)*
Helton Custom Knives LLC .... G 918 230-1773
  Claremore *(G-1633)*
▲ Hisco Inc .... F 405 524-2700
  Oklahoma City *(G-6254)*
J R Lukeman & Associates Inc .... G 405 842-6548
  Oklahoma City *(G-6338)*
JJ Perodeau Gunmaker Inc .... F 580 747-1804
  Sand Springs *(G-8195)*
▲ M W Bevins Co .... E 918 627-1273
  Tulsa *(G-10190)*
Rd Roofing and Carpentry .... G 580 341-0607
  Ada *(G-80)*
◆ Red Devil Incorporated .... F 918 585-8111
  Tulsa *(G-10629)*
Red Devil Incorporated .... G 918 825-5744
  Pryor *(G-7989)*
Sarduccis Metal Works Inc .... G 918 694-3466
  Tulsa *(G-10708)*
William L Riggs Company Inc .... G 918 437-3245
  Tulsa *(G-11125)*
William Reed .... G 918 912-8153
  Oklahoma City *(G-5324)*
Zoop-Corp .... G 405 239-8184
  Oklahoma City *(G-7489)*

3425 Hand Saws & Saw Blades

▲ H S Boyd Company Inc .... F 918 835-9359
  Tulsa *(G-9876)*
Saw Swan Service Inc .... G 918 249-3821
  Broken Arrow *(G-1043)*

3429 Hardware, NEC

Archer Technologies Intl Inc .... G 405 306-3220
  Shawnee *(G-8428)*
Beekmann Enterprises .... G 918 272-7197
  Owasso *(G-7547)*
Bert Parsons 2nd Gen Lcksmth L ..... G 918 794-7131
  Tulsa *(G-9286)*
▼ Campbell Specialty Co Inc .... F 918 756-3640
  Okmulgee *(G-7497)*
Cole Industrial Services Inc .... G 580 775-0949
  Caddo *(G-1232)*
Cook Machine Company .... E 580 252-1699
  Duncan *(G-2099)*
Crosby Group LLC .... B 918 834-4611
  Tulsa *(G-9509)*
◆ Crosby Group LLC .... F 918 834-4611
  Tulsa *(G-9510)*
Crosby Worldwide Limited .... F 918 834-4611
  Tulsa *(G-9512)*
D R Topping Saddlery .... G 918 273-2812
  Nowata *(G-5212)*
Dynamic Machine .... G 918 791-1114
  Grove *(G-3266)*
◆ Fki Industries Inc .... G 918 834-4611
  Tulsa *(G-9752)*
Genes Customized Tags & EMB .... G 580 225-8247
  Elk City *(G-2820)*
Get A Grip Inc .... G 405 286-4778
  Oklahoma City *(G-6148)*
H-V Manufacturing Company .... G 918 756-9620
  Okmulgee *(G-7509)*
Hansen Research LLC .... G 405 659-5079
  Norman *(G-5015)*
Hardin Ignition Inc .... G 405 853-4324
  Hennessey *(G-3465)*
▲ Hargrove Manufacturing Corp ...... E 918 241-7537
  Sand Springs *(G-8190)*
Integrted Lock SEC Systems LLC .... G 918 232-3436
  Jenks *(G-3708)*
Johnny Beard Co .... G 918 438-4901
  Tulsa *(G-10056)*
KB Enterprise LLC .... G 580 789-0119
  Ponca City *(G-7843)*
Key Cut Express .... G 405 353-3026
  Mustang *(G-4780)*
Key General Contractors LLC .... G 918 280-8539
  Tulsa *(G-10086)*
Keys N More .... G 405 415-1797
  Oklahoma City *(G-6410)*
Keys N More .... G 405 415-2105
  Oklahoma City *(G-6411)*
Luxe Kitchen & Bath .... G 405 471-5577
  Oklahoma City *(G-6504)*
McClure Furniture Refinishing .... G 918 587-7779
  Tulsa *(G-10230)*
OH Keys .... G 405 529-5202
  Oklahoma City *(G-6716)*
OH Keys .... G 405 378-5674
  Oklahoma City *(G-6717)*
P W Manufacturing Company Inc ..... G 918 652-4981
  Henryetta *(G-3514)*
◆ P-T Coupling Company .... E 580 237-4033
  Enid *(G-3029)*
▲ Parrish Enterprises .... D 580 233-4757
  Enid *(G-3030)*
▲ Parrish Enterprises Ltd .... E 580 237-4033
  Enid *(G-3031)*
▲ Pelco Products Inc .... C 405 340-3434
  Edmond *(G-2565)*
Pelco Products Inc .... G 405 842-6978
  Oklahoma City *(G-6822)*
Petroleum Artifacts Ltd .... G 918 949-6101
  Tulsa *(G-10504)*
Pickard Projects Inc .... G 405 321-7072
  Norman *(G-5115)*
▲ Premiere Lock Co LLC .... E 918 294-8179
  Tulsa *(G-10553)*
Punch-Lok Co .... E 580 233-4757
  Enid *(G-3040)*
▲ Sawyer Manufacturing Company .. E 918 834-2550
  Tulsa *(G-9034)*
Shur-Co LLC .... G 405 262-7600
  El Reno *(G-2757)*
Straitline Inc .... F 405 263-4604
  Lone Grove *(G-4121)*
Straitline Inc .... G 405 263-4604
  Okarche *(G-5253)*
Superior Companies Inc .... D 918 534-0755
  Dewey *(G-2033)*
T D G I .... G 405 275-8041
  Shawnee *(G-8507)*
Taylor & Sons Farms Inc .... G 405 222-0751
  Chickasha *(G-1515)*
Transponder Key .... G 405 757-3199
  Edmond *(G-2652)*
U-Change Lock Industries Inc .... E 405 376-1600
  Mustang *(G-4799)*
United Dynamics Inc .... E 405 275-8041
  Shawnee *(G-8517)*
Wayne Burt Machine .... G 918 786-4415
  Grove *(G-3293)*

34 FABRICATED METAL PRODUCTS, EXCEPT MACHINERY AND TRANSPORTATION EQUIPMENT SIC SECTION

3431 Enameled Iron & Metal Sanitary Ware

Breshears Enterprises Inc ....F 405 236-4523
Oklahoma City *(G-5624)*
Galley LLC ....G 918 794-2700
Bixby *(G-627)*
Quarry ....G 918 534-2120
Dewey *(G-2030)*
Stephen Poorboy ....G 918 373-5073
Chouteau *(G-1571)*

3432 Plumbing Fixture Fittings & Trim, Brass

A & R Plumbing and Mech LLC ....G 405 808-0671
Oklahoma City *(G-5343)*
▲ **D Vontz LLC** ....F 918 622-3600
Tulsa *(G-9540)*
Eaton Aeroquip LLC ....D 405 275-5500
Shawnee *(G-8447)*
Empire Plumbing Contrs LLC ....G 918 320-1427
Grove *(G-3267)*
Ferguson ....G 918 835-4813
Tulsa *(G-9738)*
Ferguson Enterprises LLC ....G 405 945-0107
Oklahoma City *(G-6082)*
H & K Specification & Sls LLC ....F 405 844-7456
Edmond *(G-2450)*
Heatwave Supply Inc ....G 918 333-6363
Bartlesville *(G-491)*
Norman Supply Company ....G 405 692-1191
Oklahoma City *(G-5308)*

3433 Heating Eqpt

Ahc Fabrication Co Inc ....G 918 267-5052
Beggs *(G-548)*
Alfa Laval Inc ....G 918 251-7477
Broken Arrow *(G-824)*
Alfa Lval A Cled Exchngers Inc ....G 918 251-7477
Broken Arrow *(G-825)*
◆ **Alpha Combustion LLC** ....G 918 851-1751
Tulsa *(G-9152)*
American Heating Company Inc ....G 918 246-0700
Sand Springs *(G-8159)*
Callidus Technologies LLC ....D 918 267-4920
Beggs *(G-550)*
Calvin Heaters ....G 918 367-7011
Bristow *(G-772)*
Coen Co Inc ....G 918 234-1800
Tulsa *(G-9465)*
Federal Services LLC ....G 405 239-7301
Oklahoma City *(G-6080)*
Flame Control Inc ....G 405 321-2535
Norman *(G-5001)*
Flameco Industries Inc ....E 918 832-1100
Tulsa *(G-9753)*
▲ **Gasolec America Inc** ....G 918 286-8700
Tulsa *(G-9805)*
Gastech Engineering LLC ....D 918 663-8383
Sapulpa *(G-8274)*
▲ **Hargrove Manufacturing Corp** ....E 918 241-7537
Sand Springs *(G-8190)*
Hotsy of OK Inc ....G 580 234-0608
Enid *(G-2974)*
Morton Manufacturing Co Inc ....G 918 584-0333
Tulsa *(G-10305)*
Preferred Utilities Mfg Corp ....G 203 743-6741
Tulsa *(G-10551)*
Quikwater Inc ....F 918 241-8880
Sand Springs *(G-8217)*
R & R Radiator Co ....G 405 257-3557
Wewoka *(G-11508)*
Site Distribution LLC ....G 918 625-7980
Tulsa *(G-10769)*
◆ **Tulsa Heaters Inc** ....E 918 582-9918
Tulsa *(G-10999)*
Webco Industries Inc ....C 918 241-1086
Sand Springs *(G-8238)*
◆ **Zeeco Inc** ....C 918 258-8551
Broken Arrow *(G-1179)*
▼ **Zeeco Usa LLC** ....E 918 258-8551
Broken Arrow *(G-1180)*

3441 Fabricated Structural Steel

A & J Fabricators Inc ....E 405 352-4120
Minco *(G-4475)*
Abco Steel Inc ....F 918 322-3435
Glenpool *(G-3228)*
Accurate Manufacturing Inc ....E 918 582-2585
Tulsa *(G-9090)*
Ada Iron and Welding LLC ....G 580 332-6694
Ada *(G-6)*
Adventure Manufacturing Inc ....G 405 682-3833
Oklahoma City *(G-5387)*
Afg Acquisition Group LLC ....E 918 683-5683
Muskogee *(G-4644)*
Air Duct Inc ....F 918 445-1196
Tulsa *(G-9119)*
Allison Allison Inc ....G 918 344-1768
Bixby *(G-610)*
American Tank & Cnstr Co ....G 918 254-6292
Tulsa *(G-9173)*
Amron Enterprises LLC ....F 918 224-9222
Sapulpa *(G-8249)*
Apollo Metal Specialties Inc ....F 918 341-7650
Claremore *(G-1583)*
Arbuckle Mountain Tower Corp ....G 580 223-3408
Ardmore *(G-243)*
ARC Rvals Wldg Fabrication LLC ....G 918 577-5066
Muskogee *(G-4649)*
Arcosa Wind Towers Inc ....G 918 560-4911
Tulsa *(G-9206)*
Asc Inc ....E 918 445-0260
Tulsa *(G-9215)*
Associated Stl Fabricators Inc ....E 405 787-5713
Oklahoma City *(G-5278)*
Atlantic Fbrication Design LLC ....G 405 619-7607
Oklahoma City *(G-5485)*
Avery Barron Industires LLC ....E 918 779-6903
Tulsa *(G-9229)*
Aviations Simulations Inc ....G 918 251-6880
Broken Arrow *(G-837)*
B & W Manufacturing Co Ltd ....F 918 248-5201
Tulsa *(G-8989)*
B&M Metalworks Inc ....G 918 266-5103
Catoosa *(G-1300)*
Basden Steel-Oklahoma LLC ....E 918 341-9468
Claremore *(G-1593)*
Bendco Corp ....F 918 583-1566
Tulsa *(G-9281)*
Bennett Steel Inc ....C 918 227-2564
Sapulpa *(G-8252)*
Bethesda Boys Ranch ....F 918 827-6409
Mounds *(G-4610)*
Bills Welding Coop LLC ....G 405 370-6383
Oklahoma City *(G-5567)*
Bixby Fabco Inc ....F 918 366-3446
Bixby *(G-615)*
Blm Equipment & Mfg Co Inc ....F 918 266-5282
Catoosa *(G-1304)*
▲ **Boardman LLC** ....D 405 634-5434
Oklahoma City *(G-5598)*
▼ **Bonavista Technologies Inc** ....G 918 250-3435
Tulsa *(G-9318)*
Brooks Custom Fabrication ....G 918 836-2556
Tulsa *(G-9341)*
Building Concepts Ltd ....G 405 324-5100
Oklahoma City *(G-5642)*
Butcher & Sons Steel Inds ....G 918 434-5276
Salina *(G-8133)*
By-Weld Industries Inc ....F 918 366-4850
Bixby *(G-616)*
Bynum & Company Inc ....F 580 265-7747
Stonewall *(G-8798)*
Cairns Manufacturing Inc ....G 405 947-1350
Oklahoma City *(G-5670)*
Cheshire Portable Welding ....G 405 373-4669
Piedmont *(G-7757)*
Cheyenne Innovations Inc ....G 918 793-7521
Shidler *(G-8526)*
Choctaw Mfg & Dev Corp ....D 580 326-8365
Hugo *(G-3607)*
Choctaw Mfg & Dev Corp ....D 580 326-8365
Atoka *(G-403)*
Choctaw Mfg Def Contrs Inc ....F 580 326-8365
Hugo *(G-3608)*
Choctaw Mfg Def Contrs Inc ....G 580 298-2203
Antlers *(G-215)*
Choctaw Mfg Def Contrs Inc ....G 918 426-2871
McAlester *(G-4286)*
Cnc Metal Shape Cnstr LLC ....F 405 605-5500
Oklahoma City *(G-5794)*
Coanda Company LLC ....G 214 601-4972
Norman *(G-4962)*
Connie Pirple ....G 405 375-4468
Kingfisher *(G-3792)*
Consoldted Fbrction Cnstructor ....G 918 224-3500
Tulsa *(G-8999)*
Creative Ornamental Inc ....G 918 540-1600
Miami *(G-4393)*
Cushing Truss Manufacturing ....F 918 387-2080
Yale *(G-11683)*
Custom Design Fabrication LLC ....G 918 773-5691
Vian *(G-11238)*
Custom Manufacturing Inc ....E 405 692-6311
Oklahoma City *(G-5874)*
D & Z Metal Fabrication ....G 918 456-3841
Welling *(G-11466)*
D and N Fabrication ....G 918 224-4400
Sapulpa *(G-8264)*
D Diamond Enterprises Inc ....G 918 827-4727
Mounds *(G-4612)*
D-K Metal Form Company Inc ....G 580 228-3516
Waurika *(G-11362)*
Dale Miller Group LLC ....G 580 353-4600
Lawton *(G-3917)*
Davco Fab Inc ....E 918 757-2504
Jennings *(G-3739)*
DC Exteriors & More LLC ....G 918 231-7303
Warner *(G-11307)*
Diamondback Steel Company Inc ....E 918 686-6340
Muskogee *(G-4667)*
Dmi International Inc ....G 918 438-2213
Tulsa *(G-9589)*
Doug Lee Ingenuity LLC ....G 918 542-4686
Miami *(G-4399)*
Eagleclaw Fabrication ....D 918 691-2519
Tulsa *(G-9630)*
Eastpointe Manufacturing Corp ....E 918 683-2169
Muskogee *(G-4671)*
Eco Incorporated ....G 918 258-5002
Broken Arrow *(G-894)*
Eco 2007 LLC ....G 918 258-5002
Broken Arrow *(G-895)*
Economasters LLC ....F 918 241-8244
Tulsa *(G-9640)*
Elite Manufacturing LLC ....G 918 266-1077
Catoosa *(G-1317)*
Enterprise Manufacturing LLC ....G 918 438-4455
Tulsa *(G-9691)*
Equus Metals Inc ....E 918 834-9872
Tulsa *(G-9696)*
◆ **Ernest Wiemann Iron Works** ....E 918 592-1700
Tulsa *(G-9698)*
Express Metal Fabricators LLC ....B 918 622-1420
Locust Grove *(G-4106)*
▲ **Express Metal Fabricators Inc** ....D 918 783-5129
Big Cabin *(G-603)*
EZ Carrier LLC ....G 918 827-7876
Mounds *(G-4615)*
Fabricating Specialists Inc ....F 405 476-1959
Oklahoma City *(G-6068)*
Fabrico Inc ....G 918 274-9329
Owasso *(G-7565)*
Fammco Mfg Co Inc ....G 918 437-0456
Tulsa *(G-9727)*
Fat & Happy Services Inc ....G 405 834-5782
Oklahoma City *(G-6078)*
Federal Metals Inc ....F 918 838-1725
Tulsa *(G-9731)*
Fitzgerald &SOns Steel LLC ....F 918 453-3369
Tahlequah *(G-8865)*
Five Star Steel Inc ....E 405 787-7620
Oklahoma City *(G-6086)*
Forster & Son Inc ....G 580 332-6020
Ada *(G-36)*
Friends Welding ....G 918 482-1544
Broken Arrow *(G-1127)*
Ftdm Investments Llc ....D 918 598-3430
Locust Grove *(G-4107)*
G Highfill ....G 405 598-5576
Tecumseh *(G-8915)*
G&E Power LLC ....E 918 396-2899
Skiatook *(G-8544)*
▲ **General Manufacturer Inc** ....F 918 756-3067
Okmulgee *(G-7504)*
Gerdau Ameristeel US Inc ....F 405 677-9792
Oklahoma City *(G-6147)*
Gerdau Ameristeel US Inc ....F 918 682-2600
Muskogee *(G-4679)*
Gerdau Ameristeel US Inc ....E 918 682-7806
Muskogee *(G-4680)*
Grating Company LLC ....G 918 834-8100
Tulsa *(G-9848)*
Great Plains Rebar LLC ....F 405 576-3270
Oklahoma City *(G-6183)*
Greg Butcher ....G 918 434-6892
Salina *(G-8134)*
H & H Cnstr Met Fbrication Inc ....E 405 701-1075
Norman *(G-5013)*
H & H Ornamental Iron ....G 405 634-0646
Oklahoma City *(G-6196)*

H K & S Iron Co.....E..... 405 745-2761
Oklahoma City (G-6198)
Hackney Ladish Inc.....D..... 580 237-4212
Enid (G-2967)
High Pointe Construction.....G..... 405 685-8303
Oklahoma City (G-6247)
Honeycutt Contruction Inc.....F..... 918 825-6070
Pryor (G-7969)
Insight Technologies Inc.....F..... 580 933-4109
Valliant (G-11226)
▼ Integrated Tower Systems Inc.....E..... 918 749-8535
Tulsa (G-9998)
J & D Fabricators Inc.....F..... 405 356-2243
Wellston (G-11473)
▲ J & G Steel Corporation.....C..... 918 227-3131
Sapulpa (G-8280)
J R Lukeman & Associates Inc.....G..... 405 842-6548
Oklahoma City (G-6338)
JB Metal Fabrication.....G..... 918 266-3228
Catoosa (G-1324)
Jeffery W Matlock.....G..... 918 367-9828
Bristow (G-782)
Jenco Fabricators Inc.....E..... 918 234-3364
Tulsa (G-10034)
Jerrys Dock Construction Inc.....F..... 918 256-3390
Bernice (G-567)
Johnston Test Cell Group LLC.....G..... 405 604-2804
Oklahoma City (G-6378)
Kenneth Petermann.....G..... 405 372-0111
Stillwater (G-8710)
Keymiaee Aero-Tech Inc.....F..... 405 235-5010
Oklahoma City (G-6409)
Landa Mobile Systems LLC.....G..... 571 272-3350
Tulsa (G-10121)
Laughing Water Enterprises LLC.....G..... 918 584-2080
Tulsa (G-10136)
Lbr Smith LLC.....G..... 405 601-7051
Oklahoma City (G-6458)
Lofland Co.....G..... 405 631-9555
Oklahoma City (G-6488)
Longreach Steel Inc.....F..... 405 598-5691
Tecumseh (G-8922)
M A C Manufacturing Inc.....G..... 405 527-8270
Purcell (G-8012)
Maddens Portable Buildings.....E..... 405 799-4989
Norman (G-5062)
Manufacturing Jack LLC Ram.....D..... 580 332-6694
Ada (G-63)
Martin Manufacturing Inc.....E..... 918 583-1191
Sapulpa (G-8287)
▲ Mertz Manufacturing Inc.....B..... 580 762-5646
Ponca City (G-7849)
Metal Building Services.....G..... 580 657-3339
Ardmore (G-330)
Metal Fab Inc.....G..... 580 762-2421
Ponca City (G-7850)
Metalfab LLC.....G..... 918 718-4040
Tahlequah (G-8873)
Metro Mechanical Supply Inc.....F..... 918 622-2288
Tulsa (G-10251)
Metro Mechanical Supply LLC.....E..... 918 622-2288
Tulsa (G-10252)
Midstate Mfg & Mktg Inc.....E..... 405 751-6227
Oklahoma City (G-6598)
Miller Welding & Supply.....G..... 580 492-5464
Lawton (G-3970)
Mitchco Fabrication Inc.....G..... 580 762-0256
Ponca City (G-7853)
Mobile Mini Inc.....F..... 918 582-5857
Tulsa (G-10288)
Moore Iron & Steel Corp.....D..... 918 387-2639
Yale (G-11686)
Morton Buildings Inc.....E..... 918 683-6668
Muskogee (G-4715)
Neilson Manufacturing Inc.....F..... 918 587-5548
Tulsa (G-10331)
Neisen Family LLC.....E..... 580 762-2421
Ponca City (G-7858)
OK Fabricators LLC.....E..... 918 224-3977
Tulsa (G-9023)
OK Machine and Mfg Co Inc.....E..... 918 838-1300
Tulsa (G-10390)
Oklahoma City Steel LLC.....G..... 405 235-2300
Oklahoma City (G-6743)
Oklahoma Post Tension Inc.....F..... 918 627-6013
Tulsa (G-10405)
Old World Iron Inc.....G..... 918 445-3063
Tulsa (G-10411)
▲ Orizon Arstrctures - Grove Inc.....D..... 918 786-9094
Grove (G-3284)
Ozark Steel LLC.....E..... 918 438-4330
Tulsa (G-10450)
▲ P & M Industries Inc.....E..... 918 660-0055
Tulsa (G-10451)
Pattison Metal Fab Inc.....E..... 918 251-9967
Broken Arrow (G-1000)
Pelco Structural LLC.....D..... 918 283-4004
Claremore (G-1668)
Phoenix Fabworx LLC.....G..... 918 429-8388
Quinton (G-8038)
Powder Coating of Muskogee.....G..... 918 681-4494
Muskogee (G-4736)
Power Lift Fndtn RPR OK Inc.....E..... 580 332-8282
Ada (G-75)
Precision Fabricators Inc.....F..... 918 428-7600
Tulsa (G-10544)
Premier Fabricators LLC.....G..... 580 251-9525
Duncan (G-2165)
Premier Plant Services LLC.....F..... 918 227-3131
Sapulpa (G-8300)
Premier Plant Services LLC.....G..... 918 227-1680
Sapulpa (G-8301)
Premier Steel Services LLC.....E..... 918 227-0110
Glenpool (G-3241)
Professional Fabricators Inc.....E..... 918 388-1090
Tulsa (G-10568)
Professional Metal Works Inc.....G..... 580 584-7890
Idabel (G-3644)
Pruitt Company of Ada Inc.....E..... 580 332-3523
Ada (G-78)
R&R Roustabout Services LLC.....E..... 580 883-4647
Ringwood (G-8090)
Railroad Sgnling Solutions Inc.....G..... 918 973-1888
Broken Arrow (G-1020)
Railroad Yard Inc.....E..... 405 377-8763
Stillwater (G-8743)
Rise Manufacturing LLC.....E..... 918 994-6240
Broken Arrow (G-1032)
River Bend Industries LLC.....C..... 405 703-2758
Blanchard (G-734)
Robert Mrrson Autocad Svcs LLC.....G..... 918 257-4622
Afton (G-120)
Rooks Fabrication LLC.....F..... 918 447-1990
Tulsa (G-10669)
Rt Manufacturing LLC.....F..... 405 222-7180
Chickasha (G-1504)
▲ S & T Mfg Co.....E..... 918 234-4151
Tulsa (G-10684)
S&S Fabrication.....G..... 918 447-0447
Tulsa (G-9032)
Safeco Manufacturing Inc.....F..... 918 455-0100
Broken Arrow (G-1160)
▲ Sawyer Manufacturing Company.....E..... 918 834-2550
Tulsa (G-9034)
Selman Wldg & Fabrication LLC.....G..... 580 330-0887
Weatherford (G-11440)
Shawnee Fabricators Inc.....E..... 405 275-8264
Shawnee (G-8494)
Shawnee Steel Company.....E..... 405 919-8582
Shawnee (G-8497)
Shelby Steel Service.....G..... 918 234-3098
Tulsa (G-10741)
Sooner Steel and Truss LLC.....G..... 405 232-5542
Oklahoma City (G-7167)
Source Fabrication LLC.....G..... 580 762-4114
Ponca City (G-7877)
Southwest Fabricators Inc.....F..... 580 326-3589
Hugo (G-3621)
Specialty Sales Associates.....G..... 405 495-1136
Chandler (G-1388)
Steel Thinking Inc.....F..... 405 485-2204
Washington (G-11337)
Steelfab Texas Inc.....E..... 972 562-7720
Durant (G-2262)
Storm SF Ngrnd Trnd Shltrs NC.....D..... 405 606-2563
Oklahoma City (G-7213)
Studs Unlimited LLC.....G..... 214 683-8012
Oklahoma City (G-7218)
Sufrank Corporation.....E..... 580 353-4600
Lawton (G-4006)
Supreme Mch & Stl Fabrication.....F..... 918 387-2036
Yale (G-11687)
Sweeper Metal Fabricators Corp.....E..... 918 352-9180
Drumright (G-2073)
T & D Fabrication Inc.....E..... 918 352-8031
Drumright (G-2074)
T Rowe Pipe LLC.....E..... 580 765-1500
Ponca City (G-7881)
Thorpe Plant Services Inc.....G..... 918 455-8928
Tulsa (G-10937)
Tj Services LLC.....G..... 405 596-5124
Oklahoma City (G-7295)
Tower Components Inc.....E..... 918 379-0769
Catoosa (G-1357)
Tri Red LLC.....E..... 580 476-2551
Rush Springs (G-8128)
Tulsa Metal Fab Inc.....F..... 918 451-7150
Broken Arrow (G-1175)
Tulsa Steel Mfg Company Inc.....E..... 918 227-0110
Tulsa (G-9046)
United Contracting Svcs Inc.....C..... 918 551-7659
Tulsa (G-11040)
United Holdings LLC.....G..... 405 947-3321
Oklahoma City (G-7369)
V&S Schuler Tubular Pdts LLC.....B..... 918 687-7701
Muskogee (G-4758)
Valmont Industries Inc.....D..... 918 266-2800
Claremore (G-1700)
Valmont Industries Inc.....B..... 918 583-5881
Tulsa (G-11065)
Vann Metal Products Inc.....G..... 918 341-0469
Claremore (G-1701)
Vernon Manufacturing Company.....G..... 918 224-4068
Tulsa (G-9048)
W & W Asco Steel LLC.....G..... 405 235-3621
Oklahoma City (G-7407)
W&W Steel Erectors LLC.....G..... 405 235-3621
Oklahoma City (G-7412)
W&W-Afco Steel LLC.....B..... 405 235-3621
Oklahoma City (G-7413)
Wayne Burt Machine.....G..... 918 786-4415
Grove (G-3293)
Wayne Winkler.....G..... 918 689-9745
Eufaula (G-3117)
Wedlake Fabricating Inc.....E..... 918 428-1641
Tulsa (G-11103)
Weibee Steel Inc.....F..... 405 360-7055
Norman (G-5198)
Weldco Mfg.....G..... 580 296-1585
Colbert (G-1788)
Werco Aviation Inc.....G..... 918 251-6880
Broken Arrow (G-1094)
Werco Manufacturing Inc.....E..... 918 251-6880
Broken Arrow (G-1095)
Western Frontier LLC.....E..... 918 760-4977
Locust Grove (G-4113)
Willie Dewayne Brown.....F..... 918 482-1115
Haskell (G-3403)
▲ Worldwide Steel Works Inc.....E..... 918 825-4545
Pryor (G-8000)
Wwsc Holdings LLC.....F..... 405 235-3621
Oklahoma City (G-7476)
York Metal Fabricators Inc.....E..... 405 528-7495
Oklahoma City (G-7481)
Zkc Welding.....F..... 580 220-7685
Ardmore (G-384)

3442 Metal Doors, Sash, Frames, Molding & Trim

Amarillo Chittom Airslo.....E..... 918 585-5638
Tulsa (G-9160)
Angel Ornamental Iron Works.....G..... 918 584-8726
Tulsa (G-9191)
Boomer Blinds & Shutters LLC.....G..... 918 968-2579
Stroud (G-8808)
Charles ODell.....G..... 405 745-3353
Mustang (G-4768)
Classic Shutters.....G..... 918 234-0657
Tulsa (G-9442)
Consolidated Builders Supply.....E..... 405 631-3033
Oklahoma City (G-5821)
Custom Shutters Inc.....G..... 918 924-3489
Broken Arrow (G-882)
D & M Steel Manufacturing.....G..... 405 631-5027
Oklahoma City (G-5887)
Don Young Company Incorporated.....G..... 405 947-2000
Oklahoma City (G-5966)
Dormakaba USA Inc.....G..... 405 232-6761
Oklahoma City (G-5969)
Dunlap Manufacturing Co Inc.....E..... 918 838-1383
Tulsa (G-9612)
Dynomite Custom Screens LLC.....G..... 844 396-6648
Lawton (G-3921)
Enid Insulation & Siding Inc.....G..... 580 237-5317
Enid (G-2953)
Eseco-Speedmaster.....D..... 918 225-1266
Cushing (G-1933)
Ets-Lindgren Inc.....E..... 580 434-7490
Durant (G-2230)

S I C

34 FABRICATED METAL PRODUCTS, EXCEPT MACHINERY AND TRANSPORTATION EQUIPMENT

Hirsch3667 Corp ....D....... 580 323-6966
  Clinton (G-1752)
Hughes Lumber Company ....G....... 918 266-9100
  Catoosa (G-1322)
J&S Overhead Door & Gate LLC ....G....... 405 249-0779
  Choctaw (G-1546)
Johndrow Home Improvement ....G....... 580 762-4000
  Ponca City (G-7840)
Lawton Window Co Inc ....G....... 580 353-4655
  Lawton (G-3962)
Louver & Equipment Mfrs Inc ....F....... 918 272-5600
  Owasso (G-7588)
◆ M-D Building Products Inc ....B....... 405 528-4411
  Oklahoma City (G-6510)
Maro International Corp ....G....... 918 836-7749
  Tulsa (G-10215)
▲ Mid-America Door Company ....D....... 580 765-9994
  Ponca City (G-7852)
▲ Mill Creek Lumber & Supply Co ....G....... 918 794-3600
  Tulsa (G-10279)
Mill Creek Lumber & Supply Co ....D....... 405 947-7227
  Oklahoma City (G-6609)
Moldman Kansas City ....G....... 918 921-6823
  Tulsa (G-10296)
Plantation Shutter Co ....G....... 817 703-1091
  Broken Arrow (G-1008)
Precision Shelters ....F....... 405 936-0900
  Oklahoma City (G-6883)
Security Metal Products Corp ....G....... 580 323-6966
  Clinton (G-1768)
Senox Corporation ....G....... 405 948-7464
  Oklahoma City (G-7109)
Smart Shelters Inc ....F....... 405 702-7775
  Oklahoma City (G-7151)
Southwest Shutter Co ....G....... 405 344-6406
  Purcell (G-8020)
Spade Leasing Inc ....C....... 580 653-2171
  Springer (G-8626)
Speedmaster Inc ....D....... 918 225-1266
  Cushing (G-1961)
Sweeper Metal Fabricators Corp ....E....... 918 352-9180
  Drumright (G-2073)
Taylor Storm Shelters LLC ....G....... 405 372-8130
  Stillwater (G-8765)
Titan Overhead Door LLC ....G....... 918 606-0094
  Talala (G-8904)
Vanover Metal Building Sls Inc ....F....... 918 253-6030
  Spavinaw (G-8593)
Wendell Hicks Construction ....G....... 918 520-9128
  Nowata (G-5232)

3443 Fabricated Plate Work

A R T T Corp ....G....... 405 681-0749
  Oklahoma City (G-5348)
Aerocore X LLC ....G....... 405 669-8655
  Del City (G-1994)
Affordable Dumpster OK LLC ....G....... 405 535-6644
  Oklahoma City (G-5395)
▲ Air Power Systems Co LLC ....E....... 918 622-5600
  Tulsa (G-9121)
Air-X-Hemphill LLC ....G....... 918 283-9220
  Claremore (G-1578)
Air-X-Hemphill LLC ....G....... 918 712-8268
  Tulsa (G-9123)
Airlock Pool Covers Inc ....G....... 405 373-4040
  Piedmont (G-7753)
Alfa Laval Inc ....G....... 918 251-7477
  Broken Arrow (G-823)
Amarillo Chittom Airslo ....E....... 918 585-5638
  Tulsa (G-9160)
Amercool Manufacturing Co Inc ....D....... 918 445-5366
  Tulsa (G-9162)
American Tank & Cnstr Co ....G....... 918 254-6292
  Tulsa (G-9173)
Ameripump Mfg LLC ....G....... 918 438-2953
  Tulsa (G-9178)
Arcrite Manufacturing LLC ....E....... 580 216-1050
  Woodward (G-11555)
▲ Arrow Engine Company ....D....... 918 583-5711
  Tulsa (G-9211)
AST Storage LLC ....F....... 918 208-0100
  Jay (G-3678)
Aw Specialties LLC ....G....... 918 798-9272
  Claremore (G-1584)
◆ Axh Air-Coolers LLC ....G....... 918 283-9200
  Claremore (G-1585)
Baileys Welding & Machine LLC ....F....... 405 224-6611
  Chickasha (G-1438)
Balco Inc ....E....... 316 945-9328
  Oklahoma City (G-5519)

Berry Holdings LP ....G....... 918 582-3461
  Tulsa (G-9285)
Big River Sales Inc ....G....... 580 657-4950
  Lone Grove (G-4115)
Blm Equipment & Mfg Co Inc ....F....... 918 266-5282
  Catoosa (G-1304)
Brown Minneapolis Tank ....G....... 918 224-2358
  Tulsa (G-8993)
Butner Brothers LLC ....G....... 405 321-2322
  Norman (G-4949)
Bynum & Company Inc ....F....... 580 265-7747
  Stonewall (G-8798)
Canadian Town of Inc ....G....... 918 339-2517
  Canadian (G-1261)
▼ Chart Cooler Service Co Inc ....D....... 918 834-0002
  Tulsa (G-9405)
Chart Industries Inc ....G....... 918 621-5246
  Tulsa (G-9406)
Chickasaw Energy Solutions LLC ....E....... 580 276-3306
  Marietta (G-4202)
Considilated Fabrications ....G....... 918 224-3563
  Tulsa (G-8997)
Cooling Products Inc ....E....... 918 251-8588
  Broken Arrow (G-878)
Cundiff Custom Fabrication LLC ....G....... 405 372-8204
  Stillwater (G-8673)
▼ Cust-O-Fab LLC ....E....... 918 245-6685
  Sand Springs (G-8174)
Cust-O-Fab Specialty Svcs LLC ....D....... 918 245-6685
  Sand Springs (G-8175)
Custom Manufacturing Inc ....E....... 405 692-6311
  Oklahoma City (G-5874)
▲ Custom Seating Incorporated ....C....... 918 682-4400
  Muskogee (G-4666)
D-K Metal Form Company Inc ....G....... 580 228-3516
  Waurika (G-11362)
Davco Fab Inc ....E....... 918 757-2504
  Jennings (G-3739)
Dragon ....G....... 580 653-2171
  Springer (G-8623)
Driploc Inc ....F....... 405 632-5810
  Oklahoma City (G-5982)
Dumpster Service Plus ....G....... 405 417-3707
  Oklahoma City (G-5986)
▼ E-Tech Inc ....E....... 918 665-1930
  Broken Arrow (G-1124)
Eco Incorporated ....G....... 918 258-5002
  Broken Arrow (G-894)
Eco 2007 LLC ....G....... 918 258-5002
  Broken Arrow (G-895)
El Dorado Manufacturing Co LLC ....G....... 580 318-2313
  Eldorado (G-2773)
Ellen Broach CPA ....G....... 918 665-7773
  Tulsa (G-9658)
▲ Ellis Construction Spc LLC ....E....... 405 848-4676
  Oklahoma City (G-6026)
Enerex Inc ....G....... 918 258-3573
  Broken Arrow (G-899)
Enerfin Inc ....E....... 918 258-3571
  Broken Arrow (G-900)
▲ Express Metal Fabricators Inc ....D....... 918 783-5129
  Big Cabin (G-603)
Extended Fin ....G....... 918 827-4044
  Mounds (G-4614)
▲ F C Ziegler Co ....E....... 918 587-7639
  Tulsa (G-9721)
Fab Seal Industrial Liners Inc ....F....... 405 878-0166
  Shawnee (G-8449)
▼ Fabsco Shell and Tube LLC ....D....... 918 224-7550
  Sapulpa (G-8271)
Fabwell Corporation ....E....... 918 224-9060
  Sapulpa (G-8272)
Fin Fab Incorporated ....G....... 918 227-1866
  Tulsa (G-9006)
◆ Fin-X Inc ....E....... 918 272-9546
  Owasso (G-7569)
▼ G C Broach Company ....D....... 918 627-9632
  Tulsa (G-9790)
G C Broach Company ....D....... 918 627-9632
  Tulsa (G-9791)
Genesis Metal Corporation ....F....... 918 267-5901
  Beggs (G-557)
Global Flow Products LLC ....G....... 866 267-1379
  Broken Arrow (G-919)
Global Industrial Inc ....G....... 918 266-5656
  Tulsa (G-9831)
Harsco Corporation ....E....... 918 619-8000
  Tulsa (G-9898)
Harsco Corporation ....E....... 918 619-8000
  Tulsa (G-9899)

Harsco Industrial Hammco LLC ....D....... 918 619-8000
  Tulsa (G-9900)
Harwell Industries ....G....... 405 948-7775
  Oklahoma City (G-6221)
Heartland Tank Services ....G....... 800 774-3230
  Oklahoma City (G-6234)
▼ Heat Transfer Equipment Co ....C....... 918 836-8721
  Tulsa (G-9907)
Heater Specialists LLC ....E....... 918 835-3126
  Tulsa (G-9910)
Heater Specialists LLC ....E....... 918 476-8670
  Chouteau (G-1564)
◆ Heater Specialists LLC ....D....... 918 835-3126
  Tulsa (G-9909)
Hill Metal Inc ....G....... 405 375-6284
  Kingfisher (G-3801)
Hill Steel Corporation ....E....... 918 336-2430
  Bartlesville (G-494)
Hmt LLC ....G....... 580 363-8800
  Blackwell (G-683)
◆ Hughes-Anderson Heat Exchanger .C....... 918 836-1681
  Tulsa (G-9957)
▲ Husky Portable Containment Co .....E....... 918 333-2000
  Bartlesville (G-496)
Hydro-Link Containment LLC ....G....... 580 889-4701
  Atoka (G-415)
▲ JC Fab LLC ....F....... 580 920-0878
  Durant (G-2240)
John Crane Inc ....D....... 918 664-5156
  Tulsa (G-10049)
Johnson Wldg & Fabrication LLC ....G....... 405 474-3541
  Tuttle (G-11205)
Kelvion Inc ....E....... 918 416-9058
  Catoosa (G-1326)
◆ Kelvion Inc ....C....... 918 266-9200
  Catoosa (G-1327)
▲ Koax Corp ....D....... 405 235-7178
  Oklahoma City (G-6431)
Lewis Industries Corp ....E....... 918 371-2596
  Collinsville (G-1815)
◆ Linde Engineering N Amer LLC .....C....... 918 477-1424
  Tulsa (G-10164)
Los Angeles Boiler Works Inc ....E....... 580 363-1312
  Blackwell (G-688)
Luxfer-GTM Technologies LLC ....F....... 918 439-4248
  Catoosa (G-1335)
M J & H Fabrication Inc ....F....... 580 749-5339
  Ponca City (G-7847)
Madden Steel Buildings Lawton ....G....... 580 357-1699
  Lawton (G-3968)
Matrix Service Inc ....G....... 918 425-3106
  Catoosa (G-1339)
Metal Fab Inc ....G....... 580 762-2421
  Ponca City (G-7850)
Metallic Works Inc ....G....... 918 527-6477
  Tulsa (G-10248)
Metro Mechanical Supply Inc ....F....... 918 622-2288
  Tulsa (G-10251)
Midco Fabricators Inc ....E....... 405 282-6667
  Guthrie (G-3324)
Mogar Industries ....G....... 918 445-3747
  Tulsa (G-10294)
Mountain Top Machine Inc ....G....... 918 787-5510
  Jay (G-3683)
Msc Inc ....G....... 918 425-4996
  Tulsa (G-10309)
N E O Fabrication L L C ....E....... 918 541-9203
  Miami (G-4422)
Nixon Materials Company ....G....... 580 621-3297
  Freedom (G-3208)
Okc Dumpsters Inc ....G....... 405 640-4345
  Edmond (G-2548)
Old World Iron Inc ....G....... 918 445-3063
  Tulsa (G-10411)
▲ Parker Hannifin Corporation ....F....... 918 652-7364
  Henryetta (G-3515)
Permian Tank & Mfg Inc ....E....... 405 295-2525
  El Reno (G-2747)
Phelps Machine & Fabrication ....F....... 580 662-2465
  Ringling (G-8081)
Platinum Arch Mfg & Cnstr LLC ....F....... 316 573-6814
  Stillwater (G-8739)
Prescor LLC ....G....... 918 224-6626
  Tulsa (G-9027)
Pro-Fab Industries Inc ....G....... 918 865-7590
  Mannford (G-4190)
Process Equipment Mfg Co ....G....... 817 710-2826
  Claremore (G-1675)
R & R Engineering Co Inc ....E....... 918 252-2571
  Broken Arrow (G-1018)

SIC SECTION 34 FABRICATED METAL PRODUCTS, EXCEPT MACHINERY AND TRANSPORTATION EQUIPMENT

Reading Equipment & Dist LLC............E....... 918 283-2999
Claremore *(G-1679)*
Reece-Ats Holding LLC............E....... 918 225-1010
Cushing *(G-1954)*
Rise Manufacturing LLC............E....... 918 994-6240
Broken Arrow *(G-1032)*
Royalty Fabrication LLC............G....... 405 257-6654
Wewoka *(G-11510)*
Ruby Industrial Tech LLC............G....... 580 223-9301
Ardmore *(G-352)*
Safeco Manufacturing Inc............F....... 918 455-0100
Broken Arrow *(G-1160)*
▲ Sawyer Manufacturing Company.....E....... 918 834-2550
Tulsa *(G-9034)*
Scrap Management Oklahoma Inc........F....... 405 677-7000
Oklahoma City *(G-7100)*
Seal Support Systems Inc............F....... 918 258-6484
Broken Arrow *(G-1046)*
Service Tech Coolg Towers LLC............F....... 405 222-0722
Chickasha *(G-1508)*
Sharp Metal Fabricators Inc............F....... 405 899-4849
Noble *(G-4891)*
Shelton Sanitation............G....... 918 469-3498
Kinta *(G-3836)*
Sierra Technologies Inc............F....... 918 445-1090
Tulsa *(G-10754)*
▼ Smithco Engineering Inc............E....... 918 446-4406
Tulsa *(G-10780)*
▲ Southwest Filter Company............G....... 918 835-1179
Tulsa *(G-10807)*
Southwest Filter Company............G....... 918 835-1179
Tulsa *(G-10808)*
◆ SPX Heat Transfer LLC............C....... 918 234-6000
Tulsa *(G-10827)*
Steel Creek Manufacturing LLC............G....... 918 698-3318
Tulsa *(G-10843)*
▼ Steeltek Inc............D....... 918 446-4001
Tulsa *(G-10844)*
Sufrank Corporation............E....... 580 353-4600
Lawton *(G-4006)*
Susan L Chung Chirprtr............G....... 405 773-8225
Oklahoma City *(G-7233)*
Tank Specialties Inc............F....... 918 599-8111
Tulsa *(G-10898)*
▼ Technotherm Corporation............E....... 918 446-1533
Tulsa *(G-9042)*
Tek Fins Inc............F....... 918 747-7447
Tulsa *(G-9043)*
Titan Fuel Systems LLC............G....... 405 788-2412
Norman *(G-5174)*
True Turn of Tulsa LLC............F....... 918 224-5040
Tulsa *(G-10980)*
Tsi-Enquip Inc............E....... 918 599-8111
Tulsa *(G-10983)*
Tulsa Pressure Vessels LLC............F....... 918 512-8346
Tulsa *(G-9045)*
▼ V E Enterprises Inc............E....... 580 653-2171
Springer *(G-8627)*
Vernon Manufacturing Company............G....... 918 224-4068
Tulsa *(G-9048)*
Veterans Eng Group Inc............G....... 918 864-6006
Pryor *(G-7997)*
Wagner Plate Works LLC............G....... 918 447-4488
Tulsa *(G-11090)*
Wastequip Manufacturing Co LLC........E....... 580 924-1575
Durant *(G-2272)*
Water Tank Service............G....... 918 786-7850
Grove *(G-3292)*
World Wide Exchangers LLC............E....... 918 234-3700
Skiatook *(G-8576)*
World Wide Exchangers Inc............F....... 918 240-3193
Sapulpa *(G-8327)*
Worthington Cylinder Corp............C....... 918 396-2899
Skiatook *(G-8577)*

3444 Sheet Metal Work

4-Star Trailers Inc............C....... 405 324-7827
Oklahoma City *(G-5331)*
A B Curbs Inc............G....... 405 427-1222
Oklahoma City *(G-5344)*
A-1 Sheet Metal Inc............F....... 918 835-6200
Tulsa *(G-9073)*
Acme Manufacturing Corporation.........E....... 918 266-3097
Claremore *(G-1575)*
Acme Manufacturing Corporation.........G....... 800 647-8671
Claremore *(G-1576)*
Advanced Fabrication Svcs LLC............G....... 405 339-4867
Oklahoma City *(G-5381)*
Adventure Manufacturing Inc............G....... 405 682-3833
Oklahoma City *(G-5387)*
Aeron Group LLC............F....... 918 294-1167
Broken Arrow *(G-819)*
Agilis Group LLC............E....... 918 584-3553
Tulsa *(G-9117)*
Air Duct Inc............F....... 918 445-1196
Tulsa *(G-9119)*
Airflow Solutions LLC............E....... 918 574-2748
Tulsa *(G-9129)*
All Sheet Metal Co............G....... 405 733-0039
Del City *(G-1996)*
Allen Sheet Metal Inc............G....... 918 834-2279
Tulsa *(G-9141)*
Allstate Sheet Metal Inc............F....... 405 636-1914
Oklahoma City *(G-5422)*
Always Done Right LLC............G....... 405 615-5955
Edmond *(G-2300)*
Andy Anderson Metal Works Inc..........F....... 918 245-2355
Sand Springs *(G-8161)*
Apollo Metal Specialties Inc............F....... 918 341-7650
Claremore *(G-1583)*
Archer Technologies Intl Inc............G....... 405 306-3220
Shawnee *(G-8428)*
Architectural Fabricators Inc............E....... 918 331-0393
Bartlesville *(G-448)*
Awnique............G....... 405 818-8032
Oklahoma City *(G-5497)*
Axiom Metal Solutions LLC............G....... 918 361-5982
Okmulgee *(G-7494)*
B & B Sheet Metal Heat & A Inc............G....... 918 371-1335
Collinsville *(G-1801)*
Ba Manufacturing LLC............G....... 239 246-3606
Broken Arrow *(G-842)*
Bacco Inc............G....... 918 344-3670
Claremore *(G-1587)*
Balco Inc............E....... 316 945-9328
Oklahoma City *(G-5519)*
Big River Sales Inc............G....... 580 657-4950
Lone Grove *(G-4115)*
Boxel LLC............G....... 580 239-0819
Atoka *(G-400)*
Braden Shielding Systems Const.........E....... 918 624-2888
Tulsa *(G-9327)*
Breshears Enterprises Inc............F....... 405 236-4523
Oklahoma City *(G-5624)*
Briggs Rainbow Buildings Inc............C....... 918 683-3695
Muskogee *(G-4655)*
Butchers Metal Shop............G....... 580 256-7660
Woodward *(G-11565)*
Bynum & Company Inc............F....... 580 265-7747
Stonewall *(G-8798)*
Canopies Plus Inc............G....... 918 689-7077
Eufaula *(G-3098)*
Capes Custom Welding & Fabrica........G....... 918 453-0594
Tahlequah *(G-8855)*
Captive-Aire Systems Inc............F....... 918 258-0291
Tulsa *(G-9373)*
Captive-Aire Systems Inc............D....... 918 686-6717
Muskogee *(G-4658)*
Carlsons Rural Mailbox Co............G....... 405 632-7338
Oklahoma City *(G-5704)*
CCL Acquisition LLC............D....... 918 739-4400
Catoosa *(G-1309)*
▲ Cherokee Nation Red Wing LLC.......E....... 918 430-3437
Tulsa *(G-9414)*
Choctaw Mfg & Dev Corp............D....... 580 326-8365
Hugo *(G-3607)*
Choctaw Nation of Oklahoma............D....... 580 326-8365
Hugo *(G-3610)*
Clinco Mfg LLC............G....... 580 759-3434
Ada *(G-25)*
◆ CMI Terex Corporation............A....... 405 787-6020
Oklahoma City *(G-5792)*
▼ Contech Enterprises LLC............F....... 918 341-6232
Claremore *(G-1609)*
Contech Mfg Inc............G....... 918 341-6232
Claremore *(G-1610)*
Cool Green Roofing Supply LLC..........G....... 918 860-7525
Broken Arrow *(G-877)*
Copper Accents By Jerry............G....... 918 724-8473
Bixby *(G-618)*
Council Stainless & Shtmtl............G....... 405 787-4400
Oklahoma City *(G-5842)*
Cundiff Custom Fabrication LLC..........G....... 405 372-8204
Stillwater *(G-8673)*
Custom Metal Works Inc............G....... 918 388-1881
Tulsa *(G-9529)*
Custom Storm Shelters LLC............G....... 405 209-5525
Oklahoma City *(G-5876)*
D & D Design & Mfg Inc............F....... 405 745-2126
Oklahoma City *(G-5885)*
D & L Enclosures............G....... 918 396-7355
Skiatook *(G-8538)*
Darrell Monroe............F....... 405 793-2976
Moore *(G-4513)*
David Muzny............G....... 405 681-7593
Oklahoma City *(G-5904)*
Del Nero Manufacturing Co............G....... 405 364-4800
Norman *(G-4976)*
Dilbeck Mfg Inc............E....... 918 836-1555
Tulsa *(G-9584)*
Diw Engineering Fabrication LLC..........E....... 918 534-0001
Dewey *(G-2020)*
Don Bateman Shtmtl Fabrication..........G....... 918 224-0567
Sapulpa *(G-8267)*
E F L Inc............D....... 918 665-7799
Tulsa *(G-9621)*
Earl Bannon............G....... 405 236-8829
Oklahoma City *(G-5998)*
Eastern Sheet Metal Co Inc............G....... 918 687-6231
Muskogee *(G-4669)*
Elk City Sheet Metal Inc............G....... 580 225-5844
Elk City *(G-2810)*
▲ Ellis Construction Spc LLC............E....... 405 848-4676
Oklahoma City *(G-6026)*
Empire Laser & Metal Work LLC..........F....... 918 584-6232
Broken Arrow *(G-898)*
Eric Turner............G....... 918 423-7330
McAlester *(G-4295)*
Ets-Lindgren Inc............E....... 580 434-7490
Durant *(G-2230)*
Expanded Solutions LLC............E....... 405 946-6791
Wewoka *(G-11501)*
Fabricating Specialists Inc............F....... 405 476-1959
Oklahoma City *(G-6068)*
Fabrication Dynamics............D....... 918 445-6100
Tulsa *(G-9004)*
Fabrication Dynamics Inc............G....... 918 446-1638
Tulsa *(G-9722)*
Fammco Mfg Co Inc............G....... 918 437-0456
Tulsa *(G-9727)*
Fifteen Five Gtter Sltions LLC............G....... 405 219-6741
Yukon *(G-11724)*
Gary Green Cement Construction.........G....... 405 527-5606
Purcell *(G-8008)*
Gauge Metal Fab LLC............G....... 918 794-1700
Tulsa *(G-9808)*
General Plastics Inc............F....... 405 275-3171
Shawnee *(G-8453)*
Glover Sheet Metal Inc............E....... 405 619-7117
Edmond *(G-2437)*
Hill Metal Inc............G....... 405 375-6284
Kingfisher *(G-3801)*
Hindman Metal Fabricators............G....... 918 251-3949
Broken Arrow *(G-930)*
Holman Manufacturing............F....... 918 479-5861
Locust Grove *(G-4109)*
Honeycutt Contruction Inc............F....... 918 825-6070
Pryor *(G-7969)*
Hu Don Manufacturing Co Inc............F....... 580 223-7333
Ardmore *(G-307)*
Ideas Manufacturing Inc............G....... 405 691-5525
Oklahoma City *(G-5296)*
J C Sheet Metal Fabrication............G....... 405 787-1902
Oklahoma City *(G-6335)*
▲ JC Fab LLC............F....... 580 920-0878
Durant *(G-2240)*
Johnson Welding............G....... 580 569-2231
Mountain Park *(G-4626)*
K and E Fabrication............G....... 405 635-8552
Oklahoma City *(G-6393)*
Karacon Solutions LLC............G....... 918 231-1001
Tulsa *(G-10076)*
Kenneth Petermann............G....... 405 372-0111
Stillwater *(G-8710)*
Keymiaee Aero-Tech Inc............F....... 405 235-5010
Oklahoma City *(G-6409)*
Kice Industries Inc............E....... 580 363-2850
Blackwell *(G-685)*
L & M Fabrication............G....... 918 825-7145
Pryor *(G-7973)*
L & S Seamless Guttering Inc............G....... 405 392-4487
Blanchard *(G-719)*
▲ Laser Specialities Inc............E....... 918 760-5690
Tulsa *(G-9016)*
Linde Engineering N Amer LLC............E....... 918 266-5700
Catoosa *(G-1331)*
Lockdown Ltd Co............F....... 405 605-6161
Oklahoma City *(G-6485)*
Longreach Steel Inc............F....... 405 598-5691
Tecumseh *(G-8922)*

S
I
C

34 FABRICATED METAL PRODUCTS, EXCEPT MACHINERY AND TRANSPORTATION EQUIPMENT

Los Angeles Boiler Works Inc .... E 580 363-1312
  Blackwell (G-688)
Love Air Conditioning .... G 918 341-0508
  Claremore (G-1651)
Luther Industries LLC .... G 405 819-0346
  Blanchard (G-720)
M & M Fabrication & Service .... G 405 677-1982
  Oklahoma City (G-6506)
Mac Machine .... G 405 238-7280
  Pauls Valley (G-7666)
Matherly Mechanical Contrs LLC .... C 405 737-3488
  Midwest City (G-4446)
MBI Industrial Inc .... F 405 387-4003
  Tuttle (G-11206)
McCutchen Enterprises Inc .... G 918 234-7406
  Tulsa (G-10231)
McPherson Implement Inc .... F 405 321-6292
  Norman (G-5067)
Metal Fab Inc .... G 580 762-2421
  Ponca City (G-7850)
Metal Panels Inc .... G 918 641-0641
  Tulsa (G-10246)
Metalform Inc .... F 918 585-8300
  Tulsa (G-10247)
Metallic Works Inc .... G 918 527-6477
  Tulsa (G-10248)
Metalspand Inc .... F 580 228-2393
  Waurika (G-11363)
Metaltech Inc .... F 405 659-9911
  Oklahoma City (G-6575)
Metro Mechanical Supply Inc .... F 918 622-2288
  Tulsa (G-10251)
Midco Fabricators Inc .... E 405 282-6667
  Guthrie (G-3324)
Midwest Fabricators LLC .... G 405 755-7799
  Oklahoma City (G-6603)
Midwest Precision Inc .... D 918 835-8900
  Tulsa (G-10270)
Mountain Top Machine Inc .... G 918 787-5510
  Jay (G-3683)
Mueller Supply Company Inc .... G 918 485-2034
  Wagoner (G-11288)
Nci Group Inc .... E 405 672-7676
  Oklahoma City (G-6665)
Old World Iron Inc .... G 918 445-3063
  Tulsa (G-10411)
▲ Parfab Industries LLC .... D 918 543-6310
  Inola (G-3672)
Paul G Pennington Industries .... G 405 392-2317
  Blanchard (G-726)
Penn Aluminum Inc .... G 405 476-5222
  Yukon (G-11765)
Penny Sheet Metal LLC .... F 918 251-6911
  Broken Arrow (G-1002)
Philip R Eckart .... G 580 917-3882
  Fletcher (G-3166)
Phils Ornamental Iron Inc .... G 918 786-2979
  Grove (G-3285)
▲ Phoenix Design & Mfg LLC .... G 405 418-4858
  Oklahoma City (G-6843)
Plastic Engrg Co Tulsa Inc .... E 918 622-9660
  Tulsa (G-10523)
Pro Stainless & Shtmtl LLC .... G 405 787-4400
  Oklahoma City (G-6906)
R & J Aluminum Products .... G 580 355-1809
  Lawton (G-3987)
R F Lindgren Enclosures Inc .... G 918 299-7572
  Tulsa (G-10603)
Redland Sheet Metal Inc .... G 405 673-7107
  Oklahoma City (G-6997)
Ross Dub Company Inc .... E 405 495-3611
  Oklahoma City (G-7049)
S-T Magi .... G 918 358-2312
  Cleveland (G-1733)
Sharp Metal Fabricators Inc .... F 405 899-4849
  Noble (G-4891)
Shielding Resources Group .... F 918 663-1985
  Tulsa (G-10746)
Smith Welding Fabg & Repr .... G 918 446-2293
  Tulsa (G-10779)
Sooner Machine & Equipment Co .... G 405 794-6833
  Moore (G-4572)
Southern Sheet Metal Works Inc .... G 918 584-3371
  Tulsa (G-10802)
Southern Specialties Corp .... E 918 584-3553
  Tulsa (G-10803)
◆ SPX Heat Transfer LLC .... C 918 234-6000
  Tulsa (G-10827)
Steel Queen Inc .... G 405 949-1664
  Oklahoma City (G-7199)

Storm Roofing & Cnstr LLC .... G 918 688-0165
  Owasso (G-7620)
T Town Sheet Metal .... G 918 437-4756
  Tulsa (G-10893)
Tinhorns Are US .... G 405 381-4044
  Tuttle (G-11216)
Treat Metal Stamping Inc .... G 405 275-3344
  Shawnee (G-8512)
Trojan Livestock Equipment .... G 580 772-1849
  Weatherford (G-11451)
True Steel LLC .... E 580 310-0595
  Ada (G-98)
Tulsa Copper Specialties .... G 918 249-4809
  Tulsa (G-10994)
Tulsa Sheet Metal Inc .... F 918 587-3141
  Tulsa (G-11007)
▲ Valco Inc .... E 405 228-0932
  Duncan (G-2191)
Valco Inc .... E 405 228-0932
  Oklahoma City (G-7386)
Vann Metal Products Inc .... G 918 341-0469
  Claremore (G-1701)
Ventaire LLC .... E 918 622-1191
  Tulsa (G-11070)
Ventaire Corporation .... G 918 622-1191
  Tulsa (G-11071)
Vernon Sheet Metal .... G 580 658-6778
  Marlow (G-4246)
Vogt Sheet Metal .... G 580 332-2454
  Ada (G-102)
W L Walker Co Inc .... E 918 583-3109
  Tulsa (G-11089)
Wagner Plate Works LLC .... G 918 447-4488
  Tulsa (G-11090)
Werco Manufacturing Inc .... G 918 251-6880
  Broken Arrow (G-1095)
Western Seamless Guttering .... G 580 225-7983
  Elk City (G-2890)
Westwind Sheet Metal .... G 918 437-9976
  Tulsa (G-11112)
Wright Comfort Solutions Inc .... G 580 688-3586
  Hollis (G-3572)
York Metal Fabricators Inc .... E 405 528-7495
  Oklahoma City (G-7481)
Zoe Homes LLC .... G 405 550-3563
  Oklahoma City (G-7488)

3446 Architectural & Ornamental Metal Work

Able Interior Contractor LLC .... F 918 605-2887
  Locust Grove (G-4103)
Ace Fence Co .... G 918 682-7895
  Muskogee (G-4641)
Airtech Products Inc .... E 918 241-0264
  Tulsa (G-9132)
American Fence Company Inc .... E 405 685-4800
  Oklahoma City (G-5435)
American Iron .... G 405 414-2629
  Norman (G-4908)
Ameristar Primeter SEC USA Inc .... E 918 835-0898
  Tulsa (G-9179)
Angel Ornamental Iron Works .... G 918 584-8726
  Tulsa (G-9191)
Apollo Ornamental Iron LLC .... E 405 672-5377
  Oklahoma City (G-5454)
Armstrong Products Inc .... G 405 282-7584
  Guthrie (G-3297)
Automatic Gate Systems of Okla .... G 580 920-8752
  Durant (G-2203)
B & W Manufacturing Co Ltd .... F 918 248-5201
  Tulsa (G-8989)
Balco Inc .... E 316 945-9328
  Oklahoma City (G-5519)
Beeman Products Co Inc .... G 918 251-1432
  Broken Arrow (G-845)
Berryhill Ornamental Iron LLC .... G 918 258-6531
  Broken Arrow (G-846)
Cramer Fence Company .... G 918 865-4529
  Mannford (G-4180)
Custom Design By Roberts .... G 918 664-0466
  Tulsa (G-9528)
D & M Steel Manufacturing .... G 405 631-5027
  Oklahoma City (G-5887)
Dennis Petrilla Enterprises .... G 405 364-4695
  Norman (G-4977)
Diw Engneering Fabrication LLC .... E 918 534-0001
  Dewey (G-2020)
Dover Artificial Lift .... F 918 796-1000
  Tulsa (G-9600)
Eastpointe Manufacturing Corp .... E 918 683-2169
  Muskogee (G-4671)

▲ Econofab Piping Inc .... F 918 267-5901
  Beggs (G-552)
◆ Ernest Wiemann Iron Works .... E 918 592-1700
  Tulsa (G-9698)
Goodwill Inds Centl Okla Inc .... D 405 236-4451
  Oklahoma City (G-6172)
Grating Company LLC .... G 918 834-8100
  Tulsa (G-9848)
H & H Ornamental Iron .... G 405 634-0646
  Oklahoma City (G-6196)
Henderson Ornamental Iron .... G 918 341-1089
  Claremore (G-1634)
Iron Horse Metal Works .... G 918 333-8877
  Bartlesville (G-498)
Ironcraft Urban Products LLC .... G 855 601-1647
  Oklahoma City (G-6327)
J&M Stainless Fabricators Ltd .... G 405 517-0875
  Oklahoma City (G-6340)
Jacobs Ladder Camps & Retreat .... G 405 258-5176
  Chandler (G-1381)
Kaydawn Manufacturing Co Inc .... G 918 321-5017
  Glenpool (G-3237)
L & M Fabrication .... G 918 825-7145
  Pryor (G-7973)
Liberty Fence Co Inc .... G 918 834-6553
  Tulsa (G-10156)
Longs Excavating .... G 918 782-2235
  Langley (G-3872)
Merrells Welding & Orna Ir .... G 405 321-7733
  Norman (G-5073)
Metal Fab Inc .... G 580 762-2421
  Ponca City (G-7850)
Metallic Works Inc .... G 918 527-6477
  Tulsa (G-10248)
Midland Vinyl Products Inc .... G 405 755-4972
  Oklahoma City (G-6597)
Mikes Welding .... G 918 455-7227
  Broken Arrow (G-975)
Mitchco Fabrication Inc .... G 580 762-0256
  Ponca City (G-7853)
Mitchell Ironworks Inc .... G 580 233-7925
  Enid (G-3014)
Monson Associates Inc .... G 918 298-0037
  Tulsa (G-10300)
Mosley Backhoe Service .... G 405 567-4710
  Prague (G-7931)
Oklahoma Metal Creations LLC .... G 580 917-5434
  Fletcher (G-3165)
Oklahoma Stair Craft Inc .... F 918 446-1456
  Sapulpa (G-8293)
Old World Iron .... G 405 722-0008
  Oklahoma City (G-6771)
Old World Iron Inc .... G 918 445-3063
  Tulsa (G-10411)
▼ Osiyo Medals Inc .... F 918 258-4717
  Broken Arrow (G-995)
Perryton Iron and Metal LLC .... G 580 256-5536
  Woodward (G-11620)
Phils Ornamental Iron Inc .... G 918 786-2979
  Grove (G-3285)
Premiercraft Incorporated .... F 405 600-9339
  Oklahoma City (G-6887)
Pro Stainless & Shtmtl LLC .... G 405 787-4400
  Oklahoma City (G-6906)
Royal Ironworks .... G 580 492-4265
  Edmond (G-2605)
Skiatook Statuary .... G 918 396-1309
  Skiatook (G-8570)
Top Quality Doors LLC .... G 405 579-3667
  Norman (G-5176)
Tulsa Ornamental Iron Works .... G 918 274-7253
  Owasso (G-7629)
▲ Wassco Corporation .... F 918 834-4444
  Tulsa (G-11097)
Werco Manufacturing Inc .... E 918 251-6880
  Broken Arrow (G-1095)
York Metal Fabricators Inc .... E 405 528-7495
  Oklahoma City (G-7481)
Zephyr Southwest Orna LLC .... E 918 251-4133
  Broken Arrow (G-1104)

3448 Prefabricated Metal Buildings & Cmpnts

3 PS Investment LLC .... G 918 604-1363
  Skiatook (G-8529)
Affordable Buildings LLC .... G 918 427-6005
  Muldrow (G-4630)
All American Building .... G 918 249-0515
  Tulsa (G-9136)

All Steel Carports LLC .... G 918 683-1717
Muskogee *(G-4646)*

▲ Alliance Steel Inc .... C 405 745-7500
Oklahoma City *(G-5420)*

Architectural Metal Panels LLC .... G 405 672-7407
Oklahoma City *(G-5462)*

Aztec Building Systems Inc .... E 405 329-0255
Norman *(G-4923)*

Bc Steel Buildings Inc .... D 405 324-5100
Oklahoma City *(G-5535)*

Better Bilt Portable Buildings .... G 918 224-3437
Sapulpa *(G-8255)*

Better Built Structures LLC .... G 918 224-3437
Sapulpa *(G-8256)*

◆ Braden Shielding Systems LLC .... E 918 624-2888
Tulsa *(G-9328)*

Buildings By Madden LLC .... G 405 677-0466
Oklahoma City *(G-5643)*

▲ Byers Products Group Inc .... G 405 491-8550
Oklahoma City *(G-5652)*

Circle K Steel Bldg Cnstr LLC .... F 405 932-4664
Paden *(G-7634)*

Cojac Portable Buildings Inc .... E 405 232-1229
Oklahoma City *(G-5800)*

Cojac Portable Buildings Inc .... G 405 232-1229
Oklahoma City *(G-5801)*

Cushing Truss Manufacturing .... F 918 387-2080
Yale *(G-11683)*

Davco Manufacturing .... F 918 535-2360
Ochelata *(G-5234)*

David Davis .... G 405 354-6974
El Reno *(G-2710)*

Davis Insulated Building Inc .... G 918 423-2636
McAlester *(G-4291)*

Davis Insulated Building Inc .... D 918 967-2042
Stigler *(G-8632)*

Derksen Portable Building .... G 918 636-4129
Sapulpa *(G-8266)*

Dream Buildings of Tulsa .... G 918 437-9233
Tulsa *(G-9604)*

Durnal Construction LLC .... G 405 413-5458
Perkins *(G-7716)*

Fincher & Son Pipe & Steel .... G 580 889-6778
Caddo *(G-1235)*

G & L Metal Buildings .... G 918 687-1867
Muskogee *(G-4677)*

Gideon Steel Panel Company LLC .... F 405 942-7878
Oklahoma City *(G-6153)*

Honeycutt Contruction Inc .... F 918 825-6070
Pryor *(G-7969)*

Indaco Metals LLC .... D 405 273-9200
Shawnee *(G-8462)*

James Case .... G 918 846-2884
Fairfax *(G-3119)*

L&C Metal Buildings LLC .... G 580 660-5515
Rocky *(G-8104)*

Lafes .... G 918 423-5311
McAlester *(G-4312)*

Leddy Construction .... G 580 332-3056
Ada *(G-60)*

Madden Steel Buildings Lawton .... G 580 357-1699
Lawton *(G-3968)*

Maddens Portable Buildings .... E 405 799-4989
Norman *(G-5062)*

Madison Inc of Oklahoma .... G 918 587-4501
Tulsa *(G-9017)*

▲ Marco Industries Inc .... D 918 622-4535
Tulsa *(G-10208)*

Martinez Metal Buildings .... G 580 821-2780
Elk City *(G-2848)*

McCawley Service .... G 918 484-2189
Muskogee *(G-4709)*

Meeco Sullivan LLC .... F 918 423-6833
McAlester *(G-4320)*

Metal Buildings Inc .... E 405 672-7676
Oklahoma City *(G-6572)*

Metal Panels Inc .... G 918 641-0641
Tulsa *(G-10246)*

Metro Portable Buildings .... G 405 921-5688
Oklahoma City *(G-6580)*

Midwest Portable Building .... G 918 245-9335
Tulsa *(G-10269)*

Mobile Mini Inc .... F 918 582-5857
Tulsa *(G-10288)*

Mobile Mini Inc .... E 405 682-9333
Oklahoma City *(G-6622)*

Morton Buildings Inc .... E 918 683-6668
Muskogee *(G-4715)*

Morton Buildings Inc .... E 405 288-1031
Washington *(G-11335)*

Morton Buildings Inc .... G 580 323-1172
Clinton *(G-1759)*

Nci Group Inc .... E 405 672-7676
Oklahoma City *(G-6665)*

Oakley Portable Buildings LLC .... G 405 372-6543
Stillwater *(G-8730)*

Petzold Building LLC .... F 580 563-2818
Blair *(G-697)*

Plumb Square Construction .... G 405 619-9898
Del City *(G-2006)*

Polar Insulated Sheds Oklah .... G 580 799-2265
Elk City *(G-2860)*

Quality Buildings Inc .... G 888 430-7721
Norman *(G-5126)*

Quality Buildings Inc .... E 405 364-0516
Norman *(G-5127)*

Railroad Yard Inc .... E 405 377-8763
Stillwater *(G-8743)*

Redibuilt Metal Pdts & Cnstr .... G 580 225-2829
Elk City *(G-2867)*

Rising M Enterprises .... G 918 766-4235
Stigler *(G-8643)*

Roadrunner Portable Buildings .... G 918 272-7788
Owasso *(G-7608)*

Robertson-Ceco II Corporation .... C 405 636-2010
Oklahoma City *(G-7039)*

Robertson-Ceco II Corporation .... C 405 636-2010
Oklahoma City *(G-7040)*

Ronnie Nevitt .... G 918 687-5284
Muskogee *(G-4745)*

Rons Discount Lumber Inc .... D 918 658-3857
Howe *(G-3599)*

Safe Shed .... G 580 759-3456
Stratford *(G-8807)*

▼ Star Building Systems Inc .... E 405 636-2010
Oklahoma City *(G-7193)*

TDS Portable Buildings LLC .... G 918 422-4009
Colcord *(G-1791)*

Terry Building Co Inc .... F 405 634-5777
Oklahoma City *(G-7272)*

Terry Tylor Wldg Fbrcation LLC .... G 405 205-2964
Chickasha *(G-1517)*

Texoma Sheds .... G 580 223-0000
Ardmore *(G-367)*

Tims Sheds .... G 918 506-7741
Tahlequah *(G-8888)*

Tornado Alley Armor LLC .... G 918 856-3569
Tulsa *(G-10955)*

Tornado Alley OK Storm Shlters .... G 918 706-1341
Coweta *(G-1901)*

Ventaire LLC .... E 918 622-1191
Tulsa *(G-11070)*

Whitney Manufacturing Inc .... E 918 825-6062
Pryor *(G-7998)*

Zieglers Bob Portable Bldg Sls .... G 918 486-4462
Broken Arrow *(G-1181)*

3449 Misc Structural Metal Work

Aerostar International Inc .... G 918 789-3000
Chelsea *(G-1401)*

Bennett Steel Fabrication Inc .... D 918 227-2564
Sapulpa *(G-8253)*

Bison Welding LLC .... G 580 758-3359
Bison *(G-607)*

C and C Manufacturing LLC .... G 918 288-6558
Sperry *(G-8606)*

C Johnstone Welding Fabricat .... G 580 362-2400
Newkirk *(G-4846)*

Cherokee Piping Services LLC .... G 918 931-8593
Tahlequah *(G-8856)*

Forbes Enterprises Inc .... G 580 564-2599
Kingston *(G-3828)*

Grating Company LLC .... G 918 834-8100
Tulsa *(G-9848)*

Honeycutt Contruction Inc .... F 918 825-6070
Pryor *(G-7969)*

Hurst Cnstr & Fabrication LLC .... E 580 628-2388
Tonkawa *(G-8975)*

J&K Machining Inc .... G 918 243-7936
Cleveland *(G-1725)*

J&M Stainless Fabricators Ltd .... G 405 517-0875
Oklahoma City *(G-6340)*

Ketchum Group LLC .... G 918 407-2228
Jenks *(G-3712)*

Mayhem Cstm Fbrcation Wldg LLC .... G 405 406-5160
Newalla *(G-4814)*

Phillips Prcsion Machining LLC .... F 918 914-2131
Bartlesville *(G-517)*

Post-Tension Services of Okla .... F 405 751-1582
Oklahoma City *(G-6866)*

Premier Business Solutions LLC .... G 405 650-3131
Meeker *(G-4385)*

Premiercraft Incorporated .... F 405 600-9339
Oklahoma City *(G-6887)*

Pro Piping & Fabrication LLC .... C 918 599-8218
Tulsa *(G-10565)*

Reinforcing Services Inc .... F 918 379-0090
Catoosa *(G-1350)*

Ross Fabrication & Detailing .... F 405 356-9955
Wellston *(G-11478)*

Tms International LLC .... G 918 241-0129
Sand Springs *(G-8230)*

War Metals Inc .... G 918 224-2155
Tulsa *(G-9050)*

War Metals Inc .... G 918 629-8057
Tulsa *(G-11095)*

3451 Screw Machine Prdts

▲ Badgett Corporation .... D 405 224-4138
Chickasha *(G-1437)*

Freedom Manufacturing LLC .... G 918 283-1520
Claremore *(G-1623)*

Hem Industries .... G 918 534-0579
Dewey *(G-2024)*

Kemper Valve and Fittings .... G 580 622-2048
Sulphur *(G-8836)*

Kenneth Pace .... E 405 222-1426
Chickasha *(G-1479)*

Madewell Machine Works Company .... G 918 543-2904
Inola *(G-3666)*

Psf Services LLC .... G 707 386-8805
Marlow *(G-4239)*

Rightway Mfg Solutions LLC .... E 580 252-2284
Duncan *(G-2170)*

▲ SBS Industries LLC .... C 918 836-7756
Tulsa *(G-10712)*

Slim Haney Inc .... E 918 274-1082
Tulsa *(G-10772)*

Tape-Matics Inc .... E 580 371-2510
Tishomingo *(G-8969)*

Torcsill Foundations LLC .... D 281 825-5200
Weatherford *(G-11448)*

3452 Bolts, Nuts, Screws, Rivets & Washers

▼ Gardner Industries Inc .... F 918 583-0171
Tulsa *(G-9801)*

Integrity Machine Source LLC .... G 918 230-9657
Owasso *(G-7575)*

Jasars Enterprises Inc .... G 405 808-6460
Edmond *(G-2468)*

Kennedy Restorations Llc .... G 405 761-5303
Oklahoma City *(G-5300)*

Manufacturing Solutions LLC .... G 918 951-0750
Broken Arrow *(G-1141)*

Pin Efx LLC .... G 405 341-9956
Edmond *(G-2570)*

Popefasteners Inc .... G 918 740-4801
Tulsa *(G-10532)*

Psf Services LLC .... G 707 386-8805
Marlow *(G-4239)*

◆ Refractory Anchors Inc .... E 918 455-8485
Broken Arrow *(G-1154)*

▲ SBS Industries LLC .... C 918 836-7756
Tulsa *(G-10712)*

Smith Precision Products LLC .... G 918 691-5797
Broken Arrow *(G-1165)*

Vortex Parts Washer .... G 918 582-4445
Tulsa *(G-11084)*

Witten Company Inc .... E 918 272-9567
Owasso *(G-7630)*

3462 Iron & Steel Forgings

Axels Transmissions Transfers .... G 918 425-7725
Tulsa *(G-9234)*

Crosby Group LLC .... B 918 834-4611
Tulsa *(G-9509)*

Crosby Worldwide Limited .... F 918 834-4611
Tulsa *(G-9512)*

Cundiff Custom Fabrication LLC .... G 405 372-8204
Stillwater *(G-8673)*

Ftdm Investments Llc .... D 918 598-3430
Locust Grove *(G-4107)*

Horseshoe Exploration LLC .... G 580 866-3207
Sharon *(G-8417)*

J & D Gearing & Machining Inc .... G 405 677-7667
Oklahoma City *(G-6329)*

Kloefkorn Entps Ltd Partnr .... G 580 694-2292
Manchester *(G-4167)*

Lufkin Industries LLC .... F 405 677-0567
Oklahoma City *(G-6501)*

Employee Codes: A=Over 500 employees, B=251-500
C=101-250, D=51-100, E=20-50, F=10-19, G=1-9
2020 Oklahoma Directory
of Manufacturers & Processors
471

34 FABRICATED METAL PRODUCTS, EXCEPT MACHINERY AND TRANSPORTATION EQUIPMENT

M-A Systems Inc .... F 918 824-3705
  Pryor (G-7975)
◆ Malco Incorporated .... E 918 876-1934
  Tulsa (G-10206)
◆ Mike Alexander Company Inc .... E 580 765-8085
  Tulsa (G-10276)
▲ Oklahoma Forge Inc .... E 918 446-4486
  Tulsa (G-10401)
Oklahoma Specialties Inc .... G 918 272-0931
  Owasso (G-7598)
Podunk Hunting Products LLC .... G 918 617-0358
  Quinton (G-8039)
Pro Walk Manufacturing Company .... G 580 332-5516
  Ada (G-77)
Rail Masters LLC .... G 405 840-1019
  Oklahoma City (G-6965)
Value Components Corp .... G 918 749-1689
  Tulsa (G-11066)

3463 Nonferrous Forgings

American Machine & Tool Co .... G 405 794-9820
  Wewoka (G-11497)
Hackney Ladish Inc .... D 580 237-4212
  Enid (G-2967)

3465 Automotive Stampings

Accessory and Prfmce Sls Inc .... G 918 224-5851
  Sapulpa (G-8246)
Autocraft Material Recovery .... G 405 350-3800
  Oklahoma City (G-5493)
Hart Brothers Welding .... G 918 697-5682
  Collinsville (G-1812)
Mar-K Specialized Mfg Inc .... E 405 721-7945
  Oklahoma City (G-6520)
Mike Bailey Motors Inc .... F 918 652-9637
  Henryetta (G-3512)
Nick & Pauls Quality Car Cornr .... G 918 933-4000
  Tulsa (G-10341)
Sinister Sand Sports .... G 918 521-3736
  Broken Arrow (G-1053)
Tk Aero Inc .... G 405 359-8638
  Edmond (G-2645)
Track Products .... G 918 231-9960
  Fort Gibson (G-3181)

3469 Metal Stampings, NEC

Action Spring Company .... E 918 836-9000
  Tulsa (G-9097)
All Tools Co Inc .... F 405 942-6655
  Oklahoma City (G-5416)
Arrow Tool & Gage Co Inc .... F 918 438-3600
  Tulsa (G-9212)
Avery Barron Industries .... G 918 834-6647
  Tulsa (G-9230)
Blakes Westside Tag Agency .... G 918 446-1740
  Oklahoma City (G-5585)
Braden Shielding Systems Const .... E 918 624-2888
  Tulsa (G-9327)
◆ Braden Shielding Systems LLC .... E 918 624-2888
  Tulsa (G-9328)
CCL Acquisition LLC .... D 918 739-4400
  Catoosa (G-1309)
City of Claremore .... G 918 342-2490
  Claremore (G-1606)
Coman Pattern Works .... D 918 270-1775
  Tulsa (G-9473)
▼ Component Services LP .... F 405 787-7180
  Oklahoma City (G-5813)
Croppinsville .... G 405 521-2711
  Owasso (G-7557)
D C Jones Machine Co .... G 918 786-6855
  Grove (G-3265)
Daniel W Duensing .... G 417 781-1850
  Broken Arrow (G-1120)
Enerfin Inc .... G 918 258-3571
  Broken Arrow (G-900)
Expanded Solutions LLC .... E 405 946-6791
  Wewoka (G-11501)
▼ Flanco Gasket and Mfg Inc .... E 405 672-7893
  Oklahoma City (G-6088)
▼ Gardner Industries Inc .... F 918 583-0171
  Tulsa (G-9801)
Hoel Machine Mfg Inc .... G 918 294-8895
  Broken Arrow (G-931)
Hominy Tag Agency .... G 918 885-9955
  Hominy (G-3586)
Hot Stuff Airbrush Inc .... G 918 249-0458
  Tulsa (G-9954)
Hunt Jim Sales & Mfg .... G 405 670-5663
  Oklahoma City (G-6272)

▲ Industrial Gasket Inc .... E 405 376-9393
  Mustang (G-4778)
Interstate Tool & Mfg Co .... E 918 834-6647
  Tulsa (G-10008)
Kingfisher County Drivers .... G 405 375-3711
  Kingfisher (G-3804)
Kitchen Korner Inc .... G 918 582-9951
  Tulsa (G-10093)
Mac Machine .... G 405 238-7280
  Pauls Valley (G-7666)
Marys Tag Office .... G 580 562-4745
  Burns Flat (G-1219)
Metal Fab Inc .... G 580 762-2421
  Ponca City (G-7850)
Midland Stamping and Fabg Corp .... F 918 446-1458
  Tulsa (G-10263)
Noss Machine .... G 918 358-3804
  Hominy (G-3593)
Phelps Machine & Fabrication .... F 580 662-2465
  Ringling (G-8081)
Porcelain Treasure .... G 918 230-9618
  Tulsa (G-10534)
Poteau Panel Shop Incorporated .... G 918 647-4331
  Poteau (G-7912)
Precision Metal Fab LLC .... E 580 762-2421
  Ponca City (G-7868)
Precision Tool & Die Ponca Cy .... G 580 762-2421
  Ponca City (G-7869)
Progressive Stamping LLC .... G 405 996-5347
  Oklahoma City (G-6913)
Public Safety-Drivers License .... G 918 336-0604
  Bartlesville (G-518)
Roll-Offs of America Inc .... D 580 924-6355
  Mead (G-4367)
Royal Prestige Jealpa .... G 405 602-5371
  Oklahoma City (G-7053)
Screen Tech Intl Ltd Co .... F 918 234-0010
  Broken Arrow (G-1161)
Sooner State Spring Mfg Co .... G 918 476-5707
  Chouteau (G-1570)
Ss Tag LLC .... G 918 241-3400
  Sand Springs (G-8226)
Superior Stainless Inc .... G 405 387-3414
  Blanchard (G-736)
▲ T F T Inc .... E 918 834-2366
  Tulsa (G-10889)
Tag Agent .... G 580 584-2892
  Broken Bow (G-1210)
Tag Agent .... G 918 653-2236
  Heavener (G-3433)
Tag Stillwater Agency .... G 405 624-0200
  Stillwater (G-8764)
Tags 2 Go .... G 580 335-7474
  Frederick (G-3202)
Treat Metal Stamping Inc .... G 405 275-3344
  Shawnee (G-8512)
Tulsa Pro Turn Inc .... F 918 439-9232
  Tulsa (G-11005)
Unified Brands Inc .... G 888 994-7636
  Pryor (G-7996)

3471 Electroplating, Plating, Polishing, Anodizing & Coloring

▲ Applied Indus Coatings LLC .... E 405 692-2249
  Oklahoma City (G-5455)
Brass Buff .... G 918 592-1717
  Tulsa (G-9332)
Broken Arrow Powdr Coating Inc .... G 918 251-2192
  Broken Arrow (G-856)
Buster Dorsch .... G 918 743-4509
  Tulsa (G-9353)
C & F Custom Chrome .... G 918 587-1110
  Tulsa (G-9356)
Central Metal Finishing LLC .... E 405 379-5252
  Holdenville (G-3551)
Century Plating Inc .... G 918 835-1482
  Tulsa (G-9400)
Choctaw Mfg & Dev Corp .... D 580 326-8365
  Hugo (G-3607)
Chromium Plating Company .... E 918 583-4118
  Tulsa (G-9422)
Classic Custom Plating Company .... G 405 787-3075
  Bethany (G-573)
Collins Metal Company Inc .... G 405 373-3309
  Warr Acres (G-11316)
▲ DCI Industries LLC .... E 405 947-2863
  Oklahoma City (G-5910)
Delta Plating Inc .... G 918 664-6880
  Tulsa (G-9570)

Diversified Plating Ltd .... G 405 236-0545
  Oklahoma City (G-5952)
Duracoatings Holdings LLC .... D 405 692-2249
  Oklahoma City (G-5990)
Finishing Technology Inc .... G 918 437-3820
  Tulsa (G-9746)
Friction Solutions LLC .... G 918 622-8989
  Tulsa (G-9778)
George Townsend & Co Inc .... G 405 235-1387
  Oklahoma City (G-6145)
H & H Protective Coating Co .... G 918 582-9187
  Tulsa (G-9871)
H L Custom Processing .... G 580 927-5408
  Coalgate (G-1780)
HB Brackets .... G 405 745-4417
  Oklahoma City (G-6231)
▲ LMI Finishing Inc .... D 918 438-1012
  Tulsa (G-10174)
Macs Electric Supply Company .... F 918 583-3101
  Tulsa (G-10196)
Metal Finishing of Chickasha .... F 405 224-6703
  Chickasha (G-1485)
Metcoat Inc .... G 580 255-6441
  Duncan (G-2154)
Modern Plating Co Inc .... F 918 836-5081
  Tulsa (G-10291)
Northrup Metals LLC .... G 918 225-2100
  Cushing (G-1948)
OK Products of Tulsa Inc .... G 918 445-2471
  Tulsa (G-10391)
Oklahoma High Prfmce Polsg .... G 405 787-8388
  Oklahoma City (G-6751)
Oklahoma Superior Plating LLC .... G 580 252-2787
  Duncan (G-2162)
Paysmith Processing LLC .... G 918 858-5599
  Tulsa (G-10477)
Power Services LLC .... G 405 677-7716
  Norman (G-5118)
Precision Anodizing Inc .... F 405 631-2079
  Oklahoma City (G-6880)
Precision Coatings LLC .... G 918 622-1876
  Tulsa (G-10543)
Premier Metal Finishing Inc .... G 405 947-0200
  Oklahoma City (G-6885)
Pride Plating Inc .... D 918 786-6111
  Grove (G-3286)
Protective Coatings Intl LLC .... G 405 716-4734
  Seminole (G-8395)
Quality Metal Finishing Inc .... F 405 236-1155
  Oklahoma City (G-6937)
Quality Plating Co of Tulsa .... E 918 835-2278
  Tulsa (G-10593)
Ramos Plating Co .... G 405 232-4300
  Oklahoma City (G-6970)
S&S Professional Polishing LLC .... G 405 631-7087
  Oklahoma City (G-7067)
Southwest Pickling Inc .... G 580 924-6996
  Durant (G-2259)
Sparks Plating Company .... G 918 482-5080
  Haskell (G-3401)
▲ Spray-Rite Inc .... E 479 648-3351
  Pocola (G-7786)
Ted Davis Enterprises Inc .... F 405 948-8763
  Oklahoma City (G-7263)
Topps Powder Coating .... G 405 794-2900
  Moore (G-4578)
Trios of Oklahoma LLC .... G 918 760-2734
  Edmond (G-2653)
Tulsa Metal Finishers Inc .... G 918 241-1290
  Sand Springs (G-8232)
Tulsa Metal Finishing Company .... F 918 609-5410
  Tulsa (G-11002)
Ultra Tech Ultra Tech .... G 580 351-1220
  Lawton (G-4016)
United Plating Works Inc .... G 918 835-4683
  Tulsa (G-11042)

3479 Coating & Engraving, NEC

A & B Engraving Inc .... G 918 663-7446
  Tulsa (G-9061)
AAA Galvanizing Chelsea Inc .... E 918 789-9333
  Chelsea (G-1400)
Abitl Finishing Inc .... E 918 446-5363
  Tulsa (G-8985)
Azz Inc .... E 918 379-0090
  Catoosa (G-1299)
Azz Incorporated .... E 918 584-6668
  Tulsa (G-9237)
B G Specialties Inc .... G 918 582-1165
  Tulsa (G-9243)

SIC SECTION — 34 FABRICATED METAL PRODUCTS, EXCEPT MACHINERY AND TRANSPORTATION EQUIPMENT

Be Custom Coatings ....G 405 205-9347
Harrah (G-3374)

Broken Arrow Powdr Coating Inc ....E 918 251-2192
Broken Arrow (G-856)

Broken Arrow Powdr Coating Inc ....E 918 258-1017
Broken Arrow (G-857)

Casting Coating Corp ....F 918 445-4141
Tulsa (G-8995)

Chemproof Polymers Inc ....G 918 584-0364
Tulsa (G-9410)

Coat Pro LLC ....G 405 672-0705
Oklahoma City (G-5798)

Coating Solution ....G 580 276-5432
Leon (G-4033)

Commercial Coatings Okla LLC ....G 405 226-8739
Oklahoma City (G-5805)

Copperhead Coatings LLC ....G 580 532-6243
Pond Creek (G-7889)

Custom Catings of Broken Arrow ....G 918 258-0996
Coweta (G-1876)

Custom Powder Coating & Dustle ....G 580 382-8000
Ponca City (G-7815)

Eagle Rock Coatings Inc ....G 405 948-8900
Oklahoma City (G-5996)

▲ Energy and Envmtl Svcs Inc ....G 405 843-8996
Edmond (G-2413)

Energy and Envmtl Svcs Inc ....G 405 285-8767
Edmond (G-2412)

▲ Etched In Stone ....G 918 369-0500
Bixby (G-621)

Finish Line Powder Coating ....G 918 938-6292
Tulsa (G-9744)

GE Oil & Gas Esp Inc ....E 405 527-1566
Purcell (G-8009)

Gerdau Ameristeel US Inc ....F 918 682-2600
Muskogee (G-4679)

Guthrie Industrial Coating ....G 405 377-6649
Stillwater (G-8696)

H & H Protective Coating Co ....G 918 582-9187
Tulsa (G-9871)

H-V Manufacturing Company ....G 918 756-9620
Okmulgee (G-7509)

House of Trophies ....G 918 341-2111
Claremore (G-1637)

◆ Ideal Specialty Inc ....F 918 834-1657
Tulsa (G-9967)

Industrial Coatings Oklahoma ....G 918 638-5606
Claremore (G-1640)

J&J Powder Coating & Fabr ....G 918 836-9700
Tulsa (G-10024)

Juno Companies Incorporated ....G 918 627-8868
Tulsa (G-10067)

Kuykendall Welding LLC ....G 405 905-0389
Chickasha (G-1480)

Mid-America Indus Coatings LLC ....G 580 239-9003
Atoka (G-419)

Milamar Coatings LLC ....F 405 755-8448
Oklahoma City (G-6608)

Modern Coatings LLC ....G 405 795-2633
Oklahoma City (G-5307)

Modern Plating Co Inc ....F 918 836-5081
Tulsa (G-10291)

Mtw Powder Coating ....G 918 638-4795
Coweta (G-1892)

Nacols Jewelry ....G 580 355-4280
Lawton (G-3975)

Nafcoat Inc ....G 918 367-9606
Bristow (G-789)

▲ Nameplates Inc ....D 918 584-2651
Tulsa (G-10324)

National Coating ....G 405 251-5065
Wynnewood (G-11671)

Oerlikon Blzers Cating USA Inc ....G 405 745-1026
Oklahoma City (G-6713)

Oklahoma Coating Specialists ....G 405 447-0448
Norman (G-5099)

▲ Oklahoma Cstm Cating Ltd Lblty ....E 405 382-0231
Seminole (G-8391)

Performance Coatings Inc ....G 405 525-9790
Oklahoma City (G-6829)

Pixley Coating Inc ....G 580 444-2140
Velma (G-11236)

Powder Coatings Incorporated ....G 918 627-6225
Tulsa (G-10537)

Powder Coatings Plus LLC ....F 405 232-5707
Oklahoma City (G-6868)

Precision Coatings LLC ....G 918 622-1876
Tulsa (G-10543)

Precision Metal Forming LLC ....E 405 677-3777
Oklahoma City (G-6882)

Premier Metal Finishing Inc ....G 405 947-0200
Oklahoma City (G-6885)

Protective Coatings Intl LLC ....G 405 716-4734
Seminole (G-8395)

Quality Galvanizing ....G 918 789-9333
Chelsea (G-1410)

Quality Steel Coatings Inc ....G 918 269-9104
Broken Arrow (G-1151)

Southside Powder Coating ....G 405 623-8557
Noble (G-4892)

▲ Spray-Rite Inc ....E 479 648-3351
Pocola (G-7786)

Sprayfoam Banks & Coatings ....G 580 490-6308
Overbrook (G-7539)

Sun Heat Treating Inc ....G 918 227-2188
Tulsa (G-9039)

Texoma Engraving LLC ....G 580 775-7333
Durant (G-2264)

Thompsons Metal Coating ....G 918 272-5711
Owasso (G-7624)

Topps Powder Coating ....G 405 794-2900
Moore (G-4578)

Trophies n Things ....G 405 247-9771
Anadarko (G-207)

Tulsa Powder Coating Inc ....G 918 832-1741
Tulsa (G-11004)

Twj Inc ....G 405 392-4366
Tuttle (G-11217)

Walkers Powder Coating LLC ....G 580 355-5000
Lawton (G-4018)

3482 Small Arms Ammunition

Choctaw Defense Munitions LLC ....G 918 426-7871
Mcalester (G-4284)

Hailey Ordnance Company ....G 405 813-0700
Oklahoma City (G-6203)

Johnny L Windsor ....G 405 691-3083
Oklahoma City (G-6371)

Nash Tactical LLC ....G 405 589-6425
Norman (G-5085)

Robertson Arms & Munitions Co ....G 405 376-2360
Mustang (G-4791)

Sandman Sports ....G 918 272-0862
Owasso (G-7612)

United States Dept of Army ....A 918 420-6642
McAlester (G-4348)

3484 Small Arms

Alex Arms and Instruction LLC ....G 405 351-0806
Alex (G-129)

Champlin Firearms Inc ....G 580 237-7388
Enid (G-2929)

Dark Ops Designs ....G 918 269-0049
Claremore (G-1612)

Duncan Machine Products Inc ....E 580 467-6784
Duncan (G-2110)

F&D Defense LLC ....G 512 745-6482
Seminole (G-8373)

Garys Guns ....G 405 789-6896
Bethany (G-579)

Gun World Inc ....G 405 670-5885
Del City (G-1997)

Hailey Ordnance Company ....G 405 813-0700
Oklahoma City (G-6203)

Jean Jacques Perodeau Gunmaker ....G 580 237-7388
Enid (G-2983)

JJ Perodeau Gunmaker Inc ....G 580 747-1804
Sand Springs (G-8195)

Leather Guns & Etc ....F 580 296-2616
Colbert (G-1785)

Madison Avenue Firearms LLC ....G 918 629-6910
Tulsa (G-10197)

Mike Beathe ....G 918 288-7858
Sperry (G-8610)

Newman Precision ....G 580 339-0097
Elk City (G-2856)

Oklahoma Machine Guns LLC ....G 405 418-4867
Oklahoma City (G-6754)

Old Sarges Armory LLC ....G 270 945-8324
Miami (G-4425)

Patriot Small Arms LLC ....G 405 567-7890
Tecumseh (G-8924)

Redneck Firearms Inc ....G 405 650-6605
Harrah (G-3384)

Reliance Mfg Solutions LLC ....G 405 640-9660
Oklahoma City (G-7006)

Rifle Shoppe Inc ....G 405 356-2583
Wellston (G-11477)

Rise Manufacturing LLC ....E 918 994-6240
Broken Arrow (G-1032)

Stevens & Sons LLC ....G 580 482-4142
Altus (G-169)

Three Prcent Frrms Catings LLC ....G 580 931-9908
Mead (G-4368)

Zulu 4 Tactical LLC ....G 918 978-6810
Tulsa (G-11180)

3489 Ordnance & Access, NEC

Artillery Nation LLC ....G 405 606-5080
Moore (G-4495)

Cutting Edge Arms LLC ....G 405 603-6723
Oklahoma City (G-5881)

Ducommun Labarge Tech Inc ....C 918 459-2200
Tulsa (G-9611)

Etched Ordnance LLC ....G 918 855-8779
Coweta (G-1882)

Gun World Inc ....G 405 670-5885
Del City (G-1997)

Hailey Ordnance Company ....G 405 813-0700
Oklahoma City (G-6203)

Red River Gunsmithing LLC ....G 580 770-1911
Frederick (G-3198)

Redrhino LLC ....G 405 740-5132
Blanchard (G-733)

3491 Industrial Valves

Alfa Laval Inc ....G 918 251-7477
Broken Arrow (G-824)

Alfa Lval A Cled Exchngers Inc ....G 918 251-7477
Broken Arrow (G-825)

◆ American Directional Tech ....G 405 449-3362
Wayne (G-11365)

B P S Inc ....G 918 258-7554
Broken Arrow (G-841)

B S & B Safety Systems Inc ....G 918 622-5950
Tulsa (G-9245)

▲ Balon Corporation ....A 405 677-3321
Oklahoma City (G-5522)

Balon Valves ....G 405 670-8300
Oklahoma City (G-5523)

Bellofram ....E 405 677-7222
Oklahoma City (G-5545)

Bgr LLC ....E 405 671-2000
Oklahoma City (G-5562)

BS&b Pressure Safety MGT LLC ....G 918 664-3725
Tulsa (G-9344)

◆ BS&b Safety Systems LLC ....G 918 622-5950
Tulsa (G-9345)

Cameron International Corp ....B 405 631-1321
Oklahoma City (G-5676)

Cameron International Corp ....C 405 745-2715
Oklahoma City (G-5677)

Curtiss-Wright Corporation ....G 405 515-8235
Norman (G-4973)

▲ Cyclonic Valve Company ....E 918 317-8200
Broken Arrow (G-883)

Eichler Valve ....G 405 370-6891
Edmond (G-2407)

Enviro Valve (us) Inc ....G 918 251-6103
Broken Arrow (G-902)

Flow Valve LLC ....E 580 622-2294
Sulphur (G-8832)

▲ Flow-Quip Inc ....E 918 663-3313
Tulsa (G-9758)

Fluid Controls Inc ....E 918 299-0442
Tulsa (G-9762)

Gas Products Inc ....G 918 664-5679
Tulsa (G-9804)

Kimray Inc ....C 405 525-6601
Oklahoma City (G-6417)

King Valve Inc ....F 405 672-0046
Oklahoma City (G-6421)

▲ L6 Inc ....E 918 251-5791
Broken Arrow (G-963)

▼ Mercer Valve Co Inc ....E 405 470-5213
Oklahoma City (G-6566)

▲ Ocv Control Valves LLC ....E 918 627-1942
Tulsa (G-10376)

Oklahoma Safety Eqp Co Inc ....C 918 258-5626
Broken Arrow (G-994)

▲ Omni Valve Company LLC ....E 918 687-6100
Muskogee (G-4725)

Ops Valves LLC ....G 918 273-3300
Nowata (G-5224)

Premier Valve Group ....G 918 519-4309
Broken Arrow (G-1009)

▼ Rupture Pin Technology ....E 405 789-1884
Oklahoma City (G-7062)

Turbulator Company LLC ....F 405 820-3026
Oklahoma City (G-7351)

S I C

Employee Codes: A=Over 500 employees, B=251-500
C=101-250, D=51-100, E=20-50, F=10-19, G=1-9
2020 Oklahoma Directory
of Manufacturers & Processors
473

34 FABRICATED METAL PRODUCTS, EXCEPT MACHINERY AND TRANSPORTATION EQUIPMENT

3492 Fluid Power Valves & Hose Fittings

Advent Aircraft Systems Inc ....F 918 388-5940
  Tulsa *(G-9112)*
Ameriflex Hose and ACC LLC ....G 918 437-7002
  Tulsa *(G-9176)*
Crown Products Inc ....E 918 446-4591
  Tulsa *(G-9517)*
▲ Cyclonic Valve Company ....E 918 317-8200
  Broken Arrow *(G-883)*
Devine Industrial Systems Inc ....G 405 627-3448
  Yukon *(G-11717)*
H & C Services Inc ....F 580 772-2521
  Weatherford *(G-11417)*
Horton Industries Inc ....E 918 836-3971
  Tulsa *(G-9950)*
◆ Hydraulic Specialists Inc ....E 405 752-7980
  Oklahoma City *(G-6278)*
Industrial Specialties Inc ....G 580 475-9088
  Duncan *(G-2131)*
Kims International Okla Inc ....G 918 250-9441
  Tulsa *(G-10089)*
Punch-Lok Co ....E 580 233-4757
  Enid *(G-3040)*

3493 Steel Springs, Except Wire

Action Spring Company ....E 918 836-9000
  Tulsa *(G-9097)*
Cannon & Refermat LLC ....F 405 521-0636
  Oklahoma City *(G-5688)*
Dayton Parts LLC ....D 580 931-9350
  Durant *(G-2223)*
Emco LLC ....D 918 342-3488
  Claremore *(G-1616)*
▼ Gardner Industries Inc ....F 918 583-0171
  Tulsa *(G-9801)*
Tulsa Auto Spring Co ....E 918 835-6926
  Tulsa *(G-10987)*

3494 Valves & Pipe Fittings, NEC

Aceco Valve Inc ....E 918 827-3669
  Mounds *(G-4608)*
▲ Air Power Systems Co LLC ....E 918 622-5600
  Tulsa *(G-9121)*
American Machine & Tool Co ....G 405 794-9820
  Wewoka *(G-11497)*
Apollo Engineering Company ....G 918 251-6780
  Broken Arrow *(G-830)*
▲ Badgett Corporation ....D 405 224-4138
  Chickasha *(G-1437)*
▲ Balon Corporation ....A 405 677-3321
  Oklahoma City *(G-5522)*
Barlow-Hunt Inc ....D 918 250-0828
  Tulsa *(G-9265)*
Big Elk Energy Systems LLC ....E 918 947-6800
  Tulsa *(G-9290)*
BS&b Safety Systems LLC ....C 918 622-5950
  Tulsa *(G-9346)*
▲ Carlson Company ....E 918 627-4334
  Tulsa *(G-9376)*
Closebend Inc ....F 918 445-1131
  Tulsa *(G-9456)*
Cust-O-Bend Inc ....E 918 241-0514
  Tulsa *(G-9526)*
▲ Cyclonic Valve Company ....E 918 317-8200
  Broken Arrow *(G-883)*
◆ East 74th Street Holdings Inc ....C 918 437-3037
  Tulsa *(G-9631)*
Eaton Aeroquip LLC ....D 405 275-5500
  Shawnee *(G-8447)*
Ernst Valve & Fittings ....G 918 446-0313
  Tulsa *(G-9003)*
Flowell Corporation ....F 918 224-6969
  Tulsa *(G-9007)*
Flowmatics Inc ....G 918 259-3740
  Broken Arrow *(G-911)*
Fluid Controls Inc ....E 918 299-0442
  Tulsa *(G-9762)*
Gas Products Inc ....G 918 664-5679
  Tulsa *(G-9804)*
GE Oil & Gas Pressure Ctrl LP ....E 405 273-7660
  Shawnee *(G-8451)*
Hackney Ladish Inc ....D 580 237-4212
  Enid *(G-2967)*
J P Machine & Tool Co ....F 405 677-3341
  Oklahoma City *(G-6337)*
K & S Aluminum Booms ....G 580 761-3238
  Tonkawa *(G-8976)*
King Valve Inc ....F 405 672-0046
  Oklahoma City *(G-6421)*

Lasco Fittings Inc ....G 800 776-2756
  Westville *(G-11484)*
Los Angeles Boiler Works Inc ....E 580 363-1312
  Blackwell *(G-688)*
Mayco Inc ....E 405 677-5969
  Oklahoma City *(G-6543)*
▼ Mercer Valve Co Inc ....E 405 470-5213
  Oklahoma City *(G-6566)*
Metal Goods Manufacturing Co ....F 918 336-4282
  Bartlesville *(G-512)*
Oil Capital Valve Company ....D 918 627-2474
  Tulsa *(G-10385)*
Punch-Lok Co ....E 580 233-4757
  Enid *(G-3040)*
Rotork Valvekits Inc ....F 918 259-8100
  Tulsa *(G-10677)*
Safeco Manufacturing Inc ....G 918 455-0100
  Broken Arrow *(G-1160)*
Schoeller Bleckman Energy ....G 405 672-4407
  Oklahoma City *(G-7091)*
Strope Manufacturing Inc ....G 918 835-8729
  Tulsa *(G-10861)*
Tdw (us) Inc ....G 918 447-5519
  Tulsa *(G-9040)*
Tmco Inc ....E 405 257-9373
  Wewoka *(G-11512)*
Triangle Pump Components Inc ....F 405 672-6900
  Tulsa *(G-7327)*
▼ Weamco Incorporated ....E 918 445-1141
  Sapulpa *(G-8324)*
William L Riggs Company Inc ....G 918 437-3245
  Tulsa *(G-11125)*

3495 Wire Springs

A W Bugerman Company ....G 580 237-3857
  Enid *(G-2901)*
Action Spring Company ....E 918 836-9000
  Tulsa *(G-9097)*
Cannon & Refermat LLC ....F 405 521-0636
  Oklahoma City *(G-5688)*
Cannon Racecraft Inc ....F 405 524-7223
  Oklahoma City *(G-5689)*
Ebsco Spring Co Inc ....D 918 628-1680
  Tulsa *(G-9636)*
▲ Emco Industries LLC ....D 918 342-3488
  Claremore *(G-1617)*
▼ Gardner Industries Inc ....F 918 583-0171
  Tulsa *(G-9801)*
Sooner State Spring Mfg Co ....G 918 476-5707
  Chouteau *(G-1570)*

3496 Misc Fabricated Wire Prdts

Action Spring Company ....E 918 836-9000
  Tulsa *(G-9097)*
Angel Ornamental Iron Works ....G 918 584-8726
  Tulsa *(G-9191)*
Assocted Wire Rope Fabricators ....G 918 234-7450
  Tulsa *(G-9219)*
▲ Byers Products Group Inc ....G 405 491-8550
  Oklahoma City *(G-5652)*
▼ Continental Wire Cloth LLC ....G 918 794-0334
  Jenks *(G-3701)*
Cooks Fence & Iron Co Inc ....G 405 681-2301
  Oklahoma City *(G-5827)*
Custom Design By Roberts ....G 918 664-0466
  Tulsa *(G-9528)*
D & M Steel Manufacturing ....G 405 631-5027
  Oklahoma City *(G-5887)*
Dodco of Oklahoma LLC ....G 405 314-1757
  Blanchard *(G-712)*
Eastern Okla Fabrication Inc ....G 918 654-7344
  Cameron *(G-1257)*
Fence Solutions Inc ....G 580 233-4600
  Enid *(G-2957)*
◆ Fki Industries Inc ....G 918 834-4611
  Tulsa *(G-9752)*
▼ Gardner Industries Inc ....F 918 583-0171
  Tulsa *(G-9801)*
General Wire & Supply Co Inc ....E 918 245-5961
  Tulsa *(G-9817)*
Givens Manufacturing Inc ....G 888 302-2774
  Mounds *(G-4616)*
Global Wire Cloth LLC ....G 918 836-7211
  Tulsa *(G-9834)*
Holloway Wire Rope Svcs Inc ....F 918 582-1807
  Tulsa *(G-9939)*
Industrial Splicing Sling LLC ....G 918 835-4452
  Tulsa *(G-9981)*
Kaydawn Manufacturing Co Inc ....G 918 321-5017
  Glenpool *(G-3237)*

KG Fab ....G 405 912-9938
  Moore *(G-4531)*
Liberty Fence Co Inc ....G 918 834-6553
  Tulsa *(G-10156)*
M & R Wire Works Inc ....G 580 795-4290
  Madill *(G-4153)*
Mazzella Co ....G 405 423-6283
  Oklahoma City *(G-6544)*
Mlb Welding LLC ....G 580 481-0852
  Altus *(G-162)*
Oklahoma Post Tension Inc ....F 918 627-6013
  Tulsa *(G-10405)*
Oklahoma Screen Mfg LLC ....G 918 443-6500
  Tulsa *(G-10407)*
Oklahoma Screen Mfg LLC ....F 918 443-6500
  Oologah *(G-7535)*
◆ Oklahoma Steel & Wire Co Inc ....C 580 795-7311
  Madill *(G-4160)*
P W Manufacturing Company Inc ....G 918 652-4981
  Henryetta *(G-3514)*
Sooner State Spring Mfg Co ....G 918 476-5707
  Chouteau *(G-1570)*
Southwestern Wire Inc ....C 405 447-6900
  Norman *(G-5152)*
Swc ....G 918 251-2679
  Broken Arrow *(G-1068)*
Taylor & Sons Farms Inc ....G 405 222-0751
  Chickasha *(G-1515)*
Tight Wire Fence LLC ....G 479 220-1171
  Watts *(G-11358)*
Tims Sheds ....G 918 506-7741
  Tahlequah *(G-8888)*
Titan Fence Company ....G 580 237-3412
  Enid *(G-3065)*
◆ Unarco Industries LLC ....C 918 485-9531
  Wagoner *(G-11295)*
United Slings Inc ....G 405 598-2616
  Tecumseh *(G-8930)*
Wire Cloth Manufacturers Inc ....G 918 493-9400
  Tulsa *(G-11141)*
Wizard Industries ....G 918 622-5234
  Tulsa *(G-11143)*

3498 Fabricated Pipe & Pipe Fittings

Albright Steel and Wire Co ....G 580 357-3596
  Lawton *(G-3886)*
▲ American Pipe Bending Inc ....E 918 749-2363
  Tulsa *(G-9171)*
▲ Baker Hughes Elasto Systems ....F 405 670-3354
  Oklahoma City *(G-5516)*
Bendco Corp ....F 918 583-1566
  Tulsa *(G-9281)*
Bendmasters Inc ....G 918 585-3755
  Tulsa *(G-9282)*
Cimco Industries LLC ....G 918 783-5500
  Big Cabin *(G-601)*
Coupling Specialties Inc ....F 281 457-2000
  Oklahoma City *(G-5845)*
Cust O Bend ....G 918 241-0514
  Tulsa *(G-9525)*
Cust-O-Bend Inc ....G 918 241-0514
  Tulsa *(G-9526)*
Flatlands Threading Co Inc ....G 405 677-7351
  Oklahoma City *(G-6089)*
H G Flake Company Inc ....G 918 684-9004
  Muskogee *(G-4686)*
Handy & Harman ....G 918 258-1566
  Broken Arrow *(G-1131)*
Integrity Piping Services Co ....G 918 850-0206
  Sand Springs *(G-8193)*
Ipsco Tubulars Inc ....C 918 384-6400
  Catoosa *(G-1323)*
J & J Tubulars Inc ....G 405 691-2039
  Oklahoma City *(G-6330)*
JM Eagle Co ....G 405 273-0900
  Shawnee *(G-8464)*
Kloeckner Metals Corporation ....E 918 660-2050
  Catoosa *(G-1329)*
Lewis Industries Corp ....E 918 371-2596
  Collinsville *(G-1815)*
Los Angeles Boiler Works Inc ....E 580 363-1312
  Blackwell *(G-688)*
Mayco Inc ....E 405 677-5969
  Oklahoma City *(G-6543)*
Mike Cline Inc ....F 918 592-3712
  Tulsa *(G-10277)*
MRC Global (us) Inc ....G 918 485-9511
  Wagoner *(G-11287)*
Mw Piping Fabrication LLC ....F 918 836-4200
  Tulsa *(G-10319)*

National Oilwell Varco Inc .... C 918 781-4436
  Muskogee *(G-4719)*
Nortek Air Solutions LLC .... B 405 263-7286
  Okarche *(G-5247)*
Oilfield Equipment Company .... G 405 850-1406
  Duncan *(G-2161)*
Oilfield Improvements Inc .... G 918 250-5584
  Broken Arrow *(G-993)*
Pipeline Equipment Inc .... E 918 224-4144
  Tulsa *(G-9024)*
Pro-Fab Industries Inc .... E 918 865-7590
  Mannford *(G-4190)*
Rise Manufacturing LLC .... E 918 994-6240
  Broken Arrow *(G-1032)*
Safeco Filter Products Inc .... F 918 455-0100
  Tulsa *(G-9033)*
Safeco Manufacturing Inc .... F 918 455-0100
  Broken Arrow *(G-1160)*
Sharp Metal Fabricators Inc .... F 405 899-4849
  Noble *(G-4891)*
Shaw Group Inc .... A 918 445-7744
  Tulsa *(G-10739)*
Sooner Swage & Coating Co Inc .... G 918 689-7142
  Eufaula *(G-3114)*
SUN Engineering Inc .... F 918 627-0426
  Tulsa *(G-10870)*
Superior Dynmics Fbrcation LLC .... G 918 698-9846
  Bartlesville *(G-531)*
▲ Tulsa Tube Bending Co Inc .... E 888 882-3637
  Tulsa *(G-11011)*
U S Weatherford L P .... C 580 276-5362
  Marietta *(G-4216)*
Weatherford International LLC .... E 405 773-1100
  Oklahoma City *(G-7430)*
Weatherford International LLC .... E 580 490-1476
  Wilson *(G-11545)*
Wolverine Tube Inc .... A 405 275-4850
  Shawnee *(G-8522)*
Wood Pipe Service Inc .... G 405 672-6097
  Oklahoma City *(G-7464)*
Word Inds Fabrication LLC .... E 918 382-7704
  Tulsa *(G-11152)*

3499 Fabricated Metal Prdts, NEC

Aerostar International Inc .... G 918 789-3000
  Chelsea *(G-1401)*
All-Star Trophies & Ribbon Mfg .... G 918 283-2200
  Claremore *(G-1581)*
American Intellectual LLC .... G 405 605-2378
  Oklahoma City *(G-5436)*
Automtive Cting Specialist Inc .... G 918 698-1560
  Wagoner *(G-11274)*
B Rowdy Rnch Met Fbrcation LLC ..... G 405 973-5976
  Luther *(G-4132)*
Bkw Inc .... G 918 836-6767
  Tulsa *(G-9299)*
Built Better Enterprises LLC .... G 580 492-5227
  Fletcher *(G-3161)*
▲ C&A International LLC .... E 918 872-1645
  Tulsa *(G-9362)*
C&M Enterprises .... G 918 683-4456
  Muskogee *(G-4657)*
Cheyenne Products LLC .... G 918 639-8583
  Owasso *(G-7553)*
Clark Mtal Bldngs Fbrcation LL .... G 580 695-4915
  Guthrie *(G-3309)*
Cni Manufacturing LLC .... G 580 276-3306
  Marietta *(G-4205)*
Del Nero Manufacturing Co .... G 405 364-4800
  Norman *(G-4976)*
Frog Printing & Awards Ctr LLC .... G 580 678-1114
  Lawton *(G-3931)*
Gary Mace .... G 580 654-2660
  Carnegie *(G-1276)*
Gloria Rae Travel Accessories .... G 405 848-1300
  Oklahoma City *(G-6163)*
House of Trophies .... G 918 341-2111
  Claremore *(G-1637)*
Js Metal Fabrication LLC .... G 918 428-2242
  Tulsa *(G-10063)*
Justus Fabrication .... G 918 207-5192
  Tahlequah *(G-8869)*
JW Measurement Co .... G 918 465-2605
  Wilburton *(G-11521)*
Lothrop Technologies Inc .... G 405 390-3499
  Choctaw *(G-1551)*
Mart Trophy Co Inc .... G 918 481-3388
  Tulsa *(G-10217)*
Midwest Industries Inc .... G 405 279-3595
  Meeker *(G-4382)*

▲ Mtm Recognition Corporation .... B 405 609-6900
  Oklahoma City *(G-6634)*
Oklahoma Safety Eqp Co Inc .... C 918 258-5626
  Broken Arrow *(G-994)*
RB Cnstr Met Fabrication LLC .... G 580 367-5039
  Caney *(G-1262)*
Ricks Rod Reel Svc-High .... G 405 823-7581
  Oklahoma City *(G-7022)*
River Industries LLC .... G 918 406-8991
  Collinsville *(G-1821)*
Southwest Engineering .... G 405 634-2841
  Oklahoma City *(G-7176)*
Sparks Mtal Dsign Fbrction LLC .... G 918 676-5112
  Fairland *(G-3131)*
Taraco Enterprises LLC .... G 580 679-3956
  Duke *(G-2080)*
Trinity Shtmtl Fabrication LLC .... G 918 899-6030
  Purcell *(G-8025)*
USA Metal Fabrication LLC .... G 918 845-6500
  Oklahoma City *(G-7379)*
W E Industries Inc .... G 405 949-0222
  Oklahoma City *(G-7410)*
Western Iron Works LLC .... G 405 779-1961
  Chickasha *(G-1524)*
York Metal Fabrication .... G 405 598-6239
  Tecumseh *(G-8931)*

35 INDUSTRIAL AND COMMERCIAL MACHINERY AND COMPUTER EQUIPMENT

3511 Steam, Gas & Hydraulic Turbines & Engines

◆ Bergey Windpower Company Inc .... E 405 364-4212
  Norman *(G-4930)*
Caprock Country Entps Inc .... F 580 924-1647
  Calera *(G-1239)*
Dewind Co .... G 580 338-3271
  Guymon *(G-3348)*
Integrity Power Solutions LLC .... G 918 925-9693
  Edmond *(G-2461)*
Next-Gen Wind LLC .... G 405 948-1556
  Oklahoma City *(G-6674)*
Ringside Productions .... G 818 974-2673
  Tulsa *(G-10655)*
Schock Manufacturing Inc .... E 918 609-3600
  Owasso *(G-7615)*
Siemens Energy .... G 580 254-7824
  Woodward *(G-11631)*
Solar Turbines Incorporated .... G 918 459-5100
  Broken Arrow *(G-1054)*
Suzlon Wind Energy Corporation ...... G 580 468-2641
  Guymon *(G-3367)*
Universal Pressure Pumping Inc .... B 405 262-2441
  El Reno *(G-2765)*
Vogt Power International Inc .... G 502 899-4500
  Sapulpa *(G-8321)*

3519 Internal Combustion Engines, NEC

▲ Arrow Engine Company .... D 918 583-5711
  Tulsa *(G-9211)*
Automotive Machine Shop .... G 918 775-9770
  Sallisaw *(G-8139)*
Bach Welding & Diesel Service .... G 580 593-2599
  Custer City *(G-1973)*
Cummins - Allison Corp .... F 405 321-1411
  Norman *(G-4972)*
Cummins Enterprises Inc .... G 405 232-9022
  Oklahoma City *(G-5867)*
Cummins Inc .... B 405 946-4481
  Oklahoma City *(G-5868)*
Cummins Southern Plains LLC .... E 918 234-3240
  Tulsa *(G-9522)*
Cummins Southern Plains LLC .... E 405 946-4481
  Oklahoma City *(G-5869)*
Engines Alive .... G 918 406-8149
  Broken Arrow *(G-901)*
Floyds Machine Shop .... G 918 256-8440
  Vinita *(G-11258)*
Hoss Marine Propulsion Inc .... G 918 479-5167
  Locust Grove *(G-4110)*
Hudson Bros Rmanufactured Engs ... G 405 598-2260
  Tecumseh *(G-8919)*
Independent Diesel Service .... F 580 234-0435
  Enid *(G-2977)*
Memorial Auto Supply Inc .... F 405 324-5400
  Oklahoma City *(G-6564)*

Pacific Power Group LLC .... G 405 685-4630
  Oklahoma City *(G-6793)*
Production Engine & Pump Inc .... F 405 672-3644
  Oklahoma City *(G-6910)*
Russell Baker Racing Engines .... G 918 533-3825
  Miami *(G-4429)*
Southwestern Motor Rebuilders .... G 918 585-1519
  Tulsa *(G-10811)*
Thomas H Scott Western LLC .... G 405 632-6860
  Oklahoma City *(G-7283)*
United Engines Manufacture .... G 405 601-9861
  Oklahoma City *(G-7366)*
White Dove Small Engines .... G 580 857-2201
  Allen *(G-139)*
Woltjer Engines .... G 918 258-0598
  Broken Arrow *(G-1101)*

3523 Farm Machinery & Eqpt

3 C Cattle Feeders Inc .... F 580 384-3943
  Mill Creek *(G-4465)*
Allied H2o Inc .... G 405 550-3085
  Edmond *(G-2296)*
Audio Link Inc .... G 405 359-0017
  Edmond *(G-2311)*
Baker Manufacturing Inc .... G 580 327-0234
  Alva *(G-177)*
Bermuda King LLC .... G 405 375-5000
  Ringwood *(G-8085)*
Blue Ribbon Show Supply .... G 918 288-7396
  Sperry *(G-8605)*
Blue River Ventures Inc .... G 580 920-0111
  Durant *(G-2206)*
Blue River Ventures Inc .... G 580 798-4810
  Overbrook *(G-7538)*
Blue River Ventures Inc .... G 580 920-0111
  Calera *(G-1238)*
Bramco Inc .... F 580 227-2345
  Fairview *(G-3133)*
Built Better Enterprises LLC .... G 580 492-5227
  Fletcher *(G-3161)*
Buster Par Corp .... F 918 585-8542
  Tulsa *(G-9354)*
Cammond Industries LLC .... F 580 332-9300
  Ada *(G-18)*
Cardon Trailers .... G 580 327-0701
  Alva *(G-180)*
Century Livestock Feeders Inc .... F 918 793-3382
  Shidler *(G-8524)*
Century Products LLC .... G 908 793-3382
  Kaw City *(G-3757)*
Cherokee Hart Ranch .... G 918 563-4244
  Talihina *(G-8905)*
Craigs Oklahoma Pride LLC .... G 405 224-6410
  Chickasha *(G-1451)*
Dale Case Homes Inc .... G 405 755-5055
  Oklahoma City *(G-5890)*
Davids Trading Yard .... G 918 432-5671
  Kiowa *(G-3837)*
Deans Machine & Welding Inc .... G 580 688-3374
  Hollis *(G-3564)*
Dover Products Inc .... G 918 476-5688
  Chouteau *(G-1562)*
Enterprise Grain Company LLC .... G 580 874-2286
  Kremlin *(G-3851)*
Five Star Cub Cadet .... G 918 542-4070
  Miami *(G-4404)*
Forster & Son Inc .... G 580 332-6020
  Ada *(G-36)*
▼ Garfield Inc .... E 580 242-6411
  Enid *(G-2961)*
Gilliam Cattle .... G 405 392-4204
  Newcastle *(G-4827)*
Greg E Conard .... G 580 372-7982
  Soper *(G-8587)*
Gregory Dee Spahn Trust .... G 405 826-6777
  Broken Arrow *(G-922)*
H Diamond Resources Inc .... F 580 476-3733
  Rush Springs *(G-8121)*
Heather Harjochee .... G 405 615-3273
  Oklahoma City *(G-5293)*
Heavybilt Mfg Inc .... D 580 927-3003
  Coalgate *(G-1781)*
Hidden Valley Manufacturing .... G 580 343-2303
  Corn *(G-1867)*
Johnson Welding .... G 580 569-2231
  Mountain Park *(G-4626)*
Just Plant It LLC .... G 405 226-3111
  Macomb *(G-4142)*
Kelly Labs .... G 682 367-8743
  Longdale *(G-4125)*

Lacy Lockwood ....G.... 918 456-6837
Tahlequah *(G-8871)*
Lemans Manufacturing Inc ....F.... 405 224-6410
Chickasha *(G-1481)*
Mark Armitage ....G.... 405 279-2372
Meeker *(G-4380)*
▲ Miami Industrial Supply & Mfg ....E.... 918 542-6317
Miami *(G-4415)*
Michael R Williams ....G.... 918 418-9344
Vinita *(G-11264)*
Mitchell Ironworks Inc ....G.... 580 233-7925
Enid *(G-3014)*
Murphy Products Inc ....G.... 405 842-7177
Oklahoma City *(G-6636)*
Musick Farms Inc ....G.... 580 393-4826
Sentinel *(G-8411)*
R & R Lawncare & Cleaning ....G.... 580 480-1953
Altus *(G-167)*
Red Fork Mfg LLC ....G.... 405 368-7367
Dover *(G-2044)*
Ritberger Inc ....G.... 918 271-3895
Broken Arrow *(G-1033)*
Rocky L Emmons & Judy E Sprag ....G.... 580 305-1940
Frederick *(G-3199)*
◆ Savage Equipment Incorporated ....E.... 580 795-3394
Madill *(G-4162)*
Shawnee Milling Company ....G.... 405 352-4336
Minco *(G-4481)*
Southwest Fabricators Inc ....F.... 580 326-3589
Hugo *(G-3621)*
Sullivans Grading & Sod ....G.... 580 591-2868
Lawton *(G-4007)*
Taylor & Sons Farms Inc ....G.... 405 222-0751
Chickasha *(G-1515)*
Top Secret Case LLC ....G.... 918 521-0601
Claremore *(G-1693)*
Transfer Cses Cltches Dffrntal ....G.... 405 232-9557
Oklahoma City *(G-7318)*
Trojan Livestock Equipment ....G.... 580 772-1849
Weatherford *(G-11451)*
W Flying Inc ....F.... 580 623-5566
Watonga *(G-11351)*
▼ W-W Manufacturing Co Inc ....D.... 580 661-3720
Thomas *(G-8951)*
W-W Manufacturing Co Inc ....D.... 580 661-3720
Thomas *(G-8952)*
▲ Wako LLC ....E.... 580 234-3434
Enid *(G-3072)*
Walter Shpman Dsblity Ssi Cses ....G.... 580 280-4727
Lawton *(G-4020)*

3524 Garden, Lawn Tractors & Eqpt

Bob Lowe Farm Machinery Inc ....F.... 405 224-6500
Chickasha *(G-1440)*
Day In Sun Landscaping ....G.... 580 768-4986
Durant *(G-2222)*
E & D Enterprises ....G.... 580 512-1806
Cache *(G-1226)*
Forrest Lawns Landscapes ....G.... 405 397-4679
Oklahoma City *(G-6103)*
J & N Small Engine Repair ....G.... 405 382-2792
Seminole *(G-8377)*
Juda Enterprises LLC ....G.... 405 542-3975
Hinton *(G-3531)*
Newton Equipment LLC ....F.... 918 756-3560
Okmulgee *(G-7517)*
▼ Reputation Services & Mfg LLC ....E.... 918 437-2077
Tulsa *(G-10643)*
Standard Supply Co Inc ....G.... 918 272-5014
Owasso *(G-7619)*

3531 Construction Machinery & Eqpt

A&J Mixing ....G.... 405 946-1461
Oklahoma City *(G-5349)*
A-1 Backhoe ....G.... 405 547-5452
Perkins *(G-7714)*
A-1 Backhoe Inc ....G.... 405 863-7094
Oklahoma City *(G-5350)*
Adair County Commisioners Off ....E.... 918 696-7633
Stilwell *(G-8779)*
Altec Inc ....G.... 405 577-6322
Oklahoma City *(G-5426)*
▲ American Castings LLC ....B.... 918 476-4252
Pryor *(G-7942)*
B and J Backhoe and Cnstr ....G.... 580 467-4981
Duncan *(G-2086)*
Backhoe Services Oklahoma LLC ....G.... 405 356-2712
Luther *(G-4133)*
Beller Boring Backhoe L ....G.... 405 288-6638
Washington *(G-11333)*
Billy McGill ....G.... 580 220-7097
Marietta *(G-4200)*
Bobs Backhoe Sevice ....G.... 918 391-0901
Talala *(G-8896)*
Brents Dana ....G.... 405 640-1566
Newcastle *(G-4819)*
Brown Equipment Corporation ....G.... 405 799-4000
Oklahoma City *(G-5635)*
C & C Backhoe & Tractor Inc ....G.... 405 392-4699
Blanchard *(G-703)*
Cammond Industries LLC ....F.... 580 332-9300
Ada *(G-18)*
Carl Abla ....G.... 580 526-3267
Erick *(G-3086)*
▼ Charles Machine Works Inc ....A.... 580 572-2693
Perry *(G-7728)*
Clydes Good Gruel LLC ....G.... 918 323-6143
Tulsa *(G-9458)*
CMI Terex Corporation ....G.... 405 787-6020
Oklahoma City *(G-5793)*
◆ CMI Terex Corporation ....A.... 405 787-6020
Oklahoma City *(G-5792)*
Combotronics Inc ....E.... 918 543-3300
Inola *(G-3656)*
County of Carter ....F.... 580 657-4050
Lone Grove *(G-4116)*
Crane Carrier Company ....G.... 918 286-2300
Tulsa *(G-9501)*
Cravens Backhoe Service LLC ....G.... 580 661-3652
Thomas *(G-8941)*
CRC-Evans Pipeline Intl Inc ....C.... 918 438-2100
Tulsa *(G-9504)*
Crosslands A A Rent-All Sls Co ....G.... 405 366-8878
Norman *(G-4970)*
D&S Dirtwork and Small Eqp ....G.... 580 485-8933
Atoka *(G-404)*
Dans Backhoe & Dozer Service ....G.... 580 256-0865
Woodward *(G-11576)*
◆ Darby Equipment Co ....E.... 918 582-2340
Tulsa *(G-9552)*
Dewey County ....F.... 580 995-3444
Vici *(G-11241)*
Diamond Attachments LLC ....E.... 580 889-3366
Atoka *(G-405)*
Diamond Manufacturing Inc ....E.... 580 889-6202
Atoka *(G-406)*
Dickson Industries Inc ....E.... 405 598-6547
Tecumseh *(G-8912)*
Dig-It Backhoe Trctr Svcs LLC ....G.... 405 921-2623
Harrah *(G-3376)*
Dolese Bros Co ....F.... 580 255-3046
Duncan *(G-2107)*
Don Moody Farm ....G.... 580 648-2489
Olustee *(G-7531)*
Don Wilson Pipeline Constructi ....G.... 918 225-2786
Cushing *(G-1932)*
◆ Double Life Corporation ....F.... 405 789-7867
Oklahoma City *(G-5971)*
Dougherty Forestry Mfg Ltd ....F.... 405 542-3520
Hinton *(G-3523)*
▲ Dp Manufacturing Inc ....C.... 918 250-2450
Jenks *(G-3704)*
Duck Brothers Dozer & Trucking ....G.... 580 925-3509
Konawa *(G-3845)*
E-Z Drill Inc ....G.... 405 372-0121
Perry *(G-7732)*
E-Z Drill Inc ....E.... 580 336-9874
Perry *(G-7733)*
▲ Ellis Manufacturing Co Inc ....G.... 405 528-4671
Oklahoma City *(G-6028)*
Four Feathers Transports ....G.... 405 343-9799
Crescent *(G-1915)*
Frontier Logging Corporation ....G.... 405 787-3952
Oklahoma City *(G-6122)*
G T Bynum Company ....G.... 918 587-9118
Tulsa *(G-9794)*
▼ Garfield Inc ....E.... 580 242-6411
Enid *(G-2961)*
Garrison Backhoe LLC ....G.... 580 465-2014
Ardmore *(G-294)*
George Townsend & Co Inc ....G.... 405 235-1387
Oklahoma City *(G-6145)*
George W Smith Salvage City ....G.... 580 332-2250
Ada *(G-41)*
◆ Goff Inc ....F.... 405 278-6200
Seminole *(G-8374)*
H & L Tooth Company ....D.... 918 272-0951
Tulsa *(G-9872)*
H G Jenkins Construction LLC ....E.... 580 355-9822
Lawton *(G-3938)*
Hadley-Keeney Chipping Inc ....E.... 580 835-2645
Eagletown *(G-2275)*
Horton World Solutions LLC ....F.... 817 821-8320
Broken Arrow *(G-1133)*
Ideal Crane Corporation ....F.... 800 622-6163
Tulsa *(G-9966)*
Industrial Trctr Parts Co Inc ....G.... 918 258-6580
Broken Arrow *(G-935)*
Ironwolf Manufacturing LLC ....F.... 405 872-1890
Noble *(G-4882)*
J & G Trucking ....G.... 918 693-4300
Nowata *(G-5215)*
J E Shaffer Co ....G.... 918 582-1752
Owasso *(G-7577)*
J&A Services Co Inc ....G.... 405 833-4824
Norman *(G-5040)*
Jack Sprague ....G.... 405 367-7655
Blanchard *(G-717)*
Jacks Cnstr & Backhoe Svc ....G.... 405 238-3569
Pauls Valley *(G-7661)*
▼ Jensen Mixers Intl Inc ....E.... 918 627-5770
Tulsa *(G-10035)*
Jims Backhoe LLC ....G.... 405 352-5003
Minco *(G-4476)*
John A Littleaxe ....G.... 405 365-5117
Tecumseh *(G-8921)*
K&R Backhoe and Dirt Svcs LLC ....G.... 580 239-8630
Atoka *(G-417)*
Kahn Backhoe & Trenching ....G.... 580 541-6600
Okeene *(G-5258)*
Kens Plumbing & Backhoe ....G.... 918 963-4223
Shady Point *(G-8414)*
Kevin Banks ....G.... 918 230-2142
Bristow *(G-785)*
Kinder Equipment LLC ....G.... 580 335-2363
Frederick *(G-3195)*
Kuykendal Wldg Backhoe Svc LLC ....G.... 918 372-4899
Ripley *(G-8101)*
L&M Dump Truck & Backhoe Servi ....G.... 918 798-4568
Sperry *(G-8609)*
Laney Mfg Inc ....G.... 580 335-2363
Frederick *(G-3196)*
Lincoln County Barn Dist No 3 ....E.... 405 279-3313
Meeker *(G-4379)*
Lkq Corporation ....F.... 918 428-3835
Tulsa *(G-10171)*
Majetta Tractor & Backhoe Inc ....G.... 918 272-7861
Owasso *(G-7589)*
Martys Dumptruck & Backhoe Svc ....G.... 918 869-2051
Muskogee *(G-4707)*
Mid Continent Concrete Co ....G.... 918 775-6858
Sallisaw *(G-8149)*
▲ Midwestern Manufacturing Co ....G.... 918 446-1587
Tulsa *(G-10274)*
Mike McCalip ....G.... 405 452-5730
Wetumka *(G-11495)*
Mitch Baskett ....G.... 405 324-7810
Yukon *(G-11756)*
More Boom Company ....G.... 580 226-5303
Ardmore *(G-335)*
Morgan Hauling ....G.... 580 420-3265
Broken Bow *(G-1202)*
▲ N A Blastrac Inc ....D.... 405 478-3440
Oklahoma City *(G-6645)*
Nelson Backhoe and Welding ....G.... 918 399-3426
Cushing *(G-1947)*
Okie Plumbing and Backhoe ....G.... 580 302-5018
Sulphur *(G-8840)*
Oklahoma Cement Solutions LLC ....G.... 214 802-1527
Choctaw *(G-1553)*
Ottawa County District 3 ....F.... 918 676-3227
Fairland *(G-3127)*
Paccar Inc ....C.... 918 251-8511
Broken Arrow *(G-996)*
Pennington Allen Cpitl Prtners ....E.... 918 749-6811
Tulsa *(G-10486)*
▲ Ramsey Industries Inc ....C.... 918 438-2760
Tulsa *(G-10617)*
◆ Ramsey Winch Company ....C.... 918 438-2760
Tulsa *(G-10618)*
Randys Backhoe Service ....G.... 580 227-0561
Longdale *(G-4126)*
▼ Reputation Services & Mfg LLC ....E.... 918 437-2077
Tulsa *(G-10643)*
Rick Crsslin Backhoe Dozer Svc ....G.... 918 371-7956
Mounds *(G-4624)*
Roger Key Inc ....G.... 918 423-5420
Mcalester *(G-4333)*
Roger W Boone ....G.... 580 799-0035
Elk City *(G-2868)*

SIC SECTION
35 INDUSTRIAL AND COMMERCIAL MACHINERY AND COMPUTER EQUIPMENT

Ron Griggs Backhoe & Dump .... G 918 440-1334
  Dewey *(G-2032)*
▲ Sawyer Manufacturing Company ..... E 918 834-2550
  Tulsa *(G-9034)*
◆ Simmons Tool LLC .... G 580 228-2799
  Waurika *(G-11364)*
Sjh Welding & Backhoe LLC .... G 405 833-8353
  Calumet *(G-1249)*
Smiths Backhoe and Utility .... G 405 202-7056
  Perkins *(G-7722)*
Smittys Backhoe Service LLC .... G 918 630-1090
  Tulsa *(G-10781)*
South Central Oilfld Svcs Inc .... G 580 465-4498
  Wilson *(G-11542)*
Spragues Backhoe LLC .... G 405 600-4905
  Oklahoma City *(G-7188)*
Sterling Crane LLC .... G 918 728-8613
  Tulsa *(G-10848)*
Swh Construction LLC .... F 405 317-0663
  Washington *(G-11338)*
T2t Storm Shelters .... G 580 512-4890
  Lawton *(G-4011)*
Terex Cranes .... G 405 491-2006
  Oklahoma City *(G-7269)*
Terex Mining .... G 918 296-0530
  Jenks *(G-3735)*
Terex USA LLC .... F 405 787-6020
  Oklahoma City *(G-7270)*
Thomas Appraisal Service .... G 918 341-5860
  Claremore *(G-1692)*
Toms Tree Svc & Backhoe .... G 918 865-4861
  Jennings *(G-3740)*
Tribal Consortium Inc .... G 580 332-1134
  Ada *(G-96)*
Triple C Grading & Excvtg LLC .... G 918 605-1848
  Sapulpa *(G-8317)*
▲ Tulsa Winch Inc .... G 918 298-8300
  Jenks *(G-3736)*
▼ V M I Inc .... F 918 225-7000
  Cushing *(G-1965)*
Varners Eqp Sls & Svc LLC .... G 918 367-3800
  Bristow *(G-803)*
▲ Waldon Equipment LLC .... F 580 227-3711
  Fairview *(G-3155)*
Western Fibers Inc .... E 509 679-4786
  Hollis *(G-3571)*
William L Riggs Company Inc .... G 918 437-3245
  Tulsa *(G-11125)*

3532 Mining Machinery & Eqpt

Asbury Machine Corporation .... F 580 628-3416
  Tonkawa *(G-8972)*
Audio Link Inc .... G 405 359-0017
  Edmond *(G-2311)*
Century Geophysical Corp .... E 918 838-9811
  Tulsa *(G-9399)*
Cutting Edge Technologies LLC .... G 918 284-6069
  Owasso *(G-7558)*
Dorssers Usa Inc .... G 918 422-5881
  Colcord *(G-1789)*
Enid Drill Systems Inc .... G 580 234-5971
  Enid *(G-2951)*
Flotek Industries Inc .... G 580 252-5111
  Duncan *(G-2118)*
Helvey International Usa Inc .... E 405 203-0251
  Oklahoma City *(G-6237)*
J T Harrison Construction Co .... F 918 967-2852
  Stigler *(G-8633)*
Prestige Manufacturing Co LLC .... E 405 395-0500
  Shawnee *(G-8485)*
Riverside Operations Group LLC ..... E 918 908-9480
  Broken Arrow *(G-1034)*
South Central Machine .... G 580 775-1623
  Durant *(G-2258)*
▲ Technical Manufacturing Inc .... F 918 485-0380
  Wagoner *(G-11292)*

3533 Oil Field Machinery & Eqpt

Aceco Valve Inc .... E 918 827-3669
  Mounds *(G-4608)*
Adko Inc .... G 405 677-6507
  Oklahoma City *(G-5375)*
Aether Dbs LLC .... G 918 317-2375
  Tulsa *(G-8988)*
AG Quip Inc .... G 918 536-4325
  Ramona *(G-8043)*
All States Production Eqp Co .... G 405 672-2323
  Oklahoma City *(G-5414)*
◆ American Directional Tech .... G 405 449-3362
  Wayne *(G-11365)*

American Machine & Tool Co .... G 405 794-9820
  Wewoka *(G-11497)*
Apergy Artfl Lift Intl LLC .... C 432 561-8101
  Oklahoma City *(G-9198)*
Apollo Engineering Company .... G 918 251-6780
  Broken Arrow *(G-830)*
Apollo Oilfield Supply LLC .... G 580 254-0164
  Woodward *(G-11554)*
Appli-Fab Custom Coating .... G 405 235-7039
  Chandler *(G-1375)*
APT Inc .... G 405 354-8438
  Yukon *(G-11691)*
Asbury Machine Corporation .... F 580 628-3416
  Tonkawa *(G-8972)*
Atlas Instrument & Mfg Co .... G 918 371-1976
  Collinsville *(G-1800)*
▲ Atlas Rock Bit Service Inc .... F 405 691-4848
  Oklahoma City *(G-5486)*
Axis Technologies LLC .... G 580 467-4257
  Duncan *(G-2085)*
Baker Hughes A GE Company LLC .. G 405 227-8471
  Oklahoma City *(G-5515)*
Baker Hughes A GE Company LLC .. C 918 828-1600
  Tulsa *(G-9255)*
▲ Baker Hughes Elasto Systems ..... F 405 670-3354
  Oklahoma City *(G-5516)*
Baker Hughes Incorporated .... D 918 426-6585
  McAlester *(G-4272)*
Baker Petrolite LLC .... G 918 245-2224
  Sand Springs *(G-8165)*
Bauman Machine Inc .... E 405 745-3484
  Oklahoma City *(G-5531)*
BF Machines Shop Inc .... F 580 255-5899
  Duncan *(G-2091)*
Bico Drilling Tools Inc .... G 918 872-9983
  Broken Arrow *(G-850)*
Big Iron Oilfield Services .... G 580 788-2247
  Elmore City *(G-2894)*
Borden Company Inc .... E 918 224-0816
  Sapulpa *(G-8258)*
◆ Borets US Inc .... B 918 439-7000
  Tulsa *(G-9320)*
Borets US Inc .... E 405 949-0031
  Oklahoma City *(G-5621)*
Bradshaw Home LLC .... G 918 582-5404
  Tulsa *(G-9329)*
Bri-Chem Supply Corp LLC .... G 405 200-5466
  Chickasha *(G-1444)*
◆ Bronco Manufacturing LLC .... E 918 446-7196
  Tulsa *(G-9340)*
Bynum & Company Inc .... F 580 265-7747
  Stonewall *(G-8798)*
C & C Equipment Specialist Inc .... E 405 677-3110
  Oklahoma City *(G-5655)*
C & H Safety Pin Inc .... G 405 949-5843
  Newalla *(G-4806)*
C & H Tool & Machine Inc .... G 580 332-1929
  Ada *(G-16)*
▲ C & H Tool & Machine Inc .... F 580 332-1929
  Ada *(G-17)*
C&H Safety Pin Inc .... G 405 386-3942
  McLoud *(G-4356)*
C-Star Mfg Inc .... G 405 756-1530
  Lindsay *(G-4054)*
Callaway Equipment & Mfg .... F 405 632-1870
  Oklahoma City *(G-5672)*
Cameron International Corp .... C 405 745-2715
  Oklahoma City *(G-5677)*
Cameron International Corp .... E 405 843-5578
  Oklahoma City *(G-5678)*
Cameron International Corp .... E 405 789-8065
  Oklahoma City *(G-5679)*
Cameron Technologies Inc .... G 405 682-1661
  Moore *(G-4503)*
Cameron Technologies Inc .... E 580 470-9600
  Duncan *(G-2097)*
Carl Bright Inc .... G 405 761-7129
  McLoud *(G-4357)*
▲ Centek Inc .... E 405 219-3200
  Oklahoma City *(G-5724)*
Circle B Msrment Fbrcation LLC ...... G 918 445-4488
  Tulsa *(G-9429)*
Cnc Metal Shape Cnstr LLC .... F 405 605-5500
  Oklahoma City *(G-5794)*
◆ Comanche Bit Service Inc .... G 580 439-6424
  Comanche *(G-1836)*
Compass Manufacturing LLC .... G 405 735-3518
  Oklahoma City *(G-5809)*
▲ Compressco Inc .... D 405 677-0221
  Oklahoma City *(G-5814)*

Compressco Partners Sub Inc .... C 405 677-0221
  Oklahoma City *(G-5816)*
Cougar Drilling Solutions USA .... E 405 789-4945
  Oklahoma City *(G-5841)*
CP Energy Holdings LLC .... F 405 513-6006
  Edmond *(G-2369)*
Crowley Oil & Mfg .... G 918 744-8129
  Tulsa *(G-9514)*
Crown Energy Technology Okla ...... E 405 348-9954
  Edmond *(G-2376)*
▲ Crystaltech Inc .... E 580 252-8893
  Duncan *(G-2101)*
▲ Cyclonic Valve Company .... E 918 317-8200
  Broken Arrow *(G-883)*
D C Jones Machine Co .... G 918 786-6855
  Grove *(G-3265)*
D Parks Enterprises LLC .... G 405 315-1994
  Sand Springs *(G-8177)*
D&L Manufacturing Inc .... E 918 587-3504
  Tulsa *(G-9542)*
◆ Darby Equipment Co .... E 918 582-2340
  Tulsa *(G-9552)*
Davco Fab Inc .... E 918 757-2504
  Jennings *(G-3739)*
Davis Machine Shop Inc .... F 918 756-3055
  Lindsay *(G-4059)*
Deco Development Company Inc .... G 918 747-6366
  Tulsa *(G-9566)*
◆ Den-Con Tool Co .... F 405 670-5942
  Oklahoma City *(G-5921)*
◆ Double Life Corporation .... F 405 789-7867
  Oklahoma City *(G-5971)*
▲ Downing Wellhead Equipment LLC .. E 405 486-7858
  Oklahoma City *(G-5973)*
Downing Wellhead Equipment LLC .. G 405 789-8182
  Oklahoma City *(G-5974)*
Drillers Service Center Inc .... E 405 631-3728
  Oklahoma City *(G-5980)*
Eco Oil Fill Services .... E 580 774-2240
  Weatherford *(G-11409)*
Electrotech Inc .... G 918 224-5869
  Tulsa *(G-9002)*
Energy Meter Systems LLC .... E 405 853-4976
  Hennessey *(G-3460)*
◆ Engineering Technology Inc .... E 918 492-0508
  Tulsa *(G-9687)*
Enid Mack Sales Inc .... D 580 234-0043
  Enid *(G-2954)*
Fabricating Specialists Inc .... F 405 476-1959
  Oklahoma City *(G-6068)*
Fabwell Corporation .... G 918 224-9060
  Sapulpa *(G-8272)*
Fairmount Minerals .... G 580 456-7791
  Roff *(G-8108)*
Fammco Mfg Co Inc .... G 918 437-0456
  Tulsa *(G-9727)*
Fhe USA LLC .... G 405 350-2544
  Yukon *(G-11723)*
▲ Fibre Reduction Inc .... G 580 223-3401
  Ardmore *(G-289)*
FMC Technologies Inc .... G 405 787-6301
  Oklahoma City *(G-6098)*
FMC Technologies Inc .... F 405 972-1305
  Oklahoma City *(G-6099)*
FMC Technologies Inc .... G 405 415-9532
  Oklahoma City *(G-6100)*
Forum Energy Technologies Inc ...... D 405 603-7198
  Oklahoma City *(G-6105)*
Forum Energy Technologies Inc ...... D 405 224-5779
  Chickasha *(G-1459)*
Forum Energy Technologies Inc ...... G 580 622-5058
  Davis *(G-1983)*
Forum Production Equipment .... D 580 622-5058
  Davis *(G-1984)*
Forum Us Inc .... D 580 788-2333
  Elmore City *(G-2896)*
Ftdm Investments Llc .... D 918 598-3430
  Locust Grove *(G-4107)*
G & G Quality Services LLC .... G 918 961-0288
  Miami *(G-4406)*
▼ G B E Services Corporation .... G 918 428-8665
  Tulsa *(G-9788)*
Gardner Denver Inc .... D 918 664-1151
  Tulsa *(G-9800)*
Gastech Engineering LLC .... D 918 663-8383
  Sapulpa *(G-8274)*
◆ Gator Rigs LLC .... G 405 598-3266
  Tecumseh *(G-8916)*
GE Oil & Gas Pressure Ctrl LP ...... E 405 273-7660
  Shawnee *(G-8451)*

Employee Codes: A=Over 500 employees, B=251-500
C=101-250, D=51-100, E=20-50, F=10-19, G=1-9

2020 Oklahoma Directory
of Manufacturers & Processors

35 INDUSTRIAL AND COMMERCIAL MACHINERY AND COMPUTER EQUIPMENT

Company	Code	Phone
GE Packaged Power LLC — Shawnee (G-8452)	G	405 395-0400
▼ Gefco Inc — Enid (G-2962)	C	580 243-4141
▲ General Manufacturer Inc — Okmulgee (G-7504)	F	918 756-3067
Gordon Bros Supply Inc — Stroud (G-8810)	E	918 968-2591
H-V Manufacturing Company — Glenpool (G-3235)	F	918 291-2108
Halliburton Company — Duncan (G-2121)	E	580 251-4614
Halliburton Company — Duncan (G-2122)	C	580 251-3002
Harry H Diamond Inc — Shawnee (G-8458)	G	405 275-5788
▲ Hendershot Tool Company — Oklahoma City (G-6238)	E	405 677-3386
Horizontal Well Drillers LLC — Purcell (G-8010)	G	405 527-1232
Hoss LLC — Tulsa (G-9952)	F	918 660-7220
Hunting Titan Inc — Oklahoma City (G-6273)	E	405 495-1322
Hydro Foam Technology Inc — Perkins (G-7718)	F	405 547-5800
▲ Industrial Rubber Inc — Oklahoma City (G-6300)	E	405 632-9783
Industrial Specialties LLC — Elk City (G-2826)	G	580 303-9170
▲ Industrial Vehicles Intl Inc — Tulsa (G-9983)	E	918 836-6516
▲ J A Oil Field Mfg Inc — Oklahoma City (G-6334)	E	405 672-2299
J E Shaffer Co — Owasso (G-7577)	G	918 582-1752
J P Machine & Tool Co — Oklahoma City (G-6337)	F	405 677-3341
JV Energy Services Inc — Turpin (G-11182)	F	620 482-0244
▲ Kerr Machine Co — Sulphur (G-8837)	E	580 622-4207
Kimray Inc — Oklahoma City (G-6417)	C	405 525-6601
King Valve Inc — Oklahoma City (G-6421)	F	405 672-0046
Kline Oilfield Equipment Inc — Tulsa (G-10096)	E	918 445-0588
Knight Automatics Co Inc — Tulsa (G-10097)	G	918 836-6122
Knowles Manufacturing & Mch — Moore (G-4532)	G	405 793-9339
Koby Oil Tools LLC — Cushing (G-1941)	E	405 236-3551
▲ L M S Products Inc — Perry (G-7739)	G	580 336-3555
Lahoma Production Inc — Jenks (G-3715)	G	918 298-2227
Larkin Products LLC — Tulsa (G-10129)	G	918 584-3475
▲ Lewis Friction Products LLC — Oklahoma City (G-6470)	F	405 634-5401
▲ Lewis Manufacturing Co LLC — Oklahoma City (G-6471)	G	405 634-5401
Lewis Manufacturing Co LLC — Meeker (G-4378)	E	405 279-2553
Lowery Well Heads Inc — Tulsa (G-10180)	G	918 836-1760
M & M Fabrication & Service — Oklahoma City (G-6506)	G	405 677-1982
M-I LLC — Elk City (G-2843)	E	580 225-0104
Machine Parts & Tool — Ardmore (G-326)	G	580 389-5346
Magnus Industries LLC — Edmond (G-2501)	G	405 513-8295
Mark Mullin Co LLC — Sand Springs (G-8202)	G	918 245-1426
Marple Petroleum LLC — Norman (G-5064)	G	405 360-2240
Martin-Decker Totco Inc — Yukon (G-11748)	F	405 350-7408
▲ Mathey Dearman Inc — Tulsa (G-10222)	E	918 447-1288
Mathey Dearman Inc — Tulsa (G-10223)	E	918 447-1288
Maverick Oil Tools LLC — Hennessey (G-3476)	G	405 853-5524
Mayco Inc — Oklahoma City (G-6543)	E	405 677-5969
Midco Fabricators Inc — Guthrie (G-3324)	E	405 282-6667
▲ Mingo Manufacturing Inc — Owasso (G-7593)	E	918 272-1151
Morton Grinding Works — Henryetta (G-3513)	G	918 652-8550
Morton Manufacturing Co Inc — Tulsa (G-10305)	G	918 584-0333
Mowdy Machine Inc — Duncan (G-2157)	G	580 252-9333
Murray Services Inc — Hinton (G-3534)	E	405 542-3069
N & S Flame Spray LLC — Mannford (G-4187)	E	918 865-4737
National Oilwell Varco Inc — Oklahoma City (G-6656)	D	405 745-6850
National Oilwell Varco Inc — McAlester (G-4322)	E	918 423-8000
National Oilwell Varco Inc — Oklahoma City (G-6657)	D	405 677-3386
National Oilwell Varco Inc — Tulsa (G-9022)	E	918 447-4600
National Oilwell Varco LP — Moore (G-4544)	G	405 677-2484
Natural Gas Services Group Inc — Catoosa (G-1342)	C	918 266-3330
♦ Norriseal-Wellmark Inc — Oklahoma City (G-6685)	D	405 672-6660
Oil States Energy Services LLC — Oklahoma City (G-6719)	G	405 702-6536
Oil States Energy Services LLC — Oklahoma City (G-6720)	E	405 686-1001
Oil States Industries Inc — Oklahoma City (G-6721)	D	405 671-2000
Oil States Industries Inc — Tulsa (G-10387)	E	918 250-0828
Oilfield Equipment & Mfg — Shawnee (G-8480)	F	405 275-4500
Oilfield Improvements Inc — Broken Arrow (G-993)	E	918 250-5584
OK Pump and Supply — Ratliff City (G-8059)	G	580 856-4010
Ortco Inc — Oklahoma City (G-6782)	E	405 670-2803
Ota Compression LLC — Okemah (G-5272)	C	918 623-9922
P V Valve — Ratliff City (G-8061)	G	580 856-3844
Parco Masts & Substructures — Tulsa (G-10467)	G	918 585-8221
Pcs Ferguson Inc — Stigler (G-8639)	G	918 967-3236
Penn Machine Inc — Oklahoma City (G-6824)	F	405 789-0084
Petroleum Instruments Co Inc — Oklahoma City (G-6837)	F	405 670-6200
Phil Singletary Co Inc — Broken Arrow (G-1006)	G	918 258-7733
Pipeline Equipment Inc — Tulsa (G-9024)	E	918 224-4144
Powells Waterwell Pump and Sup — Bristow (G-794)	G	918 637-9150
Process Manufacturing Co Inc — Tulsa (G-9029)	C	918 445-0909
Process Products & Service Co — Mounds (G-4623)	G	918 827-4998
Psf Services LLC — Marlow (G-4239)	E	707 386-8805
▼ Q B Johnson Mfg Inc — Moore (G-4558)	D	405 677-6676
Quality Machine Services Inc — Oklahoma City (G-6936)	E	405 495-4962
R & M Fleet Service Inc — Cleveland (G-1732)	E	918 367-9326
R&R Roustabout Services LLC — Ringwood (G-8090)	E	580 883-4647
Ralph M Thomas — Lindsay (G-4079)	G	405 756-4426
Raptor Oilfield Controls LLC — Duncan (G-2166)	G	580 251-9806
RDS Oilfield Service LLC — Cushing (G-1953)	G	918 521-9205
Reef Services LLC — Lindsay (G-4080)	E	405 756-4747
Reef Services LLC — Pawhuska (G-7694)	G	918 287-3850
▲ Reel Power Industrial Inc — Oklahoma City (G-6998)	D	405 609-3326
Reel Power Wire & Cable Inc — Oklahoma City (G-7000)	E	918 584-1000
Reliance Mfg Solutions LLC — Oklahoma City (G-7006)	G	405 640-9660
▼ Reputation Services & Mfg LLC — Tulsa (G-10643)	E	918 437-2077
Rfg Petro Systems LLC — Oklahoma City (G-7014)	G	941 487-7524
S-T Magi — Cleveland (G-1733)	G	918 358-2312
Sasco Inc — Oklahoma City (G-7085)	F	405 670-3230
▲ Scfm Inc — Tulsa (G-10713)	E	918 663-1309
▲ Screw Compression Systems Inc — Catoosa (G-1351)	C	918 266-3330
Seaboard International Inc — El Reno (G-2755)	E	405 619-3099
Serva Group LLC — Catoosa (G-1353)	E	918 266-0700
Serva Group LLC — Duncan (G-2175)	G	580 252-5111
Seventy Seven Operating LLC — Oklahoma City (G-7113)	D	405 608-7777
Sjb Linings LLC — Oklahoma City (G-7145)	G	405 225-3829
▲ Skinner Brothers Company Inc — Tulsa (G-10771)	E	918 585-5708
Solid State Controls Inc — Shawnee (G-8501)	F	405 273-9292
Sooner Swage & Coating Co Inc — Eufaula (G-3114)	G	918 689-7142
SPM Flow Control Inc — Elk City (G-2875)	C	580 225-1186
State Line Swd LLC — Reydon (G-8080)	G	580 515-1468
Step Energy Svcs Holdings Ltd — McAlester (G-4339)	E	918 423-4300
Step Energy Svcs Holdings Ltd — Tulsa (G-10845)	G	918 252-5416
Stream-Flo USA LLC — Edmond (G-2634)	G	405 330-5504
Summit Laydown Services Inc — Woodward (G-11636)	E	580 256-5700
Supreme Mch & Stl Fabrication — Yale (G-11687)	F	918 387-2036
Sydco System Inc — Foss (G-3184)	F	405 350-3161
T D Williamson Inc — Tulsa (G-10888)	E	918 447-5400
Tam Completion Systems Inc — Oklahoma City (G-7250)	G	405 601-7564
Taylor Industries LLC — Tulsa (G-10905)	G	918 266-7301
Testers Inc — Oklahoma City (G-7273)	E	405 235-9911
Tetra Technologies Inc — Oklahoma City (G-7276)	G	405 677-0221
Thompson Pump Company — Drumright (G-2075)	G	918 352-2117
♦ Thompson Pump Company — Okmulgee (G-7527)	F	918 756-6164
Tokata Oil Recovery Inc — Stillwater (G-8769)	G	405 595-0072
Tomcat Specialty Oil Tools LLC — Edmond (G-2648)	G	405 659-9222
Tri State Machine & Supply LLC — Woodward (G-11644)	G	580 256-6265
Tri-Lift Services Inc — Crescent (G-1921)	G	405 969-2069
Tularosa Inc — Oklahoma City (G-7349)	G	405 848-0408
U S Weatherford L P — Elk City (G-2886)	F	580 225-8890
U S Weatherford L P — Lindsay (G-4095)	F	405 756-4331
United Cable Tool & Supply LLC — Mannford (G-4193)	G	918 760-9012
▲ United Process Systems Corp — Wagoner (G-11296)	G	918 462-1143
▼ Upco Inc — Tulsa (G-11052)	G	918 342-1270
USA-Bops LLC — Oklahoma City (G-7381)	G	405 265-2988
Valiant Artfl Lift Sltions LLC — Oklahoma City (G-7387)	E	405 605-4567
Valiant Artfl Lift Sltions LLC — Norman (G-5191)	C	405 605-4567
Wagon Wheel Arklatex LLC — Jenks (G-3737)	G	918 528-1060
We Buy Scrap LLC — Ponca City (G-7887)	G	580 401-3083

Weatherford District Office ....G....... 405 354-7711
Yukon (G-11803)
Weatherford International LLC ....E....... 405 577-5590
Oklahoma City (G-7432)
Weatherford International LLC ....E....... 940 683-8393
Oklahoma City (G-7433)
Weatherford International LLC ....G....... 405 350-3357
Yukon (G-11804)
Weatherford International LLC ....G....... 405 853-7127
Hennessey (G-3497)
Weatherford International LLC ....F....... 405 619-7238
Oklahoma City (G-7434)
Weatherford International LLC ....E....... 405 773-1100
Oklahoma City (G-7430)
Wenco Energy Corporation ....F....... 918 252-4511
Tulsa (G-11108)
Wenzel Downhole Tools Us Inc ....G....... 405 787-4145
Oklahoma City (G-7436)
Wilco Machine & Fab Inc.......................B....... 580 658-6993
Marlow (G-4247)
Wildman Manufacturing Inc..................F....... 405 235-1264
Oklahoma City (G-7453)
▼ Woolslayer Companies Inc ....C....... 918 523-9191
Catoosa (G-1368)

3534 Elevators & Moving Stairways

American Accessibility Eqp Svc ....G....... 405 631-4142
Oklahoma City (G-5431)
▼ Hy-H Manufacturing Co Inc..............E....... 918 341-6811
Claremore (G-1638)
Travertine Inc...G....... 918 583-5210
Tulsa (G-10972)
Vasser Machine.......................................G....... 918 225-2677
Cushing (G-1966)
Wilson Products Inc ....F....... 918 224-1327
Tulsa (G-9052)

3535 Conveyors & Eqpt

Chickasaw Nation Inds Inc....................D....... 580 276-3305
Marietta (G-4203)
Clean Products Inc ....G....... 405 382-1441
Seminole (G-8364)
◆ Fki Industries Inc................................G....... 918 834-4611
Tulsa (G-9752)
Marietta Filtra Systems..........................G....... 580 276-3306
Marietta (G-4209)
Overhead Door Solutions LLC..............G....... 918 686-8847
Muskogee (G-4729)
Redback Energy Services LLC.............E....... 405 265-4608
Oklahoma City (G-6992)
Thompson Manufacturing Company ....G....... 918 585-1991
Tulsa (G-10935)

3536 Hoists, Cranes & Monorails

Ameracrane and Hoist LLC..................E....... 918 437-4775
Tulsa (G-9161)
◆ Auto Crane Company.........................C....... 918 438-2760
Tulsa (G-9226)
Boat Floaters Ind LLC.............................F....... 918 256-3330
Afton (G-113)
▲ Bridge Crane Specialists LLC..........E....... 918 321-3953
Kiefer (G-3776)
Campbell Crane and Service LLC ....G....... 405 245-8983
Oklahoma City (G-5682)
Central States Crane Hoist LLC.............F....... 918 341-2320
Claremore (G-1603)
Central States Crane Hoist LLC.............G....... 918 341-2320
Claremore (G-1604)
◆ Fki Industries Inc................................G....... 918 834-4611
Tulsa (G-9752)
▲ Gunnebo Corporation U S A ....E....... 918 832-8933
Tulsa (G-9867)
◆ Gunnebo Industries Inc ....C....... 918 832-8933
Tulsa (G-9868)
▼ Hy-H Manufacturing Co Inc..............E....... 918 341-6811
Claremore (G-1638)
Hydrohoist Boat Lifts ....G....... 918 256-8125
Bernice (G-565)
Hydrohoist Marine Group Inc ....G....... 918 256-8775
Bernice (G-566)
Kevin Davis Company ....G....... 918 280-0717
Bixby (G-639)
Konecranes Inc ....G....... 405 208-8808
Oklahoma City (G-6434)
▲ Ramsey Industries Inc.......................C....... 918 438-2760
Tulsa (G-10617)
United Slings Inc.....................................G....... 405 598-2616
Tecumseh (G-8930)

3537 Indl Trucks, Tractors, Trailers & Stackers

4-Star Trailers Inc...................................C....... 405 324-7827
Oklahoma City (G-5331)
◆ Auto Crane Company.........................C....... 918 438-2760
Tulsa (G-9226)
Becks Forklift Svc LLC..........................G....... 580 303-8038
Elk City (G-2786)
C&C Trucking and Eqp Svcs LLC.........G....... 405 567-5194
Prague (G-7922)
▼ Campbell Fbrcation Tooling Inc........G....... 918 987-0047
Stroud (G-8809)
Clark Rhyne..G....... 918 874-3563
Wardville (G-11306)
Crandell Salvage Incorporated.............F....... 918 429-0001
Mcalester (G-4287)
D & W Cupp Trucking LLC ....G....... 580 821-6844
Sayre (G-8339)
Darr Lift Main Line ....G....... 580 657-6337
Ardmore (G-273)
Ddieci Midwest LLC ....G....... 816 591-1350
Edmond (G-2386)
Dickson Industries Inc...........................E....... 405 598-6547
Tecumseh (G-8912)
Forklift Parts and Service LLC..............G....... 918 251-5119
Broken Arrow (G-913)
Green Edward DBA Ed Green Trck ....G....... 405 672-4522
Oklahoma City (G-6186)
Gurley Troy Mattingly ....G....... 580 924-3042
Durant (G-2234)
Hawkeye Fleet Services ....E....... 405 495-9939
Oklahoma City (G-6226)
Hejin Waldran ....G....... 918 408-3500
Claremore (G-1632)
▲ Industrial Vehicles Intl Inc.................E....... 918 836-6516
Tulsa (G-9983)
Karl Amanns Trucking...........................G....... 580 226-2082
Ardmore (G-320)
Kern Valley Industries ....G....... 918 868-3911
Rose (G-8118)
Kirkland Express LLC.............................G....... 405 312-3061
El Reno (G-2734)
Kremlin Welding & Fabrication.............G....... 580 874-2522
Kremlin (G-3853)
▲ Lift Technologies Inc ....G....... 918 794-8088
Tulsa (G-10159)
Mac Manufacturing Inc..........................G....... 405 527-8270
Purcell (G-8013)
Mid Continent Lift and Eqp LLC ....F....... 580 255-3867
Duncan (G-2155)
Mobile Mini Inc ....E....... 405 682-9333
Oklahoma City (G-6622)
◆ Mobile Products Inc ....G....... 580 227-3711
Fairview (G-3143)
Moblie Products Inc...............................C....... 580 227-3711
Fairview (G-3144)
OEM Systems LLC.................................G....... 405 263-7529
Okarche (G-5248)
Shelley Benefield ....G....... 580 436-0296
Ada (G-86)
▲ Vaculift Incorporated ....D....... 918 438-9875
Tulsa (G-11063)
▲ W - W Trailer Mfrs Inc ....C....... 580 795-5571
Madill (G-4166)
Walker Forklift Service LLC ....G....... 918 671-0317
Tulsa (G-11093)
Wkd Associates ....G....... 918 336-9865
Bartlesville (G-536)
Wolfe Heavy Haul and Hotshot..............G....... 918 695-7836
Tulsa (G-11146)

3541 Machine Tools: Cutting

Accu-Turn Machine LLC.........................G....... 580 704-8876
Lawton (G-3883)
Alro Steel Corporation...........................F....... 918 439-1000
Tulsa (G-9156)
American Swat Solutions LLC...............G....... 405 568-1413
Fort Gibson (G-3172)
Apache Machine Co Inc..........................G....... 918 834-0022
Tulsa (G-9196)
Bliss Industries LLC ....D....... 580 765-7787
Ponca City (G-7800)
Bryon K Barrows.....................................G....... 918 519-9369
Skiatook (G-8534)
Bullseye Boring Technology..................G....... 405 880-1878
Stillwater (G-8663)
C&D Machine Tool Svc & Parts ....G....... 405 943-6033
Oklahoma City (G-5662)
▼ Charles Machine Works Inc ....A....... 580 572-2693
Perry (G-7728)

Clicks Machine & Supply ....G....... 405 273-2497
Shawnee (G-8438)
◆ CMI Terex Corporation.......................A....... 405 787-6020
Oklahoma City (G-5792)
Cool Billet Customs................................G....... 580 216-0104
Woodward (G-11572)
Crankshaft Service Company................G....... 405 685-7553
Oklahoma City (G-5851)
CRC-Evans Pipeline Intl Inc...................C....... 918 438-2100
Tulsa (G-9504)
Cutting Edge Robotic Tech LLC ....G....... 918 247-6012
Kellyville (G-3764)
D & B Processing LLC...........................F....... 918 619-6452
Broken Arrow (G-1119)
Deans Grinding Service ....G....... 918 838-0756
Tulsa (G-9565)
Dickson Industries Inc...........................E....... 405 598-6547
Tecumseh (G-8912)
Duracoatings Holdings LLC..................D....... 405 692-2249
Oklahoma City (G-5990)
Forster & Son Inc....................................G....... 580 332-6020
Ada (G-36)
G C Broach Co ....G....... 918 369-4320
Bixby (G-626)
▲ H & M Pipe Beveling Mch Co Inc......G....... 918 582-9984
Tulsa (G-9873)
Helmco Manufacturing Inc.....................G....... 918 336-4757
Bartlesville (G-492)
◆ Hem Inc ....C....... 918 825-4821
Pryor (G-7966)
Hem Inc ....D....... 888 729-7787
Pryor (G-7967)
Hem Inc ....D....... 918 824-0800
Pryor (G-7968)
I AM Drilling LLC ....G....... 580 234-2277
Enid (G-2976)
Industrial Equipment Repair..................G....... 580 371-3361
Tishomingo (G-8966)
J & D Gearing & Machining Inc.............G....... 405 677-7667
Oklahoma City (G-6329)
J&K Machining Inc..................................G....... 918 243-7936
Cleveland (G-1725)
Kennys Machine Shop............................G....... 918 288-7241
Skiatook (G-8556)
Mfg Solutions LLC ....G....... 918 232-3503
Broken Arrow (G-1143)
Mills Machine Co.....................................E....... 405 273-4900
Shawnee (G-8475)
Precision Machine & Tool LLC ....G....... 580 256-2219
Woodward (G-11623)
Rent-A-Crane Inc.....................................G....... 405 745-2318
Oklahoma City (G-7007)
Rent-A-Crane of Okla Inc ....F....... 405 745-2318
Oklahoma City (G-7008)
▲ Sawyer Manufacturing Company.....E....... 918 834-2550
Tulsa (G-9034)
Steven Campbell......................................G....... 580 764-3469
Chester (G-1421)
Triangular Silt Dike Co Inc ....G....... 405 277-7015
Luther (G-4139)
Tulsa Trenchless Inc...............................G....... 918 321-3330
Kiefer (G-3782)
Wachob Industries Inc............................G....... 918 224-0511
Sapulpa (G-8322)
Wayne Burt Machine...............................G....... 918 786-4415
Grove (G-3293)
Wesok Drilling Corp................................G....... 580 226-2450
Ardmore (G-380)

3542 Machine Tools: Forming

Cnc Patterns & Tooling ....G....... 918 835-2344
Tulsa (G-9461)
◆ Darby Equipment Co ....E....... 918 582-2340
Tulsa (G-9552)
Delco LLC..G....... 918 527-8058
Broken Arrow (G-1122)
Dentcraft Tools...F....... 405 495-0533
Oklahoma City (G-5924)
Expanded Solutions LLC ....E....... 405 946-6791
Wewoka (G-11501)
▲ H S Boyd Company Inc ....F....... 918 835-9359
Tulsa (G-9876)
McCaskill Machining & Repair...............G....... 918 266-5186
Catoosa (G-1340)
Pritchetts Machining LLC.......................G....... 405 567-0183
Prague (G-7933)
Spencer Faith Christn Ctr Inc ....G....... 812 876-5575
Spencer (G-8601)
Strategic Armory Corps LLC ....G....... 623 780-1050
Prague (G-7936)

S I C

Employee Codes: A=Over 500 employees, B=251-500
C=101-250, D=51-100, E=20-50, F=10-19, G=1-9
2020 Oklahoma Directory
of Manufacturers & Processors
479

35 INDUSTRIAL AND COMMERCIAL MACHINERY AND COMPUTER EQUIPMENT

3543 Industrial Patterns

Cnc Patterns & Tooling ....G...... 918 835-2344
 Tulsa *(G-9461)*
Coman Pattern Works ....D...... 918 270-1775
 Tulsa *(G-9473)*
Harris Pattern & Mfg Inc ....G...... 918 227-3228
 Tulsa *(G-9011)*
J Bernardoni Pattern Co LLC ....G...... 520 390-0663
 Quinton *(G-8037)*
L & M Pattern Mfg Co Inc ....G...... 918 663-2977
 Tulsa *(G-10107)*
Lahmeyer Pattern Shop ....G...... 918 425-6008
 Tulsa *(G-10112)*
Liberty Patterns Inc ....G...... 918 234-1037
 Owasso *(G-7586)*
Sooner State Pattern Works ....G...... 580 363-1543
 Blackwell *(G-692)*
Starlite Welding Supplies ....G...... 580 252-8320
 Duncan *(G-2185)*

3544 Dies, Tools, Jigs, Fixtures & Indl Molds

AC Machine ....G...... 918 827-6552
 Mounds *(G-4607)*
Aerostar International Inc ....G...... 918 789-3000
 Chelsea *(G-1401)*
Agt Machining Co Inc ....G...... 580 774-8359
 Weatherford *(G-11388)*
Arrow Tool & Gage Co Inc ....F...... 918 438-3600
 Tulsa *(G-9212)*
Associated Tool & Machine Co ....G...... 405 670-4155
 Oklahoma City *(G-5478)*
B B Fiberglass LLC ....G...... 405 755-5895
 Guthrie *(G-3298)*
Burgess Tool & Cutter Grinding ....G...... 580 765-0954
 Ponca City *(G-7803)*
CCL Acquisition LLC ....D...... 918 739-4400
 Catoosa *(G-1309)*
Cnc Patterns & Tooling ....G...... 918 835-2344
 Tulsa *(G-9461)*
Coldren Enterprises Corp ....G...... 405 239-2205
 Oklahoma City *(G-5802)*
Custom Automotive Mfg ....F...... 918 258-2900
 Broken Arrow *(G-881)*
D and L Machine Inc ....G...... 405 433-2233
 Cashion *(G-1286)*
D B W Inc ....G...... 405 354-6211
 Yukon *(G-11714)*
Die Hard Properties LLC ....G...... 405 769-3145
 Choctaw *(G-1539)*
Die Tech Tool Machine ....G...... 918 683-3422
 Okay *(G-5257)*
Dieco Manufacturing Inc ....D...... 918 438-2193
 Tulsa *(G-9581)*
Diemasters ....G...... 800 826-2134
 Skiatook *(G-8541)*
Edmonds Fnest Mold Dmage Rmval ..G...... 405 509-9508
 Edmond *(G-2406)*
Encompass Tool & Machine Inc ....E...... 580 762-5800
 Ponca City *(G-7825)*
Engineering Tooling Svc LLC ....G...... 405 381-9322
 Tuttle *(G-11197)*
Fieldco Inc ....G...... 918 266-1815
 Claremore *(G-1620)*
Fundom Enterprises Inc ....G...... 405 557-0296
 Oklahoma City *(G-6126)*
Guthrie Guthrie Home Ch Inc ....G...... 405 600-8254
 Guthrie *(G-3316)*
Interstate Tool & Mfg Co ....E...... 918 834-6647
 Tulsa *(G-10008)*
K G Machine ....G...... 918 789-2228
 Chelsea *(G-1407)*
Lathem Tool and Machine Inc ....G...... 918 724-6655
 Broken Arrow *(G-964)*
▲ Master Kraft Tooling Corp ....E...... 918 437-2366
 Tulsa *(G-10220)*
Michael J Simmons and Die ....G...... 918 295-0057
 Tulsa *(G-10254)*
Mold Tech Inc ....G...... 918 247-6275
 Sapulpa *(G-8292)*
Nickolas Manufacturing Inc ....G...... 918 698-7109
 Tulsa *(G-10344)*
Omg Tooling Inc ....G...... 405 789-4774
 Oklahoma City *(G-6776)*
Page Tool & Machine Shop ....G...... 918 775-6766
 Sallisaw *(G-8150)*
Permocast Inc ....G...... 918 652-8812
 Henryetta *(G-3516)*
Phelps Machine & Fabrication ....F...... 580 662-2465
 Ringling *(G-8081)*

Precise Tool & Machine Company .....G...... 405 495-2001
 Oklahoma City *(G-6879)*
Precision Tool & Die Ponca Cy ....G...... 580 762-2421
 Ponca City *(G-7869)*
Progressive Tooling Inc ....G...... 918 622-0506
 Tulsa *(G-10572)*
Samco Polishing Inc ....F...... 918 789-5541
 Chelsea *(G-1412)*
Sooner Steel Rule Dies ....G...... 918 775-2668
 Sallisaw *(G-8152)*
Tech Inc ....F...... 405 547-8324
 Perkins *(G-7724)*
Tools and Troubleshooting ....G...... 580 726-5290
 Hobart *(G-3547)*
Werco Manufacturing Inc ....E...... 918 251-6880
 Broken Arrow *(G-1095)*
William L Riggs Company Inc ....G...... 918 437-3245
 Tulsa *(G-11125)*
Wrights Machine Shop ....G...... 580 363-1740
 Blackwell *(G-695)*

3545 Machine Tool Access

3d Farms & Machine L L C ....G...... 580 772-5543
 Weatherford *(G-11386)*
Bradford Boring LLC ....G...... 405 922-9344
 Chickasha *(G-1442)*
Broach Specialist Inc ....G...... 480 840-1375
 Mannford *(G-4175)*
Burgess Tool & Cutter Grinding ....G...... 580 765-0954
 Ponca City *(G-7803)*
Carlson Design Corporation ....G...... 918 438-8344
 Tulsa *(G-9377)*
Clicks Machine & Supply ....G...... 405 273-2497
 Shawnee *(G-8438)*
D & C Tool Grinding Inc ....G...... 918 689-9799
 Checotah *(G-1392)*
Diamond Manufacturing Inc ....E...... 580 889-6202
 Atoka *(G-406)*
Du-Ann Co Inc ....G...... 580 428-3315
 Coalgate *(G-1779)*
Duncan Bit Service Inc ....F...... 580 255-9787
 Duncan *(G-2109)*
Flowell Corporation ....F...... 918 224-6969
 Tulsa *(G-9007)*
Goliath Pipeline and Cnstr LLC ....G...... 512 917-9313
 Norman *(G-5008)*
Herbert Malarkey Roofing Co ....C...... 405 261-6900
 Oklahoma City *(G-6241)*
Hilti Inc ....G...... 918 252-6000
 Tulsa *(G-9931)*
Hilti of America Inc ....F...... 800 879-8000
 Tulsa *(G-9933)*
Hot Rod Machine Tool LLC ....G...... 918 508-1043
 Claremore *(G-1636)*
▲ K E Fischer LLC ....G...... 580 353-2862
 Lawton *(G-3947)*
Kanoka Ridge Services ....G...... 580 302-1561
 Lahoma *(G-3856)*
Lawyer Graphic Screen Process ....G...... 918 438-2725
 Tulsa *(G-10137)*
Linton Jim & John ....G...... 580 628-3093
 Tonkawa *(G-8978)*
M&M Precision Components LLC ....D...... 918 933-6500
 Tulsa *(G-10191)*
Metal Goods Manufacturing Co ....F...... 918 336-4282
 Bartlesville *(G-512)*
Mogar Industries ....G...... 918 445-3747
 Tulsa *(G-10294)*
Mpf Industries LLC ....G...... 918 492-0809
 Tulsa *(G-10307)*
Prelesnicks Repair Service ....G...... 580 628-3179
 Tonkawa *(G-8979)*
Rightway Mfg Solutions LLC ....E...... 580 252-2284
 Duncan *(G-2170)*
Spor Enterprises Inc ....G...... 405 745-9888
 Oklahoma City *(G-7187)*
Strope Manufacturing Inc ....G...... 918 835-8729
 Tulsa *(G-10861)*
Titan Machine Services Inc ....G...... 918 437-2411
 Tulsa *(G-10945)*
Value Components Corp ....G...... 918 749-1689
 Tulsa *(G-11066)*
WD Distributing Co Inc ....F...... 405 634-3603
 Oklahoma City *(G-7428)*

3546 Power Hand Tools

A-1 Sure Shot ....F...... 405 677-9800
 Oklahoma City *(G-5353)*
Black & Decker (us) Inc ....G...... 918 249-8641
 Tulsa *(G-9300)*

▼ Charles Machine Works Inc ....A...... 580 572-2693
 Perry *(G-7728)*
Diamond P Forrest Products Co ....F...... 918 266-2478
 Catoosa *(G-1316)*
Eastland Lawn Mower Service ....G...... 580 252-0077
 Duncan *(G-2115)*
Green Country Outdoor Eqp ....G...... 918 396-4250
 Skiatook *(G-8546)*
◆ Hilti North America Ltd ....G...... 918 252-6000
 Tulsa *(G-9932)*
▲ Jantz Supply Inc ....E...... 580 369-5503
 Davis *(G-1986)*
▼ Subsite LLC ....C...... 580 572-3700
 Perry *(G-7748)*

3547 Rolling Mill Machinery & Eqpt

CRC-Evans Pipeline Intl Inc ....C...... 918 438-2100
 Tulsa *(G-9504)*
▲ Dp Manufacturing Inc ....C...... 918 250-2450
 Jenks *(G-3704)*
G T Bynum Company ....G...... 918 587-9118
 Tulsa *(G-9794)*
Reinforced Earth Company ....E...... 918 379-0090
 Catoosa *(G-1349)*
Reinforcing Services Inc ....E...... 918 379-0090
 Catoosa *(G-1350)*
▲ Western Technologies Inc ....F...... 918 712-2406
 Tulsa *(G-11110)*

3548 Welding Apparatus

A&K Manufacturing Services LLC ......G...... 918 986-1637
 Tahlequah *(G-8849)*
Airgas Usa LLC ....F...... 580 767-1313
 Ponca City *(G-7795)*
Alltra Corp ....G...... 918 534-5100
 Dewey *(G-2014)*
Alltra Corporation ....G...... 918 534-5100
 Dewey *(G-2015)*
Barelas Welding ....G...... 580 497-7485
 Canute *(G-1266)*
Bluco Inc ....G...... 800 535-0135
 Dewey *(G-2017)*
Blue ARC Metal Specialties ....G...... 918 341-3903
 Claremore *(G-1597)*
CRC-Evans Pipeline Intl Inc ....C...... 918 438-2100
 Tulsa *(G-9504)*
Driskills Welding ....G...... 580 233-3093
 Enid *(G-2944)*
Hackney Ladish Inc ....D...... 580 237-4212
 Enid *(G-2967)*
Hat Creek Contractors Inc ....G...... 580 761-6154
 Shidler *(G-8527)*
Ledets Welding Service Inc ....G...... 405 760-8935
 Norman *(G-5057)*
Lincoln Electric Holdings Inc ....G...... 405 681-0183
 Oklahoma City *(G-6478)*
Nabors Welding & Supplies Inc ....G...... 405 756-8198
 Lindsay *(G-4075)*
Phelps Machine & Fabrication ....F...... 580 662-2465
 Ringling *(G-8081)*
Rieger Hay & Welding ....G...... 580 985-3608
 Manchester *(G-4169)*
Smith & Smith Construction ....G...... 918 297-5062
 Hartshorne *(G-3395)*
Wayne Burt Machine ....G...... 918 786-4415
 Grove *(G-3293)*
Westair Gas & Equipment LP ....G...... 580 338-6449
 Guymon *(G-3370)*

3549 Metalworking Machinery, NEC

A & W Machine LLC ....G...... 580 927-1188
 Coalgate *(G-1774)*
Clean Products Inc ....G...... 405 382-1441
 Seminole *(G-8364)*
Cse Bliss Manufacturing LLC ....G...... 580 749-4895
 Ponca City *(G-7813)*
Eastern Manufacturing Inc ....G...... 918 482-1544
 Haskell *(G-3397)*
Emmaus Group LLC ....G...... 918 834-8787
 Tulsa *(G-9673)*
▼ Jason and Ricky LLC ....G...... 580 749-4895
 Ponca City *(G-7839)*
Master Machine ....G...... 918 366-4855
 Bixby *(G-643)*
▲ Mathey Dearman Inc ....E...... 918 447-1288
 Tulsa *(G-10222)*
▲ Miami Industrial Supply & Mfg ....E...... 918 542-6317
 Miami *(G-4415)*
Morton Manufacturing Co Inc ....G...... 918 584-0333
 Tulsa *(G-10305)*

Rick Leaming Construction LLC ....G....... 580 362-2262
Newkirk (G-4852)
Rollett Mfg Inc ....G....... 405 427-9707
Oklahoma City (G-7048)
Safeco Manufacturing Inc ....F....... 918 455-0100
Broken Arrow (G-1160)
Starlite Welding Supplies ....G....... 580 252-8320
Duncan (G-2185)

3552 Textile Machinery

B Sew Inn LLC ....G....... 918 687-5762
Muskogee (G-4652)
Beckys Embroidery Design ....G....... 918 456-1235
Tahlequah (G-8852)
Creative Monogramming EMB ....G....... 580 762-6694
Ponca City (G-7812)
Gorfam Marketing Inc ....G....... 918 252-3733
Tulsa (G-9841)
House T Shirt & Silk Screening ....G....... 405 457-6321
Lookeba (G-4129)
Roses Custom ....G....... 580 252-9633
Duncan (G-2172)
United Axle ....G....... 918 344-1157
Claremore (G-1697)
World Weidner LLC ....G....... 580 765-9999
Ponca City (G-7888)

3553 Woodworking Machinery

C Easleys Touch ....G....... 918 284-9384
Tulsa (G-9360)
Classic Chisel Cabinet Shop ....G....... 405 387-2216
Blanchard (G-707)
Custom Drawers and Cabinetry ....G....... 918 322-9819
Glenpool (G-3232)
Marcy A Sharp ....G....... 405 615-9879
Asher (G-391)
Michael Allan Sharp ....G....... 405 615-3771
Asher (G-392)
Pine Creek Saw Shop Inc ....G....... 580 933-7376
Valliant (G-11231)
Tsdr LLC ....G....... 405 823-1518
Oklahoma City (G-7346)

3554 Paper Inds Machinery

Magnat-Fairview LLC ....F....... 413 593-5742
Oklahoma City (G-6517)
Marvel Photo Inc ....G....... 918 836-0741
Tulsa (G-10218)
▲ **Maxcess Americas Inc** ....G....... 405 755-1600
Oklahoma City (G-6538)
◆ **Maxcess International Corp** ....G....... 405 755-1600
Oklahoma City (G-6539)
Maxcess Intl Holdg Corp ....G....... 405 755-1600
Oklahoma City (G-6540)
Thompson Manufacturing Company ....G....... 918 585-1991
Tulsa (G-10935)
Woodward Ind Schl Dst I-1 ....G....... 580 256-5910
Woodward (G-11656)

3555 Printing Trades Machinery & Eqpt

Eagle Marketing ....G....... 580 548-8186
Enid (G-2948)
Fenimore Manufacturing Inc ....F....... 405 224-2637
Chickasha (G-1457)
▲ **H S Boyd Company Inc** ....F....... 918 835-9359
Tulsa (G-9876)
▲ **Print Finishing Systems Inc** ....G....... 405 232-1750
Oklahoma City (G-6897)
Rowmark LLC ....E....... 405 787-4542
Oklahoma City (G-7051)
Southwestern Process Supply Co ....E....... 918 582-8211
Tulsa (G-10812)
Thompson Manufacturing Company ....G....... 918 585-1991
Tulsa (G-10935)
Timothy J and Sharo Flick ....G....... 918 250-2456
Tulsa (G-10943)

3556 Food Prdts Machinery

Bar-S Foods Co ....B....... 580 510-3300
Lawton (G-3896)
Breshears Enterprises Inc ....F....... 405 236-4523
Oklahoma City (G-5624)
◆ **Burford Corp** ....D....... 405 867-4467
Maysville (G-4255)
Contact Process Piping ....G....... 405 948-9125
Oklahoma City (G-5822)
▼ **Cookshack Inc** ....E....... 580 765-3669
Ponca City (G-7810)
Doyle Dryers Inc ....G....... 918 224-4002
Tulsa (G-9601)
Forster & Son Inc ....G....... 580 332-6020
Ada (G-36)
Galaxy Distributing ....G....... 918 835-1186
Tulsa (G-9797)
Midwest Performance Pack Inc ....E....... 405 485-3567
Blanchard (G-723)
O K Restaurant Supply ....G....... 405 330-9932
Edmond (G-2543)
Rick Leaming Construction LLC ....G....... 580 362-2262
Newkirk (G-4852)
Schones Butcher Shop & Market ....G....... 580 472-3300
Canute (G-1270)
Sophisticated Sweets Inc ....G....... 580 704-8038
Cache (G-1231)
Swift Eckrich Inc ....G....... 918 258-4565
Broken Arrow (G-1069)
▲ **Unitherm Food Systems LLC** ....E....... 918 367-0197
Bristow (G-802)

3559 Special Ind Machinery, NEC

Armed Inc ....G....... 918 245-1478
Sand Springs (G-8162)
◆ **Bartec Dispensing Tech Inc** ....G....... 918 250-6496
Tulsa (G-9269)
Bolt It Hydraulic Solutions ....F....... 918 296-0202
Jenks (G-3693)
Carter Davis Machine Shop Inc ....G....... 918 437-2939
Tulsa (G-9382)
Central Sttes Shrdding Systems ....G....... 405 752-8300
Oklahoma City (G-5726)
Centrifugal Casting Mch Co Inc ....G....... 918 835-7323
Owasso (G-7552)
Chemco ....G....... 918 481-0537
Tulsa (G-9409)
Copper Kiln LLC ....G....... 918 272-5200
Owasso (G-7555)
Dathney Inc ....G....... 405 354-0481
Yukon (G-11715)
Doyle Dryers Inc ....G....... 918 224-4002
Tulsa (G-9601)
Energy Equip Sales Co ....G....... 580 276-5900
Burneyville (G-1216)
Farmers Co-Operative Gin Assn ....G....... 580 928-2664
Sayre (G-8340)
Formulated Materials LLC ....G....... 405 310-1650
Oklahoma City (G-6102)
▲ **Health Engineering System** ....G....... 405 329-6810
Norman (G-5020)
High Country Tek Inc ....E....... 530 265-3236
Tulsa (G-9928)
Hollyfrontier Corporation ....B....... 918 581-1800
Tulsa (G-9942)
J&K Machining Inc ....G....... 918 243-7936
Cleveland (G-1725)
Janes Machine Shop LLC ....G....... 580 237-4434
Enid (G-2980)
Kice Industries Inc ....E....... 580 363-2850
Blackwell (G-685)
Lam Research Corporation ....D....... 866 323-1834
Tulsa (G-10117)
Martin Bionics Innovations LLC ....G....... 405 850-2069
Oklahoma City (G-6532)
▲ **Optical Works Corporation** ....F....... 918 682-1806
Muskogee (G-4726)
◆ **Parfab Field Services LLC** ....G....... 918 543-6310
Inola (G-3671)
Powerhouse Resources Intl Inc ....D....... 405 232-7474
Oklahoma City (G-6870)
Pyrotek Incorporated ....E....... 918 224-1937
Tulsa (G-9030)
Quality Equipment Design Inc ....F....... 918 492-4019
Tulsa (G-10591)
▼ **Reputation Services & Mfg LLC** ....E....... 918 437-2077
Tulsa (G-10643)
Texas Refinery Corp ....G....... 918 455-6881
Broken Arrow (G-1073)
Tip Top Prop Shop ....G....... 580 564-3712
Kingston (G-3831)
Trace LLC ....F....... 918 510-0210
Tulsa (G-10964)
US Ferroics LLC ....G....... 601 763-1058
Ardmore (G-376)
US Shotblast Parts & Svc Corp ....G....... 405 842-6766
Oklahoma City (G-7376)
Vintage Plastics Llc ....F....... 918 439-1016
Tulsa (G-11078)
Young & New Century LLC ....G....... 281 968-0718
Norman (G-5205)

3561 Pumps & Pumping Eqpt

Accelated Artfl List Systems ....F....... 405 207-9449
Pauls Valley (G-7649)
Additive Systems Inc ....F....... 918 357-3433
Broken Arrow (G-814)
Baker Hughes A GE Company LLC ....C....... 918 828-1600
Tulsa (G-9255)
Bartling Pumps & Supplies LLC ....G....... 580 444-2227
Duncan (G-2087)
Bg & S Manufacturing ....E....... 918 396-3525
Skiatook (G-8533)
◆ **Blackhawk Industrial Dist Inc** ....C....... 918 610-4700
Broken Arrow (G-853)
Blm Equipment & Mfg Co Inc ....F....... 918 266-5282
Catoosa (G-1304)
Burleson Pump Company ....G....... 405 677-6881
Oklahoma City (G-5645)
C & B Pump Rebuilders ....G....... 405 789-4808
Oklahoma City (G-5654)
Climate Control Group Inc ....E....... 405 745-6858
Oklahoma City (G-5786)
Design Ready Controls Inc ....F....... 405 605-8234
Oklahoma City (G-5926)
Eddies Submersible Service Inc ....F....... 405 273-9292
Tecumseh (G-8913)
Excel Products ....G....... 580 216-0784
Woodward (G-11582)
Fabricating Specialists Inc ....F....... 405 476-1959
Oklahoma City (G-6068)
Flowserve Corporation ....B....... 918 627-8400
Tulsa (G-9760)
Flowserve US Inc ....C....... 918 599-6000
Tulsa (G-9761)
Floyds Machine Shop ....G....... 918 256-8440
Vinita (G-11258)
Franklin Electric Co Inc ....G....... 405 947-2511
Oklahoma City (G-6112)
Franklin Electric Co Inc ....B....... 501 455-1234
Oklahoma City (G-6113)
Franklin Electric Co Inc ....B....... 918 465-2348
Wilburton (G-11520)
Fts International Services LLC ....F....... 405 574-3900
Chickasha (G-1460)
Gardner Denver Inc ....D....... 918 664-1151
Tulsa (G-9800)
Global Oilfield Services Inc ....F....... 918 885-4024
Hominy (G-3585)
▲ **Global Oilfield Services LLC** ....E....... 405 741-0163
Oklahoma City (G-6161)
Harley Industries Inc ....G....... 918 451-2323
Tulsa (G-9892)
HEanderson Company ....F....... 918 687-4426
Muskogee (G-4688)
Hfe Process Inc ....G....... 918 663-9083
Inola (G-3661)
Ideas Manufacturing Inc ....G....... 405 691-5525
Oklahoma City (G-5296)
Idex Corporation ....D....... 405 609-1116
Oklahoma City (G-6288)
Industrial Dist Resources LLC ....G....... 239 591-3777
Tulsa (G-9979)
John Crane Inc ....D....... 918 664-5156
Tulsa (G-10049)
▲ **John Crane Lemco Inc** ....E....... 918 835-7325
Tulsa (G-10050)
K & S Pumping Unit Repair Inc ....F....... 580 237-7343
Enid (G-2991)
Kimray Inc ....C....... 405 525-6601
Oklahoma City (G-6417)
Larkin Products LLC ....G....... 918 584-3475
Tulsa (G-10129)
◆ **Little Giant Pump Company LLC** ......B....... 405 947-2511
Oklahoma City (G-6483)
Lloyd Edge ....G....... 580 726-2905
Hobart (G-3543)
Montross Tirita ....G....... 918 241-5637
Sand Springs (G-8207)
National Oilwell Varco Inc ....G....... 918 423-8000
McAlester (G-4323)
O K Plunger Service ....G....... 918 352-4269
Drumright (G-2068)
Odum Machine & Tool Inc ....G....... 918 663-6966
Tulsa (G-10377)
Oil States Industries Inc ....D....... 405 671-2000
Oklahoma City (G-6721)
Oil States Industries Inc ....G....... 918 250-0828
Tulsa (G-10387)
Perkins South Plains Inc ....E....... 405 685-4630
Oklahoma City (G-6832)

S I C

Employee Codes: A=Over 500 employees, B=251-500
C=101-250, D=51-100, E=20-50, F=10-19, G=1-9
2020 Oklahoma Directory
of Manufacturers & Processors
481

Philip Lewis G 918 850-6195
Tulsa *(G-10509)*
Pinion Manufacturing & Supply F 918 437-5428
Tulsa *(G-10516)*
Pomco Inc F 405 677-8859
Oklahoma City *(G-6863)*
▲ Practical Sales and Svc Inc G 918 446-5515
Tulsa *(G-10540)*
Premierflow LLC E 918 346-6312
Tulsa *(G-10554)*
Pump & Seal Improvements G 918 747-7742
Tulsa *(G-10582)*
Pump Shop G 918 834-8829
Tulsa *(G-10583)*
RC Pumps LLC G 580 444-2227
Ratliff City *(G-8064)*
Robbins & Myers Inc G 405 672-6793
Oklahoma City *(G-7033)*
Rod Pump Consulting LLC G 918 306-2318
Cushing *(G-1956)*
Scorpion Pump and Indus LLC G 785 285-1421
Tecumseh *(G-8927)*
Sentry Pump Units Intl LLC G 405 635-1800
Oklahoma City *(G-7110)*
▲ Sercel-Grc Corp C 918 834-9600
Tulsa *(G-10733)*
Silverback Pump & Anchor LLC G 405 756-1148
Lindsay *(G-4085)*
▲ Solar Power & Pump Company LLC F 580 225-1704
Elk City *(G-2874)*
Special Equipment Mfg Inc E 580 252-5111
Duncan *(G-2183)*
▲ Stanley Filter Company LLC G 800 545-9926
Tulsa *(G-10838)*
▲ Summit Esp LLC B 918 392-7820
Tulsa *(G-10866)*
Superior Spling Enrgy Svcs LLC G 405 613-0329
Purcell *(G-8021)*
T C Whilden Consulting Inc F 405 677-6881
Oklahoma City *(G-7243)*
Thomas Water Well Service G 580 938-2224
Shattuck *(G-8425)*
◆ Thompson Pump Company F 918 756-6164
Okmulgee *(G-7527)*
Tony Gosnell Operating G 405 756-8091
Lindsay *(G-4094)*
Total Pump and Supply LLC G 405 670-0333
Oklahoma City *(G-7309)*
Tpl Southtex Gas Utility Co LP E 918 574-3500
Tulsa *(G-10963)*
Triangle Pump Components Inc F 405 672-6900
Oklahoma City *(G-7327)*
Tulsa Rubber Co F 918 627-1371
Tulsa *(G-11006)*
Whites Welding LLC C 580 254-3766
Woodward *(G-11652)*

3562 Ball & Roller Bearings

Caster LLC G 800 255-0480
Purcell *(G-8002)*
Imak Industrial Solutions LLC G 405 406-9778
Oklahoma City *(G-6292)*
Rbc Bearings Incorporated E 405 236-2666
Oklahoma City *(G-6976)*

3563 Air & Gas Compressors

◆ A G Equipment Company A 918 250-7386
Broken Arrow *(G-809)*
Advance Eqp & Contrls LLC G 918 496-2606
Tulsa *(G-9106)*
Air Systems Pump Solutions LLC G 405 512-5100
Tulsa *(G-9122)*
Airgo Systems LLC F 405 346-5807
Oklahoma City *(G-5404)*
Airsorce LLC G 918 519-7520
Tulsa *(G-9131)*
▲ Arrow Engine Company D 918 583-5711
Tulsa *(G-9211)*
◆ Auto Crane Company C 918 438-2760
Tulsa *(G-9226)*
Berkshire Corporation G 405 677-3391
Oklahoma City *(G-5556)*
Binder Leasing LLC G 918 623-0526
Okemah *(G-5265)*
Blm Equipment & Mfg Co Inc F 918 266-5282
Catoosa *(G-1304)*
Built Right Compressor G 580 371-2007
Tishomingo *(G-8963)*
C O Hanover Bka F 918 251-8571
Broken Arrow *(G-1115)*
◆ Chase Enterprises Inc D 405 495-1722
Oklahoma City *(G-5745)*
Compressco Inc G 405 787-2808
Oklahoma City *(G-5815)*
Cook Compression F 405 677-3153
Oklahoma City *(G-5826)*
Cook Compression G 918 254-0660
Tulsa *(G-9480)*
Csi Compressco Sub Inc G 918 250-9471
Tulsa *(G-9518)*
Dresser-Rand Company E 918 835-8437
Tulsa *(G-9605)*
Dresser-Rand Group Inc G 918 695-2368
Tulsa *(G-9606)*
Dresser-Rand LLC F 918 254-4099
Tulsa *(G-9607)*
Equipment Company G 918 273-0240
Nowata *(G-5214)*
Fisher Products LLC D 918 582-2204
Tulsa *(G-9750)*
Flogistix LP D 405 536-0000
Oklahoma City *(G-6092)*
Gardner Denver Inc D 918 664-1151
Tulsa *(G-9800)*
Genreal Compressor Inc G 918 209-5499
Jenks *(G-3706)*
Green Country Comprsr Svc LLC G 918 906-6343
Claremore *(G-1628)*
Industrial Dist Resources LLC G 239 591-3777
Tulsa *(G-9979)*
Midcon Compression LLC G 405 542-6280
Hinton *(G-3533)*
Miratech Corporation G 918 622-7077
Tulsa *(G-10286)*
◆ Miratech Group LLC E 918 622-7077
Tulsa *(G-10287)*
Natural Gas Services Group Inc C 918 266-3330
Catoosa *(G-1342)*
Negative One-Eighty G 918 852-2332
Claremore *(G-1659)*
Negative One-Eighty Cryogenic G 918 261-7748
Claremore *(G-1660)*
Plateau Energy Services LLC F 580 625-3618
Beaver *(G-544)*
▲ Practical Sales and Svc Inc G 918 446-5515
Tulsa *(G-10540)*
Pressure Solutions LLC G 405 370-1830
Tuttle *(G-11208)*
▲ Screw Compression Systems Inc C 918 266-3330
Catoosa *(G-1351)*
Spangler Farm G 405 466-2536
Coyle *(G-1904)*
Spray Magnifique LLC G 918 613-6284
Broken Arrow *(G-1057)*
Thomas Energy Systems Inc E 918 665-0031
Tulsa *(G-10930)*

3564 Blowers & Fans

◆ Acme Engineering and Mfg Corp B 918 682-7791
Muskogee *(G-4642)*
Airflo Cooling Tech LLC E 918 585-5638
Tulsa *(G-9128)*
Airwolf Filter Corp G 918 561-8696
Okmulgee *(G-7493)*
Amarillo Chittom Airslo E 918 585-5638
Tulsa *(G-9160)*
▼ Andreae Team Inc F 580 223-9334
Ardmore *(G-241)*
Callidus Technologies LLC D 918 267-4920
Beggs *(G-550)*
▼ Contech Enterprises LLC F 918 341-6232
Claremore *(G-1609)*
Facet (oklahoma) LLC D 918 696-3161
Stilwell *(G-8789)*
Filter Supply and Recycling G 918 663-3143
Tulsa *(G-9742)*
▲ Flanders of Oklahoma C 580 223-5730
Ardmore *(G-291)*
Global Wire Cloth LLC E 918 836-7211
Tulsa *(G-9834)*
Good Filter Co G 580 323-5200
Clinton *(G-1751)*
Goodwill Inds Centl Okla Inc D 405 236-4451
Oklahoma City *(G-6172)*
Hu Don Manufacturing Co Inc F 580 223-7333
Ardmore *(G-307)*
Industrial Dist Resources LLC G 239 591-3777
Tulsa *(G-9979)*
L & M Fabrication G 918 825-7145
Pryor *(G-7973)*
Midco Fabricators Inc E 405 282-6667
Guthrie *(G-3324)*
Nordic Pure Inc G 918 234-2355
Tulsa *(G-10359)*
Phoenix Group Holding Company F 405 948-7788
Oklahoma City *(G-6844)*
Roth Manufacturing Co Inc G 918 743-4477
Tulsa *(G-10675)*
Royal Filter Manufacturing Co E 405 224-0229
Chickasha *(G-1503)*
Safeco Manufacturing Inc F 918 455-0100
Broken Arrow *(G-1160)*

3565 Packaging Machinery

A M & A Technical Services G 918 227-5354
Sapulpa *(G-8245)*
Bemis Company Inc C 405 207-2200
Pauls Valley *(G-7650)*
Clr Enterprises LLC G 918 298-1943
Tulsa *(G-9457)*
Emerald Manufacturing Corp G 405 235-3704
Oklahoma City *(G-6032)*
▲ Maxcess Americas Inc G 405 755-1600
Oklahoma City *(G-6538)*
◆ Maxcess International Corp G 405 755-1600
Oklahoma City *(G-6539)*
Maxcess Intl Holdg Corp G 405 755-1600
Oklahoma City *(G-6540)*
Supplyone Oklahoma City Inc C 405 947-7373
Oklahoma City *(G-7230)*

3566 Speed Changers, Drives & Gears

Hackney Ladish Inc D 580 237-4212
Enid *(G-2967)*
Machine Works LLC G 405 205-4206
Tulsa *(G-10195)*
Military Parts Plus Inc G 918 232-1581
Broken Arrow *(G-976)*
▲ Tulsa Winch Inc C 918 298-8300
Jenks *(G-3736)*

3567 Indl Process Furnaces & Ovens

Born Inc E 918 582-2186
Tulsa *(G-9322)*
◆ Callidus Technologies LLC C 918 496-7599
Tulsa *(G-9364)*
Devco Process Heaters LLC G 918 221-9629
Tulsa *(G-9577)*
Doyle Dryers Inc G 918 224-4002
Tulsa *(G-9601)*
▲ Express Metal Fabricators Inc D 918 783-5129
Big Cabin *(G-603)*
▼ G C Broach Company D 918 627-9632
Tulsa *(G-9790)*
Global Industrial Inc D 918 266-5656
Tulsa *(G-9831)*
Linde Engineering N Amer LLC G 281 717-9090
Tulsa *(G-10165)*
Linde Engineering N Amer LLC E 918 266-5700
Catoosa *(G-1331)*
Metro Outdoor Living G 918 893-2960
Tulsa *(G-10253)*
Nortek Air Solutions LLC B 405 263-7286
Okarche *(G-5247)*
Ogi Process Equipment Inc F 918 246-1600
Sand Springs *(G-8212)*
Team Inc E 918 234-9600
Tulsa *(G-10909)*

3568 Mechanical Power Transmission Eqpt, NEC

Bb Machine & Supply Inc G 580 237-8686
Enid *(G-2915)*
Drive Shafts Inc G 918 836-0111
Tulsa *(G-9608)*
H-V Manufacturing Company G 918 756-9620
Okmulgee *(G-7509)*
Imak Industrial Solutions LLC G 405 406-9778
Oklahoma City *(G-6292)*
J & D Gearing & Machining Inc G 405 677-7667
Oklahoma City *(G-6329)*
Mecco Edgemont Clutch Co Inc G 918 583-3060
Tulsa *(G-10236)*
N & S Flame Spray LLC E 918 865-4737
Mannford *(G-4187)*
Nordam Group LLC C 918 274-2742
Tulsa *(G-10356)*
Value Components Corp G 918 749-1689
Tulsa *(G-11066)*

SIC SECTION
35 INDUSTRIAL AND COMMERCIAL MACHINERY AND COMPUTER EQUIPMENT

3569 Indl Machinery & Eqpt, NEC

24 7 Machinery LLC ....G...... 580 762-8965
  Ponca City *(G-7789)*
Advance Oil Corporation ....G...... 918 321-9034
  Kiefer *(G-3775)*
Alfa Laval Inc ....G...... 918 251-7477
  Broken Arrow *(G-824)*
All American Fire Systems Inc ....F...... 918 341-6977
  Claremore *(G-1579)*
Bear Paw Manufacturing ....G...... 918 637-4775
  Wagoner *(G-11275)*
Bechtels Heavy Metal Works LLC ....G...... 580 251-1412
  Duncan *(G-2089)*
Blastpro Manufacturing Inc ....G...... 877 495-6464
  Oklahoma City *(G-5589)*
▲ Blastpro Manufacturing Inc ....E...... 405 491-6464
  Oklahoma City *(G-5590)*
Braden Filtration LLC ....G...... 918 283-4818
  Tulsa *(G-9326)*
Clear Edge Filtration Inc ....D...... 800 637-6206
  Tulsa *(G-9448)*
▲ Clear Edge Filtration Inc ....D...... 918 984-6000
  Tulsa *(G-9447)*
▲ Coyote Enterprises Inc ....F...... 918 486-8411
  Coweta *(G-1875)*
Crematory Manufacturing & Svc ....E...... 918 446-1475
  Tulsa *(G-9000)*
Crown Midstream LLC ....G...... 405 753-1955
  Oklahoma City *(G-5862)*
D & J Filter Ltd Liability Co ....G...... 405 376-5343
  Oklahoma City *(G-5886)*
Disa Holding Corp ....D...... 405 382-6900
  Seminole *(G-8369)*
Ect Services Inc ....G...... 918 691-9320
  Sand Springs *(G-8181)*
Efdyn Incorporated ....G...... 918 838-1170
  Tulsa *(G-9647)*
Evoqua Water Technologies LLC ....C...... 978 614-7233
  Tulsa *(G-9712)*
◆ Facet (oklahoma) LLC ....E...... 918 272-8700
  Tulsa *(G-9725)*
Facet (oklahoma) LLC ....C...... 918 696-3161
  Stilwell *(G-8790)*
Filter Supply and Recycling ....G...... 918 663-3143
  Tulsa *(G-9742)*
Filter Wings Corporation ....G...... 405 258-3183
  Wellston *(G-11470)*
Firetech Automatic Sprinklers ....G...... 918 633-3773
  Henryetta *(G-3506)*
Firstline Filters LLC ....G...... 918 660-8772
  Tulsa *(G-9748)*
◆ Fki Industries Inc ....G...... 918 834-4611
  Tulsa *(G-9752)*
Flanders Corporation ....G...... 580 223-1853
  Ardmore *(G-290)*
Fluid Art Technology LLC ....G...... 405 843-2009
  Oklahoma City *(G-6094)*
G T Bynum Company ....G...... 918 587-9118
  Tulsa *(G-9794)*
▲ Global Filter LLC ....F...... 319 743-0110
  Tulsa *(G-9830)*
Hipower Systems Oklahoma LLC ....G...... 918 512-6321
  Tulsa *(G-9013)*
▲ Husky Portable Containment Co ....E...... 918 333-2000
  Bartlesville *(G-496)*
Invictus Engrg Cnstr Svcs ....G...... 405 701-5622
  Norman *(G-5037)*
J&K Machining Inc ....G...... 918 243-7936
  Cleveland *(G-1725)*
Kaiser Marketing Northeast LLC ....G...... 918 494-0000
  Tulsa *(G-10073)*
Knowles Performance Engines ....G...... 580 821-4825
  Dill City *(G-2036)*
Lake Ice LLC ....G...... 405 882-7227
  Jones *(G-3750)*
Lobito Technology Group Inc ....F...... 918 619-9885
  Tulsa *(G-10175)*
Midwesco Industries Inc ....G...... 918 858-4200
  Tulsa *(G-10266)*
Mosley ....G...... 918 407-6619
  Broken Arrow *(G-982)*
▲ N A Blastrac Incorporated ....D...... 405 478-3440
  Oklahoma City *(G-6645)*
◆ Nmw Inc ....G...... 918 273-2204
  Nowata *(G-5223)*
OK Fire LLC ....G...... 918 424-1808
  McAlester *(G-4325)*
Penn Machine Inc ....F...... 405 789-0084
  Oklahoma City *(G-6824)*

Robinson Manufacturing Co ....G...... 918 251-0353
  Broken Arrow *(G-1036)*
Royal Filter Manufacturing Co ....E...... 405 224-0229
  Chickasha *(G-1503)*
Russells Machine and Fab LLC ....G...... 405 742-6818
  Stillwater *(G-8750)*
Samurai Equipment LLC ....F...... 918 878-7715
  Tulsa *(G-10701)*
Smico Manufacturing Co Inc ....E...... 405 946-1461
  Oklahoma City *(G-7153)*
Travis Quality Pdts & Sls Inc ....G...... 918 251-0115
  Broken Arrow *(G-1082)*
Turnair Fab LLC ....G...... 918 379-0796
  Catoosa *(G-1360)*
Usfilter ....G...... 405 359-7441
  Edmond *(G-2663)*
▲ Vaculift Incorporated ....D...... 918 438-9875
  Tulsa *(G-11063)*
Versum Materials Us LLC ....E...... 918 379-7101
  Catoosa *(G-1363)*
Wyatts Oil Corp ....G...... 918 287-4285
  Pawhuska *(G-7698)*

3571 Electronic Computers

ABB Inc ....C...... 918 338-4888
  Bartlesville *(G-444)*
Alpha Research & Tech Inc ....G...... 405 733-1919
  Oklahoma City *(G-5425)*
Apple Street Inc ....G...... 918 367-9898
  Bristow *(G-764)*
CIS Investors LLC ....G...... 405 370-5812
  Oklahoma City *(G-5768)*
◆ Computer Dlers Rcyclers Globl ....E...... 405 749-7989
  Oklahoma City *(G-5818)*
Eves Apple ....G...... 512 970-9016
  Norman *(G-4995)*
Innovative Technology Ltd ....F...... 580 243-1559
  Elk City *(G-2827)*
Johnny Apple Seed Store ....G...... 918 304-2055
  Okmulgee *(G-7510)*
Mc Connells Systems ....G...... 918 322-5426
  Glenpool *(G-3238)*
New X Drives Inc ....F...... 918 850-4463
  Tulsa *(G-10338)*
Oracle America Inc ....G...... 918 587-9016
  Tulsa *(G-10434)*
Stephens Scheduling Svcs Inc ....G...... 918 630-1614
  Tulsa *(G-10847)*
Visuals Tech Solutions LLC ....G...... 913 526-1775
  Edmond *(G-2674)*

3572 Computer Storage Devices

Barron and Stevenson EMC LLC ....G...... 918 804-8440
  Tulsa *(G-9268)*
Business Records Storage LLC ....E...... 405 232-7867
  Oklahoma City *(G-5649)*
EMC ....G...... 918 583-6363
  Tulsa *(G-9666)*
EMC ....G...... 405 320-5675
  Chickasha *(G-1456)*
EMC Beauty LLC ....G...... 316 655-8839
  Oklahoma City *(G-6030)*
EMC Law Pllc ....G...... 832 560-6280
  Tulsa *(G-9667)*
EMC Services LLC ....G...... 405 596-0050
  Oklahoma City *(G-6031)*
▲ Hitachi Computer Pdts Amer Inc ......B...... 405 360-5500
  Norman *(G-5024)*
Quantum Builds Company ....G...... 727 504-1628
  Oklahoma City *(G-6939)*
Seagate Technology LLC ....B...... 405 324-3000
  Oklahoma City *(G-7102)*
Seagate Technology LLC ....A...... 800 732-4283
  Oklahoma City *(G-7103)*
Vault Management Inc ....G...... 918 258-7782
  Broken Arrow *(G-1090)*

3575 Computer Terminals

Gorilla Systems Inc ....G...... 918 227-0230
  Sapulpa *(G-8275)*

3577 Computer Peripheral Eqpt, NEC

American Laser Inc ....G...... 918 234-9700
  Tulsa *(G-9168)*
Aventura Technologies Inc ....F...... 631 300-4000
  Oklahoma City *(G-5495)*
Black Box Network Services ....G...... 800 949-4039
  Tulsa *(G-9301)*

Cisco Systems Inc ....A...... 999 505-5901
  Tulsa *(G-9431)*
Colorcomm ....G...... 918 398-7777
  Tulsa *(G-9470)*
▲ Hitachi Computer Pdts Amer Inc ......B...... 405 360-5500
  Norman *(G-5024)*
Kirklind Global Inc ....G...... 580 618-2527
  El Reno *(G-2735)*
Marvel Photo Inc ....G...... 918 836-0741
  Tulsa *(G-10218)*
News OK LLC ....F...... 405 475-4000
  Oklahoma City *(G-6671)*
Onyx Imaging Corporation ....G...... 918 627-6611
  Tulsa *(G-10431)*
Order-Matic Electronics Corp ....C...... 405 672-1487
  Oklahoma City *(G-6781)*
Phx & Co LLC ....G...... 918 747-9770
  Tulsa *(G-10511)*
Poquita Circle LLC ....G...... 918 794-0750
  Tulsa *(G-10533)*
Radiotronix Inc ....E...... 405 794-7730
  Edmond *(G-2584)*
Scan To ....G...... 405 413-8015
  Yukon *(G-11776)*
Secureagent Software Inc ....E...... 918 971-1600
  Tulsa *(G-10722)*
Special Service Systems Inc ....E...... 918 582-7777
  Tulsa *(G-10816)*
Spor Enterprises Inc ....G...... 405 745-9888
  Oklahoma City *(G-7187)*
Tulsa Toner Technology ....G...... 918 838-0323
  Tulsa *(G-11009)*

3578 Calculating & Accounting Eqpt

Campaign Technologies Professi ....G...... 405 286-2686
  Oklahoma City *(G-5681)*
Cummins - Allison Corp ....F...... 405 321-1411
  Norman *(G-4972)*
Gibsons Treasures ....G...... 405 835-1109
  Oklahoma City *(G-6152)*
Integrated Payment Svcs LLC ....G...... 918 492-7094
  Tulsa *(G-9995)*
Metavante Holdings LLC ....G...... 800 554-8095
  Oklahoma City *(G-6576)*
Order-Matic Electronics Corp ....C...... 405 672-1487
  Oklahoma City *(G-6781)*
Shen Te Enterprises Inc ....G...... 918 505-7711
  Tulsa *(G-10742)*
Special Service Systems Inc ....E...... 918 582-7777
  Tulsa *(G-10816)*
Superior Federal Bank ....G...... 405 224-1021
  Chickasha *(G-1514)*
Transfund ....G...... 918 588-6707
  Tulsa *(G-10969)*

3579 Office Machines, NEC

Backup Fortress LLC ....G...... 405 314-2436
  Yukon *(G-11694)*
Clock Shop Inc ....G...... 918 583-5835
  Tulsa *(G-9455)*
Enhanced Printing Products Inc ....G...... 918 585-1991
  Tulsa *(G-9688)*
Pitney Bowes Inc ....G...... 918 779-7552
  Tulsa *(G-10521)*
Pitney Bowes Inc ....G...... 405 341-3279
  Edmond *(G-2572)*
Raf Midsouth Technologies LLC ....F...... 918 352-8300
  Tulsa *(G-10609)*

3581 Automatic Vending Machines

Anytime Propane LLC ....F...... 405 417-0222
  Chickasha *(G-1430)*
Crankshaft Service Company ....G...... 405 685-7553
  Oklahoma City *(G-5851)*
Ms Enterprises ....G...... 918 627-1824
  Tulsa *(G-10308)*

3582 Commercial Laundry, Dry Clean & Pressing Mchs

Duffy Dry Clean City LLC ....G...... 405 743-0730
  Stillwater *(G-8678)*
Hospital Linen Services LLC ....G...... 405 473-0422
  Oklahoma City *(G-6265)*

3585 Air Conditioning & Heating Eqpt

A/C Matthews & Refrigeration ....G...... 918 465-6337
  Red Oak *(G-8073)*
A1 Heat and Air ....G...... 580 832-2605
  Cordell *(G-1852)*

35 INDUSTRIAL AND COMMERCIAL MACHINERY AND COMPUTER EQUIPMENT

◆ Aaon Inc .... G 918 583-2266
Tulsa *(G-9079)*
Air Electric Inc .... G 918 406-3974
Tulsa *(G-9120)*
Air System Components Inc .... B 580 762-7521
Ponca City *(G-7794)*
Alfa Laval Inc .... G 918 251-7477
Broken Arrow *(G-824)*
Alterntive Gthrmal Sltions Inc .... G 405 948-0410
Oklahoma City *(G-5427)*
C & B Construction .... G 918 696-4476
Stilwell *(G-8782)*
▲ C&D Valve LLC .... E 405 843-5621
Oklahoma City *(G-5663)*
Clarios .... A 405 419-5400
Norman *(G-4959)*
Climacool Corp .... F 405 815-3000
Oklahoma City *(G-5785)*
◆ Climate Master Inc .... A 405 745-6000
Oklahoma City *(G-5787)*
▲ Climatecraft Inc .... C 405 415-9230
Oklahoma City *(G-5788)*
Commercial Services Corp .... F 405 634-8888
Oklahoma City *(G-5806)*
Custom Mechanical Equipment .... E 262 642-9803
Ponca City *(G-7814)*
Dallas Hermetic Company Inc .... F 214 634-1744
Oklahoma City *(G-5892)*
Everest Acqsition Holdings Inc .... F 918 770-7190
Tulsa *(G-9709)*
Everest Sciences An S T Co LLC .... F 918 770-7190
Tulsa *(G-9710)*
Harsco Corporation .... E 918 619-8000
Tulsa *(G-9899)*
◆ International Envmtl Corp .... C 405 605-5024
Oklahoma City *(G-6319)*
Jack Mangum .... G 580 658-2700
Marlow *(G-4234)*
Jim Wood Refrigeration Inc .... G 918 426-3283
McAlester *(G-4309)*
Joshua James Lennox .... G 580 739-1050
Elk City *(G-2834)*
Lennox Nas .... G 405 370-7001
Broken Arrow *(G-966)*
Lenox Leasing LLC .... G 405 664-5240
Oklahoma City *(G-5303)*
▲ Mechanical Sales Oklahoma Inc .... G 405 681-1971
Oklahoma City *(G-6554)*
Monkey Chase Banana LLC .... G 405 706-5551
Oklahoma City *(G-6626)*
National Climate Solutions .... F 844 682-4247
Tulsa *(G-10326)*
Nortek Air Solutions LLC .... B 405 525-6546
Oklahoma City *(G-6686)*
Nortek Air Solutions LLC .... B 405 263-7286
Okarche *(G-5247)*
Nortek Air Solutions LLC .... D 405 594-2811
Oklahoma City *(G-6687)*
Opportunity Center Inc .... C 580 765-6782
Ponca City *(G-7863)*
Praxair Distribution Inc .... E 918 266-3210
Claremore *(G-1673)*
Rae Corporation .... B 918 825-7222
Pryor *(G-7988)*
Refunk My Junk Inc .... G 405 990-0707
Edmond *(G-2594)*
Sierra Technologies Inc .... F 918 445-1090
Tulsa *(G-10754)*
▲ Specific Systems Ltd .... C 918 663-9321
Tulsa *(G-10817)*
Summit Esp LLC .... G 918 392-7820
Enid *(G-3064)*
Summit Esp LLC .... B 405 434-1257
Norman *(G-5165)*
Temtrol Inc .... E 405 263-7286
Okarche *(G-5254)*
Thermaclime Technologies Inc .... C 405 778-6682
Oklahoma City *(G-7280)*
Trane US Inc .... G 918 250-5522
Broken Arrow *(G-1079)*
Trane US Inc .... G 855 200-0072
Broken Arrow *(G-1080)*
Trane US Inc .... G 405 943-6600
Oklahoma City *(G-7315)*
Trane US Inc .... E 405 787-2237
Oklahoma City *(G-7316)*
Trane US Inc .... E 405 787-2237
Broken Arrow *(G-1081)*
Universal Compression Inc .... G 918 742-1801
Tulsa *(G-11047)*

Veterans Eng Group Inc .... G 918 864-6006
Pryor *(G-7997)*
Washita Refrigeration & Eqp Co .... E 800 235-9476
Milburn *(G-4464)*
York International Corporation .... D 405 364-4040
Norman *(G-5204)*
York International Corporation .... D 405 942-9675
Oklahoma City *(G-7480)*

3586 Measuring & Dispensing Pumps

◆ Bartec Dispensing Tech Inc .... G 918 250-6496
Tulsa *(G-9269)*
HEanderson Company .... F 918 687-4426
Muskogee *(G-4688)*
Integrity Pump & Supply LLC .... G 405 422-2828
El Reno *(G-2726)*

3589 Service Ind Machines, NEC

3b Industries Inc .... F 580 439-8876
Comanche *(G-1832)*
Aqua Eco Environmental Svcs .... G 952 300-0456
Broken Arrow *(G-831)*
Auto Chlor Services LLC .... G 580 657-4482
Lone Grove *(G-4114)*
Beavers High Pressure Wshg LLC .... G 580 512-3530
Apache *(G-218)*
Berkshire Corporation .... G 405 677-3391
Oklahoma City *(G-5556)*
Cairns Manufacturing Inc .... G 405 947-1350
Oklahoma City *(G-5670)*
City of Altus .... F 580 481-2270
Altus *(G-148)*
City of Weatherford .... G 580 772-5315
Weatherford *(G-11402)*
Concessions Mfg Co LLC .... G 918 786-5100
Grove *(G-3262)*
▲ Continental-Brokers & Cons Inc .... E 405 232-1534
Oklahoma City *(G-5824)*
Council Stainless & Shtmtl .... G 405 787-4400
Oklahoma City *(G-5842)*
D&R Property Services Inc .... G 405 677-2178
Oklahoma City *(G-5888)*
Dickson Industries Inc .... E 405 598-6547
Tecumseh *(G-8912)*
Easy Car Wash Systems Inc .... G 918 582-4355
Tulsa *(G-9634)*
Ecm Car Wash LLC .... E 405 590-3252
Oklahoma City *(G-6007)*
Ecohawk Advnced Wtr Rsrces LLC .... G 918 694-6011
Tulsa *(G-9639)*
Elster Amco Water Inc .... G 863 453-5336
Norman *(G-4991)*
Environmental Concepts Inc .... G 405 385-0422
Stillwater *(G-8686)*
Evoqua Water Technologies LLC .... G 978 614-7233
Tulsa *(G-9712)*
Fluid Treatment Systems Inc .... G 918 933-5678
Tulsa *(G-9763)*
Hospital Linen Services LLC .... G 405 473-0422
Oklahoma City *(G-6265)*
Industrial Commercial Entp .... G 405 681-2991
Oklahoma City *(G-6298)*
Industrial Power Wash Inc .... G 405 787-9274
Bethany *(G-582)*
Industrial Service Providers .... F 580 319-7417
Ardmore *(G-308)*
Jero Manufacturing Inc .... E 918 628-0230
Tulsa *(G-10037)*
Kenneth E Jones .... G 580 832-2227
Cordell *(G-1861)*
Kuykendall Welding LLC .... G 405 905-0389
Chickasha *(G-1480)*
Lake Tenkiller Hbr Wtr Plant .... E 918 457-4811
Park Hill *(G-7645)*
Lavi Wash .... G 405 470-0895
Oklahoma City *(G-6457)*
▲ Lindsay Manufacturing Inc .... E 580 762-2457
Ponca City *(G-7845)*
Litta Solutions LLC .... G 918 845-4854
Bixby *(G-642)*
Logic Energy Solutions LLC .... G 405 601-9037
Oklahoma City *(G-6489)*
Memories In Glass Inc .... G 405 878-9688
Shawnee *(G-8473)*
Mid America Hydro Tech .... G 405 598-1772
Macomb *(G-4143)*
Midamerica Water Technologies .... G 405 613-0250
Oklahoma City *(G-6594)*
Mighty Clean Corporation .... G 918 299-7970
Tulsa *(G-10275)*

Moms Haulin Dads Dozin Inc .... G 405 392-5508
Newcastle *(G-4832)*
Omni Water Consultants Inc .... F 918 323-0001
Vinita *(G-11266)*
Owasso Pressurewashing LLC .... G 918 557-4059
Collinsville *(G-1819)*
Pappan and Spears LLC .... G 405 742-6900
Tulsa *(G-10464)*
Phelps Ra Equipment Co Inc .... G 918 622-2724
Tulsa *(G-10508)*
Power Soak Systems Inc .... G 800 444-9624
Pryor *(G-7982)*
Preferred Fleetwash .... G 918 281-9325
Sand Springs *(G-8215)*
Pressure Point LLC .... G 918 695-8799
Tulsa *(G-10555)*
SFM Incorporated .... G 405 788-9453
Tecumseh *(G-8928)*
Star Industries Inc .... G 405 542-3041
Hinton *(G-3537)*
T S I L C .... G 918 357-5992
Broken Arrow *(G-1169)*
Veolia Water North America Ope .... G 405 354-6245
Yukon *(G-11802)*
Water Bionics Inc .... G 918 446-1988
Tulsa *(G-11098)*
◆ World Water Works Inc .... D 405 943-9000
Oklahoma City *(G-7472)*
World Water Works Holdings Inc .... G 800 607-7873
Oklahoma City *(G-7473)*
Wright Water Corporation .... G 405 224-1839
Chickasha *(G-1525)*

3592 Carburetors, Pistons, Rings & Valves

Aspen Flow Control LLC .... G 918 933-5617
Broken Arrow *(G-836)*
Cargill Valve LLC .... G 918 352-2203
Drumright *(G-2054)*
Central Valve Body .... G 918 341-0266
Claremore *(G-1605)*
King Valve Co Inc .... G 918 251-0369
Broken Arrow *(G-958)*
Oklahoma Rep Sales Inc .... G 405 794-5200
Moore *(G-4547)*
S M T Valve LLC .... G 405 512-4523
Moore *(G-4561)*
Tim Metz .... G 580 227-2456
Fairview *(G-3153)*
▲ Wilspec Technologies Inc .... E 405 495-8989
Oklahoma City *(G-7459)*

3593 Fluid Power Cylinders & Actuators

Apsco Inc .... G 918 622-5600
Tulsa *(G-9201)*
▲ Ren Holding Corporation .... F 405 533-2755
Stillwater *(G-8745)*

3594 Fluid Power Pumps & Motors

Bg & S Manufacturing .... E 918 396-3525
Skiatook *(G-8533)*
Evco Service Co Inc .... E 405 381-2172
Tuttle *(G-11198)*
▲ Hydra Service Inc .... E 918 438-3700
Tulsa *(G-9960)*
◆ Hydraulic Specialists Inc .... E 405 752-7980
Oklahoma City *(G-6278)*
National Oilwell Varco Inc .... G 713 346-7500
Oklahoma City *(G-6658)*
Pump Shop .... G 918 834-8825
Tulsa *(G-10583)*
Trojan Livestock Equipment .... G 580 772-1849
Weatherford *(G-11451)*

3596 Scales & Balances, Exc Laboratory

Base Scale Company .... G 918 523-9559
Tulsa *(G-9270)*
◆ CMI Terex Corporation .... A 405 787-6020
Oklahoma City *(G-5792)*
Sooner Scale Inc .... F 405 236-3566
Oklahoma City *(G-7165)*
Sooner Scale Inc .... F 580 925-2176
Konawa *(G-3848)*
Unibridge Scale Systems .... G 580 254-3131
Woodward *(G-11646)*
Unibridge Systems Inc .... E 580 934-3211
Knowles *(G-3841)*

35 INDUSTRIAL AND COMMERCIAL MACHINERY AND COMPUTER EQUIPMENT

3599 Machinery & Eqpt, Indl & Commercial, NEC

2012 H & H Manufacturing Inc .... G 918 838-0744
  Tulsa *(G-9056)*
3d Farms & Machine L L C .... G 580 772-5543
  Weatherford *(G-11386)*
A & E Frame Mfg Inc .... G 918 251-3343
  Broken Arrow *(G-808)*
A & M Manufacturing Co .... G 918 835-2272
  Tulsa *(G-9062)*
A and E Manufacturing Co .... F 918 583-7184
  Tulsa *(G-9065)*
A W Brueggemann Company Inc .... F 580 237-3857
  Enid *(G-2900)*
A W Pool Inc .... G 580 323-3454
  Clinton *(G-1735)*
A-1 Machine Shop Inc .... G 918 665-0706
  Tulsa *(G-9072)*
A-1 Machine Works Inc .... G 918 367-2788
  Bristow *(G-762)*
Aaron Willis President .... G 405 219-9411
  Edmond *(G-2287)*
Aberdeen Dynamics LLC .... G 918 794-0042
  Tulsa *(G-9081)*
Accent Machine Inc .... G 918 246-9695
  Sand Springs *(G-8156)*
Accu-Turn Machine LLC .... G 580 704-8876
  Lawton *(G-3883)*
Accurate Machine & Maintenance .... G 918 585-1125
  Tulsa *(G-9089)*
Aceco Valve Inc .... E 918 827-3669
  Mounds *(G-4608)*
◆ Action Machine Inc .... E 918 248-6847
  Tulsa *(G-8987)*
Action Machine Shop .... G 918 245-8308
  Sand Springs *(G-8157)*
Advanced Machining & Fabg .... E 918 664-5410
  Owasso *(G-7541)*
Advanced McHning Solutions LLC 405 208-8737
  Oklahoma City *(G-5384)*
Aero Components Inc .... E 405 631-6644
  Oklahoma City *(G-5390)*
Aero Dynamics .... F 918 258-0290
  Broken Arrow *(G-818)*
Affordable Leak Detection .... G 405 594-2341
  Oklahoma City *(G-5396)*
Agt Machining Co Inc .... G 580 774-8359
  Weatherford *(G-11388)*
Aircraft Cylinders Amer Iinc .... E 918 582-1785
  Tulsa *(G-9124)*
Airico Inc .... G 918 836-2675
  Tulsa *(G-9130)*
Alliance Machine Service Inc .... G 918 836-5588
  Tulsa *(G-9144)*
Alpha Machining & Mfg Inc .... F 918 438-2755
  Tulsa *(G-9155)*
American Machine & Tool Co .... G 405 794-9820
  Wewoka *(G-11497)*
American Machining Company LLC .... G 918 885-6194
  Hominy *(G-3574)*
American McHning Solutions LLC 405 606-7038
  Oklahoma City *(G-5439)*
American Mfg Co of Okla .... E 918 446-1968
  Tulsa *(G-9170)*
Amron Enterprises LLC .... F 918 224-9222
  Sapulpa *(G-8249)*
AMS Machining Specialists LLC .... G 918 610-2570
  Tulsa *(G-9182)*
Anson Desimone .... G 610 433-1299
  Hinton *(G-3522)*
Apache Machine Co Inc .... G 918 834-0022
  Tulsa *(G-9196)*
Apollo Engineering Company .... G 918 251-6780
  Broken Arrow *(G-830)*
Applied Indus Machining Inc .... D 405 672-2222
  Oklahoma City *(G-5456)*
Applied Indus Machining LLC .... C 405 672-2222
  Oklahoma City *(G-5457)*
Atlas Instrument & Mfg Co .... G 918 371-1976
  Collinsville *(G-1800)*
Auto-Turn Manufacturing Inc .... E 918 451-4511
  Broken Arrow *(G-1111)*
Automated Machining Co Inc .... F 918 723-3503
  Westville *(G-11480)*
Automatic & Auto Machining Inc .... G 918 775-9770
  Sallisaw *(G-8138)*
Automted McHning Solutions LLC 405 697-6234
  Mustang *(G-4762)*
B & B Machine 918 686-9900
  Muskogee *(G-4651)*

B & B Machine of Norman Inc .... F 405 799-9878
  Norman *(G-4924)*
B & C Machine Company Inc .... F 405 787-8862
  Oklahoma City *(G-5500)*
B & D Eagle Machine Shop .... F 405 787-3232
  Oklahoma City *(G-5501)*
B T Machine Inc .... E 918 834-3340
  Tulsa *(G-9246)*
B&M Machine Works LLC .... G 918 583-4067
  Tulsa *(G-9249)*
Baity Screw Products Inc .... E 405 222-1520
  Chickasha *(G-1439)*
Barker Machine Shop .... G 405 828-4683
  Dover *(G-2038)*
Barnetts .... G 405 390-3026
  Choctaw *(G-1529)*
Baskins Machined Products LLC .... G 918 284-4298
  Collinsville *(G-1802)*
Bauman Machine Inc .... E 405 745-3484
  Oklahoma City *(G-5531)*
Bb Machine & Supply Inc .... G 580 237-8686
  Enid *(G-2915)*
Benchmark Completions LLC .... F 405 691-5659
  Oklahoma City *(G-5550)*
Berry Machine & Tool Company .... G 580 536-4382
  Lawton *(G-3897)*
Best Mold Technology LLC .... G 405 659-1991
  Cache *(G-1224)*
BF Machine Shop Inc .... G 580 255-6119
  Duncan *(G-2090)*
BF Machines Shop Inc .... F 580 255-5899
  Duncan *(G-2091)*
Bobby K Birdwell .... G 580 799-2357
  Burns Flat *(G-1218)*
Boyds Auto Parts & Machine .... F 405 329-3855
  Norman *(G-4940)*
Bradley Machine & Design L L C .... F 405 224-2223
  Chickasha *(G-1443)*
Bradley Welding & Machine .... G 580 223-2250
  Ardmore *(G-260)*
Brady Welding & Machine Shop .... G 405 262-3665
  El Reno *(G-2703)*
Brady Welding & Machine Shop .... D 580 229-1168
  Healdton *(G-3408)*
▲ Branchcomb Inc .... E 918 224-8094
  Sapulpa *(G-8259)*
Brenda K Toupin .... G 918 527-6948
  Tulsa *(G-9335)*
Burgess Tool & Cutter Grinding .... G 580 765-0954
  Ponca City *(G-7803)*
Burrow Tool .... G 580 240-1045
  Temple *(G-8932)*
Bynum & Company Inc .... F 580 265-7747
  Stonewall *(G-8798)*
C & C Machine Inc .... F 918 342-1950
  Claremore *(G-1601)*
C & D Manufacturing Co Inc .... G 918 251-8535
  Broken Arrow *(G-861)*
C & M Precision Inc .... F 405 691-0984
  Oklahoma City *(G-5657)*
C & P Manufacturing Inc .... F 918 773-5060
  Sallisaw *(G-8140)*
Canfield Machine Inc .... G 580 673-2185
  Fox *(G-3190)*
Casady N Company LLC .... G 405 528-4299
  Oklahoma City *(G-5706)*
▼ Centerline Inc .... E 580 762-5451
  Ponca City *(G-7805)*
Central Machine & Tool Company .... B 580 237-4033
  Enid *(G-2927)*
Central Parts & Machine Inc .... G 405 631-5460
  Oklahoma City *(G-5725)*
Certified Machine & Design Inc .... G 405 672-9607
  Oklahoma City *(G-5731)*
Chase Industries Inc .... G 816 850-5323
  Okemah *(G-5266)*
Checos Machine Shop & General .... G 405 680-0900
  Oklahoma City *(G-5746)*
Cherokee Ntion Armred Sltons L .... E 918 696-3151
  Tulsa *(G-9415)*
Chickasha Manufacturing Co Inc .... E 405 224-0229
  Chickasha *(G-1449)*
Choctaw Nation of Oklahoma .... D 580 326-8365
  Hugo *(G-3610)*
Chromium Plating Company .... E 918 583-4118
  Tulsa *(G-9422)*
Cimarron Aerospace LLC .... G 405 260-0990
  Guthrie *(G-3308)*
Cimarron Machine Inc .... G 972 658-7051
  Bokchito *(G-750)*

Cimarron Machine Services Inc .... E 918 835-3333
  Tulsa *(G-9428)*
▼ Cimarron Machine Works Inc .... G 405 375-6452
  Kingfisher *(G-3791)*
City Machine Shop .... G 580 795-2282
  Madill *(G-4145)*
CJ Hill Inc .... G 918 251-1164
  Broken Arrow *(G-869)*
Claco Enterprises .... G 918 343-0276
  Claremore *(G-1607)*
Cline Machine Inc .... G 918 587-0126
  Tulsa *(G-9453)*
Clint Dodson Enterprises LLC .... G 580 931-9410
  Durant *(G-2216)*
Cmd Inc .... G 405 672-9607
  Oklahoma City *(G-5791)*
Conley Machine Inc .... G 918 770-3234
  Sapulpa *(G-8261)*
Contech Mfg Inc .... G 918 341-6232
  Claremore *(G-1610)*
Cox Machine and Tool .... G 405 681-1445
  Oklahoma City *(G-5848)*
Curing System Components Inc .... F 405 381-9794
  Tuttle *(G-11193)*
D & G Machine .... G 918 486-3501
  Coweta *(G-1878)*
D & V Manufacturing Inc .... F 918 245-7858
  Sand Springs *(G-8176)*
▲ D I V C O Inc .... G 918 836-9101
  Tulsa *(G-9538)*
Dads Machine & Custom Welding .... G 580 470-8334
  Duncan *(G-2103)*
Damar Manufacturing Co Inc .... G 918 445-2445
  Tulsa *(G-9549)*
Design & Mfg Inc .... G 918 576-6659
  Tulsa *(G-9575)*
Dixon & Sons Inc .... G 918 256-7455
  Vinita *(G-11253)*
DK Machine Inc .... G 918 251-1034
  Broken Arrow *(G-890)*
Duncan Machine Products Inc .... E 580 467-6784
  Duncan *(G-2110)*
Dunsworth Machine .... G 580 233-5812
  Enid *(G-2947)*
Dww Inc .... G 580 255-7886
  Duncan *(G-2114)*
Dyna-Turn of Oklahoma Inc .... F 580 243-1291
  Elk City *(G-2806)*
▼ Eastpointe Industries Inc .... E 918 683-2169
  Muskogee *(G-4670)*
Eddie Johnsons Wldg & Mch Co .... G 580 856-3418
  Ratliff City *(G-8051)*
Elastomer Specialties Inc .... F 918 485-0276
  Wagoner *(G-11281)*
Element Design & Fabrication .... G 720 372-1940
  Edmond *(G-2410)*
Elite Polishing Co .... G 405 371-5780
  Blanchard *(G-714)*
Elliott Precision Products Inc .... G 918 234-4001
  Tulsa *(G-9661)*
Elroy Machine Inc .... G 580 658-6725
  Marlow *(G-4231)*
Emp Incorporated .... G 918 756-5767
  Okmulgee *(G-7501)*
EMR Machine .... G 405 361-7991
  Noble *(G-4879)*
Ernst Valve & Fittings .... G 918 446-0313
  Tulsa *(G-9003)*
Eversharp Tool Inc .... G 918 250-9400
  Tulsa *(G-9711)*
F & F Machine Shop Inc .... G 405 680-0900
  Oklahoma City *(G-6066)*
Fabrication Solutions LLC .... F 918 398-7162
  Tulsa *(G-9723)*
Fineline Manufacturing LLC .... F 918 245-0900
  Sand Springs *(G-8184)*
Finish Line Machining LLC .... G 918 258-2944
  Broken Arrow *(G-908)*
Fisher Products LLC .... D 918 582-2204
  Tulsa *(G-9750)*
Floyds Machine Shop .... G 918 256-8440
  Vinita *(G-11258)*
Forester LLC .... G 918 835-6533
  Tulsa *(G-9765)*
Foster Machine Shop .... G 918 438-4001
  Tulsa *(G-9766)*
Frazier Mfg Co .... F 918 241-9110
  Sand Springs *(G-8186)*
Freedom Manufacturing LLC .... G 918 283-1520
  Claremore *(G-1623)*

Employee Codes: A=Over 500 employees, B=251-500
C=101-250, D=51-100, E=20-50, F=10-19, G=1-9

35 INDUSTRIAL AND COMMERCIAL MACHINERY AND COMPUTER EQUIPMENT SIC SECTION

▼ G B E Services Corporation G 918 428-8665
Tulsa *(G-9788)*

G P D Inc G 918 234-4404
Tulsa *(G-9792)*

Garnett Corporation F 918 252-2515
Tulsa *(G-9802)*

Garys Industrial Machine LLC F 580 933-4514
Valliant *(G-11225)*

Gen X Machine Technologies G 918 836-4200
Tulsa *(G-9815)*

Gen X Machine Technologies E 918 836-4200
Tulsa *(G-9816)*

Glencoe Manufacturing Co F 580 669-2555
Glencoe *(G-3222)*

Glenn Tool Inc D 405 787-1400
Oklahoma City *(G-6157)*

Gonzales Mfg & Mch Inc G 580 622-2025
Sulphur *(G-8833)*

Grace Machine Inc G 405 381-4640
Tuttle *(G-11202)*

Green Country Filter Mfg LLC F 918 455-0100
Tulsa *(G-9861)*

Grices Automotive Machine Shop G 580 924-1006
Durant *(G-2233)*

Gtsa Manufacturing Inc G 918 257-4269
Afton *(G-118)*

Guymon Motor Parts Inc E 580 338-3316
Guymon *(G-3350)*

H & B Machine & Manufacturing F 405 224-0006
Chickasha *(G-1466)*

Hailey Ordnance Company G 405 813-0700
Oklahoma City *(G-6203)*

Hancock Industries Inc F 918 835-5441
Tulsa *(G-9884)*

Haney John G 405 282-2839
Guthrie *(G-3318)*

Harrik Company LLC G 918 691-6417
Tulsa *(G-9895)*

Hart Feeds Inc G 405 224-0102
Chickasha *(G-1468)*

Hem Industries G 918 534-0579
Dewey *(G-2024)*

▲ Hendershot Tool Company E 405 677-3386
Oklahoma City *(G-6238)*

Henson Manufacturing & Sls Inc E 918 785-2153
Adair *(G-109)*

Hi-TEC Industries OK LLC F 918 455-7141
Broken Arrow *(G-1132)*

Hinsco Inc G 918 456-2138
Park Hill *(G-7643)*

Hlh Industries LLC G 918 217-0100
Skiatook *(G-8550)*

Hmt Machining Incorporated G 405 964-2054
McLoud *(G-4358)*

Hnt Welding & Machine G 405 348-8249
Edmond *(G-2456)*

Holman Manufacturing F 918 479-5861
Locust Grove *(G-4109)*

Honeygrove Machine G 580 420-3260
Idabel *(G-3638)*

Honing By Hardy G 405 919-3589
Oklahoma City *(G-6262)*

Howards Precision Mfg Inc G 918 599-7588
Tulsa *(G-9955)*

Hypro Inc E 918 549-3600
Vinita *(G-11260)*

Ideal Machine & Welding Inc G 918 352-3660
Drumright *(G-2062)*

◆ Ideal Specialty Inc F 918 834-1657
Tulsa *(G-9967)*

Industrial Enterprise Inc F 918 476-5907
Chouteau *(G-1567)*

Industrial Machine Co Inc F 405 236-5419
Oklahoma City *(G-6299)*

Industrial Manufacturing Inc G 918 787-5500
Fairland *(G-3125)*

Infinite Tool Systems Inc G 405 205-4206
Edmond *(G-2460)*

Inland Machine & Welding Co E 405 670-4355
Oklahoma City *(G-6305)*

J & D Gearing & Machining Inc G 405 677-7667
Oklahoma City *(G-6329)*

J & D Machine Inc G 918 425-5704
Tulsa *(G-10017)*

J & J Company G 918 616-2169
Muskogee *(G-4695)*

J & J Machine Shop G 918 827-6892
Mounds *(G-4618)*

J & M Machine Shop Inc G 918 650-0074
Henryetta *(G-3510)*

J & P Machine G 918 623-0005
Okemah *(G-5270)*

J & S Machine & Valve G 918 273-1582
Nowata *(G-5216)*

J & S Machine & Valve Inc E 918 273-1582
Nowata *(G-5217)*

J C & J Machine & Auto G 580 439-5919
Comanche *(G-1842)*

J F Machine LLC G 918 865-5855
Mannford *(G-4183)*

Jamesed Inc G 918 272-6775
Owasso *(G-7578)*

Jandj Machine Shop LLC G 918 827-6892
Mounds *(G-4619)*

Janeway Machine Inc E 918 224-0694
Sapulpa *(G-8282)*

Janke Products LLC F 405 677-3600
Oklahoma City *(G-6350)*

JB Machining Inc E 918 425-3337
Tulsa *(G-10032)*

Jerry D Pierce G 580 252-5354
Duncan *(G-2135)*

Jet Black Aircraft G 405 310-6556
Norman *(G-5043)*

Joel Bumpus G 580 237-5305
Enid *(G-2987)*

Johnny Beard Co G 918 438-4901
Tulsa *(G-10056)*

Johnson Machine Inc E 918 371-7537
Collinsville *(G-1814)*

Jones Machine Shop G 580 255-5784
Duncan *(G-2137)*

Jorame Inc F 918 582-5663
Tulsa *(G-10058)*

Jpm Precision Machine Inc G 918 739-4777
Tulsa *(G-10062)*

K & B Machining Inc F 918 343-2620
Claremore *(G-1647)*

K & K Manufacturing Inc G 918 247-2871
Kellyville *(G-3766)*

K G Machine G 918 789-2228
Chelsea *(G-1407)*

K-H Machine Shop G 918 273-1058
Nowata *(G-5218)*

▼ Kams Inc F 405 232-3103
Oklahoma City *(G-6396)*

Kat Industries Inc E 405 702-1387
Oklahoma City *(G-6399)*

Kat Machine Incorporated F 405 702-1387
Oklahoma City *(G-6400)*

Kenkay Machine G 918 733-2780
Morris *(G-4597)*

Kenneth H Knepper G 918 582-1954
Tulsa *(G-10083)*

Keystone Tool & Fabrication G 918 933-6100
Tulsa *(G-10088)*

Kiamichi Resources Inc G 405 364-8176
Norman *(G-5050)*

Kimberly A Johnson G 918 370-3666
Stigler *(G-8636)*

Knight Automatics Co Inc G 918 836-6122
Tulsa *(G-10097)*

Kos Machine LLC G 580 799-5042
Canute *(G-1269)*

▲ Kt Plastics Inc E 580 434-5655
Calera *(G-1241)*

L & J Welding & Machine Svc G 918 885-6666
Hominy *(G-3591)*

L & L Machine Shop G 580 357-3560
Lawton *(G-3952)*

L & S Machining G 918 543-6628
Inola *(G-3664)*

▲ L M S Products Inc G 580 336-3555
Perry *(G-7739)*

Lahmeyer Welding G 918 588-2450
Tulsa *(G-10113)*

Lanco Services LLC E 580 429-6526
Cache *(G-1229)*

Lawton Machine & Welding Works G 580 355-4678
Lawton *(G-3956)*

Lynns Auto Parts and Machine G 580 255-5190
Duncan *(G-2149)*

Lynns Machine Inc F 580 234-2051
Enid *(G-3001)*

M & BJ Farm & Machine LLC G 918 333-0430
Bartlesville *(G-507)*

M & M Machining LLC G 918 733-1337
Morris *(G-4599)*

M & P Manufacturing G 405 356-2805
Wellston *(G-11474)*

M-1 Machine LLC G 580 225-6826
Elk City *(G-2842)*

Machine Parts & Tool G 580 389-5346
Ardmore *(G-326)*

Machine Techniques G 918 396-2181
Skiatook *(G-8559)*

Machine Works LLC G 918 584-6496
Tulsa *(G-10194)*

Machining Specialists Inc G 918 386-2387
Locust Grove *(G-4112)*

Machining Technologies of OK G 918 266-1700
Catoosa *(G-1336)*

Madewell Machine Works Company G 918 543-2904
Inola *(G-3666)*

Madison Machine Companies Inc F 918 584-6496
Tulsa *(G-10199)*

Magnat-Fairview LLC F 413 593-5742
Oklahoma City *(G-6517)*

Malones Cnc Machining Inc E 918 786-7313
Grove *(G-3280)*

Mammoth Manufacturing G 580 252-4660
Duncan *(G-2151)*

Mammoth Manufacturing Inc G 405 820-8301
Bethany *(G-587)*

Martens Machine Shop G 580 227-2734
Fairview *(G-3142)*

▲ Master Kraft Tooling Corp E 918 437-2366
Tulsa *(G-10220)*

Maxx Machine Inc F 405 692-8300
Oklahoma City *(G-6542)*

Mc Machining Inc G 918 521-8945
Bixby *(G-644)*

◆ McElroy Manufacturing Inc A 918 836-8611
Tulsa *(G-10232)*

Memorial Auto Supply Inc F 405 324-5400
Oklahoma City *(G-6564)*

Metcoat Inc G 580 255-6441
Duncan *(G-2154)*

Metro Machine Works Inc F 918 446-2705
Tulsa *(G-10250)*

Mfg Specialists Inc G 918 445-9040
Tulsa *(G-9021)*

Miami Machine Shop G 918 542-1501
Miami *(G-4416)*

Micro Machine Inc G 918 836-1646
Tulsa *(G-10255)*

Mid America Machining Inc F 918 825-6202
Pryor *(G-7976)*

Midway Machine & Welding LLC G 918 968-3316
Stroud *(G-8812)*

Midwest Machine & Comprsr Co G 405 634-5454
Oklahoma City *(G-6604)*

Midwest Precision Inc D 918 835-8900
Tulsa *(G-10270)*

Mike Cline Inc F 918 592-3712
Tulsa *(G-10277)*

Milton Donaghey G 580 332-1551
Ada *(G-66)*

Mogar Industries G 918 445-3747
Tulsa *(G-10294)*

Mold Tech Inc G 918 247-6275
Sapulpa *(G-8292)*

Moonlight Machine LLC G 580 718-5111
Ponca City *(G-7855)*

Morgans Repair Shop Inc G 405 382-3114
Seminole *(G-8388)*

Moritz Inc F 918 834-1064
Sand Springs *(G-8208)*

Mostmachine LLC G 918 706-0393
Claremore *(G-1658)*

Mustang Machines Works Inc G 405 745-7545
Mustang *(G-4783)*

N & S Flame Spray LLC E 918 865-4737
Mannford *(G-4187)*

Native American Maint Svcs Inc E 918 682-5700
Muskogee *(G-4720)*

Naumann McHining Solutions Inc F 918 246-9898
Sand Springs *(G-8210)*

Newview Oklahoma Inc D 405 232-4644
Oklahoma City *(G-6672)*

Nichols Machine and Mfg LLC G 405 637-7175
Wayne *(G-11367)*

North Central Pump G 580 765-9348
Ponca City *(G-7860)*

Northeast Oklahoma Mfg G 918 663-8805
Tulsa *(G-10361)*

▲ Ocv Control Valves LLC E 918 627-1942
Tulsa *(G-10376)*

Odum Machine & Tool Inc G 918 663-6966
Tulsa *(G-10377)*

SIC SECTION 35 INDUSTRIAL AND COMMERCIAL MACHINERY AND COMPUTER EQUIPMENT

Oil Capital Valve Company......D...... 918 627-2474
Tulsa *(G-10385)*
Oilfield Equipment & Mfg......F...... 405 275-4500
Shawnee *(G-8480)*
OK Machine and Mfg Co Inc......E...... 918 838-1300
Tulsa *(G-10390)*
OK Products of Tulsa Inc......G...... 918 445-2471
Tulsa *(G-10391)*
Oklahoma Equipment Mfg PDT......G...... 405 491-6484
Oklahoma City *(G-6747)*
Oklahoma Rbr & Gasket Co Inc......F...... 918 585-3484
Tulsa *(G-10406)*
Okmulgee Automotive Machine Sp......G...... 918 756-5861
Okmulgee *(G-7518)*
Opb Pipe Bending......G...... 918 583-1566
Tulsa *(G-10432)*
Outdoor Incorporated......G...... 918 697-1402
Sapulpa *(G-8295)*
P & K Machine Inc......G...... 918 266-7815
Catoosa *(G-1345)*
▼ **Padgett Machine Shop Inc**......F...... 918 438-3444
Tulsa *(G-10455)*
Pak Electric Inc......F...... 580 482-1757
Altus *(G-166)*
▲ **Parrish Enterprises Ltd**......C...... 580 237-4033
Enid *(G-3031)*
Pats Machine......G...... 405 681-1050
Oklahoma City *(G-6810)*
Patterson Machine Shop......G...... 918 463-3600
Warner *(G-11308)*
Pattison Precision Products......E...... 918 251-9967
Broken Arrow *(G-1001)*
Paul G Pennington Industries......G...... 405 392-2317
Blanchard *(G-726)*
Paul Precision Machine Inc......F...... 918 835-6175
Tulsa *(G-10476)*
Peak Machining Group LLC......G...... 307 660-1463
Skiatook *(G-8563)*
Pennington Industries......G...... 405 392-2317
Newcastle *(G-4835)*
Performance Machine & Inductio......F...... 918 542-8740
North Miami *(G-5207)*
Phil Singletary Co Inc......G...... 918 258-7733
Broken Arrow *(G-1006)*
Pinball Doctor......G...... 918 582-3130
Tulsa *(G-10515)*
Pinion Manufacturing & Supply......F...... 918 437-5428
Tulsa *(G-10516)*
Pioneer Precision Machine Shop......F...... 580 233-1670
Enid *(G-3036)*
Pogue Machine Inc......G...... 405 677-9397
Oklahoma City *(G-6860)*
Ponca Machine Company......F...... 580 762-1031
Ponca City *(G-7867)*
Power Dyne Inc......G...... 918 587-1272
Tulsa *(G-10538)*
Precision Engrg & Mch Works......G...... 580 658-9193
Marlow *(G-4238)*
Precision Mfg & Design......E...... 918 782-2723
Langley *(G-3874)*
Precision Sintered Parts L L C......F...... 918 663-7511
Tulsa *(G-10550)*
Precison Parts Inc......G...... 918 261-6962
Tulsa *(G-9026)*
Preston-Eastin Inc......E...... 918 834-5591
Tulsa *(G-9028)*
▲ **Pro-Fab LLC**......C...... 405 495-2131
Oklahoma City *(G-6908)*
Process Manufacturing Co Inc......C...... 918 445-0909
Tulsa *(G-9029)*
Pruitt Company of Ada Inc......E...... 580 332-3523
Ada *(G-78)*
Pryer Aerospace LLC......D...... 918 835-8885
Tulsa *(G-10578)*
▲ **Pryer Machine & Tool Co Inc**......G...... 918 341-4900
Tulsa *(G-10579)*
▲ **Pryer Machine & Tool Company**......C...... 918 835-8885
Tulsa *(G-10580)*
Qmi Inc......G...... 918 456-6777
Tahlequah *(G-8879)*
Quality Machinging of Broken......G...... 918 294-1434
Broken Arrow *(G-1016)*
Quality Machining LLC......G...... 918 512-8593
Sapulpa *(G-8304)*
Quality Machining Inc......F...... 918 294-1434
Broken Arrow *(G-1017)*
Quality Parts Mfg Co Inc......G...... 918 627-3307
Tulsa *(G-10592)*
R & P Machine Shop......G...... 405 275-1321
Tecumseh *(G-8925)*
▲ **R & S Manufacturing**......G...... 918 266-2266
Catoosa *(G-1347)*
R & W Machine Shop Inc......G...... 405 632-4020
Oklahoma City *(G-6958)*
R M Machine Shop Inc......G...... 405 209-7242
Tuttle *(G-11210)*
Ram Machine Inc......G...... 918 224-8028
Tulsa *(G-10613)*
Ram Machine Products LLC......F...... 918 455-5555
Broken Arrow *(G-1152)*
Rayco Paraffin Service Inc......G...... 405 853-2055
Hennessey *(G-3482)*
RDS Manufacturing Inc......C...... 918 459-5100
Broken Arrow *(G-1027)*
Redbone Tool and Machine Inc......G...... 918 625-1617
Tulsa *(G-10632)*
Reflection Foil and Ltr Press......G...... 405 341-8660
Edmond *(G-2593)*
Reliable Manufacturing Corp......G...... 918 341-1966
Claremore *(G-1680)*
Richards Performance Machine......G...... 918 485-6393
Wagoner *(G-11289)*
Riverside Machine Inc......F...... 918 445-5141
Tulsa *(G-10658)*
Robs Magneto Service......G...... 918 367-5735
Tulsa *(G-10665)*
Rochell Machine Shop Inc......G...... 580 252-1424
Duncan *(G-2171)*
Rotork Valvekits Inc......F...... 918 259-8100
Tulsa *(G-10677)*
Rubber & Gasket Co Amer Inc......G...... 918 249-2069
Broken Arrow *(G-1039)*
Ryan Manufacturing Inc......G...... 918 482-6512
Haskell *(G-3400)*
S & J Machine Inc......G...... 580 623-8130
Watonga *(G-11349)*
Sam Yeoman......G...... 918 783-5608
Big Cabin *(G-605)*
Samco Polishing Inc......F...... 918 789-5541
Chelsea *(G-1412)*
Satterwhite Machine Shop......G...... 580 653-2821
Springer *(G-8624)*
SBS Industries......G...... 918 749-8221
Tulsa *(G-10711)*
Sdh Manufacture LLC......G...... 918 407-1065
Broken Arrow *(G-1162)*
Seminole Machine Co......G...... 405 382-0444
Seminole *(G-8399)*
Service Pipe & Supply Company......E...... 918 336-8433
Bartlesville *(G-527)*
SFM Incorporated......G...... 405 788-9453
Tecumseh *(G-8928)*
Sharps Machine Shop......G...... 918 336-2516
Bartlesville *(G-528)*
Simair Ltd......F...... 918 366-6680
Bixby *(G-659)*
Simplified Dynamics Inc......G...... 405 806-0767
Mustang *(G-4793)*
Sims Automotive Inc......G...... 405 235-1621
Oklahoma City *(G-7141)*
Sisco Specialty Products Inc......G...... 918 266-2304
Tulsa *(G-9037)*
Slim Haney Inc......E...... 918 274-1082
Tulsa *(G-10772)*
Slim Haney Machining Inc......D...... 918 274-1082
Tulsa *(G-10773)*
Slone Centerless Grinding......G...... 918 497-0654
Tulsa *(G-10774)*
Sooner Machine & Equipment Co......G...... 405 794-6833
Moore *(G-4572)*
Sooner Manufacturing Co Inc......G...... 918 835-5019
Tulsa *(G-10789)*
Sooner Manufacturing Co Inc......F...... 918 835-5019
Tulsa *(G-10790)*
Southeast Machine Inc......E...... 580 889-6418
Atoka *(G-424)*
Southern Machine Works Inc......E...... 580 255-6525
Duncan *(G-2182)*
Southern Specialties Corp......E...... 918 584-3553
Tulsa *(G-10803)*
Space Con Systems Inc......G...... 918 835-6580
Tulsa *(G-10813)*
Space Tech Inc......F...... 918 582-2616
Tulsa *(G-10814)*
Special Parts Mfg Inc......E...... 405 379-3343
Holdenville *(G-3560)*
Specialty Component Mfg......G...... 405 794-5535
Moore *(G-4573)*
Specialty Machining Inc......G...... 918 266-3626
Catoosa *(G-1355)*
Spor Enterprises Inc......G...... 405 745-9888
Oklahoma City *(G-7187)*
▲ **Spray-Rite Inc**......E...... 479 648-3351
Pocola *(G-7786)*
Srite Mechanical LLC......G...... 405 308-3182
Oklahoma City *(G-7191)*
Stahle Tool Company LLC......G...... 405 265-4360
Yukon *(G-11788)*
Standard Machine LLC......G...... 918 423-9430
McAlester *(G-4338)*
Stewart Tech......G...... 405 292-8214
Norman *(G-5158)*
Stewart Tech Incorporated......G...... 405 831-9316
Norman *(G-5159)*
Stout Manufacturing LLC......G...... 918 371-7700
Collinsville *(G-1826)*
String Up Machine Inc......G...... 936 349-0419
Perkins *(G-7723)*
Strope Manufacturing Inc......G...... 918 835-8729
Tulsa *(G-10861)*
▲ **Summit Machine Tool LLC**......F...... 405 235-2075
Oklahoma City *(G-7223)*
Sun Manufacturing Inc......G...... 580 765-4786
Ponca City *(G-7879)*
Supco Inc......C...... 918 336-5075
Bartlesville *(G-529)*
Superior Companies Inc......C...... 918 336-5075
Bartlesville *(G-530)*
Swearingen Machine Shop Inc......G...... 918 267-4308
Beggs *(G-562)*
Sweetens Prfmce Machining Inc......G...... 918 436-9882
Pocola *(G-7788)*
Synergy Sourcing Solutions LLC......G...... 918 835-5019
Tulsa *(G-10886)*
T & E Mobile Service Inc......G...... 405 990-4022
Oklahoma City *(G-7240)*
Tc Machine & Manufacturing Inc......G...... 918 986-7920
Tulsa *(G-10907)*
Ted Davis Enterprises Inc......F...... 405 948-8763
Oklahoma City *(G-7263)*
Teddy Hall......G...... 918 355-3822
Broken Arrow *(G-1170)*
Thunderbolt Machine Services......G...... 918 357-2294
Broken Arrow *(G-1172)*
Tommy Luetkemeyer......G...... 580 772-1517
Weatherford *(G-11447)*
Tool Center......F...... 918 838-7411
Tulsa *(G-10953)*
Tote Along Inc......E...... 918 542-6453
Miami *(G-4433)*
Tri State Machine & Supply LLC......G...... 580 256-6265
Woodward *(G-11644)*
Triple D Machine Inc......E...... 580 566-2284
Boswell *(G-758)*
True Turn of Tulsa LLC......F...... 918 224-5040
Tulsa *(G-10980)*
Tulsa Mch Sp & Heat Exchanger......G...... 918 224-5040
Sapulpa *(G-8319)*
Turn Quick Manufacturing LLC......G...... 918 599-0011
Tulsa *(G-11017)*
Turner Machine Co Inc......E...... 918 446-3581
Tulsa *(G-11019)*
Turning Point Industries Inc......D...... 405 401-3930
Blanchard *(G-741)*
Turning Point Mch Works LLC......G...... 918 396-2560
Skiatook *(G-8573)*
Twiggs Company......G...... 405 882-0308
Yukon *(G-11796)*
U Save Machine Shop......G...... 918 836-7163
Tulsa *(G-11030)*
Ultimate Machine Inc......G...... 918 232-6676
Tulsa *(G-11032)*
Universal Machine Inc......G...... 405 373-2248
Yukon *(G-11798)*
V W Casey Industries LLC......G...... 918 369-5205
Bixby *(G-669)*
Vasser Machine......G...... 918 225-2677
Cushing *(G-1966)*
Voight Ronnie Lynn Linda Gail......G...... 580 251-9897
Comanche *(G-1848)*
▲ **Watonga Machine & Steel Works**......G...... 580 623-5830
Watonga *(G-11352)*
Watsons Machine Shop......G...... 918 652-3414
Henryetta *(G-3517)*
Wayne Burt Machine......G...... 918 786-4415
Grove *(G-3293)*
Weatherford Machine Works......G...... 580 772-5287
Weatherford *(G-11457)*
Weins Machine Co Inc......F...... 918 865-2187
Terlton *(G-8938)*

S I C

Employee Codes: A=Over 500 employees, B=251-500
C=101-250, D=51-100, E=20-50, F=10-19, G=1-9
2020 Oklahoma Directory
of Manufacturers & Processors
487

35 INDUSTRIAL AND COMMERCIAL MACHINERY AND COMPUTER EQUIPMENT

Werco Manufacturing Inc .... E 918 251-6880
 Broken Arrow *(G-1095)*
Wheeler Frris Whl Partners LLC .... G 405 206-6612
 Oklahoma City *(G-7444)*
Whitehouse Enterprises .... G 918 224-2002
 Sapulpa *(G-8325)*
Wiedenmanns Machine Shop .... G 405 745-2682
 Mustang *(G-4801)*
Wildcat Machine Inc .... G 918 247-4220
 Kellyville *(G-3770)*
Wildman Manufacturing Inc .... F 405 235-1264
 Oklahoma City *(G-7453)*
Williams McHning Spcalists Inc .... F 918 247-1719
 Kellyville *(G-3771)*
Williamson Machine Company Inc .... F 918 625-9856
 Sapulpa *(G-8326)*
Wilson Products Inc .... F 918 224-1327
 Tulsa *(G-9052)*
Witten Company Inc .... E 918 272-9567
 Owasso *(G-7630)*
Wizard Industries .... G 918 622-5234
 Tulsa *(G-11143)*
Wolff Machine Inc .... G 405 382-3000
 Seminole *(G-8407)*
Woods Precision Products Inc .... E 918 272-9541
 Owasso *(G-7631)*
Wr Machine Shop Inc .... G 918 834-7682
 Tulsa *(G-11162)*
Wrights Machine Shop .... G 580 363-1740
 Blackwell *(G-695)*
Zeco Machine Incorporated .... E 405 282-3313
 Guthrie *(G-3342)*
Ziese Products Inc .... E 918 457-5457
 Park Hill *(G-7647)*

36 ELECTRONIC AND OTHER ELECTRICAL EQUIPMENT AND COMPONENTS, EXCEPT COMPUTER

3612 Power, Distribution & Specialty Transformers

Asc Inc .... E 918 445-0260
 Tulsa *(G-9215)*
Chemco .... G 918 481-0537
 Tulsa *(G-9409)*
D & J Enterprises .... G 918 906-3951
 Tulsa *(G-9536)*
Fluid Controls Inc .... E 918 299-0442
 Tulsa *(G-9762)*
Kimray Inc .... C 405 525-6601
 Oklahoma City *(G-6417)*
Lamar Enterprises Inc .... E 405 682-5511
 Oklahoma City *(G-6447)*
Northwest Transformer Co Inc .... E 405 636-1454
 Oklahoma City *(G-6695)*
Quick Charge Corporation .... E 405 634-2120
 Oklahoma City *(G-6944)*
Quick Start Inc .... F 405 422-3135
 El Reno *(G-2749)*
Southwest Electric Co .... E 800 364-4445
 Oklahoma City *(G-7174)*
Southwest Electric Co .... C 405 733-4700
 Oklahoma City *(G-7175)*
Wiley Transformer Co .... G 918 225-5772
 Cushing *(G-1970)*

3613 Switchgear & Switchboard Apparatus

Adv-TEC Systems Inc .... G 918 542-4710
 Quapaw *(G-8027)*
▲ Advanced Indus Dvcs Co LLC ...... D 918 445-1254
 Tulsa *(G-9110)*
Aero Solutions and Services .... G 405 308-6788
 Edmond *(G-2291)*
Aero-TEC Industries Inc .... G 405 382-8501
 Seminole *(G-8353)*
American Automation Inc .... G
 Pryor *(G-7941)*
Design Ready Controls Inc .... F 405 605-8234
 Oklahoma City *(G-5926)*
Grace Power LLC .... G 512 228-9049
 Lawton *(G-3936)*
▼ Hermetic Switch Inc .... C 405 224-4046
 Chickasha *(G-1470)*
Huber Engineered Woods LLC .... E 580 584-7000
 Broken Bow *(G-1192)*

Industrial Cntrls Slutions LLC .... G 405 601-0625
 Oklahoma City *(G-6296)*
L3 Westwood Corporation .... D 918 250-4444
 Tulsa *(G-10109)*
L3 Westwood Corporation .... C 918 252-0481
 Tulsa *(G-10110)*
▲ Norberg Industries Inc .... E 918 665-6888
 Tulsa *(G-10349)*
Paul King Company .... G 918 592-5464
 Tulsa *(G-10475)*
Poteau Panel Shop Incorporated ..... G 918 647-4331
 Poteau *(G-7912)*
Russelectric Inc .... D 918 251-7877
 Broken Arrow *(G-1040)*
Southwest Electric Co .... F 918 437-9494
 Tulsa *(G-10805)*
Tactical Power Systems Corp .... E 207 864-5528
 Hulbert *(G-3629)*
Terac Controls Inc .... E 918 622-6818
 Broken Arrow *(G-1171)*
Tranam Systems Intl Inc .... G 918 488-0007
 Tulsa *(G-10968)*
Unicorp Systems Inc .... E 918 446-1874
 Tulsa *(G-11034)*
US Pioneer Led Specialists LLC .... G 918 359-5200
 Tulsa *(G-11056)*

3621 Motors & Generators

Adaptive Corporation .... G 440 257-7460
 Tulsa *(G-9103)*
▲ Advanced Indus Dvcs Co LLC ...... D 918 445-1254
 Tulsa *(G-9110)*
Aei Corp-Okla .... G 405 236-3551
 Oklahoma City *(G-5389)*
Allied Motion Technologies Inc .... F 918 627-1845
 Tulsa *(G-9151)*
Batteries Sooner LLC .... E 405 605-1237
 Oklahoma City *(G-5530)*
Bellofram Corporation .... G 918 965-1964
 Claremore *(G-1595)*
Britton Electric Motor Inc .... C 405 842-8357
 Oklahoma City *(G-5629)*
Buttons Auto Electrical Supply .... G 580 223-3855
 Ardmore *(G-261)*
C & P Catalyst Inc .... G 918 747-8379
 Tulsa *(G-9357)*
Cpv Keenan Renewable Enrgy LLC .. G 580 698-2278
 Woodward *(G-11573)*
Electric Motor Service Company ...... G 580 223-8940
 Ardmore *(G-283)*
▲ Emoteq Corporation .... C 918 627-1845
 Tulsa *(G-9674)*
Enerfin Inc .... G 918 258-3571
 Broken Arrow *(G-900)*
Enid Electric Motor Svc Inc .... F 580 234-8622
 Enid *(G-2952)*
▲ Evans Enterprises Inc .... C 405 631-1344
 Norman *(G-4993)*
Fasco Motors Group .... G 405 387-5560
 Norman *(G-4997)*
Franklin Electric Co Inc .... B 918 465-2348
 Wilburton *(G-11520)*
Franklin Electric Co Inc .... B 501 455-1234
 Oklahoma City *(G-6113)*
G P Enterprises .... G 405 340-8986
 Edmond *(G-2428)*
General Auto Supply Inc .... G 405 329-0772
 Norman *(G-5007)*
Hipower Systems Oklahoma LLC .... G 918 512-6321
 Tulsa *(G-9013)*
Independent Diesel Service .... F 580 234-0435
 Enid *(G-2977)*
Industrial Coil Inc .... F 405 745-2030
 Oklahoma City *(G-6297)*
Interstate Electric Corp .... G 918 245-4508
 Sand Springs *(G-8194)*
Kiowa Power Partners LLC .... E 918 432-5117
 Kiowa *(G-3839)*
L3 Westwood Corporation .... C 918 250-4444
 Tulsa *(G-10108)*
L3 Westwood Corporation .... D 918 250-4444
 Tulsa *(G-10109)*
L3 Westwood Corporation .... C 918 252-0481
 Tulsa *(G-10110)*
Maggie Company Inc .... E 918 438-7800
 Tulsa *(G-10200)*
Oklahoma Emergency Generator S . G 405 735-9888
 Moore *(G-4546)*
Petrolab LLC .... G 918 459-7170
 Broken Arrow *(G-1005)*

Pipeline Coating Services LLC .... G 936 494-2919
 Tulsa *(G-10518)*
Profab .... G 918 486-4464
 Coweta *(G-1894)*
Rp Power LLC .... G 918 960-6000
 Tulsa *(G-10680)*
Sooner State Generator LLC .... G 918 927-0543
 Sperry *(G-8611)*
Southwest Electric Co .... F 918 437-9494
 Tulsa *(G-10805)*
Union Hill Electric LLC .... C 405 222-1068
 Chickasha *(G-1519)*
Windrunner Energy Inc .... G 580 841-0404
 Duke *(G-2082)*

3624 Carbon & Graphite Prdts

Continental Carbon Company .... C 580 763-8100
 Ponca City *(G-7809)*

3625 Relays & Indl Controls

3d Farms & Machine L L C .... G 580 772-5543
 Weatherford *(G-11386)*
Aae Automation Inc .... G 405 525-1100
 Oklahoma City *(G-5355)*
ABB Inc .... C 918 338-4888
 Bartlesville *(G-444)*
▲ Bob Brooks Motor Company .... C 405 681-2592
 Oklahoma City *(G-5600)*
Buttons Auto Electrical Supply .... G 580 223-3855
 Ardmore *(G-261)*
Connor-Winfield Corp .... E 405 273-1257
 Shawnee *(G-8440)*
D C Ignition Co Inc .... G 580 332-0878
 Ada *(G-28)*
Datalog Systems .... G 918 245-3939
 Tulsa *(G-9554)*
Eaton and Associates LLC .... E 405 307-9631
 Norman *(G-4987)*
Eaton Building Contractors .... G 918 273-9191
 Bartlesville *(G-478)*
▲ Enovation Controls LLC .... B 918 317-4100
 Tulsa *(G-9689)*
▲ Evans Enterprises Inc .... C 405 631-1344
 Norman *(G-4993)*
▲ Fife Corporation .... C 405 755-1600
 Oklahoma City *(G-6084)*
Fw Murphy Prod Contrls LLC .... G 918 317-4280
 Tulsa *(G-9787)*
G P Enterprises .... G 405 340-8986
 Edmond *(G-2428)*
Hetronic Usa Inc .... E 405 946-3574
 Oklahoma City *(G-6245)*
High Country Tek Inc .... E 530 265-3236
 Tulsa *(G-9928)*
Industrial Electronics Repair .... E 918 342-1160
 Claremore *(G-1641)*
John Crane Inc .... D 918 664-5156
 Tulsa *(G-10049)*
K & S Controls LLC .... G 918 363-7268
 Sand Springs *(G-8196)*
N P T Inc .... G 580 399-0306
 Ada *(G-69)*
Nations Crane Sales Inc .... G 918 836-2000
 Tulsa *(G-10327)*
Paytons Auto .... G 918 540-2501
 Miami *(G-4427)*
Poteau Panel Shop Incorporated ..... G 918 647-4331
 Poteau *(G-7912)*
Pro Battery Inc .... G 918 437-1920
 Tulsa *(G-10564)*
Process Products & Service Co ...... G 918 827-4998
 Mounds *(G-4623)*
Realtime Automation Inc .... G 918 249-9217
 Broken Arrow *(G-1028)*
▲ Remote Connections Inc .... F 918 743-3355
 Tulsa *(G-10639)*
Repair Processes Inc .... F 918 758-0863
 Okmulgee *(G-7525)*
Scudder Service & Supply Inc .... G 405 232-6069
 Oklahoma City *(G-7101)*
Southwest Electric Co .... F 918 437-9494
 Tulsa *(G-10805)*
Tulsa Brake & Clutch Co LLC .... G 918 582-2165
 Tulsa *(G-10990)*
Versatech Industries Inc .... G 918 366-7400
 Bixby *(G-670)*

3629 Electrical Indl Apparatus, NEC

Atc New Technologies .... E 405 577-9901
 Oklahoma City *(G-5482)*

36 ELECTRONIC AND OTHER ELECTRICAL EQUIPMENT AND COMPONENTS, EXCEPT COMPUTER

Better Power Inc.................................G......405 753-1192
　Oklahoma City (G-5560)
Buckley Powder Company..............F......580 384-5547
　Mill Creek (G-4467)
Crosby US Acquisition Corp..........G......918 834-4611
　Tulsa (G-9511)
Elk City Wind LLC.............................G......580 772-2080
　Sweetwater (G-8847)
Exide Technologies LLC..................F......405 745-2511
　Oklahoma City (G-6061)
Maverick Technologies LLC............F......405 680-0100
　Oklahoma City (G-6537)
Power Cable Solutions LLC............G......405 818-1993
　Tuttle (G-11207)
Quick Charge Corporation..............E......405 634-2120
　Oklahoma City (G-6944)
Sanco Enterprises Inc.....................E......405 634-2120
　Oklahoma City (G-7075)
Sunrise Systems...............................G......405 222-3816
　Blanchard (G-735)
Tsig LLC..G......405 463-7700
　Oklahoma City (G-7347)
Zentech...G......918 445-1881
　Tulsa (G-11175)

3631 Household Cooking Eqpt

▼ Hasty-Bake Inc................................F......918 665-8220
　Tulsa (G-9901)
Horizon Smoker Company..............F......580 336-2400
　Perry (G-7736)
Metro Outdoor Living......................G......918 893-2960
　Tulsa (G-10253)
Nuckolls Distributing Inc.................G......918 663-0555
　Tulsa (G-10367)
▲ Party King Grills Company LLC.....G......580 774-2828
　Weatherford (G-11432)
Southern Cooker..............................G......580 283-3982
　Achille (G-1)
▲ W C Brdly/Zebco Holdings Inc......F......706 571-6080
　Tulsa (G-11087)
Whirlpool Corporation....................B......918 274-6000
　Tulsa (G-11115)

3634 Electric Household Appliances

Belden Russell Elect Co..................G......918 791-9600
　Grove (G-3259)
DL Harmer and Company LLC........F......918 865-6993
　Mannford (G-4181)
Medical Csmtc Elctrlysis Clnic.......G......405 755-7599
　Oklahoma City (G-6557)
Sweet Puffs LLC................................G......918 367-9544
　Bristow (G-798)

3635 Household Vacuum Cleaners

Als Vacuum Repair...........................G......405 550-8599
　Norman (G-4904)
Bobs Vacuum Sewing Repair........G......918 378-1844
　Broken Arrow (G-854)
▲ Lindsay Manufacturing Inc.............E......580 762-2457
　Ponca City (G-7845)

3639 Household Appliances, NEC

Blue Speed LLC.................................G......918 856-3547
　Tulsa (G-9306)
Metro Builders Supply Inc..............E......405 751-8833
　Edmond (G-2515)

3641 Electric Lamps

Advanced Tech Solutions LLC.......G......310 591-7163
　Oklahoma City (G-5386)
C Triple Inc...G......918 664-2144
　Tulsa (G-9361)
Company De Roth............................G......405 348-3754
　Edmond (G-2362)
Optronics International LLC..........E......918 683-9514
　Muskogee (G-4727)

3643 Current-Carrying Wiring Devices

BR Electric..G......405 354-8994
　Yukon (G-11700)
Corrpro Companies Inc..................E......918 245-8791
　Sand Springs (G-8172)
Ducommun Labarge Tech Inc.......C......918 459-2200
　Tulsa (G-9611)
Hypower Inc......................................G......918 341-6811
　Claremore (G-1639)
Mid States Technical Svc LLC.......E......918 260-6912
　Skiatook (G-8561)

▲ Remote Connections Inc................F......918 743-3355
　Tulsa (G-10639)
Special Service Systems Inc..........E......918 582-7777
　Tulsa (G-10816)

3644 Noncurrent-Carrying Wiring Devices

405 R/C Raceway & Hobbies LLC....G......405 503-0364
　Oklahoma City (G-5334)
HALAQ Inc...G......405 321-7293
　Newalla (G-4810)
Lawton RC Raceway LLC...................G......580 595-0814
　Lawton (G-3960)
Neomanufacturing LLC.....................E......405 605-6581
　Kingfisher (G-3809)
Raceway Electric Inc..........................F......918 629-4252
　Catoosa (G-1348)
Reynard Promotions LLC..................G......405 793-1049
　Wellston (G-11476)
Scott Manufacturing LLC..................E......405 949-2728
　Oklahoma City (G-7096)
Wichita Raceway Park.......................G......580 704-0341
　Lawton (G-4022)

3645 Residential Lighting Fixtures

▲ Billiards of Tulsa Inc.........................E......918 835-1166
　Tulsa (G-9296)
▲ Gary Smith..F......580 762-7575
　Ponca City (G-7830)
▲ La Maison Inc....................................G......918 592-1222
　Tulsa (G-10111)
Lillian Strickler Lighting....................G......405 528-4476
　Oklahoma City (G-6477)
Petroleum Artifacts Ltd....................G......918 949-6101
　Tulsa (G-10504)
Progress Lighting...............................G......405 949-2550
　Oklahoma City (G-6911)
Roberts Step-Lite Systems Inc.......G......800 654-8268
　Oklahoma City (G-7038)

3646 Commercial, Indl & Institutional Lighting Fixtures

Antares Enterprises LLC..................G......405 329-4326
　Norman (G-4910)
Crossroads Led LLC..........................G......918 504-6595
　Collinsville (G-1807)
▲ Gary Smith..F......580 762-7575
　Ponca City (G-7830)
Petroleum Artifacts Ltd....................G......918 949-6101
　Tulsa (G-10504)
▼ Truex LLC..G......918 250-7641
　Tulsa (G-10981)
▲ US Pioneer LLC..................................E......918 359-5200
　Tulsa (G-11055)

3647 Vehicular Lighting Eqpt

Dark Peek Technologies LLC..........G......405 316-8551
　Edmond (G-2379)

3648 Lighting Eqpt, NEC

Ambassador Lighting LLC...............G......405 503-5726
　Oklahoma City (G-5428)
Channel One Lighting Systems......G......918 587-2663
　Tulsa (G-9404)
Company De Roth..............................G......405 348-3754
　Edmond (G-2362)
Crandall and Sanders Inc................G......405 375-3242
　Kingfisher (G-3794)
Flashlightz..G......918 260-5882
　Tulsa (G-9755)
Grand Avenue Lighting....................G......580 237-4656
　Enid (G-2964)
Greenlamps USA LLC........................G......580 775-2883
　Cartwright (G-1284)
Koinonia Enterprises........................G......405 275-7064
　Shawnee (G-8465)
L & L Sales LLC..................................G......580 658-3739
　Chattanooga (G-1390)
Lady Lights & Stage Inc..................G......405 376-0076
　Mustang (G-4781)
LLC Searchlight.................................G......580 699-2971
　Lawton (G-3964)
Maro International Corp.................G......918 836-7749
　Tulsa (G-10215)
Okluma LLC..G......580 716-1343
　Oklahoma City (G-6767)
Optronics International LLC..........E......918 683-9514
　Muskogee (G-4727)

Punt & Puckle LLC............................G......719 358-1419
　Oklahoma City (G-6921)
Roberts Step-Lite Systems Inc.....G......800 654-8268
　Oklahoma City (G-7038)
Searchlight Inc Jefferson................G......580 752-4374
　Hobart (G-3546)
Sheltred Work-Activity Program....E......918 683-8162
　Muskogee (G-4748)
Showtek..G......405 222-0632
　Chickasha (G-1510)
Site Distribution LLC........................G......918 625-7980
　Tulsa (G-10769)
Smith Lighting Sales Inc..................G......918 794-2525
　Tulsa (G-10778)
▲ Solutions Lucid Group LLC.............G......405 476-4332
　Oklahoma City (G-7158)
Spiro Mining LLC..............................G......918 962-5335
　Spiro (G-8619)
T Town Lighting................................G......918 693-2063
　Tulsa (G-10892)
Trailing Edge Technologies............G......580 536-0559
　Lawton (G-4014)
Unami LLC..G......405 320-5696
　Anadarko (G-208)
Viking Sales LLC................................G......918 742-7796
　Tulsa (G-11077)

3651 Household Audio & Video Eqpt

A & E Satellites.................................G......580 363-0931
　Ponca City (G-7790)
C2 Innovative Technologies Inc....G......405 388-2357
　Oklahoma City (G-5665)
▲ Cambridge Soundworks Inc...........C......405 742-6704
　Stillwater (G-8665)
Camera Guys LLC.............................G......405 310-0006
　Norman (G-4951)
Clear Tone Hearing Center Inc......E......918 838-1000
　Tulsa (G-9449)
Clear2there LLC................................G......405 605-8158
　Oklahoma City (G-5782)
Cns Audio Video Inc.........................G......405 256-8546
　Oklahoma City (G-5796)
Digital Resources Inc.......................G......866 823-6328
　Tulsa (G-9583)
Falcon Audio Video Inc...................G......918 272-3969
　Claremore (G-1619)
▲ Great Plains Audio...........................G......405 789-0221
　Oklahoma City (G-6177)
Infinity Home Solutions LLC...........G......918 704-8014
　Bixby (G-635)
Louis Systems & Products Inc......G......405 285-0950
　Edmond (G-2498)
Media Specialists Inc.......................G......918 622-0077
　Tulsa (G-10238)
R & R Media Systems LLC...............G......918 978-0578
　Tulsa (G-10601)
◆ Resonance Inc..................................E......405 239-2800
　Oklahoma City (G-7010)
Rockford Corporation......................C......405 624-6722
　Stillwater (G-8748)
Scratchout LLC.................................G......918 740-8665
　Tulsa (G-10718)
Sound Iq..G......918 442-2588
　Tulsa (G-10793)
Speaker World LLC..........................G......918 973-1700
　Tulsa (G-10815)
◆ Tactical Elec Military Sup LLC.......E......866 541-7996
　Broken Arrow (G-1070)
United Video LLC.............................D......918 488-4000
　Tulsa (G-11043)
Versatech Industries Inc.................G......918 366-7400
　Bixby (G-670)
Versitile Entertainment..................G......812 913-2677
　Seminole (G-8406)

3652 Phonograph Records & Magnetic Tape

▲ Broken Arrow Productions Inc.......E......405 360-8702
　Norman (G-4944)
Cedar Rdge Rcording Studio LLC..G......405 651-5961
　Harrah (G-3375)
Computer Solutions + LLC............G......405 259-9603
　Choctaw (G-1534)
El Jay Enterprises Inc......................G......918 836-8273
　Tulsa (G-9649)
Mark Stevens Industries Inc..........D......405 948-1077
　Edmond (G-2504)
Melody House Inc............................G......405 840-3383
　Oklahoma City (G-6562)
Mobile Laser Forces.........................G......405 259-9300
　Oklahoma City (G-6621)

On Beat Goes .... G 918 342-5654
Claremore *(G-1667)*

3661 Telephone & Telegraph Apparatus

Catoosa 2 Way .... G 918 234-0055
Tulsa *(G-9389)*
Chaddick & Associates Inc .... F 580 223-1202
Ardmore *(G-264)*
Ciena Corporation .... F 918 925-5000
Tulsa *(G-9424)*
Indian Nations Fiberoptics Inc .... G 580 355-2300
Lawton *(G-3941)*
Jesse Harbin .... G 918 734-3980
Tulsa *(G-10039)*
L3 Westwood Corporation .... C 918 250-4444
Tulsa *(G-10108)*
United Sewing Agency Inc .... G 580 924-6936
Durant *(G-2271)*
Vics Telecommunications .... G 580 512-0313
Lawton *(G-4017)*
Zeta .... G 918 664-8200
Broken Arrow *(G-1105)*
▲ Zomm LLC .... G 918 995-2233
Tulsa *(G-11179)*

3663 Radio & T V Communications, Systs & Eqpt, Broadcast/Studio

B J M Consulting Inc .... G 918 665-8737
Tulsa *(G-9244)*
Carc Inc .... G 918 266-1341
Catoosa *(G-1308)*
Channel One Lighting Systems .... G 918 587-2663
Tulsa *(G-9404)*
Ducommun Labarge Tech Inc .... C 918 459-2200
Tulsa *(G-9611)*
Gateway Com Inc .... G 405 787-0800
Edmond *(G-2432)*
His Construction .... G 405 642-4306
Oklahoma City *(G-6253)*
Josh Leeper .... G 918 618-2215
Eufaula *(G-3103)*
Lamar Systems LLC .... G 918 770-0941
Tulsa *(G-10118)*
▼ Landa Mobile Systems LLC .... F 360 474-8991
Tulsa *(G-10120)*
Logo Marketing Company Inc .... G 918 496-2989
Tulsa *(G-10176)*
Louis Systems & Products Inc .... G 405 285-0950
Edmond *(G-2498)*
Me3 Communications Company LLC ... G 405 834-8992
Oklahoma City *(G-6553)*
Microframe Corp .... F 918 258-4839
Broken Arrow *(G-973)*
Monitron Corp .... F 918 836-6831
Sand Springs *(G-8206)*
Oklahoma Community TV LLC .... G 405 808-2509
Oklahoma City *(G-6744)*
Southern Plains Cable LLC .... G 580 529-5000
Lawton *(G-4000)*
◆ Tactical Elec Military Sup LLC .... E 866 541-7996
Broken Arrow *(G-1070)*
Tribalcom Wrless Solutions LLC .... G 405 274-7245
Oklahoma City *(G-7328)*
Tulsat Inc .... G 918 587-4729
Tulsa *(G-11016)*
Tulsat Corporation .... D 918 251-2887
Broken Arrow *(G-1087)*
Tyler Enterprises .... G 405 616-5500
Oklahoma City *(G-7354)*
Versatech Industries Inc .... G 918 366-7400
Bixby *(G-670)*
Zephyrus Electronics Ltd .... F 918 437-3333
Tulsa *(G-11177)*

3669 Communications Eqpt, NEC

Ademco Inc .... G 918 663-2822
Tulsa *(G-9104)*
Ademco Inc .... G 405 681-4008
Oklahoma City *(G-5373)*
Airgo Systems LLC .... F 405 346-5807
Oklahoma City *(G-5404)*
Disan Engineering Corporation .... E 918 273-1636
Nowata *(G-5213)*
Ducommun Labarge Tech Inc .... C 918 459-2200
Tulsa *(G-9611)*
Econolite Control Products Inc .... G 405 485-2230
Blanchard *(G-713)*
Emergency Alert Response .... G 918 298-0500
Tulsa *(G-9668)*
Gades Sales Co .... G 405 720-6839
Oklahoma City *(G-6133)*
In-Tele Communication LLC .... G 580 272-0303
Ada *(G-50)*
Invictus Engrg Cnstr Svcs .... G 405 701-5622
Norman *(G-5037)*
Johnson Controls .... G 918 626-3773
Pocola *(G-7783)*
Lifetone Technology Inc .... G 405 200-1555
Oklahoma City *(G-6475)*
Midstate Traffic Control Inc .... G 405 799-0313
Moore *(G-4541)*
Newstar Netronics LLC .... G 918 932-8343
Tulsa *(G-10340)*
OK Rail Signals Inc .... G 918 378-9520
Tulsa *(G-10392)*
Order-Matic Electronics Corp .... C 405 672-1487
Oklahoma City *(G-6781)*
Railroad Sgnling Solutions Inc .... G 918 973-1888
Broken Arrow *(G-1020)*
Rapid Wireless LLC .... G 918 605-9717
Tulsa *(G-10620)*
Signaltek Inc .... G 918 583-4335
Tulsa *(G-10758)*

3671 Radio & T V Receiving Electron Tubes

All Electronic and More Llc .... G 918 557-5410
Collinsville *(G-1799)*
Time Mark Inc .... D 918 438-1220
Tulsa *(G-10942)*
Versatech Industries Inc .... G 918 366-7400
Bixby *(G-670)*

3672 Printed Circuit Boards

Advance Research & Development .... G 405 321-0550
Norman *(G-4899)*
▲ Advanced Medical Instrs Inc .... C 918 250-0566
Broken Arrow *(G-816)*
Beck Illuminations LLC .... E 918 623-2880
Okemah *(G-5264)*
Goodwill Inds Centl Okla Inc .... D 405 236-4451
Oklahoma City *(G-6172)*
Newstar Netronics LLC .... G 918 932-8343
Tulsa *(G-10340)*
Nyikos Inc .... G 918 299-3190
Tulsa *(G-10368)*
▲ Oai Electronics LLC .... D 918 836-9077
Tulsa *(G-10372)*
Steven Jackson .... G 918 813-7184
Tulsa *(G-10850)*

3674 Semiconductors

Accurate By Design .... G 918 445-0292
Tulsa *(G-8986)*
Adl Group LLC .... G 918 960-0388
Tulsa *(G-9105)*
▼ Advanced Power Inc .... F 580 774-2220
Weatherford *(G-11387)*
Amethyst Research Incorporated .... F 580 657-2575
Ardmore *(G-238)*
Clayton Macom .... G 918 967-3350
Stigler *(G-8631)*
Coorstek Inc .... B 405 601-4371
Oklahoma City *(G-5832)*
▲ Crystaltech Inc .... G 580 252-8893
Duncan *(G-2101)*
Digital Interface LLC .... G 405 201-5070
Fairland *(G-3124)*
▲ Don Tooker .... G 972 742-8515
Owasso *(G-7562)*
Downing Manufacturing Inc .... F 918 224-1116
Tulsa *(G-9001)*
Electric Green Inc .... G 405 706-1683
Oklahoma City *(G-6022)*
Green Co Corporation .... G 918 221-3997
Tulsa *(G-9859)*
Kaze LLC .... G 580 857-2707
Allen *(G-136)*
Legacy Advnced Intllctuals LLC .... G 707 358-0332
Tulsa *(G-10148)*
◆ Lektron Inc .... E 918 622-4978
Tulsa *(G-10152)*
Michael A Phillips .... G 918 251-0925
Broken Arrow *(G-972)*
New X Drive Tech Inc .... G 918 850-4463
Tulsa *(G-10337)*
Southwest Silicon Tech Corp .... E 580 223-5058
Ardmore *(G-357)*
Sun Direct Power Inc .... G 918 612-4090
Tulsa *(G-10869)*
◆ Umicore Optical Mtls USA Inc .... D 918 673-1650
Quapaw *(G-8034)*
Waylolo LLC .... G 405 714-2353
Stillwater *(G-8774)*

3676 Electronic Resistors

Okluma LLC .... G 580 716-1343
Oklahoma City *(G-6767)*

3677 Electronic Coils & Transformers

A-Line Tds Inc .... E 580 628-5371
Tonkawa *(G-8970)*

3678 Electronic Connectors

Datran Corporation .... G 918 307-2200
Broken Arrow *(G-888)*

3679 Electronic Components, NEC

All Electronic and More Llc .... G 918 557-5410
Collinsville *(G-1799)*
Ashleys Electrical Services .... G 918 825-0747
Pryor *(G-7944)*
Baron Manufacturing Inc .... G 405 947-3362
Oklahoma City *(G-5528)*
C D Connections .... G 580 248-6410
Lawton *(G-3903)*
Cherokee Medical Services LLC .... C 918 696-3151
Stilwell *(G-8783)*
Cherokee Nation .... F 918 696-3124
Stilwell *(G-8784)*
Cherokee Nation Arospc Def LLC .... G 918 430-3492
Pryor *(G-7951)*
Cherokee Nation Arospc Def LLC .... G 918 696-3151
Stilwell *(G-8785)*
Cherokee Nation Industries LLC .... E 918 696-3151
Stilwell *(G-8786)*
Cherokee Nation Red Wing LLC .... G 918 824-6050
Pryor *(G-7952)*
▲ Cherokee Nation Red Wing LLC .... E 918 430-3437
Tulsa *(G-9414)*
Connor-Winfield Corp .... E 405 273-1257
Shawnee *(G-8440)*
Csi .... G 319 274-5005
Catoosa *(G-1314)*
Ducommun Labarge Tech Inc .... C 918 459-2200
Tulsa *(G-9611)*
Duncan Overhead Door .... G 405 222-0748
Chickasha *(G-1454)*
Electranetics Inc .... G 918 960-0818
Tulsa *(G-9652)*
Electronic Assembly Corp .... G 918 286-2816
Tulsa *(G-9653)*
Hem Industries .... G 918 534-0579
Dewey *(G-2024)*
▼ Hermetic Switch Inc .... C 405 224-4046
Chickasha *(G-1470)*
Industrial Electronics Repair .... E 918 342-1160
Claremore *(G-1641)*
Inland Manufacturing LLC .... G 918 342-5733
Claremore *(G-1642)*
Interactive Cad Services Inc .... G 918 251-4470
Broken Arrow *(G-940)*
James A Brumit Jr .... G 405 924-9696
Moore *(G-4530)*
Paia Electronics Inc .... G 405 340-6300
Edmond *(G-2559)*
Qual-Tron Inc .... E 918 622-7052
Tulsa *(G-10589)*
Quick Charge Corporation .... E 405 634-2120
Oklahoma City *(G-6944)*
Sentry Manufacturing Company .... E 202 262-0225
Chickasha *(G-1507)*
Shortruncdr .... G 405 602-5555
Oklahoma City *(G-7124)*
Surface Mount Depot Inc .... D 405 948-8763
Oklahoma City *(G-7232)*
Univision Display Usa LLC .... G 918 289-6611
Tulsa *(G-11051)*
▲ Westoak Industries Inc .... E 580 526-3221
Erick *(G-3093)*
Yukon Manufacturing Inc .... G 918 850-3131
Oklahoma City *(G-7484)*

3691 Storage Batteries

Continental Battery Company .... E 918 259-0662
Broken Arrow *(G-874)*
Spiers New Technologies Inc .... E 405 464-2200
Oklahoma City *(G-7184)*

Spiers New Technologies Inc ....E 405 605-8066
Oklahoma City *(G-7185)*

3694 Electrical Eqpt For Internal Combustion Engines

▲ **Bob Brooks Motor Company** ....C 405 681-2592
Oklahoma City *(G-5600)*
Bobs Auto Electric ....G 918 687-3701
Muskogee *(G-4653)*
Buttons Auto Electrical Supply ....G 580 223-3855
Ardmore *(G-261)*
C & P Auto Electric ....G 405 799-2083
Moore *(G-4501)*
D C Ignition Co Inc ....G 580 332-0878
Ada *(G-28)*
Draeger Interlock ....G 918 270-1600
Tulsa *(G-9602)*
▲ **Enovation Controls LLC** ....B 918 317-4100
Tulsa *(G-9689)*
GC&i Global Inc ....G 918 317-4244
Tulsa *(G-9810)*
General Auto Supply Inc ....G 405 329-0772
Norman *(G-5007)*
Goodwill Inds Centl Okla Inc ....D 405 236-4451
Oklahoma City *(G-6172)*
Ignition Systems & Controls ....F 405 682-3030
Oklahoma City *(G-6291)*
Jesse Griffith Repairs ....G 580 379-0790
Elk City *(G-2832)*
Mower Parts Inc ....E 405 947-6484
Oklahoma City *(G-6631)*
Paytons Auto ....G 918 540-2501
Miami *(G-4427)*
Reggie Adudell ....G 405 631-9002
Oklahoma City *(G-7003)*
▲ **Remote Connections Inc** ....F 918 743-3355
Tulsa *(G-10639)*
Sledge Electric Inc ....G 405 793-4007
Oklahoma City *(G-5316)*
Tommy Nix Cdjr Muskogee LLC ....G 918 456-2541
Muskogee *(G-4753)*
Tri-State Elec Contrs LLC ....G 405 341-3043
Oklahoma City *(G-7324)*

3695 Recording Media

Andre Anderson ....G 405 642-3210
Moore *(G-4490)*
Benson Sound Inc ....G 405 610-7455
Oklahoma City *(G-5553)*
▲ **Broken Arrow Productions Inc** ....E 405 360-8702
Norman *(G-4944)*
▲ **Indel-Davis Inc** ....F 918 587-2151
Tulsa *(G-9976)*

3699 Electrical Machinery, Eqpt & Splys, NEC

A Bolt Electric ....G 580 510-0123
Cache *(G-1223)*
Acquire Cctv Inc ....G 405 324-1300
Yukon *(G-11689)*
Adams Electronics Inc ....G 918 622-5000
Tulsa *(G-9102)*
Airelectric Inc ....G 918 291-7531
Tulsa *(G-9127)*
Alan Beaty ....G 405 664-6768
El Reno *(G-2696)*
AMI Instruments Inc ....G 918 241-2665
Sand Springs *(G-8160)*
Amt Diversified Cnstr Inc ....G 580 279-6250
Ada *(G-8)*
Arnold Electric Inc ....G 405 605-1982
Oklahoma City *(G-5467)*
Aviation Training Devices Inc ....F 918 366-6680
Bixby *(G-613)*
Awc Inc ....G 405 601-1090
Oklahoma City *(G-5496)*
Aztec Ne Overhead Door Inc ....G 918 341-7502
Claremore *(G-1586)*
Azz Incorporated ....E 918 295-8702
Tulsa *(G-9238)*
Baby Bee Safe ....G 918 224-1104
Sapulpa *(G-8251)*
Belden Russell Elect Co ....G 918 791-9600
Grove *(G-3259)*
Bell & McCoy Companies Inc ....E 405 278-6909
Oklahoma City *(G-5543)*
Bills Electric Inc ....G 918 341-4414
Claremore *(G-1596)*
Bloom Electric Services LLC ....F 580 327-2345
Alva *(G-178)*
Broken Arrow Electric Sup Inc ....G 580 924-2237
Durant *(G-2209)*
Broken Arrow Electric Sup Inc ....G 580 436-1470
Ada *(G-13)*
Caddo Electric Corp ....G 580 774-5280
Weatherford *(G-11396)*
City Electric Supply Company ....G 918 871-2640
Tahlequah *(G-8857)*
City Electric Supply Company ....G 405 701-8544
Norman *(G-4958)*
Ckenergy Electric Co Op Inc ....G 405 247-3041
Anadarko *(G-201)*
Clement Elec ....G 580 223-6500
Ardmore *(G-267)*
Corrpro Companies Inc ....E 918 245-8791
Sand Springs *(G-8172)*
Cymstar LLC ....G 918 251-8100
Tulsa *(G-9532)*
Cymstar LLC ....C 918 251-8100
Broken Arrow *(G-884)*
D & L Enclosures ....G 918 396-7355
Skiatook *(G-8538)*
Daniel Garage Door Sales & Svc ....G 580 628-3769
Tonkawa *(G-8973)*
David Bates ....G 918 457-6169
Tahlequah *(G-8862)*
Digi Security Systems LLC ....F 918 824-2520
Tulsa *(G-9582)*
Direct Communications Inc ....E 918 291-0092
Tulsa *(G-9585)*
Dougherty Forestry Mfg Ltd ....F 405 542-3520
Hinton *(G-3523)*
Electrotech Inc ....G 918 224-5869
Tulsa *(G-9002)*
Endeavor Lser Etching Engrv LL ....G 405 202-5921
Moore *(G-4520)*
Freelance Operations Inc ....G 580 226-7051
Ardmore *(G-292)*
Icx Technologies Inc ....G 703 678-2111
Oklahoma City *(G-6286)*
Jarvis Inc ....E 918 437-1100
Tulsa *(G-10029)*
Jim Dunn ....G 918 456-3552
Tahlequah *(G-8868)*
Jjs Security Cameras Inc ....G 405 408-6096
Oklahoma City *(G-6364)*
Kingdom Alarms Inc ....F 918 627-5454
Tulsa *(G-10091)*
L3 Technologies Inc ....G 405 601-0874
Oklahoma City *(G-6442)*
L3 Technologies Inc ....C 918 258-0707
Broken Arrow *(G-962)*
L3 Technologies Inc ....E 405 739-3700
Tinker Afb *(G-8954)*
Lockdown Ltd Co ....F 405 605-6161
Oklahoma City *(G-6485)*
◆ **Lucas Holdings LLC** ....E 405 524-1811
Oklahoma City *(G-6500)*
Marietta Tag Agency ....G 580 276-2101
Marietta *(G-4210)*
Mathena Inc ....D 405 422-3600
El Reno *(G-2736)*
Maverick Technologies LLC ....F 405 680-0100
Oklahoma City *(G-6537)*
McDermott Electric LLC ....F 405 603-4665
Oklahoma City *(G-6547)*
McDonald Electric Utility Svcs ....G 580 767-8845
Ponca City *(G-7848)*
Mels Electric Contracting ....G 918 279-6036
Coweta *(G-1891)*
Millers Superior Electric LLC ....G 918 933-4006
Tulsa *(G-10283)*
Monitron Corp ....F 918 836-6831
Sand Springs *(G-8206)*
Nano Light ....G 405 579-5662
Norman *(G-5084)*
Newton Design LLC ....D 918 266-6205
Catoosa *(G-1343)*
Newton Design LLC ....G 918 381-3012
Catoosa *(G-1344)*
Oklahoma Native Electric LLC ....G 918 824-7638
Pryor *(G-7979)*
Omni Design ....G 918 495-0841
Tulsa *(G-10416)*
Power Ready LLC ....F 918 289-0088
Tulsa *(G-10539)*
Powerhouse Elec ....G 405 735-6381
Moore *(G-4553)*
▲ **Practical Sales and Svc Inc** ....G 918 446-5515
Tulsa *(G-10540)*
Prism Electric Inc ....G 918 425-2000
Tulsa *(G-10562)*
Rackley Welding ....G 580 660-1176
Mountain View *(G-4629)*
Regrid Energy LLC ....G 405 837-8707
Edmond *(G-2595)*
▲ **Safety Training Systems Inc** ....E 918 665-0125
Tulsa *(G-10688)*
Simulator Systems Intl Inc ....G 800 843-4764
Tulsa *(G-10765)*
Simulator Systems Intl Inc ....G 918 250-4500
Tulsa *(G-10766)*
◆ **Tactical Elec Military Sup LLC** ....E 866 541-7996
Broken Arrow *(G-1070)*
Total Control System Inc ....G 918 810-4004
Owasso *(G-7625)*
Total Home Controls Inc ....G 405 736-0191
Oklahoma City *(G-7308)*
Trinity Technologies LLC ....F 580 475-0900
Duncan *(G-2190)*
Trubend Systems Inc ....G 918 342-3373
Claremore *(G-1695)*
Wholesale Electric Supply Co ....G 918 647-2200
Poteau *(G-7918)*
Yandell Fire Investigations ....G 580 269-2414
Kaw City *(G-3760)*
Zebco Corporation ....A 918 836-5581
Tulsa *(G-11172)*

37 TRANSPORTATION EQUIPMENT

3711 Motor Vehicles & Car Bodies

Accurate Machine Works Inc ....F 405 615-4983
Blanchard *(G-700)*
Alpha Omega Mltary/Defence Mfg ....G 918 816-6918
Muskogee *(G-4647)*
American Street Rod Co ....G 405 373-0376
Piedmont *(G-7754)*
Antique & Rod Shop LLC ....G 405 631-3544
Oklahoma City *(G-5450)*
Broce Manufacturing Co Inc ....G 405 579-4621
Norman *(G-4943)*
Choctaw Defense Mfg LLC ....G 918 426-2871
McAlester *(G-4283)*
Choctaw Defense Mfg LLC ....E 580 326-8365
Hugo *(G-3606)*
County of Oklahoma ....G 918 456-3622
Tahlequah *(G-8859)*
Cox Motor Co Henryetta LLC ....G 918 652-0202
Henryetta *(G-3503)*
Deacon Race Cars ....G 405 348-4419
Edmond *(G-2387)*
Dials Race Shop ....G 405 382-4843
Seminole *(G-8368)*
Echota Defense Services ....G 918 384-7409
Tulsa *(G-9637)*
Elastomer Specialties Inc ....G 918 485-0276
Wagoner *(G-11282)*
Factor 1 Racing Inc ....G 918 258-7223
Broken Arrow *(G-905)*
Fat Alberts Motor Sports ....G 918 647-3069
Poteau *(G-7903)*
Federal-Mogul Chassis LLC ....F 405 672-4500
Oklahoma City *(G-6081)*
Franks Garage Auto Sls & Salv ....G 405 257-6198
Wewoka *(G-11502)*
Glenns Competition Chassis ....G 405 732-4403
Oklahoma City *(G-6158)*
Guardian Interlock of Utah ....G 580 357-8583
Lawton *(G-3937)*
Heartland Energy Options LLC ....G 405 600-6009
Piedmont *(G-7763)*
Heartland Locator ....G 580 554-0125
Pond Creek *(G-7890)*
Ic Bus of Oklahoma LLC ....A 918 833-4000
Tulsa *(G-9964)*
J J Custom Fire ....G 918 762-2102
Pawnee *(G-7705)*
James Matthews Ford LLC ....E 918 251-3673
Broken Arrow *(G-942)*
Logistics Management Company ....G 405 633-1201
Oklahoma City *(G-6490)*
Major League Sports LLC ....G 918 559-5030
Nowata *(G-5219)*
Navistar Inc ....D 918 833-4065
Tulsa *(G-10330)*
Oklahoma Dept Public Safety ....E 918 256-3388
Vinita *(G-11265)*
Paccar ....G 918 810-3810
Broken Arrow *(G-1148)*

S I C

Paccar Inc................E....... 918 756-4400
Okmulgee *(G-7521)*
Paccar Inc................E....... 405 745-3006
Oklahoma City *(G-6792)*
Patrick Michael Palazzo................G....... 918 344-3724
Tulsa *(G-10474)*
Paul Wrecker Service................G....... 918 333-9685
Bartlesville *(G-515)*
Performance Plastics Inc................G....... 918 627-9621
Tulsa *(G-10494)*
Ragsdale Wrecker Service................G....... 405 771-5544
Spencer *(G-8600)*
Ron Shanks Racing Enterprises................G....... 918 366-6050
Bixby *(G-655)*
Sky Motors LLC................F....... 918 321-2800
Sapulpa *(G-8313)*
Sportchassis LLC................D....... 580 323-4100
Clinton *(G-1770)*
Tuff Troff LLC................G....... 918 623-6091
Okemah *(G-5277)*
Welchs Wrecker................G....... 405 238-6194
Pauls Valley *(G-7674)*
Western Okla Powertrain Inc................G....... 580 243-4501
Elk City *(G-2889)*
Wheels of Past................G....... 918 225-2250
Cushing *(G-1969)*

3713 Truck & Bus Bodies

Alberts Auto & Truck Repr Inc................E....... 866 772-6065
Weatherford *(G-11389)*
Arrowhead Truck Equipment Inc................G....... 918 224-5570
Bixby *(G-612)*
◆ **Auto Crane Company**................C....... 918 438-2760
Tulsa *(G-9226)*
B&P Detailing LLC................G....... 405 684-7730
Chickasha *(G-1435)*
Big J Tank Truck Service Inc................G....... 580 336-3501
Perry *(G-7727)*
▲ **Boss Seals & Parts LLC**................G....... 918 237-6991
Tulsa *(G-9323)*
Bramco Inc................F....... 580 227-2345
Fairview *(G-3133)*
C & S Technical Services LLC................E....... 918 258-8324
Tulsa *(G-9358)*
Cadet Manufacturing Inc................E....... 918 476-8159
Chouteau *(G-1559)*
Cooper Creek Manufacturing Inc................G....... 405 729-4446
Loyal *(G-4130)*
Cooper Wrecker Service................G....... 918 639-7381
Pawnee *(G-7703)*
Crane Carrier Co................G....... 918 836-1651
Tulsa *(G-9500)*
Custom Automotive Mfg................F....... 918 258-2900
Broken Arrow *(G-881)*
Dominion Refuse Inc................G....... 918 743-8860
Tulsa *(G-9595)*
Emergency Site Protection LLC................D....... 580 699-6386
Medicine Park *(G-4370)*
Equipment Technology Inc................F....... 405 748-3841
Oklahoma City *(G-6049)*
Givens Wrecker Service................G....... 580 225-0892
Elk City *(G-2821)*
Halliburton Company................E....... 580 251-4614
Duncan *(G-2121)*
Ic Bus of Oklahoma LLC................A....... 918 833-4000
Tulsa *(G-9964)*
J & C Manufacturing Inc................F....... 580 476-3217
Rush Springs *(G-8122)*
J & I Manufacturing Inc................E....... 580 795-7377
Madill *(G-4150)*
J & J Custom Fire Inc................G....... 405 747-4442
Red Rock *(G-8079)*
Jims Truck Center................G....... 918 225-1013
Cushing *(G-1939)*
Lafaver Fiberglass Corporation................G....... 918 258-4845
Broken Arrow *(G-1137)*
Midwest Clssic Motorsports LLC................G....... 405 359-0050
Edmond *(G-2519)*
Miller Mfg Group................G....... 918 540-1600
Miami *(G-4418)*
Nix Body Shop LLC................G....... 918 797-2484
Stilwell *(G-8794)*
Pendpac Incorporated................D....... 418 831-8250
Fairview *(G-3145)*
Performance Plastics Inc................G....... 918 627-9621
Tulsa *(G-10494)*
Pfpp LP................D....... 405 946-3381
Oklahoma City *(G-6839)*
▲ **Proform Group Inc**................C....... 918 682-8666
Muskogee *(G-4739)*
Reading Equipment & Dist LLC................E....... 918 283-2999
Claremore *(G-1679)*
Robbins Salvage & Auto Sales................G....... 918 431-1000
Tahlequah *(G-8881)*
Rocky L Emmons & Judy E Sprag................G....... 580 305-1940
Frederick *(G-3199)*
Shur-Co LLC................G....... 405 262-7600
El Reno *(G-2757)*
▲ **Technical Manufacturing Inc**................F....... 918 485-0380
Wagoner *(G-11292)*
Wheels of Past................G....... 918 225-2250
Cushing *(G-1969)*

3714 Motor Vehicle Parts & Access

1 800 Radiator................G....... 405 946-9800
Oklahoma City *(G-5326)*
▲ **Advanced Racing Composites LLC**................G....... 918 760-9990
Tulsa *(G-9111)*
Aero Dynamics................F....... 918 258-0290
Broken Arrow *(G-818)*
Allen Camper Mfg Company Inc................E....... 580 857-2177
Allen *(G-133)*
◆ **Atc Drivetrain LLC**................A....... 405 577-9901
Oklahoma City *(G-5480)*
Atc Drivetrain LLC................B....... 405 350-3600
Oklahoma City *(G-5481)*
Atc Technology Corporation................A....... 405 577-9901
Oklahoma City *(G-5483)*
Auto Hail Damage Repair................G....... 405 696-6031
Edmond *(G-2312)*
Autocraft Industries................G....... 405 577-9901
Oklahoma City *(G-5492)*
B & W Diesel & Drivetrain Inc................G....... 918 427-7918
Muldrow *(G-4631)*
Blumenthal Companies LLc................G....... 405 232-9557
Oklahoma City *(G-5596)*
▲ **Blumenthal Companies LLc**................E....... 405 232-9557
Oklahoma City *(G-5595)*
Bob Howard Whl Parts Dist Ctr................G....... 405 525-4400
Oklahoma City *(G-5601)*
Boyds Auto Parts & Machine................F....... 405 329-3855
Norman *(G-4940)*
Braden Carco Gearmatic Winch................G....... 918 756-4400
Okmulgee *(G-7495)*
Brake Rebuilders Inc................F....... 918 834-0200
Tulsa *(G-9331)*
Burns Manufacturing Inc................G....... 918 622-3305
Tulsa *(G-9348)*
C & C Performance Engines................G....... 580 252-4331
Duncan *(G-2094)*
C & S Technical Services LLC................E....... 918 258-8324
Tulsa *(G-9358)*
Chevelle World Inc................F....... 405 872-3399
Noble *(G-4876)*
CNG Specialists LLC................G....... 405 677-5400
Oklahoma City *(G-5795)*
▲ **Dales Manufacturing Co**................G....... 405 631-8988
Oklahoma City *(G-5891)*
Deatschwerks LLC................G....... 405 217-0701
Oklahoma City *(G-5914)*
Dexter Axle Company................C....... 405 262-1178
El Reno *(G-2712)*
Douglas Thompson Auto Inc................G....... 405 330-6997
Edmond *(G-2393)*
Drive Shafts Inc................G....... 918 836-0111
Tulsa *(G-9608)*
Drov LLC................F....... 405 463-6562
Oklahoma City *(G-5984)*
Econtrols LLC................F....... 918 957-1000
Tulsa *(G-9642)*
▲ **Enovation Controls LLC**................B....... 918 317-4100
Tulsa *(G-9689)*
Facet (oklahoma) LLC................D....... 918 696-3161
Stilwell *(G-8789)*
Factor 1 Racing Inc................G....... 918 258-7223
Broken Arrow *(G-905)*
▲ **Flex-N-Gate Oklahoma LLC**................B....... 580 272-6700
Ada *(G-35)*
Floyds Machine Shop................G....... 918 256-8440
Vinita *(G-11258)*
▲ **Fred Jones Enterprises LLC**................E....... 800 927-7845
Oklahoma City *(G-6114)*
Gem Dirt LLC................G....... 918 298-0299
Tulsa *(G-9813)*
Genes Customized Tags & EMB................G....... 580 225-8247
Elk City *(G-2820)*
Glenns Competition Chassis................G....... 405 732-4403
Oklahoma City *(G-6158)*
Goodwill Inds Centl Okla Inc................D....... 405 236-4451
Oklahoma City *(G-6172)*
Grices Automotive Machine Shop................G....... 580 924-1006
Durant *(G-2233)*
Guymon Safety Lane................G....... 580 338-6960
Guymon *(G-3351)*
H & H Muffler Whse & Mfg Co................E....... 918 371-9633
Collinsville *(G-1811)*
Hudson Bros Rmanufactured Engs................G....... 405 598-2260
Tecumseh *(G-8919)*
Hydrogen Technologies Inc................G....... 918 645-3430
Park Hill *(G-7644)*
Ignition Systems & Controls................F....... 405 682-3030
Oklahoma City *(G-6291)*
Industrial Axle Company LLC................D....... 405 273-9315
Shawnee *(G-8463)*
▼ **Kams Inc**................F....... 405 232-3103
Oklahoma City *(G-6396)*
Kelley Repair LLC................G....... 918 456-6514
Tahlequah *(G-8870)*
Larrys Transmission Service................G....... 405 273-3432
Shawnee *(G-8468)*
Liberty Transmission Parts................G....... 405 634-3450
Oklahoma City *(G-6473)*
Liberty Transmission Parts................G....... 405 236-8749
Oklahoma City *(G-6472)*
Line X of Western Oklahoma................G....... 580 774-5000
Weatherford *(G-11425)*
Magnum Racing Components Inc................G....... 918 627-0204
Tulsa *(G-10201)*
Meritor Inc................F....... 405 224-8600
Chickasha *(G-1484)*
Mid America Automotive Pdts................E....... 918 227-1919
Sapulpa *(G-8289)*
Midwest Expdtion Otfitters LLC................G....... 918 260-1771
Tulsa *(G-10267)*
Moss Seat Cover Mfg & Sls Co................F....... 918 742-3326
Tulsa *(G-10306)*
Muncie Power Products Inc................C....... 918 838-0900
Tulsa *(G-10316)*
National Bumper & Plating................G....... 405 235-1535
Oklahoma City *(G-6655)*
Odor Control Entps Texas Inc................F....... 405 670-5600
Oklahoma City *(G-6712)*
Olmeva USA LLC................G....... 405 677-5400
Oklahoma City *(G-6772)*
Performance Machine & Inductio................F....... 918 542-8740
North Miami *(G-5207)*
Power Equipment & Engrg Inc................E....... 405 235-0531
Oklahoma City *(G-6869)*
Powertrain Company LLC................G....... 703 419-0104
Oklahoma City *(G-6871)*
Precision Drive Ltd Inc................G....... 405 495-1344
Oklahoma City *(G-6881)*
Pss Enterprises Llc................G....... 918 928-7971
Broken Arrow *(G-1150)*
Quses................E....... 817 829-1086
Oklahoma City *(G-6956)*
Raxter LLC................G....... 918 706-7987
Broken Arrow *(G-1023)*
Reggie Adudell................G....... 405 631-9002
Oklahoma City *(G-7003)*
Ride Control LLC................B....... 800 251-5932
Chickasha *(G-1502)*
Ron Shanks Racing Enterprises................G....... 918 366-6050
Bixby *(G-655)*
Ron Williams................G....... 580 772-3513
Weatherford *(G-11437)*
Royal Filter Manufacturing Co................E....... 405 224-0229
Chickasha *(G-1503)*
Rv Smart Products LLC................G....... 575 513-1712
Bixby *(G-656)*
Self Automotive & Racing Inc................G....... 580 924-5866
Durant *(G-2256)*
Seminole Machine Co................G....... 405 382-0444
Seminole *(G-8399)*
Slw Automotive Inc................E....... 918 776-3157
Sallisaw *(G-8151)*
Slyder Energy Solutions LLC................G....... 405 258-3608
Carney *(G-1280)*
Sonny Mac Industries Inc................F....... 918 261-8446
Bixby *(G-661)*
▲ **Southeast Tire Inc**................D....... 580 286-6531
Idabel *(G-3647)*
Thermal Solutions Mfg................G....... 405 272-0453
Oklahoma City *(G-7281)*
Thomas H Scott Western LLC................G....... 405 632-6860
Oklahoma City *(G-7283)*
Transmission Center................G....... 405 329-4620
Norman *(G-5182)*
Trikntrux................G....... 918 224-2116
Sapulpa *(G-8316)*

SIC SECTION
37 TRANSPORTATION EQUIPMENT

Tulsa Brake & Clutch Co LLC ....G....... 918 582-2165
Tulsa *(G-10990)*
▼ United Ford ....G....... 405 813-7300
Oklahoma City *(G-7367)*
Universal Jint Specialists Inc ....G....... 918 836-0111
Tulsa *(G-11048)*
Varco Inc ....G....... 405 732-1637
Oklahoma City *(G-7395)*
Wall Colmonoy Corporation ....E....... 405 672-1361
Oklahoma City *(G-7417)*
Weatherford Machine Works ....G....... 580 772-5287
Weatherford *(G-11457)*
Weingartner Racing LLC ....G....... 918 520-3480
Broken Arrow *(G-1176)*
Wesmar Racing Engines Inc ....G....... 918 366-7222
Bixby *(G-672)*

3715 Truck Trailers

4-Star Trailers Inc ....C....... 405 324-7827
Oklahoma City *(G-5331)*
Ardmore Dragway ....G....... 580 226-7811
Ardmore *(G-246)*
Atoka Trailer and Mfg LLC ....E....... 580 889-7270
Atoka *(G-397)*
Built Better Enterprises LLC ....G....... 580 492-5227
Fletcher *(G-3161)*
C M Trailers ....G....... 580 493-2301
Drummond *(G-2046)*
C-All Manufacturing Inc ....E....... 580 889-3351
Atoka *(G-401)*
Cherokee Industries Inc ....D....... 405 691-8222
Oklahoma City *(G-5750)*
Choctaw Global LLC ....G....... 918 426-2871
McAlester *(G-4285)*
Clubhouse Trailer Co LLC ....G....... 405 396-6747
Edmond *(G-2358)*
◆ CMI Terex Corporation ....A....... 405 787-6020
Oklahoma City *(G-5792)*
Dickson Industries Inc ....E....... 405 598-6547
Tecumseh *(G-8912)*
Diw Engineering Fabrication LLC ....E....... 918 534-0001
Dewey *(G-2020)*
Ebenezer Truck Trailer LL ....G....... 918 289-6669
Tulsa *(G-9635)*
F & F Automotive Inc ....G....... 580 933-4262
Valliant *(G-11223)*
Hart Trailer LLC ....D....... 405 224-3634
Chickasha *(G-1469)*
Haul Around ....G....... 580 353-0808
Elgin *(G-2776)*
Hejin Waldran ....G....... 918 408-3500
Claremore *(G-1632)*
J & C Manufacturing Inc ....F....... 580 476-3217
Rush Springs *(G-8122)*
Jbw Ventures LLC ....D....... 580 795-5577
Madill *(G-4152)*
Kerr-Bilt Trailers Jl Inc ....F....... 580 566-1200
Boswell *(G-757)*
Kool-Breez LLC ....G....... 918 715-3358
McAlester *(G-4311)*
Kremlin Welding & Fabrication ....G....... 580 874-2522
Kremlin *(G-3853)*
Mac Trailer of Oklahoma Inc ....G....... 817 900-2006
Davis *(G-1988)*
Oklahoma Container Corp ....G....... 405 842-8300
Oklahoma City *(G-6745)*
▼ Overbilt Trailer Company ....E....... 918 352-4474
Drumright *(G-2069)*
Pfpp LP ....D....... 405 946-3381
Oklahoma City *(G-6839)*
R N J Inc ....E....... 918 865-2781
Mannford *(G-4191)*
Sioux Leasing Company LLC ....G....... 580 772-7100
Weatherford *(G-11442)*
Spade Leasing Inc ....C....... 580 653-2171
Springer *(G-8626)*
Stahl/Scott Fetzer Company ....D....... 580 924-5575
Durant *(G-2260)*
Tall Boys Toys ....G....... 580 323-2765
Clinton *(G-1771)*
Tritan Mfg LLC ....G....... 405 375-3332
Kingfisher *(G-3819)*
Truck Bodies & Eqp Intl Inc ....G....... 918 355-6842
Broken Arrow *(G-1174)*
Tulsa Trailer LLC ....G....... 918 447-2100
Tulsa *(G-11010)*
Turnbow Trailers Inc ....F....... 918 862-3233
Oilton *(G-5241)*
Universal Trlr Holdings Corp ....G....... 405 422-7238
El Reno *(G-2766)*
▼ V E Enterprises Inc ....E....... 580 653-2171
Springer *(G-8627)*
▲ W - W Trailer Mfrs Inc ....C....... 580 795-5571
Madill *(G-4166)*

3716 Motor Homes

Grand Junction Custom Trucks ....G....... 918 245-6362
Tulsa *(G-9844)*
Heartland Energy Options LLC ....G....... 405 600-6009
Piedmont *(G-7763)*

3721 Aircraft

A&M Aerospace LLC ....G....... 405 323-6428
Harrah *(G-3373)*
Aerial Drones of Oklahoma LLC ....G....... 918 694-6523
Claremore *(G-1577)*
Aerocore X LLC ....G....... 405 669-8655
Del City *(G-1994)*
AP Jetworks LLC ....G....... 405 226-2583
Edmond *(G-2305)*
Ases LLC ....C....... 405 219-3420
Oklahoma City *(G-5473)*
Ases LLC ....C....... 405 219-3400
Oklahoma City *(G-5474)*
Black River Aerospace LLC ....G....... 386 212-3741
Moore *(G-4499)*
Boeing Arospc Operations Inc ....F....... 405 610-3100
Oklahoma City *(G-5606)*
Boeing Arospc Operations Inc ....A....... 580 481-3306
Altus *(G-145)*
Boeing Arospc Operations Inc ....D....... 580 480-4040
Altus *(G-146)*
Boeing Company ....A....... 405 622-6000
Oklahoma City *(G-5607)*
Boeing Company ....A....... 580 482-0354
Altus *(G-147)*
Boeing Company ....A....... 405 924-1385
Oklahoma City *(G-5608)*
Boeing Company ....A....... 405 622-6206
Oklahoma City *(G-5609)*
Boeing Company ....A....... 405 622-6720
Oklahoma City *(G-5610)*
Boeing Company ....G....... 405 618-2859
Oklahoma City *(G-5611)*
Boeing Company ....G....... 918 292-2707
Tulsa *(G-9316)*
Boeing Company ....F....... 316 526-3272
Oklahoma City *(G-5612)*
Boeing Company ....E....... 316 977-2121
Oklahoma City *(G-5613)*
Boeing Company ....A....... 405 736-9227
Oklahoma City *(G-5614)*
Boeing Company ....A....... 918 835-3111
Tulsa *(G-9315)*
Commander Aircraft Corporation ....G....... 405 366-6454
Norman *(G-4963)*
Concept Aircraft LLC ....G....... 405 620-1701
Edmond *(G-2364)*
CP Aerospace LLC ....G....... 580 355-5064
Lawton *(G-3912)*
Don L Gerbrandt ....G....... 580 234-3247
Enid *(G-2943)*
Drone 1 Aerial LLC ....G....... 580 704-7223
Marlow *(G-4230)*
Drone Misfits LLC ....G....... 918 810-0808
Oklahoma City *(G-5288)*
Drone Viu LLC ....G....... 405 867-4690
Tulsa *(G-9609)*
Eaglecrest Aviation LLC ....G....... 918 249-0980
Broken Arrow *(G-893)*
Ferra Aerospace Inc ....G....... 918 787-2220
Grove *(G-3269)*
Greenwood Group Inc ....G....... 580 762-2580
Ponca City *(G-7832)*
GS Restoration Services Inc ....G....... 918 408-2848
Tulsa *(G-9866)*
Helicomb International Inc ....D....... 918 835-3999
Tulsa *(G-9911)*
J Stephens LLC ....G....... 918 299-2900
Tulsa *(G-10023)*
Lockheed Martin ....G....... 405 606-3988
Oklahoma City *(G-6486)*
Lockheed Martin Corporation ....B....... 405 917-3863
Oklahoma City *(G-6487)*
Lockheed Martin Corporation ....G....... 580 357-5060
Lawton *(G-3965)*
Moog Inc ....G....... 405 732-0009
Midwest City *(G-4448)*
New Generation Drones ....G....... 918 553-8703
Tulsa *(G-10336)*
Nicola Acquisitions LLC ....G....... 405 224-0061
Chickasha *(G-1492)*
Nolan Avionics LLC ....G....... 580 924-5507
Durant *(G-2245)*
Nordam Group LLC ....C....... 918 274-2742
Tulsa *(G-10356)*
Northrop Grumman Systems Corp ....B....... 405 737-3300
Oklahoma City *(G-6690)*
Northrop Grumman Systems Corp ....C....... 405 733-1208
Oklahoma City *(G-6691)*
Oklahoma Foundation For Diges ....F....... 405 271-4602
Oklahoma City *(G-6749)*
Onefire Aerospace Services ....F....... 918 794-8804
Jenks *(G-3720)*
Red Falcon LLC ....G....... 580 647-2152
Lawton *(G-3990)*
Rise Manufacturing LLC ....E....... 918 994-6240
Broken Arrow *(G-1032)*
Skybird Sales Inc ....G....... 580 772-5100
Weatherford *(G-11443)*
Solid Path Services ....G....... 918 384-7409
Tulsa *(G-10784)*
Sparks Aerospace LLC ....G....... 580 234-7972
Enid *(G-3060)*
Strategic Mission Systems LLC ....G....... 405 595-7243
Midwest City *(G-4456)*
Tellico Engineering Services ....G....... 918 384-7409
Tulsa *(G-10919)*
Ty Giaudrone ....G....... 918 423-6499
McAlester *(G-4347)*
Unmanned Cowboys LLC ....G....... 405 744-4156
Stillwater *(G-8771)*
Vertiprime Government Svcs LLC ....G....... 844 474-2600
Duncan *(G-2192)*
Wrangler Aviation Corp ....G....... 405 364-5700
Norman *(G-5202)*
Yankee Pacific Aerospace Inc ....G....... 918 388-5940
Tulsa *(G-11167)*

3724 Aircraft Engines & Engine Parts

▲ Abbott Industries Inc ....D....... 918 756-8320
Okmulgee *(G-7492)*
Aero Component Repair LLC ....F....... 580 924-7999
Durant *(G-2200)*
Aero Solutions and Services ....G....... 405 308-6788
Edmond *(G-2291)*
AGC Manufacturing Inc ....G....... 918 258-2506
Tulsa *(G-9116)*
▲ Aircraft Specialties Svc Inc ....E....... 918 836-6872
Tulsa *(G-9125)*
Airflow Solutions LLC ....E....... 918 574-2748
Tulsa *(G-9129)*
American Airlines Inc ....A....... 918 292-2698
Tulsa *(G-9163)*
Ases LLC ....C....... 405 219-3420
Oklahoma City *(G-5473)*
Ases LLC ....C....... 405 219-3400
Oklahoma City *(G-5474)*
Baker Hughes A GE Company LLC ....G....... 518 387-7914
Oklahoma City *(G-5514)*
▲ Barrett Performance Aircraft ....G....... 918 835-1089
Tulsa *(G-9266)*
Barrett Precision Engines Inc ....G....... 918 835-1089
Tulsa *(G-9267)*
Cherokee Insights LLC ....G....... 918 430-3409
Tulsa *(G-9413)*
Consoldted Trbine Spclists LLC ....G....... 918 367-9665
Bristow *(G-774)*
Dii LLC ....G....... 405 514-7365
Purcell *(G-8005)*
Energetic Materials ....G....... 405 203-2859
Nichols Hills *(G-4860)*
Get Threaded LLC ....G....... 918 943-6156
Tulsa *(G-9823)*
Green Cntry Arcft Exhaust Inc ....E....... 918 832-1769
Tulsa *(G-9857)*
Green Country Aircraft LLC ....G....... 918 832-1769
Tulsa *(G-9860)*
H&H Aircraft Inc ....G....... 405 833-3330
Oklahoma City *(G-6200)*
Honeywell Aerospace Tulsa/Lori ....D....... 918 272-4574
Tulsa *(G-9945)*
Honeywell International Inc ....A....... 405 605-0101
Oklahoma City *(G-6261)*
J & C Enterprises Aviation ....G....... 580 661-3591
Thomas *(G-8944)*
Kyra Guffey LLC ....G....... 210 867-1374
Mannford *(G-4185)*
▲ Limco Airepair Inc ....D....... 918 445-4300
Tulsa *(G-10161)*

S I C

Employee Codes: A=Over 500 employees, B=251-500
C=101-250, D=51-100, E=20-50, F=10-19, G=1-9
2020 Oklahoma Directory
of Manufacturers & Processors
493

37 TRANSPORTATION EQUIPMENT

Micco Aircraft Company Inc .... E 918 336-4700
  Oklahoma City *(G-6586)*
▲ Mint Turbines LLC .... E 918 968-9561
  Stroud *(G-8814)*
Mission Transportation LLC .... D 405 694-4755
  Bethany *(G-591)*
Nordam Group Inc .... E 918 878-8962
  Tulsa *(G-10351)*
◆ Nordam Group LLC .... A 918 878-4000
  Tulsa *(G-10354)*
Nordam Group LLC .... B 918 476-8338
  Tulsa *(G-10358)*
◆ Orizon Arstrctres - Owasso Inc ...... B 918 274-9094
  Owasso *(G-7599)*
▲ Orizon Arstrctures - Grove Inc ...... D 918 786-9094
  Grove *(G-3284)*
Padgett Machine Shop LLC .... G 918 636-9334
  Tulsa *(G-10456)*
Pratt Whtney Mltary Aftrmrket .... G 405 622-2561
  Oklahoma City *(G-6875)*
▲ Pratt Whtney Mltary Aftrmrket ...... G 405 737-4851
  Oklahoma City *(G-6876)*
PSI Mnfacturing Operations LLC .... G 561 747-6107
  Midwest City *(G-4450)*
◆ Radial Engines Ltd .... F 405 433-2263
  Guthrie *(G-3334)*
▼ Randy Mulkey .... G 405 258-2600
  Wellston *(G-11475)*
Rival Innvtion Surfc Engrg LLC .... G 918 978-7001
  Claremore *(G-1683)*
S&J Manufacturing Inc .... G 918 636-1224
  Skiatook *(G-8567)*
Shoulders International .... G 918 728-2999
  Tulsa *(G-10751)*
Spirit Arosystems Holdings Inc .... G 918 832-2891
  Tulsa *(G-10822)*
Spirit Arosystems Holdings Inc .... F 918 832-2131
  Tulsa *(G-10823)*
Tornado Alley Turbo Inc .... D 580 332-3510
  Ada *(G-95)*
▲ Triumph Arstrctres - Tulsa LLC ..... A 615 361-2061
  Tulsa *(G-10978)*
U T C Pratt & Whitney Okla Cy .... E 405 455-2001
  Tinker Afb *(G-8956)*
Wall Colmonoy Corporation .... E 405 672-1361
  Oklahoma City *(G-7417)*
Whitney Pratt .... G 405 610-2612
  Oklahoma City *(G-7448)*

3728 Aircraft Parts & Eqpt, NEC

AAR Aircraft Services Inc .... E 405 681-3000
  Oklahoma City *(G-5356)*
AAR Aircraft Services Inc .... G 405 218-3393
  Oklahoma City *(G-5357)*
Accurate Machine Works Inc .... F 405 615-4983
  Blanchard *(G-700)*
Accurus Aerospace Corporation .... G 918 438-3121
  Tulsa *(G-9091)*
Accurus Aerospace Tulsa LLC .... C 918 438-3121
  Tulsa *(G-9092)*
◆ Advanced Aerial Services LLC ...... G 580 571-1980
  Woodward *(G-11553)*
Aero Automation LLC .... F 918 251-0987
  Broken Arrow *(G-817)*
Aero Component Repair LLC .... F 580 924-7999
  Durant *(G-2200)*
Aero Solutions and Services .... G 405 308-6788
  Edmond *(G-2291)*
Aero-TEC Industries Inc .... G 405 382-8501
  Seminole *(G-8353)*
Aerocorp International Lc .... G 405 317-5844
  Oklahoma City *(G-5392)*
Aerospace Products SE Inc .... F 405 213-1034
  Oklahoma City *(G-5393)*
Aerospace Training .... G 405 253-8343
  Oklahoma City *(G-5394)*
Aerospace Training Sy .... G 405 253-8343
  Norman *(G-4902)*
Aerostar International Inc .... G 918 789-3000
  Chelsea *(G-1401)*
Aircraft Power Service Inc .... G 405 379-2407
  Holdenville *(G-3549)*
Aircraft Structures Intl Corp .... E 580 242-5907
  Enid *(G-2908)*
Aircraft Systems .... G 918 388-5943
  Tulsa *(G-9126)*
Airofab Ltd Co .... G 918 693-1230
  Talala *(G-8895)*
American Drones LLC .... G 405 308-0866
  Moore *(G-4487)*

Apex Composites Inc .... D 580 436-6444
  Ada *(G-9)*
Archein Aerospace LLC .... E 682 499-2150
  Ponca City *(G-7798)*
ARINC Incorporated .... F 405 601-6000
  Oklahoma City *(G-5463)*
Arrowprop Inc .... G 405 279-3833
  Meeker *(G-4375)*
◆ Asco Aerospace Usa LLC .... C 405 533-5800
  Stillwater *(G-8655)*
Ases LLC .... C 405 219-3420
  Oklahoma City *(G-5473)*
Ases LLC .... C 405 219-3400
  Oklahoma City *(G-5474)*
Aviation Training Devices Inc .... F 918 366-6680
  Bixby *(G-613)*
B & C Machine Company Inc .... F 405 787-8862
  Oklahoma City *(G-5500)*
Baron Manufacturing Inc .... G 405 947-3362
  Oklahoma City *(G-5528)*
Bm .... G 405 388-3999
  Choctaw *(G-1532)*
Boeing Company .... A 918 835-3111
  Tulsa *(G-9315)*
Cat-Eyes Drone Imagery Svc LLC .... G 918 344-8324
  Tulsa *(G-9388)*
Cherokee Nation Businesses LLC ..... B 918 384-7474
  Catoosa *(G-1310)*
▲ Cherokee Nation Red Wing LLC ... E 918 430-3437
  Tulsa *(G-9414)*
Chromalloy Gas Turbine LLC .... C 845 359-4700
  Oklahoma City *(G-5764)*
Cni Aviation Advantage A Joi .... G 405 253-8200
  Norman *(G-4961)*
▼ Csi Aerospace Inc .... D 918 258-1290
  Broken Arrow *(G-880)*
Cymstar LLC .... C 918 251-8100
  Broken Arrow *(G-884)*
D C Jones Machine Co .... G 918 786-6855
  Grove *(G-3265)*
Davis Thorpe Co LLC .... G 405 585-9823
  Moore *(G-4514)*
Duncan Machine Products Inc .... E 580 467-6784
  Duncan *(G-2110)*
Dusters & Sprayers Supply Inc .... F 405 224-1201
  Chickasha *(G-1455)*
Facet (oklahoma) LLC .... D 918 696-3161
  Stilwell *(G-8789)*
Ferra Aerospace Inc .... F 918 787-2220
  Grove *(G-3268)*
Frontier Elctrnic Systems Corp .... C 405 624-7708
  Stillwater *(G-8694)*
▲ General AVI Modifications Inc ...... E 580 436-4833
  Ada *(G-40)*
Gv Aerospace LLC .... G 214 972-5055
  Okmulgee *(G-7507)*
Helicomb International Inc .... G 918 835-3999
  Tulsa *(G-9911)*
Honeywell Aerospace Tulsa/Lori .... D 918 272-4574
  Tulsa *(G-9945)*
Iap Worldwide Services Inc .... F 321 784-7100
  Oklahoma City *(G-6282)*
Ices Corporation .... E 918 358-5446
  Cleveland *(G-1724)*
JD Supply & Mfg .... G 405 517-3745
  Piedmont *(G-7765)*
Jet Tech Interiors Inc .... G 580 310-2610
  Ada *(G-53)*
Jfj Industries Inc .... G 918 342-2453
  Claremore *(G-1643)*
JH Newton LLC .... G 918 636-0423
  Catoosa *(G-1325)*
Kemmerlys Air Plus .... G 405 348-2154
  Edmond *(G-2479)*
Kern Valley Industries .... G 918 868-3911
  Rose *(G-8118)*
Keymiaee Aero-Tech Inc .... F 405 235-5010
  Oklahoma City *(G-6409)*
Kihomac Inc .... D 937 429-7744
  Midwest City *(G-4445)*
Liberty Partners Inc .... F 918 756-6474
  Okmulgee *(G-7513)*
▲ Limco Airepair Inc .... G 918 445-4300
  Tulsa *(G-10161)*
Limco-Piedmont Inc .... F 918 445-4300
  Tulsa *(G-10162)*
LMI Aerospace Inc .... G 918 271-0207
  Catoosa *(G-1332)*
▲ LMI Finishing Inc .... D 918 438-1012
  Tulsa *(G-10174)*

SIC SECTION

LMI Finishing Inc .... G 918 379-0899
  Catoosa *(G-1333)*
Magnum Aero Inc .... G 918 357-2376
  Broken Arrow *(G-1140)*
Micco Aircraft Company Inc .... E 918 336-4700
  Oklahoma City *(G-6586)*
Michael Johnson .... E 405 882-3744
  Shawnee *(G-8474)*
Neosource Inc .... G 918 622-4493
  Tulsa *(G-10334)*
Newton Design LLC .... D 918 266-6205
  Catoosa *(G-1343)*
Newton Design LLC .... G 918 381-3012
  Catoosa *(G-1344)*
Nextgen UAS Transponders LLC ...... G 405 637-7940
  Del City *(G-2003)*
Nolan Enterprises .... G 580 924-5507
  Durant *(G-2246)*
Nordam .... G 918 878-4325
  Tulsa *(G-10350)*
Nordam Group Inc .... E 918 878-8962
  Tulsa *(G-10351)*
Nordam Group LLC .... A 918 401-5000
  Tulsa *(G-10352)*
Nordam Group LLC .... G 918 878-6682
  Tulsa *(G-10353)*
Nordam Group LLC .... A 918 234-5155
  Tulsa *(G-10355)*
Nordam Group LLC .... G 918 274-2700
  Tulsa *(G-10357)*
◆ Nordam Group LLC .... A 918 878-4000
  Tulsa *(G-10354)*
Nordam Group LLC .... B 918 476-8338
  Tulsa *(G-10358)*
Nordam Group LLC .... G 918 274-2742
  Tulsa *(G-10356)*
North Amrcn Arspc Holdings LLC ..... D 316 644-2553
  Enid *(G-3020)*
Opes Industries LLC .... G 405 417-6223
  Moore *(G-4550)*
Plane Plastics Ltd .... E 580 327-1565
  Alva *(G-188)*
Precision Hose Technology Inc .... G 918 835-3660
  Tulsa *(G-10545)*
Premier Aerospace Svcs & Tech ...... G 580 327-3706
  Alva *(G-190)*
Primus International Inc .... C 918 836-6317
  Tulsa *(G-10560)*
▲ Pro-Fab LLC .... C 405 495-2131
  Oklahoma City *(G-6908)*
▲ Pryer Machine & Tool Company .... C 918 835-8885
  Tulsa *(G-10580)*
◆ Pryer Technology Group LLC .... G 918 835-8885
  Tulsa *(G-10581)*
Rajon LLC .... D 918 367-5487
  Bristow *(G-795)*
Respondair UAS LLC .... G 918 899-2113
  Owasso *(G-7607)*
S&S&d Trucking LLC .... G 405 365-3535
  Oklahoma City *(G-7069)*
▲ Safran Vntltion Systems Okla I .... C 405 382-0731
  Seminole *(G-8397)*
▼ Sertco Industries Inc .... E 918 623-0526
  Okemah *(G-5276)*
Smooth Landings LLC .... G 405 422-1822
  El Reno *(G-2758)*
Southern Aero Partners Inc .... E 918 437-7676
  Tulsa *(G-10797)*
▲ Southwest United Inds Inc .... C 918 587-4161
  Tulsa *(G-10810)*
Southwind Aviation Supply LLC .... G 405 491-0500
  Bethany *(G-595)*
Spirit Aerosystems Inc .... F 918 832-3424
  Tulsa *(G-10821)*
Spirit Aerosystems Inc .... C 918 423-6979
  McAlester *(G-4337)*
Starline Inc .... F 405 495-8274
  Bethany *(G-596)*
Stewart Industries Intl LLC .... F 405 260-0990
  Guthrie *(G-3339)*
Tellico Engineering Services .... G 918 384-7409
  Tulsa *(G-10919)*
Tinker Afb .... G 405 739-2349
  Tinker Afb *(G-8955)*
Tornado Alley Turbo Inc .... D 580 332-3510
  Ada *(G-95)*
▲ Triumph Arstrctres - Tulsa LLC .... A 615 361-2061
  Tulsa *(G-10978)*
Tulsa Turbines .... G 918 960-8918
  Bixby *(G-668)*

Turbine Aircraft Services LLC..............G....... 405 491-8995
Bethany *(G-599)*
Two Creeks Fabrication..............G....... 505 999-8798
Newalla *(G-4817)*
United Dynamics Inc..............E....... 405 275-8041
Shawnee *(G-8517)*
United Plating Works Inc..............E....... 918 835-4683
Tulsa *(G-11042)*
Valco Inc..............E....... 405 228-0932
Oklahoma City *(G-7386)*
Vertiprime Mowdy Mch JV LLC..............G....... 405 747-6668
Duncan *(G-2193)*
VIP Manufacturing Corporation..............G....... 918 244-2131
Bluejacket *(G-746)*
◆ **Waldens Machine LLC**..............B....... 918 794-0289
Tulsa *(G-11092)*
Wall Colmonoy Corporation..............E....... 405 672-1361
Oklahoma City *(G-7417)*
Werco Manufacturing Inc..............E....... 918 251-6880
Broken Arrow *(G-1095)*
Witten Company Inc..............E....... 918 272-9567
Owasso *(G-7630)*
Yankee Pacific Aerospace..............G....... 918 894-8586
Tulsa *(G-11166)*
▲ **Zivko Aeronautics Inc**..............E....... 405 282-1330
Guthrie *(G-3343)*

3731 Shipbuilding & Repairing

Burrows..............G....... 918 846-2245
Hominy *(G-3580)*
Carbon Economy LLC..............F....... 405 222-4244
Chickasha *(G-1447)*
Custom Upholstery..............G....... 918 342-3489
Claremore *(G-1611)*
Forward Oil and Gas Inc..............G....... 405 607-2247
Oklahoma City *(G-6106)*
Heath Technologies LLC..............E....... 918 342-3222
Claremore *(G-1631)*
Stiles Services LLC..............G....... 918 582-7894
Tulsa *(G-10851)*
Submersible Technical Products..............F....... 405 850-4091
Pauls Valley *(G-7673)*

3732 Boat Building & Repairing

Bkep Materials LLC..............G....... 918 266-1606
Catoosa *(G-1303)*
Brokenbow Boat Center..............G....... 580 584-5428
Broken Bow *(G-1187)*
Canyon Craft..............G....... 918 456-3552
Tahlequah *(G-8854)*
Grand Lake Detail LLC..............G....... 918 257-2174
Afton *(G-117)*
Harold Speed Jr..............G....... 580 838-2578
Hendrix *(G-3440)*
Kole Inc..............G....... 918 782-3001
Ketchum *(G-3774)*
Lilitad Boats Inc..............G....... 918 482-5992
Porter *(G-7893)*
Northfork Auto Repair..............G....... 918 689-3589
Eufaula *(G-3106)*
Offshore Extreme..............G....... 405 387-2628
Newcastle *(G-4834)*
Parks Manufacturing Inc..............C....... 405 382-0349
Seminole *(G-8393)*
Splash Marine LLC..............G....... 580 336-9874
Perry *(G-7746)*
Tip Top Prop Shop..............G....... 580 564-3712
Kingston *(G-3831)*
▼ **Tracker Marine LLC**..............G....... 918 541-2000
Miami *(G-4434)*

3743 Railroad Eqpt

Amerities Holdings LLC..............D....... 405 359-3235
Edmond *(G-2303)*
Amerities South LLC..............F....... 405 359-3235
Edmond *(G-2304)*
Big 3 Woodyard Inc..............G....... 580 298-6123
Antlers *(G-214)*
Freedom Railcar Solutions LLC..............F....... 405 256-6780
Mustang *(G-4772)*
Industrial Structures Inc..............E....... 918 341-0300
Tulsa *(G-9982)*
Integrity Rail Services Inc..............G....... 918 267-3761
Beggs *(G-558)*
Railroad Sgnling Solutions Inc..............G....... 918 973-1888
Broken Arrow *(G-1020)*
Tag Okc Inc..............G....... 405 685-7728
Oklahoma City *(G-7248)*
Trinity Tank Car Inc..............F....... 405 629-1226
Oklahoma City *(G-7335)*

3751 Motorcycles, Bicycles & Parts

ABC Choppers LLC..............G....... 405 990-8641
Oklahoma City *(G-5358)*
APS of Oklahoma LLC..............G....... 405 793-8877
Moore *(G-4492)*
Buchanan Bicycles Inc..............G....... 405 364-5513
Norman *(G-4948)*
Cannon Racecraft Inc..............F....... 405 524-7223
Oklahoma City *(G-5689)*
Cave Man Choppers..............G....... 405 672-8008
Oklahoma City *(G-5714)*
Cradduck John..............G....... 405 360-0251
Norman *(G-4968)*
DC Choppers LLC..............G....... 918 791-1846
Coweta *(G-1879)*
Eldon Valley Choppers..............G....... 918 931-2925
Tahlequah *(G-8863)*
Passion Racing Engines..............G....... 918 232-3950
Owasso *(G-7602)*
Western Mobile Glass Mirror..............G....... 913 764-7444
Guthrie *(G-3340)*

3761 Guided Missiles & Space Vehicles

Design Intelligence Inc LLC..............G....... 405 307-0397
Noble *(G-4878)*

3769 Guided Missile/Space Vehicle Parts & Eqpt, NEC

Archer Technologies Intl Inc..............G....... 405 306-3220
Shawnee *(G-8428)*
Ducommun Labarge Tech Inc..............C....... 918 459-2200
Tulsa *(G-9611)*
Frontier Elctrnic Systems Corp..............C....... 405 624-7708
Stillwater *(G-8694)*
Hurst Aerospace Inc..............G....... 918 543-6527
Inola *(G-3663)*
Spirit Aerosystems Inc..............C....... 918 423-6979
McAlester *(G-4337)*
Stewart Industries Intl LLC..............F....... 405 260-0990
Guthrie *(G-3339)*
Valco Inc..............E....... 405 228-0932
Oklahoma City *(G-7386)*

3792 Travel Trailers & Campers

Allen Camper Mfg Company Inc..............E....... 580 857-2177
Allen *(G-133)*
Complete Cooling Systems Inc..............G....... 405 272-0453
Oklahoma City *(G-5811)*
▲ **Diamond T Trailer Mfg Co**..............E....... 580 587-2432
Rattan *(G-8071)*
▲ **Gr Trailers LLC**..............G....... 405 567-0567
Prague *(G-7926)*
Industrial Axle Company LLC..............D....... 405 273-9315
Shawnee *(G-8463)*
Peak Eagles Landing..............G....... 918 636-5152
Stillwater *(G-8736)*
Resort Rv..............G....... 580 465-4428
Ardmore *(G-349)*

3795 Tanks & Tank Components

Echota Defense Services..............G....... 918 384-7409
Tulsa *(G-9637)*
Integrated Service Company LLC..............G....... 918 556-3600
Tulsa *(G-9997)*
Pelagic Tank LLC..............C....... 580 856-2182
Enid *(G-3034)*

3799 Transportation Eqpt, NEC

Backwoods Trailers LLC..............G....... 864 237-5906
Stilwell *(G-8781)*
Best Trailer Products..............G....... 580 931-3534
Durant *(G-2205)*
Cimarron Trailers Inc..............C....... 405 222-4800
Chickasha *(G-1450)*
Five A Trailers and Equipment..............G....... 580 564-2973
Kingston *(G-3827)*
Flaming Hcksaw Fabrication LLC..............G....... 479 228-0809
Westville *(G-11483)*
Frank A Hogan II Transport..............G....... 405 889-4278
Oklahoma City *(G-6111)*
Holt Trailer Mfg & Sales LLC..............F....... 405 784-2233
Asher *(G-390)*
Hourglass Transport LLC..............G....... 580 937-4569
Coleman *(G-1796)*
▲ **Millertime Manufacturing LLC**..............G....... 918 273-2040
Nowata *(G-5221)*
New Vision Manufacturing LLC..............C....... 580 677-9937
Madill *(G-4159)*

Nickolas Manufacturing Inc..............G....... 918 698-7109
Tulsa *(G-10344)*
Oasis Rv Center LLC..............G....... 580 233-9400
Enid *(G-3023)*
Polypipe Hdlg Specialists Inc..............G....... 405 330-4733
Edmond *(G-2573)*
Rv Station Ltd..............G....... 888 466-1384
Colbert *(G-1786)*
Staton Inc..............G....... 405 605-3765
Oklahoma City *(G-7197)*
Super Daves Power Sports..............G....... 918 485-9205
Wagoner *(G-11291)*
Superior Companies Inc..............D....... 918 534-0755
Dewey *(G-2033)*
Tall Boys Toys..............G....... 580 323-2765
Clinton *(G-1771)*
Timmy Pickens..............G....... 918 812-5268
Sapulpa *(G-8315)*
Tommy Biffle Lakeside Polaris..............G....... 918 485-2887
Wagoner *(G-11293)*
Vans Trailer Sales..............G....... 580 323-3999
Clinton *(G-1772)*
▲ **W - W Trailer Mfrs Inc**..............C....... 580 795-5571
Madill *(G-4166)*
Welding Shop..............G....... 580 832-5545
Cordell *(G-1864)*

38 MEASURING, ANALYZING AND CONTROLLING INSTRUMENTS; PHOTOGRAPHIC, MEDICAL AN

3812 Search, Detection, Navigation & Guidance Systs & Instrs

5 Stones Defense LLC..............G....... 405 313-9729
Tuttle *(G-11184)*
Aero Dynamics..............F....... 918 258-0290
Broken Arrow *(G-818)*
Aero-TEC Industries Inc..............G....... 405 382-8501
Seminole *(G-8353)*
Archer Technologies Intl Inc..............G....... 405 306-3220
Shawnee *(G-8428)*
Aviation Training Devices Inc..............F....... 918 366-6680
Bixby *(G-613)*
Baron Manufacturing Inc..............G....... 405 947-3362
Oklahoma City *(G-5528)*
▲ **Barrett Performance Aircraft**..............G....... 918 835-1089
Tulsa *(G-9266)*
Boeing Company..............A....... 918 835-3111
Tulsa *(G-9315)*
Bto Strategies & Solutions Inc..............G....... 405 473-8632
Norman *(G-4947)*
Cnrw Defense Service..............G....... 706 545-5088
Catoosa *(G-1312)*
COBRA Self Defense Tulsa..............G....... 918 691-0054
Sand Springs *(G-8171)*
Cole Defense LLC..............G....... 214 934-5473
Oklahoma City *(G-5803)*
Coorstek..............G....... 800 821-6110
Oklahoma City *(G-5831)*
Critical Infrastructur..............G....... 918 640-9301
Jenks *(G-3702)*
Damsel In Defense..............G....... 580 233-6609
Enid *(G-2939)*
Dark Peek Technologies LLC..............G....... 405 316-8551
Edmond *(G-2379)*
Defense Angel LLC..............G....... 405 476-4222
Yukon *(G-11716)*
Design Intelligence Inc LLC..............G....... 405 307-0397
Noble *(G-4878)*
Flightsafety International Inc..............A....... 918 259-4000
Broken Arrow *(G-910)*
Flir Detection Inc..............E....... 405 533-6618
Stillwater *(G-8689)*
Flir Systems Inc..............G....... 407 810-3634
Stillwater *(G-8691)*
Frontier Elctrnic Systems Corp..............C....... 405 624-7708
Stillwater *(G-8694)*
Girlpower Defense Llc..............G....... 918 494-9072
Tulsa *(G-9828)*
Gwacs Defense Inc..............F....... 918 794-5670
Tulsa *(G-9870)*
Halo Induction Looping LLC..............G....... 918 638-1599
Tulsa *(G-9882)*
Iball Instruments LLC..............F....... 405 366-6061
Norman *(G-5029)*
Invictus Personal Defense Llc..............G....... 918 605-1165
Owasso *(G-7576)*

SIC

Ironclad Defense....G.... 405 413-9496
Midwest City *(G-4443)*
JM Defense & Arospc Svcs LLC....G.... 918 298-2766
Jenks *(G-3710)*
Kern Valley Industries....G.... 918 868-3911
Rose *(G-8118)*
Kxd Defense and Armament....G.... 918 813-3841
Oologah *(G-7533)*
L3 Comm AMI Instruments....G.... 212 697-1111
Broken Arrow *(G-961)*
L3harris Technologies Inc....D.... 405 573-2285
Norman *(G-5055)*
Lockheed Martin Corporation....G.... 580 355-0581
Lawton *(G-3966)*
Meta Special Aerospace LLC....G.... 405 516-3357
Bethany *(G-589)*
▲ **Navico Inc**....B.... 918 437-6881
Tulsa *(G-10328)*
Navico Inc....F.... 918 437-6881
Tulsa *(G-10329)*
Nelco Defense LLC....G.... 580 471-7992
Altus *(G-164)*
Northrop Corp....G.... 580 536-9191
Lawton *(G-3976)*
Northrop Grumman Systems Corp....D.... 405 739-7875
Oklahoma City *(G-6689)*
O & L Resources Inc....G.... 918 789-5553
Chelsea *(G-1408)*
Oakley Defense LLC....G.... 918 457-8089
Tahlequah *(G-8877)*
Oklahoma Aerospace Alliance....G.... 918 527-0980
Tulsa *(G-10394)*
Oklahoma Slf-Defense Carry LLC....G.... 918 814-0122
Bixby *(G-650)*
Omada International LLC....C.... 405 495-2131
Oklahoma City *(G-6774)*
Personal Defense LLC....G.... 918 345-0075
Mounds *(G-4622)*
Physical Home Defense....G.... 405 819-0939
Oklahoma City *(G-6847)*
▲ **Pryer Machine & Tool Company**....C.... 918 835-8885
Tulsa *(G-10580)*
Qual-Tron Inc....E.... 918 622-7052
Tulsa *(G-10589)*
R C Ramsey Co....F.... 918 746-4300
Tulsa *(G-10602)*
Raytheon Company....C.... 580 351-6966
Lawton *(G-3989)*
Sextant Mineral Group LLC....G.... 918 299-5115
Tulsa *(G-10737)*
Solar View LLC....G.... 918 366-6413
Bixby *(G-660)*
Spirit Aerosystems Inc....C.... 918 423-6979
McAlester *(G-4337)*
Stewart Defense LLC....G.... 580 532-6426
Pond Creek *(G-7891)*
Tactical Ballistic System....G.... 580 254-5468
Woodward *(G-11639)*
Tech-Aid Products....G.... 918 838-8711
Tulsa *(G-10911)*
Tgv Rockets Inc....G.... 405 366-0779
Norman *(G-5173)*
Triad Personal Defense LLC....G.... 918 443-7803
Claremore *(G-1694)*

3821 Laboratory Apparatus & Furniture

Alfa Laval Inc....G.... 918 251-7477
Broken Arrow *(G-824)*
Alpha Dental Studios....G.... 405 359-2976
Edmond *(G-2298)*
Biospec Products Inc....G.... 918 336-3363
Bartlesville *(G-454)*
C & P Catalyst Inc....G.... 918 747-8379
Tulsa *(G-9357)*
Cefco Inc....G.... 918 543-8415
Inola *(G-3653)*
Chemco....G.... 918 481-0537
Tulsa *(G-9409)*
Innovative Products Inc....E.... 405 949-0040
Oklahoma City *(G-6307)*
Mc-Alipat LLC....G.... 405 370-3321
Stillwater *(G-8723)*
Metal Goods Manufacturing Co....F.... 918 336-4282
Bartlesville *(G-512)*
Miltech Lab Services Inc....G.... 918 251-4436
Broken Arrow *(G-978)*
Rambo Acquisition Company....D.... 918 627-6222
Tulsa *(G-10615)*
Refinery Supply Co Inc....G.... 918 621-1700
Tulsa *(G-10635)*
T D H Mfg Inc....G.... 918 241-8800
Sand Springs *(G-8229)*
W L Walker Co Inc....E.... 918 583-3109
Tulsa *(G-11089)*
Waid Forensics Science LLC....G.... 580 574-8692
Medicine Park *(G-4372)*

3822 Automatic Temperature Controls

Ademco Inc....G.... 918 663-2822
Tulsa *(G-9104)*
Ademco Inc....G.... 405 681-4008
Oklahoma City *(G-5373)*
▲ **Advantage Controls LLC**....D.... 918 686-6211
Muskogee *(G-4643)*
Design Systems Inc....G.... 405 341-7353
Edmond *(G-2390)*
▼ **Emerson Process Management**....C.... 918 622-6161
Tulsa *(G-9670)*
Franklin Electric Co Inc....B.... 918 465-2348
Wilburton *(G-11520)*
Hks Energy Solutions Inc....F.... 918 279-6450
Tulsa *(G-9934)*
Kimray Inc....C.... 405 525-6601
Oklahoma City *(G-6417)*
Mathena Inc....D.... 405 422-3600
El Reno *(G-2736)*
P F Services LLC....G.... 405 226-4871
Edmond *(G-2558)*
Parnel Biogas Inc....F.... 918 294-3868
Glenpool *(G-3240)*
Phoenix Group Holding Company....F.... 405 948-7788
Oklahoma City *(G-6844)*
Process Products & Service Co....G.... 918 827-4998
Mounds *(G-4623)*
Pyfi Technologies....G.... 405 816-8685
Oklahoma City *(G-6929)*
Torus Pressure Control LLC....E.... 405 670-4456
Oklahoma City *(G-7307)*

3823 Indl Instruments For Meas, Display & Control

A-1 Sure Shot....F.... 405 677-9800
Oklahoma City *(G-5353)*
ABB Inc....C.... 918 338-4888
Bartlesville *(G-444)*
◆ **AC Systems Integration Inc**....E.... 918 259-0020
Tulsa *(G-9084)*
Acl Combustion Inc....G.... 405 310-2327
Moore *(G-4484)*
Advanced Crative Solutions Inc....G.... 918 519-3651
Jenks *(G-3688)*
Advanced Processing Tech Inc....G.... 405 360-4848
Norman *(G-4901)*
Ameriflow Inc....G.... 405 603-1200
Oklahoma City *(G-5442)*
Appleton Grp LLC....F.... 918 627-5530
Tulsa *(G-9199)*
Bates Instrumentation LLC....F.... 918 441-7178
Kinta *(G-3832)*
◆ **Chandler Instruments Co LLC**....D.... 918 250-7200
Broken Arrow *(G-866)*
Control Devices Inc....E.... 918 258-6068
Broken Arrow *(G-875)*
Control Products Unlimited Inc....G.... 918 786-1801
Grove *(G-3263)*
Coretec Group Inc....G.... 918 494-0505
Tulsa *(G-9488)*
County of Tillman....G.... 580 597-3097
Chattanooga *(G-1389)*
Crane Manufacturing Inc....E.... 918 838-8800
Tulsa *(G-9502)*
▲ **Crystaltech Inc**....G.... 580 252-8893
Duncan *(G-2101)*
Du-Ann Co Inc....G.... 580 428-3315
Coalgate *(G-1779)*
▲ **Dvorak Instruments Inc**....F.... 918 447-0022
Tulsa *(G-9615)*
Eastech Flow Controls Inc....F.... 918 664-1212
Tulsa *(G-9633)*
Electronic Assembly Corp....G.... 918 286-2816
Tulsa *(G-9653)*
Enardo Inc....G.... 918 622-6161
Tulsa *(G-9679)*
Energy Meter Systems LLC....E.... 405 853-4976
Hennessey *(G-3460)*
Evoqua Water Technologies LLC....C.... 978 614-7233
Tulsa *(G-9712)*
▲ **Fife Corporation**....C.... 405 755-1600
Oklahoma City *(G-6084)*
◆ **Fki Industries Inc**....G.... 918 834-4611
Tulsa *(G-9752)*
Fluid Controls Inc....E.... 918 299-0442
Tulsa *(G-9762)*
HEanderson Company....F.... 918 687-4426
Muskogee *(G-4688)*
▼ **Hermetic Switch Inc**....C.... 405 224-4046
Chickasha *(G-1470)*
▲ **Hetronic International Inc**....F.... 405 946-3574
Oklahoma City *(G-6244)*
Hetronic Usa Inc....E.... 405 946-3574
Oklahoma City *(G-6245)*
Integrated Controls Inc....G.... 918 747-7820
Tulsa *(G-9994)*
Integrated Service Co Mfg LLC....G.... 918 234-4150
Tulsa *(G-9996)*
Jatco Inc....E.... 405 755-4100
Oklahoma City *(G-6351)*
Jnl Equipment....G.... 918 286-1951
Broken Arrow *(G-948)*
John Zink Co LLC....G.... 918 749-9345
Tulsa *(G-10054)*
◆ **John Zink Company LLC**....A.... 918 234-1800
Tulsa *(G-10055)*
Lonestar Msurement Contrls Inc....G.... 972 653-0765
Edmond *(G-2494)*
Meter Check Inc....G.... 405 790-0778
Moore *(G-4539)*
Petrolab LLC....G.... 918 459-7170
Broken Arrow *(G-1005)*
Port 40 Inc....G.... 405 360-9100
Norman *(G-5117)*
Process Products & Service Co....G.... 918 827-4998
Mounds *(G-4623)*
Q7 Inc....G.... 918 609-3251
Tulsa *(G-10587)*
Roll-2-Roll Technologies LLC....G.... 405 726-0985
Stillwater *(G-8749)*
Techtrol Inc....E.... 918 762-1050
Pawnee *(G-7712)*
Terry Company Inc....G.... 918 629-0926
Tulsa *(G-10920)*
Timbercreek Flowback & Safety....G.... 405 694-7228
El Reno *(G-2762)*
Travis Quality Pdts & Sls Inc....G.... 918 251-0115
Broken Arrow *(G-1082)*
Tsi-Enquip Inc....E.... 918 599-8111
Tulsa *(G-10983)*
Universal Combustion Corp....G.... 918 254-1828
Tulsa *(G-11046)*
▼ **Victory Energy Operations LLC**....C.... 918 274-0023
Collinsville *(G-1828)*
Victory Energy Operations LLC....E.... 918 225-2164
Cushing *(G-1967)*
William L Riggs Company Inc....G.... 918 437-3245
Tulsa *(G-11125)*
Wilnat Incorporated....G.... 918 640-0003
Collinsville *(G-1830)*
Wyatt Engineering LLC....G.... 918 824-2255
Pryor *(G-8001)*

3824 Fluid Meters & Counters

Badger Meter Inc....C.... 918 836-8411
Tulsa *(G-9253)*
Badger Meter Inc....G.... 918 628-7403
Tulsa *(G-9254)*
Fossil Fluids LLC....G.... 580 515-5402
Weatherford *(G-11416)*
Petrolab LLC....G.... 918 459-7170
Broken Arrow *(G-1005)*
Southern Specialties Corp....E.... 918 584-3553
Tulsa *(G-10803)*
Turbines Inc....E.... 580 477-3067
Altus *(G-170)*
▼ **Weamco Incorporated**....E.... 918 445-1141
Sapulpa *(G-8324)*

3825 Instrs For Measuring & Testing Electricity

Associated Research Inc....G.... 580 223-4773
Ardmore *(G-250)*
▼ **Bonavista Technologies Inc**....G.... 918 250-3435
Tulsa *(G-9318)*
Cccc Inc....F.... 405 230-0638
Oklahoma City *(G-5718)*
Custom Manufacturing & Maint....G.... 405 872-1000
Noble *(G-4877)*
D & L Enclosures....G.... 918 396-7355
Skiatook *(G-8538)*

SIC SECTION
38 MEASURING, ANALYZING AND CONTROLLING INSTRUMENTS; PHOTOGRAPHIC, MEDICAL AN

First Response Solutions LLC	G	405 284-6430
Hinton *(G-3528)*		
Hilti of America Inc	F	800 879-8000
Tulsa *(G-9933)*		
◆ Ideal Specialty Inc	F	918 834-1657
Tulsa *(G-9967)*		
Intuition Inc	G	405 361-8376
Norman *(G-5036)*		
KLA Industries LLC	G	918 994-2123
Tulsa *(G-10095)*		
▲ M W Bevins Co	E	918 627-1273
Tulsa *(G-10190)*		
Maccor Inc	D	918 445-1874
Tulsa *(G-10193)*		
N O C Supply Inc	G	405 562-7070
Edmond *(G-2526)*		
Nanna Networks LLC	G	405 833-3329
Oklahoma City *(G-6651)*		
Port 40 Inc	G	405 360-9100
Norman *(G-5117)*		
R B Watkins Inc	F	405 732-9969
Oklahoma City *(G-6960)*		
R C Ramsey Co	F	918 746-4300
Tulsa *(G-10602)*		
Southwest Electric Co	E	800 364-4445
Oklahoma City *(G-7174)*		

3826 Analytical Instruments

Dvorak Instruments	G	918 299-2223
Tulsa *(G-9614)*		
▲ Ep Scientific Products LLC	D	918 540-1507
Miami *(G-4401)*		
Eseco-Speedmaster	D	918 225-1266
Cushing *(G-1933)*		
Evoqua Water Technologies LLC	C	978 614-7233
Tulsa *(G-9712)*		
Faith Church Shawnee	G	405 948-7100
Shawnee *(G-8450)*		
Flir Detection Inc	F	703 678-2111
Stillwater *(G-8690)*		
Flir Systems Inc	F	405 372-9535
Stillwater *(G-8692)*		
Havard Industries LLC	G	405 888-0961
Edmond *(G-2453)*		
Kelix Heat Transf Systems LLC	G	918 200-0996
Tulsa *(G-10081)*		
Lakeside Polaris Inc	G	918 485-2887
Wagoner *(G-11285)*		
Leviathan Applied Sciences LLC	G	405 315-1759
Edmond *(G-2487)*		
Refinery Supply Co Inc	G	918 621-1700
Tulsa *(G-10635)*		
Rose Inc	G	918 693-2461
Sapulpa *(G-8309)*		
Thermo Fisher Scientific	F	918 540-1507
Miami *(G-4432)*		
Xplosafe LLC	G	405 334-5720
Stillwater *(G-8777)*		

3827 Optical Instruments

◆ Access Optics LLC	E	918 294-1234
Broken Arrow *(G-812)*		
Accutech Laboratories	G	405 603-2956
Warr Acres *(G-11311)*		
Doomsdaytacticalsolutions LLC	G	580 788-2412
Elmore City *(G-2895)*		
Elens	G	918 627-5395
Tulsa *(G-9654)*		
Gilmores Sports Concepts Inc	G	918 250-3910
Tulsa *(G-9827)*		
Periscope Legal	G	405 418-4155
Oklahoma City *(G-6831)*		
Plx Inc	G	918 551-6722
Tulsa *(G-10528)*		
◆ Tactical Elec Military Sup LLC	E	866 541-7996
Broken Arrow *(G-1070)*		

3829 Measuring & Controlling Devices, NEC

A-1 Sure Shot	F	405 677-9800
Oklahoma City *(G-5353)*		
Accutec-Ihs Inc	G	918 984-9838
Tulsa *(G-9093)*		
Adams Electronics Inc	G	918 622-5000
Tulsa *(G-9102)*		
▲ Barrett Performance Aircraft	G	918 835-1089
Tulsa *(G-9266)*		
Biospec Products Inc	G	918 336-3363
Bartlesville *(G-454)*		
Btm Technologies Inc	G	918 857-2855
Bristow *(G-770)*		
Carlson Design Corporation	G	918 438-8344
Tulsa *(G-9377)*		
Cefco Inc	G	918 543-8415
Inola *(G-3653)*		
Cement Test Equipment Inc	F	918 835-4454
Tulsa *(G-9395)*		
◆ Chandler Instruments Co LLC	D	918 250-7200
Broken Arrow *(G-866)*		
▼ Charles Machine Works Inc	A	580 572-2693
Perry *(G-7728)*		
Chemco	G	918 481-0537
Tulsa *(G-9409)*		
Crane Manufacturing Inc	E	918 838-8800
Tulsa *(G-9502)*		
Eastech Badger	G	918 664-1212
Tulsa *(G-9632)*		
Engius LLC	G	405 533-3770
Stillwater *(G-8685)*		
Flir Detection Inc	E	405 533-6618
Stillwater *(G-8689)*		
Fluid Technologies Inc	E	405 624-0400
Stillwater *(G-8693)*		
Garden Interlock Systems Tuls	G	918 369-9935
Tulsa *(G-9799)*		
Geo Shack	G	918 665-1880
Tulsa *(G-9820)*		
Graphic Rsources Reproductions	F	918 461-0303
Broken Arrow *(G-921)*		
Guardian Interlock Systems	G	918 369-9935
Bixby *(G-629)*		
Hometown Nrdgnstcs-Clorado LLC	G	405 286-1016
Oklahoma City *(G-6259)*		
Hydrant Repair Parts Inc	E	918 224-8713
Tulsa *(G-9014)*		
Hydro Chart	G	918 932-8586
Tulsa *(G-9961)*		
Integrated Controls Inc	G	918 747-5811
Tulsa *(G-9993)*		
Kimray Inc	C	405 525-6601
Oklahoma City *(G-6417)*		
Kimray Inc	G	405 525-4200
Oklahoma City *(G-6418)*		
Lakeside Womens Imaging	G	405 418-0302
Oklahoma City *(G-6446)*		
Lifesafer Interlock	G	800 634-3077
Oklahoma City *(G-5304)*		
Metal Goods Manufacturing Co	F	918 336-4282
Bartlesville *(G-512)*		
Midwest Equipment Company Inc	G	918 241-3672
Sand Springs *(G-8204)*		
NDC Systems	G	405 722-1101
Oklahoma City *(G-6666)*		
Parkline Systems Corporation	E	918 367-5523
Bristow *(G-792)*		
Preferred Utilities Mfg Corp	G	203 743-6741
Tulsa *(G-10551)*		
Redline Instruments Inc	F	580 622-4745
Sulphur *(G-8841)*		
Refinery Supply Co Inc	G	918 621-1700
Tulsa *(G-10635)*		
▲ Ren Holding Corporation	F	405 533-2755
Stillwater *(G-8745)*		
▲ Ren Testing Corporation	F	405 533-2700
Stillwater *(G-8745)*		
Seismic Source Company	E	580 762-8233
Ponca City *(G-7873)*		
Tech-Aid Products	G	918 838-8711
Tulsa *(G-10911)*		
Tektronix Inc	F	918 627-1500
Tulsa *(G-10918)*		
Total Systems and Controls Inc	G	918 481-9215
Tulsa *(G-10960)*		
◆ Trece Inc	F	918 785-3061
Adair *(G-112)*		
Veracity Tech Solutions LLC	G	208 821-8888
Tulsa *(G-11072)*		
Versatech Industries Inc	G	918 366-7400
Bixby *(G-670)*		
W L Walker Co Inc	E	918 583-3109
Tulsa *(G-11089)*		

3841 Surgical & Medical Instrs & Apparatus

◆ Access Optics LLC	E	918 294-1234
Broken Arrow *(G-812)*		
▲ Active-Ice Inc	F	405 310-3880
Norman *(G-4898)*		
Adroit Surgical LLC	G	425 577-2713
Nichols Hills *(G-4854)*		
▲ Advanced Medical Instrs Inc	C	918 250-0566
Broken Arrow *(G-816)*		
Anesthesia Services	G	580 536-7150
Lawton *(G-3889)*		
B & B Medical Services Inc	E	919 601-4756
Oklahoma City *(G-5499)*		
Baxter Healthcare Corporation	E	918 513-8980
Tulsa *(G-9271)*		
Biocorp Technologies Inc	G	405 990-2350
Oklahoma City *(G-5572)*		
Cardinal Health 200 LLC	C	918 865-4727
Mannford *(G-4177)*		
Carefusion Corporation	C	918 865-4727
Mannford *(G-4178)*		
Cefco Inc	G	918 543-8415
Inola *(G-3653)*		
Electronic Label Technology	G	812 875-2521
Edmond *(G-2409)*		
Howmedica Osteonics Corp	F	405 230-1340
Oklahoma City *(G-6268)*		
Immuno-Mycologics Inc	F	405 360-4669
Norman *(G-5030)*		
Immy Africa LLC	G	405 360-4669
Norman *(G-5031)*		
Integsense Inc	G	404 429-4780
Oklahoma City *(G-6317)*		
Lazarus Medical LLC	G	918 232-6915
Tulsa *(G-10140)*		
Lemco Enterprises Inc	G	580 226-7808
Ardmore *(G-324)*		
Linear Health Sciences LLC	G	415 388-2794
Oklahoma City *(G-6480)*		
McAlister Drug Corporation	G	405 354-2582
Yukon *(G-11750)*		
Medtronic Usa Inc	F	405 302-5301
Oklahoma City *(G-6559)*		
Medxpert North America LLC	G	405 285-1671
Edmond *(G-2511)*		
Nanomed Targeting Systems Inc	G	646 641-4747
Oklahoma City *(G-6652)*		
O E N T Instruments Inc	G	918 299-4343
Tulsa *(G-10369)*		
Park Dental Research Corp	F	580 226-0410
Ardmore *(G-344)*		
Pathinnovation LLC	G	405 475-9726
Oklahoma City *(G-6809)*		
Perfect Pitch Music	G	405 521-8088
Oklahoma City *(G-6828)*		
Precision Biomedical Svcs Inc	G	918 671-8091
Jenks *(G-3723)*		
Shared Services	G	405 947-0344
Oklahoma City *(G-7115)*		
Sinties Corporation	E	918 359-2000
Tulsa *(G-10768)*		
Smith & Nephew Inc	C	405 917-8500
Oklahoma City *(G-7154)*		
Sorb Technology Inc	G	405 682-1993
Oklahoma City *(G-7169)*		
Tamatha Holt Od	G	918 649-0524
Poteau *(G-7914)*		
Thomas Dist Solutions LLC	G	580 304-7741
Ponca City *(G-7883)*		

3842 Orthopedic, Prosthetic & Surgical Appliances/Splys

A Walker Electric	G	918 232-6023
Chelsea *(G-1399)*		
A X-Ceptional Quality Dntl Lab	G	918 406-1835
Tulsa *(G-9071)*		
Air Inspired Home Medical	F	918 299-3037
Glenpool *(G-3229)*		
All American Ear Mold Labs	F	405 285-2411
Edmond *(G-2295)*		
Anthony W Layton Cpo	G	580 353-8885
Lawton *(G-3890)*		
Applications For Medicine LLC	G	405 330-7910
Edmond *(G-2306)*		
Better Sound Hearing Aid Svc	G	918 995-2222
Jenks *(G-3691)*		
Body Connection LLC	G	580 745-9201
Durant *(G-2208)*		
Brace Place	G	405 858-5200
Oklahoma City *(G-5623)*		
Bruno Ind Living Aids Inc	G	405 964-5887
McLoud *(G-4355)*		
Celerity Orthotcs & Prosthetcs	G	405 605-3030
Oklahoma City *(G-5720)*		
Celerity Prosthetics LLC	G	405 605-3030
Oklahoma City *(G-5721)*		
Clear Tone Hearing Center Inc	E	918 838-1000
Tulsa *(G-9449)*		

Employee Codes: A=Over 500 employees, B=251-500
C=101-250, D=51-100, E=20-50, F=10-19, G=1-9

Clearity LLC..........G....... 918 388-9000
Tulsa *(G-9450)*
Dream Team Prosthetics LLC..........G....... 580 255-2100
Duncan *(G-2108)*
Evelyn Co Inc..........G....... 918 665-3952
Tulsa *(G-9708)*
Fenner Inc..........G....... 918 832-7768
Tulsa *(G-9737)*
Geronimo Manufacturing Inc..........G....... 580 336-5707
Perry *(G-7735)*
Get People Moving LLC..........G....... 405 529-6033
Oklahoma City *(G-6149)*
Hanger Inc..........F....... 918 742-6464
Tulsa *(G-9885)*
Hanger Prsthetcs & Ortho Inc..........G....... 580 326-6661
Hugo *(G-3611)*
Hanger Prsthetcs & Ortho Inc..........E....... 405 525-4000
Oklahoma City *(G-6213)*
Hanger Prsthetcs & Ortho Inc..........G....... 479 484-1620
Enid *(G-2968)*
Hanger Prsthetcs & Ortho Inc..........G....... 918 333-6900
Bartlesville *(G-489)*
Hanger Prsthetcs & Ortho Inc..........G....... 918 488-0400
Tulsa *(G-9886)*
Hanger Prsthetcs & Ortho Inc..........E....... 580 226-7900
Ardmore *(G-301)*
Hanger Prsthetcs & Ortho Inc..........G....... 918 423-1024
McAlester *(G-4303)*
Hanger Prsthtics Orthotics Inc..........G....... 918 687-1855
Muskogee *(G-4687)*
Hard Hat Safety and Glove LLC..........G....... 405 942-9500
Oklahoma City *(G-6217)*
Howmedica Osteonics Corp..........G....... 918 461-0152
Tulsa *(G-9956)*
Iq Surgical LLC..........F....... 918 932-2734
Tulsa *(G-10011)*
◆ **Jobri LLC**..........F....... 580 925-3500
Ada *(G-54)*
Lawton Brace & Limb Co Inc..........G....... 580 353-5525
Lawton *(G-3954)*
Lux Orthotics & Prosthetics..........G....... 417 624-2332
Wyandotte *(G-11660)*
▼ **Maris Health LLC**..........G....... 888 429-1117
Tulsa *(G-10209)*
Mobility One Transportation..........G....... 918 437-4488
Tulsa *(G-10289)*
Mondo Solutions LLC..........G....... 405 788-0056
Purcell *(G-8017)*
National Seating Mobility Inc..........G....... 918 856-3000
Oklahoma City *(G-6659)*
National Seating Mobility Inc..........G....... 405 896-3680
Oklahoma City *(G-6660)*
Orthotics Pros Inc..........G....... 918 296-3567
Jenks *(G-3721)*
Parra World Creations LLC..........G....... 918 938-2278
Tulsa *(G-10470)*
Patriot Prsthtics Orthtics Inc..........G....... 405 577-6778
Yukon *(G-11764)*
Pemco Inc..........G....... 918 341-7500
Claremore *(G-1669)*
Pipeglove LLC..........F....... 918 629-7116
Tulsa *(G-10517)*
Pro TEC Orthotics Company..........G....... 405 366-7688
Norman *(G-5123)*
Progressive Orthotic..........G....... 918 786-7701
Tulsa *(G-10570)*
Progressive Orthotic & PR..........G....... 918 681-2346
Tulsa *(G-10571)*
Prosthetics By Wade..........G....... 918 850-7544
Broken Arrow *(G-1012)*
Proud Veterans Intl Ltd..........G....... 316 209-8701
Lawton *(G-3986)*
Rowdy Hanger..........G....... 918 804-7375
Broken Arrow *(G-1038)*
Scott Sabolich Prosthetics & R..........E....... 405 841-6800
Oklahoma City *(G-7098)*
Steampunk Bnics Innvations LLC..........G....... 866 795-6645
Tulsa *(G-10842)*
Steel Systems Plus Inc..........G....... 918 286-7947
Broken Arrow *(G-1167)*
Texoma Orthtics Prsthtics Pllc..........G....... 580 699-8690
Lawton *(G-4012)*
Texoma Wheelchairs..........G....... 855 924-2525
Durant *(G-2268)*
Tgg Prosthetics Orthotics LLC..........G....... 405 285-5499
Edmond *(G-2639)*
Tim Carlton Prosthetics Inc..........G....... 405 721-7570
Oklahoma City *(G-7291)*
Total Care Orthtics Prsthtics..........G....... 918 502-5975
Tulsa *(G-10959)*
Wild Olives LLC..........G....... 580 230-1231
Duncan *(G-2199)*
Work Activity Center Inc..........E....... 405 799-6911
Moore *(G-4584)*

3843 Dental Eqpt & Splys

▲ **3M Imtec Corporation**..........C....... 800 879-9799
Ardmore *(G-233)*
Becky Welch Vacuum Forming..........G....... 918 836-7301
Tulsa *(G-9278)*
D & S Distributing..........G....... 580 763-3773
Ponca City *(G-7818)*
Dennis L Dickerson..........G....... 405 626-8630
Tuttle *(G-11196)*
Dentsply Sirona Inc..........F....... 918 878-0189
Tulsa *(G-9573)*
Dentsply Sirona Inc..........G....... 918 878-0001
Tulsa *(G-9574)*
Evelyn Co Inc..........G....... 918 665-3952
Tulsa *(G-9708)*
Happy Tooth Dental..........G....... 918 492-8793
Tulsa *(G-9889)*
Harris Discount Supplies Inc..........G....... 847 726-3800
Edmond *(G-2451)*
Jesco Products Inc..........G....... 405 943-1721
Oklahoma City *(G-6358)*
Leemark Dental Products..........G....... 918 241-6683
Sand Springs *(G-8200)*
Melton Rh..........G....... 918 968-1606
Stroud *(G-8811)*
Oklahoma Millworks Inc..........G....... 405 282-4887
Edmond *(G-2552)*
Oral Health Products Inc..........F....... 918 622-9412
Tulsa *(G-10435)*
Precision Alloy..........G....... 918 665-3952
Tulsa *(G-10542)*
Pro-Tech Dental Labs..........G....... 918 227-6407
Sapulpa *(G-8303)*
R Meyers Enterprises..........G....... 580 917-7554
Lawton *(G-3988)*
Reaux Corporation..........F....... 918 252-7660
Tulsa *(G-10626)*
Richard Brown..........G....... 918 492-1991
Tulsa *(G-10650)*

3844 X-ray Apparatus & Tubes

Desert Industrial X Ray LP..........G....... 918 650-0018
Henryetta *(G-3504)*
H & H Xray..........G....... 918 752-0966
Okmulgee *(G-7508)*
South Manufacturing Inc..........G....... 918 894-5255
Bixby *(G-662)*
Sullins International Inc..........G....... 918 258-5460
Broken Arrow *(G-1067)*
Wesco Enterprises Inc..........G....... 918 449-1081
Broken Arrow *(G-1096)*
Western X-Ray..........E....... 580 922-3166
Seiling *(G-8352)*
Xit Systems Inc..........G....... 918 259-9071
Broken Arrow *(G-1103)*

3845 Electromedical & Electrotherapeutic Apparatus

Advanced Imaging Resources Co..........G....... 918 609-5250
Broken Arrow *(G-815)*
▲ **Advanced Medical Instrs Inc**..........C....... 918 250-0566
Broken Arrow *(G-816)*
American Intrprtive Monitoring..........G....... 405 841-7826
Oklahoma City *(G-5437)*
Millennial Technologies LLC..........G....... 405 478-4351
Oklahoma City *(G-6611)*
▲ **Mms LLC**..........G....... 405 872-3486
Noble *(G-4886)*
Oto-Biomechanics LLC..........G....... 405 325-6668
Norman *(G-5105)*
Phoenix Group Holding Company..........F....... 405 948-7788
Oklahoma City *(G-6844)*
Surgiotonics LLC..........G....... 405 269-9767
Stillwater *(G-8762)*
Usut Labs Inc..........G....... 918 459-3844
Tulsa *(G-11061)*
Vadovations Inc..........E....... 405 601-5520
Oklahoma City *(G-7385)*

3851 Ophthalmic Goods

Ardmore Optical Co..........G....... 580 223-8676
Ardmore *(G-248)*
Classen Wholesale Optical Inc..........G....... 405 842-1900
Oklahoma City *(G-5777)*
Dunlaw Optical Labs Inc..........F....... 580 355-8410
Lawton *(G-3920)*
Empire Optical Inc..........E....... 918 744-8005
Tulsa *(G-9676)*
Essilor Laboratories Amer Inc..........E....... 800 568-5367
Tulsa *(G-9702)*
Gary Morgan..........G....... 405 387-4884
Newcastle *(G-4826)*
Graham Laboratories..........G....... 405 329-4413
Norman *(G-5009)*
Institute Optical Inc..........G....... 918 747-3937
Tulsa *(G-9991)*
Jeffs Optacle..........G....... 580 223-5999
Ardmore *(G-313)*
Moku LLC..........G....... 918 398-8479
Cleveland *(G-1727)*
Mustang Optical Inc..........G....... 405 376-0222
Mustang *(G-4784)*
Oakley Inc..........G....... 405 843-5447
Oklahoma City *(G-6708)*
Omega Optical Co LP..........E....... 405 703-4133
Oklahoma City *(G-6775)*
Ready Reading Glasses Inc..........G....... 405 840-4440
Oklahoma City *(G-6979)*
Rex Laboratories Inc..........G....... 918 742-9545
Tulsa *(G-10649)*
Rva..........G....... 405 608-0744
Oklahoma City *(G-7063)*
Stonewood Vision Source..........G....... 918 994-4450
Broken Arrow *(G-1065)*

3861 Photographic Eqpt & Splys

Eseco-Speedmaster..........D....... 918 225-1266
Cushing *(G-1933)*
Graphic Rsources Reproductions..........F....... 918 461-0303
Broken Arrow *(G-921)*
Gypsy Moon Studios..........G....... 918 251-7188
Broken Arrow *(G-925)*
▲ **Indel-Davis Inc**..........F....... 918 587-2151
Tulsa *(G-9976)*
Marvel Photo Inc..........G....... 918 836-0741
Tulsa *(G-10218)*
Memorabilia Corner..........G....... 405 321-8366
Norman *(G-5070)*
Miraclon Corporation..........F....... 580 772-5502
Weatherford *(G-11428)*
Mora Mora Media LLC..........G....... 918 231-6651
Owasso *(G-7594)*
Prophecy In News..........F....... 405 634-1234
Oklahoma City *(G-6917)*
Raccoon Technologies Inc..........G....... 580 399-9126
Ada *(G-79)*
Richard B Collins..........G....... 405 947-6349
Oklahoma City *(G-7015)*
Smart Office Stores LLC..........G....... 918 994-5300
Tulsa *(G-10776)*
Speedmaster Inc..........D....... 918 225-1266
Cushing *(G-1961)*
Techspeedy LLC..........G....... 918 406-0008
Tulsa *(G-10914)*
Tulsa Toner Technology..........G....... 918 838-0323
Tulsa *(G-11009)*
Vanco Systems..........G....... 405 692-4040
Oklahoma City *(G-5321)*
Waylink Systems Corporation..........G....... 405 261-9896
Stillwater *(G-8773)*
XCEL Office Solutions LLC..........G....... 580 595-9235
Lawton *(G-4024)*
Zoe Studios LLC..........G....... 918 258-4073
Broken Arrow *(G-1106)*

3873 Watch & Clock Devices & Parts

Custom Time & Neon Co Inc..........G....... 405 364-9139
Norman *(G-4974)*
Microframe Corp..........F....... 918 258-4839
Broken Arrow *(G-973)*
▲ **Mtm Recognition Corporation**..........B....... 405 609-6900
Oklahoma City *(G-6634)*
Mtm Recognition Corporation..........C....... 405 670-4545
Del City *(G-2002)*
Petroleum Artifacts Ltd..........G....... 918 949-6101
Tulsa *(G-10504)*
S & S Time Corporation..........E....... 918 437-3572
Tulsa *(G-10683)*
▲ **Selco LLC**..........E....... 918 622-6100
Tulsa *(G-10725)*

39 MISCELLANEOUS MANUFACTURING INDUSTRIES

3911 Jewelry: Precious Metal

Alans Benchworks Co ....G...... 405 222-1181
  Chickasha *(G-1427)*
Barretts Inc ....G...... 405 340-1519
  Edmond *(G-2318)*
C JS Jewelers ....G...... 405 631-0555
  Oklahoma City *(G-5659)*
Curtis Jewelry ....G...... 580 924-0041
  Durant *(G-2219)*
Diamond Dee-Lite Inc ....G...... 405 793-8166
  Moore *(G-4516)*
Elco Tech Engineering ....G...... 918 664-4646
  Tulsa *(G-9651)*
▲ F C Ziegler Co ....E...... 918 587-7639
  Tulsa *(G-9721)*
Fatt Hedz ....G...... 405 607-8484
  Oklahoma City *(G-6079)*
Fields Jewelry Inc ....G...... 405 348-2802
  Edmond *(G-2414)*
Gold Shop Custom Jewelers ....G...... 405 789-2919
  Bethany *(G-580)*
Golden Bronze Inc ....G...... 918 251-6300
  Broken Arrow *(G-920)*
▲ Graham Jewelers ....G...... 580 439-6680
  Comanche *(G-1841)*
Herff Jones LLC ....G...... 918 664-2544
  Tulsa *(G-9924)*
Herff Jones LLC ....G...... 405 794-3764
  Oklahoma City *(G-5295)*
J N B Inc ....G...... 918 786-6311
  Grove *(G-3275)*
J Thompson Custom Jewelers ....G...... 405 495-6610
  Warr Acres *(G-11323)*
Jays Jewelry ....G...... 405 224-9021
  Chickasha *(G-1475)*
Jewel Tech Mfg Inc ....F...... 918 828-9700
  Tulsa *(G-10044)*
Jewelers Bench ....G...... 405 495-1800
  Warr Acres *(G-11324)*
Jewels By James Inc ....G...... 918 745-2004
  Tulsa *(G-10045)*
Jim Griffith Custom Jeweler ....G...... 918 342-0151
  Claremore *(G-1644)*
Jims Jewelry Design ....G...... 580 336-4066
  Perry *(G-7738)*
Johnson Bvlle Fine Jwlers Pawn ....G...... 405 751-1216
  Oklahoma City *(G-6373)*
Jostens Inc ....E...... 918 274-7047
  Owasso *(G-7582)*
Massouds Fine Jwly & Artspace ....G...... 918 663-4884
  Tulsa *(G-10219)*
Moodys Jewelry Incorporated ....F...... 918 834-3371
  Tulsa *(G-10302)*
Moodys Jewelry Incorporated ....G...... 918 747-5599
  Tulsa *(G-10303)*
▲ Mtm Recognition Corporation ....B...... 405 609-6900
  Oklahoma City *(G-6634)*
Mtm Recognition Corporation ....C...... 405 670-4545
  Del City *(G-2002)*
Nature Creations ....G...... 405 848-2605
  Oklahoma City *(G-6664)*
Phoenix Industries LLC ....G...... 405 848-1688
  Oklahoma City *(G-6845)*
Plum Gold Jewelers & Designers ....G...... 918 341-4716
  Claremore *(G-1672)*
Rings Etc Fine Jewelry ....G...... 405 359-7464
  Edmond *(G-2601)*
Rosewood Designs ....G...... 405 329-0600
  Norman *(G-5135)*
Rustic Rehab ....G...... 918 314-6647
  Grove *(G-3287)*
S M Sadler Inc ....G...... 918 743-1048
  Tulsa *(G-10686)*
Samuels Jewelrey L L C ....G...... 918 241-6436
  Sand Springs *(G-8222)*
Sooner Repair ....G...... 918 742-4653
  Tulsa *(G-10791)*
Star Jewelers Inc ....G...... 918 251-9236
  Broken Arrow *(G-1061)*
Staudt Jewelers ....G...... 918 756-0517
  Okmulgee *(G-7526)*
Sueno Designs ....G...... 918 809-3027
  Owasso *(G-7621)*
Toklahoma LLC ....G...... 580 402-1243
  Oklahoma City *(G-7301)*
Treasures Custom Jewelry ....G...... 918 333-1311
  Bartlesville *(G-533)*
▲ Ultra Thin Inc ....E...... 405 794-7892
  Moore *(G-4582)*
Vintage Revival Inc ....G...... 580 379-9060
  Altus *(G-171)*
Western Metalsmith Design LLC ....G...... 580 938-2153
  Woodward *(G-11650)*
William Derrevere Designs ....G...... 918 260-5607
  Tulsa *(G-11123)*

3914 Silverware, Plated & Stainless Steel Ware

Dearinger Printing & Trophy ....F...... 405 372-5503
  Stillwater *(G-8675)*
Mtm Recognition LLC ....G...... 405 670-4545
  Oklahoma City *(G-6633)*
Trophies n Things ....G...... 405 247-9771
  Anadarko *(G-207)*
Yukon Trophy & Awards Inc ....G...... 405 354-5184
  Yukon *(G-11808)*

3915 Jewelers Findings & Lapidary Work

Alans Benchworks Co ....G...... 405 222-1181
  Chickasha *(G-1427)*
Db Unlimited LLC ....G...... 855 437-7766
  Oklahoma City *(G-9563)*
▲ Decorative Rock & Stone Inc ....G...... 405 672-2564
  Oklahoma City *(G-5916)*
Diamond Dee-Lite Inc ....G...... 405 793-8166
  Moore *(G-4516)*
J Spencer Jewelry & Gifts ....G...... 918 250-5587
  Tulsa *(G-10022)*
Jewels By James Inc ....G...... 918 745-2004
  Tulsa *(G-10045)*
Maddie & Co ....G...... 580 212-9539
  Idabel *(G-3639)*

3931 Musical Instruments

Active Violinist LLC ....G...... 612 532-1829
  Tulsa *(G-9098)*
Clubhouse Trailer Co LLC ....G...... 405 396-6747
  Edmond *(G-2358)*
Downtown Music Box LLC ....G...... 405 232-2099
  Oklahoma City *(G-5975)*
Hanson Inc ....G...... 918 447-0777
  Tulsa *(G-9888)*
Honest Rons Guitars ....G...... 405 947-3683
  Oklahoma City *(G-6260)*
Mad Dogs Emporium ....G...... 918 283-4480
  Claremore *(G-1652)*
Master Works ....G...... 580 847-2273
  Bennington *(G-564)*
Synapticgroove LLC ....G...... 405 205-6094
  Edmond *(G-2635)*
Walrus Audio LLC ....F...... 405 254-4118
  Oklahoma City *(G-7418)*

3942 Dolls & Stuffed Toys

Doodlebugs Etc Inc ....G...... 405 525-1248
  Oklahoma City *(G-5968)*
Pats World ....G...... 580 443-5751
  Milburn *(G-4463)*
Rita S Nicar ....G...... 580 492-4521
  Lawton *(G-3995)*

3944 Games, Toys & Children's Vehicles

AGS LLC ....G...... 405 605-8331
  Oklahoma City *(G-5400)*
Bill Kite Sales ....G...... 918 806-2958
  Broken Arrow *(G-851)*
Bipo Inc ....E...... 580 262-9640
  Oklahoma City *(G-5575)*
Chickasaw Nation ....G...... 405 387-6013
  Newcastle *(G-4821)*
Creative Blessings ....G...... 918 302-0734
  McAlester *(G-4289)*
Creek Nation Foundation Inc ....G...... 918 683-1825
  Muskogee *(G-4665)*
Dragonslayer Games LLC ....G...... 918 665-1472
  Tulsa *(G-9603)*
E and H Sales ....G...... 918 742-1091
  Tulsa *(G-9619)*
Fresh Monkey Fiction LLC ....G...... 405 751-3826
  Oklahoma City *(G-6118)*
Game King ....G...... 580 250-0707
  Lawton *(G-3934)*
Igg LLC ....G...... 918 607-3032
  Broken Arrow *(G-933)*
Kite Virginia ....G...... 918 747-9803
  Tulsa *(G-10094)*
Kites In Sky LLC ....G...... 405 624-6231
  Stillwater *(G-8714)*
Leisure Lane Handicrafts ....G...... 580 563-2747
  Blair *(G-696)*
Linda L Hargraves ....G...... 918 584-3442
  Tulsa *(G-10163)*
Moondog Puzzles LLC ....G...... 405 286-6881
  Oklahoma City *(G-6630)*
Music Games n Things Inc ....G...... 918 742-4349
  Tulsa *(G-10318)*
Primarily Puzzles ....G...... 918 275-8270
  Talala *(G-8902)*
Pro Darts Inc ....G...... 405 232-3552
  Oklahoma City *(G-6902)*
Puzzle Apps Inc ....G...... 918 815-6444
  Tulsa *(G-10585)*
Rocking RB Quarter Horses LLC ....F...... 405 605-9458
  Noble *(G-4890)*
Salamander Games Inc ....G...... 405 633-2725
  Yukon *(G-11774)*
Sheen Incorporated ....G...... 405 848-0881
  Oklahoma City *(G-7118)*
Solidroots LLC ....G...... 918 770-3549
  Tulsa *(G-10785)*
Toyko Toys ....G...... 405 204-7462
  Oklahoma City *(G-7313)*

3949 Sporting & Athletic Goods, NEC

2011 Ussa Limited Partnership ....F...... 918 948-7856
  Tulsa *(G-9055)*
Alluring Lures & Tackle Co LLC ....G...... 580 832-5177
  Cordell *(G-1854)*
American Iron Sports ....G...... 580 716-5662
  Tonkawa *(G-8971)*
Anita and Harold Speed ....G...... 580 838-2297
  Hendrix *(G-3438)*
Applied Oil Tools LLC ....G...... 405 670-8665
  Oklahoma City *(G-5458)*
Austin Athletic Co Inc ....F...... 405 273-8681
  Shawnee *(G-8429)*
Bedside Gunlock Products ....G...... 713 443-8172
  Tahlequah *(G-8853)*
Big Shot LLC ....G...... 918 712-7110
  Tulsa *(G-9293)*
Big Shot LLC ....G...... 918 712-7110
  Tulsa *(G-9294)*
▲ Billiards of Tulsa Inc ....E...... 918 835-1166
  Tulsa *(G-9296)*
Bills Catfish Bait ....G...... 918 224-8470
  Sapulpa *(G-8257)*
Blaze Skateboards LLC ....G...... 405 391-3838
  Choctaw *(G-1531)*
Boomerang ....G...... 405 250-6597
  Shawnee *(G-8434)*
Britter Creek Hunting Bli ....F...... 405 392-3588
  Tuttle *(G-11188)*
Buster Par Corp ....F...... 918 585-8542
  Tulsa *(G-9354)*
By Prather Inc ....G...... 580 994-2414
  Mooreland *(G-4586)*
Call ....G...... 580 789-0074
  Blackwell *(G-677)*
◆ Century LLC ....C...... 405 732-2226
  Oklahoma City *(G-5728)*
Charles Jones ....G...... 405 348-2187
  Edmond *(G-2345)*
Charleys Golf Cars Inc ....G...... 405 273-6901
  Shawnee *(G-8437)*
◆ Competitive Action Sports LLC ....G...... 405 474-7777
  Edmond *(G-2363)*
Country Leisure Inc ....E...... 405 799-7745
  Moore *(G-4511)*
Covers Plus Inc ....G...... 405 670-2221
  Oklahoma City *(G-5846)*
Dawg Pound ....G...... 580 622-2695
  Sulphur *(G-8831)*
Duggans Ann Marie Pro Shop ....G...... 405 715-2695
  Edmond *(G-2397)*
Durant ....G...... 580 920-2069
  Durant *(G-2225)*
El Reno Bowl Inc ....G...... 405 262-3611
  El Reno *(G-2714)*
Fenix Outfitters ....G...... 918 259-0099
  Broken Arrow *(G-907)*
Fish Tales Lure Company LLC ....G...... 918 814-6241
  Claremore *(G-1622)*
Floatingmats LLC ....G...... 918 504-8586
  Bixby *(G-623)*

G & H Decoy Inc....D....918 652-3314
Henryetta (G-3507)
Gear Exchange....G....405 606-3050
Oklahoma City (G-6141)
Golf Car Factory....G....405 782-0460
Oklahoma City (G-6169)
Greenlure LLC....G....918 786-9156
Grove (G-3273)
▲ Grips Etc Inc....D....405 447-2559
Norman (G-5011)
HALAQ Inc....G....405 321-7293
Newalla (G-4810)
Highnoon Tactical LLC....G....918 801-8737
Vinita (G-11259)
Instinct Performance LLC....G....405 463-7300
Oklahoma City (G-6312)
Janeway Machine Inc....E....918 224-0694
Sapulpa (G-8282)
Kick16 Skateboards LLC....G....918 869-6206
Muskogee (G-4703)
Lure Promo....G....405 664-3415
Oklahoma City (G-6502)
Majestic Marble & Granite....E....918 266-1121
Catoosa (G-1337)
Malchus Sktbard Mnistries Assn....G....405 615-6066
Edmond (G-2502)
McKinley Hardwoods LLC....G....800 522-3305
Oklahoma City (G-6548)
Miracle Recreation Eqp Co....G....918 299-1415
Bixby (G-645)
New Times Technologies Inc....D....918 872-9600
Broken Arrow (G-988)
Newell Manufacturing....G....918 782-1900
Langley (G-3873)
Next Generation....G....405 606-4455
Oklahoma City (G-6673)
Noahs Park & Playgrounds LLC....F....405 607-0714
Edmond (G-2538)
Omer Distributors LLC....G....580 695-3211
Lawton (G-3979)
Out On A Limb Mfg LLC....G....580 541-3794
Enid (G-3027)
▲ Parrish Enterprises Ltd....C....580 237-4033
Enid (G-3031)
Paul Ziert & Associates Inc....D....405 364-5344
Norman (G-5112)
Performance Surfaces LLC....G....405 463-0505
Oklahoma City (G-6830)
Pistol Wear LLC....G....918 364-5617
Tulsa (G-10519)
Plastic Research and Dev Corp....F....918 949-6291
Tulsa (G-10525)
Pony Boy Lures....G....580 327-1233
Alva (G-189)
Reagent Chemical & RES Inc....G....580 233-1024
Enid (G-3044)
Reagent Chemical & RES Inc....F....580 436-4100
Francis (G-3191)
San Juan Pools of Oklahoma....G....918 582-8169
Tulsa (G-10702)
Satterlee Teepees....G....405 255-6642
Moore (G-4563)
Sinties Corporation....E....918 359-2000
Tulsa (G-10768)
Soccer Wave LLC....G....405 361-7813
Edmond (G-2623)
SOS Pools....G....405 471-3792
Edmond (G-2624)
Sports Center....G....580 795-2993
Madill (G-4164)
Sports Vision Inc....G....918 824-7617
Pryor (G-7992)
Sportstech Quality Cardio LLC....F....918 461-9177
Tulsa (G-10825)
Stealth Mfg....G....405 843-1954
Oklahoma City (G-7198)
Steve Harrison Game Calls....G....918 688-0807
Tulsa (G-10849)
Stickem Fishing Lures Ltd....G....918 636-6179
Broken Arrow (G-1062)
Strength Tech Inc....G....405 377-7100
Stillwater (G-8760)
Tatur....G....918 244-6918
Tulsa (G-10902)
Taylor Custom Cues....G....405 317-3298
Oklahoma City (G-7257)
Tight Line Products LLC....G....918 231-0934
Tulsa (G-10940)
Tipton Company....G....580 762-0800
Ponca City (G-7884)
Tridon Composites Inc....F....918 742-0426
Kellyville (G-3768)
Trilogy Horse Ind....G....405 248-1010
Oklahoma City (G-7332)
Trilogy Horse Industries Inc....G....405 248-1010
Harrah (G-3388)
Veteran Bat Company LLC....G....580 439-5230
Comanche (G-1847)
W C Bradley Co....D....918 836-5581
Tulsa (G-11086)
Walr Corp....G....918 253-4773
Jay (G-3687)
Whitehouse Enterprises....G....918 224-2002
Sapulpa (G-8325)
Winarr Golf Tech LLC....G....918 994-2191
Tulsa (G-11136)
▲ Wohali Outdoors LLC....F....918 343-3800
Broken Arrow (G-1100)
Wombat Labs LLC....G....405 355-9662
Stillwater (G-8775)
Zebco Corporation....A....918 836-5581
Tulsa (G-11172)
▼ Zebco Sales Company LLC....G....800 588-9030
Tulsa (G-11173)

3951 Pens & Mechanical Pencils

Creative Pins....G....405 390-2038
Choctaw (G-1535)

3952 Lead Pencils, Crayons & Artist's Mtrls

Benjamin Harjo Jr....G....405 521-0246
Oklahoma City (G-5551)
Bill Glass....G....918 479-8884
Locust Grove (G-4104)
◆ Carpentree Inc....E....918 582-3600
Tulsa (G-9378)
Green Room Studios....G....580 335-5689
Frederick (G-3193)
Mulberry Tree Graphics....G....580 248-3194
Lawton (G-3974)
Oklahoma World Organiz....G....918 224-3063
Sapulpa (G-8294)

3953 Marking Devices

A-OK Rubber Stamp....G....580 357-2822
Lawton (G-3882)
Aars....G....918 313-4512
Tulsa (G-9080)
American Engraving & Trophy....G....405 360-2744
Norman (G-4906)
Beacon Stamp & Seal Co....G....918 834-2322
Tulsa (G-9276)
▼ Custom Identification Products....G....405 745-1010
Oklahoma City (G-5873)
Dsignz Custom Screen Printing....G....405 375-6806
Kingfisher (G-3796)
Layle Company Corporation....G....405 329-5143
Norman (G-5056)
Robinhood Stamp & Seal Co Inc....G....918 493-6506
Tulsa (G-10664)
Rowmark LLC....E....405 787-4542
Oklahoma City (G-7051)
Rusco Plastics....G....580 234-1596
Enid (G-3053)
▲ Southern Rubber Stamp Co Inc....G....918 587-3818
Tulsa (G-10801)
Texoma Engraving LLC....G....580 775-7333
Durant (G-2264)
Trophies n Things....G....405 247-9771
Anadarko (G-207)
▲ US Fleet Tracking LLC....E....405 726-9900
Edmond (G-2660)
Walker Stamp & Seal Co....E....405 235-5319
Oklahoma City (G-7415)

3955 Carbon Paper & Inked Ribbons

Advanced Graphics Technology....G....405 632-8600
Oklahoma City (G-5383)
Elite Creative Solutions LLC....E....918 994-5435
Broken Arrow (G-897)
Laser Source LLC....F....405 843-2528
Oklahoma City (G-6450)
Laser Source LLC....G....405 330-4442
Oklahoma City (G-6451)

3961 Costume Jewelry & Novelties

Bracelets For Baby....G....918 625-0088
Owasso (G-7549)
Brockus Creat Handcrafted Jwly....G....580 594-2215
Wakita (G-11297)
Focal Point Inc....G....405 942-2044
Oklahoma City (G-6101)
K and G Investments Inc....G....401 396-9280
Guthrie (G-3321)
Kathys Kloset Inc....G....405 524-9447
Oklahoma City (G-6401)
Kathys Kloset Inc....F....405 521-0055
Oklahoma City (G-6402)
Kosmoi LLC....G....918 520-7822
Broken Arrow (G-960)
Mary Really Nice Things....G....580 237-1177
Enid (G-3009)
Sooner Repair....G....918 742-4653
Tulsa (G-10791)
Staudt Jewelers....G....918 756-0517
Okmulgee (G-7526)

3965 Fasteners, Buttons, Needles & Pins

Midwest Automotive Fas LLC....G....918 520-6904
Broken Arrow (G-974)
Pins-N-Needles By Sandra....G....918 270-0204
Owasso (G-7603)
Truproducts LLC....G....405 830-0151
Lexington (G-4040)
WM Heitgras Company....E....918 583-3131
Tulsa (G-11144)

3991 Brooms & Brushes

▲ Da Vinci Broom LLC....G....580 224-1424
Ardmore (G-271)
Oral Health Products Inc....F....918 622-9412
Tulsa (G-10435)

3993 Signs & Advertising Displays

247 Graphx Studios Inc....G....405 677-7775
Oklahoma City (G-5329)
2911 LLC....G....405 631-2008
Oklahoma City (G-5330)
3g Sign Inc....G....918 630-5976
Broken Arrow (G-807)
4 K Kustomz Designs & Signs....G....580 226-2259
Ardmore (G-234)
405 Sign and Lighting LLC....G....405 445-8888
Oklahoma City (G-5335)
66 Sign and Light LLC....G....405 445-9212
Luther (G-4131)
A & B Quick Signs LLC....G....405 789-7446
Oklahoma City (G-5342)
A & S Graphix....G....918 640-1292
Sulphur (G-8827)
A 1 Advertising By L & H....G....918 348-2529
Muskogee (G-4639)
A Finley Sign & Lighting Co....G....405 413-5721
Oklahoma City (G-5345)
A Sign of Surprise....G....918 607-0747
Broken Arrow (G-810)
A-1 Specialties....G....405 942-1341
Oklahoma City (G-5352)
A-Max Signs Co....E....918 622-0651
Tulsa (G-9075)
A1 Vinyl Signs LLC....G....918 392-9905
Tulsa (G-9076)
AAA Sign & Supply Co....G....918 622-7883
Tulsa (G-9078)
Absolute Markings Inc....F....918 660-0600
Tulsa (G-9083)
Accent Displays & Graphics....G....918 437-4338
Tulsa (G-9087)
Ace Sign Company Inc....G....918 446-3030
Tulsa (G-9095)
Acura Neon Inc....E....918 252-2258
Broken Arrow (G-813)
Ad Tech Signs Inc....G....405 236-0551
Oklahoma City (G-5370)
Advantage Graphics....G....580 363-5734
Ponca City (G-7793)
Advertising Signs & Awngs Inc....G....405 232-7446
Oklahoma City (G-5388)
Affordable Signs & Decals Inc....G....405 942-7059
Oklahoma City (G-5397)
Al Signs & Wraps LLC....G....405 531-6938
Del City (G-1995)
Alan Thompson Signs....G....918 808-3976
Broken Arrow (G-822)
All Signs....G....918 739-3660
Tulsa (G-9137)
All-Star Trophies & Ribbon Mfg....G....918 283-2200
Claremore (G-1581)

Allem Sign Co....G....918 241-7206
Sand Springs *(G-8158)*
Allen Sign Studio LLC....G....918 542-1180
Miami *(G-4390)*
Allen Signs....G....580 688-2985
Hollis *(G-3563)*
Alphagraffix Inc....G....405 354-3000
Yukon *(G-11690)*
American Logo and Sign Inc....G....405 799-1800
Moore *(G-4488)*
American Logo and Sign Inc....F....405 799-1800
Oklahoma City *(G-5438)*
American Signworx....G....479 650-4562
Pocola *(G-7780)*
Anns Quick Print Co Inc....G....405 222-1871
Chickasha *(G-1429)*
Apple Art....G....405 691-4393
Moore *(G-4491)*
Architectural Graphics Inc....G....757 427-1900
Chickasha *(G-1432)*
Architectural Sign & Graphics....G....405 354-8829
Yukon *(G-11692)*
Arrow Sign Company Inc....F....580 353-2227
Lawton *(G-3891)*
Artworks....G....580 927-9094
Atoka *(G-396)*
Ask ME About Signs LLC....G....405 317-8157
Norman *(G-4920)*
Auto Trim Design Signs SE Okla....G....580 622-3830
Sulphur *(G-8828)*
B Bar Inc....G....580 824-8338
Waynoka *(G-11372)*
B G Specialties Inc....G....918 582-1165
Tulsa *(G-9243)*
Bad Boy Signs Graphic....D....405 224-2059
Chickasha *(G-1436)*
Bakers Sign & Design....G....405 262-5100
El Reno *(G-2700)*
Banners Signs & Business Cards....G....405 818-4371
Oklahoma City *(G-5525)*
Barbara Chaple....G....405 721-3758
Oklahoma City *(G-5526)*
Beacon Sign Company Inc....G....405 567-4886
Prague *(G-7921)*
Beacon Stamp & Seal Co....G....918 834-2322
Tulsa *(G-9276)*
Better Sign Co....G....580 242-9317
Enid *(G-2916)*
Bigfoot Prints LLC....G....918 805-0543
Collinsville *(G-1803)*
Bill Koenig....G....405 386-7979
Newalla *(G-4805)*
Billboards Etc Inc....G....580 326-1660
Hugo *(G-3603)*
Bipo Inc....E....580 262-9640
Oklahoma City *(G-5575)*
Blankenship Brothers Inc....G....405 943-3278
Oklahoma City *(G-5586)*
Blankenship Brothers Inc....G....405 943-3278
Oklahoma City *(G-5587)*
Blankenship Brothers Inc....G....918 627-3278
Tulsa *(G-9302)*
Blankenship Brothers Inc....G....405 848-7446
Oklahoma City *(G-5588)*
Bobs Sign Company....G....580 467-3646
Chickasha *(G-1441)*
Butner Brothers LLC....G....405 321-2322
Norman *(G-4949)*
▲ Bwb Sign Inc....F....405 292-3534
Oklahoma City *(G-5651)*
Byrd Signs & Designs....G....918 687-4219
Muskogee *(G-4656)*
C L and L Inc....G....405 722-9427
Oklahoma City *(G-5660)*
C M Y K Colour Corp....G....405 270-0060
Oklahoma City *(G-5661)*
Capstone Music Company Ltd....G....918 273-1888
Nowata *(G-5210)*
Carols Signs....G....405 769-5521
Oklahoma City *(G-5705)*
Chambers Signs....G....918 251-6513
Broken Arrow *(G-865)*
Checotah W T J Shoppe Inc....G....918 473-2819
Checotah *(G-1391)*
Chris Johnson....G....405 364-3879
Norman *(G-4956)*
Circle 7 Signs and Wonders....G....918 448-7744
Wilburton *(G-11519)*
Claremoresigns Com....G....918 965-1233
Claremore *(G-1608)*
Clark Signs Inc....G....918 291-3411
Kiefer *(G-3777)*
▲ Claude Neon Federal Signs Inc....D....918 587-7171
Tulsa *(G-9444)*
Claude V Sanderson Prop....G....405 232-5878
Oklahoma City *(G-5780)*
Clay Serigraphics Inc....F....918 592-2529
Tulsa *(G-9445)*
Clear Channel Outdoor Inc....E....405 528-2683
Oklahoma City *(G-5781)*
Complete Graphics Inc....G....405 232-8882
Oklahoma City *(G-5812)*
Complete Sign Service LLC....G....405 273-7567
Tecumseh *(G-8909)*
Compusign Vinyl Graphics....G....580 762-4930
Ponca City *(G-7807)*
Conyer Signs....G....405 755-0061
Edmond *(G-2366)*
Corporate Image Inc....G....918 516-8376
Owasso *(G-7556)*
Corter Enterprises LLC....G....405 326-7001
Tuttle *(G-11190)*
Crain Displays & Exhibits Inc....F....918 585-9797
Tulsa *(G-9499)*
Creative Apparel and More Inc....G....918 682-1283
Muskogee *(G-4664)*
Crown Neon Signs Inc....G....918 437-7446
Tulsa *(G-9516)*
Custom Expressignz....G....580 252-2868
Duncan *(G-2102)*
Custom Signs....G....918 225-2749
Cushing *(G-1928)*
Custom Time & Neon Co Inc....G....405 364-9139
Norman *(G-4974)*
Custom Vinyl Signs By Chas....G....580 351-4058
Lawton *(G-3914)*
Cutting Edge Signs....G....918 688-1878
Edmond *(G-2378)*
Cutting Edge Signs & Graphics....G....405 262-4300
El Reno *(G-2709)*
D Signs & Wonders LLC....F....405 932-4585
Paden *(G-7635)*
Dalmarc Enterprises Inc....D....405 942-8703
Oklahoma City *(G-5893)*
Danny Lee Signs....G....580 832-5256
Cordell *(G-1857)*
David Logan....G....918 739-4231
Catoosa *(G-1315)*
Davis Sign Co....G....580 225-3121
Elk City *(G-2801)*
Debo Dmnsons Laser Cut Engrave....G....405 843-9098
Oklahoma City *(G-5915)*
Design My Signs OK LLC....G....918 923-0175
Claremore *(G-1614)*
Designs and Signs By Jillian....G....405 409-1522
Jones *(G-3744)*
Digital Theory LLC....G....405 824-6460
Norman *(G-4980)*
Digital Theory Signs....G....405 438-0222
Norman *(G-4981)*
Dos Okies Signs & Graphics....G....918 569-7292
Clayton *(G-1709)*
Doug Strickland....G....580 436-1010
Ada *(G-33)*
Downing Manufacturing Inc....F....918 224-1116
Tulsa *(G-9001)*
Dunbar Event Signs Inc....G....918 607-9254
Owasso *(G-7564)*
Eagle Graphics....G....918 335-7777
Bartlesville *(G-477)*
Eaton-Quade Company....F....405 236-4475
Oklahoma City *(G-6002)*
Elite Media Group LLC....G....405 928-5800
Norman *(G-4989)*
Elite Sign Brokers....G....405 200-6970
Oklahoma City *(G-6025)*
Elk Valley Woodworking Inc....G....580 486-3337
Carter *(G-1281)*
▲ Elqui International Ltd Co....G....918 335-5002
Bartlesville *(G-480)*
▼ Emg Graphic Systems Inc....F....918 835-5300
Tulsa *(G-9672)*
Encinos 3d Custom Products LLC....F....918 286-8535
Tulsa *(G-9681)*
Estate Sales By Greg Earles....G....405 210-8472
Oklahoma City *(G-6052)*
◆ Excell Products Inc....E....405 390-4491
Choctaw *(G-1542)*
Express Ltg & Sign Maint LLC....G....405 378-3838
Oklahoma City *(G-6064)*
Fairchild Signs....G....405 439-3100
Moore *(G-4522)*
Fast Signs....G....918 251-0330
Broken Arrow *(G-906)*
Fastsigns....G....918 376-7870
Owasso *(G-7566)*
Fastsigns....G....405 701-2908
Norman *(G-4999)*
Fastsigns of Lawton....G....580 595-9101
Lawton *(G-3927)*
Fellers Inc....F....918 621-4412
Tulsa *(G-9735)*
▲ Fellers Inc....C....918 621-4400
Tulsa *(G-9736)*
Finley Discount Sign Ligh....G....405 445-8888
Moore *(G-4523)*
First Impressions Inc....G....918 267-4642
Beggs *(G-555)*
First Thought Inc....G....918 336-3322
Bartlesville *(G-483)*
Fixtures Express....G....405 834-1633
Edmond *(G-2415)*
Franks Signs....G....918 335-9715
Bartlesville *(G-485)*
Frederick Sommers Wstn Sign Co....F....918 587-2300
Tulsa *(G-9773)*
Freds Sign Co....G....405 235-8696
Newalla *(G-4809)*
G & S Sign Services LLC....G....405 604-3636
Oklahoma City *(G-6130)*
Galaxie Sign Co....G....580 226-2944
Ardmore *(G-293)*
Game Changing Image LLC....G....918 289-3392
Beggs *(G-556)*
George Miller....G....405 341-4097
Edmond *(G-2434)*
Good Life Concepts Inc....G....478 714-9114
Edmond *(G-2439)*
Graf-X LLC....G....405 542-6631
Hinton *(G-3529)*
Graphic Excursions....G....918 422-5318
Watts *(G-11356)*
Graphix Xpress....G....580 765-7324
Ponca City *(G-7831)*
Gss Sign & Design LLC....F....918 827-6561
Mounds *(G-4617)*
H&R Lifting & Bucket Service....G....918 446-5549
Tulsa *(G-9878)*
Happy Camper Signs....G....918 856-4279
Tulsa *(G-9010)*
Hasco Corporation....E....405 524-6366
Oklahoma City *(G-6222)*
Hays and Hays Companies Inc....G....405 624-2999
Stillwater *(G-8698)*
Hays Tent & Awning....G....918 534-1663
Dewey *(G-2023)*
Highway Man Signs....G....918 396-8024
Skiatook *(G-8548)*
Highway Man Signs LLC....G....918 534-9100
Bartlesville *(G-493)*
House of Trophies....G....918 341-2111
Claremore *(G-1637)*
House of Trophies....G....405 452-3524
Wetumka *(G-11492)*
Howdy Signs....G....918 543-2854
Inola *(G-3662)*
Htw Inc....G....918 423-4619
McAlester *(G-4305)*
Industrial Signs & Neon Inc....F....405 236-5599
Oklahoma City *(G-6301)*
Insignia Signs Inc....G....405 631-5522
Oklahoma City *(G-6309)*
Instant Signs Inc....G....405 848-8181
Oklahoma City *(G-6311)*
Integrity Signs....G....918 520-2802
Ramona *(G-8046)*
Irwin Custom Sign Company LLC....G....405 372-0657
Stillwater *(G-8704)*
Ixzibit....G....405 413-2260
Jones *(G-3748)*
Izoom Inc....G....918 836-9666
Tulsa *(G-10015)*
J & B Graphics Inc....E....405 524-7446
Oklahoma City *(G-6328)*
▲ Jack Pratt Screen-Ad Co....F....405 524-5551
Oklahoma City *(G-6342)*
Jack Stout Inc....G....918 781-1000
Muskogee *(G-4696)*
James P Compton....G....918 682-3700
Muskogee *(G-4697)*

Employee Codes: A=Over 500 employees, B=251-500
C=101-250, D=51-100, E=20-50, F=10-19, G=1-9

2020 Oklahoma Directory
of Manufacturers & Processors

501

39 MISCELLANEOUS MANUFACTURING INDUSTRIES

Jason M Haag .... G 918 369-1805
  Bixby *(G-638)*
Jelke Signs .... G 580 252-2523
  Duncan *(G-2134)*
Jerry Swanson Sales Co Inc .... G 918 712-7446
  Tulsa *(G-10038)*
Jim Did It Signs .... G 580 255-5533
  Duncan *(G-2136)*
Jim Ford Sign Co .... G 580 223-8880
  Ardmore *(G-315)*
Jim Watkins .... G 918 367-5575
  Bristow *(G-783)*
Joe Decker Signs .... G 405 630-8691
  Norman *(G-5044)*
Johnson Plastics Plus - Okla .... G 800 654-4150
  Oklahoma City *(G-6376)*
Johnson Signs Inc .... G 580 323-6454
  Arapaho *(G-224)*
Just-In-Time Signs LLC .... G 580 821-1140
  Sayre *(G-8342)*
Kaiser Sign & Graphics Co Inc .... G 580 772-3880
  Weatherford *(G-11423)*
▲ Kay Holding Co .... E 580 628-4146
  Tonkawa *(G-8977)*
Keleher Outdoor Advertising Co ...... F 918 333-8855
  Bartlesville *(G-502)*
Kennys Sign Graphx-Etchihg In .... G 580 477-4250
  Altus *(G-160)*
Kline Sign LLC .... G 580 237-0732
  Enid *(G-2995)*
Klines Signs & Crane .... G 580 256-2374
  Woodward *(G-11604)*
Krause Plastics .... G 918 835-4202
  Tulsa *(G-10100)*
Kustom Graphics .... G 405 635-8009
  Oklahoma City *(G-6436)*
Kustom Signs .... G 405 635-8009
  Oklahoma City *(G-6437)*
Lake Country Graphics Inc .... G 918 682-8849
  Muskogee *(G-4704)*
Landmark Design & Sign Corp .... G 405 387-3999
  Newcastle *(G-4830)*
Le Gravis LLC .... G 918 346-6313
  Tulsa *(G-10142)*
Led Signs of Oklahoma .... G 918 619-9798
  Tulsa *(G-10146)*
▲ Ledigital Signs LLC .... G 918 504-8506
  Tulsa *(G-10147)*
Legacy Signs .... G 580 762-2288
  Ponca City *(G-7844)*
Legacy Signs .... G 918 409-0835
  Tulsa *(G-10149)*
Lettercrafts .... G 918 584-2400
  Tulsa *(G-10154)*
Lettering Express OK Inc .... E 405 235-8999
  Oklahoma City *(G-6469)*
Liberty Signs .... G 918 409-4470
  Tulsa *(G-10157)*
Lindsey Printing .... G 580 476-2278
  Rush Springs *(G-8123)*
Luther Sign Co .... G 405 681-6535
  Oklahoma City *(G-6503)*
Lyle S Sign Contractors .... G 405 386-7443
  Newalla *(G-4812)*
Marrara Group Inc .... G 918 379-0993
  Tulsa *(G-10216)*
Marshall County Publishing Co .... F 580 795-3355
  Madill *(G-4155)*
Mart Trophy Co Inc .... G 918 481-3388
  Tulsa *(G-10217)*
McCabe Crane & Sign .... G 918 424-6381
  McAlester *(G-4318)*
McCurdy and Associates LLC .... G 405 317-4178
  Oklahoma City *(G-6546)*
Mercury Sign and Banner .... G 405 360-3303
  Norman *(G-5071)*
Mh Signs LLC .... G 580 795-2925
  Madill *(G-4156)*
Midwest Decals LLC .... G 405 787-8747
  Oklahoma City *(G-6602)*
Midwest Wraps .... G 918 624-2111
  Tulsa *(G-10273)*
Miket ADS Inc .... G 918 341-2992
  Claremore *(G-1655)*
Miketads Inc .... G 918 341-2992
  Claremore *(G-1656)*
Misaco Sign & Screen Printing .... G 918 542-4188
  Miami *(G-4419)*
ML Sign Service LLC .... G 405 386-4898
  Newalla *(G-4815)*

Mltl Enterprises LLC .... G 405 321-2224
  Norman *(G-5077)*
Modesto Vinyl Lettering Inc .... G 580 223-4262
  Ardmore *(G-334)*
Mt Designs .... G 580 317-3921
  Fort Towson *(G-3183)*
Mullins Sign Shop .... G 580 889-4772
  Atoka *(G-420)*
Multigraphic Design .... G 405 672-8201
  Oklahoma City *(G-6635)*
Myprint .... G 918 542-7672
  Miami *(G-4421)*
National Sign Market .... G 405 821-8768
  Edmond *(G-2529)*
Neon Moore and Sign .... G 405 672-6277
  Oklahoma City *(G-6670)*
New ERA Signs LLC .... G 405 926-2050
  Pauls Valley *(G-7668)*
North American Cos .... F 918 592-2000
  Tulsa *(G-10360)*
Oil Capitol Neon Inc .... G 918 582-9031
  Tulsa *(G-10386)*
Oklahoma City Frequency .... G 405 887-7115
  Oklahoma City *(G-6740)*
Oklahoma Logo Signs Inc .... G 405 840-1550
  Oklahoma City *(G-6753)*
Oklahoma Sign Association .... G 918 587-7171
  Tulsa *(G-10408)*
Oklahoma Sign Company .... G 405 620-6716
  Oklahoma City *(G-6762)*
Oklahoma Visual Graphics LLC ..... E 405 943-3278
  Oklahoma City *(G-6764)*
Order-Matic Electronics Corp .... C 405 672-1487
  Oklahoma City *(G-6781)*
Osage Neon .... G 918 583-4430
  Tulsa *(G-10443)*
Osborne Design Co .... G 918 585-3212
  Tulsa *(G-10444)*
Paul Clinton Hughes .... G 918 273-1888
  Nowata *(G-5225)*
Petes Signs .... G 580 338-2266
  Guymon *(G-3361)*
Pg13 Graphics & Design LLC .... G 405 720-8002
  Oklahoma City *(G-6840)*
Precision Image Cnversions LLC ... F 918 430-1102
  Tulsa *(G-10546)*
Precision Sign & Design .... G 918 430-1102
  Tulsa *(G-10549)*
Premier Signs & Design LLC .... G 918 825-6422
  Pryor *(G-7983)*
Prime Signs of Oklahoma Inc .... G 918 500-2213
  Tulsa *(G-10559)*
Pro-Feil Mktg Solutions LLC .... G 580 595-9101
  Lawton *(G-3985)*
R & R Signs Inc .... G 580 924-4363
  Durant *(G-2250)*
R G Enterprises .... G 580 225-2260
  Elk City *(G-2864)*
Rainbow Awnings & Signs .... G 918 249-0003
  Tulsa *(G-10610)*
Randys Signs Inc .... G 918 273-2564
  Shawnee *(G-8486)*
▲ Rbi Advertising .... G 918 592-1836
  Tulsa *(G-10624)*
Rebel Sign Company LLC .... G 405 456-9253
  Oklahoma City *(G-6982)*
Redwood Country Signs .... G 405 596-8737
  Newcastle *(G-4837)*
Reece Supply Company Houston .. F 918 556-5000
  Tulsa *(G-10634)*
Reynolds & Sons Neon Studio .... G 405 525-6366
  Oklahoma City *(G-7013)*
Rick Knight .... G 405 232-4954
  Oklahoma City *(G-7020)*
Robert Smith .... G 405 722-5188
  Oklahoma City *(G-7037)*
Robyn Holdings LLC .... E 405 722-4600
  Oklahoma City *(G-7041)*
Royal Sign & Graphic Inc .... G 918 682-6151
  Muskogee *(G-4746)*
Royal Signs LLC .... G 918 507-3303
  Hennessey *(G-3483)*
Rusty Rooster Metal .... G 918 290-9113
  Stroud *(G-8817)*
S & S Textile Inc .... F 405 632-9928
  Oklahoma City *(G-7065)*
S S Design Co .... G 918 427-3230
  Roland *(G-8113)*
Sammys Signs LLC .... G 405 320-1156
  Chickasha *(G-1506)*

Sanford Brothers Co Inc .... F 918 665-7358
  Tulsa *(G-10706)*
Semasys Inc .... E 405 525-2335
  Oklahoma City *(G-7107)*
Sheehy Signs .... G 405 623-7777
  Purcell *(G-8019)*
Sidewinder Signs .... G 918 647-5306
  Poteau *(G-7913)*
Sign & Send It LLC .... F 918 730-9309
  Tulsa *(G-10756)*
Sign A Rama Inc .... G 405 631-2008
  Oklahoma City *(G-7131)*
Sign Depot .... F 580 931-9363
  Durant *(G-2257)*
Sign Dezigns .... G 918 688-3660
  Broken Arrow *(G-1050)*
Sign Dezigns LLC .... G 580 656-0621
  Duncan *(G-2177)*
Sign Factory LLC .... G 405 401-9513
  Shawnee *(G-8498)*
Sign Gypsies Ardmore LLC .... G 512 644-6976
  Ardmore *(G-354)*
Sign Gypsies Midwest City LLC ..... G 405 259-9886
  Midwest City *(G-4453)*
Sign Innovations Inc .... G 214 234-1614
  Bokchito *(G-751)*
▲ Sign Innovations LLC .... G 405 840-1151
  Oklahoma City *(G-7132)*
Sign Language .... G 405 360-7500
  Norman *(G-5145)*
Sign Maker LLC .... G 918 728-6060
  Tulsa *(G-10757)*
Sign of Lies LLC .... G 405 618-9695
  Oklahoma City *(G-7133)*
Sign of Times .... G 405 375-4717
  Kingfisher *(G-3814)*
Sign Service .... G 405 495-0700
  Oklahoma City *(G-7134)*
Sign Solutions .... G 918 449-9439
  Broken Arrow *(G-1164)*
Sign Source .... G 580 436-1323
  Ada *(G-88)*
Sign Up For Emails .... G 405 236-3100
  Oklahoma City *(G-7135)*
Sign-A-Rama of Ok Inc .... G 405 631-2008
  Oklahoma City *(G-7136)*
Signature Graphics Corp .... G 918 294-3485
  Bixby *(G-658)*
Signco Inc .... G 405 615-7572
  Yukon *(G-11782)*
Signs & Stitches .... G 918 245-3301
  Sand Springs *(G-8224)*
Signs 405 LLC .... G 405 470-1616
  Warr Acres *(G-11329)*
Signs and T-Shirts Oklahoma Cy .... G 405 600-7080
  Oklahoma City *(G-7137)*
Signs By Dale Inc .... G 479 518-3744
  Lawton *(G-3997)*
Signs By Jade .... G 918 423-0041
  McAlester *(G-4335)*
Signs By Sikorski .... G 918 257-5164
  Afton *(G-121)*
Signs Etc .... G 918 447-1065
  Tulsa *(G-10760)*
Signs of Times .... G 918 512-6747
  Sapulpa *(G-8312)*
Signs On A Dime .... G 580 237-3078
  Enid *(G-3056)*
Signs To Go LLC .... G 405 348-8646
  Edmond *(G-2621)*
Signs-N-More .... G 918 760-5080
  Coweta *(G-1897)*
Signtec Signs Distinction Inc .... G 405 745-7555
  Oklahoma City *(G-7138)*
Skis Tees .... G 405 239-7547
  Oklahoma City *(G-7146)*
SKM Graphics & Signs .... G 405 636-1911
  Oklahoma City *(G-7147)*
Skyslate Signs .... F 405 818-0838
  Oklahoma City *(G-7149)*
Smartsigns LLC .... G 405 659-5003
  Oklahoma City *(G-7152)*
Son Signs Okc .... G 405 830-2536
  Oklahoma City *(G-7160)*
Sonburst Graphics LLC .... G 918 478-8600
  Fort Gibson *(G-3178)*
Sooner Signs .... G 405 503-8902
  Norman *(G-5151)*
Sooner State Graphics & Signs ..... G 405 837-5226
  Oklahoma City *(G-7166)*

SIC SECTION 39 MISCELLANEOUS MANUFACTURING INDUSTRIES

Southland Awards & Signs ....G.... 918 691-9141
Broken Arrow *(G-1056)*
Spraycan Creative LLC ....G.... 405 494-0321
Yukon *(G-11786)*
Srh Lighting LLC ....G.... 405 604-9414
Oklahoma City *(G-7190)*
Stansbury Noble Jr Inc ....G.... 209 847-8408
Tishomingo *(G-8968)*
Stillwater Signs Incorporated ....G.... 405 533-2828
Stillwater *(G-8758)*
Stokely Outdoor Advertising ....E.... 918 664-4724
Tulsa *(G-10852)*
Sublime Signs LLC ....G.... 405 364-1700
Norman *(G-5163)*
Superior Neon Co Inc ....E.... 405 528-5515
Oklahoma City *(G-7229)*
Susan C Willard LLC ....G.... 918 740-4630
Tulsa *(G-10882)*
Tammy Brown ....G.... 918 456-1959
Tahlequah *(G-8887)*
Tcae Enterprises Inc ....G.... 918 664-5977
Tulsa *(G-10908)*
Technology Licensing Corp ....E.... 918 836-5597
Mounds *(G-4625)*
Tfg In-Store Display LLC ....F.... 918 592-2834
Tulsa *(G-10923)*
Thinkwerx LLC ....G.... 405 590-3937
Nichols Hills *(G-4864)*
Tom Bennett Manufacturing ....F.... 405 528-5671
Oklahoma City *(G-7302)*
Tornados Screen Printing ....G.... 405 964-5339
McLoud *(G-4363)*
Trade Mark Signs ....G.... 580 242-7446
Enid *(G-3066)*
Tradeshowstuff LLC ....G.... 918 437-4338
Tulsa *(G-10967)*
Trans-Tech LLC ....F.... 405 422-5000
El Reno *(G-2763)*
Triple DS Neon Signs LLC ....G.... 817 447-2830
Jay *(G-3686)*
Trophies n Things ....G.... 405 247-9771
Anadarko *(G-207)*
Tulsa Sign Company ....G.... 918 215-7131
Tulsa *(G-11008)*
Tulsa Signs ....G.... 918 251-6262
Broken Arrow *(G-1086)*
Twj Inc ....G.... 405 392-4366
Tuttle *(G-11217)*
▲ Tyler Signs LLC ....G.... 405 631-5174
Oklahoma City *(G-7355)*
Ultra Fast Signs ....G.... 405 269-9468
Tulsa *(G-11033)*
US Safetysign & Decal LLC ....F.... 800 678-2529
Tulsa *(G-11057)*
US Signs & Led LLC ....G.... 405 819-3086
Yukon *(G-11799)*
USA Signs Inc ....G.... 918 392-5544
Tulsa *(G-11059)*
Van Horn James ....G.... 405 324-2456
Yukon *(G-11800)*
Vinyl Vikings LLC ....G.... 405 260-9022
Edmond *(G-2673)*
Walker Stamp & Seal Co ....E.... 405 235-5319
Oklahoma City *(G-7415)*
Walkers Sign Company ....G.... 580 353-7446
Lawton *(G-4019)*
▲ Warner Jwly Box Display Co LLC ....D.... 580 536-8885
Lawton *(G-4021)*
Waynoka Sign Shop ....G.... 580 824-1717
Waynoka *(G-11382)*
Whimsical Sign and Crafting Co ....G.... 918 315-4715
Roland *(G-8115)*
Whistler Media Group ....G.... 918 605-7446
Tulsa *(G-11117)*
Whistler Sign Co LLC ....F.... 918 491-7446
Tulsa *(G-11118)*
Whitecaps Inc ....G.... 405 610-7007
Midwest City *(G-4461)*
Wood Concepts Inc ....G.... 918 836-9481
Tulsa *(G-11147)*
Wyatt Earp Companies ....G.... 918 225-7770
Cushing *(G-1972)*
Yesco ....G.... 918 524-9914
Tulsa *(G-11168)*
Z Signs Inc ....F.... 405 670-1416
Oklahoma City *(G-7485)*

3995 Burial Caskets

Fright Casket ....G.... 405 602-1534
Oklahoma City *(G-6119)*
Si Precast Concrete Products ....E.... 918 446-2131
Tulsa *(G-9036)*

3996 Linoleum & Hard Surface Floor Coverings, NEC

Interstate Supply Company ....E.... 405 232-7141
Oklahoma City *(G-6322)*
Interstate Supply Company ....G.... 918 461-0177
Tulsa *(G-10007)*
Solid Rock Custom Flooring ....G.... 918 833-2884
Claremore *(G-1685)*

3999 Manufacturing Industries, NEC

1014 Industries LLC ....G.... 405 831-5351
Guthrie *(G-3295)*
2012 H & H Manufacturing Inc ....G.... 918 747-7563
Tulsa *(G-9057)*
3 D Manufacturing ....G.... 918 224-7717
Sapulpa *(G-8244)*
3I Industries ....G.... 580 788-2122
Elmore City *(G-2893)*
4 B Hunting Industries LLC ....G.... 405 823-9100
Warr Acres *(G-11309)*
4ag Mfg LLC ....G.... 580 821-9300
Elk City *(G-2780)*
A & H Manufacturing ....G.... 918 698-0987
Coweta *(G-1870)*
A Cbd Healthier Life ....G.... 405 585-0353
Shawnee *(G-8426)*
A-1 Industries LLC ....G.... 580 380-2328
Coleman *(G-1792)*
A-Z Manufacturing LLC ....G.... 918 258-2900
Broken Arrow *(G-811)*
Abby Candles Inc ....F.... 405 895-9957
Moore *(G-4483)*
Ace Grinding ....G.... 918 439-4113
Tulsa *(G-9094)*
ADC Quality Mfg ....G.... 918 808-2329
Collinsville *(G-1798)*
Adcp Industries LLC ....G.... 405 330-4728
Oklahoma City *(G-5372)*
Aguevent Industries ....G.... 580 748-0710
Cherokee *(G-1413)*
Ala Industries ....G.... 405 533-3260
Stillwater *(G-8653)*
Alan Industries Online ....G.... 405 787-1102
Oklahoma City *(G-5408)*
Alexco Manufacturing LLC ....G.... 405 274-4003
El Reno *(G-2697)*
Allpro Mfg LLC ....G.... 580 512-7248
Tipton *(G-8957)*
Always Blessed ....G.... 918 592-2200
Tulsa *(G-9159)*
Ambers Candle ....G.... 405 492-3620
Moore *(G-4486)*
American Fiber Industries ....G.... 918 335-6100
Bartlesville *(G-446)*
Amys Candles and Gifts LLC ....G.... 918 865-2827
Terlton *(G-8937)*
Ancile Industries ....G.... 405 990-5018
Moore *(G-4489)*
Anderson Rt Industries LLC ....G.... 918 607-5150
Broken Arrow *(G-828)*
Angel Delite Inc ....G.... 580 223-9777
Ardmore *(G-242)*
Antelope Oil Tool Mfg Co LLC ....G.... 405 691-2490
Oklahoma City *(G-5448)*
Architectural Models ....G.... 405 360-2828
Norman *(G-4913)*
Arrow Alliance Industries LLC ....G.... 540 273-1548
Norman *(G-4917)*
Aruze Gaming America Inc ....G.... 405 301-8140
Oklahoma City *(G-5469)*
Atrue Industries LLC ....G.... 800 782-5440
Lawton *(G-3893)*
Austinn Industries Inc Ncs LLC ....G.... 918 408-2058
Tulsa *(G-9225)*
Auto Way Manufacturing Co LLC ....G.... 405 946-3516
Oklahoma City *(G-5491)*
Axon Industries LLC ....G.... 918 313-8955
Tulsa *(G-9235)*
B & L Industries Inc ....G.... 580 591-1880
Lawton *(G-3895)*
B Brothers Manufacturing LLC ....G.... 918 625-9583
Broken Arrow *(G-840)*
Bangs ....G.... 918 338-2339
Bartlesville *(G-450)*
Barnett James ....G.... 405 833-4052
Choctaw *(G-1528)*
Bear Paw Manufacturing ....G.... 918 637-4775
Wagoner *(G-11275)*
Beaver Creek Industries LLC ....G.... 918 469-2779
Kinta *(G-3834)*
Bells and Whistles ....G.... 405 470-8400
Oklahoma City *(G-5546)*
Berridge Mfg Dist Ctr ....G.... 405 248-7404
Oklahoma City *(G-5557)*
Bill Jones Mfg ....G.... 405 392-4525
Tuttle *(G-11186)*
Biometric Identification Syste ....G.... 405 517-9641
Norman *(G-4934)*
Bisby Candles LLC ....G.... 918 408-5291
Edmond *(G-2322)*
Bkg Industries LLC ....G.... 918 694-3390
Whitefield *(G-11516)*
Black Star Manufacturing LLC ....G.... 405 315-3336
Chandler *(G-1376)*
▲ Blitz USA Inc ....B.... 918 676-3620
Miami *(G-4391)*
Boyer Industries LLC ....G.... 405 310-3015
Norman *(G-4941)*
Bpm LLC ....G.... 405 761-0911
McAlester *(G-4277)*
Brad McKinzie ....G.... 580 355-3810
Lawton *(G-3900)*
Bradley Stephen Brown ....G.... 918 639-1853
Oktaha *(G-7530)*
Brier Creek Furn Works LLC ....G.... 903 327-5602
Kingston *(G-3825)*
Bronco Manufacturing ....G.... 405 225-1909
Oklahoma City *(G-5631)*
Brooks Industries LLC ....G.... 405 305-9316
Oklahoma City *(G-5632)*
Broox Creative Industries LLC ....G.... 918 691-8834
Tulsa *(G-8992)*
Budgget Industries Inc ....G.... 918 272-6255
Owasso *(G-7550)*
Buffalo Industries ....G.... 405 720-2324
Oklahoma City *(G-5639)*
By Him Industries LLC ....G.... 918 406-0593
Jenks *(G-3696)*
C R Manufacturing ....G.... 405 780-7368
Stillwater *(G-8664)*
Cairns Manufacturing Inc ....G.... 405 636-4063
Oklahoma City *(G-5669)*
Calico Industries LLC ....G.... 405 732-0638
Midwest City *(G-4437)*
Camo Galz Candles & More ....G.... 918 399-0044
Mounds *(G-4611)*
Can-Do-Candles ....G.... 580 564-2816
Kingston *(G-3826)*
Candle Electric ....G.... 918 232-0558
Tulsa *(G-9369)*
Candles By ME ....G.... 580 798-5200
Ardmore *(G-263)*
Carters Manufacturing ....G.... 918 437-5428
Tulsa *(G-9384)*
Cbd Everything LLC ....G.... 405 605-5634
Oklahoma City *(G-5715)*
Cbd Farmacy LLC ....G.... 405 697-5245
Edmond *(G-2339)*
Cbd4help LLC ....G.... 405 206-9672
Choctaw *(G-1533)*
Centermass Industries LLC ....G.... 760 485-7405
Edmond *(G-2342)*
CFM Industries LLC ....G.... 405 213-9557
Edmond *(G-2343)*
Cg Distributors ....G.... 918 336-8882
Bartlesville *(G-460)*
Chemtica USA ....G.... 580 366-6799
Durant *(G-2213)*
Clark Creative Industries Inc ....G.... 405 473-8046
Oklahoma City *(G-5774)*
Clark Seals Ltd ....G.... 918 610-1006
Tulsa *(G-9441)*
Claw Manufacturing LLC ....G.... 918 739-4848
Catoosa *(G-1311)*
Clink Industries ....G.... 918 970-6537
Tulsa *(G-9454)*
Cobo Industries LLC ....G.... 918 574-2123
Tulsa *(G-9463)*
Code Red Industries LLC ....G.... 405 227-1552
Shawnee *(G-8439)*
Colt Ferrell Industries LLC ....G.... 580 439-6106
Comanche *(G-1835)*
Columbia Rehabilitation Svcs ....G.... 405 359-2741
Edmond *(G-2360)*
Compton Industries LLC ....G.... 405 496-6269
Yukon *(G-11712)*

Conbraco Industries Inc.......G....... 704 841-6000
Westville *(G-11482)*
Continental Industries.......G....... 918 284-9013
Tulsa *(G-9478)*
Copperhead Industries.......G....... 918 712-9927
Tulsa *(G-9485)*
Core Manufacturing LLC.......G....... 405 747-1980
Stillwater *(G-8670)*
Dakk Mfg LLC.......G....... 405 395-2139
Shawnee *(G-8443)*
Dale Rogers Training Ctr Inc.......E....... 580 481-6170
Altus *(G-153)*
Dale-Co Industries LLC.......G....... 918 864-2041
Pryor *(G-7958)*
Dashskin LLC.......G....... 918 940-8900
Broken Arrow *(G-887)*
David Combs Auto Trim.......G....... 405 799-7330
Oklahoma City *(G-5903)*
Db Unlimited LLC.......G....... 855 437-7766
Tulsa *(G-9563)*
DC Industries.......G....... 405 923-0815
Choctaw *(G-1537)*
Dean Johnson.......G....... 405 947-5736
Oklahoma City *(G-5911)*
Deborah C Montgomery.......G....... 918 527-9375
Collinsville *(G-1809)*
Diamond Game Enterprises.......E....... 405 789-5800
Oklahoma City *(G-5938)*
Diamond P Machine LLC.......G....... 918 396-7192
Skiatook *(G-8540)*
Divine Thumb Industries Inc.......G....... 405 418-7855
Oklahoma City *(G-5953)*
DMS Terms & Conditions.......G....... 580 303-7500
Duncan *(G-2106)*
Domeck Industries Inc.......G....... 260 833-0917
Tulsa *(G-9593)*
Doodlebugs Etc Inc.......G....... 405 525-1248
Oklahoma City *(G-5968)*
DR Cbd.......G....... 832 216-3301
Oklahoma City *(G-5977)*
Drake Manufacturing Inc.......G....... 405 760-5336
Shawnee *(G-8445)*
Drake Manufacturing Inc.......G....... 405 799-8157
Oklahoma City *(G-5287)*
Dreyar Industries LLC.......G....... 405 826-2454
Edmond *(G-2396)*
Duct Mate Industries.......G....... 918 340-5122
Wagoner *(G-11279)*
Duke Manufacturing.......G....... 918 653-3404
Heavener *(G-3428)*
Duncan Mannequin Inc.......G....... 580 252-5915
Duncan *(G-2111)*
▲ **Duncan Manufacturing Inc**.......G....... 580 251-2137
Duncan *(G-2112)*
Dunlap Manufacturing.......G....... 580 237-3434
Enid *(G-2946)*
Eagle Pump & Mfg LLC.......G....... 918 906-1080
Tulsa *(G-9626)*
Eastern Etching & Mfg.......G....... 918 476-6007
Chouteau *(G-1563)*
Eaves Manufacturing Inc.......G....... 580 889-3530
Atoka *(G-409)*
Eco-Bright Industries LLC.......G....... 918 728-1644
Tulsa *(G-9638)*
Edmond Coins Inc.......G....... 405 607-6800
Edmond *(G-2401)*
Element Fleet Corporation.......G....... 405 799-4775
Oklahoma City *(G-5290)*
Elevated Candles.......G....... 405 763-8223
Oklahoma City *(G-6024)*
Elliott Diversified Inds LLC.......G....... 918 293-2218
Tulsa *(G-9660)*
Elysium Industries.......G....... 405 394-3087
Midwest City *(G-4440)*
Enardo Manufacturing Co.......G....... 918 622-6161
Tulsa *(G-9680)*
Enid Cbd Company LLC.......G....... 580 297-5011
Enid *(G-2949)*
Enterprise Manufacturing LLC.......G....... 918 438-4455
Tulsa *(G-9692)*
Et Industries LLC.......G....... 918 485-3374
Wagoner *(G-11283)*
Euphoria Okc Cbd LLC.......G....... 405 412-2448
Oklahoma City *(G-6054)*
Evening Glow Candles.......G....... 918 543-2990
Inola *(G-3658)*
Excel Manufacturing LLC.......G....... 918 418-9589
Vinita *(G-11256)*
F&D Industries LLC.......G....... 918 461-0447
Broken Arrow *(G-904)*

Falcon Mx6 Manufacturing LLC.......G....... 918 647-4433
Poteau *(G-7902)*
Fashion Gear Div.......G....... 405 745-1991
Oklahoma City *(G-6076)*
Fd Products LLC.......G....... 918 698-1644
Vinita *(G-11257)*
Firepro Fire Protection Svc.......G....... 918 857-1513
Broken Arrow *(G-909)*
Flint Industries.......G....... 918 599-7162
Tulsa *(G-9756)*
Floyd Craig Company.......G....... 580 832-2597
Cordell *(G-1859)*
From Heart Candles and More.......G....... 580 334-4104
Woodward *(G-11585)*
Gardners Guns & Mfg LLC.......G....... 580 225-8884
Elk City *(G-2818)*
Garis Industries LLC.......G....... 405 639-0319
Moore *(G-4525)*
Gasoline Alley Classics Inc.......G....... 918 806-1000
Broken Arrow *(G-1128)*
Gold Rule Industries Inc.......G....... 918 682-6500
Muskogee *(G-4681)*
Goodwill Industries of SW.......G....... 580 355-2163
Lawton *(G-3935)*
Gra Enterprises Inc.......G....... 405 848-1300
Oklahoma City *(G-6173)*
Gray Eagle Industries LLC.......G....... 918 230-6652
Claremore *(G-1627)*
Green Industries.......G....... 918 825-1044
Pryor *(G-7964)*
Grey Dog Industries LLC.......G....... 405 926-0967
Edmond *(G-2446)*
Greyfox Industries LLC.......G....... 918 830-1144
Broken Arrow *(G-923)*
GTS Industries LLC.......G....... 918 706-2525
Claremore *(G-1630)*
Gwin Industries Inc.......G....... 405 795-4946
Moore *(G-4526)*
H Rockin Industries Inc.......G....... 479 285-1766
Arkoma *(G-385)*
Hacker Industries LLC.......F....... 918 272-6607
Owasso *(G-7573)*
Hadleys Industries.......G....... 405 743-0337
Stillwater *(G-8697)*
Haiku Candles LLC.......G....... 405 528-5556
Oklahoma City *(G-6202)*
Hail To Wreath.......G....... 405 659-2216
Mustang *(G-4775)*
Hamilton Industries LLC.......G....... 918 357-3862
Broken Arrow *(G-1130)*
Hannah Industries Inc.......G....... 918 430-0743
Tulsa *(G-9887)*
Harden Metalworks LLC.......G....... 405 812-2812
Norman *(G-5017)*
Hargrove Industries Inc.......G....... 918 231-7290
Sand Springs *(G-8189)*
Heavens Scent Candle Factory.......G....... 918 686-0243
Muskogee *(G-4689)*
Hem Mfg.......G....... 918 225-4600
Cushing *(G-1935)*
Hilltop Turf Inc.......G....... 918 486-4482
Coweta *(G-1884)*
Hilti Industries Inc.......G....... 918 251-7788
Broken Arrow *(G-929)*
Hix Industries.......G....... 405 640-6980
Wanette *(G-11305)*
▲ **Hodges Manufacturing**.......G....... 918 629-8723
Sand Springs *(G-8191)*
House Industries LLC.......G....... 405 761-5574
Yukon *(G-11731)*
Hts Manufacturing Corporation.......G....... 918 318-0280
Checotah *(G-1395)*
Hubbard Industries LLC.......G....... 405 388-6798
Oklahoma City *(G-6270)*
Icon Manufacturing LLC.......G....... 903 819-9091
Durant *(G-2237)*
Ikg Industries.......G....... 918 599-8417
Tulsa *(G-9969)*
Industrial Marking Co.......G....... 918 749-8851
Tulsa *(G-9980)*
Inland Manufacturing LLC.......G....... 918 697-4436
Broken Arrow *(G-938)*
Integrated Training & Mfg Tech.......G....... 918 893-2225
Broken Arrow *(G-939)*
Isabels Candles.......G....... 918 595-5358
Tulsa *(G-10013)*
Isbell Industries LLC.......G....... 405 828-7228
Dover *(G-2040)*
Issken Industries Inc.......G....... 405 623-2177
Stillwater *(G-8705)*

J T G Industries LLC.......G....... 405 285-6627
Edmond *(G-2466)*
J&C Industries Inc.......G....... 405 473-7834
Piedmont *(G-7764)*
Jacobson Fabrication Inc.......G....... 918 251-1181
Broken Arrow *(G-941)*
Jaf Industries LLC.......G....... 405 834-8362
Oklahoma City *(G-6345)*
Jay Industries LLC.......G....... 405 404-3242
Midwest City *(G-4444)*
Jedd Industries.......G....... 580 339-1500
Hinton *(G-3530)*
Jester Industries Inc.......G....... 405 919-2013
Oklahoma City *(G-6360)*
Jk Industries Inc.......G....... 405 285-9800
Edmond *(G-2470)*
JM Manufacturing.......G....... 918 261-2816
Broken Arrow *(G-947)*
Jones Power Products LLC.......G....... 405 485-2019
Blanchard *(G-718)*
Jumping Bone LLC.......G....... 918 853-2836
Tulsa *(G-10065)*
Just Bee Candles and More LLC.......G....... 918 557-5145
Chelsea *(G-1406)*
Just Dough It LLC.......G....... 918 455-0770
Broken Arrow *(G-952)*
K & D Manufacturing.......G....... 918 923-6422
Claremore *(G-1648)*
K G Hill Company LLC.......G....... 405 641-4190
Norman *(G-5046)*
K3 Industries LLC.......G....... 205 568-1252
Oklahoma City *(G-5298)*
Karis Gifts.......G....... 405 330-6428
Edmond *(G-2478)*
Kaw Nation Solutions LLC.......G....... 405 365-8900
Kaw City *(G-3759)*
Keepsake Candles Inc.......F....... 918 336-0351
Bartlesville *(G-501)*
Kid Trax.......G....... 405 366-7982
Norman *(G-5051)*
King Cbd Distributing LLC.......G....... 918 698-7118
Bixby *(G-640)*
Kjm Industries LLC.......G....... 405 340-1448
Edmond *(G-2481)*
Kmac Manufacturing LLC.......G....... 918 272-6856
Owasso *(G-7583)*
Kzb Studios LLC.......G....... 918 734-4399
Tulsa *(G-10106)*
L&L Manufacturing.......G....... 405 436-8929
Newalla *(G-4811)*
Lakelife Industries LLC.......G....... 918 618-6201
Eufaula *(G-3104)*
Language Links LLC.......G....... 918 749-7350
Tulsa *(G-10124)*
Lash Amor.......G....... 918 893-2424
Tulsa *(G-10131)*
Last Ditch Industries LLC.......G....... 405 609-2317
Oklahoma City *(G-6454)*
Lasting Impressions Gifts Inc.......G....... 405 732-2401
Oklahoma City *(G-6455)*
Laxson Industries LLC.......G....... 918 494-6677
Tulsa *(G-10138)*
Lda Industries LLC.......G....... 918 315-9758
Sallisaw *(G-8147)*
Littrell Industries LLC.......G....... 405 637-8930
Edmond *(G-2489)*
Lk Cbd LLC.......G....... 405 220-3502
Oklahoma City *(G-6484)*
Lkq Remanufacturing Yukon.......G....... 405 494-4908
Yukon *(G-11742)*
Lux Illume LLC.......G....... 405 618-4552
Moore *(G-4534)*
Mainstream Manufacturing LLC.......G....... 918 447-1008
Tulsa *(G-10203)*
Manufctring Contract Solutions.......G....... 405 229-7639
Moore *(G-4536)*
Maranatha Industries LLC.......G....... 918 336-1221
Bartlesville *(G-508)*
Mardav Industries Co LLC.......G....... 855 248-2220
Oklahoma City *(G-6522)*
Mart Trophy Co Inc.......G....... 918 481-3388
Tulsa *(G-10217)*
Martin House Candle Company.......G....... 580 504-1699
Ardmore *(G-328)*
Martinez Industries LLC.......G....... 405 503-4020
Harrah *(G-3380)*
Matin House Candle Company.......G....... 580 490-6500
Ardmore *(G-329)*
Mbs Manufacturing Inc.......G....... 918 521-6865
Broken Arrow *(G-1142)*

39 MISCELLANEOUS MANUFACTURING INDUSTRIES

McAmis Fur Company .... G 580 323-5961
  Arapaho *(G-225)*
McElroy Manufacturing Inc .... G 918 254-7182
  Broken Arrow *(G-969)*
Medline Industries .... G 405 745-9977
  Oklahoma City *(G-6558)*
Mena Manufacturing .... G 918 955-0518
  Tulsa *(G-10242)*
Metal Goods Manufacturing .... G 918 633-9069
  Tulsa *(G-10245)*
Mfg Unlimited LLC .... G 405 788-9567
  Oklahoma City *(G-6583)*
Mia Bella Candles .... G 918 470-3862
  McAlester *(G-4321)*
Mid America Vending Inc .... G 405 387-4441
  Newcastle *(G-4831)*
Midco Sand Pump Manufacturing .... G 405 824-2620
  Oklahoma City *(G-6595)*
Military Parts Mfg LLC .... G 405 301-2990
  Yukon *(G-11755)*
Mimic Manufacturing LLC .... G 918 653-7161
  Heavener *(G-3430)*
Mobility Living Inc .... G 405 672-7237
  Oklahoma City *(G-6623)*
Mostly Missiles .... G 405 808-4611
  Edmond *(G-2521)*
Mpl Manufacturing LLC .... G 918 630-9944
  Broken Arrow *(G-983)*
Mr Mfg .... G 918 352-4461
  Drumright *(G-2067)*
Mtm Inc .... G 918 824-3700
  Pryor *(G-7977)*
Mulberry Tree Graphics .... G 580 248-3194
  Lawton *(G-3974)*
Mystic Rock Miniatures .... G 817 845-1590
  El Reno *(G-2741)*
Native Cbd Distributing .... G 405 831-5270
  Meeker *(G-4384)*
Native Distributing LLC .... D 405 316-9223
  Norman *(G-5086)*
Native Remedy Cbd LLC .... G 405 285-4050
  Edmond *(G-2530)*
Nenos Homemade Candles LLC .... G 580 367-9874
  Coleman *(G-1797)*
Netpro Industries Inc .... G 918 630-3201
  Broken Arrow *(G-987)*
New U Cbd Oil .... G 405 568-8750
  Yukon *(G-11758)*
▲ Nickles Industries .... G 580 762-9300
  Ponca City *(G-7859)*
Northfork Marine Manufacturing .... G 918 689-9309
  Eufaula *(G-3107)*
Ohana Manufacturing LLC .... G 918 490-9053
  Eufaula *(G-3108)*
Oil Pro Industries .... G 405 323-6988
  Oklahoma City *(G-6718)*
Oiltech Manufacturing Div LLC .... G 918 534-3568
  Bartlesville *(G-514)*
OK Casting .... G 918 648-5300
  Burbank *(G-1215)*
Ok-1 Manufacturing Co .... G 580 482-0891
  Altus *(G-165)*
Okie Dokie Cbd Dispensary LLC .... G 405 454-5040
  Harrah *(G-3382)*
Old Town N Candles Lawton OK .... G 580 678-7608
  Lawton *(G-3978)*
Oliver Industries LLC .... G 405 314-4423
  Norman *(G-5102)*
Onpoint Manufacturing .... G 580 284-5431
  Cashion *(G-1292)*
Orcutt Machine .... G 918 629-7930
  Tulsa *(G-10438)*
Oscium .... G 719 695-0600
  Oklahoma City *(G-6786)*
Ottawa Oak Mfg .... G 918 541-8996
  Wyandotte *(G-11661)*
Outlaw Industries LLC .... G 918 569-7555
  Clayton *(G-1710)*
Paradise Pools & Hot Tubs .... G 918 938-7727
  Tulsa *(G-10465)*
Peak Industries .... G 918 289-0424
  Tulsa *(G-10479)*
Pfi Industries Ltd Co .... G 405 388-0321
  Spencer *(G-8599)*
Pierce Industries Inc .... G 405 923-4201
  Edmond *(G-2569)*
Pj Industries Inc .... G 918 682-8479
  Muskogee *(G-4735)*
Potter Industries .... G 580 775-8580
  Durant *(G-2247)*

Ppm Manufacturing LLC .... G 405 843-4448
  Oklahoma City *(G-6872)*
Precision Industries Ic T .... G 918 833-6072
  Tulsa *(G-10547)*
Prodigy Cbd Company LLC .... G 405 378-2868
  Moore *(G-4557)*
Project 3810 LLC .... G 405 834-7418
  Oklahoma City *(G-6914)*
Protrac Industries LLC .... G 405 312-5122
  Yukon *(G-11769)*
Pure Canna Cbd .... G 405 628-5119
  Oklahoma City *(G-6922)*
R K Manufacturing LLC .... G 405 626-8922
  Tuttle *(G-11209)*
R&C Industries LLC .... G 405 640-7239
  Oklahoma City *(G-6964)*
Racf Industries Inc .... G 918 258-1290
  Broken Arrow *(G-1019)*
Rank Industries LLC .... G 405 308-0503
  Blanchard *(G-730)*
Rbs Pet Products .... G 405 373-0235
  Piedmont *(G-7769)*
RCO Fabrication LLC .... G 918 225-0708
  Cushing *(G-1952)*
RDS Manufacturing .... G 918 251-0369
  Broken Arrow *(G-1026)*
Red Dirt Wreaths & Things .... G 918 809-3973
  Oklahoma City *(G-6984)*
Redbud Candles & Creations .... G 210 749-6975
  Skiatook *(G-8566)*
Redneck Candles and Gifts .... G 405 492-8987
  Lawton *(G-3992)*
Redtail Industries LLC .... G 405 933-6654
  Anadarko *(G-206)*
Rehme Mfg Inc .... F 580 658-2414
  Marlow *(G-4240)*
Rehoboth Robes .... G 918 357-1529
  Broken Arrow *(G-1155)*
Resource Mfg .... G 405 842-0999
  Oklahoma City *(G-7011)*
Rock Creek Wreaths LLC .... G 405 701-3421
  Norman *(G-5133)*
Rohm-Bolster Mfg Co LLC .... G 405 274-6915
  Oklahoma City *(G-7047)*
Royal Toga Industries LLC .... G 405 641-1643
  Broken Arrow *(G-1158)*
Rt Manufacturing Concepts LLC .... G 405 388-3999
  Oklahoma City *(G-5314)*
S&F Welding and Mfg LLC .... G 580 341-0790
  Hobart *(G-3545)*
Saber Industries .... G 405 382-3975
  Oklahoma City *(G-7071)*
Sara Smith Inc .... G 918 272-3076
  Owasso *(G-7613)*
Saunders Industries LLC .... G 405 728-3555
  Oklahoma City *(G-7086)*
SC Candles .... G 469 855-2823
  Owasso *(G-7614)*
Scotts Wldg & Fabrication LLC .... G 580 236-2990
  Broken Bow *(G-1204)*
SDS Industries LLC .... G 918 863-3740
  Tulsa *(G-10719)*
Secret Garden Candle Company .... G 918 497-8699
  Tulsa *(G-10721)*
Sentient Industries Inc .... G 918 770-0770
  Owasso *(G-7616)*
Shades of Color .... G 918 273-0001
  Nowata *(G-5229)*
Shaw Industries Group Inc .... G 405 917-5117
  Oklahoma City *(G-7116)*
Shawn Wreath .... G 580 571-2598
  Sharon *(G-8419)*
Shes Happy Hair Okc LLC .... G 405 328-3464
  Oklahoma City *(G-7122)*
Short Work Industries Inc .... G 580 774-8563
  Weatherford *(G-11441)*
Showtek .... G 405 222-0632
  Chickasha *(G-1510)*
Skyrock Industries LLC .... G 660 525-7482
  Oklahoma City *(G-7148)*
Slow Hand Manufacturing LLC .... G 580 618-0867
  Afton *(G-122)*
Slow Hand Manufacturing L .... G 918 937-3046
  Norman *(G-5148)*
Sooner Pro Assembly .... G 405 838-2838
  Norman *(G-5150)*
Southern Belles Candle Co LLC .... G 405 200-5986
  Luther *(G-4138)*
Southern Breeze Candle Co LLC .... G 918 402-4040
  Tulsa *(G-10798)*

Soy Candle Cottage LLC .... G 405 519-6827
  Jones *(G-3752)*
Spark Something Candles LLC .... G 405 872-5673
  Norman *(G-5153)*
Spiral Waves Industries LLC .... G 405 481-7685
  Shawnee *(G-8503)*
Ssec .... G 405 321-0916
  Norman *(G-5154)*
Ssg Inc .... G 405 639-2056
  Moore *(G-4574)*
Starfall Llc .... G 918 269-4364
  Coweta *(G-1898)*
Streater Industries LLC .... G 918 346-3247
  Oologah *(G-7536)*
Stroup Industries LLC .... G 405 737-4170
  Midwest City *(G-4457)*
Studio 180 .... G 405 512-2404
  Midwest City *(G-4458)*
Sub Industries LLC .... G 918 798-9712
  Elk City *(G-2879)*
Superior Steel Bldg Mfg LLC .... G 918 689-9745
  Eufaula *(G-3116)*
Susan Secor .... G 580 510-0060
  Lawton *(G-4008)*
Sweet Scent Candle .... G 918 535-3423
  Ochelata *(G-5240)*
Swift Winds Industries LLC .... G 405 600-9112
  Oklahoma City *(G-7237)*
Talking Hands Puppets .... G 918 868-5553
  Colcord *(G-1790)*
Taptec Manufacturing LLC .... G 580 467-5142
  Marlow *(G-4244)*
Tefi Tek Industries LLC .... G 918 728-7381
  Tulsa *(G-10917)*
Ten Mfg LLC .... G 405 381-3752
  Tuttle *(G-11215)*
Texas Aluminum Industries .... G 405 677-6767
  Oklahoma City *(G-7277)*
Texoma Mfg LLC .... G 580 920-0878
  Durant *(G-2265)*
Therapy For Dogs Inc .... G 405 314-7655
  Oklahoma City *(G-7278)*
Thermtech Industries LLC .... G 918 299-5473
  Tulsa *(G-10927)*
Thomas Energy Systems Inc .... E 918 665-0031
  Tulsa *(G-10930)*
Thunder Cbd LLC .... G 405 568-7235
  Edmond *(G-2641)*
Thunderbolt Machine Services .... G 918 357-2294
  Broken Arrow *(G-1172)*
Tj Trost LLC .... G 918 269-1582
  Coweta *(G-1900)*
Tom McBride Manufacturing .... G 580 239-9020
  Caney *(G-1264)*
Trb Industries LLC .... G 405 990-4159
  Choctaw *(G-1556)*
Trend To Trend Wreaths .... G 405 503-8992
  Blanchard *(G-738)*
Trinity Industries Inc .... G 405 629-1213
  Oklahoma City *(G-7334)*
Triple H Industries LLC .... G 405 201-8820
  Sulphur *(G-8845)*
Tulsa Centerless Bar Proc Inc .... E 918 438-0000
  Tulsa *(G-10992)*
Tulsa Industrial Mfg LLC .... G 918 640-3802
  Owasso *(G-7628)*
Two Candle Guys LLC .... G 918 271-5244
  Tulsa *(G-11025)*
Uncommon Touch .... G 580 276-9936
  Marietta *(G-4217)*
Up N Smoke III .... G 405 609-1702
  Oklahoma City *(G-7373)*
US Rod Manufacturing LLC .... G 636 359-9947
  Oklahoma City *(G-7375)*
Valor Industries LLC .... G 580 301-3805
  Piedmont *(G-7773)*
Venture Industries Inc .... G 918 557-8789
  Broken Arrow *(G-1091)*
Verde Industries LLC .... G 405 413-5599
  Oklahoma City *(G-7398)*
Vision Motorsports .... G 918 260-4981
  Tulsa *(G-11081)*
Waid Group Inc .... G 817 980-8985
  Medicine Park *(G-4373)*
Warrior Industries Inc .... G 918 227-3500
  Sapulpa *(G-8323)*
Wax and Hive Candle Lc .... G 918 542-6432
  Miami *(G-4436)*
Weldpro Manufacturing LLC .... G 918 724-3862
  Tulsa *(G-11106)*

Westfall Industries Inc..........G....... 520 744-2330
Arcadia *(G-232)*
Whit Industries..........G....... 405 343-1181
Ada *(G-106)*
White Shell LLC..........G....... 918 978-2767
Broken Arrow *(G-1177)*
Wichita Industries..........G....... 405 933-2162
Anadarko *(G-209)*
Wilkinson Mfg Co..........G....... 918 258-8282
Broken Arrow *(G-1097)*
Willow Creek Co LLC..........G....... 580 239-9549
Atoka *(G-427)*
Wilsdorf Manufacturing LLC..........G....... 918 369-5824
Broken Arrow *(G-1098)*
Wink Eyelash Salon..........G....... 918 949-6299
Tulsa *(G-11139)*
Withers Manufacturing Inc..........F....... 918 994-7787
Tulsa *(G-11142)*
Workhorse Industries LLC..........G....... 405 884-2023
Geary *(G-3218)*
World Weidner LLC..........G....... 580 765-9999
Ponca City *(G-7888)*
Ws Mfg LLC..........G....... 918 443-2773
Oologah *(G-7537)*
Yona Mfg Solutions LLC..........G....... 918 698-9713
Claremore *(G-1707)*
Zedco LLC..........G....... 918 521-7587
Tulsa *(G-11174)*
Zero Hour Industries Inc..........G....... 918 685-0235
Gore *(G-3253)*

73 BUSINESS SERVICES

7372 Prepackaged Software

5 Over Games LLC..........G....... 405 928-5972
Oklahoma City *(G-5336)*
Actualizing Apps LLC..........G....... 918 627-7450
Tulsa *(G-9099)*
Adjacent Creations LLC..........G....... 405 819-6507
Oklahoma City *(G-5374)*
Adtek Software Company..........G....... 815 452-2345
Oklahoma City *(G-5376)*
Advanced Micro Solutions Inc..........F....... 405 562-0112
Edmond *(G-2290)*
Al Capone Limo Corp..........G....... 405 999-3335
Oklahoma City *(G-5405)*
Aloft Software LLC..........G....... 405 633-0250
Oklahoma City *(G-5423)*
American Bank Systems Inc..........E....... 405 607-7000
Oklahoma City *(G-5432)*
Ameriinfovets Inc..........G....... 408 446-4343
Pryor *(G-7943)*
App-Solute Innovations LLC..........G....... 580 453-0055
Ada *(G-10)*
Arrowhead Software..........G....... 918 744-7239
Tulsa *(G-9213)*
At A Glance Software LLC..........G....... 405 601-3062
Oklahoma City *(G-5479)*
Axiom Automotive Tech Inc..........G....... 909 841-8200
Oklahoma City *(G-5498)*
Birddog Software Corporation..........F....... 405 794-5950
Oklahoma City *(G-5576)*
Boolean Inc..........G....... 405 341-1499
Edmond *(G-2330)*
Bottomline LLC..........G....... 918 261-2354
Tulsa *(G-9324)*
Buckelew Accnting Slutions LLC..........G....... 405 359-5887
Edmond *(G-2334)*
Businet..........F....... 918 858-4440
Tulsa *(G-9352)*
Byrum Enterprises Inc..........G....... 812 595-4598
Oklahoma City *(G-5653)*
Canvass LLC..........G....... 580 284-7896
Blanchard *(G-704)*
Catalog System Inc..........G....... 405 808-1533
Moore *(G-4507)*
Chorus Labs LLC..........G....... 405 317-2942
Oklahoma City *(G-5763)*
Christy Collins Inc..........G....... 580 305-0001
Frederick *(G-3192)*
Chrysalis Software Inc..........E....... 831 761-1307
Tulsa *(G-9423)*
Clearbay Software LLC..........G....... 405 310-9150
Norman *(G-4960)*
Compound Software LLC..........G....... 405 912-3301
Moore *(G-4509)*
Computer Assistance..........G....... 405 399-2422
Jones *(G-3743)*
Computer Technology Soltn..........G....... 918 607-2136
Broken Arrow *(G-873)*
Corona Technical Services LLC..........G....... 918 398-8052
Tulsa *(G-9490)*
Creditpoint Software LLC..........E....... 918 376-9440
Tulsa *(G-9506)*
Cura Telehealth Wellness LLC..........F....... 918 513-1062
Tulsa *(G-9523)*
Custom Software Systems Inc..........G....... 405 524-1919
Oklahoma City *(G-5875)*
Cynergy Software Corp LLC..........G....... 405 603-2953
Warr Acres *(G-11317)*
Data Systems Consultants..........G....... 405 445-0886
Oklahoma City *(G-5899)*
DCA Inc..........E....... 918 225-0346
Cushing *(G-1929)*
Delenda LLC..........G....... 918 409-1313
Owasso *(G-7561)*
Dick Hall & Associates..........G....... 405 202-4301
Norman *(G-4979)*
Digii ID LLC..........G....... 405 662-5504
Oklahoma City *(G-5946)*
Digital Doctor..........G....... 405 618-1416
Oklahoma City *(G-5947)*
Discoversoft Development LLC..........G....... 405 840-1235
Nichols Hills *(G-4859)*
Eagle Applctions Solutions Ltd..........G....... 888 511-8720
Oklahoma City *(G-5994)*
Ecapitol LLC..........G....... 405 524-2833
Oklahoma City *(G-6003)*
Ellis Enterprises Inc..........G....... 405 917-5336
Oklahoma City *(G-6027)*
Equivaq Software LLC..........G....... 405 742-0598
Stillwater *(G-8687)*
Eufrates Com LLC..........G....... 918 280-9270
Tulsa *(G-9704)*
Fjsp Inc..........G....... 405 306-0735
Oklahoma City *(G-6087)*
Genesis Financial Software..........G....... 580 252-2594
Duncan *(G-2120)*
Genesis Technologies Inc..........G....... 918 307-0098
Tulsa *(G-9818)*
Global Interface Solutions Inc..........G....... 918 971-1600
Tulsa *(G-9832)*
Goldtechs Inc..........G....... 918 856-9059
Bartlesville *(G-487)*
Hampton Software Development L..........G....... 918 607-5307
Broken Arrow *(G-926)*
Hands Down Software..........G....... 405 844-6314
Oklahoma City *(G-6212)*
High Rollers Empire LLC..........G....... 405 535-3066
Oklahoma City *(G-6248)*
Idealist Software LLC..........G....... 918 609-4364
Bixby *(G-634)*
IMS Erp Software LLC..........G....... 918 508-9544
Tulsa *(G-9975)*
Info-Sharp LLC..........G....... 520 204-5093
Norman *(G-5033)*
Innocative Computing Tech..........G....... 405 255-4453
Oklahoma City *(G-6306)*
Integrated S Mycare..........G....... 405 605-0546
Oklahoma City *(G-6314)*
Intellevue Ltd..........G....... 918 250-5561
Tulsa *(G-10001)*
International Sftwr Cons Inc..........G....... 580 924-1231
Durant *(G-2239)*
Jack Henry & Associates Inc..........F....... 405 947-6644
Oklahoma City *(G-6341)*
Jade Fire LLC..........G....... 405 295-7734
El Reno *(G-2728)*
Jansens Software..........G....... 405 692-4756
Oklahoma City *(G-5297)*
Jbr Software Development LLC..........G....... 405 872-8561
Choctaw *(G-1548)*
Jireh Software Inc..........G....... 918 294-8240
Broken Arrow *(G-945)*
Jmz Software LLC..........G....... 580 284-9551
Lawton *(G-3945)*
Juniper Networks Inc..........D....... 918 877-2642
Tulsa *(G-10066)*
Keystone Flex Admnstrators LLC..........G....... 405 285-1144
Oklahoma City *(G-6412)*
Lightbe Corporation..........G....... 918 760-6968
Tulsa *(G-10160)*
Lm Software Inc..........G....... 405 630-4663
Edmond *(G-2490)*
Martek Inc..........G....... 918 543-6477
Inola *(G-3667)*
Masters Technical Advisors Inc..........G....... 918 949-1641
Tulsa *(G-10221)*
Med-Solve LLC..........F....... 918 684-4030
Muskogee *(G-4710)*
Medexperts LLC..........F....... 918 684-4030
Muskogee *(G-4711)*
Medunison LLC..........E....... 405 271-9900
Oklahoma City *(G-6560)*
Mere Software Inc..........G....... 918 740-5018
Tulsa *(G-9020)*
Mesh Networks LLC..........G....... 832 230-8074
Oklahoma City *(G-6570)*
Microsoft Corporation..........D....... 469 775-6864
Tulsa *(G-10256)*
Monroe Gray LLC..........G....... 918 813-6588
Bixby *(G-646)*
New Vision Consulting Group..........F....... 405 796-7400
Edmond *(G-2537)*
New X Drives Inc..........F....... 918 850-4463
Tulsa *(G-10338)*
Nextthought LLC..........E....... 405 673-5588
Norman *(G-5092)*
Norman Computers..........F....... 405 292-9501
Norman *(G-5094)*
Northeast Tchnlgy Ctr- Clrmore..........E....... 918 342-8066
Claremore *(G-1663)*
Omni Lighting..........G....... 918 633-7245
Tulsa *(G-10417)*
Openlink Financial LLC..........D....... 918 594-7320
Tulsa *(G-10433)*
Paycom Software Inc..........D....... 405 722-6900
Oklahoma City *(G-6813)*
PC Net..........G....... 405 238-2001
Pauls Valley *(G-7670)*
Perfecting Software LLC..........G....... 918 250-7610
Tulsa *(G-10493)*
Perk Dynamics LLC..........G....... 405 585-2520
Asher *(G-394)*
Permian Software LLC..........G....... 405 329-6397
Norman *(G-5113)*
Phoenix Software Intl Inc..........G....... 918 491-6144
Tulsa *(G-10510)*
Pinnacle Business Systems Inc..........E....... 405 359-0121
Edmond *(G-2571)*
Pivot Medical Solutions LLC..........G....... 918 684-4030
Muskogee *(G-4734)*
Point To Point Software..........G....... 405 869-9921
Oklahoma City *(G-6861)*
Post Software International..........G....... 918 299-2158
Tulsa *(G-10535)*
Professional Datasolutions Inc..........E....... 512 218-0463
Tulsa *(G-10567)*
Quantum Trading Technologies..........G....... 918 876-3921
Bartlesville *(G-520)*
Quest Loot LLC..........G....... 405 609-4100
Edmond *(G-2580)*
Rapid Jack Solutions Inc..........G....... 405 203-3131
Norman *(G-5129)*
Ray Computer Services Intl Inc..........G....... 918 299-7262
Jenks *(G-3725)*
Rcs Corporation..........G....... 918 227-7497
Tulsa *(G-10625)*
Red River Software LLC..........G....... 405 728-8102
Oklahoma City *(G-6989)*
Red Wind Training..........G....... 918 822-0605
Park Hill *(G-7646)*
Resource Development Co LLC..........E....... 248 646-2300
Tulsa *(G-10645)*
Riggs Heinrich Media Inc..........E....... 918 492-0660
Tulsa *(G-10652)*
S4f Inc..........G....... 888 390-2224
Broken Arrow *(G-1159)*
Saltus Technologies LLC..........F....... 918 392-3900
Tulsa *(G-10690)*
Schoolware Inc..........G....... 580 745-9100
Durant *(G-2255)*
Seamless LLC..........G....... 918 743-7935
Tulsa *(G-10720)*
Seaport Software Inc..........G....... 918 258-8611
Broken Arrow *(G-1047)*
Secureagent Software Inc..........E....... 918 971-1600
Tulsa *(G-10722)*
Sequoyah Technologies LLC..........F....... 918 808-7270
Sapulpa *(G-8310)*
Shane Lee Duvall..........G....... 918 960-0506
Broken Arrow *(G-1163)*
Shave Software LLC..........G....... 405 366-2168
Norman *(G-5144)*
Shi International Corp..........G....... 918 583-4182
Tulsa *(G-10745)*
Shipzen Inc..........G....... 949 357-2127
Tulsa *(G-10748)*
Siemens Industry Software Inc..........G....... 918 505-4220
Tulsa *(G-10753)*

SIC SECTION

76 MISCELLANEOUS REPAIR SERVICES

Silvertree Solutions LLC ....G...... 405 922-7281 Yukon *(G-11783)*	A1 Quality Welding ....G...... 405 373-0066 Piedmont *(G-7752)*	Bills Welding Equipment Repr ....F...... 405 232-4799 Oklahoma City *(G-5568)*
Smartmax Software Inc ....E...... 918 388-5900 Tulsa *(G-10777)*	Able Welding ....G...... 405 760-1442 Edmond *(G-2288)*	Bison Welding LLC ....G...... 580 758-3359 Bison *(G-607)*
Software Perfection LLC ....G...... 918 266-8883 Broken Arrow *(G-1166)*	Absolute Welding Inc ....G...... 918 923-7300 Oologah *(G-7532)*	Bluearc Welding LLC ....G...... 405 341-0629 Claremore *(G-1598)*
Solutionware Ltd ....E...... 405 843-0809 Oklahoma City *(G-7159)*	Accurate Fence Contruction LLC ....G...... 580 591-3717 Lawton *(G-3884)*	Boatright Enterprises Inc ....G...... 405 612-2473 Vinita *(G-11249)*
Srifusion LLC ....G...... 774 238-7466 Lawton *(G-4003)*	Ace 1 Welding and Insptn LLC ....G...... 405 408-5370 Mustang *(G-4760)*	Bob Albauer Portable Welding ....G...... 405 789-7999 Oklahoma City *(G-5599)*
Starling Assoc Inc ....G...... 405 740-8668 Norman *(G-5156)*	Ace Welding and Mechanical LLC ....G...... 405 219-1490 Oklahoma City *(G-5365)*	Bob G Welding ....G...... 918 510-4769 Pawnee *(G-7702)*
Stonebridge Acquisition Inc ....D...... 918 663-8000 Tulsa *(G-10853)*	Acme Custom Welding ....G...... 405 288-0187 Washington *(G-11332)*	Bobby L Graham ....G...... 580 393-2247 Sentinel *(G-8410)*
Studylamp Software LLC ....G...... 918 357-1946 Broken Arrow *(G-1168)*	Action Machine Shop ....G...... 918 245-8308 Sand Springs *(G-8157)*	Bost Welding and Fabrication ....G...... 918 649-1289 Poteau *(G-7897)*
T A H Software Systems ....G...... 405 478-3962 Oklahoma City *(G-7241)*	Aero Tech Welding ....G...... 918 764-9675 Tulsa *(G-9115)*	Boyd Welding Inc ....G...... 918 485-3534 Wagoner *(G-11278)*
Taylor Accounting Systems ....G...... 405 949-9898 Oklahoma City *(G-7256)*	Ainsworth Welding ....G...... 580 512-7874 Fletcher *(G-3160)*	Bradley Welding & Machine ....G...... 580 223-2250 Ardmore *(G-260)*
Telos Payment Processing LLC ....G...... 405 321-0474 Norman *(G-5172)*	Alan Davis ....G...... 580 651-9961 Guymon *(G-3344)*	Brents Welding LLC ....G...... 918 413-1318 Pocola *(G-7781)*
Tire Soft LLC ....G...... 405 341-5070 Edmond *(G-2644)*	All Day Welding & Fabrication ....G...... 405 550-2233 El Reno *(G-2698)*	Brian Ringels ....G...... 580 927-6144 Coalgate *(G-1776)*
Tmw Systems Inc ....G...... 405 602-6055 Oklahoma City *(G-7298)*	Allens Trucking & Welding Svc ....G...... 405 341-8066 Arcadia *(G-227)*	Brians Welding and Fabrication ....G...... 405 412-7878 Norman *(G-4942)*
Top Rim Technology ....G...... 918 467-3617 Delaware *(G-2009)*	Allens Welding Service ....G...... 580 584-2375 Broken Bow *(G-1182)*	Brooks Custom Welding LLC ....G...... 580 343-2253 Corn *(G-1866)*
Trackum Inc ....G...... 405 799-4863 Norman *(G-5179)*	Always Welding ....G...... 918 426-9353 McAlester *(G-4269)*	Brother Built Welding ....G...... 918 385-1767 Hodgen *(G-3548)*
Transelearn ....G...... 405 922-4595 Oklahoma City *(G-7317)*	Ambrose Welding LLC ....G...... 580 704-0356 Elgin *(G-2774)*	Bruce Burdick Welding ....G...... 580 774-2906 Weatherford *(G-11395)*
True North Ministries Inc ....G...... 405 562-2986 Edmond *(G-2654)*	Anchor Auto & Welding Repr LLC ....G...... 918 426-7662 McAlester *(G-4270)*	Buckys Welding ....G...... 918 339-4187 Canadian *(G-1260)*
Tuxpro Software & Development ....G...... 405 812-1334 Norman *(G-5183)*	Anderson Welding ....G...... 580 355-9806 Lawton *(G-3888)*	Bull Dog Welding ....G...... 405 412-8199 Oklahoma City *(G-5644)*
Utown LLC ....G...... 918 261-3402 Tulsa *(G-11062)*	Andrews Welding ....G...... 405 990-7326 Oklahoma City *(G-5444)*	Burlington Welding LLC ....G...... 580 596-3381 Cherokee *(G-1415)*
Veritris Group Inc ....G...... 580 713-4927 Oklahoma City *(G-7399)*	Andy Anderson Metal Works Inc ....F...... 918 245-2355 Sand Springs *(G-8161)*	Burnam Welding ....G...... 580 821-0311 Elk City *(G-2789)*
Virtuoso Software LLC ....G...... 918 813-4941 Tulsa *(G-11080)*	Angel Welding Service LLC ....G...... 918 706-2237 Broken Arrow *(G-829)*	Bws Wlding Fabrictíon Svcs LLC ....G...... 918 789-3094 Chelsea *(G-1403)*
Warning Aware LLC ....G...... 405 300-8833 Edmond *(G-2681)*	Ansiels Welding & Constructio ....G...... 580 920-0573 Durant *(G-2202)*	Byfield Welding ....G...... 918 333-8100 Bartlesville *(G-459)*
Webready Software Inc ....G...... 918 808-8465 Broken Arrow *(G-1093)*	API Metallurgical ....G...... 918 266-4130 Catoosa *(G-1298)*	C & C Welding & Construction ....G...... 405 769-4924 Oklahoma City *(G-5656)*
Whiteboard Software LLC ....G...... 405 408-3326 Edmond *(G-2688)*	Apollo Metal Specialties Inc ....F...... 918 341-7650 Claremore *(G-1583)*	C & H Safety Pin Inc ....G...... 405 949-5843 Newalla *(G-4806)*
Wk Winters & Assoc ....G...... 405 341-6571 Edmond *(G-2691)*	ARC-Angel Welding ....G...... 918 838-0047 Tulsa *(G-9203)*	C V West LLC ....G...... 623 363-3529 Guthrie *(G-3305)*
Wolf Software Group Co ....G...... 405 721-0577 Warr Acres *(G-11331)*	Ares West Welding LLC ....G...... 405 534-6707 Moore *(G-4494)*	C&S Marine LLC ....G...... 918 429-2758 Indianola *(G-3651)*
Young Software ....G...... 918 290-9876 Sparks *(G-8590)*	Arthur Craig ....G...... 580 488-3398 Butler *(G-1220)*	C&S Welding & Fabrication Inc ....G...... 918 282-4122 Mannford *(G-4176)*

76 MISCELLANEOUS REPAIR SERVICES

7692 Welding Repair

3 Rivers Wldg Fabrication LLC ....G...... 918 589-2300 Jay *(G-3677)*	Atoka Welding & Fabrication ....G...... 580 889-2534 Atoka *(G-398)*	Caliber Welding Inc ....G...... 918 486-1388 Coweta *(G-1873)*
33 - Welding Company ....G...... 405 375-4468 Kingfisher *(G-3783)*	Atwood Wldg Cstm Fbrcation LLC ....G...... 918 617-7522 Eufaula *(G-3097)*	Canary Customs ....G...... 405 293-6429 Guthrie *(G-3307)*
3r Welding ....G...... 918 839-8945 Hartshorne *(G-3389)*	B&T Welding Services LLC ....G...... 580 326-4760 Hugo *(G-3602)*	Canyon Welding Service Inc ....G...... 580 371-8805 Tishomingo *(G-8964)*
4 M Welding Services Inc ....G...... 580 298-9809 Antlers *(G-212)*	B-Mac Welding Service ....G...... 918 370-0921 Broken Arrow *(G-1112)*	Capes Custom Welding & Fabrica ....G...... 918 453-0594 Tahlequah *(G-8855)*
405 Welding ....G...... 405 413-5764 Newcastle *(G-4818)*	Bach Welding & Diesel Service ....G...... 580 593-2599 Custer City *(G-1973)*	Castle Wldg & Fabrication LLC ....G...... 580 747-0218 Enid *(G-2925)*
4m Welding Inc ....G...... 405 484-7293 Pauls Valley *(G-7648)*	Backwoods Welding Inc ....G...... 405 642-5199 Maysville *(G-4254)*	Cerdafied Welding LLC ....G...... 405 578-8035 Yukon *(G-11704)*
4v Welding and Dozer LLC ....G...... 580 371-6524 Mill Creek *(G-4466)*	Bailey S Mike Welding Inc ....G...... 405 574-4489 Ninnekah *(G-4867)*	CH Mufflers & Welding LLC ....G...... 405 380-3877 Earlsboro *(G-2279)*
5r Services ....G...... 580 370-0222 Perry *(G-7725)*	Baileys Welding & Machine LLC ....F...... 405 224-6611 Chickasha *(G-1438)*	Charles Tigert Welding Sh ....G...... 580 889-3558 Atoka *(G-402)*
7b Custom Welding Fabrication ....G...... 918 850-1066 Tulsa *(G-9059)*	Baker Welding Mfg Co ....G...... 405 376-6017 Mustang *(G-4764)*	Charles Weathers Welding ....G...... 405 341-2413 Edmond *(G-2346)*
A & A Welding ....G...... 918 772-0418 Park Hill *(G-7639)*	Barnes Welding LLC ....G...... 580 774-5491 Watonga *(G-11341)*	Charlies Welding ....G...... 580 467-2266 Comanche *(G-1834)*
A & Y Enterprises Inc ....G...... 405 360-0307 Norman *(G-4894)*	▲ Barrett Performance Aircraft ....G...... 918 835-1089 Tulsa *(G-9266)*	Chc Welding LLC ....G...... 405 706-3367 Norman *(G-4955)*
A and L Welding Services LLC ....G...... 918 649-7538 Wister *(G-11547)*	Beaver Fabrication Inc ....G...... 405 360-0014 Norman *(G-4928)*	Cherokee Welding Industries ....G...... 918 247-6122 Kellyville *(G-3761)*
A T S Welding Service ....G...... 405 452-5979 Wetumka *(G-11489)*	Benchmark Completions LLC ....F...... 405 691-5659 Oklahoma City *(G-5550)*	Chris Green Greens Construct ....G...... 405 207-0690 Pauls Valley *(G-7653)*
A W Pool Inc ....G...... 580 323-3454 Clinton *(G-1735)*	Berry Holdings LP ....G...... 918 582-3461 Tulsa *(G-9285)*	Christians Welding Service ....G...... 580 674-3384 Dill City *(G-2034)*
A-Accurate Welding Inc ....G...... 918 838-1111 Tulsa *(G-9074)*	Bethel Welding Metal Building ....G...... 918 367-5776 Bristow *(G-765)*	Circle A Welding LLC ....G...... 580 890-9617 Weatherford *(G-11401)*
	BF Brandt Welding LLC ....G...... 405 657-4670 Oklahoma City *(G-5561)*	Cisper Welding ....G...... 405 665-2599 Wynnewood *(G-11665)*
	Big G Precision Welding ....G...... 918 406-2876 Tulsa *(G-9291)*	Cisper Welding Inc ....G...... 918 543-2321 Inola *(G-3654)*
	Bill Stockton Welding LLC ....G...... 918 697-7750 Chelsea *(G-1402)*	Cisper Welding of Oklahoma ....G...... 918 543-7755 Inola *(G-3655)*

Employee Codes: A=Over 500 employees, B=251-500
C=101-250, D=51-100, E=20-50, F=10-19, G=1-9

Clints Portable Welding G 405 834-4517
Oklahoma City *(G-5789)*

Clyde Welding Service G 405 222-1364
Ninnekah *(G-4868)*

CMS Welding & Fabrication G 918 676-3133
Fairland *(G-3123)*

Confederite Welding LLC G 918 407-1635
Bristow *(G-773)*

Connie Pirple G 405 375-4468
Kingfisher *(G-3792)*

Cooks Contact Welding Inc G 405 373-0059
Piedmont *(G-7758)*

Cornerstone Welding G 918 387-2538
Yale *(G-11681)*

Crane Machinery Repair G 918 349-2264
Pawhuska *(G-7683)*

Cris Choate Welding Inc G 405 853-2792
Hennessey *(G-3455)*

Ctm Welding & Fabrication LLC G 405 408-4628
Yale *(G-11682)*

Custom Metal Works G 918 231-4151
Pryor *(G-7956)*

Cwg Welding Services LLC G 580 819-1045
Weatherford *(G-11403)*

D & D Stud Welding LLC Proj G 888 965-4155
Cartwright *(G-1282)*

▲**D I V C O Inc** E 918 836-9101
Tulsa *(G-9538)*

D J Welding G 405 386-4620
Choctaw *(G-1536)*

D&P Welding Corp G 405 624-0170
Glencoe *(G-3220)*

D-A Welding & Fab LLC G 580 641-1189
Marlow *(G-4227)*

Daddy Russ Customs & Wldg LLC G 405 623-9709
Cashion *(G-1287)*

Damar Manufacturing Co Inc E 918 445-2445
Tulsa *(G-9549)*

Dandelion Welding and Fabg LLC G 405 431-8138
Oklahoma City *(G-5894)*

Darnell Services G 918 542-9236
Miami *(G-4394)*

Darrell Lewis G 405 867-5768
Maysville *(G-4257)*

Davenports Welding G 918 855-9593
Broken Arrow *(G-1121)*

Daves Welding & Dock Svc LLC G 918 773-5179
Vian *(G-11239)*

Daves Welding LLC G 580 938-2707
Shattuck *(G-8421)*

David Adkinson G 580 623-7301
Watonga *(G-11344)*

David D Kuykendall G 918 223-5055
Ripley *(G-8100)*

David Dollar G 580 965-4155
Cartwright *(G-1283)*

David Kelso Welding G 405 630-7108
Edmond *(G-2382)*

David Piatt G 405 542-6974
Lookeba *(G-4128)*

Davis Welding & Fab G 405 779-5330
Ninnekah *(G-4869)*

Davis Welding Dock Serv G 918 457-4071
Cookson *(G-1849)*

Daytons Trailer Hitch Inc G 918 744-0341
Tulsa *(G-9562)*

Deans Machine & Welding Inc G 580 688-3374
Hollis *(G-3564)*

Dennis Roberts Welding G 405 672-8285
Oklahoma City *(G-5923)*

Dennis Welding G 580 658-5669
Marlow *(G-4228)*

DH Welding LLC G 918 906-6534
Yale *(G-11684)*

Diamond Welding Mfg G 580 889-7767
Atoka *(G-407)*

Dieco Manufacturing Inc D 918 438-2193
Tulsa *(G-9581)*

Diversfied Wldg Fbrication LLC F 405 802-5487
Moore *(G-4517)*

Dixon & Sons Inc G 918 256-7455
Vinita *(G-11253)*

Dixon Auto Engine Machine Shop G 918 256-6780
Vinita *(G-11254)*

DK Machine Inc G 918 251-1034
Broken Arrow *(G-890)*

Don Bateman Shtmtl Fabrication G 918 224-0567
Sapulpa *(G-8267)*

Donerite Welding G 918 304-9594
Beggs *(G-551)*

Dosher Kennon G 580 667-5708
Tipton *(G-8959)*

Double Diamnd Wldg Fabrication G 580 445-4524
Hobart *(G-3542)*

Double H Farms Inc G 918 486-7635
Coweta *(G-1880)*

Double H Welding G 918 653-2289
Heavener *(G-3427)*

Driskills Welding G 580 233-3093
Enid *(G-2944)*

Driver & Son Welding Shop G 580 323-1714
Clinton *(G-1749)*

Drp Welding Met Buildings LLC G 405 344-6582
Alex *(G-131)*

Dry Fabrication and Welding E 580 735-2958
Buffalo *(G-1212)*

DS Welding G 580 623-4104
Fay *(G-3156)*

Dudes Welding & Etc LLC G 405 510-4786
Spencer *(G-8594)*

Durnal Construction LLC G 405 413-5458
Perkins *(G-7716)*

Dutton Welding & Construc G 918 420-5688
Bache *(G-431)*

E & E Construction Company G 918 775-6222
Sallisaw *(G-8144)*

E F L Inc D 918 665-7799
Tulsa *(G-9621)*

E-Saw Wldg & Fabrication LLC F 580 772-2448
Weatherford *(G-11407)*

Eagles Nest Welding G 405 639-8650
Oklahoma City *(G-5997)*

Eastern Okla Fabrication Inc G 918 654-7344
Cameron *(G-1257)*

Eddie Brown F 580 889-1506
Atoka *(G-411)*

Eddie Johnsons Wldg & Mch Co F 580 856-3418
Ratliff City *(G-8051)*

Eddie Ward G 405 848-3283
Oklahoma City *(G-6009)*

Elliott Precision Products Inc E 918 234-4001
Tulsa *(G-9661)*

Ellis Welding G 580 856-3907
Ratliff City *(G-8052)*

Eulitt Welding G 918 542-2635
Miami *(G-4402)*

Evans & Assoc Utility Svcs G 580 351-1800
Lawton *(G-3924)*

Evans Welding LLC G 580 470-8111
Duncan *(G-2116)*

Everetts Welding & Repair G 580 995-4942
Vici *(G-11242)*

Everything Welding & Safety In G 405 701-3711
Norman *(G-4994)*

Excalibur Welding Service LLC G 580 302-2570
Weatherford *(G-11412)*

Fab Tech Welding G 405 649-2322
Mulhall *(G-4638)*

Ferguson Welding LLC G 405 534-1517
Tuttle *(G-11199)*

Fg Welding G 405 863-8210
Oklahoma City *(G-6083)*

Fisher Welding G 580 748-0445
Enid *(G-2958)*

Fitzs Welding LLC G 405 371-1167
Mustang *(G-4771)*

Flores Welding Services LLC G 405 473-5534
Yukon *(G-11725)*

Fm2t Welding LLC G 405 837-8495
Norman *(G-5003)*

Foster Jl Welding LLC G 405 686-6090
Oklahoma City *(G-6108)*

Four Winds Field Services LLC G 918 568-1143
Eufaula *(G-3102)*

Friends Welding G 918 482-1544
Broken Arrow *(G-1127)*

Froman Wldg U0026 Fbrction Inc G 918 798-1050
Claremore *(G-1624)*

G E C Enterprises G 405 740-9365
Oklahoma City *(G-6131)*

G T Bynum Company G 918 587-9118
Tulsa *(G-9794)*

Garrison Welding G 918 331-6336
Foraker *(G-3168)*

Gary Cobb Welding LLC G 580 983-2499
Crawford *(G-1905)*

Garys Welding Inc G 918 688-2058
Broken Arrow *(G-916)*

Geralds Welding Fabrication F 405 222-5510
Chickasha *(G-1462)*

Geralds Welding 2 G 405 224-8510
Ninnekah *(G-4871)*

Giblet Welding LLC G 580 751-0104
Cordell *(G-1860)*

Gilmore Welding & Tractor Svc G 918 479-6224
Locust Grove *(G-4108)*

Glenn Hamil G 918 396-3659
Skiatook *(G-8545)*

Glenn Schlarb Welding G 580 327-3832
Alva *(G-182)*

Glenn Tool Inc D 405 787-1400
Oklahoma City *(G-6157)*

Goliath Pipeline and Cnstr LLC G 512 917-9313
Norman *(G-5008)*

Gregs Wldg & Backhoe Svc Inc F 405 222-1004
Chickasha *(G-1464)*

Grunewald Welding LLC G 580 256-2674
Woodward *(G-11589)*

Gs Specialties G 918 230-1295
Inola *(G-3660)*

Gws Welding Inc G 918 527-5776
Coweta *(G-1883)*

H & H Specialty Welding LLC G 479 322-1125
El Reno *(G-2722)*

H&H Specialty Welding G 479 252-1991
Mustang *(G-4774)*

H/H Mobile Welding LLC G 405 830-5525
Yukon *(G-11729)*

Harper Welding Design LLC G 405 396-8558
Arcadia *(G-230)*

Harpers Welding G 580 298-7165
Antlers *(G-216)*

Hart Brothers Welding G 918 697-5682
Collinsville *(G-1812)*

Hartins Welding G 580 795-5594
Madill *(G-4149)*

Hathaway & Simpson G 580 875-3177
Walters *(G-11301)*

Hayden Betchan Welding LLC G 580 863-5372
Garber *(G-3214)*

Haynes Welding Service Inc G 337 380-7126
Bethany *(G-581)*

Hays Welding & Blacksmith G 580 287-3458
Willow *(G-11530)*

HCf Welding Services G 918 907-4274
Tulsa *(G-9906)*

Heirston Welding & Cnstr G 580 657-2518
Wilson *(G-11535)*

Henrys Welding and Fab LLC G 918 535-2264
Ochelata *(G-5235)*

Hickmans Welding G 918 966-3783
Keota *(G-3772)*

Higgins Welding G 580 231-9211
Enid *(G-2971)*

Hnt Welding & Machine G 405 348-8249
Edmond *(G-2456)*

Holman Manufacturing F 918 479-5861
Locust Grove *(G-4109)*

Hoppers Welding G 918 885-6978
Hominy *(G-3587)*

Hot Rod Welding and Mech LLC G 918 754-2548
Red Oak *(G-8077)*

Hotrod Welding G 580 229-0888
Healdton *(G-3415)*

Hunts Welding Service LLC G 806 339-4591
Cushing *(G-1937)*

Hurley Welding LLC G 405 224-7332
Amber *(G-196)*

Hutson Welding Services LLC G 918 470-3673
Kiowa *(G-3838)*

Hws Hamilton Welding Svc LLC G 580 889-1725
Atoka *(G-413)*

Ideal Machine & Welding Inc G 918 352-3660
Drumright *(G-2062)*

◆**Ideal Specialty Inc** F 918 834-1657
Tulsa *(G-9967)*

Ideas Manufacturing Inc G 405 691-5525
Oklahoma City *(G-5296)*

Independence Race Works & Fabg G 918 489-2353
Gore *(G-3250)*

Industrial Enterprise Inc F 918 476-5907
Chouteau *(G-1567)*

Industrial Machine Co Inc F 405 236-5419
Oklahoma City *(G-6299)*

Industrial Pping Companies LLC D 918 825-0900
Pryor *(G-7970)*

Inland Machine & Welding Co E 405 670-4355
Oklahoma City *(G-6305)*

Inman Welding Service G 918 323-0022
Vinita *(G-11262)*

Company	Code	Phone
Iron Cowboy Welding LLC	G	580 301-3423
Lawton (G-3942)		
Iron Cowboy Welding LLC	G	580 335-2900
Frederick (G-3194)		
Iron Images	G	918 685-1514
Muskogee (G-4694)		
Ironman Welding & Mfg LLC	G	580 464-3478
Chickasha (G-1472)		
Ironman Welding Machine	G	580 791-3091
Fay (G-3157)		
Ivers Welding and Machine Shop	G	580 765-4882
Ponca City (G-7838)		
J & C Welding Co Inc	G	405 263-4967
Okarche (G-5243)		
J & M Welding	E	918 216-2090
Tulsa (G-9015)		
J B Welding	G	918 574-1806
Bartlesville (G-499)		
J Bs Welding Inc	F	580 332-6194
Ada (G-52)		
J C Sheet Metal	G	580 688-9527
Hollis (G-3566)		
J Fletcher Derrell	G	580 673-2489
Healdton (G-3416)		
J M Welding	G	918 277-4480
Sapulpa (G-8281)		
J Marrs Welding	G	918 396-2221
Skiatook (G-8552)		
J S Welding	G	405 364-1362
Norman (G-5039)		
J T Welding	G	580 504-3862
Ardmore (G-309)		
Jack Chartier Welding LLC	G	918 486-2347
Coweta (G-1888)		
Jackson Welding & Machine	G	580 472-3631
Canute (G-1268)		
Janning Welding and Supply LLC	F	580 225-6554
Elk City (G-2831)		
Jason A Bliss	G	580 304-9432
Shidler (G-8528)		
Jay Hickman Welding Inc	G	405 205-7136
Guthrie (G-3319)		
JB Fabrication	G	580 716-7524
Kaw City (G-3758)		
Jed Welding and Fabrication	G	405 420-9062
Noble (G-4883)		
Jeff Parson Welding	G	405 483-5770
Okarche (G-5244)		
Jerry Ellis	G	580 223-5649
Ardmore (G-314)		
Jerry Woods Portable Welding	G	918 272-6424
Owasso (G-7580)		
JG Welding LLC	G	405 301-3126
Tecumseh (G-8920)		
Jims Welding Service	G	405 853-4522
Hennessey (G-3469)		
Joel Bumpus	G	580 237-5305
Enid (G-2987)		
John Kennedy Welding LLC	G	580 227-2300
Fairview (G-3138)		
John Lankford	G	918 855-4417
Owasso (G-7581)		
John Patrick Raymond	G	580 481-0869
Altus (G-159)		
John Samut-Tagliaferro	G	580 284-6058
Fletcher (G-3163)		
John Ward Welding	G	580 673-2127
Healdton (G-3417)		
Johnny Blaylock	G	918 639-5951
Broken Arrow (G-949)		
Johnson Welding	G	580 569-2231
Mountain Park (G-4626)		
Jones Spclty Wldg Fbrction LLC	G	918 486-6740
Coweta (G-1889)		
Jordan Welding & Fabrication	G	918 346-7243
Claremore (G-1646)		
JP Welding	G	405 714-0232
Morrison (G-4604)		
JP Welding Fabrication	G	580 724-9104
Morrison (G-4605)		
JV Industrial Companies Ltd	G	918 591-5450
Tulsa (G-10068)		
K & J Welding LLC	G	580 541-2200
Enid (G-2990)		
K B Machine & Welding Inc	G	405 375-5888
Kingfisher (G-3803)		
K C Welding & Machine Corp	G	918 336-4560
Bartlesville (G-500)		
K G Machine	G	918 789-2228
Chelsea (G-1407)		
K-H Machine Shop	G	918 273-1058
Nowata (G-5218)		
KCR Welding Inc	G	405 619-0068
Oklahoma City (G-6403)		
Kelley Shepard Welding	G	580 234-3280
Enid (G-2994)		
Kelleys Welding Service Inc	G	405 691-5515
Oklahoma City (G-5299)		
Kelly Blake Welding Inc	G	405 756-0868
Lindsay (G-4070)		
Kenneth Petermann	G	405 372-0111
Stillwater (G-8710)		
Key Welding Inc	G	580 995-4278
Vici (G-11244)		
Kilgore Welding Inc	G	405 872-9677
Lexington (G-4037)		
▲ Kirby - Smith Machinery Inc	C	888 861-0219
Oklahoma City (G-6425)		
Kirkpatrick Welding	G	918 865-2672
Mannford (G-4184)		
Knape Fabrication & Wldg LLC	G	580 564-3107
Kingston (G-3829)		
Koda Welding LLC	G	405 443-9800
Norman (G-5053)		
Koda Welding LLC	G	405 565-1867
Noble (G-4884)		
Kremlin Welding & Fabrication	G	580 874-2522
Kremlin (G-3853)		
Kuykendall Welding LLC	G	405 905-0389
Chickasha (G-1480)		
Kwp Welding & Fabrication LLC	G	580 471-7238
Altus (G-161)		
L & C Ventures LLC	G	405 793-9353
Norman (G-5054)		
L & J Welding & Machine Svc	G	918 885-6666
Hominy (G-3591)		
L & K Seed & Manufacturing Co	G	405 663-2758
Hydro (G-3632)		
L & L Welding Inc	G	405 631-4939
Oklahoma City (G-6438)		
L & M Welding LLC	G	918 534-6864
Dewey (G-2027)		
Laird Welding LLC	G	580 995-4495
Vici (G-11245)		
Lance Easley	G	405 269-1415
Perkins (G-7719)		
Lanes Welding LLC	G	580 302-1279
Elk City (G-2836)		
Larry Bobs Welding LLC	G	405 672-7224
Del City (G-1999)		
Larry Wilcoxson	G	580 327-2110
Alva (G-185)		
Larrys Welding Service	G	918 267-4091
Bristow (G-788)		
Larrys Welding Service	G	918 432-5787
Kiowa (G-3840)		
Lawrence Welding LLC	G	580 272-3294
Ada (G-58)		
Lawton Machine & Welding Works	G	580 355-4678
Lawton (G-3956)		
Lays Custom Welding LLC	G	918 766-5227
Bartlesville (G-505)		
Lazy B Welding and Met Art LLC	G	580 512-8778
Lawton (G-3963)		
Ledets Welding Service Inc	G	405 610-2299
Oklahoma City (G-6463)		
Leviathan Inc	G	580 227-3105
Fairview (G-3141)		
Linley Welding LLC	G	405 420-5968
Elk City (G-2839)		
Lonewlf Welding	G	918 625-9128
Tulsa (G-10178)		
Longbreak Welding Service Inc	G	918 223-5976
Cushing (G-1943)		
Lonnie Williams	G	918 253-4650
Eucha (G-3094)		
Lucas Metal Works Inc	F	918 535-2726
Ochelata (G-5237)		
▲ Luckinbill Inc	D	580 233-2026
Enid (G-3000)		
Lynns Welding LLC	G	580 488-3587
Leedey (G-4029)		
M D Spoonemore Welding	G	580 233-9596
Enid (G-3003)		
M S Welding Fabrication	G	405 368-7451
Hennessey (G-3475)		
M W Machining and Welding Inc	G	918 543-8431
Inola (G-3665)		
M&M Custom Welding	G	918 231-0829
Broken Arrow (G-1139)		
Mac Machine	G	405 238-7280
Pauls Valley (G-7666)		
Mack Smotherman	G	580 526-3088
Erick (G-3088)		
Mader Welding	G	580 658-3593
Marlow (G-4235)		
Madron Welding Service	G	405 257-6161
Wewoka (G-11503)		
Maese Welding Service Llc	G	405 606-4619
Oklahoma City (G-6516)		
Mahurin General Repair LLC	G	918 676-3855
Fairland (G-3126)		
Mainline Industries	G	
Minco (G-4477)		
Mar Welding LLC	G	580 747-9967
Yukon (G-11746)		
Marcum Welding Service	G	405 485-9340
Blanchard (G-721)		
Mark Condit	G	580 656-8028
Duncan (G-2152)		
Mark Hendrix Welding LLC	G	580 657-3716
Ardmore (G-327)		
Martin Jacob Welding LLC	G	580 747-1031
Enid (G-3008)		
Martin Welding Service Inc	G	405 623-5361
Hinton (G-3532)		
Marty Watley	G	580 492-4859
Elgin (G-2777)		
Mc Iron Blacksmithing & Wldg	G	405 613-5215
Stillwater (G-8722)		
McCartney Welding LLC	G	580 542-2564
Lahoma (G-3858)		
McCrary Welding Inc	G	620 200-4733
Weatherford (G-11426)		
McCrays Manufacturing Co	G	918 426-1691
McAlester (G-4319)		
McCutchen Enterprises Inc	G	918 234-7406
Tulsa (G-10231)		
McElroys Welding Services LLC	G	405 354-2019
Yukon (G-11751)		
McKinneys Custom Welding & Fab	G	405 341-6559
Edmond (G-2508)		
McLendon Welding Llc	G	580 304-5187
Enid (G-3011)		
McMillian Welding LLC	G	918 521-6886
Claremore (G-1653)		
Mefford 4 Welding Inc	G	918 773-6326
Sallisaw (G-8148)		
Merrells Welding & Orna Ir	G	405 321-7733
Norman (G-5073)		
Metal Fab Inc	G	580 762-2421
Ponca City (G-7850)		
MG Welding LLC	G	405 365-6416
Norman (G-5074)		
Midway Machine & Welding LLC	G	918 968-3316
Stroud (G-8812)		
Midwest Welders	G	918 456-5981
Tahlequah (G-8874)		
Mike Deeds Welding LLC	G	580 863-2339
Garber (G-3215)		
Mike Macdowell Welding	G	405 354-1221
Yukon (G-11754)		
Mike S Welding	G	918 381-0273
Tulsa (G-10278)		
Mikes Welding	G	918 455-7227
Broken Arrow (G-975)		
Mikes Welding Service	G	405 387-3782
Blanchard (G-724)		
Milton Donaghey	G	580 332-1551
Ada (G-66)		
Mitchell T Widler	G	501 860-3738
Burneyville (G-1217)		
Mjs Fence Welding	G	580 320-1620
Ada (G-67)		
Mlb Portable Welding LLC	G	918 531-2414
Copan (G-1851)		
Morris Welding	G	580 486-3474
Chickasha (G-1490)		
Morton Grinding Works	G	918 652-8550
Henryetta (G-3513)		
Moss Welding LLC	G	580 216-1605
Vici (G-11246)		
Musick Welding LLC	G	405 274-1766
Chickasha (G-1491)		
Myers Metalkraft LLC	G	405 657-2084
Edmond (G-2525)		
Myers Welding LLC	G	405 277-3202
Luther (G-4136)		
Myskey Welding	G	918 371-4906
Collinsville (G-1818)		

Employee Codes: A=Over 500 employees, B=251-500, C=101-250, D=51-100, E=20-50, F=10-19, G=1-9

Nabors Welding & Supplies Inc............G....... 405 756-8198
Lindsay (G-4075)
Nbs Fabrication............G....... 918 527-5211
Chouteau (G-1568)
Nipps Welding............G....... 580 668-2915
Wilson (G-11541)
Norman Koehn............G....... 580 852-3260
Helena (G-3436)
North Welding and Construction............G....... 580 526-3260
Erick (G-3090)
Northwest Welding Inc............G....... 405 621-0201
Warr Acres (G-11325)
O K Plunger Service............G....... 918 352-4269
Drumright (G-2068)
Oakes Wldg & Fabrication LLC............G....... 918 865-2356
Mannford (G-4189)
OEM Welding LLC............G....... 918 645-8483
Sand Springs (G-8211)
Ogdens Welding Service............G....... 405 380-7649
Seminole (G-8390)
OK Machine and Mfg Co Inc............E....... 918 838-1300
Tulsa (G-10390)
Okie Newts Welding............G....... 580 564-4724
Kingston (G-3830)
Oklahoma School of Welding............G....... 405 672-1841
Del City (G-2004)
Old Town Welding Shop............G....... 918 423-8506
McAlester (G-4326)
On Site Welding & Fabrication............G....... 918 706-3339
Broken Arrow (G-1147)
Outwest Welding Services LLC............G....... 918 593-2345
Strang (G-8803)
P & L Welding and Fabrication............G....... 660 563-1775
Norman (G-5106)
Page Tool & Machine Shop............G....... 918 775-6766
Sallisaw (G-8150)
Pak Electric Inc............F....... 580 482-1757
Altus (G-166)
Palin Welding Service LLC............G....... 405 449-3541
Wayne (G-11368)
Parkers Welding Custom Work............G....... 405 341-3344
Edmond (G-2564)
Parsons Welding Inc............G....... 405 263-7495
Okarche (G-5249)
Patriot Wldg & Fabrication LLC............G....... 918 600-7147
Broken Arrow (G-999)
Patten Equipment & Welding LLC............G....... 580 334-7035
Woodward (G-11618)
Paul G Pennington Industries............G....... 405 392-2317
Blanchard (G-726)
Pearce Quinton Weld............G....... 918 559-3026
Nowata (G-5226)
Pennington Industries............G....... 405 392-2317
Newcastle (G-4835)
Perks Welding LLC............G....... 405 853-6848
Hennessey (G-3479)
Phelps Machine & Fabrication............F....... 580 662-2465
Ringling (G-8081)
Pioneer Metal & Land Svcs LLC............G....... 405 612-3575
Glencoe (G-3226)
Pioneer Precision Machine Shop............F....... 580 233-1670
Enid (G-3036)
Piping Enterprise Company Inc............B....... 918 246-7326
Sand Springs (G-8214)
Platinum Cross Welding Inc............G....... 918 623-9130
Okemah (G-5274)
Precision Mfg & Design............E....... 918 782-2723
Langley (G-3874)
Precision Welding Mfg............G....... 405 872-3530
Noble (G-4888)
Price Welding and Supply............G....... 580 668-3057
Lone Grove (G-4119)
Pritchards Welding Service............G....... 405 514-2360
Ninnekah (G-4873)
Pro Fab Welding Inc............G....... 405 470-8776
Elk City (G-2862)
Profab Welding Inc............G....... 580 488-2020
Leedey (G-4030)
R & L Mechanics & Welding............G....... 918 253-4734
Jay (G-3685)
R & W Machine Shop Inc............G....... 405 632-4020
Oklahoma City (G-6958)
R A D Welding (2)............G....... 405 206-9434
Meeker (G-4386)
Rafter H Bar Welding Svc LLC............G....... 918 210-0175
Coweta (G-1895)
Ram Machine Inc............G....... 918 224-8028
Tulsa (G-10613)
Rate My Welder............G....... 405 400-0109
Oklahoma City (G-6973)
Rays Portable Welding............G....... 405 282-3218
Guthrie (G-3335)
RC Welding & Fab LLC............G....... 580 216-1274
Oklahoma City (G-6977)
Rcw Welding Services LLC............G....... 918 852-4775
Broken Arrow (G-1153)
Red Line Welding and Services............G....... 580 591-3162
Lawton (G-3991)
Redding Welding LLC............G....... 580 883-4683
Ringwood (G-8091)
Richard Vallejos Welding Ser............G....... 405 688-0804
Oklahoma City (G-7018)
Richard Welding............G....... 405 459-6717
Pocasset (G-7778)
Richards Welding Service LLC............G....... 580 584-2831
Hugo (G-3620)
Rick Leaming Construction LLC............G....... 580 362-2262
Newkirk (G-4852)
Ricks Welding............G....... 580 470-8111
Duncan (G-2168)
Rjc Welding LLC............G....... 580 281-0516
Temple (G-8934)
Robinson Welding LLC............G....... 580 278-9363
Enid (G-3049)
Robs Welding LLC............G....... 405 596-4906
Yukon (G-11772)
Rocking C Welding LLC............G....... 405 589-8903
Yukon (G-11773)
Rocking H Welding LLC............G....... 918 966-3882
Keota (G-3773)
Rod Wiederstein............G....... 580 938-2998
Shattuck (G-8424)
Rodney Brooks Welding LLC............G....... 405 663-2256
Hydro (G-3634)
Roff Iron & Sales Inc............E....... 580 456-7850
Roff (G-8110)
Roger Magerus............G....... 405 364-7231
Norman (G-5134)
Rohlman Welding Service Inc............G....... 405 420-4033
Warr Acres (G-11328)
Rons Welding Shop............G....... 405 352-4331
Minco (G-4479)
Rotert Weld & Fab LLC............G....... 918 671-2170
Tulsa (G-10674)
Russells Welding Inc............G....... 918 245-7395
Tulsa (G-10682)
Rustys Welding & Repair............G....... 580 526-3611
Erick (G-3092)
S & S Welding LLC............G....... 405 496-1452
Hinton (G-3536)
▲ S & T Mfg Co............E....... 918 234-4151
Tulsa (G-10684)
S&W Welding and Fabrication............G....... 918 219-2565
Medford (G-4369)
S-T Magi............G....... 918 358-2312
Cleveland (G-1733)
Sam S Welding............G....... 580 470-5725
Comanche (G-1845)
Sandra Crow............G....... 580 588-2321
Apache (G-222)
Sands Weld and Fab Inc............G....... 918 419-2222
Tulsa (G-10705)
Sasco Inc............F....... 405 670-3230
Oklahoma City (G-7085)
SE Oklahoma School of Welding............G....... 918 423-9353
McAlester (G-4334)
Seiger Welding LLC............G....... 405 853-7237
Hennessey (G-3484)
Seminole Machine Co............G....... 405 382-0444
Seminole (G-8399)
Sewells Machine & Welding............G....... 580 423-7004
Texhoma (G-8939)
SF Welding and Boring LLC............G....... 405 831-8602
Norman (G-5142)
Shane Bralwey Welding LLC............G....... 936 201-9072
Oklahoma City (G-7114)
Shockey Welding LLC............G....... 405 473-1783
Moore (G-4567)
Sigman Welding............G....... 405 596-3035
Tecumseh (G-8929)
Silhouette Shop............G....... 918 257-6143
Fairland (G-3129)
Silver ARC Welding Inc............G....... 580 234-2209
Enid (G-3057)
Slavin Welding Services LLC............G....... 806 217-0429
Woodward (G-11632)
Smith Welding Co............G....... 580 335-7521
Frederick (G-3201)
Smith Welding Fabg & Repr............G....... 918 446-2293
Tulsa (G-10779)
Spencer Machine Works LLC............G....... 580 332-1551
Ada (G-91)
Stand By Personnel............G....... 918 582-0522
Tulsa (G-10834)
Standard Machine LLC............G....... 918 423-9430
McAlester (G-4338)
Stansberry Welding Inc............G....... 580 621-3211
Freedom (G-3209)
Steel Welding Inc............G....... 405 789-5713
Oklahoma City (G-7200)
Stephen Burns............G....... 580 657-3237
Wilson (G-11543)
Stout Welding LLC............G....... 580 254-2139
Woodward (G-11634)
Stouts Welding............G....... 580 243-9116
Canute (G-1271)
Stouts Welding LLC............G....... 580 339-8047
Elk City (G-2878)
Strike An ARC Wldg Fbrction LL............G....... 918 407-7964
Claremore (G-1688)
Sullivan Welding............G....... 405 301-6034
Oklahoma City (G-7222)
Summer Couch Welding LLC............G....... 405 408-3675
Moore (G-4575)
Sundance Welding Inc............G....... 918 627-4065
Tulsa (G-10872)
Superior Companies Inc............D....... 918 534-0755
Dewey (G-2033)
Superior Welding............G....... 918 439-9332
Tulsa (G-10879)
Superior Welding & Fabrication............G....... 580 641-0634
Rush Springs (G-8126)
Swink Welding LLC............G....... 405 294-0114
Norman (G-5167)
Szabo Szabi............G....... 918 697-5441
Muskogee (G-4751)
T J Construction............G....... 580 494-6500
Broken Bow (G-1209)
T&B Welding LLC............G....... 918 253-4120
Eucha (G-3096)
Taff Welding LLC............G....... 580 678-8978
Rush Springs (G-8127)
Teals Welding Inc............G....... 405 756-0615
Blanchard (G-737)
Ted Branham Welding............G....... 918 275-4431
Nowata (G-5231)
Texoma Millwright and Wldg Inc............F....... 580 931-9368
Durant (G-2266)
Thomas Welding............G....... 918 214-7657
Bartlesville (G-532)
Thomass Welding............G....... 580 821-0843
Hammon (G-3372)
Thompson Services............E....... 580 256-5005
Woodward (G-11642)
Tonys Welding............G....... 405 996-6657
Edmond (G-2650)
Toro Welding Inc............G....... 580 334-8221
Woodward (G-11643)
Town & Country Welding LLC............G....... 405 664-5361
Harrah (G-3387)
Triple T Welding............G....... 918 449-0037
Broken Arrow (G-1173)
Troutman Enterprises LLC............G....... 405 351-0665
Rush Springs (G-8129)
Trunch Bull Service LLC............F....... 580 468-1501
Guymon (G-3369)
Tsb Welding LLC............G....... 405 485-4274
Blanchard (G-740)
Tsm Industrial Welding............G....... 720 290-4431
Skiatook (G-8572)
Turn & Burn Welding Inc............G....... 918 543-7224
Inola (G-3675)
Turnair............G....... 918 267-3535
Sand Springs (G-8233)
Turner Welding Inc............F....... 405 224-3867
Amber (G-197)
Twisted Okie Welding LLC............G....... 580 335-1494
Lawton (G-4015)
Ty Slemp Dakota............G....... 405 933-2078
Gracemont (G-3254)
Universal Welding Service............G....... 918 455-3241
Broken Arrow (G-1088)
USA Energy Fabrication LLC............G....... 918 445-4792
Tulsa (G-9047)
V5 Contracting LLC............G....... 918 720-4675
Claremore (G-1699)
Vann Metal Products Inc............G....... 918 341-0469
Claremore (G-1701)
VB Welding LLC............G....... 918 695-0258
Tulsa (G-11068)

76 MISCELLANEOUS REPAIR SERVICES

Verser Welding Service ....G....... 405 352-5048
  Minco *(G-4482)*
Vision Fabrications LLC ....G....... 580 304-2444
  Ponca City *(G-7886)*
Vm Welding LLC ....G....... 405 245-2833
  Oklahoma City *(G-5322)*
Von Troutman Timothy ....G....... 580 583-7004
  Rush Springs *(G-8130)*
W&W Enterprises ....G....... 580 434-2736
  Colbert *(G-1787)*
Warren West ....G....... 580 838-2173
  Hendrix *(G-3441)*
Washingtons Welding LLC ....G....... 918 336-2111
  Bartlesville *(G-534)*
Washita Wldg & Fabrication LLC ....G....... 405 779-0140
  Chickasha *(G-1523)*
Wasinger Wasinger ....G....... 580 335-3490
  Frederick *(G-3203)*
▲ Watonga Machine & Steel Works ....G....... 580 623-5830
  Watonga *(G-11352)*
Wayne Burt Machine ....G....... 918 786-4415
  Grove *(G-3293)*
Weatherford Machine Works ....G....... 580 772-5287
  Weatherford *(G-11457)*
Weeks Welding LLC ....G....... 918 931-1167
  Enid *(G-3077)*
Weins Machine Co Inc ....F....... 918 865-2187
  Terlton *(G-8938)*
Welding Industry Services LLC ....G....... 580 479-7068
  Waukomis *(G-11361)*
Welding Shop ....G....... 580 832-5545
  Cordell *(G-1864)*
Western Welding ....G....... 580 832-2985
  Rocky *(G-8106)*
Wheelers Welding LLC ....G....... 918 246-3811
  Sand Springs *(G-8242)*
Whites Welding ....G....... 405 942-7070
  Oklahoma City *(G-7447)*
Whorton Welding ....G....... 405 610-6545
  Choctaw *(G-1557)*
Whorton Welding Inc ....G....... 405 664-7123
  Oklahoma City *(G-7449)*
Wildcat Welding LLC ....G....... 405 714-2473
  Morrison *(G-4606)*
Williams Ranch Welding LLC ....G....... 405 509-0289
  Boley *(G-756)*
Willys Fabricating & Wldg LLC ....G....... 405 250-1250
  Oklahoma City *(G-7456)*
Wilson Welding Works LLC ....F....... 580 338-7345
  Guymon *(G-3371)*

Wishon Welding LLC ....G....... 405 808-4673
  Oklahoma City *(G-7461)*
Wj Welding LLC ....G....... 580 465-4120
  Marietta *(G-4219)*
Woodall Welding ....G....... 405 736-0599
  Midwest City *(G-4462)*
Wooten Welding ....G....... 918 655-6981
  Wister *(G-11551)*
Work Horse Welding LLC ....G....... 918 530-5270
  Pryor *(G-7999)*
Wrights Machine Shop ....G....... 580 363-1740
  Blackwell *(G-695)*
Wyers Welding ....G....... 580 854-6277
  Oklahoma City *(G-7477)*
Xs Welding Company LLC ....G....... 918 346-2550
  Claremore *(G-1706)*
Yt Welding LLC ....G....... 580 799-1984
  Elk City *(G-2891)*
Zr Welding LLC ....G....... 405 602-4164
  Lexington *(G-4041)*

7694 Armature Rewinding Shops

All State Electric Motors Inc ....G....... 405 232-1129
  Oklahoma City *(G-5413)*
All State Electric Motors Inc ....G....... 918 683-6581
  Muskogee *(G-4645)*
B & B Electric Co ....G....... 918 583-6274
  Tulsa *(G-9239)*
Bartosh Electric Motor Center ....G....... 405 567-2840
  Prague *(G-7920)*
Blevins Oilfield Sls & Svc LLC ....F....... 405 619-9909
  Oklahoma City *(G-5592)*
Britton Electric Motor Inc ....G....... 405 842-8357
  Oklahoma City *(G-5629)*
Brooken Boat & Motor ....G....... 918 799-5227
  Stigler *(G-8630)*
Built Right Compressor ....G....... 580 371-2007
  Tishomingo *(G-8963)*
Capitol Electric Mtr Repr Inc ....F....... 405 235-9638
  Oklahoma City *(G-5693)*
Cecils Electric Motor Co ....G....... 918 775-3968
  Sallisaw *(G-8141)*
Doug Roberson ....G....... 405 372-2078
  Stillwater *(G-8677)*
Electric Motor Service Company ....G....... 580 223-8940
  Ardmore *(G-283)*
Enid Electric Motor Svc Inc ....F....... 580 234-8622
  Enid *(G-2952)*
Evans Enterprises ....F....... 918 587-1566
  Tulsa *(G-9705)*

Evans Enterprises Inc ....E....... 918 587-1566
  Tulsa *(G-9706)*
Evans Enterprises Inc ....G....... 918 825-2200
  Tulsa *(G-9707)*
Interstate Electric Corp ....G....... 918 245-4508
  Sand Springs *(G-8194)*
J & W Electric Motor Company ....G....... 580 357-7504
  Lawton *(G-3943)*
Johnson Service Company ....G....... 918 869-7147
  Fort Gibson *(G-3175)*
Kay Electric Motors Inc ....G....... 580 256-3254
  Woodward *(G-11598)*
Land & Lake Electric LLC ....G....... 918 791-1731
  Grove *(G-3278)*
Meyer Electric Motor Service ....G....... 580 327-1399
  Alva *(G-187)*
Miami Armature Works Inc ....G....... 918 542-2443
  Miami *(G-4413)*
Newmans Electric Motor Repair ....G....... 580 310-0151
  Ada *(G-71)*
Pak Electric Inc ....F....... 580 482-1757
  Altus *(G-166)*
Profab ....G....... 918 486-4464
  Coweta *(G-1894)*
Q E M Inc ....G....... 918 534-2000
  Ochelata *(G-5238)*
S & H Electric Motor Service ....G....... 580 924-3514
  Durant *(G-2254)*
Shawns Small Eng Eqp Repr LLC ....G....... 918 734-1565
  Tulsa *(G-10740)*
Southwest Electric Co ....F....... 918 437-9494
  Tulsa *(G-10805)*
Start Rite Auto Electric Inc ....G....... 580 924-7290
  Durant *(G-2261)*
Szabo Szabi ....G....... 918 697-5441
  Muskogee *(G-4751)*
Tank & Fuel Solutions LLC ....G....... 918 960-4361
  Claremore *(G-1691)*
Tonys Electric Inc ....G....... 405 375-4103
  Kingfisher *(G-3818)*
Tux Hard Shop ....G....... 918 885-2970
  Hominy *(G-3594)*
Victors Electric Motor S ....G....... 405 344-7339
  Blanchard *(G-743)*
W & W Electric Motor Service ....G....... 405 634-3776
  Oklahoma City *(G-7408)*
Wilson Electric Motor Svc Inc ....F....... 405 636-1515
  Oklahoma City *(G-7458)*

ALPHABETIC SECTION

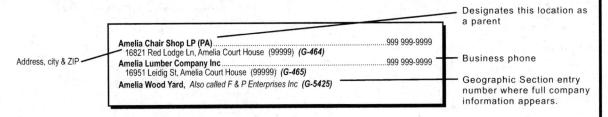

- Designates this location as a parent
- Address, city & ZIP
- Business phone
- Geographic Section entry number where full company information appears.

See footnotes for symbols and codes identification.

* Companies listed alphabetically.
* Complete physical or mailing address.

---

007 Operating LLC 580 467-2744
1098 Sheppard Rd Sulphur (73086) *(G-8826)*

1 800 Radiator 405 946-9800
4055 Nw 3rd St Oklahoma City (73107) *(G-5326)*

1014 Industries LLC 405 831-5351
8500 S Anderson Rd Guthrie (73044) *(G-3295)*

12 Acre Woodwork LLC 405 328-0655
338378 E Cedar Canyon Rd Chandler (74834) *(G-1372)*

12th Gate Publishing LLC 405 735-7611
12216 Biltmore Dr Oklahoma City (73173) *(G-5327)*

1450 Ne 2nd Ave M, Tulsa *Also called Datalog Systems* *(G-9554)*

19th Hole 405 424-0520
3401 Ne 36th St Oklahoma City (73121) *(G-5328)*

1tr3 Publishing LLC 580 350-9280
1213 Nw Arlington Ave Lawton (73507) *(G-3880)*

2 Victory Graphics Media 918 394-2665
3207 S Norwood Ave Tulsa (74135) *(G-9054)*

2011 Ussa Limited Partnership 918 948-7856
6500 E 66th St N Tulsa (74117) *(G-9055)*

2012 H & H Manufacturing Inc (PA) 918 838-0744
1711 N Sheridan Rd Tulsa (74115) *(G-9056)*

2012 H & H Manufacturing Inc 918 747-7563
1249 E 29th Pl Tulsa (74114) *(G-9057)*

209 LLC 918 584-9944
209 N Boulder Ave Tulsa (74103) *(G-9058)*

24 7 Machinery LLC 580 762-8965
3417 W North Ave Ponca City (74601) *(G-7789)*

24 Hr Inc 844 370-1726
2811 E Main St Weatherford (73096) *(G-11385)*

247 Graphx Studios Inc 405 677-7775
325 S Scott St Oklahoma City (73115) *(G-5329)*

262 LLC 918 458-5511
618 E Downing St Tahlequah (74464) *(G-8848)*

2911 LLC 405 631-2008
7111 S Western Ave Oklahoma City (73139) *(G-5330)*

2b Publishing LLC 405 209-8465
2024 Turtlecreek Rd Edmond (73013) *(G-2282)*

2by2 Industries LLC 877 234-6558
14710 Metro Plaza Blvd A Edmond (73013) *(G-2283)*

2r Schweitzer Farms, Okarche *Also called Schweitzer Gypsum & Lime* *(G-5251)*

3 C Cattle Feeders Inc 580 384-3943
103 E Main St Mill Creek (74856) *(G-4465)*

3 Cs Tees LLC 405 208-1320
16045 County Road 1590 Ada (74820) *(G-2)*

3 D Manufacturing 918 224-7717
6800 S Highway 97 Sapulpa (74066) *(G-8244)*

3 PS Investment LLC 918 604-1363
902 S John Zink St Skiatook (74070) *(G-8529)*

3 Rivers Wldg Fabrication LLC 918 589-2300
25372 State Highway 20 Jay (74346) *(G-3677)*

30 Cent Print LLC 469 408-8968
7406 N Council Rd Blanchard (73010) *(G-698)*

300 PSI Inc 918 358-5713
51249 E Highway 64 Cleveland (74020) *(G-1714)*

33 - Welding Company 405 375-4468
123 N 11th St Kingfisher (73750) *(G-3783)*

3b Backhoe Services, Yukon *Also called Mitch Baskett* *(G-11756)*

3b Industries Inc 580 439-8876
2 3b Rd St 3 Comanche (73529) *(G-1832)*

3d Cabinetry LLC 405 488-5604
12381 Sycamore Ct Lindsay (73052) *(G-4042)*

3d Farms & Machine L L C 580 772-5543
1600 E Loomis Rd Weatherford (73096) *(G-11386)*

3g Printing 918 284-9433
15389 S 273rd East Ave Coweta (74429) *(G-1869)*

3g Printing 918 346-0035
3000 E Knoxville St Broken Arrow (74014) *(G-1107)*

3g Sign Inc 918 630-5976
3304 W Galveston Pl Broken Arrow (74012) *(G-807)*

3I Industries 580 788-2122
104 S Missouri St Elmore City (73433) *(G-2893)*

3M Imtec Corporation 800 879-9799
2401 N Commerce St Ardmore (73401) *(G-233)*

3r Welding 918 839-8945
7564 Nw Bowers Rd Hartshorne (74547) *(G-3389)*

3t Oil & Gas LLC 918 758-3269
13099 Old Highway 75 Okmulgee (74447) *(G-7491)*

4 B Hunting Industries LLC 405 823-9100
6508 N Grove Ave Warr Acres (73132) *(G-11309)*

4 K Kustomz Designs & Signs 580 226-2259
904 S Commerce St Ardmore (73401) *(G-234)*

4 M Welding Services Inc 580 298-9809
185885 Us Highway 271 Antlers (74523) *(G-212)*

4-Star Trailers Inc 405 324-7827
10000 Nw 10th St Oklahoma City (73127) *(G-5331)*

405 Coatings LLC 405 822-5095
3604 Ne 143rd St Edmond (73013) *(G-2284)*

405 Magazine Inc 405 604-2623
1613 N Broadway Ave Oklahoma City (73103) *(G-5332)*

405 Plastics & Distribution 405 562-8800
3201 N Santa Fe Ave Oklahoma City (73118) *(G-5333)*

405 R/C Raceway & Hobbies LLC 405 503-0364
2905 Nw 36th St Oklahoma City (73112) *(G-5334)*

405 Sign and Lighting LLC 405 445-8888
9415 Peachtree Ln Oklahoma City (73130) *(G-5335)*

405 Welding 405 413-5764
521 Sw 5th St Newcastle (73065) *(G-4818)*

412 Comics LLC 479 414-0891
707 Howard St Pocola (74902) *(G-7779)*

4524 LLC 405 620-3711
3700 Bonaire Pl Edmond (73013) *(G-2285)*

4ag Mfg LLC 580 821-9300
11110 N 1950 Rd Elk City (73644) *(G-2780)*

4d Dozer Service Inc 580 256-2076
202683 E County Road 35 Woodward (73801) *(G-11552)*

4k Spooling Banding Sales & SE 918 766-0001
1740 Se Washington Blvd Bartlesville (74006) *(G-443)*

4m Welding Inc 405 484-7293
Rr 3 Pauls Valley (73075) *(G-7648)*

4rv Publishing LLC 405 225-7298
2912 Rankin Ter Edmond (73013) *(G-2286)*

4v Welding and Dozer LLC 580 371-6524
1191 Cyrus Harris Rd Mill Creek (74856) *(G-4466)*

5 Over Games LLC 405 928-5972
2737 Nw 140th St Apt 503 Oklahoma City (73134) *(G-5336)*

5 Stones Defense LLC 405 313-9729
874 County Street 2922 Tuttle (73089) *(G-11184)*

50th Xpress Mart 405 491-7381
5025 N Meridian Ave Warr Acres (73112) *(G-11310)*

52 Stone 918 798-9952
17520 S 4150 Rd Claremore (74017) *(G-1573)*

5a Enterprises Inc 918 260-8909
303 N Skinner Ave Drumright (74030) *(G-2049)*

5r Services 580 370-0222
26700 County Road 110 Perry (73077) *(G-7725)*

66 Oilfield Services LLC 405 735-6666
7100 S Bryant Ave Oklahoma City (73149) *(G-5337)*

66 Sign and Light LLC 405 445-9212
15455 E Coffee Creek Rd Luther (73054) *(G-4131)*

7 Up, Ponca City *Also called Seven-Up Bottling Co Inc* *(G-7874)*

7 Up Bottle 918 426-0310
4107 W Highway 31 McAlester (74501) *(G-4268)*

7b Custom Welding Fabrication 918 850-1066
4748 S 27th West Ave Tulsa (74107) *(G-9059)*

89 Energy LLC 405 600-6040
123 Nw 8th St Oklahoma City (73102) *(G-5338)*

89 Energy II LLC 405 600-6040
123 Nw 8th St Oklahoma City (73102) *(G-5339)*

(PA)=Parent Co (HQ)=Headquarters (DH)=Div Headquarters

2020 Oklahoma Directory of Manufacturers & Processors

8bit Canvas LLC 405 924-3298
9818 Skylark Rd Oklahoma City (73162) *(G-5340)*

918 Screen Printers 918 850-9542
4155 S Rockford Pl Tulsa (74105) *(G-9060)*

9800 North Oklahoma LLC 405 748-9400
9800 N Oklahoma Ave Oklahoma City (73114) *(G-5341)*

A & A Aluminum, Lawton *Also called R & J Aluminum Products (G-3987)*

A & A Welding 918 772-0418
36275 S Cherokee Dr Park Hill (74451) *(G-7639)*

A & B Engraving Inc 918 663-7446
2020 E 3rd St Tulsa (74104) *(G-9061)*

A & B Printing & Office Supply 580 889-5103
1397 S Mississippi Ave Atoka (74525) *(G-395)*

A & B Quick Signs LLC 405 789-7446
6924 Melrose Ln Ste D Oklahoma City (73127) *(G-5342)*

A & E Frame Mfg Inc 918 251-3343
1113 E Memphis St Broken Arrow (74012) *(G-808)*

A & E Satellites 580 363-0931
100 N 2nd St Ponca City (74601) *(G-7790)*

A & H Manufacturing 918 698-0987
11726 S 272nd East Ave Coweta (74429) *(G-1870)*

A & J Fabricators Inc 405 352-4120
100 S 9th St Minco (73059) *(G-4475)*

A & M Blaylock Cnstr & Parts 918 945-7081
S 7 St Mc Curtain (74944) *(G-4267)*

A & M Feeds, Perry *Also called Stillwater Milling Company LLC (G-7747)*

A & M Manufacturing Co 918 835-2272
1421 S 70th East Ave Tulsa (74112) *(G-9062)*

A & R Plumbing and Mech LLC 405 808-0671
3176 Nw Expwy Apt 313 Oklahoma City (73112) *(G-5343)*

A & S Graphix 918 640-1292
2770 Standifer Rd Sulphur (73086) *(G-8827)*

A & S Operating Inc 918 582-7205
233 S Detroit Ave Ste 200 Tulsa (74120) *(G-9063)*

A & T Oil Company 918 245-7358
14381 Shady Ln Skiatook (74070) *(G-8530)*

A & T Resources LLC 918 582-7894
5416 S Yale Ave Ste 615 Tulsa (74135) *(G-9064)*

A & W Machine LLC 580 927-1188
1410 S Highway 75 Coalgate (74538) *(G-1774)*

A & Y Enterprises Inc 405 360-0307
1100 N University Blvd Norman (73069) *(G-4894)*

A 1 Advertising By L & H 918 348-2529
2601 N Main St Muskogee (74401) *(G-4639)*

A 1 Master Print Inc 405 787-0505
8302 Nw 39th Expy Bethany (73008) *(G-571)*

A and E Manufacturing Co 918 583-7184
6468 N Yale Ave Tulsa (74117) *(G-9065)*

A and L Welding Services LLC 918 649-7538
35210 Horse Ranch Rd Wister (74966) *(G-11547)*

A B Curbs Inc 405 427-1222
6718 Ne 23rd St Oklahoma City (73141) *(G-5344)*

A B N G Inc 405 222-0024
402 W Chickasha Ave # 200 Chickasha (73018) *(G-1426)*

A B Printing 918 834-2054
4109 E 11th St Tulsa (74112) *(G-9066)*

A Bolt Electric 580 510-0123
13806 Sw Pecan Rd Cache (73527) *(G-1223)*

A Cbd Healthier Life 405 585-0353
32 W Macarthur St Shawnee (74804) *(G-8426)*

A Finley Sign & Lighting Co 405 413-5721
4712 S Blackwelder Ave Oklahoma City (73119) *(G-5345)*

A Fuller Measure 405 755-5036
2300 Belleview Ter Oklahoma City (73112) *(G-5346)*

A G Equipment Company 918 250-7386
3401 W Albany St Broken Arrow (74012) *(G-809)*

A Grease Catch, Oklahoma City *Also called Odor Control Entps Texas Inc (G-6712)*

A M & A Technical Services 918 227-5354
9693 Hickory Hill Rd Sapulpa (74066) *(G-8245)*

A Mail Call Service Inc 918 610-8533
6915 E 38th St Tulsa (74145) *(G-9067)*

A P & R Industries Inc 405 702-7661
901 Nw 89th St Oklahoma City (73114) *(G-5347)*

A Plus Printing 580 765-7752
119 N 3rd St Ponca City (74601) *(G-7791)*

A Plus Printing Inc 918 836-8659
1211 S Memorial Dr Tulsa (74112) *(G-9068)*

A Plus Printing LLC 580 765-7752
1113 Rosedale Dr Ponca City (74604) *(G-7792)*

A Plus Scrubs To You 918 691-0556
12012 E 20th Pl Tulsa (74128) *(G-9069)*

A Prior Publishing 903 882-5019
146 Nw Red Bud Rd Lawton (73507) *(G-3881)*

A Q Printing 918 438-1161
7039 E 40th St Tulsa (74145) *(G-9070)*

A R K Ramos Manufacturing Co, Oklahoma City *Also called ARk -Ramos Fndry Mfg Co Inc (G-5465)*

A R T T Corp 405 681-0749
1829 S May Ave Oklahoma City (73108) *(G-5348)*

A Royal Flush LLC 405 422-2077
213 Kingsgate Rd Yukon (73099) *(G-11688)*

A S I, Broken Arrow *Also called Additive Systems Inc (G-814)*

A Sign of Surprise 918 607-0747
709 Magnolia Ct Broken Arrow (74011) *(G-810)*

A Stitch of Art 918 638-2511
16403 E 89th St N Owasso (74055) *(G-7540)*

A T Roustabouts 405 788-0735
43335 Curtis Dr Meeker (74855) *(G-4374)*

A T S, Quapaw *Also called Adv-TEC Systems Inc (G-8027)*

A T S Welding Service 405 452-5979
8164 E 127 Wetumka (74883) *(G-11489)*

A W Brueggemann Company Inc 580 237-3857
412 N Independence St Enid (73701) *(G-2900)*

A W Bugerman Company 580 237-3857
412 N Independence St Enid (73701) *(G-2901)*

A W Pool Inc 580 323-3454
Hwy 183 Clinton (73601) *(G-1735)*

A Walker Electric 918 232-6023
7134 N 426 Chelsea (74016) *(G-1399)*

A X-Ceptional Quality Dntl Lab 918 406-1835
6333 S Memorial Dr Ste D Tulsa (74133) *(G-9071)*

A&A Tank Truck, Norman *Also called We-Go Perforators Inc (G-5197)*

A&B Home Improvement 918 341-7410
10595 E Second St Claremore (74019) *(G-1574)*

A&B Identity, Tulsa *Also called A & B Engraving Inc (G-9061)*

A&J Mixing 405 946-1461
6101 Camille Ave Oklahoma City (73149) *(G-5349)*

A&K Manufacturing Services LLC 918 986-1637
24688 Ok 51 Tahlequah (74464) *(G-8849)*

A&M Aerospace LLC 405 323-6428
1877 Church Ave Harrah (73045) *(G-3373)*

A-1 Backhoe 405 547-5452
12203 S Sangre Rd Perkins (74059) *(G-7714)*

A-1 Backhoe Inc 405 863-7094
4240 Sw 31st St Oklahoma City (73119) *(G-5350)*

A-1 Industries LLC 580 380-2328
12520 Ok Highway 48 S Coleman (73432) *(G-1792)*

A-1 Machine Shop Inc 918 665-0706
10312 E 52nd St Tulsa (74146) *(G-9072)*

A-1 Machine Works Inc 918 367-2788
624 Industrial Rd Bristow (74010) *(G-762)*

A-1 Mster Prnta/Hooper Prtg Si 518 427-0282
235 N Macarthur Blvd # 60 Oklahoma City (73127) *(G-5351)*

A-1 Quality Welding Service, Piedmont *Also called A1 Quality Welding (G-7752)*

A-1 Sheet Metal Inc 918 835-6200
5909 E 15th St Tulsa (74112) *(G-9073)*

A-1 Specialties 405 942-1341
4905 Morris Ln Oklahoma City (73112) *(G-5352)*

A-1 Sure Shot 405 677-9800
1312 Se 25th St Oklahoma City (73129) *(G-5353)*

A-1 Sure Sht-Div Ptro Instrmen, Oklahoma City *Also called A-1 Sure Shot (G-5353)*

A-Accurate Welding Inc 918 838-1111
1136 S Hudson Ave Tulsa (74112) *(G-9074)*

A-Line Tds Inc 580 628-5371
1500 N Main St Tonkawa (74653) *(G-8970)*

A-Max Signs Co 918 622-0651
9520 E 55th Pl Tulsa (74145) *(G-9075)*

A-O K Rubber Stamp Co, Lawton *Also called A-OK Rubber Stamp (G-3882)*

A-OK Printing Mill 918 775-6809
1101 E Cherokee Ave Sallisaw (74955) *(G-8136)*

A-OK Rubber Stamp 580 357-2822
701 Nw 17th St Ste D Lawton (73507) *(G-3882)*

A-Tech Paving, Oklahoma City *Also called Rdnj LLC (G-6978)*

A-Z Manufacturing LLC 918 258-2900
1116 E Memphis St Broken Arrow (74012) *(G-811)*

A. J. Acid, Blackwell *Also called Acid Inc (G-673)*

A/C Matthews & Refrigeration 918 465-6337
1351 Ne 1070th Ave Red Oak (74563) *(G-8073)*

A/Q Printing, Tulsa *Also called A Q Printing (G-9070)*

A1 Heat and Air 580 832-2605
222 E Main St Cordell (73632) *(G-1852)*

A1 Quality Welding 405 373-0066
108 L And M Dr Sw Piedmont (73078) *(G-7752)*

A1 Screen Printing 405 701-6735
102 W Eufaula St Ste 230 Norman (73069) *(G-4895)*

A1 Vinyl Signs LLC 918 392-9905
5590 S Garnett Rd Tulsa (74146) *(G-9076)*

AAA Crimstone Operating Co LP 918 445-5500
4422 W 49th St Tulsa (74107) *(G-9077)*

AAA Galvanizing Chelsea Inc 918 789-9333
6022 S Industrial Dr Chelsea (74016) *(G-1400)*

AAA Kopy 405 741-5679
709 S Air Depot Blvd A Oklahoma City (73110) *(G-5354)*

AAA Sign & Supply Co 918 622-7883
9946 E 21st St Tulsa (74129) *(G-9078)*

Aae Automation Inc 405 525-1100
3021 S High Ave Oklahoma City (73129) *(G-5355)*

ALPHABETIC SECTION

AAMCO Transm Total Car Care, Oklahoma City Also called Thomas H Scott Western LLC *(G-7283)*
Aaon Inc (PA) 918 583-2266
  2425 S Yukon Ave Tulsa (74107) *(G-9079)*
AAON HEATING AND COOLING PRODU, Tulsa Also called Aaon Inc *(G-9079)*
Aapg, Tulsa Also called American Assn Petro Geologists *(G-9164)*
AAR Aircraft Services Inc 405 681-3000
  6611 S Meridian Ave # 59100 Oklahoma City (73159) *(G-5356)*
AAR Aircraft Services Inc 405 218-3393
  6241 S Meridian Ave Oklahoma City (73159) *(G-5357)*
AAR Aircraft Services - Okla, Oklahoma City Also called AAR Aircraft Services Inc *(G-5356)*
Aaron Atencio Photography, Owasso Also called Mora Mora Media LLC *(G-7594)*
Aaron Custom Creations 580 603-0467
  2700 N Van Buren St # 93 Enid (73703) *(G-2902)*
Aaron Lance Butler 580 220-7715
  3792 Countyline Rd Ardmore (73401) *(G-235)*
Aaron Oil Inc 405 899-4138
  17650 E Etowah Rd Noble (73068) *(G-4875)*
Aaron Son Custom Cabinets 918 537-2129
  2001 Deer Run Cir Muskogee (74403) *(G-4640)*
Aaron Willis President 405 219-9411
  11780 S Sooner Rd Edmond (73034) *(G-2287)*
Aars 918 313-4512
  3171 S 129th East Ave Tulsa (74134) *(G-9080)*
Aars Notary and Tax, Tulsa Also called Aars *(G-9080)*
AB Swabbing Incorporated 219 765-3239
  914 S Ellison Ave El Reno (73036) *(G-2695)*
ABB Inc 918 338-4888
  7051 Industrial Blvd Bartlesville (74006) *(G-444)*
Abbott Industries Inc (PA) 918 756-8320
  12801 Highway 75 Okmulgee (74447) *(G-7492)*
Abbott Laboratories 405 329-5513
  404 Garland Ct Norman (73072) *(G-4896)*
Abby Candles Fundraising, Moore Also called Abby Candles Inc *(G-4483)*
Abby Candles Inc 405 895-9957
  200 Se 19th St Moore (73160) *(G-4483)*
ABC Choppers LLC 405 990-8641
  1901 N Classen Blvd Oklahoma City (73106) *(G-5358)*
ABC Printing, Coweta Also called Bill Rathbone *(G-1872)*
ABC Services LLC 580 242-1015
  4805 E Chestnut Ave Enid (73701) *(G-2903)*
Abco Printing & Office Supply 580 286-7575
  5 Se Washington St Idabel (74745) *(G-3636)*
Abco Printing & Office Sups, Idabel Also called Abco Printing & Office Supply *(G-3636)*
Abco Steel Inc 918 322-3435
  643 W 138th St Glenpool (74033) *(G-3228)*
Aberdeen Dynamics LLC 918 794-0042
  17751 E Admiral Pl Tulsa (74158) *(G-9081)*
Abitl Finishing Inc 918 446-5363
  6755 State Highway 66 Tulsa (74131) *(G-8985)*
Abla Bulldozer Service, Erick Also called Carl Abla *(G-3086)*
Able Engineering Services 918 835-3161
  227 S 72nd East Ave Tulsa (74112) *(G-9082)*
Able Interior Contractor LLC 918 605-2887
  5420 E 580 Rd Locust Grove (74352) *(G-4103)*
Able Welding 405 760-1442
  304 Longhorn Dr Edmond (73003) *(G-2288)*
Abmi Inc 405 485-9608
  211 Sw 6th St Blanchard (73010) *(G-699)*
Abng, Chickasha Also called Ouachita Exploration Inc *(G-1496)*
ABS, Oklahoma City Also called American Bank Systems Inc *(G-5432)*
Absolute Markings Inc 918 660-0600
  8710 E 41st St Tulsa (74145) *(G-9083)*
Absolute Welding Inc 918 923-7300
  220 E Nelms St Oologah (74053) *(G-7532)*
Abundant Grace Companies LLC (PA) 405 682-2589
  8801 S Kentucky Ave Oklahoma City (73159) *(G-5359)*
AC Machine 918 827-6552
  324 E 8th St Mounds (74047) *(G-4607)*
AC Nutrition LP 580 223-3900
  100 Mill St Se Ardmore (73401) *(G-236)*
AC Oil & Gas LLC 405 919-8088
  21505 E 630 Rd Hennessey (73742) *(G-3442)*
AC Systems Integration Inc 918 259-0020
  10325 E 58th St Tulsa (74146) *(G-9084)*
AC Woodworks Inc 918 298-6948
  11223 S Quebec Ave Tulsa (74137) *(G-9085)*
AC Woodworks Inc DBA Wood 918 384-0111
  6341 E 41st St Tulsa (74135) *(G-9086)*
Accelated Artfl List Systems 405 207-9449
  20310 Hwy 77 Pauls Valley (73075) *(G-7649)*
Accelerated Production Svcs 405 603-7492
  9733 Nw 6th St Oklahoma City (73127) *(G-5360)*
Accent Displays & Graphics 918 437-4338
  112 S 109th East Pl Tulsa (74128) *(G-9087)*
Accent Machine Inc 918 246-9695
  102 Wellston Park Rd Sand Springs (74063) *(G-8156)*

Access Midstream Ventures LLC 405 935-3500
  6100 N Western Ave Oklahoma City (73118) *(G-5361)*
Access Mlp Operating Llc 405 935-8000
  600 N Western Ave Oklahoma City (73106) *(G-5362)*
Access Optics LLC 918 294-1234
  2201 N Maple Ave Broken Arrow (74012) *(G-812)*
Accessories-To-Go 580 467-7408
  212 Oak Main Ave Comanche (73529) *(G-1833)*
Accessory and Prfmce Sls Inc 918 224-5851
  1013 S Moccasin Pl Sapulpa (74066) *(G-8246)*
Acco Chain & Lifting Products, Tulsa Also called Fki Industries Inc *(G-9752)*
Accord Fabrics, Oklahoma City Also called Accord Upholstery & Fabric *(G-5363)*
Accord Upholstery & Fabric 405 634-4070
  2501 S Agnew Ave Oklahoma City (73108) *(G-5363)*
Accounting Office, Oklahoma City Also called Diamondback E&P LLC *(G-5939)*
Accu Cast 918 582-3466
  3806 Charles Page Blvd Tulsa (74127) *(G-9088)*
Accu-Turn Machine LLC 580 704-8876
  3817 Nw Welch Rd Lawton (73507) *(G-3883)*
Accurate Blinds 405 396-8583
  13450 E Timberwood Ln Arcadia (73007) *(G-226)*
Accurate By Design 918 445-0292
  5800 W 68th St Tulsa (74131) *(G-8986)*
Accurate Fence Contruction LLC 580 591-3717
  6905 Se Lee Blvd Lawton (73501) *(G-3884)*
Accurate Juno Engraving Co., Tulsa Also called Juno Companies Incorporated *(G-10067)*
Accurate Machine & Maintenance 918 585-1125
  1228 S Detroit Ave Tulsa (74120) *(G-9089)*
Accurate Machine Works Inc 405 615-4983
  1266 County Street 2964 Blanchard (73010) *(G-700)*
Accurate Manufacturing Inc 918 582-2585
  2765 Dawson Rd Tulsa (74110) *(G-9090)*
Accurate Tool & Die, Oklahoma City Also called Coldren Enterprises Corp *(G-5802)*
Accurus Aerospace Corporation (PA) 918 438-3121
  12716 E Pine St Tulsa (74116) *(G-9091)*
Accurus Aerospace Tulsa LLC 918 438-3121
  12716 E Pine St Tulsa (74116) *(G-9092)*
Accutec-Ihs Inc 918 984-9838
  1408 S Denver Ave Tulsa (74119) *(G-9093)*
Accutech Laboratories 405 603-2956
  5565 Nw Expressway Warr Acres (73132) *(G-11311)*
Accutech Laboratories Inc 405 946-6446
  5565 Nw Expressway Warr Acres (73132) *(G-11312)*
Ace 1 Welding and Insptn LLC 405 408-5370
  10400 Fawn Trail Rd Mustang (73064) *(G-4760)*
Ace Completions OK 580 547-4088
  1717 S 28th St Clinton (73601) *(G-1736)*
Ace Fence Co 918 682-7895
  2337 S Cherokee St Muskogee (74403) *(G-4641)*
Ace Grinding 918 439-4113
  12515 E 11th St Tulsa (74128) *(G-9094)*
Ace Hardware 580 225-0100
  1210 S Main St Elk City (73644) *(G-2781)*
Ace Information Co 405 677-6747
  319 S Scott St Ste A Oklahoma City (73115) *(G-5364)*
Ace Lumber & Building Supply, Guthrie Also called Oklahoma Home Centers Inc *(G-3329)*
Ace NDT LLC 580 323-8601
  1430 S 14th St Clinton (73601) *(G-1737)*
Ace Sign Company Inc 918 446-3030
  5823 S 65th West Ave Tulsa (74107) *(G-9095)*
Ace Welding and Mechanical LLC 405 219-1490
  4013 Nw 32nd St Oklahoma City (73112) *(G-5365)*
Aceco Valve Inc 918 827-3669
  2300 Alt 75 Mounds (74047) *(G-4608)*
Acg Material, Mooreland Also called Harrison Gypsum LLC *(G-4591)*
Acg Materials, Bessie Also called Harrison Gypsum LLC *(G-569)*
Aci Machine & Engineering, Oklahoma City Also called Aerocorp International Lc *(G-5392)*
Aci Mfg, Claremore Also called Contech Enterprises LLC *(G-1609)*
Acid Inc 580 363-5413
  421 N 20th St Blackwell (74631) *(G-673)*
Acid Specialists LLC 432 617-2243
  14201 Caliber Dr Ste 300 Oklahoma City (73134) *(G-5366)*
Acidizing & Cementing Service 405 969-3093
  2 1/2 Mi S On Hwy 74 Crescent (73028) *(G-1907)*
Acl Combustion Inc 405 310-2327
  228 Se 8th St Moore (73160) *(G-4484)*
Acme Brick Company 918 834-3384
  4103 Dawson Rd Tulsa (74115) *(G-9096)*
Acme Brick Company 405 755-5010
  500 E Memorial Rd Oklahoma City (73114) *(G-5367)*
Acme Brick Tile & More, Tulsa Also called Acme Brick Company *(G-9096)*
Acme Custom Welding 405 288-0187
  27567 State Highway 74 Washington (73093) *(G-11332)*
Acme Engineering and Mfg Corp (PA) 918 682-7791
  1820 N York St Muskogee (74403) *(G-4642)*
Acme Manufacturing Corporation 918 266-3097
  6532 Tower Ln Claremore (74019) *(G-1575)*
Acme Manufacturing Corporation 800 647-8671
  6532 Tower Ln Claremore (74019) *(G-1576)*

Aco Inc....405 239-6863
1301 W Sheridan Ave Oklahoma City (73106) ***(G-5368)***
Acott Oil Operations....918 885-2736
604 N Katy Ave Hominy (74035) ***(G-3573)***
Acp Inc....405 249-8835
1600 Sunset Ln Oklahoma City (73127) ***(G-5369)***
Acquire Cctv Inc....405 324-1300
13101 Sw 10th St Yukon (73099) ***(G-11689)***
Acquire Video Security, Yukon *Also called Acquire Cctv Inc* ***(G-11689)***
ACS, Ardmore *Also called Ardmore Construction Sup Inc* ***(G-245)***
ACS, Crescent *Also called Acidizing & Cementing Service* ***(G-1907)***
ACS Design Services, Jenks *Also called Advanced Crative Solutions Inc* ***(G-3688)***
Act, Oklahoma City *Also called Advanced Chemical Tech Inc* ***(G-5379)***
Action Graphics Printing Inc....918 540-3336
3520 27th Ave Ne Miami (74354) ***(G-4388)***
Action Graphics Prtg & Design....918 540-3336
3520 27th Ave Ne Miami (74354) ***(G-4389)***
Action Imprints, Muskogee *Also called Jan L Jobe* ***(G-4698)***
Action Machine Inc....918 248-6847
8335 S 89th West Ave Tulsa (74131) ***(G-8987)***
Action Machine Shop....918 245-8308
403 W 2nd St Sand Springs (74063) ***(G-8157)***
Action Petroleum Services Corp....580 223-6544
1001 Timber Grv Ardmore (73401) ***(G-237)***
Action Pipe and Supply Inc....405 853-7170
400 W Jack Choate Ave Hennessey (73742) ***(G-3443)***
Action Printing Norman Inc....405 364-3615
3400 Charleston Rd Norman (73069) ***(G-4897)***
Action Signs & Banners, Norman *Also called Chris Johnson* ***(G-4956)***
Action Spring Company....918 836-9000
3003 E Apache St Tulsa (74110) ***(G-9097)***
Active Violinist LLC....612 532-1829
2101 S Boston Ave Apt 3 Tulsa (74114) ***(G-9098)***
Active-Ice Inc....405 310-3880
3650 Classen Blvd Norman (73071) ***(G-4898)***
Actualizing Apps LLC....918 627-7450
8282 E 33rd Pl Tulsa (74145) ***(G-9099)***
Acura Neon Inc....918 252-2258
1801 N Willow Ave Broken Arrow (74012) ***(G-813)***
Acura Sign, Broken Arrow *Also called Acura Neon Inc* ***(G-813)***
Acuren Inspection Inc....405 452-3337
5208 S Lawton Ave Tulsa (74107) ***(G-9100)***
Ad Tech Signs Inc....405 236-0551
2000 S Santa Fe Ave Oklahoma City (73109) ***(G-5370)***
Ad Type Inc....405 942-7951
4401 Sw 23rd St 203 Oklahoma City (73108) ***(G-5371)***
Ada Coca Cola Bottling Company....580 427-2000
1205 Cradduck Rd Ada (74820) ***(G-3)***
Ada Drilling, Ada *Also called Ada Energy Service LLC* ***(G-5)***
Ada Energy Cementing LLC....580 436-5228
13710 County Road 1550 Ada (74820) ***(G-4)***
Ada Energy Service LLC....580 436-5228
13710 County Road 1550 Ada (74820) ***(G-5)***
Ada Evening News, Ada *Also called Newspaper Holding Inc* ***(G-72)***
Ada Iron and Welding LLC (PA)....580 332-6694
13655 County Road 1570 Ada (74820) ***(G-6)***
Ada Plant, Ada *Also called Holcim (us) Inc* ***(G-48)***
Adair County Commisioners Off....918 696-7633
220 W Division St Ste 102 Stilwell (74960) ***(G-8779)***
Adair's Custom Upholstering, Edmond *Also called Adairs Sleep World Inc* ***(G-2289)***
Adairs Sleep World Inc....405 341-9468
611 W Edmond Rd Edmond (73003) ***(G-2289)***
Adams Affiliates Inc (PA)....918 582-7713
1437 S Boulder Ave Tulsa (74119) ***(G-9101)***
Adams Electronics Inc (PA)....918 622-5000
1611 S Utica Ave Pmb 408 Tulsa (74104) ***(G-9102)***
Adams Investment Company (PA)....918 335-1234
2500 Industrial Pkwy Dewey (74029) ***(G-2012)***
Adams Investment Company....918 661-2100
2500 Industrial Pkwy Dewey (74029) ***(G-2013)***
Adams Printing....580 832-2123
206 W Main St Cordell (73632) ***(G-1853)***
Adaptive Corporation....440 257-7460
4150 S 100th East Ave # 301 Tulsa (74146) ***(G-9103)***
ADC Quality Mfg....918 808-2329
12348 N 97th East Ave Collinsville (74021) ***(G-1798)***
Adcp Industries LLC....405 330-4728
2930 Nw 73rd St Oklahoma City (73116) ***(G-5372)***
Additive Systems Inc (PA)....918 357-3433
407 S Main St Broken Arrow (74012) ***(G-814)***
Ademco Inc....918 663-2822
4731 S Memorial Dr Tulsa (74145) ***(G-9104)***
Ademco Inc....405 681-4008
3801 S Moulton Dr Oklahoma City (73179) ***(G-5373)***
ADI Global Distribution, Tulsa *Also called Ademco Inc* ***(G-9104)***
ADI Global Distribution, Oklahoma City *Also called Ademco Inc* ***(G-5373)***
Adjacent Creations LLC....405 819-6507
4 Akin Dr Oklahoma City (73149) ***(G-5374)***
Adko Inc....405 677-6507
2221 S Eastern Ave Oklahoma City (73129) ***(G-5375)***
Adl Group LLC....918 960-0388
10302 E 55th Pl Ste A Tulsa (74146) ***(G-9105)***
ADM, Enid *Also called Archer-Daniels-Midland Company* ***(G-2910)***
ADM, Hooker *Also called Archer-Daniels-Midland Company* ***(G-3595)***
ADM, Enid *Also called Archer-Daniels-Midland Company* ***(G-2911)***
ADM, Tyrone *Also called Archer-Daniels-Midland Company* ***(G-11218)***
ADM, Enid *Also called Archer-Daniels-Midland Company* ***(G-2912)***
ADM, Altus *Also called Archer-Daniels-Midland Company* ***(G-143)***
ADM Milling Co....580 237-8000
1301 N 4th St Enid (73701) ***(G-2904)***
Adroit Surgical LLC....425 577-2713
7103 Nichols Rd Nichols Hills (73120) ***(G-4854)***
Adtech, Wayne *Also called American Directional Tech* ***(G-11365)***
Adtek Software Company....815 452-2345
516 Nw 20th St Oklahoma City (73103) ***(G-5376)***
Aduddlls Altrnators Starters U, Oklahoma City *Also called Reggie Adudell* ***(G-7003)***
Adv-TEC Systems Inc....918 542-4710
2201 S 700 Rd Quapaw (74363) ***(G-8027)***
Advance Eqp & Contrls LLC....918 496-2606
9428 S 68th East Ave Tulsa (74133) ***(G-9106)***
Advance Flo Systems, Tulsa *Also called Cimarron Machine Services Inc* ***(G-9428)***
Advance Food Company Inc (HQ)....800 969-2747
221 W Oxford Ave Enid (73701) ***(G-2905)***
Advance Food Company Inc....580 237-6656
201 S Raleigh Rd Enid (73701) ***(G-2906)***
Advance Graphics & Printing....405 258-0796
1113 Manvel Ave Chandler (74834) ***(G-1373)***
Advance Oil Corporation....918 321-9034
14504 S Highway 75a Kiefer (74041) ***(G-3775)***
Advance Polybag Inc....405 677-8383
4901 S I 35 Service Rd Oklahoma City (73129) ***(G-5377)***
Advance RES Chem & Mfg LLC....918 266-6789
5010 Skiatook Rd Catoosa (74015) ***(G-1293)***
Advance Research & Development....405 321-0550
2285 Industrial Blvd Norman (73069) ***(G-4899)***
Advance Research Chemicals Inc....918 266-6789
1110 Keystone Ave Catoosa (74015) ***(G-1294)***
Advance Roustabout Svcs LLC....405 612-0781
3101 S Anderson Rd Guthrie (73044) ***(G-3296)***
Advanced Aerial Services LLC (PA)....580 571-1980
9818 State Highway 34 # 28 Woodward (73801) ***(G-11553)***
Advanced Aircraft Coatings (PA)....405 495-7545
11020 Roxboro Ave Oklahoma City (73162) ***(G-5378)***
Advanced Chemical Tech Inc....405 843-2585
9608 N Robinson Ave Oklahoma City (73114) ***(G-5379)***
Advanced Comfort & Energy....405 329-2237
2810 Broce Dr Norman (73072) ***(G-4900)***
Advanced Crative Solutions Inc....918 519-3651
321 E 112th St S Jenks (74037) ***(G-3688)***
Advanced Drainage Systems....405 272-1541
1418 E Reno Ave Oklahoma City (73117) ***(G-5380)***
Advanced EMC Technologies LLC....918 994-7776
5903 S 107th East Ave # 108 Tulsa (74146) ***(G-9107)***
Advanced Fabrication Svcs LLC....405 339-4867
1217 Sw 97th St Oklahoma City (73139) ***(G-5381)***
Advanced Foot & Ankle....405 692-7114
1126 Sw 89th St Oklahoma City (73139) ***(G-5382)***
Advanced Graphic Design....918 960-0407
6605 E 19th St Apt A Tulsa (74112) ***(G-9108)***
Advanced Graphics Technology....405 632-8600
3201 S Western Ave Oklahoma City (73109) ***(G-5383)***
Advanced Hydrcrbon Strtigraphy....918 583-2474
2931 W 21st St Tulsa (74107) ***(G-9109)***
Advanced Imaging Resources Co....918 609-5250
1761 N Aspen Ave Broken Arrow (74012) ***(G-815)***
Advanced Indus Dvcs Co LLC (PA)....918 445-1254
4323 S Elwood Ave Tulsa (74107) ***(G-9110)***
Advanced Machining & Fabg....918 664-5410
11212 E 112th St N Owasso (74055) ***(G-7541)***
Advanced McHning Solutions LLC....405 208-8737
4703 Entp Dr Ste A Oklahoma City (73128) ***(G-5384)***
Advanced Medical Instrs Inc (PA)....918 250-0566
3061 W Albany St Broken Arrow (74012) ***(G-816)***
Advanced Micro Solutions Inc....405 562-0112
1709 S State St Edmond (73013) ***(G-2290)***
Advanced Power Inc....580 774-2220
1520 E Eagle Rd Weatherford (73096) ***(G-11387)***
Advanced Pressure Incorporated....405 324-5600
10300 W Reno Ave Oklahoma City (73127) ***(G-5385)***
Advanced Printing and Mktg, Edmond *Also called Biz Networks LLC* ***(G-2323)***
Advanced Processing Tech Inc....405 360-4848
405 Highland Pkwy Norman (73069) ***(G-4901)***
Advanced Pumpin Unit Service, Marlow *Also called Advanced Pumping Unit Service* ***(G-4220)***
Advanced Pumping Unit Service....580 658-2050
3812 Highway 29 Marlow (73055) ***(G-4220)***

Advanced Racing Composites LLC 918 760-9990
2720 N Sheridan Rd Tulsa (74115) ***(G-9111)***
Advanced Steel & Crane, Inc., Tulsa *Also called Asc Inc* ***(G-9215)***
Advanced Tech Solutions LLC 310 591-7163
1533 Sw 80th St Oklahoma City (73159) ***(G-5386)***
Advanced Welding & Excav LLC 918 306-2061
20304 W Highway 66 Bristow (74010) ***(G-763)***
Advancepierre Foods Inc 800 969-2747
5110 Enterprise Blvd Enid (73701) ***(G-2907)***
Advancepierre Foods Holdings, Enid *Also called Advance Food Company Inc* ***(G-2905)***
Advantage Cnstr Pdts Inc 405 372-3562
2802 S Black Oak Dr Stillwater (74074) ***(G-8651)***
Advantage Controls LLC 918 686-6211
4700 Harold Abitz Dr Muskogee (74403) ***(G-4643)***
Advantage Graphics 580 363-5734
7981 W Hubbard Rd Ponca City (74601) ***(G-7793)***
Advantage Supplements LLC 866 226-9613
4597 N 2830 Rd Hennessey (73742) ***(G-3444)***
Advent Aircraft Systems Inc 918 388-5940
8712 S Peoria Ave Tulsa (74132) ***(G-9112)***
Adventure Manufacturing Inc 405 682-3833
4012 Sw 29th St Oklahoma City (73119) ***(G-5387)***
Adventure Publishing LLC 918 270-7100
4941 S 78th East Ave Tulsa (74145) ***(G-9113)***
Adventures In Stitching LLC 918 995-7445
2821 E 102nd Pl Tulsa (74137) ***(G-9114)***
Advertising Signs & Awngs Inc 405 232-7446
6924 Melrose Ln Oklahoma City (73127) ***(G-5388)***
Advertising Specialties, Tulsa *Also called Corser Group Inc* ***(G-9492)***
Aegeos Oilfield Technology LLC 918 906-4328
9503 N 137th East Ct Owasso (74055) ***(G-7542)***
Aei Corp-Okla 405 236-3551
114 Nw 8th St Oklahoma City (73102) ***(G-5389)***
Aerial Drones of Oklahoma LLC 918 694-6523
26460 Arrowood Dr Claremore (74019) ***(G-1577)***
Aero Automation LLC 918 251-0987
5621 W Austin St Broken Arrow (74011) ***(G-817)***
Aero Component Repair LLC 580 924-7999
3625 W Arkansas St Durant (74701) ***(G-2200)***
Aero Components Inc 405 631-6644
535 Se 82nd St Oklahoma City (73149) ***(G-5390)***
Aero Dynamics 918 258-0290
905 S 11th St Broken Arrow (74012) ***(G-818)***
Aero S2, Edmond *Also called Aero Solutions and Services* ***(G-2291)***
Aero Solutions and Services 405 308-6788
14196 Meritage Dr Edmond (73034) ***(G-2291)***
Aero Tech, Oklahoma City *Also called Keymiaee Aero-Tech Inc* ***(G-6409)***
Aero Tech Welding 918 764-9675
3 S 109th East Pl Tulsa (74128) ***(G-9115)***
Aero-TEC Industries Inc 405 382-8501
11990 N Highway 99 Seminole (74868) ***(G-8353)***
Aerochem Inc 405 440-0380
212 N Falcon Dr Oklahoma City (73127) ***(G-5391)***
Aerocore X LLC 405 669-8655
4312 Se 31st St Del City (73115) ***(G-1994)***
Aerocorp International Lc 405 317-5844
8124 Sw 8th St Ste C Oklahoma City (73128) ***(G-5392)***
Aeron Group LLC 918 294-1167
1901 N Willow Ave Broken Arrow (74012) ***(G-819)***
Aerospace, Edmond *Also called AP Jetworks LLC* ***(G-2305)***
Aerospace Products SE Inc 405 213-1034
621 N Robinson Ave # 550 Oklahoma City (73102) ***(G-5393)***
Aerospace Training 405 253-8343
7919 Mid America Blvd Oklahoma City (73135) ***(G-5394)***
Aerospace Training Sy 405 253-8343
2600 John Saxon Blvd # 100 Norman (73071) ***(G-4902)***
Aerostar International Inc 918 789-3000
5869 S Ernest Pk Indus Rd Chelsea (74016) ***(G-1401)***
AES Drilling Fluids, Clinton *Also called Champion Drilling Fluids Inc* ***(G-1742)***
AES Drilling Fluids 580 225-3450
101 Falcon Rd Ste 8 Elk City (73644) ***(G-2782)***
Aether Dbs LLC (PA) 918 317-2375
8101 State Highway 66 Tulsa (74131) ***(G-8988)***
Aexco Petroleum Inc 405 844-1991
785 W Covell Rd Ste 125 Edmond (73003) ***(G-2292)***
Affinitee Graphics 580 861-2253
502 Nw Sheridan Rd Lawton (73505) ***(G-3885)***
Affordable Buildings LLC 918 427-6005
416 W Treat Rd Muldrow (74948) ***(G-4630)***
Affordable Dumpster OK LLC 405 535-6644
4113 Nw 52nd St Oklahoma City (73112) ***(G-5395)***
Affordable Leak Detection 405 594-2341
536 N Pennsylvania Ave Oklahoma City (73107) ***(G-5396)***
Affordable Restorations LLC 918 609-5399
16201 E 91st St N Owasso (74055) ***(G-7543)***
Affordable Signs & Decals Inc 405 942-7059
952 N Macarthur Blvd Oklahoma City (73127) ***(G-5397)***
Afg Acquisition Group LLC (PA) 918 366-4401
14602 S Grant St Bixby (74008) ***(G-608)***
Afg Acquisition Group LLC 918 683-5683
612 S 45th St E Muskogee (74403) ***(G-4644)***
Afton Manufacturing, Afton *Also called Gtsa Manufacturing Inc* ***(G-118)***
AG Quip Inc 918 536-4325
400261 W 3400 Rd Ramona (74061) ***(G-8043)***
AG Youth Magazine 800 599-6884
302 E Main St Sentinel (73664) ***(G-8409)***
Agape Inc 918 455-9516
1608 W Gulfport St Broken Arrow (74011) ***(G-820)***
Agave Energy Inc 918 799-6174
30039 S County Road 4300 Stigler (74462) ***(G-8628)***
AGC Inc 913 451-8900
3300 W Reno Ave Oklahoma City (73107) ***(G-5398)***
AGC Manufactoring Inc 918 258-2506
5853 S Garnett Rd Tulsa (74146) ***(G-9116)***
Age Stone Manufacturing 918 366-3270
19473 S Harvard Ave Bixby (74008) ***(G-609)***
Aggregate Materials, Tulsa *Also called Thomsons Trenching Inc* ***(G-10936)***
Agilis Group LLC 918 584-3553
7029 E Reading Pl Tulsa (74115) ***(G-9117)***
Agion Press 405 341-7477
409 Woodhollow Trl Edmond (73012) ***(G-2293)***
Agrium Advanced Tech US Inc 405 948-1084
5201 W Reno Ave Ste E Oklahoma City (73127) ***(G-5399)***
AGS LLC 405 605-8331
308 Anthony Ave Oklahoma City (73128) ***(G-5400)***
Agt Machining Co Inc 580 774-8359
4701 Engineering Way Weatherford (73096) ***(G-11388)***
Aguevent Industries 580 748-0710
820 S Oklahoma Ave Cherokee (73728) ***(G-1413)***
Ahc Fabrication Co Inc 918 267-5052
1585 Highway 16 Beggs (74421) ***(G-548)***
Ahmadys Import LLC 918 254-4094
8027 S Sheridan Rd Tulsa (74133) ***(G-9118)***
Ahmadys Persian Rugs, Tulsa *Also called Ahmadys Import LLC* ***(G-9118)***
AI Signs & Wraps LLC 405 531-6938
513 Howard Dr Del City (73115) ***(G-1995)***
Aic, Oklahoma City *Also called Applied Indus Coatings LLC* ***(G-5455)***
Ainsworth Welding 580 512-7874
14647 Ne Cline Rd Fletcher (73541) ***(G-3160)***
Air and Water, Tulsa *Also called Advanced Hydrcrbon Strtigraphy* ***(G-9109)***
Air Duct Inc 918 445-1196
4434 S Jackson Ave Tulsa (74107) ***(G-9119)***
Air Electric Inc 918 406-3974
7034 E 59th St Tulsa (74145) ***(G-9120)***
Air Inspired Home Medical 918 299-3037
519i E 141st St Glenpool (74033) ***(G-3229)***
Air Power Systems Co LLC 918 622-5600
8178 E 44th St Tulsa (74145) ***(G-9121)***
Air Products and Chemicals Inc 918 266-8800
1115 Keystone Ave Catoosa (74015) ***(G-1295)***
Air Products and Chemicals Inc 918 825-4592
4078 Hunt St Pryor (74361) ***(G-7940)***
Air Products and Chemicals Inc 580 994-2732
28052 State Highway 50 Mooreland (73852) ***(G-4585)***
Air System Components Inc 580 762-7521
900 Darr Park Dr Bldg 1 Ponca City (74601) ***(G-7794)***
Air Systems Pump Solutions LLC 405 512-5100
1119 N 105th East Pl Tulsa (74116) ***(G-9122)***
Air-X-Hemphill LLC 918 283-9220
401 E Lowry Rd Claremore (74017) ***(G-1578)***
Air-X-Hemphill LLC 918 712-8268
2230 E 49th St Ste D Tulsa (74105) ***(G-9123)***
Aircraft Cylinders Amer Iinc 918 582-1785
1006 E Independence St Tulsa (74106) ***(G-9124)***
Aircraft Group, Midwest City *Also called Moog Inc* ***(G-4448)***
Aircraft Power Service Inc 405 379-2407
Airport Rd Hngr 1 Hanger 1 Holdenville (74848) ***(G-3549)***
Aircraft Specialties Svc Inc 918 836-6872
2860 N Sheridan Rd Tulsa (74115) ***(G-9125)***
Aircraft Structures Intl Corp 580 242-5907
1026 S 66th St Enid (73701) ***(G-2908)***
Aircraft Systems 918 388-5943
8664 S Peoria Ave Bldg B Tulsa (74132) ***(G-9126)***
Airelectric Inc 918 291-7531
8815 Airport Way Unit 5 Tulsa (74132) ***(G-9127)***
Airflo Cooling Tech LLC 918 585-5638
728 S Wheeling Ave Tulsa (74104) ***(G-9128)***
Airflow Solutions LLC 918 574-2748
11541 E Pine St Tulsa (74116) ***(G-9129)***
Airgas Usa LLC 405 745-2732
7248 Sw 29th St Oklahoma City (73179) ***(G-5401)***
Airgas Usa LLC 580 767-1313
1124 N Waverly St Ponca City (74601) ***(G-7795)***
Airgas Usa LLC 405 372-7720
2607 E 6th Ave Stillwater (74074) ***(G-8652)***
Airgas Usa LLC 405 235-0009
1225 W Reno Ave Oklahoma City (73106) ***(G-5402)***
Airgo Systems 877 550-6111
13616 Railway Dr Oklahoma City (73114) ***(G-5403)***

A L P H A B E T I C

Airgo Systems LLC......405 346-5807
8232 Sw 23rd Pl Oklahoma City (73128) ***(G-5404)***
Airico Inc......918 836-2675
6530 E Independence St Tulsa (74115) ***(G-9130)***
Airinc Aerospace, Oklahoma City *Also called ARINC Incorporated* ***(G-5463)***
Airlock Pool Covers Inc......405 373-4040
5703 Ridgeroad Dr Nw Piedmont (73078) ***(G-7753)***
Airofab Ltd Co......918 693-1230
7801 S 4060 Rd Talala (74080) ***(G-8895)***
Airsorce LLC......918 519-7520
1343 N 108th East Ave Tulsa (74116) ***(G-9131)***
Airtech Products Inc......918 241-0264
1550 S 81st West Ave Tulsa (74127) ***(G-9132)***
Airwolf Filter Corp......918 561-8696
12801 Highway 75 Okmulgee (74447) ***(G-7493)***
Aj Publishers LLC......580 234-0064
117 N Washington St Enid (73701) ***(G-2909)***
Ajs Tees Inc......918 455-6751
18700 E 94th St Broken Arrow (74012) ***(G-821)***
Ajt Enterprises Inc......918 665-7083
2727 S Memorial Dr Tulsa (74129) ***(G-9133)***
Akerman Drilling Inc......580 925-3938
111 S Broadway St Konawa (74849) ***(G-3842)***
Akita Compression Services LLC......405 201-2677
14701 Glenmark Dr Edmond (73013) ***(G-2294)***
Akl Services......918 225-5533
601 E Pine St Cushing (74023) ***(G-1922)***
Akmfd, Yukon *Also called Plane Naked LLC* ***(G-11766)***
Al Capone Limo Corp......405 999-3335
8317 Nw 109th St Oklahoma City (73162) ***(G-5405)***
Al Pharma Inc......405 848-3299
7301 Broadway Ext Ste 110 Oklahoma City (73116) ***(G-5406)***
Al-S Pump & Supply, Walters *Also called Alfred N Smith* ***(G-11299)***
Ala Industries......405 533-3260
424 S Squires St Stillwater (74074) ***(G-8653)***
Aladdin Manufacturing Corp......405 943-3037
3121 Melcap Dr Ste B Oklahoma City (73179) ***(G-5407)***
Alan Beaty......405 664-6768
2409 S Dille Ave El Reno (73036) ***(G-2696)***
Alan Davis......580 651-9961
3054 Ne Hwy 54 Guymon (73942) ***(G-3344)***
Alan Industries Online......405 787-1102
7612 Nw 14th Ter Oklahoma City (73127) ***(G-5408)***
Alan L Buck......405 401-9372
960812 S Highway 18 Chandler (74834) ***(G-1374)***
Alan L Lamb......405 755-2233
11900 N Penn Ave Ste 1c Oklahoma City (73120) ***(G-5409)***
Alan Thompson Signs......918 808-3976
1516 W Phoenix Pl Broken Arrow (74011) ***(G-822)***
Alan Ware......918 658-5267
12954 Highway 77 Paoli (73074) ***(G-7637)***
Alans Benchworks Co......405 222-1181
510 S 4th St Chickasha (73018) ***(G-1427)***
Alas, Oklahoma City *Also called American Logo and Sign Inc* ***(G-5438)***
Albert J Geiger Revocable Tr......918 446-6388
3701 S 57th West Ave Tulsa (74107) ***(G-9134)***
Alberts Auto & Truck Repr Inc......866 772-6065
4900 S Frontage Rd Weatherford (73096) ***(G-11389)***
Alberts Truck Service and Sup, Weatherford *Also called Alberts Auto & Truck Repr Inc* ***(G-11389)***
Albright Steel and Wire Co (PA)......405 232-7526
12 S Virginia Ave Oklahoma City (73106) ***(G-5410)***
Albright Steel and Wire Co......580 357-3596
320 Se J Ave Lawton (73501) ***(G-3886)***
Alex Arms and Instruction LLC......405 351-0806
606 W G Ave Alex (73002) ***(G-129)***
Alex Pallets......405 414-2710
2716 S Central Ave Oklahoma City (73129) ***(G-5411)***
Alex Rogers......405 677-2306
1925 Se 29th St Oklahoma City (73129) ***(G-5412)***
Alexco Manufacturing LLC......405 274-4003
1911 E Highway 66 El Reno (73036) ***(G-2697)***
Alfa Laval Inc......918 251-7477
1201 S 9th St Broken Arrow (74012) ***(G-823)***
Alfa Laval Inc......918 251-7477
1030 E Nashville St Broken Arrow (74012) ***(G-824)***
Alfa Lval A Cled Exchngers Inc......918 251-7477
1201 S 9th St Broken Arrow (74012) ***(G-825)***
Alfalfa Dehydrating Plant Inc......918 482-3267
33090 E 211th St S Coweta (74429) ***(G-1871)***
Alfred N Smith......580 875-3317
176976 Highway 65 Walters (73572) ***(G-11299)***
Alice Kidd LLC......405 401-4391
2318 N Broadway Blvd Hinton (73047) ***(G-3520)***
Alico Embroidery Etc......405 321-2998
222 Merkle Dr Norman (73069) ***(G-4903)***
Alivecity, Sapulpa *Also called Sequoyah Technologies LLC* ***(G-8310)***
All American Bottling Cor......918 831-3800
2759 N Garnett Rd Tulsa (74116) ***(G-9135)***
All American Building......918 249-0515
11915 E 51st St Ste 25 Tulsa (74146) ***(G-9136)***
All American Ear Mold Labs......405 285-2411
625 Enterprise Dr Ste 160 Edmond (73013) ***(G-2295)***
All American Fire Systems Inc......918 341-6977
21125 E 480 Rd Claremore (74019) ***(G-1579)***
All American Mold Labs, Edmond *Also called All American Ear Mold Labs* ***(G-2295)***
All American Wrought Iron......918 213-9949
525 S Choctaw Ave Bartlesville (74003) ***(G-445)***
All Day Welding & Fabrication......405 550-2233
4503 N Highway 81 El Reno (73036) ***(G-2698)***
All Decked Out......918 313-9691
24103 S Highway 66 # 89 Claremore (74019) ***(G-1580)***
All Electronic and More Llc......918 557-5410
9742 E 182nd Pl N Collinsville (74021) ***(G-1799)***
All Music Games, Oklahoma City *Also called Pro Darts Inc* ***(G-6902)***
All Sheet Metal Co......405 733-0039
5717 Se 70th St Del City (73135) ***(G-1996)***
All Signs......918 739-3660
16401 E Admiral Pl Tulsa (74116) ***(G-9137)***
All Star Trophy Mfg, Claremore *Also called All-Star Trophies & Ribbon Mfg* ***(G-1581)***
All State Elc Mtr & Eqp Co, Muskogee *Also called All State Electric Motors Inc* ***(G-4645)***
All State Electric Motors Inc (PA)......405 232-1129
1839 Linwood Blvd Oklahoma City (73106) ***(G-5413)***
All State Electric Motors Inc......918 683-6581
1730 N 11th St Muskogee (74401) ***(G-4645)***
All States Production Eqp Co (PA)......405 672-2323
1128 Se 25th St Oklahoma City (73129) ***(G-5414)***
All Steel Carports LLC......918 683-1717
2500 S 32nd St Muskogee (74401) ***(G-4646)***
All Things Bugs LLC......352 281-3643
2211 Snapper Ln Oklahoma City (73130) ***(G-5415)***
All Tools Co Inc......405 942-6655
216 N Quapah Ave Oklahoma City (73107) ***(G-5416)***
All Wood Products Co Inc......918 585-9739
538 S Victor Ave Tulsa (74104) ***(G-9138)***
All-Star Trophies & Ribbon Mfg......918 283-2200
911 W Will Rogers Blvd Claremore (74017) ***(G-1581)***
Allan Bghs Wldg Roustabout Svc......918 625-1712
12589 S 486th West Ave Drumright (74030) ***(G-2050)***
Allan Edwards Incorporated (PA)......918 583-7184
6468 N Yale Ave Tulsa (74117) ***(G-9139)***
Allegiant Energy Production &......405 550-2331
1800 E Memorial Rd # 103 Oklahoma City (73131) ***(G-5417)***
Allegiant Precast LLC......918 486-6227
10763 S 257th East Ave Broken Arrow (74014) ***(G-1108)***
Allegra Marketing Print Mail......539 302-2229
7497 E 46th Pl Ste 1 Tulsa (74145) ***(G-9140)***
Allegra Print & Imaging, Tulsa *Also called MWH Enterprises Inc* ***(G-10320)***
Allem Sign Co......918 241-7206
4608 Redbud Dr Sand Springs (74063) ***(G-8158)***
Alleman Trim & Cabinets......405 942-7876
3800 Nw 28th St Oklahoma City (73107) ***(G-5418)***
Allen Advocate......580 857-2687
101 W Broadway Allen (74825) ***(G-132)***
Allen Brothers Feed......918 287-4379
129 E 5th St Pawhuska (74056) ***(G-7676)***
Allen Camper Mfg Company Inc......580 857-2177
29981 State Highway 1e Allen (74825) ***(G-133)***
Allen Rathole Inc......918 626-4026
19279 Us Highway 271 Spiro (74959) ***(G-8613)***
Allen Sheet Metal Inc......918 834-2279
8724 E 11th St Tulsa (74112) ***(G-9141)***
Allen Sign Studio LLC......918 542-1180
307 E Central Ave Miami (74354) ***(G-4390)***
Allen Signs......580 688-2985
305 W Washington St Hollis (73550) ***(G-3563)***
Allen Vineyards LLC......405 240-7147
6708 Nw 39th Expy Bethany (73008) ***(G-572)***
Allens Trucking & Welding Svc......405 341-8066
14585 E Old Highway 66 Arcadia (73007) ***(G-227)***
Allens Welding Service......580 584-2375
100 Silvey Rd Broken Bow (74728) ***(G-1182)***
Allens Woodcraft......918 224-8796
3020 Dogwood Ln Sapulpa (74066) ***(G-8247)***
Alliance Coal LLC (HQ)......918 295-7600
1717 S Boulder Ave # 400 Tulsa (74119) ***(G-9142)***
Alliance Holdings Gp LP (PA)......918 295-1415
1717 S Boulder Ave # 400 Tulsa (74119) ***(G-9143)***
Alliance Machine Service Inc......918 836-5588
1151 N Delaware Pl Tulsa (74110) ***(G-9144)***
Alliance Resource Finance Corp......918 295-1415
1717 S Boulder Ave # 400 Tulsa (74119) ***(G-9145)***
Alliance Resource Holdings Inc (PA)......918 295-7600
1717 S Boulder Ave Fl 6 Tulsa (74119) ***(G-9146)***
Alliance Resource Partners LP (HQ)......918 295-7600
1717 S Boulder Ave # 400 Tulsa (74119) ***(G-9147)***
Alliance Rsrce Oper Prtners LP (HQ)......918 295-7600
1717 S Boulder Ave # 600 Tulsa (74119) ***(G-9148)***

Alliance Sealants & Waterproof 405 627-9474
1205 Se 44th St Ste 1 Oklahoma City (73129) ***(G-5419)***
Alliance Steel Inc 405 745-7500
3333 S Council Rd Oklahoma City (73179) ***(G-5420)***
Alliance Steel Bldg Systems, Oklahoma City *Also called Alliance Steel Inc* ***(G-5420)***
Alliance Wor Properties LLC 918 295-7600
1717 S Boulder Ave # 400 Tulsa (74119) ***(G-9149)***
Allied Cstm Gyps Plasterworks, Mooreland *Also called Harrison Gypsum LLC* ***(G-4592)***
Allied Custom Gypsum, Norman *Also called Harrison Gypsum LLC* ***(G-5018)***
Allied Custom Gypsum 580 337-6371
17 Miles E Of Mreland Hwy Waynoka (73860) ***(G-11370)***
Allied Foam Fabricators Inc 405 946-0384
902 N Ann Arbor Ave Oklahoma City (73127) ***(G-5421)***
Allied H2o Inc 405 550-3085
1004 Woodbury Dr Edmond (73034) ***(G-2296)***
Allied Manufacturing Tech 918 899-9504
1424 S Knoxville Ave Tulsa (74112) ***(G-9150)***
Allied Motion Technologies Inc 918 627-1845
10002 E 43rd St Tulsa (74146) ***(G-9151)***
Allied Stone Inc 580 931-3388
2201 W Arkansas St Durant (74701) ***(G-2201)***
Allied Wireline Services LLC 405 445-7135
13020 S Sunnylane Rd Moore (73160) ***(G-4485)***
Allison Allison Inc 918 344-1768
11822 S 96th East Pl Bixby (74008) ***(G-610)***
Allpro Mfg LLC 580 512-7248
16775 County Road Ns 220 Tipton (73570) ***(G-8957)***
Allsbury Marketing & Pubg LLC 405 412-0809
2017 Bradford Way Edmond (73003) ***(G-2297)***
Allstate Sheet Metal Inc 405 636-1914
8605 Gateway Ter Oklahoma City (73149) ***(G-5422)***
Alltra Corp 918 534-5100
2300 Partridge Rd Dewey (74029) ***(G-2014)***
Alltra Corporation 918 534-5100
1600 Patridge Rd Dewey (74029) ***(G-2015)***
Allure Salon and Spa LLC 580 371-9333
103 N Broadway St Tishomingo (73460) ***(G-8961)***
Alluring Lures & Tackle Co LLC 580 832-5177
215 E Main St Cordell (73632) ***(G-1854)***
Allys Discount Scrubs 918 935-1359
115 E El Paso St Broken Arrow (74012) ***(G-826)***
Aloft Software LLC 405 633-0250
2706 Nw 68th St Oklahoma City (73116) ***(G-5423)***
Alpha Combustion LLC 918 851-1751
2206 E 24th St Tulsa (74114) ***(G-9152)***
Alpha Concrete Products Inc 405 769-7777
10213 Ne 23rd St Oklahoma City (73141) ***(G-5424)***
Alpha Dental Studios 405 359-2976
2300 S Broadway Ste 102 Edmond (73013) ***(G-2298)***
Alpha Investment Casting Corp (PA) 918 834-4686
6160 S New Haven Ave Tulsa (74136) ***(G-9153)***
Alpha Investment Casting LLC 918 834-4686
6160 S New Haven Ave Tulsa (74136) ***(G-9154)***
Alpha Machining & Mfg Inc 918 438-2755
1604 N 161st East Ave Tulsa (74116) ***(G-9155)***
Alpha Oilfield Services LLC 580 330-1285
704 Highland Dr Weatherford (73096) ***(G-11390)***
Alpha Omega Mltary/Defence Mfg 918 816-6918
228 N K St Muskogee (74403) ***(G-4647)***
Alpha Research & Tech Inc 405 733-1919
2601 Liberty Pkwy Oklahoma City (73110) ***(G-5425)***
Alphagraffix Inc 405 354-3000
302 W Main St Yukon (73099) ***(G-11690)***
Alpine Inc 405 507-1111
3409 S Broadway Ste 600 Edmond (73013) ***(G-2299)***
Alro Steel Corporation 918 439-1000
4321 N Garnett Rd Tulsa (74116) ***(G-9156)***
Als Vacuum Repair 405 550-8599
336 Thompson Dr Norman (73069) ***(G-4904)***
Alsate Management and Inv Co, Oklahoma City *Also called Sandridge Operating Company* ***(G-7082)***
Altec Inc 405 577-6322
9920 W Reno Ave Oklahoma City (73127) ***(G-5426)***
Alterntive Gthrmal Sltions Inc 405 948-0410
3710 N Meridian Ave Oklahoma City (73112) ***(G-5427)***
Altman Energy Inc 918 584-4781
15 W 6th St Ste 2301 Tulsa (74119) ***(G-9157)***
Altman Engineering Inc 405 368-7889
1 Mile N On Hwy 81 Kingfisher (73750) ***(G-3784)***
Altus Print Ship 580 482-6855
1701 Falcon Rd Altus (73521) ***(G-140)***
Altus Printing Co Inc 580 482-2020
421 W Broadway St Altus (73521) ***(G-141)***
Altus Ready Mix, Altus *Also called Evans & Associates Entps Inc* ***(G-155)***
Altus Ready-Mix Inc 580 482-3418
710 S Jackson St Altus (73521) ***(G-142)***
Altus Times, Altus *Also called Civitas Media LLC* ***(G-149)***
Alva Concrete Inc 580 327-2281
44223 Harmon Rd Alva (73717) ***(G-173)***
Alva Monument Works Inc (PA) 580 327-0626
724 E Oklahoma Blvd Alva (73717) ***(G-174)***
Alvin Stone 918 447-4455
2404 W 41st St Tulsa (74107) ***(G-9158)***
Always Blessed 918 592-2200
552 N 28th West Pl Tulsa (74127) ***(G-9159)***
Always Done Right LLC 405 615-5955
2228 Nw 159th Ter Edmond (73013) ***(G-2300)***
Always Welding 918 426-9353
32 E Morris Ave McAlester (74501) ***(G-4269)***
Amarillo Chittom Airslo 918 585-5638
728 S Wheeling Ave Tulsa (74104) ***(G-9160)***
Amarillo Cstm Fixs Co Inc Okla 918 266-7752
25905 E Admiral Pl Catoosa (74015) ***(G-1296)***
Amazing Grace Fudge LLC 580 883-4693
263025 E County Road 48 Ringwood (73768) ***(G-8083)***
Amazing Graze LLC 405 447-4893
2804 Belknap Ave Norman (73072) ***(G-4905)***
Amb Quick Sign Stores, Oklahoma City *Also called Advertising Signs & Awngs Inc* ***(G-5388)***
Ambassador Lighting LLC 405 503-5726
6701 N Prospect Ave Oklahoma City (73111) ***(G-5428)***
Ambers Candle 405 492-3620
821 Nw 23rd St Apt 21 Moore (73160) ***(G-4486)***
Ambiance Graphics, Broken Arrow *Also called Print N Copy Inc* ***(G-1011)***
Ambrose Welding LLC 580 704-0356
13671 Ne Cornwallis Dr Elgin (73538) ***(G-2774)***
Ambrosia Sweet Inc 405 816-2887
1400 N Broadview Dr Oklahoma City (73127) ***(G-5429)***
Amcon Resources 405 236-4100
5400 N Grand Blvd Ste 565 Oklahoma City (73112) ***(G-5430)***
Amcon Resources & Engineering, Oklahoma City *Also called Amcon Resources* ***(G-5430)***
Ameracrane and Hoist LLC 918 437-4775
16645 Eastpark St Tulsa (74116) ***(G-9161)***
Amercool Manufacturing Co Inc (PA) 918 445-5366
6312 S 39th West Ave Tulsa (74132) ***(G-9162)***
Amerex Corp 405 216-5548
933 Nw 164th St Ste 3 Edmond (73013) ***(G-2301)***
American Accessibility Eqp Svc 405 631-4142
1905 S Harvard Dr Ste C Oklahoma City (73128) ***(G-5431)***
American Airlines Inc 918 292-2698
3900 N Mingo Rd Tulsa (74116) ***(G-9163)***
American Angler Publications 918 364-4210
800 S Cherokee St C Catoosa (74015) ***(G-1297)***
American Assn Petro Geologists (PA) 918 584-2555
1444 S Boulder Ave Tulsa (74119) ***(G-9164)***
American Automation Inc ....
4592 E 480 Pryor (74361) ***(G-7941)***
American Badge & Engraving, Catoosa *Also called David Logan* ***(G-1315)***
American Bank Systems Inc 405 607-7000
14000 Parkway Commons Dr Oklahoma City (73134) ***(G-5432)***
American Beauty Manufacturing 918 671-0351
1623 E Apache St Tulsa (74106) ***(G-9165)***
American Bottling Company 405 680-5150
5200 Sw 36th St Ste 600 Oklahoma City (73179) ***(G-5433)***
American Castings LLC 918 476-4252
5265 Hunt St Pryor (74361) ***(G-7942)***
American Choral Directors Assn (PA) 405 232-8161
545 Couch Dr Oklahoma City (73102) ***(G-5434)***
American Crating Company 918 425-8787
11343 E Tecumseh St Tulsa (74116) ***(G-9166)***
American Crtfication Pull Tstg, Seminole *Also called Tx3 LLC* ***(G-8405)***
American Custom Woodworks LLC 918 344-4988
1024 E Hastain Ave Sapulpa (74066) ***(G-8248)***
American Directional Tech 405 449-3362
26426 120th St Wayne (73095) ***(G-11365)***
American Drones LLC 405 308-0866
1000 Sw 4th St Moore (73160) ***(G-4487)***
American Electric Ignition Co, Oklahoma City *Also called Aei Corp-Okla* ***(G-5389)***
American Engraving & Trophy 405 360-2744
2104 W Lindsey St Norman (73069) ***(G-4906)***
American Entps Whl Dstributers (PA) 405 273-4516
1905 E Walnut St Shawnee (74801) ***(G-8427)***
American Fence and Carport, Oklahoma City *Also called American Fence Company Inc* ***(G-5435)***
American Fence Company Inc 405 685-4800
215 N Cooley Dr Oklahoma City (73127) ***(G-5435)***
American Fiber Industries 918 335-6100
1560 Industrial Blvd Bartlesville (74006) ***(G-446)***
American Foundry Group, Bixby *Also called Afg Acquisition Group LLC* ***(G-608)***
American Foundry Group, Muskogee *Also called Afg Acquisition Group LLC* ***(G-4644)***
American Gaming Systems, Oklahoma City *Also called AGS LLC* ***(G-5400)***
American Gypsum Company LLC 580 679-3391
Highway 62 W Duke (73532) ***(G-2079)***
American Heating Company Inc 918 246-0700
11 E Broadway St Ste 200a Sand Springs (74063) ***(G-8159)***
American Industrial Inc 918 445-0627
1218 W 41st St Ste B Tulsa (74107) ***(G-9167)***
American Intellectual LLC 405 605-2378
44 Nw 44th St Oklahoma City (73118) ***(G-5436)***

ALPHABETIC

American International Ltd 405 364-1776
804 N Porter Ave Norman (73071) ***(G-4907)***
American Intl Flag Pole Map G, Norman *Also called American International Ltd* ***(G-4907)***
American Intrprtive Monitoring 405 841-7826
13401 Railway Dr Oklahoma City (73114) ***(G-5437)***
American Iron 405 414-2629
2401 Oak Forest Dr Norman (73071) ***(G-4908)***
American Iron Sports 580 716-5662
108 W Grand Ave Tonkawa (74653) ***(G-8971)***
American Iron Works, Yukon *Also called Classic Iron Works Inc* ***(G-11706)***
American Laser Inc 918 234-9700
5138 S 94th East Ave Tulsa (74145) ***(G-9168)***
American Logo and Sign Inc 405 799-1800
2631 S I 35 Service Rd Moore (73160) ***(G-4488)***
American Logo and Sign Inc (PA) 405 799-1800
12501 N Santa Fe Ave Oklahoma City (73114) ***(G-5438)***
American Machine & Tool Co 405 794-9820
36690 State Highway 270 Wewoka (74884) ***(G-11497)***
American Machining Company LLC 918 885-6194
9646 State Highway 99 Hominy (74035) ***(G-3574)***
American Manifold 580 225-1116
102 Oilfield Rd Elk City (73644) ***(G-2783)***
American Marble 918 812-7940
3815 Charles Page Blvd Tulsa (74127) ***(G-9169)***
American McHning Solutions LLC 405 606-7038
2618 S I 35 Svc Rd Ste 30 Oklahoma City (73129) ***(G-5439)***
American Mfg Co of Okla 918 446-1968
1025 W 41st St Tulsa (74107) ***(G-9170)***
American Millwork Company Inc 405 681-5347
3650 Sw 29th St Oklahoma City (73119) ***(G-5440)***
American Painting and Rmdlg, Oklahoma City *Also called A P & R Industries Inc* ***(G-5347)***
American Petro & Enviromental, Edmond *Also called American Petroleum & Envrnmntl* ***(G-2302)***
American Petro Mineral Co Inc 405 382-1255
220 Quail Creek Rd Seminole (74868) ***(G-8354)***
American Petroleum & Envrnmntl 405 513-6055
2240 Nw 164th St Edmond (73013) ***(G-2302)***
American Petroleum Corporation 580 856-3580
25525 Hwy 76 Ratliff City (73481) ***(G-8048)***
American Phoenix Inc 580 248-1488
5201 Sw 11th St Lawton (73501) ***(G-3887)***
American Pipe Bending Inc 918 749-2363
3207 Dawson Rd Tulsa (74110) ***(G-9171)***
American Pipe Bending Company, Tulsa *Also called American Pipe Bending Inc* ***(G-9171)***
American Pirate Screen, Ardmore *Also called Daniel P Wollaston* ***(G-272)***
American Signworx 479 650-4562
203 N Pocola Blvd Pocola (74902) ***(G-7780)***
American Sportswear Inc 918 665-7636
7636 E 46th St Tulsa (74145) ***(G-9172)***
American Stamp & Seal, Norman *Also called American Engraving & Trophy* ***(G-4906)***
American Street Rod Co 405 373-0376
428 Ash Ne Piedmont (73078) ***(G-7754)***
American Swat Solutions LLC 405 568-1413
5472 N 55th St E Fort Gibson (74434) ***(G-3172)***
American Tank & Cnstr Co 918 254-6292
1451 N Fulton Ave Tulsa (74115) ***(G-9173)***
American Tank Gauge Inc 405 224-7881
1801 W Carolina Ave Chickasha (73018) ***(G-1428)***
American Textile Screen Prtg, Mounds *Also called American TS* ***(G-4609)***
American Tissue Industries LLC 562 207-6814
50 N Council Rd Oklahoma City (73127) ***(G-5441)***
American Tradition 918 688-7725
5834 S 129th East Ave Tulsa (74134) ***(G-9174)***
American Traditions Clothing 918 622-8337
10306 E 52nd St Tulsa (74146) ***(G-9175)***
American TS 918 288-6682
15072 S Dogwood St Glenpool (74033) ***(G-3230)***
American TS 918 284-7685
1205 Alt 75 Mounds (74047) ***(G-4609)***
American Wheatley, Broken Arrow *Also called Global Flow Products LLC* ***(G-919)***
American Zinc Recycling Corp 918 336-7100
Hwy 123 Bartlesville (74005) ***(G-447)***
American-Chief Co 918 358-2553
212 S Broadway St Cleveland (74020) ***(G-1715)***
American-Chief Co (PA) 918 762-2552
558 Illinois St Pawnee (74058) ***(G-7699)***
American-Chief Co 918 885-2101
115 W Main St Hominy (74035) ***(G-3575)***
Americana Energy Company Inc 580 310-0084
106 N Main St Ada (74820) ***(G-7)***
Ameriflex Hose and ACC LLC 918 437-7002
12940 E Admiral Pl Tulsa (74116) ***(G-9176)***
Ameriflow Energy Services, Oklahoma City *Also called Ameriflow Inc* ***(G-5442)***
Ameriflow Inc 405 603-1200
5749 Nw 132nd St Oklahoma City (73142) ***(G-5442)***
Ameriglobe LLC 918 496-7711
1887 E 71st St Tulsa (74136) ***(G-9177)***
Ameriinfovets Inc (PA) 408 446-4343
33 Woodcreek Ln Pryor (74361) ***(G-7943)***
Ameripump Mfg LLC 918 438-2953
13759 E Apache St Tulsa (74116) ***(G-9178)***
Ameristar Primeter SEC USA Inc (HQ) 918 835-0898
1555 N Mingo Rd Tulsa (74116) ***(G-9179)***
Amerities Holdings LLC (PA) 405 359-3235
933 Nw 164th St Ste 1 Edmond (73013) ***(G-2303)***
Amerities South LLC (HQ) 405 359-3235
933 Nw 164th St Ste 1 Edmond (73013) ***(G-2304)***
Ameron International Corp 918 858-3973
4903 E 66th St N Tulsa (74117) ***(G-9180)***
Ameron Pole Products LLC 918 585-5611
2333 S Yukon Ave Tulsa (74107) ***(G-9181)***
Amerril Energy LLC 770 856-2662
411 Nw 5th St Oklahoma City (73102) ***(G-5443)***
Ametek-Chandler Instruments, Broken Arrow *Also called Chandler Instruments Co LLC* ***(G-866)***
Amethyst Research Incorporated 580 657-2575
123 Case Cir Ardmore (73401) ***(G-238)***
AMI, Broken Arrow *Also called Advanced Medical Instrs Inc* ***(G-816)***
AMI, Tulsa *Also called Amercool Manufacturing Co Inc* ***(G-9162)***
AMI Instruments Inc 918 241-2665
4116 Rustic Rd Sand Springs (74063) ***(G-8160)***
Amigos Salsa (PA) 580 224-0667
1009 S Rockford Rd Ardmore (73401) ***(G-239)***
Amigos Salsa 580 224-1424
3334 S Commerce St Ardmore (73401) ***(G-240)***
Amini's Galleria, Oklahoma City *Also called Billiards & Bar Stools Inc* ***(G-5566)***
Amron Enterprises LLC 918 224-9222
1205 N Frankoma Rd Sapulpa (74066) ***(G-8249)***
AMS, Okemah *Also called Beck Illuminations LLC* ***(G-5264)***
AMS, Edmond *Also called Advanced Micro Solutions Inc* ***(G-2290)***
AMS, Oklahoma City *Also called Advanced McHning Solutions LLC* ***(G-5384)***
AMS Machining Specialists LLC 918 610-2570
7400 E 42nd Pl Tulsa (74145) ***(G-9182)***
Amt Diversified Cnstr Inc 580 279-6250
12157 County Road 3570 Ada (74820) ***(G-8)***
Amys Candles and Gifts LLC 918 865-2827
370340 E 5605 Rd Terlton (74081) ***(G-8937)***
Anadarko Consultants Ltd 405 354-7788
1450 N Azalea Way Mustang (73064) ***(G-4761)***
Anadarko Dozer and Trckg LLC 918 496-4777
1869 E 71st St Tulsa (74136) ***(G-9183)***
Anadarko Dozer and Trckg LLC 405 542-3297
3 1/2 Miles S On Hwy 281 Hinton (73047) ***(G-3521)***
Anadarko Petroleum Corporation 405 756-4347
804 W Cherokee St Lindsay (73052) ***(G-4043)***
Anadarko Publishing Co 405 247-3331
117 E Broadway St Anadarko (73005) ***(G-199)***
Anatole Publishing LLC 405 609-0763
3613 24th Ave Se Norman (73071) ***(G-4909)***
Anchor Auto & Welding Repr LLC 918 426-7662
8 W Tyler Ave McAlester (74501) ***(G-4270)***
Anchor Exploration of Oklahoma 918 605-1005
17007 S 4102 Rd Claremore (74017) ***(G-1582)***
Anchor Gasoline Corporation (PA) 918 584-5291
2847 E 36th Pl Tulsa (74105) ***(G-9184)***
Anchor Glass Container Corp 918 652-9631
601 E Bollinger Rd Henryetta (74437) ***(G-3499)***
Anchor Paint Mfg Co (PA) 918 836-4626
6707 E 14th St Tulsa (74112) ***(G-9185)***
Anchor Paint Mfg Co 918 272-0880
401 E 2nd Ave Owasso (74055) ***(G-7544)***
Anchor Stone Co (PA) 918 599-7255
4124 S Rockford Ave # 201 Tulsa (74105) ***(G-9186)***
Anchor Stone Co 918 872-8449
14311 S 129th East Ave Broken Arrow (74011) ***(G-827)***
Anchor Stone Co 918 299-6384
11302 S Delaware Ave Tulsa (74137) ***(G-9187)***
Anchor Stone Co 918 438-1060
66 St N North Tulsa (74137) ***(G-9188)***
Ancile Industries 405 990-5018
4309 Katie Ridge Dr Moore (73160) ***(G-4489)***
Anderson Logging LLC 580 584-9898
155 Freesia Rd Broken Bow (74728) ***(G-1183)***
Anderson Rt Industries LLC 918 607-5150
2316 S Kalanchoe Ave Broken Arrow (74012) ***(G-828)***
Anderson Welding 580 355-9806
1440 Nw 40th St Lawton (73505) ***(G-3888)***
Andre Anderson 405 642-3210
3300 Paul Dr Moore (73160) ***(G-4490)***
Andrea Koenig 918 745-0828
2892 E 51st St Apt D Tulsa (74105) ***(G-9189)***
Andreae Team Inc 580 223-9334
3550 Cypert Way Ardmore (73401) ***(G-241)***
Andrews Welding 405 990-7326
13200 Se 74th St Oklahoma City (73150) ***(G-5444)***
Andrews Woodworking 918 664-6722
14217 E 33rd St Tulsa (74134) ***(G-9190)***

Andy Anderson Metal Works Inc 918 245-2355
1064 1/2 N Willow Rd Sand Springs (74063) *(G-8161)*
Andy Cross Roustabout Svc LLC 918 906-1240
10718 S 337th West Ave Mannford (74044) *(G-4174)*
Anesthesia Services 580 536-7150
7602 Nw Micklegate Blvd Lawton (73505) *(G-3889)*
Angel Delite Inc 580 223-9777
1019 Republic St Ardmore (73401) *(G-242)*
Angel Exploration 405 848-8360
3005 Nw 63rd St Oklahoma City (73116) *(G-5445)*
Angel Ornamental Iron Works 918 584-8726
1407 E 6th St Tulsa (74120) *(G-9191)*
Angel Welding Service LLC 918 706-2237
1732 S 6th St Broken Arrow (74012) *(G-829)*
Angela Lyn Sarabia 405 808-8576
1408 Sw 68th St Oklahoma City (73159) *(G-5446)*
Angus Natural Resources LLC 918 712-8487
2 W 2nd St Ste 1700 Tulsa (74103) *(G-9192)*
Anita and Harold Speed 580 838-2297
725 Carpenters Bluff Rd Hendrix (74741) *(G-3438)*
Aniti Pollution Tank, Yukon *Also called APT Inc* *(G-11691)*
Anna Lightle 405 853-4530
Rr 3 Hennessey (73742) *(G-3445)*
Annabella Oil & Gas Co LLC 405 377-8030
6610 W Coventry Dr Stillwater (74074) *(G-8654)*
Annie Printer 405 670-9640
5412 Charwood Ln Oklahoma City (73135) *(G-5447)*
Anns Quick Print Co Inc 405 222-1871
320 W Chickasha Ave Chickasha (73018) *(G-1429)*
Ansa Company Inc (PA) 918 687-1664
1200 S Main St Muskogee (74401) *(G-4648)*
Ansiels Welding & Constructio 580 920-0573
72 Moore Ln Durant (74701) *(G-2202)*
Anson Desimone 610 433-1299
20350 State Highway 37 Hinton (73047) *(G-3522)*
Anson Memorial Co 918 358-2504
606 N Division St Cleveland (74020) *(G-1716)*
Anstine-Musgrove 580 762-6355
204 E Grand Ave Ponca City (74601) *(G-7796)*
Antares Enterprises LLC 405 329-4326
2715 Aspen Cir Norman (73072) *(G-4910)*
Antelope Oil Tool Mfg Co LLC 405 691-2490
13808 S Macarthur Blvd Oklahoma City (73173) *(G-5448)*
Anthony W Layton Cpo 580 353-8885
15 Sw B Ave Lawton (73501) *(G-3890)*
Antioch Operating LLC 405 236-0080
12 E California Ave # 200 Oklahoma City (73104) *(G-5449)*
Antique & Rod Shop LLC 405 631-3544
529 Se 59th St Oklahoma City (73129) *(G-5450)*
Antlers Roof & Truss Co, Antlers *Also called Antlers Roof-Truss & Bldrs Sup* *(G-213)*
Antlers Roof-Truss & Bldrs Sup 580 298-3560
1010 Ne 5th St Antlers (74523) *(G-213)*
Antoinette Baking Co LLC 918 808-0875
207 N Main St Tulsa (74103) *(G-9193)*
Anvil House Publishers LLC 918 760-8991
10208 E 89th St N Owasso (74055) *(G-7545)*
Anvil Land and Properties Inc 580 336-4402
1959 W Fir St Perry (73077) *(G-7726)*
Anything Canvas LLC 580 658-9330
280906 E 1640 Rd Marlow (73055) *(G-4221)*
Anything Goes, Norman *Also called K A G U Inc* *(G-5045)*
Anytime Propane LLC 405 417-0222
124 Mockingbird Ln Chickasha (73018) *(G-1430)*
Anywhere Infltable Screens LLC 918 260-4146
6908 E 64th Pl Tulsa (74133) *(G-9194)*
AO Inc 918 623-1711
15 W Broadway St Okemah (74859) *(G-5263)*
AP Jetworks LLC 405 226-2583
4625 Spectacular Bid Ave Edmond (73025) *(G-2305)*
APAC Central, Vinita *Also called APAC Oklahoma Inc* *(G-11247)*
APAC Oklahoma Inc 918 256-8397
26457 S 4460 Rd Vinita (74301) *(G-11247)*
Apac-Central 918 534-1741
400251 W 1500 Rd Dewey (74029) *(G-2016)*
Apac-Central Inc 918 696-2820
Hwy 59 N Stilwell (74960) *(G-8780)*
Apac-Central Inc 918 256-7853
26457 S 4460 Rd Vinita (74301) *(G-11248)*
Apac-Central Inc 918 921-6491
4608 S Garnett Rd Ste 600 Tulsa (74146) *(G-9195)*
Apac-Central Inc 918 775-3251
1000 W Cherokee Ave 683 Sallisaw (74955) *(G-8137)*
Apac-Central Inc 918 683-1362
4997 State Hwy 251a Okay (74446) *(G-5256)*
Apache Corporation 405 222-5040
1710 Charles Allen Blvd Chickasha (73018) *(G-1431)*
Apache Machine Co Inc 918 834-0022
4316 E Pine Pl Tulsa (74115) *(G-9196)*
Apache News 580 588-3862
120 E Evans Ave Apache (73006) *(G-217)*
Apc LLC 918 587-6242
1307 S Boulder Ave # 400 Tulsa (74119) *(G-9197)*
Apergy Artfl Lift Intl LLC 405 677-3153
1315 Se 29th St Oklahoma City (73129) *(G-5451)*
Apergy Artfl Lift Intl LLC 432 561-8101
4801 W 49th St Tulsa (74107) *(G-9198)*
Apergy Artfl Lift Systems LLC 918 396-0558
19425 E 54th St S Broken Arrow (74014) *(G-1109)*
Apergy ESP Systems LLC (HQ) 918 396-0558
19425 E 54th St S Broken Arrow (74014) *(G-1110)*
Apergy ESP Systems LLC 918 536-3038
401 Wyandotte Ave Ramona (74061) *(G-8044)*
Apex Inc (PA) 405 247-7377
117 S 1st St Anadarko (73005) *(G-200)*
Apex Composites Inc 580 436-6444
414 Chamber Loop Ada (74820) *(G-9)*
Apex405 405 313-5145
1917 Atchison Dr Norman (73069) *(G-4911)*
API Enterprises Inc 713 580-4800
4901 S I 35 Service Rd Oklahoma City (73129) *(G-5452)*
API Metallurgical 918 266-4130
18501 E Admiral Pl Catoosa (74015) *(G-1298)*
Apollo Engineering Company 918 251-6780
809 W Elgin St Broken Arrow (74012) *(G-830)*
Apollo Exploration LLC 405 286-0600
1001 Nw 63rd St Ste 100 Oklahoma City (73116) *(G-5453)*
Apollo Metal Specialities, Claremore *Also called Apollo Metal Specialties Inc* *(G-1583)*
Apollo Metal Specialties Inc 918 341-7650
2605 S Highway 66 Claremore (74019) *(G-1583)*
Apollo Oilfield Supply LLC 580 254-0164
1416 46th St Woodward (73801) *(G-11554)*
Apollo Ornamental Iron LLC 405 672-5377
5400 S Hattie Ave Oklahoma City (73129) *(G-5454)*
Apothem 405 447-2345
733 Asp Ave Ste A Norman (73069) *(G-4912)*
App-Solute Innovations LLC 580 453-0055
1016 S Mississippi Ave Ada (74820) *(G-10)*
Applause Apprarel 580 762-1349
1404 N Pecan Rd Ponca City (74604) *(G-7797)*
Apple Art 405 691-4393
1007 Sw 24th St Moore (73170) *(G-4491)*
Apple Street Inc 918 367-9898
119 W 6th Ave Bristow (74010) *(G-764)*
Appleton Grp LLC 918 627-5530
9810 E 42nd St Ste 102 Tulsa (74146) *(G-9199)*
Appli-Fab Custom Coating 405 235-7039
913 Woods Ter Chandler (74834) *(G-1375)*
Applications For Medicine LLC 405 330-7910
3013 Broken Bow Cir Edmond (73013) *(G-2306)*
Applied Cntrls Sys Integration, Tulsa *Also called AC Systems Integration Inc* *(G-9084)*
Applied Indus Coatings LLC 405 692-2249
13920 S Meridian Ave Oklahoma City (73173) *(G-5455)*
Applied Indus Machining Inc 405 672-2222
2601 Nw Expwy Ste 900e Oklahoma City (73112) *(G-5456)*
Applied Indus Machining LLC 405 672-2222
1930 Se 29th St Oklahoma City (73129) *(G-5457)*
Applied Laser Systems 918 249-9025
7110 S Mingo Rd Ste 105 Tulsa (74133) *(G-9200)*
Applied Oil Tools LLC 405 670-8665
1545 Se 29th St Ste A Oklahoma City (73129) *(G-5458)*
April Oilfield Services 405 756-5688
10414 N County Road 3010 Lindsay (73052) *(G-4044)*
APS of Oklahoma LLC 405 793-8877
500 Sw 11th St Moore Moore (73160) *(G-4492)*
Apsco, Tulsa *Also called Air Power Systems Co LLC* *(G-9121)*
Apsco Inc 918 622-5600
8178 E 44th St Tulsa (74145) *(G-9201)*
Apss Inc 405 324-2071
9500 Sw 15th St Oklahoma City (73128) *(G-5459)*
APT Inc 405 354-8438
1135 Industrial Dr Yukon (73099) *(G-11691)*
Aqua Eco Environmental Svcs 952 300-0456
4004 W Twin Oaks Pl Broken Arrow (74011) *(G-831)*
ARA, Ponca City *Also called October Graphics* *(G-7861)*
Arbuckle Enterprises Inc 405 359-2815
1620 E 19th St Edmond (73013) *(G-2307)*
Arbuckle Mountain Tower Corp 580 223-3408
10 W Main St Ste 418 Ardmore (73401) *(G-243)*
Arbuckle Wireline 405 620-6739
4374 W Waterloo Rd Edmond (73025) *(G-2308)*
Arbuckle Wireline LLC 580 226-4001
2214323 Us Hwy 701 Ardmore (73401) *(G-244)*
ARC, Tulsa *Also called Advanced Racing Composites LLC* *(G-9111)*
ARC Document Solutions LLC 405 943-0378
3631 Nw 23rd St Oklahoma City (73107) *(G-5460)*
ARC Document Solutions LLC 918 663-8100
7022 E 41st St Tulsa (74145) *(G-9202)*
ARC Rvals Wldg Fabrication LLC 918 577-5066
5231 S 37th St E Muskogee (74403) *(G-4649)*

ARC-Angel Welding   ALPHABETIC SECTION

ARC-Angel Welding...918 838-0047
5961 E 12th St Tulsa (74112) *(G-9203)*
Arcadia Oil Corp...405 409-2013
4910 Clipper Xing Edmond (73013) *(G-2309)*
Arcadia Printing of Tulsa Inc.................................918 622-1875
14956 S Grant St Bixby (74008) *(G-611)*
Arcadia Resources LP..405 608-5453
301 Nw 63rd St Ste 600 Oklahoma City (73116) *(G-5461)*
Archein Aerospace LLC...682 499-2150
2501 N Waverly St Ponca City (74601) *(G-7798)*
Archer Printing Inc...405 236-1607
316 Se 6th St Moore (73160) *(G-4493)*
Archer Technologies Intl Inc (PA)............................405 306-3220
109 N Broadway Ave Ste 1 Shawnee (74801) *(G-8428)*
Archer-Daniels-Midland Company..........................580 237-8000
1301 N 4th St Enid (73701) *(G-2910)*
Archer-Daniels-Midland Company..........................580 652-3761
Rr 1 Box 65 Hooker (73945) *(G-3595)*
Archer-Daniels-Midland Company..........................580 233-3800
2502 N 16th St Enid (73701) *(G-2911)*
Archer-Daniels-Midland Company..........................580 652-2623
98-37 Mile Hooker (73945) *(G-3596)*
Archer-Daniels-Midland Company..........................580 854-6285
204 W Oklahoma St Tyrone (73951) *(G-11218)*
Archer-Daniels-Midland Company..........................580 233-5100
2309 N 10th St Ste A Enid (73701) *(G-2912)*
Archer-Daniels-Midland Company..........................580 482-7100
701 S Lee St Altus (73521) *(G-143)*
Architectural Fabricators Inc.................................918 331-0393
1034 Ne Washington Blvd Bartlesville (74006) *(G-448)*
Architectural Graphics Inc....................................757 427-1900
104 S 2nd St Chickasha (73018) *(G-1432)*
Architectural Metal Panels LLC..............................405 672-7407
1616 S Lowery St Oklahoma City (73129) *(G-5462)*
Architectural Models..405 360-2828
2801 Meadow Ave Norman (73072) *(G-4913)*
Architectural Pav Systems LLC...............................918 747-9302
3220 E 27th Pl Tulsa (74114) *(G-9204)*
Architectural Sign & Graphics................................405 354-8829
839 Industrial Dr Yukon (73099) *(G-11692)*
Architectural Sign Designs, Owasso *Also called AS Designs LLC* *(G-7546)*
Archrock Inc..580 824-0102
32728 State Highway 45 Waynoka (73860) *(G-11371)*
Archrock Inc..580 225-2091
1306 Airport Indus Rd Elk City (73644) *(G-2784)*
Archrock Inc..918 558-2216
401 E Hwy 270 Alderson (74522) *(G-127)*
Archrock Inc..918 900-4200
5727 S Lewis Ave Ste 610 Tulsa (74105) *(G-9205)*
Arcosa Acg Inc...405 366-9500
1550 Double C Dr Norman (73069) *(G-4914)*
Arcosa Wind Towers Inc..918 560-4911
15300 Tiger Switch Rd Tulsa (74116) *(G-9206)*
Arcrite Manufacturing LLC.....................................580 216-1050
6745 State Highway 15 Woodward (73801) *(G-11555)*
Arctic Blends Corporation......................................918 455-2079
2409 N Aspen Ave Broken Arrow (74012) *(G-832)*
Ardagh Glass Inc..918 224-1440
1000 N Mission St Sapulpa (74066) *(G-8250)*
Ardco, Norman *Also called Advance Research & Development* *(G-4899)*
Ardella's Pet & Garden Center, Norman *Also called Ardellas Flowers Inc* *(G-4915)*
Ardellas Flowers Inc (PA)......................................405 321-6850
1016 Woods Ave Norman (73069) *(G-4915)*
Ardmore Construction Sup Inc...............................580 223-2322
506 S Washington St Ardmore (73401) *(G-245)*
Ardmore Dragway..580 226-7811
3801 Springdale Rd Ardmore (73401) *(G-246)*
Ardmore Drilling, Ardmore *Also called Ardmore Prod & Exploration* *(G-249)*
Ardmore Inc..405 201-1288
225 Harryette Pl Ardmore (73401) *(G-247)*
Ardmore Optical Co..580 223-8676
226 W Main St Ardmore (73401) *(G-248)*
Ardmore Photo Copy Rproduction, Ardmore *Also called Johnny L Ruth* *(G-316)*
Ardmore Prod & Exploration..................................580 223-2292
301 W Main St Ste 415 Ardmore (73401) *(G-249)*
Arena Resources Inc..918 747-6060
6555 S Lewis Ave Tulsa (74136) *(G-9207)*
Ares West Welding LLC..405 534-6707
1405 Nw 14th Pl Moore (73170) *(G-4494)*
ARINC Incorporated...405 601-6000
6015 S Portland Ave Oklahoma City (73159) *(G-5463)*
Arista...405 948-1500
5221 Nw 5th St Oklahoma City (73127) *(G-5464)*
ARk -Ramos Fndry Mfg Co Inc................................405 235-5505
1321 S Walker Ave Oklahoma City (73109) *(G-5465)*
Arkansas River Press...918 744-1730
223 E 25th St Tulsa (74114) *(G-9208)*
Arkansas Surgical Supply-State, Ponca City *Also called Thomas Dist Solutions LLC* *(G-7883)*

Arkhola Sand & Gravel Co.......................................918 687-4771
3300 W 40th St N Muskogee (74401) *(G-4650)*
Arkhola Sand & Gravel Co.......................................918 456-2683
14199 W 834 Rd Tahlequah (74464) *(G-8850)*
Arkhola Sand & Gravel Co Tahle..............................918 456-6121
350 W Arkhola St Park Hill (74451) *(G-7640)*
Arkhoma Transports Inc...580 651-2682
724 W 4th St Beaver (73932) *(G-538)*
Arkoma Tanks LLC..580 622-4794
6988 Reck Rd Wilson (73463) *(G-11531)*
Arkos Field Services LP..405 262-1548
3705 S Choctaw Ave El Reno (73036) *(G-2699)*
Armacell LLC..405 494-2800
524 N Sara Rd Yukon (73099) *(G-11693)*
Armada Land LC..405 210-7554
1013 Greenway Cir Norman (73072) *(G-4916)*
Armed Inc..918 245-1478
214 N Main St Sand Springs (74063) *(G-8162)*
Armer & Quillen LLC...405 842-3222
4127 Nw 122nd St Ste A Oklahoma City (73120) *(G-5466)*
Armitage Equipment, Meeker *Also called Mark Armitage* *(G-4380)*
Armor Energy LLC..918 986-9459
4500 S Garnett Rd Ste 250 Tulsa (74146) *(G-9209)*
Armorvault, Oklahoma City *Also called Southwest Engineering* *(G-7176)*
Armour Pest Control LLC..918 489-5734
117 Kemp Rd Hendrix (74741) *(G-3439)*
Armstrong Manufacturing, Newcastle *Also called Mid America Vending Inc* *(G-4831)*
Armstrong Products Inc...405 282-7584
500 E Industrial Rd Guthrie (73044) *(G-3297)*
Arnold Electric Inc...405 605-1982
317 N Portland Ave Ste D Oklahoma City (73107) *(G-5467)*
Arnold Oil Properties LLC......................................405 842-1488
6816 N Robinson Ave Oklahoma City (73116) *(G-5468)*
Arp Sebree South LLC...918 295-1415
1717 S Boulder Ave # 400 Tulsa (74119) *(G-9210)*
Arrow Alliance Industries LLC.................................540 273-1548
3100 84th Ave Se Norman (73026) *(G-4917)*
Arrow Concrete Division, Tulsa *Also called Tulsa Dynaspan Inc* *(G-10996)*
Arrow Drilling LLC..405 749-7860
1004 Nw 139th Street Pkwy Edmond (73013) *(G-2310)*
Arrow Engine Company (HQ)..................................918 583-5711
2301 E Independence St Tulsa (74110) *(G-9211)*
Arrow Oil & Gas Inc..405 364-2601
2500 Mcgee Dr Ste 100 Norman (73072) *(G-4918)*
Arrow Sign Company Inc..580 353-2227
1344 Se 1st St Lawton (73501) *(G-3891)*
Arrow Tool & Gage Co Inc.......................................918 438-3600
14323 E Marshall St Tulsa (74116) *(G-9212)*
Arrow We Go Perforators, Ada *Also called We-Go Perforators Inc* *(G-105)*
Arrow-R Construction, Coalgate *Also called Brian Ringels* *(G-1776)*
Arrowhead Precast LLC...918 995-2227
1701 E Houston St Broken Arrow (74012) *(G-833)*
Arrowhead Software..918 744-7239
4624 E 24th St Tulsa (74114) *(G-9213)*
Arrowhead Truck Equipment Inc............................918 224-5570
12300 S Mingo Rd Bixby (74008) *(G-612)*
Arrowood Companies...405 701-3673
701 Wall St Norman (73069) *(G-4919)*
Arrowprop Inc...405 279-3833
106476 S 3440 Rd Meeker (74855) *(G-4375)*
Art, Oklahoma City *Also called Alpha Research & Tech Inc* *(G-5425)*
Art Crved Signs By WD Concepts, Tulsa *Also called Wood Concepts Inc* *(G-11147)*
Art of Manliness LLC...405 613-3340
4115 E 86th St Tulsa (74137) *(G-9214)*
Artesan Design, Broken Arrow *Also called Star Corral* *(G-1060)*
Arthur Craig..580 488-3398
20945 E 850 Rd Butler (73625) *(G-1220)*
Arthur Crews Logging..580 889-7757
7669 S Double Springs Rd Lane (74555) *(G-3870)*
Artillery Nation LLC...405 606-5080
1505 Se 8th St Moore (73160) *(G-4495)*
Artisan Custom Cabinetry Inc.................................918 645-3874
2709 W Detroit St Broken Arrow (74012) *(G-834)*
Artisan Design Inc..918 251-9795
808 S 9th St Broken Arrow (74012) *(G-835)*
Artistic Apparel..918 338-0038
401 S Dewey Ave Ste 212 Bartlesville (74003) *(G-449)*
Artistic Printing, Fairview *Also called Hammer Hoby* *(G-3137)*
Artt Wood Mfg Co, Oklahoma City *Also called A R T T Corp* *(G-5348)*
Artur Bookbinding Intl..918 478-4888
100 N Jackson St Fort Gibson (74434) *(G-3173)*
Artworks...580 927-9094
467 E A St Atoka (74525) *(G-396)*
Aruze Gaming America Inc....................................405 301-8140
6101 W Reno Ave Ste 400 Oklahoma City (73127) *(G-5469)*
Arysta Life Science Technology..............................580 871-2316
19940 County Road 480 Alva (73717) *(G-175)*
AS Designs LLC...918 381-2390
202 E 5th Ave Owasso (74055) *(G-7546)*

ALPHABETIC SECTION
Avara Pharmaceutical Tech Inc

Asbury Machine Corporation 580 628-3416
1995 N Public St Tonkawa (74653) ***(G-8972)***
Asc Inc 918 445-0260
6420 S 39th West Ave Tulsa (74132) ***(G-9215)***
Ascent Resources - Utica LLC 405 608-5544
3501 Nw 63rd St Oklahoma City (73116) ***(G-5470)***
Ascent Resources Operating LLC (PA) 405 608-5544
3501 Nw 63rd St Oklahoma City (73116) ***(G-5471)***
Ascent Rsrces Utica Hldngs LLC 405 608-5544
3501 Nw 63rd St Oklahoma City (73116) ***(G-5472)***
Asco Aerospace Usa LLC 405 533-5800
3003 N Perkins Rd Stillwater (74075) ***(G-8655)***
Ases LLC 405 219-3420
6400 Se 59th St Oklahoma City (73135) ***(G-5473)***
Ases LLC (HQ) 405 219-3400
6015 S Portland Ave Oklahoma City (73159) ***(G-5474)***
Asher Oilfield Specialty Inc 405 677-7868
1615 Se 37th St Oklahoma City (73129) ***(G-5475)***
Asher Oilfield Specialty Inc 405 568-3433
26 Ne 26th St Oklahoma City (73105) ***(G-5476)***
Ashley Cameron Building Prods 405 236-0617
2401 Sw 10th St Oklahoma City (73108) ***(G-5477)***
Ashleys Electrical Services 918 825-0747
249 Cottonwood Rd Pryor (74361) ***(G-7944)***
Ashphalt Plant, Sand Springs *Also called Dunhams Asphalt Services Inc* ***(G-8180)***
Ashton Gas Gathering LLC 918 291-3200
1030 W Main St Jenks (74037) ***(G-3689)***
Ask ME About Signs LLC 405 317-8157
1005 N Flood Ave Ste 109 Norman (73069) ***(G-4920)***
Aspect Oil Field Servvices LLC 580 774-5006
23851 Route 66 N Weatherford (73096) ***(G-11391)***
Aspect Oilfield Services LLC 504 812-5330
1803 E 17th St Tulsa (74104) ***(G-9216)***
Aspen Flow Control LLC 918 933-5617
5128 S 95th E Ave Ste C Broken Arrow (74012) ***(G-836)***
Assa Abloy Group Company, Tulsa *Also called Ameristar Primeter SEC USA Inc* ***(G-9179)***
Asset Weapon Manufacturing, Broken Arrow *Also called White Shell LLC* ***(G-1177)***
Assistance Administration, Oklahoma City *Also called Interstate Trucker Ltd* ***(G-6323)***
Associated Lithographing Co 918 663-9091
6580 E Skelly Dr Tulsa (74145) ***(G-9217)***
Associated Material Proc LLC 405 707-7301
810 N Country Club Rd Stillwater (74075) ***(G-8656)***
Associated Plastics LLC 405 390-0406
2675 Plant Dr Choctaw (73020) ***(G-1527)***
Associated Research Inc 580 223-4773
801 Hailey St Sw Ardmore (73401) ***(G-250)***
Associated Resources Inc 918 584-2111
15 E 5th St Ste 200 Tulsa (74103) ***(G-9218)***
Associated Services Printing, Seminole *Also called Bob D Berry DBA* ***(G-8360)***
Associated Stl Fabricators Inc 405 787-5713
14220 S Tulsa Dr Oklahoma City (73170) ***(G-5278)***
Associated Tool & Machine Co 405 670-4155
1126 Se 15th St Oklahoma City (73129) ***(G-5478)***
Associated Wire Line Svcs Inc 580 229-0731
203 Apple St Healdton (73438) ***(G-3407)***
Assocted Wire Rope Fabricators 918 234-7450
1369 S Garnett Rd Tulsa (74128) ***(G-9219)***
AST Storage LLC 918 208-0100
1082 E Monroe Ave Jay (74346) ***(G-3678)***
At & L Energy LLC 580 623-7265
505 W Main St Watonga (73772) ***(G-11339)***
At A Glance Software LLC 405 601-3062
3300 Nw 45th Ter Oklahoma City (73112) ***(G-5479)***
AT&I Resources LLC 918 925-0154
2900 E Apache St Tulsa (74110) ***(G-9220)***
AT&T, Tulsa *Also called Yp LLC* ***(G-11171)***
Atalaya Resources 918 949-4551
15 E 5th St Tulsa (74103) ***(G-9221)***
Atc Drivetrain LLC 405 577-9901
9901 W Reno Ave Oklahoma City (73127) ***(G-5480)***
Atc Drivetrain LLC 405 350-3600
4680 Nw 3rd St Oklahoma City (73127) ***(G-5481)***
Atc New Technologies 405 577-9901
10001 Nw 2nd St Oklahoma City (73127) ***(G-5482)***
Atc Technology Corporation 405 577-9901
9901 W Reno Ave Oklahoma City (73127) ***(G-5483)***
Atchley Resources Inc 405 848-3331
13903 Quail Pointe Dr Oklahoma City (73134) ***(G-5484)***
Atlantic Fbrication Design LLC 405 619-7607
901 Se 29th St Oklahoma City (73129) ***(G-5485)***
Atlas Concrete Inc (HQ) 580 255-7280
2112 W Bois D Arc Ave Duncan (73533) ***(G-2083)***
Atlas Instrument & Mfg Co 918 371-1976
16301 E 123rd St N Collinsville (74021) ***(G-1800)***
Atlas Pipeline, Tulsa *Also called Targa Ppline Mid-Continent LLC* ***(G-10900)***
Atlas Pipeline Mid-Continent W 918 574-3500
110 W 7th St Ste 2300 Tulsa (74119) ***(G-9222)***
Atlas Resource Partners LP 918 654-3702
27404 Walls Rd Cameron (74932) ***(G-1254)***
Atlas Rock Bit Service Inc 405 691-4848
3901 Sw 113th St Oklahoma City (73173) ***(G-5486)***
Atlas Roofing Corporation 580 226-3283
2300 P St Ne Ardmore (73401) ***(G-251)***
ATLAS TUCK CONCRETE INC, Tuttle *Also called Atlas Tuck Concrete Inc* ***(G-11185)***
Atlas Tuck Concrete Inc 580 355-8241
1601 S Sheridan Lawton (73501) ***(G-3892)***
Atlas Tuck Concrete Inc 405 224-5005
3401 S 4th St Chickasha (73018) ***(G-1433)***
Atlas Tuck Concrete Inc 405 381-2393
620 N Cimarron St Tuttle (73089) ***(G-11185)***
Atlas-Tuck Concrete Inc (HQ) 580 255-1716
2112 W Bois D Arc Ave Duncan (73533) ***(G-2084)***
Atoka Trailer and Mfg LLC 580 889-7270
677 S Jefferson Hwy Atoka (74525) ***(G-397)***
Atoka Welding & Fabrication 580 889-2534
477 N Jefferson Hwy Atoka (74525) ***(G-398)***
Atrue Industries LLC 800 782-5440
7126 Nw Birch Pl Lawton (73505) ***(G-3893)***
Attorney and Legal Publica 405 728-0392
5609 Nw 110th St 11 Oklahoma City (73162) ***(G-5487)***
Atwood Wldg Cstm Fbrcation LLC 918 617-7522
116421 S 4110 Rd Eufaula (74432) ***(G-3097)***
Aucora Breakfast Bar Backyard 405 609-8854
1704 Nw 16th St Oklahoma City (73106) ***(G-5488)***
Audio Innovations, Stillwater *Also called Rockford Corporation* ***(G-8748)***
Audio Link Inc 405 359-0017
3140 Waterloo Cir Edmond (73034) ***(G-2311)***
Audrey Parks & Associates Llc 405 328-3186
101 Park Ave Ste 101 # 101 Oklahoma City (73102) ***(G-5489)***
Aurora Innovations LLC 918 519-5356
3334 N State Highway 97 Sand Springs (74063) ***(G-8163)***
Auryn Creative 918 876-0974
1315 E 6th St Tulsa (74120) ***(G-9223)***
Aussie Built Supplies LLC 918 381-9700
386 Lone Wolf Ln Skiatook (74070) ***(G-8531)***
Austin Athletic Co Inc 405 273-8681
10987 N Kickapoo Ave Shawnee (74804) ***(G-8429)***
Austin Gas Properties LLC 405 229-2391
9609 Eagle Hill Dr Oklahoma City (73162) ***(G-5490)***
Austin Powder Co 918 835-9244
3122 N Mingo Valley Expy Tulsa (74116) ***(G-9224)***
Austinn Industries Inc Ncs LLC 918 408-2058
1566 E 22nd St Tulsa (74114) ***(G-9225)***
Auto Chlor Services LLC 580 657-4482
131 E Case Cir Lone Grove (73443) ***(G-4114)***
Auto Crane Company 918 438-2760
4707 N Mingo Rd Tulsa (74117) ***(G-9226)***
Auto Hail Damage Repair 405 696-6031
3825 Nw 166th St Ste A11 Edmond (73012) ***(G-2312)***
Auto Pride, Claremore *Also called Jfj Industries Inc* ***(G-1643)***
Auto Trim Design Signs SE Okla 580 622-3830
1400 W 1st St Sulphur (73086) ***(G-8828)***
Auto Way Manufacturing Co LLC 405 946-3516
3516 Nw 42nd St Oklahoma City (73112) ***(G-5491)***
Auto-Trim Design SE Oklahoma, Sulphur *Also called Auto Trim Design Signs SE Okla* ***(G-8828)***
Auto-Turn Manufacturing Inc 918 451-4511
9800 S 219th East Ave Broken Arrow (74014) ***(G-1111)***
Autocraft Industries 405 577-9901
9901 W Reno Ave Oklahoma City (73127) ***(G-5492)***
Autocraft Material Recovery 405 350-3800
10001 Nw 2nd St Oklahoma City (73127) ***(G-5493)***
Automated Gasket Company LLc 405 951-5301
5706 Sw 5th St Oklahoma City (73128) ***(G-5494)***
Automated Machining Co Inc 918 723-3503
107 E Main St Westville (74965) ***(G-11480)***
Automated Mail Service, Tulsa *Also called Sashay Corporate Services LLC* ***(G-10710)***
Automatic & Auto Machining Inc 918 775-9770
460 Jenkins Rd Sallisaw (74955) ***(G-8138)***
Automatic Gate Systems of Okla 580 920-8752
5580 Armstrong Rd Durant (74701) ***(G-2203)***
Automotive Machine Shop 918 775-9770
460 Jenkins Rd Sallisaw (74955) ***(G-8139)***
Automted McHning Solutions LLC 405 697-6234
1208 E Highline Ln Mustang (73064) ***(G-4762)***
Automtive Cting Specialist Inc 918 698-1560
22493 State Highway 51 Wagoner (74467) ***(G-11274)***
Avalanche Print Company 405 808-4229
1105 S Fretz Ave Edmond (73003) ***(G-2313)***
Avalon Exploration Inc 918 523-0600
15 W 6th St Ste 2300 Tulsa (74119) ***(G-9227)***
Avalon Operating LLC 918 523-0600
15 W 6th St Ste 2300 Tulsa (74119) ***(G-9228)***
Avara Pharmaceutical Services, Norman *Also called Avara Pharmaceutical Tech Inc* ***(G-4921)***
Avara Pharmaceutical Tech Inc 405 217-7670
3300 Marshall Ave Norman (73072) ***(G-4921)***

ALPHABETIC

Aventura Technologies Inc...631 300-4000
12330 Saint Andrews Dr Oklahoma City (73120) ***(G-5495)***
Avery Barron Industires LLC...918 779-6903
2102 W Skelly Dr Tulsa (74107) ***(G-9229)***
Avery Barron Industries...918 834-6647
1044 N Columbia Pl Tulsa (74110) ***(G-9230)***
Aviation Training Devices Inc...918 366-6680
613 W Needles Ave Bixby (74008) ***(G-613)***
Aviations Simulations Inc...918 251-6880
415 E Houston St Broken Arrow (74012) ***(G-837)***
Avinash Paul, Tulsa *Also called Sariel Inc* ***(G-10709)***
Avitrol Corp...918 622-7763
7644 E 46th St Tulsa (74145) ***(G-9231)***
Avpro, Norman *Also called Advanced Processing Tech Inc* ***(G-4901)***
Aw Specialties LLC...918 798-9272
18985 S 4210 Rd Claremore (74017) ***(G-1584)***
Awc Inc...405 601-1090
5600 Sw 36th St Ste A Oklahoma City (73179) ***(G-5496)***
Awesome Acres Pacas Pyrs...405 990-8205
11800 S Hiwassee Rd Oklahoma City (73165) ***(G-5279)***
Awesome Apparel Printing...918 402-3672
4412 W Oakridge St Broken Arrow (74012) ***(G-838)***
Awnings of Tulsa Inc...918 747-2050
1428 E 1st St Tulsa (74120) ***(G-9232)***
Awnings Unique...405 249-2488
906 Ne 9th St Moore (73160) ***(G-4496)***
Awnique...405 818-8032
4400 Sw 36th St Oklahoma City (73119) ***(G-5497)***
Aws LLC...405 382-1255
220 Quail Creek Rd Seminole (74868) ***(G-8355)***
Axel Royal LLC (HQ)...918 584-2671
516 S 25th West Ave Tulsa (74127) ***(G-9233)***
Axels Transmissions Transfers...918 425-7725
3244 N Lewis Ave Tulsa (74110) ***(G-9234)***
Axh Air-Coolers LLC...918 283-9200
401 E Lowry Rd Claremore (74017) ***(G-1585)***
Axiom Automotive Tech Inc...909 841-8200
101 N Robinson Ave # 710 Oklahoma City (73102) ***(G-5498)***
Axiom Metal Solutions LLC...918 361-5982
1900 N Wood Dr Okmulgee (74447) ***(G-7494)***
Axis Technologies LLC...580 467-4257
4895 W Plato Rd Duncan (73533) ***(G-2085)***
Axle Transmission & Transfers, Tulsa *Also called Axels Transmissions Transfers* ***(G-9234)***
Axon Industries LLC...918 313-8955
4115 S 33rd West Ave Tulsa (74107) ***(G-9235)***
Azimuth Spirits LLC...317 468-3931
1126 Rambling Oaks Dr Norman (73072) ***(G-4922)***
Azlin Trackhoe and Dozer Svc, Wewoka *Also called Michael S Azlin* ***(G-11505)***
Aztec Building Systems Inc...405 329-0255
3361 Deskin Dr Norman (73069) ***(G-4923)***
Aztec Manufacturing Corp...405 330-4888
6333 Boucher Dr Edmond (73034) ***(G-2314)***
Aztec Ne Overhead Door Inc...918 341-7502
221 N Owalla Ave Claremore (74017) ***(G-1586)***
Azure Energy Ltd...918 712-2727
3737 E 59th Pl Tulsa (74135) ***(G-9236)***
Azz Inc...918 379-0090
5101 Bird Creek Ave Catoosa (74015) ***(G-1299)***
Azz Incorporated...918 584-6668
2506 E 26th St Tulsa (74114) ***(G-9237)***
Azz Incorporated...918 295-8702
1800 W 21st St Tulsa (74107) ***(G-9238)***
B & A Producing LLC...405 664-3628
4700 N Westminster Rd Arcadia (73007) ***(G-228)***
B & B Butlers Custom Process...580 795-2667
N Of City Madill (73446) ***(G-4144)***
B & B Electric Co...918 583-6274
501 N Trenton Ave Tulsa (74120) ***(G-9239)***
B & B Haybeds...580 357-5083
1903 Ne 60th St Lawton (73507) ***(G-3894)***
B & B Hydroseeding LLC...580 883-5997
42666 S 264 Rd Ringwood (73768) ***(G-8084)***
B & B Log & Lumber Co Inc...580 889-2438
8592 E Highway 3 Atoka (74525) ***(G-399)***
B & B Machine...918 686-9900
2810 S 24th St W Muskogee (74401) ***(G-4651)***
B & B Machine of Norman Inc...405 799-9878
17321 S Sunnylane Rd Norman (73071) ***(G-4924)***
B & B Medical Services Inc (PA)...919 601-4756
4045 Nw 64th St Ste 250 Oklahoma City (73116) ***(G-5499)***
B & B Resources...918 495-1128
3637 E 67th St Tulsa (74136) ***(G-9240)***
B & B Sheet Metal, Oklahoma City *Also called Earl Bannon* ***(G-5998)***
B & B Sheet Metal Heat & A Inc...918 371-1335
13217 N 91st East Ave Collinsville (74021) ***(G-1801)***
B & B Tool Co Inc...405 756-4530
Hwy 76 N Lindsay (73052) ***(G-4045)***
B & C Custom Woodworks...918 830-2416
7739 E 38th St Ste B Tulsa (74145) ***(G-9241)***
B & C Machine Company Inc...405 787-8862
8301 Sw 3rd St Oklahoma City (73128) ***(G-5500)***
B & D Eagle Machine Shop...405 787-3232
8124 Sw 8th St Ste A Oklahoma City (73128) ***(G-5501)***
B & D Oil Co, Bristow *Also called Bob Pound Drilling Inc* ***(G-767)***
B & G Production Inc...580 256-5100
1010 Oklahoma Ave Woodward (73801) ***(G-11556)***
B & L Industries Inc...580 591-1880
2802 Nw Liberty Ave Lawton (73505) ***(G-3895)***
B & L Printing Inc...918 258-6655
400 S Elm Pl Ste A Broken Arrow (74012) ***(G-839)***
B & P Industrial Inc...918 665-3301
4649 S 83rd East Ave Tulsa (74145) ***(G-9242)***
B & P Logging LLC...580 584-6718
1111 Pleasant Valley Rd Broken Bow (74728) ***(G-1184)***
B & R Construction of Woodward...580 256-5522
102 E Madison Ave Woodward (73801) ***(G-11557)***
B & R Pump & Equipment Inc...405 632-3051
4001 S High Ave Oklahoma City (73129) ***(G-5502)***
B & S Light Industries, Claremore *Also called Industrial Electronics Repair* ***(G-1641)***
B & S Profab, Coweta *Also called Profab* ***(G-1894)***
B & S Roustabouts LLC...405 779-0842
1224 S 18th St Chickasha (73018) ***(G-1434)***
B & W Diesel & Drivetrain Inc...918 427-7918
303 W Treat Rd Muldrow (74948) ***(G-4631)***
B & W Exploration Inc...405 236-1807
6908 N Robinson Ave Oklahoma City (73116) ***(G-5503)***
B & W Manufacturing Co Ltd...918 248-5201
8700 S Regency Dr Tulsa (74131) ***(G-8989)***
B & W Ready Mix LLC...580 623-5059
Hwy 33 E Watonga (73772) ***(G-11340)***
B A Stevens...918 695-4362
398887 W 2700 Rd Ochelata (74051) ***(G-5233)***
B and J Backhoe and Cnstr...580 467-4981
177030 N 2950 Rd Duncan (73533) ***(G-2086)***
B B Fiberglass LLC...405 755-5895
11501 Cory Rd Guthrie (73044) ***(G-3298)***
B B M, Oklahoma City *Also called Buildings By Madden LLC* ***(G-5643)***
B B Machine & Supply, Enid *Also called Bb Machine & Supply Inc* ***(G-2915)***
B B Royalty Company...405 672-3381
3300 S High Ave Oklahoma City (73129) ***(G-5504)***
B B Sand and Gravel...405 944-1163
36827 Ew 1090 Paden (74860) ***(G-7632)***
B Bar Inc (PA)...580 824-8338
1723 E Broadway St Waynoka (73860) ***(G-11372)***
B Brothers Manufacturing LLC...918 625-9583
1293 E Kenosha St Broken Arrow (74012) ***(G-840)***
B G Specialties Inc...918 582-1165
552 S Quincy Ave Tulsa (74120) ***(G-9243)***
B J M Consulting Inc...918 665-8737
10906 E 2nd St Tulsa (74128) ***(G-9244)***
B J Printing Inc...405 372-7600
520 W 6th Ave Stillwater (74074) ***(G-8657)***
B J Printing Products Inc...918 245-6385
305 W 40th Pl Sand Springs (74063) ***(G-8164)***
B P S Inc...918 258-7554
304 N Walnut Ave Broken Arrow (74012) ***(G-841)***
B R B Roofing & Manufacturing, Muskogee *Also called Briggs Rainbow Buildings Inc* ***(G-4655)***
B R Polk Inc...405 286-9666
5715 N Western Ave Ste C Oklahoma City (73118) ***(G-5505)***
B Raye Oil Environmenta...405 818-6996
631 Hunters Way Mustang (73064) ***(G-4763)***
B Rowdy Rnch Met Fbrcation LLC...405 973-5976
22120 N Dobbs Rd Luther (73054) ***(G-4132)***
B S & B Safety Systems Inc (PA)...918 622-5950
7422 E 46th Pl Tulsa (74145) ***(G-9245)***
B Sew Inn LLC (PA)...918 687-5762
2530 Chandler Rd Muskogee (74403) ***(G-4652)***
B T Machine Inc...918 834-3340
16210 E Marshall St Tulsa (74116) ***(G-9246)***
B&C Custom Woodworks LLC...918 639-2416
2551 E 22nd Pl Tulsa (74114) ***(G-9247)***
B&G Meadery LLC...580 272-7197
36695 Old State Highway 3 Stonewall (74871) ***(G-8797)***
B&L Smoked Meats...580 641-1677
263 N Scott Rd Marlow (73055) ***(G-4222)***
B&M Digital Garment Printing...918 954-6994
1553 S 74th East Ave Tulsa (74112) ***(G-9248)***
B&M Machine Works LLC...918 583-4067
620 N Rockford Ave Tulsa (74106) ***(G-9249)***
B&M Metal Works, Catoosa *Also called B&M Metalworks Inc* ***(G-1300)***
B&M Metalworks Inc...918 266-5103
25912 E Admiral Pl Catoosa (74015) ***(G-1300)***
B&P Detailing LLC...405 684-7730
301 W Oklahoma St 19 Chickasha (73018) ***(G-1435)***
B&T Welding Services LLC...580 326-4760
1666 E 2060 Rd Hugo (74743) ***(G-3602)***

B&W Operating LLC 405 236-1807
6908 N Robinson Ave Oklahoma City (73116) **(G-5506)**
B-Mac Welding Service 918 370-0921
8424 S 353rd East Ave Broken Arrow (74014) **(G-1112)**
B.O.B. Contracting, Coalgate *Also called BOB Lumber & Grain LLC* **(G-1775)**
Ba Manufacturing LLC 239 246-3606
405 S 9th St Broken Arrow (74012) **(G-842)**
Ba Solutions, Edmond *Also called Buckelew Accnting Slutions LLC* **(G-2334)**
Babb Land & Development 405 340-1178
1900 E 15th St Ste 600b Edmond (73013) **(G-2315)**
Babe Nail Spa 918 298-2200
8102 S Lewis Ave Ste D Tulsa (74137) **(G-9250)**
Baby Bee Safe 918 224-1104
518 S Oak St Sapulpa (74066) **(G-8251)**
Bacas Oilfield Services LLC 580 461-8458
615 Douglas Ave Beaver (73932) **(G-539)**
Bacco Inc 918 344-3670
20318 E 103rd St N Claremore (74019) **(G-1587)**
Bach Welding & Diesel Service 580 593-2599
409 N Main St Custer City (73639) **(G-1973)**
Bachman Services Inc (HQ) 405 677-8296
2220 S I 35 Service Rd Oklahoma City (73129) **(G-5507)**
Back Alley Brewers & More LLC 580 716-2571
218 E Central Ave Ponca City (74601) **(G-7799)**
Back Road Oil & Gas LLC 918 932-8452
205 E 29th St Tulsa (74114) **(G-9251)**
Backbone Mountain LLC 918 295-7600
1717 S Boulder Ave # 400 Tulsa (74119) **(G-9252)**
Backhoe Services Oklahoma LLC 405 356-2712
9687 Oak Pond Dr Luther (73054) **(G-4133)**
Backup Fortress LLC 405 314-2436
11221 Nw 97th St Yukon (73099) **(G-11694)**
Backwoods Food Mfg Inc 918 458-9300
591 Main Pkwy Tahlequah (74464) **(G-8851)**
Backwoods Foods, Tahlequah *Also called Backwoods Food Mfg Inc* **(G-8851)**
Backwoods Trailers LLC 864 237-5906
84773 S 4771 Rd Stilwell (74960) **(G-8781)**
Backwoods Welding Inc 405 642-5199
23396 E County Road 1520 Maysville (73057) **(G-4254)**
Bad Boy Signs Graphic 405 224-2059
1426 S 4th St Chickasha (73018) **(G-1436)**
Badger Meter Inc 918 836-8411
6116 E 15th St Tulsa (74112) **(G-9253)**
Badger Meter Inc 918 628-7403
7420 E 46th Pl Tulsa (74145) **(G-9254)**
Badger Mining Corporation 608 864-1157
12353 N 1760 Rd Erick (73645) **(G-3085)**
Badger Pressure Control LLC 580 256-9555
1310 Airport Pkwy Rd Woodward (73802) **(G-11558)**
Badgett Corporation 405 224-4138
4009 S 4th St Chickasha (73018) **(G-1437)**
Badlands Petroleum LLC 303 921-2854
2320 Nw 59th St Oklahoma City (73112) **(G-5508)**
Bags Inc 405 427-5473
1900 N Sooner Rd Oklahoma City (73141) **(G-5509)**
Bailey Production Company 405 932-5293
95146 N 3630 Rd Paden (74860) **(G-7633)**
Bailey S Mike Welding Inc 405 574-4489
3513 County Street 2840 Ninnekah (73067) **(G-4867)**
Baileys Welding & Machine LLC 405 224-6611
3601 State Highway 92 Chickasha (73018) **(G-1438)**
Baity Screw Products Inc 405 222-1520
302 N Genevieve St Chickasha (73018) **(G-1439)**
Baker Atlas, Oklahoma City *Also called Baker Hghes Olfld Oprtions LLC* **(G-5512)**
Baker Centrilift Cable Inc 713 439-8600
200 W Stuart Roosa Dr Claremore (74017) **(G-1588)**
Baker Energy Solutions LLC 405 691-1202
11500 S Meridian Ave Oklahoma City (73173) **(G-5510)**
Baker Hghes Olfld Oprtions Inc 405 382-0003
4 N Park St Seminole (74868) **(G-8356)**
Baker Hghes Olfld Oprtions Inc 405 681-2175
12701 N Santa Fe Ave Oklahoma City (73114) **(G-5511)**
Baker Hghes Olfld Oprtions LLC 580 256-3333
12701 N Santa Fe Ave Oklahoma City (73114) **(G-5512)**
Baker Hghes Olfld Oprtions LLC 405 670-3354
6209 S Sooner Rd Oklahoma City (73135) **(G-5513)**
Baker Hghes Olfld Oprtions LLC 918 847-3296
601 S 5th St Barnsdall (74002) **(G-434)**
Baker Hghes Olfld Oprtions LLC 918 341-9600
2210 El Anderson Blvd Claremore (74017) **(G-1589)**
Baker Hghes Olfld Oprtions LLC 918 455-3000
3000 N Hemlock Cir Broken Arrow (74012) **(G-843)**
Baker Hghes Olfld Oprtions LLC 580 243-3424
521 Ed Tillery Ave Elk City (73644) **(G-2785)**
Baker Hghes Olfld Oprtions LLC 918 283-7911
844 W Lowry Rd Claremore (74017) **(G-1590)**
Baker Hghes Olfld Oprtions LLC 580 256-7471
910 Jimar Way Woodward (73801) **(G-11559)**
Baker Hghes Olfld Oprtions LLC 918 341-9600
200 W Stuart Roosa Dr Claremore (74017) **(G-1591)**
Baker Hghes Olfld Oprtions LLC 405 756-3384
Industrial Hts Lindsay (73052) **(G-4046)**
Baker Hughes A GE Company LLC 580 327-2162
3000 College Blvd Alva (73717) **(G-176)**
Baker Hughes A GE Company LLC 518 387-7914
300 Ne 9th St Oklahoma City (73104) **(G-5514)**
Baker Hughes A GE Company LLC 405 227-8471
12701 N Santa Fe Ave Oklahoma City (73114) **(G-5515)**
Baker Hughes A GE Company LLC 806 435-4096
11041 Nw 10th St Yukon (73099) **(G-11695)**
Baker Hughes A GE Company LLC 580 323-4541
1620 S 13th St Clinton (73601) **(G-1738)**
Baker Hughes A GE Company LLC 918 302-0490
2375 S George Nigh Expy Mcalester (74501) **(G-4271)**
Baker Hughes A GE Company LLC 918 828-1600
7655 E 46th St Tulsa (74145) **(G-9255)**
Baker Hughes A GE Company LLC 918 283-1957
844 W Lowry Rd Claremore (74017) **(G-1592)**
Baker Hughes Elasto Systems 405 670-3354
6417 S Sooner Rd Oklahoma City (73135) **(G-5516)**
Baker Hughes Incorporated 918 426-6585
2491 Highway 69 Byp McAlester (74501) **(G-4272)**
Baker Hughes Inteq, Oklahoma City *Also called Baker Hghes Olfld Oprtions LLC* **(G-5513)**
Baker Manufacturing Inc 580 327-0234
602 Hart St Apt 103 Alva (73717) **(G-177)**
Baker Oil Tools, Seminole *Also called Baker Hghes Olfld Oprtions Inc* **(G-8356)**
Baker Oil Tools, Broken Arrow *Also called Baker Hghes Olfld Oprtions LLC* **(G-843)**
Baker Oil Tools, Woodward *Also called Baker Hghes Olfld Oprtions LLC* **(G-11559)**
Baker Oil Tools, Oklahoma City *Also called Baker Hghes Olfld Oprtions Inc* **(G-5511)**
Baker Petrolite Inc 918 302-0490
2491 N Highway 69 Byp Bache (74501) **(G-429)**
Baker Petrolite LLC 918 847-2522
800 Birch Lake Rd Barnsdall (74002) **(G-435)**
Baker Petrolite LLC 918 245-2224
9100 W 21st St Sand Springs (74063) **(G-8165)**
Baker Petrolite LLC 918 599-8886
1818 W 21st St Tulsa (74107) **(G-9256)**
Baker Petrolite LLC 580 323-4541
1620 S 13th St Clinton (73601) **(G-1739)**
Baker Surveying LLC 918 271-5793
4677 S 83rd East Ave Tulsa (74145) **(G-9257)**
Baker Welding Mfg Co 405 376-6017
707 S Pleasant View Dr Mustang (73064) **(G-4764)**
Baker Well Service Inc 405 372-6380
406 N Bethel Rd Stillwater (74075) **(G-8658)**
Baker Wireline 405 786-3283
212 E Jack Johnson Ave Weleetka (74880) **(G-11463)**
Bakers Printing Co Inc 405 842-6944
9014 N Western Ave Oklahoma City (73114) **(G-5517)**
Bakers Sign & Design 405 262-5100
1315 S Shepard Ave El Reno (73036) **(G-2700)**
Bakery Feeds, Watts *Also called Griffin Industries LLC* **(G-11357)**
Bakken Hbt LP 405 516-8241
100 Park Ave Ste 400 Oklahoma City (73102) **(G-5518)**
Balco Inc 316 945-9328
5551 Nw 5th St Oklahoma City (73127) **(G-5519)**
Balco Metalines, Oklahoma City *Also called Balco Inc* **(G-5519)**
Balderas LLC 580 821-4134
2512 Harvest Dr Weatherford (73096) **(G-11392)**
Bale Corporation 405 848-8797
124 Nw 67th St Oklahoma City (73116) **(G-5520)**
Balero 580 221-6202
1 Valero Way Ardmore (73401) **(G-252)**
Bales Custom Woodwork Inc 918 277-6612
7100 Seay Rd Beggs (74421) **(G-549)**
Ballews Aluminum Products Inc 405 917-2225
5405 Nw 5th St Oklahoma City (73127) **(G-5521)**
Balon Corporation 405 677-3321
3245 S Hattie Ave Oklahoma City (73129) **(G-5522)**
Balon Valves 405 670-8300
3700 W Eastern Ave Oklahoma City (73129) **(G-5523)**
Bam Journal LLC 405 307-8220
333 N Sherry Ave Norman (73069) **(G-4925)**
Bama Companies Inc (PA) 918 592-0778
2745 E 11th St Tulsa (74104) **(G-9258)**
Bama Cos Inc 918 732-2640
2435 N Lewis Ave Tulsa (74110) **(G-9259)**
Bama Foods Limited Partnership 918 732-2399
5377 E 66th St N Tulsa (74117) **(G-9260)**
Bama Pie, Tulsa *Also called Bama Companies Inc* **(G-9258)**
Bama Pie Ltd 918 592-0778
2745 E 11th St Tulsa (74104) **(G-9261)**
Bandera Inc 918 747-7771
7134 S Yale Ave Ste 510 Tulsa (74136) **(G-9262)**
Bandera Petroleum, Tulsa *Also called Bandera Inc* **(G-9262)**
Bandon Oil & Gas GP LLC 405 429-5500
123 Robert S Kerr Ave Oklahoma City (73102) **(G-5524)**
Bangs 918 338-2339
128 W 2nd St Bartlesville (74003) **(G-450)**

ALPHABETIC

(PA)=Parent Co (HQ)=Headquarters (DH)=Div Headquarters

Bankers Online 888 229-8872
2541 Flint Ridge Rd Edmond (73003) ***(G-2316)***
Banks Motor Co 580 924-8883
502 Bryan Dr Durant (74701) ***(G-2204)***
Banks Son Backhoe & Dumptruck, Bristow *Also called Kevin Banks* ***(G-785)***
Banner Oil & Gas, Tulsa *Also called Pennant Oil & Gas LLC* ***(G-10485)***
Banner Oil & Gas LLC 405 642-4382
907 S Detroit Ave # 1035 Tulsa (74120) ***(G-9263)***
Banner Pipeline Company LLC 580 233-8955
302 N Independence St Enid (73701) ***(G-2913)***
Banners Signs & Business Cards 405 818-4371
45 Ne 50th St Oklahoma City (73105) ***(G-5525)***
Bar S Foods Co, Seminole *Also called Bar-S Foods Co* ***(G-8357)***
Bar-S Foods Co 580 331-1628
200 Locust Ave Clinton (73601) ***(G-1740)***
Bar-S Foods Co 580 510-3300
802 Sw Goodyear Blvd Lawton (73505) ***(G-3896)***
Bar-S Foods Co 405 303-2138
701 E Goodhope Rd Seminole (74868) ***(G-8357)***
Bar-S Foods Co 580 821-5700
500 S Bar S Blvd Altus (73521) ***(G-144)***
Baray Enterprises Inc 405 373-1800
5601 Washington Ave E Piedmont (73078) ***(G-7755)***
Barbara Chaple 405 721-3758
7030 W Wilshire Blvd Oklahoma City (73132) ***(G-5526)***
Barbara J Landreth Sewing 918 298-8141
10427 S 67th East Ave Tulsa (74133) ***(G-9264)***
Barbara J McGinnis 580 226-7675
717 N Commerce St Ardmore (73401) ***(G-253)***
Barbeque Brew Trading Company, Broken Arrow *Also called Billy Sims Barbeque LLC* ***(G-852)***
Barbour Energy Corporation 405 848-7671
3111 Quail Springs Pkwy Oklahoma City (73134) ***(G-5527)***
Barclay Contract Pumping 580 541-7439
4030 S Highway 132 Enid (73703) ***(G-2914)***
Barelas Welding 580 497-7485
10930 N 2090 Rd Canute (73626) ***(G-1266)***
Bargain Journal 918 426-5500
126 E Choctaw Ave McAlester (74501) ***(G-4273)***
Barker Machine Shop 405 828-4683
Rr 1 Dover (73734) ***(G-2038)***
Barlow Hunt, Tulsa *Also called Oil States Industries Inc* ***(G-10388)***
Barlow-Hunt Inc 918 250-0828
10322 E 58th St Tulsa (74146) ***(G-9265)***
Barnes Oil Co 918 352-2308
10015 S 433rd West Ave Drumright (74030) ***(G-2051)***
Barnes Welding LLC 580 774-5491
79317 N 2560 Rd Watonga (73772) ***(G-11341)***
Barnett James 405 833-4052
15301 Se 33rd St Choctaw (73020) ***(G-1528)***
Barnetts 405 390-3026
915 Oak Park Dr Choctaw (73020) ***(G-1529)***
Barnsdall Meat Processors Inc 918 847-2814
34 Florence Ave Barnsdall (74002) ***(G-436)***
Baroid Drilling Fluids 405 459-6611
300 S Main St Pocasset (73079) ***(G-7774)***
Baron Exploration Co Inc 405 341-1779
107 S Broadway Edmond (73034) ***(G-2317)***
Baron Manufacturing Inc 405 947-3362
3100 W I 44 Service Rd Oklahoma City (73112) ***(G-5528)***
Barrett Drilling Company 405 273-6217
1210 Gordon Cooper Dr Shawnee (74801) ***(G-8430)***
Barrett Jewelers, Edmond *Also called Barretts Inc* ***(G-2318)***
Barrett Land & Cattle Co, Shawnee *Also called Barrett Drilling Company* ***(G-8430)***
Barrett Oil Company 580 436-1896
820 Egypt Rd Ada (74820) ***(G-11)***
Barrett Performance Aircraft 918 835-1089
2870b N Sheridan Rd Tulsa (74115) ***(G-9266)***
Barrett Precision Engines Inc 918 835-1089
2870b N Sheridan Rd Tulsa (74115) ***(G-9267)***
Barretts Inc 405 340-1519
3224 S Boulevard Edmond (73013) ***(G-2318)***
Barrichem Inc 580 276-3125
Putman Rd Marietta (73448) ***(G-4199)***
Barrick Pharmacies Inc 405 273-9417
3210 Kethley Rd Shawnee (74804) ***(G-8431)***
Barron and Stevenson EMC LLC 918 804-8440
1117 S Birmingham Ave Tulsa (74104) ***(G-9268)***
Barry Fennel LLC 405 745-7645
631 N Edgewood Ter Mustang (73064) ***(G-4765)***
Bartec Dispensing Tech Inc 918 250-6496
11130 E 56th St Tulsa (74146) ***(G-9269)***
Bartlesville Custom Cabinets 918 440-5981
398681 W 2400 Rd Bartlesville (74006) ***(G-451)***
Bartlesville Print Shop 918 336-6070
120 E 2nd St Bartlesville (74003) ***(G-452)***
Bartlesville Redi-Mix Inc 580 765-6693
1500 Tuxedo Blvd Bartlesville (74006) ***(G-453)***
Bartling Pumps & Supplies LLC 580 444-2227
4310 Ashland Duncan (73533) ***(G-2087)***
Bartosh Electric Motor Center 405 567-2840
Hwy 62 Prague (74864) ***(G-7920)***
Basden Steel-Oklahoma LLC 918 341-9468
15151 S Highway 66 Claremore (74017) ***(G-1593)***
Base Scale Company 918 523-9559
6825 S Delaware Ave Tulsa (74136) ***(G-9270)***
Basic Energy Services Inc 580 227-3144
Hwy 60 N 2/5 Mi Fairview (73737) ***(G-3132)***
Basic Energy Services Inc 580 252-6200
7302 N Hwy 81 Duncan (73533) ***(G-2088)***
Basic Energy Services Inc 580 254-3600
500 Oklahoma Ave Woodward (73801) ***(G-11560)***
Basic Energy Services Inc 918 225-0161
7101 E Main St Cushing (74023) ***(G-1923)***
Basic Energy Services Inc 918 287-3388
99 Oklahoma Ave Pawhuska (74056) ***(G-7677)***
Basic Energy Services Inc 405 756-1820
401 Se 4th St Lindsay (73052) ***(G-4047)***
Basic Energy Services Inc 405 324-0848
804 S Mustang Rd Yukon (73099) ***(G-11696)***
Basic Energy Services Inc 580 758-1234
10830 S Oakwood Rd Waukomis (73773) ***(G-11359)***
Baskins Machined Products LLC 918 284-4298
12645 N 103rd East Ave Collinsville (74021) ***(G-1802)***
Bates Instrumentation LLC 918 441-7178
30949 S Cnty Rd Ste 4330 Kinta (74552) ***(G-3832)***
Batesfield GPU, Wellston *Also called Randy Mulkey* ***(G-11475)***
Bath & Body Works LLC 405 748-3197
2150 W Memorial Rd Ste A Oklahoma City (73134) ***(G-5529)***
Bath Bomb Dyes 405 406-1823
733 S Mustang Rd Yukon (73099) ***(G-11697)***
Batie Screw Machine Products, Chickasha *Also called Kenneth Pace* ***(G-1479)***
Baties Custom Saddle Tree 918 788-3686
346 S Commercial St Welch (74369) ***(G-11462)***
Batteries Plus, Oklahoma City *Also called Batteries Sooner LLC* ***(G-5530)***
Batteries Sooner LLC 405 605-1237
4100 Will Rogers Pkwy # 300 Oklahoma City (73108) ***(G-5530)***
Bauman Machine Inc 405 745-3484
6600 Sw 44th St Oklahoma City (73179) ***(G-5531)***
Baxter Health Care, Tulsa *Also called Baxter Healthcare Corporation* ***(G-9271)***
Baxter Healthcare Corporation 918 513-8980
11333 E Pine St Tulsa (74116) ***(G-9271)***
Bay, Tulsa *Also called Berry Holdings LP* ***(G-9285)***
Bayou Oil Field Service & Sup 918 398-2166
1550 N 105th East Ave Tulsa (74116) ***(G-9272)***
Bays Enterprises Inc (PA) 405 235-2297
228 Robert S Kerr Ave # 600 Oklahoma City (73102) ***(G-5532)***
Bays Exploration Inc 405 235-2297
4005 Nw Expwy St Ste 600 Oklahoma City (73116) ***(G-5533)***
Baytide Petroleum Inc (HQ) 918 585-8150
7105 E Admiral Pl Ste 200 Tulsa (74115) ***(G-9273)***
Bayville, Tulsa *Also called Emery Bay Corporation* ***(G-9671)***
Baywest Embroidery 580 626-4728
23958 Cottonwood Ln Jet (73749) ***(G-3741)***
Bb Machine & Supply Inc 580 237-8686
2317 N 11th St Enid (73701) ***(G-2915)***
Bb2 LLC 918 895-7878
3301 S Peoria Ave Tulsa (74105) ***(G-9274)***
Bb2 LLC 405 726-8300
1150 E 2nd St Edmond (73034) ***(G-2319)***
Bb2 LLC (PA) 405 232-2739
1 N Oklahoma Ave Oklahoma City (73104) ***(G-5534)***
Bbr Oil Corp (PA) 580 223-2887
10 W Main St Ste 212 Ardmore (73401) ***(G-254)***
Bbr Oil Corp 405 366-8019
330 W Gray St Ste 305 Norman (73069) ***(G-4926)***
Bc Field Services Inc 918 839-0490
13006 526th St Heavener (74937) ***(G-3425)***
Bc Steel Buildings Inc 405 324-5100
9900 Nw 10th St Oklahoma City (73127) ***(G-5535)***
Bce - Mach III LLC (PA) 405 252-8100
14201 Wireless Way # 300 Oklahoma City (73134) ***(G-5536)***
Bce-Mach II LLC 405 252-8100
14201 Wireless Way # 300 Oklahoma City (73134) ***(G-5537)***
Bce-Mach LLC (PA) 405 252-8100
14201 Wireless Way # 300 Oklahoma City (73134) ***(G-5538)***
Bce-Mach LLC 580 824-7251
103 N Missouri St Waynoka (73860) ***(G-11373)***
Bcej Company 405 470-3790
328 S Eagle Ln Ste D Oklahoma City (73128) ***(G-5539)***
BCI Barn Builders, Fort Gibson *Also called Burrow Construction LLC* ***(G-3174)***
Bcrk Limited Partnership 405 321-0089
2004 Wyckham Pl Norman (73072) ***(G-4927)***
Bdtronic, Tulsa *Also called Bartec Dispensing Tech Inc* ***(G-9269)***
Be Custom Coatings 405 205-9347
329483 E 1000 Rd Harrah (73045) ***(G-3374)***

Be-Hive Interior Drapery Fctry 918 599-0292
1343 S Harvard Ave Tulsa (74112) *(G-9275)*
Beacon Publishing Co Inc 405 232-4151
124 Sw 25th St Oklahoma City (73109) *(G-5540)*
Beacon Sign Company Inc 405 567-4886
8102 Nbu Prague (74864) *(G-7921)*
Beacon Stamp & Seal Co 918 834-2322
2521 S Sheridan Rd Tulsa (74129) *(G-9276)*
Bean Chris Oil & Gas Service 918 298-1569
543 W 112th Ct S Jenks (74037) *(G-3690)*
Bean Counter Inc 918 925-9667
2601 Holly Rd Claremore (74017) *(G-1594)*
Beane Development Corp 580 222-1150
132 Holiday Dr Ardmore (73401) *(G-255)*
Bear, Mill Creek *Also called 3 C Cattle Feeders Inc (G-4465)*
Bear Paw Manufacturing 918 637-4775
72149 S 322 Way Wagoner (74467) *(G-11275)*
Bear Productions Inc 918 768-3364
30451 W Sans Bois Rd Kinta (74552) *(G-3833)*
Bear Safes, Oklahoma City *Also called W E Industries Inc (G-7410)*
Beard Production Co, Dewey *Also called Robert C Beard (G-2031)*
Bearwood Concepts Inc 918 933-6600
6202 E 30th St N Tulsa (74115) *(G-9277)*
Beathe's Knives, Sperry *Also called Mike Beathe (G-8610)*
Beauchamp Cabinets Cstm Homes 918 476-5532
2682 W 600 Chouteau (74337) *(G-1558)*
Beav's Machine Shop, Hinton *Also called Anson Desimone (G-3522)*
Beaver Creek Industries LLC 918 469-2779
31078 W County Road 1270 Kinta (74552) *(G-3834)*
Beaver Fabrication Inc 405 360-0014
5757 York Dr Norman (73069) *(G-4928)*
Beavers High Pressure Wshg LLC 580 512-3530
15989 Nw Allison Rd Apache (73006) *(G-218)*
Beavers Independent Printe 405 205-5300
3300 Michelle Ct Moore (73160) *(G-4497)*
Becca Vermelis 405 701-1638
743 Terrace Pl Norman (73069) *(G-4929)*
Bechtels Heavy Metal Works LLC 580 251-1412
1003 E Willow Ave Duncan (73533) *(G-2089)*
Beck Illuminations LLC 918 623-2880
202 S 7th St Okemah (74859) *(G-5264)*
Beck Resources Incorporated 405 853-2736
Hwy 81 N Hennessey (73742) *(G-3446)*
Beckham and Butler 918 885-4406
1124 S Price Ave Hominy (74035) *(G-3576)*
Becks Farm Equipment Inc 405 282-1196
3650 Ne Highway 33 Guthrie (73044) *(G-3299)*
Becks Forklift Svc LLC 580 303-8038
100 Ranch Rd Elk City (73644) *(G-2786)*
Becky Welch Vacuum Forming 918 836-7301
260 S 104th East Ave Tulsa (74128) *(G-9278)*
Beckys Embroidery Design 918 456-1235
16254 E Red Fuller Rd Tahlequah (74464) *(G-8852)*
Becsul Energy Incorporated 405 789-1061
6815 Nw 10th St Ste 1 Oklahoma City (73127) *(G-5541)*
Bedford Energy Inc 405 820-2711
3555 Nw 58th St Ste 901 Oklahoma City (73112) *(G-5542)*
Bedr Fine Chocolates Factory, Davis *Also called Chickasaw Nation (G-1980)*
Bedside Gunlock Products 713 443-8172
8195 Highway 82a Tahlequah (74464) *(G-8853)*
Beefys Beastro Food Svc LLC 580 491-0325
3201 S 1st St Broken Arrow (74012) *(G-844)*
Beehive Interiors, Tulsa *Also called Be-Hive Interior Drapery Fctry (G-9275)*
Beekmann Enterprises 918 272-7197
8606 E 96th St N Owasso (74055) *(G-7547)*
Beeman Products Co Inc 918 251-1432
2228 W Oakridge St Broken Arrow (74012) *(G-845)*
Bees Knees Tees 405 370-2132
245 Woodlake Dr Choctaw (73020) *(G-1530)*
Beetle Plastics LLC (HQ) 580 389-5421
601 Beetle Dr Ardmore (73401) *(G-256)*
Beirute Consulting, Tulsa *Also called Robert M Beirute (G-10662)*
Belden Russell Elect Co 918 791-9600
63201 E 290 Rd Grove (74344) *(G-3259)*
Bell & Kinley Company 405 373-5356
13248 Nw Expressway Piedmont (73078) *(G-7756)*
Bell & McCoy Companies Inc 405 278-6909
719 N Shartel Ave Oklahoma City (73102) *(G-5543)*
Bell Printing and Advertising 405 769-6445
2408 A N W Minster St Nicoma Park (73066) *(G-4866)*
Bell Timber Inc 580 584-6902
7316 Craig Rd Broken Bow (74728) *(G-1185)*
Bella Forte Glass Studio LLC 405 659-6169
1012 Nw 81st St Oklahoma City (73114) *(G-5544)*
Belle Point Beverages Inc 918 649-3921
112 Kerr Ave Poteau (74953) *(G-7896)*
Beller Boring Backhoe L 405 288-6638
22901 Canary Ln Washington (73093) *(G-11333)*
Bellofram 405 677-7222
2221 Se 69th St Oklahoma City (73149) *(G-5545)*
Bellofram Corporation 918 965-1964
900 N Owalla Ave Claremore (74017) *(G-1595)*
Bells and Whistles 405 470-8400
340 S Vermont Ave Ste 109 Oklahoma City (73108) *(G-5546)*
Bellwood Petroleum 405 254-3113
4117 Nw 122nd St Oklahoma City (73120) *(G-5547)*
Bellylove Maternity Gifts 405 818-3339
13104 Box Canyon Rd Oklahoma City (73142) *(G-5548)*
Belport Oil Inc 918 637-5476
1719 S Boston Ave Tulsa (74119) *(G-9279)*
Bemis Company Inc 918 739-4907
905 W Verderiges Catoosa (74015) *(G-1301)*
Bemis Company Inc 405 207-2200
200 N Indian Meridian Rd Pauls Valley (73075) *(G-7650)*
Bemis-Pauls Valley, Pauls Valley *Also called Bemis Company Inc (G-7650)*
Benchmark 77 Energy 405 239-3291
777 Nw 63rd St Oklahoma City (73116) *(G-5549)*
Benchmark Completions LLC 405 691-5659
13800 S Macarthur Blvd Oklahoma City (73173) *(G-5550)*
Benchmark Monument 918 582-8600
1735 E 11th St Tulsa (74104) *(G-9280)*
Benchmark Stucco 918 810-2812
10345 N Sheridan Rd Sperry (74073) *(G-8604)*
Bendco Corp 918 583-1566
1625 E Easton St Tulsa (74120) *(G-9281)*
Bendco Pipe & Tube Bending, Tulsa *Also called Bendco Corp (G-9281)*
Bended Knee Construction LLC 918 465-4700
798 Ne 1095th Ave Red Oak (74563) *(G-8074)*
Benders 580 256-5656
120 Pen Mar Dr Woodward (73801) *(G-11561)*
Bendmasters Inc 918 585-3755
7100 Charles Page Blvd Tulsa (74127) *(G-9282)*
Benjamin Harjo Jr 405 521-0246
1516 Nw 35th St Oklahoma City (73118) *(G-5551)*
Bennett Construction 405 756-1918
505 Se 4th St Lindsay (73052) *(G-4048)*
Bennett Drilling, Poteau *Also called Clay Bennett (G-7901)*
Bennett Steel Inc 918 227-2564
2210 Industrial Rd Sapulpa (74066) *(G-8252)*
Bennett Steel Fabrication Inc 918 227-2564
2210 Industrial Rd Sapulpa (74066) *(G-8253)*
Bennett's Decal & Label, Oklahoma City *Also called Tom Bennett Manufacturing (G-7302)*
Bennie Publications LLC 918 873-0250
1809 S Grand Blvd Oklahoma City (73108) *(G-5552)*
Benson Mineral Group Inc 918 762-3651
Nw Of City Pawnee (74058) *(G-7700)*
Benson Sound Inc 405 610-7455
5717 Se 74th St Ste F Oklahoma City (73135) *(G-5553)*
Benson Sound Lights & Video, Oklahoma City *Also called Benson Sound Inc (G-5553)*
Bent Tees Screen Printing 918 734-3996
1819 S Irvington Ave Tulsa (74112) *(G-9283)*
Bentwrench Studios 918 406-8070
1602 S Main St Sapulpa (74066) *(G-8254)*
Bequettes Gourmet Foods Inc 918 946-4212
4515 E 39th St Tulsa (74135) *(G-9284)*
Beredco Inc 405 858-2326
2601 Nw Expwy Ste 1100e Oklahoma City (73112) *(G-5554)*
Berexco LLC 405 848-1165
2601 Nw Expwy Ste 1100e Oklahoma City (73112) *(G-5555)*
Berexco LLC 918 352-2588
110 N Magnolia Drumright (74030) *(G-2052)*
Bergey Windpower Company Inc 405 364-4212
2200 Industrial Blvd Norman (73069) *(G-4930)*
Berkshire Corporation (PA) 405 677-3391
1101 Se 26th St Oklahoma City (73129) *(G-5556)*
Berkshire Hathaway Inc 918 245-6634
303 N Mckinley Ave Sand Springs (74063) *(G-8166)*
Berkshire Hathaway Inc 918 272-1155
202 E 2nd Ave Ste 101 Owasso (74055) *(G-7548)*
Berkshire Hathaway Inc 918 396-1616
500 W Rogers Blvd Skiatook (74070) *(G-8532)*
Berkshire Hathaway Inc 918 486-4444
221 E Cherokee St Wagoner (74467) *(G-11276)*
Berkshire Hathaway Inc 918 485-5505
221 E Cherokee St Wagoner (74467) *(G-11277)*
Bermuda King, Ringwood *Also called Bermuda King LLC (G-8085)*
Bermuda King LLC 405 375-5000
44501 S County Road 266 Ringwood (73768) *(G-8085)*
Berridge Mfg Dist Ctr 405 248-7404
1400 Exchange Ave Oklahoma City (73108) *(G-5557)*
Berry Custom Printing LLC 918 266-3732
7 S 276th East Ave Catoosa (74015) *(G-1302)*
Berry Global Inc 812 424-2904
349 Taylor Indus Pk Rd McAlester (74501) *(G-4274)*
Berry Global Inc 918 824-4288
1 Stretch Film Way Pryor (74362) *(G-7945)*
Berry Global Inc 918 824-4400
3137 Highway 69a Pryor (74361) *(G-7946)*

Berry Global Inc 918 426-4800
349 Taylor Indus Prk Rd McAlester (74501) ***(G-4275)***
Berry Global Films LLC 918 227-1616
6940 W 76th St S Tulsa (74131) ***(G-8990)***
Berry Global Films LLC 918 446-1651
6940 W 76th St S Tulsa (74131) ***(G-8991)***
Berry Holdings LP 918 582-3461
6218 S Lewis Ave Ste 100 Tulsa (74136) ***(G-9285)***
Berry Machine & Tool Company 580 536-4382
1002 Sw Goodyear Blvd Lawton (73505) ***(G-3897)***
Berry Plastics Corporation 918 824-4400
1 Armin Rd Pryor (74361) ***(G-7947)***
Berry, Robt W, Tulsa *Also called Robert W Berry Inc* ***(G-10663)***
Berryfields Cinnamon Roll LLC 405 248-0777
3545 Nw 58th St Oklahoma City (73112) ***(G-5558)***
Berryhill Ornamental Iron LLC 918 258-6531
550 S 12th St Broken Arrow (74012) ***(G-846)***
Bert Parsons 2nd Gen Lcksmth L 918 794-7131
8132 E 9th St Tulsa (74112) ***(G-9286)***
Best Building Materials Inc 405 755-0554
14801 Bristol Park Blvd Edmond (73013) ***(G-2320)***
Best Companies (PA) 918 280-8066
4212 W Wichita St Broken Arrow (74012) ***(G-847)***
Best Mold Technology LLC 405 659-1991
17069 Sw Lee Blvd Cache (73527) ***(G-1224)***
Best Oil Field Service Inc 405 262-5060
1901 E Highway 66 El Reno (73036) ***(G-2701)***
Best Oilfield Service, El Reno *Also called Best Oil Field Service Inc* ***(G-2701)***
Best Pressure Cairns Mfg, Oklahoma City *Also called Cairns Manufacturing Inc* ***(G-5670)***
Best Printing Solution LLC 918 794-1771
1414 N 163rd East Ave Tulsa (74116) ***(G-9287)***
Best Trailer Products 580 931-3534
301 S 22nd Ave Durant (74701) ***(G-2205)***
Beta Oil Company 405 601-3389
4900 N Meridian Ave Oklahoma City (73112) ***(G-5559)***
Beta Tex, Oklahoma City *Also called Beta Oil Company* ***(G-5559)***
Bethel Welding Metal Building 918 367-5776
30515 W Highway 66 Bristow (74010) ***(G-765)***
Bethesda Adult Lf Training Ctr, Mounds *Also called Bethesda Boys Ranch* ***(G-4610)***
Bethesda Boys Ranch (PA) 918 827-6409
17477 S 49th Ave W Mounds (74047) ***(G-4610)***
Beths Bags and More LLC 918 451-7346
12220 E 131st St S Broken Arrow (74011) ***(G-848)***
Beths Baubles and Bits 405 659-3841
17910 N Harrah Rd Luther (73054) ***(G-4134)***
Better Bilt Portable Buildings 918 224-3437
301 N Main St Sapulpa (74066) ***(G-8255)***
Better Built Barns 405 547-2066
11809 S Washington Perkins (74059) ***(G-7715)***
Better Built Structures LLC 918 224-3437
301 N Main St Sapulpa (74066) ***(G-8256)***
Better Power Inc 405 753-1192
7608 N Hudson Ave Oklahoma City (73116) ***(G-5560)***
Better Sign Co 580 242-9317
1518 W Hudson Dr Enid (73703) ***(G-2916)***
Better Sound Hearing Aid Svc 918 995-2222
807 E A St Ste 117 Jenks (74037) ***(G-3691)***
Betty E Jester 580 564-9396
16939 Haircut Rd Kingston (73439) ***(G-3824)***
Bevins Co, Tulsa *Also called M W Bevins Co* ***(G-10190)***
Beyond Blinds LLC 918 935-6317
9622 E 117th Pl S Bixby (74008) ***(G-614)***
BF Brandt Welding LLC 405 657-4670
212 N Falcon Dr Oklahoma City (73127) ***(G-5561)***
BF Machine Shop Inc 580 255-6119
1603 N 5th St Duncan (73533) ***(G-2090)***
BF Machines Shop Inc 580 255-5899
1603 N 5th St Duncan (73533) ***(G-2091)***
Bg & S Manufacturing 918 396-3525
1003 S Lombard Ln Skiatook (74070) ***(G-8533)***
Bgr LLC 405 671-2000
1020 E Grand Blvd Oklahoma City (73129) ***(G-5562)***
Bible & Books Repair Center, Fort Gibson *Also called Artur Bookbinding Intl* ***(G-3173)***
Bici LLC 918 625-8811
4108 N Pine Ave Broken Arrow (74012) ***(G-849)***
Bico Drilling Tools Inc 918 872-9983
13675 E 61st St Broken Arrow (74012) ***(G-850)***
Big 3 Woodyard Inc 580 298-6123
Hc 67 Antlers (74523) ***(G-214)***
Big Buckets Rathole Drilling 580 233-9850
5915 Memorial Dr Enid (73701) ***(G-2917)***
Big Country Meat Market, Enid *Also called Janice Sue Daniel* ***(G-2982)***
Big Creek Custom Embroidery 918 446-6054
3735 S 63rd West Ave Tulsa (74107) ***(G-9288)***
Big D Industries Inc 405 682-2541
5620 Sw 29th St Oklahoma City (73179) ***(G-5563)***
Big Dipper Hot Oil Service 580 363-0168
1005 S O St Blackwell (74631) ***(G-674)***
Big Easy 918 493-6280
6533 S Peoria Ave Tulsa (74136) ***(G-9289)***
Big Elk Energy Systems LLC 918 947-6800
4140 S Galveston Ave Tulsa (74107) ***(G-9290)***
Big G Precision Welding 918 406-2876
1632 S 69th East Ave Tulsa (74112) ***(G-9291)***
Big Gas Oil LLC 405 763-9844
4900 Richmond Sq Ste 300 Oklahoma City (73118) ***(G-5564)***
Big House Specialty Prtg Inc 918 271-1414
1147 S Owasso Ave Tulsa (74120) ***(G-9292)***
Big Iron Oilfield Services 580 788-2247
22650 Highway 29 Elmore City (73433) ***(G-2894)***
Big J Tank Truck Service Inc 580 336-3501
1705 N 15th St Perry (73077) ***(G-7727)***
Big League Oil and Gas LLC 405 433-9908
26761 E 870 Rd Cashion (73016) ***(G-1285)***
Big Productions LLC 405 513-6545
2844 Nw 159th St Edmond (73013) ***(G-2321)***
Big Red Shop Inc (PA) 405 495-5551
5104 N Macarthur Blvd Warr Acres (73122) ***(G-11313)***
Big Ricks Jerky LLC 405 414-9096
9709 Lakeland Rd Oklahoma City (73162) ***(G-5565)***
Big River Sales & Mfg, Lone Grove *Also called Big River Sales Inc* ***(G-4115)***
Big River Sales Inc 580 657-4950
Hc 62 Box 3 Lone Grove (73443) ***(G-4115)***
Big Rock Foods LLC 405 269-8558
1600 N Brush Creek Rd Stillwater (74075) ***(G-8659)***
Big Shot LLC 918 712-7110
2526 E 71st St Ste G Tulsa (74136) ***(G-9293)***
Big Shot LLC (PA) 918 712-7110
7107 S Yale Ave 312 Tulsa (74136) ***(G-9294)***
Big Time Designs Screen Prtg 580 658-5000
408 N 9th St Marlow (73055) ***(G-4223)***
Big V Feeds, McAlester *Also called Big v Feeds Inc* ***(G-4276)***
Big v Feeds Inc 918 423-1565
1621 E Electric Ave McAlester (74501) ***(G-4276)***
Bigbie, Bane CPA, Ardmore *Also called Ssb Production LLC* ***(G-362)***
Bigfoot Prints LLC 918 805-0543
315 W Main St Collinsville (74021) ***(G-1803)***
Biggs Communications Inc 918 523-4425
6784 S 67th East Ave Tulsa (74133) ***(G-9295)***
Bil-Jac Pet Foods, Tulsa *Also called Win Hy Foods Inc* ***(G-9053)***
Bilco Construction Inc 405 386-5591
7810 Buckwood Rd Newalla (74857) ***(G-4804)***
Bill Durbins Mobile Home Tra 405 799-3557
10550 Se 149th St Oklahoma City (73165) ***(G-5280)***
Bill Glass 918 479-8884
8934 S 446 Locust Grove (74352) ***(G-4104)***
Bill Jones Mfg 405 392-4525
877 Squirrel Ct Tuttle (73089) ***(G-11186)***
Bill Kite Sales 918 806-2958
5309 S Hickory Ave Broken Arrow (74011) ***(G-851)***
Bill Koenig 405 386-7979
11409 Jeffery Rd Newalla (74857) ***(G-4805)***
Bill Laird Oil Company 405 289-3346
123 Town Cir Saint Louis (74866) ***(G-8131)***
Bill Rathbone 918 486-3028
304 N Broadway Coweta (74429) ***(G-1872)***
Bill Sneed Oilfield 918 358-3487
607 Miami St Nw Cleveland (74020) ***(G-1717)***
Bill Stockton Welding LLC 918 697-7750
441 W 7th St Chelsea (74016) ***(G-1402)***
Bill Weems Oil Inc 405 382-1813
2501 Hwy 9 W Seminole (74818) ***(G-8358)***
Bill's Family Shoe Store, Lawton *Also called Lawton Brace & Limb Co Inc* ***(G-3954)***
Billboards Etc Inc 580 326-1660
3004 Deer Run Hugo (74743) ***(G-3603)***
Billiards & Bar Stools Inc 405 722-2400
525 W Memorial Rd Oklahoma City (73114) ***(G-5566)***
Billiards of Tulsa Inc (PA) 918 835-1166
7813 E Admiral Pl Tulsa (74115) ***(G-9296)***
Bills Catfish Bait 918 224-8470
418 N 2nd St Sapulpa (74066) ***(G-8257)***
Bills Electric Inc 918 341-4414
24704 S Highway 66 Claremore (74019) ***(G-1596)***
Bills Marine Canvas Upholstery 405 306-2936
717 N Crawford Ave Norman (73069) ***(G-4931)***
Bills Welding Coop LLC 405 370-6383
2000 Sw 15th St Oklahoma City (73108) ***(G-5567)***
Bills Welding Equipment Repr 405 232-4799
2006 Sw 15th St Oklahoma City (73108) ***(G-5568)***
Billy Carroll 918 352-9228
10431 S 513th West Ave Drumright (74030) ***(G-2053)***
Billy Cook Harn & Saddle Mfg 580 622-5505
320 W Muskogee Ave Sulphur (73086) ***(G-8829)***
Billy Goat Ice Cream Co LLC 405 332-5508
1414 S Sangre Rd Stillwater (74074) ***(G-8660)***
Billy J Vineyard 918 246-2139
16601 W 21st St S Sand Springs (74063) ***(G-8167)***

Billy Jack Sharber Oper LLC 405 382-5740
Seminole County Konawa (74849) *(G-3843)*
Billy McGill 580 220-7097
17987 Buckeye Ln Marietta (73448) *(G-4200)*
Billy Sims Barbeque LLC 918 258-1978
2427 W Kenosha St Broken Arrow (74012) *(G-852)*
Bimbo Bakeries Usa Inc 580 234-1213
2620 N 11th St Enid (73701) *(G-2918)*
Bimbo Bakeries Usa Inc 405 273-5049
1515 N Tucker Ave Shawnee (74801) *(G-8432)*
Bimbo Bakeries Usa Inc 405 556-2135
1916 N Broadway Ave Oklahoma City (73103) *(G-5569)*
Binder Leasing LLC 918 623-0526
600 S Sertco Rd Okemah (74859) *(G-5265)*
Binger Operations LLC 405 232-0201
204 N Robinson Ave # 2300 Oklahoma City (73102) *(G-5570)*
Bint Exploration & Development 405 848-2113
5653 N Pennsylvania Ave Oklahoma City (73112) *(G-5571)*
Bio-Cide International Inc 405 364-1940
2650 Venture Dr Norman (73069) *(G-4932)*
Biocorp Technologies Inc 405 990-2350
743 Nw 99th St Oklahoma City (73114) *(G-5572)*
Biodynamics Corp 405 201-1289
1809 Atchison Dr Ste B Norman (73069) *(G-4933)*
Biometric Identification Syste 405 517-9641
311 Telstar St Norman (73069) *(G-4934)*
Biorite Acquisition Co LLC 405 701-1515
1811 Industrial Blvd # 105 Norman (73069) *(G-4935)*
Biorite Nutritionals, Norman *Also called Biorite Acquisition Co LLC* *(G-4935)*
Biospec Products Inc 918 336-3363
280 N Virginia Ave Bartlesville (74003) *(G-454)*
Biosphere Fuels LLC 713 332-5726
10601 N Penn Ave Oklahoma City (73120) *(G-5573)*
Biotech Products Inc 405 235-7575
1529 W Main St Oklahoma City (73106) *(G-5574)*
Bipo Inc 580 262-9640
12225 Candy Tuft Ln Oklahoma City (73162) *(G-5575)*
Bird Creek Resources Inc 918 582-7713
1437 S Boulder Ave # 930 Tulsa (74119) *(G-9297)*
Birddog Software Corporation 405 794-5950
8277 S Walker Ave Oklahoma City (73139) *(G-5576)*
Bisby Candles LLC 918 408-5291
16209 Monarch Field Rd Edmond (73013) *(G-2322)*
Bishop Brothers 918 367-2270
113 W 5th Ave Bristow (74010) *(G-766)*
Bishop Tadoli Products, Bristow *Also called Bishop Brothers* *(G-766)*
Bison Energy Services LLC (PA) 405 529-6577
210 Park Ave Ste 1350 Oklahoma City (73102) *(G-5577)*
Bison Materials LLC 918 333-2266
1800 W 14th St Bartlesville (74003) *(G-455)*
Bison Metals Technologies LLC 403 395-1405
41600 Wolverine Rd Shawnee (74804) *(G-8433)*
Bison Oilfield Services LLC 405 437-1485
12534 Old Highway 99 Seminole (74868) *(G-8359)*
Bison Welding LLC 580 758-3359
16128 S Van Burren Bison (73720) *(G-607)*
Bixby Fabco Inc 918 366-3446
8900 E 171st St S Bixby (74008) *(G-615)*
Biz Networks LLC 405 348-6090
500 E 2nd St Edmond (73034) *(G-2323)*
BJH Services Inc 281 686-3408
2805 Melina Dr Yukon (73099) *(G-11698)*
Bjs Oilfield Cnstr Inc 405 485-3390
722 W Veterans Mem Hwy Blanchard (73010) *(G-701)*
Bk Exploration Corporation 918 582-3855
10159 E 11th St Ste 401 Tulsa (74128) *(G-9298)*
Bk Products, Tulsa *Also called Brenda K Toupin* *(G-9335)*
Bkep Crude LLC 405 278-6452
11501 S Intrstate 44 Svce Oklahoma City (73173) *(G-5578)*
Bkep Materials LLC 918 266-1606
5645 E Channel Rd Catoosa (74015) *(G-1303)*
Bkg Industries LLC 918 694-3390
10861 W Highway 9 Whitefield (74472) *(G-11516)*
Bkw Inc (PA) 918 836-6767
2469 E King St Tulsa (74110) *(G-9299)*
Black & Decker (us) Inc 918 249-8641
11414 E 51st St Ste C Tulsa (74146) *(G-9300)*
Black & Puryear Paint Mfg Co 405 348-0447
1640 Oak Creek Dr Edmond (73034) *(G-2324)*
Black Bayou Exploration LLC 405 753-5500
1601 Nw Expreokwy 1200 Oklahoma City (73118) *(G-5579)*
Black Belt Magazine 1000 LLC 405 732-5111
1000 Century Blvd Oklahoma City (73110) *(G-5580)*
Black Box Network Services 800 949-4039
8023 E 63rd Pl Ste 225 Tulsa (74133) *(G-9301)*
Black Cat Screen Printing LLC 405 895-6635
2617 N Shields Blvd Moore (73160) *(G-4498)*
Black Chronicle Inc 405 424-4695
1528 Ne 23rd St Ste A Oklahoma City (73111) *(G-5581)*
Black Chronicle Newspaper, Oklahoma City *Also called Black Chronicle Inc* *(G-5581)*
Black Gold 918 253-3344
104 S Main St Jay (74346) *(G-3679)*
Black Gold Stone Ranch LLC 405 590-0700
4132 Castlerock Rd Norman (73072) *(G-4936)*
Black River Aerospace LLC 386 212-3741
1000 Ne 20th Pl Moore (73160) *(G-4499)*
Black Star Manufacturing LLC 405 315-3336
930290 S Highway 18 Chandler (74834) *(G-1376)*
Black Swan Oil & Gas 405 285-1996
2513 S Kelly Ave Ste 200 Edmond (73013) *(G-2325)*
Black Thunder Roofing LLC 405 473-8028
305 Nw 5th St Unit 2131 Oklahoma City (73102) *(G-5582)*
Blackburn Oil & Gas Inc 918 688-1067
49651 S 360 Rd Pawnee (74058) *(G-7701)*
Blackhawk Industrial Dist Inc (PA) 918 610-4700
1501 Sw Expressway Dr Broken Arrow (74012) *(G-853)*
Blackhawk Safety LLC 580 574-1271
129 Landon Ln Lawton (73507) *(G-3898)*
Blackhawk Wireline Services 405 238-2929
1110 W Royal Oaks Rd Pauls Valley (73075) *(G-7651)*
Blackjack Express LLC 405 462-7410
3507 County Street 2920 Bradley (73011) *(G-760)*
Blackrock Services LLC (PA) 405 254-3939
5600 N May Ave Ste 137 Oklahoma City (73112) *(G-5583)*
Blackstone Capital Partners SE 424 355-5050
1021 S El Reno Ave El Reno (73036) *(G-2702)*
Blackwell Journal-Tribune, Blackwell *Also called Lewis County Press LLC* *(G-687)*
Blackwell Wind 580 363-0553
220 N 20th St Blackwell (74631) *(G-675)*
Blaine Exploration Ltd 918 333-2115
1821 Arbor Dr Bartlesville (74006) *(G-456)*
Blair Oil Co Inc 405 263-4445
219 N 6th St Kingfisher (73750) *(G-3785)*
Blairs Oil Field Services LLC 405 698-9987
7675 N Gregory Rd Yukon (73099) *(G-11699)*
Blake Production Company Inc 405 286-9800
1601 Nw Expressway # 777 Oklahoma City (73118) *(G-5584)*
Blakes Westside Tag Agency 918 446-1740
8400 Nw 76th St Oklahoma City (73132) *(G-5585)*
Blanchard News Publishing 405 485-2311
220 N Main Blanchard (73010) *(G-702)*
Blankenship Brothers Inc 405 943-3278
1401 S Meridian Ave Oklahoma City (73108) *(G-5586)*
Blankenship Brothers Inc (PA) 405 943-3278
1401 S Meridian Ave A Oklahoma City (73108) *(G-5587)*
Blankenship Brothers Inc 918 627-3278
4735 S Memorial Dr Ste A Tulsa (74145) *(G-9302)*
Blankenship Brothers Inc 405 848-7446
2837 Nw 63rd St Oklahoma City (73116) *(G-5588)*
Blankenship Roustabout 580 791-0237
1710 W Russworm Dr Watonga (73772) *(G-11342)*
Blastpro Manufacturing Inc 877 495-6464
513 Beacon Pl Oklahoma City (73127) *(G-5589)*
Blastpro Manufacturing Inc (PA) 405 491-6464
6021 Melrose Ln Oklahoma City (73127) *(G-5590)*
Blaylock Oil and Gas LLC 918 799-6153
164 N Bk 700 Rd Stigler (74462) *(G-8629)*
Blaze Skateboards LLC 405 391-3838
4100 Maxine Dr Choctaw (73020) *(G-1531)*
Blazer Oilfield Services LLC 405 756-4800
414 E Cherokee St Lindsay (73052) *(G-4049)*
Blessettis Inc 918 830-5481
9918 S 106th East Ave Tulsa (74133) *(G-9303)*
Blessing Gravel LLC 580 513-4009
1415 E Harbert Rd Tishomingo (73460) *(G-8962)*
Blessttis Grmet Itln Psta Sces, Tulsa *Also called Blessettis Inc* *(G-9303)*
Blevins Oil Field 405 619-9909
8117 Bourbon St Oklahoma City (73128) *(G-5591)*
Blevins Oilfield Sls & Svc LLC 405 619-9909
8117 Bourbon St Oklahoma City (73128) *(G-5592)*
Bleything Oil & Gas LLC 405 535-0253
14709 Bristol Park Blvd Edmond (73013) *(G-2326)*
Blind Doctor 918 638-1487
4204 Southwest Blvd Tulsa (74107) *(G-9304)*
Blinkers & Silks Unlimited Inc 405 463-0391
8697 E Broadway Lamar (74850) *(G-3862)*
Bliss Industries LLC (PA) 580 765-7787
900 E Oakland Ave Ponca City (74601) *(G-7800)*
Blitz USA Inc 918 676-3620
309 N Main St Miami (74354) *(G-4391)*
Blm Equipment & Mfg Co Inc 918 266-5282
100 S Shawnee St Catoosa (74015) *(G-1304)*
Block Sand Co Inc 405 391-2919
329044 E 1070 Rd McLoud (74851) *(G-4352)*
Bloods Logging & Land Svcs LLC 405 314-4275
9116 E 130 Rd Lamar (74850) *(G-3863)*
Bloom Electric Services LLC 580 327-2345
46457 Howe Rd Alva (73717) *(G-178)*
Bloomin Crazy Ldscp Flral Dsig 405 238-3416
401 S Chickasaw St Pauls Valley (73075) *(G-7652)*

ALPHABETIC

Bluco Inc 800 535-0135
399258 W 1330 Dr Dewey (74029) *(G-2017)*
Blue & Gold Sausage Inc 405 399-2954
10101 N Hiwassee Rd Jones (73049) *(G-3742)*
Blue ARC Metal Specialties 918 341-3903
505 W Lowry Rd Claremore (74017) *(G-1597)*
Blue Bell Creameries LP 918 258-5100
8201 E Highway 51 Broken Arrow (74014) *(G-1113)*
Blue Bonnet Feeds LP 580 223-3010
100 Mill St Se Ardmore (73401) *(G-257)*
Blue Bridge Publishing LLC 405 533-2547
120 S Stallard St Stillwater (74074) *(G-8661)*
Blue Canvas LLC 580 327-3406
1043 8th St Alva (73717) *(G-179)*
Blue Coyote Winery 918 785-4727
9564 N 429 Rd Adair (74330) *(G-107)*
Blue Mountain Midstream LLC 281 377-8770
14000 Quail Springs Pkwy # 5200 Oklahoma City (73134) *(G-5593)*
Blue Ribbon Forms Inc 918 834-8838
1208 S Hudson Ave Ste D Tulsa (74112) *(G-9305)*
Blue Ribbon Show Supply 918 288-7396
9731 N 20th West Ave Sperry (74073) *(G-8605)*
Blue River Tractors, Durant *Also called Blue River Ventures Inc (G-2206)*
Blue River Tractors, Calera *Also called Blue River Ventures Inc (G-1238)*
Blue River Valley Winery, Caddo *Also called Diane E Dean (G-1233)*
Blue River Ventures Inc 580 920-0111
4710 W Highway 70 Durant (74701) *(G-2206)*
Blue River Ventures Inc 580 798-4810
360 Lodge Rd Overbrook (73453) *(G-7538)*
Blue River Ventures Inc 580 920-0111
8087 Hwy 69 75 Calera (74730) *(G-1238)*
Blue Rock Oil & Gas LLC 580 229-5697
235 Stanton Rd Ardmore (73401) *(G-258)*
Blue Sage Studios 405 601-2583
1218 N Western Ave Oklahoma City (73106) *(G-5594)*
Blue Sail Publishing Inc 630 851-4731
1405 4th Ave Nw Ardmore (73401) *(G-259)*
Blue Sky Digital Printing, Norman *Also called Elite Media Group LLC (G-4989)*
Blue Sky Oil Field Svcs LLC 580 491-2349
116 Oak Dr Kaw City (74641) *(G-3756)*
Blue Speed LLC 918 856-3547
7803 S Urbana Ave Tulsa (74136) *(G-9306)*
Blue Star Acid Service Inc 918 324-5350
25914 S 465th West Ave Depew (74028) *(G-2010)*
Blue Star Gas Corp 405 321-1397
1006 24th Ave Nw Ste 120 Norman (73069) *(G-4937)*
Blue Stone Operating LLC 918 392-9209
2 W 2nd St Ste 1700 Tulsa (74103) *(G-9307)*
Blue Valley Energy Corp 918 298-1032
12222 S 2nd St Jenks (74037) *(G-3692)*
Blue Wave Boats, Seminole *Also called Parks Manufacturing Inc (G-8393)*
Bluearc Welding LLC 918 341-0629
4805 E Ranch Rd Claremore (74019) *(G-1598)*
Bluegrass Energy Inc 918 743-8060
4637 E 91st St Tulsa (74137) *(G-9308)*
Bluehawk Energy Inc 405 406-1580
4000 Calm Waters Way Edmond (73034) *(G-2327)*
Bluestem Gas Services LLC 580 658-6530
4655 County Street 2970 Lindsay (73052) *(G-4050)*
Bluestem Integrated LLC 918 660-0492
5301 S 125th East Ave Tulsa (74146) *(G-9309)*
Bluestone Natural Resources, Tulsa *Also called Blue Stone Operating LLC (G-9307)*
Bluestone Natural Resources HI 918 392-9200
2 W 2nd St Ste 1700 Tulsa (74103) *(G-9310)*
Bluestone Ntral Rsurces II LLC 918 392-9200
2 W 2nd St Ste 1700 Tulsa (74103) *(G-9311)*
Bluestone Ntural Resources LLC (PA) 918 392-9200
2 W 2nd St Ste 1700 Tulsa (74103) *(G-9312)*
Bluff Service Disposal 580 438-2262
Cheyenne Vly Waynoka (73860) *(G-11374)*
Blumenthal Companies LLc (PA) 405 232-9557
301 S Western Ave Oklahoma City (73109) *(G-5595)*
Blumenthal Companies LLc 405 232-9557
504 Sw 4th St Oklahoma City (73109) *(G-5596)*
Blumenthal's Heavy Duty, Oklahoma City *Also called Blumenthal Companies LLc (G-5596)*
Blush Boutique Inc 405 701-8600
566 Buchanan Ave Ste E Norman (73069) *(G-4938)*
Bm 405 388-3999
1618 Mill Creek Blvd Choctaw (73020) *(G-1532)*
BMC Enterprise LLC 918 336-4431
3365 County Road 2706 Bartlesville (74003) *(G-457)*
BMC Petroleum Inc 580 234-3725
1209 N 30th St Enid (73701) *(G-2919)*
Bmi Management Inc 580 762-5659
1901 E Hubbard Rd Ponca City (74604) *(G-7801)*
Bo Mc Resources Corporation 580 237-2324
901 The Trails West Loop Enid (73703) *(G-2920)*
Bo-Max Industries Inc 580 256-4555
4215 Oklahoma Ave Woodward (73801) *(G-11562)*

Boadie Anderson Quarries, Ada *Also called Boadie L Anderson Quarries Inc (G-12)*
Boadie L Anderson Quarries Inc 580 436-2100
504 Rosedale Rd Ada (74820) *(G-12)*
Board of Trustees of The Teach 405 521-2387
2500 N Lincoln Blvd # 500 Oklahoma City (73105) *(G-5597)*
Boardman LLC (PA) 405 634-5434
1135 S Mckinley Ave Oklahoma City (73108) *(G-5598)*
Boardman Co, The, Oklahoma City *Also called Boardman LLC (G-5598)*
Boardwalk Distribution Co 918 551-6275
5402 S 129th East Ave Tulsa (74134) *(G-9313)*
Boat Floaters Ind LLC 918 256-3330
E Hgwy 85 Afton (74331) *(G-113)*
Boatman Marine Canvas 405 628-7844
5924 Seminole Rd Warr Acres (73132) *(G-11314)*
Boatright Enterprises Inc 405 612-2473
665 Lori Ln Vinita (74301) *(G-11249)*
Bob & Son Oil Co Inc 405 853-6261
2 One Hlf Mile S On Hwy81 Hennessey (73742) *(G-3447)*
Bob Albauer Portable Welding 405 789-7999
5909 Nw 56th St Oklahoma City (73122) *(G-5599)*
Bob Brooks Motor Company 405 681-2592
4411 Sw 19th St Oklahoma City (73108) *(G-5600)*
Bob Clemishire Oil Co 918 885-4755
2 Miles N Hominy (74035) *(G-3577)*
Bob D Berry DBA 405 382-3360
217 W Broadway Seminole (74868) *(G-8360)*
Bob G Welding 918 510-4769
1221 Harrison St Pawnee (74058) *(G-7702)*
Bob Gene Moore 918 371-4381
40401 N 4010 Rd Collinsville (74021) *(G-1804)*
Bob Howard Whl Parts Dist Ctr 405 525-4400
3501 N Santa Fe Ave Oklahoma City (73118) *(G-5601)*
Bob Lowe Farm Machinery Inc 405 224-6500
1524 E Choctaw Ave Chickasha (73018) *(G-1440)*
BOB Lumber & Grain LLC 580 927-3168
17301 Lake St Coalgate (74538) *(G-1775)*
Bob Mc Kinney & Sons 918 387-2401
8807 N Norfolk Cushing (74023) *(G-1924)*
Bob Pound Drilling Inc 918 367-6262
121 W 6th Ave Bristow (74010) *(G-767)*
Bob's Printing, Claremore *Also called Dbmac 50 Inc (G-1613)*
Bobay Nutrition LLC 405 708-0407
6313 Beaver Creek Rd Oklahoma City (73162) *(G-5602)*
Bobby Foster 580 476-3417
5 Mi N Of City Rush Springs (73082) *(G-8119)*
Bobby J Darnell 405 524-8891
2250 Nw 39th St Ste 100 Oklahoma City (73112) *(G-5603)*
Bobby Joe Cudd Company 580 515-3131
S Highway 6 Elk City (73644) *(G-2787)*
Bobby K Birdwell 580 799-2357
300 Bryan Burns Flat (73624) *(G-1218)*
Bobby L Graham 580 393-2247
20651 E 1300 Rd Sentinel (73664) *(G-8410)*
Bobby Prater 918 885-4864
199 Pope Rd Hominy (74035) *(G-3578)*
Bobrick Washroom Equipment Inc 580 924-8066
1 Gamco Pl Durant (74701) *(G-2207)*
Bobs Auto Electric 918 687-3701
1306 Gibson St Muskogee (74403) *(G-4653)*
Bobs Backhoe Sevice 918 391-0901
11531 S 4050 Rd Talala (74080) *(G-8896)*
Bobs Sign Company 580 467-3646
404 S 29th St Rm 203 Chickasha (73018) *(G-1441)*
Bobs Vacuum Sewing Repair 918 378-1844
15702 E 101st St Broken Arrow (74011) *(G-854)*
Bobs Wood Working 405 632-4894
7313 S Klein Ave Oklahoma City (73139) *(G-5604)*
Boc, Woodward *Also called Messer North America Inc (G-11608)*
Boc Gases 580 254-2259
1002 Terra Dr Woodward (73801) *(G-11563)*
Body Billboards 405 282-9922
2403 S Division St Ste G Guthrie (73044) *(G-3300)*
Body Billboards & Trophies Too, Guthrie *Also called Body Billboards (G-3300)*
Body Buddy, Edmond *Also called Useful Products Inc (G-2662)*
Body Connection LLC 580 745-9201
322 1/2 N 3rd Ave Durant (74701) *(G-2208)*
Bodycote Thermal Proc Inc 405 670-5710
6924 S Eastern Ave Oklahoma City (73149) *(G-5605)*
Bodycote Thermal Proc Inc 214 904-2420
1520 N 170th East Ave Tulsa (74116) *(G-9314)*
Boeing Arospc Operations Inc 405 610-3100
3000 Tower Dr Ste 604 Oklahoma City (73115) *(G-5606)*
Boeing Arospc Operations Inc 580 481-3306
320 N 6th St Altus (73523) *(G-145)*
Boeing Arospc Operations Inc 580 480-4040
515 S 7th St Altus (73523) *(G-146)*
Boeing Company 918 835-3111
3330 N Mingo Rd Tulsa (74116) *(G-9315)*
Boeing Company 405 622-6000
6001 S Air Depot Blvd Oklahoma City (73135) *(G-5607)*

ALPHABETIC SECTION Brandon Hyde

Boeing Company...580 482-0354
1608 Cleveland St Altus (73521) *(G-147)*
Boeing Company...405 924-1385
1332 Sw 66th St Oklahoma City (73159) *(G-5608)*
Boeing Company...405 622-6206
6001 S Air Depot Blvd Oklahoma City (73135) *(G-5609)*
Boeing Company...405 622-6720
6001 S Air Depot Blvd Oklahoma City (73135) *(G-5610)*
Boeing Company...405 618-2859
6811 Se 59th St Oklahoma City (73135) *(G-5611)*
Boeing Company...918 292-2707
3800 N Mingo Rd Tulsa (74116) *(G-9316)*
Boeing Company...316 526-3272
601 S Air Depot Blvd Oklahoma City (73110) *(G-5612)*
Boeing Company...316 977-2121
601 S Air Depot Blvd Oklahoma City (73110) *(G-5613)*
Boeing Company...405 736-9227
8121 Mid America Blvd Oklahoma City (73135) *(G-5614)*
Boelte Explorations LLC...405 285-0063
16812 Conifer Ln Edmond (73012) *(G-2328)*
Bog Resources LLC...918 592-1010
525 S Main St Ste 1120 Tulsa (74103) *(G-9317)*
Bogo Energy Corporation (PA)...405 840-1067
13933 Quail Pointe Dr Oklahoma City (73134) *(G-5615)*
Bogo Energy Corporation...580 237-3756
4100 S Van Buren St Enid (73703) *(G-2921)*
Boiler Repair Company, Oklahoma City *Also called Atlantic Fbrication Design LLC (G-5485)*
Boise City News, Boise City *Also called Mesa Black Publishing LLC (G-747)*
Boje Oil Co...918 885-2456
203 E Main St Hominy (74035) *(G-3579)*
Boley One...405 301-7692
1305 Ne 23rd St Oklahoma City (73111) *(G-5616)*
Bolt It Hydraulic Solutions...918 296-0202
2807 W Main St Jenks (74037) *(G-3693)*
Bonanza Land LLC...580 772-2680
2811 E Main St Weatherford (73096) *(G-11393)*
Bonavista Technologies Inc...918 250-3435
6004 S 118th East Ave Tulsa (74146) *(G-9318)*
Book Distribution, Edmond *Also called Mental Note LLC (G-2512)*
Book Villages LLC...719 339-8048
2800 Berrywood Cir Edmond (73034) *(G-2329)*
Books In Sight Inc...405 810-9501
4141 Nw Expwy St Ste 110 Oklahoma City (73116) *(G-5617)*
Boolean Inc...405 341-1499
2701 Hidden Valley Rd Edmond (73013) *(G-2330)*
Boomer Blinds & Shutters LLC...918 968-2579
718 W Main St Stroud (74079) *(G-8808)*
Boomer Foundations & Piers...405 799-6811
201 Se 1st St Moore (73160) *(G-4500)*
Boomer Sooie LLC...501 827-0269
1025 E Indian Hills Rd Norman (73071) *(G-4939)*
Boomerang...405 250-6597
400 W Macarthur St Shawnee (74804) *(G-8434)*
Boomerang Printing LLC...918 747-1844
3615 S Harvard Ave Tulsa (74135) *(G-9319)*
Boone Operating Inc...405 879-2332
709 Nw 54th St Oklahoma City (73118) *(G-5618)*
Boone's Backhoe Services, Elk City *Also called Roger W Boone (G-2868)*
Booth Environmental Sls & Svc, Red Oak *Also called Booth Envmtl Sls & Svc LLC (G-8075)*
Booth Envmtl Sls & Svc LLC...918 465-0214
7298 Ne Highway 270 Red Oak (74563) *(G-8075)*
Bop Ram & Iron Rental, Weatherford *Also called BOp Ram-Block Ir Rentals Inc (G-11394)*
BOp Ram-Block Ir Rentals Inc...580 772-0250
717 S Custer St Weatherford (73096) *(G-11394)*
Boral Bricks Studio, Broken Arrow *Also called Meridian Brick LLC (G-971)*
Boral Bricks Studio, Oklahoma City *Also called Meridian Brick LLC (G-6567)*
Bordeauxs Embroidery...405 227-0958
6609 S Westminster Rd Oklahoma City (73150) *(G-5619)*
Borden Company Inc...918 224-0816
205 E Line Ave Sapulpa (74066) *(G-8258)*
Borden Dairy Company Texas LLC...405 232-7955
316 N Western Ave Oklahoma City (73106) *(G-5620)*
Bordens-Meadow Gold Division, Tulsa *Also called Southern Foods Group LLC (G-10799)*
Bordon Books, Broken Arrow *Also called Bordon David & Associates LLC (G-855)*
Bordon David & Associates LLC...918 495-3508
1408 W Glendale St Broken Arrow (74011) *(G-855)*
Borets US Inc (HQ)...918 439-7000
1600 N Garnett Rd Tulsa (74116) *(G-9320)*
Borets US Inc...405 949-0031
400 N Macarthur Blvd Oklahoma City (73127) *(G-5621)*
Borg Compressed Steel Corp...918 587-2437
1032 N Lewis Ave Tulsa (74110) *(G-9321)*
Born Again Pews...918 868-7613
5750 S 545 Rd Kansas (74347) *(G-3754)*
Born Inc...918 582-2186
5400 S 49th West Ave Tulsa (74107) *(G-9322)*
Bosendorfer Oil Company...405 604-9025
5311 S Drexel Ave Oklahoma City (73119) *(G-5622)*
Boss Seals & Parts LLC...918 237-6991
8687 E 105th Ct Tulsa (74133) *(G-9323)*
Bost Welding and Fabrication...918 649-1289
36593 Kerr Mansion Rd Poteau (74953) *(G-7897)*
Bostd America LLC...580 670-0594
510 N 25th St Blackwell (74631) *(G-676)*
Bostick Service Corporation...405 969-2198
505 W Adams St Crescent (73028) *(G-1908)*
Bostick Services Corporation...405 260-0306
12700 W Highway 33 Ste 4 Guthrie (73044) *(G-3301)*
Botanicu, Jones *Also called Soy Candle Cottage LLC (G-3752)*
Bottomline LLC...918 261-2354
9721 S 70th East Ave Tulsa (74133) *(G-9324)*
Bounce Diagnostics Inc...405 740-5889
317 Antelope Trl Edmond (73012) *(G-2331)*
Bounty Transfer LLC...405 338-1531
1511 S Sangre Rd Stillwater (74074) *(G-8662)*
Boxco Trim Cabinets...918 266-4030
10105 E 576 Rd Catoosa (74015) *(G-1305)*
Boxel LLC...580 239-0819
3216 Nw Industrial Rd Atoka (74525) *(G-400)*
Boxing Bear LLC...918 606-9991
1006 W D St Jenks (74037) *(G-3694)*
Boxing Bear LLC...918 606-9991
10010 E Pin Oak Ln Claremore (74019) *(G-1599)*
Boyd Welding Inc...918 485-3534
605 Sw 15th St Wagoner (74467) *(G-11278)*
Boyds Auto Parts & Machine...405 329-3855
1202 N Flood Ave Norman (73069) *(G-4940)*
Boyds Cstm Trim Cabinetry LLC...918 724-7033
1459 E 138th St Glenpool (74033) *(G-3231)*
Boyds Racing Engines, Norman *Also called Boyds Auto Parts & Machine (G-4940)*
Boyer Industries LLC...405 310-3015
1801 Wheatland Pl Norman (73071) *(G-4941)*
Boyles & Associates Inc...580 353-7056
1908 Sw F Ave Lawton (73501) *(G-3899)*
BP America Production Company...918 465-2343
1455 Nw Highway 2 Wilburton (74578) *(G-11518)*
Bpc Industries Inc...918 584-4848
624 N Rockford Ave Tulsa (74106) *(G-9325)*
Bpi Inc...918 682-5044
2551 Port Pl Muskogee (74403) *(G-4654)*
Bpm LLC...405 761-0911
403 Edgewood Dr McAlester (74501) *(G-4277)*
BR Electric...405 354-8994
1112 S 2nd St Yukon (73099) *(G-11700)*
Brace Place...405 858-5200
409 E California Ave # 100 Oklahoma City (73104) *(G-5623)*
Bracelets For Baby...918 625-0088
8820 N 127th East Ave Owasso (74055) *(G-7549)*
Brad McKinzie...580 355-3810
902 Sw 38th St Lawton (73505) *(G-3900)*
Brad's Western & Work Wear, Ardmore *Also called Beane Development Corp (G-255)*
Braden Carco Gearmatic Winch...918 756-4400
1204 W 20th St Okmulgee (74447) *(G-7495)*
Braden Filtration LLC...918 283-4818
5199 N Mingo Rd Unit B Tulsa (74117) *(G-9326)*
Braden Shielding Systems Const...918 624-2888
9260 Broken Arrow Expy Tulsa (74145) *(G-9327)*
Braden Shielding Systems LLC...918 624-2888
9260 Broken Arrow Expy Tulsa (74145) *(G-9328)*
Bradford Boring LLC...405 922-9344
897 County Road 1405 Chickasha (73018) *(G-1442)*
Bradley Machine & Design L L C...405 224-2223
816 N 18th St Chickasha (73018) *(G-1443)*
Bradley Stephen Brown...918 639-1853
101379 S 4190 Rd Oktaha (74450) *(G-7530)*
Bradley Welding & Machine...580 223-2250
3500 S Commerce St Ardmore (73401) *(G-260)*
Bradshaw Home LLC...918 582-5404
15 E 5th St Tulsa (74103) *(G-9329)*
Brady Oil Company Inc...405 941-3368
36489 E 1420 Sasakwa (74867) *(G-8329)*
Brady Welding & Machine Shop (PA)...580 229-1168
11991 Highway 76 Healdton (73438) *(G-3408)*
Brady Welding & Machine Shop...405 262-3665
4210 S Alfadale Rd El Reno (73036) *(G-2703)*
Brainerd Chemical Midwest LLC (HQ)...918 622-1214
427 S Boston Ave Tulsa (74103) *(G-9330)*
Brake & Clutch of Tulsa, Tulsa *Also called Tulsa Brake & Clutch Co LLC (G-10990)*
Brake & Clutch Service, Tulsa *Also called Brake Rebuilders Inc (G-9331)*
Brake Rebuilders Inc...918 834-0200
7605 E 11th St Tulsa (74112) *(G-9331)*
Bramco Inc...580 227-2345
513 N Main St Fairview (73737) *(G-3133)*
Branch"n Out, Enid *Also called A W Bugerman Company (G-2901)*
Branchcomb Inc...918 224-8094
9845 S Frankoma Rd Ste B Sapulpa (74066) *(G-8259)*
Brandon Hyde...405 919-4520
490 W Chestnut Rd Goldsby (73093) *(G-3244)*

ALPHABETIC

Brass Buff — ALPHABETIC SECTION

Brass Buff 918 592-1717
9828 E 7th St Tulsa (74128) *(G-9332)*

Bratco Operating Company 918 534-2322
399258 W 1330 Dr Dewey (74029) *(G-2018)*

Braudrick Printery 405 762-2054
211 N 2nd St Ponca City (74601) *(G-7802)*

Braums Ice Cream & Dar Stores, Edmond Also called W H Braum Inc *(G-2678)*

Bravo Natural Gas LLC 918 712-7008
1323 E 71st St Ste 200 Tulsa (74136) *(G-9333)*

Brays Cabinet Shop 580 584-6771
2078 E Us Highway 70 Broken Bow (74728) *(G-1186)*

Breast & Bdy Thermography Ctr 405 596-8099
6440 Avondale Dr 20035 Nichols Hills (73116) *(G-4855)*

Breeze Investments LLC 918 492-5090
7170 S Braden Ave Ste 200 Tulsa (74136) *(G-9334)*

Brenda K Toupin 918 527-6948
5103 S Sheridan Rd Tulsa (74145) *(G-9335)*

Brenda Riggs 918 543-3530
5 E Commercial St Inola (74036) *(G-3652)*

Brennan Properties, Tulsa Also called American Traditions Clothing *(G-9175)*

Brenntag Southwest Inc 918 273-2265
1 1/2 Mi N On Hwy 169 Nowata (74048) *(G-5209)*

Brenntag Southwest Inc 918 266-2951
5702 E Channel Rd Catoosa (74015) *(G-1306)*

Brently Publishing Intl LLC 405 381-9069
4706 Lake Ridge Ct Tuttle (73089) *(G-11187)*

Brents Dana 405 640-1566
1220 Bell Dr Newcastle (73065) *(G-4819)*

Brents Welding LLC 918 413-1318
900 Gregory Ave Pocola (74902) *(G-7781)*

Breshears Enterprises Inc 405 236-4523
20 N May Ave Oklahoma City (73107) *(G-5624)*

Brett Exploration 405 842-2322
1601 Nw Exprkway Ste 1300 Oklahoma City (73118) *(G-5625)*

Brewer Media LLC 405 236-4143
429 E California Ave Oklahoma City (73104) *(G-5626)*

Brewers Union, Oklahoma City Also called Union Brewers *(G-7360)*

Brexco Inc 405 348-8124
900 Brook Frst Edmond (73034) *(G-2332)*

Brg Energy Inc 918 496-2626
7134 S Yale Ave Ste 600 Tulsa (74136) *(G-9336)*

Brg Petroleum, Enid Also called Brg Production Company *(G-2922)*

Brg Production Company (PA) 918 496-2626
7134 S Yale Ave Ste 600 Tulsa (74136) *(G-9337)*

Brg Production Company 580 233-9302
2414 S Monroe St Enid (73701) *(G-2922)*

Bri-Chem Supply Corp LLC 405 200-5466
715 N Industrial Blvd Chickasha (73018) *(G-1444)*

Brian Ringels 580 927-6144
110 N Ada St Coalgate (74538) *(G-1776)*

Brians Hot Oil Service 580 431-2070
32660 State Highway 8 Cherokee (73728) *(G-1414)*

Brians Hot Oil Service LLC 580 778-3549
Rr 2 Turpin (73950) *(G-11181)*

Brians Welding and Fabrication 405 412-7878
2909 Pinecrest Ct Norman (73071) *(G-4942)*

Brickman Fast Line 405 756-1665
1001 Se 4th St Lindsay (73052) *(G-4051)*

Bricktown Brewery, Tulsa Also called Bb2 LLC *(G-9274)*

Bricktown Brewery, Edmond Also called Bb2 LLC *(G-2319)*

Bricktown Brewery, Oklahoma City Also called Bb2 LLC *(G-5534)*

Bricktown Real Estate & Develo 405 236-4143
429 E California Ave Oklahoma City (73104) *(G-5627)*

Brides of Oklahoma, Edmond Also called Just Two Publishing Inc *(G-2476)*

Bridge Crane Specialists LLC (PA) 918 321-3953
14536 Hwy 75 Alternate Kiefer (74041) *(G-3776)*

Bridge Creek Publishing Co 405 519-6982
7676 W County Road 66 Mulhall (73063) *(G-4637)*

Brief Media, Tulsa Also called Educational Concepts LLC *(G-9644)*

Briefcase Solutions Ltd LLC 405 788-9250
19006 Walker Rd McLoud (74851) *(G-4353)*

Brier Creek Furn Works LLC 903 327-5602
20112 Highway 32 Kingston (73439) *(G-3825)*

Briggs Rainbow Buildings Inc (PA) 918 683-3695
3143 N 32nd St Muskogee (74401) *(G-4655)*

Brigham Company LLC 405 843-2660
2932 Nw 122nd St Ste 6 Oklahoma City (73120) *(G-5628)*

Brims & Accessories 580 357-2746
3801 Nw Cache Rd Ste 33 Lawton (73505) *(G-3901)*

Briscoe Oil Co 405 375-3700
406 N Main St Kingfisher (73750) *(G-3786)*

Bristol Field Services, Chouteau Also called Stephen Poorboy *(G-1571)*

Bristow 800 Kelly LLC 248 268-3289
800 S Kelly Ave Bristow (74010) *(G-768)*

Bristow Hot Oil & Steam Svc 918 367-2121
18708 S 337th West Ave Bristow (74010) *(G-769)*

Bristow News, Bristow Also called Kimberling City Publishing Co *(G-786)*

Britt Oil Co LLC 405 275-2115
19005 S Rock Creek Rd Shawnee (74801) *(G-8435)*

Britter Creek Hunting Bli 405 392-3588
2178 Fox Ln Tuttle (73089) *(G-11188)*

Britton Electric Motor Inc 405 842-8357
1001 Nw 80th St Oklahoma City (73114) *(G-5629)*

Britton Printing 405 840-3291
1337 W Britton Rd Oklahoma City (73114) *(G-5630)*

Britton Printing & Copy Center, Oklahoma City Also called Britton Printing *(G-5630)*

Britton Welding & Automotive, Oklahoma City Also called Eddie Ward *(G-6009)*

Brix Inc 918 584-6484
4657 S 83rd East Ave K Tulsa (74145) *(G-9338)*

Brix Office Products, Tulsa Also called Brix Inc *(G-9338)*

Broach Specialist Inc 480 840-1375
3051 Speck Wright Rd Mannford (74044) *(G-4175)*

Broadland Stump Removal 918 743-7014
6208 S Victor Ave Tulsa (74136) *(G-9339)*

Broce Manufacturing Co Inc 405 579-4621
205 E Main St Norman (73069) *(G-4943)*

Brockus Creat Handcrafted Jwly 580 594-2215
78262 Jefferson Rd Wakita (73771) *(G-11297)*

Broken Arrow Electric Sup Inc 580 924-2237
3119 Westside Dr Durant (74701) *(G-2209)*

Broken Arrow Electric Sup Inc 580 436-1470
300 Arlington St Ste 7 Ada (74820) *(G-13)*

Broken Arrow Powdr Coating Inc (PA) 918 251-2192
2051 Sw Expressway Dr Broken Arrow (74012) *(G-856)*

Broken Arrow Powdr Coating Inc 918 258-1017
2501 Sw Express Way Dr Broken Arrow (74012) *(G-857)*

Broken Arrow Productions Inc 405 360-8702
3209 Broce Dr Norman (73072) *(G-4944)*

Broken Arrow Quality Lube 918 258-5823
1031 N 9th St Broken Arrow (74012) *(G-858)*

Broken Arrow Woodworks 918 893-6763
2021 W Detroit St Broken Arrow (74012) *(G-859)*

Broken Bone Vnyards Winery LLC 405 585-8319
1356 S Blackberry Dr McLoud (74851) *(G-4354)*

Broken Bow, Broken Bow Also called McCurtain County News Inc *(G-1199)*

Broken Bow Redimix, Broken Bow Also called Keith Lyons *(G-1196)*

Broken Bow Sand & Gravel, Broken Bow Also called Martin Marietta Materials Inc *(G-1198)*

Brokenbow Boat Center 580 584-5428
Highway 259 S Broken Bow (74728) *(G-1187)*

Bromide Inc 405 360-2999
3200 Marshall Ave Ste 201 Norman (73072) *(G-4945)*

Bronco Manufacturing 405 225-1909
1501 Se 25th St Oklahoma City (73129) *(G-5631)*

Bronco Manufacturing LLC (PA) 918 446-7196
4953 S 48th West Ave Tulsa (74107) *(G-9340)*

Bronze Horse Inc 918 287-4433
4 Old Highway 99 Pawhuska (74056) *(G-7678)*

Brooken Boat & Motor 918 799-5227
105 E Bk 1200 Rd Stigler (74462) *(G-8630)*

Brookline Minerals LLC 405 359-0900
36 W 8th St Edmond (73003) *(G-2333)*

Brooks Custom Fabrication 918 836-2556
10604 E Ute St Tulsa (74116) *(G-9341)*

Brooks Custom Welding LLC 580 343-2253
308 W Jefferson Corn (73024) *(G-1866)*

Brooks Industries LLC 405 305-9316
3015 Nw 18th St Oklahoma City (73107) *(G-5632)*

Brookside Pottery 918 697-6364
3710 S Peoria Ave Tulsa (74105) *(G-9342)*

Broox Creative Industries LLC 918 691-8834
9999 W 81st St Tulsa (74131) *(G-8992)*

Brother Built Welding 918 385-1767
21866 Pipe Springs Rd Hodgen (74939) *(G-3548)*

Brothers Construction and Rous 405 602-3275
1523 Sw 30th St Oklahoma City (73119) *(G-5633)*

Brow Art 23 .... 405 848-3346
1901 Nw Expressway Oklahoma City (73118) *(G-5634)*

Brower Oil & Gas Co Inc 918 298-7200
505 E Main St Jenks (74037) *(G-3695)*

Brown & Borelli Inc 405 375-5788
N Hwy 81 Kingfisher (73750) *(G-3787)*

Brown & Hartman Engraving Co, Tulsa Also called B G Specialties Inc *(G-9243)*

Brown Equipment Corporation 405 799-4000
7000 S Walker Ave Apt 8 Oklahoma City (73139) *(G-5635)*

Brown Metals (PA) 405 321-6866
3121 36th Ave Se Norman (73026) *(G-4946)*

Brown Minneapolis Tank 918 224-2358
7274 W 81st St Tulsa (74131) *(G-8993)*

Brown Oil Tools Inc 580 436-0002
275 Seabrook Rd Ada (74820) *(G-14)*

Brown Printing Co Inc 918 652-9611
407 W Trudgeon St Henryetta (74437) *(G-3500)*

Brown Publishing Inc 405 842-5089
1727 Dorchester Pl Nichols Hills (73120) *(G-4856)*

Browne Bottling Co Inc (PA) 405 232-1158
2712 Tealwood Dr Oklahoma City (73120) *(G-5636)*

Browns Bakery Inc 405 232-0363
1100 N Walker Ave Oklahoma City (73103) *(G-5637)*

Browns Meat Processing 405 379-2979
7925 E 137 Rd Holdenville (74848) ***(G-3550)***
Browns Sawmill 918 617-7935
4361 N 377 Atwood (74827) ***(G-428)***
Bruce Burdick Welding 580 774-2906
604 N Loomis Rd Weatherford (73096) ***(G-11395)***
Bruce Hopson Logging Inc 580 835-7145
2300 Rd Stuffy Ln Eagletown (74734) ***(G-2274)***
Bruce Packing Company Inc 503 874-3000
1915 E Highway 70 Durant (74701) ***(G-2210)***
Bruffett Electric 918 426-1875
1803 Cardinal Ln McAlester (74501) ***(G-4278)***
Bruins Oil & Gas LLC 806 323-8353
2201 Waterford Ln Yukon (73099) ***(G-11701)***
Bruno Ind Living Aids Inc 405 964-5887
420 E Broadway Ave McLoud (74851) ***(G-4355)***
Bryon K Barrows 918 519-9369
7954 Rock School Rd Skiatook (74070) ***(G-8534)***
Bs & W Solutions LLC (HQ) 918 392-9356
6655 S Lewis Ave Ste 200 Tulsa (74136) ***(G-9343)***
Bs Oil Company 405 756-8357
801 Nw 4th St Lindsay (73052) ***(G-4052)***
BS&b Pressure Safety MGT LLC 918 664-3725
7422 E 46th Pl Tulsa (74145) ***(G-9344)***
BS&b Safety Systems LLC (HQ) 918 622-5950
7455 E 46th St Tulsa (74145) ***(G-9345)***
BS&b Safety Systems LLC 918 622-5950
7455 E 46th St Tulsa (74145) ***(G-9346)***
Btg Inc 405 604-9145
3600 S Macarthur Blvd A Oklahoma City (73179) ***(G-5638)***
Btm Technologies Inc 918 857-2855
21825 S 401st West Ave Bristow (74010) ***(G-770)***
Bto Strategies & Solutions Inc 405 473-8632
3004 Pinelake St Norman (73071) ***(G-4947)***
Bubble Bee Bakery, Tulsa *Also called Bubble Bee Bakery and Supplies* ***(G-9347)***
Bubble Bee Bakery and Supplies 918 209-8658
4712 S 74th East Pl Apt 5 Tulsa (74145) ***(G-9347)***
Buchanan Bicycles Inc 405 364-5513
561 Buchanan Ave Norman (73069) ***(G-4948)***
Buck Creek Homes Cnstr Inc 580 272-0102
15070 County Road 3539 Ada (74820) ***(G-15)***
Bucke-Tee LLC 580 747-9288
1618 Indian Dr Enid (73703) ***(G-2923)***
Buckelew Accnting Slutions LLC 405 359-5887
2700 Morrison Trl Edmond (73012) ***(G-2334)***
Buckeye Exploration Company 405 258-5428
417 Manvel Ave Chandler (74834) ***(G-1377)***
Buckley Powder Company 580 384-5547
Rr 1 Mill Creek (74856) ***(G-4467)***
Bucklingtin Pen Technology, Oklahoma City *Also called Rupture Pin Technology* ***(G-7062)***
Bucks Directional Drilling 580 276-2238
1201 N Highway 77 Marietta (73448) ***(G-4201)***
Bucky McGee Logging 918 635-0909
24178 Independence Rd Heavener (74937) ***(G-3426)***
Buckys Welding 918 339-4187
112 N Erie St Canadian (74425) ***(G-1260)***
Bud Oil Inc 580 251-1378
1032 W Main St Ste 100 Duncan (73533) ***(G-2092)***
Buddies Bars 580 254-5778
620 Main St Woodward (73801) ***(G-11564)***
Budgget Industries Inc 918 272-6255
8 S Atlanta St Unit A Owasso (74055) ***(G-7550)***
Buffalo Creek, Hartshorne *Also called Mass Brothers Inc* ***(G-3393)***
Buffalo Examiner 580 326-3926
1410 E Jefferson St Hugo (74743) ***(G-3604)***
Buffalo Industries 405 720-2324
6812 Newman Dr Oklahoma City (73162) ***(G-5639)***
Buffalo Nickel Industries LLC 918 287-3899
136 E 6th St Pawhuska (74056) ***(G-7679)***
Buffalo Nickel Press 918 287-3899
136 E 6th St Pawhuska (74056) ***(G-7680)***
Bug Reaper Pest Control, Edmond *Also called Christina Stokes* ***(G-2350)***
Bug Right 918 367-9792
637 S Maple St Bristow (74010) ***(G-771)***
Buildblock Bldg Systems LLC 405 840-3386
9705 Broadway Ext Ste 150 Oklahoma City (73114) ***(G-5640)***
Builders Firstsource Inc 405 321-2255
7401 S Sooner Rd Oklahoma City (73135) ***(G-5641)***
Builders Firstsource Inc 918 459-6872
12215 E 61st St Broken Arrow (74012) ***(G-860)***
Builders Overhead Crane, Sapulpa *Also called Martin Manufacturing Inc* ***(G-8287)***
Building Concepts Ltd 405 324-5100
9900 Nw 10th St Oklahoma City (73127) ***(G-5642)***
Buildings By Madden LLC 405 677-0466
3220 E I 240 Service Rd Oklahoma City (73135) ***(G-5643)***
Built Better Enterprises LLC 580 492-5227
410 Us Highway 277 Fletcher (73541) ***(G-3161)***
Built Right Compressor 580 371-2007
309 E 18th St Tishomingo (73460) ***(G-8963)***

Bull Dog Welding 405 412-8199
1240 Sw 15th St Oklahoma City (73108) ***(G-5644)***
Bulldog Energy Services LLC (PA) 405 919-9950
6000 E College Ave Guthrie (73044) ***(G-3302)***
Bulldog Jerky Co 580 479-5542
503 W 2nd St Grandfield (73546) ***(G-3256)***
Bullet Fence Systems LLC 918 777-3973
1001 E 20th St Okmulgee (74447) ***(G-7496)***
Bullseye Boring Technology 405 880-1878
2311 E 56th St Stillwater (74074) ***(G-8663)***
Bullseye Operating LLC 918 336-7898
301 Se Adams Blvd Bartlesville (74003) ***(G-458)***
Bullseye Precision Mfg, McAlester *Also called Bpm LLC* ***(G-4277)***
Bur-Lane, Oklahoma City *Also called Rowmark LLC* ***(G-7051)***
Burch Printing Co 580 225-3270
219 W Broadway Ave Elk City (73644) ***(G-2788)***
Burford Corp (HQ) 405 867-4467
11284 Highway 74 Maysville (73057) ***(G-4255)***
Burgess Manufacturing Okla Inc 405 282-1913
1250 Roundhouse Rd Guthrie (73044) ***(G-3303)***
Burgess Tool & Cutter Grinding 580 765-0954
1812 Potomac Dr Ponca City (74601) ***(G-7803)***
Burlane, Oklahoma City *Also called Custom Identification Products* ***(G-5873)***
Burleson Pump Company 405 677-6881
4207 S I 35 Service Rd Oklahoma City (73129) ***(G-5645)***
Burlington Welding LLC 580 596-3381
1101 Industrial Blvd Cherokee (73728) ***(G-1415)***
Burnam Welding 580 821-0311
610 S Van Buren Ave Elk City (73644) ***(G-2789)***
Burns & McDonnell Inc 405 200-0300
615 N Hudson Ave Ste 200 Oklahoma City (73102) ***(G-5646)***
Burns Manufacturing Inc 918 622-3305
1855 N 105th East Ave Tulsa (74116) ***(G-9348)***
Burns Pressure Systems, Broken Arrow *Also called B P S Inc* ***(G-841)***
Burrow Construction LLC 800 766-5793
101 Leaning Tree Rd Fort Gibson (74434) ***(G-3174)***
Burrow Tool 580 240-1045
112 N Commercial St Temple (73568) ***(G-8932)***
Burrows 918 846-2245
Hominy Rd Hominy (74035) ***(G-3580)***
Burt, Wayne Machine Shop, Grove *Also called Wayne Burt Machine* ***(G-3293)***
Burtco Enterprises LLC 918 857-1293
25910 E 19th St Catoosa (74015) ***(G-1307)***
Burton Controls Inc 405 692-7278
2164 Faurot Dr Waynoka (73860) ***(G-11375)***
Burton Controls Inc (PA) 405 692-7278
11600 S Meridian Ave Oklahoma City (73173) ***(G-5647)***
Bush Publishing 901 468-8388
20232 E 43rd St S Broken Arrow (74014) ***(G-1114)***
Bush Publishing & Assoc LLC 251 424-7298
321 S Boston Ave Tulsa (74103) ***(G-9349)***
Business Cards & More 405 235-9621
2920 N Pennsylvania Ave Oklahoma City (73107) ***(G-5648)***
Business Cards Unlimited 918 810-6265
9723 E 33rd St Apt 712 Tulsa (74146) ***(G-9350)***
Business Printing Inc 1 ......918 481-6078
5315 E 77th St Tulsa (74136) ***(G-9351)***
Business Records Storage LLC 405 232-7867
5 Ne 12th St Oklahoma City (73104) ***(G-5649)***
Businet 918 858-4440
4608 S Garnett Rd Ste 300 Tulsa (74146) ***(G-9352)***
Buster Boats, Perry *Also called Splash Marine LLC* ***(G-7746)***
Buster Dorsch 918 743-4509
3231 E 19th St Tulsa (74104) ***(G-9353)***
Buster Par Corp 918 585-8542
1209 E 3rd St Tulsa (74120) ***(G-9354)***
Busy Bee 580 661-2946
100 W South Rd Thomas (73669) ***(G-8940)***
Butaphalt Products LLC 918 740-7290
25615 Briar Dr Claremore (74019) ***(G-1600)***
Butcher & Sons Steel Inds 918 434-5276
155 S 4477 Salina (74365) ***(G-8133)***
Butcher Well Service 918 275-4439
5021 E 320 Rd Talala (74080) ***(G-8897)***
Butchers Metal Shop 580 256-7660
1206 4th St Woodward (73801) ***(G-11565)***
Butchs Processing Plant Inc 405 382-2833
12566 Ns 360 Seminole (74868) ***(G-8361)***
Butkin Oil Co LLC (PA) 580 444-2561
16 S 9th St Rm 306 Duncan (73533) ***(G-2093)***
Butner Brothers LLC 405 321-2322
3540 Wellsite Dr Norman (73069) ***(G-4949)***
Buttons Auto Electrical Supply 580 223-3855
28 S Commerce St Ardmore (73401) ***(G-261)***
Buy Rite Services LLC 580 984-1008
4511 N Van Buren Byp Enid (73701) ***(G-2924)***
Buyers Trading Designs 918 592-5477
1130 S Oxford Ave Tulsa (74112) ***(G-9355)***
Buzzi Unicem USA Inc 918 825-1937
2430 S 437 Pryor (74361) ***(G-7948)***

ALPHABETIC

Buzzi Unicem USA Inc P..............405 670-0677
4601 Ne 4th St Oklahoma City (73117) ***(G-5650)***
Bwb Sign Inc..............405 292-3534
115 E California Ave # 370 Oklahoma City (73104) ***(G-5651)***
Bws Wlding Fabriction Svcs LLC..............918 789-3094
21500 E 340 Rd Chelsea (74016) ***(G-1403)***
By Him Industries LLC..............918 406-0593
507 E E St Jenks (74037) ***(G-3696)***
By Prather Inc..............580 994-2414
200 S Main St Mooreland (73852) ***(G-4586)***
By-Weld Industries Inc..............918 366-4850
7900 E 148th St S Bixby (74008) ***(G-616)***
Byers Products Group Inc..............405 491-8550
9641 Nw 6th St Oklahoma City (73127) ***(G-5652)***
Byfield Welding..............918 333-8100
3401 Kansas Ln Bartlesville (74006) ***(G-459)***
Bynum & Company Inc..............580 265-7747
22040 County Road 1690 Stonewall (74871) ***(G-8798)***
Byrd Signs & Designs..............918 687-4219
140 W 61st St S Muskogee (74401) ***(G-4656)***
Byrum Enterprises Inc..............812 595-4598
10201 Lyndon Rd Oklahoma City (73120) ***(G-5653)***
C & B Construction..............918 696-4476
82280 S 4745 Rd Stilwell (74960) ***(G-8782)***
C & B Fabricators Inc..............918 760-6508
29717 Church House Rd Bokoshe (74930) ***(G-752)***
C & B Pump Rebuilders..............405 789-4808
8308 Sw 3rd St Ste D Oklahoma City (73128) ***(G-5654)***
C & C Backhoe & Tractor Inc..............405 392-4699
2313 County Road 1214 Blanchard (73010) ***(G-703)***
C & C Cabinets..............918 241-5249
17502 Coyote Trl Sand Springs (74063) ***(G-8168)***
C & C Equipment Specialist Inc (PA)..............405 677-3110
1141 Se Grand Blvd # 122 Oklahoma City (73129) ***(G-5655)***
C & C Machine Inc..............918 342-1950
904 W 1st St Claremore (74017) ***(G-1601)***
C & C Nitrogen LLC..............580 216-4871
203081 E County Road 35 Woodward (73801) ***(G-11566)***
C & C Performance Engines..............580 252-4331
1402 W Park Ave Duncan (73533) ***(G-2094)***
C & C Welding & Construction..............405 769-4924
10812 Ne 16th St Oklahoma City (73130) ***(G-5656)***
C & D Manufacturing Co Inc..............918 251-8535
601 S 10th St Broken Arrow (74012) ***(G-861)***
C & F Custom Chrome..............918 587-1110
1312 N Utica Ave Tulsa (74110) ***(G-9356)***
C & H Accounting, Locust Grove *Also called C & H Ranch* ***(G-4105)***
C & H Bit Company, Ada *Also called C & H Tool & Machine Inc* ***(G-16)***
C & H Bit Company, Ada *Also called C & H Tool & Machine Inc* ***(G-17)***
C & H Ranch..............918 479-8460
7 Mi E & 3 1/2 Mi S # 312 Locust Grove (74352) ***(G-4105)***
C & H Safety Pin Inc..............405 949-5843
18450 Post Oak Dr Newalla (74857) ***(G-4806)***
C & H Tool & Machine Inc..............580 332-1929
1904 N Broadway Ave Ada (74820) ***(G-16)***
C & H Tool & Machine Inc (PA)..............580 332-1929
1000 Lonnie Abbott Blvd Ada (74820) ***(G-17)***
C & J Minerals LLC..............580 504-4048
1805 Stanley St Sw Ardmore (73401) ***(G-262)***
C & J Printing Co..............580 355-3099
217 Sw C Ave Lawton (73501) ***(G-3902)***
C & J Son Machine Shop, Guthrie *Also called Haney John* ***(G-3318)***
C & J Trucks LLC..............405 382-1405
3416 N Highway 99 Seminole (74868) ***(G-8362)***
C & L Oil and Gas Corporation..............405 364-1950
1708 Topeka St Norman (73069) ***(G-4950)***
C & M Precision Inc..............405 691-0984
5700 Sw 134th St Oklahoma City (73173) ***(G-5657)***
C & P Auto Electric..............405 799-2083
815 S Sunnylane Rd Moore (73160) ***(G-4501)***
C & P Catalyst Inc..............918 747-8379
4224 S Pittsburg Ave Tulsa (74135) ***(G-9357)***
C & P Manufacturing Inc..............918 773-5060
Rr 2 Box 96 Sallisaw (74955) ***(G-8140)***
C & R Oilfield Service, Ponca City *Also called C & R Olfld Pntg Rustabout Svc* ***(G-7804)***
C & R Olfld Pntg Rustabout Svc..............620 272-6699
808 Monument Rd Ponca City (74604) ***(G-7804)***
C & R Print Shop Inc..............580 255-5656
1401 W Main St Duncan (73533) ***(G-2095)***
C & R Print Shop Inc (PA)..............405 224-7921
420 W Dakota Ave Chickasha (73018) ***(G-1445)***
C & S Technical Services LLC..............918 258-8324
1336 N 143rd East Ave Tulsa (74116) ***(G-9358)***
C & W Construction Inc (PA)..............580 625-4520
1 Fourth Mile E Of Bevr Beaver (73932) ***(G-540)***
C & W Shoes of Georgia Inc..............405 755-7112
11950 N May Ave Oklahoma City (73120) ***(G-5658)***
C 2 Supply Llc..............918 647-0430
602 N Broadway St Poteau (74953) ***(G-7898)***
C and C Manufacturing, Owasso *Also called Jamessed Inc* ***(G-7578)***
C and C Manufacturing LLC..............918 288-6558
4225 W 88th St N Sperry (74073) ***(G-8606)***
C and D Fashion Floors LLC..............918 256-8018
423 S Wilson St Vinita (74301) ***(G-11250)***
C and H Publishing Co..............918 245-9571
117 N Garfield Ave Sand Springs (74063) ***(G-8169)***
C B I, Afton *Also called Copy Box Inc* ***(G-115)***
C B S, Oklahoma City *Also called Consolidated Builders Supply* ***(G-5821)***
C C & R Construction Inc..............405 756-4710
14357 180th St Lindsay (73052) ***(G-4053)***
C C McMillin & Company Inc..............405 282-3637
6 Miles North On Hwy 77 Guthrie (73044) ***(G-3304)***
C D Adkerson Consultant Inc..............580 225-7860
2060 W 7th Pl Elk City (73644) ***(G-2790)***
C D Connections..............580 248-6410
2316 W Gore Blvd Lawton (73505) ***(G-3903)***
C D Exchange, Lawton *Also called C D Connections* ***(G-3903)***
C D I, Broken Arrow *Also called Control Devices Inc* ***(G-875)***
C E Harmon Oil Inc (PA)..............918 663-8515
5555 E 71st St Ste 9300 Tulsa (74136) ***(G-9359)***
C Easleys Touch..............918 284-9384
18503 E 31st St Tulsa (74134) ***(G-9360)***
C Johnstone Welding Fabricat..............580 362-2400
126 S Elm Ave Newkirk (74647) ***(G-4846)***
C JS Jewelers..............405 631-0555
8200 S Western Ave Oklahoma City (73139) ***(G-5659)***
C L and L Inc..............405 722-9427
7101 Nw Expressway # 100 Oklahoma City (73132) ***(G-5660)***
C M E, Ponca City *Also called Custom Mechanical Equipment* ***(G-7814)***
C M Trailers..............580 493-2301
11711 W Wood Rd Drummond (73735) ***(G-2046)***
C M Y K Colour Corp..............405 270-0060
706 N Villa Ave Oklahoma City (73107) ***(G-5661)***
C O Hanover Bka..............918 251-8571
20602 E 81st St S Broken Arrow (74014) ***(G-1115)***
C R Manufacturing..............405 780-7368
1101 W Lakeview Rd Stillwater (74075) ***(G-8664)***
C Triple Inc..............918 664-2144
1015 E 2nd St Tulsa (74120) ***(G-9361)***
C V West LLC..............623 363-3529
1831 S May Ave Guthrie (73044) ***(G-3305)***
C&A International LLC..............918 872-1645
5861c S Garnett Rd Tulsa (74146) ***(G-9362)***
C&C Trucking and Eqp Svcs LLC..............405 567-5194
357494 E 1000 Rd Prague (74864) ***(G-7922)***
C&D Machine Tool Svc & Parts..............405 943-6033
4225 Nw 48th St Oklahoma City (73112) ***(G-5662)***
C&D Valve LLC..............405 843-5621
201 Nw 67th St Oklahoma City (73116) ***(G-5663)***
C&H Safety Pin Inc..............405 386-3942
35 Walker Ln McLoud (74851) ***(G-4356)***
C&J Energy Services Inc..............405 222-8304
9636 W Reno Ave Oklahoma City (73127) ***(G-5664)***
C&J Energy Services Inc..............580 928-1300
301 Venture Rd Sayre (73662) ***(G-8337)***
C&J Well Services Inc..............405 234-9800
201 Jensen Rd E El Reno (73036) ***(G-2704)***
C&K Inc..............918 299-6307
12522 S 13th Pl Jenks (74037) ***(G-3697)***
C&M Enterprises..............918 683-4456
4002 Jefferson St Muskogee (74403) ***(G-4657)***
C&S Design..............918 455-8137
20600 E 111th St S Broken Arrow (74014) ***(G-1116)***
C&S Marine LLC..............918 429-2758
4335 Choate Prairie Rd Indianola (74442) ***(G-3651)***
C&S Welding & Fabrication Inc..............918 282-4122
169 Greenwood Ave Mannford (74044) ***(G-4176)***
C&Y Caseing Pulling Co Inc..............580 255-4453
250 S Eastland Dr Duncan (73533) ***(G-2096)***
C-All Manufacturing Inc..............580 889-3351
472 S Jefferson Hwy Atoka (74525) ***(G-401)***
C-Star Mfg Inc..............405 756-1530
13801 120th St Lindsay (73052) ***(G-4054)***
C2 Innovative Technologies Inc..............405 388-2357
10200 Se 57th St Oklahoma City (73150) ***(G-5665)***
Cabinet Cures Oklahoma LLC..............405 285-5700
129 W 1st St Edmond (73003) ***(G-2335)***
Cabinet Doors Unlimited..............918 257-5765
55450 E Highway 59 Afton (74331) ***(G-114)***
Cabinet Solutions Innovations, Tulsa *Also called Cabinet Solutions LLC* ***(G-9363)***
Cabinet Solutions LLC..............918 592-4497
1513 E Haskell St Ste A Tulsa (74106) ***(G-9363)***
Cabinetworks Inc..............405 286-1053
239 Nw 95th St Oklahoma City (73114) ***(G-5666)***
Cable Meat Center Inc..............580 658-6646
1316 S Broadway St Marlow (73055) ***(G-4224)***
Cable Printing Co Inc..............405 756-4045
117 S Main St Lindsay (73052) ***(G-4055)***
Cabot Norit Americas Inc..............918 825-8332
1432 6th St Maip Pryor (74361) ***(G-7949)***

ALPHABETIC SECTION

Cache Times 580 429-8200
　518 W C Ave Cache (73527) *(G-1225)*
Cactus Drilling Company, Oklahoma City *Also called Kaiser-Francis Oil Company (G-6395)*
Cactus Wellhead LLC 405 708-7200
　5517 Sw 29th St Oklahoma City (73179) *(G-5667)*
Caddo Electric Corp 580 774-5280
　3701 E Main St Weatherford (73096) *(G-11396)*
Cadence Energy Partners LLC 405 485-8200
　29 E Reno Ave Ste 5 Oklahoma City (73104) *(G-5668)*
Cadet Manufacturing Inc 918 476-8159
　1125 E Main St Chouteau (74337) *(G-1559)*
Cadet Truck Bodies, Chouteau *Also called Cadet Manufacturing Inc (G-1559)*
Caerus Operating LLC 580 468-3527
　1009 Ne 4th St Ste B Guymon (73942) *(G-3345)*
Cagan Land Services LLC 405 757-4046
　1900 S Broadway Ste B Edmond (73013) *(G-2336)*
Cairns Manufacturing Inc 405 636-4063
　2213 Sw 19th St Oklahoma City (73108) *(G-5669)*
Cairns Manufacturing Inc 405 947-1350
　4929 Nw 18th St Oklahoma City (73127) *(G-5670)*
Cakes & More 918 649-0451
　804 N Broadway St Ste B Poteau (74953) *(G-7899)*
Calamity Jane's Apparel, Oklahoma City *Also called Calamity Janes Funk & Junk Inc (G-5671)*
Calamity Janes Funk & Junk Inc 405 759-3383
　1537 W Main St Oklahoma City (73106) *(G-5671)*
Calebs Resources LLC 405 330-8252
　18801 Woody Creek Dr Edmond (73012) *(G-2337)*
Caliber Completion Svcs LLC 405 385-3761
　2901 Pole Rd Moore (73160) *(G-4502)*
Caliber Welding Inc 918 486-1388
　17018 Highway 51b Coweta (74429) *(G-1873)*
Caliche Resources Inc 918 492-5170
　9700 E 340 Rd Talala (74080) *(G-8898)*
Calico Dragon, Yukon *Also called Job Paper LLC (G-11737)*
Calico Industries LLC 405 732-0638
　211 Guy Dr Midwest City (73110) *(G-4437)*
Call 580 789-0074
　307 Wildwood Ln Blackwell (74631) *(G-677)*
Callaway Equipment & Mfg 405 632-1870
　8417 Gateway Ter Oklahoma City (73149) *(G-5672)*
Callidus Technologies LLC (HQ) 918 496-7599
　7130 S Lewis Ave Ste 500 Tulsa (74136) *(G-9364)*
Callidus Technologies LLC 918 267-4920
　2499 Highway 16 Beggs (74421) *(G-550)*
Callie Oil Company LLC 918 521-9292
　344442 E 790 Rd Agra (74824) *(G-124)*
Cals Plastics Designs & Fabg 405 670-1690
　4861 Se 29th St Oklahoma City (73115) *(G-5673)*
Calumet Oil Co 405 478-8770
　701 Cedar Lake Blvd Oklahoma City (73114) *(G-5674)*
Calvert Co, Tulsa *Also called Graphics Universal Inc (G-9847)*
Calvert Company 405 848-2222
　6301 N Wstn Ave Ste 110 Oklahoma City (73118) *(G-5675)*
Calvert Investment Company, Oklahoma City *Also called Calvert Company (G-5675)*
Calvin Heaters 918 367-7011
　21640 S 417th West Ave Bristow (74010) *(G-772)*
Calvin Mays Oilfield Svcs Inc 405 282-6664
　201 W County Road 72 Guthrie (73044) *(G-3306)*
Calyx Energy III LLC 918 949-4224
　6120 S Yale Ave Ste 1480 Tulsa (74136) *(G-9365)*
Calyx Energy III Holdings LLC (PA) 918 949-4224
　6120 S Yale Ave Ste 1480 Tulsa (74136) *(G-9366)*
CAM Surface Sys - Okc Plant, Oklahoma City *Also called Cameron International Corp (G-5677)*
Camargo Jacks Backhoe Service 580 926-3378
　Hwy 34 S And Black St Camargo (73835) *(G-1251)*
Cambridge Soundworks Inc (HQ) 405 742-6704
　1630 Cimarron Plz Stillwater (74075) *(G-8665)*
Camcast Corp 918 371-9966
　11231 N Memorial Dr Owasso (74055) *(G-7551)*
Camera Guys LLC 405 310-0006
　1005 N Flood Ave Norman (73069) *(G-4951)*
Cameron Glass Inc 918 254-6000
　3550 W Tacoma St Broken Arrow (74012) *(G-862)*
Cameron International Corp 405 631-1321
　845 Se 29th St Oklahoma City (73129) *(G-5676)*
Cameron International Corp 405 745-2715
　7500 Sw 29th St Bldg B Oklahoma City (73179) *(G-5677)*
Cameron International Corp 405 843-5578
　6700 N Classen Blvd Oklahoma City (73116) *(G-5678)*
Cameron International Corp 405 789-8065
　8533 Sw 2nd St Oklahoma City (73128) *(G-5679)*
Cameron Solutions Inc 405 677-8827
　1708 Se 25th St Oklahoma City (73129) *(G-5680)*
Cameron Solutions Inc 580 821-0494
　106 Robinson Pl Elk City (73644) *(G-2791)*
Cameron Technologies Inc 405 682-1661
　2101 S Broadway St Moore (73160) *(G-4503)*
Cameron Technologies Inc 580 470-9600
　7000 Nix Dr Duncan (73533) *(G-2097)*
Cameron Technologies Inc 405 703-8632
　2101 S Broadway St Moore (73160) *(G-4504)*
Camglass, Broken Arrow *Also called Cameron Glass Inc (G-862)*
Cammond Industries LLC 580 332-9300
　1920 A St Ada (74820) *(G-18)*
Camo Galz Candles & More 918 399-0044
　8443 W 176th St S Mounds (74047) *(G-4611)*
Camp Chippewa For Boys Inc 218 335-8807
　15 E 5th St Ste 4022 Tulsa (74103) *(G-9367)*
Campaign Technologies Professi 405 286-2686
　2601 Nw Expwy Ste 210w Oklahoma City (73112) *(G-5681)*
Campbell Asphalt, Oklahoma City *Also called T J Campbell Construction Co (G-7244)*
Campbell Crane and Service LLC 405 245-8983
　4104 Nw 21st St Oklahoma City (73107) *(G-5682)*
Campbell Fbrcation Tooling Inc 918 987-0047
　221 W Elm St Stroud (74079) *(G-8809)*
Campbell Metalworks, Chester *Also called Steven Campbell (G-1421)*
Campbell Specialty Co Inc 918 756-3640
　1604 W 4th St Okmulgee (74447) *(G-7497)*
Campo Alegre Foods 918 271-6775
　7633 E 63rd Pl Ste 300 Tulsa (74133) *(G-9368)*
Campus Ragz 405 329-3300
　3909 24th Ave Nw Norman (73069) *(G-4952)*
Can Global Usa Inc (PA) 405 261-0417
　4740 United Dr Oklahoma City (73179) *(G-5683)*
Can-Do-Candles 580 564-2816
　11968 Thompson Rd Kingston (73439) *(G-3826)*
Can-OK Oil Field Services Inc 405 222-2474
　887 County Road 1405 Chickasha (73018) *(G-1446)*
Canaan Energy Corp 405 604-9200
　211 N Robinson Ave N1000 Oklahoma City (73102) *(G-5684)*
Canaan Natural Gas Corp (PA) 405 604-9300
　1101 N Broadway Ave # 300 Oklahoma City (73103) *(G-5685)*
Canadian Global Mfg Ltd 405 250-1785
　4740 United Dr Oklahoma City (73179) *(G-5686)*
Canadian Pipe & Supply Co 405 794-6825
　233 Se 5th St Moore (73160) *(G-4505)*
Canadian Pwa, Canadian *Also called Canadian Town of Inc (G-1261)*
Canadian Rver Vnyrds Wnery LLC 405 872-5565
　7050 Slaughterville Rd Lexington (73051) *(G-4034)*
Canadian Town of Inc 918 339-2517
　2 Blocks North Of Po Canadian (74425) *(G-1261)*
Canary LLC 405 275-6116
　37709 45th St Shawnee (74804) *(G-8436)*
Canary Customs 405 293-6429
　3704 S Pine St Guthrie (73044) *(G-3307)*
Candle Electric 918 232-0558
　6902 W 34th St Tulsa (74107) *(G-9369)*
Candles By ME 580 798-5200
　815 A St Nw Ardmore (73401) *(G-263)*
Cane Advertising LLC 918 806-6817
　812 W Elgin St Broken Arrow (74012) *(G-863)*
Canfield Machine Inc 580 673-2185
　16096 Oklahoma 76 Fox (73435) *(G-3190)*
Canfield Ranch Energy LLC 405 272-1080
　101 Park Ave Fl 5 Oklahoma City (73102) *(G-5687)*
Cannon & Refermat LLC 405 521-0636
　4601 N Walnut Ave Oklahoma City (73105) *(G-5688)*
Cannon Oilfield Services 405 387-2644
　204 Naomi Ln Ste B Newcastle (73065) *(G-4820)*
Cannon Racecraft Inc 405 524-7223
　201 E Hill St Oklahoma City (73105) *(G-5689)*
CANNON SPRING COMPANY, Oklahoma City *Also called Cannon & Refermat LLC (G-5688)*
Cano Petroleum Inc (PA) 918 398-2728
　823 S Detroit Ave Ste 300 Tulsa (74120) *(G-9370)*
Canopies Plus Inc 918 689-7077
　420331 Texanna Rd Eufaula (74432) *(G-3098)*
Canopy Upstream LLC 620 717-3263
　2208 Valley View Rd Weatherford (73096) *(G-11397)*
Cantrell Energy Corporation 580 332-4710
　2313 N Broadway Ave Ada (74820) *(G-19)*
Canvas Sky Studios LLC 917 514-9632
　1501 W Detroit St Broken Arrow (74012) *(G-864)*
Canvass LLC 580 284-7896
　1429 Bradford Pl Blanchard (73010) *(G-704)*
Canyon Craft 918 456-3552
　119 N Muskogee Ave Tahlequah (74464) *(G-8854)*
Canyon Lakes Winery LLC 405 367-7291
　7600 Nw 134th St Oklahoma City (73142) *(G-5690)*
Canyon Oilfield Services LLC (PA) 580 225-7100
　11552 Highway 6 Elk City (73644) *(G-2792)*
Canyon Welding Service Inc 580 371-8805
　11443 S Canyon Ln Tishomingo (73460) *(G-8964)*
Capes Custom Welding & Fabrica 918 453-0594
　1005 E Lowe Dr Tahlequah (74464) *(G-8855)*
Capital Business Forms Inc 405 524-2010
　4600 N Cooper Ave Oklahoma City (73118) *(G-5691)*

Capital Risk Management Corp (PA) 405 848-5420
6301 N Wstn Ave Ste 225 Oklahoma City (73118) ***(G-5692)***
Capitalist Publishing Co 918 808-5665
3216 E 28th St Tulsa (74114) ***(G-9371)***
Capitol Electric Mtr Repr Inc (PA) 405 235-9638
2215 Sw 11th St Oklahoma City (73108) ***(G-5693)***
Capitol Hill Beacon, Oklahoma City *Also called Beacon Publishing Co Inc* ***(G-5540)***
Capitol Hill Graffix LLC 405 616-3050
330 Sw 25th St Oklahoma City (73109) ***(G-5694)***
Capitol Paint Manufacturing 405 634-3383
722 Sw 23rd St Oklahoma City (73109) ***(G-5695)***
Capitol Tube Co Inc 405 632-9901
820 Sw 27th St Oklahoma City (73109) ***(G-5696)***
Caprock Country Entps Inc 580 924-1647
19550 State Road 78 Calera (74730) ***(G-1239)***
Caprock Inc 580 255-0831
15 N 9th St Ste 208 Duncan (73533) ***(G-2098)***
Caprock Plungers LLC 580 799-1387
100 Ne Mcclary Rd Cordell (73632) ***(G-1855)***
Capstone Music Company Ltd 918 273-1888
115 N Maple St Nowata (74048) ***(G-5210)***
Capstone Oil & Gas Inc (PA) 405 853-7170
S Cemetary Rd Hennessey (73742) ***(G-3448)***
Capstone Oil & Gas Inc 405 853-7168
Cemetary Rd Hennessey (73742) ***(G-3449)***
Captive Imaging LLC 918 340-3053
5541 S Norfolk Ave Tulsa (74105) ***(G-9372)***
Captive-Aire Systems Inc 918 258-0291
12101 E 51st St Ste 101a Tulsa (74146) ***(G-9373)***
Captive-Aire Systems Inc 918 686-6717
4031 Tull Ave Muskogee (74403) ***(G-4658)***
Carboline Company 918 622-3028
S 72nd East Ave Tulsa (74145) ***(G-9374)***
Carbon Economy LLC 405 222-4244
2281 County Street 2920 Chickasha (73018) ***(G-1447)***
Carbon Economy LLC 405 222-9399
2400 S 29th St Chickasha (73018) ***(G-1448)***
Carc Inc 918 266-1341
104 W Elm St Catoosa (74015) ***(G-1308)***
Cardboard Junkeez LLC 405 990-9443
4104 Eden Ct Norman (73072) ***(G-4953)***
Cardinal Energy Inc 405 331-9206
207 S Dean A Mcgee Ave Wynnewood (73098) ***(G-11664)***
Cardinal F G Co, Durant *Also called Cardinal Glass Industries Inc* ***(G-2212)***
Cardinal Fg Glass, Durant *Also called Cardinal Glass Industries Inc* ***(G-2211)***
Cardinal Fg Minerals LLC 580 367-2123
13030 E Swamp Creek Rd Coleman (73432) ***(G-1793)***
Cardinal Glass Industries Inc 580 924-2142
515 Cardinal Pkwy Durant (74701) ***(G-2211)***
Cardinal Glass Industries Inc 580 924-2142
515 Cardinal Pkwy Durant (74701) ***(G-2212)***
Cardinal Health 200 LLC 918 865-4727
400 Foster Rd Mannford (74044) ***(G-4177)***
Cardinal Industries LLC 918 299-0396
2850 E 101st St Tulsa (74137) ***(G-9375)***
Cardinal Midstream 405 706-4161
1460 N Mustang Rd Ste 101 Mustang (73064) ***(G-4766)***
Cardinal Midstream LLC 580 927-2799
17145 Coutry Rd 3790 Coalgate (74538) ***(G-1777)***
Cardinal River Energy Co 405 606-7481
211 N Robinson Ave N200 Oklahoma City (73102) ***(G-5697)***
Cardon Trailers 580 327-0701
913 5th St Alva (73717) ***(G-180)***
Carefusion Corporation 918 865-4727
400 Foster Rd Mannford (74044) ***(G-4178)***
Carel Pumping 405 485-3495
1007 Summer Oaks Dr Blanchard (73010) ***(G-705)***
Cargill Incorporated 405 270-7011
2100 S Robinson Ave Oklahoma City (73109) ***(G-5698)***
Cargill Incorporated 580 621-3246
27565 County Road 110 Freedom (73842) ***(G-3205)***
Cargill Incorporated 405 236-0525
2100 S Robinson Ave Oklahoma City (73109) ***(G-5699)***
Cargill Heat Treat LLC 405 510-3404
1626 Se 40th St Oklahoma City (73129) ***(G-5700)***
Cargill Valve LLC 918 352-2203
507 Griffith Ave Drumright (74030) ***(G-2054)***
Carl A Nilsen 405 236-4554
3904 E Reno Ave Oklahoma City (73117) ***(G-5701)***
Carl Abla 580 526-3267
202 Ne Boundry Rd Erick (73645) ***(G-3086)***
Carl Bright Inc 405 761-7129
3210 S Arena Rd McLoud (74851) ***(G-4357)***
Carl E Gungoll Exploration LLC 405 848-7898
6 Ne 63rd St Ste 300 Oklahoma City (73105) ***(G-5702)***
Carlisle Foodservice Products, Oklahoma City *Also called CFS Brands LLC* ***(G-5732)***
Carlisle Sanitary Maintenance 405 475-5600
4711 E Hefner Rd Oklahoma City (73131) ***(G-5703)***
Carls Backhoe & Roustabout 405 893-7212
15692 N Heaston Rd Calumet (73014) ***(G-1245)***
Carls Chili Company Inc 918 227-1623
8622 S Regency Dr Tulsa (74131) ***(G-8994)***
Carlson Company 918 627-4334
4333 S 86th East Ave Tulsa (74145) ***(G-9376)***
Carlson Design Corporation 918 438-8344
539 S Trenton Ave Tulsa (74120) ***(G-9377)***
Carlsons Rural Mailbox Co 405 632-7338
301 Se 54th St Oklahoma City (73129) ***(G-5704)***
Carmen Natural Gas Measurement 580 987-2778
417 N Central Ave Carmen (73726) ***(G-1272)***
Carnegie Concrete Company 580 654-1208
Hwy 9 W Carnegie (73015) ***(G-1273)***
Carnegie Herald 580 654-1443
14 W Main St Carnegie (73015) ***(G-1274)***
Carnegie Pre-Cast Septic Tanks, Carnegie *Also called Carnegie Precast Inc* ***(G-1275)***
Carnegie Precast Inc 580 654-1718
33129 State Highway 58 Carnegie (73015) ***(G-1275)***
Carnes Oilfield Services LLC 580 309-1249
19348 E 1180 Rd Sayre (73662) ***(G-8338)***
Carnes Petroleum Corporation 918 358-2541
1315 W Caddo St Cleveland (74020) ***(G-1718)***
Carols Sgns/Hand Painted Vinyl, Oklahoma City *Also called Carols Signs* ***(G-5705)***
Carols Signs 405 769-5521
1910 N Post Rd Oklahoma City (73141) ***(G-5705)***
Carolyns Cheesecake House 918 839-5757
27444 State Highway 112 Cameron (74932) ***(G-1255)***
Carolyns Mouse House 405 354-2858
7700 N Cimarron Rd Yukon (73099) ***(G-11702)***
Carousel Kids, Oklahoma City *Also called Sheen Incorporated* ***(G-7118)***
Carpenter Co 405 634-8124
9401 Pole Rd Ste 100 Moore (73160) ***(G-4506)***
Carpentree Inc 918 582-3600
4946 E 66th St N Tulsa (74117) ***(G-9378)***
Carpet Market, Chickasha *Also called Mike McGills Carpet Inc* ***(G-1488)***
Carport City, Muskogee *Also called Ronnie Nevitt* ***(G-4745)***
Carr Graphics Inc 918 835-0605
8199 E 46th St Tulsa (74145) ***(G-9379)***
Carrera Gas Companies LLC (PA) 918 359-0980
6120 S Yale Ave Ste 1640 Tulsa (74136) ***(G-9380)***
Carter & Higgins Orthodontics 918 986-9986
3232 E 31st St Tulsa (74105) ***(G-9381)***
Carter Aerospace Mfg Co LLC 918 229-4026
901 S John Zink St Skiatook (74070) ***(G-8535)***
Carter BF 918 486-7208
31061 E 191st St S Coweta (74429) ***(G-1874)***
Carter Custom Fiberglass, Quapaw *Also called Carter Fiberglass* ***(G-8028)***
Carter Davis Machine Shop Inc 918 437-2939
102 S 111th East Ave C Tulsa (74128) ***(G-9382)***
Carter Fiberglass 918 674-2325
100 N Main St Quapaw (74363) ***(G-8028)***
Carter Production Co 918 493-7064
2526 E 71st St Ste I Tulsa (74136) ***(G-9383)***
Carters Manufacturing 918 437-5428
10835 E Admiral Pl Tulsa (74116) ***(G-9384)***
Cartridge Smart, Tulsa *Also called Applied Laser Systems* ***(G-9200)***
Cas Monogramming and Team Spt, Yukon *Also called Cas Monogramming Inc* ***(G-11703)***
Cas Monogramming Inc 405 350-6556
200 S Ranchwood Blvd # 10 Yukon (73099) ***(G-11703)***
Casa Dosa 918 243-7277
Hwy 64 Cleveland (74020) ***(G-1719)***
Casady N Company LLC 405 528-4299
2921 N Oklahoma Ave Oklahoma City (73105) ***(G-5706)***
Cascade Oil LLC 405 236-4554
1900 E 15th St Bldg 700 Edmond (73013) ***(G-2338)***
Cascade Oils, Oklahoma City *Also called Carl A Nilsen* ***(G-5701)***
Cascades Holding US Inc 918 825-0616
4826 Hunt St Pryor (74361) ***(G-7950)***
Case Wireline Services Inc 580 254-3036
105 48th St Woodward (73801) ***(G-11567)***
Casedhole Solutions, Weatherford *Also called Nextier Cmpltion Solutions Inc* ***(G-11430)***
Caseing Crews Inc 405 867-1500
300 6th St Maysville (73057) ***(G-4256)***
Casework Specialties Inc LLC 918 382-0037
1323 E 5th St Tulsa (74120) ***(G-9385)***
Cash Dept, Oklahoma City *Also called Giesecke & Devrient Amer Inc* ***(G-6154)***
Casillas Operating LLC 918 582-5310
401 S Boston Ave Ste 2400 Tulsa (74103) ***(G-9386)***
Casillas Petroleum Corp (PA) 918 582-5310
401 S Boston Ave Ste 2400 Tulsa (74103) ***(G-9387)***
Casing Crews Incorporated 580 388-4567
307 N Main Lamont (74643) ***(G-3864)***
Casing Point LLC 405 245-9855
400 Buckboard Ln Midwest City (73130) ***(G-4438)***
Cass Holdings LLC (PA) 405 755-8448
311 Nw 122nd St Ste 100 Oklahoma City (73114) ***(G-5707)***
Cass Holdings LLC 405 359-5053
500 E Russworm Dr Watonga (73772) ***(G-11343)***
Cass Polymers Inc (PA) 405 755-8448
311 Nw 122nd St Ste 100 Oklahoma City (73114) ***(G-5708)***

Cassiday Pumping Service Inc 405 969-3374
11062 W County Road 71 Crescent (73028) ***(G-1909)***
Caster LLC 800 255-0480
408 W Madison St Purcell (73080) ***(G-8002)***
Casting Coating Corp 918 445-4141
5700 W 68th St Tulsa (74131) ***(G-8995)***
Castle Rock Kitchens 405 751-1822
3017 Castlerock Rd Oklahoma City (73120) ***(G-5709)***
Castle Wldg & Fabrication LLC 580 747-0218
1805 E Oklahoma Ave Enid (73701) ***(G-2925)***
Castlerock Resources Inc 405 842-4249
3333 Nw 63rd St Ste 102a Oklahoma City (73116) ***(G-5710)***
Caston Architectural Mllwk Inc 405 843-6652
6701 N Hudson Ave Oklahoma City (73116) ***(G-5711)***
Caswell Construction Co Inc (PA) 580 225-6833
113 Panel Rd Elk City (73644) ***(G-2793)***
Cat-Eyes Drone Imagery Svc LLC 918 344-8324
7224 S Elwood Ave Apt 420 Tulsa (74132) ***(G-9388)***
Catalog System Inc 405 808-1533
1316 Nw 7th Pl Moore (73170) ***(G-4507)***
Catch 21 ....617 227-0730
12505 Blue Sage Rd Oklahoma City (73120) ***(G-5712)***
Cater County District 3, Lone Grove *Also called County of Carter* ***(G-4116)***
Cathedral Energy Services Inc 405 261-6011
4701 United Dr Oklahoma City (73179) ***(G-5713)***
Catholic Art & Gifts, Tulsa *Also called F C Ziegler Co* ***(G-9721)***
Catoosa 2 Way 918 234-0055
850 N 163rd East Ave Tulsa (74116) ***(G-9389)***
Cattleac Cattle Equipment Inc 580 774-1010
3 4 Mile S Of I On Hwy 54 Weatherford (73096) ***(G-11398)***
Caudill Components, LLC, Owasso *Also called Orizon Arstrctres - Owasso Inc* ***(G-7599)***
Caulumet Ore Co 580 673-2815
824 Convict Hill Rd Healdton (73438) ***(G-3409)***
Causley Productions Inc (PA) 405 372-0940
205 W 9th Ave Stillwater (74074) ***(G-8666)***
Cavanal Woodworks 909 649-4346
4883 Witteville Dr Poteau (74953) ***(G-7900)***
Cave Man Choppers 405 672-8008
4001 Meadowview Dr Oklahoma City (73115) ***(G-5714)***
Caveman Screen Printing 918 446-6440
3702 W 61st St Tulsa (74132) ***(G-9390)***
Caves Hot Shot Services LLC 405 397-2569
220 N Pebble Creek Ter # 202 Mustang (73064) ***(G-4767)***
CB Printing and More LLC 405 488-7107
12505 S 13th Pl Jenks (74037) ***(G-3698)***
Cbd Everything LLC 405 605-5634
8404 S Hillcrest Ter Oklahoma City (73159) ***(G-5715)***
Cbd Farmacy LLC 405 697-5245
617 N Oakridge Dr Edmond (73034) ***(G-2339)***
Cbd4help LLC 405 206-9672
601 S Henney Rd Choctaw (73020) ***(G-1533)***
Cbhc Resources Inc 405 905-9791
3000 Thorn Ridge Rd Oklahoma City (73120) ***(G-5716)***
Cbl Resources 918 551-6760
4138 S Harvard Ave Ste C1 Tulsa (74135) ***(G-9391)***
CBS Energy LLC 405 470-4644
5753 Nw 132nd St Oklahoma City (73142) ***(G-5717)***
Cccc Inc 405 230-0638
1901 Oaks Way Oklahoma City (73131) ***(G-5718)***
CCL Acquisition LLC 918 739-4400
19722 E Admiral Pl Catoosa (74015) ***(G-1309)***
Ccmco, Owasso *Also called Centrifugal Casting Mch Co Inc* ***(G-7552)***
CCS Publishing LLC 405 359-0656
1209 Rockwood Dr Edmond (73013) ***(G-2340)***
CD and More, Claremore *Also called On Beat Goes* ***(G-1667)***
CD Industrys Corporation 580 317-8448
1705 Bearden Spring Rd Hugo (74743) ***(G-3605)***
CD Services 918 341-1032
12062 Branch Rd Claremore (74017) ***(G-1602)***
Cdl Construction LLC 580 323-2847
1642 Vanessa Dr Clinton (73601) ***(G-1741)***
Cdr Global, Oklahoma City *Also called Computer Dlers Rcyclers Globl* ***(G-5818)***
Cecilias Salsas 918 984-1491
8661 E 61st St Tulsa (74133) ***(G-9392)***
Cecils Electric Motor Co 918 775-3968
28 E Interstate Cir Sallisaw (74955) ***(G-8141)***
Cedar Built USA Inc 405 794-0811
2898 N Shields Blvd Moore (73160) ***(G-4508)***
Cedar Chest 918 287-9129
134 E 6th St Pawhuska (74056) ***(G-7681)***
Cedar Gate LLC 405 640-3235
3508 French Park Dr Ste 1 Edmond (73034) ***(G-2341)***
Cedar Rdge Rcording Studio LLC 405 651-5961
2129 N Dobbs Rd Harrah (73045) ***(G-3375)***
Cedar Tree Cutter, Weatherford *Also called Larry L Williams* ***(G-11424)***
Cefco Inc 918 543-8415
16313 E 590 Rd Inola (74036) ***(G-3653)***
Cei Petroleum Inc 918 582-4284
427 S Boston Ave Ste 409 Tulsa (74103) ***(G-9393)***
Cei Pipeline LLC 405 478-8770
701 Cedar Lake Blvd Oklahoma City (73114) ***(G-5719)***
Cej & Associates, Norman *Also called Cejco Inc* ***(G-4954)***
Ceja Corporation (PA) 918 496-0770
1437 S Boulder Ave # 1250 Tulsa (74119) ***(G-9394)***
Ceja Corporation 918 648-5215
Rr 1 Burbank (74633) ***(G-1214)***
Cejco Inc 405 366-8256
3225 N Flood Ave Norman (73069) ***(G-4954)***
Celerity Orthotcs & Prosthetcs 405 605-3030
937 Sw 89th St Oklahoma City (73139) ***(G-5720)***
Celerity Prosthetics LLC 405 605-3030
8625 S Walker Ave Oklahoma City (73139) ***(G-5721)***
Cellfill LLC 918 787-2355
802 Industrial Road C Grove (74344) ***(G-3260)***
Cellofoam North America Inc 918 775-7758
1330 W Redwood Ave Sallisaw (74955) ***(G-8142)***
Cement Specialists LLC 432 617-2243
14201 Caliber Dr Ste 300 Oklahoma City (73134) ***(G-5722)***
Cement Test Equipment Inc 918 835-4454
4001 W Edison St Tulsa (74127) ***(G-9395)***
Centaur Resources Inc 405 603-8800
5500 Pulchella Ln Oklahoma City (73142) ***(G-5723)***
Centek Inc 405 219-3200
5500 Sw 36th St Oklahoma City (73179) ***(G-5724)***
Centennial Gas Liquids Ulc 918 481-1119
6120 S Yale Ave Ste 805 Tulsa (74136) ***(G-9396)***
Center Mfg, Tulsa *Also called Sooner Manufacturing Co Inc* ***(G-10790)***
Centerline Inc 580 762-5451
2110 N Ash St Ponca City (74601) ***(G-7805)***
Centermass Industries LLC 760 485-7405
4817 Blackjack Ln Edmond (73034) ***(G-2342)***
Centerpiece Custom Wdwkg LLC 405 387-9312
8418 Shadow Lake Dr Blanchard (73010) ***(G-706)***
Centerpint Enrgy Rsources Corp 580 512-5903
4262 E Us Highway 270 McAlester (74501) ***(G-4279)***
Central Burial Vaults Inc 918 224-5701
8500 W 81st St Tulsa (74131) ***(G-8996)***
Central Chemical Company 580 234-8245
222 Crestwood Enid (73701) ***(G-2926)***
Central Glass Products Inc 918 436-2401
405 W Hamon Ave Pocola (74902) ***(G-7782)***
Central Handpiece Repair, Tuttle *Also called Dennis L Dickerson* ***(G-11196)***
Central Machine & Tool Company 580 237-4033
1414 E Willow Rd Enid (73701) ***(G-2927)***
Central Machine & Tools, Enid *Also called Parrish Enterprises Ltd* ***(G-3031)***
Central Metal Finishing LLC 405 379-5252
1006 Airport Rd Holdenville (74848) ***(G-3551)***
Central Mortar and Grout LLC 918 683-3003
1300 S 43rd St E Muskogee (74403) ***(G-4659)***
Central Oil Supply, Sapulpa *Also called Inland Oil Corp* ***(G-8278)***
Central Parts & Machine Inc 405 631-5460
219 Se 29th St Oklahoma City (73129) ***(G-5725)***
Central Plains Cement Company, Tulsa *Also called Tulsa Cement LLC* ***(G-10991)***
Central Pre Past, Oklahoma City *Also called Concrete Products Inc* ***(G-5819)***
Central Sales Promo, Oklahoma City *Also called Semasys Inc* ***(G-7107)***
Central States Bus Forms Div, Dewey *Also called Adams Investment Company* ***(G-2012)***
Central States Business Forms, Dewey *Also called Adams Investment Company* ***(G-2013)***
Central States Crane Hoist LLC (PA) 918 341-2320
518 N J M Davis Blvd A Claremore (74017) ***(G-1603)***
Central States Crane Hoist LLC 918 341-2320
415 N Owalla Ave Ste A Claremore (74017) ***(G-1604)***
Central Sttes Shrdding Systems 405 752-8300
13001 Green Valley Dr Oklahoma City (73120) ***(G-5726)***
Central Supply, Kingfisher *Also called Kingfisher Office Supply Inc* ***(G-3806)***
Central Texas Ex Metalwork LLC 765 492-9058
1501 Se 66th St Ste C Oklahoma City (73149) ***(G-5727)***
Central Valve Body 918 341-0266
15551 S Highway 66 Claremore (74017) ***(G-1605)***
Centrex Operating Co Inc 918 747-9997
5550 S Lewis Ave Ste 304 Tulsa (74105) ***(G-9397)***
Centrifugal Casting Mch Co Inc 918 835-7323
7744 N Owasso Expy Ste A Owasso (74055) ***(G-7552)***
Centrilift A Baker Hughes Co, Claremore *Also called Baker Centrilift Cable Inc* ***(G-1588)***
Centrilift Division, Tulsa *Also called Baker Hughes A GE Company LLC* ***(G-9255)***
Centurion Pipeline LP 405 262-4750
2301 S Evans Rd El Reno (73036) ***(G-2705)***
Centurion Resources LLC 918 493-1110
7404 S Yale Ave Tulsa (74136) ***(G-9398)***
Century LLC (PA) 405 732-2226
1000 Century Blvd Oklahoma City (73110) ***(G-5728)***
Century Geophysical Corp (PA) 918 838-9811
1223 S 71st East Ave Tulsa (74112) ***(G-9399)***
Century Livestock Feeders Inc 918 793-3382
306 N Cosben Shidler (74652) ***(G-8524)***
Century Martial Art Supply, Oklahoma City *Also called Century LLC* ***(G-5728)***
Century Plating Inc 918 835-1482
8831 E 38th St Tulsa (74145) ***(G-9400)***

Century Printing Inc 405 942-7171
  2713 N Windsor Ter Oklahoma City (73127) *(G-5729)*
Century Products LLC 908 793-3382
  306 N Cosden Kaw City (74641) *(G-3757)*
Cep Mid-Continent LLC 918 270-9927
  1560 E 21st St Ste 215 Tulsa (74114) *(G-9401)*
Ceradyne Inc 918 673-2201
  3250 S 614 Rd Quapaw (74363) *(G-8029)*
Ceralusa LLC 405 455-7720
  7002 S Bryant Ave Oklahoma City (73149) *(G-5730)*
Cerdafied Welding LLC 405 578-8035
  10701 Sw 31st Ct Yukon (73099) *(G-11704)*
Certified Machine & Design Inc 405 672-9607
  2300 S High Ave Oklahoma City (73129) *(G-5731)*
Cesi Chemical Inc 580 658-6608
  1004 S Plainsman Rd Marlow (73055) *(G-4225)*
CFM, Blackwell *Also called Kice Industries Inc* *(G-685)*
CFM Corporation 580 363-2850
  102 S 29th St Blackwell (74631) *(G-678)*
CFM Industries LLC 405 213-9557
  508 Cloudview Pl Edmond (73003) *(G-2343)*
Cfmi LLC (PA) 918 877-5000
  3845 S 103rd East Ave # 101 Tulsa (74146) *(G-9402)*
CFS Brands LLC (HQ) 405 475-5600
  4711 E Hefner Rd Oklahoma City (73131) *(G-5732)*
CFS Brands LLC 405 397-0103
  3421 N Lincoln Blvd Oklahoma City (73105) *(G-5733)*
Cfsp Acquisition Corp (PA) 405 475-5600
  4711 E Hefner Rd Oklahoma City (73131) *(G-5734)*
Cg Distributors 918 336-8882
  2145 Mountain Dr Bartlesville (74003) *(G-460)*
Cg Printing 405 818-4371
  1125 Ne 48th St Oklahoma City (73111) *(G-5735)*
Cgshops, Oklahoma City *Also called Gibsons Treasures* *(G-6152)*
CH Mufflers & Welding LLC 405 380-3877
  35084 Highway 9 Earlsboro (74840) *(G-2279)*
Chaddick & Associates Inc 580 223-1202
  2421 Autumn Run Ste E Ardmore (73401) *(G-264)*
Chadwick Paper Inc 580 369-2807
  400 E Main St Davis (73030) *(G-1979)*
Chaffin Manufacturing, Holdenville *Also called Special Parts Mfg Inc* *(G-3560)*
Challenger Downhole Tools Inc 405 604-0096
  5353 S Hattie Ave Oklahoma City (73129) *(G-5736)*
Chambers Signs 918 251-6513
  828 N Ash Ave Broken Arrow (74012) *(G-865)*
Champion Designs & Systems LLC 405 888-8370
  701 Cedar Lake Blvd # 143 Oklahoma City (73114) *(G-5737)*
Champion Drilling Fluids Inc 580 323-0044
  3940 Custer Ave Clinton (73601) *(G-1742)*
Champion Opco LLC 405 708-6858
  417 Hudiburg Cir Ste A Oklahoma City (73108) *(G-5738)*
Champlin Exploration Inc 580 233-1155
  201 N Grand St Ste 700 Enid (73701) *(G-2928)*
Champlin Firearms Inc 580 237-7388
  Woodring Airport 66th St Enid (73701) *(G-2929)*
Chandler Instruments Co LLC (HQ) 918 250-7200
  2001 N Indianwood Ave Broken Arrow (74012) *(G-866)*
Chandler Materials Company 918 836-9151
  5519 E 15th St Tulsa (74112) *(G-9403)*
Chandler Well Services LLC 817 673-8140
  10850 Hunters Pointe Edmond (73034) *(G-2344)*
Chaney Dell Plant, Ringwood *Also called Western Gas Resources Inc* *(G-8097)*
Channel One Lighting Systems 918 587-2663
  1522 E 6th St Tulsa (74120) *(G-9404)*
Channel One Lightning Systems, Tulsa *Also called Channel One Lighting Systems* *(G-9404)*
Chaparral Energy Inc 918 793-2881
  373 Phillips Rd Ste A Shidler (74652) *(G-8525)*
Chaparral Energy Inc 918 287-2977
  447 State Highway 99 Pawhuska (74056) *(G-7682)*
Chaparral Energy Inc 580 673-2815
  824 Convict Hill Rd Healdton (73438) *(G-3410)*
Chaparral Energy Inc (PA) 405 478-8770
  701 Cedar Lake Blvd Oklahoma City (73114) *(G-5739)*
Chaparral Energy LLC (HQ) 405 478-8770
  701 Cedar Lake Blvd Oklahoma City (73114) *(G-5740)*
Chaparral Exploration LLC 405 426-4449
  701 Cedar Lake Blvd Oklahoma City (73114) *(G-5741)*
Chapman Oil Co, Velma *Also called Leland Chapman* *(G-11235)*
Chapparal Drilling Fluids, Oklahoma City *Also called Lariat Services Inc* *(G-6449)*
Chappell Supply & Equipment, Oklahoma City *Also called Chase Enterprises Inc* *(G-5745)*
Charles D Mayhue 580 436-6500
  114 S Broadway Ave Ada (74820) *(G-20)*
Charles Dale Keller 940 597-1763
  1922 Knox Rd Apt 404 Ardmore (73401) *(G-265)*
Charles E Morrison Co 405 840-1604
  6914 N Classen Blvd Oklahoma City (73116) *(G-5742)*
Charles F Doornbos Revocable T 918 336-0611
  105 1/2 Se Frank Phillips Bartlesville (74003) *(G-461)*
Charles Garrison, Foraker *Also called Garrison Welding* *(G-3168)*

Charles H Colpitt 918 371-2455
  12328 N Sheridan Rd Collinsville (74021) *(G-1805)*
Charles Jones 405 348-2187
  825 W Simmons Rd Edmond (73034) *(G-2345)*
Charles Komar & Sons Inc 918 423-3535
  400 W Chickasaw Ave McAlester (74501) *(G-4280)*
Charles Komar & Sons Inc 918 423-1227
  10 Komar Dr Mcalester (74501) *(G-4281)*
Charles Machine Works Inc (HQ) 580 572-2693
  1959 W Fir St Perry (73077) *(G-7728)*
Charles ODell 405 745-3353
  9840 Sw 44th St Mustang (73064) *(G-4768)*
Charles Service Station LLC 918 297-3308
  14365 E Us Highway 270 Hartshorne (74547) *(G-3390)*
Charles Tigert Welding Sh 580 889-3558
  151 W Highway 7 Atoka (74525) *(G-402)*
Charles Weathers Welding 405 341-2413
  616 W Main St Edmond (73003) *(G-2346)*
Charleys Golf Cars Inc 405 273-6901
  37605 45th St Shawnee (74804) *(G-8437)*
Charlie Bean Coffee LLC 405 376-4815
  4020 Will Rogers Pkwy # 900 Oklahoma City (73108) *(G-5743)*
Charlies Welding 580 467-2266
  401 Hickory Ave Comanche (73529) *(G-1834)*
Chart Cooler Service Co Inc (HQ) 918 834-0002
  5615 S 129th East Ave Tulsa (74134) *(G-9405)*
Chart Industries Inc 918 621-5246
  5615 S 129th East Ave Tulsa (74134) *(G-9406)*
Charter Oak Production Co LLC (PA) 405 286-0361
  13929 Quail Pointe Dr Oklahoma City (73134) *(G-5744)*
Chase Enterprises Inc 405 495-1722
  6509 W Reno Ave Oklahoma City (73127) *(G-5745)*
Chase Industries Inc 816 850-5323
  302 S Sertco Rd Okemah (74859) *(G-5266)*
Chastain Enterprises LLC 918 615-9355
  16410 E 50th St Tulsa (74134) *(G-9407)*
Chaston Oil & Gas LLC 580 226-2640
  100 W Main St Ardmore (73401) *(G-266)*
Chc Welding LLC 405 706-3367
  4700 Harrogate Dr Norman (73072) *(G-4955)*
Cheaper TS Inc 918 615-6262
  821 W Freeport St Broken Arrow (74012) *(G-867)*
Checos Machine Shop & General 405 680-0900
  2115 Sw 42nd St Oklahoma City (73119) *(G-5746)*
Checotah Partners LLC 918 935-2795
  2512 E 71st St Tulsa (74136) *(G-9408)*
Checotah W T J Shoppe Inc 918 473-2819
  212 Miles Ave Checotah (74426) *(G-1391)*
Cheese Factory LLC 405 375-4004
  701 Starlite Dr Kingfisher (73750) *(G-3788)*
Cheftain Royalty Company 405 767-1251
  1249 E 33rd St Edmond (73013) *(G-2347)*
Chelinos Tortilla Factory (PA) 405 631-3188
  4320 S Walker Ave Oklahoma City (73109) *(G-5747)*
Chelsea Reporter, The, Chelsea *Also called Reporter Publishing Co Inc* *(G-1411)*
Chemco 918 481-0537
  8242 S Sandusky Ave Tulsa (74137) *(G-9409)*
Chemical Dynamics Corporation 405 392-3505
  7516 E Highway 37 Tuttle (73089) *(G-11189)*
Chemical Products Inds Inc 405 745-2070
  7649 Sw 34th St Oklahoma City (73179) *(G-5748)*
Chemlink, Sand Springs *Also called Baker Petrolite LLC* *(G-8165)*
Chemoil Energy Inc 405 605-5436
  4 E Sheridan Ave Ste 400 Oklahoma City (73104) *(G-5749)*
Chemplex Advanced Mtls LLC 580 832-5288
  200 N Mcclary St Cordell (73632) *(G-1856)*
Chemproof Polymers Inc 918 584-0364
  2750 Charles Page Blvd Tulsa (74127) *(G-9410)*
Chemstation of Oklahoma, Oklahoma City *Also called E Environmental LLC* *(G-5993)*
Chemtica USA 580 366-6799
  2912 Enterprise Dr Ste A1 Durant (74701) *(G-2213)*
Chemtrade Refinery Svcs Inc 918 587-7613
  5201 W 21st St Tulsa (74107) *(G-9411)*
Cher Oil Company Inc 405 454-1575
  7317 S Ripley Rd Ripley (74062) *(G-8099)*
Chermac Energy Corporation 405 341-3506
  2909 Nw 156th St Edmond (73013) *(G-2348)*
Chernico Exploration Inc 918 587-6242
  1307 S Boulder Ave # 400 Tulsa (74119) *(G-9412)*
Cherokee Archtectural Mtls LLC 918 258-5700
  1100 E Houston St Broken Arrow (74012) *(G-868)*
Cherokee Hart Ranch 918 563-4244
  164342 Indian Hwy Talihina (74571) *(G-8905)*
Cherokee Industries Inc 405 691-8222
  11301 S Interstate 44 Svc Oklahoma City (73173) *(G-5750)*
Cherokee Insights LLC 918 430-3409
  10838 E Marshall St # 22 Tulsa (74116) *(G-9413)*
Cherokee Medical Services LLC 918 696-3151
  470739 Highway 51 Stilwell (74960) *(G-8783)*

ALPHABETIC SECTION

Cherokee Nation 918 696-3124
  217 W Oak St Stilwell (74960) *(G-8784)*
Cherokee Nation Arospc Def LLC 918 430-3492
  2777 Highway 69a Pryor (74361) *(G-7951)*
Cherokee Nation Arospc Def LLC (PA) 918 696-3151
  470739 Highway 51 Stilwell (74960) *(G-8785)*
Cherokee Nation Businesses LLC (HQ) 918 384-7474
  777 W Cherokee St Catoosa (74015) *(G-1310)*
Cherokee Nation Industries LLC (HQ) 918 696-3151
  470739 Highway 51 Stilwell (74960) *(G-8786)*
Cherokee Nation Red Wing LLC 918 824-6050
  2777 Highway 69a Pryor (74361) *(G-7952)*
Cherokee Nation Red Wing LLC (HQ) 918 430-3437
  10838 E Marshall St # 20 Tulsa (74116) *(G-9414)*
Cherokee Ntion Armred Sltons L 918 696-3151
  10838 E Marshall St # 22 Tulsa (74116) *(G-9415)*
Cherokee Piping Services LLC 918 931-8593
  24688 Highway 51 Tahlequah (74464) *(G-8856)*
Cherokee Publishing, Cherokee Also called Larry D Hammer *(G-1418)*
Cherokee Trailers, Oklahoma City Also called Cherokee Industries Inc *(G-5750)*
Cherokee Welding Industries 918 247-6122
  14643 N Maple Dr Kellyville (74039) *(G-3761)*
Cherokee Woodwork Inc 918 798-5037
  2746 E King St Tulsa (74110) *(G-9416)*
Cherry Street Print Shop Inc 918 584-0022
  608 E 3rd St Ste 7 Tulsa (74120) *(G-9417)*
Chesapeake Energy Corporation 877 245-1427
  501 S Eastern Ave Elk City (73644) *(G-2794)*
Chesapeake Energy Corporation (PA) 405 848-8000
  6100 N Western Ave Oklahoma City (73118) *(G-5751)*
Chesapeake Energy La Corp 405 848-8000
  6100 N Western Ave Oklahoma City (73118) *(G-5752)*
Chesapeake Energy Mktg LLC 877 245-1427
  6100 N Western Ave Oklahoma City (73118) *(G-5753)*
Chesapeake Exploration LLC 405 848-8000
  6100 N Western Ave Oklahoma City (73118) *(G-5754)*
Chesapeake Louisiana LP 405 848-8000
  6100 N Western Ave Oklahoma City (73118) *(G-5755)*
Chesapeake Midstream Dev LP 405 935-8000
  6100 N Western Ave Oklahoma City (73118) *(G-5756)*
Chesapeake Operating LLC 580 772-7255
  310 N State St Ste 4 Weatherford (73096) *(G-11399)*
Chesapeake Operating LLC 405 375-6755
  2110 S Main St Kingfisher (73750) *(G-3789)*
Chesapeake Operating LLC 405 375-6755
  15446 E 770 Rd Kingfisher (73750) *(G-3790)*
Chesapeake Operating LLC (HQ) 405 848-8000
  6100 N Western Ave Oklahoma City (73118) *(G-5757)*
Chesapeake Operating LLC 405 756-8700
  1407 Nw 4th St Lindsay (73052) *(G-4056)*
Cheshire Portable Welding 405 373-4669
  13001 N Cemetery Rd Piedmont (73078) *(G-7757)*
Chesser Contract Pumping LLC 405 820-7240
  9798 Musson Rd Meeker (74855) *(G-4376)*
Chester Oil Company 405 379-2600
  8163 E 131 Wetumka (74883) *(G-11490)*
Chevelle World Inc 405 872-3399
  9180 72nd St Noble (73068) *(G-4876)*
Chevron Phillips Chem Co LP 918 825-0364
  Mid American Indus Park Pryor (74361) *(G-7953)*
Chevron Phillips Chem Co LP 918 977-6846
  105 Ptc Bartlesville (74004) *(G-462)*
Chevron Phillips Chem Co LP 918 661-3317
  Highway 60 & 123 Bartlesville (74004) *(G-463)*
Chew Coast & Sons 918 333-3318
  401280 W 2460 Dr Bartlesville (74006) *(G-464)*
Cheyenne Innovations Inc 918 793-7521
  201 W Barber St Shidler (74652) *(G-8526)*
Cheyenne Petro Co Ltd Partnr (PA) 405 936-6220
  14000 Quail Springs Parkw Oklahoma City (73134) *(G-5758)*
Cheyenne Pickup Parts, Noble Also called Chevelle World Inc *(G-4876)*
Cheyenne Products LLC 918 639-8583
  8818 N 176th East Ave Owasso (74055) *(G-7553)*
Cheyenne Star 580 497-3324
  422 E Broadway Ave Cheyenne (73628) *(G-1423)*
Cheyenne Woodworks Inc 918 587-3533
  402 Heavy Traffic Way Tulsa (74127) *(G-9418)*
Chic Galleria Publications 918 671-2379
  628 Chestnut Ct Bartlesville (74003) *(G-465)*
CHICAGO BRIDGE & IRON, Tulsa Also called Shaw Group Inc *(G-10739)*
Chickasaw Defense Services Inc 405 203-0144
  6101 Camille Ave Oklahoma City (73149) *(G-5759)*
Chickasaw Energy Solutions LLC 580 276-3306
  601 N Brentwood Ave Marietta (73448) *(G-4202)*
Chickasaw Nation 405 331-2300
  37 N Colbert Rd Davis (73030) *(G-1980)*
Chickasaw Nation 405 387-6013
  2457 Hwy 62 Service Rd Newcastle (73065) *(G-4821)*
Chickasaw Nation 580 332-2796
  1005 N Country Club Rd Ada (74820) *(G-21)*

Chickasaw Nation Inds Inc 580 276-3305
  601 Ne 2nd St Marietta (73448) *(G-4203)*
Chickasaw Network Services, Marietta Also called Chickasaw Energy Solutions LLC *(G-4202)*
Chickasaw Press 580 436-7282
  1020 N Mississippi Ave Ada (74820) *(G-22)*
Chickasha Manufacturing Co Inc 405 224-0229
  5501 S 4th St Chickasha (73018) *(G-1449)*
Chief Drilling Services, Weatherford Also called Chief Drlg & Foundation Svcs *(G-11400)*
Chief Drlg & Foundation Svcs 580 302-0124
  24250 E 990 Rd Weatherford (73096) *(G-11400)*
Child Heroes LLC 757 286-8181
  6802 Lancer Ln Oklahoma City (73132) *(G-5760)*
Chips Valiant Inc 580 933-5323
  Hwy 70 Byp Valliant (74764) *(G-11222)*
Chiseled In Stone 918 813-5409
  401 S Memorial Dr Tulsa (74112) *(G-9419)*
Chisholm Oil and Gas Oper LLC 918 488-6400
  6100 S Yale Ave Ste 1700 Tulsa (74136) *(G-9420)*
Chk Cleveland Tonkawa LLC 405 848-8000
  6100 N Western Ave Oklahoma City (73118) *(G-5761)*
Chk Louisiana LLC 405 935-7871
  6100 N Western Ave Oklahoma City (73118) *(G-5762)*
Choate Publishing Inc 580 276-3255
  104 W Main St Marietta (73448) *(G-4204)*
Choc Brewing Company Inc 918 302-3002
  125 S Main St Ste 220 McAlester (74501) *(G-4282)*
Choctaw Defense, McAlester Also called Choctaw Mfg Def Contrs Inc *(G-4286)*
Choctaw Defense Mfg LLC (HQ) 918 426-2871
  3 Skyway Dr McAlester (74501) *(G-4283)*
Choctaw Defense Mfg LLC 580 326-8365
  203 Choctaw Industrial Dr Hugo (74743) *(G-3606)*
Choctaw Defense Munitions 918 426-7871
  1 Skyway Dr Mcalester Mcalester (74501) *(G-4284)*
Choctaw Gas Company 918 469-3394
  1118 Main St Quinton (74561) *(G-8035)*
Choctaw Global LLC 918 426-2871
  3 Skyway Dr Ste 103 McAlester (74501) *(G-4285)*
Choctaw Manufacturing & Dev Co 580 310-6021
  1324 Cradduck Rd Ada (74820) *(G-23)*
Choctaw Mfg & Dev Corp (HQ) 580 326-8365
  203 Choctaw Industrial Dr Hugo (74743) *(G-3607)*
Choctaw Mfg & Dev Corp 580 326-8365
  357 N Hill Rd Atoka (74525) *(G-403)*
Choctaw Mfg Def Contrs Inc 580 326-8365
  203 Choctaw Industrial Dr Hugo (74743) *(G-3608)*
Choctaw Mfg Def Contrs Inc (HQ) 580 298-2203
  209 Sw 7th St Antlers (74523) *(G-215)*
Choctaw Mfg Def Contrs Inc 918 426-2871
  3 Skyway Dr McAlester (74501) *(G-4286)*
Choctaw Mfg Def Contrs Inc 580 326-8365
  101 Ed Perry Rd Hugo (74743) *(G-3609)*
Choctaw Nation Fabricators, Atoka Also called Choctaw Mfg & Dev Corp *(G-403)*
Choctaw Nation of Oklahoma 580 326-8365
  203 Choctaw Industrial Dr Hugo (74743) *(G-3610)*
Choctaw Print Services, Durant Also called Texoma Printing Inc *(G-2267)*
Choctaw Travel Plaza 580 920-2186
  4015 Choctaw Rd Durant (74701) *(G-2214)*
Chorus Labs LLC 405 317-2942
  2205 Nw 57th St Oklahoma City (73112) *(G-5763)*
Choska Alfalfa Mills LLC 918 687-5805
  3505 Severs St Muskogee (74403) *(G-4660)*
Chouteau Fuels Company 405 249-8273
  8142 Highway 412b Chouteau (74337) *(G-1560)*
Chouteau Pallet 918 476-6098
  10451 S 430 Chouteau (74337) *(G-1561)*
Chris Bean Lcnsed Glgist 284, Jenks Also called Bean Chris Oil & Gas Service *(G-3690)*
Chris Green Greens Construct 405 207-0690
  15569 N County Road 3240 Pauls Valley (73075) *(G-7653)*
Chris Hammon Oil Properties 405 382-0250
  608 N Main St Seminole (74868) *(G-8363)*
Chris Johnson 405 364-3879
  312 E Tonhawa St Norman (73069) *(G-4956)*
Christ Centered Carriers LLC 417 850-8137
  11579 N 2080 Rd Canute (73626) *(G-1267)*
Christian Cheese Factory, Kingfisher Also called George E Christian *(G-3798)*
Christian Chronicle Inc 405 425-5070
  2801 E Memorial Rd # 102 Edmond (73013) *(G-2349)*
Christian Chronicle, The, Edmond Also called Christian Chronicle Inc *(G-2349)*
Christian Connections of Okla 405 372-2111
  9211 W 2nd Ave Stillwater (74074) *(G-8667)*
Christian Martin Lavery 405 810-0900
  6421 Avondale Dr Ste 212 Nichols Hills (73116) *(G-4857)*
Christians Welding Service 580 674-3384
  201 N Rambo Dill City (73641) *(G-2034)*
Christina Stokes 405 551-1017
  1325 Northgate Ter Edmond (73013) *(G-2350)*
Christy Collins Inc 580 305-0001
  18149 County Road Ns 234 Frederick (73542) *(G-3192)*

Christys Quilts ... 405 853-2155
7939 E 590 Rd Hennessey (73742) *(G-3450)*
Chromalloy Gas Turbine LLC ... 845 359-4700
2701 Liberty Pkwy Ste 305 Oklahoma City (73110) *(G-5764)*
Chromalloy Oklahoma, Oklahoma City Also called Chromalloy Gas Turbine LLC *(G-5764)*
Chromatech Scientific Corp ... 405 370-4466
3720 Harris Dr Edmond (73013) *(G-2351)*
Chrome River Wholesale LLC ... 918 610-0810
5412 S Mingo Rd Ste I Tulsa (74146) *(G-9421)*
Chromium Plating Company (PA) ... 918 583-4118
412 N Cheyenne Ave Tulsa (74103) *(G-9422)*
Chrysalis Software Inc ... 831 761-1307
1 W 3rd St Ste 1115 Tulsa (74103) *(G-9423)*
CHS Oil & Gas LLC ... 918 280-9368
4308 W Rogers Blvd Skiatook (74070) *(G-8536)*
Chumbolly Press LLC ... 918 607-3932
223 N Sunset Ave Sand Springs (74063) *(G-8170)*
Ciena Corporation ... 918 925-5000
100 W 5th St Ste 520 Tulsa (74103) *(G-9424)*
Cimarex Energy Co ... 918 585-1100
202 S Cheyenne Ave # 1000 Tulsa (74103) *(G-9425)*
Cimarex Energy Co ... 405 262-2966
3503 Jensen Rd E El Reno (73036) *(G-2706)*
Cimarex Energy Co ... 918 295-1638
1000 S Denver Ave # 5102 Tulsa (74119) *(G-9426)*
Cimarex Energy Co ... 580 330-0188
31990 I 40 Service Rd Clinton (73601) *(G-1743)*
Cimarron Aerospace LLC ... 405 260-0990
120 Highway 74 Guthrie (73044) *(G-3308)*
Cimarron Docs Bar-B-Que Chili ... 918 787-7881
61890 E 346 Rd Grove (74344) *(G-3261)*
Cimarron Energy Holding Co LLC (HQ) ... 405 928-7373
4190 S Harvey Ave Norman (73072) *(G-4957)*
Cimarron Energy Inc ... 405 928-2940
4190 S Harvey Newcastle (73065) *(G-4822)*
Cimarron Equine Station ... 405 373-0358
11630 N Cimarron Rd Yukon (73099) *(G-11705)*
Cimarron Equipment Company ... 918 625-1647
7828 S Granite Ave Tulsa (74136) *(G-9427)*
Cimarron Glass & Ovrhd Door Co, Cushing Also called Cimarron Glass LLC *(G-1925)*
Cimarron Glass LLC ... 918 225-6600
223 E Main St Cushing (74023) *(G-1925)*
Cimarron Machine Inc ... 972 658-7051
1740 Dodson School Rd Bokchito (74726) *(G-750)*
Cimarron Machine Services Inc ... 918 835-3333
7734 E 11th St Tulsa (74112) *(G-9428)*
Cimarron Machine Works Inc ... 405 375-6452
9 Miles East Highway 33 Kingfisher (73750) *(G-3791)*
Cimarron Pallet Mfg Co ... 405 228-0288
1430 W Sheridan Ave Oklahoma City (73106) *(G-5765)*
Cimarron Pipeline LLC ... 405 286-9797
1601 Nw Expwy St Ste 777 Oklahoma City (73118) *(G-5766)*
Cimarron River Operation Corp ... 918 633-2911
3725 Speck Wright Rd Mannford (74044) *(G-4179)*
Cimarron Screen Printing ... 405 755-8337
13716 N Lincoln Blvd Edmond (73013) *(G-2352)*
Cimarron Tank Service ... 405 853-6523
420 E 3rd St Hennessey (73742) *(G-3451)*
Cimarron Trailers Inc ... 405 222-4800
1442 Highway 62 Chickasha (73018) *(G-1450)*
Cimco Industries LLC ... 918 783-5500
32207 S Highway 69 Big Cabin (74332) *(G-601)*
Cindy Nickel Aesthetics ... 405 513-6690
200 N Bryant Ave 100 Edmond (73034) *(G-2353)*
Cindy Nickel Inc ... 405 209-1444
1816 Winding Ridge Rd Edmond (73034) *(G-2354)*
Cindys Stitching ... 405 735-7126
2112 Abbeywood Oklahoma City (73170) *(G-5281)*
Circle 7 Signs and Wonders ... 918 448-7744
5918 Se 1030th Ave Wilburton (74578) *(G-11519)*
Circle 9 Resources LLC ... 972 528-6773
2308 Nw 54th St Oklahoma City (73112) *(G-5767)*
Circle A Welding LLC ... 580 890-9617
10398 N 2385 Rd Weatherford (73096) *(G-11401)*
Circle B Msrment Fbrcation LLC (PA) ... 918 445-4488
14034 E Marshall St Tulsa (74116) *(G-9429)*
Circle D Meat ... 580 921-5500
S County Line Rd Laverne (73848) *(G-3876)*
Circle K Services Inc ... 580 254-3568
4915 Western Ave Woodward (73801) *(G-11568)*
Circle K Steel Bldg Cnstr LLC ... 405 932-4664
359071 Us Highway 62 Naple (74860) *(G-7634)*
Circle V Energy Services LLC ... 405 614-0891
10000 E Yost Rd Glencoe (74032) *(G-3219)*
Cirrus Production Company (PA) ... 580 237-0002
201 N Grand St Ste 200 Enid (73701) *(G-2930)*
CIS Investors LLC ... 405 370-5812
316 Nw 61st St Oklahoma City (73118) *(G-5768)*
Cisco Containers LLC ... 918 439-9244
17515 E Admiral Pl Tulsa (74116) *(G-9430)*

Cisco Systems Inc ... 999 505-5901
1 Memorial Pl Tulsa (74133) *(G-9431)*
Ciskoeagle Inc ... 918 622-9010
10015 E 51st St Tulsa (74146) *(G-9432)*
Cisper Welding ... 405 665-2599
906 S Powell Ave Wynnewood (73098) *(G-11665)*
Cisper Welding Inc ... 918 543-2321
36250 S 4220 Rd Inola (74036) *(G-3654)*
Cisper Welding of Oklahoma ... 918 543-7755
15681 E 590 Rd Inola (74036) *(G-3655)*
Citadel Technologies, Tulsa Also called CTI Services LLC *(G-9519)*
Citation Oil & Gas Corp ... 580 856-3014
Nw Tatums Fld Ratliff City (73481) *(G-8049)*
Citation Oil & Gas Corp ... 580 229-1756
4597 Texas St Healdton (73438) *(G-3411)*
Citation Oil & Gas Corp ... 580 265-4534
22019 County Road 1650 Stonewall (74871) *(G-8799)*
Citation Oil & Gas Corp ... 405 681-9400
9400 Broadway Ext Ste 510 Oklahoma City (73114) *(G-5769)*
Citizen Energy II LLC ... 918 949-4680
320 S Boston Ave Ste 1300 Tulsa (74103) *(G-9433)*
Citizen Energy III LLC ... 918 949-4680
320 S Boston Ave Ste 900 Tulsa (74103) *(G-9434)*
Citizen Energy Operating LLC (PA) ... 918 949-4680
320 S Boston Ave Ste 900 Tulsa (74103) *(G-9435)*
Citizen Enrgy Intermediate LLC ... 918 949-4680
320 S Boston Ave Ste 900 Tulsa (74103) *(G-9436)*
City Altus Water & Sewer Dept, Altus Also called City of Altus *(G-148)*
City Awning Company, Tulsa Also called City Tent & Awning Co Inc *(G-9437)*
City Carbonic LLC ... 405 239-2068
406 Sw 4th St Oklahoma City (73109) *(G-5770)*
City Electric Supply Company ... 918 871-2640
1598 S Park Hill Rd Tahlequah (74464) *(G-8857)*
City Electric Supply Company ... 405 701-8544
1900 Industrial Blvd Norman (73069) *(G-4958)*
City Machine Shop ... 580 795-2282
409 E Main St Madill (73446) *(G-4145)*
City of Altus ... 580 481-2270
300 E Commerce St Altus (73521) *(G-148)*
City of Claremore ... 918 342-2490
2060 S Highway 66 Claremore (74019) *(G-1606)*
City of Davis ... 580 369-2988
227 E Main St Davis (73030) *(G-1981)*
City of Tahlequah ... 918 456-8332
1851 N Douglas Ave Tahlequah (74464) *(G-8858)*
City of Weatherford ... 580 772-5315
700 S Access Rd Weatherford (73096) *(G-11402)*
City Sentinel, The, Oklahoma City Also called Frost Entertainment *(G-6125)*
City Tent & Awning Co Inc ... 918 583-5003
12234 E 60th St Tulsa (74146) *(G-9437)*
Civitas Media LLC ... 580 482-1221
218 W Commerce St Altus (73521) *(G-149)*
CJ Graphics ... 405 636-0400
636 Sw 59th St Ste B Oklahoma City (73109) *(G-5771)*
CJ Hill Inc ... 918 251-1164
2333 W Wichita St Broken Arrow (74012) *(G-869)*
Cjs Custom Apparel ... 405 340-9677
2100 S Broadway Edmond (73013) *(G-2355)*
Ckenergy Electric Co Op Inc ... 405 247-3041
311 W Petree Rd Anadarko (73005) *(G-201)*
CL Installation, Eufaula Also called Josh Leeper *(G-3103)*
Claco Enterprises ... 918 343-0276
24605 S 4150 Rd Claremore (74019) *(G-1607)*
Claras Kitchen LLC ... 229 669-1493
6036 Nw 59th St Oklahoma City (73122) *(G-5772)*
Claremore Daily Progress, Claremore Also called Newspaper Holding Inc *(G-1661)*
Claremoresigns Com ... 918 965-1233
514 N J M Davis Blvd Claremore (74017) *(G-1608)*
Clarence & Lois Parker ... 580 765-8188
300 S Silverdale Ln Ponca City (74604) *(G-7806)*
Clarion Events Inc (HQ) ... 918 835-3161
110 S Hartford Ave # 200 Tulsa (74120) *(G-9438)*
Clarios ... 405 688-3730
4730 Sw 20th St Oklahoma City (73128) *(G-5773)*
Clarios ... 918 641-0660
6533 E 46th St Tulsa (74145) *(G-9439)*
Clarios ... 405 419-5400
5005 York Rd N Norman (73069) *(G-4959)*
Clark Creative Industries Inc ... 405 473-8046
1909 Colebrook Dr Oklahoma City (73120) *(G-5774)*
Clark Ellison ... 405 525-3583
222 Ne 50th St Oklahoma City (73105) *(G-5775)*
Clark Mtal Bldngs Fbrcation LL ... 580 695-4915
11332 Coyote Run Guthrie (73044) *(G-3309)*
Clark Printing & Tag Co, Oklahoma City Also called Clark Printing Inc *(G-5776)*
Clark Printing Inc ... 405 528-5396
109 E Madison Ave Oklahoma City (73105) *(G-5776)*
Clark Rhyne ... 918 874-3563
726 E 131 West Hwy Wardville (74576) *(G-11306)*

ALPHABETIC SECTION — Cnc Metal Shape Cnstr LLC

Clark Seals LLC 918 664-0587
  3824 S 79th East Ave Tulsa (74145) *(G-9440)*
Clark Seals Ltd 918 610-1006
  7704 E 38th St Tulsa (74145) *(G-9441)*
Clark Signs Inc 918 291-3411
  306 N Main Kiefer (74041) *(G-3777)*
Clarksville Plant, Ada Also called Holcim (us) Inc *(G-49)*
Classen Wholesale Optical Inc 405 842-1900
  6600 N Olie Ave Ste C Oklahoma City (73116) *(G-5777)*
Classic Carpets Lawton Inc 580 713-0653
  1302 Sw Sheridan Rd Lawton (73505) *(G-3904)*
Classic Chisel Cabinet Shop 405 387-2216
  2280 County Road 1247 Blanchard (73010) *(G-707)*
Classic Collection, The, Lawton Also called Classic Collectn Interiors Inc *(G-3905)*
Classic Collectn Interiors Inc 580 351-0024
  838 Se 1st St Lawton (73501) *(G-3905)*
Classic Custom Plating Company 405 787-3075
  3709 N Peniel Ave Bethany (73008) *(G-573)*
Classic Design & Print LLC 580 216-0653
  107 E Broadway Vici (73859) *(G-11240)*
Classic Iron Works Inc 405 577-2877
  201 Arlington Dr Yukon (73099) *(G-11706)*
Classic Marble Design Inc 580 323-4917
  3800 Sw Commerce Clinton (73601) *(G-1744)*
Classic Overhead Doo 580 931-0340
  170 Fisher Station Rd Durant (74701) *(G-2215)*
Classic Printing Inc 405 524-6889
  2464 Nw 39th St Oklahoma City (73112) *(G-5778)*
Classic Screen Printing, Miami Also called E C Beights *(G-4400)*
Classic Shutters 918 234-0657
  10914 E 2nd St Tulsa (74128) *(G-9442)*
Classic Tile Stone & MBL LLC 405 858-8453
  117 W Wilshire Blvd Oklahoma City (73116) *(G-5779)*
Claude Neon Federal 918 585-9010
  533 S Rockford Ave Tulsa (74120) *(G-9443)*
Claude Neon Federal Signs Inc 918 587-7171
  1225 N Lansing Ave Tulsa (74106) *(G-9444)*
Claude V Sanderson Prop 405 232-5878
  1113 N Western Ave Oklahoma City (73106) *(G-5780)*
Claw Manufacturing LLC 918 739-4848
  19801 E Pine St Catoosa (74015) *(G-1311)*
Clay Bennett 918 647-9294
  212 Georgia Pl Poteau (74953) *(G-7901)*
Clay Serigraphics Inc 918 592-2529
  1433 E 6th St Tulsa (74120) *(G-9445)*
Clayton Homes Inc 918 686-0584
  2235 N 32nd St Muskogee (74401) *(G-4661)*
Clayton Homes Inc 405 341-4479
  601 Vista Ln Edmond (73034) *(G-2356)*
Clayton Homes Inc 580 237-7094
  902 Overland Trl Enid (73703) *(G-2931)*
Clayton Macom 918 967-3350
  20336 E Garland Rd Stigler (74462) *(G-8631)*
Clean Canvas Laser Tattoo Remo 580 919-5466
  1301 Nw 40th St Lawton (73505) *(G-3906)*
Clean Products Inc 405 382-1441
  11682 N Highway 99 Seminole (74868) *(G-8364)*
Cleanng LLC 918 409-0384
  10738 E 55th Pl Tulsa (74146) *(G-9446)*
Clear Channel Outdoor Inc 405 528-2683
  5205 N Santa Fe Ave Oklahoma City (73118) *(G-5781)*
Clear Edge Filtration Inc (HQ) 918 984-6000
  11607 E 43rd St N Tulsa (74116) *(G-9447)*
Clear Edge Filtration Inc 800 637-6206
  11607 E 43rd St N Tulsa (74116) *(G-9448)*
Clear Tone Hearing Center Inc 918 838-1000
  2323 S Sheridan Rd Tulsa (74129) *(G-9449)*
Clear2there LLC 405 605-8158
  4211 N Barnes Ave Oklahoma City (73112) *(G-5782)*
Clearbay Software LLC 405 310-9150
  2904 Stonebridge Ct Norman (73071) *(G-4960)*
Clearco Window Cleaning LLC 580 248-9547
  201 Sw 46th St Lawton (73505) *(G-3907)*
Clearity LLC 918 388-9000
  8408 S Delaware Ave Tulsa (74137) *(G-9450)*
Clearpoint Chemicals LLC 405 320-1719
  131 E Cardinal St Pocasset (73079) *(G-7775)*
Clearview International 580 332-2384
  1415 Sunrise Ln Ada (74820) *(G-24)*
Clearwater Enterprises 918 296-7007
  6315 E 102nd St Tulsa (74137) *(G-9451)*
Clearwter Entps LLC Ntural Gas 918 296-7007
  1914 W C St Jenks (74037) *(G-3699)*
Cleary Petroleum Corporation 405 672-4544
  10 N Broadway Edmond (73034) *(G-2357)*
Clement Elec 580 223-6500
  550 S Washington St Ardmore (73401) *(G-267)*
Clements Exploration Co 405 722-3100
  5601 Nw 72nd St Ste 354 Warr Acres (73132) *(G-11315)*

Clements Foods Co (PA) 405 842-3308
  6601 N Harvey Pl Oklahoma City (73116) *(G-5783)*
Clements Foods Co 405 842-3308
  6601 N Harvey Pl Oklahoma City (73116) *(G-5784)*
Clements Sand Gravel & Excavat 580 465-4191
  9363 State Highway 199 Ardmore (73401) *(G-268)*
Clements Vinegar, Oklahoma City Also called Clements Foods Co *(G-5784)*
Cleoptraz Scretz Hndmade Soaps 918 272-3319
  9401 E Admiral Pl Tulsa (74115) *(G-9452)*
Clevand Newspaper, Cleveland Also called Ferguson & Ferguson *(G-1723)*
Cleveland American, The, Cleveland Also called American-Chief Co *(G-1715)*
Cleveland Lease Service Inc 918 358-2791
  119 N Broadway St Cleveland (74020) *(G-1720)*
Clicks Machine & Supply 405 273-2497
  49 Bristow Ln Shawnee (74801) *(G-8438)*
Cliftton Wallcovering 918 638-4454
  1611 S Magnolia Ave Broken Arrow (74012) *(G-870)*
Climacool Corp (HQ) 405 815-3000
  15 S Virginia Ave Oklahoma City (73106) *(G-5785)*
Climate Control Group Inc (HQ) 405 745-6858
  7300 Sw 44th St Oklahoma City (73179) *(G-5786)*
Climate Master Inc (HQ) 405 745-6000
  7300 Sw 44th St Oklahoma City (73179) *(G-5787)*
Climatecraft Inc 405 415-9230
  1427 Nw 3rd St Oklahoma City (73106) *(G-5788)*
Clinco Mfg LLC 580 759-3434
  4161 County Road 1570 Ada (74820) *(G-25)*
Cline Machine Inc 918 587-0126
  1552 N 168th East Ave Tulsa (74116) *(G-9453)*
Clink Industries 918 970-6537
  6528 E 101st St Tulsa (74133) *(G-9454)*
Clint Dodson Enterprises LLC 580 931-9410
  301 S 21st Ave Durant (74701) *(G-2216)*
Clinton Daily News Company 580 323-5151
  522 Avant Ave Clinton (73601) *(G-1745)*
Clinton Daily News, The, Clinton Also called Clinton Daily News Company *(G-1745)*
Clinton Ice LLC 580 331-6060
  3750 Custer Ave Clinton (73601) *(G-1746)*
Clints Portable Welding 405 834-4517
  3309 Se 59th St Oklahoma City (73135) *(G-5789)*
Clock Shop Inc 918 583-5835
  1236 S Peoria Ave Tulsa (74120) *(G-9455)*
Close Custom Cabinets Inc 405 840-8226
  440 W Britton Rd Oklahoma City (73114) *(G-5790)*
Closebend Inc 918 445-1131
  4812 W 52nd St Tulsa (74107) *(G-9456)*
Closet Consignments LLC 405 387-3100
  1208 N Main St Newcastle (73065) *(G-4823)*
Cloverleaf Baking Co 612 708-8196
  4712 Ne Wisconsin St Bartlesville (74006) *(G-466)*
Clr Enterprises LLC 918 298-1943
  5423 E 109th Pl Tulsa (74137) *(G-9457)*
Clubbs Wood Art 918 569-4401
  60 Rte Hc 60 Box 33 6 Box Clayton (74536) *(G-1708)*
Clubhouse Trailer Co LLC 405 396-6747
  14625 Snta Fe Crssings Dr Edmond (73013) *(G-2358)*
Clubhouse Trailers, Edmond Also called Clubhouse Trailer Co LLC *(G-2358)*
Clyde Welding Service 405 222-1364
  3211 County Street 2850 Ninnekah (73067) *(G-4868)*
Clydes Good Gruel LLC 918 323-6143
  917 N Knoxville Ave Tulsa (74115) *(G-9458)*
CM Aluminum Trailers, Chickasha Also called Cimarron Trailers Inc *(G-1450)*
Cmark Resources LLC 918 492-5170
  7170 S Braden Ave Tulsa (74136) *(G-9459)*
CMC Recycling, Tulsa Also called Commercial Metals Company *(G-9474)*
CMC Steel, Durant Also called Commercial Metals Company *(G-2218)*
CMC Steel Oklahoma LLC 580 634-5092
  584 Old Highway 70 Durant (74701) *(G-2217)*
Cmd Inc 405 672-9607
  2300 S High Ave Oklahoma City (73129) *(G-5791)*
Cmg International LLC 918 493-5888
  11811 S 96th East Pl Bixby (74008) *(G-617)*
Cmg Operations LLC 580 477-0880
  212 E Broadway St Altus (73521) *(G-150)*
Cmg Operations LLC 580 353-2835
  8 Se Lee Blvd Lawton (73501) *(G-3908)*
Cmgi, Bixby Also called Cmg International LLC *(G-617)*
CMI Terex Corporation (HQ) 405 787-6020
  9528 W I 40 Service Rd Oklahoma City (73128) *(G-5792)*
CMI Terex Corporation 405 787-6020
  I-40 Morgan Rd Oklahoma City (73128) *(G-5793)*
CMS Welding & Fabrication 918 676-3133
  21150 S Highway 125 Fairland (74343) *(G-3123)*
Cmt Well Completions Inc 918 523-0600
  110 W 7th St Ste 2700 Tulsa (74119) *(G-9460)*
CNB, Catoosa Also called Cherokee Nation Businesses LLC *(G-1310)*
Cnc Metal Shape Cnstr LLC 405 605-5500
  1718 S Agnew Ave Oklahoma City (73108) *(G-5794)*

Cnc Patterns & Tooling — ALPHABETIC SECTION

Cnc Patterns & Tooling 918 835-2344
4310 E Pine Pl Tulsa (74115) *(G-9461)*

CNG Specialists LLC 405 677-5400
1211 Se 29th St Oklahoma City (73129) *(G-5795)*

Cnhi LLC 580 338-3355
515 N Ellison St Guymon (73942) *(G-3346)*

Cnhi LLC 405 238-6464
108 S Willow St Pauls Valley (73075) *(G-7654)*

Cnhi LLC 918 652-3311
302 W Main St Henryetta (74437) *(G-3501)*

Cnhi LLC 405 341-2121
123 S Broadway Edmond (73034) *(G-2359)*

Cnhi LLC 918 224-5185
16 S Park St Sapulpa (74066) *(G-8260)*

Cnhi LLC 918 825-3292
105 S Adair St Pryor (74361) *(G-7954)*

Cnhi Communications 918 723-5445
122 S Williams St Westville (74965) *(G-11481)*

Cni, Marietta Also called Chickasaw Nation Inds Inc *(G-4203)*

Cni Aviation Advantage A Joi 405 253-8200
2600 John Saxon Blvd Norman (73071) *(G-4961)*

Cni Manufacturing LLC 580 276-3306
601 N Brentwood Ave Marietta (73448) *(G-4205)*

Cnrw Defense Service 706 545-5088
777 W Cherokee St Catoosa (74015) *(G-1312)*

Cns Audio Video Inc 405 256-8546
400 S Vermont Ave Ste 100 Oklahoma City (73108) *(G-5796)*

Coal Creek Minerals LLC 918 962-5335
25858 Highline Rd Spiro (74959) *(G-8614)*

Coal Oil & Gas Company 580 332-6170
201 E Cottage St Ada (74820) *(G-26)*

Coalgate Newspaper, Coalgate Also called Coalgate Record Register *(G-1778)*

Coalgate Record Register 580 927-2355
602 E Lafayette Ave Coalgate (74538) *(G-1778)*

Coalton Road Enterprises LLC 918 652-0474
13755 Coalton Rd Henryetta (74437) *(G-3502)*

Coaltons Shavings & Feed, Henryetta Also called Coalton Road Enterprises LLC *(G-3502)*

Coanda Company LLC 214 601-4972
1000 Corbett Dr Norman (73072) *(G-4962)*

Coare Biotechnology Inc 405 227-0406
800 Research Pkwy Oklahoma City (73104) *(G-5797)*

Coast To Coast Power Spt LLC 918 712-8487
6100 S Yale Ave Ste 900 Tulsa (74136) *(G-9462)*

Coasterworks Inc 405 624-2756
2100 N Jardot Rd Stillwater (74075) *(G-8668)*

Coastline Oil & Gas LLC 405 354-6507
705 Kingston Dr Yukon (73099) *(G-11707)*

Coat Pro LLC 405 672-0705
1603 Se 25th St Oklahoma City (73129) *(G-5798)*

Coating Solution 580 276-5432
16288 Grassbur Rd Leon (73441) *(G-4033)*

Cobble Rock and Stone LLC 405 567-3552
11227 Ns 3520 Prague (74864) *(G-7923)*

Cobo Industries LLC 918 574-2123
7302 E 38th St Tulsa (74145) *(G-9463)*

Cobra Oil & Gas Corporation 580 254-2027
1211 34th St Ste 3 Woodward (73801) *(G-11569)*

COBRA Self Defense Tulsa 918 691-0054
1108 W Wekiwa Rd Sand Springs (74063) *(G-8171)*

Cobra Welding, Lookeba Also called David Piatt *(G-4128)*

Coca Cola Bottling Co 580 256-2350
3003 Lakeview Dr Woodward (73801) *(G-11570)*

Coca-Cola, Ada Also called Ada Coca Cola Bottling Company *(G-3)*

Coca-Cola, Oklahoma City Also called Great Plains Coca Cola Btlg Co *(G-6178)*

Coca-Cola, Oklahoma City Also called Great Plains Coca Cola Btlg Co *(G-6179)*

Coca-Cola, Woodward Also called Coca Cola Bottling Co *(G-11570)*

Coca-Cola Enterprises Inc 918 619-8200
14002 E 21st St Ste 800 Tulsa (74134) *(G-9464)*

Cochran Chemical Company Inc 405 382-8000
1800 Ray Davis Blvd Seminole (74868) *(G-8365)*

Cockerell Energy 405 463-7118
3160 W Britton Rd Oklahoma City (73120) *(G-5799)*

Code Red Industries LLC 405 227-1552
37802 Old Highway 270 Shawnee (74804) *(G-8439)*

Cody Mud Company Inc 580 237-5347
1122 Briar Creek Rd Enid (73703) *(G-2932)*

Coe Production 918 275-4529
6552 E 310 Rd Talala (74080) *(G-8899)*

Coen Co Inc 918 234-1800
11920 E Apache St Tulsa (74116) *(G-9465)*

Coil Chem LLC (PA) 405 445-5545
2103 E Ladd Rd Washington (73093) *(G-11334)*

Coiled Tubing Specialties LLC 918 878-7460
7404 S Yale Ave Tulsa (74136) *(G-9466)*

Cojac Building Co, Oklahoma City Also called Cojac Portable Buildings Inc *(G-5801)*

Cojac Portable Buildings Inc (PA) 405 232-1229
2820 W Reno Ave Oklahoma City (73107) *(G-5800)*

Cojac Portable Buildings Inc 405 232-1229
2820 W Reno Ave Oklahoma City (73107) *(G-5801)*

Coldren Enterprises Corp 405 239-2205
1821 Nw 6th St Oklahoma City (73106) *(G-5802)*

Cole Defense LLC 214 934-5473
413 W Britton Rd Apt 142 Oklahoma City (73114) *(G-5803)*

Cole Industrial Services Inc 580 775-0949
12469 S Woodside Dr Caddo (74729) *(G-1232)*

Coleman Heating and AC, Norman Also called York International Corporation *(G-5204)*

Coleman Press 918 437-0000
13737 E 31st Pl Tulsa (74134) *(G-9467)*

Coleman Roof Services, Coleman Also called Harrison Roof Truss Co *(G-1795)*

Collector Knives, Sulphur Also called Mike Latham *(G-8838)*

Colliers Cabinets 405 377-3508
5320 E 32nd Ave Stillwater (74074) *(G-8669)*

Collins Cnstr Fabrications LLC 918 522-4855
13191 Se 1060th Ave Talihina (74571) *(G-8906)*

Collins Copier Service, Oklahoma City Also called Richard B Collins *(G-7015)*

Collins Metal Company Inc 405 373-3309
4710 N Grove Ave Warr Acres (73122) *(G-11316)*

Collins Quality Printing 918 744-0077
3236 E 15th St Tulsa (74104) *(G-9468)*

Color Express 214 384-0887
121 Palmer Pt Mead (73449) *(G-4365)*

Color-Rite Inc 405 354-3644
600 S Ranchwood Blvd Yukon (73099) *(G-11708)*

Colorado Fuel Manufacturers 918 877-5102
3845 S 103rd East Ave # 101 Tulsa (74146) *(G-9469)*

Colorcomm 918 398-7777
4134 E 49th St Tulsa (74135) *(G-9470)*

Colpitt Charles H Oil Prod, Collinsville Also called Charles H Colpitt *(G-1805)*

Colston Building, Ardmore Also called Colston Corporation *(G-269)*

Colston Corporation 580 223-1309
10 W Main St Ste 406 Ardmore (73401) *(G-269)*

Colt Express 918 455-2658
4110 S 100th East Ave Tulsa (74146) *(G-9471)*

Colt Ferrell Industries LLC 580 439-6106
273814 E 1810 Rd Comanche (73529) *(G-1835)*

Colter Bay LLC 405 842-7622
1217 Glenbrook Ter Nichols Hills (73116) *(G-4858)*

Columbia Development Corp 918 587-5521
15 E 5th St Ste 3530 Tulsa (74103) *(G-9472)*

Columbia Rehabilitation Svcs 405 359-2741
301 S Bryant Ave Ste B100 Edmond (73034) *(G-2360)*

Coman & Associates, Tulsa Also called Protype Inc *(G-10576)*

Coman Pattern Works 918 270-1775
3806 S Granite Ave Tulsa (74135) *(G-9473)*

Comanche Bit Service Inc 580 439-6424
2 Miles North Hwy 81 Comanche (73529) *(G-1836)*

Comanche County Tag Agency, Lawton Also called County of Comanche *(G-3911)*

Comanche Exploration Co LLC 405 755-5900
6520 N Western Ave Oklahoma City (73116) *(G-5804)*

Comanche Leather Works Inc 580 439-6276
104a Village Mall Comanche (73529) *(G-1837)*

Comanche Nation Pub Info Off 580 492-3381
584 Nw Bingo Rd Lawton (73507) *(G-3909)*

Comanche Resources, Oklahoma City Also called Comanche Exploration Co LLC *(G-5804)*

Comanche Sports Group LLC 580 439-5230
281645 E 1790 Rd Comanche (73529) *(G-1838)*

Comanche Times 580 439-6500
404 N Rodeo Dr Comanche (73529) *(G-1839)*

Combined Resources Corporation 405 341-7700
1001 Medical Park Blvd Edmond (73013) *(G-2361)*

Combotronics Inc 918 543-3300
2800 Lock And Dam Rd Inola (74036) *(G-3656)*

Combs Oilfield Services Inc 580 571-2315
405 W Hanks Trl Woodward (73801) *(G-11571)*

Comfort X-Press LLC 405 382-5600
2700 N Highway 99 Seminole (74868) *(G-8366)*

Comgraphx, Broken Arrow Also called Communication Graphics Inc *(G-871)*

Commander Aircraft Corporation 405 366-6454
1600 Westheimer Dr Norman (73069) *(G-4963)*

Commerce Plastics Inc 918 675-4506
900 Main St North Miami (74358) *(G-5206)*

Commercial Brick Corporation 405 257-6613
Old Hwy 270 Wewoka (74884) *(G-11498)*

Commercial Coatings Okla LLC 405 226-8739
1421 N Fordson Dr Oklahoma City (73127) *(G-5805)*

Commercial Electronics, Broken Arrow Also called Michael A Phillips *(G-972)*

Commercial Metals Company 580 634-5046
584 Old Highway 70 Durant (74701) *(G-2218)*

Commercial Metals Company 918 437-5377
3105 E Skelly Dr Tulsa (74105) *(G-9474)*

Commercial Printing, Tulsa Also called Giles Printing Co Inc *(G-9825)*

Commercial Printing, Weatherford Also called Weatherford Press Inc *(G-11459)*

Commercial Printing Marketing 918 494-7072
608 E 3rd St Ste 5 Tulsa (74120) *(G-9475)*

Commercial Property Research 918 481-8882
8301 E 74th Pl Tulsa (74133) *(G-9476)*

Commercial Resin Division, Pryor Also called Interplastic Corporation *(G-7971)*

Commercial Services Corp 405 634-8888
6619 S Western Ave Ste A Oklahoma City (73139) *(G-5806)*
Communication Graphics Inc 918 258-6502
1765 N Juniper Ave Broken Arrow (74012) *(G-871)*
Community Publishers 918 273-1040
Hwy 169th N Nowata (74048) *(G-5211)*
Community Publishers Inc 918 259-7500
510 W Atlanta St Broken Arrow (74012) *(G-872)*
Community Racks LLC 405 210-7950
9325 Nw 75th St Yukon (73099) *(G-11709)*
Compadres Trading Co 405 816-9911
40 Ne 46th St Oklahoma City (73105) *(G-5807)*
Company De Roth 405 348-3754
2104 Hummingbird Ln Edmond (73034) *(G-2362)*
Compass Drilling, Enid *Also called Good Oil Company (G-2963)*
Compass Energy Operating LLC 405 594-4141
204 N Robinson Ave # 1300 Oklahoma City (73102) *(G-5808)*
Compass Manufacturing LLC 405 735-3518
11935 N Intrstate 44 Svce Oklahoma City (73173) *(G-5809)*
Compass Production Partners LP (PA) 405 594-4141
204 N Robinson Ave # 1300 Oklahoma City (73102) *(G-5810)*
Compass Unlimited Inc 918 824-1644
1421 W 440 Pryor (74361) *(G-7955)*
Competitive Action Sports LLC 405 474-7777
6000 Oak Tree Rd Edmond (73025) *(G-2363)*
Complete Computer Company, Oklahoma City *Also called Martindale Consultants Inc (G-6534)*
Complete Cooling Systems Inc 405 272-0453
717 Sw 4th St Oklahoma City (73109) *(G-5811)*
Complete Energy LLC 405 748-2200
220 N Sara Rd Yukon (73099) *(G-11710)*
Complete Energy Services Inc 405 748-2211
220 N Sara Rd Yukon (73099) *(G-11711)*
Complete Energy Services Inc 580 249-3200
302 N Independence St # 12 Enid (73701) *(G-2933)*
Complete Graphics Inc 405 232-8882
1010 Sw 3rd St Oklahoma City (73109) *(G-5812)*
Complete Graphics Service, Oklahoma City *Also called Complete Graphics Inc (G-5812)*
Complete Sign Service LLC 405 273-7567
133 Betty Dr Tecumseh (74873) *(G-8909)*
Complete Wireline Svcs Ltd Co 405 317-0001
3207 N 9th Ave Purcell (73080) *(G-8003)*
Completion Oil Tools LLC 580 478-6263
1802 N Grand St Enid (73701) *(G-2934)*
Completion Services, Oklahoma City *Also called Superior Energy Services LLC (G-7228)*
Component Services LP 405 787-7180
8316 Sw 8th St Oklahoma City (73128) *(G-5813)*
Compound Software LLC 405 912-3301
3600 S Bryant Ave Moore (73160) *(G-4509)*
Compressco Inc (HQ) 405 677-0221
1313 Se 25th St Oklahoma City (73129) *(G-5814)*
Compressco Inc 405 787-2808
8224 Sw 3rd St Oklahoma City (73128) *(G-5815)*
Compressco Partners Sub Inc (HQ) 405 677-0221
101 Park Ave Ste 1200 Oklahoma City (73102) *(G-5816)*
Comptech Computer Tech Inc 937 228-2667
2601 Liberty Pkwy Ste 102 Oklahoma City (73110) *(G-5817)*
Compton Industries LLC 405 496-6269
720 Greenfield Dr Yukon (73099) *(G-11712)*
Compusign Vinyl Graphics 580 762-4930
2704 Canterbury Ave Ponca City (74604) *(G-7807)*
Computalog Wireline Inc 918 225-1187
Rr 2 Box 2020 Cushing (74023) *(G-1926)*
Computer Assistance 405 399-2422
10413 N Indian Meridian Jones (73049) *(G-3743)*
Computer Dlers Rcyclers Globl 405 749-7989
615 W Wilshire Blvd # 11 Oklahoma City (73116) *(G-5818)*
Computer Solutions + LLC (PA) 405 259-9603
12228 Ne 23rd St Choctaw (73020) *(G-1534)*
Computer Technology Soltn 918 607-2136
1825 S Umbrella Ct Broken Arrow (74012) *(G-873)*
Computer Xpressions, Tulsa *Also called Linda L Hargraves (G-10163)*
Conbraco Industries Inc 704 841-6000
300 N Industrial Pkwy Westville (74965) *(G-11482)*
Concept Aircraft LLC 405 620-1701
818 Hawthorne Pl Edmond (73003) *(G-2364)*
Concessions Mfg Co LLC 918 786-5100
34320 S 620 Rd Grove (74344) *(G-3262)*
Concorde Resource Corporation 918 689-9510
111 S Main St Eufaula (74432) *(G-3099)*
Concorde Resources Corporation 918 291-3200
1030 W Main St Jenks (74037) *(G-3700)*
Concrete Products Inc 405 427-8686
2107 Ne 10th St Oklahoma City (73117) *(G-5819)*
Concrete Supply House, Norman *Also called Construction Supply House Inc (G-4964)*
Cone Solvents, Oklahoma City *Also called Frontier Logistical Svcs LLC (G-6123)*
Confed Oil Incorporated (PA) 918 582-0018
2121 S Columbia Ave # 200 Tulsa (74114) *(G-9477)*
Confederite Welding LLC 918 407-1635
508 W 10th Ave Bristow (74010) *(G-773)*
Conley Machine Inc 918 770-3234
19553 S 145th West Ave Sapulpa (74066) *(G-8261)*
Connelly Paving Company, Oklahoma City *Also called Connelly Ready-Mix Con LLC (G-5820)*
Connelly Ready-Mix Con LLC 405 943-8388
917 N Tulsa Ave Ste A Oklahoma City (73107) *(G-5820)*
Conner Industries Inc 918 696-5885
Us Hwy 59 N Stilwell (74960) *(G-8787)*
Connie Pirple 405 375-4468
123 N 11th St Kingfisher (73750) *(G-3792)*
Connor-Winfield Corp 405 273-1257
41001 Wolverine Rd Shawnee (74804) *(G-8440)*
Conoco Inc 580 767-3456
100 S Pine St Ponca City (74601) *(G-7808)*
Conocophillips 918 977-6002
315 S Johnstone Ave Bartlesville (74003) *(G-467)*
Conocophillips Company 580 243-6000
909 S Main St Elk City (73644) *(G-2795)*
Conocophillips Company 281 293-1000
315 S Johnstone Ave Bartlesville (74003) *(G-468)*
Conrady, Jeffery L, Kingfisher *Also called Sign of Times (G-3814)*
Considilated Fabrications 918 224-3563
7963 S Regency Dr Tulsa (74131) *(G-8997)*
Consoldted Fabrication Constrs 918 224-3500
7963 S Regency Dr Tulsa (74131) *(G-8998)*
Consoldted Fbrction Cnstructor 918 224-3500
7963 S Regency Dr Tulsa (74131) *(G-8999)*
Consoldted Trbine Spclists LLC 918 367-9665
24323 S 385th West Ave Bristow (74010) *(G-774)*
Consolidated Builders Supply 405 631-3033
1450 Exchange Ave Oklahoma City (73108) *(G-5821)*
Constien and Associates Inc 918 272-9099
7750 N Owasso Expy Ste A Owasso (74055) *(G-7554)*
Construction Supply House Inc 405 214-9366
1013 Hearthstone Norman (73072) *(G-4964)*
Contact Process Piping 405 948-9125
100 N Quapah Ave Ste D Oklahoma City (73107) *(G-5822)*
Contech Enterprises LLC (PA) 918 341-6232
14241 E 450 Rd Claremore (74017) *(G-1609)*
Contech Mfg Inc 918 341-6232
14241 E 450 Rd Claremore (74017) *(G-1610)*
Contemporary Cabinets Inc 405 330-4592
308 Westland Dr Edmond (73013) *(G-2365)*
Continental Battery Company 918 259-0662
509 N Redbud Ave Ste G Broken Arrow (74012) *(G-874)*
Continental Carbon Company 580 763-8100
1006 E Oakland Ave Ponca City (74601) *(G-7809)*
Continental Industries 918 284-9013
2416 S Joplin Ave Tulsa (74114) *(G-9478)*
Continental Oil & Refining Co 918 266-4420
E Of City Catoosa (74015) *(G-1313)*
Continental Resources Inc (PA) 405 234-9000
20 N Broadway Oklahoma City (73102) *(G-5823)*
Continental Resources Inc 580 883-2838
3 S Of Ringwood Ringwood (73768) *(G-8086)*
Continental Stoneworks Inc 918 835-6725
10026a S Mingo Rd Ste 168 Tulsa (74133) *(G-9479)*
Continental Wire Cloth LLC (PA) 918 794-0334
11240 S James Ave Jenks (74037) *(G-3701)*
Continental-Brokers & Cons Inc 405 232-1534
1530 W Main St Oklahoma City (73106) *(G-5824)*
Continntal Oil Gas Enrgy Ntwrk 214 636-2401
7121 S Santa Fe Ave Oklahoma City (73139) *(G-5825)*
Control Devices Inc 918 258-6068
1801 N Juniper Ave Broken Arrow (74012) *(G-875)*
Control Devices Intl Inc 918 258-6068
1801 N Juniper Ave Broken Arrow (74012) *(G-876)*
Control Products Unlimited Inc 918 786-1801
24570 S 647 Rd Grove (74344) *(G-3263)*
Conway Custom Marble Co 580 357-3757
202 Se Park Ave Lawton (73501) *(G-3910)*
Conyer Signs 405 755-0061
809 Nw 143rd St Edmond (73013) *(G-2366)*
Cook Compression 405 677-3153
6836 Pat Ave Oklahoma City (73149) *(G-5826)*
Cook Compression 918 254-0660
5411 S 125th East Ave Tulsa (74146) *(G-9480)*
Cook Machine Company 580 252-1699
3920 S 13th St Duncan (73533) *(G-2099)*
Cook Oil Company, Wewoka *Also called Doyle Cook (G-11500)*
Cook Processing 918 542-5796
2603 E St Sw Miami (74354) *(G-4392)*
Cook Roustabout LLC 405 410-7951
6574 S Kelly Ave Guthrie (73044) *(G-3310)*
Cook's Portable Shop Welding, Piedmont *Also called Cooks Contact Welding Inc (G-7758)*
Cooks Contact Welding Inc 405 373-0059
14832 Nw Expressway Piedmont (73078) *(G-7758)*

ALPHABETIC

(PA)=Parent Co (HQ)=Headquarters (DH)=Div Headquarters
2020 Oklahoma Directory of Manufacturers & Processors
543

Cooks Fence & Iron Co Inc 405 681-2301
3725 S Meridian Ave Oklahoma City (73119) ***(G-5827)***
Cookshack Inc 580 765-3669
2405 Sykes Blvd Ponca City (74601) ***(G-7810)***
Cookson Hills Publishers Inc 918 775-4433
111 N Oak St Sallisaw (74955) ***(G-8143)***
Cool Baby Inc 405 755-1100
16800 Kingsley Rd Edmond (73012) ***(G-2367)***
Cool Billet Customs 580 216-0104
2133 3rd St Woodward (73801) ***(G-11572)***
Cool Green Roofing Supply LLC 918 860-7525
712 S 8th St Broken Arrow (74012) ***(G-877)***
Cool Hard Hat Inc 918 812-7636
2511 S Cincinnati Ave Tulsa (74114) ***(G-9481)***
Coolbodispa 405 420-9785
111 24th Ave Nw Ste 120-A Norman (73069) ***(G-4965)***
Cooley Creek Printing 918 835-8200
6825 E 15th St Tulsa (74112) ***(G-9482)***
Cooley Enterprises Inc 918 437-6900
10755 E Admiral Pl Tulsa (74116) ***(G-9483)***
Cooling Products Inc 918 251-8588
500 N Pecan Ave Broken Arrow (74012) ***(G-878)***
Coop's Buttons, Oklahoma City *Also called Barbara Chaple* ***(G-5526)***
Cooper Cabinet Systems Inc 405 528-7220
4019 N Walnut Ave Oklahoma City (73105) ***(G-5828)***
Cooper Cabinets Inc 405 528-7220
4019 N Walnut Ave Oklahoma City (73105) ***(G-5829)***
Cooper Consulting LLC 918 427-7171
472440 E 1070 Rd Muldrow (74948) ***(G-4632)***
Cooper Contract Pumping Svc 580 487-3552
Rr 1 Box 101 Forgan (73938) ***(G-3169)***
Cooper Creek Manufacturing Inc 405 729-4446
Rr 1 Box 97a Loyal (73756) ***(G-4130)***
Cooper Machinery Services Inc 713 354-4068
2216 Se 15th St Oklahoma City (73129) ***(G-5830)***
Cooper Marketing Solutions, Tulsa *Also called Adventure Publishing LLC* ***(G-9113)***
Cooper Wrecker Service 918 639-7381
52500 S 34900 Rd Pawnee (74058) ***(G-7703)***
Cooperton Plant, Mountain View *Also called Dolese Bros Co* ***(G-4627)***
Coorstek 800 821-6110
7700 S Bryant Ave Oklahoma City (73149) ***(G-5831)***
Coorstek Inc 405 601-4371
7700 S Bryant Ave Oklahoma City (73149) ***(G-5832)***
Coorstek Oklahoma City, Oklahoma City *Also called Coorstek Inc* ***(G-5832)***
Cope Plastics Inc 405 528-5697
310 Ne 31st St Oklahoma City (73105) ***(G-5833)***
Copeland Hot Oil Service LLC 405 853-2179
526 N Oak Ave Hennessey (73742) ***(G-3452)***
Copes Woodworking 918 698-2104
9928 S 107th East Ave Tulsa (74133) ***(G-9484)***
Coppedge Septic Tank 918 371-4549
Highway 169 & 156th St N Collinsville (74021) ***(G-1806)***
Copper Accents By Jerry 918 724-8473
12808 S Memorial Dr # 107 Bixby (74008) ***(G-618)***
Copper Cup Images 918 337-2781
117 W 5th St Ste 410 Bartlesville (74003) ***(G-469)***
Copper Kiln LLC 918 272-5200
122 S Main St Owasso (74055) ***(G-7555)***
Copperhead Coatings LLC 580 532-6243
419 E Ash St Pond Creek (73766) ***(G-7889)***
Copperhead Industries 918 712-9927
2651 E 21st St Ste 405 Tulsa (74114) ***(G-9485)***
Copy Box Inc 918 257-8000
56414 E 230 Rd Afton (74331) ***(G-115)***
Copy Fast Printing Inc 405 947-7468
3629 Nw 50th St Oklahoma City (73112) ***(G-5834)***
Copy Write Incorporated 918 224-1148
1602 S Main St Sapulpa (74066) ***(G-8262)***
Copypasta Publishing 580 236-4071
904 N Park Dr Broken Bow (74728) ***(G-1188)***
Copyshop Printing Downtown, Tulsa *Also called Litgistix LLC* ***(G-10167)***
Cord & Pleat Design Inc 918 622-7676
24212 E Highway 51 Broken Arrow (74014) ***(G-1117)***
Cordell Beacon The, Cordell *Also called Wesner Publications Company* ***(G-1865)***
Cordray Candle Company, Oklahoma City *Also called Lasting Impressions Gifts Inc* ***(G-6455)***
Core Laboratories LP 918 834-2337
4616 N Mingo Rd Tulsa (74117) ***(G-9486)***
Core Manufacturing LLC 405 747-1980
3623 N Star Dr Stillwater (74075) ***(G-8670)***
Coreslab Structures Okla Inc 405 632-4944
817 Se 55th St Oklahoma City (73129) ***(G-5835)***
Coreslab Structures Oklahoma 405 672-2325
7000 S Sunnylane Rd Oklahoma City (73135) ***(G-5836)***
Coreslab Structures Tulsa Inc 918 438-0230
3206 N 129th East Ave Tulsa (74116) ***(G-9487)***
Coretec Group Inc (PA) 918 494-0505
6804 S Canton Ave Ste 150 Tulsa (74136) ***(G-9488)***
Cork and Bottle Wine and 405 318-6842
9621 High Noon Rd Yukon (73099) ***(G-11713)***
Cornelius Oil Inc 918 247-6743
21301 W 191st St S Kellyville (74039) ***(G-3762)***
Cornelius Peteroleum, Kellyville *Also called Cornelius Oil Inc* ***(G-3762)***
Corner Copy & Printing LLC 405 801-2020
770 Deans Row Ave Norman (73069) ***(G-4966)***
Cornerstone Leather 817 598-0367
179867 N 2800 Rd Comanche (73529) ***(G-1840)***
Cornerstone Petroleum Oper LLC 817 730-5200
20 E 5th St Ste 1300 Tulsa (74103) ***(G-9489)***
Cornerstone Quarries Inc 918 647-2117
16511 Mckeown Rd Cameron (74932) ***(G-1256)***
Cornerstone Welding 918 387-2538
1609 S Underwood Yale (74085) ***(G-11681)***
Corona Technical Services LLC 918 398-8052
6914 S Yorktown Ave # 115 Tulsa (74136) ***(G-9490)***
Coronado Petroleum Corporation 405 232-9700
105 N Hudson Ave Ste 800 Oklahoma City (73102) ***(G-5837)***
Coronado Resources MGT LLC 918 591-3500
4745 E 91st St Ste 200 Tulsa (74137) ***(G-9491)***
Corp Comm Oil & Gas Div 405 375-5570
101 S 6th St Kingfisher (73750) ***(G-3793)***
Corpo Commission OK 580 332-3441
1318 Cradduck Rd Ada (74820) ***(G-27)***
Corpo Commission OK 405 521-4683
2101 N Lincoln Blvd # 480 Oklahoma City (73105) ***(G-5838)***
Corporate Image Inc 918 516-8376
10305 E 94th Ct N Owasso (74055) ***(G-7556)***
Corporate Image Apparel LLC 405 659-8264
11100 Roxboro Ave # 2314 Oklahoma City (73162) ***(G-5839)***
Corporate To Causal Screen 918 686-6688
1305 N Main St Muskogee (74401) ***(G-4662)***
Corporate To Csual Screen Prtg 918 686-6688
1305 N Main St Muskogee (74401) ***(G-4663)***
Corrpro Companies Inc 918 245-8791
11616 W 59th St S Sand Springs (74063) ***(G-8172)***
Corrugated Services LP 405 672-1695
7216 S Bryant Ave Oklahoma City (73149) ***(G-5840)***
Corser Group Inc 918 749-6456
2849 E 35th St Tulsa (74105) ***(G-9492)***
Corter Enterprises LLC 405 326-7001
1472 County Road 1190 Tuttle (73089) ***(G-11190)***
Costume Fun House, Oklahoma City *Also called Dean Johnson* ***(G-5911)***
Cotton Candi Creations LLC 580 471-6550
927 E Broadway St Altus (73521) ***(G-151)***
Cougar Drilling Solutions USA 405 789-4945
9505 W Reno Ave Oklahoma City (73127) ***(G-5841)***
Coulter Oil Field Services LLC 580 504-0813
567 Pinewood Trails Dr Ardmore (73401) ***(G-270)***
Council Oak Resources LLC 918 513-0900
1 W 3rd St Ste 1000 Tulsa (74103) ***(G-9493)***
Council Stainless & Shtmtl 405 787-4400
7918 Nw 10th St Oklahoma City (73127) ***(G-5842)***
Council Stainless and Shtmtl, Oklahoma City *Also called Pro Stainless & Shtmtl LLC* ***(G-6906)***
Counter Canter Inc 405 321-8326
2500 Mcgee Dr Ste 147 Norman (73072) ***(G-4967)***
Counterbattery Press LLC 405 794-2885
2216 Ne 8th St Moore (73160) ***(G-4510)***
Countertop Werks Inc 405 943-1988
3800 Nw 39th St Oklahoma City (73112) ***(G-5843)***
Countrstrike Lghtning Prtction 405 863-8480
2421 Sw 90th Pl Oklahoma City (73159) ***(G-5844)***
Country Connection News Inc 405 797-3648
315 Main St Eakly (73033) ***(G-2278)***
Country Crafts 918 247-6144
236 And A Half W Buffalo Kellyville (74039) ***(G-3763)***
Country Home Meat Company 405 341-0267
2775 E Waterloo Rd Edmond (73034) ***(G-2368)***
Country Leisure Inc 405 799-7745
3001 N Service Rd Moore (73160) ***(G-4511)***
County Democrat 405 273-8888
226 N Broadway Ave Shawnee (74801) ***(G-8441)***
County of Carter 580 657-4050
Hwy 70 Lone Grove (73443) ***(G-4116)***
County of Comanche 580 355-3810
902 Sw 38th St Lawton (73505) ***(G-3911)***
County of Oklahoma 918 456-3622
5102 S Muskogee Ave Tahlequah (74464) ***(G-8859)***
County of Tillman 580 597-3097
204 3rd St Chattanooga (73528) ***(G-1389)***
Countywide News Inc 405 598-3793
108 E Washington St Tecumseh (74873) ***(G-8910)***
Coupling Specialties Inc 281 457-2000
1300 S Meridian Ave # 501 Oklahoma City (73108) ***(G-5845)***
Cove Petroleum Corporation 918 584-5291
114 E 5th St Ste 300 Tulsa (74103) ***(G-9494)***
Covercraft Industries LLC (PA) 405 238-9651
100 Enterprise Pauls Valley (73075) ***(G-7655)***
Covers Plus Inc 405 670-2221
1200 Se 34th St Ste 1 Oklahoma City (73129) ***(G-5846)***

ALPHABETIC SECTION
Crosby Custom Woodwork

Covia Holdings Corporation ... 580 456-7772
3rd & Walling St Roff (74865) **(G-8107)**
Covington Aircrafts, Okmulgee *Also called Abbott Industries Inc* **(G-7492)**
Covington Oil Co Inc ... 405 842-8727
901 Nw 63rd St Ste 102 Oklahoma City (73116) **(G-5847)**
Cowan Printing & Litho Inc ... 405 789-1961
803 Schumann Ct Tuttle (73089) **(G-11191)**
Cowans Millwork Inc ... 918 357-3725
24620 E 91st St S Broken Arrow (74014) **(G-1118)**
Cowboy Compost ... 405 853-0462
17067 E 672 Rd Hennessey (73742) **(G-3453)**
Cowboy Copy Center (PA) ... 405 372-8099
514 S Washington St Stillwater (74074) **(G-8671)**
Cowboy Covers Inc ... 405 624-2270
5601 W 6th Ave Stillwater (74074) **(G-8672)**
Cowboy Pmpg Unit Sls Repr LLC ... 405 853-7170
600 W Jack Choate Ave Hennessey (73742) **(G-3454)**
Coweta American, Wagoner *Also called Berkshire Hathaway Inc* **(G-11276)**
Cox Machine & Tool, Oklahoma City *Also called Cox Machine and Tool* **(G-5848)**
Cox Machine and Tool ... 405 681-1445
5301 Sw 25th St Oklahoma City (73128) **(G-5848)**
Cox Motor Co Henryetta LLC ... 918 652-0202
1007 N 5th St Henryetta (74437) **(G-3503)**
Coyote Enterprises Inc ... 918 486-8411
27301 E 121st St S Coweta (74429) **(G-1875)**
Coyote Run Vineyard LLC ... 918 785-4727
9564 N 429 Rd Adair (74330) **(G-108)**
Cozy Cub Products LLP ... 405 386-2879
19112 Newsom Rd Newalla (74857) **(G-4807)**
CP & C Services ... 918 497-6606
443954 E 340 Rd Vinita (74301) **(G-11251)**
CP Aerospace LLC ... 580 355-5064
2202 Se 165th St Lawton (73501) **(G-3912)**
CP Energy Holdings LLC (PA) ... 405 513-6006
317 Lilac Dr Ste 200 Edmond (73034) **(G-2369)**
CP Energy LLC ... 405 513-6006
317 Lilac Dr Ste 200 Edmond (73034) **(G-2370)**
CP Industries Inc ... 918 468-2230
500 Industrial Rd Grove (74344) **(G-3264)**
CP Kelco US Inc ... 918 758-2600
1200 W 20th St Okmulgee (74447) **(G-7498)**
CP Solutions Inc ... 918 664-6642
2757 S Memorial Dr Tulsa (74129) **(G-9495)**
Cpk Manufacturing LLC ... 405 290-7788
5400 Nw 5th St Oklahoma City (73127) **(G-5849)**
Cplp LLC ... 580 355-5515
212 Se Park Ave Lawton (73501) **(G-3913)**
Cpv Keenan Renewable Enrgy LLC ... 580 698-2278
197352 E County Road 51 Woodward (73801) **(G-11573)**
Cr Services LLC ... 918 295-7600
1717 S Boulder Ave # 400 Tulsa (74119) **(G-9496)**
Cr Stripes Ltd Co ... 405 946-8577
3636 Nw 51st St Oklahoma City (73112) **(G-5850)**
Crackshot Corporation ... 918 838-1272
3616 N Columbia Ave Tulsa (74110) **(G-9497)**
Craco Truss Post Frame Sup LLC ... 918 457-1111
30257 S Sizemore Rd Park Hill (74451) **(G-7641)**
Cradduck John ... 405 360-0251
9004 E Franklin Rd Norman (73026) **(G-4968)**
Cradduck Manufacturing Company, Norman *Also called Cradduck John* **(G-4968)**
Craft Printed Envelopes Inc ... 918 249-8887
5663 N Mingo Rd Tulsa (74117) **(G-9498)**
Crafty Manatees LLC ... 405 630-5415
938 Timber Xing Blanchard (73010) **(G-708)**
Craig Elder Oil and Gas LLC ... 405 917-7860
1004 Nw 139th Street Pkwy Edmond (73013) **(G-2371)**
Craig Welding, Butler *Also called Arthur Craig* **(G-1220)**
Craigs Oklahoma Pride LLC ... 405 224-6410
1301 S 3rd St Chickasha (73018) **(G-1451)**
Crain Displays & Exhibits Inc ... 918 585-9797
1510 S Memorial Dr Tulsa (74112) **(G-9499)**
Cramer Fence Company ... 918 865-4529
93 Lake Country Mannford (74044) **(G-4180)**
Crandall and Sanders Inc ... 405 375-3242
110 N Main St Kingfisher (73750) **(G-3794)**
Crandall Sanders Plbg Elec Eng, Kingfisher *Also called Crandall and Sanders Inc* **(G-3794)**
Crandell Salvage Incorporated ... 918 429-0001
904 Old Highway 69 Mcalester (74501) **(G-4287)**
Crane Carrier Co ... 918 836-1651
1925 N Sheridan Rd Tulsa (74115) **(G-9500)**
Crane Carrier Company ... 918 286-2300
5874 S Mingo Rd Tulsa (74146) **(G-9501)**
Crane Machinery Repair ... 918 349-2264
48176 State Highway 99 Pawhuska (74056) **(G-7683)**
Crane Manufacturing Inc ... 918 838-8800
5531 E Admiral Pl Tulsa (74115) **(G-9502)**
Crankshaft Service Company ... 405 685-7553
4600 S Macarthur Blvd Oklahoma City (73179) **(G-5851)**
Cravens Backhoe Service LLC ... 580 661-3652
844 N 15th St Thomas (73669) **(G-8941)**
Crawford Cabinetry & Cnstr Inc ... 918 453-0164
17877 W Murrel Rd Tahlequah (74464) **(G-8860)**
Crawford Granite Works ... 918 423-3020
Rr 6 Box 5 McAlester (74501) **(G-4288)**
Crawley Petroleum Corporation (PA) ... 405 232-9700
105 N Hudson Ave Ste 800 Oklahoma City (73102) **(G-5852)**
Crawson Corporation ... 918 427-8400
110872 S 4760 Rd Muldrow (74948) **(G-4633)**
Crazy Socks Productions Inc ... 580 618-1228
4374 Gddard Youth Camp Rd Sulphur (73086) **(G-8830)**
CRC Evans Weighting Systems ... 918 438-2100
10700 E Independence St Tulsa (74116) **(G-9503)**
CRC-Evans Pipeline Intl Inc ... 918 438-2100
10700 E Independence St Tulsa (74116) **(G-9504)**
Crd Oil Corp ... 918 885-4527
401 N Price Ave Hominy (74035) **(G-3581)**
Creative Apparel and More Inc ... 918 682-1283
1116 W Broadway St Muskogee (74401) **(G-4664)**
Creative Blessings ... 918 302-0734
2755 Krebs Lake Rd McAlester (74501) **(G-4289)**
Creative Cabinets ... 580 762-9500
126 E Hartford Ave Ponca City (74601) **(G-7811)**
Creative Jewelry Designers, Tulsa *Also called Jewel Tech Mfg Inc* **(G-10044)**
Creative Marketing Promotion, Edmond *Also called 4524 LLC* **(G-2285)**
Creative Media ... 918 245-3779
712 N Cleveland Ave Sand Springs (74063) **(G-8173)**
Creative Monogramming EMB ... 580 762-6694
108 N 2nd St Ponca City (74601) **(G-7812)**
Creative Ornamental Inc ... 918 540-1600
58250 E 100 Rd Miami (74354) **(G-4393)**
Creative Packaging Inc ... 918 587-0347
2837 Charles Page Blvd Tulsa (74127) **(G-9505)**
Creative Pins ... 405 390-2038
1147 Whisper Ln Choctaw (73020) **(G-1535)**
Creative Printing, Norman *Also called Liv3design LLC* **(G-5060)**
Creative Pultrusions Inc ... 405 979-2141
11935 S Intrstate 44 Svc Oklahoma City (73173) **(G-5853)**
Creative Quilting, Tulsa *Also called Doris Winford* **(G-9598)**
Creative Spaces ... 405 341-8710
6400 Industrial Blvd Edmond (73034) **(G-2372)**
Creative Stitches By C S ... 918 418-9049
50991 E 243 Rd Afton (74331) **(G-116)**
Creativestitch LLC ... 405 664-1144
1312 Nw 172nd St Edmond (73012) **(G-2373)**
Creditmaster Software, Tulsa *Also called Creditpoint Software LLC* **(G-9506)**
Creditpoint Software LLC ... 918 376-9440
20 E 5th St Ste 900 Tulsa (74103) **(G-9506)**
Creek International Rig Corp ... 918 585-8221
8 E 3rd St Tulsa (74103) **(G-9507)**
Creek Nation Foundation Inc ... 918 683-1825
3420 W Peak Blvd Muskogee (74401) **(G-4665)**
Creekside Woodworks ... 405 528-5432
4421 N Barnes Ave Oklahoma City (73112) **(G-5854)**
Crematory Manufacturing & Svc ... 918 446-1475
6802 S 65th West Ave Tulsa (74131) **(G-9000)**
Crescent Companies LLC ... 405 721-5511
5749 Nw 132nd St Oklahoma City (73142) **(G-5855)**
Crescent Ready Mix Inc ... 405 853-1599
14417 W Cooksey Rd Crescent (73028) **(G-1910)**
Crescent Services LLC (PA) ... 405 603-1200
5721 Nw 132nd St Oklahoma City (73142) **(G-5856)**
Crescent Services LLC ... 580 225-4346
200 Hughes Access Rd Elk City (73644) **(G-2796)**
Crest Energy, Tulsa *Also called Crest Resources Inc* **(G-9508)**
Crest Resources Inc ... 918 585-2900
15 E 5th St Ste 3650 Tulsa (74103) **(G-9508)**
Crimson Hot Shot Service LLC ... 469 358-2005
1110 Missouri St Norman (73071) **(G-4969)**
Cris Choate Welding Inc ... 405 853-2792
432 N Oak Ave Hennessey (73742) **(G-3455)**
Critical Components Inc ... 405 212-9166
2400 Purdue Dr Oklahoma City (73128) **(G-5857)**
Critical Components-Oil & Gas, Oklahoma City *Also called Critical Components Inc* **(G-5857)**
Critical Infrastructur ... 918 640-9301
11258 S Franklin Ave Jenks (74037) **(G-3702)**
Crm Energy Inc ... 405 848-5420
600 N Walker Ave Ste 201 Oklahoma City (73102) **(G-5858)**
Croan Custom Woodworks LLC ... 405 227-2067
134 W Lily Ln Edmond (73025) **(G-2374)**
Crochetangel ... 918 282-3056
8316 S Kalanchoe Ave Broken Arrow (74011) **(G-879)**
Cromwells Inc ... 580 234-6561
302 E Maine Ave Enid (73701) **(G-2935)**
Cromwells Press, Enid *Also called Cromwells Inc* **(G-2935)**
Croppinsville ... 405 521-2711
208 W 17th St Owasso (74055) **(G-7557)**
Crosby Custom Woodwork ... 405 802-9615
1016 Nw 8th St Moore (73160) **(G-4512)**

ALPHABETIC

Crosby Group LLC — ALPHABETIC SECTION

Crosby Group LLC 918 834-4611
2857 Dawson Rd Tulsa (74110) *(G-9509)*

Crosby Group LLC (PA) 918 834-4611
2801 Dawson Rd Tulsa (74110) *(G-9510)*

Crosby US Acquisition Corp (HQ) 918 834-4611
2801 Dawson Rd Tulsa (74110) *(G-9511)*

Crosby Worldwide Limited 918 834-4611
2801 Dawson Rd Tulsa (74110) *(G-9512)*

Cross Roll Inc (PA) 405 348-9663
2604 Nw 159th St Edmond (73013) *(G-2375)*

Cross Shadows Inc 405 262-9777
1502 Ridgecrest Dr El Reno (73036) *(G-2707)*

Cross Timbers Operating Co 405 232-4011
210 Park Ave Ste 2350 Oklahoma City (73102) *(G-5859)*

Crossfire Production Svcs LLC 580 254-3766
46005 S County Road 202 Woodward (73801) *(G-11574)*

Crosslands A A Rent-All Sls Co 405 366-8878
2451 E Imhoff Rd Norman (73071) *(G-4970)*

Crossroad Holsters LLC 405 317-7405
2216 Nw 118th St Oklahoma City (73120) *(G-5860)*

Crossroads Led LLC 918 504-6595
10710 E 119th Ct N Collinsville (74021) *(G-1807)*

Crosstimbers Hot Shot Svcs LLC 405 740-2900
4200 E Highway 37 Tuttle (73089) *(G-11192)*

Crow Creek Energy LLC 918 970-6706
11920 S Erie Ave Tulsa (74137) *(G-9513)*

Crowley Oil & Mfg 918 744-8129
5312 E 26th St Tulsa (74114) *(G-9514)*

Crown Energy Company 405 526-0111
1117 Nw 24th St Oklahoma City (73106) *(G-5861)*

Crown Energy Technology Okla 405 348-9954
6024 Nw 178th St Edmond (73012) *(G-2376)*

Crown Geochemistry Inc 918 392-0334
427 S Boston Ave Tulsa (74103) *(G-9515)*

Crown Midstream LLC 405 753-1955
701 Cedar Lake Blvd 210 Oklahoma City (73114) *(G-5862)*

Crown Neon Signs Inc 918 437-7446
5676 S 107th East Ave Tulsa (74146) *(G-9516)*

Crown Oil Field Services LLC 580 363-0269
2103 Ridgeway Rd Blackwell (74631) *(G-679)*

Crown Paint Co., Oklahoma City *Also called Crown Paint Company (G-5863)*

Crown Paint Company (PA) 405 232-8580
1801 W Sheridan Ave Oklahoma City (73106) *(G-5863)*

Crown Products Inc (PA) 918 446-4591
912 W Skelly Dr Tulsa (74107) *(G-9517)*

Crucible LLC 405 579-2700
110 E Tonhawa St Norman (73069) *(G-4971)*

Cryogas Services LLC 580 252-6200
7024 N Highway 81 Duncan (73533) *(G-2100)*

Crystal Lake Farms, Jay *Also called Liberty Free Range Poultry LLC (G-3682)*

Crystal River Operating Co LLC 405 510-0440
100 Park Ave Ste 400 Oklahoma City (73102) *(G-5864)*

Crystal Tech, Duncan *Also called Crystaltech Inc (G-2101)*

Crystal Works, Shawnee *Also called Connor-Winfield Corp (G-8440)*

Crystaltech Inc 580 252-8893
1601 N 5th St Duncan (73533) *(G-2101)*

CSC Inc (PA) 580 994-6110
202 N Main St Mooreland (73852) *(G-4587)*

CSC Inc 580 938-2533
329 S Main St Shattuck (73858) *(G-8420)*

CSC Inc 580 256-2409
202 N Main St Mooreland (73852) *(G-4588)*

CSC Oil Co 918 287-1138
2803 Cleo Ln Pawhuska (74056) *(G-7684)*

CSC Oil Company, Pawhuska *Also called CSC Oil Co (G-7684)*

Cse Bliss Manufacturing LLC 580 749-4895
1415 W Summit Ave Ponca City (74601) *(G-7813)*

Csi 319 274-5005
8455 E 590 Rd Catoosa (74015) *(G-1314)*

Csi Aerospace Inc 918 258-1290
2020 W Detroit St Ste 1 Broken Arrow (74012) *(G-880)*

Csi Compressco Sub Inc 918 250-9471
6140 S 104th East Ave Tulsa (74133) *(G-9518)*

Csi Measurement LLC 580 234-4979
3730 Cactus Flts Enid (73703) *(G-2936)*

CTI Services LLC (HQ) 918 584-2220
1261 E 25th St Tulsa (74114) *(G-9519)*

Ctm Welding & Fabrication LLC 405 408-4628
824 W Beaumont Ave Yale (74085) *(G-11682)*

Ctsa LLC 405 478-3501
14004 Pecan Hollow Ter Edmond (73013) *(G-2377)*

Cudd Energy Services, Krebs *Also called Cudd Pressure Control Inc (G-3849)*

Cudd Energy Services 405 756-4344
1210 Nw 4th St Lindsay (73052) *(G-4057)*

Cudd Holdings, Oklahoma City *Also called Cudd Operating Corp (G-5865)*

Cudd Operating Corp 405 841-1144
6305 Waterford Blvd # 130 Oklahoma City (73118) *(G-5865)*

Cudd Pressure Control, Lindsay *Also called Cudd Energy Services (G-4057)*

Cudd Pressure Control Inc 580 243-5890
6001 Oklahoma 6 Elk City (73644) *(G-2797)*

Cudd Pressure Control Inc 405 756-4337
1210 Se 4th St Lindsay (73052) *(G-4058)*

Cudd Pressure Control Inc 580 225-6922
900 S Merritt Rd Elk City (73644) *(G-2798)*

Cudd Pressure Control Inc 405 382-2803
1701 Ray Davis Blvd Seminole (74868) *(G-8367)*

Cudd Pressure Control Inc 918 423-0160
405 A Highway 270 E Krebs (74554) *(G-3849)*

Cudd Pumping Services, Seminole *Also called Cudd Pressure Control Inc (G-8367)*

Cudd Pumping Services 580 256-7000
2627 3rd St Woodward (73801) *(G-11575)*

Cuesta Petroleum 405 878-0744
23 E 9th St Ste 403 Shawnee (74801) *(G-8442)*

Culbreath Oil & Gas Co Inc 918 749-3508
3501 S Yale Ave Tulsa (74135) *(G-9520)*

Culligan, Chickasha *Also called Wright Water Corporation (G-1525)*

Cumberland Pipeline Co LLC 918 359-0980
6100 S Yale Ave Ste 2050 Tulsa (74136) *(G-9521)*

Cummings Oil Company 405 948-1818
4917 N Portland Ave Oklahoma City (73112) *(G-5866)*

Cummins - Allison Corp 405 321-1411
680 24th Ave Sw Norman (73069) *(G-4972)*

Cummins Construction Co, Ada *Also called RLC Holding Co Inc (G-82)*

Cummins Construction Co Inc (HQ) 580 233-6000
1420 W Chestnut Ave Enid (73703) *(G-2937)*

Cummins Construction Company, Enid *Also called RLC Holding Co Inc (G-3048)*

Cummins Enterprises Inc 405 232-9022
202 E Sheridan Ave Oklahoma City (73104) *(G-5867)*

Cummins Inc 405 946-4481
5800 W Reno Ave Oklahoma City (73127) *(G-5868)*

Cummins Southern Plains LLC 918 234-3240
16525 E Skelly Dr Tulsa (74116) *(G-9522)*

Cummins Southern Plains LLC 405 946-4481
5800 W Reno Ave Oklahoma City (73127) *(G-5869)*

Cundiff Custom Fabrication LLC 405 372-8204
318 E Harned Ave Stillwater (74075) *(G-8673)*

Cunningham Graphics Inc 918 337-9100
1209 Sw Frank Phllips Blv Bartlesville (74003) *(G-470)*

Cupcake-A-Licious, Oklahoma City *Also called Enchanted Delights LLC (G-6034)*

Cupcakes & Sweets Galore 405 641-7760
8301 Willow Creek Blvd Oklahoma City (73162) *(G-5870)*

Cupcakes By Lu 918 671-0599
12681 S 88th East Ave Bixby (74008) *(G-619)*

Cupid Foundations Inc 580 363-1935
318 N 29th St Blackwell (74631) *(G-680)*

Cura Telehealth Wellness LLC 918 513-1062
4920 E 113th St Tulsa (74137) *(G-9523)*

Curing System Components Inc 405 381-9794
2916 E Highway 37 Tuttle (73089) *(G-11193)*

Current Alternative News Advg 918 431-0392
328 E Downing St Tahlequah (74464) *(G-8861)*

Curry Shades LLC 918 779-3902
3116 E 45th St Tulsa (74105) *(G-9524)*

Curtis Jewelry 580 924-0041
207 W Main St Durant (74701) *(G-2219)*

Curtiss-Wright Corporation 405 515-8235
1012 24th Ave Nw Ste 100 Norman (73069) *(G-4973)*

Curzon Operating Company Ltd 405 235-8180
4509 N Classen Blvd # 20 Oklahoma City (73118) *(G-5871)*

Cushing Screen Printing LLC 646 267-3513
1024 E Leland St Cushing (74023) *(G-1927)*

Cushing Truss Manufacturing 918 387-2080
1010 N Highway 18 Yale (74085) *(G-11683)*

Cust O Bend 918 241-0514
1350 S 74th West Ave Tulsa (74127) *(G-9525)*

Cust-O-Bend Inc 918 241-0514
7512 Charles Page Blvd Tulsa (74127) *(G-9526)*

Cust-O-Fab LLC (PA) 918 245-6685
8888 W 21st St Sand Springs (74063) *(G-8174)*

Cust-O-Fab Specialty Svcs LLC (HQ) 918 245-6685
8888 W 21st St Sand Springs (74063) *(G-8175)*

Custer Enterprises Inc 580 371-9588
450 W Broadway Mannsville (73447) *(G-4195)*

Custom 4 X 4 Fabrication 405 799-7599
11825 Se 109th St Oklahoma City (73165) *(G-5282)*

Custom Automotive Mfg 918 258-2900
1116 E Memphis St Broken Arrow (74012) *(G-881)*

Custom Cabinet Services 918 340-9015
5328 E Admiral Pl Tulsa (74115) *(G-9527)*

Custom Carbide Application LLC 580 799-5575
19848 E 1160 Rd Elk City (73644) *(G-2799)*

Custom Catings of Broken Arrow 918 258-0996
27100 E 111th St S Coweta (74429) *(G-1876)*

Custom Components & Logistics, Catoosa *Also called CCL Acquisition LLC (G-1309)*

Custom Cutting Millwork Inc 405 942-3196
3905 Amelia Ave Oklahoma City (73112) *(G-5872)*

Custom Design By Roberts 918 664-0466
9756 E 55th Pl Tulsa (74146) *(G-9528)*

Custom Design Fabrication LLC 918 773-5691
450122 Highway 64 Vian (74962) *(G-11238)*
Custom Drawers and Cabinetry 918 322-9819
1243 E 142nd St Glenpool (74033) *(G-3232)*
Custom EMB & More By Rose, Broken Arrow *Also called Jlm2 LLC (G-946)*
Custom Embriodary, Grove *Also called First Impression Custom EMB (G-3270)*
Custom Embroidery & Gifts LLC 405 240-7950
950852 S 3360 Rd Wellston (74881) *(G-11468)*
Custom Expressignz 580 252-2868
1306 W Sycamore Ave Duncan (73533) *(G-2102)*
Custom Generator Power, Noble *Also called Custom Manufacturing & Maint (G-4877)*
Custom Graphics 580 477-4597
521 N Main St Altus (73521) *(G-152)*
Custom Identification Products 405 745-1010
3131 S Council Rd Oklahoma City (73179) *(G-5873)*
Custom Jewelry By Robert Ellis, Tulsa *Also called Elco Tech Engineering (G-9651)*
Custom Lea Sad & Cowboy Decor 918 335-2277
401300 Us Highway 60 Bartlesville (74006) *(G-471)*
Custom Manufacturing Inc 405 692-6311
4101 Sw 113th St Oklahoma City (73173) *(G-5874)*
Custom Manufacturing & Maint 405 872-1000
427 S Front St Noble (73068) *(G-4877)*
Custom Mechanical Equipment 262 642-9803
2101 Hall Blvd Ponca City (74601) *(G-7814)*
Custom Metal Fab, Fairfax *Also called James Case (G-3119)*
Custom Metal Works 918 231-4151
2333 E 450 Pryor (74361) *(G-7956)*
Custom Metal Works Inc 918 388-1881
1830 N 106th East Ave Tulsa (74116) *(G-9529)*
Custom Molding Services Inc 918 333-4872
3509 Minnesota St Bartlesville (74006) *(G-472)*
Custom Monograms & Lettering 405 495-8586
7801 Nw 23rd St Bethany (73008) *(G-574)*
Custom Mser Lvstk Pre Mix Whse 580 336-2053
9 Memorial Dr Perry (73077) *(G-7729)*
Custom Mser Lvstk Pre-Mix Whse, Perry *Also called Custom Mser Lvstk Pre Mix Whse (G-7729)*
Custom Picture Framing, Clinton *Also called Southwest Interiors Inc (G-1769)*
Custom Powder Coating & Dustle 580 382-8000
2101 Hall Blvd Ponca City (74601) *(G-7815)*
Custom Products Company, Cyril *Also called James D Johnson (G-1975)*
Custom Screen Printers 918 423-3696
502 E Wyandotte Ave McAlester (74501) *(G-4290)*
Custom Seating Incorporated 918 682-4400
341 S 41st St E Muskogee (74403) *(G-4666)*
Custom Shutters Inc 918 924-3489
1904 W Albany St Broken Arrow (74012) *(G-882)*
Custom Signs 918 225-2749
947 E Main St Cushing (74023) *(G-1928)*
Custom Signs By Jade, McAlester *Also called Signs By Jade (G-4335)*
Custom Software Systems Inc 405 524-1919
2250 Nw 39th St Ste 103 Oklahoma City (73112) *(G-5875)*
Custom Stainless, Oklahoma City *Also called Breshears Enterprises Inc (G-5624)*
Custom Storm Shelters LLC 405 209-5525
7225 Nw 16th St Oklahoma City (73127) *(G-5876)*
Custom Tile & Marble Inc 405 810-8515
8220 N Western Ave Oklahoma City (73114) *(G-5877)*
Custom Time & Neon Co Inc 405 364-9139
1809 Atchison Dr Norman (73069) *(G-4974)*
Custom Upholstery 918 342-3489
1618 N Chambers Ter Claremore (74017) *(G-1611)*
Custom Upholstery Contracting 405 236-3505
1209 W Main St Oklahoma City (73106) *(G-5878)*
Custom Vinyl Signs By Chas 580 351-4058
1722 Jesse L Davenport St Lawton (73501) *(G-3914)*
Custom WD Fbers Cdar Mulch LLC 405 745-2270
616 N Macarthur Blvd Oklahoma City (73127) *(G-5879)*
Custom Wood Craft Construction 405 262-5228
2424 Sunset Dr El Reno (73036) *(G-2708)*
Custom Wood Creations 580 512-6994
507 Ne Carver Ave Lawton (73507) *(G-3915)*
Custom Wood Creations LLC 405 517-8689
17068 W County Road 76 Crescent (73028) *(G-1911)*
Custom Wood Works 918 279-1333
11741 S 305th East Ave Coweta (74429) *(G-1877)*
Custom Woodcraft, El Reno *Also called Custom Wood Craft Construction (G-2708)*
Custom Woodwork Inc 918 224-4276
221 E Hobson Ave Sapulpa (74066) *(G-8263)*
Custom Yarmuck Scrap Proc LLC 580 354-9134
907 Sw Rr St Lawton (73501) *(G-3916)*
Customized Fctry Interiors LLC 405 848-9999
8320 S Shields Blvd Oklahoma City (73149) *(G-5880)*
Cuts Custom Butchering LLC 918 534-1382
Highway 75 Dewey (74029) *(G-2019)*
Cutting Edge Arms LLC 405 603-6723
6840 Nw 11th St Oklahoma City (73127) *(G-5881)*
Cutting Edge Industries Corp 918 523-7373
6931 S 66th St East Ave Tulsa (74133) *(G-9530)*
Cutting Edge Machine Inc 580 658-5036
115 E Main St Marlow (73055) *(G-4226)*
Cutting Edge Robotic Tech LLC 918 247-6012
50 E Buffalo St Kellyville (74039) *(G-3764)*
Cutting Edge Signs 918 688-1878
3012 Aerie Dr Edmond (73013) *(G-2378)*
Cutting Edge Signs & Graphics 405 262-4300
1302 S Choctaw Ave El Reno (73036) *(G-2709)*
Cutting Edge Technologies LLC 918 284-6069
8913 N 151st East Ave Owasso (74055) *(G-7558)*
Cutting Edge Woodwork LLC 918 706-1143
820 W 5th St Skiatook (74070) *(G-8537)*
Cvr Energy 405 286-0341
14000 Quail Springs Pkwy Oklahoma City (73134) *(G-5882)*
Cvr Energy Inc 913 982-0500
113 E Robert S Kerr Blvd Wynnewood (73098) *(G-11666)*
Cwg Welding Services LLC 580 819-1045
23983 E 1013 Rd Weatherford (73096) *(G-11403)*
Cws Wireline LLC 405 828-4225
600 S Hwy 81 Dover (73734) *(G-2039)*
Cyanostar Energy Inc 918 582-2069
616 S Boston Ave Ste 402 Tulsa (74119) *(G-9531)*
Cyber Stitchery 405 329-6018
2702 S Pickard Ave Norman (73072) *(G-4975)*
Cyclonic Valve Company 918 317-8200
2349 W Vancouver St Broken Arrow (74012) *(G-883)*
Cymstar LLC 918 251-8100
12214 E 55th St Tulsa (74146) *(G-9532)*
Cymstar LLC (PA) 918 251-8100
1700 W Albany St Ste 500 Broken Arrow (74012) *(G-884)*
Cynergy Software Corp LLC 405 603-2953
5770 Nw Expressway Warr Acres (73132) *(G-11317)*
Cypress Energy Holdings LLC (PA) 918 748-3900
5727 S Lewis Ave Ste 300 Tulsa (74105) *(G-9533)*
Cypress Energy Holdings II LLC (HQ) 918 748-3900
5727 S Lewis Ave Ste 500 Tulsa (74105) *(G-9534)*
Cypress Energy Partners LP (PA) 918 748-3900
5727 S Lewis Ave Ste 300 Tulsa (74105) *(G-9535)*
Cypress Scents 918 629-8610
17405 Tracy Rd Inola (74036) *(G-3657)*
Cytec Industrial Mtls OK Inc 918 252-3922
2514 N Hemlock Cir Broken Arrow (74012) *(G-885)*
Cytovance Biologics Inc 405 319-8310
100 Ne 30th St Oklahoma City (73105) *(G-5883)*
D & B Oil Field Services Inc 580 883-2897
223 W Melrose St Ringwood (73768) *(G-8087)*
D & B Printing Inc 405 632-0055
9124 S Walker Ave Oklahoma City (73139) *(G-5884)*
D & B Processing LLC 918 619-6452
9750 S 219th East Ave Broken Arrow (74014) *(G-1119)*
D & C Tool Grinding Inc 918 689-9799
114500 Dogwood Gln Checotah (74426) *(G-1392)*
D & D Design & Mfg Inc 405 745-2126
5701 S Rockwell St Oklahoma City (73179) *(G-5885)*
D & D Stud Welding, Cartwright *Also called David Dollar (G-1283)*
D & D Stud Welding LLC Proj 888 965-4155
1242 Boat Club Rd Cartwright (74731) *(G-1282)*
D & G Machine 918 486-3501
13746 S 337th East Ave Coweta (74429) *(G-1878)*
D & J Enterprises 918 906-3951
10902 S 77th East Ave Tulsa (74133) *(G-9536)*
D & J Filter Ltd Liability Co 405 376-5343
2320 S Portland Ave Oklahoma City (73108) *(G-5886)*
D & L Enclosures 918 396-7355
14630 N 56th West Ave Skiatook (74070) *(G-8538)*
D & L Printing, Cushing *Also called Leda Grimm (G-1942)*
D & M Directional Drilling LLC 405 221-2959
1722 Seran Dr Wewoka (74884) *(G-11499)*
D & M Oil Flds Svc Csing Crews 918 623-0492
Intersection Hwy48& Hwy56 Okemah (74859) *(G-5267)*
D & M Steel Manufacturing 405 631-5027
2320 S Agnew Ave Oklahoma City (73108) *(G-5887)*
D & P Tank Service Inc (PA) 580 762-4526
3833 Highway 60 Ponca City (74604) *(G-7816)*
D & P Tank Service Inc 580 762-4526
1000 S Pine St Ponca City (74601) *(G-7817)*
D & S Distributing 580 763-3773
520 N Elm St Ponca City (74601) *(G-7818)*
D & S Refinishing 580 233-4351
1915 W Maine Ave Enid (73703) *(G-2938)*
D & S Surveying, Broken Arrow *Also called David Lacy (G-889)*
D & T Swabbing & Well Service 405 853-7045
Rr 3 Hennessey (73742) *(G-3456)*
D & V Manufacturing Inc 918 245-7858
105 Wellston Park Rd Sand Springs (74063) *(G-8176)*
D & W Cupp Trucking LLC 580 821-6844
317 E Kennemer Sayre (73662) *(G-8339)*
D & Z Metal Fabrication 918 456-3841
19334 S Welling Rd Welling (74471) *(G-11466)*

ALPHABETIC

D and L Machine Inc..405 433-2233
  1 123a Cashion (73016) *(G-1286)*
D and M Resources Inc..405 375-4602
  1617 Anna Pl Kingfisher (73750) *(G-3795)*
D and N Fabrication...918 224-4400
  230 E Jackson Ave N Sapulpa (74066) *(G-8264)*
D and R Directional Drilling....................................405 208-1399
  13525 Cimarron Dr Crescent (73028) *(G-1912)*
D B R Construction, Alva Also called Dbr Construction Services Inc *(G-181)*
D B W Inc..405 354-6211
  201 Oak Ave Yukon (73099) *(G-11714)*
D C A, Cushing Also called DCA Inc *(G-1929)*
D C Ignition Co Inc..580 332-0878
  412 W Main St Ada (74820) *(G-28)*
D C Jones Machine Co..918 786-6855
  818 Industrial Rd Grove (74344) *(G-3265)*
D D R, Oklahoma City Also called Direct Downhole Rentals LLC *(G-5948)*
D Diamond Enterprises Inc......................................918 827-4727
  6490 Creager Rd Mounds (74047) *(G-4612)*
D E M Operations Inc...580 388-4315
  16489 County Road 1060 Lamont (74643) *(G-3865)*
D E Ziegler Art Craft Supply...................................918 584-2217
  6 N Lewis Ave Tulsa (74110) *(G-9537)*
D Gala..580 468-4980
  707 N Main St Guymon (73942) *(G-3347)*
D I V C O Inc..918 836-9101
  2806 N Sheridan Rd Tulsa (74115) *(G-9538)*
D J Welding...405 386-4620
  15232 Se 104th St Choctaw (73020) *(G-1536)*
D Lloyd Hollingsworth..918 587-3533
  5 N Cheyenne Ave Tulsa (74103) *(G-9539)*
D Parks Enterprises LLC..405 315-1994
  234 Dotson Dr Sand Springs (74063) *(G-8177)*
D R Topping Saddlery..918 273-2812
  1223 E Cherokee Ave Nowata (74048) *(G-5212)*
D Signs & Wonders LLC...405 932-4585
  108 E 9th St Paden (74860) *(G-7635)*
D Vontz LLC..918 622-3600
  7208 E 38th St Tulsa (74145) *(G-9540)*
D Willams Pipe Insptn Poly Ll................................405 426-7776
  947 Blue Bird Ter Purcell (73080) *(G-8004)*
D&L Manufacturing Inc...918 587-3504
  1924 S 49th West Ave Tulsa (74107) *(G-9541)*
D&L Manufacturing Inc...918 587-3504
  1915 S 49th West Ave Tulsa (74107) *(G-9542)*
D&L Oil Tools, Tulsa Also called D&L Manufacturing Inc *(G-9542)*
D&P Welding Corp..405 624-0170
  12520 E Airport Rd Glencoe (74032) *(G-3220)*
D&R Property Services Inc.......................................405 677-2178
  817 Se 88th St Ste 10 Oklahoma City (73149) *(G-5888)*
D&S Dirtwork and Small Eqp..................................580 485-8933
  3351 E Allison Rd Atoka (74525) *(G-404)*
D-A Welding & Fab LLC..580 641-1189
  10705 Highway 29 Marlow (73055) *(G-4227)*
D-K Metal Form Company Inc................................580 228-3516
  122 W D Ave Waurika (73573) *(G-11362)*
Da Bomb Cupcakes...918 261-3595
  6722 S 110th East Ave Tulsa (74133) *(G-9543)*
Da Vinci Broom LLC..580 224-1424
  710 Franklin Ct Ardmore (73401) *(G-271)*
Da/Pro Rubber Inc (PA)..918 258-9386
  601 N Poplar Ave Broken Arrow (74012) *(G-886)*
Da/Pro Rubber Inc...918 272-7799
  6712 N Canton Ave Tulsa (74117) *(G-9544)*
Da/Pro Rubber Inc...918 299-5480
  4505 E 100th St Tulsa (74137) *(G-9545)*
Dad's Guide To Wdw, Edmond Also called Ctsa LLC *(G-2377)*
Daddy Hinkles Inc..918 358-2129
  2000 W Caddo St Cleveland (74020) *(G-1721)*
Daddy Russ Customs & Wldg LLC..........................405 623-9709
  16562 W Camp Dr Cashion (73016) *(G-1287)*
Dads Machine & Custom Welding.........................580 470-8334
  105 E Bois D Arc Ave Duncan (73533) *(G-2103)*
Dagwood Energy Inc..918 582-6604
  427 S Boston Ave Ste 604 Tulsa (74103) *(G-9546)*
Daily Dental Solutions Inc......................................405 373-3299
  1213 Piedmont Rd N # 108 Piedmont (73078) *(G-7759)*
Daily OCollegian...405 744-7371
  106 Paul Miller Building Stillwater (74078) *(G-8674)*
Daily Perk LLC...405 567-5491
  101731 S Highway 99 Prague (74864) *(G-7924)*
Daily Stop..405 495-5556
  108 S Rockwell Ave Oklahoma City (73127) *(G-5889)*
Daily Times...918 825-3292
  105 S Adair St Pryor (74361) *(G-7957)*
Dakk Mfg LLC..405 395-2139
  14102 Highway 177 Shawnee (74804) *(G-8443)*
Dakota Exploration LLC...918 806-8687
  110 W 7th St 210 Tulsa (74119) *(G-9547)*

Dale Case Homes Inc..405 755-5055
  13424 Railway Dr Oklahoma City (73114) *(G-5890)*
Dale E Dyer...918 519-0189
  3530 S 39th West Ave Tulsa (74107) *(G-9548)*
Dale Kreimeyer Co..405 789-9499
  3211 N Wilburn Ave Bethany (73008) *(G-575)*
Dale Miller Group LLC (PA)....................................580 353-4600
  102 Se B Ave Lawton (73501) *(G-3917)*
Dale P Jackson..580 332-1988
  222 E 9th St Ada (74820) *(G-29)*
Dale Rogers Training Ctr Inc..................................580 481-6170
  Altus Air Force Base Altus (73522) *(G-153)*
Dale-Co Industries LLC...918 864-2041
  6170 Country Dr Pryor (74361) *(G-7958)*
Dales Manufacturing Co...405 631-8988
  8717 S I 35 Service Rd Oklahoma City (73149) *(G-5891)*
Dallas Hermetic Company Inc................................214 634-1744
  4101 Se 85th St Oklahoma City (73135) *(G-5892)*
Dallas Morning News, Oklahoma City Also called Dmn Inc *(G-5954)*
Dalmarc Enterprises Inc..405 942-8703
  4040 S I 35 Service Rd Oklahoma City (73129) *(G-5893)*
Dalmarc Signs, Oklahoma City Also called Dalmarc Enterprises Inc *(G-5893)*
Damar Manufacturing Co Inc................................918 445-2445
  3332 W 45th Pl Tulsa (74107) *(G-9549)*
Damsel In Defense..580 233-6609
  4209 Lexington Pl Enid (73703) *(G-2939)*
Dan Abney..405 527-0675
  25507 State Highway 59 Wayne (73095) *(G-11366)*
Dan Andrews Limited, Oklahoma City Also called Andrews Welding *(G-5444)*
Dan Quyen Newspaper...405 691-2522
  1320 Sw 116th Pl Oklahoma City (73170) *(G-5283)*
Dancey-Meador Publishing Co...............................580 762-9359
  118 N Oak St Ponca City (74601) *(G-7819)*
Danco Inspection Service Inc.................................405 691-5752
  1324 Sw 155th St Oklahoma City (73170) *(G-5284)*
Danco Machine, Broken Arrow Also called Daniel W Duensing *(G-1120)*
Dandee Donuts..580 332-7700
  109 S Mississippi Ave Ada (74820) *(G-30)*
Dandelion Welding and Fabg LLC..........................405 431-8138
  7921 Nw 83rd St Oklahoma City (73132) *(G-5894)*
Dandy Donuts..580 924-7872
  111 N 8th Ave Durant (74701) *(G-2220)*
Daniel E and Marl Newport....................................918 445-9129
  1103 W 49th St Tulsa (74107) *(G-9550)*
Daniel Garage Door Sales & Svc.............................580 628-3769
  1011 E Oklahoma Ave Tonkawa (74653) *(G-8973)*
Daniel H Finnefrock..918 585-3350
  427 S Boston Ave Ste 614 Tulsa (74103) *(G-9551)*
Daniel P Wollaston..580 768-4694
  6 W Main St Ardmore (73401) *(G-272)*
Daniel R Willits Offices..580 227-2592
  120 N Main St Fairview (73737) *(G-3134)*
Daniel W Duensing...417 781-1850
  3404 E Jersey St Broken Arrow (74014) *(G-1120)*
Danlin Industries Corp...405 853-2559
  431 W Oklahoma St Hennessey (73742) *(G-3457)*
Danlin Industries LLC (PA).....................................580 661-3248
  801 Marshall Rd Clinton (73601) *(G-1747)*
Danny Bowen...405 618-3377
  337215 E 1010 Rd Meeker (74855) *(G-4377)*
Danny Lee Signs..580 832-5256
  11973 N 2240 Rd Cordell (73632) *(G-1857)*
Dannys Bop LLC..405 815-4041
  727 N Morgan Rd Oklahoma City (73127) *(G-5895)*
Dannys Oilfield Services Inc...................................918 645-1651
  605 E 5th Ave Bristow (74010) *(G-775)*
Dans Backhoe & Dozer Service...............................580 256-0865
  20145 E 29 Rd Woodward (73801) *(G-11576)*
Dans Custom Awnings LLC....................................405 601-2703
  3309 E Reno Ave Oklahoma City (73117) *(G-5896)*
Dans Custom Canvas..405 525-2419
  545 Nw 33rd St Oklahoma City (73118) *(G-5897)*
Darby Equipment Co (PA).......................................918 582-2340
  2940 N Toledo Ave Tulsa (74115) *(G-9552)*
Dark Horse Oil Field Svcs LLC................................580 229-0626
  13152 Highway 76 Healdton (73438) *(G-3412)*
Dark Ops Designs..918 269-0049
  26520 Foxen Dr Claremore (74019) *(G-1612)*
Dark Peek Technologies LLC..................................405 316-8551
  2011 W Danforth Rd # 137 Edmond (73003) *(G-2379)*
Darling Ingredients Inc...918 371-2528
  915 N 5th St Collinsville (74021) *(G-1808)*
Darling Oil Corp..580 388-4567
  307 N Main Lamont (74643) *(G-3866)*
Darling Oil Corporation...580 388-6681
  317 N Main St Lamont (74643) *(G-3867)*
Darnell Drilling Inc...405 524-8816
  2250 Nw 39th St Ste 100 Oklahoma City (73112) *(G-5898)*
Darnell Services...918 542-9236
  506 S Main St Miami (74354) *(G-4394)*

ALPHABETIC SECTION

Darr Lift Main Line 580 657-6337
266 Case Cir Ardmore (73401) *(G-273)*

Darrell Lewis 405 867-5768
Rr 2 Box 146 Maysville (73057) *(G-4257)*

Darrell Monroe 405 793-2976
9700 S Sunnylane Rd G Moore (73160) *(G-4513)*

Darrells Drilling Inc 580 925-3854
N Of City On Hwy 9 A Konawa (74849) *(G-3844)*

Darren McIninch 405 912-8403
14000 Sauna Ln Oklahoma City (73165) *(G-5285)*

Dartmouth Journal Service 918 286-3513
6606 S 77th East Ave Tulsa (74133) *(G-9553)*

Dasa Investments Inc 405 820-7703
1900 S Broadway Edmond (73013) *(G-2380)*

Dashskin LLC 918 940-8900
606 N Redbud Ave Broken Arrow (74012) *(G-887)*

Dastar Inc 580 786-8833
511 N 10th St Duncan (73533) *(G-2104)*

Data Systems Consultants 405 445-0886
11332 Marbella Dr Oklahoma City (73173) *(G-5899)*

Data Video Systems, Muskogee *Also called Grw Inc* *(G-4685)*

Databadge, Tulsa *Also called Marvel Photo Inc* *(G-10218)*

Datalog Lwt Inc 405 286-0418
228 Nw 59th St Oklahoma City (73118) *(G-5900)*

Datalog Systems 918 245-3939
410 W 7th St Apt 1428 Tulsa (74119) *(G-9554)*

Datapages Inc 918 584-2555
1444 S Boulder Ave Tulsa (74119) *(G-9555)*

Datebox Inc Okc 253 678-1173
7501 Sw 29th St Oklahoma City (73179) *(G-5901)*

Dathney Inc 405 354-0481
717 Vickery Ave Yukon (73099) *(G-11715)*

Datran Corporation 918 307-2200
4211 W Wichita St Broken Arrow (74012) *(G-888)*

Daube Company 580 223-7403
5 S Commerce St Ste 21 Ardmore (73401) *(G-274)*

Davco Fab Inc 918 757-2504
921 N Main St Jennings (74038) *(G-3739)*

Davco Manufacturing 918 535-2360
724 County Road 2466 Ochelata (74051) *(G-5234)*

Davco Productions Inc 405 266-9832
25980 State Highway 53 Springer (73458) *(G-8621)*

Dave Bolton 205 637-1402
3413 Stone Brook Ct Oklahoma City (73120) *(G-5902)*

Dave's Welding, Watonga *Also called David Adkinson* *(G-11344)*

Davenport Cloaks Inc 918 932-8600
716 S Troost Ave Tulsa (74120) *(G-9556)*

Davenport Oilfield Services 580 465-0314
3075 Meridian Rd Ardmore (73401) *(G-275)*

Davenport Roustabout Service 918 377-2987
349358 E 910 Rd Chandler (74834) *(G-1378)*

Davenports Welding 918 855-9593
10210 S 257th East Ave Broken Arrow (74014) *(G-1121)*

Daves Welding & Dock Svc LLC 918 773-5179
97113 S 4536 Rd Vian (74962) *(G-11239)*

Daves Welding LLC 580 938-2707
218 S Sylvania St Shattuck (73858) *(G-8421)*

David Adkinson 580 623-7301
Rr 1 Watonga (73772) *(G-11344)*

David Bates 918 457-6169
721 E Ward St Tahlequah (74464) *(G-8862)*

David Combs Auto Trim 405 799-7330
813 Nw 8th St Oklahoma City (73106) *(G-5903)*

David D Kuykendall 918 223-5055
8414 W Grandstaff Ripley (74062) *(G-8100)*

David Davis 405 354-6974
16547 W Us Highway 66 El Reno (73036) *(G-2710)*

David Denham Interiors 918 585-3161
1540 S Peoria Ave Tulsa (74120) *(G-9557)*

David Dodd Inc 405 216-5412
2701 Coltrane Pl Ste 6 Edmond (73034) *(G-2381)*

David Dollar 580 965-4155
1463 4th Ave Cartwright (74731) *(G-1283)*

David Gormley 918 845-0443
1609 E Thompson Ave Sapulpa (74066) *(G-8265)*

David Greens Office 918 335-3855
2407 Nowata Pl Ste 304 Bartlesville (74006) *(G-473)*

David Kelso Welding 405 630-7108
304 W Main St Edmond (73003) *(G-2382)*

David Kempe 580 924-6798
3805 W Main St Durant (74701) *(G-2221)*

David L Greene Inc 918 335-3855
2407 Nowata Pl Ste 304 Bartlesville (74006) *(G-474)*

David Lacy 918 519-1873
1233 S Aspen Ct Broken Arrow (74012) *(G-889)*

David Logan 918 739-4231
3510 Crestview Ln Catoosa (74015) *(G-1315)*

David Muzny 405 681-7593
2148 Sw 46th St Oklahoma City (73119) *(G-5904)*

David Piatt 405 542-6974
12101 County Road 1110 Lookeba (73053) *(G-4128)*

David Smith 580 229-1195
189 Golf Course Rd Healdton (73438) *(G-3413)*

David Stevens Cabinetmaker, Tulsa *Also called David Stevens Cabinets & Trim* *(G-9558)*

David Stevens Cabinets & Trim 918 234-0656
10914 E 2nd St Tulsa (74128) *(G-9558)*

David W and Abbe Belcher 918 376-9816
9508 N 139th East Ct Owasso (74055) *(G-7559)*

David W Potts Land Exploration 580 226-3633
301 W Main St Ste 545 Ardmore (73401) *(G-276)*

Davids Trading Yard 918 432-5671
16918 Taft Us Hwy 69 Kiowa (74553) *(G-3837)*

Davidson Oil, Perry *Also called Gerald W Davidson LLC* *(G-7734)*

Davis Bros Oil Producers Inc (PA) 918 584-3581
110 W 7th St Ste 1000 Tulsa (74119) *(G-9559)*

Davis Building, Stigler *Also called Davis Insulated Building Inc* *(G-8632)*

Davis Cabinet Shop 405 391-5527
21001 Se 59th St Newalla (74857) *(G-4808)*

Davis Cnstr Rcvery Sltions LLC 580 500-7527
7428 Nw 131st St Oklahoma City (73142) *(G-5905)*

Davis Gulf Coast Inc 918 587-7782
401 S Boston Ave Ste 2800 Tulsa (74103) *(G-9560)*

Davis Hudson Inc 405 203-0604
2024 Woodland Rd Edmond (73013) *(G-2383)*

Davis Insulated Building Inc (PA) 918 967-2042
300 Sw A St Stigler (74462) *(G-8632)*

Davis Insulated Building Inc 918 423-2636
1539 S Main St McAlester (74501) *(G-4291)*

Davis Machine Shop Inc 405 756-3055
901 State Hwy 76 N Lindsay (73052) *(G-4059)*

Davis Morgan International 405 598-2380
31365 Rattlesnake Hill Rd Macomb (74852) *(G-4141)*

Davis News, The, Davis *Also called Chadwick Paper Inc* *(G-1979)*

Davis Oil Co 918 333-5871
399232 W 1800 Rd Bartlesville (74006) *(G-475)*

Davis Operating Company 918 587-7782
1924 S Utica Ave Ste 1218 Tulsa (74104) *(G-9561)*

Davis Pakeing Co and Bldg Stor, McAlester *Also called Davis Insulated Building Inc* *(G-4291)*

Davis Pipe Testing Company 918 358-5272
Se Of City Cleveland (74020) *(G-1722)*

Davis Printing Company Inc 580 225-2902
217 S Jefferson Ave Elk City (73644) *(G-2800)*

Davis Sign Co 580 225-3121
11112 N 1967 Rd Elk City (73644) *(G-2801)*

Davis Thorpe Co LLC 405 585-9823
216 Se 8th St Moore (73160) *(G-4514)*

Davis Welding, Guymon *Also called Alan Davis* *(G-3344)*

Davis Welding & Fab 405 779-5330
3656 County Street 2850 Ninnekah (73067) *(G-4869)*

Davis Welding Dock Serv 918 457-4071
33333 Highway 82 Cookson (74427) *(G-1849)*

Dawg Pound 580 622-2695
1904 W Broadway Ave Sulphur (73086) *(G-8831)*

Dawson Geophysical Company 405 848-7512
1001 Nw 63rd St Ste 210 Oklahoma City (73116) *(G-5906)*

Dawson-Markwell Exploration Co 405 232-0418
1000 Sw 5th St Oklahoma City (73109) *(G-5907)*

Day Concrete Block Company 580 223-3317
1401 Monroe St Ne Ardmore (73401) *(G-277)*

Day In Sun Landscaping 580 768-4986
757 Church Rd Durant (74701) *(G-2222)*

Daybreak Screen Printing LLC 405 919-6386
2525 Sw 102nd St Oklahoma City (73159) *(G-5908)*

Daylight Donuts, Edmond *Also called Legend Enterprises Inc* *(G-2486)*

Daylight Donuts 918 256-6236
425 S Wilson St Vinita (74301) *(G-11252)*

Daylight Donuts 405 598-8707
421 E Walnut St Tecumseh (74873) *(G-8911)*

Daylight Donuts 580 279-6560
300 S Mississippi Ave Ada (74820) *(G-31)*

Daylight Donuts Inc 405 359-9016
400 S Santa Fe Ave Edmond (73003) *(G-2384)*

Days Wood Products Inc 405 238-6477
220 S Earl St Pauls Valley (73075) *(G-7656)*

Dayton Parts LLC 580 931-9350
1811 W Arkansas St Durant (74701) *(G-2223)*

Daytons Trailer Hitch Inc 918 744-0341
2920 S Yale Ave Tulsa (74114) *(G-9562)*

Db Unlimited LLC 855 437-7766
2876 E 49th St Tulsa (74105) *(G-9563)*

Db Wireline Services Inc 918 389-5038
12558 W Us Highway 270 McAlester (74501) *(G-4292)*

Dbk Contract Pumping 580 225-2009
20208 E 1070 Rd Elk City (73644) *(G-2802)*

Dbmac 50 Inc 918 342-5590
117 W Blue Starr Dr Claremore (74017) *(G-1613)*

Dbr Construction Services Inc 580 327-4335
1704 Oklahoma Blvd Alva (73717) *(G-181)*
Dbr Publishing Co LLC (PA) 918 250-1984
18706 E Stonebridge Dr Owasso (74055) *(G-7560)*
DC Choppers LLC 918 791-1846
30288 E 169th St S Coweta (74429) *(G-1879)*
DC Consulting Inc 405 833-4856
1408 Carltoe Oklahoma City (73143) *(G-5909)*
DC Custom Framing 918 549-8754
405 S Broadway St Skiatook (74070) *(G-8539)*
DC Exteriors & More LLC 918 231-7303
101 Warmac St Warner (74469) *(G-11307)*
DC Industries 405 923-0815
5320 Hart Ln Choctaw (73020) *(G-1537)*
DC Metal Fab, Warner *Also called DC Exteriors & More LLC (G-11307)*
DCA Inc 918 225-0346
1515 E Pine St Cushing (74023) *(G-1929)*
DCI Industries LLC 405 947-2863
13920 S Meridian Ave Oklahoma City (73173) *(G-5910)*
Dcp Midstream 580 653-2641
11272 State Highway 53 Springer (73458) *(G-8622)*
Dcp Midstream LLC 405 362-2200
2609 E Tyler Dr Tuttle (73089) *(G-11194)*
Dcp Midstream LLC 405 705-7400
2445 Nw 164th St Edmond (73013) *(G-2385)*
DDB Unlimited Incorporated (PA) 405 665-2876
8445 Highway 77 N Wynnewood (73098) *(G-11667)*
DDB Unlimited Incorporated 800 753-8459
Rr 1 Box 14 Wynnewood (73098) *(G-11668)*
DDB Unlimited Incorporated 800 753-8459
8580 Highway 77 N Wynnewood (73098) *(G-11669)*
Ddieci Midwest LLC 816 591-1350
3855 S Boulevard Edmond (73013) *(G-2386)*
Deacon Race Cars 405 348-4419
5419 Butte Rd Edmond (73025) *(G-2387)*
Deal USA Today LLC 918 825-7835
9646 W 520 Pryor (74361) *(G-7959)*
Dealers Market 405 789-6455
4409 N State St Warr Acres (73122) *(G-11318)*
Dean Foods Company 918 587-2471
215 N Denver Ave Tulsa (74103) *(G-9564)*
Dean Johnson 405 947-5736
4917 Nw 23rd St Oklahoma City (73127) *(G-5911)*
Dean Printing 580 782-3777
210 E Lincoln St Mangum (73554) *(G-4170)*
Dean's Motor Co, Hollis *Also called Deans Machine & Welding Inc (G-3564)*
Dean's Printing, Mangum *Also called Dean Printing (G-4170)*
Deangel Farms & Winery LLC 405 996-0914
3041 S County Line Ave Blanchard (73010) *(G-709)*
Deans Casing Service 405 379-3495
222 W Main St Holdenville (74848) *(G-3552)*
Deans Grinding Service 918 838-0756
9201 E Admiral Ct Tulsa (74115) *(G-9565)*
Deans Machine & Welding Inc 580 688-3374
1122 E Broadway St Hollis (73550) *(G-3564)*
Deans Typesetting Service 405 842-7247
7416 Broadway Ext Ste J Oklahoma City (73116) *(G-5912)*
Dear John Denim Inc 580 334-6637
7316 Nw 120th St Oklahoma City (73162) *(G-5913)*
Dearinger Printing & Trophy 405 372-5503
605 S Lewis St Stillwater (74074) *(G-8675)*
Deatschwerks LLC 405 217-0701
415 E Hill St Oklahoma City (73105) *(G-5914)*
Debbie Do EMB & Screen Prtg 580 353-2606
207 Sw H Ave Lawton (73501) *(G-3918)*
Debo Dmnsons Laser Cut Engrave 405 843-9098
7210 Broadway Ext Ste 203 Oklahoma City (73116) *(G-5915)*
Debon Energy Oil & Gas, Oklahoma City *Also called Devon Energy Corporation (G-5930)*
Deborah C Montgomery 918 527-9375
15710 E 146th St N Collinsville (74021) *(G-1809)*
Decal Shop 918 783-5206
432332 E 330 Rd Big Cabin (74332) *(G-602)*
Deco Development Company Inc 918 747-6366
2809 E 29th St Tulsa (74114) *(G-9566)*
Decorative Rock & Stone 405 341-8900
501 S Broadway Edmond (73034) *(G-2388)*
Decorative Rock & Stone Inc 405 672-2564
305 Tinker Diagonal St Oklahoma City (73129) *(G-5916)*
Decorator Drapery Mfg Inc 405 942-5613
428 N Ann Arbor Ave Oklahoma City (73127) *(G-5917)*
Dee-Jay Exploration 405 773-8500
5909 Nw Expressway # 500 Oklahoma City (73132) *(G-5918)*
Deep Branch Winery LLC 918 519-5490
20827 W 887 Rd Cookson (74427) *(G-1850)*
Deep Well Tubular Services Inc 405 850-5826
8080 Glade Ave Bldg B Oklahoma City (73132) *(G-5919)*
Deeprock Oil Operating LLC 918 225-7100
321 E Broadway St Cushing (74023) *(G-1930)*
Deeprock Tank Oper Colo LLC 918 225-7100
321 E Broadway St Cushing (74023) *(G-1931)*
Deepwater Chemicals Inc 580 256-0500
196122 E County Road 40 Woodward (73801) *(G-11577)*
Defense Angel LLC 405 476-4222
4013 Chase Cir Yukon (73099) *(G-11716)*
Degge, Bill Oil Field Service, Okemah *Also called Degges Oil Field Service (G-5268)*
Degges Oil Field Service 918 623-1373
711 W Date St Okemah (74859) *(G-5268)*
Dehart Company 580 223-7792
115 4th Ave Sw Ardmore (73401) *(G-278)*
Deisenroth Gas Products Inc 918 742-4769
1924 S Utica Ave Ste 540 Tulsa (74104) *(G-9567)*
Dejay Oil & Gas Inc 405 390-0906
13700 Ne 50th St Choctaw (73020) *(G-1538)*
Del Nero Manufacturing Co 405 364-4800
4801 Pleasant Hill Ln Norman (73026) *(G-4976)*
Del Technical Coatings Inc 405 672-1431
1801 W Reno Ave Oklahoma City (73106) *(G-5920)*
Delaware County Journal Inc 918 253-4322
254 N 5th St Jay (74346) *(G-3680)*
Delco LLC 918 527-8058
9107 S 241st East Ave Broken Arrow (74014) *(G-1122)*
Delenda LLC 918 409-1313
10005 E 100th Pl N Owasso (74055) *(G-7561)*
Delphi International Inc 918 749-9401
1924 S Utica Ave Ste 1201 Tulsa (74104) *(G-9568)*
Delphia Publishing LLC 918 232-8709
129 E Broadway St Drumright (74030) *(G-2055)*
Delson Properties Ltd 405 262-5005
2517 Sw Holloway St El Reno (73036) *(G-2711)*
Delta Oil and Gas LLC 918 599-9800
601 S Boulder Ave # 1310 Tulsa (74119) *(G-9569)*
Delta Plating Inc 918 664-6880
1923 W 48th St Tulsa (74107) *(G-9570)*
Delta Well Logging Svc 405 381-2954
Rr Rt Tuttle (73089) *(G-11195)*
Demco Oil & Gas Company 580 363-4223
1335 S 6th St Blackwell (74631) *(G-681)*
Demco Printing Inc 405 273-8888
226 N Broadway Ave Shawnee (74801) *(G-8444)*
Democrat Chief Publishing Co 580 726-3333
407 S Main St Hobart (73651) *(G-3541)*
Democrat Journal, Stilwell *Also called Indian Nations Communications (G-8791)*
Den-Con Tool Co 405 670-5942
5354 S I 35 Service Rd Oklahoma City (73129) *(G-5921)*
Denali Incorporated (HQ) 713 627-0933
9910 E 56th St N Tulsa (74117) *(G-9571)*
Denham Operating Co 918 585-3161
1540 S Peoria Ave Tulsa (74120) *(G-9572)*
Denham, David Design, Tulsa *Also called Denham Operating Co (G-9572)*
Denneny Oil and Gas LLC 405 229-4885
1201 River Chase Dr Edmond (73025) *(G-2389)*
Dennis Beyer Consulting, Owasso *Also called Master Movers Incorporated (G-7590)*
Dennis Farms Soap Company, Mustang *Also called Melanie Margaret Dennis (G-4782)*
Dennis Grothe Water Svc 405 651-5353
8112 Sw 8th St Oklahoma City (73128) *(G-5922)*
Dennis L Dickerson 405 626-8630
1709 Riviera Dr Tuttle (73089) *(G-11196)*
Dennis Petrilla Enterprises 405 364-4695
813 E Mosier St Norman (73071) *(G-4977)*
Dennis Ranch, Grady *Also called Don Dennis (G-3255)*
Dennis Roberts Welding 405 672-8285
2801 S Eastern Ave Oklahoma City (73129) *(G-5923)*
Dennis Welding 580 658-5669
Nw Of City Marlow (73055) *(G-4228)*
Dentcraft Tools 405 495-0533
8118 Glade Ave Oklahoma City (73132) *(G-5924)*
Dentsply International, Tulsa *Also called Dentsply Sirona Inc (G-9573)*
Dentsply Sirona Inc 918 878-0189
5100 E Skelly Dr Ste 300 Tulsa (74135) *(G-9573)*
Dentsply Sirona Inc 918 878-0001
2131 S Lewis Ave Tulsa (74114) *(G-9574)*
Dereks Pit LLC 405 485-2562
922 S Rockwell Ave Blanchard (73010) *(G-710)*
Derksen Portable Building 918 636-4129
14905 W 96th St S Sapulpa (74066) *(G-8266)*
Dermamedics LLC 405 319-8130
3000 United Founders Blvd # 145 Oklahoma City (73112) *(G-5925)*
Derrick Hoppes 580 667-4373
310 E Main St Tipton (73570) *(G-8958)*
Desert Industrial X Ray LP 918 650-0018
902 E Robertson Hwy Henryetta (74437) *(G-3504)*
Desert Moon Enterprises 918 540-0333
826 K St Nw Miami (74354) *(G-4395)*
Design & Mfg Inc 918 576-6659
1174 N 169th East Ave Tulsa (74116) *(G-9575)*
Design Intelligence Inc LLC (PA) 405 307-0397
8901 72nd St Noble (73068) *(G-4878)*
Design It 405 756-3635
304 S Main St Lindsay (73052) *(G-4060)*

Design My Signs OK LLC 918 923-0175
605 N Lynn Riggs Blvd Claremore (74017) *(G-1614)*
Design Ready Controls Inc 405 605-8234
3512 S Lakeside Dr Oklahoma City (73179) *(G-5926)*
Design Resources, Oklahoma City *Also called Interior Designers Supply Inc (G-6318)*
Design Systems Inc 405 341-7353
1800 Hardy Dr Edmond (73013) *(G-2390)*
Design-It Advertising, Lindsay *Also called Design It (G-4060)*
Designs and Signs By Jillian 405 409-1522
9131 N Midwest Blvd Jones (73049) *(G-3744)*
Designs By Lex LLC 580 280-2557
7 Sw D Ave Lawton (73501) *(G-3919)*
Desired Size 405 314-3704
1148 Ne 5th Ter Oklahoma City (73117) *(G-5927)*
Destin Corporation 580 242-6627
Rr 5 Enid (73701) *(G-2940)*
Destiny Petroleum LLC 281 362-2833
2524 N Broadway St Moore (73160) *(G-4515)*
Devault Enterprises Inc 918 249-1595
7440 E 46th Pl Tulsa (74145) *(G-9576)*
Devco Process Heaters LLC 918 221-9629
2504 E 71st St Ste A Tulsa (74136) *(G-9577)*
Devilbiss Coring Service Inc 405 392-2515
2373 County Road 1207 Blanchard (73010) *(G-711)*
Devine Industrial Systems Inc 405 627-3448
10108 Thompson Ave Yukon (73099) *(G-11717)*
Deviney Contract Pumping LLC 405 428-2192
12607 N County Road 3110 Maysville (73057) *(G-4258)*
Deviney Paraffin Scraping 405 867-5945
Rr 2 Maysville (73057) *(G-4259)*
Devon Energy Corporation 405 235-7798
20 N Broadway Ave # 1500 Oklahoma City (73102) *(G-5928)*
Devon Energy Corporation (PA) 405 235-3611
333 W Sheridan Ave Oklahoma City (73102) *(G-5929)*
Devon Energy Corporation (HQ) 405 235-3611
333 W Sheridan Ave Oklahoma City (73102) *(G-5930)*
Devon Energy International Co (HQ) 405 235-3611
20 N Broadway Ave # 1500 Oklahoma City (73102) *(G-5931)*
Devon Energy Production Co LP (HQ) 405 235-3611
333 W Sheridan Ave Oklahoma City (73102) *(G-5932)*
Devon Gas Services LP (HQ) 405 235-3611
333 W Sheridan Ave Oklahoma City (73102) *(G-5933)*
Devon Gas Services LP 405 228-7543
20 N Broadway Oklahoma City (73102) *(G-5934)*
Devon Industries Inc 405 943-3881
7510 Melrose Ln Oklahoma City (73127) *(G-5935)*
Devon Lube Center Equipment, Oklahoma City *Also called Devon Industries Inc (G-5935)*
Devon Oei Operating Inc (HQ) 405 235-3611
20 N Broadway Oklahoma City (73102) *(G-5936)*
Dewaynes Bbq Sauce Catering 580 363-3394
5700 W Adobe Rd Newkirk (74647) *(G-4847)*
Dewey Chemical Inc 405 848-8611
5801 Broadway Ext Ste 305 Oklahoma City (73118) *(G-5937)*
Dewey County 580 995-3444
Hwy 60 E Vici (73859) *(G-11241)*
Dewey County District 3, Vici *Also called Dewey County (G-11241)*
Dewind Co 580 338-3271
810 Ne 6th St Guymon (73942) *(G-3348)*
Dewitt Trucking & Excavation 580 669-2534
4601 N West Point Rd Glencoe (74032) *(G-3221)*
Dexter Axle Company 405 262-1178
500 Se 27th St El Reno (73036) *(G-2712)*
Dexxon Inc 918 321-9331
732 E Indiana Kiefer (74041) *(G-3778)*
Dgmi.com, Oklahoma City *Also called Mark W McGuffee Inc (G-6528)*
DH Cabinet and Trim Inc 405 376-1709
1350 N Bettys Way Mustang (73064) *(G-4769)*
DH Welding LLC 918 906-6534
26810 E 19th St Yale (74085) *(G-11684)*
Dharma Inc 405 366-1336
3750 W Main St Ste A Norman (73072) *(G-4978)*
Dhr Manufacturing, Rush Springs *Also called H Diamond Resources Inc (G-8121)*
Dhs Tees 405 397-0274
2421 Nw 161st St Edmond (73013) *(G-2391)*
Diabetic Pure Skin Therapy, Oklahoma City *Also called Marie Anastasia Labs Inc (G-6524)*
Diagnostic Center, Tulsa *Also called Hilti Inc (G-9931)*
Dials Race Shop 405 382-4843
3504 N Highway 3 Seminole (74868) *(G-8368)*
Diamond Attachments LLC 580 889-3366
4381 S Mississippi Ave A Atoka (74525) *(G-405)*
Diamond Catchment, Atoka *Also called Diamond Manufacturing Inc (G-406)*
Diamond Cnstr Co Shattuck Inc (PA) 580 256-3385
4220 Oklahoma Ave Woodward (73801) *(G-11578)*
Diamond Dee-Lite Inc 405 793-8166
308 Se 4th St Moore (73160) *(G-4516)*
Diamond Dee-Lite Jewelry, Moore *Also called Diamond Dee-Lite Inc (G-4516)*
Diamond Energy Services LP (PA) 918 764-4000
406 S Boulder Ave Ste 708 Tulsa (74103) *(G-9578)*
Diamond Game Enterprises 405 789-5800
6100 Nw 2nd St Ste 1600 Oklahoma City (73127) *(G-5938)*
Diamond Gypsum LLC 580 623-2868
E0790 Rd Watonga (73772) *(G-11345)*
Diamond Manufacturing Inc 580 889-6202
2801 S Mkokippi Ave Ste A Atoka (74525) *(G-406)*
Diamond Oil Field Services Inc 405 863-1052
6521 Lois Ln Yukon (73099) *(G-11718)*
Diamond Oilfield Services Inc 405 243-7113
7941 N Richland Rd Yukon (73099) *(G-11719)*
Diamond P Forrest Products Co 918 266-2478
10707 E 590 Rd Catoosa (74015) *(G-1316)*
Diamond P Machine LLC 918 396-7192
3875 W 178th St N Skiatook (74070) *(G-8540)*
Diamond R Saddle Shop 918 479-6279
8134 S 448 Rd Rose (74364) *(G-8117)*
Diamond R Wireline LLC 405 361-7933
2901 W Royal Oaks Rd Pauls Valley (73075) *(G-7657)*
Diamond Services, Woodward *Also called Diamond Cnstr Co Shattuck Inc (G-11578)*
Diamond T Trailer Mfg Co 580 587-2432
429157 State Highway 3 Rattan (74562) *(G-8071)*
Diamond Tees 918 665-0815
8335 E 51st St Ste J Tulsa (74145) *(G-9579)*
Diamond Welding Mfg 580 889-7767
Highway 69 S Atoka (74525) *(G-407)*
Diamondback E&P LLC 432 221-7400
515 Central Park Dr Oklahoma City (73105) *(G-5939)*
Diamondback Energy Inc 405 600-0711
9400 Broadway Ext Ste 600 Oklahoma City (73114) *(G-5940)*
Diamondback Energy Services 405 242-4080
14301 Caliber Dr Ste 200 Oklahoma City (73134) *(G-5941)*
Diamondback Energy Svcs LLC (HQ) 405 789-3499
14201 Caliber Dr Ste 300 Oklahoma City (73134) *(G-5942)*
Diamondback Operating LP 918 477-7755
6660 S Sheridan Rd # 250 Tulsa (74133) *(G-9580)*
Diamondback Steel Company Inc 918 686-6340
419 S Cherokee St Muskogee (74403) *(G-4667)*
Diane Barcheers 918 649-0440
821 Byington School Rd McAlester (74501) *(G-4293)*
Diane E Dean 580 775-4203
3633 Sawmill Rd Caddo (74729) *(G-1233)*
Diane Oil Co 405 528-5100
47 Ne 37th St Oklahoma City (73105) *(G-5943)*
Dib 718 LLC 405 525-2151
617 Nw 16th St Oklahoma City (73103) *(G-5944)*
Dicaperl Minerals, Noble *Also called Noble Acquisition LLC (G-4887)*
Dick Hall & Associates 405 202-4301
416 Terrace Pl Norman (73069) *(G-4979)*
Dickson Industries Inc 405 598-6547
Rr 1 Box 234 Tecumseh (74873) *(G-8912)*
Die Block, Skiatook *Also called Diemasters (G-8541)*
Die Hard Properties LLC 405 769-3145
14458 Autumn Dr Choctaw (73020) *(G-1539)*
Die Tech Tool Machine 918 683-3422
1000 S Hwy 251a Okay (74446) *(G-5257)*
Dieco Manufacturing Inc 918 438-2193
15715 E Pine St Tulsa (74116) *(G-9581)*
Diemasters 800 826-2134
77777 Superdie Indus Park Skiatook (74070) *(G-8541)*
Diemer Construction Co LLC 580 628-3052
14211 S 13th St Tonkawa (74653) *(G-8974)*
Dig It Rocks LLC 580 362-6211
638 E Furguson Ave Ponca City (74601) *(G-7820)*
Dig-It Backhoe Trctr Svcs LLC 405 921-2623
1035 Timberridge Rd Harrah (73045) *(G-3376)*
Digger Oil & Gas Co 405 567-2288
815 W 1st St Prague (74864) *(G-7925)*
Digger Oil & Gas Producers, Prague *Also called Digger Oil & Gas Co (G-7925)*
Digi Print LLC (PA) 405 947-0099
4222 N May Ave Oklahoma City (73112) *(G-5945)*
Digi Security Systems LLC (PA) 918 824-2520
11333 E 51st Pl Tulsa (74146) *(G-9582)*
Digii ID LLC 405 662-5504
5534 N Portland Ave Oklahoma City (73112) *(G-5946)*
Digiprint, Oklahoma City *Also called Ross Printing LLC (G-7050)*
Digital Design, Oklahoma City *Also called Resonance Inc (G-7010)*
Digital Doctor 405 618-1416
1950 Nw 16th St Oklahoma City (73106) *(G-5947)*
Digital Interface LLC 405 201-5070
19600b S 609 Rd Fairland (74343) *(G-3124)*
Digital Print Communications, Oklahoma City *Also called Digi Print LLC (G-5945)*
Digital Prints Plus Inc 918 520-7630
5966 E 138th St N Collinsville (74021) *(G-1810)*
Digital Resources Inc 866 823-6328
12626 E 60th St Tulsa (74146) *(G-9583)*
Digital Theory LLC 405 824-6460
425 Golden Oaks Dr Norman (73072) *(G-4980)*
Digital Theory Signs 405 438-0222
3540 Wellsite Dr Norman (73069) *(G-4981)*

ALPHABETIC

Dii, Noble Also called Design Intelligence Inc LLC *(G-4878)*
Dii LLC 405 514-7365
132 W Main St Purcell (73080) *(G-8005)*
Dilbeck Mfg Inc 918 836-1555
1871 N 106th East Ave Tulsa (74116) *(G-9584)*
Dill City Embroidery 580 674-3989
Highway 152 Dill City (73641) *(G-2035)*
Dinks Monogramming & EMB LLC 580 541-4371
718 W Broadway Ave Ste 12 Enid (73701) *(G-2941)*
Direct Communications Inc 918 291-0092
11063 S Memorial Dr Ste D Tulsa (74133) *(G-9585)*
Direct Downhole Rentals LLC 281 531-8881
10005 S Penn Ave Ste C Oklahoma City (73159) *(G-5948)*
Direct Oilfield Services LLC 405 385-4743
633 N Husband St Stillwater (74075) *(G-8676)*
Direct Tank Services, Stillwater Also called Direct Oilfield Services LLC *(G-8676)*
Directional Boring Inc 405 842-8850
5001 N Pennsylvania Ave Oklahoma City (73112) *(G-5949)*
Directional Fluid Disposals 405 626-3261
6801 Camille Ave Oklahoma City (73149) *(G-5950)*
Disa Holding Corp 405 382-6900
1 Pleasant Grove Rd Seminole (74868) *(G-8369)*
Disan Engineering Corporation 918 273-1636
101 Mohawk Dr Nowata (74048) *(G-5213)*
Discoversoft Development LLC 405 840-1235
6602 Trenton Rd Nichols Hills (73116) *(G-4859)*
Discovery Plastics LLC 918 540-2822
3607 28th Ave Ne Miami (74354) *(G-4396)*
Display With Honor Wdwkg LLC 405 659-9894
2724 Sw 115th St Oklahoma City (73170) *(G-5286)*
Distinctive Decor LLC 580 252-9494
901 W Main St Duncan (73533) *(G-2105)*
Distribution Div, Tulsa Also called Webco Industries Inc *(G-11100)*
Distribution Systems Oklahoma, Oklahoma City Also called Oklahoma Publishing Co of Okla *(G-6759)*
District 1, Bristow Also called Oklahoma Comm On Consmr Cr *(G-791)*
Divco Supply, Tulsa Also called D I V C O Inc *(G-9538)*
Diversfied Wldg Fbrication LLC 405 802-5487
1825 Briarhill St Moore (73160) *(G-4517)*
Diversified Energy Svcs LLC 405 775-0414
3141 Nw 63rd St Ste 4 Oklahoma City (73116) *(G-5951)*
Diversified Geosynthetics Inc 580 395-0041
49600 Highway 3e Earlsboro (74840) *(G-2280)*
Diversified Plastics Inds LLC 918 245-0770
1606 W Timber Dr Sand Springs (74063) *(G-8178)*
Diversified Plating Ltd 405 236-0545
2109 W Sheridan Ave Oklahoma City (73107) *(G-5952)*
Diversified Printing Inc 918 665-2275
10021 E 44th Pl Tulsa (74146) *(G-9586)*
Diversified Rubber Pdts Inc 918 241-0193
7650 Charles Page Blvd Tulsa (74127) *(G-9587)*
Divine Cultured Marble 918 836-2121
1831 N 105th East Ave Tulsa (74116) *(G-9588)*
Divine Thumb Industries Inc 405 418-7855
2112 Churchill Pl Oklahoma City (73120) *(G-5953)*
Division Harris Mud Chem Inc, Cleveland Also called 300 PSI Inc *(G-1714)*
Division Order Beginnings (PA) 918 477-4559
15248 S 337th East Ave Porter (74454) *(G-7892)*
Diw Engneering Fabrication LLC 918 534-0001
1220 Industrial Pkwy Dewey (74029) *(G-2020)*
Dixie Wireline 405 853-5402
7248 Us Highway 81 Hennessey (73742) *(G-3458)*
Dixon & Sons Inc 918 256-7455
441469 E 270 Rd Vinita (74301) *(G-11253)*
Dixon Auto Engine Machine Shop 918 256-6780
27155 S 4380 Rd Vinita (74301) *(G-11254)*
Dixon Construction Co 405 665-5515
110 N Dean A Mcgee Ave Wynnewood (73098) *(G-11670)*
Dizzy Lizzy Cupcakery LLC 405 263-7667
980 206th St Nw Okarche (73762) *(G-5242)*
Djf Services Inc 405 380-7273
3231 N 3715 Rd Holdenville (74848) *(G-3553)*
DK Machine Inc 918 251-1034
820 W Elgin St Broken Arrow (74012) *(G-890)*
DK&k Energy LLC 540 395-2400
501 S Seminole Ave Okmulgee (74447) *(G-7499)*
DL Harmer and Company LLC 918 865-6993
44 N Basin Rd Mannford (74044) *(G-4181)*
Dla Document Services 405 734-2177
3420 D Ave Ste 105 Tinker Afb (73145) *(G-8953)*
Dlubak Galss, Okmulgee Also called Dlubak Glass Company *(G-7500)*
Dlubak Glass Company 918 752-0226
1018 W 14th St Okmulgee (74447) *(G-7500)*
Dmi, Tulsa Also called Downing Manufacturing Inc *(G-9001)*
Dmi International Inc 918 438-2213
15615 E Pine St Tulsa (74116) *(G-9589)*
Dmn Inc 405 848-9401
1000 W Wilshire Blvd # 3 Oklahoma City (73116) *(G-5954)*

DMS Terms & Conditions 580 303-7500
750 Ridley Rd Duncan (73533) *(G-2106)*
Do It Best Hardware 580 482-8898
500 N Market Rd Altus (73521) *(G-154)*
Doane Pet Care, Miami Also called Mars Petcare Us Inc *(G-4412)*
Dobbs & Crowder Inc 918 452-3211
111 S Main St Eufaula (74432) *(G-3100)*
Dobbs J Mark & Associates, Eufaula Also called Dobbs & Crowder Inc *(G-3100)*
Doco Development Corp 405 321-7493
2705 Poplar Ln Norman (73072) *(G-4982)*
Doctors Optical Supply Inc (PA) 918 256-6416
613 N Wilson St Vinita (74301) *(G-11255)*
Document Centre Inc 405 879-1101
333 W Wilshire Blvd Ste B Oklahoma City (73116) *(G-5955)*
Document Imging Ntwrk Slutions 405 818-3888
713 E Frolich Dr Oklahoma City (73110) *(G-5956)*
Dodco of Oklahoma LLC 405 314-1757
1041 Parrish Pl Blanchard (73010) *(G-712)*
Dog Dish LLC 918 624-2600
1778 Utica Sq Tulsa (74114) *(G-9590)*
Dolese Bros Co (PA) 405 235-2311
20 Nw 13th St Oklahoma City (73103) *(G-5957)*
Dolese Bros Co 580 795-3549
401 S 4th St Madill (73446) *(G-4146)*
Dolese Bros Co 405 947-7085
5600 W Reno Ave Oklahoma City (73127) *(G-5958)*
Dolese Bros Co 580 924-4944
3305 N Washington Ave Durant (74701) *(G-2224)*
Dolese Bros Co 580 237-2650
805 W Southgate Rd Enid (73701) *(G-2942)*
Dolese Bros Co 405 454-2478
21500 E Reno Ave Harrah (73045) *(G-3377)*
Dolese Bros Co 580 639-2237
Rr 2 Mountain View (73062) *(G-4627)*
Dolese Bros Co 918 437-6535
13521 E 11th St Tulsa (74108) *(G-9591)*
Dolese Bros Co 580 332-0820
1727 N Mississippi Ave Ada (74820) *(G-32)*
Dolese Bros Co 405 382-2060
1600 Wills Rd Seminole (74868) *(G-8370)*
Dolese Bros Co 405 795-9757
4727 N Midwest Blvd Oklahoma City (73141) *(G-5959)*
Dolese Bros Co 580 369-2834
Hwy 77 S Davis (73030) *(G-1982)*
Dolese Bros Co 580 576-9478
15129 N 2220 Rd Roosevelt (73564) *(G-8116)*
Dolese Bros Co 580 761-0022
1300 W Cowboy Hill Rd Ponca City (74601) *(G-7821)*
Dolese Bros Co 918 423-1061
1620 S George Nigh Expy McAlester (74501) *(G-4294)*
Dolese Bros Co 580 323-1202
S Highway 183 Clinton (73601) *(G-1748)*
Dolese Bros Co 580 225-1247
1201 S Pioneer Rd Elk City (73644) *(G-2803)*
Dolese Bros Co 580 255-3046
1109 S 2nd St Duncan (73533) *(G-2107)*
Dolese Bros Co 580 889-6033
2791 N Highway 69 Atoka (74525) *(G-408)*
Dolese Bros Co 405 247-2564
1800 S Mission St Anadarko (73005) *(G-202)*
Dolese Bros Co 405 262-0226
305 Se 22nd St El Reno (73036) *(G-2713)*
Dolese Bros Co 918 297-2376
S Of Hartshorne Hartshorne (74547) *(G-3391)*
Dolese Bros Co 580 937-4889
13982 W Crusher Rd Coleman (73432) *(G-1794)*
Dolese Bros Co 405 235-2311
315 S Broadway St Weatherford (73096) *(G-11404)*
Dolese Bros Co 405 235-1515
3028 W Country Club Rd Chickasha (73018) *(G-1452)*
Dolese Bros Co 405 794-0546
310 Industrial Blvd Moore (73160) *(G-4518)*
Dolese Bros Co 580 832-2720
106 S Grant St Cordell (73632) *(G-1858)*
Dolese Bros Co 405 282-2153
5740 N Hway 77 Guthrie (73044) *(G-3311)*
Dolese Bros Co 405 672-4577
901 N Sooner Rd Oklahoma City (73117) *(G-5960)*
Dolese Bros Co 405 732-0909
10625 Se 29th St Oklahoma City (73130) *(G-5961)*
Dolese Bros Co 580 492-4771
375 Nw Dolese Rd Elgin (73538) *(G-2775)*
Dolese Bros Co 405 670-9626
7100 S Sunnylane Rd Oklahoma City (73135) *(G-5962)*
Dolese Bros Co 405 373-2102
6013 Edmond Rd Ne Piedmont (73078) *(G-7760)*
Dolese Bros Co 405 232-1228
120 N Lottie Ave Oklahoma City (73117) *(G-5963)*
Dolese Bros Co 405 324-2944
10700 Nw 10th St Yukon (73099) *(G-11720)*

Dolese Bros Co 580 223-2243
115 N Plainview Rd Ardmore (73401) *(G-279)*
Dolese Bros Co 580 226-8737
164 Dolese Rd Ardmore (73401) *(G-280)*
Dolese Bros Co 405 949-2278
24 N Mccormick St Oklahoma City (73127) *(G-5964)*
Dolese Sand Plant, Guthrie *Also called Dolese Bros Co* *(G-3311)*
Dolese Trucking Co, Davis *Also called Dolese Bros Co* *(G-1982)*
Dolphin Blue Production LLC 405 285-5388
13120 N Macarthur Blvd Oklahoma City (73142) *(G-5965)*
Dome Blue Operating LLC 918 583-3333
15 E 5th St Ste 3300 Tulsa (74103) *(G-9592)*
Domeck Industries Inc 260 833-0917
3031 W 101st St Tulsa (74132) *(G-9593)*
Dominance Industries Inc 580 584-6247
610 W State Highway 3 A Broken Bow (74728) *(G-1189)*
Dominion Corp 918 270-1722
4444 S Lewis Ave Tulsa (74105) *(G-9594)*
Dominion Refuse Inc 918 743-8860
4444 S Lewis Ave Tulsa (74105) *(G-9595)*
Don Bateman Shtmtl Fabrication 918 224-0567
107 E Hobson Ave Sapulpa (74066) *(G-8267)*
Don Betchan 580 336-5954
19401 County Road 70 Perry (73077) *(G-7730)*
Don Dennis 580 662-3163
423 N Main Grady (73569) *(G-3255)*
Don Hume Company LLC 918 542-6604
500 26th Ave Nw Miami (74354) *(G-4397)*
Don Hume Leathergoods Inc 918 542-6604
500 26th Ave Nw Miami (74354) *(G-4398)*
Don L Gerbrandt 580 234-3247
3201 N Lincoln St Enid (73703) *(G-2943)*
Don Moody Farm 580 648-2489
302 E 6th St Olustee (73560) *(G-7531)*
Don Regier 580 772-3510
10152 Highway 54 Weatherford (73096) *(G-11405)*
Don Scott 405 969-3649
200 E Adams St Crescent (73028) *(G-1913)*
Don Tooker 972 742-8515
15510 E 87th Pl N Owasso (74055) *(G-7562)*
Don Wilmut 405 785-9192
705 S Main St Alex (73002) *(G-130)*
Don Wilson Pipeline Constructi 918 225-2786
780454 S Highway 99 Cushing (74023) *(G-1932)*
Don Young Company Incorporated 405 947-2000
901 Enterprise Ave Ste 13 Oklahoma City (73128) *(G-5966)*
Don-Nan Pump and Supply Co Inc 432 682-7742
1548 Old Highway 7 Ratliff City (73481) *(G-8050)*
Donald L Stafford Co 918 492-0324
7824 S Evanston Ave Tulsa (74136) *(G-9596)*
Donald Standridge 580 298-3760
4701 W 187th St S Mounds (74047) *(G-4613)*
Donald W Cox 918 471-8967
4712 E 308th St S Porum (74455) *(G-7895)*
Donerite Welding 918 304-9594
5410 Harreld Rd Beggs (74421) *(G-551)*
Donmar Industries LLC 918 688-7277
14080 N 44th West Ave Skiatook (74070) *(G-8542)*
Donnie Gaines Wldg Fabrication 580 668-3249
Hwy 70 & 76 N Wilson (73463) *(G-11532)*
Donray Petroleum LLC 405 418-4348
2525 Nw Expwy Ste 640 Oklahoma City (73112) *(G-5967)*
Donut Shop 580 276-3910
401 S Highway 77 Marietta (73448) *(G-4206)*
Doodle and Peck Publishing 405 354-7422
413 Cedarburg Ct Yukon (73099) *(G-11721)*
Doodlebugs Etc Inc 405 525-1248
625 Nw 18th St Oklahoma City (73103) *(G-5968)*
Doomsdaytacticalsolutions LLC 580 788-2412
27494 E County Road 1650 Elmore City (73433) *(G-2895)*
Dorada Foods, Ponca City *Also called Dorada Poultry LLC* *(G-7822)*
Dorada Poultry LLC 580 718-4700
2000 Hall Blvd Ponca City (74601) *(G-7822)*
Dorado E&P Partners LLC (PA) 720 402-3700
1 W 3rd St Ste 1000 Tulsa (74103) *(G-9597)*
Dorians Foods Inc 580 658-3022
1020 County Road 1586 Marlow (73055) *(G-4229)*
Doric Vaults, Tulsa *Also called Central Burial Vaults Inc* *(G-8996)*
Doris Winford 918 599-8931
4905 W 7th St Tulsa (74127) *(G-9598)*
Dormakaba USA Inc 405 232-6761
701 N Ann Arbor Ave Oklahoma City (73127) *(G-5969)*
Dorssers Usa Inc 918 422-5881
3350 Highway 412 Colcord (74338) *(G-1789)*
Dos Okies Signs & Graphics 918 569-7292
436 S 6th St Clayton (74536) *(G-1709)*
Dos Tees LLC 405 323-2382
16720 N Pennsylvania Ave Edmond (73012) *(G-2392)*
Dosher Kennon 580 667-5708
423 Nw 2nd St Tipton (73570) *(G-8959)*
Double C Oil and Gas LLC 918 518-5047
11204 S 26th West Ave Jenks (74037) *(G-3703)*
Double D Foods Inc 405 245-8909
7300 Sw 29th St Oklahoma City (73179) *(G-5970)*
Double D Horse Stalls, Catoosa *Also called Elite Manufacturing LLC* *(G-1317)*
Double D Sand and Gravel LLC 405 207-8050
106 N Spruce Stratford (74872) *(G-8804)*
Double Diamnd Wldg Fabrication 580 445-4524
401 S Washington St Hobart (73651) *(G-3542)*
Double H Farms Inc 918 486-7635
14279 S 385th East Ave Coweta (74429) *(G-1880)*
Double H Welding 918 653-2289
Highway 59 N Frrest Hl Rd Heavener (74937) *(G-3427)*
Double J Beef Jerky 580 476-2465
430 County St 2820 Rush Springs (73082) *(G-8120)*
Double J Production LLC 918 691-4060
601 Meadowood Dr Broken Arrow (74011) *(G-891)*
Double Life Corporation 405 789-7867
200 N Rockwell Ave Oklahoma City (73127) *(G-5971)*
Double R Oilfield Services LLC 580 388-4567
307 N Main Lamont (74643) *(G-3868)*
Double R Services Company Inc 580 883-4637
46953 S County Road 267 Ringwood (73768) *(G-8088)*
Double S Tank Truck Service 580 863-5231
Garber Rd Garber (73738) *(G-3212)*
Doug Butler Enterprises Inc 918 425-3565
1111 E 32nd St N Tulsa (74105) *(G-9599)*
Doug Lee Ingenuity LLC 918 542-4686
9201 S 650 Rd Miami (74354) *(G-4399)*
Doug Roberson 405 372-2078
1023 S Perkins Rd Stillwater (74074) *(G-8677)*
Doug Strickland 580 436-1010
930 Industrial Blvd Ada (74820) *(G-33)*
Doug Troxell 405 387-3574
1000 Springlake Rd Newcastle (73065) *(G-4824)*
Doug's Automotive Garage, Edmond *Also called Douglas Thompson Auto Inc* *(G-2393)*
Doug's Sand & Gravel, Newcastle *Also called Doug Troxell* *(G-4824)*
Dougherty Forestry Mfg Ltd 405 542-3520
211 W Canyon Run Hinton (73047) *(G-3523)*
Doughnut Palace, The, Purcell *Also called Dounut Palace* *(G-8006)*
Douglas A Pharr 405 200-4983
2972 County Street 2910 Ninnekah (73067) *(G-4870)*
Douglas Group LLC 405 946-6853
4625 Nw 35th St Oklahoma City (73122) *(G-5972)*
Douglas Rose Custom Tailoring 918 366-6002
17115 E 176th St S Bixby (74008) *(G-620)*
Douglas Thompson Auto Inc 405 330-6997
16120 Silverado Dr Edmond (73013) *(G-2393)*
Douglass Rose Custom Clothing, Bixby *Also called Douglas Rose Custom Tailoring* *(G-620)*
Dounut Palace 405 527-5746
403 S Green Ave Purcell (73080) *(G-8006)*
Dover Artificial Lift 918 796-1000
4801 W 49th St Tulsa (74107) *(G-9600)*
Dover Products Inc 918 476-5688
5321 W 570 Chouteau (74337) *(G-1562)*
Dovetail Enterprises LLC 405 476-3953
6417 Nw 31st St Bethany (73008) *(G-576)*
Dowell Schlumberger, El Reno *Also called Schlumberger Technology Corp* *(G-2753)*
Dowell Schlumberger, El Reno *Also called Schlumberger Technology Corp* *(G-2754)*
Downhole Hinton Services LLC 580 302-4129
315 W Tom Stafford St Weatherford (73096) *(G-11406)*
Downhole Wireline Special 580 254-3842
43718 S County Road 206 Woodward (73801) *(G-11579)*
Downing Manufacturing Inc (PA) 918 224-1116
8504 S Regency Dr Tulsa (74131) *(G-9001)*
Downing Wellhead Equipment LLC (HQ) 405 486-7858
2601 Nw Expwy Ste 900e Oklahoma City (73112) *(G-5973)*
Downing Wellhead Equipment LLC 405 789-8182
8528 Sw 2nd St Oklahoma City (73128) *(G-5974)*
Downtown Music Box LLC 405 232-2099
535 N Ann Arbor Ave Oklahoma City (73127) *(G-5975)*
Downtown Pub 918 274-8202
106 S Atlanta St Owasso (74055) *(G-7563)*
Downtown Threads, Enid *Also called Munger and Krout Inc* *(G-3016)*
Doyle Cook 405 257-3301
120 W 2nd St Wewoka (74884) *(G-11500)*
Doyle Dryers Inc 918 224-4002
1404 S Quaker Ave Tulsa (74120) *(G-9601)*
Dp Manufacturing Inc (PA) 918 250-2450
11135 S James Ave Jenks (74037) *(G-3704)*
DPM Group LLC 405 682-3468
1910 S Nicklas Ave Oklahoma City (73128) *(G-5976)*
Dps Printing Services Inc 405 285-4614
6121 Stonecreek Way Edmond (73025) *(G-2394)*
Dps Printing Services of 918 794-7755
3419 E 116th St N Sperry (74073) *(G-8607)*
Dr Cannabis LLC 918 277-1105
6234 S 123rd West Ave Sapulpa (74066) *(G-8268)*

ALPHABETIC

DR Cbd | ALPHABETIC SECTION

DR Cbd 832 216-3301
   2711 W Britton Rd Apt 85 Oklahoma City (73120) *(G-5977)*
Dr G W Clay Optomotrist, Ardmore Also called Ardmore Optical Co *(G-248)*
Dr Pepper Bottling Co 580 256-2350
   3003 Lakeview Dr Woodward (73801) *(G-11580)*
Dr Pepper Bottling Co Elk City 580 225-3186
   322 S Jefferson Ave Elk City (73644) *(G-2804)*
Dr Pepper Co 580 765-6468
   1200 N Union St Ponca City (74601) *(G-7823)*
Dr Pepper Snapple Group 405 680-5150
   5200 Sw 36th St Ste 600 Oklahoma City (73179) *(G-5978)*
Dr Pepper-Royal Crown Btlg Co 405 224-1260
   205 W Kansas Ave Chickasha (73018) *(G-1453)*
Draeger Interlock 918 270-1600
   4125 S 68th East Ave P Tulsa (74145) *(G-9602)*
Draft2digital LLC 405 708-7894
   9400 Broadway Ext Ste 410 Oklahoma City (73114) *(G-5979)*
Dragon 580 653-2171
   10834 State Highway 53 Springer (73458) *(G-8623)*
Dragonfly Publishing Inc 405 359-6952
   2440 Twin Ridge Dr Edmond (73034) *(G-2395)*
Dragonslayer Games LLC 918 665-1472
   3929 S Granite Ave Tulsa (74135) *(G-9603)*
Drake Manufacturing Inc 405 760-5336
   41101 Wolverine Rd Shawnee (74804) *(G-8445)*
Drake Manufacturing Inc 405 799-8157
   4601 Se 139th St Oklahoma City (73165) *(G-5287)*
Drc Service Co 580 661-3300
   401 N 1st St Thomas (73669) *(G-8942)*
Dream Buildings of Tulsa 918 437-9233
   11212 E Admiral Pl Tulsa (74116) *(G-9604)*
Dream Green International LLC 814 616-7800
   133 24th Ave Nw 290 Norman (73069) *(G-4983)*
Dream Team Prosthetics LLC 580 255-2100
   7111 Nix Dr Duncan (73533) *(G-2108)*
Dreamers Screen Print and More 580 761-4376
   105 S Main St Blackwell (74631) *(G-682)*
Dreams Reflected, Norman Also called Pickard Projects Inc *(G-5115)*
Dresser-Rand Arrow, Kiefer Also called Dresser-Rand Services LLC *(G-3779)*
Dresser-Rand Company 918 835-8437
   1354 S Sheridan Rd Tulsa (74112) *(G-9605)*
Dresser-Rand Group Inc 918 695-2368
   1354 S Sheridan Rd Tulsa (74112) *(G-9606)*
Dresser-Rand LLC 918 254-4099
   1354 S Sheridan Rd Tulsa (74112) *(G-9607)*
Dresser-Rand Repair Center, Tulsa Also called Dresser-Rand Company *(G-9605)*
Dresser-Rand Services LLC 918 321-3690
   14963 S 49th Ave W Kiefer (74041) *(G-3779)*
Dreyar Industries LLC 405 826-2454
   904 Oak Tree Dr Edmond (73025) *(G-2396)*
Drillers Service Center Inc 405 631-3728
   2620 S Central Ave Oklahoma City (73129) *(G-5980)*
Drilling Fluids Technology 580 225-1009
   106 Panel Rd Elk City (73644) *(G-2805)*
DRILLING FLUIDS TECHNOLOGY INC, Elk City Also called Drilling Fluids Technology *(G-2805)*
Drilling Tools Intl Inc 405 604-2763
   2525 S Ann Arbor Ave Oklahoma City (73128) *(G-5981)*
Drillworx Directional Drlg LLC 405 386-3380
   16533 Se 89th St Choctaw (73020) *(G-1540)*
Driploc Inc 405 632-5810
   2213 Sw 19th St Oklahoma City (73108) *(G-5982)*
Driskills Welding 580 233-3093
   717 N 30th St Enid (73701) *(G-2944)*
Drive Shafts Inc 918 836-0111
   6960 E 11th St Tulsa (74112) *(G-9608)*
Driver & Son Welding Shop 580 323-1714
   2 Miles N On Hwy 183 Clinton (73601) *(G-1749)*
Driver Examiner Div 580 762-1728
   1015 W South Ave Ponca City (74601) *(G-7824)*
Drivetrain, Oklahoma City Also called Atc Technology Corporation *(G-5483)*
Drivin Printing By Aaron 405 609-9608
   2701 Nw 63rd St Oklahoma City (73116) *(G-5983)*
Drone 1 Aerial LLC 580 704-7223
   280075 Hlavaty Rd Marlow (73055) *(G-4230)*
Drone Misfits LLC 918 810-0808
   5816 Se 144th St Oklahoma City (73165) *(G-5288)*
Drone Viu LLC 405 867-4690
   6120 S Yale Ave Ste 500 Tulsa (74136) *(G-9609)*
Drov LLC 405 463-6562
   13832 Wireless Way # 100 Oklahoma City (73134) *(G-5984)*
Drov Technologies, Oklahoma City Also called Drov LLC *(G-5984)*
Drov Technologies, Oklahoma City Also called Airgo Systems LLC *(G-5404)*
Drovers Trail Land Company LLC 405 702-6300
   500 N Broadway Ave # 350 Oklahoma City (73102) *(G-5985)*
Drp Welding Met Buildings LLC 405 344-6582
   2498 County Road 1400 Alex (73002) *(G-131)*
Drug Warehouse 918 592-4545
   1437 S Boulder Ave # 1050 Tulsa (74119) *(G-9610)*

Drumright Gusher Inc 918 352-2284
   129 E Broadway St Drumright (74030) *(G-2056)*
Drumright Oil Well Servic 918 704-0252
   1501 W Main St Henryetta (74437) *(G-3505)*
Drumright Oilwell Services LLC 918 352-9646
   501 Ok 99 Drumright (74030) *(G-2057)*
Drumright Tar 918 352-4000
   1103 E Broadway St Drumright (74030) *(G-2058)*
Dry Fabrication and Welding 580 735-2958
   405 N Hoy St Buffalo (73834) *(G-1212)*
Dryvit Systems Inc 918 245-0216
   5850 S 116th West Ave Sand Springs (74063) *(G-8179)*
DS Welding 580 623-4104
   Block 1 Box 210 Fay (73646) *(G-3156)*
DSA Designs LLC 580 493-2723
   9512 S Logan Rd Drummond (73735) *(G-2047)*
Dsignz Custom Screen Printing 405 375-6806
   108 W Miles Ave Kingfisher (73750) *(G-3796)*
Du Pont Delaware Inc 918 476-5825
   5532 Hunt St Pryor (74361) *(G-7960)*
Du-Ann Co Inc (PA) 580 428-3315
   8 Mi W Of Town On Hwy 31 Coalgate (74538) *(G-1779)*
Duane Durkee Pumping Svc 405 820-3256
   1916 Lake View Dr Perry (73077) *(G-7731)*
Duane Waugh 580 596-2485
   N Of Town Cherokee (73728) *(G-1416)*
Dub's Sheet Metal, Moore Also called Darrell Monroe *(G-4513)*
Dublin Petroleum Corp 580 234-7718
   2500 N 11th St Enid (73701) *(G-2945)*
Duck Brothers Dozer & Trucking 580 925-3509
   34826 Ew 1420 Konawa (74849) *(G-3845)*
Ducommun Labarge Tech Inc 918 459-2200
   11616 E 51st St Tulsa (74146) *(G-9611)*
Duct Mate Industries 918 340-5122
   301 Se 15th St Wagoner (74467) *(G-11279)*
Dudes Welding & Etc LLC 405 510-4786
   8400 Ne 34th St Spencer (73084) *(G-8594)*
Dudz and Things Inc 918 321-9443
   10132 W 161st St S Sapulpa (74066) *(G-8269)*
Duffens Optical, Tulsa Also called Essilor Laboratories Amer Inc *(G-9702)*
Duffy Dry Clean City LLC 405 743-0730
   2203 W 6th Ave Stillwater (74074) *(G-8678)*
Duggans Ann Marie Pro Shop 405 715-2695
   3501 S Boulevard Edmond (73013) *(G-2397)*
Duke Manufacturing 918 653-3404
   907 W Highway 270 Heavener (74937) *(G-3428)*
Dulaney's Retail Liquor Store, Stillwater Also called Dulaneys Liquor Store *(G-8679)*
Dulaneys Liquor Store 405 377-9007
   2012 N Boomer Rd Stillwater (74075) *(G-8679)*
Dumpster Service Plus 405 417-3707
   4217 S May Ave Ste 1 Oklahoma City (73119) *(G-5986)*
Dunbar Event Signs Inc 918 607-9254
   9204 N 96th East Ave Owasso (74055) *(G-7564)*
Duncan Inc Walter 405 272-1800
   100 Park Ave Ste 1200 Oklahoma City (73102) *(G-5987)*
Duncan Banner, Duncan Also called Newspaper Holding Inc *(G-2159)*
Duncan Bit Service Inc 580 255-9787
   2501 S Highway 81 Duncan (73533) *(G-2109)*
Duncan Industrial Solutions, Broken Arrow Also called Blackhawk Industrial Dist Inc *(G-853)*
Duncan Machine Products Inc 580 467-6784
   1003 S 2nd St Duncan (73533) *(G-2110)*
Duncan Mannequin & Mfg, Duncan Also called Duncan Mannequin Inc *(G-2111)*
Duncan Mannequin Inc 580 252-5915
   2525 S Highway 81 Duncan (73533) *(G-2111)*
Duncan Manufacturing Inc 580 251-2137
   100 E Hwy 7 Receiving Duncan (73536) *(G-2112)*
Duncan Oil & Gas Inc 405 360-2183
   4604 Laurelbrook Ct Norman (73072) *(G-4984)*
Duncan Oil & Gas Inc (PA) 405 214-1108
   23 E 9th St Ste 213 Shawnee (74801) *(G-8446)*
Duncan Oil Properties Inc 405 272-1800
   100 Park Ave Ste 1200 Oklahoma City (73102) *(G-5988)*
Duncan Overhead Door 405 222-0748
   513 W Choctaw Ave Chickasha (73018) *(G-1454)*
Duncan Ticking Inc (PA) 405 528-5480
   1421 Nw 23rd St Oklahoma City (73106) *(G-5989)*
Duncan Wood Works LLC 580 641-1190
   1225 W Park Ave Duncan (73533) *(G-2113)*
Dunhams Asphalt Services Inc 918 246-9210
   8387 W 21st St Sand Springs (74063) *(G-8180)*
Dunlap & Company 580 223-8181
   100 W Main St Ardmore (73401) *(G-281)*
Dunlap Drilling Producing Inc 918 237-0015
   16950 S 9th West Ave Glenpool (74033) *(G-3233)*
Dunlap Manufacturing 580 237-3434
   3022 N Van Buren St Enid (73703) *(G-2946)*
Dunlap Manufacturing Co Inc 918 838-1383
   3250 N Sheridan Rd Tulsa (74115) *(G-9612)*
Dunlap Oil Tools 918 885-6353
   300 E Main St Hominy (74035) *(G-3582)*

Dunlap Well Service Inc ... 918 367-2660
21 W First St Bristow (74010) *(G-776)*
Dunlaw Optical Labs Inc ... 580 355-8410
1313 Sw A Ave Lawton (73501) *(G-3920)*
Dunns Tank Service Inc ... 580 465-1687
300637 State Highway 29 Foster (73434) *(G-3185)*
Dunsworth Machine ... 580 233-5812
701 N Independence St Enid (73701) *(G-2947)*
Dupont, Pryor *Also called Du Pont Delaware Inc (G-7960)*
Dura-Line Corporation ... 918 302-0330
10 Steven Taylor Blvd Bache (74501) *(G-430)*
Duracoatings, Oklahoma City *Also called DCI Industries LLC (G-5910)*
Duracoatings Holdings LLC ... 405 692-2249
13920 S Meridian Ave Oklahoma City (73173) *(G-5990)*
Durant ... 580 920-2069
142 W Main St Durant (74701) *(G-2225)*
Durant Iron & Metal Inc ... 580 924-0595
11 W Locust St Durant (74701) *(G-2226)*
Durant Plastics & Mfg ... 580 745-9430
301 Gerlach Dr Durant (74701) *(G-2227)*
Durant Printing ... 580 924-2271
401 N 3rd Ave Durant (74701) *(G-2228)*
Durnal Construction LLC ... 405 413-5458
12415 S Fairgrounds Perkins (74059) *(G-7716)*
Dust Cutter ... 405 615-7788
3813 Danfield Ln Norman (73072) *(G-4985)*
Dusters & Sprayers Supply Inc ... 405 224-1201
2163 Highway 81 Chickasha (73018) *(G-1455)*
Dustin Holbird ... 918 448-7687
46145 Bengal Rd Wister (74966) *(G-11548)*
Dusty Trunk ... 918 446-4203
8515 S 33rd West Ave Tulsa (74132) *(G-9613)*
Dustys Jerky LLC ... 405 702-8016
628 Se 82nd St Oklahoma City (73149) *(G-5991)*
Dutton Welding & Construc ... 918 420-5688
2831 N Main St Bache (74501) *(G-431)*
Dvm Nutrion Pets Corp Inc ... 918 686-6111
1410 S Cherokee St Muskogee (74403) *(G-4668)*
Dvorak Instruments ... 918 299-2223
6818 E 96th Pl Tulsa (74133) *(G-9614)*
Dvorak Instruments Inc ... 918 447-0022
9402 E 55th St Tulsa (74145) *(G-9615)*
Dw-Natnal Stndrd-Stllwater LLC ... 405 377-5050
3602 N Perkins Rd Stillwater (74075) *(G-8680)*
Dww Inc ... 580 255-7886
750 Ridley Rd Duncan (73533) *(G-2114)*
Dyco Petroleum Corporation ... 918 591-1917
2 W 2nd St Ste 1500 Tulsa (74103) *(G-9616)*
Dylans Precision Stainless LLC ... 918 207-9149
13509 E 655 Rd Hulbert (74441) *(G-3623)*
Dyna-Turn of Oklahoma Inc ... 580 243-1291
116 Meadow Ridge Dr Elk City (73644) *(G-2806)*
Dynamic Brands Inc ... 918 630-7083
7223 S 285th East Pl Broken Arrow (74014) *(G-1123)*
Dynamic Machine ... 918 791-1114
2001 E Industrial 5 Rd Grove (74344) *(G-3266)*
Dynamic Mapping Solutions Inc ... 918 446-7803
3021 W 68th Pl Tulsa (74132) *(G-9617)*
Dyne Exploration Company ... 405 245-0624
5100 E Skelly Dr Ste 650 Tulsa (74135) *(G-9618)*
Dynegy, Waukomis *Also called Tri Resources Inc (G-11360)*
Dynegy, Blackwell *Also called Tri Resources Inc (G-694)*
Dynex, Tulsa *Also called Dyne Exploration Company (G-9618)*
Dynomite Custom Screens LLC ... 844 396-6648
1421 Nw Great Plains Blvd E Lawton (73505) *(G-3921)*
Dynosaw Inc ... 405 418-6060
9008 N Walker Ave Oklahoma City (73114) *(G-5992)*
Dywy Spooling LLC ... 405 469-4148
38601 110th St Byars (74831) *(G-1222)*
E & D Enterprises ... 580 512-1806
1249 Nw Airport Rd Cache (73527) *(G-1226)*
E & E Construction Company ... 918 775-6222
1700 W Ruth Ave Sallisaw (74955) *(G-8144)*
E & K Oilfield Services Inc ... 580 994-2442
604 Se 2nd St Mooreland (73852) *(G-4589)*
E & P Wire Line, Moore *Also called Schlumberger Technology Corp (G-4564)*
E and H Sales ... 918 742-1091
3539 S Fulton Ave Tulsa (74135) *(G-9619)*
E C Beights ... 918 674-2773
60151 E 66 Rd Miami (74354) *(G-4400)*
E C Carman Casing Gauge Co ... 918 605-5093
9220 E 77th St Tulsa (74133) *(G-9620)*
E E Sewing Inc ... 918 789-5881
21601 E 340 Rd Chelsea (74016) *(G-1404)*
E E Sewing Inc ... 918 214-5343
2377 London Ln Bartlesville (74006) *(G-476)*
E Environmental LLC ... 405 604-0000
101 Ne 24th St Oklahoma City (73105) *(G-5993)*
E F L Inc ... 918 665-7799
9401 E 54th St Tulsa (74145) *(G-9621)*
E H Publishing Inc ... 405 258-0877
109 Clador Dr Chandler (74834) *(G-1379)*
E J Higgins Interior Design ... 405 387-3434
2224 Nw 32nd St Newcastle (73065) *(G-4825)*
E J R Enterprises LLC ... 580 623-0051
802 N Noble Ave Watonga (73772) *(G-11346)*
E Lyle Johnson Inc (PA) ... 405 470-2047
7100 Nw 63rd St Ste 1703 Bethany (73008) *(G-577)*
E M S, Hennessey *Also called Energy Meter Systems LLC (G-3460)*
E S E C O Speed Master, Cushing *Also called Speedmaster Inc (G-1961)*
E S P, Oklahoma City *Also called GE Oil & Gas Esp Inc (G-6140)*
E&M Solutions LLC ... 918 551-9515
12317 E 13th Pl Tulsa (74128) *(G-9622)*
E-Saw Wldg & Fabrication LLC ... 580 772-2448
1200 E Loomis Rd Weatherford (73096) *(G-11407)*
E-Tech Inc ... 918 665-1930
20701 E 81st St S Ste 103 Broken Arrow (74014) *(G-1124)*
E-Z Drill Inc (PA) ... 405 372-0121
610 Cedar St Perry (73077) *(G-7732)*
E-Z Drill Inc ... 580 336-9874
321 Ash St Perry (73077) *(G-7733)*
EAC, Tulsa *Also called Electronic Assembly Corp (G-9653)*
Eagle Applctions Solutions Ltd ... 888 511-8720
2501 Ne 23rd St Ste A Oklahoma City (73111) *(G-5994)*
Eagle Chief Midstream LLC (PA) ... 405 888-5585
2575 Kelley Pointe Pkwy # 340 Edmond (73013) *(G-2398)*
Eagle Drilling LLC ... 405 447-8181
1126 Rambling Oaks Dr Norman (73072) *(G-4986)*
Eagle Electronics, Tulsa *Also called Navico Inc (G-10329)*
Eagle Energy Company LLC ... 918 746-1350
2488 E 81st St Ste 2000 Tulsa (74137) *(G-9623)*
Eagle Exploration Prod LLC ... 918 746-1350
2488 E 81st St Ste 2000 Tulsa (74137) *(G-9624)*
Eagle Explrtion Oprting GP LLC ... 918 746-1350
6100 S Yale Ave Ste 700 Tulsa (74136) *(G-9625)*
Eagle Graphics ... 918 335-7777
1000 Ne Washington Blvd Bartlesville (74006) *(G-477)*
Eagle Imaging Management ... 405 286-4114
3600 Nw 138th St Ste 102 Oklahoma City (73134) *(G-5995)*
Eagle Marketing ... 580 548-8186
227 W Broadway Ave Enid (73701) *(G-2948)*
Eagle Oilfield Service LLC ... 580 774-2240
300 S Access Rd Weatherford (73096) *(G-11408)*
Eagle Pump & Mfg LLC ... 918 906-1080
1013 N Columbia Ave Tulsa (74110) *(G-9626)*
Eagle Redi-Mix Concrete LLC ... 918 355-5700
2761 E Skelly Dr Ste 300 Tulsa (74105) *(G-9627)*
Eagle Resources Inc ... 918 342-5733
8202 E 485 Rd Claremore (74019) *(G-1615)*
Eagle River Energy Corporation ... 918 494-8928
3701 S Orange Cir Broken Arrow (74011) *(G-892)*
Eagle Road Oil LLC ... 844 211-2961
321 S Boston Ave Ste 700 Tulsa (74103) *(G-9628)*
Eagle Rock Coatings Inc ... 405 948-8900
6424 N Santa Fe Ave Ste B Oklahoma City (73116) *(G-5996)*
Eagle Rock Energy Partners LP ... 281 408-1467
1717 S Boulder Ave # 100 Tulsa (74119) *(G-9629)*
Eagle Urns Inc ... 918 469-3024
412 Etchison Rd Quinton (74561) *(G-8036)*
Eagle Web Design, Lawton *Also called Harry A Lippert Jr (G-3939)*
Eagleclaw Fabrication ... 918 691-2519
11818 S Oswego Ave Tulsa (74137) *(G-9630)*
Eaglecrest Aviation LLC ... 918 249-0980
54 Cedar Ridge Rd Broken Arrow (74011) *(G-893)*
Eagles Nest Welding ... 405 639-8650
6408 Nw 24th St Oklahoma City (73127) *(G-5997)*
Earl Bannon ... 405 236-8829
1221 N Portland Ave Oklahoma City (73107) *(G-5998)*
Earl-Le Dozer Service LLC ... 918 352-2072
51266 W Highway 33 Drumright (74030) *(G-2059)*
Earlsboro Energies Corp ... 405 282-5007
7424 S Westminster Rd Guthrie (73044) *(G-3312)*
Earlsboro Energies Corporation ... 405 848-2829
3007 Nw 63rd St Ste 205 Oklahoma City (73116) *(G-5999)*
Early Bird Express, Newcastle *Also called Newcastle Pacer Inc (G-4833)*
Earlywine Press LLC ... 405 820-8208
3048 Sw 127th St Oklahoma City (73170) *(G-5289)*
Earnheart Crescent LLC ... 888 536-8703
12782 W County Road 60 Marshall (73056) *(G-4250)*
Earth Data Graphics, Edmond *Also called Greenbriar Resources Corp (G-2444)*
Earthgrains Companies, Oklahoma City *Also called Bimbo Bakeries Usa Inc (G-5569)*
Easley Welding, Perkins *Also called Lance Easley (G-7719)*
Easleys Performance Wear Inc ... 918 357-2400
6818 S 245th East Ave Broken Arrow (74014) *(G-1125)*
East 74th Street Holdings Inc ... 918 437-3037
1140 N 129th East Ave Tulsa (74116) *(G-9631)*
East Hill Car Wash, Cordell *Also called Kenneth E Jones (G-1861)*
East Texas Exploration LLC ... 405 245-6568
755 W Covell Rd Ste 100 Edmond (73003) *(G-2399)*

ALPHABETIC

Eastech Badger — ALPHABETIC SECTION

Eastech Badger 918 664-1212
4250 S 76th East Ave Tulsa (74145) *(G-9632)*
Eastech Flow Controls Inc 918 664-1212
4250 S 76th East Ave Tulsa (74145) *(G-9633)*
Eastern Etching & Mfg 918 476-6007
420 E Loy St Chouteau (74337) *(G-1563)*
Eastern Manufacturing Inc 918 482-1544
100 E South Pr Haskell (74436) *(G-3397)*
Eastern Oil Well Services 405 947-1091
5400 N Grand Blvd Ste 450 Oklahoma City (73112) *(G-6000)*
Eastern Okla Fabrication Inc 918 654-7344
27355 State Highway 112 Cameron (74932) *(G-1257)*
Eastern Red Cedar Products LLC 405 780-7520
6310 W Devonshire Rd Stillwater (74074) *(G-8681)*
Eastern Sheet Metal Co Inc 918 687-6231
2301 N Main St Muskogee (74401) *(G-4669)*
Eastland Lawn Mower Service 580 252-0077
1105 S Highway 81 Duncan (73533) *(G-2115)*
Easton Land Services 405 842-1930
6600 N Meridian Ave # 242 Oklahoma City (73116) *(G-6001)*
Eastpointe Industries Inc 918 683-2169
4020 Tull Ave Muskogee (74403) *(G-4670)*
Eastpointe Manufacturing Corp 918 683-2169
4020 Tull Ave Muskogee (74403) *(G-4671)*
Eastside Septic Tank 918 486-2290
11614 S 272nd East Ave Coweta (74429) *(G-1881)*
Easy Car Wash Systems Inc 918 582-4355
2302 Charles Page Blvd Tulsa (74127) *(G-9634)*
Eat It Up LLC 405 853-2313
114 S Main St Hennessey (73742) *(G-3459)*
Eaton Aeroquip LLC 405 275-5500
8701 N Harrison Shawnee (74804) *(G-8447)*
Eaton and Associates LLC 405 307-9631
300 Victory Ct Norman (73072) *(G-4987)*
Eaton Building Contractors 918 273-9191
3820 Se Kentucky St Ste 6 Bartlesville (74006) *(G-478)*
Eaton-Quade Company 405 236-4475
1116 W Main St Oklahoma City (73106) *(G-6002)*
Eaton-Quade Plastics, Oklahoma City Also called Eaton-Quade Company *(G-6002)*
Eaves Manufacturing Inc 580 889-3530
677 S Jefferson Hwy Atoka (74525) *(G-409)*
Eaves Stones Products 580 889-7858
925 W 13th St Atoka (74525) *(G-410)*
Ebenezer Truck Trailer LL 918 289-6669
45 S Fulton Ave Tulsa (74112) *(G-9635)*
Ebsco Spring Co Inc 918 628-1680
4949 S 83rd East Ave Tulsa (74145) *(G-9636)*
Ecapitol LLC 405 524-2833
113 Nw 13th St Apt 101 Oklahoma City (73103) *(G-6003)*
Echo E&P LLC 405 753-4232
120 Robert S Kerr Ave Oklahoma City (73102) *(G-6004)*
Echo Energy LLC (PA) 405 753-4232
120 Robert S Kerr Ave Oklahoma City (73102) *(G-6005)*
Echota Defense Services 918 384-7409
10838 E Marshall St Ste 2 Tulsa (74116) *(G-9637)*
Eckroat Seed Co 405 427-2484
1106 N Martin L King Ave Oklahoma City (73117) *(G-6006)*
Ecm Car Wash LLC 405 590-3252
325 W Memorial Rd Oklahoma City (73114) *(G-6007)*
Eco Incorporated 918 258-5002
3101 N Hemlock Cir 110f Broken Arrow (74012) *(G-894)*
Eco 2007 LLC 918 258-5002
3101 N Hemlock Cir 110f Broken Arrow (74012) *(G-895)*
Eco Elite, Broken Arrow Also called Elite Creative Solutions LLC *(G-897)*
Eco Oil Fill Services 580 774-2240
1200 E Loomis Rd Weatherford (73096) *(G-11409)*
Eco-Bright Industries LLC 918 728-1644
3835 E 56th Pl Tulsa (74135) *(G-9638)*
Eco-Lift Energy Services Inc 580 772-5157
1450 E Loomis Rd Weatherford (73096) *(G-11410)*
Eco-Tech Inc 405 542-6483
1212 S Broadway Ave Hinton (73047) *(G-3524)*
Ecohawk Advnced Wtr Rsrces LLC 918 694-6011
1620 S Lewis Ave Tulsa (74104) *(G-9639)*
Econo Biogasoline Corporation 918 347-5408
414 Se Wash Blvd Ste 215 Bartlesville (74006) *(G-479)*
Econofab Piping Inc 918 267-5901
8255 Highway 16 Beggs (74421) *(G-552)*
Econolite Control Products Inc 405 485-2230
Rr 5 Box 977 Blanchard (73010) *(G-713)*
Economasters LLC 918 241-8244
3209 W 21st St Tulsa (74107) *(G-9640)*
Economy Lumber Company Inc 918 835-4933
4221 E Pine St Tulsa (74115) *(G-9641)*
Econtrols LLC 918 957-1000
4646 S Harvard Ave # 100 Tulsa (74135) *(G-9642)*
Ecowood Solutions, Norman Also called Elm Creek Gravel LLC *(G-4990)*
Ect Services Inc 918 691-9320
10475 Lance Ln Sand Springs (74063) *(G-8181)*

Ed F Davis Inc 580 265-4210
20987 County Road 1597 Stonewall (74871) *(G-8800)*
Ed Prentice 580 857-2713
7581 County Road 3700 Allen (74825) *(G-134)*
Edc AG Products Company LLC 405 235-4546
3503 Nw 63rd St Ste 500 Oklahoma City (73116) *(G-6008)*
Eddie Brown 580 889-1506
718 W 13th St Atoka (74525) *(G-411)*
Eddie Johnson's Crane Service, Ratliff City Also called Eddie Johnsons Wldg & Mch Co *(G-8051)*
Eddie Johnsons Wldg & Mch Co 580 856-3418
75a Kirkpatrick Curv Ratliff City (73481) *(G-8051)*
Eddie Ward 405 848-3283
737 Nw 92nd St Oklahoma City (73114) *(G-6009)*
Eddies Submersible Service Inc 405 273-9292
1019 N Broadway St Tecumseh (74873) *(G-8913)*
Eden Clinic Inc (PA) 405 579-4673
1807 W Lindsey St Norman (73069) *(G-4988)*
Eden Pharmaceuticals 405 455-7200
7550 Se 15th St Midwest City (73110) *(G-4439)*
Edge One Signs, Bixby Also called Jason M Haag *(G-638)*
Edge Services Inc 580 254-3216
4420 Anderson Rd Woodward (73801) *(G-11581)*
Edinger Engineering Inc 405 232-6315
105 N Hudson Ave Ste 600 Oklahoma City (73102) *(G-6010)*
Editorial Annex 405 474-2114
3113 Carriage Park Ln Edmond (73003) *(G-2400)*
Editorial Grama Inc 918 744-9502
100 W 5th St Ste 701 Tulsa (74103) *(G-9643)*
Edmond Coins Inc 405 607-6800
3409 S Broadway Ste 650 Edmond (73013) *(G-2401)*
Edmond Glass 405 751-5900
13778 N Lincoln Blvd Edmond (73013) *(G-2402)*
Edmond Life & Leisure 405 340-3311
107 S Broadway Edmond (73034) *(G-2403)*
Edmond Printing Co, Edmond Also called Edmond Printings *(G-2404)*
Edmond Printings 405 341-4330
13 S Broadway Edmond (73034) *(G-2404)*
Edmond Screen Printing, Edmond Also called Cimarron Screen Printing *(G-2352)*
Edmond Sun, Edmond Also called Cnhi LLC *(G-2359)*
Edmond Trophy Co 405 341-4631
401 W 15th St Edmond (73013) *(G-2405)*
Edmonds Fnest Mold Dmage Rmval 405 509-9508
1708 S Broadway Edmond (73013) *(G-2406)*
Edrio Oil Co 405 621-1300
13300 N Macarthur Blvd Oklahoma City (73142) *(G-6011)*
EDS Inc 405 416-6700
2401 Nw 23rd St Ste 11 Oklahoma City (73107) *(G-6012)*
Education Oklahoma Department 405 743-5531
1201 N Western Rd Stillwater (74075) *(G-8682)*
Educational Concepts LLC 918 749-0118
2021 S Lewis Ave Ste 760 Tulsa (74104) *(G-9644)*
Edward C Lawson Properties 918 584-5155
401 S Boston Ave Ste 2100 Tulsa (74103) *(G-9645)*
Edwards Canvas Inc 405 238-7551
17499 Highway 77 Pauls Valley (73075) *(G-7658)*
Edwards Pipeline Services LLC 918 627-8288
7647b E 46th Pl Tulsa (74145) *(G-9646)*
Edwards Trust, Duncan Also called Stagestand Ranch *(G-2184)*
Efdyn Incorporated 918 838-1170
7734 E 11th St Tulsa (74112) *(G-9647)*
Efficient Fuel Solutions Llc 713 466-1400
350 Nails Crossing Rd Caddo (74729) *(G-1234)*
Egr Construction Inc 405 943-0900
601 N Miller Blvd Oklahoma City (73107) *(G-6013)*
Egret Operating Company Inc 918 687-8665
124 S 4th St Muskogee (74401) *(G-4672)*
Ehrle's Party Supply, Tulsa Also called Ehrles Carnival & Party Sups *(G-9648)*
Ehrles Carnival & Party Sups 918 622-5266
5150 S Sheridan Rd Tulsa (74145) *(G-9648)*
Eichler Valve 405 370-6891
11 Stony Trl Edmond (73034) *(G-2407)*
Ej Usa Inc 231 536-2261
270 Redwing Rd Ardmore (73401) *(G-282)*
Ejiw Ardmore Foundry, Ardmore Also called Ej Usa Inc *(G-282)*
Ek Exploration LLC 405 285-1220
3501 French Park Dr Ste A Edmond (73034) *(G-2408)*
El Capora Tortilleria 405 662-0427
4608 S May Ave Oklahoma City (73119) *(G-6014)*
El Dorado Chemical Company (HQ) 405 235-4546
3503 Nw 63rd St Ste 500 Oklahoma City (73116) *(G-6015)*
El Dorado Manufacturing Co LLC 580 318-2313
110 N Lloyd St Eldorado (73537) *(G-2773)*
El Jay Enterprises Inc 918 836-8273
5905 E 26th St Tulsa (74114) *(G-9649)*
El Latino American Inc 405 632-1934
8870 S Western Ave Oklahoma City (73139) *(G-6016)*
El Mojado 918 492-1138
6827 S Peoria Ave Tulsa (74136) *(G-9650)*

ALPHABETIC SECTION

El Nacional 405 632-4531
  2328 S Harvey Ave Oklahoma City (73109) *(G-6017)*
El Nacional News Inc 405 632-4531
  300 Sw 25th St Oklahoma City (73109) *(G-6018)*
El Paso Prod Oil Gas Texas LP 580 994-2171
  3 Mi East On Hwy 412 Mooreland (73852) *(G-4590)*
El Reno Bowl Inc 405 262-3611
  2412 Sunset Dr El Reno (73036) *(G-2714)*
El Reno Tribune, El Reno Also called Tribune Corp *(G-2764)*
El Reno Tribune 405 262-7231
  801 Thompson Dr El Reno (73036) *(G-2715)*
El Toro Resources LLC 405 242-2777
  14301 Caliber Dr Ste 200 Oklahoma City (73134) *(G-6019)*
El-Jayvideoaudio.com, Tulsa Also called El Jay Enterprises Inc *(G-9649)*
Elanco Animal Health, Broken Arrow Also called Eli Lilly and Company *(G-896)*
Elanco Animal Health, Tulsa Also called Eli Lilly and Company *(G-9655)*
Eland Energy Inc 405 840-9885
  2601 Nw Expressway St 1200w Oklahoma City (73112) *(G-6020)*
Elastech Technologies LLC 405 470-1539
  200 N Rockwell Ave Oklahoma City (73127) *(G-6021)*
Elastomer Specialties Inc 800 786-4244
  25981 State Highway 51 Wagoner (74467) *(G-11280)*
Elastomer Specialties Inc (PA) 918 485-0276
  2210 S Highway 69 Wagoner (74467) *(G-11281)*
Elastomer Specialties Inc 918 485-0276
  902 S Adams Ave Wagoner (74467) *(G-11282)*
Elco Tech Engineering 918 664-4646
  5256 S Irvington Pl Tulsa (74135) *(G-9651)*
Eldon Valley Choppers 918 931-2925
  25976 Highway 62 Tahlequah (74464) *(G-8863)*
Electranetics Inc 918 960-0818
  1811 S Baltimore Ave Tulsa (74119) *(G-9652)*
Electric Green Inc 405 706-1683
  2737 Nw 24th St Oklahoma City (73107) *(G-6022)*
Electric Motor Service Company 580 223-8940
  808 K St Nw Ardmore (73401) *(G-283)*
Electronic Assembly Corp 918 286-2816
  8120 E 12th St Ste A Tulsa (74112) *(G-9653)*
Electronic Label Technology 812 875-2521
  425 Centennial Blvd Edmond (73013) *(G-2409)*
Electrotech Inc 918 224-5869
  7221 S 81st West Pl Tulsa (74131) *(G-9002)*
Element Design & Fabrication 720 372-1940
  1915 Genova Ct Edmond (73034) *(G-2410)*
Element Fleet Corporation 405 799-4775
  14312 Se 110th St Oklahoma City (73165) *(G-5290)*
Elemetal 405 605-2402
  1000 Cornell Pkwy Ste 800 Oklahoma City (73108) *(G-6023)*
Elens 918 627-5395
  4138 S 88th East Ave Tulsa (74145) *(G-9654)*
Elevated Candles 405 763-8223
  2701 N Lyon Blvd Oklahoma City (73107) *(G-6024)*
Eli Lilly and Company 918 250-6848
  3611 W Boston Ct Broken Arrow (74012) *(G-896)*
Eli Lilly and Company 918 459-4540
  7633 E 63rd Pl Ste 300 Tulsa (74133) *(G-9655)*
Elite Cabinets 918 794-0757
  11320 E 20th St Tulsa (74128) *(G-9656)*
Elite Creative Solutions LLC 918 994-5435
  2502 N Hemlock Cir Broken Arrow (74012) *(G-897)*
Elite Fabricators LLC 918 824-4528
  49 N 435 Pryor (74361) *(G-7961)*
Elite Manufacturing LLC 918 266-1077
  950 Verdigris Pkwy Catoosa (74015) *(G-1317)*
Elite Media Group LLC 405 928-5800
  2700 Technology Pl Norman (73071) *(G-4989)*
Elite Polishing Co 405 371-5780
  114 Nw 3rd St Blanchard (73010) *(G-714)*
Elite Sign Brokers 405 200-6970
  8921 Nw 85th St Oklahoma City (73132) *(G-6025)*
Elite Wood Creations LLC 580 220-1153
  15 W Broadway St Ardmore (73401) *(G-284)*
Elk Citian 580 799-0925
  120 S Main St Elk City (73644) *(G-2807)*
Elk City Daily News Inc 580 225-3000
  109 W Broadway Ave Elk City (73644) *(G-2808)*
Elk City Forklift Service Inc 580 225-0855
  19482 E 1140 Rd Elk City (73644) *(G-2809)*
Elk City Sheet Metal Inc 580 225-5844
  217 N Main St Elk City (73644) *(G-2810)*
Elk City Sheet Metal Works, Elk City Also called Elk City Sheet Metal Inc *(G-2810)*
Elk City Wind LLC 580 772-2080
  17265 E 1070 Rd Sweetwater (73666) *(G-8847)*
Elk Valley Woodworking Inc 580 486-3337
  12334 N 2000 Rd Carter (73627) *(G-1281)*
Elkhorn Energy, Tulsa Also called Elkhorn Operating Company *(G-9657)*
Elkhorn Operating Company (PA) 918 492-4418
  4613 S 91st St Tulsa (74137) *(G-9657)*
Elkouri Land Services LLC 405 604-5580
  3116 White Cedar Dr Moore (73160) *(G-4519)*

Ellen Broach CPA 918 665-7773
  8123 E 48th St Tulsa (74145) *(G-9658)*
Elliot Enterprises 918 742-9916
  2761 E Skelly Dr Ste 700e Tulsa (74105) *(G-9659)*
Elliott Diversified Inds LLC 918 293-2218
  4171 E 47th St Tulsa (74135) *(G-9660)*
Elliott Precision Products Inc 918 234-4001
  16309 E Latimer St Tulsa (74116) *(G-9661)*
Elliott, Lloyd S, Tulsa Also called Elliot Enterprises *(G-9659)*
Ellis Bridal LLC 501 247-8698
  8931 S Yale Ave Tulsa (74137) *(G-9662)*
Ellis Construction Spc LLC 405 848-4676
  12409 Holmboe Ave Oklahoma City (73114) *(G-6026)*
Ellis County Capital 580 885-7788
  323 E Renfrow Ave Arnett (73832) *(G-387)*
Ellis Enterprise 405 826-3572
  3000 S 9th Ave Trlr 106 Purcell (73080) *(G-8007)*
Ellis Enterprises Inc 405 917-5336
  5100 N Brookline Ave # 465 Oklahoma City (73112) *(G-6027)*
Ellis Manufacturing Co Inc 405 528-4671
  4803 N Cooper Ave Oklahoma City (73118) *(G-6028)*
Ellis Welding 580 856-3907
  Hc 1 Ratliff City (73481) *(G-8052)*
Ellison Clark Irevocable Trust, Oklahoma City Also called Clark Ellison *(G-5775)*
Elm Creek Gravel LLC 405 360-7300
  1529 24th Ave Sw Norman (73072) *(G-4990)*
Elqui International Ltd Co 918 335-5002
  330 Sw Watson Ave Bartlesville (74003) *(G-480)*
Elroy Machine Inc 580 658-6725
  4414 E York Rd Marlow (73055) *(G-4231)*
Elson Oil Co 918 584-5225
  20 E 5th St Ste 1404 Tulsa (74103) *(G-9663)*
Elster Amco Water Inc 863 453-5336
  417 Misty Ridge Dr Norman (73071) *(G-4991)*
Elvis S Seshie 405 887-3050
  11216 Sw 37th St Mustang (73064) *(G-4770)*
Elynx Technologies LLC (PA) 877 643-5969
  2431 E 6th St Tulsa (74104) *(G-9664)*
Elysium Industries 405 394-3087
  710 Esther Ave Midwest City (73130) *(G-4440)*
Embrodred Mnograms Designs LLC 918 335-5055
  137 Ne Washington Blvd Bartlesville (74006) *(G-481)*
Embroidery By Stacie 580 656-5232
  42 Sonora St Ardmore (73401) *(G-285)*
Embroidery Creations 405 728-1355
  8117 Nw 118th St Oklahoma City (73162) *(G-6029)*
Embroidery For You, Holdenville Also called Webber Kathryn *(G-3562)*
Embroidery Plus 918 652-2117
  116025 Highway 124 Weleetka (74880) *(G-11464)*
Embroidme of Tulsa 918 459-6699
  7115 S Mingo Rd Tulsa (74133) *(G-9665)*
Embroidme- Yukon, Mustang Also called Girlinghouse Unlimited LLC *(G-4773)*
EMC 918 583-6363
  1437 S Boulder Ave # 940 Tulsa (74119) *(G-9666)*
EMC 405 320-5675
  1728 Frisco Ave Chickasha (73018) *(G-1456)*
EMC Beauty LLC 316 655-8839
  123 Ne 2nd St Apt 179 Oklahoma City (73104) *(G-6030)*
EMC Law Pllc 832 560-6280
  1132 E 21st St Tulsa (74114) *(G-9667)*
EMC Services LLC 405 596-0050
  1400 Sw 56th St Oklahoma City (73119) *(G-6031)*
Emco LLC 918 342-3488
  24625 Amah Pkwy Claremore (74019) *(G-1616)*
Emco Industries LLC 918 342-3488
  24625 Amah Pkwy Claremore (74019) *(G-1617)*
Emco Spring, Claremore Also called Emco Industries LLC *(G-1617)*
Emco Springs, Claremore Also called Emco LLC *(G-1616)*
Emerald Film System, Oklahoma City Also called Emerald Manufacturing Corp *(G-6032)*
Emerald Isle of Midwest Inc 405 802-0092
  3891 N Choctaw Rd Choctaw (73020) *(G-1541)*
Emerald Manufacturing Corp 405 235-3704
  515 E California Ave Oklahoma City (73104) *(G-6032)*
Emerald Quest 580 920-5917
  2015 W Liveoak St Durant (74701) *(G-2229)*
Emergency Alert Response 918 298-0500
  6725 E 102nd St Tulsa (74133) *(G-9668)*
Emergency Site Protection LLC 580 699-6386
  191 W Lake Dr Medicine Park (73557) *(G-4370)*
Emerging Fuels Technology LLC 918 286-6802
  6024 S 116th East Ave Tulsa (74146) *(G-9669)*
Emerson Process Management 918 622-6161
  9932 E 58th St Tulsa (74146) *(G-9670)*
Emert Enterprises LLC 580 495-5511
  326 E Valliant St Bennington (74723) *(G-563)*
Emery Bay Corporation (PA) 918 494-2988
  4938 E 73rd St Tulsa (74136) *(G-9671)*
Emg Graphic Systems Inc 918 835-5300
  1110 N Iroquois Ave Tulsa (74106) *(G-9672)*

(PA)=Parent Co (HQ)=Headquarters (DH)=Div Headquarters

Emjo Operations Inc 580 658-6457
  4754 County Street 2950 Marlow (73055) *(G-4232)*
Emmaus Group LLC 918 834-8787
  2202 N 170th East Ave Tulsa (74116) *(G-9673)*
Emoteq Corporation (HQ) 918 627-1845
  10002 E 43rd St Tulsa (74146) *(G-9674)*
Emp Incorporated 918 756-5767
  5030 N Wood Dr Okmulgee (74447) *(G-7501)*
Empire Laser & Metal Work LLC 918 584-6232
  4151 W Albany St Broken Arrow (74012) *(G-898)*
Empire Louisiana LLC 539 444-8002
  1203 E 33rd St Ste 250 Tulsa (74105) *(G-9675)*
Empire Louisiana LLC Delaware, Tulsa *Also called Empire Louisiana LLC (G-9675)*
Empire Optical Inc 918 744-8005
  3220 E 21st St Tulsa (74114) *(G-9676)*
Empire Petroleum Corporation (PA) 539 444-8002
  1203 E 33rd St Ste 250 Tulsa (74105) *(G-9677)*
Empire Plumbing Contrs LLC 918 320-1427
  307 N 3rd St Grove (74344) *(G-3267)*
Empowered Life Stores LLC 918 523-5700
  7498 E 46th Pl Tulsa (74145) *(G-9678)*
EMR Machine 405 361-7991
  4224 Cemetery Rd Noble (73068) *(G-4879)*
En-Fab Corp 918 251-9647
  8200 S 202nd East Ave Broken Arrow (74014) *(G-1126)*
Enable Midstream Partners LP 580 225-7190
  1316 Airport Indus Rd Elk City (73644) *(G-2811)*
Enable Okla Intrstate Trnsm LL (HQ) 405 525-7788
  499 W Sheridan Ave # 1500 Oklahoma City (73102) *(G-6033)*
Enable Okla Intrstate Trnsm LL 405 969-3906
  15400 W Cooksey Rd Crescent (73028) *(G-1914)*
Enable Oklahoma Int Transm LLC 405 356-4060
  500 Ash St Wellston (74881) *(G-11469)*
Enable Oklahoma Int Transm LLC 580 661-2266
  23584 E 880 Rd Thomas (73669) *(G-8943)*
Enable Oklahoma Int Transm LLC 580 323-7450
  5 Mile E 1 And One Half S Clinton (73601) *(G-1750)*
Enardo, Tulsa *Also called Emerson Process Management (G-9670)*
Enardo Inc 918 622-6161
  4470 S 70th East Ave Tulsa (74145) *(G-9679)*
Enardo Manufacturing Co 918 622-6161
  9932 E 58th St Tulsa (74146) *(G-9680)*
Enchanted Delights LLC 405 202-5782
  2322 Sw 48th St Oklahoma City (73119) *(G-6034)*
Encinos 3d Custom Products LLC 918 286-8535
  9810 E 58th St Tulsa (74146) *(G-9681)*
Encompass Media LLC 405 823-8081
  1715 N Midwest Blvd Oklahoma City (73141) *(G-6035)*
Encompass Tool & Machine Inc 580 762-5800
  2402 Sykes Blvd Ponca City (74601) *(G-7825)*
Encore Cnstr Solutions LLC 405 542-3316
  31200 I 40 Service Rd 3 Hinton (73047) *(G-3525)*
Endeavor Lser Etching Engrv LL 405 202-5921
  617 Cross Timbers Dr Moore (73160) *(G-4520)*
Endico Inc 405 340-8009
  2000 E 15th St Ste 450 Edmond (73013) *(G-2411)*
Endurance Publishing LLC 405 332-5273
  5811 Trenton Ave Stillwater (74074) *(G-8683)*
Ener-Corr Solutions LLC 405 509-9291
  2136 Huntleigh Dr Oklahoma City (73120) *(G-6036)*
Enerex Inc 918 258-3573
  1217 E Houston St Broken Arrow (74012) *(G-899)*
Enerfin Inc 918 258-3571
  1217 E Houston St Broken Arrow (74012) *(G-900)*
Enerfin Resources Company 918 492-8686
  2250 E 73rd St Ste 410 Tulsa (74136) *(G-9682)*
Enerfin Resources I Ltd Partnr 405 382-3049
  400 N Harvey Rd Seminole (74868) *(G-8371)*
Energas Corp (PA) 405 879-1752
  800 Ne 63rd St Ste 300 Oklahoma City (73105) *(G-6037)*
Energes 580 339-8044
  610 S Van Buren Ave Elk City (73644) *(G-2812)*
Energetic Materials 405 203-2859
  1604 Norwood Pl Nichols Hills (73120) *(G-4860)*
Energy and Envmtl Svcs Inc 405 285-8767
  6701 Boucher Dr Edmond (73034) *(G-2412)*
Energy and Envmtl Svcs Inc (PA) 405 843-8996
  6300 Boucher Dr Edmond (73034) *(G-2413)*
Energy Annastin 405 810-5460
  701 N Broadway Ave # 120 Oklahoma City (73102) *(G-6038)*
Energy Control System Inc 918 481-3244
  1787 E 71st St Tulsa (74136) *(G-9683)*
Energy Equip Sales Co 580 276-5900
  72 Golf Club Dr Burneyville (73430) *(G-1216)*
Energy Financial & Physcl EFP, Oklahoma City *Also called Energy Financial and Physcl LP (G-6039)*
Energy Financial and Physcl LP 405 702-4700
  105 N Hudson Ave Ste 206 Oklahoma City (73102) *(G-6039)*
Energy Innovation Ctr N Amer, Oklahoma City *Also called Baker Hughes A GE Company LLC (G-5514)*

Energy Meter Systems LLC 405 853-4976
  1161 S Main St Hennessey (73742) *(G-3460)*
Energy Partners 405 573-9064
  1020 24th Ave Nw Norman (73069) *(G-4992)*
Energyvest Inc 918 549-1838
  8211 E Regal Pl Ste 103 Tulsa (74133) *(G-9684)*
Enerlabs Inc 405 879-1752
  6300 Nw Expressway Oklahoma City (73132) *(G-6040)*
Enerquest Oil & Gas LLC 405 478-3300
  12368 Market Dr Oklahoma City (73114) *(G-6041)*
Enersource Petroleum Inc 918 446-8028
  4550 W 57th St Tulsa (74107) *(G-9685)*
Engatech Inc (PA) 918 599-7500
  233 S Detroit Ave Ste 300 Tulsa (74120) *(G-9686)*
Engineered Food Processes LLC 405 377-7320
  1010 W Osage Dr Stillwater (74075) *(G-8684)*
Engineering Automation Tech, Tulsa *Also called Engatech Inc (G-9686)*
Engineering Consultant, Ardmore *Also called Spring Harry A Geological Engr (G-361)*
Engineering Technology Inc 918 492-0508
  11920 E Apache St Tulsa (74116) *(G-9687)*
Engineering Tooling Svc LLC 405 381-9322
  5911 Aero Dr Tuttle (73089) *(G-11197)*
Engines Alive 918 406-8149
  1637 S Birch Ave Broken Arrow (74012) *(G-901)*
Engius LLC 405 533-3770
  712 Eastgate St Stillwater (74074) *(G-8685)*
Engraving Designs LLC 580 763-4228
  7879 Lake Rd Ponca City (74604) *(G-7826)*
Enhanced Printing Products, Tulsa *Also called Thompson Manufacturing Company (G-10935)*
Enhanced Printing Products Inc 918 585-1991
  6315 E 12th St Tulsa (74112) *(G-9688)*
Enid Cbd Company LLC 580 297-5011
  721 S Oakwood Rd Enid (73703) *(G-2949)*
Enid Concrete Co Inc 580 237-7766
  621 W Birch Ave Enid (73701) *(G-2950)*
Enid Drill Systems Inc 580 234-5971
  1611 W Chestnut Ave Enid (73703) *(G-2951)*
Enid Electric Motor Svc Inc 580 234-8622
  3311 N 4th St Enid (73701) *(G-2952)*
Enid Insulation & Siding Inc 580 237-5317
  808 W Willow Rd Enid (73703) *(G-2953)*
Enid Mack Sales Inc 580 234-0043
  5913 E Owen K Garriott Rd Enid (73701) *(G-2954)*
Enid News and Eagle, The, Enid *Also called Newspaper Holding Inc (G-3018)*
Enid Packing Co, Enid *Also called Janice Sue Daniel (G-2981)*
Enogex Services Corporation (HQ) 405 525-7788
  515 Central Park Dr # 408 Oklahoma City (73105) *(G-6042)*
Enogex Services Corporation 405 893-2267
  18005 W 192nd St Calumet (73014) *(G-1246)*
Enos Kauk 580 488-3375
  203737 E 820 Rd Leedey (73654) *(G-4028)*
Enovation Controls LLC (HQ) 918 317-4100
  5311 S 122nd East Ave Tulsa (74146) *(G-9689)*
Enterprise Energy Production, Tulsa *Also called Enterprise Exploration Inc (G-9690)*
Enterprise Exploration Inc 918 481-2125
  6528 D 1 Ste 392 Tulsa (74133) *(G-9690)*
Enterprise Grain Company LLC (PA) 580 874-2286
  Po Box 68 Kremlin (73753) *(G-3851)*
Enterprise Ice Inc 580 237-4015
  416 S Independence St Enid (73701) *(G-2955)*
Enterprise Manufacturing LLC 918 438-4455
  16309 E Latimer St Tulsa (74116) *(G-9691)*
Enterprise Manufacturing LLC 918 438-4455
  1720 N 161st East Ave Tulsa (74116) *(G-9692)*
Entransco Inc 916 628-6835
  112 N Delaware St Dewey (74029) *(G-2021)*
Entwined Vines Winery LLC 405 320-0452
  17134 County Road 1340 Anadarko (73005) *(G-203)*
Entz Ground Sterilant Inc 405 542-3174
  910 S Broadway Hinton (73047) *(G-3526)*
Entz Oilfield Chemicals Inc (PA) 405 542-3174
  S Hwy 281 Hinton (73047) *(G-3527)*
Envia Energy Oklahoma City LLC 405 427-0790
  3500 N Sooner Rd Oklahoma City (73141) *(G-6043)*
Envirnmental Toxin Removal LLC 405 757-4099
  2410 W Memorial Rd Oklahoma City (73134) *(G-6044)*
Envirnmntal Tchncians Okla LLC 580 772-7805
  720 N Wilson Rd Weatherford (73096) *(G-11411)*
Envirnmntal Tchncians Okla LLC 580 227-2521
  3 And A Half Mile N Fairview (73737) *(G-3135)*
Enviro Clean, Oklahoma City *Also called Enviro-Clean Services L L C (G-6045)*
Enviro Clean 918 207-9779
  19150 E Flournory Rd Park Hill (74451) *(G-7642)*
Enviro Log Operating LLC 405 834-1417
  15305 N Richland Rd Piedmont (73078) *(G-7761)*
Enviro Valve (us) Inc 918 251-6103
  807 N Sycamore Ave Broken Arrow (74012) *(G-902)*

ALPHABETIC SECTION

Enviro-Clean Services L L C 405 373-4545
525 Central Park Dr # 500 Oklahoma City (73105) *(G-6045)*
Enviro-Tech Products, Choctaw *Also called Lothrop Technologies Inc* *(G-1551)*
Environmate Inc 817 707-5282
16171 Redbud Dr Catoosa (74015) *(G-1318)*
Environmental Compliance LLC 405 949-0103
2333 Nw 3rd St Oklahoma City (73107) *(G-6046)*
Environmental Concepts Inc 405 385-0422
6911 S Prairie Rd Stillwater (74074) *(G-8686)*
Environmental Remediation 405 235-9999
4625 S Rockwell St Oklahoma City (73179) *(G-6047)*
Environmental Tstg & Oil Lab, Oklahoma City *Also called Oilab Inc* *(G-6723)*
Enxnet Inc 918 494-6663
7450 S Winston Ave Tulsa (74136) *(G-9693)*
Eog Resources Inc 580 225-8314
105 Stout Dr Elk City (73644) *(G-2813)*
Eog Resources Inc 405 246-3100
14701 Hrtz Qail Sprng Pkw Oklahoma City (73134) *(G-6048)*
Ep Scientific Products LLC 918 540-1507
520 N Main St Miami (74354) *(G-4401)*
Eppingers 580 248-1442
2106 One Half Nw Fort Sil Lawton (73507) *(G-3922)*
Equal Energy US Inc 405 242-6000
15 W 6th St Ste 1201 Tulsa (74119) *(G-9694)*
Equidae, Bartlesville *Also called American Zinc Recycling Corp* *(G-447)*
Equipment Company 918 273-0240
830 S Ash St Nowata (74048) *(G-5214)*
Equipment Technology Inc 405 748-3841
341 Nw 122nd St Oklahoma City (73114) *(G-6049)*
Equivaq Software LLC 405 742-0598
1414 S Sangre Rd Stillwater (74074) *(G-8687)*
Equus Metalcraft Llc 918 832-0956
303 S 123rd East Pl Tulsa (74128) *(G-9695)*
Equus Metals Inc 918 834-9872
303 S 123rd East Pl Tulsa (74128) *(G-9696)*
Ergon Inc 918 266-7070
5850 Arkansas Rd Catoosa (74015) *(G-1319)*
Ergon A E Lawton 580 536-0098
9301 Sw Koch St Lawton (73505) *(G-3923)*
Ergon Ardmore 580 223-8010
2500 Refinery Rd Ardmore (73401) *(G-286)*
Ergon Asphalt & Emulsions Inc 918 683-1732
2501 Port Pl Muskogee (74403) *(G-4673)*
Eric Adams Trim 405 570-5931
402 Beebe St Jones (73049) *(G-3745)*
Eric Turner 918 423-7330
820 N Main St McAlester (74501) *(G-4295)*
Erik Democrat, Sayre *Also called Spitzer Publishing* *(G-8347)*
Erik Robins 580 371-1470
237 Killarney Lake Rd Ardmore (73401) *(G-287)*
Erik Robins Woodworks, Ardmore *Also called Erik Robins* *(G-287)*
Erin Turner Custom EMB LLC 918 869-6481
5426 E 110th Pl Tulsa (74137) *(G-9697)*
Ernest Wiemann Iron Works 918 592-1700
639 W 41st St Tulsa (74107) *(G-9698)*
Ernst Valve & Fittings 918 446-0313
6503 S 57th West Ave Tulsa (74131) *(G-9003)*
Ershigs Inc 918 477-9371
9910 E 56th St N Tulsa (74117) *(G-9699)*
Es2-Tulsa, Tulsa *Also called Hks Energy Solutions Inc* *(G-9934)*
Esb Sales Inc 918 227-0378
408 Pioneer Rd Sapulpa (74066) *(G-8270)*
Escher Corp 405 751-2893
2932 Nw 122nd St Ste G Oklahoma City (73120) *(G-6050)*
Eseco-Speedmaster 918 225-1266
730 E Eseco Rd Cushing (74023) *(G-1933)*
Eskridge Production Co Inc 918 836-3058
412 S Allegheny Ave Tulsa (74112) *(G-9700)*
Esperanza Resources Corp 918 497-1231
7170 S Braden Ave Ste 200 Tulsa (74136) *(G-9701)*
Espiritu Miki 405 213-5167
6025 Se 87th St Oklahoma City (73135) *(G-6051)*
Essex Energy Inc 405 350-1351
11141 Nw 10th St Yukon (73099) *(G-11722)*
Essilor Laboratories Amer Inc 800 568-5367
7633 E 63rd Pl Ste 300 Tulsa (74133) *(G-9702)*
Estate Sales By Greg Earles 405 210-8472
12609 Redstone Ct Oklahoma City (73142) *(G-6052)*
Estee Lauder Companies Inc 405 949-9757
3030 Nw Expressway Oklahoma City (73112) *(G-6053)*
Estey Cabinet Door Co 405 771-3004
9100 Ne 40th St Spencer (73084) *(G-8595)*
Et Industries LLC 918 485-3374
603 W Cherokee St Wagoner (74467) *(G-11283)*
Etched In Stone 918 369-0500
8303 E 111th St S Ste A Bixby (74008) *(G-621)*
Etched Ordnance LLC 918 855-8779
26387 E 115th Pl S Coweta (74429) *(G-1882)*
Etr Fabricators, Oklahoma City *Also called Equipment Technology Inc* *(G-6049)*

Ets-Lindgren Inc 580 434-7490
1016 Waldron Dr Durant (74701) *(G-2230)*
Etx Energy LLC (PA) 918 728-3020
6100 S Yale Ave Ste 500 Tulsa (74136) *(G-9703)*
Eubankswoodworks LLC 918 245-7835
1201 E 8th St Sand Springs (74063) *(G-8182)*
Eufrates Com LLC 918 280-9270
9810 E 42nd St Ste 102 Tulsa (74146) *(G-9704)*
Eulitt Welding 918 542-2635
50300 E 120 Rd Miami (74354) *(G-4402)*
Euphoria Okc Cbd LLC 405 412-2448
1618 N Blackwelder Ave Oklahoma City (73106) *(G-6054)*
Eurecat U S Incorporated 918 423-5800
100 Steven Taylor Blvd McAlester (74501) *(G-4296)*
Eurocraft Ltd 918 322-5500
16052 S Broadway St Glenpool (74033) *(G-3234)*
Evan & Sons Inc 405 756-2704
512 Industrial Park Lindsay (73052) *(G-4061)*
Evans & Assoc Utility Svcs 580 351-1800
2208 Sw F Ave Lawton (73501) *(G-3924)*
Evans & Associates Cnstr Co 580 765-6693
3320 N 14th St Ponca City (74601) *(G-7827)*
Evans & Associates Entps Inc 580 482-3418
710 S Jackson St Altus (73521) *(G-155)*
Evans & Associates Entps Inc (PA) 580 765-6693
3320 N 14th St Ponca City (74601) *(G-7828)*
Evans Asphalt Co Inc (HQ) 580 765-6693
3320 N 14th St Ponca City (74601) *(G-7829)*
Evans Coal Company 405 202-3239
15008 Gaillardia Dr Oklahoma City (73142) *(G-6055)*
Evans Concrete Co Inc 580 765-6693
4000 W 133rd St N Skiatook (74070) *(G-8543)*
Evans Electric Motors, Tulsa *Also called Evans Enterprises Inc* *(G-9707)*
Evans Enterprises 918 587-1566
2020 Southwest Blvd Tulsa (74107) *(G-9705)*
Evans Enterprises Inc (PA) 405 631-1344
6707 N Interstate Dr Norman (73069) *(G-4993)*
Evans Enterprises Inc 918 587-1566
2002 Southwest Blvd Tulsa (74107) *(G-9706)*
Evans Enterprises Inc 918 825-2200
2002 Southwest Blvd Tulsa (74107) *(G-9707)*
Evans Tool Co Inc 580 889-5770
301 S Bond St Atoka (74525) *(G-412)*
Evans Welding LLC 580 470-8111
615 E Willow Ave Duncan (73533) *(G-2116)*
Evco Service Co Inc 405 381-2172
1317 County St Ste 2910 Tuttle (73089) *(G-11198)*
Eve Breathe 918 454-2866
53100 S 34800 Rd Pawnee (74058) *(G-7704)*
Evelyn Co Inc 918 665-3952
7401 E 46th Pl Tulsa (74145) *(G-9708)*
Evening Glow Candles 918 543-2990
9371 W 600 Rd Inola (74036) *(G-3658)*
Eventsigns.biz, Owasso *Also called Dunbar Event Signs Inc* *(G-7564)*
Everest Acqsition Holdings Inc 918 770-7190
7737 E 42nd Pl Ste H Tulsa (74145) *(G-9709)*
Everest Sciences An S T Co LLC 918 770-7190
17411 E Pine St Tulsa (74116) *(G-9710)*
Everetts Welding & Repair 580 995-4942
412 E Broadway Vici (73859) *(G-11242)*
Everhart Publishing LLC 405 370-4850
2929 Fennel Rd Oklahoma City (73128) *(G-6056)*
Eversharp Tool Inc 918 250-9400
11350 E 60th Pl Tulsa (74146) *(G-9711)*
Every Nook & Cranny 580 332-3899
110 E Main St Ada (74820) *(G-34)*
Everyday Foods LLC 918 299-7939
412 N Juniper St Jenks (74037) *(G-3705)*
Everything Welding & Safety In 405 701-3711
3451 N Flood Ave Norman (73069) *(G-4994)*
Eves Apple 512 970-9016
1107 W Apache St Norman (73069) *(G-4995)*
Evoqua Water Technologies LLC 978 614-7233
9410 E 51st St Tulsa (74145) *(G-9712)*
Ewing Electric Company, Stillwater *Also called Doug Roberson* *(G-8677)*
Ex-Press Vac LLC 580 606-0799
1625 E Bois D Arc Ave Duncan (73533) *(G-2117)*
Excalibur Cast Stone LLC 405 702-4314
1601 Sw 89th St Ste B400 Oklahoma City (73159) *(G-6057)*
Excalibur Stoneworks LLC 405 702-4314
3820 Nw 39th St Oklahoma City (73112) *(G-6058)*
Excalibur Welding Service LLC 580 302-2570
1800 Pleasant Ln Weatherford (73096) *(G-11412)*
Excel Manufacturing LLC 918 418-9589
435426 E 300 Rd Vinita (74301) *(G-11256)*
Excel Mining LLC (HQ) 918 295-7600
1717 S Boulder Ave Tulsa (74119) *(G-9713)*
Excel Paralubes LLC 800 527-3236
411 S Keeler Ave Bartlesville (74003) *(G-482)*

(PA)=Parent Co (HQ)=Headquarters (DH)=Div Headquarters

Excel Products — 202573 E County Road 43 # 13 Woodward (73801) *(G-11582)* 580 216-0784

Excell Products Inc — 2500 Enterprise Blvd Choctaw (73020) *(G-1542)* 405 390-4491

Excellence Logging — 7136 S Yale Ave Ste 420 Tulsa (74136) *(G-9714)* 815 272-7622

Exco Mid Continent Division, Tulsa *Also called Exco Resources Inc* *(G-9715)*

Exco Midcontinent Division, Lindsay *Also called Exco Resources Inc* *(G-4062)*

Exco Resources Inc — 804 W Cherokee St Lindsay (73052) *(G-4062)* 405 756-4347

Exco Resources Inc — 2100 One Williams Ctr Tulsa (74172) *(G-9715)* 918 592-7300

Executive Coffee Service Co (PA) — 11 Ne 11th St Oklahoma City (73104) *(G-6059)* 405 236-3932

Executive Forms & Supplies (PA) — 3848 Nw 10th St Oklahoma City (73107) *(G-6060)* 817 423-9088

Exide Battery, Oklahoma City *Also called Exide Technologies LLC* *(G-6061)*

Exide Technologies LLC — 6000 Nw 2nd St Ste 100 Oklahoma City (73127) *(G-6061)* 405 745-2511

Exok Inc — 6410 N Santa Fe Ave Ste B Oklahoma City (73116) *(G-6062)* 405 840-9196

Expanded Solutions LLC — 300 N Wewoka Ave Wewoka (74884) *(G-11501)* 405 946-6791

Exponent Energy LLC — 1560 E 21st St Ste 215 Tulsa (74114) *(G-9716)* 918 906-6045

Express Bus Inc — 6333 E Apache St Tulsa (74115) *(G-9717)* 918 835-2040

Express Energy Svcs Oper LP — 2704 S Meridian Ave Oklahoma City (73108) *(G-6063)* 405 763-5850

Express Exterminators, Oklahoma City *Also called Darren McIninch* *(G-5285)*

Express Home Help — 3903 N Harrison St Shawnee (74804) *(G-8448)* 405 214-6400

Express Ltg & Sign Maint LLC — 4311 Sw 119th St Oklahoma City (73173) *(G-6064)* 405 378-3838

Express Metal Fabricators LLC — 9490 E Highway 412 Locust Grove (74352) *(G-4106)* 918 622-1420

Express Metal Fabricators Inc — 32207 S Highway 69 Big Cabin (74332) *(G-603)* 918 783-5129

Express Personnel Services, Shawnee *Also called Express Home Help* *(G-8448)*

Expro Americas LLC — 4404 Sw 134th St Oklahoma City (73173) *(G-6065)* 405 378-6762

Extended Fin — 7219 Ferguson Rd Mounds (74047) *(G-4614)* 918 827-4044

Exterran, Elk City *Also called Archrock Inc* *(G-2784)*

Extract Production Svcs LLC — 1336 N 143rd East Ave Tulsa (74116) *(G-9718)* 918 938-6828

Extract Surface Systems LLC — 1336 N 143rd East Ave Tulsa (74116) *(G-9719)* 918 938-6828

Extract Touch-Up LLC — 505 E Reno Pl Broken Arrow (74012) *(G-903)* 918 639-4011

Extraordinary Woodworks — 4402 Oakcrest Ave Enid (73703) *(G-2956)* 801 995-0906

EZ Carrier, Mounds *Also called Givens Manufacturing Inc* *(G-4616)*

EZ Carrier LLC — 975 Highway 75 Mounds (74047) *(G-4615)* 918 827-7876

EZ Mail Express — 1621 N Main St Miami (74354) *(G-4403)* 918 542-2057

Ezekiel Chrles Pblications LLC — 8709 S 70th East Ave Tulsa (74133) *(G-9720)* 918 747-8841

F & F Automotive Inc — 1 And A Half Mi E On Hwy Valliant (74764) *(G-11223)* 580 933-4262

F & F Machine Shop Inc — 2115 Sw 42nd St Oklahoma City (73119) *(G-6066)* 405 680-0900

F & F Production Eqp Svcs LLC — 25640 Winding Trail Rd Bokoshe (74930) *(G-753)* 479 414-2772

F & F Tool Co (PA) — 1819 E Highway 270 Seminole (74868) *(G-8372)* 405 382-0009

F A Highly Counter Top Werks, Oklahoma City *Also called Countertop Werks Inc* *(G-5843)*

F C Witt Associates Ltd — 2211 El Anderson Blvd Claremore (74017) *(G-1618)* 918 342-0083

F C Ziegler Co (PA) — 2111 E 11th St Ste A-B Tulsa (74104) *(G-9721)* 918 587-7639

F G Sawmill LLC — 723 Hwy 51 Stilwell (74960) *(G-8788)* 918 905-1132

F M C Energy Systems, Oklahoma City *Also called FMC Technologies Inc* *(G-6099)*

F W Grubb Oilfield Service — Corner Of Rlrad Apache St Garber (73738) *(G-3213)* 580 863-2395

F&D Defense LLC — 201 W Oak Ave Seminole (74868) *(G-8373)* 512 745-6482

F&D Industries LLC — 4800 W Houston St Broken Arrow (74012) *(G-904)* 918 461-0447

Fab Seal Industrial Liners Inc — 6121 Highway 177 Shawnee (74804) *(G-8449)* 405 878-0166

Fab Tech Welding — 17535 Bow Rd Mulhall (73063) *(G-4638)* 405 649-2322

Fabric Factory — 1421 Nw 23rd St Oklahoma City (73106) *(G-6067)* 405 521-1694

Fabricating Specialists Inc — 1915 Se 29th St Oklahoma City (73129) *(G-6068)* 405 476-1959

Fabrication Dynamics — 6611 State Highway 66 Tulsa (74131) *(G-9004)* 918 445-6100

Fabrication Dynamics Inc — 2102 W Skelly Dr Tulsa (74107) *(G-9722)* 918 446-1638

Fabrication Solutions LLC — 109 S 122nd East Ave Tulsa (74128) *(G-9723)* 918 398-7162

Fabrico Inc — 408 W 2nd Ave Owasso (74055) *(G-7565)* 918 274-9329

Fabricut Inc — S Of City On Hwy 69 Pryor (74361) *(G-7962)* 918 825-4400

Fabricut Inc — 9303 E 46th St Tulsa (74145) *(G-9724)* 918 622-7700

Fabsco Shell and Tube LLC — 2410 Industrial Rd Sapulpa (74066) *(G-8271)* 918 224-7550

Fabwell Corporation — 10611 W Houston St Sapulpa (74066) *(G-8272)* 918 224-9060

Facet (oklahoma) LLC (HQ) — 11607 E 43rd St N Tulsa (74116) *(G-9725)* 918 272-8700

Facet (oklahoma) LLC — 470555 E 868 Rd Stilwell (74960) *(G-8789)* 918 696-3161

Facet (oklahoma) LLC — 470555 E 868 Rd Stilwell (74960) *(G-8790)* 918 696-3161

Facet USA, Stilwell *Also called Facet (oklahoma) LLC* *(G-8789)*

Factor 1 Racing Inc — 805 W Freeport St Broken Arrow (74012) *(G-905)* 918 258-7223

Fadco, Tulsa *Also called Fixtures & Drywall Co Okla Inc* *(G-9751)*

Fadco of Arkansas LLC — 5531 E Admiral Pl Tulsa (74115) *(G-9726)* 918 832-1641

Faded Canvas Barber Studio — 105 N Eastern Ave Moore (73160) *(G-4521)* 405 735-7105

Fairchild Signs — 505 Messenger Ln Moore (73160) *(G-4522)* 405 439-3100

Fairfax Chief — 100 N 2nd St Fairfax (74637) *(G-3118)* 918 642-3814

Fairmount Minerals — 8834 Mayfield Rd Roff (74865) *(G-8108)* 580 456-7791

Fairmount Minerals — 910 S Eastern Ave Elk City (73644) *(G-2814)* 580 303-9160

Fairview Production Co, Muldrow *Also called Morris Richardson* *(G-4634)*

Fairview Ready Mix, Fairview *Also called Green Valley Enterprises Inc* *(G-3136)*

Fairway E&P LLC — 14322 S 50th East Ave Bixby (74008) *(G-622)* 918 284-5322

Fairway Energy LLC — 1601 Nw Expwy St Ste 777 Oklahoma City (73118) *(G-6069)* 405 286-9796

Fairwind LLC — 6862 Nw Meers Porter Hl Lawton (73507) *(G-3925)* 580 492-5209

Faith Church Shawnee — 130 S Oklahoma Ave Shawnee (74801) *(G-8450)* 405 948-7100

Fake Bake LLC — 210 W Wilshire Blvd C3 Oklahoma City (73116) *(G-6070)* 405 843-9660

Falcon Audio Video Inc (PA) — 13560 E 463 Rd Claremore (74017) *(G-1619)* 918 272-3969

Falcon Audio Video East, Claremore *Also called Falcon Audio Video Inc* *(G-1619)*

Falcon Field Service Inc — 150 County Road 1705 Hominy (74035) *(G-3583)* 918 885-2244

Falcon Flowback Services LLC — 1708 Se 25th St Oklahoma City (73129) *(G-6071)* 405 563-0163

Falcon Mx6 Manufacturing LLC — 110 S Witte St Poteau (74953) *(G-7902)* 918 647-4433

Falcon Oil Properties — Hwy 66 And Turner Tpke Bristow (74010) *(G-777)* 918 367-5596

Family Tree Corporation — 1000 E Seneca Ave McAlester (74501) *(G-4297)* 307 850-4147

Family Tree Oil & Gas, McAlester *Also called Family Tree Corporation* *(G-4297)*

Fammco Mfg Co Inc — 17309 E Pine St Tulsa (74116) *(G-9727)* 918 437-0456

Fancy Cakes — 404 W Main St Norman (73069) *(G-4996)* 405 701-3434

Fancy Dancer Leather Designs — 302 W Alabama Ave Anadarko (73005) *(G-204)* 405 247-7030

Fancy Stitch — 1421 Nw Great Plains Blvd A Lawton (73505) *(G-3926)* 580 699-2112

Far West Development LLC — 1410 Nw 44th St Oklahoma City (73118) *(G-6072)* 405 557-1384

Farallon Petroleum LLC — 1425 Nw 37th St Oklahoma City (73118) *(G-6073)* 405 225-1009

Farley Redfield — 20874 Rock Creek Rd Tecumseh (74873) *(G-8914)* 405 275-2266

Farmer Bros Co — 13131 Broadway Ext Oklahoma City (73114) *(G-6074)* 405 751-7222

Farmer Bros Co — 11529 E Pine St Tulsa (74116) *(G-9728)* 918 439-9262

Farmer/Rancher, Ninnekah *Also called Douglas A Pharr* *(G-4870)*

Farmers Brothers Coffee, Oklahoma City *Also called Farmer Bros Co* *(G-6074)*

Farmers Brothers Coffee, Tulsa *Also called Farmer Bros Co* *(G-9728)*

Farmers Co Op (PA) — 1501 S Parkhill Rd Tahlequah (74464) *(G-8864)* 918 456-0557

Farmers Co-Operative Gin Assn — 109 S 6th St Sayre (73662) *(G-8340)* 580 928-2664

ALPHABETIC SECTION — Firetech Automatic Sprinklers

Farmers Coop (PA) 580 772-3334
300 E Clark Ave Weatherford (73096) *(G-11413)*

Farmers Coop Gin of Martha 580 266-3222
304 N Walnut St Martha (73556) *(G-4251)*

Farmers Energy Corp 918 587-6756
1 W 3rd St Ste 918 Tulsa (74103) *(G-9729)*

Farmers Royalty Company 405 521-9685
3829 N Classen Blvd Oklahoma City (73118) *(G-6075)*

Farmers Union Co-Operative Gin 580 482-5136
2109 Afthalt Rd Altus (73521) *(G-156)*

Farrier Livingston Technology 580 657-3469
7300 Myall Rd Ardmore (73401) *(G-288)*

Fascast Inc 918 445-7405
7835 State Highway 66 Tulsa (74131) *(G-9005)*

Fasco Directional Drilling LLC 918 224-2756
1925 Timberton Rd Sapulpa (74066) *(G-8273)*

Fasco Motors Group 405 387-5560
2913 Se 44th St Norman (73072) *(G-4997)*

Fashion Gear Div 405 745-1991
7507 Sw 44th St Oklahoma City (73179) *(G-6076)*

Fashion Sports By Sia Inc 405 524-9990
1300 Nw 23rd St Oklahoma City (73106) *(G-6077)*

Fashionable Medical Covers 405 414-1147
121 Sandstone Dr Norman (73071) *(G-4998)*

Fast Fuel LLC 405 375-6666
100 Mitchell Blvd Kingfisher (73750) *(G-3797)*

Fast Signs 918 251-0330
927 N Elm Pl Broken Arrow (74012) *(G-906)*

Fastcurbs, Claremore Also called Acme Manufacturing Corporation *(G-1575)*

Fastsigns, Broken Arrow Also called Fast Signs *(G-906)*

Fastsigns, Oklahoma City Also called Blankenship Brothers Inc *(G-5586)*

Fastsigns, Oklahoma City Also called Oklahoma Visual Graphics LLC *(G-6764)*

Fastsigns, Oklahoma City Also called Blankenship Brothers Inc *(G-5587)*

Fastsigns, Tulsa Also called Blankenship Brothers Inc *(G-9302)*

Fastsigns, Oklahoma City Also called Blankenship Brothers Inc *(G-5588)*

Fastsigns 918 376-7870
8751 N 117th East Ave D Owasso (74055) *(G-7566)*

Fastsigns 405 701-2908
900 24th Ave Nw Norman (73069) *(G-4999)*

Fastsigns of Lawton 580 595-9101
301 Se Wallock St Lawton (73501) *(G-3927)*

Fat & Happy Services Inc 405 834-5782
4001 Sw 113th St Oklahoma City (73173) *(G-6078)*

Fat Alberts Motor Sports 918 647-3069
28871 N Side Ln Poteau (74953) *(G-7903)*

Fatt Hedz 405 607-8484
2 W Memorial Rd Oklahoma City (73114) *(G-6079)*

Fatutyi Adeshola 785 424-4208
7301 Sw Lee Blvd Apt 602 Lawton (73505) *(G-3928)*

Fd Products LLC 918 698-1644
36154 S Highway 82 Vinita (74301) *(G-11257)*

Fdnd Oil and Gas LLC 918 583-9960
124 E 4th St Tulsa (74103) *(G-9730)*

Featherston Publishing LLC 918 289-7877
7504 E 84th St N Owasso (74055) *(G-7567)*

Federal Metals Inc 918 838-1725
2107 E 48th St Tulsa (74105) *(G-9731)*

Federal Services LLC 405 239-7301
120 E Main St Oklahoma City (73104) *(G-6080)*

Federal-Mogul Chassis LLC 405 672-4500
5600 S Hattie Ave Oklahoma City (73129) *(G-6081)*

Fedex Office & Print Svcs Inc 918 492-6701
1324 E 71st St Tulsa (74136) *(G-9732)*

Fedex Office & Print Svcs Inc 918 252-3757
8228 E 61st St Ste 105 Tulsa (74133) *(G-9733)*

Fedex Office Print & Ship, Tulsa Also called Fedex Office & Print Svcs Inc *(G-9732)*

Fehr Foods Inc 580 276-4100
600 N Highway 77 Marietta (73448) *(G-4207)*

Felini's Cookies & Deli, Tulsa Also called Felinis Cookies Inc *(G-9734)*

Felinis Cookies Inc (PA) 918 742-3638
3533 S Harvard Ave Tulsa (74135) *(G-9734)*

Felkins Enterprises LLC 918 272-3456
9924 N Garnett Rd Owasso (74055) *(G-7568)*

Fellers Inc 918 621-4412
7101 E 38th St Unit 7184 Tulsa (74145) *(G-9735)*

Fellers Inc (PA) 918 621-4400
6566 E Skelly Dr Tulsa (74145) *(G-9736)*

Fence Solutions Inc 580 233-4600
217 W Oxford Ave Enid (73701) *(G-2957)*

Fenimore Manufacturing Inc 405 224-2637
900 N 18th St Chickasha (73018) *(G-1457)*

Fenix Outfitters 918 259-0099
904 S Main St Broken Arrow (74012) *(G-907)*

Fenner Inc 918 832-7768
10338 E 21st St Tulsa (74129) *(G-9737)*

Fenton Office Mart, Stillwater Also called Fenton Office Supply Co *(G-8688)*

Fenton Office Supply Co 405 372-5555
111 W Mcelroy Rd Stillwater (74075) *(G-8688)*

Ferguson 918 835-4813
231 S Memorial Dr Tulsa (74112) *(G-9738)*

Ferguson & Ferguson 918 358-2553
212 S Broadway St Cleveland (74020) *(G-1723)*

Ferguson Enterprises LLC 405 945-0107
3950 Nw 3rd St Oklahoma City (73107) *(G-6082)*

Ferguson Welding LLC 405 534-1517
2178 Fox Ln Tuttle (73089) *(G-11199)*

Ferra Aerospace Inc 918 787-2220
64353 E 290 Rd Grove (74344) *(G-3268)*

Ferra Aerospace Inc (PA) 918 787-2220
64353 E 290 Rd Grove (74344) *(G-3269)*

Ferra Holdings Limited, Grove Also called Ferra Aerospace Inc *(G-3269)*

Fg Welding 405 863-8210
3313 Sw 21st St Oklahoma City (73108) *(G-6083)*

Fhe USA LLC 405 350-2544
12451 Nw 10th St Yukon (73099) *(G-11723)*

Fhl Hot Shot Trucking Services 405 615-6658
16905 Sw 29th St El Reno (73036) *(G-2716)*

Fiber Glass Systems LP 918 245-6651
25 S Main St Sand Springs (74063) *(G-8183)*

Fiber Pad Inc (PA) 918 438-7430
17260 Tiger Switch Rd Tulsa (74116) *(G-9739)*

Fiber Pad Inc 918 438-7430
2201 N 170th East Ave Tulsa (74116) *(G-9740)*

Fibre Reduction Inc 580 223-3401
112 2nd Ave Se Ardmore (73401) *(G-289)*

Fidgets Oilfield Services LLC 918 473-2765
2213 N Broadway St Checotah (74426) *(G-1393)*

Field Aerospace, Oklahoma City Also called Ases LLC *(G-5473)*

Field Aerospace, Oklahoma City Also called Ases LLC *(G-5474)*

Field Services 580 256-3338
N Of City Woodward (73801) *(G-11583)*

Fieldco Inc 918 266-1815
9155 E Misty Dr Claremore (74019) *(G-1620)*

Fieldpoint Energy Services LLC 918 691-3427
7030 S Yale Ave Ste 100 Tulsa (74136) *(G-9741)*

Fields Inc 405 238-7381
100 Fields Row Pauls Valley (73075) *(G-7659)*

Fields Jewelry Inc 405 348-2802
12 S Broadway Edmond (73034) *(G-2414)*

Fife, Oklahoma City Also called Maxcess Americas Inc *(G-6538)*

Fife Corporation (HQ) 405 755-1600
222 W Memorial Rd Oklahoma City (73114) *(G-6084)*

Fifteen Five Gtter Sltions LLC 405 219-6741
3601 Mustang Creek Cir Yukon (73099) *(G-11724)*

Fifth Quarter Printing LLC 918 471-9390
224 S 3rd St McAlester (74501) *(G-4298)*

Filter Supply and Recycling 918 663-3143
4214 S 76th East Ave Tulsa (74145) *(G-9742)*

Filter Wings Corporation 405 258-3183
930554 S 3390 Rd Wellston (74881) *(G-11470)*

Fin Fab Incorporated 918 227-1866
8315 S 89th West Ave Tulsa (74131) *(G-9006)*

Fin-X Inc 918 272-9546
402 W 2nd Ave Owasso (74055) *(G-7569)*

Fincher & Son Pipe & Steel 580 889-6778
13289 S Chisolm Rd Caddo (74729) *(G-1235)*

Fincher & Son Steel Buildings, Caddo Also called Fincher & Son Pipe & Steel *(G-1235)*

Fine Arts Engraving Co Inc 918 835-6400
6716 E 12th St Tulsa (74112) *(G-9743)*

Fineline Manufacturing LLC 918 245-0900
5816 S 116th West Ave A Sand Springs (74063) *(G-8184)*

Finish Line Machining LLC 918 258-2944
800 S 12th St Broken Arrow (74012) *(G-908)*

Finish Line of Oklahoma Inc 918 341-8291
15593 E 523 Rd Claremore (74019) *(G-1621)*

Finish Line Powder Coating 918 938-6292
191 S 122nd East Ave Tulsa (74128) *(G-9744)*

Finished Seam 918 742-4727
3611 S Atlanta Pl Tulsa (74105) *(G-9745)*

Finishing Technology Inc 918 437-3820
11384 E Tecumseh St Tulsa (74116) *(G-9746)*

Finity Enterprises Inc 580 699-2640
605 Sw E Ave Lawton (73501) *(G-3929)*

Finity Marketing Group, Lawton Also called Finity Enterprises Inc *(G-3929)*

Finley Discount Sign Ligh 405 445-8888
1105 Teak Ct Moore (73160) *(G-4523)*

Finley Welding and Fencing, Lawton Also called William B Finley *(G-4023)*

Fire Protection Pubs, Stillwater Also called Oklahoma State University *(G-8733)*

Fire Song Publishing 405 799-2799
621 Sw 27th St Moore (73160) *(G-4524)*

Firecracker Joe, Shawnee Also called American Entps Whl Dstributers *(G-8427)*

Firefly Custom Laser Engrv LLC 405 664-4145
2234 Ravenwood Ln Norman (73071) *(G-5000)*

Firepro Fire Protection Svc 918 857-1513
4812 N Poplar Ave Broken Arrow (74012) *(G-909)*

Firetech Automatic Sprinklers 918 633-3773
12745 New Lake Rd Henryetta (74437) *(G-3506)*

(PA)=Parent Co (HQ)=Headquarters (DH)=Div Headquarters

2020 Oklahoma Directory of Manufacturers & Processors

First Circle, Oklahoma City *Also called Warren Ramsey Inc (G-7422)*
First Class Outlet..918 808-3405
1 E Chickasaw Ave McAlester (74501) *(G-4299)*
First Impression Custom EMB...........................918 787-4182
62311 E 252 Rd Grove (74344) *(G-3270)*
First Impression Prtg Co Inc (PA).....................918 749-5446
11 E Main Beggs (74421) *(G-553)*
First Impression Prtg Co Inc.............................918 749-5446
111 E Main St Beggs (74421) *(G-554)*
First Impressions Inc..918 267-4642
111 E Main St Beggs (74421) *(G-555)*
First Place Sports Center, Pryor *Also called Tim Dees (G-7995)*
First Response Solutions LLC...........................405 284-6430
13400 S Maple Rd Hinton (73047) *(G-3528)*
First Stuart Corporation....................................918 744-5222
2431 E 61st St Ste 600 Tulsa (74136) *(G-9747)*
First Thought Inc..918 336-3322
114 Se Frank Phllips Blvd Bartlesville (74003) *(G-483)*
Firstline Filters LLC...918 660-8772
2201 S Jackson Ave Tulsa (74107) *(G-9748)*
Fis Operations LLC..918 246-7100
2100 S Utica Ave Ste 200 Tulsa (74114) *(G-9749)*
Fish Tale Winery...580 494-6115
17 Oak Leaf Ln Broken Bow (74728) *(G-1190)*
Fish Tales Lure Company LLC..........................918 814-6241
24103 S Highway 66 Claremore (74019) *(G-1622)*
Fisher AG Enterprises Inc..................................918 367-6382
14 Mi S E Of Town Bristow (74010) *(G-778)*
Fisher Products LLC..918 582-2204
1320 W 22nd Pl Tulsa (74107) *(G-9750)*
Fisher Welding..580 748-0445
1618 N Van Buren St Enid (73703) *(G-2958)*
Fisher Wireline Services Inc..............................918 885-6564
11402 County Rd 1701 Hominy (74035) *(G-3584)*
Fisher's Eggs & Grain, Bristow *Also called Fisher AG Enterprises Inc (G-778)*
Fittstone, Fittstown *Also called Jennings Stone Company Inc (G-3159)*
Fittstone Inc...580 777-2808
County Rd 1670 Fittstown (74842) *(G-3158)*
Fitzgerald &SOns Steel LLC..............................918 453-3369
13435 Highway 62 Tahlequah (74464) *(G-8865)*
Fitzs Welding LLC..405 371-1167
627 S Shepherd Dr Mustang (73064) *(G-4771)*
Five A Trailers and Equipment.........................580 564-2973
Hwy 70 N Kingston (73439) *(G-3827)*
Five F Publishing..405 732-1050
4004 Twisted Trail Rd Oklahoma City (73150) *(G-6085)*
Five Point Services Inc......................................580 856-3670
28217 State Highway 76 Ratliff City (73481) *(G-8053)*
Five Star Cub Cadet...918 542-4070
58610 E 100 Rd Miami (74354) *(G-4404)*
Five Star Equipment LLC..................................918 637-0200
404 Wyandotte Ave Ramona (74061) *(G-8045)*
Five Star Steel Inc..405 787-7620
6412 Melrose Ln Oklahoma City (73127) *(G-6086)*
Five Star Technologies, Tulsa *Also called Multiprint Corp (G-10315)*
Fixtures & Drywall Co Okla Inc........................918 832-1641
5531 E Admiral Pl Tulsa (74115) *(G-9751)*
Fixtures Express...405 834-1633
3425 Cheyenne Dr Edmond (73013) *(G-2415)*
Fizz-O-Water Co, Tulsa *Also called O Fizz Inc (G-10370)*
Fjsp Inc..405 306-0735
13001 Twisted Oak Rd Oklahoma City (73120) *(G-6087)*
Fki Industries Inc (HQ)......................................918 834-4611
2801 Dawson Rd Tulsa (74110) *(G-9752)*
Flagship Vapor Company, Oklahoma City *Also called Treehouse Vapor Co LLC (G-7322)*
Flame Control Inc...405 321-2535
1011 W Tecumseh Rd Norman (73069) *(G-5001)*
Flameco Industries Inc.......................................918 832-1100
5943 E 13th St Tulsa (74112) *(G-9753)*
Flaming Hcksaw Fabrication LLC....................479 228-0809
476086 E 740 Rd Westville (74965) *(G-11483)*
Flaming Hope LLC...405 924-4380
9850 E Maguire Rd Noble (73068) *(G-4880)*
Flamingo Media Inc...405 620-5889
12529 Crick Hollow Ct Oklahoma City (73170) *(G-5291)*
Flanagan Energy..580 357-1227
217 N Broadway St Walters (73572) *(G-11300)*
Flanco Gasket and Mfg Inc................................405 672-7893
1010 Se 36th Grand Blvd Oklahoma City (73129) *(G-6088)*
Flanders Corporation..580 223-1853
3500 Flanders Dr Ardmore (73401) *(G-290)*
Flanders of Oklahoma, Ardmore *Also called Flanders Corporation (G-290)*
Flanders of Oklahoma..580 223-5730
3500 Flanders Dr Ardmore (73401) *(G-291)*
Flare Industries...918 376-7811
15008 E 89th St N Owasso (74055) *(G-7570)*
Flash Flood Print Studios LLC..........................918 794-3527
2421 E Admiral Blvd Tulsa (74110) *(G-9754)*
Flashlightz..918 260-5882
7122 S Sheridan Rd 2-546 Tulsa (74133) *(G-9755)*
Flatlands Threading Co Inc................................405 677-7351
1621 E Grand Blvd Oklahoma City (73129) *(G-6089)*
Flatrock Energy Advisers...................................405 341-9993
3856 S Boulevard Ste 210 Edmond (73013) *(G-2416)*
Fleet Service of Tulsa, Tulsa *Also called Reputation Services & Mfg LLC (G-10643)*
Fletcher Lewis Engineering................................405 840-5675
605 N Sweetgum Ave Oklahoma City (73127) *(G-6090)*
Fletcher Welding, Healdton *Also called J Fletcher Derrell (G-3416)*
Flex Chem Corporation (PA).............................580 772-2386
700 N Wilson Rd Weatherford (73096) *(G-11414)*
Flex-Ability Concepts LLC................................405 996-5343
5500 W Reno Ave Ste 300 Oklahoma City (73127) *(G-6091)*
Flex-Chem Services Corporation.......................580 772-2386
700 N Wilson Rd Weatherford (73096) *(G-11415)*
Flex-Kote, Ada *Also called National Coating Mfg Inc (G-70)*
Flex-N-Gate Oklahoma LLC..............................580 272-6700
1 General St Ada (74820) *(G-35)*
Flexx Wireline Services LLC.............................405 990-1593
2729 M And K Ln El Reno (73036) *(G-2717)*
Flightsafety International Inc.............................918 259-4000
700 N 9th St Broken Arrow (74012) *(G-910)*
Flint Energy Services Inc...................................580 856-3251
3 Miles S Highway 76 Ratliff City (73481) *(G-8054)*
Flint Industries...918 599-7162
322 E Archer St Tulsa (74120) *(G-9756)*
Flir Detection Inc...405 533-6618
1024 S Innovation Way Stillwater (74074) *(G-8689)*
Flir Detection Inc (HQ)......................................703 678-2111
1024 S Innovation Way Stillwater (74074) *(G-8690)*
Flir Systems Inc..407 810-3634
1110 S Innovation Way Stillwater (74074) *(G-8691)*
Flir Systems Inc..405 372-9535
1024 S Innovation Way Stillwater (74074) *(G-8692)*
Floatingmats LLC...918 504-8586
13330 S 19th St Bixby (74008) *(G-623)*
Flogistix LP (PA)..405 536-0000
6529 N Classen Blvd Oklahoma City (73116) *(G-6092)*
Flooring Outfitters..580 286-3030
501 Ne Lincoln Rd Idabel (74745) *(G-3637)*
Flores Welding Services LLC............................405 473-5534
11857 Sw 4th St Yukon (73099) *(G-11725)*
Flotek Chemistry LLC..713 849-9911
1004 S Plainsman Rd Marlow (73055) *(G-4233)*
Flotek Industries Inc...580 252-5111
3600 S 13th St Duncan (73533) *(G-2118)*
Flow Measurement Company Inc......................918 493-3443
1214 S Joplin Ave Tulsa (74112) *(G-9757)*
Flow Testing Inc..918 423-0017
1125 W Washington Ave Krebs (74554) *(G-3850)*
Flow Valve LLC...580 622-2294
2214 W 14th St Sulphur (73086) *(G-8832)*
Flow-Quip Inc..918 663-3313
4433 W 49th St Ste D Tulsa (74107) *(G-9758)*
Flowco Energy Service LLC..............................405 385-1062
605b Methodist Ave Perkins (74059) *(G-7717)*
Flowell Corporation..918 224-6969
8308 S Regency Dr Tulsa (74131) *(G-9007)*
Flowers Bakery Outlet, McAlester *Also called Franklin Baking Company LLC (G-4300)*
Flowers Baking Co Denton LLC.......................405 366-2175
5741 Huettner Ct Norman (73069) *(G-5002)*
Flowers Bkg Co Lynchburg LLC.......................918 270-1182
12787 E 41st St Tulsa (74146) *(G-9759)*
Flowers Foods Inc..405 270-7880
301 N Rhode Island Ave Oklahoma City (73117) *(G-6093)*
Flowmatics Inc..918 259-3740
2342 W Vancouver St Broken Arrow (74012) *(G-911)*
Flowserve Corporation..918 627-8400
4501 S 86th East Ave Tulsa (74145) *(G-9760)*
Flowserve US Inc..918 599-6000
724 W 41st St Tulsa (74107) *(G-9761)*
Floyd Craig Company...580 832-2597
404 S Market St Cordell (73632) *(G-1859)*
Floyd's Automotive Machine, Vinita *Also called Floyds Machine Shop (G-11258)*
Floyds Machine Shop..918 256-8440
415 S Wilson St Vinita (74301) *(G-11258)*
Fluid Art Technology LLC.................................405 843-2009
8100 N Clken Blvd Ste 115 Oklahoma City (73114) *(G-6094)*
Fluid Controls Inc...918 299-0442
10050 S 33rd West Ave Tulsa (74132) *(G-9762)*
Fluid Lift Inc..405 853-6876
Hwy 81 S Hennessey (73742) *(G-3461)*
Fluid Management, Yukon *Also called Complete Energy LLC (G-11710)*
Fluid Technologies Inc.......................................405 624-0400
1016 E Airport Rd Stillwater (74075) *(G-8693)*
Fluid Treatment Systems Inc.............................918 933-5678
5123 S 103rd East Ave Tulsa (74146) *(G-9763)*
Fluidart, Oklahoma City *Also called Fluid Art Technology LLC (G-6094)*

Flying W Livestock Equipment, Watonga *Also called W Flying Inc* ***(G-11351)***
Flywheel Energy LLC (PA)...405 702-6991
621 N Robinson Ave # 400 Oklahoma City (73102) ***(G-6095)***
Flywheel Energy Management LLC...405 702-6991
621 N Robinson Ave # 400 Oklahoma City (73102) ***(G-6096)***
Flywheel Energy Operating LLC (PA)...405 702-6991
621 N Robinson Ave # 400 Oklahoma City (73102) ***(G-6097)***
Fm2t Welding LLC...405 837-8495
3614 Stonebrook Dr Norman (73072) ***(G-5003)***
FMC Technologies Inc...405 787-6301
8624 Sw 2nd St Oklahoma City (73128) ***(G-6098)***
FMC Technologies Inc...405 972-1305
8624 Sw 2nd St Oklahoma City (73128) ***(G-6099)***
FMC Technologies Inc...405 415-9532
3400 Melcat Dr Oklahoma City (73179) ***(G-6100)***
Fo Mac, Tulsa *Also called Texre Inc* ***(G-10922)***
Foam Unit Inc...580 921-3366
172 Ns 19 2 Ew Laverne (73848) ***(G-3877)***
Foamtech Inc...580 256-3979
4515 Western Ave Woodward (73801) ***(G-11584)***
Focal Point Inc...405 942-2044
3417 Nw 42nd St Oklahoma City (73112) ***(G-6101)***
Food Mech, Stillwater *Also called Engineered Food Processes LLC* ***(G-8684)***
Food Svcs Auth of Quapaw Tribe...918 542-1853
5681 S 630 Rd Quapaw (74363) ***(G-8030)***
For His Glory Cutting Boards...918 633-7233
6539 E 46th St Tulsa (74145) ***(G-9764)***
Forbes Enterprises Inc...580 564-2599
6300 Hummingbird Ln Kingston (73439) ***(G-3828)***
Ford Energy Corporation...405 224-3620
2802 S 4th St Chickasha (73018) ***(G-1458)***
Ford Exploration Inc...405 341-7502
5 S Broadway Ste 200 Edmond (73034) ***(G-2417)***
Foresee Ready-Mix Concrete Inc (PA)...918 689-3951
710 S Main St Eufaula (74432) ***(G-3101)***
Forester LLC...918 835-6533
6929 E 15th St Tulsa (74112) ***(G-9765)***
Forester Machine & Mfg, Tulsa *Also called Forester LLC* ***(G-9765)***
Forged By Creation LLC...918 798-0051
822 W Elgin St Broken Arrow (74012) ***(G-912)***
Forklift Parts and Service LLC...918 251-5119
305 N Redbud Ave Broken Arrow (74012) ***(G-913)***
Formulated Materials LLC...405 310-1650
3010 Nw 149th St 100 Oklahoma City (73134) ***(G-6102)***
Forrest Lawns Landscapes...405 397-4679
3916 Nw 15th St Oklahoma City (73107) ***(G-6103)***
Forrest Valentine...580 309-2190
8705 N 2220 Rd Custer City (73639) ***(G-1974)***
Forster & Son Inc...580 332-6020
1900 B St Ada (74820) ***(G-36)***
Forsythe Oilfield Service Inc...580 668-3371
7183 Dillard Rd Wilson (73463) ***(G-11533)***
Fort Cobb Locker Plant...405 643-2355
100 Mopope St Fort Cobb (73038) ***(G-3171)***
Fort Thunder Harley-Davidson, Moore *Also called APS of Oklahoma LLC* ***(G-4492)***
Forterra Pipe & Precast LLC...405 677-8811
6504 Interpace St Oklahoma City (73135) ***(G-6104)***
Fortiflex Inc...918 540-3131
1410 Goodrich Blvd Ste A Miami (74354) ***(G-4405)***
Fortis Solutions Group...918 258-8321
19014 E Admiral Pl Catoosa (74015) ***(G-1320)***
Fortress Whitetails...405 401-5533
2951 S Post Rd Guthrie (73044) ***(G-3313)***
Forum Energy Technologies Inc...405 603-7198
1610 Se 66th St Oklahoma City (73149) ***(G-6105)***
Forum Energy Technologies Inc...405 224-5779
1175 State Highway 19 Chickasha (73018) ***(G-1459)***
Forum Energy Technologies Inc...580 622-5058
5015 Highway 7 W Davis (73030) ***(G-1983)***
Forum Flow Equipment, Davis *Also called Forum Energy Technologies Inc* ***(G-1983)***
Forum Oilfield Technologies, Oklahoma City *Also called Forum Energy Technologies Inc* ***(G-6105)***
Forum Production Equipment, Guthrie *Also called Forum Us Inc* ***(G-3314)***
Forum Production Equipment...580 622-5058
5015 Highway 7 W Davis (73030) ***(G-1984)***
Forum Us Inc...580 788-2333
22568 Highway 29 Elmore City (73433) ***(G-2896)***
Forum Us Inc...405 260-7800
3110 W Noble Ave Guthrie (73044) ***(G-3314)***
Forward Oil and Gas Inc...405 607-2247
6801 Broadway Ext Ste 100 Oklahoma City (73116) ***(G-6106)***
Fossil Creek Energy Corp...405 949-0880
4216 N Portland Ave # 206 Oklahoma City (73112) ***(G-6107)***
Fossil Fluids LLC...580 515-5402
9742 N 2350 Rd Weatherford (73096) ***(G-11416)***
Foster Feed & Produce Company, Rush Springs *Also called Bobby Foster* ***(G-8119)***
Foster Jl Welding LLC...405 686-6090
3209 Sw 85th St Oklahoma City (73159) ***(G-6108)***
Foster Machine Shop...918 438-4001
15856 E Pine St Tulsa (74116) ***(G-9766)***
Foti Directional LLC...352 848-5281
4624 Crestmere Ln Edmond (73025) ***(G-2418)***
Foundation Energy Company LLC...918 585-1650
15 E 5th St Ste 1200 Tulsa (74103) ***(G-9767)***
Foundation Energy MGT LLC...918 526-5521
15 E 5th St Ste 1200 Tulsa (74103) ***(G-9768)***
Four Feathers Transports...405 343-9799
15383 W County Road 71 Crescent (73028) ***(G-1915)***
Four Star Crating Co...918 663-6689
9911 E 54th St Ste D Tulsa (74146) ***(G-9769)***
Four State Meat Processing LLC...918 783-5556
440439 E 320 Rd Big Cabin (74332) ***(G-604)***
Four Winds Field Services LLC...918 568-1143
413299 E 1210 Rd Eufaula (74432) ***(G-3102)***
Four-O-One Corporation...405 848-0425
14000 N Western Ave Edmond (73013) ***(G-2419)***
Fourpoint Energy LLC...580 225-8556
501 S Eastern Ave Elk City (73644) ***(G-2815)***
Fox Northeastern Oil Gas Corp...918 331-7791
1723 W Hensley Blvd Bartlesville (74003) ***(G-484)***
Foxborough Energy Company LLC...405 286-3526
6501 Broadway Ext Ste 220 Oklahoma City (73116) ***(G-6109)***
Foxhead Oil & Gas Company...918 582-2124
320 S Boston Ave Ste 1104 Tulsa (74103) ***(G-9770)***
Frac Specialists LLC...432 617-3722
14201 Caliber Dr Ste 300 Oklahoma City (73134) ***(G-6110)***
Fracdogs...918 786-9797
28860 S 595 Cir Grove (74344) ***(G-3271)***
Fractal, Norman *Also called Bbr Oil Corp* ***(G-4926)***
Fractal Oil & Gas, Ardmore *Also called Bbr Oil Corp* ***(G-254)***
Fractalsoft LLC...405 330-3555
19109 Saddle River Dr Edmond (73012) ***(G-2420)***
Frahm John...213 500-0741
302 W 39th St Sand Springs (74063) ***(G-8185)***
Frame Builders & Brokerage, Sand Springs *Also called Frahm John* ***(G-8185)***
Francis Oil & Gas Inc...918 491-4253
6733 S Yale Ave Ste 202 Tulsa (74136) ***(G-9771)***
Frank A Hogan II Transport...405 889-4278
3920 E Reno Ave Oklahoma City (73117) ***(G-6111)***
Frank G Love Envelopes Inc (PA)...214 637-5900
10733 E Ute St Tulsa (74116) ***(G-9772)***
Frank G Love Envelopes Inc...405 720-9177
5601 Nw 72nd St Ste 342 Warr Acres (73132) ***(G-11319)***
Frank K Young Oil Properties...405 340-2500
1320 E 9th St Ste 6 Edmond (73034) ***(G-2421)***
Frank Priegel Co...918 756-3161
907 E 6th St Okmulgee (74447) ***(G-7502)***
Frank T Fleet Inc...580 332-1422
920 N Mississippi Ave Ada (74820) ***(G-37)***
Franklin Baking Company LLC...918 423-2888
460 S Main St McAlester (74501) ***(G-4300)***
Franklin Digital Inc...918 687-6149
3103 S Cherokee Dr Muskogee (74403) ***(G-4674)***
Franklin Electric Co Inc...918 465-2348
1301 W Stovall Rd Wilburton (74578) ***(G-11520)***
Franklin Electric Co Inc...405 947-2511
301 N Macarthur Blvd Oklahoma City (73127) ***(G-6112)***
Franklin Electric Co Inc...501 455-1234
301 N Macarthur Blvd Oklahoma City (73127) ***(G-6113)***
Franklin Graphics Inc...918 687-6149
3103 S Cherokee Dr Muskogee (74403) ***(G-4675)***
Franks Garage Auto Sls & Salv...405 257-6198
12297 Ns 3650 Wewoka (74884) ***(G-11502)***
Franks Signs...918 335-9715
746 Ne Washington Blvd Bartlesville (74006) ***(G-485)***
Fraser Oilfield Service LLC...918 716-0665
379060 E 1070 Rd Okemah (74859) ***(G-5269)***
Frazier Mfg Co...918 241-9110
200 Wellston Park Rd Sand Springs (74063) ***(G-8186)***
Fred Jones Enterprises LLC (PA)...800 927-7845
6200 Sw 29th St Oklahoma City (73179) ***(G-6114)***
Fred M Buxton...405 840-4331
6402 N Santa Fe Ave Ste B Oklahoma City (73116) ***(G-6115)***
Frederick Sommers & Wstn Sign, Tulsa *Also called Frederick Sommers Wstn Sign Co* ***(G-9773)***
Frederick Sommers Wstn Sign Co...918 587-2300
10017 E 46th Pl Tulsa (74146) ***(G-9773)***
Fredrick F Drummond...918 287-4400
100 W Main St Pawhuska (74056) ***(G-7685)***
Freds Rat Hole Service Inc...405 756-4300
211 Ne 3rd St Lindsay (73052) ***(G-4063)***
Freds Sign Co...405 235-8696
14425 Melody Ln Newalla (74857) ***(G-4809)***
Free Ranger LLC...918 253-4223
1st & Dial St Jay (74346) ***(G-3681)***
Free Spirit Embroidery...918 429-4552
200 E Choctaw Ave McAlester (74501) ***(G-4301)***

A L P H A B E T I C

Freedom Bell Inc

Freedom Bell Inc...918 671-1089
 2607 N Quincy Ave Tulsa (74106) *(G-9774)*
Freedom Bell Wireless, Tulsa Also called Freedom Bell Inc *(G-9774)*
Freedom Call LLC..580 621-3578
 512 Main St Freedom (73842) *(G-3206)*
Freedom Embroidery LLC.....................................580 540-8504
 2918 Dona Kaye Dr Enid (73701) *(G-2959)*
Freedom Energy Ltd..405 285-2682
 1015 Waterwood Pkwy Edmond (73034) *(G-2422)*
Freedom Homes...918 728-2277
 9516 E Admiral Pl Tulsa (74115) *(G-9775)*
Freedom Manufacturing LLC.................................918 283-1520
 24055 Amah Pkwy Claremore (74019) *(G-1623)*
Freedom Midstream Services LLC.........................918 582-5313
 20 E 5th St Ste 1403 Tulsa (74103) *(G-9776)*
Freedom Railcar Solutions LLC (PA)......................405 256-6780
 250 S Castlerock Ln Mustang (73064) *(G-4772)*
Freedom Rubber LLC...918 250-4673
 3081 W Albany St Ste 103 Broken Arrow (74012) *(G-914)*
Freedom Stone Company LLC...............................918 649-0021
 24075 Picturerock Rd Poteau (74953) *(G-7904)*
Freelance Operations Inc....................................580 226-7051
 5605 Prairie Valley Rd Ardmore (73401) *(G-292)*
Freeman Ice LLC..580 263-0021
 Rr 3 Box 30n Madill (73446) *(G-4147)*
Freeman Products Inc (PA)..................................918 258-8861
 1912 W Kenosha St Broken Arrow (74012) *(G-915)*
Freepoint Pipe & Supply Inc.................................405 341-1913
 5624 Industrial Blvd Edmond (73034) *(G-2423)*
Freestyle Embroidery...405 802-5838
 5236 Coble St Oklahoma City (73135) *(G-6116)*
French Nail Spa LLC...405 843-2080
 1841 Belle Isle Blvd L3 Oklahoma City (73118) *(G-6117)*
French Oil..580 248-3131
 2401 Se 45th St Lawton (73501) *(G-3930)*
French Printing Inc..405 381-4057
 408 E Main St Tuttle (73089) *(G-11200)*
Frenches Quarter..918 691-2553
 10622 E 17th Pl Tulsa (74128) *(G-9777)*
Frenchs Blue River Cnstr....................................580 274-3444
 19 E 7th St Longdale (73755) *(G-4123)*
Fresh Monkey Fiction LLC...................................405 751-3826
 11825 Blue Sage Rd Oklahoma City (73120) *(G-6118)*
Fresh Promise Foods Inc....................................561 703-4659
 3416 Shadybrook Dr Midwest City (73110) *(G-4441)*
Friction Solutions LLC..918 622-8989
 7427 E 46th Pl Tulsa (74145) *(G-9778)*
Friday Newspaper, Oklahoma City Also called Nichols Hills Publishing Co *(G-6678)*
Friedel Petroleum Corporation............................405 359-1285
 2817 Sweetbriar Edmond (73034) *(G-2424)*
Friends Welding..918 482-1544
 20219 E 83rd St S Broken Arrow (74014) *(G-1127)*
Fright Casket...405 602-1534
 3010 N Mckinley Ave Oklahoma City (73106) *(G-6119)*
Frisco Energy LLC..918 742-5200
 4124 S Rockford Ave # 102 Tulsa (74105) *(G-9779)*
Frog Printing & Awards Ctr LLC...........................580 678-1114
 1005 Sw F Ave Lawton (73501) *(G-3931)*
From Heart..405 348-3009
 1701 Westwood Ln Edmond (73013) *(G-2425)*
From Heart Candles and More.............................580 334-4104
 122 Oklahoma Ave Woodward (73801) *(G-11585)*
Froman Wldg U0026 Fbrction Inc.........................918 798-1050
 8032 E 480 Rd Claremore (74017) *(G-1624)*
Frontier Drilling LLC..405 745-7700
 13800 S Meridian Ave Oklahoma City (73173) *(G-6120)*
Frontier Drilling LLC (PA)...................................405 745-7700
 4801 Richmond Sq Oklahoma City (73118) *(G-6121)*
Frontier Elctrnic Systems Corp...........................405 624-7708
 4500 W 6th Ave Stillwater (74074) *(G-8694)*
Frontier Elevator Inc...888 421-9400
 731 Kerr Research Dr Ada (74820) *(G-38)*
Frontier Energy Leasing Svc, Tulsa Also called Frontier Land Co Inc *(G-9783)*
Frontier Energy Services LLC.............................918 754-2226
 4200 E Skelly Dr Ste 700 Tulsa (74135) *(G-9780)*
Frontier Energy Services LLC (PA)......................918 388-8438
 4200 E Skelly Dr Ste 400 Tulsa (74135) *(G-9781)*
Frontier Gas Services LLC..................................918 388-8438
 4200 E Skelly Dr Ste 400 Tulsa (74135) *(G-9782)*
Frontier Integrity Solutions, Tulsa Also called Fis Operations LLC *(G-9749)*
Frontier Land Co Inc..918 584-2050
 601 S Boulder Ave Ste 810 Tulsa (74119) *(G-9783)*
Frontier Land Surveying LLC...............................405 285-0433
 600 W 18th St Edmond (73013) *(G-2426)*
Frontier Logging Corporation.............................405 787-3952
 7221 Nw 3rd St Oklahoma City (73127) *(G-6122)*
Frontier Logistical Svcs LLC...............................405 232-4401
 600 N Bryant Ave Oklahoma City (73117) *(G-6123)*
Frontier Midstream LLC.....................................918 388-8438
 4200 E Skelly Dr Ste 400 Tulsa (74135) *(G-9784)*

ALPHABETIC SECTION

Frontier Plastic Fabricators................................918 445-5208
 4518 W 56th St Tulsa (74107) *(G-9785)*
Frontier Resource Development..........................918 682-6571
 240 North St Muskogee (74403) *(G-4676)*
Fronttoback Studio LLC.....................................405 788-4400
 10802 Quail Plaza Dr # 120 Oklahoma City (73120) *(G-6124)*
Frost Entertainment...405 834-8484
 434 Nw 18th St Oklahoma City (73103) *(G-6125)*
Frozen Mesa Winery LLC....................................405 281-5962
 16322 Sandstone Cir Choctaw (73020) *(G-1543)*
Fs & J Music Publishing LLC...............................918 369-6010
 8805 E 106th St Tulsa (74133) *(G-9786)*
Ft Sill Tees & Embroidery...................................580 248-8484
 2609 Nw Sheridan Rd Lawton (73505) *(G-3932)*
Ftdm Investments Llc..918 598-3430
 14302 S 442 Rd Locust Grove (74352) *(G-4107)*
Fts International Services LL.............................405 574-3900
 2500 Highway 62 W Chickasha (73018) *(G-1460)*
Fudgenomics 101 LLC..405 401-3832
 1220 E Robinson St Norman (73071) *(G-5004)*
Fuel..903 948-3125
 4856 Berryhill Dr Woodward (73801) *(G-11586)*
Fuel Haulers LLC...405 830-3385
 210 N Buffalo Ave Guthrie (73044) *(G-3315)*
Fuel Inc...580 583-5202
 1620 Se Indiana Ave Lawton (73501) *(G-3933)*
Fuels Marketing Inc..405 433-9935
 19550 Lakeview Dr Cashion (73016) *(G-1288)*
Fullerton Building Systems Inc............................918 246-9995
 8645 W 21st St Sand Springs (74063) *(G-8187)*
Fullerton Finish Systems, Sand Springs Also called Fullerton Building Systems Inc *(G-8187)*
Fundom Enterprises Inc.....................................405 557-0296
 12 Ne 29th St Oklahoma City (73105) *(G-6126)*
Fungo Designs..405 348-9922
 629 Redstone Ave Edmond (73013) *(G-2427)*
Funk..405 329-7571
 239 Crestmont Ave Norman (73069) *(G-5005)*
Furrs Custom Woodwork....................................918 406-7021
 18237 S 132nd East Ave Bixby (74008) *(G-624)*
Furseth G N Oil & Gas Producer...........................405 848-1232
 901 Nw 63rd St Ste 201 Oklahoma City (73116) *(G-6127)*
Future Foam Inc...405 948-0001
 1101 Metropolitan Ave Oklahoma City (73108) *(G-6128)*
Fw Murphy Prod Contrls LLC...............................918 317-4280
 4646 S Harvard Ave # 100 Tulsa (74135) *(G-9787)*
G & D Industries Inc..918 369-2648
 11448 S 99th East Ave Bixby (74008) *(G-625)*
G & G Quality Services LLC.................................918 961-0288
 9902 S Highway 137 Miami (74354) *(G-4406)*
G & G Steam Service Inc (PA)............................580 225-4254
 120 W 12th St Elk City (73644) *(G-2816)*
G & H Decoy Inc..918 652-3314
 601 N Highway 75 Henryetta (74437) *(G-3507)*
G & L Metal Buildings...918 687-1867
 3246 N 32nd St Muskogee (74401) *(G-4677)*
G & L Tool, Yukon Also called Basic Energy Services Inc *(G-11696)*
G & S Printing Inc..405 789-6813
 7706 Nw 3rd St Ste B Oklahoma City (73127) *(G-6129)*
G & S Sign Services LLC.....................................405 604-3636
 1019 E Grand Blvd Oklahoma City (73129) *(G-6130)*
G A P Roofing Inc (PA).......................................918 825-5200
 4444 Hunt St Pryor (74361) *(G-7963)*
G B E Services Corporation................................918 428-8665
 6011 N Yorktown Ave Tulsa (74130) *(G-9788)*
G B K Holdings Inc (PA)......................................918 494-0000
 6733 S Yale Ave Tulsa (74136) *(G-9789)*
G C A, Tulsa Also called Green Cntry Arcft Exhaust Inc *(G-9857)*
G C Broach Co...918 369-4320
 11323 S 109th East Ave Bixby (74008) *(G-626)*
G C Broach Company (PA)..................................918 627-9632
 7667 E 46th Pl Tulsa (74145) *(G-9790)*
G C Broach Company...918 627-9632
 8199 E 44th St Tulsa (74145) *(G-9791)*
G C I, Spiro Also called Georges Colliers Inc *(G-8615)*
G Design, Sapulpa Also called David Gormley *(G-8265)*
G E C Enterprises..405 740-9365
 512 Country Club Ter Oklahoma City (73110) *(G-6131)*
G Highfill...405 598-5576
 36492 Rattlesnake Hill Rd Tecumseh (74873) *(G-8915)*
G L B Exploration Inc...405 787-0049
 7716 Melrose Ln Oklahoma City (73127) *(G-6132)*
G M C Oil & Gas...405 701-5515
 2900 W Lindsey St Norman (73072) *(G-5006)*
G M I, Tulsa Also called Gorfam Marketing Inc *(G-9842)*
G P D Inc...918 234-4404
 16712 E Admiral Pl Tulsa (74116) *(G-9792)*
G P Enterprises..405 340-8986
 2629 Broadway Ct Edmond (73013) *(G-2428)*
G PC Inc (PA)...918 582-0018
 2121 S Columbia Ave # 200 Tulsa (74114) *(G-9793)*

ALPHABETIC SECTION — Gear Exchange

G T Bynum Company 918 587-9118
  1116 N Peoria Ave Tulsa (74106) (G-9794)
G T R Newspapers Inc 918 254-1515
  7116 S Mingo Rd Ste 103 Tulsa (74133) (G-9795)
G&E Power LLC 918 396-2899
  679 W 136th St N Skiatook (74070) (G-8544)
G&G Logging LLC 918 635-5988
  15695 Gap Creek Rd Poteau (74953) (G-7905)
G&J Enterprises 580 237-2029
  2601 N 30th St Enid (73701) (G-2960)
G&J Measurement Inc 580 560-3190
  2004 Townsend St Duncan (73533) (G-2119)
G-T Engineering, Shawnee Also called Prestige Manufacturing Co LLC (G-8485)
G2solutions, Oklahoma City Also called Michael Gipson LLC (G-6587)
Gabriel Ride Control Products, Chickasha Also called Ride Control LLC (G-1502)
Gades Sales Co 405 720-6839
  7216 Nw 111th St Oklahoma City (73162) (G-6133)
Gage Locker Service 580 923-7661
  611 N Main St Gage (73843) (G-3210)
Gage Record, Arnett Also called Ellis County Capital (G-387)
Gail Evans Embroidery 918 605-1013
  5757 E 97th Pl Tulsa (74137) (G-9796)
Gainsville Pallet Company, Kingston Also called Betty E Jester (G-3824)
Galaxie Sign Co 580 226-2944
  414 A St Ne Ardmore (73401) (G-293)
Galaxy Chemicals LLC 918 379-0820
  6472 Tower Ln Claremore (74019) (G-1625)
Galaxy Distributing, Tulsa Also called Billiards of Tulsa Inc (G-9296)
Galaxy Distributing 918 835-1186
  7813 E Admiral Pl Tulsa (74115) (G-9797)
Galaxy Energy, Stigler Also called Roye Realty & Developing Inc (G-8644)
Gallaher Printing, Comanche Also called Paula Gallaher (G-1844)
Galley LLC 918 794-2700
  12626 S Memorial Dr Bixby (74008) (G-627)
Gallium Compounds LLC 918 673-2511
  3225 S 625 Rd Quapaw (74363) (G-8031)
Galmor's, Elk City Also called G & G Steam Service Inc (G-2816)
Galmors Inc 580 225-4254
  120 W 12th St Elk City (73644) (G-2817)
Gambill Oilfield Services LLC 580 471-1451
  324 E Cleveland St Mangum (73554) (G-4171)
Game Changing Image LLC 918 289-3392
  6843 N 120 Rd Beggs (74421) (G-556)
Game King 580 250-0707
  2332 W Gore Blvd Lawton (73505) (G-3934)
Game Time Designs LLC 405 702-1318
  8000 S Shields Blvd Oklahoma City (73149) (G-6134)
Gameday Screen Printing 405 570-0176
  8717 Nw 73rd St Oklahoma City (73132) (G-6135)
Gameday Screen Prtg Promotions 405 637-8577
  5008 N Rockwell Ave Bethany (73008) (G-578)
Gami, Ada Also called General AVI Modifications Inc (G-40)
Ganoa Imports 918 622-3788
  2121 S Garnett Rd Tulsa (74129) (G-9798)
Garage Storage Cabinets LLC 405 743-0133
  2805 E 6th Ave Stillwater (74074) (G-8695)
Garbage To Garden Compost Inc 918 260-4463
  8617 E 132nd St S Bixby (74008) (G-628)
Garbrecht, Robt A, Oklahoma City Also called Ogp Energy L P (G-6715)
Garden Interlock Systems Tuls 918 369-9935
  5130 S 94th East Ave Tulsa (74145) (G-9799)
Gardner Denver Inc 918 664-1151
  4747 S 83rd East Ave Tulsa (74145) (G-9800)
Gardner Industries Inc 918 583-0171
  1115 N Utica Ave Tulsa (74110) (G-9801)
Gardner Spring, Tulsa Also called Gardner Industries Inc (G-9801)
Gardners Guns & Mfg LLC 580 225-8884
  1901 E 20th St Elk City (73644) (G-2818)
Garfield Inc (PA) 580 242-6411
  500 W Southgate Rd Enid (73701) (G-2961)
Garfield Equipment, Enid Also called Garfield Inc (G-2961)
Garis Industries LLC 405 639-0319
  106 N Santa Fe Ave Moore (73160) (G-4525)
Garner Packaging, Pocola Also called Stan-Mel Industries Inc (G-7787)
Garnett Corporation 918 252-2515
  7070 S Garnett Rd Tulsa (74133) (G-9802)
Garrett Book Co, Ada Also called Garrett Educational Corp (G-39)
Garrett Educational Corp 580 332-6884
  130 E 13th St Ada (74820) (G-39)
Garrett Petroleum Inc (PA) 918 492-3239
  8801 S Yale Ave Ste 240 Tulsa (74137) (G-9803)
Garrison Backhoe LLC 580 465-2014
  4204 12th Ave Nw Ardmore (73401) (G-294)
Garrison Welding 918 331-6336
  135 County Road 4657 Foraker (74652) (G-3168)
Gary Cobb Welding LLC 580 983-2499
  18388 E 850 Rd Crawford (73638) (G-1905)

Gary D Adams Geologist 405 691-5380
  2632 Sw 105th St Oklahoma City (73170) (G-5292)
Gary Green Cement Construction 405 527-5606
  301 W Main St Purcell (73080) (G-8008)
Gary L Deaton Corporation (PA) 405 521-8811
  2520 N Oklahoma Ave Oklahoma City (73105) (G-6136)
Gary Land Services Inc 580 226-9808
  10 W Main St Ste 401 Ardmore (73401) (G-295)
Gary M Lake & Company 405 340-6138
  18700 Aerial Rd Edmond (73012) (G-2429)
Gary Mace 580 654-2660
  Hwy 9 E Carnegie (73015) (G-1276)
Gary Morgan 405 387-4884
  3383 N Meridian Ave Newcastle (73065) (G-4826)
Gary Moss 580 286-1359
  969 Cotton Moss Rd Valliant (74764) (G-11224)
Gary Moss Trucking, Valliant Also called Gary Moss (G-11224)
Gary Rumsey 405 330-5732
  33 Greenmore Dr Edmond (73034) (G-2430)
Gary Smith 580 762-7575
  2501 N Ash St Ponca City (74601) (G-7830)
Gary Underwood 405 341-0935
  2 E 11th St Ste 209 Edmond (73034) (G-2431)
Garys Guns 405 789-6896
  30th Terr St Bethany (73008) (G-579)
Garys Industrial Machine LLC 580 933-4514
  202 Roady Rd Valliant (74764) (G-11225)
Garys Welding Inc 918 688-2058
  312 E Washington St Broken Arrow (74012) (G-916)
Gas Development Corporation 918 523-9090
  908 S 11th St Broken Arrow (74012) (G-917)
Gas Field Compressor Sales, Tulsa Also called Dresser-Rand LLC (G-9607)
Gas Products Inc 918 664-5679
  4530 S Sheridan Rd # 219 Tulsa (74145) (G-9804)
Gas Turbine Applications, Calera Also called Caprock Country Entps Inc (G-1239)
Gasolec America Inc 918 286-8700
  5818 S 129th East Ave Tulsa (74134) (G-9805)
Gasoline Alley Classics Inc 918 806-1000
  9820 Swan Dr Broken Arrow (74014) (G-1128)
Gastar Exploration Inc 405 772-1500
  6100 S Yale Ave Ste 1700 Tulsa (74136) (G-9806)
Gastech Engineering LLC 918 663-8383
  2110 Industrial Rd Sapulpa (74066) (G-8274)
Gaston H L III Oil Properties 918 758-0008
  114 N Grand Ave Okmulgee (74447) (G-7503)
Gaston Services Inc 580 328-5647
  217239 E 750 Rd Camargo (73835) (G-1252)
Gatehuse Mdia Okla Hldings Inc 585 598-0030
  117 W Broadway St Ardmore (73401) (G-296)
Gateway Com Inc 405 787-0800
  1605 E 2nd St Ste 5 Edmond (73034) (G-2432)
Gateway Directional Drilling 405 752-4230
  13911 N Harvey Ave Edmond (73013) (G-2433)
Gateway International Inc 918 747-8393
  6506 S Lewis Ave Ste 112 Tulsa (74136) (G-9807)
Gateway Resources USA Inc 918 333-2115
  1821 Arbor Dr Bartlesville (74006) (G-486)
Gateway Services Group, Shawnee Also called McGuire Gateway Holdings LLC (G-8471)
Gator Hyde Bedliners, Wagoner Also called Elastomer Specialties Inc (G-11282)
Gator Rigs LLC 405 598-3266
  26531 Old Highway 18 Tecumseh (74873) (G-8916)
Gauge Metal Fab LLC 918 794-1700
  1004 N Victor Ave Tulsa (74110) (G-9808)
Gaylan Adams Inc 405 751-9668
  13524 Railway Dr Ste E Oklahoma City (73114) (G-6137)
Gayly 405 496-0011
  1406 Nw 15th St Oklahoma City (73106) (G-6138)
Gazette Media Inc 405 528-6000
  3701 N Shartel Ave Oklahoma City (73118) (G-6139)
Gb Energy Inc 405 224-8634
  124 S 4th St Chickasha (73018) (G-1461)
Gbg Earthmovers LLC 580 243-5662
  19338 Highway 6 Elk City (73644) (G-2819)
Gbk Corporation (PA) 918 494-0000
  6733 S Yale Ave Tulsa (74136) (G-9809)
GC&I Global Inc 918 317-4244
  3511 122nd E Ave Tulsa (74146) (G-9810)
Gcc Ready Mix LLC 918 582-8111
  431 W 23rd St Tulsa (74107) (G-9811)
GE Oil & Gas Esp Inc (HQ) 405 670-1431
  5500 Se 59th St Oklahoma City (73135) (G-6140)
GE Oil & Gas Esp Inc 405 527-1566
  1739 Hardcastle Blvd Purcell (73080) (G-8009)
GE Oil & Gas Pressure Ctrl LP 405 273-7660
  14311 Highway 177 Shawnee (74804) (G-8451)
GE Packaged Power LLC 405 395-0400
  14311 Highway 177 Shawnee (74804) (G-8452)
Gear Exchange 405 606-3050
  3401 Nw 36th St Oklahoma City (73112) (G-6141)

Geary Star   ALPHABETIC SECTION

Geary Star 405 884-2424
114 W Main St Geary (73040) *(G-3216)*

Gefco Inc 580 243-4141
2215 S Van Buren St Enid (73703) *(G-2962)*

Geiger Printing & Promotion 918 810-2833
4512 E 51st St Tulsa (74135) *(G-9812)*

Gem Asset Acquisition LLC 405 200-1992
1628 S Kelham Ave Oklahoma City (73129) *(G-6142)*

Gem Dirt LLC 918 298-0299
2526 W 101st St Tulsa (74132) *(G-9813)*

Gemini Coatings, El Reno Also called Gemini Industries Inc *(G-2719)*

Gemini Coatings Inc (HQ) 405 262-5710
421 Se 27th St El Reno (73036) *(G-2718)*

Gemini Industries Inc (PA) 405 262-5710
421 Se 27th St El Reno (73036) *(G-2719)*

Gemini Oil Co Inc 918 582-3935
427 S Boston Ave Ste 320 Tulsa (74103) *(G-9814)*

Gemini Woodworks 405 630-8586
421 Sw 6th St Jones (73049) *(G-3746)*

Gemseal Pvments Pdts - Okla Cy, Oklahoma City Also called Gem Asset Acquisition LLC *(G-6142)*

Gen X Machine Technologies 918 836-4200
4470 S 70th East Ave Tulsa (74145) *(G-9815)*

Gen X Machine Technologies 918 836-4200
4470 S 70th East Ave Tulsa (74145) *(G-9816)*

Gene Cook Inc 580 256-5335
4325 Oil Patch Dr Woodward (73801) *(G-11587)*

Gene Higgins Interiors, Newcastle Also called E J Higgins Interior Design *(G-4825)*

Gene Larew, Tulsa Also called Plastic Research and Dev Corp *(G-10525)*

General Inc 580 921-3365
N Edge Of City Laverne (73848) *(G-3878)*

General Auto Supply Inc 405 329-0772
319 E Comanche St Norman (73069) *(G-5007)*

General AVI Modifications Inc 580 436-4833
2800 Airport Rd Hngr A Ada (74820) *(G-40)*

General Clamp and Tong, Okmulgee Also called General Manufacturer Inc *(G-7504)*

General Manufacturer Inc (PA) 918 756-3067
701 W 4th St Okmulgee (74447) *(G-7504)*

General Plastics Inc 405 275-3171
3500 N Harrison St Shawnee (74804) *(G-8453)*

General Wire & Supply Co Inc (PA) 918 245-5961
1800 S 81st West Ave Tulsa (74127) *(G-9817)*

Genes Customized Tags & EMB 580 225-8247
122 S Main St Elk City (73644) *(G-2820)*

Genesis Financial Software 580 252-2594
15 N 9th St Ste 105 Duncan (73533) *(G-2120)*

Genesis Metal Corporation 918 267-5901
8255 Highway 16 Beggs (74421) *(G-557)*

Genesis Oil Tool International 403 298-2430
5353 S Hattie Ave Oklahoma City (73129) *(G-6143)*

Genesis Technologies Inc 918 307-0098
5812 S 129th East Ave Tulsa (74134) *(G-9818)*

Genie Oil & Gas Corporation 918 747-3675
2424 E 21st St Ste 500 Tulsa (74114) *(G-9819)*

Genie Well Service Inc 405 969-2141
7507 N Meridian Ave Crescent (73028) *(G-1916)*

Genral Enquries 918 749-1301
3081 W Albany St Ste 111 Broken Arrow (74012) *(G-918)*

Genreal Compressor Inc 918 209-5499
395 W K Pl Jenks (74037) *(G-3706)*

Geo Shack 918 665-1880
5125 S Garnett Rd Ste A Tulsa (74146) *(G-9820)*

Geoamerican Resources Inc 918 428-8665
6011 N Yorktown Ave Tulsa (74130) *(G-9821)*

Geodyne Production Company 918 583-1791
2 W 2nd St Tulsa (74103) *(G-9822)*

Geolog LLC 405 745-2197
9412 Sw 33rd St Oklahoma City (73179) *(G-6144)*

George B Hughes 405 784-5575
43138 Tooley Rd Asher (74826) *(G-389)*

George E Christian 405 375-6711
13th And Airport Rd Kingfisher (73750) *(G-3798)*

George Miller 405 341-4097
7321 Shannon Cir Edmond (73034) *(G-2434)*

George Townsend & Co Inc 405 235-1387
629 N Blackwelder Ave Oklahoma City (73106) *(G-6145)*

George W Smith Salvage City 580 332-2250
12521 State Highway 3w Ada (74820) *(G-41)*

Georges Colliers Inc 918 962-2202
22279 Us Highway 271 Spiro (74959) *(G-8615)*

Georges Gun Shop, Choctaw Also called Computer Solutions + LLC *(G-1534)*

Georgia-Pacific LLC 405 536-0070
204 N Robinson Ave # 300 Oklahoma City (73102) *(G-6146)*

Georgia-Pacific LLC 918 687-9800
4901 Chandler Rd Muskogee (74403) *(G-4678)*

Georgia-Pacific LLC 580 549-7100
16850 Ne 135th St Fletcher (73541) *(G-3162)*

Gerald W Davidson LLC 580 336-9303
621 Delaware St Perry (73077) *(G-7734)*

Geralds Welding Fabrication 405 222-5510
150 Quail Rd Chickasha (73018) *(G-1462)*

Geralds Welding 2 .... 405 224-8510
178 W Quail Rd Ninnekah (73067) *(G-4871)*

Gerbrant Agency, Enid Also called Don L Gerbrandt *(G-2943)*

Gerdau Ameristeel US Inc 918 241-7762
404 S Main St Sand Springs (74063) *(G-8188)*

Gerdau Ameristeel US Inc 405 677-9792
3200 Se 59th St Oklahoma City (73135) *(G-6147)*

Gerdau Ameristeel US Inc 918 682-2600
2301a Anderson Dr Muskogee (74403) *(G-4679)*

Gerdau Ameristeel US Inc 918 682-7806
1921 Anderson Dr Muskogee (74403) *(G-4680)*

Geronimo Manufacturing Inc 580 336-5707
612 Cedar St Perry (73077) *(G-7735)*

Get A Grip Inc 405 286-4778
5225 N Shartel Ave # 200 Oklahoma City (73118) *(G-6148)*

Get People Moving LLC 405 529-6033
4504 Gaylord Dr Apt D Oklahoma City (73162) *(G-6149)*

Get Threaded LLC 918 943-6156
10846 S Memorial Dr # 112 Tulsa (74133) *(G-9823)*

Gh Co 918 488-0014
6033 S 66th East Ave Tulsa (74145) *(G-9824)*

Gh Land Co 405 947-5500
4216 N Portland Ave # 104 Oklahoma City (73112) *(G-6150)*

Gh Printing Solutions Inc 405 630-0609
22900 Bailey Cir Edmond (73025) *(G-2435)*

Ghk Company LLC 405 858-9800
6305 Waterford Blvd # 470 Oklahoma City (73118) *(G-6151)*

Ghost Town Press 405 396-2166
13100 E Old Highway 66 Arcadia (73007) *(G-229)*

Giblet Welding LLC 580 751-0104
212 N Massingale Dr Cordell (73632) *(G-1860)*

Gibsons Treasures 405 835-1109
6001 N Brookline Ave # 1207 Oklahoma City (73112) *(G-6152)*

Gideon Steel Panel Company LLC 405 942-7878
814 Overhead Dr Oklahoma City (73128) *(G-6153)*

Giesecke & Devrient Amer Inc 405 270-8400
226 Dean A Mcgee Ave Oklahoma City (73102) *(G-6154)*

Gifford Monument Works Inc (PA) 580 332-1271
900 N Broadway Ave Ada (74820) *(G-42)*

Gilchrist Construction Inc 580 886-2540
102 W Main St Canton (73724) *(G-1265)*

Gilded Gate 405 590-3139
2617 Nw 61st St Oklahoma City (73112) *(G-6155)*

Giles Printing Co Inc 918 584-1583
520a S Peoria Ave Tulsa (74120) *(G-9825)*

Gill Operating Company 918 756-1873
209 W 7th St Okmulgee (74447) *(G-7505)*

Gill Royalty, Okmulgee Also called Gill Operating Company *(G-7505)*

Gill X-Stream Investments LLC 918 743-8379
4972 S Detroit Ave Tulsa (74105) *(G-9826)*

Gillham Oil & Gas Inc 405 997-8549
301 E Wanda Jackson Blvd Maud (74854) *(G-4252)*

Gillham Oil Co, Maud Also called Gillham Oil & Gas Inc *(G-4252)*

Gilliam Cattle 405 392-4204
1937 Hwy 76 Newcastle Newcastle (73065) *(G-4827)*

Gilliland Fluid Corporation 405 853-7188
Rr 1 Hennessey (73742) *(G-3462)*

Gilliland Oil & Gas Inc 405 853-7116
601 N Cheyenne St Hennessey (73742) *(G-3463)*

Gilmore Welding & Tractor Svc 918 479-6224
10371 S 437 Locust Grove (74352) *(G-4108)*

Gilmores Sports Concepts Inc 918 250-3910
5949 S Garnett Rd Tulsa (74146) *(G-9827)*

Girlinghouse Unlimited LLC 405 265-3330
528 W State Highway 152 # 1 Mustang (73064) *(G-4773)*

Girlpower Defense Llc 918 494-9072
7017 E 63rd St Tulsa (74133) *(G-9828)*

Girls Gone Wine 580 494-6243
471 Old Broken Bow Hwy Broken Bow (74728) *(G-1191)*

Givens Manufacturing Inc 888 302-2774
975 Highway 75 Mounds (74047) *(G-4616)*

Givens Wrecker Service 580 225-0892
1212 W 5th St Elk City (73644) *(G-2821)*

Gj Leather LLC 405 795-2998
404 S Main St Newcastle (73065) *(G-4828)*

Glacier Petroleum Co of Okla 405 840-2625
14000 N Western Ave Edmond (73013) *(G-2436)*

Glass, Bill Studio, Locust Grove Also called Bill Glass *(G-4104)*

Glencoe Manufacturing Co 580 669-2555
401 S Excel Ave Glencoe (74032) *(G-3222)*

Glencoe Mfg Roofg Installation, Glencoe Also called Glencoe Manufacturing Co *(G-3222)*

Glenn Brents Sales Inc 405 733-4960
2904 Mockingbird Ln Oklahoma City (73110) *(G-6156)*

Glenn Hamil 918 396-3659
18300 N Peoria Ave Skiatook (74070) *(G-8545)*

Glenn Schlarb Welding 580 327-3832
1322 Mill St Alva (73717) *(G-182)*

Glenn Tool Inc 405 787-1400
5940 Nw 5th St Oklahoma City (73127) **(G-6157)**
Glenna F Kirk 580 497-3435
19450 E 1100 Rd Cheyenne (73628) **(G-1424)**
Glenns Competition Chassis 405 732-4403
423 N Douglas Blvd Oklahoma City (73130) **(G-6158)**
Glimp Oil Company LLC 918 352-2978
Se Of City Drumright (74030) **(G-2060)**
Glitter Gear LLC 405 321-4327
420 N Pennsylvania Ave Oklahoma City (73107) **(G-6159)**
Glm Energy Inc 405 470-2873
5732 Nw 132nd St Oklahoma City (73142) **(G-6160)**
Glo Press 405 275-1038
3911 N Chapman Ave Shawnee (74804) **(G-8454)**
Global Artificial Lift, Oklahoma City *Also called Global Oilfield Services LLC* **(G-6161)**
Global Bearings Inc 918 664-8902
3818 S 79th East Ave Tulsa (74145) **(G-9829)**
Global Filter LLC (PA) 319 743-0110
11607 E 43rd St N Tulsa (74116) **(G-9830)**
Global Flow Products LLC 866 267-1379
2701 W Concord St Broken Arrow (74012) **(G-919)**
Global Industrial Inc 918 266-5656
19801 E 6th St Tulsa (74108) **(G-9831)**
Global Interface Solutions, Tulsa *Also called Secureagent Software Inc* **(G-10722)**
Global Interface Solutions Inc 918 971-1600
2448 E 81st St Ste 2000 Tulsa (74137) **(G-9832)**
Global Machine Company, Muskogee *Also called Native American Maint Svcs Inc* **(G-4720)**
Global Oil Gas Fields Okla LLC 918 392-3345
9726 E 42nd St Ste 230 Tulsa (74146) **(G-9833)**
Global Oilfield Services Inc 918 885-4024
10912 State Highway 99 Hominy (74035) **(G-3585)**
Global Oilfield Services LLC (HQ) 405 741-0163
6917 S Air Depot Blvd Oklahoma City (73135) **(G-6161)**
Global Sealcoating Inc 918 283-2040
9603 Alawhe Dr Claremore (74019) **(G-1626)**
Global Sign Solutions, Mounds *Also called Technology Licensing Corp* **(G-4625)**
Global Wire Cloth LLC 918 836-7211
1550 N 105th East Ave Tulsa (74116) **(G-9834)**
Globe Marketing Services Inc 800 742-6787
133 Nw 122nd St Oklahoma City (73114) **(G-6162)**
Globe Mfg Company-OK LLC 580 272-9400
2000 B St Ada (74820) **(G-43)**
Gloria Corp Inc 580 332-4050
830 N Broadway Ave Ada (74820) **(G-44)**
Gloria Rae Travel Accessories 405 848-1300
917 Nw 79th St Oklahoma City (73114) **(G-6163)**
Glover Sheet Metal Inc 405 619-7117
2817 Perth Dr Edmond (73013) **(G-2437)**
Gmg Oil & Gas Corporation 918 756-5308
15648 Banyan Rd Morris (74445) **(G-4596)**
Gms Lalos Custom Wheels Ltd Co 918 622-3616
3927 S 123rd East Pl Tulsa (74146) **(G-9835)**
GNC Concrete Products Inc 918 438-1182
2100 N 161st East Ave Tulsa (74116) **(G-9836)**
Go Print USA 405 708-7000
719 Garden Grv Yukon (73099) **(G-11726)**
Go Rowdy Girl Screen Print EMB 580 668-2545
204 Mulberry Ln Wilson (73463) **(G-11534)**
GOAT Beef Jerky Co LLC 405 627-5096
9617 Sw 18th St Oklahoma City (73128) **(G-6164)**
Goddard's Concrete, Oklahoma City *Also called Goddards Ready Mix Con Inc* **(G-6165)**
Goddards Ready Mix Con Inc (PA) 405 424-4383
3101 Ne 10th St Oklahoma City (73117) **(G-6165)**
Goddards Ready Mix Concrete 405 424-4383
10100 Ne 10th St Oklahoma City (73130) **(G-6166)**
Godfrey Oil Properties (PA) 580 795-3087
901 E Main St Madill (73446) **(G-4148)**
Godiva Chocolatier Inc 918 459-2635
7021 S Memorial Dr 235a Tulsa (74133) **(G-9837)**
Goff Inc 405 278-6200
12216 Ns 3520 Seminole (74868) **(G-8374)**
Goff Associates Inc 615 750-2900
9608 S Allen Dr Oklahoma City (73139) **(G-6167)**
Goff Division, Seminole *Also called Disa Holding Corp* **(G-8369)**
Gold Rule Industries Inc 918 682-6500
627 Elgin St Muskogee (74401) **(G-4681)**
Gold Shop Custom Jewelers 405 789-2919
7005 Nw 50th St Bethany (73008) **(G-580)**
Gold Star Graphics Inc 405 677-1529
8812 S Bryant Ave Oklahoma City (73149) **(G-6168)**
Gold Strike Chili 405 606-1819
5901 Nw 41st St Warr Acres (73122) **(G-11320)**
Golden Bronze Inc 918 251-6300
613 N Aspen Ave Broken Arrow (74012) **(G-920)**
Golden Gas Service Co 918 582-0139
2502 E 21st St Ste B Tulsa (74114) **(G-9838)**
Golden Plaines Publishing, Laverne *Also called Leader Tribune* **(G-3879)**
Golden Trend Gas Gathering LLC 405 749-7860
1004 Nw 139th Street Pkwy Edmond (73013) **(G-2438)**
Goldtechs Inc 918 856-9059
1525 Saddle Ln Ste B Bartlesville (74006) **(G-487)**
Golf Advisors 918 645-6179
3701 S Harvard Ave Ste A Tulsa (74135) **(G-9839)**
Golf Car Factory 405 782-0460
6922 Melrose Ln Ste A Oklahoma City (73127) **(G-6169)**
Goliath Pipeline and Cnstr LLC 512 917-9313
2116 138th Ave Se Norman (73026) **(G-5008)**
Golsen Petroleum Corp 405 232-7033
16 S Pennsylvania Ave Oklahoma City (73107) **(G-6170)**
Gomaco Inc (PA) 918 585-8077
415 S Boston Ave Ste 500 Tulsa (74103) **(G-9840)**
Gonzales Mfg & Mch Inc 580 622-2025
2410 W Broadway Ave Sulphur (73086) **(G-8833)**
Gonzo LLC 405 373-1715
15750 Nw Expressway Yukon (73099) **(G-11727)**
Goobers Drilling LLC 918 846-2732
415 W 7th St Wynona (74084) **(G-11678)**
Good Filter Co 580 323-5200
505 Frisco Ave Clinton (73601) **(G-1751)**
Good Life Concepts Inc 478 714-9114
23000 N May Ave Edmond (73025) **(G-2439)**
Good Oil Company 580 233-3899
3801 N Oakwood Rd Enid (73703) **(G-2963)**
Good Printing Co Inc 405 235-9593
1910 S Nicklas Ave Oklahoma City (73128) **(G-6171)**
Good Springs Energy LLC 580 257-9762
1234 N Kemp Ave Tishomingo (73460) **(G-8965)**
Gooden Studios 405 375-3432
123 W Thompson Dr Kingfisher (73750) **(G-3799)**
Goodtimes Beef Jerky 405 387-5448
3613 N Country Club Rd Newcastle (73065) **(G-4829)**
Goodwill Inds Centl Okla Inc (PA) 405 236-4451
316 S Blackwelder Ave Oklahoma City (73108) **(G-6172)**
Goodwill Industries of SW 580 355-2163
1210 Sw Summit Ave Lawton (73501) **(G-3935)**
Goprints 918 798-0643
15499 Ash Rd Okmulgee (74447) **(G-7506)**
Gordon Bros Supply Inc 918 968-2591
5498 Hwy 66 W Stroud (74079) **(G-8810)**
Gordon White Lumber, Warr Acres *Also called White Gordon Lbr Co of Lindsay* **(G-11330)**
Gore Exploration LLC 580 922-4673
1208 Mary Lee Ln Edmond (73034) **(G-2440)**
Gore Nitrogen 405 381-4928
1202 Prairie Hills Dr Tuttle (73089) **(G-11201)**
Gore Nitrogen Pumping Svc LLC 580 922-4660
916 N Elm St Seiling (73663) **(G-8349)**
Gorfam Marketing Inc 918 252-3733
5666 S 122nd East Ave Tulsa (74146) **(G-9841)**
Gorfam Marketing Inc 918 388-9935
9495 E 55th St Tulsa (74145) **(G-9842)**
Gorilla Systems Inc 918 227-0230
815 E Bryan Ave Sapulpa (74066) **(G-8275)**
Gothic Production LLC 918 749-5666
6120 S Yale Ave Ste 1200 Tulsa (74136) **(G-9843)**
Gourdin Consulting LLC 918 207-9825
153 High Point St McAlester (74501) **(G-4302)**
Gourley Royalty Company LLC 580 223-8783
1112 S Rockford Rd Ardmore (73401) **(G-297)**
Gpe Competition Starters, Edmond *Also called G P Enterprises* **(G-2428)**
Gps Woodworks LLC 405 399-2369
6501 Deer Creek Trl Jones (73049) **(G-3747)**
Gr Trailers LLC 405 567-0567
1422 E Main St Prague (74864) **(G-7926)**
Gra Enterprises Inc 405 848-1300
115 Nw 44th St Oklahoma City (73118) **(G-6173)**
Gra Services International LP 405 672-8885
5540 Ne 2nd St Oklahoma City (73117) **(G-6174)**
Grace Allen Design - Custom 405 509-5164
1329 Sims Ave Edmond (73013) **(G-2441)**
Grace Fibrgls & Composites LLC 405 233-3203
9677 N Harrah Rd Harrah (73045) **(G-3378)**
Grace Machine Inc 405 381-4640
213 S Mustang Rd Tuttle (73089) **(G-11202)**
Grace Power LLC 512 228-9049
8645 Nw 4 Mile Rd Lawton (73507) **(G-3936)**
Graco Fishing & Rental Tls Inc 405 382-0009
1819 E Highway 270 Seminole (74868) **(G-8375)**
Graco Oilfield Services, Seminole *Also called Graco Fishing & Rental Tls Inc* **(G-8375)**
Graduate Services, Tulsa *Also called Herff Jones LLC* **(G-9924)**
Graf-X LLC 405 542-6631
109 W Main St Hinton (73047) **(G-3529)**
Graham Jewelers 580 439-6680
219 Oak Main Ave Comanche (73529) **(G-1841)**
Graham Laboratories 405 329-4413
2033 24th Ave Sw Norman (73072) **(G-5009)**
Graham Packaging Company LP 918 680-7900
102 Kaad St Muskogee (74401) **(G-4682)**
Grahams Bakery & Cafe 918 543-4244
25 N Broadway Inola (74036) **(G-3659)**

ALPHABETIC

Grain and Grit Woodworks LLC 405 250-6824
117 Sw 99th St Oklahoma City (73139) *(G-6175)*
Grand Avenue Lighting 580 237-4656
323 S Grand St Enid (73701) *(G-2964)*
Grand Junction Custom Trucks 918 245-6362
8100 Charles Page Blvd Tulsa (74127) *(G-9844)*
Grand Lake Detail LLC 918 257-2174
450672 E 338 Rd Afton (74331) *(G-117)*
Grand Resources Inc 918 492-2366
2448 E 81st St Ste 4040 Tulsa (74137) *(G-9845)*
Grand River Chronicle-Grove 918 786-8722
1627 S Main St Grove (74344) *(G-3272)*
Grande Oil & Gas Inc 405 348-8135
19 W 1st St Ste 4 Edmond (73003) *(G-2442)*
Granna's, Bessie *Also called S and J Foods LLC (G-570)*
Grannas LLC 580 337-6360
412 Main St Bessie (73622) *(G-568)*
Granola Shirts 918 592-5477
1130 S Oxford Ave Ste B Tulsa (74112) *(G-9846)*
Graphic Excursions 918 422-5318
1576 S Highway 59 Watts (74964) *(G-11356)*
Graphic Resources Reproduction, Broken Arrow *Also called Graphic Rsources Reproductions (G-921)*
Graphic Rsources Reproductions 918 461-0303
4251 W Albany St Broken Arrow (74012) *(G-921)*
Graphics Etc 918 274-4744
6905 N 129th East Ave Owasso (74055) *(G-7571)*
Graphics Universal Inc 918 461-0609
12437 E 60th St Tulsa (74146) *(G-9847)*
Graphix Xpress 580 765-7324
512 N 1st St Ponca City (74601) *(G-7831)*
Grating Company LLC 918 834-8100
2443 Dawson Rd Tulsa (74110) *(G-9848)*
Gravel Group LLC 405 359-4932
7601 Sunset Sail Ave Edmond (73034) *(G-2443)*
Gravel Road LLC 918 766-6368
3820 Silver Lake Vw Bartlesville (74006) *(G-488)*
Graves Cos Michael L 918 293-1500
4880 S Lewis Ave Tulsa (74105) *(G-9849)*
Gravley Companies Inc (PA) 405 842-1404
3401 Nw Expressway Oklahoma City (73112) *(G-6176)*
Gravley Companies Inc 918 743-6619
1919 S Harvard Ave Tulsa (74112) *(G-9850)*
Gray & Sons Sawmill & Sup LLC 580 924-2941
44 Sawmill Rd Durant (74701) *(G-2231)*
Gray Eagle Industries LLC 918 230-6652
18974 E 480 Rd Claremore (74019) *(G-1627)*
Gray Mud Disposal 580 635-2225
14701 N Garland Rd Kremlin (73753) *(G-3852)*
Gray Wireline 580 256-3775
4100 Oklahoma Ave Woodward (73801) *(G-11588)*
Grayfox Vineyards LLC 918 378-2214
6745 N Gregory Rd Yukon (73099) *(G-11728)*
Grayhorse Energy LLC 918 382-9201
20 E 5th St Ste 320 Tulsa (74103) *(G-9851)*
Grayhorse Operating, Tulsa *Also called Grayhorse Energy LLC (G-9851)*
Grays Sawmill Inc 580 924-2941
44 Sawmill Rd Durant (74701) *(G-2232)*
Grayson Creek, Ada *Also called Shelley Benefield (G-86)*
Grayson Investments LLC 580 421-9770
19264 State Rte 1 E Ada (74820) *(G-45)*
GRB Resources Inc 918 587-0036
1789 E 71st St Tulsa (74136) *(G-9852)*
Great Guns Logging, Hominy *Also called Fisher Wireline Services Inc (G-3584)*
Great Plains Audio 405 789-0221
7127 Nw 3rd St Oklahoma City (73127) *(G-6177)*
Great Plains Coca Cola Btlg Co 405 503-9328
12112 Skyway Ave Oklahoma City (73162) *(G-6178)*
Great Plains Coca Cola Btlg Co 405 280-2000
600 N May Ave Oklahoma City (73107) *(G-6179)*
Great Plains Coca-Cola Btlg Co 918 439-3013
1224 N Lewis Ave Tulsa (74110) *(G-9853)*
Great Plains Coca-Cola Btlg Co (HQ) 405 280-2000
600 N May Ave Oklahoma City (73107) *(G-6180)*
Great Plains Coca-Cola Btlg Co 405 280-2700
227 N Quapah Ave Oklahoma City (73107) *(G-6181)*
Great Plains Coca-Cola Btlg Co 800 753-2653
11333 E Pine St Ste 141 Tulsa (74116) *(G-9854)*
Great Plains Design 405 943-9018
3340 Nw 19th St Oklahoma City (73107) *(G-6182)*
Great Plains Oilfld Rentl LLC 405 422-2873
3401 S Radio Rd El Reno (73036) *(G-2720)*
Great Plains Rebar LLC (PA) 405 576-3270
13800 S Macarthur Blvd Oklahoma City (73173) *(G-6183)*
Great Plins Grphics Shwnee LLC 405 273-4263
414 W Federal St Shawnee (74804) *(G-8455)*
Great Salt Plains Midstream 405 608-8569
14000 Quail Springs Pkwy Oklahoma City (73134) *(G-6184)*
Great White Well Control, Oklahoma City *Also called Qes Pressure Control LLC (G-6930)*
Greater Tlsa Rprter Newspapers 918 743-3458
5341 S Yorktown Ave Tulsa (74105) *(G-9855)*
Greater Tlsa Rprter Newspapers 918 254-1515
5401 S Sheridan Rd # 302 Tulsa (74145) *(G-9856)*
Grecian Marble & Granite LLC 405 632-3802
919 Nw 74th St Oklahoma City (73116) *(G-6185)*
Green Bay Packaging Inc 405 222-2306
1800 Charles Allen Blvd Chickasha (73018) *(G-1463)*
Green Bay Packaging Inc 918 446-3341
6106 W 68th St Tulsa (74131) *(G-9008)*
Green Cntry Arcft Exhaust Inc 918 832-1769
1876 N 106th East Ave Tulsa (74116) *(G-9857)*
Green Cntry Cstm Woodworks LLC 918 585-1040
2323 S 49th West Ave Tulsa (74107) *(G-9858)*
Green Cntry Orthtic Prsthetics, Bartlesville *Also called Hanger Prsthetcs & Ortho Inc (G-489)*
Green Cntry Trophy Screen Prtg 918 647-2923
201 Hughes Dr Poteau (74953) *(G-7906)*
Green Co Corporation 918 221-3997
7424 E 46th St Tulsa (74145) *(G-9859)*
Green Country Aircraft LLC 918 832-1769
1876 N 106th East Ave Tulsa (74116) *(G-9860)*
Green Country Comprsr Svc LLC 918 906-6343
11974 E 530 Rd Claremore (74019) *(G-1628)*
Green Country Filter Mfg LLC 918 455-0100
1415 S 70th East Ave Tulsa (74112) *(G-9861)*
Green Country Outdoor Eqp 918 396-4250
542 E Chestnut St Skiatook (74070) *(G-8546)*
Green Country S Inc 918 224-8244
14177 W Highway 66 Sapulpa (74066) *(G-8276)*
Green Country Wireline Inc 918 534-2107
8 3/4 Mi Ne On Road 11 Dewey (74029) *(G-2022)*
Green Edward DBA Ed Green Trck 405 672-4522
3409 Lazy Ln Ste 4 Oklahoma City (73115) *(G-6186)*
Green Horizons LLC 405 364-9921
4700 168th Ave Ne Norman (73026) *(G-5010)*
Green Industries 918 825-1044
6471 S Highway 69 Pryor (74361) *(G-7964)*
Green Operating Company Inc 918 746-1700
2222 S Utica Pl Ste 200 Tulsa (74114) *(G-9862)*
Green Ox Pallet Technology LLC 720 276-8013
12352 Market Dr Oklahoma City (73114) *(G-6187)*
Green River Operating Co 405 872-9616
201 Cemetery Rd Noble (73068) *(G-4881)*
Green Room Studios 580 335-5689
521 N 12th St Frederick (73542) *(G-3193)*
Green Valley Distillery LLC 918 413-5199
501 Se 1160th Ave Red Oak (74563) *(G-8076)*
Green Valley Enterprises Inc 580 227-4938
201 W Central St Fairview (73737) *(G-3136)*
Greenbriar Resources Corp 405 348-7114
2204 Tredington Way Edmond (73034) *(G-2444)*
Greenhill Materials LLC 918 274-6560
14701 E Hwy 266 Owasso (74055) *(G-7572)*
Greenlamps USA LLC 580 775-2883
107 Red Oak Rd Cartwright (74731) *(G-1284)*
Greenleaf Energy Corporation 405 239-7763
101 Park Ave Ste 310 Oklahoma City (73102) *(G-6188)*
Greenlure LLC 918 786-9156
2633 Shasten St Grove (74344) *(G-3273)*
Greenstar Energy LLC (PA) 205 349-2852
101 Park Ave Ste 1000 Oklahoma City (73102) *(G-6189)*
Greenstar Energy LLC 405 604-0781
123 S Hudson Ave Oklahoma City (73102) *(G-6190)*
Greenwood Group Inc 580 762-2580
2117 N Waverly St Ponca City (74601) *(G-7832)*
Greer Oil Company 580 762-6355
724 Monument Rd Ponca City (74604) *(G-7833)*
Greg Butcher 918 434-6892
923 County Road 487 Salina (74365) *(G-8134)*
Greg E Conard 580 372-7982
Hc 71 Box 53-2 Soper (74759) *(G-8587)*
Greg Hall Oil & Gas LLC 405 330-6238
2940 Nw 156th St Edmond (73013) *(G-2445)*
Greg Riepl 405 232-6818
200 N Harvey Ave Apt 404 Oklahoma City (73102) *(G-6191)*
Greg Tucker Construction 405 756-3958
915 Se 4th St Lindsay (73052) *(G-4064)*
Gregath Publishing Company (PA) 918 542-4148
61101 E 140 Rd Miami (74354) *(G-4407)*
Gregory Dee Spahn Trust 405 826-6777
7305 S 2nd St Broken Arrow (74011) *(G-922)*
Gregory Prizzell P & R M Inc 405 752-0782
11317 Twisted Oak Rd Oklahoma City (73120) *(G-6192)*
Gregs Press 405 356-4156
990221 S Highway 102 Wellston (74881) *(G-11471)*
Gregs Wldg & Backhoe Svc Inc 405 222-1004
1388 E Highway 19 Chickasha (73018) *(G-1464)*
Gretchen Cagle Publications 918 342-1080
1199 W Country Club Rd Claremore (74017) *(G-1629)*

Grey Dog Industries LLC 405 926-0967
528 Nw 170th St Edmond (73012) **(G-2446)**
Greyfox Industries LLC 918 830-1144
1805 N 14th St Broken Arrow (74012) **(G-923)**
Greystone Logistics Inc (PA) 918 583-7441
1613 E 15th St Tulsa (74120) **(G-9863)**
Grice's Machine Shop, Durant *Also called Grices Automotive Machine Shop* **(G-2233)**
Grices Automotive Machine Shop 580 924-1006
2501 Rodeo Rd Durant (74701) **(G-2233)**
Griffin Food, Muskogee *Also called Griffin Holdings Inc* **(G-4684)**
Griffin Food Company 918 687-6311
111 S Cherokee St Muskogee (74403) **(G-4683)**
Griffin Holdings Inc (PA) 918 687-6311
111 S Cherokee St Muskogee (74403) **(G-4684)**
Griffin Industries LLC 918 422-4790
Hwy 59 Watts (74964) **(G-11357)**
Griffin Oil Properties LLC 580 226-0461
1320 W Broadway St Ardmore (73401) **(G-298)**
Griffin Resources 405 853-4688
805 E Jack Choate Ave Hennessey (73742) **(G-3464)**
Grip Jar Opener LLC 918 766-2711
36 E Cameron St Tulsa (74103) **(G-9864)**
Grips Etc Inc 405 447-2559
3214 Bart Conner Dr Norman (73072) **(G-5011)**
Grisham Services Incorporated 918 307-7635
800 S 11th St Broken Arrow (74012) **(G-924)**
Griswold Trucking Randy 580 476-3590
1398 County Road 1500 Ninnekah (73067) **(G-4872)**
Grizzly Grin Printing LLC 918 351-9066
8280 S Yorktown Ct Apt B Tulsa (74137) **(G-9865)**
Groves Oil Investments 405 341-8828
4312 Red Bud Pl Edmond (73013) **(G-2447)**
Groves, James R, Edmond *Also called Groves Oil Investments* **(G-2447)**
Grs Hot Shot Trucking LLC 580 353-9449
2005 County Road 1199 Tuttle (73089) **(G-11203)**
Grunewald Welding LLC 580 256-2674
4921 Pleasant View St Woodward (73801) **(G-11589)**
Grw Inc 918 681-3282
3105 Azalea Park Dr Muskogee (74401) **(G-4685)**
Gryphon Oilfield Solutions 405 446-8065
479 E Highway 19 Chickasha (73018) **(G-1465)**
GS Restoration Services Inc 918 408-2848
8815 Airport Way Unit 6 Tulsa (74132) **(G-9866)**
Gs Specialties 918 230-1295
36895 S 4215 Rd Inola (74036) **(G-3660)**
GSC, Stillwater *Also called Garage Storage Cabinets LLC* **(G-8695)**
Gss Sign & Design LLC 918 827-6561
17424 S Union Ave Mounds (74047) **(G-4617)**
Gtbco LLC, Tulsa *Also called G T Bynum Company* **(G-9794)**
GTS Ind., Claremore *Also called GTS Industries LLC* **(G-1630)**
GTS Industries LLC 918 706-2525
1607 Forest Hill Dr Claremore (74017) **(G-1630)**
Gtsa Manufacturing Inc 918 257-4269
1 S Maple Ave Afton (74331) **(G-118)**
Guard Exploration Partnership 580 234-3229
502 S Fillmore St Enid (73703) **(G-2965)**
Guardian Interlock of Utah 580 357-8583
4120 Nw Currell Dr Lawton (73505) **(G-3937)**
Guardian Interlock Systems 918 369-9935
8311 E 111th St S Ste G Bixby (74008) **(G-629)**
Guardian Tubular Services Inc 405 262-3800
8208 E Us Highway 66 El Reno (73036) **(G-2721)**
Guest Petroleum Incorporated 405 341-8698
1600 E 19th St Ste 204 Edmond (73013) **(G-2448)**
Gulf Exploration LLC 405 840-3381
9701 Broadway Ext Oklahoma City (73114) **(G-6193)**
Gulfport Energy Corporation (PA) 405 252-4600
3001 Quail Springs Pkwy Oklahoma City (73134) **(G-6194)**
Gulfport Energy Corporation 405 756-0060
401 Industrial Park Lindsay (73052) **(G-4065)**
Gun World Inc 405 670-5885
3420 S Sunnylane Rd Del City (73115) **(G-1997)**
Gunnebo Corporation U S A 918 832-8933
1240 N Harvard Ave Tulsa (74115) **(G-9867)**
Gunnebo Industries Inc (HQ) 918 832-8933
1240 N Harvard Ave Tulsa (74115) **(G-9868)**
Gunnebo Johnson, Tulsa *Also called Gunnebo Corporation U S A* **(G-9867)**
Gunnebo Johnson Corporation, Tulsa *Also called Gunnebo Industries Inc* **(G-9868)**
Gunter Peanut Co 405 656-2398
401 S Broadway Binger (73009) **(G-606)**
Gurley Custom Woodwork 580 235-3350
219 S Johnston St Ada (74820) **(G-46)**
Gurley Troy Mattingly 580 924-3042
28 W Ward Rd Durant (74701) **(G-2234)**
Gust Media LLC 641 715-3900
3126 S Boulevard Unit 139 Edmond (73013) **(G-2449)**
Guthrie Darin Cabinet Shop 918 773-8444
456556 E 1080 Rd Sallisaw (74955) **(G-8145)**
Guthrie Guthrie Home Ch Inc 405 600-8254
116 Sw 19th St Guthrie (73044) **(G-3316)**
Guthrie Industrial Coating 405 377-6649
1905 Birchwood Ct Stillwater (74075) **(G-8696)**
Guy W Logsdon 918 743-2171
4645 S Columbia Ave Tulsa (74105) **(G-9869)**
Guymon Daily Herald, Guymon *Also called Cnhi LLC* **(G-3346)**
Guymon Extracts Inc 580 338-2624
3001 Tumbleweed Dr Guymon (73942) **(G-3349)**
Guymon Motor Parts Inc 580 338-3316
1313 Ne Highway 54 Guymon (73942) **(G-3350)**
Guymon Safety Lane 580 338-6960
203 N Crumley St Guymon (73942) **(G-3351)**
Guys Wise 405 801-3339
1200 W Main St Norman (73069) **(G-5012)**
Gv Aerospace LLC 214 972-5055
1007 Oakwood Dr Okmulgee (74447) **(G-7507)**
Gwacs Defense Inc 918 794-5670
7130 S Lewis Ave Ste 300 Tulsa (74136) **(G-9870)**
Gwin Industries Inc 405 795-4946
1017 Nw 25th St Moore (73160) **(G-4526)**
Gws Welding Inc 918 527-5776
16255 S 225th East Ave Coweta (74429) **(G-1883)**
Gypsy Moon Studios 918 251-7188
1412 W Kenosha St Broken Arrow (74012) **(G-925)**
Gypsy Twang Publishing 918 398-3116
14578 S Gary Pl Bixby (74008) **(G-630)**
Gyrodata Incorporated 405 677-0200
421 S Eagle Ln Oklahoma City (73128) **(G-6195)**
H & B Machine & Manufacturing 405 224-0006
1003 Quail Ln Chickasha (73018) **(G-1466)**
H & C Service & Supply, Weatherford *Also called H & C Services Inc* **(G-11417)**
H & C Services Inc 580 772-2521
400 S Access Rd Weatherford (73096) **(G-11417)**
H & H Cnstr Met Fbrication Inc 405 701-1075
1301 Quality Ave Norman (73071) **(G-5013)**
H & H Manufacturing and Distrg, Hinton *Also called Star Industries Inc* **(G-3537)**
H & H Muffler Whse & Mfg Co 918 371-9633
10301 E 126th St N Collinsville (74021) **(G-1811)**
H & H Ornamental Iron 405 634-0646
2205 S Agnew Ave Oklahoma City (73108) **(G-6196)**
H & H Protective Coating Co 918 582-9187
4849 W 21st St Tulsa (74107) **(G-9871)**
H & H Specialty Welding LLC 479 322-1125
2727 M And K Ln El Reno (73036) **(G-2722)**
H & H Xray 918 752-0966
1113 N Griffin Ave Okmulgee (74447) **(G-7508)**
H & J Services 580 237-4613
3312 N 16th St Enid (73701) **(G-2966)**
H & K Specification & Sls LLC 405 844-7456
633 Enterprise Dr Ste 160 Edmond (73013) **(G-2450)**
H & L Forge, Tulsa *Also called H & L Tooth Company* **(G-9872)**
H & L Tooth Company 918 272-0951
10055 E 56th St N Tulsa (74117) **(G-9872)**
H & M Energy Services LLC 405 428-0740
200 Sheperds Way Blanchard (73010) **(G-715)**
H & M Pipe Beveling Mch Co Inc 918 582-9984
311 E 3rd St Tulsa (74120) **(G-9873)**
H & P Drilling, Oklahoma City *Also called Helmerich & Payne Intl Drlg Co* **(G-6236)**
H & P Finco 918 742-5531
1437 S Bulgar Tulsa (74119) **(G-9874)**
H & S Drilling Co 918 794-9944
320 S Boston Ave Ste 1910 Tulsa (74103) **(G-9875)**
H 5 C Pumping Inc 580 487-3869
621 Main Forgan (73938) **(G-3170)**
H C E Inc 405 745-2145
8100 Sw 15th St Oklahoma City (73128) **(G-6197)**
H C Rustin Corporation (HQ) 580 924-3260
50 E Main St Durant (74701) **(G-2235)**
H C Rustin Corporation 580 224-2672
1948 Cooper Dr Ardmore (73401) **(G-299)**
H Diamond Resources Inc 580 476-3733
S Hwy 81 Rush Springs (73082) **(G-8121)**
H G Flake Company Inc 918 684-9004
3007 Kimberlea Dr Muskogee (74403) **(G-4686)**
H G Jenkins Construction LLC 580 355-9822
1630 Sw Railroad St Lawton (73501) **(G-3938)**
H G P Industries, Shawnee *Also called Oldcastle Buildingenvelope Inc* **(G-8481)**
H Gellar 617 834-0602
5830 Nw Expressway Warr Acres (73132) **(G-11321)**
H K & S Iron Co 405 745-2761
6801 S Council Rd Oklahoma City (73169) **(G-6198)**
H L Custom Processing 580 927-5408
17208 County Road 3760 Coalgate (74538) **(G-1780)**
H Petro R Inc 405 242-4400
5530 N Western Ave # 100 Oklahoma City (73118) **(G-6199)**
H Rockin Industries Inc 479 285-1766
113 Oak St Arkoma (74901) **(G-385)**
H Rockn Inc 405 323-6593
106 Rosewood Dr Chickasha (73018) **(G-1467)**

ALPHABETIC

H S Boyd Company Inc 918 835-9359
6915 E 14th St Tulsa (74112) ***(G-9876)***
H S I, Tulsa *Also called Heater Specialists LLC* ***(G-9909)***
H S Milam 918 789-2666
341 W 6th St Chelsea (74016) ***(G-1405)***
H W Allen Co LLC 918 747-8700
4835 S Peoria Ave Ste 20 Tulsa (74105) ***(G-9877)***
H&A Shirt Cafe Cstm Screen Prt 918 357-1115
7839 S Townsend Ave Broken Arrow (74014) ***(G-1129)***
H&H Aircraft Inc 405 833-3330
3828 Nw 67th St Oklahoma City (73116) ***(G-6200)***
H&H Ornamental Ironworks, Oklahoma City *Also called H & H Ornamental Iron* ***(G-6196)***
H&H Printer Services, Bixby *Also called H&H Retail Services LLC* ***(G-631)***
H&H Retail Services LLC 918 369-4055
12816 S Memorial Dr # 110 Bixby (74008) ***(G-631)***
H&H Specialty Welding 479 252-1991
717 E Lydia Ter Mustang (73064) ***(G-4774)***
H&P Technologies, Tulsa *Also called Helmerich & Payne Tech LLC* ***(G-9918)***
H&R Lifting & Bucket Service 918 446-5549
7411 S Jackson Ave Tulsa (74132) ***(G-9878)***
H-I-S Paint Mfg Co Inc (PA) 405 232-2077
1801 W Reno Ave Oklahoma City (73106) ***(G-6201)***
H-V Manufacturing Company (PA) 918 291-2108
138th & Hwy 75 Glenpool (74033) ***(G-3235)***
H-V Manufacturing Company 918 756-9620
2950 N Wood Dr Okmulgee (74447) ***(G-7509)***
H.S., Oklahoma City *Also called Hobby Supermarket Inc* ***(G-6256)***
H/H Mobile Welding LLC 405 830-5525
14525 W Frisco Dr Yukon (73099) ***(G-11729)***
H2 Services LLC 405 388-9049
4700 Highway 105 Guthrie (73044) ***(G-3317)***
H2s Safety Plus Inc 580 622-4796
1133 Fletcher Rd Sulphur (73086) ***(G-8834)***
H2szero LLC 918 384-9600
14724 Lone Star Rd Sapulpa (74066) ***(G-8277)***
H3 Custom Wood Moldings LLC 918 250-8746
12933 E Apache St Tulsa (74116) ***(G-9879)***
Hacker Industries LLC 918 272-6607
11505 E 76th St N Owasso (74055) ***(G-7573)***
Hackney Ladish Inc 580 237-4212
400 E Willow Rd Enid (73701) ***(G-2967)***
Hadley-Keeney Chipping Inc 580 835-2645
3631 Cascade Creek Rd Eagletown (74734) ***(G-2275)***
Hadleys Industries 405 743-0337
3505 S Jardot Rd Stillwater (74074) ***(G-8697)***
Haiku Candles LLC 405 528-5556
910 Nw 32nd St Oklahoma City (73118) ***(G-6202)***
Hail To Wreath 405 659-2216
119 E Forster Ln Mustang (73064) ***(G-4775)***
Hailey Ordnance Company 405 813-0700
1661 Exchange Ave Oklahoma City (73108) ***(G-6203)***
Hailey Spcalty Tls Div Testers, Oklahoma City *Also called Testers Inc* ***(G-7273)***
Haken Dozer Service 580 669-2211
14004 E Richmond Rd Glencoe (74032) ***(G-3223)***
HALAQ Inc 405 321-7293
19912 S Dobbs Rd Newalla (74857) ***(G-4810)***
Halcon Operating Co Inc 832 649-4015
5100 E Skelly Dr Ste 650 Tulsa (74135) ***(G-9880)***
Hale Exploration LLC 405 273-8000
130 N Broadway Ave Shawnee (74801) ***(G-8456)***
Hale Publications 405 632-2450
740 Sw 39th St Oklahoma City (73109) ***(G-6204)***
Haley Specialty Tools, Elk City *Also called Testers Inc* ***(G-2881)***
Hall & Anderson Services Inc 580 319-5624
14867 Us Highway 70 Ardmore (73401) ***(G-300)***
Hall Energy 405 231-2490
9225 Lake Hefner Pkwy # 200 Oklahoma City (73120) ***(G-6205)***
Hall Painting and Wall Cvg 405 373-2724
3555 Washington Ave E Piedmont (73078) ***(G-7762)***
Hallco, Broken Arrow *Also called Teddy Hall* ***(G-1170)***
Halliburton Company 580 251-4614
100 E Halliburton Blvd Duncan (73536) ***(G-2121)***
Halliburton Company 580 251-3002
1015 W Bois D Arc Ave Duncan (73533) ***(G-2122)***
Halliburton Company 580 251-3379
1310 N Hwy 81 Duncan (73533) ***(G-2123)***
Halliburton Company 580 251-3420
6917 S Air Depot Blvd Oklahoma City (73135) ***(G-6206)***
Halliburton Company 580 251-2847
215 E Bois D Arc Ave Duncan (73533) ***(G-2124)***
Halliburton Company 918 587-3117
1 W 3rd St Ste 1400 Tulsa (74103) ***(G-9881)***
Halliburton Company 405 278-9685
215 E Bois D Arc Ave Duncan (73533) ***(G-2125)***
Halliburton Company 580 251-4421
1409 S 13th St 718 Duncan (73533) ***(G-2126)***
Halliburton Company 405 231-1800
210 Park Ave Ste 2000 Oklahoma City (73102) ***(G-6207)***
Halliburton Company 806 665-0005
215 E Bois D Arc Ave Duncan (73533) ***(G-2127)***
Halliburton Company 405 459-6611
Hwy 81 N Pocasset (73079) ***(G-7776)***
Halliburton Company 580 251-3406
2600 S 2nd St Duncan (73536) ***(G-2128)***
Halliburton Company 405 459-6611
300 N Main St Pocasset (73079) ***(G-7777)***
Halliburton Company 405 552-8520
210 Park Ave Ste 1950 Oklahoma City (73102) ***(G-6208)***
Halliburton Company 405 805-2200
9800 W Reno Ave Oklahoma City (73127) ***(G-6209)***
Halliburton Company 580 251-3760
1015 W Bois D Arcade Ave Duncan (73533) ***(G-2129)***
Halliburton Company 405 231-1800
9500 Pole Rd Moore (73160) ***(G-4527)***
Halliburton Energy Services, Duncan *Also called Halliburton Company* ***(G-2121)***
Halliburton Energy Services, Duncan *Also called Halliburton Company* ***(G-2122)***
Halliburton Energy Services, Duncan *Also called Halliburton Company* ***(G-2123)***
Halliburton Energy Services, Tulsa *Also called Halliburton Company* ***(G-9881)***
Halliburton Energy Services, Duncan *Also called Halliburton Company* ***(G-2127)***
Halliburton Energy Services, Pocasset *Also called Halliburton Company* ***(G-7776)***
Halliburton Service Division, Duncan *Also called Halliburton Company* ***(G-2125)***
Halo Induction Looping LLC 918 638-1599
4564 S Harvard Ave Ste A Tulsa (74135) ***(G-9882)***
Ham Ventures LLC 918 277-9500
8119 E 48th St Tulsa (74145) ***(G-9883)***
Hamil Service LLC 405 375-3815
15748 Beverly Dr Kingfisher (73750) ***(G-3800)***
Hamilton Industries LLC 918 357-3862
8112 S Winwood Ln Broken Arrow (74014) ***(G-1130)***
Hamm & Phillips Services, Enid *Also called Complete Energy Services Inc* ***(G-2933)***
Hamm and Phillips Services Co 580 256-8686
1010 E Hanks Trl Woodward (73801) ***(G-11590)***
Hammer Construction Inc (PA) 405 310-3160
4320 Adams Rd Norman (73069) ***(G-5014)***
Hammer Hoby 580 227-2100
112 N Main St Fairview (73737) ***(G-3137)***
Hampton Software Development L 918 607-5307
4704 W El Paso St Broken Arrow (74012) ***(G-926)***
Hancock Industries Inc 918 835-5441
6533 E Independence St Tulsa (74115) ***(G-9884)***
Handi-Sak Inc 405 789-3001
8300 Nw 3rd St Oklahoma City (73127) ***(G-6210)***
Handle LLC 405 822-9312
2410 W Memorial Rd Oklahoma City (73134) ***(G-6211)***
Handle It 3d Printing LLC 405 788-9471
33109 Hardesty Rd Shawnee (74801) ***(G-8457)***
Hands Down Software 405 844-6314
516 Nw 20th St Oklahoma City (73103) ***(G-6212)***
Handy & Harman 918 258-1566
21808 E Highway 51 Broken Arrow (74014) ***(G-1131)***
Handy Grocery, Pawhuska *Also called Moores Hardware and Home Ctr* ***(G-7689)***
Handy Mart Inc 580 254-5889
1201 Oklahoma Ave Woodward (73801) ***(G-11591)***
Haney John 405 282-2839
1501 S Post Rd Guthrie (73044) ***(G-3318)***
Hanger Inc 918 742-6464
2116 E 15th St Tulsa (74104) ***(G-9885)***
Hanger Clinic, Enid *Also called Hanger Prsthetcs & Ortho Inc* ***(G-2968)***
Hanger Prsthetcs & Ortho Inc 580 326-6661
103 S Broadway St Hugo (74743) ***(G-3611)***
Hanger Prsthetcs & Ortho Inc 405 525-4000
4207 W Memorial Rd Oklahoma City (73134) ***(G-6213)***
Hanger Prsthetcs & Ortho Inc 479 484-1620
330 S 5th St Ste 102 Enid (73701) ***(G-2968)***
Hanger Prsthetcs & Ortho Inc 918 333-6900
1904 Se Washington Blvd Bartlesville (74006) ***(G-489)***
Hanger Prsthetcs & Ortho Inc 918 488-0400
6052 S Sheridan Rd Tulsa (74145) ***(G-9886)***
Hanger Prsthetcs & Ortho Inc 580 226-7900
1109 Walnut Dr Ardmore (73401) ***(G-301)***
Hanger Prsthetcs & Ortho Inc 918 423-1024
1611 N Strong Blvd McAlester (74501) ***(G-4303)***
Hanger Prsthtics Orthotics Inc 918 687-1855
737 S 32nd St Muskogee (74401) ***(G-4687)***
Hanlock-Causeway Company LLC 918 446-1450
6802 S 65th West Ave Tulsa (74131) ***(G-9009)***
Hannah Industries Inc 918 430-0743
6525 N 57th West Ave Tulsa (74126) ***(G-9887)***
Hanor Company of Wisconsin LLC 580 237-3255
3025 S Van Buren St Enid (73703) ***(G-2969)***
Hanor Feed Mill, Enid *Also called Hanor Company of Wisconsin LLC* ***(G-2969)***
Hansen Millwork & Trim Inc 405 239-2564
812 Sw 6th St Oklahoma City (73109) ***(G-6214)***
Hansen Research LLC 405 659-5079
7510 E Lindsey St Norman (73026) ***(G-5015)***
Hanson Inc 918 447-0777
209 N Main St Tulsa (74103) ***(G-9888)***

Hanson Aggregates Wrp Inc 580 369-3773
6.5 Mles W Of I 35 On Hwy Davis (73030) ***(G-1985)***
Hansons Stone & Landscape 580 310-0071
2129 1/2 Woodland Dr Ada (74820) ***(G-47)***
Happy Camper Signs 918 856-4279
9400 W 61st St Tulsa (74131) ***(G-9010)***
Happy Carpet Cleaning, Lawton *Also called Johnsonm3 LLC* ***(G-3946)***
Happy Tooth Dental 918 492-8793
7104 S Sheridan Rd Ste 8 Tulsa (74133) ***(G-9889)***
Harbison-Fischer Inc 405 677-3393
1606 S Jordan Ave Oklahoma City (73129) ***(G-6215)***
Harbison-Fischer Sales Co, Oklahoma City *Also called Harbison-Fischer Inc* ***(G-6215)***
Harbisonwalker Intl Inc 918 825-1044
6471 S Highway 69 Pryor (74361) ***(G-7965)***
Harbor Light Hospice LLC 405 949-1200
1009 N Meridian Ave Oklahoma City (73107) ***(G-6216)***
Harbour AC & Refrigration, Wilburton *Also called Southeastern Ice* ***(G-11524)***
Hard Edge Design Inc 405 360-9714
1007 N University Blvd Norman (73069) ***(G-5016)***
Hard Hat Safety and Glove LLC (PA) 405 942-9500
6015 S I 35 Service Rd Oklahoma City (73149) ***(G-6217)***
Hard Hat Services, Tulsa *Also called Aether Dbs LLC* ***(G-8988)***
Harden Metalworks LLC 405 812-2812
3001 28th Ave Ne Norman (73071) ***(G-5017)***
Hardesty Company Inc (HQ) 918 585-3100
4141 N Memorial Dr Tulsa (74115) ***(G-9890)***
Hardesty Press Inc 918 582-5306
1317 E 11th St Tulsa (74120) ***(G-9891)***
Hardin Ignition Inc 405 853-4324
210 S Main St Hennessey (73742) ***(G-3465)***
Hardin Ignition Magneto Shop, Hennessey *Also called Hardin Ignition Inc* ***(G-3465)***
Harding & Shelton Inc 405 236-0080
12 E California Ave Oklahoma City (73104) ***(G-6218)***
Hardtimes Real Beef Jerky Inc 580 497-7695
3533 Jensen Rd E El Reno (73036) ***(G-2723)***
Hardwood Innovations Inc 405 722-5588
8025 N Wilshire Ct Ste C Oklahoma City (73132) ***(G-6219)***
Hargrove Industries Inc 918 231-7290
6211 Merrimack Dr Sand Springs (74063) ***(G-8189)***
Hargrove Manufacturing Corp 918 241-7537
207 Wellston Park Rd Sand Springs (74063) ***(G-8190)***
Harley Industries Inc (HQ) 918 451-2323
4530 S Sheridan Rd # 218 Tulsa (74145) ***(G-9892)***
Harley Valve & Instrument, Tulsa *Also called Harley Industries Inc* ***(G-9892)***
Harold Speed Jr 580 838-2578
635 Carpenters Bluff Rd Hendrix (74741) ***(G-3440)***
Harold's Vibration Control, Enid *Also called Enid Electric Motor Svc Inc* ***(G-2952)***
Harper County Journal 580 735-2526
3 W Turner Ave Buffalo (73834) ***(G-1213)***
Harper Welding Design LLC 405 396-8558
11316 E 15th St Arcadia (73007) ***(G-230)***
Harpers Welding 580 298-7165
1207 Se 3rd St Antlers (74523) ***(G-216)***
Harrell Energy Co 918 587-2750
15 W 6th St Ste 2510 Tulsa (74119) ***(G-9893)***
Harrell Exploration 580 226-8887
5 S Commerce St Ste 32 Ardmore (73401) ***(G-302)***
Harrell Exploration Corp 918 587-2750
15 W 6th St Ste 2510 Tulsa (74119) ***(G-9894)***
Harrell Petroleum, Oklahoma City *Also called Harrell Verlan W Oil & Gas Co* ***(G-6220)***
Harrell Verlan W Oil & Gas Co 405 272-9345
101 Park Ave Ste 310 Oklahoma City (73102) ***(G-6220)***
Harrik Company LLC 918 691-6417
5317 E 5th Pl Tulsa (74112) ***(G-9895)***
Harris Discount Supplies Inc 847 726-3800
1318 Fretz Dr Edmond (73003) ***(G-2451)***
Harris Pattern & Mfg Inc 918 227-3228
8200 S 89th West Ave Tulsa (74131) ***(G-9011)***
Harrison Gypsum LLC (HQ) 405 366-9500
1550 Double C Dr Norman (73069) ***(G-5018)***
Harrison Gypsum LLC 580 994-6048
10930 Us Highway 412 Mooreland (73852) ***(G-4591)***
Harrison Gypsum LLC 580 994-6050
801 Sw 6th St Mooreland (73852) ***(G-4592)***
Harrison Gypsum LLC 580 337-6371
1113 Main St Bessie (73622) ***(G-569)***
Harrison Gypsum Holdings LLC (HQ) 405 366-9500
1550 Double C Dr Norman (73069) ***(G-5019)***
Harrison House Inc 918 582-2126
1029 N Utica Ave Tulsa (74110) ***(G-9896)***
Harrison Logging Lc 580 245-2179
3161 Ferguson Rd Haworth (74740) ***(G-3404)***
Harrison Manufacturing Co Inc 918 838-9961
6130 E 13th St Tulsa (74112) ***(G-9897)***
Harrison Roof Truss Co 580 937-4900
9240 Ok Highway 48 S Coleman (73432) ***(G-1795)***
Harry A Lippert Jr 512 705-1248
1717 Nw Ozmun Ave Lawton (73507) ***(G-3939)***
Harry H Diamond Inc 405 275-5788
116 N Bell Ave Shawnee (74801) ***(G-8458)***
Harsco Corporation 918 619-8000
5555 S 129th East Ave Tulsa (74134) ***(G-9898)***
Harsco Corporation 918 619-8000
5615 S 129th East Ave Tulsa (74134) ***(G-9899)***
Harsco Indus Air-X-Changers, Tulsa *Also called Harsco Corporation* ***(G-9898)***
Harsco Indus Air-X-Changers, Tulsa *Also called Harsco Corporation* ***(G-9899)***
Harsco Industrial Hammco LLC 918 619-8000
5615 S 129th East Ave Tulsa (74134) ***(G-9900)***
Hart Brothers Welding 918 697-5682
17315 N Memorial Dr Collinsville (74021) ***(G-1812)***
Hart Feeds Inc 405 224-0102
2301 W Country Club Rd Chickasha (73018) ***(G-1468)***
Hart Trailer LLC 405 224-3634
3909 S 4th St Chickasha (73018) ***(G-1469)***
Hart, Elzie, Collinsville *Also called Hart Brothers Welding* ***(G-1812)***
Hartco Metal Products Inc 405 471-2784
6300 N Coltrane Rd Edmond (73034) ***(G-2452)***
Hartins Welding 580 795-5594
7376 Four Corners Rd Madill (73446) ***(G-4149)***
Hartshorne Sun, Hartshorne *Also called Newspaper Holding Inc* ***(G-3394)***
Harvey Kates 918 225-2567
920 E Maple St Cushing (74023) ***(G-1934)***
Harvey's Vacuum Service, Cushing *Also called Harvey Kates* ***(G-1934)***
Harwell Industries 405 948-7775
100 N Quapah Ave Ste B Oklahoma City (73107) ***(G-6221)***
Hasco Corporation 405 524-6366
6220 S I 35 Service Rd Oklahoma City (73149) ***(G-6222)***
Haskell Lemon Construction Co (PA) 405 947-6069
3800 Sw 10th St Oklahoma City (73108) ***(G-6223)***
Haskell Lemon Construction Co 405 236-2701
1400 Ne 2nd St Oklahoma City (73117) ***(G-6224)***
Haskell News 918 482-5619
108 E Main St Haskell (74436) ***(G-3398)***
Hassler Hot Oil Service LLC 405 756-0448
202 Se 4th St Lindsay (73052) ***(G-4066)***
Hasty Bake Charcoal Ovens, Tulsa *Also called Hasty-Bake Inc* ***(G-9901)***
Hasty-Bake Inc 918 665-8220
1313 S Lewis Ave Tulsa (74104) ***(G-9901)***
Hat Creek Contractors Inc 580 761-6154
737 S Cosden Ave Shidler (74652) ***(G-8527)***
Hathaway & Simpson 580 875-3177
528 W Missouri St Walters (73572) ***(G-11301)***
Haub Oil and Gas LLC 580 765-3585
135 Road Runner Dr Ponca City (74604) ***(G-7834)***
Haul Around 580 353-0808
12714 Ne Townley Rd Elgin (73538) ***(G-2776)***
Haus Bioceuticals Inc 405 295-5257
755 Research Pkwy Ste 460 Oklahoma City (73104) ***(G-6225)***
Hausner's, Drumright *Also called Hausners Precast Con Pdts Inc* ***(G-2061)***
Hausners Limited 580 924-6988
8883 Us 70 Mead (73449) ***(G-4366)***
Hausners Precast Con Pdts Inc 918 352-3479
505 Griffith Ave Drumright (74030) ***(G-2061)***
Havard Industries LLC 405 888-0961
704 Nw 139th St Edmond (73013) ***(G-2453)***
Hawk Ammo, Edmond *Also called Havard Industries LLC* ***(G-2453)***
Hawkeye Fleet Services 405 495-9939
924 S Morgan Rd Oklahoma City (73128) ***(G-6226)***
Hawkeye Printing Co 918 744-0158
2707 E 15th St Tulsa (74104) ***(G-9902)***
Hawkeye Signs & Printing 918 864-2035
3865 Suthridge Cir Apt 12 Tahlequah (74464) ***(G-8866)***
Hawkins International Inc 918 592-4422
427 S Boston Ave Ste 210 Tulsa (74103) ***(G-9903)***
Hawkins Oil Co LLc 918 382-7743
427 S Boston Ave Ste 915 Tulsa (74103) ***(G-9904)***
Hawley & Co 918 587-0510
702 S Utica Ave Tulsa (74104) ***(G-9905)***
Hawley Design Furnishings, Tulsa *Also called Hawley & Co* ***(G-9905)***
Hawley Hot Oil LLC 580 839-2416
24986 County Road 800 Nash (73761) ***(G-4803)***
Hawthorne Resources 405 840-1928
5225 N Shartel Ave Oklahoma City (73118) ***(G-6227)***
Hayden Betchan Welding LLC 580 863-5372
1309 S Knox Rd Garber (73738) ***(G-3214)***
Haynes Welding Service Inc 337 380-7126
7921 Nw 39th St Bethany (73008) ***(G-581)***
Hays and Hays Companies Inc 405 624-2999
504 W 6th Ave Stillwater (74074) ***(G-8698)***
Hays Awning, Dewey *Also called Hays Tent & Awning* ***(G-2023)***
Hays Publishing 918 456-7717
21922 Sequoyah Club Dr Tahlequah (74464) ***(G-8867)***
Hays Tent & Awning 918 534-1663
512 S Osage Ave Dewey (74029) ***(G-2023)***
Hays Welding & Blacksmith 580 287-3458
201 S Stepp Ave Willow (73673) ***(G-11530)***

Hazelwood Inc..405 848-6884
  6801 Broadway Ext Ste 320 Oklahoma City (73116) *(G-6228)*
Hazelwood Prod Exploration LLC..............................405 848-6884
  6801 Broadway Ext Ste 320 Oklahoma City (73116) *(G-6229)*
Hazelwood Oil & Gas Co Inc....................................405 631-3532
  5350 S Western Ave # 608 Oklahoma City (73109) *(G-6230)*
HB Brackets...405 745-4417
  6625 Sw 104th St Oklahoma City (73169) *(G-6231)*
Hbi, Broken Arrow Also called Houston Brothers Inc *(G-1134)*
HCf Welding Services...918 907-4274
  2305 S 96th East Ave B Tulsa (74129) *(G-9906)*
Head Country Inc..580 762-1227
  2116 N Ash St Ponca City (74601) *(G-7835)*
Heady Trucking..580 326-2739
  242 N 4290 Rd Sawyer (74756) *(G-8334)*
Healdton Herald, Healdton Also called Hilton Herald Corp Oklahoma *(G-3414)*
Health Engineering System....................................405 329-6810
  2600 Technology Pl Norman (73071) *(G-5020)*
HEanderson Company...918 687-4426
  2025 Anderson Dr Muskogee (74403) *(G-4688)*
Hear My Heart Publishing LLC...............................918 510-1483
  313 E Oak St Skiatook (74070) *(G-8547)*
Heart 2 Heart Embroidery.......................................405 401-7408
  5004 N Cromwell Ave Oklahoma City (73112) *(G-6232)*
Heartbeat Designs LLC...918 333-0833
  3383 State St Ste 100 Bartlesville (74003) *(G-490)*
Heartland Energy Options LLC.............................405 600-6009
  4981 Moffat Rd Nw Piedmont (73078) *(G-7763)*
Heartland Locator...580 554-0125
  501 W Broadway St Pond Creek (73766) *(G-7890)*
Heartland Mobility, Piedmont Also called Heartland Energy Options LLC *(G-7763)*
Heartland Oil & Gas LLC...405 848-8099
  7100 N Classen Blvd # 400 Oklahoma City (73116) *(G-6233)*
Heartland Precious Metals......................................405 254-6870
  307 E Danforth Rd Ste 150 Edmond (73034) *(G-2454)*
Heartland Tank Services..800 774-3230
  5200 S Hattie Ave Oklahoma City (73129) *(G-6234)*
Heartland Vaccines LLC..716 848-9251
  1201 S Innovation Way Stillwater (74074) *(G-8699)*
Heat Transfer Equipment Co..................................918 836-8721
  1515 N 93rd East Ave Tulsa (74115) *(G-9907)*
Heater Fabricators Tulsa LLC.................................918 430-1127
  5426 S 49th West Ave Tulsa (74107) *(G-9908)*
Heater Specialists LLC (HQ)..................................918 835-3126
  3171 N Toledo Ave Tulsa (74115) *(G-9909)*
Heater Specialists   LLC..918 835-3126
  5500 E Independence St Tulsa (74115) *(G-9910)*
Heater Specialists   LLC..918 476-8670
  303 S Main St Chouteau (74337) *(G-1564)*
Heath Technologies LLC...918 342-3222
  2405 S Hwy 66 Claremore (74017) *(G-1631)*
Heather Harjochee..405 615-3273
  1213 Sw 105th St Oklahoma City (73170) *(G-5293)*
Heatwave Supply Inc..918 333-6363
  332 Ne Katherine Ave Bartlesville (74006) *(G-491)*
Heavener Ledger...918 653-2425
  507 E 1st St Heavener (74937) *(G-3429)*
Heavens Scent Candle Factory...............................918 686-0243
  2410 N 32nd St Muskogee (74401) *(G-4689)*
Heavybilt Mfg Inc...580 927-3003
  38038 Us Highway 75 Coalgate (74538) *(G-1781)*
Hefner Co Inc..405 236-4404
  1 Ne 2nd St Ste 207 Oklahoma City (73104) *(G-6235)*
Heintzelman Cons & Rofing...................................405 409-8954
  9601 Bluewater Cir Oklahoma City (73165) *(G-5294)*
Heirston Welding & Cnstr......................................580 657-2518
  6309 Oil City Rd Wilson (73463) *(G-11535)*
Heister Custom Cabinets Inc.................................405 329-6318
  4915 W Tecumseh Rd Norman (73072) *(G-5021)*
Hejin Waldran..918 408-3500
  9583 E Highway 88 Claremore (74017) *(G-1632)*
Helen Murphy Colpitt Trust....................................918 371-9930
  118 S 11th St Collinsville (74021) *(G-1813)*
Helena Agri-Enterprises LLC...................................580 477-0986
  20369 E County Road 158 Altus (73521) *(G-157)*
Helicomb International Inc....................................918 835-3999
  1402 S 69th East Ave Tulsa (74112) *(G-9911)*
Helmco Manufacturing Inc.....................................918 336-4757
  Hwy 123 Sw 14th Lkout Ave Bartlesville (74003) *(G-492)*
Helmerich & Payne Inc (PA)...................................918 742-5531
  1437 S Boulder Ave # 1400 Tulsa (74119) *(G-9912)*
Helmerich & Payne Inc..918 447-2630
  6105 W 68th St Tulsa (74131) *(G-9012)*
Helmerich & Payne Inc..918 447-8692
  5416 S 49th West Ave Tulsa (74107) *(G-9913)*
Helmerich & Payne Inc..918 835-6071
  3003 N Sheridan Rd Tulsa (74115) *(G-9914)*
Helmerich & Payne De Venezuela.........................918 742-5531
  1437 S Boulder Ave # 1400 Tulsa (74119) *(G-9915)*

Helmerich & Payne Intl Drlg Co (HQ)....................918 742-5531
  1437 S Boulder Ave # 1400 Tulsa (74119) *(G-9916)*
Helmerich & Payne Intl Drlg Co.............................918 742-5531
  5401 S Hattie Ave Oklahoma City (73129) *(G-6236)*
Helmerich & Payne Rasco Inc (HQ).......................918 742-5531
  1437 S Boulder Ave # 1400 Tulsa (74119) *(G-9917)*
Helmerich & Payne Tech LLC.................................918 742-5531
  1437 S Boulder Ave # 1400 Tulsa (74119) *(G-9918)*
Helmerich Payne Argentina Drlg...........................918 742-5531
  1437 S Boulder Ave # 1400 Tulsa (74119) *(G-9919)*
Helmerich Payne Boulder Drlg (HQ).....................918 742-5531
  1437 S Boulder Ave # 1400 Tulsa (74119) *(G-9920)*
Helmerich Payne Columbia Drlg............................918 742-5531
  1437 S Boulder Ave # 1400 Tulsa (74119) *(G-9921)*
Helmerich Payne Trinidad Drlg..............................918 742-5531
  1437 S Boulder Ave # 1400 Tulsa (74119) *(G-9922)*
Helmerich/Payne Intrntnl Drll, Tulsa Also called Helmerich Payne Trinidad Drlg *(G-9922)*
Help Housing...918 258-7252
  945 N Elm Pl Broken Arrow (74012) *(G-927)*
Helton Custom Knives LLC....................................918 230-1773
  18633 S Fern Pl Claremore (74019) *(G-1633)*
Helvey International Usa Inc.................................405 203-0251
  330 Se 29th St Oklahoma City (73129) *(G-6237)*
Hem Inc (PA)...918 825-4821
  4065 Main St Pryor (74361) *(G-7966)*
Hem Inc..888 729-7787
  4174 Zarrow St Pryor (74361) *(G-7967)*
Hem Inc..918 824-0800
  302 S Hunt Pryor (74361) *(G-7968)*
Hem East, Pryor Also called Hem Inc *(G-7968)*
Hem Industries..918 534-0579
  13280 N 3990 Rd Dewey (74029) *(G-2024)*
Hem Mfg..918 225-4600
  7101 E Main St Cushing (74023) *(G-1935)*
Hem-Saw, Pryor Also called Hem Inc *(G-7966)*
Hembree Lewis A Production Co..........................405 273-6137
  1501 N Shawnee Ave Shawnee (74804) *(G-8459)*
Hemispheres (PA)...405 773-8410
  5561 Nw Expressway Warr Acres (73132) *(G-11322)*
Henderhan Recognition Award, Lawton Also called Cplp LLC *(G-3913)*
Hendershot Tool Company (PA)............................405 677-3386
  1008 Se 29th St Oklahoma City (73129) *(G-6238)*
Henderson Coffee Corp..918 682-8751
  3421 S 24th St W Muskogee (74401) *(G-4690)*
Henderson Feeds LLC...580 574-5375
  18332 E 1300 Rd Sayre (73662) *(G-8341)*
Henderson Ornamental Iron..................................918 341-1089
  2001 College Park Rd Claremore (74017) *(G-1634)*
Henderson Truss Incorporated..............................918 473-5573
  423225 E 1100 Rd Checotah (74426) *(G-1394)*
Hendrie Resources Ltd...405 948-4459
  4361 Nw 50th St Ste E Oklahoma City (73112) *(G-6239)*
Hendryx Printing Brokerage LLC...........................405 532-1255
  2725 Flagstone Ln Edmond (73003) *(G-2455)*
Henke Petroleum Corp...405 878-0909
  1421 E 45th St Shawnee (74804) *(G-8460)*
Henley Sealants Inc...405 235-7325
  200 N Wisconsin Ave Oklahoma City (73117) *(G-6240)*
Hennessey Clipper..405 853-4888
  117 S Main St Hennessey (73742) *(G-3466)*
Hennessey Ready Mix Concrete............................405 853-4473
  507 S Dunlap St Hennessey (73742) *(G-3467)*
Henry & Son Roustabouts LLC..............................580 747-8400
  13533 E 630 Rd Hennessey (73742) *(G-3468)*
Henry Gungoll Operating Inc.................................580 234-2302
  2208 W Willow Rd Enid (73703) *(G-2970)*
Henryetta Free Lance, Henryetta Also called Cnhi LLC *(G-3501)*
Henryetta Pallet Company.....................................918 652-9897
  999 E Industry Rd Henryetta (74437) *(G-3508)*
Henrys Welding and Fab LLC.................................918 535-2264
  24521 N 3940 Rd Ochelata (74051) *(G-5235)*
Henson Manufacturing & Sls Inc...........................918 785-2153
  612 E Main St Adair (74330) *(G-109)*
Herald Democrat, The, Beaver Also called Joe Brent Lansden *(G-541)*
Herald James M and Teresa..................................918 437-7016
  15326 E 13th St Tulsa (74108) *(G-9923)*
Herald Publishing Co (PA).....................................580 875-3326
  112 S Broadway St Walters (73572) *(G-11302)*
Herald Wakita...580 594-2440
  104 W Main St Wakita (73771) *(G-11298)*
Herbalife, Moore Also called Pats Custom Draperies *(G-4551)*
Herbert Malarkey Roofing Co................................405 261-6900
  3400 S Council Rd Oklahoma City (73179) *(G-6241)*
Herff Jones LLC...918 664-2544
  1640 S Boston Ave Tulsa (74119) *(G-9924)*
Herff Jones LLC...405 794-3764
  541 Sw 154th Ct Oklahoma City (73170) *(G-5295)*
Heritage, El Reno Also called Delson Properties Ltd *(G-2711)*

Heritage Burial Park 405 692-5503
4000 Sw 119th St Oklahoma City (73173) *(G-6242)*
Heritage Petroleum Inc 405 377-2689
1225 N Perkins Rd Ste C Stillwater (74075) *(G-8700)*
Hermann Jermey 918 200-2604
17823 E Brady St Catoosa (74015) *(G-1321)*
Hermans Chili Mix Inc 918 743-1832
1251 E 31st Pl Tulsa (74105) *(G-9925)*
Hermetic Switch Inc (PA) 405 224-4046
3100 S Norge Rd Chickasha (73018) *(G-1470)*
Hernandez Pallets 405 636-0503
2401 S Shartel Ave Oklahoma City (73109) *(G-6243)*
Hero Flare LLC 512 772-5744
14842 N Maple Dr Kellyville (74039) *(G-3765)*
Hero Printworks, Tulsa *Also called Paper House Productions LLC (G-10463)*
Herriman Oilfield Services 580 925-2144
13998 Ns 3520 Konawa (74849) *(G-3846)*
Herring Rowsey Properties, Muskogee *Also called Jcr Exploration Inc (G-4699)*
Hetronic International, Oklahoma City *Also called Hetronic Usa Inc (G-6245)*
Hetronic International Inc (PA) 405 946-3574
3905 Nw 36th St Oklahoma City (73112) *(G-6244)*
Hetronic Usa Inc 405 946-3574
3905 Nw 36th St Oklahoma City (73112) *(G-6245)*
Hewitt Mineral Corp 580 223-3619
10 W Main St Ste 522 Ardmore (73401) *(G-303)*
Hewitt Mineral Corporation 580 223-6565
10 W Main St Ardmore (73401) *(G-304)*
Hewlett-Packard Entp Svcs 918 939-4072
11618 S Hudson Pl Tulsa (74137) *(G-9926)*
Hext Trucking LLC 580 821-6150
17871 E 1200 Rd Erick (73645) *(G-3087)*
Heyman Stephen J Operating Co, Tulsa *Also called Stephen J Heyman (G-10846)*
Hfe Process Inc 918 663-9083
490 Summerlin Dr Inola (74036) *(G-3661)*
Hg Screen Printing 580 623-3638
201 Rice Dr Watonga (73772) *(G-11347)*
Hl Pro Feeds Inc 580 497-2219
402 N Ll Males Cheyenne (73628) *(G-1425)*
Hi-TEC Industries OK LLC 918 455-7141
19701 E 91st St S Broken Arrow (74014) *(G-1132)*
Hickmans Welding 918 966-3783
20337 N County Road 4560 Keota (74941) *(G-3772)*
Hidden Pearls LLC 405 707-0851
4700 Sherman Lake Dr Stillwater (74074) *(G-8701)*
Hidden Valley Manufacturing 580 343-2303
23849 Highway 152 Corn (73024) *(G-1867)*
Hidden Whiteboard, The, Weatherford *Also called Wooden Concepts LLC (G-11461)*
Hide-Away Ironing Boards, Tulsa *Also called C&A International LLC (G-9362)*
Hifi.com, Stillwater *Also called Cambridge Soundworks Inc (G-8665)*
Higgins & Sons Roof, Truss, Tecumseh *Also called Higgins & Sons Truss Company (G-8918)*
Higgins & Sons Truss Company 405 997-5455
20923 Rock Creek Rd Tecumseh (74873) *(G-8917)*
Higgins & Sons Truss Company (PA) 405 997-5455
E On Hwy 9 Tecumseh (74873) *(G-8918)*
Higgins Welding 580 231-9211
730 N Malone St Enid (73701) *(G-2971)*
Higgs-Palmer Technologies LLC (PA) 918 585-3775
3206 S Darlington Ave Tulsa (74135) *(G-9927)*
High Caliper Growing Inc 405 842-7700
7000 N Robinson Ave Oklahoma City (73116) *(G-6246)*
High Country Tek Inc 530 265-3236
5311 S 122nd East Ave Tulsa (74146) *(G-9928)*
High Five Graphics 918 636-3312
3904 Keystone Loop Mannford (74044) *(G-4182)*
High Plains Services Inc 580 225-7388
2615 W 20th St Elk City (73644) *(G-2822)*
High Pointe Construction 405 685-8303
2256 Laneway Cir Oklahoma City (73159) *(G-6247)*
High Rollers Empire LLC 405 535-3066
11325 N Markwell Dr Oklahoma City (73162) *(G-6248)*
High Times Tulsa 918 600-2110
7030 S Lewis Ave Ste C Tulsa (74136) *(G-9929)*
Highfill Welding & Fabrication, Tecumseh *Also called G Highfill (G-8915)*
Highlands Publishing LLC 405 596-8391
11201 Mystic Isle Norman (73026) *(G-5022)*
Highnoon Tactical LLC 918 801-8737
232 N Thompson St Vinita (74301) *(G-11259)*
Highway Man Signs 918 396-8024
603 W Rogers Blvd Skiatook (74070) *(G-8548)*
Highway Man Signs LLC 918 534-9100
1037 Ne Washington Blvd Bartlesville (74006) *(G-493)*
Hiland Dairy Foods Company LLC 405 258-3100
1100 Thunderbird Rd Chandler (74834) *(G-1380)*
Hiland Dairy Foods Company LLC 405 321-3191
302 S Porter Ave Norman (73071) *(G-5023)*
Hiland Lp LLC (HQ) 713 369-9000
302 N Independence St # 100 Enid (73701) *(G-2972)*
Hill Metal & Supply, Kingfisher *Also called Hill Metal Inc (G-3801)*
Hill Metal Inc 405 375-6284
421 N 4th St Kingfisher (73750) *(G-3801)*
Hill Pipe and Supply, Broken Arrow *Also called Hillenburg Oil Co LLC (G-928)*
Hill Steel Corporation 918 336-2430
1800 W 14th St Bartlesville (74003) *(G-494)*
Hillenburg Oil Co LLC (PA) 918 455-4444
11600 S Lynn Lane Rd Broken Arrow (74011) *(G-928)*
Hillsboro Co 918 481-0484
8016 S Joplin Ave Tulsa (74136) *(G-9930)*
Hillshire Brands Company 405 751-7222
13131 Broadway Ext Oklahoma City (73114) *(G-6249)*
Hilltop Custom Processing 405 527-7048
11651 Duffy Rd Lexington (73051) *(G-4035)*
Hilltop Turf Inc 918 486-4482
14412 S State Highway 51 Coweta (74429) *(G-1884)*
Hilti Inc 918 252-6000
10660 E 31st St Tulsa (74146) *(G-9931)*
Hilti Industries Inc 918 251-7788
305 S 2nd St Broken Arrow (74012) *(G-929)*
Hilti North America Ltd (HQ) 918 252-6000
5400 S 122nd East Ave Tulsa (74146) *(G-9932)*
Hilti of America Inc 800 879-8000
5400 S 122nd East Ave Tulsa (74146) *(G-9933)*
Hilton Herald Corp Oklahoma 580 229-0132
11204 Highway 76 Healdton (73438) *(G-3414)*
Hinderliter Heat Treating Inc 405 670-5710
6924 S Eastern Ave Oklahoma City (73149) *(G-6250)*
Hindman Metal Fabricators 918 251-3949
6998 S 145th East Ave Broken Arrow (74012) *(G-930)*
Hinkle Oil and Gas (PA) 405 848-0924
5600 N May Ave Ste 295 Oklahoma City (73112) *(G-6251)*
Hinkle Printing & Office Sup 405 238-9308
110 E Paul Ave Pauls Valley (73075) *(G-7660)*
Hinsco Inc 918 456-2138
22518 Highway 82 Park Hill (74451) *(G-7643)*
Hinton Record, Watonga *Also called Watonga Republican Inc (G-11354)*
Hipower Systems Oklahoma LLC 918 512-6321
7249 State Highway 66 Tulsa (74131) *(G-9013)*
Hipsleys Litho & Prtg Co LLC 405 528-2686
313 Ne 36th St Oklahoma City (73105) *(G-6252)*
Hirsch3667 Corp 580 323-6966
1749 S Highway 183 Clinton (73601) *(G-1752)*
His Coatings, Oklahoma City *Also called H-I-S Paint Mfg Co Inc (G-6201)*
His Construction 405 642-4306
3400 S Kelley Ave Oklahoma City (73129) *(G-6253)*
His Publishing LLC 405 390-0518
15210 Scottsdale Ln Choctaw (73020) *(G-1544)*
Hisco Inc 405 524-2700
4320 N Cooper Ave Oklahoma City (73118) *(G-6254)*
Hitachi Computer Pdts Amer Inc (HQ) 405 360-5500
1800 E Imhoff Rd Norman (73071) *(G-5024)*
Hitch Enterprises Inc 580 338-6510
2 Miles North Of Optima Hooker (73945) *(G-3597)*
Hitch Mills, Hooker *Also called Hitch Enterprises Inc (G-3597)*
Hitch N Post LLC 918 396-9480
5265 W Rogers Blvd Ste A Skiatook (74070) *(G-8549)*
Hite Plastics Inc (PA) 405 297-9818
201 N Wisconsin Ave Oklahoma City (73117) *(G-6255)*
Hix Industries 405 640-6980
Rr 2 Box 303a Wanette (74878) *(G-11305)*
Hjd Gas, Norman *Also called Octagon Resources Inc (G-5097)*
Hks Energy Solutions Inc 918 279-6450
10404 E 55th Pl Ste E Tulsa (74146) *(G-9934)*
Hl Wirick Jr LLP 918 587-4548
907 S Detroit Ave Tulsa (74120) *(G-9935)*
Hlh Industries LLC 918 217-0100
5435 W Oak St Skiatook (74070) *(G-8550)*
Hman Global Solutions LLC 405 338-5348
301 Echo Ln Morrison (73061) *(G-4603)*
Hmh Publishing 405 788-5589
161 Fairway Dr Elk City (73644) *(G-2823)*
Hmt LLC 580 363-8800
1545 W Doolin Ave Blackwell (74631) *(G-683)*
Hmt Machining Incorporated 405 964-2054
3108 S Arena Rd McLoud (74851) *(G-4358)*
Hnt Welding & Machine 405 348-8249
27 W 4th St Edmond (73003) *(G-2456)*
Hobby Supermarket Inc 405 239-6864
1301 W Sheridan Ave Oklahoma City (73106) *(G-6256)*
Hodgden Operating Company Inc 580 233-2870
1005 The Trails West Loop Enid (73703) *(G-2973)*
Hodges Manufacturing 918 629-8723
106 Wellston Park Rd Sand Springs (74063) *(G-8191)*
Hodges Materials Inc 580 223-3317
1401 Monroe St Ne Ardmore (73401) *(G-305)*
Hoel Machine Mfg Inc 918 294-8895
2220 N Yellowood Ave Broken Arrow (74012) *(G-931)*
Hoffman Essentials 918 485-4679
71559 S 230 Rd Wagoner (74467) *(G-11284)*
Hoffman Fixture Company, Tulsa *Also called Hoffman Fixtures Company (G-9936)*

ALPHABETIC

Hoffman Fixtures Company (PA) 918 252-0451
6031 S 129th East Ave B Tulsa (74134) ***(G-9936)***
Hoffman Printing LLC 918 682-8341
1409 W Shawnee St Muskogee (74401) ***(G-4691)***
Hogan Assessment Systems Inc (PA) 918 293-2300
11 S Greenwood Ave Tulsa (74120) ***(G-9937)***
Hoggard Welding & Backhoe Svc 580 856-3934
1952 Pelton Rd Ratliff City (73481) ***(G-8055)***
Hoke James T Jr Oil Producer 405 341-1779
107 S Broadway Edmond (73034) ***(G-2457)***
Holasek Oil & Gas Co LLC 405 321-6663
6378 Harold Way Ne Norman (73026) ***(G-5025)***
Holbrook Printing 918 835-5950
6351 E Newton St Tulsa (74115) ***(G-9938)***
Holbrook Tribune-News, Edmond *Also called Northern Arizona Newspaper* ***(G-2540)***
Holcim (us) Inc 580 332-1512
14500 County Road 1550 Ada (74820) ***(G-48)***
Holcim (us) Inc 573 242-3571
14500 County Road 1550 Ada (74820) ***(G-49)***
Holden Energy Corp (PA) 580 226-3960
301 W Main St Ste 600 Ardmore (73401) ***(G-306)***
Holdenville News 405 379-5411
112 S Creek St Holdenville (74848) ***(G-3554)***
Holick Family LLC 580 765-3209
201 S Oak St Ponca City (74601) ***(G-7836)***
Holiday Car Care Center, Oklahoma City *Also called Berkshire Corporation* ***(G-5556)***
Holiday Creek Prticipation LLC 405 275-1045
130 N Broadway Ave # 200 Shawnee (74801) ***(G-8461)***
Holiday Lighting Specialist, Tonkawa *Also called Kay Holding Co* ***(G-8977)***
Holland Services LLC 405 842-9393
1200 Nw 63rd St Oklahoma City (73116) ***(G-6257)***
Hollands Mobile Homes 918 476-5663
116 N 2nd St Chouteau (74337) ***(G-1565)***
Holliday Sand & Gravel Co 918 486-1413
17402 S 305th East Ave Coweta (74429) ***(G-1885)***
Holliday Sand Gravel Co LLC 918 369-8850
14389 S Mingo Rd Bixby (74008) ***(G-632)***
Hollis Cotton Oil Mill Inc 580 688-3394
201 S Glover St Hollis (73550) ***(G-3565)***
Hollis Home Made Salsa LLC 405 464-6249
717 Small Oaks Midwest City (73110) ***(G-4442)***
Holloway Technical Svcs LLC 405 223-9352
7576 N Highway 81 Ste 12 Duncan (73533) ***(G-2130)***
Holloway Wire Rope Svcs Inc 918 582-1807
14620 E Pine St Tulsa (74116) ***(G-9939)***
Holloway's Blue Print Co, Muskogee *Also called Holloways Bluprt & Copy Sp Inc* ***(G-4692)***
Holloways Bluprt & Copy Sp Inc 918 682-0280
810 Eastside Blvd Muskogee (74403) ***(G-4692)***
Hollrah Exploration Company 405 773-5440
8104 Nw 122nd St Oklahoma City (73142) ***(G-6258)***
Holly Ref & Mktg - Tulsa LLC 918 445-0056
1307 W 35th St Tulsa (74107) ***(G-9940)***
Holly Ref & Mktg - Tulsa LLC (HQ) 918 594-6000
902 W 25th St Tulsa (74107) ***(G-9941)***
Hollyfrontier Corporation 918 581-1800
1700 S Union Ave Tulsa (74107) ***(G-9942)***
Hollyfrontier Corporation 918 594-6000
907 S Detroit Ave Tulsa (74120) ***(G-9943)***
Hollyfrontier Ref & Mktg LLC 918 588-1142
1700 S Union Ave Tulsa (74107) ***(G-9944)***
Hollywood Express Oklahoma Inc 405 324-8111
14700 Nw 10th St Yukon (73099) ***(G-11730)***
Holman Manufacturing 918 479-5861
302 E Main St Locust Grove (74352) ***(G-4109)***
Holman Oil and Gas 405 567-3528
104447 S 3580 Rd Prague (74864) ***(G-7927)***
Holmes Exparation, Tulsa *Also called Panther Energy Company LLC* ***(G-10461)***
Holt Trailer Mfg & Sales LLC 405 784-2233
901 Us Highway 177 Asher (74826) ***(G-390)***
Hom Kitchen Bath, Edmond *Also called Warhall Designs LLC* ***(G-2680)***
Homer Rinehart Company (PA) 405 756-2785
15914 Hwy 19 Lindsay (73052) ***(G-4067)***
Homer Rinehart Company 405 756-2785
Highway 19 E Lindsay (73052) ***(G-4068)***
Hometown Bottled Water LLC 918 786-4426
63651 E 290 Rd Grove (74344) ***(G-3274)***
Hometown Nrdgnstcs-Clorado LLC 405 286-1016
11900 N Macarthur Blvd # 200 Oklahoma City (73162) ***(G-6259)***
Hometown Water, Grove *Also called Hometown Bottled Water LLC* ***(G-3274)***
Hominy News Progress, Pawnee *Also called American-Chief Co* ***(G-7699)***
Hominy Tag Agency 918 885-9955
113 W Main St Hominy (74035) ***(G-3586)***
Honest Rons Guitars 405 947-3683
1129 N May Ave Oklahoma City (73107) ***(G-6260)***
Honeycutt Construction, Pryor *Also called Honeycutt Contruction Inc* ***(G-7969)***
Honeycutt Contruction Inc 918 825-6070
2750 W 530 Pryor (74361) ***(G-7969)***
Honeygrove Machine 580 420-3260
382 White Rock Rd Idabel (74745) ***(G-3638)***
Honeywell Aerospace Tulsa/Lori 918 272-4574
6930 N Lakewood Ave Tulsa (74117) ***(G-9945)***
Honeywell Ecc Callidus, Tulsa *Also called Callidus Technologies LLC* ***(G-9364)***
Honeywell International Inc 405 605-0101
804 W I 240 Service Rd Oklahoma City (73139) ***(G-6261)***
Honing By Hardy 405 919-3589
2313 Sw 82nd St Oklahoma City (73159) ***(G-6262)***
Hooker Advance & Office Supply 580 652-2476
108 W Glaydas Hooker (73945) ***(G-3598)***
Hooper Printing, Bethany *Also called A 1 Master Print Inc* ***(G-571)***
Hooper Printing Company Inc (PA) 405 321-4288
301 W Gray St Norman (73069) ***(G-5026)***
Hoot of Loot 918 743-9802
1322 S Guthrie Ave Tulsa (74119) ***(G-9946)***
Hooty Creek Alpacas 918 284-5025
23005 S Hooty Creek Rd Claremore (74019) ***(G-1635)***
Hope Minerals International 405 452-3529
7333 E 119 Wetumka (74883) ***(G-11491)***
Hopkins County Coal LLC 918 295-7600
1717 S Boulder Ave # 400 Tulsa (74119) ***(G-9947)***
Hopkins Manufacturing Corp 918 961-8722
2400 Industrial Pkwy Miami (74354) ***(G-4408)***
Hoppers Welding 918 885-6978
606 S Haines Ave Hominy (74035) ***(G-3587)***
Hoppes Oil Field Svc, Tipton *Also called Derrick Hoppes* ***(G-8958)***
Hoppis Interiors 405 390-2963
540 S Choctaw Rd Choctaw (73020) ***(G-1545)***
Horizon Energy Services LLC 405 533-4800
115 E 80th St Stillwater (74074) ***(G-8702)***
Horizon Energy Services LLC 918 392-9351
5727 S Lewis Ave Ste 550 Tulsa (74105) ***(G-9948)***
Horizon Natural Resources Inc 918 494-0790
2131 W 73rd St Tulsa (74132) ***(G-9949)***
Horizon Smoker Company 580 336-2400
802 N 15th St Perry (73077) ***(G-7736)***
Horizon Smokers, Perry *Also called Horizon Smoker Company* ***(G-7736)***
Horizon Well Servicing LLC 580 482-7500
300 Pintail Cir Altus (73521) ***(G-158)***
Horizon Welltesting LLC 918 429-1200
3635 E Us Hwy 270 Mcalester (74501) ***(G-4304)***
Horizontal Well Drillers LLC (PA) 405 527-1232
2915 Highway 74 Purcell (73080) ***(G-8010)***
Hornbeek and Wadley 405 604-2874
100 N Broadway Ave Oklahoma City (73102) ***(G-6263)***
Horsepower Printing Inc 405 631-3800
7113 Ashby Ter Oklahoma City (73149) ***(G-6264)***
Horseshoe Exploration LLC 580 866-3207
27583 State Highway 34 Sharon (73857) ***(G-8417)***
Horton Industries Inc 918 836-3971
2001 N 69th East Ave Tulsa (74115) ***(G-9950)***
Horton Mfg, Tulsa *Also called Horton Industries Inc* ***(G-9950)***
Horton Tool Company 918 885-6941
215 W Main St Hominy (74035) ***(G-3588)***
Horton Tool Corporation 918 885-6941
108 N Katy Ave Hominy (74035) ***(G-3589)***
Horton World Solutions LLC 817 821-8320
5971 S 301st East Ave Broken Arrow (74014) ***(G-1133)***
Hoskins Gypsum Company LLC 580 274-3446
4959 S Hwy 58 Longdale (73755) ***(G-4124)***
Hoskins Wireline LLC 580 303-9101
1320 Airport Indus Rd Elk City (73644) ***(G-2824)***
Hospice Pharmacy Providers LLC 918 633-6229
9213 N 98th East Ct Owasso (74055) ***(G-7574)***
Hospital Linen Services LLC 405 473-0422
2121 Sw 71st St Oklahoma City (73159) ***(G-6265)***
Hospital Products Oklahoma LLC 918 271-7169
1323 E 53rd Pl Ste A Tulsa (74105) ***(G-9951)***
Hoss LLC 918 660-7220
4405 S 74th East Ave Tulsa (74145) ***(G-9952)***
Hoss Consulting Serv 405 324-5543
13125 Sw 47th St Mustang (73064) ***(G-4776)***
Hoss Directional Service Inc 405 822-0551
1405 Jami Dr Norman (73071) ***(G-5027)***
Hoss Marine Propellers, Locust Grove *Also called Hoss Marine Propulsion Inc* ***(G-4110)***
Hoss Marine Propulsion Inc 918 479-5167
Highway 82 Locust Grove (74352) ***(G-4110)***
Hoswel, Fletcher *Also called Built Better Enterprises LLC* ***(G-3161)***
Hot Off Press 918 492-2313
6047 S Sheridan Rd Tulsa (74145) ***(G-9953)***
Hot Oil Units Inc 580 256-6461
4616 Oil Patch Dr Woodward (73801) ***(G-11592)***
Hot Rod Hot Shot Service Inc 405 834-5591
2104 W Glen Eagle Edmond (73025) ***(G-2458)***
Hot Rod Machine Tool LLC 918 508-1043
13052 S Pine Ave Claremore (74017) ***(G-1636)***
Hot Rod Shirts & Stuff 580 669-2531
6800 N Rose Rd Glencoe (74032) ***(G-3224)***
Hot Rod Welding and Mech LLC 918 754-2548
1597 Se 1108th Ave Red Oak (74563) ***(G-8077)***

Hot Stuff Airbrush Inc ... 918 249-0458
7021 S Memorial Dr Tulsa (74133) **(G-9954)**
Hotco, Cushing *Also called Hough Oilfield Service Inc* **(G-1936)**
Hotrod City USA, Bixby *Also called Sonny Mac Industries Inc* **(G-661)**
Hotrod Welding ... 580 229-0888
10837 Highway 76 Healdton (73438) **(G-3415)**
Hotsy of OK Inc ... 580 234-0608
1627 N Van Buren St Enid (73703) **(G-2974)**
Hough Oilfield Service Inc ... 918 225-1851
711 W Cherry St Cushing (74023) **(G-1936)**
Hourglass Transport LLC ... 580 937-4569
9805 Ok Highway 48 S Coleman (73432) **(G-1796)**
House Dog Industries LLC ... 405 761-5576
701 Thompson Dr El Reno (73036) **(G-2724)**
House Industries LLC ... 405 761-5574
16100 W Britton Rd Yukon (73099) **(G-11731)**
House of Bedlam LLC ... 405 946-3100
3100 S Meridian Ave Oklahoma City (73119) **(G-6266)**
House of Trophies ... 405 452-3524
115 N Main St Wetumka (74883) **(G-11492)**
House of Trophies ... 918 341-2111
127 W Blue Starr Dr Claremore (74017) **(G-1637)**
House T Shirt & Silk Screening ... 405 457-6321
111 N Second St Lookeba (73053) **(G-4129)**
Housing USA ... 405 631-3653
6100 S Shields Blvd Oklahoma City (73149) **(G-6267)**
Houston Brothers Inc ... 918 449-1175
19465 E 131st St S Broken Arrow (74014) **(G-1134)**
How To Build A Flagstone Patio ... 405 478-1200
12300 S Mingo Rd Bixby (74008) **(G-633)**
Howard Engineering ... 918 396-3463
1109 E 176th St N Skiatook (74070) **(G-8551)**
Howards Precision Mfg Inc ... 918 599-7588
2730 Charles Page Blvd Tulsa (74127) **(G-9955)**
Howdy Signs ... 918 543-2854
16644 E Kings Pl Inola (74036) **(G-3662)**
Howells Well Service Inc ... 918 846-2531
203 E 6th St Wynona (74084) **(G-11679)**
Howes Ltg & Win Blinds LLC ... 918 791-4101
627 Se Wilshire Ave Bartlesville (74006) **(G-495)**
Howmedica Osteonics Corp ... 405 230-1340
1141 N Robinson Ave Oklahoma City (73103) **(G-6268)**
Howmedica Osteonics Corp ... 918 461-0152
11811 E 51st St Tulsa (74146) **(G-9956)**
HP Field Services LLC ... 580 763-1428
3210 W Lakeview Rd Stillwater (74075) **(G-8703)**
HS Field Services Inc ... 918 534-9121
397781 W 1400 Rd Dewey (74029) **(G-2025)**
Hsi, Oklahoma City *Also called Hydraulic Specialists Inc* **(G-6278)**
Hsi Sensing, Chickasha *Also called Hermetic Switch Inc* **(G-1470)**
Hte, Tulsa *Also called Heat Transfer Equipment Co* **(G-9907)**
Hts Manufacturing Corporation ... 918 318-0280
317 W Gentry Ave Checotah (74426) **(G-1395)**
Htw Inc ... 918 423-4619
18 W Cherokee Ave McAlester (74501) **(G-4305)**
Hu Don Manufacturing Co Inc ... 580 223-7333
159 C St Se Ardmore (73401) **(G-307)**
Hub Oil & Gas Inc ... 405 236-3354
110 N Robinson Ave # 400 Oklahoma City (73102) **(G-6269)**
Hubbard ... 918 785-2000
412 W Main St Adair (74330) **(G-110)**
Hubbard Industries LLC ... 405 388-6798
2009 Nw 18th St Oklahoma City (73106) **(G-6270)**
Huber Engineered Woods LLC ... 580 584-7000
1070 W State Highway 3 Broken Bow (74728) **(G-1192)**
Hudgins Co Pipe Testing, Sapulpa *Also called L Dean Hudgins Inc* **(G-8284)**
Hudson Bros Rmanufactured Engs ... 405 598-2260
38434 Highway 9 Tecumseh (74873) **(G-8919)**
Huerecas Woodworking LLC ... 580 302-2687
515 N 8th St Weatherford (73096) **(G-11418)**
Hughes County Publishing Co ... 405 452-3294
501 E Highway 9 Wetumka (74883) **(G-11493)**
Hughes County Times, Wetumka *Also called Hughes County Publishing Co* **(G-11493)**
Hughes Electric, Cleveland *Also called Oklahoma Cellulose Inc* **(G-1730)**
Hughes Exploration Consulting ... 918 486-3188
13232 S 275th East Ave Coweta (74429) **(G-1886)**
Hughes Gas Measurement Inc (PA) ... 405 227-0904
2919 Highway 75 Wetumka (74883) **(G-11494)**
Hughes Lumber Company ... 918 266-9100
5615 Bird Creek Ave Catoosa (74015) **(G-1322)**
Hughes Trucking ... 580 244-3731
24005 State Highway 144 Smithville (74957) **(G-8578)**
Hughes-Anderson Heat Exchanger ... 918 836-1681
1001 N Fulton Ave Tulsa (74115) **(G-9957)**
Hugo Daily News, Hugo *Also called Hugo Publishing Company* **(G-3612)**
Hugo Publishing Company ... 580 326-3311
128 E Jackson St Hugo (74743) **(G-3612)**
Hugo Sash & Door Inc ... 580 326-5569
Old Highway 70 W Hugo (74743) **(G-3613)**
Hugo Wyrick Lumber ... 580 326-5569
Old Hwy 70 W Hugo (74743) **(G-3614)**
Hulen Operating Company ... 405 848-5252
205 Nw 63rd St Ste 140 Oklahoma City (73116) **(G-6271)**
Hull Contract Pumping ... 580 824-0440
1646 Santa Fe St Waynoka (73860) **(G-11376)**
Hulls Oilfield LLC ... 580 668-2619
3001 State Highway 76 Wilson (73463) **(G-11536)**
Humphreys Coop, Altus *Also called Farmers Union Co-Operative Gin* **(G-156)**
Humps N Horns Bull Riding News, Chouteau *Also called Humps N Hrns Bull Rdng Nws LLC* **(G-1566)**
Humps N Horns Bull Riding News ... 918 872-9713
3004 S Birch Ave Broken Arrow (74012) **(G-932)**
Humps N Hrns Bull Rdng Nws LLC ... 918 476-8213
105 E Orr St Chouteau (74337) **(G-1566)**
Hungerford Oil & Gas Inc ... 580 852-3288
3rd Main St Helena (73741) **(G-3434)**
Hunt Jim Sales & Mfg ... 405 670-5663
2809 N Sterling Ave Oklahoma City (73127) **(G-6272)**
Hunter Steel LLC ... 918 684-9600
3704 River Bend Rd Muskogee (74403) **(G-4693)**
Hunter's Horn, Sand Springs *Also called C and H Publishing Co* **(G-8169)**
Hunters Laser Cartridges ... 918 740-8164
1126 S Evanston Ave Tulsa (74104) **(G-9958)**
Hunting Titan Inc ... 405 495-1322
8600 W Reno Ave Oklahoma City (73127) **(G-6273)**
Huntington Energy LLC ... 405 840-9876
908 Nw 71st St Oklahoma City (73116) **(G-6274)**
Huntington Energy USA Inc ... 580 772-3644
23900 E 1020 Rd Weatherford (73096) **(G-11419)**
Hunton Oil and Gas Corp ... 405 848-5545
6416 N Santa Fe Ave Oklahoma City (73116) **(G-6275)**
Hunts Welding Service LLC ... 806 339-4591
1306 W Dunkin Rd Cushing (74023) **(G-1937)**
Hurd Oil Inc ... 918 846-2725
2 Mi North Of City Wynona (74084) **(G-11680)**
Hurley Welding LLC ... 405 224-7332
104 Holly Amber (73004) **(G-196)**
Huron Ventures, Tulsa *Also called Cano Petroleum Inc* **(G-9370)**
Hurricane Gas Process Plant ... 918 492-4418
4613 E 91st St Tulsa (74137) **(G-9959)**
Hurst Aerospace Inc ... 918 543-6527
21247 E 630 Rd Inola (74036) **(G-3663)**
Hurst Cnstr & Fabrication LLC ... 580 628-2388
207 S 7th St Tonkawa (74653) **(G-8975)**
Husky Portable Containment Co ... 918 333-2000
7202 Se International Ct Bartlesville (74006) **(G-496)**
Husky Ventures Inc ... 405 600-9393
5800 Nw 135th St Oklahoma City (73142) **(G-6276)**
Huston Energy Corporation ... 580 233-6030
2414 Heritage Trl Ste B Enid (73703) **(G-2975)**
Hutchinson Products Company ... 405 946-4403
3900 N Tulsa Ave Oklahoma City (73112) **(G-6277)**
Hutson Welding Services LLC ... 918 470-3673
268 Haynes Ln Kiowa (74553) **(G-3838)**
Hutton Inc ... 580 225-0225
19676 Route 66 N Elk City (73644) **(G-2825)**
Hwd, Purcell *Also called Horizontal Well Drillers LLC* **(G-8010)**
Hws Hamilton Welding Svc LLC ... 580 889-1725
6757 S Sawmill Rd Atoka (74525) **(G-413)**
Hy-H Manufacturing Co Inc ... 918 341-6811
915 W Blue Starr Dr Claremore (74017) **(G-1638)**
Hyatt Ladona ... 580 889-0199
9398 S Sawmill Rd Atoka (74525) **(G-414)**
Hybrid Tool Solutions LLC ... 405 756-1408
12509 State Highway 76 Lindsay (73052) **(G-4069)**
Hyde Sand & Gravel, Goldsby *Also called Brandon Hyde* **(G-3244)**
Hydra Rig, Duncan *Also called National Oilwell Varco Inc* **(G-2158)**
Hydra Service Inc ... 918 438-3700
12332 E 1st St Tulsa (74128) **(G-9960)**
Hydra-Walk, Lindsay *Also called Key Energy Services Inc* **(G-4071)**
Hydrant Repair Parts Inc ... 918 224-8713
7835 State Highway 66 Tulsa (74131) **(G-9014)**
Hydraulic Specialists Inc ... 405 752-7980
12100 N Santa Fe Ave Oklahoma City (73114) **(G-6278)**
Hydro Chart ... 918 932-8586
7709 E 42nd Pl Ste 104 Tulsa (74145) **(G-9961)**
Hydro Foam Technology Inc ... 405 547-5800
4321 E 122nd St Perkins (74059) **(G-7718)**
Hydro Hoist, Claremore *Also called Hy-H Manufacturing Co Inc* **(G-1638)**
Hydro-Link Containment LLC ... 580 889-4701
4757 S Crestview Rd Atoka (74525) **(G-415)**
Hydrogen On Demand ... 405 618-6644
425 W Wilshire Blvd Oklahoma City (73116) **(G-6279)**
Hydrogen Technologies Inc ... 918 645-3430
15803 W Deer Run Rd Park Hill (74451) **(G-7644)**
Hydrohoist Boat Lifts ... 918 256-8125
453265 E Highway 85a Bernice (74331) **(G-565)**

ALPHABETIC

Hydrohoist Marine Group Inc 918 256-8775
  453265 E Highway 85a Bernice (74331) *(G-566)*
Hydrostatic Engineers Inc 405 677-7169
  2328 Se 13th St Oklahoma City (73129) *(G-6280)*
Hyperion Energy LP 918 321-3350
  14530 S 49th West Ave Kiefer (74041) *(G-3780)*
Hypower Inc 918 341-6811
  24012 Amah Pkwy Claremore (74019) *(G-1639)*
Hypro Inc 918 549-3600
  1100 Industrial Ave Vinita (74301) *(G-11260)*
Hytorc Central, Jenks *Also called Bolt It Hydraulic Solutions* *(G-3693)*
I & Gn Resources Inc 918 481-7927
  6585 S Yale Ave Ste 900 Tulsa (74136) *(G-9962)*
I AM Drilling LLC 580 234-2277
  3521 Lisa Ln Enid (73703) *(G-2976)*
I Chemex Corporation (PA) 405 947-0764
  5700 N Portland Ave # 301 Oklahoma City (73112) *(G-6281)*
I E S Raglin, Ponca City *Also called Industrial Equipment Services* *(G-7837)*
I Enrg 405 360-4600
  1624 24th Ave Sw Norman (73072) *(G-5028)*
I M I, Fairland *Also called Industrial Manufacturing Inc* *(G-3125)*
I M R, Tulsa *Also called Interntnal Mktg Resources Corp* *(G-10005)*
I-Mac Petroleum Service Inc 918 348-9400
  11726 S Sandusky Ave Tulsa (74137) *(G-9963)*
Iap Worldwide Services Inc 321 784-7100
  5400 Se 44th St Ste B Oklahoma City (73135) *(G-6282)*
Iball Instruments LLC 405 366-6061
  3540 National Dr Norman (73069) *(G-5029)*
IBP, Woodward *Also called Foamtech Inc* *(G-11584)*
Ic Bus of Oklahoma LLC 918 833-4000
  2322 N Mingo Rd Tulsa (74116) *(G-9964)*
Icandee Refinishings LLC 405 923-4956
  8001 N Wilshire Ct Ste F Oklahoma City (73132) *(G-6283)*
Ice Global, Tulsa *Also called Steven Jackson* *(G-10850)*
Ice-T King LLC 405 206-1185
  905 Nw 6th St Oklahoma City (73106) *(G-6284)*
ICEE Company 405 685-7739
  2804 Purdue Dr Oklahoma City (73128) *(G-6285)*
ICEE Company 800 423-3872
  2642 Mohawk Blvd Tulsa (74110) *(G-9965)*
Ices Corporation 918 358-5446
  50152 Highway Dr Cleveland (74020) *(G-1724)*
Icon Construction Inc 580 931-3806
  2917 Big Lots Rd Durant (74701) *(G-2236)*
Icon Manufacturing LLC 903 819-9091
  2917 Big Lots Rd Ste B Durant (74701) *(G-2237)*
Icon Roofing and Cnstr LLC 405 403-6615
  1824 W Crossbow Way Mustang (73064) *(G-4777)*
Icx Biodefense, Stillwater *Also called Flir Detection Inc* *(G-8689)*
Icx Technologies Inc 703 678-2111
  800 Research Pkwy Oklahoma City (73104) *(G-6286)*
ID Solutions LLC (PA) 405 677-8833
  3821 S Robinson Ave Oklahoma City (73109) *(G-6287)*
Idabel Plant, Idabel *Also called Martin Marietta Materials Inc* *(G-3640)*
Ideal Crane Corporation 800 622-6163
  4632 S Lakewood Ave Tulsa (74135) *(G-9966)*
Ideal Machine & Welding Inc 918 352-3660
  405 N Harley Ave Drumright (74030) *(G-2062)*
Ideal Specialty Inc 918 834-1657
  2531 E Independence St Tulsa (74110) *(G-9967)*
Idealist Software LLC 918 609-4364
  18003 S 72nd East Ave Bixby (74008) *(G-634)*
Ideas Manufacturing Inc 405 691-5525
  11821 S Walker Ave Oklahoma City (73170) *(G-5296)*
Identity & Tanning Salon 412 269-7879
  1301 Antler Rdg Tuttle (73089) *(G-11204)*
Identity Hair & Tanning Salon, Tuttle *Also called Identity & Tanning Salon* *(G-11204)*
Idex Corporation 405 609-1116
  3805 Nw 36th St Oklahoma City (73112) *(G-6288)*
Idle Time Creations, Skiatook *Also called Kelly L Young* *(G-8555)*
Idle Time Rv Sales & Service, Allen *Also called Allen Camper Mfg Company Inc* *(G-133)*
IEC, Oklahoma City *Also called International Envmtl Corp* *(G-6319)*
Ifco Systems 405 491-9300
  8812 Sheringham Dr Oklahoma City (73132) *(G-6289)*
Ifco Systems Us LLC (HQ) 405 681-8090
  2211 S May Ave Oklahoma City (73108) *(G-6290)*
IFE Ndt LLC 405 642-4899
  14698 Clair Ct W Yukon (73099) *(G-11732)*
Iffia, Tulsa *Also called Interfaceflor LLC* *(G-10003)*
Igg LLC 918 607-3032
  913 S Willow Ave Broken Arrow (74012) *(G-933)*
Igg Screen Printing, El Reno *Also called Inspired Gifts & Graphics LLC* *(G-2725)*
Ignition Systems & Controls 405 682-3030
  3612 S Moulton Dr Oklahoma City (73179) *(G-6291)*
II L W Barrett 918 496-8309
  3727 E 56th St Tulsa (74135) *(G-9968)*
Ikg Industries 918 599-8417
  1514 Sheldon Rd Tulsa (74120) *(G-9969)*

Illbird Press 918 859-7789
  4426 E 14th St Tulsa (74112) *(G-9970)*
Illinois Refining Co 918 367-5562
  210 E 9th Ave Bristow (74010) *(G-779)*
Im Stitched & Stoned 918 418-9107
  431224 E 273 Rd Vinita (74301) *(G-11261)*
Image Print & Promo LLC 405 408-6763
  605 Aberdeen Rd Edmond (73025) *(G-2459)*
Imagen Latino Americana Mag, Tulsa *Also called Editorial Grama Inc* *(G-9643)*
Images Ink, Tulsa *Also called Nameplates Inc* *(G-10325)*
Imagine Durant Inc 580 380-0743
  215 N 4th Ave Durant (74701) *(G-2238)*
Imaging Concepts 918 534-1761
  516 E Don Tyler Ave Dewey (74029) *(G-2026)*
Imak Industrial Solutions LLC 405 406-9778
  8816 S Hillcrest Dr Oklahoma City (73159) *(G-6292)*
Imco, Oklahoma City *Also called Industrial Machine Co Inc* *(G-6299)*
Imel Woodworks Inc 405 356-2505
  910480 S 3340 Rd Wellston (74881) *(G-11472)*
Imirus, Tulsa *Also called Riggs Heinrich Media Inc* *(G-10652)*
Immuno-Mycologics Inc 405 360-4669
  2701 Corporate Centre Dr Norman (73069) *(G-5030)*
Immy Africa LLC 405 360-4669
  2701 Corporate Centre Dr Norman (73069) *(G-5031)*
Imoco LLC 918 459-8366
  6404 S 110th East Ave Tulsa (74133) *(G-9971)*
Impac Exploration Services Inc (PA) 580 772-3117
  1501 Lera Ste 3 Weatherford (73096) *(G-11420)*
Impact Casing Services LLC 580 216-1159
  1419 Ctr Dr Woodward (73802) *(G-11593)*
Impact Energy Services, Alderson *Also called Select Energy Services LLC* *(G-128)*
Impact Screen Printing 918 258-8337
  720 W Elgin St Broken Arrow (74012) *(G-934)*
Imperial Inc 580 357-8300
  815 Se 2nd St Lawton (73501) *(G-3940)*
Imperial LLC (PA) 918 437-1300
  2020 N Mingo Rd Tulsa (74116) *(G-9972)*
Imperial Molding LLC 580 362-3412
  122 E 7th St Nwkirk Ok Newkirk (74647) *(G-4848)*
Imperial Plastics Inc 580 362-3412
  101 N Chestnut Ave Newkirk (74647) *(G-4849)*
Imperial Printing Inc 918 663-1302
  4153 S 87th East Ave Tulsa (74145) *(G-9973)*
Impressions In Stone LLC 918 828-9745
  1415 S Joplin Ave Tulsa (74112) *(G-9974)*
Impressions Printing A 405 722-2442
  2241 W I 44 Service Rd Oklahoma City (73112) *(G-6293)*
Improved Cnstr Methods Inc 405 235-2609
  4127 W Reno Ave Oklahoma City (73107) *(G-6294)*
IMS Erp Software LLC 918 508-9544
  401 S Boston Ave Ste 500 Tulsa (74103) *(G-9975)*
In His Name Screenprinting LLC 405 756-8911
  24260 E County Road 1560 Maysville (73057) *(G-4260)*
In-Tele Communication LLC 580 272-0303
  111 W Main St Ada (74820) *(G-50)*
Inboard Hammock Light, Drummond *Also called DSA Designs LLC* *(G-2047)*
Incor, Muskogee *Also called Sheltred Work-Activity Program* *(G-4748)*
Indaco Metals LLC 405 273-9200
  3 American Way Shawnee (74804) *(G-8462)*
Indel-Davis Inc (PA) 918 587-2151
  4401 S Jackson Ave Tulsa (74107) *(G-9976)*
Independence Race Works & Fabg 918 489-2353
  306 Ray Fine Dr Gore (74435) *(G-3250)*
Independent Diesel Parts & Svc, Enid *Also called Independent Diesel Service* *(G-2977)*
Independent Diesel Service 580 234-0435
  4524 E Market St Enid (73701) *(G-2977)*
Independent Machine, McAlester *Also called Eric Turner* *(G-4295)*
Independent School 918 245-2622
  138 Oak St Sand Springs (74063) *(G-8192)*
Independent Trucking Co Inc 918 352-2539
  902 N Smather Ave Drumright (74030) *(G-2063)*
Indian Creek Gas Processing LP 918 359-0980
  6100 S Yale Ave Ste 2050 Tulsa (74136) *(G-9977)*
Indian Exploration Company LLC 405 231-2476
  123 S Hudson Ave Oklahoma City (73102) *(G-6295)*
Indian Nations Communications 918 696-2228
  118 N 2nd St Stilwell (74960) *(G-8791)*
Indian Nations Fiber Optics, Lawton *Also called Indian Nations Fiberoptics Inc* *(G-3941)*
Indian Nations Fiberoptics Inc 580 355-2300
  9 Sw 21st St Lawton (73501) *(G-3941)*
Indigo Streams Publishing LLC 918 293-0247
  5138 E 30th Pl Tulsa (74114) *(G-9978)*
Industrial Axle Company LLC 405 273-9315
  301 N Kennedy Ave Shawnee (74801) *(G-8463)*
Industrial City Press 918 299-2767
  103 E F St Jenks (74037) *(G-3707)*
Industrial Cntrls Slutions LLC 405 601-0625
  1005 Metropolitan Ave Oklahoma City (73108) *(G-6296)*

Industrial Coatings Oklahoma....918 638-5606
903 Star St Claremore (74017) *(G-1640)*
Industrial Coil Inc....405 745-2030
4305 Beacon Dr Oklahoma City (73179) *(G-6297)*
Industrial Coil Shop, Oklahoma City *Also called Industrial Coil Inc (G-6297)*
Industrial Commercial Entp....405 681-2991
3120 S Ann Arbor Ave Oklahoma City (73179) *(G-6298)*
Industrial Dist Resources LLC....239 591-3777
7255 E 46th St Tulsa (74145) *(G-9979)*
Industrial Electronics Repair....918 342-1160
24905 S Highway 66 Claremore (74019) *(G-1641)*
Industrial Enterprise Inc....918 476-5907
65 Lakeside Dr Chouteau (74337) *(G-1567)*
Industrial Equipment Repair....580 371-3361
1509 Industrial Ln Tishomingo (73460) *(G-8966)*
Industrial Equipment Services....580 765-5544
1809 Princeton Ave Ponca City (74604) *(G-7837)*
Industrial Gasket Inc....405 376-9393
720 S Sara Rd Mustang (73064) *(G-4778)*
Industrial Ignition Supply, Duncan *Also called Vincent Enterprises Inc (G-2194)*
Industrial Machine Co Inc....405 236-5419
1546 W Reno Ave Oklahoma City (73106) *(G-6299)*
Industrial Manufacturing Inc....918 787-5500
57530 E Highway 59 Fairland (74343) *(G-3125)*
Industrial Marking Co....918 749-8851
6216 S Lewis Ave Ste 136 Tulsa (74136) *(G-9980)*
Industrial Metal Fab and Sup, Oklahoma City *Also called Lockdown Ltd Co (G-6485)*
Industrial Oils Unlimited, Tulsa *Also called Oils Unlimited LLC (G-10389)*
Industrial Powder Coatings, Oklahoma City *Also called Powder Coatings Plus LLC (G-6868)*
Industrial Power Wash Inc....405 787-9274
7608 Nw 40th St Bethany (73008) *(G-582)*
Industrial Pping Companies LLC....918 825-0900
1933 S Elliott St Pryor (74361) *(G-7970)*
Industrial Rubber Inc....405 632-9783
11801 S Meridian Ave Oklahoma City (73173) *(G-6300)*
Industrial Service Providers (PA)....580 319-7417
619 Interstate Dr Ardmore (73401) *(G-308)*
Industrial Signs & Neon Inc....405 236-5599
101 S Villa Ave Oklahoma City (73107) *(G-6301)*
Industrial Specialties LLC....580 303-9170
315 W 20th St Elk City (73644) *(G-2826)*
Industrial Specialties Inc....580 475-9088
508 And A Half S Hwy 81 Duncan (73533) *(G-2131)*
Industrial Splicing Sling LLC (PA)....918 835-4452
1842 N 109th East Ave Tulsa (74116) *(G-9981)*
Industrial Structures Inc....918 341-0300
1931 N 170th East Ave Tulsa (74116) *(G-9982)*
Industrial Tractor Parts Tulsa, Broken Arrow *Also called Industrial Trctr Parts Co Inc (G-935)*
Industrial Trctr Parts Co Inc....918 258-6580
2251 N Indianwood Ave Broken Arrow (74012) *(G-935)*
Industrial Vehicles Intl Inc (PA)....918 836-6516
6737 E 12th St Tulsa (74112) *(G-9983)*
Infinite Composites Tech, Tulsa *Also called Cleanng LLC (G-9446)*
Infinite Tool Systems Inc....405 205-4206
1009 Hunters Pointe Rd Edmond (73003) *(G-2460)*
Infinitee By Mars LLC....405 474-6505
919 W Britton Rd Oklahoma City (73114) *(G-6302)*
Infinity Home Solutions LLC....918 704-8014
12806 S Memorial Dr # 113 Bixby (74008) *(G-635)*
Infinity Resources Company....405 701-3229
2740 Washington Dr Norman (73069) *(G-5032)*
Infinity Resources LLC....405 767-3519
6301 Waterford Blvd Oklahoma City (73118) *(G-6303)*
Infinity Screenprinting LLC....405 485-3203
1899 Doc Bar Ave Blanchard (73010) *(G-716)*
Info-Sharp LLC....520 204-5093
1808 Parkridge Dr Norman (73071) *(G-5033)*
Infocus Print Co LLC....918 465-5572
502 E Chickasaw Ave McAlester (74501) *(G-4306)*
Ingels Vineyard LLC....405 321-1008
2310 Ravenwood Ln Norman (73071) *(G-5034)*
Ingersoll-Rand Air Solutio....918 451-9747
6613 S Birch Ave Broken Arrow (74011) *(G-936)*
Ingevity....918 704-6423
1540 N 107th East Ave Tulsa (74116) *(G-9984)*
Inglesrud Corp....405 429-7928
5104 N Francis Ave A600 Oklahoma City (73118) *(G-6304)*
Ingram Exploration Inc....405 382-2040
2 One Half Mi S On Hwy99 Seminole (74868) *(G-8376)*
Ingredion Incorporated....539 292-4369
810 S Cincinnati Ave Tulsa (74119) *(G-9985)*
Initially Yours Inc....918 832-9889
1539 N 105th East Ave Tulsa (74116) *(G-9986)*
Ink & Toner Outlet, Tulsa *Also called Smart Office Stores LLC (G-10776)*
Ink Images Inc....918 828-0300
4305 S Mingo Rd Ste C Tulsa (74146) *(G-9987)*
Ink Masters Screen Printing....918 399-5220
1421 E Moses St Cushing (74023) *(G-1938)*
Ink Spot Tttoo Bdy Percing LLC....918 637-2897
27108 E 82nd St S Broken Arrow (74014) *(G-1135)*
Inkana Publishing....937 760-8446
406 Winchester Ave Ada (74820) *(G-51)*
Inkana Publishing LLC....937 725-1296
4235 Macys Pl Moore (73160) *(G-4528)*
Inked Custom Printing....918 872-6544
2234 W Houston St Ste A Broken Arrow (74012) *(G-937)*
Inklahoma Screen Prtg & EMB....405 206-0500
317 N Trade Center Ter # 2 Mustang (73064) *(G-4779)*
Inkling Design....405 495-5575
5508 N Rockwell Ave Ste B Bethany (73008) *(G-583)*
Inkspot....405 793-7200
216 W Main St Moore (73160) *(G-4529)*
Inkwell Printing....918 508-3634
4195 S 69th West Ave Tulsa (74107) *(G-9988)*
Inland Machine & Welding Co....405 670-4355
2133 Se 15th St Oklahoma City (73129) *(G-6305)*
Inland Manufacturing LLC....918 697-4436
2701 W Montgomery St Broken Arrow (74012) *(G-938)*
Inland Manufacturing LLC....918 342-5733
6852 E Highway 20 Claremore (74019) *(G-1642)*
Inland Oil Corp....918 227-1180
14920 W Highway 66 Sapulpa (74066) *(G-8278)*
Inman Welding Service....918 323-0022
23580 S 4430 Rd Vinita (74301) *(G-11262)*
Inman Well Service....918 440-3151
23530 N 4025 Rd Bartlesville (74006) *(G-497)*
Innocative Computing Tech....405 255-4453
8524 S Wstn Ave Ste 114 Oklahoma City (73139) *(G-6306)*
Innovasia, Tulsa *Also called Rsga Incorporated (G-10681)*
Innovation Controls, Tulsa *Also called GC&i Global Inc (G-9810)*
Innovationone, LLC, Marietta *Also called Cni Manufacturing LLC (G-4205)*
Innovative Oilfield Svcs LLC....918 521-8317
5828 Ne Highway 270 Red Oak (74563) *(G-8078)*
Innovative Production Inc....918 729-9312
4602 W 51st St Tulsa (74107) *(G-9989)*
Innovative Products Inc....405 949-0040
520 Beacon Pl Oklahoma City (73127) *(G-6307)*
Innovative Technology Ltd....580 243-1559
105 Carter Rd Elk City (73644) *(G-2827)*
Innovex Downhole Solutions Inc....405 491-2658
2709 S Ann Arbor Ave Oklahoma City (73128) *(G-6308)*
Inprint Publishing, Oklahoma City *Also called Metro Family Magazine (G-6579)*
Inserv's, Tulsa *Also called Integrated Service Company LLC (G-9997)*
Insight Publishing Group....918 493-1718
4739 E 91st St Ste 210 Tulsa (74137) *(G-9990)*
Insight Technologies Inc....580 933-4109
52 E Wilson St Valliant (74764) *(G-11226)*
Insignia Signs Inc....405 631-5522
809 Se 83rd St Oklahoma City (73149) *(G-6309)*
Inspiration Logos Inc....405 741-5646
1810 S Midwest Blvd Oklahoma City (73110) *(G-6310)*
Inspired Gifts & Graphics LLC....405 295-1669
1605 E Us Highway 66 El Reno (73036) *(G-2725)*
Instant Signs Inc....405 848-8181
227 Nw 63rd St Oklahoma City (73116) *(G-6311)*
Instinct Performance LLC....405 463-7300
7 Ne 6th St 30 Oklahoma City (73104) *(G-6312)*
Institute Optical Inc....918 747-3937
1717 S Utica Ave Ste 105 Tulsa (74104) *(G-9991)*
Insul-Vest Inc (PA)....918 445-2279
6417 S 39th West Ave Tulsa (74132) *(G-9992)*
Integral Geophysics Inc....405 848-4573
3037 Nw 63rd St Ste 158w Oklahoma City (73116) *(G-6313)*
Integrated Controls Inc....918 747-5811
1537 S Harvard Ave Tulsa (74112) *(G-9993)*
Integrated Controls Inc....918 747-7820
5236 S Zunis Ave Tulsa (74105) *(G-9994)*
Integrated Fluid Systems....405 418-2897
3 Honda Ln Chickasha (73018) *(G-1471)*
Integrated Fluid Systems LLC....580 323-8431
22456 E 1078 Rd Clinton (73601) *(G-1753)*
Integrated Payment Svcs LLC....918 492-7094
1703 E Skelly Dr Ste 105 Tulsa (74105) *(G-9995)*
Integrated Production Services....580 225-5667
1602 Enterprise Rd Elk City (73644) *(G-2828)*
Integrated S Mycare....405 605-0546
5401 N Portland Ave A Oklahoma City (73112) *(G-6314)*
Integrated Service Co Mfg LLC....918 234-4150
1900 N 161st East Ave Tulsa (74116) *(G-9996)*
Integrated Service Company LLC....918 556-3600
4300 E 36th St N Tulsa (74115) *(G-9997)*
Integrated Tower Systems Inc....918 749-8535
2703 Dawson Rd Tulsa (74110) *(G-9998)*
Integrated Training & Mfg Tech....918 893-2225
1300 E Fort Worth St Broken Arrow (74012) *(G-939)*
Integriteezv, Tulsa *Also called Integrity Screen Works Inc (G-9999)*
Integrity Custom Mill Works....405 495-9732
9115 Ne 36th St Trlr 1 Spencer (73084) *(G-8596)*

ALPHABETIC

Integrity Directional Svcs LLC (PA)...817 731-8881
119 N Robinson Ave # 400 Oklahoma City (73102) ***(G-6315)***
Integrity Machine Source LLC...918 230-9657
15405 E 114th St N Owasso (74055) ***(G-7575)***
Integrity Piping Services Co...918 850-0206
4801 Bermuda Cir Sand Springs (74063) ***(G-8193)***
Integrity Power Solutions LLC...918 925-9693
2708 Cumberland Dr Edmond (73034) ***(G-2461)***
Integrity Pump & Supply LLC...405 422-2828
301 S Bickford Ave El Reno (73036) ***(G-2726)***
Integrity Rail Services Inc...918 267-3761
7828 Highway 16 Beggs (74421) ***(G-558)***
Integrity Rmdlg Cnstr Svcs LLC...405 754-9836
708 Nw 25th St Oklahoma City (73103) ***(G-6316)***
Integrity Screen Works Inc...918 663-8339
6580 E Skelly Dr Tulsa (74145) ***(G-9999)***
Integrity Signs...918 520-2802
399700 W 3100 Rd Ramona (74061) ***(G-8046)***
Integrity Tech & Svcs LLC...405 482-9206
15716 Hyde Parke Dr Edmond (73013) ***(G-2462)***
Integrity Trckg Cnstr Svcs Inc...580 361-2387
Rr 2 Box 17 Balko (73931) ***(G-432)***
Integrity Woodcrafters LLC...918 664-1041
8809 E 34th St Tulsa (74145) ***(G-10000)***
Integrted Lock SEC Systems LLC...918 232-3436
1239 W 111th St S Jenks (74037) ***(G-3708)***
Integsense Inc...404 429-4780
3030 Nw Expwy Ste 200b Oklahoma City (73112) ***(G-6317)***
Intellevue Ltd...918 250-5561
11102 E 75th Pl Tulsa (74133) ***(G-10001)***
Intensity Midstream LLC (PA)...918 949-9098
320 S Boston Ave Ste 705 Tulsa (74103) ***(G-10002)***
Interactive Cad Services Inc...918 251-4470
2101 N Yellowood Ave Broken Arrow (74012) ***(G-940)***
Interfaceflor LLC...918 746-0501
4207 S Wheeling Ave Tulsa (74105) ***(G-10003)***
Interior Designers Supply Inc...405 521-1551
7720 N Robinson Ave B3 Oklahoma City (73116) ***(G-6318)***
International Energy Corp...918 743-7300
1801 E 71st St Tulsa (74136) ***(G-10004)***
International Envmtl Corp...405 605-5024
5000 W I 40 Service Rd Oklahoma City (73128) ***(G-6319)***
International Gymnast Magazine...405 447-9988
3214 Bart Conner Dr Norman (73072) ***(G-5035)***
International Gymnastic Mag, Norman *Also called Paul Ziert & Associates Inc* ***(G-5112)***
International Journal of Ph...405 330-0094
122 N Bryant Ave Ste B4 Edmond (73034) ***(G-2463)***
International Journal Phrm Com, Edmond *Also called International Journal of Ph* ***(G-2463)***
INTERNATIONAL ORDER OF THE RAI, McAlester *Also called Rainbow Spreme Assmbly I O R G* ***(G-4331)***
International Paper Company...405 745-5800
4901 Westpoint Blvd Oklahoma City (73179) ***(G-6320)***
International Paper Company...580 933-7211
890 International Ppr Ln Valliant (74764) ***(G-11227)***
International Pro Rodeo Assn...405 235-6540
1412 S Agnew Ave Oklahoma City (73108) ***(G-6321)***
International Sftwr Cons Inc (PA)...580 924-1231
402 N 1st Ave Durant (74701) ***(G-2239)***
Interntnal Mktg Resources Corp...918 270-1200
1200 N Peoria Ave Tulsa (74106) ***(G-10005)***
Interplastic Corporation...918 825-2755
5019 Hunt St Pryor (74361) ***(G-7971)***
Interplastic Corporation...918 592-0205
1012 E Oklahoma St Tulsa (74106) ***(G-10006)***
Interplastic Dist Group, Tulsa *Also called Interplastic Corporation* ***(G-10006)***
Interstate Electric Corp...918 245-4508
196 E Morrow Rd Sand Springs (74063) ***(G-8194)***
Interstate Supply Company...405 232-7141
5600 Sw 36th St Ste C Oklahoma City (73179) ***(G-6322)***
Interstate Supply Company...918 461-0177
11915 E 51st St Ste 57 Tulsa (74146) ***(G-10007)***
Interstate Tool & Mfg Co...918 834-6647
1044 N Columbia Pl Tulsa (74110) ***(G-10008)***
Interstate Trucker Ltd...405 948-6576
1101 Sovereign Row Ste A Oklahoma City (73108) ***(G-6323)***
Intrepid Directional Drilling...405 607-0422
205 Nw 63rd St Oklahoma City (73116) ***(G-6324)***
Intuition Inc...405 361-8376
613 Coopers Hawk Dr Norman (73072) ***(G-5036)***
Invia Pavement Tech LLC...918 878-7890
1540 N 107th East Ave Tulsa (74116) ***(G-10009)***
Invictus Engrg Cnstr Svcs...405 701-5622
800 W Rock Creek Rd # 115 Norman (73069) ***(G-5037)***
Invictus Personal Defense Llc...918 605-1165
9117 N 137th East Ave Owasso (74055) ***(G-7576)***
Invisible Element LLC...918 296-7562
12203 S 4th St Jenks (74037) ***(G-3709)***
Invitation, Edmond *Also called Pueblo Motors Inc* ***(G-2577)***
Inviting Place...918 488-0525
3525 S Harvard Ave Tulsa (74135) ***(G-10010)***
Iochem Corporation (PA)...405 848-8611
5801 Broadway Ext Ste 305 Oklahoma City (73118) ***(G-6325)***
Iochem Corporation...580 995-3198
3 Miles East Hwy 60 Vici (73859) ***(G-11243)***
Iofina Natural Gas...580 871-2316
19940 County Road 480 Alva (73717) ***(G-183)***
Ips, Elk City *Also called Integrated Production Services* ***(G-2828)***
Ips...405 722-0896
7408 Nw 83rd St Oklahoma City (73132) ***(G-6326)***
Ipsco Tubulars Inc...918 384-6400
5610 Bird Creek Ave Catoosa (74015) ***(G-1323)***
Ipsco Tubulars OK, Catoosa *Also called Ipsco Tubulars Inc* ***(G-1323)***
Iq Surgical LLC...918 932-2734
22 S Lewis Ave Tulsa (74104) ***(G-10011)***
Ira E Rongey...918 227-0046
621 Countrywood Way Sapulpa (74066) ***(G-8279)***
Iron Bear Jewelry & Lea Co LLC...918 289-1420
6527 N Trenton Ave Tulsa (74126) ***(G-10012)***
Iron Cowboy Welding LLC...580 301-3423
25 Baylee Creek Cir Lawton (73501) ***(G-3942)***
Iron Cowboy Welding LLC...580 335-2900
22325 State Highway 5 Frederick (73542) ***(G-3194)***
Iron Decor, Tulsa *Also called Laughing Water Enterprises LLC* ***(G-10136)***
Iron Gate Tubular Services...580 303-9046
11118 N 1967 Rd Elk City (73644) ***(G-2829)***
Iron Horse Metal Works...918 333-8877
3908 Minnesota St Bartlesville (74006) ***(G-498)***
Iron Horse Roustabout Svcs LLC...918 352-8586
34251 W 161st St S Bristow (74010) ***(G-780)***
Iron Images...918 685-1514
5010 Elm Grove Rd Muskogee (74403) ***(G-4694)***
Iron Post Winery LLC...918 479-3600
9797 Se 560 Dr Locust Grove (74352) ***(G-4111)***
Ironclad Defense...405 413-9496
437 W Fairchild Dr Midwest City (73110) ***(G-4443)***
Ironcraft Urban Products LLC...855 601-1647
5401 5405 Nw 5th St Oklahoma City (73127) ***(G-6327)***
Ironman Welding & Mfg LLC...580 464-3478
203 Christopher Dr Chickasha (73018) ***(G-1472)***
Ironman Welding Machine...580 791-3091
81594 Wild Goose Cir Fay (73646) ***(G-3157)***
Ironwolf Manufacturing LLC...405 872-1890
9000 S Highway 77 Noble (73068) ***(G-4882)***
Irw, Gore *Also called Independence Race Works & Fabg* ***(G-3250)***
Irwin Custom Sign Company LLC...405 372-0657
415 E 14th Ave Stillwater (74074) ***(G-8704)***
Isabels Candles...918 595-5358
1746 W Young St Tulsa (74127) ***(G-10013)***
Isbell Industries LLC...405 828-7228
10602 N 2850 Rd Dover (73734) ***(G-2040)***
ISC, Oklahoma City *Also called Ignition Systems & Controls* ***(G-6291)***
ISC Computers, Durant *Also called International Sftwr Cons Inc* ***(G-2239)***
ISC Surfaces LLC, Oklahoma City *Also called Interstate Supply Company* ***(G-6322)***
ISI, Tulsa *Also called Industrial Structures Inc* ***(G-9982)***
Island Disc Golf Course...541 337-8668
22005 State Highway 99 Pawhuska (74056) ***(G-7686)***
Island Palm LLC...405 321-1056
2817 Cynthia Cir Norman (73072) ***(G-5038)***
Issken Industries Inc...405 623-2177
205 S Main St Stillwater (74074) ***(G-8705)***
Itero Energy, Inc., Tulsa *Also called Lakewood Energy Solutions LLC* ***(G-10115)***
Its In Print...918 493-4141
6131 S Joplin Ave Tulsa (74136) ***(G-10014)***
Ivers Welding and Machine Shop...580 765-4882
715 S 1st St Ponca City (74601) ***(G-7838)***
Ixzibit...405 413-2260
11120 Ne 141st St Jones (73049) ***(G-3748)***
Izoom Graphics, Tulsa *Also called Izoom Inc* ***(G-10015)***
Izoom Inc...918 836-9666
9015 S 48th West Ave Tulsa (74132) ***(G-10015)***
J & A Hot Oilers Inc...405 341-7600
9 W 9th St Edmond (73003) ***(G-2464)***
J & A Peanut, Caddo *Also called Joa Inc* ***(G-1236)***
J & B Deep Discount...918 622-7600
6525 E 51st St Tulsa (74145) ***(G-10016)***
J & B Graphics Inc...405 524-7446
1811 Nw 1st St Oklahoma City (73106) ***(G-6328)***
J & C Enterprises Aviation...580 661-3591
721 N Missouri St Thomas (73669) ***(G-8944)***
J & C Manufacturing Inc...580 476-3217
Hwy 81 S Rush Springs (73082) ***(G-8122)***
J & C Welding Co Inc...405 263-4967
506 N 1st St Okarche (73762) ***(G-5243)***
J & D Fabricators Inc...405 356-2243
334760 E Highway 66 Wellston (74881) ***(G-11473)***
J & D Gearing & Machining Inc...405 677-7667
1900 E Grand Blvd Oklahoma City (73129) ***(G-6329)***
J & D Machine Inc...918 425-5704
2700 N Erie Ave Tulsa (74115) ***(G-10017)***

J & D Potter Oil LLC 405 375-6303
1203 W Fay Ave Kingfisher (73750) *(G-3802)*
J & F Oil Co 918 652-7957
22420 S 250 Rd Henryetta (74437) *(G-3509)*
J & G Steel Corporation 918 227-3131
2429 Industrial Rd Sapulpa (74066) *(G-8280)*
J & G Trucking 918 693-4300
Rr 2 Box 202-10 Nowata (74048) *(G-5215)*
J & I Manufacturing Inc 580 795-7377
16967 Highway 99c Madill (73446) *(G-4150)*
J & J Company 918 616-2169
5611 Sally Brown Rd Muskogee (74403) *(G-4695)*
J & J Custom Fire Inc 405 747-4442
22274 Valley Red Rock (74651) *(G-8079)*
J & J Machine, Enid *Also called Joel Bumpus (G-2987)*
J & J Machine Shop 918 827-6892
7660 Adams Rd Mounds (74047) *(G-4618)*
J & J Oil Tools LLC 580 523-1995
Rr 2 Box 106a Guymon (73942) *(G-3352)*
J & J Services Inc 580 265-9466
22527 County Road 3 Dr Stonewall (74871) *(G-8801)*
J & J Solutions LLC 580 336-3050
6990 Independence Perry (73077) *(G-7737)*
J & J Tubulars Inc 405 691-2039
14024 S Meridian Ave Oklahoma City (73173) *(G-6330)*
J & Js Wdwrk HM Decor & Gifts 918 420-9411
32 E Cherokee Ave McAlester (74501) *(G-4307)*
J & L Exploration LLC 405 842-6876
6412 N Santa Fe Ave Oklahoma City (73116) *(G-6331)*
J & L Oil Field Services LLC 580 938-2205
2100 S Main St Shattuck (73858) *(G-8422)*
J & L Tool Co Inc 918 835-8484
63 N Yale Ave Tulsa (74115) *(G-10018)*
J & M Investment 405 848-3755
901 Nw 84th St Oklahoma City (73114) *(G-6332)*
J & M Machine Shop Inc 918 650-0074
511 E Gum St Henryetta (74437) *(G-3510)*
J & M Pipe & Supply, Watonga *Also called John Thompson Enterprises Inc (G-11348)*
J & M Welding 918 216-2090
7862 S Regency Dr Tulsa (74131) *(G-9015)*
J & N Small Engine Repair 405 382-2792
1905 Boren Blvd Seminole (74868) *(G-8377)*
J & P Machine 918 623-0005
E Of City Okemah (74859) *(G-5270)*
J & R Service Inc 580 256-6461
4230 Oklahoma Ave Woodward (73801) *(G-11594)*
J & R Transport, Woodward *Also called Hot Oil Units Inc (G-11592)*
J & S Fittings Inc 918 324-5777
21284 Milfay Rd Depew (74028) *(G-2011)*
J & S Machine & Valve 918 273-1582
125 Vinita Rd Nowata (74048) *(G-5216)*
J & S Machine & Valve Inc 918 273-1582
131 Vinita Rd Nowata (74048) *(G-5217)*
J & S of Enid Inc 580 237-6152
1913 N 10th St Enid (73701) *(G-2978)*
J & S Woodworking Inc 405 619-9910
1033 Se 40th St Oklahoma City (73129) *(G-6333)*
J & W Electric Motor Company 580 357-7504
19 Se F Ave Lawton (73501) *(G-3943)*
J A Oil Field Mfg Inc (PA) 405 672-2299
2101 Se 67th St Oklahoma City (73149) *(G-6334)*
J and S Trucking Company 580 216-7213
1023 Oak Ave Woodward (73801) *(G-11595)*
J B Granite Countertops 580 771-6894
2413 Nw 28th St Lawton (73505) *(G-3944)*
J B Hot Oil and Steam Co Inc 918 366-3872
18134 S Harvard Ave Bixby (74008) *(G-636)*
J B Welding, Ada *Also called J Bs Welding Inc (G-52)*
J B Welding 918 574-1806
806 Belmont Rd Bartlesville (74006) *(G-499)*
J B Woodworking 918 760-2399
17525 S 273rd West Ave Bristow (74010) *(G-781)*
J Bernardoni Pattern Co LLC 520 390-0663
17165 E State Highway 31 Quinton (74561) *(G-8037)*
J BS Donuts 918 486-4022
13743 S State Highway 51 Coweta (74429) *(G-1887)*
J Bs Welding Inc 580 332-6194
120 Armory Rd Ada (74820) *(G-52)*
J C & J Machine & Auto 580 439-5919
9950 E 1880 Rd Comanche (73529) *(G-1842)*
J C N Petroleum Corp 405 341-8179
1625 E Coffee Creek Rd Edmond (73034) *(G-2465)*
J C Petroleum Inc 405 222-1412
3010 S 4th St Chickasha (73018) *(G-1473)*
J C Sheet Metal 580 688-9527
202 N 4th St Hollis (73550) *(G-3566)*
J C Sheet Metal Fabrication 405 787-1902
7233 Nw 3rd St Oklahoma City (73127) *(G-6335)*
J D'S Machine Shop, Duncan *Also called Jerry D Pierce (G-2135)*
J Davids Jeweler, Broken Arrow *Also called Golden Bronze Inc (G-920)*
J Duke Logan Family Trust 918 256-7511
101 S Wilson St Vinita (74301) *(G-11263)*
J E & L E Mabee Foundation (PA) 918 584-4286
401 S Boston Ave Ste 3001 Tulsa (74103) *(G-10019)*
J E Shaffer Co 918 582-1752
8410 N 66th East Ave Owasso (74055) *(G-7577)*
J F Machine LLC 918 865-5855
6810 N Three Fnger Bay Rd Mannford (74044) *(G-4183)*
J Fletcher Derrell 580 673-2489
27970 State Highway 53 Healdton (73438) *(G-3416)*
J Franklin Publishers Inc 628 400-3382
4926 S Boston Pl Tulsa (74105) *(G-10020)*
J Grantham Drilling Inc 918 647-8926
305 Dees Rd Poteau (74953) *(G-7907)*
J H B & Company Inc 405 354-6709
809 Lancaster Dr Yukon (73099) *(G-11733)*
J J Custom Fire 918 762-2102
1300 N Sewell Dr Pawnee (74058) *(G-7705)*
J L'S Retipping, Tonkawa *Also called Linton Jim & John (G-8978)*
J M A Resources Inc 405 947-4322
1021 Nw Grand Blvd Oklahoma City (73118) *(G-6336)*
J M Eagle, Tulsa *Also called J-M Manufacturing Company Inc (G-10025)*
J M Welding 918 277-4480
9887 S Frankoma Rd Sapulpa (74066) *(G-8281)*
J Marrs Welding 918 396-2221
4001 W Munson Rd Skiatook (74070) *(G-8552)*
J Mottos Italian Ice Sorbet, Tulsa *Also called J Mottos LLC (G-10021)*
J Mottos LLC 918 760-3866
8759 S Lewis Ave Ste A Tulsa (74137) *(G-10021)*
J N B Inc 918 786-6311
62042 E 278 Rd Grove (74344) *(G-3275)*
J P Machine & Tool Co 405 677-3341
1534 Se 29th St Oklahoma City (73129) *(G-6337)*
J Price Energy Services LLC 580 795-6106
221 Plaza Madill (73446) *(G-4151)*
J R Lukeman & Associates Inc 405 842-6548
3017 Hemingford Ln Oklahoma City (73120) *(G-6338)*
J Rose Printing LLC 210 875-0947
301 Pointe Parkway Blvd # 1402 Yukon (73099) *(G-11734)*
J S Welding 405 364-1362
4000 48th Ave Nw Norman (73072) *(G-5039)*
J Scott Inc 405 262-5900
12215 Reuter Rd W El Reno (73036) *(G-2727)*
J Spencer Jewelry & Gifts (PA) 918 250-5587
8303 S Memorial Dr Tulsa (74133) *(G-10022)*
J Stephens LLC 918 299-2900
5415 E 109th Pl Tulsa (74137) *(G-10023)*
J T G Industries LLC 405 285-6627
3324 Findhorn Dr Edmond (73034) *(G-2466)*
J T Harrison Construction Co 918 967-2852
20289 N Airport Rd Stigler (74462) *(G-8633)*
J T Industries, Owasso *Also called Don Tooker (G-7562)*
J T Jewelers, Grove *Also called J N B Inc (G-3275)*
J T Welding 580 504-3862
53 Walnut Hill St Ardmore (73401) *(G-309)*
J Thompson Custom Jewelers 405 495-6610
5770 Nw Expressway # 101 Warr Acres (73132) *(G-11323)*
J W Companies (PA) 405 789-2460
3709 N Grant Ave Bethany (73008) *(G-584)*
J Walter Duncan Jr Oil Inc 405 272-1800
100 Park Ave Ste 1200 Oklahoma City (73102) *(G-6339)*
J&A Services Co Inc 405 833-4824
401 W Johnson St Norman (73069) *(G-5040)*
J&C Industries Inc 405 473-7834
3582 Southridge Ln Ne Piedmont (73078) *(G-7764)*
J&J Logging LLC 580 933-7218
1356 Pine Creek Rd Valliant (74764) *(G-11228)*
J&J Powder Coating & Fabr 918 836-9700
6410 E Archer St Tulsa (74115) *(G-10024)*
J&Js Woodwork and More 918 429-9704
429 W Osage Ave McAlester (74501) *(G-4308)*
J&K Machining Inc 918 243-7936
1232 E Scenic Blf Cleveland (74020) *(G-1725)*
J&K Rstbout Weed Ctrl Svcs LLC 918 429-2392
4071 S Pine Hollow Rd Stuart (74570) *(G-8825)*
J&M Stainless Fabricators Ltd 405 517-0875
744 Sw 23rd St Oklahoma City (73109) *(G-6340)*
J&N Small Engines, Seminole *Also called J & N Small Engine Repair (G-8377)*
J&S Overhead Door & Gate LLC 405 249-0779
274 Murray Dr Choctaw (73020) *(G-1546)*
J-A-G Construction Company 580 338-3188
913 Ne 14th St Guymon (73942) *(G-3353)*
J-B Oilfield Services LLC 580 388-4484
1227 Main Lamont (74643) *(G-3869)*
J-M Farms Inc 918 540-1567
7001 S 580 Rd Miami (74354) *(G-4409)*
J-M Manufacturing Company Inc 918 446-4471
4501 W 49th St Tulsa (74107) *(G-10025)*
J-Tech, Tulsa *Also called Donald L Stafford Co (G-9596)*

ALPHABETIC

J-W Power Company 580 254-5663
1307 46th St Woodward (73801) ***(G-11596)***
Ja Marrs Oil Co Inc 918 352-2798
206 E Pine St Drumright (74030) ***(G-2064)***
Jabjr Technology, Moore *Also called James A Brumit Jr* ***(G-4530)***
Jacckson Techinical, Broken Arrow *Also called Webready Software Inc* ***(G-1093)***
Jack Chartier Welding LLC 918 486-2347
16818 S 305th East Ave Coweta (74429) ***(G-1888)***
Jack Exploration Inc 580 621-3679
409 S Kansas Ave Cherokee (73728) ***(G-1417)***
Jack Exploration Inc (PA) 580 622-2310
812 W 11th St Sulphur (73086) ***(G-8835)***
Jack Henry & Associates Inc 405 947-6644
4248 Highline Blvd Oklahoma City (73108) ***(G-6341)***
Jack Mangum 580 658-2700
1106 S 9th St Marlow (73055) ***(G-4234)***
Jack Oil Company 580 255-2310
1032 W Main St Ste 100 Duncan (73533) ***(G-2132)***
Jack Pratt Screen-Ad Co 405 524-5551
409 Ne 40th St Oklahoma City (73105) ***(G-6342)***
Jack Sprague 405 367-7655
1035 County Street 2982 Blanchard (73010) ***(G-717)***
Jack Stout Inc 918 781-1000
515 S Main St Muskogee (74401) ***(G-4696)***
Jack Warner Fireworks 580 234-3827
Southgate Rd Enid (73702) ***(G-2979)***
Jacks Backhoe & Roustabout Svc, Camargo *Also called Jacks Backhoe Service* ***(G-1253)***
Jacks Backhoe Service 580 926-3378
Hwy 34 In Town Camargo (73835) ***(G-1253)***
Jacks Cnstr & Backhoe Svc 405 238-3569
Rr 1 Box 268 Pauls Valley (73075) ***(G-7661)***
Jacks Flex Pipe 405 382-5740
35585 Ew 1270 Seminole (74868) ***(G-8378)***
Jackson Clip Co Inc 918 476-8331
2 And A Half Mile W Mazie (74337) ***(G-4264)***
Jackson Holdings LLC 405 842-8903
922 Nw 70th St Oklahoma City (73116) ***(G-6343)***
Jackson Powder Coating, Chouteau *Also called Sooner State Spring Mfg Co* ***(G-1570)***
Jackson Welding & Machine 580 472-3631
124 Willard Canute (73626) ***(G-1268)***
Jacmac Energy Corp 405 224-1284
114 Mockingbird Ln Chickasha (73018) ***(G-1474)***
Jacmor Inc 405 843-0203
8028 N May Ave Ste 202 Oklahoma City (73120) ***(G-6344)***
Jaco Energy Company Inc 918 967-8889
20292 E Highway 9 Stigler (74462) ***(G-8634)***
Jacob Manufacturing Inc 918 787-6606
499 Industrial Road A Grove (74344) ***(G-3276)***
Jacobs Ladder Camps & Retreat 405 258-5176
880876 S 3390 Rd Chandler (74834) ***(G-1381)***
Jacobs Manufacturing, Grove *Also called Jacob Manufacturing Inc* ***(G-3276)***
Jacobson Fabrication Inc 918 251-1181
1500 N Poplar Ave Broken Arrow (74012) ***(G-941)***
Jacobson Ready Mixed Concrete, Pauls Valley *Also called L A Jacobson Inc* ***(G-7664)***
Jade Fire LLC 405 295-7734
2604 S Reno Ave El Reno (73036) ***(G-2728)***
Jaf Industries LLC 405 834-8362
5909 Nw Expressway # 269 Oklahoma City (73132) ***(G-6345)***
Jag Fuels Company Inc 580 465-3256
2744 Brock Rd Ardmore (73401) ***(G-310)***
Jag Machine Inc 918 791-0004
340 Industrial Road A Grove (74344) ***(G-3277)***
Jaguar Meter Service Inc 405 670-2327
1605 Se 37th St Oklahoma City (73129) ***(G-6346)***
Jak D Up Tees Inc 405 260-0007
301 W Waterloo Rd Bldg C Edmond (73025) ***(G-2467)***
Jalex LLC 405 627-7856
6583 E 122nd St S Bixby (74008) ***(G-637)***
James A Brumit Jr 405 924-9696
1901 Se 13th St Moore (73160) ***(G-4530)***
James A Taylor 918 724-3121
22005 State Highway 99 Pawhuska (74056) ***(G-7687)***
James B Read Operating Inc 580 226-0055
5 A St Sw Ste 300 Ardmore (73401) ***(G-311)***
James Bethell 918 677-2328
48521 Us Highway 271 Wister (74966) ***(G-11549)***
James Case 918 846-2884
3248 Fairfax Lake Rd Fairfax (74637) ***(G-3119)***
James D Johnson 580 464-3299
Highway 8 Cyril (73029) ***(G-1975)***
James D Pate Jr 405 942-3647
3625 Goodger Dr Ste D Oklahoma City (73112) ***(G-6347)***
James H Milligan Enterprises 405 525-8331
5400 N Grand Blvd Ste 545 Oklahoma City (73112) ***(G-6348)***
James Jeremy Burcham 580 420-3243
247 Ogden Rd Broken Bow (74728) ***(G-1193)***
James K Anderson Inc (PA) 405 329-7414
903 Chautauqua Ave Norman (73069) ***(G-5041)***
James Land Residual Assets LLC 405 842-2828
11316 Cedar Hollow Rd Oklahoma City (73162) ***(G-6349)***
James Matthews Ford LLC 918 251-3673
1101 Sw Expressway Dr Broken Arrow (74012) ***(G-942)***
James P Compton 918 682-3700
4159 S 65th St E Muskogee (74403) ***(G-4697)***
James Porter Shorty 580 326-0592
2321 E 2000 Rd Hugo (74743) ***(G-3615)***
James R Biddick 918 587-1551
427 S Boston Ave Ste 1036 Tulsa (74103) ***(G-10026)***
James Roy Hopson 580 835-2288
555 Skipjack Rd Eagletown (74734) ***(G-2276)***
James S Jim Vanway 580 223-8962
303 C St Sw Ardmore (73401) ***(G-312)***
Jamessed Inc 918 272-6775
14411 E 56th St N Owasso (74055) ***(G-7578)***
Jamey H Voorhees 479 599-9921
724 S Jefferson St Apt 4 Stillwater (74074) ***(G-8706)***
Jan Farha 405 848-1388
400 Poplar Ave Yukon (73099) ***(G-11735)***
Jan Farha Interiors, Yukon *Also called Jan Farha* ***(G-11735)***
Jan L Jobe 918 683-0404
107 S Edmond Pl Muskogee (74403) ***(G-4698)***
Jandj Machine Shop LLC 918 827-6892
7660 Adams Rd Mounds (74047) ***(G-4619)***
Janes Machine Shop LLC 580 237-4434
421 S Grand St Enid (73701) ***(G-2980)***
Janet D Redd 580 243-0595
202 Ramsey Dr Elk City (73644) ***(G-2830)***
Janeway Machine Inc 918 224-0694
6228 S 161st West Ave Sapulpa (74066) ***(G-8282)***
Janice Sue Daniel (PA) 580 237-2695
2424 N Madison St Enid (73701) ***(G-2981)***
Janice Sue Daniel 580 233-8666
606 W Willow Rd Enid (73701) ***(G-2982)***
Janimals 918 587-4799
7803 S 28th West Ave Tulsa (74132) ***(G-10027)***
Janke Products LLC 405 677-3600
1600 Se 37th St Oklahoma City (73129) ***(G-6350)***
Janning Welding and Supply LLC 580 225-6554
918 N Van Buren Ave Elk City (73644) ***(G-2831)***
Jans Digitizing & EMB LLC 970 587-2834
15023 Scottsdale Ln Choctaw (73020) ***(G-1547)***
Jansens Software 405 692-4756
1112 Sw 132nd St Oklahoma City (73170) ***(G-5297)***
Jantz Supply Inc 580 369-5503
309 W Main St Davis (73030) ***(G-1986)***
Japa Corp 918 893-6763
1304 W Phoenix St Broken Arrow (74011) ***(G-943)***
Jarrt Holdings Inc 918 664-0931
6112 E 32nd Pl Tulsa (74135) ***(G-10028)***
Jarvis Inc 918 437-1100
8321 E 61st St Ste 201 Tulsa (74133) ***(G-10029)***
Jasars Enterprises Inc 405 808-6460
7416 Ne 133rd St Edmond (73013) ***(G-2468)***
Jason A Bliss 580 304-9432
737 S Cosden Ave Shidler (74652) ***(G-8528)***
Jason and Ricky LLC 580 749-4895
1415 W Summit Ave Ponca City (74601) ***(G-7839)***
Jason M Haag 918 369-1805
8230 E 111th Pl S Ste C Bixby (74008) ***(G-638)***
Jatco Inc 405 755-4100
244 Nw 111th St Oklahoma City (73114) ***(G-6351)***
Jatco Environmental Equipment, Oklahoma City *Also called Jatco Inc* ***(G-6351)***
Jath Oil Co (PA) 580 252-5580
1202 N 10th St Duncan (73533) ***(G-2133)***
Java Daves Executive Cof Svc, Tulsa *Also called Tulsa Coffee Service Inc* ***(G-10993)***
Jay Hickman Welding Inc 405 205-7136
2002 Polly Pl Guthrie (73044) ***(G-3319)***
Jay Industries LLC 405 404-3242
9429 Se 29th St Trlr 133 Midwest City (73130) ***(G-4444)***
Jay Rambo Co Hahn Showroom 918 615-3370
6710 S 105th East Ave Tulsa (74133) ***(G-10030)***
Jays Jewelry 405 224-9021
327 W Chickasha Ave Ste 1 Chickasha (73018) ***(G-1475)***
JB Books Unlimited LLC 918 954-8308
4823 S Sheridan Rd 305a Tulsa (74145) ***(G-10031)***
JB Fabrication 580 716-7524
709 Morgan Sq Kaw City (74641) ***(G-3758)***
JB Machining Inc 918 425-3337
6227 N Peoria Ave Tulsa (74126) ***(G-10032)***
JB Metal Fabrication 918 266-3228
9878 E 570 Rd Catoosa (74015) ***(G-1324)***
JB Oil Field Services 580 363-3030
421 N 20th St Blackwell (74631) ***(G-684)***
Jbk Well Service LLC 918 695-6062
8689 State Highway 11 Barnsdall (74002) ***(G-437)***
Jbr Software Development LLC 405 872-8561
17550 Tall Oak Rd Choctaw (73020) ***(G-1548)***
Jbs Graphic Repair 918 272-3522
7918 N 120th East Ave Owasso (74055) ***(G-7579)***

Jbw Ventures LLC 580 795-5577
200 County Rd Madill (73446) *(G-4152)*
JC Fab LLC 580 920-0878
1325 Highway 78 S Durant (74701) *(G-2240)*
JC Hot Shot Services Inc 918 782-7922
13827 S Elm St Glenpool (74033) *(G-3236)*
JC Sheet Metal Fabrication, Oklahoma City *Also called J C Sheet Metal Fabrication* *(G-6335)*
Jcl & Jfl Oil & Gas 405 360-1620
1005 N Flood Ave Norman (73069) *(G-5042)*
Jcr Exploration Inc 918 682-8200
124 S 4th St Ste A Muskogee (74401) *(G-4699)*
JD Supply & Mfg 405 517-3745
5974 Tracy Ln Piedmont (73078) *(G-7765)*
Jdw Hotshot Services 918 407-8787
5206 S Harvard Ave # 308 Tulsa (74135) *(G-10033)*
Jean Jacques Perodeau Gunmaker 580 237-7388
Woodring Airport 66th St Enid (73701) *(G-2983)*
Jec Operating, Oklahoma City *Also called Johnson Exploration Company* *(G-6375)*
Jec Operating LLC 405 235-4454
921 E Britton Rd Oklahoma City (73114) *(G-6352)*
Jec Production LLC 405 235-4454
921 W Britton Rd Oklahoma City (73114) *(G-6353)*
Jed Welding and Fabrication 405 420-9062
4300 Banner Rd Noble (73068) *(G-4883)*
Jedd Industries 580 339-1500
5905 S Methodist Rd Hinton (73047) *(G-3530)*
Jeff Mc Kenzie & Co Inc 405 236-5848
630 W Sheridan Ave Oklahoma City (73102) *(G-6354)*
Jeff Parson Welding 405 483-5770
28334 N 2860 Rd Okarche (73762) *(G-5244)*
Jeffery Mariott 580 320-5474
27800 County Road 3500 Roff (74865) *(G-8109)*
Jeffery W Matlock 918 367-9828
35000 W Highway 66 Bristow (74010) *(G-782)*
Jeffrey C James 405 728-8145
6804 Newman Dr Oklahoma City (73162) *(G-6355)*
Jeffries Pumping Service Inc 580 628-2769
525 Broadway Guthrie (73044) *(G-3320)*
Jeffs Optacle 580 223-5999
2617 N Commerce St Ste C Ardmore (73401) *(G-313)*
Jelke Signs 580 252-2523
1112 N 5th St Duncan (73533) *(G-2134)*
Jemison Denna 405 922-7830
2624 W Park Pl Oklahoma City (73107) *(G-6356)*
Jenco Fabricators Inc 918 234-3364
1850 N 170th East Ave Tulsa (74116) *(G-10034)*
Jenkins Quary 580 588-3020
616 W Evans Ave Apache (73006) *(G-219)*
Jennings Stone Company Inc 580 777-2880
17330 County Road 1670 Fittstown (74842) *(G-3159)*
Jensen Mixers Intl Inc 918 627-5770
5354 S Garnett Rd Tulsa (74146) *(G-10035)*
Jer-Co Industries, Locust Grove *Also called Ftdm Investments Llc* *(G-4107)*
Jeremy Hart Music Inc 918 687-3605
1213 S 64th St W Muskogee (74401) *(G-4700)*
Jeremys Rustabouts Backhoe Inc 580 772-5157
23986 E 1013 Rd Weatherford (73096) *(G-11421)*
Jericho Oil (oklahoma) Corp 215 383-2433
321 S Boston Ave Ste 300 Tulsa (74103) *(G-10036)*
Jero Manufacturing Inc 918 628-0230
5117 S 100th East Ave Tulsa (74146) *(G-10037)*
Jeroco Inc 405 222-1179
2908 Lacey Dr Chickasha (73018) *(G-1476)*
Jerry Beagley Braiding Company 580 924-4995
3569 Caney Creek Rd Calera (74730) *(G-1240)*
Jerry Bendorf Trustee 405 840-9900
3300 S High Ave Oklahoma City (73129) *(G-6357)*
Jerry D Pierce 580 252-5354
Rr 4 Duncan (73533) *(G-2135)*
Jerry Dunkin Well Services 580 237-6152
1913 N 10th St Enid (73701) *(G-2984)*
Jerry Ellis 580 223-5649
275 Woodstock Ln Ardmore (73401) *(G-314)*
Jerry Sanner Oil Properties 580 233-2442
1202 W Willow Rd Ste B Enid (73703) *(G-2985)*
Jerry Scott Drilling Co Inc 405 382-2202
Hwy 99 N Seminole (74868) *(G-8379)*
Jerry Swanson Sales Co Inc 918 712-7446
3229 S Harvard Ave Tulsa (74135) *(G-10038)*
Jerry Woods Portable Welding 918 272-6424
209 E 4th Ave Owasso (74055) *(G-7580)*
Jerrys Dock Construction Inc 918 256-3390
321 Hwy 85 A Bernice (74331) *(G-567)*
Jesco Products Inc 405 943-1721
304 N Meridian Ave Ste B Oklahoma City (73107) *(G-6358)*
Jess Harris Inc 405 840-3271
2601 Nw Expwy Ste 200e Oklahoma City (73112) *(G-6359)*
Jesse Griffith Repairs 580 379-0790
101 E 20th St Elk City (73644) *(G-2832)*
Jesse Harbin 918 734-3980
9346 S 94th East Ave Tulsa (74133) *(G-10039)*
Jessie Shaw 918 587-6329
1041 N Madison Ave Tulsa (74106) *(G-10040)*
Jester Industries Inc 405 919-2013
11212 Sturbridge Rd Oklahoma City (73162) *(G-6360)*
Jet Black Aircraft 405 310-6556
2206 Research Park Blvd Norman (73069) *(G-5043)*
Jet Printing Co Inc 405 732-1262
7017 Se 15th St Oklahoma City (73110) *(G-6361)*
Jet Set Screen Printing I 918 294-1053
2107 W Greeley St Broken Arrow (74012) *(G-944)*
Jet Tech Interiors Inc 580 310-2610
10729 County Road 3600 Ada (74820) *(G-53)*
Jet Vistor, Fairview *Also called Larry D Hammer* *(G-3140)*
Jett Oil and Gas LLC 918 995-7430
10319 S 67th East Ave Tulsa (74133) *(G-10041)*
Jetta Corporation 918 574-2151
9515 E 51st St Ste E Tulsa (74145) *(G-10042)*
Jetta Corporation (PA) 405 340-6661
425 Centennial Blvd Edmond (73013) *(G-2469)*
Jetta of Tulsa, Tulsa *Also called Jetta Corporation* *(G-10042)*
Jetta Production Company Inc 918 299-0107
10949 S Urbana Ave Tulsa (74137) *(G-10043)*
Jewel Tech Mfg Inc 918 828-9700
8223 S Marion Ave Tulsa (74137) *(G-10044)*
Jewelers Bench 405 495-1800
4716 N Macarthur Blvd Warr Acres (73122) *(G-11324)*
Jewell Jordan Publishing LLC (PA) 405 496-2672
3212 Ne Overbrook Dr Oklahoma City (73121) *(G-6362)*
Jewels By James Inc 918 745-2004
3329 E 31st St Tulsa (74135) *(G-10045)*
Jewels By James.com, Tulsa *Also called Jewels By James Inc* *(G-10045)*
Jfj Industries Inc 918 342-2453
2301 El Anderson Blvd Claremore (74017) *(G-1643)*
JG Welding LLC 405 301-3126
505 Mark St Tecumseh (74873) *(G-8920)*
JH Newton LLC 918 636-0423
29343 S 4130 Rd Catoosa (74015) *(G-1325)*
Jiggs Smokehouse 580 323-5641
10635 N 2230 Rd Clinton (73601) *(G-1754)*
Jim Campbell & Associates Rlty 405 372-9225
1776 W Lakeview Rd Stillwater (74075) *(G-8707)*
Jim Did It Signs 580 255-5533
802 S 1st St Duncan (73533) *(G-2136)*
Jim Dunn 918 456-3552
119 N Muskogee Ave Tahlequah (74464) *(G-8868)*
Jim Ford Sign Co 580 223-8880
672 Dove Ln Ardmore (73401) *(G-315)*
Jim Giles Safe Rooms 918 639-8102
2214 Industrial Rd Sapulpa (74066) *(G-8283)*
Jim Griffith Custom Jeweler 918 342-0151
3207 Club St Claremore (74019) *(G-1644)*
Jim Haynes 918 733-2517
4280 N 320 Rd Haskell (74436) *(G-3399)*
Jim Haynes Oil Company, Haskell *Also called Jim Haynes* *(G-3399)*
Jim Norton Ford, Broken Arrow *Also called James Matthews Ford LLC* *(G-942)*
Jim Roth 405 235-4100
101 N Robinson Ave Oklahoma City (73102) *(G-6363)*
Jim Watkins 918 367-5575
109 S Main St Bristow (74010) *(G-783)*
Jim Wood Refrigeration Inc 918 426-3283
200 E Wyandotte Ave McAlester (74501) *(G-4309)*
Jim's Jewerly Design, Perry *Also called Jims Jewelry Design* *(G-7738)*
Jim's Used Oilfield Equipment, Bartlesville *Also called Fox Northeastern Oil Gas Corp* *(G-484)*
Jimco Sign Company, Muskogee *Also called James P Compton* *(G-4697)*
Jimmy Fuchs 580 225-7784
1019 S Main St Elk City (73644) *(G-2833)*
Jims Backhoe LLC 405 352-5003
871 County Road 1170 Minco (73059) *(G-4476)*
Jims Jewelry Design 580 336-4066
320 N 1st St Perry (73077) *(G-7738)*
Jims Truck Center 918 225-1013
601 N Steele Ave Cushing (74023) *(G-1939)*
Jims Welding Service 405 853-4522
S 81 Hwy Hennessey (73742) *(G-3469)*
Jireh Software Inc 918 294-8240
3901 W South Park Blvd Broken Arrow (74011) *(G-945)*
JJ Perodeau Gunmaker Inc 580 747-1804
711 S 263rd West Ave Sand Springs (74063) *(G-8195)*
Jjs Security Cameras Inc 405 408-6096
3717 Se 45th St Oklahoma City (73135) *(G-6364)*
Jk Industries Inc 405 285-9800
6250 Industrial Blvd Edmond (73034) *(G-2470)*
JKJ Processing Inc 405 606-9711
12204 W Reno Ave Ste B Yukon (73099) *(G-11736)*
Jlm2 LLC 918 258-0239
816 W Elgin St Broken Arrow (74012) *(G-946)*

ALPHABETIC

JM Defense & Arospc Svcs LLC 918 298-2766
2405 W 108th St S Jenks (74037) ***(G-3710)***
JM Eagle Co 405 273-0900
7901 N Kickapoo Ave Shawnee (74804) ***(G-8464)***
JM Huber, Okmulgee *Also called CP Kelco US Inc* ***(G-7498)***
JM Huber Corporation 580 584-7002
1070 W State Highway 3 Broken Bow (74728) ***(G-1194)***
JM Manufacturing 918 261-2816
1712 E Edgewater St Broken Arrow (74012) ***(G-947)***
JM Oilfield Services Inc 501 589-4044
1502 Oakhill Cir Enid (73703) ***(G-2986)***
JM Publications LLC 405 639-9472
11305 N Markwell Dr Oklahoma City (73162) ***(G-6365)***
JM Publishing LLC 405 684-0450
101 W 5th St Edmond (73003) ***(G-2471)***
Jma Energy Company LLC 405 418-2853
1021 Nw Grand Blvd Oklahoma City (73118) ***(G-6366)***
Jmd Properties 405 848-5722
1201 W Britton Rd Oklahoma City (73114) ***(G-6367)***
Jmi, Collinsville *Also called Johnson Machine Inc* ***(G-1814)***
JMJ Petroleum Inc 918 209-5913
2914 W 117th St S Jenks (74037) ***(G-3711)***
Jmz Software LLC 580 284-9551
6926 Sw Forest Ave Lawton (73505) ***(G-3945)***
Jnl Equipment 918 286-1951
1721 N 10th St Broken Arrow (74012) ***(G-948)***
Jo Rose Fine Cabinets Inc 918 832-1500
1810 N 75th East Ave Tulsa (74115) ***(G-10046)***
Jo Sco Environmental 405 340-5499
3027 Willowood Rd Ste 110 Edmond (73034) ***(G-2472)***
Joa Inc 580 367-2616
605 Buffalo St Caddo (74729) ***(G-1236)***
Joanie's Upholstery, Lawton *Also called L & L Machine Shop* ***(G-3952)***
Joans Print Shop Inc 918 624-5858
5505 S Mingo Rd Ste A Tulsa (74146) ***(G-10047)***
Job Paper LLC 405 242-4804
113 W Olympic Dr Yukon (73099) ***(G-11737)***
Jobri LLC 580 925-3500
305 Lake Dr Ada (74820) ***(G-54)***
Joco Assembly LLC 918 622-5111
1575 N 93rd East Ave Tulsa (74115) ***(G-10048)***
Joe Brent Lansden 580 625-3241
108 Douglas Ave Beaver (73932) ***(G-541)***
Joe Decker Signs 405 630-8691
3216 Dove Hollow Ln Norman (73072) ***(G-5044)***
Joe Martin 918 850-2776
27108 E 82nd St S Broken Arrow (74014) ***(G-1136)***
Joe's Hand Cleaner, Oklahoma City *Also called Kleen Products Inc* ***(G-6428)***
Joel Bumpus 580 237-5305
4520 N 4th St Enid (73701) ***(G-2987)***
John A Littleaxe 405 365-5117
29223 Sunshine Dr Tecumseh (74873) ***(G-8921)***
John C Parks II Energy LLC 918 885-6197
1616 County Road 5245 Hominy (74035) ***(G-3590)***
John Clark 918 853-8286
4215 E 106th St N Sperry (74073) ***(G-8608)***
John Crane Inc 918 664-5156
2931 E Apache St Tulsa (74110) ***(G-10049)***
John Crane Lemco, Tulsa *Also called John Crane Inc* ***(G-10049)***
John Crane Lemco Inc 918 835-7325
2931 E Apache St Tulsa (74110) ***(G-10050)***
John E Rougeot Oil & Gas 918 494-9978
8187 S Harvard Ave Tulsa (74137) ***(G-10051)***
John H Booth Inc 918 481-0383
1787 E 71st St Tulsa (74136) ***(G-10052)***
John Henley Cstm Cabinets LLC 405 535-9143
13909 N Everest Ave Edmond (73013) ***(G-2473)***
John Kennedy Welding LLC 580 227-2300
56526 S County Road 256 Fairview (73737) ***(G-3138)***
John L Lewis 405 941-3224
Half Mile E Of Hwy 56 Sasakwa (74867) ***(G-8330)***
John Lankford 918 855-4417
11505 E 112th Pl N Owasso (74055) ***(G-7581)***
John M Beard 405 751-2727
12316 Saint Andrews Dr A Oklahoma City (73120) ***(G-6368)***
John Patrick Raymond 580 481-0869
21 Constitution Ave Altus (73521) ***(G-159)***
John R Little Jr 405 751-5227
2601 Kings Way Oklahoma City (73120) ***(G-6369)***
John R Warren 405 843-9402
50 Penn Pl 410 Oklahoma City (73118) ***(G-6370)***
John R Warren Revocable Trust, Oklahoma City *Also called John R Warren* ***(G-6370)***
John Samut-Tagliaferro 580 284-6058
15801 Ne North Dr Fletcher (73541) ***(G-3163)***
John Scoggins Company Inc 918 775-2748
Hwy 64 E Sallisaw (74955) ***(G-8146)***
John Thompson Enterprises Inc (PA) 580 623-5820
W Highway 33 Watonga (73772) ***(G-11348)***
John W Stone Oil Distributing 918 744-8168
2825 E Skelly Dr Tulsa (74105) ***(G-10053)***
John Ward Welding 580 673-2127
4065 Inwood Rd Healdton (73438) ***(G-3417)***
John Zink Co LLC 918 749-9345
3914 E 51st Pl Tulsa (74135) ***(G-10054)***
John Zink Company LLC (HQ) 918 234-1800
11920 E Apache St Tulsa (74116) ***(G-10055)***
John Zink Hamworthy Combustion, Tulsa *Also called John Zink Company LLC* ***(G-10055)***
Johndrow Home Improvement 580 762-4000
710 S 1st St Ponca City (74601) ***(G-7840)***
Johndrow Termite & Pest Ctrl, Ponca City *Also called Johndrow Home Improvement* ***(G-7840)***
Johnnie & Lonnie Smith 580 933-4323
1970 Rufe Rd Valliant (74764) ***(G-11229)***
Johnny Apple Seed Store 918 304-2055
320 S Wood Dr Okmulgee (74447) ***(G-7510)***
Johnny Beard Co 918 438-4901
14308 E 11th St Tulsa (74108) ***(G-10056)***
Johnny Blaylock 918 639-5951
12106 E 131st St S Broken Arrow (74011) ***(G-949)***
Johnny L Ruth (PA) 580 223-3061
11 W Main St Ardmore (73401) ***(G-316)***
Johnny L Windsor 405 691-3083
2624 Sw 102nd St Oklahoma City (73159) ***(G-6371)***
Johns Manville Corporation 405 552-4115
812 N Bryant Ave Oklahoma City (73117) ***(G-6372)***
Johns Professional Sharpening 405 313-7027
316 Partridge Run Rd Yukon (73099) ***(G-11738)***
Johnson Bvlle Fine Jwlers Pawn 405 751-1216
9344 N May Ave Oklahoma City (73120) ***(G-6373)***
Johnson Controls, Oklahoma City *Also called Clarios* ***(G-5773)***
Johnson Controls, Tulsa *Also called Clarios* ***(G-9439)***
Johnson Controls 918 626-3773
1507b Highway 112 N Pocola (74902) ***(G-7783)***
Johnson Crating Services LLC 405 672-7964
5354 S I 35 Oklahoma City (73143) ***(G-6374)***
Johnson Exploration Company 405 235-4454
921 E Britton Rd Oklahoma City (73114) ***(G-6375)***
Johnson Kendall Cnstr Co 580 223-5954
1410 Kings Rd Ardmore (73401) ***(G-317)***
Johnson Lumber Company Inc 918 253-8786
3174 State Highway 20 Spavinaw (74366) ***(G-8591)***
Johnson Machine Inc 918 371-7537
226 S 2nd St Collinsville (74021) ***(G-1814)***
Johnson Marcum Oil and Gas LLC 918 949-8901
1320 N Mill St Ste 128 Muskogee (74401) ***(G-4701)***
Johnson Minford 580 772-0430
128 Jackson Ave Weatherford (73096) ***(G-11422)***
Johnson Otey Properties Inc 580 226-8425
5 A St Sw Ardmore (73401) ***(G-318)***
Johnson Plastics Plus - Okla 800 654-4150
6100 Nw 2nd St Ste 1600 Oklahoma City (73127) ***(G-6376)***
Johnson Service Company 918 869-7147
8199 W 800 Rd Fort Gibson (74434) ***(G-3175)***
Johnson Signs Inc 580 323-6454
10057 N 2250 Rd Arapaho (73620) ***(G-224)***
Johnson Welding 580 569-2231
114 Spruce St Mountain Park (73559) ***(G-4626)***
Johnson Well Logging Inc 405 721-5989
6112 N State St Oklahoma City (73122) ***(G-6377)***
Johnson Wldg & Fabrication LLC 405 474-3541
206 Sw 3rd St Tuttle (73089) ***(G-11205)***
Johnson Woodcraft 918 693-2388
16210 S 4110 Rd Claremore (74017) ***(G-1645)***
Johnsonm3 LLC 580 353-5550
6732 Nw Eisenhower Dr Lawton (73505) ***(G-3946)***
Johnsons Spring Crest Drpery C 405 238-7341
301 W Paul Ave Pauls Valley (73075) ***(G-7662)***
Johnsonwoodworks 918 407-7747
8525 E 41st St 1017 Tulsa (74145) ***(G-10057)***
Johnston Test Cell Group LLC 405 604-2804
1300 Se Grand Blvd Oklahoma City (73129) ***(G-6378)***
Jolen Operating Company (PA) 405 235-8444
100 N Broadway Ave # 2460 Oklahoma City (73102) ***(G-6379)***
Jolen Production Company (PA) 405 235-8444
100 N Broadway Ave # 2460 Oklahoma City (73102) ***(G-6380)***
Jolliff Coffee Company, Wilson *Also called Minnette Company Ltd* ***(G-11538)***
Jomaga House 918 455-0794
4520 S Redbud Ave Broken Arrow (74011) ***(G-950)***
Jon A Belonoik 405 258-4131
213 E 1st St Chandler (74834) ***(G-1382)***
Jon's Cabinet Shop, Chandler *Also called Jon A Belonoik* ***(G-1382)***
Jones & Jackson Cabinets 580 889-8978
551 N Texhoma Ave Atoka (74525) ***(G-416)***
Jones Energy Inc 405 832-5100
8308 N May Ave Ste 100 Oklahoma City (73120) ***(G-6381)***
Jones Energy Inc (PA) 512 328-2953
14301 Caliber Dr Ste 110 Oklahoma City (73134) ***(G-6382)***
Jones Energy Finance Corp 512 328-2953
14301 Caliber Dr Ste 110 Oklahoma City (73134) ***(G-6383)***

Jones Energy Holdings LLC (HQ)....512 328-2953
14301 Caliber Dr Ste 110 Oklahoma City (73134) ***(G-6384)***
Jones Energy Limited, Oklahoma City *Also called Jones Energy Holdings LLC* ***(G-6384)***
Jones Jerseys and Tees LLC....405 264-6151
104524 S 3520 Rd Prague (74864) ***(G-7928)***
Jones Machine Shop....580 255-5784
1501 Shadybrook Ln Duncan (73533) ***(G-2137)***
Jones Monuments Co....580 255-2276
701 W Willow Ave Duncan (73533) ***(G-2138)***
Jones Oil Co LLC....580 255-9400
16 S 9th St Rm 302 Duncan (73533) ***(G-2139)***
Jones Oil Co The, Duncan *Also called Jones Oil Co LLC* ***(G-2139)***
Jones Power Products LLC....405 485-2019
3415 Hunters Ridge Ln Blanchard (73010) ***(G-718)***
Jones Spclty Wldg Fbrction LLC....918 486-7740
12066 S 257th East Ave Coweta (74429) ***(G-1889)***
Jones, D C Machine Co, Grove *Also called D C Jones Machine Co* ***(G-3265)***
Jones-Kalkman Mineral Co....580 223-3101
425 1st Ave Sw Ardmore (73401) ***(G-319)***
Jorame Inc....918 582-5663
1605 N 168th East Ave Tulsa (74116) ***(G-10058)***
Jordan Services Inc....405 748-3997
3129 Brookhollow Rd Oklahoma City (73120) ***(G-6385)***
Jordan Welding & Fabrication....918 346-7243
14325 S 4170 Rd Claremore (74017) ***(G-1646)***
Jos Lamerton Woodworking LLC....580 336-8448
2020 Willow Run Enid (73703) ***(G-2988)***
Josefy, Jerry, Grandfield *Also called Bulldog Jerky Co* ***(G-3256)***
Josh Leeper....918 618-2215
121316 S 4083 Rd Eufaula (74432) ***(G-3103)***
Joshi Technologies Intl Inc (PA)....918 665-6419
5801 E 41st St Ste 603 Tulsa (74135) ***(G-10059)***
Joshua Coal Company....918 652-3023
205 Perryman Rd Henryetta (74437) ***(G-3511)***
Joshua James Lennox....580 739-1050
710 E 7th St Elk City (73644) ***(G-2834)***
Joshua Oil & Gas LLC....620 672-5505
14646 Sw Bishop Rd Cache (73527) ***(G-1227)***
Joshua Promotions....405 590-8894
2335 Janene St Harrah (73045) ***(G-3379)***
Jostens Inc....918 274-7047
7762 N Owasso Expy B Owasso (74055) ***(G-7582)***
Joullian Vineyards Ltd (PA)....405 848-4585
5653 N Pennsylvania Ave Oklahoma City (73112) ***(G-6386)***
Journal Record....405 524-7777
2300 N Lincoln Blvd Oklahoma City (73105) ***(G-6387)***
Journal Record Publishing Co....405 278-2848
101 N Robinson Ave # 101 Oklahoma City (73102) ***(G-6388)***
Joyeaux Inc....918 252-7660
9802 E 58th St Tulsa (74146) ***(G-10060)***
Joys Uniforms Boutique Ltd (PA)....918 747-4114
1518 S Harvard Ave Tulsa (74112) ***(G-10061)***
JP Welding....405 714-0232
22801 Independence Morrison (73061) ***(G-4604)***
JP Welding Fabrication....580 724-9104
22851 County Road 230 Morrison (73061) ***(G-4605)***
Jpm Precision Machine Inc....918 739-4777
19715 E 6th St Tulsa (74108) ***(G-10062)***
Jps Creations....580 892-3455
414 4th St Allen (74825) ***(G-135)***
JPS LLC....405 535-5136
8401 Timberwood Ln Oklahoma City (73135) ***(G-6389)***
Jr Alpacas LLC....405 771-2636
13301 N Douglas Blvd Jones (73049) ***(G-3749)***
Jr Custom Welding & Repair, Altus *Also called John Patrick Raymond* ***(G-159)***
Jr Sand & Gravel Inc....405 474-8730
2825 Charleston Rd Edmond (73025) ***(G-2474)***
Js Metal Fabrication LLC....918 428-2242
4686 N Boston Pl Tulsa (74126) ***(G-10063)***
JS Oilfield Services LLC....580 542-7822
807 W Cherokee Ave Enid (73701) ***(G-2989)***
Jti, Tulsa *Also called Joshi Technologies Intl Inc* ***(G-10059)***
Jts Woodworks LLC....918 640-1791
700 W Fredericksburg St Broken Arrow (74011) ***(G-951)***
Ju Ju Jams....918 230-6650
2440 E 29th St Tulsa (74114) ***(G-10064)***
Juan Manzo Custom Refinishing....405 848-3843
9215 N Western Ave Oklahoma City (73114) ***(G-6390)***
Juda Enterprises LLC....405 542-3975
1106 N Broadway Hinton (73047) ***(G-3531)***
Judies Custom Creations, Woodward *Also called Judy Airson* ***(G-11597)***
Judy Airson....580 254-9076
2727 Oklahoma Ave Woodward (73801) ***(G-11597)***
Judy Tomlinson....580 252-2559
755 Oakridge Dr Duncan (73533) ***(G-2140)***
Juice Blendz Cafe....405 285-0133
1200 W Covell Rd Ste 132 Edmond (73003) ***(G-2475)***
July Gas Ltd Liability Co....918 367-2831
27301 W 201st St S Bristow (74010) ***(G-784)***
Jumping Bone LLC....918 853-2836
2825 S 124th East Ave Tulsa (74129) ***(G-10065)***
Juniper Networks Inc....918 877-2642
1831 E 71st St Tulsa (74136) ***(G-10066)***
Juniper Ridge Inc....405 762-2555
3805 W Rutledge Dr Stillwater (74075) ***(G-8708)***
Junk N Leslies Trunk LLC....405 748-6702
3429 Partridge Rd Oklahoma City (73120) ***(G-6391)***
Juno Companies Incorporated....918 627-8868
8702 E 41st St Tulsa (74145) ***(G-10067)***
Jupiter Sulphur LLC....580 762-1130
200 Jupiter Pkwy Ponca City (74601) ***(G-7841)***
Just Bee Candles and More LLC....918 557-5145
8495 N 4270 Rd Chelsea (74016) ***(G-1406)***
Just Breathe Publishing LLC....405 633-0160
9801 Ne 30th St Spencer (73084) ***(G-8597)***
Just Dough It LLC....918 455-0770
11375 E 61st St Broken Arrow (74012) ***(G-952)***
Just Plant It Grnhse & Nurs, Macomb *Also called Just Plant It LLC* ***(G-4142)***
Just Plant It LLC....405 226-3111
20301 Palomino Way Macomb (74852) ***(G-4142)***
Just Two Publishing Inc....405 607-2902
14013 N Eastern Ave Edmond (73013) ***(G-2476)***
Just-In-Time Signs LLC....580 821-1140
18767 E 1210 Rd Sayre (73662) ***(G-8342)***
Justice....405 842-7180
1901 Nw Expwy St Ste 2086 Oklahoma City (73118) ***(G-6392)***
Justus Fabrication....918 207-5192
1841 W Choctaw St Tahlequah (74464) ***(G-8869)***
JV Energy Services Inc....620 482-0244
240 Quail Cir Turpin (73950) ***(G-11182)***
JV Industrial Companies Ltd....918 591-5450
2642 E 21st St Ste 170 Tulsa (74114) ***(G-10068)***
Jvh Marketing, Yukon *Also called Van Horn James* ***(G-11800)***
JW Measurement Co....918 465-5605
1210 W Main St Wilburton (74578) ***(G-11521)***
JW Nutritional LLC....214 221-0404
1607 S Main St Broken Arrow (74012) ***(G-953)***
K & B Machining Inc....918 343-2620
24055 Amah Pkwy Claremore (74019) ***(G-1647)***
K & C Manufacturing Inc....580 362-2979
1025 N Waverly St Ponca City (74601) ***(G-7842)***
K & D Manufacturing....918 923-6422
816 W 1st St Claremore (74017) ***(G-1648)***
K & H Well Service Inc....405 382-2762
1901 N Harvey Rd Seminole (74868) ***(G-8380)***
K & J Welding LLC....580 541-2200
1418 Beverly Dr Enid (73703) ***(G-2990)***
K & K Manufacturing Inc....918 247-2871
19155 W 141st St S Kellyville (74039) ***(G-3766)***
K & K Wood Products....918 396-4004
17000 N Cincinnati Ave Skiatook (74070) ***(G-8553)***
K & M Outfitters, Claremore *Also called Hejin Waldran* ***(G-1632)***
K & S Aluminum Booms....580 761-3238
9825 S 44th St Tonkawa (74653) ***(G-8976)***
K & S Controls LLC....918 363-7268
4408 S 209th West Ave Sand Springs (74063) ***(G-8196)***
K & S Hotshot Services LLC....918 899-2649
998 W Oak Grove Rd Cleveland (74020) ***(G-1726)***
K & S Pumping Unit Repair Inc....580 237-7343
722 Morningside Pl Enid (73701) ***(G-2991)***
K & W Well Service Inc....918 225-7855
Hwy 33 E 3 Miles Cushing (74023) ***(G-1940)***
K A G U Inc....405 364-4637
3517 National Dr Norman (73069) ***(G-5045)***
K and E Fabrication....405 635-8552
6401 Se 74th St Oklahoma City (73135) ***(G-6393)***
K and G Investments Inc....401 396-9280
8924 Morningside Rd Guthrie (73044) ***(G-3321)***
K and G Sand & Gravel LLC....580 369-2244
5140 Sunshine Rd Davis (73030) ***(G-1987)***
K B Machine & Welding Inc....405 375-5888
Un Known Kingfisher (73750) ***(G-3803)***
K C Welding & Machine Corp....918 336-4560
428 W 8th St Bartlesville (74003) ***(G-500)***
K D Typesetting....405 302-0799
14024 Choctaw Dr Edmond (73013) ***(G-2477)***
K E Fischer LLC....580 353-2862
2512 Sw 38th St Lawton (73505) ***(G-3947)***
K G Hill Company LLC....405 641-4190
1857 Danfield Dr Norman (73072) ***(G-5046)***
K G Machine....918 789-2228
21571 E 340 Rd Chelsea (74016) ***(G-1407)***
K Oil Company....405 382-0891
S Of City Seminole (74868) ***(G-8381)***
K S Oil Company Inc....405 634-5115
3100 S Berry Rd Ste 210 Norman (73072) ***(G-5047)***
K V I, Rose *Also called Kern Valley Industries* ***(G-8118)***
K W B Inc (PA)....918 583-8300
20 E 5th St Ste 1100 Tulsa (74103) ***(G-10069)***

A L P H A B E T I C

K W B Oil Property Management (HQ)....918 583-8300
20 E 5th St Ste 1100 Tulsa (74103) *(G-10070)*
K&K Hardwood, Roff *Also called Jeffery Mariott (G-8109)*
K&R Backhoe and Dirt Svcs LLC....580 239-8630
4618 E Boggy Depot Rd Atoka (74525) *(G-417)*
K-Dub LLC....580 353-6899
106 Se D Ave Lawton (73501) *(G-3948)*
K-H Machine Shop....918 273-1058
922 E Cherokee Ave Nowata (74048) *(G-5218)*
K2 Bath Salts Online....405 445-4295
2613 Nw 35th St Oklahoma City (73112) *(G-6394)*
K3 Industries LLC....205 568-1252
11617 Se 156th St Oklahoma City (73165) *(G-5298)*
K3 LLC....580 231-2040
1323 W Poplar Ave Enid (73703) *(G-2992)*
K9 Media....504 233-2576
3401 Vickie Dr Del City (73115) *(G-1998)*
Kactus Rose LLC....405 830-7551
6512 Foreman Rd E El Reno (73036) *(G-2729)*
Kahn Backhoe & Trenching....580 541-6600
263584 E County Road 57 Okeene (73763) *(G-5258)*
Kaiser Energy Ltd....918 494-0000
6733 S Yale Ave Tulsa (74136) *(G-10071)*
Kaiser Francis Gulf Coast LLC....918 491-4490
5001 E 68th St Tulsa (74136) *(G-10072)*
Kaiser Francis Oil Co, Tulsa *Also called Kaiser Energy Ltd (G-10071)*
Kaiser Investment....918 245-4719
3112 S Nassau Ave Sand Springs (74063) *(G-8197)*
Kaiser Marketing Northeast LLC....918 494-0000
6733 S Yale Ave Tulsa (74136) *(G-10073)*
Kaiser Outdoor Advertising, Weatherford *Also called Kaiser Sign & Graphics Co Inc (G-11423)*
Kaiser Sign & Graphics Co Inc....580 772-3880
820 W Main St Weatherford (73096) *(G-11423)*
Kaiser-Francis Oil Company, Tulsa *Also called Gbk Corporation (G-9809)*
Kaiser-Francis Oil Company....405 577-5347
8300 Sw 15th St Oklahoma City (73128) *(G-6395)*
Kaiser-Francis Oil Company (HQ)....918 494-0000
6733 S Yale Ave Tulsa (74136) *(G-10074)*
Kaiser-Francis Oil Company....580 668-2335
11832 Memorial Rd Wilson (73463) *(G-11537)*
Kaiser-Francis Oil Company....405 262-5511
4101 E Highway 66 El Reno (73036) *(G-2730)*
Kalamar Inc....580 242-5121
1405 E Willow Rd Enid (73701) *(G-2993)*
Kams Inc....405 232-3103
1831 Nw 4th Dr Oklahoma City (73106) *(G-6396)*
Kane/Miller Book Publishers....918 346-6118
10302 E 55th Pl Tulsa (74146) *(G-10075)*
Kanoka Ridge Services....580 302-1561
340 E Lahoma Rd Lahoma (73754) *(G-3856)*
Kansas MB Project LLC....760 212-0606
1102 N Lenapah Ave Skiatook (74070) *(G-8554)*
Kaonohi Woodworks....918 893-4661
1009 W Decatur St Broken Arrow (74011) *(G-954)*
Kar Glo Tuffy....405 631-4091
2618 S I 35 Service Rd # 106 Oklahoma City (73129) *(G-6397)*
Karacon Solutions LLC....918 231-1001
3123 E 48th St Tulsa (74105) *(G-10076)*
Karchmer Pipe & Supply Co Inc....405 236-3568
2100 Ne 4th St Oklahoma City (73117) *(G-6398)*
Karen E Hopson....580 584-7221
413 Darlene Dr Broken Bow (74728) *(G-1195)*
Karis Gifts....405 330-6428
1500 Turtlecreek Rd Edmond (73013) *(G-2478)*
Karl Amanns Trucking....580 226-2082
1520 Dogwood Rd Ardmore (73401) *(G-320)*
Karlin Company....405 542-6991
10111 Old 66 Rd Hydro (73048) *(G-3631)*
Kasm Publishing LLC....918 798-8908
5200 S Yale Ave Tulsa (74135) *(G-10077)*
Kasper, Oklahoma City *Also called Nine West Holdings Inc (G-6683)*
Kat Industries Inc....405 702-1387
5209 Sw 23rd St Oklahoma City (73128) *(G-6399)*
Kat Machine, Oklahoma City *Also called Kat Industries Inc (G-6399)*
Kat Machine Incorporated....405 702-1387
5209 Sw 23rd St Oklahoma City (73128) *(G-6400)*
Katahdin Cedar Log Homes OK....918 473-7020
109930 Highway 150 Checotah (74426) *(G-1396)*
Kathy Tim Lowery....580 925-2171
35037 Ew 1370 Konawa (74849) *(G-3847)*
Kathy's Clothing, Oklahoma City *Also called Kathys Kloset Inc (G-6401)*
Kathy's On Paseo, Oklahoma City *Also called Kathys Kloset Inc (G-6402)*
Kathys Kloset Inc....405 524-9447
1209 Nw 23rd St Oklahoma City (73106) *(G-6401)*
Kathys Kloset Inc (PA)....405 521-0055
530 Nw 27th St Oklahoma City (73103) *(G-6402)*
Kautzs Pumping Inc....580 661-3397
121 N 11th St Thomas (73669) *(G-8945)*
Kaw Nation Solutions LLC....405 365-8900
698 Grandview Dr Kaw City (74641) *(G-3759)*
Kay Electric, Altus *Also called Pak Electric Inc (G-166)*
Kay Electric Motors Inc....580 256-3254
810 48th St Woodward (73801) *(G-11598)*
Kay Holding Co....580 628-4146
100 Holiday Ln Tonkawa (74653) *(G-8977)*
Kay Production Co Inc....405 398-4254
35833 Hi Way 59 E Bowlegs (74830) *(G-759)*
Kay Production Services Inc....405 398-3109
35833 Highway 59 E Seminole (74868) *(G-8382)*
Kaydawn Manufacturing Co Inc....918 321-5017
5224 W 151st St Glenpool (74033) *(G-3237)*
Kaze LLC....580 857-2707
28561 County Road 1470 Allen (74825) *(G-136)*
KB Enterprise LLC....580 789-0119
3408 Crown St Ponca City (74604) *(G-7843)*
Kc Woodwork & Fixture Inc....918 582-5300
1131 E Easton St Tulsa (74120) *(G-10078)*
Kcc, Miami *Also called Blitz USA Inc (G-4391)*
KCR Welding Inc....405 619-0068
108 Se 24th St Oklahoma City (73129) *(G-6403)*
Kdl Print Production Svcs LLC....918 254-8150
3801 W Urbana St Broken Arrow (74012) *(G-955)*
Ke-Fab Manufacturing, Frederick *Also called Wasinger Wasinger (G-3203)*
Kechi Energy LLC....405 222-1412
3010 S 4th St Chickasha (73018) *(G-1477)*
Keck Oil & Gas LLC....918 756-6688
15485 Old Morris Hwy Okmulgee (74447) *(G-7511)*
Keco Store, Oklahoma City *Also called H C E Inc (G-6197)*
Keen Development Co, Watonga *Also called Watonga Machine & Steel Works (G-11352)*
Keenan II, Woodward *Also called Cpv Keenan Renewable Enrgy LLC (G-11573)*
Keener Oil & Gas Company....918 587-4154
1648 S Boston Ave Ste 200 Tulsa (74119) *(G-10079)*
Keepa LLC....405 235-4968
101 N Robinson Ave # 1000 Oklahoma City (73102) *(G-6404)*
Keepsake Candles Inc....918 336-0351
263 County Road 3022 Bartlesville (74003) *(G-501)*
Keifer Oil & Gas Co, Sapulpa *Also called Ira E Rongey (G-8279)*
Keith F Walker Oil Gas Co LLC (PA)....580 223-1575
219 Stanley St Sw Ardmore (73401) *(G-321)*
Keith Lyons....580 584-3360
1300 S Park Dr Broken Bow (74728) *(G-1196)*
Kel-Crete Industries Inc....918 744-0800
1257 E 29th St Tulsa (74114) *(G-10080)*
Kel-Tech Mid-Con, Clinton *Also called Danlin Industries LLC (G-1747)*
Keleher Outdoor Advertising Co....918 333-8855
523 S Virginia Ave Bartlesville (74003) *(G-502)*
Kelix Heat Transf Systems LLC....918 200-0996
4725b S Memorial Dr Tulsa (74145) *(G-10081)*
Keller Custom Cabinets & Trim, Ardmore *Also called Charles Dale Keller (G-265)*
Kelley Retha....580 317-7483
1705 N 4290 Rd Grant (74738) *(G-3258)*
Kelley Printing....405 238-4848
202 S Chickasaw St Pauls Valley (73075) *(G-7663)*
Kelley Publications LLC....405 585-7210
321 Jan Dr Stratford (74872) *(G-8805)*
Kelley Repair LLC....918 456-6514
1111 E Allen Rd Tahlequah (74464) *(G-8870)*
Kelley Shepard Welding....580 234-3280
2658 Rock Island Blvd Enid (73701) *(G-2994)*
Kelleyo, Grant *Also called Kelley Retha (G-3258)*
Kelleys Welding Service Inc....405 691-5515
11505 S Miller Ave Oklahoma City (73170) *(G-5299)*
Kelly Blake Welding Inc....405 756-0868
15453 E County Road 1554 Lindsay (73052) *(G-4070)*
Kelly L Young....918 859-1046
509 S Creek St Skiatook (74070) *(G-8555)*
Kelly Labs....682 367-8743
103 S Oak Longdale (73755) *(G-4125)*
Kelly Loyd....405 740-2345
17525 County Road 3545 Ada (74820) *(G-55)*
Kelly Monument, Muskogee *Also called Muskogee Marble & Granite LLC (G-4716)*
Kelly-Moore Paint Company Inc....405 350-2375
1224 Garth Brooks Blvd Yukon (73099) *(G-11739)*
Kellyville Training Center, Kellyville *Also called Schlumberger Technology Corp (G-3767)*
Kelmar Oil Co....405 222-2364
Mid First Bank Bldg 606 Chickasha (73018) *(G-1478)*
Kelvion Inc....918 416-9058
990 Keystone Ave Catoosa (74015) *(G-1326)*
Kelvion Inc (HQ)....918 266-9200
5202 W Channel Rd Catoosa (74015) *(G-1327)*
Kemah Oil & Gas Co LLC....405 364-3899
4600 Timberidge Cir Norman (73072) *(G-5048)*
Kemmerlys Air Plus....405 348-2154
22106 Ole Barn Rd Edmond (73025) *(G-2479)*
Kemp Quarries, Pryor *Also called Kemp Stone Inc (G-7972)*

Kemp Stone Inc (PA)	918 825-3370
1050 E 520 Pryor (74361) *(G-7972)*	
Kemp Stone Inc	918 772-3366
17801 Highway 80 Hulbert (74441) *(G-3624)*	
Kemper Valve and Fittings	580 622-2048
2733 Industrial Dr Sulphur (73086) *(G-8836)*	
Ken's Welding, Stillwater *Also called Kenneth Petermann (G-8710)*	
Kencan Flowback LLC	580 429-8913
21501 Sw Coombs Rd Cache (73527) *(G-1228)*	
Kendol Resources LLC	405 627-3523
3239 Elmwood Ave Oklahoma City (73116) *(G-6405)*	
Kenkay Machine	918 733-2780
18550 Ash Rd Morris (74445) *(G-4597)*	
Kenmar Energy Services LLC	405 844-2500
6288 Boucher Dr Edmond (73034) *(G-2480)*	
Kennedy Restorations Llc	405 761-5303
150098 Kyle Dr Unit A Oklahoma City (73170) *(G-5300)*	
Kennel and Crate LLC	405 624-0062
9521 Perfect Dr Stillwater (74074) *(G-8709)*	
Kenneth A Weikel	918 582-7205
233 S Detroit Ave Ste 200 Tulsa (74120) *(G-10082)*	
Kenneth D Jewell	580 244-7450
1948 Plunketville Rd Watson (74963) *(G-11355)*	
Kenneth D Jewell Logging, Watson *Also called Kenneth D Jewell (G-11355)*	
Kenneth E Jones	580 832-2227
615 E Ollie St Cordell (73632) *(G-1861)*	
Kenneth H Knepper	918 582-1954
1001 N Wheeling Ave Tulsa (74110) *(G-10083)*	
Kenneth Pace	405 222-1426
124 Bowerwood Dr Chickasha (73018) *(G-1479)*	
Kenneth Petermann	405 372-0111
2812 E 56th St Stillwater (74074) *(G-8710)*	
Kenneth Valliquette Inc	405 969-3317
Rr 1 Crescent (73028) *(G-1917)*	
Kenny's Graphx, Altus *Also called Kennys Sign Graphx-Etcihhg In (G-160)*	
Kennys Machine Shop	918 288-7241
11027 N Cincinnati Ave Skiatook (74070) *(G-8556)*	
Kennys Sign Graphx-Etcihhg In	580 477-4250
1000 N Park Ln Altus (73521) *(G-160)*	
Kens Advertising	405 527-6030
11400 Bryant Rd Lexington (73051) *(G-4036)*	
Kens Handcrafted Leather Gds	918 616-5804
1001 Georgia Pl Muskogee (74403) *(G-4702)*	
Kens Hot Oil & Steam Service	405 382-3052
35355 Highway 99a Earlsboro (74840) *(G-2281)*	
Kens Plumbing & Backhoe	918 963-4223
27087 247th Ave Shady Point (74956) *(G-8414)*	
Kent Engineering Inc	405 364-2207
5 Burlington Pl Norman (73072) *(G-5049)*	
Kenton Knorpp	918 629-0968
13142 E 44th St Tulsa (74134) *(G-10084)*	
Kenwood Industries, Salina *Also called Greg Butcher (G-8134)*	
Kern Valley Industries	918 868-3911
6248 E 526 Rd Rose (74364) *(G-8118)*	
Kerns Asphalt Company Inc (PA)	405 372-2750
1805 S Perkins Rd Stillwater (74074) *(G-8711)*	
Kerns Construction Inc	405 372-2750
1805 S Perkins Rd Stillwater (74074) *(G-8712)*	
Kerns Ready Mixed Concrete Inc	405 372-2750
1805 S Perkins Rd Stillwater (74074) *(G-8713)*	
Kerr Machine Co	580 622-4207
2214 W 14th St Sulphur (73086) *(G-8837)*	
Kerr Pump, Sulphur *Also called Kerr Machine Co (G-8837)*	
Kerr Sail Makers, Tulsa *Also called Kerr Salesmakers & Marine Inc (G-10085)*	
Kerr Salesmakers & Marine Inc	918 437-0544
11429 E 20th St Tulsa (74128) *(G-10085)*	
Kerr Well Service Inc (PA)	620 629-0400
704 N Florence Tyrone (73951) *(G-11219)*	
Kerr-Bilt Trailers Jl Inc	580 566-1200
491 E 2060 Rd Boswell (74727) *(G-757)*	
Kesc Enterprises Inc	918 297-2501
1008 Pennsylvania Ave Hartshorne (74547) *(G-3392)*	
Keta Oil Rural	580 537-2443
610 5th St Loco (73442) *(G-4102)*	
Ketcherside Custom Cabinets	580 254-2672
1404 19th St Woodward (73801) *(G-11599)*	
Ketchum Group LLC	918 407-2228
12228 S 18th Ave E Jenks (74037) *(G-3712)*	
Kevin Banks	918 230-2142
1020 E Tejon Ave Bristow (74010) *(G-785)*	
Kevin Davis Company	918 280-0717
9919 E 46th Pl Bixby (74008) *(G-639)*	
Kevin Heidebrecht, Moore *Also called Ultimate Chemicals LLC (G-4581)*	
Key Cut Express	405 353-3026
949 E State Highway 152 Mustang (73064) *(G-4780)*	
Key Energy Services Inc	405 262-1231
4009 Oklahoma Ave Woodward (73801) *(G-11600)*	
Key Energy Services Inc	405 853-4327
Hwy 81 Hennessey (73742) *(G-3470)*	
Key Energy Services Inc	405 843-6854
4334 Nw Expwy St Ste 235 Oklahoma City (73116) *(G-6406)*	
Key Energy Services Inc	405 262-1190
3801 Valley Park Dr Ste A El Reno (73036) *(G-2731)*	
Key Energy Services Inc	713 651-4300
1328 Se 25th St Oklahoma City (73129) *(G-6407)*	
Key Energy Services Inc	580 256-7413
206 48th St Woodward (73801) *(G-11601)*	
Key Energy Services Inc	918 302-0372
142 Powell Rd McAlester (74501) *(G-4310)*	
Key Energy Services Inc	580 338-0664
2202 Yucca Blvd Guymon (73942) *(G-3354)*	
Key Energy Services Inc	806 435-5583
4009 Oklahoma Ave Woodward (73801) *(G-11602)*	
Key Energy Services Inc	806 323-8361
3611 W 3rd St Elk City (73644) *(G-2835)*	
Key Energy Services Inc	405 262-1231
4000 Valley Park Dr El Reno (73036) *(G-2732)*	
Key Energy Services Inc	405 756-3347
603 Industrial Park Lindsay (73052) *(G-4071)*	
Key General Contractors LLC	918 280-8539
8166 S Memorial Dr Tulsa (74133) *(G-10086)*	
Key Magazine	405 602-3300
25 S Oklahoma Ave Ste 112 Oklahoma City (73104) *(G-6408)*	
Key To Natures Blessings LLC	405 603-8200
8282 Nw 39th Expy Bethany (73008) *(G-585)*	
Key Welding Inc	580 995-4278
608 N Wells St Vici (73859) *(G-11244)*	
Keymiaee Aero-Tech Inc	405 235-5010
1300 Ne 4th St Ste 2 Oklahoma City (73117) *(G-6409)*	
Keys N More	405 415-1797
900 W Reno Ave Oklahoma City (73106) *(G-6410)*	
Keys N More	405 415-2105
7420 S Shields Blvd Oklahoma City (73149) *(G-6411)*	
Keystone Flex Admnstrators LLC	405 285-1144
2932 Nw 122nd St Ste 1 Oklahoma City (73120) *(G-6412)*	
Keystone Gas Corporation (PA)	918 352-2443
101 E Broadway St Drumright (74030) *(G-2065)*	
Keystone Gas Corporation	918 352-2443
1106 N Smather Ave Drumright (74030) *(G-2066)*	
Keystone Labels LLC	405 631-2341
5501 Sw 29th St Oklahoma City (73179) *(G-6413)*	
Keystone Production Co	580 255-2162
1730 W Camelback Rd Duncan (73533) *(G-2141)*	
Keystone Rock & Excavation LLC	405 608-7777
777 Nw 63rd St Oklahoma City (73116) *(G-6414)*	
Keystone Sand & Gravel	918 241-0415
1430 N 209th West Ave Sand Springs (74063) *(G-8198)*	
Keystone Tape & Label Inc	405 631-2341
5501 Sw 29th St Oklahoma City (73179) *(G-6415)*	
Keystone Test Facility LLC	405 213-5965
2111 S Atlanta Pl Tulsa (74114) *(G-10087)*	
Keystone Tool & Fabrication	918 933-6100
6033 E Tecumseh St Tulsa (74115) *(G-10088)*	
Kfm Inc	580 342-6293
201 E Main St Temple (73568) *(G-8933)*	
KG Fab	405 912-9938
1004 Stadium Rd Moore (73160) *(G-4531)*	
Kh Publishing LLC	405 378-7539
1436 Sw 129th St Oklahoma City (73170) *(G-5301)*	
Khody Land & Minerals Company	405 949-2221
210 Park Ave Ste 900 Oklahoma City (73102) *(G-6416)*	
Ki Ho Mltary Acqstion Cnslting, Midwest City *Also called Kihomac Inc (G-4445)*	
Ki Inc	918 289-0200
118 S Main St Broken Arrow (74012) *(G-956)*	
Kiamichi Resources Inc	405 364-8176
4771 E Rock Creek Rd Norman (73026) *(G-5050)*	
Kice Industries Inc	580 363-2850
102 S 29th St Blackwell (74631) *(G-685)*	
Kick16 Skateboards LLC	918 869-6206
1902 Quail Run Muskogee (74403) *(G-4703)*	
Kid Trax	405 366-7982
2345 Heatherfield Ln Norman (73071) *(G-5051)*	
Kiester Operating Company	580 255-4020
1226 N Grand Blvd Duncan (73533) *(G-2142)*	
Kihomac Inc	937 429-7744
2801 Parklawn Dr Ste 500 Midwest City (73110) *(G-4445)*	
Kilgore Meat Processing Plant	918 967-2613
908 Se E St Stigler (74462) *(G-8635)*	
Kilgore Welding Inc	405 872-9677
6851 Slaughterville Rd Lexington (73051) *(G-4037)*	
Kimball Ready Mix Inc	580 922-4444
503 S Main Seiling (73663) *(G-8350)*	
Kimbel Oil, Tulsa *Also called G PC Inc (G-9793)*	
Kimberling City Publishing Co	918 367-2282
112 W 6th Ave Bristow (74010) *(G-786)*	
Kimberling City Publishing Co	918 756-3600
320 W 6th St Okmulgee (74447) *(G-7512)*	
Kimberly A Johnson	918 370-3666
324 Yellow Rock Rd Stigler (74462) *(G-8636)*	

Kimberly-Clark Corporation 918 366-5000
13219 S Kimberly Clark Pl Jenks (74037) ***(G-3713)***
Kimbrel Oil, Tulsa *Also called Confed Oil Incorporated* ***(G-9477)***
Kimbro Furniture LLC 580 351-7304
1303 Ne 75th St Lawton (73507) ***(G-3949)***
Kimray Inc (PA) 405 525-6601
52 Nw 42nd St Oklahoma City (73118) ***(G-6417)***
Kimray Inc 405 525-4200
4305 N Santa Fe Ave Oklahoma City (73118) ***(G-6418)***
Kims International Okla Inc 918 250-9441
11516 E 58th St Tulsa (74146) ***(G-10089)***
Kinda Wilson LLC 405 880-5308
2950 E 76th Pl Tulsa (74136) ***(G-10090)***
Kinder Equipment LLC 580 335-2363
22146 County Road Ew 183 Frederick (73542) ***(G-3195)***
Kinder's Shutter Shop, Clinton *Also called Leon Kinder* ***(G-1756)***
Kindrick & Co Prtg & Copy Svc, Ada *Also called Kindrick Co Prtg & Copying Svc* ***(G-56)***
Kindrick Co Prtg & Copying Svc 580 332-1022
1320 Cradduck Rd Ada (74820) ***(G-56)***
King Cbd Distributing LLC 918 698-7118
9012 E 138th St S Bixby (74008) ***(G-640)***
King Design & Printing LLC 580 661-3061
623 E Hughes St Thomas (73669) ***(G-8946)***
King Energy LLC 405 463-0909
7025 N Robinson Ave Oklahoma City (73116) ***(G-6419)***
King Graphics Inc 405 232-2369
1821 Linwood Blvd Oklahoma City (73106) ***(G-6420)***
King Kopy LLC 405 321-0202
119 W Boyd St Ste 112 Norman (73069) ***(G-5052)***
King Properties Inc 918 366-6868
14 N Armstrong St Bixby (74008) ***(G-641)***
King Screen Co 405 258-0416
109 W 11th St Chandler (74834) ***(G-1383)***
King Screens 918 845-0004
2103 W Greeley St Broken Arrow (74012) ***(G-957)***
King Valve Co Inc 918 251-0369
304 N Redbud Ave Broken Arrow (74012) ***(G-958)***
King Valve Inc 405 672-0046
4015 Se 29th St Oklahoma City (73115) ***(G-6421)***
Kingdom Alarms Inc 918 627-5454
1044 E Pine St Tulsa (74106) ***(G-10091)***
Kingdom Printing 580 512-3789
1328 Nw Elm Ave Lawton (73507) ***(G-3950)***
Kingery Drilling Company Inc (PA) 580 223-6823
210 W Broadway St Ardmore (73401) ***(G-322)***
Kingery Drilling Company Inc 580 229-0716
1217 W Like Rd Healdton (73438) ***(G-3418)***
Kingfisher County Drivers 405 375-3711
101 S Main St Ste 4 Kingfisher (73750) ***(G-3804)***
Kingfisher Midstream LLC 281 655-3200
1833 S Morgan Rd Oklahoma City (73128) ***(G-6422)***
Kingfisher Newspaper Inc 405 375-3220
323 N Main St Kingfisher (73750) ***(G-3805)***
Kingfisher Office Supply Inc 405 375-3404
317 N Main St Kingfisher (73750) ***(G-3806)***
Kingfisher Pipe Sales and Svc 405 262-4422
9016 Lehman Rd El Reno (73036) ***(G-2733)***
Kingfisher Resources Inc 580 323-6097
123 S 6th St Clinton (73601) ***(G-1755)***
Kingfisher Times & Free Press, Kingfisher *Also called Kingfisher Newspaper Inc* ***(G-3805)***
Kings Remnant Ministry Inc 918 207-0866
18767 S Welling Rd Welling (74471) ***(G-11467)***
Kings Well Service 580 363-3912
4008 W Doolin Ave Blackwell (74631) ***(G-686)***
Kingston Flooring LLC 405 470-3494
100 N Rockwell Ave Ste 76 Oklahoma City (73127) ***(G-6423)***
Kingsview Freewill Baptist Ch 405 692-1554
14200 S May Ave Oklahoma City (73170) ***(G-5302)***
Kinkos Inc 303 449-9247
732 W New Orleans St # 150 Broken Arrow (74011) ***(G-959)***
Kinrich 405 842-4307
8604 N Classen Blvd Oklahoma City (73114) ***(G-6424)***
Kiowa County Democrat 580 569-2684
530 E St Snyder (73566) ***(G-8581)***
Kiowa Power Partners LLC 918 432-5117
Milepost 69 Hwy 69 S Kiowa (74553) ***(G-3839)***
Kirby - Smith Machinery Inc (PA) 888 861-0219
6715 W Reno Ave Oklahoma City (73127) ***(G-6425)***
Kirk Tank Trucks Inc 918 733-4503
100 E Ozark St Morris (74445) ***(G-4598)***
Kirkland Express LLC 405 312-3061
2624 Homestead Dr El Reno (73036) ***(G-2734)***
Kirklind Global Inc 580 618-2527
2719 M&K Ln El Reno (73036) ***(G-2735)***
Kirkpatrick Oil Company Inc (PA) 405 840-2882
1001 W Wilshire Blvd # 202 Oklahoma City (73116) ***(G-6426)***
Kirkpatrick Oil Company Inc 405 853-2922
Hwy 81 Hennessey (73742) ***(G-3471)***
Kirkpatrick Welding 918 865-2672
37723 W Highway 51 Mannford (74044) ***(G-4184)***
Kirks Contract Pumping 580 541-6405
1228 Ridge Pl Lahoma (73754) ***(G-3857)***
Kirtz Shutters, Stillwater *Also called Shutter Mill Inc* ***(G-8754)***
Kiska Oil Company 918 584-4251
6 E 5th St Ste 300 Tulsa (74103) ***(G-10092)***
Kitchen Korner Inc 918 582-9951
1408 S Peoria Ave Tulsa (74120) ***(G-10093)***
Kite Virginia 918 747-9803
3429 E 56th Pl Tulsa (74135) ***(G-10094)***
Kites In Sky LLC 405 624-6231
1024 S Mcdonald St Stillwater (74074) ***(G-8714)***
Kittys Chicken, Apache *Also called Rath Inc* ***(G-221)***
Kize Concepts Inc 405 226-0701
1740 Nw 3rd St Oklahoma City (73106) ***(G-6427)***
Kj's Const Co, Ardmore *Also called Johnson Kendall Cnstr Co* ***(G-317)***
Kjm Industries LLC 405 340-1448
7090 Orchard Trl Edmond (73025) ***(G-2481)***
KLA Industries LLC 918 994-2123
9802 E 45th Pl Tulsa (74146) ***(G-10095)***
Klabzuba Royalty Company 405 567-3031
814 9th St Prague (74864) ***(G-7929)***
Klassen Enterprises Inc 918 342-1850
910 N J M Davis Blvd Claremore (74017) ***(G-1649)***
Kleen Oilfield Services Co 580 657-3967
Hwy 70 W Lone Grove (73443) ***(G-4117)***
Kleen Products Inc 405 495-1168
8136 Sw 8th St Oklahoma City (73128) ***(G-6428)***
Kline Materials Inc 580 256-2062
Ne Of City Woodward (73802) ***(G-11603)***
Kline Oilfield Equipment Inc 918 445-0588
8531 E 44th St Tulsa (74145) ***(G-10096)***
Kline Sign LLC 580 237-0732
3005 S Van Buren St Enid (73703) ***(G-2995)***
Klines Signs & Crane 580 256-2374
626 E Oklahoma Ave Woodward (73801) ***(G-11604)***
Kloeckner Metals Corporation 918 266-1666
5250 Bird Creek Ave Catoosa (74015) ***(G-1328)***
Kloeckner Metals Corporation 918 660-2050
5151 Skiatook Rd Catoosa (74015) ***(G-1329)***
Kloefkorn Entps Ltd Partnr 580 694-2292
Main & Hwy 132 Manchester (73758) ***(G-4167)***
Klx Energy Services 580 824-0955
942 Main St Waynoka (73860) ***(G-11377)***
Klx Energy Services LLC 405 838-1230
10625 Nw 4th St Oklahoma City (73127) ***(G-6429)***
Km Metal Polishing 918 397-2221
5915 Baylor Dr Bartlesville (74006) ***(G-503)***
Kmac Manufacturing LLC 918 272-6856
13809 E 87th St N Owasso (74055) ***(G-7583)***
Kmh Enterprises Inc 405 722-4600
7717 W Britton Rd Oklahoma City (73132) ***(G-6430)***
Kmh Labs, Oklahoma City *Also called Kmh Enterprises Inc* ***(G-6430)***
Knape Fabrication & Wldg LLC 580 564-3107
13299 Cliff Rd Kingston (73439) ***(G-3829)***
Knepper Kenneth H Mfg Co, Tulsa *Also called Kenneth H Knepper* ***(G-10083)***
Knight Automatics Co Inc 918 836-6122
6527 E Independence St Tulsa (74115) ***(G-10097)***
Knl Screenprinting 580 654-5394
20 E 4th St Carnegie (73015) ***(G-1277)***
Knock On Wood Custom 918 261-6948
501 W Lowry Rd Claremore (74017) ***(G-1650)***
Knotted Rope Winery LLC 918 839-1464
85 N Lukfata Trail Rd Broken Bow (74728) ***(G-1197)***
Knowcando Ltd 918 599-8600
5918 E 31st St Tulsa (74135) ***(G-10098)***
Knowles Manufacturing & Mch 405 793-9339
9600 S Sunnylane Rd Ste B Moore (73160) ***(G-4532)***
Knowles Performance Engines 580 821-4825
11828 N 2120 Rd Dill City (73641) ***(G-2036)***
Knox Laboratory Services Inc 918 331-9982
2232 Se Wash Blvd Ste 203 Bartlesville (74006) ***(G-504)***
Koax Corp 405 235-7178
510 N Indiana Ave Oklahoma City (73106) ***(G-6431)***
Kobe Express LLC 580 920-0444
1428 W University Blvd Durant (74701) ***(G-2241)***
Kobe Express LLC (PA) 580 889-2420
544 N Hickory St Atoka (74525) ***(G-418)***
Koby Oil Company LLC 405 236-3551
114 Nw 8th St Oklahoma City (73102) ***(G-6432)***
Koby Oil Tools LLC 405 236-3551
900 N Little Ave Cushing (74023) ***(G-1941)***
Koch Fertilizer Enid LLC 580 249-4870
1619 S 78th St Enid (73701) ***(G-2996)***
Koch Industries Inc 580 233-3900
1619 S 78th St Enid (73701) ***(G-2997)***
Koch Industries Inc 918 266-7070
5850 Arkansas Rd Catoosa (74015) ***(G-1330)***
Koda Welding LLC 405 443-9800
202 S Mercedes Dr Norman (73069) ***(G-5053)***

ALPHABETIC SECTION — La-Z-Boy Incorporated

Koda Welding LLC 405 565-1867
4800 Memelou Ln Noble (73068) *(G-4884)*

Kodiak Corp 405 478-1900
9500 Cedar Lake Ave Oklahoma City (73114) *(G-6433)*

Kodiak Production Company 405 350-6465
505 W Main St Yukon (73099) *(G-11740)*

Kog Production LLC 580 621-3510
1121 Tumbleweed Ln Po Freedom (73842) *(G-3207)*

Kohns Doors & Woodworking LLC 405 596-8245
1608 Rolling Ct Nw Piedmont (73078) *(G-7766)*

Koinonia Enterprises 405 275-7064
237 S Draper Ave Shawnee (74801) *(G-8465)*

Koko-Best Inc 918 836-2400
2030 N Mingo Rd Tulsa (74116) *(G-10099)*

Kolb Type Service Incorporated 405 341-0984
3009 S Ripley Rd Agra (74824) *(G-125)*

Kolb's Printing & Type Service, Agra Also called Kolb Type Service Incorporated *(G-125)*

Kole Inc 918 782-3001
Grand Lake Of Cherokee Ketchum (74349) *(G-3774)*

Kommunitees LLC 405 203-2491
4825 Elk Run Yukon (73099) *(G-11741)*

Konecranes Inc 405 208-8808
3208 E I 240 Service Rd Oklahoma City (73135) *(G-6434)*

Kool-Breez LLC 918 715-3358
1507 N 1st St McAlester (74501) *(G-4311)*

Koons Gas Measurement, Collinsville Also called Wilnat Incorporated *(G-1830)*

Kopco Inc 405 743-3290
818 S Main St Stillwater (74074) *(G-8715)*

Kopps On Run LLC 580 326-9400
2689 Us Highway 70 Hugo (74743) *(G-3616)*

Kormondy Enterprises Inc 918 274-8787
301 E 5th Ave Owasso (74055) *(G-7584)*

Kos Engineering & Machine, Canute Also called Kos Machine LLC *(G-1269)*

Kos Machine LLC 580 799-5042
500 Willard St Canute (73626) *(G-1269)*

Kosmoi LLC 918 520-7822
221 S Yellowood Ave Broken Arrow (74012) *(G-960)*

Kp Designs LLC 865 776-7769
1521 Nw 31st St Lawton (73505) *(G-3951)*

Kpj Enterprises, Fort Gibson Also called Johnson Service Company *(G-3175)*

Kratos Unmnned Arial Systems I 405 248-9545
7501 Sw 29th St Ste 200 Oklahoma City (73179) *(G-6435)*

Krause Plastics (PA) 918 835-4202
7412 E 11th St Tulsa (74112) *(G-10100)*

Krebs Brewing Co Inc 918 740-9293
3733 S Wheeling Ave Tulsa (74105) *(G-10101)*

Krebs Brewing Co Inc 918 488-8910
9435 S Hudson Ave Tulsa (74137) *(G-10102)*

Kremlin Welding & Fabrication 580 874-2522
Main St Kremlin (73753) *(G-3853)*

Krispy Kreme 918 294-5293
10128 E 71st St Tulsa (74133) *(G-10103)*

Krumme Oil Company LLP 918 367-5562
210 E 9th Ave Bristow (74010) *(G-787)*

Ksquared Woodworks LLC 918 496-3681
6119 S Joplin Ave Tulsa (74136) *(G-10104)*

Kt Plastics Inc 580 434-5655
132 Gantry Ln Calera (74730) *(G-1241)*

Ktak Corporation 918 492-0505
2019 E 81st St Tulsa (74137) *(G-10105)*

Kully Chaha Native Stone LLC 918 654-3005
13253 Duboise Rd Cameron (74932) *(G-1258)*

Kustom Graphics 405 635-8009
1223 Sw 59th St Oklahoma City (73109) *(G-6436)*

Kustom Signs 405 635-8009
1223 Sw 59th St Oklahoma City (73109) *(G-6437)*

Kuykendal Wldg Backhoe Svc LLC 918 372-4899
8414 W Grandstaff Ripley (74062) *(G-8101)*

Kuykendall Welding LLC 405 905-0389
1711 S 15th St Chickasha (73018) *(G-1480)*

Kwik Kopy Printing, Tulsa Also called Cooley Enterprises Inc *(G-9483)*

Kwp Welding & Fabrication LLC 580 471-7238
1025 Darla Ave Altus (73521) *(G-161)*

Kxd Defense and Armament 918 813-3841
13096 Horseshoe Bnd Oologah (74053) *(G-7533)*

Kxok TV, Oklahoma City Also called Me3 Communications Company LLC *(G-6553)*

Kyra Guffey LLC 210 867-1374
33778 W 51st St S Mannford (74044) *(G-4185)*

Kzb Studios LLC 918 734-4399
5724 E 30th St Tulsa (74114) *(G-10106)*

L & B Pipe & Fabrication Inc 580 234-0712
10801 Bluestem Dr Enid (73701) *(G-2998)*

L & C Ventures LLC 405 793-9753
530 Opportunity Dr Norman (73071) *(G-5054)*

L & J Welding & Machine Svc 918 885-6666
214 N Eastern Ave Hominy (74035) *(G-3591)*

L & K Seed & Manufacturing Co 405 663-2758
246432 E 990 Rd Hydro (73048) *(G-3632)*

L & L Hot Shot Service, Wilburton Also called Luke Mitchell *(G-11523)*

L & L Machine Shop 580 357-3560
2802 E Gore Blvd Lawton (73501) *(G-3952)*

L & L Sales LLC 580 658-3739
404 3rd St Chattanooga (73528) *(G-1390)*

L & L Welding Inc 405 631-4939
4201 S High Ave Oklahoma City (73129) *(G-6438)*

L & M Exploration 405 359-6060
1600 E 19th St Edmond (73013) *(G-2482)*

L & M Fabrication 918 825-7145
Hc 4 Box 111 Pryor (74361) *(G-7973)*

L & M Pattern Mfg Co Inc 918 663-2977
10031 E 52nd St Tulsa (74146) *(G-10107)*

L & M Welding LLC 918 534-6864
12700 N 3990 Rd Dewey (74029) *(G-2027)*

L & O Pump and Supply Inc 405 756-3877
201 Se 3rd St Lindsay (73052) *(G-4072)*

L & R Properties Inc 405 263-7404
114 N 4th St Okarche (73762) *(G-5245)*

L & S Machining 918 543-6628
191 Kayo Mullen Inola (74036) *(G-3664)*

L & S Seamless Guttering Inc 405 392-4487
834 S County Line Rd Blanchard (73010) *(G-719)*

L A Jacobson Inc (PA) 405 238-9313
102 E Bethlehem Rd Pauls Valley (73075) *(G-7664)*

L and A Filtration LLC 580 380-2976
2467 Folsom Rd Durant (74701) *(G-2242)*

L C B Resources 405 375-3718
406 N Main St Kingfisher (73750) *(G-3807)*

L C D Embroidery 405 379-6083
322 S Hinckley St Holdenville (74848) *(G-3555)*

L Dean Hudgins Inc 918 224-6236
12 W Goodykoontz Ave Sapulpa (74066) *(G-8284)*

L E Jones Drilling LLC 580 255-3532
15 S 10th St Ste A Duncan (73533) *(G-2143)*

L E Jones Production Co (PA) 580 255-1191
15 S 10th St Ste A Duncan (73533) *(G-2144)*

L E Jones Production Company, Duncan Also called L E Jones Production Co *(G-2144)*

L I B Ventures Company Inc 405 659-8800
5821 Nw Grand Blvd Ste B Oklahoma City (73118) *(G-6439)*

L L Wilkins E and O Co 405 273-3008
23 E 9th St Shawnee (74801) *(G-8466)*

L M R General Contracting LLC 405 605-6547
3801 S Eastern Ave Oklahoma City (73129) *(G-6440)*

L M S Products Inc 580 336-3555
6500 Independence 164 Perry (73077) *(G-7739)*

L S Marann Publishing 405 751-9369
2608 Abbey Rd Oklahoma City (73120) *(G-6441)*

L W Duncan Printing Inc 580 355-6229
1312 Nw Lawton Ave Lawton (73507) *(G-3953)*

L Z Williams Energy Inc 918 296-3555
513 W Main St Jenks (74037) *(G-3714)*

L&C Metal Buildings Inc 580 660-5515
22380 E 1250 Rd Rocky (73661) *(G-8104)*

L&E Hot Shot LLC 918 839-2419
25758 370th St Wister (74966) *(G-11550)*

L&L Manufacturing 405 436-8929
15000 Choctaw Hills Rd Newalla (74857) *(G-4811)*

L&M Dump Truck & Backhoe Servi 918 798-4568
9571 N 68th West Ave Sperry (74073) *(G-8609)*

L&S Fuels LLC 580 227-0999
120 Cedar Springs Rd Fairview (73737) *(G-3139)*

L-3 Cmmnications Westwood Corp, Tulsa Also called L3 Westwood Corporation *(G-10110)*

L3 AMI, Broken Arrow Also called L3 Technologies Inc *(G-962)*

L3 Comm AMI Instruments 212 697-1111
1914 W Reno St Ste A Broken Arrow (74012) *(G-961)*

L3 Technologies Inc 405 601-0874
6700 Se 59th St Oklahoma City (73135) *(G-6442)*

L3 Technologies Inc 918 258-0707
3724 W Vancouver St Broken Arrow (74012) *(G-962)*

L3 Technologies Inc 405 739-3700
7641 Mercury Rd 830162 Tinker Afb (73145) *(G-8954)*

L3 Westwood Corporation 918 250-4444
12402 E 60th St Tulsa (74146) *(G-10108)*

L3 Westwood Corporation 918 250-4444
12402 E 60th St Tulsa (74146) *(G-10109)*

L3 Westwood Corporation (HQ) 918 252-0481
12402 E 60th St Tulsa (74146) *(G-10110)*

L3harris Technologies Inc 405 573-2285
600 W Rock Creek Rd Norman (73069) *(G-5055)*

L6 Inc (PA) 918 251-5791
1300 E Memphis St Broken Arrow (74012) *(G-963)*

La Boiler Works, Blackwell Also called Los Angeles Boiler Works Inc *(G-688)*

La Faver Fiberglass Supply, Broken Arrow Also called Lafaver Fiberglass Corporation *(G-1137)*

La Maison Inc 918 592-1222
1736 E 11th St Tulsa (74104) *(G-10111)*

La-Z-Boy Incorporated 405 417-5704
3400 W Memorial Rd Oklahoma City (73120) *(G-6443)*

La-Z-Boy Incorporated 405 951-1437
3738 W Reno Ave Oklahoma City (73107) *(G-6444)*

(PA)=Parent Co (HQ)=Headquarters (DH)=Div Headquarters

Labarge Inc Electronics Div, Tulsa *Also called Ducommun Labarge Tech Inc* ***(G-9611)***
Labarge Rolled & Welded Plant, Wagoner *Also called MRC Global (us) Inc* ***(G-11287)***
Label Stable Inc 580 223-2037
102 W Main St Ardmore (73401) ***(G-323)***
Lacebark Inc 405 377-3539
2104 N Cottonwood Rd Stillwater (74075) ***(G-8716)***
Lackey William H Oil Gas Oper 405 275-4164
624 W Independence St # 107 Shawnee (74804) ***(G-8467)***
Lacy Lockwood 918 456-6837
15198 W 850 Rd Tahlequah (74464) ***(G-8871)***
Ladder Energy Co 918 467-3323
Rr 1 Delaware (74027) ***(G-2008)***
Lady Lights & Stage Inc 405 376-0076
7400 Country Ln Mustang (73064) ***(G-4781)***
Lady Love Gifts, Oklahoma City *Also called Gra Enterprises Inc* ***(G-6173)***
Ladybugs and Lollipops LLC 405 919-8555
11274 Kim Cir Guthrie (73044) ***(G-3322)***
Lafarge North America Inc 405 686-0320
2728 Sw 20th St Oklahoma City (73108) ***(G-6445)***
Lafaver Fiberglass Corporation 918 258-4845
19955 E Highway 51 Broken Arrow (74014) ***(G-1137)***
Lafes 918 423-5311
3402 N Robin St McAlester (74501) ***(G-4312)***
Lahmeyer Pattern Shop 918 425-6008
2715 N Madison Ave Tulsa (74106) ***(G-10112)***
Lahmeyer Welding 918 588-2450
65 N Madison Ave Tulsa (74120) ***(G-10113)***
Lahoma Production Inc 918 298-2227
240 1/2 St Se Jenks (74037) ***(G-3715)***
Laird Welding LLC 580 995-4495
61606 N 2070 Rd Vici (73859) ***(G-11245)***
Lake Country Beverage Inc 918 426-0310
4107 W Highway 31 McAlester (74501) ***(G-4313)***
Lake Country Drilling, Ardmore *Also called Morgan Drilling Co* ***(G-336)***
Lake Country Graphics Inc 918 682-8849
1321 N Main St Muskogee (74401) ***(G-4704)***
Lake Ice LLC 405 882-7227
13604 Silver Meadows Rd Jones (73049) ***(G-3750)***
Lake Oil Company Inc 580 332-1737
111 N Turner St Ada (74820) ***(G-57)***
Lake Oologah Leader LLC 918 443-2428
109 S Maple St Oologah (74053) ***(G-7534)***
Lake Tenkiller Hbr Wtr Plant 918 457-4811
14977 W Forest Rd Park Hill (74451) ***(G-7645)***
Lakelife Industries LLC 918 618-6201
139 N Main St Eufaula (74432) ***(G-3104)***
Lakeside Polaris Inc 918 485-2887
33508 State Highway 51 Wagoner (74467) ***(G-11285)***
Lakeside Womens Imaging 405 418-0302
10900 Hefner Pointe Dr # 501 Oklahoma City (73120) ***(G-6446)***
Lakewood Cabinetry Inc 918 782-2203
Hwy 82 Langley (74350) ***(G-3871)***
Lakewood Disposal LLC 918 392-9356
6655 S Lewis Ave Ste 200 Tulsa (74136) ***(G-10114)***
Lakewood Energy Solutions LLC (HQ) 918 392-9356
6655 S Lewis Ave Ste 200 Tulsa (74136) ***(G-10115)***
Lakewood Energy Solutions LLC 918 392-9356
216 County Road 1290 Verden (73092) ***(G-11237)***
Lakey Printing Co 918 744-0158
2707 E 15th St Tulsa (74104) ***(G-10116)***
Lalye, Norman *Also called Layle Company Corporation* ***(G-5056)***
Lam Research Corporation 866 323-1834
521 S Boston Ave Tulsa (74103) ***(G-10117)***
Lamamco Drilling Co 580 856-3561
3100 Continental Rd Ratliff City (73481) ***(G-8056)***
Lamamco Drilling Company 580 336-3524
13250 Deer Rdg Perry (73077) ***(G-7740)***
Lamamco Drilling LLC 918 396-3020
4444 E 146th St N Skiatook (74070) ***(G-8557)***
Lamar Enterprises Inc 405 682-5511
4300 W River Park Dr Oklahoma City (73108) ***(G-6447)***
Lamar Systems LLC 918 770-0941
1224 S 141st East Ave Tulsa (74108) ***(G-10118)***
Lamima Corp 918 491-6846
2940 E 76th St Tulsa (74136) ***(G-10119)***
Lance Easley 405 269-1415
330135 E 760 Rd Perkins (74059) ***(G-7719)***
Lanco Services LLC 580 429-6526
15016 Sw Lee Blvd Cache (73527) ***(G-1229)***
Land & Lake Electric LLC 918 791-1731
29530 S 585 Trl Grove (74344) ***(G-3278)***
Land Run Alpacas 405 226-9005
780596 S Highway 18 Agra (74824) ***(G-126)***
Landa Mobile Systems LLC (PA) 360 474-8991
2239 S Jackson Ave Tulsa (74107) ***(G-10120)***
Landa Mobile Systems LLC 571 272-3350
2211 S Jackson Ave Tulsa (74107) ***(G-10121)***
Landers & Musgroves Oil & Gas (PA) 918 623-2740
3884 Old Bridge Ln Tulsa (74132) ***(G-10122)***
Landmark Design & Sign Corp 405 387-3999
1411 N Main St Newcastle (73065) ***(G-4830)***
Landmark Energy LLC 405 382-3951
319 N Harvey Rd Seminole (74868) ***(G-8383)***
Lane Victory Screen Printing 580 924-3556
316 W Main St Durant (74701) ***(G-2243)***
Lanes Welding LLC 580 302-1279
1902 Bell Ave Elk City (73644) ***(G-2836)***
Laney Mfg Inc 580 335-2363
1007 Rebecca Rd Frederick (73542) ***(G-3196)***
Langdon Publishing Co Inc 918 585-9924
1603 S Boulder Ave Tulsa (74119) ***(G-10123)***
Language Links LLC 918 749-7350
2459 E 23rd St Tulsa (74114) ***(G-10124)***
Lanie Farms 580 694-2259
80574 Mcclain Rd Manchester (73758) ***(G-4168)***
Lankford Welding, Owasso *Also called John Lankford* ***(G-7581)***
Lansing Building Products Inc 405 943-2493
500 N Ann Arbor Ave Oklahoma City (73127) ***(G-6448)***
Laredo Midstream Services LLC 918 513-4570
15 W 6th St Ste 1800 Tulsa (74119) ***(G-10125)***
Laredo Petroleum Inc (PA) 918 513-4570
15 W 6th St Ste 900 Tulsa (74119) ***(G-10126)***
Laredo Petroleum LLC (PA) 918 513-4570
15 W 6th St Ste 1800 Tulsa (74119) ***(G-10127)***
Laredo Petroleum-Dallas Inc 469 522-7800
15 W 6th St Ste 1800 Tulsa (74119) ***(G-10128)***
Lariat Services Inc 580 977-5050
2300 E Oklahoma Blvd Alva (73717) ***(G-184)***
Lariat Services Inc (HQ) 405 753-5500
123 Robert S Kerr Ave Oklahoma City (73102) ***(G-6449)***
Lario Oil & Gas Company 405 238-5609
3 Mi W Of Pauls Vly Pauls Valley (73075) ***(G-7665)***
Larkin Energy Inc 405 941-3224
1 2 Mile Of Hwy 56 Sasakwa (74867) ***(G-8331)***
Larkin Products LLC (PA) 918 584-3475
3105 Charles Page Blvd Tulsa (74127) ***(G-10129)***
Larrance Steel & Door, Lawton *Also called Sufrank Corporation* ***(G-4006)***
Larry Bobs Welding LLC 405 672-7224
4712 Michael Dr Del City (73115) ***(G-1999)***
Larry Campbell Ofc 918 682-1209
2940 S York St Muskogee (74403) ***(G-4705)***
Larry Chinn Oil 918 336-4269
138 County Road 3304 Pawhuska (74056) ***(G-7688)***
Larry D Hammer (PA) 580 227-2100
112 N Main St Fairview (73737) ***(G-3140)***
Larry D Hammer 580 596-3344
216 S Grand Ave Cherokee (73728) ***(G-1418)***
Larry L Williams 580 772-3303
10125 N 2350 Rd Weatherford (73096) ***(G-11424)***
Larry Mustin Construction 918 995-7055
2926 E 93rd Pl Apt 2101 Tulsa (74137) ***(G-10130)***
Larry Sherman Oil LLC 405 258-0816
340604 E 870 Rd Chandler (74834) ***(G-1384)***
Larry Wilcoxson 580 327-2110
44934 Jefferson Rd Alva (73717) ***(G-185)***
Larry's Machine Shop, Perry *Also called L M S Products Inc* ***(G-7739)***
Larrys Transm Parts & Svc, Shawnee *Also called Larrys Transmission Service* ***(G-8468)***
Larrys Transmission Service 405 273-3432
306 E 7th St Shawnee (74801) ***(G-8468)***
Larrys Welding Service 918 432-5787
5 Miles South On Hwy 131 Kiowa (74553) ***(G-3840)***
Larrys Welding Service 918 267-4091
31653 S 193rd West Ave Bristow (74010) ***(G-788)***
Lasco Fittings Inc 800 776-2756
300 Industrial Park Rd Westville (74965) ***(G-11484)***
Laser Ennovation and Engrg, Tulsa *Also called E F L Inc* ***(G-9621)***
Laser Source LLC (PA) 405 843-2528
7925 N Hudson Ave Ste C Oklahoma City (73114) ***(G-6450)***
Laser Source LLC 405 330-4442
4937 Nw 29th St Oklahoma City (73127) ***(G-6451)***
Laser Specialities Inc 918 760-5690
6611 State Highway 66 Tulsa (74131) ***(G-9016)***
Lash Amor 918 893-2424
5840 S Memorial Dr # 203 Tulsa (74145) ***(G-10131)***
Laska LLC 405 820-7617
1212 Pine Oak Cir Edmond (73034) ***(G-2483)***
Lasser Inc 405 842-4010
3244 Nw Grand Blvd Oklahoma City (73116) ***(G-6452)***
Lasso Oil & Gas LLC 405 753-5300
14313 N May Ave Ste 100 Oklahoma City (73134) ***(G-6453)***
Last Ditch Industries LLC 405 609-2317
744 Culbertson Dr Oklahoma City (73105) ***(G-6454)***
Last Stitch Studio 918 200-5859
5309 S Irvington Ave Tulsa (74135) ***(G-10132)***
Laster/Castor Corporation (PA) 918 234-7777
1101 N 161st East Ave Tulsa (74116) ***(G-10133)***
Lasting Impressions Gifts Inc 405 732-2401
3900 S Noma Rd Oklahoma City (73150) ***(G-6455)***

ALPHABETIC SECTION
Lemans Manufacturing Inc

Lata Group 918 535-2147
  320 E Main St Ochelata (74051) *(G-5236)*
Lateesha D Hunter PC 405 534-2200
  1230 Sw 89th St Ste A Oklahoma City (73139) *(G-6456)*
Lathem Tool and Machine Inc 918 724-6655
  701 S 11th St A Broken Arrow (74012) *(G-964)*
Latigo Drilling Corporation 580 255-1674
  4550 Odom Dr Duncan (73533) *(G-2145)*
Latigo Oil & Gas Inc 580 256-1416
  5815 Oklahoma Ave Woodward (73801) *(G-11605)*
Latimer County News Tribune 918 465-2321
  111 W Ada Ave Wilburton (74578) *(G-11522)*
Latimer County Today, Wilburton Also called Tri County Publications Inc *(G-11526)*
Latimers Barbeque 918 425-1242
  1533 N Frankfort Pl Tulsa (74106) *(G-10134)*
Latshaw Drilling, Stillwater Also called Mustang Heavy Haul LLC *(G-8726)*
Latshaw Drilling Company LLC 918 355-4380
  4500 S 129th East Ave Tulsa (74134) *(G-10135)*
Lattimore Materials Company LP 580 276-4631
  4 Miles N 2 Miles Wof Bac Marietta (73448) *(G-4208)*
Laughing Rabbit Soap 405 737-7413
  12732 Se 38th St Choctaw (73020) *(G-1549)*
Laughing Water Enterprises LLC 918 584-2080
  1131 E Archer St Tulsa (74120) *(G-10136)*
Lavi Wash 405 470-0895
  9124 N Council Rd Oklahoma City (73132) *(G-6457)*
Lavishea LLC 303 805-0805
  4103 S 193rd East Ave Broken Arrow (74014) *(G-1138)*
Lawrence County Newspapers LLC 918 224-5185
  16 S Park St Sapulpa (74066) *(G-8285)*
Lawrence Welding LLC 580 272-3294
  804 E Main St Ada (74820) *(G-58)*
Lawton Brace & Limb Co Inc 580 353-5525
  2724 W Gore Blvd Lawton (73505) *(G-3954)*
Lawton Constitution, The, Lawton Also called Lawton Newspapers LLC *(G-3959)*
Lawton Council of The Blind 580 536-1650
  7127 Nw Ash Ave Lawton (73505) *(G-3955)*
Lawton Ice Co, Lawton Also called K-Dub LLC *(G-3948)*
Lawton Machine & Welding Works 580 355-4678
  611 Se 2nd St Lawton (73501) *(G-3956)*
Lawton Machine and Wldg Work, Lawton Also called Lawton Machine & Welding Works *(G-3956)*
Lawton Meat Processing 580 353-6448
  603 Se F Ave Lawton (73501) *(G-3957)*
Lawton Media Inc 580 355-8920
  21 Nw 44th St Lawton (73505) *(G-3958)*
Lawton Newspapers LLC 580 585-5115
  102 Sw 3rd St Lawton (73501) *(G-3959)*
Lawton RC Raceway LLC 580 595-0814
  7807 Se Lee Blvd Lawton (73501) *(G-3960)*
Lawton Transit Mix Inc (HQ) 580 353-6900
  2208 Sw F Ave Lawton (73501) *(G-3961)*
Lawton Transit Mix Inc 580 569-4333
  16725 County Rd N S 219 Snyder (73566) *(G-8582)*
Lawton Window Co Inc 580 353-4655
  604 Sw Sheridan Rd Lawton (73505) *(G-3962)*
Lawyer Graphic Screen Process 918 438-2725
  11332a E 19th St Ste A Tulsa (74128) *(G-10137)*
Laxson Industries LLC 918 494-6677
  6750 S Lewis Ave Tulsa (74136) *(G-10138)*
Layle Company Corporation 405 329-5143
  110 S University Blvd Norman (73069) *(G-5056)*
Lays Custom Welding LLC 918 766-5227
  300 S Quapaw Ave Bartlesville (74003) *(G-505)*
Layton & Smallwood 918 446-6945
  3730 S 63rd West Ave Tulsa (74107) *(G-10139)*
Layton, Tony Clinic, Lawton Also called Anthony W Layton Cpo *(G-3890)*
Lazarus Medical LLC 918 232-6915
  10805 S Marion Ave Tulsa (74137) *(G-10140)*
Lazy B Welding and Met Art LLC 580 512-8778
  4108 Nw Currell Dr Lawton (73505) *(G-3963)*
Lb Machine & Mfg., Skiatook Also called Bryon K Barrows *(G-8534)*
Lbr Smith LLC 405 601-7051
  2205 S Agnew Ave Oklahoma City (73108) *(G-6458)*
Lbz Prints 405 905-1607
  11941 N Pennsylvania Ave Oklahoma City (73120) *(G-6459)*
Ld Consultants LLC 432 230-1098
  2 W 2nd St Ste 1205 Tulsa (74103) *(G-10141)*
Lda Industries LLC 918 315-9758
  1502 W Chickasaw Ave # 3 Sallisaw (74955) *(G-8147)*
LDS Building Specialties LLC 405 917-9901
  5229 Nw 5th St Ste A Oklahoma City (73127) *(G-6460)*
Le Gravis LLC 918 346-6213
  8270 E 41st St Tulsa (74145) *(G-10142)*
Leachco Inc 580 436-1142
  130 E 10th St Ada (74820) *(G-59)*
Lead Babies, Cordell Also called Alluring Lures & Tackle Co LLC *(G-1854)*
Leader Tribune 580 921-3391
  205 S Broadway Laverne (73848) *(G-3879)*

Leadership Training Academy 405 551-8059
  13800 Benson Rd Ste 206 Edmond (73013) *(G-2484)*
Leam Drilling Systems 918 794-3457
  7136 S Yale Ave Ste 206 Tulsa (74136) *(G-10143)*
Leam Drilling Systems LLC 405 440-9436
  9733 Nw 4th St Oklahoma City (73127) *(G-6461)*
Leamco Ruthco Division, Hennessey Also called Weatherford Artificia *(G-3496)*
Leamco Ruthco Division, Oklahoma City Also called Weatherford Artificia *(G-7429)*
Leaming Manufacturing & Cnstr, Newkirk Also called Rick Leaming Construction LLC *(G-4852)*
Leasehold Management Corp (PA) 405 670-5535
  1141 Se Grand Blvd # 101 Oklahoma City (73129) *(G-6462)*
Leather Doctor 918 271-4600
  501 S 10th St Broken Arrow (74012) *(G-965)*
Leather Guns & Etc 580 296-2616
  216 S Collins St Colbert (74733) *(G-1785)*
Leather Our Way 918 214-2036
  249 County Road 3309 Bartlesville (74003) *(G-506)*
Leather Stone, Sand Springs Also called Leather Store *(G-8199)*
Leather Store 918 245-8676
  11 W 41st St Sand Springs (74063) *(G-8199)*
Leatherseats.com, Oklahoma City Also called Customized Fctry Interiors LLC *(G-5880)*
Leche Express, Tulsa Also called Leche Lounge Llc *(G-10144)*
Leche Lounge Llc 918 409-5426
  125 W 3rd St Fl 1 Tulsa (74103) *(G-10144)*
Lechhner Wallcovering 918 744-1742
  2536 E 55th Pl Tulsa (74105) *(G-10145)*
Led Signs of Oklahoma 918 619-9798
  10101 E 46th Pl Tulsa (74146) *(G-10146)*
Leda Grimm 918 225-0507
  742 E Main St Cushing (74023) *(G-1942)*
Leddy Construction 580 332-3056
  3421 N Broadway Ave Ada (74820) *(G-60)*
Ledets Welding Service Inc 405 760-8935
  8100 Bert Ln Norman (73026) *(G-5057)*
Ledets Welding Service Inc 405 610-2299
  4725 Se 59th St Oklahoma City (73135) *(G-6463)*
Ledford Oil & Gas LLC 580 467-0593
  2206 Fairway Dr Duncan (73533) *(G-2146)*
Ledigital Signs LLC 918 504-8506
  8922 E 88th St Tulsa (74133) *(G-10147)*
Ledusa, Tulsa Also called Viking Sales LLC *(G-11077)*
Lee C Moore, Catoosa Also called Woolslayer Companies Inc *(G-1368)*
Leemark Dental Products 918 241-6683
  10331 Edgewood Dr Sand Springs (74063) *(G-8200)*
Legacy Advnced Intllctuals LLC 707 358-0332
  7433 E 3rd St Tulsa (74112) *(G-10148)*
Legacy Metalcraft LLC 918 612-0001
  1209 Sw 9th St Wagoner (74467) *(G-11286)*
Legacy Resources LLC 405 359-1080
  15625 Bald Cypress Cv Edmond (73013) *(G-2485)*
Legacy Signs 580 762-2288
  2208 W South Ave Ponca City (74601) *(G-7844)*
Legacy Signs 918 409-0835
  3023 S Harvard Ave Ste G Tulsa (74114) *(G-10149)*
Legal News 918 259-7500
  315 S Boulder Ave Tulsa (74103) *(G-10150)*
Legend Energy Services LLC 580 225-4500
  2115 W 20th St Elk City (73644) *(G-2837)*
Legend Energy Services LLC (PA) 405 600-1264
  5801 Broadway Ext Ste 210 Oklahoma City (73118) *(G-6464)*
Legend Enterprises Inc 405 340-0410
  1700 S Kelly Ave Ste A Edmond (73013) *(G-2486)*
Legend Lighting, Ponca City Also called Gary Smith *(G-7830)*
Legendary Lube and Oil LLC 918 351-5312
  1619 Houston St Muskogee (74403) *(G-4706)*
Legends Hair Studio 580 237-5524
  1014 N Van Buren St Enid (73703) *(G-2999)*
Legends Vineyard & Winery 405 823-8265
  12955 Meridian Ave Lindsay (73052) *(G-4073)*
Leggett & Platt 0004, Oklahoma City Also called Leggett & Platt Incorporated *(G-6465)*
Leggett & Platt Incorporated 405 787-1212
  6828 Melrose Ln Oklahoma City (73127) *(G-6465)*
Legion Energy LLC 918 895-8785
  8801 S Yale Ave Ste 100 Tulsa (74137) *(G-10151)*
Leisure Lane Handicrafts 580 563-2747
  115 W 9th Blair (73526) *(G-696)*
Lejones Operating Inc 580 255-3532
  15 S 10th St Duncan (73533) *(G-2147)*
Lektron Inc 918 622-4978
  4111 S 74th East Ave Tulsa (74145) *(G-10152)*
Lektron Led Technology, Tulsa Also called Lektron Inc *(G-10152)*
Leland Chapman 580 444-2511
  Old Hwy 7 Industrial Park Velma (73491) *(G-11235)*
Lema Petroleum Inc 405 379-6678
  111 N Oak St Holdenville (74848) *(G-3556)*
Lemans Manufacturing Inc 405 224-6410
  1301 S 3rd St Chickasha (73018) *(G-1481)*

(PA)=Parent Co (HQ)=Headquarters (DH)=Div Headquarters

Lemco Enterprises Inc.....580 226-7808
3204 Hale Rd Ardmore (73401) ***(G-324)***
Lemi, Owasso *Also called Louver & Equipment Mfrs Inc* ***(G-7588)***
Lennox Nas.....405 370-7001
2301 N Sweet Gum Ave Broken Arrow (74012) ***(G-966)***
Lenora Elizabeth Brown.....918 797-2034
475633 E 810 Rd Stilwell (74960) ***(G-8792)***
Lenox Leasing LLC.....405 664-5240
16113 Raindust Dr Oklahoma City (73170) ***(G-5303)***
Leon Kinder.....580 323-0365
1514 Neptune Dr Clinton (73601) ***(G-1756)***
Leonard Mountain Inc.....800 822-7700
4401 S 72nd East Ave Tulsa (74145) ***(G-10153)***
Leonard Skodak Distributors.....405 787-8044
2516 N Adams Ave Oklahoma City (73127) ***(G-6466)***
Les Well Service, Saint Louis *Also called Bill Laird Oil Company* ***(G-8131)***
Letica Corporation.....405 745-2781
7428 Sw 29th St Oklahoma City (73179) ***(G-6467)***
Lettercrafts.....918 584-2400
4148 S 70th East Ave Tulsa (74145) ***(G-10154)***
Lettering Express.....405 260-9022
241 W Wilshire Blvd Ste A Oklahoma City (73116) ***(G-6468)***
Lettering Express OK Inc.....405 235-8999
2130 W Reno Ave Oklahoma City (73107) ***(G-6469)***
Level Up Publishing LLC.....405 771-4372
8900 Ne 51st St Spencer (73084) ***(G-8598)***
Levelops Inc.....405 602-8040
7000 Nw 39th St Bethany (73008) ***(G-586)***
Leviathan Inc.....580 227-3105
1925 Industrial Blvd Fairview (73737) ***(G-3141)***
Leviathan Applied Sciences LLC.....405 315-1759
904 Posados Dr Edmond (73012) ***(G-2487)***
Lew Graphics Inc.....405 743-0890
4724 W Village Ct Stillwater (74074) ***(G-8717)***
Lewis County Press LLC.....580 363-3370
523 S Main St Blackwell (74631) ***(G-687)***
Lewis Friction Products LLC.....405 634-5401
3601 S Byers Ave Oklahoma City (73129) ***(G-6470)***
Lewis Industries Corp.....918 371-2596
816 N 5th St Collinsville (74021) ***(G-1815)***
Lewis Manufacturing Co LLC (PA).....405 634-5401
3601 S Byers Ave Oklahoma City (73129) ***(G-6471)***
Lewis Manufacturing Co LLC.....405 279-2553
705 W Carl Hubbell Blvd Meeker (74855) ***(G-4378)***
Lewis Oil & Gas Inc.....918 272-1278
10704 E 99th St N Owasso (74055) ***(G-7585)***
Lewis Oil Corporation.....405 377-6556
1905 Cedardale Ln Stillwater (74075) ***(G-8718)***
Lewis Oil Properties, Ratliff City *Also called American Petroleum Corporation* ***(G-8048)***
Lewis Printing & Office Supply.....405 379-5124
114 N Broadway St Holdenville (74848) ***(G-3557)***
Lewis Well Service, Sasakwa *Also called John L Lewis* ***(G-8330)***
Lewis, Darrell Welding, Maysville *Also called Darrell Lewis* ***(G-4257)***
Lexington Gas & Go.....405 527-4009
326 W Broadway Purcell (73080) ***(G-8011)***
Lexso T Shirt Printing.....918 861-0772
10863 E 15th St Tulsa (74128) ***(G-10155)***
Liberty Bit Co.....580 255-6400
7414 N Highway 81 Duncan (73533) ***(G-2148)***
Liberty Fence Co Inc (PA).....918 834-6553
6901 E 11th St Tulsa (74112) ***(G-10156)***
Liberty Free Range Poultry LLC.....319 627-6000
234 E Dial St Jay (74346) ***(G-3682)***
Liberty Minerals LLC (PA).....405 317-8107
1405 4th Ave Nw Ardmore (73401) ***(G-325)***
Liberty Operating Inc.....405 329-6200
1827 Atchison Dr Norman (73069) ***(G-5058)***
Liberty Partners Inc.....918 756-6474
812 W 9th St Okmulgee (74447) ***(G-7513)***
Liberty Patterns Inc.....918 234-1037
105 E 3rd St Owasso (74055) ***(G-7586)***
Liberty Signs.....918 409-4470
3109 S Jamestown Ave Tulsa (74135) ***(G-10157)***
Liberty Swabbing Inc.....405 828-4427
19762 E 700 Rd Dover (73734) ***(G-2041)***
Liberty Transmission Parts (HQ).....405 236-8749
301 N Western Ave Oklahoma City (73106) ***(G-6472)***
Liberty Transmission Parts.....405 634-3450
701 Sw 89th St Oklahoma City (73139) ***(G-6473)***
Liberty Transportation LLC.....580 225-2784
522 N Van Buren Ave Elk City (73644) ***(G-2838)***
Life Impact Publishing LLC.....918 407-9938
9916 S 107th East Ave Tulsa (74133) ***(G-10158)***
Life Lift Systems Inc.....904 635-8231
2805 S Purdue Ave Oklahoma City (73128) ***(G-6474)***
Lifes Adult Day Services.....918 664-9000
3106 S Juniper Ave Broken Arrow (74012) ***(G-967)***
Lifesafer Interlock.....800 634-3077
3424 Lakeside Dr Oklahoma City (73160) ***(G-5304)***
Lifetone Technology Inc.....405 200-1555
755 Research Pkwy Ste 125 Oklahoma City (73104) ***(G-6475)***
Lift Technologies Inc.....918 794-8088
5162 S 24th West Ave Tulsa (74107) ***(G-10159)***
Lightbe Corporation.....918 760-6968
2713 S 79th East Ave Tulsa (74129) ***(G-10160)***
Lightfoot Ready Mix LLC.....405 714-5539
332469 E 780 Rd Perkins (74059) ***(G-7720)***
Lighthouse Graphics.....405 635-0022
212 Corona Dr Oklahoma City (73149) ***(G-6476)***
Lightle Sand & Construction Co, Hennessey *Also called Anna Lightle* ***(G-3445)***
Lightninb Saddlery, Stilwell *Also called Lenora Elizabeth Brown* ***(G-8792)***
Lightning Services Inc.....405 853-6669
708 E 4th St Hennessey (73742) ***(G-3472)***
Lightstitching.....405 210-7645
4124 Moorgate Cir Norman (73072) ***(G-5059)***
Lilitad Boats Inc.....918 482-5992
32558 E 241st St S Porter (74454) ***(G-7893)***
Lillian Strickler Lighting.....405 528-4476
617 Nw 23rd St Oklahoma City (73103) ***(G-6477)***
Limbsaw Company.....580 272-3194
340 N 84th St Noble (73068) ***(G-4885)***
Limco Airepair Inc (HQ).....918 445-4300
5304 S Lawton Ave Tulsa (74107) ***(G-10161)***
Limco-Piedmont Inc (HQ).....918 445-4300
5304 S Lawton Ave Tulsa (74107) ***(G-10162)***
Lincoln County Barn Dist No 3.....405 279-3313
1408 Veteran Dr Meeker (74855) ***(G-4379)***
Lincoln County News, The, Chandler *Also called Lincoln County Publishing Co* ***(G-1385)***
Lincoln County Publishing Co.....405 258-1818
718 Manvel Ave Chandler (74834) ***(G-1385)***
Lincoln Electric Holdings Inc.....405 681-0183
3860 Harmon Ave Oklahoma City (73179) ***(G-6478)***
Linda L Hargraves.....918 584-3442
828 S Wheeling Ave # 207 Tulsa (74104) ***(G-10163)***
Linda Sullivan.....918 629-7223
9901 N 114th East Ct Owasso (74055) ***(G-7587)***
Linde Engineering Americas, Catoosa *Also called Linde Engineering N Amer LLC* ***(G-1331)***
Linde Engineering N Amer LLC (HQ).....918 477-1424
6100 S Yale Ave Ste 1200 Tulsa (74136) ***(G-10164)***
Linde Engineering N Amer LLC.....281 717-9090
6100 S Yale Ave Ste 1200 Tulsa (74136) ***(G-10165)***
Linde Engineering N Amer LLC.....918 266-5700
945 Keystone Ave Catoosa (74015) ***(G-1331)***
Linder Screen Printing.....405 558-1275
2418 N Moore Ave Moore (73160) ***(G-4533)***
Linderer Printing Co Inc.....580 323-2102
221 Regency Dr Clinton (73601) ***(G-1757)***
Lindmark Outdoor Advertising, Oklahoma City *Also called Bwb Sign Inc* ***(G-5651)***
Lindsay Gauge & Instrument, Lindsay *Also called Ralph M Thomas* ***(G-4079)***
Lindsay Manufacturing Inc (PA).....580 762-2457
3 Darr Park Dr Ponca City (74601) ***(G-7845)***
Lindsay Woodworks.....405 370-9712
13290 Ne 36th St Choctaw (73020) ***(G-1550)***
Lindsey Printing.....580 476-2278
207 W Blakely St Rush Springs (73082) ***(G-8123)***
Lindsey Webb Press.....405 756-9551
305 S Main St Lindsay (73052) ***(G-4074)***
Lindzco, Duncan *Also called Wetzel Producing Company* ***(G-2198)***
Line X of Stillwater.....405 743-0911
5703 E 6th Ave Stillwater (74074) ***(G-8719)***
Line X of Western Oklahoma.....580 774-5000
2200 S Frontage Rd Weatherford (73096) ***(G-11425)***
Line X Prtctive Ctngs Okla LLC.....405 232-4994
4928 W I 40 Service Rd Oklahoma City (73128) ***(G-6479)***
Linear Health Sciences LLC.....415 388-2794
5333 Wisteria Dr Oklahoma City (73142) ***(G-6480)***
Link Oil Company.....918 585-8343
427 S Boston Ave Ste 1000 Tulsa (74103) ***(G-10166)***
Linley Welding LLC.....405 420-5968
1216 Crestview Dr Elk City (73644) ***(G-2839)***
Linn Energy, Kingfisher *Also called Riviera Operating LLC* ***(G-3813)***
Linn Energy.....405 273-1185
624 W Independence St # 102 Shawnee (74804) ***(G-8469)***
Linn Energy Inc.....405 241-2100
14000 Quail Springs Pkwy # 5000 Oklahoma City (73134) ***(G-6481)***
Linn Energy LLC.....281 605-4100
216 N 20th St Collinsville (74021) ***(G-1816)***
Linn Operating LLC.....918 642-1265
10599 County Road 5451 Fairfax (74637) ***(G-3120)***
Linsay Perkins Development, Tulsa *Also called Perkins Development Corp* ***(G-10495)***
Linton Jim & John.....580 628-3093
307 Thunderbird Rd Tonkawa (74653) ***(G-8978)***
Lipstick Chica.....405 432-6399
2249 Flint Ridge Rd Edmond (73003) ***(G-2488)***
Liquefied Petro Gas Bd Okla.....405 521-2458
3815 N Santa Fe Ave # 117 Oklahoma City (73118) ***(G-6482)***
Lisa Snell.....918 708-5838
14113 Ranch Acres Dr Tahlequah (74464) ***(G-8872)***

ALPHABETIC SECTION — Lucas Metal Works Inc

Litgistix LLC 918 585-5875
5 E 5th St Tulsa (74103) *(G-10167)*

Lithaprint Inc 918 587-7746
802 W 1st St Tulsa (74127) *(G-10168)*

Litta Solutions LLC 918 845-4854
14242 E 208th St S Bixby (74008) *(G-642)*

Little Giant Pump Company LLC 405 947-2511
301 N Macarthur Blvd Oklahoma City (73127) *(G-6483)*

Little Sahara Powers Store, Waynoka Also called Little Sahara Sandsports LLC *(G-11378)*

Little Sahara Sandsports LLC 580 824-0569
137 Main St Waynoka (73860) *(G-11378)*

Littrell Industries LLC 405 637-8930
900 Jupiter Rd Edmond (73003) *(G-2489)*

Litzenberger Exploration Inc 580 824-9351
515 Main St Waynoka (73860) *(G-11379)*

Liv3design LLC 432 296-1968
330 E Gray St Norman (73069) *(G-5060)*

Lively Printing 918 582-3668
6365 E 41st St Tulsa (74135) *(G-10169)*

Liverpool Production Company 918 523-9595
2642 E 21st St Ste 288 Tulsa (74114) *(G-10170)*

Lk Cbd LLC 405 220-3502
8117 N Classen Blvd Oklahoma City (73114) *(G-6484)*

Lkq Corporation 918 428-3835
7600 Charles Page Blvd Tulsa (74127) *(G-10171)*

Lkq Remanufacturing Yukon 405 494-4908
600 N Sara Rd Yukon (73099) *(G-11742)*

Lkq Self Service, Tulsa Also called Lkq Corporation *(G-10171)*

LLC Searchlight 580 699-2971
5802 Nw Elm Ave Lawton (73505) *(G-3964)*

Lloyd Edge 580 726-2905
902 W 11th St Hobart (73651) *(G-3543)*

Lloyd Freeman Creations LLC 918 245-4921
935 S 177th West Ave Sand Springs (74063) *(G-8201)*

Lloyd Provence Logging 580 245-1170
998 Geode Hill Rd Haworth (74740) *(G-3405)*

Lloyd Words LLC 918 457-6852
5906 S Knoxville Ave Tulsa (74135) *(G-10172)*

Lm Software Inc 405 630-4663
2008 Mill Creek Rd Edmond (73025) *(G-2490)*

LMI Aerospace Inc 918 281-0124
16900 Tiger Switch Rd Tulsa (74116) *(G-10173)*

LMI Aerospace Inc 918 271-0207
5270 Skiatook Rd Catoosa (74015) *(G-1332)*

LMI Distributing, Catoosa Also called LMI Finishing Inc *(G-1333)*

LMI Finishing Inc 918 438-1012
2104 N 170th East Ave Tulsa (74116) *(G-10174)*

LMI Finishing Inc 918 379-0899
5270 Skiatook Rd Catoosa (74015) *(G-1333)*

Lobar Oil Co 405 330-7938
3500 S Boulevard Edmond (73013) *(G-2491)*

Lobito Technology Group Inc 918 619-9885
11605 E 27th St N Ste B Tulsa (74116) *(G-10175)*

Local Hometown Publishing Inc 405 273-3838
17809 Deer Trl McLoud (74851) *(G-4359)*

Local Telephone Directory 580 762-9359
118 N Oak St Ste 4 Ponca City (74601) *(G-7846)*

Lockdown Ltd Co 405 605-6161
301 Nw 70th St Ste B Oklahoma City (73116) *(G-6485)*

Lockheed Martin 405 606-3988
F35 Ppe Oak Holow Industr Oklahoma City (73149) *(G-6486)*

Lockheed Martin Corporation 405 917-3863
4243 Will Rogers Pkwy Oklahoma City (73108) *(G-6487)*

Lockheed Martin Corporation 580 357-5060
528 Sw D Ave 402 Lawton (73501) *(G-3965)*

Lockheed Martin Corporation 580 355-0581
1614 W Gore Blvd 2 Lawton (73501) *(G-3966)*

Lodestone Letterpress LLC 405 269-9111
116 W 10th Pl Edmond (73003) *(G-2492)*

Lofland Co 405 631-9555
2101 S Villa Ave Oklahoma City (73108) *(G-6488)*

Log Cutters 580 371-8349
1455 N Elks Rd Tishomingo (73460) *(G-8967)*

Logan County Asphalt Co 405 282-3711
2905 Commerce Blvd Guthrie (73044) *(G-3323)*

Logging Contractor Inc 580 244-3571
Hc 15 Smithville (74957) *(G-8579)*

Logic Energy Solutions LLC 405 601-9037
3939 N Walnut Ave Oklahoma City (73105) *(G-6489)*

Logistics Management Company 405 633-1201
7626 Sw 89th St Oklahoma City (73169) *(G-6490)*

Logo Marketing Company Inc 918 496-2989
3730 E 82nd St Tulsa (74137) *(G-10176)*

London Montin Harbert Inc 405 879-1900
6303 Waterford Blvd # 220 Oklahoma City (73118) *(G-6491)*

Lone Grove Ledger 580 657-6492
Hwy 70 W Lone Grove (73443) *(G-4118)*

Lone Star Industries Inc 405 670-0677
4601 Ne 4th St Oklahoma City (73117) *(G-6492)*

Lone Star Industries Inc 918 825-1937
2430 N 437 Pryor (74361) *(G-7974)*

Lone Star Industries Inc 918 492-2121
8242 S Harvard Ave Ste D Tulsa (74137) *(G-10177)*

Lonestar Gphysical Surveys LLC 405 726-8626
441 Fretz Ave Edmond (73003) *(G-2493)*

Lonestar Msurement Contrls Inc 972 653-0765
520 Harrier Hawk Edmond (73003) *(G-2494)*

Lonewlf Welding 918 625-9128
13005 E 30th St Tulsa (74134) *(G-10178)*

Longbreak Welding Service Inc 918 223-5976
5212 W Eseco Rd Cushing (74023) *(G-1943)*

Longhorn Energy Services LLC 918 302-7610
616 Macy Ln Stillwater (74075) *(G-8720)*

Longhorn Express, Alex Also called Don Wilmut *(G-130)*

Longhorn Service Company LLC 405 853-7170
S Cemetery Rd Hennessey (73742) *(G-3473)*

Longreach Steel Inc 405 598-5691
38174 Hwy 9 Tecumseh (74873) *(G-8922)*

Longs Excavating 918 782-2235
Second & Osage Langley (74350) *(G-3872)*

Lonnie B Nickels Jr 918 756-3426
450 Alder Rd Okmulgee (74447) *(G-7514)*

Lonnie Williams 918 253-4650
4319 E 400 Rd Eucha (74342) *(G-3094)*

Lopez Foods Inc 405 499-0131
9500 Nw 4th St Oklahoma City (73127) *(G-6493)*

Lopez Foods Inc (PA) 405 789-7500
3817 Nw Expwy Ste 900 Oklahoma City (73112) *(G-6494)*

Lopez Foods Inc 405 789-7500
9500 Nw 4th St Oklahoma City (73127) *(G-6495)*

Loporchio Silk Screen 323 258-6459
731 S Oak Ave Ada (74820) *(G-61)*

Loporchios Silk Screening, Ada Also called Loporchio Silk Screen *(G-61)*

Lorraine Oil Co Inc 405 853-2715
2760 Us Highway 81 Hennessey (73742) *(G-3474)*

Lortz R Michael Office 405 236-3230
200 N Harvey Ave Ste 617 Oklahoma City (73102) *(G-6496)*

Los Angeles Boiler Works Inc 580 363-1312
707 N 20th St Blackwell (74631) *(G-688)*

Los Quesitos De Mama LLC 312 276-2638
8020 Nw 159th St Edmond (73013) *(G-2495)*

Lost River Oilfield Services L 208 670-5787
501 S Coltrane Rd Ste 1 Edmond (73034) *(G-2496)*

Lost Treasure Inc 918 786-2182
5500 Us Highway 59 Grove (74344) *(G-3279)*

Lothrop Technologies Inc 405 390-3499
17171 Se 29th St Choctaw (73020) *(G-1551)*

Lou Ann Amstutz, Tulsa Also called Alpha Machining & Mfg Inc *(G-9155)*

Loud City Pharmaceutical 405 259-9014
9113 Ne 23rd St Oklahoma City (73141) *(G-6497)*

Loud Graphic Studios LLC 405 520-5349
2417 Nw 162nd Ter Edmond (73013) *(G-2497)*

Loud Gs, Edmond Also called Loud Graphic Studios LLC *(G-2497)*

Louis McKee Ford Living Trust, Edmond Also called Ford Exploration Inc *(G-2417)*

Louis Systems & Products Inc 405 285-0950
8234 Gold Circle Dr Edmond (73025) *(G-2498)*

Louver & Equipment Mfrs Inc 918 272-5600
7007 N 115th East Ave Owasso (74055) *(G-7588)*

Love Air Conditioning 918 341-0508
122 W Will Rogers Blvd Claremore (74017) *(G-1651)*

Love Heating & AC, Claremore Also called Love Air Conditioning *(G-1651)*

Love Letters Monogramming LLC 918 231-6691
5507 E 109th St Tulsa (74137) *(G-10179)*

Lowery Well Heads Inc 918 836-1760
5908 E Tecumseh St Tulsa (74115) *(G-10180)*

Lowrance Smrad B G Gfree Brnds, Tulsa Also called Navico Inc *(G-10328)*

Lowry Baker Hughes, Claremore Also called Baker Hghes Olfld Oprtions LLC *(G-1590)*

Lowry Exploration Inc 918 587-5094
616 S Boston Ave Ste 402 Tulsa (74119) *(G-10181)*

Lps Specialty Products Inc 918 893-5486
5505 Bird Creek Ave Catoosa (74015) *(G-1334)*

Lps Specialty Tubing, Catoosa Also called Lps Specialty Products Inc *(G-1334)*

LSB Chemical LLC (HQ) 405 235-4546
3503 Nw 63rd St Ste 500 Oklahoma City (73116) *(G-6498)*

LSB Industries Inc (PA) 405 235-4546
3503 Nw 63rd St Ste 500 Oklahoma City (73116) *(G-6499)*

LSB Strategic Accounts, Oklahoma City Also called Climate Control Group Inc *(G-5786)*

Lsgs, Edmond Also called Lonestar Gphysical Surveys LLC *(G-2493)*

LSI, Tulsa Also called Laser Specialities Inc *(G-9016)*

Lube Power, Broken Arrow Also called Seal Support Systems Inc *(G-1046)*

Lubri Flange LLC 580 303-9139
3511 S Highway 6 Elk City (73644) *(G-2840)*

Lucas Color Card, Oklahoma City Also called Lucas Holdings LLC *(G-6500)*

Lucas Holdings LLC 405 524-1811
4900 N Santa Fe Ave Oklahoma City (73118) *(G-6500)*

Lucas Metal Works Inc 918 535-2726
396281 W 3000 Rd Ochelata (74051) *(G-5237)*

(PA)=Parent Co (HQ)=Headquarters (DH)=Div Headquarters

2020 Oklahoma Directory of Manufacturers & Processors

Lucas Oil & Gas Service Inc ... 580 225-3006
1303 S Main St Elk City (73644) ***(G-2841)***
Lucas Trading Company, Oklahoma City *Also called Espiritu Miki* ***(G-6051)***
Luckinbill Inc (PA) ... 580 233-2026
304 E Broadway Ave Enid (73701) ***(G-3000)***
Lucky 13 Motorcycle Shop ... 816 808-0985
636 W 14th St Tulsa (74127) ***(G-10182)***
Lucky 13 Salvage, Tulsa *Also called Lucky 13 Motorcycle Shop* ***(G-10182)***
Lucky Four Oil Company ... 405 941-3307
1721 Rt Sasakwa (74867) ***(G-8332)***
Lufkin Industries LLC ... 405 677-0567
2300 S I 35 Service Rd Oklahoma City (73129) ***(G-6501)***
Luke Mitchell ... 918 429-0373
1314 Nw Highway 2 Wilburton (74578) ***(G-11523)***
Lumen Energy Corporation (HQ) ... 918 584-0052
4200 E Skelly Dr Ste 760 Tulsa (74135) ***(G-10183)***
Lumen Midstream Partnership, Tulsa *Also called Lumen Energy Corporation* ***(G-10183)***
Luna Logging ... 580 933-7517
156 Wading Bird Ln Valliant (74764) ***(G-11230)***
Lure Promo ... 405 664-3415
8520 Nw 118th St Oklahoma City (73162) ***(G-6502)***
Luther Industries LLC ... 405 819-0346
2450 County Road 1341 Blanchard (73010) ***(G-720)***
Luther Mill and Farm Supply ... 405 277-3221
300 N Ash St Luther (73054) ***(G-4135)***
Luther Sign Co ... 405 681-6535
4425 Sw 34th St Oklahoma City (73119) ***(G-6503)***
Lux Grooming Quarters LLC ... 918 259-9910
1821 W Queen St Tulsa (74127) ***(G-10184)***
Lux Illume LLC ... 405 618-4552
2204 Se 8th St Moore (73160) ***(G-4534)***
Lux Orthotics & Prosthetics ... 417 624-2332
9100 S 680 Rd Wyandotte (74370) ***(G-11660)***
Luxe Kitchen & Bath ... 405 471-5577
219 W Wilshire Blvd 101a Oklahoma City (73116) ***(G-6504)***
Luxfer-GTM Technologies LLC ... 918 439-4248
5785 Bird Creek Ave Catoosa (74015) ***(G-1335)***
Lvm Oil Production LLC ... 918 387-2822
16010 E Mcelroy Yale (74085) ***(G-11685)***
Lw Duncan Printing, Lawton *Also called L W Duncan Printing Inc* ***(G-3953)***
Lw Publications ... 405 203-6740
1100 Oak Tree Ave Norman (73072) ***(G-5061)***
Lyle S Sign Contractors ... 405 386-7443
11415 S Peebly Rd Newalla (74857) ***(G-4812)***
Lynns Auto Parts and Machine ... 580 255-5190
1101 E Plato Rd Duncan (73533) ***(G-2149)***
Lynns Machine Inc ... 580 234-2051
3616 E Market St Enid (73701) ***(G-3001)***
Lynns Welding LLC ... 580 488-3587
20185 Highway 47 Leedey (73654) ***(G-4029)***
Lynxsystems LLC ... 918 728-6000
11415 E 19th St Ste B Tulsa (74128) ***(G-10185)***
Lyons & Lyons Inc ... 918 587-2497
1519 S Baltimore Ave Tulsa (74119) ***(G-10186)***
M & BJ Farm & Machine LLC ... 918 333-0430
403260 W 2380 Dr Bartlesville (74006) ***(G-507)***
M & D Oilfield Services ... 405 677-5720
1607 Se 25th St Oklahoma City (73129) ***(G-6505)***
M & L Oil LLC ... 918 798-4511
4444 E 146th St N Skiatook (74070) ***(G-8558)***
M & M Custom Butchering ... 918 542-6421
54420 E 110 Rd Miami (74354) ***(G-4410)***
M & M Electric ... 580 233-8999
11219 W Fox Dr Enid (73703) ***(G-3002)***
M & M Fabrication & Service ... 405 677-1982
1033 Se 36th St Oklahoma City (73129) ***(G-6506)***
M & M Machining LLC ... 918 733-1337
419 N 6th St Morris (74445) ***(G-4599)***
M & M Mattress Company ... 918 834-2033
717 N Sheridan Rd Tulsa (74115) ***(G-10187)***
M & P Manufacturing ... 405 356-2805
960205 S Highway 102 Wellston (74881) ***(G-11474)***
M & R Wire Works Inc ... 580 795-4290
1320 Smiley Rd Madill (73446) ***(G-4153)***
M & W Oilfield Service LLC ... 580 927-2200
Inman Rd Hwy 75 N Coalgate (74538) ***(G-1782)***
M A C Manufacturing Inc ... 405 527-8270
23336 State Highway 74 Purcell (73080) ***(G-8012)***
M and V Resources Inc ... 405 969-2338
108 N Grand Crescent (73028) ***(G-1918)***
M Craig Deisenroth Oil & Gas ... 918 742-4769
1924 S Utica Ave Ste 540 Tulsa (74104) ***(G-10188)***
M D Spoonemore Welding ... 580 233-9596
5306 N 16th St Enid (73701) ***(G-3003)***
M E Klein & Associates Inc ... 405 288-2804
143 Airport Rd Goldsby (73093) ***(G-3245)***
M I Swaco, Elk City *Also called M-I LLC* ***(G-2844)***
M J & H Fabrication Inc ... 580 749-5339
2120 Hall Blvd Ponca City (74601) ***(G-7847)***
M L S Oil Properties ... 405 720-8867
12101 N Macarthur Blvd # 171 Oklahoma City (73162) ***(G-6507)***
M M Energy Inc ... 405 463-3355
13927 Qail Pinte Dr Ste A Oklahoma City (73134) ***(G-6508)***
M P Ready Mix Inc ... 405 631-6814
5800 S High Ave Oklahoma City (73129) ***(G-6509)***
M P Ready Mix Inc (PA) ... 405 354-8824
1400 Holly Ave Yukon (73099) ***(G-11743)***
M S Welding Fabrication ... 405 368-7451
Rr 1 Hennessey (73742) ***(G-3475)***
M Shawn Anderson Rph PC ... 580 595-9500
5366 Nw Cache Rd Ste 1 Lawton (73505) ***(G-3967)***
M T H Inc ... 918 445-9235
2526 W 68th Pl Tulsa (74132) ***(G-10189)***
M T M Mfg, Nowata *Also called Millertime Manufacturing LLC* ***(G-5221)***
M T P Drilling, Tulsa *Also called Mt Percussion Drilling LLC* ***(G-10310)***
M W Bevins Co ... 918 627-1273
9903 E 54th St Tulsa (74146) ***(G-10190)***
M W Machining and Welding Inc ... 918 543-8431
18455 E 640 Rd Inola (74036) ***(G-3665)***
M&M Custom Welding ... 918 231-0829
29350 E 19th St S Broken Arrow (74014) ***(G-1139)***
M&M Hot Oil Service LLC ... 580 651-1746
102 S Ellison St Guymon (73942) ***(G-3355)***
M&M Precision Components LLC ... 918 933-6500
13914 E Admiral Pl Ste A Tulsa (74116) ***(G-10191)***
M&T Production Co ... 918 227-1528
4412 W 91st St Tulsa (74132) ***(G-10192)***
M-1 Machine LLC ... 580 225-6826
3833 W 3rd St Elk City (73644) ***(G-2842)***
M-A Systems Inc ... 918 824-3705
4811 Ne 1st St Pryor (74361) ***(G-7975)***
M-D Building Products Inc (PA) ... 405 528-4411
4041 N Santa Fe Ave Oklahoma City (73118) ***(G-6510)***
M-D Plastics Group ... 503 981-3726
4041 N Santa Fe Ave Oklahoma City (73118) ***(G-6511)***
M-I LLC ... 580 225-0104
100 S Monroe St Ste 9 Elk City (73644) ***(G-2843)***
M-I LLC ... 580 225-2482
524 S Woodward St Elk City (73644) ***(G-2844)***
M-I LLC ... 405 224-4170
110 S Grand Ave Chickasha (73018) ***(G-1482)***
M-O Masonry LLC ... 405 219-4220
413 Sw 64th Pl Oklahoma City (73139) ***(G-6512)***
M.M.C. I., Tulsa *Also called Madison Machine Companies Inc* ***(G-10199)***
M/D Totco, Elk City *Also called Martin-Decker Totco Inc* ***(G-2847)***
M1 Woodworks ... 405 923-4144
157 Barrett Pl Edmond (73003) ***(G-2499)***
M2print LLC ... 505 263-7999
2248 Timber Xing Yukon (73099) ***(G-11744)***
Mabels Fashion Alteration ... 405 605-4558
5603 S Western Ave Oklahoma City (73109) ***(G-6513)***
Mac Industries Inc ... 405 631-8553
2119 N Eastern Ave Moore (73160) ***(G-4535)***
Mac Machine ... 405 238-7280
17509 Highway 77 Pauls Valley (73075) ***(G-7666)***
Mac Manufacturing Inc ... 405 527-8270
23336 State Highway 74 Purcell (73080) ***(G-8013)***
Mac Oil & Gas ... 405 375-5619
104 W Chisholm Dr Kingfisher (73750) ***(G-3808)***
Mac Publishing Company LLC ... 405 964-3576
333244 E 1070 Rd McLoud (74851) ***(G-4360)***
Mac Trailer of Oklahoma Inc ... 817 900-2006
8304 Mckee Industrial Rd Davis (73030) ***(G-1988)***
Maccor Inc ... 918 445-1874
4322 S 49th West Ave Tulsa (74107) ***(G-10193)***
Mach Resources LLC ... 405 252-8100
14201 Wireless Way # 300 Oklahoma City (73134) ***(G-6514)***
Machine Parts & Tool ... 580 389-5346
620 Happy Trails Rd Ardmore (73401) ***(G-326)***
Machine Shop, Yukon *Also called Twiggs Company* ***(G-11796)***
Machine Techniques ... 918 396-2181
110 N Choctaw Rd Skiatook (74070) ***(G-8559)***
Machine Works LLC ... 918 584-6496
220 N Boston Ave Tulsa (74103) ***(G-10194)***
Machine Works LLC ... 405 205-4206
6767 E Virgin St Tulsa (74115) ***(G-10195)***
Machining Specialists Inc ... 918 386-2387
224 Sw 629 Locust Grove (74352) ***(G-4112)***
Machining Technologies of OK ... 918 266-1700
2003 N 193rd East Ave Catoosa (74015) ***(G-1336)***
Macho Muffler, Oklahoma City *Also called Liberty Transmission Parts* ***(G-6473)***
Mack Energy Co ... 580 856-3705
3730 Samedan Rd Ratliff City (73481) ***(G-8057)***
Mack Energy Co ... 580 252-5580
1202 N 10th St Duncan (73533) ***(G-2150)***
Mack Smotherman ... 580 526-3089
101 N Sheb Wooley Ave Erick (73645) ***(G-3088)***
Mackellar Inc ... 405 433-2658
74 S County Line Rd Cashion (73016) ***(G-1289)***

Mackellar Services Inc (HQ) 405 848-2877
7100 N Classen Blvd # 100 Oklahoma City (73116) *(G-6515)*
Mackellar Services Inc 580 237-9383
1101 Sooner Trend Enid (73701) *(G-3004)*
Macks Welding, Erick *Also called Mack Smotherman* *(G-3088)*
Macs Electric Supply Company (PA) 918 583-3101
1624 E 3rd St Tulsa (74120) *(G-10196)*
Mad Dogs Emporium 918 283-4480
103 N Cherokee Ave Claremore (74017) *(G-1652)*
Madden Steel Buildings Lawton 580 357-1699
502 Sw Mckinley Ave Lawton (73501) *(G-3968)*
Madden's Buildings, Ada *Also called Leddy Construction* *(G-60)*
Maddens Portable Buildings 405 799-4989
1161 Bluestem Norman (73069) *(G-5062)*
Maddie & Co 580 212-9539
1409 Garfield St Idabel (74745) *(G-3639)*
Made By ME Publications, Oklahoma City *Also called Marie Thierrey Lucinda* *(G-6525)*
Mader Welding 580 658-3593
816 W Clampitt Rd Marlow (73055) *(G-4235)*
Madewell Machine Works Company 918 543-2904
30205 S 4230 Rd Inola (74036) *(G-3666)*
Madill Gas Processing Co LLC 580 795-7396
3449 Neafus Rd Madill (73446) *(G-4154)*
Madill Record, The, Madill *Also called Marshall County Publishing Co* *(G-4155)*
Madison Avenue Firearms LLC 918 629-6910
3111 S Madison Ave Tulsa (74105) *(G-10197)*
Madison Filter, Tulsa *Also called Clear Edge Filtration Inc* *(G-9447)*
Madison Filter Incorporated 315 685-3466
11607 E 43rd St N Tulsa (74116) *(G-10198)*
Madison Inc of Oklahoma 918 587-4501
8301 State Highway 66 Tulsa (74131) *(G-9017)*
Madison Machine Companies Inc 918 584-6496
65 N Madison Ave Tulsa (74120) *(G-10199)*
Madron Welding Service 405 257-6161
423 S Okfuskee Ave Wewoka (74884) *(G-11503)*
Maese Welding Service Llc 405 606-4619
2513 Pine Ave Oklahoma City (73128) *(G-6516)*
Maf Seismic LLC 405 285-6444
4600 Avalon Pl Edmond (73034) *(G-2500)*
Magerus Welding & Trucking, Norman *Also called Roger Magerus* *(G-5134)*
Maggard Supply and Oil Co Inc 918 865-4333
Hwy 48 S Mannford (74044) *(G-4186)*
Maggie Company Inc 918 438-7800
5109 W 31st St N Tulsa (74127) *(G-10200)*
Magic Circle Energy Corp 405 275-1666
601 N Broadway Ave Shawnee (74801) *(G-8470)*
Magic T'S T-Shirts, Ada *Also called Magic TS* *(G-62)*
Magic TS 580 332-6675
407 Nw J A Rchardson Loop Ada (74820) *(G-62)*
Magnat-Fairview LLC 413 593-5742
222 W Memorial Rd Oklahoma City (73114) *(G-6517)*
Magnesium Products Inc 918 587-9930
5105 W 66th Pl Tulsa (74131) *(G-9018)*
Magnum Aero Inc 918 357-2376
8256 Wright Pl Broken Arrow (74014) *(G-1140)*
Magnum Diversified Services 405 391-9653
5800 S Harrah Rd Newalla (74857) *(G-4813)*
Magnum Energy Inc 405 360-2784
3111 Broce Dr Norman (73072) *(G-5063)*
Magnum Racing Components Inc 918 627-0204
4632 S 102nd East Ave Tulsa (74146) *(G-10201)*
Magnum Racing Componets, Tulsa *Also called Magnum Racing Components Inc* *(G-10201)*
Magnum Screen Print Inc 918 665-7636
7636 E 46th St Tulsa (74145) *(G-10202)*
Magnum Screen Printing, Tulsa *Also called Magnum Screen Print Inc* *(G-10202)*
Magnus Industries LLC 405 513-8295
5608 Industrial Blvd Edmond (73034) *(G-2501)*
Magpro Chlor-Alkali LLC 918 587-9930
5105 W 66th Pl Tulsa (74131) *(G-9019)*
Mah Industries LLC 918 540-0656
429 K St Nw Miami (74354) *(G-4411)*
Mahurin General Repair LLC 918 676-3855
1799 Taft Hwy 125 Fairland (74343) *(G-3126)*
Main Street Vapors, Bristow *Also called Sweet Puffs LLC* *(G-798)*
Mainline Industries ....
5015 Sw Clayton Rd Minco (73059) *(G-4477)*
Mainstream Manufacturing LLC 918 447-1008
8170 S 40th West Ave Tulsa (74132) *(G-10203)*
Majeska & Associates LLC 918 576-6878
1540 N 107th East Ave Tulsa (74116) *(G-10204)*
Majestic Marble & Granite 918 266-1121
2930 N S Highway 167 Catoosa (74015) *(G-1337)*
Majetta Tractor & Backhoe Inc 918 272-7861
107 W 4th Ave Owasso (74055) *(G-7589)*
Major Lab Mfg, Oklahoma City *Also called Melton Co Inc* *(G-6563)*
Major League Sports LLC 918 559-5030
347 N Ash St Nowata (74048) *(G-5219)*
Make Ready Mobiles, Broken Arrow *Also called Joe Martin* *(G-1136)*
Makeba Design & Prints LLC 405 719-0104
13908 Teagen Ln Yukon (73099) *(G-11745)*
Makefield Oil Co 918 492-1463
7170 S Braden Ave Tulsa (74136) *(G-10205)*
Malarkey Roofing Products, Oklahoma City *Also called Herbert Malarkey Roofing Co* *(G-6241)*
Malchus Sktbard Mnistries Assn 405 615-6066
1035 Riley Rdg Edmond (73025) *(G-2502)*
Malco, Tulsa *Also called Mike Alexander Company Inc* *(G-10276)*
Malco Incorporated 918 876-1934
1120 E 1st St Tulsa (74120) *(G-10206)*
Malone Contract Pumping Inc 918 767-2450
51575 E 45 Pawnee (74058) *(G-7706)*
Malones Cnc Machining Inc 918 786-7313
2015 E Industrial 5 Rd Grove (74344) *(G-3280)*
Mammoth Energy Partners LLC (PA) 405 265-4600
14201 Caliber Dr Ste 300 Oklahoma City (73134) *(G-6518)*
Mammoth Energy Services Inc (HQ) 405 608-6007
14201 Caliber Dr Ste 300 Oklahoma City (73134) *(G-6519)*
Mammoth Manufacturing 580 252-4660
2000 N 5th St Duncan (73533) *(G-2151)*
Mammoth Manufacturing Inc 405 820-8301
591 Philip J Rhoads Ave Bethany (73008) *(G-587)*
Manford Oilfield Services LLC 918 424-3280
2257 Green Meadows Cir McAlester (74501) *(G-4314)*
Mangum Brick 405 410-4478
1409 Cedar Ridge Rd Edmond (73013) *(G-2503)*
Mangum Brick Company, Mangum *Also called MB Holdings LLC* *(G-4172)*
Mangum Equipment Company, Marlow *Also called Jack Mangum* *(G-4234)*
Mangum Star News, Mangum *Also called Paxton Publishing Co* *(G-4173)*
Manila Foods 580 262-9900
110 S Main St Blackwell (74631) *(G-689)*
Mann Solvents Inc 918 626-3733
100 Phoenix Ave Arkoma (74901) *(G-386)*
Mannsville AG Center, Mannsville *Also called Custer Enterprises Inc* *(G-4195)*
Manufacturer, Norman *Also called Native Distributing LLC* *(G-5086)*
Manufacturing, Oklahoma City *Also called Automated Gasket Company LLc* *(G-5494)*
Manufacturing Jack LLC Ram 580 332-6694
13655 County Road 1570 Ada (74820) *(G-63)*
Manufacturing Solutions LLC 918 951-0750
20665 E 46th St S Broken Arrow (74014) *(G-1141)*
Manufacturing/ Wholesaler, Duncan *Also called Wild Olives LLC* *(G-2199)*
Manufctring Contract Solutions 405 229-7639
3113 White Cedar Dr Moore (73160) *(G-4536)*
Map Exploration Inc 405 527-6038
505 N 4th Ave Purcell (73080) *(G-8014)*
Mar Welding LLC 580 747-9967
3209 Canton Trl Yukon (73099) *(G-11746)*
Mar-K Specialized Mfg Inc 405 721-7945
6625 W Wilshire Blvd Oklahoma City (73132) *(G-6520)*
Maranatha Industries LLC 918 336-1221
526 S Seminole Ave Bartlesville (74003) *(G-508)*
Marathon Electric Co, Oklahoma City *Also called Lamar Enterprises Inc* *(G-6447)*
Marathon Oil Company 866 323-1836
15 E 5th St Ste 1100 Tulsa (74103) *(G-10207)*
Marathon Oil Company 318 624-0874
7301 Nw Expressway # 225 Oklahoma City (73132) *(G-6521)*
Marcelle Publishing LLC 405 288-2317
2585 E Redbud Rd Purcell (73080) *(G-8015)*
Marco Industries Inc (PA) 918 622-4535
4150 S 100th East Ave # 301 Tulsa (74146) *(G-10208)*
Marcum Welding Service 405 485-9340
14148 State Highway 74b Blanchard (73010) *(G-721)*
Marcy A Sharp 405 615-9879
41423 Saint Louis Rd Asher (74826) *(G-391)*
Mardav Industries Co LLC 855 248-2220
3030 Nw Expwy Ste 200 Oklahoma City (73112) *(G-6522)*
Marexco Inc 405 286-5657
3033 Nw 63rd St Ste 151 Oklahoma City (73116) *(G-6523)*
Margarita Man Hq LLC 830 336-4252
601 S Washington St 303 Stillwater (74074) *(G-8721)*
Maria Raes Inc 580 242-3342
2517 N Van Buren St Enid (73703) *(G-3005)*
Marie Anastasia Labs Inc 405 840-0123
6520 N Western Ave # 100 Oklahoma City (73116) *(G-6524)*
Marie Thierrey Lucinda 405 623-9431
414 Betty Ln Oklahoma City (73110) *(G-6525)*
Marietta Filtra Systems 580 276-3306
601 N Brentwood Ave Marietta (73448) *(G-4209)*
Marietta Monitor, Marietta *Also called Choate Publishing Inc* *(G-4204)*
Marietta Tag Agency 580 276-2101
112 W Main St Ste J10 Marietta (73448) *(G-4210)*
Maris Health LLC 888 429-1117
6936 E 13th St Tulsa (74112) *(G-10209)*
Marjo Advertising LLC 918 500-3108
6167 W Hilton Rd Sapulpa (74066) *(G-8286)*
Marjo Oil Company Inc 918 583-0241
427 S Boston Ave Tulsa (74103) *(G-10210)*

ALPHABETIC

(PA)=Parent Co (HQ)=Headquarters (DH)=Div Headquarters
2020 Oklahoma Directory of Manufacturers & Processors
593

Marjo Operating Co Inc 918 583-0241
427 S Boston Ave Ste 240 Tulsa (74103) ***(G-10211)***
Mark 4 Technologies, Broken Arrow *Also called Shane Lee Duvall* ***(G-1163)***
Mark A Holkum LLC 405 735-3463
109 Sw 132nd St Oklahoma City (73170) ***(G-5305)***
Mark Armitage 405 279-2372
425 E Maker Meeker (74855) ***(G-4380)***
Mark C Blakley 405 245-3606
9200 S Villa Ave Oklahoma City (73159) ***(G-6526)***
Mark Condit 580 656-8028
178884 N 2910 Rd Duncan (73533) ***(G-2152)***
Mark Cromwell Inc 580 233-7992
119 N Washington St Enid (73701) ***(G-3006)***
Mark Hendrix Welding LLC 580 657-3716
998 Memorial Rd Ardmore (73401) ***(G-327)***
Mark Holloway Inc 405 833-7947
100 S Vermont Ave Oklahoma City (73107) ***(G-6527)***
Mark Mullin Co LLC 918 245-1426
201 Wellston Park Rd Sand Springs (74063) ***(G-8202)***
Mark Mullin Company, Sand Springs *Also called Mark Mullin Co LLC* ***(G-8202)***
Mark Stevens Industries Inc 405 948-1077
2504 Nw 159th St Edmond (73013) ***(G-2504)***
Mark W McGuffee Inc (PA) 405 603-8113
11408 N Grove Ave Oklahoma City (73162) ***(G-6528)***
Mark West, Elk City *Also called Markwest Oklahoma Gas Co LLC* ***(G-2846)***
Mark West Hydrocarbon Inc 800 730-8388
2448 E 81st St Ste 5400 Tulsa (74137) ***(G-10212)***
Mark's Sand & Gravel, Oklahoma City *Also called Mark C Blakley* ***(G-6526)***
Markenia Foods LLC 405 751-8616
125 Deer Creek Rd Edmond (73012) ***(G-2505)***
Market 54, Weatherford *Also called Don Regier* ***(G-11405)***
Marketing & Embroidery Magic 405 340-9677
3900 S Broadway Ste 6e Edmond (73013) ***(G-2506)***
Marketing Office, Tulsa *Also called Jetta Production Company Inc* ***(G-10043)***
Markwest Eastern, McAlester *Also called Markwest Enrgy E Texas Gas LP* ***(G-4315)***
Markwest Energy Partners LP 580 225-5400
905 S Eastern Ave Elk City (73644) ***(G-2845)***
Markwest Enrgy E Texas Gas LP 918 389-5100
9725 W Us Highway 270 McAlester (74501) ***(G-4315)***
Markwest Enrgy E Texas Gas LP (HQ) 918 477-8000
2448 E 81st St Ste 5400 Tulsa (74137) ***(G-10213)***
Markwest Hydrocarbon Inc 580 664-5282
8718 N 2120 Rd Butler (73625) ***(G-1221)***
Markwest Oklahoma Gas Co LLC 580 225-5400
905 S Eastern Ave Elk City (73644) ***(G-2846)***
Markwest Pioneer LLC 918 477-8000
2448 E 81st St Ste 5400 Tulsa (74137) ***(G-10214)***
Marlin Oil Corporation 405 478-1900
9500 Cedar Lake Ave Oklahoma City (73114) ***(G-6529)***
Marlow Review, Marlow *Also called Review Printing Company Inc* ***(G-4241)***
Marmac Resources Company 918 846-2293
S Of Hwy 99 E 11 Jct Barnsdall (74002) ***(G-438)***
Maro International Corp (PA) 918 836-7749
3250 N Sheridan Rd Tulsa (74115) ***(G-10215)***
Marple Petroleum LLC 405 360-2240
412 Flint Ridge Ct Norman (73072) ***(G-5064)***
Marpro Label Inc 405 672-3344
1612 Se Grand Blvd Ste A Oklahoma City (73129) ***(G-6530)***
Marrara Group Inc 918 379-0993
5150 S 94th East Ave Tulsa (74145) ***(G-10216)***
Mars Petcare Us Inc 918 540-0045
2020 6th Ave Se Miami (74354) ***(G-4412)***
Marsau 580 432-5000
161909 State Highway 76 Foster (73434) ***(G-3186)***
Marsau Enterprises Inc 580 233-3910
1209 N 30th St Enid (73701) ***(G-3007)***
Marsh Oil & Gas Co 405 238-9660
111 N Chickasaw St Pauls Valley (73075) ***(G-7667)***
Marshall County Publishing Co 580 795-3355
211 Plaza Madill (73446) ***(G-4155)***
Marshall Minerals LLC 405 848-5715
2825 Nw Grand Blvd Apt 23 Oklahoma City (73116) ***(G-6531)***
Marshall Printing 405 883-6122
11120 Nw 111th St Yukon (73099) ***(G-11747)***
Mart Trophy Co Inc 918 481-3388
2901 E 73rd St Tulsa (74136) ***(G-10217)***
Martek Inc 918 543-6477
32848 S 4230 Rd Inola (74036) ***(G-3667)***
Martens Machine Shop 580 227-2734
1414 N Main St Fairview (73737) ***(G-3142)***
Martin Bionics Innovations LLC 405 850-2069
214 E Main St Oklahoma City (73104) ***(G-6532)***
Martin Broadcasting Corp 580 327-1510
620 Choctaw St Alva (73717) ***(G-186)***
Martin House Candle Company 580 504-1699
786 Comet Rd Ardmore (73401) ***(G-328)***
Martin Jacob Welding LLC 580 747-1031
1717 N Adams St Enid (73701) ***(G-3008)***
Martin Manufacturing Inc (PA) 918 583-1191
6917 S Highway 97 Sapulpa (74066) ***(G-8287)***
Martin Marietta Materials Inc 580 326-7709
Hc 66 Box 1135 Sawyer (74756) ***(G-8335)***
Martin Marietta Materials Inc 405 799-7799
8524 S Wstn Ave Ste 118 Oklahoma City (73139) ***(G-6533)***
Martin Marietta Materials Inc 580 384-3574
11662 W Txi Mill Creek Rd Mill Creek (74856) ***(G-4468)***
Martin Marietta Materials Inc 580 369-2706
Hwy 7 W Interstate 35 Davis (73030) ***(G-1989)***
Martin Marietta Materials Inc 580 384-5246
7 Mi N Of Ravia Highway 1 Mill Creek (74856) ***(G-4469)***
Martin Marietta Materials Inc 580 326-9671
3239 E 2000 Rd Sawyer (74756) ***(G-8336)***
Martin Marietta Materials Inc 580 286-3290
4401 Ne Lincoln Rd Idabel (74745) ***(G-3640)***
Martin Marietta Materials Inc 580 569-2393
Rr 1 Snyder (73566) ***(G-8583)***
Martin Marietta Materials Inc 580 835-7311
500 River Rock Rd Broken Bow (74728) ***(G-1198)***
Martin Monument Co, Okmulgee *Also called Okmulgee Monuments Inc* ***(G-7519)***
Martin Oil Properties, Nichols Hills *Also called Christian Martin Lavery* ***(G-4857)***
Martin Service Company, Tulsa *Also called Msc Inc* ***(G-10309)***
Martin Tank Trck Csing Pulling 918 225-2388
2626 N Little Ave Cushing (74023) ***(G-1944)***
Martin Thomas Enterprises Inc 918 739-4015
19014 E Admiral Pl Catoosa (74015) ***(G-1338)***
Martin Welding Service Inc 405 623-5361
16533 State Highway 37 Hinton (73047) ***(G-3532)***
Martin-Decker Totco Inc 580 225-8980
990 S Merritt Rd Elk City (73644) ***(G-2847)***
Martin-Decker Totco Inc 405 350-7408
888 17th St Yukon (73099) ***(G-11748)***
Martindale Consultants Inc 405 728-3003
4242 N Meridian Ave Oklahoma City (73112) ***(G-6534)***
Martinez Fencing Construction 580 309-2046
301 N 4th St Clinton (73601) ***(G-1758)***
Martinez Industries LLC 405 503-4020
21213 Se 37th St Harrah (73045) ***(G-3380)***
Martinez Metal Buildings 580 821-2780
3605 W Country Club Blvd Elk City (73644) ***(G-2848)***
Marty Watley 580 492-4859
108 Green Way Elgin (73538) ***(G-2777)***
Martys Dumptruck & Backhoe Svc 918 869-2051
1517 Out Of Bounds Dr Muskogee (74403) ***(G-4707)***
Marvel Photo Inc (PA) 918 836-0741
1720 N Sheridan Rd Tulsa (74115) ***(G-10218)***
Mary K Rose Inc 405 324-5612
632 Westridge Dr Yukon (73099) ***(G-11749)***
Mary Really Nice Things 580 237-1177
1126 Hillcrest Dr Enid (73701) ***(G-3009)***
Marys Tag Office 580 562-4745
312 State Rt 44 Burns Flat (73624) ***(G-1219)***
Mascots Etc Inc 405 722-3406
7212 Walnut Creek Dr Oklahoma City (73142) ***(G-6535)***
Mason Enterprises Group LLC 918 230-5782
14473 S 302nd East Ave B Coweta (74429) ***(G-1890)***
Mason Pipe & Supply Company 405 942-6926
3212 Nw 50th St Oklahoma City (73112) ***(G-6536)***
Masons Pecans & Peanuts Inc 405 329-7828
4913 Se 44th St Norman (73072) ***(G-5065)***
Mass Brothers Inc 918 527-3753
1116 Lehigh Ave Hartshorne (74547) ***(G-3393)***
Massive Graphic Screen Prtg 405 364-3594
2895 Broce Dr Norman (73072) ***(G-5066)***
Massouds A Fine Jwly Dsign Std, Tulsa *Also called Massouds Fine Jwly & Artspace* ***(G-10219)***
Massouds Fine Jwly & Artspace 918 663-4884
6540 E 51st St Tulsa (74145) ***(G-10219)***
Master Kraft Tooling Corp 918 437-2366
425 S 122nd East Ave Tulsa (74128) ***(G-10220)***
Master Machine 918 366-4855
16552 S 129th East Ave Bixby (74008) ***(G-643)***
Master Movers Incorporated 918 408-1490
9030 N Memorial Dr Ste A Owasso (74055) ***(G-7590)***
Master Works 580 847-2273
36613 Us Highway 70 Bennington (74723) ***(G-564)***
Mastercraft Millwork Inc 405 895-6050
811 S Sunnylane Rd Ste B Moore (73160) ***(G-4537)***
Mastermind Comics 315 308-0593
4308 Se 12th St Del City (73115) ***(G-2000)***
Masters Technical Advisors Inc 918 949-1641
12002 S Pittsburg Ave Tulsa (74137) ***(G-10221)***
Mat Assembly , The, Tulsa *Also called Jessie Shaw* ***(G-10040)***
Matador Processing LLC 405 485-3567
1820 N Council Aka Hwy 76 Blanchard (73010) ***(G-722)***
Mathena Inc (HQ) 405 422-3600
3900 S Hwy 81 Service Rd El Reno (73036) ***(G-2736)***
Matherly Mechanical Contrs LLC 405 737-3488
1520 Ocama Blvd Midwest City (73110) ***(G-4446)***

ALPHABETIC SECTION — McLemore Monument Services

Matheson Tri-Gas Inc 580 536-2965
  1302 Sw 112th St Lawton (73505) *(G-3969)*
Mathey Dearman Inc 918 447-1288
  10541 E Ute St Tulsa (74116) *(G-10222)*
Mathey Dearman Inc 918 447-1288
  1851 N 106th East Ave Tulsa (74116) *(G-10223)*
Mathis Printing & Copy Center, Muskogee *Also called Mathis Printing Inc (G-4708)*
Mathis Printing Inc 918 682-2999
  109 S 5th St Muskogee (74401) *(G-4708)*
Matin House Candle Company 580 490-6500
  4735 State Highway 199 Ardmore (73401) *(G-329)*
Matrix Print & Promo LLC 918 994-1943
  1006 Arbor Dr Bartlesville (74006) *(G-509)*
Matrix Service Inc 918 425-3106
  5725 Kaw Lake Rd Catoosa (74015) *(G-1339)*
Mattison Ave, Edmond *Also called West Mattison Publishing Inc (G-2684)*
Mattocks Printing Co LLC 405 794-2307
  325 N Service Rd Moore (73160) *(G-4538)*
Mauvaisterre Publishing LLC 918 492-3846
  5727 E 62nd St Tulsa (74136) *(G-10224)*
Maverick Bros Resources LLC 580 233-4701
  1710 W Willow Rd Enid (73703) *(G-3010)*
Maverick Energy Group Ltd (PA) 918 764-4081
  406 S Boulder Ave Ste 708 Tulsa (74103) *(G-10225)*
Maverick Machinery LLC 918 584-2504
  2301 N Aspen Ave Broken Arrow (74012) *(G-968)*
Maverick Oil Tools LLC 405 853-5524
  600 N Cheyenne St Hennessey (73742) *(G-3476)*
Maverick Tarkets, Edmond *Also called Charles Jones (G-2345)*
Maverick Technologies LLC 405 680-0100
  2800 Purdue Dr Oklahoma City (73128) *(G-6537)*
Max Dubs & Machine, Duncan *Also called Oilfield Equipment Company (G-2161)*
Maxcess Americas Inc (HQ) 405 755-1600
  222 W Memorial Rd Oklahoma City (73114) *(G-6538)*
Maxcess International Corp (HQ) 405 755-1600
  222 W Memorial Rd Oklahoma City (73114) *(G-6539)*
Maxcess Intl Holdg Corp (HQ) 405 755-1600
  222 W Memorial Rd Oklahoma City (73114) *(G-6540)*
Maxim Energy Corp 405 348-9669
  721 S Boulevard Edmond (73034) *(G-2507)*
Maximus Exploration LLC 405 239-2829
  13903 Quail Pointe Dr Oklahoma City (73134) *(G-6541)*
Maxx Machine Inc 405 692-8300
  3940 Sw 113th St Oklahoma City (73173) *(G-6542)*
Mayabb Oil Co Inc 918 396-2654
  1721 S Broadway St Skiatook (74070) *(G-8560)*
Mayco Inc 405 677-5969
  3501 E Reno Ave Oklahoma City (73117) *(G-6543)*
Mayco Fixture Co Inc 918 428-5305
  2400 N Lewis Ave Tulsa (74110) *(G-10226)*
Mayco Resources LLC 918 241-3392
  1124 N Woodland Pl Sand Springs (74063) *(G-8203)*
Mayhem Cstm Fbrcation Wldg LLC 405 406-5160
  19001 Wolf Dr Newalla (74857) *(G-4814)*
Maysville News, Maysville *Also called Maysville Publishing Co (G-4261)*
Maysville Publishing Co 405 867-4457
  402 Williams Maysville (73057) *(G-4261)*
Mazzella Co 405 423-6283
  301 S Eagle Ln Oklahoma City (73128) *(G-6544)*
MB Holdings LLC 580 782-2324
  2316 N Louis Tittle Ave Mangum (73554) *(G-4172)*
MBC Graphics 918 585-2321
  316 S Rockford Ave Tulsa (74120) *(G-10227)*
MBI Industrial Inc 405 387-4003
  323 W Main St Tuttle (73089) *(G-11206)*
Mbm, Oklahoma City *Also called McLane Foodservice Dist Inc (G-6549)*
Mbs Manufacturing Inc 918 521-6865
  26319 E Highway 51 Broken Arrow (74014) *(G-1142)*
Mc Alester Food Warehouse 580 436-4302
  1601 N Broadway Ave Ada (74820) *(G-64)*
Mc Clain County Publishing Co 405 527-2126
  225 W Main St Purcell (73080) *(G-8016)*
Mc Connells Systems 918 322-5426
  15089 S Yukon Ave Glenpool (74033) *(G-3238)*
Mc Ferrons Quality Meats Inc 918 273-2892
  Rr 1 Box 374 Nowata (74048) *(G-5220)*
Mc II Electric Division, Tulsa *Also called L3 Westwood Corporation (G-10108)*
Mc Iron Blacksmithing & Wldg 405 613-5215
  2405 W 44th St Stillwater (74074) *(G-8722)*
Mc Machining Inc 918 521-8945
  16416 S 129th East Ave Bixby (74008) *(G-644)*
Mc Mahon Operating Company, Tulsa *Also called Petroleum International Inc (G-10506)*
Mc-Alipat LLC 405 370-3321
  1004 W Connell Ave Stillwater (74075) *(G-8723)*
McAbery Acquistion, Bartlesville *Also called Metal Goods Manufacturing Co (G-512)*
McAdams Energy LLC 918 758-0308
  1406 E 10th St Okmulgee (74447) *(G-7515)*
McAlester Army Ammun Plant, McAlester *Also called United States Dept of Army (G-4348)*

McAlester Democrat Inc 918 423-1700
  500 S 2nd St McAlester (74501) *(G-4316)*
McAlester Monument Co Inc 918 423-1647
  320 E Choctaw Ave McAlester (74501) *(G-4317)*
McAlister Drug Corporation 405 354-2582
  948 S Yukon Pkwy Yukon (73099) *(G-11750)*
McAllister Farms 580 512-9009
  17362 E 1560 Rd Hollis (73550) *(G-3567)*
McAmis Fur Company 580 323-5961
  209 S 14th St Arapaho (73620) *(G-225)*
McCabe Crane & Sign 918 424-6381
  801 E Miami Ave McAlester (74501) *(G-4318)*
McCabe Industrial Minerals (PA) 918 252-5090
  7225 S 85th East Ave # 400 Tulsa (74133) *(G-10228)*
McCabe Industrial Minerals 580 369-3660
  1444 Woodland Rd Davis (73030) *(G-1990)*
McCabe Industrial Mnrl Corp 918 252-5090
  7225 S 85th East Ave # 400 Tulsa (74133) *(G-10229)*
McCabe Roustabout Service 918 534-3131
  11783 Us Highway 75 Dewey (74029) *(G-2028)*
McCartney Welding LLC 580 542-2564
  121 Anthony Dr Lahoma (73754) *(G-3858)*
McCaskill Machining & Repair 918 266-5186
  24454 S Keetonville Rd Catoosa (74015) *(G-1340)*
McCasland Mercantile LLC 580 252-5580
  905 W Peach Ave Duncan (73533) *(G-2153)*
McCawley Service 918 484-2189
  704 Kershaw Dr Muskogee (74401) *(G-4709)*
McClarin Plastics Llc 877 912-6297
  3949 Nw 36th St Oklahoma City (73112) *(G-6545)*
McClure Furniture Refinishing 918 587-7779
  4107 S 72nd East Ave Tulsa (74145) *(G-10230)*
McCollum Custom Cabinets 580 548-5851
  6411 County Road 650 Helena (73741) *(G-3435)*
McCormick & Associates LLC 405 747-9991
  1212 S Range Rd Stillwater (74074) *(G-8724)*
McCrary Welding Inc 620 200-4733
  1424 Plains Ave Weatherford (73096) *(G-11426)*
McCrays Manufacturing Co 918 426-1691
  500 W Brewer Ave McAlester (74501) *(G-4319)*
McCullough Printing 580 286-7681
  301 Nw Lincoln Rd Idabel (74745) *(G-3641)*
McCullough Sales Co, Tulsa *Also called Industrial Marking Co (G-9980)*
McCurdy and Associates LLC 405 317-4178
  11300 N Penn Ave Apt 175 Oklahoma City (73120) *(G-6546)*
McCurtain County News Inc (PA) 580 286-3321
  107 S Central Ave Idabel (74745) *(G-3642)*
McCurtain County News Inc 580 584-6210
  108 N Broadway St Broken Bow (74728) *(G-1199)*
McCurtain Daily Gazette, Idabel *Also called McCurtain County News Inc (G-3642)*
McCutchen Enterprises Inc 918 234-7406
  17408 E Pine St Tulsa (74116) *(G-10231)*
McCutchen Welding, Tulsa *Also called McCutchen Enterprises Inc (G-10231)*
McDermott Electric LLC 405 603-4665
  328 S Eagle Ln Ste F Oklahoma City (73128) *(G-6547)*
McDonald Electric Utility Svcs 580 767-8845
  904 S Waverly St Ponca City (74601) *(G-7848)*
McDonald Safety Anchor Inc 405 574-4151
  520 S 7th St Chickasha (73018) *(G-1483)*
McElroy Manufacturing Inc (PA) 918 836-8611
  833 N Fulton Ave Tulsa (74115) *(G-10232)*
McElroy Manufacturing Inc 918 254-7182
  311 S Redwood Ave Broken Arrow (74012) *(G-969)*
McElroys Welding Services LLC 405 354-2019
  13008 Nw 91st St Yukon (73099) *(G-11751)*
McElyea Custom Woodworking LLC 918 332-7651
  1207 May Ln Bartlesville (74006) *(G-510)*
McF Services Inc 918 481-1620
  8177 S Harvard Ave Tulsa (74137) *(G-10233)*
McFarland Cascade 580 584-3511
  305 Silvey Rd Broken Bow (74728) *(G-1200)*
McFarland Cascade Holdings Inc 580 584-2272
  611 N Bock St Broken Bow (74728) *(G-1201)*
McGonigal Ted Oil and Well Svc 918 299-5250
  124 N 6th St Jenks (74037) *(G-3716)*
McGuire Gateway Holdings LLC 405 285-5884
  42005 Moccasin Trl Shawnee (74804) *(G-8471)*
McIntosh County Democrat 918 473-2313
  300 S Broadway St Ste D Checotah (74426) *(G-1397)*
McIntyre Transports Inc 580 526-3121
  12248 N 1790 Rd Erick (73645) *(G-3089)*
McKay's Interior Design Center, Cache *Also called Patricia McKay (G-1230)*
McKinley Hardwoods LLC 800 522-3305
  1815 S Agnew Ave Oklahoma City (73108) *(G-6548)*
McKinneys Custom Welding & Fab 405 341-6559
  1350 Echo Dr Edmond (73034) *(G-2508)*
McLane Foodservice Dist Inc 405 632-0118
  1301 Se 89th St Oklahoma City (73149) *(G-6549)*
McLemore Monument Services 405 788-0164
  5803 N Reformatory Rd El Reno (73036) *(G-2737)*

McLendon Welding Llc ...580 304-5187
5405 Fountain Head Dr Enid (73703) ***(G-3011)***
McMillian Welding LLC ...918 521-6886
25010 Singletree Ln Claremore (74019) ***(G-1653)***
McMur Oil and Gas LLC ...405 834-2221
1643 Nw 164th Cir Edmond (73013) ***(G-2509)***
McMurtry Cabinet Shop ...405 627-3275
1429 Sw 54th St Oklahoma City (73119) ***(G-6550)***
McNally and Associates Inc ...918 587-7068
505 S Quaker Ave Tulsa (74120) ***(G-10234)***
McNally Printing, Tulsa *Also called McNally and Associates Inc* ***(G-10234)***
McPherson Implement Inc ...405 321-6292
I 35 Hwy 9 W Norman (73072) ***(G-5067)***
McPherson Machine, Norman *Also called McPherson Implement Inc* ***(G-5067)***
McSmith Creations LLC ...405 596-2301
5508 N Rockwell Ave Ste B Bethany (73008) ***(G-588)***
McSpadden Bookbindery ...405 275-7788
911 W Benedict St Shawnee (74801) ***(G-8472)***
McWI Inc ...405 360-2277
4510 Green Field Cir Norman (73072) ***(G-5068)***
Md-Advantages LLC ...405 996-6125
5300 Ryan Dr Oklahoma City (73135) ***(G-6551)***
ME Oil Co ...405 232-9541
105 N Hudson Ave Ste 310 Oklahoma City (73102) ***(G-6552)***
Me3 Communications Company LLC ...405 834-8992
13121 Box Canyon Rd Oklahoma City (73142) ***(G-6553)***
Meade Energy, Oklahoma City *Also called Penn-OK Gathering Systems Inc* ***(G-6825)***
Meadowbrook Oil Corp of Okla ...405 672-0240
3612 Epperly Dr Del City (73115) ***(G-2001)***
Meadows Oil Gas Corp ...405 285-8500
609 S Kelly Ave Ste G3 Edmond (73003) ***(G-2510)***
Meagher Energy Advisors Inc ...918 481-5900
1731 E 71st St Tulsa (74136) ***(G-10235)***
Measurement Control Specialist, Elk City *Also called Lucas Oil & Gas Service Inc* ***(G-2841)***
Measurement Systems, Duncan *Also called Cameron Technologies Inc* ***(G-2097)***
Meatlovers, Muskogee *Also called Dvm Nutrion Pets Corp Inc* ***(G-4668)***
Mecco Edgemont Clutch Co Inc ...918 583-3060
308 S Lansing Ave Tulsa (74120) ***(G-10236)***
Mechanical Contractors, Enid *Also called Luckinbill Inc* ***(G-3000)***
Mechanical Sales Oklahoma Inc ...405 681-1971
5229 Nw 5th St Ste B Oklahoma City (73127) ***(G-6554)***
Mechanics Plus, Crescent *Also called Don Scott* ***(G-1913)***
Med-Solve LLC ...918 684-4030
4495 E Hancock St Muskogee (74403) ***(G-4710)***
Medallion Petroleum Inc ...918 582-1320
2021 S Lewis Ave Tulsa (74104) ***(G-10237)***
Medcraft LLC ...918 938-0642
1312 Commercial Ave Mounds (74047) ***(G-4620)***
Medexperts LLC ...918 684-4030
4495 E Hancock St Muskogee (74403) ***(G-4711)***
Media Resources Inc ...405 682-4400
3731 Sw 29th St Oklahoma City (73119) ***(G-6555)***
Media Specialists Inc ...918 622-0077
5333 S Mingo Rd Ste E Tulsa (74146) ***(G-10238)***
Media Technology, Oklahoma City *Also called Media Resources Inc* ***(G-6555)***
Media Technology Incorporated ...405 682-4400
3731 Sw 29th St Oklahoma City (73119) ***(G-6556)***
Medical Csmtc Elctrlysis Clnic ...405 755-7599
9809 Lakeshore Dr Oklahoma City (73120) ***(G-6557)***
Medina Exploration Inc ...405 579-4200
2600 Banburen St Ste 2636 Norman (73072) ***(G-5069)***
Medline Industries ...405 745-9977
8001 Sw 47th St Ste B Oklahoma City (73179) ***(G-6558)***
Medtronic Usa Inc ...405 302-5301
14000 Quail Springs Pkwy Oklahoma City (73134) ***(G-6559)***
Medunison LLC ...405 271-9900
701 Ne 10th St Ste 302 Oklahoma City (73104) ***(G-6560)***
Medxpert North America LLC ...405 285-1671
609 S Kelly Ave Ste H1 Edmond (73003) ***(G-2511)***
Meeco Sullivan LLC (PA) ...918 423-6833
1501 E Electric Ave McAlester (74501) ***(G-4320)***
Meeker Football Press Box ...405 279-1075
214 E Carl Hubbell Blvd Meeker (74855) ***(G-4381)***
Meeks Group, Tulsa *Also called Meeks Lithographing Company* ***(G-10240)***
Meeks Group, Tulsa *Also called Meeks Lithographing Company* ***(G-10241)***
Meeks Group, Prepress Division, Tulsa *Also called Meeks Lithographing Company* ***(G-10239)***
Meeks Lithographing Company ...918 838-9900
6913 E 13th St Tulsa (74112) ***(G-10239)***
Meeks Lithographing Company (PA) ...918 836-0900
6913 E 13th St Tulsa (74112) ***(G-10240)***
Meeks Lithographing Company ...918 836-0900
6913 E 13th St Tulsa (74112) ***(G-10241)***
Mefford 4 Welding Inc ...918 773-6326
108530 S 4550 Rd Sallisaw (74955) ***(G-8148)***
Mega Tek Steel Fabricators, Haskell *Also called Willie Dewayne Brown* ***(G-3403)***
MEI Labels, Catoosa *Also called Martin Thomas Enterprises Inc* ***(G-1338)***
Mekusukey Oil Co Inc ...405 257-5431
201 S Wewoka Ave Wewoka (74884) ***(G-11504)***
Mel Robinson ...405 843-7529
21 Ne 65th St Oklahoma City (73105) ***(G-6561)***
Melanie Margaret Dennis ...405 760-1978
310 S Mustang Rd Mustang (73064) ***(G-4782)***
Melbre Southern Stitches LLC ...918 399-4966
501 S Linwood Ave Cushing (74023) ***(G-1945)***
Melmark Services Inc ...405 324-6999
12228 Sw 26th St Yukon (73099) ***(G-11752)***
Melody House Inc ...405 840-3383
819 Nw 92nd St Oklahoma City (73114) ***(G-6562)***
Mels Construction Inc ...405 853-4621
1216 S Main St Hennessey (73742) ***(G-3477)***
Mels Electric Contracting ...918 279-6036
29827 E State Highway 51 Coweta (74429) ***(G-1891)***
Melton Co Inc ...405 524-2281
4408 N Sewell Ave Oklahoma City (73118) ***(G-6563)***
Melton Dental Lab ...580 369-2448
309 E Freeman Ave Davis (73030) ***(G-1991)***
Melton Rh ...918 968-1606
401 W Main St Stroud (74079) ***(G-8811)***
Melton, Bill, Davis *Also called Melton Dental Lab* ***(G-1991)***
Memorabilia Corner ...405 321-8366
1312 Mckinley Ave Norman (73072) ***(G-5070)***
Memorial Auto Supply Inc ...405 324-5400
709 N Morgan Rd Oklahoma City (73127) ***(G-6564)***
Memories In Glass Inc ...405 878-9688
7 Limousin Ln Shawnee (74804) ***(G-8473)***
Memories N Glass Studio, Shawnee *Also called Memories In Glass Inc* ***(G-8473)***
Mena Manufacturing ...918 955-0518
1735 S Gary Ave Tulsa (74104) ***(G-10242)***
Mental Note LLC ...405 301-4182
401 W Covell Rd Apt 1334 Edmond (73003) ***(G-2512)***
Mentorhope LLC ...405 752-0940
5915 Nw 23rd St Oklahoma City (73127) ***(G-6565)***
Mentorhope Publishing, Oklahoma City *Also called Mentorhope LLC* ***(G-6565)***
Menz Printing Service LLC ...405 620-3673
20922 Se 29th St Harrah (73045) ***(G-3381)***
Mercer Petroleum Management ...405 341-1110
1600 E 19th St Ste 102 Edmond (73013) ***(G-2513)***
Mercer Valve Co Inc (PA) ...405 470-5213
9609 Nw 4th St Oklahoma City (73127) ***(G-6566)***
Mercer, Ronald G, Edmond *Also called Mercer Petroleum Management* ***(G-2513)***
Mercury Press, Okc Digital Sol, Oklahoma City *Also called DPM Group LLC* ***(G-5976)***
Mercury Sign and Banner ...405 360-3303
123 24th Ave Nw Norman (73069) ***(G-5071)***
Mere Minerals ...918 902-3156
1313 W Quinton St Broken Arrow (74011) ***(G-970)***
Mere Software Inc ...918 740-5018
8538 Gary Dr Tulsa (74131) ***(G-9020)***
Meridian Brick LLC ...918 687-6734
3101 W 53rd St S Muskogee (74401) ***(G-4712)***
Meridian Brick LLC ...918 258-7533
225 N Aspen Ave Broken Arrow (74012) ***(G-971)***
Meridian Brick LLC ...405 749-9900
2912 W Hefner Rd Oklahoma City (73120) ***(G-6567)***
Meridian Contracting Inc ...405 928-5959
17500 S Sooner Rd Norman (73071) ***(G-5072)***
Meridian Contracting Co, Norman *Also called Meridian Contracting Inc* ***(G-5072)***
Meridian Press Publications ...405 751-2342
2932 Nw 122nd St Ste H Oklahoma City (73120) ***(G-6568)***
Meritor Inc ...405 224-8600
700 N Industrial Blvd Chickasha (73018) ***(G-1484)***
Merrells Welding & Orna Ir ...405 321-7733
2219 60th Ave Ne Norman (73026) ***(G-5073)***
Merrick Printing ...918 876-6264
4006 Fairview Rd Bartlesville (74006) ***(G-511)***
Merritt's Bakery, Tulsa *Also called Tulsa Baking Inc* ***(G-10989)***
Merritts Monograms LLC ...918 346-2757
2608 Nw 69th St Oklahoma City (73116) ***(G-6569)***
Mertz Manufacturing Inc ...580 762-5646
1701 N Waverly St Ponca City (74601) ***(G-7849)***
Mesa Black Production LLC ...918 933-4454
401 S Boston Ave Ste 450 Tulsa (74103) ***(G-10243)***
Mesa Black Publishing LLC ...580 544-2222
105 W Main St Boise City (73933) ***(G-747)***
Mesh Networks LLC ...832 230-8074
6701 Broadway Ext Ste 310 Oklahoma City (73116) ***(G-6570)***
Mesquite Minerals Inc ...405 848-7551
6801 Broadway Ext Ste 300 Oklahoma City (73116) ***(G-6571)***
Messer LLC ...580 254-2259
1002 Terra Dr Woodward (73801) ***(G-11606)***
Messer LLC ...580 254-2929
802 Jimar Way Woodward (73801) ***(G-11607)***
Messer North America Inc ...580 254-2929
802 Jimar Way Woodward (73801) ***(G-11608)***
Meta Special Aerospace LLC ...405 516-3357
5600 Philip J Rhoads Ave Bethany (73008) ***(G-589)***

Metal Building Components Mbci, Oklahoma City *Also called Nci Group Inc* ***(G-6665)***
Metal Building Services......580 657-3339
300 Case Cir Ardmore (73401) ***(G-330)***
Metal Buildings Inc......405 672-7676
7000 S Eastern Ave Oklahoma City (73149) ***(G-6572)***
Metal Check Inc......405 636-1916
5700 S High Ave Oklahoma City (73129) ***(G-6573)***
Metal Container Corporation......405 680-3140
3713 Harmon Ave Oklahoma City (73179) ***(G-6574)***
Metal Dynamics Corp......918 582-0124
1145 N Iroquois Ave Tulsa (74106) ***(G-10244)***
Metal Fab Inc......580 762-2421
2200 N Ash St Ponca City (74601) ***(G-7850)***
Metal Finishing of Chickasha......405 224-6703
402 N 6th St Chickasha (73018) ***(G-1485)***
Metal Finishings, Chickasha *Also called Metal Finishing of Chickasha* ***(G-1485)***
Metal Goods Manufacturing......918 633-9069
1732 S Yorktown Ave Tulsa (74104) ***(G-10245)***
Metal Goods Manufacturing Co......918 336-4282
309 W Hensley Blvd Bartlesville (74003) ***(G-512)***
Metal Panels Inc......918 641-0641
131 S 147th East Ave Tulsa (74116) ***(G-10246)***
Metalfab LLC......918 718-4040
14553 Highway 62 Tahlequah (74464) ***(G-8873)***
Metalform Inc......918 585-8300
1346 E Haskell St Tulsa (74106) ***(G-10247)***
Metallic Works Inc......918 527-6477
1228 S Erie Ave Tulsa (74112) ***(G-10248)***
Metals USA Plates and Shap......918 682-7833
2800 N 43rd St E Muskogee (74403) ***(G-4713)***
Metalspand Inc......580 228-2393
1000 E G Ave Waurika (73573) ***(G-11363)***
Metalspand By Niles, Waurika *Also called Metalspand Inc* ***(G-11363)***
Metaltech Inc......405 659-9911
7700 Melrose Ln Oklahoma City (73127) ***(G-6575)***
Metavante Holdings LLC......800 554-8095
1200 Sovereign Row Oklahoma City (73108) ***(G-6576)***
Metcel LLC......405 334-7846
3901 Sea Ray Channel Edmond (73013) ***(G-2514)***
Metco Inc......580 233-6717
1522 S Imo Rd Enid (73703) ***(G-3012)***
Metco Provers, Enid *Also called Metco Inc* ***(G-3012)***
Metcoat Inc......580 255-6441
1619 N 5th St Duncan (73533) ***(G-2154)***
Meter Check Inc......405 790-0778
2501 S I 35 Service Rd Moore (73160) ***(G-4539)***
Metheny Concrete Products Inc......405 947-5566
504 N Sunnylane Rd Oklahoma City (73117) ***(G-6577)***
Metheny Concrete Products Inc (PA)......405 947-5566
1617 S Lowery St Oklahoma City (73129) ***(G-6578)***
Metro Builders Supply Inc......405 751-8833
220 Ne 150th St Edmond (73013) ***(G-2515)***
Metro Family Magazine......405 601-2081
318 Nw 13th St Oklahoma City (73103) ***(G-6579)***
Metro Graphic Systems......918 744-0308
1545 S Harvard Ave A Tulsa (74112) ***(G-10249)***
Metro Machine Works Inc......918 446-2705
5204 S 49th West Ave Tulsa (74107) ***(G-10250)***
Metro Mechanical Supply Inc......918 622-2288
9900 E 47th Pl Tulsa (74146) ***(G-10251)***
Metro Mechanical Supply LLC......918 622-2288
9900 E 47th Pl Tulsa (74146) ***(G-10252)***
Metro Outdoor Living......918 893-2960
6235 S Mingo Rd Tulsa (74133) ***(G-10253)***
Metro Portable Buildings......405 921-5688
8201 S Shartel Ave Oklahoma City (73139) ***(G-6580)***
Metro Publishing LLC......405 631-5100
4501 N Classen Blvd # 10 Oklahoma City (73118) ***(G-6581)***
Metro Publishing LLC......405 593-1335
916 Preston Park Dr Yukon (73099) ***(G-11753)***
Metzger Oil Tools, Hominy *Also called Boje Oil Co* ***(G-3579)***
Metzger Oil Tools Inc......918 885-2456
203 E Main St Hominy (74035) ***(G-3592)***
Mewbourne Oil Company......405 235-6374
211 N Robinson Ave N2000 Oklahoma City (73102) ***(G-6582)***
Mewbourne Oil Company......903 561-2900
6535 State Highway 15 Woodward (73801) ***(G-11609)***
Mexco Energy Corporation......405 330-4042
1019 Waterwood Pkwy Ste E Edmond (73034) ***(G-2516)***
Meyer Electric Motor Service......580 327-1399
Hwy 281 N Alva (73717) ***(G-187)***
Mez Woodworks LLC......405 589-5408
1700 Nw 164th Cir Edmond (73013) ***(G-2517)***
Mfg Solutions LLC......918 232-3503
9806 S 236th East Ave Broken Arrow (74014) ***(G-1143)***
Mfg Specialists Inc......918 445-9040
5770 W 68th St Tulsa (74131) ***(G-9021)***
Mfg Unlimited LLC......405 788-9567
3101 S Council Rd Oklahoma City (73179) ***(G-6583)***
Mfp Petroleum Ltd Partnership......405 728-5588
430 Nw 5th St Ste A Oklahoma City (73102) ***(G-6584)***
MG Welding LLC......405 365-6416
2829 Creekview Ter Norman (73071) ***(G-5074)***
Mh Signs LLC......580 795-2925
15762 W Highway 70 Madill (73446) ***(G-4156)***
Mh Woodworking LLC......405 799-2661
1704 Se 16th St Moore (73160) ***(G-4540)***
Mht Luxury Alloys, Oklahoma City *Also called Mobile Hightech* ***(G-6620)***
MI SA Co Sign, Miami *Also called Misaco Sign and Screen Prtg* ***(G-4420)***
Mia Bella Candles......918 470-3862
117 E South Ave McAlester (74501) ***(G-4321)***
Miami Armature Works Inc......918 542-2443
1925 N Main St Miami (74354) ***(G-4413)***
Miami Concrete, Miami *Also called Neo Concrete & Materials Inc* ***(G-4423)***
Miami Designs......918 542-9553
1601 N Main St Miami (74354) ***(G-4414)***
Miami Industrial Supply & Mfg......918 542-6317
7251 S Highway 69a Miami (74354) ***(G-4415)***
Miami Machine Shop......918 542-1501
135 D St Ne Miami (74354) ***(G-4416)***
Miami News-Record, Miami *Also called Miami Newspapers Inc* ***(G-4417)***
Miami Newspapers Inc......918 542-5533
14 1st Ave Nw Miami (74354) ***(G-4417)***
Micahel A Sleem......405 947-6288
6303 N Portland Ave Oklahoma City (73112) ***(G-6585)***
Micco Aircraft Company Inc......918 336-4700
1302 Nw 84th St Oklahoma City (73114) ***(G-6586)***
Michael A Phillips......918 251-0925
801 N 15th St Broken Arrow (74012) ***(G-972)***
Michael Allan Sharp......405 615-3771
41423 Saint Louis Rd Asher (74826) ***(G-392)***
Michael and Mary Seever......405 808-2494
7119 Nw 45th St Bethany (73008) ***(G-590)***
Michael Feezel......580 332-5544
808 E Main St Ada (74820) ***(G-65)***
Michael Gipson LLC......405 819-6349
4820 Casper Dr Oklahoma City (73111) ***(G-6587)***
Michael J Simmons and Die......918 295-0057
315 N Santa Fe Ave Tulsa (74127) ***(G-10254)***
Michael Johnson......405 882-3744
37600 Old Highway 270 # 5 Shawnee (74804) ***(G-8474)***
Michael Nelson......580 922-5074
228070 E County Road 56 Chester (73838) ***(G-1420)***
Michael R Williams......918 418-9344
33784 S 4440 Rd Vinita (74301) ***(G-11264)***
Michael S Azlin......405 257-3581
12725 Ns 3665 Wewoka (74884) ***(G-11505)***
Michael Sherry Alpert......405 912-0062
11800 S Hiwassee Rd Oklahoma City (73165) ***(G-5306)***
Micheal T Robinson......580 767-9414
6491 E Tower Rd Ponca City (74604) ***(G-7851)***
Michelangelo Properties LLC......918 341-4771
16881 S 4200 Rd Claremore (74017) ***(G-1654)***
Michelin North America Inc......580 226-1200
1101 Michelin Rd Ardmore (73401) ***(G-331)***
Micro Machine Inc......918 836-1646
5937 E 12th St Tulsa (74112) ***(G-10255)***
Microframe Corp......918 258-4839
604 S 12th St Broken Arrow (74012) ***(G-973)***
Microsoft Corporation......469 775-6864
7633 E 63rd Pl Tulsa (74133) ***(G-10256)***
Mid America Alloys LLC......918 224-3446
2210 Industrial Rd Sapulpa (74066) ***(G-8288)***
Mid America Automotive Pdts......918 227-1919
519 W Dewey Ave Sapulpa (74066) ***(G-8289)***
Mid America Farm & Ranch......918 275-4984
308 S Elm St Talala (74080) ***(G-8900)***
Mid America Hydro Tech......405 598-1772
36376 Anderson Rd Macomb (74852) ***(G-4143)***
Mid America Machining Inc......918 825-6202
1141 2nd St Maip Pryor (74361) ***(G-7976)***
Mid America Vending Inc......405 387-4441
811 Nw 36th St Newcastle (73065) ***(G-4831)***
Mid American Stl & Wire Co LLC......580 795-2559
1327 Smiley Rd Madill (73446) ***(G-4157)***
Mid Continent Completion, Clinton *Also called Newpark Drilling Fluids LLC* ***(G-1761)***
Mid Continent Concrete Co......918 775-6858
1515 W Redwood Ave Sallisaw (74955) ***(G-8149)***
Mid Continent Concrete Company......918 647-0550
34500 Us Highway 59 S Poteau (74953) ***(G-7908)***
Mid Continent Lift and Eqp LLC......580 255-3867
517 W Bois D Arc Ave Duncan (73533) ***(G-2155)***
Mid Continent Minerals Inc......405 272-0204
120 N Robinson Ave 1350w Oklahoma City (73102) ***(G-6588)***
Mid Continent Well Log Svcs (PA)......405 360-7333
717 26th Ave Nw Norman (73069) ***(G-5075)***
Mid States Technical Svc LLC......918 260-6912
8560 Battle Creek Ct Skiatook (74070) ***(G-8561)***
Mid West Printing, Sapulpa *Also called Mid-West Printing & Pubg Co* ***(G-8291)***

ALPHABETIC

Mid-America Door Company 580 765-9994
1001 W Hartford Ave Ponca City (74601) ***(G-7852)***
Mid-America Indus Coatings LLC 580 239-9003
4757 S Crestview Rd Atoka (74525) ***(G-419)***
Mid-America Midstream Gas 405 935-8000
6100 N Western Ave Oklahoma City (73118) ***(G-6589)***
Mid-American Oil Co Inc 405 848-7551
6801 Broadway Ext Ste 300 Oklahoma City (73116) ***(G-6590)***
Mid-Central Energy Svcs LLC 405 815-4041
727 N Morgan Rd Oklahoma City (73127) ***(G-6591)***
Mid-Con Data Services Inc 405 478-1234
13431 Broadway Ext # 115 Oklahoma City (73114) ***(G-6592)***
Mid-Con Energy Gp LLC 972 479-5980
2431 E 61st St Ste 850 Tulsa (74136) ***(G-10257)***
Mid-Con Energy II LLC 918 743-7575
2431 E 61st St Ste 850 Tulsa (74136) ***(G-10258)***
Mid-Con Energy Operating LLC (PA) 918 743-7575
2431 E 61st St Ste 850 Tulsa (74136) ***(G-10259)***
Mid-Con Energy Partners LP (PA) 918 743-7575
2431 E 61st St Ste 850 Tulsa (74136) ***(G-10260)***
Mid-Con Energy Properties LLC 918 743-7575
2431 E 61st St Ste 850 Tulsa (74136) ***(G-10261)***
Mid-Con Exploration LLC 580 571-7929
2816 Oak Hollow Rd Woodward (73801) ***(G-11610)***
Mid-Continent Concrete Co Inc 918 758-0200
13449 Birch Rd Okmulgee (74447) ***(G-7516)***
Mid-Continent Concrete Co Inc 918 224-4122
201 S Walnut St Sapulpa (74066) ***(G-8290)***
Mid-Continent Conductor LLC 580 254-3232
199584 E County Road 39 Woodward (73801) ***(G-11611)***
Mid-Continent Fuel Co Inc 918 266-1923
5550 E Channel Rd Catoosa (74015) ***(G-1341)***
Mid-Continent Packaging Inc 580 234-5200
1200 N 54th St Enid (73701) ***(G-3013)***
Mid-South Metals LLC 918 835-8055
1031 N Columbia Pl Tulsa (74110) ***(G-10262)***
Mid-States Minerals LLC 405 298-7043
1014 Camelot St Weatherford (73096) ***(G-11427)***
Mid-States Oilfield Machine, El Reno *Also called Nomac Drilling LLC* ***(G-2743)***
Mid-States Oilfield Mch LLC 405 605-5656
6501 Interpace St Oklahoma City (73135) ***(G-6593)***
Mid-West Division, Miami *Also called Gregath Publishing Company* ***(G-4407)***
Mid-West Printing & Pubg Co 918 224-3666
1227 N 9th St Sapulpa (74066) ***(G-8291)***
Midamerica Water Technologies 405 613-0250
8003 N Wilshire Ct Ste E Oklahoma City (73132) ***(G-6594)***
Midcentral Completion Services 405 445-5979
901 Se 35th St El Reno (73036) ***(G-2738)***
Midco Fabricators Inc 405 282-6667
3110 W Noble Ave Guthrie (73044) ***(G-3324)***
Midco Ready Mix, Sallisaw *Also called Mid Continent Concrete Co* ***(G-8149)***
Midco Sand Pump Manufacturing 405 824-2620
1200 Se 34th St Ste 44 Oklahoma City (73129) ***(G-6595)***
Midcon Compression LLC 405 542-6280
325 W Canyon Run Hinton (73047) ***(G-3533)***
Midcon Energy, Tulsa *Also called Olmstead Oil Company* ***(G-10415)***
Midcon Energy, Tulsa *Also called Mid-Con Energy Operating LLC* ***(G-10259)***
Midcon Midstream LP 405 429-5500
123 Robert S Kerr Ave Oklahoma City (73102) ***(G-6596)***
Midcontinent Concrete Co, Okmulgee *Also called Mid-Continent Concrete Co Inc* ***(G-7516)***
Midland Carriers, Edmond *Also called Polypipe Hdlg Specialists Inc* ***(G-2573)***
Midland Stamping and Fabg Corp 918 446-1458
1010 W 37th Pl Tulsa (74107) ***(G-10263)***
Midland Vinyl Products Inc 405 755-4972
11607 N Santa Fe Ave A Oklahoma City (73114) ***(G-6597)***
Midstate Mfg & Mktg Inc 405 751-6227
12501 N Santa Fe Ave Oklahoma City (73114) ***(G-6598)***
Midstate Traffic Control Inc 405 799-0313
9215 S Shields Blvd Moore (73160) ***(G-4541)***
Midtown Printing Inc 918 295-0090
5110 S 95th East Ave Tulsa (74145) ***(G-10264)***
Midtown Printing Services, Tulsa *Also called Midtown Printing Inc* ***(G-10264)***
Midtown Ventures LLC 918 728-3102
3311 S Peoria Ave Tulsa (74105) ***(G-10265)***
Midway Machine & Welding LLC 918 968-3316
Hwy 66 W Stroud (74079) ***(G-8812)***
Midway Services LLC 405 820-8850
5709 Lakewood Ridge Rd Edmond (73013) ***(G-2518)***
Midwesco Industries Inc 918 858-4200
2119 S Union Ave Tulsa (74107) ***(G-10266)***
Midwest Automotive Fas LLC 918 520-6904
1704 W Baton Rouge Cir Broken Arrow (74011) ***(G-974)***
Midwest Bakers Supply Co Inc 405 942-3489
2716 Nw 10th St Oklahoma City (73107) ***(G-6599)***
Midwest City Pub Schools I-52 405 739-1665
607 W Rickenbacker Dr Oklahoma City (73110) ***(G-6600)***
Midwest Clssic Motorsports LLC 405 359-0050
6177 Boucher Dr Edmond (73034) ***(G-2519)***
Midwest Cooling Towers Inc 580 389-5421
601 Beetle Dr Ardmore (73401) ***(G-332)***
Midwest Cooling Towers Inc (PA) 405 224-4622
1156 E Highway 19 Chickasha (73018) ***(G-1486)***
Midwest Copy and Printing 405 737-8311
7031 E Reno Ave Oklahoma City (73110) ***(G-6601)***
Midwest Decals LLC 405 787-8747
6001 Sw 12th St Apt 1328 Oklahoma City (73128) ***(G-6602)***
Midwest Enterprises Inc 405 433-2419
17980 W Prairie Grove Rd Cashion (73016) ***(G-1290)***
Midwest Equipment Company Inc 918 241-3672
3208 Rawson Rd Sand Springs (74063) ***(G-8204)***
Midwest Expdtion Otfitters LLC 918 260-1771
5508 E 11th St Tulsa (74112) ***(G-10267)***
Midwest Fabricators LLC 405 755-7799
10521 N Garnett St Oklahoma City (73114) ***(G-6603)***
Midwest Industries Inc (PA) 405 279-3595
614 W Carl Hubbell Blvd Meeker (74855) ***(G-4382)***
Midwest Industries Inc 405 279-2706
701 W Main St Meeker (74855) ***(G-4383)***
Midwest Logging & Perforating 405 382-4200
2220 N Harvey Rd Seminole (74868) ***(G-8384)***
Midwest Machine & Comprsr Co 405 634-5454
601 Se 29th St Oklahoma City (73129) ***(G-6604)***
Midwest Marble Co 918 587-8193
510 S Quincy Ave Tulsa (74120) ***(G-10268)***
Midwest Med Istpes Nclear Phrm 405 604-4438
5401 N Portland Ave # 330 Oklahoma City (73112) ***(G-6605)***
Midwest Performance Pack Inc 405 485-3567
1820 N Council Blanchard (73010) ***(G-723)***
Midwest Pole Barns & Buildings, Tulsa *Also called Midwest Portable Building* ***(G-10269)***
Midwest Portable Building 918 245-9335
6800 Charles Page Blvd Tulsa (74127) ***(G-10269)***
Midwest Precision Inc 918 835-8900
9725 E Admiral Pl Tulsa (74116) ***(G-10270)***
Midwest Publication 405 948-6506
500 N Meridian Ave Oklahoma City (73107) ***(G-6606)***
Midwest Publishing Co 405 282-1890
100 E College Ave Guthrie (73044) ***(G-3325)***
Midwest Publishing Co Inc 918 582-2000
2230 E 49th St Ste E Tulsa (74105) ***(G-10271)***
Midwest Ready Mix 580 625-4477
20 Avenue G Beaver (73932) ***(G-542)***
Midwest Ready Mix Concrete, Beaver *Also called Midwest Ready Mix* ***(G-542)***
Midwest Urethane Inc 918 445-2277
6417 S 39th West Ave Tulsa (74132) ***(G-10272)***
Midwest Welders 918 456-5981
5971 N 510 Rd Tahlequah (74464) ***(G-8874)***
Midwest Wraps 918 624-2111
6417 E 53rd St Tulsa (74135) ***(G-10273)***
Midwestern Manufacturing Co 918 446-1587
2119 S Union Ave Tulsa (74107) ***(G-10274)***
Midwestern Pet Foods Inc 405 224-2691
913 N 9th St Chickasha (73018) ***(G-1487)***
Midwestern Pipe Line Pdts Co, Tulsa *Also called Midwesco Industries Inc* ***(G-10266)***
Mighty Clean Corporation 918 299-7970
10050 S 33rd West Ave Tulsa (74132) ***(G-10275)***
Mighty Clean, The, Tulsa *Also called Mighty Clean Corporation* ***(G-10275)***
Miid Del Print Shop, Oklahoma City *Also called Midwest City Pub Schools I-52* ***(G-6600)***
Mike Alexander Company Inc 580 765-8085
1120 E 1st St Tulsa (74120) ***(G-10276)***
Mike Bailey Motors Inc 918 652-9637
Hwy 75 & Industrial Henryetta (74437) ***(G-3512)***
Mike Beathe 918 288-7858
3214 E 106th St N Sperry (74073) ***(G-8610)***
Mike Cline Inc 918 592-3712
4704 Charles Page Blvd Tulsa (74127) ***(G-10277)***
Mike Deeds Welding LLC 580 863-2339
21715 E Centennial Rd Garber (73738) ***(G-3215)***
Mike Latham 580 622-6980
2175 Leveridge Rd Sulphur (73086) ***(G-8838)***
Mike Macdowell Welding 405 354-1221
14540 W Wilshire Blvd Yukon (73099) ***(G-11754)***
Mike McCalip 405 452-5730
515 S Washita St Wetumka (74883) ***(G-11495)***
Mike McGills Carpet Inc 405 222-0899
426 W Chickasha Ave Chickasha (73018) ***(G-1488)***
Mike Pung 405 736-6282
1108 Loftin Dr Oklahoma City (73130) ***(G-6607)***
Mike S Welding 918 381-0273
6930 E Newton St Tulsa (74115) ***(G-10278)***
Mikes Custom Woodworking, Oklahoma City *Also called Mike Pung* ***(G-6607)***
Mikes Famous Beef Jerky 405 414-7501
102 W Kansas Ave Chickasha (73018) ***(G-1489)***
Mikes Trucking Co 580 256-5063
5015 Western Ave Woodward (73801) ***(G-11612)***
Mikes Welding 918 455-7227
18819 E 141st St Broken Arrow (74011) ***(G-975)***
Mikes Welding Service 405 387-3782
7756 N County Line Ave Blanchard (73010) ***(G-724)***

ALPHABETIC SECTION

Miket ADS Inc...918 341-2992
218 N Missouri Ave Claremore (74017) *(G-1655)*

Miketads Inc..918 341-2992
218 N Missouri Ave Claremore (74017) *(G-1656)*

Milam Engineering, Oklahoma City Also called Inglesrud Corp *(G-6304)*

Milamar Coatings LLC (HQ).......................405 755-8448
311 Nw 122nd St Ste 100 Oklahoma City (73114) *(G-6608)*

Milamar/Polymax, Oklahoma City Also called Milamar Coatings LLC *(G-6608)*

Milestones Learning Center, Owasso Also called Hacker Industries LLC *(G-7573)*

Military Parts Mfg LLC................................405 301-2990
420 Winding Creek Rd Yukon (73099) *(G-11755)*

Military Parts Plus Inc (PA)........................918 232-1581
2320 W Mobile Pl Broken Arrow (74011) *(G-976)*

Mill Creek Granite & Stone, Tulsa Also called Wood Systems Inc *(G-11148)*

Mill Creek Lumber & Supply Co (PA)............918 794-3600
6974 E 38th St Tulsa (74145) *(G-10279)*

Mill Creek Lumber & Supply Co...................405 947-7227
5251 W Reno Ave Ste E Oklahoma City (73127) *(G-6609)*

Mill Creek Quarry, Mill Creek Also called Martin Marietta Materials Inc *(G-4469)*

Mill Work Specialties LLC..........................918 639-8385
712 N 95th East Pl # 293 Tulsa (74115) *(G-10280)*

Millbrae Energy LLC..................................405 286-1941
770 E Britton Rd Oklahoma City (73114) *(G-6610)*

Millennial Technologies LLC.......................405 478-4351
6701 N Bryant Ave Oklahoma City (73121) *(G-6611)*

Millennium Prod Explrtion Corp..................405 495-3311
229 S Eagle Ln Oklahoma City (73128) *(G-6612)*

Miller Bros Wldg & Roustabout..................918 968-1611
314 W Main St Stroud (74079) *(G-8813)*

Miller Graphics...580 824-2698
1111 Church St Waynoka (73860) *(G-11380)*

Miller Mfg Group.......................................918 540-1600
410 A St Ne Miami (74354) *(G-4418)*

Miller Printing Company Inc......................918 749-0981
4932 S Peoria Ave Tulsa (74105) *(G-10281)*

Miller Pump Systems Inc...........................918 455-4556
6301 S 5th St Broken Arrow (74011) *(G-977)*

Miller Sales Wholesale Distr.......................918 629-4064
6224 S Victor Ave Tulsa (74136) *(G-10282)*

Miller Welding & Supply............................580 492-5464
4700 Nw Wolf Rd Lawton (73507) *(G-3970)*

Millers Marble and Granite.........................580 357-1348
19106 Se Woodlawn Rd Lawton (73501) *(G-3971)*

Millers Superior Electric LLC......................918 933-4006
8 S 109th East Pl Tulsa (74128) *(G-10283)*

Millertime Manufacturing LLC....................918 273-2040
Rr 2 Box 354 Nowata (74048) *(G-5221)*

Mills Enterprises Inc.................................405 236-4470
2709 Sw 52nd St Oklahoma City (73119) *(G-6613)*

Mills Machine Co......................................405 273-4900
201 N Oklahoma Ave Shawnee (74801) *(G-8475)*

Mills Roof Truss Co, Oklahoma City Also called Mills Enterprises Inc *(G-6613)*

Mills Well Service Inc................................405 382-4107
12525 Ns 356 Seminole (74868) *(G-8385)*

Milot James Residence Cnstr......................405 433-2661
16371 W Forrest Hills Rd Cashion (73016) *(G-1291)*

Miltech Lab Services Inc............................918 251-4436
2225 W Atlanta St Ste B Broken Arrow (74012) *(G-978)*

Milton Donaghey......................................580 332-1551
224 N Rennie St Ada (74820) *(G-66)*

Milton Nichols Inc....................................405 769-2216
232 N Tunbridge Rd Oklahoma City (73130) *(G-6614)*

Mimic Manufacturing LLC.........................918 653-7161
102 Pitchford Ln Heavener (74937) *(G-3430)*

Minco Grain & Feed, Minco Also called Shawnee Milling Company *(G-4481)*

Mineral Resource Tech Inc.........................918 683-7671
4901 Chandler Rd Muskogee (74403) *(G-4714)*

Mineral Resources Company......................405 234-9000
20 N Broadway Oklahoma City (73102) *(G-6615)*

Minexco, Norman Also called Montgomery Exploration Company *(G-5080)*

Mingo Aerospace LLC..............................918 272-7371
8141 N 116th East Ave Owasso (74055) *(G-7591)*

Mingo Aerospace LLC..............................918 272-7371
8121 N 116th Ave Owasso (74055) *(G-7592)*

Mingo Manufacturing Inc...........................918 272-1151
8091 N 115th East Ave Owasso (74055) *(G-7593)*

Minick Materials Company (PA)..................405 789-2068
326 N Council Rd Oklahoma City (73127) *(G-6616)*

Minko Design Architecture, Tulsa Also called Minko Design LLC *(G-10285)*

Minko Design LLC (PA)..............................918 895-6498
1131 E Easton St Tulsa (74120) *(G-10284)*

Minko Design LLC....................................918 895-6498
108 N Greenwood Ave Tulsa (74120) *(G-10285)*

Minko Design-Millwork, Tulsa Also called Minko Design LLC *(G-10284)*

Minnette Company Ltd.............................580 226-2929
1161 Us Highway 70a Wilson (73463) *(G-11538)*

Minor Printing Company............................580 795-3745
1201 Wiggs Ave Madill (73446) *(G-4158)*

Mint Turbines LLC....................................918 968-9561
2915 N Highway 99 Stroud (74079) *(G-8814)*

Minuteman Press.....................................405 942-5595
300 N Ann Arbor Ave Oklahoma City (73127) *(G-6617)*

Miracle Production Inc..............................405 324-2216
9500 Sw 15th St Oklahoma City (73128) *(G-6618)*

Miracle Recreation Eqp Co.........................918 299-1415
14221 S Urbana Ave Bixby (74008) *(G-645)*

Miraclon Corporation (PA).........................580 772-5502
2720 S Frontage Rd Weatherford (73096) *(G-11428)*

Miratech Corporation................................918 622-7077
420 S 145th East Ave A Tulsa (74108) *(G-10286)*

Miratech Group LLC (PA)..........................918 622-7077
420 S 145th East Ave Tulsa (74108) *(G-10287)*

Misaco Sign & Screen Printing....................918 542-4188
424 Henley St Miami (74354) *(G-4419)*

Misaco Sign and Screen Prtg......................918 542-4188
424 Henley St Miami (74354) *(G-4420)*

Misco, Yale Also called Moore Iron & Steel Corp *(G-11686)*

Miss Priss Monograms & EMB....................918 697-9468
4888 E 360 Rd Talala (74080) *(G-8901)*

Mission Transportation LLC......................405 694-4755
7200 Nw 63rd St Bethany (73008) *(G-591)*

Misson Fluid King Oil Field........................405 670-8771
1501 Se 25th St Oklahoma City (73129) *(G-6619)*

Mitch Baskett..405 324-7810
11704 Sw 4th St Yukon (73099) *(G-11756)*

Mitchco Fabrication Inc............................580 762-0256
2104 N Ash St Ponca City (74601) *(G-7853)*

Mitchell Ironworks Inc..............................580 233-7925
3825 E Willow Rd Enid (73701) *(G-3014)*

Mitchell Oil Company................................918 652-9175
900 W Vandever Blvd Broken Arrow (74012) *(G-979)*

Mitchell T Widler......................................501 860-3738
10434 Brug Hartman Rd Burneyville (73430) *(G-1217)*

Mitchells Sausage Rolls............................918 342-5852
9459 Alawhe Dr Claremore (74019) *(G-1657)*

Mitchells Tank Truck Service......................580 229-1880
12546 Highway 76 Healdton (73438) *(G-3419)*

Mito Material Solutions Inc.......................855 344-6486
1414 S Sangre Rd 103 Stillwater (74074) *(G-8725)*

Mitre Box Frame Shop..............................580 338-2319
507 N Main St Guymon (73942) *(G-3356)*

Mixon Brothers Wood Prsv Co....................580 286-9494
1202 Nw 16th St Idabel (74745) *(G-3643)*

MJ&h Fabrication, Ponca City Also called M J & H Fabrication Inc *(G-7847)*

MJM Resources Inc..................................405 579-4455
4003 Potomac Dr Norman (73072) *(G-5076)*

Mjs Crafts...405 598-8105
38763 New Hope Rd Tecumseh (74873) *(G-8923)*

Mjs Fence Welding...................................580 320-1620
17302 County Road 3540 Ada (74820) *(G-67)*

ML Sign Service LLC.................................405 386-4898
11601 S Triple Rd Newalla (74857) *(G-4815)*

Mlb Consulting LLC..................................405 285-8559
3075 Willowood Rd Edmond (73034) *(G-2520)*

Mlb Consulting LLC (PA)...........................580 225-2717
213 N Jefferson Ave Elk City (73644) *(G-2849)*

Mlb Consulting LLC..................................580 504-8810
620 General Dr Ste 5 Ardmore (73401) *(G-333)*

Mlb Portable Welding LLC.........................918 531-2414
399551 W 400 Rd Copan (74022) *(G-1851)*

Mlb Welding LLC......................................580 481-0852
2112 N Canary Ln Altus (73521) *(G-162)*

Mltl Enterprises LLC.................................405 321-2224
231 E Robinson St Norman (73069) *(G-5077)*

Mms LLC...405 872-3486
1101 E Maguire Rd Noble (73068) *(G-4886)*

MMS Sales, Noble Also called Mms LLC *(G-4886)*

MO Money Minerals LLC...........................405 262-2457
824 N Calumet Rd Calumet (73014) *(G-1247)*

MO Publishing LLC...................................580 284-3719
30 Nw Sandy Trail Ln Lawton (73505) *(G-3972)*

Mobetta..580 588-9222
104 E Evans Ave Apache (73006) *(G-220)*

Mobile Express..405 395-9378
4901 N Kickapoo Ave Shawnee (74804) *(G-8476)*

Mobile Hightech.......................................405 942-4600
1001 Enterprise Ave Ste 9 Oklahoma City (73128) *(G-6620)*

Mobile Laser Forces.................................405 259-9300
10009 Ne 23rd St Oklahoma City (73141) *(G-6621)*

Mobile Mini LLC.......................................918 582-5857
12044 E Pine St Tulsa (74116) *(G-10288)*

Mobile Mini Inc..405 682-9333
14120 S Meridian Ave Oklahoma City (73173) *(G-6622)*

Mobile PC Manager LLC............................574 551-4521
606 E 119th St S Jenks (74037) *(G-3717)*

Mobile Products Inc..................................580 227-3711
201 W Oklahoma Ave Fairview (73737) *(G-3143)*

Mobility Living Inc 405 672-7237
  1215 Se 44th St Oklahoma City (73129) *(G-6623)*
Mobility One Transportation 918 437-4488
  17520 E Pine St Unit C Tulsa (74116) *(G-10289)*
Moblie Products Inc 580 227-3711
  201 W Oklahoma Ave Fairview (73737) *(G-3144)*
Mobonoto Automotive LLC 580 480-0410
  400 W Broadway St Altus (73521) *(G-163)*
Moccasin Trail Company 405 380-8221
  359188 E 1090 Rd Paden (74860) *(G-7636)*
Moccasins of Hope Society 605 431-3738
  7447 E Coleman Rd Ponca City (74604) *(G-7854)*
Mock Brothers Saddlery Inc 918 245-7259
  17441 W 9th St S Sand Springs (74063) *(G-8205)*
Modern Bindery Inc 918 250-9486
  5408 S 103rd East Ave Tulsa (74146) *(G-10290)*
Modern Coatings LLC 405 795-2633
  10600 S Pennsylvania Ave Oklahoma City (73170) *(G-5307)*
Modern Plating Co Inc (PA) 918 836-5081
  1125 S Norwood Ave Tulsa (74112) *(G-10291)*
Modernblox LLC 405 673-6215
  1305 N Louisville Ave Tulsa (74115) *(G-10292)*
Modesto Signs, Ardmore Also called Modesto Vinyl Lettering Inc *(G-334)*
Modesto Vinyl Lettering Inc 580 223-4262
  604 W Broadway St Ardmore (73401) *(G-334)*
Modular Services Company 405 521-9923
  12501 E Coffee Creek Rd Arcadia (73007) *(G-231)*
Modular Squad LLC 918 695-0114
  2864 S Gary Ave Tulsa (74114) *(G-10293)*
Moe Mark of Excellence LLC 405 650-9898
  1112 Nw 5th St Oklahoma City (73106) *(G-6624)*
Moeder Oil & Gas LLC 405 286-9192
  14208 Gaillardia Pl Oklahoma City (73142) *(G-6625)*
Moes Portable Steam Co Inc 580 432-5467
  28252 N County Road 3070 Foster (73434) *(G-3187)*
Mogar Industries 918 445-3747
  6440 S 39th West Ave Tulsa (74132) *(G-10294)*
Mohawk Industries 214 309-4652
  2504 W Owen K Garriott Rd Enid (73703) *(G-3015)*
Mohawk Materials, Oklahoma City Also called Handi-Sak Inc *(G-6210)*
Mohawk Materials Co Inc (PA) 918 584-2707
  2521 Charles Page Blvd Tulsa (74127) *(G-10295)*
Moi Oil & Gas Inc 580 753-4266
  274410 E County Road 56 Ames (73718) *(G-198)*
Mojo Sports LLC 405 390-8935
  6001 Se 15th St Midwest City (73110) *(G-4447)*
Moku LLC 918 398-8479
  110 E Delaware St Cleveland (74020) *(G-1727)*
Mold Tech Inc 918 247-6275
  22239 W Highway 33 Sapulpa (74066) *(G-8292)*
Molded Products Incorporated 918 254-9061
  21920 E 96th St S Broken Arrow (74014) *(G-1144)*
Moldman Kansas City 918 921-6823
  3315 E 39th St Tulsa (74135) *(G-10296)*
Molitor Design & Cnstr LLC 405 802-8302
  1404 Sw 25th St Moore (73170) *(G-4542)*
Mollycoddled Hash Slinger LLC 918 236-1196
  118 Se Railroad Fort Gibson (74434) *(G-3176)*
Molycorp Rare Metals 918 673-2511
  3225 S 625 Rd Quapaw (74363) *(G-8032)*
Mom Hustle Tee Co 417 658-6450
  4001 S Ash Ave Broken Arrow (74011) *(G-980)*
Momentum Completion 918 364-9444
  4302 E 116th Pl Tulsa (74137) *(G-10297)*
Moms Haulin Dads Dozin Inc 405 392-5508
  2705 Nw 16th St Newcastle (73065) *(G-4832)*
Monarch Foods, Inc., Muskogee Also called Henderson Coffee Corp *(G-4690)*
Mondo Solutions LLC 405 788-0056
  911 N 4th Ave Purcell (73080) *(G-8017)*
Mongoose Energy LLC 918 884-3508
  1 W 3rd St Ste 1700 Tulsa (74103) *(G-10298)*
Mongrel Empire Press LLC 405 459-0042
  133 24th Ave Nw Norman (73069) *(G-5078)*
Monitron Corp 918 836-6831
  733 Greenview Cir Sand Springs (74063) *(G-8206)*
Monkey Chase Banana LLC 405 706-5551
  1705 Dublin Rd Oklahoma City (73120) *(G-6626)*
Monod Bloc Inc 918 622-8132
  5556 S Mingo Rd Tulsa (74146) *(G-10299)*
Monogram Hut 214 707-4196
  124 N Cedar St Jenks (74037) *(G-3718)*
Monograms Elite Inc 580 353-1635
  2422 Sw Jefferson Ave Lawton (73505) *(G-3973)*
Monroe Gray LLC (PA) 918 813-6588
  122 W Breckenridge Ave Bixby (74008) *(G-646)*
Monroe Natural Gas Inc 405 321-5647
  501 Okmulgee St Norman (73071) *(G-5079)*
Monson Associates Inc 918 298-0037
  6014 E 101st St Tulsa (74137) *(G-10300)*

Montello Inc 918 665-1170
  6106 E 32nd Pl Ste 100 Tulsa (74135) *(G-10301)*
Montgomery Exploration Company 405 232-1169
  2600 Van Buren St # 2636 Norman (73072) *(G-5080)*
Montgomery Mattress 580 255-8979
  5101 N Hwy 81 Duncan (73533) *(G-2156)*
Montgomery Mattress Factory, Duncan Also called Montgomery Mattress *(G-2156)*
Monticello Cabinets Doors Inc 405 228-4900
  512 Sw 3rd St Oklahoma City (73109) *(G-6627)*
Montross Tirita 918 241-5637
  21 W 41st St Sand Springs (74063) *(G-8207)*
Monty L Hott Production Corp 405 495-3311
  7925 N Wilshire Ct Oklahoma City (73132) *(G-6628)*
Monumental Rocks 918 240-8398
  1001 S Desert Palm Ave Broken Arrow (74012) *(G-981)*
Moodys Jewelry Incorporated (PA) 918 834-3371
  1137 S Harvard Ave Tulsa (74112) *(G-10302)*
Moodys Jewelry Incorporated 918 747-5599
  1812 Utica Sq Tulsa (74114) *(G-10303)*
Moog Inc 405 732-0009
  2501 Liberty Pkwy Ste 500 Midwest City (73110) *(G-4448)*
Moon Chemical Products Co 405 602-6678
  409 N Ann Arbor Ave Oklahoma City (73127) *(G-6629)*
Moondog Puzzles LLC 405 286-6881
  2748 Nw Grand Blvd Oklahoma City (73116) *(G-6630)*
Mooney Oilfield Services LLC 580 660-5203
  2109 Ez Go Dr Weatherford (73096) *(G-11429)*
Moonlight Machine LLC 580 718-5111
  3908 Santa Fe St Ponca City (74601) *(G-7855)*
Moore Contract Pumping 918 372-4645
  11906 E 68th St Ripley (74062) *(G-8102)*
Moore Iron & Steel Corp 918 387-2639
  201 W Charleston Ave Yale (74085) *(G-11686)*
Moore Oil & Gas, Collinsville Also called Bob Gene Moore *(G-1804)*
Moore Printing Co Inc 417 866-6696
  604 S Classen Ave Moore (73160) *(G-4543)*
Moore Scents LLC 405 642-5472
  10637 Sw 36th St Yukon (73099) *(G-11757)*
Moores Hardware and Home Ctr 918 287-4458
  521 E Main St Pawhuska (74056) *(G-7689)*
Mora Mora Media LLC 918 231-6651
  18390 E Red Fox Trl Owasso (74055) *(G-7594)*
Moran Equipment 405 262-1422
  2614 Sunset Dr El Reno (73036) *(G-2739)*
Moran Equipment LLC 580 225-2575
  305 Industrial Pkwy Elk City (73644) *(G-2850)*
MORAN OIL ENTERPRISES, Seminole Also called Moran-K Oil LLC *(G-8387)*
Moran Oil Enterprises 405 382-6001
  222 N 2nd St Seminole (74868) *(G-8386)*
Moran-K Oil, Seminole Also called Moran Oil Enterprises *(G-8386)*
Moran-K Oil LLC 405 382-6001
  222 N 2nd St Seminole (74868) *(G-8387)*
More Boom Company 580 226-5303
  1823 Stanley St Sw Ardmore (73401) *(G-335)*
More Than Wood Sawmill, Asher Also called Michael Allan Sharp *(G-392)*
Morgan Drilling Co 580 657-3659
  2308 Foxden Rd Ardmore (73401) *(G-336)*
Morgan Hauling 580 420-3265
  1550 Morgan Rd Broken Bow (74728) *(G-1202)*
Morgan Well Service Inc 405 567-2288
  815 W 1st St Prague (74864) *(G-7930)*
Morgans Bakery 918 456-3731
  131 N Muskogee Ave Tahlequah (74464) *(G-8875)*
Morgans Repair Shop Inc 405 382-3114
  398 Boren Blvd Seminole (74868) *(G-8388)*
Morgn Graphic Design, McAlester Also called Bargain Journal *(G-4273)*
Moritz Inc 918 834-1064
  877 Creek Rd Sand Springs (74063) *(G-8208)*
Moritz Machine Shop, Sand Springs Also called Moritz Inc *(G-8208)*
Morning Fax 918 357-5245
  24010 Lamb Ter Broken Arrow (74014) *(G-1145)*
Morrill & Assoc Inc 918 481-1055
  6011 S Sheridan Rd Tulsa (74145) *(G-10304)*
Morris Communications Co LLC 405 273-4200
  215 N Bell Ave Shawnee (74801) *(G-8477)*
Morris Monuments 580 924-1323
  1517 Cemetery Rd Durant (74701) *(G-2244)*
Morris News 918 733-4898
  421 E Ozark St Ste A Morris (74445) *(G-4600)*
Morris Richardson 918 427-7323
  Rr 2 Box 135 Muldrow (74948) *(G-4634)*
Morris Welding 580 486-3474
  1644 County Road 1380 Chickasha (73018) *(G-1490)*
Morrow Wood Products Inc 405 579-5200
  6851 72nd Ave Ne Norman (73026) *(G-5081)*
Morton Buildings Inc 918 683-6668
  4021 Old Shawnee Rd Muskogee (74403) *(G-4715)*
Morton Buildings Inc 580 323-1172
  I40 W At Parkersburg Rd Clinton (73601) *(G-1759)*

Morton Buildings Inc...405 288-1031
527 E Center Rd Washington (73093) *(G-11335)*
Morton Grinding Works...918 652-8550
25980 S 290 Rd Henryetta (74437) *(G-3513)*
Morton Leases Inc...918 733-2331
16360 N 280 Rd Morris (74445) *(G-4601)*
Morton Manufacturing Co Inc...918 584-0333
839 N Wheeling Ave Tulsa (74110) *(G-10305)*
Mosley...918 407-6619
2916 N Hickory Ave Broken Arrow (74012) *(G-982)*
Mosley Backhoe Service...405 567-4710
2 1/2 E Centerview Prague (74864) *(G-7931)*
Moss Seat Cover Mfg & Sls Co...918 742-3326
4954 S Peoria Ave Tulsa (74105) *(G-10306)*
Moss Seat Covers, Tulsa *Also called Moss Seat Cover Mfg & Sls Co (G-10306)*
Moss Welding LLC...580 216-1605
204225 E County Road 57 Vici (73859) *(G-11246)*
Mostly Missiles...405 808-4611
1404 Nw 141st St Edmond (73013) *(G-2521)*
Mostmachine LLC...918 706-0393
327 S Cherokee Ave Claremore (74017) *(G-1658)*
Mother Earth Eco Entps LLC...785 250-8706
17814 County Road 1499 Ct Ada (74820) *(G-68)*
Mounds Printing...918 827-6573
17257 S 89th West Ave Mounds (74047) *(G-4621)*
Mountain Country Foods LLC...580 822-4130
201 Industrial Ave Okeene (73763) *(G-5259)*
Mountain Top Machine Inc...918 787-5510
35999 S 568 Rd Jay (74346) *(G-3683)*
Mountain View News, Mountain View *Also called Mountain View Printing Company (G-4628)*
Mountain View Printing Company...580 347-2231
319 Main St Mountain View (73062) *(G-4628)*
Mountaintop Tees LLC...918 508-6208
10483 Lance Ln Sand Springs (74063) *(G-8209)*
Mowdy Machine Inc...580 252-9333
1245 Boren Rd Duncan (73533) *(G-2157)*
Mower Parts Inc...405 947-6484
4110 Nw 10th St Oklahoma City (73107) *(G-6631)*
Mpf Industries LLC...918 492-0809
2448 E 81st St Ste 4550 Tulsa (74137) *(G-10307)*
Mpi Davis Quarry, Davis *Also called Martin Marietta Materials Inc (G-1989)*
Mpl Manufacturing LLC...918 630-9944
13555 S 129th East Ave Broken Arrow (74011) *(G-983)*
Mpress Cards...405 590-5393
3405 Bright St Norman (73072) *(G-5082)*
Mpt, Ardmore *Also called Machine Parts & Tool (G-326)*
Mr Bill Sign Design & Graphics, Newalla *Also called Bill Koenig (G-4805)*
Mr Mfg...918 352-4461
9931 S Highway 99 Drumright (74030) *(G-2067)*
Mr Windshield Repair, Oklahoma City *Also called Mel Robinson (G-6561)*
MRC Global (us) Inc...405 491-7392
2010 S Radio Rd El Reno (73036) *(G-2740)*
MRC Global (us) Inc...918 485-9511
1300 N Labarge Ave Wagoner (74467) *(G-11287)*
Mrs Smiths Bakery of Stillwell, Stilwell *Also called Sfc Global Supply Chain Inc (G-8795)*
Mrsdish LLC...405 447-3813
1025 E Indian Hills Rd Norman (73071) *(G-5083)*
Mrt - Muskogee Plant TP, Muskogee *Also called Mineral Resource Tech Inc (G-4714)*
MRW Technologies Inc...918 827-6030
2301 W 171st St S Glenpool (74033) *(G-3239)*
Ms 3 Oil & Gas LLC...580 465-7354
374 Santa Fe Rd Wilson (73463) *(G-11539)*
Ms Enterprises...918 627-1824
3823 S 99th East Ave Tulsa (74146) *(G-10308)*
Msc Inc...918 425-4996
3123 N Lewis Ave Tulsa (74110) *(G-10309)*
MSI Inspection Service LLC...405 265-2121
1306 Sovereign Row Oklahoma City (73108) *(G-6632)*
Mt Designs...580 317-3921
194541 N 4360 Rd Fort Towson (74735) *(G-3183)*
Mt Percussion Drilling LLC...918 232-5472
6237 S Indianapolis Pl Tulsa (74136) *(G-10310)*
Mt Vernon Coal Transfer Co (HQ)...918 295-7600
1717 S Boulder Ave Tulsa (74119) *(G-10311)*
Mtds, Sand Springs *Also called Montross Tirita (G-8207)*
Mtm Inc...918 824-3700
4811 Ne 1st St Pryor (74361) *(G-7977)*
Mtm Recognition LLC...405 670-4545
3501 Se 29th St Oklahoma City (73115) *(G-6633)*
Mtm Recognition Corporation (PA)...405 609-6900
3201 Se 29th St Oklahoma City (73115) *(G-6634)*
Mtm Recognition Corporation...405 670-4545
3405 Se 29th St Del City (73115) *(G-2002)*
Mtw Powder Coating...918 638-4795
11283 S 285th East Ave Coweta (74429) *(G-1892)*
Mud Haulers LLC...580 338-3830
102 S East St Guymon (73942) *(G-3357)*
Mud Mixers LLC...580 243-7826
201 W Broadway Ave # 203 Elk City (73644) *(G-2851)*
Mudd Print & Promo LLC...405 501-6107
1701 Signal Ridge Dr # 15 Edmond (73013) *(G-2522)*
Mueggs Hot Shot Service LLC...405 368-8362
210 Stroh Ave Okarche (73762) *(G-5246)*
Mueller Supply Company Inc...918 485-2034
2110 S Highway 69 Wagoner (74467) *(G-11288)*
Muirfield Production Co Inc...918 744-5604
2627 E 21st St Tulsa (74114) *(G-10312)*
Muirfield Resources, Tulsa *Also called Muirfield Production Co Inc (G-10312)*
Muirfield Resources Company (PA)...918 744-5604
2642 E 21st St Ste 285 Tulsa (74114) *(G-10313)*
Mulberry Tree Graphics...580 248-3194
5527 Nw Eisenhower Dr Lawton (73505) *(G-3974)*
Mule Hunting Clothes Inc...601 856-5169
19723 E 126th St N Collinsville (74021) *(G-1817)*
Mullins Salvage Inc...918 352-9612
7304 E Main St Cushing (74023) *(G-1946)*
Mullins Sign Shop...580 889-4772
2700 S Mississippi Ave Atoka (74525) *(G-420)*
Multigraphic Design...405 672-8201
3517 Ridglea Ct Oklahoma City (73115) *(G-6635)*
Multiples Inc...918 584-7982
110 S Norfolk Ave Tulsa (74120) *(G-10314)*
Multiprint Corp...918 832-0300
6915 E 38th St Tulsa (74145) *(G-10315)*
Muncie Power Products Inc...918 838-0900
7217 E Pine St Tulsa (74115) *(G-10316)*
Munger and Krout Inc...580 237-7060
101 S Grand St Enid (73701) *(G-3016)*
Munoz Oilfield Services LLC...580 799-5857
103 Mary Dr Elk City (73644) *(G-2852)*
Muras Energy Inc...405 751-0442
25 Nw 144th Cir Ste B Edmond (73013) *(G-2523)*
Murphy Products Inc...405 842-7177
2512 Exchange Ave Oklahoma City (73108) *(G-6636)*
Murphy Wallbed USA LLC...918 836-5833
1835 N 105th East Ave Tulsa (74116) *(G-10317)*
Murray Services Inc...405 542-3069
3209 N Vernon Ave Hinton (73047) *(G-3534)*
Musgrove Energy Inc...580 765-7314
1121 N Prentice Rd Ponca City (74604) *(G-7856)*
Music Games n Things Inc...918 742-4349
1556 E 37th St Tulsa (74105) *(G-10318)*
Musick Farms Cattle Co, Sentinel *Also called Musick Farms Inc (G-8411)*
Musick Farms Inc...580 393-4826
12692 N 2090 Rd Sentinel (73664) *(G-8411)*
Musick Welding LLC...405 274-1766
4401 S 16th St Chickasha (73018) *(G-1491)*
Musicware Press...405 627-1894
409 Sw 64th St Oklahoma City (73139) *(G-6637)*
Muskie Proppant LLC (HQ)...405 233-3558
14201 Caliber Dr Ste 300 Oklahoma City (73134) *(G-6638)*
Muskogee Marble & Granite LLC (PA)...918 682-0064
1525 N York St Muskogee (74403) *(G-4716)*
Muskogee Pallet, Muskogee *Also called Prime Pallet LLC (G-4737)*
Muskogee Phoenix, Muskogee *Also called Newspaper Holding Inc (G-4722)*
Muskogee Ready Mix Inc...918 682-3403
4400 Callery Dr Muskogee (74403) *(G-4717)*
Muskogee Sand Company Inc...918 683-1766
3202 W 50th St N Porter (74454) *(G-7894)*
Mustang Extreme Environmental...405 681-1800
2425 S Ann Arbor Ave Oklahoma City (73128) *(G-6639)*
Mustang Fuel Corporation...580 446-5552
3214 N 42nd St Enid (73701) *(G-3017)*
Mustang Fuel Corporation...405 748-9400
9800 N Oklahoma Ave Oklahoma City (73114) *(G-6640)*
Mustang Fuel Corporation (PA)...405 884-2092
9800 N Oklahoma Ave Oklahoma City (73114) *(G-6641)*
Mustang Gas Proc In Texas, Oklahoma City *Also called Mustang Fuel Corporation (G-6640)*
Mustang Gas Products LLC...405 748-9400
9800 N Oklahoma Ave Oklahoma City (73114) *(G-6642)*
Mustang Heavy Haul LLC...405 743-0085
4905 S Perkins Rd Stillwater (74074) *(G-8726)*
Mustang Land & Cattle Co, Oklahoma City *Also called Dave Bolton (G-5902)*
Mustang Machines Works Inc...405 745-7545
1516 E State Highway 152 Mustang (73064) *(G-4783)*
Mustang Manufacturing, Sapulpa *Also called Outdoor Incorporated (G-8295)*
Mustang News, The, Mustang *Also called News Enterprises Inc (G-4787)*
Mustang Optical Inc...405 376-0222
123 N Mustang Rd Mustang (73064) *(G-4784)*
Mustang Times...405 606-1023
4557 W Memorial Rd Oklahoma City (73142) *(G-6643)*
Mustang Ventures Company...405 748-9400
13439 Broadway Ext Oklahoma City (73114) *(G-6644)*
Mustard Seed Screen Printing...918 687-6290
3620 S Country Club Rd Muskogee (74403) *(G-4718)*
Muzny Sheet Metal Works, Oklahoma City *Also called David Muzny (G-5904)*
Mv Pipeline Company...918 689-5600
111 S Main St Eufaula (74432) *(G-3105)*

ALPHABETIC

Mvp, Oklahoma City *Also called Midland Vinyl Products Inc* ***(G-6597)***
Mw Engineering Co 405 273-0370
23 E 9th St Ste 406 Shawnee (74801) ***(G-8478)***
Mw Piping Fabrication LLC 918 836-4200
5001 W 21st St Tulsa (74107) ***(G-10319)***
Mwd Services LLC 918 698-6109
8404 E 80th St N Owasso (74055) ***(G-7595)***
MWH Enterprises Inc 918 665-0944
7707 E 38th St Tulsa (74145) ***(G-10320)***
My Man Tees LLC 580 695-9474
20077 Ne Wolf Rd Fletcher (73541) ***(G-3164)***
Myers & Myers Inc 405 341-5861
1616 E 19th St Ste 500 Edmond (73013) ***(G-2524)***
Myers Metalkraft LLC 405 657-2084
1201 Allens Trl Edmond (73012) ***(G-2525)***
Myers Welding LLC 405 277-3202
18220 E Highway 66 Luther (73054) ***(G-4136)***
Myprint 918 542-7672
218 E Central Ave Ste D Miami (74354) ***(G-4421)***
Myskey Welding 918 371-4906
16718 N 137th East Ave Collinsville (74021) ***(G-1818)***
Mystic Rock Miniatures 817 845-1590
16101 Sw 25th St El Reno (73036) ***(G-2741)***
Mystik River Woodworks 580 606-0071
711 Church Ave Comanche (73529) ***(G-1843)***
Mythic Press 918 516-8255
2015 E 3rd St Tulsa (74104) ***(G-10321)***
Mzmouze Embroidery Creat LLP 405 696-6545
215 S 17th St Guthrie (73044) ***(G-3326)***
N & S Flame Spray LLC 918 865-4737
2158 S Highway 48 Mannford (74044) ***(G-4187)***
N A Blastrac Inc 405 478-3440
13201 N Santa Fe Ave Oklahoma City (73114) ***(G-6645)***
N E O Fabrication L L C 918 541-9203
604 Henley St Miami (74354) ***(G-4422)***
N M & O Operating Company 918 584-3802
15 E 5th St Ste 3000 Tulsa (74103) ***(G-10322)***
N O C Supply Inc 405 562-7070
1326 S Fretz Ave Edmond (73003) ***(G-2526)***
N P T Inc 580 399-0306
227 E 26th St Ada (74820) ***(G-69)***
N2r Media LLC 405 301-0188
3126 S Boulevard Ste 127 Edmond (73013) ***(G-2527)***
Nabi Biomedical Center, Tulsa *Also called Vaxart Inc* ***(G-11067)***
Nabors Completion Prod Svcs Co 580 323-0058
22096 Highway 73 Clinton (73601) ***(G-1760)***
Nabors Drilling Tech USA Inc 580 243-4000
100 Panel Rd Elk City (73644) ***(G-2853)***
Nabors Drilling Tech USA Inc 405 324-8081
10100 Nw 10th St Oklahoma City (73127) ***(G-6646)***
Nabors Drilling Tech USA Inc 405 745-3457
5500 S Rockwell St Oklahoma City (73179) ***(G-6647)***
Nabors Drilling Usa LP 580 225-0072
1501 S Merritt Rd Elk City (73644) ***(G-2854)***
Nabors Welding & Supplies Inc 405 756-8198
202 W Cherokee St Lindsay (73052) ***(G-4075)***
Nabors Well Services Ltd 405 262-6262
4301 Us 66 E El Reno (73036) ***(G-2742)***
Nacols Jewelry 580 355-4280
3801 Nw Cache Rd Ste 33 Lawton (73505) ***(G-3975)***
Nadel & Gussman Anadarko, Tulsa *Also called Nadel and Gussman LLC* ***(G-10323)***
Nadel and Gussman LLC (PA) 918 583-3333
15 E 5th St Ste 3300 Tulsa (74103) ***(G-10323)***
Nafcoat Inc 918 367-9606
20963 W Highway 16 Bristow (74010) ***(G-789)***
Nafta Mud Inc 405 751-6261
4324 Nw Expressway 202 Oklahoma City (73116) ***(G-6648)***
Nafta Mud LLC (PA) 405 751-6261
4334 Nw Expwy St Ste 202 Oklahoma City (73116) ***(G-6649)***
Naked Wood Works 918 864-0229
509 N Redbud Ave Ste E Broken Arrow (74012) ***(G-984)***
Nameplates Inc (PA) 918 584-2651
325 S Quincy Ave Tulsa (74120) ***(G-10324)***
Nameplates Inc 918 561-8732
325 S Quincy Ave Tulsa (74120) ***(G-10325)***
Nance Precast Concrete Pdts, Piedmont *Also called Baray Enterprises Inc* ***(G-7755)***
Nance Solutions Inc 918 804-9301
5800 Sycamore Pond Dr Mustang (73064) ***(G-4785)***
Nancy Dalrymple 405 525-7544
1949 Nw 14th St Oklahoma City (73106) ***(G-6650)***
Nancy Nelson & Associates 580 765-0115
7879 Lake Rd Ponca City (74604) ***(G-7857)***
Nancy W Gravel 405 348-4409
4708 Blackjack Ln Edmond (73034) ***(G-2528)***
Nancys Trunk 405 413-5037
9211 W Main St Ripley (74062) ***(G-8103)***
Nanna Networks LLC 405 833-3329
3324 Green Wing Ct Oklahoma City (73120) ***(G-6651)***
Nano Light 405 579-5662
4625 Timberidge Cir Norman (73072) ***(G-5084)***
Nanomed Targeting Systems Inc 646 641-4747
4901 Richmond Sq Ste 103 Oklahoma City (73118) ***(G-6652)***
NAPA Auto Parts, Guymon *Also called Guymon Motor Parts Inc* ***(G-3350)***
NAPA Auto Parts, Owasso *Also called Standard Supply Co Inc* ***(G-7619)***
Napcus, Tulsa *Also called Petroflow Energy Ltd* ***(G-10503)***
Narcomey LLC 405 473-1350
150 Sw 10th St Oklahoma City (73109) ***(G-6653)***
Nash Custom Cabinets 405 919-7711
8329 Sw 92nd Cir Oklahoma City (73169) ***(G-6654)***
Nash Tactical LLC 405 589-6425
2716 Cimarron Dr Norman (73071) ***(G-5085)***
Natco, Oklahoma City *Also called Cameron Solutions Inc* ***(G-5680)***
Natco, Elk City *Also called Cameron Solutions Inc* ***(G-2791)***
National Bumper & Plating 405 235-1535
717 Sw 4th St Oklahoma City (73109) ***(G-6655)***
National Climate Solutions 844 682-4247
1418 E 71st St Tulsa (74136) ***(G-10326)***
National Coating 405 251-5065
25679 Highway 77 N Wynnewood (73098) ***(G-11671)***
National Coating Mfg Inc 580 332-8751
13707 County Road 3500 Ada (74820) ***(G-70)***
National Oilwell Varco Inc 580 251-6900
1200 E Highway 7 Duncan (73533) ***(G-2158)***
National Oilwell Varco Inc 405 745-6850
6602 Newcastle Rd Oklahoma City (73179) ***(G-6656)***
National Oilwell Varco Inc 918 423-8000
501 N George Nigh Expy McAlester (74501) ***(G-4322)***
National Oilwell Varco Inc 918 423-8000
401 Steven Taylor Blvd McAlester (74501) ***(G-4323)***
National Oilwell Varco Inc 405 677-3386
1008 Se 29th St Oklahoma City (73129) ***(G-6657)***
National Oilwell Varco Inc 713 346-7500
6440 Sw 44th St Oklahoma City (73179) ***(G-6658)***
National Oilwell Varco Inc 580 225-4136
S Hwy 6 Elk City (73648) ***(G-2855)***
National Oilwell Varco Inc 918 781-4436
3820 Port Pl Muskogee (74403) ***(G-4719)***
National Oilwell Varco Inc 918 447-4600
6750 S 57th West Ave Tulsa (74131) ***(G-9022)***
National Oilwell Varco LP 405 677-2484
9525b Pole Rd Moore (73160) ***(G-4544)***
National Petro Chem, Ada *Also called Technology Management Inc* ***(G-93)***
National Quality Cooling Pdts, Oklahoma City *Also called National Bumper & Plating* ***(G-6655)***
National Seating Mobility Inc 918 856-3000
3401 N May Ave Ste B Oklahoma City (73112) ***(G-6659)***
National Seating Mobility Inc 405 896-3680
3401 N May Ave Oklahoma City (73112) ***(G-6660)***
National Sign Market 405 821-8768
18409 Agua Dr Edmond (73012) ***(G-2529)***
National Steak & Poultry, Owasso *Also called Kormondy Enterprises Inc* ***(G-7584)***
National Steak and Poultry, Owasso *Also called National Steak Processors LLC* ***(G-7596)***
National Steak Processors LLC 918 274-8787
301 E 5th Ave Owasso (74055) ***(G-7596)***
National Swage, Tulsa *Also called Crosby Group LLC* ***(G-9510)***
Nations Crane Sales Inc 918 836-2000
3101 N Toledo Ave Tulsa (74115) ***(G-10327)***
Native American Capital LLC 918 289-7489
1932 S Desert Palm Ave Broken Arrow (74012) ***(G-985)***
Native American Maint Svcs Inc 918 682-5700
2000 Anderson Dr Muskogee (74403) ***(G-4720)***
Native American Times, Tahlequah *Also called Lisa Snell* ***(G-8872)***
Native Cbd Distributing 405 831-5270
980998 S 3390 Rd Meeker (74855) ***(G-4384)***
Native Distributing LLC 405 316-9223
3300 Deskin Dr Norman (73069) ***(G-5086)***
Native Exploration Mnrl LLC 405 603-5520
909 Nw 63rd St Oklahoma City (73116) ***(G-6661)***
Native Explration Holdings LLC 405 603-5520
909 Nw 63rd St Oklahoma City (73116) ***(G-6662)***
Native Explrtion Operating LLC 405 603-5520
921 Nw 63rd St Oklahoma City (73116) ***(G-6663)***
Native Remedy Cbd LLC 405 285-4050
5712 Industrial Blvd Edmond (73034) ***(G-2530)***
Native Spirits Winery LLC 405 329-9942
10500 E Lindsey St Norman (73026) ***(G-5087)***
Natural Care Solution LLC 405 919-1982
9716 S Gregory Rd Mustang (73064) ***(G-4786)***
Natural Fusion Energy, Tulsa *Also called New X Drive Tech Inc* ***(G-10337)***
Natural Gas Commpression Corp 918 243-7500
102 N Elm St Cleveland (74020) ***(G-1728)***
Natural Gas Services Group Inc 918 266-3330
5725 Bird Creek Ave Catoosa (74015) ***(G-1342)***
Natural Resources Oper LLC 405 997-3869
1831 E Imhoff Rd Ste 100 Norman (73071) ***(G-5088)***
Natural Stone Interiors 918 851-3451
611 W Breckenridge Ave Bixby (74008) ***(G-647)***

Naturalock Solutions LLC 405 812-9058
3201 Crystal Spring Dr Norman (73072) *(G-5089)*
Nature Creations 405 848-2605
1901 Nw Expressway Oklahoma City (73118) *(G-6664)*
Nature's Choice, Tulsa *Also called Supply Company Inc (G-10880)*
Natures Light LLC 925 209-1766
2420 S Sowegel Ave Broken Arrow (74012) *(G-986)*
Natures Rx Inc 405 484-7302
62 Rr 1 Paoli (73074) *(G-7638)*
Naumann McHining Solutions Inc 918 246-9898
11308 W 57th Pl S Sand Springs (74063) *(G-8210)*
Navajo County Publishers Inc 928 524-6203
1920 E 2nd St Apt 4011 Edmond (73034) *(G-2531)*
Navico Inc (PA) 918 437-6881
4500 S 129th East Ave # 200 Tulsa (74134) *(G-10328)*
Navico Inc 918 437-6881
4500 S 129th East Ave # 200 Tulsa (74134) *(G-10329)*
Navistar Inc 918 833-4065
2322 N Mingo Rd Tulsa (74116) *(G-10330)*
Nayfa Publications Inc 405 373-1616
414 Piedmont Rd N Ste A Piedmont (73078) *(G-7767)*
NBC Chemical Co Inc 580 256-2627
1603 9th St Woodward (73801) *(G-11613)*
Nbs Fabrication 918 527-5211
13537 S 4328 Chouteau (74337) *(G-1568)*
Nci Group Inc 405 672-7676
7000 S Eastern Ave Oklahoma City (73149) *(G-6665)*
NDC Systems 405 722-1101
5420 Nw 112th St Oklahoma City (73162) *(G-6666)*
Ndn Enterprises LLC 703 772-6635
134 E 6th St Pawhuska (74056) *(G-7690)*
Ndn Ink Works LLC 918 708-9250
418 W Main St Hulbert (74441) *(G-3625)*
Neco Industries Inc 405 682-3003
3345 S Ann Arbor Ave Oklahoma City (73179) *(G-6667)*
Nedley Publishing Co 580 223-5980
1045 15th Ave Nw Ardmore (73401) *(G-337)*
Needham Royalty Company LLC 405 297-0177
722 N Broadway Ave Oklahoma City (73102) *(G-6668)*
Negative One-Eighty 918 852-2332
24747 S Highway 66 Unit A Claremore (74019) *(G-1659)*
Negative One-Eighty Cryogenic 918 261-7748
24747 S Highway 66 Unit A Claremore (74019) *(G-1660)*
Neighbors Quality House Coffee, Oklahoma City *Also called Executive Coffee Service Co (G-6059)*
Neilson Manufacturing Inc (PA) 918 587-5548
3517 Charles Page Blvd Tulsa (74127) *(G-10331)*
Neisen Family LLC 580 762-2421
2200 N Ash St Ponca City (74601) *(G-7858)*
Nelco Defense LLC 580 471-7992
220 Buena Vista St Altus (73521) *(G-164)*
Nell Gavin LLC 972 935-6692
1524 Mountain Rd Bartlesville (74003) *(G-513)*
Nellis Vineyards LLC 405 826-5279
21204 Bogie Rd Edmond (73012) *(G-2532)*
Nelson Backhoe and Welding 918 399-3426
1513 S Linwood Ave Cushing (74023) *(G-1947)*
Nelson Exploration Corp 405 853-6933
1567 S Timber Rd Cleveland (74020) *(G-1729)*
Nelson Incorporated 918 812-5876
209 E 19th St Tulsa (74119) *(G-10332)*
Nelson's Pumping Service, Chester *Also called Michael Nelson (G-1420)*
Neminis Inc 918 582-8083
1350 S Boulder Ave # 400 Tulsa (74119) *(G-10333)*
Nenos Homemade Candles LLC 580 367-9874
13085 E Egypt Rd Coleman (73432) *(G-1797)*
Neo Concrete & Materials Inc 918 542-4456
2840 G St Nw Miami (74354) *(G-4423)*
Neo Rare Metals Oklahoma LLC 918 673-2511
3225 S 625 Rd Quapaw (74363) *(G-8033)*
Neo Sign Company 918 456-1959
23761 N 7 Mile Rd Fort Gibson (74434) *(G-3177)*
Neoinsulation LLC 405 605-6518
3900 E I 240 Scc Rd Oklahoma City (73135) *(G-6669)*
Neok Production Company 918 273-5662
1223 E Cherokee Ave Nowata (74048) *(G-5222)*
Neomanufacturing LLC 405 605-6581
202 N 6th St Apt 4 Kingfisher (73750) *(G-3809)*
Neon Creative LLC 405 837-0178
801 Nw 189th Cir Edmond (73012) *(G-2533)*
Neon Moore and Sign 405 672-6277
3501 Se 89th St Oklahoma City (73135) *(G-6670)*
Neosource Inc 918 622-4493
9422 E 55th Pl Tulsa (74145) *(G-10334)*
Ness Energy International 405 285-1140
1900 E 15th St Bldg 600 Edmond (73013) *(G-2534)*
Nestle Purina Factory, Edmond *Also called Nestle Purina Petcare Company (G-2535)*
Nestle Purina Petcare Company 405 751-4550
13900 N Lincoln Blvd Edmond (73013) *(G-2535)*
Netpro Industries Inc 918 630-3201
2604 S Beech Ave Broken Arrow (74012) *(G-987)*
New Day Creations LLC 918 576-9619
12345 S Memorial Dr # 120 Bixby (74008) *(G-648)*
New Dominion LLC 405 567-3034
11822 N Highway 99 Seminole (74868) *(G-8389)*
New Dominion LLC (PA) 918 587-6242
1307 S Boulder Ave # 400 Tulsa (74119) *(G-10335)*
New ERA 918 377-2259
209 N Broadway St Davenport (74026) *(G-1978)*
New ERA Newspaper, Davenport *Also called New ERA (G-1978)*
New ERA Signs LLC 405 926-2050
501 N Pecan St Pauls Valley (73075) *(G-7668)*
New Forums Press Inc 405 372-6158
1018 S Lewis St Stillwater (74074) *(G-8727)*
New Generation Drones 918 553-8703
18579 E 3rd St Tulsa (74108) *(G-10336)*
New Moon Vineyard 405 364-8655
4717 Tanglewood Ct Norman (73072) *(G-5090)*
New Ngc Inc 918 825-0142
4189 Hunt St Pryor (74361) *(G-7978)*
New Plains Review 405 974-5613
100 N University Dr Edmond (73034) *(G-2536)*
New Times Technologies Inc 918 872-9600
2600 W Albany St Ste A Broken Arrow (74012) *(G-988)*
New Tongs 580 335-3030
715 S Main St Frederick (73542) *(G-3197)*
New U Cbd Oil 405 568-8750
7605 Harold Dr Yukon (73099) *(G-11758)*
New Vision Consulting Group 405 796-7400
14711 Bristol Park Blvd Edmond (73013) *(G-2537)*
New Vision Manufacturing LLC 580 677-9937
1000 N Industrial Rd Madill (73446) *(G-4159)*
New X Drive Tech Inc 918 850-4463
613 E Young Pl Tulsa (74106) *(G-10337)*
New X Drives Inc 918 850-4463
613 E Young Pl Tulsa (74106) *(G-10338)*
Newcastle Gaming, Newcastle *Also called Chickasaw Nation (G-4821)*
Newcastle Pacer Inc 405 387-5277
120 Ne 2nd St Ste 102 Newcastle (73065) *(G-4833)*
Newcomb T Shirts and Promos, Oklahoma City *Also called Tony Newcomb Sportswear Inc (G-7303)*
Newell Manufacturing 918 782-1900
39026 S Hwy 82 Langley (74350) *(G-3873)*
Newell Wood Products 918 686-8060
6290 Highway 69 Muskogee (74402) *(G-4721)*
Newfield Exploration 2003 Inc 918 495-0598
7134 S Yale Ave Ste 430 Tulsa (74136) *(G-10339)*
Newfield Explrtion Md-Cntinent, Tulsa *Also called Newfield Exploration 2003 Inc (G-10339)*
Newkirk Herald Journal, Newkirk *Also called Newkirk Herald Journal (G-4850)*
Newkirk Herald Journal 580 362-2140
121 N Main St Newkirk (74647) *(G-4850)*
Newman Precision 580 339-0097
119 Rainbow Dr Elk City (73644) *(G-2856)*
Newmans Electric Motor Repair 580 310-0151
18032 County Road 1558 Ada (74820) *(G-71)*
Newpark Drilling Fluids LLC 580 323-1612
3600 S Hwy 183 Clinton (73601) *(G-1761)*
News Capital & Democrat, McAlester *Also called Newspaper Holding Inc (G-4324)*
News Enterprises Inc 405 376-4571
290 N Trade Center Ter Mustang (73064) *(G-4787)*
News OK LLC 405 475-4000
100 W Main St Ste 100 # 100 Oklahoma City (73102) *(G-6671)*
Newsgram, Alva *Also called Martin Broadcasting Corp (G-186)*
Newspaper Holding Inc 918 456-8833
106 W 2nd St Tahlequah (74464) *(G-8876)*
Newspaper Holding Inc 580 233-6600
227 W Broadway Ave Enid (73701) *(G-3018)*
Newspaper Holding Inc 580 255-5354
1001 W Elm Ave Duncan (73533) *(G-2159)*
Newspaper Holding Inc 580 256-2200
904 Oklahoma Ave Woodward (73801) *(G-11614)*
Newspaper Holding Inc 580 332-4433
116 N Broadway Ave Ada (74820) *(G-72)*
Newspaper Holding Inc 405 372-5000
211 W 9th Ave Stillwater (74074) *(G-8728)*
Newspaper Holding Inc 918 423-1700
500 S 2nd St McAlester (74501) *(G-4324)*
Newspaper Holding Inc 405 321-1800
215 E Comanche St Norman (73069) *(G-5091)*
Newspaper Holding Inc 918 341-1101
315 W Will Rogers Blvd Claremore (74017) *(G-1661)*
Newspaper Holding Inc 918 297-2544
1101 Pennsylvania Ave Hartshorne (74547) *(G-3394)*
Newspaper Holding Inc 918 684-2922
214 Wall St Muskogee (74401) *(G-4722)*
Newspaper Holding Inc 918 696-2228
118 N 2nd St Stilwell (74960) *(G-8793)*

Newspaper Sales LLC....918 357-5070
27109 E 82nd St S Broken Arrow (74014) ***(G-1146)***
Newspaper Services....918 283-1564
521 S Pine St Claremore (74017) ***(G-1662)***
Newspress Inc....405 372-5000
211 W 9th Ave Stillwater (74074) ***(G-8729)***
Newstar Netronics LLC....918 932-8343
3926 E 3rd St Tulsa (74112) ***(G-10340)***
Newton Design LLC....918 266-6205
26015 E Admiral Pl Catoosa (74015) ***(G-1343)***
Newton Design LLC....918 381-3012
26015 E Admiral Pl Catoosa (74015) ***(G-1344)***
Newton Equipment LLC....918 756-3560
12751 Highway 75 Okmulgee (74447) ***(G-7517)***
Newview Oklahoma Inc (PA)....405 232-4644
501 N Douglas Ave Oklahoma City (73106) ***(G-6672)***
Nexstreem Reclaim Plant....580 657-4580
10472 Dillard Rd Wilson (73463) ***(G-11540)***
Next Generation....405 606-4455
1533 Se 66th St Oklahoma City (73149) ***(G-6673)***
Next-Gen Wind LLC....405 948-1556
210 Park Ave Ste 2820 Oklahoma City (73102) ***(G-6674)***
Nextgen UAS Transponders LLC....405 637-7940
213 Howard Dr Del City (73115) ***(G-2003)***
Nextier Cmpltion Solutions Inc....580 772-3100
1720 N Airport Rd Weatherford (73096) ***(G-11430)***
Nextstep Custom Printing....580 678-4331
7126 S Hillside Dr Duncan (73533) ***(G-2160)***
Nextstream Heavy Oil LLC....405 808-5435
300 Ne 9th St Oklahoma City (73104) ***(G-6675)***
Nextthought LLC....405 673-5588
301 David Boren Ste 3030 Norman (73072) ***(G-5092)***
Nexus Alliance Editorial &, Oklahoma City *Also called Omni LLC* ***(G-6777)***
Ng Discovery LLC....405 945-0940
5121 Gaillardia Corp Pl Oklahoma City (73142) ***(G-6676)***
Niagara Bottling LLC....909 230-5000
500 N Sara Rd Oklahoma City (73127) ***(G-6677)***
Nice Printing Co....405 673-9437
9217 Forest Cove Cir Midwest City (73130) ***(G-4449)***
Nichols Hills Publishing Co....405 755-3311
10801 Quail Plaza Dr Oklahoma City (73120) ***(G-6678)***
Nichols Land Services Inc....405 840-1344
1025 N Broadway Ave Oklahoma City (73102) ***(G-6679)***
Nichols Machine and Mfg LLC....405 637-7175
31058 State Highway 59 Wayne (73095) ***(G-11367)***
Nicholson Monument Co....580 323-7513
638 N 6th St Clinton (73601) ***(G-1762)***
Nick & Pauls Quality Car Cornr....918 933-4000
7658 E 46th Pl Tulsa (74145) ***(G-10341)***
Nick and Paul's, Tulsa *Also called Nick & Pauls Quality Car Cornr* ***(G-10341)***
Nickel & Company LLC....918 744-6384
5807 S Garnett Rd Ste J Tulsa (74146) ***(G-10342)***
Nickel 8 LLC....405 721-7945
1200 Nw 63rd St Oklahoma City (73116) ***(G-6680)***
Nickel Creek Photography....918 447-2688
7370 S 26th West Ave Tulsa (74132) ***(G-10343)***
Nickel Saver, Ada *Also called Mc Alester Food Warehouse* ***(G-64)***
Nickles Industries....580 762-9300
600 S 1st St Ponca City (74601) ***(G-7859)***
Nickolas Manufacturing Inc....918 698-7109
11311 E 4th St Tulsa (74128) ***(G-10344)***
Nicnik Woodworks....703 474-7994
8617 Mercato St Choctaw (73020) ***(G-1552)***
Nicola Acquisitions LLC....405 224-0061
709 W Country Club Rd Chickasha (73018) ***(G-1492)***
Nightowl Publications Main Off....405 603-8130
10216 Mantle Dr Oklahoma City (73162) ***(G-6681)***
Nike Exploration LLC....918 878-7410
7404 S Yale Ave Tulsa (74136) ***(G-10345)***
Nine Energy Service....405 601-5336
2817 S Ann Arbor Ave Oklahoma City (73128) ***(G-6682)***
Nine West Holdings Inc....405 810-8568
1901 Nw Exprkway Ste 1017 Oklahoma City (73118) ***(G-6683)***
Nipps Welding....580 668-2915
8863 Buck Skin Rd Wilson (73463) ***(G-11541)***
Nitro Lift Holdings LLC....405 620-3274
8980 Ok Highway 1 S Mill Creek (74856) ***(G-4470)***
Nitro Lift Technologies LLC (PA)....580 371-3700
8980 Ok Highway 1 S Mill Creek (74856) ***(G-4471)***
Nitro Lift Technologies LLC....405 618-3026
4009 S Harvey Ave Norman (73072) ***(G-5093)***
Nitrogen Lifting Technologies, Norman *Also called Nitro Lift Technologies LLC* ***(G-5093)***
Nix Body Shop LLC....918 797-2484
413 W Blackjack St Stilwell (74960) ***(G-8794)***
Nixon Materials Company....580 621-3297
511 Sandbur Ln Freedom (73842) ***(G-3208)***
NMB Manufacturing LLC....918 943-6633
8453 E 151st St S Bixby (74008) ***(G-649)***
Nmp Division, Tulsa *Also called L3 Westwood Corporation* ***(G-10109)***
Nmsi, Sand Springs *Also called Naumann McHining Solutions Inc* ***(G-8210)***
Nmw Inc....918 273-2204
428 N Elm St Nowata (74048) ***(G-5223)***
No Mans Land Beef Jerky, Boise City *Also called No Mans Land Foods LLC* ***(G-748)***
No Mans Land Foods LLC....580 297-5142
1016 E Main St Boise City (73933) ***(G-748)***
Noahs Park & Playgrounds LLC....405 607-0714
14710 Metro Plaza Blvd A Edmond (73013) ***(G-2538)***
Noble Acquisition LLC....405 872-5660
312 W Chestnut Noble (73068) ***(G-4887)***
Noble Resources Inc....918 865-3301
134 Evans Ave B Mannford (74044) ***(G-4188)***
Noble Signs, Tishomingo *Also called Stansbury Noble Jr Inc* ***(G-8968)***
Noco Investment Co Inc....918 582-0090
16 E 16th St Ste 300 Tulsa (74119) ***(G-10346)***
Nolan Avionics LLC....580 924-5507
8 Waldron Dr Durant (74701) ***(G-2245)***
Nolan Custom Woodwork....918 576-1158
4132 E Admiral Pl Tulsa (74115) ***(G-10347)***
Nolan Enterprises....580 924-5507
8 Waldron Dr Hngr 24-C Durant (74701) ***(G-2246)***
Nomac Drilling....405 242-4444
16217 N May Ave Edmond (73013) ***(G-2539)***
Nomac Drilling LLC (HQ)....405 422-2754
3400 S Radio Rd El Reno (73036) ***(G-2743)***
Nomaco Inc....405 494-2800
524 N Sara Rd Yukon (73099) ***(G-11759)***
Nomad Defense LLC....405 808-4325
101 E Mesa Verde St Yukon (73099) ***(G-11760)***
Non Deplume, Norman *Also called Hard Edge Design Inc* ***(G-5016)***
Nonni's, Tulsa *Also called Nonnis Foods LLC* ***(G-10348)***
Nonnis Foods LLC (PA)....918 621-1200
3920 E Pine St Tulsa (74115) ***(G-10348)***
Nonovels Press LLC....325 721-2577
6213 Se 80th St Oklahoma City (73135) ***(G-6684)***
Norberg Industries Inc....918 665-6888
4237 S 74th East Ave Tulsa (74145) ***(G-10349)***
Norco-Northeastern Okla Roll, Tulsa *Also called Chromium Plating Company* ***(G-9422)***
Nordam....918 878-4325
11153 E Newton St Tulsa (74116) ***(G-10350)***
Nordam Group Inc....918 878-8962
11200 E Pine St Tulsa (74116) ***(G-10351)***
Nordam Group LLC....918 401-5000
6910 Whirlpool Dr Tulsa (74117) ***(G-10352)***
Nordam Group LLC....918 878-6682
11200 E Pine St Tulsa (74116) ***(G-10353)***
Nordam Group LLC (PA)....918 878-4000
6910 Whirlpool Dr Tulsa (74117) ***(G-10354)***
Nordam Group LLC....918 234-5155
11200 E Pine St Tulsa (74116) ***(G-10355)***
Nordam Group LLC....918 274-2742
1050 E Archer St Tulsa (74120) ***(G-10356)***
Nordam Group LLC....918 274-2700
7018 N Lakewood Ave Tulsa (74117) ***(G-10357)***
Nordam Group LLC....918 476-8338
6911 Whirlpool Dr Tulsa (74117) ***(G-10358)***
Nordam Intriors Structures Div, Tulsa *Also called Nordam Group LLC* ***(G-10352)***
Nordam Nacelle & Thrust Revers, Tulsa *Also called Nordam Group LLC* ***(G-10358)***
Nordam Repair Division, Tulsa *Also called Nordam Group LLC* ***(G-10354)***
Nordam Repair Division, Tulsa *Also called Nordam Group LLC* ***(G-10355)***
Nordam Transparency Division, Tulsa *Also called Nordam Group LLC* ***(G-10356)***
Nordic Pure Inc....918 234-2355
14602 Clean Air Dr Tulsa (74116) ***(G-10359)***
Norman Computers....405 292-9501
916 W Main St Norman (73069) ***(G-5094)***
Norman Koehn....580 852-3260
103 W 2nd St Helena (73741) ***(G-3436)***
Norman Moore....405 941-3220
3 Miles W 2 S 1/4 E Sasakwa (74867) ***(G-8333)***
Norman Supply Company....405 692-1191
11901 S Portland Ave Oklahoma City (73170) ***(G-5308)***
Norman Transcript, Norman *Also called Newspaper Holding Inc* ***(G-5091)***
Norman's Tank Truck Service, Sasakwa *Also called Norman Moore* ***(G-8333)***
Norman's Welding & Repair, Helena *Also called Norman Koehn* ***(G-3436)***
Norris Rods, Tulsa *Also called Apergy Artfl Lift Intl LLC* ***(G-9198)***
Norriseal-Wellmark Inc....405 672-6660
1903 Se 29th St Oklahoma City (73129) ***(G-6685)***
Nortek Air Solutions LLC....405 525-6546
4841 N Sewell Ave Oklahoma City (73118) ***(G-6686)***
Nortek Air Solutions LLC....405 263-7286
106 N Industrial Blvd Okarche (73762) ***(G-5247)***
Nortek Air Solutions LLC....405 594-2811
5510 Sw 29th St Oklahoma City (73179) ***(G-6687)***
North Amercn Precision Cast Co....580 237-4033
1414 E Willow Rd Enid (73701) ***(G-3019)***
North American Cos....918 592-2000
2400 N Lewis Ave Tulsa (74110) ***(G-10360)***
North American Van Lines, Stillwater *Also called Stillwater Transfer & Stor Co* ***(G-8759)***

ALPHABETIC SECTION Oakley Inc

North Amrcn Arspc Holdings LLC......316 644-2553
4002 Twilight Ave Enid (73703) ***(G-3020)***
North Amrcn Brine Rsources LLC......405 828-7123
2415 S Garland Rd Enid (73703) ***(G-3021)***
North Central Pump......580 765-9348
3912 Santa Fe St Ponca City (74601) ***(G-7860)***
North Star Publishing LLC......405 415-2400
6801 Sandlewood Dr Oklahoma City (73132) ***(G-6688)***
North Star Well Services Inc......580 256-5644
502 48th St Woodward (73801) ***(G-11615)***
North Welding and Construction......580 526-3260
17433 E 1190 Rd Erick (73645) ***(G-3090)***
Northeast Oklahoma Mfg......918 663-8805
10730 E 55th Pl Tulsa (74146) ***(G-10361)***
Northeast Tchnlgy Ctr- Clrmore......918 342-8066
1901 N Highway 88 Claremore (74017) ***(G-1663)***
Northern Arizona Newspaper......928 524-6203
1920 E 2nd St Apt 4011 Edmond (73034) ***(G-2540)***
Northfork Auto Repair......918 689-3589
Highway 69 Eufaula (74432) ***(G-3106)***
Northfork Marine Manufacturing......918 689-9309
417797 E 1145 Rd Eufaula (74432) ***(G-3107)***
Northport Production Co Inc......405 848-1212
3501 French Park Dr Ste B Edmond (73034) ***(G-2541)***
Northrop Corp......580 536-9191
1 Sw 11th St Lawton (73501) ***(G-3976)***
Northrop Grumman Integrated, Oklahoma City *Also called Northrop Grumman Systems Corp* ***(G-6691)***
Northrop Grumman Systems Corp......405 739-7875
6400 Se 59th St Ste A Oklahoma City (73135) ***(G-6689)***
Northrop Grumman Systems Corp......405 737-3300
6401 S Air Depot Blvd Oklahoma City (73135) ***(G-6690)***
Northrop Grumman Systems Corp......405 733-1208
5600 Liberty Pkwy Ste 101 Oklahoma City (73110) ***(G-6691)***
Northrup Metals LLC......918 225-2100
322 W Grandstaff Cushing (74023) ***(G-1948)***
Northshore Corp......405 329-8026
2503 S Berry Rd Norman (73072) ***(G-5095)***
Northstar Energy LLC......231 941-0073
3211 S Lakewood Ave Tulsa (74135) ***(G-10362)***
Northwest Alpacas Ltd......903 450-1999
5804 Wilson Dr Edmond (73034) ***(G-2542)***
Northwest Measurement......580 822-3528
202 S Main St Okeene (73763) ***(G-5260)***
Northwest Oil Gas Explrtn......405 974-0165
125 Park Ave Ste Ll Oklahoma City (73102) ***(G-6692)***
Northwest Oklahoman, Shattuck *Also called CSC Inc* ***(G-8420)***
Northwest Printing Inc......580 234-0953
120 N Independence St Enid (73701) ***(G-3022)***
Northwest Royalty LLC......405 241-9707
125 Park Ave Ste Ll Oklahoma City (73102) ***(G-6693)***
Northwest Rubber......405 681-2667
3501 Melcat Dr Ste B Oklahoma City (73179) ***(G-6694)***
Northwest Transformer Co Inc......405 636-1454
8 Sw 29th St Oklahoma City (73109) ***(G-6695)***
Northwest Truss......580 496-2420
Hwy 45 Newell St Goltry (73739) ***(G-3248)***
Northwest Welding Inc......405 621-0201
5717 Nw 64th St Warr Acres (73132) ***(G-11325)***
Northwood Publishing LLC......918 451-9388
507 W Los Angeles Pl Broken Arrow (74011) ***(G-989)***
Norville Oil Co LLC......405 286-9100
901 E Britton Rd Oklahoma City (73114) ***(G-6696)***
Norwesco Inc......405 275-2034
201 N Kennedy Ave Shawnee (74801) ***(G-8479)***
Norwood Custom Cabinets......918 478-2462
20181 S 410 Rd Hulbert (74441) ***(G-3626)***
Nosley Scoop LLC......512 328-2953
14301 Caliber Dr Ste 110 Oklahoma City (73134) ***(G-6697)***
Noss Machine......918 358-3804
1715 Boston Pool Rd Hominy (74035) ***(G-3593)***
Note-Able Workshop LLC......918 801-2725
4600 Us Highway 59 Grove (74344) ***(G-3281)***
Note-Able Workshop LLC......918 801-2725
24501 S 613 Rd Grove (74344) ***(G-3282)***
Nov Downhole......405 688-5000
6602 Newcastle Rd Oklahoma City (73179) ***(G-6698)***
Nov Rig Systems, McAlester *Also called National Oilwell Varco Inc* ***(G-4323)***
Nov Tuboscope Inc......405 677-8889
1800 Se 44th St Oklahoma City (73129) ***(G-6699)***
Nov-Tuboscope-Machining Svcs, Oklahoma City *Also called Hendershot Tool Company* ***(G-6238)***
Novalco Inc......405 528-2711
130 Ne 31st St Oklahoma City (73105) ***(G-6700)***
Novartis Corporation......918 845-0906
3737 E 37th Pl Tulsa (74135) ***(G-10363)***
Novo Oil & Gas......405 286-4391
1001 W Wilshire Blvd # 2 Oklahoma City (73116) ***(G-6701)***
Novo Oil & Gas LLC......405 609-1625
105 N Hudson Ave Ste 500 Oklahoma City (73102) ***(G-6702)***
Nowata Printing Co West, Nowata *Also called Community Publishers* ***(G-5211)***
Nprocess Technology, Ada *Also called N P T Inc* ***(G-69)***
NRG Wireline LLC......918 768-3210
203 N King St Kinta (74552) ***(G-3835)***
Nsi Fracturing LLC......918 496-2072
7030 S Yale Ave Ste 502 Tulsa (74136) ***(G-10364)***
Ntu Pipeline LLC......918 392-9255
2 W 2nd St Ste 1700 Tulsa (74103) ***(G-10365)***
Nu-Tier Brands Inc......918 550-8026
8282 S Memorial Dr # 302 Tulsa (74133) ***(G-10366)***
Nubs Well Servicing Inc......580 856-3887
25627 State Highway 76 Ratliff City (73481) ***(G-8058)***
Nuckolls Distributing Inc......918 663-0555
9513 E 55th St Ste B Tulsa (74145) ***(G-10367)***
Nucleic Products LLC......818 419-9176
63225 E 290 Rd Grove (74344) ***(G-3283)***
Nuestra Comunidad......405 685-3822
2524 Sw 44th St Oklahoma City (73119) ***(G-6703)***
Nupocket LLC......918 850-1903
3400 W Washington St Broken Arrow (74012) ***(G-990)***
Nut House......918 266-1604
26677 S Highway 66 Claremore (74019) ***(G-1664)***
Nutech Energy Alliance Ltd......405 388-4236
11301 Gateshead Dr Oklahoma City (73170) ***(G-5309)***
Nutopia Nuts & More......405 663-2330
206 W Main St Hydro (73048) ***(G-3633)***
Nuttall Trailers, Atoka *Also called C-All Manufacturing Inc* ***(G-401)***
Nutting Custom Trikes......918 257-8795
21507 S Highway 69 Afton (74331) ***(G-119)***
Nuyaka Creek Winery LLC......918 756-8485
35230 S 177th West Ave Bristow (74010) ***(G-790)***
Nxt Lvl Woodworking LLC......405 613-6637
19421 8 A St Norman (73026) ***(G-5096)***
Nxtnano LLC......918 923-4824
2201 El Anderson Blvd Claremore (74017) ***(G-1665)***
Nye Investment Co LLC......405 923-7155
9520 N May Ave Ste 320 Oklahoma City (73120) ***(G-6704)***
Nye J Marshall, Oklahoma City *Also called Nye Oil Co* ***(G-6705)***
Nye Oil Co......405 843-6609
5805 Nw Grand Blvd Ste C Oklahoma City (73118) ***(G-6705)***
Nyes Cabinet Shop......580 622-6323
4990 N Us Highway 177 Sulphur (73086) ***(G-8839)***
Nyikos Inc......918 299-3190
4815 S Harvard Ave # 360 Tulsa (74135) ***(G-10368)***
O & L Resources Inc......918 789-5553
400 E 1st St Chelsea (74016) ***(G-1408)***
O C & Associates Inc......918 251-0971
509 N Walnut Ave Ste C Broken Arrow (74012) ***(G-991)***
O E N T Instruments Inc......918 299-4343
9021 S Gary Ave Tulsa (74137) ***(G-10369)***
O Fizz Inc......918 834-3691
809 N Lewis Ave Tulsa (74110) ***(G-10370)***
O H S N Inc......580 248-1299
201 Se Lee Blvd Lawton (73501) ***(G-3977)***
O K Country Donut Shoppe......918 493-6455
8048 S Yale Ave Tulsa (74136) ***(G-10371)***
O K Distributions and Trnsp, Muldrow *Also called O K Foods Inc* ***(G-4635)***
O K Foods Inc......918 427-7000
100 N Wilson Rock Rd Muldrow (74948) ***(G-4635)***
O K Foods Inc......918 653-1640
Hwy 128 E Heavener (74937) ***(G-3431)***
O K Foods Inc......918 653-2819
1000 Old Pike Rd Heavener (74937) ***(G-3432)***
O K Plunger Service......918 352-4269
Highway 33 W Drumright (74030) ***(G-2068)***
O K Restaurant Supply......405 330-9932
6176 Boucher Dr Edmond (73034) ***(G-2543)***
O K Staudt Jewelers, Okmulgee *Also called Staudt Jewelers* ***(G-7526)***
O K Tank Trucks Inc......918 396-3043
13801 N Cincinnati Ave Skiatook (74070) ***(G-8562)***
O Klahoma Sign Co, Tahlequah *Also called Tammy Brown* ***(G-8887)***
O S R Inc......281 422-7206
14265 E 590 Rd Inola (74036) ***(G-3668)***
O2 Concepts LLC (PA)......877 867-4008
6303 Waterford Blvd # 150 Oklahoma City (73118) ***(G-6706)***
Oai Electronics LLC......918 836-9077
6960 E 12th St Tulsa (74112) ***(G-10372)***
Oak Hill Petroleum Corporation......405 842-1568
1611 Randel Rd Nichols Hills (73116) ***(G-4861)***
Oak Tree Natural Resources LLC......405 775-0987
10900 Hefner Pointe Dr # 401 Oklahoma City (73120) ***(G-6707)***
Oak Tree Sales......405 224-9332
1103 N Industrial Blvd Chickasha (73018) ***(G-1493)***
Oakes Wldg & Fabrication LLC......918 865-2356
169 Greenwood Ave Mannford (74044) ***(G-4189)***
Oakland Petroleum Operating Co......918 496-3027
7318 S Yale Ave Ste A Tulsa (74136) ***(G-10373)***
Oakley Inc......405 843-5447
1901 Nw Expwy St Ste 1045 Oklahoma City (73118) ***(G-6708)***

ALPHABETIC

Oakley Defense LLC...918 457-8089
508 Talley St Tahlequah (74464) *(G-8877)*
Oakley Portable Buildings LLC...405 372-6543
2623 E 6th Ave Stillwater (74074) *(G-8730)*
Oakridge Estates, Edmond *Also called Clayton Homes Inc (G-2356)*
Oakwood Graphics, Tulsa *Also called Marrara Group Inc (G-10216)*
Oasis Rv Center LLC...580 233-9400
1610 N Van Buren St Enid (73703) *(G-3023)*
Oatskc Granola Company LLC...405 834-6159
6 Ne 63rd St Ste 220 Oklahoma City (73105) *(G-6709)*
Oba, Oklahoma City *Also called Oklahoma Bankers (G-6736)*
OBrien Oil Corporation...405 282-6500
201 W Oklahoma Ave # 233 Guthrie (73044) *(G-3327)*
Occidental Petroleum Corp...918 610-1990
110 W 7th St Ste 1600 Tulsa (74119) *(G-10374)*
Occuscreen Associates LLC...918 292-8865
1044 N Sheridan Rd Tulsa (74115) *(G-10375)*
Oconnell Woodworks LLC...918 805-7233
2100 S Aster Ave Broken Arrow (74012) *(G-992)*
Octagon Resources Inc...405 842-3322
6801 Broadway Ext Ste 204 Oklahoma City (73116) *(G-6710)*
Octagon Resources Inc (PA)...405 366-8885
1831 E Imhoff Rd Ste 100 Norman (73071) *(G-5097)*
Octapharma Plasma...405 686-9226
2962 Sw 59th St Oklahoma City (73119) *(G-6711)*
October Graphics...580 765-5089
2300 E Hubbard Rd Ponca City (74604) *(G-7861)*
Ocubrite LLC...405 250-2084
14901 Carlingford Way Edmond (73013) *(G-2544)*
Ocv Control Valves LLC...918 627-1942
7400 E 42nd Pl Tulsa (74145) *(G-10376)*
Odor Control Entps Texas Inc...405 670-5600
1610 Se 37th St Oklahoma City (73129) *(G-6712)*
Odum Machine & Tool Inc...918 663-6966
9933 E 44th Pl Tulsa (74146) *(G-10377)*
OEM Systems LLC...405 263-7529
308 N Industrial Blvd Okarche (73762) *(G-5248)*
OEM Welding LLC...918 645-8483
14139 W 31st St S Sand Springs (74063) *(G-8211)*
Oerlikon Blzers Cating USA Inc...405 745-1026
7124 Sw 29th St Ste 101 Oklahoma City (73179) *(G-6713)*
Oex-1 LLC...918 492-0254
4870 S Lewis Ave Ste 240 Tulsa (74105) *(G-10378)*
Office Concepts, Ardmore *Also called Chaddick & Associates Inc (G-264)*
Office Everything, Claremore *Also called Offices Etc (G-1666)*
Offices Etc...918 342-1501
436 S Lynn Riggs Blvd Claremore (74017) *(G-1666)*
Offshore Extreme...405 387-2628
3060 Highway 62 Svc Rd Newcastle (73065) *(G-4834)*
Ofs Inc...405 424-1101
4901 Ne 23rd St Oklahoma City (73121) *(G-6714)*
Og Sawmill...918 598-3464
13065 E 645 Rd Hulbert (74441) *(G-3627)*
Ogci, Tulsa *Also called Oil & Gas Consultants Intl Inc (G-10381)*
Ogci Building Fund LLC...918 828-2500
2930 S Yale Ave Tulsa (74114) *(G-10379)*
Ogdens Welding Service...405 380-7649
12916 S Highway 99 Seminole (74868) *(G-8390)*
Oge Energy, Oklahoma City *Also called Enable Okla Intrstate Trnsm LL (G-6033)*
Ogi Process Equipment Inc...918 246-1600
8939 W 21st St Sand Springs (74063) *(G-8212)*
Ogp Energy L P...405 235-9571
211 N Robinson Ave N1520 Oklahoma City (73102) *(G-6715)*
OH Keys...405 529-5202
14101 N Pennsylvania Ave Oklahoma City (73134) *(G-6716)*
OH Keys...405 378-5674
9001 S May Ave Oklahoma City (73159) *(G-6717)*
Ohana Manufacturing LLC...918 490-9053
116785 S 4214 Rd Eufaula (74432) *(G-3108)*
Ohana Oil & Gas LLC...405 341-8822
1800 Canyon Park Cir # 201 Edmond (73013) *(G-2545)*
Ohgoodygoodycom...315 727-5960
1616 S Peoria Ave Apt 3 Tulsa (74120) *(G-10380)*
Oil & Gas Conservation Div, Ada *Also called Corpo Commission OK (G-27)*
Oil & Gas Consultants Intl Inc (PA)...918 828-2500
2930 S Yale Ave Tulsa (74114) *(G-10381)*
Oil & Gas Division...918 581-2296
440 S Houston Ave Ste 114 Tulsa (74127) *(G-10382)*
Oil & Gas Optimization Special...432 685-0029
2601 E 74th Pl Tulsa (74136) *(G-10383)*
Oil Capital Land Exploration, Tulsa *Also called Oil Capital Land Exploration (G-10384)*
Oil Capital Land Exploration...918 582-2603
320 S Boston Ave Ste 807 Tulsa (74103) *(G-10384)*
Oil Capital Valve Company, Tulsa *Also called Ocv Control Valves LLC (G-10376)*
Oil Capital Valve Company...918 627-2474
7400 E 42nd Pl Tulsa (74145) *(G-10385)*
Oil Capitol Neon Inc...918 582-9031
4419 W 55th Pl Tulsa (74107) *(G-10386)*
Oil Office, Edmond *Also called Guest Petroleum Incorporated (G-2448)*
Oil Pro Industries...405 323-6988
3536 S Meridian Ave Oklahoma City (73119) *(G-6718)*
Oil State, Oklahoma City *Also called Stinger Wllhead Protection Inc (G-7206)*
Oil States Energy Services LLC...405 702-6536
3120 Melcat Dr Oklahoma City (73179) *(G-6719)*
Oil States Energy Services LLC...405 686-1001
5300 Sw 33rd St Oklahoma City (73179) *(G-6720)*
Oil States Industries Inc...405 671-2000
1020 E Grand Blvd Oklahoma City (73129) *(G-6721)*
Oil States Industries Inc...918 250-0828
5563 S 104th East Ave Tulsa (74146) *(G-10387)*
Oil States Industries Inc...918 250-0828
10322 E 58th St Tulsa (74146) *(G-10388)*
Oil States Piper Valves, Oklahoma City *Also called Oil States Industries Inc (G-6721)*
Oil Tools Rentals Inc...580 242-1140
1029 N 54th St Enid (73701) *(G-3024)*
Oil Well Cementers Inc (PA)...580 229-1776
189 Golf Course Rd Healdton (73438) *(G-3420)*
Oil-Law Records Corporation...405 840-1631
8 Nw 65th St Oklahoma City (73116) *(G-6722)*
Oilab Inc...405 528-8378
4619 N Santa Fe Ave Oklahoma City (73118) *(G-6723)*
Oilfield Dstrbtons Spclsts LLC...580 237-1237
4025 Shady Ln Enid (73701) *(G-3025)*
Oilfield Equipment & Mfg...405 275-4500
7801 N Harrison Shawnee (74804) *(G-8480)*
Oilfield Equipment Company...405 850-1406
4 1/2 Mi W Twn Beach Rd Duncan (73533) *(G-2161)*
Oilfield Fresh Wtr Mud Dsposal, El Reno *Also called J Scott Inc (G-2727)*
Oilfield Improvements Inc...918 250-5584
1902 N Yellowood Ave Broken Arrow (74012) *(G-993)*
Oilfield Lease Maintenance...405 348-1562
2917 Cedarbend Ct Edmond (73003) *(G-2546)*
Oilfield R T...405 238-2026
30980 E County Road 1585 Pauls Valley (73075) *(G-7669)*
Oilfield Services, Cherokee *Also called Duane Waugh (G-1416)*
Oilfield Technical Svcs LLC...405 603-4288
7412 Nw 83rd St Oklahoma City (73132) *(G-6724)*
Oils Unlimited LLC (PA)...918 583-1155
3621 W 5th St Tulsa (74127) *(G-10389)*
Oiltech Manufacturing Div LLC...918 534-3568
2601 E Durham Rd Bartlesville (74006) *(G-514)*
Oilwell Tech & Enhancement...405 202-9720
3030 Nw Expressway Oklahoma City (73112) *(G-6725)*
OK Brand, Madill *Also called Oklahoma Steel & Wire Co Inc (G-4160)*
OK Casting...918 648-5300
1716 Remington Rd Burbank (74633) *(G-1215)*
OK Contract Services LLC...918 352-5369
11587 W Indian Rd Braman (74632) *(G-761)*
OK Fab and Machining, Tulsa *Also called OK Fabricators LLC (G-9023)*
OK Fabricators LLC...918 224-3977
8630 S Regency Dr Tulsa (74131) *(G-9023)*
OK Fire LLC...918 424-1808
400 N Main St McAlester (74501) *(G-4325)*
OK Machine and Mfg Co Inc...918 838-1300
2522 N Columbia Pl Tulsa (74110) *(G-10390)*
OK Print and Promo, Edmond *Also called V O Inc (G-2664)*
OK Products of Tulsa Inc...918 445-2471
4925 W 50th St Tulsa (74107) *(G-10391)*
OK Pump and Supply...580 856-4010
1 Mile Hwy 776 Ratliff City (73481) *(G-8059)*
OK Quality Printing Inc...405 624-2925
901 N Boomer Rd Stillwater (74075) *(G-8731)*
OK Rail Signals Inc...918 378-9520
1515 W 36th Pl Tulsa (74107) *(G-10392)*
OK Swabbing Inc...405 853-6953
400 E Jack Taute Ave Hennessey (73742) *(G-3478)*
Ok-1 Manufacturing Co...580 482-0891
709 S Veterans Dr Altus (73521) *(G-165)*
Ok-Red Land Energy, Edmond *Also called Red Land Energy LLC (G-2589)*
Okarche Grain, Okarche *Also called Shawnee Milling Company (G-5252)*
Okay See Ltd Co...405 562-3154
4700 Nw 157th Ter Edmond (73013) *(G-2547)*
Okc Allergy Supplies Inc...405 235-1451
1005 Sw 2nd St Oklahoma City (73109) *(G-6726)*
Okc Boys of Leather...318 564-0312
3612 Altadena Ave Oklahoma City (73112) *(G-6727)*
Okc Dumpsters Inc...405 640-4345
14900 Kurdson Way Edmond (73013) *(G-2548)*
Okc Energy Corporation...405 330-5586
10804 Quail Plaza Dr # 100 Oklahoma City (73120) *(G-6728)*
Okc Fabric Market...405 531-0546
10956 N May Ave Oklahoma City (73120) *(G-6729)*
Okc Soda Co LLC...405 628-9543
6516 Westrock Dr Oklahoma City (73132) *(G-6730)*
Okeen Motel...580 822-4491
806 W Oklahoma Okeene (73763) *(G-5261)*
Okemah Leader...918 623-0123
115 W Broadway St Okemah (74859) *(G-5271)*

Okemah News Leader, Okemah *Also called Okemah Leader* ***(G-5271)***
Okie Crude Company, Tulsa *Also called Okie Operating Co Ltd* ***(G-10393)***
Okie Dokie Cbd Dispensary LLC 405 454-5040
20107 Ne 23rd St Harrah (73045) ***(G-3382)***
Okie Dough LLC 580 606-0142
9119 N 153rd East Ave Owasso (74055) ***(G-7597)***
Okie Ferments 405 310-9724
44 Ne 51st St Ste A Oklahoma City (73105) ***(G-6731)***
Okie Ink Screenprinting LLC 918 681-0736
7910 S 13th St E Muskogee (74403) ***(G-4723)***
Okie Newts Welding 580 564-4724
401 Highway 70 N Kingston (73439) ***(G-3830)***
Okie Operating Co Ltd 918 582-2594
401 S Boston Ave Ste 715 Tulsa (74103) ***(G-10393)***
Okie Plumbing and Backhoe 580 302-5018
1501 W Broadway Ave Sulphur (73086) ***(G-8840)***
Okie Roasters LLC 405 699-2007
1540 Debbie Dr Guthrie (73044) ***(G-3328)***
Okiewood LLC 405 245-5257
3817 Nw 51st Pl Oklahoma City (73112) ***(G-6732)***
Okki Industries LLC 405 204-6357
2925 Chapel Hill Rd Oklahoma City (73120) ***(G-6733)***
Okla Casing Co 580 432-5311
27244 Highway 76 Foster (73434) ***(G-3188)***
Okla Hi-Tech. Equipment, Oklahoma City *Also called Johnny L Windsor* ***(G-6371)***
Okla Royalty, Oklahoma City *Also called Royalok Royalty LLC* ***(G-7055)***
Oklahoma AAA Pallet Company (PA) 405 670-1414
1901 S Skyline Dr Oklahoma City (73129) ***(G-6734)***
Oklahoma Academy Publishing 405 454-6211
18509 Ne 63rd St Harrah (73045) ***(G-3383)***
Oklahoma Aerospace Alliance 918 527-0980
1800 S Baltimore Ave # 830 Tulsa (74119) ***(G-10394)***
Oklahoma Assn of Elc Coop 405 478-1455
2325 E I 44 Service Rd Oklahoma City (73111) ***(G-6735)***
Oklahoma Aztec Co Inc 405 784-2475
44701 Tooley Rd Asher (74826) ***(G-393)***
Oklahoma Bankers 405 424-5252
643 Ne 41st St Oklahoma City (73105) ***(G-6736)***
Oklahoma Bar Foundation Inc 405 416-7000
1901 N Lincoln Blvd Oklahoma City (73105) ***(G-6737)***
Oklahoma Basic Economy Corp 580 332-4710
2313 N Broadway Ave Ada (74820) ***(G-73)***
Oklahoma Bindery Inc 405 235-4802
2832 W Lindley Ave Oklahoma City (73107) ***(G-6738)***
Oklahoma Biorefining Corp 405 201-1824
1611 Southern Heights Ave Norman (73072) ***(G-5098)***
Oklahoma Cellulose Inc 918 706-5279
733 N Cimarron Valley Rd Cleveland (74020) ***(G-1730)***
Oklahoma Cement Solutions LLC 214 802-1527
13133 Chinkapin Oak Pl Choctaw (73020) ***(G-1553)***
Oklahoma Cementing Cushing LLC 918 225-0688
1115 N Euchee Valley Rd Cushing (74023) ***(G-1949)***
Oklahoma Center For Athletes, Edmond *Also called Columbia Rehabilitation Svcs* ***(G-2360)***
Oklahoma City Blazers 405 543-2922
119 N Robinson Ave Oklahoma City (73102) ***(G-6739)***
Oklahoma City Frequency 405 887-7115
5201 Se 56th St Oklahoma City (73135) ***(G-6740)***
Oklahoma City Herald 405 842-7827
7416 Broadway Ext Oklahoma City (73116) ***(G-6741)***
Oklahoma City Reinforcing Stl, Oklahoma City *Also called Gerdau Ameristeel US Inc* ***(G-6147)***
Oklahoma City Shutter Co Inc 405 787-1234
210 S Alliance Blvd Oklahoma City (73128) ***(G-6742)***
Oklahoma City Steel LLC 405 235-2300
100 Se 17th St Oklahoma City (73129) ***(G-6743)***
Oklahoma City's Nursing Times, Oklahoma City *Also called Metro Publishing LLC* ***(G-6581)***
Oklahoma Co Op, Jay *Also called Oklahoma State University* ***(G-3684)***
Oklahoma Coating Specialists 405 447-0448
1900 Robin Ridge Dr Norman (73072) ***(G-5099)***
Oklahoma Comm On Consmr Cr 918 367-3396
115 W 6th Ave Bristow (74010) ***(G-791)***
Oklahoma Community TV LLC 405 808-2509
7401 N Kelley Ave Oklahoma City (73111) ***(G-6744)***
Oklahoma Container Corp 405 842-8300
9545 N I 35 Service Rd Oklahoma City (73131) ***(G-6745)***
Oklahoma Cstm Cating Ltd Lblty (PA) 405 382-0231
1801 Boren Blvd Seminole (74868) ***(G-8391)***
Oklahoma Custom Canvas Pdts 918 438-4040
2 S 109th East Pl Tulsa (74128) ***(G-10395)***
Oklahoma Custom Rubber Co 405 634-3943
2117 N Lincoln Ave Moore (73160) ***(G-4545)***
Oklahoma Dep't of Career Tech, Stillwater *Also called Education Oklahoma Department* ***(G-8682)***
Oklahoma Department of Mines 918 485-3999
4845 S Sheridan Rd # 514 Tulsa (74145) ***(G-10396)***
Oklahoma Dept Public Safety 918 256-3388
441276 E Highway 60 Vinita (74301) ***(G-11265)***
Oklahoma Distilling Company 918 505-4861
1724 E 7th St Tulsa (74104) ***(G-10397)***
Oklahoma Document Solutions, Warr Acres *Also called Printer Store LLC* ***(G-11326)***
Oklahoma Eagle LLC 918 582-7124
624 E Archer St Tulsa (74120) ***(G-10398)***
Oklahoma Eagle Publishing Co 918 582-7124
624 E Archer St Tulsa (74120) ***(G-10399)***
Oklahoma Eagle, The, Tulsa *Also called Oklahoma Eagle LLC* ***(G-10398)***
Oklahoma Electric Cooperative (PA) 405 321-2024
242 24th Ave Nw Norman (73069) ***(G-5100)***
Oklahoma EMB Sup & Design 405 359-2741
13821 N Harvey Ave Edmond (73013) ***(G-2549)***
Oklahoma Emergency Generator S 405 735-9888
2219 N Moore Ave Moore (73160) ***(G-4546)***
Oklahoma Energy Source LLC 918 307-8142
7136 S Yale Ave Ste 210 Tulsa (74136) ***(G-10400)***
Oklahoma Envelope Company LLC 405 946-2169
5621 W Reno Ave Ste B Oklahoma City (73127) ***(G-6746)***
Oklahoma Equipment Mfg PDT 405 491-6484
2401 Purdue Dr Oklahoma City (73128) ***(G-6747)***
Oklahoma Executive Printing 405 948-8136
1017 S Meridian Ave Oklahoma City (73108) ***(G-6748)***
Oklahoma Ferrious Services, Oklahoma City *Also called Ofs Inc* ***(G-6714)***
Oklahoma Flding Crton Prtg Inc 405 352-9920
118 Nw Main St Minco (73059) ***(G-4478)***
Oklahoma Forge Inc 918 446-4486
5259 S 49th West Ave Tulsa (74107) ***(G-10401)***
Oklahoma Foundation For Diges 405 271-4602
711 Stanton L Young Blvd Oklahoma City (73104) ***(G-6749)***
Oklahoma Fuel Athletics LLC 405 286-3144
14712 Bristol Park Blvd Edmond (73013) ***(G-2550)***
Oklahoma Gazette, Oklahoma City *Also called Gazette Media Inc* ***(G-6139)***
Oklahoma Grocers Association 405 525-9419
25 Ne 52nd St Oklahoma City (73105) ***(G-6750)***
Oklahoma Hand Pours 580 669-2520
10309 E Tower Ests Glencoe (74032) ***(G-3225)***
Oklahoma Heartland Inc 918 914-3124
9302 E Leisure Ln Stillwater (74075) ***(G-8732)***
Oklahoma High Prfmce Polsg 405 787-8388
117 N Council Rd Ste B Oklahoma City (73127) ***(G-6751)***
Oklahoma Highway Patrol, Vinita *Also called Oklahoma Dept Public Safety* ***(G-11265)***
Oklahoma Home Centers Inc 405 260-7625
5103 S Division St Guthrie (73044) ***(G-3329)***
Oklahoma Hot Shot Service 405 605-0464
1225 Se 29th St Oklahoma City (73129) ***(G-6752)***
Oklahoma Industrial Silver 405 341-6021
2700 Coltrane Pl Ste 6 Edmond (73034) ***(G-2551)***
Oklahoma Interpak, Muskogee *Also called Professional Packaging Inc* ***(G-4738)***
Oklahoma Interpak Inc 918 687-1681
2424 N Main St Muskogee (74401) ***(G-4724)***
Oklahoma Leather Products Inc 918 542-6651
500 26th St Ave Nw Miami (74354) ***(G-4424)***
Oklahoma Led, Tulsa *Also called Adl Group LLC* ***(G-9105)***
Oklahoma Living Publication, Oklahoma City *Also called Oklahoma Assn of Elc Coop* ***(G-6735)***
Oklahoma Logo Signs Inc 405 840-1550
4334 Nw Expwy St Ste 169 Oklahoma City (73116) ***(G-6753)***
Oklahoma Machine Guns LLC 405 418-4867
615 W Wilshire Blvd Ste 1 Oklahoma City (73116) ***(G-6754)***
Oklahoma Magazine 918 744-6205
1609 S Boston Ave Tulsa (74119) ***(G-10402)***
Oklahoma Metal Creations LLC 580 917-5434
10185 Ne Wolf Rd Fletcher (73541) ***(G-3165)***
Oklahoma Millworks Inc 405 282-4887
2019 Ruhl Dr Guthrie (73044) ***(G-3330)***
Oklahoma Millworks Inc 405 282-4887
2019 Ruoh Dr Edmond (73003) ***(G-2552)***
Oklahoma Mobil Concrete Inc 918 622-3930
10313 E 48th St Tulsa (74146) ***(G-10403)***
Oklahoma Native Electric LLC 918 824-7638
325 S Mill St Pryor (74361) ***(G-7979)***
Oklahoma Natural Gas, Tulsa *Also called Oneok Inc* ***(G-10422)***
Oklahoma Newspaper 405 475-3989
100 W Main St Ste 100 # 100 Oklahoma City (73102) ***(G-6755)***
Oklahoma Newspaper Foundation 405 499-0020
3601 N Lincoln Blvd Oklahoma City (73105) ***(G-6756)***
Oklahoma Ntry Svc A Div of M- 405 948-8900
3627 Nw 50th St Oklahoma City (73112) ***(G-6757)***
Oklahoma Offset Veba Inc 918 582-0921
1415 S Quincy Ave Tulsa (74120) ***(G-10404)***
Oklahoma Oil Gas Management 405 341-1856
1721 W 33rd St Edmond (73013) ***(G-2553)***
Oklahoma Optical, Ada *Also called Chickasaw Nation* ***(G-21)***
Oklahoma Post Tension Inc 918 627-6013
4119 S 88th East Ave Tulsa (74145) ***(G-10405)***
Oklahoma Pride Mfg, Chickasha *Also called Craigs Oklahoma Pride LLC* ***(G-1451)***
Oklahoma Prime Energy LLC 580 226-2373
301 W Main St Ste 430 Ardmore (73401) ***(G-338)***
Oklahoma Promo LLC 918 248-8145
512 W 127th Pl S Jenks (74037) ***(G-3719)***

ALPHABETIC

Oklahoma Propane Gas Assn ALPHABETIC SECTION

Oklahoma Propane Gas Assn 405 424-1775
4200 N Lindsay Ave Oklahoma City (73105) **(G-6758)**
Oklahoma Publishing Co of Okla 405 475-3585
3901 N Harvard Ave Oklahoma City (73122) **(G-6759)**
Oklahoma Publishing Company 405 475-4040
7015 N Robinson Ave Oklahoma City (73116) **(G-6760)**
Oklahoma Rbr & Gasket Co Inc 918 585-3484
3216 Charles Page Blvd Tulsa (74127) **(G-10406)**
Oklahoma Rep Sales Inc 405 794-5200
214 Ne 12th St Ste A Moore (73160) **(G-4547)**
Oklahoma Restaurant Assn 405 942-8181
3800 N Portland Ave Oklahoma City (73112) **(G-6761)**
Oklahoma Safety Eqp Co Inc (HQ) 918 258-5626
1701 W Tacoma St Broken Arrow (74012) **(G-994)**
Oklahoma School of Welding 405 672-1841
321 S Scott St Del City (73115) **(G-2004)**
Oklahoma Screen Mfg LLC 918 443-6500
10838 E Marshall St 102 Tulsa (74116) **(G-10407)**
Oklahoma Screen Mfg LLC (PA) 918 443-6500
7287 E Highway 88 Oologah (74053) **(G-7535)**
Oklahoma Sign Association 918 587-7171
533 S Rockford Ave Tulsa (74120) **(G-10408)**
Oklahoma Sign Company 405 620-6716
5913 Se 67th St Oklahoma City (73135) **(G-6762)**
Oklahoma Slf-Defense Carry LLC 918 814-0122
10317 E 112th Pl S Bixby (74008) **(G-650)**
Oklahoma Soc Prof Engineers 405 528-1435
201 Ne 27th St Rm 125 Oklahoma City (73105) **(G-6763)**
Oklahoma Specialties Inc 918 272-0931
7007 N 115th East Ave Owasso (74055) **(G-7598)**
Oklahoma Stair Craft Inc 918 446-1456
2214 Industrial Rd Sapulpa (74066) **(G-8293)**
Oklahoma State University 405 744-5723
930 N Willis St Stillwater (74078) **(G-8733)**
Oklahoma State University 918 253-4332
38267 Us Hwy 59 Jay (74346) **(G-3684)**
Oklahoma Steel & Wire Co Inc (PA) 580 795-7311
1042 S 1st St Madill (73446) **(G-4160)**
Oklahoma Stone 405 721-6775
9311 Nw Expressway Yukon (73099) **(G-11761)**
Oklahoma Sub Surfc Pump & Sup 405 382-7311
2536 Hwy 99 S Seminole (74868) **(G-8392)**
Oklahoma Superior Plating LLC 580 252-2787
602 S 2nd St Duncan (73533) **(G-2162)**
Oklahoma Territory Land Co LLC 405 329-1142
2007 Trailview Ct Norman (73072) **(G-5101)**
Oklahoma Tool & Machine 405 262-2624
401 E Foreman St El Reno (73036) **(G-2744)**
Oklahoma Visual Graphics LLC 405 943-3278
1401 S Meridian Ave Oklahoma City (73108) **(G-6764)**
Oklahoma World Organiz 918 224-3063
1811 Glendale Rd Sapulpa (74066) **(G-8294)**
Oklahoman Media Company 405 475-3311
100 W Main St Ste 100 # 100 Oklahoma City (73102) **(G-6765)**
Oklahomans For Vaccine 918 606-9213
6011 E 115th St Tulsa (74137) **(G-10409)**
Okland Oil Company (PA) 405 236-3046
110 N Robinson Ave # 400 Oklahoma City (73102) **(G-6766)**
Okluma LLC 580 716-1343
434 Nw 35th St Oklahoma City (73118) **(G-6767)**
Okmulgee Automotive Machine Sp 918 756-5861
205 N Alabama Ave Okmulgee (74447) **(G-7518)**
Okmulgee Daily Times, Okmulgee *Also called Kimberling City Publishing Co* **(G-7512)**
Okmulgee Monuments Inc 918 756-6619
2200 S Wood Dr Okmulgee (74447) **(G-7519)**
Okmulgee Ready Mix Concrete Co 918 756-6005
300 N Comanche Ave Okmulgee (74447) **(G-7520)**
Okrusticwoodworks 405 562-0371
5424 Fawn Run Guthrie (73044) **(G-3331)**
Okstyle Publishing LLC 405 816-3338
220 W Wilshire Blvd F2 Oklahoma City (73116) **(G-6768)**
Okt Resources LLC 405 285-1140
1900 E 15th St Ste 600c Edmond (73013) **(G-2554)**
Oky Investments Inc 405 850-4533
600 Nw 149th St Edmond (73013) **(G-2555)**
Olam Publishing LLC 918 200-9770
8525 E 75th St Tulsa (74133) **(G-10410)**
Old Epp Inc 866 408-2837
2425 S Ann Arbor Ave Oklahoma City (73128) **(G-6769)**
Old Farm Publishing LLC 405 237-1153
2119 Riverwalk Dr Moore (73160) **(G-4548)**
Old Inc 405 840-3017
901 Nw 63rd St Ste 100 Oklahoma City (73116) **(G-6770)**
Old Sarges Armory LLC 270 945-8324
713 G St Nw Miami (74354) **(G-4425)**
Old Town N Candles Lawton OK 580 678-7608
611 Nw Bell Ave Lawton (73507) **(G-3978)**
Old Town Welding Shop 918 423-8506
509 W Coal Ave McAlester (74501) **(G-4326)**
Old West Cabinets Inc 580 762-7474
122 S Pine St Ponca City (74601) **(G-7862)**
Old World Iron 405 722-0008
8405 Mantle Ave Oklahoma City (73132) **(G-6771)**
Old World Iron Inc 918 445-3063
4718 S 25th West Ave Tulsa (74107) **(G-10411)**
Old Wrld Msters Div Bldg Pdts 918 230-0340
2651 E 21st St Tulsa (74114) **(G-10412)**
Oldcastle Buildingenvelope Inc 405 275-5510
10000 N Harrison Shawnee (74804) **(G-8481)**
Oldcastle Materials Inc 918 978-0459
4150 S 100th East Ave # 300 Tulsa (74146) **(G-10413)**
Olh Moore LLC 405 703-0250
660 Sw 19th St Ste D Moore (73160) **(G-4549)**
Olifant Energy LLC 918 984-9074
15 W 6th St Ste 2200 Tulsa (74119) **(G-10414)**
Oliver & Olivia Apparel 405 300-8906
3825 Nw 166th St Ste C3 Edmond (73012) **(G-2556)**
Oliver Industries LLC 405 314-4423
3901 24th Ave Se Apt 1 Norman (73071) **(G-5102)**
Olmeva USA LLC 405 677-5400
1211 Se 29th St Oklahoma City (73129) **(G-6772)**
Olmstead Oil Company 918 743-2360
2431 E 61st St Ste 850 Tulsa (74136) **(G-10415)**
Olpco, Miami *Also called Oklahoma Leather Products Inc* **(G-4424)**
Olson Packaging Service 405 224-5577
2500 Highway 62 W Chickasha (73018) **(G-1494)**
Olympia Oil Inc 405 726-8400
4808 Rose Rock Dr Oklahoma City (73111) **(G-6773)**
Omada International LLC 405 495-2131
910 N Morgan Rd Oklahoma City (73127) **(G-6774)**
Omada International OK Cy Div, Oklahoma City *Also called Pro-Fab LLC* **(G-6908)**
Omega Optical Co LP 405 703-4133
713 Nw 119th St Oklahoma City (73114) **(G-6775)**
Omer Distributors LLC 580 695-3211
2323 Nw Nottingham Rd Lawton (73505) **(G-3979)**
Omg Tooling Inc 405 789-4774
8000 Sw 8th St Oklahoma City (73128) **(G-6776)**
Omni LLC 405 246-9252
3105 Huntleigh Dr Oklahoma City (73120) **(G-6777)**
Omni Design 918 495-0841
6131 S Oswego Ave Tulsa (74136) **(G-10416)**
Omni Lighting 918 633-7245
212 N Main St Tulsa (74103) **(G-10417)**
Omni Valve Company LLC 918 687-6100
4520 Chandler Rd Muskogee (74403) **(G-4725)**
Omni Water Consultants Inc 918 323-0001
1580 Industrial Ave Vinita (74301) **(G-11266)**
On Beat Goes 918 342-5654
9652 E Shadowview Dr Claremore (74017) **(G-1667)**
On Site Welding & Fabrication 918 706-3339
20219 E 83rd St S Broken Arrow (74014) **(G-1147)**
On The Go Hot Shot Svcs LLC 405 471-2055
612 Earl A Rodkey Dr Edmond (73003) **(G-2557)**
One Gas Inc (PA) 918 947-7000
15 E 5th St Tulsa (74103) **(G-10418)**
One Gas Inc 918 831-8218
5848 E 15th St Tulsa (74112) **(G-10419)**
One Grand Center 580 234-6600
201 N Grand St Ste 700 Enid (73701) **(G-3026)**
One Moore Embroidery Place 580 328-5755
66205 N 2170 Rd Taloga (73667) **(G-8907)**
One Oaks Field Service 580 816-4500
605 N Loomis Rd Weatherford (73096) **(G-11431)**
Onedoc Managed Print Svcs LLC 405 633-3050
6505 Nw 114th St Oklahoma City (73162) **(G-6778)**
Onefire Aerospace Services 918 794-8804
300 Riverwalk Ter Ste 280 Jenks (74037) **(G-3720)**
Onegas 918 947-7000
100 W 5th St Tulsa (74103) **(G-10420)**
Oneok Inc 405 878-6267
621 W Independence St Shawnee (74804) **(G-8482)**
Oneok Inc (PA) 918 588-7000
100 W 5th St Ste Ll Tulsa (74103) **(G-10421)**
Oneok Inc 918 588-7000
205 E Pine St Ste 2 Tulsa (74106) **(G-10422)**
Oneok Field Services Co LLC (HQ) 918 588-7000
100 W 5th St Ste Ll Tulsa (74103) **(G-10423)**
Oneok Gas Processing LLC 918 588-7000
100 W 5th St Ste Ll Tulsa (74103) **(G-10424)**
Oneok Gas Transportation, Shawnee *Also called Oneok Inc* **(G-8482)**
Oneok Gas Transportation LLC 918 588-7000
100 W 5th St Md14-5 Tulsa (74103) **(G-10425)**
Oneok Midstream Gas Supply LLC 918 588-7000
100 W 5th St Ste 450 Tulsa (74103) **(G-10426)**
Oneok Partners LP (HQ) 918 588-7000
100 W 5th St Ste Ll Tulsa (74103) **(G-10427)**
Oneok Producer Services Co 918 588-7000
100 W 5th St Ste Ll Tulsa (74103) **(G-10428)**
Oneok Resources Company (HQ) 918 588-7000
100 W 5th St Ste 450 Tulsa (74103) **(G-10429)**

Oneok Texas Field Services LP (PA)....918 588-7000
100 W 5th St Ste Ll Tulsa (74103) ***(G-10430)***
Onesource LLC....580 434-6250
11 W Main St Calera (74730) ***(G-1242)***
Online Packaging....580 389-5373
575 Waterplant Rd Ardmore (73401) ***(G-339)***
Onpoint Manufacturing....580 284-5431
25586 N 2980 Rd Cashion (73016) ***(G-1292)***
Onsite Oil Tools Inc....580 856-3367
1390 Old Hwy 7 Ratliff City (73481) ***(G-8060)***
Onsite Stress Relieving Svc....918 234-1222
14265 E 590 Rd Inola (74036) ***(G-3669)***
Onyx Imaging Corporation....918 627-6611
7446 E 46th Pl Tulsa (74145) ***(G-10431)***
Op Nail....405 222-1829
1716 S 1st St Chickasha (73018) ***(G-1495)***
Opb Pipe Bending....918 583-1566
1625 E Easton St Tulsa (74120) ***(G-10432)***
Openlink Financial LLC....918 594-7320
320 S Boston Ave Ste 600 Tulsa (74103) ***(G-10433)***
Opes Industries LLC....405 417-6223
4000 Turtle Crk Moore (73160) ***(G-4550)***
Opp Liquidating Company Inc (PA)....918 825-0616
4826 Hunt St Pryor (74361) ***(G-7980)***
Opportunity Center Inc....580 765-6782
3007 N Union St Ponca City (74601) ***(G-7863)***
Ops Sales Company....918 534-3760
14861 N 3980 Rd Dewey (74029) ***(G-2029)***
Ops Valves LLC....918 273-3300
3.8 Miles Nowata (74048) ***(G-5224)***
Optical Works Corporation....918 682-1806
7259 Border Ave Muskogee (74401) ***(G-4726)***
Optionone LLC....405 548-4848
14000 N Portland Ave Oklahoma City (73134) ***(G-6779)***
Options Inc (PA)....918 473-2614
1129 White Stag Ave Checotah (74426) ***(G-1398)***
Optronics International LLC....918 683-9514
401 S 41st St E Muskogee (74403) ***(G-4727)***
Opubco Development Co....405 475-3311
100 W Main St Ste 100 # 100 Oklahoma City (73102) ***(G-6780)***
Oracle America Inc....918 587-9016
321 S Boston Ave Ste 600 Tulsa (74103) ***(G-10434)***
Oral Health Products Inc....918 622-9412
6855 E 40th St Tulsa (74145) ***(G-10435)***
Oral Rbrts Evnglistic Assn Inc (PA)....918 591-2000
6201 E 43rd St Tulsa (74135) ***(G-10436)***
Orange Oil LLC....405 701-3505
2401 Tee Cir Ste 203 Norman (73069) ***(G-5103)***
Orca Operating Company LLC....918 587-1312
427 S Boston Ave Ste 400 Tulsa (74103) ***(G-10437)***
Orchids, Pryor *Also called Opp Liquidating Company Inc* ***(G-7980)***
Orcutt Machine....918 629-7930
3129 Charles Page Blvd Tulsa (74127) ***(G-10438)***
Order Here Tulsa LLC....888 633-9905
2217 Arline St Muskogee (74401) ***(G-4728)***
Order-Matic Electronics Corp....405 672-1487
340 S Eckroat St Oklahoma City (73129) ***(G-6781)***
Oremus Press & Publishing....405 368-4645
24212 E 680 Rd Dover (73734) ***(G-2042)***
Orica USA Inc....918 437-1644
12502 E 36th St N Tulsa (74116) ***(G-10439)***
Original Productions Pubg LLC....405 420-9559
612 Leopard Lily Dr Norman (73069) ***(G-5104)***
Orion Exploration LLC....918 492-0254
4870 S Lewis Ave Ste 240 Tulsa (74105) ***(G-10440)***
Orizon Arstrctres - Owasso Inc....918 274-9094
209 E 5th Ave Owasso (74055) ***(G-7599)***
Orizon Arstrctures - Grove Inc....918 786-9094
500 Industrial Rd Grove (74344) ***(G-3284)***
Ormca....918 296-7711
2526 E 71st St Ste H Tulsa (74136) ***(G-10441)***
Oro Woodworks....405 334-7445
6814 Walnut Crk Stillwater (74074) ***(G-8734)***
Orr Oil & Gas E & P Inc....580 224-9290
5 S Commerce St Ardmore (73401) ***(G-340)***
Ortco Inc....405 670-2803
1317 Se 25th St Oklahoma City (73129) ***(G-6782)***
Orthotics Pros Inc....918 296-3567
11709 S Ivy St Jenks (74037) ***(G-3721)***
Orthwein Petroleum....405 478-7663
925 E Britton Rd Oklahoma City (73114) ***(G-6783)***
Osage County Treasurer....918 287-3101
611 Grandview Ave Pawhuska (74056) ***(G-7691)***
Osage Door Co Inc....918 542-7281
7200 S 580th Rd Miami (74354) ***(G-4426)***
Osage Land Company....405 946-8402
1800 Cyn Pk Cir Ste 201 Oklahoma City (73156) ***(G-6784)***
Osage Leather Inc....918 745-0772
3220 S Peoria Ave Ste 202 Tulsa (74105) ***(G-10442)***
Osage Neon....918 583-4430
915 N 33rd West Ave Tulsa (74127) ***(G-10443)***
Osage Oil and Gas Property....405 841-7600
9520 N May Ave Ste 301 Oklahoma City (73120) ***(G-6785)***
Osage Surveying Service....918 287-4029
100 W Main St Ste 210 Pawhuska (74056) ***(G-7692)***
Osage Trading Co Inc (PA)....918 287-4544
153 John Dahl Ave Pawhuska (74056) ***(G-7693)***
Osage Wireline Service Inc....918 358-5155
2 Miles S Of Cy On Hwy 64 Cleveland (74020) ***(G-1731)***
Osborne Design Co....918 585-3212
4524 W 21st St Tulsa (74107) ***(G-10444)***
Oscium....719 695-0600
5909 Nw Expressway # 269 Oklahoma City (73132) ***(G-6786)***
Oseco, Broken Arrow *Also called Oklahoma Safety Eqp Co Inc* ***(G-994)***
Osiyo Medals Inc....918 258-4717
1801 N Indianwood Ave Broken Arrow (74012) ***(G-995)***
Osr Services LP....918 234-1222
14265 E 590 Rd Inola (74036) ***(G-3670)***
OSteen Meat Specialties Inc....405 236-1952
2126 N Broadway Ave Oklahoma City (73103) ***(G-6787)***
Ota Compression LLC....918 623-9922
401 E Columbia St Okemah (74859) ***(G-5272)***
Otc Petroleum Corporation....405 840-2255
3244 Nw Grand Blvd Oklahoma City (73116) ***(G-6788)***
Oto-Biomechanics LLC....405 325-6668
201 Stephenson Pkwy # 130 Norman (73072) ***(G-5105)***
Ottawa County District 3....918 676-3227
7 S Main St Fairland (74343) ***(G-3127)***
Ottawa Oak Mfg....918 541-8996
15604 S Highway 10 Wyandotte (74370) ***(G-11661)***
Ou Press, Norman *Also called University of Oklahoma* ***(G-5186)***
Ouachita Exploration Inc....405 222-0024
402 W Chickasha Ave # 200 Chickasha (73018) ***(G-1496)***
Oustanding Lady Oil & Gas,, Oklahoma City *Also called S S & L Oil and Gas Properties* ***(G-7066)***
Out N Back Hot Shot LLC....405 201-3576
4608 Deer Creek Ct Yukon (73099) ***(G-11762)***
Out On A Limb Mfg LLC....580 541-3794
5710 N Us Highway 81 Enid (73701) ***(G-3027)***
Out On A Limb Publishing, Tulsa *Also called Out On Limb Publishing* ***(G-10445)***
Out On Limb Publishing....918 743-4408
1810 E 51st St Ste C Tulsa (74105) ***(G-10445)***
Outback Laboratories....405 527-6355
13110 Us Highway 77 Lexington (73051) ***(G-4038)***
Outdoor Incorporated....918 697-1402
7757 S 145th West Ave Sapulpa (74066) ***(G-8295)***
Outlaw Industries LLC....918 569-7555
168344 N 4280 Rd Clayton (74536) ***(G-1710)***
Outlaw Oilfield Supply LLC....580 526-3792
12292 Highway 30 Erick (73645) ***(G-3091)***
Outsource Group LLC....918 307-0110
15 E 5th St Ste 2221 Tulsa (74103) ***(G-10446)***
Outwest Welding Services LLC....918 593-2345
6123 N 4435 Strang (74367) ***(G-8803)***
Over 60 LLC....405 224-0711
4007 Hickory Stick Dr Chickasha (73018) ***(G-1497)***
Overbilt Trailer Company....918 352-4474
1115 E Broadway St Drumright (74030) ***(G-2069)***
Overhead Door Solutions LLC....918 686-8847
10648 S Highway 64 Muskogee (74403) ***(G-4729)***
Overland Federal LLC....469 269-2303
534 Us Highway 77 Ardmore (73401) ***(G-341)***
Overland Materials and Mfg Inc....580 223-8432
534 Us Highway 77 Ardmore (73401) ***(G-342)***
Overstreet Building & Supply....580 234-5666
2613 Mcgill Dr Enid (73703) ***(G-3028)***
Ovintiv Exploration Inc....580 927-9064
5505 S Us Highway 69 McAlester (74501) ***(G-4327)***
Ovintiv Exploration Inc....918 740-1400
110 W 7th St Tulsa (74119) ***(G-10447)***
Ovintiv Exploration Inc....580 243-4101
2001 E 20th St Elk City (73644) ***(G-2857)***
Ovintiv Exploration Inc....918 420-5086
5111 S Highway 69 Mc Alester (74501) ***(G-4265)***
Ovintiv Mid-Continent Inc (HQ)....918 582-2690
101 E 2nd St Tulsa (74103) ***(G-10448)***
Ovintiv Mid-Continent Inc....580 243-4101
106 Panel Rd Elk City (73644) ***(G-2858)***
Owasso Glass....918 272-4490
304 S Birch St Owasso (74055) ***(G-7600)***
Owasso Pressurewashing LLC....918 557-4059
10956 E 176th St N Collinsville (74021) ***(G-1819)***
Owasso Reporter, Owasso *Also called Berkshire Hathaway Inc* ***(G-7548)***
Owen Oil Tools LP....405 495-4441
9616 Nw 6th St Oklahoma City (73127) ***(G-6789)***
Owens Corning Sales LLC....405 235-2491
3400 Ne 4th St Oklahoma City (73117) ***(G-6790)***
Owens-Brockway Glass Cont Inc....918 684-4526
2401 Old Shawnee Rd Muskogee (74403) ***(G-4730)***
Owner Value News....918 828-9600
5800 E Skelly Dr Ste 708 Tulsa (74135) ***(G-10449)***

Oxbow Calcining LLC 580 874-2201
11826 N 30th St Kremlin (73753) ***(G-3854)***
OXY Inc 580 338-6593
2810 Tumbleweed Dr Guymon (73942) ***(G-3358)***
Ozark Steel LLC 918 438-4330
908 W 41st St Tulsa (74107) ***(G-10450)***
Ozmo Design and Print LLC 417 655-5615
919 Mike Ave Tahlequah (74464) ***(G-8878)***
P & H Construction Inc 405 257-3307
125 W Park St Wewoka (74884) ***(G-11506)***
P & K Machine Inc 918 266-7815
401 N Cherokee St Catoosa (74015) ***(G-1345)***
P & L Welding and Fabrication 660 563-1775
2021 Alameda St Apt 712 Norman (73071) ***(G-5106)***
P & M Industries Inc 918 660-0055
4450 S Mingo Rd Tulsa (74146) ***(G-10451)***
P /Masters C Inc 405 293-9777
1700 E Seward Rd Guthrie (73044) ***(G-3332)***
P C Concrete Co Inc 580 762-1302
3320 Lake Rd Ponca City (74604) ***(G-7864)***
P C S, Tulsa *Also called Pipeline Coating Services LLC* ***(G-10518)***
P D I Inc 405 232-9700
105 N Hudson Ave Ste 800 Oklahoma City (73102) ***(G-6791)***
P F Beeler LLC 405 364-0799
1012 Nottingham Cir Norman (73072) ***(G-5107)***
P F Services LLC 405 226-4871
921 Glacier Ln Edmond (73003) ***(G-2558)***
P H C Explorations Inc 918 298-2008
11111 S Fulton Ave Tulsa (74137) ***(G-10452)***
P H D Oil & Gas Inc 580 476-3005
223 W Blakely St Rush Springs (73082) ***(G-8124)***
P I Speakers 918 663-2131
10608 E 18th St Tulsa (74128) ***(G-10453)***
P M Graphics 405 525-8789
11901 Se 157th St Oklahoma City (73165) ***(G-5310)***
P M I, Moore *Also called Paving Materials Inc* ***(G-4552)***
P O H, Tulsa *Also called Oral Health Products Inc* ***(G-10435)***
P S Improvements, Tulsa *Also called Pump & Seal Improvements* ***(G-10582)***
P V Valve 580 856-3844
22727 State Highway 76 Ratliff City (73481) ***(G-8061)***
P W Manufacturing Company Inc 918 652-4981
610 High St Henryetta (74437) ***(G-3514)***
P&D's, Porum *Also called Donald W Cox* ***(G-7895)***
P&W Wrhuse Lgstic Srvices- Okc, Oklahoma City *Also called Pratt Whtney Mltary Aftrmrket* ***(G-6875)***
P-Americas LLC 580 326-8333
200 Pepsi Cola Ave Hugo (74743) ***(G-3617)***
P-F Unlimited, Tulsa *Also called Promotions - Forms Unlimited* ***(G-10573)***
P-T Coupling Company (HQ) 580 237-4033
1414 E Willow Rd Enid (73701) ***(G-3029)***
P.E.S., Bokoshe *Also called F & F Production Eqp Svcs LLC* ***(G-753)***
Paccar 918 810-3810
4841 S 197th East Ave Broken Arrow (74014) ***(G-1148)***
Paccar Inc 918 756-4400
1204 W 20th St Okmulgee (74447) ***(G-7521)***
Paccar Inc 918 251-8511
800 E Dallas St Broken Arrow (74012) ***(G-996)***
Paccar Inc 405 745-3006
5700 S Council Rd Oklahoma City (73179) ***(G-6792)***
Pace Printing Inc 918 585-5664
611 E 4th St Tulsa (74120) ***(G-10454)***
Pacific Oil & Gas LLC 405 835-2790
16300 W Highway 66 Yukon (73099) ***(G-11763)***
Pacific Power Group LLC 405 685-4630
4253 Will Rogers Pkwy Oklahoma City (73108) ***(G-6793)***
Pacific Power Products, Oklahoma City *Also called Pacific Power Group LLC* ***(G-6793)***
Padgett Machine, Jenks *Also called Onefire Aerospace Services* ***(G-3720)***
Padgett Machine Shop Inc 918 438-3444
1226 N 143rd East Ave Tulsa (74116) ***(G-10455)***
Padgett Machine Shop LLC 918 636-9334
1226 N 143rd East Ave Tulsa (74116) ***(G-10456)***
Page Tool & Machine Shop 918 775-6766
3009 N Wheeler Ave Sallisaw (74955) ***(G-8150)***
Paia Electronics Inc 405 340-6300
3200 Teakwood Ln Edmond (73013) ***(G-2559)***
Paige 1 Publishing 918 706-4359
12350 E 138th St S Broken Arrow (74011) ***(G-997)***
Paige Publishing 405 527-3245
518 Se 6th St Lexington (73051) ***(G-4039)***
Paint Handy LLC 918 734-3422
8303 E 111th St S Ste E Bixby (74008) ***(G-651)***
Paint On Canvas 405 574-6689
624 W Chickasha Ave Chickasha (73018) ***(G-1498)***
Paint Pros Inc 405 226-8898
2009 Westbrooke Ter Norman (73072) ***(G-5108)***
Pak Electric Inc (PA) 580 482-1757
1101 W Broadway St Altus (73521) ***(G-166)***
PAK Oilfield Services LLC 580 504-7049
179 Stone Bridge Ln Ardmore (73401) ***(G-343)***
Pal-Serv Oklahoma City LLC 405 672-1155
1432 W Main St Oklahoma City (73106) ***(G-6794)***
Paladin Geological Svcs LLC 405 463-3270
13832 Snta Fe Crssings Dr Edmond (73013) ***(G-2560)***
Paladin Land Group LLC 918 582-5404
15 E 5th St Ste 1602 Tulsa (74103) ***(G-10457)***
Paladin Surface Logging, Edmond *Also called Paladin Geological Svcs LLC* ***(G-2560)***
Paleo Inc 405 942-1546
6303 N Portland Ave # 203 Oklahoma City (73112) ***(G-6795)***
Palin Welding Service LLC 405 449-3541
15243 Hopping Ave Wayne (73095) ***(G-11368)***
Pallet Liquidations Okc LLC 405 843-0402
12017 Brookhollow Rd Oklahoma City (73120) ***(G-6796)***
Pallet Logistics of America 405 670-1414
1901 S Skyline Dr Oklahoma City (73129) ***(G-6797)***
Pallet Supply Co, Tulsa *Also called Doug Butler Enterprises Inc* ***(G-9599)***
Pallets Plus LLC 580 513-4090
100 E Ferguson Ave Davis (73030) ***(G-1992)***
Palm Operating LLC 918 968-0574
509 N 2nd Ave Stroud (74079) ***(G-8815)***
Palm Vault Co Inc 580 332-7565
401 Arlington St Ada (74820) ***(G-74)***
Paloma Partners IV 405 295-6755
221 N Rock Island Ave El Reno (73036) ***(G-2745)***
Paluca Petroleum Inc 405 379-5656
225 Kingsberry Rd Holdenville (74848) ***(G-3558)***
Pan Pacific Products, Broken Bow *Also called Dominance Industries Inc* ***(G-1189)***
Panda Screen Printing Entps 918 622-3601
3927 E Admiral Pl Tulsa (74115) ***(G-10458)***
Panderia La Guadalupana 918 764-9000
1126 E 61st St Tulsa (74136) ***(G-10459)***
Panhandle Construction Svcs 580 338-7667
Hwy 64 Rd T Guymon (73942) ***(G-3359)***
Panhandle Corrosion LLC 580 651-3208
717 Jackson St Goodwell (73939) ***(G-3249)***
Panhandle Oil and Gas Inc (PA) 405 948-1560
5400 N Grand Blvd Ste 300 Oklahoma City (73112) ***(G-6798)***
Panhandle Oilfield Service Com (PA) 405 608-5330
14000 Quail Springs Pkwy # 300 Oklahoma City (73134) ***(G-6799)***
Panhandle Pipe Supply, Oklahoma City *Also called Panhandle Oilfield Service Com* ***(G-6799)***
Panhandle Printing 580 338-1633
315 Ne 4th St Guymon (73942) ***(G-3360)***
Panhandle Royalty Co 405 945-6100
5400 N Grand Blvd Ste 300 Oklahoma City (73112) ***(G-6800)***
Panoak Oil & Gas Corporation (PA) 918 857-4929
403 S Cheyenne Ave # 1000 Tulsa (74103) ***(G-10460)***
Panther Drilling Systems LLC 405 896-9300
14301 Caliber Dr Ste 220 Oklahoma City (73134) ***(G-6801)***
Panther Energy Company LLC 918 583-1396
6100 S Yale Ave Ste 600 Tulsa (74136) ***(G-10461)***
Panther Energy Company II LLC 918 583-1396
6100 S Yale Ave Ste 600 Tulsa (74136) ***(G-10462)***
Panthera Roustabout Svcs LLC 405 826-8466
1601 Brook Bank Dr Jones (73049) ***(G-3751)***
Papa Har's Pickles, Lahoma *Also called Plainview Winery* ***(G-3859)***
Paper 918 825-2860
3 N Adair St Ste 7 Pryor (74361) ***(G-7981)***
Paper Concierge 405 286-3322
1717 W 33rd St Edmond (73013) ***(G-2561)***
Paper House Productions LLC 918 835-0172
6103 E Admiral Blvd Tulsa (74115) ***(G-10463)***
Paper Plus 405 948-1120
290 S Quadrum Dr Oklahoma City (73108) ***(G-6802)***
Paperwork Company 918 369-1014
11 E Dawes Ave Bixby (74008) ***(G-652)***
Pappan and Spears LLC 405 742-6900
11108 E Admiral Pl Tulsa (74116) ***(G-10464)***
Pappe Court Jr Office 405 375-5450
204 N Main St Kingfisher (73750) ***(G-3810)***
Paradise Construction LLC 918 967-9991
110 W Main St Stigler (74462) ***(G-8637)***
Paradise Doughnuts 405 224-2907
601 S 4th St Chickasha (73018) ***(G-1499)***
Paradise Pools & Hot Tubs 918 938-7727
6353 E 41st St Tulsa (74135) ***(G-10465)***
Paragon Films Inc (PA) 918 250-3456
3500 W Tacoma St Broken Arrow (74012) ***(G-998)***
Paragon Industries Inc 918 781-1430
4632 Harold Scoggins Dr Muskogee (74403) ***(G-4731)***
Paragon Industries Inc (PA) 918 291-4459
3378 W Highway 117 Sapulpa (74066) ***(G-8296)***
Paragon Press Inc 405 681-5757
3029 S Ann Arbor Ave Oklahoma City (73179) ***(G-6803)***
Paragon Production Co 405 348-1116
1300 E 15th St Ste 100 Edmond (73013) ***(G-2562)***
Parallel Energy LP 918 712-7008
1323 E 71st St Ste 200 Tulsa (74136) ***(G-10466)***
Paramount Building Pdts LLC 405 470-5073
6924 Nw 80th St Oklahoma City (73132) ***(G-6804)***

Parco Masts & Substructures 918 585-8221
8 E 3rd St Tulsa (74103) *(G-10467)*
Parfab Field Services LLC 918 543-6310
15615 E 590 Rd Inola (74036) *(G-3671)*
Parfab Industries LLC (PA) 918 543-6310
15615 E 590 Rd Inola (74036) *(G-3672)*
Park Dental Research Corp 580 226-0410
2401 N Commerce St Ste D Ardmore (73401) *(G-344)*
Park Energy Services LLC 918 617-4350
1408 N Country Ridge Dr Stigler (74462) *(G-8638)*
Park Oil, Sperry *Also called William M Park* *(G-8612)*
Parker & Parsley Petroleum 405 756-1912
302 W Pawnee St Lindsay (73052) *(G-4076)*
Parker Drilling Company 918 281-2708
2021 S Lewis Ave Ste 410 Tulsa (74104) *(G-10468)*
Parker Energy Services Co 918 626-4982
401 Rose Dr Pocola (74902) *(G-7784)*
Parker Hannifin Corporation 918 652-7364
26220 S 220 Rd Henryetta (74437) *(G-3515)*
Parker Kustom Woodworking 405 414-2820
4209 Angela Dr Del City (73115) *(G-2005)*
Parker Plastics Inc 918 241-0350
101 S Woodland Dr Sand Springs (74063) *(G-8213)*
Parkers Custom Hardwoods Inc 405 341-9663
17 N Fretz Ave Edmond (73003) *(G-2563)*
Parkers Welding Custom Work 405 341-3344
309 W Main St Edmond (73003) *(G-2564)*
Parkerville USA EMB & More 918 636-0048
7890 N Owasso Expy Owasso (74055) *(G-7601)*
Parking Drilling Company Intl 281 406-2000
8 E 3rd St Tulsa (74103) *(G-10469)*
Parkline Arrow, Bristow *Also called Parkline Systems Corporation* *(G-792)*
Parkline Systems Corporation 918 367-5523
23630 S 369th West Ave Bristow (74010) *(G-792)*
Parks Custom Cabinets LLC 918 789-2694
7454 S Highway 28 Chelsea (74016) *(G-1409)*
Parks Manufacturing Inc 405 382-0349
711 Boren Blvd Seminole (74868) *(G-8393)*
Parks Oil Tools LLC 405 485-9515
703 S Tyler Ave Blanchard (73010) *(G-725)*
Parnel Biogas Inc 918 294-3868
13701 S Hwy 75 Glenpool (74033) *(G-3240)*
Parra World Creations LLC 918 938-2278
8001 S Mingo Rd Apt 1901 Tulsa (74133) *(G-10470)*
Parrish Enterprises 580 233-4757
3005 N Emerson St Enid (73701) *(G-3030)*
Parrish Enterprises Ltd (PA) 580 237-4033
1414 E Willow Rd Enid (73701) *(G-3031)*
Parsage Oil Company LLC 918 846-2358
1821 E 71st St Tulsa (74136) *(G-10471)*
Parson Welding, Okarche *Also called Parsons Welding Inc* *(G-5249)*
Parsons Welding Inc 405 263-7495
28334 N 2860 Rd Okarche (73762) *(G-5249)*
Partical Rent A Car, Cushing *Also called Jims Truck Center* *(G-1939)*
Partners Oilfield Services LLC 580 625-2239
1 Mile South Of Beaver Beaver (73932) *(G-543)*
Party King Grills Company LLC 580 774-2828
400 E Main St Ste B Weatherford (73096) *(G-11432)*
Party Station, Grove *Also called Two K Enterprises LLC* *(G-3290)*
Parwest Land Exploration Inc 405 843-1917
2601 Nw Expwy Ste 707w Oklahoma City (73112) *(G-6805)*
Paschall Land Management 405 842-1391
6424 N Santa Fe Ave Ste A Oklahoma City (73116) *(G-6806)*
Paseo Pottery 405 525-3017
3017 Paseo Oklahoma City (73103) *(G-6807)*
Passion Berri 405 310-6669
1204 N Interstate Dr Norman (73072) *(G-5109)*
Passion Racing Engines 918 232-3950
14911 E 94th St N Owasso (74055) *(G-7602)*
Pasta Pizzaz Inc 405 848-9966
8121 N Classen Blvd Ste C Oklahoma City (73114) *(G-6808)*
Pat McVicker Oilfield Services 580 256-1577
131 Spruce Dr Woodward (73801) *(G-11616)*
Pathinnovation LLC 405 475-9726
133 Lake Aluma Dr Oklahoma City (73121) *(G-6809)*
Pathkiller, Tuttle *Also called Twj Inc* *(G-11217)*
Patricia Lyons 850 445-4782
12530 S Ash Ave Jenks (74037) *(G-3722)*
Patricia McKay 580 355-2739
6 Mountain View Dr Cache (73527) *(G-1230)*
Patrick A McGinley 918 583-3267
1105 E 21st Pl Tulsa (74114) *(G-10472)*
Patrick Energy Group 918 477-7755
7380 S Olympia Ave Tulsa (74132) *(G-10473)*
Patrick McVicker 580 256-1577
2728 Williams Ave Woodward (73801) *(G-11617)*
Patrick Michael Palazzo 918 344-3724
577 E 32nd St N Apt C Tulsa (74106) *(G-10474)*
Patrick Petroleum, Tulsa *Also called Patrick Energy Group* *(G-10473)*
Patriot Chemicals & Svcs LLC 580 856-3114
11506 State Highway 7 Ratliff City (73481) *(G-8062)*
Patriot Directional Drlg LLC 405 831-0085
2417 N Marine Rd Ste 3 Stillwater (74075) *(G-8735)*
Patriot Prsthtics Orthtics Inc 405 577-6778
1804 Commons Cir Ste A Yukon (73099) *(G-11764)*
Patriot Small Arms LLC 405 567-7890
19208 Patterson Rd Tecumseh (74873) *(G-8924)*
Patriot Wldg & Fabrication LLC 918 600-7147
305 N Redbud Ave Broken Arrow (74012) *(G-999)*
Pats Custom Draperies 405 794-1019
2721 Little Ln Moore (73160) *(G-4551)*
Pats Machine 405 681-1050
2229 Sw 42nd St Oklahoma City (73119) *(G-6810)*
Pats Phase II Hair & Nail Sln 405 232-4746
120 N Robinson Ave B38e Oklahoma City (73102) *(G-6811)*
Pats World 580 443-5751
7100 E Egypt Rd Milburn (73450) *(G-4463)*
Patten Equipment & Welding LLC 580 334-7035
41791 S County Road 200 # 9 Woodward (73801) *(G-11618)*
Patternwork Veneering Inc 405 447-1800
303 E Main St Norman (73069) *(G-5110)*
Patterson Machine Shop 918 463-3600
3805 E 153rd St S Warner (74469) *(G-11308)*
Patterson Oil Company Inc 405 257-3241
201 S Wewoka Ave Wewoka (74884) *(G-11507)*
Pattison Metal Fab Inc 918 251-9967
701 N 15th St Broken Arrow (74012) *(G-1000)*
Pattison Precision Products 918 251-9967
701 N 15th St Broken Arrow (74012) *(G-1001)*
Paul Clinton Hughes 918 273-1888
115 N Maple St Nowata (74048) *(G-5225)*
Paul E Kloberdanz 405 947-5570
100 N Broadway Ave # 3150 Oklahoma City (73102) *(G-6812)*
Paul G Pennington Industries (PA) 405 392-2317
2325 Fox Ln Blanchard (73010) *(G-726)*
Paul King Company 918 592-5464
1030 N Owasso Ave Tulsa (74106) *(G-10475)*
Paul Philp Gchmical Conslt LLC 405 325-4469
4212 Brookfield Dr Norman (73072) *(G-5111)*
Paul Precision Machine Inc 918 835-6175
5908 E 12th St Tulsa (74112) *(G-10476)*
Paul Wrecker Service 918 333-9685
731 Ne Washington Blvd Bartlesville (74006) *(G-515)*
Paul Ziert & Associates Inc (PA) 405 364-5344
3214 Bart Conner Dr Norman (73072) *(G-5112)*
Paul Zirt & Associates, Norman *Also called International Gymnast Magazine* *(G-5035)*
Paula Gallaher 580 439-6484
185939 N 2810 Rd Comanche (73529) *(G-1844)*
Paulaura Cattle Co 918 682-6030
1852 W 63rd St N Muskogee (74403) *(G-4732)*
Pauline Oil and Gas Co 405 842-4213
1321 Sherwood Ln Nichols Hills (73116) *(G-4862)*
Pauls Pallet Co 918 435-4321
37419 County Road 492 Eucha (74342) *(G-3095)*
Pauls Valley Daily Democrat, Pauls Valley *Also called Cnhi LLC* *(G-7654)*
Paving Materials Inc 405 799-9880
140 Industrial Blvd Moore (73160) *(G-4552)*
Paving Materials Southern Okla, Enid *Also called Cummins Construction Co Inc* *(G-2937)*
Pawnee Millworks LLC 918 767-2565
51752 E 43 Rd Pawnee (74058) *(G-7707)*
Pawnee Ready Mix Inc 918 762-3437
2000 S 9th St Pawnee (74058) *(G-7708)*
Paxton McMillin Chrisanna 918 734-5753
15495 Linda Ln Sapulpa (74066) *(G-8297)*
Paxton Publishing Co 580 782-3321
121 S Oklahoma Ave Mangum (73554) *(G-4173)*
Paycom Software Inc (PA) 405 722-6900
7501 W Memorial Rd Oklahoma City (73142) *(G-6813)*
Payne Farms 580 661-2351
8890 N 2445 Rd Thomas (73669) *(G-8947)*
Payrock II LLC 405 608-8077
3200 Quail Springs Pkwy Oklahoma City (73134) *(G-6814)*
Paysmith Processing LLC 918 858-5599
4500 S 129th East Ave # 175 Tulsa (74134) *(G-10477)*
Paytons Auto 918 540-2501
817 D St Ne Miami (74354) *(G-4427)*
Payzone Completion Svcs LLC 405 772-7184
837 Se 82nd St Oklahoma City (73149) *(G-6815)*
PC Net 405 238-2001
1700 S Chickasaw St Pauls Valley (73075) *(G-7670)*
Pcs Ferguson Inc 918 967-3236
1212 E Main St Stigler (74462) *(G-8639)*
Pcs Ferguson Inc 580 256-1317
3510 Williams Ave Woodward (73801) *(G-11619)*
PDC, Tulsa *Also called Petroleum Development Company* *(G-10505)*
Pdi, Tulsa *Also called Professional Datasolutions Inc* *(G-10567)*
PDQ Printing LLC 580 233-3241
131 E Maine Ave Enid (73701) *(G-3032)*

Pdqlipprints LLC...580 233-3241
131 E Maine Ave Enid (73701) ***(G-3033)***
Pdrx Pharmaceutica, Oklahoma City *Also called Trimark Labs* ***(G-7333)***
Peabody & Kent Designs Inc...918 439-4300
6935 E 13th St Tulsa (74112) ***(G-10478)***
Peabodys Printing & A Brush Sp...580 248-8317
709 Sw Lee Blvd Lawton (73501) ***(G-3980)***
Peabodys Prtg & Airbrush Sp, Lawton *Also called Peabodys Printing & A Brush Sp* ***(G-3980)***
Peak Cement Piedmont...405 373-2086
1823 Susanna Rd Ne Piedmont (73078) ***(G-7768)***
Peak Eagles Landing...918 636-5152
810 S Jardot Rd Trlr 58 Stillwater (74074) ***(G-8736)***
Peak Industries...918 289-0424
9955 E 55th Pl Tulsa (74146) ***(G-10479)***
Peak Machining Group LLC (PA)...307 660-1463
1900 S Osage St Skiatook (74070) ***(G-8563)***
Peak Oilfield Services...405 884-2379
26460 Highway 281 Spur Geary (73040) ***(G-3217)***
Peak Operating LLC...405 343-7590
1601 Nw Expwy St Ste 1600 Oklahoma City (73118) ***(G-6816)***
Peak Sulfur Inc...918 587-7613
5201 W 21st St Tulsa (74107) ***(G-10480)***
Peake Fuel Solutions LLC...405 935-8000
6100 N Western Ave Oklahoma City (73118) ***(G-6817)***
Peanut Products Co Inc...580 296-4888
26 Spivey Dr Calera (74730) ***(G-1243)***
Peanut Shoppe, The, Calera *Also called Peanut Products Co Inc* ***(G-1243)***
Pearce Quinton Weld...918 559-3026
706 S Ash St Nowata (74048) ***(G-5226)***
Pearl District Embroidery LLC...918 269-3347
716 S Troost Ave Tulsa (74120) ***(G-10481)***
Pearl Energy Group LLC...281 799-7459
9201 Via Del Vis Oklahoma City (73131) ***(G-6818)***
Pearl Petroleum Inc...580 355-6477
3202 Se 165th St Lawton (73501) ***(G-3981)***
Pearson Pumping Inc...918 486-2386
18505 Highway 51b Coweta (74429) ***(G-1893)***
Pecan Creek Winery LLC...918 683-1087
8510 Fern Mountain Rd Muskogee (74401) ***(G-4733)***
Pechiney Plastic Packaging...918 739-4900
905 Verdigris Pkwy Catoosa (74015) ***(G-1346)***
Peco, Sand Springs *Also called Piping Enterprise Company Inc* ***(G-8214)***
Pecos Pipeline LLC...918 574-3500
110 W 7th St Ste 2300 Tulsa (74119) ***(G-10482)***
Pedestal Oil Company Inc...405 236-8596
204 N Robinson Ave # 1700 Oklahoma City (73102) ***(G-6819)***
Pedros Cstm Cabinets Trim LLC...580 656-3982
205 N I St Duncan (73533) ***(G-2163)***
Pegleg Publishing LLC...405 618-7740
1612 Nw 20th St Oklahoma City (73106) ***(G-6820)***
PEL Company LLC...405 816-6553
2805 N Windsor Ter Oklahoma City (73127) ***(G-6821)***
Pelagic Tank LLC...580 856-2182
301 S 54th St Enid (73701) ***(G-3034)***
Pelco Products Inc...405 340-3434
320 W 18th St Edmond (73013) ***(G-2565)***
Pelco Products Inc...405 842-6978
1025 Nw Grand Blvd Oklahoma City (73118) ***(G-6822)***
Pelco Structural LLC...918 283-4004
1501 N Industrial Blvd Claremore (74017) ***(G-1668)***
Pelican Energy LLC...405 418-8000
301 Nw 63rd St Ste 600 Oklahoma City (73116) ***(G-6823)***
Pemco Inc...918 341-7500
15201 S Highway 66 Claremore (74017) ***(G-1669)***
Pendleton Woolen Mills Inc...918 712-8545
1828 Utica Sq Tulsa (74114) ***(G-10483)***
Pendpac Incorporated...418 831-8250
124 E Broadway Ste 4 Fairview (73737) ***(G-3145)***
Penielite Ggg Press...405 850-5795
407 Jarman Dr McLoud (74851) ***(G-4361)***
Penielite Press, McLoud *Also called Penielite Ggg Press* ***(G-4361)***
Penloyd LLC...918 836-3794
2900 E Apache St Tulsa (74110) ***(G-10484)***
Penn Aluminum Inc...405 476-5222
4121 Lake Dr Yukon (73099) ***(G-11765)***
Penn Machine Inc...405 789-0084
8513 Sw 2nd St Oklahoma City (73128) ***(G-6824)***
Penn-OK Gathering Systems Inc...405 843-1544
5605 N Classen Blvd Oklahoma City (73118) ***(G-6825)***
Pennant Oil & Gas LLC...405 642-4382
907 S Detroit Ave # 1035 Tulsa (74120) ***(G-10485)***
Penner Energy Inc...405 751-7504
3336 Rock Hollow Rd Oklahoma City (73120) ***(G-6826)***
Pennington Allen Cpitl Prtners...918 749-6811
5100 E Skelly Dr Tulsa (74135) ***(G-10486)***
Pennington Industries...405 392-2317
7512 E Hwy 37 Tuttle Newcastle (73065) ***(G-4835)***
Pennmark Energy LLC...405 840-9885
2601 Nw Expwy Ste 1200w Oklahoma City (73112) ***(G-6827)***
Pennsylvania Chernicky LLC...918 587-6242
1307 S Boulder Ave # 400 Tulsa (74119) ***(G-10487)***
Pennwell Corporation, Tulsa *Also called Clarion Events Inc* ***(G-9438)***
Penny Sheet Metal LLC...918 251-6911
1910 W Detroit St Broken Arrow (74012) ***(G-1002)***
Penterra Services LLC...405 726-2762
15314 N May Ave Edmond (73013) ***(G-2566)***
Pepper Creek Farms Inc...580 536-1300
1002 Sw Ard St Lawton (73505) ***(G-3982)***
Pepper Land Inc...918 691-7241
4645 S 189th East Ave Tulsa (74134) ***(G-10488)***
Pepsi Cola Btlg Clinton Okla...580 323-1666
712 Frisco Ave Clinton (73601) ***(G-1763)***
Pepsi Cola Company...918 446-6601
510 W Skelly Dr Tulsa (74107) ***(G-10489)***
Pepsi-Cola, Clinton *Also called Pepsi Cola Btlg Clinton Okla* ***(G-1763)***
Pepsi-Cola Btlg McAlester Inc (PA)...918 423-2360
1528 E Electric Ave McAlester (74501) ***(G-4328)***
Pepsi-Cola Btlg McAlester Inc...918 446-6601
510 W Skelly Dr Tulsa (74107) ***(G-10490)***
Pepsi-Cola Metro Btlg Co Inc...580 326-8333
200 Pepsi Cola Ave Hugo (74743) ***(G-3618)***
Pepsi-Cola Metro Btlg Co Inc...580 585-6281
209 Se Simpson St Lawton (73501) ***(G-3983)***
Pepsico, Tulsa *Also called Pepsi-Cola Btlg McAlester Inc* ***(G-10490)***
Pepsico, Tulsa *Also called Pepsi Cola Company* ***(G-10489)***
Pepsico, Hugo *Also called P-Americas LLC* ***(G-3617)***
Perceptions...405 964-7000
1927 N Fishmarket Rd McLoud (74851) ***(G-4362)***
Peregrine Products LLC...918 361-4304
5510 S Lewis Ave Ste 201 Tulsa (74105) ***(G-10491)***
Perfect Circle Publishing Inc...918 629-0061
10026a S Mingo Rd Ste 440 Tulsa (74133) ***(G-10492)***
Perfect Pitch Music...405 521-8088
412 Nw 23rd St Oklahoma City (73103) ***(G-6828)***
Perfecting Software LLC...918 250-7610
10707 E 76th St Tulsa (74133) ***(G-10493)***
Performance Coatings Inc...405 525-9790
201 E Hill St Oklahoma City (73105) ***(G-6829)***
Performance Machine & Inductio...918 542-8740
701 N Main St North Miami (74358) ***(G-5207)***
Performance Operating Co LLC...918 847-3830
3993 State Hiwy 123 Barnsdall (74002) ***(G-439)***
Performance Petroleum Co...918 847-2531
Ne Cor Intrs Hwy 11123 Barnsdall (74002) ***(G-440)***
Performance Pipe Div, Pryor *Also called Chevron Phillips Chem Co LP* ***(G-7953)***
Performance Plastics Inc...918 627-9621
4747 S 102nd East Ave Tulsa (74146) ***(G-10494)***
Performance Screen Printing...405 247-9891
401 E Central Blvd Anadarko (73005) ***(G-205)***
Performance Surfaces LLC...405 463-0505
821 W Wilshire Blvd Oklahoma City (73116) ***(G-6830)***
Performance Technologies LLC (HQ)...405 262-2441
3715 S Radio Rd El Reno (73036) ***(G-2746)***
Periscope Legal...405 418-4155
128 W Hefner Rd Oklahoma City (73114) ***(G-6831)***
Perk Dynamics LLC...405 585-2520
37500 Us Highway 177 Asher (74826) ***(G-394)***
Perkins Cabinet Trim...918 476-6567
11207 S 432 Chouteau (74337) ***(G-1569)***
Perkins Development Corp...918 749-2152
2223 E Skelly Dr 10 Tulsa (74105) ***(G-10495)***
Perkins Energy Co...580 255-5400
903 W Peach Ave Duncan (73533) ***(G-2164)***
Perkins Production Service, Seminole *Also called Kay Production Services Inc* ***(G-8382)***
Perkins Sand LLC...405 240-7870
335754 E 794 Rd Carney (74832) ***(G-1279)***
Perkins South Plains Inc...405 685-4630
4253 Will Rogers Pkwy Oklahoma City (73108) ***(G-6832)***
Perks Welding LLC...405 853-6848
8384 E 600 Rd Hennessey (73742) ***(G-3479)***
Perma-Strong Wood Products Inc...405 449-3376
Rr 1 Wayne (73095) ***(G-11369)***
Permac Inc (HQ)...918 295-7600
1717 S Boulder Ave Tulsa (74119) ***(G-10496)***
Permian Basin Banding...432 238-1483
3166 S 57th West Ave Tulsa (74107) ***(G-10497)***
Permian Resources Holdings LLC (PA)...405 418-8000
301 Nw 63rd St Oklahoma City (73116) ***(G-6833)***
Permian Software LLC...405 329-6397
626 Cedarbrook Dr Norman (73072) ***(G-5113)***
Permian Tank & Mfg Inc...405 295-2525
2309 E Highway 66 El Reno (73036) ***(G-2747)***
Permian Well Service, Ringwood *Also called Phil Lack* ***(G-8089)***
Permocast Inc...918 652-8812
Hwy 75 N Henryetta (74437) ***(G-3516)***
Peroxychem LLC...918 626-8020
900 Highway 112 N Pocola (74902) ***(G-7785)***

Perry Broadcasting Company 405 427-5877
1528 Ne 23rd St Ste A Oklahoma City (73111) *(G-6834)*
Perry Dailey Journal Inc 580 336-2222
714 Delaware St Perry (73077) *(G-7741)*
Perry Ready Mix Inc 580 336-5575
910 Ash St Perry (73077) *(G-7742)*
Perryton Iron and Metal LLC 580 256-5536
1002 5th St Woodward (73801) *(G-11620)*
Personal Defense LLC 918 345-0075
15695 Hectorville Rd Mounds (74047) *(G-4622)*
Personal Expressions 918 406-4581
1129 S Tamarack Ave Broken Arrow (74012) *(G-1003)*
Personal Expressions Inc 918 660-0494
4107 S Yale Ave Ste 120 Tulsa (74135) *(G-10498)*
Personal Expressions Inc 918 660-0494
8009 S Sheridan Rd Unit D Tulsa (74133) *(G-10499)*
Personal Touch, The, Durant *Also called Curtis Jewelry* *(G-2219)*
Personali Tees LLC 580 759-2188
48128 E County Road 1510 Stratford (74872) *(G-8806)*
Pestco Inc 405 485-8060
606 N Monroe Ave Blanchard (73010) *(G-727)*
Peters Oil & Gas 405 315-6378
33820 W 261st St S Bristow (74010) *(G-793)*
Petes Signs 580 338-2266
805 N Quinn St Guymon (73942) *(G-3361)*
Petnet Solutions Inc 918 259-0899
2341 W Albany St Ste H Broken Arrow (74012) *(G-1004)*
Petra Solutions LLC 316 554-6586
4551 Hillside Ln Edmond (73025) *(G-2567)*
Petro Mac Corporation 918 585-5853
20 E 5th St Ste 710 Tulsa (74103) *(G-10500)*
Petro Source Consultants 405 751-0474
2400 Nw 120th St Oklahoma City (73120) *(G-6835)*
Petro Speed Inc 405 364-6785
4900 Pullin Ln Norman (73069) *(G-5114)*
Petrocorp Incorporated 918 491-4500
6733 S Yale Ave Tulsa (74136) *(G-10501)*
Petroflow Energy Corporation (PA) 918 592-1010
114 E 5th St Ste 300 Tulsa (74103) *(G-10502)*
Petroflow Energy Ltd 918 592-1010
114 E 5th St Ste 300 Tulsa (74103) *(G-10503)*
Petrolab LLC (HQ) 918 459-7170
2001 N Indianwood Ave Broken Arrow (74012) *(G-1005)*
Petroleum Artifacts Ltd 918 949-6101
32 E 25th St Tulsa (74114) *(G-10504)*
Petroleum Development Company 918 583-7434
401 S Boston Ave Ste 1850 Tulsa (74103) *(G-10505)*
Petroleum Elastomers 405 672-0900
1400 Se 25th St Oklahoma City (73129) *(G-6836)*
Petroleum Instruments Co Inc 405 670-6200
1312 Se 25th St Oklahoma City (73129) *(G-6837)*
Petroleum International Inc 918 712-1840
1818 E 42nd St Tulsa (74105) *(G-10506)*
Petroleum Storage Tank Div, Oklahoma City *Also called Corpo Commission OK* *(G-5838)*
Petroleum Strategies Unlimited 405 720-0200
13120 Box Canyon Rd Oklahoma City (73142) *(G-6838)*
Petroskills LLC (PA) 918 828-2500
2930 S Yale Ave Tulsa (74114) *(G-10507)*
Pettit Motor Co, Hartshorne *Also called William Pettit* *(G-3396)*
Pettitt Wireline Service LLC 580 234-0550
5710 N Us Highway 81 Enid (73701) *(G-3035)*
Petzold Buildings LLC 580 563-2818
15319 Us Highway 283 Blair (73526) *(G-697)*
Pfi, Tulsa *Also called Precision Fabricators Inc* *(G-10544)*
Pfi, Tulsa *Also called Professional Fabricators Inc* *(G-10568)*
Pfl Industries Ltd Co 405 388-0321
7021 N Post Rd Spencer (73084) *(G-8599)*
Pfpp LP 405 946-3381
2800 W I 44 Service Rd Oklahoma City (73112) *(G-6839)*
Pg13 Graphics & Design LLC 405 720-8002
8324 Picnic Ln Oklahoma City (73127) *(G-6840)*
Pham Thuy 918 623-0700
517 S Woody Guthrie St Okemah (74859) *(G-5273)*
Phelps Machine & Fabrication 580 662-2465
1000 W Pine St Ringling (73456) *(G-8081)*
Phelps Ra Equipment Co Inc (PA) 918 622-2724
3220 S 85th East Ave Tulsa (74145) *(G-10508)*
Phelps Sculpture Studio 405 752-9512
3 N Ellison Ave Oklahoma City (73106) *(G-6841)*
Phil C Cook's & C Performance, Duncan *Also called C & C Performance Engines* *(G-2094)*
Phil Lack 580 883-4945
S Main St Ringwood (73768) *(G-8089)*
Phil Singletary Co Inc 918 258-7733
500 S 12th St Broken Arrow (74012) *(G-1006)*
Phil-Good Products Inc 405 942-5527
3500 W Reno Ave Oklahoma City (73107) *(G-6842)*
Philip H Brewer 580 657-8029
2236 Deese Rd Ardmore (73401) *(G-345)*
Philip Lewis 918 850-6195
3508 E 70th St Tulsa (74136) *(G-10509)*
Philip R Eckart 580 917-3882
8166 Ne Watts Rd Fletcher (73541) *(G-3166)*
Phillips & Company 714 663-6324
311 Nw Chickasaw St Millerton (74750) *(G-4473)*
Phillips 66, Bartlesville *Also called Conocophillips* *(G-467)*
Phillips 66 Company 580 767-3456
1000 S Pine St Ponca City (74601) *(G-7865)*
Phillips 66 Spectrum Corp 918 977-7909
411 S Keeler Ave Bartlesville (74003) *(G-516)*
Phillips Prcsion Machining LLC 918 914-2131
1321 Industrial Blvd Bartlesville (74006) *(G-517)*
Phillips Printing Co 918 266-3373
7363 E Ridgeview Way Claremore (74019) *(G-1670)*
Phils Ornamental Iron Inc 918 786-2979
10732 Us Highway 59 Grove (74344) *(G-3285)*
Phoenix Design & Mfg LLC 405 418-4858
6215 Aluma Valley Dr Oklahoma City (73121) *(G-6843)*
Phoenix Fabworx LLC 918 429-8388
5389 Bascum Rd Quinton (74561) *(G-8038)*
Phoenix Group Holding Company 405 948-7788
5725 Sw 21st St Oklahoma City (73128) *(G-6844)*
Phoenix Industries LLC 405 848-1688
6517 N May Ave Oklahoma City (73116) *(G-6845)*
Phoenix Mining Company 918 256-7873
310 S Scraper St Vinita (74301) *(G-11267)*
Phoenix Oil and Gas Inc 405 382-0935
35863 E Highway 270 Seminole (74868) *(G-8394)*
Phoenix Products, Tulsa *Also called Enhanced Printing Products Inc* *(G-9688)*
Phoenix Software Intl Inc 918 491-6144
6660 S Sheridan Rd # 202 Tulsa (74133) *(G-10510)*
Phoenix Trade Publication 405 948-6555
3108 Nw 54th St Oklahoma City (73112) *(G-6846)*
Phx & Co LLC 918 747-9770
2121 S Yorktown Ave # 904 Tulsa (74114) *(G-10511)*
Physical Home Defense 405 819-0939
10316 Greenbriar Pl Ste 7 Oklahoma City (73159) *(G-6847)*
Pickard Projects Inc 405 321-7072
545 S Pickard Ave Norman (73069) *(G-5115)*
Pickering Metal Casting LLC 806 747-3411
2729 Charles Page Blvd Tulsa (74127) *(G-10512)*
Pickles of Edmond Inc 405 285-4342
921 E Danforth Rd Edmond (73034) *(G-2568)*
Pie In Sky Publishing Co LLC 918 762-3310
415 Denver St Pawnee (74058) *(G-7709)*
Pie In Sky Tulsa LLc 918 527-5855
7912 E 27th Pl Tulsa (74129) *(G-10513)*
Piedmont-Surrey Gazette, Piedmont *Also called Nayfa Publications Inc* *(G-7767)*
Pierce Industries Inc 405 923-4201
21353 Backhorn Rd Edmond (73012) *(G-2569)*
Pierco Petroleum Inc 405 379-0038
225 Kingsberry Rd Holdenville (74848) *(G-3559)*
Pierpont Lamont LLC 918 592-1705
320 S Boston Ave Ste 2200 Tulsa (74103) *(G-10514)*
Pigeon Debut 405 686-0412
3341 Sw 49th St Oklahoma City (73119) *(G-6848)*
Pilcrow & Caret, Jenks *Also called Patricia Lyons* *(G-3722)*
Pilgrim Drilling Co, Tulsa *Also called Kaiser-Francis Oil Company* *(G-10074)*
Pillow Walks, Allen *Also called Jps Creations* *(G-135)*
Pin Efx LLC 405 341-9956
3801 Pawnee Edmond (73013) *(G-2570)*
Pinball Doctor 918 582-3130
2831 E 1st St Tulsa (74104) *(G-10515)*
Pine Cove Jerky LLC 918 872-1138
431 Stone Wood Dr Broken Arrow (74012) *(G-1007)*
Pine Creek Saw Shop Inc 580 933-7376
267 Gray Jay Rd Valliant (74764) *(G-11231)*
Pinecliffe Prtrs of Tecumseh 405 273-1292
1815 N Harrison St Ste 1 Shawnee (74804) *(G-8483)*
Pinion Manufacturing & Supply 918 437-5428
1319 N Mingo Rd Tulsa (74116) *(G-10516)*
Pink Petals Flowers Gifts LLC 580 317-8200
401 E Bluff St Hugo (74743) *(G-3619)*
Pinnacle Business Systems Inc (PA) 405 359-0121
3824 S Boulevard Ste 200 Edmond (73013) *(G-2571)*
Pinnacle Energy Services LLC (PA) 405 810-9151
9420 Cedar Lake Ave Oklahoma City (73114) *(G-6849)*
Pinnacle Fuel Additives LLC 405 658-3744
535 W Geronimo Court Way Mustang (73064) *(G-4788)*
Pinpoint Monograms Inc 405 228-0600
280 S Quadrum Dr Oklahoma City (73108) *(G-6850)*
Pinpoint Wire Technologies LLC 405 447-6900
3505 N Interstate Dr Norman (73069) *(G-5116)*
Pins-N-Needles By Sandra 918 270-0204
11901 E 113th Pl N Owasso (74055) *(G-7603)*
Pinson Well Logging 405 604-5036
25 N Cooley Dr Oklahoma City (73127) *(G-6851)*
Pioneer Drectional Drlg II LLC 405 533-1552
4815 S Perkins Rd Stillwater (74074) *(G-8737)*
Pioneer Metal & Land Svcs LLC 405 612-3575
14509 E Mcelroy Glencoe (74032) *(G-3226)*

ALPHABETIC

Pioneer Oilfield Services Inc ...580 243-4000
2020 N Randall Ave Elk City (73644) ***(G-2859)***
Pioneer Precision Machine Shop ...580 233-1670
4502 E Market St Enid (73701) ***(G-3036)***
Pioneer Printing Inc ...918 542-5521
18 W Central Ave Miami (74354) ***(G-4428)***
Pioneer Services, Elk City *Also called Pioneer Oilfield Services Inc* ***(G-2859)***
Pioneer Sport Floors LLC ...214 460-6921
166 Allison Rd Calera (74730) ***(G-1244)***
Pioneer Wireline Services ...405 601-8755
1535 Se 25th St Oklahoma City (73129) ***(G-6852)***
Pipeglove LLC ...918 629-7116
2915 E 74th St Tulsa (74136) ***(G-10517)***
Pipeline Coating Services LLC ...936 494-2919
2940 N Toledo Ave Tulsa (74115) ***(G-10518)***
Pipeline Equipment Inc ...918 224-4144
8403 S 89th West Ave Tulsa (74131) ***(G-9024)***
Pipes Plus LLC ...405 942-7473
920 N Meridian Ave Oklahoma City (73107) ***(G-6853)***
Piping Enterprise Company Inc ...918 246-7326
1520 S 129th West Ave Sand Springs (74063) ***(G-8214)***
Piranha Proppant LLC ...715 642-4192
14201 Caliber Dr Ste 200 Oklahoma City (73134) ***(G-6854)***
Pistol Drilling LLC ...580 256-9371
4420 Anderson Rd Woodward (73801) ***(G-11621)***
Pistol Wear LLC (PA) ...918 364-5617
11063 S Memorial Dr 337d Tulsa (74133) ***(G-10519)***
Pitezel's Screen Printing, Tulsa *Also called Pitezels Ink & Print Inc* ***(G-10520)***
Pitezels Ink & Print Inc ...918 663-2393
8943 E 76th St Tulsa (74133) ***(G-10520)***
Pitney Bowes Inc ...918 779-7552
5115 S 122nd East Ave # 20 Tulsa (74146) ***(G-10521)***
Pitney Bowes Inc ...405 341-3279
3224 Teakwood Ln Ste 120 Edmond (73013) ***(G-2572)***
Pivot Medical Solutions LLC ...918 684-4030
207 Lancelot Ct Muskogee (74403) ***(G-4734)***
Pivot Point Publishing ...918 347-5415
3106 N Water St Sapulpa (74066) ***(G-8298)***
Pixel Park LLC ...405 613-0924
10712 Hinshaw Dr Mustang (73064) ***(G-4789)***
Pixley Coating Inc ...580 444-2140
Velma Industrial Park Dr Velma (73491) ***(G-11236)***
Pj Industries Inc ...918 682-8479
3007 River Oaks Dr Muskogee (74403) ***(G-4735)***
Plains Nitrogen LLC ...405 418-8426
2601 Nw Exprkway Ste 411w Oklahoma City (73112) ***(G-6855)***
Plains Nitrogen LLC ...918 429-0041
4997 W State Highway 31 McAlester (74501) ***(G-4329)***
Plainsman Technology Inc (HQ) ...580 658-6608
1004 S Plainsman Rd Marlow (73055) ***(G-4236)***
Plainview Winery ...580 796-2902
321 W Lahoma Rd Lahoma (73754) ***(G-3859)***
Plan Bible ...918 254-6983
10026 S Mingo Rd Ste A Tulsa (74133) ***(G-10522)***
Plane Naked LLC ...405 317-7661
950 E Wagner Rd Yukon (73099) ***(G-11766)***
Plane Plastics Ltd ...580 327-1565
3161 College Blvd Alva (73717) ***(G-188)***
Plant 1, Tulsa *Also called Berry Global Films LLC* ***(G-8991)***
Plant 4, Tulsa *Also called Berry Global Films LLC* ***(G-8990)***
Plantation Shutter Co ...817 703-1091
304 N Redbud Ave Broken Arrow (74012) ***(G-1008)***
Plas-Tech Inc ...918 649-0065
28718 State Highway 112 Poteau (74953) ***(G-7909)***
Plasma Bionics LLC ...405 564-5333
1508 W 15th Ave Unit 2 Stillwater (74074) ***(G-8738)***
Plasma Solutions 1 ...918 543-2178
28644 S 4240 Rd Inola (74036) ***(G-3673)***
Plastic Designs Inc ...918 224-9187
6809 S 124th West Ave Sapulpa (74066) ***(G-8299)***
Plastic Engrg Co Tulsa Inc ...918 622-9660
6801 E 44th St Tulsa (74145) ***(G-10523)***
Plastic Fabricators Inc ...918 836-6611
8822 E Admiral Pl Tulsa (74115) ***(G-10524)***
Plastic Research and Dev Corp ...918 949-6291
10702 E 11th St Tulsa (74128) ***(G-10525)***
Plastic Sup & Fabrication Co ...918 622-8430
7328 E 38th St Tulsa (74145) ***(G-10526)***
Plasticon Fluid Systems Inc ...918 477-9371
7134 S Yale Ave Ste 560 Tulsa (74136) ***(G-10527)***
Plateau Energy Services LLC ...580 625-3618
1 M S Of Bevr E 4 10 Snto Beaver (73932) ***(G-544)***
Platinum Arch Mfg & Cnstr LLC ...316 573-6814
15 E 80th St Stillwater (74074) ***(G-8739)***
Platinum Cross Welding Inc ...918 623-9130
379054 E 1130 Rd Okemah (74859) ***(G-5274)***
Platinum Machine, Durant *Also called Clint Dodson Enterprises LLC* ***(G-2216)***
Platt Energy Corporation ...405 840-5081
11600 Broadway Ext # 250 Oklahoma City (73114) ***(G-6856)***
Play 2 Win Athletics ...918 341-9500
514 N J M Davis Blvd Claremore (74017) ***(G-1671)***
Pleasant Expressions, Collinsville *Also called Deborah C Montgomery* ***(G-1809)***
Pleasing Ptnts/Bttrbody Cmpny/, Ada *Also called Jobri LLC* ***(G-54)***
Pletcher Oil Company ...580 657-4221
473 Gateway Rd Ardmore (73401) ***(G-346)***
Plow Technologies LLC ...405 265-6072
8925 Nw 10th St Oklahoma City (73127) ***(G-6857)***
Plum Gold Jewelers & Designers ...918 341-4716
418 S Lynn Riggs Blvd Claremore (74017) ***(G-1672)***
Plumb Square Construction ...405 619-9898
3112 Del View Dr Del City (73115) ***(G-2006)***
Plummer Energy Inc ...405 238-9132
17808 N County Road 3190 Pauls Valley (73075) ***(G-7671)***
Plx Inc ...918 551-6722
7030 S Yale Ave Ste 402 Tulsa (74136) ***(G-10528)***
Plymouth Resources Inc (PA) ...918 599-1880
2200 S Utica Pl Ste 430 Tulsa (74114) ***(G-10529)***
Plymouth Valley Cellars Inc ...580 227-0348
57442 S County Road 255 Fairview (73737) ***(G-3146)***
PMI, North Miami *Also called Performance Machine & Inductio* ***(G-5207)***
Pml Exploration Services LLC ...405 606-2701
5600 Se 11th St Oklahoma City (73128) ***(G-6858)***
Png Operating Company, Oklahoma City *Also called Prentice Napier & Green Inc* ***(G-6888)***
Png Operation ...405 470-4333
5704 Nw 132nd St Oklahoma City (73142) ***(G-6859)***
Poage Sand & Dirt, Oklahoma City *Also called Miracle Production Inc* ***(G-6618)***
Podunk Hunting Products LLC ...918 617-0358
30707 S Lone Valley Rd Quinton (74561) ***(G-8039)***
Pogue Machine Inc ...405 677-9397
3700 S High Ave Oklahoma City (73129) ***(G-6860)***
Point To Point Software ...405 869-9921
8901 S Anderson Rd Oklahoma City (73150) ***(G-6861)***
Pointer Waddell & Associates ...405 942-5600
5400 N Grand Blvd Ste 560 Oklahoma City (73112) ***(G-6862)***
Polar Insulated Sheds Oklah ...580 799-2265
112 Meadow Ridge Dr Elk City (73644) ***(G-2860)***
Polish Kitchen LLC ...580 583-5970
2801 Se 165th St Lawton (73501) ***(G-3984)***
Polisher, The, Tulsa *Also called Buster Dorsch* ***(G-9353)***
Polk Appliances Co ...918 592-6858
1511 E Admiral Blvd Tulsa (74120) ***(G-10530)***
Polycor Oklahoma Inc ...770 735-2611
97065 S 4610 Rd Marble City (74945) ***(G-4197)***
Polydyne LLC ...918 649-0065
28718 State Highway 112 Poteau (74953) ***(G-7910)***
Polypipe Hdlg Specialists Inc ...405 330-4733
6992 E Waterloo Indus Rd Edmond (73034) ***(G-2573)***
Polyvision Corporation ...918 756-7392
4301 N Wood Dr Okmulgee (74447) ***(G-7522)***
Pomco Inc (PA) ...405 677-8859
17 Se 55th St Oklahoma City (73129) ***(G-6863)***
Ponca City News, The, Ponca City *Also called Ponca City Publishing Co Inc* ***(G-7866)***
Ponca City Publishing Co Inc ...580 765-3311
300 N 3rd St Ponca City (74601) ***(G-7866)***
Ponca City Refinery, Ponca City *Also called Phillips 66 Company* ***(G-7865)***
Ponca Machine Company ...580 762-1031
3913 Santa Fe St Ponca City (74601) ***(G-7867)***
Pondliner.com, Shawnee *Also called Unit Liner Company* ***(G-8516)***
Pontiki Coal, Tulsa *Also called Excel Mining LLC* ***(G-9713)***
Pontotoc Gathering LLC ...918 742-5835
1345 E 29th St Tulsa (74114) ***(G-10531)***
Pontotoc Sands Company LLC (PA) ...580 777-2735
18644 County Road 1720 Stonewall (74871) ***(G-8802)***
Pony Boy Lures ...580 327-1233
600 Mimosa Dr Alva (73717) ***(G-189)***
Pony Express Printing LLC ...405 375-5064
103 N 6th St Kingfisher (73750) ***(G-3811)***
Popefasteners Inc ...918 740-4801
8159 S 39th West Ave Tulsa (74132) ***(G-10532)***
Poquita Circle LLC ...918 794-0750
5825 E 78th Pl Tulsa (74136) ***(G-10533)***
Porcelain Treasure ...918 230-9618
1127 S Quebec Ave Tulsa (74112) ***(G-10534)***
Port 40 Inc ...405 360-9100
317 Towry Dr Norman (73069) ***(G-5117)***
Portable Building Sales, Howe *Also called Rons Discount Lumber Inc* ***(G-3599)***
Porters Custom Meat Processing, Hugo *Also called James Porter Shorty* ***(G-3615)***
Portman Minerals LLC ...405 843-4063
2424 Nw 55th Pl Oklahoma City (73112) ***(G-6864)***
Post Construction Company ...580 928-5983
1802 N 4th St Sayre (73662) ***(G-8343)***
Post Oak Oil Co ...405 621-1300
13300 N Macarthur Blvd Oklahoma City (73142) ***(G-6865)***
Post Oak Petroleum LLC ...918 245-9919
14054 Rock School Rd Skiatook (74070) ***(G-8564)***
Post Software International ...918 299-2158
11722 S Erie Ave Tulsa (74137) ***(G-10535)***

Post-Tension Services of Okla 405 751-1582
209 Nw 111th St Oklahoma City (73114) *(G-6866)*
Poteau Daily News 918 647-3335
804 N Broadway St Ste C Poteau (74953) *(G-7911)*
Poteau Panel Shop Incorporated 918 647-4331
505 N Mckenna St Poteau (74953) *(G-7912)*
Poteau Vision Source, Poteau *Also called Tamatha Holt Od (G-7914)*
Poteet Oil Co Inc (PA) 405 756-4530
Hwy 76 N Lindsay (73052) *(G-4077)*
Potions By Pier LLC 580 658-2900
163352 6 Mile Rd Marlow (73055) *(G-4237)*
Potoco LLC 405 600-3065
1141 N Robinson Ave # 301 Oklahoma City (73103) *(G-6867)*
Potter Industries 580 775-8580
503 E Georgia St Durant (74701) *(G-2247)*
Powder Blue 918 835-2629
7203 E Reading Pl Tulsa (74115) *(G-10536)*
Powder Coating of Muskogee 918 681-4494
13 Tantalum Pl Muskogee (74403) *(G-4736)*
Powder Coatings Incorporated (PA) 918 627-6225
9832 E 58th St Tulsa (74146) *(G-10537)*
Powder Coatings Plus LLC 405 232-5707
513 N Indiana Ave Oklahoma City (73106) *(G-6868)*
Powell Services Inc 580 225-9017
Rr 2 Box 305 Elk City (73644) *(G-2861)*
Powells Waterwell Pump and Sup 918 637-9150
46427 W 154th Bristow (74010) *(G-794)*
Power Cable Solutions LLC 405 818-1993
832 County Street 2920 Tuttle (73089) *(G-11207)*
Power Dyne Inc 918 587-1272
3628 S Elwood Ave Tulsa (74107) *(G-10538)*
Power Equipment & Engrg Inc (PA) 405 235-0531
1739 W Main St Oklahoma City (73106) *(G-6869)*
Power Lift Fndtn RPR OK Inc 580 332-8282
120 Armory Rd Ada (74820) *(G-75)*
Power Ready LLC 918 289-0088
4121 S Sheridan Rd Tulsa (74145) *(G-10539)*
Power Rig LLC 580 254-3232
199584 E County Road 39 Woodward (73801) *(G-11622)*
Power Services LLC 405 677-7716
6700 103rd Ave Ne Norman (73026) *(G-5118)*
Power Soak Systems Inc 800 444-9624
4650 54th St Maip Pryor (74361) *(G-7982)*
Power Transformer, Oklahoma City *Also called Southwest Electric Co (G-7175)*
Powerco Seismic Services LLC 918 424-3745
3537 Mt Moriah McAlester (74501) *(G-4330)*
Powerhouse Elec 405 735-6381
601 Messenger Ln Ste B Moore (73160) *(G-4553)*
Powerhouse Resources Intl Inc 405 232-7474
6 Ne 6th St Oklahoma City (73104) *(G-6870)*
Powers Drilling Inc 580 343-2444
11163 Highway 54 Weatherford (73096) *(G-11433)*
Powertrain Company LLC 703 419-0104
400 S Lee Ave Oklahoma City (73109) *(G-6871)*
Ppm Manufacturing LLC 405 843-4448
3333 Nw 63rd St Ste 104 Oklahoma City (73116) *(G-6872)*
Ppr LLC 574 516-1131
205 W Mcelroy Rd Ste 1 Stillwater (74075) *(G-8740)*
Practical Sales and Svc Inc 918 446-5515
4411 S Elwood Ave Tulsa (74107) *(G-10540)*
Prague Times Herald 405 567-3933
1123 N Jim Thorpe Blvd Prague (74864) *(G-7932)*
Prairie Exploration Co 405 360-7077
100 N Santa Fe Ave # 200 Norman (73069) *(G-5119)*
Prairie Graphics & Sportswear 405 789-0028
6600 Nw 36th St Ste A Bethany (73008) *(G-592)*
Prairie Gypsies Inc 405 525-3013
411 Nw 30th St Oklahoma City (73118) *(G-6873)*
Prairie Oil & Gas 405 464-6060
330 W Gray St Ste 180 Norman (73069) *(G-5120)*
Prairie Rose Processing Inc 405 224-6429
830 County Road 1310 Chickasha (73018) *(G-1500)*
Prairie Supply Co, Cleveland *Also called Spess Drilling Company (G-1734)*
Prather Cues, Mooreland *Also called By Prather Inc (G-4586)*
Pratt Industries USA Inc 405 787-3500
305 N Rockwell Ave Oklahoma City (73127) *(G-6874)*
Pratt Whtney Mltary Aftrmrket, Oklahoma City *Also called Pratt Whtney Mltary Aftrmrket (G-6876)*
Pratt Whtney Mltary Aftrmrket 405 622-2561
8120 Mid America Blvd # 3 Oklahoma City (73135) *(G-6875)*
Pratt Whtney Mltary Aftrmrket 405 737-4851
2701 Liberty Pkwy Ste 301 Oklahoma City (73110) *(G-6876)*
Praxair Distribution Inc 918 266-3210
5101 Sw Alliance Dr Claremore (74017) *(G-1673)*
Pre Mc Inc 580 857-2408
304 E Broadway Allen (74825) *(G-137)*
Pre-Press Graphics Inc 918 582-2775
1307 E 11th St Tulsa (74120) *(G-10541)*
Precast Solutions LLC 580 819-2455
1809 Grainer St Yukon (73099) *(G-11767)*
Precast Trtmnt Solutions LLC 405 455-5303
13525 Se 74th St Oklahoma City (73150) *(G-6877)*
Precious Memories By M L 405 427-7007
3801 Quail Dr Oklahoma City (73121) *(G-6878)*
Precise Tool & Machine Company 405 495-2001
8124 Sw 8th St Ste E Oklahoma City (73128) *(G-6879)*
Precision Alloy 918 665-3952
5436 S Mingo Rd Ste K Tulsa (74146) *(G-10542)*
Precision Anodizing Inc 405 631-2079
800 804 Se 82nd St Oklahoma City (73149) *(G-6880)*
Precision Biomedical Svcs Inc 918 671-8091
10712 S Gum St Jenks (74037) *(G-3723)*
Precision Coatings LLC 918 622-1876
7448 E 42nd Pl Tulsa (74145) *(G-10543)*
Precision Drive Ltd Inc 405 495-1344
6201 Sw 15th St Oklahoma City (73128) *(G-6881)*
Precision Engrg & Mch Works 580 658-9193
219 N Railroad St Marlow (73055) *(G-4238)*
Precision Fabricators Inc 918 428-7600
3928 N Osage Dr Tulsa (74127) *(G-10544)*
Precision Heat Treating 918 445-7424
6300 S 57th West Ave Tulsa (74131) *(G-9025)*
Precision Hose Technology Inc 918 835-3660
2702 N Sheridan Rd Bldg D Tulsa (74115) *(G-10545)*
Precision Image Cnversions LLC 918 430-1102
195 S 122nd East Ave Tulsa (74128) *(G-10546)*
Precision Industries Ic T 918 833-6072
2322 N Mingo Rd D Tulsa (74116) *(G-10547)*
Precision Machine & Mfg, Grove *Also called Orizon Arstrctures - Grove Inc (G-3284)*
Precision Machine & Tool LLC 580 256-2219
819 48th St Woodward (73801) *(G-11623)*
Precision Metal Fab LLC 580 762-2421
2200 N Ash St Ponca City (74601) *(G-7868)*
Precision Metal Forming LLC 405 677-3777
7000 S Bryant Ave Oklahoma City (73149) *(G-6882)*
Precision Metals LLC 918 266-2202
19504 E 6th St Tulsa (74108) *(G-10548)*
Precision Mfg & Design 918 782-2723
1690 N 3rd St Langley (74350) *(G-3874)*
Precision Mfg. & Design, Langley *Also called Precision Mfg & Design (G-3874)*
Precision Printing Corporation 405 794-2500
2500 N Moore Ave Moore (73160) *(G-4554)*
Precision Products, Sapulpa *Also called Mold Tech Inc (G-8292)*
Precision Prts Remanufacturing, Oklahoma City *Also called Bob Brooks Motor Company (G-5600)*
Precision Punch 405 340-7546
2116 Castle Rock Edmond (73003) *(G-2574)*
Precision Rotational Molding 580 362-3262
600 S Main St Newkirk (74647) *(G-4851)*
Precision Screen Manufacturing, Oologah *Also called Oklahoma Screen Mfg LLC (G-7535)*
Precision Shelters 405 936-0900
13612 Gentry Dr Oklahoma City (73142) *(G-6883)*
Precision Sign & Design 918 430-1102
195 S 122nd East Ave Tulsa (74128) *(G-10549)*
Precision Sintered Parts L L C 918 663-7511
9902 E 46th Pl Tulsa (74146) *(G-10550)*
Precision Stone 405 214-2224
17501 Highway 102 Shawnee (74801) *(G-8484)*
Precision Tool & Die Ponca Cy 580 762-2421
2200 N Ash St Ponca City (74601) *(G-7869)*
Precision Welding Mfg 405 872-3530
4700 Brookwood Dr Noble (73068) *(G-4888)*
Precision Wireline LLC 580 233-0033
2402 S Monroe St Enid (73701) *(G-3037)*
Precison Parts Inc 918 261-6962
7207 W 81st St Tulsa (74131) *(G-9026)*
Preferred Fleetwash 918 281-9325
16615 W Coyote Trl Sand Springs (74063) *(G-8215)*
Preferred Utilities Mfg Corp 203 743-6741
10001 E 44th Pl Ste A Tulsa (74146) *(G-10551)*
Pregis LLC 918 439-9916
10838 E Marshall St # 14 Tulsa (74116) *(G-10552)*
Prelesnicks Repair Service 580 628-3179
117 N Public St Tonkawa (74653) *(G-8979)*
Premeir Companies Inc 405 895-7100
132 E Main St Moore (73160) *(G-4555)*
Premier Aerospace Svcs & Tech 580 327-3706
1601 Oklahoma Blvd Alva (73717) *(G-190)*
Premier Business Solutions LLC 405 650-3131
344142 E 1000 Rd Meeker (74855) *(G-4385)*
Premier Catering, Moore *Also called Premeir Companies Inc (G-4555)*
Premier Chem & Oilfld Sup LLC 405 893-2321
302 N Independence St # 1500 Enid (73701) *(G-3038)*
Premier Energy LLC 405 286-0615
3700 N Classen Blvd # 220 Oklahoma City (73118) *(G-6884)*
Premier Fabricators LLC 580 251-9525
1251 Mccurdy Rd Duncan (73533) *(G-2165)*
Premier Iron Works, Meeker *Also called Premier Business Solutions LLC (G-4385)*

A L P H A B E T I C

Premier Metal Finishing Inc — 405 947-0200
640 N Meridian Ave Oklahoma City (73107) *(G-6885)*
Premier Plant Services LLC (PA) — 918 227-3131
2429 Industrial Rd Sapulpa (74066) *(G-8300)*
Premier Plant Services LLC — 918 227-1680
8984 Frankoma Rd Sapulpa (74066) *(G-8301)*
Premier Printing — 405 632-1132
320 Sw 89th St Oklahoma City (73139) *(G-6886)*
Premier Printing & Stamp, Oklahoma City Also called Premier Printing *(G-6886)*
Premier Signs & Design LLC — 918 825-6422
210 S Mill St Pryor (74361) *(G-7983)*
Premier Steel Services LLC — 918 227-0110
16420 S Highway 75 Glenpool (74033) *(G-3241)*
Premier Valve Group — 918 519-4309
1401 W Plymouth St Broken Arrow (74012) *(G-1009)*
Premiercraft Incorporated — 405 600-9339
1316 Se Grand Blvd Oklahoma City (73129) *(G-6887)*
Premiere Inc — 405 262-1554
4004 W 10th St El Reno (73036) *(G-2748)*
Premiere Lock Co LLC — 918 294-8179
10203 E 61st St Ste A Tulsa (74133) *(G-10553)*
Premiere Press & Graphics, Tulsa Also called Ajt Enterprises Inc *(G-9133)*
Premierflow LLC — 918 346-6312
2716 E Apache St Tulsa (74110) *(G-10554)*
Prentice Napier & Green Inc — 405 752-7680
14000 Quail Springs Pkwy Oklahoma City (73134) *(G-6888)*
Prescor LLC (PA) — 918 224-6626
8601 State Highway 66 Tulsa (74131) *(G-9027)*
Prescription Care LLC — 405 310-9230
800 W Rock Creek Rd # 117 Norman (73069) *(G-5121)*
Presley Operating LLC — 405 526-3000
101 Park Ave Ste 670 Oklahoma City (73102) *(G-6889)*
Press — 405 464-6181
1610 N Gatewood Ave Oklahoma City (73106) *(G-6890)*
Press Go — 580 889-2399
107 N Ohio Ave Atoka (74525) *(G-421)*
Press Group, The, Tulsa Also called TWI Industries Inc *(G-11022)*
Pressburg LLC (HQ) — 405 896-8050
14701 Hrtz Qail Sprng Pkw Oklahoma City (73134) *(G-6891)*
Pressley Press N Prod Fcilty — 405 752-5700
13919 S Harvey Ave Oklahoma City (73170) *(G-5311)*
Pressure Point LLC — 918 695-8799
4127 S 185th East Ave Tulsa (74134) *(G-10555)*
Pressure Solutions LLC — 405 370-1830
12 Nw 4th St Tuttle (73089) *(G-11208)*
Prestige Manufacturing Co LLC — 405 395-0500
7 American Way Shawnee (74804) *(G-8485)*
Preston-Eastin Inc — 918 834-5591
9490 N Ridgeway St Tulsa (74131) *(G-9028)*
Preview Magazine, Tulsa Also called Preview of Green Country Inc *(G-10556)*
Preview of Green Country Inc — 918 745-1190
4150 S 100th East Ave # 200 Tulsa (74146) *(G-10556)*
Priam Oil, Tulsa Also called Liverpool Production Company *(G-10170)*
Price Prints Inc — 580 832-2492
300 N Mcclary St Cordell (73632) *(G-1862)*
Price Welding and Supply — 580 668-3057
Hc 62 Box 39c Lone Grove (73443) *(G-4119)*
Price's Printing, Durant Also called Prices Quality Printing Inc *(G-2248)*
Prices Quality Printing Inc — 580 924-2271
401 N 3rd Ave Durant (74701) *(G-2248)*
Pride Energy Company — 918 524-9200
4641 E 91st St Tulsa (74137) *(G-10557)*
Pride Plating Inc — 918 786-6111
2900 E Highway 10 Grove (74344) *(G-3286)*
Priegel Real Estate, Okmulgee Also called Frank Priegel Co *(G-7502)*
Primarily Puzzles — 918 275-8270
7915 S Country Ln Talala (74080) *(G-8902)*
Primary Natural Resources III, Tulsa Also called Resolute Wyoming Inc *(G-10644)*
Primary Ntral Rsources III LLC — 918 495-0598
7134 S Yale Ave Ste 430 Tulsa (74136) *(G-10558)*
Prime Conduit Inc — 405 670-6132
6500 Interpace St Oklahoma City (73135) *(G-6892)*
Prime Operating, Oklahoma City Also called Primeenergy Corporation *(G-6894)*
Prime Operating Company — 405 947-1091
5400 N Grand Blvd Ste 360 Oklahoma City (73112) *(G-6893)*
Prime Pallet LLC (PA) — 918 683-0907
921 S Cherokee St Muskogee (74403) *(G-4737)*
Prime Signs of Oklahoma Inc — 918 500-2213
5840 S Memorial Dr Tulsa (74145) *(G-10559)*
Primedia, Tulsa Also called Rentpath LLC *(G-10642)*
Primeenergy Corporation — 405 942-2897
5400 N Grand Blvd Ste 450 Oklahoma City (73112) *(G-6894)*
Primeenergy Corporation — 405 375-5203
5400 N Grand Blvd Ste 450 Oklahoma City (73112) *(G-6895)*
Primo Redimix LLC — 580 494-7649
9627 N Us Highway 259 Broken Bow (74728) *(G-1203)*
Primus International Inc — 918 836-6317
3030 N Erie Ave Tulsa (74115) *(G-10560)*

Princo Press Corp — 405 760-6064
19525 Talavera Ln Edmond (73012) *(G-2575)*
Pringle Publications Corp — 405 848-4859
1601 Nw Expressway Oklahoma City (73118) *(G-6896)*
Print Finishing Systems Inc — 405 232-1750
7116 Nw 79th St Oklahoma City (73132) *(G-6897)*
Print Happy Fundraising — 918 355-4368
21440 E 39th Pl S Broken Arrow (74014) *(G-1149)*
Print Happy LLC — 918 270-1300
1015 E Lansing St Broken Arrow (74012) *(G-1010)*
Print Imaging Group LLC — 405 235-4888
607 N Western Ave Oklahoma City (73106) *(G-6898)*
Print Master General LLC — 580 442-2474
13293 Ne Kleeman Rd Elgin (73538) *(G-2778)*
Print Monkey LLC — 405 735-8999
114 N Broadway St Moore (73160) *(G-4556)*
Print Monkey LLC — 405 249-6926
9300 S Pennsylvania Ave Oklahoma City (73159) *(G-6899)*
Print N Copy Inc — 918 258-8200
921 N Elm Pl Broken Arrow (74012) *(G-1011)*
Print Party — 405 206-2191
4904 Butte Rd Edmond (73025) *(G-2576)*
Print People USA — 918 346-2560
11259 N 177th East Ave Owasso (74055) *(G-7604)*
Print Plus OK LLC — 405 371-5365
314 Nw 7th St Blanchard (73010) *(G-728)*
Print Shop — 918 342-3993
910 N J M Davis Blvd Claremore (74017) *(G-1674)*
Print Shoppe Etc, Tulsa Also called Two Lees Inc *(G-11027)*
Print This — 918 693-5581
813 E 6th St Okmulgee (74447) *(G-7523)*
Printed Products Inc — 918 295-9950
1144 E Haskell St Tulsa (74106) *(G-10561)*
Printer Store LLC — 405 782-0755
5107 N Macarthur Blvd Warr Acres (73122) *(G-11326)*
Printers Bindery Inc — 405 236-8423
4417 Brookfield Dr Norman (73072) *(G-5122)*
Printers of Oklahoma LLC — 405 943-8855
1601 N Portland Ave Oklahoma City (73107) *(G-6900)*
Printing, Oklahoma City Also called North Star Publishing LLC *(G-6688)*
Printing and Design — 580 871-2396
859 Main St Dacoma (73731) *(G-1976)*
Printing Center — 405 681-5303
1423 Sw 59th St Oklahoma City (73119) *(G-6901)*
Printing Plus, Claremore Also called Klassen Enterprises Inc *(G-1649)*
Printing Solutions Inc — 580 421-6446
205 Arlington St Ada (74820) *(G-76)*
Prior Creek Publishing, Pryor Also called Paper *(G-7981)*
Priority Artificial Lift — 405 265-1696
1509 Commerce Yukon (73099) *(G-11768)*
Priority Dodge, Coalgate Also called Du-Ann Co Inc *(G-1779)*
Priority Printworks Inc — 918 825-6397
7 N Adair St Pryor (74361) *(G-7984)*
Prism Electric Inc — 918 425-2000
6558 E 40th St Tulsa (74145) *(G-10562)*
Prism Energy Inc — 918 248-4177
4523 Edgewood Sapulpa (74066) *(G-8302)*
Pritchards Welding Service — 405 514-2360
2525 W Highway 277 Ninnekah (73067) *(G-4873)*
Pritchetts Machining LLC — 405 567-0183
48955 Moccasin Trail Rd Prague (74864) *(G-7933)*
Prl Manufacturing Inc — 918 280-1090
4946 E 66th St N Tulsa (74117) *(G-10563)*
Pro Battery Inc — 918 437-1920
1731 N 168th East Ave Tulsa (74116) *(G-10564)*
Pro Darts Inc — 405 232-3552
1500 Linwood Blvd Oklahoma City (73106) *(G-6902)*
Pro Directional — 405 200-1450
2908 S Ann Arbor Ave Oklahoma City (73128) *(G-6903)*
Pro Fab Welding Inc — 405 470-8776
11740 N 1970 Rd Elk City (73644) *(G-2862)*
Pro Ject Chemicals — 580 445-4345
900 Sw 4th St Weatherford (73096) *(G-11434)*
Pro Oilfield Services LLC — 405 778-8844
2704 S Meridian Ave Oklahoma City (73108) *(G-6904)*
Pro Pallets — 405 679-8076
2228 Sw 20th St Oklahoma City (73108) *(G-6905)*
Pro Piping & Fabrication LLC — 918 599-8218
1925 S 33rd West Ave Tulsa (74107) *(G-10565)*
PRO RODEO WORLD, Oklahoma City Also called International Pro Rodeo Assn *(G-6321)*
Pro Stainless & Shtmtl LLC — 405 787-4400
7918 Nw 10th St Oklahoma City (73127) *(G-6906)*
Pro TEC Orthotics Company — 405 366-7688
4505 Beckett Ct Norman (73072) *(G-5123)*
Pro Technics International — 405 680-5560
4300 Sw 33rd St Oklahoma City (73119) *(G-6907)*
Pro Walk Manufacturing Company — 580 332-5516
1115 W Main St Ada (74820) *(G-77)*
Pro-Fab LLC — 405 495-2131
910 N Morgan Rd Oklahoma City (73127) *(G-6908)*

ALPHABETIC SECTION

Pure Digital Print

Pro-Fab Industries Inc..918 865-7590
   2235 N Hwy 48 Mannford (74044) *(G-4190)*
Pro-Feil Mktg Solutions LLC..580 595-9101
   301 Se Wallock St Lawton (73501) *(G-3985)*
Pro-Grass By University Center, Lawton Also called Brad McKinzie *(G-3900)*
Pro-Tech Dental Labs...918 227-6407
   9703 W 66th Pl S Sapulpa (74066) *(G-8303)*
Pro-Tech Mobile Solutions, Tulsa Also called Stephens Scheduling Svcs Inc *(G-10847)*
Probuilt Manufacturing, Eufaula Also called Probuilt Spincasting LLC *(G-3109)*
Probuilt Spincasting LLC..918 617-9053
   420267 E 1140 Rd Eufaula (74432) *(G-3109)*
Process Equipment Mfg Co...817 710-2826
   15151 S Highway 66 Claremore (74017) *(G-1675)*
Process Manufacturing Co Inc.....................................918 445-0909
   5800 W 68th St Tulsa (74131) *(G-9029)*
Process Products & Service Co....................................918 827-4998
   1115 Commercial St Mounds (74047) *(G-4623)*
Process Service & Mfg, Tulsa Also called Process Manufacturing Co Inc *(G-9029)*
Prochem Energy Services Inc......................................580 465-1737
   9396 Highway 76 Healdton (73438) *(G-3421)*
Prodigy Cbd Company LLC..405 378-2868
   811 Sw 19th St Moore (73160) *(G-4557)*
Producers Cooperative Oil Mill....................................405 232-7555
   2500 S Council Rd Oklahoma City (73128) *(G-6909)*
Producers Oil Company Inc..918 582-1188
   427 S Boston Ave Ste 711 Tulsa (74103) *(G-10566)*
Producing Lamamco III L P...918 396-3020
   4444 E 146th St N M Skiatook (74070) *(G-8565)*
Production Engine & Pump Inc.....................................405 672-3644
   3115 Se 67th St Oklahoma City (73135) *(G-6910)*
Production String Services..580 747-4017
   1410 S Van Buren St Enid (73703) *(G-3039)*
Productive Clutter Inc...405 447-3839
   753 Asp Ave Norman (73069) *(G-5124)*
Profab...918 486-4464
   29861 E State Highway 51 Coweta (74429) *(G-1894)*
Profab Welding Inc...580 488-2020
   601 S Main Leedey (73654) *(G-4030)*
Professional Communications....................................580 745-9838
   3016 Quail Ridge Cir Durant (74701) *(G-2249)*
Professional Datasolutions Inc....................................512 218-0463
   5147 S Garnett Rd Ste D Tulsa (74146) *(G-10567)*
Professional Fabricators Inc.......................................918 388-1090
   2765 Dawson Rd Tulsa (74110) *(G-10568)*
Professional Image Inc..918 461-0609
   12437 E 60th St Tulsa (74146) *(G-10569)*
Professional Marble Company....................................918 225-5364
   802 E Brissy St Cushing (74023) *(G-1950)*
Professional Metal Works Inc.....................................580 584-7890
   1100 Ne Avenue B Idabel (74745) *(G-3644)*
Professional Packaging Inc..918 682-9531
   2424 N Main St Muskogee (74401) *(G-4738)*
Professional Prtg Norman LLC....................................405 823-3383
   913 Golden Eagle Dr Norman (73072) *(G-5125)*
Profishing Equipment, Pryor Also called Deal USA Today LLC *(G-7959)*
Proform Group Inc (PA)...918 682-8666
   4400 Don Cayo Dr Muskogee (74403) *(G-4739)*
Progress Lighting...405 949-2550
   1217 Sovereign Row Ste 10 Oklahoma City (73108) *(G-6911)*
Progressive Industries Inc..405 843-0597
   816 Nw 70th St Oklahoma City (73116) *(G-6912)*
Progressive O & P Services, Tulsa Also called Progressive Orthotic *(G-10570)*
Progressive Orthotic...918 786-7701
   9511 E 46th St Ste 1 Tulsa (74145) *(G-10570)*
Progressive Orthotic & PR..918 681-2346
   9511 E 46th St Ste 1 Tulsa (74145) *(G-10571)*
Progressive Stamping LLC..405 996-5347
   5500 W Reno Ave Ste 300 Oklahoma City (73127) *(G-6913)*
Progressive Tooling & Mfg, Tulsa Also called Progressive Tooling Inc *(G-10572)*
Progressive Tooling Inc...918 622-0506
   7739 E 38th St Ste C Tulsa (74145) *(G-10572)*
Progressive Windows Inc..580 227-9915
   Rr 2 Box 296 Fairview (73737) *(G-3147)*
Progrssive Stmping Fabrication, Oklahoma City Also called Progressive Stamping LLC *(G-6913)*
Project 3810 LLC..405 834-7418
   11132 Blue Stem Back Rd Oklahoma City (73162) *(G-6914)*
Prometheus Publications LLC....................................717 460-4881
   125 E Euclid Vinita (74301) *(G-11268)*
Promo Print 4 U LLC..405 259-6721
   4220 Nw 23rd St Oklahoma City (73107) *(G-6915)*
Promos Advertising Pdts Inc......................................918 343-9675
   224 E 8th St Claremore (74017) *(G-1676)*
Promotions - Forms Unlimited...................................918 627-8800
   8644 S Peoria Ave Tulsa (74132) *(G-10573)*
Promoz Screen Printing Inc..918 439-4030
   1345 N 108th East Ave Tulsa (74116) *(G-10574)*
Pronto Chemical Co, Hennessey Also called Capstone Oil & Gas Inc *(G-3449)*

Pronto Print Inc..580 223-1612
   1020 N Washington St Ardmore (73401) *(G-347)*
Propak Logistics Inc..405 694-4441
   11300 Partnr Dr Ste C Oklahoma City (73131) *(G-6916)*
Prophecy In News..405 634-1234
   1145 W I 240 Service Rd B100 Oklahoma City (73139) *(G-6917)*
Prosthetics By Wade..918 850-7544
   12920 S 126th East Ave Broken Arrow (74011) *(G-1012)*
Protechnics Okc Chemical Off....................................405 601-3078
   4307 Sw 34th St Oklahoma City (73119) *(G-6918)*
Protective Coatings Intl LLC.......................................405 716-4734
   1801 Boren Blvd Seminole (74868) *(G-8395)*
Protege Energy III LLC..918 286-2457
   4509 S Yellow Pine Ave Broken Arrow (74011) *(G-1013)*
Protege Energy III LLC (PA)..918 728-3092
   2200 S Utica Pl Ste 400 Tulsa (74114) *(G-10575)*
Proto Daily News, Poteau Also called Poteau Daily News *(G-7911)*
Protrac Industries LLC...405 312-5122
   10020 Leeds Dr Yukon (73099) *(G-11769)*
Protype Inc...918 743-4408
   2208 E 14th St Tulsa (74104) *(G-10576)*
Proud Veterans Intl Ltd...316 209-8701
   2325 Sw Pennsylvania Ave Lawton (73505) *(G-3986)*
Proven Torque LLC...780 982-7597
   9949 Us Highway 412 Mooreland (73852) *(G-4593)*
Providence Energy Corp..918 747-3675
   2424 E 21st St Ste 500 Tulsa (74114) *(G-10577)*
Pruett Cabinet and Trim LLC......................................405 692-1552
   13120 Turtle Creek Dr Oklahoma City (73170) *(G-5312)*
Pruitt Care, Ada Also called Pruitt Company of Ada Inc *(G-78)*
Pruitt Company of Ada Inc..580 332-3523
   402 E 12th St Ada (74820) *(G-78)*
Pruitt Oil Company LLc..580 889-2413
   1171 S Mississippi Ave Atoka (74525) *(G-422)*
Pryer Aerospace LLC...918 835-8885
   2230 N Sheridan Rd Tulsa (74115) *(G-10578)*
Pryer Machine & Tool Co Inc......................................918 341-4900
   2230 N Sheridan Rd Tulsa (74115) *(G-10579)*
Pryer Machine & Tool Company.................................918 835-8885
   2230 N Sheridan Rd Tulsa (74115) *(G-10580)*
Pryer Technology Group LLC......................................918 835-8885
   2230 N Sheridan Rd Tulsa (74115) *(G-10581)*
Pryor Chemical Company..918 825-3383
   4463 Hunt St Pryor (74361) *(G-7985)*
Pryor Daily Times, Pryor Also called Cnhi LLC *(G-7954)*
Pryor Printing Inc...918 825-2888
   15 S Vann St Pryor (74361) *(G-7986)*
Pryor Protein Plant, Pryor Also called Solae LLC *(G-7991)*
Pryor Prtg Print & Copy Ctr, Pryor Also called Pryor Printing Inc *(G-7986)*
Pryor Sand & Redi-Mix Inc..918 484-2150
   Highway 2 Whitefield (74472) *(G-11517)*
Pryor Stone Inc..918 825-3370
   1050 E 520 Pryor (74361) *(G-7987)*
Ps Tees LLC..405 694-7979
   1104 Ne 5th St Oklahoma City (73117) *(G-6919)*
Psa, Chandler Also called Alan L Buck *(G-1374)*
Psf Services LLC..707 386-8805
   109 W Cherokee St Marlow (73055) *(G-4239)*
PSI Mnfacturing Operations LLC................................561 747-6107
   8911 Se 29th St Ste B Midwest City (73110) *(G-4450)*
Pss Enterprises Llc...918 928-7971
   508 S 62nd St Broken Arrow (74014) *(G-1150)*
PTL Prop Solutions LLC..405 848-8000
   6100 N Western Ave Oklahoma City (73118) *(G-6920)*
Public Safety-Drivers License....................................918 336-0604
   1816 W Hensley Blvd Bartlesville (74003) *(G-518)*
Publics Water Company, Tahlequah Also called Tahlequah Public Works Auth *(G-8886)*
Pueblo Motors Inc..520 297-3244
   14709 Glenmark Dr Edmond (73013) *(G-2577)*
Pump & Seal Improvements.......................................918 747-7742
   3336 E 32nd St Ste 220 Tulsa (74135) *(G-10582)*
Pump Shop..918 834-8829
   802 N Lewis Pl Tulsa (74110) *(G-10583)*
Punch-Lok Co, Enid Also called Parrish Enterprises *(G-3030)*
Punch-Lok Co..580 233-4757
   3001 N 4th St Enid (73701) *(G-3040)*
Punkin Hollerwood...918 456-9640
   13870 N Pumpkin Holw Proctor (74457) *(G-7939)*
Punt & Puckle LLC..719 358-1419
   7201 S Klein Ave Oklahoma City (73139) *(G-6921)*
Purcell Jack Oil Gas Cnsulting...................................580 256-2040
   3319 Hidden Ridge Rd Woodward (73801) *(G-11624)*
Purcell Register, Purcell Also called Mc Clain County Publishing Co *(G-8016)*
Pure Canna Cbd..405 628-5119
   127 Nw 16th St Oklahoma City (73103) *(G-6922)*
Pure Creativity LLC..918 272-3152
   7160 Bluebird Ct Owasso (74055) *(G-7605)*
Pure Digital Print..918 899-2000
   5301 S 125th East Ave Tulsa (74146) *(G-10584)*

Pure Mountain 918 254-2225
  108 E El Paso St Broken Arrow (74012) *(G-1014)*
Pure Protein LLC 405 271-3838
  655 Research Pkwy Ste 556 Oklahoma City (73104) *(G-6923)*
Pure Republic, Owasso Also called Pure Creativity LLC *(G-7605)*
Pure Transplant Solutions LLC 512 697-8144
  655 Research Pkwy Ste 556 Oklahoma City (73104) *(G-6924)*
Purina Animal Nutrition LLC 405 232-6171
  1108 Nw 3rd St Oklahoma City (73106) *(G-6925)*
Purina Mills LLC 405 232-6171
  1108 Nw 3rd St Oklahoma City (73106) *(G-6926)*
Purpose Publishing 405 808-1332
  3600 Ne 50th St Oklahoma City (73121) *(G-6927)*
Put On Your Armor Inc 918 259-5000
  1000 E Memphis St Broken Arrow (74012) *(G-1015)*
Puzzle Apps Inc 918 815-6444
  1432 S Trenton Ave Tulsa (74120) *(G-10585)*
Pv Publishing Inc 405 409-1799
  5030 N May Ave 353 Oklahoma City (73112) *(G-6928)*
Pvintl, Lawton Also called Proud Veterans Intl Ltd *(G-3986)*
Pvr Midstreem LLC 580 837-5265
  Rr 2 Box 82 Beaver (73932) *(G-545)*
Pyfi Technologies 405 816-8685
  1113 W Wilshire Blvd Oklahoma City (73116) *(G-6929)*
Pyr Energy Corporation (HQ) 918 591-1791
  2 W 2nd St Ste 1500 Tulsa (74103) *(G-10586)*
Pyramid Printing 918 514-4073
  104 W 2nd St Sand Springs (74063) *(G-8216)*
Pyrotek Incorporated 918 224-1937
  8521 S Regency Dr Tulsa (74131) *(G-9030)*
Q B Johnson Mfg Inc 405 677-6676
  9000 S Sunnylane Rd Moore (73160) *(G-4558)*
Q E M Inc 918 534-2000
  394640 Gap Rd Ochelata (74051) *(G-5238)*
Q7 Inc 918 609-3251
  2940 E 26th St Tulsa (74114) *(G-10587)*
Q7 Services, Tulsa Also called Q7 Inc *(G-10587)*
Qep Energy Company 405 263-4831
  600 W Oklahoma Okarche (73762) *(G-5250)*
Qes Pressure Control LLC 580 885-7885
  14658 Us Highway 60 Arnett (73832) *(G-388)*
Qes Pressure Control LLC 580 243-6622
  2003 S Merritt Rd Elk City (73644) *(G-2863)*
Qes Pressure Control LLC (HQ) 405 605-2700
  4500 Se 59th St Oklahoma City (73135) *(G-6930)*
Qes Pressure Pumping LLC 918 338-0808
  155 County Rd Bartlesville (74003) *(G-519)*
Qes Pressure Pumping LLC 405 483-8000
  701 Main St Union City (73090) *(G-11220)*
Qg LLC 405 742-2222
  100 W Airport Rd Stillwater (74075) *(G-8741)*
Qmi Inc 918 456-6777
  1195 E Allen Rd Tahlequah (74464) *(G-8879)*
Qp Broadway EXT 405 843-9820
  401 W Wilshire Blvd Oklahoma City (73116) *(G-6931)*
Quad/Graphics Inc 405 264-4341
  6801 S Air Depot Blvd Oklahoma City (73135) *(G-6932)*
Quad/Graphics Inc 405 264-4000
  6801 S Sunnylane Rd Oklahoma City (73135) *(G-6933)*
Quail Creek Companies, Oklahoma City Also called Quail Creek Oil Corporation *(G-6934)*
Quail Creek Oil Corporation (PA) 405 755-7419
  13831 Quail Pointe Dr Oklahoma City (73134) *(G-6934)*
Quail Creek Production Company 405 755-7419
  13831 Quail Pointe Dr Oklahoma City (73134) *(G-6935)*
Quail Tools LP 918 994-4695
  11811 E 51st St Tulsa (74146) *(G-10588)*
Qual-Tron Inc 918 622-7052
  9409 E 55th Pl Tulsa (74145) *(G-10589)*
Qualgen LLC 405 551-8216
  301 Enterprise Dr Edmond (73013) *(G-2578)*
Qualgen LLC 405 551-8216
  301 Enterprise Dr Edmond (73013) *(G-2579)*
Quality Bakery Products LLC 609 871-7393
  20 East St Ste 620 Tulsa (74103) *(G-10590)*
Quality Buildings Inc 888 430-7721
  714 E 34th St Norman (73070) *(G-5126)*
Quality Buildings Inc 405 364-0516
  2450 W Robinson St Norman (73069) *(G-5127)*
Quality Cabinet Company 918 299-2721
  817 N Elm St Jenks (74037) *(G-3724)*
Quality Cabinetry 918 469-2119
  N Highway 71 Quinton (74561) *(G-8040)*
Quality Electric Motors, Ochelata Also called Q E M Inc *(G-5238)*
Quality Equipment Design Inc 918 492-4019
  4246 S 74th East Ave Tulsa (74145) *(G-10591)*
Quality Exhaust Sales, Collinsville Also called H & H Muffler Whse & Mfg Co *(G-1811)*
Quality Galvanizing 918 789-9333
  6022 S Industrial Dr Chelsea (74016) *(G-1410)*
Quality In Counters Inc 405 664-2744
  6611 Central Rd Guthrie (73044) *(G-3333)*

Quality Line Truss Inc 918 783-5227
  434557 E 350 Rd Adair (74330) *(G-111)*
Quality Liquid Feeds Inc 918 683-7215
  2530 Port Pl Muskogee (74403) *(G-4740)*
Quality Machine Services Inc 405 495-4962
  8412 Sw 8th St Oklahoma City (73128) *(G-6936)*
Quality Machinging of Broken 918 294-1434
  12320 E 126th St S Broken Arrow (74011) *(G-1016)*
Quality Machining LLC 918 512-8593
  2400 Industrial Rd Sapulpa (74066) *(G-8304)*
Quality Machining Inc 918 294-1434
  12320 E 126th St S Broken Arrow (74011) *(G-1017)*
Quality Metal Finishing Inc 405 236-1155
  15 Sw 25th St Oklahoma City (73109) *(G-6937)*
Quality Parts Mfg Co Inc 918 627-3307
  10218 E 47th Pl Tulsa (74146) *(G-10592)*
Quality Plating Co of Tulsa 918 835-2278
  2665 N Darlington Ave Tulsa (74115) *(G-10593)*
Quality Production Co Stigler 918 967-4383
  20292 E Highway 9 Stigler (74462) *(G-8640)*
Quality Prtg & Graphic Design, Lone Grove Also called Lone Grove Ledger *(G-4118)*
Quality Steel Coatings Inc 918 269-9104
  7528 E Galveston Pl Broken Arrow (74014) *(G-1151)*
Quality Stone, Atoka Also called Eaves Stones Products *(G-410)*
Quality Stone Quarries LLC 918 967-5195
  108 S Broadway St Stigler (74462) *(G-8641)*
Quality Tank Manufacturing 405 756-1188
  202 Se 4th St Lindsay (73052) *(G-4078)*
Quality Truss Co Inc 918 543-2077
  14852 E 530 Rd Claremore (74019) *(G-1677)*
Quality Wholesale Millwork Inc 405 681-6575
  2320 S May Ave Oklahoma City (73108) *(G-6938)*
Quality Woodworks Inc 918 944-3314
  3451 Southern Heights Dr Muskogee (74401) *(G-4741)*
Quantum Builds Company 727 504-1628
  14616 Brinklee Way Oklahoma City (73142) *(G-6939)*
Quantum Forms Corporation (PA) 918 665-1320
  6000 Nw 2nd St Ste 300 Oklahoma City (73127) *(G-6940)*
Quantum Trading Technologies 918 876-3921
  401 S Dewey Ave Ste 503 Bartlesville (74003) *(G-520)*
Quapaw Company 918 225-0580
  7312 E Main St Cushing (74023) *(G-1951)*
Quapaw Company Inc 918 352-2533
  Hwy 33 2 One Half Mi E Drumright (74030) *(G-2070)*
Quapaw Company Inc 918 767-2985
  45551 S 354 Rd Pawnee (74058) *(G-7710)*
Quapaw Food Services, Quapaw Also called Food Svcs Auth of Quapaw Tribe *(G-8030)*
Quapaw Rock Co, Pawnee Also called Quapaw Company Inc *(G-7710)*
Quarry, Hulbert Also called Kemp Stone Inc *(G-3624)*
Quarry 918 534-2120
  2001 N Osage Ave Dewey (74029) *(G-2030)*
Quarry Custom Cultured Marble, Dewey Also called Quarry *(G-2030)*
Quarry Services, Poteau Also called Freedom Stone Company LLC *(G-7904)*
Quarter Midgets of America 918 371-9410
  310 S Avenue G Collinsville (74021) *(G-1820)*
Quest, Oklahoma City Also called William Reed *(G-5324)*
Quest Cherokee LLC (HQ) 405 371-1653
  5901 N Western Ave # 200 Oklahoma City (73118) *(G-6941)*
Quest Energy Partners LP 405 600-7704
  210 Park Ave Ste 2750 Oklahoma City (73102) *(G-6942)*
Quest Loot LLC 405 609-4100
  509 Country Side Trl Edmond (73012) *(G-2580)*
Quest Midstream Partners LP 405 702-7410
  210 Park Ave Ste 2750 Oklahoma City (73102) *(G-6943)*
Quest Property Inc 405 722-7530
  11117 Folkstone Wheatland (73097) *(G-11515)*
Quick Charge, Oklahoma City Also called Sanco Enterprises Inc *(G-7075)*
Quick Charge Corporation 405 634-2120
  1032 Sw 22nd St Oklahoma City (73109) *(G-6944)*
Quick Print, Tulsa Also called Quik Print of Tulsa Inc *(G-10595)*
Quick Start Inc 405 422-3135
  3700 S Highway 81 Svc Rd El Reno (73036) *(G-2749)*
Quickcharge, Oklahoma City Also called Sanco Products Inc *(G-7076)*
Quik Print, Oklahoma City Also called Quik-Print of Oklahoma City *(G-6946)*
Quik Print, Oklahoma City Also called Quik-Print of Oklahoma City *(G-6949)*
Quik Print of Tulsa Inc 918 250-5466
  6111 S Mingo Rd Ste A Tulsa (74133) *(G-10594)*
Quik Print of Tulsa Inc (PA) 918 665-6246
  3711 S Sheridan Rd Tulsa (74145) *(G-10595)*
Quik Print of Tulsa Inc 918 582-1825
  402 S Main St Tulsa (74103) *(G-10596)*
Quik Print of Tulsa Inc 918 491-9292
  6620 S Lewis Ave Tulsa (74136) *(G-10597)*
Quik Print Oklahoma City Inc (PA) 405 840-3275
  3403 Nw Expressway Oklahoma City (73112) *(G-6945)*
Quik-Print 1405, Oklahoma City Also called Quik-Print of Oklahoma City *(G-6947)*
Quik-Print of Oklahoma City (PA) 405 842-1404
  3401 Nw Expressway St Oklahoma City (73112) *(G-6946)*

Quik-Print of Oklahoma City....405 843-9820
7206 N Western Ave Oklahoma City (73116) *(G-6947)*
Quik-Print of Oklahoma City....405 232-7579
119 N Robinson Ave # 100 Oklahoma City (73102) *(G-6948)*
Quik-Print of Oklahoma City....405 943-3222
4233 Charter Ave Oklahoma City (73108) *(G-6949)*
Quik-Print of Oklahoma City....405 840-3275
3403 Nw Expwy Oklahoma City (73112) *(G-6950)*
Quik-Print of Oklahoma City....405 528-7976
406 Nw 23rd St Oklahoma City (73103) *(G-6951)*
Quik-Print of Oklahoma City....405 751-5315
10637 N May Ave Oklahoma City (73120) *(G-6952)*
Quikrete Companies LLC....405 787-2050
8000 Melrose Ln Oklahoma City (73127) *(G-6953)*
Quikrete Companies LLC....918 835-4441
6204 E 11th St Tulsa (74112) *(G-10598)*
Quikrete Holdings Inc....405 354-8824
1400 Holly Ave Ste 100 Yukon (73099) *(G-11770)*
Quiktrip Corporation (PA)....918 615-7700
4705 S 129th East Ave Tulsa (74134) *(G-10599)*
Quikwater Inc....918 241-8880
8939 W 21st St Sand Springs (74063) *(G-8217)*
Quikwater.com, Sand Springs *Also called Quikwater Inc* *(G-8217)*
Quilts Unlimited....580 746-2770
201 S Choctaw Millerton (74750) *(G-4474)*
Quinque Operating Company....405 840-9876
908 Nw 71st St Oklahoma City (73116) *(G-6954)*
Quintella Printing Company Inc....405 631-6566
130 Se 44th St Ste 300 Oklahoma City (73129) *(G-6955)*
Quintin Little Company Inc....580 226-7600
2007 N Commerce St Ardmore (73401) *(G-348)*
Quses....817 829-1086
1224 Nw 4th St Oklahoma City (73106) *(G-6956)*
Quses Manufacturing, Oklahoma City *Also called Quses* *(G-6956)*
R & B Sports, Atoka *Also called Shops of Standing Rock Inc* *(G-423)*
R & D Mud Logging Services LLP....405 969-2587
602 S Pine St Crescent (73028) *(G-1919)*
R & J Aluminum Products....580 355-1809
1415 Nw Taylor Ave Lawton (73507) *(G-3987)*
R & J Food Tulsa LLC....918 520-0484
1232 E 2nd St Tulsa (74120) *(G-10600)*
R & J Oil and Gas Royalty LLC....405 562-3334
689 Outer Banks Way Edmond (73034) *(G-2581)*
R & L Endeavors LLC....405 826-8226
6912 Lakepointe Dr Oklahoma City (73116) *(G-6957)*
R & L Mechanics & Welding....918 253-4734
804 S 17th St Jay (74346) *(G-3685)*
R & M Energy System, Oklahoma City *Also called Robbins & Myers Inc* *(G-7033)*
R & M Fleet Service Inc....918 367-9326
543 N Meadowood Pl Cleveland (74020) *(G-1732)*
R & M Packer Inc....580 863-2242
31 Sunset Dr Sand Springs (74063) *(G-8218)*
R & P Machine Shop....405 275-1321
19705 Gordon Cooper Dr Tecumseh (74873) *(G-8925)*
R & R Engineering Co Inc....918 252-2571
12585 E 61st St Broken Arrow (74012) *(G-1018)*
R & R Lawncare & Cleaning....580 480-1953
2104 N Robin St Altus (73521) *(G-167)*
R & R Media Systems LLC....918 978-0578
5332 E 21st Pl Tulsa (74114) *(G-10601)*
R & R Radiator Co....405 257-3557
207 E 2nd St Wewoka (74884) *(G-11508)*
R & R Signs Inc....580 924-4363
1325 Highway 78 S Durant (74701) *(G-2250)*
R & R Well Service Inc....580 254-3068
507 48th St Woodward (73801) *(G-11625)*
R & S Manufacturing....918 266-2266
3010 N Highway 167 Catoosa (74015) *(G-1347)*
R & S Swabbing Inc....405 853-5445
318 S Oak Ave Hennessey (73742) *(G-3480)*
R & W Machine Shop Inc....405 632-4020
6209 S Shields Blvd Oklahoma City (73149) *(G-6958)*
R A Bodenhame Assoc Inc....918 855-1964
604 W 36th St Sand Springs (74063) *(G-8219)*
R A D Welding (2)....405 206-9434
105366 S 3410 Rd Meeker (74855) *(G-4386)*
R A I, Broken Arrow *Also called Refractory Anchors Inc* *(G-1154)*
R and P Cabinetry LLC....405 230-0495
540 Nw 42nd St Oklahoma City (73118) *(G-6959)*
R B Watkins Inc....405 732-9969
617 S Margene Dr Oklahoma City (73130) *(G-6960)*
R C Ramsey Co....918 746-4300
2916 E 21st St Tulsa (74114) *(G-10602)*
R C Taylor Companies Inc....405 840-2700
5661 N Classen Blvd Oklahoma City (73118) *(G-6961)*
R Collins Woodwork, Owasso *Also called Affordable Restorations LLC* *(G-7543)*
R D Davis & Associates Inc....405 720-2882
13212 N Mcarthur Blvd A Oklahoma City (73142) *(G-6962)*
R E Blaik Inc....405 285-8000
1616 E 19th St Ste 201 Edmond (73013) *(G-2582)*
R E G Energy....405 842-4249
3333 Nw 63rd St Oklahoma City (73116) *(G-6963)*
R F Lindgren Enclosures Inc....918 299-7572
8751 S College Pl Tulsa (74137) *(G-10603)*
R G A Rubber & Gasket Co Amer, Broken Arrow *Also called Rubber & Gasket Co Amer Inc* *(G-1039)*
R G Berry Co....918 587-0036
1789 E 71st St Tulsa (74136) *(G-10604)*
R G Enterprises....580 225-2260
806 S Randall Ave Elk City (73644) *(G-2864)*
R K Manufacturing LLC....405 626-8922
1884 County Road 1250 Tuttle (73089) *(G-11209)*
R M Machine Shop Inc....405 209-7242
1227 County Street 2960 Tuttle (73089) *(G-11210)*
R M Swabbing LLC....405 828-7213
17199 E 715 Rd Dover (73734) *(G-2043)*
R Meyers Enterprises....580 917-7554
2402 Sw Lee Blvd Unit 2 Lawton (73505) *(G-3988)*
R N J Inc....918 865-2781
34289 W Highway 51 Mannford (74044) *(G-4191)*
R P Small Corp....918 712-2226
1585 E 22nd St Tulsa (74114) *(G-10605)*
R R Donnelley, Tulsa *Also called R R Donnelley & Sons Company* *(G-10606)*
R R Donnelley & Sons Company....405 743-2124
3100 N Husband St Stillwater (74075) *(G-8742)*
R R Donnelley & Sons Company....918 749-6496
2757 S Memorial Dr Tulsa (74129) *(G-10606)*
R Squared Chemicals LLC....918 520-2384
1350 N Louisville Ave # 1 Tulsa (74115) *(G-10607)*
R T C Resources LLP....580 774-2313
316 W Kee St Weatherford (73096) *(G-11435)*
R W D 9 Mayes County....918 434-5000
3134 E 523 Salina (74365) *(G-8135)*
R&C Industries LLC....405 640-7239
2113 N Gatewood Ave Oklahoma City (73106) *(G-6964)*
R&D Labs LLC....405 875-9937
2518 Countrywood Ln Edmond (73012) *(G-2583)*
R&L Custom Cycles, Jay *Also called R & L Mechanics & Welding* *(G-3685)*
R&R Roustabout Rental Services, Ringwood *Also called R&R Roustabout Services LLC* *(G-8090)*
R&R Roustabout Services LLC....580 883-4647
220 N Main St Ringwood (73768) *(G-8090)*
R-5 Caps & Tees....580 256-3579
43151 S County Road 203 Woodward (73801) *(G-11626)*
R360 Oklahoma LLC....405 262-5900
12000 Reuter Rd W El Reno (73036) *(G-2750)*
Ra Graphix....405 703-3599
214 Ne 12th St Ste C Moore (73160) *(G-4559)*
Ra Jac Inc....405 701-5222
1614 Wilshire Ave Norman (73072) *(G-5128)*
Raber Renovations Inc....918 499-3030
5605 E 109th St Tulsa (74137) *(G-10608)*
Rabid....580 234-3632
2302 W Willow Rd Enid (73703) *(G-3041)*
Raccoon Technologies Inc....580 399-9126
130 N Country Club Rd Ada (74820) *(G-79)*
Raceway Electric Inc....918 629-4252
119 N Cherokee St Catoosa (74015) *(G-1348)*
Racf Industries Inc....918 258-1290
102 W Norman St Broken Arrow (74012) *(G-1019)*
Rackley Welding....580 660-1176
12827 N 2410 Rd Mountain View (73062) *(G-4629)*
RAD Welding Svc, Meeker *Also called R A D Welding (2)* *(G-4386)*
Radial Engines Ltd....405 433-2263
11701 W Forrest Hills Rd Guthrie (73044) *(G-3334)*
Radiotronix Inc....405 794-7730
2117 Shadow Lake Dr Edmond (73025) *(G-2584)*
Rae Corporation (PA)....918 825-7222
4492 Hunt St Pryor (74361) *(G-7988)*
Raf Midsouth Technologies LLC....918 352-8300
2728 Charles Page Blvd Tulsa (74127) *(G-10609)*
Rafter H Bar Welding Svc LLC....918 210-0175
121 N Broadway Coweta (74429) *(G-1895)*
Rafter H Operating LLC....405 295-2100
219 N Bickford Ave El Reno (73036) *(G-2751)*
Ragan Petroleum, Muskogee *Also called Tridon Oil Inc* *(G-4754)*
Ragsdale Wrecker Service....405 771-5544
3728 Spencer Rd Spencer (73084) *(G-8600)*
Ragtops Athletics Inc....918 274-3575
9100 N Garnett Rd Ste Dd Owasso (74055) *(G-7606)*
Rail Masters LLC....405 840-1019
7301 Broadway Ext Ste 228 Oklahoma City (73116) *(G-6965)*
Railroad Sgnling Solutions Inc....918 973-1888
1103 E Houston St Broken Arrow (74012) *(G-1020)*
Railroad Yard Inc....405 377-8763
5915 S Perkins Rd Stillwater (74074) *(G-8743)*
Rainbo Service Co (PA)....405 677-5353
1839 Se 25th St Oklahoma City (73129) *(G-6966)*

ALPHABETIC

Rainbow Awnings & Signs 918 249-0003
6422 S 112th East Ave Tulsa (74133) ***(G-10610)***
Rainbow Concrete Company 918 234-9044
13521 E 11th St Tulsa (74108) ***(G-10611)***
Rainbow Creations 405 942-6207
3252 N Nesbitt Ave Oklahoma City (73112) ***(G-6967)***
Rainbow Oil & Gas Inc 918 335-2188
5800 Harvard Dr Bartlesville (74006) ***(G-521)***
Rainbow Pennant Inc 405 524-1577
148 Ne 48th St Oklahoma City (73105) ***(G-6968)***
Rainbow Spreme Assmbly I O R G 918 423-1328
315 E Carl Albert Pkwy McAlester (74501) ***(G-4331)***
Rainbow Studies International, El Reno *Also called Cross Shadows Inc* ***(G-2707)***
Rainey Oil, Tulsa *Also called Tek Fins Inc* ***(G-9043)***
Rajon LLC 918 367-5487
23800 S 369th West Ave Bristow (74010) ***(G-795)***
Ralph Lynn Szatkowski, Lawton *Also called Accu-Turn Machine LLC* ***(G-3883)***
Ralph M Thomas 405 756-4426
109 Nw 2nd St Lindsay (73052) ***(G-4079)***
Ralphs Packing Company 405 547-2464
500 W Freeman Ave Perkins (74059) ***(G-7721)***
Ralston Purina 405 751-4550
13700 N Lincoln Blvd Edmond (73013) ***(G-2585)***
Ram Design Inc 918 342-4051
24454 S Orange Cv Claremore (74019) ***(G-1678)***
Ram Energy LLC 918 947-6300
2100 S Utica Ave Ste 165 Tulsa (74114) ***(G-10612)***
Ram Internet Media 405 614-0641
4603 White Oak Dr Stillwater (74074) ***(G-8744)***
Ram Machine Inc 918 224-8028
9312 S 46th West Ave Tulsa (74132) ***(G-10613)***
Ram Machine Products LLC 918 455-5555
9818 S 219th East Ave Broken Arrow (74014) ***(G-1152)***
Ram Oilfield Services LLC 918 639-2827
5858 S 129th East Ave Tulsa (74134) ***(G-10614)***
Rambler Energy Services Inc 580 242-7447
114 E Broadway Ave # 207 Enid (73701) ***(G-3042)***
Rambo Acquisition Company (PA) 918 627-6222
8401 E 41st St Tulsa (74145) ***(G-10615)***
Rambo, Jay Company, Tulsa *Also called Rambo Acquisition Company* ***(G-10615)***
Ramcco Concrete Cnstr LLC 918 266-3838
19548 E 6th St Tulsa (74108) ***(G-10616)***
Ramcco Trucking, Tulsa *Also called Ramcco Concrete Cnstr LLC* ***(G-10616)***
Ramco, Mustang *Also called Robertson Arms & Munitions Co* ***(G-4791)***
Ramco Packers 405 485-8804
Hwy 76 S Blanchard (73010) ***(G-729)***
Ramey Oil, Kiefer *Also called Rameys Welding & Roustabout* ***(G-3781)***
Rameys Welding & Roustabout 918 321-3156
11 S A St Kiefer (74041) ***(G-3781)***
Ramiiisol Vineyards LLC 405 858-9800
6305 Waterford Blvd Oklahoma City (73118) ***(G-6969)***
Ramon & Bennett Roustabout 580 625-4092
107 Douglas Ave Beaver (73932) ***(G-546)***
Ramos Plating Co 405 232-4300
1320 S Walker Ave Oklahoma City (73109) ***(G-6970)***
Ramsey Industries Inc (HQ) 918 438-2760
4707 N Mingo Rd Tulsa (74117) ***(G-10617)***
Ramsey Property Management LLC 405 302-6200
2932 Nw 122nd St Ste 4 Oklahoma City (73120) ***(G-6971)***
Ramsey Winch Company 918 438-2760
4707 N Mingo Rd Tulsa (74117) ***(G-10618)***
Ranch Acres Car Care 918 742-3902
3003 S Harvard Ave Tulsa (74114) ***(G-10619)***
Ranch Acres Texaco, Tulsa *Also called Ranch Acres Car Care* ***(G-10619)***
Rand Trans Inc 580 866-3355
54979 S County Road 205 Sharon (73857) ***(G-8418)***
Randall Reed Ford, Oklahoma City *Also called Pfpp LP* ***(G-6839)***
Randy Mulkey 405 258-2600
930335 S Pilot Dr Wellston (74881) ***(G-11475)***
Randy Wyrick 918 848-0117
58495 E 160 Rd Fairland (74343) ***(G-3128)***
Randys Backhoe Service 580 227-0561
2382 State Highway 58 Longdale (73755) ***(G-4126)***
Randys Construction 405 387-3568
800 Springlake Rd Newcastle (73065) ***(G-4836)***
Randys Signs Inc 405 273-2564
34305 Waco Rd Shawnee (74801) ***(G-8486)***
Range Energy Services Company 580 227-3762
253632 E County Road 49 Fairview (73737) ***(G-3148)***
Range Production Co, Fairview *Also called Range Energy Services Company* ***(G-3148)***
Range Production Company 580 628-3700
303 Thunderbird Rd Tonkawa (74653) ***(G-8980)***
Range Rsurces-Midcontinent LLC 405 810-7359
5600 N May Ave Ste 100 Oklahoma City (73112) ***(G-6972)***
Ranger Oilfield Services Corp 405 853-7279
1801 N Hwy 81 Hennessey (73742) ***(G-3481)***
Ranger Rentals LLC 580 541-4242
723 W Randolph Ave Ste 8 Enid (73701) ***(G-3043)***
Rank Industries LLC 405 308-0503
10808 270th St Blanchard (73010) ***(G-730)***
Rapid Application Group LLC 918 760-1242
13105 E 61st St Ste A Broken Arrow (74012) ***(G-1021)***
Rapid Jack Solutions Inc 405 203-3131
4101 Stonehurst St Norman (73072) ***(G-5129)***
Rapid Wireless LLC 918 605-9717
8221 S 69th East Ave Tulsa (74133) ***(G-10620)***
Raptor Oilfield Controls LLC 580 251-9806
7025 Nix Dr Duncan (73533) ***(G-2166)***
Rar Wood Works LLC 205 233-2920
2612 S Walnut Ave Broken Arrow (74012) ***(G-1022)***
Rate My Welder 405 400-0109
131 Dean A Mcgee Ave Oklahoma City (73102) ***(G-6973)***
Rath Inc 580 588-3064
908 E Apache Trail Rd Apache (73006) ***(G-221)***
Rauh Oilfield Services Co 580 796-2128
1622 S Higway 132 Lahoma (73754) ***(G-3860)***
Raven Resources LLC 405 773-7340
2575 Kelley Pointe Pkwy # 380 Edmond (73013) ***(G-2586)***
Raven Services, Mustang *Also called Elvis S Seshie* ***(G-4770)***
Raw Elements LLC 918 392-4957
2510 E 15th St Ste 102 Tulsa (74104) ***(G-10621)***
Rawhide Custom Leather 918 273-0511
116 S Chase St Nowata (74048) ***(G-5227)***
Rawhide Dirt Works 580 367-5242
37427 State Highway 31 Coalgate (74538) ***(G-1783)***
Rawhide N Rustics 580 307-9941
115 W Main St Weatherford (73096) ***(G-11436)***
Raxter LLC 918 706-7987
3820 W El Paso St Broken Arrow (74012) ***(G-1023)***
Ray Clour Well Service Inc 580 856-3905
23932 State Highway 76 Ratliff City (73481) ***(G-8063)***
Ray Computer Services Intl Inc 918 299-7262
381 E Main St Jenks (74037) ***(G-3725)***
Ray Harrington Draperies 405 789-6710
6710 Nw 29th St Bethany (73008) ***(G-593)***
Ray Lu Petroleum LLC 405 424-4006
5300 N Bryant Ave Oklahoma City (73121) ***(G-6974)***
Ray McClain Inc 918 363-7350
6310 Merrimack Dr Sand Springs (74063) ***(G-8220)***
Ray Meat Market 580 256-6031
3605 Williams Ave Woodward (73801) ***(G-11627)***
Rayco Paraffin Service Inc 405 853-2055
S Metro Rd Hennessey (73742) ***(G-3482)***
Raydon Exploration Inc 405 478-8585
1601 Nw Expwy St Ste 1300 Oklahoma City (73118) ***(G-6975)***
Raymac Corp 918 752-0002
1015 E 13th St Okmulgee (74447) ***(G-7524)***
Raymond L Weil Pblications LLC 580 323-4594
2717 Owen Dr Clinton (73601) ***(G-1764)***
Raymonds Donut Shop 918 660-0644
4955 S Memorial Dr Ste H Tulsa (74145) ***(G-10622)***
Rays Portable Welding 405 282-3218
2750 Browne Ave Guthrie (73044) ***(G-3335)***
Raytheon Company 580 351-6966
1 Sw 11th St Ste 290 Lawton (73501) ***(G-3989)***
Razor Oilfield Services LLC 405 661-0008
3520 N Vernon Ave Hinton (73047) ***(G-3535)***
RB Cnstr Met Fabrication LLC 580 367-5039
2436 E Folsom Rd Caney (74533) ***(G-1262)***
Rbc Bearings Incorporated 405 236-2666
5001 Sw 20th St Oklahoma City (73128) ***(G-6976)***
Rbc Exploration Company (PA) 918 744-5607
2627 E 21st St Ste 200 Tulsa (74114) ***(G-10623)***
Rbi Advertising 918 592-1836
1637 S Boston Ave 310 Tulsa (74119) ***(G-10624)***
Rbi Company, Tulsa *Also called Rbi Advertising* ***(G-10624)***
Rbs Pet Products 405 373-0235
320 Piedmont Rd N Piedmont (73078) ***(G-7769)***
RC Custom Woodwork 405 414-1162
905 Eagle Cliff Dr Norman (73072) ***(G-5130)***
RC Pumps LLC 580 444-2227
721 Old Hwy 76 Ratliff City (73481) ***(G-8064)***
RC Welding & Fab LLC 580 216-1274
9701 Lakeshore Dr Oklahoma City (73120) ***(G-6977)***
Rccs Woodworking LLC 405 694-9680
4625 Vista Valley Ln Edmond (73025) ***(G-2587)***
RCO Fabrication LLC 918 225-0708
8221 E 9th St Cushing (74023) ***(G-1952)***
RCP Print Solutions 918 341-1950
1018 N 6th St Broken Arrow (74012) ***(G-1024)***
RCP Printing 918 341-1950
1018 N 6th St Broken Arrow (74012) ***(G-1025)***
Rcr Construction 918 682-9033
1918 N 11th St Muskogee (74401) ***(G-4742)***
Rcs Corporation 918 227-7497
9231 S 36th West Ave Tulsa (74132) ***(G-10625)***
Rcw Welding Services LLC 918 852-4775
29606 E 68th St S Broken Arrow (74014) ***(G-1153)***

ALPHABETIC SECTION

Rd Logging..918 666-2556
   69998 E 152 Rd Wyandotte (74370) *(G-11662)*
Rd Roofing and Carpentry................................580 341-0607
   11025 County Road 3502 Ada (74820) *(G-80)*
Rdnj LLC...405 418-4741
   500 N Vickie Dr Oklahoma City (73117) *(G-6978)*
RDS Manufacturing..918 251-0369
   304 N Redbud Ave Broken Arrow (74012) *(G-1026)*
RDS Manufacturing Inc...918 459-5100
   4217 W Seattle St Broken Arrow (74012) *(G-1027)*
RDS Oilfield Service LLC...................................918 521-9205
   910 Whispering Oaks Cushing (74023) *(G-1953)*
Reach Wireline..405 872-8828
   8530 Enterprise Ave Noble (73068) *(G-4889)*
Reading Equipment & Dist LLC...........................918 283-2999
   2800 N Lynn Riggs Blvd Claremore (74017) *(G-1679)*
Reading Glasses To Go, Oklahoma City Also called Ready Reading Glasses Inc *(G-6979)*
Ready Reading Glasses Inc..................................405 840-4440
   9223 N Pennsylvania Pl Oklahoma City (73120) *(G-6979)*
Reagan Resources Inc.......................................405 848-2707
   2601 Nw Expwy Ste 801w Oklahoma City (73112) *(G-6980)*
Reagent Chemical & RES Inc................................580 233-1024
   5520 E Market St Enid (73701) *(G-3044)*
Reagent Chemical & RES Inc................................580 436-4100
   201 W 5th St Francis (74844) *(G-3191)*
Real Alloy Recycling LLC..................................918 224-4746
   1508 N 8th St Sapulpa (74066) *(G-8305)*
Real Cabinets...918 336-0255
   717 W 5th St Bartlesville (74003) *(G-522)*
Real Time Pain Relief, Edmond Also called Rtpr LLC *(G-2607)*
Realtime Automation Inc....................................918 249-9217
   1401 W Detroit St Broken Arrow (74012) *(G-1028)*
Reasor Enterprises..918 633-1746
   1600 S Fir Ave Broken Arrow (74012) *(G-1029)*
Reasor Fiberglass, Broken Arrow Also called Reasor Enterprises *(G-1029)*
Reaux Corporation...918 252-7660
   9802 E 58th St Tulsa (74146) *(G-10626)*
Reaux Medical Molding, Tulsa Also called Reaux Corporation *(G-10626)*
Reba Tidwell Beck, Comanche Also called Accessories-To-Go *(G-1833)*
Rebel Oil Company...405 848-2208
   6500 N Classen Blvd Oklahoma City (73116) *(G-6981)*
Rebel Press, Tulsa Also called Lloyd Words LLC *(G-10172)*
Rebel Sign Company LLC....................................405 456-9253
   7109 W Hefner Rd G2525 Oklahoma City (73162) *(G-6982)*
Rebellion Energy LLC..918 779-3163
   5416 S Yale Ave Ste 300 Tulsa (74135) *(G-10627)*
Rebellion Energy II LLC.....................................918 779-3163
   5416 S Yale Ave Ste 300 Tulsa (74135) *(G-10628)*
Reclaimed Oil & Gas Prpts LLC...........................580 234-8085
   2421 Rockwood Rd Enid (73703) *(G-3045)*
Recognition Place, Bartlesville Also called First Thought Inc *(G-483)*
Recoil Energy Rental LLC....................................405 650-1373
   8177 Skyline Dr Blanchard (73010) *(G-731)*
Recoil Oilfield Services LLC...............................405 227-4198
   8177 Skyline Dr Blanchard (73010) *(G-732)*
Reconnect Mfg, Stigler Also called Kimberly A Johnson *(G-8636)*
Rector Fire Works...918 681-0513
   4751 S 32nd St W Muskogee (74401) *(G-4743)*
Red Bluff Resources Oper LLC............................405 605-8360
   3030 Nw Expwy Ste 650 Oklahoma City (73112) *(G-6983)*
Red Bone Services LLC (HQ)..............................580 225-1200
   1700 Enterprise Rd Elk City (73644) *(G-2865)*
Red Bud Glass Inc..405 685-3331
   733 Maple Brook Ln Vinita (74301) *(G-11269)*
Red Bud Resources..580 227-2592
   120 N Main St Fairview (73737) *(G-3149)*
Red Cedar Creations..580 227-3198
   249839 E County Road 58 Longdale (73755) *(G-4127)*
Red Collar Pet Foods Inc...................................580 323-3359
   1 Mars Rd Clinton (73601) *(G-1765)*
Red Devil Incorporated (PA).................................918 585-8111
   1437 S Boulder Ave # 750 Tulsa (74119) *(G-10629)*
Red Devil Incorporated..918 825-5744
   4175 Webb St Pryor (74361) *(G-7989)*
Red Dirt Msurement Contrls LLC..........................405 422-5085
   2742 M And K Ln El Reno (73036) *(G-2752)*
Red Dirt Wood Works LLC...................................918 640-5917
   109 E 21st St Edmond (73013) *(G-2588)*
Red Dirt Wreaths & Things.................................918 809-3973
   4036 Nw 60th St Oklahoma City (73112) *(G-6984)*
Red Dog Press LLC...405 703-2896
   209 S Wyndemere Lakes Dr Moore (73160) *(G-4560)*
Red Earth Farm Store Inc...................................405 478-3424
   2301 E I 44 Service Rd Oklahoma City (73111) *(G-6985)*
Red Falcon LLC..580 647-2152
   6302 Sw Oakmont Lawton (73505) *(G-3990)*
Red Fork Mfg LLC...405 368-7367
   11921 N 2850 Rd Dover (73734) *(G-2044)*

Red Fork Motor Co...918 587-2778
   5015 W 27th St Tulsa (74107) *(G-10630)*
Red Fork USA Investments Inc..........................918 270-2941
   1437 S Boulder Ave # 700 Tulsa (74119) *(G-10631)*
Red Hills Hot Shot Inc..580 225-8686
   19023 E 1140 Rd Sayre (73662) *(G-8344)*
Red Land Energy LLC..405 520-1205
   1600 E 19th St Ste 103 Edmond (73013) *(G-2589)*
Red Line Welding and Services.........................580 591-3162
   2395 Se 45th St Lawton (73501) *(G-3991)*
Red Mountain Energy LLC..................................405 842-4500
   5901 N Western Ave # 200 Oklahoma City (73118) *(G-6986)*
Red Mountain Operating LLC.............................405 842-9200
   5901 N Western Ave # 200 Oklahoma City (73118) *(G-6987)*
Red Plains Oil & Gas LLC...................................405 375-3377
   508 W Chisholm Dr Kingfisher (73750) *(G-3812)*
Red River Cold Storage LLC..............................580 795-9948
   600 E Industrial Rd Madill (73446) *(G-4161)*
Red River Custom Camo & Hydro.....................580 745-5262
   3825 N 1st Ave Durant (74701) *(G-2251)*
Red River Gunsmithing LLC................................580 770-1911
   112 N Main St Frederick (73542) *(G-3198)*
Red River Imaging LP...405 308-4545
   5601 Nw 72nd St Ste 232 Warr Acres (73132) *(G-11327)*
Red River Oilfield Svcs LLC...............................405 802-4280
   19401 Stubblefield Ln Edmond (73012) *(G-2590)*
Red River Printing Corp....................................405 685-1794
   5300 Sw 23rd St Oklahoma City (73128) *(G-6988)*
Red River Software LLC......................................405 728-8102
   11100 Roxboro Ave # 2303 Oklahoma City (73162) *(G-6989)*
Red River Specialties LLC..................................580 436-0883
   1906 N Broadway Ave Ada (74820) *(G-81)*
Red Rock Fabrication...405 602-4602
   417 Westland Dr Edmond (73013) *(G-2591)*
Red Rocks Oil & Gas Operating, Oklahoma City Also called Red Rocks Resources LLC *(G-6990)*
Red Rocks Resources LLC..................................405 600-3065
   1321 N Robinson Ave Oklahoma City (73103) *(G-6990)*
Red Seal Feeds LLC..918 423-3710
   1400 E Washington Ave McAlester (74501) *(G-4332)*
Red Wind Simulations, Park Hill Also called Red Wind Training *(G-7646)*
Red Wind Training...918 822-0605
   22349 E 843 Rd Park Hill (74451) *(G-7646)*
Red Wolf Customs, Lawton Also called Grace Power LLC *(G-3936)*
Redback Coil Tubing LLC (HQ)............................405 265-4600
   14201 Caliber Dr Ste 300 Oklahoma City (73134) *(G-6991)*
Redback Energy Services LLC (PA)....................405 265-4608
   14201 Caliber Dr Ste 300 Oklahoma City (73134) *(G-6992)*
Redbird Woodworks..918 227-5938
   1001 Hickory Hill Rd Sapulpa (74066) *(G-8306)*
Redbone Tool and Machine Inc..........................918 625-1617
   10837 E Marshall St # 10 Tulsa (74116) *(G-10632)*
Redbud Candles & Creations.............................210 749-6975
   10099 Lakewood Rd Skiatook (74070) *(G-8566)*
Redbud E&P Inc..918 469-3600
   100 E Main St Quinton (74561) *(G-8041)*
Redbud Soil Company LLC.................................405 476-0429
   4217 Nw 144th Ter Oklahoma City (73134) *(G-6993)*
Redbud Woodworks..316 765-4079
   9821 Lloyd Dr Midwest City (73130) *(G-4451)*
Redding Welding LLC..580 883-4683
   42015 S 264 Rd Ringwood (73768) *(G-8091)*
Reddirt Oilfield Services....................................580 665-9321
   703 S Oliver Ave Elk City (73644) *(G-2866)*
Reddy Ice Corporation..918 682-2471
   541 N Cherokee St Muskogee (74403) *(G-4744)*
Reddy Ice Corporation..405 681-2892
   5525 Sw 29th St Oklahoma City (73179) *(G-6994)*
Reddy Ice Corporation..580 323-3080
   106 W Gary Blvd Clinton (73601) *(G-1766)*
Reddy Ice Corporation..918 836-8223
   8904 E Admiral Pl Tulsa (74115) *(G-10633)*
Redfield Refrigeration, Tecumseh Also called Farley Redfield *(G-8914)*
Redfork Energy, Tulsa Also called Red Fork USA Investments Inc *(G-10631)*
Redhawk Pressure Control LLC..........................405 605-1958
   5400 N Grand Blvd Ste 210 Oklahoma City (73112) *(G-6995)*
Redibuilt Metal Pdts & Cnstr..............................580 225-2829
   3830 W Highway 66 Elk City (73644) *(G-2867)*
Redland Resources Inc......................................405 789-7104
   6001 Nw 23rd St Oklahoma City (73127) *(G-6996)*
Redland Sheet Metal Inc....................................405 673-7107
   7500 Melrose Ln Oklahoma City (73127) *(G-6997)*
Redline Constructn Sand Dirt............................405 380-6994
   36416 Us Highway 270b Wewoka (74884) *(G-11509)*
Redline Gaskets LLC..918 845-7700
   124 Shawnee Rd Sand Springs (74063) *(G-8221)*
Redline Instruments Inc (PA).............................580 622-4745
   1091 Fletcher Rd Sulphur (73086) *(G-8841)*
Redneck Candles and Gifts................................405 492-8987
   6908 Nw Sprucewood Dr Lawton (73505) *(G-3992)*

Redneck Firearms Inc 405 650-6605
19891 Se 15th St Harrah (73045) ***(G-3384)***
Redrhino LLC 405 740-5132
547 Chippingham Ln Blanchard (73010) ***(G-733)***
Redsky Land LLC 405 470-2015
1501 Renaissance Blvd Edmond (73013) ***(G-2592)***
Redtail Industries LLC 405 933-6654
131 E Central Blvd Anadarko (73005) ***(G-206)***
Redwood Country Signs 405 596-8737
2016 N Rockwell Ave Newcastle (73065) ***(G-4837)***
Redzone Coil Tubing LLC 580 237-3663
1201 Sooner Trend Enid (73701) ***(G-3046)***
Reece Supply Company Houston 918 556-5000
3148 S 108th East Ave # 130 Tulsa (74146) ***(G-10634)***
Reece-Ats Holding LLC 918 225-1010
613 N Euchee Vly Cushing (74023) ***(G-1954)***
Reeds Power Tongs Inc 405 382-2762
1901 N Harvey Rd Seminole (74868) ***(G-8396)***
Reef Services LLC 405 756-4747
Hwy 76 N Lindsay (73052) ***(G-4080)***
Reef Services LLC 918 287-3850
876 Old Highway 99 Pawhuska (74056) ***(G-7694)***
Reel Power Industrial Inc (HQ) 405 609-3326
5101 S Council Rd Ste 100 Oklahoma City (73179) ***(G-6998)***
Reel Power International Corp (PA) 405 609-3326
5101 S Council Rd Ste 100 Oklahoma City (73179) ***(G-6999)***
Reel Power Wire & Cable Inc 918 584-1000
5101 S Council Rd Ste 100 Oklahoma City (73179) ***(G-7000)***
Refinery Supply Co Inc 918 621-1700
1104 N 105th East Ave Tulsa (74116) ***(G-10635)***
Reflection Carl Mles Phtgraphy, Edmond *Also called Reflection Foil and Ltr Press* ***(G-2593)***
Reflection Foil and Ltr Press 405 341-8660
3909 E 30th St Edmond (73013) ***(G-2593)***
Reflective Edge Screenprinting 405 917-7837
200 N Ann Arbor Ave Oklahoma City (73127) ***(G-7001)***
Refractory Anchors Inc 918 455-8485
9836 S 219th East Ave Broken Arrow (74014) ***(G-1154)***
Refrigeration Systems Division, Pryor *Also called Rae Corporation* ***(G-7988)***
Refuge Lifestyle 918 366-6650
4221 S 68th East Ave Tulsa (74145) ***(G-10636)***
Refunk My Junk Inc 405 990-0707
2520 Antelope Trl Edmond (73012) ***(G-2594)***
Regency Gas 580 487-3862
8 Miles E Of Forgan Hwy Beaver (73932) ***(G-547)***
Regency Labels Inc 405 682-3460
4303 Sw 44th St Oklahoma City (73119) ***(G-7002)***
Reggie Adudell 405 631-9002
820 Sw 23rd St Oklahoma City (73109) ***(G-7003)***
Regrid Energy LLC 405 837-8707
528 Nw 141st St Edmond (73013) ***(G-2595)***
Rehme Mfg Inc 580 658-2414
100 E Cherokee St Marlow (73055) ***(G-4240)***
Rehoboth Robes 918 357-1529
400 N Forest Ridge Blvd Broken Arrow (74014) ***(G-1155)***
Reid Communications LLC 918 285-5555
202 N Harrison Ave Cushing (74023) ***(G-1955)***
Reid Manufacturing LLC 405 606-7006
212 N Ann Arbor Ave Oklahoma City (73127) ***(G-7004)***
Reid Printing Inc 405 348-0066
3120 S Boulevard Edmond (73013) ***(G-2596)***
Reinforced Earth Company 918 379-0090
5101 Bird Creek Ave Ste A Catoosa (74015) ***(G-1349)***
Reinforcing Services Inc 918 379-0090
5101 Bird Creek Ave Catoosa (74015) ***(G-1350)***
Relay Creative Group, Tulsa *Also called Chastain Enterprises LLC* ***(G-9407)***
Relevant Products LLC 405 524-5250
407 Ne 48th St Oklahoma City (73105) ***(G-7005)***
Relf Upholstery 405 454-3295
10975 N Luther Rd Luther (73054) ***(G-4137)***
Reliable Manufacturing Corp 918 341-1966
9688 Alawhe Dr Claremore (74019) ***(G-1680)***
Reliance Mfg Solutions LLC 405 640-9660
13509 Railway Dr Oklahoma City (73114) ***(G-7006)***
Reliance Ofs 303 317-6565
2 W 2nd St Tulsa (74103) ***(G-10637)***
Reliance Oilfield Services LLC (PA) 918 392-9000
2 W 2nd St Fl 15 Tulsa (74103) ***(G-10638)***
Reliance Pressure Control 405 320-5074
4845 Se 44th St Norman (73072) ***(G-5131)***
Relyassist LLC 918 260-6517
4059 S 213th East Ave Broken Arrow (74014) ***(G-1156)***
Remote Connections Inc 918 743-3355
1809 E 11th St Tulsa (74104) ***(G-10639)***
Rempel Rock-N-Ready Mix Inc 405 275-1107
1200 N Leo Ave Shawnee (74801) ***(G-8487)***
Rempels Rock & Ready Mix, Prague *Also called Rempels Rock & Ready Mix Inc* ***(G-7934)***
Rempels Rock & Ready Mix Inc 405 567-3991
Hwy 62 W Prague (74864) ***(G-7934)***
Remwood Products, Tulsa *Also called B & P Industrial Inc* ***(G-9242)***
Remwood Products Co 918 251-8399
501 N Redbud Ave Ste G Broken Arrow (74012) ***(G-1030)***
Ren Holding Corporation (PA) 405 533-2755
5900 S Perkins Rd Stillwater (74074) ***(G-8745)***
Ren Testing Corporation 405 533-2700
5900 S Perkins Rd Stillwater (74074) ***(G-8746)***
Renal Solutions, Oklahoma City *Also called Sorb Technology Inc* ***(G-7169)***
Renavotio Infratech Inc 504 722-7402
601 S Boulder Ave Ste 600 Tulsa (74119) ***(G-10640)***
Renegade Services 580 254-2828
22154 Us Highway 270 Woodward (73801) ***(G-11628)***
Rent-A-Crane Inc 405 745-2318
8020 Sw 74th St Oklahoma City (73169) ***(G-7007)***
Rent-A-Crane of Okla Inc 405 745-2318
8020 Sw 74th St Oklahoma City (73169) ***(G-7008)***
Rental Ready 918 500-6922
1217 E Admiral Blvd Tulsa (74120) ***(G-10641)***
Rentpath LLC 918 307-8980
5125 S Garnett Rd Ste A Tulsa (74146) ***(G-10642)***
Repair Processes Inc 918 758-0863
5401 N Wood Dr Okmulgee (74447) ***(G-7525)***
Reporter Publishing Co Inc 918 789-2331
245 W 6th St Chelsea (74016) ***(G-1411)***
Republic Paperboard Co LLC 580 510-2200
8801 Sw Lee Blvd Lawton (73505) ***(G-3993)***
Reputation Services & Mfg LLC 918 437-2077
15855 E Pine St Tulsa (74116) ***(G-10643)***
Resco Enterprises Inc 918 298-0052
1917 W C St Jenks (74037) ***(G-3726)***
Rescue Lumber & Wdwkg LLC 405 650-4637
7801 Tangle Vine Dr Edmond (73034) ***(G-2597)***
Research America, Tulsa *Also called Commercial Property Research* ***(G-9476)***
Reserve Management Inc 918 227-0894
10195 S 49th West Ave Sapulpa (74066) ***(G-8307)***
Reserve Petroleum Company 405 848-7551
6801 Broadway Ext Ste 300 Oklahoma City (73116) ***(G-7009)***
Resolute Wyoming Inc 918 495-0598
7134 S Yale Ave Ste 430 Tulsa (74136) ***(G-10644)***
Resonance Inc 405 239-2800
4025 Nw 36th St Oklahoma City (73112) ***(G-7010)***
Resort Rv 580 465-4428
26 Kingfisher Rd Ardmore (73401) ***(G-349)***
Resource Development Co LLC (HQ) 248 646-2300
2930 S Yale Ave Tulsa (74114) ***(G-10645)***
Resource Mfg 405 842-0999
4334 Nw Expressway Oklahoma City (73116) ***(G-7011)***
Resource Oil and Gas LLC 405 878-7336
1421 E 45th St Shawnee (74804) ***(G-8488)***
Resource One, Tulsa *Also called Worldwide Printing & Dist Inc* ***(G-11154)***
Resource Services Inc 918 799-6174
30039 S County Road 4300 Stigler (74462) ***(G-8642)***
Resourceone Communications Inc 918 295-0112
2900 E Apache St Tulsa (74110) ***(G-10646)***
Resources Operating Company 580 237-7744
2428 Wagon Trl Enid (73703) ***(G-3047)***
Respondair UAS LLC 918 899-2113
9101 N 130th East Ave Owasso (74055) ***(G-7607)***
Response Solutions Inc 918 508-7022
5800 E Skelly Dr Ste 830 Tulsa (74135) ***(G-10647)***
Restaurant Equipment & Sup LLC 918 664-1778
9070 E 31st St Tulsa (74145) ***(G-10648)***
Resthaven & Sunset, Ponca City *Also called Bmi Management Inc* ***(G-7801)***
Reveille Energy Innovation LLC 405 577-6438
9940 W Reno Ave Oklahoma City (73127) ***(G-7012)***
Review News Co 405 354-5264
335 S Mustang Rd Ste F Yukon (73099) ***(G-11771)***
Review Printing Company Inc 580 658-6657
316 W Main St Marlow (73055) ***(G-4241)***
Rex B Benway 918 366-3626
16401 S Yale Ave Bixby (74008) ***(G-653)***
Rex Laboratories Inc 918 742-9545
1320 S Wheeling Ave Tulsa (74104) ***(G-10649)***
Rex Ross 580 835-7244
737 Tablerville Rd Eagletown (74734) ***(G-2277)***
Rex Ross Logging, Eagletown *Also called Rex Ross* ***(G-2277)***
Rexbo Energy Co 405 359-0458
819 Sunny Brook Dr Edmond (73034) ***(G-2598)***
Reynard Promotions LLC 405 793-1049
940163 S Highway 177 Wellston (74881) ***(G-11476)***
Reynolds & Sons Neon Studio 405 525-6366
1201 Nw 38th St Oklahoma City (73118) ***(G-7013)***
Reynolds Custom Woodworks 918 595-5988
9488 E Mulberry Ln Claremore (74019) ***(G-1681)***
Rfg Petro Systems LLC 941 487-7524
6724 Pat Ave Oklahoma City (73149) ***(G-7014)***
Rhinestone Cowgirl 405 564-0512
223 S Knoblock St Stillwater (74074) ***(G-8747)***
Rhinestone Cowgirl 405 387-3111
200 N Main St Newcastle (73065) ***(G-4838)***

Rhino Oil & Gas Inc 405 657-2999
22906 Crossfield Ct Edmond (73025) *(G-2599)*
Rhodes Printing 918 445-7444
207 N Broadway Coweta (74429) *(G-1896)*
Rhodes Printing 918 965-1005
1820 N Sioux Ave Claremore (74017) *(G-1682)*
Rhodes Printing Inc 918 457-7801
1106 S Muskogee Ave Tahlequah (74464) *(G-8880)*
Rhyneco, Wardville *Also called Clark Rhyne (G-11306)*
Rice Welding Inc 580 776-2584
3 Miles So 1/2 Mile E # 12 Meno (73760) *(G-4387)*
Richard B Collins 405 947-6349
3009 Cashion Pl Oklahoma City (73112) *(G-7015)*
Richard Bolusky 918 381-5694
3500 W Tacoma St Broken Arrow (74012) *(G-1031)*
Richard Brown 918 492-1991
7115 S Yale Ave Tulsa (74136) *(G-10650)*
Richard Douglas Co 405 577-6626
220 S Alliance Ct Oklahoma City (73128) *(G-7016)*
Richard Exploration Co Inc 405 840-0101
4141 Nw Expwy St Ste 343 Oklahoma City (73116) *(G-7017)*
Richard Spur Plant, Elgin *Also called Dolese Bros Co (G-2775)*
Richard Vallejos Welding Ser 405 688-0804
2144 Sw 82nd St Oklahoma City (73159) *(G-7018)*
Richard Welding 405 459-6717
240 Adams Cir Pocasset (73079) *(G-7778)*
Richards Performance Machine 918 485-6393
126 N Main St Wagoner (74467) *(G-11289)*
Richards Printing Co 405 224-8640
2200 S 29th St Chickasha (73018) *(G-1501)*
Richards Welding Service LLC 580 584-2831
667 N 4180 Rd Hugo (74743) *(G-3620)*
Richardson Wellsite Services 918 807-7105
539 Pioneer Rd Sapulpa (74066) *(G-8308)*
Richland Resources Corporation (PA) 405 732-0045
917 Cedar Lake Blvd Oklahoma City (73114) *(G-7019)*
Rick Crsslin Backhoe Dozer Svc 918 371-7956
7675 W 183rd St S Mounds (74047) *(G-4624)*
Rick Davis 918 733-4760
800 S 1st St Morris (74445) *(G-4602)*
Rick Knight 405 232-4954
1106 S Robinson Ave Oklahoma City (73109) *(G-7020)*
Rick Leaming Construction LLC 580 362-2262
4525 N Pleasant Vw Newkirk (74647) *(G-4852)*
Rick Woodten 580 786-5050
715 W Main St Duncan (73533) *(G-2167)*
Ricks Rig Service 405 619-9193
1200 S Eastern Ave Oklahoma City (73129) *(G-7021)*
Ricks Rod Reel Svc-High 405 823-7581
4901 Nw 58th St Oklahoma City (73122) *(G-7022)*
Ricks Welding 580 470-8111
615 E Willow Ave Duncan (73533) *(G-2168)*
Rico Woodworking LLC 918 743-0741
171 E 57th St Tulsa (74105) *(G-10651)*
Riddle Construction Co Inc 580 256-8109
3110 Robin Ridge Rd Woodward (73801) *(G-11629)*
Riddle Corporation 405 728-7504
6301 Paschall Ct Oklahoma City (73132) *(G-7023)*
Ride Control LLC 800 251-5932
700 N Industrial Blvd Chickasha (73018) *(G-1502)*
Ridleys Butcher Shop Inc 580 255-9330
416 W Main St Duncan (73533) *(G-2169)*
Rieger Hay & Welding 580 985-3608
Rr 1 Box 125a Manchester (73758) *(G-4169)*
Rifle Shoppe Inc 405 356-2583
870740 S Highway 177 Wellston (74881) *(G-11477)*
Rifle Tool Company 580 856-3030
W Hwy 7 Ratliff City (73481) *(G-8065)*
Rig Chasers LLC 580 254-3830
202672 E County Road 44 # 2 Woodward (73801) *(G-11630)*
Riggs Heinrich Media Inc 918 492-0660
7715 E 111th St Ste 111 Tulsa (74133) *(G-10652)*
Riggs Tag Agency, Inola *Also called Brenda Riggs (G-3652)*
Right Mix 580 704-8904
12 Sw River Bend Rd Lawton (73505) *(G-3994)*
Rightway Mfg Solutions LLC 580 252-2284
5615 N Hwy 81 Unit 100 Duncan (73533) *(G-2170)*
Rigyard Publications LLC 405 330-1456
304 Carmel Valley Way Edmond (73025) *(G-2600)*
Riley Exploration LLC 405 485-8200
29 E Reno Ave Ste 5 Oklahoma City (73104) *(G-7024)*
Riley Exploration Group LLC (PA) 405 485-8200
29 E Reno Ave Ste 5 Oklahoma City (73104) *(G-7025)*
Riley Explration - Permian LLC (PA) 405 415-8699
29 E Reno Ave Ste 500 Oklahoma City (73104) *(G-7026)*
Riley Exporation, Oklahoma City *Also called Cadence Energy Partners LLC (G-5668)*
Riley Permian Operating Co LLC 405 415-8699
29 E Reno Ave Ste 5 Oklahoma City (73104) *(G-7027)*
Rim Molded Products Co 918 438-7070
1222 N Garnett Rd Tulsa (74116) *(G-10653)*
Ring Energy Inc 918 499-3880
6555 S Lewis Ave Ste 200 Tulsa (74136) *(G-10654)*
Ringling Eagle 580 662-2221
103 E Main St Ringling (73456) *(G-8082)*
Rings Etc Fine Jewelry 405 359-7464
225 S Broadway Edmond (73034) *(G-2601)*
Ringside Productions 818 974-2673
2222 S 85th East Ave Tulsa (74129) *(G-10655)*
Rinker Materials Concrete Pipe 405 745-3404
6200 Sw 44th St Oklahoma City (73179) *(G-7028)*
Rio Vista Operating LLC 918 689-5600
120702 S 4104 Rd Eufaula (74432) *(G-3110)*
Rise Manufacturing LLC 918 994-6240
1605 E Lola St Broken Arrow (74012) *(G-1032)*
Rising M Enterprises 918 766-4235
1308 Ne H St Stigler (74462) *(G-8643)*
Rita S Nicar 580 492-4521
10956 Nw 4 Mile Rd Lawton (73507) *(G-3995)*
Ritberger Inc 918 271-3895
523 E Madison St Broken Arrow (74012) *(G-1033)*
Rival Innvtion Surfc Engrg LLC 918 978-7001
18307 S Quail Meadow Dr Claremore (74017) *(G-1683)*
River Bend Industries LLC 405 703-2758
1700 Crystal Lk Blanchard (73010) *(G-734)*
River Industries LLC 918 406-8991
12610 N Garnett Rd Collinsville (74021) *(G-1821)*
River Ridge Logging LLC 580 380-2948
929 Hoover Rd Durant (74701) *(G-2252)*
River Rock Energy LLC 405 606-7481
211 N Robinson Ave S1525 Oklahoma City (73102) *(G-7029)*
Rivers Edge Countertops Inc 405 387-2930
3066 Highway 62 Svc Rd Newcastle (73065) *(G-4839)*
Rivers Edge Countertops Inc 405 532-3180
632 Wildwood Dr Tuttle (73089) *(G-11211)*
Rivers Edge Publications 918 855-9469
4636 W 43rd St Tulsa (74107) *(G-10656)*
Riverside Laboratories Inc 918 585-3064
516 S 25th West Ave Tulsa (74127) *(G-10657)*
Riverside Machine Inc 918 445-5141
2313 W 41st St Tulsa (74107) *(G-10658)*
Riverside Machine Works, Tulsa *Also called Riverside Machine Inc (G-10658)*
Riverside Mdstream Prtners LLC 918 949-4224
6120 S Yale Ave Ste 1480 Tulsa (74136) *(G-10659)*
Riverside Operations Group LLC 918 908-9480
1700 W Albany St Ste 100 Broken Arrow (74012) *(G-1034)*
Riverside Ranch LLC (PA) 405 360-7300
2630 12th Ave Nw Norman (73069) *(G-5132)*
Rives Enterprises Inc 918 671-4099
1735 E 11th St Tulsa (74104) *(G-10660)*
Riviera Operating LLC 405 375-6065
Rr 24 Box B Kingfisher (73750) *(G-3813)*
Rjc Welding LLC 580 281-0516
186119 N 2700 Rd Temple (73568) *(G-8934)*
Rkb Woodworks 405 919-4149
10020 S Allen Dr Oklahoma City (73139) *(G-7030)*
Rkk Production Company 405 376-2223
5501 Stuart Dr Mustang (73064) *(G-4790)*
Rl Hudson, Broken Arrow *Also called RL Hudson & Company (G-1035)*
RL Hudson & Company (PA) 918 259-6600
2000 W Tacoma St Broken Arrow (74012) *(G-1035)*
RLC Holding Co Inc 580 332-3080
4 Miles N Ada Ada (74821) *(G-82)*
RLC Holding Co Inc (PA) 580 233-6000
1420 W Chestnut Ave Enid (73703) *(G-3048)*
RMH Survey LLC 918 927-8868
41755 E Highway 60 Vinita (74301) *(G-11270)*
RMR Energy, Pawhuska *Also called James A Taylor (G-7687)*
Rn Concrete Products 405 564-3020
4600 Independence Perry (73077) *(G-7743)*
Road Science LLC (HQ) 918 960-3800
6502 S Yale Ave Tulsa (74136) *(G-10661)*
Roadrunner Apparel, Oklahoma City *Also called Hendrie Resources Ltd (G-6239)*
Roadrunner Marketing, Oklahoma City *Also called Robert Smith (G-7037)*
Roadrunner Portable Buildings 918 272-7788
6835 N 115th East Ave Owasso (74055) *(G-7608)*
Roadrunner Press 405 524-6205
122 Nw 32nd St Oklahoma City (73118) *(G-7031)*
Roan Resources LLC (HQ) 405 241-2271
14701 Hrtz Qail Sprng Pkw Oklahoma City (73134) *(G-7032)*
Roan Resources, Inc., Oklahoma City *Also called Pressburg LLC (G-6891)*
Roasters Exchange, Oklahoma City *Also called Continental-Brokers & Cons Inc (G-5824)*
Robbins & Myers Inc 405 672-6793
2100 E Grand Blvd Oklahoma City (73129) *(G-7033)*
Robbins Salvage & Auto Sales 918 431-1000
23591 Highway 51 Tahlequah (74464) *(G-8881)*
Roberson Oil Co Inc 580 332-6170
201 E Cottage St Ada (74820) *(G-83)*
Roberson, David A, Ada *Also called Roberson Oil Co Inc (G-83)*

ALPHABETIC

Robert C Beard 918 534-2020
  423 E 9th St Dewey (74029) *(G-2031)*
Robert C Brooks Inc 405 478-0260
  12707 N Bryant Ave Edmond (73013) *(G-2602)*
Robert L Scott Co 405 235-5345
  101 Park Ave Ste 620 Oklahoma City (73102) *(G-7034)*
Robert M Beirute 918 299-4259
  10104 S Urbana Ave Tulsa (74137) *(G-10662)*
Robert M Cobb Oil Feld Eqp Sls, Oklahoma City Also called Robert M Cobb Oilfield Eqp Sls *(G-7035)*
Robert M Cobb Oilfield Eqp Sls 405 840-2902
  4201 S High Ave Oklahoma City (73129) *(G-7035)*
Robert Mrrson Autocad Svcs LLC 918 257-4622
  28805 S 563 Rd Afton (74331) *(G-120)*
Robert R Cantrell 580 332-9495
  11330 County Road 3560 Ada (74820) *(G-84)*
Robert S Cargile 405 732-7915
  10633 Quail Run Rd Oklahoma City (73130) *(G-7036)*
Robert Smith 405 722-5188
  5030 N May Ave Ste 315 Oklahoma City (73112) *(G-7037)*
Robert W Berry Inc (PA) 918 492-1140
  2200 S Utica Pl Ste 410 Tulsa (74114) *(G-10663)*
Roberts Step-Lite Systems Inc 800 654-8268
  8100 Sw 15th St Oklahoma City (73128) *(G-7038)*
Robertson Arms & Munitions Co 405 376-2360
  10700 Hames Blvd Mustang (73064) *(G-4791)*
Robertson-Ceco II Corporation 405 636-2010
  8600 S I 35 Service Rd Oklahoma City (73149) *(G-7039)*
Robertson-Ceco II Corporation 405 636-2010
  8600 S Interstate 35 Oklahoma City (73149) *(G-7040)*
Robertsons Hams Inc 580 276-3395
  110 Wanda St Marietta (73448) *(G-4211)*
Robinhood Stamp & Seal Co Inc 918 493-6506
  2323 E 71st St Tulsa (74136) *(G-10664)*
Robinowitz Oil Company 918 557-1544
  419 W Main St Bixby (74008) *(G-654)*
Robinson Manufacturing Co 918 251-0353
  604 S 10th St Broken Arrow (74012) *(G-1036)*
Robinson Publishing Company, Holdenville Also called Lewis Printing & Office Supply *(G-3557)*
Robinson Welding LLC 580 278-9363
  5105 Ridgeview Ave Enid (73703) *(G-3049)*
Robinson, Bill & Dayna, Allen Also called Allen Advocate *(G-132)*
Robinson, Kurt, Muskogee Also called Egret Operating Company Inc *(G-4672)*
Robison Solar Systems, Weatherford Also called Advanced Power Inc *(G-11387)*
Robs Magneto Service 918 367-5735
  144 E 1st St Tulsa (74103) *(G-10665)*
Robs Welding LLC 405 596-4906
  10304 Nw 39th St Yukon (73099) *(G-11772)*
Robyn Holdings LLC 405 722-4600
  7717 W Britton Rd Oklahoma City (73132) *(G-7041)*
Robyn Promotions & Printing, Oklahoma City Also called Robyn Holdings LLC *(G-7041)*
Rochell Machine Shop Inc 580 252-1424
  Terry Rd & Old 81 Duncan (73534) *(G-2171)*
Rock Creek Distillery LLC 580 254-1407
  1204 S Summer St Shattuck (73858) *(G-8423)*
Rock Creek Land and Energy 405 358-6090
  15212 Bay Ridge Dr Oklahoma City (73165) *(G-5313)*
Rock Creek Wreaths LLC 405 701-3421
  3025 Yosemite Dr Norman (73071) *(G-5133)*
Rock Island Exploration LLC 405 232-7077
  500 W Main St Apt 200 Oklahoma City (73102) *(G-7042)*
Rock Oil Co 918 357-1188
  27089 E 89th St S Broken Arrow (74014) *(G-1157)*
Rock Producers Inc 918 963-2111
  26496 255th Ave Shady Point (74956) *(G-8415)*
Rock Producers Inc 918 969-2100
  24275 Mine Rd Bokoshe (74930) *(G-754)*
Rock Riverer Investments, Oklahoma City Also called Robert L Scott Co *(G-7034)*
Rocket Color Copies, Oklahoma City Also called Rocket Color Inc *(G-7043)*
Rocket Color Inc 405 842-6001
  6905 N May Ave Oklahoma City (73116) *(G-7043)*
Rocket Science Labs Inc 972 454-0412
  14300 S Rockwell Ave Oklahoma City (73173) *(G-7044)*
Rockford Corporation 405 624-6722
  2805 E 6th Ave Stillwater (74074) *(G-8748)*
Rockford Energy Partner 918 592-0679
  15 E 5th St Ste 2800 Tulsa (74103) *(G-10666)*
Rockford Exploration Inc 918 582-1320
  2021 S Lewis Ave Tulsa (74104) *(G-10667)*
Rockin Dolls Denim 918 402-6151
  10759 E 122nd St N Collinsville (74021) *(G-1822)*
Rockin L-H Asparagus Farms 918 689-5086
  11800 S 4120 Rd Eufaula (74432) *(G-3111)*
Rockin Wood LLC 405 673-5171
  700 Se 59th St Oklahoma City (73129) *(G-7045)*
Rocking C Welding LLC 405 589-8903
  316 Yuhoma Dr Yukon (73099) *(G-11773)*
Rocking Chair Enterprises LLC 918 455-3744
  4328 S Dogwood Ave Broken Arrow (74011) *(G-1037)*
Rocking H Welding LLC 918 966-3882
  40824 E County Road 1240 Keota (74941) *(G-3773)*
Rocking P Sales & Services LLC 580 530-0028
  101 N Highland Ave Hobart (73651) *(G-3544)*
Rocking RB Quarter Horses LLC 405 605-9458
  8301 E Etowah Rd Noble (73068) *(G-4890)*
Rockland Oil Co 580 223-0960
  310 W Main St Ste 309 Ardmore (73401) *(G-350)*
Rockwater Energy Solutions, Springer Also called Select Energy Solutions Rw LLC *(G-8625)*
Rocky Farmers Cooperative Inc (PA) 580 666-2440
  105 N Main St Rocky (73661) *(G-8105)*
Rocky Farmers Cooperative Inc 580 674-3356
  702 S Rambo Dill City (73641) *(G-2037)*
Rocky L Emmons & Judy E Sprag 580 305-1940
  18417 Ste Hwy 54 Frederick (73542) *(G-3199)*
Rocky Mountain Prod Co LLC 405 720-2000
  7250 Nw Expressway Oklahoma City (73132) *(G-7046)*
Rocky Mtn Mdstream Hldings LLC 918 573-2000
  1 Williams Ctr Tulsa (74172) *(G-10668)*
Rocky Top Energy LLC 918 273-7444
  701 E Modoc Ave Nowata (74048) *(G-5228)*
Rocky Top Winery LLC 580 857-2869
  7569 E West 148 Allen (74825) *(G-138)*
Rod Pump Consulting LLC 918 306-2318
  2707 Schlegel 1st Cushing (74023) *(G-1956)*
Rod Pumps Inc 918 968-4369
  817 S 8th Ave Stroud (74079) *(G-8816)*
Rod Wiederstein 580 938-2998
  212 S Olive St Shattuck (73858) *(G-8424)*
Rod's Welding Service, Shattuck Also called Rod Wiederstein *(G-8424)*
Rodney Brooks Welding LLC 405 663-2256
  5138 County Road 1040 Hydro (73048) *(G-3634)*
Roff Iron & Sales Inc 580 456-7850
  7010 County Road 1650 Roff (74865) *(G-8110)*
Roger Key Inc 918 423-5420
  2600 Standard Rd Mcalester (74501) *(G-4333)*
Roger Magerus 405 364-7231
  1602 Paso De Vaca Dr Norman (73026) *(G-5134)*
Roger W Boone 580 799-0035
  11076 N 1960 Rd Elk City (73644) *(G-2868)*
Rogers Locker Plant, Oklahoma City Also called Alex Rogers *(G-5412)*
Rogers Resources Inc (PA) 580 237-7744
  2428 Wagon Trl Enid (73703) *(G-3050)*
Rogue Industrial LLC 580 832-7060
  311 W 7th St Cordell (73632) *(G-1863)*
Rohlman Welding Service Inc 405 420-4033
  5713 Nw 46th St Warr Acres (73122) *(G-11328)*
Rohm-Bolster Mfg Co LLC 405 274-6915
  8324 John Robert Dr Oklahoma City (73135) *(G-7047)*
Rolco Energy Services LLC 580 657-2602
  308 Case Cir Ardmore (73401) *(G-351)*
Roll-2-Roll Technologies LLC 405 726-0985
  1110 S Innovation Way Stillwater (74074) *(G-8749)*
Roll-Offs of America Inc 580 924-6355
  8567 Us Hwy 70 Mead (73449) *(G-4367)*
Roll-Offs USA, Mead Also called Roll-Offs of America Inc *(G-4367)*
Rolled Alloys Inc 918 594-2600
  6555 S 57th West Ave Tulsa (74131) *(G-9031)*
Rollett Mfg Inc 405 427-9707
  4101 Woodnoll St Oklahoma City (73121) *(G-7048)*
Rolling Thunder Oilfield 580 303-4587
  918 N Van Buren Ave Elk City (73644) *(G-2869)*
Romayne - Baker Oil & Gas Ltd 580 237-1626
  108 N Washington St Enid (73701) *(G-3051)*
Romine Oil & Gas Ltd 405 273-1171
  23 E 9th St Ste 223 Shawnee (74801) *(G-8489)*
Ron Griggs Backhoe & Dump 918 440-1334
  600 W 9th St Dewey (74029) *(G-2032)*
Ron Shanks Racing Enterprises 918 366-6050
  15303 E 161st St S Bixby (74008) *(G-655)*
Ron Williams 580 772-3513
  24086 E 990 Rd Weatherford (73096) *(G-11437)*
Ronnie Nevitt 918 687-5284
  1113 Fredonia St Muskogee (74403) *(G-4745)*
Rons Discount Lumber Inc 918 658-3857
  37850 Us Highway 59 Howe (74940) *(G-3599)*
Rons Welding Shop 405 352-4331
  Hwy 81 N Minco (73059) *(G-4479)*
Rooks Fabrication LLC 918 447-1990
  6500 S 39th West Ave Tulsa (74132) *(G-10669)*
Roper Product 580 795-2293
  411 Hagood Rd Lebanon (73440) *(G-4027)*
Rosa & Unis LLC 918 445-4204
  4141 S Galveston Ave Tulsa (74107) *(G-10670)*
Rose Inc 918 693-2461
  14170 W Line St Sapulpa (74066) *(G-8309)*
Rose Rock Midstream Corp 918 524-8100
  6120 S Yale Ave Ste 700 Tulsa (74136) *(G-10671)*

Rose Rock Midstream Field Svcs 918 524-7700
2 Warren Pl 6120 S Yal Tulsa (74136) *(G-10672)*
Rose Rock Midstream Oper LLC 918 524-7700
6120 S Yale Ave Ste 700 Tulsa (74136) *(G-10673)*
Rose Rock Petroleum LLC 405 212-6987
1712 Nw 195th Cir Edmond (73012) *(G-2603)*
Rose Rock Resources Inc (PA) 918 752-0511
5060 N 240 Rd Beggs (74421) *(G-559)*
Rosemon Martin LLC 918 272-7145
17892 E 101st Pl N Owasso (74055) *(G-7609)*
Roserock Creations Inc 405 209-6005
13525 S Western Ave Edmond (73025) *(G-2604)*
Roses Custom 580 252-9633
3930 Country Ests Duncan (73533) *(G-2172)*
Rosewood Designs 405 329-0600
2278 Industrial Blvd # 105 Norman (73069) *(G-5135)*
Ross C Byrd III Signs Designs, Muskogee *Also called Byrd Signs & Designs (G-4656)*
Ross Dub Company Inc 405 495-3611
6300 Melrose Ln Oklahoma City (73127) *(G-7049)*
Ross Fabrication & Detailing 405 356-9955
98053 S Hwy 177 Wellston (74881) *(G-11478)*
Ross Honey Co 405 352-4125
1309 Sw 3rd St Minco (73059) *(G-4480)*
Ross Printing LLC 405 947-0099
4222 N May Ave Oklahoma City (73112) *(G-7050)*
Rosson Wheel Service, Muskogee *Also called Spencer L Rosson (G-4750)*
Rotational Technologies Inc 918 343-1350
915 W Blue Starr Dr Claremore (74017) *(G-1684)*
Rotek, Claremore *Also called Rotational Technologies Inc (G-1684)*
Rotert Weld & Fab LLC 918 671-2170
1565 N 166th East Ave Tulsa (74116) *(G-10674)*
Roth Manufacturing Co Inc (PA) 918 743-4477
1379 E 45th St Tulsa (74105) *(G-10675)*
Rotocolor Inc 510 785-7686
7221 S Gary Pl Tulsa (74136) *(G-10676)*
Rotork Valvekits Inc 918 259-8100
4433 W 49th St Ste D Tulsa (74107) *(G-10677)*
Rotork Valvekits USA, Tulsa *Also called Rotork Valvekits Inc (G-10677)*
Rougeot Oil & Gas Corp 918 288-2022
8177 S Harvard Ave # 734 Tulsa (74137) *(G-10678)*
Round House Manufacturing LLC 405 273-0510
1 American Way Shawnee (74804) *(G-8490)*
Round House Overalls, Shawnee *Also called Round House Manufacturing LLC (G-8490)*
Round Springs Water Co LLC 918 253-8188
41624 S 540 Rd Spavinaw (74366) *(G-8592)*
Rovill Biodiesel Solution LLC 580 339-6815
220 Ridgecrest Dr Apt 80 Elk City (73644) *(G-2870)*
Rowdy Hanger 918 804-7375
2218 W Houston St Broken Arrow (74012) *(G-1038)*
Rowe Wireline Services LLC 580 541-5086
3801 Whippoorwill Ln Enid (73703) *(G-3052)*
Rowlands Proc & Cattle Co 580 924-2560
524 Lee Ave Durant (74701) *(G-2253)*
Rowmark LLC 405 787-4542
6100 W Reno Ave Oklahoma City (73127) *(G-7051)*
Rox Exploration Inc 405 329-0009
2416 Palmer Cir Norman (73069) *(G-5136)*
Roxtec Inc (HQ) 918 254-9872
10127 E Admiral Pl Tulsa (74116) *(G-10679)*
Roy Hopson Logging, Eagletown *Also called James Roy Hopson (G-2276)*
Roy Putnam 918 333-5642
2733 Oxford Ct Bartlesville (74006) *(G-523)*
Roy Slagel Keno 580 585-0283
13883 Ne Townley Rd Elgin (73538) *(G-2779)*
Royal Cup Inc 405 943-6088
901 Enterprise Ave Ste 8a Oklahoma City (73128) *(G-7052)*
Royal Filter Manufacturing Co 405 224-0229
4327 S 4th St Chickasha (73018) *(G-1503)*
Royal Ironworks 580 492-4265
14801 Metro Plaza Blvd # 7 Edmond (73013) *(G-2605)*
Royal Prestige Jealpa 405 602-5371
2612 Sw 44th St Oklahoma City (73119) *(G-7053)*
Royal Printing & Copy Center, Broken Arrow *Also called B & L Printing Inc (G-839)*
Royal Printing Co Inc 405 235-8581
1830 Nw 4th Dr Oklahoma City (73106) *(G-7054)*
Royal Sign & Graphic Inc 918 682-6151
103 Kaad St Muskogee (74401) *(G-4746)*
Royal Signs LLC 918 507-3303
7177 Us Highway 81 Hennessey (73742) *(G-3483)*
Royal Toga Industries LLC 405 641-1643
10355 S 261st East Ave Broken Arrow (74014) *(G-1158)*
Royal Vista Plastics, Tulsa *Also called W J L S Inc (G-11088)*
Royalok Royalty LLC 405 721-9771
6601 Briarcreek Dr Oklahoma City (73162) *(G-7055)*
Royalty Fabrication LLC 405 257-6654
12828 Ns 3650 Wewoka (74884) *(G-11510)*
Royce Dublin Inc 219 324-7995
4509 N Classen Blvd # 200 Oklahoma City (73118) *(G-7056)*
Roye Realty & Developing Inc 918 967-4888
603 W Main St Stigler (74462) *(G-8644)*
Rp Power LLC 918 960-6000
1111 N 105th East Ave Tulsa (74116) *(G-10680)*
Rp Window Washing 405 341-0065
625 Oak Springs Dr Edmond (73034) *(G-2606)*
Rpc Inc 580 225-0843
723 S Merritt Rd Elk City (73644) *(G-2871)*
RPI, Tulsa *Also called Red Devil Incorporated (G-10629)*
RPI, Okmulgee *Also called Repair Processes Inc (G-7525)*
Rs Fuel LLC 405 748-4277
3300 W Memorial Rd Oklahoma City (73120) *(G-7057)*
RSC Scientific Lab Products, Tulsa *Also called Refinery Supply Co Inc (G-10635)*
Rsga Incorporated 918 978-6800
10496 S 86th East Ave Tulsa (74133) *(G-10681)*
Rt Manufacturing Concepts LLC 405 388-3999
13233 Se 104th St Oklahoma City (73165) *(G-5314)*
Rt Manufacturing LLC 405 222-7180
501 W Michigan Ave Chickasha (73018) *(G-1504)*
Rta Systems Incorporated (PA) 405 388-6802
14260 Whippoorwill Vis Choctaw (73020) *(G-1554)*
Rtpr LLC 877 787-7180
129 W 1st St Ste A Edmond (73003) *(G-2607)*
RTS Energy Services LLC 432 617-2243
14201 Caliber Dr Ste 300 Oklahoma City (73134) *(G-7058)*
Rubber & Gasket Co Amer Inc 918 249-2069
1751 N Indianwood Ave Broken Arrow (74012) *(G-1039)*
Rubber Mold Company 405 673-7177
6200 S Bryant Ave Oklahoma City (73149) *(G-7059)*
Ruby Industrial Tech LLC 580 223-9301
2601 Crossroads Dr Ardmore (73401) *(G-352)*
Ruffel Lance Oil & Gas Corp 405 239-7036
210 Park Ave Ste 2150 Oklahoma City (73102) *(G-7060)*
Rufnex Oilfield Services LLC 405 741-8322
3120 S Meridian Ave Oklahoma City (73119) *(G-7061)*
Rugged Roustabout LLC 918 225-0700
740384 S 3480 Rd Cushing (74023) *(G-1957)*
Rupp Drilling Inc 580 336-4717
1701 Parklane St Perry (73077) *(G-7744)*
Rupture Pin Technology 405 789-1884
8230 Sw 8th St Oklahoma City (73128) *(G-7062)*
Rusco Plastics 580 234-1596
3125 Chisholm Trl Enid (73701) *(G-3053)*
Rush Springs Gazette 580 476-2525
220 W Blakely St Rush Springs (73082) *(G-8125)*
Russelectric Inc 918 251-7877
1215 E Houston St Broken Arrow (74012) *(G-1040)*
Russell Baker Racing Engines 918 533-3825
9295 S 490 Rd Miami (74354) *(G-4429)*
Russell Chemical Sales & Svc 580 234-2100
901 Sooner Trend Enid (73701) *(G-3054)*
Russell Oil Inc 405 752-7600
904 Nw 139th Street Pkwy Edmond (73013) *(G-2608)*
Russell Publishing Company 405 665-4333
40752 Highway 29 Wynnewood (73098) *(G-11672)*
Russell Sales, Tulsa *Also called Gas Products Inc (G-9804)*
Russell W Mackey 580 571-7595
Rr 1 Box 17 Gage (73843) *(G-3211)*
Russells Machine and Fab LLC 405 742-6818
133 S Stallard St Stillwater (74074) *(G-8750)*
Russells Welding Inc 918 245-7395
7756 Charles Page Blvd Tulsa (74127) *(G-10682)*
Rustic Rehab 918 314-6647
3633 Us Highway 59 Grove (74344) *(G-3287)*
Rustin Concrete, Durant *Also called H C Rustin Corporation (G-2235)*
Rusty Nail Winery 580 622-8466
218 W Muskogee Ave Sulphur (73086) *(G-8842)*
Rusty Rooster Metal 918 290-9113
2023 Briarwood St Stroud (74079) *(G-8817)*
Rusty's Ornamental Iron, Co, Lawton *Also called Lawton Window Co Inc (G-3962)*
Rustys Welding & Repair 580 526-3611
Old Hgwy 66 Erick (73645) *(G-3092)*
Rutherford Lterary Group L L C 405 623-9031
1205 S Air Depot Blvd # 135 Midwest City (73110) *(G-4452)*
Ruttman Printing, Mooreland *Also called CSC Inc (G-4587)*
Ruttman Printing, Mooreland *Also called CSC Inc (G-4588)*
Rv Smart Products LLC 575 513-1712
14759 S Grant St Bixby (74008) *(G-656)*
Rv Station Ltd 888 466-1384
411 Sherrard St Colbert (74733) *(G-1786)*
Rva 405 608-0744
13904 Quailbrook Dr Oklahoma City (73134) *(G-7063)*
Rwdesign Publishing 918 924-8865
828 W Midway St Broken Arrow (74012) *(G-1041)*
Ryan Manufacturing Inc 918 482-6512
19212 Oklahoma 104 Haskell (74436) *(G-3400)*
S & H Electric Motor Service 580 924-3514
1903 W Arkansas St Durant (74701) *(G-2254)*

ALPHABETIC

S & H Tank Service Inc 405 756-3121
103 W Cherokee St Lindsay (73052) ***(G-4081)***
S & H Tank Service of Oklahoma 405 756-3121
Hwy 76 N Lindsay (73052) ***(G-4082)***
S & H Trailer, Madill *Also called Jbw Ventures LLC* ***(G-4152)***
S & J Machine Inc 580 623-8130
E On Hwy 33 Watonga (73772) ***(G-11349)***
S & S Farm Center 405 273-6907
302 S Beard Ave Shawnee (74801) ***(G-8491)***
S & S Foods Inc 405 256-6557
1209 E Highline Ln Mustang (73064) ***(G-4792)***
S & S Promotions Inc 405 631-6516
1717 S Pennsylvania Ave Oklahoma City (73108) ***(G-7064)***
S & S Textile Inc 405 632-9928
2400 S Western Ave Oklahoma City (73109) ***(G-7065)***
S & S Time Corporation 918 437-3572
8909 E 21st St Tulsa (74129) ***(G-10683)***
S & S Watches & Clocks, Tulsa *Also called S & S Time Corporation* ***(G-10683)***
S & S Welding LLC 405 496-1452
10761 Juniper St Hinton (73047) ***(G-3536)***
S & S Woodworks Inc 405 627-8195
2417 Horse Trail Rd Edmond (73012) ***(G-2609)***
S & T Mfg Co (PA) 918 234-4151
17411 E Pine St Tulsa (74116) ***(G-10684)***
S & T Rose Inc 580 657-4906
192 Rounsaville Ave Lone Grove (73443) ***(G-4120)***
S and J Foods LLC 580 337-6360
412 Main St Bessie (73622) ***(G-570)***
S and W Embroidery 580 654-2929
26 W Main St Carnegie (73015) ***(G-1278)***
S C S, Catoosa *Also called Screw Compression Systems Inc* ***(G-1351)***
S Coker Custom Woodworks 918 638-3443
731 W Freeport St Broken Arrow (74012) ***(G-1042)***
S E & M Monogramming 405 377-9677
906 S Main St Stillwater (74074) ***(G-8751)***
S E A Y Manufacturing LLC 405 454-2328
20747 Prairie Hills Dr Harrah (73045) ***(G-3385)***
S K Warren Resourses LLC 918 491-5900
6585 S Yale Ave Ste 900 Tulsa (74136) ***(G-10685)***
S Kat Embroidery & Quilting 405 200-6283
3119 S 9th St Chickasha (73018) ***(G-1505)***
S M Sadler Inc 918 743-1048
1423 E 41st St Tulsa (74105) ***(G-10686)***
S M T Valve LLC 405 512-4523
405 Sw 145th St Moore (73170) ***(G-4561)***
S R G, Tulsa *Also called Shielding Resources Group* ***(G-10746)***
S S & L Oil and Gas Properties 405 603-6996
5700 Nw 135th St Ste 200 Oklahoma City (73142) ***(G-7066)***
S S Design Co 918 427-3230
420 W Ray Fine Blvd Roland (74954) ***(G-8113)***
S T S, Tulsa *Also called Safety Training Systems Inc* ***(G-10688)***
S U M Professional, Durham *Also called Sum Professionals Inc* ***(G-2273)***
S&F Welding and Mfg LLC 580 341-0790
22406 E 1430 Rd Hobart (73651) ***(G-3545)***
S&H Tank Service of Oklahoma, Lindsay *Also called S & H Tank Service Inc* ***(G-4081)***
S&J Manufacturing Inc 918 636-1224
1898 S Osage St Skiatook (74070) ***(G-8567)***
S&S Canvas & Upholstery 580 231-2587
10510 Highway 58 Ringwood (73768) ***(G-8092)***
S&S Custom Wood Moldings LLC (PA) 214 995-8710
14625 S Grant St Bixby (74008) ***(G-657)***
S&S Fabrication 918 447-0447
9635 W 71st St Tulsa (74131) ***(G-9032)***
S&S Printing, Shawnee *Also called Suggs Orel* ***(G-8505)***
S&S Professional Polishing LLC 405 631-7087
129 Se 27th St Oklahoma City (73129) ***(G-7067)***
S&S Star Operating LLC 817 676-1638
13182 N Macarthur Blvd Oklahoma City (73142) ***(G-7068)***
S&S&d Trucking LLC 405 365-3535
6128 Se 86th St Oklahoma City (73135) ***(G-7069)***
S&W Welding and Fabrication 918 219-2565
311 N 3rd St Medford (73759) ***(G-4369)***
S-T Magi 918 358-2312
53195 S 36700 Rd Cleveland (74020) ***(G-1733)***
S.B.c, Tulsa *Also called Skinner Brothers Company Inc* ***(G-10771)***
S4f Inc 888 390-2224
4804 S 194th East Ave Broken Arrow (74014) ***(G-1159)***
Saan World LLC 405 494-1282
2324 N Macarthur Blvd Oklahoma City (73127) ***(G-7070)***
Saber Industries 405 382-3975
2601 Nw Expressway Oklahoma City (73112) ***(G-7071)***
Sable Exploration, Broken Arrow *Also called Gas Development Corporation* ***(G-917)***
Safe Child IDS, Norman *Also called Biometric Identification Syste* ***(G-4934)***
Safe Harbor Docks Inc 918 376-2756
302 E 5th Ave Owasso (74055) ***(G-7610)***
Safe Harbor Products LLC 918 376-2756
7845 E 86th St N Owasso (74055) ***(G-7611)***
Safe Shed 580 759-3456
12482 Highway 177 Stratford (74872) ***(G-8807)***
Safeco Filter Products Inc 918 455-0100
6440 S 57th West Ave Tulsa (74131) ***(G-9033)***
Safeco Manufacturing Inc 918 455-0100
21200 E 91st St S Broken Arrow (74014) ***(G-1160)***
Safetac Publishing LLC 559 640-7233
1209 S Frankfort Ave 200a Tulsa (74120) ***(G-10687)***
Safety Plus USA LLC 580 622-4796
1091 Fletcher Rd Sulphur (73086) ***(G-8843)***
Safety Training Systems Inc 918 665-0125
7373 E 38th St Tulsa (74145) ***(G-10688)***
Safetyco LLC 405 603-3306
3200 N May Ave Ste 112 Oklahoma City (73112) ***(G-7072)***
Safran Vntltion Systems Okla I 405 382-0731
12037 N Highway 99 Seminole (74868) ***(G-8397)***
Saga Card Co Inc 918 967-0333
1707 N Broadway St Stigler (74462) ***(G-8645)***
Sage Brush Junction 580 227-3434
15154 Highway 60 Fairview (73737) ***(G-3150)***
Sage Natural Resources LLC 940 539-2225
6100 S Yale Ave Ste 900 Tulsa (74136) ***(G-10689)***
Sage Premium Denim Bar 405 288-1503
2538 S Ladd Ave Goldsby (73093) ***(G-3246)***
Sagebrush Building Systems, Tulsa *Also called Ventaire LLC* ***(G-11070)***
Sagebrush Pipeline LLC 405 753-5500
1601 Nw Expressway Oklahoma City (73118) ***(G-7073)***
Sailing Horse Enterprises LLC 918 618-4824
412887 Highway 9 Eufaula (74432) ***(G-3112)***
Saint Louis Well Service Inc 405 289-3314
1 Main St Saint Louis (74866) ***(G-8132)***
Salamander Games Inc 405 633-2725
10805 Nw 118th Pl Yukon (73099) ***(G-11774)***
Salina Journal 785 822-1470
17214 E 119th St N Collinsville (74021) ***(G-1823)***
Sallee Meat Processing Inc 405 282-1241
7901 S Sooner Rd Guthrie (73044) ***(G-3336)***
Sallee Oil Corp 918 371-2290
2115 W Broadway St Collinsville (74021) ***(G-1824)***
Salt Soothers LLC (PA) 405 201-2020
2702 Princeton Ave Edmond (73034) ***(G-2610)***
Saltfork Service 580 716-1022
8560 S Ranch Dr Ponca City (74601) ***(G-7870)***
Saltus Technologies LLC 918 392-3900
907 S Detroit Ave Ste 820 Tulsa (74120) ***(G-10690)***
Sam Dee Custom Draperies 405 631-6128
6700 Sears Ter Oklahoma City (73149) ***(G-7074)***
Sam S Welding 580 470-5725
274255 E 1800 Rd Comanche (73529) ***(G-1845)***
Sam W Mays Jr 918 382-9170
427 S Boston Ave Ste 1207 Tulsa (74103) ***(G-10691)***
Sam Yeoman 918 783-5608
287 W Main St Big Cabin (74332) ***(G-605)***
Samco Anchors 806 435-6870
22035 Highway 73 Clinton (73601) ***(G-1767)***
Samco Polishing Inc 918 789-5541
Ew 34 W Of Hwy 66 Chelsea (74016) ***(G-1412)***
Samedan Oil Corp 580 856-3705
3730 Samedan Rd Ratliff City (73481) ***(G-8066)***
Samhill LLC 580 761-1255
312 S 3rd St Tonkawa (74653) ***(G-8981)***
Sammys Signs LLC 405 320-1156
925 Vermont St Chickasha (73018) ***(G-1506)***
Sampson Brothers Inc 580 994-2464
822 S Laird St Mooreland (73852) ***(G-4594)***
Sams Well Service Inc 580 762-6355
1216 E Hartford Ave 1b Ponca City (74601) ***(G-7871)***
Samson Contour, Tulsa *Also called Samson Resources Company* ***(G-10696)***
Samson Energy Company LLC (PA) 918 879-0279
110 W 7th St Ste 2000 Tulsa (74119) ***(G-10692)***
Samson Exploration LLC 918 879-0279
110 W 7th St Ste 2000 Tulsa (74119) ***(G-10693)***
Samson Investment Company (HQ) 918 583-1791
2 W 2nd St Ste 1500 Tulsa (74103) ***(G-10694)***
Samson Natural Gas Company 918 583-1791
2 W 2nd St Ste 1500 Tulsa (74103) ***(G-10695)***
Samson Production Services, Tulsa *Also called Samson Natural Gas Company* ***(G-10695)***
Samson Publishing Company LLC 918 344-7416
11024 Ferguson Rd Beggs (74421) ***(G-560)***
Samson Resources Company (HQ) 918 583-1791
2 W 2nd St Ste 1500 Tulsa (74103) ***(G-10696)***
Samson Resources Company 580 225-4272
320 Industrial Pkwy Elk City (73644) ***(G-2872)***
Samson Resources Corporation (PA) 918 591-1791
15 E 5th St Ste 1000 Tulsa (74103) ***(G-10697)***
Samson Resources II LLC 918 591-1791
15 E 5th St Ste 1000 Tulsa (74103) ***(G-10698)***
Samson Resources II Opco LLC 918 591-1791
15 E 5th St Ste 1000 Tulsa (74103) ***(G-10699)***
Samson-International Ltd (HQ) 918 583-1791
2 W 2nd St Ste 1800 Tulsa (74103) ***(G-10700)***

Samuels Jewelrey L L C...918 241-6436
1138 E Charles Page Blvd Sand Springs (74063) ***(G-8222)***
Samurai Equipment LLC...918 878-7715
15627 E Pine St Tulsa (74116) ***(G-10701)***
Samut Welding, Fletcher *Also called John Samut-Tagliaferro* ***(G-3163)***
San Juan Pools of Oklahoma...918 582-8169
1518 E 5th Ct Tulsa (74120) ***(G-10702)***
San-Dee's Custom Draperies, Oklahoma City *Also called Sam Dee Custom Draperies* ***(G-7074)***
Sanchez Cnstr & Rmdlg LLC...405 443-8324
101 S 8th Ave Purcell (73080) ***(G-8018)***
Sanco Enterprises Inc (PA)...405 634-2120
1032 Sw 22nd St Oklahoma City (73109) ***(G-7075)***
Sanco Products Inc...405 634-2120
1032 Sw 22nd St Oklahoma City (73109) ***(G-7076)***
Sand Creek Custom Cabinets LLC...580 822-1269
314 N 4th Ave Fairview (73737) ***(G-3151)***
Sand Hill Vineyards LLC...405 760-1268
12767 N Courtney Rd Calumet (73014) ***(G-1248)***
Sand Point LLC...405 728-2111
5909 Nw Expressway # 540 Oklahoma City (73132) ***(G-7077)***
Sand Resources LLC (PA)...405 573-0242
3334 W Main St Pmb 154 Norman (73072) ***(G-5137)***
Sand Run LLC...918 296-3205
3328 E 99th St Tulsa (74137) ***(G-10703)***
Sand Springs Leader, Sand Springs *Also called Berkshire Hathaway Inc* ***(G-8166)***
Sand Tech Screening and EMB...918 458-0312
120 N Water Ave Tahlequah (74464) ***(G-8882)***
Sander Sporting Gds & Atvs LLC...580 922-4930
610 N Main St Seiling (73663) ***(G-8351)***
Sanders Electric...405 377-1691
3503 N Park Dr Stillwater (74075) ***(G-8752)***
Sanders Laboratories Inc...405 598-2131
402 W Highland St Tecumseh (74873) ***(G-8926)***
Sanders Sawmill & Forest Pdts...405 799-0899
3020 N Eastern Ave Moore (73160) ***(G-4562)***
Sanderson Custom Woodworks...918 361-1921
112 N 46th West Ave Tulsa (74127) ***(G-10704)***
Sanderson Signs, Oklahoma City *Also called Claude V Sanderson Prop* ***(G-5780)***
Sandman Sports...918 272-0862
11809 E 81st St N Owasso (74055) ***(G-7612)***
Sandollar Exploration Co LLC...405 513-7715
2600 Still Meadow Rd Edmond (73013) ***(G-2611)***
Sandra Crow...580 588-2321
45200 County Street 2540 Apache (73006) ***(G-222)***
Sandridge Co2 LLC...405 429-5500
123 Robert S Kerr Ave Oklahoma City (73102) ***(G-7078)***
Sandridge Energy Inc...580 430-4500
2300 E Oklahoma Blvd Alva (73717) ***(G-191)***
Sandridge Energy Inc...405 354-2727
410 Maple St Yukon (73099) ***(G-11775)***
Sandridge Energy Inc (PA)...405 429-5500
123 Robert S Kerr Ave Oklahoma City (73102) ***(G-7079)***
Sandridge Exploration Prod LLC...405 429-5734
123 Robert S Kerr Ave Oklahoma City (73102) ***(G-7080)***
Sandridge Offshore LLC...405 429-5500
1601 Nw Expwy St Ste 1600 Oklahoma City (73118) ***(G-7081)***
Sandridge Operating Company...405 753-5500
123 Robert S Kerr Ave Oklahoma City (73102) ***(G-7082)***
Sands Weld and Fab Inc (PA)...918 419-2222
7905 W 18th St Tulsa (74127) ***(G-10705)***
Sandstar Custom Cabinets LLC...918 456-2964
419 E Fuller St Tahlequah (74464) ***(G-8883)***
Sandstone Enrgy Acqstions Corp...405 239-2150
101 N Robinson Ave # 810 Oklahoma City (73102) ***(G-7083)***
Sandy Childress Inc...405 748-4949
14709 Glenmark Dr Edmond (73013) ***(G-2612)***
Sandy Creek Millworks Inc...405 288-0670
5475 Se 12th Ave Washington (73093) ***(G-11336)***
Sandy Petroleum Inc...405 273-9289
19109 Highway 102 Shawnee (74801) ***(G-8492)***
Sanford Brothers Co Inc...918 665-7358
3801 S 79th East Ave Tulsa (74145) ***(G-10706)***
Sanguine Gas Exploration LLC...405 285-1904
3404 E 2nd St Edmond (73034) ***(G-2613)***
Sanguine Ltd...918 494-6070
110 W 7th St Ste 2700 Tulsa (74119) ***(G-10707)***
Santana Inc...405 826-8817
13140 Eastvalley Rd Oklahoma City (73170) ***(G-5315)***
Sapulpa Daily Herald, Sapulpa *Also called Cnhi LLC* ***(G-8260)***
Sara Oil & Gas Inc...405 721-2117
6016 Kingsbridge Dr Oklahoma City (73162) ***(G-7084)***
Sara Smith Inc...918 272-3076
8254 N 128th East Ave Owasso (74055) ***(G-7613)***
Sarduccis Metal Works Inc...918 694-3466
8820 S 33rd West Ave Tulsa (74132) ***(G-10708)***
Sariel Inc...918 855-1400
7723 S Yale Ave Apt 206 Tulsa (74136) ***(G-10709)***
Sarvam Solutions Corporation...918 346-9502
6105 Nowata Rd 4 Bartlesville (74006) ***(G-524)***
Sasco Inc...405 670-3230
2101 S Eastern Ave Oklahoma City (73129) ***(G-7085)***
Sasco Rental Tools and Mch Sp, Oklahoma City *Also called Sasco Inc* ***(G-7085)***
Sashay Corporate Services LLC...918 664-2507
6915 E 38th St Tulsa (74145) ***(G-10710)***
Saskas Sweets...580 772-3476
501 E Main St Weatherford (73096) ***(G-11438)***
Satin Siren LLC...918 803-6351
4215 S 440 Pryor (74361) ***(G-7990)***
Satterlee Teepees...405 255-6642
304 S Bristow Ave Moore (73160) ***(G-4563)***
Satterlee, Louis, Moore *Also called Satterlee Teepees* ***(G-4563)***
Satterwhite Machine Shop...580 653-2821
2288 Hereford Rd Springer (73458) ***(G-8624)***
Saturn Land Co Inc...405 275-4406
624 W Independence St # 107 Shawnee (74804) ***(G-8493)***
Saunders Industries LLC...405 728-3555
8401 Mantle Ave Oklahoma City (73132) ***(G-7086)***
Sav-On Printing & Signs, Owasso *Also called Felkins Enterprises LLC* ***(G-7568)***
Savage Equipment Incorporated...580 795-3394
1020 N Industrial Rd Madill (73446) ***(G-4162)***
Savoy Leather LLC...405 786-2296
110027 Us Highway 75 S Weleetka (74880) ***(G-11465)***
Saw Swan Service Inc...918 249-3821
2200 N Yellowood Ave Broken Arrow (74012) ***(G-1043)***
Sawdust Ltd...918 809-3456
509 N Walnut Ave Ste A Broken Arrow (74012) ***(G-1044)***
Sawyer Manufacturing Company...918 834-2550
7799 S Regency Dr Tulsa (74131) ***(G-9034)***
Sawyer Plant, Sawyer *Also called Martin Marietta Materials Inc* ***(G-8336)***
Saxet Energy...405 752-9544
4205 Nw 146th Ter Oklahoma City (73134) ***(G-7087)***
Sayre Record...580 928-5540
112 E Main St Sayre (73662) ***(G-8345)***
Sb Consulting LLC...405 926-7177
5135 Sw 29th St Oklahoma City (73179) ***(G-7088)***
Sb Directional Services, Oklahoma City *Also called Sb Consulting LLC* ***(G-7088)***
Sb Wholesale, Moore *Also called Andre Anderson* ***(G-4490)***
SBS Industries...918 749-8221
191 S 122nd East Ave Tulsa (74128) ***(G-10711)***
SBS Industries LLC (HQ)...918 836-7756
10541 E Ute St Tulsa (74116) ***(G-10712)***
SC Candles...469 855-2823
13314 E 89th St N Owasso (74055) ***(G-7614)***
Scan To...405 413-8015
353 E Main St Yukon (73099) ***(G-11776)***
Scarab Woodworking LLC...405 612-2111
7213 N Western Rd Stillwater (74075) ***(G-8753)***
Scare Innovations, Bokchito *Also called Sign Innovations Inc* ***(G-751)***
Scents In Soy Naturals...918 269-8322
105 E Main St Jenks (74037) ***(G-3727)***
Scepter Manufacturing LLC...918 544-2222
404 26th Ave Nw Miami (74354) ***(G-4430)***
Scfm Inc...918 663-1309
3701 S Maybelle Ave Tulsa (74107) ***(G-10713)***
Schatz Publishing Group LLC...580 628-4607
11950 W Highland Ave Blackwell (74631) ***(G-690)***
Schatz Strategy Group, Blackwell *Also called Schatz Publishing Group LLC* ***(G-690)***
Schlumberger Technology Corp...405 789-1515
10546 Nw 10th St Oklahoma City (73127) ***(G-7089)***
Schlumberger Technology Corp...405 422-8700
560 Jensen Rd W El Reno (73036) ***(G-2753)***
Schlumberger Technology Corp...580 762-2481
1405 N Waverly St Ponca City (74601) ***(G-7872)***
Schlumberger Technology Corp...405 942-0002
5200 W I 40 Service Rd Oklahoma City (73128) ***(G-7090)***
Schlumberger Technology Corp...918 661-2000
509 W Hensley Blvd Bartlesville (74003) ***(G-525)***
Schlumberger Technology Corp...918 584-6651
525 S Main St Ste 1000 Tulsa (74103) ***(G-10714)***
Schlumberger Technology Corp...405 306-8244
2901 Pole Rd Moore (73160) ***(G-4564)***
Schlumberger Technology Corp...580 252-3355
3445 Us 81 Duncan (73533) ***(G-2173)***
Schlumberger Technology Corp...580 774-7557
1620 N Airport Rd Weatherford (73096) ***(G-11439)***
Schlumberger Technology Corp...580 225-0730
560 Jensen Rd W El Reno (73036) ***(G-2754)***
Schlumberger Technology Corp...918 247-1300
16879 W 141st St S Kellyville (74039) ***(G-3767)***
Schlumberger Technology Corp...405 682-2284
10546 Nw 10th St Yukon (73099) ***(G-11777)***
Schmidt Farms At Strlng Ridge...580 919-2111
133 Ne Grandview St Fletcher (73541) ***(G-3167)***
Schmoldt Engineering Services...918 336-1221
526 S Seminole Ave Bartlesville (74003) ***(G-526)***
Schock Manufacturing LLC...918 609-3600
6901 N 115th East Ave Owasso (74055) ***(G-7615)***

ALPHABETIC

Schoeller Bleckman Energy 405 672-4407
1901 Se 22nd St Oklahoma City (73129) *(G-7091)*
Schones Butcher Shop & Market 580 472-3300
Old Hwy 66 Canute (73626) *(G-1270)*
Schoolware Inc 580 745-9100
2912 Enterprise Dr Ste C1 Durant (74701) *(G-2255)*
Schultz Roof Truss Inc 405 364-6530
1037 W Adkins Hill Rd Norman (73072) *(G-5138)*
Schuman Publishing Company 918 744-6205
1609 S Boston Ave Tulsa (74119) *(G-10715)*
Schwarz Asphalt LLC 405 789-7203
8251 W Reno Ave Oklahoma City (73127) *(G-7092)*
Schwarz Ready Mix, Yukon Also called Srm Inc *(G-11787)*
Schwarz Ready Mix, Yukon Also called M P Ready Mix Inc *(G-11743)*
Schwarz Ready Mix of Okc 405 354-6671
1400 Holly Ave Yukon (73099) *(G-11778)*
Schwarz Sand 405 789-7914
7475 Sw 15th St Oklahoma City (73128) *(G-7093)*
Schweitzer Gypsum & Lime (PA) 405 263-7967
21139 N Calumet Rd Okarche (73762) *(G-5251)*
Scientific Drilling Intl 405 787-3663
11220 Nw 10th St Yukon (73099) *(G-11779)*
Scientific Drilling Intl Inc 405 787-3663
11220 Nw 10th St Yukon (73099) *(G-11780)*
Scipio Creek Livestock Feed, McAlester Also called Diane Barcheers *(G-4293)*
Scissor Tail Custom Holster 405 595-6315
1501 Morland Ave Norman (73071) *(G-5139)*
Scissortail Distillery LLC 405 326-5466
2318 N Moore Ave Moore (73160) *(G-4565)*
Scissortail Energy LLC (HQ) 918 588-5000
8811 S Yale Ave Ste 200 Tulsa (74137) *(G-10716)*
Scissortail Energy LLC 918 968-0422
222 S Allied Rd Stroud (74079) *(G-8818)*
Scissortail Graphics Inc 580 255-2914
117 S 10th St Duncan (73533) *(G-2174)*
Scissortail Printing, Duncan Also called Scissortail Graphics Inc *(G-2174)*
Scissortail Tees 405 706-6371
8000 S Shields Blvd Oklahoma City (73149) *(G-7094)*
Scoggins Production Co, Cleo Springs Also called Tim Scoggins *(G-1712)*
Scoozies Coneys & Frz Custard 918 396-1500
1529 W Rogers Blvd Ste A Skiatook (74070) *(G-8568)*
Scorpion Pump and Indus LLC 785 285-1421
37515 New Hope Rd Tecumseh (74873) *(G-8927)*
Scott Craig Consulting LLC 580 571-4199
203476 E 720 Rd Leedey (73654) *(G-4031)*
Scott Greer Sales Inc 405 670-4654
1818 Se 22nd St Oklahoma City (73129) *(G-7095)*
Scott Manufacturing 405 949-2728
900 E Grand Blvd Oklahoma City (73129) *(G-7096)*
Scott Manufacturing of Ky 405 949-2728
900 E Grand Blvd Oklahoma City (73129) *(G-7097)*
Scott Sabolich Prosthetics & R (PA) 405 841-6800
10201 Broadway Ext Oklahoma City (73114) *(G-7098)*
Scotts Printing & Copying Inc 405 236-0821
801 N Western Ave Oklahoma City (73106) *(G-7099)*
Scotts Wldg & Fabrication LLC 580 236-2990
7087 W State Highway 3 Broken Bow (74728) *(G-1204)*
Scout Guide Tulsa LLC 918 693-1198
3701 S Harvard Ave Tulsa (74135) *(G-10717)*
Scrap Management Oklahoma Inc 405 677-7000
5200 Se 59th St Oklahoma City (73135) *(G-7100)*
Scrapworx 918 259-9547
1430 W Kenosha St Broken Arrow (74012) *(G-1045)*
Scratchout LLC 918 740-8665
6216 S Lewis Ave Ste 200 Tulsa (74136) *(G-10718)*
Screen Tech Intl Ltd Co 918 234-0010
26319 E Highway 51 Broken Arrow (74014) *(G-1161)*
Screw Compression Systems Inc 918 266-3330
5725 Bird Creek Ave Catoosa (74015) *(G-1351)*
Scriptorium 405 203-5943
313 Nw 2nd St Moore (73160) *(G-4566)*
Scudder Service & Supply Inc 405 232-6069
4410 Sw 34th St Oklahoma City (73119) *(G-7101)*
Scurlock Industries Miami Inc 918 542-1884
600 Newman Rd North Miami (74358) *(G-5208)*
Sdh Manufacture LLC 918 407-1065
29500 E 68th St S Broken Arrow (74014) *(G-1162)*
SDS Industries LLC 918 863-3740
2705 S 117th East Ave Tulsa (74129) *(G-10719)*
SDS Services, Eufaula Also called Shawn Schaeffer *(G-3113)*
SE Oklahoma School of Welding 918 423-9353
1710 E College Ave McAlester (74501) *(G-4334)*
Seaboard Corporation 580 468-3790
3291 Desert Rd Guymon (73942) *(G-3362)*
Seaboard Energy Guymon, Guymon Also called Seaboard Corporation *(G-3362)*
Seaboard Farms Inc 580 338-4900
2801 Hurliman Rd Guymon (73942) *(G-3363)*
Seaboard Farms Inc 580 338-3311
2700 Ne 28th St Guymon (73942) *(G-3364)*

Seaboard Foods LLC 580 338-4900
2801 Hurliman Rd Guymon (73942) *(G-3365)*
Seaboard Gas Company 405 341-1779
107 S Broadway Edmond (73034) *(G-2614)*
Seaboard International Inc 405 619-3099
3900 S Highway 81 Svc Rd El Reno (73036) *(G-2755)*
Seagate Technology LLC 405 324-3000
10321 W Reno Ave Oklahoma City (73127) *(G-7102)*
Seagate Technology LLC 800 732-4283
401 E Memorial Rd Ste 500 Oklahoma City (73114) *(G-7103)*
Seahawk Manufacturing, Tulsa Also called Joyeaux Inc *(G-10060)*
Seal Company Enterprises Inc 405 947-3307
100 Ne 34th St Oklahoma City (73105) *(G-7104)*
Seal Masters Inc 580 369-2393
2244 Highway 77 S 134 Davis (73030) *(G-1993)*
Seal Seismic Service LLC 405 603-2121
6905 W Wilshire Blvd Oklahoma City (73132) *(G-7105)*
Seal Support Systems Inc 918 258-6484
432 N Pecan Ave Broken Arrow (74012) *(G-1046)*
Seal Tight Doors & Windows, Mustang Also called Charles ODell *(G-4768)*
Sealmaster, Davis Also called Seal Masters Inc *(G-1993)*
Seamless LLC 918 743-7935
2250 E 73rd St Tulsa (74136) *(G-10720)*
Seamless Ehr, Tulsa Also called Seamless LLC *(G-10720)*
Seamprufe, McAlester Also called Charles Komar & Sons Inc *(G-4280)*
Sean Josephson LLC 918 606-9677
7885 W 75th St Tulsa (74131) *(G-9035)*
Seaport Software Inc 918 258-8611
3700 W Iola St Broken Arrow (74012) *(G-1047)*
Searchlight Inc Jefferson 580 752-4374
215 S Jefferson St Hobart (73651) *(G-3546)*
Sebo Lanila Lynn 479 719-5612
21454 Aes Rd Spiro (74959) *(G-8616)*
SEC Production Inc 405 715-0088
3206 Teakwood Ln Edmond (73013) *(G-2615)*
Secret Garden Candle Company 918 497-8699
9999 S Mingo Rd Ste Q Tulsa (74133) *(G-10721)*
Secure Agent Software, Tulsa Also called Global Interface Solutions Inc *(G-9832)*
Secure Operations Group LLC 918 642-3444
39 Little Star Dr Fairfax (74637) *(G-3121)*
Secure Screen LLC 918 294-4444
3101 W Albany St Broken Arrow (74012) *(G-1048)*
Secureagent Software Inc 918 971-1600
2448 E 81st St Ste 2000 Tulsa (74137) *(G-10722)*
Security Metal Products Corp 580 323-6966
1749 S Highway 183 Clinton (73601) *(G-1768)*
Security Solutions, Mustang Also called U-Change Lock Industries Inc *(G-4799)*
Sedona Energy LLC 405 973-7366
4611 Churchill Downs Dr Norman (73069) *(G-5140)*
Seiger Welding LLC 405 853-7237
2443 Us Highway 81 Hennessey (73742) *(G-3484)*
Seismic Drilling Services LLC 918 587-2225
1437 S Boulder Ave # 930 Tulsa (74119) *(G-10723)*
Seismic Exchange Inc 918 712-7186
2021 S Lewis Ave Ste 580 Tulsa (74104) *(G-10724)*
Seismic Source Company 580 762-8233
2391 E Coleman Rd Ponca City (74604) *(G-7873)*
Selco LLC 918 622-6100
8909 E 21st St Tulsa (74129) *(G-10725)*
Select Coatings Inc 405 745-9011
2517 S Vermont Ave Oklahoma City (73108) *(G-7106)*
Select Energy Services LLC 405 295-2566
1900 Sw 27th St El Reno (73036) *(G-2756)*
Select Energy Services LLC 918 302-0069
104 9th St Alderson (74522) *(G-128)*
Select Energy Solutions Rw LLC 580 653-2167
11079 State Highway 53 Springer (73458) *(G-8625)*
Self Automotive & Racing Inc 580 924-5866
54 W Locust St Durant (74701) *(G-2256)*
Self Printing Inc 918 838-2113
10021 E 44th Pl Tulsa (74146) *(G-10726)*
Self-Suspending Proppant LLC 580 456-7791
Cr 1650 & 14th St Roff (74865) *(G-8111)*
Sell Well Servicing Company 918 287-1711
N Of Cy On E 21st St Pawhuska (74056) *(G-7695)*
Selman Wldg & Fabrication LLC 580 330-0887
4701 Engineering Way Weatherford (73096) *(G-11440)*
Semasys Inc 405 525-2335
130 Ne 50th St Oklahoma City (73105) *(G-7107)*
Semcrude LP (HQ) 918 524-8100
6120 S Yale Ave Ste 700 Tulsa (74136) *(G-10727)*
Semgroup Corporation (HQ) 918 524-8100
6120 S Yale Ave Ste 1500 Tulsa (74136) *(G-10728)*
Semgroup Corporation 918 225-7758
3710 N Little Ave Cushing (74023) *(G-1958)*
Semgroup Corporation 405 945-6300
3030 Nw Expwy Ste 1100 Oklahoma City (73112) *(G-7108)*
Seminole County Publishing 405 382-1125
2514 Northwood Dr Seminole (74868) *(G-8398)*

Seminole Machine Co 405 382-0444
1 1/2 Miles South On Old Seminole (74868) ***(G-8399)***
Seminole Oilfield Supply 918 623-9900
503 S 9th St Okemah (74859) ***(G-5275)***
Semmaterials LP 918 683-1732
2501 Port Pl Muskogee (74403) ***(G-4747)***
Semmaterials LP 580 223-8010
2500 Refinery Rd Ardmore (73401) ***(G-353)***
Semmaterials LP 580 536-0098
9301 Sw Koch St Lawton (73505) ***(G-3996)***
Semmaterials LP 918 266-1606
5645 E Channel Rd Catoosa (74015) ***(G-1352)***
Semmaterials LP (HQ) 918 524-8100
6520 S Yale Ave Ste 700 Tulsa (74136) ***(G-10729)***
Semmexico LLC 918 524-8100
6120 S Yale Ave Tulsa (74136) ***(G-10730)***
Senax Inc 918 494-0681
1844 E 31st Pl Tulsa (74105) ***(G-10731)***
Sendee Sales Inc 918 427-3318
107 W Treat Rd Muldrow (74948) ***(G-4636)***
Senox Corporation 405 948-7464
1340 Metropolitan Ave Oklahoma City (73108) ***(G-7109)***
Sentient Industries Inc 918 770-0770
8406 N 156th East Ave Owasso (74055) ***(G-7616)***
Sentinel Leader 580 393-4348
701 E Main St Sentinel (73664) ***(G-8412)***
Sentry Manufacturing Company 202 262-0225
1201 Crystal Park Chickasha (73018) ***(G-1507)***
Sentry Pump Units Intl LLC 405 635-1800
4101 S High Ave Oklahoma City (73129) ***(G-7110)***
Seo Bio, Valliant *Also called F & F Automotive Inc* ***(G-11223)***
Sequoia Custom Cabinets LLC 801 830-2741
12135 E 11th St Ste E Tulsa (74128) ***(G-10732)***
Sequoia Natural Resources LLC 405 463-0355
6900 N Classen Blvd Oklahoma City (73116) ***(G-7111)***
Sequoyah County Times, Sallisaw *Also called Cookson Hills Publishers Inc* ***(G-8143)***
Sequoyah Fuels Corporation 918 489-5511
I-40 Hwy 10 Gore (74435) ***(G-3251)***
Sequoyah Technologies LLC 918 808-7270
201 E Hobson Ave Sapulpa (74066) ***(G-8310)***
Sercel-Grc Corp 918 834-9600
13914 E Admiral Pl Ste B Tulsa (74116) ***(G-10733)***
Sertco Industries Inc (PA) 918 623-0526
600 S Sertco Rd Okemah (74859) ***(G-5276)***
Serva Group LLC 918 266-0700
1045 Keystone Ave Catoosa (74015) ***(G-1353)***
Serva Group LLC 580 252-5111
3600b S 13th St Duncan (73533) ***(G-2175)***
Service Pipe & Supply Company 918 336-8433
389 Cr 3007 Bartlesville (74003) ***(G-527)***
Service Tech Coolg Towers LLC 405 222-0722
801 S 29th St Chickasha (73018) ***(G-1508)***
Servicios Petroleros Flint CA 918 587-7131
1625 W 21st St Tulsa (74107) ***(G-10734)***
Setco Inc 580 286-6531
1803 Nw Seminole Ave Idabel (74745) ***(G-3645)***
Setco Solid Tire & Rim, Idabel *Also called Southeast Tire Inc* ***(G-3647)***
Setco Solid Tire & Rim, Idabel *Also called Setco Inc* ***(G-3645)***
Seth W Herndon Jr 918 744-4072
6440 S Lewis Ave Ste 2200 Tulsa (74136) ***(G-10735)***
Seven-Up Bottling Co Inc 580 765-6468
1200 N Union St Ponca City (74601) ***(G-7874)***
Seventy Seven Energy Inc., Oklahoma City *Also called Seventy Seven Energy LLC* ***(G-7112)***
Seventy Seven Energy LLC (HQ) 405 608-7777
777 Nw 63rd St Oklahoma City (73116) ***(G-7112)***
Seventy Seven Operating LLC (HQ) 405 608-7777
777 Nw 63rd St Oklahoma City (73116) ***(G-7113)***
Sew Glam Monogram LLC 918 606-2644
6227 S Date Pl Broken Arrow (74011) ***(G-1049)***
Sew Graphics Plus Inc 405 364-1707
1323 Spruce Dr Norman (73072) ***(G-5141)***
Sew Much Fun 405 359-1544
5817 Dundee Ct Edmond (73025) ***(G-2616)***
Sew N Saw 405 282-2241
9924 S Kelly Ave Guthrie (73044) ***(G-3337)***
Sew Stylish Embroidery LLC 580 238-8797
10748 Red Oaks Rd Marietta (73448) ***(G-4212)***
Sew Tulsa 918 627-1577
5412 S Mingo Rd Ste G Tulsa (74146) ***(G-10736)***
Sewcool Embroidery LLC 405 326-2854
8124 Ne 139th St Edmond (73013) ***(G-2617)***
Sewells Machine & Welding 580 423-7004
122 S 2nd St Texhoma (73949) ***(G-8939)***
Sewfly Embroidery 580 477-1957
2000 E Tamarack Rd # 607 Altus (73521) ***(G-168)***
Sextant Mineral Group LLC 918 299-5115
5308 E 102nd St Tulsa (74137) ***(G-10737)***
SF Welding and Boring LLC 405 831-8602
18501 Valley Dr Norman (73026) ***(G-5142)***
Sfc Global Supply Chain Inc 918 696-8325
5 E Walnut St Stilwell (74960) ***(G-8795)***
SFM Incorporated 405 788-9453
37515 New Hope Rd Tecumseh (74873) ***(G-8928)***
Shabby Chicks Natural Product, Duncan *Also called Shabby Chicks Smart Clean LLC* ***(G-2176)***
Shabby Chicks Smart Clean LLC 405 414-8938
8100 N Hwy 81 Ste 16 Duncan (73533) ***(G-2176)***
Shack Little Glass 405 364-2649
110 Lakeside Dr Norman (73026) ***(G-5143)***
Shades of Color 918 273-0001
107 W Delaware Ave Nowata (74048) ***(G-5229)***
Shading Concepts, Stillwater *Also called Cowboy Covers Inc* ***(G-8672)***
Shadowkast Screen Printing LLC 405 808-5148
2704 Nw 160th Ter Edmond (73013) ***(G-2618)***
Shafer Kline & Warren Inc 918 499-6000
7615 E 63rd Pl Ste 210 Tulsa (74133) ***(G-10738)***
Shane Bralwey Welding LLC 936 201-9072
9714 Sw 17th St Oklahoma City (73128) ***(G-7114)***
Shane Lee Duvall 918 960-0506
22333 E 66th St S Broken Arrow (74014) ***(G-1163)***
Shared Services 405 947-0344
3433 Nw 56th St Ste 560 Oklahoma City (73112) ***(G-7115)***
Sharp Cuts Custom Cabinets 405 282-3657
1418 Chapco Dr Guthrie (73044) ***(G-3338)***
Sharp Metal Fabricators Inc 405 899-4849
8401 156th St Noble (73068) ***(G-4891)***
Sharps Machine Shop 918 336-2516
103 N Kaw Ave Bartlesville (74003) ***(G-528)***
Sharpshooters Inc 580 332-3109
12698 State Highway 3w Ada (74820) ***(G-85)***
Shave Software LLC 405 366-2168
1004 Bentbrook Pl Norman (73072) ***(G-5144)***
Shaw Group Inc 918 445-7744
626 W 41st St Tulsa (74107) ***(G-10739)***
Shaw Industries Group Inc 405 917-5117
4601 Nw 3rd St Oklahoma City (73127) ***(G-7116)***
Shaw Wireline LLC 405 853-2168
501 S Arapaho St Hennessey (73742) ***(G-3485)***
Shawn Gibson 580 584-5537
N Hwy 259 1/4 W Sweethome Broken Bow (74728) ***(G-1205)***
Shawn Gibson Logging, Broken Bow *Also called Shawn Gibson* ***(G-1205)***
Shawn Schaeffer 918 689-6781
414938 E 1203 Rd Eufaula (74432) ***(G-3113)***
Shawn Wreath 580 571-2598
48802 S County Road 210 Sharon (73857) ***(G-8419)***
Shawnee Fabricators Inc 405 275-8264
5 American Way Shawnee (74804) ***(G-8494)***
Shawnee Milling Company 580 822-4415
302 W Oklahoma Ave Okeene (73763) ***(G-5262)***
Shawnee Milling Company 405 263-4566
20625 N Calumet Rd Okarche (73762) ***(G-5252)***
Shawnee Milling Company 405 352-4336
826 Nw 3rd St Minco (73059) ***(G-4481)***
Shawnee News Star, Shawnee *Also called Morris Communications Co LLC* ***(G-8477)***
Shawnee News-Star 405 273-4200
215 N Bell Ave Shawnee (74801) ***(G-8495)***
Shawnee Sawmill LLC 405 788-6186
511 E Highland St Shawnee (74801) ***(G-8496)***
Shawnee Steel Company 405 919-8582
41508 Hardesty Rd Shawnee (74801) ***(G-8497)***
Shawnee Tubing Industries, Shawnee *Also called Bison Metals Technologies LLC* ***(G-8433)***
Shawns Small Eng Eqp Repr LLC 918 734-1565
101 N Garnett Rd Apt 331 Tulsa (74116) ***(G-10740)***
Shebester Bechtel Inc 405 577-2700
400 S Jernivan Blvd Oklahoma City (73128) ***(G-7117)***
Shebester Bechtel Inc 405 513-8580
2948 Via Esperanza Edmond (73013) ***(G-2619)***
Shebester Bechtel Inc (PA) 580 363-4124
605 N 29th St Blackwell (74631) ***(G-691)***
Shebester Bechtel Inc 580 242-4876
4210 S Van Buren St Enid (73703) ***(G-3055)***
Sheehy Signs 405 623-7777
218 W Main St Purcell (73080) ***(G-8019)***
Sheen Incorporated 405 848-0881
2625 W Country Club Dr Oklahoma City (73116) ***(G-7118)***
Sheet Metal Contractors Assn 405 848-3683
3801 Willow Springs Ave Oklahoma City (73112) ***(G-7119)***
Shelburne Oil Company 405 843-1352
901 Nw 63rd St Ste 201 Oklahoma City (73116) ***(G-7120)***
Shelby Steel Service 918 234-3098
16850 E Pine St Tulsa (74116) ***(G-10741)***
Shelby Trailer Service LLC 580 252-2922
282066 E 1790 Rd Comanche (73529) ***(G-1846)***
Shell Creek Vineyards LLC 214 415-4741
15400 Kyles Cir Yukon (73099) ***(G-11781)***
Shellback Woodworks 918 851-3992
321 E 5th Ave Bristow (74010) ***(G-796)***
Shelley Benefield 580 436-0296
9085 County Road 3510 Ada (74820) ***(G-86)***

ALPHABETIC

Shelton Sanitation 918 469-3498
31387 Scr 4330 Kinta (74552) *(G-3836)*
Sheltred Work-Activity Program 918 683-8162
920 N 43rd St E Muskogee (74403) *(G-4748)*
Shen Te Enterprises Inc 918 505-7711
5888 W 55th St Tulsa (74107) *(G-10742)*
Shepherds Heart Music Inc 918 781-1200
7804 Fern Mountain Rd Muskogee (74401) *(G-4749)*
Shepprds Retreat Bed Breakfast, Oklahoma City Also called Nancy Dalrymple *(G-6650)*
Sheridan Production Co LLC 405 756-4347
804 W Cherokee St Lindsay (73052) *(G-4083)*
Sheridan Production Co LLC 405 453-7860
1656 County Street 2780 Chickasha (73018) *(G-1509)*
Sherman Oil and Gas Company 405 258-5932
820 Manvel Ave Chandler (74834) *(G-1386)*
Sherrell Steel LLC 580 436-4322
12625 State Highway 19 Ada (74820) *(G-87)*
Sherri Burch 405 720-9021
768 N Main Ave Oklahoma City (73116) *(G-7121)*
Sherri's Fashions & Accesories, Oklahoma City Also called Sherri Burch *(G-7121)*
Sherrif 918 663-3705
12629 E 31st Ct Tulsa (74146) *(G-10743)*
Sheryls Print Services 918 724-2452
13225 E 32nd Ct Tulsa (74134) *(G-10744)*
Shes Happy Hair Okc LLC 405 328-3464
1618 Nw 23rd St Ste A Oklahoma City (73106) *(G-7122)*
Shi International Corp 918 583-4182
307 W Young St Tulsa (74106) *(G-10745)*
Shielding Resources Group 918 663-1985
9512 E 55th St Tulsa (74145) *(G-10746)*
Shields Operating Inc 405 341-7607
411 W Waterloo Rd Edmond (73025) *(G-2620)*
Shields Operating Inc (PA) 479 785-1222
5661 N Classen Blvd Oklahoma City (73118) *(G-7123)*
Shine On Designs 918 224-7439
105 S Water St Sapulpa (74066) *(G-8311)*
Shineon Designs, Sapulpa Also called Shine On Designs *(G-8311)*
Shipman Home Improvement Inc 918 514-0049
724 N Willow Rd Sand Springs (74063) *(G-8223)*
Shiprock Midstream LLC (PA) 918 289-2949
15 W 6th St Ste 2901 Tulsa (74119) *(G-10747)*
Shipzen Inc 949 357-2127
36 E Cameron St Tulsa (74103) *(G-10748)*
Shirt Nutz LLC 918 900-2362
10226 N 151st East Ave Owasso (74055) *(G-7617)*
Shirts & Stuff 918 445-0323
4222 S 73rd West Ave Tulsa (74107) *(G-10749)*
Shoberts Feed Supplements, Hennessey Also called Advantage Supplements LLC *(G-3444)*
Shockey Welding LLC 405 473-1783
943 Nw 1st St Moore (73160) *(G-4567)*
Shoe Gallery, Oklahoma City Also called C & W Shoes of Georgia Inc *(G-5658)*
Shofner Custom Wood 405 787-5768
7804 Nw 33rd St Bethany (73008) *(G-594)*
Shopper News Note 405 756-3169
318 S Main St Lindsay (73052) *(G-4084)*
Shops of Standing Rock Inc 580 364-0834
2783 S Mississippi Ave Atoka (74525) *(G-423)*
Short Oil Co 918 747-8200
2536 E 51st St Tulsa (74105) *(G-10750)*
Short Oil Co Yard 918 287-2925
N Of City Pawhuska (74056) *(G-7696)*
Short Work Industries Inc 580 774-8563
1404 E Quail Ave Weatherford (73096) *(G-11441)*
Shortruncdr 405 602-5555
1810 Ne 67th St Oklahoma City (73111) *(G-7124)*
Shortys Hattery 405 232-4287
1007 S Agnew Ave Oklahoma City (73108) *(G-7125)*
Shoulders International 918 728-2999
4714 S 176th East Pl Tulsa (74134) *(G-10751)*
Show and Tell Times Inc 918 225-4111
1047 E Main St Cushing (74023) *(G-1959)*
Showstring USA Inc 580 335-7171
1000 S Main St Frederick (73542) *(G-3200)*
Showtek 405 222-0632
727 Reding Rd Chickasha (73018) *(G-1510)*
Showtime Display & Graphics, Oklahoma City Also called C M Y K Colour Corp *(G-5661)*
Shur-Co LLC 405 262-7600
1604 E Us Highway 66 El Reno (73036) *(G-2757)*
Shurco of Oklahoma, El Reno Also called Shur-Co LLC *(G-2757)*
Shutter Mill Inc 405 377-6455
8517 S Perkins Rd Stillwater (74074) *(G-8754)*
Shutters Unlimited Ltd 405 843-7762
900 Nw 85th St Oklahoma City (73114) *(G-7126)*
Si Precast Concrete Products 918 446-2131
6505 S 57th West Ave Tulsa (74131) *(G-9036)*
Sidekick Embroidery Works, Tulsa Also called Sew Tulsa *(G-10736)*
Sides Screenprinting More LLC 580 772-8888
350 S Vermont Ave Ste 216 Oklahoma City (73108) *(G-7127)*

Sidewinder Signs 918 647-5306
2300 N Broadway St Poteau (74953) *(G-7913)*
Siegfried Companies Inc 918 747-3411
1924 S Utica Ave Ste 1120 Tulsa (74104) *(G-10752)*
Siemens Energy 580 254-7824
1123 Airpark Rd Woodward (73801) *(G-11631)*
Siemens Industry Software Inc 918 505-4220
7645 E 63rd St Ste 105 Tulsa (74133) *(G-10753)*
Sierra Hamilton LLC 405 843-5566
3101 S Lakeside Dr Oklahoma City (73179) *(G-7128)*
Sierra Madera Co2 Pipeline LLC 405 753-5500
1601 Nw Expwy St Oklahoma City (73118) *(G-7129)*
Sierra Resources Inc 405 946-2242
5121 Gaillardia Corp Pl Oklahoma City (73142) *(G-7130)*
Sierra Technologies Inc 918 445-1090
5124 E Archer St Tulsa (74115) *(G-10754)*
Sightglass, Oklahoma City Also called Monkey Chase Banana LLC *(G-6626)*
Sigma Extruding Corp 918 446-6265
4035 W 49th St Tulsa (74107) *(G-10755)*
Sigma Stretch Film, Tulsa Also called Sigma Extruding Corp *(G-10755)*
Sigman Welding 405 596-3035
43360 Hickory Dr Tecumseh (74873) *(G-8929)*
Sign & Banner Express, Bartlesville Also called Elqui International Ltd Co *(G-480)*
Sign & Send It LLC 918 730-9309
8033 S Mingo Rd Tulsa (74133) *(G-10756)*
Sign A Rama Inc 405 631-2008
7111 S Western Ave Oklahoma City (73139) *(G-7131)*
Sign Depot 580 931-9363
44 W Evergreen St Durant (74701) *(G-2257)*
Sign Dezigns 918 688-3660
317 E New Orleans St Broken Arrow (74011) *(G-1050)*
Sign Dezigns LLC 580 656-0621
603 S Highway 81 Duncan (73533) *(G-2177)*
Sign Factory LLC 405 401-9513
136 W Macarthur St Shawnee (74804) *(G-8498)*
Sign Gypsies Ardmore LLC 512 644-6976
135 Chaparral St Ardmore (73401) *(G-354)*
Sign Gypsies Midwest City LLC 405 259-9886
12305 Jaycie Cir Midwest City (73130) *(G-4453)*
Sign Innovations Inc 214 234-1614
27490 Us 70 Bokchito (74726) *(G-751)*
Sign Innovations LLC 405 840-1151
1333 Se 38th St Oklahoma City (73129) *(G-7132)*
Sign Language 405 360-7500
220 N Crawford Ave Norman (73069) *(G-5145)*
Sign Maker LLC 918 728-6060
10926 E 55th Pl Tulsa (74146) *(G-10757)*
Sign of Lies LLC 405 618-9695
3821 Nw 17th St Oklahoma City (73107) *(G-7133)*
Sign of Times 405 375-4717
305 Seay Ave Kingfisher (73750) *(G-3814)*
Sign Service 405 495-0700
8308 Sw 3rd St Ste B Oklahoma City (73128) *(G-7134)*
Sign Solutions 918 449-9439
15534 S 193rd East Ave Broken Arrow (74014) *(G-1164)*
Sign Source 580 436-1323
531 N Broadway Ave Ada (74820) *(G-88)*
Sign Up For Emails 405 236-3100
415 Couch Dr Oklahoma City (73102) *(G-7135)*
Sign-A-Rama, Oklahoma City Also called Sign A Rama Inc *(G-7131)*
Sign-A-Rama of Ok Inc 405 631-2008
7111 S Western Ave Oklahoma City (73139) *(G-7136)*
Signaltek Inc 918 583-4335
1502 W 37th Pl Tulsa (74107) *(G-10758)*
Signarama Okc, Oklahoma City Also called 2911 LLC *(G-5330)*
Signature Cabinets LLC 918 636-3433
8196 E 46th St Tulsa (74145) *(G-10759)*
Signature Graphics Corp 918 294-3485
11110 S 82nd East Pl D Bixby (74008) *(G-658)*
Signco Inc 405 615-7572
810 Lancaster Dr Yukon (73099) *(G-11782)*
Signfxr Sign Superstore, Oklahoma City Also called Hasco Corporation *(G-6222)*
Signs & Stitches 918 245-3301
200 N Garfield Ave Sand Springs (74063) *(G-8224)*
Signs 405 LLC 405 470-1616
4307 N Meridian Ave Warr Acres (73112) *(G-11329)*
Signs and T-Shirts Oklahoma Cy 405 600-7080
8805 S Western Ave Oklahoma City (73139) *(G-7137)*
Signs By Dale Inc 479 518-3744
202 Se B Ave Lawton (73501) *(G-3997)*
Signs By Jade 918 423-0041
343 E Choctaw Ave McAlester (74501) *(G-4335)*
Signs By Sikorski 918 257-5164
55015 E 70th Rd Afton (74331) *(G-121)*
Signs By Tomorrow, Midwest City Also called Whitecaps Inc *(G-4461)*
Signs Etc 918 447-1065
8274 E 71st St Tulsa (74133) *(G-10760)*
Signs For The Times, Muskogee Also called Lake Country Graphics Inc *(G-4704)*
Signs Now, Stillwater Also called Hays and Hays Companies Inc *(G-8698)*

Signs Now, Oklahoma City *Also called C L and L Inc* ***(G-5660)***
Signs Now, Tulsa *Also called Jerry Swanson Sales Co Inc* ***(G-10038)***
Signs Now 373, Norman *Also called Mltl Enterprises LLC* ***(G-5077)***
Signs of Times 918 512-6747
18 E Hobson Ave Sapulpa (74066) ***(G-8312)***
Signs On A Dime 580 237-3078
1212 W Oklahoma Ave Enid (73703) ***(G-3056)***
Signs To Go LLC 405 348-8646
3130 S Boulevard Edmond (73013) ***(G-2621)***
Signs Today, Tulsa *Also called Sanford Brothers Co Inc* ***(G-10706)***
Signs-N-More 918 760-5080
27721 E 146th St S Coweta (74429) ***(G-1897)***
Signtec Signs Distinction Inc 405 745-7555
4805 Nw 10th St Oklahoma City (73127) ***(G-7138)***
Silas Salsa Company LLC 469 556-9762
2340 W Britton Rd Oklahoma City (73120) ***(G-7139)***
Silex LLC 844 239-4056
9502 S Eastern Ave Moore (73160) ***(G-4568)***
Silex Interiors Inc (PA) 918 836-5454
10011 E 51st St Tulsa (74146) ***(G-10761)***
Silhouette Shop 918 257-6143
57301 E Highway 59 Fairland (74343) ***(G-3129)***
Silsby Media LLC 405 733-9727
2425 S Douglas Blvd Midwest City (73130) ***(G-4454)***
Silvan Oil, Tulsa *Also called Farmers Energy Corp* ***(G-9729)***
Silver ARC Welding Inc 580 234-2209
3809 E Willow Rd Enid (73701) ***(G-3057)***
Silver City Excavating LLC 405 673-3062
613 S Portland Ave Newcastle (73065) ***(G-4840)***
Silver Cliff Resourse 405 842-8698
3112 Nw 62nd St Oklahoma City (73112) ***(G-7140)***
Silver Creek Logging 580 241-7717
Hc 72 Box 737 Broken Bow (74728) ***(G-1206)***
Silver Dollar Custom Boats, Hendrix *Also called Harold Speed Jr* ***(G-3440)***
Silver Dollar Grocery Store, Hendrix *Also called Anita and Harold Speed* ***(G-3438)***
Silver Lining Creative, Sapulpa *Also called Pivot Point Publishing* ***(G-8298)***
Silver Quill LLC 405 735-9191
194 Ne 12th St Ste A Moore (73160) ***(G-4569)***
Silver Star Cleaners, Tulsa *Also called Super Saver Dry Cleaning* ***(G-10876)***
Silver-Line Plastics Corp 828 252-8755
8801 Sw Neal Blvd Lawton (73505) ***(G-3998)***
Silverado Oil & Gas LLP 918 592-3060
320 S Boston Ave Ste 1504 Tulsa (74103) ***(G-10762)***
Silverback Pump & Anchor LLC 405 756-1148
207 Ne 4th St Lindsay (73052) ***(G-4085)***
Silverstone LLC 918 371-3622
4931 Redbud Dr Sand Springs (74063) ***(G-8225)***
Silverstone LLC 918 373-2437
740 W Elgin St Broken Arrow (74012) ***(G-1051)***
Silvertree Solutions LLC 405 922-7281
424 Sage Brush Rd Yukon (73099) ***(G-11783)***
Simair Ltd 918 366-6680
613 W Needles Ave Bixby (74008) ***(G-659)***
Simek Oil Properties Inc 405 567-4606
619 Jim Phorte Blvd Prague (74864) ***(G-7935)***
Simer Pallet Recycling Inc 405 224-8583
3000 Industrial Blvd Chickasha (73018) ***(G-1511)***
Simmons Foods Inc 918 676-3285
1010 Industrial Park Fairland (74343) ***(G-3130)***
Simmons Foods Inc 918 791-0010
69605 E 300 Rd Grove (74344) ***(G-3288)***
Simmons Tool LLC 580 228-2799
804 E Florida Ave Waurika (73573) ***(G-11364)***
Simplified Dynamics Inc 405 806-0767
1810 E Dowden Ln Mustang (73064) ***(G-4793)***
Simply Scentsational 918 691-8027
925 W Quincy St Broken Arrow (74012) ***(G-1052)***
Simply Vintage Tees LLC 405 239-0444
3313 Valley Mdw Norman (73071) ***(G-5146)***
Simpson Enterprises LLC 918 495-1819
7108 S Sleepy Hollow Dr Tulsa (74136) ***(G-10763)***
Simpson Photographics Tulsa 918 630-1134
7335 S Lewis Ave Tulsa (74136) ***(G-10764)***
Sims Automotive Inc 405 235-1621
1628 Nw 6th St Oklahoma City (73106) ***(G-7141)***
Sims Electric of Oklahoma Inc 580 338-8932
1104 S East St Guymon (73942) ***(G-3366)***
Simulation Systems Division, Broken Arrow *Also called Flightsafety International Inc* ***(G-910)***
Simulator Systems Intl Inc 800 843-4764
11130 E 56th St Tulsa (74146) ***(G-10765)***
Simulator Systems Intl Inc (HQ) 918 250-4500
5358 S 125th East Ave D Tulsa (74146) ***(G-10766)***
Sinclair Companies 405 637-8444
301 E Highland St Shawnee (74801) ***(G-8499)***
Sine Qua Non LLC 405 478-2539
9105 Oakmont Dr Oklahoma City (73131) ***(G-7142)***
Singer Bros 405 236-8596
204 N Robinson Ave # 1700 Oklahoma City (73102) ***(G-7143)***
Singer Bros (PA) 918 582-6237
4124 S Rockford Ave # 101 Tulsa (74105) ***(G-10767)***
Singer Oil Company LLC 405 853-6807
203 Exxon Rd Hennessey (73742) ***(G-3486)***
Singing Wire Cedar 918 607-8643
12250 Grimes Rd Beggs (74421) ***(G-561)***
Sinister Sand Sports 918 521-3736
2013 W Detroit St Broken Arrow (74012) ***(G-1053)***
Sintertec Div, Muskogee *Also called Bpi Inc* ***(G-4654)***
Sinties Corporation 918 359-2000
5151 S 110th East Ave Tulsa (74146) ***(G-10768)***
Siosi Oil Co 918 492-1400
Rr 1 Box 310 Skiatook (74070) ***(G-8569)***
Sioux Leasing Company LLC 580 772-7100
23807 Route 66 N Weatherford (73096) ***(G-11442)***
Sirrah Investments 405 853-4909
12707 E 630 Rd Hennessey (73742) ***(G-3487)***
Sisco Specialty Products Inc 918 266-2304
8403 S 89th West Ave Tulsa (74131) ***(G-9037)***
Sisk Construction Co 405 375-5318
1009 S Main St Kingfisher (73750) ***(G-3815)***
Site Distribution LLC (PA) 918 625-7980
5314 S Yale Ave Ste 510 Tulsa (74135) ***(G-10769)***
Site Solar, Tulsa *Also called Site Distribution LLC* ***(G-10769)***
Sitrin Petroleum Corp 918 747-1111
5910 S Delaware Ave Tulsa (74105) ***(G-10770)***
Six S Energy Group LLC 405 819-8053
2617 Nw 61st St Oklahoma City (73112) ***(G-7144)***
Sjb Linings LLC 405 225-3829
410 S Eagle Ln Oklahoma City (73128) ***(G-7145)***
Sjh Welding & Backhoe LLC 405 833-8353
18210 N Red Rock Rd Calumet (73014) ***(G-1249)***
Sjl Oil and Gas Inc 405 853-2044
Highway 81 S Hennessey (73742) ***(G-3488)***
Sjl Well Service LLC 405 853-2044
7553 Us Highway 81 Hennessey (73742) ***(G-3489)***
Skate-Reation, Poteau *Also called Green Cntry Trophy Screen Prtg* ***(G-7906)***
Skd Craft Embroidery, Henryetta *Also called J & M Machine Shop Inc* ***(G-3510)***
Skiatook Journal, Skiatook *Also called Berkshire Hathaway Inc* ***(G-8532)***
Skiatook Statuary 918 396-1309
100 N Quapaw St Skiatook (74070) ***(G-8570)***
Skinner Brothers Company Inc 918 585-5708
1317 E 5th Pl Tulsa (74120) ***(G-10771)***
Skis Tees 405 239-7547
1014 Nw 1st St Oklahoma City (73106) ***(G-7146)***
SKM Graphics & Signs 405 636-1911
4601 S Shields Blvd Oklahoma City (73129) ***(G-7147)***
Sky Motors LLC 918 321-2800
17 S Spruce St Sapulpa (74066) ***(G-8313)***
Sky Tech, Skiatook *Also called Skiatook Statuary* ***(G-8570)***
Skybird Sales Inc 580 772-5100
10289 N 2422 Cir Weatherford (73096) ***(G-11443)***
Skykae Kreations 405 250-4055
3336 Smokey Bend Rdg Piedmont (73078) ***(G-7770)***
Skyline Drctonal Drillling LLC 405 429-4050
9620 Pole Rd Moore (73160) ***(G-4570)***
Skyrock Industries LLC 660 525-7482
12101 N Macarthur Blvd Oklahoma City (73162) ***(G-7148)***
Skyslate Signs 405 818-0838
1116 Ne 5th Ter Oklahoma City (73117) ***(G-7149)***
Skyview Products Inc 405 745-6064
305 S Spring Ln Mustang (73064) ***(G-4794)***
Skyy Screen Printing 405 412-4646
3920 W Indian Hills Rd Norman (73072) ***(G-5147)***
Slapsok LLC 405 845-2299
2309 Brenton Dr Edmond (73012) ***(G-2622)***
Slavin Welding Services LLC 806 217-0429
206493 E County Road 46 Woodward (73801) ***(G-11632)***
Sledge Electric Inc 405 793-4007
10616 Fairway Ave Oklahoma City (73170) ***(G-5316)***
Sleeve It Handles 405 250-2419
33109 Hardesty Rd Shawnee (74801) ***(G-8500)***
Slim Haney Inc 918 274-1082
5615 N Mingo Rd Tulsa (74117) ***(G-10772)***
Slim Haney Machining Inc 918 274-1082
5615 N Mingo Rd Tulsa (74117) ***(G-10773)***
Slone Centerless Grinding 918 497-0654
5434 S 99th East Ave Tulsa (74146) ***(G-10774)***
Slow Hand Manufacturing LLC 580 618-0867
32128 Pine Vly Afton (74331) ***(G-122)***
Slow Hand Manufacturing L 918 937-3046
980 Bluestem Norman (73069) ***(G-5148)***
Slow N Low Smoked Meats 918 946-6894
11451 E 37th Pl Tulsa (74146) ***(G-10775)***
Slpt Global Pump Group, Sallisaw *Also called Slw Automotive Inc* ***(G-8151)***
Slw Automotive Inc 918 776-3157
1300 S Opdyke St Sallisaw (74955) ***(G-8151)***
Slyder Energy Solutions LLC 405 258-3608
901 S Neva St Carney (74832) ***(G-1280)***

ALPHABETIC

SM Oil & Gas Inc 918 629-2151
4444 E 146th St N Skiatook (74070) *(G-8571)*
SMA Surface Logging LLC 405 301-3375
8224 Nw 92nd St Oklahoma City (73132) *(G-7150)*
Small Potato Tees LLC 405 264-6330
2402 S 13th St Chickasha (73018) *(G-1512)*
Smallwood Building LLC 918 424-9378
426 S Main St McAlester (74501) *(G-4336)*
Smart Batch Systems, Oklahoma City *Also called Formulated Materials LLC (G-6102)*
Smart Office Stores LLC 918 994-5300
7107 S Memorial Dr Tulsa (74133) *(G-10776)*
Smart Oilfield Solutions LLC 580 243-9571
11580 Highway 6 Elk City (73644) *(G-2873)*
Smart Shelters Inc 405 702-7775
4000 S I 35 Service Rd Oklahoma City (73129) *(G-7151)*
Smartmax Software Inc 918 388-5900
8801 S Yale Ave Ste 460 Tulsa (74137) *(G-10777)*
Smartsigns LLC 405 659-5003
905 Nw 74th St Oklahoma City (73116) *(G-7152)*
SMC Technologies Inc 405 737-3740
1517 Ocama Blvd Midwest City (73110) *(G-4455)*
SMD, Oklahoma City *Also called Surface Mount Depot Inc (G-7232)*
Smeac Group International LLC 580 574-4092
121 Melodie Ln Lawton (73507) *(G-3999)*
Smico Manufacturing Co Inc 405 946-1461
6101 Camille Ave Oklahoma City (73149) *(G-7153)*
Smith & Nephew Inc 405 917-8500
76 S Meridian Ave Oklahoma City (73107) *(G-7154)*
Smith & Smith Construction 918 297-5062
2624 Hartshorne Lake Rd Hartshorne (74547) *(G-3395)*
Smith & Sons Salvage 580 342-6218
Rr 1 Temple (73568) *(G-8935)*
Smith Brothers Logging, Valliant *Also called Johnnie & Lonnie Smith (G-11229)*
Smith Construction Inc 580 226-2159
2720 Refinery Rd Ardmore (73401) *(G-355)*
SMITH DISTRIBUTING, Oklahoma City *Also called Mower Parts Inc (G-6631)*
Smith Drilling & Completions, Oklahoma City *Also called Smith International Inc (G-7155)*
Smith Energy Services 580 596-2104
201 E 2nd St Cherokee (73728) *(G-1419)*
Smith Fibercast, Sand Springs *Also called Fiber Glass Systems LP (G-8183)*
Smith International Inc 405 670-7200
6912 S Bryant Ave Oklahoma City (73149) *(G-7155)*
Smith International Inc 580 252-3355
3445 N Hwy 81 Bldg J Duncan (73533) *(G-2178)*
Smith International Inc 800 654-6461
1405 N Waverly St Ponca City (74601) *(G-7875)*
Smith Lighting Sales Inc 918 794-2525
1221 E 33rd St Tulsa (74105) *(G-10778)*
Smith Office Supply, Lindsay *Also called Shopper News Note (G-4084)*
Smith Petroleum Inc 918 638-1301
401 W Main St Barnsdall (74002) *(G-441)*
Smith Precision Products LLC 918 691-5797
7150 S 305th East Ave Broken Arrow (74014) *(G-1165)*
Smith Pump & Supply, Chandler *Also called Smith Pump Supply (G-1387)*
Smith Pump Supply 405 258-0834
709 Manvel Ave Chandler (74834) *(G-1387)*
Smith Septic Tank Inc 918 456-8741
18050 S Muskogee Ave Tahlequah (74464) *(G-8884)*
Smith Welding Co 580 335-7521
503 S 8th St Frederick (73542) *(G-3201)*
Smith Welding Fabg & Repr 918 446-2293
5301 S Union Ave Tulsa (74107) *(G-10779)*
Smithco Engineering Inc (HQ) 918 446-4406
5615 S 129th East Ave Tulsa (74134) *(G-10780)*
Smiths Backhoe and Utility 405 202-7056
1190 S Fairgrounds Perkins (74059) *(G-7722)*
Smiths Welding & Fabg Repr, Tulsa *Also called Smith Welding Fabg & Repr (G-10779)*
Smittys Backhoe Service LLC 918 630-1090
6204 E Latimer Pl Tulsa (74115) *(G-10781)*
Smooth Landings LLC 405 422-1822
2735 M And K Ln El Reno (73036) *(G-2758)*
Smurfit Kappa 405 672-1695
7216 S Bryant Ave Oklahoma City (73149) *(G-7156)*
Smurfit Kappa North Amer LLC 405 672-1695
7216 S Bryant Ave Oklahoma City (73149) *(G-7157)*
Smyth Land Services 918 745-9210
3829 E 51st Pl Tulsa (74135) *(G-10782)*
Snapbacks & Flatbills, Ada *Also called Kelly Loyd (G-55)*
Sneaky Ts Salsa LLC 405 323-7244
1011 Buchanan Ave Piedmont (73078) *(G-7771)*
Snider Farms Peanut Barn LLC 580 471-3470
15651 N 1730 Rd Hollis (73550) *(G-3568)*
Snider Printing & Office Sup 405 257-3402
210 S Wewoka St Wewoka (74884) *(G-11511)*
Snuffy Scents LLC 405 850-6889
606 N Songbird Way Mustang (73064) *(G-4795)*
Snuffys Oilfield Services 405 368-9333
8528 N 2830 Rd Hennessey (73742) *(G-3490)*

Snwellservice Llc 580 430-9346
15314 County Road 490 Dacoma (73731) *(G-1977)*
Snyder Plant, Snyder *Also called Martin Marietta Materials Inc (G-8583)*
Snyder Printing Inc 405 682-8880
10904 Gateshead Dr Oklahoma City (73170) *(G-5317)*
Snyder's Doughnuts, Chickasha *Also called Paradise Doughnuts (G-1499)*
Snyder's Printing, Oklahoma City *Also called Snyder Printing Inc (G-5317)*
Snyders Stucco and Stone 580 421-9747
6065 State Highway 99n Ada (74820) *(G-89)*
Soccer Wave LLC 405 361-7813
16720 Crest Vly Edmond (73012) *(G-2623)*
Sock Monkey Bizz LLC 918 462-7392
70076 S 336 Ct Wagoner (74467) *(G-11290)*
Software Perfection LLC 918 266-8883
30175 E 36th St S Broken Arrow (74014) *(G-1166)*
Solae LLC 918 476-5825
5532 Hunt St Pryor (74361) *(G-7991)*
Solar Exploration OK LLC 918 252-2203
7867 S 95th East Ave Tulsa (74133) *(G-10783)*
Solar Power & Pump Company LLC 580 225-1704
301 W 12th St Elk City (73644) *(G-2874)*
Solar Turbines Incorporated 918 459-5100
4217 W Seattle St Broken Arrow (74012) *(G-1054)*
Solar View LLC 918 366-6413
18622 S 62nd East Ave Bixby (74008) *(G-660)*
Solid Path Services 918 384-7409
10838 E Marshall St 200f Tulsa (74116) *(G-10784)*
Solid Rock Custom Flooring 918 833-2884
14309 E 500 Rd Claremore (74019) *(G-1685)*
Solid State Controls Inc 405 273-9292
35431 Hardesty Rd Shawnee (74801) *(G-8501)*
Solidroots LLC 918 770-3549
1119 N Main St Tulsa (74106) *(G-10785)*
Solidtech Animal Health Inc 405 387-3300
812 Ne 24th St Newcastle (73065) *(G-4841)*
Solitaire Holdings LLC 580 252-6060
7232 Nickles Rd Duncan (73533) *(G-2179)*
Solitaire Homes Inc (PA) 580 252-6060
7232 Nickles Rd Duncan (73533) *(G-2180)*
Solo Cup Operating Corporation 580 436-1500
401 Ne Richardson Loop Ada (74820) *(G-90)*
Soltow Business Supply (PA) 918 786-4465
810 Industrial Rd Grove (74344) *(G-3289)*
Solutions Lighting, Oklahoma City *Also called Solutions Lucid Group LLC (G-7158)*
Solutions Lucid Group LLC 405 476-4332
701 Ne 15th St 11 Oklahoma City (73104) *(G-7158)*
Solutionware Ltd 405 843-0809
10400 Vineyard Blvd Ste F Oklahoma City (73120) *(G-7159)*
Something Printed 918 967-9188
112 N Broadway St Stigler (74462) *(G-8646)*
Something Special, Idabel *Also called Stuart Beverly & (G-3648)*
Son Signs Okc 405 830-2536
350 S Vermont Ave Ste 204 Oklahoma City (73108) *(G-7160)*
Sonburst Graphics LLC 918 478-8600
116 W Poplar Fort Gibson (74434) *(G-3178)*
Sonny Mac Industries Inc (PA) 918 261-8446
12806 S Memorial Dr Bixby (74008) *(G-661)*
Sonoco Industrial Products, Tulsa *Also called Sonoco Products Company (G-10786)*
Sonoco Products Company 918 622-3370
10008 E 52nd St Tulsa (74146) *(G-10786)*
SOO & Associates 405 397-5072
4029 Sam Gordon Dr Norman (73072) *(G-5149)*
Sooner Bindery Inc 405 232-4764
4335 Se 28th St Ste A Del City (73115) *(G-2007)*
Sooner Cabinet & Trim Inc 405 820-2920
208 S Ramblin Oaks Dr Moore (73160) *(G-4571)*
Sooner Cnc LLC 918 261-5231
6912 E 66th St Tulsa (74133) *(G-10787)*
Sooner Coca-Cola Bottling Co 918 423-0911
1610 E Van Buren Ave McAlester (74501) *(G-4266)*
Sooner Completions Inc 405 273-4599
810 W Ayre St Shawnee (74801) *(G-8502)*
Sooner Denim Inc 405 641-4720
2817 Sw 88th St Oklahoma City (73159) *(G-7161)*
Sooner Energy Services Inc (HQ) 405 579-3200
1004 S Plainsman Rd Marlow (73055) *(G-4242)*
Sooner Food Group LLC 703 791-9069
15101 Se 139th St Newalla (74857) *(G-4816)*
Sooner Holdings Inc (HQ) 918 592-7900
5416 S Yale Ave Ste 400 Tulsa (74135) *(G-10788)*
Sooner Hot Oil Service 580 762-2586
56 Prospect Rd Ponca City (74604) *(G-7876)*
Sooner Industries Inc 918 540-2422
16 N Main St Miami (74354) *(G-4431)*
Sooner Machine & Equipment Co 405 794-6833
233 Se 5th St Moore (73160) *(G-4572)*
Sooner Manufacturing Co Inc (PA) 918 835-5019
1529 N 168th East Ave Tulsa (74116) *(G-10789)*
Sooner Manufacturing Co Inc 918 835-5019
1019 N Columbia Ave Tulsa (74110) *(G-10790)*

Sooner Millwork, Ada *Also called Dale P Jackson* ***(G-29)***
Sooner Neon 918 269-5250
202 Waterford St Catoosa (74015) ***(G-1354)***
Sooner Pallet Services Inc 918 342-9663
18215 Quail Creek Rd Claremore (74017) ***(G-1686)***
Sooner Press 405 382-8351
619 N Milt Phillips Ave Seminole (74868) ***(G-8400)***
Sooner Print Imaging 405 272-0600
900 Nw 6th St Oklahoma City (73106) ***(G-7162)***
Sooner Printing, Miami *Also called Sooner Industries Inc* ***(G-4431)***
Sooner Pro Assembly 405 838-2838
203 Keith St Norman (73069) ***(G-5150)***
Sooner Production Services Inc 580 256-1155
3921 Oklahoma Ave Woodward (73801) ***(G-11633)***
Sooner Publishing Inc 580 233-8400
412 N Van Buren St Enid (73703) ***(G-3058)***
Sooner Ready Mix 405 670-3300
8420 S Bryant Ave Oklahoma City (73149) ***(G-7163)***
Sooner Ready Mix LLC 405 692-5595
13996 S Macarthur Blvd Oklahoma City (73173) ***(G-7164)***
Sooner Repair 918 742-4653
1146 E 61st St Tulsa (74136) ***(G-10791)***
Sooner Rubber Products Company 918 461-1391
5833 S Garnett Rd Tulsa (74146) ***(G-10792)***
Sooner Sandblasting, Norman *Also called Power Services LLC* ***(G-5118)***
Sooner Scale Inc 405 236-3566
2428 Sw 14th St Oklahoma City (73108) ***(G-7165)***
Sooner Scale Inc 580 925-2176
14082 Ns 3500 Konawa (74849) ***(G-3848)***
Sooner Signs 405 503-8902
2533 Hollywood Ave Norman (73072) ***(G-5151)***
Sooner State Generator LLC 918 927-0543
9839 N Lewis Ave Sperry (74073) ***(G-8611)***
Sooner State Graphics & Signs 405 837-5226
1909 Breakers West Blvd Oklahoma City (73128) ***(G-7166)***
Sooner State Pattern Works 580 363-1543
2701 W Dewey St Blackwell (74631) ***(G-692)***
Sooner State Spring Mfg Co 918 476-5707
9799 S 432 Chouteau (74337) ***(G-1570)***
Sooner Steel & Truss, Oklahoma City *Also called Sooner Steel and Truss LLC* ***(G-7167)***
Sooner Steel and Truss LLC 405 232-5542
801 S Agnew Ave Oklahoma City (73108) ***(G-7167)***
Sooner Steel Rule Dies 918 775-2668
460538 E 1000 Rd Sallisaw (74955) ***(G-8152)***
Sooner Swabbing Services Inc 580 233-4347
2120 W Willow Rd Enid (73703) ***(G-3059)***
Sooner Swage & Coating Co Inc 918 689-7142
Hc 62 Box A3 Eufaula (74432) ***(G-3114)***
Sooner Tool Company (PA) 918 352-4440
1 Mile W Of City Hwy 33 Drumright (74030) ***(G-2071)***
Sooner Trend Exploration Inc 405 375-3405
1202 Regency Ct Kingfisher (73750) ***(G-3816)***
Sooner Welding Inspection, Duncan *Also called Mark Condit* ***(G-2152)***
Sooner Wiping Rags LLC 405 670-3100
301 N Rhode Island Ave # 109 Oklahoma City (73117) ***(G-7168)***
Sophisticated Sweets Inc 580 704-8038
514 W C Ave Cache (73527) ***(G-1231)***
Sorb Technology Inc 405 682-1993
3631 Sw 54th St Oklahoma City (73119) ***(G-7169)***
Sorrels Ventures LLC 903 556-2941
2168 Belpine Loop Broken Bow (74728) ***(G-1207)***
Sorrels, Larry, Kiowa *Also called Larrys Welding Service* ***(G-3840)***
SOS Pools 405 471-3792
625 Evergreen St Edmond (73003) ***(G-2624)***
Sothwestern Exploration Cons 405 767-0041
6305 Waterford Blvd # 405 Oklahoma City (73118) ***(G-7170)***
Sound Ink 2 Publishing LLC 918 605-6026
8220 Gary Dr Tulsa (74131) ***(G-9038)***
Sound Iq 918 442-2588
3105 S Harvard Ave Tulsa (74135) ***(G-10793)***
Sounds Impossible, Lawton *Also called Trailing Edge Technologies* ***(G-4014)***
Souno LLC 918 495-1771
6737 S 85th East Ave Tulsa (74133) ***(G-10794)***
Source Fabrication LLC 580 762-4114
2101 Hall Blvd Ponca City (74601) ***(G-7877)***
Source Rock Enrgy Partners LLC 918 728-3116
1714 S Boston Ave Tulsa (74119) ***(G-10795)***
Souter Limestone and Mnrl LLC 918 489-5589
445501 E 987 Rd Gore (74435) ***(G-3252)***
South Central Coal Company Inc (PA) 918 962-2544
904 W Broadway St Spiro (74959) ***(G-8617)***
South Central Golf Inc 918 280-0787
6218 S Lewis Ave Ste 102 Tulsa (74136) ***(G-10796)***
South Central Machine 580 775-1623
3376 S Mclean Rd Durant (74701) ***(G-2258)***
South Central Oilfld Svcs Inc 580 465-4498
251 Locust Rd Wilson (73463) ***(G-11542)***
South Central Publications, Tulsa *Also called South Central Golf Inc* ***(G-10796)***

South Edge 918 286-4936
7850 S Elm Pl Broken Arrow (74011) ***(G-1055)***
South Manufacturing Inc 918 894-5255
11640 S Memorial Dr Bixby (74008) ***(G-662)***
South Tulsa Hot Shot Svcs LLC 918 299-7373
724 W 108th Pl S Jenks (74037) ***(G-3728)***
Southeast Machine Inc 580 889-6418
4375 S Mississippi Ave Atoka (74525) ***(G-424)***
Southeast Times 580 286-2628
110 S Central Ave Idabel (74745) ***(G-3646)***
Southeast Tire Inc 580 286-6531
1803 Nw Seminole Ave Idabel (74745) ***(G-3647)***
Southeastern Drilling 918 469-3489
N Of Town Quinton (74561) ***(G-8042)***
Southeastern Ice 918 465-2500
1202 W Stovall Rd 1 Wilburton (74578) ***(G-11524)***
Southeastern Oklahoma Pubg Co, Idabel *Also called Southeast Times* ***(G-3646)***
Southern Aero Partners Inc 918 437-7676
4085 Southwest Blvd Tulsa (74107) ***(G-10797)***
Southern Belles Candle Co LLC 405 200-5986
329425 E 950 Rd Luther (73054) ***(G-4138)***
Southern Box Company 580 255-7969
908 W Main St Duncan (73533) ***(G-2181)***
Southern Boys Clay Gravel LLC 580 584-6711
211 Mountain Goat Trl Broken Bow (74728) ***(G-1208)***
Southern Breeze Candle Co LLC 918 402-4040
4606 W 90th St Tulsa (74132) ***(G-10798)***
Southern Cooker 580 283-3982
117 Hwy 78 Achille (74720) ***(G-1)***
Southern Foods Group LLC 918 587-2471
215 N Denver Ave Tulsa (74103) ***(G-10799)***
Southern International Inc 405 943-5288
4200 Perimeter Center Dr # 205 Oklahoma City (73112) ***(G-7171)***
Southern Lace Stitchery 405 414-3550
8712 Ally Way Yukon (73099) ***(G-11784)***
Southern Machine Works Inc 580 255-6525
907 E Bois D Arc Ave Duncan (73533) ***(G-2182)***
Southern Millwork Inc 918 585-8125
525 S Troost Ave Tulsa (74120) ***(G-10800)***
Southern Okie LLC 405 657-7765
2009 Bridgeview Blvd Edmond (73003) ***(G-2625)***
Southern Plains Cable LLC 580 529-5000
22937 State Highway 58 Lawton (73507) ***(G-4000)***
Southern Plains Enrgy Svcs LLC 918 225-3570
5405 S Country Club Rd Cushing (74023) ***(G-1960)***
Southern Plains Enrgy Svcs LLC 580 336-7444
13200 John Wayne Perry (73077) ***(G-7745)***
Southern Plains Power, Tulsa *Also called Cummins Southern Plains LLC* ***(G-9522)***
Southern Plastics LLC 918 274-6767
408 W 2nd Ave Owasso (74055) ***(G-7618)***
Southern Qlf, Muskogee *Also called Quality Liquid Feeds Inc* ***(G-4740)***
Southern Resources Inc 405 601-1322
4509 N Classen Blvd # 201 Oklahoma City (73118) ***(G-7172)***
Southern Rubber Stamp Co Inc 918 587-3818
2637 E Marshall St Tulsa (74110) ***(G-10801)***
Southern Sheet Metal Works Inc 918 584-3371
1225 E 2nd St Tulsa (74120) ***(G-10802)***
Southern Specialties Corp 918 584-3553
1828 N 105th East Ave Tulsa (74116) ***(G-10803)***
Southern Style Custom Cookers, Achille *Also called Southern Cooker* ***(G-1)***
Southland Awards & Signs 918 691-9141
914 S Nyssa Pl Broken Arrow (74012) ***(G-1056)***
Southside Powder Coating 405 623-8557
9161 48th Ave Se Noble (73068) ***(G-4892)***
Southstar Energy Corp 580 223-1553
301 W Main St Ste 500 Ardmore (73401) ***(G-356)***
Southwest Business Pdts LLC 580 765-4401
1032 N Union St Ponca City (74601) ***(G-7878)***
Southwest Business Unit, Mill Creek *Also called U S Silica Company* ***(G-4472)***
Southwest Cnstr News Svc (PA) 405 948-7474
3616 Nw 58th St Oklahoma City (73112) ***(G-7173)***
Southwest Cnstr News Svc 918 493-5066
7170 S Braden Ave Ste 180 Tulsa (74136) ***(G-10804)***
Southwest Corset Corporation 580 363-1935
318 N 29th St Blackwell (74631) ***(G-693)***
Southwest Cupid, Blackwell *Also called Southwest Corset Corporation* ***(G-693)***
Southwest Electric Co (PA) 800 364-4445
6503 Se 74th St Oklahoma City (73135) ***(G-7174)***
Southwest Electric Co 918 437-9494
1304 N 143rd East Ave Tulsa (74116) ***(G-10805)***
Southwest Electric Co 405 733-4700
6501 Se 74th St Oklahoma City (73135) ***(G-7175)***
Southwest Energy LP 918 779-0699
1869 E 71st St Tulsa (74136) ***(G-10806)***
Southwest Engineering 405 634-2841
729 Se 29th St Oklahoma City (73129) ***(G-7176)***
Southwest Fabricators Inc 580 326-3589
503 S Industrial Blvd Hugo (74743) ***(G-3621)***
Southwest Filter Company (PA) 918 835-1179
7435 E Reading St Tulsa (74115) ***(G-10807)***

ALPHABETIC

Southwest Filter Company.....918 835-1179
1534 N 75th East Ave Tulsa (74115) ***(G-10808)***
Southwest Interiors Inc.....580 323-3050
421 Frisco Ave Clinton (73601) ***(G-1769)***
Southwest Latex LLC.....405 420-0018
210 Jones St Marlow (73055) ***(G-4243)***
Southwest Oil Field Cnstr, Oklahoma City *Also called Primeenergy Corporation* ***(G-6895)***
Southwest Oilfield Service.....580 302-4069
115 Bluestem St Weatherford (73096) ***(G-11444)***
Southwest Petroleum Corp.....918 352-2700
4815 S Harvard Ave # 460 Tulsa (74135) ***(G-10809)***
Southwest Pickling Inc.....580 924-6996
68 Waldron Dr Durant (74701) ***(G-2259)***
Southwest Ready Mix (PA).....580 248-4709
800 Se 1st St Lawton (73501) ***(G-4001)***
Southwest Ready Mix.....580 355-2093
8 Se I Ave Lawton (73501) ***(G-4002)***
Southwest Readymix, Lawton *Also called Southwest Ready Mix* ***(G-4002)***
Southwest Shutter Co.....405 344-6406
21197 Fir Ln Purcell (73080) ***(G-8020)***
Southwest Silicon Tech Corp.....580 223-5058
18 Interstate Dr Ardmore (73401) ***(G-357)***
Southwest Tile Distributor, Oklahoma City *Also called Young Brothers Inc* ***(G-7482)***
Southwest Tube Mfg Div, Sand Springs *Also called Webco Industries Inc* ***(G-8237)***
Southwest United Inds Inc (HQ).....918 587-4161
422 S Saint Louis Ave Tulsa (74120) ***(G-10810)***
Southwestern Motor Rebuilders.....918 585-1519
2201 E 3rd St Tulsa (74104) ***(G-10811)***
Southwestern Process Supply Co (PA).....918 582-8211
325 S Quincy Ave Tulsa (74120) ***(G-10812)***
Southwestern State Sand Corp.....580 569-4333
16725 Ns County Road 219 Snyder (73566) ***(G-8584)***
Southwestern Sty & Bnk Sup Inc.....405 525-9411
4500 N Santa Fe Ave Oklahoma City (73118) ***(G-7177)***
Southwestern Wire Inc (PA).....405 447-6900
3505 N Interstate Dr Norman (73069) ***(G-5152)***
Southwind Aviation Supply LLC.....405 491-0500
5700 N Rockwell Ave Bethany (73008) ***(G-595)***
Southwstern Group of Companies.....405 525-9411
4500 N Santa Fe Ave Oklahoma City (73118) ***(G-7178)***
Southwstern Stationary Bnk Sup, Oklahoma City *Also called Southwstern Group of Companies* ***(G-7178)***
Soy Candle Cottage LLC.....405 519-6827
8500 E Memorial Rd Jones (73049) ***(G-3752)***
Space Con Systems Inc.....918 835-6580
6567 E 21st Pl Ste A Tulsa (74129) ***(G-10813)***
Space Tech Inc.....918 582-2616
1535 E Marshall St Tulsa (74106) ***(G-10814)***
Spacebar Publishing LLC.....918 852-6311
8133 E 485 Rd Claremore (74019) ***(G-1687)***
Spade Leasing Inc.....580 653-2171
1376 Mount Vica Rd Springer (73458) ***(G-8626)***
Spangenhelm Publishing.....405 430-6464
1000 Cornwell Dr Apt 307 Yukon (73099) ***(G-11785)***
Spangler Farm.....405 466-2536
11208 S Coyle Rd Coyle (73027) ***(G-1904)***
Spanish Lady Oil Co.....405 659-3515
200 Shortgrass Rd Edmond (73003) ***(G-2626)***
Spark Something Candles LLC.....405 872-5673
1734 W Robinson St Norman (73069) ***(G-5153)***
Sparks Greg Operating Co.....918 633-8807
8307 E 111th St S Ste N Bixby (74008) ***(G-663)***
Sparks Aerospace LLC.....580 234-7972
3501 Elm Pl Enid (73703) ***(G-3060)***
Sparks Mtal Dsign Fbrction LLC.....918 676-5112
21100 S 625 Rd Fairland (74343) ***(G-3131)***
Sparks Plating Company.....918 482-5080
201 N Broadway Haskell (74436) ***(G-3401)***
Sparks Vineyard & Winery Inc.....918 866-2529
351310 E 970 Rd Sparks (74869) ***(G-8589)***
Sparlin Hot Oil Service Inc.....580 795-2513
Hwy 99 3 Main St Ne Madill (73446) ***(G-4163)***
Spartan Resources LLC (PA).....405 843-0420
4013 Nw Expwy St Ste 690 Oklahoma City (73116) ***(G-7179)***
Spartan Resources LLC.....580 226-2400
216 1st Ave Sw Ardmore (73401) ***(G-358)***
Speaker World LLC.....918 973-1700
2032 E 12th St Tulsa (74104) ***(G-10815)***
Spearhead Services.....405 756-8615
708 Se 4th St Lindsay (73052) ***(G-4086)***
Special Equipment Mfg Inc.....580 252-5111
3600 S 13th St Duncan (73533) ***(G-2183)***
Special Parts Mfg Inc.....405 379-3343
1001 S Echo St Holdenville (74848) ***(G-3560)***
Special Service Systems Inc.....918 582-7777
4627 E 56th Pl Tulsa (74135) ***(G-10816)***
Specialty Advertising Co Inc.....405 495-3838
1400 N Mcmillan Ave Oklahoma City (73127) ***(G-7180)***
Specialty Component Mfg.....405 794-5535
2200 Pole Rd Moore (73160) ***(G-4573)***
Specialty Machining Inc.....918 266-3626
19100 E Pine St Catoosa (74015) ***(G-1355)***
Specialty Plastics Inc.....580 237-1018
2302 N 11th St Enid (73701) ***(G-3061)***
Specialty Prosthetic, Tulsa *Also called Fenner Inc* ***(G-9737)***
Specialty Sales Associates.....405 495-1136
840481 S 3420 Rd Chandler (74834) ***(G-1388)***
Specific Systems Ltd (PA).....918 663-9321
439 W 41st St Tulsa (74107) ***(G-10817)***
Spectrum Distributing, Norman *Also called Broken Arrow Productions Inc* ***(G-4944)***
Spectrum Lng LLC (PA).....918 298-6660
8605 S Elwood Ave Ste B12 Tulsa (74132) ***(G-10818)***
Spectrum Paint & Decorating, Oklahoma City *Also called Spectrum Paint Company Inc* ***(G-7181)***
Spectrum Paint Company Inc.....405 525-6519
709 Nw 36th St Oklahoma City (73118) ***(G-7181)***
Spectrum Tracer Services LLC (HQ).....405 470-5566
9111 E Pine St Ste 104 Tulsa (74115) ***(G-10819)***
Spectrumfx Inc.....918 392-9799
9733 E 54th St Tulsa (74146) ***(G-10820)***
Speedmaster Inc (PA).....918 225-1266
1 E Eseco Rd Cushing (74023) ***(G-1961)***
Speedys TS & More LLC.....580 748-0067
29864 County Road 452 Alva (73717) ***(G-192)***
Speer Cushion Co.....970 854-2911
9513 E 117th St S Bixby (74008) ***(G-664)***
Speller Oil Corporation.....405 942-7869
3535 Nw 58th St Ste 900 Oklahoma City (73112) ***(G-7182)***
Speller Petroleum Corporation.....405 942-7869
3535 Nw 58th St Ste 900 Oklahoma City (73112) ***(G-7183)***
Spencer Faith Christn Ctr Inc.....812 876-5575
5401 N Westminster Rd Spencer (73084) ***(G-8601)***
Spencer L Rosson.....918 682-4291
526 W Okmulgee St Muskogee (74401) ***(G-4750)***
Spencer Machine Works LLC.....580 332-1551
224 N Rennie St Ada (74820) ***(G-91)***
Spencers Contract Pumping LLC.....405 238-6363
42607 E County Road 1570 Wynnewood (73098) ***(G-11673)***
Spencers Custom Cabinets.....918 598-3208
Hwy 82 Peggs (74452) ***(G-7713)***
Spess Drilling Company (PA).....918 358-5831
200 S Broadway St Cleveland (74020) ***(G-1734)***
Spiers New Technologies Inc (PA).....405 464-2200
1500 Se 89th St Oklahoma City (73149) ***(G-7184)***
Spiers New Technologies Inc.....405 605-8066
3228 N Santa Fe Ave Oklahoma City (73118) ***(G-7185)***
Spin Doctor, The, Oklahoma City *Also called Tsdr LLC* ***(G-7346)***
Spinnaker Oil Company LLC.....405 345-9556
3675 S Alfadale Rd El Reno (73036) ***(G-2759)***
Spinning Star Design.....405 359-3965
513 Joni Deanne Ct Edmond (73034) ***(G-2627)***
Spiral Exploration LLC.....330 936-4689
1609 N Blackwelder Ave Oklahoma City (73106) ***(G-7186)***
Spiral Waves Industries LLC.....405 481-7685
2204 Ellis Dr Shawnee (74804) ***(G-8503)***
Spirit Aerosystems Inc.....918 832-3424
11333 E Pine St Tulsa (74116) ***(G-10821)***
Spirit Aerosystems Inc.....918 423-6979
1900 E Electric Ave McAlester (74501) ***(G-4337)***
Spirit Arosystems Holdings Inc.....918 832-2891
1541 N Garnett Rd Tulsa (74116) ***(G-10822)***
Spirit Arosystems Holdings Inc.....918 832-2131
2035 N 85th East Ave Tulsa (74115) ***(G-10823)***
Spirit Spot, Tulsa *Also called Joys Uniforms Boutique Ltd* ***(G-10061)***
Spiro Graphic.....918 962-2075
212 S Main St Spiro (74959) ***(G-8618)***
Spiro Mining LLC.....918 962-5335
25858 Highline Rd Spiro (74959) ***(G-8619)***
Spitzer Printing.....580 928-5540
112 E Main St Sayre (73662) ***(G-8346)***
Spitzer Publishing.....580 928-5540
112 E Main St Sayre (73662) ***(G-8347)***
Splash Marine LLC.....580 336-9874
321 Ash St Perry (73077) ***(G-7746)***
SPM Flow Control Inc.....580 225-1186
1600 S Merritt Rd Elk City (73644) ***(G-2875)***
Spor Enterprises Inc.....405 745-9888
5600 Hardy Dr Oklahoma City (73179) ***(G-7187)***
Sport Signs, Tulsa *Also called Lettercrafts* ***(G-10154)***
Sportchassis LLC.....580 323-4100
2300 S 13th St Clinton (73601) ***(G-1770)***
Sportees.....918 618-6201
139 N Main St Eufaula (74432) ***(G-3115)***
Sports & Stress Marketing.....580 327-3463
1710 College Blvd B Alva (73717) ***(G-193)***
Sports Center.....580 795-2993
502 N 1st St Madill (73446) ***(G-4164)***
Sports Fitnes Publications LLC.....918 587-7223
2448 E 81st St Ste 2051 Tulsa (74137) ***(G-10824)***

ALPHABETIC SECTION

Sports Vision Inc 918 824-7617
   109 Ne 1st St Pryor (74361) *(G-7992)*

Sportstech Quality Cardio LLC 918 461-9177
   10909c E 56th St Tulsa (74146) *(G-10825)*

Spot My Bag LLC 918 895-8810
   1722 E King Pl Tulsa (74110) *(G-10826)*

Spragues Backhoe LLC 405 600-4905
   8424 Nw 92nd St Oklahoma City (73132) *(G-7188)*

Spray Magnifique LLC 918 613-6284
   2509 W Iola St Broken Arrow (74012) *(G-1057)*

Spray-Rite Inc 479 648-3351
   201 Durham Pocola (74902) *(G-7786)*

Spraycan Creative LLC 405 494-0321
   420 W Main St Yukon (73099) *(G-11786)*

Sprayfoam Banks & Coatings 580 490-6308
   574 Abner Rd Overbrook (73453) *(G-7539)*

Spread Tech LLC 580 994-2506
   417 Sw 7th St Mooreland (73852) *(G-4595)*

Sprekelmeyer Printing Company 580 223-5100
   12 C St Sw Ardmore (73401) *(G-359)*

Spring Drilling Corp 580 226-3800
   911 W Broadway St Ardmore (73401) *(G-360)*

Spring Energy Co 405 340-6811
   201 E Campbell St Edmond (73034) *(G-2628)*

Spring Harry A Geological Engr 580 226-1910
   911 W Broadway St Ardmore (73401) *(G-361)*

Spring Hollow Feed Mill Inc 918 453-9933
   13243 W Killabrew Rd Hulbert (74441) *(G-3628)*

Springcrest Drapery Center 918 258-5644
   2004 W Nashville St Broken Arrow (74012) *(G-1058)*

Springdale Food Co Inc 580 928-2598
   209 N 5th St Sayre (73662) *(G-8348)*

Springmaker, Oklahoma City *Also called Cannon Racecraft Inc (G-5689)*

Spsc, Mounds *Also called Medcraft LLC (G-4620)*

Spurlock Co Satellite Mapping 405 495-8628
   6017 1/2 Nw 16th St 3 Oklahoma City (73127) *(G-7189)*

SPX Heat Transfer LLC (HQ) 918 234-6000
   2121 N 161st East Ave Tulsa (74116) *(G-10827)*

Spyglass Energy Group LLC 918 582-9900
   15 E 5th St Ste 4000 Tulsa (74103) *(G-10828)*

Srh Lighting LLC 405 604-9414
   2328 Nw 12th St Oklahoma City (73107) *(G-7190)*

Srifusion LLC 774 238-7466
   5406 Nw Wilfred Dr Lawton (73505) *(G-4003)*

Srite Mechanical LLC 405 308-3182
   2704 Nw 65th St Oklahoma City (73116) *(G-7191)*

Srm Inc (PA) 405 354-8824
   1400 S Holly St Yukon (73099) *(G-11787)*

Srm Inc 405 475-1746
   4004a S Kelly Ave Edmond (73013) *(G-2629)*

Ss Roustabout Services 405 320-2183
   3096 County Street 2800 Ninnekah (73067) *(G-4874)*

Ss Tag LLC 918 241-3400
   414 Plaza Ct Sand Springs (74063) *(G-8226)*

Ssb Production LLC 580 226-7000
   1505 N Commerce St # 201 Ardmore (73401) *(G-362)*

Ssec 405 321-0916
   3360 Allspice Run Norman (73026) *(G-5154)*

Ssg Inc 405 639-2056
   1700 S Broadway St Ste J Moore (73160) *(G-4574)*

Ssi Technologies Inc 918 451-6160
   8405 S 7th St Broken Arrow (74011) *(G-1059)*

St Bonaventure Press Ltd 918 770-8546
   2232 E 45th Pl Tulsa (74105) *(G-10829)*

St John 405 364-1917
   9701 Brush Creek Rd Norman (73026) *(G-5155)*

Stableridge LLC 918 968-2568
   2016 Rte 66 W Stroud (74079) *(G-8819)*

Stableridge Vineyards, Stroud *Also called Stableridge LLC (G-8819)*

Stabor Sporting Goods, Newalla *Also called HALAQ Inc (G-4810)*

Stacey Oil Services 918 427-3940
   479273 Us Highway 64 Roland (74954) *(G-8114)*

Stadia Energy Partners LLC 918 812-6169
   10804 S 93rd East Ave Tulsa (74133) *(G-10830)*

Stagestand Ranch 580 255-1161
   1214 N Hwy 81 Ste 116 Duncan (73533) *(G-2184)*

Staghorn Energy LLC 918 584-2558
   1 W 3rd St Ste 1000 Tulsa (74103) *(G-10831)*

Staghorn Petroleum LLC 918 584-2558
   1 W 3rd St Ste 1000 Tulsa (74103) *(G-10832)*

Staghorn Petroleum II LLC 918 584-2558
   1 W 3rd St Ste 1000 Tulsa (74103) *(G-10833)*

Stahl/Scott Fetzer Company 580 924-5575
   92 Waldron Dr Durant (74701) *(G-2260)*

Stahle Tool Company LLC 405 265-4360
   825 Preston Park Dr Yukon (73099) *(G-11788)*

Stallion Oilfield Services Ltd 580 225-5800
   319 Industrial Pkwy Elk City (73644) *(G-2876)*

Stallion Oilfield Services Ltd 580 225-8990
   108 Oilfield Rd Elk City (73644) *(G-2877)*

Stallion Oilfield Services Ltd 580 856-3169
   24130 State Highway 76 Ratliff City (73481) *(G-8067)*

Stan Clark Co 405 377-0799
   516 W Elm Ave Stillwater (74074) *(G-8755)*

Stan-Mel Industries Inc 918 436-0056
   1 Archery Ln Pocola (74902) *(G-7787)*

Stand By Personnel 918 582-0522
   1530 E 1st St Tulsa (74120) *(G-10834)*

Standard Machine 918 423-9430
   5610 S Us Highway 69 McAlester (74501) *(G-4338)*

Standard Machine & Wldg Works, McAlester *Also called Standard Machine LLC (G-4338)*

Standard Materials Group 479 587-3300
   4608 S Garnett Rd Ste 600 Tulsa (74146) *(G-10835)*

Standard Materials Group Inc 918 582-8111
   4608 S Garnett Rd Ste 600 Tulsa (74146) *(G-10836)*

Standard Panel LLC 918 984-1717
   1355 N Louisville Ave Tulsa (74115) *(G-10837)*

Standard Printing Co Inc 405 840-0001
   905 Nw 74th St Oklahoma City (73116) *(G-7192)*

Standard Supply Co Inc 918 272-5014
   6602b N Owasso Expy Owasso (74055) *(G-7619)*

Stanley Filter Company LLC 800 545-9926
   8189 E 44th St Tulsa (74145) *(G-10838)*

Stansberry Welding Inc 580 621-3211
   5 Miles Ne On Hwy 64 Freedom (73842) *(G-3209)*

Stansbury Noble Jr Inc 209 847-8408
   10650 Canada Ln Tishomingo (73460) *(G-8968)*

Stanton Sand & Gravel Inc 580 229-3353
   1887 Memorial Rd Ardmore (73401) *(G-363)*

Stanton's Custom Prints, Lawton *Also called Stantons Apparel Inc (G-4004)*

Stantons Apparel Inc 580 353-1777
   3708 Sw J Ave Lawton (73505) *(G-4004)*

Star Building Systems, Oklahoma City *Also called Robertson-Ceco II Corporation (G-7040)*

Star Building Systems Inc 405 636-2010
   8600 S I 35 Service Rd A Oklahoma City (73149) *(G-7193)*

Star Center Tube, Sand Springs *Also called Webco Industries Inc (G-8236)*

Star Corral 918 251-9795
   808 S 9th St Broken Arrow (74012) *(G-1060)*

Star Industries 580 977-4576
   1721 N Grand St Enid (73701) *(G-3062)*

Star Industries Inc 405 542-3041
   124 W Main St Hinton (73047) *(G-3537)*

Star Jewelers Inc 918 251-9236
   120 S Main St Broken Arrow (74012) *(G-1061)*

Star Nowata 918 273-2446
   126 E Cherokee Ave Nowata (74048) *(G-5230)*

Star Pipe Service Inc 405 672-6688
   7100 S Bryant Ave Oklahoma City (73149) *(G-7194)*

Star Royalty Co 405 748-5070
   13112 Oakcliff Rd Oklahoma City (73120) *(G-7195)*

Star Well Services Inc 405 222-4606
   5401 Glenwood Dr Chickasha (73018) *(G-1513)*

Starfall Llc 918 269-4364
   13142 S 267th East Ave Coweta (74429) *(G-1898)*

Starfall Press LLC 405 343-2369
   6677 Valley Ridge Dr Edmond (73034) *(G-2630)*

Starline Inc 405 495-8274
   5412 N Rockwell Ave Bethany (73008) *(G-596)*

Starling Assoc Inc 405 740-8668
   1324 Brookside Dr Norman (73072) *(G-5156)*

Starlite Welding Supplies 580 252-8320
   506 S Industrial Ave Duncan (73533) *(G-2185)*

Stars Restaurants LLC (PA) 405 947-1396
   2941 Nw 156th St Edmond (73013) *(G-2631)*

Stars Stripes Construction 405 387-4847
   721 Grigsby St Newcastle (73065) *(G-4842)*

Start Rite Auto Electric Inc (PA) 580 924-7290
   805 S 9th Ave Durant (74701) *(G-2261)*

State Line Swd LLC 580 515-1468
   9473 N 1690 Rd Reydon (73660) *(G-8080)*

State of Oklahoma, Tahlequah *Also called County of Oklahoma (G-8859)*

State Oil Company, Ardmore *Also called Tripledee Drilling Co Inc (G-374)*

Stateline Processing LLC 855 979-2012
   3500 One Williams Ctr Tulsa (74172) *(G-10839)*

Stateline Water LLC 855 979-2012
   3500 One Williams Ctr Tulsa (74172) *(G-10840)*

Statewide Roustabouts Inc 405 262-5934
   5910 N Radio Rd El Reno (73036) *(G-2760)*

Station 7 .... 405 470-4317
   5900 W Memorial Rd Oklahoma City (73142) *(G-7196)*

Staton Inc 405 605-3765
   3310 S Brunson St Oklahoma City (73119) *(G-7197)*

Staudt Jewelers 918 756-0517
   113 W 6th St Okmulgee (74447) *(G-7526)*

Stealth Mfg 405 843-1954
   3204 Nw 66th St Oklahoma City (73116) *(G-7198)*

Steamport LLC 918 295-7600
   1717 S Boulder Ave # 400 Tulsa (74119) *(G-10841)*

Steampunk Bnics Innvations LLC 866 795-6645
   28 S Lakewood Ave Tulsa (74112) *(G-10842)*

Steden Oil Corp 405 364-7611
330 W Gray St Norman (73069) *(G-5157)*

Steel Creek Manufacturing LLC 918 698-3318
2972 E 76th St Tulsa (74136) *(G-10843)*

Steel Queen Inc 405 949-1664
1740 Nw 5th St Oklahoma City (73106) *(G-7199)*

Steel Systems Plus Inc 918 286-7947
10540 S 213th East Ave Broken Arrow (74014) *(G-1167)*

Steel Thinking Inc 405 485-2204
27699 Western Ave Washington (73093) *(G-11337)*

Steel Welding Inc 405 789-5713
5600 N Tulsa Ave Oklahoma City (73112) *(G-7200)*

Steeley D Upshaw Pubg LLC 405 948-7802
3730 Newport St Oklahoma City (73112) *(G-7201)*

Steelfab Texas Inc 972 562-7720
446 Country Club Rd Durant (74701) *(G-2262)*

Steeltek Inc 918 446-4001
4141 S Jackson Ave Tulsa (74107) *(G-10844)*

Stellar Art Publishing Inc 918 277-3325
5765 E 140th St S Bixby (74008) *(G-665)*

Step Energy Svcs Holdings Ltd 918 423-4300
7319 E Us Highway 270 McAlester (74501) *(G-4339)*

Step Energy Svcs Holdings Ltd 918 252-5416
12607 E 60th St Tulsa (74146) *(G-10845)*

Stephen Burns 580 657-3237
1421 Woodland Rd Wilson (73463) *(G-11543)*

Stephen J Heyman 918 583-3333
15 E 5th St Ste 3300 Tulsa (74103) *(G-10846)*

Stephen Poorboy 918 373-5073
31875 E 668 Rd Chouteau (74337) *(G-1571)*

Stephens & Johnson Oper Co 405 619-1866
6100 S Hattie Ave Oklahoma City (73149) *(G-7202)*

Stephens Custom Woodworks 405 938-7065
22399 Sutherly Farms Blvd Edmond (73025) *(G-2632)*

Stephens Oil & Gas Exploration 214 773-5898
3555 Nw 58th St Ste 1000 Oklahoma City (73112) *(G-7203)*

Stephens Scheduling Svcs Inc 918 630-1614
11063 S Memorial Dr Ste D Tulsa (74133) *(G-10847)*

Sterling Cabinetry & Trim LLC 918 928-9982
606 Ne F St Stigler (74462) *(G-8647)*

Sterling Crane LLC 918 728-8613
5104 W 21st St Tulsa (74107) *(G-10848)*

Sterling Properties 580 357-6095
9910 E Gore Blvd Lawton (73501) *(G-4005)*

Steve Harrison Game Calls 918 688-0807
3714 Silver Oak Ct Tulsa (74107) *(G-10849)*

Steven Campbell 580 764-3469
237289 E County Road 58 Chester (73838) *(G-1421)*

Steven Jackson 918 813-7184
9759 E 4th St Tulsa (74128) *(G-10850)*

Stevens & Sons LLC 580 482-4142
113 S Main St Altus (73521) *(G-169)*

Steveos Custom Wood-Work LLC 405 532-1863
5202 N Rockwell Ave Bethany (73008) *(G-597)*

Steves Bindery Service Inc 405 946-2183
1000 N Virginia Dr Oklahoma City (73107) *(G-7204)*

Steves Construction Company 580 432-5398
680 Pernell Pl Elmore City (73433) *(G-2897)*

Stewart Defense LLC 580 532-6426
315 N Biloxi Pond Creek (73766) *(G-7891)*

Stewart Industries Intl LLC (PA) 405 260-0990
120 Highway 74 Guthrie (73044) *(G-3339)*

Stewart Martin Equipment, Okmulgee *Also called Newton Equipment LLC (G-7517)*

Stewart Stone Inc 918 225-2704
1016 N Elm Creek Rd Cushing (74023) *(G-1962)*

Stewart Tech 405 292-8214
1331 Quality Ave Norman (73071) *(G-5158)*

Stewart Tech Incorporated 405 831-9316
2112 Natchez Dr Norman (73071) *(G-5159)*

Stich This and More 405 207-9922
123 E Grant Ave Pauls Valley (73075) *(G-7672)*

Stickem Fishing Lures Ltd 918 636-6179
9 Royal Dublin Ln Broken Arrow (74011) *(G-1062)*

Stigler Digital 918 967-8383
116 E Main St Stigler (74462) *(G-8648)*

Stigler Stone Company Inc 918 967-3316
910377 W 9 Hwy Stigler (74462) *(G-8649)*

Stiles Services LLC 918 582-7894
15 E 5th St Ste 3650 Tulsa (74103) *(G-10851)*

Stillwater Brewing Company LLC 405 614-2520
519 S Husband St Stillwater (74074) *(G-8756)*

Stillwater Milling Company LLC (PA) 405 372-2766
512 E 6th Ave Stillwater (74074) *(G-8757)*

Stillwater Milling Company LLC 580 369-2354
205 Gene Taylor St Perry (73077) *(G-7747)*

Stillwater News Press, Stillwater *Also called Newspress Inc (G-8729)*

Stillwater News Press, Stillwater *Also called Newspaper Holding Inc (G-8728)*

Stillwater Screenprinting, Stillwater *Also called B J Printing Inc (G-8657)*

Stillwater Signs Incorporated 405 533-2828
1225 N Perkins Rd Stillwater (74075) *(G-8758)*

Stillwater Transfer & Stor Co 405 372-0577
2005 E 6th Ave Stillwater (74074) *(G-8759)*

Stillwell Democrat Journal, Stilwell *Also called Newspaper Holding Inc (G-8793)*

Stinebrings Custom Processing 405 828-4247
308 S Barr St Dover (73734) *(G-2045)*

Stinger Wllhead Protection Inc (HQ) 405 702-6575
4301 Will Rogers Pkwy # 600 Oklahoma City (73108) *(G-7205)*

Stinger Wllhead Protection Inc 405 684-2940
3300 S Ann Arbor Ave Oklahoma City (73179) *(G-7206)*

Stingray Cmnting Acidizing LLC 432 617-2243
14201 Caliber Dr Ste 300 Oklahoma City (73134) *(G-7207)*

Stingray Pressure Pumping LLC 405 242-4998
14201 Caliber Dr Ste 200 Oklahoma City (73134) *(G-7208)*

Stink Free Inc 405 273-0006
9 Country Club Rd Shawnee (74801) *(G-8504)*

Stitch Boom Ba LLC 918 518-5859
12523 S 18th Cir E Jenks (74037) *(G-3729)*

Stitch Design 405 350-0126
300 S Ranchwood Blvd # 4 Yukon (73099) *(G-11789)*

Stitch N Print 405 789-8862
450 N Rockwell Ave Oklahoma City (73127) *(G-7209)*

Stitch N Sew Embroidery 432 741-0433
27455 N 3979 Dr Ochelata (74051) *(G-5239)*

Stitch N Stuff Embroidery Shop 918 465-3036
114 E Main St Wilburton (74578) *(G-11525)*

Stitch Witch 918 371-3568
2411 Black Jack Ct Collinsville (74021) *(G-1825)*

Stitch Wizard 405 816-6356
525 W Carson Dr Mustang (73064) *(G-4796)*

Stitchabella LLC 405 562-3316
5008 Kelly Lakes Dr Edmond (73025) *(G-2633)*

Stitched By Shayna 405 708-8614
3112 N Bartell Rd Oklahoma City (73121) *(G-7210)*

Stitchin Acres 405 740-6035
7618 W Keowee Rd Kremlin (73753) *(G-3855)*

Stitchin Stitches 918 251-9696
118 E Jackson St Broken Arrow (74012) *(G-1063)*

Stitchsumm LLC 918 201-2148
161 W M St Jenks (74037) *(G-3730)*

Stockmans Mill & Grain Inc 918 762-3459
600 Kansas St Pawnee (74058) *(G-7711)*

Stockmans Supply Company 580 255-7762
3733 N Highway 81 Duncan (73533) *(G-2186)*

Stockmans Tack & Supply, Duncan *Also called Stockmans Supply Company (G-2186)*

Stockton Transports Inc 580 227-3793
253920 E County Road 49 Fairview (73737) *(G-3152)*

Stokely Outdoor Advertising 918 664-4724
10111 E 45th Pl Tulsa (74146) *(G-10852)*

Stokes Production 405 485-2402
Hwy 99 S Seminole (74868) *(G-8401)*

Stone Creek Operating LLC 405 395-4313
6301 Waterford Blvd # 115 Oklahoma City (73118) *(G-7211)*

Stone Mill Inc 918 812-4438
740 State Highway 10 Kansas (74347) *(G-3755)*

Stone Oak Operating LLC 888 606-4744
10900 Hefner Pointe Dr Oklahoma City (73120) *(G-7212)*

Stone Splitters Inc 479 651-8873
300 E Vine Ave Sallisaw (74955) *(G-8153)*

Stone Warehouse 918 250-0800
9251 S Garnett Rd Broken Arrow (74012) *(G-1064)*

Stonebridge Acquisition Inc (PA) 918 663-8000
4200 E Skelly Dr Ste 1000 Tulsa (74135) *(G-10853)*

Stonebridge Partnership 1 LP 918 747-7594
4815 S Harvard Ave # 450 Tulsa (74135) *(G-10854)*

Stonecoat of Tulsa LLC 918 551-6868
5423 S 101st East Ave Tulsa (74146) *(G-10855)*

Stonehouse Marketing Svcs LLC 405 360-5674
2039 Industrial Blvd Norman (73069) *(G-5160)*

Stonemen Granite & Marble 918 851-3400
4702 S 103rd East Ave Tulsa (74146) *(G-10856)*

Stonewood Vision Source 918 994-4450
433 Stone Wood Dr Broken Arrow (74012) *(G-1065)*

Stoney Point Mine 580 362-3916
6901 E Brake Rd Newkirk (74647) *(G-4853)*

Store 1500, Tulsa *Also called Gravley Companies Inc (G-9850)*

Store 6, Tulsa *Also called Moodys Jewelry Incorporated (G-10303)*

Storehouse Printing 918 286-7222
5666 S 122nd East Ave B-5 Tulsa (74146) *(G-10857)*

Storm Haven Alpaca LLC 405 391-2767
2301 S Peebly Rd Choctaw (73020) *(G-1555)*

Storm Roofing & Cnstr LLC 918 688-0165
19450 E 72nd St N Owasso (74055) *(G-7620)*

Storm SF Ngrnd Trnd Shltrs NC 405 606-2563
6101 Camille Ave Oklahoma City (73149) *(G-7213)*

Stout Manufacturing LLC 918 371-7700
10903 E 166th St N Collinsville (74021) *(G-1826)*

Stout Welding LLC 580 254-2139
4832 Berryhill Dr Woodward (73801) *(G-11634)*

Stouts Welding 580 243-9116
20778 E 1160 Rd Canute (73626) *(G-1271)*

Stouts Welding LLC 580 339-8047
713 N Van Buren Ave Elk City (73644) ***(G-2878)***
Straight Edge Sawmill 405 401-7798
12200 S Country Club Rd Union City (73090) ***(G-11221)***
Straitline Inc 405 263-4604
11899 Prairie Valley Rd Lone Grove (73443) ***(G-4121)***
Straitline Inc 405 263-4604
108 N Industrial Blvd Okarche (73762) ***(G-5253)***
Straits Steel and Wire LLC 231 843-3416
5525 E 13th St Tulsa (74112) ***(G-10858)***
Strat Land Exploration Co (PA) 918 584-3844
15 E 5th St Ste 2020 Tulsa (74103) ***(G-10859)***
Strata Minerals Inc 405 722-3227
12028 N Pennsylvania Ave Oklahoma City (73120) ***(G-7214)***
Strata View Operating LLC 405 364-1613
1601 36th Ave Nw Ste 210 Norman (73072) ***(G-5161)***
Strategic Armory Corps LLC (PA) 623 780-1050
48955 Moccasin Trail Rd Prague (74864) ***(G-7936)***
Strategic Mission Systems LLC 405 595-7243
2501 Liberty Pkwy Ste 200 Midwest City (73110) ***(G-4456)***
Stratford Times, The, Stratford *Also called Kelley Publications LLC* ***(G-8805)***
Strawberry Valley Press LLC 405 237-1893
13601 Se 104th St Oklahoma City (73165) ***(G-5318)***
Stream Energy 405 272-1080
8241 S Walker Ave Ste C Oklahoma City (73139) ***(G-7215)***
Stream Energy Inc (PA) 405 272-1080
101 Park Ave Ste 500 Oklahoma City (73102) ***(G-7216)***
Stream Line 405 756-4422
903 Se 3rd St Lindsay (73052) ***(G-4087)***
Stream-Flo USA LLC 405 330-5504
5712 Industrial Blvd Edmond (73034) ***(G-2634)***
Streater Industries LLC 918 346-3247
15102 S 4060 Rd Oologah (74053) ***(G-7536)***
Strebel Creek Vineyard 405 720-7779
11521 N Macarthur Blvd Oklahoma City (73162) ***(G-7217)***
Strength Tech Inc 405 377-7100
1512 N Hightower St Stillwater (74075) ***(G-8760)***
Strictly Hardwoods 405 269-1026
6711 Lilly Ln Stillwater (74074) ***(G-8761)***
Stride Well Service 580 883-4931
Hwy 60 58 12 Mile St Ringwood (73768) ***(G-8093)***
Stride Well Service Inc 580 254-2353
1010 E Hanks Trl Woodward (73801) ***(G-11635)***
Stride Well Service Inc (HQ) 580 242-7300
615 E Ponca St Lindsay (73052) ***(G-4088)***
Stride Well Service Inc 405 375-4129
205 W Maple Ave Ste 600 Enid (73701) ***(G-3063)***
Strike An ARC Wldg Fbrction LL 918 407-7964
19496 Helt Rd Claremore (74017) ***(G-1688)***
String Up Machine Inc 936 349-0419
10819 S Rose Rd Perkins (74059) ***(G-7723)***
Striper Tinting 918 636-4043
4763 E 486 Rd Claremore (74019) ***(G-1689)***
Stroheim Romann Upholstery 918 622-7700
9303 E 46th St Tulsa (74145) ***(G-10860)***
Strong Service LP 405 756-1716
601 Nw 4th St Lindsay (73052) ***(G-4089)***
Strop Shoppe LLc 775 557-8767
110 W Dale St Norman (73069) ***(G-5162)***
Strope Manufacturing Inc 918 835-8729
1240 S Joplin Ave Tulsa (74112) ***(G-10861)***
Stroud American Inc 918 968-2310
315 W Main St Stroud (74079) ***(G-8820)***
Stroud Corridor LLC 405 823-7561
518 W Main St Stroud (74079) ***(G-8821)***
Stroup Industries LLC 405 737-4170
3629 Rolling Lane Cir Midwest City (73110) ***(G-4457)***
Stryker Service, Tulsa *Also called Sean Josephson LLC* ***(G-9035)***
STS Logging Services LLC 918 933-5653
9111 E Pine St Tulsa (74115) ***(G-10862)***
Stuart Beverly & 580 286-5586
1449 Se Washington St Idabel (74745) ***(G-3648)***
Stucco 2 Stone 918 770-2944
2623 E 1st St Tulsa (74104) ***(G-10863)***
Studio 180 405 512-2404
7901 Ne 10th St Ste C223 Midwest City (73110) ***(G-4458)***
Studs Unlimited LLC 214 683-8012
809 S Agnew Ave Ste D Oklahoma City (73108) ***(G-7218)***
Studylamp Software LLC 918 357-1946
7529 S Shelby Ln Broken Arrow (74014) ***(G-1168)***
Sturdevant Ice, Enid *Also called Enterprise Ice Inc* ***(G-2955)***
Sturgeon Acquisitions LLC (HQ) 405 608-6007
14201 Caliber Dr Ste 300 Oklahoma City (73134) ***(G-7219)***
Stutzman Consulting Service, Shawnee *Also called Terry Stutzmann* ***(G-8510)***
Suans Inc 405 413-1751
4716 Dove Tree Ln Oklahoma City (73162) ***(G-7220)***
Sub Industries LLC 918 798-9712
118 Mitchell Dr Elk City (73644) ***(G-2879)***
Sub Zero Ice Services LLC 405 387-2224
1840 S Highway 76 Newcastle (73065) ***(G-4843)***

Sublime Signs LLC 405 364-1700
912 N Flood Ave Norman (73069) ***(G-5163)***
Submersible Technical Products 405 850-4091
2301 S Highway 77 Pauls Valley (73075) ***(G-7673)***
Subsite LLC 580 572-3700
1950 W Fir St Perry (73077) ***(G-7748)***
Subsite Electronics, Perry *Also called Subsite LLC* ***(G-7748)***
Subtledemon Publishing LLC 405 670-3471
12231 S May Ave Oklahoma City (73170) ***(G-5319)***
Suburban Cabinet Shop 405 231-3110
128 Se 21st St Oklahoma City (73129) ***(G-7221)***
Sueno Designs 918 809-3027
16518 E 93rd St N Owasso (74055) ***(G-7621)***
Sues Monogramming 918 455-1011
12829 E 133rd St S Broken Arrow (74011) ***(G-1066)***
Sufrank Corporation 580 353-4600
102 Se B Ave Lawton (73501) ***(G-4006)***
Sugar Loaf Quarries Inc 918 647-4244
Arnall Rd & Highway 59 Shady Point (74956) ***(G-8416)***
Sugar Pills Apparel 580 277-0231
202 E Main St Ardmore (73401) ***(G-364)***
Sugar Sisters LLC 405 722-9266
2832 W Wilshire Blvd # 101 Nichols Hills (73116) ***(G-4863)***
Sugar Trading, Ravia *Also called West Texas By Products LP* ***(G-8072)***
Sugarwood Digital Printing 918 378-5771
706 W 119th Pl S Jenks (74037) ***(G-3731)***
Suggs Orel 405 275-6159
35109 Clearpond Rd Shawnee (74801) ***(G-8505)***
Sullins International Inc 918 258-5460
801 E Jackson Pl Broken Arrow (74012) ***(G-1067)***
Sullivan and Company LLC 918 584-4288
1437 S Boulder Ave # 700 Tulsa (74119) ***(G-10864)***
Sullivan Welding 405 301-6034
1706 Everglade Ct Oklahoma City (73128) ***(G-7222)***
Sullivans Custom Cabinetry 918 445-9191
5235 S 43rd West Ave Tulsa (74107) ***(G-10865)***
Sullivans Grading & Sod 580 591-2868
4728 Se Tinney Rd Lawton (73501) ***(G-4007)***
Sulphur Times Democrat, Sulphur *Also called Times-Democrat Company Inc* ***(G-8844)***
Sum Professionals Inc 580 983-2379
7725 N 1740 Rd Durham (73642) ***(G-2273)***
Summer Couch Welding LLC 405 408-3675
128 Sw 15th St Moore (73160) ***(G-4575)***
Summerside Vineyards & Winery 918 256-3000
1611 N Morgan Rd Tuttle (73089) ***(G-11212)***
Summerside Winery & Meadery 405 514-6360
1611 N Morgan Rd Tuttle (73089) ***(G-11213)***
Summit Casing Services, Woodward *Also called Summit Laydown Services Inc* ***(G-11636)***
Summit Energy Explorations LLC 918 396-3020
8198 N 70th East Ave Owasso (74055) ***(G-7622)***
Summit Energy Services Inc 405 366-9999
1013 N University Blvd Norman (73069) ***(G-5164)***
Summit Esp LLC 918 392-7820
103 S 42nd St Enid (73701) ***(G-3064)***
Summit Esp LLC 405 434-1257
2720 Classen Blvd Norman (73071) ***(G-5165)***
Summit Esp LLC (HQ) 918 392-7820
835 W 41st St Tulsa (74107) ***(G-10866)***
Summit Exploration LLC 918 583-0933
2530 E 71st St Ste K Tulsa (74136) ***(G-10867)***
Summit Labels Inc 918 936-4950
5420 E 9th St Tulsa (74112) ***(G-10868)***
Summit Laydown Services Inc 580 256-5700
207694 E County Road 40 Woodward (73801) ***(G-11636)***
Summit Machine Tool LLC 405 235-2075
518 N Indiana Ave Oklahoma City (73106) ***(G-7223)***
Summit Oil Company Inc 405 842-7896
7011 N Robinson Ave Oklahoma City (73116) ***(G-7224)***
Summit Sand & Gravel LLC 405 256-6029
628 W State Highway 152 Mustang (73064) ***(G-4797)***
Summit Well Servicing LLC 580 467-0886
3100 Continental Rd Ratliff City (73481) ***(G-8068)***
Sun Direct Power Inc 918 612-4090
6730 W Archer St Tulsa (74127) ***(G-10869)***
SUN Engineering Inc 918 627-0426
10031 E 52nd St Tulsa (74146) ***(G-10870)***
Sun Heat Treating Inc 918 227-2188
8500 S 89th West Ave Tulsa (74131) ***(G-9039)***
Sun Manufacturing Inc 580 765-4786
2401 N Ash St Ponca City (74601) ***(G-7879)***
Sun Materials Testing, Tulsa *Also called Sun Heat Treating Inc* ***(G-9039)***
Sun Microsystems, Tulsa *Also called Oracle America Inc* ***(G-10434)***
Sun of A Beach 918 938-6219
6848 S 32nd West Ave Tulsa (74132) ***(G-10871)***
Sun Proecision Machine, Ponca City *Also called Sun Manufacturing Inc* ***(G-7879)***
Sun West Mud Company Inc 580 256-2865
1107 Lakeview Dr Woodward (73801) ***(G-11637)***
Sunbelt Industries Inc 405 843-1275
8017 N Walker Ave Oklahoma City (73114) ***(G-7225)***

A L P H A B E T I C

(PA)=Parent Co (HQ)=Headquarters (DH)=Div Headquarters
2020 Oklahoma Directory of Manufacturers & Processors
637

Sundance Welding Inc 918 627-4065
5410 S 108th East Ave Tulsa (74146) *(G-10872)*

Sunflower Embroidery LLC 918 869-9646
1404 Richmond Dr Fort Gibson (74434) *(G-3179)*

Sunglow, Tulsa Also called Tcae Enterprises Inc *(G-10908)*

Sunoco (R&m) LLC 918 586-6246
907 S Detroit Ave # 1025 Tulsa (74120) *(G-10873)*

Sunoco Logistics Partners LP 918 352-9442
907 S Detroit Drumright (74030) *(G-2072)*

Sunrise Sheds 405 831-0904
1126 E Main St Prague (74864) *(G-7937)*

Sunrise Systems 405 222-3816
2126 County Road 1386 Blanchard (73010) *(G-735)*

Sunrotor Solar Products, Elk City Also called Solar Power & Pump Company LLC *(G-2874)*

Sunset Ridge Vineyard, Duncan Also called Judy Tomlinson *(G-2140)*

Sunshine Printing 918 951-6349
4523 N Hartford Ave Tulsa (74106) *(G-10874)*

Suntime Products Inc 918 664-8330
5566 S 79th East Pl Tulsa (74145) *(G-10875)*

Sunwest Mud 405 631-2101
6601 S I 35 Service Rd Oklahoma City (73149) *(G-7226)*

Supco, Bartlesville Also called Superior Companies Inc *(G-530)*

Supco Inc 918 336-5075
101 N Johnstone Ave Bartlesville (74003) *(G-529)*

Super Cuts 918 245-3320
430 W Wekiwa Rd Ste D Sand Springs (74063) *(G-8227)*

Super Daves Power Sports 918 485-9205
25981 State Highway 51 Wagoner (74467) *(G-11291)*

Super Flow Testers Inc 405 756-8795
400 Industrial Park Ste A Lindsay (73052) *(G-4090)*

Super Heaters LLC 580 225-3196
1701 E 20th St Elk City (73644) *(G-2880)*

Super Saver Dry Cleaning 918 296-7168
2036 E 81st St Ste 110 Tulsa (74137) *(G-10876)*

Super Signs & Printing LLC 405 842-7070
2838 Guilford Ln Oklahoma City (73120) *(G-7227)*

Supercuts, Sand Springs Also called Super Cuts *(G-8227)*

Supercuts Inc 918 775-6389
1108 W Ruth Ave Sallisaw (74955) *(G-8154)*

Superheat Fgh Services Inc 580 762-8538
3287 S 7th St Ponca City (74601) *(G-7880)*

Superior Companies Inc (PA) 918 336-5075
101 N Johnstone Ave Bartlesville (74003) *(G-530)*

Superior Companies Inc 918 534-0755
1000 E 14th St Dewey (74029) *(G-2033)*

Superior Dynmics Fbrcation LLC 918 698-9846
1800 W 14th St Bartlesville (74003) *(G-531)*

Superior Energy Services LLC 405 722-0896
7408 Nw 83rd St Ste E Oklahoma City (73132) *(G-7228)*

Superior Federal Bank 405 224-1021
1927 S 4th St Chickasha (73018) *(G-1514)*

Superior Graphics & Signs, Muskogee Also called Jack Stout Inc *(G-4696)*

Superior Honing and Grinding, Tulsa Also called Jorame Inc *(G-10058)*

Superior Manufacturing, Dewey Also called Superior Companies Inc *(G-2033)*

Superior Neon Co Inc 405 528-5515
2515 N Oklahoma Ave Oklahoma City (73105) *(G-7229)*

Superior Oil and Gas Co 405 884-2069
844 S Walbaum Rd Calumet (73014) *(G-1250)*

Superior Pellet Fuels LLC 918 494-0790
2131 W 73rd St Tulsa (74132) *(G-10877)*

Superior Pipeline Texas LLC 918 382-7200
8200 S Unit Dr Tulsa (74132) *(G-10878)*

Superior Resources 580 393-4314
218 E Main St Sentinel (73664) *(G-8413)*

Superior Sign Company, Oklahoma City Also called Superior Neon Co Inc *(G-7229)*

Superior Sign Shop, Ada Also called Doug Strickland *(G-33)*

Superior Solutions Welding & F 405 623-0104
1251 Golden Hills Ln Piedmont (73078) *(G-7772)*

Superior Spling Enrgy Svcs LLC 405 613-0329
2630 N 9th Ave Purcell (73080) *(G-8021)*

Superior Spooling LLC 405 613-0329
508 W Pierce St Purcell (73080) *(G-8022)*

Superior Stainless Inc 405 387-3414
1076 S Sara Rd Blanchard (73010) *(G-736)*

Superior Steel Bldg Mfg LLC 918 689-9745
710 Birkes Rd Eufaula (74432) *(G-3116)*

Superior Steel Buildings Mfg, Eufaula Also called Wayne Winkler *(G-3117)*

Superior Tool Services Inc 918 640-5503
26400 S Highway 48 Bristow (74010) *(G-797)*

Superior Vegetation Solutions, Braman Also called OK Contract Services LLC *(G-761)*

Superior Welding 918 439-9332
1606 N 168th East Ave Tulsa (74116) *(G-10879)*

Superior Welding & Fabrication 580 641-0634
4245 County Street 2845 Rush Springs (73082) *(G-8126)*

Supply Company Inc 918 585-2863
6924 E 38th St Tulsa (74145) *(G-10880)*

Supplyone Oklahoma City Inc (HQ) 405 947-7373
3801 Nw 3rd St Oklahoma City (73107) *(G-7230)*

Supplyone Oklahoma City Inc 918 446-4428
10590 E Pine St Tulsa (74116) *(G-10881)*

Supreme Mch & Stl Fabrication 918 387-2036
305 S Main St Yale (74085) *(G-11687)*

Sureshot Cans Inc 580 698-2800
194234 E County Road 50 Woodward (73801) *(G-11638)*

Surface Mount Depot Inc 405 789-0670
6003 Nw 5th St Oklahoma City (73127) *(G-7231)*

Surface Mount Depot Inc (PA) 405 948-8763
4001 Will Rogers Pkwy Oklahoma City (73108) *(G-7232)*

Surgiotonics LLC 405 269-9767
1105 S Stoneybrook St Stillwater (74074) *(G-8762)*

Susan C Willard LLC 918 740-4630
6009 S Atlanta Ct Tulsa (74105) *(G-10882)*

Susan L Chung Chirprtr 405 773-8225
7213 Nw 111th Ter Oklahoma City (73162) *(G-7233)*

Susan Secor 580 510-0060
1609 Sw Sandra Cir Lawton (73505) *(G-4008)*

Susan's Framing, Lawton Also called Susan Secor *(G-4008)*

Sutherland Well Service Inc (PA) 580 229-1338
S On Hwy 76 Healdton (73438) *(G-3422)*

Sutherland Well Service Inc 580 795-5525
1300 Industrial Blvd Madill (73446) *(G-4165)*

Sutherland Well Service Inc 580 856-3538
207 W Hwy 7 Ratliff City (73481) *(G-8069)*

Suzlon Wind Energy Corporation 580 468-2641
507 Sw Highway 54 Guymon (73942) *(G-3367)*

Suzy's Creations, Norman Also called Productive Clutter Inc *(G-5124)*

Swabbing Johns LLC 405 756-8141
Hwy 76 N Lindsay (73052) *(G-4091)*

Swabbing Johns Inc 405 756-8141
Hwy 76 N Lindsay (73052) *(G-4092)*

Swaim Serum Company 918 241-4363
13602 W 51st St S Sand Springs (74063) *(G-8228)*

Swan Brothers Dairy Inc 918 341-2069
938 E 5th St Claremore (74017) *(G-1690)*

Swan Plastics 405 275-4826
6500 N Kickapoo Ave Shawnee (74804) *(G-8506)*

Swanderland Associates LLC 918 621-6533
5153 E 51st St Ste 110 Tulsa (74135) *(G-10883)*

Swash Car Wash, Oklahoma City Also called Ecm Car Wash LLC *(G-6007)*

Swc 918 251-2679
604 N Redbud Ave Broken Arrow (74012) *(G-1068)*

Swc Production Inc 405 948-1559
210 Park Ave Ste 2820 Oklahoma City (73102) *(G-7234)*

Swearingen Machine Shop Inc 918 267-4308
71216 E Beggs (74421) *(G-562)*

Sweeper Metal Fabricators Corp 918 352-9180
Hwy 99 Truck Byp Drumright (74030) *(G-2073)*

Sweet Memories By Heather LLC 360 608-1600
821 Holmes Ave Cushing (74023) *(G-1963)*

Sweet Organic Scrubs & More 203 465-2683
1529 Ne 34th St Oklahoma City (73111) *(G-7235)*

Sweet Puffs LLC 918 367-9544
214 S Main St Bristow (74010) *(G-798)*

Sweet Sap Extracts Inc 405 205-8706
9120 N Harrah Rd Harrah (73045) *(G-3386)*

Sweet Scent Candle 918 535-3423
394661 W 2800 Rd Ochelata (74051) *(G-5240)*

Sweet Scrubs LLC 918 513-1176
7455 S Yale Ave Apt 137 Tulsa (74136) *(G-10884)*

Sweetandsassytinytees LLC 405 470-1170
9825 Nw 100th St Yukon (73099) *(G-11790)*

Sweetens Prfmce Machining Inc 918 436-9882
2701 S Pocola Blvd Pocola (74902) *(G-7788)*

Sweetiesrite Baking 405 400-6581
2201 Nw 35th St Oklahoma City (73112) *(G-7236)*

Sweetwater Exploration LLC 405 329-1967
121 S Santa Fe Ave Ste A Norman (73069) *(G-5166)*

Swh Construction LLC 405 317-0663
468 Sw 24th Ave Washington (73093) *(G-11338)*

Swift Eckrich Inc 918 258-4565
1901 W Iola St Broken Arrow (74012) *(G-1069)*

Swift Winds Industries LLC 405 600-9112
400 N Walker Ave Ste 125 Oklahoma City (73102) *(G-7237)*

Swiftwater Energy Services LLC 405 820-7612
9211 Lake Hefner Pkwy # 200 Oklahoma City (73120) *(G-7238)*

Swink Welding LLC 405 294-0114
4209 Snowy Owl Dr Norman (73072) *(G-5167)*

Sydco System Inc (PA) 405 350-3161
10879 Highway 44 Foss (73647) *(G-3184)*

Sydnis Shag Socks 405 664-5333
930319 S 3330 Rd Wellston (74881) *(G-11479)*

Sylvan Croft Woodworks 405 329-6668
7900 E Rock Creek Rd Norman (73026) *(G-5168)*

Sylvan Oil Operating Company 918 267-3764
1 W 3rd St Ste 918 Tulsa (74103) *(G-10885)*

Synapticgroove LLC 405 205-6094
3601 Lea Ct Edmond (73013) *(G-2635)*

Synergex Inc (PA)........405 748-5050
3705 W Memorial Rd # 1401 Oklahoma City (73134) ***(G-7239)***
Synergy Gas Bartlesville 1141, Tulsa *Also called Titan Propane LLC* ***(G-10946)***
Synergy Maintenance LLC........580 574-7355
6104 Nw Ferris Ave Lawton (73505) ***(G-4009)***
Synergy Petroleum LLC........918 456-9991
104 S Muskogee Ave Tahlequah (74464) ***(G-8885)***
Synergy Sourcing Solutions LLC........918 835-5019
1529 N 168th East Ave Tulsa (74116) ***(G-10886)***
Syntroleum, Tulsa *Also called Sooner Holdings Inc* ***(G-10788)***
Szabo Szabi........918 697-5441
1303 Sallie St Muskogee (74403) ***(G-4751)***
Szabo's Construction Services, Muskogee *Also called Szabo Szabi* ***(G-4751)***
T & A Gasket Co Inc........918 664-7600
3148 S 108th East Ave # 100 Tulsa (74146) ***(G-10887)***
T & C Construction........580 432-5413
Oklahoma 76 Foster (73434) ***(G-3189)***
T & D Fabrication Inc........918 352-8031
54440 W Highway 16 Drumright (74030) ***(G-2074)***
T & E Mobile Service Inc........405 990-4022
5325 S Madera St Oklahoma City (73129) ***(G-7240)***
T & G Construction Inc........580 355-6655
800 Se 1st St Lawton (73501) ***(G-4010)***
T & K Oil Inc........405 382-5241
11609 Ns 357 Seminole (74868) ***(G-8402)***
T & L Foundry Inc........918 322-3310
515 W 138th St Glenpool (74033) ***(G-3242)***
T A C, Tulsa *Also called Tulsa Auto Core* ***(G-10986)***
T A H Software Systems........405 478-3962
3400 Ne 115th St Oklahoma City (73131) ***(G-7241)***
T A T Inc........405 942-0489
2910 N Macarthur Blvd Oklahoma City (73127) ***(G-7242)***
T A T Oil Co, Oklahoma City *Also called T A T Inc* ***(G-7242)***
T and A Sawmill LLC........580 309-3100
235171 E 815 Rd Thomas (73669) ***(G-8948)***
T and L Embroidery........580 493-2239
418 Nebraska Ave Drummond (73735) ***(G-2048)***
T C Craighead & Company........580 223-7470
310 W Main St Ste 311 Ardmore (73401) ***(G-365)***
T C I N A, Seminole *Also called Tcina Holding Company Ltd* ***(G-8404)***
T C Whilden Consulting Inc (PA)........405 677-6881
4207 S Prospect Oklahoma City (73129) ***(G-7243)***
T D Craighead........405 329-2229
100 N Santa Fe Ave # 100 Norman (73069) ***(G-5169)***
T D Crghead Oil Gas Invstments, Norman *Also called T D Craighead* ***(G-5169)***
T D G I........405 275-8041
41901 Wolverine Rd Shawnee (74804) ***(G-8507)***
T D H Mfg Inc........918 241-8800
20520 W Wekiwa Rd Sand Springs (74063) ***(G-8229)***
T D Williamson Inc........918 447-5400
10727 E 55th Pl Tulsa (74146) ***(G-10888)***
T F T Inc........918 834-2366
2991 N Osage Dr Tulsa (74127) ***(G-10889)***
T H I, Tulsa *Also called Tulsa Heaters Inc* ***(G-10999)***
T J Campbell Construction Co (PA)........405 672-6800
6900 S Sunnylane Rd Oklahoma City (73135) ***(G-7244)***
T J Construction........580 494-6500
8041 N Us Highway 259 Broken Bow (74728) ***(G-1209)***
T John Co Inc........405 761-3460
2705 E Highway 37 Tuttle (73089) ***(G-11214)***
T K Drilling Corp........918 270-1084
8131 E 49th St Tulsa (74145) ***(G-10890)***
T K Exploration Co........405 239-7006
204 N Robinson Ave # 2350 Oklahoma City (73102) ***(G-7245)***
T K Publishing Inc........918 582-8504
1622 S Denver Ave Tulsa (74119) ***(G-10891)***
T K Stanley Inc........405 745-3479
6504 Sw 29th St Bldg B Oklahoma City (73179) ***(G-7246)***
T P I, Marietta *Also called Tasler Pallet Inc* ***(G-4213)***
T R S, Wellston *Also called Rifle Shoppe Inc* ***(G-11477)***
T R Tack Supply........918 299-5880
636 W Main St Jenks (74037) ***(G-3732)***
T Rowe Pipe LLC........580 765-1500
900 E Oakland Ave Ponca City (74601) ***(G-7881)***
T S & H EMB & Screen Prtg........405 214-7701
414 W Chicago St Shawnee (74804) ***(G-8508)***
T S & H Shirt Co Inc........405 382-3731
130 N Milt Phillips Ave Seminole (74868) ***(G-8403)***
T S I, Tulsa *Also called Tank Specialties Inc* ***(G-10898)***
T S I L C........918 357-5992
7420 E Forest Ridge Blvd Broken Arrow (74014) ***(G-1169)***
T Shirt & Signs, Durant *Also called Texoma Engraving LLC* ***(G-2264)***
T Town Lighting........918 693-2063
6918 E 19th St Tulsa (74112) ***(G-10892)***
T Town Sheet Metal........918 437-4756
1920 S 129th East Ave A Tulsa (74108) ***(G-10893)***
T W G, Jenks *Also called Tulsa Winch Inc* ***(G-3736)***

T&B Welding LLC........918 253-4120
4763 E 400 Rd Eucha (74342) ***(G-3096)***
T&K Auto, Sapulpa *Also called Timmy Pickens* ***(G-8315)***
T&M Roustabout Services LLC........580 796-2478
101 Oklahoma St Lahoma (73754) ***(G-3861)***
T&T Forklift Service Inc........405 756-3451
G Brown Ave Lindsay (73052) ***(G-4093)***
T-Birds Custom Screenprinting........918 521-3996
5206 S Harvard Ave # 333 Tulsa (74135) ***(G-10894)***
T-N-T Machine, Weatherford *Also called Tommy Luetkemeyer* ***(G-11447)***
T-Shirts & Hoodies Print Shop........918 861-0772
10318 E 21st St Tulsa (74129) ***(G-10895)***
T-Shirts & Hoodies Print Shop........918 861-0772
10318 E 21st St Tulsa (74129) ***(G-10896)***
T-Shirts Unlimited........580 286-5223
2103 E Washington St B Idabel (74745) ***(G-3649)***
T1 Box 190, Snyder *Also called Lawton Transit Mix Inc* ***(G-8582)***
T2t Storm Shelters........580 512-4890
2201 Se Flower Mound Rd Lawton (73501) ***(G-4011)***
T3 Energy LLC........405 677-8051
11900 N Macarthur Blvd Oklahoma City (73162) ***(G-7247)***
Tack Designs........918 825-1211
1355 Horkey St Maip Pryor (74361) ***(G-7993)***
Tactical Ballistic System........580 254-5468
1703 8th St Woodward (73801) ***(G-11639)***
Tactical Elec Military Sup LLC (PA)........866 541-7996
2200 N Hemlock Ave Broken Arrow (74012) ***(G-1070)***
Tactical Power Systems Corp........207 864-5528
19375 S Coos Thompson Rd Hulbert (74441) ***(G-3629)***
Taff Welding LLC........580 678-8978
24805 Ne Welch Rd Rush Springs (73082) ***(G-8127)***
Tag Agent........580 584-2892
32 Main St Broken Bow (74728) ***(G-1210)***
Tag Agent........918 653-2236
103 E Avenue C Heavener (74937) ***(G-3433)***
Tag Okc Inc........405 685-7728
5201 S Meridian Ave Ste 5 Oklahoma City (73119) ***(G-7248)***
Tag Petroleum Inc........405 377-6185
6519 W Coventry Dr Stillwater (74074) ***(G-8763)***
Tag Stillwater Agency........405 624-0200
702 S Western Rd Stillwater (74074) ***(G-8764)***
Tags 2 Go........580 335-7474
102 W Grand Ave Frederick (73542) ***(G-3202)***
Tah Software Systems, Oklahoma City *Also called T A H Software Systems* ***(G-7241)***
Tahlequah Daily Press, Tahlequah *Also called Newspaper Holding Inc* ***(G-8876)***
Tahlequah Printing, Tahlequah *Also called 262 LLC* ***(G-8848)***
Tahlequah Public Works Auth........918 456-9251
1410 E Powell Rd Tahlequah (74464) ***(G-8886)***
Tahlequah Solid Waste Services, Tahlequah *Also called City of Tahlequah* ***(G-8858)***
Tajour Specialty Products LLC........479 684-7445
65294 S 4710 Rd Westville (74965) ***(G-11485)***
Takeda Phrmceuticals N Amer In........405 317-7495
4405 Vincent St Norman (73072) ***(G-5170)***
Talking Hands Puppets........918 868-5553
10342 E 550 Rd Colcord (74338) ***(G-1790)***
Tall Boys Toys........580 323-2765
2410 W Commerce Rd Clinton (73601) ***(G-1771)***
Tall Chief LLC........918 783-8255
23 Cypress Cir Pryor (74361) ***(G-7994)***
Tall Chief Smoke Shop, Pryor *Also called Tall Chief LLC* ***(G-7994)***
Tall Oak Woodford LLC........405 888-5585
2575 Kelley Pointe Pkwy # 340 Edmond (73013) ***(G-2636)***
Taloga Times Advocate........580 328-5619
Broadway Taloga (73667) ***(G-8908)***
Talon/Lpe Ltd........806 467-0607
5909 Nw Expressway G185 Oklahoma City (73132) ***(G-7249)***
Tam Completion Systems Inc........405 601-7564
6809 Camille Ave Oklahoma City (73149) ***(G-7250)***
Tamatha Holt Od........918 649-0524
1104 Dewey Ave Poteau (74953) ***(G-7914)***
Tamco Plunger & Lift Inc........405 853-6195
Hwy 81 S Hennessey (73742) ***(G-3491)***
Tami Wheeler LLC........405 759-2239
741 Sw 101st St Oklahoma City (73139) ***(G-7251)***
Tammy Brown........918 456-1959
17954 S Muskogee Ave Tahlequah (74464) ***(G-8887)***
Tangier Explorations........918 585-3350
427 S Boston Ave Tulsa (74103) ***(G-10897)***
Tank & Fuel Solutions LLC........918 960-4361
14800 S 4220 Rd Claremore (74017) ***(G-1691)***
Tank Division, Catoosa *Also called Matrix Service Inc* ***(G-1339)***
Tank Masters........580 332-3325
120 Armory Rd Ada (74820) ***(G-92)***
Tank Specialties Inc........918 599-8111
3319 N Lewis Ave Tulsa (74110) ***(G-10898)***
Tank Trucks Inc........918 224-7515
14473 S Hwy 75a Sapulpa (74066) ***(G-8314)***
Taos Exploration........405 840-5398
6412 N Santa Fe Ave Oklahoma City (73116) ***(G-7252)***

A L P H A B E T I C

Tap Woodworks LLC 580 819-0455
  23982 E 1047 Rd Weatherford (73096) *(G-11445)*
Tape-Matics Inc 580 371-2510
  1539 Industrial Ln Tishomingo (73460) *(G-8969)*
Tapoil Inc 580 788-4576
  Hwy 2974 2 1/2 Miles N Elmore City (73433) *(G-2898)*
Tapstone Energy LLC 405 702-1600
  100 E Main St Ste 101 Oklahoma City (73104) *(G-7253)*
Taptec Manufacturing LLC 580 467-5142
  913 Silverwood Marlow (73055) *(G-4244)*
Taraco Enterprises LLC 580 679-3956
  101 W 2nd St Duke (73532) *(G-2080)*
Targa Pipeline Mid-Continent W 918 574-3500
  110 W 7th St Ste 2300 Tulsa (74119) *(G-10899)*
Targa Ppline Mid-Continent LLC 580 435-2267
  38348 Craig Rd Alva (73717) *(G-194)*
Targa Ppline Mid-Continent LLC (HQ) 918 574-3500
  110 W 7th St Ste 2300 Tulsa (74119) *(G-10900)*
Targa Ppline Mid-Continent LLC 580 883-2273
  3196 Highway 58 Ringwood (73768) *(G-8094)*
Targa Resources Corp 580 883-2273
  3196 Highway 58 Ringwood (73768) *(G-8095)*
Target Completions LLC 918 872-6115
  1700 N Indianwood Ave Broken Arrow (74012) *(G-1071)*
Target Pipe Line, Tulsa *Also called Tpl Southtex Gas Utility Co LP (G-10963)*
Tarhay LLC 940 655-4210
  16091 N 1720 Rd Hollis (73550) *(G-3569)*
Tarheel Oil & Gas LLC 405 823-9965
  9116 Woodrock Dr Oklahoma City (73169) *(G-7254)*
Tasler Pallet Inc 580 276-9800
  9196 Peanut Rd Marietta (73448) *(G-4213)*
Tatco Metals Inc 918 853-4663
  2025 W 121st St S Jenks (74037) *(G-3733)*
Tatermash Oilcloth LLC 918 743-3888
  3101 S Jamestown Ave Tulsa (74135) *(G-10901)*
Tates Flow Back LLC 405 663-2179
  711 N Hunt Ave Hydro (73048) *(G-3635)*
Tatur 918 244-6918
  13839 E 28th St Tulsa (74134) *(G-10902)*
Taxes Print Shop 405 521-3165
  511 Ne 31st St Oklahoma City (73105) *(G-7255)*
Taylor & Sons Farms Inc 405 222-0751
  2222 County Street 2900 Chickasha (73018) *(G-1515)*
Taylor & Sons Pipe and Stl Inc 405 222-0751
  2479 County Street 2865 Chickasha (73018) *(G-1516)*
Taylor Accounting Systems 405 949-9898
  3401 Nw 36th St Oklahoma City (73112) *(G-7256)*
Taylor Custom Cues 405 317-3298
  4619 Nw 10th St Oklahoma City (73127) *(G-7257)*
Taylor Energy LLC 918 481-1241
  7170 S Braden Ave Ste 200 Tulsa (74136) *(G-10903)*
Taylor Foam Inc 405 787-5811
  370 N Rockwell Ave Oklahoma City (73127) *(G-7258)*
Taylor Forge Engineered 918 280-1183
  6333 N Erie Ave Tulsa (74117) *(G-10904)*
Taylor Frac LLC (HQ) 405 293-4208
  14201 Caliber Dr Ste 300 Oklahoma City (73134) *(G-7259)*
Taylor Industries LLC 918 266-7301
  6015 N Xanthus Ave Tulsa (74130) *(G-10905)*
Taylor International Inc 918 352-9511
  8701 E Main Cushing (74023) *(G-1964)*
Taylor Resources 405 850-2283
  3001 Quail Creek Rd Oklahoma City (73120) *(G-7260)*
Taylor Rig LLC 918 266-7301
  6015 N Xanthus Ave Tulsa (74130) *(G-10906)*
Taylor Storm Shelters LLC 405 372-8130
  624 N Shallow Brk Stillwater (74075) *(G-8765)*
Taylormade Cbntry Cntrtops LLC 405 227-4063
  9205 Nyswonger Rd Jones (73049) *(G-3753)*
Tazz Too Embroidery 580 334-7373
  1120 6th St Woodward (73801) *(G-11640)*
Tbk Industries LLC 405 789-6940
  6656 Nw 39th Expy Ste 101 Bethany (73008) *(G-598)*
Tc Machine & Manufacturing Inc 918 986-7920
  7657 E 46th Pl Tulsa (74145) *(G-10907)*
Tcaacp LLC 918 251-6655
  511 S Aspen Ave Broken Arrow (74012) *(G-1072)*
Tcae Enterprises Inc 918 664-5977
  3801 S 79th East Ave Tulsa (74145) *(G-10908)*
Tcina Holding Company Ltd 405 382-0399
  201 N 2nd St Seminole (74868) *(G-8404)*
Tcj Oilfield Services LLC 580 687-4454
  237 Barr Ave Elmer (73539) *(G-2892)*
TCS Systems, Tulsa *Also called Clock Shop Inc (G-9455)*
Tdk Ferrites Corporation 405 275-2100
  5900 N Harrison Shawnee (74804) *(G-8509)*
Tdp Energy Company LLC 580 226-6700
  16 E St Se Ardmore (73401) *(G-366)*
TDS Portable Buildings LLC 918 422-4009
  21239 Us Highway 412 Colcord (74338) *(G-1791)*

Tdw (us) Inc 918 447-5519
  6645 S 61st West Ave Tulsa (74131) *(G-9040)*
Tdw Services Inc (HQ) 918 447-5000
  6801 S 65th West Ave Tulsa (74131) *(G-9041)*
Te-Ray Energy Inc 405 232-4121
  13208 N Macarthur Blvd Oklahoma City (73142) *(G-7261)*
Te-Ray Resources, Oklahoma City *Also called Te-Ray Energy Inc (G-7261)*
Te-Ray Resources Inc 405 792-7486
  13208 N Macarthur Blvd Oklahoma City (73142) *(G-7262)*
Teals Welding Inc 405 756-0615
  2093 County Road 1400 Blanchard (73010) *(G-737)*
Team Inc 918 234-9600
  12204 E Admiral Pl Tulsa (74116) *(G-10909)*
Team Duffens Optical, Oklahoma City *Also called Omega Optical Co LP (G-6775)*
Team Spirit Sales 918 296-5620
  502 E Main St Jenks (74037) *(G-3734)*
Tech Inc 405 547-8324
  511 E Highway 33 Perkins (74059) *(G-7724)*
Tech Pack Inc 918 836-8493
  6947 E 13th St Tulsa (74112) *(G-10910)*
Tech-Aid Products 918 838-8711
  2708 N Sheridan Rd Tulsa (74115) *(G-10911)*
Tech-Mesh Apparel LLC 918 492-1193
  7494 S Sleepy Hollow Dr Tulsa (74136) *(G-10912)*
Technical Energy Services Inc 405 329-8196
  6301 E Cedar Lane Rd Norman (73026) *(G-5171)*
Technical Manufacturing Inc 918 485-0380
  305 Se 11th St Wagoner (74467) *(G-11292)*
Technisand Inc 580 456-7791
  900 S Hickory Roff (74865) *(G-8112)*
Technisand Plant 2, Roff *Also called Technisand Inc (G-8112)*
Technology Licensing Corp 918 836-5597
  17424 S Union Ave Mounds (74047) *(G-4625)*
Technology Management Inc 580 332-8615
  529 Seabrook Rd Ada (74820) *(G-93)*
Technotherm Corporation 918 446-1533
  5505 W 66th Pl Tulsa (74131) *(G-9042)*
Techsico Entp Solutions Inc 918 585-2347
  910 S Hudson Ave Tulsa (74112) *(G-10913)*
Techspeedy LLC 918 406-0008
  6368 S 80th East Ave C Tulsa (74133) *(G-10914)*
Techtrol Inc 918 762-1050
  1310 N Sewell Dr Pawnee (74058) *(G-7712)*
Tecolote Energy LLC 918 513-4100
  2 W 2nd St Ste 1700 Tulsa (74103) *(G-10915)*
Tecolote Energy Operating LLC 918 513-4121
  2 W 2nd St Ste 1700 Tulsa (74103) *(G-10916)*
Tecolote Operating, Tulsa *Also called Tecolote Energy Operating LLC (G-10916)*
Tecumseh County Wide News, Tecumseh *Also called Countywide News Inc (G-8910)*
Ted Branham Welding 918 275-4431
  Rr 2 Box 48-2 Nowata (74048) *(G-5231)*
Ted Davis Enterprise, Oklahoma City *Also called Surface Mount Depot Inc (G-7231)*
Ted Davis Enterprises Inc 405 948-8763
  4001 Will Rogers Pkwy Oklahoma City (73108) *(G-7263)*
Ted S Cabinet 580 668-5207
  366 Tabor Rd Wilson (73463) *(G-11544)*
Ted Smith 405 677-8402
  4004 S Highland Park Dr Oklahoma City (73129) *(G-7264)*
Ted Smith Wire Rope Spooling, Oklahoma City *Also called Ted Smith (G-7264)*
Teddy Hall 918 355-3822
  20937 E 37th Pl S Broken Arrow (74014) *(G-1170)*
Tee For Soul 405 237-3186
  2500 S Service Rd Moore (73160) *(G-4576)*
Teeds Up Printing 918 279-1018
  13779 S State Highway 51 Coweta (74429) *(G-1899)*
Tees For Soul 405 844-7685
  507 S Coltrane Rd Edmond (73034) *(G-2637)*
Tees Q Usbs Llc 405 414-3264
  6600 N Meridian Ave # 160 Oklahoma City (73116) *(G-7265)*
Teeters Asphalt & Materials 918 673-1243
  57221 E 30th Rd Picher (74360) *(G-7751)*
Tefi Tek Industries LLC 918 728-7381
  2222 W Newton St Tulsa (74127) *(G-10917)*
Teg Solutions LLC (PA) 405 354-1951
  2490 Auction Pkwy El Reno (73036) *(G-2761)*
Tek Fins Inc 918 747-7447
  8301 State Highway 66 Tulsa (74131) *(G-9043)*
Tektronix Inc 918 627-1500
  9902 E 43rd St Ste D Tulsa (74146) *(G-10918)*
Teletronics Co, Mounds *Also called Process Products & Service Co (G-4623)*
Tellico Engineering Services 918 384-7409
  10838 E Marshall St Tulsa (74116) *(G-10919)*
Telos Payment Processing LLC 405 321-0474
  205 E Main St Norman (73069) *(G-5172)*
Templar Energy LLC (HQ) 405 548-1200
  4700 Gaillardia Pkwy # 200 Oklahoma City (73142) *(G-7266)*
Templar Operating LLC 405 548-1200
  4700 Gaillardia Pkwy # 200 Oklahoma City (73142) *(G-7267)*

Temple Custom Slaughter & Proc 580 342-5031
521 W Central St Temple (73568) *(G-8936)*
Temple Meat Processing, Temple *Also called Temple Custom Slaughter & Proc (G-8936)*
Temtrol, Okarche *Also called Nortek Air Solutions LLC (G-5247)*
Temtrol Inc 405 263-7286
106 N Industrial Blvd Okarche (73762) *(G-5254)*
Ten Mfg LLC 405 381-3752
414 Case Tuttle (73089) *(G-11215)*
Tenderette Steak Co Inc 405 634-5655
2200 S Central Ave Oklahoma City (73129) *(G-7268)*
Tendertte Old Fashioned Mt Mkt, Oklahoma City *Also called Tenderette Steak Co Inc (G-7268)*
Terac Controls Inc 918 622-6818
9600 S 219th East Ave Broken Arrow (74014) *(G-1171)*
Terac Manufacturing, Broken Arrow *Also called Terac Controls Inc (G-1171)*
Terex Cranes 405 491-2006
9528 W I 40 Service Rd Oklahoma City (73128) *(G-7269)*
Terex Mining 918 296-0530
302 W 120th St S Jenks (74037) *(G-3735)*
Terex Roadbuilding, Oklahoma City *Also called CMI Terex Corporation (G-5792)*
Terex USA LLC 405 787-6020
9528 W 140 Service Rd Oklahoma City (73128) *(G-7270)*
Terra Nitrogen 580 256-8651
1000 Terra Dr Woodward (73801) *(G-11641)*
Terra Pilot Mwd Tools LLC 405 603-2200
5 N Cooley Dr Oklahoma City (73127) *(G-7271)*
Terra Star Inc (PA) 405 200-1336
1515 S 7th St Ste 300 Kingfisher (73750) *(G-3817)*
Terraco Production Leasing LLC 580 658-3000
842 County Road 1610 Marlow (73055) *(G-4245)*
Terraquest Corporation 405 359-0773
1015 Waterwood Pkwy Ste J Edmond (73034) *(G-2638)*
Terrico Advertising, Beggs *Also called First Impressions Inc (G-555)*
Terrico Printing, Beggs *Also called First Impression Prtg Co Inc (G-554)*
Territory Cellars LLC 918 987-1800
1521 N Highway 99 Apt 1 Stroud (74079) *(G-8822)*
Territory Resources LLC (PA) 405 533-1300
1511 S Sangre Rd Stillwater (74074) *(G-8766)*
Terry Belknap & Sons Logging 580 244-3303
Hwy 259 Smithville (74957) *(G-8580)*
Terry Building Co Inc 405 634-5777
7621 S Shields Blvd Oklahoma City (73149) *(G-7272)*
Terry Company Inc 918 629-0926
2433 E 31st St Tulsa (74105) *(G-10920)*
Terry Hall 817 271-4838
760 Chickadee Ln Valliant (74764) *(G-11232)*
Terry Stutzmann 405 481-3853
9 Magnolia Hills Ln Shawnee (74801) *(G-8510)*
Terry Tylor Wldg Fbrcation LLC 405 205-2964
2489 County Street 2865 Chickasha (73018) *(G-1517)*
Terry's Acoustics, Valliant *Also called Terry Hall (G-11232)*
Terrys Contract Pumping 580 554-2387
21625 E Wood Rd Covington (73730) *(G-1868)*
Terrys Pump & Supply Inc 405 853-6550
112 N Main St Hennessey (73742) *(G-3492)*
Tesprinting LLC 405 708-7000
719 Garden Grv Yukon (73099) *(G-11791)*
Tessenderlo Kerley Inc 405 665-2544
307 W South St Wynnewood (73098) *(G-11674)*
Tessenderlo Kerley Inc 580 762-1130
200 Jupiter Pkwy Ponca City (74601) *(G-7882)*
Testco Inc 580 623-4900
1 Half Mile W On Hwy 33 Watonga (73772) *(G-11350)*
Testers Inc 580 243-0148
100 Robinson Pl Elk City (73644) *(G-2881)*
Testers Inc (PA) 405 235-9911
1661 Exchange Ave Oklahoma City (73108) *(G-7273)*
Tetherex Pharmaceuticals Corp 405 206-7843
840 Research Pkwy Ste 516 Oklahoma City (73104) *(G-7274)*
Tetra Technologies Inc 405 542-5461
31970 I 40 Service Rd Hinton (73047) *(G-3538)*
Tetra Technologies Inc 405 606-8600
119 N Robinson Ave # 700 Oklahoma City (73102) *(G-7275)*
Tetra Technologies Inc 405 677-0221
101 Park Ave Ste 1200 Oklahoma City (73102) *(G-7276)*
Tetrachem Seal Company Inc 580 924-1717
9660 W Highway 70 Durant (74701) *(G-2263)*
Tex Star AG LLC 580 579-9877
16774 County Road 3820 Coalgate (74538) *(G-1784)*
Texas Aluminum Industries 405 677-6767
2221 Se 69th St Oklahoma City (73149) *(G-7277)*
Texas Refinery Corp 918 455-6881
2205 W Canton Pl Broken Arrow (74012) *(G-1073)*
Texas Transco Inc 903 857-9136
10118 Mink Ln Marietta (73448) *(G-4214)*
Texhoma Fiber LLC 918 747-7000
1 Big Rock Blvd Medicine Park (73557) *(G-4371)*
Texhoma Limestone 580 889-8808
1102 S Highway 69 75 Rd Caney (74533) *(G-1263)*
Texhoma Truss, Durant *Also called David Kempe (G-2221)*
Texoak Petro Holdings LLC 918 592-1010
114 E 5th St Ste 300 Tulsa (74103) *(G-10921)*
Texoma Engraving LLC 580 775-7333
3509 W Arkansas St Durant (74701) *(G-2264)*
Texoma Materials 580 367-2339
1975 Bandit Trl Caddo (74729) *(G-1237)*
Texoma Mfg LLC 580 920-0878
3324 N 1st Ave Durant (74701) *(G-2265)*
Texoma Millwright and Wldg Inc 580 931-9368
1325 Se 3rd Ave Durant (74701) *(G-2266)*
Texoma O & P, Lawton *Also called Texoma Orthtics Prsthtics Pllc (G-4012)*
Texoma Orthtics Prsthtics Pllc 580 699-8690
1915 W Gore Blvd Ste 1 Lawton (73501) *(G-4012)*
Texoma Printing Inc 580 924-1120
2712 Enterprise Dr Durant (74701) *(G-2267)*
Texoma Pumping Unit Svc Inc 580 856-4024
119 Doral Rd Ratliff City (73481) *(G-8070)*
Texoma Sheds 580 223-0000
1411 4th Ave Nw Ardmore (73401) *(G-367)*
Texoma Tractor LLC 918 640-7949
10780 S 4050 Rd Talala (74080) *(G-8903)*
Texoma Wheelchairs 855 924-2525
1400 Bryan Dr Durant (74701) *(G-2268)*
Texre Inc 918 425-5524
2621 N Iroquois Ave Tulsa (74106) *(G-10922)*
Tfg In-Store Display LLC 918 592-2834
1507 E 7th St Tulsa (74120) *(G-10923)*
Tgg Prosthetics Orthotics LLC 405 285-5499
125 E 3rd St Ste C Edmond (73034) *(G-2639)*
TGI Enterprises Inc 918 835-4330
1219 S Hudson Ave Tulsa (74112) *(G-10924)*
Tgs Plastics Inc 918 252-3636
12528 E 60th St Tulsa (74146) *(G-10925)*
Tgv Rockets Inc 405 366-0779
2420 Springer Dr Ste 100 Norman (73069) *(G-5173)*
The Machine Shop, Tulsa *Also called A-1 Machine Shop Inc (G-9072)*
The Oklahoman Online, Oklahoma City *Also called Oklahoma Newspaper (G-6755)*
Therapy For Dogs Inc 405 314-7655
3001 Pine Ridge Rd Oklahoma City (73120) *(G-7278)*
Thermaclime LLC 405 235-4546
3503 Nw 63rd St Ste 500 Oklahoma City (73116) *(G-7279)*
Thermaclime Technologies Inc 405 778-6682
5000 Interstate 40 W Oklahoma City (73101) *(G-7280)*
Thermal Solutions, Catoosa *Also called Kelvion Inc (G-1327)*
Thermal Solutions Mfg 405 272-0453
717 Sw 4th St Oklahoma City (73109) *(G-7281)*
Thermal Specialties LLC (PA) 918 836-4800
6314 E 15th St Tulsa (74112) *(G-10926)*
Thermal Specialties LLC 970 532-3796
10116 E 93rd St N Owasso (74055) *(G-7623)*
Thermal Specialties LLC 918 227-4800
8181 S 88th West Ave Tulsa (74131) *(G-9044)*
Thermal Specialties LLC 405 681-4400
5001 Sw 20th St Oklahoma City (73128) *(G-7282)*
Thermo Fisher Scientific 918 540-1507
520 N Main St Miami (74354) *(G-4432)*
Thermoweld, Tulsa *Also called East 74th Street Holdings Inc (G-9631)*
Thermtech Industries LLC 918 299-5473
8526 S Elwood Ave Tulsa (74132) *(G-10927)*
Think Ability Inc 580 252-8000
1301 W Main St Duncan (73533) *(G-2187)*
Think Healthy Systems 918 384-0555
5321 S Sheridan Rd Tulsa (74145) *(G-10928)*
Think Screenprinting LLC 405 590-5131
2713 Ne 129th St Edmond (73013) *(G-2640)*
Thinkwerx LLC 405 590-3937
1609 Norwood Pl Nichols Hills (73120) *(G-4864)*
Third Rock Construction LLC 918 429-2011
308 E Camp Loop McAlester (74501) *(G-4340)*
Thirty Three Welding, Kingfisher *Also called Connie Pirple (G-3792)*
Thomas Appraisal Service 918 341-5860
18303 S 4200 Claremore (74017) *(G-1692)*
Thomas Cabinet Company 580 588-9231
128 S Hillside Rd Apache (73006) *(G-223)*
Thomas Companies, Claremore *Also called Thomas Appraisal Service (G-1692)*
Thomas Digital LLC 918 836-1540
6817 E 65th Pl Tulsa (74133) *(G-10929)*
Thomas Dist Solutions LLC 580 304-7741
2015 N Ash St Ste 113 Ponca City (74601) *(G-7883)*
Thomas Energy Systems Inc (PA) 918 665-0031
8525 E 46th St Tulsa (74145) *(G-10930)*
Thomas Engineering Co Inc 918 587-6649
1224 N Utica Ave Tulsa (74110) *(G-10931)*
Thomas Exploration Company 918 496-1414
7159 S Braden Ave Tulsa (74136) *(G-10932)*
Thomas H Scott Western LLC 405 632-6860
8817 S Western Ave Oklahoma City (73139) *(G-7283)*

ALPHABETIC

Thomas Millwork Inc 405 769-5618
2421 N Westminster Rd Spencer (73084) ***(G-8602)***
Thomas N Berry & Company 405 372-5252
S On Hwy 177 Stillwater (74076) ***(G-8767)***
Thomas Oil Tools LLC 580 252-4672
293833 E 1760 Rd Duncan (73533) ***(G-2188)***
Thomas P Harris Jr 918 742-6414
1503 E 19th St Tulsa (74120) ***(G-10933)***
Thomas P Shaw 918 742-4673
5721 S Delaware Ave Tulsa (74105) ***(G-10934)***
Thomas Processing Plant, Thomas *Also called Enable Oklahoma Int Transm LLC* ***(G-8943)***
Thomas Pv Shell, Tulsa *Also called Thomas P Shaw* ***(G-10934)***
Thomas Tribute Inc 580 661-3524
115 W Orient St Thomas (73669) ***(G-8949)***
Thomas Water Well Service 580 938-2224
Rr 2 Shattuck (73858) ***(G-8425)***
Thomas Welding 918 214-7657
5711 Harvard Dr Bartlesville (74006) ***(G-532)***
Thomass Welding 580 821-0843
20062 E 950 Rd Hammon (73650) ***(G-3372)***
Thomco Cabinet Co 405 627-1445
2650 Nw 13th St Oklahoma City (73107) ***(G-7284)***
Thompson Manufacturing Company 918 585-1991
6315 E 12th St Tulsa (74112) ***(G-10935)***
Thompson Pump Company (PA) 918 756-6164
801 W 20th St Okmulgee (74447) ***(G-7527)***
Thompson Pump Company 918 352-2117
409 E Federal St Drumright (74030) ***(G-2075)***
Thompson Services 580 256-5005
202201 E County Road 434 Woodward (73801) ***(G-11642)***
Thompson Woodworks 405 269-6480
1517 Hanson Cir Stillwater (74075) ***(G-8768)***
Thompsons Custom Butcher Barn 918 476-5508
6878 W 590 Chouteau (74337) ***(G-1572)***
Thompsons Metal Coating 918 272-5711
15358 E 91st St N Owasso (74055) ***(G-7624)***
Thomsons Trenching Inc (PA) 918 745-1030
4124 S Rockford Ave # 201 Tulsa (74105) ***(G-10936)***
Thorpe Plant Services Inc 918 455-8928
5125 S Garnett Rd Ste E Tulsa (74146) ***(G-10937)***
Three B Land & Cattle Company 580 332-9480
201 W 14th St Ada (74820) ***(G-94)***
Three Prcent Frrms Catings LLC 580 931-9908
2104 S Ranchette Rd Mead (73449) ***(G-4368)***
Three Rivers Corp 918 492-3239
8801 S Yale Ave Ste 240 Tulsa (74137) ***(G-10938)***
Three Rivers Custom Cabinets 918 537-2311
240 North St Muskogee (74403) ***(G-4752)***
Three Sands Oil Inc 580 336-2410
633 Delaware St Perry (73077) ***(G-7749)***
Throop Rock Bits, Tonkawa *Also called Asbury Machine Corporation* ***(G-8972)***
Thru Tubing Solutions 405 692-1900
200 Ne 16th St Newcastle (73065) ***(G-4844)***
Thru Tubing Solutions Inc 918 429-7700
225 Sw Haileyville Ave McAlester (74501) ***(G-4341)***
Thru Tubing Solutions Inc (HQ) 405 692-1900
11515 S Portland Ave Oklahoma City (73170) ***(G-5320)***
Thru Tubing Solutions Inc 580 225-6977
1501 E 20th St Elk City (73644) ***(G-2882)***
Thunder Cbd LLC 405 568-7235
500 Seville Dr Edmond (73034) ***(G-2641)***
Thunder Oil & Gas LLC 580 226-3800
911 W Broadway St Ardmore (73401) ***(G-368)***
Thunder Road Magazine Oklahoma 405 612-3844
2940 Nw 34th St Oklahoma City (73112) ***(G-7285)***
Thunderbird Energy Resources 918 627-5433
4786 S Irvington Ave Tulsa (74135) ***(G-10939)***
Thunderbolt Machine Services 918 357-2294
24787 E 51st St S Broken Arrow (74014) ***(G-1172)***
Thundrbird Rsources Equity Inc (PA) 405 600-0711
6300 Oak Tree Cir Edmond (73025) ***(G-2642)***
Thurmond-Mcglothlin LLC 580 774-2659
3301 E Main St Weatherford (73096) ***(G-11446)***
Thurmond-Mcglothlin LLC 405 853-2248
Hwy 81 S Hennessey (73742) ***(G-3493)***
Thurmond-Mcglothlin LLC 580 223-9632
34 Broadlawn Vlg Ardmore (73401) ***(G-369)***
Tidal School Winery 918 352-4900
500 N Bristow Ave Drumright (74030) ***(G-2076)***
Tier Lvel Thrads Stuff Screen 918 808-7290
1904 W Iola St Ste 106 Broken Arrow (74012) ***(G-1074)***
Ties Oilfield Service Inc 405 306-2655
4225 Bridle Path Yukon (73099) ***(G-11792)***
Tietsort LLC 405 664-7353
1500 Ne 4th St Ste 100 Oklahoma City (73117) ***(G-7286)***
Tiger Mountain Gas & Oil 405 605-1181
4305 Nw 46th St Oklahoma City (73112) ***(G-7287)***
Tiger Town Tees 918 409-4282
309 N Aspen Ave Broken Arrow (74012) ***(G-1075)***
Tigers Den By Dreamcatcher 918 478-4873
131 S Lee St Fort Gibson (74434) ***(G-3180)***
Tigers Express 918 251-0118
701 S 9th St Broken Arrow (74012) ***(G-1076)***
Tight Line Enterprises, Tulsa *Also called Tight Line Products LLC* ***(G-10940)***
Tight Line Products LLC 918 231-0934
9014 S Gary Ave Tulsa (74137) ***(G-10940)***
Tight Wire Fence LLC 479 220-1171
59168 S 4720 Rd Watts (74964) ***(G-11358)***
Tile & Design Concepts Inc 405 842-8551
310 W Wilshire Blvd Oklahoma City (73116) ***(G-7288)***
Tile Shop LLC 580 920-1570
1800 W Arkansas St Durant (74701) ***(G-2269)***
Tilford Pinson Exploration LLC 405 348-7201
841 S Kelly Ave Ste 130 Edmond (73003) ***(G-2643)***
Tilley Oil & Gas Inc 405 608-4970
12311 N May Ave Oklahoma City (73120) ***(G-7289)***
Tillison Cabinet Company LLC 405 793-2940
137 Se 4th St Moore (73160) ***(G-4577)***
Tilman Woodworks LLC 405 441-3324
2904 N Harvard Ave Oklahoma City (73127) ***(G-7290)***
Tim Carlton Prosthetics Inc 405 721-7570
9414 Westgate Rd Ste B Oklahoma City (73162) ***(G-7291)***
Tim Dees 918 825-1211
116 E Graham Ave Pryor (74361) ***(G-7995)***
Tim E Hutcheson 918 313-5710
1135 S Fulton Ave Tulsa (74112) ***(G-10941)***
Tim Metz 580 227-2456
707 S 13th Ave Fairview (73737) ***(G-3153)***
Tim Scoggins 580 438-2476
Highway 8 Cleo Springs (73729) ***(G-1712)***
Timber Ridge Spray Foam 405 608-5995
8401 N Walker Ave Oklahoma City (73114) ***(G-7292)***
Timbercreek Flowback & Safety 405 694-7228
1708 E Woodson St El Reno (73036) ***(G-2762)***
Timberlake Trussworks LLC 580 852-3660
12177 State Highway 58 Helena (73741) ***(G-3437)***
Timco Blasting & Coatings (PA) 918 367-1700
200 N Main St Bristow (74010) ***(G-799)***
Timco Blasting & Coatings 918 605-1179
34081 W 241st St S Bristow (74010) ***(G-800)***
Timco Blasting & Coatings 918 605-1179
820 E Highway 66 Stroud (74079) ***(G-8823)***
Timco Blasting & Coatings 918 605-1179
31188 S Highway 48 Bristow (74010) ***(G-801)***
Timco Blasting & Coatings 918 608-1179
301 S Allied Rd Track 103 Stroud (74079) ***(G-8824)***
Time Mark Inc 918 438-1220
11440 E Pine St Tulsa (74116) ***(G-10942)***
Times Star 918 710-5740
1122 W Main St Ste A Collinsville (74021) ***(G-1827)***
Times-Democrat Company Inc 580 622-2102
115 W Muskogee Ave Sulphur (73086) ***(G-8844)***
Timmy Pickens 918 812-5268
9925 W 91st St S Lot 61 Sapulpa (74066) ***(G-8315)***
Timothy J and Sharo Flick 918 250-2456
6407 S 73rd East Ave Tulsa (74133) ***(G-10943)***
Timothy Publishing Services 918 924-6246
3409 W Gary St Broken Arrow (74012) ***(G-1077)***
Tims Sheds 918 506-7741
14490 U S 62 Tahlequah (74464) ***(G-8888)***
Tin Roof Quilting LLC 918 551-7282
3106 E 26th Pl Tulsa (74114) ***(G-10944)***
Tinhorns Are US (PA) 405 381-4044
1884 County Rd Ste 1250 Tuttle (73089) ***(G-11216)***
Tinker Afb 405 739-2349
3301 F Ave Dr 22 Tinker Afb (73145) ***(G-8955)***
Tip Top Prop Shop 580 564-3712
Hc 72 Box 235 Kingston (73439) ***(G-3831)***
Tipton Company 580 762-0800
8725 S R St Ponca City (74601) ***(G-7884)***
Tipton Oil Tools LLC 405 964-3030
7575 Highway 177 Shawnee (74804) ***(G-8511)***
Tiptop Energy Prod US LLC 405 821-0796
3817 Nw Expwy Ste 950 Oklahoma City (73112) ***(G-7293)***
Tire Soft LLC 405 341-5070
3325 French Park Dr Ste 4 Edmond (73034) ***(G-2644)***
Titan Chemical 918 420-5990
5034 E Us Highway 270 McAlester (74501) ***(G-4342)***
Titan Fence Company 580 237-3412
5110 E Market St Enid (73701) ***(G-3065)***
Titan Fuel Systems LLC 405 788-2412
2201 Tecumseh Dr Norman (73069) ***(G-5174)***
Titan Machine Services Inc 918 437-2411
124 S 147th East Ave Tulsa (74116) ***(G-10945)***
Titan Overhead Door LLC 918 606-0094
5175 S 4110 Rd Talala (74080) ***(G-8904)***
Titan Propane LLC 918 838-8804
3602 N Mingo Valley Expy Tulsa (74116) ***(G-10946)***
Titan Resources Limited 918 298-1811
11114 S Yale Ave Ste B Tulsa (74137) ***(G-10947)***

Titan Specialties, Oklahoma City *Also called Hunting Titan Inc (G-6273)*
Titanium Nutrition LLC 918 697-1012
1301 Oakwood Dr Broken Arrow (74011) *(G-1078)*
Titanium Phoenix Inc 405 305-1304
1205 S Air Depot Blvd Oklahoma City (73110) *(G-7294)*
Tj Services LLC 405 596-5124
1300 Se Grand Blvd Oklahoma City (73129) *(G-7295)*
Tj Trost LLC 918 269-1582
14515 S 209th East Ave Coweta (74429) *(G-1900)*
Tjk Molded Products LLC (PA) 409 200-1007
1649 Fernwood Rd Ardmore (73401) *(G-370)*
Tjk Molded Products LLC 409 200-1007
1405 4th Ave Nw Ste 103 Ardmore (73401) *(G-371)*
Tk Aero Inc 405 359-8638
312 Saint James Dr Edmond (73034) *(G-2645)*
Tking Energy Solutions LLC 740 827-4599
671 Ne Addiebeth Rd Lawton (73507) *(G-4013)*
Tlp Energy LLC 405 241-1800
4747 Gaillardia Pkwy # 100 Oklahoma City (73142) *(G-7296)*
Tlr Well Services Inc 580 225-4096
Hwy 6 & Lakeview Rd Elk City (73644) *(G-2883)*
Tmco Inc 405 257-9373
108 W Cedar St Wewoka (74884) *(G-11512)*
Tmg Service Company LLC 405 213-4317
8000 Se Linda Ln Oklahoma City (73149) *(G-7297)*
Tmk Ipsco International LLC 918 384-6400
5610 Bird Creek Ave Catoosa (74015) *(G-1356)*
Tms International LLC 918 241-0129
2300 S Highway 97 Sand Springs (74063) *(G-8230)*
Tmw Systems Inc 405 602-6055
4300 Highline Blvd Oklahoma City (73108) *(G-7298)*
Tng Construction, Carnegie *Also called Carnegie Concrete Company (G-1273)*
TNT Sand & Gravel LLC 580 277-0640
7189 Prairie Valley Rd Ardmore (73401) *(G-372)*
TO Digital Media LLC 405 639-8219
1915 N Classen Blvd Oklahoma City (73106) *(G-7299)*
To Market LLC 405 236-2878
1131 Entp Ave Ste 5a Oklahoma City (73128) *(G-7300)*
Todd J Nightengale 580 227-2646
17557 Highway 8 Fairview (73737) *(G-3154)*
Together Tulsa Publications 918 269-1085
2631 S Boston Pl Tulsa (74114) *(G-10948)*
Tokata Oil Recovery Inc 405 595-0072
1414 S Sangre Rd Stillwater (74074) *(G-8769)*
Toklahoma LLC 580 402-1243
300 Smmit Ridge Dr Apt A4 Oklahoma City (73114) *(G-7301)*
Toklan Oil and Gas Corporation 918 582-5400
7404 S Yale Ave Tulsa (74136) *(G-10949)*
Toland & Johnston Inc 405 330-2006
3324 French Park Dr Ste C Edmond (73034) *(G-2646)*
Tom Bennett Manufacturing 405 528-5671
18 Ne 48th St Oklahoma City (73105) *(G-7302)*
Tom McBride Manufacturing 580 239-9020
100 E Smith St Caney (74533) *(G-1264)*
Tom Meason Oil Ventures 918 587-3492
427 S Boston Ave Lbby Tulsa (74103) *(G-10950)*
Tom-Stack LLC 405 888-5585
2575 Kelley Pointe Pkwy Edmond (73013) *(G-2647)*
Toma's Tanning, Oklahoma City *Also called Fake Bake LLC (G-6070)*
Tomcat Specialty Oil Tools LLC 405 659-9222
6304 Blackberry Rd Edmond (73034) *(G-2648)*
Tommy Biffle Lakeside Polaris 918 485-2887
33508 State Highway 51 Wagoner (74467) *(G-11293)*
Tommy Higle Publishers 580 276-5136
9052 Aztec Rd Marietta (73448) *(G-4215)*
Tommy Luetkemeyer 580 772-1517
24069 E 1040 Rd Weatherford (73096) *(G-11447)*
Tommy Nix Cdjr Muskogee LLC 918 456-2541
1711 W Shawnee St Muskogee (74401) *(G-4753)*
Tompc LLC 405 888-5585
2575 Kelley Pointe Pkwy Edmond (73013) *(G-2649)*
Toms Hot Shot Service 580 243-4300
Rr 4 Box 204a Elk City (73644) *(G-2884)*
Toms Tree Svc & Backhoe 918 865-4861
43851 W 61st St S Jennings (74038) *(G-3740)*
Toner Express 405 517-8817
2624 Butler Dr Norman (73069) *(G-5175)*
Tongs 580 875-2053
129 W Missouri St Walters (73572) *(G-11303)*
Tonis Stitches-N-Stuff Inc 580 688-2697
210 W Broadway St Hollis (73550) *(G-3570)*
Tonkawa Foundry Inc 580 628-2575
510 S 7th St Tonkawa (74653) *(G-8982)*
Tonkawa Meat Processing 580 628-4550
707 S Public St Tonkawa (74653) *(G-8983)*
Tonkawa News 580 628-2532
108 N 7th St Tonkawa (74653) *(G-8984)*
Tony Gosnell Operating 405 756-8091
4148 County St Lindsay (73052) *(G-4094)*
Tony Newcomb Sportswear Inc (PA) 405 232-0022
1824 Linwood Blvd Oklahoma City (73106) *(G-7303)*
Tony Oil Company 918 493-1882
6821 S Richmond Pl Tulsa (74136) *(G-10951)*
Tony Smallwood 918 402-9267
2016 W Ute St Tulsa (74127) *(G-10952)*
Tony's, Tulsa *Also called Tony Smallwood (G-10952)*
Tonys Electric Inc 405 375-4103
102 E Schroeder Dr Kingfisher (73750) *(G-3818)*
Tonys Welding 405 996-6657
6933 E Waterloo Rd Edmond (73034) *(G-2650)*
Tool Center 918 838-7411
1447 N Yale Ave Tulsa (74115) *(G-10953)*
Toolbox Oil Gas Consulting Inc 432 234-2067
1201 N 13th St Duncan (73533) *(G-2189)*
Tools and Troubleshooting 580 726-5290
425 S Main St Hobart (73651) *(G-3547)*
Toomey Oil Company Inc 918 583-1166
1126 S Frankfort Ave # 200 Tulsa (74120) *(G-10954)*
Top O Texas Oilfield Services 806 662-5206
1353 W Highway 7 Atoka (74525) *(G-425)*
Top Quality Doors LLC 405 579-3667
427 Highland Pkwy Norman (73069) *(G-5176)*
Top Rim Technology 918 467-3617
319 E Delaware Delaware (74027) *(G-2009)*
Top Secret Case LLC 918 521-0601
25567 Blackberry Blvd Claremore (74019) *(G-1693)*
Topco Oilsite Products USA Inc (HQ) 405 491-8521
8200 W Reno Ave Oklahoma City (73127) *(G-7304)*
Topog-E Gasket Company, Tulsa *Also called Thomas Engineering Co Inc (G-10931)*
Topps Powder Coating 405 794-2900
2132 Pole Rd Moore (73160) *(G-4578)*
Torbett Printing Co & Off Sup 918 756-5789
109 N Morton Ave Okmulgee (74447) *(G-7528)*
Torbett Prntg Co, Okmulgee *Also called Torbett Printing Co & Off Sup (G-7528)*
Torcsill Foundations LLC 281 825-5200
404 N Wilson Rd Weatherford (73096) *(G-11448)*
Tornado Alley Armor LLC 918 856-3569
9300 Broken Arrow Expy B Tulsa (74145) *(G-10955)*
Tornado Alley OK Storm Shlters 918 706-1341
11851 S State Highway 51 Coweta (74429) *(G-1901)*
Tornado Alley Turbo Inc 580 332-3510
300 Airport Rd Ada (74820) *(G-95)*
Tornados Screen Printing 405 964-5339
1 Whispering Oaks Dr McLoud (74851) *(G-4363)*
Toro Welding Inc 580 334-8221
321 E Oklahoma Ave Woodward (73801) *(G-11643)*
Tortilla Velasquez 580 468-6753
409 Ne 4th St Guymon (73942) *(G-3368)*
Tortilleria Azteca Inc 405 632-5382
2400 Sw 29th St Oklahoma City (73119) *(G-7305)*
Tortilleria Lupita Inc 405 232-2760
235 Sw 25th St Ste D Oklahoma City (73109) *(G-7306)*
Tortilleria Milagro 918 895-8225
6314 S Peoria Ave Tulsa (74136) *(G-10956)*
Tortilleria Milargo 918 439-9977
2128 S Garnett Rd Tulsa (74129) *(G-10957)*
Tortilleria Puebla Inc 918 610-8816
3118 S Mingo Rd Tulsa (74146) *(G-10958)*
Torus Pressure Control LLC 405 670-4456
1715 S Lowery St Oklahoma City (73129) *(G-7307)*
Total Beverage Services LLC 405 366-1344
2451 Van Buren St Norman (73072) *(G-5177)*
Total Care Orthtics Prsthtics 918 502-5975
6565 S Yale Ave Ste 909 Tulsa (74136) *(G-10959)*
Total Control System Inc 918 810-4004
7524 N 119th East Ave Owasso (74055) *(G-7625)*
Total Flow Products Div, Bartlesville *Also called ABB Inc (G-444)*
Total Home Controls Inc 405 736-0191
10925 Rowlett Ave Oklahoma City (73150) *(G-7308)*
Total Pump and Supply LLC 405 670-0333
2800 S High Ave Oklahoma City (73129) *(G-7309)*
Total Restaurant Interiors 405 535-6348
3936 E I 240 Service Rd Oklahoma City (73135) *(G-7310)*
Total Rod Concepts Inc 405 677-0585
7001 S Eastern Ave Oklahoma City (73149) *(G-7311)*
Total Systems and Controls Inc 918 481-9215
5122 E 84th Pl Tulsa (74137) *(G-10960)*
Total Valve Systems, Broken Arrow *Also called L6 Inc (G-963)*
Total Well Solutions LLC 918 392-9352
5727 S Lewis Ave Ste 550 Tulsa (74105) *(G-10961)*
Tote Along Inc 918 542-6453
51701 E 110 Rd Miami (74354) *(G-4433)*
Tote4me 405 664-1144
1312 Nw 172nd St Edmond (73012) *(G-2651)*
Touch Up Unlimited 405 527-5609
23759 180th St Purcell (73080) *(G-8023)*
Tourkick LLC 918 409-2543
12324 E 86th St N Owasso (74055) *(G-7626)*

ALPHABETIC

Tower Cafe Inc — ALPHABETIC SECTION

Tower Cafe Inc 405 263-4853
  Hwy 81 S Okarche (73762) *(G-5255)*
Tower Components Inc 918 379-0769
  4730 N 193rd East Ave Catoosa (74015) *(G-1357)*
Tower Inn, Okarche Also called Tower Cafe Inc *(G-5255)*
Tower Sealants LLC 405 528-4411
  4041 N Santa Fe Ave Oklahoma City (73118) *(G-7312)*
Tower Tech, Oklahoma City Also called Cpk Manufacturing LLC *(G-5849)*
Town & Country Hardware 918 865-2888
  104 Industrial Dr Mannford (74044) *(G-4192)*
Town & Country Welding LLC 405 664-5361
  21800 Martin Rd Harrah (73045) *(G-3387)*
TOWN HALL, Goldsby Also called Town of Goldsby *(G-3247)*
Town of Goldsby 405 288-6675
  100 E Center Rd Goldsby (73093) *(G-3247)*
Towne Publishing LLC 405 473-7436
  4017 Nw Pioneer Cir Norman (73072) *(G-5178)*
Townsend Marketing Inc 918 496-9222
  8315 E 111th St S Ste J Bixby (74008) *(G-666)*
Toyko Toys 405 204-7462
  3805 Nw 57th St Oklahoma City (73112) *(G-7313)*
Tpi Petroleum Inc 580 221-6288
  E Hwy 142 Byp Ardmore (73401) *(G-373)*
Tpl Arkoma Midstream LLC (HQ) 918 574-3500
  110 W 7th St Ste 2300 Tulsa (74119) *(G-10962)*
Tpl Southtex Gas Utility Co LP 918 574-3500
  110 W 7th St Ste 2300 Tulsa (74119) *(G-10963)*
Tpx, Edmond Also called Tilford Pinson Exploration LLC *(G-2643)*
Tr Tack Supply 918 543-4095
  29022 S 4230 Rd Inola (74036) *(G-3674)*
Trace LLC 918 510-0210
  7101 S Yale Ave Ste 348 Tulsa (74136) *(G-10964)*
Trace Oil 405 222-4449
  2931 County Street 2773 Chickasha (73018) *(G-1518)*
Trace Oil Co, Crescent Also called Tracy Tarrent *(G-1920)*
Tracey Gregory 580 819-0057
  24219 E 1040 Rd Weatherford (73096) *(G-11449)*
Traceys Window Boutique Inc 918 495-1806
  4206 E 80th Pl Tulsa (74136) *(G-10965)*
Traci Rae Woolman 580 544-2521
  118 W Main St Boise City (73933) *(G-749)*
Track Products 918 231-9960
  101 E Railroad St S Fort Gibson (74434) *(G-3181)*
Tracker Marine LLC 918 541-2000
  3807 Tahoe Way Miami (74354) *(G-4434)*
Tracker Marine Group, Miami Also called Tracker Marine LLC *(G-4434)*
Trackum Inc 405 799-4863
  1525 Camden Way Norman (73069) *(G-5179)*
Trackum Software, Norman Also called Trackum Inc *(G-5179)*
Tracy Tarrent 405 969-2343
  7 Appleridge Rd Crescent (73028) *(G-1920)*
Tracy Wood Shop, Tulsa Also called Tracys Wood Shop Inc *(G-10966)*
Tracy's Graphics, Tulsa Also called TGI Enterprises Inc *(G-10924)*
Tracys Wood Shop Inc 918 587-4860
  1338 E 2nd St Tulsa (74120) *(G-10966)*
Trade Mark Signs 580 242-7446
  1610 N Van Buren St Enid (73703) *(G-3066)*
Trade Trucking LLC 405 443-5375
  2316 Nw 32nd St Oklahoma City (73112) *(G-7314)*
Tradeshowstuff LLC 918 437-4338
  112 S 109th East Pl Tulsa (74128) *(G-10967)*
Trailing Edge Technologies 580 536-0559
  7109 Nw Birch Pl Lawton (73505) *(G-4014)*
Tranam Systems Intl Inc 918 488-0007
  6131 E 32nd Pl Tulsa (74135) *(G-10968)*
Trane US Inc 918 250-5522
  2201 N Willow Ave Broken Arrow (74012) *(G-1079)*
Trane US Inc 855 200-0072
  2205 N Willow Ave Ste A Broken Arrow (74012) *(G-1080)*
Trane US Inc 405 943-6600
  3450 S Macarthur Blvd B Oklahoma City (73179) *(G-7315)*
Trane US Inc 405 787-2237
  305 Hudiburg Cir Oklahoma City (73108) *(G-7316)*
Trane US Inc 405 787-2237
  2201 N Willow Ave Ste A Broken Arrow (74012) *(G-1081)*
Trans-Tech LLC 405 422-5000
  1600 Grider Ave El Reno (73036) *(G-2763)*
Trans-Tel Central Inc (PA) 405 447-5025
  2851 N Flood Ave Norman (73069) *(G-5180)*
Transcontinental Holding Corp 918 739-4907
  905 Verdigris Pkwy Catoosa (74015) *(G-1358)*
Transcontinental US LLC 918 739-4906
  905 Verdigris Pkwy Catoosa (74015) *(G-1359)*
Transcript Press Inc 405 360-7999
  222 E Eufaula St Norman (73069) *(G-5181)*
Transelearn 405 922-4595
  10333 Buccaneer Dr Oklahoma City (73159) *(G-7317)*
Transfer Cses Cltches Dffrntal 405 232-9557
  301 S Western Ave Oklahoma City (73109) *(G-7318)*
Transfund 918 588-6707
  1 Williams Ctr Bsmt 1 # 1 Tulsa (74172) *(G-10969)*
Transmission Center 405 329-4620
  4015 60th Ave Ne Norman (73026) *(G-5182)*
Transponder Key 405 757-3199
  15001 N Kelly Ave Edmond (73013) *(G-2652)*
Transtate Castings Inc 405 232-3936
  1424 Nw 1st St Oklahoma City (73106) *(G-7319)*
Transtrade LLC 918 521-7271
  4404 S Maybelle Ave Tulsa (74107) *(G-10970)*
Transwestern Pipeline Co LLC 918 492-7272
  8801 S Yale Ave Ste 310 Tulsa (74137) *(G-10971)*
Travertine Inc (PA) 918 583-5210
  1325 E 35th Pl Tulsa (74105) *(G-10972)*
Travertine Elevator Interiors, Tulsa Also called Travertine Inc *(G-10972)*
Travis Quality Pdts & Sls Inc 918 251-0115
  1404 W Detroit St Broken Arrow (74012) *(G-1082)*
Trb Industries LLC 405 990-4159
  700 N Peebly Rd Choctaw (73020) *(G-1556)*
TRC Rod Services of Oklahoma 405 677-0585
  7001 S Eastern Ave Oklahoma City (73149) *(G-7320)*
Treasures Custom Jewelry 918 333-1311
  2245 Se Wash Blvd Ste D Bartlesville (74006) *(G-533)*
Treat Metal Stamping Inc 405 275-3344
  37609 Old Highway 270 Shawnee (74804) *(G-8512)*
Treatment Systems, Broken Arrow Also called T S I L C *(G-1169)*
Treble Services LLC 405 401-1217
  4329 Nw 18th St Oklahoma City (73107) *(G-7321)*
Trece Inc (PA) 918 785-3061
  7569 Highway 28 W Adair (74330) *(G-112)*
Treehouse Embroidery 580 667-4322
  17419 County Road Ns 212 Tipton (73570) *(G-8960)*
Treehouse Private Brands Inc 270 365-5505
  400 Industrial Blvd Poteau (74953) *(G-7915)*
Treehouse Vapor Co LLC 405 601-6867
  8101 Nw 10th St Ste D Oklahoma City (73127) *(G-7322)*
Trees Oil Co 918 257-5050
  56351 E 307 Rd Afton (74331) *(G-123)*
Trenary Publishing LLC 918 607-3280
  1100 S Yellowood Ave Broken Arrow (74012) *(G-1083)*
Trend To Trend Wreaths 405 503-8992
  2309 County Road 1268 Blanchard (73010) *(G-738)*
Trendy Tees 405 620-3673
  305 Teri Ln McLoud (74851) *(G-4364)*
Trepco Inc 405 722-1400
  9320 Nw Expressway Yukon (73099) *(G-11793)*
Trepco Production Co Inc 405 722-1400
  9320 Nw Expressway Yukon (73099) *(G-11794)*
Tres Suenos, Luther Also called Twiss Sueons Winery Inc *(G-4140)*
Tri County Publications Inc (PA) 918 465-3851
  134 E Main St Wilburton (74578) *(G-11526)*
Tri D Cattle Farming, Morris Also called Rick Davis *(G-4602)*
Tri Production Inc 580 229-1280
  Hwy 76 S Healdton (73438) *(G-3423)*
Tri Red LLC 580 476-2551
  4624 Highway 81 Rush Springs (73082) *(G-8128)*
Tri Resources Inc 580 363-0243
  14500 W Adobe Rd Blackwell (74631) *(G-694)*
Tri Resources Inc 580 493-2249
  Rr 1 Box 112 Waukomis (73773) *(G-11360)*
Tri State Industrial 918 286-8110
  314 N Redbud Ave Broken Arrow (74012) *(G-1084)*
Tri State Machine & Supply LLC 580 256-6265
  220 48th St Woodward (73801) *(G-11644)*
Tri-Co Testing 580 772-8829
  114 Clover Ln Weatherford (73096) *(G-11450)*
Tri-Lift Services Inc 405 969-2069
  5325 N Highway 74 Crescent (73028) *(G-1921)*
Tri-State Con Foundations LLC 405 341-3043
  7608 N Harvey Ave Oklahoma City (73116) *(G-7323)*
Tri-State Elec Contrs LLC 405 341-3043
  7608 N Harvey Ave Oklahoma City (73116) *(G-7324)*
Tri-State Industries Inc 918 938-6004
  8620 E 46th St Tulsa (74145) *(G-10973)*
Triad Energy Inc (PA) 405 842-4312
  6 Ne 63rd St Ste 220 Oklahoma City (73105) *(G-7325)*
Triad Operating Corporation 405 842-4312
  6 Ne 63rd St Ste 220 Oklahoma City (73105) *(G-7326)*
Triad Personal Defense LLC 918 443-7803
  18833 S 4185 Rd Claremore (74017) *(G-1694)*
Triad Precision Products Inc 918 584-3543
  888 E Marshall St Tulsa (74106) *(G-10974)*
Triangle Pump Components Inc 405 672-6900
  1600 Se 23rd St Oklahoma City (73129) *(G-7327)*
Triangular Silt Dike Co Inc 405 277-7015
  18505 E Highway 66 Luther (73054) *(G-4139)*
Tribal Complex Office, Stilwell Also called Cherokee Nation *(G-8784)*
Tribal Consortium Inc 580 332-1134
  6950 County Road 3610 Ada (74820) *(G-96)*

Tribalcom Wrless Solutions LLC 405 274-7245
100 N Broadway Ave # 2550 Oklahoma City (73102) ***(G-7328)***
Tribune, Thomas *Also called Thomas Tribute Inc* ***(G-8949)***
Tribune Corp 405 262-5180
102 E Wade St El Reno (73036) ***(G-2764)***
Tribune-Review, Bethany *Also called Wesner Publications Company* ***(G-600)***
Tricat Inc 918 423-5800
103 Taylar Rd McAlester (74501) ***(G-4343)***
Tricked Out Pony 918 931-2646
17587 N Baker Rd Tahlequah (74464) ***(G-8889)***
Trickser Native Apparel Co, Catoosa *Also called Hermann Jermey* ***(G-1321)***
Tricon Unlmited Cnstr Svcs LLC 405 473-9186
3917 Nw 16th St Oklahoma City (73107) ***(G-7329)***
Tridon Composites Inc 918 742-0426
18987 W Highway 66 Kellyville (74039) ***(G-3768)***
Tridon Oil Inc 918 682-6801
111 And A Half S York St Muskogee (74403) ***(G-4754)***
Triguard of Oklahoma 580 243-8015
1701 E 20th St Elk City (73644) ***(G-2885)***
Trikntrux 918 224-2116
408 N Mission St Sapulpa (74066) ***(G-8316)***
Trillium CNG, Oklahoma City *Also called Trillium Trnsp Fuels LLC* ***(G-7330)***
Trillium Trnsp Fuels LLC (PA) 800 920-1166
10601 N Pennsylvania Ave Oklahoma City (73120) ***(G-7330)***
Trillium Trnsp Fuels LLC 405 302-6500
10601 N Pennsylvania Ave Oklahoma City (73120) ***(G-7331)***
Trilogy Horse Ind 405 248-1010
2840 Linda Ln Oklahoma City (73115) ***(G-7332)***
Trilogy Horse Industries Inc 405 248-1010
2169 Copperridge Ln Harrah (73045) ***(G-3388)***
Trim Line Cabinets Inc 405 664-1439
910 S 6th Ave Purcell (73080) ***(G-8024)***
Trim Rite Moldings Inc 918 423-2525
2303 N Main St McAlester (74501) ***(G-4344)***
Trimark Labs 405 942-3289
727 N Ann Arbor Ave Oklahoma City (73127) ***(G-7333)***
Trinity Gas Corporation (PA) 580 233-1155
201 N Grand St Ste 700 Enid (73701) ***(G-3067)***
Trinity Industries Inc 405 629-1213
2100 S Pennsylvania Ave Oklahoma City (73108) ***(G-7334)***
Trinity Scrnprntng/Dmond Awrds 580 364-3752
5692 S Mockingbird Ln Atoka (74525) ***(G-426)***
Trinity Shtmtl Fabrication LLC 918 899-6030
23670 240th St Purcell (73080) ***(G-8025)***
Trinity Tank Car Inc 405 629-1226
2100 S Pennsylvania Ave Oklahoma City (73108) ***(G-7335)***
Trinity Technologies LLC 580 475-0900
1710 W Terry Rd Duncan (73533) ***(G-2190)***
Trinity Wood Works 918 619-3959
7290 River Ridge Rd Muskogee (74403) ***(G-4755)***
Trio Di Vino LLC 405 494-1954
712 N Broadway Ave Oklahoma City (73102) ***(G-7336)***
Trios of Oklahoma LLC 918 760-2734
10 N Grand Fork Dr Edmond (73003) ***(G-2653)***
Triple B Media LLC 405 732-7577
9075 Harmony Dr Midwest City (73130) ***(G-4459)***
Triple C Grading & Excvtg LLC 918 605-1848
19495 W 101st St S Sapulpa (74066) ***(G-8317)***
Triple Crown Energy-Bh LLC 918 518-5422
2201 S Utica Pl Ste 100 Tulsa (74114) ***(G-10975)***
Triple D Machine Inc 580 566-2284
406 6th St Boswell (74727) ***(G-758)***
Triple DS Neon Signs LLC 817 447-2830
55801 E 350 Rd Jay (74346) ***(G-3686)***
Triple Elite LLC 405 610-5200
5717 Se 74th St Ste C Oklahoma City (73135) ***(G-7337)***
Triple H Industries LLC 405 201-8820
4685 Highway 177 N Sulphur (73086) ***(G-8845)***
Triple M 580 488-3468
75000 N 2090 Rd Leedey (73654) ***(G-4032)***
Triple M Roustabouts LLC 918 619-7610
15 E 5th St Ste 3000 Tulsa (74103) ***(G-10976)***
Triple T Hotshot 405 745-6698
9524 Kickapoo Dr Mustang (73064) ***(G-4798)***
Triple T Printing 405 912-1212
116 N Broadway St Moore (73160) ***(G-4579)***
Triple T Welding 918 449-0037
10875 S 209th East Ave Broken Arrow (74014) ***(G-1173)***
Tripledee Drilling Co Inc (PA) 580 223-8181
100 W Main St Ardmore (73401) ***(G-374)***
Tripower Resources LLC 580 226-6700
16 E St Sw Ste 200 Ardmore (73401) ***(G-375)***
Trism's Home School, Tulsa *Also called Trisms Inc* ***(G-10977)***
Trisms Inc 918 585-2778
1203 S Delaware Pl Tulsa (74104) ***(G-10977)***
Tritan Mfg LLC 405 375-3332
1512 S 10th St Kingfisher (73750) ***(G-3819)***
Triumph Arstrctres - Tulsa LLC 615 361-2061
3330 N Mingo Rd Tulsa (74116) ***(G-10978)***
Triumph Energy Partners LLC 918 986-8283
8908 S Yale Ave Ste 2 Tulsa (74137) ***(G-10979)***
Triumph Resources Inc 405 478-8770
701 Cedar Lake Blvd Oklahoma City (73114) ***(G-7338)***
Troglin Tank Gauge Svcs LLC 806 275-0010
125 Prairie Hawk Ln Blanchard (73010) ***(G-739)***
Trojan Livestock Equipment 580 772-1849
24169 Lawter Rd Weatherford (73096) ***(G-11451)***
Trojan Oil and Gas LLC 918 606-0260
6478 Mandy Ct Sapulpa (74066) ***(G-8318)***
Tronox Incorporated 580 921-5411
1222 10th St Ste 115 Woodward (73801) ***(G-11645)***
Tronox Incorporated 405 775-5000
3301 Nw 150th St Oklahoma City (73134) ***(G-7339)***
Tronox LLC 405 775-5000
3301 Nw 150th St Oklahoma City (73134) ***(G-7340)***
Tronox Pigments LLC 405 775-5000
3301 Nw 150th St Oklahoma City (73134) ***(G-7341)***
Tronox US Holdings Inc (HQ) 405 775-5000
3301 Nw 150th St Oklahoma City (73134) ***(G-7342)***
Tronox Worldwide LLC (HQ) 405 775-5000
3301 Nw 150th St Oklahoma City (73134) ***(G-7343)***
Trooper Trap, El Reno *Also called Alan Beaty* ***(G-2696)***
Trophies n Things 405 247-9771
121 W Broadway St Anadarko (73005) ***(G-207)***
Tropical Minerals Inc 405 236-2700
11032 Quail Creek Rd Oklahoma City (73120) ***(G-7344)***
Trotter Custom Woodworks LLC 918 698-5231
4039 S 177th West Ave Sand Springs (74063) ***(G-8231)***
Troutman Dragline Service, Rush Springs *Also called Troutman Enterprises LLC* ***(G-8129)***
Troutman Enterprises LLC 405 351-0665
4401 County Street 2760 Rush Springs (73082) ***(G-8129)***
Troy Hulett 580 922-5298
252334 E County Road 39 Cleo Springs (73729) ***(G-1713)***
Troy Wesnidge Inc 405 387-4720
2024 S Main St Newcastle (73065) ***(G-4845)***
Trpr Oilfield Services LLC 405 853-1988
2221 Berry Ave Weatherford (73096) ***(G-11452)***
Trs Cabinets & Trim LLC 405 234-7276
110 Asbill Ave Yukon (73099) ***(G-11795)***
Trubend Systems Inc 918 342-3373
15505 E 520 Rd Claremore (74019) ***(G-1695)***
Truck Bodies & Eqp Intl Inc 918 355-6842
6112 New Sapulpa Rd Broken Arrow (74014) ***(G-1174)***
True Energy Services LLC (HQ) 580 421-9808
329 S Rennie St Ada (74820) ***(G-97)***
True North Ministries Inc (PA) 405 562-2986
14033 N Eastern Ave Fl 2 Edmond (73013) ***(G-2654)***
True Steel LLC 580 310-0595
19380 County Road 1590 Ada (74820) ***(G-98)***
True Turn of Tulsa LLC 918 224-5040
423 N Boulder Ave Tulsa (74103) ***(G-10980)***
Truevine Operating LLC 580 427-7919
2612 Arlington St Ada (74820) ***(G-99)***
Truex LLC 918 250-7641
11108 E 56th St Tulsa (74146) ***(G-10981)***
Truex Lighting, Tulsa *Also called Truex LLC* ***(G-10981)***
Trulite GL Alum Solutions LLC 918 665-6655
4363 S 86th East Ave Tulsa (74145) ***(G-10982)***
Truman F Logsdon 405 348-4504
1616 E 19th St Ste 403 Edmond (73013) ***(G-2655)***
Trunch Bull Service LLC 580 468-1501
3235 Ne Highway 54 Guymon (73942) ***(G-3369)***
Truproducts LLC 405 830-0151
8700 Banner Rd Lexington (73051) ***(G-4040)***
Trusty Willow LLC 253 241-0520
21637 Carters Lake Rd Bokoshe (74930) ***(G-755)***
Tsalta Corporation 405 607-4141
821 W Wilshire Blvd Oklahoma City (73116) ***(G-7345)***
Tsalta Oil, Oklahoma City *Also called Tsalta Corporation* ***(G-7345)***
Tsb Welding LLC 405 485-4274
1510 Ladderback Ln Blanchard (73010) ***(G-740)***
Tsdr LLC 405 823-1518
1712 Nw 5th St Oklahoma City (73106) ***(G-7346)***
Tsi Heat Treating, Tulsa *Also called Thermal Specialties LLC* ***(G-9044)***
Tsi-Enquip Inc 918 599-8111
3319 N Lewis Ave Tulsa (74110) ***(G-10983)***
Tsig LLC 405 463-7700
7608 N Harvey Ave Oklahoma City (73116) ***(G-7347)***
Tsm Industrial Welding 720 290-4431
16363 N 36th West Ave Skiatook (74070) ***(G-8572)***
Tts Embroiderys Plus 918 770-3515
14915 Courtney Ln Glenpool (74033) ***(G-3243)***
Tubacex Durant Inc 724 646-4301
362 Country Club Rd Durant (74701) ***(G-2270)***
Tuboscope Pipeline Svcs Inc 405 478-2441
3600 S Kelly Ave Edmond (73013) ***(G-2656)***
Tuboscope Vetco International, Edmond *Also called Tuboscope Pipeline Svcs Inc* ***(G-2656)***
Tucker Construction Co, Lindsay *Also called Greg Tucker Construction* ***(G-4064)***

A L P H A B E T I C

Tucker Energy Services Inc 918 806-5647
12607 E 60th St Tulsa (74146) **(G-10984)**
Tucker Slaughter House, Durant *Also called Rowlands Proc & Cattle Co* **(G-2253)**
Tuff Shed Inc 405 272-1011
1250 E Reno Ave Oklahoma City (73117) **(G-7348)**
Tuff Shed Inc 405 788-4143
14120 Highway 177 Shawnee (74804) **(G-8513)**
Tuff Troff LLC 918 623-6091
378181 E 1000 Rd Okemah (74859) **(G-5277)**
Tuffroots LLC 580 728-0000
6909 Old 21 Rd Idabel (74745) **(G-3650)**
Tularosa Inc 405 848-0408
6424 N Santa Fe Ave Ste A Oklahoma City (73116) **(G-7349)**
Tulsa American Shaman 918 938-0718
5455 S Mingo Rd Tulsa (74146) **(G-10985)**
Tulsa Asphalt LLC 918 445-2684
14901 E 66th St N Owasso (74055) **(G-7627)**
Tulsa Auto Core 918 584-5899
1130 N Lewis Ave Tulsa (74110) **(G-10986)**
Tulsa Auto Spring Co 918 835-6926
6545 E 21st Pl Tulsa (74129) **(G-10987)**
Tulsa Baking Inc 918 712-2918
3202 E 15th St Tulsa (74104) **(G-10988)**
Tulsa Baking Inc (PA) 918 747-2301
7712 E 11th St Tulsa (74112) **(G-10989)**
Tulsa Beacon, Tulsa *Also called Biggs Communications Inc* **(G-9295)**
Tulsa Brake & Clutch Co LLC 918 582-2165
129 N Lewis Ave Tulsa (74110) **(G-10990)**
Tulsa Casting Inc 918 366-1272
15250 S 76th East Ave Bixby (74008) **(G-667)**
Tulsa Cement LLC 918 437-3902
2609 N 145th East Ave Tulsa (74116) **(G-10991)**
Tulsa Centerless Bar Proc Inc 918 438-0000
1605 N 168th East Ave Tulsa (74116) **(G-10992)**
Tulsa Coffee Service Inc (PA) 918 836-5570
6239 E 15th St Tulsa (74112) **(G-10993)**
Tulsa Copper Specialties 918 249-4809
5910 S 107th East Ave Tulsa (74146) **(G-10994)**
Tulsa County Medical Society 918 743-6184
5315 S Lewis Ave Tulsa (74105) **(G-10995)**
Tulsa Dynaspan Inc 918 258-8693
1241 E 29th Pl Tulsa (74114) **(G-10996)**
Tulsa Fin Tube, Tulsa *Also called T F T Inc* **(G-10889)**
Tulsa Gamma Ray Inc 918 425-3112
3487 N Osage Dr Tulsa (74127) **(G-10997)**
Tulsa Gas Oil, Tulsa *Also called Shawns Small Eng Eqp Repr LLC* **(G-10740)**
Tulsa Glass Blowing Studio Inc 918 582-4527
7440 E 7th St Tulsa (74112) **(G-10998)**
Tulsa Heaters Inc 918 582-9918
1215 S Boulder Ave # 1200 Tulsa (74119) **(G-10999)**
Tulsa Hose & Fittings Inc 918 485-0348
305 Se 11th St Wagoner (74467) **(G-11294)**
Tulsa Industrial Mfg LLC 918 640-3802
8410 N 66th East Ave Owasso (74055) **(G-7628)**
Tulsa Instant Printing 918 627-0730
6380 E 31st St Ste D Tulsa (74135) **(G-11000)**
Tulsa Kids Magazine, Tulsa *Also called T K Publishing Inc* **(G-10891)**
Tulsa Litho Co Consolidat 918 582-8185
2757 S Memorial Dr Tulsa (74129) **(G-11001)**
Tulsa Masurement Gauge Lab Div, Tulsa *Also called William L Riggs Company Inc* **(G-11125)**
Tulsa Mch Sp & Heat Exchanger 918 224-5040
2240 Industrial Rd Sapulpa (74066) **(G-8319)**
Tulsa Metal Fab Inc 918 451-7150
9805 S 219th East Ave Broken Arrow (74014) **(G-1175)**
Tulsa Metal Finishers Inc 918 241-1290
Hwy 97 Sand Springs (74063) **(G-8232)**
Tulsa Metal Finishing Company 918 609-5410
1705 N 166th East Ave Tulsa (74116) **(G-11002)**
Tulsa Ornamental Iron Works 918 274-7253
101 E 21st St Owasso (74055) **(G-7629)**
Tulsa Packing Specialist Inc 918 459-8991
4245 S Jackson Ave Tulsa (74107) **(G-11003)**
Tulsa Plastics, Tulsa *Also called Jarrt Holdings Inc* **(G-10028)**
Tulsa Powder Coating Inc 918 832-1741
1815 N 75th East Ave Tulsa (74115) **(G-11004)**
Tulsa Power, Oklahoma City *Also called Reel Power Industrial Inc* **(G-6998)**
Tulsa Power, Oklahoma City *Also called Reel Power Wire & Cable Inc* **(G-7000)**
Tulsa Pressure Vessels LLC 918 512-8346
7861 S Regency Dr Tulsa (74131) **(G-9045)**
Tulsa Pro Turn Inc 918 439-9232
16803 E Pine St Tulsa (74116) **(G-11005)**
Tulsa Rubber Co 918 627-1371
401 S Boston Ave Ste 2200 Tulsa (74103) **(G-11006)**
Tulsa Screen Printing 918 488-1331
1310 N Elm Pl Broken Arrow (74012) **(G-1085)**
Tulsa Sheet Metal Inc 918 587-3141
42 N Quincy Ave Tulsa (74120) **(G-11007)**
Tulsa Sign Company 918 215-7131
12121 E 51st St Ste 106 Tulsa (74146) **(G-11008)**
Tulsa Signs 918 251-6262
2437 N Aspen Ave Broken Arrow (74012) **(G-1086)**
Tulsa Steel Mfg Company Inc 918 227-0110
7600 New Sapulpa Rd Tulsa (74131) **(G-9046)**
Tulsa Toner Technology 918 838-0323
2122 S 67th East Ave C Tulsa (74129) **(G-11009)**
Tulsa Trailer LLC 918 447-2100
4231 S Elwood Ave Tulsa (74107) **(G-11010)**
Tulsa Trenchless Inc 918 321-3330
4457 W 151st St S Kiefer (74041) **(G-3782)**
Tulsa Tube Bending Co Inc 888 882-3637
4192 S Galveston Ave Tulsa (74107) **(G-11011)**
Tulsa Turbines 918 960-8918
8303 E 111th St S Ste Q Bixby (74008) **(G-668)**
Tulsa Wilbert Vault Co, Tulsa *Also called Wilbert Funeral Services Inc* **(G-9051)**
Tulsa Winch Inc (HQ) 918 298-8300
11135 S James Ave Jenks (74037) **(G-3736)**
Tulsa Wood Arts LLC 918 576-6142
1108 S Atlanta Ave Tulsa (74104) **(G-11012)**
Tulsa World 918 664-8683
5915 E 28th St Tulsa (74114) **(G-11013)**
Tulsa World 918 582-5921
214 W Oklahoma St Tulsa (74106) **(G-11014)**
Tulsa World Capitol Bureau 405 528-2465
State Capital Bldg Rm 430 Oklahoma City (73105) **(G-7350)**
Tulsapets Magazine 918 834-1252
1439 S Marion Ave Tulsa (74112) **(G-11015)**
Tulsat Inc 918 587-4729
1513 S Boston Ave Tulsa (74119) **(G-11016)**
Tulsat Corporation 918 251-2887
1221 E Houston St Broken Arrow (74012) **(G-1087)**
Tumbleweed Creek Cottage 580 242-2767
112 N Independence St Enid (73701) **(G-3068)**
Tumbleweed Embroidery and Scre 580 371-9742
14000 S Church Rd Mannsville (73447) **(G-4196)**
Tuna Spot Tees LLC 918 931-9586
3116 W Shiloh Creek Ave Stillwater (74074) **(G-8770)**
Tunbridge Enterprises, Oklahoma City *Also called Milton Nichols Inc* **(G-6614)**
Tunnell Chance 580 245-2422
174 Log Spur Rd Haworth (74740) **(G-3406)**
Turben & Associates Affiliate, Tulsa *Also called T & A Gasket Co Inc* **(G-10887)**
Turbine Aircraft Services LLC 405 491-8995
7101 Mllonaire Dr Bethany Bethany (73008) **(G-599)**
Turbines Inc 580 477-3067
15935 Us Highway 283 Altus (73521) **(G-170)**
Turbulator Company LLC 405 820-3026
8705 Gateway Ter Oklahoma City (73149) **(G-7351)**
Turn & Burn Welding Inc 918 543-7224
30184 Gale Ave Inola (74036) **(G-3675)**
Turn Quick Manufacturing LLC 918 599-0011
5302 W 21st St Tulsa (74107) **(G-11017)**
Turnair 918 267-3535
11315 W 57th Pl S Sand Springs (74063) **(G-8233)**
Turnair Fab LLC 918 379-0796
28102 E Admiral Pl Catoosa (74015) **(G-1360)**
Turnbow Trailers Inc 918 862-3233
115 W Broadway St Oilton (74052) **(G-5241)**
Turnbow-Kiker Ltd 918 481-8871
5504 E 89th Ct Tulsa (74137) **(G-11018)**
Turner Electric Communications, Oklahoma City *Also called Cccc Inc* **(G-5718)**
Turner Falls Park, Davis *Also called City of Davis* **(G-1981)**
Turner Machine Co Inc 918 446-3581
5311 Southwest Blvd Tulsa (74107) **(G-11019)**
Turner Oil & Gas Properties (PA) 405 752-8000
3232 W Britton Rd Ste 200 Oklahoma City (73120) **(G-7352)**
Turner Resources Inc 405 853-6275
105 E Exxon Rd Hwy 81 Hennessey (73742) **(G-3494)**
Turner Welding Inc 405 224-3867
1496 County Road 1280 Amber (73004) **(G-197)**
Turner Welding and Steel Sups, Amber *Also called Turner Welding Inc* **(G-197)**
Turney Bros Oilfld Svcs & Pp 918 470-6937
401 Oklahoma Ave McAlester (74501) **(G-4345)**
Turning Point Industries Inc 405 401-3930
3180 Greystone Dr Blanchard (73010) **(G-741)**
Turning Point Mch Works LLC 918 396-2560
17300 N Cincinnati Ave Skiatook (74070) **(G-8573)**
Tuun Leh Zua Printing Services 918 809-7925
7702 S Victor Ave Tulsa (74136) **(G-11020)**
Tux Hard Shop 918 885-2970
1104 S Price Ave Hominy (74035) **(G-3594)**
Tuxpro Software & Development 405 812-1334
517 Trinidad Dr Norman (73072) **(G-5183)**
Twelve States Oil & Gas Co LLC 918 296-7625
5714 E 108th St Tulsa (74137) **(G-11021)**
Twenty-Twenty Oil & Gas Co 405 853-4607
115 S Main St Hennessey (73742) **(G-3495)**
TWI Industries Inc 918 663-6655
8605 S Elwood Ave B108 Tulsa (74132) **(G-11022)**
Twiggs Company 405 882-0308
633 W Vandament Ave # 164 Yukon (73099) **(G-11796)**

ALPHABETIC SECTION

Twin Cities Ready Mix Inc (PA)..........918 423-8855
102 W Ashland Ave McAlester (74501) *(G-4346)*

Twin Cities Ready Mix Inc..........918 647-8218
1710 S Broadway Ave Poteau (74953) *(G-7916)*

Twin Cities Ready Mix Inc..........918 967-3391
1400 Industrial Rd Stigler (74462) *(G-8650)*

Twin Cities Ready Mix Inc..........918 465-2555
1004 W Stovall Rd Wilburton (74578) *(G-11527)*

Twin Cities Ready Mix Inc..........918 682-8181
2601 S 6th St Muskogee (74401) *(G-4756)*

Twin Cities Ready Mix Inc..........918 458-0323
4612 S Muskogee Ave Tahlequah (74464) *(G-8890)*

Twin Cities Ready Mix Inc..........918 438-8888
1818 N 127th East Ave Tulsa (74116) *(G-11023)*

Twin Eagle Midstream LLC..........918 459-4548
7633 E 63rd Pl Ste 316 Tulsa (74133) *(G-11024)*

Twiss Sueons Winery Inc..........405 277-7089
19691 E Charter Oak Rd Luther (73054) *(G-4140)*

Twist A Stitch..........918 514-0143
23 E 34th St Sand Springs (74063) *(G-8234)*

Twisted B Industries, Choctaw Also called Barnett James *(G-1528)*

Twisted Oak Foods LLC..........405 720-7059
5209 Nw 111th Ter Oklahoma City (73162) *(G-7353)*

Twisted Okie Welding LLC..........580 335-1494
2302 Ne 9th St Lawton (73507) *(G-4015)*

Twisters Distillery..........405 237-3499
2322 N Moore Ave Moore (73160) *(G-4580)*

Twj Inc..........405 392-4366
2413 County Road 1196 Tuttle (73089) *(G-11217)*

Two Brothers Sand Grave..........405 923-6762
11200 Sundance Dr Yukon (73099) *(G-11797)*

Two Candle Guys LLC..........918 271-5244
9402 E 55th Pl Ste B Tulsa (74145) *(G-11025)*

Two Creeks Fabrication..........505 999-8798
21245 Se 97th Pl Newalla (74857) *(G-4817)*

Two Guys Bowtie Company LLC..........405 612-0116
623 S Peoria Ave Ste B Tulsa (74120) *(G-11026)*

Two K Enterprises LLC..........918 964-7004
1400 Kayla St Grove (74344) *(G-3290)*

Two Lees Inc..........918 663-2390
6915 E 38th St Tulsa (74145) *(G-11027)*

Two Socks LLC..........405 535-4753
3914 Warwick Dr Norman (73072) *(G-5184)*

Two Territories Trading Co LLC..........580 679-4701
16249 State Highway 34 Duke (73532) *(G-2081)*

Tx3 LLC..........405 382-2270
1501 N Harvey Rd Seminole (74868) *(G-8405)*

Ty Giaudrone..........918 423-6499
290 Baileys Bend Rd McAlester (74501) *(G-4347)*

Ty Slemp Dakota..........405 933-2078
25100 County Road 1260 Gracemont (73042) *(G-3254)*

Tyler Enterprises..........405 616-5500
5101 S Shields Blvd Oklahoma City (73129) *(G-7354)*

Tyler McIntyre, Erick Also called McIntyre Transports Inc *(G-3089)*

Tyler Signs LLC..........405 631-5174
5107 S Shields Blvd Oklahoma City (73129) *(G-7355)*

Type House Inc..........918 492-8513
3224 E 69th St Tulsa (74136) *(G-11028)*

Tyson Foods Inc..........918 723-5494
Hwy 59 N Westville (74965) *(G-11486)*

Tyson Foods Inc..........580 584-9191
Hwy 259 S Broken Bow (74728) *(G-1211)*

Tyson Foods Inc..........918 696-4530
N Hwy 59 Stilwell (74960) *(G-8796)*

Tyson Foods Inc..........918 723-5091
67378 S 4744 Rd Westville (74965) *(G-11487)*

Tyson Foods Inc..........405 379-7241
201 Kingsberry Rd Holdenville (74848) *(G-3561)*

U and S Wire Rope..........580 421-1077
120 Jade Ln Shawnee (74801) *(G-8514)*

U Big TS Designs Inc..........405 401-4327
905 Nw 6th St Ste 100 Oklahoma City (73106) *(G-7356)*

U S Poly Company (HQ)..........918 446-4471
4501 W 49th St Tulsa (74107) *(G-11029)*

U S Silica Company..........580 384-5241
Hwy 7 N Mill Creek (74856) *(G-4472)*

U S Weatherford L P..........580 225-8890
1505 S Main St Elk City (73644) *(G-2886)*

U S Weatherford L P..........405 756-4331
1 2 Mile N Hwy 76 Lindsay (73052) *(G-4095)*

U S Weatherford L P..........580 276-5362
1000 N Highway 77 Marietta (73448) *(G-4216)*

U S Weatherford L P..........405 756-4389
Hwy 76 N 1/2 Mile Lindsay (73052) *(G-4096)*

U S Weatherford L P..........918 465-2311
6525 N Meridian Ave # 201 Oklahoma City (73116) *(G-7357)*

U Save Machine Shop..........918 836-7163
510 S Sheridan Rd Tulsa (74112) *(G-11030)*

U T C Pratt & Whitney Okla Cy..........405 455-2001
3001 Staff Dr Tinker Afb (73145) *(G-8956)*

U-Change Lock Industries Inc..........405 376-1600
1640 W State Highway 152 Mustang (73064) *(G-4799)*

U.s Safety Sign and Decal, Tulsa Also called Clay Serigraphics Inc *(G-9445)*

Uc, Stillwater Also called Unmanned Cowboys LLC *(G-8771)*

UC Oil & Gas LLC..........918 270-2383
4634 S Norwood Ave Tulsa (74135) *(G-11031)*

Ufp Shawnee LLC..........405 273-1533
8702 N Harrison Shawnee (74804) *(G-8515)*

Ulterra Drilling Tech LP..........405 751-6212
13913 Qail Pinte Dr Ste A Oklahoma City (73134) *(G-7358)*

Ultimate Chemicals LLC..........405 703-2771
821 Nw 27th St Ste A Moore (73160) *(G-4581)*

Ultimate Machine Inc..........918 232-6676
1238 E 41st St Ste E Tulsa (74107) *(G-11032)*

Ultra Botanica LLC..........405 694-4175
120 Ne 26th St Oklahoma City (73105) *(G-7359)*

Ultra Fast Signs..........405 269-9468
1808 E 66th Pl Unit D301 Tulsa (74136) *(G-11033)*

Ultra Tech Ultra Tech..........580 351-1220
105 Sw 2nd St Lawton (73501) *(G-4016)*

Ultra Thin Inc..........405 794-7892
1720 S Broadway St Moore (73160) *(G-4582)*

Ultrasound Solutions, Sapulpa Also called Rose Inc *(G-8309)*

Ultrathin Ribbons & Metals, Moore Also called Ultra Thin Inc *(G-4582)*

Umicore Autocat USA Inc..........918 266-8923
1301 W Main Pkwy Catoosa (74015) *(G-1361)*

Umicore Optical Mtls USA Inc (HQ)..........918 673-1650
2976 S 614 Rd Quapaw (74363) *(G-8034)*

Umicore Precious Metals..........918 266-1400
1305 W Main Pkwy Catoosa (74015) *(G-1362)*

Unami LLC..........405 320-5696
1617 Industrial Rd Anadarko (73005) *(G-208)*

Unarco Industries LLC (HQ)..........918 485-9531
400 Se 15th St Wagoner (74467) *(G-11295)*

Uncommon Touch..........580 276-9936
Hc 67 Box 189b Marietta (73448) *(G-4217)*

Underground Printing, Norman Also called A1 Screen Printing *(G-4895)*

Underwood, Gary Oil & Gas, Edmond Also called Gary Underwood *(G-2431)*

Unibridge Scale Systems..........580 254-3131
4902 Oklahoma Ave Woodward (73801) *(G-11646)*

Unibridge Systems Inc (PA)..........580 934-3211
4th & Oklahoma St Knowles (73844) *(G-3841)*

Unicorn Woodworking..........580 762-0004
1901 El Camino St Ponca City (74604) *(G-7885)*

Unicorp Systems Inc..........918 446-1874
2625 W 40th Pl Tulsa (74107) *(G-11034)*

Unified Brands Inc..........888 994-7636
4650 54th St Pryor (74361) *(G-7996)*

Uniforms Etc, Ardmore Also called Barbara J McGinnis *(G-253)*

Union Bndary Grter Tlsa Rprter, Tulsa Also called Greater Tlsa Rprter Newspapers *(G-9856)*

Union Brewers..........405 604-8989
520 N Meridian Ave Oklahoma City (73107) *(G-7360)*

Union Hill Electric LLC..........405 222-1068
1232 County Road 1390 Chickasha (73018) *(G-1519)*

Union Valley Petroleum Corp..........580 237-3959
10422 Pinto Ln Enid (73701) *(G-3069)*

Unipro, Wagoner Also called United Process Systems Corp *(G-11296)*

Unique Designs Studio More LLC..........580 237-0034
1814 N Grand St Enid (73701) *(G-3070)*

Unique Printing Inc (PA)..........405 842-3966
1625 Broadview Cir Oklahoma City (73127) *(G-7361)*

Unique Stitches Inc..........918 794-5494
9435 E 51st St Ste B Tulsa (74145) *(G-11035)*

Unique Wireless, Tulsa Also called Jesse Harbin *(G-10039)*

Unique Wood Works Inc..........405 249-6615
13877 Sooner Ave Maysville (73057) *(G-4262)*

Uniquely Yours LLC..........918 283-2228
411 N Owalla Ave Ste B Claremore (74017) *(G-1696)*

Unit Corp..........405 222-6441
4413 S 4th St Chickasha (73018) *(G-1520)*

Unit Corporation..........580 774-5200
1635 E Loomis Rd Weatherford (73096) *(G-11453)*

Unit Corporation..........918 493-7700
8200 S U Dr 74132 Tulsa (74132) *(G-11036)*

Unit Corporation (PA)..........918 493-7700
8200 S Unit Dr Tulsa (74132) *(G-11037)*

Unit Drilling Co..........281 446-6889
7101 Sw 29th St Oklahoma City (73179) *(G-7362)*

Unit Drilling Company..........580 256-8688
1623 Downs Ave Woodward (73801) *(G-11647)*

Unit Drilling Company..........405 745-4948
7101 Sw 29th St Oklahoma City (73179) *(G-7363)*

Unit Drilling Company (HQ)..........918 493-7700
8200 S U Dr Tulsa (74132) *(G-11038)*

Unit Drilling Company..........405 745-4948
7101 Sw 29th St Oklahoma City (73179) *(G-7364)*

Unit Energy Company, Tulsa Also called James R Biddick *(G-10026)*

Unit Liner Company..........405 275-4600
7901 N Kickapoo Ave Shawnee (74804) *(G-8516)*

Unit Petroleum Company (HQ).....918 493-7700
8200 S U Dr Tulsa (74132) *(G-11039)*
Unit Texas Drilling, Oklahoma City *Also called Unit Drilling Company (G-7363)*
Unit Texas Drilling LLC.....281 446-6889
7101 Sw 29th St Oklahoma City (73179) *(G-7365)*
United Airparts, Shawnee *Also called Michael Johnson (G-8474)*
United Axle.....918 344-1157
24850 Amah Pkwy Claremore (74019) *(G-1697)*
United Cable Tool & Supply LLC.....918 760-9012
34679 W 31st St S Mannford (74044) *(G-4193)*
United Contracting Svcs Inc.....918 551-7659
5114 W 46th St Tulsa (74107) *(G-11040)*
United Dynamics Inc.....405 275-8041
41001 Wolverine Rd Shawnee (74804) *(G-8517)*
United Energy Exploration, Ada *Also called Michael Feezel (G-65)*
United Energy Technologies, Norman *Also called Intuition Inc (G-5036)*
United Energy Trading LLC.....918 392-8444
7645 E 63rd St Ste 103 Tulsa (74133) *(G-11041)*
United Engines Manufacture.....405 601-9861
1545 Se 29th St Oklahoma City (73129) *(G-7366)*
United Ford.....405 813-7300
1231 Sovereign Row Ste A2 Oklahoma City (73108) *(G-7367)*
United Fuels & Energy.....405 945-7400
533 N Portland Ave Oklahoma City (73107) *(G-7368)*
United Fuels Energy.....580 332-5222
301 N Broadway Ave Ada (74820) *(G-100)*
United Holdings LLC (HQ).....405 947-3321
5 N Mccormick St Ste 200 Oklahoma City (73127) *(G-7369)*
United Land Co LLC.....405 840-2666
6801 Broadway Ext Ste 105 Oklahoma City (73116) *(G-7370)*
United Millwork Inc.....405 670-3999
1718 E Grand Blvd Oklahoma City (73129) *(G-7371)*
United Pallet, Tulsa *Also called Tim E Hutcheson (G-10941)*
United Plating Works Inc.....918 835-4683
4118 N Mingo Rd Tulsa (74116) *(G-11042)*
United Process Systems Corp.....918 462-1143
68912 S 313 Ct Wagoner (74467) *(G-11296)*
United Production Co L L C.....405 728-8900
1001 Nw 139th Street Pkwy Edmond (73013) *(G-2657)*
United Services Limited.....580 256-5335
4325 Oil Patch Dr Woodward (73801) *(G-11648)*
United Sewing Agency Inc.....580 924-6936
2929 W Main St Durant (74701) *(G-2271)*
United Slings Inc.....405 598-2616
110 E Washington St Tecumseh (74873) *(G-8930)*
United States Aviation, Tulsa *Also called Hardesty Company Inc (G-9890)*
United States Dept of Army.....918 420-6642
1 C Tree Rd McAlester (74501) *(G-4348)*
United States Gypsum Company.....580 822-6100
Hwy 51a Southard (73770) *(G-8588)*
United Utlties Specialists LLC.....918 342-0840
17211 S 4170 Rd Claremore (74017) *(G-1698)*
United Video LLC.....918 488-4000
7140 S Lewis Ave Tulsa (74136) *(G-11043)*
United We Stand Inc.....918 382-1766
205 E Pine St Ste 16 Tulsa (74106) *(G-11044)*
Unitherm Food Systems LLC (PA).....918 367-0197
502 Industrial Rd Bristow (74010) *(G-802)*
Unity Press Inc.....405 232-8910
10733 E Ute St Tulsa (74116) *(G-11045)*
Universal Combustion Corp.....918 254-1828
8312 S 75th East Ave Tulsa (74133) *(G-11046)*
Universal Compression Inc.....918 742-1801
5727 S Lewis Ave Ste 610 Tulsa (74105) *(G-11047)*
Universal Forest Products, Shawnee *Also called Ufp Shawnee LLC (G-8515)*
Universal Jint Specialists Inc.....918 836-0111
6960 E 11th St Tulsa (74112) *(G-11048)*
Universal Land Services LLC.....918 712-9038
1323 E 71st St Ste 400 Tulsa (74136) *(G-11049)*
Universal Machine Inc.....405 373-2248
15511 Hwy 3 & Cimarron Rd Yukon (73099) *(G-11798)*
Universal Pressure Pumping Inc.....405 608-7346
777 Nw 63rd St Oklahoma City (73116) *(G-7372)*
Universal Pressure Pumping Inc.....405 262-2441
3715 S Radio Rd El Reno (73036) *(G-2765)*
Universal Rig Service Corp.....918 585-8221
8 E 3rd St Tulsa (74103) *(G-11050)*
Universal Sign Company, Nowata *Also called Paul Clinton Hughes (G-5225)*
Universal Trlr Holdings Corp.....405 422-7238
900 E Trail Blvd El Reno (73036) *(G-2766)*
Universal Welding Service.....918 455-3241
7401 S Birch Ave Broken Arrow (74011) *(G-1088)*
University of Oklahoma.....405 325-4531
3000 Chautauqua Ave # 111 Norman (73072) *(G-5185)*
University of Oklahoma.....405 325-3189
1005 Asp Ave Rm 117 Norman (73019) *(G-5186)*
University of Oklahoma.....405 325-3276
4100 28th Ave Nw Norman (73069) *(G-5187)*
University of Oklahoma.....405 325-3666
860 Van Vleet Oval 149a Norman (73019) *(G-5188)*
University of Oklahoma Press.....405 325-2000
2800 Venture Dr Norman (73069) *(G-5189)*
Univision Display Usa LLC.....918 289-6611
10203 E 61st St Ste B Tulsa (74133) *(G-11051)*
Unmanned Cowboys LLC.....405 744-4156
1201 S Innovation Way Stillwater (74074) *(G-8771)*
Unrau Meat Co Inc.....918 543-8245
9415 W 590 Rd Inola (74036) *(G-3676)*
Up N Smoke III.....405 609-1702
4424 Se 44th St Oklahoma City (73135) *(G-7373)*
Upco Inc.....918 342-1270
4801 W 49th St Tulsa (74107) *(G-11052)*
Uplands Resources Inc.....918 592-0305
427 S Boston Ave Ste 800 Tulsa (74103) *(G-11053)*
Uponor Aldyl Co Inc.....918 446-4471
4501 W 49th St Tulsa (74107) *(G-11054)*
Upper Room.....
5909 Nw Expressway # 365 Oklahoma City (73132) *(G-7374)*
UPS Store 6206.....580 248-7800
1712 Macomb Rd Ste 300 Fort Sill (73503) *(G-3182)*
Urban Okie Custom Woodwork.....405 420-1176
1000 W 15th St Edmond (73013) *(G-2658)*
Urban Okie Custom Woodwork LLC.....405 635-7800
1615 Ketch Pl Edmond (73003) *(G-2659)*
Urban Worm Compost LLC.....918 557-9255
3112 W Pittsburg Pl Broken Arrow (74012) *(G-1089)*
Urbane Commercial Contrs LLC.....405 534-1677
12429 Goldsborough Rd Midwest City (73130) *(G-4460)*
US Casing Service OK Inc.....701 713-0047
1710 N Airport Rd Weatherford (73096) *(G-11454)*
US Concrete, Lawton *Also called Atlas Tuck Concrete Inc (G-3892)*
US Ferroics LLC.....601 763-1058
123 Case Cir Ardmore (73401) *(G-376)*
US Fleet Tracking LLC (PA).....405 726-9900
2912 Nw 156th St Edmond (73013) *(G-2660)*
US Lime Company - St Clair.....918 775-4466
98054 S 4610 Rd Marble City (74945) *(G-4198)*
US Oil Tools Inc.....580 256-6874
6699 S 8th St Woodward (73801) *(G-11649)*
US Pioneer LLC.....918 359-5200
4450 S 70th East Ave Tulsa (74145) *(G-11055)*
US Pioneer Led Specialists LLC.....918 359-5200
4450 S 70th East Ave Tulsa (74145) *(G-11056)*
US Rod Manufacturing LLC.....636 359-9947
13212 N Macarthur Blvd Oklahoma City (73142) *(G-7375)*
US Safetysign & Decal LLC.....800 678-2529
1433 E 6th St Tulsa (74120) *(G-11057)*
US Shooting Academy, Tulsa *Also called 2011 Ussa Limited Partnership (G-9055)*
US Shotblast Parts & Svc Corp.....405 842-6766
207 Nw 59th St Oklahoma City (73118) *(G-7376)*
US Signs & Led LLC.....405 819-3086
912 Justin Dr Yukon (73099) *(G-11799)*
US Whip Inc.....918 542-6453
51701 E 110 Rd Miami (74354) *(G-4435)*
USA Compression.....405 790-0300
14504 Hrtz Qail Sprng Pkw Oklahoma City (73134) *(G-7377)*
USA Compression Partners LLC.....918 742-6548
5801 E 41st St Ste 505 Tulsa (74135) *(G-11058)*
USA Compression Partners LLC.....405 234-3850
14504 Hertz Quail Spgs Pa Oklahoma City (73134) *(G-7378)*
USA Energy Fabrication LLC.....918 445-4792
6444 S 57th West Ave Tulsa (74131) *(G-9047)*
USA Industries Oklahoma Inc.....405 840-5577
3126 S Boulevard Ste 208 Edmond (73013) *(G-2661)*
USA Metal Fabrication LLC.....918 845-6500
1838 Nw 1st St Unit C Oklahoma City (73106) *(G-7379)*
USA Screen Prtg & EMB Co Inc.....405 946-3100
101 S Mickey Mantle Dr Oklahoma City (73104) *(G-7380)*
USA Signs Inc.....918 392-5544
9242 S Sheridan Rd Ste D Tulsa (74133) *(G-11059)*
USA-Bops LLC.....405 265-2988
9910 W Reno Ave Oklahoma City (73127) *(G-7381)*
Useful Products Inc.....405 715-2639
1605 Kings Rd Edmond (73013) *(G-2662)*
User Friendly, Ponca City *Also called Nancy Nelson & Associates (G-7857)*
User Friendly Phone Book LLC.....918 384-0224
4150 S 100th East Ave # 106 Tulsa (74146) *(G-11060)*
Usfilter.....405 359-7441
16208 Acoma Pl Edmond (73013) *(G-2663)*
Usher Corporation.....405 495-2125
1 N Hudson Ave Ste 190 Oklahoma City (73102) *(G-7382)*
Usut Labs Inc.....918 459-3844
12505 E 55th St Ste A Tulsa (74146) *(G-11061)*
Utec Corporation LLC.....405 928-7061
222 E Eufaula St Ste 120 Norman (73069) *(G-5190)*
Utown LLC.....918 261-3402
36 E Cameron St Tulsa (74103) *(G-11062)*
V E Enterprises, Springer *Also called Spade Leasing Inc (G-8626)*

V E Enterprises Inc (HQ).......580 653-2171
10834 State Highway 53 Springer (73458) ***(G-8627)***
V J Stone LLC.......405 840-2255
3244 Nw Grand Blvd Oklahoma City (73116) ***(G-7383)***
V M I Inc.......918 225-7000
1125 N Maitlen Dr Cushing (74023) ***(G-1965)***
V M Publishing Co.......405 533-1883
205 W 7th Ave Ste 201e Stillwater (74074) ***(G-8772)***
V M Star.......918 781-4400
3800 Port Pl Muskogee (74403) ***(G-4757)***
V O Inc.......405 659-0654
509 Clermont Dr Edmond (73003) ***(G-2664)***
V W Casey Industries LLC.......918 369-5205
8312 E 132nd St S Bixby (74008) ***(G-669)***
V&H Coatings Co.......405 819-4163
500 Se 14th St Oklahoma City (73129) ***(G-7384)***
V&S Schuler Tubular Pdts LLC.......918 687-7701
420 Frankfort Ave Muskogee (74403) ***(G-4758)***
V5 Contracting LLC.......918 720-4675
20632 E 440 Rd Claremore (74017) ***(G-1699)***
Vaculift Incorporated (PA).......918 438-9875
10105 E 55th Pl Tulsa (74146) ***(G-11063)***
Vacuworx International, Tulsa *Also called Vaculift Incorporated* ***(G-11063)***
Vadovations Inc.......405 601-5520
1333 Cornell Pkwy Oklahoma City (73108) ***(G-7385)***
Valco Inc.......405 228-0932
4524 Enterprise Pl Oklahoma City (73128) ***(G-7386)***
Valco Inc (PA).......405 228-0932
1009 Boren Rd Duncan (73533) ***(G-2191)***
Valco Manufacturing Company, Duncan *Also called Valco Inc* ***(G-2191)***
Valence Surface Technologies, Grove *Also called Pride Plating Inc* ***(G-3286)***
Valero Refining-Texas LP.......580 223-0534
718 Cameron St Ardmore (73401) ***(G-377)***
Valet, Ponca City *Also called Lindsay Manufacturing Inc* ***(G-7845)***
Valhoma Corporation.......918 836-7135
1617 N 93rd East Ave Tulsa (74115) ***(G-11064)***
Valiant Artfl Lift Sltions LLC (PA).......405 605-4567
1 Leadership Sq N Oklahoma City (73102) ***(G-7387)***
Valiant Artfl Lift Sltions LLC.......405 605-4567
5729 Huettner Ct Norman (73069) ***(G-5191)***
Valiant Artfl Lift Systems, Oklahoma City *Also called Valiant Artfl Lift Sltions LLC* ***(G-7387)***
Valiant Midstream LLC.......405 286-5580
16420 Muirfield Pl Edmond (73013) ***(G-2665)***
Valley Stone Inc.......918 647-2388
19782 Gardenhire Rd Howe (74940) ***(G-3600)***
Valliant Leader, Valliant *Also called Wilson-Monroe Publishing Co* ***(G-11234)***
Valliant Leader Inc.......580 933-4570
119 N Dalton St Valliant (74764) ***(G-11233)***
Valliant Leader, The, Valliant *Also called Valliant Leader Inc* ***(G-11233)***
Vallouret, Muskogee *Also called V M Star* ***(G-4757)***
Valmont Coatings, Claremore *Also called Valmont Industries Inc* ***(G-1700)***
Valmont Industries Inc.......918 266-2800
25055 Alliance Dr Claremore (74019) ***(G-1700)***
Valmont Industries Inc.......918 583-5881
801 N Xanthus Ave Tulsa (74110) ***(G-11065)***
Valmont/Tulsa, Tulsa *Also called Valmont Industries Inc* ***(G-11065)***
Valor Energy Services LLC (PA).......405 513-5043
111 N Broadway Ste B Edmond (73034) ***(G-2666)***
Valor Energy Services LLC.......405 209-6081
120 W 12th St Elk City (73644) ***(G-2887)***
Valor Industries LLC.......580 301-3805
12005 Nw 135th St Piedmont (73078) ***(G-7773)***
Value Added Products.......580 327-0400
2101 College Blvd Alva (73717) ***(G-195)***
Value Components Corp.......918 749-1689
308 S Lansing Ave Tulsa (74120) ***(G-11066)***
Vam Usa LLC.......405 720-2200
7424 Nw 84th St Oklahoma City (73132) ***(G-7388)***
Van Brunt Lumber.......405 567-3776
Mbu 4002 Prague (74864) ***(G-7938)***
Van Eaton C W.......580 223-4374
108 D St Sw Ardmore (73401) ***(G-378)***
Van Eaton Ready Mix Inc.......405 912-4825
17301 S Sunnylane Rd Norman (73071) ***(G-5192)***
Van Eaton Ready Mix Inc.......405 364-2028
2905 Water View Ct Norman (73071) ***(G-5193)***
Van Eaton Ready Mix Inc.......405 844-2900
2547 E Waterloo Indus Rd Edmond (73034) ***(G-2667)***
Van Eaton Ready Mix Inc.......405 789-1795
401 N Council Rd Oklahoma City (73127) ***(G-7389)***
Van Eaton Ready Mix Inc (PA).......405 214-7450
8 Timber Pond Shawnee (74804) ***(G-8518)***
Van Horn James.......405 324-2456
10124 Thompson Ave Yukon (73099) ***(G-11800)***
Vance Brothers Inc.......405 427-1389
4908 N Bryant Ave Oklahoma City (73121) ***(G-7390)***
Vanco Systems.......405 692-4040
11308 Gateshead Dr Oklahoma City (73170) ***(G-5321)***
Vande Lune Packaging LLC.......405 517-0098
12009 Somerville Dr Yukon (73099) ***(G-11801)***
Vanderbilt Cabinet & Trim.......405 376-3876
234 E Hillcrest Ln Mustang (73064) ***(G-4800)***
Vaneaton & Vaneaton, Ardmore *Also called Van Eaton C W* ***(G-378)***
Vanhoose Wood Creations.......405 443-0454
1514 Jacy Ln Blanchard (73010) ***(G-742)***
Vann Metal Products Inc.......918 341-0469
74754 Amah Pkwy Claremore (74017) ***(G-1701)***
Vann Systems, Duncan *Also called Halliburton Company* ***(G-2128)***
Vanover Metal Building Sls Inc.......918 253-6030
540 State Highway 20 Spavinaw (74366) ***(G-8593)***
Vans Inc.......405 843-5286
1901 Nw Expwy St Ste 2009 Oklahoma City (73118) ***(G-7391)***
Vans Inc.......405 787-9992
7628 W Reno Ave Ste 100 Oklahoma City (73127) ***(G-7392)***
Vans Printing Service.......918 786-9496
423 S Hazel St Grove (74344) ***(G-3291)***
Vans Trailer Sales.......580 323-3999
1012 Scissortail Dr Clinton (73601) ***(G-1772)***
Vantage Plane Plastics, Alva *Also called Plane Plastics Ltd* ***(G-188)***
Varco LP.......405 677-8889
1800 Se 44th St Oklahoma City (73129) ***(G-7393)***
Varco LP.......405 478-3400
3216 Aluma Valley Dve Oklahoma City (73121) ***(G-7394)***
Varco Inc.......405 732-1637
8200 S Anderson Rd Oklahoma City (73150) ***(G-7395)***
Varners Eqp Sls & Svc LLC.......918 367-3800
921 S Roland St Bristow (74010) ***(G-803)***
Vassal Well Services LLC.......580 279-1579
808 E Main St Ada (74820) ***(G-101)***
Vasser Machine.......918 225-2677
2115 W Old Highway 33 Cushing (74023) ***(G-1966)***
Vault, Owasso *Also called Downtown Pub* ***(G-7563)***
Vault Management Inc.......918 258-7782
1805 W Detroit St Broken Arrow (74012) ***(G-1090)***
Vaxart Inc.......918 582-4346
824 S Cheyenne Ave Tulsa (74119) ***(G-11067)***
VB Welding LLC.......918 695-0258
11718 E Admiral Pl Tulsa (74116) ***(G-11068)***
Vector Exploration Inc.......405 340-5373
223 N Broadway Edmond (73034) ***(G-2668)***
Veem Jade Oil & Gas LLC.......918 298-1555
11417 S Granite Ave Tulsa (74137) ***(G-11069)***
Ventaire LLC.......918 622-1191
909 N Wheeling Ave Tulsa (74110) ***(G-11070)***
Ventaire Corporation.......918 622-1191
909 N Wheeling Ave Tulsa (74110) ***(G-11071)***
Ventana Exploration & Prod LLC.......405 754-5000
13832 Wireless Way # 100 Oklahoma City (73134) ***(G-7396)***
Ventura LLC (PA).......405 418-0300
6100 N Western Ave Oklahoma City (73118) ***(G-7397)***
Ventura LLC.......580 661-2924
24322 E 910 Rd Thomas (73669) ***(G-8950)***
Venture Industries Inc.......918 557-8789
1812 W Phoenix Pl Broken Arrow (74011) ***(G-1091)***
Venture Properties, Tulsa *Also called H W Allen Co LLC* ***(G-9877)***
Veolia Water North America Ope.......405 354-6245
501 W Wagner Rd Yukon (73099) ***(G-11802)***
Veracity Tech Solutions LLC (PA).......208 821-8888
11331 E 20th St Ste A Tulsa (74128) ***(G-11072)***
Verallia.......918 224-1440
1000 N Mission St Sapulpa (74066) ***(G-8320)***
Verdavia Press LLC.......405 254-5030
208 Nw 142nd St Edmond (73013) ***(G-2669)***
Verde Industries LLC.......405 413-5599
9213 Sunnymeade Pl Oklahoma City (73120) ***(G-7398)***
Verexco Inc.......405 341-4302
111 N Broadway Edmond (73034) ***(G-2670)***
Veritris Group Inc.......580 713-4927
2828 Nw 57th St Ste 207 Oklahoma City (73112) ***(G-7399)***
Vernon E Faulconer Inc.......580 883-2892
7122 Highway 58 Ringwood (73768) ***(G-8096)***
Vernon L Smith & Assoc Inc (PA).......405 360-3374
3940 W Tecumseh Rd Norman (73072) ***(G-5194)***
Vernon Manufacturing Company.......918 224-4068
8403 S 89th West Ave Tulsa (74131) ***(G-9048)***
Vernon Sheet Metal.......580 658-6778
1010 Black Rd Marlow (73055) ***(G-4246)***
Versatech Industries Inc.......918 366-7400
14750 S Grant St Bixby (74008) ***(G-670)***
Verser Welding Service.......405 352-5048
103 E 3rd St Minco (73059) ***(G-4482)***
Versitile Entertainment.......812 913-2677
35679 Ew 1250 Seminole (74868) ***(G-8406)***
Versitile Entertainment Group, Seminole *Also called Versitile Entertainment* ***(G-8406)***
Versum Materials Us LLC.......918 379-7101
1115 Keystone Ave Catoosa (74015) ***(G-1363)***
Vertical Aerospace, Bristow *Also called Rajon LLC* ***(G-795)***

ALPHABETIC

(PA)=Parent Co (HQ)=Headquarters (DH)=Div Headquarters
2020 Oklahoma Directory of Manufacturers & Processors
649

Vertical Limit LLC

ALPHABETIC SECTION

Vertical Limit LLC 918 409-1633
   1660 E 71st St Ste O Tulsa (74136) *(G-11073)*
Vertiprime Aerospace, Duncan Also called Vertiprime Government Svcs LLC *(G-2192)*
Vertiprime Government Svcs LLC 844 474-2600
   7576 N Highway 81 Duncan (73533) *(G-2192)*
Vertiprime Mowdy Mch JV LLC 405 747-6668
   1245 Boren Rd Duncan (73533) *(G-2193)*
Vesta Midstream Partners LLC 918 986-9520
   2431 E 61st St Ste 310 Tulsa (74136) *(G-11074)*
Veteran Bat Company LLC 580 439-5230
   281645 E 1790 Rd Comanche (73529) *(G-1847)*
Veterans Eng Group Inc 918 864-6006
   33 Woodcreek Ln Pryor (74361) *(G-7997)*
Vickers Construction Inc 405 756-4386
   1102 Cherokee Pl Lindsay (73052) *(G-4097)*
Vickers Sand and Gravel 405 573-1989
   3976 S Harvey Ave Norman (73072) *(G-5195)*
Vics Telecommunications 580 512-0313
   387 Sunset St Lawton (73507) *(G-4017)*
Victors Electric Motor S 405 344-7339
   23822 State Highway 76 Blanchard (73010) *(G-743)*
Victortees LLC 405 889-7763
   1860 W Robinson St Apt B Norman (73069) *(G-5196)*
Victory Energy Operations LLC Inc 918 274-0023
   10701 E 126th St N Collinsville (74021) *(G-1828)*
Victory Energy Operations LLC 918 225-2164
   1200 N Maitlen Dr Cushing (74023) *(G-1967)*
Victory Garden Homestead LLC 405 306-0308
   1058 County Street 2965 Blanchard (73010) *(G-744)*
Victory Glass Co Inc 405 232-5114
   2404 S Robinson Ave Oklahoma City (73109) *(G-7400)*
Victory House Inc (PA) 918 747-5009
   6506 S Lewis Ave Ste 114 Tulsa (74136) *(G-11075)*
Victory Oil Field Services Co 405 694-0468
   11025 Bramblewood Ln Noble (73068) *(G-4893)*
Victory Shooting Steel, Oklahoma City Also called Rohm-Bolster Mfg Co LLC *(G-7047)*
Viersen Oil & Gas Co 918 742-1979
   7130 S Lewis Ave Ste 200 Tulsa (74136) *(G-11076)*
Viking Packing Specialists, Catoosa Also called Weilert Enterprises Inc *(G-1365)*
Viking Pipe and Supply LLC 405 262-9337
   1911 E Highway 66 El Reno (73036) *(G-2767)*
Viking Rain Covers 405 359-1850
   1409 Devonshire Ct Edmond (73034) *(G-2671)*
Viking Sales LLC 918 742-7796
   1849 N 105th East Ave Tulsa (74116) *(G-11077)*
Viking Software Solutions, Tulsa Also called Phoenix Software Intl Inc *(G-10510)*
VILLAGE SCREENPRINT EMBROIDERY, Ponca City Also called Opportunity Center Inc *(G-7863)*
Vima, Oklahoma City Also called Instinct Performance LLC *(G-6312)*
Vincent Enterprises Inc 580 252-1322
   3209 Lansbrook Ct Duncan (73533) *(G-2194)*
Vinces Lease Service 405 542-3908
   321 N Noble Ave Hinton (73047) *(G-3539)*
Vineyard Plating & Sup Co Tx 918 342-0083
   2211 El Anderson Blvd Claremore (74017) *(G-1702)*
Vinita Daily Journal, Vinita Also called Vinita Printing Co Inc *(G-11271)*
Vinita Printing Co Inc 918 256-6422
   140 S Wilson St Vinita (74301) *(G-11271)*
Vinson James R Linda F Co 405 478-1330
   2216 Red Elm Dr Edmond (73013) *(G-2672)*
Vintage Accessory Reproduction, Oklahoma City Also called Varco Inc *(G-7395)*
Vintage Aero Parts, Guthrie Also called Radial Engines Ltd *(G-3334)*
Vintage Plastics Llc 918 439-1016
   1305 N 143rd East Ave Tulsa (74116) *(G-11078)*
Vintage Revival Inc 580 379-9060
   313 Falcon Rd Altus (73521) *(G-171)*
Vintage Vault 918 619-9954
   1134 S Harvard Ave Tulsa (74112) *(G-11079)*
Vinyl Vikings LLC 405 260-9022
   2101 Rambling Rd Edmond (73025) *(G-2673)*
VIP Manufacturing Corporation 918 244-2131
   13356 S 4440th Rd Bluejacket (74333) *(G-746)*
Viper Products, Tahlequah Also called David Bates *(G-8862)*
Viridian Coffee LLC 405 795-0773
   1441 W Willow Duncan Duncan (73533) *(G-2195)*
Virtuoso Software LLC 918 813-4941
   6415 S 110th East Ave Tulsa (74133) *(G-11080)*
Vision Energy Group LLC 405 848-3933
   5600 N May Ave Ste 137 Oklahoma City (73112) *(G-7401)*
Vision Fabrications LLC 580 304-2444
   900 Throup Blvd Ponca City (74601) *(G-7886)*
Vision Motorsports 918 260-4981
   6863 E 40th St Tulsa (74145) *(G-11081)*
Vision Print PPG 405 519-4047
   9717 Nw 10th St Trlr 103 Oklahoma City (73127) *(G-7402)*
Vision Type & Design Inc 918 252-3817
   6329 S 109th East Ave Tulsa (74133) *(G-11082)*
Visions Innovated Products, McAlester Also called Webcoat Inc *(G-4350)*

Vista Disposal Solutions LLC 918 623-0333
   4124 St Tulsa (74105) *(G-11083)*
Visuals Tech Solutions LLC 913 526-1775
   2501 E Memorial Rd Edmond (73013) *(G-2674)*
Vita, Oklahoma City Also called Vmebus Intl Trade Assn *(G-7405)*
Vita-Source Inc 918 407-9525
   3963 S State Highway 97 Sand Springs (74063) *(G-8235)*
Vitol Inc 405 228-8100
   201 Nw 10th St Ste 105 Oklahoma City (73103) *(G-7403)*
Vitruvian II Woodford LLC 405 428-2491
   401 Industrial Park Lindsay (73052) *(G-4098)*
VITs Screen Printing 405 531-6012
   180 W 15th St Ste 180 # 180 Edmond (73013) *(G-2675)*
Vm Arkoma Stack LLC 405 286-5580
   14612 Hertz Quail Spg Oklahoma City (73134) *(G-7404)*
Vm Welding LLC 405 245-2833
   13100 Cloverleaf Ln Oklahoma City (73170) *(G-5322)*
Vmebus Intl Trade Assn 480 577-1916
   9100 Paseo Del Vita Oklahoma City (73131) *(G-7405)*
Vogt Power International Inc 502 899-4500
   2110 Industrial Rd Sapulpa (74066) *(G-8321)*
Vogt Sheet Metal 580 332-2454
   10140 State Highway 99n Ada (74820) *(G-102)*
Voight Manufacturing, Comanche Also called Voight Ronnie Lynn Linda Gail *(G-1848)*
Voight Ronnie Lynn Linda Gail 580 251-9897
   7249 S 13th St Comanche (73529) *(G-1848)*
Von Troutman Timothy 580 583-7004
   472 County Road 1560 Rush Springs (73082) *(G-8130)*
Vortex Fluid Systems Inc 918 810-7798
   7108 W 76th St S Tulsa (74131) *(G-9049)*
Vortex Manufacturing, Tulsa Also called Vortex Fluid Systems Inc *(G-9049)*
Vortex Parts Washer 918 582-4445
   427 S Boston Ave Ste 353 Tulsa (74103) *(G-11084)*
Vox Printing Incorporated (PA) 800 654-8437
   4000 E Britton Rd Oklahoma City (73131) *(G-7406)*
Vus Fabrics LLC 405 330-9050
   340 S Kelly Ave Edmond (73003) *(G-2676)*
Vvc Dry Cleaning & Laundry 580 255-2121
   1015 W Oak Ave Duncan (73533) *(G-2196)*
Vype High School Spt Mag LLC 918 495-1771
   8282 S Memorial Dr # 300 Tulsa (74133) *(G-11085)*
W & S Oil Co, Pawhuska Also called Wachtman-Schroeder *(G-7697)*
W & W Asco Steel LLC (HQ) 405 235-3621
   1730 W Reno Ave Oklahoma City (73106) *(G-7407)*
W & W Custom Cabinets 405 222-1410
   102 Todd Estate Dr Chickasha (73018) *(G-1521)*
W & W Electric Motor Service 405 634-3776
   24 Se 29th St Oklahoma City (73129) *(G-7408)*
W - W Trailer Mfrs Inc 580 795-5571
   Hwy 199 W Madill (73446) *(G-4166)*
W 2 Enterprises LLC 918 429-8793
   13618 Sw Highway 2 Tuskahoma (74574) *(G-11183)*
W A A, Tulsa Also called Nordam Group LLC *(G-10353)*
W A Waterman and Co Inc 405 632-5631
   8101 S Walker Ave Ste B Oklahoma City (73139) *(G-7409)*
W C Bradley Co 918 836-5581
   6101 E Apache St Tulsa (74115) *(G-11086)*
W C Bradley Co 918 379-6238
   6505 Tower Ln Claremore (74019) *(G-1703)*
W C Brdly/Zebco Holdings Inc (HQ) 706 571-6080
   6105 E Apache St Tulsa (74115) *(G-11087)*
W E Industries Inc 405 949-0222
   4500 Nw 16th St Oklahoma City (73127) *(G-7410)*
W E O C Inc 918 367-5918
   121 E 6th Ave Bristow (74010) *(G-804)*
W F D Oil Corporation 405 715-3130
   16800 Conifer Ln Edmond (73012) *(G-2677)*
W Flying Inc 580 623-5566
   922 W Russworm Dr Watonga (73772) *(G-11351)*
W H Braum Inc 405 340-9288
   2410 W Edmond Rd Edmond (73012) *(G-2678)*
W J L S Inc 918 252-3636
   12528 E 60th St Tulsa (74146) *(G-11088)*
W K Linduff Inc 918 225-6000
   1101 S Thompson Ave Cushing (74023) *(G-1968)*
W L Walker Co Inc (PA) 918 583-3109
   330 N Boulder Ave Tulsa (74103) *(G-11089)*
W R Meat Co 580 622-2494
   2354 Highway 7 E Sulphur (73086) *(G-8846)*
W R Western Company Inc (PA) 405 605-5586
   4915 Nw 10th St Oklahoma City (73127) *(G-7411)*
W&W Enterprises 580 434-2736
   261 Elnora Ln Colbert (74733) *(G-1787)*
W&W Steel Erectors LLC 405 235-3621
   1730 W Reno Ave Oklahoma City (73106) *(G-7412)*
W&W-Afco Steel LLC (HQ) 405 235-3621
   1730 W Reno Ave Oklahoma City (73106) *(G-7413)*
W-W Manufacturing Co Inc (HQ) 580 661-3720
   8832 State Highway 54 Thomas (73669) *(G-8951)*

W-W Manufacturing Co Inc 580 661-3720
108 S Main St Thomas (73669) *(G-8952)*
Wachob Industries Inc 918 224-0511
2786 E Highway 117 Sapulpa (74066) *(G-8322)*
Wachtman-Schroeder 918 287-3122
2400 Mckenzie Rd Pawhuska (74056) *(G-7697)*
Wacky Logging LLC 918 457-9393
7919 N 450 Rd Hulbert (74441) *(G-3630)*
Waddell Vineyards LLC 580 421-6933
11533 County Road 3570 Ada (74820) *(G-103)*
Wades Cabinet Door Shop 918 868-2516
18403 E 626 Rd Tahlequah (74464) *(G-8891)*
Wadley Bill & Son Drilling Co 918 756-4650
11461 Smith Rd Okmulgee (74447) *(G-7529)*
Waggoner Oil & Gas 580 234-0030
3114 Wren Ln Enid (73703) *(G-3071)*
Wagner Plate Works LLC 918 447-4488
4142 W 49th St Tulsa (74107) *(G-11090)*
Wagner Tribune, Wagoner *Also called Berkshire Hathaway Inc (G-11277)*
Wagon Wheel Arklatex LLC 918 528-1060
100 S Riverfront Dr Ste 4 Jenks (74037) *(G-3737)*
Wagon Wheel Exploration LLC 918 746-7477
100 Suth Rvrfront Dr Ste Jenks (74037) *(G-3738)*
Wagon Wheel Production Co 580 983-2371
8167 N 1815 Rd Crawford (73638) *(G-1906)*
Wagoner Field Office, Tulsa *Also called Oklahoma Department of Mines (G-10396)*
Waid Forensics Science LLC 580 574-8692
115 E Lake Dr Medicine Park (73557) *(G-4372)*
Waid Group Inc 817 980-8985
115 E Lk Dr Mdcine Park Medicine Medicine Park (73557) *(G-4373)*
Wajo Chemical Inc 580 255-1191
15 S 10th St Duncan (73533) *(G-2197)*
Wako LLC 580 234-3434
5606 N Us Highway 81 Enid (73701) *(G-3072)*
Walden Energy LLC 918 488-8663
5115 E 84th Pl Tulsa (74137) *(G-11091)*
Waldens Machine LLC 918 794-0289
3030 N Erie Ave Tulsa (74115) *(G-11092)*
Waldon Equipment LLC 580 227-3711
201 W Oklahoma Ave Fairview (73737) *(G-3155)*
Walke Brothers Meats Inc 918 341-3236
9815 E 520 Rd Unit B Claremore (74019) *(G-1704)*
Walker Companies, Oklahoma City *Also called Walker Stamp & Seal Co (G-7415)*
Walker Forklift Service LLC 918 671-0317
5944 W 43rd St Tulsa (74107) *(G-11093)*
Walker Resources Inc 405 751-5357
12308 Val Verde Dr Oklahoma City (73142) *(G-7414)*
Walker Stamp & Seal Co 405 235-5319
121 Nw 6th St Oklahoma City (73102) *(G-7415)*
Walker Unlimited, Oklahoma City *Also called Walker Woods Inc (G-7416)*
Walker Woods Inc 208 266-1601
14201 N Kentucky Ave # 308 Oklahoma City (73134) *(G-7416)*
Walker's Publishing, Norman *Also called Dharma Inc (G-4978)*
Walkers Powder Coating LLC 580 355-5000
804 Se 135th St Lawton (73501) *(G-4018)*
Walkers Sign Company 580 353-7446
804 Se 135th St Lawton (73501) *(G-4019)*
Walkup Wellhead 580 320-5913
1806 N 4th Ave Purcell (73080) *(G-8026)*
Wall Colmonoy Corporation 405 672-1361
4700 Se 59th St Oklahoma City (73135) *(G-7417)*
Wallace Energy, Tulsa *Also called Cfmi LLC (G-9402)*
Wallace Printing Company 580 326-6323
509 S 10th St Hugo (74743) *(G-3622)*
Waller Exploration LLC 405 359-2050
1616 E 19th St Ste 202 Edmond (73013) *(G-2679)*
Wallis Printing Inc 580 223-7473
28 N Washington St Ardmore (73401) *(G-379)*
Walr Corp 918 253-4773
2010 W Cedar St Jay (74346) *(G-3687)*
Walrus Audio LLC 405 254-4118
7801 N Robinson Ave D8 Oklahoma City (73116) *(G-7418)*
Walter Baker 580 233-7820
1510 N Tyler St Enid (73703) *(G-3073)*
Walter Shpman Dsblity Ssi Cses 580 280-4727
605 W Gore Blvd Lawton (73501) *(G-4020)*
Walters Herald, Walters *Also called Herald Publishing Co (G-11302)*
Walters Oil 580 432-5294
630 Pernell Pl Elmore City (73433) *(G-2899)*
Walters Oilwell Service Inc 580 875-2601
623 N 3rd St Walters (73572) *(G-11304)*
Waltman Oil & Gas 405 374-2694
46659 Romulus Rd Maud (74854) *(G-4253)*
Wanderlust Pen Company 918 551-6809
1254 E 29th Pl Tulsa (74114) *(G-11094)*
Wapco Inc 405 489-3212
605 N Main St Cement (73017) *(G-1370)*
War Metals Inc 918 224-2155
5375 W Canyon Rd Tulsa (74131) *(G-9050)*
War Metals Inc 918 629-8057
6306 S 40th West Ave Tulsa (74132) *(G-11095)*
Ward Brothers Printing 918 465-5551
102 W Main St Wilburton (74578) *(G-11528)*
Ward Petroleum Corporation (PA) 580 234-3229
502 S Fillmore St Enid (73703) *(G-3074)*
Ward Petroleum Corporation 405 242-4188
14000 Quail Springs Pkwy # 5000 Oklahoma City (73134) *(G-7419)*
Ward Wood Products Inc 405 681-5522
5401 Sw 33rd St Oklahoma City (73179) *(G-7420)*
Ware's The Bucks, Paoli *Also called Alan Ware (G-7637)*
Warehouse, Norman *Also called Bio-Cide International Inc (G-4932)*
Warhall Designs LLC 405 330-0907
14350 N Lincoln Blvd # 210 Edmond (73013) *(G-2680)*
Warner Jwly Box Display Co LLC 580 536-8885
1002 Sw Ard St Lawton (73505) *(G-4021)*
Warning Aware LLC 405 300-8833
1050 E 2nd St Ste 117 Edmond (73034) *(G-2681)*
Warrant Divisions Inc 918 962-4800
19346 Us Highway 271 Spiro (74959) *(G-8620)*
Warren American Oil Company (PA) 918 481-7990
6585 S Yale Ave Ste 800 Tulsa (74136) *(G-11096)*
Warren American Oil Company 918 846-2294
7326 County Road 2420 Barnsdall (74002) *(G-442)*
Warren Products Inc 405 947-5676
1233 Sovereign Row Ste B1 Oklahoma City (73108) *(G-7421)*
Warren Ramsey Inc 405 528-2828
218 Ne 38th St Oklahoma City (73105) *(G-7422)*
Warren West 580 838-2173
2297 Kemp Rd Hendrix (74741) *(G-3441)*
Warren, Bill, Office Products, Oklahoma City *Also called Warren Products Inc (G-7421)*
Warren, Robert H & Assoc, Oklahoma City *Also called Mfp Petroleum Ltd Partnership (G-6584)*
Warrens Screen Prtg EMB L L C 405 422-3900
1307 Fairfax Ln El Reno (73036) *(G-2768)*
Warrior Industries Inc 918 227-3500
13902 W 171st St S Sapulpa (74066) *(G-8323)*
Warwick Energy Group LLC (PA) 405 607-3400
900 W Wilshire Blvd Oklahoma City (73116) *(G-7423)*
Warwick Energy Group LLC 972 351-2740
6608 N Western Ave 417 Oklahoma City (73116) *(G-7424)*
Warwick Energy Inv Group LLC 405 607-3400
2802 W Country Club Dr Oklahoma City (73116) *(G-7425)*
Washingtons Welding LLC 918 336-2111
1340 S Virginia Ave Bartlesville (74003) *(G-534)*
Washita Flow Testers Inc 405 756-3397
Hwy 76 N Lindsay (73052) *(G-4099)*
Washita Refrigeration & Eqp Co 800 235-9476
8725 S Callen Rd Milburn (73450) *(G-4464)*
Washita Valley Enterprises 405 568-4525
5605 S Eastern Ave Oklahoma City (73129) *(G-7426)*
Washita Valley Enterprises Inc 580 540-9277
4411 Shady Ln Enid (73701) *(G-3075)*
Washita Valley Enterprises Inc (PA) 405 670-5338
1705 Se 59th St Oklahoma City (73129) *(G-7427)*
Washita Valley Enterprises Inc 918 429-0186
387 Alderson Rd McAlester (74501) *(G-4349)*
Washita Valley Weekly 405 224-7467
920 S 4th St Chickasha (73018) *(G-1522)*
Washita Wldg & Fabrication LLC 405 779-0140
115 N 29th St Chickasha (73018) *(G-1523)*
Wasinger Wasinger 580 335-3490
17972 County Road Ns 222 Frederick (73542) *(G-3203)*
Wassco Bottling Company, Tulsa *Also called Wassco Corporation (G-11097)*
Wassco Corporation 918 834-4444
515 S 25th West Ave Tulsa (74127) *(G-11097)*
Wastequip Manufacturing Co LLC 580 924-1575
101 Waldron Dr Durant (74701) *(G-2272)*
Water Bionics Inc 918 446-1988
4207 S 33rd West Ave Tulsa (74107) *(G-11098)*
Water Tank Service 918 786-7850
66500 E 255 Rd Grove (74344) *(G-3292)*
Waters Edge Winery, Oklahoma City *Also called Trio Di Vino LLC (G-7336)*
Waters Edge Winery On Rose 918 286-0086
116 S Main St Broken Arrow (74012) *(G-1092)*
Waterwood Parkway LLC 405 341-5077
3820 Woodshadow Rd Edmond (73003) *(G-2682)*
Watkins Cabinet Doors LLC 580 320-6301
416 E Broadway Ada (74820) *(G-104)*
Watkins Products, Oklahoma City *Also called Leonard Skodak Distributors (G-6466)*
Watkins Sand Co 918 369-5238
14376 S Mingo Rd Bixby (74008) *(G-671)*
Watkins Trucking & Sand, Bixby *Also called Watkins Sand Co (G-671)*
Watley's Welding Service, Elgin *Also called Marty Watley (G-2777)*
Watonga Cheese Plant 580 623-5915
Rr 2 Box 114 Balko (73931) *(G-433)*
Watonga Machine & Steel Works 580 623-5830
12855 Us Highway 270 Watonga (73772) *(G-11352)*

ALPHABETIC

Watonga Printing & Office Sups 580 623-4989
108 E Main St Watonga (73772) ***(G-11353)***
Watonga Republican Inc 580 623-4922
104 E Main St Watonga (73772) ***(G-11354)***
Watson Well Solutions 580 772-3059
9851 N 2430 Rd Weatherford (73096) ***(G-11455)***
Watsons Machine Shop 918 652-3414
28885 S 196 Rd Henryetta (74437) ***(G-3517)***
Wave On Flags and Banners LLC 918 782-3330
2165 N 3rd St Langley (74350) ***(G-3875)***
Wax and Hive Candle Lc 918 542-6432
49721 E 95 Rd Miami (74354) ***(G-4436)***
Way-Wear LLC 405 410-8367
15276 E 770 Rd Kingfisher (73750) ***(G-3820)***
Wayland Woodworks LLC 918 799-6196
18668 S 344th West Ave Bristow (74010) ***(G-805)***
Waylink Systems Corporation 405 261-9896
1414 S Sangre Rd Stillwater (74074) ***(G-8773)***
Waylolo LLC 405 714-2353
3412 W 29th Ave Stillwater (74074) ***(G-8774)***
Wayman Hugh Rev, Oklahoma City *Also called Auto Way Manufacturing Co LLC* ***(G-5491)***
Wayne Burt Machine 918 786-4415
510 Industrial Rd Grove (74344) ***(G-3293)***
Wayne Winkler 918 689-9745
710 Birkes Rd Eufaula (74432) ***(G-3117)***
Waynoka Pubg Co Woods Cnty 580 824-2171
1643 Main St Waynoka (73860) ***(G-11381)***
Waynoka Sign Shop 580 824-1717
1511 Missouri St Waynoka (73860) ***(G-11382)***
WD Distributing Co Inc (PA) 405 634-3603
807 Se 83rd St Oklahoma City (73149) ***(G-7428)***
WD Sales Inc 580 237-1220
3520 Edgewater Dr Enid (73703) ***(G-3076)***
Wdks, Oklahoma City *Also called Liberty Transmission Parts* ***(G-6472)***
We Buy Scrap LLC 580 401-3083
4423 S Union St Ponca City (74601) ***(G-7887)***
We-Go Perforators Inc (PA) 580 332-1346
8717 County Road 3470 Ada (74820) ***(G-105)***
We-Go Perforators Inc 405 364-3618
2500 Mackie Dr Ste 100 Norman (73072) ***(G-5197)***
Weamco Incorporated 918 445-1141
2350 Industrial Rd Sapulpa (74066) ***(G-8324)***
Weamcometric, Sapulpa *Also called Weamco Incorporated* ***(G-8324)***
Wear-Tech 918 663-2009
6945 E 38th St Ste C Tulsa (74145) ***(G-11099)***
Weatherford Artificia 405 853-7181
Hwy 81 S Hennessey (73742) ***(G-3496)***
Weatherford Artificia 405 677-2410
2836 Se 15th St Oklahoma City (73129) ***(G-7429)***
Weatherford Cabinets 580 772-7511
201 S Custer St Weatherford (73096) ***(G-11456)***
Weatherford Cementation, Elk City *Also called U S Weatherford L P* ***(G-2886)***
Weatherford Daily News, The, Weatherford *Also called Weatherford News Inc* ***(G-11458)***
Weatherford District Office 405 354-7711
3500 N Cimarron Rd Yukon (73099) ***(G-11803)***
Weatherford International LLC 405 773-1100
857 S Scott St Oklahoma City (73115) ***(G-7430)***
Weatherford International LLC 580 225-1237
104 Harless Elk City (73644) ***(G-2888)***
Weatherford International LLC 405 773-1100
7725 W Reno Ave Ste 220 Oklahoma City (73127) ***(G-7431)***
Weatherford International LLC 405 577-5590
717 N Morgan Rd Ste 69 Oklahoma City (73127) ***(G-7432)***
Weatherford International LLC 580 490-1476
Us Hwy 70 E Wilson (73463) ***(G-11545)***
Weatherford International LLC 940 683-8393
2800 S Meridian Ave Oklahoma City (73108) ***(G-7433)***
Weatherford International LLC 405 350-3357
11133 Nw 10th St Yukon (73099) ***(G-11804)***
Weatherford International LLC 405 853-7127
34th St 557 Hennessey (73742) ***(G-3497)***
Weatherford International LLC 405 619-7238
808 Se 84th St Oklahoma City (73149) ***(G-7434)***
Weatherford Jar Repair, Elk City *Also called Weatherford International LLC* ***(G-2888)***
Weatherford Machine Works 580 772-5287
110 N Custer St Weatherford (73096) ***(G-11457)***
Weatherford News Inc (PA) 580 772-3301
118 S Broadway St Weatherford (73096) ***(G-11458)***
Weatherford Press Inc 580 772-5300
114 S Broadway St Weatherford (73096) ***(G-11459)***
Weatherford Sewage Plant, Weatherford *Also called City of Weatherford* ***(G-11402)***
Weatherford Submersible, Pauls Valley *Also called Submersible Technical Products* ***(G-7673)***
Weaver Energy Corporation 405 853-6068
600 N Cheyenne St Hennessey (73742) ***(G-3498)***
Weavers Meat Processing Inc 918 647-9832
34842 Us Highway 59 S Poteau (74953) ***(G-7917)***
Webber Kathryn 405 379-3872
7749 Highway 270 Holdenville (74848) ***(G-3562)***
Webco Industries Inc 918 581-0900
13701 W Highway 51 Sand Springs (74063) ***(G-8236)***
Webco Industries Inc (PA) 918 245-2211
9101 W 21st St Sand Springs (74063) ***(G-8237)***
Webco Industries Inc 865 388-5001
307 Waterford St Catoosa (74015) ***(G-1364)***
Webco Industries Inc 918 241-1086
201 S Woodland Dr Sand Springs (74063) ***(G-8238)***
Webco Industries Inc 918 865-6215
501 Foster Rd Mannford (74044) ***(G-4194)***
Webco Industries Inc 918 245-9521
8911 W 21st St Sand Springs (74063) ***(G-8239)***
Webco Industries Inc 918 865-6215
18256 W Highway 66 Kellyville (74039) ***(G-3769)***
Webco Industries Inc 918 836-1188
3116 E 31st St N Tulsa (74110) ***(G-11100)***
Webcoat Inc 918 426-5100
1801 E College Ave McAlester (74501) ***(G-4350)***
Weber Root Beer, Tulsa *Also called Webers Superior Root Beer Inc* ***(G-11101)***
Webers Superior Root Beer Inc 918 742-1082
3817 S Peoria Ave Tulsa (74105) ***(G-11101)***
Webready Software Inc 918 808-8465
200 S Desert Palm Ave Broken Arrow (74012) ***(G-1093)***
Webster County Coal LLC 918 295-7600
1717 S Boulder Ave # 400 Tulsa (74119) ***(G-11102)***
Webster Drilling Services LLC 405 517-5585
13817 May Ave Lindsay (73052) ***(G-4100)***
Wecktees 580 747-5363
7311 E Airport Rd Glencoe (74032) ***(G-3227)***
Weddle Signs, McAlester *Also called Htw Inc* ***(G-4305)***
Wedlake Fabricating Inc 918 428-1641
3989 N Osage Dr Tulsa (74127) ***(G-11103)***
Weekly Leader 918 458-8001
1596 S Muskogee Ave Tahlequah (74464) ***(G-8892)***
Weeks Welding LLC 918 931-1167
3502 N Grant St Enid (73703) ***(G-3077)***
Wehlu Producers Inc 405 844-9487
708 W 15th St Edmond (73013) ***(G-2683)***
Weibee Steel Inc 405 360-7055
5009 Se 44th St Norman (73072) ***(G-5198)***
Weilert Enterprises Inc 918 252-5515
5505 Bird Creek Ave Catoosa (74015) ***(G-1365)***
Weingartner Racing LLC 918 520-3480
20211 E 45th St S Broken Arrow (74014) ***(G-1176)***
Weinkauf Exploration 918 749-8383
6540 S Lewis Ave Tulsa (74136) ***(G-11104)***
Weinkauf Petroleum Inc (PA) 918 749-8383
6540 S Lewis Ave Tulsa (74136) ***(G-11105)***
Weins Machine Co Inc 918 865-2187
3 One Half Mi N On Hwy 48 Terlton (74081) ***(G-8938)***
Weir Oil Gas 580 225-2381
3900 S Highway 81 Svc Rd El Reno (73036) ***(G-2769)***
Welchs Twing Rcovery Trck Auto, Pauls Valley *Also called Welchs Wrecker* ***(G-7674)***
Welchs Wrecker 405 238-6194
2001 W Airline Rd Pauls Valley (73075) ***(G-7674)***
Weldco Mfg 580 296-1585
350 S Franklin St Colbert (74733) ***(G-1788)***
Welding Co-Op, The, Oklahoma City *Also called Bills Welding Coop LLC* ***(G-5567)***
Welding Industry Services LLC 580 479-7068
307 Highland Dr Waukomis (73773) ***(G-11361)***
Welding Shop 580 832-5545
202 W Main St Cordell (73632) ***(G-1864)***
Weldpro Manufacturing LLC 918 724-3862
5306 W 31st St Tulsa (74107) ***(G-11106)***
Well Completions Inc 918 654-3030
16578 Knot Hole Rd Cameron (74932) ***(G-1259)***
Well Solutions Inc 580 775-2373
13658 Sinclair Ln Marietta (73448) ***(G-4218)***
Wellhead Equipment Division, Oklahoma City *Also called FMC Technologies Inc* ***(G-6098)***
Wellstar Downhole Services LLC 580 542-6982
2504 W Owen K Garriott Rd # 301 Enid (73703) ***(G-3078)***
Wellston Plant, Wellston *Also called Enable Oklahoma Int Transm LLC* ***(G-11469)***
Welltec Inc 918 585-6122
320 S Boston Ave Tulsa (74103) ***(G-11107)***
Welton Acquisitions LLC 918 850-7981
4006 S Bermuda Ave Sand Springs (74063) ***(G-8240)***
Wenco Energy Corporation 918 252-4511
11102 E 56th St Ste D Tulsa (74146) ***(G-11108)***
Wendell Hicks Construction 918 520-9128
125 N Sycamore St Nowata (74048) ***(G-5232)***
Wentworth Operating Co 405 341-6122
11900 N Macarthur Blvd E1 Oklahoma City (73162) ***(G-7435)***
Wenzel Downhole Tools Us Inc 405 787-4145
100 S Cooley Dr Oklahoma City (73127) ***(G-7436)***
Wepadit, Oklahoma City *Also called Environmental Compliance LLC* ***(G-6046)***
Werco Aviation Inc 918 251-6880
415 E Houston St Broken Arrow (74012) ***(G-1094)***
Werco Manufacturing Inc 918 251-6880
415 E Houston St Broken Arrow (74012) ***(G-1095)***

ALPHABETIC SECTION

Wesco Enterprises Inc..918 449-1081
  1907 W Detroit St Broken Arrow (74012) *(G-1096)*
Weslock, Tulsa *Also called Premiere Lock Co LLC* *(G-10553)*
Wesmar Racing Engines Inc..................................918 366-7222
  14502 S Lewis Ave Bixby (74008) *(G-672)*
Wesner Publications Company..............................405 789-1962
  6728 Nw 38th St Bethany (73008) *(G-600)*
Wesner Publications Company (PA).......................580 832-3333
  115 E Main St Cordell (73632) *(G-1865)*
Wesok Drilling Corp..580 226-2450
  911 W Broadway St Ardmore (73401) *(G-380)*
West Mattison Publishing Inc................................405 842-2266
  320 N Broadway Ste 201 Edmond (73034) *(G-2684)*
West OK Disposal, Tulsa *Also called Lakewood Disposal LLC* *(G-10114)*
West Texas By Products LP...................................580 371-9413
  108 N Easton Ravia (73455) *(G-8072)*
West Valbel Corporation.......................................580 223-3494
  10 W Main St Ardmore (73401) *(G-381)*
West Worldwide Services Inc...............................405 601-9877
  5500 W Reno Ave Ste 500 Oklahoma City (73127) *(G-7437)*
Westair Gas & Equipment LP................................580 338-6449
  502 Ne 4th St Guymon (73942) *(G-3370)*
Westech, Tulsa *Also called Western Technologies Inc* *(G-11110)*
Westenergy..405 607-6604
  5651 N Classen Blvd # 200 Oklahoma City (73118) *(G-7438)*
Western Cartoons..405 275-1054
  115 Maggies Pl Shawnee (74801) *(G-8519)*
Western Fibers Inc..509 679-4786
  1601 E Broadway St 62e Hollis (73550) *(G-3571)*
Western Frontier LLC..918 760-4977
  6968 E 610 Rd Locust Grove (74352) *(G-4113)*
Western Gas Resources Inc.................................580 883-2273
  3 N Hwy 58 Ringwood (73768) *(G-8097)*
Western Gas Resources Inc.................................580 764-3397
  225695 E County Road 53 Chester (73838) *(G-1422)*
Western Hull Sacking Inc.....................................580 335-2144
  Rr 2 Frederick (73542) *(G-3204)*
Western Industries Corporation (PA)....................405 419-3100
  5500 S Hattie Ave Oklahoma City (73129) *(G-7439)*
Western Iron Works LLC......................................405 779-1961
  1691 Highway 62 Chickasha (73018) *(G-1524)*
Western Metalsmith Design LLC...........................580 938-2153
  199416 E County Road 39 Woodward (73801) *(G-11650)*
Western Mobile Glass Mirror................................913 764-7444
  424 Sigma Pl Guthrie (73044) *(G-3340)*
Western Oil and Gas Dev Corp.............................405 235-4590
  420 Nw 13th St Ste 200 Oklahoma City (73103) *(G-7440)*
Western Okla Powertrain Inc...............................580 243-4501
  19485 E 1130 Rd Elk City (73644) *(G-2889)*
Western Plastics LLC...405 235-7272
  1819 Nw 5th St Oklahoma City (73106) *(G-7441)*
Western Portable Building, El Reno *Also called David Davis* *(G-2710)*
Western Prnting Company Inc..............................918 665-2874
  5129 S 95th East Ave Tulsa (74145) *(G-11109)*
Western Producers Cooperative, Dill City *Also called Rocky Farmers Cooperative Inc* *(G-2037)*
Western Seamless Guttering................................580 225-7983
  2001 E Highway 66 Elk City (73644) *(G-2890)*
Western Technologies Inc (PA)............................918 712-2406
  4404 S Maybelle Ave Tulsa (74107) *(G-11110)*
Western Web Envelope Co Inc (PA)......................405 682-0207
  3711 Sw 29th St Oklahoma City (73119) *(G-7442)*
Western Welding...580 832-2985
  22444 E 1240 Rd Rocky (73661) *(G-8106)*
Western X-Ray..580 922-3166
  409 N Elm St Seiling (73663) *(G-8352)*
Westfall Industries Inc..520 744-2330
  10233 Beaupre Dr Arcadia (73007) *(G-232)*
Westfall Producing Company................................918 743-1192
  2610 S Birmingham Pl Tulsa (74114) *(G-11111)*
Westoak Industries Inc..580 526-3221
  110 N Sheb Wooley Ave Erick (73645) *(G-3093)*
Westoak Production Svcs Inc...............................580 254-3568
  4915 Western Ave Woodward (73801) *(G-11651)*
Westport Oil Company Inc...................................405 239-2829
  5800 Nw 135th St Oklahoma City (73142) *(G-7443)*
Westrock Cp LLC...918 245-5102
  200 W Morrow Rd Sand Springs (74063) *(G-8241)*
Weststar Oil and Gas Inc.....................................405 341-2338
  1601 E 19th St Edmond (73013) *(G-2685)*
Westville Reporter The, Westville *Also called Cnhi Communications* *(G-11481)*
Westway Feed Products LLC................................918 266-5911
  5450 E Channel Rd Catoosa (74015) *(G-1366)*
Westwind Sheet Metal...918 437-9976
  152 S 122nd East Ave Tulsa (74128) *(G-11112)*
Westwood Cabinets & Furniture, Tulsa *Also called Westwood Furniture Inc* *(G-11113)*
Westwood Furniture Inc.......................................918 508-7657
  5744 E 30th Pl Tulsa (74114) *(G-11113)*

Westwood Printing Center....................................405 366-8961
  2403 N Porter Ave Norman (73071) *(G-5199)*
Wet Willies Screen Print & CU..............................405 262-6076
  705 N Rock Island Ave El Reno (73036) *(G-2770)*
Wetzel Producing Company..................................580 255-2929
  18 N 8th St Duncan (73533) *(G-2198)*
Wewoka Times..405 257-3341
  210 S Wewoka Ave Wewoka (74884) *(G-11513)*
Wewoka Window Works LLC.................................405 257-3109
  1024 S Eufaula Ave Wewoka (74884) *(G-11514)*
Wfwoodworks LLC...405 740-8920
  1912 Grassland Dr Norman (73072) *(G-5200)*
Wh International Casting LLC...............................562 521-0727
  117 E Airport Rd Haskell (74436) *(G-3402)*
What Print Now...580 649-7996
  1705 Oxford Dr Altus (73521) *(G-172)*
Wheeler & Sons Oil and Gas.................................405 375-4613
  406 N Main St Kingfisher (73750) *(G-3821)*
Wheeler Energy Corporation.................................918 587-7474
  4835 S Peoria Ave Ste 4 Tulsa (74105) *(G-11114)*
Wheeler Frris Whl Partners LLC............................405 206-6612
  223 S Walker Ave Oklahoma City (73109) *(G-7444)*
Wheelers Welding LLC...918 246-3811
  5905 S 170th West Ave Sand Springs (74063) *(G-8242)*
Wheels of Past..918 225-2250
  2320 S Agra Rd Cushing (74023) *(G-1969)*
Whimsical Sign and Crafting Co...........................918 315-4715
  512 Carson Rd Roland (74954) *(G-8115)*
Whiptail Midstream, Tulsa *Also called Shiprock Midstream LLC* *(G-10747)*
Whirlpool Corporation...918 274-6000
  7301 Whirlpool Dr Tulsa (74117) *(G-11115)*
Whispering Vines Vinyrd Winery..........................918 447-0808
  7374 W 51st St Tulsa (74107) *(G-11116)*
Whispring Mdows Vnyards Winery.......................918 423-9463
  34 E Choctaw Ave McAlester (74501) *(G-4351)*
Whistle Stop Bedding & More (PA)......................405 620-5749
  7205 Nw 210th St Edmond (73012) *(G-2686)*
Whistler Media Group..918 605-7446
  6304 E 102nd St Tulsa (74137) *(G-11117)*
Whistler Sign Co LLC..918 491-7446
  11063 S Memorial Dr Ste D Tulsa (74133) *(G-11118)*
Whit Industries..405 343-1181
  1312 Willow Brook St Ada (74820) *(G-106)*
Whitacre Glass Works LLC...................................918 366-6646
  8177 E 44th St Tulsa (74145) *(G-11119)*
White Bffalo Cstm Wdwrk Rnvtio........................405 387-3278
  5005 Eagle Nest Dr Blanchard (73010) *(G-745)*
White County Coal LLC..918 295-7600
  1717 S Boulder Ave # 400 Tulsa (74119) *(G-11120)*
White Dove Small Engines...................................580 857-2201
  28396 State Highway 1e Allen (74825) *(G-139)*
White Gordon Lbr Co of Lindsay...........................405 946-9032
  5801 Nw 36th St Warr Acres (73122) *(G-11330)*
White Operating Company....................................405 735-8419
  1627 Sw 96th St Oklahoma City (73159) *(G-7445)*
White Sail Energy LLC..405 255-4669
  3024 Katie Ln Edmond (73012) *(G-2687)*
White Shell LLC..918 978-2767
  11233 S 212th East Ave Broken Arrow (74014) *(G-1177)*
White Stone LLC...580 824-3271
  15639 State Highway 14 Waynoka (73860) *(G-11383)*
Whiteboard Software LLC....................................405 408-3326
  1015 Waterwood Pkwy Ste F Edmond (73034) *(G-2688)*
Whitecaps Inc...405 610-7007
  1932 S Air Depot Blvd Midwest City (73110) *(G-4461)*
Whitehouse Enterprises.......................................918 224-2002
  12082 S Whitehouse Dr Sapulpa (74066) *(G-8325)*
Whiteman Industries Inc......................................405 879-0077
  2601 Nw Expressway Oklahoma City (73112) *(G-7446)*
Whiterock Oil & Gas LLC......................................580 307-5565
  202 E Tower Ave Perry (73077) *(G-7750)*
Whites Roustabout Service Inc............................405 489-7126
  401 E 5th St Cement (73017) *(G-1371)*
Whites Welding...405 942-7070
  5400 N Grand Blvd Oklahoma City (73112) *(G-7447)*
Whites Welding LLC..580 254-3766
  46005 S County Road 202 Woodward (73801) *(G-11652)*
Whitetail Bath Bombs..405 474-8017
  808 Allison Pl El Reno (73036) *(G-2771)*
Whitetail Well Testing LLC..................................580 225-4200
  13574 N 2040 Rd Lone Wolf (73655) *(G-4122)*
Whiting Petroleum Corporation............................580 234-5554
  418 Chisholm Crk Enid (73701) *(G-3079)*
Whitlock Saw Mill...918 652-4410
  Rick Hill Addition Henryetta (74437) *(G-3518)*
Whitney Buildings, Pryor *Also called Whitney Manufacturing Inc* *(G-7998)*
Whitney Manufacturing Inc..................................918 825-6062
  4304 Ne 1st St Pryor (74361) *(G-7998)*
Whitney Pratt...405 610-2612
  3000 S Douglas Blvd Oklahoma City (73150) *(G-7448)*

Whitson Services, Elk City *Also called Liberty Transportation LLC* ***(G-2838)***
Whitten, J D Jr, Duncan *Also called Keystone Production Co* ***(G-2141)***
Whittle & Neher Company, Oklahoma City *Also called Bellofram* ***(G-5545)***
Whm Granite Products Inc (PA) 580 535-2184
900 Quarry Dr Granite (73547) ***(G-3257)***
Wholesale, Oklahoma City *Also called Tees Q Usbs Llc* ***(G-7265)***
Wholesale Electric Supply Co 918 647-2200
106 Ben Klutz Blvd Poteau (74953) ***(G-7918)***
Whorton Welding 405 610-6545
14113 Se 29th St Choctaw (73020) ***(G-1557)***
Whorton Welding Inc 405 664-7123
14220 Se 76th Pl Oklahoma City (73150) ***(G-7449)***
Wichita Industries 405 933-2162
1503 S Mission St Ste 4 Anadarko (73005) ***(G-209)***
Wichita Raceway Park 580 704-0341
1709 Nw Lake Ave Lawton (73507) ***(G-4022)***
Wicho Leather Creations LLC 405 885-8644
6209 Greenwood Ln Oklahoma City (73132) ***(G-7450)***
Wide Area Directory, Nichols Hills *Also called Brown Publishing Inc* ***(G-4856)***
Widler Welding, Burneyville *Also called Mitchell T Widler* ***(G-1217)***
Wiedenmanns Machine Shop 405 745-2682
10601 S County Line Rd Mustang (73064) ***(G-4801)***
Wiemann Ironworks, Tulsa *Also called Ernest Wiemann Iron Works* ***(G-9698)***
Wilbert Funeral Services Inc 918 446-2131
6505 S 57th West Ave Tulsa (74131) ***(G-9051)***
Wilbert Funeral Services Inc 405 752-9033
345 W Hefner Rd Oklahoma City (73114) ***(G-7451)***
Wilco Machine & Fab Inc 580 658-6993
1326 S Broadway St Marlow (73055) ***(G-4247)***
Wild Horse Distrubuting LLC 405 691-0755
11816 Chelsea Chase Oklahoma City (73170) ***(G-5323)***
Wild Leaf Screen Prtg & Design 918 440-4945
398408 W 4000 Rd Ramona (74061) ***(G-8047)***
Wild Olives LLC 580 230-1231
7 Miller Ave Duncan (73533) ***(G-2199)***
Wild Well Control Inc 405 686-0330
6125 W Reno Ave Ste 300 Oklahoma City (73127) ***(G-7452)***
Wild West Creations 405 542-6507
28789 Reuter Rd W Hinton (73047) ***(G-3540)***
Wildcat Field Services LLC 918 606-6217
123b N 14th St Collinsville (74021) ***(G-1829)***
Wildcat Machine Inc 918 247-4220
19083 W Highway 66 Kellyville (74039) ***(G-3770)***
Wildcat Minerals 580 254-0141
110 22nd St Woodward (73801) ***(G-11653)***
Wildcat Welding LLC 405 714-2273
405 W Highway 64 Morrison (73061) ***(G-4606)***
Wildcat Welding & Fabrications, Elgin *Also called Roy Slagel Keno* ***(G-2779)***
Wildcate Drilling Services Inc 580 254-3306
605 Martin Rd Woodward (73801) ***(G-11654)***
Wildhorse Exploration Prod LLC 918 396-3736
18744 N Javine Hill Rd Skiatook (74070) ***(G-8574)***
Wildhorse Oil & Gas Corp 580 223-0936
301 W Main St Ste 540 Ardmore (73401) ***(G-382)***
Wildkat Manufacturing, Oktaha *Also called Bradley Stephen Brown* ***(G-7530)***
Wildman Manufacturing Inc 405 235-1264
301 N Virginia Ave Oklahoma City (73106) ***(G-7453)***
Wildwood Fine Cabinet Doors 918 331-0007
211 Ne Debell Ave Bartlesville (74006) ***(G-535)***
Wiley Transformer Co 918 225-5772
6624 E Main St Cushing (74023) ***(G-1970)***
Wiljackal LLC 918 252-2663
5910 E 87th St Tulsa (74137) ***(G-11121)***
Wilkins L L E & O Company 405 273-0370
23 E 9th St Ste 406 Shawnee (74801) ***(G-8520)***
Wilkinson Mfg Co 918 258-8282
808 S 8th St Broken Arrow (74012) ***(G-1097)***
Will Robinson Logging LLC 918 569-4248
171272 N 4250 Rd Clayton (74536) ***(G-1711)***
Willco Hollow Metal, Clinton *Also called Hirsch3667 Corp* ***(G-1752)***
William B Finley 580 512-7573
4916 Nw Wolf Rd Lawton (73507) ***(G-4023)***
William B Hugos 405 810-0909
909 Nw 71st St Oklahoma City (73116) ***(G-7454)***
William C Jackson 918 742-0602
1762 S Utica Ave Tulsa (74104) ***(G-11122)***
William Cloud Oil 405 751-8422
12008 Quail Creek Rd Oklahoma City (73120) ***(G-7455)***
William Derrevere Designs 918 260-5607
1347 E 19th St Tulsa (74120) ***(G-11123)***
William H Davis 918 587-7782
1924 S Utica Ave Ste 1218 Tulsa (74104) ***(G-11124)***
William L Riggs Company Inc 918 437-3245
600 S 129th East Ave Tulsa (74108) ***(G-11125)***
William M Park 918 288-7752
211a W 113 St N Sperry (74073) ***(G-8612)***
William Pettit 918 297-2564
800 Pennsylvania Ave Hartshorne (74547) ***(G-3396)***
William Reed 405 912-8153
9500 Fendrych Dr Oklahoma City (73165) ***(G-5324)***
William W McClure Jr 918 747-6094
427 S Boston Ave Ste 952 Tulsa (74103) ***(G-11126)***
Williams 3g Ranch, Vinita *Also called Michael R Williams* ***(G-11264)***
Williams Companies Inc (PA) 918 573-2000
1 Williams Ctr Tulsa (74172) ***(G-11127)***
Williams Companies, The, Tulsa *Also called Williams Energy Resources LLC* ***(G-11128)***
Williams Energy Resources LLC 918 573-2000
1 Williams Ctr Bsmt 2 Tulsa (74172) ***(G-11128)***
Williams Field Services Co LLC (HQ) 918 573-2000
1 Williams Ctr Tulsa (74172) ***(G-11129)***
Williams Gas Pipeline Co LLC (HQ) 918 573-2000
1 Williams Ctr Bsmt 2 Tulsa (74172) ***(G-11130)***
Williams MBL Bay Prod Svcs LLC 918 573-2000
1 Williams Ctr Tulsa (74172) ***(G-11131)***
Williams McHning Spcalists Inc 918 247-1719
18750 W 141st St S Kellyville (74039) ***(G-3771)***
Williams Monuments 918 225-1344
1445 E Main St Cushing (74023) ***(G-1971)***
Williams Partners LP (HQ) 918 573-2000
1 Williams Ctr Tulsa (74172) ***(G-11132)***
Williams Prod Appalachia LLC 918 573-2000
1 One Williams Ctr Tulsa (74172) ***(G-11133)***
Williams Ranch Welding LLC 405 509-0289
367103 Us Highway 62 Boley (74829) ***(G-756)***
Williams Water Well Co 405 250-8531
700 Applewood Enid (73701) ***(G-3080)***
Williams Welding, Eucha *Also called Lonnie Williams* ***(G-3094)***
Williamson Machine Company Inc 918 625-9856
660 E Lakeview Dr Sapulpa (74066) ***(G-8326)***
Willie Dewayne Brown 918 482-1115
2315 Haskell Blvd Haskell (74436) ***(G-3403)***
Williford Energy Company (PA) 918 495-2700
6060 S American Plz Tulsa (74135) ***(G-11134)***
Williford Resources LLC 918 712-8828
6506 S Lewis Ave Ste 102 Tulsa (74136) ***(G-11135)***
Willis Bros Land & Cattle Co 580 569-2698
904 G St Snyder (73566) ***(G-8585)***
Willis Contruction, Moore *Also called Diversfied Wldg Fbrication LLC* ***(G-4517)***
Willis Granite Products, Granite *Also called Whm Granite Products Inc* ***(G-3257)***
Willischild Oil & Gas Corp 580 569-2598
621 E St Snyder (73566) ***(G-8586)***
Willoughby Pharmacy Svcs LLC 580 214-1043
600 W Arlington Ave # 18 Weatherford (73096) ***(G-11460)***
Willow Creek Co LLC 580 239-9549
5563 S Katy Rd Atoka (74525) ***(G-427)***
Willow Park Marina, Ketchum *Also called Kole Inc* ***(G-3774)***
Willys Fabricating & Wldg LLC 405 250-1250
1813 Nw 36th St Oklahoma City (73118) ***(G-7456)***
Wilnat Incorporated 918 640-0003
15332 N 149th East Ave Collinsville (74021) ***(G-1830)***
Wilsdorf Manufacturing LLC 918 369-5824
11409 E 130th St S Broken Arrow (74011) ***(G-1098)***
Wilshire Cabinet & Company LLC 405 286-6282
320 W Wilshire Blvd Oklahoma City (73116) ***(G-7457)***
Wilson & Wilson 405 375-5194
804 Clark Dr Kingfisher (73750) ***(G-3822)***
Wilson Electric Motor Svc Inc 405 636-1515
2208 S Agnew Ave Oklahoma City (73108) ***(G-7458)***
Wilson II Geary Wayne 405 330-4888
6333 Boucher Dr Edmond (73034) ***(G-2689)***
Wilson Patriot, Edmond *Also called Wilson II Geary Wayne* ***(G-2689)***
Wilson Pinstar Co 580 255-5899
284539 E 1690 Rd Marlow (73055) ***(G-4248)***
Wilson Products Inc 918 224-1327
8250 S 89th West Ave Tulsa (74131) ***(G-9052)***
Wilson Welding Works LLC 580 338-7345
3101 Tumbleweed Dr Guymon (73942) ***(G-3371)***
Wilson-Monroe Publishing Co 580 933-4579
119 N Dalton St Valliant (74764) ***(G-11234)***
Wilspec Technologies Inc (PA) 405 495-8989
4801 S Council Rd Oklahoma City (73179) ***(G-7459)***
Win Hy Foods Inc 918 227-0004
8620 S Regency Dr Tulsa (74131) ***(G-9053)***
Winarr Golf Tech LLC 918 994-2191
6912 E 12th St Tulsa (74112) ***(G-11136)***
Windor Supply & Mfg Inc 918 664-4017
6537 E 46th St Tulsa (74145) ***(G-11137)***
Windrunner Energy Inc 580 841-0404
19016 Us Highway 62 Duke (73532) ***(G-2082)***
Winds of Heartland 405 947-8558
3625 Goodger Dr Ste C Oklahoma City (73112) ***(G-7460)***
Windsor Quality Food Co Ltd 918 628-0277
9016 E 46th St Tulsa (74145) ***(G-11138)***
Wine Press 580 540-8913
3604 W Owen K Garriott Rd Enid (73703) ***(G-3081)***
Winfield Solutions LLC 580 237-2456
3225 E Willow Rd Enid (73701) ***(G-3082)***

ALPHABETIC SECTION

Wing-It Concepts 405 691-8053
 11324 S Shartel Ave Oklahoma City (73170) *(G-5325)*
Wink Eyelash Salon 918 949-6299
 3807 S Peoria Ave Tulsa (74105) *(G-11139)*
Winkles Woodworks Ltd 918 486-5022
 119 E Chestnut St Coweta (74429) *(G-1902)*
Winston Company Inc 800 331-9099
 3824 S 79th East Ave Tulsa (74145) *(G-11140)*
Winter Creek Drilling LLC 405 321-1200
 2419 Wilcox Dr Norman (73069) *(G-5201)*
Winter Hawk Pipe Line Services, Tulsa Also called SUN Engineering Inc *(G-10870)*
Winzeler Family LLC 405 218-2829
 709 Aberdeen Rd Edmond (73025) *(G-2690)*
Wire Cloth Manufacturers Inc 918 493-9400
 7136 S Yale Ave Ste 300 Tulsa (74136) *(G-11141)*
Wire Twisters Inc 405 376-0052
 1813 W Cedar Ridge Dr Mustang (73064) *(G-4802)*
Wise Foamco Inc 918 839-4784
 304 Kerr Ave Poteau (74953) *(G-7919)*
Wishon Welding LLC 405 808-4673
 7408 Nw 131st St Oklahoma City (73142) *(G-7461)*
Wister Lake Feed Inc 918 655-7954
 25096 Nobles Rd Howe (74940) *(G-3601)*
Withers Manufacturing Inc 918 994-7787
 5811 S Mingo Rd Tulsa (74146) *(G-11142)*
Withers Trucking Co 580 668-2320
 3 1/2 S On S W 8th St Healdton (73438) *(G-3424)*
Witt Lining Systems, Claremore Also called F C Witt Associates Ltd *(G-1618)*
Witten Company Inc 918 272-9567
 8199 N 116th East Ave Owasso (74055) *(G-7630)*
Witten Fasteners, Owasso Also called Witten Company Inc *(G-7630)*
Witter Marketing Inc 918 369-8639
 11716 E 133rd St S Broken Arrow (74011) *(G-1099)*
Witty Ideas Inc 918 367-9528
 115 S Main St Bristow (74010) *(G-806)*
Wizard Industries 918 622-5234
 10150 E 47th Pl Tulsa (74146) *(G-11143)*
Wj Welding LLC 580 465-4120
 801 W Main St Marietta (73448) *(G-4219)*
Wk Winters & Assoc 405 341-6571
 21 S Easy St Edmond (73012) *(G-2691)*
Wkd Associates 918 336-9865
 401 S Dewey Ave Bartlesville (74003) *(G-536)*
Wkp Compost, Boise City Also called Traci Rae Woolman *(G-749)*
WM Heitgras Company 918 583-3131
 1316 N Osage Dr 18 Tulsa (74106) *(G-11144)*
Wmi, Tulsa Also called Waldens Machine LLC *(G-11092)*
Wndells Woodturning 918 775-1124
 465172 E 1060 Rd Sallisaw (74955) *(G-8155)*
WO&w, Sand Springs Also called WOW Metallizing & Hard *(G-8243)*
Wohali Outdoors LLC (PA) 918 343-3800
 2466 W New Orleans St Broken Arrow (74011) *(G-1100)*
Wohler, Guthrie Also called Wolher Company *(G-3341)*
Wolf Creek Enterprises Inc 580 254-3361
 1222 10th St Ste 109n Woodward (73801) *(G-11655)*
Wolf Publishing 918 500-9921
 5946 E 26th Pl Tulsa (74114) *(G-11145)*
Wolf Software Group Co 405 721-0577
 6117 Covington Ln Warr Acres (73132) *(G-11331)*
Wolfe Heavy Haul and Hotshot 918 695-7836
 9133 E Newton St Tulsa (74115) *(G-11146)*
Wolff Machine Inc 405 382-3000
 404 Boren Blvd Seminole (74868) *(G-8407)*
Wolher Company 405 282-6210
 509 W Oklahoma Ave Guthrie (73044) *(G-3341)*
Woltjer Engines 918 258-0598
 805 W Elgin St Broken Arrow (74012) *(G-1101)*
Wolverine Tube Inc 405 275-4850
 41600 Wolverine Rd Shawnee (74804) *(G-8521)*
Wolverine Tube Inc 405 275-4850
 500 Walverine Rd Shawnee (74801) *(G-8522)*
Womack, Dana Typesetting, Tulsa Also called Vision Type & Design Inc *(G-11082)*
Wombat Labs LLC 405 355-9662
 1414 S Sangre Rd Stillwater (74074) *(G-8775)*
Wood Concepts Inc 918 836-9481
 2640 N Darlington Ave Tulsa (74115) *(G-11147)*
Wood Creations By Rod LLC 405 235-2222
 215 N Western Ave Oklahoma City (73106) *(G-7462)*
Wood Creations By Rod LLC 405 912-8099
 2601 Crystal Dr Moore (73160) *(G-4583)*
Wood Finishers Supply & Gemini, El Reno Also called Wood Finishers Supply Inc *(G-2772)*
Wood Finishers Supply Inc 405 422-1025
 2300 Sw Holloway St El Reno (73036) *(G-2772)*
Wood Flowline Products, L.L.C., Davis Also called Forum Production Equipment *(G-1984)*
Wood Group Pressure Control, Shawnee Also called GE Oil & Gas Pressure Ctrl LP *(G-8451)*
Wood Oil Company 405 948-1560
 5400 N Grand Blvd Ste 300 Oklahoma City (73112) *(G-7463)*

Wood Pipe Service Inc 405 672-6097
 8400 S Bryant Ave Oklahoma City (73149) *(G-7464)*
Wood Systems Inc 918 388-0900
 4706 W 46th St Tulsa (74107) *(G-11148)*
Wood Tech Structures 918 678-2108
 66301 E Highway 60 Wyandotte (74370) *(G-11663)*
Wood Working, Tulsa Also called D Lloyd Hollingsworth *(G-9539)*
Woodall Welding 405 736-0599
 411 W Ercoupe Dr Midwest City (73110) *(G-4462)*
Woodbine Financial Corporation 918 584-5309
 427 S Boston Ave Ste 303 Tulsa (74103) *(G-11149)*
Woodcrest Litho Inc 918 357-1676
 24814 E 71st St S Broken Arrow (74014) *(G-1178)*
Wooden Concepts LLC 405 459-0411
 11142 N 2370 Rd Weatherford (73096) *(G-11461)*
Wooden Solutions LLC 918 396-0774
 5433 W Oak St Skiatook (74070) *(G-8575)*
Woodford Express LLC 405 437-0857
 301 Nw 63rd St 200 Oklahoma City (73116) *(G-7465)*
Woodland Park Vineyards 405 743-2442
 3023 N Jardot Rd Stillwater (74075) *(G-8776)*
Woods and Waters Holdings LLC 405 347-3000
 17153 Cty Rd 1380 Anadarko (73005) *(G-210)*
Woods County Enterprise, Waynoka Also called Waynoka Pubg Co Woods Cnty *(G-11381)*
Woods County Enterprise 580 824-2171
 1543 Main St Waynoka (73860) *(G-11384)*
Woods Precision Products Inc 918 272-9541
 11501 N 109th East Ave Owasso (74055) *(G-7631)*
Woods Pumping Service Inc 405 449-3485
 13612 State Highway 74 Maysville (73057) *(G-4263)*
Woods Saddlery 918 723-5503
 70246 S 4760 Rd Westville (74965) *(G-11488)*
Woods Waters Winery Vineyards, Anadarko Also called Woods and Waters Holdings LLC *(G-210)*
Woods Wters Wnery Vneyards LLC (PA) 405 247-3000
 17153 County Road 1380 Anadarko (73005) *(G-211)*
Woodshed 918 256-9868
 111 N 1st St Vinita (74301) *(G-11272)*
Woodshop Cstm Cbinets Trim LLC 405 673-7139
 20 Sw 66th St Oklahoma City (73139) *(G-7466)*
Woodshop Ltd 405 922-3789
 4425 Deason Dr Edmond (73013) *(G-2692)*
Woodstock Cabinet LLC 918 834-4840
 4129 S 72nd East Ave Tulsa (74145) *(G-11150)*
Woodstock Sawmill & Timbers Co 405 673-7966
 1117 Exchange Ave Oklahoma City (73108) *(G-7467)*
Woodward Concrete, Woodward Also called Bo-Max Industries Inc *(G-11562)*
Woodward Ind Schl Dst I-1 .... 580 256-5910
 1023 10th St Woodward (73801) *(G-11656)*
Woodward Iodine Corporation 580 254-3311
 205865 E County Rd 54 Woodward (73801) *(G-11657)*
Woodward News, Woodward Also called Newspaper Holding Inc *(G-11614)*
Woodward News 580 256-2200
 904 Oklahoma Ave Woodward (73801) *(G-11658)*
Woodward Prffsion Developement, Woodward Also called Woodward Ind Schl Dst I-1 *(G-11656)*
Woodwork Productions LLC 918 639-3167
 18441 Woodcrest Ln Catoosa (74015) *(G-1367)*
Woodwright Woodworking LLC 918 254-6577
 2518 S Gardenia Pl Broken Arrow (74012) *(G-1102)*
Woody Candy Company, Oklahoma City Also called Jackson Holdings LLC *(G-6343)*
Woody Candy Company Inc 405 842-8903
 922 Nw 70th St Oklahoma City (73116) *(G-7468)*
Woody Creek Ranch 580 658-5448
 Rr 4 Box 59 Marlow (73055) *(G-4249)*
Wooldridge Oil Co Inc 918 465-3073
 250 Nw 1014th Ave Wilburton (74578) *(G-11529)*
Woolslayer Companies Inc 918 523-9191
 5002 Bird Creek Ave Catoosa (74015) *(G-1368)*
Wooten Pumping Service 918 642-5312
 192 Littlechief Ranch Rd Fairfax (74637) *(G-3122)*
Wooten Ranch, Fairfax Also called Wooten Pumping Service *(G-3122)*
Wooten Welding 918 655-6981
 29032 Pocohontas Rd Wister (74966) *(G-11551)*
Word Among US 918 812-5254
 7521 S 69th East Pl Tulsa (74133) *(G-11151)*
Word Exploration LP 580 234-3229
 502 S Fillmore St Enid (73703) *(G-3083)*
Word Inds Fabrication LLC 918 382-7704
 1150a N Peoria Ave Tulsa (74106) *(G-11152)*
Word Inds Piping Fabrication, Tulsa Also called Mw Piping Fabrication LLC *(G-10319)*
Work Activity Center Inc 405 799-6911
 203 E Main St Moore (73160) *(G-4584)*
Work Horse Welding LLC 918 530-5270
 212 S Gaither Rd Pryor (74361) *(G-7999)*
Workhorse Industries LLC 405 884-2023
 93497 N 2630 Rd Geary (73040) *(G-3218)*
World Arts Press LLC 405 314-2578
 1716 Huntington Ave Nichols Hills (73116) *(G-4865)*

World Energy Resources Inc 405 375-6484
6th & Miles St Kingfisher (73750) *(G-3823)*
World Imports At Wholesale Inc 405 947-7710
3935 W Reno Ave Oklahoma City (73107) *(G-7469)*
World Literature Today, Norman *Also called University of Oklahoma (G-5185)*
World Organization China Pntrs (PA) 405 521-1234
2700 N Portland Ave Oklahoma City (73107) *(G-7470)*
World Publishing Company Veba 918 582-0921
1415 S Quincy Ave Tulsa (74120) *(G-11153)*
World Trading Company Inc 405 787-1982
6754 Melrose Ln Oklahoma City (73127) *(G-7471)*
World Water Works Inc 405 943-9000
4000 Sw 113th St Oklahoma City (73173) *(G-7472)*
World Water Works Holdings Inc (PA) 800 607-7873
4000 Sw 113th St Oklahoma City (73173) *(G-7473)*
World Weidner LLC 580 765-9999
1001 Knight St Ponca City (74601) *(G-7888)*
World Wide Air Coolers, Sapulpa *Also called World Wide Exchangers Inc (G-8327)*
World Wide Exchangers LLC (HQ) 918 234-3700
601 W 136th St N Skiatook (74070) *(G-8576)*
World Wide Exchangers Inc 918 240-3193
6917 S Highway 97 Sapulpa (74066) *(G-8327)*
Worldwide Printing & Dist Inc (HQ) 918 295-0112
2900 E Apache St Tulsa (74110) *(G-11154)*
Worldwide Steel Works Inc 918 825-4545
650 Highway 69a Pryor (74361) *(G-8000)*
Worstell Oil 918 371-5425
10116 E 156th St N Collinsville (74021) *(G-1831)*
Worthington Cylinder Corp 918 396-2899
679 W 136th St N Skiatook (74070) *(G-8577)*
Worthington Industries Inc 614 438-3048
5215 Arkansas Rd Catoosa (74015) *(G-1369)*
WOW Metallizing & Hard 918 245-9922
100 Wellston Park Rd Sand Springs (74063) *(G-8243)*
Wpx Energy Inc (PA) 855 979-2012
3500 One Williams Ctr Tulsa (74172) *(G-11155)*
Wpx Energy Appalachia LLC 866 326-3190
1 Williams Ctr Ste 4700 Tulsa (74172) *(G-11156)*
Wpx Energy Keystone LLC 918 573-2000
1 Williams Ctr Tulsa (74172) *(G-11157)*
Wpx Energy Marketing LLC 918 573-0068
11005 S Granite Ave Tulsa (74137) *(G-11158)*
Wpx Energy Marketing LLC (HQ) 918 573-2000
1 One Williams Ctr Tulsa (74172) *(G-11159)*
Wpx Energy Permian LLC 855 979-2102
3500 One Williams Ctr Tulsa (74172) *(G-11160)*
Wpx Energy Rm Company 918 573-2000
1 Williams Ctr Tulsa (74172) *(G-11161)*
Wr Machine Shop Inc 918 834-7682
6514 E Independence St Tulsa (74115) *(G-11162)*
Wrangler Aviation Corp 405 364-5700
1700 Lexington Ave # 208 Norman (73069) *(G-5202)*
WRB Refining LP 918 977-6600
411 S Keeler Ave Bartlesville (74003) *(G-537)*
Wrg Management Services, Oklahoma City *Also called Writers Research Group LLC (G-7474)*
Wright Comfort Solutions Inc (PA) 580 688-3586
302 W Broadway St Hollis (73550) *(G-3572)*
Wright Lease Services 806 857-9116
1116 Quail Ridge Rd Enid (73703) *(G-3084)*
Wright Water Corporation 405 224-1839
1001 S 3rd St Chickasha (73018) *(G-1525)*
Wright Way Screen Printing 918 787-7898
25890 S 621 Rd Grove (74344) *(G-3294)*
Wrights Heating & Air, Hollis *Also called Wright Comfort Solutions Inc (G-3572)*
Wrights Machine Shop 580 363-1740
2245 S Main St Blackwell (74631) *(G-695)*
Write Green Light 405 722-7823
9109 Nw 101st St Yukon (73099) *(G-11805)*
Writers Research Group LLC 405 682-2589
8801 S Kentucky Ave Oklahoma City (73159) *(G-7474)*
Ws Mfg LLC 918 443-2773
12745 S Old Highway 169 Oologah (74053) *(G-7537)*
Wsnusa, Tulsa *Also called Green Co Corporation (G-9859)*
Wtl Oil LLC 405 608-6007
14201 Caliber Dr Ste 300 Oklahoma City (73134) *(G-7475)*
Ww Livestock Systems, Thomas *Also called W-W Manufacturing Co Inc (G-8951)*
Wwsc Holdings LLC (HQ) 405 235-3621
1730 W Reno Ave Oklahoma City (73106) *(G-7476)*
Wyatt Earp Companies 918 225-7770
112 S Highway 99 Cushing (74023) *(G-1972)*
Wyatt Engineering LLC 918 824-2255
439 S Wood St Pryor (74361) *(G-8001)*
Wyatts Oil Corp 918 287-4285
731 W 6th St Pawhuska (74056) *(G-7698)*
Wyers Welding 580 854-6277
4024 N Barr Ave Oklahoma City (73122) *(G-7477)*
Wyndham Tulsa 918 627-5000
10918 E 41st St Tulsa (74146) *(G-11163)*
Wynn Wynn Media 918 283-1834
2105 Walnut Hill Ln Claremore (74019) *(G-1705)*
Wynnewood 1500 LLC 248 268-3289
1500 E Kerr Blvd Wynnewood (73098) *(G-11675)*
Wynnewood Gazette, Wynnewood *Also called Russell Publishing Company (G-11672)*
Wynnewood LLC 248 268-3289
1500 E Kerr Blvd Wynnewood (73098) *(G-11676)*
Wynnewood Refining Company LLC 405 665-6565
906 S Powell Ave Wynnewood (73098) *(G-11677)*
Wyoming Casing Service Inc 580 256-1222
1020 Energy Rd Woodward (73801) *(G-11659)*
Wyoming Casing Service In 701 456-0136
401 E Highway 19 Chickasha (73018) *(G-1526)*
Wyrick Lumber Hugo, Hugo *Also called Hugo Wyrick Lumber (G-3614)*
X-Tra Oil Field Svcs & Cnstr, Drumright *Also called Xtra Oil Field & Cnstr Co (G-2077)*
Xae Corp 405 452-5735
915 N Alex Noon St Wetumka (74883) *(G-11496)*
Xanadu Exploration Company 918 584-3802
320 S Boston Ave Tulsa (74103) *(G-11164)*
XCEL Office Solutions LLC 580 595-9235
500 N Merridian Lawton (73501) *(G-4024)*
Xgp LLC 405 584-1444
545 W Strothers Ave Seminole (74868) *(G-8408)*
Xit Systems Inc 918 259-9071
803 E Jackson Pl Broken Arrow (74012) *(G-1103)*
Xpect Energy Services LLC 405 641-7537
609 Westland Dr Edmond (73013) *(G-2693)*
Xplorer Midstream LLC (HQ) 918 237-5885
301 Nw 63rd St Ste 200 Oklahoma City (73116) *(G-7478)*
Xplosafe LLC 405 334-5720
712 Eastgate St Stillwater (74074) *(G-8777)*
Xposure Inc 918 581-8900
20 E 5th St Ste 400 Tulsa (74103) *(G-11165)*
Xs Welding Company LLC 918 346-2550
16144 E 460 Rd Claremore (74017) *(G-1706)*
Xto Energy, Oklahoma City *Also called Cross Timbers Operating Co (G-5859)*
Xto Energy Inc 580 883-2253
501 S Highway 58 Ringwood (73768) *(G-8098)*
Xto Energy Inc 580 668-2332
8871 Dillard Rd Wilson (73463) *(G-11546)*
Xto Energy Inc 580 653-3200
15948 Us Highway 77 Ardmore (73401) *(G-383)*
Xtra Oil Field & Cnstr Co 918 352-3722
113 N Skinner Ave Drumright (74030) *(G-2077)*
Xtreme Energy Company 405 273-1185
624 W Independence St # 10 Shawnee (74804) *(G-8523)*
Xzeno Productions 405 974-4016
100 N University Dr Edmond (73034) *(G-2694)*
Xzube Tees 405 249-9506
2848 Classen Blvd Norman (73071) *(G-5203)*
Yandell Fire Investigations 580 269-2414
11 Acker Hill Rd Kaw City (74641) *(G-3760)*
Yandells Well Service 405 756-3407
610 Se 4th St Lindsay (73052) *(G-4101)*
Yankee Pacific Aerospace 918 894-8586
8664 S Peoria Ave Tulsa (74132) *(G-11166)*
Yankee Pacific Aerospace Inc 918 388-5940
4325 E 51st St Ste 116 Tulsa (74135) *(G-11167)*
Ydf Inc 405 324-2216
9500 Sw 15th Yukon (73085) *(G-11806)*
Ye Olde Woodshop 918 224-1603
7425 S 161st West Ave Sapulpa (74066) *(G-8328)*
Yellow Bird Communication 405 238-6260
619 N Pine St Pauls Valley (73075) *(G-7675)*
Yellow Rose Firing Range, Altus *Also called Stevens & Sons LLC (G-169)*
Yeomans Mch Sp & Auto Parts, Big Cabin *Also called Sam Yeoman (G-605)*
Yesco 918 524-9914
4312 S Mingo Rd Tulsa (74146) *(G-11168)*
Yester Year Carousel 405 427-5863
4949 N Coltrane Rd Oklahoma City (73121) *(G-7479)*
Yippee Ay-O-K Winery 580 515-8214
420 S 3rd St Clinton (73601) *(G-1773)*
Ymf, Oklahoma City *Also called York Metal Fabricators Inc (G-7481)*
Yocham Custom Saddlery, Bartlesville *Also called Custom Lea Sad & Cowboy Decor (G-471)*
Yolanda Olmos 918 850-8334
514 S 78th East Ave Tulsa (74112) *(G-11169)*
Yona Mfg Solutions LLC 918 698-9713
1102 N Oklahoma Ave Claremore (74017) *(G-1707)*
York International Corporation 405 364-4040
5005 York Dr Norman (73069) *(G-5204)*
York International Corporation 405 942-9675
257 N Harvard Ave Oklahoma City (73127) *(G-7480)*
York Metal Fabrication 405 598-6239
311 Debbie Ln Tecumseh (74873) *(G-8931)*
York Metal Fabricators Inc 405 528-7495
27 Ne 26th St Oklahoma City (73105) *(G-7481)*
Yorkshire Publishing LLC 918 394-2665
3207 S Norwood Ave Tulsa (74135) *(G-11170)*

ALPHABETIC SECTION

You Are Here Curriculum 918 650-8586
   910 N 14th St Henryetta (74437) *(G-3519)*
Young & New Century LLC 281 968-0718
   3521 Glisten St Norman (73072) *(G-5205)*
Young Brothers Inc 405 272-0821
   100 N Classen Blvd Oklahoma City (73106) *(G-7482)*
Young Construction Supply LLC 918 456-3250
   1506 W Choctaw St Tahlequah (74464) *(G-8893)*
Young Software 918 290-9876
   353573 E 980 Rd Sparks (74869) *(G-8590)*
Young Tool Company LLC 918 352-2213
   49698 W Highway 33 Drumright (74030) *(G-2078)*
Young, Frank K, Edmond Also called Frank K Young Oil Properties *(G-2421)*
Youngman Rock Inc (PA) 918 682-7070
   2401 S 6th St W Muskogee (74401) *(G-4759)*
Yp LLC 918 835-8600
   10159 E 11th St Ste 600 Tulsa (74128) *(G-11171)*
Yt Welding LLC 580 799-1984
   19953 E 1070 Rd Elk City (73644) *(G-2891)*
Yukon Door and Plywood Inc 405 354-4861
   900 S 17th St Yukon (73099) *(G-11807)*
Yukon Drilling Fluid Inc 405 324-8876
   9500 Sw 15th St Oklahoma City (73128) *(G-7483)*
Yukon Manufacturing Inc 918 850-3131
   3900 Ne Plum Creek Cir Oklahoma City (73131) *(G-7484)*
Yukon Review, Yukon Also called Review News Co *(G-11771)*
Yukon Stone Yard, Yukon Also called Dolese Bros Co *(G-11720)*
Yukon Trophy & Awards Inc 405 354-5184
   1007 W Main St Yukon (73099) *(G-11808)*
Z Signs Inc 405 670-1416
   2101 S Missouri Ave Oklahoma City (73129) *(G-7485)*
Zara Group Inc 918 782-4473
   32244 S 4470 Rd Vinita (74301) *(G-11273)*
Zebco, Tulsa Also called W C Bradley Co *(G-11086)*
Zebco, Claremore Also called W C Bradley Co *(G-1703)*
Zebco Corporation 918 836-5581
   6101 E Apache St Tulsa (74115) *(G-11172)*
Zebco Sales Company LLC 800 588-9030
   6101 E Apache St Tulsa (74115) *(G-11173)*
Zeco Machine Incorporated 405 282-3313
   1800 E Seward Rd Guthrie (73044) *(G-3342)*
Zedco LLC 918 521-7587
   2121 S Columbia Ave # 210 Tulsa (74114) *(G-11174)*
Zeeco Inc (HQ) 918 258-8551
   22151 E 91st St S Broken Arrow (74014) *(G-1179)*
Zeeco Usa LLC (PA) 918 258-8551
   22151 E 91st St S Broken Arrow (74014) *(G-1180)*
Zeigler Publishing 405 771-8754
   9401 Ne 45th St Spencer (73084) *(G-8603)*
Zentech 918 445-1881
   3744 S Jackson Ave Tulsa (74107) *(G-11175)*
Zentech LLC 918 585-8200
   1030 N Iroquois Ave Tulsa (74106) *(G-11176)*
Zephyr Operating Co LLC 405 286-4771
   5225 N Shartel Ave # 200 Oklahoma City (73118) *(G-7486)*
Zephyr Operating Company, Oklahoma City Also called Zephyr Operating Co LLC *(G-7486)*
Zephyr Southwest Orna LLC 918 251-4133
   600 S 10th St Broken Arrow (74012) *(G-1104)*
Zephyrus Electronics Ltd 918 437-3333
   168 S 122nd East Ave Tulsa (74128) *(G-11177)*
Zephyrus Manufacturing, Tulsa Also called Zephyrus Electronics Ltd *(G-11177)*
Zero Hour Industries Inc 918 685-0235
   97791 S 4433 Rd Gore (74435) *(G-3253)*
Zeta 918 664-8200
   1814 W Tacoma St Broken Arrow (74012) *(G-1105)*
Zieglers Bob Portable Bldg Sls 918 486-4462
   10295 S State Highway 51 Broken Arrow (74014) *(G-1181)*
Ziese Products Inc 918 457-5457
   23374 E 878 Rd Park Hill (74451) *(G-7647)*
Zimmermans Custom Design Inc 918 486-4179
   14048 S 302nd East Ave Coweta (74429) *(G-1903)*
Zinke & Trumbo Inc 918 488-6400
   6100 S Yale Ave Ste 1700 Tulsa (74136) *(G-11178)*
Zip ME Up Please LLC 405 614-2778
   1602 S Hillside Ct Stillwater (74074) *(G-8778)*
Zivko Aeronautics Inc 405 282-1330
   502 Airport Rd Hngr 6 Guthrie (73044) *(G-3343)*
Zkc Welding 580 220-7685
   538 Case Cir Ardmore (73401) *(G-384)*
Zlb Behring 405 521-9204
   716 Nw 23rd St Oklahoma City (73103) *(G-7487)*
Zlb Bio Services 580 248-4851
   1216 Nw Sheridan Rd Lawton (73505) *(G-4025)*
Zoe Homes LLC 405 550-3563
   4320 Nw 63rd St Oklahoma City (73116) *(G-7488)*
Zoe Studios LLC 918 258-4073
   920 S Lions Ave Broken Arrow (74012) *(G-1106)*
Zomm LLC 918 995-2233
   8620 S Peoria Ave Tulsa (74132) *(G-11179)*
Zon Graphics, Tahlequah Also called Zon Inc *(G-8894)*
Zon Inc 918 458-5511
   618 E Downing St Tahlequah (74464) *(G-8894)*
Zoo Too 580 250-1088
   2002 Sw Lee Blvd Lawton (73501) *(G-4026)*
Zoop-Corp 405 239-8184
   2512 Ashley Dr Oklahoma City (73120) *(G-7489)*
Zr Welding LLC 405 602-4164
   11800 Duffy Rd Lexington (73051) *(G-4041)*
Zulu 4 Tactical LLC 918 978-6810
   4108 E 47th St Tulsa (74135) *(G-11180)*
Zzw Global Inc (PA) 405 388-8720
   13109 Nw 7th St Yukon (73099) *(G-11809)*
Zzw Global Inc 405 985-8759
   11300 N Pennsylvania Ave Oklahoma City (73120) *(G-7490)*

PRODUCT INDEX

• Product categories are listed in alphabetical order.

A

ABRASIVES
ACADEMY
ACCELERATORS: Particle, High Voltage
ACCOUNTING MACHINES & CASH REGISTERS
ACCOUNTING SVCS: Certified Public
ACIDS: Hydrochloric
ACIDS: Hydrofluoric
ACIDS: Inorganic
ACIDS: Nitric
ACIDS: Sulfuric, Oleum
ADDITIVE BASED PLASTIC MATERIALS: Plasticizers
ADHESIVES
ADHESIVES & SEALANTS
ADHESIVES: Adhesives, paste
ADHESIVES: Epoxy
ADULT DAYCARE CENTERS
ADVERTISING AGENCIES
ADVERTISING AGENCIES: Consultants
ADVERTISING DISPLAY PRDTS
ADVERTISING MATERIAL DISTRIBUTION
ADVERTISING REPRESENTATIVES: Electronic Media
ADVERTISING REPRESENTATIVES: Magazine
ADVERTISING REPRESENTATIVES: Newspaper
ADVERTISING REPRESENTATIVES: Television & Radio Time Sales
ADVERTISING SPECIALTIES, WHOLESALE
ADVERTISING SVCS, NEC
ADVERTISING SVCS: Billboards
ADVERTISING SVCS: Direct Mail
ADVERTISING SVCS: Display
ADVERTISING SVCS: Outdoor
AEROBIC DANCE & EXERCISE CLASSES
AGENTS, BROKERS & BUREAUS: Personal Service
AGRICULTURAL DISINFECTANTS
AGRICULTURAL EQPT: BARN, SILO, POULTRY, DAIRY/LIVESTOCK MACH
AGRICULTURAL EQPT: Elevators, Farm
AGRICULTURAL EQPT: Fertilizing Machinery
AGRICULTURAL EQPT: Fertilizng, Sprayng, Dustng/Irrigatn Mach
AGRICULTURAL EQPT: Greens Mowing Eqpt
AGRICULTURAL EQPT: Grounds Mowing Eqpt
AGRICULTURAL EQPT: Harvesters, Fruit, Vegetable, Tobacco
AGRICULTURAL EQPT: Storage Bins, Crop
AGRICULTURAL EQPT: Tractors, Farm
AGRICULTURAL EQPT: Trailers & Wagons, Farm
AGRICULTURAL EQPT: Turf & Grounds Eqpt
AGRICULTURAL MACHINERY & EQPT REPAIR
AGRICULTURAL MACHINERY & EQPT: Wholesalers
AIR CLEANING SYSTEMS
AIR CONDITIONING & VENTILATION EQPT & SPLYS: Wholesales
AIR CONDITIONING EQPT
AIR CONDITIONING UNITS: Complete, Domestic Or Indl
AIR COOLERS: Metal Plate
AIR POLLUTION CONTROL EQPT & SPLYS WHOLESALERS
AIR TRAFFIC CONTROL SYSTEMS & EQPT
AIRCRAFT & AEROSPACE FLIGHT INSTRUMENTS & GUIDANCE SYSTEMS
AIRCRAFT & HEAVY EQPT REPAIR SVCS
AIRCRAFT ASSEMBLY PLANTS
AIRCRAFT CONTROL SYSTEMS:
AIRCRAFT DEALERS
AIRCRAFT ELECTRICAL EQPT REPAIR SVCS
AIRCRAFT ENG/ENG PART: Extrnl Pwr Unt, Hand Inertia Starter
AIRCRAFT ENGINES & ENGINE PARTS: Air Scoops
AIRCRAFT ENGINES & ENGINE PARTS: Exhaust Systems
AIRCRAFT ENGINES & ENGINE PARTS: Jet Asstd Takeoff Devices
AIRCRAFT ENGINES & ENGINE PARTS: Mount Parts
AIRCRAFT ENGINES & ENGINE PARTS: Research & Development, Mfr
AIRCRAFT ENGINES & ENGINE PARTS: Rocket Motors
AIRCRAFT ENGINES & PARTS
AIRCRAFT HANGAR OPERATION SVCS
AIRCRAFT MAINTENANCE & REPAIR SVCS
AIRCRAFT PARTS & AUXILIARY EQPT: Accumulators, Propeller
AIRCRAFT PARTS & AUXILIARY EQPT: Aircraft Training Eqpt
AIRCRAFT PARTS & AUXILIARY EQPT: Assys, Subassemblies/Parts
AIRCRAFT PARTS & AUXILIARY EQPT: Bodies
AIRCRAFT PARTS & AUXILIARY EQPT: Body & Wing Assys & Parts
AIRCRAFT PARTS & AUXILIARY EQPT: Body Assemblies & Parts
AIRCRAFT PARTS & AUXILIARY EQPT: Fins
AIRCRAFT PARTS & AUXILIARY EQPT: Gears, Power Transmission
AIRCRAFT PARTS & AUXILIARY EQPT: Military Eqpt & Armament
AIRCRAFT PARTS & AUXILIARY EQPT: Refueling Eqpt, In Flight
AIRCRAFT PARTS & AUXILIARY EQPT: Research & Development, Mfr
AIRCRAFT PARTS & AUXILIARY EQPT: Wing Assemblies & Parts
AIRCRAFT PARTS & EQPT, NEC
AIRCRAFT PARTS WHOLESALERS
AIRCRAFT PARTS/AUX EQPT: Airframe Assy, Exc Guided Missiles
AIRCRAFT SERVICING & REPAIRING
AIRCRAFT TURBINES
AIRCRAFT: Airplanes, Fixed Or Rotary Wing
AIRCRAFT: Motorized
AIRCRAFT: Research & Development, Manufacturer
AIRLOCKS
AIRPORT TERMINAL SVCS
ALARM SYSTEMS WHOLESALERS
ALARMS: Burglar
ALARMS: Fire
ALCOHOL, ETHYL: For Beverage Purposes
ALCOHOL: Butyl & Butanol
ALCOHOL: Methyl & Methanol, Synthetic
ALKALIES & CHLORINE
ALLOYS: Additive, Exc Copper Or Made In Blast Furnaces
ALTERNATORS & GENERATORS: Battery Charging
ALTERNATORS: Automotive
ALUMINUM
ALUMINUM PRDTS
ALUMINUM: Rolling & Drawing
AMMONIA & AMMONIUM SALTS
AMMONIUM NITRATE OR AMMONIUM SULFATE
AMMUNITION: Small Arms
AMPLIFIERS
AMUSEMENT & RECREATION SVCS: Art Gallery, Commercial
AMUSEMENT & RECREATION SVCS: Aviation Club, Membership
AMUSEMENT & RECREATION SVCS: Juke Box
AMUSEMENT MACHINES: Coin Operated
AMUSEMENT PARK DEVICES & RIDES: Carnival Mach & Eqpt, NEC
AMUSEMENT PARK DEVICES & RIDES: Ferris Wheels
ANALYZERS: Network
ANALYZERS: Respiratory
ANESTHESIA EQPT
ANIMAL BASED MEDICINAL CHEMICAL PRDTS
ANIMAL FEED & SUPPLEMENTS: Livestock & Poultry
ANIMAL FEED: Wholesalers
ANIMAL FOOD & SUPPLEMENTS: Dog
ANIMAL FOOD & SUPPLEMENTS: Dog & Cat
ANIMAL FOOD & SUPPLEMENTS: Feed Concentrates
ANIMAL FOOD & SUPPLEMENTS: Feed Supplements
ANIMAL FOOD & SUPPLEMENTS: Livestock
ANIMAL FOOD & SUPPLEMENTS: Mineral feed supplements
ANIMAL FOOD & SUPPLEMENTS: Pet, Exc Dog & Cat, Dry
ANIMAL FOOD & SUPPLEMENTS: Poultry
ANIMAL FOOD & SUPPLEMENTS: Stock Feeds, Dry
ANODIZING SVC
ANTI-GLARE MATERIAL
ANTIQUE & CLASSIC AUTOMOBILE RESTORATION
ANTIQUE AUTOMOBILE DEALERS
ANTIQUE FURNITURE RESTORATION & REPAIR
ANTIQUE REPAIR & RESTORATION SVCS, EXC FURNITURE & AUTOS
ANTIQUE SHOPS
APATITE MINING
APPAREL ACCESS STORES
APPLIANCES, HOUSEHOLD: Kitchen, Major, Exc Refrigs & Stoves
APPLIANCES, HOUSEHOLD: Sweepers, Electric
APPLIANCES: Household, NEC
APPLIANCES: Major, Cooking
APPLIANCES: Small, Electric
APPLICATIONS SOFTWARE PROGRAMMING
ARCHITECTURAL SVCS
ARCHITECTURAL SVCS: Engineering
ARMATURE REPAIRING & REWINDING SVC
ART & ORNAMENTAL WARE: Pottery
ART DEALERS & GALLERIES
ART DESIGN SVCS
ART GOODS & SPLYS WHOLESALERS
ART RELATED SVCS
ART SPLY STORES
ARTISTS' MATERIALS: Boards, Drawing
ARTISTS' MATERIALS: Canvas Board
ARTISTS' MATERIALS: Colors, Water & Oxide Ceramic Glass
ARTISTS' MATERIALS: Frames, Artists' Canvases
ARTISTS' MATERIALS: Paints, China Painting
ARTWORK: Framed
ASPHALT & ASPHALT PRDTS
ASPHALT COATINGS & SEALERS
ASPHALT PLANTS INCLUDING GRAVEL MIX TYPE
ASSEMBLING SVC: Clocks
ASSEMBLING SVC: Plumbing Fixture Fittings, Plastic
ASSOCIATION FOR THE HANDICAPPED
ASSOCIATIONS: Bar
ASSOCIATIONS: Fraternal
ASSOCIATIONS: Trade
ATOMIZERS
AUDIO & VIDEO EQPT, EXC COMMERCIAL
AUDIO ELECTRONIC SYSTEMS
AUDITING SVCS
AUTO & HOME SUPPLY STORES: Auto & Truck Eqpt & Parts
AUTO & HOME SUPPLY STORES: Auto Air Cond Eqpt, Sell/Install
AUTO & HOME SUPPLY STORES: Automotive Access
AUTO & HOME SUPPLY STORES: Automotive parts
AUTO & HOME SUPPLY STORES: Batteries, Automotive & Truck
AUTO & HOME SUPPLY STORES: Speed Shops, Incl Race Car Splys
AUTO & HOME SUPPLY STORES: Truck Eqpt & Parts
AUTOMATIC REGULATING CONTROL: Building Svcs Monitoring, Auto
AUTOMATIC REGULATING CONTROLS: Pressure, Air-Cond Sys
AUTOMATIC REGULATING CONTROLS: Surface Burner, Temperature
AUTOMATIC REGULATING CONTROLS: Vapor Heating
AUTOMATIC TELLER MACHINES
AUTOMOBILES & OTHER MOTOR VEHICLES WHOLESALERS
AUTOMOTIVE & TRUCK GENERAL REPAIR SVC
AUTOMOTIVE BATTERIES WHOLESALERS
AUTOMOTIVE BODY SHOP
AUTOMOTIVE BODY, PAINT & INTERIOR REPAIR & MAINTENANCE SVC
AUTOMOTIVE CUSTOMIZING SVCS, NONFACTORY BASIS
AUTOMOTIVE GLASS REPLACEMENT SHOPS
AUTOMOTIVE PAINT SHOP
AUTOMOTIVE PARTS, ACCESS & SPLYS
AUTOMOTIVE PARTS: Plastic
AUTOMOTIVE RADIATOR REPAIR SHOPS
AUTOMOTIVE REPAIR SHOPS: Alternators/Generator, Rebuild/Rpr
AUTOMOTIVE REPAIR SHOPS: Diesel Engine Repair
AUTOMOTIVE REPAIR SHOPS: Electrical Svcs
AUTOMOTIVE REPAIR SHOPS: Engine Rebuilding

PRODUCT INDEX

AUTOMOTIVE REPAIR SHOPS: Engine Repair
AUTOMOTIVE REPAIR SHOPS: Engine Repair, Exc Diesel
AUTOMOTIVE REPAIR SHOPS: Machine Shop
AUTOMOTIVE REPAIR SHOPS: Trailer Repair
AUTOMOTIVE REPAIR SHOPS: Truck Engine Repair, Exc Indl
AUTOMOTIVE REPAIR SHOPS: Wheel Alignment
AUTOMOTIVE REPAIR SVC
AUTOMOTIVE REPAIR SVCS, MISCELLANEOUS
AUTOMOTIVE SPLYS & PARTS, NEW, WHOLESALE: Brakes
AUTOMOTIVE SPLYS & PARTS, NEW, WHOLESALE: Engines/Eng Parts
AUTOMOTIVE SPLYS & PARTS, NEW, WHOLESALE: Pumps, Oil & Gas
AUTOMOTIVE SPLYS & PARTS, NEW, WHOLESALE: Radiators
AUTOMOTIVE SPLYS & PARTS, NEW, WHOLESALE: Trailer Parts
AUTOMOTIVE SPLYS & PARTS, USED, WHOLESALE
AUTOMOTIVE SPLYS & PARTS, USED, WHOLESALE: Engines
AUTOMOTIVE SPLYS & PARTS, WHOLESALE, NEC
AUTOMOTIVE SPLYS, USED, WHOLESALE & RETAIL
AUTOMOTIVE SPLYS/PARTS, NEW, WHOL: Body Rpr/Paint Shop Splys
AUTOMOTIVE SVCS
AUTOMOTIVE SVCS, EXC REPAIR & CARWASHES: Glass Tinting
AUTOMOTIVE SVCS, EXC REPAIR & CARWASHES: Insp & Diagnostic
AUTOMOTIVE SVCS, EXC REPAIR & CARWASHES: Maintenance
AUTOMOTIVE SVCS, EXC REPAIR & CARWASHES: Sun Roof Install
AUTOMOTIVE SVCS, EXC REPAIR & CARWASHES: Trailer Maintenance
AUTOMOTIVE SVCS, EXC REPAIR: Carwash, Automatic
AUTOMOTIVE SVCS, EXC REPAIR: Washing & Polishing
AUTOMOTIVE SVCS, EXC RPR/CARWASHES: High Perf Auto Rpr/Svc
AUTOMOTIVE TOWING SVCS
AUTOMOTIVE TRANSMISSION REPAIR SVC
AUTOMOTIVE WELDING SVCS
AUTOMOTIVE: Bodies
AUTOMOTIVE: Seating
AWNING REPAIR SHOP
AWNINGS & CANOPIES
AWNINGS & CANOPIES: Awnings, Fabric, From Purchased Matls
AWNINGS & CANOPIES: Canopies, Fabric, From Purchased Matls
AWNINGS & CANOPIES: Fabric
AXLES

B

BABBITT (METAL)
BACKHOES
BADGES, WHOLESALE
BAGS: Food Storage & Frozen Food, Plastic
BAGS: Garment, Plastic Film, Made From Purchased Materials
BAGS: Plastic
BAGS: Plastic, Made From Purchased Materials
BAGS: Textile
BAKERIES, COMMERCIAL: On Premises Baking Only
BAKERIES: On Premises Baking & Consumption
BAKERY FOR HOME SVC DELIVERY
BAKERY MACHINERY
BAKERY PRDTS: Bakery Prdts, Partially Cooked, Exc frozen
BAKERY PRDTS: Biscuits, Baked, Baking Powder & Raised
BAKERY PRDTS: Bread, All Types, Fresh Or Frozen
BAKERY PRDTS: Cakes, Bakery, Exc Frozen
BAKERY PRDTS: Cakes, Bakery, Frozen
BAKERY PRDTS: Cones, Ice Cream
BAKERY PRDTS: Cookies
BAKERY PRDTS: Cookies & crackers
BAKERY PRDTS: Crackers
BAKERY PRDTS: Doughnuts, Exc Frozen
BAKERY PRDTS: Dry
BAKERY PRDTS: Frozen
BAKERY PRDTS: Pies, Bakery, Frozen
BAKERY PRDTS: Wholesalers
BAKERY: Wholesale Or Wholesale & Retail Combined
BALERS

BARBECUE EQPT
BARRELS: Shipping, Metal
BARS & BAR SHAPES: Steel, Hot-Rolled
BARS: Concrete Reinforcing, Fabricated Steel
BASKETS, WHOLESALE
BATH SALTS
BATHROOM ACCESS & FITTINGS: Vitreous China & Earthenware
BATHROOM FIXTURES: Plastic
BATTERIES: Storage
BATTERY CHARGERS
BATTERY REPAIR & SVCS
BEARINGS: Ball & Roller
BEAUTY & BARBER SHOP EQPT
BEAUTY & BARBER SHOP EQPT & SPLYS WHOLESALERS
BEAUTY SALONS
BED & BREAKFAST INNS
BED SHEETING, COTTON
BEDDING, BEDSPREADS, BLANKETS & SHEETS
BEDDING, BEDSPREADS, BLANKETS & SHEETS: Comforters & Quilts
BEDS & ACCESS STORES
BEDSPREADS & BED SETS, FROM PURCHASED MATERIALS
BEER & ALE WHOLESALERS
BEER, WINE & LIQUOR STORES: Hard Liquor
BEER, WINE & LIQUOR STORES: Wine
BELLOWS
BELTS & BELT PRDTS
BELTS: Bandoleers
BENZENE
BEVERAGE BASES & SYRUPS
BEVERAGE PRDTS: Brewers' Grain
BEVERAGES, ALCOHOLIC: Beer
BEVERAGES, ALCOHOLIC: Beer & Ale
BEVERAGES, ALCOHOLIC: Cocktails
BEVERAGES, ALCOHOLIC: Distilled Liquors
BEVERAGES, ALCOHOLIC: Liquors, Malt
BEVERAGES, ALCOHOLIC: Scotch Whiskey
BEVERAGES, ALCOHOLIC: Wines
BEVERAGES, NONALCOHOLIC: Bottled & canned soft drinks
BEVERAGES, NONALCOHOLIC: Carbonated
BEVERAGES, NONALCOHOLIC: Carbonated, Canned & Bottled, Etc
BEVERAGES, NONALCOHOLIC: Flavoring extracts & syrups, nec
BEVERAGES, NONALCOHOLIC: Lemonade, Bottled & Canned, Etc
BEVERAGES, NONALCOHOLIC: Soft Drinks, Canned & Bottled, Etc
BEVERAGES, NONALCOHOLIC: Tea, Iced, Bottled & Canned, Etc
BEVERAGES, WINE & DISTILLED ALCOHOLIC, WHOLESALE: Wine
BEVERAGES, WINE/DISTILLED ALCOHOLIC, WHOL: Bttlg Wine/Liquor
BICYCLE REPAIR SHOP
BICYCLE SHOPS
BILLIARD & POOL TABLES & SPLYS
BILLING & BOOKKEEPING SVCS
BINDING SVC: Books & Manuals
BINDING SVC: Magazines
BINDING SVC: Trade
BINS: Prefabricated, Sheet Metal
BIOLOGICAL PRDTS: Blood Derivatives
BIOLOGICAL PRDTS: Exc Diagnostic
BIOLOGICAL PRDTS: Extracts
BIOLOGICAL PRDTS: Serums
BIOLOGICAL PRDTS: Toxins
BIOLOGICAL PRDTS: Vaccines
BIOLOGICAL PRDTS: Vaccines & Immunizing
BIOLOGICAL PRDTS: Veterinary
BLACKSMITH SHOP
BLADES: Knife
BLADES: Saw, Hand Or Power
BLANKBOOKS & LOOSELEAF BINDERS
BLANKBOOKS: Scrapbooks
BLAST SAND MINING
BLASTING SVC: Sand, Metal Parts
BLINDS & SHADES: Mini
BLINDS & SHADES: Vertical
BLINDS : Window
BLINDS, WOOD
BLOCK & BRICK: Sand Lime

BLOCKS & BRICKS: Concrete
BLOCKS: Chimney Or Fireplace, Concrete
BLOCKS: Insulating, Concrete
BLOCKS: Landscape Or Retaining Wall, Concrete
BLOCKS: Paving, Concrete
BLOCKS: Standard, Concrete Or Cinder
BLOOD BANK
BLOWER FILTER UNITS: Furnace Blowers
BLOWERS & FANS
BLUEPRINTING SVCS
BOAT BUILDING & REPAIR
BOAT BUILDING & REPAIRING: Fiberglass
BOAT BUILDING & REPAIRING: Motorboats, Inboard Or Outboard
BOAT BUILDING & REPAIRING: Motorized
BOAT BUILDING & RPRG: Fishing, Small, Lobster, Crab, Oyster
BOAT DEALERS
BOAT LIFTS
BOAT REPAIR SVCS
BOAT YARD: Boat yards, storage & incidental repair
BODIES: Truck & Bus
BODY PARTS: Automobile, Stamped Metal
BOILER & HEATING REPAIR SVCS
BOILER REPAIR SHOP
BOILERS & BOILER SHOP WORK
BOOK STORES
BOOK STORES: Religious
BOOKS, WHOLESALE
BOTTLE CAPS & RESEALERS: Plastic
BOTTLES: Plastic
BOUTIQUE STORES
BOXES & CRATES: Rectangular, Wood
BOXES & SHOOK: Nailed Wood
BOXES: Corrugated
BOXES: Paperboard, Folding
BOXES: Paperboard, Set-Up
BOXES: Tool Chests, Wood
BOXES: Wooden
BOYS' CAMPS
BRACKETS, ARCHITECTURAL: Plaster
BRAKES & BRAKE PARTS
BRAKES: Electromagnetic
BRASS & BRONZE PRDTS: Die-casted
BRASS GOODS, WHOLESALE
BRICK, STONE & RELATED PRDTS WHOLESALERS
BRICKS & BLOCKS: Structural
BRICKS: Clay
BRICKS: Concrete
BRIEFCASES
BROADCASTING & COMMS EQPT: Antennas, Transmitting/Comms
BROADCASTING & COMMUNICATIONS EQPT: Cellular Radio Telephone
BROADCASTING & COMMUNICATIONS EQPT: Transmitting, Radio/TV
BROADCASTING STATIONS, RADIO: Music Format
BROKERS' SVCS
BROKERS: Business
BROKERS: Food
BROKERS: Mortgage, Arranging For Loans
BROKERS: Printing
BRONZE FOUNDRY, NEC
BROOMS & BRUSHES: Push
BUILDING & STRUCTURAL WOOD MBRS: Timbers, Struct, Lam Lumber
BUILDING & STRUCTURAL WOOD MEMBERS
BUILDING COMPONENTS: Structural Steel
BUILDING INSPECTION SVCS
BUILDING MAINTENANCE SVCS, EXC REPAIRS
BUILDING PRDTS & MATERIALS DEALERS
BUILDING PRDTS: Stone
BUILDING STONE, ARTIFICIAL: Concrete
BUILDINGS & COMPONENTS: Prefabricated Metal
BUILDINGS, PREFABRICATED: Wholesalers
BUILDINGS: Chicken Coops, Prefabricated, Wood
BUILDINGS: Farm, Prefabricated Or Portable, Wood
BUILDINGS: Portable
BUILDINGS: Prefabricated, Metal
BUILDINGS: Prefabricated, Plastic
BUILDINGS: Prefabricated, Wood
BUILDINGS: Prefabricated, Wood
BULLETPROOF VESTS
BUMPERS: Motor Vehicle
BURIAL VAULTS: Concrete Or Precast Terrazzo

PRODUCT INDEX

BURNERS: Gas, Domestic
BURNERS: Gas, Indl
BUSINESS ACTIVITIES: Non-Commercial Site
BUSINESS FORMS WHOLESALERS
BUSINESS FORMS: Printed, Continuous
BUSINESS FORMS: Printed, Manifold
BUSINESS SUPPORT SVCS
BUSINESS TRAINING SVCS

C

CABINETS & CASES: Show, Display & Storage, Exc Wood
CABINETS: Bathroom Vanities, Wood
CABINETS: Entertainment
CABINETS: Entertainment Units, Household, Wood
CABINETS: Factory
CABINETS: Kitchen, Wood
CABINETS: Office, Wood
CABINETS: Show, Display, Etc, Wood, Exc Refrigerated
CABLE & PAY TELEVISION SVCS: Closed Circuit
CABLE TELEVISION PRDTS
CABLE: Fiber
CABLE: Fiber Optic
CABLE: Nonferrous, Shipboard
CABLE: Ropes & Fiber
CAGES: Wire
CALCULATING & ACCOUNTING EQPT
CALIBRATING SVCS, NEC
CAMPERS: Truck Mounted
CAN LIDS & ENDS
CANDLE SHOPS
CANDLES
CANDLES: Wholesalers
CANDY & CONFECTIONS: Candy Bars, Including Chocolate Covered
CANDY & CONFECTIONS: Fudge
CANDY & CONFECTIONS: Nuts, Candy Covered
CANDY, NUT & CONFECTIONERY STORES: Confectionery
CANDY, NUT & CONFECTIONERY STORES: Nuts
CANDY: Hard
CANNED SPECIALTIES
CANOPIES: Sheet Metal
CANS: Composite Foil-Fiber, Made From Purchased Materials
CANS: Fiber
CANS: Garbage, Stamped Or Pressed Metal
CANS: Metal
CANS: Oil, Metal
CANVAS PRDTS
CANVAS PRDTS: Air Cushions & Mattresses
CAPACITORS & CONDENSERS
CAR WASH EQPT
CARBIDES
CARBON & GRAPHITE PRDTS, NEC
CARBON BLACK
CARDS, PLASTIC, UNPRINTED, WHOLESALE
CARDS: Greeting
CARDS: Identification
CARPET & UPHOLSTERY CLEANING SVCS
CARPET & UPHOLSTERY CLEANING SVCS: Carpet/Furniture, On Loc
CARPETS & RUGS: Tufted
CARPETS, RUGS & FLOOR COVERING
CARPORTS: Prefabricated Metal
CARS: Electric
CASEMENTS: Aluminum
CASES: Carrying, Clothing & Apparel
CASES: Jewelry
CASES: Shipping, Nailed Or Lock Corner, Wood
CASH REGISTERS WHOLESALERS
CASINGS: Storage, Missile & Missile Components
CASKETS & ACCESS
CAST STONE: Concrete
CASTERS
CASTING BUREAU, MOTION PICTURE
CASTINGS GRINDING: For The Trade
CASTINGS: Aerospace Investment, Ferrous
CASTINGS: Aerospace, Aluminum
CASTINGS: Aerospace, Nonferrous, Exc Aluminum
CASTINGS: Aluminum
CASTINGS: Brass, NEC, Exc Die
CASTINGS: Bronze, NEC, Exc Die
CASTINGS: Commercial Investment, Ferrous
CASTINGS: Die, Aluminum
CASTINGS: Die, Copper & Copper Alloy
CASTINGS: Die, Magnesium & Magnesium-Base Alloy
CASTINGS: Die, Zinc
CASTINGS: Ductile
CASTINGS: Gray Iron
CASTINGS: Machinery, Brass
CASTINGS: Machinery, Nonferrous, Exc Die or Aluminum Copper
CASTINGS: Precision
CATALOG SALES
CATALYSTS: Chemical
CATERERS
CAULKING COMPOUNDS
CEMENT & CONCRETE RELATED PRDTS & EQPT: Bituminous
CEMENT ROCK: Crushed & Broken
CEMENT: Clay Refractory
CEMENT: Hydraulic
CEMENT: Masonry
CEMENT: Natural
CEMENT: Portland
CEMETERY MEMORIAL DEALERS
CERAMIC FIBER
CERAMIC FLOOR & WALL TILE WHOLESALERS
CHAIN: Welded, Made From Purchased Wire
CHAINS: Forged
CHANDELIERS: Commercial
CHANDELIERS: Residential
CHART & GRAPH DESIGN SVCS
CHASSIS: Automobile Trailer
CHASSIS: Motor Vehicle
CHEMICAL PROCESSING MACHINERY & EQPT
CHEMICAL SPLYS FOR FOUNDRIES
CHEMICAL: Sodm Compnds/Salts, Inorg, Exc Rfnd Sodm Chloride
CHEMICALS & ALLIED PRDTS WHOLESALERS, NEC
CHEMICALS & ALLIED PRDTS, WHOLESALE: Chemicals, Indl
CHEMICALS & ALLIED PRDTS, WHOLESALE: Chemicals, Indl & Heavy
CHEMICALS & ALLIED PRDTS, WHOLESALE: Detergent/Soap
CHEMICALS & ALLIED PRDTS, WHOLESALE: Essential Oils
CHEMICALS & ALLIED PRDTS, WHOLESALE: Indl Gases
CHEMICALS & ALLIED PRDTS, WHOLESALE: Oil Additives
CHEMICALS & ALLIED PRDTS, WHOLESALE: Oxygen
CHEMICALS & ALLIED PRDTS, WHOLESALE: Plastics Materials, NEC
CHEMICALS & ALLIED PRDTS, WHOLESALE: Plastics Prdts, NEC
CHEMICALS & ALLIED PRDTS, WHOLESALE: Sealants
CHEMICALS & OTHER PRDTS DERIVED FROM COKING
CHEMICALS, AGRICULTURE: Wholesalers
CHEMICALS: Agricultural
CHEMICALS: Anhydrous Ammonia
CHEMICALS: Brine
CHEMICALS: Fire Retardant
CHEMICALS: High Purity Grade, Organic
CHEMICALS: High Purity, Refined From Technical Grade
CHEMICALS: Hydrogen Peroxide
CHEMICALS: Inorganic, NEC
CHEMICALS: Iodine, Elemental
CHEMICALS: Magnesium Compounds Or Salts, Inorganic
CHEMICALS: Medicinal, Organic, Uncompounded, Bulk
CHEMICALS: NEC
CHEMICALS: Organic, NEC
CHEMICALS: Sodium Hyposulfite & Sodium Hydrosulfite
CHEMICALS: Sulfur, Incl Rcvrd/Refined, Fm Sour Natural Gas
CHEMICALS: Tanning Agents, Synthetic Inorganic
CHEMICALS: Water Treatment
CHICKEN SLAUGHTERING & PROCESSING
CHILD DAY CARE SVCS
CHLOROPRENE RUBBER: Neoprene
CHOCOLATE, EXC CANDY FROM BEANS: Chips, Powder, Block, Syrup
CHOCOLATE, EXC CANDY FROM PURCH CHOC: Chips, Powder, Block
CHUTES: Mail, Sheet Metal
CIGARETTE & CIGAR PRDTS & ACCESS
CIRCUIT BOARDS, PRINTED: Television & Radio
CIRCUITS: Electronic
CLAMPS & COUPLINGS: Hose
CLAMPS: Metal
CLAY PRDTS: Structural
CLEANING & DESCALING SVC: Metal Prdts
CLEANING EQPT: Blast, Dustless
CLEANING EQPT: Commercial
CLEANING EQPT: Dirt Sweeping Units, Indl
CLEANING EQPT: High Pressure
CLEANING OR POLISHING PREPARATIONS, NEC
CLEANING PRDTS: Ammonia, Household
CLEANING PRDTS: Degreasing Solvent
CLEANING PRDTS: Deodorants, Nonpersonal
CLEANING PRDTS: Drain Pipe Solvents Or Cleaners
CLEANING PRDTS: Laundry Preparations
CLEANING PRDTS: Metal Polish
CLEANING PRDTS: Sanitation Preparations
CLEANING PRDTS: Sanitation Preps, Disinfectants/Deodorants
CLEANING PRDTS: Specialty
CLEANING PRDTS: Window Cleaning Preparations
CLEANING SVCS
CLEANING SVCS: Industrial Or Commercial
CLOCK REPAIR SVCS
CLOTHING & ACCESS STORES
CLOTHING & ACCESS, WOMEN, CHILD & INFANT, WHOL: Blouses
CLOTHING & ACCESS, WOMEN, CHILD & INFANT, WHOLESALE: Sets
CLOTHING & ACCESS, WOMEN, CHILDREN & INFANT, WHOL: Uniforms
CLOTHING & ACCESS, WOMEN, CHILDREN/INFANT, WHOL: Baby Goods
CLOTHING & ACCESS: Handicapped
CLOTHING & ACCESS: Men's Miscellaneous Access
CLOTHING & ACCESS: Regalia
CLOTHING & APPAREL STORES: Custom
CLOTHING & FURN, MENS & BOYS, WHOLESALE: Robes, Under/Night
CLOTHING & FURNISHINGS, MEN'S & BOYS', WHOLESALE: Shirts
CLOTHING & FURNISHINGS, MEN'S & BOYS', WHOLESALE: Uniforms
CLOTHING & FURNISHINGS, MENS & BOYS, WHOL: Sportswear/Work
CLOTHING STORES: Shirts, Custom Made
CLOTHING STORES: T-Shirts, Printed, Custom
CLOTHING STORES: Unisex
CLOTHING: Access
CLOTHING: Access, Women's & Misses'
CLOTHING: Athletic & Sportswear, Men's & Boys'
CLOTHING: Athletic & Sportswear, Women's & Girls'
CLOTHING: Belts
CLOTHING: Brassieres
CLOTHING: Bridal Gowns
CLOTHING: Children & Infants'
CLOTHING: Coats & Suits, Men's & Boys'
CLOTHING: Coats, Hunting & Vests, Men's
CLOTHING: Costumes
CLOTHING: Dresses
CLOTHING: Gowns & Dresses, Wedding
CLOTHING: Hats & Caps, NEC
CLOTHING: Hats & Caps, Uniform
CLOTHING: Hats & Headwear, Knit
CLOTHING: Hosiery, Anklets
CLOTHING: Hospital, Men's
CLOTHING: Knit Underwear & Nightwear
CLOTHING: Leather & sheep-lined clothing
CLOTHING: Maternity
CLOTHING: Outerwear, Women's & Misses' NEC
CLOTHING: Overalls & Coveralls
CLOTHING: Robes & Dressing Gowns
CLOTHING: Shirts
CLOTHING: Shirts & T-Shirts, Knit
CLOTHING: Shirts, Dress, Men's & Boys'
CLOTHING: Shirts, Uniform, From Purchased Materials
CLOTHING: Sleeping Garments, Men's & Boys'
CLOTHING: Sleeping Garments, Women's & Children's
CLOTHING: Socks
CLOTHING: T-Shirts & Tops, Knit
CLOTHING: T-Shirts & Tops, Women's & Girls'
CLOTHING: Tailored Suits & Formal Jackets
CLOTHING: Ties, Bow, Men's & Boys', From Purchased Materials
CLOTHING: Tuxedos, From Purchased Materials
CLOTHING: Underwear, Women's & Children's
CLOTHING: Uniforms, Firemen's, From Purchased Materials
CLOTHING: Uniforms, Men's & Boys'
CLOTHING: Uniforms, Work
CLOTHING: Waterproof Outerwear
CLOTHING: Work Apparel, Exc Uniforms
CLUTCHES, EXC VEHICULAR
COAL & OTHER MINERALS & ORES WHOLESALERS

PRODUCT INDEX

COAL GASIFICATION
COAL MINING EXPLORATION & TEST BORING SVC
COAL MINING EXPLORATION SVCS: Anthracite
COAL MINING SERVICES
COAL MINING SVCS: Bituminous, Contract Basis
COAL MINING: Anthracite
COAL MINING: Bituminous & Lignite Surface
COAL MINING: Bituminous Coal & Lignite-Surface Mining
COAL MINING: Bituminous Underground
COAL MINING: Underground, Semibituminous
COAL PREPARATION PLANT: Bituminous or Lignite
COATING SVC
COATING SVC: Aluminum, Metal Prdts
COATING SVC: Hot Dip, Metals Or Formed Prdts
COATING SVC: Metals & Formed Prdts
COATING SVC: Metals, With Plastic Or Resins
COATING SVC: Rust Preventative
COATINGS: Air Curing
COATINGS: Epoxy
COFFEE SVCS
COILS & TRANSFORMERS
COILS: Electric Motors Or Generators
COILS: Pipe
COIN-OPERATED MACHINES & MECHANISMS, WHOLESALE
COINS & TOKENS: Non-Currency
COLOR SEPARATION: Photographic & Movie Film
COLORS: Pigments, Inorganic
COMBINATION UTILITIES, NEC
COMMERCIAL ART & GRAPHIC DESIGN SVCS
COMMERCIAL COOKING EQPT WHOLESALERS
COMMERCIAL EQPT WHOLESALERS, NEC
COMMERCIAL EQPT, WHOLESALE: Bakery Eqpt & Splys
COMMERCIAL EQPT, WHOLESALE: Coffee Brewing Eqpt & Splys
COMMERCIAL EQPT, WHOLESALE: Comm Cooking & Food Svc Eqpt
COMMERCIAL EQPT, WHOLESALE: Display Eqpt, Exc Refrigerated
COMMERCIAL EQPT, WHOLESALE: Restaurant, NEC
COMMERCIAL EQPT, WHOLESALE: Scales, Exc Laboratory
COMMERCIAL PRINTING & NEWSPAPER PUBLISHING COMBINED
COMMERCIAL SECTOR REG, LICENSING/INSP, GOVT: Prof Occupation
COMMODITY INVESTORS
COMMON SAND MINING
COMMUNICATIONS EQPT & SYSTEMS, NEC
COMMUNICATIONS EQPT WHOLESALERS
COMMUNICATIONS SVCS: Cellular
COMMUNICATIONS SVCS: Data
COMMUNICATIONS SVCS: Internet Connectivity Svcs
COMMUNICATIONS SVCS: Internet Host Svcs
COMMUNICATIONS SVCS: Phone Cable, Svcs, Land Or Submarine
COMMUNICATIONS SVCS: Telegraph
COMMUNICATIONS SVCS: Telephone Or Video
COMMUNICATIONS SVCS: Telephone, Local & Long Distance
COMPACT LASER DISCS: Prerecorded
COMPOSITION STONE: Plastic
COMPOST
COMPRESSORS: Air & Gas
COMPRESSORS: Air & Gas, Including Vacuum Pumps
COMPRESSORS: Refrigeration & Air Conditioning Eqpt
COMPRESSORS: Repairing
COMPRESSORS: Wholesalers
COMPUTER & COMPUTER SOFTWARE STORES
COMPUTER & COMPUTER SOFTWARE STORES: Printers & Plotters
COMPUTER & COMPUTER SOFTWARE STORES: Software & Access
COMPUTER & COMPUTER SOFTWARE STORES: Software, Bus/Non-Game
COMPUTER & OFFICE MACHINE MAINTENANCE & REPAIR
COMPUTER & SFTWR STORE: Modem, Monitor, Terminal/Disk Drive
COMPUTER FACILITIES MANAGEMENT SVCS
COMPUTER FORMS
COMPUTER GRAPHICS SVCS
COMPUTER INTERFACE EQPT: Indl Process
COMPUTER PERIPHERAL EQPT, NEC
COMPUTER PERIPHERAL EQPT, WHOLESALE
COMPUTER PERIPHERAL EQPT: Encoders

COMPUTER PROGRAMMING SVCS
COMPUTER PROGRAMMING SVCS: Custom
COMPUTER RELATED MAINTENANCE SVCS
COMPUTER SOFTWARE DEVELOPMENT
COMPUTER SOFTWARE DEVELOPMENT & APPLICATIONS
COMPUTER SOFTWARE SYSTEMS ANALYSIS & DESIGN: Custom
COMPUTER SOFTWARE WRITERS
COMPUTER STORAGE DEVICES, NEC
COMPUTER SYSTEMS ANALYSIS & DESIGN
COMPUTER-AIDED DESIGN SYSTEMS SVCS
COMPUTERS, NEC
COMPUTERS, NEC, WHOLESALE
COMPUTERS, PERIPHERALS & SOFTWARE, WHOLESALE: Keying Eqpt
COMPUTERS, PERIPHERALS & SOFTWARE, WHOLESALE: Printers
COMPUTERS, PERIPHERALS & SOFTWARE, WHOLESALE: Software
COMPUTERS: Mainframe
COMPUTERS: Mini
COMPUTERS: Personal
CONCENTRATES, DRINK
CONCRETE CURING & HARDENING COMPOUNDS
CONCRETE PLANTS
CONCRETE PRDTS
CONCRETE PRDTS, PRECAST, NEC
CONCRETE: Dry Mixture
CONCRETE: Ready-Mixed
CONDENSERS & CONDENSING UNITS: Air Conditioner
CONDENSERS: Heat Transfer Eqpt, Evaporative
CONDENSERS: Steam
CONFECTIONS & CANDY
CONFINEMENT SURVEILLANCE SYS MAINTENANCE & MONITORING SVCS
CONNECTORS: Electronic
CONSTRUCTION & MINING MACHINERY WHOLESALERS
CONSTRUCTION EQPT REPAIR SVCS
CONSTRUCTION EQPT: Attachments
CONSTRUCTION EQPT: Attachments, Backhoe Mounted, Hyd Pwrd
CONSTRUCTION EQPT: Backhoes, Tractors, Cranes & Similar Eqpt
CONSTRUCTION EQPT: Bulldozers
CONSTRUCTION EQPT: Crane Carriers
CONSTRUCTION EQPT: Cranes
CONSTRUCTION EQPT: Dozers, Tractor Mounted, Material Moving
CONSTRUCTION EQPT: Graders, Road
CONSTRUCTION EQPT: Hammer Mills, Port, Incl Rock/Ore Crush
CONSTRUCTION EQPT: Ladder Ditchers, Vertical Boom Or Wheel
CONSTRUCTION EQPT: Rakes, Land Clearing, Mechanical
CONSTRUCTION EQPT: Tractors, Crawler
CONSTRUCTION EQPT: Wrecker Hoists, Automobile
CONSTRUCTION MATERIALS WHOLESALERS
CONSTRUCTION MATERIALS, WHOL: Concrete/Cinder Bldg Prdts
CONSTRUCTION MATERIALS, WHOLESALE: Architectural Metalwork
CONSTRUCTION MATERIALS, WHOLESALE: Asphalt Felts & coating
CONSTRUCTION MATERIALS, WHOLESALE: Building Stone
CONSTRUCTION MATERIALS, WHOLESALE: Building Stone, Marble
CONSTRUCTION MATERIALS, WHOLESALE: Cement
CONSTRUCTION MATERIALS, WHOLESALE: Drywall Materials
CONSTRUCTION MATERIALS, WHOLESALE: Glass
CONSTRUCTION MATERIALS, WHOLESALE: Gravel
CONSTRUCTION MATERIALS, WHOLESALE: Metal Buildings
CONSTRUCTION MATERIALS, WHOLESALE: Molding, All Materials
CONSTRUCTION MATERIALS, WHOLESALE: Pallets, Wood
CONSTRUCTION MATERIALS, WHOLESALE: Paving Materials
CONSTRUCTION MATERIALS, WHOLESALE: Prefabricated Structures
CONSTRUCTION MATERIALS, WHOLESALE: Roof, Asphalt/Sheet Metal
CONSTRUCTION MATERIALS, WHOLESALE: Sand

CONSTRUCTION MATERIALS, WHOLESALE: Septic Tanks
CONSTRUCTION MATERIALS, WHOLESALE: Stone, Crushed Or Broken
CONSTRUCTION MATERIALS, WHOLESALE: Trim, Sheet Metal
CONSTRUCTION MATERIALS, WHOLESALE: Windows
CONSTRUCTION MATL, WHOLESALE: Structural Assy, Prefab, Wood
CONSTRUCTION MATLS, WHOL: Composite Board Prdts, Woodbeard
CONSTRUCTION MATLS, WHOL: Lumber, Rough, Dressed/Finished
CONSTRUCTION SAND MINING
CONSTRUCTION: Agricultural Building
CONSTRUCTION: Apartment Building
CONSTRUCTION: Athletic & Recreation Facilities
CONSTRUCTION: Bridge
CONSTRUCTION: Commercial & Institutional Building
CONSTRUCTION: Commercial & Office Building, New
CONSTRUCTION: Dock
CONSTRUCTION: Electric Power Line
CONSTRUCTION: Elevated Highway
CONSTRUCTION: Foundation & Retaining Wall
CONSTRUCTION: Greenhouse
CONSTRUCTION: Heavy Highway & Street
CONSTRUCTION: Indl Building & Warehouse
CONSTRUCTION: Indl Building, Prefabricated
CONSTRUCTION: Indl Buildings, New, NEC
CONSTRUCTION: Indl Plant
CONSTRUCTION: Mausoleum
CONSTRUCTION: Nonresidential Buildings, Custom
CONSTRUCTION: Oil & Gas Pipeline Construction
CONSTRUCTION: Pharmaceutical Manufacturing Plant
CONSTRUCTION: Pipeline, NEC
CONSTRUCTION: Pond
CONSTRUCTION: Power & Communication Transmission Tower
CONSTRUCTION: Pumping Station
CONSTRUCTION: Refineries
CONSTRUCTION: Residential, Nec
CONSTRUCTION: Roads, Gravel or Dirt
CONSTRUCTION: Sewer Line
CONSTRUCTION: Single-Family Housing
CONSTRUCTION: Single-family Housing, New
CONSTRUCTION: Steel Buildings
CONSTRUCTION: Street Surfacing & Paving
CONSTRUCTION: Utility Line
CONSTRUCTION: Waste Disposal Plant
CONSTRUCTION: Water Main
CONSULTING SVC: Actuarial
CONSULTING SVC: Business, NEC
CONSULTING SVC: Chemical
CONSULTING SVC: Computer
CONSULTING SVC: Engineering
CONSULTING SVC: Management
CONSULTING SVC: Marketing Management
CONSULTING SVC: Online Technology
CONSULTING SVC: Radio
CONSULTING SVC: Telecommunications
CONSULTING SVCS, BUSINESS: Agricultural
CONSULTING SVCS, BUSINESS: Communications
CONSULTING SVCS, BUSINESS: Environmental
CONSULTING SVCS, BUSINESS: Sys Engnrg, Exc Computer/Prof
CONSULTING SVCS, BUSINESS: Systems Analysis & Engineering
CONSULTING SVCS, BUSINESS: Systems Analysis Or Design
CONSULTING SVCS: Geological
CONSULTING SVCS: Oil
CONSUMER ELECTRONICS STORE: Video & Disc Recorder/Player
CONTACT LENSES
CONTAINERS, GLASS: Food
CONTAINERS: Cargo, Wood & Metal Combination
CONTAINERS: Corrugated
CONTAINERS: Food, Wood Wirebound
CONTAINERS: Glass
CONTAINERS: Liquid Tight Fiber, From Purchased Materials
CONTAINERS: Metal
CONTAINERS: Plastic
CONTAINERS: Sanitary, Food
CONTAINERS: Shipping & Mailing, Fiber
CONTAINERS: Shipping, Wood
CONTAINERS: Wood

PRODUCT INDEX

CONTAINMENT VESSELS: Reactor, Metal Plate
CONTRACTORS: Antenna Installation
CONTRACTORS: Asphalt
CONTRACTORS: Awning Installation
CONTRACTORS: Blasting, Exc Building Demolition
CONTRACTORS: Building Eqpt & Machinery Installation
CONTRACTORS: Building Front Installation, Metal
CONTRACTORS: Building Sign Installation & Mntnce
CONTRACTORS: Caisson Drilling
CONTRACTORS: Carpentry Work
CONTRACTORS: Carpentry, Cabinet & Finish Work
CONTRACTORS: Carpentry, Cabinet Building & Installation
CONTRACTORS: Carpentry, Finish & Trim Work
CONTRACTORS: Carpet Laying
CONTRACTORS: Chimney Construction & Maintenance
CONTRACTORS: Coating, Caulking & Weather, Water & Fire
CONTRACTORS: Commercial & Office Building
CONTRACTORS: Computer Power Conditioning Svcs
CONTRACTORS: Computerized Controls Installation
CONTRACTORS: Concrete
CONTRACTORS: Construction Site Cleanup
CONTRACTORS: Construction Site Metal Structure Coating
CONTRACTORS: Core Drilling & Cutting
CONTRACTORS: Corrosion Control Installation
CONTRACTORS: Countertop Installation
CONTRACTORS: Demolition, Building & Other Structures
CONTRACTORS: Directional Oil & Gas Well Drilling Svc
CONTRACTORS: Dock Eqpt Installation, Indl
CONTRACTORS: Drapery Track Installation
CONTRACTORS: Drywall
CONTRACTORS: Electric Power Systems
CONTRACTORS: Electrical
CONTRACTORS: Energy Management Control
CONTRACTORS: Erection & Dismantling, Poured Concrete Forms
CONTRACTORS: Excavating
CONTRACTORS: Excavating Slush Pits & Cellars Svcs
CONTRACTORS: Fence Construction
CONTRACTORS: Fiber Optic Cable Installation
CONTRACTORS: Fiberglass Work
CONTRACTORS: Fire Sprinkler System Installation Svcs
CONTRACTORS: Floor Laying & Other Floor Work
CONTRACTORS: Flooring
CONTRACTORS: Foundation Building
CONTRACTORS: Garage Doors
CONTRACTORS: Gas Detection & Analysis Svcs
CONTRACTORS: Gas Field Svcs, NEC
CONTRACTORS: Gasoline Condensation Removal Svcs
CONTRACTORS: General Electric
CONTRACTORS: Glass Tinting, Architectural & Automotive
CONTRACTORS: Glass, Glazing & Tinting
CONTRACTORS: Gutters & Downspouts
CONTRACTORS: Heating & Air Conditioning
CONTRACTORS: Heating Systems Repair & Maintenance Svc
CONTRACTORS: Highway & Street Construction, General
CONTRACTORS: Highway & Street Paving
CONTRACTORS: Home & Office Intrs Finish, Furnish/Remodel
CONTRACTORS: Hot Shot Svcs
CONTRACTORS: Hotel & Motel Renovation
CONTRACTORS: Hydraulic Eqpt Installation & Svcs
CONTRACTORS: Hydraulic Well Fracturing Svcs
CONTRACTORS: Indl Building Renovation, Remodeling & Repair
CONTRACTORS: Irrigation Land Leveling
CONTRACTORS: Kitchen & Bathroom Remodeling
CONTRACTORS: Lighting Syst
CONTRACTORS: Machinery Installation
CONTRACTORS: Marble Installation, Interior
CONTRACTORS: Mechanical
CONTRACTORS: Office Furniture Installation
CONTRACTORS: Oil & Gas Aerial Geophysical Exploration Svcs
CONTRACTORS: Oil & Gas Building, Repairing & Dismantling Svc
CONTRACTORS: Oil & Gas Field Fire Fighting Svcs
CONTRACTORS: Oil & Gas Field Geological Exploration Svcs
CONTRACTORS: Oil & Gas Field Geophysical Exploration Svcs
CONTRACTORS: Oil & Gas Field Salt Water Impound/Storing Svc
CONTRACTORS: Oil & Gas Field Tools Fishing Svcs
CONTRACTORS: Oil & Gas Well Casing Cement Svcs
CONTRACTORS: Oil & Gas Well Drilling Svc
CONTRACTORS: Oil & Gas Well Flow Rate Measurement Svcs
CONTRACTORS: Oil & Gas Well Foundation Grading Svcs
CONTRACTORS: Oil & Gas Well On-Site Foundation Building Svcs
CONTRACTORS: Oil & Gas Well Plugging & Abandoning Svcs
CONTRACTORS: Oil & Gas Well Redrilling
CONTRACTORS: Oil & Gas Well reworking
CONTRACTORS: Oil & Gas Wells Pumping Svcs
CONTRACTORS: Oil & Gas Wells Svcs
CONTRACTORS: Oil Field Haulage Svcs
CONTRACTORS: Oil Field Lease Tanks: Erectg, Clng/Rprg Svcs
CONTRACTORS: Oil Field Mud Drilling Svcs
CONTRACTORS: Oil Field Pipe Testing Svcs
CONTRACTORS: Oil Sampling Svcs
CONTRACTORS: Oil/Gas Field Casing,Tube/Rod Running,Cut/Pull
CONTRACTORS: Oil/Gas Well Construction, Rpr/Dismantling Svcs
CONTRACTORS: On-Site Welding
CONTRACTORS: Ornamental Metal Work
CONTRACTORS: Paint & Wallpaper Stripping
CONTRACTORS: Painting & Wall Covering
CONTRACTORS: Painting, Commercial
CONTRACTORS: Painting, Indl
CONTRACTORS: Painting, Residential
CONTRACTORS: Parking Lot Maintenance
CONTRACTORS: Patio & Deck Construction & Repair
CONTRACTORS: Petroleum Storage Tank Install, Underground
CONTRACTORS: Petroleum Storage Tanks, Pumping & Draining
CONTRACTORS: Pipe & Boiler Insulating
CONTRACTORS: Playground Construction & Eqpt Installation
CONTRACTORS: Plumbing
CONTRACTORS: Pollution Control Eqpt Installation
CONTRACTORS: Power Generating Eqpt Installation
CONTRACTORS: Precast Concrete Struct Framing & Panel Placing
CONTRACTORS: Prefabricated Window & Door Installation
CONTRACTORS: Protective Lining Install, Underground Sewage
CONTRACTORS: Refractory or Acid Brick Masonry
CONTRACTORS: Refrigeration
CONTRACTORS: Renovation, Aircraft Interiors
CONTRACTORS: Roof Repair
CONTRACTORS: Roofing
CONTRACTORS: Roofing & Gutter Work
CONTRACTORS: Roustabout Svcs
CONTRACTORS: Sandblasting Svc, Building Exteriors
CONTRACTORS: Seismograph Survey Svcs
CONTRACTORS: Septic System
CONTRACTORS: Sheet Metal Work, NEC
CONTRACTORS: Sheet metal Work, Architectural
CONTRACTORS: Shoring & Underpinning
CONTRACTORS: Siding
CONTRACTORS: Single-family Home General Remodeling
CONTRACTORS: Skylight Installation
CONTRACTORS: Sound Eqpt Installation
CONTRACTORS: Stone Masonry
CONTRACTORS: Storage Tank Erection, Metal
CONTRACTORS: Structural Steel Erection
CONTRACTORS: Svc Well Drilling Svcs
CONTRACTORS: Target Systems Installation
CONTRACTORS: Tile Installation, Ceramic
CONTRACTORS: Trenching
CONTRACTORS: Underground Utilities
CONTRACTORS: Warm Air Heating & Air Conditioning
CONTRACTORS: Water Well Drilling
CONTRACTORS: Well Acidizing Svcs
CONTRACTORS: Well Bailing, Cleaning, Swabbing & Treating Svc
CONTRACTORS: Well Casings Perforating Svcs
CONTRACTORS: Well Chemical Treating Svcs
CONTRACTORS: Well Cleaning Svcs
CONTRACTORS: Well Logging Svcs
CONTRACTORS: Well Swabbing Svcs
CONTRACTORS: Window Treatment Installation
CONTRACTORS: Windows & Doors
CONTRACTORS: Wrecking & Demolition
CONTROL CIRCUIT DEVICES
CONTROL EQPT: Electric
CONTROL PANELS: Electrical
CONTROLS & ACCESS: Indl, Electric
CONTROLS & ACCESS: Motor
CONTROLS: Automatic Temperature
CONTROLS: Crane & Hoist, Including Metal Mill
CONTROLS: Electric Motor
CONTROLS: Environmental
CONTROLS: Hydronic
CONTROLS: Relay & Ind
CONTROLS: Truck, Indl Battery
CONVENIENCE STORES
CONVERTERS: Data
CONVERTERS: Power, AC to DC
CONVEYOR SYSTEMS: Belt, General Indl Use
CONVEYORS & CONVEYING EQPT
CONVEYORS: Overhead
COOKING & FOOD WARMING EQPT: Commercial
COOKING & FOODWARMING EQPT: Coffee Brewing
COOKING & FOODWARMING EQPT: Popcorn Machines, Commercial
COOKING EQPT, HOUSEHOLD: Ranges, Gas
COOLERS & ICE CHESTS: Polystyrene Foam
COOLING TOWERS: Metal
COOLING TOWERS: Wood
COOPERAGE STOCK PRODUCTS
COPPER: Rolling & Drawing
COPY MACHINES WHOLESALERS
CORK & CORK PRDTS: Bottle
CORRUGATED PRDTS: Boxes, Partition, Display Items, Sheet/Pad
COSMETIC PREPARATIONS
COSMETICS & TOILETRIES
COSTUME JEWELRY & NOVELTIES: Apparel, Exc Precious Metals
COSTUME JEWELRY & NOVELTIES: Bracelets, Exc Precious Metals
COSTUME JEWELRY & NOVELTIES: Exc Semi & Precious
COSTUME JEWELRY STORES
COSTUMES & WIGS STORES
COUNCIL FOR SOCIAL AGENCY
COUNTER & SINK TOPS
COUNTERS OR COUNTER DISPLAY CASES, WOOD
COUPLINGS: Pipe
COURIER SVCS: Ground
COURT REPORTING SVCS
COVERS: Automobile Seat
CRACKED CASTING REPAIR SVCS
CRANE & AERIAL LIFT SVCS
CRANES & MONORAIL SYSTEMS
CRANES: Indl Plant
CRANES: Indl Truck
CRANES: Overhead
CRANKSHAFTS & CAMSHAFTS: Machining
CREDIT AGENCIES: Farmers Home Administration
CREDIT CARD SVCS
CREDIT INSTITUTIONS: Short-Term Business
CRUDE PETROLEUM & NATURAL GAS PRODUCTION
CRUDE PETROLEUM & NATURAL GAS PRODUCTION
CRUDE PETROLEUM PRODUCTION
CRUDES: Cyclic, Organic
CULVERTS: Sheet Metal
CUPS: Plastic Exc Polystyrene Foam
CURTAIN & DRAPERY FIXTURES: Poles, Rods & Rollers
CURTAINS & BEDDING: Knit
CUSHIONS & PILLOWS
CUSHIONS & PILLOWS: Bed, From Purchased Materials
CUSHIONS: Textile, Exc Spring & Carpet
CUSTOMIZING SVCS
CUT STONE & STONE PRODUCTS
CUTLERY
CYCLIC CRUDES & INTERMEDIATES
CYLINDER & ACTUATORS: Fluid Power
CYLINDERS: Pressure

D

DAIRY PRDTS STORE: Cheese
DAIRY PRDTS STORE: Ice Cream, Packaged
DAIRY PRDTS WHOLESALERS: Fresh
DAIRY PRDTS: Cheese
DAIRY PRDTS: Custard, Frozen
DAIRY PRDTS: Dietary Supplements, Dairy & Non-Dairy Based
DAIRY PRDTS: Farmers' Cheese
DAIRY PRDTS: Frozen Desserts & Novelties

PRODUCT INDEX

DAIRY PRDTS: Ice Cream, Packaged, Molded, On Sticks, Etc.
DAIRY PRDTS: Milk & Cream, Cultured & Flavored
DAIRY PRDTS: Milk, Fluid
DAIRY PRDTS: Milk, Processed, Pasteurized, Homogenized/Btld
DAIRY PRDTS: Natural Cheese
DAIRY PRDTS: Yogurt, Exc Frozen
DAIRY PRDTS: Yogurt, Frozen
DATA PROCESSING & PREPARATION SVCS
DATA PROCESSING SVCS
DATABASE INFORMATION RETRIEVAL SVCS
DECALS, WHOLESALE
DECORATIVE WOOD & WOODWORK
DEFENSE SYSTEMS & EQPT
DENTAL EQPT & SPLYS
DENTAL EQPT & SPLYS WHOLESALERS
DENTAL EQPT & SPLYS: Cabinets
DENTAL EQPT & SPLYS: Compounds
DENTAL EQPT & SPLYS: Dental Hand Instruments, NEC
DENTAL EQPT & SPLYS: Dental Materials
DENTAL EQPT & SPLYS: Denture Materials
DENTAL EQPT & SPLYS: Enamels
DENTAL EQPT & SPLYS: Gold
DENTAL INSTRUMENT REPAIR SVCS
DEPARTMENT STORES
DEPARTMENT STORES: Surplus & Salvage
DERRICKS: Oil & Gas Field
DESALTER KITS: Sea Water
DESIGN SVCS, NEC
DESIGN SVCS: Commercial & Indl
DESIGN SVCS: Computer Integrated Systems
DETECTION APPARATUS: Electronic/Magnetic Field, Light/Heat
DIAGNOSTIC SUBSTANCES
DIAGNOSTIC SUBSTANCES OR AGENTS: In Vivo
DIAGNOSTIC SUBSTANCES OR AGENTS: Microbiology & Virology
DIAGNOSTIC SUBSTANCES OR AGENTS: Radioactive
DIE SETS: Presses, Metal Stamping
DIES & TOOLS: Special
DIES: Plastic Forming
DIES: Steel Rule
DIODES: Light Emitting
DIODES: Solid State, Germanium, Silicon, Etc
DIRECT SELLING ESTABLISHMENTS, NEC
DIRECT SELLING ESTABLISHMENTS: Food Svcs
DIRECT SELLING ESTABLISHMENTS: Home Related Prdts
DISHWASHING EQPT: Commercial
DISINFECTING & DEODORIZING SVCS
DISINFECTING & PEST CONTROL SERVICES
DISINFECTING SVCS
DISK DRIVES: Computer
DISPENSING EQPT & PARTS, BEVERAGE: Coolers, Milk/Water, Elec
DISPLAY LETTERING SVCS
DISTILLERS DRIED GRAIN & SOLUBLES
DOCKS: Floating, Wood
DOCKS: Prefabricated Metal
DOCUMENT DESTRUCTION SVC
DOLLIES: Industrial
DOOR FRAMES: Wood
DOOR OPERATING SYSTEMS: Electric
DOORS & WINDOWS WHOLESALERS: All Materials
DOORS & WINDOWS: Screen & Storm
DOORS & WINDOWS: Storm, Metal
DOORS, LOUVER: Metal
DOORS: Combination Screen & Storm, Wood
DOORS: Garage, Overhead, Metal
DOORS: Garage, Overhead, Wood
DOORS: Hangar, Metal
DOORS: Wooden
DRAFTING SPLYS WHOLESALERS
DRAFTING SVCS
DRAPERIES & CURTAINS
DRAPERIES: Plastic & Textile, From Purchased Materials
DRAPERY & UPHOLSTERY STORES: Draperies
DRAPES & DRAPERY FABRICS, FROM MANMADE FIBER
DRILL BITS
DRILLING MACHINERY & EQPT: Oil & Gas
DRILLING MACHINERY & EQPT: Water Well
DRILLING MUD COMPOUNDS, CONDITIONERS & ADDITIVES
DRILLS & DRILLING EQPT: Mining
DRILLS: Rock, Portable

DRINKING PLACES: Saloon
DRIVE SHAFTS
DRIVE-A-WAY AUTOMOBILE SVCS
DRUG STORES
DRUG TESTING KITS: Blood & Urine
DRUGS & DRUG PROPRIETARIES, WHOL: Biologicals/Allied Prdts
DRUGS & DRUG PROPRIETARIES, WHOLESALE
DRUMS: Shipping, Metal
DRYCLEANING & LAUNDRY SVCS: Commercial & Family
DRYERS & REDRYERS: Indl
DUCTS: Sheet Metal
DUMPSTERS: Garbage

E

EARTH SCIENCE SVCS
EATING PLACES
ECONOMIZERS, BOILER
EDITING SVCS
EDITORIAL SVCS
EDUCATIONAL PROGRAM ADMINISTRATION, GOVERNMENT: State
EDUCATIONAL SVCS
EDUCATIONAL SVCS, NONDEGREE GRANTING: Continuing Education
EGG WHOLESALERS
ELECTRIC & OTHER SERVICES COMBINED
ELECTRIC MOTOR REPAIR SVCS
ELECTRIC POWER DISTRIBUTION TO CONSUMERS
ELECTRIC SERVICES
ELECTRICAL APPARATUS & EQPT WHOLESALERS
ELECTRICAL CURRENT CARRYING WIRING DEVICES
ELECTRICAL EQPT & SPLYS
ELECTRICAL EQPT FOR ENGINES
ELECTRICAL EQPT REPAIR & MAINTENANCE
ELECTRICAL EQPT REPAIR SVCS: High Voltage
ELECTRICAL EQPT: Automotive, NEC
ELECTRICAL GOODS, WHOL: Antennas, Receiving/Satellite Dishes
ELECTRICAL GOODS, WHOLESALE: Batteries, Storage, Indl
ELECTRICAL GOODS, WHOLESALE: Electrical Appliances, Major
ELECTRICAL GOODS, WHOLESALE: Electronic Parts
ELECTRICAL GOODS, WHOLESALE: Fire Alarm Systems
ELECTRICAL GOODS, WHOLESALE: Generators
ELECTRICAL GOODS, WHOLESALE: Motors
ELECTRICAL GOODS, WHOLESALE: Security Control Eqpt & Systems
ELECTRICAL GOODS, WHOLESALE: Svc Entrance Eqpt
ELECTRICAL GOODS, WHOLESALE: Switches, Exc Electronic, NEC
ELECTRICAL GOODS, WHOLESALE: Transformer & Transmission Eqpt
ELECTRICAL GOODS, WHOLESALE: Transformers
ELECTRICAL GOODS, WHOLESALE: Wire & Cable
ELECTRICAL INDL APPARATUS, NEC
ELECTRICAL SPLYS
ELECTRICAL SUPPLIES: Porcelain
ELECTRICAL WIRING TOOLS: Fish Wire
ELECTROLYSIS & EPILATORY SVCS
ELECTROMEDICAL EQPT
ELECTRON TUBES
ELECTRON TUBES: Parts
ELECTRONIC COMPONENTS
ELECTRONIC DEVICES: Solid State, NEC
ELECTRONIC EQPT REPAIR SVCS
ELECTRONIC PARTS & EQPT WHOLESALERS
ELECTRONIC TRAINING DEVICES
ELECTROPLATING & PLATING SVC
ELEMENTARY & SECONDARY SCHOOLS, PUBLIC
ELEVATOR: Grain, Storage Only
ELEVATORS & EQPT
ELEVATORS: Automobile
EMBLEMS: Embroidered
EMBROIDERING & ART NEEDLEWORK FOR THE TRADE
EMBROIDERING SVC
EMBROIDERING SVC: Schiffli Machine
EMBROIDERY ADVERTISING SVCS
EMBROIDERY KITS
EMERGENCY ALARMS
EMPLOYEE LEASING SVCS
EMPLOYMENT AGENCY SVCS
ENCLOSURES: Electronic
ENCLOSURES: Screen
ENGINE PARTS & ACCESS: Internal Combustion

ENGINE REBUILDING: Diesel
ENGINE REBUILDING: Gas
ENGINEERING HELP SVCS
ENGINEERING SVCS
ENGINEERING SVCS: Aviation Or Aeronautical
ENGINEERING SVCS: Building Construction
ENGINEERING SVCS: Chemical
ENGINEERING SVCS: Construction & Civil
ENGINEERING SVCS: Electrical Or Electronic
ENGINEERING SVCS: Fire Protection
ENGINEERING SVCS: Industrial
ENGINEERING SVCS: Mechanical
ENGINEERING SVCS: Petroleum
ENGINEERING SVCS: Pollution Control
ENGINEERING SVCS: Professional
ENGINEERING SVCS: Sanitary
ENGINES: Gasoline, NEC
ENGINES: Internal Combustion, NEC
ENGRAVING SVC, NEC
ENGRAVING SVC: Jewelry & Personal Goods
ENGRAVING SVCS
ENGRAVING SVCS: Tombstone
ENGRAVINGS: Plastic
ENTERTAINERS & ENTERTAINMENT GROUPS
ENTERTAINMENT SVCS
ENVELOPES
ENVIRONMENTAL QUALITY PROGS ADMIN, GOVT: Waste Mgmt
ENZYMES
EQUIPMENT: Rental & Leasing, NEC
ETCHING & ENGRAVING SVC
EXCAVATING MACHINERY & EQPT WHOLESALERS
EXERCISE EQPT STORES
EXPLORATION, METAL MINING
EXPLOSIVES
EXTERMINATING PRDTS: Household Or Indl Use
EXTRACTS, FLAVORING
EYEGLASSES
EYEGLASSES: Sunglasses
EYELASHES, ARTIFICIAL
Ethylene Glycols

F

FABRIC STORES
FABRICATED METAL PRODUCTS, NEC
FABRICS: Alpacas, Cotton
FABRICS: Alpacas, Mohair, Woven
FABRICS: Apparel & Outerwear, Cotton
FABRICS: Apparel & Outerwear, From Manmade Fiber Or Silk
FABRICS: Automotive, Cotton
FABRICS: Broadwoven, Cotton
FABRICS: Broadwoven, Synthetic Manmade Fiber & Silk
FABRICS: Broadwoven, Wool
FABRICS: Canvas
FABRICS: Coated Or Treated
FABRICS: Denims
FABRICS: Fiberglass, Broadwoven
FABRICS: Nonwoven
FABRICS: Oilcloth
FABRICS: Satin
FABRICS: Scrub Cloths
FABRICS: Trimmings
FABRICS: Wool, Broadwoven
FABRICS: Woven, Narrow Cotton, Wool, Silk
FACIAL SALONS
FACILITIES SUPPORT SVCS
FACILITY RENTAL & PARTY PLANNING SVCS
FACSIMILE COMMUNICATION EQPT
FAMILY CLOTHING STORES
FANS, BLOWING: Indl Or Commercial
FARM & GARDEN MACHINERY WHOLESALERS
FARM MACHINERY REPAIR SVCS
FARM PRDTS, RAW MATERIAL, WHOLESALE: Tobacco & Tobacco Prdts
FARM PRDTS, RAW MATERIALS, WHOLESALE: Farm Animals
FARM PRDTS, RAW MTRLS, WHOL: Nuts, Unprocessed/Shelled Only
FARM PRDTS, RAW MTRLS, WHOLESALE: Peanuts, Unroasted, Bulk
FARM SPLY STORES
FARM SPLYS WHOLESALERS
FARM SPLYS, WHOLESALE: Equestrian Eqpt
FARM SPLYS, WHOLESALE: Feed
FARM SPLYS, WHOLESALE: Herbicides

PRODUCT INDEX

FARM SPLYS, WHOLESALE: Saddlery
FARM SPLYS, WHOLESALE: Soil, Potting & Planting
FASTENERS: Metal
FASTENERS: Notions, NEC
FASTENERS: Wire, Made From Purchased Wire
FENCE POSTS: Iron & Steel
FENCES & FENCING MATERIALS
FENCES OR POSTS: Ornamental Iron Or Steel
FENCING DEALERS
FENCING MATERIALS: Plastic
FENCING: Chain Link
FERTILIZER, AGRICULTURAL: Wholesalers
FERTILIZERS: NEC
FERTILIZERS: Nitrogenous
FERTILIZERS: Phosphatic
FIBER & FIBER PRDTS: Synthetic Cellulosic
FIBER & FIBER PRDTS: Vinyl
FILM & SHEET: Unsuppported Plastic
FILM DEVELOPING & PRINTING SVCS
FILTERS
FILTERS & STRAINERS: Pipeline
FILTERS: Air
FILTERS: Air Intake, Internal Combustion Engine, Exc Auto
FILTERS: Gasoline, Internal Combustion Engine, Exc Auto
FILTERS: General Line, Indl
FILTERS: Motor Vehicle
FILTERS: Oil, Internal Combustion Engine, Exc Auto
FINANCIAL INVEST ACTS: Mineral, Oil & Gas Leasing & Royalty
FINANCIAL INVESTMENT ADVICE
FINISHING SVCS
FIRE ALARM MAINTENANCE & MONITORING SVCS
FIRE ARMS, SMALL: Guns Or Gun Parts, 30 mm & Below
FIRE ARMS, SMALL: Pistols Or Pistol Parts, 30 mm & below
FIRE ARMS, SMALL: Revolvers Or Revolver Parts, 30 mm & Below
FIRE ARMS, SMALL: Rifles Or Rifle Parts, 30 mm & below
FIRE ARMS, SMALL: Shotguns Or Shotgun Parts, 30 mm & Below
FIRE CONTROL OR BOMBING EQPT: Electronic
FIRE EXTINGUISHERS, WHOLESALE
FIRE EXTINGUISHERS: Portable
FIRE OR BURGLARY RESISTIVE PRDTS
FIRE PROTECTION EQPT
FIRE PROTECTION SVCS: Contracted
FIREARMS & AMMUNITION, EXC SPORTING, WHOLESALE
FIREARMS: Small, 30mm or Less
FIREPLACE & CHIMNEY MATERIAL: Concrete
FIREPLACES: Concrete
FIREWORKS
FIREWORKS SHOPS
FISH FOOD
FISHING EQPT: Lures
FITTINGS & ASSEMBLIES: Hose & Tube, Hydraulic Or Pneumatic
FITTINGS & SPECIALTIES: Steam
FITTINGS: Pipe
FITTINGS: Pipe, Fabricated
FIXTURES & EQPT: Kitchen, Metal, Exc Cast Aluminum
FIXTURES & EQPT: Kitchen, Porcelain Enameled
FLAGS: Fabric
FLAGSTONES
FLARES
FLAT GLASS: Building
FLAT GLASS: Skylight
FLAT GLASS: Spectacle
FLAT GLASS: Window, Clear & Colored
FLOOR COVERING STORES
FLOOR COVERING STORES: Carpets
FLOOR COVERINGS WHOLESALERS
FLOOR COVERINGS: Aircraft & Automobile
FLOOR COVERINGS: Art Squares
FLOOR COVERINGS: Textile Fiber
FLOOR COVERINGS: Twisted Paper, Grass, Reed, Coir, Etc
FLOORING & GRATINGS: Open, Construction Applications
FLOORING & SIDING: Metal
FLOORING: Hard Surface
FLOORING: Hardwood
FLOORING: Rubber
FLORIST: Flowers, Fresh
FLORISTS
FLUID METERS & COUNTING DEVICES
FLUID POWER PUMPS & MOTORS
FLUID POWER VALVES & HOSE FITTINGS
FLUXES

FOAM RUBBER
FOOD PRDTS, BREAKFAST: Cereal, Granola & Muesli
FOOD PRDTS, BREAKFAST: Cereal, Hulled Corn
FOOD PRDTS, CANNED, NEC
FOOD PRDTS, CANNED: Barbecue Sauce
FOOD PRDTS, CANNED: Chili
FOOD PRDTS, CANNED: Fruits
FOOD PRDTS, CANNED: Jams, Jellies & Preserves
FOOD PRDTS, CANNED: Jellies, Edible, Including Imitation
FOOD PRDTS, CANNED: Mexican, NEC
FOOD PRDTS, CANNED: Soups
FOOD PRDTS, CANNED: Spaghetti & Other Pasta Sauce
FOOD PRDTS, CANNED: Vegetables
FOOD PRDTS, FROZEN: Fruit Juice, Concentrates
FOOD PRDTS, FROZEN: NEC
FOOD PRDTS, MEAT & MEAT PRDTS, WHOLESALE: Brokers
FOOD PRDTS, MEAT & MEAT PRDTS, WHOLESALE: Cured Or Smoked
FOOD PRDTS, MEAT & MEAT PRDTS, WHOLESALE: Fresh
FOOD PRDTS, POULTRY, WHOLESALE: Live/Dressed/Frozen, Unpkgd
FOOD PRDTS, WHOL: Canned Goods, Fruit, Veg, Seafood/Meats
FOOD PRDTS, WHOLESALE: Baking Splys
FOOD PRDTS, WHOLESALE: Beans, Inedible
FOOD PRDTS, WHOLESALE: Coffee & Tea
FOOD PRDTS, WHOLESALE: Coffee, Green Or Roasted
FOOD PRDTS, WHOLESALE: Dog Food
FOOD PRDTS, WHOLESALE: Dried or Canned Foods
FOOD PRDTS, WHOLESALE: Flavorings & Fragrances
FOOD PRDTS, WHOLESALE: Grain Elevators
FOOD PRDTS, WHOLESALE: Spices & Seasonings
FOOD PRDTS, WHOLESALE: Water, Mineral Or Spring, Bottled
FOOD PRDTS: Almond Pastes
FOOD PRDTS: Animal & marine fats & oils
FOOD PRDTS: Box Lunches, For Sale Off Premises
FOOD PRDTS: Breakfast Bars
FOOD PRDTS: Chicken, Processed, Cooked
FOOD PRDTS: Chicken, Processed, NEC
FOOD PRDTS: Chicken, Slaughtered & Dressed
FOOD PRDTS: Chili Pepper Or Powder
FOOD PRDTS: Cocoa & Cocoa Prdts
FOOD PRDTS: Coffee
FOOD PRDTS: Coffee Roasting, Exc Wholesale Grocers
FOOD PRDTS: Dessert Mixes & Fillings
FOOD PRDTS: Dips, Exc Cheese & Sour Cream Based
FOOD PRDTS: Dough, Pizza, Prepared
FOOD PRDTS: Dressings, Salad, Raw & Cooked Exc Dry Mixes
FOOD PRDTS: Dried & Dehydrated Fruits, Vegetables & Soup Mix
FOOD PRDTS: Edible fats & oils
FOOD PRDTS: Emulsifiers
FOOD PRDTS: Flavored Ices, Frozen
FOOD PRDTS: Flour & Other Grain Mill Products
FOOD PRDTS: Flour Mixes & Doughs
FOOD PRDTS: Fruits & Vegetables, Pickled
FOOD PRDTS: Granular Wheat Flour
FOOD PRDTS: Nuts & Seeds
FOOD PRDTS: Peanut Butter
FOOD PRDTS: Poultry, Processed, NEC
FOOD PRDTS: Preparations
FOOD PRDTS: Relishes, Fruit & Vegetable
FOOD PRDTS: Seasonings & Spices
FOOD PRDTS: Soup Mixes
FOOD PRDTS: Spices, Including Ground
FOOD PRDTS: Starches
FOOD PRDTS: Syrups
FOOD PRDTS: Tea
FOOD PRDTS: Tortilla Chips
FOOD PRDTS: Tortillas
FOOD PRDTS: Vinegar
FOOD PRODUCTS MACHINERY
FOOD STORES: Convenience, Chain
FOOD STORES: Grocery, Independent
FOOTWEAR: Cut Stock
FORESTRY RELATED EQPT
FORGINGS
FORGINGS: Anchors
FORGINGS: Gear & Chain
FORGINGS: Iron & Steel
FORGINGS: Machinery, Ferrous
FORMAL WRITING SVCS

FORMS: Concrete, Sheet Metal
FOUNDRIES: Aluminum
FOUNDRIES: Brass, Bronze & Copper
FOUNDRIES: Gray & Ductile Iron
FOUNDRIES: Iron
FOUNDRIES: Nonferrous
FOUNDRIES: Steel
FOUNDRIES: Steel Investment
FOUNDRY MACHINERY & EQPT
FRAMES & HANDLES: Handbag & Luggage
FREIGHT TRANSPORTATION ARRANGEMENTS
FRUITS & VEGETABLES WHOLESALERS: Fresh
FUEL ADDITIVES
FUEL OIL DEALERS
FUELS & RADIOACTIVE COMPOUNDS
FUELS: Diesel
FUELS: Ethanol
FUELS: Gas, Liquefied
FUELS: Oil
FUNDRAISING SVCS
FUNGICIDES OR HERBICIDES
FURNACE BLACK
FURNACES & OVENS: Indl
FURNACES: Warm Air, Electric
FURNITURE & CABINET STORES: Cabinets, Custom Work
FURNITURE & CABINET STORES: Custom
FURNITURE & FIXTURES Factory
FURNITURE REFINISHING SVCS
FURNITURE STORES
FURNITURE STORES: Bar Fixtures, Eqpt & Splys
FURNITURE STORES: Cabinets, Kitchen, Exc Custom Made
FURNITURE STORES: Office
FURNITURE, OFFICE: Wholesalers
FURNITURE: Altars, Cut Stone
FURNITURE: Bed Frames & Headboards, Wood
FURNITURE: Beds, Household, Incl Folding & Cabinet, Metal
FURNITURE: Bedsprings, Assembled
FURNITURE: Bookcases, Wood
FURNITURE: Cabinets & Filing Drawers, Office, Exc Wood
FURNITURE: Chests, Cedar
FURNITURE: Church
FURNITURE: Club Room, Wood
FURNITURE: Desks & Tables, Office, Exc Wood
FURNITURE: Foundations & Platforms
FURNITURE: Game Room
FURNITURE: Game Room, Wood
FURNITURE: Garden, Metal
FURNITURE: High Chairs, Children's, Wood
FURNITURE: Hospital
FURNITURE: Hotel
FURNITURE: Household, Metal
FURNITURE: Household, NEC
FURNITURE: Household, Upholstered, Exc Wood Or Metal
FURNITURE: Household, Wood
FURNITURE: Institutional, Exc Wood
FURNITURE: Living Room, Upholstered On Wood Frames
FURNITURE: Mattresses, Box & Bedsprings
FURNITURE: Mattresses, Innerspring Or Box Spring
FURNITURE: NEC
FURNITURE: Office, Exc Wood
FURNITURE: Office, Wood
FURNITURE: Pews, Church
FURNITURE: Picnic Tables Or Benches, Park
FURNITURE: Restaurant
FURNITURE: Serving Carts & Tea Wagons, Metal
FURNITURE: Storage Chests, Household, Wood
FURNITURE: Table Tops, Marble
FURNITURE: Tables, Office, Wood
FURNITURE: Upholstered
FUSES: Electric
Furs

G

GAMES & TOYS: Board Games, Children's & Adults'
GAMES & TOYS: Craft & Hobby Kits & Sets
GAMES & TOYS: Darts & Dart Games
GAMES & TOYS: Dollhouses & Furniture
GAMES & TOYS: Electronic
GAMES & TOYS: Game Machines, Exc Coin-Operated
GAMES & TOYS: Miniature Dolls, Collectors'
GAMES & TOYS: Puzzles
GAMES & TOYS: Rocking Horses
GARAGE DOOR REPAIR SVCS
GAS & HYDROCARBON LIQUEFACTION FROM COAL
GAS & OIL FIELD EXPLORATION SVCS

PRODUCT INDEX

GAS & OIL FIELD SVCS, NEC
GAS APPLIANCE REPAIR SVCS
GAS FIELD MACHINERY & EQPT
GAS PROCESSING SVC
GAS PRODUCTION & DISTRIBUTION
GAS STATIONS
GAS WELDING RODS, MADE FROM PURCHASED WIRE
GAS: Refinery
GASES & LIQUIFIED PETROLEUM GASES
GASES: Carbon Dioxide
GASES: Hydrogen
GASES: Indl
GASES: Neon
GASES: Nitrogen
GASES: Oxygen
GASKETS
GASKETS & SEALING DEVICES
GASOLINE BLENDING PLANT
GASOLINE FILLING STATIONS
GASOLINE WHOLESALERS
GASTROINTESTINAL OR GENITOURINARY SYSTEM DRUGS
GATES: Ornamental Metal
GAUGES
GEARS
GEARS: Power Transmission, Exc Auto
GENERAL COUNSELING SVCS
GENERAL MERCHANDISE, NONDURABLE, WHOLESALE
GENERATION EQPT: Electronic
GENERATOR REPAIR SVCS
GENERATORS: Electric
GENERATORS: Electrochemical, Fuel Cell
GENERATORS: Gas
GENERATORS: Storage Battery Chargers
GIFT SHOP
GIFT WRAP: Paper, Made From Purchased Materials
GIFT, NOVELTY & SOUVENIR STORES: Gifts & Novelties
GIFT, NOVELTY & SOUVENIR STORES: Party Favors
GIFTS & NOVELTIES: Wholesalers
GLASS & GLASS CERAMIC PRDTS, PRESSED OR BLOWN: Tableware
GLASS FABRICATORS
GLASS PRDTS, FROM PURCHASED GLASS: Glassware
GLASS PRDTS, FROM PURCHASED GLASS: Insulating
GLASS PRDTS, FROM PURCHASED GLASS: Mirrored
GLASS PRDTS, FROM PURCHASED GLASS: Windshields
GLASS PRDTS, PRESSED OR BLOWN: Optical
GLASS PRDTS, PRESSED OR BLOWN: Vases
GLASS PRDTS, PURCHD GLASS: Furniture Top, Cut, Beveld/Polshd
GLASS PRDTS, PURCHSD GLASS: Ornamental, Cut, Engraved/Décor
GLASS STORES
GLASS, AUTOMOTIVE: Wholesalers
GLASS: Flat
GLASS: Pressed & Blown, NEC
GLASS: Tempered
GLOVES: Safety
GO-CART DEALERS
GOLF CARTS: Wholesalers
GOLF EQPT
GOURMET FOOD STORES
GOVERNMENT, EXECUTIVE & LEGISLATIVE OFFICES COMBINED: County
GOVERNMENT, EXECUTIVE OFFICES: City & Town Managers' Offices
GOVERNMENT, EXECUTIVE OFFICES: Mayors'
GOVERNMENT, GENERAL: Administration
GOVERNMENT, GENERAL: Administration, Level Of Government
GOVERNMENT, GENERAL: Administration, State
GRAIN & FIELD BEANS WHOLESALERS
GRANITE: Crushed & Broken
GRANITE: Cut & Shaped
GRANITE: Dimension
GRAPHIC ARTS & RELATED DESIGN SVCS
GRASSES: Artificial & Preserved
GRATINGS: Tread, Fabricated Metal
GREASES & INEDIBLE FATS, RENDERED
GREENHOUSES: Prefabricated Metal
GREETING CARD SHOPS
GRIPS OR HANDLES: Rubber
GRITS: Crushed & Broken
GROCERIES WHOLESALERS, NEC
GROCERIES, GENERAL LINE WHOLESALERS

GUARD SVCS
GUIDED MISSILES & SPACE VEHICLES: Research & Development
GUIDED MISSILES/SPACE VEHICLE PARTS/AUX EQPT: Research/Devel
GUN SIGHTS: Optical
GUNNING EQPT: Concrete
GUNSMITHS
GUTTERS: Sheet Metal
GYMNASTICS INSTRUCTION
GYPSUM MINING
GYPSUM PRDTS

H

HAIR & HAIR BASED PRDTS
HAIR CARE PRDTS
HAIR CARE PRDTS: Hair Coloring Preparations
HAIR CURLERS: Beauty Shop
HAIR DRESSING, FOR THE TRADE
HAND TOOLS, NEC: Wholesalers
HANDBAGS
HANDBAGS: Women's
HANDLES: Wood
HANDYMAN SVCS
HARDWARE
HARDWARE & BUILDING PRDTS: Plastic
HARDWARE & EQPT: Stage, Exc Lighting
HARDWARE STORES
HARDWARE STORES: Builders'
HARDWARE STORES: Chainsaws
HARDWARE STORES: Tools, Power
HARDWARE WHOLESALERS
HARDWARE, WHOLESALE: Bolts
HARDWARE, WHOLESALE: Nuts
HARDWARE, WHOLESALE: Security Devices, Locks
HARDWARE: Aircraft
HARDWARE: Aircraft & Marine, Incl Pulleys & Similar Items
HARDWARE: Builders'
HARDWARE: Cabinet
HARDWARE: Furniture
HARDWARE: Furniture, Builders' & Other Household
HARDWARE: Locking Systems, Security Cable
HARDWARE: Plastic
HARDWARE: Rubber
HARDWARE: Saddlery
HARNESS ASSEMBLIES: Cable & Wire
HARNESSES, HALTERS, SADDLERY & STRAPS
HEALTH & ALLIED SERVICES, NEC
HEALTH AIDS: Exercise Eqpt
HEALTH FOOD & SUPPLEMENT STORES
HEARING AIDS
HEAT EXCHANGERS
HEAT EXCHANGERS: After Or Inter Coolers Or Condensers, Etc
HEAT TREATING: Metal
HEATERS: Unit, Domestic
HEATING & AIR CONDITIONING EQPT & SPLYS WHOLESALERS
HEATING & AIR CONDITIONING UNITS, COMBINATION
HEATING EQPT & SPLYS
HEATING EQPT: Complete
HEATING SYSTEMS: Radiant, Indl Process
HEATING UNITS & DEVICES: Indl, Electric
HEATING UNITS: Gas, Infrared
HELP SUPPLY SERVICES
HERMETICS REPAIR SVCS
HIGHWAY & STREET MAINTENANCE SVCS
HITCHES: Trailer
HOBBY, TOY & GAME STORES: Dolls & Access
HOBBY, TOY & GAME STORES: Toys & Games
HOISTS
HOLDERS, PAPER TOWEL, GROCERY BAG, ETC: Plastic
HOLDING COMPANIES: Investment, Exc Banks
HOME CENTER STORES
HOME DELIVERY NEWSPAPER ROUTES
HOME ENTERTAINMENT EQPT: Electronic, NEC
HOME HEALTH CARE SVCS
HOMEBUILDERS & OTHER OPERATIVE BUILDERS
HOMEFURNISHING STORES: Pottery
HOMEFURNISHING STORES: Towels
HOMEFURNISHING STORES: Venetian Blinds
HOMEFURNISHING STORES: Window Shades, NEC
HOMEFURNISHINGS & SPLYS, WHOLESALE: Decorative
HOMEFURNISHINGS, WHOLESALE: Blinds, Venetian
HOMEFURNISHINGS, WHOLESALE: Decorating Splys

HOMEFURNISHINGS, WHOLESALE: Draperies
HOMEFURNISHINGS, WHOLESALE: Window Shades
HOMES: Log Cabins
HONEYCOMB CORE & BOARD: Made From Purchased Materials
HOODS: Range, Sheet Metal
HORSE & PET ACCESSORIES: Textile
HORSE ACCESS: Harnesses & Riding Crops, Etc, Exc Leather
HORSE ACCESS: Saddle Cloth
HORSES WHOLESALERS
HORSESHOES
HOSE: Fabric
HOSE: Flexible Metal
HOSE: Plastic
HOSE: Rubber
HOSES & BELTING: Rubber & Plastic
HOSPITAL EQPT REPAIR SVCS
HOT TUBS
HOT TUBS: Plastic & Fiberglass
HOTELS & MOTELS
HOUSEHOLD APPLIANCE STORES
HOUSEHOLD ARTICLES: Metal
HOUSEHOLD FURNISHINGS, NEC
HOUSEWARES, ELECTRIC: Lighters, Cigarette
HOUSEWARES, ELECTRIC: Massage Machines, Exc Beauty/Barber
HOUSEWARES, ELECTRIC: Radiators
HOUSEWARES: Dishes, Plastic
HOUSEWARES: Pots & Pans, Glass
HYDRAULIC EQPT REPAIR SVC
Hard Rubber & Molded Rubber Prdts

I

ICE
ICE CREAM & ICES WHOLESALERS
ICE WHOLESALERS
IDENTIFICATION TAGS, EXC PAPER
IGNEOUS ROCK: Crushed & Broken
IGNITION CONTROLS: Gas Appliance
IGNITION SYSTEMS: Internal Combustion Engine
INCINERATORS
INDL & PERSONAL SVC PAPER, WHOL: Boxes, Corrugtd/Solid Fiber
INDL & PERSONAL SVC PAPER, WHOL: Container, Paper/Plastic
INDL & PERSONAL SVC PAPER, WHOLESALE: Cardboard & Prdts
INDL & PERSONAL SVC PAPER, WHOLESALE: Press Sensitive Tape
INDL & PERSONAL SVC PAPER, WHOLESALE: Towels, Paper
INDL CONTRACTORS: Exhibit Construction
INDL EQPT CLEANING SVCS
INDL EQPT SVCS
INDL GASES WHOLESALERS
INDL MACHINERY & EQPT WHOLESALERS
INDL MACHINERY REPAIR & MAINTENANCE
INDL PATTERNS: Foundry Patternmaking
INDL PROCESS INSTRUMENTS: Boiler Controls, Power & Marine
INDL PROCESS INSTRUMENTS: Control
INDL PROCESS INSTRUMENTS: Controllers, Process Variables
INDL PROCESS INSTRUMENTS: Digital Display, Process Variables
INDL PROCESS INSTRUMENTS: Elements, Primary
INDL PROCESS INSTRUMENTS: Fluidic Devices, Circuit & Systems
INDL PROCESS INSTRUMENTS: Indl Flow & Measuring
INDL PROCESS INSTRUMENTS: Water Quality Monitoring/Cntrl Sys
INDL SPLYS WHOLESALERS
INDL SPLYS, WHOL: Fasteners, Incl Nuts, Bolts, Screws, Etc
INDL SPLYS, WHOLESALE: Abrasives
INDL SPLYS, WHOLESALE: Bearings
INDL SPLYS, WHOLESALE: Filters, Indl
INDL SPLYS, WHOLESALE: Fittings
INDL SPLYS, WHOLESALE: Gaskets
INDL SPLYS, WHOLESALE: Rubber Goods, Mechanical
INDL SPLYS, WHOLESALE: Seals
INDL SPLYS, WHOLESALE: Signmaker Eqpt & Splys
INDL SPLYS, WHOLESALE: Springs
INDL SPLYS, WHOLESALE: Tools
INDL SPLYS, WHOLESALE: Tools, NEC

PRODUCT INDEX

INDL SPLYS, WHOLESALE: Valves & Fittings
INDL TOOL GRINDING SVCS
INDUSTRIAL & COMMERCIAL EQPT INSPECTION SVCS
INFORMATION RETRIEVAL SERVICES
INK OR WRITING FLUIDS
INK: Printing
INK: Screen process
INNER TUBES: Truck Or Bus
INSECTICIDES
INSECTICIDES & PESTICIDES
INSPECTION & TESTING SVCS
INSTR, MEASURE & CONTROL: Gauge, Oil Pressure & Water Temp
INSTRUMENTS, LABORATORY: Analyzers, Thermal
INSTRUMENTS, LABORATORY: Polariscopes
INSTRUMENTS, MEASURING & CNTRG: Plotting, Drafting/Map Rdg
INSTRUMENTS, MEASURING & CNTRLG: Aircraft & Motor Vehicle
INSTRUMENTS, MEASURING & CNTRLG: Thermometers/Temp Sensors
INSTRUMENTS, MEASURING & CNTRLNG: Humidity, Exc Indl Process
INSTRUMENTS, MEASURING & CONTROLLING: Anamometers
INSTRUMENTS, MEASURING & CONTROLLING: Breathalyzers
INSTRUMENTS, MEASURING & CONTROLLING: Map Plotting
INSTRUMENTS, MEASURING/CNTRL: Gauging, Ultrasonic Thickness
INSTRUMENTS, MEASURING/CNTRLNG: Med Diagnostic Sys, Nuclear
INSTRUMENTS, OPTICAL: Lenses, All Types Exc Ophthalmic
INSTRUMENTS, SURGICAL & MEDICAL: Blood & Bone Work
INSTRUMENTS, SURGICAL & MEDICAL: IV Transfusion
INSTRUMENTS, SURGICAL & MEDICAL: Inhalation Therapy
INSTRUMENTS, SURGICAL & MEDICAL: Muscle Exercise, Ophthalmic
INSTRUMENTS, SURGICAL & MEDICAL: Optometers
INSTRUMENTS, SURGICAL & MEDICAL: Physiotherapy, Electrical
INSTRUMENTS: Analytical
INSTRUMENTS: Combustion Control, Indl
INSTRUMENTS: Endoscopic Eqpt, Electromedical
INSTRUMENTS: Flow, Indl Process
INSTRUMENTS: Indl Process Control
INSTRUMENTS: Laser, Scientific & Engineering
INSTRUMENTS: Measurement, Indl Process
INSTRUMENTS: Measuring & Controlling
INSTRUMENTS: Measuring Electricity
INSTRUMENTS: Measuring, Electrical Power
INSTRUMENTS: Medical & Surgical
INSTRUMENTS: Meters, Integrating Electricity
INSTRUMENTS: Optical, Analytical
INSTRUMENTS: Pressure Measurement, Indl
INSTRUMENTS: Radio Frequency Measuring
INSTRUMENTS: Standards & Calibration, Electrical Measuring
INSTRUMENTS: Temperature Measurement, Indl
INSTRUMENTS: Test, Electronic & Electric Measurement
INSTRUMENTS: Transformers, Portable
INSTRUMENTS: Vibration
INSULATING COMPOUNDS
INSULATION & CUSHIONING FOAM: Polystyrene
INSULATION & ROOFING MATERIALS: Wood, Reconstituted
INSULATION: Fiberglass
INSULATORS & INSULATION MATERIALS: Electrical
INSURANCE CARRIERS: Direct Accident & Health
INSURANCE CARRIERS: Life
INSURANCE CLAIM PROCESSING, EXC MEDICAL
INSURANCE INFORMATION & CONSULTING SVCS
INSURANCE: Agents, Brokers & Service
INTEGRATED CIRCUITS, SEMICONDUCTOR NETWORKS, ETC
INTERCOMMUNICATIONS SYSTEMS: Electric
INTERIOR DECORATING SVCS
INTERIOR DESIGN SVCS, NEC
INTERIOR DESIGNING SVCS
INTERMEDIATE CARE FACILITY
INTRAVENOUS SOLUTIONS
INVESTMENT COUNSELORS
INVESTMENT FUNDS: Open-Ended
INVESTORS, NEC
INVESTORS: Real Estate, Exc Property Operators
IRON & STEEL PRDTS: Hot-Rolled
IRONING BOARDS

J

JACKS: Floor, Metal
JACKS: Hydraulic
JANITORIAL & CUSTODIAL SVCS
JEWELERS' FINDINGS & MATERIALS
JEWELRY APPAREL
JEWELRY FINDINGS & LAPIDARY WORK
JEWELRY REPAIR SVCS
JEWELRY STORES
JEWELRY STORES: Clocks
JEWELRY STORES: Precious Stones & Precious Metals
JEWELRY, PRECIOUS METAL: Cigar & Cigarette Access
JEWELRY, PRECIOUS METAL: Earrings
JEWELRY, PRECIOUS METAL: Medals, Precious Or Semi-precious
JEWELRY, PRECIOUS METAL: Rings, Finger
JEWELRY, WHOLESALE
JEWELRY: Decorative, Fashion & Costume
JEWELRY: Precious Metal
JOB PRINTING & NEWSPAPER PUBLISHING COMBINED
JOB TRAINING & VOCATIONAL REHABILITATION SVCS
JOB TRAINING SVCS
JOISTS: Long-Span Series, Open Web Steel
JUNIOR OR SENIOR HIGH SCHOOLS, NEC
JUVENILE CORRECTIONAL HOME

K

KAOLIN & BALL CLAY MINING
KITCHEN & COOKING ARTICLES: Pottery
KITCHEN CABINET STORES, EXC CUSTOM
KITCHEN CABINETS WHOLESALERS
KITCHEN UTENSILS: Food Handling & Processing Prdts, Wood
KITCHEN UTENSILS: Wooden
KITCHENWARE STORES

L

LABELS: Paper, Made From Purchased Materials
LABORATORIES, TESTING: Pollution
LABORATORIES, TESTING: X-ray Inspection Svc, Indl
LABORATORIES: Biological Research
LABORATORIES: Commercial Nonphysical Research
LABORATORIES: Dental
LABORATORIES: Electronic Research
LABORATORIES: Environmental Research
LABORATORIES: Neurological
LABORATORIES: Noncommercial Research
LABORATORIES: Physical Research, Commercial
LABORATORIES: Testing
LABORATORY APPARATUS & FURNITURE
LABORATORY APPARATUS, EXC HEATING & MEASURING
LABORATORY CHEMICALS: Organic
LABORATORY EQPT, EXC MEDICAL: Wholesalers
LABORATORY EQPT: Clinical Instruments Exc Medical
LABORATORY INSTRUMENT REPAIR SVCS
LADDERS: Permanent Installation, Metal
LAMINATED PLASTICS: Plate, Sheet, Rod & Tubes
LAMP & LIGHT BULBS & TUBES
LAMP BULBS & TUBES, ELECTRIC: Light, Complete
LAMP STORES
LAMPS: Boudoir, Residential
LAND SUBDIVISION & DEVELOPMENT
LASER SYSTEMS & EQPT
LASERS: Welding, Drilling & Cutting Eqpt
LAUNDRY & DRYCLEANING SVCS, EXC COIN-OPERATED: Pickup
LAUNDRY & GARMENT SVCS, NEC: Garment Alteration & Repair
LAUNDRY & GARMENT SVCS, NEC: Garment Making, Alter & Repair
LAUNDRY & GARMENT SVCS: Tailor Shop, Exc Custom/Merchant
LAUNDRY EQPT: Commercial
LAUNDRY SVC: Flame & Heat Resistant Clothing Sply
LAWN & GARDEN EQPT
LAWN & GARDEN EQPT STORES
LAWN & GARDEN EQPT: Grass Catchers, Lawn Mower
LAWN & GARDEN EQPT: Tractors & Eqpt
LAWN MOWER REPAIR SHOP
LEAD & ZINC ORES
LEAD PENCILS & ART GOODS
LEASING & RENTAL SVCS: Cranes & Aerial Lift Eqpt
LEASING & RENTAL SVCS: Earth Moving Eqpt
LEASING & RENTAL SVCS: Oil Field Eqpt
LEASING & RENTAL SVCS: Oil Well Drilling
LEASING & RENTAL: Computers & Eqpt
LEASING & RENTAL: Construction & Mining Eqpt
LEASING & RENTAL: Medical Machinery & Eqpt
LEASING & RENTAL: Mobile Home Sites
LEASING & RENTAL: Office Machines & Eqpt
LEASING & RENTAL: Other Real Estate Property
LEASING & RENTAL: Trucks, Without Drivers
LEASING: Residential Buildings
LEASING: Shipping Container
LEATHER & CUT STOCK WHOLESALERS
LEATHER GOODS: Cases
LEATHER GOODS: Harnesses Or Harness Parts
LEATHER GOODS: Holsters
LEATHER GOODS: Mill Strapping, Textile Mills
LEATHER GOODS: NEC
LEATHER GOODS: Personal
LEATHER GOODS: Riding Crops
LEATHER GOODS: Saddles Or Parts
LEATHER GOODS: Safety Belts
LEATHER GOODS: Vanity Cases
LEATHER GOODS: Whipstocks
LEATHER TANNING & FINISHING
LEATHER: Accessory Prdts
LEATHER: Artificial
LEATHER: Equestrian Prdts
LEATHER: Rawhide
LEATHER: Saddlery
LECTURING SVCS
LEGAL & TAX SVCS
LEGAL OFFICES & SVCS
LEGAL SVCS: General Practice Attorney or Lawyer
LEGAL SVCS: General Practice Law Office
LICENSE TAGS: Automobile, Stamped Metal
LIGHTING EQPT: Flashlights
LIGHTING EQPT: Floodlights
LIGHTING EQPT: Miners' Lamps
LIGHTING EQPT: Motor Vehicle, Dome Lights
LIGHTING EQPT: Reflectors, Metal, For Lighting Eqpt
LIGHTING EQPT: Searchlights
LIGHTING EQPT: Strobe Lighting Systems
LIGHTING FIXTURES WHOLESALERS
LIGHTING FIXTURES, NEC
LIGHTING FIXTURES: Airport
LIGHTING FIXTURES: Indl & Commercial
LIGHTING FIXTURES: Ornamental, Commercial
LIGHTING FIXTURES: Residential
LIGHTING FIXTURES: Residential, Electric
LIME
LIMESTONE: Crushed & Broken
LIMESTONE: Cut & Shaped
LIMESTONE: Dimension
LIMESTONE: Ground
LIMOUSINE SVCS
LINERS & COVERS: Fabric
LIPSTICK
LIQUEFIED PETROLEUM GAS WHOLESALERS
LIQUID CRYSTAL DISPLAYS
LIVESTOCK WHOLESALERS, NEC
LOCKS
LOCKS: Safe & Vault, Metal
LOCKSMITHS
LOCOMOTIVES & PARTS
LOG SPLITTERS
LOGGING
LOGGING CAMPS & CONTRACTORS
LOGGING: Stump Harvesting
LOGGING: Timber, Cut At Logging Camp
LOGGING: Wooden Logs
LOGS: Gas, Fireplace
LOTIONS OR CREAMS: Face
LOUDSPEAKERS
LOUVERS: Ventilating
LUBRICANTS: Corrosion Preventive
LUBRICATING EQPT: Indl
LUBRICATING OIL & GREASE WHOLESALERS
LUGGAGE & BRIEFCASES
LUGGAGE & LEATHER GOODS STORES: Leather, Exc Luggage & Shoes
LUMBER & BLDG MATLS DEALER, RET: Garage Doors, Sell/Install

PRODUCT INDEX

LUMBER & BLDG MTRLS DEALERS, RET: Closets, Interiors/Access
LUMBER & BLDG MTRLS DEALERS, RET: Doors, Storm, Wood/Metal
LUMBER & BLDG MTRLS DEALERS, RET: Planing Mill Prdts/Lumber
LUMBER & BLDG MTRLS DEALERS, RET: Windows, Storm, Wood/Metal
LUMBER & BUILDING MATERIAL DEALERS, RETAIL: Roofing Material
LUMBER & BUILDING MATERIALS DEALER, RET: Door & Window Prdts
LUMBER & BUILDING MATERIALS DEALER, RET: Masonry Matls/Splys
LUMBER & BUILDING MATERIALS DEALERS, RET: Solar Heating Eqpt
LUMBER & BUILDING MATERIALS DEALERS, RETAIL: Brick
LUMBER & BUILDING MATERIALS DEALERS, RETAIL: Cement
LUMBER & BUILDING MATERIALS DEALERS, RETAIL: Lime & Plaster
LUMBER & BUILDING MATERIALS DEALERS, RETAIL: Sand & Gravel
LUMBER & BUILDING MATERIALS DEALERS, RETAIL: Siding
LUMBER & BUILDING MATERIALS DEALERS, RETAIL: Tile, Ceramic
LUMBER & BUILDING MATERIALS RET DEALERS: Millwork & Lumber
LUMBER & BUILDING MATLS DEALERS, RET: Concrete/Cinder Block
LUMBER & BUILDING MTRLS DEALERS, RET: Insulation Mtrl, Bldg
LUMBER: Fiberboard
LUMBER: Furniture Dimension Stock, Softwood
LUMBER: Hardwood Dimension
LUMBER: Hardwood Dimension & Flooring Mills
LUMBER: Kiln Dried
LUMBER: Plywood, Hardwood
LUMBER: Posts, Treated
LUMBER: Resawn, Small Dimension
LUMBER: Treated

M

MACHINE PARTS: Stamped Or Pressed Metal
MACHINE SHOPS
MACHINE TOOL ACCESS: Broaches
MACHINE TOOL ACCESS: Cams
MACHINE TOOL ACCESS: Cutting
MACHINE TOOL ACCESS: Diamond Cutting, For Turning, Etc
MACHINE TOOL ACCESS: Tools & Access
MACHINE TOOLS & ACCESS
MACHINE TOOLS, METAL CUTTING: Drilling
MACHINE TOOLS, METAL CUTTING: Drilling & Boring
MACHINE TOOLS, METAL CUTTING: Grind, Polish, Buff, Lapp
MACHINE TOOLS, METAL CUTTING: Numerically Controlled
MACHINE TOOLS, METAL CUTTING: Pipe Cutting & Threading
MACHINE TOOLS, METAL CUTTING: Plasma Process
MACHINE TOOLS, METAL CUTTING: Tool Replacement & Rpr Parts
MACHINE TOOLS, METAL CUTTING: Turret Lathes
MACHINE TOOLS, METAL FORMING: Bending
MACHINE TOOLS: Metal Cutting
MACHINE TOOLS: Metal Forming
MACHINERY & EQPT, AGRICULTURAL, WHOL: Farm Eqpt Parts/Splys
MACHINERY & EQPT, AGRICULTURAL, WHOLESALE: Agricultural, NEC
MACHINERY & EQPT, AGRICULTURAL, WHOLESALE: Cultivating
MACHINERY & EQPT, AGRICULTURAL, WHOLESALE: Farm Implements
MACHINERY & EQPT, AGRICULTURAL; WHOLESALE: Lawn & Garden
MACHINERY & EQPT, AGRICULTURAL, WHOLESALE: Livestock Eqpt
MACHINERY & EQPT, INDL, WHOL: Controlling Instruments/Access
MACHINERY & EQPT, INDL, WHOL: Environ Pollution Cntrl, Air
MACHINERY & EQPT, INDL, WHOL: Environ Pollution Cntrl, Water
MACHINERY & EQPT, INDL, WHOL: Indicating Instruments/Access
MACHINERY & EQPT, INDL, WHOLESALE: Conveyor Systems
MACHINERY & EQPT, INDL, WHOLESALE: Drilling Bits
MACHINERY & EQPT, INDL, WHOLESALE: Drilling, Exc Bits
MACHINERY & EQPT, INDL, WHOLESALE: Engines & Parts, Diesel
MACHINERY & EQPT, INDL, WHOLESALE: Engines, Gasoline
MACHINERY & EQPT, INDL, WHOLESALE: Hydraulic Systems
MACHINERY & EQPT, INDL, WHOLESALE: Indl Machine Parts
MACHINERY & EQPT, INDL, WHOLESALE: Instruments & Cntrl Eqpt
MACHINERY & EQPT, INDL, WHOLESALE: Machine Tools & Access
MACHINERY & EQPT, INDL, WHOLESALE: Machine Tools & Metalwork
MACHINERY & EQPT, INDL, WHOLESALE: Measure/Test, Electric
MACHINERY & EQPT, INDL, WHOLESALE: Petroleum Industry
MACHINERY & EQPT, INDL, WHOLESALE: Processing & Packaging
MACHINERY & EQPT, INDL, WHOLESALE: Trailers, Indl
MACHINERY & EQPT, INDL, WHOLESALE: Water Pumps
MACHINERY & EQPT, WHOLESALE: Construction & Mining, Pavers
MACHINERY & EQPT, WHOLESALE: Construction, General
MACHINERY & EQPT, WHOLESALE: Contractors Materials
MACHINERY & EQPT, WHOLESALE: Oil Field Eqpt
MACHINERY & EQPT: Electroplating
MACHINERY & EQPT: Farm
MACHINERY & EQPT: Gas Producers, Generators/Other Rltd Eqpt
MACHINERY & EQPT: Metal Finishing, Plating Etc
MACHINERY & EQPT: Petroleum Refinery
MACHINERY BASES
MACHINERY, COMMERCIAL LAUNDRY: Dryers, Incl Coin-Operated
MACHINERY, FOOD PRDTS: Flour Mill
MACHINERY, FOOD PRDTS: Food Processing, Smokers
MACHINERY, FOOD PRDTS: Ovens, Bakery
MACHINERY, MAILING: Mailing
MACHINERY, MAILING: Postage Meters
MACHINERY, METALWORKING: Cutting & Slitting
MACHINERY, OFFICE: Time Clocks &Time Recording Devices
MACHINERY, PAPER INDUSTRY: Converting, Die Cutting & Stampng
MACHINERY, PRINTING TRADES: Bookbinding Machinery
MACHINERY, PRINTING TRADES: Bronzing Or Dusting
MACHINERY, PRINTING TRADES: Mats, Advertising & Newspaper
MACHINERY, PRINTING TRADES: Printing Trade Parts & Attchts
MACHINERY, PRINTING TRADES: Rules
MACHINERY, SERVICING: Coin-Operated, Exc Dry Clean & Laundry
MACHINERY, SEWING: Sewing & Hat & Zipper Making
MACHINERY, TEXTILE: Embroidery
MACHINERY, TEXTILE: Silk Screens
MACHINERY, WOODWORKING: Bandsaws
MACHINERY, WOODWORKING: Cabinet Makers'
MACHINERY, WOODWORKING: Shapers
MACHINERY/EQPT, INDL, WHOL: Cleaning, High Press, Sand/Steam
MACHINERY: Assembly, Exc Metalworking
MACHINERY: Automotive Maintenance
MACHINERY: Automotive Related
MACHINERY: Banking
MACHINERY: Blasting, Electrical
MACHINERY: Centrifugal
MACHINERY: Concrete Prdts
MACHINERY: Construction
MACHINERY: Cotton Ginning
MACHINERY: Custom
MACHINERY: Dredging
MACHINERY: Electrical Discharge Erosion
MACHINERY: Electronic Component Making
MACHINERY: Electronic Teaching Aids
MACHINERY: Fiber Optics Strand Coating
MACHINERY: Gas Producers
MACHINERY: General, Industrial, NEC
MACHINERY: Glassmaking
MACHINERY: Grinding
MACHINERY: Ice Crushers
MACHINERY: Industrial, NEC
MACHINERY: Kilns
MACHINERY: Labeling
MACHINERY: Logging Eqpt
MACHINERY: Metalworking
MACHINERY: Milling
MACHINERY: Mining
MACHINERY: Nuclear Reactor Control Rod & Drive Mechanism
MACHINERY: Optical Lens
MACHINERY: Packaging
MACHINERY: Paper Industry Miscellaneous
MACHINERY: Photographic Reproduction
MACHINERY: Plastic Working
MACHINERY: Recycling
MACHINERY: Road Construction & Maintenance
MACHINERY: Robots, Molding & Forming Plastics
MACHINERY: Saw & Sawing
MACHINERY: Screening Eqpt, Electric
MACHINERY: Semiconductor Manufacturing
MACHINERY: Service Industry, NEC
MACHINERY: Sifting & Screening
MACHINERY: Specialty
MACHINERY: Tire Shredding
MACHINERY: Woodworking
MACHINES: Forming, Sheet Metal
MACHINISTS' TOOLS: Measuring, Precision
MACHINISTS' TOOLS: Precision
MAGAZINE STAND
MAGAZINES, WHOLESALE
MAGNETIC RESONANCE IMAGING DEVICES: Nonmedical
MAGNETIC TAPE, AUDIO: Prerecorded
MAGNETS: Ceramic
MAGNETS: Permanent
MAIL-ORDER HOUSE, NEC
MAIL-ORDER HOUSES: Collectibles & Antiques
MAIL-ORDER HOUSES: Jewelry
MAIL-ORDER HOUSES: Tools & Hardware
MAILBOX RENTAL & RELATED SVCS
MAILING SVCS, NEC
MANAGEMENT CONSULTING SVCS: Banking & Finance
MANAGEMENT CONSULTING SVCS: Business
MANAGEMENT CONSULTING SVCS: Business Planning & Organizing
MANAGEMENT CONSULTING SVCS: Construction Project
MANAGEMENT CONSULTING SVCS: Distribution Channels
MANAGEMENT CONSULTING SVCS: Industrial
MANAGEMENT CONSULTING SVCS: Industrial & Labor
MANAGEMENT CONSULTING SVCS: Information Systems
MANAGEMENT CONSULTING SVCS: Management Engineering
MANAGEMENT CONSULTING SVCS: Manufacturing
MANAGEMENT CONSULTING SVCS: Planning
MANAGEMENT CONSULTING SVCS: Real Estate
MANAGEMENT CONSULTING SVCS: Restaurant & Food
MANAGEMENT SERVICES
MANAGEMENT SVCS, FACILITIES SUPPORT: Environ Remediation
MANAGEMENT SVCS: Business
MANAGEMENT SVCS: Construction
MANHOLES COVERS: Concrete
MANICURE PREPARATIONS
MANNEQUINS
MANUFACTURED & MOBILE HOME DEALERS
MANUFACTURING INDUSTRIES, NEC
MAPS
MARBLE, BUILDING: Cut & Shaped
MARINAS
MARINE BASIN OPERATIONS
MARINE CARGO HANDLING SVCS: Loading
MARINE REPORTING SVCS
MARKETS: Meat & fish
MARKING DEVICES
MARKING DEVICES: Date Stamps, Hand, Rubber Or Metal
MARKING DEVICES: Embossing Seals & Hand Stamps
MARKING DEVICES: Screens, Textile Printing
MARKING DEVICES: Seal Presses, Notary & Hand
MARKING DEVICES: Time Stamps, Hand, Rubber Or Metal
MASSAGE PARLORS
MASTIC ROOFING COMPOSITION
MATERIAL GRINDING & PULVERIZING SVCS NEC

PRODUCT INDEX

MATERIALS HANDLING EQPT WHOLESALERS
MATTRESS RENOVATING & REPAIR SHOP
MATTRESS STORES
MEAT & MEAT PRDTS WHOLESALERS
MEAT CUTTING & PACKING
MEAT MARKETS
MEAT PRDTS: Cooked Meats, From Purchased Meat
MEAT PRDTS: Cured, From Slaughtered Meat
MEAT PRDTS: Dried Beef, From Purchased Meat
MEAT PRDTS: Pork, From Slaughtered Meat
MEAT PRDTS: Prepared Beef Prdts From Purchased Beef
MEAT PRDTS: Sausages, From Purchased Meat
MEAT PRDTS: Smoked
MEAT PRDTS: Snack Sticks, Incl Jerky, From Purchased Meat
MEAT PROCESSED FROM PURCHASED CARCASSES
MEAT PROCESSING MACHINERY
MECHANISMS: Coin-Operated Machines
MEDIA BUYING AGENCIES
MEDIA: Magnetic & Optical Recording
MEDICAL & HOSPITAL EQPT WHOLESALERS
MEDICAL & SURGICAL SPLYS: Braces, Orthopedic
MEDICAL & SURGICAL SPLYS: Hydrotherapy
MEDICAL & SURGICAL SPLYS: Limbs, Artificial
MEDICAL & SURGICAL SPLYS: Orthopedic Appliances
MEDICAL & SURGICAL SPLYS: Personal Safety Eqpt
MEDICAL & SURGICAL SPLYS: Prosthetic Appliances
MEDICAL & SURGICAL SPLYS: Respiratory Protect Eqpt, Personal
MEDICAL & SURGICAL SPLYS: Supports, Abdominal, Ankle, Etc
MEDICAL & SURGICAL SPLYS: Technical Aids, Handicapped
MEDICAL & SURGICAL SPLYS: Trusses, Orthopedic & Surgical
MEDICAL & SURGICAL SPLYS: Walkers
MEDICAL & SURGICAL SPLYS: Welders' Hoods
MEDICAL CENTERS
MEDICAL EQPT: Diagnostic
MEDICAL EQPT: Electrotherapeutic Apparatus
MEDICAL EQPT: MRI/Magnetic Resonance Imaging Devs, Nuclear
MEDICAL EQPT: Patient Monitoring
MEDICAL EQPT: Ultrasonic, Exc Cleaning
MEDICAL EQPT: X-Ray Apparatus & Tubes, Radiographic
MEDICAL FIELD ASSOCIATION
MEDICAL, DENTAL & HOSPITAL EQPT, WHOL: Hosptl Eqpt/Furniture
MEDICAL, DENTAL & HOSPITAL EQPT, WHOLESALE: Hearing Aids
MEDICAL, DENTAL & HOSPITAL EQPT, WHOLESALE: Med Eqpt & Splys
MEDICAL, DENTAL & HOSPITAL EQPT, WHOLESALE: Oxygen Therapy
MEDICAL, DENTAL & HOSPITAL EQPT, WHOLESALE: Safety
MEDICAL, DENTAL & HOSPITAL EQPT, WHOLESALE: Therapy
MEMBERSHIP ORGANIZATIONS, BUSINESS: Contractors' Association
MEMBERSHIP ORGANIZATIONS, BUSINESS: Merchants' Association
MEMBERSHIP ORGANIZATIONS, BUSINESS: Public Utility Assoc
MEMBERSHIP ORGANIZATIONS, NEC: Charitable
MEMBERSHIP ORGANIZATIONS, PROF: Education/Teacher Assoc
MEMBERSHIP ORGANIZATIONS, RELIGIOUS: Baptist Church
MEN'S & BOYS' CLOTHING ACCESS STORES
MEN'S & BOYS' CLOTHING WHOLESALERS, NEC
MEN'S & BOYS' SPORTSWEAR CLOTHING STORES
MEN'S & BOYS' SPORTSWEAR WHOLESALERS
MERCHANDISING MACHINE OPERATORS: Vending
METAL & STEEL PRDTS: Abrasive
METAL CUTTING SVCS
METAL FABRICATORS: Architechtural
METAL FABRICATORS: Plate
METAL FABRICATORS: Sheet
METAL FABRICATORS: Structural, Ship
METAL FINISHING SVCS
METAL MINING SVCS
METAL SERVICE CENTERS & OFFICES
METAL STAMPING, FOR THE TRADE
METAL STAMPINGS: Ornamental
METAL STAMPINGS: Patterned

METALS SVC CENTERS & WHOL: Structural Shapes, Iron Or Steel
METALS SVC CENTERS & WHOLESALERS: Pipe & Tubing, Steel
METALS SVC CENTERS & WHOLESALERS: Reinforcement Mesh, Wire
METALS SVC CENTERS & WHOLESALERS: Rope, Wire, Exc Insulated
METALS SVC CENTERS & WHOLESALERS: Steel
METALS SVC CENTERS & WHOLESALERS: Tubing, Metal
METALS SVC CENTERS/WHOL: Forms, Steel Concrete Construction
METALS SVC CTRS & WHOLESALERS: Aluminum Bars, Rods, Etc
METALS: Precious NEC
METALS: Precious, Secondary
METALS: Primary Nonferrous, NEC
METALWORK: Miscellaneous
METALWORK: Ornamental
METALWORKING MACHINERY WHOLESALERS
METERS: Liquid
MGMT CONSULTING SVCS: Matls, Incl Purch, Handle & Invntry
MICROPROCESSORS
MICROPUBLISHER
MILITARY INSIGNIA, TEXTILE
MILLING: Chemical
MILLING: Grains, Exc Rice
MILLWORK
MINE & QUARRY SVCS: Nonmetallic Minerals
MINE DEVELOPMENT SVCS: Nonmetallic Minerals
MINE EXPLORATION SVCS: Nonmetallic Minerals
MINERAL PIGMENT MINING
MINERAL PRODUCTS
MINERAL WOOL
MINERAL WOOL INSULATION PRDTS
MINERALS: Ground Or Otherwise Treated
MINERALS: Ground or Treated
MINIATURES
MINING MACHINES & EQPT: Feeders, Ore & Aggregate
MINING MACHINES & EQPT: Pellet Mills
MINING: Oil Sand
MINING: Oil Shale
MINING: Sand & Shale Oil
MISCELLANEOUS FIN INVEST ACTVTS: Mineral Royalty Dealer
MISCELLANEOUS FINANCIAL INVEST ACT: Oil/Gas Lease Brokers
MISCELLANEOUS FINANCIAL INVEST ACTIVITIES: Oil Royalties
MISSILE GUIDANCE SYSTEMS & EQPT
MIXING EQPT
MIXTURES & BLOCKS: Asphalt Paving
MOBILE COMMUNICATIONS EQPT
MOBILE HOME PARTS & ACCESS, WHOLESALE
MOBILE HOMES
MOBILE HOMES: Personal Or Private Use
MODELS: General, Exc Toy
MODULES: Computer Logic
MOLDED RUBBER PRDTS
MOLDING COMPOUNDS
MOLDINGS: Picture Frame
MOLDS: Indl
MOLDS: Plastic Working & Foundry
MONUMENTS & GRAVE MARKERS, EXC TERRAZZO
MONUMENTS & GRAVE MARKERS, WHOLESALE
MONUMENTS: Concrete
MONUMENTS: Cut Stone, Exc Finishing Or Lettering Only
MORTAR
MOTEL
MOTION PICTURE & VIDEO PRODUCTION SVCS
MOTION PICTURE & VIDEO PRODUCTION SVCS: Cartoon
MOTOR & GENERATOR PARTS: Electric
MOTOR REBUILDING SVCS, EXC AUTOMOTIVE
MOTOR REPAIR SVCS
MOTOR VEHICLE ASSEMBLY, COMPLETE: Ambulances
MOTOR VEHICLE ASSEMBLY, COMPLETE: Autos, Incl Specialty
MOTOR VEHICLE ASSEMBLY, COMPLETE: Fire Department Vehicles
MOTOR VEHICLE ASSEMBLY, COMPLETE: Military Motor Vehicle
MOTOR VEHICLE ASSEMBLY, COMPLETE: Patrol Wagons
MOTOR VEHICLE ASSEMBLY, COMPLETE: Truck & Tractor Trucks

MOTOR VEHICLE ASSEMBLY, COMPLETE: Trucks, Pickup
MOTOR VEHICLE ASSEMBLY, COMPLETE: Universal Carriers, Mil
MOTOR VEHICLE ASSEMBLY, COMPLETE: Wreckers, Tow Truck
MOTOR VEHICLE ASSY, COMPLETE: Street Sprinklers & Sweepers
MOTOR VEHICLE DEALERS: Automobiles, New & Used
MOTOR VEHICLE DEALERS: Cars, Used Only
MOTOR VEHICLE DEALERS: Trucks, Tractors/Trailers, New & Used
MOTOR VEHICLE PARTS & ACCESS: Body Components & Frames
MOTOR VEHICLE PARTS & ACCESS: Cleaners, air
MOTOR VEHICLE PARTS & ACCESS: Cylinder Heads
MOTOR VEHICLE PARTS & ACCESS: Engines & Parts
MOTOR VEHICLE PARTS & ACCESS: Engs & Trans,Factory, Rebuilt
MOTOR VEHICLE PARTS & ACCESS: Fuel Pipes
MOTOR VEHICLE PARTS & ACCESS: Fuel Pumps
MOTOR VEHICLE PARTS & ACCESS: Lifting Mechanisms, Dump Truck
MOTOR VEHICLE PARTS & ACCESS: Mufflers, Exhaust
MOTOR VEHICLE PARTS & ACCESS: Pickup Truck Bed Liners
MOTOR VEHICLE PARTS & ACCESS: Pumps, Hydraulic Fluid Power
MOTOR VEHICLE PARTS & ACCESS: Tie Rods
MOTOR VEHICLE PARTS & ACCESS: Transmissions
MOTOR VEHICLE PARTS & ACCESS: Wipers, Windshield
MOTOR VEHICLE SPLYS & PARTS WHOLESALERS: New
MOTOR VEHICLE SPLYS & PARTS WHOLESALERS: Used
MOTOR VEHICLE: Hardware
MOTOR VEHICLE: Radiators
MOTOR VEHICLES & CAR BODIES
MOTOR VEHICLES, WHOLESALE: Trailers for passenger vehicles
MOTOR VEHICLES, WHOLESALE: Trailers, Truck, New & Used
MOTOR VEHICLES, WHOLESALE: Trucks, commercial
MOTORCYCLE & BICYCLE PARTS: Frames
MOTORCYCLE DEALERS
MOTORCYCLE PARTS & ACCESS DEALERS
MOTORCYCLE PARTS: Wholesalers
MOTORCYCLES & RELATED PARTS
MOTORS: Electric
MOTORS: Generators
MOTORS: Starting, Automotive & Aircraft
MOVING SVC: Local
MOWERS & ACCESSORIES
MUSEUMS & ART GALLERIES
MUSIC BROADCASTING SVCS
MUSIC DISTRIBUTION APPARATUS
MUSIC RECORDING PRODUCER
MUSICAL ENTERTAINERS
MUSICAL INSTRUMENT PARTS & ACCESS, WHOLESALE
MUSICAL INSTRUMENT REPAIR
MUSICAL INSTRUMENTS & ACCESS: NEC
MUSICAL INSTRUMENTS & SPLYS STORES
MUSICAL INSTRUMENTS WHOLESALERS
MUSICAL INSTRUMENTS: Guitars & Parts, Electric & Acoustic
MUSICAL INSTRUMENTS: Violins & Parts

N

NAIL SALONS
NAME PLATES: Engraved Or Etched
NATIONAL SECURITY FORCES
NATIONAL SECURITY, GOVERNMENT: Army
NATURAL BUTANE PRODUCTION
NATURAL GAS COMPRESSING SVC, On-Site
NATURAL GAS DISTRIBUTION TO CONSUMERS
NATURAL GAS LIQUID FRACTIONATING SVC
NATURAL GAS LIQUIDS PRODUCTION
NATURAL GAS LIQUIDS PRODUCTION
NATURAL GAS PRODUCTION
NATURAL GAS TRANSMISSION
NATURAL GAS TRANSMISSION & DISTRIBUTION
NATURAL GASOLINE PRODUCTION
NATURAL LIQUEFIED PETROLEUM GAS PRODUCTION
NATURAL PROPANE PRODUCTION
NAVIGATIONAL SYSTEMS & INSTRUMENTS
NEW & USED CAR DEALERS
NEWSPAPERS, WHOLESALE
NEWSSTAND

PRODUCT INDEX

NICKEL ALLOY
NONDURABLE GOODS WHOLESALERS, NEC
NONFERROUS: Rolling & Drawing, NEC
NONMETALLIC MINERALS: Support Activities, Exc Fuels
NOTARIES PUBLIC
NOTIONS: Pins & Needles
NOVELTIES
NOVELTIES: Plastic
NOVELTY SHOPS
NOZZLES: Spray, Aerosol, Paint Or Insecticide
NURSERIES & LAWN & GARDEN SPLY STORE, RET: Fountain, Outdoor
NURSERIES & LAWN & GARDEN SPLY STORES, RETAIL: Fertilizer
NURSERIES & LAWN & GARDEN SPLY STORES, RETAIL: Top Soil
NURSERIES & LAWN/GARDEN SPLY STORE, RET: Lawnmowers/Tractors
NURSERIES & LAWN/GARDEN SPLY STORES, RET: Garden Splys/Tools
NURSERIES/LAWN/GRDN SPLY STORE, RET: Nursery Stck, Seed/Bulb

O

OFFICE EQPT WHOLESALERS
OFFICE EQPT, WHOLESALE: Photocopy Machines
OFFICE MACHINES, NEC
OFFICE MANAGEMENT SVCS
OFFICE SPLY & STATIONERY STORES
OFFICE SPLY & STATIONERY STORES: Notary & Corporate Seals
OFFICE SPLY & STATIONERY STORES: Office Forms & Splys
OFFICE SPLYS, NEC, WHOLESALE
OFFICES & CLINICS OF HEALTH PRACTITIONERS: Nurse & Med Asst
OFFICES & CLINICS OF OPTOMETRISTS: Specialist, Contact Lens
OIL & GAS FIELD EQPT: Drill Rigs
OIL & GAS FIELD MACHINERY
OIL BURNER REPAIR SVCS
OIL FIELD MACHINERY & EQPT
OIL FIELD SVCS, NEC
OIL LEASES, BUYING & SELLING ON OWN ACCOUNT
OIL ROYALTY TRADERS
OIL TREATING COMPOUNDS
OILS & GREASES: Lubricating
OILS: Lubricating
OILS: Lubricating
OILS: Orange
OLEFINS
ON-LINE DATABASE INFORMATION RETRIEVAL SVCS
OPERATOR: Apartment Buildings
OPERATOR: Nonresidential Buildings
OPHTHALMIC GOODS
OPHTHALMIC GOODS WHOLESALERS
OPHTHALMIC GOODS, NEC, WHOLESALE: Lenses
OPHTHALMIC GOODS: Frames, Lenses & Parts, Eyeglasses
OPHTHALMIC GOODS: Lenses, Ophthalmic
OPTICAL GOODS STORES
OPTICAL GOODS STORES: Opticians
OPTICAL INSTRUMENTS & APPARATUS
OPTICAL INSTRUMENTS & LENSES
OPTOMETRIC EQPT & SPLYS WHOLESALERS
OPTOMETRISTS' OFFICES
ORDNANCE
ORGANIZATIONS: Civic & Social
ORGANIZATIONS: Professional
ORGANIZATIONS: Religious
ORGANIZATIONS: Research Institute
ORNAMENTS: Christmas Tree, Exc Electrical & Glass
ORTHODONTIST
OSCILLATORS
OSICIZERS: Inorganic
OUTBOARD MOTORS & PARTS
OUTBOARD MOTORS: Electric
OVENS: Cremating
OVENS: Distillation, Charcoal & Coke

P

PACKAGED FROZEN FOODS WHOLESALERS, NEC
PACKAGING & LABELING SVCS
PACKAGING MATERIALS, WHOLESALE
PACKAGING MATERIALS: Paper
PACKAGING MATERIALS: Paper, Coated Or Laminated
PACKAGING MATERIALS: Paperboard Backs For Blister/Skin Pkgs
PACKAGING MATERIALS: Polystyrene Foam
PACKING & CRATING SVC
PACKING SVCS: Shipping
PADDING: Foamed Plastics
PAGERS: One-way
PAINT STORE
PAINTING SVC: Metal Prdts
PAINTS & ADDITIVES
PAINTS & ALLIED PRODUCTS
PAINTS, VARNISHES & SPLYS WHOLESALERS
PAINTS, VARNISHES & SPLYS, WHOLESALE: Colors & Pigments
PAINTS, VARNISHES & SPLYS, WHOLESALE: Lacquers
PAINTS, VARNISHES & SPLYS, WHOLESALE: Paints
PAINTS: Oil Or Alkyd Vehicle Or Water Thinned
PAINTS: Waterproof
PALLET REPAIR SVCS
PALLETS
PALLETS & SKIDS: Wood
PALLETS: Plastic
PALLETS: Wooden
PANEL & DISTRIBUTION BOARDS & OTHER RELATED APPARATUS
PANELS: Building, Metal
PANELS: Building, Wood
PAPER & BOARD: Die-cut
PAPER CONVERTING
PAPER MANUFACTURERS: Exc Newsprint
PAPER PRDTS: Facial Tissue
PAPER PRDTS: Infant & Baby Prdts
PAPER PRDTS: Napkins, Sanitary, Made From Purchased Material
PAPER PRDTS: Sanitary
PAPER PRDTS: Sanitary Tissue Paper
PAPER: Absorbent
PAPER: Adhesive
PAPER: Cardboard
PAPER: Coated & Laminated, NEC
PAPER: Packaging
PAPER: Printer
PAPER: Wallpaper
PAPER: Wrapping & Packaging
PAPERBOARD
PAPERBOARD CONVERTING
PARKING METERS
PARTITIONS & FIXTURES: Except Wood
PARTITIONS: Wood & Fixtures
PARTS: Metal
PATTERNS: Indl
PAVERS
PAVING MIXTURES
PAWN SHOPS
PAYROLL SVCS
PENS: Meter
PERISCOPES
PERLITE MINING SVCS
PERSONAL & HOUSEHOLD GOODS REPAIR, NEC
PERSONAL DOCUMENT & INFORMATION SVCS
PERSONAL INVESTIGATION SVCS
PERSONAL ITEM CARE & STORAGE SVCS
PERSONAL SVCS, NEC
PESTICIDES
PET SPLYS
PET SPLYS WHOLESALERS
PETROLEUM & PETROLEUM PRDTS, WHOL Svc Station Splys, Petro
PETROLEUM & PETROLEUM PRDTS, WHOLESALE Crude Oil
PETROLEUM & PETROLEUM PRDTS, WHOLESALE Diesel Fuel
PETROLEUM & PETROLEUM PRDTS, WHOLESALE Fuel Oil
PETROLEUM & PETROLEUM PRDTS, WHOLESALE Gases
PETROLEUM & PETROLEUM PRDTS, WHOLESALE Petroleum Brokers
PETROLEUM & PETROLEUM PRDTS, WHOLESALE: Bulk Stations
PETROLEUM BULK STATIONS & TERMINALS
PETROLEUM PRDTS WHOLESALERS
PHARMACEUTICAL PREPARATIONS: Druggists' Preparations
PHARMACEUTICAL PREPARATIONS: Emulsions
PHARMACEUTICAL PREPARATIONS: Medicines, Capsule Or Ampule
PHARMACEUTICAL PREPARATIONS: Powders
PHARMACEUTICAL PREPARATIONS: Proprietary Drug PRDTS
PHARMACEUTICAL PREPARATIONS: Solutions
PHARMACEUTICALS
PHARMACEUTICALS: Medicinal & Botanical Prdts
PHARMACIES & DRUG STORES
PHOTOCONDUCTIVE CELLS
PHOTOCOPY MACHINES
PHOTOCOPYING & DUPLICATING SVCS
PHOTOENGRAVING SVC
PHOTOGRAPHIC EQPT & SPLY: Sound Recordg/Reprod Eqpt, Motion
PHOTOGRAPHIC EQPT & SPLYS
PHOTOGRAPHIC EQPT & SPLYS: Blueprint Reproduction Mach/Eqpt
PHOTOGRAPHIC EQPT & SPLYS: Cameras, Aerial
PHOTOGRAPHIC EQPT & SPLYS: Cameras, Still & Motion Pictures
PHOTOGRAPHIC EQPT & SPLYS: Densitometers
PHOTOGRAPHIC EQPT & SPLYS: Printing Eqpt
PHOTOGRAPHIC EQPT & SPLYS: Toners, Prprd, Not Chem Plnts
PHOTOGRAPHY SVCS: Commercial
PHOTOGRAPHY SVCS: Passport
PHOTOGRAPHY SVCS: Portrait Studios
PHOTOGRAPHY: Aerial
PHYSICAL EXAMINATION & TESTING SVCS
PHYSICIANS' OFFICES & CLINICS: Medical doctors
PICTURE FRAMES: Wood
PIECE GOODS, NOTIONS & DRY GOODS, WHOL: Fabrics Broadwoven
PIECE GOODS, NOTIONS & DRY GOODS, WHOLESALE: Tape, Textile
PIECE GOODS, NOTIONS & OTHER DRY GOODS, WHOL: Flags/Banners
PIECE GOODS, NOTIONS/DRY GOODS, WHOL: Drapery Mtrl, Woven
PIGMENTS, INORGANIC: Chrome Green, Chrome Yellow, Zinc Yellw
PIGMENTS, INORGANIC: White
PILOT SVCS: Aviation
PINS
PINS: Cotter
PIPE & FITTING: Fabrication
PIPE & FITTINGS: Cast Iron
PIPE & FITTINGS: Pressure, Cast Iron
PIPE & TUBES: Seamless
PIPE FITTINGS: Plastic
PIPE SECTIONS, FABRICATED FROM PURCHASED PIPE
PIPE, CAST IRON: Wholesalers
PIPE, CYLINDER: Concrete, Prestressed Or Pretensioned
PIPE, SEWER: Concrete
PIPE: Concrete
PIPE: Plastic
PIPE: Sheet Metal
PIPE: Water, Cast Iron
PIPELINE & POWER LINE INSPECTION SVCS
PIPELINES: Crude Petroleum
PIPELINES: Natural Gas
PIPELINES: Refined Petroleum
PIPES & TUBES
PIPES & TUBES: Steel
PIPES & TUBES: Welded
PIPES OR FITTINGS: Sewer, Clay
PIPES: Steel & Iron
PLAQUES: Picture, Laminated
PLASMAPHEROUS CENTER
PLASMAS
PLASTER, ACOUSTICAL: Gypsum
PLASTIC PRDTS
PLASTICS FILM & SHEET
PLASTICS FILM & SHEET: Polyethylene
PLASTICS FILM & SHEET: Polyvinyl
PLASTICS MATERIAL & RESINS
PLASTICS MATERIALS, BASIC FORMS & SHAPES WHOLESALERS
PLASTICS PROCESSING
PLASTICS SHEET: Packing Materials
PLASTICS: Blow Molded
PLASTICS: Cast
PLASTICS: Extruded
PLASTICS: Finished Injection Molded

PRODUCT INDEX

PLASTICS: Injection Molded
PLASTICS: Molded
PLASTICS: Polystyrene Foam
PLATE WORK: Metalworking Trade
PLATEMAKING SVC: Color Separations, For The Printing Trade
PLATEMAKING SVC: Letterpress
PLATES
PLATES: Aluminum
PLATING & POLISHING SVC
PLATING SVC: Chromium, Metals Or Formed Prdts
PLATING SVC: Electro
PLATING SVC: NEC
PLAYGROUND EQPT
PLEATING & STITCHING FOR THE TRADE: Decorative & Novelty
PLEATING & STITCHING SVC
PLUGS: Electric
PLUMBING & HEATING EQPT & SPLY, WHOL: Htg Eqpt/Panels, Solar
PLUMBING & HEATING EQPT & SPLY, WHOLESALE: Hydronic Htg Eqpt
PLUMBING & HEATING EQPT & SPLYS WHOLESALERS
PLUMBING & HEATING EQPT & SPLYS, WHOL: Plumbing Fitting/Sply
PLUMBING & HEATING EQPT & SPLYS, WHOL: Water Purif Eqpt
PLUMBING & HEATING EQPT, WHOLESALE: Water Heaters/Purif
PLUMBING FIXTURES
PLUMBING FIXTURES: Brass, Incl Drain Cocks, Faucets/Spigots
PLUMBING FIXTURES: Plastic
PLUMBING FIXTURES: Vitreous
POINT OF SALE DEVICES
POLES & POSTS: Concrete
POLISHING SVC: Metals Or Formed Prdts
POLYPROPYLENE RESINS
POLYVINYL CHLORIDE RESINS
PORCELAIN ENAMELED PRDTS & UTENSILS
POSTERS
POTTERY
POULTRY & POULTRY PRDTS WHOLESALERS
POULTRY & SMALL GAME SLAUGHTERING & PROCESSING
POWDER: Metal
POWER GENERATORS
POWER HAND TOOLS WHOLESALERS
POWER SUPPLIES: All Types, Static
POWER TOOL REPAIR SVCS
POWER TRANSMISSION EQPT: Mechanical
POWERED GOLF CART DEALERS
PRECAST TERRAZZO OR CONCRETE PRDTS
PRECIOUS METALS WHOLESALERS
PRECIOUS STONE MINING SVCS, NEC
PRECIOUS STONES & METALS, WHOLESALE
PRECISION INSTRUMENT REPAIR SVCS
PREFABRICATED BUILDING DEALERS
PRENATAL INSTRUCTION
PRERECORDED TAPE, COMPACT DISC & RECORD STORES: Compact Disc
PRESTRESSED CONCRETE PRDTS
PRIMARY METAL PRODUCTS
PRINT CARTRIDGES: Laser & Other Computer Printers
PRINTED CIRCUIT BOARDS
PRINTERS' SVCS: Folding, Collating, Etc
PRINTERS: Computer
PRINTING & BINDING: Books
PRINTING & ENGRAVING: Invitation & Stationery
PRINTING & ENGRAVING: Plateless
PRINTING & ENGRAVING: Poster & Decal
PRINTING & ENGRAVING: Rolls, Textile Printing
PRINTING & STAMPING: Fabric Articles
PRINTING & WRITING PAPER WHOLESALERS
PRINTING INKS WHOLESALERS
PRINTING MACHINERY
PRINTING TRADES MACHINERY & EQPT REPAIR SVCS
PRINTING, COMMERCIAL: Business Forms, NEC
PRINTING, COMMERCIAL: Calendars, NEC
PRINTING, COMMERCIAL: Decals, NEC
PRINTING, COMMERCIAL: Envelopes, NEC
PRINTING, COMMERCIAL: Imprinting
PRINTING, COMMERCIAL: Invitations, NEC
PRINTING, COMMERCIAL: Labels & Seals, NEC
PRINTING, COMMERCIAL: Letterpress & Screen

PRINTING, COMMERCIAL: Literature, Advertising, NEC
PRINTING, COMMERCIAL: Magazines, NEC
PRINTING, COMMERCIAL: Promotional
PRINTING, COMMERCIAL: Publications
PRINTING, COMMERCIAL: Screen
PRINTING, COMMERCIAL: Stamps, Trading, NEC
PRINTING, LITHOGRAPHIC: Advertising Posters
PRINTING, LITHOGRAPHIC: Decals
PRINTING, LITHOGRAPHIC: Forms, Business
PRINTING, LITHOGRAPHIC: Letters, Circular Or Form
PRINTING, LITHOGRAPHIC: Offset & photolithographic printing
PRINTING, LITHOGRAPHIC: On Metal
PRINTING, LITHOGRAPHIC: Posters & Decals
PRINTING, LITHOGRAPHIC: Promotional
PRINTING, LITHOGRAPHIC: Tickets
PRINTING: Books
PRINTING: Commercial, NEC
PRINTING: Flexographic
PRINTING: Gravure, Business Form & Card
PRINTING: Gravure, Job
PRINTING: Gravure, Rotogravure
PRINTING: Laser
PRINTING: Letterpress
PRINTING: Lithographic
PRINTING: Offset
PRINTING: Overprinting, Man Fiber & Silk, Broadwoven Fabric
PRINTING: Photolithographic
PRINTING: Screen, Broadwoven Fabrics, Cotton
PRINTING: Screen, Fabric
PRINTING: Screen, Manmade Fiber & Silk, Broadwoven Fabric
PRINTING: Thermography
PRODUCT STERILIZATION SVCS
PROFESSIONAL EQPT & SPLYS, WHOLESALE: Optical Goods
PROFESSIONAL EQPT & SPLYS, WHOLESALE: Scientific & Engineerg
PROFESSIONAL INSTRUMENT REPAIR SVCS
PROGRAM ADMIN, GOVT: Air, Water & Solid Waste Mgmt, Cnty
PROGRAM ADMIN, GOVT: Air, Water & Solid Waste Mgmt, State
PROPERTY DAMAGE INSURANCE
PROTECTION EQPT: Lightning
PROTECTIVE FOOTWEAR: Rubber Or Plastic
PUBLIC ADDRESS SYSTEMS
PUBLIC ORDER & SAFETY OFFICES, GOVERNMENT: State
PUBLIC RELATIONS SVCS
PUBLISHERS: Book
PUBLISHERS: Books, No Printing
PUBLISHERS: Catalogs
PUBLISHERS: Directories, NEC
PUBLISHERS: Directories, Telephone
PUBLISHERS: Guides
PUBLISHERS: Magazines, No Printing
PUBLISHERS: Miscellaneous
PUBLISHERS: Music Book & Sheet Music
PUBLISHERS: Newsletter
PUBLISHERS: Newspaper
PUBLISHERS: Newspapers, No Printing
PUBLISHERS: Pamphlets, No Printing
PUBLISHERS: Periodicals, Magazines
PUBLISHERS: Periodicals, No Printing
PUBLISHERS: Racing Forms & Programs
PUBLISHERS: Sheet Music
PUBLISHERS: Shopping News
PUBLISHERS: Technical Manuals & Papers
PUBLISHERS: Technical Papers
PUBLISHERS: Telephone & Other Directory
PUBLISHERS: Television Schedules, No Printing
PUBLISHERS: Textbooks, No Printing
PUBLISHERS: Trade journals, No Printing
PUBLISHING & BROADCASTING: Internet Only
PUBLISHING & PRINTING: Books
PUBLISHING & PRINTING: Catalogs
PUBLISHING & PRINTING: Comic Books
PUBLISHING & PRINTING: Directories, NEC
PUBLISHING & PRINTING: Directories, Telephone
PUBLISHING & PRINTING: Magazines: publishing & printing
PUBLISHING & PRINTING: Newsletters, Business Svc
PUBLISHING & PRINTING: Newspapers
PUBLISHING & PRINTING: Pamphlets

PUBLISHING & PRINTING: Periodical Statistical Reports
PUBLISHING & PRINTING: Trade Journals
PULLEYS: Metal
PULP MILLS: Kraft Sulfate Pulp
PULP MILLS: Mechanical & Recycling Processing
PULP MILLS: Soda Pulp
PUMP JACKS & OTHER PUMPING EQPT: Indl
PUMPS
PUMPS & PARTS: Indl
PUMPS & PUMPING EQPT REPAIR SVCS
PUMPS & PUMPING EQPT WHOLESALERS
PUMPS, HEAT: Electric
PUMPS: Domestic, Water Or Sump
PUMPS: Hydraulic Power Transfer
PUMPS: Measuring & Dispensing
PUMPS: Oil Well & Field
PURIFIERS: Centrifugal
PURSES: Women's

Q

QUARTZ CRYSTALS: Electronic
QUILTING SVC
QUILTING SVC & SPLYS, FOR THE TRADE
QUILTING: Individuals

R

RACEWAYS
RADAR SYSTEMS & EQPT
RADIATORS, EXC ELECTRIC
RADIO & TELEVISION COMMUNICATIONS EQUIPMENT
RADIO BROADCASTING & COMMUNICATIONS EQPT
RADIO BROADCASTING STATIONS
RADIO, TELEVISION & CONSUMER ELECTRONICS STORES: Eqpt, NEC
RADIO, TELEVISION/CONSUMER ELEC STORES: Video Cameras/Access
RADIO, TV & CONSUMER ELEC STORES: Automotive Sound Eqpt
RADIO, TV & CONSUMER ELEC STORES: High Fidelity Stereo Eqpt
RAILINGS: Prefabricated, Metal
RAILROAD CARGO LOADING & UNLOADING SVCS
RAILROAD EQPT
RAILROAD EQPT, EXC LOCOMOTIVES
RAILROAD EQPT: Cars, Maintenance
RAILROAD EQPT: Cars, Tank Freight & Eqpt
RAILROAD MAINTENANCE & REPAIR SVCS
REAL ESTATE AGENCIES & BROKERS
REAL ESTATE AGENCIES: Leasing & Rentals
REAL ESTATE AGENCIES: Residential
REAL ESTATE AGENTS & MANAGERS
REAL ESTATE OPERATORS, EXC DEVELOPERS: Commercial/Indl Bldg
RECORDS & TAPES: Prerecorded
RECORDS OR TAPES: Masters
RECOVERY OR EXTRACTION SVCS: Explosives
RECOVERY SVC: Silver, From Used Photographic Film
RECREATIONAL VEHICLE DEALERS
RECTIFIERS: Electrical Apparatus
RECYCLABLE SCRAP & WASTE MATERIALS WHOLESALERS
RECYCLING: Paper
REFINERS & SMELTERS: Aluminum
REFINERS & SMELTERS: Babbit Metal, Secondary
REFINERS & SMELTERS: Germanium, Primary
REFINERS & SMELTERS: Nonferrous Metal
REFINERS & SMELTERS: Silver
REFINERS & SMELTERS: Zinc, Primary, Including Slabs & Dust
REFINING: Petroleum
REFRACTORIES: Brick
REFRACTORIES: Cement, nonclay
REFRACTORIES: Clay
REFRACTORIES: Nonclay
REFRACTORY MATERIALS WHOLESALERS
REFRIGERATION & HEATING EQUIPMENT
REFRIGERATION EQPT & SPLYS WHOLESALERS
REFRIGERATION EQPT & SPLYS, WHOLESALE: Ice Making Machines
REFRIGERATION EQPT: Complete
REFRIGERATION REPAIR SVCS
REFRIGERATION SVC & REPAIR
REFUSE SYSTEMS
REGULATORS: Transmission & Distribution Voltage
REMOTE DATABASE INFORMATION RETRIEVAL SVCS

PRODUCT INDEX

REMOVERS & CLEANERS
REMOVERS: Paint
RENT-A-CAR SVCS
RENTAL CENTERS: Tools
RENTAL SVCS: Business Machine & Electronic Eqpt
RENTAL SVCS: Costume
RENTAL SVCS: Invalid Splys
RENTAL SVCS: Mobile Communication Eqpt
RENTAL SVCS: Mobile Home, Exc On Site
RENTAL SVCS: Office Facilities & Secretarial Svcs
RENTAL SVCS: Oil Eqpt
RENTAL SVCS: Photographic Eqpt
RENTAL SVCS: Propane Eqpt
RENTAL SVCS: Trailer
REPAIR SERVICES, NEC
REPRODUCTION SVCS: Video Tape Or Disk
RESEARCH, DEVELOPMENT & TEST SVCS, COMM: Cmptr Hardware Dev
RESEARCH, DEVELOPMENT & TEST SVCS, COMM: Research, Exc Lab
RESEARCH, DEVELOPMENT & TESTING SVCS, COMM: Agricultural
RESEARCH, DEVELOPMENT & TESTING SVCS, COMM: Research Lab
RESEARCH, DEVELOPMENT & TESTING SVCS, COMMERCIAL: Education
RESEARCH, DVLPT & TEST SVCS, COMM: Mkt Analysis or Research
RESIDENTIAL CARE FOR THE HANDICAPPED
RESIDENTIAL REMODELERS
RESIDUES
RESINS: Custom Compound Purchased
RESISTORS
RESTAURANT EQPT: Carts
RESTAURANT EQPT: Food Wagons
RESTAURANT EQPT: Sheet Metal
RESTAURANTS: Delicatessen
RESTAURANTS:Full Svc, American
RESTAURANTS:Full Svc, Barbecue
RESTAURANTS:Full Svc, Italian
RESTAURANTS:Full Svc, Steak & Barbecue
RESTAURANTS:Limited Svc, Coffee Shop
RESTAURANTS:Limited Svc, Drive-In
RESTAURANTS:Limited Svc, Grill
RESTAURANTS:Limited Svc, Soft Drink Stand
RETAIL BAKERY: Bread
RETAIL BAKERY: Cakes
RETAIL BAKERY: Doughnuts
RETAIL FIREPLACE STORES
RETAIL LUMBER YARDS
RETAIL STORES, NEC
RETAIL STORES: Alcoholic Beverage Making Eqpt & Splys
RETAIL STORES: Artificial Limbs
RETAIL STORES: Audio-Visual Eqpt & Splys
RETAIL STORES: Banners
RETAIL STORES: Batteries, Non-Automotive
RETAIL STORES: Canvas Prdts
RETAIL STORES: Cleaning Eqpt & Splys
RETAIL STORES: Communication Eqpt
RETAIL STORES: Concrete Prdts, Precast
RETAIL STORES: Decals
RETAIL STORES: Drafting Eqpt & Splys
RETAIL STORES: Educational Aids & Electronic Training Mat
RETAIL STORES: Electronic Parts & Eqpt
RETAIL STORES: Engine & Motor Eqpt & Splys
RETAIL STORES: Farm Eqpt & Splys
RETAIL STORES: Farm Machinery, NEC
RETAIL STORES: Foam & Foam Prdts
RETAIL STORES: Hearing Aids
RETAIL STORES: Ice
RETAIL STORES: Maps & Charts
RETAIL STORES: Medical Apparatus & Splys
RETAIL STORES: Monuments, Finished To Custom Order
RETAIL STORES: Motors, Electric
RETAIL STORES: Orthopedic & Prosthesis Applications
RETAIL STORES: Perfumes & Colognes
RETAIL STORES: Pet Splys
RETAIL STORES: Picture Frames, Ready Made
RETAIL STORES: Safety Splys & Eqpt
RETAIL STORES: Spas & Hot Tubs
RETAIL STORES: Telephone Eqpt & Systems
RETAIL STORES: Welding Splys
REUPHOLSTERY & FURNITURE REPAIR
REUPHOLSTERY SVCS
RIPRAP QUARRYING
ROAD CONSTRUCTION EQUIPMENT WHOLESALERS
ROBOTS: Assembly Line
RODS: Plastic
RODS: Steel & Iron, Made In Steel Mills
RODS: Welding
ROLLING MILL EQPT: Galvanizing Lines
ROLLING MILL MACHINERY
ROLLING MILL ROLLS: Cast Steel
ROOF DECKS
ROOFING GRANULES
ROOFING MATERIALS: Asphalt
ROOFING MATERIALS: Sheet Metal
RUBBER
RUBBER PRDTS: Automotive, Mechanical
RUBBER PRDTS: Mechanical
RUBBER PRDTS: Oil & Gas Field Machinery, Mechanical
RUBBER STAMP, WHOLESALE
RUGS : Hand & Machine Made

S

SADDLERY STORES
SAFES & VAULTS: Metal
SAFETY EQPT & SPLYS WHOLESALERS
SAILS
SALT
SAND & GRAVEL
SAND MINING
SAND: Hygrade
SAND: Silica
SANDBLASTING EQPT
SANDSTONE: Crushed & Broken
SANITARY SVCS: Environmental Cleanup
SANITARY SVCS: Liquid Waste Collection & Disposal
SANITARY SVCS: Rubbish Collection & Disposal
SANITARY SVCS: Waste Materials, Recycling
SANITARY WARE: Metal
SANITATION CHEMICALS & CLEANING AGENTS
SASHES: Door Or Window, Metal
SATELLITE COMMUNICATIONS EQPT
SATELLITES: Communications
SAW BLADES
SAWING & PLANING MILLS
SAWING & PLANING MILLS: Custom
SAWS & SAWING EQPT
SCAFFOLDS: Mobile Or Stationary, Metal
SCALE REPAIR SVCS
SCALES & BALANCES, EXC LABORATORY
SCALES: Indl
SCALES: Railroad Track
SCALES: Truck
SCHOOLS & EDUCATIONAL SVCS, NEC
SCHOOLS: Vocational, NEC
SCRAP & WASTE MATERIALS, WHOLESALE: Ferrous Metal
SCRAP & WASTE MATERIALS, WHOLESALE: Metal
SCRAP & WASTE MATERIALS, WHOLESALE: Paper
SCRAP & WASTE MATERIALS, WHOLESALE: Paper & Cloth Materials
SCREENS: Window, Metal
SCREENS: Woven Wire
SCREW MACHINE PRDTS
SEALANTS
SEALS: Oil, Rubber
SEARCH & NAVIGATION SYSTEMS
SECURE STORAGE SVC: Document
SECURITIES DEALING
SECURITY CONTROL EQPT & SYSTEMS
SECURITY DEVICES
SECURITY EQPT STORES
SECURITY PROTECTIVE DEVICES MAINTENANCE & MONITORING SVCS
SECURITY SYSTEMS SERVICES
SEEDS: Coated Or Treated, From Purchased Seeds
SELF-PROPELLED AIRCRAFT DEALER
SEMICONDUCTOR & RELATED DEVICES: Random Access Memory Or RAM
SEMICONDUCTORS & RELATED DEVICES
SENSORS: Radiation
SEPTIC TANK CLEANING SVCS
SEPTIC TANKS: Concrete
SEWAGE & WATER TREATMENT EQPT
SEWAGE TREATMENT SYSTEMS & EQPT
SEWING CONTRACTORS
SEWING MACHINE STORES
SEWING MACHINES & PARTS: Indl
SEWING, NEEDLEWORK & PIECE GOODS STORES: Fabric, Remnants
SEWING, NEEDLEWORK & PIECE GOODS STORES: Sewing & Needlework
SEWING, NEEDLEWORK & PIECE GOODS STORES: Sewing Splys
SEXTANTS
SHALE: Expanded
SHAPES & PILINGS, STRUCTURAL: Steel
SHAPES: Extruded, Aluminum, NEC
SHAVING PREPARATIONS
SHEET METAL SPECIALTIES, EXC STAMPED
SHEETING: Window, Plastic
SHEETS & STRIPS: Aluminum
SHELLAC
SHELTERED WORKSHOPS
SHIP BLDG & RPRG: Drilling & Production Platforms, Oil/Gas
SHIP BLDG/RPRG: Submersible Marine Robots, Manned/Unmanned
SHIP BUILDING & REPAIRING: Lighters, Marine
SHOE MATERIALS: Counters
SHOE MATERIALS: Quarters
SHOE MATERIALS: Rands
SHOE MATERIALS: Uppers
SHOE STORES: Athletic
SHOE STORES: Men's
SHOE STORES: Orthopedic
SHOES: Canvas, Rubber Soled
SHOES: Moccasins
SHOES: Women's, Dress
SHUTTERS, DOOR & WINDOW: Metal
SHUTTERS: Door, Wood
SHUTTERS: Window, Wood
SIDING & STRUCTURAL MATERIALS: Wood
SIDING, INSULATING: Impregnated, From Purchased Materials
SIDING: Sheet Metal
SIGN LETTERING & PAINTING SVCS
SIGN PAINTING & LETTERING SHOP
SIGNALING APPARATUS: Electric
SIGNALING DEVICES: Sound, Electrical
SIGNALS: Railroad, Electric
SIGNALS: Traffic Control, Electric
SIGNALS: Transportation
SIGNS & ADVERTISING SPECIALTIES
SIGNS & ADVERTISING SPECIALTIES: Artwork, Advertising
SIGNS & ADVERTISING SPECIALTIES: Letters For Signs, Metal
SIGNS & ADVERTISING SPECIALTIES: Novelties
SIGNS & ADVERTISING SPECIALTIES: Signs
SIGNS & ADVERTSG SPECIALTIES: Displays/Cutouts Window/Lobby
SIGNS, EXC ELECTRIC, WHOLESALE
SIGNS: Electrical
SIGNS: Neon
SILICA MINING
SILICON WAFERS: Chemically Doped
SILK SCREEN DESIGN SVCS
SILO STAVES: Concrete Or Cast Stone
SILVER ORES
SILVERWARE & PLATED WARE
SIMULATORS: Flight
SIZES
SIZES: Rosin
SKATING RINKS: Roller
SKILL TRAINING CENTER
SKYLIGHTS
SLAB & TILE: Precast Concrete, Floor
SLAUGHTERING & MEAT PACKING
SLINGS: Lifting, Made From Purchased Wire
SLOT MACHINES
SNACK & NONALCOHOLIC BEVERAGE BARS
SOAPS & DETERGENTS
SOAPS & DETERGENTS: Textile
SOCIAL SVCS: Individual & Family
SOFTWARE PUBLISHERS: Application
SOFTWARE PUBLISHERS: Business & Professional
SOFTWARE PUBLISHERS: Education
SOFTWARE PUBLISHERS: NEC
SOFTWARE PUBLISHERS: Operating Systems
SOFTWARE PUBLISHERS: Publisher's
SOIL CONDITIONERS
SOLAR CELLS
SOLAR HEATING EQPT
SOLDERING EQPT: Electrical, Handheld

PRODUCT INDEX

SOLVENTS
SOUND RECORDING STUDIOS
SOUND REPRODUCING EQPT
SOYBEAN PRDTS
SPACE FLIGHT OPERATIONS, EXC GOVERNMENT
SPACE VEHICLE EQPT
SPEAKER SYSTEMS
SPECIALTY FOOD STORES: Coffee
SPECIALTY FOOD STORES: Dried Fruit
SPECIALTY FOOD STORES: Soft Drinks
SPINDLES: Textile
SPORTING & ATHLETIC GOODS: Boomerangs
SPORTING & ATHLETIC GOODS: Bowling Alleys & Access
SPORTING & ATHLETIC GOODS: Carts, Golf, Hand
SPORTING & ATHLETIC GOODS: Cases, Gun & Rod
SPORTING & ATHLETIC GOODS: Decoys, Duck & Other Game Birds
SPORTING & ATHLETIC GOODS: Fishing Bait, Artificial
SPORTING & ATHLETIC GOODS: Fishing Eqpt
SPORTING & ATHLETIC GOODS: Fishing Tackle, General
SPORTING & ATHLETIC GOODS: Football Eqpt & Splys, NEC
SPORTING & ATHLETIC GOODS: Game Calls
SPORTING & ATHLETIC GOODS: Hunting Eqpt
SPORTING & ATHLETIC GOODS: Pools, Swimming, Exc Plastic
SPORTING & ATHLETIC GOODS: Pools, Swimming, Plastic
SPORTING & ATHLETIC GOODS: Rods & Rod Parts, Fishing
SPORTING & ATHLETIC GOODS: Shooting Eqpt & Splys, General
SPORTING & ATHLETIC GOODS: Skateboards
SPORTING & ATHLETIC GOODS: Target Shooting Eqpt
SPORTING & ATHLETIC GOODS: Targets, Archery & Rifle Shooting
SPORTING & ATHLETIC GOODS: Track & Field Athletic Eqpt
SPORTING & ATHLETIC GOODS: Treadmills
SPORTING & RECREATIONAL GOODS & SPLYS WHOLESALERS
SPORTING & RECREATIONAL GOODS, WHOLESALE: Fishing Tackle
SPORTING & RECREATIONAL GOODS, WHOLESALE: Golf
SPORTING & RECREATIONAL GOODS, WHOLESALE: Gymnasium
SPORTING GOODS
SPORTING GOODS STORES, NEC
SPORTING GOODS STORES: Firearms
SPORTING GOODS STORES: Playground Eqpt
SPORTING GOODS STORES: Pool & Billiard Tables
SPORTING GOODS STORES: Team sports Eqpt
SPORTING GOODS: Archery
SPORTING GOODS: Hammocks & Other Net Prdts
SPORTS APPAREL STORES
SPORTS CLUBS, MANAGERS & PROMOTERS
SPRAYING & DUSTING EQPT
SPRINGS: Leaf, Automobile, Locomotive, Etc
SPRINGS: Precision
SPRINGS: Steel
SPRINGS: Wire
SPRINKLER SYSTEMS: Field
SPRINKLING SYSTEMS: Fire Control
STAGE LIGHTING SYSTEMS
STAINLESS STEEL
STAMPED ART GOODS FOR EMBROIDERING
STAMPING: Fabric Articles
STAMPINGS: Automotive
STAMPINGS: Metal
STARTERS & CONTROLLERS: Motor, Electric
STARTERS: Motor
STATIONERY & OFFICE SPLYS WHOLESALERS
STATIONERY PRDTS
STATORS REWINDING SVCS
STEEL FABRICATORS
STEEL MILLS
STEEL, COLD-ROLLED: Strip NEC, From Purchased Hot-Rolled
STEEL: Cold-Rolled
STEERING SYSTEMS & COMPONENTS
STITCHING SVCS
STITCHING SVCS: Custom
STONE: Cast Concrete
STONE: Crushed & Broken, NEC
STONE: Dimension, NEC
STONE: Quarrying & Processing, Own Stone Prdts
STONEWARE PRDTS: Pottery
STORE FIXTURES, EXC REFRIGERATED: Wholesalers

STORE FIXTURES: Wood
STORES: Auto & Home Supply
STORES: Drapery & Upholstery
STRAINERS: Line, Piping Systems
STRAPPING
STRAWS: Drinking, Made From Purchased Materials
STRUCTURAL SUPPORT & BUILDING MATERIAL: Concrete
STUCCO
STUDIOS: Artist's
STUDIOS: Artists & Artists' Studios
STUDIOS: Sculptor's
STYLING SVCS: Wigs
SUBDIVIDERS & DEVELOPERS: Real Property, Cemetery Lots Only
SUNDRIES & RELATED PRDTS: Medical & Laboratory, Rubber
SUPERMARKETS & OTHER GROCERY STORES
SURFACE ACTIVE AGENTS
SURGICAL & MEDICAL INSTRUMENTS WHOLESALERS
SURGICAL APPLIANCES & SPLYS
SURGICAL IMPLANTS
SURVEYING & MAPPING: Land Parcels
SURVEYING SVCS: Aerial Digital Imaging
SURVEYING SVCS: Photogrammetric Engineering
SVC ESTABLISHMENT EQPT, WHOL: Concrete Burial Vaults & Boxes
SVC ESTABLISHMENT EQPT, WHOLESALE: Engraving Eqpt & Splys
SVC ESTABLISHMENT EQPT, WHOLESALE: Restaurant Splys
SVC ESTABLISHMENT EQPT, WHOLESALE: Vending Machines & Splys
SWEEPING COMPOUNDS
SWIMMING POOL ACCESS: Leaf Skimmers Or Pool Rakes
SWIMMING POOL EQPT: Filters & Water Conditioning Systems
SWITCHES: Electronic
SWITCHGEAR & SWITCHBOARD APPARATUS
SWITCHGEAR & SWITCHGEAR ACCESS, NEC
SYNTHETIC RESIN FINISHED PRDTS, NEC
SYRUPS, FLAVORING, EXC DRINK
SYSTEMS ENGINEERING: Computer Related
SYSTEMS INTEGRATION SVCS: Local Area Network
SYSTEMS INTEGRATION SVCS: Office Computer Automation

T

TABLE OR COUNTERTOPS, PLASTIC LAMINATED
TAGS & LABELS: Paper
TAGS: Paper, Blank, Made From Purchased Paper
TANK & BOILER CLEANING SVCS
TANK COMPONENTS: Military, Specialized
TANK REPAIR & CLEANING SVCS
TANK REPAIR SVCS
TANK TOWERS: Metal Plate
TANKS & OTHER TRACKED VEHICLE CMPNTS
TANKS: For Tank Trucks, Metal Plate
TANKS: Fuel, Including Oil & Gas, Metal Plate
TANKS: Lined, Metal
TANKS: Plastic & Fiberglass
TANKS: Standard Or Custom Fabricated, Metal Plate
TANKS: Storage, Farm, Metal Plate
TANKS: Water, Metal Plate
TANNING SALONS
TAR
TARGET DRONES
TARPAULINS
TAX REFUND DISCOUNTING
TAX RETURN PREPARATION SVCS
TECHNICAL MANUAL PREPARATION SVCS
TELECOMMUNICATION SYSTEMS & EQPT
TELECOMMUNICATIONS CARRIERS & SVCS: Wireless
TELEPHONE EQPT INSTALLATION
TELEPHONE SVCS
TELEPHONE SWITCHING EQPT
TELEPHONE: Fiber Optic Systems
TELEVISION BROADCASTING & COMMUNICATIONS EQPT
TELEVISION SETS
TEMPORARY HELP SVCS
TERMITE CONTROL SVCS
TEST KITS: Pregnancy
TESTERS: Battery
TESTERS: Liquid, Exc Indl Process
TESTERS: Physical Property
TEXTILE & APPAREL SVCS

TEXTILE FABRICATORS
TEXTILE PRDTS: Hand Woven & Crocheted
TEXTILE: Finishing, Cotton Broadwoven
TEXTILES: Jute & Flax Prdts
TEXTILES: Linen Fabrics
TEXTILES: Mill Waste & Remnant
THERMITE
THREAD: Embroidery
TIE SHOPS
TILE: Brick & Structural, Clay
TILE: Clay, Roof
TIMBER DRIVING & BOOMING
TIMBER PRDTS WHOLESALERS
TIMING DEVICES: Electronic
TINCTURE OF IODINE
TINSEL
TINSMITHING, REPAIR WORK
TIRE DEALERS
TIRE INFLATORS: Hand Or Compressor Operated
TIRE SUNDRIES OR REPAIR MATERIALS: Rubber
TIRES & INNER TUBES
TIRES & TUBES WHOLESALERS
TIRES & TUBES, WHOLESALE: Truck
TIRES: Auto
TIRES: Cushion Or Solid Rubber
TIRES: Motorcycle, Pneumatic
TITANIUM MILL PRDTS
TITLE SEARCH COMPANIES
TOBACCO STORES & STANDS
TOBACCO: Chewing
TOBACCO: Chewing & Snuff
TOBACCO: Smoking
TOILET PREPARATIONS
TOILETS: Portable Chemical, Plastics
TOOL & DIE STEEL
TOOLS & EQPT: Used With Sporting Arms
TOOLS: Carpenters', Including Levels & Chisels, Exc Saws
TOOLS: Hand
TOOLS: Hand, Power
TOOLS: Hand, Shovels Or Spades
TOOTHBRUSHES: Exc Electric
TOWELS: Fabric & Nonwoven, Made From Purchased Materials
TOWERS, SECTIONS: Transmission, Radio & Television
TOYS
TOYS & HOBBY GOODS & SPLYS, WHOL: Toy Novelties & Amusements
TOYS & HOBBY GOODS & SPLYS, WHOLESALE: Board Games
TOYS, HOBBY GOODS & SPLYS WHOLESALERS
TOYS: Dolls, Stuffed Animals & Parts
TOYS: Kites
TOYS: Video Game Machines
TRACTOR REPAIR SVCS
TRAILERS & PARTS: Boat
TRAILERS & PARTS: Horse
TRAILERS & PARTS: Truck & Semi's
TRAILERS & TRAILER EQPT
TRAILERS OR VANS: Horse Transportation, Fifth-Wheel Type
TRAILERS: Bodies
TRAILERS: Demountable Cargo Containers
TRAILERS: House, Exc Permanent Dwellings
TRAILERS: Semitrailers, Truck Tractors
TRAILERS: Truck, Chassis
TRANS PROG REG & ADMIN, GOVT: Motor Vehicle Licensing & Insp
TRANSDUCERS: Electrical Properties
TRANSFORMERS: Power Related
TRANSFORMERS: Specialty
TRANSMISSIONS: Motor Vehicle
TRANSPORTATION EPQT & SPLYS, WHOL: Aircraft Engs/Eng Parts
TRANSPORTATION EQPT & SPLYS WHOLESALERS, NEC
TRANSPORTATION SVCS, NEC
TRANSPORTATION: Air, Nonscheduled, NEC
TRANSPORTATION: Local Passenger, NEC
TRAP ROCK: Dimension
TRAPS: Animal, Iron Or Steel
TRAVEL AGENCIES
TRAVEL TRAILERS & CAMPERS
TROPHIES, NEC
TROPHIES, SILVER
TROPHIES: Metal, Exc Silver
TROPHY & PLAQUE STORES
TRUCK & BUS BODIES: Ambulance

PRODUCT INDEX

TRUCK & BUS BODIES: Automobile Wrecker Truck
TRUCK & BUS BODIES: Car Carrier
TRUCK & BUS BODIES: Farm Truck
TRUCK & BUS BODIES: Garbage Or Refuse Truck
TRUCK & BUS BODIES: Tank Truck
TRUCK & BUS BODIES: Truck Beds
TRUCK & BUS BODIES: Truck Tops
TRUCK & BUS BODIES: Truck, Motor Vehicle
TRUCK BODIES: Body Parts
TRUCK GENERAL REPAIR SVC
TRUCK PAINTING & LETTERING SVCS
TRUCK PARTS & ACCESSORIES: Wholesalers
TRUCKING & HAULING SVCS: Animal & Farm Prdt
TRUCKING & HAULING SVCS: Building Materials
TRUCKING & HAULING SVCS: Contract Basis
TRUCKING & HAULING SVCS: Heavy, NEC
TRUCKING & HAULING SVCS: Liquid Petroleum, Exc Local
TRUCKING & HAULING SVCS: Liquid, Local
TRUCKING & HAULING SVCS: Lumber & Timber
TRUCKING & HAULING SVCS: Petroleum, Local
TRUCKING, AUTOMOBILE CARRIER
TRUCKING, DUMP
TRUCKING: Except Local
TRUCKING: Local, With Storage
TRUCKING: Local, Without Storage
TRUCKS & TRACTORS: Industrial
TRUCKS: Forklift
TRUCKS: Indl
TRUNKS
TRUSSES & FRAMING: Prefabricated Metal
TRUSSES: Wood, Floor
TRUSSES: Wood, Roof
TUB CONTAINERS: Plastic
TUBE & TUBING FABRICATORS
TUBES: Boiler, Wrought
TUBES: Finned, For Heat Transfer
TUBES: Fins
TUBES: Paper
TUBES: Steel & Iron
TUBING: Copper
TUBING: Seamless
TURBINES & TURBINE GENERATOR SET UNITS: Gas, Complete
TURBINES & TURBINE GENERATOR SETS
TURBINES: Hydraulic, Complete
TYPESETTING SVC

U

UNIFORM STORES
UNISEX HAIR SALONS
UNIVERSITY
UNSUPPORTED PLASTICS: Floor Or Wall Covering
UPHOLSTERY WORK SVCS
URNS: Cut Stone
USED CAR DEALERS
USED MERCHANDISE STORES
UTILITY TRAILER DEALERS

V

VACUUM CLEANERS: Household
VACUUM CLEANERS: Indl Type
VALUE-ADDED RESELLERS: Computer Systems
VALVE REPAIR SVCS, INDL
VALVES
VALVES & PIPE FITTINGS

VALVES & REGULATORS: Pressure, Indl
VALVES: Aerosol, Metal
VALVES: Aircraft, Hydraulic
VALVES: Fluid Power, Control, Hydraulic & pneumatic
VALVES: Indl
VALVES: Plumbing & Heating
VAN CONVERSIONS
VAN CONVERSIONS
VARIETY STORES
VASES: Pottery
VAULTS & SAFES WHOLESALERS
VEHICLES: All Terrain
VEHICLES: Recreational
VENDING MACHINE OPERATORS: Sandwich & Hot Food
VENDING MACHINE REPAIR SVCS
VENDING MACHINES & PARTS
VENTILATING EQPT: Metal
VENTILATING EQPT: Sheet Metal
VENTURE CAPITAL COMPANIES
VESSELS: Process, Indl, Metal Plate
VIDEO & AUDIO EQPT, WHOLESALE
VIDEO CAMERA-AUDIO RECORDERS: Household Use
VIDEO EQPT
VOCATIONAL REHABILITATION AGENCY
VOCATIONAL TRAINING AGENCY

W

WAREHOUSING & STORAGE FACILITIES, NEC
WAREHOUSING & STORAGE, REFRIGERATED: Cold Storage Or Refrig
WAREHOUSING & STORAGE, REFRIGERATED: Frozen Or Refrig Goods
WAREHOUSING & STORAGE: Farm Prdts
WAREHOUSING & STORAGE: General
WAREHOUSING & STORAGE: General
WAREHOUSING & STORAGE: Miniwarehouse
WAREHOUSING & STORAGE: Oil & Gasoline, Caverns For Hire
WARFARE COUNTER-MEASURE EQPT
WARM AIR HEATING & AC EQPT & SPLYS, WHOLESALE Furnaces
WASHERS
WASTE CLEANING SVCS
WATCHES & PARTS, WHOLESALE
WATER HEATERS WHOLESALERS EXCEPT ELECTRIC
WATER SOFTENING WHOLESALERS
WATER SUPPLY
WATER TREATMENT EQPT: Indl
WATER: Distilled
WATER: Pasteurized & Mineral, Bottled & Canned
WATER: Pasteurized, Canned & Bottled, Etc
WAVEGUIDE STRUCTURES: Accelerating
WAX REMOVERS
WAXES: Mineral, Natural
WAXES: Petroleum, Not Produced In Petroleum Refineries
WEATHER STRIPS: Metal
WELDING & CUTTING APPARATUS & ACCESS, NEC
WELDING EQPT
WELDING EQPT & SPLYS WHOLESALERS
WELDING EQPT & SPLYS: Electrodes
WELDING EQPT & SPLYS: Generators, Arc Welding, AC & DC
WELDING EQPT & SPLYS: Resistance, Electric
WELDING EQPT & SPLYS: Spot, Electric
WELDING EQPT: Electric

WELDING MACHINES & EQPT: Ultrasonic
WELDING REPAIR SVC
WELDING SPLYS, EXC GASES: Wholesalers
WELDMENTS
WELL LOGGING EQPT
WESTERN APPAREL STORES
WHEELBARROWS
WHEELCHAIR LIFTS
WHEELCHAIRS
WHEELS: Current Collector, Trolley Rigging
WHEY: Raw, Liquid
WHISTLES
WIGS & HAIRPIECES
WINCHES
WINDMILLS: Electric Power Generation
WINDMILLS: Farm Type
WINDOW & DOOR FRAMES
WINDOW CLEANING SVCS
WINDOW FRAMES & SASHES: Plastic
WINDOW FRAMES, MOLDING & TRIM: Vinyl
WINDSHIELDS: Plastic
WINE & DISTILLED ALCOHOLIC BEVERAGES WHOLESALERS
WINE CELLARS, BONDED: Wine, Blended
WIRE
WIRE & CABLE: Aluminum
WIRE & WIRE PRDTS
WIRE CLOTH & WOVEN WIRE PRDTS, MADE FROM PURCHASED WIRE
WIRE MATERIALS: Steel
WIRE PRDTS: Steel & Iron
WOMEN'S & CHILDREN'S CLOTHING WHOLESALERS, NEC
WOMEN'S & GIRLS' SPORTSWEAR WHOLESALERS
WOMEN'S CLOTHING STORES
WOMEN'S CLOTHING STORES: Ready-To-Wear
WOOD CARVINGS, WHOLESALE
WOOD CHIPS, PRODUCED AT THE MILL
WOOD PRDTS
WOOD PRDTS: Applicators
WOOD PRDTS: Baskets, Fruit & Veg, Round Stave, Till, Etc
WOOD PRDTS: Flagpoles
WOOD PRDTS: Knobs
WOOD PRDTS: Laundry
WOOD PRDTS: Moldings, Unfinished & Prefinished
WOOD PRDTS: Panel Work
WOOD PRDTS: Porch Columns
WOOD PRDTS: Porch Work
WOOD PRDTS: Saddle Trees
WOOD PRDTS: Signboards
WOOD PRDTS: Trophy Bases
WOOD PRODUCTS: Reconstituted
WOOD SHAVINGS BALES, MULCH TYPE, WHOLESALE
WOOD TREATING: Structural Lumber & Timber
WOODWORK: Carved & Turned
WOODWORK: Interior & Ornamental, NEC
WOODWORK: Ornamental, Cornices, Mantels, Etc.
WOVEN WIRE PRDTS, NEC
WREATHS: Artificial

X

X-RAY EQPT & TUBES

Y

YARN: Embroidery, Spun

PRODUCT SECTION

Product category — **BOXES: Folding**
Edgar & Son Paperboard ....G...... 999 999-9999
  Yourtown *(G-11480)*
Ready Box Co............................E...... 999 999-9999
  Anytown *(G-7097)*
City

Indicates approximate employment figure
A = Over 500 employees, B = 251-500
C = 101-250, D = 51-100, E = 20-50
F = 10-19, G = 1-9
Business phone
Geographic Section entry number where full company information appears.

See footnotes for symbols and codes identification.
• Refer to the Industrial Product Index preceding this section to locate product headings.

ABRASIVES
Jesco Products Inc ....G...... 405 943-1721
  Oklahoma City *(G-6358)*
Sunbelt Industries Inc ....G...... 405 843-1275
  Oklahoma City *(G-7225)*

ACADEMY
2011 Ussa Limited Partnership ....F...... 918 948-7856
  Tulsa *(G-9055)*
Leadership Training Academy ....G...... 405 551-8059
  Edmond *(G-2484)*

ACCELERATORS: Particle, High Voltage
Amt Diversified Cnstr Inc ....G...... 580 279-6250
  Ada *(G-8)*

ACCOUNTING MACHINES & CASH REGISTERS
Campaign Technologies Professi ....G...... 405 286-2686
  Oklahoma City *(G-5681)*

ACCOUNTING SVCS: Certified Public
Wentworth Operating Co ....F...... 405 341-6122
  Oklahoma City *(G-7435)*

ACIDS: Hydrochloric
B & B Hydroseeding LLC ....F...... 580 883-5997
  Ringwood *(G-8084)*
Brainerd Chemical Midwest LLC ....G...... 918 622-1214
  Tulsa *(G-9330)*

ACIDS: Hydrofluoric
Acid Specialists LLC ....G...... 432 617-2243
  Oklahoma City *(G-5366)*

ACIDS: Inorganic
Edc AG Products Company LLC ....D...... 405 235-4546
  Oklahoma City *(G-6008)*
El Dorado Chemical Company ....G...... 405 235-4546
  Oklahoma City *(G-6015)*
Tronox LLC ....A...... 405 775-5000
  Oklahoma City *(G-7340)*
Tronox Worldwide LLC ....F...... 405 775-5000
  Oklahoma City *(G-7343)*

ACIDS: Nitric
LSB Chemical LLC ....F...... 405 235-4546
  Oklahoma City *(G-6498)*

ACIDS: Sulfuric, Oleum
LSB Chemical LLC ....F...... 405 235-4546
  Oklahoma City *(G-6498)*
Peak Sulfur Inc ....C...... 918 587-7613
  Tulsa *(G-10480)*
Tronox US Holdings Inc ....E...... 405 775-5000
  Oklahoma City *(G-7342)*

ADDITIVE BASED PLASTIC MATERIALS: Plasticizers
Rapid Application Group LLC ....G...... 918 760-1242
  Broken Arrow *(G-1021)*

ADHESIVES
Self-Suspending Proppant LLC ....E...... 580 456-7791
  Roff *(G-8111)*
Versum Materials Us LLC ....E...... 918 379-7101
  Catoosa *(G-1363)*

ADHESIVES & SEALANTS
Appli-Fab Custom Coating ....G...... 405 235-7039
  Chandler *(G-1375)*
CRC Evans Weighting Systems ....G...... 918 438-2100
  Tulsa *(G-9503)*
Henley Sealants Inc ....G...... 405 235-7325
  Oklahoma City *(G-6240)*
Line X Prtctive Ctngs Okla LLC ....F...... 405 232-4994
  Oklahoma City *(G-6479)*
National Coating Mfg Inc ....F...... 580 332-8751
  Ada *(G-70)*
Seal Support Systems Inc ....F...... 918 258-6484
  Broken Arrow *(G-1046)*

ADHESIVES: Adhesives, paste
Tile Shop LLC ....F...... 580 920-1570
  Durant *(G-2269)*

ADHESIVES: Epoxy
Havard Industries LLC ....G...... 405 888-0961
  Edmond *(G-2453)*
Mito Material Solutions Inc ....G...... 855 344-6486
  Stillwater *(G-8725)*

ADULT DAYCARE CENTERS
Think Ability Inc ....C...... 580 252-8000
  Duncan *(G-2187)*

ADVERTISING AGENCIES
AAA Sign & Supply Co ....G...... 918 622-7883
  Tulsa *(G-9078)*
Comanche Bit Service Inc ....G...... 580 439-6424
  Comanche *(G-1836)*
Dancey-Meador Publishing Co ....G...... 580 762-9359
  Ponca City *(G-7819)*
Humps N Horns Bull Riding News ....G...... 918 872-9713
  Broken Arrow *(G-932)*

ADVERTISING AGENCIES: Consultants
Christy Collins Inc ....G...... 580 305-0001
  Frederick *(G-3192)*

ADVERTISING DISPLAY PRDTS
Just Dough It LLC ....G...... 918 455-0770
  Broken Arrow *(G-952)*

ADVERTISING MATERIAL DISTRIBUTION
Community Racks LLC ....F...... 405 210-7950
  Yukon *(G-11709)*

ADVERTISING REPRESENTATIVES: Electronic Media
Oklahoma Eagle LLC ....G...... 918 582-7124
  Tulsa *(G-10398)*

ADVERTISING REPRESENTATIVES: Magazine
Oklahoma Magazine ....F...... 918 744-6205
  Tulsa *(G-10402)*

ADVERTISING REPRESENTATIVES: Newspaper
Cache Times ....G...... 580 429-8200
  Cache *(G-1225)*
Cnhi LLC ....E...... 405 341-2121
  Edmond *(G-2359)*
Newspaper Holding Inc ....E...... 918 341-1101
  Claremore *(G-1661)*
Northern Arizona Newspaper ....F...... 928 524-6203
  Edmond *(G-2540)*

ADVERTISING REPRESENTATIVES: Television & Radio Time Sales
Sariel Inc ....G...... 918 855-1400
  Tulsa *(G-10709)*

ADVERTISING SPECIALTIES, WHOLESALE
A-1 Specialties ....G...... 405 942-1341
  Oklahoma City *(G-5352)*
Corser Group Inc ....G...... 918 749-6456
  Tulsa *(G-9492)*
Dearinger Printing & Trophy ....F...... 405 372-5503
  Stillwater *(G-8675)*
First Thought Inc ....G...... 918 336-3322
  Bartlesville *(G-483)*
Graphix Xpress ....G...... 580 765-7324
  Ponca City *(G-7831)*
Initially Yours Inc ....G...... 918 832-9889
  Tulsa *(G-9986)*
J W Companies ....G...... 405 789-2460
  Bethany *(G-584)*
Oklahoma Promo LLC ....G...... 918 248-8145
  Jenks *(G-3719)*
Robyn Holdings LLC ....E...... 405 722-4600
  Oklahoma City *(G-7041)*
TGI Enterprises Inc ....E...... 918 835-4330
  Tulsa *(G-10924)*
Townsend Marketing Inc ....G...... 918 496-9222
  Bixby *(G-666)*
Walker Stamp & Seal Co ....E...... 405 235-5319
  Oklahoma City *(G-7415)*

ADVERTISING SVCS, NEC
American Tradition ....G...... 918 688-7725
  Tulsa *(G-9174)*

ADVERTISING SVCS: Billboards
Clear Channel Outdoor Inc ....E...... 405 528-2683
  Oklahoma City *(G-5781)*
Kaiser Sign & Graphics Co Inc ....G...... 580 772-3880
  Weatherford *(G-11423)*
Keleher Outdoor Advertising Co ....F...... 918 333-8855
  Bartlesville *(G-502)*
Stokely Outdoor Advertising ....E...... 918 664-4724
  Tulsa *(G-10852)*

ADVERTISING SVCS: Direct Mail
262 LLC ....F...... 918 458-5511
  Tahlequah *(G-8848)*
Worldwide Printing & Dist Inc ....C...... 918 295-0112
  Tulsa *(G-11154)*

ADVERTISING SVCS: Display
Delson Properties Ltd ....D...... 405 262-5005
  El Reno *(G-2711)*

ADVERTISING SVCS: Outdoor

Oklahoma Logo Signs Inc .... G 405 840-1550
Oklahoma City *(G-6753)*
Osborne Design Co .... G 918 585-3212
Tulsa *(G-10444)*
R & R Signs Inc .... G 580 924-4363
Durant *(G-2250)*
Sidewinder Signs .... G 918 647-5306
Poteau *(G-7913)*

AEROBIC DANCE & EXERCISE CLASSES

Montross Tirita .... G 918 241-5637
Sand Springs *(G-8207)*

AGENTS, BROKERS & BUREAUS: Personal Service

Flir Systems Inc .... F 405 372-9535
Stillwater *(G-8692)*
Scott Manufacturing LLC .... E 405 949-2728
Oklahoma City *(G-7096)*

AGRICULTURAL DISINFECTANTS

Integrity Tech & Svcs LLC .... G 405 482-9206
Edmond *(G-2462)*

AGRICULTURAL EQPT: BARN, SILO, POULTRY, DAIRY/LIVESTOCK MACH

W Flying Inc .... F 580 623-5566
Watonga *(G-11351)*

AGRICULTURAL EQPT: Elevators, Farm

Forster & Son Inc .... G 580 332-6020
Ada *(G-36)*

AGRICULTURAL EQPT: Fertilizing Machinery

Wako LLC .... E 580 234-3434
Enid *(G-3072)*

AGRICULTURAL EQPT: Fertilizng, Sprayng, Dustng/Irrigatn Mach

Allied H2o Inc .... G 405 550-3085
Edmond *(G-2296)*

AGRICULTURAL EQPT: Greens Mowing Eqpt

Ritberger Inc .... G 918 271-3895
Broken Arrow *(G-1033)*

AGRICULTURAL EQPT: Grounds Mowing Eqpt

Kelly Labs .... G 682 367-8743
Longdale *(G-4125)*
Sullivans Grading & Sod .... G 580 591-2868
Lawton *(G-4007)*

AGRICULTURAL EQPT: Harvesters, Fruit, Vegetable, Tobacco

Heather Harjochee .... G 405 615-3273
Oklahoma City *(G-5293)*
Michael R Williams .... G 918 418-9344
Vinita *(G-11264)*
Savage Equipment Incorporated .... E 580 795-3394
Madill *(G-4162)*

AGRICULTURAL EQPT: Storage Bins, Crop

Heavybilt Mfg Inc .... D 580 927-3003
Coalgate *(G-1781)*

AGRICULTURAL EQPT: Tractors, Farm

Blue River Ventures Inc .... G 580 920-0111
Durant *(G-2206)*
Blue River Ventures Inc .... G 580 920-0111
Calera *(G-1238)*

AGRICULTURAL EQPT: Trailers & Wagons, Farm

Cardon Trailers .... G 580 327-0701
Alva *(G-180)*

AGRICULTURAL EQPT: Turf & Grounds Eqpt

Buster Par Corp .... F 918 585-8542
Tulsa *(G-9354)*
Murphy Products Inc .... G 405 842-7177
Oklahoma City *(G-6636)*

AGRICULTURAL MACHINERY & EQPT REPAIR

Built Better Enterprises LLC .... G 580 492-5227
Fletcher *(G-3161)*
Norman Koehn .... G 580 852-3260
Helena *(G-3436)*

AGRICULTURAL MACHINERY & EQPT: Wholesalers

Bob Lowe Farm Machinery Inc ...... F 405 224-6500
Chickasha *(G-1440)*
Lanco Services LLC .... E 580 429-6526
Cache *(G-1229)*

AIR CLEANING SYSTEMS

Andreae Team Inc .... F 580 223-9334
Ardmore *(G-241)*

AIR CONDITIONING & VENTILATION EQPT & SPLYS: Wholesales

Dallas Hermetic Company Inc .... F 214 634-1744
Oklahoma City *(G-5892)*

AIR CONDITIONING EQPT

Air System Components Inc .... B 580 762-7521
Ponca City *(G-7794)*
C&D Valve LLC .... E 405 843-5621
Oklahoma City *(G-5663)*
Climacool Corp .... F 405 815-3000
Oklahoma City *(G-5785)*
Nortek Air Solutions LLC .... D 405 594-2811
Oklahoma City *(G-6687)*

AIR CONDITIONING UNITS: Complete, Domestic Or Indl

Aaon Inc .... G 918 583-2266
Tulsa *(G-9079)*
Everest Acqsition Holdings Inc ...... F 918 770-7190
Tulsa *(G-9709)*
Nortek Air Solutions LLC .... B 405 525-6546
Oklahoma City *(G-6686)*
Nortek Air Solutions LLC .... E 405 263-7286
Okarche *(G-5247)*
Temtrol Inc .... E 405 263-7286
Okarche *(G-5254)*
York International Corporation ...... D 405 364-4040
Norman *(G-5204)*

AIR COOLERS: Metal Plate

Cooling Products Inc .... E 918 251-8588
Broken Arrow *(G-878)*
Fin-X Inc .... E 918 272-9546
Owasso *(G-7569)*
Harsco Industrial Hammco LLC .... D 918 619-8000
Tulsa *(G-9900)*
World Wide Exchangers Inc .... F 918 240-3193
Sapulpa *(G-8327)*

AIR POLLUTION CONTROL EQPT & SPLYS WHOLESALERS

AC Systems Integration Inc .... E 918 259-0020
Tulsa *(G-9084)*

AIR TRAFFIC CONTROL SYSTEMS & EQPT

Solar View LLC .... G 918 366-6413
Bixby *(G-660)*

AIRCRAFT & AEROSPACE FLIGHT INSTRUMENTS & GUIDANCE SYSTEMS

Design Intelligence Inc LLC .... G 405 307-0397
Noble *(G-4878)*
Northrop Grumman Systems Corp .. D 405 739-7875
Oklahoma City *(G-6689)*
Oklahoma Aerospace Alliance 918 527-0980
Tulsa *(G-10394)*

Omada International LLC .... C 405 495-2131
Oklahoma City *(G-6774)*

AIRCRAFT & HEAVY EQPT REPAIR SVCS

Aero Component Repair LLC .... F 580 924-7999
Durant *(G-2200)*
Dixon Auto Engine Machine Shop .. G 918 256-6780
Vinita *(G-11254)*
Helicomb International Inc .... D 918 835-3999
Tulsa *(G-9911)*
Honeywell Aerospace Tulsa/Lori ... D 918 272-4574
Tulsa *(G-9945)*

AIRCRAFT ASSEMBLY PLANTS

A&M Aerospace LLC .... G 405 323-6428
Harrah *(G-3373)*
Aerocore X LLC .... C 405 669-8655
Del City *(G-1994)*
AP Jetworks LLC .... G 405 226-2583
Edmond *(G-2305)*
Ases LLC .... C 405 219-3400
Oklahoma City *(G-5474)*
Black River Aerospace LLC .... G 386 212-3741
Moore *(G-4499)*
Boeing Arospc Operations Inc ...... F 405 610-3100
Oklahoma City *(G-5606)*
Boeing Arospc Operations Inc ...... A 580 481-3306
Altus *(G-145)*
Boeing Arospc Operations Inc ...... D 580 480-4040
Altus *(G-146)*
Boeing Company .... A 405 622-6000
Oklahoma City *(G-5607)*
Boeing Company .... A 405 622-6206
Oklahoma City *(G-5609)*
Boeing Company .... G 405 618-2859
Oklahoma City *(G-5611)*
Boeing Company .... G 918 292-2707
Tulsa *(G-9316)*
Boeing Company .... F 316 526-3272
Oklahoma City *(G-5612)*
Concept Aircraft LLC .... G 405 620-1701
Edmond *(G-2364)*
CP Aerospace LLC .... G 580 355-5064
Lawton *(G-3912)*
Don L Gerbrandt .... G 580 234-3247
Enid *(G-2943)*
Eaglecrest Aviation LLC .... G 918 249-0980
Broken Arrow *(G-893)*
Ferra Aerospace Inc .... G 918 787-2220
Grove *(G-3269)*
Greenwood Group Inc .... G 580 762-2580
Ponca City *(G-7832)*
GS Restoration Services Inc .... G 918 408-2848
Tulsa *(G-9866)*
Helicomb International Inc .... D 918 835-3999
Tulsa *(G-9911)*
J Stephens LLC .... G 918 299-2900
Tulsa *(G-10023)*
Lockheed Martin .... G 405 606-3988
Oklahoma City *(G-6486)*
Lockheed Martin Corporation .... G 580 357-5060
Lawton *(G-3965)*
Moog Inc .... G 405 732-0009
Midwest City *(G-4448)*
Nicola Acquisitions LLC .... G 405 224-0061
Chickasha *(G-1492)*
Nolan Avionics LLC .... G 580 924-5507
Durant *(G-2245)*
Nordam Group LLC .... C 918 274-2742
Tulsa *(G-10356)*
Northrop Grumman Systems Corp .. C 405 733-1208
Oklahoma City *(G-6691)*
Onefire Aerospace Services .... F 918 794-8804
Jenks *(G-3720)*
Red Falcon LLC 580 647-2152
Lawton *(G-3990)*
Rise Manufacturing LLC .... E 918 994-6240
Broken Arrow *(G-1032)*
Skybird Sales Inc .... G 580 772-5100
Weatherford *(G-11443)*
Solid Path Services .... G 918 384-7409
Tulsa *(G-10784)*
Sparks Aerospace LLC .... G 580 234-7972
Enid *(G-3060)*
Tellico Engineering Services .... G 918 384-7409
Tulsa *(G-10919)*
Vertiprime Government Svcs LLC .. G 844 474-2600
Duncan *(G-2192)*
Wrangler Aviation Corp .... G 405 364-5700
Norman *(G-5202)*

PRODUCT SECTION

AIRCRAFT PARTS & AUXILIARY EQPT: Wing Assemblies & Parts

Yankee Pacific Aerospace Inc ....G....... 918 388-5940
  Tulsa *(G-11167)*

AIRCRAFT CONTROL SYSTEMS:

Coorstek ....G....... 800 821-6110
  Oklahoma City *(G-5831)*

AIRCRAFT DEALERS

Eaglecrest Aviation LLC ....G....... 918 249-0980
  Broken Arrow *(G-893)*
Tk Aero Inc ....G....... 405 359-8638
  Edmond *(G-2645)*

AIRCRAFT ELECTRICAL EQPT REPAIR SVCS

Unicorp Systems Inc ....E....... 918 446-1874
  Tulsa *(G-11034)*

AIRCRAFT ENG/ENG PART: Extrnl Pwr Unt, Hand Inertia Starter

Randy Mulkey ....G....... 405 258-2600
  Wellston *(G-11475)*

AIRCRAFT ENGINES & ENGINE PARTS: Air Scoops

Airflow Solutions LLC ....E....... 918 574-2748
  Tulsa *(G-9129)*
Ases LLC ....C....... 405 219-3420
  Oklahoma City *(G-5473)*
Ases LLC ....C....... 405 219-3400
  Oklahoma City *(G-5474)*

AIRCRAFT ENGINES & ENGINE PARTS: Exhaust Systems

Wall Colmonoy Corporation ....E....... 405 672-1361
  Oklahoma City *(G-7417)*

AIRCRAFT ENGINES & ENGINE PARTS: Jet Asstd Takeoff Devices

Nordam Group LLC ....B....... 918 476-8338
  Tulsa *(G-10358)*

AIRCRAFT ENGINES & ENGINE PARTS: Mount Parts

Spirit Arosystems Holdings Inc ....G....... 918 832-2891
  Tulsa *(G-10822)*
Spirit Arosystems Holdings Inc ....F....... 918 832-2131
  Tulsa *(G-10823)*

AIRCRAFT ENGINES & ENGINE PARTS: Research & Development, Mfr

Baker Hughes A GE Company LLC ....G....... 518 387-7914
  Oklahoma City *(G-5514)*
Cherokee Insights LLC ....G....... 918 430-3409
  Tulsa *(G-9413)*
Dii LLC ....G....... 405 514-7365
  Purcell *(G-8005)*

AIRCRAFT ENGINES & ENGINE PARTS: Rocket Motors

Energetic Materials ....G....... 405 203-2859
  Nichols Hills *(G-4860)*

AIRCRAFT ENGINES & PARTS

Abbott Industries Inc ....D....... 918 756-8320
  Okmulgee *(G-7492)*
Aero Component Repair LLC ....F....... 580 924-7999
  Durant *(G-2200)*
AGC Manufacturing Inc ....G....... 918 258-2506
  Tulsa *(G-9116)*
Aircraft Specialties Svc Inc ....E....... 918 836-6872
  Tulsa *(G-9125)*
American Airlines Inc ....A....... 918 292-2698
  Tulsa *(G-9163)*
Barrett Performance Aircraft ....G....... 918 835-1089
  Tulsa *(G-9266)*
Barrett Precision Engines Inc ....G....... 918 835-1089
  Tulsa *(G-9267)*
Get Threaded LLC ....G....... 918 943-6156
  Tulsa *(G-9823)*

Green Cntry Arcft Exhaust Inc ....E....... 918 832-1769
  Tulsa *(G-9857)*
Green Country Aircraft LLC ....G....... 918 832-1769
  Tulsa *(G-9860)*
H&H Aircraft Inc ....G....... 405 833-3330
  Oklahoma City *(G-6200)*
Honeywell Aerospace Tulsa/Lori ....D....... 918 272-4574
  Tulsa *(G-9945)*
Honeywell International Inc ....A....... 405 605-0101
  Oklahoma City *(G-6261)*
J & C Enterprises Aviation ....G....... 580 661-3591
  Thomas *(G-8944)*
Kyra Guffey LLC ....G....... 210 867-1374
  Mannford *(G-4185)*
Limco Airepair Inc ....D....... 918 445-4300
  Tulsa *(G-10161)*
Micco Aircraft Company Inc ....E....... 918 336-4700
  Oklahoma City *(G-6586)*
Mint Turbines LLC ....E....... 918 968-9561
  Stroud *(G-8814)*
Mission Transportation LLC ....D....... 405 694-4755
  Bethany *(G-591)*
Nordam Group Inc ....E....... 918 878-8962
  Tulsa *(G-10351)*
Nordam Group LLC ....A....... 918 878-4000
  Tulsa *(G-10354)*
Orizon Arstrctres - Owasso Inc ....B....... 918 274-9094
  Owasso *(G-7599)*
Orizon Arstrctures - Grove Inc ....D....... 918 786-9094
  Grove *(G-3284)*
Padgett Machine Shop LLC ....G....... 918 636-9334
  Tulsa *(G-10456)*
Pratt Whtney Mltary Aftrmrket ....G....... 405 622-2561
  Oklahoma City *(G-6875)*
Pratt Whtney Mltary Aftrmrket ....G....... 405 737-4851
  Oklahoma City *(G-6876)*
PSI Mnfacturing Operations LLC ....G....... 561 747-6107
  Midwest City *(G-4450)*
Radial Engines Ltd ....F....... 405 433-2263
  Guthrie *(G-3334)*
Rival Innvtion Surfc Engrg LLC ....G....... 918 978-7001
  Claremore *(G-1683)*
S&J Manufacturing Inc ....G....... 918 636-1224
  Skiatook *(G-8567)*
Shoulders International ....G....... 918 728-2999
  Tulsa *(G-10751)*
Tornado Alley Turbo Inc ....D....... 580 332-3510
  Ada *(G-95)*
Triumph Arstrctres - Tulsa LLC ....A....... 615 361-2061
  Tulsa *(G-10978)*
U T C Pratt & Whitney Okla Cy ....E....... 405 455-2001
  Tinker Afb *(G-8956)*
Whitney Pratt ....G....... 405 610-2612
  Oklahoma City *(G-7448)*

AIRCRAFT HANGAR OPERATION SVCS

Airelectric Inc ....E....... 918 291-7531
  Tulsa *(G-9127)*

AIRCRAFT MAINTENANCE & REPAIR SVCS

Ases LLC ....C....... 405 219-3400
  Oklahoma City *(G-5474)*
Limco-Piedmont Inc ....F....... 918 445-4300
  Tulsa *(G-10162)*
Mission Transportation LLC ....D....... 405 694-4755
  Bethany *(G-591)*
Powerhouse Resources Intl Inc ....D....... 405 232-7474
  Oklahoma City *(G-6870)*

AIRCRAFT PARTS & AUXILIARY EQPT: Accumulators, Propeller

Aircraft Structures Intl Corp ....E....... 580 242-5907
  Enid *(G-2908)*
North Amrcn Arspc Holdings LLC ....D....... 316 644-2553
  Enid *(G-3020)*

AIRCRAFT PARTS & AUXILIARY EQPT: Aircraft Training Eqpt

Aviation Training Devices Inc ....F....... 918 366-6680
  Bixby *(G-613)*
Newton Design LLC ....D....... 918 266-6205
  Catoosa *(G-1343)*
Newton Design LLC ....G....... 918 381-3012
  Catoosa *(G-1344)*

AIRCRAFT PARTS & AUXILIARY EQPT: Assys, Subassemblies/Parts

AAR Aircraft Services Inc ....E....... 405 681-3000
  Oklahoma City *(G-5356)*
Accurate Machine Works Inc ....F....... 405 615-4983
  Blanchard *(G-700)*
Accurus Aerospace Tulsa LLC ....C....... 918 438-3121
  Tulsa *(G-9092)*
Apex Composites Inc ....D....... 580 436-6444
  Ada *(G-9)*
Ices Corporation ....E....... 918 358-5446
  Cleveland *(G-1724)*
Starline Inc ....F....... 405 495-8274
  Bethany *(G-596)*
Stewart Industries Intl LLC ....F....... 405 260-0990
  Guthrie *(G-3339)*
Zivko Aeronautics Inc ....G....... 405 282-1330
  Guthrie *(G-3343)*

AIRCRAFT PARTS & AUXILIARY EQPT: Bodies

Advanced Aerial Services LLC ....G....... 580 571-1980
  Woodward *(G-11553)*
Nordam Group LLC ....A....... 918 878-4000
  Tulsa *(G-10354)*
VIP Manufacturing Corporation ....G....... 918 244-2131
  Bluejacket *(G-746)*

AIRCRAFT PARTS & AUXILIARY EQPT: Body & Wing Assys & Parts

Aero-TEC Industries Inc ....G....... 405 382-8501
  Seminole *(G-8353)*
Primus International Inc ....C....... 918 836-6317
  Tulsa *(G-10560)*
Triumph Arstrctres - Tulsa LLC ....A....... 615 361-2061
  Tulsa *(G-10978)*
Valco Inc ....E....... 405 228-0932
  Oklahoma City *(G-7386)*

AIRCRAFT PARTS & AUXILIARY EQPT: Body Assemblies & Parts

Dusters & Sprayers Supply Inc ....F....... 405 224-1201
  Chickasha *(G-1455)*

AIRCRAFT PARTS & AUXILIARY EQPT: Fins

Ases LLC ....C....... 405 219-3400
  Oklahoma City *(G-5474)*

AIRCRAFT PARTS & AUXILIARY EQPT: Gears, Power Transmission

Smooth Landings LLC ....G....... 405 422-1822
  El Reno *(G-2758)*

AIRCRAFT PARTS & AUXILIARY EQPT: Military Eqpt & Armament

Ases LLC ....C....... 405 219-3420
  Oklahoma City *(G-5473)*
Cherokee Nation Red Wing LLC ....E....... 918 430-3437
  Tulsa *(G-9414)*
Kemmerlys Air Plus ....G....... 405 348-2154
  Edmond *(G-2479)*
Liberty Partners Inc ....F....... 918 756-6474
  Okmulgee *(G-7513)*
Tinker Afb ....G....... 405 739-2349
  Tinker Afb *(G-8955)*

AIRCRAFT PARTS & AUXILIARY EQPT: Refueling Eqpt, In Flight

Magnum Aero Inc ....G....... 918 357-2376
  Broken Arrow *(G-1140)*

AIRCRAFT PARTS & AUXILIARY EQPT: Research & Development, Mfr

Archein Aerospace LLC ....E....... 682 499-2150
  Ponca City *(G-7798)*

AIRCRAFT PARTS & AUXILIARY EQPT: Wing Assemblies & Parts

Two Creeks Fabrication ....G....... 505 999-8798
  Newalla *(G-4817)*

Employee Codes: A=Over 500 employees, B=251-500
C=101-250, D=51-100, E=20-50, F=10-19, G=1-9

AIRCRAFT PARTS & EQPT, NEC

AIRCRAFT PARTS & EQPT, NEC

Company		Phone
AAR Aircraft Services Inc	G	405 218-3393
Oklahoma City *(G-5357)*		
Accurus Aerospace Corporation	G	918 438-3121
Tulsa *(G-9091)*		
Aero Automation LLC	F	918 251-0987
Broken Arrow *(G-817)*		
Aero Component Repair LLC	F	580 924-7999
Durant *(G-2200)*		
Aero Solutions and Services	G	405 308-6788
Edmond *(G-2291)*		
Aerocorp International Lc	G	405 317-5844
Oklahoma City *(G-5392)*		
Aerospace Products SE Inc	F	405 213-1034
Oklahoma City *(G-5393)*		
Aerospace Training	G	405 253-8343
Oklahoma City *(G-5394)*		
Aerospace Training Sy	G	405 253-8343
Norman *(G-4902)*		
Aerostar International Inc	G	918 789-3000
Chelsea *(G-1401)*		
Aircraft Power Service Inc	G	405 379-2407
Holdenville *(G-3549)*		
Aircraft Systems	G	918 388-5943
Tulsa *(G-9126)*		
Airofab Ltd Co	G	918 693-1230
Talala *(G-8895)*		
ARINC Incorporated	F	405 601-6000
Oklahoma City *(G-5463)*		
Arrowprop Inc	G	405 279-3833
Meeker *(G-4375)*		
Asco Aerospace Usa LLC	C	405 533-5800
Stillwater *(G-8655)*		
B & C Machine Company Inc	F	405 787-8862
Oklahoma City *(G-5500)*		
Baron Manufacturing Inc	G	405 947-3362
Oklahoma City *(G-5528)*		
Bm	G	405 388-3999
Choctaw *(G-1532)*		
Boeing Company	A	918 835-3111
Tulsa *(G-9315)*		
Cat-Eyes Drone Imagery Svc LLC	G	918 344-8324
Tulsa *(G-9388)*		
Cherokee Nation Businesses LLC	B	918 384-7474
Catoosa *(G-1310)*		
Chromalloy Gas Turbine LLC	C	845 359-4700
Oklahoma City *(G-5764)*		
Cni Aviation Advantage A Joi	G	405 253-8200
Norman *(G-4961)*		
Csi Aerospace Inc	D	918 258-1290
Broken Arrow *(G-880)*		
Cymstar LLC	C	918 251-8100
Broken Arrow *(G-884)*		
D C Jones Machine Co	G	918 786-6855
Grove *(G-3265)*		
Davis Thorpe Co LLC	G	405 585-9823
Moore *(G-4514)*		
Duncan Machine Products Inc	E	580 467-6784
Duncan *(G-2110)*		
Facet (oklahoma) LLC	D	918 696-3161
Stilwell *(G-8789)*		
Ferra Aerospace Inc	F	918 787-2220
Grove *(G-3268)*		
Frontier Elctrnc Systems Corp	C	405 624-7708
Stillwater *(G-8694)*		
General AVI Modifications Inc	E	580 436-4833
Ada *(G-40)*		
Gv Aerospace LLC	G	214 972-5055
Okmulgee *(G-7507)*		
Helicomb International Inc	D	918 835-3999
Tulsa *(G-9911)*		
Honeywell Aerospace Tulsa/Lori	D	918 272-4574
Tulsa *(G-9945)*		
Iap Worldwide Services Inc	F	321 784-7100
Oklahoma City *(G-6282)*		
JD Supply & Mfg	G	405 517-3745
Piedmont *(G-7765)*		
Jet Tech Interiors Inc	G	580 310-2610
Ada *(G-53)*		
Jfj Industries Inc	G	918 342-2453
Claremore *(G-1643)*		
JH Newton LLC	G	918 636-0423
Catoosa *(G-1325)*		
Kern Valley Industries	G	918 868-3911
Rose *(G-8118)*		
Keymiaee Aero-Tech Inc	F	405 235-5010
Oklahoma City *(G-6409)*		
Kihomac Inc	D	937 429-7744
Midwest City *(G-4445)*		
Limco Airepair Inc	D	918 445-4300
Tulsa *(G-10161)*		
Limco-Piedmont Inc	F	918 445-4300
Tulsa *(G-10162)*		
LMI Aerospace Inc	G	918 271-0207
Catoosa *(G-1332)*		
LMI Finishing Inc	D	918 438-1012
Tulsa *(G-10174)*		
LMI Finishing Inc	G	918 379-0899
Catoosa *(G-1333)*		
Micco Aircraft Company Inc	E	918 336-4700
Oklahoma City *(G-6586)*		
Michael Johnson	E	405 882-3744
Shawnee *(G-8474)*		
Nextgen UAS Transponders LLC	G	405 637-7940
Del City *(G-2003)*		
Nolan Enterprises	G	580 924-5507
Durant *(G-2246)*		
Nordam	G	918 878-4325
Tulsa *(G-10350)*		
Nordam Group Inc	E	918 878-8962
Tulsa *(G-10351)*		
Nordam Group LLC	A	918 401-5000
Tulsa *(G-10352)*		
Nordam Group LLC	A	918 878-6682
Tulsa *(G-10353)*		
Nordam Group LLC	A	918 234-5155
Tulsa *(G-10355)*		
Nordam Group LLC	C	918 274-2700
Tulsa *(G-10357)*		
Nordam Group LLC	B	918 476-8338
Tulsa *(G-10358)*		
Nordam Group LLC	C	918 274-2742
Tulsa *(G-10356)*		
Opes Industries LLC	G	405 417-6223
Moore *(G-4550)*		
Plane Plastics Ltd	E	580 327-1565
Alva *(G-188)*		
Precision Hose Technology Inc	G	918 835-3660
Tulsa *(G-10545)*		
Premier Aerospace Svcs & Tech	G	580 327-3706
Alva *(G-190)*		
Pro-Fab LLC	C	405 495-2131
Oklahoma City *(G-6908)*		
Pryer Machine & Tool Company	C	918 835-8885
Tulsa *(G-10580)*		
Pryer Technology Group LLC	C	918 835-8885
Tulsa *(G-10581)*		
Rajon LLC	D	918 367-5487
Bristow *(G-795)*		
Respondair UAS LLC	G	918 899-2113
Owasso *(G-7607)*		
S&S&d Trucking LLC	C	405 365-3535
Oklahoma City *(G-7069)*		
Safran Vntltion Systems Okla I	C	405 382-0731
Seminole *(G-8397)*		
Sertco Industries Inc	E	918 623-0526
Okemah *(G-5276)*		
Southern Aero Partners Inc	E	918 437-7676
Tulsa *(G-10797)*		
Southwest United Inds Inc	C	918 587-4161
Tulsa *(G-10810)*		
Southwind Aviation Supply LLC	G	405 491-0500
Bethany *(G-595)*		
Spirit Aerosystems Inc	F	918 832-3424
Tulsa *(G-10821)*		
Spirit Aerosystems Inc	C	918 423-6979
McAlester *(G-4337)*		
Tellico Engineering Services	G	918 384-7409
Tulsa *(G-10919)*		
Tornado Alley Turbo Inc	D	580 332-3510
Ada *(G-95)*		
Tulsa Turbines	G	918 960-8918
Bixby *(G-668)*		
Turbine Aircraft Services LLC	G	405 491-8995
Bethany *(G-599)*		
United Dynamics Inc	E	405 275-8041
Shawnee *(G-8517)*		
United Plating Works Inc	E	918 835-4683
Tulsa *(G-11042)*		
Vertiprime Mowdy Mch JV LLC	G	405 747-6668
Duncan *(G-2193)*		
Waldens Machine LLC	B	918 794-0289
Tulsa *(G-11092)*		
Wall Colmonoy Corporation	E	405 672-1361
Oklahoma City *(G-7417)*		
Werco Manufacturing Inc	E	918 251-6880
Broken Arrow *(G-1095)*		
Witten Company Inc	E	918 272-9567
Owasso *(G-7630)*		
Yankee Pacific Aerospace	G	918 894-8586
Tulsa *(G-11166)*		

AIRCRAFT PARTS WHOLESALERS

Company		Phone
J & C Enterprises Aviation	G	580 661-3591
Thomas *(G-8944)*		
JD Supply & Mfg	G	405 517-3745
Piedmont *(G-7765)*		

AIRCRAFT PARTS/AUX EQPT: Airframe Assy, Exc Guided Missiles

Company		Phone
Neosource Inc	G	918 622-4493
Tulsa *(G-10334)*		

AIRCRAFT SERVICING & REPAIRING

Company		Phone
Aircraft Power Service Inc	G	405 379-2407
Holdenville *(G-3549)*		
Aircraft Structures Intl Corp	E	580 242-5907
Enid *(G-2908)*		
Turbine Aircraft Services LLC	G	405 491-8995
Bethany *(G-599)*		

AIRCRAFT TURBINES

Company		Phone
Aero Solutions and Services	G	405 308-6788
Edmond *(G-2291)*		
Consoldted Trbine Spclists LLC	G	918 367-9665
Bristow *(G-774)*		

AIRCRAFT: Airplanes, Fixed Or Rotary Wing

Company		Phone
Boeing Company	A	580 482-0354
Altus *(G-147)*		
Boeing Company	A	405 924-1385
Oklahoma City *(G-5608)*		
Boeing Company	A	405 622-6720
Oklahoma City *(G-5610)*		
Boeing Company	E	316 977-2121
Oklahoma City *(G-5613)*		
Boeing Company	A	405 736-9227
Oklahoma City *(G-5614)*		
Boeing Company	A	918 835-3111
Tulsa *(G-9315)*		
Commander Aircraft Corporation	G	405 366-6454
Norman *(G-4963)*		
Northrop Grumman Systems Corp	B	405 737-3300
Oklahoma City *(G-6690)*		
Strategic Mission Systems LLC	G	405 595-7243
Midwest City *(G-4456)*		
Unmanned Cowboys LLC	G	405 744-4156
Stillwater *(G-8771)*		

AIRCRAFT: Motorized

Company		Phone
Aerial Drones of Oklahoma LLC	G	918 694-6523
Claremore *(G-1577)*		
Ases LLC	C	405 219-3420
Oklahoma City *(G-5473)*		
Drone 1 Aerial LLC	G	580 704-7223
Marlow *(G-4230)*		
Drone Misfits LLC	G	918 810-0808
Oklahoma City *(G-5288)*		
Drone Viu LLC	G	405 867-4690
Tulsa *(G-9609)*		
New Generation Drones	G	918 553-8703
Tulsa *(G-10336)*		
Ty Giaudrone	G	918 423-6499
McAlester *(G-4347)*		

AIRCRAFT: Research & Development, Manufacturer

Company		Phone
Lockheed Martin Corporation	B	405 917-3863
Oklahoma City *(G-6487)*		
Oklahoma Foundation For Diges	F	405 271-4602
Oklahoma City *(G-6749)*		

AIRLOCKS

Company		Phone
Airlock Pool Covers Inc	G	405 373-4040
Piedmont *(G-7753)*		

AIRPORT TERMINAL SVCS

Company		Phone
American Airlines Inc	A	918 292-2698
Tulsa *(G-9163)*		

ALARM SYSTEMS WHOLESALERS

Company		Phone
Ademco Inc	G	405 681-4008
Oklahoma City *(G-5373)*		

PRODUCT SECTION

ANIMAL FOOD & SUPPLEMENTS: Dog & Cat

ALARMS: Burglar
In-Tele Communication LLC .... G 580 272-0303
  Ada *(G-50)*

ALARMS: Fire
Invictus Engrg Cnstr Svcs .... G 405 701-5622
  Norman *(G-5037)*

ALCOHOL, ETHYL: For Beverage Purposes
Scissortail Distillery LLC .... G 405 326-5466
  Moore *(G-4565)*

ALCOHOL: Butyl & Butanol
Trusty Willow LLC .... G 253 241-0520
  Bokoshe *(G-755)*

ALCOHOL: Methyl & Methanol, Synthetic
Bluehawk Energy Inc .... G 405 406-1580
  Edmond *(G-2327)*

ALKALIES & CHLORINE
Brenntag Southwest Inc .... E 918 273-2265
  Nowata *(G-5209)*

ALLOYS: Additive, Exc Copper Or Made In Blast Furnaces
Cutting Edge Machine Inc .... G 580 658-5036
  Marlow *(G-4226)*

ALTERNATORS & GENERATORS: Battery Charging
Mower Parts Inc .... E 405 947-6484
  Oklahoma City *(G-6631)*

ALTERNATORS: Automotive
Bob Brooks Motor Company .... C 405 681-2592
  Oklahoma City *(G-5600)*
General Auto Supply Inc .... G 405 329-0772
  Norman *(G-5007)*
Reggie Adudell .... G 405 631-9002
  Oklahoma City *(G-7003)*
Tommy Nix Cdjr Muskogee LLC .... G 918 456-2541
  Muskogee *(G-4753)*

ALUMINUM
Fortiflex Inc .... F 918 540-3131
  Miami *(G-4405)*

ALUMINUM PRDTS
Acme Manufacturing Corporation .... E 918 266-3097
  Claremore *(G-1575)*
Armstrong Products Inc .... G 405 282-7584
  Guthrie *(G-3297)*
Ballews Aluminum Products Inc .... G 405 917-2225
  Oklahoma City *(G-5521)*
Custom Design By Roberts .... G 918 664-0466
  Tulsa *(G-9528)*
Dunlap Manufacturing Co Inc .... E 918 838-1383
  Tulsa *(G-9612)*
Herbert Malarkey Roofing Co .... C 405 261-6900
  Oklahoma City *(G-6241)*
Trulite GL Alum Solutions LLC .... G 918 665-6655
  Tulsa *(G-10982)*

ALUMINUM: Rolling & Drawing
Nixon Materials Company .... G 580 621-3297
  Freedom *(G-3208)*

AMMONIA & AMMONIUM SALTS
Tessenderlo Kerley Inc .... E 405 665-2544
  Wynnewood *(G-11674)*
Tessenderlo Kerley Inc .... F 580 762-1130
  Ponca City *(G-7882)*

AMMONIUM NITRATE OR AMMONIUM SULFATE
Pryor Chemical Company .... C 918 825-3383
  Pryor *(G-7985)*

AMMUNITION: Small Arms
Choctaw Defense Munitions LLC .... G 918 426-7871
  Mcalester *(G-4284)*
Hailey Ordnance Company .... G 405 813-0700
  Oklahoma City *(G-6203)*
Johnny L Windsor .... G 405 691-3083
  Oklahoma City *(G-6371)*
Nash Tactical LLC .... G 405 589-6425
  Norman *(G-5085)*
Robertson Arms & Munitions Co .... G 405 376-2360
  Mustang *(G-4791)*
Sandman Sports .... G 918 272-0862
  Owasso *(G-7612)*
United States Dept of Army .... A 918 420-6642
  McAlester *(G-4348)*

AMPLIFIERS
Resonance Inc .... E 405 239-2800
  Oklahoma City *(G-7010)*

AMUSEMENT & RECREATION SVCS: Art Gallery, Commercial
Narcomey LLC .... G 405 473-1350
  Oklahoma City *(G-6653)*

AMUSEMENT & RECREATION SVCS: Aviation Club, Membership
Airflow Solutions LLC .... E 918 574-2748
  Tulsa *(G-9129)*

AMUSEMENT & RECREATION SVCS: Juke Box
Pinball Doctor .... G 918 582-3130
  Tulsa *(G-10515)*

AMUSEMENT MACHINES: Coin Operated
Aruze Gaming America Inc .... G 405 301-8140
  Oklahoma City *(G-5469)*

AMUSEMENT PARK DEVICES & RIDES: Carnival Mach & Eqpt, NEC
Pinball Doctor .... G 918 582-3130
  Tulsa *(G-10515)*

AMUSEMENT PARK DEVICES & RIDES: Ferris Wheels
Wheeler Frris Whl Partners LLC .... G 405 206-6612
  Oklahoma City *(G-7444)*

ANALYZERS: Network
N O C Supply Inc .... G 405 562-7070
  Edmond *(G-2526)*
Nanna Networks LLC .... G 405 833-3329
  Oklahoma City *(G-6651)*

ANALYZERS: Respiratory
Mms LLC .... G 405 872-3486
  Noble *(G-4886)*

ANESTHESIA EQPT
Anesthesia Services .... G 580 536-7150
  Lawton *(G-3889)*

ANIMAL BASED MEDICINAL CHEMICAL PRDTS
Hillsboro Co .... G 918 481-0484
  Tulsa *(G-9930)*

ANIMAL FEED & SUPPLEMENTS: Livestock & Poultry
Alfalfa Dehydrating Plant Inc .... G 918 482-3267
  Coweta *(G-1871)*
Allen Brothers Feed .... G 918 287-4379
  Pawhuska *(G-7676)*
Big v Feeds Inc .... D 918 423-1565
  McAlester *(G-4276)*
Cargill Incorporated .... D 405 270-7011
  Oklahoma City *(G-5698)*
Cargill Incorporated .... E 405 236-0525
  Oklahoma City *(G-5699)*
Choska Alfalfa Mills LLC .... G 918 687-5805
  Muskogee *(G-4660)*
Compass Unlimited Inc .... G 918 824-1644
  Pryor *(G-7955)*
Darling Ingredients Inc .... E 918 371-2528
  Collinsville *(G-1808)*
Douglas A Pharr .... G 405 200-4983
  Ninnekah *(G-4870)*
Farmers Co Op .... F 918 456-0557
  Tahlequah *(G-8864)*
Farmers Coop .... F 580 772-3334
  Weatherford *(G-11413)*
Fisher AG Enterprises Inc .... F 918 367-6382
  Bristow *(G-778)*
Griffin Industries LLC .... E 918 422-4790
  Watts *(G-11357)*
Hanor Company of Wisconsin LLC .... E 580 237-3255
  Enid *(G-2969)*
Hart Feeds Inc .... G 405 224-0102
  Chickasha *(G-1468)*
HI Pro Feeds Inc .... F 580 497-2219
  Cheyenne *(G-1425)*
Hubbard .... G 918 785-2000
  Adair *(G-110)*
Kfm Inc .... F 580 342-6293
  Temple *(G-8933)*
Luther Mill and Farm Supply .... G 405 277-3221
  Luther *(G-4135)*
Marshall Minerals LLC .... G 405 848-5715
  Oklahoma City *(G-6531)*
Midwestern Pet Foods Inc .... F 405 224-2691
  Chickasha *(G-1487)*
Nestle Purina Petcare Company .... D 405 751-4550
  Edmond *(G-2535)*
Purina Animal Nutrition LLC .... E 405 232-6171
  Oklahoma City *(G-6925)*
Purina Mills LLC .... E 405 232-6171
  Oklahoma City *(G-6926)*
Rocky Farmers Cooperative Inc .... F 580 666-2440
  Rocky *(G-8105)*
Rocky Farmers Cooperative Inc .... G 580 674-3356
  Dill City *(G-2037)*
S & S Farm Center .... F 405 273-6907
  Shawnee *(G-8491)*
Shawnee Milling Company .... G 405 352-4336
  Minco *(G-4481)*
Stockmans Mill & Grain Inc .... G 918 762-3459
  Pawnee *(G-7711)*
Westway Feed Products LLC .... G 918 266-5911
  Catoosa *(G-1366)*

ANIMAL FEED: Wholesalers
Shawnee Milling Company .... G 405 352-4336
  Minco *(G-4481)*
Wister Lake Feed Inc .... G 918 655-7954
  Howe *(G-3601)*

ANIMAL FOOD & SUPPLEMENTS: Dog
Dog Dish LLC .... G 918 624-2600
  Tulsa *(G-9590)*
House Dog Industries LLC .... G 405 761-5576
  El Reno *(G-2724)*
Mars Petcare Us Inc .... E 918 540-0045
  Miami *(G-4412)*
Midwestern Pet Foods Inc .... F 405 224-2691
  Chickasha *(G-1487)*
Nestle Purina Petcare Company .... D 405 751-4550
  Edmond *(G-2535)*
Red Collar Pet Foods Inc .... D 580 323-3359
  Clinton *(G-1765)*
Win Hy Foods Inc .... F 918 227-0004
  Tulsa *(G-9053)*

ANIMAL FOOD & SUPPLEMENTS: Dog & Cat
Big v Feeds Inc .... D 918 423-1565
  McAlester *(G-4276)*
Blue Bonnet Feeds LP .... D 580 223-3010
  Ardmore *(G-257)*
Farmers Co Op .... F 918 456-0557
  Tahlequah *(G-8864)*
Mountain Country Foods LLC .... E 580 822-4130
  Okeene *(G-5259)*
Ralston Purina .... G 405 751-4550
  Edmond *(G-2585)*
Rbs Pet Products .... G 405 373-0235
  Piedmont *(G-7769)*

Employee Codes: A=Over 500 employees, B=251-500
C=101-250, D=51-100, E=20-50, F=10-19, G=1-9

2020 Oklahoma Directory of Manufacturers & Processors

ANIMAL FOOD & SUPPLEMENTS: Feed Concentrates

ANIMAL FOOD & SUPPLEMENTS: Feed Concentrates

Winfield Solutions LLC ....G..... 580 237-2456
  Enid *(G-3082)*

ANIMAL FOOD & SUPPLEMENTS: Feed Supplements

Custom Mser Lvstk Pre Mix Whse ....G..... 580 336-2053
  Perry *(G-7729)*
Eve Breathe ....G..... 918 454-2866
  Pawnee *(G-7704)*
Frontier Elevator Inc ....G..... 888 421-9400
  Ada *(G-38)*
Hitch Enterprises Inc ....G..... 580 338-6510
  Hooker *(G-3597)*
Ultra Botanica LLC ....G..... 405 694-4175
  Oklahoma City *(G-7359)*
West Texas By Products LP ....F..... 580 371-9413
  Ravia *(G-8072)*

ANIMAL FOOD & SUPPLEMENTS: Livestock

AC Nutrition LP ....F..... 580 223-3900
  Ardmore *(G-236)*
Blue Bonnet Feeds LP ....D..... 580 223-3010
  Ardmore *(G-257)*
Diane Barcheers ....G..... 918 649-0440
  McAlester *(G-4293)*
Espiritu Miki ....G..... 405 213-5167
  Oklahoma City *(G-6051)*
Hollis Cotton Oil Mill Inc ....F..... 580 688-3394
  Hollis *(G-3565)*
Mid America Farm & Ranch ....G..... 918 275-4984
  Talala *(G-8900)*
Oklahoma Tool & Machine ....G..... 405 262-2624
  El Reno *(G-2744)*
Red Seal Feeds LLC ....G..... 918 423-3710
  McAlester *(G-4332)*
Spring Hollow Feed Mill Inc ....G..... 918 453-9933
  Hulbert *(G-3628)*
Stillwater Milling Company LLC ....D..... 405 372-2766
  Stillwater *(G-8757)*

ANIMAL FOOD & SUPPLEMENTS: Mineral feed supplements

Advantage Supplements LLC ....G..... 866 226-9613
  Hennessey *(G-3444)*
C & H Ranch ....G..... 918 479-8460
  Locust Grove *(G-4105)*

ANIMAL FOOD & SUPPLEMENTS: Pet, Exc Dog & Cat, Dry

Dvm Nutrion Pets Corp Inc ....F..... 918 686-6111
  Muskogee *(G-4668)*
Mountain Country Foods LLC ....E..... 580 822-4130
  Okeene *(G-5259)*

ANIMAL FOOD & SUPPLEMENTS: Poultry

O K Foods Inc ....A..... 918 653-1640
  Heavener *(G-3431)*

ANIMAL FOOD & SUPPLEMENTS: Stock Feeds, Dry

Bobby Foster ....G..... 580 476-3417
  Rush Springs *(G-8119)*
Henderson Feeds LLC ....G..... 580 574-5375
  Sayre *(G-8341)*

ANODIZING SVC

Century Plating Inc ....G..... 918 835-1482
  Tulsa *(G-9400)*

ANTI-GLARE MATERIAL

Biotech Products Inc ....G..... 405 235-7575
  Oklahoma City *(G-5574)*

ANTIQUE & CLASSIC AUTOMOBILE RESTORATION

Wheels of Past ....G..... 918 225-2250
  Cushing *(G-1969)*

ANTIQUE AUTOMOBILE DEALERS

Antique & Rod Shop LLC ....G..... 405 631-3544
  Oklahoma City *(G-5450)*

ANTIQUE FURNITURE RESTORATION & REPAIR

Buster Dorsch ....G..... 918 743-4509
  Tulsa *(G-9353)*

ANTIQUE REPAIR & RESTORATION SVCS, EXC FURNITURE & AUTOS

Antique & Rod Shop LLC ....G..... 405 631-3544
  Oklahoma City *(G-5450)*
Bws Wlding Fabriction Svcs LLC ....G..... 918 789-3094
  Chelsea *(G-1403)*

ANTIQUE SHOPS

Juan Manzo Custom Refinishing ....G..... 405 848-3843
  Oklahoma City *(G-6390)*
Rustic Rehab ....G..... 918 314-6647
  Grove *(G-3287)*
Warren Ramsey Inc ....G..... 405 528-2828
  Oklahoma City *(G-7422)*

APATITE MINING

D and M Resources Inc ....G..... 405 375-4602
  Kingfisher *(G-3795)*

APPAREL ACCESS STORES

Flaming Hope LLC ....G..... 405 924-4380
  Noble *(G-4880)*

APPLIANCES, HOUSEHOLD: Kitchen, Major, Exc Refrigs & Stoves

Metro Builders Supply Inc ....E..... 405 751-8833
  Edmond *(G-2515)*

APPLIANCES, HOUSEHOLD: Sweepers, Electric

Lindsay Manufacturing Inc ....E..... 580 762-2457
  Ponca City *(G-7845)*

APPLIANCES: Household, NEC

Blue Speed LLC ....G..... 918 856-3547
  Tulsa *(G-9306)*

APPLIANCES: Major, Cooking

Metro Outdoor Living ....G..... 918 893-2960
  Tulsa *(G-10253)*

APPLIANCES: Small, Electric

Belden Russell Elect Co ....G..... 918 791-9600
  Grove *(G-3259)*

APPLICATIONS SOFTWARE PROGRAMMING

Airgo Systems LLC ....F..... 405 346-5807
  Oklahoma City *(G-5404)*
Canopy Upstream LLC ....G..... 620 717-3263
  Weatherford *(G-11397)*
Cutting Edge Technologies LLC ....G..... 918 284-6069
  Owasso *(G-7558)*
Dancey-Meador Publishing Co ....G..... 580 762-9359
  Ponca City *(G-7819)*
Fronttoback Studio LLC ....G..... 405 788-4400
  Oklahoma City *(G-6124)*
Vertiprime Government Svcs LLC ....G..... 844 474-2600
  Duncan *(G-2192)*

ARCHITECTURAL SVCS

Burns & McDonnell Inc ....G..... 405 200-0300
  Oklahoma City *(G-5646)*
Minko Design LLC ....G..... 918 895-6498
  Tulsa *(G-10284)*
Minko Design LLC ....G..... 918 895-6498
  Tulsa *(G-10285)*

ARCHITECTURAL SVCS: Engineering

Dream Green International LLC ....G..... 814 616-7800
  Norman *(G-4983)*

ARMATURE REPAIRING & REWINDING SVC

Electric Motor Service Company ....G..... 580 223-8940
  Ardmore *(G-283)*
Profab ....G..... 918 486-4464
  Coweta *(G-1894)*

ART & ORNAMENTAL WARE: Pottery

Brookside Pottery ....G..... 918 697-6364
  Tulsa *(G-9342)*
Roserock Creations Inc ....G..... 405 209-6005
  Edmond *(G-2604)*

ART DEALERS & GALLERIES

Green Room Studios ....G..... 580 335-5689
  Frederick *(G-3193)*

ART DESIGN SVCS

Dearinger Printing & Trophy ....F..... 405 372-5503
  Stillwater *(G-8675)*

ART GOODS & SPLYS WHOLESALERS

F C Ziegler Co ....E..... 918 587-7639
  Tulsa *(G-9721)*

ART RELATED SVCS

Crucible LLC ....F..... 405 579-2700
  Norman *(G-4971)*

ART SPLY STORES

D E Ziegler Art Craft Supply ....E..... 918 584-2217
  Tulsa *(G-9537)*

ARTISTS' MATERIALS: Boards, Drawing

Green Room Studios ....G..... 580 335-5689
  Frederick *(G-3193)*

ARTISTS' MATERIALS: Canvas Board

Benjamin Harjo Jr ....G..... 405 521-0246
  Oklahoma City *(G-5551)*

ARTISTS' MATERIALS: Colors, Water & Oxide Ceramic Glass

Bill Glass ....G..... 918 479-8884
  Locust Grove *(G-4104)*

ARTISTS' MATERIALS: Frames, Artists' Canvases

Carpentree Inc ....E..... 918 582-3600
  Tulsa *(G-9378)*

ARTISTS' MATERIALS: Paints, China Painting

Oklahoma World Organiz ....G..... 918 224-3063
  Sapulpa *(G-8294)*

ARTWORK: Framed

Susan Secor ....G..... 580 510-0060
  Lawton *(G-4008)*

ASPHALT & ASPHALT PRDTS

Caswell Construction Co Inc ....D..... 580 225-6833
  Elk City *(G-2793)*
Cummins Construction Co Inc ....E..... 580 233-6000
  Enid *(G-2937)*
Evans & Associates Entps Inc ....E..... 580 765-6693
  Ponca City *(G-7828)*
Haskell Lemon Construction Co ....G..... 405 236-2701
  Oklahoma City *(G-6224)*
Kerns Asphalt Company Inc ....E..... 405 372-2750
  Stillwater *(G-8711)*
Logan County Asphalt Co ....E..... 405 282-3711
  Guthrie *(G-3323)*
RLC Holding Co Inc ....D..... 580 233-6000
  Enid *(G-3048)*
T & G Construction Inc ....C..... 580 355-6655
  Lawton *(G-4010)*
T J Campbell Construction Co ....C..... 405 672-6800
  Oklahoma City *(G-7244)*
Vance Brothers Inc ....G..... 405 427-1389
  Oklahoma City *(G-7390)*

PRODUCT SECTION

AUTOMOTIVE BODY, PAINT & INTERIOR REPAIR & MAINTENANCE SVC

ASPHALT COATINGS & SEALERS

Acme Manufacturing Corporation .... E 918 266-3097
  Claremore *(G-1575)*
Butaphalt Products LLC .... G 918 740-7290
  Claremore *(G-1600)*
Global Sealcoating Inc .... G 918 283-2040
  Claremore *(G-1626)*
McCabe Industrial Minerals .... G 918 252-5090
  Tulsa *(G-10228)*
McCabe Industrial Minerals .... F 580 369-3660
  Davis *(G-1990)*
Schwarz Asphalt LLC .... E 405 789-7203
  Oklahoma City *(G-7092)*
Vance Brothers Inc .... G 405 427-1389
  Oklahoma City *(G-7390)*

ASPHALT PLANTS INCLUDING GRAVEL MIX TYPE

CMI Terex Corporation .... A 405 787-6020
  Oklahoma City *(G-5792)*
H G Jenkins Construction LLC .... E 580 355-9822
  Lawton *(G-3938)*

ASSEMBLING SVC: Clocks

Petroleum Artifacts Ltd .... G 918 949-6101
  Tulsa *(G-10504)*

ASSEMBLING SVC: Plumbing Fixture Fittings, Plastic

A & R Plumbing and Mech LLC .... G 405 808-0671
  Oklahoma City *(G-5343)*

ASSOCIATION FOR THE HANDICAPPED

Sheltred Work-Activity Program .... E 918 683-8162
  Muskogee *(G-4748)*

ASSOCIATIONS: Bar

Oklahoma Bar Foundation Inc .... E 405 416-7000
  Oklahoma City *(G-6737)*

ASSOCIATIONS: Fraternal

Rainbow Spreme Assmbly I O R G ..... G 918 423-1328
  McAlester *(G-4331)*

ASSOCIATIONS: Trade

Oklahoma Bankers .... E 405 424-5252
  Oklahoma City *(G-6736)*
Oklahoma Grocers Association .... F 405 525-9419
  Oklahoma City *(G-6750)*
Vmebus Intl Trade Assn .... G 480 577-1916
  Oklahoma City *(G-7405)*

ATOMIZERS

Bkg Industries LLC .... G 918 694-3390
  Whitefield *(G-11516)*
Gardners Guns & Mfg LLC .... G 580 225-8884
  Elk City *(G-2818)*
Jk Industries Inc .... G 405 285-9800
  Edmond *(G-2470)*
Thermtech Industries LLC .... G 918 299-5473
  Tulsa *(G-10927)*
Trinity Industries Inc .... G 405 629-1213
  Oklahoma City *(G-7334)*

AUDIO & VIDEO EQPT, EXC COMMERCIAL

C2 Innovative Technologies Inc .... G 405 388-2357
  Oklahoma City *(G-5665)*
Cambridge Soundworks Inc .... C 405 742-6704
  Stillwater *(G-8665)*
Clear Tone Hearing Center Inc .... E 918 838-1000
  Tulsa *(G-9449)*
Clear2there LLC .... G 405 605-8158
  Oklahoma City *(G-5782)*
Digital Resources Inc .... G 866 823-6328
  Tulsa *(G-9583)*
United Video LLC .... D 918 488-4000
  Tulsa *(G-11243)*
Versatech Industries Inc .... G 918 366-7400
  Bixby *(G-670)*

AUDIO ELECTRONIC SYSTEMS

Falcon Audio Video Inc .... G 918 272-3969
  Claremore *(G-1619)*

Great Plains Audio .... G 405 789-0221
  Oklahoma City *(G-6177)*
Sound Iq .... G 918 442-2588
  Tulsa *(G-10793)*

AUDITING SVCS

Terry Stutzmann .... G 405 481-3853
  Shawnee *(G-8510)*

AUTO & HOME SUPPLY STORES: Auto & Truck Eqpt & Parts

Guymon Motor Parts Inc .... E 580 338-3316
  Guymon *(G-3350)*

AUTO & HOME SUPPLY STORES: Auto Air Cond Eqpt, Sell/Install

Carc Inc .... G 918 266-1341
  Catoosa *(G-1308)*

AUTO & HOME SUPPLY STORES: Automotive Access

Daytons Trailer Hitch Inc .... G 918 744-0341
  Tulsa *(G-9562)*
Performance Machine & Inductio .... F 918 542-8740
  North Miami *(G-5207)*

AUTO & HOME SUPPLY STORES: Automotive parts

Alberts Auto & Truck Repr Inc .... E 866 772-6065
  Weatherford *(G-11389)*
Boyds Auto Parts & Machine .... F 405 329-3855
  Norman *(G-4940)*
Chevelle World Inc .... F 405 872-3399
  Noble *(G-4876)*
Demco Oil & Gas Company .... G 580 363-4223
  Blackwell *(G-681)*
Drive Shafts Inc .... G 918 836-0111
  Tulsa *(G-9608)*
General Auto Supply Inc .... G 405 329-0772
  Norman *(G-5007)*
Hot Rod Shirts & Stuff .... G 580 669-2531
  Glencoe *(G-3224)*
Lanco Services LLC .... E 580 429-6526
  Cache *(G-1229)*
Larrys Transmission Service .... G 405 273-3432
  Shawnee *(G-8468)*
Lkq Corporation .... F 918 428-3835
  Tulsa *(G-10171)*
Lynns Auto Parts and Machine .... G 580 255-5190
  Duncan *(G-2149)*
Timmy Pickens .... G 918 812-5268
  Sapulpa *(G-8315)*

AUTO & HOME SUPPLY STORES: Batteries, Automotive & Truck

Batteries Sooner LLC .... E 405 605-1237
  Oklahoma City *(G-5530)*
Liberty Transmission Parts .... G 405 236-8749
  Oklahoma City *(G-6472)*

AUTO & HOME SUPPLY STORES: Speed Shops, Incl Race Car Splys

Dunsworth Machine .... G 580 233-5812
  Enid *(G-2947)*
G P Enterprises .... G 405 340-8986
  Edmond *(G-2428)*

AUTO & HOME SUPPLY STORES: Truck Eqpt & Parts

Enid Mack Sales Inc .... D 580 234-0043
  Enid *(G-2954)*

AUTOMATIC REGULATING CONTROL: Building Svcs Monitoring, Auto

Pyfi Technologies .... G 405 816-8685
  Oklahoma City *(G-6929)*

AUTOMATIC REGULATING CONTROLS: Pressure, Air-Cond Sys

Torus Pressure Control LLC .... E 405 670-4456
  Oklahoma City *(G-7307)*

AUTOMATIC REGULATING CONTROLS: Surface Burner, Temperature

Mathena Inc .... D 405 422-3600
  El Reno *(G-2736)*

AUTOMATIC REGULATING CONTROLS: Vapor Heating

Emerson Process Management .... C 918 622-6161
  Tulsa *(G-9670)*

AUTOMATIC TELLER MACHINES

Cummins - Allison Corp .... F 405 321-1411
  Norman *(G-4972)*
Superior Federal Bank .... G 405 224-1021
  Chickasha *(G-1514)*
Transfund .... G 918 588-6707
  Tulsa *(G-10969)*

AUTOMOBILES & OTHER MOTOR VEHICLES WHOLESALERS

Elvis S Seshie .... G 405 887-3050
  Mustang *(G-4770)*
Guardian Interlock of Utah .... G 580 357-8583
  Lawton *(G-3937)*
Logistics Management Company .... G 405 633-1201
  Oklahoma City *(G-6490)*

AUTOMOTIVE & TRUCK GENERAL REPAIR SVC

Anchor Auto & Welding Repr LLC ...... G 918 426-7662
  McAlester *(G-4270)*
C & C Performance Engines .... G 580 252-4331
  Duncan *(G-2094)*
Carc Inc .... G 918 266-1341
  Catoosa *(G-1308)*
Charles Service Station LLC .... G 918 297-3308
  Hartshorne *(G-3390)*
Dixon Auto Engine Machine Shop ..... G 918 256-6780
  Vinita *(G-11254)*
Douglas Thompson Auto Inc .... G 405 330-6997
  Edmond *(G-2393)*
Guymon Safety Lane .... G 580 338-6960
  Guymon *(G-3351)*
Hawkeye Fleet Services .... E 405 495-9939
  Oklahoma City *(G-6226)*
James Matthews Ford LLC .... E 918 251-3673
  Broken Arrow *(G-942)*
L & K Seed & Manufacturing Co .... G 405 663-2758
  Hydro *(G-3632)*
Northfork Auto Repair .... G 918 689-3589
  Eufaula *(G-3106)*
Paytons Auto .... G 918 540-2501
  Miami *(G-4427)*
R & P Machine Shop .... G 405 275-1321
  Tecumseh *(G-8925)*
Self Automotive & Racing Inc .... G 580 924-5866
  Durant *(G-2256)*
Tulsa Auto Spring Co .... E 918 835-6926
  Tulsa *(G-10987)*

AUTOMOTIVE BATTERIES WHOLESALERS

Exide Technologies LLC .... F 405 745-2511
  Oklahoma City *(G-6061)*

AUTOMOTIVE BODY SHOP

Ronnie Nevitt .... G 918 687-5284
  Muskogee *(G-4745)*

AUTOMOTIVE BODY, PAINT & INTERIOR REPAIR & MAINTENANCE SVC

David Combs Auto Trim .... G 405 799-7330
  Oklahoma City *(G-5903)*
Topps Powder Coating .... G 405 794-2900
  Moore *(G-4578)*

AUTOMOTIVE CUSTOMIZING SVCS, NONFACTORY BASIS

Auto Trim Design Signs SE Okla ....G....... 580 622-3830
　Sulphur *(G-8828)*

AUTOMOTIVE GLASS REPLACEMENT SHOPS

Owasso Glass ....G....... 918 272-4490
　Owasso *(G-7600)*

AUTOMOTIVE PAINT SHOP

Nix Body Shop LLC ....G....... 918 797-2484
　Stilwell *(G-8794)*

AUTOMOTIVE PARTS, ACCESS & SPLYS

Aero Dynamics ....F....... 918 258-0290
　Broken Arrow *(G-818)*
Allen Camper Mfg Company Inc ....E....... 580 857-2177
　Allen *(G-133)*
Auto Hail Damage Repair ....G....... 405 696-6031
　Edmond *(G-2312)*
Autocraft Industries ....G....... 405 577-9901
　Oklahoma City *(G-5492)*
B & W Diesel & Drivetrain Inc ....G....... 918 427-7918
　Muldrow *(G-4631)*
Bob Howard Whl Parts Dist Ctr ....G....... 405 525-4400
　Oklahoma City *(G-5601)*
Boyds Auto Parts & Machine ....F....... 405 329-3855
　Norman *(G-4940)*
Braden Carco Gearmatic Winch ....G....... 918 756-4400
　Okmulgee *(G-7495)*
Burns Manufacturing Inc ....G....... 918 622-3305
　Tulsa *(G-9348)*
C & S Technical Services LLC ....E....... 918 258-8324
　Tulsa *(G-9358)*
Chevelle World Inc ....F....... 405 872-3399
　Noble *(G-4876)*
CNG Specialists LLC ....G....... 405 677-5400
　Oklahoma City *(G-5795)*
Dales Manufacturing Co ....G....... 405 631-8988
　Oklahoma City *(G-5891)*
Drive Shafts Inc ....G....... 918 836-0111
　Tulsa *(G-9608)*
Drov LLC ....F....... 405 463-6562
　Oklahoma City *(G-5984)*
Factor 1 Racing Inc ....G....... 918 258-7223
　Broken Arrow *(G-905)*
Flex-N-Gate Oklahoma LLC ....B....... 580 272-6700
　Ada *(G-35)*
Floyds Machine Shop ....G....... 918 256-8440
　Vinita *(G-11258)*
Fred Jones Enterprises LLC ....E....... 800 927-7845
　Oklahoma City *(G-6114)*
Genes Customized Tags & EMB ....G....... 580 225-8247
　Elk City *(G-2820)*
Glenns Competition Chassis ....G....... 405 732-4403
　Oklahoma City *(G-6158)*
Goodwill Inds Centl Okla Inc ....D....... 405 236-4451
　Oklahoma City *(G-6172)*
Grices Automotive Machine Shop ....G....... 580 924-1006
　Durant *(G-2233)*
Guymon Safety Lane ....G....... 580 338-6960
　Guymon *(G-3351)*
Hudson Bros Rmanufactured Engs ....G....... 405 598-2260
　Tecumseh *(G-8919)*
Hydrogen Technologies Inc ....G....... 918 645-3430
　Park Hill *(G-7644)*
Ignition Systems & Controls ....F....... 405 682-3030
　Oklahoma City *(G-6291)*
Kams Inc ....F....... 405 232-3103
　Oklahoma City *(G-6396)*
Magnum Racing Components Inc ....G....... 918 627-0204
　Tulsa *(G-10201)*
Meritor Inc ....F....... 405 224-8600
　Chickasha *(G-1484)*
Midwest Expdtion Otfitters LLC ....G....... 918 260-1771
　Tulsa *(G-10267)*
Moss Seat Cover Mfg & Sls Co ....F....... 918 742-3326
　Tulsa *(G-10306)*
National Bumper & Plating ....G....... 405 235-1535
　Oklahoma City *(G-6655)*
Olmeva USA LLC ....G....... 405 677-5400
　Oklahoma City *(G-6772)*
Performance Machine & Inductio ....F....... 405 542-8740
　North Miami *(G-5207)*
Power Equipment & Engrg Inc ....E....... 405 235-0531
　Oklahoma City *(G-6869)*
Powertrain Company LLC ....G....... 703 419-0104
　Oklahoma City *(G-6871)*
Pss Enterprises Llc ....G....... 918 928-7971
　Broken Arrow *(G-1150)*
Raxter LLC ....G....... 918 706-7987
　Broken Arrow *(G-1023)*
Reggie Adudell ....G....... 405 631-9002
　Oklahoma City *(G-7003)*
Ron Shanks Racing Enterprises ....G....... 918 366-6050
　Bixby *(G-655)*
Royal Filter Manufacturing Co ....E....... 405 224-0229
　Chickasha *(G-1503)*
Rv Smart Products LLC ....G....... 575 513-1712
　Bixby *(G-656)*
Self Automotive & Racing Inc ....G....... 580 924-5866
　Durant *(G-2256)*
Seminole Machine Co ....G....... 405 382-0444
　Seminole *(G-8399)*
Southeast Tire Inc ....D....... 580 286-6531
　Idabel *(G-3647)*
Thermal Solutions Mfg ....G....... 405 272-0453
　Oklahoma City *(G-7281)*
Trikntrux ....G....... 918 224-2116
　Sapulpa *(G-8316)*
United Ford ....G....... 405 813-7300
　Oklahoma City *(G-7367)*
Universal Jint Specialists Inc ....G....... 918 836-0111
　Tulsa *(G-11048)*
Wall Colmonoy Corporation ....E....... 405 672-1361
　Oklahoma City *(G-7417)*
Weatherford Machine Works ....G....... 580 772-5287
　Weatherford *(G-11457)*

AUTOMOTIVE PARTS: Plastic

Banks Motor Co ....G....... 580 924-8883
　Durant *(G-2204)*
Hopkins Manufacturing Corp ....F....... 918 961-8722
　Miami *(G-4408)*
Magnum Racing Components Inc ....G....... 918 627-0204
　Tulsa *(G-10201)*
Surface Mount Depot Inc ....G....... 405 789-0670
　Oklahoma City *(G-7231)*

AUTOMOTIVE RADIATOR REPAIR SHOPS

R & R Radiator Co ....G....... 405 257-3557
　Wewoka *(G-11508)*

AUTOMOTIVE REPAIR SHOPS: Alternators/Generator, Rebuild/Rpr

Hipower Systems Oklahoma LLC ....G....... 918 512-6321
　Tulsa *(G-9013)*

AUTOMOTIVE REPAIR SHOPS: Diesel Engine Repair

B & W Diesel & Drivetrain Inc ....G....... 918 427-7918
　Muldrow *(G-4631)*
Cummins Southern Plains LLC ....E....... 918 234-3240
　Tulsa *(G-9522)*
United Holdings LLC ....G....... 405 947-3321
　Oklahoma City *(G-7369)*

AUTOMOTIVE REPAIR SHOPS: Electrical Svcs

Carc Inc ....G....... 918 266-1341
　Catoosa *(G-1308)*
Fred Jones Enterprises LLC ....E....... 800 927-7845
　Oklahoma City *(G-6114)*
Start Rite Auto Electric Inc ....G....... 580 924-7290
　Durant *(G-2261)*
Tonys Electric Inc ....G....... 405 375-4103
　Kingfisher *(G-3818)*
Tsig LLC ....G....... 405 463-7700
　Oklahoma City *(G-7347)*

AUTOMOTIVE REPAIR SHOPS: Engine Rebuilding

Floyds Machine Shop ....G....... 918 256-8440
　Vinita *(G-11258)*
Southwestern Motor Rebuilders ....G....... 918 585-1519
　Tulsa *(G-10811)*
Woltjer Engines ....G....... 918 258-0598
　Broken Arrow *(G-1101)*

AUTOMOTIVE REPAIR SHOPS: Engine Repair

Cummins Southern Plains LLC ....E....... 405 946-4481
　Oklahoma City *(G-5869)*
D C Ignition Co Inc ....G....... 580 332-0878
　Ada *(G-28)*

AUTOMOTIVE REPAIR SHOPS: Engine Repair, Exc Diesel

Alberts Auto & Truck Repr Inc ....E....... 866 772-6065
　Weatherford *(G-11389)*
Independent Diesel Service ....F....... 580 234-0435
　Enid *(G-2977)*

AUTOMOTIVE REPAIR SHOPS: Machine Shop

Crankshaft Service Company ....G....... 405 685-7553
　Oklahoma City *(G-5851)*
Dunsworth Machine ....G....... 580 233-5812
　Enid *(G-2947)*
Hartco Metal Products Inc ....G....... 405 471-2784
　Edmond *(G-2452)*
McCaskill Machining & Repair ....G....... 918 266-5186
　Catoosa *(G-1340)*
Richards Performance Machine ....G....... 918 485-6393
　Wagoner *(G-11289)*
Stephen Poorboy ....G....... 918 373-5073
　Chouteau *(G-1571)*

AUTOMOTIVE REPAIR SHOPS: Trailer Repair

Five A Trailers and Equipment ....G....... 580 564-2973
　Kingston *(G-3827)*
Gr Trailers LLC ....G....... 405 567-0567
　Prague *(G-7926)*
Mac Trailer of Oklahoma Inc ....G....... 817 900-2006
　Davis *(G-1988)*
Old Town Welding Shop ....G....... 918 423-8506
　McAlester *(G-4326)*
Turnbow Trailers Inc ....F....... 918 862-3233
　Oilton *(G-5241)*

AUTOMOTIVE REPAIR SHOPS: Truck Engine Repair, Exc Indl

Bach Welding & Diesel Service ....G....... 580 593-2599
　Custer City *(G-1973)*
Enid Mack Sales Inc ....D....... 580 234-0043
　Enid *(G-2954)*

AUTOMOTIVE REPAIR SHOPS: Wheel Alignment

Dobbs & Crowder Inc ....G....... 918 452-3211
　Eufaula *(G-3100)*
Spencer L Rosson ....G....... 918 682-4291
　Muskogee *(G-4750)*

AUTOMOTIVE REPAIR SVC

Axels Transmissions Transfers ....G....... 918 425-7725
　Tulsa *(G-9234)*
Drive Shafts Inc ....G....... 918 836-0111
　Tulsa *(G-9608)*
L & M Fabrication ....G....... 918 825-7145
　Pryor *(G-7973)*
Precision Drive Ltd Inc ....G....... 405 495-1344
　Oklahoma City *(G-6881)*
R & L Mechanics & Welding ....G....... 918 253-4734
　Jay *(G-3685)*
Tcae Enterprises Inc ....G....... 918 664-5977
　Tulsa *(G-10908)*

AUTOMOTIVE REPAIR SVCS, MISCELLANEOUS

Johnny Blaylock ....G....... 918 639-5951
　Broken Arrow *(G-949)*

AUTOMOTIVE SPLYS & PARTS, NEW, WHOLESALE: Brakes

Tulsa Brake & Clutch Co LLC ....G....... 918 582-2165
　Tulsa *(G-10990)*

PRODUCT SECTION

AUTOMOTIVE SPLYS & PARTS, NEW, WHOLESALE: Engines/Eng Parts
Blumenthal Companies LLc..................E....... 405 232-9557
  Oklahoma City (G-5595)

AUTOMOTIVE SPLYS & PARTS, NEW, WHOLESALE: Pumps, Oil & Gas
Ameripump Mfg LLC...........................G....... 918 438-2953
  Tulsa (G-9178)

AUTOMOTIVE SPLYS & PARTS, NEW, WHOLESALE: Radiators
1 800 Radiator..................................G....... 405 946-9800
  Oklahoma City (G-5326)

AUTOMOTIVE SPLYS & PARTS, NEW, WHOLESALE: Trailer Parts
Daytons Trailer Hitch Inc.....................G....... 918 744-0341
  Tulsa (G-9562)

AUTOMOTIVE SPLYS & PARTS, USED, WHOLESALE
Dale Kreimeyer Co.............................G....... 405 789-9499
  Bethany (G-575)

AUTOMOTIVE SPLYS & PARTS, USED, WHOLESALE: Engines
Tulsa Auto Core.................................G....... 918 584-5899
  Tulsa (G-10986)

AUTOMOTIVE SPLYS & PARTS, WHOLESALE, NEC
Bob Howard Whl Parts Dist Ctr............G....... 405 525-4400
  Oklahoma City (G-5601)
Buttons Auto Electrical Supply............G....... 580 223-3855
  Ardmore (G-261)
Chevelle World Inc............................F....... 405 872-3399
  Noble (G-4876)
Drive Shafts Inc................................G....... 918 836-0111
  Tulsa (G-9608)
Larrys Transmission Service...............G....... 405 273-3432
  Shawnee (G-8468)
Lynns Auto Parts and Machine............G....... 580 255-5190
  Duncan (G-2149)
United Holdings LLC..........................G....... 405 947-3321
  Oklahoma City (G-7369)

AUTOMOTIVE SPLYS, USED, WHOLESALE & RETAIL
Gibsons Treasures............................G....... 405 835-1109
  Oklahoma City (G-6152)

AUTOMOTIVE SPLYS/PARTS, NEW, WHOL: Body Rpr/Paint Shop Splys
B & W Diesel & Drivetrain Inc..............G....... 918 427-7918
  Muldrow (G-4631)

AUTOMOTIVE SVCS
Lakeside Polaris Inc..........................G....... 918 485-2887
  Wagoner (G-11285)

AUTOMOTIVE SVCS, EXC REPAIR & CARWASHES: Glass Tinting
Tcae Enterprises Inc.........................G....... 918 664-5977
  Tulsa (G-10908)

AUTOMOTIVE SVCS, EXC REPAIR & CARWASHES: Insp & Diagnostic
Carc Inc..G....... 918 266-1341
  Catoosa (G-1308)

AUTOMOTIVE SVCS, EXC REPAIR & CARWASHES: Maintenance
Cook Machine Company....................E....... 580 252-1699
  Duncan (G-2099)

AUTOMOTIVE SVCS, EXC REPAIR & CARWASHES: Sun Roof Install
Auto Trim Design Signs SE Okla..........G....... 580 622-3830
  Sulphur (G-8828)

AUTOMOTIVE SVCS, EXC REPAIR & CARWASHES: Trailer Maintenance
Turnbow Trailers Inc..........................F....... 918 862-3233
  Oilton (G-5241)

AUTOMOTIVE SVCS, EXC REPAIR: Carwash, Automatic
Berkshire Corporation.......................G....... 405 677-3391
  Oklahoma City (G-5556)

AUTOMOTIVE SVCS, EXC REPAIR: Washing & Polishing
Bendmasters Inc...............................G....... 918 585-3755
  Tulsa (G-9282)

AUTOMOTIVE SVCS, EXC RPR/CARWASHES: High Perf Auto Rpr/Svc
Self Automotive & Racing Inc.............G....... 580 924-5866
  Durant (G-2256)

AUTOMOTIVE TOWING SVCS
Alberts Auto & Truck Repr Inc.............E....... 866 772-6065
  Weatherford (G-11389)
Bach Welding & Diesel Service...........G....... 580 593-2599
  Custer City (G-1973)
Sky Motors LLC................................F....... 918 321-2800
  Sapulpa (G-8313)

AUTOMOTIVE TRANSMISSION REPAIR SVC
Axels Transmissions Transfers............G....... 918 425-7725
  Tulsa (G-9234)
Custom Upholstery............................G....... 918 342-3489
  Claremore (G-1611)
Fat Alberts Motor Sports....................G....... 918 647-3069
  Poteau (G-7903)
Liberty Transmission Parts.................G....... 405 634-3450
  Oklahoma City (G-6473)
Thomas H Scott Western LLC............G....... 405 632-6860
  Oklahoma City (G-7283)
Transmission Center.........................G....... 405 329-4620
  Norman (G-5182)
United Holdings LLC..........................G....... 405 947-3321
  Oklahoma City (G-7369)

AUTOMOTIVE WELDING SVCS
Stouts Welding.................................G....... 580 243-9116
  Canute (G-1271)
Twisted Okie Welding LLC.................G....... 580 335-1494
  Lawton (G-4015)

AUTOMOTIVE: Bodies
Factor 1 Racing Inc...........................G....... 918 258-7223
  Broken Arrow (G-905)

AUTOMOTIVE: Seating
Clarios..G....... 405 688-3730
  Oklahoma City (G-5773)
Clarios..G....... 918 641-0660
  Tulsa (G-9439)

AWNING REPAIR SHOP
Elk City Sheet Metal Inc.....................G....... 580 225-5844
  Elk City (G-2810)
Hays Tent & Awning..........................G....... 918 534-1663
  Dewey (G-2023)

AWNINGS & CANOPIES
Karacon Solutions LLC......................G....... 918 231-1001
  Tulsa (G-10076)

AWNINGS & CANOPIES: Awnings, Fabric, From Purchased Matls
Awnings of Tulsa Inc.........................G....... 918 747-2050
  Tulsa (G-9232)

BACKHOES

Irwin Custom Sign Company LLC........G....... 405 372-0657
  Stillwater (G-8704)
Oklahoma Custom Canvas Pdts..........F....... 918 438-4040
  Tulsa (G-10395)

AWNINGS & CANOPIES: Canopies, Fabric, From Purchased Matls
City Tent & Awning Co Inc..................G....... 918 583-5003
  Tulsa (G-9437)

AWNINGS & CANOPIES: Fabric
Awnings Unique................................G....... 405 249-2488
  Moore (G-4496)
Dans Custom Awnings LLC................G....... 405 601-2703
  Oklahoma City (G-5896)
Karacon Solutions LLC......................G....... 918 231-1001
  Tulsa (G-10076)

AXLES
Dexter Axle Company........................C....... 405 262-1178
  El Reno (G-2712)
Douglas Thompson Auto Inc..............G....... 405 330-6997
  Edmond (G-2393)

BABBITT (METAL)
Probuilt Spincasting LLC....................G....... 918 617-9053
  Eufaula (G-3109)

BACKHOES
A-1 Backhoe....................................G....... 405 547-5452
  Perkins (G-7714)
A-1 Backhoe Inc...............................G....... 405 863-7094
  Oklahoma City (G-5350)
B and J Backhoe and Cnstr...............G....... 580 467-4981
  Duncan (G-2086)
Backhoe Services Oklahoma LLC.......G....... 405 356-2712
  Luther (G-4133)
Beller Boring Backhoe L....................G....... 405 288-6638
  Washington (G-11333)
Billy McGill......................................G....... 580 220-7097
  Marietta (G-4200)
Bobs Backhoe Sevice........................G....... 918 391-0901
  Talala (G-8896)
Brents Dana....................................G....... 405 640-1566
  Newcastle (G-4819)
C & C Backhoe & Tractor Inc.............G....... 405 392-4699
  Blanchard (G-703)
Cravens Backhoe Service LLC...........G....... 580 661-3652
  Thomas (G-8941)
Dans Backhoe & Dozer Service.........G....... 580 256-0865
  Woodward (G-11576)
Dig-It Backhoe Trctr Svcs LLC...........G....... 405 921-2623
  Harrah (G-3376)
Garrison Backhoe LLC......................G....... 580 465-2014
  Ardmore (G-294)
Jack Sprague..................................G....... 405 367-7655
  Blanchard (G-717)
Jacks Cnstr & Backhoe Svc...............G....... 405 238-3569
  Pauls Valley (G-7661)
Jims Backhoe LLC............................G....... 405 352-5003
  Minco (G-4476)
K&R Backhoe and Dirt Svcs LLC........G....... 580 239-8630
  Atoka (G-417)
Kahn Backhoe & Trenching...............G....... 580 541-6600
  Okeene (G-5258)
Kens Plumbing & Backhoe.................G....... 918 963-4223
  Shady Point (G-8414)
Kevin Banks....................................G....... 918 230-2142
  Bristow (G-785)
Kuykendal Wldg Backhoe Svc LLC....G....... 918 372-4899
  Ripley (G-8101)
L&M Dump Truck & Backhoe Servi.....G....... 918 798-4568
  Sperry (G-8609)
Majetta Tractor & Backhoe Inc...........G....... 918 272-7861
  Owasso (G-7589)
Martys Dumptruck & Backhoe Svc.....G....... 918 869-2051
  Muskogee (G-4707)
Mike McCalip...................................G....... 405 452-5730
  Wetumka (G-11495)
Mitch Baskett..................................G....... 405 324-7810
  Yukon (G-11756)
Nelson Backhoe and Welding.............G....... 918 399-3426
  Cushing (G-1947)
Okie Plumbing and Backhoe..............G....... 580 302-5018
  Sulphur (G-8840)
Randys Backhoe Service...................G....... 580 227-0561
  Longdale (G-4126)

BACKHOES

Rick Crsslin Backhoe Dozer Svc..........G...... 918 371-7956
  Mounds *(G-4624)*
Roger W Boone..G...... 580 799-0035
  Elk City *(G-2868)*
Ron Griggs Backhoe & Dump................G...... 918 440-1334
  Dewey *(G-2032)*
Sjh Welding & Backhoe LLC..................G...... 405 833-8353
  Calumet *(G-1249)*
Smiths Backhoe and Utility...................G...... 405 202-7056
  Perkins *(G-7722)*
Smittys Backhoe Service LLC...............G...... 918 630-1090
  Tulsa *(G-10781)*
Spragues Backhoe LLC...........................G...... 405 600-4905
  Oklahoma City *(G-7188)*
T2t Storm Shelters...................................G...... 580 512-4890
  Lawton *(G-4011)*
Toms Tree Svc & Backhoe......................G...... 918 865-4861
  Jennings *(G-3740)*

BADGES, WHOLESALE

David Logan..G...... 918 739-4231
  Catoosa *(G-1315)*

BAGS: Food Storage & Frozen Food, Plastic

Richard Bolusky......................................G...... 918 381-5694
  Broken Arrow *(G-1031)*

BAGS: Garment, Plastic Film, Made From Purchased Materials

Sigma Extruding Corp............................F...... 918 446-6265
  Tulsa *(G-10755)*

BAGS: Plastic

Advance Polybag Inc..............................G...... 405 677-8383
  Oklahoma City *(G-5377)*
Transcontinental Holding Corp.............F...... 918 739-4907
  Catoosa *(G-1358)*
Transcontinental US LLC........................D...... 918 739-4906
  Catoosa *(G-1359)*

BAGS: Plastic, Made From Purchased Materials

API Enterprises Inc.................................C...... 713 580-4800
  Oklahoma City *(G-5452)*
Bags Inc...E...... 405 427-5473
  Oklahoma City *(G-5509)*
Tech Pack Inc..G...... 918 836-8493
  Tulsa *(G-10910)*

BAGS: Textile

Beths Bags and More LLC.....................G...... 918 451-7346
  Broken Arrow *(G-848)*
Fashionable Medical Covers.................G...... 405 414-1147
  Norman *(G-4998)*
Madison Filter Incorporated................G...... 315 685-3466
  Tulsa *(G-10198)*

BAKERIES, COMMERCIAL: On Premises Baking Only

Angela Lyn Sarabia.................................G...... 405 808-8576
  Oklahoma City *(G-5446)*
Antoinette Baking Co LLC.....................G...... 918 808-0875
  Tulsa *(G-9193)*
Bama Foods Limited Partnership.........C...... 918 732-2399
  Tulsa *(G-9260)*
Berryfields Cinnamon Roll LLC............G...... 405 248-0777
  Oklahoma City *(G-5558)*
Bimbo Bakeries Usa Inc........................G...... 405 273-5049
  Shawnee *(G-8432)*
Browns Bakery Inc..................................E...... 405 232-0363
  Oklahoma City *(G-5637)*
Cloverleaf Baking Co..............................G...... 612 708-8196
  Bartlesville *(G-466)*
Cupcakes & Sweets Galore...................G...... 405 641-7760
  Oklahoma City *(G-5870)*
Cupcakes By Lu......................................G...... 918 671-0599
  Bixby *(G-619)*
Da Bomb Cupcakes................................G...... 405 261-3595
  Tulsa *(G-9543)*
Dandee Donuts..G...... 580 332-7700
  Ada *(G-30)*
Dizzy Lizzy Cupcakery LLC..................G...... 405 263-7667
  Okarche *(G-5242)*
Felinis Cookies Inc.................................G...... 918 742-3638
  Tulsa *(G-9734)*
Flowers Baking Co Denton LLC............G...... 405 366-2175
  Norman *(G-5002)*
Flowers Bkg Co Lynchburg LLC...........G...... 918 270-1182
  Tulsa *(G-9759)*
Flowers Foods Inc..................................G...... 405 270-7880
  Oklahoma City *(G-6093)*
Franklin Baking Company LLC..............G...... 918 423-2888
  McAlester *(G-4300)*
Mc Alester Food Warehouse................D...... 580 436-4302
  Ada *(G-64)*
Nut House...G...... 918 266-1604
  Claremore *(G-1664)*
Quality Bakery Products LLC................F...... 609 871-7393
  Tulsa *(G-10590)*
Sfc Global Supply Chain Inc................C...... 918 696-8325
  Stilwell *(G-8795)*
Tower Cafe Inc..F...... 405 263-4853
  Okarche *(G-5255)*
Tulsa Baking Inc......................................D...... 918 712-2918
  Tulsa *(G-10988)*
Tulsa Baking Inc......................................E...... 918 747-2301
  Tulsa *(G-10989)*

BAKERIES: On Premises Baking & Consumption

Browns Bakery Inc..................................E...... 405 232-0363
  Oklahoma City *(G-5637)*
Dandee Donuts..G...... 580 332-7700
  Ada *(G-30)*
Donut Shop..G...... 580 276-3910
  Marietta *(G-4206)*
Morgans Bakery.......................................G...... 918 456-3731
  Tahlequah *(G-8875)*
O K Country Donut Shoppe..................G...... 918 493-6455
  Tulsa *(G-10371)*
Raymonds Donut Shop..........................G...... 918 660-0644
  Tulsa *(G-10622)*

BAKERY FOR HOME SVC DELIVERY

Order Here Tulsa LLC............................G...... 888 633-9905
  Muskogee *(G-4728)*
Sweetiesrite Baking................................G...... 405 400-6581
  Oklahoma City *(G-7236)*

BAKERY MACHINERY

Burford Corp..D...... 405 867-4467
  Maysville *(G-4255)*

BAKERY PRDTS: Bakery Prdts, Partially Cooked, Exc frozen

Grahams Bakery & Cafe........................G...... 918 543-4244
  Inola *(G-3659)*
Jemison Denna..G...... 405 922-7830
  Oklahoma City *(G-6356)*

BAKERY PRDTS: Biscuits, Baked, Baking Powder & Raised

Bama Companies Inc.............................A...... 918 592-0778
  Tulsa *(G-9258)*

BAKERY PRDTS: Bread, All Types, Fresh Or Frozen

Morgans Bakery.......................................G...... 918 456-3731
  Tahlequah *(G-8875)*

BAKERY PRDTS: Cakes, Bakery, Exc Frozen

Ambrosia Sweet Inc...............................G...... 405 816-2887
  Oklahoma City *(G-5429)*
Bubble Bee Bakery and Supplies.........G...... 918 209-8658
  Tulsa *(G-9347)*
Cakes & More..G...... 918 649-0451
  Poteau *(G-7899)*
Key To Natures Blessings LLC.............G...... 405 603-8200
  Bethany *(G-585)*
Mitchells Sausage Rolls.........................G...... 918 342-5852
  Claremore *(G-1657)*
Panderia La Guadalupana....................G...... 918 764-9000
  Tulsa *(G-10459)*
Precious Memories By M L...................G...... 405 427-7007
  Oklahoma City *(G-6878)*
Sophisticated Sweets Inc.....................G...... 580 704-8038
  Cache *(G-1231)*

BAKERY PRDTS: Cakes, Bakery, Frozen

Enchanted Delights LLC........................G...... 405 202-5782
  Oklahoma City *(G-6034)*

BAKERY PRDTS: Cones, Ice Cream

Billy Goat Ice Cream Co LLC................G...... 405 332-5508
  Stillwater *(G-8660)*

BAKERY PRDTS: Cookies

Fehr Foods Inc..E...... 580 276-4100
  Marietta *(G-4207)*

BAKERY PRDTS: Cookies & crackers

Dandee Donuts..G...... 580 332-7700
  Ada *(G-30)*
Felinis Cookies Inc.................................G...... 918 742-3638
  Tulsa *(G-9734)*
Masons Pecans & Peanuts Inc.............G...... 405 329-7828
  Norman *(G-5065)*
Pure Creativity LLC................................G...... 918 272-3152
  Owasso *(G-7605)*
Tulsa Baking Inc......................................D...... 918 712-2918
  Tulsa *(G-10988)*
Tulsa Baking Inc......................................E...... 918 747-2301
  Tulsa *(G-10989)*

BAKERY PRDTS: Crackers

Treehouse Private Brands Inc..............C...... 270 365-5505
  Poteau *(G-7915)*

BAKERY PRDTS: Doughnuts, Exc Frozen

Dandy Donuts...G...... 580 924-7872
  Durant *(G-2220)*
Daylight Donuts.......................................G...... 918 256-6236
  Vinita *(G-11252)*
Daylight Donuts.......................................G...... 405 598-8707
  Tecumseh *(G-8911)*
Daylight Donuts.......................................G...... 580 279-6560
  Ada *(G-31)*
Daylight Donuts Inc................................G...... 405 359-9016
  Edmond *(G-2384)*
Donut Shop..G...... 580 276-3910
  Marietta *(G-4206)*
Dounut Palace...G...... 405 527-5746
  Purcell *(G-8006)*
J B S Donuts..G...... 918 486-4022
  Coweta *(G-1887)*
Krispy Kreme..G...... 918 294-5293
  Tulsa *(G-10103)*
Legend Enterprises Inc.........................G...... 405 340-0410
  Edmond *(G-2486)*
O K Country Donut Shoppe..................G...... 918 493-6455
  Tulsa *(G-10371)*
Paradise Doughnuts...............................G...... 405 224-2907
  Chickasha *(G-1499)*
Raymonds Donut Shop..........................G...... 918 660-0644
  Tulsa *(G-10622)*
Saskas Sweets...G...... 580 772-3476
  Weatherford *(G-11438)*

BAKERY PRDTS: Dry

Nonnis Foods LLC..................................D...... 918 621-1200
  Tulsa *(G-10348)*

BAKERY PRDTS: Frozen

Nonnis Foods LLC..................................D...... 918 621-1200
  Tulsa *(G-10348)*

BAKERY PRDTS: Pies, Bakery, Frozen

Bama Companies Inc.............................A...... 918 592-0778
  Tulsa *(G-9258)*
Bama Pie Ltd...A...... 918 592-0778
  Tulsa *(G-9261)*
Fields Inc..E...... 405 238-7381
  Pauls Valley *(G-7659)*

BAKERY PRDTS: Wholesalers

Browns Bakery Inc..................................E...... 405 232-0363
  Oklahoma City *(G-5637)*

PRODUCT SECTION   BEVERAGES, ALCOHOLIC: Beer & Ale

BAKERY: Wholesale Or Wholesale & Retail Combined

Bimbo Bakeries Usa Inc	G	580 234-1213
Enid (G-2918)		
Bimbo Bakeries Usa Inc	B	405 556-2135
Oklahoma City (G-5569)		
Sweet Memories By Heather LLC	G	360 608-1600
Cushing (G-1963)		

BALERS

Bramco Inc	F	580 227-2345
Fairview (G-3133)		
Musick Farms Inc	G	580 393-4826
Sentinel (G-8411)		

BARBECUE EQPT

Hasty-Bake Inc	F	918 665-8220
Tulsa (G-9901)		
Horizon Smoker Company	F	580 336-2400
Perry (G-7736)		
Party King Grills Company LLC	G	580 774-2828
Weatherford (G-11432)		
Southern Cooker	G	580 283-3982
Achille (G-1)		
W C Brdly/Zebco Holdings Inc	F	706 571-6080
Tulsa (G-11087)		

BARRELS: Shipping, Metal

Davco Manufacturing	F	918 535-2360
Ochelata (G-5234)		

BARS & BAR SHAPES: Steel, Hot-Rolled

Commercial Metals Company	F	918 437-5377
Tulsa (G-9474)		

BARS: Concrete Reinforcing, Fabricated Steel

Bennett Steel Fabrication Inc	D	918 227-2564
Sapulpa (G-8253)		
Bison Welding LLC	G	580 758-3359
Bison (G-607)		
C Johnstone Welding Fabricat	G	580 362-2400
Newkirk (G-4846)		
Cherokee Piping Services LLC	G	918 931-8593
Tahlequah (G-8856)		
Grating Company LLC	G	918 834-8100
Tulsa (G-9848)		
Hurst Prcsion & Fabrication LLC	E	580 628-2388
Tonkawa (G-8975)		
Ketchum Group LLC	G	918 407-2228
Jenks (G-3712)		
Phillips Prcsion Machining LLC	F	918 914-2131
Bartlesville (G-517)		
Post-Tension Services of Okla	F	405 751-1582
Oklahoma City (G-6866)		
Pro Piping & Fabrication LLC	C	918 599-8218
Tulsa (G-10565)		
Reinforcing Services Inc	F	918 379-0090
Catoosa (G-1350)		
Ross Fabrication & Detailing	F	405 356-9955
Wellston (G-11478)		

BASKETS, WHOLESALE

Miller Sales Wholesale Distr	G	918 629-4064
Tulsa (G-10282)		

BATH SALTS

Bath Bomb Dyes	G	405 406-1823
Yukon (G-11697)		
K2 Bath Salts Online	G	405 445-4295
Oklahoma City (G-6394)		
Salt Soothers LLC	G	405 201-2020
Edmond (G-2610)		
Tony Smallwood	G	918 402-9267
Tulsa (G-10952)		
Whitetail Bath Bombs	G	405 474-8017
El Reno (G-2771)		

BATHROOM ACCESS & FITTINGS: Vitreous China & Earthenware

Bobrick Washroom Equipment Inc	F	580 924-8066
Durant (G-2207)		

BATHROOM FIXTURES: Plastic

G & D Industries Inc	G	918 369-2648
Bixby (G-625)		

BATTERIES: Storage

Continental Battery Company	E	918 259-0662
Broken Arrow (G-874)		
Spiers New Technologies Inc	E	405 464-2200
Oklahoma City (G-7184)		
Spiers New Technologies Inc	E	405 605-8066
Oklahoma City (G-7185)		

BATTERY CHARGERS

Atc New Technologies	E	405 577-9901
Oklahoma City (G-5482)		
Exide Technologies LLC	F	405 745-2511
Oklahoma City (G-6061)		
Quick Charge Corporation	E	405 634-2120
Oklahoma City (G-6944)		

BATTERY REPAIR & SVCS

Hardin Ignition Inc	G	405 853-4324
Hennessey (G-3465)		

BEARINGS: Ball & Roller

Imak Industrial Solutions LLC	G	405 406-9778
Oklahoma City (G-6292)		
Rbc Bearings Incorporated	E	405 236-2666
Oklahoma City (G-6976)		

BEAUTY & BARBER SHOP EQPT

Bronco Manufacturing	G	405 225-1909
Oklahoma City (G-5631)		
Element Fleet Corporation	G	405 799-4775
Oklahoma City (G-5290)		
Greyfox Industries LLC	G	918 830-1144
Broken Arrow (G-923)		
Jones Power Products LLC	G	405 485-2019
Blanchard (G-718)		
Medline Industries	G	405 745-9977
Oklahoma City (G-6558)		
Racf Industries Inc	G	918 258-1290
Broken Arrow (G-1019)		
Shaw Industries Group Inc	G	405 917-5117
Oklahoma City (G-7116)		
Ssg Inc	G	405 639-2056
Moore (G-4574)		
Thomas Energy Systems Inc	E	918 665-0031
Tulsa (G-10930)		
Thunderbolt Machine Services	G	918 357-2294
Broken Arrow (G-1172)		
Venture Industries Inc	G	918 557-8789
Broken Arrow (G-1091)		

BEAUTY & BARBER SHOP EQPT & SPLYS WHOLESALERS

Ssg Inc	G	405 639-2056
Moore (G-4574)		

BEAUTY SALONS

Allure Salon and Spa LLC	G	580 371-9333
Tishomingo (G-8961)		
Ssg Inc	G	405 639-2056
Moore (G-4574)		

BED & BREAKFAST INNS

Nancy Dalrymple	G	405 525-7544
Oklahoma City (G-6650)		

BED SHEETING, COTTON

Burns & McDonnell Inc	G	405 200-0300
Oklahoma City (G-5646)		

BEDDING, BEDSPREADS, BLANKETS & SHEETS

Whistle Stop Bedding & More	G	405 620-5749
Edmond (G-2686)		

BEDDING, BEDSPREADS, BLANKETS & SHEETS: Comforters & Quilts

Quilts Unlimited	G	580 746-2770
Millerton (G-4474)		

BEDS & ACCESS STORES

Life Lift Systems Inc	F	904 635-8231
Oklahoma City (G-6474)		
Mobility Living Inc	G	405 672-7237
Oklahoma City (G-6623)		

BEDSPREADS & BED SETS, FROM PURCHASED MATERIALS

Fabricut Inc	F	918 825-4400
Pryor (G-7962)		
Interior Designers Supply Inc	F	405 521-1551
Oklahoma City (G-6318)		

BEER & ALE WHOLESALERS

Stillwater Brewing Company LLC	G	405 614-2520
Stillwater (G-8756)		

BEER, WINE & LIQUOR STORES: Hard Liquor

Dulaneys Liquor Store	G	405 377-9007
Stillwater (G-8679)		

BEER, WINE & LIQUOR STORES: Wine

Native Spirits Winery LLC	G	405 329-9942
Norman (G-5087)		
Rocky Top Winery LLC	G	580 857-2869
Allen (G-138)		
Tidal School Winery	G	918 352-4900
Drumright (G-2076)		
Whispering Vines Vinyrd Winery	G	918 447-0808
Tulsa (G-11116)		

BELLOWS

Oklahoma Equipment Mfg PDT	G	405 491-6484
Oklahoma City (G-6747)		

BELTS & BELT PRDTS

Sooner Rubber Products Company	G	918 461-1391
Tulsa (G-10792)		

BELTS: Bandoleers

South Central Machine	G	580 775-1623
Durant (G-2258)		

BENZENE

Sunoco (R&m) LLC	F	918 586-6246
Tulsa (G-10873)		

BEVERAGE BASES & SYRUPS

Margarita Man Hq LLC	G	830 336-4252
Stillwater (G-8721)		

BEVERAGE PRDTS: Brewers' Grain

Brewer Media LLC	G	405 236-4143
Oklahoma City (G-5626)		

BEVERAGES, ALCOHOLIC: Beer

Dulaneys Liquor Store	G	405 377-9007
Stillwater (G-8679)		
Ed F Davis Inc	G	580 265-4210
Stonewall (G-8800)		
Union Brewers	G	405 604-8989
Oklahoma City (G-7360)		

BEVERAGES, ALCOHOLIC: Beer & Ale

Back Alley Brewers & More LLC	G	580 716-2571
Ponca City (G-7799)		
Bb2 LLC	G	918 895-7878
Tulsa (G-9274)		
Bb2 LLC	G	405 726-8300
Edmond (G-2319)		
Bb2 LLC	E	405 232-2739
Oklahoma City (G-5534)		
Choc Brewing Company Inc	G	918 302-3002
McAlester (G-4282)		
Krebs Brewing Co Inc	F	918 740-9293
Tulsa (G-10101)		
Krebs Brewing Co Inc	F	918 488-8910
Tulsa (G-10102)		
Stillwater Brewing Company LLC	G	405 614-2520
Stillwater (G-8756)		

Employee Codes: A=Over 500 employees, B=251-500
C=101-250, D=51-100, E=20-50, F=10-19, G=1-9

BEVERAGES, ALCOHOLIC: Cocktails

19th Hole	G	405 424-0520

Oklahoma City (G-5328)

BEVERAGES, ALCOHOLIC: Distilled Liquors

Oklahoma Distilling Company .... G 918 505-4861
  Tulsa (G-10397)
Rock Creek Distillery LLC .... G 580 254-1407
  Shattuck (G-8423)

BEVERAGES, ALCOHOLIC: Liquors, Malt

Azimuth Spirits LLC .... G 317 468-3931
  Norman (G-4922)

BEVERAGES, ALCOHOLIC: Scotch Whiskey

Green Valley Distillery LLC .... G 918 413-5199
  Red Oak (G-8076)

BEVERAGES, ALCOHOLIC: Wines

Allen Vineyards LLC .... G 405 240-7147
  Bethany (G-572)
B&G Meadery LLC .... G 580 272-7197
  Stonewall (G-8797)
Billy J Vineyard .... G 918 246-2139
  Sand Springs (G-8167)
Blue Coyote Winery .... G 918 785-4727
  Adair (G-107)
Boardwalk Distribution Co .... F 918 551-6275
  Tulsa (G-9313)
Broken Bone Vnyards Winery LLC ..... G 405 585-8319
  McLoud (G-4354)
Canadian Rver Vnyrds Wnery LLC ..... G 405 872-5565
  Lexington (G-4034)
Canyon Lakes Winery LLC .... G 405 367-7291
  Oklahoma City (G-5690)
Coyote Run Vineyard LLC .... G 918 785-4727
  Adair (G-108)
Deangel Farms & Winery LLC .... G 405 996-0914
  Blanchard (G-709)
Deep Branch Winery LLC .... G 918 519-5490
  Cookson (G-1850)
Diane E Dean .... G 580 775-4203
  Caddo (G-1233)
Entwined Vines Winery LLC .... G 405 320-0452
  Anadarko (G-203)
Fish Tale Winery .... G 580 494-6115
  Broken Bow (G-1190)
Frozen Mesa Winery LLC .... G 405 281-5962
  Choctaw (G-1543)
Girls Gone Wine .... E 580 494-6243
  Broken Bow (G-1191)
Grayfox Vineyards LLC .... G 918 378-2214
  Yukon (G-11728)
Ingels Vineyard LLC .... G 405 321-1008
  Norman (G-5034)
Iron Post Winery LLC .... G 918 479-3600
  Locust Grove (G-4111)
J & B Deep Discount .... G 918 622-7600
  Tulsa (G-10016)
Joullian Vineyards Ltd .... E 405 848-4585
  Oklahoma City (G-6386)
Judy Tomlinson .... G 580 252-2559
  Duncan (G-2140)
Knotted Rope Winery LLC .... G 918 839-1464
  Broken Bow (G-1197)
Legends Vineyard & Winery .... G 405 823-8265
  Lindsay (G-4073)
Native Spirits Winery LLC .... G 405 329-9942
  Norman (G-5087)
Nellis Vineyards LLC .... G 405 826-5279
  Edmond (G-2532)
New Moon Vineyard .... G 405 364-8655
  Norman (G-5090)
Nuyaka Creek Winery LLC .... G 918 756-8485
  Bristow (G-790)
Pecan Creek Winery LLC .... G 918 683-1087
  Muskogee (G-4733)
Plainview Winery .... G 580 796-2902
  Lahoma (G-3859)
Plymouth Valley Cellars Inc .... G 580 227-0348
  Fairview (G-3146)
Ramiiisol Vineyards LLC .... G 405 858-9800
  Oklahoma City (G-6969)
Rocky Top Winery LLC .... G 580 857-2869
  Allen (G-138)
Rusty Nail Winery .... G 580 622-8466
  Sulphur (G-8842)
Sailing Horse Enterprises LLC .... G 918 618-4824
  Eufaula (G-3112)
Shell Creek Vineyards LLC .... G 214 415-4741
  Yukon (G-11781)
Sine Qua Non LLC .... G 405 478-2539
  Oklahoma City (G-7142)
Sparks Vineyard & Winery Inc .... G 918 866-2529
  Sparks (G-8589)
Stableridge LLC .... F 918 968-2568
  Stroud (G-8819)
Strebel Creek Vineyard .... G 405 720-7779
  Oklahoma City (G-7217)
Summerside Vineyards & Winery ...... F 918 256-3000
  Tuttle (G-11212)
Summerside Winery & Meadery .... G 405 514-6360
  Tuttle (G-11213)
Territory Cellars LLC .... G 918 987-1800
  Stroud (G-8822)
Tidal School Winery .... G 918 352-4900
  Drumright (G-2076)
Twiss Sueons Winery Inc .... E 405 277-7089
  Luther (G-4140)
Waddell Vineyards LLC .... G 580 421-6933
  Ada (G-103)
Waters Edge Winery On Rose .... G 918 286-0086
  Broken Arrow (G-1092)
Whispering Vines Vinyrd Winery .... G 918 447-0808
  Tulsa (G-11116)
Whispring Mdows Vnyards Winery ... G 918 423-9463
  McAlester (G-4351)
Woodland Park Vineyards .... G 405 743-2442
  Stillwater (G-8776)
Woods and Waters Holdings LLC ..... F 405 347-3000
  Anadarko (G-210)
Woods Wters Wnery Vneyards LLC .. G 405 247-3000
  Anadarko (G-211)
Yippee Ay-O-K Winery .... G 580 515-8214
  Clinton (G-1773)

BEVERAGES, NONALCOHOLIC: Bottled & canned soft drinks

7 Up Bottle .... G 918 426-0310
  McAlester (G-4268)
Ada Coca Cola Bottling Company ..... D 580 427-2000
  Ada (G-3)
All American Bottling Cor .... G 918 831-3800
  Tulsa (G-9135)
Coca Cola Bottling Co .... G 580 256-2350
  Woodward (G-11570)
Coca-Cola Enterprises Inc .... G 918 619-8200
  Tulsa (G-9464)
Dr Pepper Snapple Group .... G 405 680-5150
  Oklahoma City (G-5978)
Fresh Promise Foods Inc .... G 561 703-4659
  Midwest City (G-4441)
Great Plains Coca Cola Btlg Co .... G 405 503-9328
  Oklahoma City (G-6178)
Great Plains Coca Cola Btlg Co .... B 405 280-2000
  Oklahoma City (G-6179)
Great Plains Coca-Cola Btlg Co .... D 918 439-3013
  Tulsa (G-9853)
Great Plains Coca-Cola Btlg Co .... D 405 280-2000
  Oklahoma City (G-6180)
Great Plains Coca-Cola Btlg Co .... C 405 280-2700
  Oklahoma City (G-6181)
Great Plains Coca-Cola Btlg Co .... C 800 753-2653
  Tulsa (G-9854)
Great Plains Design .... G 405 943-9018
  Oklahoma City (G-6182)
Lake Country Beverage Inc .... G 918 426-0310
  McAlester (G-4313)
Pure Mountain .... G 918 254-2225
  Broken Arrow (G-1014)
Seven-Up Bottling Co Inc .... F 580 765-6468
  Ponca City (G-7874)
Sooner Coca-Cola Bottling Co .... G 918 423-0911
  Mc Alester (G-4266)

BEVERAGES, NONALCOHOLIC: Carbonated

P-Americas LLC .... G 580 326-8333
  Hugo (G-3617)
Pepsi Cola Btlg Clinton Okla .... E 580 323-1666
  Clinton (G-1763)
Pepsi Cola Company .... B 918 446-6601
  Tulsa (G-10489)
Pepsi-Cola Btlg McAlester Inc .... E 918 423-2360
  McAlester (G-4328)
Pepsi-Cola Btlg McAlester Inc .... G 918 446-6601
  Tulsa (G-10490)
Pepsi-Cola Metro Btlg Co Inc .... C 580 326-8333
  Hugo (G-3618)
Pepsi-Cola Metro Btlg Co Inc .... E 580 585-6281
  Lawton (G-3983)

BEVERAGES, NONALCOHOLIC: Carbonated, Canned & Bottled, Etc

American Bottling Company .... D 405 680-5150
  Oklahoma City (G-5433)
Belle Point Beverages Inc .... G 918 649-3921
  Poteau (G-7896)
Vita-Source Inc .... G 918 407-9525
  Sand Springs (G-8235)

BEVERAGES, NONALCOHOLIC: Flavoring extracts & syrups, nec

Cesi Chemical Inc .... B 580 658-6608
  Marlow (G-4225)
Griffin Food Company .... D 918 687-6311
  Muskogee (G-4683)
Midwest Bakers Supply Co Inc .... G 405 942-3489
  Oklahoma City (G-6599)
Pepper Creek Farms Inc .... G 580 536-1300
  Lawton (G-3982)
Webers Superior Root Beer Inc .... G 918 742-1082
  Tulsa (G-11101)

BEVERAGES, NONALCOHOLIC: Lemonade, Bottled & Canned, Etc

Dust Cutter .... E 405 615-7788
  Norman (G-4985)

BEVERAGES, NONALCOHOLIC: Soft Drinks, Canned & Bottled, Etc

Browne Bottling Co Inc .... F 405 232-1158
  Oklahoma City (G-5636)
Dr Pepper Bottling Co .... G 580 256-2350
  Woodward (G-11580)
Dr Pepper Bottling Co Elk City .... F 580 225-3186
  Elk City (G-2804)
Dr Pepper Co .... G 580 765-6468
  Ponca City (G-7823)
Dr Pepper-Royal Crown Btlg Co .... F 405 224-1260
  Chickasha (G-1453)

BEVERAGES, NONALCOHOLIC: Tea, Iced, Bottled & Canned, Etc

Ice-T King LLC .... G 405 206-1185
  Oklahoma City (G-6284)

BEVERAGES, WINE & DISTILLED ALCOHOLIC, WHOLESALE: Wine

Trio Di Vino LLC .... F 405 494-1954
  Oklahoma City (G-7336)

BEVERAGES, WINE/DISTILLED ALCOHOLIC, WHOL: Bttlg Wine/Liquor

Native Spirits Winery LLC .... G 405 329-9942
  Norman (G-5087)

BICYCLE REPAIR SHOP

Buchanan Bicycles Inc .... G 405 364-5513
  Norman (G-4948)

BICYCLE SHOPS

Buchanan Bicycles Inc .... G 405 364-5513
  Norman (G-4948)

BILLIARD & POOL TABLES & SPLYS

By Prather Inc .... G 580 994-2414
  Mooreland (G-4586)

BILLING & BOOKKEEPING SVCS

Aars .... G 918 313-4512
  Tulsa (G-9080)

BINDING SVC: Books & Manuals

A 1 Master Print Inc .... G 405 787-0505
  Bethany (G-571)

PRODUCT SECTION

BROADCASTING & COMMS EQPT: Antennas, Transmitting/Comms

Hy-H Manufacturing Co Inc ....E...... 918 341-6811
  Claremore *(G-1638)*
Hydrohoist Boat Lifts ....G...... 918 256-8125
  Bernice *(G-565)*
Hydrohoist Marine Group Inc ....G...... 918 256-8775
  Bernice *(G-566)*

BOAT REPAIR SVCS

Tip Top Prop Shop ....G...... 580 564-3712
  Kingston *(G-3831)*

BOAT YARD: Boat yards, storage & incidental repair

Beaver Fabrication Inc ....G...... 405 360-0014
  Norman *(G-4928)*

BODIES: Truck & Bus

Arrowhead Truck Equipment Inc..........G...... 918 224-5570
  Bixby *(G-612)*
Bramco Inc ....F...... 580 227-2345
  Fairview *(G-3133)*
Cooper Creek Manufacturing Inc ....G...... 405 729-4446
  Loyal *(G-4130)*
Crane Carrier Co ....G...... 918 836-1651
  Tulsa *(G-9500)*
Custom Automotive Mfg ....F...... 918 258-2900
  Broken Arrow *(G-881)*
Halliburton Company ....E...... 580 251-4614
  Duncan *(G-2121)*
Ic Bus of Oklahoma LLC ....A...... 918 833-4000
  Tulsa *(G-9964)*
J & J Custom Fire Inc ....G...... 405 747-4442
  Red Rock *(G-8079)*
Nix Body Shop LLC ....G...... 918 797-2484
  Stilwell *(G-8794)*
Performance Plastics Inc ....G...... 918 627-9621
  Tulsa *(G-10494)*
Shur-Co LLC ....G...... 405 262-7600
  El Reno *(G-2757)*
Wheels of Past ....G...... 918 225-2250
  Cushing *(G-1969)*

BODY PARTS: Automobile, Stamped Metal

Accessory and Prfmce Sls Inc ....G...... 918 224-5851
  Sapulpa *(G-8246)*
Autocraft Material Recovery ....G...... 405 350-3800
  Oklahoma City *(G-5493)*
Hart Brothers Welding ....G...... 918 697-5682
  Collinsville *(G-1812)*
Mar-K Specialized Mfg Inc ....E...... 405 721-7945
  Oklahoma City *(G-6520)*
Mike Bailey Motors Inc ....F...... 918 652-9637
  Henryetta *(G-3512)*
Nick & Pauls Quality Car Cornr ....G...... 918 933-4000
  Tulsa *(G-10341)*
Sinister Sand Sports ....G...... 918 521-3736
  Broken Arrow *(G-1053)*
Track Products ....G...... 918 231-9960
  Fort Gibson *(G-3181)*

BOILER & HEATING REPAIR SVCS

Zoe Homes LLC ....G...... 405 550-3563
  Oklahoma City *(G-7488)*

BOILER REPAIR SHOP

JV Industrial Companies Ltd ....G...... 918 591-5450
  Tulsa *(G-10068)*

BOILERS & BOILER SHOP WORK

Technotherm Corporation ....E...... 918 446-1533
  Tulsa *(G-9042)*
Veterans Eng Group Inc ....G...... 918 864-6006
  Pryor *(G-7997)*

BOOK STORES

JB Books Unlimited LLC ....G...... 918 954-8308
  Tulsa *(G-10031)*

BOOK STORES: Religious

Cross Shadows Inc ....G...... 405 262-9777
  El Reno *(G-2707)*
F C Ziegler Co ....E...... 918 587-7639
  Tulsa *(G-9721)*
Gregory Prizzell P & R M Inc ....G...... 405 752-0782
  Oklahoma City *(G-6192)*

Harper County Journal ....G...... 580 735-2526
  Buffalo *(G-1213)*
Watonga Printing & Office Sups ....G...... 580 623-4989
  Watonga *(G-11353)*

BOOKS, WHOLESALE

Cross Shadows Inc ....G...... 405 262-9777
  El Reno *(G-2707)*
Garrett Educational Corp ....E...... 580 332-6884
  Ada *(G-39)*
JB Books Unlimited LLC ....G...... 918 954-8308
  Tulsa *(G-10031)*

BOTTLE CAPS & RESEALERS: Plastic

Berry Global Inc ....F...... 812 424-2904
  McAlester *(G-4274)*
Berry Global Inc ....F...... 918 824-4288
  Pryor *(G-7945)*
Berry Global Inc ....D...... 918 824-4400
  Pryor *(G-7946)*
Berry Global Inc ....C...... 918 426-4800
  McAlester *(G-4275)*

BOTTLES: Plastic

405 Plastics & Distribution ....G...... 405 562-8800
  Oklahoma City *(G-5333)*
Ansa Company Inc ....F...... 918 687-1664
  Muskogee *(G-4648)*
Blitz USA Inc ....B...... 918 676-3620
  Miami *(G-4391)*
Cleanng LLC ....G...... 918 409-0384
  Tulsa *(G-9446)*
J-M Manufacturing Company Inc ....D...... 918 446-4471
  Tulsa *(G-10025)*
Parker Plastics Inc ....D...... 918 241-0350
  Sand Springs *(G-8213)*
Relyassist LLC ....G...... 918 260-6517
  Broken Arrow *(G-1156)*
Uponor Aldyl Co Inc ....G...... 918 446-4471
  Tulsa *(G-11054)*

BOUTIQUE STORES

Blush Boutique Inc ....G...... 405 701-8600
  Norman *(G-4938)*

BOXES & CRATES: Rectangular, Wood

Four Star Crating Co ....G...... 918 663-6689
  Tulsa *(G-9769)*
Johnson Crating Services LLC ....G...... 405 672-7964
  Oklahoma City *(G-6374)*

BOXES & SHOOK: Nailed Wood

Johnson Crating Services LLC ....G...... 405 672-7964
  Oklahoma City *(G-6374)*
Tulsa Packing Specialist Inc ....F...... 918 459-8991
  Tulsa *(G-11003)*

BOXES: Corrugated

Creative Packaging Inc ....G...... 918 587-0347
  Tulsa *(G-9505)*
Georgia-Pacific LLC ....C...... 580 549-7100
  Fletcher *(G-3162)*
Green Bay Packaging Inc ....E...... 405 222-2306
  Chickasha *(G-1463)*
Green Bay Packaging Inc ....C...... 918 446-3341
  Tulsa *(G-9008)*
Pratt Industries USA Inc ....B...... 405 787-3500
  Oklahoma City *(G-6874)*
Smurfit Kappa ....G...... 405 672-1695
  Oklahoma City *(G-7156)*
Smurfit Kappa North Amer LLC ....B...... 405 672-1695
  Oklahoma City *(G-7157)*
Southern Box Company ....G...... 580 255-7969
  Duncan *(G-2181)*
Supplyone Oklahoma City Inc ....C...... 405 947-7373
  Oklahoma City *(G-7230)*
Westrock Cp LLC ....C...... 918 245-5102
  Sand Springs *(G-8241)*

BOXES: Paperboard, Folding

Artur Bookbinding Intl ....G...... 918 478-4888
  Fort Gibson *(G-3173)*
International Paper Company ....D...... 580 933-7211
  Valliant *(G-11227)*
Warner Jwly Box Display Co LLC ....D...... 580 536-8885
  Lawton *(G-4021)*

BOXES: Paperboard, Set-Up

Professional Image Inc ....E...... 918 461-0609
  Tulsa *(G-10569)*

BOXES: Tool Chests, Wood

Sunrise Sheds ....G...... 405 831-0904
  Prague *(G-7937)*

BOXES: Wooden

Pratt Industries USA Inc ....B...... 405 787-3500
  Oklahoma City *(G-6874)*

BOYS' CAMPS

Camp Chippewa For Boys Inc ....E...... 218 335-8807
  Tulsa *(G-9367)*

BRACKETS, ARCHITECTURAL: Plaster

CD Industrys Corporation ....G...... 580 317-8448
  Hugo *(G-3605)*

BRAKES & BRAKE PARTS

Brake Rebuilders Inc ....F...... 918 834-0200
  Tulsa *(G-9331)*
Tulsa Brake & Clutch Co LLC ....G...... 918 582-2165
  Tulsa *(G-10990)*

BRAKES: Electromagnetic

Tulsa Brake & Clutch Co LLC ....G...... 918 582-2165
  Tulsa *(G-10990)*

BRASS & BRONZE PRDTS: Die-casted

Cutting Edge Machine Inc ....G...... 580 658-5036
  Marlow *(G-4226)*

BRASS GOODS, WHOLESALE

Buster Dorsch ....G...... 918 743-4509
  Tulsa *(G-9353)*
Eaton Aeroquip LLC ....D...... 405 275-5500
  Shawnee *(G-8447)*
Outlaw Oilfield Supply LLC ....E...... 580 526-3792
  Erick *(G-3091)*

BRICK, STONE & RELATED PRDTS WHOLESALERS

Altus Ready-Mix Inc ....F...... 580 482-3418
  Altus *(G-142)*
Evans & Associates Entps Inc ....E...... 580 765-6693
  Ponca City *(G-7828)*
M P Ready Mix Inc ....E...... 405 354-8824
  Yukon *(G-11743)*
McAlester Monument Co Inc ....G...... 918 423-1647
  McAlester *(G-4317)*
RLC Holding Co Inc ....E...... 580 332-3080
  Ada *(G-82)*
Twin Cities Ready Mix Inc ....G...... 918 465-2555
  Wilburton *(G-11527)*

BRICKS & BLOCKS: Structural

Acme Brick Company ....D...... 405 755-5010
  Oklahoma City *(G-5367)*

BRICKS: Clay

MB Holdings LLC ....D...... 580 782-2324
  Mangum *(G-4172)*

BRICKS: Concrete

Stone Splitters Inc ....G...... 479 651-8873
  Sallisaw *(G-8153)*
Tri-State Con Foundations LLC ....E...... 405 341-3043
  Oklahoma City *(G-7323)*

BRIEFCASES

Briefcase Solutions Ltd LLC ....G...... 405 788-9250
  McLoud *(G-4353)*

BROADCASTING & COMMS EQPT: Antennas, Transmitting/Comms

B J M Consulting Inc ....G...... 918 665-8737
  Tulsa *(G-9244)*

BROADCASTING & COMMS EQPT: Antennas, Transmitting/Comms — PRODUCT SECTION

Landa Mobile Systems LLC ....F....... 360 474-8991
Tulsa (G-10120)

BROADCASTING & COMMUNICATIONS EQPT: Cellular Radio Telephone

Gateway Com Inc ....G....... 405 787-0800
Edmond (G-2432)
Logo Marketing Company Inc ....G....... 918 496-2989
Tulsa (G-10176)
Tribalcom Wrless Solutions LLC ....G....... 405 274-7245
Oklahoma City (G-7328)

BROADCASTING & COMMUNICATIONS EQPT: Transmitting, Radio/TV

Tactical Elec Military Sup LLC ....E....... 866 541-7996
Broken Arrow (G-1070)

BROADCASTING STATIONS, RADIO: Music Format

Versitile Entertainment ....G....... 812 913-2677
Seminole (G-8406)

BROKERS' SVCS

U-Change Lock Industries Inc ....E....... 405 376-1600
Mustang (G-4799)

BROKERS: Business

Frahm John ....G....... 213 500-0741
Sand Springs (G-8185)

BROKERS: Food

McLane Foodservice Dist Inc ....C....... 405 632-0118
Oklahoma City (G-6549)

BROKERS: Mortgage, Arranging For Loans

United Sewing Agency Inc ....G....... 580 924-6936
Durant (G-2271)

BROKERS: Printing

247 Graphx Studios Inc ....G....... 405 677-7775
Oklahoma City (G-5329)

BRONZE FOUNDRY, NEC

Transtate Castings Inc ....G....... 405 232-3936
Oklahoma City (G-7319)

BROOMS & BRUSHES: Push

Da Vinci Broom LLC ....G....... 580 224-1424
Ardmore (G-271)

BUILDING & STRUCTURAL WOOD MBRS: Timbers, Struct, Lam Lumber

McFarland Cascade ....G....... 580 584-3511
Broken Bow (G-1200)

BUILDING & STRUCTURAL WOOD MEMBERS

Builders Firstsource Inc ....D....... 918 459-6872
Broken Arrow (G-860)
Builders Firstsource Inc ....E....... 405 321-2255
Oklahoma City (G-5641)
Coreslab Structures Okla Inc ....C....... 405 632-4944
Oklahoma City (G-5835)
Northwest Truss ....G....... 580 496-2420
Goltry (G-3248)
Sawdust Ltd ....G....... 918 809-3456
Broken Arrow (G-1044)
Zara Group Inc ....F....... 918 782-4473
Vinita (G-11273)

BUILDING COMPONENTS: Structural Steel

Accurate Manufacturing Inc ....E....... 918 582-2585
Tulsa (G-9090)
Afg Acquisition Group LLC ....E....... 918 683-5683
Muskogee (G-4644)
Bills Welding Coop LLC ....G....... 405 370-6383
Oklahoma City (G-5567)
Economasters LLC ....F....... 918 241-8244
Tulsa (G-9640)
Fitzgerald &SOns Steel LLC ....F....... 918 453-3369
Tahlequah (G-8865)
Ftdm Investments Llc ....D....... 918 598-3430
Locust Grove (G-4107)
Gerdau Ameristeel US Inc ....F....... 918 682-2600
Muskogee (G-4679)
Gerdau Ameristeel US Inc ....E....... 918 682-7806
Muskogee (G-4680)
H K & S Iron Co ....E....... 405 745-2761
Oklahoma City (G-6198)
Insight Technologies Inc ....F....... 580 933-4109
Valliant (G-11226)
Jeffery W Matlock ....G....... 918 367-9828
Bristow (G-782)
Jenco Fabricators Inc ....E....... 918 234-3364
Tulsa (G-10034)
Maddens Portable Buildings ....E....... 405 799-4989
Norman (G-5062)
River Bend Industries LLC ....C....... 405 703-2758
Blanchard (G-734)
Shawnee Fabricators Inc ....E....... 405 275-8264
Shawnee (G-8494)
Specialty Sales Associates ....G....... 405 495-1136
Chandler (G-1388)
Studs Unlimited LLC ....G....... 214 683-8012
Oklahoma City (G-7218)
Sweeper Metal Fabricators Corp ....E....... 918 352-9180
Drumright (G-2073)
Thorpe Plant Services Inc ....G....... 918 455-8928
Tulsa (G-10937)
W & W Asco Steel LLC ....E....... 918 235-3621
Oklahoma City (G-7407)
Wayne Winkler ....G....... 918 689-9745
Eufaula (G-3117)
Weibee Steel Inc ....F....... 405 360-7055
Norman (G-5198)
Worldwide Steel Works Inc ....E....... 918 825-4545
Pryor (G-8000)

BUILDING INSPECTION SVCS

Firepro Fire Protection Svc ....G....... 918 857-1513
Broken Arrow (G-909)

BUILDING MAINTENANCE SVCS, EXC REPAIRS

Commercial Services Corp ....F....... 405 634-8888
Oklahoma City (G-5806)

BUILDING PRDTS & MATERIALS DEALERS

Altus Ready-Mix Inc ....F....... 580 482-3418
Altus (G-142)
Antlers Roof-Truss & Bldrs Sup ....G....... 580 298-3560
Antlers (G-213)
Davis Insulated Building Inc ....G....... 918 423-2636
McAlester (G-4291)
Dolese Bros Co ....F....... 580 255-3046
Duncan (G-2107)
H & H Ornamental Iron ....G....... 405 634-0646
Oklahoma City (G-6196)
Higgins & Sons Truss Company ....F....... 405 997-5455
Tecumseh (G-8918)
MB Holdings LLC ....D....... 580 782-2324
Mangum (G-4172)
Mill Creek Lumber & Supply Co ....D....... 918 794-3600
Tulsa (G-10279)
Mill Creek Lumber & Supply Co ....D....... 405 947-7227
Oklahoma City (G-6609)
Railroad Yard Inc ....E....... 405 377-8763
Stillwater (G-8743)
Rons Discount Lumber Inc ....D....... 918 658-3857
Howe (G-3599)
Sugar Loaf Quarries Inc ....E....... 918 647-4244
Shady Point (G-8416)
Twin Cities Ready Mix Inc ....G....... 918 967-3391
Stigler (G-8650)
Yukon Door and Plywood Inc ....E....... 405 354-4861
Yukon (G-11807)

BUILDING PRDTS: Stone

Sugar Loaf Quarries Inc ....E....... 918 647-4244
Shady Point (G-8416)

BUILDING STONE, ARTIFICIAL: Concrete

Eaves Stones Products ....F....... 580 889-7858
Atoka (G-410)
Stone Mill Inc ....F....... 918 812-4438
Kansas (G-3755)

BUILDINGS & COMPONENTS: Prefabricated Metal

3 PS Investment LLC ....G....... 918 604-1363
Skiatook (G-8529)
All American Building ....G....... 918 249-0515
Tulsa (G-9136)
All Steel Carports LLC ....G....... 918 683-1717
Muskogee (G-4646)
Alliance Steel Inc ....C....... 405 745-7500
Oklahoma City (G-5420)
Aztec Building Systems Inc ....E....... 405 329-0255
Norman (G-4923)
Bc Steel Buildings Inc ....D....... 405 324-5100
Oklahoma City (G-5535)
Cojac Portable Buildings Inc ....G....... 405 232-1229
Oklahoma City (G-5801)
Davco Manufacturing ....F....... 918 535-2360
Ochelata (G-5234)
Davis Insulated Building Inc ....D....... 918 967-2042
Stigler (G-8632)
Dream Buildings of Tulsa ....G....... 918 437-9233
Tulsa (G-9604)
Durnal Construction LLC ....G....... 405 413-5458
Perkins (G-7716)
Fincher & Son Pipe & Steel ....G....... 580 889-6778
Caddo (G-1235)
G & L Metal Buildings ....G....... 918 687-1867
Muskogee (G-4677)
Gideon Steel Panel Company LLC .....F....... 405 942-7878
Oklahoma City (G-6153)
L&C Metal Buildings LLC ....G....... 580 660-5515
Rocky (G-8104)
Leddy Construction ....G....... 580 332-3056
Ada (G-60)
Madden Steel Buildings Lawton ....G....... 580 357-1699
Lawton (G-3968)
Madison Inc of Oklahoma ....G....... 918 587-4501
Tulsa (G-9017)
Marco Industries Inc ....D....... 918 622-4535
Tulsa (G-10208)
Metal Buildings Inc ....E....... 405 672-7676
Oklahoma City (G-6572)
Midwest Portable Building ....G....... 918 245-9335
Tulsa (G-10269)
Morton Buildings Inc ....E....... 405 288-1031
Washington (G-11335)
Morton Buildings Inc ....G....... 580 323-1172
Clinton (G-1759)
Plumb Square Construction ....G....... 405 619-9898
Del City (G-2006)
Railroad Yard Inc ....E....... 405 377-8763
Stillwater (G-8743)
Redibuilt Metal Pdts & Cnstr ....G....... 580 225-2829
Elk City (G-2867)
Rons Discount Lumber Inc ....D....... 918 658-3857
Howe (G-3599)
Star Building Systems Inc ....E....... 405 636-2010
Oklahoma City (G-7193)
TDS Portable Buildings LLC ....G....... 918 422-4009
Colcord (G-1791)
Terry Tylor Wldg Fbrcation LLC ....G....... 405 205-2964
Chickasha (G-1517)
Texoma Sheds ....G....... 580 223-0000
Ardmore (G-367)
Tornado Alley Armor LLC ....G....... 918 856-3569
Tulsa (G-10955)
Tornado Alley OK Storm Shlters ....G....... 918 706-1341
Coweta (G-1901)
Ventaire LLC ....E....... 918 622-1191
Tulsa (G-11070)

BUILDINGS, PREFABRICATED: Wholesalers

Morton Buildings Inc ....G....... 580 323-1172
Clinton (G-1759)

BUILDINGS: Chicken Coops, Prefabricated, Wood

Victory Garden Homestead LLC ....G....... 405 306-0308
Blanchard (G-744)

BUILDINGS: Farm, Prefabricated Or Portable, Wood

Burrow Construction LLC ....E....... 800 766-5793
Fort Gibson (G-3174)

A B Printing G 918 834-2054
Tulsa (G-9066)
A Plus Printing G 580 765-7752
Ponca City (G-7791)
A Plus Printing Inc G 918 836-8659
Tulsa (G-9068)
A Q Printing G 918 438-1161
Tulsa (G-9070)
A-OK Printing Mill G 918 775-6809
Sallisaw (G-8136)
AAA Kopy G 405 741-5679
Oklahoma City (G-5354)
Abco Printing & Office Supply G 580 286-7575
Idabel (G-3636)
Adams Printing G 580 832-2123
Cordell (G-1853)
Advance Graphics & Printing G 405 258-0796
Chandler (G-1373)
Ajt Enterprises Inc F 918 665-7083
Tulsa (G-9133)
Altus Printing Co Inc G 580 482-2020
Altus (G-141)
Anns Quick Print Co Inc G 405 222-1871
Chickasha (G-1429)
B & L Printing Inc G 918 258-6655
Broken Arrow (G-839)
Bartlesville Print Shop G 918 336-6070
Bartlesville (G-452)
Bell Printing and Advertising G 405 769-6445
Nicoma Park (G-4866)
Bill Rathbone G 918 486-3028
Coweta (G-1872)
Britton Printing G 405 840-3291
Oklahoma City (G-5630)
Brown Printing Co Inc G 918 652-9611
Henryetta (G-3500)
Burch Printing Co G 580 225-3270
Elk City (G-2788)
C & J Printing Co G 580 355-3099
Lawton (G-3902)
C & R Print Shop Inc G 405 224-7921
Chickasha (G-1445)
Carr Graphics Inc G 918 835-0605
Tulsa (G-9379)
Cherry Street Print Shop Inc G 918 584-0022
Tulsa (G-9417)
Choate Publishing Inc F 580 276-3255
Marietta (G-4204)
Clark Printing Inc G 405 528-5396
Oklahoma City (G-5776)
Collins Quality Printing G 918 744-0077
Tulsa (G-9468)
Cooley Enterprises Inc G 918 437-6900
Tulsa (G-9483)
Copy Fast Printing Inc F 405 947-7468
Oklahoma City (G-5834)
Cowan Printing & Litho Inc F 405 789-1961
Tuttle (G-11191)
Cowboy Copy Center F 405 372-8099
Stillwater (G-8671)
CP Solutions Inc D 918 664-6642
Tulsa (G-9495)
Cromwells Inc G 580 234-6561
Enid (G-2935)
CSC Inc G 580 994-6110
Mooreland (G-4587)
Davis Printing Company Inc G 580 225-2902
Elk City (G-2800)
Dbmac 50 Inc G 918 342-5590
Claremore (G-1613)
Demco Printing Inc F 405 273-8888
Shawnee (G-8444)
Digi Print LLC G 405 947-0099
Oklahoma City (G-5945)
Diversified Printing Inc F 918 665-2275
Tulsa (G-9586)
Edmond Printings G 405 341-4330
Edmond (G-2404)
Education Oklahoma Department F 405 743-5531
Stillwater (G-8682)
Ellis County Capital G 580 885-7788
Arnett (G-387)
Fedex Office & Print Svcs Inc F 918 492-6701
Tulsa (G-9732)
Fedex Office & Print Svcs Inc E 918 252-3757
Tulsa (G-9733)
Felkins Enterprises LLC G 918 272-3456
Owasso (G-7568)
First Impression Prtg Co Inc G 918 749-5446
Beggs (G-553)
Franklin Graphics Inc F 918 687-6149
Muskogee (G-4675)
French Printing Inc G 405 381-4057
Tuttle (G-11200)
G & S Printing Inc G 405 789-6813
Oklahoma City (G-6129)
Giles Printing Co Inc G 918 584-1583
Tulsa (G-9825)
Gravley Companies Inc G 918 743-6619
Tulsa (G-9850)
Gregath Publishing Company G 918 542-4148
Miami (G-4407)
Hammer Hoby G 580 227-2100
Fairview (G-3137)
Hardesty Press Inc F 918 582-5306
Tulsa (G-9891)
Heavener Ledger G 918 653-2425
Heavener (G-3429)
Hinkle Printing & Office Sup G 405 238-9308
Pauls Valley (G-7660)
Hipsleys Litho & Prtg Co LLC G 405 528-2686
Oklahoma City (G-6252)
Hoffman Printing LLC F 918 682-8341
Muskogee (G-4691)
Holbrook Printing G 918 835-5950
Tulsa (G-9938)
Hooper Printing Company Inc F 405 321-4288
Norman (G-5026)
Imperial Printing Inc G 918 663-1302
Tulsa (G-9973)
Ink Images Inc G 918 828-0300
Tulsa (G-9987)
Jet Printing Co Inc G 405 732-1262
Oklahoma City (G-6361)
Joans Print Shop Inc G 918 624-5858
Tulsa (G-10047)
Kelley Printing G 405 238-4848
Pauls Valley (G-7663)
Kindrick Co Prtg & Copying Svc G 580 332-1022
Ada (G-56)
King Kopy LLC G 405 321-0202
Norman (G-5052)
Kingfisher Office Supply Inc G 405 375-3404
Kingfisher (G-3806)
Krause Plastics G 918 835-4202
Tulsa (G-10100)
L W Duncan Printing Inc G 580 355-6229
Lawton (G-3953)
Larry D Hammer F 580 227-2100
Fairview (G-3140)
Leda Grimm G 918 225-0507
Cushing (G-1942)
Linderer Printing Co Inc F 580 323-2102
Clinton (G-1757)
Litgistix LLC E 918 585-5875
Tulsa (G-10167)
Lithaprint Inc F 918 587-7746
Tulsa (G-10168)
Mattocks Printing Co LLC G 405 794-2307
Moore (G-4538)
McCullough Printing G 580 286-7681
Idabel (G-3641)
Meeks Lithographing Company G 918 838-9900
Tulsa (G-10239)
Meeks Lithographing Company G 918 836-0900
Tulsa (G-10241)
Mesa Black Publishing LLC G 580 544-2222
Boise City (G-747)
Mid-West Printing & Pubg Co F 918 224-3666
Sapulpa (G-8291)
Midtown Printing Inc G 918 295-0090
Tulsa (G-10264)
Midwest Publishing Co G 405 282-1890
Guthrie (G-3325)
Minor Printing Company G 580 795-3745
Madill (G-4158)
Minuteman Press G 405 942-5595
Oklahoma City (G-6617)
Multiprint Corp G 918 832-0300
Tulsa (G-10315)
Nancy Nelson & Associates G 580 765-0115
Ponca City (G-7857)
North Star Publishing LLC D 405 415-2400
Oklahoma City (G-6688)
Northwest Printing Inc G 580 234-0953
Enid (G-3022)
OK Quality Printing Inc G 405 624-2925
Stillwater (G-8731)
Pace Printing Inc G 918 585-5664
Tulsa (G-10454)
Peabodys Printing & A Brush Sp G 580 248-8317
Lawton (G-3980)
Pinecliffe Prtrs of Tecumseh G 405 273-1292
Shawnee (G-8483)
Pioneer Printing Inc G 918 542-5521
Miami (G-4428)
Pony Express Printing LLC G 405 375-5064
Kingfisher (G-3811)
Premier Printing G 405 632-1132
Oklahoma City (G-6886)
Prices Quality Printing Inc G 580 924-2271
Durant (G-2248)
Print N Copy Inc G 918 258-8200
Broken Arrow (G-1011)
Print Shop G 918 342-3993
Claremore (G-1674)
Printers of Oklahoma LLC G 405 943-8855
Oklahoma City (G-6900)
Printing Center G 405 681-5303
Oklahoma City (G-6901)
Priority Printworks Inc G 918 825-6397
Pryor (G-7984)
Pronto Print Inc G 580 223-1612
Ardmore (G-347)
Pryor Printing Inc G 918 825-2888
Pryor (G-7986)
Quantum Forms Corporation F 918 665-1320
Oklahoma City (G-6940)
Quik Print of Tulsa Inc G 918 250-5466
Tulsa (G-10594)
Quik Print of Tulsa Inc E 918 665-6246
Tulsa (G-10595)
Quik Print of Tulsa Inc G 918 582-1825
Tulsa (G-10596)
Quik-Print of Oklahoma City G 405 843-9820
Oklahoma City (G-6947)
Quik-Print of Oklahoma City G 405 528-7976
Oklahoma City (G-6951)
Quik-Print of Oklahoma City G 405 842-1404
Oklahoma City (G-6946)
Quik-Print of Oklahoma City G 405 840-3275
Oklahoma City (G-6950)
Reid Printing Inc G 405 348-0066
Edmond (G-2596)
Review Printing Company Inc F 580 658-6657
Marlow (G-4241)
Self Printing Inc G 918 838-2113
Tulsa (G-10726)
Signature Graphics Corp G 918 294-3485
Bixby (G-658)
Silver Quill LLC G 405 735-9191
Moore (G-4569)
Snider Printing & Office Sup G 405 257-3402
Wewoka (G-11511)
Snyder Printing Inc F 405 682-8880
Oklahoma City (G-5317)
Sooner Industries Inc G 918 540-2422
Miami (G-4431)
Sooner Press G 405 382-8351
Seminole (G-8400)
Sprekelmeyer Printing Company G 580 223-5100
Ardmore (G-359)
Standard Printing Co Inc G 405 840-0001
Oklahoma City (G-7192)
Torbett Printing Co & Off Sup G 918 756-5789
Okmulgee (G-7528)
Transcript Press Inc E 405 360-7999
Norman (G-5181)
Tulsa Instant Printing G 918 627-0730
Tulsa (G-11000)
Unique Printing Inc G 405 842-3966
Oklahoma City (G-7361)
Usher Corporation G 405 495-2125
Oklahoma City (G-7382)
Wallace Printing Company G 580 326-6323
Hugo (G-3622)
Wallis Printing Inc G 580 223-7473
Ardmore (G-379)
Wilson-Monroe Publishing Co G 580 933-4579
Valliant (G-11234)
Work Activity Center Inc E 405 799-6911
Moore (G-4584)

BINDING SVC: Magazines

Current Alternative News Advg G 918 431-0392
Tahlequah (G-8861)

BINDING SVC: Trade

Printers Bindery Inc E 405 236-8423
Norman (G-5122)

PRODUCT

Employee Codes: A=Over 500 employees, B=251-500
C=101-250, D=51-100, E=20-50, F=10-19, G=1-9

2020 Oklahoma Directory
of Manufacturers & Processors

687

BINS: Prefabricated, Sheet Metal
Hill Metal Inc..G....... 405 375-6284
Kingfisher *(G-3801)*

BIOLOGICAL PRDTS: Blood Derivatives
Vaxart Inc..G....... 918 582-4346
Tulsa *(G-11067)*

BIOLOGICAL PRDTS: Exc Diagnostic
Coare Biotechnology Inc........................G....... 405 227-0406
Oklahoma City *(G-5797)*

BIOLOGICAL PRDTS: Extracts
Dr Cannabis LLC...................................G....... 918 277-1105
Sapulpa *(G-8268)*
Extract Surface Systems LLC................G....... 918 938-6828
Tulsa *(G-9719)*
Extract Touch-Up LLC............................G....... 918 639-4011
Broken Arrow *(G-903)*
Leonard Skodak Distributors..................G....... 405 787-8044
Oklahoma City *(G-6466)*
Sweet Sap Extracts Inc..........................G....... 405 205-8706
Harrah *(G-3386)*

BIOLOGICAL PRDTS: Serums
Swaim Serum Company........................G....... 918 241-4363
Sand Springs *(G-8228)*

BIOLOGICAL PRDTS: Toxins
Envirnmental Toxin Removal LLC...........G....... 405 757-4099
Oklahoma City *(G-6044)*

BIOLOGICAL PRDTS: Vaccines
Heartland Vaccines LLC........................G....... 716 848-9251
Stillwater *(G-8699)*
Oklahomans For Vaccine......................G....... 918 606-9213
Tulsa *(G-10409)*

BIOLOGICAL PRDTS: Vaccines & Immunizing
M Shawn Anderson Rph PC..................G....... 580 595-9500
Lawton *(G-3967)*
Pure Protein LLC...................................G....... 405 271-3838
Oklahoma City *(G-6923)*

BIOLOGICAL PRDTS: Veterinary
Jimmy Fuchs..G....... 580 225-7784
Elk City *(G-2833)*
Solidtech Animal Health Inc...................F....... 405 387-3300
Newcastle *(G-4841)*

BLACKSMITH SHOP
Hays Welding & Blacksmith...................G....... 580 287-3458
Willow *(G-11530)*

BLADES: Knife
Mike Latham..G....... 580 622-6980
Sulphur *(G-8838)*

BLADES: Saw, Hand Or Power
Saw Swan Service Inc...........................G....... 918 249-3821
Broken Arrow *(G-1043)*

BLANKBOOKS & LOOSELEAF BINDERS
Scrapworx..G....... 918 259-9547
Broken Arrow *(G-1045)*

BLANKBOOKS: Scrapbooks
Tumbleweed Creek Cottage..................G....... 580 242-2767
Enid *(G-3068)*

BLAST SAND MINING
Mohawk Materials Co Inc......................G....... 918 584-2707
Tulsa *(G-10295)*

BLASTING SVC: Sand, Metal Parts
George Townsend & Co Inc...................G....... 405 235-1387
Oklahoma City *(G-6145)*
Power Services LLC..............................G....... 405 677-7716
Norman *(G-5118)*

Precision Coatings LLC.........................G....... 918 622-1876
Tulsa *(G-10543)*

BLINDS & SHADES: Mini
Classic Collectn Interiors Inc..................G....... 580 351-0024
Lawton *(G-3905)*
Patricia McKay......................................G....... 580 355-2739
Cache *(G-1230)*

BLINDS & SHADES: Vertical
Vertical Limit LLC..................................G....... 918 409-1633
Tulsa *(G-11073)*

BLINDS : Window
Beyond Blinds LLC................................G....... 918 935-6317
Bixby *(G-614)*
Blind Doctor...G....... 918 638-1487
Tulsa *(G-9304)*
Carolyns Cheesecake House................G....... 918 839-5757
Cameron *(G-1255)*
Curry Shades LLC.................................G....... 918 779-3902
Tulsa *(G-9524)*
Grace Allen Design - Custom................G....... 405 509-5164
Edmond *(G-2441)*
Howes Ltg & Win Blinds LLC.................G....... 918 791-4101
Bartlesville *(G-495)*
Lawton Council of The Blind..................G....... 580 536-1650
Lawton *(G-3955)*

BLINDS, WOOD
Accurate Blinds.....................................G....... 405 396-8583
Arcadia *(G-226)*
R and P Cabinetry LLC..........................G....... 405 230-0495
Oklahoma City *(G-6959)*
Secure Screen LLC...............................G....... 918 294-4444
Broken Arrow *(G-1048)*
Shutter Mill Inc......................................D....... 405 377-6455
Stillwater *(G-8754)*

BLOCK & BRICK: Sand Lime
Blessing Gravel LLC.............................G....... 580 513-4009
Tishomingo *(G-8962)*

BLOCKS & BRICKS: Concrete
Alpha Concrete Products Inc.................F....... 405 769-7777
Oklahoma City *(G-5424)*
Dolese Bros Co.....................................E....... 405 670-9626
Oklahoma City *(G-5962)*
Meridian Brick LLC................................E....... 918 687-6734
Muskogee *(G-4712)*

BLOCKS: Chimney Or Fireplace, Concrete
Boomer Foundations & Piers.................G....... 405 799-6811
Moore *(G-4500)*

BLOCKS: Insulating, Concrete
Buildblock Bldg Systems LLC................G....... 405 840-3386
Oklahoma City *(G-5640)*

BLOCKS: Landscape Or Retaining Wall, Concrete
Arrowhead Precast LLC........................D....... 918 995-2227
Broken Arrow *(G-833)*
Baray Enterprises Inc............................E....... 405 373-1800
Piedmont *(G-7755)*

BLOCKS: Paving, Concrete
Rdnj LLC..G....... 405 418-4741
Oklahoma City *(G-6978)*

BLOCKS: Standard, Concrete Or Cinder
Chandler Materials Company.................E....... 918 836-9151
Tulsa *(G-9403)*
Day Concrete Block Company...............F....... 580 223-3317
Ardmore *(G-277)*

BLOOD BANK
McAlister Drug Corporation...................G....... 405 354-2582
Yukon *(G-11750)*

BLOWER FILTER UNITS: Furnace Blowers
Nordic Pure Inc......................................G....... 918 234-2355
Tulsa *(G-10359)*

BLOWERS & FANS
Amarillo Chittom Airslo..........................E....... 918 585-5638
Tulsa *(G-9160)*
Callidus Technologies LLC....................D....... 918 267-4920
Beggs *(G-550)*
Facet (oklahoma) LLC...........................D....... 918 696-3161
Stilwell *(G-8789)*
Global Wire Cloth LLC...........................E....... 918 836-7211
Tulsa *(G-9834)*
Goodwill Inds Centl Okla Inc..................D....... 405 236-4451
Oklahoma City *(G-6172)*
Hu Don Manufacturing Co Inc................F....... 580 223-7333
Ardmore *(G-307)*
Industrial Dist Resources LLC...............G....... 239 591-3777
Tulsa *(G-9979)*
L & M Fabrication..................................G....... 918 825-7145
Pryor *(G-7973)*
Midco Fabricators Inc............................E....... 405 282-6667
Guthrie *(G-3324)*
Phoenix Group Holding Company.........F....... 405 948-7788
Oklahoma City *(G-6844)*
Safeco Manufacturing Inc......................F....... 918 455-0100
Broken Arrow *(G-1160)*

BLUEPRINTING SVCS
ARC Document Solutions LLC...............F....... 405 943-0378
Oklahoma City *(G-5460)*
ARC Document Solutions LLC...............E....... 918 663-8100
Tulsa *(G-9202)*
Cowboy Copy Center............................F....... 405 372-8099
Stillwater *(G-8671)*
Johnny L Ruth.......................................G....... 580 223-3061
Ardmore *(G-316)*

BOAT BUILDING & REPAIR
Brokenbow Boat Center........................G....... 580 584-5428
Broken Bow *(G-1187)*
Grand Lake Detail LLC..........................G....... 918 257-2174
Afton *(G-117)*
Kole Inc..G....... 918 782-3001
Ketchum *(G-3774)*
Lilitad Boats Inc.....................................G....... 918 482-5992
Porter *(G-7893)*
Northfork Auto Repair............................G....... 918 689-3589
Eufaula *(G-3106)*
Offshore Extreme..................................G....... 405 387-2628
Newcastle *(G-4834)*
Tip Top Prop Shop.................................G....... 580 564-3712
Kingston *(G-3831)*
Tracker Marine LLC...............................G....... 918 541-2000
Miami *(G-4434)*

BOAT BUILDING & REPAIRING: Fiberglass
Parks Manufacturing Inc........................C....... 405 382-0349
Seminole *(G-8393)*

BOAT BUILDING & REPAIRING: Motorboats, Inboard Or Outboard
Bkep Materials LLC...............................G....... 918 266-1606
Catoosa *(G-1303)*

BOAT BUILDING & REPAIRING: Motorized
Canyon Craft..G....... 918 456-3552
Tahlequah *(G-8854)*
Harold Speed Jr.....................................G....... 580 838-2578
Hendrix *(G-3440)*

BOAT BUILDING & RPRG: Fishing, Small, Lobster, Crab, Oyster
Splash Marine LLC................................G....... 580 336-9874
Perry *(G-7746)*

BOAT DEALERS
Splash Marine LLC................................G....... 580 336-9874
Perry *(G-7746)*

BOAT LIFTS
Boat Floaters Ind LLC............................F....... 918 256-3330
Afton *(G-113)*

PRODUCT SECTION

BUILDINGS: Portable

Company	Code	Phone
Better Bilt Portable Buildings	G	918 224-3437
Sapulpa (G-8255)		
Better Built Structures LLC	G	918 224-3437
Sapulpa (G-8256)		
Braden Shielding Systems LLC	E	918 624-2888
Tulsa (G-9328)		
Cojac Portable Buildings Inc	E	405 232-1229
Oklahoma City (G-5800)		
David Davis	G	405 354-6974
El Reno (G-2710)		
Davis Insulated Building Inc	G	918 423-2636
McAlester (G-4291)		
Derksen Portable Building	G	918 636-4129
Sapulpa (G-8266)		
Indaco Metals LLC	D	405 273-9200
Shawnee (G-8462)		
Maddens Portable Buildings	E	405 799-4989
Norman (G-5062)		
Martinez Metal Buildings	G	580 821-2780
Elk City (G-2848)		
Metro Portable Buildings	G	405 921-5688
Oklahoma City (G-6580)		
Mobile Mini Inc	F	918 582-5857
Tulsa (G-10288)		
Mobile Mini Inc	E	405 682-9333
Oklahoma City (G-6622)		
Morton Buildings Inc	E	918 683-6668
Muskogee (G-4715)		
Nci Group Inc	E	405 672-7676
Oklahoma City (G-6665)		
Oakley Portable Buildings LLC	G	405 372-6543
Stillwater (G-8730)		
Petzold Buildings LLC	F	580 563-2818
Blair (G-697)		
Polar Insulated Sheds Oklah	G	580 799-2265
Elk City (G-2860)		
Quality Buildings Inc	G	888 430-7721
Norman (G-5126)		
Quality Buildings Inc	E	405 364-0516
Norman (G-5127)		
Roadrunner Portable Buildings	G	918 272-7788
Owasso (G-7608)		
Robertson-Ceco II Corporation	C	405 636-2010
Oklahoma City (G-7039)		
Safe Shed	G	580 759-3456
Stratford (G-8807)		
Whitney Manufacturing Inc	E	918 825-6062
Pryor (G-7998)		
Zieglers Bob Portable Bldg Sls	G	918 486-4462
Broken Arrow (G-1181)		

BUILDINGS: Prefabricated, Metal

Company	Code	Phone
Buildings By Madden LLC	G	405 677-0466
Oklahoma City (G-5643)		
Honeycutt Contruction Inc	F	918 825-6070
Pryor (G-7969)		
James Case	G	918 846-2884
Fairfax (G-3119)		
Robertson-Ceco II Corporation	C	405 636-2010
Oklahoma City (G-7040)		
Tims Sheds	G	918 506-7741
Tahlequah (G-8888)		

BUILDINGS: Prefabricated, Plastic

Company	Code	Phone
Leche Lounge Llc	G	918 409-5426
Tulsa (G-10144)		

BUILDINGS: Prefabricated, Wood

Company	Code	Phone
Better Built Barns	G	405 547-2066
Perkins (G-7715)		
Cedar Built USA Inc	G	405 794-0811
Moore (G-4508)		
David Davis	G	405 354-6974
El Reno (G-2710)		
Flex-Ability Concepts LLC	G	405 996-5343
Oklahoma City (G-6091)		
Icon Construction Inc	F	580 931-3806
Durant (G-2236)		
Midwest Cooling Towers Inc	C	405 224-4622
Chickasha (G-1486)		
Midwest Portable Building	G	918 245-9335
Tulsa (G-10269)		
Molitor Design & Cnstr LLC	G	405 802-8302
Moore (G-4542)		
Morton Buildings Inc	G	580 323-1172
Clinton (G-1759)		
Morton Buildings Inc	E	918 683-6668
Muskogee (G-4715)		
Roadrunner Portable Buildings	G	918 272-7788
Owasso (G-7608)		
Solitaire Holdings LLC	G	580 252-6060
Duncan (G-2179)		
Solitaire Homes Inc	E	580 252-6060
Duncan (G-2180)		
Standard Panel LLC	G	918 984-1717
Tulsa (G-10837)		
Tuff Shed Inc	G	405 272-1011
Oklahoma City (G-7348)		
Tuff Shed Inc	G	405 788-4143
Shawnee (G-8513)		
Wood Tech Structures	G	918 678-2108
Wyandotte (G-11663)		

BUILDINGS: Prefabricated, Wood

Company	Code	Phone
Fullerton Building Systems Inc	E	918 246-9995
Sand Springs (G-8187)		
Rons Discount Lumber Inc	D	918 658-3857
Howe (G-3599)		

BULLETPROOF VESTS

Company	Code	Phone
Mondo Solutions LLC	G	405 788-0056
Purcell (G-8017)		

BUMPERS: Motor Vehicle

Company	Code	Phone
Mid America Automotive Pdts	E	918 227-1919
Sapulpa (G-8289)		

BURIAL VAULTS: Concrete Or Precast Terrazzo

Company	Code	Phone
Allegiant Precast LLC	F	918 486-6227
Broken Arrow (G-1108)		
Downtown Pub	F	918 274-8202
Owasso (G-7563)		
Heritage Burial Park	G	405 692-5503
Oklahoma City (G-6242)		
Palm Vault Co Inc	G	580 332-7565
Ada (G-74)		
Vintage Vault	G	918 619-9954
Tulsa (G-11079)		
Wilbert Funeral Services Inc	G	918 446-2131
Tulsa (G-9051)		

BURNERS: Gas, Domestic

Company	Code	Phone
Flameco Industries Inc	E	918 832-1100
Tulsa (G-9753)		

BURNERS: Gas, Indl

Company	Code	Phone
Alpha Combustion LLC	G	918 851-1751
Tulsa (G-9152)		
Preferred Utilities Mfg Corp	G	203 743-6741
Tulsa (G-10551)		
Zeeco Inc	C	918 258-8551
Broken Arrow (G-1179)		
Zeeco Usa LLC	E	918 258-8551
Broken Arrow (G-1180)		

BUSINESS ACTIVITIES: Non-Commercial Site

Company	Code	Phone
412 Comics LLC	G	479 414-0891
Pocola (G-7779)		
A & R Plumbing and Mech LLC	G	405 808-0671
Oklahoma City (G-5343)		
Aaron Oil Inc	G	405 899-4138
Noble (G-4875)		
Accessory and Prfmce Sls Inc	G	918 224-5851
Sapulpa (G-8246)		
Adjacent Creations LLC	G	405 819-6507
Oklahoma City (G-5374)		
American Custom Woodworks LLC	G	918 344-4988
Sapulpa (G-8248)		
Ameriinfovets Inc	G	408 446-4343
Pryor (G-7943)		
Aqua Eco Environmental Svcs	G	952 300-0456
Broken Arrow (G-831)		
Archer Technologies Intl Inc	G	405 306-3220
Shawnee (G-8428)		
Baker Surveying LLC	G	918 271-5793
Tulsa (G-9257)		
Bankers Online	G	888 229-8872
Edmond (G-2316)		
Barelas Welding	G	580 497-7485
Canute (G-1266)		
Beefys Beastro Food Svc LLC	G	580 491-0325
Broken Arrow (G-844)		
Big Productions LLC	G	405 513-6545
Edmond (G-2321)		
Campbell Crane and Service LLC	G	405 245-8983
Oklahoma City (G-5682)		
Charles Jones	G	405 348-2187
Edmond (G-2345)		
Chorus Labs LLC	G	405 317-2942
Oklahoma City (G-5763)		
Christina Stokes	G	405 551-1017
Edmond (G-2350)		
Chromatech Scientific Corp	G	405 370-4466
Edmond (G-2351)		
Cimarron River Operation Corp	G	918 633-2911
Mannford (G-4179)		
Cole Industrial Services Inc	G	580 775-0949
Caddo (G-1232)		
Competitive Action Sports LLC	G	405 474-7777
Edmond (G-2363)		
Control Products Unlimited Inc	G	918 786-1801
Grove (G-3263)		
Cool Hard Hat Inc	G	918 812-7636
Tulsa (G-9481)		
Corporate Image Inc	G	918 516-8376
Owasso (G-7556)		
Corporate Image Apparel LLC	G	405 659-8264
Oklahoma City (G-5839)		
Ctsa LLC	G	405 478-3501
Edmond (G-2377)		
Cura Telehealth Wellness LLC	F	918 513-1062
Tulsa (G-9523)		
Da Vinci Broom LLC	G	580 224-1424
Ardmore (G-271)		
Deep Well Tubular Services Inc	F	405 850-5826
Oklahoma City (G-5919)		
Del Nero Manufacturing Co	G	405 364-4800
Norman (G-4976)		
Delenda LLC	G	918 409-1313
Owasso (G-7561)		
Digii ID LLC	G	405 662-5504
Oklahoma City (G-5946)		
Douglas Group LLC	G	405 946-6853
Oklahoma City (G-5972)		
Downhole Hinton Services LLC	G	580 302-4129
Weatherford (G-11406)		
Durnal Construction LLC	G	405 413-5458
Perkins (G-7716)		
Frontier Land Surveying LLC	F	405 285-0433
Edmond (G-2426)		
Fw Murphy Prod Contrls LLC	G	918 317-4280
Tulsa (G-9787)		
Good Springs Energy LLC	G	580 257-9762
Tishomingo (G-8965)		
Harry A Lippert Jr	G	512 705-1248
Lawton (G-3939)		
Hejin Waldran	G	918 408-3500
Claremore (G-1632)		
High Five Graphics	G	918 636-3312
Mannford (G-4182)		
Icon Roofing and Cnstr LLC	G	405 403-6615
Mustang (G-4777)		
Igg LLC	G	918 607-3032
Broken Arrow (G-933)		
Integrity Power Solutions LLC	G	918 925-9693
Edmond (G-2461)		
Integrity Rmdlg Cnstr Svcs LLC	G	405 754-9836
Oklahoma City (G-6316)		
Intuition Inc	G	405 361-8376
Norman (G-5036)		
Jade Fire LLC	G	405 295-7734
El Reno (G-2728)		
James A Taylor	G	918 724-3121
Pawhuska (G-7687)		
JB Fabrication	G	580 716-7524
Kaw City (G-3758)		
Jemison Denna	G	405 922-7830
Oklahoma City (G-6356)		
Jjs Security Cameras Inc	G	405 408-6096
Oklahoma City (G-6364)		
Johns Professional Sharpening	G	405 313-7027
Yukon (G-11738)		
Johnson Wldg & Fabrication LLC	G	405 474-3541
Tuttle (G-11205)		
Jumping Bone LLC	G	918 853-2836
Tulsa (G-10065)		
Kelly Labs	G	682 367-8743
Longdale (G-4125)		

Employee Codes: A=Over 500 employees, B=251-500
C=101-250, D=51-100, E=20-50, F=10-19, G=1-9

2020 Oklahoma Directory of Manufacturers & Processors

Kingfisher Pipe Sales and Svc ....G....... 405 262-4422
El Reno (G-2733)
Larry Mustin Construction ....G....... 918 995-7055
Tulsa (G-10130)
Lenora Elizabeth Brown ....G....... 918 797-2034
Stilwell (G-8792)
Leviathan Applied Sciences LLC ....G....... 405 315-1759
Edmond (G-2487)
Lisa Snell ....G....... 918 708-5838
Tahlequah (G-8872)
Logistics Management Company..........G....... 405 633-1201
Oklahoma City (G-6490)
Lonestar Gphysical Surveys LLC..........D....... 405 726-8626
Edmond (G-2493)
Loud Graphic Studios LLC ....G....... 405 520-5349
Edmond (G-2497)
Manufacturing Solutions LLC...............G....... 918 951-0750
Broken Arrow (G-1141)
Mc-Alipat LLC...G....... 405 370-3321
Stillwater (G-8723)
McCurdy and Associates LLC ....G....... 405 317-4178
Oklahoma City (G-6546)
Md-Advantages LLC ....G....... 405 996-6125
Oklahoma City (G-6551)
Neo Rare Metals Oklahoma LLC............F........ 918 673-2511
Quapaw (G-8033)
Newstar Netronics LLC ....G....... 918 932-8343
Tulsa (G-10340)
Nomad Defense LLC...............................G....... 405 808-4325
Yukon (G-11760)
Oklahoma Territory Land Co LLC..........G....... 405 329-1142
Norman (G-5101)
Olam Publishing LLC.............................G....... 918 200-9770
Tulsa (G-10410)
Perfect Circle Publishing Inc ....G....... 918 629-0061
Tulsa (G-10492)
Pioneer Sport Floors LLC ....G....... 214 460-6921
Calera (G-1244)
Plateau Energy Services LLC ....F 580 625-3618
Beaver (G-544)
Plummer Energy Inc ....G....... 405 238-9132
Pauls Valley (G-7671)
Pueblo Motors Inc...................................G....... 520 297-3244
Edmond (G-2577)
R & S Swabbing Inc ....G....... 405 853-5445
Hennessey (G-3480)
Ram Internet Media.................................G....... 405 614-0641
Stillwater (G-8744)
Rapid Application Group LLC................G....... 918 760-1242
Broken Arrow (G-1021)
Reasor Enterprises..................................G....... 918 633-1746
Broken Arrow (G-1029)
Redline Instruments Inc ....F 580 622-4745
Sulphur (G-8841)
Rita S Nicar..G....... 580 492-4521
Lawton (G-3995)
Rowmark LLC...E....... 405 787-4542
Oklahoma City (G-7051)
S & T Rose Inc..G....... 580 657-4906
Lone Grove (G-4120)
Sarduccis Metal Works Inc ....G....... 918 694-3466
Tulsa (G-10708)
Schmidt Farms At Strlng Ridge..............G....... 580 919-2111
Fletcher (G-3167)
Sean Josephson LLC ....G....... 918 606-9677
Tulsa (G-9035)
Sebo Lanila Lynn ....G....... 479 719-5612
Spiro (G-8616)
SFM Incorporated ....G....... 405 788-9453
Tecumseh (G-8928)
Six S Energy Group LLC ....G....... 405 819-8053
Oklahoma City (G-7144)
Skyslate Signs...F 405 818-0838
Oklahoma City (G-7149)
Smith & Smith Construction ....G....... 918 297-5062
Hartshorne (G-3395)
Smith Precision Products LLC ....G....... 918 691-5797
Broken Arrow (G-1165)
Snwellservice Llc ....G....... 580 430-9346
Dacoma (G-1977)
Solidroots LLC...G....... 918 770-3549
Tulsa (G-10785)
Sooner Food Group LLC ....G....... 703 791-9069
Newalla (G-4816)
Spencers Contract Pumping LLC...........G....... 405 238-6363
Wynnewood (G-11673)
Steel Creek Manufacturing LLC.............G....... 918 698-3318
Tulsa (G-10843)
Sullivans Grading & Sod ....G....... 580 591-2868
Lawton (G-4007)

Superior Solutions Welding & F ....G....... 405 623-0104
Piedmont (G-7772)
Tajour Specialty Products LLC.............G....... 479 684-7445
Westville (G-11485)
Tex Star AG LLC.......................................G....... 580 579-9877
Coalgate (G-1784)
Twisted Okie Welding LLC ....G....... 580 335-1494
Lawton (G-4015)
Veterans Eng Group Inc ....G....... 918 864-6006
Pryor (G-7997)
W 2 Enterprises LLC...............................G....... 918 429-8793
Tuskahoma (G-11183)
We Buy Scrap LLC...................................G....... 580 401-3083
Ponca City (G-7887)

BUSINESS FORMS WHOLESALERS

Brown Printing Co Inc ....G....... 918 652-9611
Henryetta (G-3500)
Dps Printing Services Inc.......................G....... 405 285-4614
Edmond (G-2394)
Media Technology Incorporated...........E....... 405 682-4400
Oklahoma City (G-6556)
Metro Graphic Systems...........................G....... 918 744-0308
Tulsa (G-10249)
Quantum Forms Corporation.................F 918 665-1320
Oklahoma City (G-6940)

BUSINESS FORMS: Printed, Continuous

Printed Products Inc...............................F 918 295-9950
Tulsa (G-10561)

BUSINESS FORMS: Printed, Manifold

Adams Investment Company.................D....... 918 335-1234
Dewey (G-2012)
Blue Ribbon Forms Inc............................G....... 918 834-8838
Tulsa (G-9305)
Media Technology Incorporated...........E....... 405 682-4400
Oklahoma City (G-6556)
Mid-West Printing & Pubg Co.................F 918 224-3666
Sapulpa (G-8291)
Promotions - Forms Unlimited ....G....... 918 627-8800
Tulsa (G-10573)
R R Donnelley & Sons Company...........B....... 405 743-2124
Stillwater (G-8742)

BUSINESS SUPPORT SVCS

Ross Honey Co ....G....... 405 352-4125
Minco (G-4480)

BUSINESS TRAINING SVCS

Downtown Music Box LLC.......................G....... 405 232-2099
Oklahoma City (G-5975)

CABINETS & CASES: Show, Display & Storage, Exc Wood

E J Higgins Interior Design.....................G....... 405 387-3434
Newcastle (G-4825)
Garage Storage Cabinets LLC...............F 405 743-0133
Stillwater (G-8695)
Perceptions ....G....... 405 964-7000
McLoud (G-4362)

CABINETS: Bathroom Vanities, Wood

Beauchamp Cabinets Cstm Homes ......G....... 918 476-5532
Chouteau (G-1558)
Dynosaw Inc ....G....... 405 418-6060
Oklahoma City (G-5992)
Trim Line Cabinets Inc............................F 405 664-1439
Purcell (G-8024)

CABINETS: Entertainment

Beauchamp Cabinets Cstm Homes ......G....... 918 476-5532
Chouteau (G-1558)
Contemporary Cabinets Inc...................D....... 405 330-4592
Edmond (G-2365)
Creative Spaces ....G....... 405 341-8710
Edmond (G-2372)
Ketcherside Custom Cabinets...............G....... 580 254-2672
Woodward (G-11599)
P I Speakers...G....... 918 663-2131
Tulsa (G-10453)
Rambo Acquisition Company................D....... 918 627-6222
Tulsa (G-10615)
United Millwork Inc ....G....... 405 670-3999
Oklahoma City (G-7371)

Weatherford Cabinets.............................G....... 580 772-7511
Weatherford (G-11456)

CABINETS: Entertainment Units, Household, Wood

Parkers Custom Hardwoods Inc............G....... 405 341-9663
Edmond (G-2563)

CABINETS: Factory

Affordable Restorations LLC ....G....... 918 609-5399
Owasso (G-7543)
Creative Spaces ....G....... 405 341-8710
Edmond (G-2372)
Ketcherside Custom Cabinets...............G....... 580 254-2672
Woodward (G-11599)
Milot James Residence Cnstr................G....... 405 433-2661
Cashion (G-1291)
Rambo Acquisition Company................D....... 918 627-6222
Tulsa (G-10615)

CABINETS: Kitchen, Wood

3d Cabinetry LLC ....G....... 405 488-5604
Lindsay (G-4042)
Aaron Son Custom Cabinets ....G....... 918 537-2129
Muskogee (G-4640)
Alleman Trim & Cabinets........................G....... 405 942-7876
Oklahoma City (G-5418)
Artisan Custom Cabinetry Inc ....G....... 918 645-3874
Broken Arrow (G-834)
Bartlesville Custom Cabinets ....G....... 918 440-5981
Bartlesville (G-451)
Becca Vermelis...G....... 405 701-1638
Norman (G-4929)
Boxco Trim Cabinets ....G....... 918 266-4030
Catoosa (G-1305)
Boyds Cstm Trim Cabinetry LLC...........G....... 918 724-7033
Glenpool (G-3231)
Brays Cabinet Shop.................................G....... 580 584-6771
Broken Bow (G-1186)
Broken Arrow Woodworks......................F 918 893-6763
Broken Arrow (G-859)
C & C Cabinets..G....... 918 241-5249
Sand Springs (G-8168)
Cabinet Cures Oklahoma LLC ....G....... 405 285-5700
Edmond (G-2335)
Cabinet Doors Unlimited.........................F 918 257-5765
Afton (G-114)
Cabinet Solutions LLC ....G....... 918 592-4497
Tulsa (G-9363)
Cabinetworks Inc ....G....... 405 286-1053
Oklahoma City (G-5666)
Casework Specialties Inc LLC...............G....... 918 382-0037
Tulsa (G-9385)
Charles Dale Keller..................................G....... 940 597-1763
Ardmore (G-265)
Classic Marble Design Inc.......................G....... 580 323-4917
Clinton (G-1744)
Close Custom Cabinets Inc ....E....... 405 840-8226
Oklahoma City (G-5790)
Colliers Cabinets......................................G....... 405 377-3508
Stillwater (G-8669)
Contemporary Cabinets Inc...................D....... 405 330-4592
Edmond (G-2365)
Cooper Cabinet Systems Inc ....D....... 405 528-7220
Oklahoma City (G-5828)
Cooper Cabinets Inc ....E....... 405 528-7220
Oklahoma City (G-5829)
Crawford Cabinetry & Cnstr Inc ....G....... 918 453-0164
Tahlequah (G-8860)
Creative Cabinets.....................................G....... 580 762-9500
Ponca City (G-7811)
Creative Spaces ....G....... 405 341-8710
Edmond (G-2372)
Custom Cabinet Services........................G....... 918 340-9015
Tulsa (G-9527)
Custom Wood Craft Construction.........G....... 405 262-5228
El Reno (G-2708)
Custom Woodwork Inc.............................F 918 224-4276
Sapulpa (G-8263)
Dale P Jackson..F 580 332-1988
Ada (G-29)
David Stevens Cabinets & Trim ....G....... 918 234-0656
Tulsa (G-9558)
Davis Cabinet Shop ....G....... 405 391-5527
Newalla (G-4808)
DH Cabinet and Trim Inc ....G....... 405 376-1709
Mustang (G-4769)
E&M Solutions LLC...................................G....... 918 551-9515
Tulsa (G-9622)

PRODUCT SECTION

CANDLES

Elite Cabinets .... G 918 794-0757
  Tulsa (G-9656)
Enviro Clean .... G 918 207-9779
  Park Hill (G-7642)
Guthrie Darin Cabinet Shop .... G 918 773-8444
  Sallisaw (G-8145)
Hawley & Co .... G 918 587-0510
  Tulsa (G-9905)
Heister Custom Cabinets Inc .... G 405 329-6318
  Norman (G-5021)
Hugo Wyrick Lumber .... E 580 326-5569
  Hugo (G-3614)
Imel Woodworks Inc .... G 405 356-2505
  Wellston (G-11472)
Jay Rambo Co Hahn Showroom .... G 918 615-3370
  Tulsa (G-10030)
Jo Rose Fine Cabinets Inc .... E 918 832-1500
  Tulsa (G-10046)
John Henley Cstm Cabinets LLC .... G 405 535-9143
  Edmond (G-2473)
Johnson Kendall Cnstr Co .... G 580 223-5954
  Ardmore (G-317)
Jon A Belonoik .... G 405 258-4131
  Chandler (G-1382)
Jones & Jackson Cabinets .... G 580 889-8978
  Atoka (G-416)
Kc Woodwork & Fixture Inc .... G 918 582-5300
  Tulsa (G-10078)
Ketcherside Custom Cabinets .... G 580 254-2672
  Woodward (G-11599)
Lakewood Cabinetry Inc .... F 918 782-2203
  Langley (G-3871)
Majestic Marble & Granite .... E 918 266-1121
  Catoosa (G-1337)
Mass Brothers Inc .... G 918 527-3753
  Hartshorne (G-3393)
Mastercraft Millwork Inc .... G 405 895-6050
  Moore (G-4537)
McCollum Custom Cabinets .... G 580 548-5851
  Helena (G-3435)
Monticello Cabinets Doors Inc .... G 405 228-4900
  Oklahoma City (G-6627)
Morrow Wood Products Inc .... G 405 579-5200
  Norman (G-5081)
Nash Custom Cabinets .... G 405 919-7711
  Oklahoma City (G-6654)
Norwood Custom Cabinets .... G 918 478-2462
  Hulbert (G-3626)
Nyes Cabinet Shop .... G 580 622-6323
  Sulphur (G-8839)
Oak Tree Sales .... G 405 224-9332
  Chickasha (G-1493)
Oklahoma Millworks Inc .... D 405 282-4887
  Guthrie (G-3330)
Old West Cabinets Inc .... G 580 762-7474
  Ponca City (G-7862)
Old Wrld Msters Div Bldg Pdts .... G 918 230-0340
  Tulsa (G-10412)
Paradise Construction LLC .... G 918 967-9991
  Stigler (G-8637)
Parks Custom Cabinets LLC .... G 918 789-2694
  Chelsea (G-1409)
Pedros Cstm Cabinets Trim LLC .... G 580 656-3982
  Duncan (G-2163)
Perkins Cabinet Trim .... G 918 476-6567
  Chouteau (G-1569)
Pruett Cabinet and Trim LLC .... G 405 692-1552
  Oklahoma City (G-5312)
Quality Cabinet Company .... G 918 299-2721
  Jenks (G-3724)
Quality Cabinetry .... G 918 469-2119
  Quinton (G-8040)
Quarry .... G 918 534-2120
  Dewey (G-2030)
R and P Cabinetry LLC .... G 405 230-0495
  Oklahoma City (G-6959)
Raber Renovations Inc .... G 918 499-3030
  Tulsa (G-10608)
Rambo Acquisition Company .... D 918 627-6222
  Tulsa (G-10615)
Real Cabinets .... G 918 336-0255
  Bartlesville (G-522)
Reid Manufacturing LLC .... G 405 606-7006
  Oklahoma City (G-7004)
Richard Douglas Co .... G 405 577-6626
  Oklahoma City (G-7016)
Sand Creek Custom Cabinets LLC .... G 580 822-1269
  Fairview (G-3151)
Sandstar Custom Cabinets LLC .... G 918 456-2964
  Tahlequah (G-8883)

Sequoia Custom Cabinets LLC .... G 801 830-2741
  Tulsa (G-10732)
Sharp Cuts Custom Cabinets .... G 405 282-3657
  Guthrie (G-3338)
Signature Cabinets LLC .... G 918 636-3433
  Tulsa (G-10759)
Sooner Cabinet & Trim Inc .... E 405 820-2920
  Moore (G-4571)
Spencers Custom Cabinets .... G 918 598-3208
  Peggs (G-7713)
Sterling Cabinetry & Trim LLC .... G 918 928-9982
  Stigler (G-8647)
Suburban Cabinet Shop .... E 405 231-3110
  Oklahoma City (G-7221)
Sullivans Custom Cabinetry .... G 918 445-9191
  Tulsa (G-10865)
Taylormade Cbntry Cntrtops LLC .... G 405 227-4063
  Jones (G-3753)
Ted S Cabinet .... G 580 668-5207
  Wilson (G-11544)
Thomas Cabinet Company .... G 580 588-9231
  Apache (G-223)
Thomas Millwork Inc .... F 405 769-5618
  Spencer (G-8602)
Thomco Cabinet Co .... G 405 627-1445
  Oklahoma City (G-7284)
Three Rivers Custom Cabinets .... G 918 537-2311
  Muskogee (G-4752)
Tillison Cabinet Company LLC .... E 405 793-2940
  Moore (G-4577)
Trs Cabinets & Trim LLC .... G 405 234-7276
  Yukon (G-11795)
United Millwork Inc .... G 405 670-3999
  Oklahoma City (G-7371)
Vanderbilt Cabinet & Trim .... G 405 376-3876
  Mustang (G-4800)
W & W Custom Cabinets .... G 405 222-1410
  Chickasha (G-1521)
Wades Cabinet Door Shop .... G 918 868-2516
  Tahlequah (G-8891)
Ward Wood Products Inc .... D 405 681-5522
  Oklahoma City (G-7420)
Watkins Cabinet Doors LLC .... G 580 320-6301
  Ada (G-104)
WD Sales Inc .... F 580 237-1220
  Enid (G-3076)
Weatherford Cabinets .... G 580 772-7511
  Weatherford (G-11456)
Wildwood Fine Cabinet Doors .... G 918 331-0007
  Bartlesville (G-535)
Wilshire Cabinet & Company LLC .... G 405 286-6282
  Oklahoma City (G-7457)
Wolher Company .... G 405 282-6210
  Guthrie (G-3341)
Wood Systems Inc .... D 918 388-0900
  Tulsa (G-11148)
Wooden Solutions LLC .... E 918 396-0774
  Skiatook (G-8575)
Woodshop Cstm Cbinets Trim LLC .... G 405 673-7139
  Oklahoma City (G-7466)
Woodstock Cabinet LLC .... F 918 834-4840
  Tulsa (G-11150)
Woodwrk Productions LLC .... G 918 639-3167
  Catoosa (G-1367)
Ye Olde Woodshop .... G 918 224-1603
  Sapulpa (G-8328)
Young Construction Supply LLC .... G 918 456-3250
  Tahlequah (G-8893)

CABINETS: Office, Wood

Bearwood Concepts Inc .... D 918 933-6600
  Tulsa (G-9277)
Days Wood Products Inc .... F 405 238-6477
  Pauls Valley (G-7656)
Woodstock Cabinet LLC .... F 918 834-4840
  Tulsa (G-11150)

CABINETS: Show, Display, Etc, Wood, Exc Refrigerated

All Wood Products Co Inc .... E 918 585-9739
  Tulsa (G-9138)
Dale P Jackson .... F 580 332-1988
  Ada (G-29)
Estey Cabinet Door Co .... E 405 771-3004
  Spencer (G-8595)

CABLE & PAY TELEVISION SVCS: Closed Circuit

Green Co Corporation .... G 918 221-3997
  Tulsa (G-9859)

CABLE TELEVISION PRDTS

Tulsat Inc .... G 918 587-4729
  Tulsa (G-11016)

CABLE: Fiber

Lynxsystems LLC .... G 918 728-6000
  Tulsa (G-10185)
Surface Mount Depot Inc .... D 405 948-8763
  Oklahoma City (G-7232)

CABLE: Fiber Optic

Grw Inc .... F 918 681-3282
  Muskogee (G-4685)
Holloway Technical Svcs LLC .... G 405 223-9352
  Duncan (G-2130)
Techsico Entp Solutions Inc .... D 918 585-2347
  Tulsa (G-10913)

CABLE: Nonferrous, Shipboard

US Pioneer LLC .... E 918 359-5200
  Tulsa (G-11055)

CABLE: Ropes & Fiber

Texhoma Fiber LLC .... G 918 747-7000
  Medicine Park (G-4371)

CAGES: Wire

Tims Sheds .... G 918 506-7741
  Tahlequah (G-8888)

CALCULATING & ACCOUNTING EQPT

Shen Te Enterprises Inc .... E 918 505-7711
  Tulsa (G-10742)
Special Service Systems Inc .... E 918 582-7777
  Tulsa (G-10816)

CALIBRATING SVCS, NEC

Csi Measurement LLC .... G 580 234-4979
  Enid (G-2936)

CAMPERS: Truck Mounted

Allen Camper Mfg Company Inc .... E 580 857-2177
  Allen (G-133)

CAN LIDS & ENDS

Metal Container Corporation .... C 405 680-3140
  Oklahoma City (G-6574)

CANDLE SHOPS

Heavens Scent Candle Factory .... G 918 686-0243
  Muskogee (G-4689)
Keepsake Candles Inc .... F 918 336-0351
  Bartlesville (G-501)
Lasting Impressions Gifts Inc .... G 405 732-2401
  Oklahoma City (G-6455)

CANDLES

Abby Candles Inc .... F 405 895-9957
  Moore (G-4483)
Ambers Candle .... G 405 492-3620
  Moore (G-4486)
Amys Candles and Gifts LLC .... G 918 865-2827
  Terlton (G-8937)
Angel Delite Inc .... G 580 223-9777
  Ardmore (G-242)
Bisby Candles LLC .... G 918 408-5291
  Edmond (G-2322)
Camo Galz Candles & More .... G 918 399-0044
  Mounds (G-4611)
Can-Do-Candles .... G 580 564-2816
  Kingston (G-3826)
Candle Electric .... G 918 232-0558
  Tulsa (G-9369)
Candles By ME .... G 580 798-5200
  Ardmore (G-263)
Elevated Candles .... G 405 763-8223
  Oklahoma City (G-6024)

Employee Codes: A=Over 500 employees, B=251-500
C=101-250, D=51-100, E=20-50, F=10-19, G=1-9

2020 Oklahoma Directory of Manufacturers & Processors

CANDLES

PRODUCT SECTION

Evening Glow Candles .... G 918 543-2990
  Inola *(G-3658)*
From Heart Candles and More .... G 580 334-4104
  Woodward *(G-11585)*
Haiku Candles LLC .... G 405 528-5556
  Oklahoma City *(G-6202)*
Heavens Scent Candle Factory .... G 918 686-0243
  Muskogee *(G-4689)*
Isabels Candles .... G 918 595-5358
  Tulsa *(G-10013)*
Just Bee Candles and More LLC .... G 918 557-5145
  Chelsea *(G-1406)*
Keepsake Candles Inc .... F 918 336-0351
  Bartlesville *(G-501)*
Lasting Impressions Gifts Inc .... G 405 732-2401
  Oklahoma City *(G-6455)*
Lux Illume LLC .... G 405 618-4552
  Moore *(G-4534)*
Martin House Candle Company .... G 580 504-1699
  Ardmore *(G-328)*
Matin House Candle Company .... G 580 490-6500
  Ardmore *(G-329)*
Mia Bella Candles .... G 918 470-3862
  McAlester *(G-4321)*
Nenos Homemade Candles LLC .... G 580 367-9874
  Coleman *(G-1797)*
Old Town N Candles Lawton OK .... G 580 678-7608
  Lawton *(G-3978)*
Redbud Candles & Creations .... G 210 749-6975
  Skiatook *(G-8566)*
Redneck Candles and Gifts .... G 405 492-8987
  Lawton *(G-3992)*
SC Candles .... G 469 855-2823
  Owasso *(G-7614)*
Secret Garden Candle Company .... G 918 497-8699
  Tulsa *(G-10721)*
Southern Belles Candle Co LLC .... G 405 200-5986
  Luther *(G-4138)*
Southern Breeze Candle Co LLC .... G 918 402-4040
  Tulsa *(G-10798)*
Soy Candle Cottage LLC .... G 405 519-6827
  Jones *(G-3752)*
Spark Something Candles LLC .... G 405 872-5673
  Norman *(G-5153)*
Sweet Scent Candle .... G 918 535-3423
  Ochelata *(G-5240)*
Two Candle Guys LLC .... G 918 271-5244
  Tulsa *(G-11025)*
Wax and Hive Candle Lc .... G 918 542-6432
  Miami *(G-4436)*
Willow Creek Co LLC .... G 580 239-9549
  Atoka *(G-427)*

CANDLES: Wholesalers

Heavens Scent Candle Factory .... G 918 686-0243
  Muskogee *(G-4689)*

CANDY & CONFECTIONS: Candy Bars, Including Chocolate Covered

Big Easy .... G 918 493-6280
  Tulsa *(G-9289)*
Zoo Too .... G 580 250-1088
  Lawton *(G-4026)*

CANDY & CONFECTIONS: Fudge

Amazing Grace Fudge LLC .... G 580 883-4693
  Ringwood *(G-8083)*
Fudgenomics 101 LLC .... G 405 401-3832
  Norman *(G-5004)*

CANDY & CONFECTIONS: Nuts, Candy Covered

Peanut Products Co Inc .... F 580 296-4888
  Calera *(G-1243)*

CANDY, NUT & CONFECTIONERY STORES: Confectionery

Mollycoddled Hash Slinger LLC .... G 918 236-1196
  Fort Gibson *(G-3176)*

CANDY, NUT & CONFECTIONERY STORES: Nuts

Masons Pecans & Peanuts Inc .... G 405 329-7828
  Norman *(G-5065)*

Nut House .... G 918 266-1604
  Claremore *(G-1664)*

CANDY: Hard

Ladybugs and Lollipops LLC .... G 405 919-8555
  Guthrie *(G-3322)*

CANNED SPECIALTIES

Cable Meat Center Inc .... F 580 658-6646
  Marlow *(G-4224)*
Head Country Inc .... F 580 762-1227
  Ponca City *(G-7835)*
Rockin L-H Asparagus Farms .... G 918 689-5086
  Eufaula *(G-3111)*
S & S Foods Inc .... F 405 256-6557
  Mustang *(G-4792)*

CANOPIES: Sheet Metal

Canopies Plus Inc .... G 918 689-7077
  Eufaula *(G-3098)*

CANS: Composite Foil-Fiber, Made From Purchased Materials

Mito Material Solutions Inc .... G 855 344-6486
  Stillwater *(G-8725)*

CANS: Fiber

Sureshot Cans Inc .... G 580 698-2800
  Woodward *(G-11638)*

CANS: Garbage, Stamped Or Pressed Metal

Roll-Offs of America Inc .... D 580 924-6355
  Mead *(G-4367)*

CANS: Metal

Herbert Malarkey Roofing Co .... C 405 261-6900
  Oklahoma City *(G-6241)*
Keymiaee Aero-Tech Inc .... F 405 235-5010
  Oklahoma City *(G-6409)*
Mullins Salvage Inc .... G 918 352-9612
  Cushing *(G-1946)*

CANS: Oil, Metal

Blitz USA Inc .... B 918 676-3620
  Miami *(G-4391)*

CANVAS PRDTS

Dobbs & Crowder Inc .... G 918 452-3211
  Eufaula *(G-3100)*
Roper Product .... G 580 795-2293
  Lebanon *(G-4027)*
Shur-Co LLC .... G 405 262-7600
  El Reno *(G-2757)*

CANVAS PRDTS: Air Cushions & Mattresses

Jessie Shaw .... G 918 587-6329
  Tulsa *(G-10040)*

CAPACITORS & CONDENSERS

Tsig LLC .... G 405 463-7700
  Oklahoma City *(G-7347)*

CAR WASH EQPT

3b Industries Inc .... F 580 439-8876
  Comanche *(G-1832)*
Berkshire Corporation .... G 405 677-3391
  Oklahoma City *(G-5556)*
Easy Car Wash Systems Inc .... G 918 582-4355
  Tulsa *(G-9634)*
Ecm Car Wash LLC .... E 405 590-3252
  Oklahoma City *(G-6007)*
Industrial Power Wash Inc .... G 405 787-9274
  Bethany *(G-582)*
Kenneth E Jones .... G 580 832-2227
  Cordell *(G-1861)*
Lavi Wash .... G 405 470-0895
  Oklahoma City *(G-6457)*
Pappan and Spears LLC .... G 405 742-6900
  Tulsa *(G-10464)*
Preferred Fleetwash .... G 918 281-9325
  Sand Springs *(G-8215)*
Star Industries Inc .... G 405 542-3041
  Hinton *(G-3537)*

CARBIDES

Custom Carbide Application LLC .... G 580 799-5575
  Elk City *(G-2799)*

CARBON & GRAPHITE PRDTS, NEC

Continental Carbon Company .... C 580 763-8100
  Ponca City *(G-7809)*

CARBON BLACK

Cabot Norit Americas Inc .... D 918 825-8332
  Pryor *(G-7949)*
Continental Carbon Company .... C 580 763-8100
  Ponca City *(G-7809)*

CARDS, PLASTIC, UNPRINTED, WHOLESALE

Lucas Holdings LLC .... E 405 524-1811
  Oklahoma City *(G-6500)*

CARDS: Greeting

Saga Card Co Inc .... G 918 967-0333
  Stigler *(G-8645)*

CARDS: Identification

Stonehouse Marketing Svcs LLC .... D 405 360-5674
  Norman *(G-5160)*

CARPET & UPHOLSTERY CLEANING SVCS

Clearco Window Cleaning LLC .... G 580 248-9547
  Lawton *(G-3907)*

CARPET & UPHOLSTERY CLEANING SVCS: Carpet/Furniture, On Loc

Johnsonm3 LLC .... G 580 353-5550
  Lawton *(G-3946)*

CARPETS & RUGS: Tufted

Interfaceflor LLC .... G 918 746-0501
  Tulsa *(G-10003)*
Mohawk Industries .... G 214 309-4652
  Enid *(G-3015)*

CARPETS, RUGS & FLOOR COVERING

Ahmadys Import LLC .... G 918 254-4094
  Tulsa *(G-9118)*
Aladdin Manufacturing Corp .... F 405 943-3037
  Oklahoma City *(G-5407)*
Burtco Enterprises LLC .... G 918 857-1293
  Catoosa *(G-1307)*
Classic Carpets Lawton Inc .... G 580 713-0653
  Lawton *(G-3904)*
Moss Seat Cover Mfg & Sls Co .... F 918 742-3326
  Tulsa *(G-10306)*
Oklahoma Interpak Inc .... E 918 687-1681
  Muskogee *(G-4724)*

CARPORTS: Prefabricated Metal

Affordable Buildings LLC .... G 918 427-6005
  Muldrow *(G-4630)*
Lafes .... G 918 423-5311
  McAlester *(G-4312)*
Rising M Enterprises .... G 918 766-4235
  Stigler *(G-8643)*
Ronnie Nevitt .... G 918 687-5284
  Muskogee *(G-4745)*

CARS: Electric

Cox Motor Co Henryetta LLC .... G 918 652-0202
  Henryetta *(G-3503)*
Guardian Interlock of Utah .... G 580 357-8583
  Lawton *(G-3937)*

CASEMENTS: Aluminum

Mill Creek Lumber & Supply Co .... D 918 794-3600
  Tulsa *(G-10279)*
Mill Creek Lumber & Supply Co .... D 405 947-7227
  Oklahoma City *(G-6609)*

CASES: Carrying, Clothing & Apparel

D Gala .... G 580 468-4980
  Guymon *(G-3347)*

PRODUCT SECTION

Frenches Quarter .... G....... 918 691-2553
  Tulsa (G-9777)
Titanium Phoenix Inc .... G....... 405 305-1304
  Oklahoma City (G-7294)

CASES: Jewelry

Warner Jwly Box Display Co LLC .... D....... 580 536-8885
  Lawton (G-4021)

CASES: Shipping, Nailed Or Lock Corner, Wood

American Crating Company .... E....... 918 425-8787
  Tulsa (G-9166)

CASH REGISTERS WHOLESALERS

Juno Companies Incorporated .... G....... 918 627-8868
  Tulsa (G-10067)

CASINGS: Storage, Missile & Missile Components

Frontier Elctrnic Systems Corp .... C....... 405 624-7708
  Stillwater (G-8694)

CASKETS & ACCESS

Fright Casket .... G....... 405 602-1534
  Oklahoma City (G-6119)
Si Precast Concrete Products .... E....... 918 446-2131
  Tulsa (G-9036)

CAST STONE: Concrete

52 Stone .... G....... 918 798-9952
  Claremore (G-1573)
Excalibur Cast Stone LLC .... E....... 405 702-4314
  Oklahoma City (G-6057)
Excalibur Stoneworks LLC .... D....... 405 702-4314
  Oklahoma City (G-6058)

CASTERS

Caster LLC .... G....... 800 255-0480
  Purcell (G-8002)

CASTING BUREAU, MOTION PICTURE

American Castings LLC .... B....... 918 476-4252
  Pryor (G-7942)

CASTINGS GRINDING: For The Trade

Airico Inc .... G....... 918 836-2675
  Tulsa (G-9130)
Chromium Plating Company .... E....... 918 583-4118
  Tulsa (G-9422)
Honing By Hardy .... G....... 405 919-3589
  Oklahoma City (G-6262)
Slone Centerless Grinding .... G....... 918 497-0654
  Tulsa (G-10774)

CASTINGS: Aerospace Investment, Ferrous

Carter Aerospace Mfg Co LLC .... G....... 918 229-4026
  Skiatook (G-8535)
Mingo Aerospace LLC .... F....... 918 272-7371
  Owasso (G-7591)
Mingo Aerospace LLC .... G....... 918 272-7371
  Owasso (G-7592)

CASTINGS: Aerospace, Aluminum

Jag Machine Inc .... F....... 918 791-0004
  Grove (G-3277)
Neco Industries Inc .... E....... 405 682-3003
  Oklahoma City (G-6667)

CASTINGS: Aerospace, Nonferrous, Exc Aluminum

LMI Aerospace Inc .... E....... 918 281-0124
  Tulsa (G-10173)

CASTINGS: Aluminum

Hurst Aerospace Inc .... G....... 918 543-6527
  Inola (G-3663)
Pickering Metal Casting LLC .... E....... 806 747-3411
  Tulsa (G-10512)

CASTINGS: Brass, NEC, Exc Die

ARk -Ramos Fndry Mfg Co Inc .... D....... 405 235-5505
  Oklahoma City (G-5465)

CASTINGS: Bronze, NEC, Exc Die

Bronze Horse Inc .... G....... 918 287-4433
  Pawhuska (G-7678)

CASTINGS: Commercial Investment, Ferrous

North Amercn Precision Cast Co .... D....... 580 237-4033
  Enid (G-3019)

CASTINGS: Die, Aluminum

Mold Tech Inc .... G....... 918 247-6275
  Sapulpa (G-8292)
Transtate Castings Inc .... G....... 405 232-3936
  Oklahoma City (G-7319)

CASTINGS: Die, Copper & Copper Alloy

Alpha Investment Casting Corp .... E....... 918 834-4686
  Tulsa (G-9153)
Alpha Investment Casting LLC .... E....... 918 834-4686
  Tulsa (G-9154)

CASTINGS: Die, Magnesium & Magnesium-Base Alloy

Diemasters .... G....... 800 826-2134
  Skiatook (G-8541)

CASTINGS: Die, Zinc

Mid America Alloys LLC .... E....... 918 224-3446
  Sapulpa (G-8288)

CASTINGS: Ductile

Supco Inc .... C....... 918 336-5075
  Bartlesville (G-529)
Superior Companies Inc .... C....... 918 336-5075
  Bartlesville (G-530)

CASTINGS: Gray Iron

CFM Corporation .... F....... 580 363-2850
  Blackwell (G-678)
Ej Usa Inc .... C....... 231 536-2261
  Ardmore (G-282)
Fascast Inc .... E....... 918 445-7405
  Tulsa (G-9005)

CASTINGS: Machinery, Brass

Maverick Machinery LLC .... G....... 918 584-2504
  Broken Arrow (G-968)

CASTINGS: Machinery, Nonferrous, Exc Die or Aluminum Copper

Metal Dynamics Corp .... E....... 918 582-0124
  Tulsa (G-10244)

CASTINGS: Precision

Nordam Group LLC .... C....... 918 274-2742
  Tulsa (G-10356)

CATALOG SALES

Cambridge Soundworks Inc .... C....... 405 742-6704
  Stillwater (G-8665)
Gibsons Treasures .... G....... 405 835-1109
  Oklahoma City (G-6152)

CATALYSTS: Chemical

Bilco Construction Inc .... G....... 405 386-5591
  Newalla (G-4804)
C & P Catalyst Inc .... G....... 918 747-8379
  Tulsa (G-9357)
Eurecat U S Incorporated .... G....... 918 423-5800
  McAlester (G-4296)
Tricat Inc .... E....... 918 423-5800
  McAlester (G-4343)

CATERERS

Prairie Gypsies Inc. .... G....... 405 525-3013
  Oklahoma City (G-6873)

CAULKING COMPOUNDS

Color-Rite Inc .... F....... 405 354-3644
  Yukon (G-11708)
Tower Sealants LLC .... F....... 405 528-4411
  Oklahoma City (G-7312)

CEMENT & CONCRETE RELATED PRDTS & EQPT: Bituminous

Ellis Manufacturing Co Inc .... G....... 405 528-4671
  Oklahoma City (G-6028)
G T Bynum Company .... G....... 918 587-9118
  Tulsa (G-9794)
Oklahoma Cement Solutions LLC .... G....... 214 802-1527
  Choctaw (G-1553)

CEMENT ROCK: Crushed & Broken

Jenkins Quary .... G....... 580 588-3020
  Apache (G-219)
Stewart Stone Inc .... F....... 918 225-2704
  Cushing (G-1962)

CEMENT: Clay Refractory

Heater Specialists LLC .... G....... 918 835-3126
  Tulsa (G-9909)

CEMENT: Hydraulic

Holcim (us) Inc .... C....... 580 332-1512
  Ada (G-48)
Holcim (us) Inc .... C....... 573 242-3571
  Ada (G-49)

CEMENT: Masonry

Tulsa Cement LLC .... B....... 918 437-3902
  Tulsa (G-10991)

CEMENT: Natural

Peak Cement Piedmont .... G....... 405 373-2086
  Piedmont (G-7768)

CEMENT: Portland

Buzzi Unicem USA Inc .... E....... 918 825-1937
  Pryor (G-7948)
Buzzi Unicem USA Inc P .... G....... 405 670-0677
  Oklahoma City (G-5650)
Lone Star Industries Inc .... G....... 405 670-0677
  Oklahoma City (G-6492)
Lone Star Industries Inc .... G....... 918 825-1937
  Pryor (G-7974)
Lone Star Industries Inc .... G....... 918 492-2121
  Tulsa (G-10177)

CEMETERY MEMORIAL DEALERS

Eddie Brown .... F....... 580 889-1506
  Atoka (G-411)
Eurocraft Ltd .... E....... 918 322-5500
  Glenpool (G-3234)
Whm Granite Products Inc .... F....... 580 535-2184
  Granite (G-3257)

CERAMIC FIBER

Insul-Vest Inc .... G....... 918 445-2279
  Tulsa (G-9992)
To Market LLC .... G....... 405 236-2878
  Oklahoma City (G-7300)

CERAMIC FLOOR & WALL TILE WHOLESALERS

Tile & Design Concepts Inc .... E....... 405 842-8551
  Oklahoma City (G-7288)
Young Brothers Inc .... E....... 405 272-0821
  Oklahoma City (G-7482)

CHAIN: Welded, Made From Purchased Wire

Fki Industries Inc .... G....... 918 834-4611
  Tulsa (G-9752)

CHAINS: Forged

Kloefkorn Entps Ltd Partnr .... G....... 580 694-2292
  Manchester (G-4167)

Employee Codes: A=Over 500 employees, B=251-500
C=101-250, D=51-100, E=20-50, F=10-19, G=1-9

CHANDELIERS: Commercial
Gary Smith .... F 580 762-7575
  Ponca City (G-7830)

CHANDELIERS: Residential
Gary Smith .... F 580 762-7575
  Ponca City (G-7830)

CHART & GRAPH DESIGN SVCS
Peabodys Printing & A Brush Sp .... G 580 248-8317
  Lawton (G-3980)

CHASSIS: Automobile Trailer
Frank A Hogan II Transport .... G 405 889-4278
  Oklahoma City (G-6111)

CHASSIS: Motor Vehicle
Antique & Rod Shop LLC .... G 405 631-3544
  Oklahoma City (G-5450)
Federal-Mogul Chassis LLC .... F 405 672-4500
  Oklahoma City (G-6081)
Glenns Competition Chassis .... G 405 732-4403
  Oklahoma City (G-6158)

CHEMICAL PROCESSING MACHINERY & EQPT
Dathney Inc .... G 405 354-0481
  Yukon (G-11715)

CHEMICAL SPLYS FOR FOUNDRIES
Technology Management Inc .... F 580 332-8615
  Ada (G-93)
Umicore Precious Metals .... E 918 266-1400
  Catoosa (G-1362)

CHEMICAL: Sodm Compnds/Salts, Inorg, Exc Rfnd Sodm Chloride
Tronox Pigments LLC .... G 405 775-5000
  Oklahoma City (G-7341)

CHEMICALS & ALLIED PRDTS WHOLESALERS, NEC
Energy and Envmtl Svcs Inc .... G 405 843-8996
  Edmond (G-2413)
Gra Services International LP .... G 405 672-8885
  Oklahoma City (G-6174)
Laster/Castor Corporation .... G 918 234-7777
  Tulsa (G-10133)
Plainsman Technology Inc .... F 580 658-6608
  Marlow (G-4236)
Westair Gas & Equipment LP .... G 580 338-6449
  Guymon (G-3370)

CHEMICALS & ALLIED PRDTS, WHOLESALE: Chemicals, Indl
Biotech Products Inc .... G 405 235-7575
  Oklahoma City (G-5574)
Brenntag Southwest Inc .... E 918 266-2951
  Catoosa (G-1306)
Coil Chem LLC .... F 405 445-5545
  Washington (G-11334)
Fairwind LLC .... E 580 492-5209
  Lawton (G-3925)
John Scoggins Company Inc .... E 918 775-2748
  Sallisaw (G-8146)
Russell Chemical Sales & Svc .... G 580 234-2100
  Enid (G-3054)

CHEMICALS & ALLIED PRDTS, WHOLESALE: Chemicals, Indl & Heavy
Brenntag Southwest Inc .... E 918 273-2265
  Nowata (G-5209)
Chemical Dynamics Corporation .... G 405 392-3505
  Tuttle (G-11189)

CHEMICALS & ALLIED PRDTS, WHOLESALE: Detergent/Soap
3b Industries Inc .... F 580 439-8876
  Comanche (G-1832)

CHEMICALS & ALLIED PRDTS, WHOLESALE: Essential Oils
Rustic Rehab .... G 918 314-6647
  Grove (G-3287)

CHEMICALS & ALLIED PRDTS, WHOLESALE: Indl Gases
Boc Gases .... G 580 254-2259
  Woodward (G-11563)

CHEMICALS & ALLIED PRDTS, WHOLESALE: Oil Additives
Energy and Envmtl Svcs Inc .... G 405 285-8767
  Edmond (G-2412)
Entz Oilfield Chemicals Inc .... F 405 542-3174
  Hinton (G-3527)

CHEMICALS & ALLIED PRDTS, WHOLESALE: Oxygen
Airgas Usa LLC .... G 405 745-2732
  Oklahoma City (G-5401)

CHEMICALS & ALLIED PRDTS, WHOLESALE: Plastics Materials, NEC
Handy & Harman .... E 918 258-1566
  Broken Arrow (G-1131)

CHEMICALS & ALLIED PRDTS, WHOLESALE: Plastics Prdts, NEC
Diversified Plastics Inds LLC .... G 918 245-0770
  Sand Springs (G-8178)
Plastic Engrg Co Tulsa Inc .... E 918 622-9660
  Tulsa (G-10523)
Rowmark LLC .... G 405 787-4542
  Oklahoma City (G-7051)

CHEMICALS & ALLIED PRDTS, WHOLESALE: Sealants
George Townsend & Co Inc .... G 405 235-1387
  Oklahoma City (G-6145)

CHEMICALS & OTHER PRDTS DERIVED FROM COKING
Danlin Industries LLC .... C 580 661-3248
  Clinton (G-1747)

CHEMICALS, AGRICULTURE: Wholesalers
Custer Enterprises Inc .... F 580 371-9588
  Mannsville (G-4195)
Winfield Solutions LLC .... G 580 237-2456
  Enid (G-3082)

CHEMICALS: Agricultural
Armour Pest Control LLC .... G 918 489-5734
  Hendrix (G-3439)
Avitrol Corp .... G 918 622-7763
  Tulsa (G-9231)
Bug Right .... G 918 367-9792
  Bristow (G-771)
Chromatech Scientific Corp .... G 405 370-4466
  Edmond (G-2351)
Deepwater Chemicals Inc .... E 580 256-0500
  Woodward (G-11577)
Houston Brothers Inc .... G 918 449-1175
  Broken Arrow (G-1134)
Tex Star AG LLC .... G 580 579-9877
  Coalgate (G-1784)

CHEMICALS: Anhydrous Ammonia
Koch Industries Inc .... D 580 233-3900
  Enid (G-2997)

CHEMICALS: Brine
Tetra Technologies Inc .... G 405 606-8600
  Oklahoma City (G-7275)

CHEMICALS: Fire Retardant
OK Fire LLC .... G 918 424-1808
  McAlester (G-4325)

Spectrumfx Inc .... G 918 392-9799
  Tulsa (G-10820)

CHEMICALS: High Purity Grade, Organic
H2szero LLC .... G 918 384-9600
  Sapulpa (G-8277)

CHEMICALS: High Purity, Refined From Technical Grade
Flotek Chemistry LLC .... G 713 849-9911
  Marlow (G-4233)

CHEMICALS: Hydrogen Peroxide
Peroxychem LLC .... F 918 626-8020
  Pocola (G-7785)

CHEMICALS: Inorganic, NEC
Advance RES Chem & Mfg LLC .... G 918 266-6789
  Catoosa (G-1293)
Advance Research Chemicals Inc .... D 918 266-6789
  Catoosa (G-1294)
Air Products and Chemicals Inc .... E 918 266-8800
  Catoosa (G-1295)
Airgas Usa LLC .... G 405 235-0009
  Oklahoma City (G-5402)
American Zinc Recycling Corp .... D 918 336-7100
  Bartlesville (G-447)
Associated Material Proc LLC .... G 405 707-7301
  Stillwater (G-8656)
Bpi Inc .... G 918 682-5044
  Muskogee (G-4654)
Brenntag Southwest Inc .... E 918 273-2265
  Nowata (G-5209)
Cabot Norit Americas Inc .... D 918 825-8332
  Pryor (G-7949)
Cardinal Fg Minerals LLC .... E 580 367-2123
  Coleman (G-1793)
Ceradyne Inc .... D 918 673-2201
  Quapaw (G-8029)
Chemplex Advanced Mtls LLC .... G 580 832-5288
  Cordell (G-1856)
Chemtrade Refinery Svcs Inc .... F 918 587-7613
  Tulsa (G-9411)
Galaxy Chemicals LLC .... F 918 379-0820
  Claremore (G-1625)
Ingevity .... G 918 704-6423
  Tulsa (G-9984)
Invia Pavement Tech LLC .... F 918 878-7890
  Tulsa (G-10009)
Invisible Element LLC .... E 918 296-7562
  Jenks (G-3709)
Jupiter Sulphur LLC .... E 580 762-1130
  Ponca City (G-7841)
Neo Rare Metals Oklahoma LLC .... F 918 673-2511
  Quapaw (G-8033)
Raw Elements LLC .... G 918 392-4957
  Tulsa (G-10621)
Sequoyah Fuels Corporation .... G 918 489-5511
  Gore (G-3251)
Sooner Energy Services Inc .... G 405 579-3200
  Marlow (G-4242)
Sunbelt Industries Inc .... G 405 843-1275
  Oklahoma City (G-7225)
Thermaclime LLC .... G 405 235-4546
  Oklahoma City (G-7279)
Tronox Incorporated .... D 405 775-5000
  Oklahoma City (G-7339)
U S Silica Company .... D 580 384-5241
  Mill Creek (G-4472)
Ultimate Chemicals LLC .... G 405 703-2771
  Moore (G-4581)
Umicore Autocat USA Inc .... D 918 266-8923
  Catoosa (G-1361)

CHEMICALS: Iodine, Elemental
Deepwater Chemicals Inc .... E 580 256-0500
  Woodward (G-11577)
Dewey Chemical Inc .... G 405 848-8611
  Oklahoma City (G-5937)
Iochem Corporation .... E 405 848-8611
  Oklahoma City (G-6325)
Iochem Corporation .... E 580 995-3198
  Vici (G-11243)
Woodward Iodine Corporation .... E 580 254-3311
  Woodward (G-11657)

PRODUCT SECTION • CLEANING EQPT: High Pressure

CHEMICALS: Magnesium Compounds Or Salts, Inorganic

Magnesium Products Inc ....F....... 918 587-9930
 Tulsa *(G-9018)*

CHEMICALS: Medicinal, Organic, Uncompounded, Bulk

Environmate Inc ....G....... 817 707-5282
 Catoosa *(G-1318)*

CHEMICALS: NEC

Advanced Chemical Tech Inc ....G....... 405 843-2585
 Oklahoma City *(G-5379)*
Bachman Services Inc ....E....... 405 677-8296
 Oklahoma City *(G-5507)*
Baker Petrolite LLC ....C....... 918 245-2224
 Sand Springs *(G-8165)*
Best Building Materials Inc ....G....... 405 755-0554
 Edmond *(G-2320)*
Brenntag Southwest Inc ....E....... 918 273-2265
 Nowata *(G-5209)*
C & P Catalyst Inc ....G....... 918 747-8379
 Tulsa *(G-9357)*
Callidus Technologies LLC ....D....... 918 267-4920
 Beggs *(G-550)*
Ceralusa LLC ....G....... 405 455-7720
 Oklahoma City *(G-5730)*
Chemical Products Inds Inc ....G....... 405 745-2070
 Oklahoma City *(G-5748)*
Corrpro Companies Inc ....E....... 918 245-8791
 Sand Springs *(G-8172)*
Deepwater Chemicals Inc ....E....... 580 256-0500
 Woodward *(G-11577)*
Dennis Grothe Water Svc ....G....... 405 651-5353
 Oklahoma City *(G-5922)*
Galaxy Chemicals LLC ....F....... 918 379-0820
 Claremore *(G-1625)*
Gallium Compounds LLC ....F....... 918 673-2511
 Quapaw *(G-8031)*
Kel-Crete Industries Inc ....G....... 918 744-0800
 Tulsa *(G-10080)*
Magnesium Products Inc ....F....... 918 587-9930
 Tulsa *(G-9018)*
Mid-Continent Packaging Inc ....D....... 580 234-5200
 Enid *(G-3013)*
Molycorp Rare Metals ....F....... 918 673-2511
 Quapaw *(G-8032)*
Moon Chemical Products Co ....G....... 405 602-6678
 Oklahoma City *(G-6629)*
Plainsman Technology Inc ....F....... 580 658-6608
 Marlow *(G-4236)*
Quikrete Companies LLC ....E....... 405 787-2050
 Oklahoma City *(G-6953)*
R Squared Chemicals LLC ....G....... 918 520-2384
 Tulsa *(G-10607)*
Russell Chemical Sales & Svc ....E....... 580 234-2100
 Enid *(G-3054)*
Schmoldt Engineering Services ....F....... 918 336-1221
 Bartlesville *(G-526)*
Silex LLC ....G....... 844 239-4056
 Moore *(G-4568)*
Sooner Energy Services Inc ....G....... 405 579-3200
 Marlow *(G-4242)*

CHEMICALS: Organic, NEC

Bio-Cide International Inc ....G....... 405 364-1940
 Norman *(G-4932)*
Biosphere Fuels LLC ....G....... 713 332-5726
 Oklahoma City *(G-5573)*
Brenntag Southwest Inc ....E....... 918 266-2951
 Catoosa *(G-1306)*
C & P Catalyst Inc ....G....... 918 747-8379
 Tulsa *(G-9357)*
Fairwind LLC ....E....... 580 492-5209
 Lawton *(G-3925)*
Galaxy Chemicals LLC ....F....... 918 379-0820
 Claremore *(G-1625)*
Iochem Corporation ....E....... 580 995-3198
 Vici *(G-11243)*
Magpro Chlor-Alkali LLC ....G....... 918 587-9930
 Tulsa *(G-9019)*
Oklahoma Biorefining Corp ....G....... 405 201-1824
 Norman *(G-5098)*
Plainsman Technology Inc ....F....... 580 658-6608
 Marlow *(G-4236)*
Premier Chem & Oilfld Sup LLC ....F....... 405 893-2321
 Enid *(G-3038)*

CHEMICALS: Sodium Hyposulfite & Sodium Hydrosulfite

Tessenderlo Kerley Inc ....E....... 405 665-2544
 Wynnewood *(G-11674)*
Tessenderlo Kerley Inc ....F....... 580 762-1130
 Ponca City *(G-7882)*

CHEMICALS: Sulfur, Incl Rcvrd/Refined, Fm Sour Natural Gas

Reagent Chemical & RES Inc ....G....... 580 233-1024
 Enid *(G-3044)*
Reagent Chemical & RES Inc ....F....... 580 436-4100
 Francis *(G-3191)*

CHEMICALS: Tanning Agents, Synthetic Inorganic

Fake Bake LLC ....E....... 405 843-9660
 Oklahoma City *(G-6070)*

CHEMICALS: Water Treatment

Bici LLC ....F....... 918 625-8811
 Broken Arrow *(G-849)*
Coil Chem LLC ....F....... 405 445-5545
 Washington *(G-11334)*
Interntnal Mktg Resources Corp ....G....... 918 270-1200
 Tulsa *(G-10005)*
Ofs Inc ....F....... 405 424-1101
 Oklahoma City *(G-6714)*
SMC Technologies Inc ....F....... 405 737-3740
 Midwest City *(G-4455)*
Tahlequah Public Works Auth ....F....... 918 456-9251
 Tahlequah *(G-8886)*
Think Healthy Systems ....G....... 918 384-0555
 Tulsa *(G-10928)*
Town of Goldsby ....F....... 405 288-6675
 Goldsby *(G-3247)*

CHICKEN SLAUGHTERING & PROCESSING

Dorada Poultry LLC ....E....... 580 718-4700
 Ponca City *(G-7822)*
Liberty Free Range Poultry LLC ....C....... 319 627-6000
 Jay *(G-3682)*

CHILD DAY CARE SVCS

Creek Nation Foundation Inc ....G....... 918 683-1825
 Muskogee *(G-4665)*

CHLOROPRENE RUBBER: Neoprene

Neoinsulation LLC ....G....... 405 605-6518
 Oklahoma City *(G-6669)*

CHOCOLATE, EXC CANDY FROM BEANS: Chips, Powder, Block, Syrup

Castle Rock Kitchens ....G....... 405 751-1822
 Oklahoma City *(G-5709)*
Chickasaw Nation ....G....... 405 331-2300
 Davis *(G-1980)*
Nut House ....G....... 918 266-1604
 Claremore *(G-1664)*

CHOCOLATE, EXC CANDY FROM PURCH CHOC: Chips, Powder, Block

Godiva Chocolatier Inc ....G....... 918 459-2635
 Tulsa *(G-9837)*

CHUTES: Mail, Sheet Metal

Carlsons Rural Mailbox Co ....G....... 405 632-7338
 Oklahoma City *(G-5704)*

CIGARETTE & CIGAR PRDTS & ACCESS

Up N Smoke III ....G....... 405 609-1702
 Oklahoma City *(G-7373)*

CIRCUIT BOARDS, PRINTED: Television & Radio

Oai Electronics LLC ....D....... 918 836-9077
 Tulsa *(G-10372)*
Steven Jackson ....G....... 918 813-7184
 Tulsa *(G-10850)*

CIRCUITS: Electronic

All Electronic and More Llc ....G....... 918 557-5410
 Collinsville *(G-1799)*
Baron Manufacturing Inc ....G....... 405 947-3362
 Oklahoma City *(G-5528)*
Cherokee Nation Arospc Def LLC ....G....... 918 430-3492
 Pryor *(G-7951)*
Cherokee Nation Arospc Def LLC ....G....... 918 696-3151
 Stilwell *(G-8785)*
Ducommun Labarge Tech Inc ....C....... 918 459-2200
 Tulsa *(G-9611)*
Electranetics Inc ....G....... 918 960-0818
 Tulsa *(G-9652)*
Electronic Assembly Corp ....G....... 918 286-2816
 Tulsa *(G-9653)*
Hem Industries ....G....... 918 534-0579
 Dewey *(G-2024)*
Industrial Electronics Repair ....E....... 918 342-1160
 Claremore *(G-1641)*
Interactive Cad Services Inc ....G....... 918 251-4470
 Broken Arrow *(G-940)*
Paia Electronics Inc ....G....... 405 340-6300
 Edmond *(G-2559)*
Qual-Tron Inc ....E....... 918 622-7052
 Tulsa *(G-10589)*
Surface Mount Depot Inc ....D....... 405 948-8763
 Oklahoma City *(G-7232)*
Westoak Industries Inc ....E....... 580 526-3221
 Erick *(G-3093)*

CLAMPS & COUPLINGS: Hose

Parrish Enterprises Ltd ....C....... 580 237-4033
 Enid *(G-3031)*
Punch-Lok Co ....E....... 580 233-4757
 Enid *(G-3040)*

CLAMPS: Metal

Get A Grip Inc ....G....... 405 286-4778
 Oklahoma City *(G-6148)*
Sawyer Manufacturing Company ....E....... 918 834-2550
 Tulsa *(G-9034)*
Wayne Burt Machine ....G....... 918 786-4415
 Grove *(G-3293)*

CLAY PRDTS: Structural

MO Money Minerals LLC ....G....... 405 262-2457
 Calumet *(G-1247)*

CLEANING & DESCALING SVC: Metal Prdts

Trios of Oklahoma LLC ....G....... 918 760-2734
 Edmond *(G-2653)*

CLEANING EQPT: Blast, Dustless

Blastpro Manufacturing Inc ....G....... 877 495-6464
 Oklahoma City *(G-5589)*
Blastpro Manufacturing Inc ....E....... 405 491-6464
 Oklahoma City *(G-5590)*
Coyote Enterprises Inc ....F....... 918 486-8411
 Coweta *(G-1875)*
Disa Holding Corp ....D....... 405 382-6900
 Seminole *(G-8369)*
N A Blastrac Inc ....D....... 405 478-3440
 Oklahoma City *(G-6645)*

CLEANING EQPT: Commercial

Power Soak Systems Inc ....G....... 800 444-9624
 Pryor *(G-7982)*

CLEANING EQPT: Dirt Sweeping Units, Indl

Jero Manufacturing Inc ....E....... 918 628-0230
 Tulsa *(G-10037)*
Moms Haulin Dads Dozin Inc ....G....... 405 392-5508
 Newcastle *(G-4832)*

CLEANING EQPT: High Pressure

Beavers High Pressure Wshg LLC ....G....... 580 512-3530
 Apache *(G-218)*
Cairns Manufacturing Inc ....G....... 405 947-1350
 Oklahoma City *(G-5670)*
D&R Property Services Inc ....G....... 405 677-2178
 Oklahoma City *(G-5888)*
Mighty Clean Corporation ....G....... 918 299-7970
 Tulsa *(G-10275)*
Owasso Pressurewashing LLC ....G....... 918 557-4059
 Collinsville *(G-1819)*

CLEANING EQPT: High Pressure

Pressure Point LLC..................G...... 918 695-8799
Tulsa *(G-10555)*

CLEANING OR POLISHING PREPARATIONS, NEC

Plane Naked LLC......................G...... 405 317-7661
Yukon *(G-11766)*

CLEANING PRDTS: Ammonia, Household

Versum Materials Us LLC..............E...... 918 379-7101
Catoosa *(G-1363)*

CLEANING PRDTS: Degreasing Solvent

Chemical Products Inds Inc...........G...... 405 745-2070
Oklahoma City *(G-5748)*

CLEANING PRDTS: Deodorants, Nonpersonal

Big D Industries Inc.................E...... 405 682-2541
Oklahoma City *(G-5563)*

CLEANING PRDTS: Drain Pipe Solvents Or Cleaners

Empire Plumbing Contrs LLC...........G...... 918 320-1427
Grove *(G-3267)*

CLEANING PRDTS: Laundry Preparations

Super Saver Dry Cleaning.............G...... 918 296-7168
Tulsa *(G-10876)*
Vvc Dry Cleaning & Laundry...........G...... 580 255-2121
Duncan *(G-2196)*

CLEANING PRDTS: Metal Polish

Km Metal Polishing...................G...... 918 397-2221
Bartlesville *(G-503)*

CLEANING PRDTS: Sanitation Preparations

Carlisle Sanitary Maintenance........G...... 405 475-5600
Oklahoma City *(G-5703)*
City of Tahlequah....................E...... 918 456-8332
Tahlequah *(G-8858)*

CLEANING PRDTS: Sanitation Preps, Disinfectants/Deodorants

Integrity Tech & Svcs LLC............G...... 405 482-9206
Edmond *(G-2462)*
Mother Earth Eco Entps LLC...........G...... 785 250-8706
Ada *(G-68)*
Stink Free Inc.......................G...... 405 273-0006
Shawnee *(G-8504)*

CLEANING PRDTS: Specialty

Johnsonm3 LLC........................G...... 580 353-5550
Lawton *(G-3946)*
Supply Company Inc...................G...... 918 585-2863
Tulsa *(G-10880)*
Todd J Nightengale...................G...... 580 227-2646
Fairview *(G-3154)*

CLEANING PRDTS: Window Cleaning Preparations

Rp Window Washing....................G...... 405 341-0065
Edmond *(G-2606)*

CLEANING SVCS

Fairwind LLC.........................E...... 580 492-5209
Lawton *(G-3925)*

CLEANING SVCS: Industrial Or Commercial

D & P Tank Service Inc...............G...... 580 762-4526
Ponca City *(G-7816)*

CLOCK REPAIR SVCS

Clock Shop Inc.......................G...... 918 583-5835
Tulsa *(G-9455)*

CLOTHING & ACCESS STORES

Applause Apparel.....................G...... 580 762-1349
Ponca City *(G-7797)*

Caveman Screen Printing..............G...... 918 446-6440
Tulsa *(G-9390)*
Prairie Graphics & Sportswear........G...... 405 789-0028
Bethany *(G-592)*

CLOTHING & ACCESS, WOMEN, CHILD & INFANT, WHOL: Blouses

Mobetta..............................G...... 580 588-9222
Apache *(G-220)*

CLOTHING & ACCESS, WOMEN, CHILD & INFANT, WHOLESALE: Sets

Slapsok LLC..........................G...... 405 845-2299
Edmond *(G-2622)*

CLOTHING & ACCESS, WOMEN, CHILDREN & INFANT, WHOL: Uniforms

Graphix Xpress.......................G...... 580 765-7324
Ponca City *(G-7831)*

CLOTHING & ACCESS, WOMEN, CHILDREN/INFANT, WHOL: Baby Goods

Ansa Company Inc.....................F...... 918 687-1664
Muskogee *(G-4648)*

CLOTHING & ACCESS: Handicapped

Little Sahara Sandsports LLC.........G...... 580 824-0569
Waynoka *(G-11378)*

CLOTHING & ACCESS: Men's Miscellaneous Access

Apex Inc.............................E...... 405 247-7377
Anadarko *(G-200)*
Flaming Hope LLC.....................G...... 405 924-4380
Noble *(G-4880)*
Mtm Recognition Corporation..........B...... 405 609-6900
Oklahoma City *(G-6634)*
Sherri Burch.........................G...... 405 720-9021
Oklahoma City *(G-7121)*

CLOTHING & ACCESS: Regalia

Apothem..............................G...... 405 447-2345
Norman *(G-4912)*
Rainbow Spreme Assmbly I O R G.......G...... 918 423-1328
McAlester *(G-4331)*

CLOTHING & APPAREL STORES: Custom

A & B Engraving Inc..................G...... 918 663-7446
Tulsa *(G-9061)*
Campus Ragz..........................G...... 405 329-3300
Norman *(G-4952)*
Custom Screen Printers...............G...... 918 423-3696
McAlester *(G-4290)*
Girlinghouse Unlimited LLC...........G...... 405 265-3330
Mustang *(G-4773)*
Titanium Phoenix Inc.................G...... 405 305-1304
Oklahoma City *(G-7294)*

CLOTHING & FURN, MENS & BOYS, WHOLESALE: Robes, Under/Night

Gorfam Marketing Inc.................F...... 918 388-9935
Tulsa *(G-9842)*

CLOTHING & FURNISHINGS, MEN'S & BOYS', WHOLESALE: Shirts

Apothem..............................G...... 405 447-2345
Norman *(G-4912)*
Mobetta..............................G...... 580 588-9222
Apache *(G-220)*
Slapsok LLC..........................G...... 405 845-2299
Edmond *(G-2622)*

CLOTHING & FURNISHINGS, MEN'S & BOYS', WHOLESALE: Uniforms

Graphix Xpress.......................G...... 580 765-7324
Ponca City *(G-7831)*

CLOTHING & FURNISHINGS, MENS & BOYS, WHOL: Sportswear/Work

Sandy Childress Inc..................G...... 405 748-4949
Edmond *(G-2612)*

CLOTHING STORES: Shirts, Custom Made

Mobetta..............................G...... 580 588-9222
Apache *(G-220)*
Shirts & Stuff.......................G...... 918 445-0323
Tulsa *(G-10749)*
Tigers Den By Dreamcatcher...........G...... 918 478-4873
Fort Gibson *(G-3180)*

CLOTHING STORES: T-Shirts, Printed, Custom

Apothem..............................G...... 405 447-2345
Norman *(G-4912)*
Play 2 Win Athletics.................G...... 918 341-9500
Claremore *(G-1671)*
T-Shirts Unlimited...................G...... 580 286-5223
Idabel *(G-3649)*
Texoma Engraving LLC.................G...... 580 775-7333
Durant *(G-2264)*
Townsend Marketing Inc...............G...... 918 496-9222
Bixby *(G-666)*
U Big TS Designs Inc.................G...... 405 401-4327
Oklahoma City *(G-7356)*
Wear-Tech............................G...... 918 663-2009
Tulsa *(G-11099)*

CLOTHING STORES: Unisex

Cas Monogramming Inc.................G...... 405 350-6556
Yukon *(G-11703)*
Joys Uniforms Boutique Ltd...........G...... 918 747-4114
Tulsa *(G-10061)*

CLOTHING: Access

Applause Apparel.....................G...... 580 762-1349
Ponca City *(G-7797)*
Brims & Accessories..................G...... 580 357-2746
Lawton *(G-3901)*
Mrsdish LLC..........................G...... 405 447-3813
Norman *(G-5083)*
Rainbow Creations....................G...... 405 942-6207
Oklahoma City *(G-6967)*
Renavotio Infratech Inc..............G...... 504 722-7402
Tulsa *(G-10640)*
Witter Marketing Inc.................G...... 918 369-8639
Broken Arrow *(G-1099)*

CLOTHING: Access, Women's & Misses'

Flaming Hope LLC.....................G...... 405 924-4380
Noble *(G-4880)*
Jps Creations........................G...... 580 892-3455
Allen *(G-135)*
Titanium Phoenix Inc.................G...... 405 305-1304
Oklahoma City *(G-7294)*

CLOTHING: Athletic & Sportswear, Men's & Boys'

Anvil Land and Properties Inc........G...... 580 336-4402
Perry *(G-7726)*
Creative Apparel and More Inc........G...... 918 682-1283
Muskogee *(G-4664)*

CLOTHING: Athletic & Sportswear, Women's & Girls'

Jan Farha............................G...... 405 848-1388
Yukon *(G-11735)*
Mule Hunting Clothes Inc.............G...... 601 856-5169
Collinsville *(G-1817)*
Ndn Enterprises LLC..................G...... 703 772-6635
Pawhuska *(G-7690)*
Rustic Rehab.........................G...... 918 314-6647
Grove *(G-3287)*

CLOTHING: Belts

Gilmores Sports Concepts Inc.........G...... 918 250-3910
Tulsa *(G-9827)*

PRODUCT SECTION

CLOTHING: Brassieres
Cupid Foundations Inc ....C 580 363-1935
  Blackwell (G-680)

CLOTHING: Bridal Gowns
Ellis Bridal LLC ....G 501 247-8698
  Tulsa (G-9662)
Fancy Cakes ....G 405 701-3434
  Norman (G-4996)

CLOTHING: Children & Infants'
Closet Consignments LLC ....G 405 387-3100
  Newcastle (G-4823)
Justice ....G 405 842-7180
  Oklahoma City (G-6392)

CLOTHING: Coats & Suits, Men's & Boys'
Mobetta ....G 580 588-9222
  Apache (G-220)

CLOTHING: Coats, Hunting & Vests, Men's
Mule Hunting Clothes Inc ....G 601 856-5169
  Collinsville (G-1817)

CLOTHING: Costumes
Blush Boutique Inc ....G 405 701-8600
  Norman (G-4938)
Easleys Performance Wear Inc ....G 918 357-2400
  Broken Arrow (G-1125)
Mascots Etc Inc ....G 405 722-3406
  Oklahoma City (G-6535)

CLOTHING: Dresses
Glitter Gear LLC ....F 405 321-4327
  Oklahoma City (G-6159)
Mobetta ....G 580 588-9222
  Apache (G-220)

CLOTHING: Gowns & Dresses, Wedding
Bricktown Real Estate & Develo ....G 405 236-4143
  Oklahoma City (G-5627)
Captive Imaging LLC ....G 918 340-3053
  Tulsa (G-9372)
Esb Sales Inc ....G 918 227-0378
  Sapulpa (G-8270)
Pixel Park LLC ....G 405 613-0924
  Mustang (G-4789)
Sandy Childress Inc ....G 405 748-4949
  Edmond (G-2612)

CLOTHING: Hats & Caps, NEC
M T H Inc ....G 918 445-9235
  Tulsa (G-10189)
Shortys Hattery ....G 405 232-4287
  Oklahoma City (G-7125)

CLOTHING: Hats & Caps, Uniform
Cool Hard Hat Inc ....G 918 812-7636
  Tulsa (G-9481)

CLOTHING: Hats & Headwear, Knit
Kelly Loyd ....G 405 740-2345
  Ada (G-55)

CLOTHING: Hosiery, Anklets
Advanced Foot & Ankle ....G 405 692-7114
  Oklahoma City (G-5382)

CLOTHING: Hospital, Men's
Barbara J McGinnis ....G 580 226-7675
  Ardmore (G-253)

CLOTHING: Knit Underwear & Nightwear
Hyatt Ladona ....G 580 889-0199
  Atoka (G-414)

CLOTHING: Leather & sheep-lined clothing
Ganoa Imports ....G 918 622-3788
  Tulsa (G-9798)
Leather Store ....G 918 245-8676
  Sand Springs (G-8199)

CLOTHING: Maternity
Bellylove Maternity Gifts ....G 405 818-3339
  Oklahoma City (G-5548)

CLOTHING: Outerwear, Women's & Misses' NEC
Ajs Tees Inc ....G 918 455-6751
  Broken Arrow (G-821)
Charles Komar & Sons Inc ....B 918 423-3535
  McAlester (G-4280)
First Class Outlet ....G 918 808-3405
  McAlester (G-4299)
St John ....G 405 364-1917
  Norman (G-5155)
Team Spirit Sales ....G 918 296-5620
  Jenks (G-3734)

CLOTHING: Overalls & Coveralls
Round House Manufacturing LLC ....D 405 273-0510
  Shawnee (G-8490)

CLOTHING: Robes & Dressing Gowns
Charles Komar & Sons Inc ....B 918 423-3535
  McAlester (G-4280)

CLOTHING: Shirts
Apex405 ....G 405 313-5145
  Norman (G-4911)
Emery Bay Corporation ....G 918 494-2988
  Tulsa (G-9671)
Finish Line of Oklahoma Inc ....G 918 341-8291
  Claremore (G-1621)
Mobetta ....G 580 588-9222
  Apache (G-220)

CLOTHING: Shirts & T-Shirts, Knit
House of Bedlam LLC ....G 405 946-3100
  Oklahoma City (G-6266)
Uniquely Yours LLC ....G 918 283-2228
  Claremore (G-1696)

CLOTHING: Shirts, Dress, Men's & Boys'
Slapsok LLC ....G 405 845-2299
  Edmond (G-2622)

CLOTHING: Shirts, Uniform, From Purchased Materials
Synergy Maintenance LLC ....G 580 574-7355
  Lawton (G-4009)

CLOTHING: Sleeping Garments, Men's & Boys'
Synergy Maintenance LLC ....G 580 574-7355
  Lawton (G-4009)

CLOTHING: Sleeping Garments, Women's & Children's
Charles Komar & Sons Inc ....G 918 423-1227
  Mcalester (G-4281)

CLOTHING: Socks
Crazy Socks Productions Inc ....G 580 618-1228
  Sulphur (G-8830)
Sock Monkey Bizz LLC ....G 918 462-7392
  Wagoner (G-11290)
Sydnis Shag Socks ....G 405 664-5333
  Wellston (G-11479)
Two Socks LLC ....G 405 535-4753
  Norman (G-5184)

CLOTHING: T-Shirts & Tops, Knit
Calamity Janes Funk & Junk Inc ....G 405 759-3383
  Oklahoma City (G-5671)
Gorfam Marketing Inc ....F 918 388-9935
  Tulsa (G-9842)

CLOTHING: T-Shirts & Tops, Women's & Girls'
Relevant Products LLC ....E 405 524-5250
  Oklahoma City (G-7005)

COAL MINING SERVICES

U Big TS Designs Inc ....G 405 401-4327
  Oklahoma City (G-7356)

CLOTHING: Tailored Suits & Formal Jackets
Douglas Rose Custom Tailoring ....G 918 366-6002
  Bixby (G-620)

CLOTHING: Ties, Bow, Men's & Boys', From Purchased Materials
Two Guys Bowtie Company LLC ....G 405 612-0116
  Tulsa (G-11026)

CLOTHING: Tuxedos, From Purchased Materials
Sage Brush Junction ....G 580 227-3434
  Fairview (G-3150)

CLOTHING: Underwear, Women's & Children's
Southwest Corset Corporation ....C 580 363-1935
  Blackwell (G-693)

CLOTHING: Uniforms, Firemen's, From Purchased Materials
Globe Mfg Company-OK LLC ....E 580 272-9400
  Ada (G-43)

CLOTHING: Uniforms, Men's & Boys'
Synergy Maintenance LLC ....G 580 574-7355
  Lawton (G-4009)

CLOTHING: Uniforms, Work
Synergy Maintenance LLC ....G 580 574-7355
  Lawton (G-4009)

CLOTHING: Waterproof Outerwear
Wohali Outdoors LLC ....F 918 343-3800
  Broken Arrow (G-1100)

CLOTHING: Work Apparel, Exc Uniforms
Beane Development Corp ....G 580 222-1150
  Ardmore (G-255)
Corporate Image Inc ....G 918 516-8376
  Owasso (G-7556)

CLUTCHES, EXC VEHICULAR
Mecco Edgemont Clutch Co Inc ....G 918 583-3060
  Tulsa (G-10236)
Value Components Corp ....G 918 749-1689
  Tulsa (G-11066)

COAL & OTHER MINERALS & ORES WHOLESALERS
Sariel Inc ....G 918 855-1400
  Tulsa (G-10709)

COAL GASIFICATION
Seth W Herndon Jr ....G 918 744-4072
  Tulsa (G-10735)

COAL MINING EXPLORATION & TEST BORING SVC
Oklahoma Department of Mines ....G 918 485-3999
  Tulsa (G-10396)

COAL MINING EXPLORATION SVCS: Anthracite
James D Pate Jr ....G 405 942-3647
  Oklahoma City (G-6347)

COAL MINING SERVICES
Alliance Resource Partners LP ....C 918 295-7600
  Tulsa (G-9147)
Coal Creek Minerals LLC ....E 918 962-5335
  Spiro (G-8614)
Evans Coal Company ....G 405 202-3239
  Oklahoma City (G-6055)

COAL MINING SERVICES

Warrant Divisions Inc .... G 918 962-4800
Spiro *(G-8620)*
Webster County Coal LLC .... B 918 295-7600
Tulsa *(G-11102)*

COAL MINING SVCS: Bituminous, Contract Basis

South Central Coal Company Inc .... G 918 962-2544
Spiro *(G-8617)*

COAL MINING: Anthracite

Walter Baker .... G 580 233-7820
Enid *(G-3073)*

COAL MINING: Bituminous & Lignite Surface

Alliance Coal LLC .... D 918 295-7600
Tulsa *(G-9142)*
Alliance Resource Holdings Inc .... G 918 295-7600
Tulsa *(G-9146)*
Joshua Coal Company .... G 918 652-3023
Henryetta *(G-3511)*
Mt Vernon Coal Transfer Co .... F 918 295-7600
Tulsa *(G-10311)*
Permac Inc .... G 918 295-7600
Tulsa *(G-10496)*

COAL MINING: Bituminous Coal & Lignite-Surface Mining

Alliance Holdings Gp LP .... C 918 295-1415
Tulsa *(G-9143)*
Alliance Resource Finance Corp .... G 918 295-1415
Tulsa *(G-9145)*
Alliance Rsrce Oper Prtners LP .... G 918 295-7600
Tulsa *(G-9148)*
Alliance Wor Properties LLC .... E 918 295-7600
Tulsa *(G-9149)*
Arp Sebree South LLC .... E 918 295-1415
Tulsa *(G-9210)*
Excel Mining LLC .... G 918 295-7600
Tulsa *(G-9713)*
Georges Colliers Inc .... E 918 962-2202
Spiro *(G-8615)*
Phoenix Mining Company .... D 918 256-7873
Vinita *(G-11267)*
Southeastern Drilling .... G 918 469-3489
Quinton *(G-8042)*
Steamport LLC .... G 918 295-7600
Tulsa *(G-10841)*

COAL MINING: Bituminous Underground

Alliance Coal LLC .... D 918 295-7600
Tulsa *(G-9142)*
Alliance Holdings Gp LP .... C 918 295-1415
Tulsa *(G-9143)*
Alliance Resource Holdings Inc .... G 918 295-7600
Tulsa *(G-9146)*
Alliance Resource Partners LP .... C 918 295-7600
Tulsa *(G-9147)*
Backbone Mountain LLC .... C 918 295-7600
Tulsa *(G-9252)*

COAL MINING: Underground, Semibituminous

Dig It Rocks LLC .... G 580 362-6211
Ponca City *(G-7820)*

COAL PREPARATION PLANT: Bituminous or Lignite

Alliance Resource Partners LP .... C 918 295-7600
Tulsa *(G-9147)*
Cr Services LLC .... E 918 295-7600
Tulsa *(G-9496)*
Hopkins County Coal LLC .... D 918 295-7600
Tulsa *(G-9947)*
White County Coal LLC .... G 918 295-7600
Tulsa *(G-11120)*

COATING SVC

Be Custom Coatings .... G 405 205-9347
Harrah *(G-3374)*
Commercial Coatings Okla LLC .... G 405 226-8739
Oklahoma City *(G-5805)*
Copperhead Coatings LLC .... G 580 532-6243
Pond Creek *(G-7889)*
Custom Powder Coating & Dustle .... G 580 382-8000
Ponca City *(G-7815)*
Guthrie Industrial Coating .... G 405 377-6649
Stillwater *(G-8696)*
House of Trophies .... G 918 341-2111
Claremore *(G-1637)*
Industrial Coatings Oklahoma .... G 918 638-5606
Claremore *(G-1640)*
Modern Coatings LLC .... G 405 795-2633
Oklahoma City *(G-5307)*
Mtw Powder Coating .... G 918 638-4795
Coweta *(G-1892)*
Nafcoat Inc. .... G 918 367-9606
Bristow *(G-789)*
Quality Steel Coatings Inc .... G 918 269-9104
Broken Arrow *(G-1151)*
Southside Powder Coating .... G 405 623-8557
Noble *(G-4892)*
Sprayfoam Banks & Coatings .... G 580 490-6308
Overbrook *(G-7539)*

COATING SVC: Aluminum, Metal Prdts

Performance Coatings Inc .... G 405 525-9790
Oklahoma City *(G-6829)*

COATING SVC: Hot Dip, Metals Or Formed Prdts

Premier Metal Finishing Inc .... G 405 947-0200
Oklahoma City *(G-6885)*

COATING SVC: Metals & Formed Prdts

Abitl Finishing Inc .... E 918 446-5363
Tulsa *(G-8985)*
Broken Arrow Powdr Coating Inc .... E 918 251-2192
Broken Arrow *(G-856)*
Broken Arrow Powdr Coating Inc .... E 918 258-1017
Broken Arrow *(G-857)*
Casting Coating Corp .... F 918 445-4141
Tulsa *(G-8995)*
Chemproof Polymers Inc .... G 918 584-0364
Tulsa *(G-9410)*
Coat Pro LLC .... G 405 672-0705
Oklahoma City *(G-5798)*
Coating Solution .... G 580 276-5432
Leon *(G-4033)*
Custom Catings of Broken Arrow .... G 918 258-0996
Coweta *(G-1876)*
Eagle Rock Coatings Inc .... G 405 948-8900
Oklahoma City *(G-5996)*
Finish Line Powder Coating .... G 918 938-6292
Tulsa *(G-9744)*
GE Oil & Gas Esp Inc .... G 405 527-1566
Purcell *(G-8009)*
Gerdau Ameristeel US Inc .... F 918 682-2600
Muskogee *(G-4679)*
H & H Protective Coating Co .... G 918 582-9187
Tulsa *(G-9871)*
J&J Powder Coating & Fabr .... G 918 836-9700
Tulsa *(G-10024)*
Mid-America Indus Coatings LLC .... G 580 239-9003
Atoka *(G-419)*
Milamar Coatings LLC .... F 405 755-8448
Oklahoma City *(G-6608)*
National Coating .... G 405 251-5065
Wynnewood *(G-11671)*
Oerlikon Blzers Cating USA Inc .... G 405 745-1026
Oklahoma City *(G-6713)*
Oklahoma Coating Specialists .... G 405 447-0448
Norman *(G-5099)*
Oklahoma Cstm Cating Ltd Lblty .... E 405 382-0231
Seminole *(G-8391)*
Powder Coatings Incorporated .... G 918 627-6225
Tulsa *(G-10537)*
Powder Coatings Plus LLC .... F 405 232-5707
Oklahoma City *(G-6868)*
Precision Coatings LLC .... G 918 622-1876
Tulsa *(G-10543)*
Precision Metal Forming LLC .... E 405 677-3777
Oklahoma City *(G-6882)*
Spray-Rite Inc. .... E 479 648-3351
Pocola *(G-7786)*
Thompsons Metal Coating .... G 918 272-5711
Owasso *(G-7624)*
Tulsa Powder Coating Inc .... G 918 832-1741
Tulsa *(G-11004)*

COATING SVC: Metals, With Plastic Or Resins

Pixley Coating Inc .... G 580 444-2140
Velma *(G-11236)*

COATING SVC: Rust Preventative

Energy and Envmtl Svcs Inc .... G 405 843-8996
Edmond *(G-2413)*
Sun Heat Treating Inc .... G 918 227-2188
Tulsa *(G-9039)*

COATINGS: Air Curing

American Industrial Inc .... G 918 445-0627
Tulsa *(G-9167)*
National Coating Mfg Inc .... F 580 332-8751
Ada *(G-70)*
Powder Blue .... F 918 835-2629
Tulsa *(G-10536)*

COATINGS: Epoxy

CTI Services LLC .... G 918 584-2220
Tulsa *(G-9519)*
Gra Services International LP .... G 405 672-8885
Oklahoma City *(G-6174)*

COFFEE SVCS

Executive Coffee Service Co .... D 405 236-3932
Oklahoma City *(G-6059)*

COILS & TRANSFORMERS

A-Line Tds Inc .... E 580 628-5371
Tonkawa *(G-8970)*

COILS: Electric Motors Or Generators

Industrial Coil Inc .... F 405 745-2030
Oklahoma City *(G-6297)*

COILS: Pipe

Integrity Piping Services Co .... G 918 850-0206
Sand Springs *(G-8193)*
Kloeckner Metals Corporation .... E 918 660-2050
Catoosa *(G-1329)*
Superior Dynmics Fbrcation LLC .... G 918 698-9846
Bartlesville *(G-531)*
Tulsa Tube Bending Co Inc .... E 888 882-3637
Tulsa *(G-11011)*

COIN-OPERATED MACHINES & MECHANISMS, WHOLESALE

Billiards of Tulsa Inc .... E 918 835-1166
Tulsa *(G-9296)*

COINS & TOKENS: Non-Currency

Edmond Coins Inc .... G 405 607-6800
Edmond *(G-2401)*

COLOR SEPARATION: Photographic & Movie Film

C M Y K Colour Corp .... G 405 270-0060
Oklahoma City *(G-5661)*
Graphics Universal Inc .... G 918 461-0609
Tulsa *(G-9847)*

COLORS: Pigments, Inorganic

Performance Coatings Inc .... G 405 525-9790
Oklahoma City *(G-6829)*

COMBINATION UTILITIES, NEC

Fairwind LLC .... E 580 492-5209
Lawton *(G-3925)*

COMMERCIAL ART & GRAPHIC DESIGN SVCS

American Logo and Sign Inc .... G 405 799-1800
Moore *(G-4488)*
American Logo and Sign Inc .... F 405 799-1800
Oklahoma City *(G-5438)*
Apple Art .... G 405 691-4393
Moore *(G-4491)*

PRODUCT SECTION

COMPRESSORS: Air & Gas

Chastain Enterprises LLC .... G 918 615-9355
  Tulsa *(G-9407)*
Copper Cup Images .... G 918 337-2781
  Bartlesville *(G-469)*
Digi Print LLC .... G 405 947-0099
  Oklahoma City *(G-5945)*
Flash Flood Print Studios LLC .... G 918 794-3527
  Tulsa *(G-9754)*
Kaiser Sign & Graphics Co Inc .... G 580 772-3880
  Weatherford *(G-11423)*
King Graphics Inc .... G 405 232-2369
  Oklahoma City *(G-6420)*
L C D Embroidery .... G 405 379-6083
  Holdenville *(G-3555)*
Quik-Print of Oklahoma City .... G 405 943-3222
  Oklahoma City *(G-6949)*

COMMERCIAL COOKING EQPT WHOLESALERS

Hasty-Bake Inc .... F 918 665-8220
  Tulsa *(G-9901)*

COMMERCIAL EQPT WHOLESALERS, NEC

C&A International LLC .... E 918 872-1645
  Tulsa *(G-9362)*

COMMERCIAL EQPT, WHOLESALE: Bakery Eqpt & Splys

Midwest Bakers Supply Co Inc .... G 405 942-3489
  Oklahoma City *(G-6599)*

COMMERCIAL EQPT, WHOLESALE: Coffee Brewing Eqpt & Splys

Continental-Brokers & Cons Inc .... E 405 232-1534
  Oklahoma City *(G-5824)*

COMMERCIAL EQPT, WHOLESALE: Comm Cooking & Food Svc Eqpt

McLane Foodservice Dist Inc .... C 405 632-0118
  Oklahoma City *(G-6549)*

COMMERCIAL EQPT, WHOLESALE: Display Eqpt, Exc Refrigerated

C M Y K Colour Corp .... G 405 270-0060
  Oklahoma City *(G-5661)*

COMMERCIAL EQPT, WHOLESALE: Restaurant, NEC

Breshears Enterprises Inc .... F 405 236-4523
  Oklahoma City *(G-5624)*

COMMERCIAL EQPT, WHOLESALE: Scales, Exc Laboratory

Unibridge Scale Systems .... G 580 254-3131
  Woodward *(G-11646)*

COMMERCIAL PRINTING & NEWSPAPER PUBLISHING COMBINED

Beacon Publishing Co Inc .... G 405 232-4151
  Oklahoma City *(G-5540)*
Berkshire Hathaway Inc .... G 918 272-1155
  Owasso *(G-7548)*
Clinton Daily News Company .... F 580 323-5151
  Clinton *(G-1745)*
Cnhi LLC .... E 918 224-5185
  Sapulpa *(G-8260)*
CSC Inc .... G 580 994-6110
  Mooreland *(G-4587)*
Demco Printing Inc .... F 405 273-8888
  Shawnee *(G-8444)*
Elk Citian .... G 580 799-0925
  Elk City *(G-2807)*
Elk City Daily News Inc .... F 580 225-3000
  Elk City *(G-2808)*
Gatehuse Mdia Okla Hldings Inc 585 598-0030
  Ardmore *(G-296)*
Marshall County Publishing Co .... F 580 795-3355
  Madill *(G-4155)*
Mc Clain County Publishing Co .... E 405 527-2126
  Purcell *(G-8016)*
Mesa Black Publishing LLC .... G 580 544-2222
  Boise City *(G-747)*
Newspaper Holding Inc .... E 580 256-2200
  Woodward *(G-11614)*
Newspaper Holding Inc .... D 405 372-5000
  Stillwater *(G-8728)*
Newspaper Holding Inc .... D 405 321-1800
  Norman *(G-5091)*
Nichols Hills Publishing Co .... F 405 755-3311
  Oklahoma City *(G-6678)*
Oklahoma City Herald .... G 405 842-7827
  Oklahoma City *(G-6741)*
Perry Broadcasting Company .... F 405 427-5877
  Oklahoma City *(G-6834)*
Premier Printing .... G 405 632-1132
  Oklahoma City *(G-6886)*
Tribune Corp .... E 405 262-5180
  El Reno *(G-2764)*
Valliant Leader Inc .... G 580 933-4570
  Valliant *(G-11233)*
Weatherford News Inc .... E 580 772-3301
  Weatherford *(G-11458)*

COMMERCIAL SECTOR REG, LICENSING/INSP, GOVT: Prof Occupation

RMH Survey LLC .... G 918 927-8868
  Vinita *(G-11270)*

COMMODITY INVESTORS

C & J Minerals LLC .... G 580 504-4048
  Ardmore *(G-262)*

COMMON SAND MINING

Watkins Sand Co .... E 918 369-5238
  Bixby *(G-671)*

COMMUNICATIONS EQPT & SYSTEMS, NEC

Midstate Traffic Control Inc .... G 405 799-0313
  Moore *(G-4541)*
Railroad Sgnling Solutions Inc .... G 918 973-1888
  Broken Arrow *(G-1020)*
Rapid Wireless LLC .... G 918 605-9717
  Tulsa *(G-10620)*

COMMUNICATIONS EQPT WHOLESALERS

Redline Instruments Inc .... F 580 622-4745
  Sulphur *(G-8841)*

COMMUNICATIONS SVCS: Cellular

New X Drive Tech Inc .... G 918 850-4463
  Tulsa *(G-10337)*

COMMUNICATIONS SVCS: Data

Gorilla Systems Inc .... G 918 227-0230
  Sapulpa *(G-8275)*

COMMUNICATIONS SVCS: Internet Connectivity Svcs

Veritris Group Inc .... G 580 713-4927
  Oklahoma City *(G-7399)*

COMMUNICATIONS SVCS: Internet Host Svcs

Fronttoback Studio LLC .... G 405 788-4400
  Oklahoma City *(G-6124)*

COMMUNICATIONS SVCS: Phone Cable, Svcs, Land Or Submarine

Lynxsystems LLC .... G 918 728-6000
  Tulsa *(G-10185)*
T John Co Inc .... G 405 761-3460
  Tuttle *(G-11214)*

COMMUNICATIONS SVCS: Telegraph

Stuart Beverly & .... G 580 286-5586
  Idabel *(G-3648)*

COMMUNICATIONS SVCS: Telephone Or Video

Trans-Tel Central Inc .... C 405 447-5025
  Norman *(G-5180)*
Unami LLC .... G 405 320-5696
  Anadarko *(G-208)*

COMMUNICATIONS SVCS: Telephone, Local & Long Distance

Tribalcom Wrless Solutions LLC .... G 405 274-7245
  Oklahoma City *(G-7328)*

COMPACT LASER DISCS: Prerecorded

Mobile Laser Forces .... G 405 259-9300
  Oklahoma City *(G-6621)*
On Beat Goes .... G 918 342-5654
  Claremore *(G-1667)*

COMPOSITION STONE: Plastic

Quarry .... G 918 534-2120
  Dewey *(G-2030)*

COMPOST

Bloomin Crazy Ldscp Flral Dsig .... G 405 238-3416
  Pauls Valley *(G-7652)*
Cowboy Compost .... G 405 853-0462
  Hennessey *(G-3453)*
Traci Rae Woolman .... G 580 544-2521
  Boise City *(G-749)*
Urban Worm Compost LLC .... G 918 557-9255
  Broken Arrow *(G-1089)*

COMPRESSORS: Air & Gas

A G Equipment Company .... A 918 250-7386
  Broken Arrow *(G-809)*
Advance Eqp & Contrls LLC .... G 918 496-2606
  Tulsa *(G-9106)*
Air Systems Pump Solutions LLC .... G 405 512-5100
  Tulsa *(G-9122)*
Airsorce LLC .... G 918 519-7520
  Tulsa *(G-9131)*
Arrow Engine Company .... D 918 583-5711
  Tulsa *(G-9211)*
Auto Crane Company .... C 918 438-2760
  Tulsa *(G-9226)*
Berkshire Corporation .... G 405 677-3391
  Oklahoma City *(G-5556)*
Binder Leasing LLC .... G 918 623-0526
  Okemah *(G-5265)*
Blm Equipment & Mfg Co Inc .... F 918 266-5282
  Catoosa *(G-1304)*
Built Right Compressor .... G 580 371-2007
  Tishomingo *(G-8963)*
C O Hanover Bka .... F 918 251-8571
  Broken Arrow *(G-1115)*
Compressco Inc .... G 405 787-2808
  Oklahoma City *(G-5815)*
Cook Compression .... F 405 677-3153
  Oklahoma City *(G-5826)*
Cook Compression .... G 918 254-0660
  Tulsa *(G-9480)*
Csi Compressco Sub Inc .... G 918 250-9471
  Tulsa *(G-9518)*
Dresser-Rand Company .... E 918 835-8437
  Tulsa *(G-9605)*
Dresser-Rand Group Inc .... G 918 695-2368
  Tulsa *(G-9606)*
Dresser-Rand LLC .... F 918 254-4099
  Tulsa *(G-9607)*
Equipment Company .... G 918 273-0240
  Nowata *(G-5214)*
Gardner Denver Inc .... D 918 664-1151
  Tulsa *(G-9800)*
Genreal Compressor Inc .... G 918 209-5499
  Jenks *(G-3706)*
Green Country Comprsr Svc LLC .... G 918 906-6343
  Claremore *(G-1628)*
Industrial Dist Resources LLC .... G 239 591-3777
  Tulsa *(G-9979)*
Midcon Compression LLC .... G 405 542-6280
  Hinton *(G-3533)*
Miratech Corporation .... G 918 622-7077
  Tulsa *(G-10286)*
Miratech Group LLC .... E 918 622-7077
  Tulsa *(G-10287)*
Natural Gas Services Group Inc .... C 918 266-3330
  Catoosa *(G-1342)*
Negative One-Eighty .... G 918 852-2332
  Claremore *(G-1659)*
Negative One-Eighty Cryogenic .... G 918 261-7748
  Claremore *(G-1660)*
Plateau Energy Services LLC .... F 580 625-3618
  Beaver *(G-544)*

Employee Codes: A=Over 500 employees, B=251-500
C=101-250, D=51-100, E=20-50, F=10-19, G=1-9

COMPRESSORS: Air & Gas

Practical Sales and Svc Inc .... G 918 446-5515
 Tulsa (G-10540)
Pressure Solutions LLC .... G 405 370-1830
 Tuttle (G-11208)
Screw Compression Systems Inc .... C 918 266-3330
 Catoosa (G-1351)
Spray Magnifique LLC .... G 918 613-6284
 Broken Arrow (G-1057)

COMPRESSORS: Air & Gas, Including Vacuum Pumps

Flogistix LP .... D 405 536-0000
 Oklahoma City (G-6092)
Spangler Farm .... G 405 466-2536
 Coyle (G-1904)
Thomas Energy Systems Inc .... E 918 665-0031
 Tulsa (G-10930)

COMPRESSORS: Refrigeration & Air Conditioning Eqpt

Dallas Hermetic Company Inc .... F 214 634-1744
 Oklahoma City (G-5892)
Opportunity Center Inc .... C 580 765-6782
 Ponca City (G-7863)

COMPRESSORS: Repairing

Built Right Compressor .... G 580 371-2007
 Tishomingo (G-8963)
Caprock Country Entps Inc .... F 580 924-1647
 Calera (G-1239)

COMPRESSORS: Wholesalers

Archrock Inc .... F 580 225-2091
 Elk City (G-2784)
Compass Manufacturing LLC .... G 405 735-3518
 Oklahoma City (G-5809)

COMPUTER & COMPUTER SOFTWARE STORES

Gorilla Systems Inc .... G 918 227-0230
 Sapulpa (G-8275)
Innovative Technology Ltd .... F 580 243-1559
 Elk City (G-2827)
Nancy Nelson & Associates .... G 580 765-0115
 Ponca City (G-7857)
Norman Computers .... F 405 292-9501
 Norman (G-5094)

COMPUTER & COMPUTER SOFTWARE STORES: Printers & Plotters

Advanced Graphics Technology .... G 405 632-8600
 Oklahoma City (G-5383)
Graphic Rsources Reproductions ..... F 918 461-0303
 Broken Arrow (G-921)

COMPUTER & COMPUTER SOFTWARE STORES: Software & Access

International Sftwr Cons Inc .... G 580 924-1231
 Durant (G-2239)

COMPUTER & COMPUTER SOFTWARE STORES: Software, Bus/Non-Game

Boolean Inc .... G 405 341-1499
 Edmond (G-2330)

COMPUTER & OFFICE MACHINE MAINTENANCE & REPAIR

International Sftwr Cons Inc .... G 580 924-1231
 Durant (G-2239)
Nancy Nelson & Associates .... G 580 765-0115
 Ponca City (G-7857)
Norman Computers .... F 405 292-9501
 Norman (G-5094)
Treble Services LLC .... G 405 401-1217
 Oklahoma City (G-7321)
Tulsa Toner Technology .... G 918 838-0323
 Tulsa (G-11009)

COMPUTER & SFTWR STORE: Modem, Monitor, Terminal/Disk Drive

Cedar Rdge Rcording Studio LLC ..... G 405 651-5961
 Harrah (G-3375)
Computer Solutions + LLC .... G 405 259-9603
 Choctaw (G-1534)

COMPUTER FACILITIES MANAGEMENT SVCS

Kihomac Inc .... D 937 429-7744
 Midwest City (G-4445)
Smeac Group International LLC .... G 580 574-4092
 Lawton (G-3999)

COMPUTER FORMS

262 LLC .... F 918 458-5511
 Tahlequah (G-8848)

COMPUTER GRAPHICS SVCS

Dancey-Meador Publishing Co .... G 580 762-9359
 Ponca City (G-7819)
Pivot Point Publishing .... G 918 347-5415
 Sapulpa (G-8298)
Way-Wear LLC .... G 405 410-8367
 Kingfisher (G-3820)

COMPUTER INTERFACE EQPT: Indl Process

Electronic Assembly Corp .... G 918 286-2816
 Tulsa (G-9653)
Port 40 Inc .... G 405 360-9100
 Norman (G-5117)

COMPUTER PERIPHERAL EQPT, NEC

American Laser Inc .... G 918 234-9700
 Tulsa (G-9168)
Aventura Technologies Inc .... F 631 300-4000
 Oklahoma City (G-5495)
Black Box Network Services .... G 800 949-4039
 Tulsa (G-9301)
Cisco Systems Inc .... A 999 505-5901
 Tulsa (G-9431)
Hitachi Computer Pdts Amer Inc ...... B 405 360-5500
 Norman (G-5024)
Marvel Photo Inc .... G 918 836-0741
 Tulsa (G-10218)
Onyx Imaging Corporation .... G 918 627-6611
 Tulsa (G-10431)
Order-Matic Electronics Corp .... C 405 672-1487
 Oklahoma City (G-6781)
Phx & Co LLC .... G 918 747-9770
 Tulsa (G-10511)
Poquita Circle LLC .... G 918 794-0750
 Tulsa (G-10533)
Scan To .... G 405 413-8015
 Yukon (G-11776)
Secureagent Software Inc .... E 918 971-1600
 Tulsa (G-10722)
Special Service Systems Inc .... E 918 582-7777
 Tulsa (G-10816)
Spor Enterprises Inc .... G 405 745-9888
 Oklahoma City (G-7187)
Tulsa Toner Technology .... G 918 838-0323
 Tulsa (G-11009)

COMPUTER PERIPHERAL EQPT, WHOLESALE

DCA Inc .... E 918 225-0346
 Cushing (G-1929)

COMPUTER PERIPHERAL EQPT: Encoders

Radiotronix Inc .... E 405 794-7730
 Edmond (G-2584)

COMPUTER PROGRAMMING SVCS

Harry A Lippert Jr .... G 512 705-1248
 Lawton (G-3939)
Kihomac Inc .... D 937 429-7744
 Midwest City (G-4445)
New Vision Consulting Group .... F 405 796-7400
 Edmond (G-2537)
Oklahoma EMB Sup & Design .... G 405 359-2741
 Edmond (G-2549)
Paycom Software Inc .... D 405 722-6900
 Oklahoma City (G-6813)
Port 40 Inc .... G 405 360-9100
 Norman (G-5117)
Rapid Jack Solutions Inc .... G 405 203-3131
 Norman (G-5129)
Secureagent Software Inc .... E 918 971-1600
 Tulsa (G-10722)
Sequoyah Technologies LLC .... F 918 808-7270
 Sapulpa (G-8310)
Shane Lee Duvall .... G 918 960-0506
 Broken Arrow (G-1163)
Stonebridge Acquisition Inc .... D 918 663-8000
 Tulsa (G-10853)
Tourkick LLC .... G 918 409-2543
 Owasso (G-7626)

COMPUTER PROGRAMMING SVCS: Custom

New X Drive Tech Inc .... G 918 850-4463
 Tulsa (G-10337)

COMPUTER RELATED MAINTENANCE SVCS

Elvis S Seshie .... G 405 887-3050
 Mustang (G-4770)
Solutions Lucid Group LLC .... G 405 476-4332
 Oklahoma City (G-7158)
Unami LLC .... G 405 320-5696
 Anadarko (G-208)

COMPUTER SOFTWARE DEVELOPMENT

Hughes Gas Measurement Inc .... G 405 227-0904
 Wetumka (G-11494)
Joshi Technologies Intl Inc .... F 918 665-6419
 Tulsa (G-10059)
Jumping Bone LLC .... G 918 853-2836
 Tulsa (G-10065)
Medunison LLC .... E 405 271-9900
 Oklahoma City (G-6560)
Oil & Gas Consultants Intl Inc .... G 918 828-2500
 Tulsa (G-10381)
Phoenix Software Intl Inc .... G 918 491-6144
 Tulsa (G-10510)

COMPUTER SOFTWARE DEVELOPMENT & APPLICATIONS

Ameriinfovets Inc .... G 408 446-4343
 Pryor (G-7943)
Chrysalis Software Inc .... E 831 761-1307
 Tulsa (G-9423)
Resource Development Co LLC .... E 248 646-2300
 Tulsa (G-10645)
Shipzen Inc .... G 949 357-2127
 Tulsa (G-10748)
Subsite LLC .... C 580 572-3700
 Perry (G-7748)

COMPUTER SOFTWARE SYSTEMS ANALYSIS & DESIGN: Custom

Adjacent Creations LLC .... G 405 819-6507
 Oklahoma City (G-5374)
B Sew Inn LLC .... G 918 687-5762
 Muskogee (G-4652)
DCA Inc .... E 918 225-0346
 Cushing (G-1929)
Masters Technical Advisors Inc .... G 918 949-1641
 Tulsa (G-10221)
Norman Computers .... F 405 292-9501
 Norman (G-5094)
Pyfi Technologies .... G 405 816-8685
 Oklahoma City (G-6929)
Srifusion LLC .... G 774 238-7466
 Lawton (G-4003)
Trackum Inc .... G 405 799-4863
 Norman (G-5179)

COMPUTER SOFTWARE WRITERS

Info-Sharp LLC .... G 520 204-5093
 Norman (G-5033)
Lightbe Corporation .... G 918 760-6968
 Tulsa (G-10160)

COMPUTER STORAGE DEVICES, NEC

Barron and Stevenson EMC LLC .... G 918 804-8440
 Tulsa (G-9268)
Business Records Storage LLC .... E 405 232-7867
 Oklahoma City (G-5649)

PRODUCT SECTION

CONCRETE: Ready-Mixed

EMC .... G 918 583-6363
  Tulsa *(G-9666)*
EMC .... G 405 320-5675
  Chickasha *(G-1456)*
EMC Beauty LLC .... G 316 655-8839
  Oklahoma City *(G-6030)*
EMC Law Pllc .... G 832 560-6280
  Tulsa *(G-9667)*
EMC Services LLC .... G 405 596-0050
  Oklahoma City *(G-6031)*
Hitachi Computer Pdts Amer Inc ..... B 405 360-5500
  Norman *(G-5024)*
Quantum Builds Company .... G 727 504-1628
  Oklahoma City *(G-6939)*
Vault Management Inc .... G 918 258-7782
  Broken Arrow *(G-1090)*

COMPUTER SYSTEMS ANALYSIS & DESIGN

New X Drive Tech Inc .... G 918 850-4463
  Tulsa *(G-10337)*

COMPUTER-AIDED DESIGN SYSTEMS SVCS

David Gormley .... G 918 845-0443
  Sapulpa *(G-8265)*

COMPUTERS, NEC

ABB Inc .... C 918 338-4888
  Bartlesville *(G-444)*
Alpha Research & Tech Inc .... G 405 733-1919
  Oklahoma City *(G-5425)*
CIS Investors LLC .... G 405 370-5812
  Oklahoma City *(G-5768)*
Innovative Technology Ltd .... F 580 243-1559
  Elk City *(G-2827)*
New X Drives Inc .... F 918 850-4463
  Tulsa *(G-10338)*
Stephens Scheduling Svcs Inc .... G 918 630-1614
  Tulsa *(G-10847)*
Visuals Tech Solutions LLC .... G 913 526-1775
  Edmond *(G-2674)*

COMPUTERS, NEC, WHOLESALE

Innovative Technology Ltd .... F 580 243-1559
  Elk City *(G-2827)*
Onedoc Managed Print Svcs LLC ... G 405 633-3050
  Oklahoma City *(G-6778)*

COMPUTERS, PERIPHERALS & SOFTWARE, WHOLESALE: Keying Eqpt

Marjo Advertising LLC .... G 918 500-3108
  Sapulpa *(G-8286)*

COMPUTERS, PERIPHERALS & SOFTWARE, WHOLESALE: Printers

Cedar Rdge Rcording Studio LLC ... G 405 651-5961
  Harrah *(G-3375)*
Chaddick & Associates Inc .... F 580 223-1202
  Ardmore *(G-264)*
Computer Solutions + LLC .... G 405 259-9603
  Choctaw *(G-1534)*

COMPUTERS, PERIPHERALS & SOFTWARE, WHOLESALE: Software

American Bank Systems Inc .... E 405 607-7000
  Oklahoma City *(G-5432)*
New Times Technologies Inc .... D 918 872-9600
  Broken Arrow *(G-988)*

COMPUTERS: Mainframe

Mc Connells Systems .... G 918 322-5426
  Glenpool *(G-3238)*

COMPUTERS: Mini

Oracle America Inc .... G 918 587-9016
  Tulsa *(G-10434)*

COMPUTERS: Personal

Apple Street Inc .... G 918 367-9898
  Bristow *(G-764)*
Eves Apple .... G 512 970-9016
  Norman *(G-4995)*
Johnny Apple Seed Store .... G 918 304-2055
  Okmulgee *(G-7510)*

CONCENTRATES, DRINK

Arctic Blends Corporation .... G 918 455-2079
  Broken Arrow *(G-832)*

CONCRETE CURING & HARDENING COMPOUNDS

Chandler Materials Company .... E 918 836-9151
  Tulsa *(G-9403)*

CONCRETE PLANTS

Mid Continent Concrete Co .... G 918 775-6858
  Sallisaw *(G-8149)*

CONCRETE PRDTS

Accurate Fence Construction LLC .. G 580 591-3717
  Lawton *(G-3884)*
Architectural Pav Systems LLC ...... G 918 747-9302
  Tulsa *(G-9204)*
Blackstone Capital Partners SE ...... G 424 355-5050
  El Reno *(G-2702)*
Bmi Management Inc .... G 580 762-5659
  Ponca City *(G-7801)*
Central Burial Vaults Inc .... E 918 224-5701
  Tulsa *(G-8996)*
Construction Supply House Inc ...... G 405 214-9366
  Norman *(G-4964)*
Coppedge Septic Tank .... G 918 371-4549
  Collinsville *(G-1806)*
Coreslab Structures Oklahoma .... F 405 672-2325
  Oklahoma City *(G-5836)*
CRC Evans Weighting Systems ...... G 918 438-2100
  Tulsa *(G-9503)*
Dolese Bros Co .... F 580 225-1247
  Elk City *(G-2803)*
Dolese Bros Co .... E 405 670-9626
  Oklahoma City *(G-5962)*
Dover Products Inc .... G 918 476-5688
  Chouteau *(G-1562)*
Forterra Pipe & Precast LLC .... G 405 677-8811
  Oklahoma City *(G-6104)*
Haskell Lemon Construction Co ..... C 405 947-6069
  Oklahoma City *(G-6223)*
Improved Cnstr Methods Inc .... G 405 235-2609
  Oklahoma City *(G-6294)*
Jim Giles Safe Rooms .... G 918 639-8102
  Sapulpa *(G-8283)*
Keith Lyons .... F 580 584-3360
  Broken Bow *(G-1196)*
Kel-Crete Industries Inc .... G 918 744-0800
  Tulsa *(G-10080)*
McF Services Inc .... G 918 481-1620
  Tulsa *(G-10233)*
Quikrete Companies LLC .... E 918 835-4441
  Tulsa *(G-10598)*
Quikrete Holdings Inc .... G 405 354-8824
  Yukon *(G-11770)*
Rinker Materials Concrete Pipe ...... G 918 745-3404
  Oklahoma City *(G-7028)*
Schwarz Sand .... G 405 789-7914
  Oklahoma City *(G-7093)*
Tricon Unlmited Cnstr Svcs LLC .... G 405 473-9186
  Oklahoma City *(G-7329)*
Triguard of Oklahoma .... G 580 243-8015
  Elk City *(G-2885)*
Twin Cities Ready Mix Inc .... G 918 465-2555
  Wilburton *(G-11527)*
V&H Coatings Co .... G 405 819-4163
  Oklahoma City *(G-7384)*
Wilbert Funeral Services Inc .... E 405 752-9033
  Oklahoma City *(G-7451)*

CONCRETE PRDTS, PRECAST, NEC

Allan Edwards Incorporated .... G 918 583-7184
  Tulsa *(G-9139)*
Arrowhead Precast LLC .... D 918 995-2227
  Broken Arrow *(G-833)*
Carnegie Precast Inc .... F 580 654-1718
  Carnegie *(G-1275)*
Coreslab Structures Tulsa Inc .... E 918 438-0230
  Tulsa *(G-9487)*
Impressions In Stone LLC .... G 918 828-9745
  Tulsa *(G-9974)*
Rn Concrete Products .... G 405 564-3020
  Perry *(G-7743)*
Spencer L Rosson .... G 918 682-4291
  Muskogee *(G-4750)*

Stonecoat of Tulsa LLC .... G 918 551-6868
  Tulsa *(G-10855)*
Tulsa Casting Inc .... G 918 366-1272
  Bixby *(G-667)*

CONCRETE: Dry Mixture

Handi-Sak Inc .... E 405 789-3001
  Oklahoma City *(G-6210)*

CONCRETE: Ready-Mixed

Altus Ready-Mix Inc .... F 580 482-3418
  Altus *(G-142)*
Alva Concrete Inc .... B 580 327-2281
  Alva *(G-173)*
Apac-Central Inc .... G 918 696-2820
  Stilwell *(G-8780)*
Apac-Central Inc .... G 918 921-6491
  Tulsa *(G-9195)*
Apac-Central Inc .... G 918 775-3251
  Sallisaw *(G-8137)*
Atlas Concrete Inc .... G 580 255-7280
  Duncan *(G-2083)*
Atlas Tuck Concrete Inc .... F 580 355-8241
  Lawton *(G-3892)*
Atlas Tuck Concrete Inc .... G 405 224-5005
  Chickasha *(G-1433)*
Atlas Tuck Concrete Inc .... G 405 381-2393
  Tuttle *(G-11185)*
Atlas-Tuck Concrete Inc .... G 580 255-1716
  Duncan *(G-2084)*
B & W Ready Mix LLC .... G 580 623-5059
  Watonga *(G-11340)*
Bartlesville Redi-Mix Inc .... F 580 765-6693
  Bartlesville *(G-453)*
Block Sand Co Inc .... E 405 391-2919
  McLoud *(G-4352)*
Bo-Max Industries Inc .... F 580 256-4555
  Woodward *(G-11562)*
Carnegie Concrete Company .... G 580 654-1208
  Carnegie *(G-1273)*
Caswell Construction Co Inc .... D 580 225-6833
  Elk City *(G-2793)*
Connelly Ready-Mix Con LLC .... D 405 943-8388
  Oklahoma City *(G-5820)*
Crescent Ready Mix Inc .... G 405 853-1599
  Crescent *(G-1910)*
Day Concrete Block Company .... F 580 223-3317
  Ardmore *(G-277)*
Dolese Bros Co .... C 405 235-2311
  Oklahoma City *(G-5957)*
Dolese Bros Co .... F 580 795-3549
  Madill *(G-4146)*
Dolese Bros Co .... G 405 947-7085
  Oklahoma City *(G-5958)*
Dolese Bros Co .... G 580 924-4944
  Durant *(G-2224)*
Dolese Bros Co .... G 580 237-2650
  Enid *(G-2942)*
Dolese Bros Co .... G 405 454-2478
  Harrah *(G-3377)*
Dolese Bros Co .... E 580 639-2237
  Mountain View *(G-4627)*
Dolese Bros Co .... F 918 437-6535
  Tulsa *(G-9591)*
Dolese Bros Co .... F 580 332-0820
  Ada *(G-32)*
Dolese Bros Co .... G 405 382-2060
  Seminole *(G-8370)*
Dolese Bros Co .... G 405 795-9757
  Oklahoma City *(G-5959)*
Dolese Bros Co .... E 580 369-2834
  Davis *(G-1982)*
Dolese Bros Co .... G 580 576-9478
  Roosevelt *(G-8116)*
Dolese Bros Co .... G 580 761-0022
  Ponca City *(G-7821)*
Dolese Bros Co .... G 918 423-1061
  McAlester *(G-4294)*
Dolese Bros Co .... G 580 323-1202
  Clinton *(G-1748)*
Dolese Bros Co .... G 580 889-6033
  Atoka *(G-408)*
Dolese Bros Co .... G 405 247-2564
  Anadarko *(G-202)*
Dolese Bros Co .... G 405 262-0226
  El Reno *(G-2713)*
Dolese Bros Co .... G 918 297-2376
  Hartshorne *(G-3391)*
Dolese Bros Co .... G 405 235-2311
  Weatherford *(G-11404)*

CONCRETE: Ready-Mixed

Dolese Bros Co ....F 405 235-1515
  Chickasha (G-1452)
Dolese Bros Co ....E 405 794-0546
  Moore (G-4518)
Dolese Bros Co ....E 580 832-2720
  Cordell (G-1858)
Dolese Bros Co ....G 405 282-2153
  Guthrie (G-3311)
Dolese Bros Co ....G 405 672-4577
  Oklahoma City (G-5960)
Dolese Bros Co ....G 405 732-0909
  Oklahoma City (G-5961)
Dolese Bros Co ....G 405 670-9626
  Oklahoma City (G-5962)
Dolese Bros Co ....G 405 373-2102
  Piedmont (G-7760)
Dolese Bros Co ....F 405 232-1228
  Oklahoma City (G-5963)
Dolese Bros Co ....G 405 324-2944
  Yukon (G-11720)
Dolese Bros Co ....F 580 223-2243
  Ardmore (G-279)
Dolese Bros Co ....E 405 949-2278
  Oklahoma City (G-5964)
Dolese Bros Co ....F 580 225-1247
  Elk City (G-2803)
Dolese Bros Co ....F 580 255-3046
  Duncan (G-2107)
Eagle Redi-Mix Concrete LLC ....G 918 355-5700
  Tulsa (G-9627)
Enid Concrete Co Inc ....B 580 237-7766
  Enid (G-2950)
Evans & Associates Entps Inc ....F 580 482-3418
  Altus (G-155)
Evans & Associates Entps Inc ....E 580 765-6693
  Ponca City (G-7828)
Evans Asphalt Co Inc ....G 580 765-6693
  Ponca City (G-7829)
Evans Concrete Co Inc ....G 580 765-6693
  Skiatook (G-8543)
Foresee Ready-Mix Concrete Inc ....F 918 689-3951
  Eufaula (G-3101)
Gcc Ready Mix LLC ....G 918 582-8111
  Tulsa (G-9811)
Goddards Ready Mix Con Inc ....F 405 424-4383
  Oklahoma City (G-6165)
Goddards Ready Mix Concrete ....G 405 424-4383
  Oklahoma City (G-6166)
Green Valley Enterprises Inc ....G 580 227-4938
  Fairview (G-3136)
H C Rustin Corporation ....E 580 924-3260
  Durant (G-2235)
H C Rustin Corporation ....G 580 224-2672
  Ardmore (G-299)
Hardesty Company Inc ....E 918 585-3100
  Tulsa (G-9890)
Hennessey Ready Mix Concrete ....G 405 853-4473
  Hennessey (G-3467)
Hodges Materials Inc ....G 580 223-3317
  Ardmore (G-305)
J-A-G Construction Company ....G 580 338-3188
  Guymon (G-3353)
Joe Martin ....G 918 850-2776
  Broken Arrow (G-1136)
Karlin Company ....G 405 542-6991
  Hydro (G-3631)
Keith Lyons ....F 580 584-3360
  Broken Bow (G-1196)
Kerns Construction Inc ....E 405 372-2750
  Stillwater (G-8712)
Kerns Ready Mixed Concrete Inc ....F 405 372-2750
  Stillwater (G-8713)
Kimball Ready Mix Inc ....G 580 922-4444
  Seiling (G-8350)
Kline Materials Inc ....F 580 256-2062
  Woodward (G-11603)
L A Jacobson Inc ....E 405 238-9313
  Pauls Valley (G-7664)
Lafarge North America Inc ....G 405 686-0320
  Oklahoma City (G-6445)
Larry Campbell Ofc ....G 918 682-1209
  Muskogee (G-4705)
Lawton Transit Mix Inc ....E 580 353-6900
  Lawton (G-3961)
M P Ready Mix Inc ....G 405 631-6814
  Oklahoma City (G-6509)
M P Ready Mix Inc ....E 405 354-8824
  Yukon (G-11743)
Metheny Concrete Products Inc ....E 405 947-5566
  Oklahoma City (G-6577)

Metheny Concrete Products Inc ....D 405 947-5566
  Oklahoma City (G-6578)
Mid Continent Concrete Co ....G 918 775-6858
  Sallisaw (G-8149)
Mid Continent Concrete Company ....E 918 647-0550
  Poteau (G-7908)
Mid-Continent Concrete Co Inc ....G 918 758-0200
  Okmulgee (G-7516)
Mid-Continent Concrete Co Inc ....F 918 224-4122
  Sapulpa (G-8290)
Midwest Ready Mix ....G 580 625-4477
  Beaver (G-542)
Mineral Resource Tech Inc ....G 918 683-7671
  Muskogee (G-4714)
Muskogee Ready Mix Inc ....F 918 682-3403
  Muskogee (G-4717)
Neo Concrete & Materials Inc ....E 918 542-4456
  Miami (G-4423)
Nixon Materials Company ....G 580 621-3297
  Freedom (G-3208)
Oklahoma Mobil Concrete Inc ....G 918 622-3930
  Tulsa (G-10403)
Okmulgee Ready Mix Concrete Co ....F 918 756-6005
  Okmulgee (G-7520)
Ormca ....G 918 296-7711
  Tulsa (G-10441)
P C Concrete Co Inc ....B 580 762-1302
  Ponca City (G-7864)
Pawnee Ready Mix Inc ....G 918 762-3437
  Pawnee (G-7708)
Perry Ready Mix Inc ....B 580 336-5575
  Perry (G-7742)
Primo Redimix LLC ....F 580 494-7649
  Broken Bow (G-1203)
Quikrete Companies LLC ....E 405 787-2050
  Oklahoma City (G-6953)
Rainbow Concrete Company ....D 918 234-9044
  Tulsa (G-10611)
Randys Construction ....G 405 387-3568
  Newcastle (G-4836)
Rempel Rock-N-Ready Mix Inc ....G 405 275-1107
  Shawnee (G-8487)
Rempels Rock & Ready Mix Inc ....F 405 567-3991
  Prague (G-7934)
Rental Ready ....G 918 500-6922
  Tulsa (G-10641)
Right Mix ....G 580 704-8904
  Lawton (G-3994)
Schwarz Ready Mix of Okc ....G 405 354-6671
  Yukon (G-11778)
Sooner Ready Mix ....G 405 670-3300
  Oklahoma City (G-7163)
Sooner Ready Mix LLC ....E 405 692-5595
  Oklahoma City (G-7164)
Southwest Ready Mix ....F 580 248-4709
  Lawton (G-4001)
Southwest Ready Mix ....E 580 355-2093
  Lawton (G-4002)
Srm Inc ....F 405 354-8824
  Yukon (G-11787)
Srm Inc ....B 405 475-1746
  Edmond (G-2629)
Standard Materials Group ....F 479 587-3300
  Tulsa (G-10835)
Standard Materials Group Inc ....G 918 582-8111
  Tulsa (G-10836)
Tulsa Dynaspan Inc ....C 918 258-8693
  Tulsa (G-10996)
Twin Cities Ready Mix Inc ....E 918 423-8855
  McAlester (G-4346)
Twin Cities Ready Mix Inc ....G 918 647-8218
  Poteau (G-7916)
Twin Cities Ready Mix Inc ....G 918 967-3391
  Stigler (G-8650)
Twin Cities Ready Mix Inc ....G 918 465-2555
  Wilburton (G-11527)
Twin Cities Ready Mix Inc ....E 918 682-8181
  Muskogee (G-4756)
Twin Cities Ready Mix Inc ....G 918 458-0323
  Tahlequah (G-8890)
Twin Cities Ready Mix Inc ....E 918 438-8888
  Tulsa (G-11023)
Van Eaton Ready Mix Inc ....G 405 912-4825
  Norman (G-5192)
Van Eaton Ready Mix Inc ....G 405 364-2028
  Norman (G-5193)
Van Eaton Ready Mix Inc ....E 405 844-2900
  Edmond (G-2667)
Van Eaton Ready Mix Inc ....E 405 789-1795
  Oklahoma City (G-7389)

Van Eaton Ready Mix Inc ....D 405 214-7450
  Shawnee (G-8518)
Withers Trucking Co ....G 580 668-2320
  Healdton (G-3424)

CONDENSERS & CONDENSING UNITS: Air Conditioner

Climatecraft Inc ....C 405 415-9230
  Oklahoma City (G-5788)
Custom Mechanical Equipment ....E 262 642-9803
  Ponca City (G-7814)

CONDENSERS: Heat Transfer Eqpt, Evaporative

Harsco Corporation ....E 918 619-8000
  Tulsa (G-9899)

CONDENSERS: Steam

SPX Heat Transfer LLC ....C 918 234-6000
  Tulsa (G-10827)

CONFECTIONS & CANDY

Castle Rock Kitchens ....G 405 751-1822
  Oklahoma City (G-5709)
Cotton Candi Creations LLC ....G 580 471-6550
  Altus (G-151)
Jackson Holdings LLC ....E 405 842-8903
  Oklahoma City (G-6343)
Masons Pecans & Peanuts Inc ....G 405 329-7828
  Norman (G-5065)
Mollycoddled Hash Slinger LLC ....G 918 236-1196
  Fort Gibson (G-3176)
Nutopia Nuts & More ....G 405 663-2330
  Hydro (G-3633)
Woody Candy Company Inc ....G 405 842-8903
  Oklahoma City (G-7468)

CONFINEMENT SURVEILLANCE SYS MAINTENANCE & MONITORING SVCS

Jarvis Inc ....E 918 437-1100
  Tulsa (G-10029)
Pyfi Technologies ....G 405 816-8685
  Oklahoma City (G-6929)

CONNECTORS: Electronic

Datran Corporation ....G 918 307-2200
  Broken Arrow (G-888)

CONSTRUCTION & MINING MACHINERY WHOLESALERS

B & B Log & Lumber Co Inc ....F 580 889-2438
  Atoka (G-399)
Broken Arrow Electric Sup Inc ....G 580 436-1470
  Ada (G-13)
Harsco Corporation ....E 918 619-8000
  Tulsa (G-9899)
Oil States Energy Services LLC ....G 405 702-6536
  Oklahoma City (G-6719)

CONSTRUCTION EQPT REPAIR SVCS

Industrial Machine Co Inc ....F 405 236-5419
  Oklahoma City (G-6299)

CONSTRUCTION EQPT: Attachments

Diamond Manufacturing Inc ....E 580 889-6202
  Atoka (G-406)

CONSTRUCTION EQPT: Attachments, Backhoe Mounted, Hyd Pwrd

J&A Services Co Inc ....G 405 833-4824
  Norman (G-5040)

CONSTRUCTION EQPT: Backhoes, Tractors, Cranes & Similar Eqpt

Diamond Attachments LLC ....E 580 889-3366
  Atoka (G-405)
Don Wilson Pipeline Constructi ....G 918 225-2786
  Cushing (G-1932)
Garfield Inc ....E 580 242-6411
  Enid (G-2961)

PRODUCT SECTION

CONSTRUCTION MATL, WHOLESALE: Structural Assy, Prefab, Wood

H & L Tooth Company ....D...... 918 272-0951
  Tulsa *(G-9872)*
J & G Trucking ....G...... 918 693-4300
  Nowata *(G-5215)*
Terex Cranes ....G...... 405 491-2006
  Oklahoma City *(G-7269)*
Waldon Equipment LLC ....F...... 580 227-3711
  Fairview *(G-3155)*

CONSTRUCTION EQPT: Bulldozers

Carl Abla ....G...... 580 526-3267
  Erick *(G-3086)*
Don Moody Farm ....G...... 580 648-2489
  Olustee *(G-7531)*
Roger Key Inc ....G...... 918 423-5420
  Mcalester *(G-4333)*

CONSTRUCTION EQPT: Crane Carriers

Crane Carrier Company ....G...... 918 286-2300
  Tulsa *(G-9501)*

CONSTRUCTION EQPT: Cranes

Sterling Crane LLC ....G...... 918 728-8613
  Tulsa *(G-10848)*

CONSTRUCTION EQPT: Dozers, Tractor Mounted, Material Moving

Duck Brothers Dozer & Trucking ....G...... 580 925-3509
  Konawa *(G-3845)*

CONSTRUCTION EQPT: Graders, Road

Laney Mfg Inc ....G...... 580 335-2363
  Frederick *(G-3196)*

CONSTRUCTION EQPT: Hammer Mills, Port, Incl Rock/Ore Crush

Pennington Allen Cpitl Prtners ....E....... 918 749-6811
  Tulsa *(G-10486)*

CONSTRUCTION EQPT: Ladder Ditchers, Vertical Boom Or Wheel

More Boom Company ....G...... 580 226-5303
  Ardmore *(G-335)*

CONSTRUCTION EQPT: Rakes, Land Clearing, Mechanical

D&S Dirtwork and Small Eqp ....G...... 580 485-8933
  Atoka *(G-404)*

CONSTRUCTION EQPT: Tractors, Crawler

Midwestern Manufacturing Co ....G...... 918 446-1587
  Tulsa *(G-10274)*
Varners Eqp Sls & Svc LLC ....G...... 918 367-3800
  Bristow *(G-803)*

CONSTRUCTION EQPT: Wrecker Hoists, Automobile

George W Smith Salvage City ....G...... 580 332-2250
  Ada *(G-41)*
Lkq Corporation ....F....... 918 428-3835
  Tulsa *(G-10171)*

CONSTRUCTION MATERIALS WHOLESALERS

Decorative Rock & Stone ....G...... 405 341-8900
  Edmond *(G-2388)*
Iron Horse Metal Works ....G...... 918 333-8877
  Bartlesville *(G-498)*

CONSTRUCTION MATERIALS, WHOL: Concrete/Cinder Bldg Prdts

Decorative Rock & Stone Inc ....G...... 405 672-2564
  Oklahoma City *(G-5916)*
Reinforced Earth Company ....E....... 918 379-0090
  Catoosa *(G-1349)*

CONSTRUCTION MATERIALS, WHOLESALE: Architectural Metalwork

Beeman Products Co Inc ....G....... 918 251-1432
  Broken Arrow *(G-845)*
H & H Ornamental Iron ....G....... 405 634-0646
  Oklahoma City *(G-6196)*

CONSTRUCTION MATERIALS, WHOLESALE: Asphalt Felts & coating

Vance Brothers Inc ....G....... 405 427-1389
  Oklahoma City *(G-7390)*

CONSTRUCTION MATERIALS, WHOLESALE: Building Stone

Impressions In Stone LLC ....G....... 918 828-9745
  Tulsa *(G-9974)*
Texhoma Limestone ....G....... 580 889-8808
  Caney *(G-1263)*

CONSTRUCTION MATERIALS, WHOLESALE: Building Stone, Marble

Classic Tile Stone & MBL LLC ....F....... 405 858-8453
  Oklahoma City *(G-5779)*
Custom Tile & Marble Inc ....F....... 405 810-8515
  Oklahoma City *(G-5877)*
Eurocraft Ltd ....E....... 918 322-5500
  Glenpool *(G-3234)*
Stonemen Granite & Marble ....G....... 918 851-3400
  Tulsa *(G-10856)*

CONSTRUCTION MATERIALS, WHOLESALE: Cement

Holcim (us) Inc ....C....... 573 242-3571
  Ada *(G-49)*

CONSTRUCTION MATERIALS, WHOLESALE: Drywall Materials

Freeman Products Inc ....E....... 918 258-8861
  Broken Arrow *(G-915)*

CONSTRUCTION MATERIALS, WHOLESALE: Glass

Ardagh Glass Inc ....E....... 918 224-1440
  Sapulpa *(G-8250)*
Oldcastle Buildingenvelope Inc ....D....... 405 275-5510
  Shawnee *(G-8481)*

CONSTRUCTION MATERIALS, WHOLESALE: Gravel

Evans & Associates Entps Inc ....F....... 580 482-3418
  Altus *(G-155)*
Lawton Transit Mix Inc ....G....... 580 569-4333
  Snyder *(G-8582)*

CONSTRUCTION MATERIALS, WHOLESALE: Metal Buildings

Champion Designs & Systems LLC .....G....... 405 888-8370
  Oklahoma City *(G-5737)*
H & C Services Inc ....F....... 580 772-2521
  Weatherford *(G-11417)*
T J Construction ....G....... 580 494-6500
  Broken Bow *(G-1209)*
Vanover Metal Building Sls Inc ....F....... 918 253-6030
  Spavinaw *(G-8593)*

CONSTRUCTION MATERIALS, WHOLESALE: Molding, All Materials

Diversified Rubber Pdts Inc ....E....... 918 241-0193
  Tulsa *(G-9587)*

CONSTRUCTION MATERIALS, WHOLESALE: Pallets, Wood

Henryetta Pallet Company ....E....... 918 652-9897
  Henryetta *(G-3508)*

CONSTRUCTION MATERIALS, WHOLESALE: Paving Materials

Dunhams Asphalt Services Inc ....G....... 918 246-9210
  Sand Springs *(G-8180)*
Haskell Lemon Construction Co ....C....... 405 947-6069
  Oklahoma City *(G-6223)*
Paving Materials Inc ....G....... 405 799-9880
  Moore *(G-4552)*
Quapaw Company Inc ....E....... 918 352-2533
  Drumright *(G-2070)*

CONSTRUCTION MATERIALS, WHOLESALE: Prefabricated Structures

A-Accurate Welding Inc ....G....... 918 838-1111
  Tulsa *(G-9074)*
Morton Buildings Inc ....E....... 918 683-6668
  Muskogee *(G-4715)*

CONSTRUCTION MATERIALS, WHOLESALE: Roof, Asphalt/Sheet Metal

Cool Green Roofing Supply LLC ....G....... 918 860-7525
  Broken Arrow *(G-877)*
Storm Roofing & Cnstr LLC ....G....... 918 688-0165
  Owasso *(G-7620)*

CONSTRUCTION MATERIALS, WHOLESALE: Sand

Alva Concrete Inc ....B....... 580 327-2281
  Alva *(G-173)*
Block Sand Co Inc ....E....... 405 391-2919
  McLoud *(G-4352)*
Karlin Company ....G....... 405 542-6991
  Hydro *(G-3631)*
Kline Materials Inc ....F....... 580 256-2062
  Woodward *(G-11603)*
Lawton Transit Mix Inc ....E....... 580 353-6900
  Lawton *(G-3961)*
Minick Materials Company ....E....... 405 789-2068
  Oklahoma City *(G-6616)*
Muskogee Sand Company Inc ....G....... 918 683-1766
  Porter *(G-7894)*
T & G Construction Inc ....C....... 580 355-6655
  Lawton *(G-4010)*

CONSTRUCTION MATERIALS, WHOLESALE: Septic Tanks

Coppedge Septic Tank ....G....... 918 371-4549
  Collinsville *(G-1806)*

CONSTRUCTION MATERIALS, WHOLESALE: Stone, Crushed Or Broken

Apac-Central Inc ....F....... 918 683-1362
  Okay *(G-5256)*
Dolese Bros Co ....F....... 580 937-4889
  Coleman *(G-1794)*
Dolese Bros Co ....E....... 580 226-8737
  Ardmore *(G-280)*
Dolese Bros Co ....E....... 405 247-2564
  Anadarko *(G-202)*
Hanson Aggregates Wrp Inc ....E....... 580 369-3773
  Davis *(G-1985)*

CONSTRUCTION MATERIALS, WHOLESALE: Trim, Sheet Metal

Cool Green Roofing Supply LLC ....G....... 918 860-7525
  Broken Arrow *(G-877)*

CONSTRUCTION MATERIALS, WHOLESALE: Windows

Consolidated Builders Supply ....E....... 405 631-3033
  Oklahoma City *(G-5821)*

CONSTRUCTION MATL, WHOLESALE: Structural Assy, Prefab, Wood

Timberlake Trussworks LLC ....G....... 580 852-3660
  Helena *(G-3437)*

CONSTRUCTION MATLS, WHOL: Composite Board Prdts, Woodboard

Paramount Building Pdts LLC .... G 405 470-5073
  Oklahoma City *(G-6804)*

CONSTRUCTION MATLS, WHOL: Lumber, Rough, Dressed/Finished

B & B Log & Lumber Co Inc .... F 580 889-2438
  Atoka *(G-399)*
Builders Firstsource Inc .... E 405 321-2255
  Oklahoma City *(G-5641)*
Diamond P Forrest Products Co .... F 918 266-2478
  Catoosa *(G-1316)*
Oak Tree Sales .... G 405 224-9332
  Chickasha *(G-1493)*
Oklahoma Home Centers Inc .... E 405 260-7625
  Guthrie *(G-3329)*
Van Brunt Lumber .... G 405 567-3776
  Prague *(G-7938)*
Yukon Door and Plywood Inc .... E 405 354-4861
  Yukon *(G-11807)*

CONSTRUCTION SAND MINING

Dolese Bros Co .... C 405 235-2311
  Oklahoma City *(G-5957)*
Evans & Associates Entps Inc .... E 580 765-6693
  Ponca City *(G-7828)*
Meridian Contracting Inc .... D 405 928-5959
  Norman *(G-5072)*
Perkins Sand LLC .... G 405 240-7870
  Carney *(G-1279)*
Southwestern State Sand Corp .... E 580 569-4333
  Snyder *(G-8584)*

CONSTRUCTION: Agricultural Building

Burrow Construction LLC .... E 800 766-5793
  Fort Gibson *(G-3174)*

CONSTRUCTION: Apartment Building

Hardesty Company Inc .... E 918 585-3100
  Tulsa *(G-9890)*
Resco Enterprises Inc .... G 918 298-0052
  Jenks *(G-3726)*

CONSTRUCTION: Athletic & Recreation Facilities

Cramer Fence Company .... G 918 865-4529
  Mannford *(G-4180)*
DS Welding .... G 580 623-4104
  Fay *(G-3156)*

CONSTRUCTION: Bridge

Oldcastle Materials Inc .... C 918 978-0459
  Tulsa *(G-10413)*

CONSTRUCTION: Commercial & Institutional Building

C-Star Mfg Inc .... G 405 756-1530
  Lindsay *(G-4054)*
Dream Buildings of Tulsa .... G 918 437-9233
  Tulsa *(G-9604)*
Iron Horse Metal Works .... G 918 333-8877
  Bartlesville *(G-498)*
Leddy Construction .... G 580 332-3056
  Ada *(G-60)*
Martinez Metal Buildings .... G 580 821-2780
  Elk City *(G-2848)*
Roff Iron & Sales Inc .... E 580 456-7850
  Roff *(G-8110)*

CONSTRUCTION: Commercial & Office Building, New

Aztec Building Systems Inc .... E 405 329-0255
  Norman *(G-4923)*
Hardesty Company Inc .... E 918 585-3100
  Tulsa *(G-9890)*
Larry Mustin Construction .... G 918 995-7055
  Tulsa *(G-10130)*
Molitor Design & Cnstr LLC .... G 405 802-8302
  Moore *(G-4542)*

CONSTRUCTION: Dock

Beaver Fabrication Inc .... G 405 360-0014
  Norman *(G-4928)*
Jerrys Dock Construction Inc .... F 918 256-3390
  Bernice *(G-567)*
Meeco Sullivan LLC .... F 918 423-6833
  McAlester *(G-4320)*

CONSTRUCTION: Electric Power Line

Red Dirt Msurement Contrls LLC .... E 405 422-5085
  El Reno *(G-2752)*

CONSTRUCTION: Elevated Highway

Earl-Le Dozer Service LLC .... D 918 352-2072
  Drumright *(G-2059)*
Haken Dozer Service .... G 580 669-2211
  Glencoe *(G-3223)*

CONSTRUCTION: Foundation & Retaining Wall

Power Lift Fndtn RPR OK Inc .... E 580 332-8282
  Ada *(G-75)*

CONSTRUCTION: Greenhouse

Skyview Products Inc .... G 405 745-6064
  Mustang *(G-4794)*

CONSTRUCTION: Heavy Highway & Street

Meridian Contracting Inc .... D 405 928-5959
  Norman *(G-5072)*
Overland Federal LLC .... F 469 269-2303
  Ardmore *(G-341)*

CONSTRUCTION: Indl Building & Warehouse

Industrial Structures Inc .... E 918 341-0300
  Tulsa *(G-9982)*
Project 3810 LLC .... G 405 834-7418
  Oklahoma City *(G-6914)*
Tj Services LLC .... G 405 596-5124
  Oklahoma City *(G-7295)*
Unami LLC .... G 405 320-5696
  Anadarko *(G-208)*

CONSTRUCTION: Indl Building, Prefabricated

Oklahoma Metal Creations LLC .... G 580 917-5434
  Fletcher *(G-3165)*

CONSTRUCTION: Indl Buildings, New, NEC

Madden Steel Buildings Lawton .... G 580 357-1699
  Lawton *(G-3968)*

CONSTRUCTION: Indl Plant

Shaw Group Inc .... A 918 445-7744
  Tulsa *(G-10739)*
Trans-Tel Central Inc .... C 405 447-5025
  Norman *(G-5180)*

CONSTRUCTION: Mausoleum

Gifford Monument Works Inc .... F 580 332-1271
  Ada *(G-42)*

CONSTRUCTION: Nonresidential Buildings, Custom

North American Cos .... F 918 592-2000
  Tulsa *(G-10360)*
Shielding Resources Group .... F 918 663-1985
  Tulsa *(G-10746)*

CONSTRUCTION: Oil & Gas Pipeline Construction

007 Operating LLC .... G 580 467-2744
  Sulphur *(G-8826)*
Industrial Machine Co Inc .... F 405 236-5419
  Oklahoma City *(G-6299)*
Jeremys Rustabouts Backhoe Inc .... F 580 772-5157
  Weatherford *(G-11421)*
Luckinbill Inc .... D 580 233-2026
  Enid *(G-3000)*
P & H Construction Inc .... G 405 257-3307
  Wewoka *(G-11506)*

CONSTRUCTION: Panhandle

Panhandle Construction Svcs .... F 580 338-7667
  Guymon *(G-3359)*
Sisk Construction Co .... G 405 375-5318
  Kingfisher *(G-3815)*
United Contracting Svcs Inc .... C 918 551-7659
  Tulsa *(G-11040)*
W 2 Enterprises LLC .... G 918 429-8793
  Tuskahoma *(G-11183)*

CONSTRUCTION: Pharmaceutical Manufacturing Plant

Chickasaw Defense Services Inc .... G 405 203-0144
  Oklahoma City *(G-5759)*

CONSTRUCTION: Pipeline, NEC

Diamond Cnstr Co Shattuck Inc .... C 580 256-3385
  Woodward *(G-11578)*
Greg Tucker Construction .... E 405 756-3958
  Lindsay *(G-4064)*
Midwesco Industries Inc .... G 918 858-4200
  Tulsa *(G-10266)*

CONSTRUCTION: Pond

007 Operating LLC .... G 580 467-2744
  Sulphur *(G-8826)*
Booth Envmtl Sls & Svc LLC .... E 918 465-0214
  Red Oak *(G-8075)*

CONSTRUCTION: Power & Communication Transmission Tower

B J M Consulting Inc .... G 918 665-8737
  Tulsa *(G-9244)*
Trans-Tel Central Inc .... C 405 447-5025
  Norman *(G-5180)*

CONSTRUCTION: Pumping Station

Solar Power & Pump Company LLC .... F 580 225-1704
  Elk City *(G-2874)*

CONSTRUCTION: Refineries

Best Oil Field Service Inc .... E 405 262-5060
  El Reno *(G-2701)*
Post Construction Company .... G 580 928-5983
  Sayre *(G-8343)*
Vickers Construction Inc .... D 405 756-4386
  Lindsay *(G-4097)*

CONSTRUCTION: Residential, Nec

Bennett Construction .... G 405 756-1918
  Lindsay *(G-4048)*
Bilco Construction Inc .... G 405 386-5591
  Newalla *(G-4804)*
Harry A Lippert Jr .... G 512 705-1248
  Lawton *(G-3939)*
Jackson Welding & Machine .... G 580 472-3631
  Canute *(G-1268)*
Sands Weld and Fab Inc .... G 918 419-2222
  Tulsa *(G-10705)*

CONSTRUCTION: Roads, Gravel or Dirt

007 Operating LLC .... G 580 467-2744
  Sulphur *(G-8826)*
Integrity Trckg Cnstr Svcs Inc .... E 580 361-2387
  Balko *(G-432)*

CONSTRUCTION: Sewer Line

Improved Cnstr Methods Inc .... G 405 235-2609
  Oklahoma City *(G-6294)*

CONSTRUCTION: Single-Family Housing

Bennett Construction .... G 405 756-1918
  Lindsay *(G-4048)*
Chris Green Greens Construct .... G 405 207-0690
  Pauls Valley *(G-7653)*
Dennis Petrilla Enterprises .... G 405 364-4695
  Norman *(G-4977)*
Heintzelman Cons & Rofing .... G 405 409-8954
  Oklahoma City *(G-5294)*
Karacon Solutions LLC .... G 918 231-1001
  Tulsa *(G-10076)*
Paradise Construction LLC .... G 918 967-9991
  Stigler *(G-8637)*
Storm Roofing & Cnstr LLC .... G 918 688-0165
  Owasso *(G-7620)*

PRODUCT SECTION

CONSULTING SVCS: Oil

Swh Construction LLC ....F...... 405 317-0663
  Washington (G-11338)
T J Construction ....G...... 580 494-6500
  Broken Bow (G-1209)

CONSTRUCTION: Single-family Housing, New

B & W Ready Mix LLC ....G...... 580 623-5059
  Watonga (G-11340)
Mike Pung ....G...... 405 736-6282
  Oklahoma City (G-6607)
Resco Enterprises Inc ....G...... 918 298-0052
  Jenks (G-3726)

CONSTRUCTION: Steel Buildings

Briggs Rainbow Buildings Inc .....C....... 918 683-3695
  Muskogee (G-4655)
Circle K Steel Bldg Cnstr LLC ....F....... 405 932-4664
  Paden (G-7634)

CONSTRUCTION: Street Surfacing & Paving

High Pointe Construction ....G....... 405 685-8303
  Oklahoma City (G-6247)
Logan County Asphalt Co ....E....... 405 282-3711
  Guthrie (G-3323)

CONSTRUCTION: Utility Line

Evans & Associates Cnstr Co ....D....... 580 765-6693
  Ponca City (G-7827)
Montross Tirita ....G....... 918 241-5637
  Sand Springs (G-8207)

CONSTRUCTION: Waste Disposal Plant

Town of Goldsby ....F....... 405 288-6675
  Goldsby (G-3247)

CONSTRUCTION: Water Main

Dixon Construction Co ....E....... 405 665-5515
  Wynnewood (G-11670)

CONSULTING SVC: Actuarial

Buckelew Accnting Slutions LLC ....G....... 405 359-5887
  Edmond (G-2334)
Lariat Services Inc ....G....... 580 977-5050
  Alva (G-184)

CONSULTING SVC: Business, NEC

American Bank Systems Inc ....E....... 405 607-7000
  Oklahoma City (G-5432)
Archein Aerospace LLC ....E....... 682 499-2150
  Ponca City (G-7798)
Burns & McDonnell Inc ....G....... 405 200-0300
  Oklahoma City (G-5646)
David Gormley ....G....... 918 845-0443
  Sapulpa (G-8265)
Engineering Technology Inc ....E....... 918 492-0508
  Tulsa (G-9687)
Fifteen Five Gtter Sltions LLC ....G....... 405 219-6741
  Yukon (G-11724)
Goff Associates Inc ....G....... 615 750-2900
  Oklahoma City (G-6167)
Png Operation ....G....... 405 470-4333
  Oklahoma City (G-6859)
Ramsey Property Management LLC .....G....... 405 302-6200
  Oklahoma City (G-6971)
Stan Clark Co ....G....... 405 377-0799
  Stillwater (G-8755)
Sublime Signs LLC ....G....... 405 364-1700
  Norman (G-5163)
Troutman Enterprises LLC ....G....... 405 351-0665
  Rush Springs (G-8129)

CONSULTING SVC: Chemical

Dathney Inc ....G....... 405 354-0481
  Yukon (G-11715)

CONSULTING SVC: Computer

Greenbriar Resources Corp ....G....... 405 348-7114
  Edmond (G-2444)
Hitachi Computer Pdts Amer Inc .....B....... 405 360-5500
  Norman (G-5024)
Srifusion LLC 774 238-7466
  Lawton (G-4003)

Visuals Tech Solutions LLC ....G....... 913 526-1775
  Edmond (G-2674)

CONSULTING SVC: Engineering

Chermac Energy Corporation ....F....... 405 341-3506
  Edmond (G-2348)
Elco Tech Engineering ....G....... 918 664-4646
  Tulsa (G-9651)
Engatech Inc ....F....... 918 599-7500
  Tulsa (G-9686)
Interactive Cad Services Inc ....G....... 918 251-4470
  Broken Arrow (G-940)
Ren Holding Corporation ....F....... 405 533-2755
  Stillwater (G-8745)
Shielding Resources Group ....F....... 918 663-1985
  Tulsa (G-10746)
Spring Harry A Geological Engr ....G....... 580 226-1910
  Ardmore (G-361)
Troutman Enterprises LLC ....G....... 405 351-0665
  Rush Springs (G-8129)
Universal Combustion Corp ....G....... 918 254-1828
  Tulsa (G-11046)

CONSULTING SVC: Management

Asher Oilfield Specialty Inc ....G....... 405 677-7868
  Oklahoma City (G-5475)
Associated Resources Inc ....E....... 918 584-2111
  Tulsa (G-9218)
Cargill Incorporated ....D....... 405 270-7011
  Oklahoma City (G-5698)
Frontier Logging Corporation ......G....... 405 787-3952
  Oklahoma City (G-6122)
Goff Associates Inc ....G....... 615 750-2900
  Oklahoma City (G-6167)
Greenbriar Resources Corp ....G....... 405 348-7114
  Edmond (G-2444)
Lightbe Corporation ....G....... 918 760-6968
  Tulsa (G-10160)
Martindale Consultants Inc ....E....... 405 728-3003
  Oklahoma City (G-6534)
Ndn Enterprises LLC ....G....... 703 772-6635
  Pawhuska (G-7690)
Nordam Group LLC ....C....... 918 274-2700
  Tulsa (G-10357)
Richardson Wellsite Services ......G....... 918 807-7105
  Sapulpa (G-8308)

CONSULTING SVC: Marketing Management

Archein Aerospace LLC ....E....... 682 499-2150
  Ponca City (G-7798)
Christy Collins Inc ....G....... 580 305-0001
  Frederick (G-3192)
Majeska & Associates LLC ....F....... 918 576-6878
  Tulsa (G-10204)
Osage Land Company ....F....... 405 946-8402
  Oklahoma City (G-6784)
Tourkick LLC ....G....... 918 409-2543
  Owasso (G-7626)
Woodbine Financial Corporation .....G....... 918 584-5309
  Tulsa (G-11149)

CONSULTING SVC: Online Technology

Ameriinfovets Inc ....G....... 408 446-4343
  Pryor (G-7943)
Sequoyah Technologies LLC ....F....... 918 808-7270
  Sapulpa (G-8310)

CONSULTING SVC: Radio

Native American Capital LLC ....G....... 918 289-7489
  Broken Arrow (G-985)

CONSULTING SVC: Telecommunications

Freedom Bell Inc ....G....... 918 671-1089
  Tulsa (G-9774)

CONSULTING SVCS, BUSINESS: Agricultural

Lacebark Inc ....G....... 405 377-3539
  Stillwater (G-8716)

CONSULTING SVCS, BUSINESS: Communications

B J M Consulting Inc ....G....... 918 665-8737
  Tulsa (G-9244)

CONSULTING SVCS, BUSINESS: Environmental

Accutec-lhs Inc ....G....... 918 984-9838
  Tulsa (G-9093)
Havard Industries LLC ....G....... 405 888-0961
  Edmond (G-2453)
Paul Philp Gchmical Conslt LLC .....G....... 405 325-4469
  Norman (G-5111)
Phoenix Group Holding Company ...F....... 405 948-7788
  Oklahoma City (G-6844)
Talon/Lpe Ltd ....G....... 806 467-0607
  Oklahoma City (G-7249)

CONSULTING SVCS, BUSINESS: Sys Engnrg, Exc Computer/Prof

Chaddick & Associates Inc ....F....... 580 223-1202
  Ardmore (G-264)
Lightbe Corporation ....G....... 918 760-6968
  Tulsa (G-10160)

CONSULTING SVCS, BUSINESS: Systems Analysis & Engineering

Digital Interface LLC ....G....... 405 201-5070
  Fairland (G-3124)
RMH Survey LLC ....G....... 918 927-8868
  Vinita (G-11270)

CONSULTING SVCS, BUSINESS: Systems Analysis Or Design

Paia Electronics Inc ....G....... 405 340-6300
  Edmond (G-2559)
Pyfi Technologies ....G....... 405 816-8685
  Oklahoma City (G-6929)

CONSULTING SVCS: Geological

Greenbriar Resources Corp ....G....... 405 348-7114
  Edmond (G-2444)
Greg Riepl ....G....... 405 232-6818
  Oklahoma City (G-6191)
Shields Operating Inc ....G....... 405 341-7607
  Edmond (G-2620)
Tilford Pinson Exploration LLC .....F....... 405 348-7201
  Edmond (G-2643)

CONSULTING SVCS: Oil

Anadarko Consultants Ltd ....G....... 405 354-7788
  Mustang (G-4761)
Arcadia Oil Corp ....G....... 405 409-2013
  Edmond (G-2309)
Austin Gas Properties LLC ....G....... 405 229-2391
  Oklahoma City (G-5490)
Blazer Oilfield Services LLC ....E....... 405 756-4800
  Lindsay (G-4049)
Bluestem Gas Services LLC ....F....... 580 658-6530
  Lindsay (G-4050)
Britt Oil Co LLC ....G....... 405 275-2115
  Shawnee (G-8435)
C D Adkerson Consultant Inc ......G....... 580 225-7860
  Elk City (G-2790)
Chandler Well Services LLC ....G....... 817 673-8140
  Edmond (G-2344)
Dan Abney ....G....... 405 527-0675
  Wayne (G-11366)
Dasa Investments Inc ....G....... 405 820-7703
  Edmond (G-2380)
DC Consulting Inc ....G....... 405 833-4856
  Oklahoma City (G-5909)
DK&k Energy LLC ....G....... 540 395-2400
  Okmulgee (G-7499)
Donald L Stafford Co ....G....... 918 492-0324
  Tulsa (G-9596)
Drovers Trail Land Company LLC .....G....... 405 702-6300
  Oklahoma City (G-5985)
Echo E&P LLC ....D....... 405 753-4232
  Oklahoma City (G-6004)
Elliot Enterprises ....G....... 918 742-9916
  Tulsa (G-9659)
Ener-Corr Solutions LLC ....G....... 405 509-9291
  Oklahoma City (G-6036)
Fletcher Lewis Engineering ....G....... 405 840-5675
  Oklahoma City (G-6090)
Gourdin Consulting LLC ....G....... 918 207-9825
  McAlester (G-4302)
Greenbriar Resources Corp ....G....... 405 348-7114
  Edmond (G-2444)

CONSULTING SVCS: Oil

Higgs-Palmer Technologies LLC .... G 918 585-3775
 Tulsa *(G-9927)*
Il L W Barrett .... G 918 496-8309
 Tulsa *(G-9968)*
Joshi Technologies Intl Inc .... F 918 665-6419
 Tulsa *(G-10059)*
Kent Engineering Inc .... G 405 364-2207
 Norman *(G-5049)*
Ld Consultants LLC .... G 432 230-1098
 Tulsa *(G-10141)*
Linda Sullivan .... G 918 629-7223
 Owasso *(G-7587)*
Lyons & Lyons Inc .... G 918 587-2497
 Tulsa *(G-10186)*
Mark A Holkum LLC .... G 405 735-3463
 Oklahoma City *(G-5305)*
Martindale Consultants Inc .... E 405 728-3003
 Oklahoma City *(G-6534)*
Mary K Rose Inc .... G 405 324-5612
 Yukon *(G-11749)*
Master Movers Incorporated .... G 918 408-1490
 Owasso *(G-7590)*
McCormick & Associates LLC .... G 405 747-9991
 Stillwater *(G-8724)*
ME Oil Co .... G 405 232-9541
 Oklahoma City *(G-6552)*
Meagher Energy Advisors Inc .... F 918 481-5900
 Tulsa *(G-10235)*
Mlb Consulting LLC .... G 580 225-2717
 Elk City *(G-2849)*
Mlb Consulting LLC .... D 580 504-8810
 Ardmore *(G-333)*
Morrill & Assoc Inc .... G 918 481-1055
 Tulsa *(G-10304)*
Osage Land Company .... F 405 946-8402
 Oklahoma City *(G-6784)*
Panhandle Corrosion LLC .... G 580 651-3208
 Goodwell *(G-3249)*
Paul Philp Gchmical Conslt LLC .... G 405 325-4469
 Norman *(G-5111)*
Penterra Services LLC .... G 405 726-2762
 Edmond *(G-2566)*
Petro Source Consultants .... G 405 751-0474
 Oklahoma City *(G-6835)*
Purcell Jack Oil Gas Cnsulting .... G 580 256-2040
 Woodward *(G-11624)*
Rex B Benway .... G 918 366-3626
 Bixby *(G-653)*
Robert M Beirute .... G 918 299-4259
 Tulsa *(G-10662)*
S & T Rose Inc .... G 580 657-4906
 Lone Grove *(G-4120)*
Santana Inc .... G 405 826-8817
 Oklahoma City *(G-5315)*
Scott Craig Consulting LLC .... G 580 571-4199
 Leedey *(G-4031)*
Snwellservice Llc .... G 580 430-9346
 Dacoma *(G-1977)*
SOO & Associates .... G 405 397-5072
 Norman *(G-5149)*
Southern International Inc .... F 405 943-5288
 Oklahoma City *(G-7171)*
Step Energy Svcs Holdings Ltd .... E 918 423-4300
 McAlester *(G-4339)*
Step Energy Svcs Holdings Ltd .... G 918 252-5416
 Tulsa *(G-10845)*
Stephens & Johnson Oper Co .... G 405 619-1866
 Oklahoma City *(G-7202)*
Tami Wheeler LLC .... G 405 759-2239
 Oklahoma City *(G-7251)*
Tiptop Energy Prod US LLC .... G 405 821-0796
 Oklahoma City *(G-7293)*
Two K Enterprises LLC .... G 918 964-7004
 Grove *(G-3290)*
Vortex Fluid Systems Inc .... G 918 810-7798
 Tulsa *(G-9049)*
W 2 Enterprises LLC .... G 918 429-8793
 Tuskahoma *(G-11183)*
Waid Group Inc .... G 817 980-8985
 Medicine Park *(G-4373)*
Wright Lease Services .... G 806 857-9116
 Enid *(G-3084)*
Xtreme Energy Company .... G 405 273-1185
 Shawnee *(G-8523)*

CONSUMER ELECTRONICS STORE: Video & Disc Recorder/Player

Dobbs & Crowder Inc .... G 918 452-3211
 Eufaula *(G-3100)*

Game King .... G 580 250-0707
 Lawton *(G-3934)*

CONTACT LENSES

Graham Laboratories .... G 405 329-4413
 Norman *(G-5009)*
Rex Laboratories Inc .... G 918 742-9545
 Tulsa *(G-10649)*
Stonewood Vision Source .... G 918 994-4450
 Broken Arrow *(G-1065)*

CONTAINERS, GLASS: Food

Ardagh Glass Inc .... E 918 224-1440
 Sapulpa *(G-8250)*

CONTAINERS: Cargo, Wood & Metal Combination

Cisco Containers LLC .... G 918 439-9244
 Tulsa *(G-9430)*
Frahm John .... G 213 500-0741
 Sand Springs *(G-8185)*

CONTAINERS: Corrugated

Corrugated Services LP .... G 405 672-1695
 Oklahoma City *(G-5840)*
International Paper Company .... D 405 745-5800
 Oklahoma City *(G-6320)*
Oklahoma Interpak Inc .... E 918 687-1681
 Muskogee *(G-4724)*
Supplyone Oklahoma City Inc .... E 918 446-4428
 Tulsa *(G-10881)*
Vande Lune Packaging LLC .... G 405 517-0098
 Yukon *(G-11801)*

CONTAINERS: Food, Wood Wirebound

Burgess Manufacturing Okla Inc .... E 405 282-1913
 Guthrie *(G-3303)*

CONTAINERS: Glass

Anchor Glass Container Corp .... B 918 652-9631
 Henryetta *(G-3499)*
Owens-Brockway Glass Cont Inc .... C 918 684-4526
 Muskogee *(G-4730)*
Verallia .... G 918 224-1440
 Sapulpa *(G-8320)*

CONTAINERS: Liquid Tight Fiber, From Purchased Materials

High Caliper Growing Inc .... D 405 842-7700
 Oklahoma City *(G-6246)*

CONTAINERS: Metal

B A Stevens .... G 918 695-4362
 Ochelata *(G-5233)*
Custom Manufacturing Inc .... E 405 692-6311
 Oklahoma City *(G-5874)*
Keymiaee Aero-Tech Inc .... F 405 235-5010
 Oklahoma City *(G-6409)*
Pratt Industries USA Inc .... B 405 787-3500
 Oklahoma City *(G-6874)*

CONTAINERS: Plastic

Ameriglobe LLC .... E 918 496-7711
 Tulsa *(G-9177)*
Carlsons Rural Mailbox Co .... G 405 632-7338
 Oklahoma City *(G-5704)*
CFS Brands LLC .... F 405 397-0103
 Oklahoma City *(G-5733)*
CFS Brands LLC .... B 405 475-5600
 Oklahoma City *(G-5732)*
Cfsp Acquisition Corp .... G 405 475-5600
 Oklahoma City *(G-5734)*
Fiber Pad Inc .... E 405 438-7430
 Tulsa *(G-9740)*
Gooden Studios .... G 405 375-3432
 Kingfisher *(G-3799)*
Graham Packaging Company LP .... G 918 680-7900
 Muskogee *(G-4682)*
Lacebark Inc .... G 405 377-3539
 Stillwater *(G-8716)*
Letica Corporation .... C 405 745-2781
 Oklahoma City *(G-6467)*
McClarin Plastics Llc .... E 877 912-6297
 Oklahoma City *(G-6545)*

CONTAINERS: Sanitary, Food

Hobby Supermarket Inc .... E 405 239-6864
 Oklahoma City *(G-6256)*

CONTAINERS: Shipping & Mailing, Fiber

EZ Mail Express .... G 918 542-2057
 Miami *(G-4403)*

CONTAINERS: Shipping, Wood

Economy Lumber Company Inc .... G 918 835-4933
 Tulsa *(G-9641)*

CONTAINERS: Wood

Choctaw Mfg Def Contrs Inc .... G 580 326-8365
 Hugo *(G-3609)*
Van Brunt Lumber .... G 405 567-3776
 Prague *(G-7938)*
Weilert Enterprises Inc .... E 918 252-5515
 Catoosa *(G-1365)*
Western Industries Corporation .... C 405 419-3100
 Oklahoma City *(G-7439)*

CONTAINMENT VESSELS: Reactor, Metal Plate

Driploc Inc .... F 405 632-5810
 Oklahoma City *(G-5982)*
Hydro-Link Containment LLC .... G 580 889-4701
 Atoka *(G-415)*

CONTRACTORS: Antenna Installation

A & M Blaylock Cnstr & Parts .... G 918 945-7081
 Mc Curtain *(G-4267)*
B J M Consulting Inc .... G 918 665-8737
 Tulsa *(G-9244)*

CONTRACTORS: Asphalt

Quapaw Company .... F 918 225-0580
 Cushing *(G-1951)*

CONTRACTORS: Awning Installation

R & J Aluminum Products .... G 580 355-1809
 Lawton *(G-3987)*

CONTRACTORS: Blasting, Exc Building Demolition

Utec Corporation LLC .... G 405 928-7061
 Norman *(G-5190)*

CONTRACTORS: Building Eqpt & Machinery Installation

Tulsa Dynaspan Inc .... C 918 258-8693
 Tulsa *(G-10996)*

CONTRACTORS: Building Front Installation, Metal

Pioneer Metal & Land Svcs LLC .... G 405 612-3575
 Glencoe *(G-3226)*
Tietsort LLC .... G 405 664-7353
 Oklahoma City *(G-7286)*

CONTRACTORS: Building Sign Installation & Mntnce

A-Max Signs Co .... E 918 622-0651
 Tulsa *(G-9075)*
Acura Neon Inc .... E 918 252-2258
 Broken Arrow *(G-813)*
American Logo and Sign Inc .... F 405 799-1800
 Oklahoma City *(G-5438)*
Architectural Sign & Graphics .... G 405 354-8829
 Yukon *(G-11692)*
Encinos 3d Custom Products LLC .... F 918 286-8535
 Tulsa *(G-9681)*
Johnson Signs Inc .... G 580 323-6454
 Arapaho *(G-224)*
Klines Signs & Crane .... G 580 256-2374
 Woodward *(G-11604)*
Landmark Design & Sign Corp .... G 405 387-3999
 Newcastle *(G-4830)*

PRODUCT SECTION

CONTRACTORS: Caisson Drilling

Chief Drlg & Foundation Svcs .... G 580 302-0124
  Weatherford *(G-11400)*

CONTRACTORS: Carpentry Work

Charles ODell .... G 405 745-3353
  Mustang *(G-4768)*
Lawton Window Co Inc .... G 580 353-4655
  Lawton *(G-3962)*
Sooner Cabinet & Trim Inc .... E 405 820-2920
  Moore *(G-4571)*

CONTRACTORS: Carpentry, Cabinet & Finish Work

Dale P Jackson .... F 580 332-1988
  Ada *(G-29)*
Dennis Petrilla Enterprises .... G 405 364-4695
  Norman *(G-4977)*
Dynosaw Inc .... G 405 418-6060
  Oklahoma City *(G-5992)*
Oak Tree Sales .... G 405 224-9332
  Chickasha *(G-1493)*
Pawnee Millworks LLC .... G 918 767-2565
  Pawnee *(G-7707)*
Reid Manufacturing LLC .... G 405 606-7006
  Oklahoma City *(G-7004)*
W & W Custom Cabinets .... G 405 222-1410
  Chickasha *(G-1521)*

CONTRACTORS: Carpentry, Cabinet Building & Installation

Custom Woodwork Inc .... F 918 224-4276
  Sapulpa *(G-8263)*
Parks Custom Cabinets LLC .... G 918 789-2694
  Chelsea *(G-1409)*
Trim Line Cabinets Inc .... F 405 664-1439
  Purcell *(G-8024)*
Ye Olde Woodshop .... G 918 224-1603
  Sapulpa *(G-8328)*

CONTRACTORS: Carpentry, Finish & Trim Work

Minko Design LLC .... G 918 895-6498
  Tulsa *(G-10284)*
Minko Design LLC .... G 918 895-6498
  Tulsa *(G-10285)*
United Millwork Inc .... G 405 670-3999
  Oklahoma City *(G-7371)*

CONTRACTORS: Carpet Laying

American Millwork Company Inc .... E 405 681-5347
  Oklahoma City *(G-5440)*

CONTRACTORS: Chimney Construction & Maintenance

Samson Energy Company LLC .... F 918 879-0279
  Tulsa *(G-10692)*

CONTRACTORS: Coating, Caulking & Weather, Water & Fire

Elastomer Specialties Inc .... F 918 485-0276
  Wagoner *(G-11281)*

CONTRACTORS: Commercial & Office Building

Boyles & Associates Inc .... G 580 353-7056
  Lawton *(G-3899)*
Mason Enterprises Group LLC .... G 918 230-5782
  Coweta *(G-1890)*

CONTRACTORS: Computer Power Conditioning Svcs

Ashleys Electrical Services .... G 918 825-0747
  Pryor *(G-7944)*

CONTRACTORS: Computerized Controls Installation

American Automation Inc .... G
  Pryor *(G-7941)*

CONTRACTORS: Concrete

CRC Evans Weighting Systems .... G 918 438-2100
  Tulsa *(G-9503)*
Forterra Pipe & Precast LLC .... G 405 677-8811
  Oklahoma City *(G-6104)*
Lightfoot Ready Mix LLC .... G 405 714-5539
  Perkins *(G-7720)*
Martinez Fencing Construction .... F 580 309-2046
  Clinton *(G-1758)*
Mosley Backhoe Service .... G 405 567-4710
  Prague *(G-7931)*
Overland Federal LLC .... F 469 269-2303
  Ardmore *(G-341)*
Pryor Sand & Redi-Mix Inc .... G 918 484-2150
  Whitefield *(G-11517)*
Randys Construction .... G 405 387-3568
  Newcastle *(G-4836)*
Sooner Ready Mix .... G 405 670-3300
  Oklahoma City *(G-7163)*
Stallion Oilfield Services Ltd .... D 580 856-3169
  Ratliff City *(G-8067)*
Taylor Storm Shelters LLC .... G 405 372-8130
  Stillwater *(G-8765)*

CONTRACTORS: Construction Site Cleanup

Integrity Rmdlg Cnstr Svcs LLC .... G 405 754-9836
  Oklahoma City *(G-6316)*

CONTRACTORS: Construction Site Metal Structure Coating

Finish Line Powder Coating .... G 918 938-6292
  Tulsa *(G-9744)*

CONTRACTORS: Core Drilling & Cutting

American Fence Company Inc .... E 405 685-4800
  Oklahoma City *(G-5435)*

CONTRACTORS: Corrosion Control Installation

Energy and Envmtl Svcs Inc .... G 405 285-8767
  Edmond *(G-2412)*
Panhandle Corrosion LLC .... G 580 651-3208
  Goodwell *(G-3249)*

CONTRACTORS: Countertop Installation

Continental Stoneworks Inc .... F 918 835-6725
  Tulsa *(G-9479)*
Eurocraft Ltd .... E 918 322-5500
  Glenpool *(G-3234)*
Zimmermans Custom Design Inc .... G 918 486-4179
  Coweta *(G-1903)*

CONTRACTORS: Demolition, Building & Other Structures

Molitor Design & Cnstr LLC .... G 405 802-8302
  Moore *(G-4542)*

CONTRACTORS: Directional Oil & Gas Well Drilling Svc

Angus Natural Resources LLC .... G 918 712-8487
  Tulsa *(G-9192)*
Arrow Drilling LLC .... E 405 749-7860
  Edmond *(G-2310)*
Big Buckets Rathole Drilling .... G 580 233-9850
  Enid *(G-2917)*
Bucks Directional Drilling .... G 580 276-2238
  Marietta *(G-4201)*
Cathedral Energy Services Inc .... D 405 261-6011
  Oklahoma City *(G-5713)*
Cleary Petroleum Corporation .... F 405 672-4544
  Edmond *(G-2357)*
D & M Directional Drilling LLC .... G 405 221-2959
  Wewoka *(G-11499)*
D and R Directional Drilling .... G 405 208-1399
  Crescent *(G-1912)*
David Dodd Inc .... G 405 216-5412
  Edmond *(G-2381)*
Directional Boring Inc .... G 405 842-8850
  Oklahoma City *(G-5949)*
Directional Fluid Disposals .... G 405 626-3261
  Oklahoma City *(G-5950)*
Downing Manufacturing Inc .... F 918 224-1116
  Tulsa *(G-9001)*
Drillworx Directional Drlg LLC .... G 405 386-3380
  Choctaw *(G-1540)*
Fasco Directional Drilling LLC .... G 918 224-2756
  Sapulpa *(G-8273)*
Foti Directional LLC .... G 352 848-5281
  Edmond *(G-2418)*
Gateway Directional Drilling .... G 405 752-4230
  Edmond *(G-2433)*
Helmerich & Payne Inc .... F 918 447-2630
  Tulsa *(G-9012)*
Helmerich & Payne Intl Drlg Co .... B 918 742-5531
  Tulsa *(G-9916)*
Helmerich & Payne Intl Drlg Co .... B 918 742-5531
  Oklahoma City *(G-6236)*
Hoss Directional Service Inc .... G 405 822-0551
  Norman *(G-5027)*
Inglesrud Corp .... G 405 429-7928
  Oklahoma City *(G-6304)*
Integrity Directional Svcs LLC .... F 817 731-8881
  Oklahoma City *(G-6315)*
Intrepid Directional Drilling .... G 405 607-0422
  Oklahoma City *(G-6324)*
Jack Exploration Inc .... G 580 621-3679
  Cherokee *(G-1417)*
Leam Drilling Systems .... G 918 794-3457
  Tulsa *(G-10143)*
Nabors Drilling Tech USA Inc .... E 405 745-3457
  Oklahoma City *(G-6647)*
Panther Drilling Systems LLC .... E 405 896-9300
  Oklahoma City *(G-6801)*
Patriot Directional Drlg LLC .... G 405 831-0085
  Stillwater *(G-8735)*
Pioneer Drectional Drlg II LLC .... G 405 533-1552
  Stillwater *(G-8737)*
Robert R Cantrell .... F 580 332-9495
  Ada *(G-84)*
Scientific Drilling Intl Inc .... D 405 787-3663
  Yukon *(G-11780)*

CONTRACTORS: Dock Eqpt Installation, Indl

T&T Forklift Service Inc .... G 405 756-3451
  Lindsay *(G-4093)*

CONTRACTORS: Drapery Track Installation

Ray Harrington Draperies .... G 405 789-6710
  Bethany *(G-593)*

CONTRACTORS: Drywall

Dryvit Systems Inc .... E 918 245-0216
  Sand Springs *(G-8179)*
Terry Hall .... E 817 271-4838
  Valliant *(G-11232)*

CONTRACTORS: Electric Power Systems

Mid States Technical Svc LLC .... E 918 260-6912
  Skiatook *(G-8561)*

CONTRACTORS: Electrical

Arnold Electric Inc .... G 405 605-1982
  Oklahoma City *(G-5467)*
Bills Electric Inc .... G 918 341-4414
  Claremore *(G-1596)*
City Electric Supply Company .... G 918 871-2640
  Tahlequah *(G-8857)*
City Electric Supply Company .... G 405 701-8544
  Norman *(G-4958)*
Millers Superior Electric LLC .... G 918 933-4006
  Tulsa *(G-10283)*
Prism Electric Inc .... G 918 425-2000
  Tulsa *(G-10562)*
Union Hill Electric LLC .... G 405 222-1068
  Chickasha *(G-1519)*

CONTRACTORS: Energy Management Control

Hks Energy Solutions Inc .... F 918 279-6450
  Tulsa *(G-9934)*

CONTRACTORS: Erection & Dismantling, Poured Concrete Forms

Szabo Szabi .... G 918 697-5441
  Muskogee *(G-4751)*

Employee Codes: A=Over 500 employees, B=251-500
C=101-250, D=51-100, E=20-50, F=10-19, G=1-9

CONTRACTORS: Excavating

CONTRACTORS: Excavating

Company		Phone
Anna Lightle	G	405 853-4530
Hennessey *(G-3445)*		
Dixon Construction Co	E	405 665-5515
Wynnewood *(G-11670)*		
Don Wilson Pipeline Constructi	G	918 225-2786
Cushing *(G-1932)*		
Earl-Le Dozer Service LLC	D	918 352-2072
Drumright *(G-2059)*		
Evans & Assoc Utility Svcs	G	580 351-1800
Lawton *(G-3924)*		
Gbg Earthmovers LLC	G	580 243-5662
Elk City *(G-2819)*		
Haken Dozer Service	G	580 669-2211
Glencoe *(G-3223)*		
Jacks Backhoe Service	G	580 926-3378
Camargo *(G-1253)*		
Michael S Azlin	G	405 257-3581
Wewoka *(G-11505)*		
Mosley Backhoe Service	G	405 567-4710
Prague *(G-7931)*		
Panhandle Oilfield Service Com	D	405 608-5330
Oklahoma City *(G-6799)*		
Rdnj LLC	G	405 418-4741
Oklahoma City *(G-6978)*		
Stallion Oilfield Services Ltd	D	580 856-3169
Ratliff City *(G-8067)*		
Timco Blasting & Coatings	E	918 367-1700
Bristow *(G-799)*		
Timco Blasting & Coatings	F	918 605-1179
Bristow *(G-800)*		
Timco Blasting & Coatings	G	918 605-1179
Stroud *(G-8823)*		
Timco Blasting & Coatings	G	918 605-1179
Bristow *(G-801)*		
Timco Blasting & Coatings	G	918 608-1179
Stroud *(G-8824)*		
W&W Enterprises	G	580 434-2736
Colbert *(G-1787)*		

CONTRACTORS: Excavating Slush Pits & Cellars Svcs

Company		Phone
4d Dozer Service Inc	G	580 256-2076
Woodward *(G-11552)*		
Silver City Excavating LLC	G	405 673-3062
Newcastle *(G-4840)*		

CONTRACTORS: Fence Construction

Company		Phone
Accurate Fence Contruction LLC	G	580 591-3717
Lawton *(G-3884)*		
Ace Fence Co	G	918 682-7895
Muskogee *(G-4641)*		
Ameristar Primeter SEC USA Inc	E	918 835-0898
Tulsa *(G-9179)*		
Berryhill Ornamental Iron LLC	G	918 258-6531
Broken Arrow *(G-846)*		
Bullet Fence Systems LLC	G	918 777-3973
Okmulgee *(G-7496)*		
Cooks Fence & Iron Co Inc	F	405 681-2301
Oklahoma City *(G-5827)*		
Fence Solutions Inc	G	580 233-4600
Enid *(G-2957)*		
Liberty Fence Co Inc	G	918 834-6553
Tulsa *(G-10156)*		
Martinez Fencing Construction	F	580 309-2046
Clinton *(G-1758)*		
Mitchell Ironworks Inc	G	580 233-7925
Enid *(G-3014)*		
Molitor Design & Cnstr LLC	G	405 802-8302
Moore *(G-4542)*		
Old World Iron Inc	G	918 445-3063
Tulsa *(G-10411)*		
Zoe Homes LLC	G	405 550-3563
Oklahoma City *(G-7488)*		

CONTRACTORS: Fiber Optic Cable Installation

Company		Phone
Holloway Technical Svcs LLC	G	405 223-9352
Duncan *(G-2130)*		
Trans-Tel Central Inc	C	405 447-5025
Norman *(G-5180)*		

CONTRACTORS: Fiberglass Work

Company		Phone
Custom Seating Incorporated	C	918 682-4400
Muskogee *(G-4666)*		

CONTRACTORS: Fire Sprinkler System Installation Svcs

Company		Phone
All American Fire Systems Inc	F	918 341-6977
Claremore *(G-1579)*		

CONTRACTORS: Floor Laying & Other Floor Work

Company		Phone
Beeman Products Co Inc	G	918 251-1432
Broken Arrow *(G-845)*		
Performance Surfaces LLC	G	405 463-0505
Oklahoma City *(G-6830)*		

CONTRACTORS: Flooring

Company		Phone
Kingston Flooring LLC	G	405 470-3494
Oklahoma City *(G-6423)*		
Mill Creek Lumber & Supply Co	D	918 794-3600
Tulsa *(G-10279)*		
Mill Creek Lumber & Supply Co	D	405 947-7227
Oklahoma City *(G-6609)*		
Pioneer Sport Floors LLC	G	214 460-6921
Calera *(G-1244)*		

CONTRACTORS: Foundation Building

Company		Phone
Diemer Construction Co LLC	E	580 628-3052
Tonkawa *(G-8974)*		

CONTRACTORS: Garage Doors

Company		Phone
Aztec Ne Overhead Door Inc	G	918 341-7502
Claremore *(G-1586)*		
Cimarron Glass LLC	G	918 225-6600
Cushing *(G-1925)*		

CONTRACTORS: Gas Detection & Analysis Svcs

Company		Phone
Advanced Hydrcrbon Strtigraphy	G	918 583-2474
Tulsa *(G-9109)*		
Diamondback Energy Svcs LLC	F	405 789-3499
Oklahoma City *(G-5942)*		
Oil & Gas Consultants Intl Inc	E	918 828-2500
Tulsa *(G-10381)*		
Petroskills LLC	E	918 828-2500
Tulsa *(G-10507)*		

CONTRACTORS: Gas Field Svcs, NEC

Company		Phone
Alan L Buck	G	405 401-9372
Chandler *(G-1374)*		
B & G Production Inc	G	580 256-5100
Woodward *(G-11556)*		
Bc Field Services Inc	G	918 839-0490
Heavener *(G-3425)*		
Blackrock Services LLC	G	405 254-3939
Oklahoma City *(G-5583)*		
BMC Petroleum Inc	G	580 234-3725
Enid *(G-2919)*		
Canadian Global Mfg Ltd	G	405 250-1785
Oklahoma City *(G-5686)*		
Chesapeake Energy Mktg LLC	C	877 245-1427
Oklahoma City *(G-5753)*		
Cumberland Pipeline Co LLC	G	918 359-0980
Tulsa *(G-9521)*		
Helmerich & Payne Inc	A	918 742-5531
Tulsa *(G-9912)*		
Lexington Gas & Go	G	405 527-4009
Purcell *(G-8011)*		
Magnum Diversified Services	F	405 391-9653
Newalla *(G-4813)*		
OK Contract Services LLC	G	918 352-5369
Braman *(G-761)*		
Oklahoma Energy Source LLC	G	918 307-8142
Tulsa *(G-10400)*		
Oklahoma Prime Energy LLC	G	580 226-2373
Ardmore *(G-338)*		
Pecos Pipeline LLC	G	918 574-3500
Tulsa *(G-10482)*		
Red Bud Resources	G	580 227-2592
Fairview *(G-3149)*		
Reserve Management Inc	G	918 227-0894
Sapulpa *(G-8307)*		
Rocky Mtn Mdstream Hldings LLC	G	918 573-2000
Tulsa *(G-10668)*		
Thurmond-Mcglothlin LLC	G	580 223-9632
Ardmore *(G-369)*		
Tmg Service Company LLC	E	405 213-4317
Oklahoma City *(G-7297)*		
Tri State Industrial	F	918 286-8110
Broken Arrow *(G-1084)*		
Truevine Operating LLC	G	580 427-7919
Ada *(G-99)*		

CONTRACTORS: Gasoline Condensation Removal Svcs

Company		Phone
Complete Wireline Svcs Ltd Co	G	405 317-0001
Purcell *(G-8003)*		
Diamond R Wireline LLC	G	405 361-7933
Pauls Valley *(G-7657)*		
Dixie Wireline	G	405 853-5402
Hennessey *(G-3458)*		
Downhole Wireline Special	G	580 254-3842
Woodward *(G-11579)*		
Gray Wireline	G	580 256-3775
Woodward *(G-11588)*		
Precision Wireline LLC	F	580 233-0033
Enid *(G-3037)*		
Shaw Wireline LLC	G	405 853-2168
Hennessey *(G-3485)*		

CONTRACTORS: General Electric

Company		Phone
Belden Russell Elect Co	G	918 791-9600
Grove *(G-3259)*		
BR Electric	G	405 354-8994
Yukon *(G-11700)*		
Cccc Inc	F	405 230-0638
Oklahoma City *(G-5718)*		
Custom Manufacturing & Maint	G	405 872-1000
Noble *(G-4877)*		
Industrial Service Providers	F	580 319-7417
Ardmore *(G-308)*		
Insight Technologies Inc	F	580 933-4109
Valliant *(G-11226)*		
Luckinbill Inc	D	580 233-2026
Enid *(G-3000)*		
M & M Electric	G	580 233-8999
Enid *(G-3002)*		
Miami Armature Works Inc	G	918 542-2443
Miami *(G-4413)*		
Sanders Electric	G	405 377-1691
Stillwater *(G-8752)*		
Tonys Electric Inc	G	405 375-4103
Kingfisher *(G-3818)*		
Tri-State Elec Contrs LLC	G	405 341-3043
Oklahoma City *(G-7324)*		

CONTRACTORS: Glass Tinting, Architectural & Automotive

Company		Phone
Auto Trim Design Signs SE Okla	G	580 622-3830
Sulphur *(G-8828)*		

CONTRACTORS: Glass, Glazing & Tinting

Company		Phone
Cimarron Glass LLC	G	918 225-6600
Cushing *(G-1925)*		
Lawton Window Co Inc	G	580 353-4655
Lawton *(G-3962)*		
Owasso Glass	G	918 272-4490
Owasso *(G-7600)*		
Proud Veterans Intl Ltd	G	316 209-8701
Lawton *(G-3986)*		
Sanford Brothers Co Inc	F	918 665-7358
Tulsa *(G-10706)*		
Victory Glass Co Inc	G	405 232-5114
Oklahoma City *(G-7400)*		
Whitacre Glass Works LLC	G	918 366-6646
Tulsa *(G-11119)*		

CONTRACTORS: Gutters & Downspouts

Company		Phone
Fifteen Five Gtter Sltions LLC	G	405 219-6741
Yukon *(G-11724)*		
R & J Aluminum Products	G	580 355-1809
Lawton *(G-3987)*		
Western Seamless Guttering	G	580 225-7983
Elk City *(G-2890)*		

CONTRACTORS: Heating & Air Conditioning

Company		Phone
Glover Sheet Metal Inc	E	405 619-7117
Edmond *(G-2437)*		
Industrial Service Providers	F	580 319-7417
Ardmore *(G-308)*		
Monkey Chase Banana LLC	G	405 706-5551
Oklahoma City *(G-6626)*		

PRODUCT SECTION

CONTRACTORS: Heating Systems Repair & Maintenance Svc

Hks Energy Solutions Inc .... F 918 279-6450
Tulsa *(G-9934)*

CONTRACTORS: Highway & Street Construction, General

Oldcastle Materials Inc .... C 918 978-0459
Tulsa *(G-10413)*

CONTRACTORS: Highway & Street Paving

Evans & Associates Cnstr Co .... D 580 765-6693
Ponca City *(G-7827)*
Evans & Associates Entps Inc .... E 580 765-6693
Ponca City *(G-7828)*
H G Jenkins Construction LLC .... E 580 355-9822
Lawton *(G-3938)*
Haskell Lemon Construction Co .... C 405 947-6069
Oklahoma City *(G-6223)*
T & G Construction Inc .... C 580 355-6655
Lawton *(G-4010)*
T J Campbell Construction Co .... C 405 672-6800
Oklahoma City *(G-7244)*

CONTRACTORS: Home & Office Intrs Finish, Furnish/Remodel

CD Industrys Corporation .... G 580 317-8448
Hugo *(G-3605)*
Rustic Rehab .... G 918 314-6647
Grove *(G-3287)*

CONTRACTORS: Hot Shot Svcs

Caves Hot Shot Services LLC .... G 405 397-2569
Mustang *(G-4767)*
Crimson Hot Shot Service LLC .... G 469 358-2005
Norman *(G-4969)*
Crosstimbers Hot Shot Svcs LLC .... G 405 740-2900
Tuttle *(G-11192)*
Fhl Hot Shot Trucking Services .... G 405 615-6658
El Reno *(G-2716)*
Grs Hot Shot Trucking LLC .... G 580 353-9449
Tuttle *(G-11203)*
Harbor Light Hospice LLC .... F 405 949-1200
Oklahoma City *(G-6216)*
Hot Rod Hot Shot Service Inc .... G 405 834-5591
Edmond *(G-2458)*
JC Hot Shot Services Inc .... G 918 782-7922
Glenpool *(G-3236)*
Jdw Hotshot Services .... G 918 407-8787
Tulsa *(G-10033)*
K & S Hotshot Services LLC .... G 918 899-2649
Cleveland *(G-1726)*
L&E Hot Shot LLC .... G 918 839-2419
Wister *(G-11550)*
Luke Mitchell .... G 918 429-0373
Wilburton *(G-11523)*
Mueggs Hot Shot Service LLC .... G 405 368-8362
Okarche *(G-5246)*
Oklahoma Hot Shot Service .... G 405 605-0464
Oklahoma City *(G-6752)*
On The Go Hot Shot Svcs LLC .... G 405 471-2055
Edmond *(G-2557)*
Out N Back Hot Shot LLC .... G 405 201-3576
Yukon *(G-11762)*
South Tulsa Hot Shot Svcs LLC .... G 918 299-7373
Jenks *(G-3728)*

CONTRACTORS: Hotel & Motel Renovation

Trans-Tel Central Inc .... C 405 447-5025
Norman *(G-5180)*

CONTRACTORS: Hydraulic Eqpt Installation & Svcs

Mid Continent Lift and Eqp LLC .... F 580 255-3867
Duncan *(G-2155)*

CONTRACTORS: Hydraulic Well Fracturing Svcs

Seventy Seven Energy LLC .... D 405 608-7777
Oklahoma City *(G-7112)*
Seventy Seven Operating LLC .... D 405 608-7777
Oklahoma City *(G-7113)*

Universal Pressure Pumping Inc .... G 405 608-7346
Oklahoma City *(G-7372)*

CONTRACTORS: Indl Building Renovation, Remodeling & Repair

Heintzelman Cons & Rofing .... G 405 409-8954
Oklahoma City *(G-5294)*

CONTRACTORS: Irrigation Land Leveling

Sullivans Grading & Sod .... G 580 591-2868
Lawton *(G-4007)*

CONTRACTORS: Kitchen & Bathroom Remodeling

A P & R Industries Inc .... F 405 702-7661
Oklahoma City *(G-5347)*

CONTRACTORS: Lighting Syst

Optronics International LLC .... E 918 683-9514
Muskogee *(G-4727)*

CONTRACTORS: Machinery Installation

Torcsill Foundations LLC .... D 281 825-5200
Weatherford *(G-11448)*

CONTRACTORS: Marble Installation, Interior

Hoffman Fixtures Company .... E 918 252-0451
Tulsa *(G-9936)*
Natural Stone Interiors .... F 918 851-3451
Bixby *(G-647)*
Professional Marble Company .... G 918 225-5364
Cushing *(G-1950)*
Warhall Designs LLC .... F 405 330-0907
Edmond *(G-2680)*

CONTRACTORS: Mechanical

Allstate Sheet Metal Inc .... F 405 636-1914
Oklahoma City *(G-5422)*
Custom Mechanical Equipment .... G 262 642-9803
Ponca City *(G-7814)*
Matherly Mechanical Contrs LLC .... C 405 737-3488
Midwest City *(G-4446)*
Specific Systems Ltd .... C 918 663-9321
Tulsa *(G-10817)*

CONTRACTORS: Office Furniture Installation

Narcomey LLC .... G 405 473-1350
Oklahoma City *(G-6653)*

CONTRACTORS: Oil & Gas Aerial Geophysical Exploration Svcs

Bean Chris Oil & Gas Service .... G 918 298-1569
Jenks *(G-3690)*
El Toro Resources LLC .... E 405 242-2777
Oklahoma City *(G-6019)*
Lamamco Drilling Company .... G 580 336-3524
Perry *(G-7740)*
R P Small Corp .... G 918 712-2226
Tulsa *(G-10605)*
Samson Exploration LLC .... F 918 879-0279
Tulsa *(G-10693)*
True Energy Services LLC .... G 580 421-9808
Ada *(G-97)*

CONTRACTORS: Oil & Gas Building, Repairing & Dismantling Svc

Allegiant Energy Production & .... F 405 550-2331
Oklahoma City *(G-5417)*
Bcej Company .... G 405 470-3790
Oklahoma City *(G-5539)*
Bill Laird Oil Company .... G 405 289-3346
Saint Louis *(G-8131)*
Cimarron Pipeline LLC .... G 405 286-9797
Oklahoma City *(G-5766)*
Cmt Well Completions Inc .... G 918 523-0600
Tulsa *(G-9460)*
Critical Components Inc .... G 405 212-9166
Oklahoma City *(G-5857)*
Cws Wireline LLC .... E 405 828-4225
Dover *(G-2039)*
Gilchrist Construction Inc .... G 580 886-2540
Canton *(G-1265)*

Industrial Equipment Services .... G 580 765-5544
Ponca City *(G-7837)*
Oil States Industries Inc .... D 405 671-2000
Oklahoma City *(G-6721)*
Oil States Industries Inc .... G 918 250-0828
Tulsa *(G-10387)*
Panhandle Oilfield Service Com .... D 405 608-5330
Oklahoma City *(G-6799)*
Presley Operating LLC .... G 405 526-3000
Oklahoma City *(G-6889)*
Ray Clour Well Service Inc .... E 580 856-3905
Ratliff City *(G-8063)*
Rice Welding Inc .... G 580 776-2584
Meno *(G-4387)*
Robert M Cobb Oilfield Eqp Sls .... G 405 840-2902
Oklahoma City *(G-7035)*
Well Completions Inc .... E 918 654-3030
Cameron *(G-1259)*
Ydf Inc .... G 405 324-2216
Yukon *(G-11806)*

CONTRACTORS: Oil & Gas Field Fire Fighting Svcs

Wild Well Control Inc .... G 405 686-0330
Oklahoma City *(G-7452)*

CONTRACTORS: Oil & Gas Field Geological Exploration Svcs

A & S Operating Inc .... G 918 582-7205
Tulsa *(G-9063)*
Belport Oil Inc .... E 918 637-5476
Tulsa *(G-9279)*
Calebs Resources LLC .... G 405 330-8252
Edmond *(G-2337)*
Caliche Resources Inc .... G 918 492-5170
Talala *(G-8898)*
Citizen Energy II LLC .... F 918 949-4680
Tulsa *(G-9433)*
Citizen Enrgy Intermediate LLC .... G 918 949-4680
Tulsa *(G-9436)*
Craig Elder Oil and Gas LLC .... G 405 917-7860
Edmond *(G-2371)*
Etx Energy LLC .... D 918 728-3020
Tulsa *(G-9703)*
F & F Production Eqp Svcs LLC .... G 479 414-2772
Bokoshe *(G-753)*
James R Biddick .... G 918 587-1551
Tulsa *(G-10026)*
Kenton Knorpp .... G 918 629-0968
Tulsa *(G-10084)*
Mach Resources LLC .... E 405 252-8100
Oklahoma City *(G-6514)*
Maximus Exploration LLC .... G 405 239-2829
Oklahoma City *(G-6541)*
OK Contract Services LLC .... G 918 352-5369
Braman *(G-761)*
Rogue Industrial LLC .... G 580 832-7060
Cordell *(G-1863)*
Rox Exploration Inc .... G 405 329-0009
Norman *(G-5136)*
United Land Co LLC .... G 405 840-2666
Oklahoma City *(G-7370)*

CONTRACTORS: Oil & Gas Field Geophysical Exploration Svcs

Century Geophysical Corp .... E 918 838-9811
Tulsa *(G-9399)*
Lonestar Gphysical Surveys LLC .... D 405 726-8626
Edmond *(G-2493)*
M E Klein & Associates Inc .... G 405 288-2804
Goldsby *(G-3245)*
Native American Capital LLC .... G 918 289-7489
Broken Arrow *(G-985)*
Rockford Exploration Inc .... G 918 582-1320
Tulsa *(G-10667)*
Russell Oil Inc .... G 405 752-7600
Edmond *(G-2608)*

CONTRACTORS: Oil & Gas Field Salt Water Impound/Storing Svc

Cypress Energy Holdings LLC .... F 918 748-3900
Tulsa *(G-9533)*
Cypress Energy Holdings II LLC .... G 918 748-3900
Tulsa *(G-9534)*
Cypress Energy Partners LP .... G 918 748-3900
Tulsa *(G-9535)*

CONTRACTORS: Oil & Gas Field Salt Water Impound/Storing Svc

Lakewood Disposal LLC .... E 918 392-9356
  Tulsa *(G-10114)*
Swiftwater Energy Services LLC .... G 405 820-7612
  Oklahoma City *(G-7238)*

CONTRACTORS: *Oil & Gas Field Tools Fishing Svcs*

Arkhoma Transports Inc .... G 580 651-2682
  Beaver *(G-538)*
F & F Tool Co .... G 405 382-0009
  Seminole *(G-8372)*
Graco Fishing & Rental Tls Inc .... F 405 382-0009
  Seminole *(G-8375)*
Hough Oilfield Service Inc .... E 918 225-1851
  Cushing *(G-1936)*
Kalamar Inc .... F 580 242-5121
  Enid *(G-2993)*
Klx Energy Services LLC .... G 405 838-1230
  Oklahoma City *(G-6429)*
Onsite Oil Tools Inc .... F 580 856-3367
  Ratliff City *(G-8060)*

CONTRACTORS: *Oil & Gas Well Casing Cement Svcs*

Ada Energy Cementing LLC .... G 580 436-5228
  Ada *(G-4)*
Butcher Well Service .... G 918 275-4439
  Talala *(G-8897)*
Casing Point LLC .... G 405 245-9855
  Midwest City *(G-4438)*
Cooper Machinery Services Inc .... C 713 354-4068
  Oklahoma City *(G-5830)*
Crossfire Production Svcs LLC .... G 580 254-3766
  Woodward *(G-11574)*
D & M Oil Flds Svc Csing Crews 918 623-0492
  Okemah *(G-5267)*
Eco-Tech Inc .... F 405 542-6483
  Hinton *(G-3524)*
Halliburton Company .... C 580 251-2847
  Duncan *(G-2124)*
Hamil Service LLC .... F 405 375-3815
  Kingfisher *(G-3800)*
Impact Casing Services LLC .... F 580 216-1159
  Woodward *(G-11593)*
Johnson Otey Properties Inc .... G 580 226-8425
  Ardmore *(G-318)*
Legend Energy Services LLC .... E 580 225-4500
  Elk City *(G-2837)*
Mlb Consulting LLC .... G 405 285-8559
  Edmond *(G-2520)*
Mud Mixers LLC .... F 580 243-7826
  Elk City *(G-2851)*
Oil Well Cementers Inc .... F 580 229-1776
  Healdton *(G-3420)*
Okla Casing Co .... G 580 432-5311
  Foster *(G-3188)*
Oklahoma Cementing Cushing LLC 918 225-0688
  Cushing *(G-1949)*
Outlaw Oilfield Supply LLC .... E 580 526-3792
  Erick *(G-3091)*
Pearl Energy Group LLC .... G 281 799-7459
  Oklahoma City *(G-6818)*
Rafter H Operating LLC .... G 405 295-2100
  El Reno *(G-2751)*
Red Dirt Msurement Contrls LLC .... E 405 422-5085
  El Reno *(G-2752)*
Reeds Power Tongs Inc .... E 405 382-2762
  Seminole *(G-8396)*
Samson Exploration LLC .... F 918 879-0279
  Tulsa *(G-10693)*
Terra Star Inc .... E 405 200-1336
  Kingfisher *(G-3817)*
Triple Crown Energy-Bh LLC .... G 918 518-5422
  Tulsa *(G-10975)*
US Casing Service OK Inc .... G 701 713-0047
  Weatherford *(G-11454)*

CONTRACTORS: *Oil & Gas Well Drilling Svc*

Agave Energy Inc .... G 918 799-6174
  Stigler *(G-8628)*
Akerman Drilling Inc .... G 580 925-3938
  Konawa *(G-3842)*
Allen Rathole Inc .... G 918 626-4026
  Spiro *(G-8613)*
Ardmore Prod & Exploration .... G 580 223-2292
  Ardmore *(G-249)*
At & L Energy LLC .... G 580 623-7265
  Watonga *(G-11339)*
Badlands Petroleum LLC .... G 303 921-2854
  Oklahoma City *(G-5508)*
Bailey Production Company .... G 405 932-5293
  Paden *(G-7633)*
Baker Hghes Olfld Oprtions LLC .... G 918 341-9600
  Claremore *(G-1589)*
Bays Enterprises Inc .... G 405 235-2297
  Oklahoma City *(G-5532)*
Bays Exploration Inc .... G 405 235-2297
  Oklahoma City *(G-5533)*
Bill Sneed Oilfield .... G 918 358-3487
  Cleveland *(G-1717)*
Bird Creek Resources Inc .... G 918 582-7713
  Tulsa *(G-9297)*
Bison Energy Services LLC .... F 405 529-6577
  Oklahoma City *(G-5577)*
Black Gold Stone Ranch LLC .... G 405 590-0700
  Norman *(G-4936)*
Blazer Oilfield Services LLC .... E 405 756-4800
  Lindsay *(G-4049)*
Bob Pound Drilling Inc .... F 918 367-6262
  Bristow *(G-767)*
Boone Operating Inc .... G 405 879-2332
  Oklahoma City *(G-5618)*
Brexco Inc .... G 405 348-8124
  Edmond *(G-2332)*
Canfield Ranch Energy LLC .... G 405 272-1080
  Oklahoma City *(G-5687)*
Cardinal River Energy Co .... G 405 606-7481
  Oklahoma City *(G-5697)*
Carel Pumping .... G 405 485-3495
  Blanchard *(G-705)*
Casillas Operating LLC .... E 918 582-5310
  Tulsa *(G-9386)*
Chesapeake Energy La Corp .... G 405 848-8000
  Oklahoma City *(G-5752)*
Circle V Energy Services LLC 405 614-0891
  Glencoe *(G-3219)*
Clay Bennett .... G 918 647-9294
  Poteau *(G-7901)*
Combs Oilfield Services Inc .... G 580 571-2315
  Woodward *(G-11571)*
Continental Resources Inc .... G 580 883-2838
  Ringwood *(G-8086)*
Creek International Rig Corp .... G 918 585-8221
  Tulsa *(G-9507)*
Crown Energy Company .... E 405 526-0111
  Oklahoma City *(G-5861)*
Crown Geochemistry Inc .... G 918 392-0334
  Tulsa *(G-9515)*
Cuesta Petroleum .... G 405 878-0744
  Shawnee *(G-8442)*
Dakota Exploration LLC .... G 918 806-8687
  Tulsa *(G-9547)*
Darling Oil Corp .... G 580 388-4567
  Lamont *(G-3866)*
Darrells Drilling Inc .... G 580 925-3854
  Konawa *(G-3844)*
Destiny Petroleum LLC .... F 281 362-2833
  Moore *(G-4515)*
Diamondback Energy Inc .... G 405 600-0711
  Oklahoma City *(G-5940)*
Dunlap Drilling Producing Inc .... G 918 237-0015
  Glenpool *(G-3233)*
Eagle Drilling LLC .... G 405 447-8181
  Norman *(G-4986)*
Edge Services Inc .... E 580 254-3216
  Woodward *(G-11581)*
Farallon Petroleum LLC .... G 405 225-1009
  Oklahoma City *(G-6073)*
Foam Unit Inc .... G 580 921-3366
  Laverne *(G-3877)*
Frontier Drilling LLC .... C 405 745-7700
  Oklahoma City *(G-6120)*
Frontier Drilling LLC .... D 405 745-7700
  Oklahoma City *(G-6121)*
G B K Holdings Inc .... G 918 494-0000
  Tulsa *(G-9789)*
George B Hughes .... G 405 784-5575
  Asher *(G-389)*
Gillham Oil & Gas Inc .... G 405 997-8549
  Maud *(G-4252)*
Goobers Drilling LLC .... G 918 846-2732
  Wynona *(G-11678)*
Great Plains Oilfld Rentl LLC .... A 405 422-2873
  El Reno *(G-2720)*
H & P Finco .... D 918 742-5531
  Tulsa *(G-9874)*
H Rockn Inc .... G 405 323-6593
  Chickasha *(G-1467)*
Halliburton Company .... C 580 251-2847
  Duncan *(G-2124)*
Helmerich & Payne Inc .... A 918 742-5531
  Tulsa *(G-9912)*
Helmerich & Payne Inc .... G 918 447-8692
  Tulsa *(G-9913)*
Helmerich & Payne Inc .... G 918 835-6071
  Tulsa *(G-9914)*
Helmerich & Payne De Venezuela .... C 918 742-5531
  Tulsa *(G-9915)*
Helmerich & Payne Rasco Inc 918 742-5531
  Tulsa *(G-9917)*
Helmerich & Payne Tech LLC 918 742-5531
  Tulsa *(G-9918)*
Helmerich Payne Argentina Drlg .... B 918 742-5531
  Tulsa *(G-9919)*
Helmerich Payne Boulder Drlg 918 742-5531
  Tulsa *(G-9920)*
Helmerich Payne Columbia Drlg .... B 918 742-5531
  Tulsa *(G-9921)*
Helmerich Payne Trinidad Drlg .... B 918 742-5531
  Tulsa *(G-9922)*
Hendershot Tool Company .... E 405 677-3386
  Oklahoma City *(G-6238)*
Hewitt Mineral Corp .... G 580 223-3619
  Ardmore *(G-303)*
Holiday Creek Prticipation LLC .... G 405 275-1045
  Shawnee *(G-8461)*
Horizon Energy Services LLC .... B 405 533-4800
  Stillwater *(G-8702)*
Horizon Energy Services LLC .... F 918 392-9351
  Tulsa *(G-9948)*
Horizontal Well Drillers LLC .... G 405 527-1232
  Purcell *(G-8010)*
Hulen Operating Company .... G 405 848-5252
  Oklahoma City *(G-6271)*
Huntington Energy LLC .... F 405 840-9876
  Oklahoma City *(G-6274)*
Hybrid Tool Solutions LLC .... G 405 756-1408
  Lindsay *(G-4069)*
J Grantham Drilling Inc .... G 918 647-8926
  Poteau *(G-7907)*
J H B & Company Inc .... G 405 354-6709
  Yukon *(G-11733)*
Ja Marrs Oil Co Inc .... G 918 352-2798
  Drumright *(G-2064)*
Jbk Well Service LLC .... F 918 695-6062
  Barnsdall *(G-437)*
Jeffries Pumping Service Inc .... F 580 628-2769
  Guthrie *(G-3320)*
JMJ Petroleum Inc .... G 918 209-5913
  Jenks *(G-3711)*
Jordan Services Inc .... G 405 748-3997
  Oklahoma City *(G-6385)*
K & H Well Service Inc .... F 405 382-2762
  Seminole *(G-8380)*
Kaiser Energy Ltd .... G 918 494-0000
  Tulsa *(G-10071)*
Kaiser Francis Gulf Coast LLC .... G 918 491-4490
  Tulsa *(G-10072)*
Kay Production Services Inc .... F 405 398-3109
  Seminole *(G-8382)*
Key Energy Services Inc .... E 405 843-6854
  Oklahoma City *(G-6406)*
Koby Oil Company .... G 405 236-3551
  Oklahoma City *(G-6432)*
L E Jones Drilling LLC .... G 580 255-3532
  Duncan *(G-2143)*
Latigo Drilling Corporation .... G 580 255-1674
  Duncan *(G-2145)*
Latshaw Drilling Company LLC 918 355-4380
  Tulsa *(G-10135)*
Layton & Smallwood .... G 918 446-6945
  Tulsa *(G-10139)*
Leam Drilling Systems LLC .... F 405 440-9436
  Oklahoma City *(G-6461)*
Lejones Operating Inc .... F 580 255-3532
  Duncan *(G-2147)*
Liberty Bit Co .... G 580 255-6400
  Duncan *(G-2148)*
Liberty Minerals LLC .... G 405 317-8107
  Ardmore *(G-325)*
Mammoth Energy Partners LLC .... F 405 265-4600
  Oklahoma City *(G-6518)*
Marmac Resources Company 918 846-2293
  Barnsdall *(G-438)*
Millbrae Energy LLC .... G 405 286-1941
  Oklahoma City *(G-6610)*
Mitchell Oil Company .... G 918 652-9175
  Broken Arrow *(G-979)*

Mustang Heavy Haul LLC ....A 405 743-0085
Stillwater *(G-8726)*
Nabors Drilling Tech USA Inc ....E 405 324-8081
Oklahoma City *(G-6646)*
Nabors Drilling Usa LP ....G 580 225-0072
Elk City *(G-2854)*
Natural Gas Commpression Corp ....G 918 243-7500
Cleveland *(G-1728)*
Neminis Inc ....G 918 582-8083
Tulsa *(G-10333)*
Noble Resources Inc ....G 918 865-3301
Mannford *(G-4188)*
Nomac Drilling ....G 405 242-4444
Edmond *(G-2539)*
Nomac Drilling LLC ....G 405 422-2754
El Reno *(G-2743)*
Oneok Inc ....E 918 588-7000
Tulsa *(G-10422)*
Oneok Partners LP ....E 918 588-7000
Tulsa *(G-10427)*
Osage Land Company ....F 405 946-8402
Oklahoma City *(G-6784)*
Ouachita Exploration Inc ....G 405 222-0024
Chickasha *(G-1496)*
Palm Operating LLC ....G 918 968-0574
Stroud *(G-8815)*
Parker Drilling Company ....G 918 281-2708
Tulsa *(G-10468)*
Parking Drilling Company Intl ....C 281 406-2000
Tulsa *(G-10469)*
Pearl Petroleum Inc ....G 580 355-6477
Lawton *(G-3981)*
Petroflow Energy Ltd ....E 918 592-1010
Tulsa *(G-10503)*
Petroleum Development Company ....G 918 583-7434
Tulsa *(G-10505)*
Phil Lack ....E 580 883-4945
Ringwood *(G-8089)*
Pistol Drilling LLC ....G 580 256-9371
Woodward *(G-11621)*
Plymouth Resources Inc ....G 918 599-1880
Tulsa *(G-10529)*
Png Operation ....G 405 470-4333
Oklahoma City *(G-6859)*
Poteet Oil Co Inc ....G 405 756-4530
Lindsay *(G-4077)*
Powers Drilling Inc ....G 580 343-2444
Weatherford *(G-11433)*
Prairie Exploration Co ....G 405 360-7077
Norman *(G-5119)*
Qes Pressure Control LLC ....E 580 885-7885
Arnett *(G-388)*
Qes Pressure Control LLC ....D 580 243-6622
Elk City *(G-2863)*
Quest Cherokee LLC ....G 405 371-1653
Oklahoma City *(G-6941)*
Ra Jac Inc ....G 405 701-5222
Norman *(G-5128)*
Ricks Rig Service ....G 405 619-9193
Oklahoma City *(G-7021)*
Robert C Beard ....G 918 534-2020
Dewey *(G-2031)*
Romine Oil & Gas Ltd ....G 405 273-1171
Shawnee *(G-8489)*
Rose Rock Petroleum LLC ....G 405 212-6987
Edmond *(G-2603)*
Rowe Wireline Services LLC ....G 580 541-5086
Enid *(G-3052)*
Rupp Drilling Inc ....G 580 336-4717
Perry *(G-7744)*
Samson Natural Gas Company ....B 918 583-1791
Tulsa *(G-10695)*
Sb Consulting LLC ....F 405 926-7177
Oklahoma City *(G-7088)*
Scientific Drilling Intl ....G 405 787-3663
Yukon *(G-11779)*
Southeastern Drilling ....G 918 469-3489
Quinton *(G-8042)*
Spring Drilling Corp ....G 580 226-3800
Ardmore *(G-360)*
Talon/Lpe Ltd ....G 806 467-0607
Oklahoma City *(G-7249)*
Taylor Resources ....G 405 850-2283
Oklahoma City *(G-7260)*
Thunderbird Energy Resources ....G 918 627-5433
Tulsa *(G-10939)*
Titan Resources Limited ....G 918 298-1811
Tulsa *(G-10947)*
Topco Oilsite Products USA Inc ....F 405 491-8521
Oklahoma City *(G-7304)*
Unit Corporation ....C 580 774-5200
Weatherford *(G-11453)*
Unit Corporation ....G 918 493-7700
Tulsa *(G-11036)*
Unit Corporation ....D 918 493-7700
Tulsa *(G-11037)*
Unit Drilling Co ....E 281 446-6889
Oklahoma City *(G-7362)*
Unit Drilling Company ....C 580 256-8688
Woodward *(G-11647)*
Unit Drilling Company ....F 405 745-4948
Oklahoma City *(G-7364)*
Unit Texas Drilling LLC ....G 281 446-6889
Oklahoma City *(G-7365)*
Universal Rig Service Corp ....G 918 585-8221
Tulsa *(G-11050)*
Vernon L Smith & Assoc Inc ....G 405 360-3374
Norman *(G-5194)*
W F D Oil Corporation ....G 405 715-3130
Edmond *(G-2677)*
Wagon Wheel Production Co ....G 580 983-2371
Crawford *(G-1906)*
White Stone LLC ....G 580 824-3271
Waynoka *(G-11383)*
Wildcate Drilling Services Inc ....E 580 254-3306
Woodward *(G-11654)*
Willischild Oil & Gas Corp ....G 580 569-2598
Snyder *(G-8586)*
Winter Creek Drilling LLC ....G 405 321-1200
Norman *(G-5201)*
Woody Creek Ranch ....G 580 658-5448
Marlow *(G-4249)*

CONTRACTORS: Oil & Gas Well Flow Rate Measurement Svcs

Carmen Natural Gas Measurement ....G 580 987-2778
Carmen *(G-1272)*
Flow Measurement Company Inc ....G 918 493-3443
Tulsa *(G-9757)*
Hughes Gas Measurement Inc ....G 405 227-0904
Wetumka *(G-11494)*
Ogci Building Fund LLC ....G 918 828-2500
Tulsa *(G-10379)*
Toolbox Oil Gas Consulting Inc ....G 432 234-2067
Duncan *(G-2189)*
Well Solutions Inc ....G 580 775-2373
Marietta *(G-4218)*

CONTRACTORS: Oil & Gas Well Foundation Grading Svcs

Diamond Cnstr Co Shattuck Inc ....C 580 256-3385
Woodward *(G-11578)*
Diemer Construction Co LLC ....E 580 628-3052
Tonkawa *(G-8974)*
Moran Equipment ....G 405 262-1422
El Reno *(G-2739)*
S&S Star Operating LLC ....G 817 676-1638
Oklahoma City *(G-7068)*
Smeac Group International LLC ....G 580 574-4092
Lawton *(G-3999)*
Spencer Machine Works LLC ....G 580 332-1551
Ada *(G-91)*

CONTRACTORS: Oil & Gas Well On-Site Foundation Building Svcs

Atalaya Resources ....G 918 949-4551
Tulsa *(G-9221)*
Booth Envmtl Sls & Svc LLC ....E 918 465-0214
Red Oak *(G-8075)*
Chesapeake Operating LLC ....A 405 848-8000
Oklahoma City *(G-5757)*
Glenn Brents Sales Inc ....G 405 733-4960
Oklahoma City *(G-6156)*
P & H Construction Inc ....G 405 257-3307
Wewoka *(G-11506)*
Rocky Top Energy LLC ....G 918 273-7444
Nowata *(G-5228)*
Samson Energy Company LLC ....F 918 879-0279
Tulsa *(G-10692)*
Tim Scoggins ....G 580 438-2476
Cleo Springs *(G-1712)*

CONTRACTORS: Oil & Gas Well Plugging & Abandoning Svcs

Mason Pipe & Supply Company ....G 405 942-6926
Oklahoma City *(G-6536)*
McIntyre Transports Inc ....E 580 526-3121
Erick *(G-3089)*
Superior Energy Services LLC ....E 405 722-0896
Oklahoma City *(G-7228)*

CONTRACTORS: Oil & Gas Well Redrilling

Unit Drilling Company ....C 405 745-4948
Oklahoma City *(G-7363)*
Unit Drilling Company ....C 918 493-7700
Tulsa *(G-11038)*

CONTRACTORS: Oil & Gas Well reworking

Atchley Resources Inc ....G 405 848-3331
Oklahoma City *(G-5484)*
Mason Enterprises Group LLC ....G 918 230-5782
Coweta *(G-1890)*

CONTRACTORS: Oil & Gas Wells Pumping Svcs

Apergy ESP Systems LLC ....D 918 396-0558
Broken Arrow *(G-1110)*
Barclay Contract Pumping ....G 580 541-7439
Enid *(G-2914)*
Beck Resources Incorporated ....E 405 853-2736
Hennessey *(G-3446)*
Bobby Prater ....G 918 885-4864
Hominy *(G-3578)*
Brg Production Company ....G 580 233-9302
Enid *(G-2922)*
Cassiday Pumping Service Inc ....G 405 969-3374
Crescent *(G-1909)*
Chesser Contract Pumping LLC ....G 405 820-7240
Meeker *(G-4376)*
Circle K Services Inc ....F 580 254-3568
Woodward *(G-11568)*
Cowboy Pmpg Unit Sls Repr LLC ....G 405 853-7170
Hennessey *(G-3454)*
Dbk Contract Pumping ....G 580 225-2009
Elk City *(G-2802)*
Deviney Contract Pumping LLC ....G 405 428-2192
Maysville *(G-4258)*
Don Betchan ....G 580 336-5954
Perry *(G-7730)*
Eagle Road Oil LLC ....G 844 211-2961
Tulsa *(G-9628)*
Elkouri Land Services LLC ....G 405 604-5580
Moore *(G-4519)*
Extract Production Svcs LLC ....C 918 938-6828
Tulsa *(G-9718)*
Griswold Trucking Randy ....G 580 476-3590
Ninnekah *(G-4872)*
H 5 C Pumping Inc ....G 580 487-3869
Forgan *(G-3170)*
Harbison-Fischer Inc ....G 405 677-3393
Oklahoma City *(G-6215)*
Hull Contract Pumping ....G 580 824-0440
Waynoka *(G-11376)*
Jaco Energy Company Inc ....G 918 967-8889
Stigler *(G-8634)*
Kirks Contract Pumping ....G 580 541-6405
Lahoma *(G-3857)*
Legacy Resources LLC ....G 405 359-1080
Edmond *(G-2485)*
Malone Contract Pumping Inc ....G 918 767-2450
Pawnee *(G-7706)*
Miller Pump Systems Inc ....G 918 455-4556
Broken Arrow *(G-977)*
Monroe Natural Gas Inc ....G 405 321-5647
Norman *(G-5079)*
Morris Richardson ....G 918 427-7323
Muldrow *(G-4634)*
Performance Technologies LLC ....D 405 262-2441
El Reno *(G-2746)*
Post Construction Company ....G 580 928-5983
Sayre *(G-8343)*
Quality Production Co Stigler ....D 918 967-4383
Stigler *(G-8640)*
Russell W Mackey ....G 580 571-7595
Gage *(G-3211)*
Sand Resources LLC ....G 405 573-0242
Norman *(G-5137)*
Sander Sporting Gds & Atvs LLC ....G 580 922-4930
Seiling *(G-8351)*
Saxet Energy ....G 405 752-9544
Oklahoma City *(G-7087)*
Siosi Oil Co ....G 918 492-1400
Skiatook *(G-8569)*
Smith Petroleum LLC ....G 918 638-1301
Barnsdall *(G-441)*

Employee Codes: A=Over 500 employees, B=251-500
C=101-250, D=51-100, E=20-50, F=10-19, G=1-9

2020 Oklahoma Directory
of Manufacturers & Processors

713

CONTRACTORS: Oil & Gas Wells Pumping Svcs

Company		Phone
Spencers Contract Pumping LLC	G	405 238-6363
Wynnewood (G-11673)		
Terrys Contract Pumping	G	580 554-2387
Covington (G-1868)		
Texoma Pumping Unit Svc Inc	E	580 856-4024
Ratliff City (G-8070)		
Thomas P Harris Jr	G	918 742-6414
Tulsa (G-10933)		
Ties Oilfield Service Inc	G	405 306-2655
Yukon (G-11792)		
Tracy Tarrent	G	405 969-2343
Crescent (G-1920)		
Triple M	G	580 488-3468
Leedey (G-4032)		
Waltman Oil & Gas	G	405 374-2694
Maud (G-4253)		

CONTRACTORS: Oil & Gas Wells Svcs

Company		Phone
Ashton Gas Gathering LLC	G	918 291-3200
Jenks (G-3689)		
Baker Hghes Olfld Oprtions LLC	G	580 243-3424
Elk City (G-2785)		
Bjs Oilfield Cnstr Inc	E	405 485-3390
Blanchard (G-701)		
Boomer Sooie LLC	E	501 827-0269
Norman (G-4939)		
Bristow Hot Oil & Steam Svc	G	918 367-2121
Bristow (G-769)		
Bs Oil Company	G	405 756-8357
Lindsay (G-4052)		
Coe Production	F	918 275-4529
Talala (G-8899)		
Concorde Resources Corporation	G	918 291-3200
Jenks (G-3700)		
Dcp Midstream	G	580 653-2641
Springer (G-8622)		
Degges Oil Field Service	G	918 623-1373
Okemah (G-5268)		
Drumright Oilwell Services LLC	D	918 352-9646
Drumright (G-2057)		
Elvis S Seshie	G	405 887-3050
Mustang (G-4770)		
Entz Oilfield Chemicals Inc	F	405 542-3174
Hinton (G-3527)		
Flint Energy Services Inc	G	580 856-3251
Ratliff City (G-8054)		
G & G Steam Service Inc	C	580 225-4254
Elk City (G-2816)		
Galmors Inc	G	580 225-4254
Elk City (G-2817)		
H & M Energy Services LLC	G	405 428-0740
Blanchard (G-715)		
HS Field Services Inc	E	918 534-9121
Dewey (G-2025)		
Jericho Oil (oklahoma) Corp	G	215 383-2433
Tulsa (G-10036)		
Jim Haynes	G	918 733-2517
Haskell (G-3399)		
K & H Well Service Inc	F	405 382-2762
Seminole (G-8380)		
Key Energy Services Inc	D	405 853-4327
Hennessey (G-3470)		
Key Energy Services Inc	G	713 651-4300
Oklahoma City (G-6407)		
Key Energy Services Inc	G	580 256-7413
Woodward (G-11601)		
Key Energy Services Inc	G	918 302-0372
McAlester (G-4310)		
Key Energy Services Inc	E	806 323-8361
Elk City (G-2835)		
Key Energy Services Inc	G	405 262-1231
El Reno (G-2732)		
Kodiak Corp	G	405 478-1900
Oklahoma City (G-6433)		
Kog Production LLC	G	580 621-3510
Freedom (G-3207)		
Lucas Oil & Gas Service Inc	G	580 225-3006
Elk City (G-2841)		
Mackellar Inc	F	405 433-2658
Cashion (G-1289)		
Mackellar Services Inc	G	405 848-2877
Oklahoma City (G-6515)		
Mackellar Services Inc	G	580 237-9383
Enid (G-3004)		
Mid-Central Energy Svcs LLC	D	405 815-4041
Oklahoma City (G-6591)		
Moes Portable Steam Co Inc	G	580 432-5467
Foster (G-3187)		
Morgan Well Service Inc	E	405 567-2288
Prague (G-7930)		
Quinque Operating Company	G	405 840-9876
Oklahoma City (G-6954)		
R & R Well Service Inc	G	580 254-3068
Woodward (G-11625)		
Ramco Packers	G	405 485-8804
Blanchard (G-729)		
Saint Louis Well Service Inc	E	405 289-3314
Saint Louis (G-8132)		
Sjl Well Service LLC	G	405 853-2044
Hennessey (G-3489)		
Southern Plains Enrgy Svcs LLC	F	580 336-7444
Perry (G-7745)		
Stride Well Service Inc	F	580 242-7300
Lindsay (G-4088)		
Stride Well Service Inc	G	405 375-4129
Enid (G-3063)		
Sutherland Well Service Inc	G	580 795-5525
Madill (G-4165)		
Tapoil Inc	G	580 788-4576
Elmore City (G-2898)		
Tarhay LLC	G	940 655-4210
Hollis (G-3569)		
Trade Trucking LLC	G	405 443-5375
Oklahoma City (G-7314)		
Valor Energy Services LLC	E	405 209-6081
Elk City (G-2887)		
Walters Oilwell Service Inc	G	580 875-2601
Walters (G-11304)		
Wilson & Wilson	G	405 375-5194
Kingfisher (G-3822)		

CONTRACTORS: Oil Field Haulage Svcs

Company		Phone
Blairs Oil Field Services LLC	G	405 698-9987
Yukon (G-11699)		
Burton Controls Inc	G	405 692-7278
Waynoka (G-11375)		
D & P Tank Service Inc	E	580 762-4526
Ponca City (G-7817)		
D & P Tank Service Inc	G	580 762-4526
Ponca City (G-7816)		
Dunns Tank Service Inc	E	580 465-1687
Foster (G-3185)		
F W Grubb Oilfield Service	G	580 863-2395
Garber (G-3213)		
Gore Nitrogen Pumping Svc LLC	G	580 922-4660
Seiling (G-8349)		
Hext Trucking LLC	G	580 821-6150
Erick (G-3087)		
Mikes Trucking Co	E	580 256-5063
Woodward (G-11612)		
Rainbo Service Co	G	405 677-5353
Oklahoma City (G-6966)		
Ranger Oilfield Services Corp	E	405 853-7279
Hennessey (G-3481)		
Rolling Thunder Oilfield	G	580 303-4587
Elk City (G-2869)		
Troglin Tank Gauge Svcs LLC	G	806 275-0010
Blanchard (G-739)		
Zzw Global Inc	G	405 388-8720
Yukon (G-11809)		

CONTRACTORS: Oil Field Lease Tanks: Erectg, Clng/Rprg Svcs

Company		Phone
Action Petroleum Services Corp	G	580 223-6544
Ardmore (G-237)		
C & J Trucks LLC	F	405 382-1405
Seminole (G-8362)		
Caprock Plungers LLC	F	580 799-1387
Cordell (G-1855)		
Crd Oil Corp	G	918 885-4527
Hominy (G-3581)		
Kenmar Energy Services LLC	F	405 844-2500
Edmond (G-2480)		
Samco Anchors	G	806 435-6870
Clinton (G-1767)		
Smith Construction Inc	E	580 226-2159
Ardmore (G-355)		
Westoak Production Svcs Inc	E	580 254-3568
Woodward (G-11651)		

CONTRACTORS: Oil Field Mud Drilling Svcs

Company		Phone
C&J Well Services Inc	G	405 234-9800
El Reno (G-2704)		
Geolog LLC	G	405 745-2197
Oklahoma City (G-6144)		
Mud Haulers LLC	G	580 338-3830
Guymon (G-3357)		
Nafta Mud Inc	G	405 751-6261
Oklahoma City (G-6648)		
Nafta Mud LLC	G	405 751-6261
Oklahoma City (G-6649)		
Pml Exploration Services LLC	E	405 606-2701
Oklahoma City (G-6858)		
Spinnaker Oil Company LLC	E	405 345-9556
El Reno (G-2759)		
Sun West Mud Company Inc	G	580 256-2865
Woodward (G-11637)		
Williams Water Well Co	G	405 250-8531
Enid (G-3080)		

CONTRACTORS: Oil Field Pipe Testing Svcs

Company		Phone
Control Devices Intl Inc	G	918 258-6068
Broken Arrow (G-876)		
Crescent Companies LLC	G	405 721-5511
Oklahoma City (G-5855)		
Crescent Services LLC	D	580 225-4346
Elk City (G-2796)		
Davis Pipe Testing Company	F	918 358-5272
Cleveland (G-1722)		
Dbr Construction Services Inc	G	580 327-4335
Alva (G-181)		
Edwards Pipeline Services LLC	C	918 627-8288
Tulsa (G-9646)		
Fis Operations LLC	C	918 246-7100
Tulsa (G-9749)		
Hydrostatic Engineers Inc	G	405 677-7169
Oklahoma City (G-6280)		
K3 LLC	G	580 231-2040
Enid (G-2992)		
L & B Pipe & Fabrication Inc	G	580 234-0712
Enid (G-2998)		
Northwest Measurement	G	580 822-3528
Okeene (G-5260)		
Shafer Kline & Warren Inc	E	918 499-6000
Tulsa (G-10738)		
Tall Oak Woodford LLC	G	405 888-5585
Edmond (G-2636)		
TRC Rod Services of Oklahoma	F	405 677-0585
Oklahoma City (G-7320)		
Tx3 LLC	G	405 382-2270
Seminole (G-8405)		
Wildcat Field Services LLC	G	918 606-6217
Collinsville (G-1829)		

CONTRACTORS: Oil Sampling Svcs

Company		Phone
Badger Pressure Control LLC	G	580 256-9555
Woodward (G-11558)		
Direct Downhole Rentals LLC	G	281 531-8881
Oklahoma City (G-5948)		
Riverside Laboratories Inc	G	918 585-3064
Tulsa (G-10657)		
Walters Oil	G	580 432-5294
Elmore City (G-2899)		

CONTRACTORS: Oil/Gas Field Casing,Tube/Rod Running,Cut/Pull

Company		Phone
Howells Well Service Inc	G	918 846-2531
Wynona (G-11679)		
J & S of Enid Inc	E	580 237-6152
Enid (G-2978)		
Martin Tank Trck Csing Pulling	F	918 225-2388
Cushing (G-1944)		

CONTRACTORS: Oil/Gas Well Construction, Rpr/Dismantling Svcs

Company		Phone
A P & R Industries Inc	F	405 702-7661
Oklahoma City (G-5347)		
Apergy ESP Systems LLC	G	918 536-3038
Ramona (G-8044)		
Aussie Built Supplies LLC	G	918 381-9700
Skiatook (G-8531)		
Aws LLC	G	405 382-1255
Seminole (G-8355)		
Bended Knee Construction LLC	G	918 465-4700
Red Oak (G-8074)		
Brady Welding & Machine Shop	D	580 229-1168
Healdton (G-3408)		
Bravo Natural Gas LLC	G	918 712-7008
Tulsa (G-9333)		
Bull Dog Welding	G	405 412-8199
Oklahoma City (G-5644)		
C & W Construction Inc	F	580 625-4520
Beaver (G-540)		
Circle V Energy Services LLC	G	405 614-0891
Glencoe (G-3219)		

Custom Manufacturing Inc....E....405 692-6311
Oklahoma City *(G-5874)*
Davis Cnstr Rcvery Sltions LLC....F....580 500-7527
Oklahoma City *(G-5905)*
Dewitt Trucking & Excavation....G....580 669-2534
Glencoe *(G-3221)*
Dexxon Inc....G....918 321-9331
Kiefer *(G-3778)*
Diamondback Energy Services....G....405 242-4080
Oklahoma City *(G-5941)*
Diversified Geosynthetics Inc....G....580 395-0041
Earlsboro *(G-2280)*
Downhole Hinton Services LLC....G....580 302-4129
Weatherford *(G-11406)*
Dresser-Rand Services LLC....G....918 321-3690
Kiefer *(G-3779)*
Drilling Fluids Technology....G....580 225-1009
Elk City *(G-2805)*
Encore Cnstr Solutions LLC....F....405 542-3316
Hinton *(G-3525)*
Evan & Sons Inc....G....405 756-2704
Lindsay *(G-4061)*
Family Tree Corporation....G....307 850-4147
McAlester *(G-4297)*
Fieldpoint Energy Services LLC....G....918 691-3427
Tulsa *(G-9741)*
Flowco Energy Service LLC....G....405 385-1062
Perkins *(G-7717)*
Gbg Earthmovers LLC....G....580 243-5662
Elk City *(G-2819)*
Hoggard Welding & Backhoe Svc....G....580 856-3934
Ratliff City *(G-8055)*
Integrity Rmdlg Cnstr Svcs LLC....G....405 754-9836
Oklahoma City *(G-6316)*
Ira E Rongey....G....918 227-0046
Sapulpa *(G-8279)*
J & D Potter Oil LLC....G....405 375-6303
Kingfisher *(G-3802)*
J & J Oil Tools LLC....G....580 523-1995
Guymon *(G-3352)*
J Price Energy Services LLC....F....580 795-6106
Madill *(G-4151)*
Kemper Valve and Fittings....G....580 622-2048
Sulphur *(G-8836)*
Key Energy Services Inc....D....580 338-0664
Guymon *(G-3354)*
Kleen Oilfield Services Co....F....580 657-3967
Lone Grove *(G-4117)*
Lamamco Drilling Company....G....580 336-3524
Perry *(G-7740)*
Larry Mustin Construction....G....918 995-7055
Tulsa *(G-10130)*
M & L Oil LLC....G....918 798-4511
Skiatook *(G-8558)*
M M Energy Inc....G....405 463-3355
Oklahoma City *(G-6508)*
Mammoth Energy Partners LLC....F....405 265-4600
Oklahoma City *(G-6518)*
Mammoth Energy Services Inc....F....405 608-6007
Oklahoma City *(G-6519)*
Martinez Fencing Construction....F....580 309-2046
Clinton *(G-1758)*
Midcentral Completion Services....G....405 445-5979
El Reno *(G-2738)*
Mills Well Service Inc....D....405 382-4107
Seminole *(G-8385)*
MRW Technologies Inc....E....918 827-6030
Glenpool *(G-3239)*
Nabors Completion Prod Svcs Co....E....580 323-0058
Clinton *(G-1760)*
New Tongs....G....580 335-3030
Frederick *(G-3197)*
Nine Energy Service....G....405 601-5336
Oklahoma City *(G-6682)*
Nov Downhole....G....405 688-5000
Oklahoma City *(G-6698)*
Nsi Fracturing LLC....G....918 496-2072
Tulsa *(G-10364)*
Orca Operating Company LLC....G....918 587-1312
Tulsa *(G-10437)*
Paschall Land Management....G....405 842-1391
Oklahoma City *(G-6806)*
Payzone Completion Svcs LLC....D....405 772-7184
Oklahoma City *(G-6815)*
Prime Operating Company....G....405 947-1091
Oklahoma City *(G-6893)*
Prochem Energy Services Inc....F....580 465-1737
Healdton *(G-3421)*
R&R Roustabout Services LLC....E....580 883-4647
Ringwood *(G-8090)*
Ray McClain Inc....G....918 363-7350
Sand Springs *(G-8220)*
Redzone Coil Tubing LLC....G....580 237-3663
Enid *(G-3046)*
Reputation Services & Mfg LLC....E....918 437-2077
Tulsa *(G-10643)*
Riddle Construction Co Inc....G....580 256-8109
Woodward *(G-11629)*
Robert S Cargile....G....405 732-7915
Oklahoma City *(G-7036)*
Rod Pumps Inc....G....918 968-4369
Stroud *(G-8816)*
Sanchez Cnstr & Rmdlg LLC....G....405 443-8324
Purcell *(G-8018)*
Secure Operations Group LLC....G....918 642-3444
Fairfax *(G-3121)*
Select Energy Solutions Rw LLC....G....580 653-2167
Springer *(G-8625)*
Seminole Oilfield Supply....G....918 623-9900
Okemah *(G-5275)*
Shebester Bechtel Inc....D....405 513-8580
Edmond *(G-2619)*
Stars Stripes Construction....G....405 387-4847
Newcastle *(G-4842)*
Stride Well Service....E....580 883-4931
Ringwood *(G-8093)*
Synergy Petroleum LLC....G....918 456-9991
Tahlequah *(G-8885)*
T & C Construction....G....580 432-5413
Foster *(G-3189)*
Tetra Technologies Inc....G....405 542-5461
Hinton *(G-3538)*
Texoma Tractor LLC....G....918 640-7949
Talala *(G-8903)*
Tking Energy Solutions LLC....G....740 827-4599
Lawton *(G-4013)*
Tongs....G....580 875-2053
Walters *(G-11303)*
Wagon Wheel Exploration LLC....G....918 746-7477
Jenks *(G-3738)*
Wellstar Downhole Services LLC....G....580 542-6982
Enid *(G-3078)*

CONTRACTORS: On-Site Welding

33 - Welding Company....G....405 375-4468
Kingfisher *(G-3783)*
A&K Manufacturing Services LLC....G....918 986-1637
Tahlequah *(G-8849)*
A-Accurate Welding Inc....G....918 838-1111
Tulsa *(G-9074)*
ARC Rvals Wldg Fabrication LLC....G....918 577-5066
Muskogee *(G-4649)*
Blue ARC Metal Specialties....G....918 341-3903
Claremore *(G-1597)*
Bob Albauer Portable Welding....G....405 789-7999
Oklahoma City *(G-5599)*
Boyd Welding Inc....G....918 485-3534
Wagoner *(G-11278)*
Capes Custom Welding & Fabrica....G....918 453-0594
Tahlequah *(G-8855)*
Christians Welding Service....G....580 674-3384
Dill City *(G-2034)*
Clicks Machine & Supply....G....405 273-2497
Shawnee *(G-8438)*
D & Z Metal Fabrication....G....918 456-3841
Welling *(G-11466)*
Darrell Lewis....G....405 867-5768
Maysville *(G-4257)*
Don Bateman Shtmtl Fabrication....G....918 224-0567
Sapulpa *(G-8267)*
Durnal Construction LLC....G....405 413-5458
Perkins *(G-7716)*
G Highfill....G....405 598-5576
Tecumseh *(G-8915)*
Gary Green Cement Construction....G....405 527-5606
Purcell *(G-8008)*
Greg Tucker Construction....E....405 756-3958
Lindsay *(G-4064)*
Hathaway & Simpson....G....580 875-3177
Walters *(G-11301)*
J & C Welding Co Inc....G....405 263-4967
Okarche *(G-5243)*
Jerry Woods Portable Welding....G....918 272-6424
Owasso *(G-7580)*
Kay Holding Co....E....580 628-4146
Tonkawa *(G-8977)*
Kenneth Petermann....G....405 372-0111
Stillwater *(G-8710)*
Kuykendall Welding LLC....G....405 905-0389
Chickasha *(G-1480)*
L & C Ventures LLC....G....405 793-9353
Norman *(G-5054)*
Larrys Welding Service....G....918 432-5787
Kiowa *(G-3840)*
Lynns Welding LLC....G....580 488-3587
Leedey *(G-4029)*
Marty Watley....G....580 492-4859
Elgin *(G-2777)*
McCutchen Enterprises Inc....G....918 234-7406
Tulsa *(G-10231)*
McPherson Implement Inc....F....405 321-6292
Norman *(G-5067)*
Midway Machine & Welding LLC....G....918 968-3316
Stroud *(G-8812)*
Mikes Welding....G....918 455-7227
Broken Arrow *(G-975)*
Oakes Wldg & Fabrication LLC....G....918 865-2356
Mannford *(G-4189)*
Old Town Welding Shop....G....918 423-8506
McAlester *(G-4326)*
R & L Mechanics & Welding....G....918 253-4734
Jay *(G-3685)*
R & S Manufacturing....G....918 266-2266
Catoosa *(G-1347)*
Rays Portable Welding....G....405 282-3218
Guthrie *(G-3335)*
Rice Welding Inc....G....580 776-2584
Meno *(G-4387)*
Russells Welding Inc....G....918 245-7395
Tulsa *(G-10682)*
S & J Machine Inc....G....580 623-8130
Watonga *(G-11349)*
Shelby Steel Service....G....918 234-3098
Tulsa *(G-10741)*
Stansberry Welding Inc....G....580 621-3211
Freedom *(G-3209)*
Terry Tylor Wldg Fbrcation LLC....G....405 205-2964
Chickasha *(G-1517)*
Troutman Enterprises LLC....G....405 351-0665
Rush Springs *(G-8129)*
Whites Welding LLC....C....580 254-3766
Woodward *(G-11652)*
Wilson Welding Works LLC....F....580 338-7345
Guymon *(G-3371)*
Zeco Machine Incorporated....E....405 282-3313
Guthrie *(G-3342)*

CONTRACTORS: Ornamental Metal Work

Custom Design By Roberts....G....918 664-0466
Tulsa *(G-9528)*
D & M Steel Manufacturing....G....405 631-5027
Oklahoma City *(G-5887)*
Diw Engneering Fabrication LLC....E....918 534-0001
Dewey *(G-2020)*
Equus Metalcraft Llc....G....918 832-0956
Tulsa *(G-9695)*
Oklahoma Metal Creations LLC....G....580 917-5434
Fletcher *(G-3165)*
Zephyr Southwest Orna LLC....E....918 251-4133
Broken Arrow *(G-1104)*

CONTRACTORS: Paint & Wallpaper Stripping

Timco Blasting & Coatings....E....918 367-1700
Bristow *(G-799)*
Timco Blasting & Coatings....F....918 605-1179
Bristow *(G-800)*
Timco Blasting & Coatings....G....918 605-1179
Stroud *(G-8823)*
Timco Blasting & Coatings....G....918 605-1179
Bristow *(G-801)*
Timco Blasting & Coatings....G....918 608-1179
Stroud *(G-8824)*

CONTRACTORS: Painting & Wall Covering

National Coating Mfg Inc....F....580 332-8751
Ada *(G-70)*

CONTRACTORS: Painting, Commercial

Martinez Fencing Construction....F....580 309-2046
Clinton *(G-1758)*

CONTRACTORS: Painting, Indl

Choctaw Nation of Oklahoma....D....580 326-8365
Hugo *(G-3610)*
Metaltech Inc....F....405 659-9911
Oklahoma City *(G-6575)*
Power Services LLC....G....405 677-7716
Norman *(G-5118)*

Employee Codes: A=Over 500 employees, B=251-500
C=101-250, D=51-100, E=20-50, F=10-19, G=1-9
2020 Oklahoma Directory
of Manufacturers & Processors
715

CONTRACTORS: Painting, Residential
Chickasaw Defense Services Inc ....G....... 405 203-0144
  Oklahoma City *(G-5759)*

CONTRACTORS: Parking Lot Maintenance
High Pointe Construction.......................G....... 405 685-8303
  Oklahoma City *(G-6247)*

CONTRACTORS: Patio & Deck Construction & Repair
Sawdust Ltd..G....... 918 809-3456
  Broken Arrow *(G-1044)*

CONTRACTORS: Petroleum Storage Tank Install, Underground
Red Dirt Msurement Contrls LLC ....E....... 405 422-5085
  El Reno *(G-2752)*

CONTRACTORS: Petroleum Storage Tanks, Pumping & Draining
Extract Production Svcs LLC ....C....... 918 938-6828
  Tulsa *(G-9718)*

CONTRACTORS: Pipe & Boiler Insulating
Elite Fabricators LLC..............................E....... 918 824-4528
  Pryor *(G-7961)*

CONTRACTORS: Playground Construction & Eqpt Installation
Noahs Park & Playgrounds LLC..............F....... 405 607-0714
  Edmond *(G-2538)*

CONTRACTORS: Plumbing
A Royal Flush LLC ....G....... 405 422-2077
  Yukon *(G-11688)*
Empire Plumbing Contrs LLC.................G....... 918 320-1427
  Grove *(G-3267)*
Kens Plumbing & Backhoe ....G....... 918 963-4223
  Shady Point *(G-8814)*
Luckinbill Inc ....D....... 580 233-2026
  Enid *(G-3000)*

CONTRACTORS: Pollution Control Eqpt Installation
AC Systems Integration Inc ....E....... 918 259-0020
  Tulsa *(G-9084)*

CONTRACTORS: Power Generating Eqpt Installation
Electric Green Inc ....G....... 405 706-1683
  Oklahoma City *(G-6022)*

CONTRACTORS: Precast Concrete Struct Framing & Panel Placing
Coreslab Structures Okla Inc.................C....... 405 632-4944
  Oklahoma City *(G-5835)*

CONTRACTORS: Prefabricated Window & Door Installation
R & J Aluminum Products.......................G....... 580 355-1809
  Lawton *(G-3987)*
Shipman Home Improvement Inc...........G....... 918 514-0049
  Sand Springs *(G-8223)*

CONTRACTORS: Protective Lining Install, Underground Sewage
Montross Tirita......................................G....... 918 241-5637
  Sand Springs *(G-8207)*

CONTRACTORS: Refractory or Acid Brick Masonry
Thermal Specialties LLC ....F....... 918 836-4800
  Tulsa *(G-10926)*

CONTRACTORS: Refrigeration
Farley Redfield ....G....... 405 275-2266
  Tecumseh *(G-8914)*

CONTRACTORS: Renovation, Aircraft Interiors
Jet Tech Interiors Inc............................G....... 580 310-2610
  Ada *(G-53)*
Liberty Partners Inc...............................F....... 918 756-6474
  Okmulgee *(G-7513)*

CONTRACTORS: Roof Repair
Rd Roofing and Carpentry ....G....... 580 341-0607
  Ada *(G-80)*

CONTRACTORS: Roofing
Briggs Rainbow Buildings Inc................C....... 918 683-3695
  Muskogee *(G-4655)*
Heintzelman Cons & Rofing....................G....... 405 409-8954
  Oklahoma City *(G-5294)*

CONTRACTORS: Roofing & Gutter Work
Storm Roofing & Cnstr LLC....................G....... 918 688-0165
  Owasso *(G-7620)*

CONTRACTORS: Roustabout Svcs
A T Roustabouts....................................G....... 405 788-0735
  Meeker *(G-4374)*
Advance Roustabout Svcs LLC..............G....... 405 612-0781
  Guthrie *(G-3296)*
Allan Bghs Wldg Roustabout Svc ....G....... 918 625-1712
  Drumright *(G-2050)*
Andy Cross Roustabout Svc LLC ....G....... 918 906-1240
  Mannford *(G-4174)*
B & S Roustabouts LLC ....G....... 405 779-0842
  Chickasha *(G-1434)*
Blankenship Roustabout........................G....... 580 791-0237
  Watonga *(G-11342)*
Brothers Construction and Rous ....G....... 405 602-3275
  Oklahoma City *(G-5633)*
Bruce Burdick Welding ....G....... 580 774-2906
  Weatherford *(G-11395)*
Buy Rite Services LLC...........................F....... 580 984-1008
  Enid *(G-2924)*
C C & R Construction Inc ....G....... 405 756-4710
  Lindsay *(G-4053)*
Carls Backhoe & Roustabout ....G....... 405 893-7212
  Calumet *(G-1245)*
Christ Centered Carriers LLC................E....... 417 850-8137
  Canute *(G-1267)*
Cook Roustabout LLC............................G....... 405 410-7951
  Guthrie *(G-3310)*
Coulter Oil Field Services LLC ....G....... 580 504-0813
  Ardmore *(G-270)*
Davenport Roustabout Service ....G....... 918 377-2987
  Chandler *(G-1378)*
H2s Safety Plus Inc...............................E....... 580 622-4796
  Sulphur *(G-8834)*
Henry & Son Roustabouts LLC ....G....... 580 747-8400
  Hennessey *(G-3468)*
Iron Horse Roustabout Svcs LLC..........G....... 918 352-8586
  Bristow *(G-780)*
J&K Rstbout Weed Ctrl Svcs LLC ....G....... 918 429-2392
  Stuart *(G-8825)*
Jacks Backhoe Service ....G....... 580 926-3378
  Camargo *(G-1253)*
James K Anderson Inc ....G....... 405 329-7414
  Norman *(G-5041)*
John Thompson Enterprises Inc............F....... 580 623-5820
  Watonga *(G-11348)*
Mels Construction Inc ....G....... 405 853-4621
  Hennessey *(G-3477)*
Panthera Roustabout Svcs LLC ....G....... 405 826-8466
  Jones *(G-3751)*
Pioneer Oilfield Services Inc..................E....... 580 243-4000
  Elk City *(G-2859)*
Powell Services Inc...............................G....... 580 225-9017
  Elk City *(G-2861)*
Ramon & Bennett Roustabout...............E....... 580 625-4092
  Beaver *(G-546)*
Recoil Energy Rental LLC ....G....... 405 650-1373
  Blanchard *(G-731)*
Rugged Roustabout LLC.......................F....... 918 225-0700
  Cushing *(G-1957)*
Ss Roustabout Services........................G....... 405 320-2183
  Ninnekah *(G-4874)*
Stallion Oilfield Services Ltd ....D....... 580 856-3169
  Ratliff City *(G-8067)*
Statewide Roustabouts Inc ....G....... 405 262-5934
  El Reno *(G-2760)*
T&M Roustabout Services LLC ....G....... 580 796-2478
  Lahoma *(G-3861)*
Triple M Roustabouts LLC ....G....... 918 619-7610
  Tulsa *(G-10976)*
Whites Roustabout Service Inc ....G....... 405 489-7126
  Cement *(G-1371)*

CONTRACTORS: Sandblasting Svc, Building Exteriors
Aw Specialties LLC ....G....... 918 798-9272
  Claremore *(G-1584)*
Bull Dog Welding ....G....... 405 412-8199
  Oklahoma City *(G-5644)*
Iron Horse Metal Works.........................G....... 918 333-8877
  Bartlesville *(G-498)*
Powder Coating of Muskogee ....G....... 918 681-4494
  Muskogee *(G-4736)*
Power Services LLC ....G....... 405 677-7716
  Norman *(G-5118)*
Premier Metal Finishing Inc...................G....... 405 947-0200
  Oklahoma City *(G-6885)*
Texoma Tractor LLC ....G....... 580 640-7949
  Talala *(G-8903)*

CONTRACTORS: Seismograph Survey Svcs
Baker Hghes Olfld Oprtions LLC............E....... 580 256-3333
  Oklahoma City *(G-5512)*
Maf Seismic LLC ....G....... 405 285-6444
  Edmond *(G-2500)*
Mid-Con Data Services Inc....................E....... 405 478-1234
  Oklahoma City *(G-6592)*
Powerco Seismic Services LLC.............G....... 918 424-3745
  McAlester *(G-4330)*
Seal Seismic Service LLC ....G....... 405 603-2121
  Oklahoma City *(G-7105)*
Seismic Exchange Inc ....E....... 918 712-7186
  Tulsa *(G-10724)*

CONTRACTORS: Septic System
Carnegie Precast Inc ....F....... 580 654-1718
  Carnegie *(G-1275)*
Dover Products Inc ....G....... 918 476-5688
  Chouteau *(G-1562)*
Haken Dozer Service ....G....... 580 669-2211
  Glencoe *(G-3223)*

CONTRACTORS: Sheet Metal Work, NEC
A & Y Enterprises Inc............................G....... 405 360-0307
  Norman *(G-4894)*
David Muzny ....G....... 405 681-7593
  Oklahoma City *(G-5904)*
Eastern Sheet Metal Co Inc...................G....... 918 687-6231
  Muskogee *(G-4669)*
Elk City Sheet Metal Inc........................G....... 580 225-5844
  Elk City *(G-2810)*
Glover Sheet Metal Inc ....E....... 405 619-7117
  Edmond *(G-2437)*
J C Sheet Metal Fabrication ....G....... 405 787-1902
  Oklahoma City *(G-6335)*
Pattison Metal Fab Inc ....E....... 918 251-9967
  Broken Arrow *(G-1000)*
Rick Leaming Construction LLC ....G....... 580 362-2262
  Newkirk *(G-4852)*
SFM Incorporated ....G....... 405 788-9453
  Tecumseh *(G-8928)*

CONTRACTORS: Sheet metal Work, Architectural
Penny Sheet Metal LLC ....F....... 918 251-6911
  Broken Arrow *(G-1002)*

CONTRACTORS: Shoring & Underpinning
American Logo and Sign Inc ....G....... 405 799-1800
  Moore *(G-4488)*

CONTRACTORS: Siding
A&B Home Improvement........................G....... 918 341-7410
  Claremore *(G-1574)*
Shipman Home Improvement Inc ....G....... 918 514-0049
  Sand Springs *(G-8223)*

PRODUCT SECTION

CONTRACTORS: Single-family Home General Remodeling

A&B Home Improvement	G	918 341-7410	
Claremore (G-1574)			
Buck Creek Homes Cnstr Inc	F	580 272-0102	
Ada (G-15)			
Milot James Residence Cnstr	G	405 433-2661	
Cashion (G-1291)			
Sooner Cabinet & Trim Inc	E	405 820-2920	
Moore (G-4571)			

CONTRACTORS: Skylight Installation

Skyview Products Inc .... G 405 745-6064
  Mustang (G-4794)

CONTRACTORS: Sound Eqpt Installation

Benson Sound Inc .... G 405 610-7455
  Oklahoma City (G-5553)

CONTRACTORS: Stone Masonry

Decorative Rock & Stone Inc .... G 405 672-2564
  Oklahoma City (G-5916)

CONTRACTORS: Storage Tank Erection, Metal

Hmt LLC .... G 580 363-8800
  Blackwell (G-683)
Platinum Arch Mfg & Cnstr LLC .... F 316 573-6814
  Stillwater (G-8739)

CONTRACTORS: Structural Steel Erection

Bennett Steel Inc .... C 918 227-2564
  Sapulpa (G-8252)
Double H Welding .... G 918 653-2289
  Heavener (G-3427)
Ketchum Group LLC .... G 918 407-2228
  Jenks (G-3712)
Martin Manufacturing Inc .... E 918 583-1191
  Sapulpa (G-8287)
Redibuilt Metal Pdts & Cnstr .... G 580 225-2829
  Elk City (G-2867)
Wasinger Wasinger .... G 580 335-3490
  Frederick (G-3203)

CONTRACTORS: Svc Well Drilling Svcs

Baker Energy Solutions LLC .... G 405 691-1202
  Oklahoma City (G-5510)
Can Global Usa Inc .... F 405 261-0417
  Oklahoma City (G-5683)
L and A Filtration LLC .... G 580 380-2976
  Durant (G-2242)
Seismic Drilling Services LLC .... D 918 587-2225
  Tulsa (G-10723)
Sutherland Well Service Inc .... F 580 856-3538
  Ratliff City (G-8069)
Troy Hulett .... G 580 922-5298
  Cleo Springs (G-1713)
Vassal Well Services LLC .... F 580 279-1579
  Ada (G-101)
Woolslayer Companies Inc .... C 918 523-9191
  Catoosa (G-1368)

CONTRACTORS: Target Systems Installation

Charles Jones .... G 405 348-2187
  Edmond (G-2345)

CONTRACTORS: Tile Installation, Ceramic

American Millwork Company Inc .... E 405 681-5347
  Oklahoma City (G-5440)
Silex Interiors Inc .... G 918 836-5454
  Tulsa (G-10761)
Young Brothers Inc .... E 405 272-0821
  Oklahoma City (G-7482)

CONTRACTORS: Trenching

Heirston Welding & Cnstr .... G 580 657-2518
  Wilson (G-11235)

CONTRACTORS: Underground Utilities

Caswell Construction Co Inc .... D 580 225-6833
  Elk City (G-2793)
Evans & Assoc Utility Svcs .... G 580 351-1800
  Lawton (G-3924)

CONTRACTORS: Warm Air Heating & Air Conditioning

Butchers Metal Shop .... G 580 256-7660
  Woodward (G-11565)
Love Air Conditioning .... G 918 341-0508
  Claremore (G-1651)
Vogt Sheet Metal .... G 580 332-2454
  Ada (G-102)
Wright Comfort Solutions Inc .... G 580 688-3586
  Hollis (G-3572)

CONTRACTORS: Water Well Drilling

A W Pool Inc .... G 580 323-3454
  Clinton (G-1735)
Downing Manufacturing Inc .... F 918 224-1116
  Tulsa (G-9001)
Freds Rat Hole Service Inc .... F 405 756-4300
  Lindsay (G-4063)
Halliburton Company .... C 580 251-2847
  Duncan (G-2124)
J Grantham Drilling Inc .... G 918 647-8926
  Poteau (G-7907)
Karlin Company .... G 405 542-6991
  Hydro (G-3631)
Lamamco Drilling Co .... G 580 856-3561
  Ratliff City (G-8056)
Morgan Drilling Co .... G 580 657-3659
  Ardmore (G-336)

CONTRACTORS: Well Acidizing Svcs

Acid Inc .... E 580 363-5413
  Blackwell (G-673)
Acidizing & Cementing Service .... F 405 969-3093
  Crescent (G-1907)

CONTRACTORS: Well Bailing, Cleaning, Swabbing & Treating Svc

4k Spooling Banding Sales & SE .... F 918 766-0001
  Bartlesville (G-443)
AB Swabbing Incorporated .... G 219 765-3239
  El Reno (G-2695)
Dywy Spooling LLC .... G 405 469-4148
  Byars (G-1222)
R & S Swabbing Inc .... G 405 853-5445
  Hennessey (G-3480)
R M Swabbing LLC .... G 405 828-7213
  Dover (G-2043)
Sooner Swabbing Services Inc .... G 580 233-4347
  Enid (G-3059)
Superior Spooling LLC .... G 405 613-0329
  Purcell (G-8022)

CONTRACTORS: Well Casings Perforating Svcs

Computalog Wireline Inc .... G 918 225-1187
  Cushing (G-1926)
Midwest Logging & Perforating .... G 405 382-4200
  Seminole (G-8384)
Sharpshooters Inc .... G 580 332-3109
  Ada (G-85)

CONTRACTORS: Well Chemical Treating Svcs

Resource Services Inc .... G 918 799-6174
  Stigler (G-8642)

CONTRACTORS: Well Cleaning Svcs

Tank Trucks Inc .... G 918 224-7515
  Sapulpa (G-8314)

CONTRACTORS: Well Logging Svcs

Arbuckle Wireline .... G 405 620-6739
  Edmond (G-2308)
Datalog Lwt Inc .... G 405 286-0418
  Oklahoma City (G-5900)
Drumright Oil Well Servic .... G 918 704-0252
  Henryetta (G-3505)
Frontier Logging Corporation .... G 405 787-3952
  Oklahoma City (G-6122)
Halliburton Company .... C 580 251-3002
  Duncan (G-2122)
Johnson Well Logging Inc .... G 405 721-5989
  Oklahoma City (G-6377)

CONTRACTORS: Well Swabbing Svcs

D & T Swabbing & Well Service .... G 405 853-7045
  Hennessey (G-3456)
Liberty Swabbing Inc .... G 405 828-4427
  Dover (G-2041)
Rayco Paraffin Service Inc .... G 405 853-2055
  Hennessey (G-3482)
Swabbing Johns LLC .... F 405 756-8141
  Lindsay (G-4091)

CONTRACTORS: Window Treatment Installation

Solar View LLC .... G 918 366-6413
  Bixby (G-660)

CONTRACTORS: Windows & Doors

Woodwork Productions LLC .... G 918 639-3167
  Catoosa (G-1367)

CONTRACTORS: Wrecking & Demolition

Fat & Happy Services Inc .... G 405 834-5782
  Oklahoma City (G-6078)
W&W Enterprises .... G 580 434-2736
  Colbert (G-1787)

CONTROL CIRCUIT DEVICES

Scudder Service & Supply Inc .... G 405 232-6069
  Oklahoma City (G-7101)

CONTROL EQPT: Electric

High Country Tek Inc .... E 530 265-3236
  Tulsa (G-9928)
K & S Controls LLC .... G 918 363-7268
  Sand Springs (G-8196)

CONTROL PANELS: Electrical

Adv-TEC Systems Inc .... G 918 542-4710
  Quapaw (G-8027)
Grace Power LLC .... G 512 228-9049
  Lawton (G-3936)
Industrial Cntrls Slutions LLC .... G 405 601-0625
  Oklahoma City (G-6296)
Paul King Company .... G 918 592-5464
  Tulsa (G-10475)
Poteau Panel Shop Incorporated .... G 918 647-4331
  Poteau (G-7912)
Terac Controls Inc .... E 918 622-6818
  Broken Arrow (G-1171)
Unicorp Systems Inc .... E 918 446-1874
  Tulsa (G-11034)

CONTROLS & ACCESS: Indl, Electric

Aae Automation Inc .... G 405 525-1100
  Oklahoma City (G-5355)

CONTROLS & ACCESS: Motor

Eaton Building Contractors .... G 918 273-9191
  Bartlesville (G-478)

CONTROLS: Automatic Temperature

Design Systems Inc .... G 405 341-7353
  Edmond (G-2390)
Hks Energy Solutions Inc .... F 918 279-6450
  Tulsa (G-9934)

CONTROLS: Crane & Hoist, Including Metal Mill

Nations Crane Sales Inc .... G 918 836-2000
  Tulsa (G-10327)

CONTROLS: Electric Motor

N P T Inc .... G 580 399-0306
  Ada (G-69)

CONTROLS: Environmental

Ademco Inc .... G 918 663-2822
  Tulsa (G-9104)
Ademco Inc .... G 405 681-4008
  Oklahoma City (G-5373)
Franklin Electric Co Inc .... B 918 465-2348
  Wilburton (G-11520)

Employee Codes: A=Over 500 employees, B=251-500
C=101-250, D=51-100, E=20-50, F=10-19, G=1-9

CONTROLS: Environmental

Kimray Inc	C	405 525-6601
Oklahoma City *(G-6417)*		
P F Services LLC	G	405 226-4871
Edmond *(G-2558)*		
Parnel Biogas Inc	F	918 294-3868
Glenpool *(G-3240)*		
Phoenix Group Holding Company	F	405 948-7788
Oklahoma City *(G-6844)*		

CONTROLS: Hydronic

Advantage Controls LLC	D	918 686-6211
Muskogee *(G-4643)*		

CONTROLS: Relay & Ind

3d Farms & Machine L L C	G	580 772-5543
Weatherford *(G-11386)*		
ABB Inc	C	918 338-4888
Bartlesville *(G-444)*		
Bob Brooks Motor Company	C	405 681-2592
Oklahoma City *(G-5600)*		
Buttons Auto Electrical Supply	G	580 223-3855
Ardmore *(G-261)*		
D C Ignition Co Inc	G	580 332-0878
Ada *(G-28)*		
Datalog Systems	G	918 245-3939
Tulsa *(G-9554)*		
Eaton and Associates LLC	G	405 307-9631
Norman *(G-4987)*		
Evans Enterprises Inc	C	405 631-1344
Norman *(G-4993)*		
Fife Corporation	C	405 755-1600
Oklahoma City *(G-6084)*		
Fw Murphy Prod Contrls LLC	G	918 317-4280
Tulsa *(G-9787)*		
G P Enterprises	G	405 340-8986
Edmond *(G-2428)*		
Hetronic Usa Inc	E	405 946-3574
Oklahoma City *(G-6245)*		
John Crane Inc	D	918 664-5156
Tulsa *(G-10049)*		
Paytons Auto	G	918 540-2501
Miami *(G-4427)*		
Poteau Panel Shop Incorporated	G	918 647-4331
Poteau *(G-7912)*		
Process Products & Service Co	G	918 827-4998
Mounds *(G-4623)*		
Realtime Automation Inc	G	918 249-9217
Broken Arrow *(G-1028)*		
Remote Connections Inc	F	918 743-3355
Tulsa *(G-10639)*		
Repair Processes Inc	F	918 758-0863
Okmulgee *(G-7525)*		
Southwest Electric Co	F	918 437-9494
Tulsa *(G-10805)*		
Versatech Industries Inc	G	918 366-7400
Bixby *(G-670)*		

CONTROLS: Truck, Indl Battery

Pro Battery Inc	G	918 437-1920
Tulsa *(G-10564)*		

CONVENIENCE STORES

50th Xpress Mart	G	405 491-7381
Warr Acres *(G-11310)*		
Anchor Gasoline Corporation	D	918 584-5291
Tulsa *(G-9184)*		
Mobonoto Automotive LLC	G	580 480-0410
Altus *(G-163)*		
Quiktrip Corporation	B	918 615-7700
Tulsa *(G-10599)*		

CONVERTERS: Data

News OK LLC	F	405 475-4000
Oklahoma City *(G-6671)*		

CONVERTERS: Power, AC to DC

Better Power Inc	G	405 753-1192
Oklahoma City *(G-5560)*		
Maverick Technologies LLC	F	405 680-0100
Oklahoma City *(G-6537)*		

CONVEYOR SYSTEMS: Belt, General Indl Use

Fki Industries Inc	G	918 834-4611
Tulsa *(G-9752)*		

CONVEYORS & CONVEYING EQPT

Chickasaw Nation Inds Inc	D	580 276-3305
Marietta *(G-4203)*		
Clean Products Inc	G	405 382-1441
Seminole *(G-8364)*		
Marietta Filtra Systems	G	580 276-3306
Marietta *(G-4209)*		
Redback Energy Services LLC	E	405 265-4608
Oklahoma City *(G-6992)*		
Thompson Manufacturing Company	G	918 585-1991
Tulsa *(G-10935)*		

CONVEYORS: Overhead

Overhead Door Solutions LLC	G	918 686-8847
Muskogee *(G-4729)*		

COOKING & FOOD WARMING EQPT: Commercial

Council Stainless & Shtmtl	G	405 787-4400
Oklahoma City *(G-5842)*		
Industrial Service Providers	F	580 319-7417
Ardmore *(G-308)*		

COOKING & FOODWARMING EQPT: Coffee Brewing

Continental-Brokers & Cons Inc	E	405 232-1534
Oklahoma City *(G-5824)*		

COOKING & FOODWARMING EQPT: Popcorn Machines, Commercial

Concessions Mfg Co LLC	G	918 786-5100
Grove *(G-3262)*		

COOKING EQPT, HOUSEHOLD: Ranges, Gas

Nuckolls Distributing Inc	G	918 663-0555
Tulsa *(G-10367)*		
Whirlpool Corporation	B	918 274-6000
Tulsa *(G-11115)*		

COOLERS & ICE CHESTS: Polystyrene Foam

Taylor Foam Inc	G	405 787-5811
Oklahoma City *(G-7258)*		
Tbk Industries LLC	G	405 789-6940
Bethany *(G-598)*		

COOLING TOWERS: Metal

Service Tech Coolg Towers LLC	F	405 222-0722
Chickasha *(G-1508)*		

COOLING TOWERS: Wood

Midwest Cooling Towers Inc	G	580 389-5421
Ardmore *(G-332)*		
Midwest Cooling Towers Inc	C	405 224-4622
Chickasha *(G-1486)*		

COOPERAGE STOCK PRODUCTS

Farmers Coop Gin of Martha	G	580 266-3222
Martha *(G-4251)*		

COPPER: Rolling & Drawing

Albright Steel and Wire Co	F	405 232-7526
Oklahoma City *(G-5410)*		

COPY MACHINES WHOLESALERS

Chaddick & Associates Inc	F	580 223-1202
Ardmore *(G-264)*		

CORK & CORK PRDTS: Bottle

Cork and Bottle Wine and	G	405 318-6842
Yukon *(G-11713)*		

CORRUGATED PRDTS: Boxes, Partition, Display Items, Sheet/Pad

Stan-Mel Industries Inc	E	918 436-0056
Pocola *(G-7787)*		

COSMETIC PREPARATIONS

Snuffy Scents LLC	G	405 850-6889
Mustang *(G-4795)*		

COSMETICS & TOILETRIES

A Plus Scrubs To You	G	918 691-0556
Tulsa *(G-9069)*		
American Beauty Manufacturing	G	918 671-0351
Tulsa *(G-9165)*		
Bath & Body Works LLC	E	405 748-3197
Oklahoma City *(G-5529)*		
Cleoptraz Scretz Hndmade Soaps	G	918 272-3319
Tulsa *(G-9452)*		
Coolbodispa	G	405 420-9785
Norman *(G-4965)*		
Cypress Scents	G	918 629-8610
Inola *(G-3657)*		
Estee Lauder Companies Inc	G	405 949-9757
Oklahoma City *(G-6053)*		
Hoffman Essentials	G	918 485-4679
Wagoner *(G-11284)*		
Lavishea LLC	G	303 805-0805
Broken Arrow *(G-1138)*		
Mah Industries LLC	G	918 540-0656
Miami *(G-4411)*		
Mere Minerals	G	918 902-3156
Broken Arrow *(G-970)*		
Moore Scents LLC	G	405 642-5472
Yukon *(G-11757)*		
Natures Light LLC	G	925 209-1766
Broken Arrow *(G-986)*		
Outback Laboratories	G	405 527-6355
Lexington *(G-4038)*		
Pointer Waddell & Associates	G	405 942-5600
Oklahoma City *(G-6862)*		
Raymac Corp	G	918 752-0002
Okmulgee *(G-7524)*		
Scents In Soy Naturals	G	918 269-8322
Jenks *(G-3727)*		
Simply Scentsational	G	918 691-8027
Broken Arrow *(G-1052)*		
Sugar Sisters LLC	G	405 722-9266
Nichols Hills *(G-4863)*		
Sweet Organic Scrubs & More	G	203 465-2683
Oklahoma City *(G-7235)*		
Sweet Scrubs LLC	G	918 513-1176
Tulsa *(G-10884)*		
Valhoma Corporation	E	918 836-7135
Tulsa *(G-11064)*		

COSTUME JEWELRY & NOVELTIES: Apparel, Exc Precious Metals

Kathys Kloset Inc	G	405 524-9447
Oklahoma City *(G-6401)*		
Kathys Kloset Inc	F	405 521-0055
Oklahoma City *(G-6402)*		

COSTUME JEWELRY & NOVELTIES: Bracelets, Exc Precious Metals

Bracelets For Baby	G	918 625-0088
Owasso *(G-7549)*		

COSTUME JEWELRY & NOVELTIES: Exc Semi & Precious

Staudt Jewelers	G	918 756-0517
Okmulgee *(G-7526)*		

COSTUME JEWELRY STORES

Accessories-To-Go	G	580 467-7408
Comanche *(G-1833)*		
Curtis Jewelry	G	580 924-0041
Durant *(G-2219)*		

COSTUMES & WIGS STORES

Dean Johnson	G	405 947-5736
Oklahoma City *(G-5911)*		

COUNCIL FOR SOCIAL AGENCY

Newview Oklahoma Inc	D	405 232-4644
Oklahoma City *(G-6672)*		

COUNTER & SINK TOPS

Breshears Enterprises Inc	F	405 236-4523
Oklahoma City *(G-5624)*		
Continental Stoneworks Inc	F	918 835-6725
Tulsa *(G-9479)*		
Countertop Werks Inc	E	405 943-1988
Oklahoma City *(G-5843)*		

PRODUCT SECTION

Eurocraft Ltd ..... E 918 322-5500
  Glenpool (G-3234)
Red Rock Fabrication ..... G 405 602-4602
  Edmond (G-2591)
Rivers Edge Countertops Inc ..... G 405 532-3180
  Tuttle (G-11211)
Zimmermans Custom Design Inc ..... G 918 486-4179
  Coweta (G-1903)

COUNTERS OR COUNTER DISPLAY CASES, WOOD

Hoffman Fixtures Company ..... E 918 252-0451
  Tulsa (G-9936)

COUPLINGS: Pipe

Coupling Specialties Inc ..... F 281 457-2000
  Oklahoma City (G-5845)

COURIER SVCS: Ground

Quik-Print of Oklahoma City ..... G 405 840-3275
  Oklahoma City (G-6950)

COURT REPORTING SVCS

Wild Horse Distrubuting LLC ..... G 405 691-0755
  Oklahoma City (G-5323)

COVERS: Automobile Seat

Moss Seat Cover Mfg & Sls Co ..... F 918 742-3326
  Tulsa (G-10306)
Speer Cushion Co ..... G 970 854-2911
  Bixby (G-664)

CRACKED CASTING REPAIR SVCS

S & T Mfg Co ..... E 918 234-4151
  Tulsa (G-10684)

CRANE & AERIAL LIFT SVCS

Central States Crane Hoist LLC ..... F 918 341-2320
  Claremore (G-1603)
Eddie Johnsons Wldg & Mch Co ..... F 580 856-3418
  Ratliff City (G-8051)
R&R Roustabout Services LLC ..... E 580 883-4647
  Ringwood (G-8090)

CRANES & MONORAIL SYSTEMS

Ameracrane and Hoist LLC ..... E 918 437-4775
  Tulsa (G-9161)

CRANES: Indl Plant

Ramsey Industries Inc ..... C 918 438-2760
  Tulsa (G-10617)

CRANES: Indl Truck

Auto Crane Company ..... C 918 438-2760
  Tulsa (G-9226)

CRANES: Overhead

Central States Crane Hoist LLC ..... F 918 341-2320
  Claremore (G-1603)

CRANKSHAFTS & CAMSHAFTS: Machining

Accu-Turn Machine LLC ..... G 580 704-8876
  Lawton (G-3883)
Automted McHning Solutions LLC ..... G 405 697-6234
  Mustang (G-4762)
Kams Inc ..... F 405 232-3103
  Oklahoma City (G-6396)
SFM Incorporated ..... G 405 788-9453
  Tecumseh (G-8928)
Swearingen Machine Shop Inc ..... G 918 267-4308
  Beggs (G-562)
Synergy Sourcing Solutions LLC ..... G 918 835-5019
  Tulsa (G-10886)

CREDIT AGENCIES: Farmers Home Administration

McAllister Farms ..... G 580 512-9009
  Hollis (G-3567)

CREDIT CARD SVCS

Special Service Systems Inc ..... E 918 582-7777
  Tulsa (G-10816)

CREDIT INSTITUTIONS: Short-Term Business

Adams Affiliates Inc ..... F 918 582-7713
  Tulsa (G-9101)

CRUDE PETROLEUM & NATURAL GAS PRODUCTION

Arena Resources Inc ..... D 918 747-6060
  Tulsa (G-9207)
Bce - Mach III LLC ..... D 405 252-8100
  Oklahoma City (G-5536)
Bce-Mach II LLC ..... D 405 252-8100
  Oklahoma City (G-5537)
Bromide Inc ..... G 405 360-2999
  Norman (G-4945)
Ceja Corporation ..... E 918 648-5215
  Burbank (G-1214)
Cimarex Energy Co ..... G 580 330-0188
  Clinton (G-1743)
Compass Energy Operating LLC ..... D 405 594-4141
  Oklahoma City (G-5808)
David L Greene Inc ..... G 918 335-3855
  Bartlesville (G-474)
Djf Services Inc ..... G 405 380-7273
  Holdenville (G-3553)
Equal Energy US Inc ..... D 405 242-6000
  Tulsa (G-9694)
Gary L Deaton Corporation ..... G 405 521-8811
  Oklahoma City (G-6136)
Gulfport Energy Corporation ..... F 405 756-0060
  Lindsay (G-4065)
Heritage Petroleum Inc ..... G 405 377-2689
  Stillwater (G-8700)
Hinkle Oil and Gas ..... F 405 848-0924
  Oklahoma City (G-6251)
Horizon Natural Resources Inc ..... F 918 494-0790
  Tulsa (G-9949)
Inland Oil Corp ..... G 918 227-1180
  Sapulpa (G-8278)
J-W Power Company ..... G 580 254-5663
  Woodward (G-11596)
James R Biddick ..... G 918 587-1551
  Tulsa (G-10026)
Johnson Marcum Oil and Gas LLC ..... F 918 949-8901
  Muskogee (G-4701)
Jones Energy Inc ..... E 512 328-2953
  Oklahoma City (G-6382)
Knowcando Ltd ..... G 918 599-8600
  Tulsa (G-10098)
L & R Properties Inc ..... G 405 263-7404
  Okarche (G-5245)
Lamamco Drilling Company ..... G 580 336-3524
  Perry (G-7740)
Lamima Corp ..... G 918 491-6846
  Tulsa (G-10119)
Laredo Midstream Services LLC ..... B 918 513-4570
  Tulsa (G-10125)
Laredo Petroleum Inc ..... E 918 513-4570
  Tulsa (G-10126)
Larkin Energy Inc ..... F 405 941-3224
  Sasakwa (G-8331)
Liverpool Production Company ..... G 918 523-9595
  Tulsa (G-10170)
M Craig Deisenroth Oil & Gas ..... G 918 742-4769
  Tulsa (G-10188)
Madill Gas Processing Co LLC ..... F 580 795-7396
  Madill (G-4154)
Mexco Energy Corporation ..... G 405 330-4042
  Edmond (G-2516)
Ovintiv Exploration Inc ..... G 918 420-5086
  Mc Alester (G-4265)
Pelican Energy LLC ..... G 405 418-8000
  Oklahoma City (G-6823)
Performance Petroleum Co ..... E 918 847-2531
  Barnsdall (G-440)
Qep Energy Company ..... G 405 263-4831
  Okarche (G-5250)
R T C Resources LLP ..... G 580 774-2313
  Weatherford (G-11435)
Rainbow Oil & Gas Inc ..... G 918 335-2188
  Bartlesville (G-521)
Range Energy Services Company ..... F 580 227-3762
  Fairview (G-3148)
Romine Oil & Gas Ltd ..... G 405 273-1171
  Shawnee (G-8489)
Sandstone Enrgy Acqstions Corp ..... G 405 239-2150
  Oklahoma City (G-7083)
Semgroup Corporation ..... G 918 225-7758
  Cushing (G-1958)
Stream Line ..... G 405 756-4422
  Lindsay (G-4087)
Sunoco Logistics Partners LP ..... G 918 352-9442
  Drumright (G-2072)
Tilley Oil & Gas Inc ..... G 405 608-4970
  Oklahoma City (G-7289)
Truman F Logsdon ..... G 405 348-4504
  Edmond (G-2655)
Valiant Midstream LLC ..... G 405 286-5580
  Edmond (G-2665)
W F D Oil Corporation ..... G 405 715-3130
  Edmond (G-2677)
Walker Resources Inc ..... G 405 751-5357
  Oklahoma City (G-7414)
Warren American Oil Company ..... G 918 846-2294
  Barnsdall (G-442)
William W McClure Jr ..... G 918 747-6094
  Tulsa (G-11126)
Xto Energy Inc ..... G 580 668-2332
  Wilson (G-11546)

CRUDE PETROLEUM & NATURAL GAS PRODUCTION

A B N G Inc ..... F 405 222-0024
  Chickasha (G-1426)
Access Midstream Ventures LLC ..... E 405 935-3500
  Oklahoma City (G-5361)
Access Mlp Operating LLc ..... G 405 935-8000
  Oklahoma City (G-5362)
Aegeos Oilfield Technology LLC ..... G 918 906-4328
  Owasso (G-7542)
Agape Inc ..... G 918 455-9516
  Broken Arrow (G-820)
Angel Exploration ..... G 405 848-8360
  Oklahoma City (G-5445)
Avalon Operating LLC ..... G 918 523-0600
  Tulsa (G-9228)
B & B Resources ..... G 918 495-1128
  Tulsa (G-9240)
Bandon Oil & Gas GP LLC ..... G 405 429-5500
  Oklahoma City (G-5524)
Banner Pipeline Company LLC ..... G 580 233-8955
  Enid (G-2913)
Billy Carroll ..... G 918 352-9228
  Drumright (G-2053)
Black Bayou Exploration LLC ..... G 405 753-5500
  Oklahoma City (G-5579)
Blackburn Oil & Gas Inc ..... G 918 688-1067
  Pawnee (G-7701)
Blue Mountain Midstream LLC ..... G 281 377-8770
  Oklahoma City (G-5593)
Bog Resources LLC ..... G 918 592-1010
  Tulsa (G-9317)
Brians Hot Oil Service ..... G 580 431-2070
  Cherokee (G-1414)
Calyx Energy III LLC ..... F 918 949-4224
  Tulsa (G-9365)
Cbhc Resources Inc ..... G 405 905-9791
  Oklahoma City (G-5716)
Centerpint Enrgy Rsources Corp ..... G 580 512-5903
  McAlester (G-4279)
Centurion Pipeline LP ..... G 405 262-4750
  El Reno (G-2705)
Choctaw Travel Plaza ..... G 580 920-2186
  Durant (G-2214)
Cimarron River Operation Corp ..... G 918 633-2911
  Mannford (G-4179)
Clark Ellison ..... G 405 525-3583
  Oklahoma City (G-5775)
Clearwter Entps LLC Ntural Gas ..... G 918 296-7007
  Jenks (G-3699)
Colston Corporation ..... G 580 223-1309
  Ardmore (G-269)
Columbia Development Corp ..... G 918 587-5521
  Tulsa (G-9472)
Conocophillips Company ..... F 580 243-6000
  Elk City (G-2795)
Continental Oil & Refining Co ..... G 918 266-4420
  Catoosa (G-1313)
Cornerstone Petroleum Oper LLC ..... G 817 730-5200
  Tulsa (G-9489)
Cyanostar Energy Inc ..... G 918 582-2069
  Tulsa (G-9531)

David Denham Interiors.....G..... 918 585-3161
Tulsa *(G-9557)*
Deeprock Oil Operating LLC.....G..... 918 225-7100
Cushing *(G-1930)*
Devon Energy Corporation.....F..... 405 235-3611
Oklahoma City *(G-5930)*
Diamondback E&P LLC.....E..... 432 221-7400
Oklahoma City *(G-5939)*
Dome Blue Operating LLC.....G..... 918 583-3333
Tulsa *(G-9592)*
E Lyle Johnson Inc.....G..... 405 470-2047
Bethany *(G-577)*
Eagle Rock Energy Partners LP.....G..... 281 408-1467
Tulsa *(G-9629)*
Enable Midstream Partners LP.....G..... 580 225-7190
Elk City *(G-2811)*
Enable Oklahoma Int Transm LLC.....G..... 580 661-2266
Thomas *(G-8943)*
Enerfin Resources I Ltd Partnr.....E..... 405 382-3049
Seminole *(G-8371)*
Energyvest Inc.....F..... 918 549-1838
Tulsa *(G-9684)*
Enerlabs Inc.....G..... 405 879-1752
Oklahoma City *(G-6040)*
Flywheel Energy LLC.....G..... 405 702-6991
Oklahoma City *(G-6095)*
Flywheel Energy Operating LLC.....G..... 405 702-6991
Oklahoma City *(G-6097)*
Fox Northeastern Oil Gas Corp.....G..... 918 331-7791
Bartlesville *(G-484)*
Fred M Buxton.....G..... 405 840-4331
Oklahoma City *(G-6115)*
French Oil.....G..... 580 248-3131
Lawton *(G-3930)*
Gary M Lake & Company.....G..... 405 340-6138
Edmond *(G-2429)*
Gh Land Co.....G..... 405 947-5500
Oklahoma City *(G-6150)*
H S Milam.....G..... 918 789-2666
Chelsea *(G-1405)*
Haub Oil and Gas LLC.....G..... 580 765-3585
Ponca City *(G-7834)*
Infinity Resources LLC.....G..... 405 767-3519
Oklahoma City *(G-6303)*
Jones Energy Inc.....G..... 405 832-5100
Oklahoma City *(G-6381)*
Jones Energy Finance Corp.....G..... 512 328-2953
Oklahoma City *(G-6383)*
Kaiser Investment.....G..... 918 245-4719
Sand Springs *(G-8197)*
Kaiser-Francis Oil Company.....F..... 405 577-5347
Oklahoma City *(G-6395)*
Kaiser-Francis Oil Company.....C..... 918 494-0000
Tulsa *(G-10074)*
Kay Production Co Inc.....G..... 405 398-4254
Bowlegs *(G-759)*
Kencan Flowback LLC.....G..... 580 429-8913
Cache *(G-1228)*
King Properties Inc.....G..... 918 366-6868
Bixby *(G-641)*
Kopco Inc.....G..... 405 743-3290
Stillwater *(G-8715)*
L L Wilkins E and O Co.....G..... 405 273-3008
Shawnee *(G-8466)*
Lakewood Energy Solutions LLC.....F..... 918 392-9356
Tulsa *(G-10115)*
Lakewood Energy Solutions LLC.....G..... 918 392-9356
Verden *(G-11237)*
Laredo Petroleum LLC.....E..... 918 513-4570
Tulsa *(G-10127)*
Linn Energy Inc.....D..... 405 241-2100
Oklahoma City *(G-6481)*
Lucky Four Oil Company.....G..... 405 941-3307
Sasakwa *(G-8332)*
Lyons & Lyons Inc.....G..... 918 587-2497
Tulsa *(G-10186)*
M&T Production Co.....G..... 918 227-1528
Tulsa *(G-10192)*
Markwest Energy Partners LP.....G..... 580 225-5400
Elk City *(G-2845)*
Markwest Oklahoma Gas Co LLC.....E..... 580 225-5400
Elk City *(G-2846)*
Mayabb Oil Co Inc.....G..... 918 396-2654
Skiatook *(G-8560)*
Mercer Petroleum Management.....G..... 405 341-1110
Edmond *(G-2513)*
Mid-Con Energy Gp LLC.....D..... 972 479-5980
Tulsa *(G-10257)*
Mineral Resources Company.....G..... 405 234-9000
Oklahoma City *(G-6615)*
Monty L Hott Production Corp.....G..... 405 495-3311
Oklahoma City *(G-6628)*
MRC Global (us) Inc.....F..... 405 491-7392
El Reno *(G-2740)*
Musgrove Energy Inc.....G..... 580 765-7314
Ponca City *(G-7856)*
Mw Engineering Co.....G..... 405 273-0370
Shawnee *(G-8478)*
Noco Investment Co Inc.....G..... 918 582-0090
Tulsa *(G-10346)*
Nosley Scoop LLC.....G..... 512 328-2953
Oklahoma City *(G-6697)*
Oilfield R T.....G..... 405 238-2026
Pauls Valley *(G-7669)*
Oky Investments Inc.....G..... 405 850-4533
Edmond *(G-2555)*
Oneok Inc.....A..... 918 588-7000
Tulsa *(G-10421)*
Oneok Gas Processing LLC.....G..... 918 588-7000
Tulsa *(G-10424)*
Oneok Gas Transportation LLC.....C..... 918 588-7000
Tulsa *(G-10425)*
Perkins Development Corp.....G..... 918 749-2152
Tulsa *(G-10495)*
Pressburg LLC.....G..... 405 896-8050
Oklahoma City *(G-6891)*
Primeenergy Corporation.....F..... 405 942-2897
Oklahoma City *(G-6894)*
Primeenergy Corporation.....E..... 405 375-5203
Oklahoma City *(G-6895)*
Red Fork Motor Co.....G..... 918 587-2778
Tulsa *(G-10630)*
Rick Davis.....G..... 918 733-4760
Morris *(G-4602)*
Rocky Mountain Prod Co LLC.....G..... 405 720-2000
Oklahoma City *(G-7046)*
Rose Rock Midstream Corp.....G..... 918 524-8100
Tulsa *(G-10671)*
Rose Rock Midstream Oper LLC.....G..... 918 524-7700
Tulsa *(G-10673)*
Samedan Oil Corp.....G..... 580 856-3705
Ratliff City *(G-8066)*
Sams Well Service Inc.....F..... 580 762-6355
Ponca City *(G-7871)*
Samson Resources II LLC.....G..... 918 591-1791
Tulsa *(G-10698)*
Samson Resources II Opco LLC.....G..... 918 591-1791
Tulsa *(G-10699)*
Sariel Inc.....G..... 918 855-1400
Tulsa *(G-10709)*
Scissortail Energy LLC.....F..... 918 588-5000
Tulsa *(G-10716)*
Scissortail Energy LLC.....G..... 918 968-0422
Stroud *(G-8818)*
Sierra Madera Co2 Pipeline LLC.....G..... 405 753-5500
Oklahoma City *(G-7129)*
Spyglass Energy Group LLC.....G..... 918 582-9900
Tulsa *(G-10828)*
Ssb Production LLC.....G..... 580 226-7000
Ardmore *(G-362)*
Stateline Processing LLC.....E..... 855 979-2012
Tulsa *(G-10839)*
Stateline Water LLC.....E..... 855 979-2012
Tulsa *(G-10840)*
Stonebridge Partnership 1 LP.....G..... 918 747-7594
Tulsa *(G-10854)*
T & K Oil Inc.....G..... 405 382-5241
Seminole *(G-8402)*
Technical Energy Services Inc.....G..... 405 329-8196
Norman *(G-5171)*
Templar Operating LLC.....F..... 405 548-1200
Oklahoma City *(G-7267)*
Total Well Solutions LLC.....G..... 918 392-9352
Tulsa *(G-10961)*
Tpi Petroleum Inc.....C..... 580 221-6288
Ardmore *(G-373)*
Tri Resources Inc.....E..... 580 493-2249
Waukomis *(G-11360)*
Triad Operating Corporation.....F..... 405 842-4312
Oklahoma City *(G-7326)*
Twin Eagle Midstream LLC.....G..... 918 459-4548
Tulsa *(G-11024)*
Wachtman-Schroeder.....G..... 918 287-3122
Pawhuska *(G-7697)*
Warwick Energy Group LLC.....E..... 972 351-2740
Oklahoma City *(G-7424)*
Warwick Energy Inv Group LLC.....E..... 405 607-3400
Oklahoma City *(G-7425)*
Weaver Energy Corporation.....G..... 405 853-6068
Hennessey *(G-3498)*
Westfall Producing Company.....G..... 918 743-1192
Tulsa *(G-11111)*
Wildhorse Oil & Gas Corp.....G..... 580 223-0936
Ardmore *(G-382)*
William Pettit.....F..... 918 297-2564
Hartshorne *(G-3396)*
Williams Field Services Co LLC.....C..... 918 573-2000
Tulsa *(G-11129)*
Williams MBL Bay Prod Svcs LLC.....G..... 918 573-2000
Tulsa *(G-11131)*
Wpx Energy Inc.....D..... 855 979-2012
Tulsa *(G-11155)*
Wpx Energy Keystone LLC.....F..... 918 573-2000
Tulsa *(G-11157)*
Wpx Energy Rm Company.....F..... 918 573-2000
Tulsa *(G-11161)*
Xae Corp.....G..... 405 452-5735
Wetumka *(G-11496)*
Xplorer Midstream LLC.....F..... 918 237-5885
Oklahoma City *(G-7478)*
Yukon Drilling Fluid Inc.....G..... 405 324-8876
Oklahoma City *(G-7483)*

CRUDE PETROLEUM PRODUCTION

A & T Oil Company.....G..... 918 245-7358
Skiatook *(G-8530)*
Acott Oil Operations.....G..... 918 885-2736
Hominy *(G-3573)*
Adams Affiliates Inc.....F..... 918 582-7713
Tulsa *(G-9101)*
Alan L Lamb.....G..... 405 755-2233
Oklahoma City *(G-5409)*
Albert J Geiger Revocable Tr.....G..... 918 446-6388
Tulsa *(G-9134)*
Altman Energy Inc.....G..... 918 584-4781
Tulsa *(G-9157)*
American Petro Mineral Co Inc.....G..... 405 382-1255
Seminole *(G-8354)*
American Petroleum Corporation.....F..... 580 856-3580
Ratliff City *(G-8048)*
Americana Energy Company Inc.....G..... 580 310-0084
Ada *(G-7)*
Anstine-Musgrove.....G..... 580 762-6355
Ponca City *(G-7796)*
Apache Corporation.....E..... 405 222-5040
Chickasha *(G-1431)*
Apc LLC.....G..... 918 587-6242
Tulsa *(G-9197)*
Arbuckle Enterprises Inc.....G..... 405 359-2815
Edmond *(G-2307)*
Ardmore Prod & Exploration.....G..... 580 223-2292
Ardmore *(G-249)*
Arnold Oil Properties LLC.....F..... 405 842-1488
Oklahoma City *(G-5468)*
Arrow Oil & Gas Inc.....G..... 405 364-2601
Norman *(G-4918)*
Avalon Exploration Inc.....F..... 918 523-0600
Tulsa *(G-9227)*
Azure Energy Ltd.....G..... 918 712-2727
Tulsa *(G-9236)*
B B Royalty Company.....G..... 405 672-3381
Oklahoma City *(G-5504)*
B R Polk Inc.....G..... 405 286-9666
Oklahoma City *(G-5505)*
Bale Corporation.....G..... 405 848-8797
Oklahoma City *(G-5520)*
Banner Oil & Gas LLC.....G..... 405 642-4382
Tulsa *(G-9263)*
Barbour Energy Corporation.....G..... 405 848-7671
Oklahoma City *(G-5527)*
Barnes Oil Co.....G..... 918 352-2308
Drumright *(G-2051)*
Baron Exploration Co Inc.....G..... 405 341-1779
Edmond *(G-2317)*
Barrett Drilling Company.....G..... 405 273-6217
Shawnee *(G-8430)*
Barrett Oil Company.....G..... 580 436-1896
Ada *(G-11)*
Bays Enterprises Inc.....G..... 405 235-2297
Oklahoma City *(G-5532)*
Baytide Petroleum Inc.....F..... 918 585-8150
Tulsa *(G-9273)*
Bbr Oil Corp.....G..... 580 223-2887
Ardmore *(G-254)*
Beck Resources Incorporated.....E..... 405 853-2736
Hennessey *(G-3446)*
Beckham and Butler.....G..... 918 885-4406
Hominy *(G-3576)*
Becks Farm Equipment Inc.....G..... 405 282-1196
Guthrie *(G-3299)*

Bell & Kinley Company..........G....... 405 373-5356
Piedmont *(G-7756)*
Benson Mineral Group Inc..........G....... 918 762-3651
Pawnee *(G-7700)*
Berexco LLC..........F....... 918 352-2588
Drumright *(G-2052)*
Beta Oil Company..........G....... 405 601-3389
Oklahoma City *(G-5559)*
Bill Weems Oil Inc..........G....... 405 382-1813
Seminole *(G-8358)*
Binger Operations LLC..........G....... 405 232-0201
Oklahoma City *(G-5570)*
Bkep Crude LLC..........B....... 405 278-6452
Oklahoma City *(G-5578)*
Blair Oil Co Inc..........G....... 405 263-4445
Kingfisher *(G-3785)*
Blake Production Company Inc..........G....... 405 286-9800
Oklahoma City *(G-5584)*
Bluegrass Energy Inc..........G....... 918 743-8060
Tulsa *(G-9308)*
Bo Mc Resources Corporation..........G....... 580 237-2324
Enid *(G-2920)*
Bob & Son Oil Co Inc..........G....... 405 853-6261
Hennessey *(G-3447)*
Bob Clemishire Oil Co..........G....... 918 885-4755
Hominy *(G-3577)*
Bob Gene Moore..........G....... 918 371-4381
Collinsville *(G-1804)*
Bobby J Darnell..........G....... 405 524-8891
Oklahoma City *(G-5603)*
Bogo Energy Corporation..........G....... 405 840-1067
Oklahoma City *(G-5615)*
Bogo Energy Corporation..........G....... 580 237-3756
Enid *(G-2921)*
Boje Oil Co..........G....... 918 885-2456
Hominy *(G-3579)*
Boyles & Associates Inc..........G....... 580 353-7056
Lawton *(G-3899)*
BP America Production Company..........F....... 918 465-2343
Wilburton *(G-11518)*
Brady Oil Company Inc..........G....... 405 941-3368
Sasakwa *(G-8329)*
Bratco Operating Company..........F....... 918 534-2322
Dewey *(G-2018)*
Breeze Investments LLC..........G....... 918 492-5090
Tulsa *(G-9334)*
Brg Production Company..........E....... 918 496-2626
Tulsa *(G-9337)*
Brg Production Company..........G....... 580 233-9302
Enid *(G-2922)*
Briscoe Oil Co..........G....... 405 375-3700
Kingfisher *(G-3786)*
Brower Oil & Gas Co Inc..........G....... 918 298-7200
Jenks *(G-3695)*
Brown & Borelli Inc..........G....... 405 375-5788
Kingfisher *(G-3787)*
Bud Oil Inc..........G....... 580 251-1378
Duncan *(G-2092)*
Bullseye Operating LLC..........G....... 918 336-7898
Bartlesville *(G-458)*
Butkin Oil Co LLC..........F....... 580 444-2561
Duncan *(G-2093)*
C & L Oil and Gas Corporation..........G....... 405 364-1950
Norman *(G-4950)*
C C McMillin & Company Inc..........G....... 405 282-3637
Guthrie *(G-3304)*
C E Harmon Oil Inc..........F....... 918 663-8515
Tulsa *(G-9359)*
C&Y Caseing Pulling Co Inc..........G....... 580 255-4453
Duncan *(G-2096)*
Calumet Oil Co..........G....... 405 478-8770
Oklahoma City *(G-5674)*
Calvert Company..........G....... 405 848-2222
Oklahoma City *(G-5675)*
Canaan Natural Gas Corp..........F....... 405 604-9300
Oklahoma City *(G-5685)*
Capital Risk Management Corp..........G....... 405 848-5420
Oklahoma City *(G-5692)*
Caprock Inc..........G....... 580 255-0831
Duncan *(G-2098)*
Carl A Nilsen..........G....... 405 236-4554
Oklahoma City *(G-5701)*
Carl E Gungoll Exploration LLC..........F....... 405 848-7898
Oklahoma City *(G-5702)*
Carnes Petroleum Corporation..........G....... 918 358-2541
Cleveland *(G-1718)*
Cascade Oil LLC..........G....... 405 236-4554
Edmond *(G-2338)*
Castlerock Resources Inc..........G....... 405 842-4249
Oklahoma City *(G-5710)*
Cei Petroleum Inc..........G....... 918 582-4284
Tulsa *(G-9393)*
Ceja Corporation..........E....... 918 496-0770
Tulsa *(G-9394)*
Centaur Resources Inc..........G....... 405 603-8800
Oklahoma City *(G-5723)*
Centrex Operating Co Inc..........G....... 918 747-9997
Tulsa *(G-9397)*
Champlin Exploration Inc..........G....... 580 233-1155
Enid *(G-2928)*
Chaparral Energy Inc..........E....... 918 793-2881
Shidler *(G-8525)*
Chaparral Energy Inc..........F....... 918 287-2977
Pawhuska *(G-7682)*
Chaparral Energy Inc..........E....... 580 673-2815
Healdton *(G-3410)*
Chaparral Energy Inc..........D....... 405 478-8770
Oklahoma City *(G-5739)*
Chaparral Energy LLC..........C....... 405 478-8770
Oklahoma City *(G-5740)*
Chaparral Exploration LLC..........G....... 405 426-4449
Oklahoma City *(G-5741)*
Charles F Doornbos Revocable T..........G....... 918 336-0611
Bartlesville *(G-461)*
Charles H Colpitt..........G....... 918 371-2455
Collinsville *(G-1805)*
Cher Oil Company Inc..........G....... 405 454-1575
Ripley *(G-8099)*
Chermac Energy Corporation..........F....... 405 341-3506
Edmond *(G-2348)*
Chesapeake Energy Corporation..........E....... 877 245-1427
Elk City *(G-2794)*
Chesapeake Energy Corporation..........A....... 405 848-8000
Oklahoma City *(G-5751)*
Chesapeake Exploration LLC..........B....... 405 848-8000
Oklahoma City *(G-5754)*
Chesapeake Louisiana LP..........B....... 405 848-8000
Oklahoma City *(G-5755)*
Chesapeake Midstream Dev LP..........G....... 405 935-8000
Oklahoma City *(G-5756)*
Chesapeake Operating LLC..........E....... 580 772-7255
Weatherford *(G-11399)*
Chesapeake Operating LLC..........F....... 405 375-6755
Kingfisher *(G-3789)*
Chesapeake Operating LLC..........F....... 405 375-6755
Kingfisher *(G-3790)*
Chesapeake Operating LLC..........A....... 405 848-8000
Oklahoma City *(G-5757)*
Chesapeake Operating LLC..........E....... 405 756-8700
Lindsay *(G-4056)*
Chester Oil Company..........G....... 405 379-2600
Wetumka *(G-11490)*
Chew Coast & Sons..........G....... 918 333-3318
Bartlesville *(G-464)*
Cheyenne Petro Co Ltd Partnr..........E....... 405 936-6220
Oklahoma City *(G-5758)*
Chk Cleveland Tonkawa LLC..........G....... 405 848-8000
Oklahoma City *(G-5761)*
Chk Louisiana LLC..........G....... 405 935-7871
Oklahoma City *(G-5762)*
Chris Hammon Oil Properties..........G....... 405 382-0250
Seminole *(G-8363)*
Christian Martin Lavery..........G....... 405 810-0900
Nichols Hills *(G-4857)*
Cirrus Production Company..........G....... 580 237-0002
Enid *(G-2930)*
Ciskoeagle Inc..........F....... 918 622-9010
Tulsa *(G-9432)*
Citation Oil & Gas Corp..........G....... 580 856-3014
Ratliff City *(G-8049)*
Citation Oil & Gas Corp..........E....... 580 229-1756
Healdton *(G-3411)*
Citation Oil & Gas Corp..........E....... 580 265-4534
Stonewall *(G-8799)*
Clements Exploration Co..........G....... 405 722-3100
Warr Acres *(G-11315)*
Coal Oil & Gas Company..........G....... 580 332-6170
Ada *(G-26)*
Cobra Oil & Gas Corporation..........G....... 580 254-2027
Woodward *(G-11569)*
Combined Resources Corporation..........G....... 405 341-7700
Edmond *(G-2361)*
Concorde Resource Corporation..........G....... 918 689-9510
Eufaula *(G-3099)*
Confed Oil Incorporated..........G....... 918 582-0018
Tulsa *(G-9477)*
Continental Resources Inc..........C....... 405 234-9000
Oklahoma City *(G-5823)*
Cornelius Oil Inc..........G....... 918 247-6743
Kellyville *(G-3762)*
Coronado Petroleum Corporation..........E....... 405 232-9700
Oklahoma City *(G-5837)*
Cove Petroleum Corporation..........G....... 918 584-5291
Tulsa *(G-9494)*
Covington Oil Co Inc..........G....... 405 842-8727
Oklahoma City *(G-5847)*
Crawley Petroleum Corporation..........C....... 405 232-9700
Oklahoma City *(G-5852)*
Crm Energy Inc..........G....... 405 848-5420
Oklahoma City *(G-5858)*
Cross Timbers Operating Co..........E....... 405 232-4011
Oklahoma City *(G-5859)*
CSC Oil Co..........G....... 918 287-1138
Pawhuska *(G-7684)*
Cummings Oil Company..........G....... 405 948-1818
Oklahoma City *(G-5866)*
Curzon Operating Company Ltd..........G....... 405 235-8180
Oklahoma City *(G-5871)*
D E M Operations Inc..........G....... 580 388-4315
Lamont *(G-3865)*
Darling Oil Corporation..........G....... 580 388-6681
Lamont *(G-3867)*
Darnell Drilling Inc..........G....... 405 524-8816
Oklahoma City *(G-5898)*
Daube Company..........F....... 580 223-7403
Ardmore *(G-274)*
Davco Productions Inc..........G....... 405 266-9832
Springer *(G-8621)*
Davis Bros Oil Producers Inc..........G....... 918 584-3581
Tulsa *(G-9559)*
Davis Gulf Coast Inc..........G....... 918 587-7782
Tulsa *(G-9560)*
Davis Oil Co..........G....... 918 333-5871
Bartlesville *(G-475)*
Dawson-Markwell Exploration Co..........G....... 405 232-0418
Oklahoma City *(G-5907)*
Deco Development Company Inc..........G....... 918 747-6366
Tulsa *(G-9566)*
Dehart Company..........G....... 580 223-7792
Ardmore *(G-278)*
Delphi International Inc..........G....... 918 749-9401
Tulsa *(G-9568)*
Demco Oil & Gas Company..........G....... 580 363-4223
Blackwell *(G-681)*
Denham Operating Co..........G....... 918 585-3161
Tulsa *(G-9572)*
Destin Corporation..........G....... 580 242-6627
Enid *(G-2940)*
Devon Energy Corporation..........C....... 405 235-3611
Oklahoma City *(G-5929)*
Devon Energy Production Co LP..........A....... 405 235-3611
Oklahoma City *(G-5932)*
Devon Gas Services LP..........G....... 405 228-7543
Oklahoma City *(G-5934)*
Devon Oei Operating Inc..........A....... 405 235-3611
Oklahoma City *(G-5936)*
Digger Oil & Gas Co..........G....... 405 567-2288
Prague *(G-7925)*
Doco Development Corp..........G....... 405 321-7493
Norman *(G-4982)*
Don Dennis..........G....... 580 662-3163
Grady *(G-3255)*
Doyle Cook..........F....... 405 257-3301
Wewoka *(G-11500)*
Dublin Petroleum Corp..........G....... 580 234-7718
Enid *(G-2945)*
Duncan Inc Walter..........E....... 405 272-1800
Oklahoma City *(G-5987)*
Duncan Oil & Gas Inc..........G....... 405 214-1108
Shawnee *(G-8446)*
Duncan Oil Properties Inc..........E....... 405 272-1800
Oklahoma City *(G-5988)*
Dunlap & Company..........G....... 580 223-8181
Ardmore *(G-281)*
Dyco Petroleum Corporation..........F....... 918 591-1917
Tulsa *(G-9616)*
Dyne Exploration Company..........G....... 405 245-0624
Tulsa *(G-9618)*
Eagle Resources Inc..........G....... 918 342-5733
Claremore *(G-1615)*
Eagle River Energy Corporation..........G....... 918 494-8928
Broken Arrow *(G-892)*
Earlsboro Energies Corporation..........G....... 405 848-2829
Oklahoma City *(G-5999)*
Ed Prentice..........G....... 580 857-2713
Allen *(G-134)*
Edinger Engineering Inc..........G....... 405 232-6315
Oklahoma City *(G-6010)*
Edward C Lawson Properties..........G....... 918 584-5155
Tulsa *(G-9645)*

Employee Codes: A=Over 500 employees, B=251-500
C=101-250, D=51-100, E=20-50, F=10-19, G=1-9
2020 Oklahoma Directory
of Manufacturers & Processors
721

Elson Oil Co....G.... 918 584-5225
Tulsa *(G-9663)*
Enable Okla Intrstate Trnsm LL....F.... 405 969-3906
Crescent *(G-1914)*
Energas Corp....E.... 405 879-1752
Oklahoma City *(G-6037)*
Enersource Petroleum Inc....G.... 918 446-8028
Tulsa *(G-9685)*
Eog Resources Inc....E.... 405 246-3100
Oklahoma City *(G-6048)*
Escher Corp....G.... 405 751-2893
Oklahoma City *(G-6050)*
Eskridge Production Co Inc....G.... 918 836-3058
Tulsa *(G-9700)*
Evans & Associates Entps Inc....E.... 580 765-6693
Ponca City *(G-7828)*
Exco Resources Inc....D.... 918 592-7300
Tulsa *(G-9715)*
Exok Inc....G.... 405 840-9196
Oklahoma City *(G-6062)*
Falcon Oil Properties....G.... 918 367-5596
Bristow *(G-777)*
Farmers Energy Corp....G.... 918 587-6756
Tulsa *(G-9729)*
Farmers Royalty Company....G.... 405 521-9685
Oklahoma City *(G-6075)*
First Stuart Corporation....G.... 918 744-5222
Tulsa *(G-9747)*
Ford Energy Corporation....G.... 405 224-3620
Chickasha *(G-1458)*
Forward Oil and Gas Inc....G.... 405 607-2247
Oklahoma City *(G-6106)*
Fossil Creek Energy Corp....G.... 405 949-0880
Oklahoma City *(G-6107)*
Four-O-One Corporation....G.... 405 848-0425
Edmond *(G-2419)*
Francis Oil & Gas Inc....G.... 918 491-4253
Tulsa *(G-9771)*
Frank K Young Oil Properties....G.... 405 340-2500
Edmond *(G-2421)*
Frank Priegel Co....G.... 918 756-3161
Okmulgee *(G-7502)*
Frank T Fleet Inc....G.... 580 332-1422
Ada *(G-37)*
Fredrick F Drummond....G.... 918 287-4400
Pawhuska *(G-7685)*
Frisco Energy LLC....G.... 918 742-5200
Tulsa *(G-9779)*
Frontier Land Co Inc....G.... 918 584-2050
Tulsa *(G-9783)*
Furseth G N Oil & Gas Producer....G.... 405 848-1232
Oklahoma City *(G-6127)*
G PC Inc....G.... 918 582-0018
Tulsa *(G-9793)*
Gbk Corporation....F.... 918 494-0000
Tulsa *(G-9809)*
Gemini Oil Co Inc....G.... 918 582-3935
Tulsa *(G-9814)*
Genie Oil & Gas Corporation....G.... 918 747-3675
Tulsa *(G-9819)*
Geoamerican Resources Inc....G.... 918 428-8665
Tulsa *(G-9821)*
Geodyne Production Company....G.... 918 583-1791
Tulsa *(G-9822)*
Gerald W Davidson LLC....G.... 580 336-9303
Perry *(G-7734)*
Ghk Company LLC....E.... 405 858-9800
Oklahoma City *(G-6151)*
Gill Operating Company....G.... 918 756-1873
Okmulgee *(G-7505)*
Gilliland Oil & Gas Inc....F.... 405 853-7116
Hennessey *(G-3463)*
Glacier Petroleum Co of Okla....G.... 405 840-2625
Edmond *(G-2436)*
Gloria Corp Inc....G.... 580 332-4050
Ada *(G-44)*
Godfrey Oil Properties....F.... 580 795-3087
Madill *(G-4148)*
Golsen Petroleum Corp....F.... 405 232-7033
Oklahoma City *(G-6170)*
Gomaco Inc....G.... 918 585-8077
Tulsa *(G-9840)*
Good Oil Company....F.... 580 233-3899
Enid *(G-2963)*
Gothic Production LLC....E.... 918 749-5666
Tulsa *(G-9843)*
Grand Resources Inc....E.... 918 492-2366
Tulsa *(G-9845)*
GRB Resources Inc....G.... 918 587-0036
Tulsa *(G-9852)*
Green Operating Company Inc....E.... 918 746-1700
Tulsa *(G-9862)*
Greer Oil Company....G.... 580 762-6355
Ponca City *(G-7833)*
Griffin Oil Properties LLC....G.... 580 226-0461
Ardmore *(G-298)*
Griffin Resources....G.... 405 853-4688
Hennessey *(G-3464)*
Guest Petroleum Incorporated....F.... 405 341-8698
Edmond *(G-2448)*
H & S Drilling Co....G.... 918 794-9944
Tulsa *(G-9875)*
H W Allen Co LLC....E.... 918 747-8700
Tulsa *(G-9877)*
Halcon Operating Co Inc....G.... 832 649-4015
Tulsa *(G-9880)*
Harding & Shelton Inc....F.... 405 236-0080
Oklahoma City *(G-6218)*
Harrell Energy Co....G.... 918 587-2750
Tulsa *(G-9893)*
Harrell Exploration Corp....G.... 918 587-2750
Tulsa *(G-9894)*
Harrell Verlan W Oil & Gas Co....G.... 405 272-9345
Oklahoma City *(G-6220)*
Hawkins International Inc....G.... 918 592-4422
Tulsa *(G-9903)*
Hawkins Oil Co LLc....G.... 918 382-7743
Tulsa *(G-9904)*
Hazelwood Inc....G.... 405 848-6884
Oklahoma City *(G-6228)*
Hazelwood Prod Exploration LLC....G.... 405 848-6884
Oklahoma City *(G-6229)*
Hazlewood Oil & Gas Co Inc....G.... 405 631-3532
Oklahoma City *(G-6230)*
Helen Murphy Colpitt Trust....G.... 918 371-9930
Collinsville *(G-1813)*
Hembree Lewis A Production Co....G.... 405 273-6137
Shawnee *(G-8459)*
Hendrie Resources Ltd....G.... 405 948-4459
Oklahoma City *(G-6239)*
Hillenburg Oil Co LLC....G.... 918 455-4444
Broken Arrow *(G-928)*
Hl Wirick Jr LLP....G.... 918 587-4548
Tulsa *(G-9935)*
Hodgden Operating Company Inc....G.... 580 233-2870
Enid *(G-2973)*
Hoke James T Jr Oil Producer....G.... 405 341-1779
Edmond *(G-2457)*
Holden Energy Corp....E.... 580 226-3960
Ardmore *(G-306)*
Hollrah Exploration Company....G.... 405 773-5440
Oklahoma City *(G-6258)*
Howard Engineering....G.... 918 396-3463
Skiatook *(G-8551)*
Hunton Oil and Gas Corp....G.... 405 848-5545
Oklahoma City *(G-6275)*
Hurd Oil Inc....G.... 918 846-2725
Wynona *(G-11680)*
Huston Energy Corporation....G.... 580 233-6030
Enid *(G-2975)*
Illinois Refining Co....G.... 918 367-5562
Bristow *(G-779)*
Ingram Exploration Inc....G.... 405 382-2040
Seminole *(G-8376)*
Ips....G.... 405 722-0896
Oklahoma City *(G-6326)*
J & F Oil Co....G.... 918 652-7957
Henryetta *(G-3509)*
J & M Investment....G.... 405 848-3755
Oklahoma City *(G-6332)*
J C N Petroleum Corp....G.... 405 341-8179
Edmond *(G-2465)*
J C Petroleum Inc....G.... 405 222-1412
Chickasha *(G-1473)*
J E & L E Mabee Foundation....F.... 918 584-4286
Tulsa *(G-10019)*
J M A Resources Inc....G.... 405 947-4322
Oklahoma City *(G-6336)*
J Walter Duncan Jr Oil Inc....E.... 405 272-1800
Oklahoma City *(G-6339)*
Jack Oil Company....G.... 580 255-2310
Duncan *(G-2132)*
James B Read Operating Inc....G.... 580 226-0055
Ardmore *(G-311)*
James H Milligan Enterprises....G.... 405 525-8331
Oklahoma City *(G-6348)*
James K Anderson Inc....G.... 405 329-7414
Norman *(G-5041)*
Jath Oil Co....C.... 580 252-5580
Duncan *(G-2133)*
Jerry Bendorf Trustee....G.... 405 840-9900
Oklahoma City *(G-6357)*
Jerry Sanner Oil Properties....G.... 580 233-2442
Enid *(G-2985)*
Jerry Scott Drilling Co Inc....G.... 405 382-2202
Seminole *(G-8379)*
Jetta Production Company Inc....G.... 918 299-0107
Tulsa *(G-10043)*
Jim Campbell & Associates Rlty....G.... 405 372-9225
Stillwater *(G-8707)*
Jim Haynes....G.... 918 733-2517
Haskell *(G-3399)*
John E Rougeot Oil & Gas....G.... 918 494-9978
Tulsa *(G-10051)*
John H Booth Inc....G.... 918 481-0383
Tulsa *(G-10052)*
John L Lewis....G.... 405 941-3224
Sasakwa *(G-8330)*
John M Beard....G.... 405 751-2727
Oklahoma City *(G-6368)*
John R Warren....G.... 405 843-9402
Oklahoma City *(G-6370)*
Johnson Exploration Company....G.... 405 235-4454
Oklahoma City *(G-6375)*
Jolen Operating Company....F.... 405 235-8444
Oklahoma City *(G-6379)*
Jolen Production Company....G.... 405 235-8444
Oklahoma City *(G-6380)*
Jones Energy Holdings LLC....E.... 512 328-2953
Oklahoma City *(G-6384)*
Jones Oil Co LLC....F.... 580 255-9400
Duncan *(G-2139)*
Jones-Kalkman Mineral Co....G.... 580 223-3101
Ardmore *(G-319)*
Joshi Technologies Intl Inc....F.... 918 665-6419
Tulsa *(G-10059)*
K Oil Company....G.... 405 382-0891
Seminole *(G-8381)*
K S Oil Company Inc....G.... 405 634-5115
Norman *(G-5047)*
K W B Inc....E.... 918 583-8300
Tulsa *(G-10069)*
Kaiser-Francis Oil Company....F.... 580 668-2335
Wilson *(G-11537)*
Kaiser-Francis Oil Company....G.... 405 262-5511
El Reno *(G-2730)*
Kechi Energy LLC....G.... 405 222-1412
Chickasha *(G-1477)*
Keener Oil & Gas Company....G.... 918 587-4154
Tulsa *(G-10079)*
Keith F Walker Oil Gas Co LLC....G.... 580 223-1575
Ardmore *(G-321)*
Kiamichi Resources Inc....G.... 405 364-8176
Norman *(G-5050)*
Kingery Drilling Company Inc....G.... 580 223-6823
Ardmore *(G-322)*
Kingery Drilling Company Inc....G.... 580 229-0716
Healdton *(G-3418)*
Kingfisher Resources Inc....G.... 580 323-6097
Clinton *(G-1755)*
Kirkpatrick Oil Company Inc....F.... 405 840-2882
Oklahoma City *(G-6426)*
Kirkpatrick Oil Company Inc....G.... 405 853-2922
Hennessey *(G-3471)*
Kiska Oil Company....G.... 918 584-4251
Tulsa *(G-10092)*
Krumme Oil Company LLP....F.... 918 367-5562
Bristow *(G-787)*
L C B Resources....G.... 405 375-3718
Kingfisher *(G-3807)*
L E Jones Production Co....G.... 580 255-1191
Duncan *(G-2144)*
L I B Ventures Company Inc....G.... 405 659-8800
Oklahoma City *(G-6439)*
Lackey William H Oil Gas Oper....G.... 405 275-4164
Shawnee *(G-8467)*
Lake Oil Company Inc....G.... 580 332-1737
Ada *(G-57)*
Lamamco Drilling LLC....G.... 918 396-3020
Skiatook *(G-8557)*
Landers & Musgroves Oil & Gas....G.... 918 623-2740
Tulsa *(G-10122)*
Laredo Petroleum-Dallas Inc....E.... 469 522-7800
Tulsa *(G-10128)*
Lario Oil & Gas Company....G.... 405 238-5609
Pauls Valley *(G-7665)*
Larry Chinn Oil....G.... 918 336-4269
Pawhuska *(G-7688)*
Larry Sherman Oil LLC....G.... 405 258-0816
Chandler *(G-1384)*

PRODUCT SECTION

CRUDE PETROLEUM PRODUCTION

Latigo Oil & Gas Inc..............................F.......580 256-1416
  Woodward *(G-11605)*
Leasehold Management Corp.............G.......405 670-5535
  Oklahoma City *(G-6462)*
Lema Petroleum Inc...............................G.......405 379-6678
  Holdenville *(G-3556)*
Lewis Oil Corporation.............................G.......405 377-6556
  Stillwater *(G-8718)*
Liberty Operating Inc.............................G.......405 329-6200
  Norman *(G-5058)*
Link Oil Company...................................G.......918 585-8343
  Tulsa *(G-10166)*
Linn Energy..G.......405 273-1185
  Shawnee *(G-8469)*
Litzenberger Exploration Inc..................G.......580 824-9351
  Waynoka *(G-11379)*
Lobar Oil Co...G.......405 330-7938
  Edmond *(G-2491)*
Lorraine Oil Co Inc.................................G.......405 853-2715
  Hennessey *(G-3474)*
Lvm Oil Production LLC........................G.......918 387-2822
  Yale *(G-11685)*
M and V Resources Inc.........................G.......405 969-2338
  Crescent *(G-1918)*
Mack Energy Co.....................................G.......580 856-3705
  Ratliff City *(G-8057)*
Mack Energy Co.....................................C.......580 252-5580
  Duncan *(G-2150)*
Maggard Supply and Oil Co Inc............G.......918 865-4333
  Mannford *(G-4186)*
Marjo Oil Company Inc..........................G.......918 583-0241
  Tulsa *(G-10210)*
Marjo Operating Co Inc.........................G.......918 583-0241
  Tulsa *(G-10211)*
Mark Holloway Inc..................................G.......405 833-7947
  Oklahoma City *(G-6527)*
Marlin Oil Corporation............................E.......405 478-1900
  Oklahoma City *(G-6529)*
Marsh Oil & Gas Co...............................G.......405 238-9660
  Pauls Valley *(G-7667)*
Maxim Energy Corp...............................G.......405 348-9669
  Edmond *(G-2507)*
McCasland Mercantile LLC...................G.......580 252-5580
  Duncan *(G-2153)*
McGonigal Ted Oil and Well Svc..........G.......918 299-5250
  Jenks *(G-3716)*
Meadowbrook Oil Corp of Okla.............G.......405 672-0240
  Del City *(G-2001)*
Medallion Petroleum Inc........................G.......918 582-1320
  Tulsa *(G-10237)*
Metzger Oil Tools Inc.............................G.......918 885-2456
  Hominy *(G-3592)*
Mfp Petroleum Ltd Partnership.............G.......405 728-5588
  Oklahoma City *(G-6584)*
Mid-American Oil Co Inc.......................G.......405 848-7551
  Oklahoma City *(G-6590)*
Mid-Con Energy Operating LLC...........F.......918 743-7575
  Tulsa *(G-10259)*
Mid-Con Energy Partners LP...............D.......918 743-7575
  Tulsa *(G-10260)*
Mid-Con Energy Properties LLC..........G.......918 743-7575
  Tulsa *(G-10261)*
Midcon Midstream LP...........................G.......405 429-5500
  Oklahoma City *(G-6596)*
Midwest Enterprises Inc........................G.......405 433-2419
  Cashion *(G-1290)*
Miracle Production Inc..........................F.......405 324-2216
  Oklahoma City *(G-6618)*
MJM Resources Inc...............................G.......405 579-4455
  Norman *(G-5076)*
Montgomery Exploration Company......G.......405 232-1169
  Norman *(G-5080)*
Moran Oil Enterprises...........................G.......405 382-6001
  Seminole *(G-8386)*
Moran-K Oil LLC...................................F.......405 382-6001
  Seminole *(G-8387)*
Muirfield Production Co Inc..................F.......918 744-5604
  Tulsa *(G-10312)*
Muirfield Resources Company.............F.......918 744-5604
  Tulsa *(G-10313)*
Mustang Fuel Corporation....................D.......405 884-2092
  Oklahoma City *(G-6641)*
N M & O Operating Company..............G.......918 584-3802
  Tulsa *(G-10322)*
Nadel and Gussman LLC....................E.......918 583-3333
  Tulsa *(G-10323)*
Nelson Exploration Corp......................G.......405 853-6933
  Cleveland *(G-1729)*
New Dominion LLC..............................E.......918 587-6242
  Tulsa *(G-10335)*

Northport Production Co Inc................G.......405 848-1212
  Edmond *(G-2541)*
Norville Oil Co LLC................................G.......405 286-9100
  Oklahoma City *(G-6696)*
Nubs Well Servicing Inc.......................F.......580 856-3887
  Ratliff City *(G-8058)*
Nye Oil Co...G.......405 843-6609
  Oklahoma City *(G-6705)*
Oak Hill Petroleum Corporation...........G.......405 842-1568
  Nichols Hills *(G-4861)*
Oakland Petroleum Operating Co.......G.......918 496-3027
  Tulsa *(G-10373)*
Occidental Petroleum Corp.................F.......918 610-1990
  Tulsa *(G-10374)*
Octagon Resources Inc.......................G.......405 366-8885
  Norman *(G-5097)*
Ogp Energy L P...................................G.......405 235-9571
  Oklahoma City *(G-6715)*
OK Swabbing Inc.................................G.......405 853-6953
  Hennessey *(G-3478)*
Okc Energy Corporation......................G.......405 330-5586
  Oklahoma City *(G-6728)*
Okie Operating Co Ltd.........................G.......918 582-2594
  Tulsa *(G-10393)*
Oklahoma Basic Economy Corp.........F.......580 332-4710
  Ada *(G-73)*
Okland Oil Company...........................E.......405 236-3046
  Oklahoma City *(G-6766)*
Olmstead Oil Company.......................G.......918 743-2360
  Tulsa *(G-10415)*
Olympia Oil Inc....................................G.......405 726-8400
  Oklahoma City *(G-6773)*
Oneok Inc..E.......918 588-7000
  Tulsa *(G-10422)*
Oneok Producer Services Co............G.......918 588-7000
  Tulsa *(G-10428)*
Oneok Resources Company..............G.......918 588-7000
  Tulsa *(G-10429)*
Osage Surveying Service...................G.......918 287-4029
  Pawhuska *(G-7692)*
Otc Petroleum Corporation.................G.......405 840-2255
  Oklahoma City *(G-6788)*
Ouachita Exploration Inc....................G.......405 222-0024
  Chickasha *(G-1496)*
Ovintiv Exploration Inc........................G.......580 927-9064
  McAlester *(G-4327)*
Ovintiv Mid-Continent Inc...................C.......918 582-2690
  Tulsa *(G-10448)*
OXY Inc..G.......580 338-6593
  Guymon *(G-3358)*
P D I Inc...E.......405 232-9700
  Oklahoma City *(G-6791)*
P F Beeler LLC....................................G.......405 364-0799
  Norman *(G-5107)*
P H D Oil & Gas Inc.............................G.......580 476-3005
  Rush Springs *(G-8124)*
Paleo Inc...G.......405 942-1546
  Oklahoma City *(G-6795)*
Paloma Partners IV.............................G.......405 295-6755
  El Reno *(G-2745)*
Panhandle Royalty Co........................G.......405 945-6100
  Oklahoma City *(G-6800)*
Panoak Oil & Gas Corporation...........G.......918 857-4929
  Tulsa *(G-10460)*
Pappe Court Jr Office.........................G.......405 375-5450
  Kingfisher *(G-3810)*
Paragon Production Co......................G.......405 348-1116
  Edmond *(G-2562)*
Parsage Oil Company LLC.................G.......918 846-2358
  Tulsa *(G-10471)*
Patrick A McGinley..............................G.......918 583-3267
  Tulsa *(G-10472)*
Patterson Oil Company Inc................G.......405 257-3241
  Wewoka *(G-11507)*
Paul E Kloberdanz..............................G.......405 947-5570
  Oklahoma City *(G-6812)*
Paulaura Cattle Co.............................G.......918 682-6030
  Muskogee *(G-4732)*
Pauline Oil and Gas Co.....................G.......405 842-4213
  Nichols Hills *(G-4862)*
Payne Farms......................................G.......580 661-2351
  Thomas *(G-8947)*
Peake Fuel Solutions LLC.................G.......405 935-8000
  Oklahoma City *(G-6817)*
Pedestal Oil Company Inc.................F.......405 236-8596
  Oklahoma City *(G-6819)*
Pennant Oil & Gas LLC......................G.......405 642-4382
  Tulsa *(G-10485)*
Penner Energy Inc.............................G.......405 751-7504
  Oklahoma City *(G-6826)*

Performance Operating Co LLC.........F.......918 847-3830
  Barnsdall *(G-439)*
Perkins Energy Co...............................G.......580 255-5400
  Duncan *(G-2164)*
Petro Speed Inc...................................G.......405 364-6785
  Norman *(G-5114)*
Petrocorp Incorporated.......................G.......918 491-4500
  Tulsa *(G-10501)*
Petroflow Energy Corporation............F.......918 592-1010
  Tulsa *(G-10502)*
Petroleum International Inc................G.......918 712-1840
  Tulsa *(G-10506)*
Phoenix Oil and Gas Inc....................F.......405 382-0935
  Seminole *(G-8394)*
Platt Energy Corporation...................G.......405 840-5081
  Oklahoma City *(G-6856)*
Pletcher Oil Company........................G.......580 657-4221
  Ardmore *(G-346)*
Plymouth Resources Inc...................G.......918 599-1880
  Tulsa *(G-10529)*
Portman Minerals LLC......................G.......405 843-4063
  Oklahoma City *(G-6864)*
Post Oak Oil Co................................G.......405 621-1300
  Oklahoma City *(G-6865)*
Post Oak Petroleum LLC..................G.......918 245-9919
  Skiatook *(G-8564)*
Pre Mc Inc...G.......580 857-2408
  Allen *(G-137)*
Prentice Napier & Green Inc............F.......405 752-7680
  Oklahoma City *(G-6888)*
Producers Oil Company Inc..............E.......918 582-1188
  Tulsa *(G-10566)*
Producing Lamamco III L P..............C.......918 396-3020
  Skiatook *(G-8565)*
Providence Energy Corp...................G.......918 747-3675
  Tulsa *(G-10577)*
Quail Creek Oil Corporation.............E.......405 755-7419
  Oklahoma City *(G-6934)*
Quail Creek Production Company....G.......405 755-7419
  Oklahoma City *(G-6935)*
Quest Property Inc............................G.......405 722-7530
  Wheatland *(G-11515)*
Quintin Little Company Inc...............E.......580 226-7600
  Ardmore *(G-348)*
R C Taylor Companies Inc...............G.......405 840-2700
  Oklahoma City *(G-6961)*
R E Blaik Inc.....................................G.......405 285-8000
  Edmond *(G-2582)*
R E G Energy...................................G.......405 842-4249
  Oklahoma City *(G-6963)*
R G Berry Co...................................G.......918 587-0036
  Tulsa *(G-10604)*
Ramsey Property Management LLC....G.......405 302-6200
  Oklahoma City *(G-6971)*
Raven Resources LLC....................G.......405 773-7340
  Edmond *(G-2586)*
Ray Lu Petroleum LLC...................G.......405 424-4006
  Oklahoma City *(G-6974)*
Raydon Exploration Inc..................G.......405 478-8585
  Oklahoma City *(G-6975)*
Rbc Exploration Company..............G.......918 744-5607
  Tulsa *(G-10623)*
Rebel Oil Company.........................G.......405 848-2208
  Oklahoma City *(G-6981)*
Reclaimed Oil & Gas Prpts LLC......G.......580 234-8085
  Enid *(G-3045)*
Red Plains Oil & Gas LLC...............G.......405 375-3377
  Kingfisher *(G-3812)*
Redland Resources Inc..................G.......405 789-7104
  Oklahoma City *(G-6996)*
Reserve Petroleum Company.........G.......405 848-7551
  Oklahoma City *(G-7009)*
Resources Operating Company.....G.......580 237-7744
  Enid *(G-3047)*
Richard Exploration Co Inc............G.......405 840-0101
  Oklahoma City *(G-7017)*
Richland Resources Corporation...F.......405 732-0045
  Oklahoma City *(G-7019)*
Riviera Operating LLC...................E.......405 375-6065
  Kingfisher *(G-3813)*
Rkk Production Company..............G.......405 376-2223
  Mustang *(G-4790)*
Roberson Oil Co Inc.......................G.......580 332-6170
  Ada *(G-83)*
Robert W Berry Inc........................G.......918 492-1140
  Tulsa *(G-10663)*
Rockland Oil Co.............................G.......580 223-0960
  Ardmore *(G-350)*
Rogers Resources Inc..................G.......580 237-7744
  Enid *(G-3050)*

Employee Codes: A=Over 500 employees, B=251-500
C=101-250, D=51-100, E=20-50, F=10-19, G=1-9

CRUDE PETROLEUM PRODUCTION

Romayne - Baker Oil & Gas Ltd ....G..... 580 237-1626
  Enid *(G-3051)*
Rougeot Oil & Gas Corp ....G..... 918 288-2022
  Tulsa *(G-10678)*
Rox Exploration Inc ....G..... 405 329-0009
  Norman *(G-5136)*
Royalok Royalty LLC ....G..... 405 721-9771
  Oklahoma City *(G-7055)*
Roye Realty & Developing Inc ....G..... 918 967-4888
  Stigler *(G-8644)*
Ruffel Lance Oil & Gas Corp ....F..... 405 239-7036
  Oklahoma City *(G-7060)*
Sallee Oil Corp ....G..... 918 371-2290
  Collinsville *(G-1824)*
Sam W Mays Jr ....G..... 918 382-9170
  Tulsa *(G-10691)*
Samson Investment Company ....B..... 918 583-1791
  Tulsa *(G-10694)*
Samson Natural Gas Company ....B..... 918 583-1791
  Tulsa *(G-10695)*
Samson Resources Company ....D..... 918 583-1791
  Tulsa *(G-10696)*
Samson Resources Corporation ....F..... 918 591-1791
  Tulsa *(G-10697)*
Sandridge Co2 LLC ....G..... 405 429-5500
  Oklahoma City *(G-7078)*
Sandridge Energy Inc ....G..... 580 430-4500
  Alva *(G-191)*
Sandridge Energy Inc ....A..... 405 354-2727
  Yukon *(G-11775)*
Sandridge Energy Inc ....C..... 405 429-5500
  Oklahoma City *(G-7079)*
Sandridge Exploration Prod LLC ....G..... 405 429-5734
  Oklahoma City *(G-7080)*
Sandridge Offshore LLC ....G..... 405 429-5500
  Oklahoma City *(G-7081)*
Sandridge Operating Company ....C..... 405 753-5500
  Oklahoma City *(G-7082)*
Sandy Petroleum Inc ....G..... 405 273-9289
  Shawnee *(G-8492)*
Seaboard Gas Company ....G..... 405 341-1779
  Edmond *(G-2614)*
SEC Production Inc ....G..... 405 715-0088
  Edmond *(G-2615)*
Sell Well Servicing Company ....G..... 918 287-1711
  Pawhuska *(G-7695)*
Semgroup Corporation ....E..... 405 945-6300
  Oklahoma City *(G-7108)*
Senax Inc ....G..... 918 494-0681
  Tulsa *(G-10731)*
Servicios Petroleros Flint CA ....E..... 918 587-7131
  Tulsa *(G-10734)*
Shelburne Oil Company ....G..... 405 843-1352
  Oklahoma City *(G-7120)*
Sherman Oil and Gas Company ....G..... 405 258-5932
  Chandler *(G-1386)*
Shields Operating Inc ....G..... 405 341-7607
  Edmond *(G-2620)*
Short Oil Co ....E..... 918 747-8200
  Tulsa *(G-10750)*
Short Oil Co Yard ....G..... 918 287-2925
  Pawhuska *(G-7696)*
Siegfried Companies Inc ....G..... 918 747-3411
  Tulsa *(G-10752)*
Simek Oil Properties Inc ....G..... 405 567-4606
  Prague *(G-7935)*
Singer Bros ....G..... 918 582-6237
  Tulsa *(G-10767)*
Singer Oil Company LLC ....G..... 405 853-6807
  Hennessey *(G-3486)*
Sitrin Petroleum Corp ....G..... 918 747-1111
  Tulsa *(G-10770)*
Solar Exploration OK LLC ....G..... 918 252-2203
  Tulsa *(G-10783)*
Sooner Tool Company ....G..... 918 352-4440
  Drumright *(G-2071)*
Sooner Trend Exploration Inc ....G..... 405 375-3405
  Kingfisher *(G-3816)*
Southern Resources Inc ....G..... 405 601-1322
  Oklahoma City *(G-7172)*
Southwest Energy LP ....G..... 918 779-0699
  Tulsa *(G-10806)*
Southwest Petroleum Corp ....E..... 918 352-2700
  Tulsa *(G-10809)*
Speller Oil Corporation ....F..... 405 942-7869
  Oklahoma City *(G-7182)*
Speller Petroleum Corporation ....G..... 405 942-7869
  Oklahoma City *(G-7183)*
Spess Drilling Company ....F..... 918 358-5831
  Cleveland *(G-1734)*

Spiral Exploration LLC ....G..... 330 936-4689
  Oklahoma City *(G-7186)*
Spring Harry A Geological Engr ....G..... 580 226-1910
  Ardmore *(G-361)*
Stadia Energy Partners LLC ....G..... 918 812-6169
  Tulsa *(G-10830)*
Stagestand Ranch ....G..... 580 255-1161
  Duncan *(G-2184)*
Stars Restaurants LLC ....E..... 405 947-1396
  Edmond *(G-2631)*
Stephen J Heyman ....G..... 918 583-3333
  Tulsa *(G-10846)*
Stokes Production ....G..... 405 485-2402
  Seminole *(G-8401)*
Strat Land Exploration Co ....F..... 918 584-3844
  Tulsa *(G-10859)*
Strata Minerals Inc ....G..... 405 722-3227
  Oklahoma City *(G-7214)*
Stream Energy Inc ....F..... 405 272-1080
  Oklahoma City *(G-7216)*
Sullivan and Company LLC ....F..... 918 584-4288
  Tulsa *(G-10864)*
Summit Oil Company Inc ....G..... 405 842-7896
  Oklahoma City *(G-7224)*
Sutherland Well Service Inc ....D..... 580 229-1338
  Healdton *(G-3422)*
Sweetwater Exploration LLC ....G..... 405 329-1967
  Norman *(G-5166)*
Sylvan Oil Operating Company ....G..... 918 267-3764
  Tulsa *(G-10885)*
Synergex Inc ....E..... 405 748-5050
  Oklahoma City *(G-7239)*
T A T Inc ....G..... 405 942-0489
  Oklahoma City *(G-7242)*
T C Craighead & Company ....F..... 580 223-7470
  Ardmore *(G-365)*
T K Drilling Corp ....G..... 918 270-1084
  Tulsa *(G-10890)*
Tag Petroleum Inc ....G..... 405 377-6185
  Stillwater *(G-8763)*
Taylor International Inc ....G..... 918 352-9511
  Cushing *(G-1964)*
Tcina Holding Company Ltd ....G..... 405 382-0399
  Seminole *(G-8404)*
Thomas Exploration Company ....G..... 918 496-1414
  Tulsa *(G-10932)*
Thomas N Berry & Company ....G..... 405 372-5252
  Stillwater *(G-8767)*
Thomas P Shaw ....G..... 918 742-4673
  Tulsa *(G-10934)*
Three B Land & Cattle Company ....G..... 580 332-9480
  Ada *(G-94)*
Three Sands Oil Inc ....G..... 580 336-2410
  Perry *(G-7749)*
Thunderbird Energy Resources ....G..... 918 627-5433
  Tulsa *(G-10939)*
Thundrbird Rsources Equity Inc ....F..... 405 600-0711
  Edmond *(G-2642)*
Toklan Oil and Gas Corporation ....F..... 918 582-5400
  Tulsa *(G-10949)*
Toland & Johnston Inc ....G..... 405 330-2006
  Edmond *(G-2646)*
Tom Meason Oil Ventures ....G..... 918 587-3492
  Tulsa *(G-10950)*
Tony Oil Company ....G..... 918 493-1882
  Tulsa *(G-10951)*
Toomey Oil Company Inc ....G..... 918 583-1166
  Tulsa *(G-10954)*
Trace Oil ....G..... 405 222-4449
  Chickasha *(G-1518)*
Trees Oil Co ....G..... 918 257-5050
  Afton *(G-123)*
Trepco Production Co Inc ....G..... 405 722-1400
  Yukon *(G-11794)*
Tri Production Inc ....G..... 580 229-1280
  Healdton *(G-3423)*
Tripledee Drilling Co Inc ....G..... 580 223-8181
  Ardmore *(G-374)*
Tripower Resources LLC ....F..... 580 226-6700
  Ardmore *(G-375)*
Tsalta Corporation ....G..... 405 607-4141
  Oklahoma City *(G-7345)*
Turner Resources Inc ....G..... 405 853-6275
  Hennessey *(G-3494)*
Twenty-Twenty Oil & Gas Co ....G..... 405 853-4607
  Hennessey *(G-3495)*
Union Valley Petroleum Corp ....G..... 580 237-3959
  Enid *(G-3069)*
Unit Corporation ....D..... 918 493-7700
  Tulsa *(G-11037)*

PRODUCT SECTION

Unit Petroleum Company ....C..... 918 493-7700
  Tulsa *(G-11039)*
United Production Co L L C ....G..... 405 728-8900
  Edmond *(G-2657)*
Uplands Resources Inc ....G..... 918 592-0305
  Tulsa *(G-11053)*
Van Eaton C W ....G..... 580 223-4374
  Ardmore *(G-378)*
Vernon E Faulconer Inc ....G..... 580 883-2892
  Ringwood *(G-8096)*
Wadley Bill & Son Drilling Co ....G..... 918 756-4650
  Okmulgee *(G-7529)*
Walden Energy LLC ....G..... 918 488-8663
  Tulsa *(G-11091)*
Warren American Oil Company ....E..... 918 481-7990
  Tulsa *(G-11096)*
Warwick Energy Group LLC ....F..... 405 607-3400
  Oklahoma City *(G-7423)*
Wehlu Producers Inc ....G..... 405 844-9487
  Edmond *(G-2683)*
Weinkauf Petroleum Inc ....F..... 918 749-8383
  Tulsa *(G-11105)*
West Valbel Corporation ....G..... 580 223-3494
  Ardmore *(G-381)*
Western Gas Resources Inc ....E..... 580 883-2273
  Ringwood *(G-8097)*
Western Oil and Gas Dev Corp ....F..... 405 235-4590
  Oklahoma City *(G-7440)*
Wetzel Producing Company ....G..... 580 255-2929
  Duncan *(G-2198)*
Wheeler & Sons Oil and Gas ....G..... 405 375-4613
  Kingfisher *(G-3821)*
Wheeler Energy Corporation ....G..... 918 587-7474
  Tulsa *(G-11114)*
White Operating Company ....G..... 405 735-8419
  Oklahoma City *(G-7445)*
Whiteman Industries Inc ....G..... 405 879-0077
  Oklahoma City *(G-7446)*
Wildhorse Exploration Prod LLC ....G..... 918 396-3736
  Skiatook *(G-8574)*
Wilkins L L E & O Company ....G..... 405 273-0370
  Shawnee *(G-8520)*
William C Jackson ....G..... 918 742-0602
  Tulsa *(G-11122)*
William Cloud Oil ....G..... 405 751-8422
  Oklahoma City *(G-7455)*
William H Davis ....G..... 918 587-7782
  Tulsa *(G-11124)*
William M Park ....G..... 918 288-7752
  Sperry *(G-8612)*
Williford Energy Company ....F..... 918 495-2700
  Tulsa *(G-11134)*
Willis Bros Land & Cattle Co ....G..... 580 569-2698
  Snyder *(G-8585)*
Wolf Creek Enterprises Inc ....G..... 580 254-3361
  Woodward *(G-11655)*
Wood Oil Company ....F..... 405 948-1560
  Oklahoma City *(G-7463)*
Woodbine Financial Corporation ....G..... 918 584-5309
  Tulsa *(G-11149)*
Worstell Oil ....G..... 918 371-5425
  Collinsville *(G-1831)*
Xanadu Exploration Company ....G..... 918 584-3802
  Tulsa *(G-11164)*
Xto Energy Inc ....E..... 580 883-2253
  Ringwood *(G-8098)*
Xto Energy Inc ....D..... 580 653-3200
  Ardmore *(G-383)*
Zephyr Operating Co LLC ....G..... 405 286-4771
  Oklahoma City *(G-7486)*
Zinke & Trumbo Inc ....F..... 918 488-6400
  Tulsa *(G-11178)*

CRUDES: Cyclic, Organic

Baker Hughes A GE Company LLC ....C..... 918 828-1600
  Tulsa *(G-9255)*

CULVERTS: Sheet Metal

Tinhorns Are US ....G..... 405 381-4044
  Tuttle *(G-11216)*

CUPS: Plastic Exc Polystyrene Foam

Solo Cup Operating Corporation ....C..... 580 436-1500
  Ada *(G-90)*

PRODUCT SECTION

CURTAIN & DRAPERY FIXTURES: Poles, Rods & Rollers
Cowboy Covers Inc ....G....... 405 624-2270
  Stillwater *(G-8672)*
Johnsons Spring Crest Drpery C ....G....... 405 238-7341
  Pauls Valley *(G-7662)*

CURTAINS & BEDDING: Knit
E E Sewing Inc ....E 918 789-5881
  Chelsea *(G-1404)*

CUSHIONS & PILLOWS
Cozy Cub Products LLP ....G....... 405 386-2879
  Newalla *(G-4807)*
Leachco Inc ....E 580 436-1142
  Ada *(G-59)*

CUSHIONS & PILLOWS: Bed, From Purchased Materials
Life Lift Systems Inc ....F 904 635-8231
  Oklahoma City *(G-6474)*

CUSHIONS: Textile, Exc Spring & Carpet
Pestco Inc ....G....... 405 485-8060
  Blanchard *(G-727)*
Speer Cushion Co ....G....... 970 854-2911
  Bixby *(G-664)*

CUSTOMIZING SVCS
Custom Automotive Mfg ....F 918 258-2900
  Broken Arrow *(G-881)*

CUT STONE & STONE PRODUCTS
Alva Monument Works Inc ....G....... 580 327-0626
  Alva *(G-174)*
Anson Memorial Co ....G....... 918 358-2504
  Cleveland *(G-1716)*
Benchmark Monument ....G....... 918 582-8600
  Tulsa *(G-9280)*
Classic Tile Stone & MBL LLC ....F 405 858-8453
  Oklahoma City *(G-5779)*
Decorative Rock & Stone Inc ....G....... 405 672-2564
  Oklahoma City *(G-5916)*
Divine Cultured Marble ....G....... 918 836-2121
  Tulsa *(G-9588)*
Eaves Stones Products ....F 580 889-7858
  Atoka *(G-410)*
Eurocraft Ltd ....E 918 322-5500
  Glenpool *(G-3234)*
Freedom Stone Company LLC ....G....... 918 649-0021
  Poteau *(G-7904)*
Jones Monuments Co ....G....... 580 255-2276
  Duncan *(G-2138)*
Majestic Marble & Granite ....E 918 266-1121
  Catoosa *(G-1337)*
McAlester Monument Co Inc ....G....... 918 423-1647
  McAlester *(G-4317)*
Morris Monuments ....G....... 580 924-1323
  Durant *(G-2244)*
Muskogee Marble & Granite LLC ....E 918 682-0064
  Muskogee *(G-4716)*
Okmulgee Monuments Inc ....G....... 918 756-6619
  Okmulgee *(G-7519)*
Stigler Stone Company Inc ....F 918 967-3316
  Stigler *(G-8649)*
Tile & Design Concepts Inc ....E 405 842-8551
  Oklahoma City *(G-7288)*
Warhall Designs LLC ....F 405 330-0907
  Edmond *(G-2680)*

CUTLERY
Solo Cup Operating Corporation ....C....... 580 436-1500
  Ada *(G-90)*

CYCLIC CRUDES & INTERMEDIATES
Brenntag Southwest Inc ....E 918 273-2265
  Nowata *(G-5209)*

CYLINDER & ACTUATORS: Fluid Power
Apsco Inc ....G....... 918 622-5600
  Tulsa *(G-9201)*
Ren Holding Corporation ....F 405 533-2755
  Stillwater *(G-8745)*

CYLINDERS: Pressure
Air Power Systems Co LLC ....E 918 622-5600
  Tulsa *(G-9121)*
Worthington Cylinder Corp ....C....... 918 396-2899
  Skiatook *(G-8577)*

DAIRY PRDTS STORE: Cheese
Watonga Cheese Plant ....G....... 580 623-5915
  Balko *(G-433)*

DAIRY PRDTS STORE: Ice Cream, Packaged
W H Braum Inc ....E 405 340-9288
  Edmond *(G-2678)*

DAIRY PRDTS WHOLESALERS: Fresh
Hiland Dairy Foods Company LLC ....D....... 405 321-3191
  Norman *(G-5023)*

DAIRY PRDTS: Cheese
George E Christian ....G....... 405 375-6711
  Kingfisher *(G-3798)*
Los Quesitos De Mama LLC ....G....... 312 276-2638
  Edmond *(G-2495)*
Watonga Cheese Plant ....G....... 580 623-5915
  Balko *(G-433)*

DAIRY PRDTS: Custard, Frozen
Scoozies Coneys & Frz Custard ....G....... 918 396-1500
  Skiatook *(G-8568)*

DAIRY PRDTS: Dietary Supplements, Dairy & Non-Dairy Based
24 Hr Inc ....G...... 844 370-1726
  Weatherford *(G-11385)*
All Things Bugs LLC ....G....... 352 281-3643
  Oklahoma City *(G-5415)*
Biorite Acquisition Co LLC ....G....... 405 701-1515
  Norman *(G-4935)*
Juice Blendz Cafe ....G....... 405 285-0133
  Edmond *(G-2475)*
JW Nutritional LLC ....G....... 214 221-0404
  Broken Arrow *(G-953)*
Native Distributing LLC ....D....... 405 316-9223
  Norman *(G-5086)*
Natures Rx Inc ....G....... 405 484-7302
  Paoli *(G-7638)*
Nucleic Products LLC ....G....... 818 419-9176
  Grove *(G-3283)*
Sanders Laboratories Inc ....G....... 405 598-2131
  Tecumseh *(G-8926)*
Ultra Botanica LLC ....G....... 405 694-4175
  Oklahoma City *(G-7359)*

DAIRY PRDTS: Farmers' Cheese
McAllister Farms ....G....... 580 512-9009
  Hollis *(G-3567)*

DAIRY PRDTS: Frozen Desserts & Novelties
C&K Inc ....G....... 918 299-6307
  Jenks *(G-3697)*
Hiland Dairy Foods Company LLC ....B....... 405 258-3100
  Chandler *(G-1380)*
W H Braum Inc ....E 405 340-9288
  Edmond *(G-2678)*
Wiljackal LLC ....F 918 252-2663
  Tulsa *(G-11121)*

DAIRY PRDTS: Ice Cream, Packaged, Molded, On Sticks, Etc.
Blue Bell Creameries LP ....B....... 918 258-5100
  Broken Arrow *(G-1113)*

DAIRY PRDTS: Milk & Cream, Cultured & Flavored
Hiland Dairy Foods Company LLC ....B....... 405 258-3100
  Chandler *(G-1380)*

DAIRY PRDTS: Milk, Fluid
Borden Dairy Company Texas LLC ....G....... 405 232-7955
  Oklahoma City *(G-5620)*
Dean Foods Company ....G....... 918 587-2471
  Tulsa *(G-9564)*
Hiland Dairy Foods Company LLC ....D....... 405 321-3191
  Norman *(G-5023)*
Southern Foods Group LLC ....C....... 918 587-2471
  Tulsa *(G-10799)*
Swan Brothers Dairy Inc ....G....... 918 341-2069
  Claremore *(G-1690)*

DAIRY PRDTS: Milk, Processed, Pasteurized, Homogenized/Btld
James Porter Shorty ....G....... 580 326-0592
  Hugo *(G-3615)*

DAIRY PRDTS: Natural Cheese
Cheese Factory LLC ....G....... 405 375-4004
  Kingfisher *(G-3788)*
Swan Brothers Dairy Inc ....G....... 918 341-2069
  Claremore *(G-1690)*

DAIRY PRDTS: Yogurt, Exc Frozen
Passion Berri ....G....... 405 310-6669
  Norman *(G-5109)*

DAIRY PRDTS: Yogurt, Frozen
M-O Masonry LLC ....G....... 405 219-4220
  Oklahoma City *(G-6512)*
Olh Moore LLC ....G....... 405 703-0250
  Moore *(G-4549)*

DATA PROCESSING & PREPARATION SVCS
Abundant Grace Companies LLC ....F 405 682-2589
  Oklahoma City *(G-5359)*
Smeac Group International LLC ....G....... 580 574-4092
  Lawton *(G-3999)*

DATA PROCESSING SVCS
MWH Enterprises Inc ....F 918 665-0944
  Tulsa *(G-10320)*
Writers Research Group LLC ....F 405 682-2589
  Oklahoma City *(G-7474)*

DATABASE INFORMATION RETRIEVAL SVCS
Oklahoma Publishing Co of Okla ....E 405 475-3585
  Oklahoma City *(G-6759)*
Okland Oil Company ....E 405 236-3046
  Oklahoma City *(G-6766)*

DECALS, WHOLESALE
Regency Labels Inc ....E 405 682-3460
  Oklahoma City *(G-7002)*
Trans-Tech LLC ....F 405 422-5000
  El Reno *(G-2763)*

DECORATIVE WOOD & WOODWORK
Artisan Design Inc ....G....... 918 251-9795
  Broken Arrow *(G-835)*
D & S Refinishing ....G....... 580 233-4351
  Enid *(G-2938)*
Desert Moon Enterprises ....G....... 918 540-0333
  Miami *(G-4395)*
Eric Adams Trim ....G....... 405 570-5931
  Jones *(G-3745)*
Hardwood Innovations Inc ....F 405 722-5588
  Oklahoma City *(G-6219)*
Kactus Rose LLC ....G....... 405 830-7551
  El Reno *(G-2729)*
Patternwork Veneering Inc ....G....... 405 447-1800
  Norman *(G-5110)*
Red Cedar Creations ....G....... 580 227-3198
  Longdale *(G-4127)*
Tulsa Wood Arts LLC ....G....... 918 576-6142
  Tulsa *(G-11012)*
Welton Acquisitions LLC ....G....... 918 850-7981
  Sand Springs *(G-8240)*

DEFENSE SYSTEMS & EQPT
5 Stones Defense LLC ....G....... 405 313-9729
  Tuttle *(G-11184)*
Archer Technologies Intl Inc ....G....... 405 306-3220
  Shawnee *(G-11176)*
Bto Strategies & Solutions Inc ....G....... 405 473-8632
  Norman *(G-4947)*
Cnrw Defense Service ....G....... 706 545-5080
  Catoosa *(G-1312)*

Employee Codes: A=Over 500 employees, B=251-500
C=101-250, D=51-100, E=20-50, F=10-19, G=1-9

2020 Oklahoma Directory of Manufacturers & Processors

DEFENSE SYSTEMS & EQPT

COBRA Self Defense Tulsa ....G...... 918 691-0054
  Sand Springs *(G-8171)*
Cole Defense LLC ....G...... 214 934-5473
  Oklahoma City *(G-5803)*
Damsel In Defense ....G...... 580 233-6609
  Enid *(G-2939)*
Defense Angel LLC ....G...... 405 476-4222
  Yukon *(G-11716)*
Girlpower Defense Llc ....G...... 918 494-9072
  Tulsa *(G-9828)*
Invictus Personal Defense Llc ....G...... 918 605-1165
  Owasso *(G-7576)*
Ironclad Defense ....G...... 405 413-9496
  Midwest City *(G-4443)*
JM Defense & Arospc Svcs LLC ....G...... 918 298-2766
  Jenks *(G-3710)*
Kxd Defense and Armament ....G...... 918 813-3841
  Oologah *(G-7533)*
Nelco Defense LLC ....G...... 580 471-7992
  Altus *(G-164)*
Northrop Corp ....G...... 580 536-9191
  Lawton *(G-3976)*
Oakley Defense LLC ....G...... 918 457-8089
  Tahlequah *(G-8877)*
Oklahoma Slf-Defense Carry LLC ....G...... 918 814-0122
  Bixby *(G-650)*
Personal Defense LLC ....G...... 918 345-0075
  Mounds *(G-4622)*
Physical Home Defense ....G...... 405 819-0939
  Oklahoma City *(G-6847)*
Stewart Defense LLC ....G...... 580 532-6426
  Pond Creek *(G-7891)*
Tactical Ballistic System ....G...... 580 254-5468
  Woodward *(G-11639)*
Triad Personal Defense LLC ....G...... 918 443-7803
  Claremore *(G-1694)*

DENTAL EQPT & SPLYS

Becky Welch Vacuum Forming ....G...... 918 836-7301
  Tulsa *(G-9278)*
D & S Distributing ....G...... 580 763-3773
  Ponca City *(G-7818)*
Dentsply Sirona Inc ....F...... 918 878-0189
  Tulsa *(G-9573)*
Dentsply Sirona Inc ....G...... 918 878-0001
  Tulsa *(G-9574)*
Evelyn Co Inc ....G...... 918 665-3952
  Tulsa *(G-9708)*
Leemark Dental Products ....G...... 918 241-6683
  Sand Springs *(G-8200)*
Precision Alloy ....G...... 918 665-3952
  Tulsa *(G-10542)*
R Meyers Enterprises ....G...... 580 917-7554
  Lawton *(G-3988)*
Reaux Corporation ....F...... 918 252-7660
  Tulsa *(G-10626)*

DENTAL EQPT & SPLYS WHOLESALERS

Evelyn Co Inc ....G...... 918 665-3952
  Tulsa *(G-9708)*
Precision Alloy ....G...... 918 665-3952
  Tulsa *(G-10542)*

DENTAL EQPT & SPLYS: Cabinets

Oklahoma Millworks Inc ....G...... 405 282-4887
  Edmond *(G-2552)*

DENTAL EQPT & SPLYS: Compounds

Jesco Products Inc ....G...... 405 943-1721
  Oklahoma City *(G-6358)*

DENTAL EQPT & SPLYS: Dental Hand Instruments, NEC

Dennis L Dickerson ....G...... 405 626-8630
  Tuttle *(G-11196)*

DENTAL EQPT & SPLYS: Dental Materials

3M Imtec Corporation ....C...... 800 879-9799
  Ardmore *(G-233)*
Oral Health Products Inc ....F...... 918 622-9412
  Tulsa *(G-10435)*

DENTAL EQPT & SPLYS: Denture Materials

Pro-Tech Dental Labs ....G...... 918 227-6407
  Sapulpa *(G-8303)*

DENTAL EQPT & SPLYS: Enamels

Happy Tooth Dental ....G...... 918 492-8793
  Tulsa *(G-9889)*
Melton Rh ....G...... 918 968-1606
  Stroud *(G-8811)*
Richard Brown ....G...... 918 492-1991
  Tulsa *(G-10650)*

DENTAL EQPT & SPLYS: Gold

Harris Discount Supplies Inc ....G...... 847 726-3800
  Edmond *(G-2451)*

DENTAL INSTRUMENT REPAIR SVCS

Dennis L Dickerson ....G...... 405 626-8630
  Tuttle *(G-11196)*

DEPARTMENT STORES

Distinctive Decor LLC ....F...... 580 252-9494
  Duncan *(G-2105)*

DEPARTMENT STORES: Surplus & Salvage

Lkq Corporation ....F...... 918 428-3835
  Tulsa *(G-10171)*
Mullins Salvage Inc ....G...... 918 352-9612
  Cushing *(G-1946)*

DERRICKS: Oil & Gas Field

State Line Swd LLC ....G...... 580 515-1468
  Reydon *(G-8080)*

DESALTER KITS: Sea Water

Midamerica Water Technologies ....G...... 405 613-0250
  Oklahoma City *(G-6594)*

DESIGN SVCS, NEC

Creative Packaging Inc ....G...... 918 587-0347
  Tulsa *(G-9505)*
Media Technology Incorporated ....E...... 405 682-4400
  Oklahoma City *(G-6556)*
Minko Design LLC ....G...... 918 895-6498
  Tulsa *(G-10284)*
Minko Design LLC ....G...... 918 895-6498
  Tulsa *(G-10285)*
S S Design Co ....G...... 918 427-3230
  Roland *(G-8113)*
Spinning Star Design ....G...... 405 359-3965
  Edmond *(G-2627)*
Stroud Corridor LLC ....G...... 405 823-7561
  Stroud *(G-8821)*
Sueno Designs ....G...... 918 809-3027
  Owasso *(G-7621)*

DESIGN SVCS: Commercial & Indl

Accurate By Design ....G...... 918 445-0292
  Tulsa *(G-8986)*
Industrial Electronics Repair ....E...... 918 342-1160
  Claremore *(G-1641)*
Liberty Partners Inc ....F...... 918 756-6474
  Okmulgee *(G-7513)*

DESIGN SVCS: Computer Integrated Systems

Ameriinfovets Inc ....G...... 408 446-4343
  Pryor *(G-7943)*
Norman Computers ....F...... 405 292-9501
  Norman *(G-5094)*
Stonebridge Acquisition Inc ....D...... 918 663-8000
  Tulsa *(G-10853)*
Versatech Industries Inc ....G...... 918 366-7400
  Bixby *(G-670)*

DETECTION APPARATUS: Electronic/Magnetic Field, Light/Heat

Dark Peek Technologies LLC ....G...... 405 316-8551
  Edmond *(G-2379)*
Flir Detection Inc ....E...... 405 533-6618
  Stillwater *(G-8689)*
Halo Induction Looping LLC ....G...... 918 638-1599
  Tulsa *(G-9882)*
Qual-Tron Inc ....E...... 918 622-7052
  Tulsa *(G-10589)*

DIAGNOSTIC SUBSTANCES

Immuno-Mycologics Inc ....F...... 405 360-4669
  Norman *(G-5030)*

DIAGNOSTIC SUBSTANCES OR AGENTS: In Vivo

Bounce Diagnostics Inc ....G...... 405 740-5889
  Edmond *(G-2331)*

DIAGNOSTIC SUBSTANCES OR AGENTS: Microbiology & Virology

Sarvam Solutions Corporation ....G...... 918 346-9502
  Bartlesville *(G-524)*

DIAGNOSTIC SUBSTANCES OR AGENTS: Radioactive

Petnet Solutions Inc ....G...... 918 259-0899
  Broken Arrow *(G-1004)*

DIE SETS: Presses, Metal Stamping

Precision Tool & Die Ponca Cy ....G...... 580 762-2421
  Ponca City *(G-7869)*

DIES & TOOLS: Special

AC Machine ....G...... 918 827-6552
  Mounds *(G-4607)*
Arrow Tool & Gage Co Inc ....F...... 918 438-3600
  Tulsa *(G-9212)*
Die Hard Properties LLC ....G...... 405 769-3145
  Choctaw *(G-1539)*
Die Tech Tool Machine ....G...... 918 683-3422
  Okay *(G-5257)*
Dieco Manufacturing Inc ....D...... 918 438-2193
  Tulsa *(G-9581)*
Diemasters ....G...... 800 826-2134
  Skiatook *(G-8541)*
Engineering Tooling Svc LLC ....G...... 405 381-9322
  Tuttle *(G-11197)*
Fundom Enterprises Inc ....G...... 405 557-0296
  Oklahoma City *(G-6126)*
Interstate Tool & Mfg Co ....E...... 918 834-6647
  Tulsa *(G-10008)*
Michael J Simmons and Die ....G...... 918 295-0057
  Tulsa *(G-10254)*
Precise Tool & Machine Company ......G...... 405 495-2001
  Oklahoma City *(G-6879)*
Progressive Tooling Inc ....G...... 918 622-0506
  Tulsa *(G-10572)*

DIES: Plastic Forming

Tools and Troubleshooting ....G...... 580 726-5290
  Hobart *(G-3547)*

DIES: Steel Rule

Fieldco Inc ....G...... 918 266-1815
  Claremore *(G-1620)*

DIODES: Light Emitting

Adl Group LLC ....G...... 918 960-0388
  Tulsa *(G-9105)*
Green Co Corporation ....G...... 918 221-3997
  Tulsa *(G-9859)*
Lektron Inc ....E...... 918 622-4978
  Tulsa *(G-10152)*

DIODES: Solid State, Germanium, Silicon, Etc

Umicore Optical Mtls USA Inc ....D...... 918 673-1650
  Quapaw *(G-8034)*

DIRECT SELLING ESTABLISHMENTS, NEC

Fort Cobb Locker Plant ....G...... 405 643-2355
  Fort Cobb *(G-3171)*
Hejin Waldran ....G...... 918 408-3500
  Claremore *(G-1632)*

DIRECT SELLING ESTABLISHMENTS: Food Svcs

Felinis Cookies Inc ....G...... 918 742-3638
  Tulsa *(G-9734)*

PRODUCT SECTION

DIRECT SELLING ESTABLISHMENTS: Home Related Prdts
Gibsons Treasures..................................G....... 405 835-1109
Oklahoma City *(G-6152)*

DISHWASHING EQPT: Commercial
Auto Chlor Services LLC.......................G....... 580 657-4482
Lone Grove *(G-4114)*

DISINFECTING & DEODORIZING SVCS
Bio-Cide International Inc ....G....... 405 364-1940
Norman *(G-4932)*

DISINFECTING & PEST CONTROL SERVICES
Darren McIninch......................................G....... 405 912-8403
Oklahoma City *(G-5285)*

DISINFECTING SVCS
Mother Earth Eco Entps LLC ....G....... 785 250-8706
Ada *(G-68)*

DISK DRIVES: Computer
Seagate Technology LLC ....B....... 405 324-3000
Oklahoma City *(G-7102)*
Seagate Technology LLC ....A....... 800 732-4283
Oklahoma City *(G-7103)*

DISPENSING EQPT & PARTS, BEVERAGE: Coolers, Milk/Water, Elec
Refunk My Junk Inc ....G....... 405 990-0707
Edmond *(G-2594)*

DISPLAY LETTERING SVCS
Chambers Signs......................................G....... 918 251-6513
Broken Arrow *(G-865)*
Frederick Sommers Wstn Sign Co ....F....... 918 587-2300
Tulsa *(G-9773)*
Lettering Express OK Inc ....E....... 405 235-8999
Oklahoma City *(G-6469)*

DISTILLERS DRIED GRAIN & SOLUBLES
Twisters Distillery ....G....... 405 237-3499
Moore *(G-4580)*

DOCKS: Floating, Wood
Safe Harbor Docks Inc ....G....... 918 376-2756
Owasso *(G-7610)*
Safe Harbor Products LLC ....G....... 918 376-2756
Owasso *(G-7611)*

DOCKS: Prefabricated Metal
Meeco Sullivan LLC ....F....... 918 423-6833
McAlester *(G-4320)*

DOCUMENT DESTRUCTION SVC
Mid-Con Data Services Inc ....E....... 405 478-1234
Oklahoma City *(G-6592)*

DOLLIES: Industrial
Mac Manufacturing Inc ....G....... 405 527-8270
Purcell *(G-8013)*
Shelley Benefield ....G....... 580 436-0296
Ada *(G-86)*

DOOR FRAMES: Wood
Osage Door Co Inc ....G....... 918 542-7281
Miami *(G-4426)*

DOOR OPERATING SYSTEMS: Electric
Aztec Ne Overhead Door Inc................G....... 918 341-7502
Claremore *(G-1586)*
Daniel Garage Door Sales & Svc ....G....... 580 628-3769
Tonkawa *(G-8973)*

DOORS & WINDOWS WHOLESALERS: All Materials
Cimarron Glass LLC ....G....... 918 225-6600
Cushing *(G-1925)*

Sufrank Corporation..............................E....... 580 353-4600
Lawton *(G-4006)*

DOORS & WINDOWS: Screen & Storm
Precision Shelters..................................F....... 405 936-0900
Oklahoma City *(G-6883)*
Smart Shelters Inc ....F....... 405 702-7775
Oklahoma City *(G-7151)*

DOORS & WINDOWS: Storm, Metal
Charles ODell ....G....... 405 745-3353
Mustang *(G-4768)*
Enid Insulation & Siding Inc ....G....... 580 237-5317
Enid *(G-2953)*
Taylor Storm Shelters LLC ....G....... 405 372-8130
Stillwater *(G-8765)*

DOORS, LOUVER: Metal
Maro International Corp ....G....... 918 836-7749
Tulsa *(G-10215)*

DOORS: Combination Screen & Storm, Wood
Ardmore Construction Sup Inc............G....... 580 223-2322
Ardmore *(G-245)*

DOORS: Garage, Overhead, Metal
Mid-America Door Company................D....... 580 765-9994
Ponca City *(G-7852)*

DOORS: Garage, Overhead, Wood
Classic Overhead Doo..........................G....... 580 931-0340
Durant *(G-2215)*

DOORS: Hangar, Metal
Dormakaba USA Inc..............................G....... 405 232-6761
Oklahoma City *(G-5969)*

DOORS: Wooden
Hugo Sash & Door Inc ....F....... 580 326-5569
Hugo *(G-3613)*
Hutchinson Products Company ....E....... 405 946-4403
Oklahoma City *(G-6277)*
LDS Building Specialties LLC ....G....... 405 917-9901
Oklahoma City *(G-6460)*
Quality Wholesale Millwork Inc ....G....... 405 681-6575
Oklahoma City *(G-6938)*
Southern Millwork Inc...........................E....... 918 585-8125
Tulsa *(G-10800)*
Windor Supply & Mfg Inc ....E....... 918 664-4017
Tulsa *(G-11137)*

DRAFTING SPLYS WHOLESALERS
Johnny L Ruth ....G....... 580 223-3061
Ardmore *(G-316)*

DRAFTING SVCS
Interactive Cad Services Inc ....G....... 918 251-4470
Broken Arrow *(G-940)*
Rapid Jack Solutions Inc ....G....... 405 203-3131
Norman *(G-5129)*

DRAPERIES & CURTAINS
Be-Hive Interior Drapery Fctry.............G....... 918 599-0292
Tulsa *(G-9275)*
Clearco Window Cleaning LLC............G....... 580 248-9547
Lawton *(G-3907)*
Cord & Pleat Design Inc ....G....... 918 622-7676
Broken Arrow *(G-1117)*
Curry Shades LLC.................................G....... 918 779-3902
Tulsa *(G-9524)*
Finished Seam ....G....... 918 742-4727
Tulsa *(G-9745)*
Hoppis Interiors ....G....... 405 390-2963
Choctaw *(G-1545)*
Interior Designers Supply Inc ....F....... 405 521-1551
Oklahoma City *(G-6318)*
Pats Custom Draperies ....G....... 405 794-1019
Moore *(G-4551)*
Ray Harrington Draperies ....G....... 405 789-6710
Bethany *(G-593)*
Springcrest Drapery Center ....G....... 918 258-5644
Broken Arrow *(G-1058)*
Traceys Window Boutique Inc ....G....... 918 495-1806
Tulsa *(G-10965)*

Vus Fabrics LLC.....................................G....... 405 330-9050
Edmond *(G-2676)*

DRAPERIES: Plastic & Textile, From Purchased Materials
Decorator Drapery Mfg Inc ....E....... 405 942-5613
Oklahoma City *(G-5917)*
Fabricut Inc..F....... 918 825-4400
Pryor *(G-7962)*
Johnsons Spring Crest Drpery C ....G....... 405 238-7341
Pauls Valley *(G-7662)*
Patricia McKay ....G....... 580 355-2739
Cache *(G-1230)*
Sam Dee Custom Draperies ....G....... 405 631-6128
Oklahoma City *(G-7074)*

DRAPERY & UPHOLSTERY STORES: Draperies
Hoppis Interiors ....G....... 405 390-2963
Choctaw *(G-1545)*
Johnsons Spring Crest Drpery C ....G....... 405 238-7341
Pauls Valley *(G-7662)*
Patricia McKay ....G....... 580 355-2739
Cache *(G-1230)*
Pats Custom Draperies ....G....... 405 794-1019
Moore *(G-4551)*
Sam Dee Custom Draperies ....G....... 405 631-6128
Oklahoma City *(G-7074)*
Warren Ramsey Inc...............................G....... 405 528-2828
Oklahoma City *(G-7422)*

DRAPES & DRAPERY FABRICS, FROM MANMADE FIBER
Ray Harrington Draperies ....G....... 405 789-6710
Bethany *(G-593)*

DRILL BITS
Duncan Bit Service Inc.........................F....... 580 255-9787
Duncan *(G-2109)*
Kanoka Ridge Services ....G....... 580 302-1561
Lahoma *(G-3856)*
Linton Jim & John.................................G....... 580 628-3093
Tonkawa *(G-8978)*
Prelesnicks Repair Service ....G....... 580 628-3179
Tonkawa *(G-8979)*

DRILLING MACHINERY & EQPT: Oil & Gas
Asbury Machine Corporation................F....... 580 628-3416
Tonkawa *(G-8972)*
CP Energy Holdings LLC ....F....... 405 513-6006
Edmond *(G-2369)*
Den-Con Tool Co ....F....... 405 670-5942
Oklahoma City *(G-5921)*
Eco Oil Fill Services...............................E....... 580 774-2240
Weatherford *(G-11409)*
Engineering Technology Inc ....E....... 918 492-0508
Tulsa *(G-9687)*
Gator Rigs LLC.....................................G....... 405 598-3266
Tecumseh *(G-8916)*
Horizontal Well Drillers LLC................G....... 405 527-1232
Purcell *(G-8010)*
JV Energy Services Inc ....F....... 620 482-0244
Turpin *(G-11182)*
Magnus Industries LLC ....G....... 405 513-8295
Edmond *(G-2501)*
Maverick Oil Tools LLC ....G....... 405 853-5524
Hennessey *(G-3476)*
Mowdy Machine Inc ....G....... 580 252-9333
Duncan *(G-2157)*
OK Pump and Supply ....G....... 580 856-4010
Ratliff City *(G-8059)*
Raptor Oilfield Controls LLC ....G....... 580 251-9806
Duncan *(G-2166)*
Reef Services LLC ....E....... 405 756-4747
Lindsay *(G-4080)*
Reef Services LLC ....G....... 918 287-3850
Pawhuska *(G-7694)*
Reel Power Industrial Inc ....D....... 405 609-3326
Oklahoma City *(G-6998)*
Reel Power Wire & Cable Inc ....E....... 918 584-1000
Oklahoma City *(G-7000)*
Reputation Services & Mfg LLC ....E....... 918 437-2077
Tulsa *(G-10643)*
Taylor Industries LLC ....G....... 918 266-7301
Tulsa *(G-10905)*

Employee Codes: A=Over 500 employees, B=251-500
C=101-250, D=51-100, E=20-50, F=10-19, G=1-9

DRILLING MACHINERY & EQPT: Oil & Gas

USA-Bops LLC .... G 405 265-2988
Oklahoma City *(G-7381)*

DRILLING MACHINERY & EQPT: Water Well

Powells Waterwell Pump and Sup .... G 918 637-9150
Bristow *(G-794)*
United Cable Tool & Supply LLC .... G 918 760-9012
Mannford *(G-4193)*

DRILLING MUD COMPOUNDS, CONDITIONERS & ADDITIVES

Adko Inc .... G 405 677-6507
Oklahoma City *(G-5375)*
Custer Enterprises Inc .... F 580 371-9588
Mannsville *(G-4195)*
Montello Inc .... G 918 665-1170
Tulsa *(G-10301)*
Western Hull Sacking Inc .... G 580 335-2144
Frederick *(G-3204)*

DRILLS & DRILLING EQPT: Mining

Flotek Industries Inc .... G 580 252-5111
Duncan *(G-2118)*
Helvey International Usa Inc .... E 405 203-0251
Oklahoma City *(G-6237)*
Technical Manufacturing Inc .... F 918 485-0380
Wagoner *(G-11292)*

DRILLS: Rock, Portable

J T Harrison Construction Co .... F 918 967-2852
Stigler *(G-8633)*
Riverside Operations Group LLC .... E 918 908-9480
Broken Arrow *(G-1034)*

DRINKING PLACES: Saloon

Shes Happy Hair Okc LLC .... G 405 328-3464
Oklahoma City *(G-7122)*

DRIVE SHAFTS

Muncie Power Products Inc .... C 918 838-0900
Tulsa *(G-10316)*
Precision Drive Ltd Inc .... G 405 495-1344
Oklahoma City *(G-6881)*

DRIVE-A-WAY AUTOMOBILE SVCS

Mike Bailey Motors Inc .... F 918 652-9637
Henryetta *(G-3512)*

DRUG STORES

Natures Rx Inc .... G 405 484-7302
Paoli *(G-7638)*

DRUG TESTING KITS: Blood & Urine

Knox Laboratory Services Inc .... G 918 331-9982
Bartlesville *(G-504)*
Kopps On Run LLC .... G 580 326-9400
Hugo *(G-3616)*

DRUGS & DRUG PROPRIETARIES, WHOL: Biologicals/Allied Prdts

Solidtech Animal Health Inc .... F 405 387-3300
Newcastle *(G-4841)*

DRUGS & DRUG PROPRIETARIES, WHOLESALE

Prescription Care LLC .... G 405 310-9230
Norman *(G-5121)*

DRUMS: Shipping, Metal

Mobile Mini Inc .... F 918 582-5857
Tulsa *(G-10288)*

DRYCLEANING & LAUNDRY SVCS: Commercial & Family

Industrial Power Wash Inc .... G 405 787-9274
Bethany *(G-582)*

DRYERS & REDRYERS: Indl

Doyle Dryers Inc .... G 918 224-4002
Tulsa *(G-9601)*

DUCTS: Sheet Metal

Air Duct Inc .... F 918 445-1196
Tulsa *(G-9119)*
Council Stainless & Shtmtl .... G 405 787-4400
Oklahoma City *(G-5842)*
Gauge Metal Fab LLC .... G 918 794-1700
Tulsa *(G-9808)*
Southern Sheet Metal Works Inc .... E 918 584-3371
Tulsa *(G-10802)*

DUMPSTERS: Garbage

Affordable Dumpster OK LLC .... G 405 535-6644
Oklahoma City *(G-5395)*
Canadian Town of Inc .... G 918 339-2517
Canadian *(G-1261)*
Dumpster Service Plus .... G 405 417-3707
Oklahoma City *(G-5986)*
Hill Steel Corporation .... E 918 336-2430
Bartlesville *(G-494)*
N E O Fabrication L L C .... G 918 541-9203
Miami *(G-4422)*
Okc Dumpsters Inc .... G 405 640-4345
Edmond *(G-2548)*
Shelton Sanitation .... G 918 469-3498
Kinta *(G-3836)*

EARTH SCIENCE SVCS

Bromide Inc .... G 405 360-2999
Norman *(G-4945)*

EATING PLACES

Cakes & More .... G 918 649-0451
Poteau *(G-7899)*
Castle Rock Kitchens .... G 405 751-1822
Oklahoma City *(G-5709)*
Donut Shop .... G 580 276-3910
Marietta *(G-4206)*
Glencoe Manufacturing Co .... F 580 669-2555
Glencoe *(G-3222)*
Imperial LLC .... B 918 437-1300
Tulsa *(G-9972)*
Macs Electric Supply Company .... F 918 583-3101
Tulsa *(G-10196)*
Ridleys Butcher Shop Inc .... G 580 255-9330
Duncan *(G-2169)*
Southwest Corset Corporation .... C 580 363-1935
Blackwell *(G-693)*
Tower Cafe Inc .... F 405 263-4853
Okarche *(G-5255)*
W H Braum Inc .... E 405 340-9288
Edmond *(G-2678)*

ECONOMIZERS, BOILER

Eco Incorporated .... G 918 258-5002
Broken Arrow *(G-894)*
Eco 2007 LLC .... G 918 258-5002
Broken Arrow *(G-895)*
Enerex Inc .... G 918 258-3573
Broken Arrow *(G-899)*

EDITING SVCS

Patricia Lyons .... G 850 445-4782
Jenks *(G-3722)*

EDITORIAL SVCS

Oklahoma Eagle LLC .... G 918 582-7124
Tulsa *(G-10398)*

EDUCATIONAL PROGRAM ADMINISTRATION, GOVERNMENT: State

Education Oklahoma Department .... F 405 743-5531
Stillwater *(G-8682)*

EDUCATIONAL SVCS

Hman Global Solutions LLC .... G 405 338-5348
Morrison *(G-4603)*
Oral Rbrts Evnglistic Assn Inc .... D 918 591-2000
Tulsa *(G-10436)*
University of Oklahoma .... E 405 325-3276
Norman *(G-5187)*

EDUCATIONAL SVCS, NONDEGREE GRANTING: Continuing Education

Oil & Gas Consultants Intl Inc .... E 918 828-2500
Tulsa *(G-10381)*

EGG WHOLESALERS

Fisher AG Enterprises Inc .... F 918 367-6382
Bristow *(G-778)*

ELECTRIC & OTHER SERVICES COMBINED

Tank & Fuel Solutions LLC .... G 918 960-4361
Claremore *(G-1691)*

ELECTRIC MOTOR REPAIR SVCS

All State Electric Motors Inc .... G 405 232-1129
Oklahoma City *(G-5413)*
All State Electric Motors Inc .... G 918 683-6581
Muskogee *(G-4645)*
Bartosh Electric Motor Center .... G 405 567-2840
Prague *(G-7920)*
Brooken Boat & Motor .... G 918 799-5227
Stigler *(G-8630)*
Built Right Compressor .... G 580 371-2007
Tishomingo *(G-8963)*
Capitol Electric Mtr Repr Inc .... F 405 235-9638
Oklahoma City *(G-5693)*
Cecils Electric Motor Co .... G 918 775-3968
Sallisaw *(G-8141)*
Doug Roberson .... G 405 372-2078
Stillwater *(G-8677)*
Enid Electric Motor Svc Inc .... F 580 234-8622
Enid *(G-2952)*
Evans Enterprises .... G 918 587-1566
Tulsa *(G-9705)*
Evans Enterprises Inc .... E 918 587-1566
Tulsa *(G-9706)*
Evans Enterprises Inc .... G 918 825-2200
Tulsa *(G-9707)*
Interstate Electric Corp .... G 918 245-4508
Sand Springs *(G-8194)*
J & W Electric Motor Company .... G 580 357-7504
Lawton *(G-3943)*
Kay Electric Motors Inc .... G 580 256-3254
Woodward *(G-11598)*
Land & Lake Electric LLC .... G 918 791-1731
Grove *(G-3278)*
Meyer Electric Motor Service .... G 580 327-1399
Alva *(G-187)*
Miami Armature Works Inc .... G 918 542-2443
Miami *(G-4413)*
Newmans Electric Motor Repair .... G 580 310-0151
Ada *(G-71)*
Pak Electric Inc .... F 580 482-1757
Altus *(G-166)*
Q E M Inc .... G 918 534-2000
Ochelata *(G-5238)*
Southwest Electric Co .... F 918 437-9494
Tulsa *(G-10805)*
Start Rite Auto Electric Inc .... G 580 924-7290
Durant *(G-2261)*
Tonys Electric Inc .... G 405 375-4103
Kingfisher *(G-3818)*
Tux Hard Shop .... G 918 885-2970
Hominy *(G-3594)*
Victors Electric Motor S .... G 405 344-7339
Blanchard *(G-743)*
W & W Electric Motor Service .... G 405 634-3776
Oklahoma City *(G-7408)*

ELECTRIC POWER DISTRIBUTION TO CONSUMERS

Ckenergy Electric Co Op Inc .... G 405 247-3041
Anadarko *(G-201)*
Grace Power LLC .... G 512 228-9049
Lawton *(G-3936)*
Oklahoma Electric Cooperative .... D 405 321-2024
Norman *(G-5100)*

ELECTRIC SERVICES

City Electric Supply Company .... G 918 871-2640
Tahlequah *(G-8857)*
City Electric Supply Company .... G 405 701-8544
Norman *(G-4958)*
Foundation Energy Company LLC .... F 918 585-1650
Tulsa *(G-9767)*

PRODUCT SECTION

ELECTRICAL GOODS, WHOLESALE: Svc Entrance Eqpt

Parker & Parsley Petroleum ....G...... 405 756-1912
 Lindsay (G-4076)
Rolco Energy Services LLC ....G...... 580 657-2602
 Ardmore (G-351)
Xtreme Energy Company ....G...... 405 273-1185
 Shawnee (G-8523)

ELECTRICAL APPARATUS & EQPT WHOLESALERS

Ademco Inc ....G...... 918 663-2822
 Tulsa (G-9104)
Awc Inc ....G...... 405 601-1090
 Oklahoma City (G-5496)
City Electric Supply Company ....G...... 918 871-2640
 Tahlequah (G-8857)
Lifetone Technology Inc ....G...... 405 200-1555
 Oklahoma City (G-6475)
Oklahoma Home Centers Inc ....E...... 405 260-7625
 Guthrie (G-3329)
Wholesale Electric Supply Co ....G...... 918 647-2200
 Poteau (G-7918)
Wilspec Technologies Inc ....E...... 405 495-8989
 Oklahoma City (G-7459)

ELECTRICAL CURRENT CARRYING WIRING DEVICES

Corrpro Companies Inc ....E...... 918 245-8791
 Sand Springs (G-8172)
Ducommun Labarge Tech Inc ....C...... 918 459-2200
 Tulsa (G-9611)
Hypower Inc ....G...... 918 341-6811
 Claremore (G-1639)
Remote Connections Inc ....F...... 918 743-3355
 Tulsa (G-10639)
Special Service Systems Inc ....E...... 918 582-7777
 Tulsa (G-10816)

ELECTRICAL EQPT & SPLYS

A Bolt Electric ....G...... 580 510-0123
 Cache (G-1223)
AMI Instruments Inc ....G...... 918 241-2665
 Sand Springs (G-8160)
Arnold Electric Inc ....G...... 405 605-1982
 Oklahoma City (G-5467)
Aviation Training Devices Inc ....F...... 918 366-6680
 Bixby (G-613)
Awc Inc ....G...... 405 601-1090
 Oklahoma City (G-5496)
Azz Incorporated ....E...... 918 295-8702
 Tulsa (G-9238)
Belden Russell Elect Co ....G...... 918 791-9600
 Grove (G-3259)
Bell & McCoy Companies Inc ....E...... 405 278-6909
 Oklahoma City (G-5543)
Bills Electric Inc ....G...... 918 341-4414
 Claremore (G-1596)
Bloom Electric Services LLC ....F...... 580 327-2345
 Alva (G-178)
Broken Arrow Electric Sup Inc ....G...... 580 924-2237
 Durant (G-2209)
Broken Arrow Electric Sup Inc ....G...... 580 436-1470
 Ada (G-13)
Caddo Electric Corp ....G...... 580 774-5280
 Weatherford (G-11396)
City Electric Supply Company ....G...... 918 871-2640
 Tahlequah (G-8857)
City Electric Supply Company ....G...... 405 701-8544
 Norman (G-4958)
Ckenergy Electric Co Op Inc ....G...... 405 247-3041
 Anadarko (G-201)
Clement Elec ....G...... 580 223-6500
 Ardmore (G-267)
Corrpro Companies Inc ....E...... 918 245-8791
 Sand Springs (G-8172)
D & L Enclosures ....G...... 918 396-7355
 Skiatook (G-8538)
Dougherty Forestry Mfg Ltd ....F...... 405 542-3520
 Hinton (G-3523)
Electrotech Inc ....G...... 918 224-5869
 Tulsa (G-9002)
Icx Technologies Inc ....G...... 703 678-2111
 Oklahoma City (G-6286)
L3 Technologies Inc ....C...... 918 258-0707
 Broken Arrow (G-962)
Marietta Tag Agency ....G...... 580 276-2101
 Marietta (G-4210)
Maverick Technologies LLC ....F...... 405 680-0100
 Oklahoma City (G-6537)

McDermott Electric LLC ....F...... 405 603-4665
 Oklahoma City (G-6547)
McDonald Electric Utility Svcs ....G...... 580 767-8845
 Ponca City (G-7848)
Mels Electric Contracting ....G...... 918 279-6036
 Coweta (G-1891)
Millers Superior Electric LLC ....G...... 918 933-4006
 Tulsa (G-10283)
Monitron Corp ....F...... 918 836-6831
 Sand Springs (G-8206)
Newton Design LLC ....D...... 918 266-6205
 Catoosa (G-1343)
Newton Design LLC ....G...... 918 381-3012
 Catoosa (G-1344)
Oklahoma Native Electric LLC ....G...... 918 824-7638
 Pryor (G-7979)
Omni Design ....G...... 918 495-0841
 Tulsa (G-10416)
Power Ready LLC ....F...... 918 289-0088
 Tulsa (G-10539)
Powerhouse Elec ....G...... 405 735-6381
 Moore (G-4553)
Practical Sales and Svc Inc ....G...... 918 446-5515
 Tulsa (G-10540)
Prism Electric Inc ....G...... 918 425-2000
 Tulsa (G-10562)
Total Control System Inc ....G...... 918 810-4004
 Owasso (G-7625)
Wholesale Electric Supply Co ....G...... 918 647-2200
 Poteau (G-7918)

ELECTRICAL EQPT FOR ENGINES

D C Ignition Co Inc ....G...... 580 332-0878
 Ada (G-28)
Draeger Interlock ....G...... 918 270-1600
 Tulsa (G-9602)
GC&i Global Inc ....G...... 918 317-4244
 Tulsa (G-9810)
Goodwill Inds Centl Okla Inc ....D...... 405 236-4451
 Oklahoma City (G-6172)
Ignition Systems & Controls ....F...... 405 682-3030
 Oklahoma City (G-6291)
Jesse Griffith Repairs ....G...... 580 379-0790
 Elk City (G-2832)
Paytons Auto ....G...... 918 540-2501
 Miami (G-4427)
Remote Connections Inc ....F...... 918 743-3355
 Tulsa (G-10639)

ELECTRICAL EQPT REPAIR & MAINTENANCE

Advance Research & Development ....G...... 405 321-0550
 Norman (G-4899)
Cecils Electric Motor Co ....G...... 918 775-3968
 Sallisaw (G-8141)
Dormakaba USA Inc ....G...... 405 232-6761
 Oklahoma City (G-5969)
Drillers Service Center Inc ....G...... 405 631-3728
 Oklahoma City (G-5980)
Evans Enterprises Inc ....G...... 405 631-1344
 Norman (G-4993)
Industrial Machine Co Inc ....F...... 405 236-5419
 Oklahoma City (G-6299)
K E Fischer LLC ....G...... 580 353-2862
 Lawton (G-3947)
L & J Welding & Machine Svc ....G...... 918 885-6666
 Hominy (G-3591)
Michael A Phillips ....G...... 918 251-0925
 Broken Arrow (G-972)
Nelson Incorporated ....G...... 918 812-5876
 Tulsa (G-10332)
Osage Neon ....G...... 918 583-4430
 Tulsa (G-10443)
Robs Magneto Service ....G...... 918 367-5735
 Tulsa (G-10665)
Sharps Machine Shop ....G...... 918 336-2516
 Bartlesville (G-528)
Wolff Machine Inc ....G...... 918 382-3000
 Seminole (G-8407)
Wood Pipe Service Inc ....G...... 405 672-6097
 Oklahoma City (G-7464)

ELECTRICAL EQPT REPAIR SVCS: High Voltage

Lamar Enterprises Inc ....E...... 405 682-5511
 Oklahoma City (G-6447)
Northwest Transformer Co Inc ....E...... 405 636-1454
 Oklahoma City (G-6695)

Southwest Electric Co ....C...... 405 733-4700
 Oklahoma City (G-7175)

ELECTRICAL EQPT: Automotive, NEC

Bobs Auto Electric ....G...... 918 687-3701
 Muskogee (G-4653)
Sledge Electric Inc ....G...... 405 793-4007
 Oklahoma City (G-5316)
Tri-State Elec Contrs LLC ....G...... 405 341-3043
 Oklahoma City (G-7324)

ELECTRICAL GOODS, WHOL: Antennas, Receiving/Satellite Dishes

Tulsat Corporation ....D...... 918 251-2887
 Broken Arrow (G-1087)

ELECTRICAL GOODS, WHOLESALE: Batteries, Storage, Indl

Exide Technologies LLC ....F...... 405 745-2511
 Oklahoma City (G-6061)

ELECTRICAL GOODS, WHOLESALE: Electrical Appliances, Major

Metro Builders Supply Inc ....E...... 405 751-8833
 Edmond (G-2515)
Whirlpool Corporation ....B...... 918 274-6000
 Tulsa (G-11115)

ELECTRICAL GOODS, WHOLESALE: Electronic Parts

Beck Illuminations LLC ....E...... 918 623-2880
 Okemah (G-5264)

ELECTRICAL GOODS, WHOLESALE: Fire Alarm Systems

Trinity Technologies LLC ....F...... 580 475-0900
 Duncan (G-2190)

ELECTRICAL GOODS, WHOLESALE: Generators

Custom Manufacturing & Maint ......G...... 405 872-1000
 Noble (G-4877)
Oklahoma Emergency Generator S ......G...... 405 735-9888
 Moore (G-4546)

ELECTRICAL GOODS, WHOLESALE: Motors

Aei Corp-Okla ....G...... 405 236-3551
 Oklahoma City (G-5389)
B & B Electric Co ....G...... 918 583-6274
 Tulsa (G-9239)
Britton Electric Motor Inc ....G...... 405 842-8357
 Oklahoma City (G-5629)
Electric Motor Service Company ...G...... 580 223-8940
 Ardmore (G-283)
Enid Electric Motor Svc Inc ....F...... 580 234-8622
 Enid (G-2952)
Evans Enterprises Inc ....E...... 918 587-1566
 Tulsa (G-9706)
Kay Electric Motors Inc ....G...... 580 256-3254
 Woodward (G-11598)
Newmans Electric Motor Repair .....G...... 580 310-0151
 Ada (G-71)
Wilson Electric Motor Svc Inc ....F...... 405 636-1515
 Oklahoma City (G-7458)

ELECTRICAL GOODS, WHOLESALE: Security Control Eqpt & Systems

Lucas Holdings LLC ....E...... 405 524-1811
 Oklahoma City (G-6500)
Scudder Service & Supply Inc ....G...... 405 232-6069
 Oklahoma City (G-7101)
Trinity Technologies LLC ....F...... 580 475-0900
 Duncan (G-2190)

ELECTRICAL GOODS, WHOLESALE: Svc Entrance Eqpt

Proud Veterans Intl Ltd ....G...... 316 209-8701
 Lawton (G-3986)

Employee Codes: A=Over 500 employees, B=251-500
C=101-250, D=51-100, E=20-50, F=10-19, G=1-9

ELECTRICAL GOODS, WHOLESALE: Switches, Exc Electronic, NEC

Remote Connections Inc .... F 918 743-3355
Tulsa *(G-10639)*

ELECTRICAL GOODS, WHOLESALE: Transformer & Transmission Eqpt

R C Ramsey Co .... F 918 746-4300
Tulsa *(G-10602)*

ELECTRICAL GOODS, WHOLESALE: Transformers

Wiley Transformer Co .... G 918 225-5772
Cushing *(G-1970)*

ELECTRICAL GOODS, WHOLESALE: Wire & Cable

United Slings Inc .... G 405 598-2616
Tecumseh *(G-8930)*

ELECTRICAL INDL APPARATUS, NEC

Zentech .... G 918 445-1881
Tulsa *(G-11175)*

ELECTRICAL SPLYS

Belden Russell Elect Co .... G 918 791-9600
Grove *(G-3259)*
Bell & McCoy Companies Inc .... E 405 278-6909
Oklahoma City *(G-5543)*
Broken Arrow Electric Sup Inc .... G 580 924-2237
Durant *(G-2209)*
Broken Arrow Electric Sup Inc .... G 580 436-1470
Ada *(G-13)*
City Electric Supply Company .... G 405 701-8544
Norman *(G-4958)*
Crandall and Sanders Inc .... G 405 375-3242
Kingfisher *(G-3794)*
Macs Electric Supply Company .... F 918 583-3101
Tulsa *(G-10196)*
Pak Electric Inc .... F 580 482-1757
Altus *(G-166)*
Tech Inc .... F 405 547-8324
Perkins *(G-7724)*

ELECTRICAL SUPPLIES: Porcelain

Coorstek Inc .... B 405 601-4371
Oklahoma City *(G-5832)*

ELECTRICAL WIRING TOOLS: Fish Wire

HALAQ Inc .... G 405 321-7293
Newalla *(G-4810)*

ELECTROLYSIS & EPILATORY SVCS

Medical Csmtc Elctrlysis Clnic .... G 405 755-7599
Oklahoma City *(G-6557)*

ELECTROMEDICAL EQPT

Advanced Medical Instrs Inc .... C 918 250-0566
Broken Arrow *(G-816)*
Oto-Biomechanics LLC .... G 405 325-6668
Norman *(G-5105)*
Phoenix Group Holding Company .... F 405 948-7788
Oklahoma City *(G-6844)*
Vadovations Inc .... E 405 601-5520
Oklahoma City *(G-7385)*

ELECTRON TUBES

All Electronic and More Llc .... G 918 557-5410
Collinsville *(G-1799)*
Versatech Industries Inc .... G 918 366-7400
Bixby *(G-670)*

ELECTRON TUBES: Parts

Time Mark Inc .... D 918 438-1220
Tulsa *(G-10942)*

ELECTRONIC COMPONENTS

Csi .... G 319 274-5005
Catoosa *(G-1314)*
Duncan Overhead Door .... G 405 222-0748
Chickasha *(G-1454)*
James A Brumit Jr .... G 405 924-9696
Moore *(G-4530)*
Yukon Manufacturing Inc .... G 918 850-3131
Oklahoma City *(G-7484)*

ELECTRONIC DEVICES: Solid State, NEC

Downing Manufacturing Inc .... F 918 224-1116
Tulsa *(G-9001)*

ELECTRONIC EQPT REPAIR SVCS

Combotronics Inc .... E 918 543-3300
Inola *(G-3656)*
Nyikos Inc .... G 918 299-3190
Tulsa *(G-10368)*
WD Distributing Co Inc .... F 405 634-3603
Oklahoma City *(G-7428)*

ELECTRONIC PARTS & EQPT WHOLESALERS

Hetronic Usa Inc .... E 405 946-3574
Oklahoma City *(G-6245)*
Media Specialists Inc .... G 918 622-0077
Tulsa *(G-10238)*
Tulsat Corporation .... D 918 251-2887
Broken Arrow *(G-1087)*

ELECTRONIC TRAINING DEVICES

Trubend Systems Inc .... G 918 342-3373
Claremore *(G-1695)*

ELECTROPLATING & PLATING SVC

Duracoatings Holdings LLC .... D 405 692-2249
Oklahoma City *(G-5990)*
Macs Electric Supply Company .... F 918 583-3101
Tulsa *(G-10196)*
Premier Metal Finishing Inc .... G 405 947-0200
Oklahoma City *(G-6885)*
Protective Coatings Intl LLC .... G 405 716-4734
Seminole *(G-8395)*
Spray-Rite Inc .... E 479 648-3351
Pocola *(G-7786)*

ELEMENTARY & SECONDARY SCHOOLS, PUBLIC

Independent School .... E 918 245-2622
Sand Springs *(G-8192)*

ELEVATOR: Grain, Storage Only

Luther Mill and Farm Supply .... G 405 277-3221
Luther *(G-4135)*

ELEVATORS & EQPT

Travertine Inc .... G 918 583-5210
Tulsa *(G-10972)*

ELEVATORS: Automobile

Vasser Machine .... G 918 225-2677
Cushing *(G-1966)*

EMBLEMS: Embroidered

Dudz and Things Inc .... G 918 321-9443
Sapulpa *(G-8269)*
Sew Tulsa .... G 918 627-1577
Tulsa *(G-10736)*
USA Industries Oklahoma Inc .... G 405 840-5577
Edmond *(G-2661)*

EMBROIDERING & ART NEEDLEWORK FOR THE TRADE

Adventures In Stitching LLC .... G 918 995-7445
Tulsa *(G-9114)*
Bordeauxs Embroidery .... G 405 227-0958
Oklahoma City *(G-5619)*
Carolyns Mouse House .... G 405 354-2858
Yukon *(G-11702)*
Causley Productions Inc .... F 405 372-0940
Stillwater *(G-8666)*
Christys Quilts .... G 405 853-2155
Hennessey *(G-3450)*
Cindys Stitching .... G 405 735-7126
Oklahoma City *(G-5281)*
Corporate Image Apparel LLC .... G 405 659-8264
Oklahoma City *(G-5839)*
Creative Stitches By C S .... G 918 418-9049
Afton *(G-116)*
Creativestitch LLC .... G 405 664-1144
Edmond *(G-2373)*
Custom Embroidery & Gifts LLC ...... G 405 240-7950
Wellston *(G-11468)*
Dinks Monogramming & EMB LLC ..... G 580 541-4371
Enid *(G-2941)*
Embroidery By Stacie .... G 580 656-5232
Ardmore *(G-285)*
Embroidery Creations .... G 405 728-1355
Oklahoma City *(G-6029)*
Embroidery Plus .... G 918 652-2117
Weleetka *(G-11464)*
Embroidme of Tulsa .... G 918 459-6699
Tulsa *(G-9665)*
Erin Turner Custom EMB LLC .... G 918 869-6481
Tulsa *(G-9697)*
Fashion Sports By Sia Inc .... F 405 524-9990
Oklahoma City *(G-6077)*
Free Spirit Embroidery .... G 918 429-4552
McAlester *(G-4301)*
Freedom Embroidery LLC .... G 580 540-8504
Enid *(G-2959)*
Freestyle Embroidery .... G 405 802-5838
Oklahoma City *(G-6116)*
Heart 2 Heart Embroidery .... G 405 401-7408
Oklahoma City *(G-6232)*
Im Stitched & Stoned .... G 918 418-9107
Vinita *(G-11261)*
Jans Digitzing & EMB LLC .... G 970 587-2834
Choctaw *(G-1547)*
Judy Airson .... G 580 254-9076
Woodward *(G-11597)*
K A G U Inc .... G 405 364-4637
Norman *(G-5045)*
L C D Embroidery .... G 405 379-6083
Holdenville *(G-3555)*
Lane Victory Screen Printing .... G 580 924-3556
Durant *(G-2243)*
Last Stitch Studio .... G 918 200-5859
Tulsa *(G-10132)*
Lightstitching .... G 405 210-7645
Norman *(G-5059)*
Love Letters Monogramming LLC ..... G 918 231-6691
Tulsa *(G-10179)*
Melbre Southern Stitches LLC .... G 918 399-4966
Cushing *(G-1945)*
Merritts Monograms LLC .... G 918 346-2757
Oklahoma City *(G-6569)*
Miss Priss Monograms & EMB .... G 918 697-9468
Talala *(G-8901)*
Monogram Hut .... G 214 707-4196
Jenks *(G-3718)*
Mulberry Tree Graphics .... G 580 248-3194
Lawton *(G-3974)*
Munger and Krout Inc .... F 580 237-7060
Enid *(G-3016)*
Mzmouze Embroidery Creat LLP ...... G 405 696-6545
Guthrie *(G-3326)*
One Moore Embroidery Place .... G 580 328-5755
Taloga *(G-8907)*
Parkerville USA EMB & More .... G 918 636-0048
Owasso *(G-7601)*
Pinpoint Monograms Inc .... F 405 228-0600
Oklahoma City *(G-6850)*
R-5 Caps & Tees .... G 580 256-3579
Woodward *(G-11626)*
S and W Embroidery .... G 580 654-2929
Carnegie *(G-1278)*
Sand Tech Screening and EMB .... G 918 458-0312
Tahlequah *(G-8882)*
Sebo Lanila Lynn .... G 479 719-5612
Spiro *(G-8616)*
Sew Glam Monogram LLC .... G 918 606-2644
Broken Arrow *(G-1049)*
Sew Much Fun .... G 405 359-1544
Edmond *(G-2616)*
Sew Stylish Embroidery LLC .... G 580 238-8797
Marietta *(G-4212)*
Sewcool Embroidery LLC .... G 405 326-2854
Edmond *(G-2617)*
Shirts & Stuff .... G 918 445-0323
Tulsa *(G-10749)*
Shops of Standing Rock Inc .... G 580 364-0834
Atoka *(G-423)*
Southern Lace Stitchery .... G 405 414-3550
Yukon *(G-11784)*

PRODUCT SECTION

ENGINEERING SVCS: Construction & Civil

Star Corral ....G....... 918 251-9795
 Broken Arrow *(G-1060)*
Stitch Boom Ba LLC ....G....... 918 518-5859
 Jenks *(G-3729)*
Stitch Design ....G....... 405 350-0126
 Yukon *(G-11789)*
Stitch N Sew Embroidery ....G....... 432 741-0433
 Ochelata *(G-5239)*
Stitch Witch ....G....... 918 371-3568
 Collinsville *(G-1825)*
Stitch Wizard ....G....... 405 816-6356
 Mustang *(G-4796)*
Stitchabella LLC ....G....... 405 562-3316
 Edmond *(G-2633)*
Stitched By Shayna ....G....... 405 708-8614
 Oklahoma City *(G-7210)*
Stitchin Acres ....G....... 405 740-6035
 Kremlin *(G-3855)*
Stitchin Stitches ....G....... 918 251-9696
 Broken Arrow *(G-1063)*
Stitchsumm LLC ....G....... 918 201-2148
 Jenks *(G-3730)*
Sues Monogramming ....G....... 918 455-1011
 Broken Arrow *(G-1066)*
Sunflower Embroidery LLC ....G....... 918 869-9646
 Fort Gibson *(G-3179)*
T and L Embroidery ....G....... 580 493-2239
 Drummond *(G-2048)*
Tazz Too Embroidery ....G....... 580 334-7373
 Woodward *(G-11640)*
Tony Newcomb Sportswear Inc ....G....... 405 232-0022
 Oklahoma City *(G-7303)*
Tts Embroiderys Plus ....G....... 918 770-3515
 Glenpool *(G-3243)*
Tumbleweed Embroidery and Scre ....G....... 580 371-9742
 Mannsville *(G-4196)*
Twist A Stitch ....G....... 918 514-0143
 Sand Springs *(G-8234)*
Unique Stitches Inc ....G....... 918 794-5494
 Tulsa *(G-11035)*
Webber Kathryn ....G....... 405 379-3872
 Holdenville *(G-3562)*

EMBROIDERING SVC

A Stitch of Art ....G....... 918 638-2511
 Owasso *(G-7540)*
Alico Embroidery Etc ....G....... 405 321-2998
 Norman *(G-4903)*
American TS ....G....... 918 288-6682
 Glenpool *(G-3230)*
Apothem ....G....... 405 447-2345
 Norman *(G-4912)*
Corporate Image Inc ....G....... 918 516-8376
 Owasso *(G-7556)*
Corser Group Inc ....G....... 918 749-6456
 Tulsa *(G-9492)*
Creative Apparel and More Inc ....G....... 918 682-1283
 Muskogee *(G-4664)*
Debbie Do EMB & Screen Prtg ....G....... 580 353-2606
 Lawton *(G-3918)*
Embrodred Mnograms Designs LLC ....G....... 918 335-5055
 Bartlesville *(G-481)*
Fancy Stitch ....G....... 580 699-2112
 Lawton *(G-3926)*
First Impression Custom EMB ....G....... 918 787-4182
 Grove *(G-3270)*
Ft Sill Tees & Embroidery ....G....... 580 248-8484
 Lawton *(G-3932)*
Gail Evans Embroidery ....G....... 918 605-1013
 Tulsa *(G-9796)*
Gold Star Graphics Inc ....F....... 405 677-1529
 Oklahoma City *(G-6168)*
Great Plins Grphics Shwnee LLC ....G....... 405 273-4263
 Shawnee *(G-8455)*
Initially Yours Inc ....G....... 918 832-9889
 Tulsa *(G-9986)*
Integrity Screen Works Inc ....E....... 918 663-8339
 Tulsa *(G-9999)*
JIm2 LLC ....G....... 918 258-0239
 Broken Arrow *(G-946)*
Marketing & Embroidery Magic ....G....... 405 340-9677
 Edmond *(G-2506)*
Monograms Elite Inc ....G....... 580 353-1635
 Lawton *(G-3973)*
Oklahoma EMB Sup & Design ....G....... 405 359-2741
 Edmond *(G-2549)*
Peabody & Kent Designs Inc ....G....... 405 439-4300
 Tulsa *(G-10478)*
Personal Expressions ....G....... 918 406-4581
 Broken Arrow *(G-1003)*

Personal Expressions Inc ....G....... 918 660-0494
 Tulsa *(G-10498)*
Personal Expressions Inc ....G....... 918 660-0494
 Tulsa *(G-10499)*
Play 2 Win Athletics ....G....... 918 341-9500
 Claremore *(G-1671)*
Precision Punch ....G....... 405 340-7546
 Edmond *(G-2574)*
Productive Clutter Inc ....G....... 405 447-3839
 Norman *(G-5124)*
S E & M Monogramming ....G....... 405 377-9677
 Stillwater *(G-8751)*
Sewfly Embroidery ....G....... 580 477-1957
 Altus *(G-168)*
Showstring USA Inc ....G....... 580 335-7171
 Frederick *(G-3200)*
Stitch N Stuff Embroidery Shop ....G....... 918 465-3036
 Wilburton *(G-11525)*
Tonis Stitches-N-Stuff Inc ....G....... 580 688-2697
 Hollis *(G-3570)*

EMBROIDERING SVC: Schiffli Machine

Baywest Embroidery ....G....... 580 626-4728
 Jet *(G-3741)*
Big Creek Custom Embroidery ....G....... 918 446-6054
 Tulsa *(G-9288)*
C&S Design ....G....... 918 455-8137
 Broken Arrow *(G-1116)*

EMBROIDERY ADVERTISING SVCS

Girlinghouse Unlimited LLC ....G....... 405 265-3330
 Mustang *(G-4773)*
S E & M Monogramming ....G....... 405 377-9677
 Stillwater *(G-8751)*
Safetyco LLC ....G....... 405 603-3306
 Oklahoma City *(G-7072)*

EMBROIDERY KITS

Columbia Rehabilitation Svcs ....G....... 405 359-2741
 Edmond *(G-2360)*
World Weidner LLC ....G....... 580 765-9999
 Ponca City *(G-7888)*

EMERGENCY ALARMS

Ademco Inc ....G....... 918 663-2822
 Tulsa *(G-9104)*
Ademco Inc ....G....... 405 681-4008
 Oklahoma City *(G-5373)*
Ducommun Labarge Tech Inc ....C....... 918 459-2200
 Tulsa *(G-9611)*
Emergency Alert Response ....G....... 918 298-0500
 Tulsa *(G-9668)*
Johnson Controls ....G....... 918 626-3773
 Pocola *(G-7783)*
Lifetone Technology Inc ....G....... 405 200-1555
 Oklahoma City *(G-6475)*

EMPLOYEE LEASING SVCS

Cook Machine Company ....E....... 580 252-1699
 Duncan *(G-2099)*

EMPLOYMENT AGENCY SVCS

Optronics International LLC ....E....... 918 683-9514
 Muskogee *(G-4727)*

ENCLOSURES: Electronic

All Tools Co Inc ....F....... 405 942-6655
 Oklahoma City *(G-5416)*
Poteau Panel Shop Incorporated ....G....... 918 647-4331
 Poteau *(G-7912)*

ENCLOSURES: Screen

Byers Products Group Inc ....G....... 405 491-8550
 Oklahoma City *(G-5652)*

ENGINE PARTS & ACCESS: Internal Combustion

Arrow Engine Company ....D....... 918 583-5711
 Tulsa *(G-9211)*

ENGINE REBUILDING: Diesel

Memorial Auto Supply Inc ....F....... 405 324-5400
 Oklahoma City *(G-6564)*

Pacific Power Group LLC ....G....... 405 685-4630
 Oklahoma City *(G-6793)*

ENGINE REBUILDING: Gas

Hudson Bros Rmanufactured Engs .....G....... 405 598-2260
 Tecumseh *(G-8919)*
Production Engine & Pump Inc ....F....... 405 672-3644
 Oklahoma City *(G-6910)*
Thomas H Scott Western LLC ....G....... 405 632-6860
 Oklahoma City *(G-7283)*

ENGINEERING HELP SVCS

Bonavista Technologies Inc ....G....... 918 250-3435
 Tulsa *(G-9318)*

ENGINEERING SVCS

BS&b Safety Systems LLC ....C....... 918 622-5950
 Tulsa *(G-9346)*
Camcast Corp ....C....... 918 371-9966
 Owasso *(G-7551)*
Corrpro Companies Inc ....E....... 918 245-8791
 Sand Springs *(G-8172)*
Datalog Systems ....G....... 918 245-3939
 Tulsa *(G-9554)*
H K & S Iron Co ....E....... 405 745-2761
 Oklahoma City *(G-6198)*
Hansen Research LLC ....G....... 405 659-5079
 Norman *(G-5015)*
Iap Worldwide Services Inc ....F....... 321 784-7100
 Oklahoma City *(G-6282)*
Innovative Products Inc ....E....... 405 949-0040
 Oklahoma City *(G-6307)*
Innovative Technology Ltd ....F....... 580 243-1559
 Elk City *(G-2827)*
Kihomac Inc ....D....... 937 429-7744
 Midwest City *(G-4445)*
Linde Engineering N Amer LLC ....C....... 918 477-1424
 Tulsa *(G-10164)*
Mingo Aerospace LLC ....F....... 918 272-7371
 Owasso *(G-7591)*
Oilfield Improvements Inc ....G....... 918 250-5584
 Broken Arrow *(G-993)*
Pinnacle Energy Services LLC ....G....... 405 810-9151
 Oklahoma City *(G-6849)*
Precision Engrg & Mch Works ....G....... 580 658-9193
 Marlow *(G-4238)*
Quality Equipment Design Inc ....F....... 918 492-4019
 Tulsa *(G-10591)*
Rapid Jack Solutions Inc ....G....... 405 203-3131
 Norman *(G-5129)*
Schmoldt Engineering Services ....F....... 918 336-1221
 Bartlesville *(G-526)*
Southwest Engineering ....G....... 405 634-2841
 Oklahoma City *(G-7176)*
Techtrol Inc ....E....... 918 762-1050
 Pawnee *(G-7712)*
Unami LLC ....G....... 405 320-5696
 Anadarko *(G-208)*

ENGINEERING SVCS: Aviation Or Aeronautical

Archein Aerospace LLC ....E....... 682 499-2150
 Ponca City *(G-7798)*
Ases LLC ....C....... 405 219-3420
 Oklahoma City *(G-5473)*
Ases LLC ....C....... 405 219-3400
 Oklahoma City *(G-5474)*
Crown Products Inc ....E....... 918 446-4591
 Tulsa *(G-9517)*
Inglesrud Corp ....G....... 405 429-7928
 Oklahoma City *(G-6304)*
Zivko Aeronautics Inc ....E....... 405 282-1330
 Guthrie *(G-3343)*

ENGINEERING SVCS: Building Construction

Chickasaw Defense Services Inc ....G....... 405 203-0144
 Oklahoma City *(G-5759)*

ENGINEERING SVCS: Chemical

Fts International Services LLC ....F....... 405 574-3900
 Chickasha *(G-1460)*

ENGINEERING SVCS: Construction & Civil

Martinez Fencing Construction ....F....... 580 309-2046
 Clinton *(G-1758)*

Employee Codes: A=Over 500 employees, B=251-500
C=101-250, D=51-100, E=20-50, F=10-19, G=1-9

2020 Oklahoma Directory
of Manufacturers & Processors

ENGINEERING SVCS: Construction & Civil

Montross Tirita ....G....... 918 241-5637
  Sand Springs *(G-8207)*
RMH Survey LLC ....G....... 918 927-8868
  Vinita *(G-11270)*
Shaw Group Inc ....A....... 918 445-7744
  Tulsa *(G-10739)*
Sutherland Well Service Inc ....F....... 580 856-3538
  Ratliff City *(G-8069)*

ENGINEERING SVCS: Electrical Or Electronic

Advance Research & Development.......G....... 405 321-0550
  Norman *(G-4899)*
Advanced Crative Solutions Inc...........G....... 918 519-3651
  Jenks *(G-3688)*
Fluid Technologies Inc ....E....... 405 624-0400
  Stillwater *(G-8693)*
Shen Te Enterprises Inc ....E....... 918 505-7711
  Tulsa *(G-10742)*
Unicorp Systems Inc ....E....... 918 446-1874
  Tulsa *(G-11034)*

ENGINEERING SVCS: Fire Protection

Invictus Engrg Cnstr Svcs ....G....... 405 701-5622
  Norman *(G-5037)*

ENGINEERING SVCS: Industrial

Linde Engineering N Amer LLC............G....... 281 717-9090
  Tulsa *(G-10165)*

ENGINEERING SVCS: Mechanical

Axiom Metal Solutions LLC ....G....... 918 361-5982
  Okmulgee *(G-7494)*
Born Inc ....E....... 918 582-2186
  Tulsa *(G-9322)*
Diw Engneering Fabrication LLC ....E....... 918 534-0001
  Dewey *(G-2020)*
Enovation Controls LLC ....B....... 918 317-4100
  Tulsa *(G-9689)*
Madison Avenue Firearms LLC ....G....... 918 629-6910
  Tulsa *(G-10197)*
Sky Motors LLC..................................F....... 918 321-2800
  Sapulpa *(G-8313)*
Wombat Labs LLC ....G....... 405 355-9662
  Stillwater *(G-8775)*

ENGINEERING SVCS: Petroleum

Escher Corp......................................G....... 405 751-2893
  Oklahoma City *(G-6050)*
Fred M Buxton ....G....... 405 840-4331
  Oklahoma City *(G-6115)*
Heritage Petroleum Inc......................G....... 405 377-2689
  Stillwater *(G-8700)*
Hinkle Oil and Gas ....F....... 405 848-0924
  Oklahoma City *(G-6251)*
Marjo Operating Co Inc ....G....... 918 583-0241
  Tulsa *(G-10211)*
Png Operation ....G....... 405 470-4333
  Oklahoma City *(G-6859)*
Prentice Napier & Green Inc ....F....... 405 752-7680
  Oklahoma City *(G-6888)*

ENGINEERING SVCS: Pollution Control

AC Systems Integration Inc ....E....... 918 259-0020
  Tulsa *(G-9084)*

ENGINEERING SVCS: Professional

Bonavista Technologies Inc................G....... 918 250-3435
  Tulsa *(G-9318)*
Centek Inc ....E....... 405 219-3200
  Oklahoma City *(G-5724)*
Fletcher Lewis Engineering ....G....... 405 840-5675
  Oklahoma City *(G-6090)*

ENGINEERING SVCS: Sanitary

Thomas Energy Systems Inc ....E....... 918 665-0031
  Tulsa *(G-10930)*

ENGINES: Gasoline, NEC

Automotive Machine Shop..................G....... 918 775-9770
  Sallisaw *(G-8139)*

ENGINES: Internal Combustion, NEC

Bach Welding & Diesel Service ....G....... 580 593-2599
  Custer City *(G-1973)*
Cummins - Allison Corp ....F....... 405 321-1411
  Norman *(G-4972)*
Cummins Enterprises Inc....................G....... 405 232-9022
  Oklahoma City *(G-5867)*
Cummins Inc ....B....... 405 946-4481
  Oklahoma City *(G-5868)*
Cummins Southern Plains LLC.............E....... 918 234-3240
  Tulsa *(G-9522)*
Cummins Southern Plains LLC.............E....... 405 946-4481
  Oklahoma City *(G-5869)*
Engines Alive ....G....... 918 406-8149
  Broken Arrow *(G-901)*
Floyds Machine Shop ....G....... 918 256-8440
  Vinita *(G-11258)*
Russell Baker Racing Engines ....G....... 918 533-3825
  Miami *(G-4429)*
Southwestern Motor Rebuilders ....G....... 918 585-1519
  Tulsa *(G-10811)*
United Engines Manufacture ....G....... 405 601-9861
  Oklahoma City *(G-7366)*
White Dove Small Engines ....G....... 580 857-2201
  Allen *(G-139)*
Woltjer Engines ....G....... 918 258-0598
  Broken Arrow *(G-1101)*

ENGRAVING SVC, NEC

Firefly Custom Laser Engrv LLC..........G....... 405 664-4145
  Norman *(G-5000)*

ENGRAVING SVC: Jewelry & Personal Goods

B G Specialties Inc ....G....... 918 582-1165
  Tulsa *(G-9243)*
Juno Companies Incorporated ....G....... 918 627-8868
  Tulsa *(G-10067)*
Nacols Jewelry ....G....... 580 355-4280
  Lawton *(G-3975)*
Trophies n Things ....G....... 405 247-9771
  Anadarko *(G-207)*

ENGRAVING SVCS

David Logan ....G....... 918 739-4231
  Catoosa *(G-1315)*
Initially Yours Inc ....G....... 918 832-9889
  Tulsa *(G-9986)*
Rusco Plastics ....G....... 580 234-1596
  Enid *(G-3053)*

ENGRAVING SVCS: Tombstone

Anson Memorial Co ....G....... 918 358-2504
  Cleveland *(G-1716)*
Whm Granite Products Inc ....F....... 580 535-2184
  Granite *(G-3257)*

ENGRAVINGS: Plastic

Krause Plastics ....G....... 918 835-4202
  Tulsa *(G-10100)*
Layle Company Corporation................G....... 405 329-5143
  Norman *(G-5056)*

ENTERTAINERS & ENTERTAINMENT GROUPS

A-1 Mster Prnta/Hooper Prtg Si ....G....... 518 427-0282
  Oklahoma City *(G-5351)*
Dean Johnson ....G....... 405 947-5736
  Oklahoma City *(G-5911)*

ENTERTAINMENT SVCS

Infinity Home Solutions LLC................G....... 918 704-8014
  Bixby *(G-635)*

ENVELOPES

Frank G Love Envelopes Inc...............D....... 214 637-5900
  Tulsa *(G-9772)*
Frank G Love Envelopes Inc...............G....... 405 720-9177
  Warr Acres *(G-11319)*
Response Solutions Inc ....G....... 918 508-7022
  Tulsa *(G-10647)*
Unity Press Inc ....E....... 405 232-8910
  Tulsa *(G-11045)*
Western Web Envelope Co Inc ....F....... 405 682-0207
  Oklahoma City *(G-7442)*

ENVIRONMENTAL QUALITY PROGS ADMIN, GOVT: Waste Mgmt

Trusty Willow LLC ....G....... 253 241-0520
  Bokoshe *(G-755)*

ENZYMES

Winston Company Inc ....E....... 800 331-9099
  Tulsa *(G-11140)*

EQUIPMENT: Rental & Leasing, NEC

Apss Inc ....G....... 405 324-2071
  Oklahoma City *(G-5459)*
BOp Ram-Block Ir Rentals Inc ....D....... 580 772-0250
  Weatherford *(G-11394)*
Cook Machine Company ....E....... 580 252-1699
  Duncan *(G-2099)*
Crain Displays & Exhibits Inc ....F....... 918 585-9797
  Tulsa *(G-9499)*
Harsco Corporation ....E....... 918 619-8000
  Tulsa *(G-9899)*
Klines Signs & Crane.........................G....... 580 256-2374
  Woodward *(G-11604)*

ETCHING & ENGRAVING SVC

A & B Engraving Inc ....G....... 918 663-7446
  Tulsa *(G-9061)*
Etched In Stone ....G....... 918 369-0500
  Bixby *(G-621)*
H-V Manufacturing Company..............G....... 918 756-9620
  Okmulgee *(G-7509)*
Ideal Specialty Inc.............................F....... 918 834-1657
  Tulsa *(G-9967)*
Texoma Engraving LLC ....G....... 580 775-7333
  Durant *(G-2264)*
Twj Inc ....G....... 405 392-4366
  Tuttle *(G-11217)*
Walkers Powder Coating LLC ....G....... 580 355-5000
  Lawton *(G-4018)*

EXCAVATING MACHINERY & EQPT WHOLESALERS

BOB Lumber & Grain LLC ....F....... 580 927-3168
  Coalgate *(G-1775)*
CRC-Evans Pipeline Intl Inc ....C....... 918 438-2100
  Tulsa *(G-9504)*

EXERCISE EQPT STORES

Gorfam Marketing Inc ....F....... 918 388-9935
  Tulsa *(G-9842)*

EXPLORATION, METAL MINING

Eagle Exploration Prod LLC ....G....... 918 746-1350
  Tulsa *(G-9624)*
Eagle Explrtion Oprting GP LLC...........G....... 918 746-1350
  Tulsa *(G-9625)*

EXPLOSIVES

All Decked Out ....G....... 918 313-9691
  Claremore *(G-1580)*
Austin Powder Co ....G....... 918 835-9244
  Tulsa *(G-9224)*
El Dorado Chemical Company.............G....... 405 235-4546
  Oklahoma City *(G-6015)*
Hman Global Solutions LLC ....G....... 405 338-5348
  Morrison *(G-4603)*
LSB Chemical LLC ....F....... 405 235-4546
  Oklahoma City *(G-6498)*
Orica USA Inc ....G....... 918 437-1644
  Tulsa *(G-10439)*
Utec Corporation LLC ....G....... 405 928-7061
  Norman *(G-5190)*

EXTERMINATING PRDTS: Household Or Indl Use

Christina Stokes................................G....... 405 551-1017
  Edmond *(G-2350)*
Darren McIninch ....G....... 405 912-8403
  Oklahoma City *(G-5285)*

EXTRACTS, FLAVORING

Big Rock Foods LLC............................G....... 405 269-8558
  Stillwater *(G-8659)*

PRODUCT SECTION FABRICS: Trimmings

EYEGLASSES
Classen Wholesale Optical Inc .... G 405 842-1900
  Oklahoma City *(G-5777)*
Gary Morgan .... G 405 387-4884
  Newcastle *(G-4826)*
Moku LLC .... G 918 398-8479
  Cleveland *(G-1727)*
Omega Optical Co LP .... E 405 703-4133
  Oklahoma City *(G-6775)*

EYEGLASSES: Sunglasses
Jeffs Optacle .... G 580 223-5999
  Ardmore *(G-313)*

EYELASHES, ARTIFICIAL
Lash Amor .... G 918 893-2424
  Tulsa *(G-10131)*
Wink Eyelash Salon .... G 918 949-6299
  Tulsa *(G-11139)*

Ethylene Glycols
Sunoco (R&m) LLC .... F 918 586-6246
  Tulsa *(G-10873)*

FABRIC STORES
Fabric Factory .... F 405 521-1694
  Oklahoma City *(G-6067)*

FABRICATED METAL PRODUCTS, NEC
American Intellectual LLC .... G 405 605-2378
  Oklahoma City *(G-5436)*
Automtive Cting Specialist Inc .... G 918 698-1560
  Wagoner *(G-11274)*
B Rowdy Rnch Met Fbrcation LLC .... G 405 973-5976
  Luther *(G-4132)*
Clark Mtal Bldngs Fbrcation LL .... G 580 695-4915
  Guthrie *(G-3309)*
Gary Mace .... G 580 654-2660
  Carnegie *(G-1276)*
House of Trophies .... G 918 341-2111
  Claremore *(G-1637)*
Js Metal Fabrication LLC .... G 918 428-2242
  Tulsa *(G-10063)*
Justus Fabrication .... G 918 207-5192
  Tahlequah *(G-8869)*
JW Measurement Co .... G 918 465-5605
  Wilburton *(G-11521)*
RB Cnstr Met Fabrication LLC .... G 580 367-5039
  Caney *(G-1262)*
Ricks Rod Reel Svc-High .... G 405 823-7581
  Oklahoma City *(G-7022)*
Sparks Mtal Dsign Fbrction LLC .... G 918 676-5112
  Fairland *(G-3131)*
Trinity Shtmtl Fabrication LLC .... G 918 899-6030
  Purcell *(G-8025)*
USA Metal Fabrication LLC .... G 918 845-6500
  Oklahoma City *(G-7379)*
Western Iron Works LLC .... G 405 779-1961
  Chickasha *(G-1524)*

FABRICS: Alpacas, Cotton
Awesome Acres Pacas Pyrs .... G 405 990-8205
  Oklahoma City *(G-5279)*
Michael Sherry Alpert .... G 405 912-0062
  Oklahoma City *(G-5306)*

FABRICS: Alpacas, Mohair, Woven
Hooty Creek Alpacas .... G 918 284-5025
  Claremore *(G-1635)*
Jr Alpacas LLC .... G 405 771-2636
  Jones *(G-3749)*
Land Run Alpacas .... G 405 226-9005
  Agra *(G-126)*
Storm Haven Alpaca LLC .... G 405 391-2767
  Choctaw *(G-1555)*

FABRICS: Apparel & Outerwear, Cotton
Wohali Outdoors LLC .... F 918 343-3800
  Broken Arrow *(G-1100)*

FABRICS: Apparel & Outerwear, From Manmade Fiber Or Silk
Okc Fabric Market .... G 405 531-0546
  Oklahoma City *(G-6729)*

Rsga Incorporated .... G 918 978-6800
  Tulsa *(G-10681)*

FABRICS: Automotive, Cotton
Custom 4 X 4 Fabrication .... G 405 799-7599
  Oklahoma City *(G-5282)*

FABRICS: Broadwoven, Cotton
Duncan Ticking Inc .... F 405 528-5480
  Oklahoma City *(G-5989)*
Stroheim Romann Upholstery .... G 918 622-7700
  Tulsa *(G-10860)*

FABRICS: Broadwoven, Synthetic Manmade Fiber & Silk
Jerry Beagley Braiding Company .... G 580 924-4995
  Calera *(G-1240)*

FABRICS: Broadwoven, Wool
Northwest Alpacas Ltd .... G 903 450-1999
  Edmond *(G-2542)*

FABRICS: Canvas
8bit Canvas LLC .... G 405 924-3298
  Oklahoma City *(G-5340)*
Anything Canvas LLC .... G 580 658-9330
  Marlow *(G-4221)*
Bills Marine Canvas Upholstery .... G 405 306-2936
  Norman *(G-4931)*
Blue Canvas LLC .... G 580 327-3406
  Alva *(G-179)*
Boatman Marine Canvas .... G 405 628-7844
  Warr Acres *(G-11314)*
Canvas Sky Studios LLC .... G 917 514-9632
  Broken Arrow *(G-864)*
Clean Canvas Laser Tattoo Remo .... G 580 919-5466
  Lawton *(G-3906)*
Dans Custom Canvas .... G 405 525-2419
  Oklahoma City *(G-5897)*
Faded Canvas Barber Studio .... G 405 735-7105
  Moore *(G-4521)*
Paint On Canvas .... G 405 574-6689
  Chickasha *(G-1498)*
S&S Canvas & Upholstery .... G 580 231-2587
  Ringwood *(G-8092)*

FABRICS: Coated Or Treated
Clear Edge Filtration Inc .... D 918 984-6000
  Tulsa *(G-9447)*
Clear Edge Filtration Inc .... D 800 637-6206
  Tulsa *(G-9448)*

FABRICS: Denims
Dear John Denim Inc .... G 580 334-6637
  Oklahoma City *(G-5913)*
Rockin Dolls Denim .... G 918 402-6151
  Collinsville *(G-1822)*
Sage Premium Denim Bar .... G 405 288-1503
  Goldsby *(G-3246)*
Sooner Denim Inc .... G 405 641-4720
  Oklahoma City *(G-7161)*

FABRICS: Fiberglass, Broadwoven
B B Fiberglass LLC .... G 405 755-5895
  Guthrie *(G-3298)*
Carter Fiberglass .... G 918 674-2325
  Quapaw *(G-8028)*
Insul-Vest Inc .... G 918 445-2279
  Tulsa *(G-9992)*
Jacob Manufacturing Inc .... F 918 787-6606
  Grove *(G-3276)*
Wing-It Concepts .... G 405 691-8053
  Oklahoma City *(G-5325)*

FABRICS: Nonwoven
Nxtnano LLC .... E 918 923-4824
  Claremore *(G-1665)*

FABRICS: Oilcloth
Tatermash Oilcloth LLC .... G 918 743-3888
  Tulsa *(G-10901)*

FABRICS: Satin
Satin Siren LLC .... G 918 803-6351
  Pryor *(G-7990)*

FABRICS: Scrub Cloths
Allys Discount Scrubs .... G 918 935-1359
  Broken Arrow *(G-826)*
Salt Soothers LLC .... G 405 201-2020
  Edmond *(G-2610)*

FABRICS: Trimmings
4524 LLC .... G 405 620-3711
  Edmond *(G-2285)*
All-Star Trophies & Ribbon Mfg .... G 918 283-2200
  Claremore *(G-1581)*
B J Printing Inc .... F 405 372-7600
  Stillwater *(G-8657)*
Bartlesville Print Shop .... G 918 336-6070
  Bartlesville *(G-452)*
Beacon Sign Company Inc .... G 405 567-4886
  Prague *(G-7921)*
Big Red Shop Inc .... G 405 495-5551
  Warr Acres *(G-11313)*
Caveman Screen Printing .... G 918 446-6440
  Tulsa *(G-9390)*
Cimarron Screen Printing .... G 405 755-8337
  Edmond *(G-2352)*
Complete Graphics Inc .... G 405 232-8882
  Oklahoma City *(G-5812)*
CP Solutions Inc .... D 918 664-6642
  Tulsa *(G-9495)*
Cr Stripes Ltd Co .... G 405 946-8577
  Oklahoma City *(G-5850)*
Creative Apparel and More Inc .... G 918 682-1283
  Muskogee *(G-4664)*
Cunningham Graphics Inc .... G 918 337-9100
  Bartlesville *(G-470)*
Custom Monograms & Lettering .... G 405 495-8586
  Bethany *(G-574)*
Custom Screen Printers .... G 918 423-3696
  McAlester *(G-4290)*
Customized Fctry Interiors LLC .... G 405 848-9999
  Oklahoma City *(G-5880)*
D & B Printing Inc .... G 405 632-0055
  Oklahoma City *(G-5884)*
Dean Printing .... G 580 782-3777
  Mangum *(G-4170)*
Design It .... G 405 756-3635
  Lindsay *(G-4060)*
Ehrles Carnival & Party Sups .... G 918 622-5266
  Tulsa *(G-9648)*
First Impression Prtg Co Inc .... G 918 749-5446
  Beggs *(G-553)*
Gold Star Graphics Inc .... F 405 677-1529
  Oklahoma City *(G-6168)*
Great Plins Grphics Shwnee LLC .... G 405 273-4263
  Shawnee *(G-8455)*
Green Cntry Trophy Screen Prtg .... G 918 647-2923
  Poteau *(G-7906)*
Ham Ventures LLC .... G 918 277-9500
  Tulsa *(G-9883)*
Holloways Bluprt & Copy Sp Inc .... G 918 682-0280
  Muskogee *(G-4692)*
House of Trophies .... G 405 452-3524
  Wetumka *(G-11492)*
House of Trophies .... G 918 341-2111
  Claremore *(G-1637)*
House T Shirt & Silk Screening .... G 405 457-6321
  Lookeba *(G-4129)*
Imaging Concepts .... G 918 534-1761
  Dewey *(G-2026)*
Impact Screen Printing .... G 918 258-8337
  Broken Arrow *(G-934)*
Inkling Design .... G 405 495-5575
  Bethany *(G-583)*
Jeff Mc Kenzie & Co Inc .... G 405 236-5848
  Oklahoma City *(G-6354)*
Joys Uniforms Boutique Ltd .... G 918 747-4114
  Tulsa *(G-10061)*
Label Stable Inc .... G 580 223-2037
  Ardmore *(G-323)*
Lawyer Graphic Screen Process .... G 918 438-2725
  Tulsa *(G-10137)*
Leda Grimm .... G 918 225-0507
  Cushing *(G-1942)*
Magic TS .... G 580 332-6675
  Ada *(G-62)*
Magnum Screen Print Inc .... G 918 665-7636
  Tulsa *(G-10202)*

FABRICS: Trimmings

Massive Graphic Screen Prtg ....F..... 405 364-3594
  Norman *(G-5066)*
MBC Graphics ....G..... 918 585-2321
  Tulsa *(G-10227)*
Midwest Decals LLC ....G..... 405 787-8747
  Oklahoma City *(G-6602)*
Midwest Publishing Co ....G..... 405 282-1890
  Guthrie *(G-3325)*
Misaco Sign & Screen Printing ....G..... 918 542-4188
  Miami *(G-4419)*
Mobonoto Automotive LLC ....G..... 580 480-0410
  Altus *(G-163)*
Opportunity Center Inc ....C..... 580 765-6782
  Ponca City *(G-7863)*
Options Inc ....F..... 918 473-2614
  Checotah *(G-1398)*
Peabodys Printing & A Brush Sp ....G..... 580 248-8317
  Lawton *(G-3980)*
Performance Screen Printing ....G..... 405 247-9891
  Anadarko *(G-205)*
Pinpoint Monograms Inc ....F..... 405 228-0600
  Oklahoma City *(G-6850)*
Pitezels Ink & Print Inc ....G..... 918 663-2393
  Tulsa *(G-10520)*
Prairie Graphics & Sportswear ....G..... 405 789-0028
  Bethany *(G-592)*
Print Imaging Group LLC ....E..... 405 235-4888
  Oklahoma City *(G-6898)*
Quantum Forms Corporation ....F..... 918 665-1320
  Oklahoma City *(G-6940)*
R-5 Caps & Tees ....G..... 580 256-3579
  Woodward *(G-11626)*
Reflective Edge Screenprinting ....G..... 405 917-7837
  Oklahoma City *(G-7001)*
Relevant Products LLC ....E..... 405 524-5250
  Oklahoma City *(G-7005)*
Sand Tech Screening and EMB ....G..... 918 458-0312
  Tahlequah *(G-8882)*
Semasys Inc ....E..... 405 525-2335
  Oklahoma City *(G-7107)*
Shine On Designs ....G..... 918 224-7439
  Sapulpa *(G-8311)*
Stan Clark Co ....G..... 405 377-0799
  Stillwater *(G-8755)*
T S & H EMB & Screen Prtg ....G..... 405 214-7701
  Shawnee *(G-8508)*
T-Shirts Unlimited ....G..... 580 286-5223
  Idabel *(G-3649)*
Tim Dees ....G..... 918 825-1211
  Pryor *(G-7995)*
Tom Bennett Manufacturing ....F..... 405 528-5671
  Oklahoma City *(G-7302)*
Tony Newcomb Sportswear Inc ....G..... 405 232-0022
  Oklahoma City *(G-7303)*
Ultra Thin Inc ....E..... 405 794-7892
  Moore *(G-4582)*
Wallis Printing Inc ....G..... 580 223-7473
  Ardmore *(G-379)*
Wear-Tech ....G..... 918 663-2009
  Tulsa *(G-11099)*
Witty Ideas Inc ....G..... 918 367-9528
  Bristow *(G-806)*

FABRICS: Wool, Broadwoven

Pendleton Woolen Mills Inc ....D..... 918 712-8545
  Tulsa *(G-10483)*

FABRICS: Woven, Narrow Cotton, Wool, Silk

Central Texas Ex Metalwork LLC ......G..... 765 492-9058
  Oklahoma City *(G-5727)*
Dill City Embroidery ....G..... 580 674-3989
  Dill City *(G-2035)*
Jerry Beagley Braiding Company ......G..... 580 924-4995
  Calera *(G-1240)*

FACIAL SALONS

Lash Amor ....G..... 918 893-2424
  Tulsa *(G-10131)*
Wink Eyelash Salon ....G..... 918 949-6299
  Tulsa *(G-11139)*

FACILITIES SUPPORT SVCS

Iap Worldwide Services Inc ....F..... 321 784-7100
  Oklahoma City *(G-6282)*
Port 40 Inc ....G..... 405 360-9100
  Norman *(G-5117)*

FACILITY RENTAL & PARTY PLANNING SVCS

Rocky Top Winery LLC ....G..... 580 857-2869
  Allen *(G-138)*

FACSIMILE COMMUNICATION EQPT

Chaddick & Associates Inc ....F..... 580 223-1202
  Ardmore *(G-264)*

FAMILY CLOTHING STORES

Speedys TS & More LLC ....G..... 580 748-0067
  Alva *(G-192)*
Stockmans Supply Company ....G..... 580 255-7762
  Duncan *(G-2186)*

FANS, BLOWING: Indl Or Commercial

Airflo Cooling Tech LLC ....E..... 918 585-5638
  Tulsa *(G-9128)*
Roth Manufacturing Co Inc ....G..... 918 743-4477
  Tulsa *(G-10675)*

FARM & GARDEN MACHINERY WHOLESALERS

Dougherty Forestry Mfg Ltd ....F..... 405 542-3520
  Hinton *(G-3523)*
Honeygrove Machine ....G..... 580 420-3260
  Idabel *(G-3638)*
Newton Equipment LLC ....F..... 918 756-3560
  Okmulgee *(G-7517)*

FARM MACHINERY REPAIR SVCS

Bob Lowe Farm Machinery Inc ....F..... 405 224-6500
  Chickasha *(G-1440)*
Lanco Services LLC ....E..... 580 429-6526
  Cache *(G-1229)*

FARM PRDTS, RAW MATERIAL, WHOLESALE: Tobacco & Tobacco Prdts

Green Co Corporation ....G..... 918 221-3997
  Tulsa *(G-9859)*

FARM PRDTS, RAW MATERIALS, WHOLESALE: Farm Animals

Rocky L Emmons & Judy E Sprag ...G..... 580 305-1940
  Frederick *(G-3199)*

FARM PRDTS, RAW MTRLS, WHOL: Nuts, Unprocessed/Shelled Only

Masons Pecans & Peanuts Inc ....G..... 405 329-7828
  Norman *(G-5065)*

FARM PRDTS, RAW MTRLS, WHOLESALE: Peanuts, Unroasted, Bulk

Gunter Peanut Co ....E..... 405 656-2398
  Binger *(G-606)*
Nutopia Nuts & More ....G..... 405 663-2330
  Hydro *(G-3633)*
Peanut Products Co Inc ....F..... 580 296-4888
  Calera *(G-1243)*

FARM SPLY STORES

Coalton Road Enterprises LLC ....G..... 918 652-0474
  Henryetta *(G-3502)*
Farmers Co Op ....F..... 918 456-0557
  Tahlequah *(G-8864)*
S & S Farm Center ....F..... 405 273-6907
  Shawnee *(G-8491)*
Spring Hollow Feed Mill Inc ....G..... 918 453-9933
  Hulbert *(G-3628)*
Stillwater Milling Company LLC ....D..... 405 372-2766
  Stillwater *(G-8757)*
Wister Lake Feed Inc ....G..... 918 655-7954
  Howe *(G-3601)*

FARM SPLYS WHOLESALERS

Cargill Incorporated ....E..... 405 236-0525
  Oklahoma City *(G-5699)*
Compass Unlimited Inc ....G..... 918 824-1644
  Pryor *(G-7955)*
Stockmans Mill & Grain Inc ....G..... 918 762-3459
  Pawnee *(G-7711)*
Valhoma Corporation ....E..... 918 836-7135
  Tulsa *(G-11064)*
Win Hy Foods Inc ....F..... 918 227-0004
  Tulsa *(G-9053)*

FARM SPLYS, WHOLESALE: Equestrian Eqpt

Finish Line of Oklahoma Inc ....G..... 918 341-8291
  Claremore *(G-1621)*

FARM SPLYS, WHOLESALE: Feed

Farmers Co-Operative Gin Assn ......G..... 580 928-2664
  Sayre *(G-8340)*
Farmers Coop ....F..... 580 772-3334
  Weatherford *(G-11413)*
Fisher AG Enterprises Inc ....G..... 918 367-6382
  Bristow *(G-778)*
Luther Mill and Farm Supply ....G..... 405 277-3221
  Luther *(G-4135)*
Rocky Farmers Cooperative Inc ......F..... 580 666-2440
  Rocky *(G-8105)*
Rocky Farmers Cooperative Inc ......G..... 580 674-3356
  Dill City *(G-2037)*
S & S Farm Center ....F..... 405 273-6907
  Shawnee *(G-8491)*
Stillwater Milling Company LLC ....F..... 580 369-2354
  Perry *(G-7747)*
Stockmans Supply Company ....G..... 580 255-7762
  Duncan *(G-2186)*

FARM SPLYS, WHOLESALE: Herbicides

Texoma Tractor LLC ....G..... 918 640-7949
  Talala *(G-8903)*

FARM SPLYS, WHOLESALE: Saddlery

Blinkers & Silks Unlimited Inc ....G..... 405 463-0391
  Lamar *(G-3862)*
Tipton Company ....G..... 580 762-0800
  Ponca City *(G-7884)*

FARM SPLYS, WHOLESALE: Soil, Potting & Planting

Minick Materials Company ....E..... 405 789-2068
  Oklahoma City *(G-6616)*

FASTENERS: Metal

Archer Technologies Intl Inc ....G..... 405 306-3220
  Shawnee *(G-8428)*
Hilti Inc ....G..... 918 252-6000
  Tulsa *(G-9931)*

FASTENERS: Notions, NEC

Midwest Automotive Fas LLC ....G..... 918 520-6904
  Broken Arrow *(G-974)*
WM Heitgras Company ....E..... 918 583-3131
  Tulsa *(G-11144)*

FASTENERS: Wire, Made From Purchased Wire

Sooner State Spring Mfg Co ....G..... 918 476-5707
  Chouteau *(G-1570)*

FENCE POSTS: Iron & Steel

Bucke-Tee LLC ....G..... 580 747-9288
  Enid *(G-2923)*
Bullet Fence Systems LLC ....G..... 918 777-3973
  Okmulgee *(G-7496)*

FENCES & FENCING MATERIALS

Fence Solutions Inc ....G..... 580 233-4600
  Enid *(G-2957)*
General Wire & Supply Co Inc ....E..... 918 245-5961
  Tulsa *(G-9817)*
Oklahoma Steel & Wire Co Inc ....C..... 580 795-7311
  Madill *(G-4160)*
Tight Wire Fence LLC ....G..... 479 220-1171
  Watts *(G-11358)*

PRODUCT SECTION — FIRE ARMS, SMALL: Shotguns Or Shotgun Parts, 30 mm & Below

FENCES OR POSTS: Ornamental Iron Or Steel
Skiatook Statuary .... G 918 396-1309
  Skiatook *(G-8570)*

FENCING DEALERS
Old World Iron Inc .... G 918 445-3063
  Tulsa *(G-10411)*

FENCING MATERIALS: Plastic
2by2 Industries LLC .... G 877 234-6558
  Edmond *(G-2283)*
American Fence Company Inc .... E 405 685-4800
  Oklahoma City *(G-5435)*
Ameristar Primeter SEC USA Inc .... E 918 835-0898
  Tulsa *(G-9179)*

FENCING: Chain Link
William B Finley .... G 580 512-7573
  Lawton *(G-4023)*

FERTILIZER, AGRICULTURAL: Wholesalers
Bloomin Crazy Ldscp Flrl Dsig .... G 405 238-3416
  Pauls Valley *(G-7652)*
Murphy Products Inc .... G 405 842-7177
  Oklahoma City *(G-6636)*

FERTILIZERS: NEC
Eckroat Seed Co .... F 405 427-2484
  Oklahoma City *(G-6006)*
Edc AG Products Company LLC .... D 405 235-4546
  Oklahoma City *(G-6008)*
El Dorado Chemical Company .... D 405 235-4546
  Oklahoma City *(G-6015)*
Farmers Union Co-Operative Gin .... G 580 482-5136
  Altus *(G-156)*
Garbage To Garden Compost Inc .... G 918 260-4463
  Bixby *(G-628)*
Stillwater Milling Company LLC .... F 580 369-2354
  Perry *(G-7747)*
Stockmans Mill & Grain Inc .... G 918 762-3459
  Pawnee *(G-7711)*

FERTILIZERS: Nitrogenous
Agrium Advanced Tech US Inc .... F 405 948-1084
  Oklahoma City *(G-5399)*
I Chemex Corporation .... G 405 947-0764
  Oklahoma City *(G-6281)*
Koch Fertilizer Enid LLC .... A 580 249-4870
  Enid *(G-2996)*
LSB Industries Inc .... E 405 235-4546
  Oklahoma City *(G-6499)*

FERTILIZERS: Phosphatic
Dib 718 LLC .... G 405 525-2151
  Oklahoma City *(G-5944)*
Tessenderlo Kerley Inc .... E 405 665-2544
  Wynnewood *(G-11674)*
Tessenderlo Kerley Inc .... F 580 762-1130
  Ponca City *(G-7882)*

FIBER & FIBER PRDTS: Synthetic Cellulosic
Western Hull Sacking Inc .... G 580 335-2144
  Frederick *(G-3204)*

FIBER & FIBER PRDTS: Vinyl
Midland Vinyl Products Inc .... G 405 755-4972
  Oklahoma City *(G-6597)*
Progressive Windows Inc .... G 580 227-9915
  Fairview *(G-3147)*

FILM & SHEET: Unsuppported Plastic
Bags Inc .... E 405 427-5473
  Oklahoma City *(G-5509)*
Berry Global Inc .... F 918 824-4288
  Pryor *(G-7945)*
Berry Global Inc .... D 918 824-4400
  Pryor *(G-7946)*
Berry Global Inc .... C 918 426-4800
  McAlester *(G-4275)*
High Caliper Growing Inc .... D 405 842-7700
  Oklahoma City *(G-6246)*

Midwest Urethane Inc .... F 918 445-2277
  Tulsa *(G-10272)*
Sigma Extruding Corp .... F 918 446-6265
  Tulsa *(G-10755)*
Taylor Foam Inc .... G 405 787-5811
  Oklahoma City *(G-7258)*

FILM DEVELOPING & PRINTING SVCS
Miraclon Corporation .... F 580 772-5502
  Weatherford *(G-11428)*

FILTERS
Braden Filtration LLC .... G 918 283-4818
  Tulsa *(G-9326)*
D & J Filter Ltd Liability Co .... G 405 376-5343
  Oklahoma City *(G-5886)*
Filter Supply and Recycling .... G 918 663-3143
  Tulsa *(G-9742)*
Filter Wings Corporation .... G 405 258-3183
  Wellston *(G-11470)*
Flanders Corporation .... G 580 223-1853
  Ardmore *(G-290)*
Fluid Art Technology LLC .... G 405 843-2009
  Oklahoma City *(G-6094)*
Nmw Inc .... G 918 273-2204
  Nowata *(G-5223)*

FILTERS & STRAINERS: Pipeline
Midwesco Industries Inc .... G 918 858-4200
  Tulsa *(G-10266)*
Samurai Equipment LLC .... F 918 878-7715
  Tulsa *(G-10701)*
Travis Quality Pdts & Sls Inc .... G 918 251-0115
  Broken Arrow *(G-1082)*
Vaculift Incorporated .... D 918 438-9875
  Tulsa *(G-11063)*

FILTERS: Air
Acme Engineering and Mfg Corp .... B 918 682-7791
  Muskogee *(G-4642)*
Airwolf Filter Corp .... G 918 561-8696
  Okmulgee *(G-7493)*
Contech Enterprises LLC .... F 918 341-6232
  Claremore *(G-1609)*
Filter Supply and Recycling .... G 918 663-3143
  Tulsa *(G-9742)*
Flanders of Oklahoma .... C 580 223-5730
  Ardmore *(G-291)*
Good Filter Co .... G 580 323-5200
  Clinton *(G-1751)*
Royal Filter Manufacturing Co .... G 405 224-0229
  Chickasha *(G-1503)*

FILTERS: Air Intake, Internal Combustion Engine, Exc Auto
Harrik Company LLC .... G 918 691-6417
  Tulsa *(G-9895)*

FILTERS: Gasoline, Internal Combustion Engine, Exc Auto
Apollo Engineering Company .... G 918 251-6780
  Broken Arrow *(G-830)*
Green Country Filter Mfg LLC .... F 918 455-0100
  Tulsa *(G-9861)*

FILTERS: General Line, Indl
Clear Edge Filtration Inc .... D 800 637-6206
  Tulsa *(G-9448)*
Clear Edge Filtration Inc .... D 918 984-6000
  Tulsa *(G-9447)*
Evoqua Water Technologies LLC .... C 978 614-7233
  Tulsa *(G-9712)*
Facet (oklahoma) LLC .... E 918 272-8700
  Tulsa *(G-9725)*
Facet (oklahoma) LLC .... C 918 696-3161
  Stilwell *(G-8790)*
Firstline Filters LLC .... G 918 660-8772
  Tulsa *(G-9748)*
Global Filter LLC .... F 319 743-0110
  Tulsa *(G-9830)*
Royal Filter Manufacturing Co .... E 405 224-0229
  Chickasha *(G-1503)*

FILTERS: Motor Vehicle
Facet (oklahoma) LLC .... D 918 696-3161
  Stilwell *(G-8789)*

FILTERS: Oil, Internal Combustion Engine, Exc Auto
Peak Machining Group LLC .... G 307 660-1463
  Skiatook *(G-8563)*

FINANCIAL INVEST ACTS: Mineral, Oil & Gas Leasing & Royalty
Chaston Oil & Gas LLC .... G 580 226-2640
  Ardmore *(G-266)*

FINANCIAL INVESTMENT ADVICE
Chaston Oil & Gas LLC .... G 580 226-2640
  Ardmore *(G-266)*

FINISHING SVCS
Thermal Specialties LLC .... F 918 836-4800
  Tulsa *(G-10926)*

FIRE ALARM MAINTENANCE & MONITORING SVCS
All American Fire Systems Inc .... F 918 341-6977
  Claremore *(G-1579)*
Trinity Technologies LLC .... G 580 475-0900
  Duncan *(G-2190)*

FIRE ARMS, SMALL: Guns Or Gun Parts, 30 mm & Below
Alex Arms and Instruction LLC .... G 405 351-0806
  Alex *(G-129)*
Duncan Machine Products Inc .... E 580 467-6784
  Duncan *(G-2110)*
F&D Defense LLC .... G 512 745-6482
  Seminole *(G-8373)*
Jean Jacques Perodeau Gunmaker ... G 580 237-7388
  Enid *(G-2983)*
Leather Guns & Etc .... F 580 296-2616
  Colbert *(G-1785)*
Madison Avenue Firearms LLC .... G 918 629-6910
  Tulsa *(G-10197)*
Mike Beathe .... G 918 288-7858
  Sperry *(G-8610)*
Oklahoma Machine Guns LLC .... G 405 418-4867
  Oklahoma City *(G-6754)*
Reliance Mfg Solutions LLC .... G 405 640-9660
  Oklahoma City *(G-7006)*
Three Prcent Frrms Catings LLC .... G 580 931-9908
  Mead *(G-4368)*
Zulu 4 Tactical LLC .... G 918 978-6810
  Tulsa *(G-11180)*

FIRE ARMS, SMALL: Pistols Or Pistol Parts, 30 mm & below
Gun World Inc .... G 405 670-5885
  Del City *(G-1997)*

FIRE ARMS, SMALL: Revolvers Or Revolver Parts, 30 mm & Below
Rifle Shoppe Inc .... G 405 356-2583
  Wellston *(G-11477)*

FIRE ARMS, SMALL: Rifles Or Rifle Parts, 30 mm & below
Champlin Firearms Inc .... G 580 237-7388
  Enid *(G-2929)*
Newman Precision .... G 580 339-0097
  Elk City *(G-2856)*

FIRE ARMS, SMALL: Shotguns Or Shotgun Parts, 30 mm & Below
JJ Perodeau Gunmaker Inc .... G 580 747-1804
  Sand Springs *(G-8195)*

FIRE CONTROL OR BOMBING EQPT: Electronic

Tactical Elec Military Sup LLC .... E 866 541-7996
Broken Arrow *(G-1070)*
Yandell Fire Investigations .... G 580 269-2414
Kaw City *(G-3760)*

FIRE EXTINGUISHERS, WHOLESALE

Firepro Fire Protection Svc .... G 918 857-1513
Broken Arrow *(G-909)*
Spectrumfx Inc .... G 918 392-9799
Tulsa *(G-10820)*

FIRE EXTINGUISHERS: Portable

Firepro Fire Protection Svc .... G 918 857-1513
Broken Arrow *(G-909)*

FIRE OR BURGLARY RESISTIVE PRDTS

Bkw Inc .... G 918 836-6767
Tulsa *(G-9299)*
C&M Enterprises .... G 918 683-4456
Muskogee *(G-4657)*
York Metal Fabrication .... G 405 598-6239
Tecumseh *(G-8931)*

FIRE PROTECTION EQPT

Husky Portable Containment Co .... E 918 333-2000
Bartlesville *(G-496)*
OK Fire LLC .... G 918 424-1808
McAlester *(G-4325)*

FIRE PROTECTION SVCS: Contracted

Master Movers Incorporated .... G 918 408-1490
Owasso *(G-7590)*

FIREARMS & AMMUNITION, EXC SPORTING, WHOLESALE

Wholesale Electric Supply Co .... G 918 647-2200
Poteau *(G-7918)*

FIREARMS: Small, 30mm or Less

Dark Ops Designs .... G 918 269-0049
Claremore *(G-1612)*
Garys Guns .... G 405 789-6896
Bethany *(G-579)*
Hailey Ordnance Company .... G 405 813-0700
Oklahoma City *(G-6203)*
Old Sarges Armory LLC .... G 270 945-8324
Miami *(G-4425)*
Patriot Small Arms LLC .... G 405 567-7890
Tecumseh *(G-8924)*
Redneck Firearms Inc .... E 405 650-6605
Harrah *(G-3384)*
Rise Manufacturing LLC .... E 918 994-6240
Broken Arrow *(G-1032)*
Stevens & Sons LLC .... G 580 482-4142
Altus *(G-169)*

FIREPLACE & CHIMNEY MATERIAL: Concrete

Age Stone Manufacturing .... G 918 366-3270
Bixby *(G-609)*

FIREPLACES: Concrete

Advanced Comfort & Energy .... F 405 329-2237
Norman *(G-4900)*

FIREWORKS

American Entps Whl Dstributers .... G 405 273-4516
Shawnee *(G-8427)*
Jack Warner Fireworks .... G 580 234-3827
Enid *(G-2979)*
Rector Fire Works .... G 918 681-0513
Muskogee *(G-4743)*

FIREWORKS SHOPS

American Entps Whl Dstributers .... G 405 273-4516
Shawnee *(G-8427)*

FISH FOOD

W C Bradley Co .... G 918 379-6238
Claremore *(G-1703)*

FISHING EQPT: Lures

Plastic Research and Dev Corp .... F 918 949-6291
Tulsa *(G-10525)*
Pony Boy Lures .... G 580 327-1233
Alva *(G-189)*
Stickem Fishing Lures Ltd .... G 918 636-6179
Broken Arrow *(G-1062)*

FITTINGS & ASSEMBLIES: Hose & Tube, Hydraulic Or Pneumatic

Ameriflex Hose and ACC LLC .... G 918 437-7002
Tulsa *(G-9176)*
H & C Services Inc .... F 580 772-2521
Weatherford *(G-11417)*
Industrial Specialties Inc .... G 580 475-9088
Duncan *(G-2131)*
Kims International Okla Inc .... G 918 250-9441
Tulsa *(G-10089)*

FITTINGS & SPECIALTIES: Steam

Flowmatics Inc .... G 918 259-3740
Broken Arrow *(G-911)*

FITTINGS: Pipe

East 74th Street Holdings Inc .... C 918 437-3037
Tulsa *(G-9631)*

FITTINGS: Pipe, Fabricated

H G Flake Company Inc .... G 918 684-9004
Muskogee *(G-4686)*
Los Angeles Boiler Works Inc .... E 580 363-1312
Blackwell *(G-688)*
Mw Piping Fabrication LLC .... F 918 836-4200
Tulsa *(G-10319)*

FIXTURES & EQPT: Kitchen, Metal, Exc Cast Aluminum

Superior Stainless Inc .... G 405 387-3414
Blanchard *(G-736)*

FIXTURES & EQPT: Kitchen, Porcelain Enameled

Kitchen Korner Inc .... G 918 582-9951
Tulsa *(G-10093)*
Royal Prestige Jealpa .... G 405 602-5371
Oklahoma City *(G-7053)*

FLAGS: Fabric

Rainbow Pennant Inc .... E 405 524-1577
Oklahoma City *(G-6968)*

FLAGSTONES

How To Build A Flagstone Patio 405 478-1200
Bixby *(G-633)*

FLARES

Flare Industries .... G 918 376-7811
Owasso *(G-7570)*
Hero Flare LLC .... E 512 772-5744
Kellyville *(G-3765)*

FLAT GLASS: Building

Whitacre Glass Works LLC .... G 918 366-6646
Tulsa *(G-11119)*

FLAT GLASS: Skylight

Skyview Products Inc .... G 405 745-6064
Mustang *(G-4794)*

FLAT GLASS: Spectacle

Doctors Optical Supply Inc .... G 918 256-6416
Vinita *(G-11255)*

FLAT GLASS: Window, Clear & Colored

Edmond Glass .... G 405 751-5900
Edmond *(G-2402)*

Guys Wise .... G 405 801-3339
Norman *(G-5012)*
Striper Tinting .... G 918 636-4043
Claremore *(G-1689)*

FLOOR COVERING STORES

Conway Custom Marble Co .... G 580 357-3757
Lawton *(G-3910)*
Warren Ramsey Inc .... G 405 528-2828
Oklahoma City *(G-7422)*

FLOOR COVERING STORES: Carpets

Hemispheres .... G 405 773-8410
Warr Acres *(G-11322)*

FLOOR COVERINGS WHOLESALERS

Conway Custom Marble Co .... G 580 357-3757
Lawton *(G-3910)*

FLOOR COVERINGS: Aircraft & Automobile

Triumph Arstrctres - Tulsa LLC .... A 615 361-2061
Tulsa *(G-10978)*

FLOOR COVERINGS: Art Squares

Brow Art 23 .... G 405 848-3346
Oklahoma City *(G-5634)*

FLOOR COVERINGS: Textile Fiber

Kingston Flooring LLC .... G 405 470-3494
Oklahoma City *(G-6423)*

FLOOR COVERINGS: Twisted Paper, Grass, Reed, Coir, Etc

Mike McGills Carpet Inc .... G 405 222-0899
Chickasha *(G-1488)*

FLOORING & GRATINGS: Open, Construction Applications

Monson Associates Inc .... G 918 298-0037
Tulsa *(G-10300)*

FLOORING & SIDING: Metal

Architectural Fabricators Inc .... E 918 331-0393
Bartlesville *(G-448)*

FLOORING: Hard Surface

Interstate Supply Company .... E 405 232-7141
Oklahoma City *(G-6322)*
Interstate Supply Company .... G 918 461-0177
Tulsa *(G-10007)*
Solid Rock Custom Flooring .... G 918 833-2884
Claremore *(G-1685)*

FLOORING: Hardwood

Flooring Outfitters .... G 580 286-3030
Idabel *(G-3637)*
Pioneer Sport Floors LLC .... G 214 460-6921
Calera *(G-1244)*
Strictly Hardwoods 405 269-1026
Stillwater *(G-8761)*

FLOORING: Rubber

C and D Fashion Floors LLC .... G 918 256-8018
Vinita *(G-11250)*

FLORIST: Flowers, Fresh

Ardellas Flowers Inc .... F 405 321-6850
Norman *(G-4915)*

FLORISTS

Mc Alester Food Warehouse .... D 580 436-4302
Ada *(G-64)*

FLUID METERS & COUNTING DEVICES

Badger Meter Inc .... C 918 836-8411
Tulsa *(G-9253)*
Badger Meter Inc .... G 918 628-7403
Tulsa *(G-9254)*
Fossil Fluids LLC .... G 580 515-5402
Weatherford *(G-11416)*

PRODUCT SECTION

FOOD PRDTS: Box Lunches, For Sale Off Premises

Petrolab LLC .... G 918 459-7170
  Broken Arrow *(G-1005)*
Turbines Inc .... E 580 477-3067
  Altus *(G-170)*

FLUID POWER PUMPS & MOTORS

Bg & S Manufacturing .... E 918 396-3525
  Skiatook *(G-8533)*
Hydra Service Inc .... E 918 438-3700
  Tulsa *(G-9960)*
Pump Shop .... G 918 834-8829
  Tulsa *(G-10583)*
Trojan Livestock Equipment .... G 580 772-1849
  Weatherford *(G-11451)*

FLUID POWER VALVES & HOSE FITTINGS

Cyclonic Valve Company .... E 918 317-8200
  Broken Arrow *(G-883)*
Hydraulic Specialists Inc .... E 405 752-7980
  Oklahoma City *(G-6278)*
Punch-Lok Co .... E 580 233-4757
  Enid *(G-3040)*

FLUXES

Blue ARC Metal Specialties .... G 918 341-3903
  Claremore *(G-1597)*
Roy Slagel Keno .... G 580 585-0283
  Elgin *(G-2779)*
Superior Solutions Welding & F .... G 405 623-0104
  Piedmont *(G-7772)*

FOAM RUBBER

Jessie Shaw .... G 918 587-6329
  Tulsa *(G-10040)*

FOOD PRDTS, BREAKFAST: Cereal, Granola & Muesli

Granola Shirts .... G 918 592-5477
  Tulsa *(G-9846)*
Oatskc Granola Company LLC .... G 405 834-6159
  Oklahoma City *(G-6709)*

FOOD PRDTS, BREAKFAST: Cereal, Hulled Corn

Alan Ware .... G 918 658-5267
  Paoli *(G-7637)*

FOOD PRDTS, CANNED, NEC

Manila Foods .... G 580 262-9900
  Blackwell *(G-689)*
Polish Kitchen LLC .... G 580 583-5970
  Lawton *(G-3984)*

FOOD PRDTS, CANNED: Barbecue Sauce

Bequettes Gourmet Foods Inc .... G 918 946-4212
  Tulsa *(G-9284)*
Billy Sims Barbeque LLC .... E 918 258-1978
  Broken Arrow *(G-852)*
Dewaynes Bbq Sauce Catering .... G 580 363-3394
  Newkirk *(G-4847)*

FOOD PRDTS, CANNED: Chili

Carls Chili Company Inc .... G 918 227-1623
  Tulsa *(G-8994)*

FOOD PRDTS, CANNED: Fruits

Claras Kitchen LLC 229 669-1493
  Oklahoma City *(G-5772)*
Maria Raes Inc .... G 580 242-3342
  Enid *(G-3005)*
Okie Ferments 405 310-9724
  Oklahoma City *(G-6731)*
Two Territories Trading Co LLC .... G 580 679-4701
  Duke *(G-2081)*

FOOD PRDTS, CANNED: Jams, Jellies & Preserves

Ju Ju Jams .... G 918 230-6650
  Tulsa *(G-10064)*
Pepper Creek Farms Inc .... G 580 536-1300
  Lawton *(G-3982)*

Prairie Gypsies Inc .... G 405 525-3013
  Oklahoma City *(G-6873)*
Southern Okie LLC .... G 405 657-7765
  Edmond *(G-2625)*
Suans Inc .... G 405 413-1751
  Oklahoma City *(G-7220)*

FOOD PRDTS, CANNED: Jellies, Edible, Including Imitation

Dorians Foods Inc .... G 580 658-3022
  Marlow *(G-4229)*
Griffin Food Company .... D 918 687-6311
  Muskogee *(G-4683)*

FOOD PRDTS, CANNED: Mexican, NEC

El Mojado .... G 918 492-1138
  Tulsa *(G-9650)*
Silas Salsa Company LLC .... G 469 556-9762
  Oklahoma City *(G-7139)*

FOOD PRDTS, CANNED: Soups

Grannas LLC .... F 580 337-6360
  Bessie *(G-568)*

FOOD PRDTS, CANNED: Spaghetti & Other Pasta Sauce

Blessettis Inc .... G 918 830-5481
  Tulsa *(G-9303)*

FOOD PRDTS, CANNED: Vegetables

Leonard Mountain Inc .... E 800 822-7700
  Tulsa *(G-10153)*

FOOD PRDTS, FROZEN: Fruit Juice, Concentrates

ICEE Company .... G 405 685-7739
  Oklahoma City *(G-6285)*

FOOD PRDTS, FROZEN: NEC

Guymon Extracts Inc .... E 580 338-2624
  Guymon *(G-3349)*
ICEE Company .... G 800 423-3872
  Tulsa *(G-9965)*
Sfc Global Supply Chain Inc .... C 918 696-8325
  Stilwell *(G-8795)*
Windsor Quality Food Co Ltd 918 628-0277
  Tulsa *(G-11138)*

FOOD PRDTS, MEAT & MEAT PRDTS, WHOLESALE: Brokers

McLane Foodservice Dist Inc .... C 405 632-0118
  Oklahoma City *(G-6549)*

FOOD PRDTS, MEAT & MEAT PRDTS, WHOLESALE: Cured Or Smoked

Bulldog Jerky Co .... G 580 479-5542
  Grandfield *(G-3256)*

FOOD PRDTS, MEAT & MEAT PRDTS, WHOLESALE: Fresh

Alex Rogers .... G 405 677-2306
  Oklahoma City *(G-5412)*
Barnsdall Meat Processors Inc .... G 918 847-2814
  Barnsdall *(G-436)*
Butchs Processing Plant Inc .... G 405 382-2833
  Seminole *(G-8361)*
Cable Meat Center Inc .... F 580 658-6646
  Marlow *(G-4224)*
OSteen Meat Specialties Inc .... D 405 236-1952
  Oklahoma City *(G-6787)*
Tenderette Steak Co Inc .... F 405 634-5655
  Oklahoma City *(G-7268)*
Thompsons Custom Butcher Barn .... G 918 476-5508
  Chouteau *(G-1572)*

FOOD PRDTS, POULTRY, WHOLESALE: Live/Dressed/Frozen, Unpkgd

OSteen Meat Specialties Inc .... D 405 236-1952
  Oklahoma City *(G-6787)*

FOOD PRDTS, WHOL: Canned Goods, Fruit, Veg, Seafood/Meats

S & S Foods Inc .... F 405 256-6557
  Mustang *(G-4792)*

FOOD PRDTS, WHOLESALE: Baking Splys

Bishop Brothers .... G 918 367-2270
  Bristow *(G-766)*

FOOD PRDTS, WHOLESALE: Beans, Inedible

Eckroat Seed Co .... F 405 427-2484
  Oklahoma City *(G-6006)*

FOOD PRDTS, WHOLESALE: Coffee & Tea

Farmer Bros Co .... G 405 751-7222
  Oklahoma City *(G-6074)*
Minnette Company Ltd .... G 580 226-2929
  Wilson *(G-11538)*

FOOD PRDTS, WHOLESALE: Coffee, Green Or Roasted

Henderson Coffee Corp .... E 918 682-8751
  Muskogee *(G-4690)*
Tulsa Coffee Service Inc .... E 918 836-5570
  Tulsa *(G-10993)*

FOOD PRDTS, WHOLESALE: Dog Food

House Dog Industries LLC .... G 405 761-5576
  El Reno *(G-2724)*

FOOD PRDTS, WHOLESALE: Dried or Canned Foods

Leonard Mountain Inc .... E 800 822-7700
  Tulsa *(G-10153)*

FOOD PRDTS, WHOLESALE: Flavorings & Fragrances

Midwest Bakers Supply Co Inc .... G 405 942-3489
  Oklahoma City *(G-6599)*

FOOD PRDTS, WHOLESALE: Grain Elevators

Farmers Coop .... F 580 772-3334
  Weatherford *(G-11413)*
Rocky Farmers Cooperative Inc .... F 580 666-2440
  Rocky *(G-8105)*
Rocky Farmers Cooperative Inc .... G 580 674-3356
  Dill City *(G-2037)*
S & S Farm Center .... F 405 273-6907
  Shawnee *(G-8491)*
Shawnee Milling Company .... G 405 352-4336
  Minco *(G-4481)*
Stillwater Milling Company LLC .... F 580 369-2354
  Perry *(G-7747)*

FOOD PRDTS, WHOLESALE: Spices & Seasonings

Daddy Hinkles Inc .... G 918 358-2129
  Cleveland *(G-1721)*

FOOD PRDTS, WHOLESALE: Water, Mineral Or Spring, Bottled

O Fizz Inc .... F 918 834-3691
  Tulsa *(G-10370)*

FOOD PRDTS: Almond Pastes

Nut House .... G 918 266-1604
  Claremore *(G-1664)*

FOOD PRDTS: Animal & marine fats & oils

Griffin Industries LLC .... E 918 422-4790
  Watts *(G-11357)*
Oklahoma Heartland Inc .... G 918 914-3124
  Stillwater *(G-8732)*

FOOD PRDTS: Box Lunches, For Sale Off Premises

Kize Concepts Inc .... F 405 226-0701
  Oklahoma City *(G-6427)*

Employee Codes: A=Over 500 employees, B=251-500
C=101-250, D=51-100, E=20-50, F=10-19, G=1-9

FOOD PRDTS: Breakfast Bars

Aucora Breakfast Bar Backyard ....G...... 405 609-8854
  Oklahoma City *(G-5488)*

FOOD PRDTS: Chicken, Processed, Cooked

Advance Food Company Inc................C...... 800 969-2747
  Enid *(G-2905)*

FOOD PRDTS: Chicken, Processed, NEC

Rath Inc..F...... 580 588-3064
  Apache *(G-221)*

FOOD PRDTS: Chicken, Slaughtered & Dressed

Free Ranger LLC ....C...... 918 253-4223
  Jay *(G-3681)*

FOOD PRDTS: Chili Pepper Or Powder

Pepper Land Inc ....G...... 918 691-7241
  Tulsa *(G-10488)*

FOOD PRDTS: Cocoa & Cocoa Prdts

Executive Coffee Service Co ....D...... 405 236-3932
  Oklahoma City *(G-6059)*

FOOD PRDTS: Coffee

Charlie Bean Coffee LLC....................F...... 405 376-4815
  Oklahoma City *(G-5743)*
Farmer Bros Co ....G...... 405 751-7222
  Oklahoma City *(G-6074)*
Henderson Coffee Corp......................E...... 918 682-8751
  Muskogee *(G-4690)*
Hillshire Brands Company ....C...... 405 751-7222
  Oklahoma City *(G-6249)*
Imperial Inc ....F...... 580 357-8300
  Lawton *(G-3940)*
Imperial LLC ....B...... 918 437-1300
  Tulsa *(G-9972)*
Okie Roasters LLC ....G...... 405 699-2007
  Guthrie *(G-3328)*
Royal Cup Inc ....G...... 405 943-6088
  Oklahoma City *(G-7052)*
Tulsa Coffee Service Inc....................E...... 918 836-5570
  Tulsa *(G-10993)*
Viridian Coffee LLC............................G...... 405 795-0773
  Duncan *(G-2195)*

FOOD PRDTS: Coffee Roasting, Exc Wholesale Grocers

Compadres Trading Co ....G...... 405 816-9911
  Oklahoma City *(G-5807)*
Executive Coffee Service Co ....D...... 405 236-3932
  Oklahoma City *(G-6059)*
Farmer Bros Co ....G...... 918 439-9262
  Tulsa *(G-9728)*
Minnette Company Ltd......................G...... 580 226-2929
  Wilson *(G-11538)*

FOOD PRDTS: Dessert Mixes & Fillings

JKJ Processing Inc..............................G...... 405 606-9711
  Yukon *(G-11736)*

FOOD PRDTS: Dips, Exc Cheese & Sour Cream Based

Hollis Home Made Salsa LLC..............G...... 405 464-6249
  Midwest City *(G-4442)*
Sneaky Ts Salsa LLC ....G...... 405 323-7244
  Piedmont *(G-7771)*

FOOD PRDTS: Dough, Pizza, Prepared

Bama Companies Inc..........................A...... 918 592-0778
  Tulsa *(G-9258)*

FOOD PRDTS: Dressings, Salad, Raw & Cooked Exc Dry Mixes

Griffin Food Company ....D...... 918 687-6311
  Muskogee *(G-4683)*

FOOD PRDTS: Dried & Dehydrated Fruits, Vegetables & Soup Mix

Alfalfa Dehydrating Plant Inc..............G...... 918 482-3267
  Coweta *(G-1871)*

FOOD PRDTS: Edible fats & oils

Davis Hudson Inc................................G...... 405 203-0604
  Edmond *(G-2383)*
Rock Oil Co ....G...... 918 357-1188
  Broken Arrow *(G-1157)*

FOOD PRDTS: Emulsifiers

S and J Foods LLC ....E...... 580 337-6360
  Bessie *(G-570)*

FOOD PRDTS: Flavored Ices, Frozen

J Mottos LLC ....G...... 918 760-3866
  Tulsa *(G-10021)*

FOOD PRDTS: Flour & Other Grain Mill Products

ADM Milling Co..................................D...... 580 237-8000
  Enid *(G-2904)*
Archer-Daniels-Midland Company ......D...... 580 237-8000
  Enid *(G-2910)*
Archer-Daniels-Midland Company ......G...... 580 652-3761
  Hooker *(G-3595)*
Archer-Daniels-Midland Company ......G...... 580 233-3800
  Enid *(G-2911)*
Archer-Daniels-Midland Company ......G...... 580 652-2623
  Hooker *(G-3596)*
Archer-Daniels-Midland Company ......G...... 580 854-6285
  Tyrone *(G-11218)*
Archer-Daniels-Midland Company ......G...... 580 233-5100
  Enid *(G-2912)*
Archer-Daniels-Midland Company ......G...... 580 482-7100
  Altus *(G-143)*
Big v Feeds Inc...................................D...... 918 423-1565
  McAlester *(G-4276)*
Shawnee Milling Company ....E...... 580 822-4415
  Okeene *(G-5262)*
Shawnee Milling Company ....G...... 405 263-4566
  Okarche *(G-5252)*

FOOD PRDTS: Flour Mixes & Doughs

Bama Cos Inc ....G...... 918 732-2640
  Tulsa *(G-9259)*
Okie Dough LLC ....G...... 580 606-0142
  Owasso *(G-7597)*

FOOD PRDTS: Fruits & Vegetables, Pickled

Pickles of Edmond Inc........................G...... 405 285-4342
  Edmond *(G-2568)*

FOOD PRDTS: Granular Wheat Flour

Lanie Farms ....G...... 580 694-2259
  Manchester *(G-4168)*

FOOD PRDTS: Nuts & Seeds

Gunter Peanut Co ....E...... 405 656-2398
  Binger *(G-606)*
Masons Pecans & Peanuts Inc ....G...... 405 329-7828
  Norman *(G-5065)*
Nutopia Nuts & More ....G...... 405 663-2330
  Hydro *(G-3633)*
Peanut Products Co Inc ....F...... 580 296-4888
  Calera *(G-1243)*

FOOD PRDTS: Peanut Butter

Peanut Products Co Inc ....F...... 580 296-4888
  Calera *(G-1243)*
Snider Farms Peanut Barn LLC...........G...... 580 471-3470
  Hollis *(G-3568)*

FOOD PRDTS: Poultry, Processed, NEC

Bar-S Foods Co ....A...... 580 331-1628
  Clinton *(G-1740)*
O K Foods Inc ....A...... 918 653-2819
  Heavener *(G-3432)*
Tyson Foods Inc.................................A...... 580 584-9191
  Broken Bow *(G-1211)*

FOOD PRDTS: Preparations

Advance Food Company Inc................C...... 800 969-2747
  Enid *(G-2905)*
Advancepierre Foods Inc ....F...... 800 969-2747
  Enid *(G-2907)*
Amigos Salsa ....G...... 580 224-1424
  Ardmore *(G-240)*
Bishop Brothers ....G...... 918 367-2270
  Bristow *(G-766)*
Campo Alegre Foods ....G...... 918 271-6775
  Tulsa *(G-9368)*
Cecilias Salsas ....G...... 918 984-1491
  Tulsa *(G-9392)*
Designs By Lex LLC ....G...... 580 280-2557
  Lawton *(G-3919)*
Du Pont Delaware Inc ....G...... 918 476-5825
  Pryor *(G-7960)*
Everyday Foods LLC ....G...... 918 299-7939
  Jenks *(G-3705)*
Gold Strike Chili ....G...... 405 606-1819
  Warr Acres *(G-11320)*
Griffin Holdings Inc ....D...... 918 687-6311
  Muskogee *(G-4684)*
H Gellar ....G...... 617 834-0602
  Warr Acres *(G-11321)*
Hermans Chili Mix Inc........................G...... 918 743-1832
  Tulsa *(G-9925)*
Hillshire Brands Company ....C...... 405 751-7222
  Oklahoma City *(G-6249)*
J-M Farms Inc....................................G...... 918 540-1567
  Miami *(G-4409)*
Maria Raes Inc...................................G...... 580 242-3342
  Enid *(G-3005)*
Markenia Foods LLC...........................G...... 405 751-8616
  Edmond *(G-2505)*
Matador Processing LLC ....E...... 405 485-3567
  Blanchard *(G-722)*
Midwest Bakers Supply Co Inc...........G...... 405 942-3489
  Oklahoma City *(G-6599)*
O K Foods Inc ....B...... 918 427-7000
  Muldrow *(G-4635)*
Pepper Creek Farms Inc.....................G...... 580 536-1300
  Lawton *(G-3982)*
Pie In Sky Tulsa LLc ....G...... 918 527-5855
  Tulsa *(G-10513)*
Premeir Companies Inc ....F...... 405 895-7100
  Moore *(G-4555)*
Quality Bakery Products LLC ....F...... 609 871-7393
  Tulsa *(G-10590)*
R & J Food Tulsa LLC.........................G...... 918 520-0484
  Tulsa *(G-10600)*
Ross Honey Co ....G...... 405 352-4125
  Minco *(G-4480)*
Twisted Oak Foods LLC ....G...... 405 720-7059
  Oklahoma City *(G-7353)*

FOOD PRDTS: Relishes, Fruit & Vegetable

Dorians Foods Inc..............................G...... 580 658-3022
  Marlow *(G-4229)*

FOOD PRDTS: Seasonings & Spices

Big Productions LLC ....G...... 405 513-6545
  Edmond *(G-2321)*
Tajour Specialty Products LLC............G...... 479 684-7445
  Westville *(G-11485)*

FOOD PRDTS: Soup Mixes

Leonard Mountain Inc ....E...... 800 822-7700
  Tulsa *(G-10153)*

FOOD PRDTS: Spices, Including Ground

Cimarron Docs Bar-B-Que Chili ....G...... 918 787-7881
  Grove *(G-3261)*

FOOD PRDTS: Starches

Ingredion Incorporated......................G...... 539 292-4369
  Tulsa *(G-9985)*

FOOD PRDTS: Syrups

Griffin Food Company ....D...... 918 687-6311
  Muskogee *(G-4683)*

FOOD PRDTS: Tea

Executive Coffee Service Co ....D...... 405 236-3932
  Oklahoma City *(G-6059)*

PRODUCT SECTION

Royal Cup Inc .... G 405 943-6088
  Oklahoma City (G-7052)

FOOD PRDTS: Tortilla Chips

Tortilleria Lupita Inc .... G 405 232-2760
  Oklahoma City (G-7306)

FOOD PRDTS: Tortillas

Chelinos Tortilla Factory .... F 405 631-3188
  Oklahoma City (G-5747)
El Capora Tortilleria .... G 405 662-0427
  Oklahoma City (G-6014)
Tortilla Velasquez .... G 580 468-6753
  Guymon (G-3368)
Tortilleria Azteca Inc .... G 405 632-5382
  Oklahoma City (G-7305)
Tortilleria Milagro .... G 918 895-8225
  Tulsa (G-10956)
Tortilleria Milargo .... G 918 439-9977
  Tulsa (G-10957)
Tortilleria Puebla Inc .... G 918 610-8816
  Tulsa (G-10958)

FOOD PRDTS: Vinegar

Clements Foods Co .... G 405 842-3308
  Oklahoma City (G-5784)
Springdale Food Co Inc .... G 580 928-2598
  Sayre (G-8348)

FOOD PRODUCTS MACHINERY

Breshears Enterprises Inc .... F 405 236-4523
  Oklahoma City (G-5624)
Contact Process Piping .... G 405 948-9125
  Oklahoma City (G-5822)
Doyle Dryers Inc .... G 918 224-4002
  Tulsa (G-9601)
Galaxy Distributing .... G 918 835-1186
  Tulsa (G-9797)
O K Restaurant Supply .... G 405 330-9932
  Edmond (G-2543)
Rick Leaming Construction LLC .... G 580 362-2262
  Newkirk (G-4852)
Unitherm Food Systems LLC .... E 918 367-0197
  Bristow (G-802)

FOOD STORES: Convenience, Chain

Sunoco (R&m) LLC .... F 918 586-6246
  Tulsa (G-10873)

FOOD STORES: Grocery, Independent

Mc Alester Food Warehouse .... D 580 436-4302
  Ada (G-64)

FOOTWEAR: Cut Stock

Quarter Midgets of America .... G 918 371-9410
  Collinsville (G-1820)

FORESTRY RELATED EQPT

Dougherty Forestry Mfg Ltd .... F 405 542-3520
  Hinton (G-3523)
Reputation Services & Mfg LLC .... E 918 437-2077
  Tulsa (G-10643)

FORGINGS

Axels Transmissions Transfers .... G 918 425-7725
  Tulsa (G-9234)
Crosby Group LLC .... B 918 834-4611
  Tulsa (G-9509)
Crosby Worldwide Limited .... F 918 834-4611
  Tulsa (G-9512)
Cundiff Custom Fabrication LLC .... G 405 372-8204
  Stillwater (G-8673)
Ftdm Investments Llc .... D 918 598-3430
  Locust Grove (G-4107)
Oklahoma Forge Inc .... E 918 446-4486
  Tulsa (G-10401)
Rail Masters LLC .... G 405 840-1019
  Oklahoma City (G-6965)
Value Components Corp .... G 918 749-1689
  Tulsa (G-11066)

FORGINGS: Anchors

Malco Incorporated .... E 918 876-1934
  Tulsa (G-10206)

Mike Alexander Company Inc .... E 580 765-8085
  Tulsa (G-10276)

FORGINGS: Gear & Chain

J & D Gearing & Machining Inc .... G 405 677-7667
  Oklahoma City (G-6329)
Lufkin Industries LLC .... F 405 677-0567
  Oklahoma City (G-6501)

FORGINGS: Iron & Steel

Carlson Company .... E 918 627-4334
  Tulsa (G-9376)

FORGINGS: Machinery, Ferrous

M-A Systems Inc .... F 918 824-3705
  Pryor (G-7975)

FORMAL WRITING SVCS

Writers Research Group LLC .... F 405 682-2589
  Oklahoma City (G-7474)

FORMS: Concrete, Sheet Metal

Ellis Construction Spc LLC .... E 405 848-4676
  Oklahoma City (G-6026)

FOUNDRIES: Aluminum

Accu Cast .... G 918 582-3466
  Tulsa (G-9088)
Camcast Corp .... C 918 371-9966
  Owasso (G-7551)
CP Industries Inc .... G 918 468-2230
  Grove (G-3264)
Lahmeyer Pattern Shop .... G 918 425-6008
  Tulsa (G-10112)
Permocast Inc .... G 918 652-8812
  Henryetta (G-3516)
Transtate Castings Inc .... G 405 232-3936
  Oklahoma City (G-7319)

FOUNDRIES: Brass, Bronze & Copper

Custom Design By Roberts .... G 918 664-0466
  Tulsa (G-9528)
Fancy Dancer Leather Designs .... G 405 247-7030
  Anadarko (G-204)
T & L Foundry Inc .... D 918 322-3310
  Glenpool (G-3242)
Tonkawa Foundry Inc .... E 580 628-2575
  Tonkawa (G-8982)

FOUNDRIES: Gray & Ductile Iron

American Castings LLC .... B 918 476-4252
  Pryor (G-7942)
Camcast Corp .... C 918 371-9966
  Owasso (G-7551)
Concessions Mfg Co LLC .... G 918 786-5100
  Grove (G-3262)
Wh International Casting LLC .... G 562 521-0727
  Haskell (G-3402)

FOUNDRIES: Iron

American Castings LLC .... B 918 476-4252
  Pryor (G-7942)
Ej Usa Inc .... C 231 536-2261
  Ardmore (G-282)
Mid-South Metals LLC .... G 918 835-8055
  Tulsa (G-10262)
R & L Endeavors LLC .... G 405 826-8226
  Oklahoma City (G-6957)

FOUNDRIES: Nonferrous

Camcast Corp .... C 918 371-9966
  Owasso (G-7551)
Crucible LLC .... F 405 579-2700
  Norman (G-4971)
Mold Tech Inc .... G 918 247-6275
  Sapulpa (G-8292)
Tatco Metals Inc .... G 918 853-4663
  Jenks (G-3733)

FOUNDRIES: Steel

Alpha Investment Casting Corp .... E 918 834-4686
  Tulsa (G-9153)
Consoldted Fabrication Constrs .... G 918 224-3500
  Tulsa (G-8998)

Southwest Pickling Inc .... G 580 924-6996
  Durant (G-2259)

FOUNDRIES: Steel Investment

Afg Acquisition Group LLC .... B 918 366-4401
  Bixby (G-608)
Alpha Investment Casting Corp .... E 918 834-4686
  Tulsa (G-9153)
Camcast Corp .... C 918 371-9966
  Owasso (G-7551)
Metal Dynamics Corp .... E 918 582-0124
  Tulsa (G-10244)
Parrish Enterprises Ltd .... C 580 237-4033
  Enid (G-3031)

FOUNDRY MACHINERY & EQPT

Centrifugal Casting Mch Co Inc .... G 918 835-7323
  Owasso (G-7552)
Kice Industries Inc .... E 580 363-2850
  Blackwell (G-685)

FRAMES & HANDLES: Handbag & Luggage

Floyd Craig Company .... G 580 832-2597
  Cordell (G-1859)

FREIGHT TRANSPORTATION ARRANGEMENTS

Atc Drivetrain LLC .... A 405 577-9901
  Oklahoma City (G-5480)

FRUITS & VEGETABLES WHOLESALERS: Fresh

Johnny Apple Seed Store .... G 918 304-2055
  Okmulgee (G-7510)
Victory Garden Homestead LLC .... G 405 306-0308
  Blanchard (G-744)

FUEL ADDITIVES

Pinnacle Fuel Additives LLC .... G 405 658-3744
  Mustang (G-4788)

FUEL OIL DEALERS

Hough Oilfield Service Inc .... E 918 225-1851
  Cushing (G-1936)
Outlaw Oilfield Supply LLC .... E 580 526-3792
  Erick (G-3091)

FUELS & RADIOACTIVE COMPOUNDS

Kesc Enterprises LLC .... G 918 297-2501
  Hartshorne (G-3392)

FUELS: Diesel

Tank & Fuel Solutions LLC .... G 918 960-4361
  Claremore (G-1691)

FUELS: Ethanol

Chouteau Fuels Company .... G 405 249-8273
  Chouteau (G-1560)
Colorado Fuel Manufacturers .... G 918 877-5102
  Tulsa (G-9469)
Efficient Fuel Solutions Llc .... G 713 466-1400
  Caddo (G-1234)
Emerging Fuels Technology LLC .... F 918 286-6802
  Tulsa (G-9669)
Fast Fuel LLC .... G 405 375-6666
  Kingfisher (G-3797)
Fuel .... G 903 948-3125
  Woodward (G-11586)
Fuel Haulers LLC .... G 405 830-3385
  Guthrie (G-3315)
Fuel Inc .... G 580 583-5202
  Lawton (G-3933)
Fuels Marketing Inc .... G 405 433-9935
  Cashion (G-1288)
Grayson Investments LLC .... G 580 421-9770
  Ada (G-45)
Jag Fuels Company Inc .... G 580 465-3256
  Ardmore (G-310)
Johnson Minford .... G 580 772-0430
  Weatherford (G-11422)
L&S Fuels LLC .... G 580 227-0999
  Fairview (G-3139)
Mid-Continent Fuel Co Inc .... G 918 266-1923
  Catoosa (G-1341)

Employee Codes: A=Over 500 employees, B=251-500
C=101-250, D=51-100, E=20-50, F=10-19, G=1-9

FUELS: Ethanol

Oklahoma Fuel Athletics LLC ....G...... 405 286-3144
  Edmond *(G-2550)*
Pruitt Oil Company LLc ....G...... 580 889-2413
  Atoka *(G-422)*
Rovill Biodiesel Solution LLC ....G...... 580 339-6815
  Elk City *(G-2870)*
Rs Fuel LLC ....G...... 405 748-4277
  Oklahoma City *(G-7057)*
Station 7 ....G...... 405 470-4317
  Oklahoma City *(G-7196)*
Superior Pellet Fuels LLC ....G...... 918 494-0790
  Tulsa *(G-10877)*
United Fuels & Energy ....G...... 405 945-7400
  Oklahoma City *(G-7368)*
United Fuels Energy ....G...... 580 332-5222
  Ada *(G-100)*

FUELS: Gas, Liquefied

Marathon Oil Company ....E...... 318 624-0874
  Oklahoma City *(G-6521)*

FUELS: Oil

Aaron Oil Inc ....G...... 405 899-4138
  Noble *(G-4875)*
Earnheart Crescent LLC ....G...... 888 536-8703
  Marshall *(G-4250)*
H Petro R Inc ....G...... 405 242-4400
  Oklahoma City *(G-6199)*
Jec Production LLC ....G...... 405 235-4454
  Oklahoma City *(G-6353)*
NMB Manufacturing LLC ....F...... 918 943-6633
  Bixby *(G-649)*
Plummer Energy Inc ....G...... 405 238-9132
  Pauls Valley *(G-7671)*
Pruitt Oil Company LLc ....G...... 580 889-2413
  Atoka *(G-422)*
Roy Putnam ....G...... 918 333-5642
  Bartlesville *(G-523)*

FUNDRAISING SVCS

William C Jackson ....G...... 918 742-0602
  Tulsa *(G-11122)*

FUNGICIDES OR HERBICIDES

Shawn Schaeffer ....G...... 918 689-6781
  Eufaula *(G-3113)*

FURNACE BLACK

Thermal Specialties LLC ....F...... 918 836-4800
  Tulsa *(G-10926)*

FURNACES & OVENS: Indl

Born Inc ....E...... 918 582-2186
  Tulsa *(G-9322)*
Devco Process Heaters LLC ....G...... 918 221-9629
  Tulsa *(G-9577)*
Express Metal Fabricators Inc ....D...... 918 783-5129
  Big Cabin *(G-603)*
Global Industrial Inc ....D...... 918 266-5656
  Tulsa *(G-9831)*
Nortek Air Solutions LLC ....B...... 405 263-7286
  Okarche *(G-5247)*

FURNACES: Warm Air, Electric

Veterans Eng Group Inc ....G...... 918 864-6006
  Pryor *(G-7997)*

FURNITURE & CABINET STORES: Cabinets, Custom Work

McMurtry Cabinet Shop ....G...... 405 627-3275
  Oklahoma City *(G-6550)*
Tracys Wood Shop Inc ....G...... 918 587-4860
  Tulsa *(G-10966)*
Wades Cabinet Door Shop ....G...... 918 868-2516
  Tahlequah *(G-8891)*
Wolher Company ....G...... 405 282-6210
  Guthrie *(G-3341)*

FURNITURE & CABINET STORES: Custom

Ironcraft Urban Products LLC ....G...... 855 601-1647
  Oklahoma City *(G-6327)*

FURNITURE & FIXTURES Factory

Polk Appliances Co ....G...... 918 592-6858
  Tulsa *(G-10530)*

FURNITURE REFINISHING SVCS

D & S Refinishing ....G...... 580 233-4351
  Enid *(G-2938)*
Juan Manzo Custom Refinishing ......G...... 405 848-3843
  Oklahoma City *(G-6390)*

FURNITURE STORES

Jobri LLC ....F...... 580 925-3500
  Ada *(G-54)*
Murphy Wallbed USA LLC ....G...... 918 836-5833
  Tulsa *(G-10317)*
Think Ability Inc ....C...... 580 252-8000
  Duncan *(G-2187)*
Warren Ramsey Inc ....G...... 405 528-2828
  Oklahoma City *(G-7422)*
Weatherford Cabinets ....G...... 580 772-7511
  Weatherford *(G-11456)*

FURNITURE STORES: Bar Fixtures, Eqpt & Splys

Restaurant Equipment & Sup LLC ....G...... 918 664-1778
  Tulsa *(G-10648)*

FURNITURE STORES: Cabinets, Kitchen, Exc Custom Made

Woodstock Cabinet LLC ....F...... 918 834-4840
  Tulsa *(G-11150)*

FURNITURE STORES: Office

Benders ....G...... 580 256-5656
  Woodward *(G-11561)*
Fenton Office Supply Co ....E...... 405 372-5555
  Stillwater *(G-8688)*
Sooner Industries Inc ....G...... 918 540-2422
  Miami *(G-4431)*
Southwest Business Pdts LLC ....G...... 580 765-4401
  Ponca City *(G-7878)*
Southwestern Sty & Bnk Sup Inc .....D...... 405 525-9411
  Oklahoma City *(G-7177)*
Twj Inc ....G...... 405 392-4366
  Tuttle *(G-11217)*
Warren Products Inc ....F...... 405 947-5676
  Oklahoma City *(G-7421)*

FURNITURE, OFFICE: Wholesalers

Hooker Advance & Office Supply .....G...... 580 652-2476
  Hooker *(G-3598)*
Kingfisher Office Supply Inc ....G...... 405 375-3404
  Kingfisher *(G-3806)*
Pioneer Printing Inc ....G...... 918 542-5521
  Miami *(G-4428)*

FURNITURE: Altars, Cut Stone

Buck Creek Homes Cnstr Inc ....F...... 580 272-0102
  Ada *(G-15)*

FURNITURE: Bed Frames & Headboards, Wood

Fabric Factory ....F...... 405 521-1694
  Oklahoma City *(G-6067)*
Kennel and Crate LLC ....G...... 405 624-0062
  Stillwater *(G-8709)*

FURNITURE: Beds, Household, Incl Folding & Cabinet, Metal

Life Lift Systems Inc ....F...... 904 635-8231
  Oklahoma City *(G-6474)*
Melton Co Inc ....G...... 405 524-2281
  Oklahoma City *(G-6563)*

FURNITURE: Bedsprings, Assembled

Leggett & Platt Incorporated ....G...... 405 787-1212
  Oklahoma City *(G-6465)*

FURNITURE: Bookcases, Wood

Punkin Hollerwood ....G...... 918 456-9640
  Proctor *(G-7939)*

FURNITURE: Cabinets & Filing Drawers, Office, Exc Wood

Close Custom Cabinets Inc ....E...... 405 840-8226
  Oklahoma City *(G-5790)*

FURNITURE: Chests, Cedar

Cedar Chest ....G...... 918 287-9129
  Pawhuska *(G-7681)*

FURNITURE: Church

Kingsview Freewill Baptist Ch ....G...... 405 692-1554
  Oklahoma City *(G-5302)*

FURNITURE: Club Room, Wood

Donmar Industries LLC ....G...... 918 688-7277
  Skiatook *(G-8542)*

FURNITURE: Desks & Tables, Office, Exc Wood

Michael Gipson LLC ....G...... 405 819-6349
  Oklahoma City *(G-6587)*

FURNITURE: Foundations & Platforms

Tote4me ....G...... 405 664-1144
  Edmond *(G-2651)*

FURNITURE: Game Room

Billiards & Bar Stools Inc ....F...... 405 722-2400
  Oklahoma City *(G-5566)*

FURNITURE: Game Room, Wood

Billiards & Bar Stools Inc ....F...... 405 722-2400
  Oklahoma City *(G-5566)*

FURNITURE: Garden, Metal

Webcoat Inc ....C...... 918 426-5100
  McAlester *(G-4350)*

FURNITURE: High Chairs, Children's, Wood

Days Wood Products Inc ....F...... 405 238-6477
  Pauls Valley *(G-7656)*

FURNITURE: Hospital

Braden Shielding Systems Const .....E...... 918 624-2888
  Tulsa *(G-9327)*
Md-Advantages LLC ....G...... 405 996-6125
  Oklahoma City *(G-6551)*
Modular Services Company ....G...... 405 521-9923
  Arcadia *(G-231)*

FURNITURE: Hotel

Accord Upholstery & Fabric ....G...... 405 634-4070
  Oklahoma City *(G-5363)*

FURNITURE: Household, Metal

Angel Ornamental Iron Works ....G...... 918 584-8726
  Tulsa *(G-9191)*
Chris Green Greens Construct ....G...... 405 207-0690
  Pauls Valley *(G-7653)*
Glenn Schlarb Welding ....G...... 580 327-3832
  Alva *(G-182)*
Ironcraft Urban Products LLC ....G...... 855 601-1647
  Oklahoma City *(G-6327)*
Legacy Metalcraft LLC ....G...... 918 612-0001
  Wagoner *(G-11286)*
Pro Stainless & Shtmtl LLC ....G...... 405 787-4400
  Oklahoma City *(G-6906)*

FURNITURE: Household, NEC

Murphy Wallbed USA LLC ....G...... 918 836-5833
  Tulsa *(G-10317)*

FURNITURE: Household, Upholstered, Exc Wood Or Metal

Hemispheres ....G...... 405 773-8410
  Warr Acres *(G-11322)*
World Imports At Wholesale Inc ......G...... 405 947-7710
  Oklahoma City *(G-7469)*

FURNITURE: Household, Wood

American Custom Woodworks LLC .....G....... 918 344-4988
　Sapulpa *(G-8248)*
Breshears Enterprises Inc ....F....... 405 236-4523
　Oklahoma City *(G-5624)*
Close Custom Cabinets Inc ....E....... 405 840-8226
　Oklahoma City *(G-5790)*
Creative Spaces ....G....... 405 341-8710
　Edmond *(G-2372)*
Desert Moon Enterprises ....G....... 918 540-0333
　Miami *(G-4395)*
Hawley & Co ....G....... 918 587-0510
　Tulsa *(G-9905)*
Imel Woodworks Inc ....G....... 405 356-2505
　Wellston *(G-11472)*
Johnson Woodcraft ....G....... 918 693-2388
　Claremore *(G-1645)*
Jos Lamerton Woodworking LLC ....G....... 580 336-8448
　Enid *(G-2988)*
Juan Manzo Custom Refinishing ....G....... 405 848-3843
　Oklahoma City *(G-6390)*
Kc Woodwork & Fixture Inc ....G....... 918 582-5300
　Tulsa *(G-10078)*
Legacy Metalcraft LLC ....G....... 918 612-0001
　Wagoner *(G-11286)*
Mass Brothers Inc ....G....... 918 527-3753
　Hartshorne *(G-3393)*
Milot James Residence Cnstr ....G....... 405 433-2661
　Cashion *(G-1291)*
Refuge Lifestyle ....F....... 918 366-6650
　Tulsa *(G-10636)*
Troy Wesnidge Inc ....E....... 405 387-4720
　Newcastle *(G-4845)*
United Millwork Inc ....G....... 405 670-3999
　Oklahoma City *(G-7371)*
Weatherford Cabinets ....G....... 580 772-7511
　Weatherford *(G-11456)*
Westwood Furniture Inc ....G....... 918 508-7657
　Tulsa *(G-11113)*
Winkles Woodworks Ltd ....F....... 918 486-5022
　Coweta *(G-1902)*
Woodshop Ltd ....G....... 405 922-3789
　Edmond *(G-2692)*
Young Construction Supply LLC ....G....... 918 456-3250
　Tahlequah *(G-8893)*

FURNITURE: Institutional, Exc Wood

Aviation Training Devices Inc ....F....... 918 366-6680
　Bixby *(G-613)*
Moss Seat Cover Mfg & Sls Co ....F....... 918 742-3326
　Tulsa *(G-10306)*
Sweeper Metal Fabricators Corp ....E....... 918 352-9180
　Drumright *(G-2073)*

FURNITURE: Living Room, Upholstered On Wood Frames

Sendee Sales Inc ....E....... 918 427-3318
　Muldrow *(G-4636)*

FURNITURE: Mattresses, Box & Bedsprings

Adairs Sleep World Inc ....F....... 405 341-9468
　Edmond *(G-2289)*
B & B Haybeds ....G....... 580 357-5083
　Lawton *(G-3894)*
Melton Co Inc ....G....... 405 524-2281
　Oklahoma City *(G-6563)*
Montgomery Mattress ....G....... 580 255-8979
　Duncan *(G-2156)*
Treble Services LLC ....G....... 405 401-1217
　Oklahoma City *(G-7321)*

FURNITURE: Mattresses, Innerspring Or Box Spring

M & M Mattress Company ....G....... 918 834-2033
　Tulsa *(G-10187)*

FURNITURE: NEC

Ki Inc ....G....... 918 289-0200
　Broken Arrow *(G-956)*
Kimbro Furniture LLC ....G....... 580 351-7304
　Lawton *(G-3949)*

FURNITURE: Office, Exc Wood

CSC Inc ....G....... 580 938-2533
　Shattuck *(G-8420)*
Fixtures & Drywall Co Okla Inc ....F....... 918 832-1641
　Tulsa *(G-9751)*
Melton Co Inc ....G....... 405 524-2281
　Oklahoma City *(G-6563)*
Rambo Acquisition Company ....D....... 918 627-6222
　Tulsa *(G-10615)*
Sweeper Metal Fabricators Corp ....E....... 918 352-9180
　Drumright *(G-2073)*

FURNITURE: Office, Wood

Beauchamp Cabinets Cstm Homes .....G....... 918 476-5532
　Chouteau *(G-1558)*
D Lloyd Hollingsworth ....G....... 918 587-3533
　Tulsa *(G-9539)*
Dale P Jackson ....F....... 580 332-1988
　Ada *(G-29)*
Kc Woodwork & Fixture Inc ....G....... 918 582-5300
　Tulsa *(G-10078)*
Ketcherside Custom Cabinets ....G....... 580 254-2672
　Woodward *(G-11599)*
Narcomey LLC ....G....... 405 473-1350
　Oklahoma City *(G-6653)*
Penloyd LLC ....G....... 918 836-3794
　Tulsa *(G-10484)*
Rambo Acquisition Company ....D....... 918 627-6222
　Tulsa *(G-10615)*
Thomas Millwork Inc ....F....... 405 769-5618
　Spencer *(G-8602)*
Winkles Woodworks Ltd ....F....... 918 486-5022
　Coweta *(G-1902)*
Wolher Company ....G....... 405 282-6210
　Guthrie *(G-3341)*
Ye Olde Woodshop ....G....... 918 224-1603
　Sapulpa *(G-8328)*
Young Construction Supply LLC ....G....... 918 456-3250
　Tahlequah *(G-8893)*

FURNITURE: Pews, Church

Born Again Pews ....F....... 918 868-7613
　Kansas *(G-3754)*

FURNITURE: Picnic Tables Or Benches, Park

City of Davis ....E....... 580 369-2988
　Davis *(G-1981)*

FURNITURE: Restaurant

J&M Stainless Fabricators Ltd ....G....... 405 517-0875
　Oklahoma City *(G-6340)*

FURNITURE: Serving Carts & Tea Wagons, Metal

J&M Stainless Fabricators Ltd ....G....... 405 517-0875
　Oklahoma City *(G-6340)*

FURNITURE: Storage Chests, Household, Wood

Stillwater Transfer & Stor Co ....F....... 405 372-0577
　Stillwater *(G-8759)*

FURNITURE: Table Tops, Marble

Forged By Creation LLC ....G....... 918 798-0051
　Broken Arrow *(G-912)*
Young Brothers Inc ....E....... 405 272-0821
　Oklahoma City *(G-7482)*

FURNITURE: Tables, Office, Wood

Polyvision Corporation ....F....... 918 756-7392
　Okmulgee *(G-7522)*

FURNITURE: Upholstered

Custom Lea Sad & Cowboy Decor ....G....... 918 335-2277
　Bartlesville *(G-471)*
Custom Upholstery Contracting ....F....... 405 236-3505
　Oklahoma City *(G-5878)*
Davenport Cloaks Inc ....G....... 918 932-8600
　Tulsa *(G-9556)*
James D Johnson ....G....... 580 464-3299
　Cyril *(G-1975)*
La-Z-Boy Incorporated ....G....... 405 417-5704
　Oklahoma City *(G-6443)*
La-Z-Boy Incorporated ....G....... 405 951-1437
　Oklahoma City *(G-6444)*
Patricia McKay ....G....... 580 355-2739
　Cache *(G-1230)*
Relf Upholstery ....G....... 405 454-3295
　Luther *(G-4137)*
Warren Ramsey Inc ....G....... 405 528-2828
　Oklahoma City *(G-7422)*

FUSES: Electric

Norberg Industries Inc ....E....... 918 665-6888
　Tulsa *(G-10349)*

Furs

McAmis Fur Company ....G....... 580 323-5961
　Arapaho *(G-225)*
Talking Hands Puppets ....G....... 918 868-5553
　Colcord *(G-1790)*

GAMES & TOYS: Board Games, Children's & Adults'

Music Games n Things Inc ....G....... 918 742-4349
　Tulsa *(G-10318)*

GAMES & TOYS: Craft & Hobby Kits & Sets

Creative Blessings ....G....... 918 302-0734
　McAlester *(G-4289)*
Leisure Lane Handicrafts ....G....... 580 563-2747
　Blair *(G-696)*
Linda L Hargraves ....G....... 918 584-3442
　Tulsa *(G-10163)*

GAMES & TOYS: Darts & Dart Games

Pro Darts Inc ....G....... 405 232-3552
　Oklahoma City *(G-6902)*

GAMES & TOYS: Dollhouses & Furniture

E and H Sales ....G....... 918 742-1091
　Tulsa *(G-9619)*

GAMES & TOYS: Electronic

Chickasaw Nation ....G....... 405 387-6013
　Newcastle *(G-4821)*
Creek Nation Foundation Inc ....G....... 918 683-1825
　Muskogee *(G-4665)*
Salamander Games Inc ....G....... 405 633-2725
　Yukon *(G-11774)*

GAMES & TOYS: Game Machines, Exc Coin-Operated

AGS LLC ....G....... 405 605-8331
　Oklahoma City *(G-5400)*

GAMES & TOYS: Miniature Dolls, Collectors'

Pats World ....G....... 580 443-5751
　Milburn *(G-4463)*

GAMES & TOYS: Puzzles

Moondog Puzzles LLC ....G....... 405 286-6881
　Oklahoma City *(G-6630)*
Primarily Puzzles ....G....... 918 275-8270
　Talala *(G-8902)*
Puzzle Apps Inc ....G....... 918 815-6444
　Tulsa *(G-10585)*

GAMES & TOYS: Rocking Horses

Rocking RB Quarter Horses LLC ....G....... 405 605-9458
　Noble *(G-4890)*

GARAGE DOOR REPAIR SVCS

Aztec Ne Overhead Door Inc ....G....... 918 341-7502
　Claremore *(G-1586)*

GAS & HYDROCARBON LIQUEFACTION FROM COAL

Enxnet Inc ....G....... 918 494-6663
　Tulsa *(G-9693)*
Northstar Energy LLC ....D....... 231 941-0073
　Tulsa *(G-10362)*

GAS & OIL FIELD EXPLORATION SVCS

89 Energy LLC ....F....... 405 600-6040
　Oklahoma City *(G-5338)*

89 Energy II LLC ....F....... 405 600-6040
Oklahoma City *(G-5339)*
9800 North Oklahoma LLC ....G....... 405 748-9400
Oklahoma City *(G-5341)*
A & T Resources LLC ....G....... 918 582-7894
Tulsa *(G-9064)*
Ada Energy Service LLC ....D....... 580 436-5228
Ada *(G-5)*
Aexco Petroleum Inc ....G....... 405 844-1991
Edmond *(G-2292)*
Alpine Inc ....G....... 405 507-1111
Edmond *(G-2299)*
Amazing Graze LLC ....G....... 405 447-4893
Norman *(G-4905)*
Amcon Resources ....G....... 405 236-4100
Oklahoma City *(G-5430)*
Amerex Corp ....G....... 405 216-5548
Edmond *(G-2301)*
American Manifold ....G....... 580 225-1116
Elk City *(G-2783)*
American Petroleum & Envrnmntl ....G....... 405 513-6055
Edmond *(G-2302)*
Amerril Energy LLC ....G....... 770 856-2662
Oklahoma City *(G-5443)*
Anadarko Petroleum Corporation ....E....... 405 756-4347
Lindsay *(G-4043)*
Anchor Exploration of Oklahoma ....G....... 918 605-1005
Claremore *(G-1582)*
Annabella Oil & Gas Co LLC ....G....... 405 377-8030
Stillwater *(G-8654)*
Antioch Operating LLC ....G....... 405 236-0080
Oklahoma City *(G-5449)*
Apollo Exploration LLC ....G....... 405 286-0600
Oklahoma City *(G-5453)*
Apss Inc ....G....... 405 324-2071
Oklahoma City *(G-5459)*
Arcadia Resources LP ....D....... 405 608-5453
Oklahoma City *(G-5461)*
Arena Resources Inc ....D....... 918 747-6060
Tulsa *(G-9207)*
Arkos Field Services LP ....G....... 405 262-1548
El Reno *(G-2699)*
Armor Energy LLC ....G....... 918 986-9459
Tulsa *(G-9209)*
Arnold Oil Properties LLC ....F....... 405 842-1488
Oklahoma City *(G-5468)*
Arrowood Companies ....G....... 405 701-3673
Norman *(G-4919)*
Ascent Resources - Utica LLC ....D....... 405 608-5544
Oklahoma City *(G-5470)*
Ascent Resources Operating LLC ....F....... 405 608-5544
Oklahoma City *(G-5471)*
Ascent Rsrces Utica Hldngs LLC ....G....... 405 608-5544
Oklahoma City *(G-5472)*
Aspect Oilfield Services LLC ....G....... 504 812-5330
Tulsa *(G-9216)*
Associated Resources Inc ....E....... 918 584-2111
Tulsa *(G-9218)*
B & W Exploration Inc ....G....... 405 236-1807
Oklahoma City *(G-5503)*
B R Polk Inc ....G....... 405 286-9666
Oklahoma City *(G-5505)*
B Raye Oil Environmenta ....G....... 405 818-6996
Mustang *(G-4763)*
B&W Operating LLC ....G....... 405 236-1807
Oklahoma City *(G-5506)*
Babb Land & Development ....G....... 405 340-1178
Edmond *(G-2315)*
Bailey Production Company ....G....... 405 932-5293
Paden *(G-7633)*
Baker Hghes Olfld Oprtions LLC ....C....... 405 670-3354
Oklahoma City *(G-5513)*
Bakken Hbt LP ....G....... 405 516-8241
Oklahoma City *(G-5518)*
Bandera Inc ....G....... 918 747-7771
Tulsa *(G-9262)*
Barbour Energy Corporation ....G....... 405 848-7671
Oklahoma City *(G-5527)*
Bbr Oil Corp ....G....... 405 366-8019
Norman *(G-4926)*
Bce-Mach II LLC ....D....... 405 252-8100
Oklahoma City *(G-5537)*
Bce-Mach LLC ....D....... 405 252-8100
Oklahoma City *(G-5538)*
Bce-Mach LLC ....C....... 580 824-7251
Waynoka *(G-11373)*
Becsul Energy Incorporated ....G....... 405 789-1061
Oklahoma City *(G-5541)*
Bedford Energy Inc ....G....... 405 820-2711
Oklahoma City *(G-5542)*
Bellwood Petroleum ....G....... 405 254-3113
Oklahoma City *(G-5547)*
Benchmark 77 Energy ....G....... 405 239-3291
Oklahoma City *(G-5549)*
Beredco Inc ....C....... 405 858-2326
Oklahoma City *(G-5554)*
Berexco LLC ....G....... 405 848-1165
Oklahoma City *(G-5555)*
Beta Oil Company ....G....... 405 601-3389
Oklahoma City *(G-5559)*
Billy Jack Sharber Oper LLC ....G....... 405 382-5740
Konawa *(G-3843)*
Bint Exploration & Development ....G....... 405 848-2113
Oklahoma City *(G-5571)*
Bison Oilfield Services LLC ....E....... 405 437-1485
Seminole *(G-8359)*
Bk Exploration Corporation ....G....... 918 582-3855
Tulsa *(G-9298)*
Black Swan Oil & Gas ....G....... 405 285-1996
Edmond *(G-2325)*
Blaine Exploration Ltd ....G....... 918 333-2115
Bartlesville *(G-456)*
Blue Star Gas Corp ....G....... 405 321-1397
Norman *(G-4937)*
Blue Stone Operating LLC ....D....... 918 392-9209
Tulsa *(G-9307)*
Blue Valley Energy Corp ....G....... 918 298-1032
Jenks *(G-3692)*
Bluestone Natural Resources HI ....G....... 918 392-9200
Tulsa *(G-9310)*
Bluestone Ntral Rsurces II LLC ....G....... 918 392-9200
Tulsa *(G-9311)*
Bluestone Ntural Resources LLC ....F....... 918 392-9200
Tulsa *(G-9312)*
Bob Pound Drilling Inc ....F....... 918 367-6262
Bristow *(G-767)*
Boelte Explorations LLC ....G....... 405 285-0063
Edmond *(G-2328)*
Boone Operating Inc ....G....... 405 879-2332
Oklahoma City *(G-5618)*
Bosendorfer Oil Company ....G....... 405 604-9025
Oklahoma City *(G-5622)*
Bounty Transfer LLC ....F....... 405 338-1531
Stillwater *(G-8662)*
Brett Exploration ....G....... 405 842-2322
Oklahoma City *(G-5625)*
Brg Energy Inc ....G....... 918 496-2626
Tulsa *(G-9336)*
Brigham Company LLC ....G....... 405 843-2660
Oklahoma City *(G-5628)*
Brookline Minerals LLC ....G....... 405 359-0900
Edmond *(G-2333)*
Bs & W Solutions LLC ....G....... 918 392-9356
Tulsa *(G-9343)*
Buckeye Exploration Company ....G....... 405 258-5428
Chandler *(G-1377)*
C & J Minerals LLC ....G....... 580 504-4048
Ardmore *(G-262)*
Cadence Energy Partners LLC ....E....... 405 485-8200
Oklahoma City *(G-5668)*
Caerus Operating LLC ....G....... 580 468-3527
Guymon *(G-3345)*
Cagan Land Services LLC ....G....... 405 757-4046
Edmond *(G-2336)*
Caliber Completion Svcs LLC ....G....... 405 385-3761
Moore *(G-4502)*
Callie Oil Company LLC ....G....... 918 521-9292
Agra *(G-124)*
Calyx Energy III Holdings LLC ....G....... 918 949-4224
Tulsa *(G-9366)*
Canaan Energy Corp ....G....... 405 604-9200
Oklahoma City *(G-5684)*
Cano Petroleum Inc ....F....... 918 398-2728
Tulsa *(G-9370)*
Cantrell Energy Corporation ....G....... 580 332-4710
Ada *(G-19)*
Capstone Oil & Gas Inc ....G....... 405 853-7170
Hennessey *(G-3448)*
Cardinal Energy Inc ....G....... 405 331-9206
Wynnewood *(G-11664)*
Cardinal Midstream ....G....... 405 706-4161
Mustang *(G-4766)*
Cardinal Midstream LLC ....G....... 580 927-2799
Coalgate *(G-1777)*
Cardinal River Energy Co ....G....... 405 606-7481
Oklahoma City *(G-5697)*
Carter Production Co ....G....... 918 493-7064
Tulsa *(G-9383)*
Casillas Petroleum Corp ....G....... 918 582-5310
Tulsa *(G-9387)*
Cbl Resources ....G....... 918 551-6760
Tulsa *(G-9391)*
CBS Energy LLC ....G....... 405 470-4644
Oklahoma City *(G-5717)*
Cep Mid-Continent LLC ....G....... 918 270-9927
Tulsa *(G-9401)*
Cfmi LLC ....G....... 918 877-5000
Tulsa *(G-9402)*
Chaparral Energy Inc ....D....... 405 478-8770
Oklahoma City *(G-5739)*
Chaparral Energy LLC ....C....... 405 478-8770
Oklahoma City *(G-5740)*
Charles D Mayhue ....G....... 580 436-6500
Ada *(G-20)*
Charter Oak Production Co LLC ....F....... 405 286-0361
Oklahoma City *(G-5744)*
Chaston Oil & Gas LLC ....G....... 580 226-2640
Ardmore *(G-266)*
Cheftain Royalty Company ....G....... 405 767-1251
Edmond *(G-2347)*
Chernico Exploration Inc ....G....... 918 587-6242
Tulsa *(G-9412)*
Chesapeake Energy Corporation ....E....... 877 245-1427
Elk City *(G-2794)*
Cheyenne Petro Co Ltd Partnr ....E....... 405 936-6220
Oklahoma City *(G-5758)*
Cimarex Energy Co ....C....... 918 585-1100
Tulsa *(G-9425)*
Cimarex Energy Co ....F....... 405 262-2966
El Reno *(G-2706)*
Cimarex Energy Co ....D....... 918 295-1638
Tulsa *(G-9426)*
Cimarex Energy Co ....G....... 580 330-0188
Clinton *(G-1743)*
Circle 9 Resources LLC ....F....... 972 528-6773
Oklahoma City *(G-5767)*
Citation Oil & Gas Corp ....F....... 405 681-9400
Oklahoma City *(G-5769)*
Citizen Energy III LLC ....G....... 918 949-4680
Tulsa *(G-9434)*
Citizen Energy Operating LLC ....G....... 918 949-4680
Tulsa *(G-9435)*
Clearwater Enterprises ....G....... 918 296-7007
Tulsa *(G-9451)*
Cobra Oil & Gas Corporation ....G....... 580 254-2027
Woodward *(G-11569)*
Cockerell Energy ....G....... 405 463-7118
Oklahoma City *(G-5799)*
Colter Bay LLC ....G....... 405 842-7622
Nichols Hills *(G-4858)*
Comanche Exploration Co LLC ....E....... 405 755-5900
Oklahoma City *(G-5804)*
Concorde Resource Corporation ....G....... 918 689-9510
Eufaula *(G-3099)*
Conocophillips Company ....E....... 281 293-1000
Bartlesville *(G-468)*
Coronado Resources MGT LLC ....G....... 918 591-3500
Tulsa *(G-9491)*
Corp Comm Oil & Gas Div ....G....... 405 375-5570
Kingfisher *(G-3793)*
Council Oak Resources LLC ....F....... 918 513-0900
Tulsa *(G-9493)*
CP Energy LLC ....F....... 405 513-6006
Edmond *(G-2370)*
Crest Resources Inc ....G....... 918 585-2900
Tulsa *(G-9508)*
Crow Creek Energy LLC ....G....... 918 970-6706
Tulsa *(G-9513)*
Crystal River Operating Co LLC ....G....... 405 510-0440
Oklahoma City *(G-5864)*
Cudd Pressure Control Inc ....E....... 405 756-4337
Lindsay *(G-4058)*
Cudd Pressure Control Inc ....E....... 580 225-6922
Elk City *(G-2798)*
Culbreath Oil & Gas Co Inc ....G....... 918 749-3508
Tulsa *(G-9520)*
Cummings Oil Company ....G....... 405 948-1818
Oklahoma City *(G-5866)*
Cyanostar Energy Inc ....G....... 918 582-2069
Tulsa *(G-9531)*
Dagwood Energy Inc ....G....... 918 582-6604
Tulsa *(G-9546)*
Daniel H Finnefrock ....G....... 918 585-3350
Tulsa *(G-9551)*
Daniel R Willits Offices ....G....... 580 227-2592
Fairview *(G-3134)*
Danlin Industries Corp ....G....... 405 853-2559
Hennessey *(G-3457)*
Dannys Bop LLC ....D....... 405 815-4041
Oklahoma City *(G-5895)*

David Greens Office G 918 335-3855
Bartlesville *(G-473)*
David W Potts Land Exploration G 580 226-3633
Ardmore *(G-276)*
Davis Operating Company G 918 587-7782
Tulsa *(G-9561)*
Dawson Geophysical Company F 405 848-7512
Oklahoma City *(G-5906)*
Dee-Jay Exploration G 405 773-8500
Oklahoma City *(G-5918)*
Delphi International Inc G 918 749-9401
Tulsa *(G-9568)*
Delta Oil and Gas LLC G 918 599-9800
Tulsa *(G-9569)*
Devon Energy Corporation C 405 235-3611
Oklahoma City *(G-5929)*
Devon Gas Services LP G 405 235-3611
Oklahoma City *(G-5933)*
Diamondback Operating LP F 918 477-7755
Tulsa *(G-9580)*
Diversified Energy Svcs LLC G 405 775-0414
Oklahoma City *(G-5951)*
Division Order Beginnings G 918 477-4559
Porter *(G-7892)*
Djf Services Inc G 405 380-7273
Holdenville *(G-3553)*
Dolphin Blue Production LLC G 405 285-5388
Oklahoma City *(G-5965)*
Dominion Corp G 918 270-1722
Tulsa *(G-9594)*
Donray Petroleum LLC E 405 418-4348
Oklahoma City *(G-5967)*
Double J Production LLC G 918 691-4060
Broken Arrow *(G-891)*
Drug Warehouse G 918 592-4545
Tulsa *(G-9610)*
Duncan Inc Walter E 405 272-1800
Oklahoma City *(G-5987)*
Duncan Oil & Gas Inc G 405 360-2183
Norman *(G-4984)*
Duncan Oil Properties Inc E 405 272-1800
Oklahoma City *(G-5988)*
Eagle Chief Midstream LLC E 405 888-5585
Edmond *(G-2398)*
Eagle Energy Company LLC G 918 746-1350
Tulsa *(G-9623)*
Earlsboro Energies Corp G 405 282-5007
Guthrie *(G-3312)*
East Texas Exploration LLC G 405 245-6568
Edmond *(G-2399)*
Easton Land Services G 405 842-1930
Oklahoma City *(G-6001)*
Echo Energy LLC D 405 753-4232
Oklahoma City *(G-6005)*
Edinger Engineering Inc G 405 232-6315
Oklahoma City *(G-6010)*
Edrio Oil Co G 405 621-1300
Oklahoma City *(G-6011)*
Egret Operating Company Inc G 918 687-8665
Muskogee *(G-4672)*
Ek Exploration LLC G 405 285-1220
Edmond *(G-2408)*
Eland Energy Inc F 405 840-9885
Oklahoma City *(G-6020)*
Empire Louisiana LLC G 539 444-8002
Tulsa *(G-9675)*
Empire Petroleum Corporation G 539 444-8002
Tulsa *(G-9677)*
Encompass Media LLC G 405 823-8081
Oklahoma City *(G-6035)*
Endico Inc G 405 340-8009
Edmond *(G-2411)*
Enerfin Resources Company G 918 492-8686
Tulsa *(G-9682)*
Energy Annastin G 405 810-5460
Oklahoma City *(G-6038)*
Energy Control System Inc G 918 481-3244
Tulsa *(G-9683)*
Energy Partners G 405 573-9064
Norman *(G-4992)*
Enerlabs Inc G 405 879-1752
Oklahoma City *(G-6040)*
Enerquest Oil & Gas LLC F 405 478-3300
Oklahoma City *(G-6041)*
Enterprise Exploration Inc G 918 481-2125
Tulsa *(G-9690)*
Entransco Inc G 916 628-6835
Dewey *(G-2021)*
Eog Resources Inc F 580 225-8314
Elk City *(G-2813)*
Eog Resources Inc E 405 246-3100
Oklahoma City *(G-6048)*
Esperanza Resources Corp G 918 497-1231
Tulsa *(G-9701)*
Essex Energy Inc G 405 350-1351
Yukon *(G-11722)*
Exco Resources Inc G 405 756-4347
Lindsay *(G-4062)*
Exok Inc G 405 840-9196
Oklahoma City *(G-6062)*
Fairway Energy LLC G 405 286-9796
Oklahoma City *(G-6069)*
Flanagan Energy G 580 357-1227
Walters *(G-11300)*
Flatrock Energy Advisers G 405 341-9993
Edmond *(G-2416)*
Flexx Wireline Services LLC G 405 990-1593
El Reno *(G-2717)*
Ford Exploration Inc G 405 341-7502
Edmond *(G-2417)*
Forum Us Inc G 405 260-7800
Guthrie *(G-3314)*
Forward Oil and Gas Inc G 405 607-2247
Oklahoma City *(G-6106)*
Fossil Creek Energy Corp G 405 949-0880
Oklahoma City *(G-6107)*
Foundation Energy Company LLC F 918 585-1650
Tulsa *(G-9767)*
Foundation Energy MGT LLC G 918 526-5521
Tulsa *(G-9768)*
Fourpoint Energy LLC G 580 225-8556
Elk City *(G-2815)*
Foxborough Energy Company LLC G 405 286-3526
Oklahoma City *(G-6109)*
Foxhead Oil & Gas Company G 918 582-2124
Tulsa *(G-9770)*
Freedom Energy Ltd G 405 285-2682
Edmond *(G-2422)*
Friedel Petroleum Corporation G 405 359-1285
Edmond *(G-2424)*
Funk G 405 329-7571
Norman *(G-5005)*
G B K Holdings Inc G 918 494-0000
Tulsa *(G-9789)*
G L B Exploration Inc G 405 787-0049
Oklahoma City *(G-6132)*
G M C Oil & Gas G 405 701-5515
Norman *(G-5006)*
Garrett Petroleum Inc G 918 492-3239
Tulsa *(G-9803)*
Gary D Adams Geologist G 405 691-5380
Oklahoma City *(G-5292)*
Gary L Deaton Corporation G 405 521-8811
Oklahoma City *(G-6136)*
Gary Land Services Inc G 580 226-9808
Ardmore *(G-295)*
Gary Rumsey G 405 330-5732
Edmond *(G-2430)*
Gary Underwood G 405 341-0935
Edmond *(G-2431)*
Gas Development Corporation G 918 523-9090
Broken Arrow *(G-917)*
Gastar Exploration Inc E 405 772-1500
Tulsa *(G-9806)*
Gaston H L III Oil Properties G 918 758-0008
Okmulgee *(G-7503)*
Gateway Resources USA Inc G 918 333-2115
Bartlesville *(G-486)*
Gaylan Adams Inc G 405 751-9668
Oklahoma City *(G-6137)*
Gb Energy Inc G 405 224-8634
Chickasha *(G-1461)*
Gh Co G 918 488-0014
Tulsa *(G-9824)*
Glenna F Kirk G 580 497-3435
Cheyenne *(G-1424)*
Glm Energy Inc G 405 470-2873
Oklahoma City *(G-6160)*
Global Oil Gas Fields Okla LLC G 918 392-3345
Tulsa *(G-9833)*
Gmg Oil & Gas Corporation G 918 756-5308
Morris *(G-4596)*
Golden Gas Service Co G 918 582-0139
Tulsa *(G-9838)*
Golden Trend Gas Gathering LLC G 405 749-7860
Edmond *(G-2438)*
Good Springs Energy LLC G 580 257-9762
Tishomingo *(G-8965)*
Gore Exploration LLC G 580 922-4673
Edmond *(G-2440)*
Gourley Royalty Company LLC G 580 223-8783
Ardmore *(G-297)*
Grande Oil & Gas Inc G 405 348-8135
Edmond *(G-2442)*
Graves Cos Michael L G 918 293-1500
Tulsa *(G-9849)*
Grayhorse Energy LLC G 918 382-9201
Tulsa *(G-9851)*
Great Salt Plains Midstream G 405 608-8569
Oklahoma City *(G-6184)*
Greenleaf Energy Corporation G 405 239-7763
Oklahoma City *(G-6188)*
Greenstar Energy LLC G 205 349-2852
Oklahoma City *(G-6189)*
Greenstar Energy LLC G 405 604-0781
Oklahoma City *(G-6190)*
Greg Hall Oil & Gas LLC G 405 330-6238
Edmond *(G-2445)*
Greg Riepl G 405 232-6818
Oklahoma City *(G-6191)*
Groves Oil Investments G 405 341-8828
Edmond *(G-2447)*
Guard Exploration Partnership G 580 234-3229
Enid *(G-2965)*
Gulf Exploration LLC F 405 840-3381
Oklahoma City *(G-6193)*
Gulfport Energy Corporation D 405 252-4600
Oklahoma City *(G-6194)*
Hale Exploration LLC G 405 273-8000
Shawnee *(G-8456)*
Halliburton Company C 405 231-1800
Oklahoma City *(G-6207)*
Harrell Exploration G 580 226-8887
Ardmore *(G-302)*
Hawthorne Resources G 405 840-1928
Oklahoma City *(G-6227)*
Hazelwood Prod Exploration LLC G 405 848-6884
Oklahoma City *(G-6229)*
Hefner Co Inc G 405 236-4404
Oklahoma City *(G-6235)*
Holden Energy Corp E 580 226-3960
Ardmore *(G-306)*
Hollrah Exploration Company G 405 773-5440
Oklahoma City *(G-6258)*
Hornbeek and Wadley G 405 604-2874
Oklahoma City *(G-6263)*
Hub Oil & Gas Inc G 405 236-3354
Oklahoma City *(G-6269)*
Hughes Exploration Consulting G 918 486-3188
Coweta *(G-1886)*
Hungerford Oil & Gas Inc G 580 852-3288
Helena *(G-3434)*
Huntington Energy USA Inc G 580 772-3644
Weatherford *(G-11419)*
Hunton Oil and Gas Corp G 405 848-5545
Oklahoma City *(G-6275)*
Husky Ventures Inc G 405 600-9393
Oklahoma City *(G-6276)*
I-Mac Petroleum Service Inc G 918 348-9400
Tulsa *(G-9963)*
Indian Exploration Company LLC G 405 231-2476
Oklahoma City *(G-6295)*
Infinity Resources Company G 405 701-3229
Norman *(G-5032)*
Ingram Exploration Inc G 405 382-2040
Seminole *(G-8376)*
Innovative Production Inc G 918 729-9312
Tulsa *(G-9989)*
Integral Geophysics Inc G 405 848-4573
Oklahoma City *(G-6313)*
International Energy Corp F 918 743-7300
Tulsa *(G-10004)*
J & L Exploration LLC G 405 842-6876
Oklahoma City *(G-6331)*
J & S of Enid Inc E 580 237-6152
Enid *(G-2978)*
J Walter Duncan Jr Oil Inc E 405 272-1800
Oklahoma City *(G-6339)*
Jack Exploration Inc G 580 622-2310
Sulphur *(G-8835)*
Jacks Flex Pipe F 405 382-5740
Seminole *(G-8378)*
Jalex LLC G 405 627-7856
Bixby *(G-637)*
James S Jim Vanway G 580 223-8962
Ardmore *(G-312)*
Jath Oil Co C 580 252-5580
Duncan *(G-2133)*
Jcl & Jfl Oil & Gas G 405 360-1620
Norman *(G-5042)*

PRODUCT

Employee Codes: A=Over 500 employees, B=251-500
C=101-250, D=51-100, E=20-50, F=10-19, G=1-9

Jcr Exploration Inc ....G 918 682-8200
Muskogee *(G-4699)*
Jeroco Inc ....G 405 222-1179
Chickasha *(G-1476)*
Jetta Production Company Inc ....G 918 299-0107
Tulsa *(G-10043)*
Jma Energy Company LLC ....E 405 418-2853
Oklahoma City *(G-6366)*
Jmd Properties ....G 405 848-5722
Oklahoma City *(G-6367)*
Jo Sco Environmental ....G 405 340-5499
Edmond *(G-2472)*
John C Parks II Energy LLC ....G 918 885-6197
Hominy *(G-3590)*
Jones Energy Holdings LLC ....E 512 328-2953
Oklahoma City *(G-6384)*
Kaiser Energy Ltd ....G 918 494-0000
Tulsa *(G-10071)*
Kaiser-Francis Oil Company ....F 405 577-5347
Oklahoma City *(G-6395)*
Kaiser-Francis Oil Company ....C 918 494-0000
Tulsa *(G-10074)*
Kansas MB Project LLC ....G 760 212-0606
Skiatook *(G-8554)*
Keepa LLC ....G 405 235-4968
Oklahoma City *(G-6404)*
Kelmar Oil Co ....G 405 222-2364
Chickasha *(G-1478)*
Kendol Resources LLC ....G 405 627-3523
Oklahoma City *(G-6405)*
Kenneth A Weikel ....G 918 582-7205
Tulsa *(G-10082)*
Kenneth Valliquette Inc ....G 405 969-3317
Crescent *(G-1917)*
Kerr Well Service Inc ....G 620 629-0400
Tyrone *(G-11219)*
Key Energy Services Inc ....D 580 338-0664
Guymon *(G-3354)*
Keystone Gas Corporation ....E 918 352-2443
Drumright *(G-2065)*
Keystone Gas Corporation ....E 918 352-2443
Drumright *(G-2066)*
Keystone Production Co ....G 580 255-2162
Duncan *(G-2141)*
Keystone Test Facility LLC ....G 405 213-5965
Tulsa *(G-10087)*
Khody Land & Minerals Company ....G 405 949-2221
Oklahoma City *(G-6416)*
King Energy LLC ....G 405 463-0909
Oklahoma City *(G-6419)*
Klabzuba Royalty Company ....G 405 567-3031
Prague *(G-7929)*
Kodiak Corp ....G 405 478-1900
Oklahoma City *(G-6433)*
Kodiak Production Company ....G 405 350-6465
Yukon *(G-11740)*
L & M Exploration ....G 405 359-6060
Edmond *(G-2482)*
L Z Williams Energy Inc ....G 918 296-3555
Jenks *(G-3714)*
Ladder Energy Co ....G 918 467-3323
Delaware *(G-2008)*
Lariat Services Inc ....E 405 753-5500
Oklahoma City *(G-6449)*
Lariat Services Inc ....G 580 977-5050
Alva *(G-184)*
Lasser Inc ....G 405 842-4010
Oklahoma City *(G-6452)*
Lasso Oil & Gas LLC ....G 405 753-5300
Oklahoma City *(G-6453)*
Lata Group ....F 918 535-2147
Ochelata *(G-5236)*
Levelops Inc ....E 405 602-8040
Bethany *(G-586)*
Linn Energy LLC ....G 281 605-4100
Collinsville *(G-1816)*
Linn Operating LLC ....G 918 642-1265
Fairfax *(G-3120)*
London Montin Harbert Inc ....G 405 879-1900
Oklahoma City *(G-6491)*
Longhorn Energy Services LLC ....G 918 302-7610
Stillwater *(G-8720)*
Lortz R Michael Office ....G 405 236-3230
Oklahoma City *(G-6496)*
Lowry Exploration Inc ....G 918 587-5094
Tulsa *(G-10181)*
M L S Oil Properties ....G 405 720-8867
Oklahoma City *(G-6507)*
Mack Energy Co ....C 580 252-5580
Duncan *(G-2150)*
Magic Circle Energy Corp ....F 405 275-1666
Shawnee *(G-8470)*
Makefield Oil Co ....G 918 492-1463
Tulsa *(G-10205)*
Map Exploration Inc ....G 405 527-6038
Purcell *(G-8014)*
Marathon Oil Company ....G 866 323-1836
Tulsa *(G-10207)*
Marexco Inc ....G 405 286-5657
Oklahoma City *(G-6523)*
Mark Cromwell Inc ....G 580 233-7992
Enid *(G-3006)*
Markwest Enrgy E Texas Gas LP ....G 918 389-5100
McAlester *(G-4315)*
Markwest Enrgy E Texas Gas LP ....F 918 477-8000
Tulsa *(G-10213)*
Markwest Oklahoma Gas Co LLC ....E 580 225-5400
Elk City *(G-2846)*
Maverick Bros Resources LLC ....G 580 233-4701
Enid *(G-3010)*
Maverick Energy Group Ltd ....E 918 764-4081
Tulsa *(G-10225)*
Maxim Energy Corp ....G 405 348-9669
Edmond *(G-2507)*
Mayco Resources LLC ....G 918 241-3392
Sand Springs *(G-8203)*
McGuire Gateway Holdings LLC ....G 405 285-5884
Shawnee *(G-8471)*
McMur Oil and Gas LLC ....G 405 834-2221
Edmond *(G-2509)*
Meadows Oil Gas Corp ....F 405 285-8500
Edmond *(G-2510)*
Medina Exploration Inc ....G 405 579-4200
Norman *(G-5069)*
Mekusukey Oil Co Inc ....G 405 257-5431
Wewoka *(G-11504)*
Melmark Services Inc ....G 405 324-6999
Yukon *(G-11752)*
Mesa Black Production LLC ....G 918 933-4454
Tulsa *(G-10243)*
Mewbourne Oil Company ....F 405 235-6374
Oklahoma City *(G-6582)*
Mewbourne Oil Company ....F 903 561-2900
Woodward *(G-11609)*
Micahel A Sleem ....G 405 947-6288
Oklahoma City *(G-6585)*
Michael Feezel ....G 580 332-5544
Ada *(G-65)*
Michael Nelson ....G 580 922-5074
Chester *(G-1420)*
Mid Continent Minerals Inc ....G 405 272-0204
Oklahoma City *(G-6588)*
Mid-Con Exploration LLC ....G 580 571-7929
Woodward *(G-11610)*
Mid-Continent Conductor LLC ....G 580 254-3232
Woodward *(G-11611)*
Mid-States Minerals LLC ....G 405 298-7043
Weatherford *(G-11427)*
Millennium Prod Explrtion Corp ....G 405 495-3311
Oklahoma City *(G-6612)*
Milton Nichols Inc ....G 405 769-2216
Oklahoma City *(G-6614)*
Moeder Oil & Gas LLC ....G 405 286-9192
Oklahoma City *(G-6625)*
Moi Oil & Gas Inc ....G 580 753-4266
Ames *(G-198)*
Mongoose Energy LLC ....G 918 884-3508
Tulsa *(G-10298)*
Montgomery Exploration Company ....G 405 232-1169
Norman *(G-5080)*
Morgan Drilling Co ....G 580 657-3659
Ardmore *(G-336)*
Mustang Gas Products LLC ....E 405 748-9400
Oklahoma City *(G-6642)*
Mustang Ventures Company ....G 405 748-9400
Oklahoma City *(G-6644)*
Myers & Myers Inc ....G 405 341-5861
Edmond *(G-2524)*
National Oilwell Varco Inc ....E 580 225-4136
Elk City *(G-2855)*
Native Exploration Mnrl LLC ....G 405 603-5520
Oklahoma City *(G-6661)*
Native Explration Holdings LLC ....G 405 603-5520
Oklahoma City *(G-6662)*
Native Explrtion Operating LLC ....G 405 603-5520
Oklahoma City *(G-6663)*
Natural Resources Oper LLC ....F 405 997-3869
Norman *(G-5088)*
Needham Royalty Company LLC ....G 405 297-0177
Oklahoma City *(G-6668)*
Nelson Exploration Corp ....G 405 853-6933
Cleveland *(G-1729)*
Neok Production Company ....G 918 273-5662
Nowata *(G-5222)*
Ness Energy International ....G 405 285-1140
Edmond *(G-2534)*
New Dominion LLC ....G 405 567-3034
Seminole *(G-8389)*
Newfield Exploration 2003 Inc ....E 918 495-0598
Tulsa *(G-10339)*
Ng Discovery LLC ....G 405 945-0940
Oklahoma City *(G-6676)*
Nichols Land Services Inc ....G 405 840-1344
Oklahoma City *(G-6679)*
Nike Exploration LLC ....G 918 878-7410
Tulsa *(G-10345)*
Northshore Corp ....G 405 329-8026
Norman *(G-5095)*
Northwest Oil Gas Explrtn ....G 405 974-0165
Oklahoma City *(G-6692)*
Northwest Royalty LLC ....G 405 241-9707
Oklahoma City *(G-6693)*
Novo Oil & Gas ....G 405 286-4391
Oklahoma City *(G-6701)*
Novo Oil & Gas LLC ....F 405 609-1625
Oklahoma City *(G-6702)*
Nye Investment Co LLC ....G 405 923-7155
Oklahoma City *(G-6704)*
Oak Tree Natural Resources LLC ....C 405 775-0987
Oklahoma City *(G-6707)*
OBrien Oil Corporation ....G 405 282-6500
Guthrie *(G-3327)*
Oex-1 LLC ....G 918 492-0254
Tulsa *(G-10378)*
Oil & Gas Consultants Intl Inc ....E 918 828-2500
Tulsa *(G-10381)*
Oil & Gas Division ....G 918 581-2296
Tulsa *(G-10382)*
Oil-Law Records Corporation ....E 405 840-1631
Oklahoma City *(G-6722)*
Oilwell Tech & Enhancement ....G 405 202-9720
Oklahoma City *(G-6725)*
Okki Industries LLC ....G 405 204-6357
Oklahoma City *(G-6733)*
Oklahoma Comm On Consmr Cr ....F 918 367-3396
Bristow *(G-791)*
Oklahoma Oil Gas Management ....G 405 341-1856
Edmond *(G-2553)*
Oklahoma Territory Land Co LLC ....G 405 329-1142
Norman *(G-5101)*
Okland Oil Company ....E 405 236-3046
Oklahoma City *(G-6766)*
Okt Resources LLC ....G 405 285-1140
Edmond *(G-2554)*
Old Inc ....G 405 840-3017
Oklahoma City *(G-6770)*
Olifant Energy LLC ....G 918 984-9074
Tulsa *(G-10414)*
One Grand Center ....G 580 234-6600
Enid *(G-3026)*
Onegas ....G 918 947-7000
Tulsa *(G-10420)*
Orion Exploration LLC ....G 918 492-0254
Tulsa *(G-10440)*
Orr Oil & Gas E & P Inc ....G 580 224-9290
Ardmore *(G-340)*
Orthwein Petroleum ....G 405 478-7663
Oklahoma City *(G-6783)*
Osage Oil and Gas Property ....G 405 841-7600
Oklahoma City *(G-6785)*
Otc Petroleum Corporation ....G 405 840-2255
Oklahoma City *(G-6788)*
Ovintiv Exploration Inc ....G 918 740-1400
Tulsa *(G-10447)*
Ovintiv Mid-Continent Inc ....E 580 243-4101
Elk City *(G-2858)*
P H C Explorations Inc ....G 918 298-2008
Tulsa *(G-10452)*
Pacific Oil & Gas LLC ....G 405 835-2790
Yukon *(G-11763)*
Paladin Land Group LLC ....G 918 582-5404
Tulsa *(G-10457)*
Paluca Petroleum Inc ....G 405 379-5656
Holdenville *(G-3558)*
Panhandle Oil and Gas Inc ....F 405 948-1560
Oklahoma City *(G-6798)*
Panther Energy Company LLC ....D 918 583-1396
Tulsa *(G-10461)*
Panther Energy Company II LLC ....F 918 583-1396
Tulsa *(G-10462)*

Parker & Parsley Petroleum....G....... 405 756-1912
Lindsay *(G-4076)*
Parwest Land Exploration Inc....G....... 405 843-1917
Oklahoma City *(G-6805)*
Patrick Energy Group....G....... 918 477-7755
Tulsa *(G-10473)*
Peak Operating LLC....G....... 405 343-7590
Oklahoma City *(G-6816)*
Penn-OK Gathering Systems Inc....E....... 405 843-1544
Oklahoma City *(G-6825)*
Pennmark Energy LLC....G....... 405 840-9885
Oklahoma City *(G-6827)*
Pennsylvania Chernicky LLC....G....... 918 587-6242
Tulsa *(G-10487)*
Peregrine Products LLC....G....... 918 361-4304
Tulsa *(G-10491)*
Permian Resources Holdings LLC....G....... 405 418-8000
Oklahoma City *(G-6833)*
Petro Mac Corporation....G....... 918 585-5853
Tulsa *(G-10500)*
Petrocorp Incorporated....G....... 918 491-4500
Tulsa *(G-10501)*
Petroleum Development Company....G....... 918 583-7434
Tulsa *(G-10505)*
Petroleum Strategies Unlimited....F....... 405 720-0200
Oklahoma City *(G-6838)*
Pierco Petroleum Inc....G....... 405 379-0038
Holdenville *(G-3559)*
Piranha Proppant LLC....G....... 715 642-4192
Oklahoma City *(G-6854)*
Plow Technologies LLC....E....... 405 265-6072
Oklahoma City *(G-6857)*
Potoco LLC....G....... 405 600-3065
Oklahoma City *(G-6867)*
Prairie Oil & Gas....G....... 405 464-6060
Norman *(G-5120)*
Premier Energy LLC....G....... 405 286-0615
Oklahoma City *(G-6884)*
Prentice Napier & Green Inc....F....... 405 752-7680
Oklahoma City *(G-6888)*
Pride Energy Company....E....... 918 524-9200
Tulsa *(G-10557)*
Primary Ntral Rsources III LLC....G....... 918 495-0598
Tulsa *(G-10558)*
Primeenergy Corporation....F....... 405 942-2897
Oklahoma City *(G-6894)*
Protege Energy III LLC....G....... 918 286-2457
Broken Arrow *(G-1013)*
Protege Energy III LLC....F....... 918 728-3092
Tulsa *(G-10575)*
Pyr Energy Corporation....G....... 918 591-1791
Tulsa *(G-10586)*
Qep Energy Company....E....... 405 263-4831
Okarche *(G-5250)*
Quest Cherokee LLC....G....... 405 371-1653
Oklahoma City *(G-6941)*
Quest Energy Partners LP....G....... 405 600-7704
Oklahoma City *(G-6942)*
Quest Midstream Partners LP....D....... 405 702-7410
Oklahoma City *(G-6943)*
Quest Property Inc....G....... 405 722-7530
Wheatland *(G-11515)*
R D Davis & Associates Inc....G....... 405 720-2882
Oklahoma City *(G-6962)*
Ram Energy LLC....F....... 918 947-6300
Tulsa *(G-10612)*
Rambler Energy Services Inc....E....... 580 242-7447
Enid *(G-3042)*
Range Production Company....G....... 580 628-3700
Tonkawa *(G-8980)*
Reagan Resources Inc....G....... 405 848-2707
Oklahoma City *(G-6980)*
Rebellion Energy LLC....G....... 918 779-3163
Tulsa *(G-10627)*
Rebellion Energy II LLC....G....... 918 779-3163
Tulsa *(G-10628)*
Red Bluff Resources Oper LLC....G....... 405 605-8360
Oklahoma City *(G-6983)*
Red Fork USA Investments Inc....G....... 918 270-2941
Tulsa *(G-10631)*
Red Land Energy LLC....G....... 405 520-1205
Edmond *(G-2589)*
Red River Imaging LP....G....... 405 308-4545
Warr Acres *(G-11327)*
Red Rocks Resources LLC....F....... 405 600-3065
Oklahoma City *(G-6990)*
Redback Coil Tubing LLC....E....... 405 265-4600
Oklahoma City *(G-6991)*
Redbud E&P Inc....E....... 918 469-3600
Quinton *(G-8041)*
Redhawk Pressure Control LLC....F....... 405 605-1958
Oklahoma City *(G-6995)*
Redsky Land LLC....D....... 405 470-2015
Edmond *(G-2592)*
Regency Gas....G....... 580 487-3862
Beaver *(G-547)*
Resco Enterprises Inc....G....... 918 298-0052
Jenks *(G-3726)*
Resolute Wyoming Inc....E....... 918 495-0598
Tulsa *(G-10644)*
Resource Oil and Gas LLC....G....... 405 878-7336
Shawnee *(G-8488)*
Reveille Energy Innovation LLC....E....... 405 577-6438
Oklahoma City *(G-7012)*
Rhino Oil & Gas Inc....G....... 405 657-2999
Edmond *(G-2599)*
Riddle Corporation....G....... 405 728-7504
Oklahoma City *(G-7023)*
Riley Exploration LLC....D....... 405 485-8200
Oklahoma City *(G-7024)*
Riley Exploration Group LLC....F....... 405 485-8200
Oklahoma City *(G-7025)*
Riley Explration - Permian LLC....G....... 405 415-8699
Oklahoma City *(G-7026)*
Riley Permian Operating Co LLC....E....... 405 415-8699
Oklahoma City *(G-7027)*
Ring Energy Inc....G....... 918 499-3880
Tulsa *(G-10654)*
Rio Vista Operating LLC....D....... 918 689-5600
Eufaula *(G-3110)*
River Rock Energy LLC....D....... 405 606-7481
Oklahoma City *(G-7029)*
Riverside Mdstream Prtners LLC....F....... 918 949-4224
Tulsa *(G-10659)*
Roan Resources LLC....E....... 405 241-2271
Oklahoma City *(G-7032)*
Robert L Scott Co....G....... 405 235-5345
Oklahoma City *(G-7034)*
Robinowitz Oil Company....G....... 918 557-1544
Bixby *(G-654)*
Rock Creek Land and Energy....G....... 405 358-6090
Oklahoma City *(G-5313)*
Rock Island Exploration LLC....G....... 405 232-7077
Oklahoma City *(G-7042)*
Rockford Energy Partner....G....... 918 592-0679
Tulsa *(G-10666)*
Rose Rock Resources Inc....G....... 918 752-0511
Beggs *(G-559)*
Royce Dublin Inc....G....... 219 324-7995
Oklahoma City *(G-7056)*
RTS Energy Services LLC....F....... 432 617-2243
Oklahoma City *(G-7058)*
S K Warren Resourses LLC....G....... 918 491-5900
Tulsa *(G-10685)*
S S & L Oil and Gas Properties....G....... 405 603-6996
Oklahoma City *(G-7066)*
Saint Louis Well Service Inc....E....... 405 289-3314
Saint Louis *(G-8132)*
Samson Resources Company....E....... 580 225-4272
Elk City *(G-2872)*
Samson-International Ltd....E....... 918 583-1791
Tulsa *(G-10700)*
Sand Point LLC....G....... 405 728-2111
Oklahoma City *(G-7077)*
Sandollar Exploration Co LLC....G....... 405 513-7715
Edmond *(G-2611)*
Sanguine Gas Exploration LLC....G....... 405 285-1904
Edmond *(G-2613)*
Sanguine Ltd....G....... 918 494-6070
Tulsa *(G-10707)*
Sara Oil & Gas Inc....G....... 405 721-2117
Oklahoma City *(G-7084)*
Saturn Land Co Inc....G....... 405 275-4406
Shawnee *(G-8493)*
Schlumberger Technology Corp....C....... 405 422-8700
El Reno *(G-2753)*
Scientific Drilling Intl Inc....D....... 405 787-3663
Yukon *(G-11780)*
SEC Production Inc....G....... 405 715-0088
Edmond *(G-2615)*
Sedona Energy LLC....G....... 405 973-7366
Norman *(G-5140)*
Sequoia Natural Resources LLC....G....... 405 463-0355
Oklahoma City *(G-7111)*
Sheridan Production Co LLC....D....... 405 756-4347
Lindsay *(G-4083)*
Sheridan Production Co LLC....G....... 405 453-7860
Chickasha *(G-1509)*
Shields Operating Inc....G....... 479 785-1222
Oklahoma City *(G-7123)*
Shiprock Midstream LLC....G....... 918 289-2949
Tulsa *(G-10747)*
Sierra Hamilton LLC....G....... 405 843-5566
Oklahoma City *(G-7128)*
Sierra Resources Inc....E....... 405 946-2242
Oklahoma City *(G-7130)*
Silverado Oil & Gas LLP....G....... 918 592-3060
Tulsa *(G-10762)*
Simpson Enterprises LLC....G....... 918 495-1819
Tulsa *(G-10763)*
Simpson Photographics Tulsa....G....... 918 630-1134
Tulsa *(G-10764)*
Six S Energy Group LLC....G....... 405 819-8053
Oklahoma City *(G-7144)*
Smart Oilfield Solutions LLC....G....... 580 243-9571
Elk City *(G-2873)*
Smyth Land Services....G....... 918 745-9210
Tulsa *(G-10782)*
Snuffys Oilfield Services....G....... 405 368-9333
Hennessey *(G-3490)*
Sothwestern Exploration Cons....G....... 405 767-0041
Oklahoma City *(G-7170)*
Source Rock Enrgy Partners LLC....G....... 918 728-3116
Tulsa *(G-10795)*
Southern Resources Inc....G....... 405 601-1322
Oklahoma City *(G-7172)*
Spanish Lady Oil Co....G....... 405 659-3515
Edmond *(G-2626)*
Sparks Greg Operating Co....F....... 918 633-8807
Bixby *(G-663)*
Spartan Resources LLC....G....... 405 843-0420
Oklahoma City *(G-7179)*
Spartan Resources LLC....G....... 580 226-2400
Ardmore *(G-358)*
Spring Energy Co....G....... 405 340-6811
Edmond *(G-2628)*
Staghorn Energy LLC....G....... 918 584-2558
Tulsa *(G-10831)*
Staghorn Petroleum LLC....G....... 918 584-2558
Tulsa *(G-10832)*
Staghorn Petroleum II LLC....G....... 918 584-2558
Tulsa *(G-10833)*
Star Royalty Co....G....... 405 748-5070
Oklahoma City *(G-7195)*
Steden Oil Corp....G....... 405 364-7611
Norman *(G-5157)*
Stingray Cmnting Acidizing LLC....G....... 432 617-2243
Oklahoma City *(G-7207)*
Stingray Pressure Pumping LLC....C....... 405 242-4998
Oklahoma City *(G-7208)*
Stone Creek Operating LLC....G....... 405 395-4313
Oklahoma City *(G-7211)*
Stone Oak Operating LLC....G....... 888 606-4744
Oklahoma City *(G-7212)*
Stream Energy....G....... 405 272-1080
Oklahoma City *(G-7215)*
Sturgeon Acquisitions LLC....G....... 405 608-6007
Oklahoma City *(G-7219)*
Summit Energy Explorations LLC....G....... 918 396-3020
Owasso *(G-7622)*
Summit Exploration LLC....G....... 918 583-0933
Tulsa *(G-10867)*
Superior Oil and Gas Co....G....... 405 884-2069
Calumet *(G-1250)*
Superior Pipeline Texas LLC....E....... 918 382-7200
Tulsa *(G-10878)*
Superior Resources....F....... 580 393-4314
Sentinel *(G-8413)*
Swanderland Associates LLC....G....... 918 621-6533
Tulsa *(G-10883)*
Swc Production Inc....G....... 405 948-1559
Oklahoma City *(G-7234)*
Sweetwater Exploration LLC....G....... 405 329-1967
Norman *(G-5166)*
T A T Inc....G....... 405 942-0489
Oklahoma City *(G-7242)*
T K Exploration Co....G....... 405 239-7006
Oklahoma City *(G-7245)*
Tangier Explorations....G....... 918 585-3350
Tulsa *(G-10897)*
Taos Exploration....G....... 405 840-5398
Oklahoma City *(G-7252)*
Tapstone Energy LLC....E....... 405 702-1600
Oklahoma City *(G-7253)*
Tates Flow Back LLC....G....... 405 663-2179
Hydro *(G-3635)*
Taylor Energy LLC....G....... 918 481-1241
Tulsa *(G-10903)*
Tdp Energy Company LLC....F....... 580 226-6700
Ardmore *(G-366)*

Employee Codes: A=Over 500 employees, B=251-500
C=101-250, D=51-100, E=20-50, F=10-19, G=1-9
2020 Oklahoma Directory
of Manufacturers & Processors
745

GAS & OIL FIELD EXPLORATION SVCS

Tdw Services Inc .... E 918 447-5000
  Tulsa *(G-9041)*
Te-Ray Energy Inc .... G 405 232-4121
  Oklahoma City *(G-7261)*
Te-Ray Resources Inc .... G 405 792-7486
  Oklahoma City *(G-7262)*
Tecolote Energy LLC .... G 918 513-4100
  Tulsa *(G-10915)*
Tecolote Energy Operating LLC .... G 918 513-4121
  Tulsa *(G-10916)*
Templar Energy LLC .... G 405 548-1200
  Oklahoma City *(G-7266)*
Templar Operating LLC .... F 405 548-1200
  Oklahoma City *(G-7267)*
Terraquest Corporation .... E 405 359-0773
  Edmond *(G-2638)*
Territory Resources LLC .... G 405 533-1300
  Stillwater *(G-8766)*
Testers Inc .... G 580 243-0148
  Elk City *(G-2881)*
Thomas Oil Tools LLC .... G 580 252-4672
  Duncan *(G-2188)*
Thunder Oil & Gas LLC .... G 580 226-3800
  Ardmore *(G-368)*
Tilford Pinson Exploration LLC .... F 405 348-7201
  Edmond *(G-2643)*
Titan Resources Limited .... G 918 298-1811
  Tulsa *(G-10947)*
Tlp Energy LLC .... G 405 241-1800
  Oklahoma City *(G-7296)*
Tompc LLC .... E 405 888-5585
  Edmond *(G-2649)*
Tracey Gregory .... G 580 819-0057
  Weatherford *(G-11449)*
Trepco Inc .... G 405 722-1400
  Yukon *(G-11793)*
Triad Energy Inc .... F 405 842-4312
  Oklahoma City *(G-7325)*
Triple Crown Energy-Bh LLC .... G 918 518-5422
  Tulsa *(G-10975)*
Triumph Energy Partners LLC .... G 918 986-8283
  Tulsa *(G-10979)*
Triumph Resources Inc .... G 405 478-8770
  Oklahoma City *(G-7338)*
Trojan Oil and Gas LLC .... G 918 606-0260
  Sapulpa *(G-8318)*
Tropical Minerals Inc .... G 405 236-2700
  Oklahoma City *(G-7344)*
Turnbow-Kiker Ltd .... G 918 481-8871
  Tulsa *(G-11018)*
Turner Oil & Gas Properties .... G 405 752-8000
  Oklahoma City *(G-7352)*
Unit Corp .... G 405 222-6441
  Chickasha *(G-1520)*
Unit Corporation .... D 918 493-7700
  Tulsa *(G-11037)*
Valiant Midstream LLC .... G 405 286-5580
  Edmond *(G-2665)*
Vector Exploration Inc .... G 405 340-5373
  Edmond *(G-2668)*
Ventana Exploration & Prod LLC .... F 405 754-5000
  Oklahoma City *(G-7396)*
Verexco Inc .... G 405 341-4302
  Edmond *(G-2670)*
Vesta Midstream Partners LLC .... G 918 986-9520
  Tulsa *(G-11074)*
Viersen Oil & Gas Co .... F 918 742-1979
  Tulsa *(G-11076)*
Vision Energy Group LLC .... G 405 848-3933
  Oklahoma City *(G-7401)*
Vitol Inc .... G 405 228-8100
  Oklahoma City *(G-7403)*
Vitruvian II Woodford LLC .... G 405 428-2491
  Lindsay *(G-4098)*
Waggoner Oil & Gas .... G 580 234-0030
  Enid *(G-3071)*
Waller Exploration LLC .... G 405 359-2050
  Edmond *(G-2679)*
Ward Petroleum Corporation .... D 580 234-3229
  Enid *(G-3074)*
Ward Petroleum Corporation .... G 405 242-4188
  Oklahoma City *(G-7419)*
Watson Well Solutions .... G 580 772-3059
  Weatherford *(G-11455)*
We Buy Scrap LLC .... G 580 401-3083
  Ponca City *(G-7887)*
Weinkauf Exploration .... F 918 749-8383
  Tulsa *(G-11104)*
Weinkauf Petroleum Inc .... F 918 749-8383
  Tulsa *(G-11105)*

Weir Oil Gas .... G 580 225-2381
  El Reno *(G-2769)*
Wentworth Operating Co .... F 405 341-6122
  Oklahoma City *(G-7435)*
Westenergy .... G 405 607-6604
  Oklahoma City *(G-7438)*
Westport Oil Company Inc .... G 405 239-2829
  Oklahoma City *(G-7443)*
Weststar Oil and Gas Inc .... G 405 341-2338
  Oklahoma City *(G-2685)*
Wheeler Energy Corporation .... G 918 587-7474
  Tulsa *(G-11114)*
White Sail Energy LLC .... G 405 255-4669
  Edmond *(G-2687)*
William B Hugos .... G 405 810-0909
  Oklahoma City *(G-7454)*
Williams Prod Appalachia LLC .... D 918 573-2000
  Tulsa *(G-11133)*
Williford Resources LLC .... G 918 712-8828
  Tulsa *(G-11135)*
Winzeler Family LLC .... G 405 218-2829
  Edmond *(G-2690)*
Word Exploration LP .... D 580 234-3229
  Enid *(G-3083)*
World Energy Resources Inc .... G 405 375-6484
  Kingfisher *(G-3823)*
Wpx Energy Appalachia LLC .... F 866 326-3190
  Tulsa *(G-11156)*
Wpx Energy Permian LLC .... E 855 979-2102
  Tulsa *(G-11160)*
Xpect Energy Services LLC .... G 405 641-7537
  Edmond *(G-2693)*
Zinke & Trumbo Inc .... F 918 488-6400
  Tulsa *(G-11178)*

GAS & OIL FIELD SVCS, NEC

3t Oil & Gas LLC .... G 918 758-3269
  Okmulgee *(G-7491)*
AC Oil & Gas LLC .... G 405 919-8088
  Hennessey *(G-3442)*
Advanced Welding & Excav LLC .... G 918 306-2061
  Bristow *(G-763)*
AES Drilling Fluids .... G 580 225-3450
  Elk City *(G-2782)*
Alpha Oilfield Services LLC .... G 580 330-1285
  Weatherford *(G-11390)*
B & A Producing LLC .... G 405 664-3628
  Arcadia *(G-228)*
B & R Construction of Woodward ...... G 580 256-5522
  Woodward *(G-11557)*
Back Road Oil & Gas LLC .... G 918 932-8452
  Tulsa *(G-9251)*
Baker Hghes Olfld Oprtions LLC .... G 918 283-7911
  Claremore *(G-1590)*
Bennett Construction .... G 405 756-1918
  Lindsay *(G-4048)*
Big Gas Oil LLC .... G 405 763-9844
  Oklahoma City *(G-5564)*
Blaylock Oil and Gas LLC .... G 918 799-6153
  Stigler *(G-8629)*
Bleything Oil & Gas LLC .... G 405 535-0253
  Edmond *(G-2326)*
Blue Rock Oil & Gas LLC .... G 580 229-5697
  Ardmore *(G-258)*
Bluff Service Disposal .... G 580 438-2262
  Waynoka *(G-11374)*
Bonanza Land LLC .... G 580 772-2680
  Weatherford *(G-11393)*
Brickman Fast Line .... G 405 756-1665
  Lindsay *(G-4051)*
Bruins Oil & Gas LLC .... G 806 323-8353
  Yukon *(G-11701)*
C & R Olfld Pntg Rustabout Svc .... G 620 272-6699
  Ponca City *(G-7804)*
Canopy Upstream LLC .... G 620 717-3263
  Weatherford *(G-11397)*
CHS Oil & Gas LLC .... G 918 280-9368
  Skiatook *(G-8536)*
Clearview International .... G 580 332-2384
  Ada *(G-24)*
Cmark Resources LLC .... G 918 492-5170
  Tulsa *(G-9459)*
Coastline Oil & Gas LLC .... G 405 354-6507
  Yukon *(G-11707)*
Cochran Chemical Company Inc .... E 405 382-8000
  Seminole *(G-8365)*
Contintnal Oil Gas Enrgy Ntwrk .... G 214 636-2401
  Oklahoma City *(G-5825)*
Dale E Dyer .... G 918 519-0189
  Tulsa *(G-9548)*

Dark Horse Oil Field Svcs LLC .... G 580 229-0626
  Healdton *(G-3412)*
David Smith .... G 580 229-1195
  Healdton *(G-3413)*
Dejay Oil & Gas Inc .... G 405 390-0906
  Choctaw *(G-1538)*
Denneny Oil and Gas LLC .... G 405 229-4885
  Edmond *(G-2389)*
Dorado E&P Partners LLC .... F 720 402-3700
  Tulsa *(G-9597)*
Double C Oil and Gas LLC .... G 918 518-5047
  Jenks *(G-3703)*
Douglas Group LLC .... G 405 946-6853
  Oklahoma City *(G-5972)*
Fdnd Oil and Gas LLC .... G 918 583-9960
  Tulsa *(G-9730)*
Flex-Chem Services Corporation .... E 580 772-2386
  Weatherford *(G-11415)*
Flywheel Energy Management LLC ... D 405 702-6991
  Oklahoma City *(G-6096)*
Fracdogs .... G 918 786-9797
  Grove *(G-3271)*
Freedom Midstream Services LLC ..... G 918 582-5313
  Tulsa *(G-9776)*
Gb Energy Inc .... G 405 224-8634
  Chickasha *(G-1461)*
Glm Energy Inc .... G 405 470-2873
  Oklahoma City *(G-6160)*
Heartland Oil & Gas LLC .... G 405 848-8099
  Oklahoma City *(G-6233)*
Holasek Oil & Gas Co LLC .... G 405 321-6663
  Norman *(G-5025)*
Holman Oil and Gas .... G 405 567-3528
  Prague *(G-7927)*
Huntington Energy USA Inc .... G 580 772-3644
  Weatherford *(G-11419)*
I & Gn Resources Inc .... G 918 481-7927
  Tulsa *(G-9962)*
I Enrg .... G 405 360-4600
  Norman *(G-5028)*
Jett Oil and Gas LLC .... G 918 995-7430
  Tulsa *(G-10041)*
Joshua Oil & Gas LLC .... G 620 672-5505
  Cache *(G-1227)*
Keck Oil & Gas LLC .... G 918 756-6688
  Okmulgee *(G-7511)*
Kemah Oil & Gas Co LLC .... G 405 364-3899
  Norman *(G-5048)*
Keta Oil Rural .... G 580 537-2443
  Loco *(G-4102)*
Klx Energy Services .... G 580 824-0955
  Waynoka *(G-11377)*
Ledford Oil & Gas LLC .... G 580 467-0593
  Duncan *(G-2146)*
Lewis Oil & Gas Inc .... G 918 272-1278
  Owasso *(G-7585)*
Mac Oil & Gas .... G 405 375-5619
  Kingfisher *(G-3808)*
McAdams Energy LLC .... G 918 758-0308
  Okmulgee *(G-7515)*
Morton Leases Inc .... G 918 733-2331
  Morris *(G-4601)*
Ms 3 Oil & Gas LLC .... G 580 465-7354
  Wilson *(G-11539)*
Mv Pipeline Company .... G 918 689-5600
  Eufaula *(G-3105)*
Nance Solutions Inc .... G 918 804-9301
  Mustang *(G-4785)*
Nitro Lift Holdings LLC .... D 405 620-3274
  Mill Creek *(G-4470)*
Ohana Oil & Gas LLC .... G 405 341-8822
  Edmond *(G-2545)*
Oil & Gas Optimization Special .... G 432 685-0029
  Tulsa *(G-10383)*
Peters Oil & Gas .... G 405 315-6378
  Bristow *(G-793)*
Pierpont Lamont LLC .... G 918 592-1705
  Tulsa *(G-10514)*
Pioneer Wireline Services .... G 405 601-8755
  Oklahoma City *(G-6852)*
Prism Energy Inc .... G 918 248-4177
  Sapulpa *(G-8302)*
R & J Oil and Gas Royalty LLC .... G 405 562-3334
  Edmond *(G-2581)*
R A Bodenhame Assoc Inc .... G 918 855-1964
  Sand Springs *(G-8219)*
Reach Wireline .... G 405 872-8828
  Noble *(G-4889)*
Richardson Wellsite Services .... G 918 807-7105
  Sapulpa *(G-8308)*

PRODUCT SECTION
GASOLINE FILLING STATIONS

Rolco Energy Services LLC ....G....... 580 657-2602
  Ardmore *(G-351)*
Semmexico LLC ....G....... 918 524-8100
  Tulsa *(G-10730)*
Sequoia Natural Resources LLC ......G....... 405 463-0355
  Oklahoma City *(G-7111)*
Silver Cliff Resourse ....G....... 405 842-8698
  Oklahoma City *(G-7140)*
Smith Energy Services ....G....... 580 596-2104
  Cherokee *(G-1419)*
Star Industries ....G....... 580 977-4576
  Enid *(G-3062)*
Stephens Oil & Gas Exploration ....G....... 214 773-5898
  Oklahoma City *(G-7203)*
Strata View Operating LLC ....G....... 405 364-1613
  Norman *(G-5161)*
Summit Energy Services Inc ....G....... 405 366-9999
  Norman *(G-5164)*
Sunwest Mud ....G....... 405 631-2101
  Oklahoma City *(G-7226)*
Swanderland Associates LLC ....G....... 918 621-6533
  Tulsa *(G-10883)*
Tarheel Oil & Gas LLC ....G....... 405 823-9965
  Oklahoma City *(G-7254)*
Thru Tubing Solutions ....G....... 405 692-1900
  Newcastle *(G-4844)*
Tiger Mountain Gas & Oil ....G....... 405 605-1181
  Oklahoma City *(G-7287)*
Twelve States Oil & Gas Co LLC ......G....... 918 296-7625
  Tulsa *(G-11021)*
UC Oil & Gas LLC ....G....... 918 270-2383
  Tulsa *(G-11031)*
Universal Land Services LLC ....G....... 918 712-9038
  Tulsa *(G-11049)*
Veem Jade Oil & Gas LLC ....G....... 918 298-1555
  Tulsa *(G-11069)*
W E O C Inc ....G....... 918 367-5918
  Bristow *(G-804)*
Walkup Wellhead ....G....... 580 320-5913
  Purcell *(G-8026)*
Webster Drilling Services LLC ....G....... 405 517-5585
  Lindsay *(G-4100)*
Whiterock Oil & Gas LLC ....G....... 580 307-5565
  Perry *(G-7750)*
Wild Horse Distrubuting LLC ....G....... 405 691-0755
  Oklahoma City *(G-5323)*
Zzw Global Inc ....G....... 405 985-8759
  Oklahoma City *(G-7490)*

GAS APPLIANCE REPAIR SVCS

Crown Energy Technology Okla ....E....... 405 348-9954
  Edmond *(G-2376)*

GAS FIELD MACHINERY & EQPT

Compressco Inc ....D....... 405 677-0221
  Oklahoma City *(G-5814)*
Compressco Partners Sub Inc ....C....... 405 677-0221
  Oklahoma City *(G-5816)*
Energy Meter Systems LLC ....E....... 405 853-4976
  Hennessey *(G-3460)*
Forum Energy Technologies Inc ....D....... 405 224-5779
  Chickasha *(G-1459)*
Natural Gas Services Group Inc ....C....... 918 266-3330
  Catoosa *(G-1342)*
Q B Johnson Mfg Inc ....D....... 405 677-6676
  Moore *(G-4558)*
Screw Compression Systems Inc ....C....... 918 266-3330
  Catoosa *(G-1351)*
T D Williamson Inc ....E....... 918 447-5400
  Tulsa *(G-10888)*
Tetra Technologies Inc ....G....... 405 677-0221
  Oklahoma City *(G-7276)*
Weatherford District Office ....G....... 405 354-7711
  Yukon *(G-11803)*

GAS PROCESSING SVC

Atlas Pipeline Mid-Continent W ....B....... 918 574-3500
  Tulsa *(G-9222)*
Carrera Gas Companies LLC ....G....... 918 359-0980
  Tulsa *(G-9380)*
Indian Creek Gas Processing LP .....G....... 918 359-0980
  Tulsa *(G-9977)*
Kingfisher Midstream LLC ....G....... 281 655-3200
  Oklahoma City *(G-6422)*
Mustang Fuel Corporation ....G....... 580 446-5552
  Enid *(G-3017)*
Targa Pipeline Mid-Continent W ....F....... 918 574-3500
  Tulsa *(G-10899)*

Targa Ppline Mid-Continent LLC ......E....... 580 435-2267
  Alva *(G-194)*
Targa Ppline Mid-Continent LLC ......C....... 918 574-3500
  Tulsa *(G-10900)*
Targa Ppline Mid-Continent LLC ......D....... 580 883-2273
  Ringwood *(G-8094)*

GAS PRODUCTION & DISTRIBUTION

Oneok Partners LP ....E....... 918 588-7000
  Tulsa *(G-10427)*
Panhandle Royalty Co ....G....... 405 945-6100
  Oklahoma City *(G-6800)*
Xto Energy Inc ....G....... 580 668-2332
  Wilson *(G-11546)*

GAS STATIONS

Marathon Oil Company ....G....... 866 323-1836
  Tulsa *(G-10207)*
Marathon Oil Company ....E....... 318 624-0874
  Oklahoma City *(G-6521)*
Oklahoma Oil Gas Management ....G....... 405 341-1856
  Edmond *(G-2553)*
Quiktrip Corporation ....B....... 918 615-7700
  Tulsa *(G-10599)*

GAS WELDING RODS, MADE FROM PURCHASED WIRE

Mlb Welding LLC ....G....... 580 481-0852
  Altus *(G-162)*

GAS: Refinery

Devon Energy International Co ....A....... 405 235-3611
  Oklahoma City *(G-5931)*
Econo Biogasoline Corporation ....G....... 918 347-5408
  Bartlesville *(G-479)*
Holly Ref & Mktg - Tulsa LLC ....E....... 918 594-6000
  Tulsa *(G-9941)*
Hollyfrontier Corporation ....G....... 918 594-6000
  Tulsa *(G-9943)*
Hollyfrontier Ref & Mktg LLC ....A....... 918 588-1142
  Tulsa *(G-9944)*
Nextstream Heavy Oil LLC ....G....... 405 808-5435
  Oklahoma City *(G-6675)*
Ventura LLC ....G....... 405 418-0300
  Oklahoma City *(G-7397)*
Ventura LLC ....E....... 580 661-2924
  Thomas *(G-8950)*

GASES & LIQUIFIED PETROLEUM GASES

Dcp Midstream LLC ....F....... 405 362-2200
  Tuttle *(G-11194)*
Deisenroth Gas Products Inc ....G....... 918 742-4769
  Tulsa *(G-9567)*
Ergon Inc ....F....... 918 266-7070
  Catoosa *(G-1319)*
Hurricane Gas Process Plant ....G....... 918 492-4418
  Tulsa *(G-9959)*
July Gas Ltd Liability Co ....G....... 918 367-2831
  Bristow *(G-784)*
Octagon Resources Inc ....G....... 405 842-3322
  Oklahoma City *(G-6710)*
Octagon Resources Inc ....F....... 405 366-8885
  Norman *(G-5097)*
Western Gas Resources Inc ....G....... 580 764-3397
  Chester *(G-1422)*

GASES: Carbon Dioxide

Messer LLC ....F....... 580 254-2259
  Woodward *(G-11606)*
Praxair Distribution Inc ....E....... 918 266-3210
  Claremore *(G-1673)*

GASES: Hydrogen

Hydrogen On Demand ....G....... 405 618-6644
  Oklahoma City *(G-6279)*

GASES: Indl

Air Products and Chemicals Inc ......D....... 918 825-4592
  Pryor *(G-7940)*
Air Products and Chemicals Inc ......E....... 918 266-8800
  Catoosa *(G-1295)*
Airgas Usa LLC ....G....... 405 745-2732
  Oklahoma City *(G-5401)*
Airgas Usa LLC ....F....... 580 767-1313
  Ponca City *(G-7795)*

Airgas Usa LLC ....G....... 405 372-7720
  Stillwater *(G-8652)*
Airgas Usa LLC ....G....... 405 235-0009
  Oklahoma City *(G-5402)*
Boc Gases ....G....... 580 254-2259
  Woodward *(G-11563)*
City Carbonic LLC ....G....... 405 239-2068
  Oklahoma City *(G-5770)*
Exponent Energy LLC ....G....... 918 906-6045
  Tulsa *(G-9716)*
Lincoln Electric Holdings Inc ....G....... 405 681-0183
  Oklahoma City *(G-6478)*
Messer LLC ....F....... 580 254-2929
  Woodward *(G-11607)*
Messer North America Inc ....G....... 580 254-2929
  Woodward *(G-11608)*
Nextstream Heavy Oil LLC ....G....... 405 808-5435
  Oklahoma City *(G-6675)*
Nitro Lift Technologies LLC ....G....... 405 618-3026
  Norman *(G-5093)*
Oil Capital Land Exploration ....G....... 918 582-2603
  Tulsa *(G-10384)*

GASES: Neon

Claude Neon Federal ....G....... 918 585-9010
  Tulsa *(G-9443)*
Neon Creative LLC ....G....... 405 837-0178
  Edmond *(G-2533)*
Sooner Neon ....G....... 918 269-5250
  Catoosa *(G-1354)*

GASES: Nitrogen

C & C Nitrogen LLC ....G....... 580 216-4871
  Woodward *(G-11566)*
Matheson Tri-Gas Inc ....F....... 580 536-2965
  Lawton *(G-3969)*
Nitro Lift Technologies LLC ....D....... 580 371-3700
  Mill Creek *(G-4471)*
Terra Nitrogen ....G....... 580 256-8651
  Woodward *(G-11641)*

GASES: Oxygen

Air Products and Chemicals Inc ......F....... 580 994-2732
  Mooreland *(G-4585)*
O2 Concepts LLC ....E....... 877 867-4008
  Oklahoma City *(G-6706)*

GASKETS

Automated Gasket Company LLc .....F....... 405 951-5301
  Oklahoma City *(G-5494)*
Flanco Gasket and Mfg Inc ....E....... 405 672-7893
  Oklahoma City *(G-6088)*
Freedom Rubber LLC ....G....... 918 250-4673
  Broken Arrow *(G-914)*
Harrison Manufacturing Co Inc ....F....... 918 838-9961
  Tulsa *(G-9897)*
Industrial Gasket Inc ....E....... 405 376-9393
  Mustang *(G-4778)*
Thomas Engineering Co Inc ....E....... 918 587-6649
  Tulsa *(G-10931)*
Triad Precision Products Inc ....E....... 918 584-3543
  Tulsa *(G-10974)*

GASKETS & SEALING DEVICES

Hunt Jim Sales & Mfg ....G....... 405 670-5663
  Oklahoma City *(G-6272)*
John Crane Inc ....D....... 918 664-5156
  Tulsa *(G-10049)*
John Crane Lemco Inc ....E....... 918 835-7325
  Tulsa *(G-10050)*
Kt Plastics Inc ....E....... 580 434-5655
  Calera *(G-1241)*
Oklahoma Rbr & Gasket Co Inc ....F....... 918 585-3484
  Tulsa *(G-10406)*
Redline Gaskets LLC ....G....... 918 845-7700
  Sand Springs *(G-8221)*

GASOLINE BLENDING PLANT

Valero Refining-Texas LP ....C....... 580 223-0534
  Ardmore *(G-377)*

GASOLINE FILLING STATIONS

Charles Service Station LLC ....G....... 918 297-3308
  Hartshorne *(G-3390)*
Conocophillips Company ....F....... 580 243-6000
  Elk City *(G-2795)*

Employee Codes: A=Over 500 employees, B=251-500
C=101-250, D=51-100, E=20-50, F=10-19, G=1-9

GASOLINE FILLING STATIONS

Conocophillips Company............E...... 281 293-1000
  Bartlesville *(G-468)*
Sunoco (R&m) LLC.....................F...... 918 586-6246
  Tulsa *(G-10873)*

GASOLINE WHOLESALERS

HP Field Services LLC..................G...... 580 763-1428
  Stillwater *(G-8703)*

GASTROINTESTINAL OR GENITOURINARY SYSTEM DRUGS

Tetherex Pharmaceuticals Corp........G...... 405 206-7843
  Oklahoma City *(G-7274)*

GATES: Ornamental Metal

Automatic Gate Systems of Okla.......G...... 580 920-8752
  Durant *(G-2203)*
Top Quality Doors LLC..................G...... 405 579-3667
  Norman *(G-5176)*

GAUGES

Du-Ann Co Inc..............................G...... 580 428-3315
  Coalgate *(G-1779)*

GEARS

Podunk Hunting Products LLC..........G...... 918 617-0358
  Quinton *(G-8039)*

GEARS: Power Transmission, Exc Auto

Tulsa Winch Inc............................C...... 918 298-8300
  Jenks *(G-3736)*

GENERAL COUNSELING SVCS

Kings Remnant Ministry Inc.............G...... 918 207-0866
  Welling *(G-11467)*

GENERAL MERCHANDISE, NONDURABLE, WHOLESALE

Fd Products LLC............................G...... 918 698-1644
  Vinita *(G-11257)*
Omer Distributors LLC....................G...... 580 695-3211
  Lawton *(G-3979)*

GENERATION EQPT: Electronic

Sanco Enterprises Inc....................E...... 405 634-2120
  Oklahoma City *(G-7075)*
Sunrise Systems............................G...... 405 222-3816
  Blanchard *(G-735)*

GENERATOR REPAIR SVCS

Oklahoma Emergency Generator S.....G...... 405 735-9888
  Moore *(G-4546)*
Wilson Electric Motor Svc Inc...........F...... 405 636-1515
  Oklahoma City *(G-7458)*

GENERATORS: Electric

Kiowa Power Partners LLC...............E...... 918 432-5117
  Kiowa *(G-3839)*
Oklahoma Emergency Generator S.....G...... 405 735-9888
  Moore *(G-4546)*
Rp Power LLC...............................G...... 918 960-6000
  Tulsa *(G-10680)*

GENERATORS: Electrochemical, Fuel Cell

Elk City Wind LLC..........................G...... 580 772-2080
  Sweetwater *(G-8847)*

GENERATORS: Gas

Hipower Systems Oklahoma LLC.......G...... 918 512-6321
  Tulsa *(G-9013)*

GENERATORS: Storage Battery Chargers

Batteries Sooner LLC....................E...... 405 605-1237
  Oklahoma City *(G-5530)*

GIFT SHOP

Apothem.......................................G...... 405 447-2345
  Norman *(G-4912)*
Causley Productions Inc.................F...... 405 372-0940
  Stillwater *(G-8666)*

Curtis Jewelry...............................G...... 580 924-0041
  Durant *(G-2219)*
Distinctive Decor LLC....................F...... 580 252-9494
  Duncan *(G-2105)*
Ehrles Carnival & Party Sups..........G...... 918 622-5266
  Tulsa *(G-9648)*
F C Ziegler Co..............................E...... 918 587-7639
  Tulsa *(G-9721)*
Joys Uniforms Boutique Ltd............G...... 918 747-4114
  Tulsa *(G-10061)*
Kathys Kloset Inc..........................F...... 405 521-0055
  Oklahoma City *(G-6402)*
Productive Clutter Inc...................G...... 405 447-3839
  Norman *(G-5124)*
Southern Box Company..................G...... 580 255-7969
  Duncan *(G-2181)*
Stuart Beverly &...........................G...... 580 286-5586
  Idabel *(G-3648)*
Trophies n Things.........................G...... 405 247-9771
  Anadarko *(G-207)*

GIFT WRAP: Paper, Made From Purchased Materials

Pink Petals Flowers Gifts LLC..........G...... 580 317-8200
  Hugo *(G-3619)*

GIFT, NOVELTY & SOUVENIR STORES: Gifts & Novelties

Allens Woodcraft..........................G...... 918 224-8796
  Sapulpa *(G-8247)*
B Bar Inc.....................................G...... 580 824-8338
  Waynoka *(G-11372)*
Carpentree Inc.............................E...... 918 582-3600
  Tulsa *(G-9378)*
Green Co Corporation....................G...... 918 221-3997
  Tulsa *(G-9859)*

GIFT, NOVELTY & SOUVENIR STORES: Party Favors

Two K Enterprises LLC...................G...... 918 964-7004
  Grove *(G-3290)*

GIFTS & NOVELTIES: Wholesalers

Gloria Rae Travel Accessories.........G...... 405 848-1300
  Oklahoma City *(G-6163)*
Joys Uniforms Boutique Ltd............G...... 918 747-4114
  Tulsa *(G-10061)*

GLASS & GLASS CERAMIC PRDTS, PRESSED OR BLOWN: Tableware

Distinctive Decor LLC....................F...... 580 252-9494
  Duncan *(G-2105)*

GLASS FABRICATORS

Cardinal Glass Industries Inc..........C...... 580 924-2142
  Durant *(G-2212)*
Central Glass Products Inc.............F...... 918 436-2401
  Pocola *(G-7782)*
Dlubak Glass Company...................F...... 918 752-0226
  Okmulgee *(G-7500)*
Hourglass Transport LLC................G...... 580 937-4569
  Coleman *(G-1796)*
Michael and Mary Seever...............G...... 405 808-2494
  Bethany *(G-590)*
Shack Little Glass.........................G...... 405 364-2649
  Norman *(G-5143)*
Victory Glass Co Inc......................G...... 405 232-5114
  Oklahoma City *(G-7400)*
Zephyr Southwest Orna LLC...........E...... 918 251-4133
  Broken Arrow *(G-1104)*

GLASS PRDTS, FROM PURCHASED GLASS: Glassware

Memories In Glass Inc....................G...... 405 878-9688
  Shawnee *(G-8473)*
Professional Packaging Inc.............E...... 918 682-9531
  Muskogee *(G-4738)*

GLASS PRDTS, FROM PURCHASED GLASS: Insulating

Cardinal Glass Industries Inc..........C...... 580 924-2142
  Durant *(G-2211)*

PRODUCT SECTION

Red Bud Glass Inc.........................E...... 405 685-3331
  Vinita *(G-11269)*

GLASS PRDTS, FROM PURCHASED GLASS: Mirrored

Whitacre Glass Works LLC..............G...... 918 366-6646
  Tulsa *(G-11119)*

GLASS PRDTS, FROM PURCHASED GLASS: Windshields

Mel Robinson...............................G...... 405 843-7529
  Oklahoma City *(G-6561)*

GLASS PRDTS, PRESSED OR BLOWN: Optical

Chickasaw Nation..........................G...... 580 332-2796
  Ada *(G-21)*

GLASS PRDTS, PRESSED OR BLOWN: Vases

Miller Sales Wholesale Distr............G...... 918 629-4064
  Tulsa *(G-10282)*

GLASS PRDTS, PURCHD GLASS: Furniture Top, Cut, Beveld/Polshd

Cimarron Glass LLC.......................G...... 918 225-6600
  Cushing *(G-1925)*
Owasso Glass...............................G...... 918 272-4490
  Owasso *(G-7600)*

GLASS PRDTS, PURCHSD GLASS: Ornamental, Cut, Engraved/Décor

Oklahoma Metal Creations LLC........G...... 580 917-5434
  Fletcher *(G-3165)*

GLASS STORES

Cimarron Glass LLC.......................G...... 918 225-6600
  Cushing *(G-1925)*
Owasso Glass...............................G...... 918 272-4490
  Owasso *(G-7600)*

GLASS, AUTOMOTIVE: Wholesalers

Dale Kreimeyer Co.........................G...... 405 789-9499
  Bethany *(G-575)*

GLASS: Flat

Oldcastle Buildingenvelope Inc........D...... 405 275-5510
  Shawnee *(G-8481)*
Tietsort LLC.................................G...... 405 664-7353
  Oklahoma City *(G-7286)*

GLASS: Pressed & Blown, NEC

Accutech Laboratories Inc..............F...... 405 946-6446
  Warr Acres *(G-11312)*
Bella Forte Glass Studio LLC..........G...... 405 659-6169
  Oklahoma City *(G-5544)*
Blue Sage Studios.........................G...... 405 601-2583
  Oklahoma City *(G-5594)*
Dlubak Glass Company...................F...... 918 752-0226
  Okmulgee *(G-7500)*
Dunlaw Optical Labs Inc.................F...... 580 355-8410
  Lawton *(G-3920)*
Essilor Laboratories Amer Inc.........E...... 800 568-5367
  Tulsa *(G-9702)*
Petroleum Artifacts Ltd..................G...... 918 949-6101
  Tulsa *(G-10504)*
Tulsa Glass Blowing Studio Inc........G...... 918 582-4527
  Tulsa *(G-10998)*

GLASS: Tempered

Cameron Glass Inc........................D...... 918 254-6000
  Broken Arrow *(G-862)*
Oldcastle Buildingenvelope Inc........D...... 405 275-5510
  Shawnee *(G-8481)*

GLOVES: Safety

Pipeglove LLC...............................F...... 918 629-7116
  Tulsa *(G-10517)*

PRODUCT SECTION

GO-CART DEALERS
Lahmeyer Pattern Shop.................................G....... 918 425-6008
  Tulsa *(G-10112)*

GOLF CARTS: Wholesalers
Charleys Golf Cars Inc ....G....... 405 273-6901
  Shawnee *(G-8437)*

GOLF EQPT
Golf Car Factory.......................................G....... 405 782-0460
  Oklahoma City *(G-6169)*
Winarr Golf Tech LLC ....G....... 918 994-2191
  Tulsa *(G-11136)*

GOURMET FOOD STORES
Maria Raes Inc...G....... 580 242-3342
  Enid *(G-3005)*

GOVERNMENT, EXECUTIVE & LEGISLATIVE OFFICES COMBINED: County
Chickasaw Nation ....G....... 405 331-2300
  Davis *(G-1980)*
Chickasaw Nation ....G....... 405 387-6013
  Newcastle *(G-4821)*
Chickasaw Nation ....G....... 580 332-2796
  Ada *(G-21)*

GOVERNMENT, EXECUTIVE OFFICES: City & Town Managers' Offices
County of Oklahoma.................................G....... 918 456-3622
  Tahlequah *(G-8859)*

GOVERNMENT, EXECUTIVE OFFICES: Mayors'
City of Altus..F 580 481-2270
  Altus *(G-148)*
City of Davis..E 580 369-2988
  Davis *(G-1981)*

GOVERNMENT, GENERAL: Administration
Corpo Commission OK ....F 580 332-3441
  Ada *(G-27)*
Oklahoma Comm On Consmr Cr............F 918 367-3396
  Bristow *(G-791)*

GOVERNMENT, GENERAL: Administration, Level Of Government
Dewey County ....F 580 995-3444
  Vici *(G-11241)*

GOVERNMENT, GENERAL: Administration, State
Corpo Commission OK ....F 405 521-4683
  Oklahoma City *(G-5838)*
Liquefied Petro Gas Bd Okla ....F 405 521-2458
  Oklahoma City *(G-6482)*

GRAIN & FIELD BEANS WHOLESALERS
Cargill Incorporated...............................E 405 236-0525
  Oklahoma City *(G-5699)*

GRANITE: Crushed & Broken
Blessing Gravel LLC................................G....... 580 513-4009
  Tishomingo *(G-8962)*
Martin Marietta Materials Inc................E 580 384-5246
  Mill Creek *(G-4469)*
Martin Marietta Materials Inc................E 580 326-9671
  Sawyer *(G-8336)*
Thomsons Trenching Inc........................G....... 918 745-1030
  Tulsa *(G-10936)*
Youngman Rock Inc.................................F 918 682-7070
  Muskogee *(G-4759)*

GRANITE: Cut & Shaped
Custom Tile & Marble Inc......................F 405 810-8515
  Oklahoma City *(G-5877)*
J B Granite Countertops ....G....... 580 771-6894
  Lawton *(G-3944)*
Midwest Marble Co ....G....... 918 587-8193
  Tulsa *(G-10268)*

Natural Stone Interiors...........................F 918 851-3451
  Bixby *(G-647)*
Rivers Edge Countertops Inc................F 405 387-2930
  Newcastle *(G-4839)*
Rives Enterprises Inc.............................G....... 918 671-4099
  Tulsa *(G-10660)*
Silex Interiors Inc....................................G....... 918 836-5454
  Tulsa *(G-10761)*

GRANITE: Dimension
Grecian Marble & Granite LLC..............F 405 632-3802
  Oklahoma City *(G-6185)*
Stonemen Granite & Marble...................G....... 918 851-3400
  Tulsa *(G-10856)*

GRAPHIC ARTS & RELATED DESIGN SVCS
Ad Type Inc...G....... 405 942-7951
  Oklahoma City *(G-5371)*
Compusign Vinyl Graphics ....G....... 580 762-4930
  Ponca City *(G-7807)*
Cunningham Graphics Inc ....G....... 918 337-9100
  Bartlesville *(G-470)*
Graphics Etc..G....... 918 274-4744
  Owasso *(G-7571)*
Graphix Xpress..G....... 580 765-7324
  Ponca City *(G-7831)*
Miami Designs..G....... 918 542-9553
  Miami *(G-4414)*

GRASSES: Artificial & Preserved
Hilltop Turf Inc..G....... 918 486-4482
  Coweta *(G-1884)*

GRATINGS: Tread, Fabricated Metal
Grating Company LLC............................G....... 918 834-8100
  Tulsa *(G-9848)*

GREASES & INEDIBLE FATS, RENDERED
Darling Ingredients Inc..........................E 918 371-2528
  Collinsville *(G-1808)*

GREENHOUSES: Prefabricated Metal
McCawley Service...................................G....... 918 484-2189
  Muskogee *(G-4709)*

GREETING CARD SHOPS
Ardellas Flowers Inc..............................F 405 321-6850
  Norman *(G-4915)*
Saga Card Co Inc ....G....... 918 967-0333
  Stigler *(G-8645)*

GRIPS OR HANDLES: Rubber
Grip Jar Opener LLC...............................G....... 918 766-2711
  Tulsa *(G-9864)*

GRITS: Crushed & Broken
Hoskins Gypsum Company LLC............F 580 274-3446
  Longdale *(G-4124)*

GROCERIES WHOLESALERS, NEC
Archer-Daniels-Midland Company ......D....... 580 237-8000
  Enid *(G-2910)*
Quality Bakery Products LLC................F 609 871-7393
  Tulsa *(G-10590)*
Royal Cup Inc...G....... 405 943-6088
  Oklahoma City *(G-7052)*
Seven-Up Bottling Co Inc......................F 580 765-6468
  Ponca City *(G-7874)*

GROCERIES, GENERAL LINE WHOLESALERS
Charlie Bean Coffee LLC........................F 405 376-4815
  Oklahoma City *(G-5743)*
Quiktrip Corporation..............................B....... 918 615-7700
  Tulsa *(G-10599)*

GUARD SVCS
Hman Global Solutions LLC ....G....... 405 338-5348
  Morrison *(G-4603)*

GUIDED MISSILES & SPACE VEHICLES: Research & Development
Design Intelligence Inc LLC ....G....... 405 307-0397
  Noble *(G-4878)*

GUIDED MISSILES/SPACE VEHICLE PARTS/AUX EQPT: Research/Devel
Archer Technologies Intl Inc.................G....... 405 306-3220
  Shawnee *(G-8428)*

GUN SIGHTS: Optical
Gilmores Sports Concepts Inc ....G....... 918 250-3910
  Tulsa *(G-9827)*
Tactical Elec Military Sup LLC ....E 866 541-7996
  Broken Arrow *(G-1070)*

GUNNING EQPT: Concrete
E-Z Drill Inc..E 580 336-9874
  Perry *(G-7733)*

GUNSMITHS
Gun World Inc..G....... 405 670-5885
  Del City *(G-1997)*

GUTTERS: Sheet Metal
Acme Manufacturing Corporation........E 918 266-3097
  Claremore *(G-1575)*
Always Done Right LLC ....G....... 405 615-5955
  Edmond *(G-2300)*
Fifteen Five Gtter Sltions LLC ....G....... 405 219-6741
  Yukon *(G-11724)*
L & S Seamless Guttering Inc................G....... 405 392-4487
  Blanchard *(G-719)*

GYMNASTICS INSTRUCTION
Paul Ziert & Associates Inc....................D....... 405 364-5344
  Norman *(G-5112)*

GYPSUM MINING
Allied Custom Gypsum ....F 580 337-6371
  Waynoka *(G-11370)*
Diamond Gypsum LLC ....G....... 580 623-2868
  Watonga *(G-11345)*
Harrison Gypsum LLC ....F 405 366-9500
  Norman *(G-5018)*
Harrison Gypsum LLC ....E 580 994-6048
  Mooreland *(G-4591)*
Harrison Gypsum LLC ....F 580 994-6050
  Mooreland *(G-4592)*
Harrison Gypsum Holdings LLC ....C....... 405 366-9500
  Norman *(G-5019)*
Schweitzer Gypsum & Lime...................G....... 405 263-7967
  Okarche *(G-5251)*

GYPSUM PRDTS
American Gypsum Company LLC.........C....... 580 679-3391
  Duke *(G-2079)*
Diamond Gypsum LLC ....G....... 580 623-2868
  Watonga *(G-11345)*
Georgia-Pacific LLC................................G....... 405 536-0070
  Oklahoma City *(G-6146)*
Harrison Gypsum LLC ....E 580 337-6371
  Bessie *(G-569)*
New Ngc Inc..D....... 918 825-0142
  Pryor *(G-7978)*
United States Gypsum Company ....B....... 580 822-6100
  Southard *(G-8588)*

HAIR & HAIR BASED PRDTS
Db Unlimited LLC....................................G....... 855 437-7766
  Tulsa *(G-9563)*

HAIR CARE PRDTS
Legends Hair Studio...............................G....... 580 237-5524
  Enid *(G-2999)*

HAIR CARE PRDTS: Hair Coloring Preparations
Supercuts Inc...G....... 918 775-6389
  Sallisaw *(G-8154)*

HAIR CURLERS: Beauty Shop

Always Blessed............................G...... 918 592-2200
  Tulsa (G-9159)
Bangs..G...... 918 338-2339
  Bartlesville (G-450)
Shades of Color..........................G...... 918 273-0001
  Nowata (G-5229)
Studio 180..................................G...... 405 512-2404
  Midwest City (G-4458)

HAIR DRESSING, FOR THE TRADE

Kzb Studios LLC..........................G...... 918 734-4399
  Tulsa (G-10106)

HAND TOOLS, NEC: Wholesalers

Hilti North America Ltd................G...... 918 252-6000
  Tulsa (G-9932)
Hisco Inc.....................................F...... 405 524-2700
  Oklahoma City (G-6254)
Scorpion Pump and Indus LLC...G...... 785 285-1421
  Tecumseh (G-8927)

HANDBAGS

Accessories-To-Go......................G...... 580 467-7408
  Comanche (G-1833)

HANDBAGS: Women's

Job Paper LLC.............................G...... 405 242-4804
  Yukon (G-11737)

HANDLES: Wood

Handle LLC..................................G...... 405 822-9312
  Oklahoma City (G-6211)

HANDYMAN SVCS

Sledge Electric Inc......................G...... 405 793-4007
  Oklahoma City (G-5316)

HARDWARE

Cook Machine Company..............E...... 580 252-1699
  Duncan (G-2099)
Crosby Group LLC......................B...... 918 834-4611
  Tulsa (G-9509)
Crosby Group LLC......................F...... 918 834-4611
  Tulsa (G-9510)
Crosby Worldwide Limited..........F...... 918 834-4611
  Tulsa (G-9512)
Genes Customized Tags & EMB.G...... 580 225-8247
  Elk City (G-2820)
H-V Manufacturing Company......G...... 918 756-9620
  Okmulgee (G-7509)
Hansen Research LLC................G...... 405 659-5079
  Norman (G-5015)
Hardin Ignition Inc......................G...... 405 853-4324
  Hennessey (G-3465)
Hargrove Manufacturing Corp....E...... 918 241-7537
  Sand Springs (G-8190)
Johnny Beard Co........................G...... 918 438-4901
  Tulsa (G-10056)
P-T Coupling Company...............E...... 580 237-4033
  Enid (G-3029)
Pelco Products Inc.....................C...... 405 340-3434
  Edmond (G-2565)
Pelco Products Inc.....................G...... 405 842-6978
  Oklahoma City (G-6822)
Petroleum Artifacts Ltd...............G...... 918 949-6101
  Tulsa (G-10504)
Premiere Lock Co LLC................E...... 918 294-8179
  Tulsa (G-10553)
Superior Companies Inc.............D...... 918 534-0755
  Dewey (G-2033)
T D G I..G...... 405 275-8041
  Shawnee (G-8507)
Taylor & Sons Farms Inc............G...... 405 222-0751
  Chickasha (G-1515)
United Dynamics Inc..................E...... 405 275-8041
  Shawnee (G-8517)

HARDWARE & BUILDING PRDTS: Plastic

Amarillo Chittom Airslo...............E...... 918 585-5638
  Tulsa (G-9160)
Diversified Plastics Inds LLC......G...... 918 245-0770
  Sand Springs (G-8178)

HARDWARE & EQPT: Stage, Exc Lighting

Showtek.......................................G...... 405 222-0632
  Chickasha (G-1510)

HARDWARE STORES

Ace Hardware..............................G...... 580 225-0100
  Elk City (G-2781)
H & C Services Inc.....................F...... 580 772-2521
  Weatherford (G-11417)
Moores Hardware and Home Ctr.G...... 918 287-4458
  Pawhuska (G-7689)
Oklahoma Home Centers Inc.....E...... 405 260-7625
  Guthrie (G-3329)

HARDWARE STORES: Builders'

LDS Building Specialties LLC....G...... 405 917-9901
  Oklahoma City (G-6460)
Oak Tree Sales............................G...... 405 224-9332
  Chickasha (G-1493)
Town & Country Hardware..........G...... 918 865-2888
  Mannford (G-4192)

HARDWARE STORES: Chainsaws

Morgans Repair Shop Inc...........G...... 405 382-3114
  Seminole (G-8388)

HARDWARE STORES: Tools, Power

Jantz Supply Inc.........................E...... 580 369-5503
  Davis (G-1986)

HARDWARE WHOLESALERS

Kay Electric Motors Inc..............G...... 580 256-3254
  Woodward (G-11598)
Mid-America Door Company......D...... 580 765-9994
  Ponca City (G-7852)

HARDWARE, WHOLESALE: Bolts

Bolt It Hydraulic Solutions..........F...... 918 296-0202
  Jenks (G-3693)
Bpc Industries Inc......................E...... 918 584-4848
  Tulsa (G-9325)

HARDWARE, WHOLESALE: Nuts

SBS Industries LLC....................C...... 918 836-7756
  Tulsa (G-10712)

HARDWARE, WHOLESALE: Security Devices, Locks

U-Change Lock Industries Inc...E...... 405 376-1600
  Mustang (G-4799)

HARDWARE: Aircraft

Beekmann Enterprises................G...... 918 272-7197
  Owasso (G-7547)
Dynamic Machine........................G...... 918 791-1114
  Grove (G-3266)

HARDWARE: Aircraft & Marine, Incl Pulleys & Similar Items

Archer Technologies Intl Inc......G...... 405 306-3220
  Shawnee (G-8428)
KB Enterprise LLC.......................G...... 580 789-0119
  Ponca City (G-7843)

HARDWARE: Builders'

Straitline Inc...............................F...... 405 263-4604
  Lone Grove (G-4121)
Straitline Inc...............................G...... 405 263-4604
  Okarche (G-5253)

HARDWARE: Cabinet

Cole Industrial Services Inc.......G...... 580 775-0949
  Caddo (G-1232)
Luxe Kitchen & Bath...................G...... 405 471-5577
  Oklahoma City (G-6504)

HARDWARE: Furniture

Fki Industries Inc.......................G...... 918 834-4611
  Tulsa (G-9752)

HARDWARE: Furniture, Builders' & Other Household

McClure Furniture Refinishing....G...... 918 587-7779
  Tulsa (G-10230)
Pickard Projects Inc...................G...... 405 321-7072
  Norman (G-5115)

HARDWARE: Locking Systems, Security Cable

Integrted Lock SEC Systems LLC.G...... 918 232-3436
  Jenks (G-3708)

HARDWARE: Plastic

Cpk Manufacturing LLC..............E...... 405 290-7788
  Oklahoma City (G-5849)
Creative Pultrusions Inc.............G...... 405 979-2141
  Oklahoma City (G-5853)
SUN Engineering Inc..................F...... 918 627-0426
  Tulsa (G-10870)

HARDWARE: Rubber

Custom Identification Products...G...... 405 745-1010
  Oklahoma City (G-5873)

HARDWARE: Saddlery

D R Topping Saddlery.................G...... 918 273-2812
  Nowata (G-5212)

HARNESS ASSEMBLIES: Cable & Wire

Cherokee Medical Services LLC.C...... 918 696-3151
  Stilwell (G-8783)
Cherokee Nation.........................F...... 918 696-3124
  Stilwell (G-8784)
Cherokee Nation Industries LLC.E...... 918 696-3151
  Stilwell (G-8786)
Cherokee Nation Red Wing LLC.G...... 918 824-6050
  Pryor (G-7952)
Cherokee Nation Red Wing LLC.E...... 918 430-3437
  Tulsa (G-9414)
Inland Manufacturing LLC...........G...... 918 342-5733
  Claremore (G-1642)

HARNESSES, HALTERS, SADDLERY & STRAPS

Custom Lea Sad & Cowboy Decor.G...... 918 335-2277
  Bartlesville (G-471)
Jerry Beagley Braiding Company.G...... 580 924-4995
  Calera (G-1240)
Lenora Elizabeth Brown...............G...... 918 797-2034
  Stilwell (G-8792)
Mock Brothers Saddlery Inc.......G...... 918 245-7259
  Sand Springs (G-8205)
W R Western Company Inc........G...... 405 605-5586
  Oklahoma City (G-7411)

HEALTH & ALLIED SERVICES, NEC

Cura Telehealth Wellness LLC....F...... 918 513-1062
  Tulsa (G-9523)

HEALTH AIDS: Exercise Eqpt

Sinties Corporation....................E...... 918 359-2000
  Tulsa (G-10768)
Sportstech Quality Cardio LLC...F...... 918 461-9177
  Tulsa (G-10825)
Strength Tech Inc......................G...... 405 377-7100
  Stillwater (G-8760)

HEALTH FOOD & SUPPLEMENT STORES

Winds of Heartland.....................G...... 405 947-8558
  Oklahoma City (G-7460)

HEARING AIDS

All American Ear Mold Labs.......F...... 405 285-2411
  Edmond (G-2295)
Better Sound Hearing Aid Svc...G...... 918 995-2222
  Jenks (G-3691)
Clear Tone Hearing Center Inc..E...... 918 838-1000
  Tulsa (G-9449)
Clearity LLC................................G...... 918 388-9000
  Tulsa (G-9450)

HEAT EXCHANGERS

Aerocore X LLC .... G 405 669-8655
  Del City *(G-1994)*
Cust-O-Fab Specialty Svcs LLC .... D 918 245-6685
  Sand Springs *(G-8175)*
Enerfin Inc .... G 918 258-3571
  Broken Arrow *(G-900)*

HEAT EXCHANGERS: After Or Inter Coolers Or Condensers, Etc

Alfa Laval Inc .... G 918 251-7477
  Broken Arrow *(G-823)*
Amarillo Chittom Airslo .... E 918 585-5638
  Tulsa *(G-9160)*
Amercool Manufacturing Co Inc .... D 918 445-5366
  Tulsa *(G-9162)*
Axh Air-Coolers LLC .... G 918 283-9200
  Claremore *(G-1585)*
Fabsco Shell and Tube LLC .... D 918 224-7550
  Sapulpa *(G-8271)*
Heat Transfer Equipment Co .... C 918 836-8721
  Tulsa *(G-9907)*
Hughes-Anderson Heat Exchanger ...... C 918 836-1681
  Tulsa *(G-9957)*
Kelvion Inc .... C 918 266-9200
  Catoosa *(G-1327)*
Tek Fins Inc .... F 918 747-7447
  Tulsa *(G-9043)*

HEAT TREATING: Metal

Bodycote Thermal Proc Inc .... F 405 670-5710
  Oklahoma City *(G-5605)*
Bodycote Thermal Proc Inc .... G 214 904-2420
  Tulsa *(G-9314)*
Cargill Heat Treat LLC .... G 405 510-3404
  Oklahoma City *(G-5700)*
Casting Coating Corp .... F 918 445-4141
  Tulsa *(G-8995)*
Hinderliter Heat Treating Inc .... G 405 670-5710
  Oklahoma City *(G-6250)*
National Oilwell Varco Inc .... C 918 781-4436
  Muskogee *(G-4719)*
O S R Inc .... G 281 422-7206
  Inola *(G-3668)*
Onsite Stress Relieving Svc .... E 918 234-1222
  Inola *(G-3669)*
Osr Services LP .... F 918 234-1222
  Inola *(G-3670)*
Precision Heat Treating .... G 918 445-7424
  Tulsa *(G-9025)*
Q B Johnson Mfg Inc .... D 405 677-6676
  Moore *(G-4558)*
Smith Welding Fabg & Repr .... G 918 446-2293
  Tulsa *(G-10779)*
Superheat Fgh Services Inc .... G 580 762-8538
  Ponca City *(G-7880)*
Team Inc .... E 918 234-9600
  Tulsa *(G-10909)*
Thermal Specialties LLC .... G 970 532-3796
  Owasso *(G-7623)*
Thermal Specialties LLC .... F 918 227-4800
  Tulsa *(G-9044)*
Thermal Specialties LLC .... G 405 681-4400
  Oklahoma City *(G-7282)*
Tulsa Gamma Ray Inc .... G 918 425-3112
  Tulsa *(G-10997)*
V M Star .... C 918 781-4400
  Muskogee *(G-4757)*
Zentech LLC .... F 918 585-8200
  Tulsa *(G-11176)*

HEATERS: Unit, Domestic

Calvin Heaters .... G 918 367-7011
  Bristow *(G-772)*

HEATING & AIR CONDITIONING EQPT & SPLYS WHOLESALERS

Captive-Aire Systems Inc .... D 918 686-6717
  Muskogee *(G-4658)*
Thermaclime LLC .... E 405 235-4546
  Oklahoma City *(G-7279)*

HEATING & AIR CONDITIONING UNITS, COMBINATION

A1 Heat and Air .... G 580 832-2605
  Cordell *(G-1852)*

Air Electric Inc .... G 918 406-3974
  Tulsa *(G-9120)*
Commercial Services Corp .... F 405 634-8888
  Oklahoma City *(G-5806)*
Monkey Chase Banana LLC .... G 405 706-5551
  Oklahoma City *(G-6626)*

HEATING EQPT & SPLYS

Ahc Fabrication Co Inc .... G 918 267-5052
  Beggs *(G-548)*
Alfa Laval Inc .... G 918 251-7477
  Broken Arrow *(G-824)*
Alfa Lval A Cled Exchngers Inc .... G 918 251-7477
  Broken Arrow *(G-825)*
American Heating Company Inc .... G 918 246-0700
  Sand Springs *(G-8159)*
Callidus Technologies LLC .... D 918 267-4920
  Beggs *(G-550)*
Coen Co Inc .... G 918 234-1800
  Tulsa *(G-9465)*
Gastech Engineering LLC .... D 918 663-8383
  Sapulpa *(G-8274)*
Hotsy of OK Inc .... G 580 234-0608
  Enid *(G-2974)*
Quikwater Inc .... F 918 241-8880
  Sand Springs *(G-8217)*
Tulsa Heaters Inc .... E 918 582-9918
  Tulsa *(G-10999)*
Webco Industries Inc .... C 918 241-1086
  Sand Springs *(G-8238)*

HEATING EQPT: Complete

Thermaclime Technologies Inc .... C 405 778-6682
  Oklahoma City *(G-7280)*

HEATING SYSTEMS: Radiant, Indl Process

G C Broach Company .... D 918 627-9632
  Tulsa *(G-9790)*

HEATING UNITS & DEVICES: Indl, Electric

Team Inc .... E 918 234-9600
  Tulsa *(G-10909)*

HEATING UNITS: Gas, Infrared

Gasolec America Inc .... G 918 286-8700
  Tulsa *(G-9805)*

HELP SUPPLY SERVICES

Belle Point Beverages Inc .... G 918 649-3921
  Poteau *(G-7896)*

HERMETICS REPAIR SVCS

Johnson Service Company .... G 918 869-7147
  Fort Gibson *(G-3175)*

HIGHWAY & STREET MAINTENANCE SVCS

Unami LLC .... G 405 320-5696
  Anadarko *(G-208)*

HITCHES: Trailer

Welding Shop .... G 580 832-5545
  Cordell *(G-1864)*

HOBBY, TOY & GAME STORES: Dolls & Access

E and H Sales .... G 918 742-1091
  Tulsa *(G-9619)*

HOBBY, TOY & GAME STORES: Toys & Games

Fresh Monkey Fiction LLC .... G 405 751-3826
  Oklahoma City *(G-6118)*

HOISTS

United Slings Inc .... G 405 598-2616
  Tecumseh *(G-8930)*

HOLDERS, PAPER TOWEL, GROCERY BAG, ETC: Plastic

Green Co Corporation .... G 918 221-3997
  Tulsa *(G-9859)*

HOLDING COMPANIES: Investment, Exc Banks

Ascent Resources Operating LLC .... F 405 608-5544
  Oklahoma City *(G-5471)*
Crosby Worldwide Limited .... F 918 834-4611
  Tulsa *(G-9512)*
Maxcess International Corp .... G 405 755-1600
  Oklahoma City *(G-6539)*
Maxcess Intl Holdg Corp .... G 405 755-1600
  Oklahoma City *(G-6540)*
Rocky Mtn Mdstream Hldings LLC ...... G 918 573-2000
  Tulsa *(G-10668)*
Sinties Corporation .... E 918 359-2000
  Tulsa *(G-10768)*
Sturgeon Acquisitions LLC .... G 405 608-6007
  Oklahoma City *(G-7219)*
World Water Works Holdings Inc .... G 800 607-7873
  Oklahoma City *(G-7473)*

HOME CENTER STORES

Economy Lumber Company Inc .... G 918 835-4933
  Tulsa *(G-9641)*

HOME DELIVERY NEWSPAPER ROUTES

Lewis County Press LLC .... G 580 363-3370
  Blackwell *(G-687)*

HOME ENTERTAINMENT EQPT: Electronic, NEC

A & E Satellites .... G 580 363-0931
  Ponca City *(G-7790)*
Infinity Home Solutions LLC .... G 918 704-8014
  Bixby *(G-635)*
R & R Media Systems LLC .... G 918 978-0578
  Tulsa *(G-10601)*

HOME HEALTH CARE SVCS

Maris Health LLC .... G 888 429-1117
  Tulsa *(G-10209)*
Onesource LLC .... G 580 434-6250
  Calera *(G-1242)*
Optionone LLC .... E 405 548-4848
  Oklahoma City *(G-6779)*

HOMEBUILDERS & OTHER OPERATIVE BUILDERS

Molitor Design & Cnstr LLC .... G 405 802-8302
  Moore *(G-4542)*

HOMEFURNISHING STORES: Pottery

Brookside Pottery .... G 918 697-6364
  Tulsa *(G-9342)*
Paseo Pottery .... G 405 525-3017
  Oklahoma City *(G-6807)*

HOMEFURNISHING STORES: Towels

S E & M Monogramming .... G 405 377-9677
  Stillwater *(G-8751)*

HOMEFURNISHING STORES: Venetian Blinds

Boomer Blinds & Shutters LLC .... G 918 968-2579
  Stroud *(G-8808)*

HOMEFURNISHING STORES: Window Shades, NEC

Ray Harrington Draperies .... G 405 789-6710
  Bethany *(G-593)*

HOMEFURNISHINGS & SPLYS, WHOLESALE: Decorative

Emery Bay Corporation .... G 918 494-2988
  Tulsa *(G-9671)*
Lasting Impressions Gifts Inc .... G 405 732-2401
  Oklahoma City *(G-6455)*

HOMEFURNISHINGS, WHOLESALE: Blinds, Venetian

Interior Designers Supply Inc .... F 405 521-1551
  Oklahoma City *(G-6318)*

HOMEFURNISHINGS, WHOLESALE: Decorating Splys

HOMEFURNISHINGS, WHOLESALE: Decorating Splys
Accessories-To-Go .... G 580 467-7408
  Comanche *(G-1833)*

HOMEFURNISHINGS, WHOLESALE: Draperies
Cowboy Covers Inc .... G 405 624-2270
  Stillwater *(G-8672)*

HOMEFURNISHINGS, WHOLESALE: Window Shades
Solar View LLC .... G 918 366-6413
  Bixby *(G-660)*

HOMES: Log Cabins
Katahdin Cedar Log Homes OK .... G 918 473-7020
  Checotah *(G-1396)*

HONEYCOMB CORE & BOARD: Made From Purchased Materials
Metcel LLC .... G 405 334-7846
  Edmond *(G-2514)*

HOODS: Range, Sheet Metal
Lockdown Ltd Co .... F 405 605-6161
  Oklahoma City *(G-6485)*

HORSE & PET ACCESSORIES: Textile
Casa Dosa .... G 918 243-7277
  Cleveland *(G-1719)*
Tr Tack Supply .... G 918 543-4095
  Inola *(G-3674)*

HORSE ACCESS: Harnesses & Riding Crops, Etc, Exc Leather
Cimarron Equine Station .... G 405 373-0358
  Yukon *(G-11705)*
Lenora Elizabeth Brown .... G 918 797-2034
  Stilwell *(G-8792)*
Red Earth Farm Store Inc .... F 405 478-3424
  Oklahoma City *(G-6985)*
Valhoma Corporation .... E 918 836-7135
  Tulsa *(G-11064)*

HORSE ACCESS: Saddle Cloth
United We Stand Inc .... G 918 382-1766
  Tulsa *(G-11044)*

HORSES WHOLESALERS
Tr Tack Supply .... G 918 543-4095
  Inola *(G-3674)*

HORSESHOES
Horseshoe Exploration LLC .... G 580 866-3207
  Sharon *(G-8417)*
Pro Walk Manufacturing Company .... G 580 332-5516
  Ada *(G-77)*

HOSE: Fabric
Mammoth Manufacturing Inc .... G 405 820-8301
  Bethany *(G-587)*

HOSE: Flexible Metal
Oklahoma Rbr & Gasket Co Inc .... F 918 585-3484
  Tulsa *(G-10406)*

HOSE: Plastic
Tulsa Hose & Fittings Inc .... G 918 485-0348
  Wagoner *(G-11294)*

HOSE: Rubber
Power Cable Solutions LLC .... G 405 818-1993
  Tuttle *(G-11207)*

HOSES & BELTING: Rubber & Plastic
Miami Industrial Supply & Mfg .... E 918 542-6317
  Miami *(G-4415)*

Precision Hose Technology Inc .... G 918 835-3660
  Tulsa *(G-10545)*

HOSPITAL EQPT REPAIR SVCS
B & B Medical Services Inc .... E 919 601-4756
  Oklahoma City *(G-5499)*

HOT TUBS
Paradise Pools & Hot Tubs .... G 918 938-7727
  Tulsa *(G-10465)*

HOT TUBS: Plastic & Fiberglass
Country Leisure Inc .... E 405 799-7745
  Moore *(G-4511)*

HOTELS & MOTELS
Tower Cafe Inc .... F 405 263-4853
  Okarche *(G-5255)*

HOUSEHOLD APPLIANCE STORES
Hasty-Bake Inc .... F 918 665-8220
  Tulsa *(G-9901)*
Kitchen Korner Inc .... G 918 582-9951
  Tulsa *(G-10093)*

HOUSEHOLD ARTICLES: Metal
Aerostar International Inc .... G 918 789-3000
  Chelsea *(G-1401)*
River Industries LLC .... G 918 406-8991
  Collinsville *(G-1821)*

HOUSEHOLD FURNISHINGS, NEC
Adairs Sleep World Inc .... F 405 341-9468
  Edmond *(G-2289)*
Decorator Drapery Mfg Inc .... E 405 942-5613
  Oklahoma City *(G-5917)*
Doris Winford .... G 918 599-8931
  Tulsa *(G-9598)*
E E Sewing Inc .... E 918 789-5881
  Chelsea *(G-1404)*
Gilded Gate .... G 405 590-3139
  Oklahoma City *(G-6155)*
Hoppis Interiors .... G 405 390-2963
  Choctaw *(G-1545)*
Jobri LLC .... F 580 925-3500
  Ada *(G-54)*
Patricia McKay .... G 580 355-2739
  Cache *(G-1230)*
Ray Harrington Draperies .... G 405 789-6710
  Bethany *(G-593)*
Tuffroots LLC .... G 580 728-0000
  Idabel *(G-3650)*

HOUSEWARES, ELECTRIC: Lighters, Cigarette
Sweet Puffs LLC .... G 918 367-9544
  Bristow *(G-798)*

HOUSEWARES, ELECTRIC: Massage Machines, Exc Beauty/Barber
Medical Csmtc Elctrlysis Clnic .... G 405 755-7599
  Oklahoma City *(G-6557)*

HOUSEWARES, ELECTRIC: Radiators
DL Harmer and Company LLC .... F 918 865-6993
  Mannford *(G-4181)*

HOUSEWARES: Dishes, Plastic
Coasterworks Inc .... G 405 624-2756
  Stillwater *(G-8668)*

HOUSEWARES: Pots & Pans, Glass
Help Housing .... G 918 258-7252
  Broken Arrow *(G-927)*

HYDRAULIC EQPT REPAIR SVC
Evco Service Co Inc .... E 405 381-2172
  Tuttle *(G-11198)*
G T Bynum Company .... G 918 587-9118
  Tulsa *(G-9794)*
Hydraulic Specialists Inc .... E 405 752-7980
  Oklahoma City *(G-6278)*

Mid Continent Lift and Eqp LLC .... F 580 255-3867
  Duncan *(G-2155)*
Standard Machine LLC .... G 918 423-9430
  McAlester *(G-4338)*

Hard Rubber & Molded Rubber Prdts
Northwest Rubber .... G 405 681-2667
  Oklahoma City *(G-6694)*

ICE
Clinton Ice LLC .... F 580 331-6060
  Clinton *(G-1746)*
Enterprise Ice Inc .... G 580 237-4015
  Enid *(G-2955)*
Freeman Ice LLC .... G 580 263-0021
  Madill *(G-4147)*
K-Dub LLC .... G 580 353-6899
  Lawton *(G-3948)*
Reddy Ice Corporation .... F 918 682-2471
  Muskogee *(G-4744)*
Reddy Ice Corporation .... E 405 681-2892
  Oklahoma City *(G-6994)*
Reddy Ice Corporation .... G 580 323-3080
  Clinton *(G-1766)*
Reddy Ice Corporation .... E 918 836-8223
  Tulsa *(G-10633)*
Southeastern Ice .... E 918 465-2500
  Wilburton *(G-11524)*
Sub Zero Ice Services LLC .... G 405 387-2224
  Newcastle *(G-4843)*

ICE CREAM & ICES WHOLESALERS
Blue Bell Creameries LP .... B 918 258-5100
  Broken Arrow *(G-1113)*
J Mottos LLC .... G 918 760-3866
  Tulsa *(G-10021)*

ICE WHOLESALERS
K-Dub LLC .... G 580 353-6899
  Lawton *(G-3948)*
Sub Zero Ice Services LLC .... G 405 387-2224
  Newcastle *(G-4843)*

IDENTIFICATION TAGS, EXC PAPER
Industrial Marking Co .... G 918 749-8851
  Tulsa *(G-9980)*
Kid Trax .... G 405 366-7982
  Norman *(G-5051)*

IGNEOUS ROCK: Crushed & Broken
Hanson Aggregates Wrp Inc .... E 580 369-3773
  Davis *(G-1985)*
Kemp Stone Inc .... F 918 825-3370
  Pryor *(G-7972)*

IGNITION CONTROLS: Gas Appliance
Process Products & Service Co .... G 918 827-4998
  Mounds *(G-4623)*

IGNITION SYSTEMS: Internal Combustion Engine
C & P Auto Electric .... G 405 799-2083
  Moore *(G-4501)*
Enovation Controls LLC .... B 918 317-4100
  Tulsa *(G-9689)*

INCINERATORS
Callidus Technologies LLC .... C 918 496-7599
  Tulsa *(G-9364)*
Linde Engineering N Amer LLC .... G 281 717-9090
  Tulsa *(G-10165)*
Linde Engineering N Amer LLC .... E 918 266-5700
  Catoosa *(G-1331)*

INDL & PERSONAL SVC PAPER, WHOL: Boxes, Corrugtd/Solid Fiber
Green Bay Packaging Inc .... E 405 222-2306
  Chickasha *(G-1463)*
International Paper Company .... E 405 745-5800
  Oklahoma City *(G-6320)*
Supplyone Oklahoma City Inc .... E 918 446-4428
  Tulsa *(G-10881)*

PRODUCT SECTION

INDL SPLYS, WHOLESALE: Gaskets

INDL & PERSONAL SVC PAPER, WHOL: Container, Paper/Plastic

Weilert Enterprises Inc .... E 918 252-5515
  Catoosa *(G-1365)*

INDL & PERSONAL SVC PAPER, WHOLESALE: Cardboard & Prdts

Green Ox Pallet Technology LLC .... G 720 276-8013
  Oklahoma City *(G-6187)*

INDL & PERSONAL SVC PAPER, WHOLESALE: Press Sensitive Tape

Industrial Marking Co .... G 918 749-8851
  Tulsa *(G-9980)*

INDL & PERSONAL SVC PAPER, WHOLESALE: Towels, Paper

Tulsa Coffee Service Inc .... E 918 836-5570
  Tulsa *(G-10993)*

INDL CONTRACTORS: Exhibit Construction

Crain Displays & Exhibits Inc .... F 918 585-9797
  Tulsa *(G-9499)*
North American Cos .... F 918 592-2000
  Tulsa *(G-10360)*

INDL EQPT CLEANING SVCS

Enviro-Clean Services L L C .... E 405 373-4545
  Oklahoma City *(G-6045)*
Southwest Pickling Inc .... G 580 924-6996
  Durant *(G-2259)*

INDL EQPT SVCS

A M & A Technical Services .... G 918 227-5354
  Sapulpa *(G-8245)*
AC Systems Integration Inc .... E 918 259-0020
  Tulsa *(G-9084)*
Bull Dog Welding .... G 405 412-8199
  Oklahoma City *(G-5644)*
Crematory Manufacturing & Svc .... E 918 446-1475
  Tulsa *(G-9000)*
Csi Compressco Sub Inc .... G 918 250-9471
  Tulsa *(G-9518)*
Cust-O-Fab LLC .... C 918 245-6685
  Sand Springs *(G-8174)*
Evans Enterprises Inc .... C 405 631-1344
  Norman *(G-4993)*
Hetronic Usa Inc .... E 405 946-3574
  Oklahoma City *(G-6245)*
Hilti North America Ltd .... G 918 252-6000
  Tulsa *(G-9932)*
J A Oil Field Mfg Inc .... E 405 672-2299
  Oklahoma City *(G-6334)*
Practical Sales and Svc Inc .... G 918 446-5515
  Tulsa *(G-10540)*

INDL GASES WHOLESALERS

Airgas Usa LLC .... G 405 235-0009
  Oklahoma City *(G-5402)*
City Carbonic LLC .... G 405 239-2068
  Oklahoma City *(G-5770)*
Gore Nitrogen Pumping Svc LLC .... G 580 922-4660
  Seiling *(G-8349)*

INDL MACHINERY & EQPT WHOLESALERS

All State Electric Motors Inc .... G 918 683-6581
  Muskogee *(G-4645)*
Ameripump Mfg LLC .... G 918 438-2953
  Tulsa *(G-9178)*
Blackhawk Industrial Dist Inc .... C 918 610-4700
  Broken Arrow *(G-853)*
City Carbonic LLC .... G 405 239-2068
  Oklahoma City *(G-5770)*
Curing System Components Inc .... F 405 381-9794
  Tuttle *(G-11193)*
Design Ready Controls Inc .... F 405 605-8234
  Oklahoma City *(G-5926)*
Evans Enterprises Inc .... E 918 587-1566
  Tulsa *(G-9706)*
Fluid Art Technology LLC .... G 405 843-2009
  Oklahoma City *(G-6094)*
Halliburton Company .... G 405 459-6611
  Pocasset *(G-7776)*
Honeywell Aerospace Tulsa/Lori .... D 918 272-4574
  Tulsa *(G-9945)*
Hydra Service Inc .... E 918 438-3700
  Tulsa *(G-9960)*
Industrial Dist Resources LLC .... G 239 591-3777
  Tulsa *(G-9979)*
Industrial Splicing Sling LLC .... F 918 835-4452
  Tulsa *(G-9981)*
K E Fischer LLC .... G 580 353-2862
  Lawton *(G-3947)*
Kay Electric Motors Inc .... G 580 256-3254
  Woodward *(G-11598)*
Paul G Pennington Industries .... G 405 392-2317
  Blanchard *(G-726)*
Pump Shop .... G 918 834-8829
  Tulsa *(G-10583)*
Ralph M Thomas .... G 405 756-4426
  Lindsay *(G-4079)*
Rotork Valvekits Inc .... F 918 259-8100
  Tulsa *(G-10677)*
Westair Gas & Equipment LP .... G 580 338-6449
  Guymon *(G-3370)*

INDL MACHINERY REPAIR & MAINTENANCE

Downing Wellhead Equipment LLC .... E 405 486-7858
  Oklahoma City *(G-5973)*
F & F Automotive Inc .... G 580 933-4262
  Valliant *(G-11223)*
Hydra Service Inc .... E 918 438-3700
  Tulsa *(G-9960)*
Midway Machine & Welding LLC .... G 918 968-3316
  Stroud *(G-8812)*
Petroleum Instruments Co Inc .... F 405 670-6200
  Oklahoma City *(G-6837)*
Tape-Matics Inc .... G 580 371-2510
  Tishomingo *(G-8969)*
Titan Machine Services Inc .... G 918 437-2411
  Tulsa *(G-10945)*

INDL PATTERNS: Foundry Patternmaking

Harris Pattern & Mfg Inc .... G 918 227-3228
  Tulsa *(G-9011)*
Lahmeyer Pattern Shop .... G 918 425-6008
  Tulsa *(G-10112)*
Sooner State Pattern Works .... G 580 363-1543
  Blackwell *(G-692)*

INDL PROCESS INSTRUMENTS: Boiler Controls, Power & Marine

Victory Energy Operations LLC .... C 918 274-0023
  Collinsville *(G-1828)*
Victory Energy Operations LLC .... E 918 225-2164
  Cushing *(G-1967)*

INDL PROCESS INSTRUMENTS: Control

Fki Industries Inc .... G 918 834-4611
  Tulsa *(G-9752)*
Integrated Service Co Mfg LLC .... G 918 234-4150
  Tulsa *(G-9996)*
Roll-2-Roll Technologies LLC .... G 405 726-0985
  Stillwater *(G-8749)*

INDL PROCESS INSTRUMENTS: Controllers, Process Variables

ABB Inc .... C 918 338-4888
  Bartlesville *(G-444)*
Advanced Processing Tech Inc .... G 405 360-4848
  Norman *(G-4901)*
Control Devices Inc .... E 918 258-6068
  Broken Arrow *(G-875)*

INDL PROCESS INSTRUMENTS: Digital Display, Process Variables

Coretec Group Inc .... G 918 494-0505
  Tulsa *(G-9488)*

INDL PROCESS INSTRUMENTS: Elements, Primary

Travis Quality Pdts & Sls Inc .... G 918 251-0115
  Broken Arrow *(G-1082)*

INDL PROCESS INSTRUMENTS: Fluidic Devices, Circuit & Systems

Fluid Controls Inc .... E 918 299-0442
  Tulsa *(G-9762)*

INDL PROCESS INSTRUMENTS: Indl Flow & Measuring

AC Systems Integration Inc .... E 918 259-0020
  Tulsa *(G-9084)*
Ameriflow Inc .... G 405 603-1200
  Oklahoma City *(G-5442)*
Timbercreek Flowback & Safety .... G 405 694-7228
  El Reno *(G-2762)*

INDL PROCESS INSTRUMENTS: Water Quality Monitoring/Cntrl Sys

Control Products Unlimited Inc .... G 918 786-1801
  Grove *(G-3263)*
County of Tillman .... G 580 597-3097
  Chattanooga *(G-1389)*
Evoqua Water Technologies LLC .... C 978 614-7233
  Tulsa *(G-9712)*
Meter Check Inc .... G 405 790-0778
  Moore *(G-4539)*

INDL SPLYS WHOLESALERS

Airgas Usa LLC .... F 580 767-1313
  Ponca City *(G-7795)*
Balon Corporation .... A 405 677-3321
  Oklahoma City *(G-5522)*
Blackhawk Industrial Dist Inc .... C 918 610-4700
  Broken Arrow *(G-853)*
Cyclonic Valve Company .... E 918 317-8200
  Broken Arrow *(G-883)*
Imak Industrial Solutions LLC .... G 405 406-9778
  Oklahoma City *(G-6292)*
Industrial Dist Resources LLC .... G 239 591-3777
  Tulsa *(G-9979)*
Mohawk Materials Co Inc .... G 918 584-2707
  Tulsa *(G-10295)*
Practical Sales and Svc Inc .... G 918 446-5515
  Tulsa *(G-10540)*
WM Heitgras Company .... G 918 583-3131
  Tulsa *(G-11144)*

INDL SPLYS, WHOL: Fasteners, Incl Nuts, Bolts, Screws, Etc

Aerospace Products SE Inc .... F 405 213-1034
  Oklahoma City *(G-5393)*
Cherokee Nation Businesses LLC .... B 918 384-7474
  Catoosa *(G-1310)*
Harrison Manufacturing Co Inc .... F 918 838-9961
  Tulsa *(G-9897)*

INDL SPLYS, WHOLESALE: Abrasives

N A Blastrac Inc .... D 405 478-3440
  Oklahoma City *(G-6645)*

INDL SPLYS, WHOLESALE: Bearings

Global Bearings Inc .... E 918 664-8902
  Tulsa *(G-9829)*
Lawton Machine & Welding Works .... G 580 355-4678
  Lawton *(G-3956)*

INDL SPLYS, WHOLESALE: Filters, Indl

Kiamichi Resources Inc .... G 405 364-8176
  Norman *(G-5050)*

INDL SPLYS, WHOLESALE: Fittings

Sooner Swage & Coating Co Inc .... G 918 689-7142
  Eufaula *(G-3114)*

INDL SPLYS, WHOLESALE: Gaskets

Automated Gasket Company LLc .... F 405 951-5301
  Oklahoma City *(G-5494)*
Crown Products Inc .... E 918 446-4591
  Tulsa *(G-9517)*
Pomco Inc .... F 405 677-8859
  Oklahoma City *(G-6863)*

Employee Codes: A=Over 500 employees, B=251-500
C=101-250, D=51-100, E=20-50, F=10-19, G=1-9

INDL SPLYS, WHOLESALE: Rubber Goods, Mechanical

Oklahoma Custom Rubber Co..............G...... 405 634-3943
  Moore (G-4545)
Oklahoma Rbr & Gasket Co Inc...........F...... 918 585-3484
  Tulsa (G-10406)
RL Hudson & Company....................C...... 918 259-6600
  Broken Arrow (G-1035)

INDL SPLYS, WHOLESALE: Seals

Clark Seals LLC..........................E...... 918 664-0587
  Tulsa (G-9440)

INDL SPLYS, WHOLESALE: Signmaker Eqpt & Splys

A 1 Advertising By L & H................G...... 918 348-2529
  Muskogee (G-4639)

INDL SPLYS, WHOLESALE: Springs

Action Spring Company...................E...... 918 836-9000
  Tulsa (G-9097)
Gardner Industries Inc..................F...... 918 583-0171
  Tulsa (G-9801)

INDL SPLYS, WHOLESALE: Tools

Scorpion Pump and Indus LLC............G...... 785 285-1421
  Tecumseh (G-8927)

INDL SPLYS, WHOLESALE: Tools, NEC

Metzger Oil Tools Inc...................G...... 918 885-2456
  Hominy (G-3592)

INDL SPLYS, WHOLESALE: Valves & Fittings

GE Oil & Gas Pressure Ctrl LP..........E...... 405 273-7660
  Shawnee (G-8451)
L6 Inc..................................E...... 918 251-5791
  Broken Arrow (G-963)
P V Valve...............................G...... 580 856-3844
  Ratliff City (G-8061)

INDL TOOL GRINDING SVCS

J & L Tool Co Inc.......................G...... 918 835-8484
  Tulsa (G-10018)
Superior Tool Services Inc..............G...... 918 640-5503
  Bristow (G-797)

INDUSTRIAL & COMMERCIAL EQPT INSPECTION SVCS

Hmt LLC.................................G...... 580 363-8800
  Blackwell (G-683)

INFORMATION RETRIEVAL SERVICES

Mid-Con Data Services Inc...............E...... 405 478-1234
  Oklahoma City (G-6592)
Oil & Gas Consultants Intl Inc..........E...... 918 828-2500
  Tulsa (G-10381)

INK OR WRITING FLUIDS

Ndn Ink Works LLC.......................G...... 918 708-9250
  Hulbert (G-3625)

INK: Printing

Applied Laser Systems...................G...... 918 249-9025
  Tulsa (G-9200)
Caveman Screen Printing.................G...... 918 446-6440
  Tulsa (G-9390)
H&H Retail Services LLC.................F...... 918 369-4055
  Bixby (G-631)

INK: Screen process

Southwestern Process Supply Co..........E...... 918 582-8211
  Tulsa (G-10812)

INNER TUBES: Truck Or Bus

West Worldwide Services Inc............G...... 405 601-9877
  Oklahoma City (G-7437)

INSECTICIDES

Red River Specialties LLC...............G...... 580 436-0883
  Ada (G-81)

INSECTICIDES & PESTICIDES

Redbud Soil Company LLC.................G...... 405 476-0429
  Oklahoma City (G-6993)

INSPECTION & TESTING SVCS

Advanced Aerial Services LLC............G...... 580 571-1980
  Woodward (G-11553)
Industrial Pping Companies LLC..........D...... 918 825-0900
  Pryor (G-7970)
JW Measurement Co.......................G...... 918 465-5605
  Wilburton (G-11521)
MSI Inspection Service LLC..............G...... 405 265-2121
  Oklahoma City (G-6632)
Panhandle Oilfield Service Com..........D...... 405 608-5330
  Oklahoma City (G-6799)

INSTR, MEASURE & CONTROL: Gauge, Oil Pressure & Water Temp

Redline Instruments Inc.................F...... 580 622-4745
  Sulphur (G-8841)

INSTRUMENTS, LABORATORY: Analyzers, Thermal

Kelix Heat Transf Systems LLC...........G...... 918 200-0996
  Tulsa (G-10081)

INSTRUMENTS, LABORATORY: Polariscopes

Lakeside Polaris Inc....................G...... 918 485-2887
  Wagoner (G-11285)

INSTRUMENTS, MEASURING & CNTRG: Plotting, Drafting/Map Rdg

Graphic Rsources Reproductions..........F...... 918 461-0303
  Broken Arrow (G-921)

INSTRUMENTS, MEASURING & CNTRLG: Aircraft & Motor Vehicle

Tech-Aid Products.......................G...... 918 838-8711
  Tulsa (G-10911)
Total Systems and Controls Inc..........G...... 918 481-9215
  Tulsa (G-10960)

INSTRUMENTS, MEASURING & CNTRLG: Thermometers/Temp Sensors

Btm Technologies Inc....................G...... 918 857-2855
  Bristow (G-770)

INSTRUMENTS, MEASURING & CNTRLNG: Humidity, Exc Indl Process

Accutec-Ihs Inc.........................G...... 918 984-9838
  Tulsa (G-9093)

INSTRUMENTS, MEASURING & CONTROLLING: Anamometers

Flir Detection Inc......................E...... 405 533-6618
  Stillwater (G-8689)

INSTRUMENTS, MEASURING & CONTROLLING: Breathalyzers

Garden Interlock Systems Tuls...........G...... 918 369-9935
  Tulsa (G-9799)
Guardian Interlock Systems..............G...... 918 369-9935
  Bixby (G-629)

INSTRUMENTS, MEASURING & CONTROLLING: Map Plotting

Carlson Design Corporation..............G...... 918 438-8344
  Tulsa (G-9377)

INSTRUMENTS, MEASURING/CNTRL: Gauging, Ultrasonic Thickness

Cement Test Equipment Inc...............F...... 918 835-4454
  Tulsa (G-9395)

INSTRUMENTS, MEASURING/CNTRLNG: Med Diagnostic Sys, Nuclear

Hometown Nrdgnstcs-Clorado LLC..........G...... 405 286-1016
  Oklahoma City (G-6259)
Lakeside Womens Imaging.................G...... 405 418-0302
  Oklahoma City (G-6446)

INSTRUMENTS, OPTICAL: Lenses, All Types Exc Ophthalmic

Access Optics LLC.......................E...... 918 294-1234
  Broken Arrow (G-812)

INSTRUMENTS, SURGICAL & MEDICAL: Blood & Bone Work

O E N T Instruments Inc.................G...... 918 299-4343
  Tulsa (G-10369)
Sorb Technology Inc.....................E...... 405 682-1993
  Oklahoma City (G-7169)

INSTRUMENTS, SURGICAL & MEDICAL: IV Transfusion

Linear Health Sciences LLC..............G...... 415 388-2794
  Oklahoma City (G-6480)

INSTRUMENTS, SURGICAL & MEDICAL: Inhalation Therapy

Active-Ice Inc..........................F...... 405 310-3880
  Norman (G-4898)
Medxpert North America LLC..............G...... 405 285-1671
  Edmond (G-2511)

INSTRUMENTS, SURGICAL & MEDICAL: Muscle Exercise, Ophthalmic

McAlister Drug Corporation..............G...... 405 354-2582
  Yukon (G-11750)

INSTRUMENTS, SURGICAL & MEDICAL: Optometers

Tamatha Holt Od.........................G...... 918 649-0524
  Poteau (G-7914)

INSTRUMENTS, SURGICAL & MEDICAL: Physiotherapy, Electrical

Cefco Inc...............................G...... 918 543-8415
  Inola (G-3653)

INSTRUMENTS: Analytical

Dvorak Instruments......................G...... 918 299-2223
  Tulsa (G-9614)
Ep Scientific Products LLC..............D...... 918 540-1507
  Miami (G-4401)
Eseco-Speedmaster.......................D...... 918 225-1266
  Cushing (G-1933)
Faith Church Shawnee....................G...... 405 948-7100
  Shawnee (G-8450)
Flir Systems Inc........................F...... 405 372-9535
  Stillwater (G-8692)
Havard Industries LLC...................G...... 405 888-0961
  Edmond (G-2453)
Thermo Fisher Scientific................F...... 918 540-1507
  Miami (G-4432)
Xplosafe LLC............................G...... 405 334-5720
  Stillwater (G-8777)

INSTRUMENTS: Combustion Control, Indl

John Zink Company LLC...................A...... 918 234-1800
  Tulsa (G-10055)
Universal Combustion Corp...............G...... 918 254-1828
  Tulsa (G-11046)

INSTRUMENTS: Endoscopic Eqpt, Electromedical

Surgiotonics LLC........................G...... 405 269-9767
  Stillwater (G-8762)

INSTRUMENTS: Flow, Indl Process

Crane Manufacturing Inc.................E...... 918 838-8800
  Tulsa (G-9502)

PRODUCT SECTION

INSTRUMENTS: Indl Process Control

A-1 Sure Shot ....F 405 677-9800
  Oklahoma City *(G-5353)*
Acl Combustion Inc ....G 405 310-2327
  Moore *(G-4484)*
Advanced Crative Solutions Inc ....G 918 519-3651
  Jenks *(G-3688)*
Appleton Grp LLC ....F 918 627-5530
  Tulsa *(G-9199)*
Chandler Instruments Co LLC ....D 918 250-7200
  Broken Arrow *(G-866)*
Crystaltech Inc ....G 580 252-8893
  Duncan *(G-2101)*
Du-Ann Co Inc ....G 580 428-3315
  Coalgate *(G-1779)*
Dvorak Instruments Inc ....F 918 447-0022
  Tulsa *(G-9615)*
Eastech Flow Controls Inc ....F 918 664-1212
  Tulsa *(G-9633)*
Enardo Inc ....G 918 622-6161
  Tulsa *(G-9679)*
Energy Meter Systems LLC ....E 405 853-4976
  Hennessey *(G-3460)*
Fife Corporation ....C 405 755-1600
  Oklahoma City *(G-6084)*
HEanderson Company ....F 918 687-4426
  Muskogee *(G-4688)*
Hermetic Switch Inc ....C 405 224-4046
  Chickasha *(G-1470)*
Hetronic International Inc ....E 405 946-3574
  Oklahoma City *(G-6244)*
Hetronic Usa Inc ....E 405 946-3574
  Oklahoma City *(G-6245)*
Integrated Controls Inc ....G 918 747-7820
  Tulsa *(G-9994)*
Jatco Inc ....E 405 755-4100
  Oklahoma City *(G-6351)*
Jnl Equipment ....G 918 286-1951
  Broken Arrow *(G-948)*
John Zink Co LLC ....G 918 749-9345
  Tulsa *(G-10054)*
Lonestar Msurement Contrls Inc ....G 972 653-0765
  Edmond *(G-2494)*
Petrolab LLC ....G 918 459-7170
  Broken Arrow *(G-1005)*
Process Products & Service Co ....G 918 827-4998
  Mounds *(G-4623)*
Techtrol Inc ....E 918 762-1050
  Pawnee *(G-7712)*
Terry Company Inc ....G 918 629-0926
  Tulsa *(G-10920)*
Tsi-Enquip Inc ....E 918 599-8111
  Tulsa *(G-10983)*
William L Riggs Company Inc ....G 918 437-3245
  Tulsa *(G-11125)*
Wilnat Incorporated ....G 918 640-0003
  Collinsville *(G-1830)*

INSTRUMENTS: Laser, Scientific & Engineering

Leviathan Applied Sciences LLC ....G 405 315-1759
  Edmond *(G-2487)*

INSTRUMENTS: Measurement, Indl Process

Q7 Inc ....G 918 609-3251
  Tulsa *(G-10587)*

INSTRUMENTS: Measuring & Controlling

A-1 Sure Shot ....F 405 677-9800
  Oklahoma City *(G-5353)*
Adams Electronics Inc ....G 918 622-5000
  Tulsa *(G-9102)*
Barrett Performance Aircraft ....G 918 835-1089
  Tulsa *(G-9266)*
Biospec Products Inc ....G 918 336-3363
  Bartlesville *(G-454)*
Cefco Inc ....G 918 543-8415
  Inola *(G-3653)*
Chandler Instruments Co LLC ....D 918 250-7200
  Broken Arrow *(G-866)*
Charles Machine Works Inc ....A 580 572-2693
  Perry *(G-7728)*
Chemco ....G 918 481-0537
  Tulsa *(G-9409)*
Crane Manufacturing Inc ....E 918 838-8800
  Tulsa *(G-9502)*
Eastech Badger ....G 918 664-1212
  Tulsa *(G-9632)*

Fluid Technologies Inc ....E 405 624-0400
  Stillwater *(G-8693)*
Geo Shack ....G 918 665-1880
  Tulsa *(G-9820)*
Hydrant Repair Parts Inc ....E 918 224-8713
  Tulsa *(G-9014)*
Hydro Chart ....G 918 932-8586
  Tulsa *(G-9961)*
Integrated Controls Inc ....G 918 747-5811
  Tulsa *(G-9993)*
Kimray Inc ....F 405 525-6601
  Oklahoma City *(G-6417)*
Kimray Inc ....F 405 525-4200
  Oklahoma City *(G-6418)*
Lifesafer Interlock ....G 800 634-3077
  Oklahoma City *(G-5304)*
Metal Goods Manufacturing Co ....F 918 336-4282
  Bartlesville *(G-512)*
NDC Systems ....G 405 722-1101
  Oklahoma City *(G-6666)*
Parkline Systems Corporation ....E 918 367-5523
  Bristow *(G-792)*
Preferred Utilities Mfg Corp ....G 203 743-6741
  Tulsa *(G-10551)*
Refinery Supply Co Inc ....G 918 621-1700
  Tulsa *(G-10635)*
Ren Holding Corporation ....F 405 533-2755
  Stillwater *(G-8745)*
Ren Testing Corporation ....F 405 533-2700
  Stillwater *(G-8746)*
Seismic Source Company ....E 580 762-8233
  Ponca City *(G-7873)*
Tektronix Inc ....F 918 627-1500
  Tulsa *(G-10918)*
Trece Inc ....F 918 785-3061
  Adair *(G-112)*
Veracity Tech Solutions LLC ....G 208 821-8888
  Tulsa *(G-11072)*
Versatech Industries Inc ....G 918 366-7400
  Bixby *(G-670)*
W L Walker Co Inc ....E 918 583-3109
  Tulsa *(G-11089)*

INSTRUMENTS: Measuring Electricity

Associated Research Inc ....G 580 223-4773
  Ardmore *(G-250)*
Bonavista Technologies Inc ....G 918 250-3435
  Tulsa *(G-9318)*
Intuition Inc ....G 405 361-8376
  Norman *(G-5036)*
KLA Industries LLC ....G 918 994-2123
  Tulsa *(G-10095)*
M W Bevins Co ....E 918 627-1273
  Tulsa *(G-10190)*
Port 40 Inc ....G 405 360-9100
  Norman *(G-5117)*
R C Ramsey Co ....F 918 746-4300
  Tulsa *(G-10602)*

INSTRUMENTS: Measuring, Electrical Power

Cccc Inc ....F 405 230-0638
  Oklahoma City *(G-5718)*

INSTRUMENTS: Medical & Surgical

Access Optics LLC ....E 918 294-1234
  Broken Arrow *(G-812)*
Adroit Surgical LLC ....G 425 577-2713
  Nichols Hills *(G-4854)*
B & B Medical Services Inc ....E 919 601-4756
  Oklahoma City *(G-5499)*
Baxter Healthcare Corporation ....E 918 513-8980
  Tulsa *(G-9271)*
Biocorp Technologies Inc ....G 405 990-2350
  Oklahoma City *(G-5572)*
Cardinal Health 200 LLC ....C 918 865-4727
  Mannford *(G-4177)*
Carefusion Corporation ....G 918 865-4727
  Mannford *(G-4178)*
Electronic Label Technology ....G 812 875-2521
  Edmond *(G-2409)*
Howmedica Osteonics Corp ....G 405 230-1340
  Oklahoma City *(G-6268)*
Integsense Inc ....G 404 429-4780
  Oklahoma City *(G-6317)*
Lazarus Medical LLC ....G 918 232-6915
  Tulsa *(G-10140)*
Lemco Enterprises Inc ....G 580 226-7808
  Ardmore *(G-324)*

Medtronic Usa Inc ....F 405 302-5301
  Oklahoma City *(G-6559)*
Nanomed Targeting Systems Inc ....G 646 641-4747
  Oklahoma City *(G-6652)*
Park Dental Research Corp ....F 580 226-0410
  Ardmore *(G-344)*
Pathinnovation LLC ....G 405 475-9726
  Oklahoma City *(G-6809)*
Perfect Pitch Music ....G 405 521-8088
  Oklahoma City *(G-6828)*
Precision Biomedical Svcs Inc ....G 918 671-8091
  Jenks *(G-3723)*
Shared Services ....G 405 947-0344
  Oklahoma City *(G-7115)*
Smith & Nephew Inc ....G 405 917-8500
  Oklahoma City *(G-7154)*
Thomas Dist Solutions LLC ....G 580 304-7741
  Ponca City *(G-7883)*

INSTRUMENTS: Meters, Integrating Electricity

First Response Solutions LLC ....G 405 284-6430
  Hinton *(G-3528)*

INSTRUMENTS: Optical, Analytical

Flir Detection Inc ....F 703 678-2111
  Stillwater *(G-8690)*

INSTRUMENTS: Pressure Measurement, Indl

Bates Instrumentation LLC ....F 918 441-7178
  Kinta *(G-3832)*

INSTRUMENTS: Radio Frequency Measuring

D & L Enclosures ....G 918 396-7355
  Skiatook *(G-8538)*

INSTRUMENTS: Standards & Calibration, Electrical Measuring

Hilti of America Inc ....F 800 879-8000
  Tulsa *(G-9933)*
Ideal Specialty Inc ....F 918 834-1657
  Tulsa *(G-9967)*

INSTRUMENTS: Temperature Measurement, Indl

Wyatt Engineering LLC ....G 918 824-2255
  Pryor *(G-8001)*

INSTRUMENTS: Test, Electronic & Electric Measurement

Custom Manufacturing & Maint ....G 405 872-1000
  Noble *(G-4877)*

INSTRUMENTS: Transformers, Portable

R B Watkins Inc ....F 405 732-9969
  Oklahoma City *(G-6960)*
Southwest Electric Co ....E 800 364-4445
  Oklahoma City *(G-7174)*

INSTRUMENTS: Vibration

Midwest Equipment Company Inc ....G 918 241-3672
  Sand Springs *(G-8204)*

INSULATING COMPOUNDS

Glencoe Manufacturing Co ....F 580 669-2555
  Glencoe *(G-3222)*

INSULATION & CUSHIONING FOAM: Polystyrene

Atlas Roofing Corporation ....C 580 226-3283
  Ardmore *(G-251)*
Carpenter Co ....F 405 634-8124
  Moore *(G-4506)*
Emerald Isle of Midwest Inc ....G 405 802-0092
  Choctaw *(G-1541)*
Future Foam Inc ....E 405 948-0001
  Oklahoma City *(G-6128)*

Employee Codes: A=Over 500 employees, B=251-500
C=101-250, D=51-100, E=20-50, F=10-19, G=1-9

INSULATION & ROOFING MATERIALS: Wood, Reconstituted

Company		Phone
Black Thunder Roofing LLC	G	405 473-8028
Oklahoma City *(G-5582)*		
Heintzelman Cons & Rofing	G	405 409-8954
Oklahoma City *(G-5294)*		
Icon Roofing and Cnstr LLC	G	405 403-6615
Mustang *(G-4777)*		

INSULATION: Fiberglass

Scott Manufacturing of Ky .... E 405 949-2728
Oklahoma City *(G-7097)*

INSULATORS & INSULATION MATERIALS: Electrical

Neomanufacturing LLC .... E 405 605-6581
Kingfisher *(G-3809)*
Scott Manufacturing LLC .... E 405 949-2728
Oklahoma City *(G-7096)*

INSURANCE CARRIERS: Direct Accident & Health

Don L Gerbrandt .... G 580 234-3247
Enid *(G-2943)*

INSURANCE CARRIERS: Life

Oral Rbrts Evnglistic Assn Inc .... D 918 591-2000
Tulsa *(G-10436)*

INSURANCE CLAIM PROCESSING, EXC MEDICAL

Keystone Flex Admnstrators LLC .... G 405 285-1144
Oklahoma City *(G-6412)*

INSURANCE INFORMATION & CONSULTING SVCS

Goff Associates Inc .... G 615 750-2900
Oklahoma City *(G-6167)*

INSURANCE: Agents, Brokers & Service

County of Comanche .... G 580 355-3810
Lawton *(G-3911)*

INTEGRATED CIRCUITS, SEMICONDUCTOR NETWORKS, ETC

Advanced Power Inc .... F 580 774-2220
Weatherford *(G-11387)*
Digital Interface LLC .... G 405 201-5070
Fairland *(G-3124)*

INTERCOMMUNICATIONS SYSTEMS: Electric

Disan Engineering Corporation .... E 918 273-1636
Nowata *(G-5213)*
Order-Matic Electronics Corp .... C 405 672-1487
Oklahoma City *(G-6781)*

INTERIOR DECORATING SVCS

David Denham Interiors .... G 918 585-3161
Tulsa *(G-9557)*
Patricia McKay .... G 580 355-2739
Cache *(G-1230)*

INTERIOR DESIGN SVCS, NEC

Be-Hive Interior Drapery Fctry .... G 918 599-0292
Tulsa *(G-9275)*
Classic Collectn Interiors Inc .... G 580 351-0024
Lawton *(G-3905)*
Narcomey LLC .... G 405 473-1350
Oklahoma City *(G-6653)*
Natural Stone Interiors .... F 918 851-3451
Bixby *(G-647)*
Silex Interiors Inc .... G 918 836-5454
Tulsa *(G-10761)*

INTERIOR DESIGNING SVCS

Accord Upholstery & Fabric .... G 405 634-4070
Oklahoma City *(G-5363)*
E J Higgins Interior Design .... G 405 387-3434
Newcastle *(G-4825)*
Hemispheres .... G 405 773-8410
Warr Acres *(G-11322)*
Jan Farha .... G 405 848-1388
Yukon *(G-11735)*
Warren Ramsey Inc .... G 405 528-2828
Oklahoma City *(G-7422)*

INTERMEDIATE CARE FACILITY

Think Ability Inc .... C 580 252-8000
Duncan *(G-2187)*

INTRAVENOUS SOLUTIONS

Carter & Higgins Orthodontics .... G 918 986-9986
Tulsa *(G-9381)*

INVESTMENT COUNSELORS

Adams Affiliates Inc .... F 918 582-7713
Tulsa *(G-9101)*

INVESTMENT FUNDS: Open-Ended

Capital Risk Management Corp .... G 405 848-5420
Oklahoma City *(G-5692)*

INVESTORS, NEC

Golsen Petroleum Corp .... F 405 232-7033
Oklahoma City *(G-6170)*
Hardesty Company Inc .... E 918 585-3100
Tulsa *(G-9890)*
Helen Murphy Colpitt Trust .... G 918 371-9930
Collinsville *(G-1813)*
Oil Capital Land Exploration .... G 918 582-2603
Tulsa *(G-10384)*
Permian Resources Holdings LLC .... G 405 418-8000
Oklahoma City *(G-6833)*

INVESTORS: Real Estate, Exc Property Operators

Amazing Graze LLC .... G 405 447-4893
Norman *(G-4905)*
Black Gold Stone Ranch LLC .... G 405 590-0700
Norman *(G-4936)*
First Stuart Corporation .... G 918 744-5222
Tulsa *(G-9747)*
Kiamichi Resources Inc .... G 405 364-8176
Norman *(G-5050)*

IRON & STEEL PRDTS: Hot-Rolled

Gerdau Ameristeel US Inc .... G 918 241-7762
Sand Springs *(G-8188)*
S E A Y Manufacturing LLC .... G 405 454-2328
Harrah *(G-3385)*

IRONING BOARDS

C&A International LLC .... E 918 872-1645
Tulsa *(G-9362)*

JACKS: Floor, Metal

J R Lukeman & Associates Inc .... G 405 842-6548
Oklahoma City *(G-6338)*

JACKS: Hydraulic

Efdyn Incorporated .... G 918 838-1170
Tulsa *(G-9647)*
G T Bynum Company .... G 918 587-9118
Tulsa *(G-9794)*

JANITORIAL & CUSTODIAL SVCS

Elvis S Seshie .... G 405 887-3050
Mustang *(G-4770)*
Mother Earth Eco Entps LLC .... G 785 250-8706
Ada *(G-68)*
Sheltred Work-Activity Program .... E 918 683-8162
Muskogee *(G-4748)*

JEWELERS' FINDINGS & MATERIALS

J Spencer Jewelry & Gifts .... G 918 250-5587
Tulsa *(G-10022)*

JEWELRY APPAREL

Jewels By James Inc .... G 918 745-2004
Tulsa *(G-10045)*
Rustic Rehab .... G 918 314-6647
Grove *(G-3287)*

JEWELRY FINDINGS & LAPIDARY WORK

Alans Benchworks Co .... G 405 222-1181
Chickasha *(G-1427)*
Db Unlimited LLC 855 437-7766
Tulsa *(G-9563)*
Decorative Rock & Stone Inc .... G 405 672-2564
Oklahoma City *(G-5916)*
Diamond Dee-Lite Inc .... G 405 793-8166
Moore *(G-4516)*
Jewels By James Inc .... G 918 745-2004
Tulsa *(G-10045)*
Maddie & Co .... G 580 212-9539
Idabel *(G-3639)*

JEWELRY REPAIR SVCS

Alans Benchworks Co .... G 405 222-1181
Chickasha *(G-1427)*
Curtis Jewelry .... G 580 924-0041
Durant *(G-2219)*
Diamond Dee-Lite Inc .... G 405 793-8166
Moore *(G-4516)*
J N B Inc .... G 918 786-6311
Grove *(G-3275)*
Jim Griffith Custom Jeweler .... G 918 342-0151
Claremore *(G-1644)*
Massouds Fine Jwly & Artspace .... G 918 663-4884
Tulsa *(G-10219)*
Moodys Jewelry Incorporated .... G 918 747-5599
Tulsa *(G-10303)*
Nacols Jewelry .... G 580 355-4280
Lawton *(G-3975)*
Rings Etc Fine Jewelry .... G 405 359-7464
Edmond *(G-2601)*
Staudt Jewelers 918 756-0517
Okmulgee *(G-7526)*

JEWELRY STORES

Checotah W T J Shoppe Inc .... G 918 473-2819
Checotah *(G-1391)*
J N B Inc .... G 918 786-6311
Grove *(G-3275)*
J Spencer Jewelry & Gifts .... G 918 250-5587
Tulsa *(G-10022)*
Jim Griffith Custom Jeweler .... G 918 342-0151
Claremore *(G-1644)*
Jims Jewelry Design .... G 580 336-4066
Perry *(G-7738)*
Kathys Kloset Inc .... G 405 524-9447
Oklahoma City *(G-6401)*
Moodys Jewelry Incorporated .... G 918 747-5599
Tulsa *(G-10303)*
Nacols Jewelry .... G 580 355-4280
Lawton *(G-3975)*
Phoenix Industries LLC .... G 405 848-1688
Oklahoma City *(G-6845)*
Samuels Jewelrey L L C .... G 918 241-6436
Sand Springs *(G-8222)*
Treasures Custom Jewelry .... G 918 333-1311
Bartlesville *(G-533)*

JEWELRY STORES: Clocks

Moodys Jewelry Incorporated .... F 918 834-3371
Tulsa *(G-10302)*

JEWELRY STORES: Precious Stones & Precious Metals

Alans Benchworks Co .... G 405 222-1181
Chickasha *(G-1427)*
Barretts Inc .... G 405 340-1519
Edmond *(G-2318)*
C JS Jewelers .... G 405 631-0555
Oklahoma City *(G-5659)*
Curtis Jewelry .... G 580 924-0041
Durant *(G-2219)*
Diamond Dee-Lite Inc .... G 405 793-8166
Moore *(G-4516)*
Fields Jewelry Inc .... G 405 348-2802
Edmond *(G-2414)*
Gold Shop Custom Jewelers .... G 405 789-2919
Bethany *(G-580)*

PRODUCT SECTION

Golden Bronze Inc .... G 918 251-6300
Broken Arrow *(G-920)*
Graham Jewelers .... G 580 439-6680
Comanche *(G-1841)*
Iron Bear Jewelry & Lea Co LLC .... G 918 289-1420
Tulsa *(G-10012)*
Jays Jewelry .... G 405 224-9021
Chickasha *(G-1475)*
Jewel Tech Mfg Inc .... F 918 828-9700
Tulsa *(G-10044)*
Jewelers Bench .... G 405 495-1800
Warr Acres *(G-11324)*
Johnson Bvlle Fine Jwlers Pawn .... G 405 751-1216
Oklahoma City *(G-6373)*
Massouds Fine Jwly & Artspace .... G 918 663-4884
Tulsa *(G-10219)*
Plum Gold Jewelers & Designers .... G 918 341-4716
Claremore *(G-1672)*
Rings Etc Fine Jewelry .... G 405 359-7464
Edmond *(G-2601)*
Star Jewelers Inc .... G 918 251-9236
Broken Arrow *(G-1061)*
Staudt Jewelers .... G 918 756-0517
Okmulgee *(G-7526)*

JEWELRY, PRECIOUS METAL: Cigar & Cigarette Access

Fatt Hedz .... G 405 607-8484
Oklahoma City *(G-6079)*
Toklahoma LLC .... G 580 402-1243
Oklahoma City *(G-7301)*

JEWELRY, PRECIOUS METAL: Earrings

Fields Jewelry Inc .... G 405 348-2802
Edmond *(G-2414)*

JEWELRY, PRECIOUS METAL: Medals, Precious Or Semiprecious

Ultra Thin Inc .... E 405 794-7892
Moore *(G-4582)*

JEWELRY, PRECIOUS METAL: Rings, Finger

Herff Jones LLC .... G 918 664-2544
Tulsa *(G-9924)*
Herff Jones LLC .... G 405 794-3764
Oklahoma City *(G-5295)*
Jostens Inc .... E 918 274-7047
Owasso *(G-7582)*

JEWELRY, WHOLESALE

Jewel Tech Mfg Inc .... F 918 828-9700
Tulsa *(G-10044)*
Plum Gold Jewelers & Designers .... G 918 341-4716
Claremore *(G-1672)*
Sooner Repair .... G 918 742-4653
Tulsa *(G-10791)*

JEWELRY: Decorative, Fashion & Costume

Brockus Creat Handcrafted Jwly .... G 580 594-2215
Wakita *(G-11297)*
Focal Point Inc .... G 405 942-2044
Oklahoma City *(G-6101)*
K and G Investments Inc .... G 401 396-9280
Guthrie *(G-3321)*
Kosmoi LLC .... G 918 520-7822
Broken Arrow *(G-960)*
Mary Really Nice Things .... G 580 237-1177
Enid *(G-3009)*
Sooner Repair .... G 918 742-4653
Tulsa *(G-10791)*

JEWELRY: Precious Metal

Alans Benchworks Co .... G 405 222-1181
Chickasha *(G-1427)*
Barretts Inc .... G 405 340-1519
Edmond *(G-2318)*
C JS Jewelers .... G 405 631-0555
Oklahoma City *(G-5659)*
Curtis Jewelry .... G 580 924-0041
Durant *(G-2219)*
Diamond Dee-Lite Inc .... G 405 793-8166
Moore *(G-4516)*
Elco Tech Engineering .... G 918 664-4646
Tulsa *(G-9651)*

F C Ziegler Co .... E 918 587-7639
Tulsa *(G-9721)*
Gold Shop Custom Jewelers .... G 405 789-2919
Bethany *(G-580)*
Golden Bronze Inc .... G 918 251-6300
Broken Arrow *(G-920)*
Graham Jewelers .... G 580 439-6680
Comanche *(G-1841)*
J N B Inc .... G 918 786-6311
Grove *(G-3275)*
J Thompson Custom Jewelers .... G 405 495-6610
Warr Acres *(G-11323)*
Jays Jewelry .... G 405 224-9021
Chickasha *(G-1475)*
Jewel Tech Mfg Inc .... F 918 828-9700
Tulsa *(G-10044)*
Jewelers Bench .... G 405 495-1800
Warr Acres *(G-11324)*
Jim Griffith Custom Jeweler .... G 918 342-0151
Claremore *(G-1644)*
Jims Jewelry Design .... G 580 336-4066
Perry *(G-7738)*
Johnson Bvlle Fine Jwlers Pawn .... G 405 751-1216
Oklahoma City *(G-6373)*
Massouds Fine Jwly & Artspace .... G 918 663-4884
Tulsa *(G-10219)*
Moodys Jewelry Incorporated .... F 918 834-3371
Tulsa *(G-10302)*
Moodys Jewelry Incorporated .... G 918 747-5599
Tulsa *(G-10303)*
Mtm Recognition Corporation .... B 405 609-6900
Oklahoma City *(G-6634)*
Mtm Recognition Corporation .... C 405 670-4545
Del City *(G-2002)*
Nature Creations .... G 405 848-2605
Oklahoma City *(G-6664)*
Phoenix Industries LLC .... G 405 848-1688
Oklahoma City *(G-6845)*
Plum Gold Jewelers & Designers .... G 918 341-4716
Claremore *(G-1672)*
Rings Etc Fine Jewelry .... G 405 359-7464
Edmond *(G-2601)*
Rosewood Designs .... G 405 329-0600
Norman *(G-5135)*
S M Sadler Inc .... G 918 743-1048
Tulsa *(G-10686)*
Samuels Jewelrey L L C .... G 918 241-6436
Sand Springs *(G-8222)*
Sooner Repair .... G 918 742-4653
Tulsa *(G-10791)*
Star Jewelers Inc .... G 918 251-9236
Broken Arrow *(G-1061)*
Staudt Jewelers .... G 918 756-0517
Okmulgee *(G-7526)*
Sueno Designs .... G 918 809-3027
Owasso *(G-7621)*
Treasures Custom Jewelry .... G 918 333-1311
Bartlesville *(G-533)*
Vintage Revival Inc .... G 580 379-9060
Altus *(G-171)*
Western Metalsmith Design LLC .... G 580 938-2153
Woodward *(G-11650)*
William Derrevere Designs .... G 918 260-5607
Tulsa *(G-11123)*

JOB PRINTING & NEWSPAPER PUBLISHING COMBINED

Adams Investment Company .... D 918 661-2100
Dewey *(G-2013)*
Cookson Hills Publishers Inc .... E 918 775-4433
Sallisaw *(G-8143)*
Haskell News .... G 918 482-5619
Haskell *(G-3398)*
Hennessey Clipper .... G 405 853-4888
Hennessey *(G-3466)*
Joe Brent Lansden .... G 580 625-3241
Beaver *(G-541)*
Larry D Hammer .... F 580 227-2100
Fairview *(G-3140)*
McAlester Democrat Inc .... G 918 423-1700
McAlester *(G-4316)*
Woods County Enterprise .... G 580 824-2171
Waynoka *(G-11384)*

JOB TRAINING & VOCATIONAL REHABILITATION SVCS

Alltra Corp .... G 918 534-5100
Dewey *(G-2014)*

LABORATORIES: Biological Research

Alltra Corporation .... C 918 534-5100
Dewey *(G-2015)*
Ndn Enterprises LLC .... G 703 772-6635
Pawhuska *(G-7690)*
Work Activity Center Inc .... E 405 799-6911
Moore *(G-4584)*

JOB TRAINING SVCS

Goodwill Inds Centl Okla Inc .... D 405 236-4451
Oklahoma City *(G-6172)*
Veracity Tech Solutions LLC .... G 208 821-8888
Tulsa *(G-11072)*

JOISTS: Long-Span Series, Open Web Steel

Dale Miller Group LLC .... G 580 353-4600
Lawton *(G-3917)*
Sufrank Corporation .... E 580 353-4600
Lawton *(G-4006)*

JUNIOR OR SENIOR HIGH SCHOOLS, NEC

HS Field Services Inc .... E 918 534-9121
Dewey *(G-2025)*

JUVENILE CORRECTIONAL HOME

Bethesda Boys Ranch .... F 918 827-6409
Mounds *(G-4610)*

KAOLIN & BALL CLAY MINING

JM Huber Corporation .... C 580 584-7002
Broken Bow *(G-1194)*

KITCHEN & COOKING ARTICLES: Pottery

Paseo Pottery .... G 405 525-3017
Oklahoma City *(G-6807)*

KITCHEN CABINET STORES, EXC CUSTOM

W & W Custom Cabinets .... G 405 222-1410
Chickasha *(G-1521)*

KITCHEN CABINETS WHOLESALERS

W & W Custom Cabinets .... G 405 222-1410
Chickasha *(G-1521)*
Wades Cabinet Door Shop .... G 918 868-2516
Tahlequah *(G-8891)*

KITCHEN UTENSILS: Food Handling & Processing Prdts, Wood

Engineered Food Processes LLC .... G 405 377-7320
Stillwater *(G-8684)*

KITCHEN UTENSILS: Wooden

D Lloyd Hollingsworth .... G 918 587-3533
Tulsa *(G-9539)*

KITCHENWARE STORES

Mike Beathe .... G 918 288-7858
Sperry *(G-8610)*

LABELS: Paper, Made From Purchased Materials

Rotocolor Inc .... F 510 785-7686
Tulsa *(G-10676)*

LABORATORIES, TESTING: Pollution

Shaw Group Inc .... A 918 445-7744
Tulsa *(G-10739)*

LABORATORIES, TESTING: X-ray Inspection Svc, Indl

Tulsa Gamma Ray Inc .... G 918 425-3112
Tulsa *(G-10997)*

LABORATORIES: Biological Research

Drilling Fluids Technology .... G 580 225-1009
Elk City *(G-2805)*
Tetra Technologies Inc .... G 405 542-5461
Hinton *(G-3538)*

Employee Codes: A=Over 500 employees, B=251-500
C=101-250, D=51-100, E=20-50, F=10-19, G=1-9

LABORATORIES: Commercial Nonphysical Research

Commercial Property Research ....G..... 918 481-8882
Tulsa *(G-9476)*

LABORATORIES: Dental

Melton Dental Lab ....G..... 580 369-2448
Davis *(G-1991)*
Pro-Tech Dental Labs ....G..... 918 227-6407
Sapulpa *(G-8303)*

LABORATORIES: Electronic Research

Datalog Systems ....G..... 918 245-3939
Tulsa *(G-9554)*

LABORATORIES: Environmental Research

Oilab Inc ....G..... 405 528-8378
Oklahoma City *(G-6723)*

LABORATORIES: Neurological

Hometown Nrdgnstcs-Clorado LLC ......G..... 405 286-1016
Oklahoma City *(G-6259)*

LABORATORIES: Noncommercial Research

Thurmond-Mcglothlin LLC ....G..... 580 774-2659
Weatherford *(G-11446)*

LABORATORIES: Physical Research, Commercial

American Assn Petro Geologists ....D..... 918 584-2555
Tulsa *(G-9164)*
Martin Bionics Innovations LLC ....G..... 405 850-2069
Oklahoma City *(G-6532)*
Miltech Lab Services Inc ....G..... 918 251-4436
Broken Arrow *(G-978)*
Tactical Ballistic System ....G..... 580 254-5468
Woodward *(G-11639)*

LABORATORIES: Testing

Accutech Laboratories ....G..... 405 603-2956
Warr Acres *(G-11311)*
C & P Catalyst Inc ....G..... 918 747-8379
Tulsa *(G-9357)*
Callidus Technologies LLC ....D..... 918 267-4920
Beggs *(G-550)*
City Carbonic LLC ....G..... 405 239-2068
Oklahoma City *(G-5770)*
Fluid Technologies Inc ....E..... 405 624-0400
Stillwater *(G-8693)*
Lanco Services LLC ....E..... 580 429-6526
Cache *(G-1229)*
Liberty Partners Inc ....F..... 918 756-6474
Okmulgee *(G-7513)*
Miltech Lab Services Inc ....G..... 918 251-4436
Broken Arrow *(G-978)*
Oilab Inc ....G..... 405 528-8378
Oklahoma City *(G-6723)*
Veracity Tech Solutions LLC ....G..... 208 821-8888
Tulsa *(G-11072)*

LABORATORY APPARATUS & FURNITURE

Alfa Laval Inc ....G..... 918 251-7477
Broken Arrow *(G-824)*
C & P Catalyst Inc ....G..... 918 747-8379
Tulsa *(G-9357)*
Cefco Inc ....G..... 918 543-8415
Inola *(G-3653)*
Chemco ....G..... 918 481-0537
Tulsa *(G-9409)*
Innovative Products Inc ....E..... 405 949-0040
Oklahoma City *(G-6307)*
Metal Goods Manufacturing Co ....F..... 918 336-4282
Bartlesville *(G-512)*
Miltech Lab Services Inc ....G..... 918 251-4436
Broken Arrow *(G-978)*
Rambo Acquisition Company ....D..... 918 627-6222
Tulsa *(G-10615)*
Refinery Supply Co Inc ....G..... 918 621-1700
Tulsa *(G-10635)*
W L Walker Co Inc ....E..... 918 583-3109
Tulsa *(G-11089)*

LABORATORY APPARATUS, EXC HEATING & MEASURING

Mc-Alipat LLC ....G..... 405 370-3321
Stillwater *(G-8723)*
T D H Mfg Inc ....G..... 918 241-8800
Sand Springs *(G-8229)*
Waid Forensics Science LLC ....G..... 580 574-8692
Medicine Park *(G-4372)*

LABORATORY CHEMICALS: Organic

Melton Dental Lab ....G..... 580 369-2448
Davis *(G-1991)*
Titan Chemical ....G..... 918 420-5990
McAlester *(G-4342)*

LABORATORY EQPT, EXC MEDICAL: Wholesalers

Relyassist LLC ....G..... 918 260-6517
Broken Arrow *(G-1156)*

LABORATORY EQPT: Clinical Instruments Exc Medical

Alpha Dental Studios ....G..... 405 359-2976
Edmond *(G-2298)*

LABORATORY INSTRUMENT REPAIR SVCS

Q7 Inc ....G..... 918 609-3251
Tulsa *(G-10587)*

LADDERS: Permanent Installation, Metal

Jacobs Ladder Camps & Retreat ....G..... 405 258-5176
Chandler *(G-1381)*

LAMINATED PLASTICS: Plate, Sheet, Rod & Tubes

Bostd America LLC ....E..... 580 670-0594
Blackwell *(G-676)*
Ershigs Inc ....E..... 918 477-9371
Tulsa *(G-9699)*
Old Epp Inc ....G..... 866 408-2837
Oklahoma City *(G-6769)*
Patternwork Veneering Inc ....G..... 405 447-1800
Norman *(G-5110)*
Plasticon Fluid Systems Inc ....C..... 918 477-9371
Tulsa *(G-10527)*

LAMP & LIGHT BULBS & TUBES

Advanced Tech Solutions LLC ....G..... 310 591-7163
Oklahoma City *(G-5386)*
C Triple Inc ....G..... 918 664-2144
Tulsa *(G-9361)*
Optronics International LLC ....E..... 918 683-9514
Muskogee *(G-4727)*

LAMP BULBS & TUBES, ELECTRIC: Light, Complete

Company De Roth ....G..... 405 348-3754
Edmond *(G-2362)*

LAMP STORES

Lillian Strickler Lighting ....G..... 405 528-4476
Oklahoma City *(G-6477)*

LAMPS: Boudoir, Residential

La Maison Inc ....G..... 918 592-1222
Tulsa *(G-10111)*

LAND SUBDIVISION & DEVELOPMENT

Boyles & Associates Inc ....G..... 580 353-7056
Lawton *(G-3899)*
Hathaway & Simpson ....G..... 580 875-3177
Walters *(G-11301)*
Platt Energy Corporation ....G..... 405 840-5081
Oklahoma City *(G-6856)*

LASER SYSTEMS & EQPT

Endeavor Lser Etching Engrv LL ....G..... 405 202-5921
Moore *(G-4520)*
Jim Dunn ....G..... 918 456-3552
Tahlequah *(G-8868)*

Nano Light ....G..... 405 579-5662
Norman *(G-5084)*

LASERS: Welding, Drilling & Cutting Eqpt

Rackley Welding ....G..... 580 660-1176
Mountain View *(G-4629)*

LAUNDRY & DRYCLEANING SVCS, EXC COIN-OPERATED: Pickup

Duffy Dry Clean City LLC ....G..... 405 743-0730
Stillwater *(G-8678)*
Hospital Linen Services LLC ....G..... 405 473-0422
Oklahoma City *(G-6265)*

LAUNDRY & GARMENT SVCS, NEC: Garment Alteration & Repair

Productive Clutter Inc ....G..... 405 447-3839
Norman *(G-5124)*

LAUNDRY & GARMENT SVCS, NEC: Garment Making, Alter & Repair

Rollett Mfg Inc ....G..... 405 427-9707
Oklahoma City *(G-7048)*

LAUNDRY & GARMENT SVCS: Tailor Shop, Exc Custom/Merchant

United We Stand Inc ....G..... 918 382-1766
Tulsa *(G-11044)*

LAUNDRY EQPT: Commercial

Duffy Dry Clean City LLC ....G..... 405 743-0730
Stillwater *(G-8678)*

LAUNDRY SVC: Flame & Heat Resistant Clothing Sply

Hard Hat Safety and Glove LLC ....G..... 405 942-9500
Oklahoma City *(G-6217)*

LAWN & GARDEN EQPT

E & D Enterprises ....G..... 580 512-1806
Cache *(G-1226)*
J & N Small Engine Repair ....G..... 405 382-2792
Seminole *(G-8377)*
Newton Equipment LLC ....F..... 918 756-3560
Okmulgee *(G-7517)*
Standard Supply Co Inc ....G..... 918 272-5014
Owasso *(G-7619)*

LAWN & GARDEN EQPT STORES

Bloomin Crazy Ldscp Flral Dsig ....G..... 405 238-3416
Pauls Valley *(G-7652)*
Bob Lowe Farm Machinery Inc ....F..... 405 224-6500
Chickasha *(G-1440)*
Tux Hard Shop ....G..... 918 885-2970
Hominy *(G-3594)*

LAWN & GARDEN EQPT: Grass Catchers, Lawn Mower

Juda Enterprises LLC ....G..... 405 542-3975
Hinton *(G-3531)*

LAWN & GARDEN EQPT: Tractors & Eqpt

Bob Lowe Farm Machinery Inc ....F..... 405 224-6500
Chickasha *(G-1440)*
Reputation Services & Mfg LLC ....E..... 918 437-2077
Tulsa *(G-10643)*

LAWN MOWER REPAIR SHOP

Morgans Repair Shop Inc ....G..... 405 382-3114
Seminole *(G-8388)*

LEAD & ZINC ORES

American Zinc Recycling Corp ....D..... 918 336-7100
Bartlesville *(G-447)*

LEAD PENCILS & ART GOODS

Mulberry Tree Graphics ....G..... 580 248-3194
Lawton *(G-3974)*

PRODUCT SECTION

LEASING & RENTAL SVCS: Cranes & Aerial Lift Eqpt

H&R Lifting & Bucket Service .... G 918 446-5549
  Tulsa *(G-9878)*
Rent-A-Crane Inc .... G 405 745-2318
  Oklahoma City *(G-7007)*
Rent-A-Crane of Okla Inc .... F 405 745-2318
  Oklahoma City *(G-7008)*
Rig Chasers LLC .... E 580 254-3830
  Woodward *(G-11630)*

LEASING & RENTAL SVCS: Earth Moving Eqpt

V M I Inc .... F 918 225-7000
  Cushing *(G-1965)*

LEASING & RENTAL SVCS: Oil Field Eqpt

Adams Affiliates Inc .... F 918 582-7713
  Tulsa *(G-9101)*
Big J Tank Truck Service Inc .... G 580 336-3501
  Perry *(G-7727)*
Can-OK Oil Field Services Inc .... E 405 222-2474
  Chickasha *(G-1446)*
Downing Wellhead Equipment LLC ..... E 405 486-7858
  Oklahoma City *(G-5973)*
Downing Wellhead Equipment LLC ..... G 405 789-8182
  Oklahoma City *(G-5974)*
GE Oil & Gas Esp Inc .... C 405 670-1431
  Oklahoma City *(G-6140)*
GE Oil & Gas Esp Inc .... E 405 527-1566
  Purcell *(G-8009)*
Halliburton Company .... C 405 231-1800
  Oklahoma City *(G-6207)*
High Plains Services Inc .... D 580 225-7388
  Elk City *(G-2822)*
Kalamar Inc .... F 580 242-5121
  Enid *(G-2993)*
Metzger Oil Tools Inc .... G 918 885-2456
  Hominy *(G-3592)*
Petroleum Instruments Co Inc .... F 405 670-6200
  Oklahoma City *(G-6837)*
Pioneer Oilfield Services Inc .... E 580 243-4000
  Elk City *(G-2859)*
Samson Investment Company .... B 918 583-1791
  Tulsa *(G-10694)*
Samson Natural Gas Company .... B 918 583-1791
  Tulsa *(G-10695)*
Sydco System Inc .... F 405 350-3161
  Foss *(G-3184)*
Valiant Artfl Lift Sltions LLC .... E 405 605-4567
  Oklahoma City *(G-7387)*
Valiant Artfl Lift Sltions LLC .... C 405 605-4567
  Norman *(G-5191)*

LEASING & RENTAL SVCS: Oil Well Drilling

J A Oil Field Mfg Inc .... E 405 672-2299
  Oklahoma City *(G-6334)*
Phil Lack .... E 580 883-4945
  Ringwood *(G-8089)*

LEASING & RENTAL: Computers & Eqpt

Special Service Systems Inc .... E 918 582-7777
  Tulsa *(G-10816)*

LEASING & RENTAL: Construction & Mining Eqpt

Darby Equipment Co .... E 918 582-2340
  Tulsa *(G-9552)*
Diamond Attachments LLC .... E 580 889-3566
  Atoka *(G-405)*
H G Jenkins Construction LLC .... E 580 355-9822
  Lawton *(G-3938)*
Harsco Corporation .... E 918 619-8000
  Tulsa *(G-9899)*
Kirby - Smith Machinery Inc .... C 888 861-0219
  Oklahoma City *(G-6425)*
Site Distribution LLC .... G 918 625-7980
  Tulsa *(G-10769)*

LEASING & RENTAL: Medical Machinery & Eqpt

B & B Medical Services Inc .... E 919 601-4756
  Oklahoma City *(G-5499)*
Precision Biomedical Svcs Inc .... G 918 671-8091
  Jenks *(G-3723)*
Pruitt Company of Ada Inc .... E 580 332-3523
  Ada *(G-78)*

LEASING & RENTAL: Mobile Home Sites

Bob Gene Moore .... G 918 371-4381
  Collinsville *(G-1804)*
Jim Campbell & Associates Rlty .... G 405 372-9225
  Stillwater *(G-8707)*

LEASING & RENTAL: Office Machines & Eqpt

Chaddick & Associates Inc .... F 580 223-1202
  Ardmore *(G-264)*

LEASING & RENTAL: Other Real Estate Property

Prime Operating Company .... G 405 947-1091
  Oklahoma City *(G-6893)*

LEASING & RENTAL: Trucks, Without Drivers

Douglas Thompson Auto Inc .... G 405 330-6997
  Edmond *(G-2393)*
Jims Truck Center .... G 918 225-1013
  Cushing *(G-1939)*
Mobonoto Automotive LLC .... G 580 480-0410
  Altus *(G-163)*
SUN Engineering Inc .... F 918 627-0426
  Tulsa *(G-10870)*

LEASING: Residential Buildings

Bob Gene Moore .... G 918 371-4381
  Collinsville *(G-1804)*

LEASING: Shipping Container

Mobile Mini Inc .... F 918 582-5857
  Tulsa *(G-10288)*

LEATHER & CUT STOCK WHOLESALERS

Osage Leather Inc .... G 918 745-0772
  Tulsa *(G-10442)*

LEATHER GOODS: Cases

Harry A Lippert Jr .... G 512 705-1248
  Lawton *(G-3939)*

LEATHER GOODS: Harnesses Or Harness Parts

T R Tack Supply .... G 918 299-5880
  Jenks *(G-3732)*

LEATHER GOODS: Holsters

Crossroad Holsters LLC .... G 405 317-7405
  Oklahoma City *(G-5860)*
Don Hume Company LLC .... E 918 542-6604
  Miami *(G-4397)*
Scissor Tail Custom Holster .... G 405 595-6315
  Norman *(G-5139)*

LEATHER GOODS: Mill Strapping, Textile Mills

Don Hume Leathergoods Inc .... D 918 542-6604
  Miami *(G-4398)*

LEATHER GOODS: NEC

Comanche Leather Works Inc .... G 580 439-6276
  Comanche *(G-1837)*
Cornerstone Leather .... G 817 598-0367
  Comanche *(G-1840)*
Gj Leather LLC .... G 405 795-2998
  Newcastle *(G-4828)*
Johnny Beard Co .... G 918 438-4901
  Tulsa *(G-10056)*
Kens Handcrafted Leather Gds .... G 918 616-5804
  Muskogee *(G-4702)*
Leather Doctor .... G 918 271-4600
  Broken Arrow *(G-965)*
Okc Boys of Leather .... G 318 564-0312
  Oklahoma City *(G-6727)*
Wicho Leather Creations LLC .... G 405 885-8644
  Oklahoma City *(G-7450)*

LEATHER GOODS: Personal

Leather Our Way .... G 918 214-2036
  Bartlesville *(G-506)*
Savoy Leather LLC .... G 405 786-2296
  Weleetka *(G-11465)*
Tipton Company .... G 580 762-0800
  Ponca City *(G-7884)*

LEATHER GOODS: Riding Crops

Finish Line of Oklahoma Inc .... G 918 341-8291
  Claremore *(G-1621)*

LEATHER GOODS: Saddles Or Parts

Billy Cook Harn & Saddle Mfg .... D 580 622-5505
  Sulphur *(G-8829)*
D R Topping Saddlery .... G 918 273-2812
  Nowata *(G-5212)*
Woods Saddlery .... G 918 723-5503
  Westville *(G-11488)*

LEATHER GOODS: Safety Belts

Geronimo Manufacturing Inc .... G 580 336-5707
  Perry *(G-7735)*
Lewis Manufacturing Co LLC .... E 405 279-2553
  Meeker *(G-4378)*
Lewis Manufacturing Co LLC .... G 405 634-5401
  Oklahoma City *(G-6471)*

LEATHER GOODS: Vanity Cases

Nupocket LLC .... F 918 850-1903
  Broken Arrow *(G-990)*

LEATHER GOODS: Whipstocks

US Whip Inc .... E 918 542-6453
  Miami *(G-4435)*

LEATHER TANNING & FINISHING

Osage Leather Inc .... G 918 745-0772
  Tulsa *(G-10442)*

LEATHER: Accessory Prdts

Iron Bear Jewelry & Lea Co LLC .... G 918 289-1420
  Tulsa *(G-10012)*
Oklahoma Leather Products Inc .... D 918 542-6651
  Miami *(G-4424)*
Tricked Out Pony .... G 918 931-2646
  Tahlequah *(G-8889)*

LEATHER: Artificial

Leather Guns & Etc .... F 580 296-2616
  Colbert *(G-1785)*

LEATHER: Equestrian Prdts

Lenora Elizabeth Brown .... G 918 797-2034
  Stilwell *(G-8792)*

LEATHER: Rawhide

Rawhide Custom Leather .... G 918 273-0511
  Nowata *(G-5227)*
Rawhide Dirt Works .... G 580 367-5242
  Coalgate *(G-1783)*
Rawhide N Rustics .... G 580 307-9941
  Weatherford *(G-11436)*

LEATHER: Saddlery

Blinkers & Silks Unlimited Inc .... G 405 463-0391
  Lamar *(G-3862)*
Diamond R Saddle Shop .... G 918 479-6279
  Rose *(G-8117)*
Stockmans Supply Company .... G 580 255-7762
  Duncan *(G-2186)*

LECTURING SVCS

Master Movers Incorporated .... G 918 408-1490
  Owasso *(G-7590)*

LEGAL & TAX SVCS

Hominy Tag Agency .... G 918 885-9955
  Hominy *(G-3586)*

Employee Codes: A=Over 500 employees, B=251-500
C=101-250, D=51-100, E=20-50, F=10-19, G=1-9

LEGAL OFFICES & SVCS

LEGAL OFFICES & SVCS
Charles D Mayhue .... G 580 436-6500
 Ada *(G-20)*
Oklahoma Bar Foundation Inc .... E 405 416-7000
 Oklahoma City *(G-6737)*

LEGAL SVCS: General Practice Attorney or Lawyer
Dobbs & Crowder Inc .... G 918 452-3211
 Eufaula *(G-3100)*
William C Jackson .... G 918 742-0602
 Tulsa *(G-11122)*

LEGAL SVCS: General Practice Law Office
Interstate Trucker Ltd .... E 405 948-6576
 Oklahoma City *(G-6323)*

LICENSE TAGS: Automobile, Stamped Metal
Blakes Westside Tag Agency .... G 918 446-1740
 Oklahoma City *(G-5585)*
City of Claremore .... G 918 342-2490
 Claremore *(G-1606)*
Hominy Tag Agency .... G 918 885-9955
 Hominy *(G-3586)*
Kingfisher County Drivers .... G 405 375-3711
 Kingfisher *(G-3804)*
Marys Tag Office .... G 580 562-4745
 Burns Flat *(G-1219)*
Public Safety-Drivers License .... G 918 336-0604
 Bartlesville *(G-518)*
Ss Tag LLC .... G 918 241-3400
 Sand Springs *(G-8226)*
Tag Agent .... G 580 584-2892
 Broken Bow *(G-1210)*
Tag Agent .... G 918 653-2236
 Heavener *(G-3433)*
Tag Stillwater Agency .... G 405 624-0200
 Stillwater *(G-8764)*
Tags 2 Go .... G 580 335-7474
 Frederick *(G-3202)*

LIGHTING EQPT: Flashlights
Okluma LLC .... G 580 716-1343
 Oklahoma City *(G-6767)*

LIGHTING EQPT: Floodlights
Site Distribution LLC .... G 918 625-7980
 Tulsa *(G-10769)*

LIGHTING EQPT: Miners' Lamps
Spiro Mining LLC .... G 918 962-5335
 Spiro *(G-8619)*

LIGHTING EQPT: Motor Vehicle, Dome Lights
Dark Peek Technologies LLC .... G 405 316-8551
 Edmond *(G-2379)*

LIGHTING EQPT: Reflectors, Metal, For Lighting Eqpt
Crandall and Sanders Inc .... G 405 375-3242
 Kingfisher *(G-3794)*

LIGHTING EQPT: Searchlights
LLC Searchlight .... G 580 699-2971
 Lawton *(G-3964)*
Searchlight Inc Jefferson .... G 580 752-4374
 Hobart *(G-3546)*

LIGHTING EQPT: Strobe Lighting Systems
Viking Sales LLC .... G 918 742-7796
 Tulsa *(G-11077)*

LIGHTING FIXTURES WHOLESALERS
Progress Lighting .... G 405 949-2550
 Oklahoma City *(G-6911)*
Viking Sales LLC .... G 918 742-7796
 Tulsa *(G-11077)*

LIGHTING FIXTURES, NEC
Ambassador Lighting LLC .... G 405 503-5726
 Oklahoma City *(G-5428)*

Channel One Lighting Systems .... G 918 587-2663
 Tulsa *(G-9404)*
Company De Roth .... G 405 348-3754
 Edmond *(G-2362)*
Flashlightz .... G 918 260-5882
 Tulsa *(G-9755)*
Grand Avenue Lighting .... G 580 237-4656
 Enid *(G-2964)*
Greenlamps USA LLC .... G 580 775-2883
 Cartwright *(G-1284)*
Koinonia Enterprises .... G 405 275-7064
 Shawnee *(G-8465)*
L & L Sales LLC .... G 580 658-3739
 Chattanooga *(G-1390)*
Optronics International LLC .... E 918 683-9514
 Muskogee *(G-4727)*
Punt & Puckle LLC .... G 719 358-1419
 Oklahoma City *(G-6921)*
Roberts Step-Lite Systems Inc .... G 800 654-8268
 Oklahoma City *(G-7038)*
Sheltred Work-Activity Program .... E 918 683-8162
 Muskogee *(G-4748)*
Showtek .... G 405 222-0632
 Chickasha *(G-1510)*
Solutions Lucid Group LLC .... G 405 476-4332
 Oklahoma City *(G-7158)*
T Town Lighting .... G 918 693-2063
 Tulsa *(G-10892)*
Unami LLC .... G 405 320-5696
 Anadarko *(G-208)*

LIGHTING FIXTURES: Airport
Maro International Corp .... G 918 836-7749
 Tulsa *(G-10215)*

LIGHTING FIXTURES: Indl & Commercial
Antares Enterprises LLC .... G 405 329-4326
 Norman *(G-4910)*
Petroleum Artifacts Ltd .... G 918 949-6101
 Tulsa *(G-10504)*
Truex LLC .... G 918 250-7641
 Tulsa *(G-10981)*
US Pioneer LLC .... E 918 359-5200
 Tulsa *(G-11055)*

LIGHTING FIXTURES: Ornamental, Commercial
Crossroads Led LLC .... G 918 504-6595
 Collinsville *(G-1807)*

LIGHTING FIXTURES: Residential
Lillian Strickler Lighting .... G 405 528-4476
 Oklahoma City *(G-6477)*
Petroleum Artifacts Ltd .... G 918 949-6101
 Tulsa *(G-10504)*
Progress Lighting .... G 405 949-2550
 Oklahoma City *(G-6911)*
Roberts Step-Lite Systems Inc .... G 800 654-8268
 Oklahoma City *(G-7038)*

LIGHTING FIXTURES: Residential, Electric
Smith Lighting Sales Inc .... G 918 794-2525
 Tulsa *(G-10778)*

LIME
Schweitzer Gypsum & Lime .... G 405 263-7967
 Okarche *(G-5251)*

LIMESTONE: Crushed & Broken
Anchor Stone Co .... G 918 872-8449
 Broken Arrow *(G-827)*
Anchor Stone Co .... D 918 438-1060
 Tulsa *(G-9188)*
Apac-Central Inc .... E 918 256-7853
 Vinita *(G-11248)*
Apac-Central Inc .... F 918 683-1362
 Okay *(G-5256)*
Dolese Bros Co .... C 405 235-2311
 Oklahoma City *(G-5957)*
Dolese Bros Co .... D 580 492-4771
 Elgin *(G-2775)*
Dolese Bros Co .... E 405 670-9626
 Oklahoma City *(G-5962)*
Dolese Bros Co .... E 580 226-8737
 Ardmore *(G-280)*

Dolese Bros Co .... F 580 937-4889
 Coleman *(G-1794)*
Dream Green International LLC .... G 814 616-7800
 Norman *(G-4983)*
Jennings Stone Company Inc .... E 580 777-2880
 Fittstown *(G-3159)*
Kemp Stone Inc .... F 918 772-3366
 Hulbert *(G-3624)*
Martin Marietta Materials Inc .... G 405 799-7799
 Oklahoma City *(G-6533)*
Martin Marietta Materials Inc .... E 580 369-2706
 Davis *(G-1989)*
Martin Marietta Materials Inc .... G 580 286-3290
 Idabel *(G-3640)*
Martin Marietta Materials Inc .... F 580 569-2393
 Snyder *(G-8583)*
Martin Marietta Materials Inc .... G 580 835-7311
 Broken Bow *(G-1198)*
Muskogee Sand Company Inc .... G 918 683-1766
 Porter *(G-7894)*
Pryor Stone Inc .... G 918 825-3370
 Pryor *(G-7987)*
Quality Stone Quarries LLC .... G 918 967-5195
 Stigler *(G-8641)*
Quapaw Company Inc .... E 918 767-2985
 Pawnee *(G-7710)*
Rock Producers Inc .... G 918 963-2111
 Shady Point *(G-8415)*
Schweitzer Gypsum & Lime .... G 405 263-7967
 Okarche *(G-5251)*
Souter Limestone and Mnrl LLC .... F 918 489-5589
 Gore *(G-3252)*
US Lime Company - St Clair .... D 918 775-4466
 Marble City *(G-4198)*

LIMESTONE: Cut & Shaped
Dolese Bros Co .... D 580 492-4771
 Elgin *(G-2775)*

LIMESTONE: Dimension
Apac-Central Inc .... E 918 256-7853
 Vinita *(G-11248)*
Bison Materials LLC .... G 918 333-2266
 Bartlesville *(G-455)*
Martin Marietta Materials Inc .... E 580 326-7709
 Sawyer *(G-8335)*
Polycor Oklahoma Inc .... G 770 735-2611
 Marble City *(G-4197)*

LIMESTONE: Ground
Anchor Stone Co .... F 918 599-7255
 Tulsa *(G-9186)*
Anchor Stone Co .... G 918 299-6384
 Tulsa *(G-9187)*

LIMOUSINE SVCS
Al Capone Limo Corp .... G 405 999-3335
 Oklahoma City *(G-5405)*

LINERS & COVERS: Fabric
Covercraft Industries LLC .... C 405 238-9651
 Pauls Valley *(G-7655)*
Covers Plus Inc .... G 405 670-2221
 Oklahoma City *(G-5846)*

LIPSTICK
Lipstick Chica .... G 405 432-6399
 Edmond *(G-2488)*

LIQUEFIED PETROLEUM GAS WHOLESALERS
Dcp Midstream LLC .... F 405 362-2200
 Tuttle *(G-11194)*

LIQUID CRYSTAL DISPLAYS
C D Connections .... G 580 248-6410
 Lawton *(G-3903)*
Shortruncdr .... G 405 602-5555
 Oklahoma City *(G-7124)*
Univision Display Usa LLC .... G 918 289-6611
 Tulsa *(G-11051)*

LIVESTOCK WHOLESALERS, NEC
Mid America Farm & Ranch .... G 918 275-4984
 Talala *(G-8900)*

PRODUCT SECTION

LUMBER & BUILDING MATERIALS DEALERS, RET: Solar Heating Eqpt

LOCKS

Bert Parsons 2nd Gen Lcksmth L ....G....... 918 794-7131
  Tulsa *(G-9286)*
U-Change Lock Industries Inc ....E....... 405 376-1600
  Mustang *(G-4799)*

LOCKS: Safe & Vault, Metal

Del Nero Manufacturing Co.................G....... 405 364-4800
  Norman *(G-4976)*

LOCKSMITHS

Cooper Wrecker Service ....G....... 918 639-7381
  Pawnee *(G-7703)*

LOCOMOTIVES & PARTS

Integrity Rail Services Inc ....G....... 918 267-3761
  Beggs *(G-558)*

LOG SPLITTERS

John A Littleaxe ....G....... 405 365-5117
  Tecumseh *(G-8921)*

LOGGING

Anderson Logging LLC ....G....... 580 584-9898
  Broken Bow *(G-1183)*
B & B Log & Lumber Co Inc ....F....... 580 889-2438
  Atoka *(G-399)*
B & P Logging LLC ....G....... 580 584-6718
  Broken Bow *(G-1184)*
Bloods Logging & Land Svcs LLC ....G....... 405 314-4275
  Lamar *(G-3863)*
Bucky McGee Logging ....G....... 918 635-0909
  Heavener *(G-3426)*
Donald Standridge ....G....... 580 298-3760
  Mounds *(G-4613)*
Dustin Holbird ....G....... 918 448-7687
  Wister *(G-11548)*
Excellence Logging ....G....... 815 272-7622
  Tulsa *(G-9714)*
Fortress Whitetails ....G....... 405 401-5533
  Guthrie *(G-3313)*
Hadley-Keeney Chipping Inc ....E....... 580 835-2645
  Eagletown *(G-2275)*
J&J Logging LLC ....G....... 580 933-7218
  Valliant *(G-11228)*
James Jeremy Burcham ....G....... 580 420-3243
  Broken Bow *(G-1193)*
James Roy Hopson ....G....... 580 835-2288
  Eagletown *(G-2276)*
Johnnie & Lonnie Smith ....G....... 580 933-4323
  Valliant *(G-11229)*
Kenneth D Jewell ....G....... 580 244-7450
  Watson *(G-11355)*
Larry L Williams ....G....... 580 772-3303
  Weatherford *(G-11424)*
Lucky 13 Motorcycle Shop ....F....... 816 808-0985
  Tulsa *(G-10182)*
Luna Logging ....G....... 580 933-7517
  Valliant *(G-11230)*
Midwest Logging & Perforating ....G....... 405 382-4200
  Seminole *(G-8384)*
Mixon Brothers Wood Prsv Co ....F....... 580 286-9494
  Idabel *(G-3643)*
Nancy Dalrymple ....G....... 405 525-7544
  Oklahoma City *(G-6650)*
Paladin Geological Svcs LLC ....F....... 405 463-3270
  Edmond *(G-2560)*
River Ridge Logging LLC ....G....... 580 380-2948
  Durant *(G-2252)*
SMA Surface Logging LLC ....G....... 405 301-3375
  Oklahoma City *(G-7150)*
STS Logging Services LLC ....G....... 918 933-5653
  Tulsa *(G-10862)*
Tunnell Chance ....G....... 580 245-2422
  Haworth *(G-3406)*
Walker Woods Inc ....G....... 208 266-1601
  Oklahoma City *(G-7416)*
Will Robinson Logging LLC ....G....... 918 569-4248
  Clayton *(G-1711)*

LOGGING CAMPS & CONTRACTORS

Arthur Crews Logging ....G....... 580 889-7757
  Lane *(G-3870)*
Bruce Hopson Logging Inc ....G....... 580 835-7145
  Eagletown *(G-2274)*

F G Sawmill LLC...................................G....... 918 905-1132
  Stilwell *(G-8788)*
G&G Logging LLC ....G....... 918 635-5988
  Poteau *(G-7905)*
Harrison Logging Lc ....G....... 580 245-2179
  Haworth *(G-3404)*
Impac Exploration Services Inc ....G....... 580 772-3117
  Weatherford *(G-11420)*
Karen E Hopson ....G....... 580 584-7221
  Broken Bow *(G-1195)*
Lloyd Provence Logging ....G....... 580 245-1170
  Haworth *(G-3405)*
Logging Contractor Inc ....F....... 580 244-3571
  Smithville *(G-8579)*
R & D Mud Logging Services LLP .....G....... 405 969-2587
  Crescent *(G-1919)*
Rd Logging ....F....... 918 666-2556
  Wyandotte *(G-11662)*
Shawn Gibson ....E....... 580 584-5537
  Broken Bow *(G-1205)*
Silver Creek Logging ....G....... 580 241-7717
  Broken Bow *(G-1206)*
Terry Belknap & Sons Logging..............G....... 580 244-3303
  Smithville *(G-8580)*
Wacky Logging LLC ....G....... 918 457-9393
  Hulbert *(G-3630)*

LOGGING: Stump Harvesting

Broadland Stump Removal ....G....... 918 743-7014
  Tulsa *(G-9339)*

LOGGING: Timber, Cut At Logging Camp

Gary Moss..G....... 580 286-1359
  Valliant *(G-11224)*
J Duke Logan Family Trust ....G....... 918 256-7511
  Vinita *(G-11263)*

LOGGING: Wooden Logs

Erik Robins..G....... 580 371-1470
  Ardmore *(G-287)*

LOGS: Gas, Fireplace

Flame Control Inc..................................G....... 405 321-2535
  Norman *(G-5001)*
Hargrove Manufacturing Corp ....E....... 918 241-7537
  Sand Springs *(G-8190)*

LOTIONS OR CREAMS: Face

Useful Products Inc ....G....... 405 715-2639
  Edmond *(G-2662)*

LOUDSPEAKERS

Speaker World LLC ....G....... 918 973-1700
  Tulsa *(G-10815)*

LOUVERS: Ventilating

Airtech Products Inc..............................E....... 918 241-0264
  Tulsa *(G-9132)*

LUBRICANTS: Corrosion Preventive

Rocket Science Labs Inc......................G....... 972 454-0412
  Oklahoma City *(G-7044)*

LUBRICATING EQPT: Indl

Turnair Fab LLC ....G....... 918 379-0796
  Catoosa *(G-1360)*

LUBRICATING OIL & GREASE WHOLESALERS

John Scoggins Company Inc................E....... 918 775-2748
  Sallisaw *(G-8146)*
Oils Unlimited LLC ....D....... 918 583-1155
  Tulsa *(G-10389)*
Phillips 66 Spectrum Corp ....F....... 918 977-7909
  Bartlesville *(G-516)*
Veterans Eng Group Inc ....G....... 918 864-6006
  Pryor *(G-7997)*

LUGGAGE & BRIEFCASES

Floyd Craig Company ....G....... 580 832-2597
  Cordell *(G-1859)*
Gra Enterprises Inc ....G....... 405 848-1300
  Oklahoma City *(G-6173)*

Spot My Bag LLC ....G....... 918 895-8810
  Tulsa *(G-10826)*
W L Walker Co Inc ....E....... 918 583-3109
  Tulsa *(G-11089)*

LUGGAGE & LEATHER GOODS STORES: Leather, Exc Luggage & Shoes

Leather Store...G....... 918 245-8676
  Sand Springs *(G-8199)*

LUMBER & BLDG MATLS DEALER, RET: Garage Doors, Sell/Install

Aztec Ne Overhead Door Inc................G....... 918 341-7502
  Claremore *(G-1586)*
Cimarron Glass LLC ....G....... 918 225-6600
  Cushing *(G-1925)*
Daniel Garage Door Sales & Svc ....G....... 580 628-3769
  Tonkawa *(G-8973)*

LUMBER & BLDG MTRLS DEALERS, RET: Closets, Interiors/Access

Boxel LLC ....G....... 580 239-0819
  Atoka *(G-400)*

LUMBER & BLDG MTRLS DEALERS, RET: Doors, Storm, Wood/Metal

Charles ODell ....G....... 405 745-3353
  Mustang *(G-4768)*

LUMBER & BLDG MTRLS DEALERS, RET: Planing Mill Prdts/Lumber

Van Brunt Lumber ....G....... 405 567-3776
  Prague *(G-7938)*

LUMBER & BLDG MTRLS DEALERS, RET: Windows, Storm, Wood/Metal

Johndrow Home Improvement ....G....... 580 762-4000
  Ponca City *(G-7840)*

LUMBER & BUILDING MATERIAL DEALERS, RETAIL: Roofing Material

Henderson Truss Incorporated.............F....... 918 473-5573
  Checotah *(G-1394)*

LUMBER & BUILDING MATERIALS DEALER, RET: Door & Window Prdts

Estey Cabinet Door Co ....E....... 405 771-3004
  Spencer *(G-8595)*
Oklahoma City Shutter Co Inc ....F....... 405 787-1234
  Oklahoma City *(G-6742)*
Windor Supply & Mfg Inc ....E....... 918 664-4017
  Tulsa *(G-11137)*

LUMBER & BUILDING MATERIALS DEALER, RET: Masonry Matls/Splys

Coppedge Septic Tank ....G....... 918 371-4549
  Collinsville *(G-1806)*
Dolese Bros Co ....G....... 405 247-2564
  Anadarko *(G-202)*
Dolese Bros Co ....F....... 580 937-4889
  Coleman *(G-1794)*
J-A-G Construction Company ....G....... 580 338-3188
  Guymon *(G-3353)*
Mid Continent Concrete Company ......G....... 918 647-0550
  Poteau *(G-7908)*
Southwest Ready Mix ....E....... 580 355-2093
  Lawton *(G-4002)*
Stigler Stone Company Inc ....G....... 918 967-3316
  Stigler *(G-8649)*

LUMBER & BUILDING MATERIALS DEALERS, RET: Solar Heating Eqpt

Advanced Power Inc ....F....... 580 774-2220
  Weatherford *(G-11387)*
Site Distribution LLC ....G....... 918 625-7980
  Tulsa *(G-10769)*

Employee Codes: A=Over 500 employees, B=251-500
C=101-250, D=51-100, E=20-50, F=10-19, G=1-9

LUMBER & BUILDING MATERIALS DEALERS, RETAIL: Brick

LUMBER & BUILDING MATERIALS DEALERS, RETAIL: Brick

Company		Phone
Acme Brick Company Tulsa (G-9096)	D	918 834-3384
Meridian Brick LLC Broken Arrow (G-971)	G	918 258-7533
Meridian Brick LLC Oklahoma City (G-6567)	G	405 749-9900
Meridian Brick LLC Muskogee (G-4712)	E	918 687-6734

LUMBER & BUILDING MATERIALS DEALERS, RETAIL: Cement

Sooner Ready Mix .... G 405 670-3300
Oklahoma City (G-7163)

LUMBER & BUILDING MATERIALS DEALERS, RETAIL: Lime & Plaster

Texhoma Limestone .... G 580 889-8808
Caney (G-1263)

LUMBER & BUILDING MATERIALS DEALERS, RETAIL: Sand & Gravel

Evans & Associates Entps Inc .... F 580 482-3418
Altus (G-155)
Karlin Company .... G 405 542-6991
Hydro (G-3631)
Lawton Transit Mix Inc .... G 580 569-4333
Snyder (G-8582)
Minick Materials Company .... E 405 789-2068
Oklahoma City (G-6616)
Oklahoma Aztec Co Inc .... G 405 784-2475
Asher (G-393)

LUMBER & BUILDING MATERIALS DEALERS, RETAIL: Siding

Enid Insulation & Siding Inc .... G 580 237-5317
Enid (G-2953)
Lansing Building Products Inc .... G 405 943-2493
Oklahoma City (G-6448)

LUMBER & BUILDING MATERIALS DEALERS, RETAIL: Tile, Ceramic

Silex Interiors Inc .... G 918 836-5454
Tulsa (G-10761)
Tile & Design Concepts Inc .... E 405 842-8551
Oklahoma City (G-7288)

LUMBER & BUILDING MATERIALS RET DEALERS: Millwork & Lumber

Contemporary Cabinets Inc .... D 405 330-4592
Edmond (G-2365)
Hugo Sash & Door Inc .... F 580 326-5569
Hugo (G-3613)
Mastercraft Millwork Inc .... G 405 895-6050
Moore (G-4537)
Shutter Mill Inc .... D 405 377-6455
Stillwater (G-8754)
United Millwork Inc .... G 405 670-3999
Oklahoma City (G-7371)
Young Construction Supply LLC .... G 918 456-3250
Tahlequah (G-8893)

LUMBER & BUILDING MATLS DEALERS, RET: Concrete/Cinder Block

H C Rustin Corporation .... E 580 924-3260
Durant (G-2235)
Pawnee Ready Mix Inc .... G 918 762-3437
Pawnee (G-7708)

LUMBER & BUILDING MTRLS DEALERS, RET: Insulation Mtrl, Bldg

Diversified Plastics Inds LLC .... G 918 245-0770
Sand Springs (G-8178)

LUMBER: Fiberboard

Dominance Industries Inc .... C 580 584-6247
Broken Bow (G-1189)
Riverside Ranch LLC .... F 405 360-7300
Norman (G-5132)

LUMBER: Furniture Dimension Stock, Softwood

Shelley Benefield .... G 580 436-0296
Ada (G-86)

LUMBER: Hardwood Dimension

Johnson Lumber Company Inc .... E 918 253-8786
Spavinaw (G-8591)
Moores Hardware and Home Ctr .... G 918 287-4458
Pawhuska (G-7689)

LUMBER: Hardwood Dimension & Flooring Mills

B & B Log & Lumber Co Inc .... F 580 889-2438
Atoka (G-399)
Conner Industries Inc .... E 918 696-5885
Stilwell (G-8787)
Diamond P Forrest Products Co .... G 918 266-2478
Catoosa (G-1316)
Grays Sawmill Inc .... F 580 924-2941
Durant (G-2232)
Hugo Wyrick Lumber .... E 580 326-5569
Hugo (G-3614)
Juan Manzo Custom Refinishing .... G 405 848-3843
Oklahoma City (G-6390)
Ram Design Inc .... G 918 342-4051
Claremore (G-1678)
Rd Logging .... F 918 666-2556
Wyandotte (G-11662)
White Gordon Lbr Co of Lindsay ...... G 405 946-9032
Warr Acres (G-11330)
Zara Group Inc .... F 918 782-4473
Vinita (G-11273)

LUMBER: Kiln Dried

Newview Oklahoma Inc .... D 405 232-4644
Oklahoma City (G-6672)

LUMBER: Plywood, Hardwood

Hugo Wyrick Lumber .... E 580 326-5569
Hugo (G-3614)
Morton Buildings Inc .... G 918 683-6668
Muskogee (G-4715)

LUMBER: Posts, Treated

Mixon Brothers Wood Prsv Co .... F 580 286-9494
Idabel (G-3643)

LUMBER: Resawn, Small Dimension

Conner Industries Inc .... E 918 696-5885
Stilwell (G-8787)

LUMBER: Treated

McFarland Cascade Holdings Inc ...... G 580 584-2272
Broken Bow (G-1201)

MACHINE PARTS: Stamped Or Pressed Metal

D C Jones Machine Co .... G 918 786-6855
Grove (G-3265)
Daniel W Duensing 417 781-1850
Broken Arrow (G-1120)
Hoel Machine Mfg Inc .... G 918 294-8895
Broken Arrow (G-931)
Mac Machine .... G 405 238-7280
Pauls Valley (G-7666)
Noss Machine 918 358-3804
Hominy (G-3593)
Phelps Machine & Fabrication .... F 918 662-2465
Ringling (G-8081)
Screen Tech Intl Ltd Co 918 234-0010
Broken Arrow (G-1161)
Tulsa Pro Turn Inc .... F 918 439-9232
Tulsa (G-11005)

MACHINE SHOPS

Aceco Valve Inc .... E 918 827-3669
Mounds (G-4608)
Automatic & Auto Machining Inc ...... G 918 775-9770
Sallisaw (G-8138)
Benchmark Completions LLC .... F 405 691-5659
Oklahoma City (G-5550)
Burrow Tool .... G 580 240-1045
Temple (G-8932)
Centerline Inc .... E 580 762-5451
Ponca City (G-7805)
Cherokee Ntion Armred Sltons L .... E 918 696-3151
Tulsa (G-9415)
Claco Enterprises .... G 918 343-0276
Claremore (G-1607)
Cox Machine and Tool .... G 405 681-1445
Oklahoma City (G-5848)
Dixon & Sons Inc .... G 918 256-7455
Vinita (G-11253)
Element Design & Fabrication 720 372-1940
Edmond (G-2410)
Elroy Machine Inc .... G 580 658-6725
Marlow (G-4231)
Fineline Manufacturing LLC .... F 918 245-0900
Sand Springs (G-8184)
Freedom Manufacturing LLC .... G 918 283-1520
Claremore (G-1623)
Gonzales Mfg & Mch Inc .... G 580 622-2025
Sulphur (G-8833)
Hailey Ordnance Company .... G 405 813-0700
Oklahoma City (G-6203)
Kimberly A Johnson .... G 918 370-3666
Stigler (G-8636)
Metcoat Inc .... G 580 255-6441
Duncan (G-2154)
Newview Oklahoma Inc .... D 405 232-4644
Oklahoma City (G-6672)
Pryer Machine & Tool Company .... C 918 835-8885
Tulsa (G-10580)
R & S Manufacturing .... G 918 266-2266
Catoosa (G-1347)
Redbone Tool and Machine Inc .... G 918 625-1617
Tulsa (G-10632)
Sdh Manufacture LLC .... G 918 407-1065
Broken Arrow (G-1162)
Simplified Dynamics Inc .... G 405 806-0767
Mustang (G-4793)
Spray-Rite Inc .... E 479 648-3351
Pocola (G-7786)
T & E Mobile Service Inc .... G 405 990-4022
Oklahoma City (G-7240)
Tc Machine & Manufacturing Inc ...... G 918 986-7920
Tulsa (G-10907)
Teddy Hall .... G 918 355-3822
Broken Arrow (G-1170)
Ultimate Machine Inc .... G 918 232-6676
Tulsa (G-11032)
Wildman Manufacturing Inc .... F 405 235-1264
Oklahoma City (G-7453)

MACHINE TOOL ACCESS: Broaches

Broach Specialist Inc .... G 480 840-1375
Mannford (G-4175)

MACHINE TOOL ACCESS: Cams

Herbert Malarkey Roofing Co .... C 405 261-6900
Oklahoma City (G-6241)

MACHINE TOOL ACCESS: Cutting

D & C Tool Grinding Inc .... G 918 689-9799
Checotah (G-1392)
K E Fischer LLC .... G 580 353-2862
Lawton (G-3947)

MACHINE TOOL ACCESS: Diamond Cutting, For Turning, Etc

Bradford Boring LLC .... G 405 922-9344
Chickasha (G-1442)

MACHINE TOOL ACCESS: Tools & Access

3d Farms & Machine L L C .... G 580 772-5543
Weatherford (G-11386)
Hilti Inc .... G 918 252-6000
Tulsa (G-9931)

MACHINE TOOLS & ACCESS

Burgess Tool & Cutter Grinding .... G 580 765-0954
Ponca City (G-7803)
Carlson Design Corporation 918 438-8344
Tulsa (G-9377)
Clicks Machine & Supply .... G 405 273-2497
Shawnee (G-8438)
Diamond Manufacturing Inc .... E 580 889-6202
Atoka (G-406)
Flowell Corporation .... F 918 224-6969
Tulsa (G-9007)

PRODUCT SECTION

MACHINERY & EQPT, INDL, WHOLESALE: Engines, Gasoline

Goliath Pipeline and Cnstr LLC .... G 512 917-9313
  Norman *(G-5008)*
Hot Rod Machine Tool LLC .... G 918 508-1043
  Claremore *(G-1636)*
Lawyer Graphic Screen Process .... G 918 438-2725
  Tulsa *(G-10137)*
Metal Goods Manufacturing Co .... F 918 336-4282
  Bartlesville *(G-512)*
Mogar Industries .... G 918 445-3747
  Tulsa *(G-10294)*
Mpf Industries LLC .... G 918 492-0809
  Tulsa *(G-10307)*
Spor Enterprises Inc .... G 405 745-9888
  Oklahoma City *(G-7187)*
Strope Manufacturing Inc .... G 918 835-8729
  Tulsa *(G-10861)*
Titan Machine Services Inc .... G 918 437-2411
  Tulsa *(G-10945)*
Value Components Corp .... G 918 749-1689
  Tulsa *(G-11066)*
WD Distributing Co Inc .... F 405 634-3603
  Oklahoma City *(G-7428)*

MACHINE TOOLS, METAL CUTTING: Drilling

Precision Machine & Tool LLC .... G 580 256-2219
  Woodward *(G-11623)*

MACHINE TOOLS, METAL CUTTING: Drilling & Boring

Bullseye Boring Technology .... G 405 880-1878
  Stillwater *(G-8663)*
Charles Machine Works Inc .... A 580 572-2693
  Perry *(G-7728)*
I AM Drilling LLC .... G 580 234-2277
  Enid *(G-2976)*
Tulsa Trenchless Inc .... G 918 321-3330
  Kiefer *(G-3782)*
Wesok Drilling Corp .... G 580 226-2450
  Ardmore *(G-380)*

MACHINE TOOLS, METAL CUTTING: Grind, Polish, Buff, Lapp

Duracoatings Holdings LLC .... D 405 692-2249
  Oklahoma City *(G-5990)*

MACHINE TOOLS, METAL CUTTING: Numerically Controlled

Mfg Solutions LLC .... G 918 232-3503
  Broken Arrow *(G-1143)*

MACHINE TOOLS, METAL CUTTING: Pipe Cutting & Threading

H & M Pipe Beveling Mch Co Inc .... G 918 582-9984
  Tulsa *(G-9873)*
Sawyer Manufacturing Company .... E 918 834-2550
  Tulsa *(G-9034)*
Wachob Industries Inc .... G 918 224-0511
  Sapulpa *(G-8322)*

MACHINE TOOLS, METAL CUTTING: Plasma Process

Cutting Edge Robotic Tech LLC .... G 918 247-6012
  Kellyville *(G-3764)*
D & B Processing LLC .... F 918 619-6452
  Broken Arrow *(G-1119)*
Steven Campbell .... G 580 764-3469
  Chester *(G-1421)*

MACHINE TOOLS, METAL CUTTING: Tool Replacement & Rpr Parts

Alro Steel Corporation .... F 918 439-1000
  Tulsa *(G-9156)*
C&D Machine Tool Svc & Parts .... G 405 943-6033
  Oklahoma City *(G-5662)*
Industrial Equipment Repair .... G 580 371-3361
  Tishomingo *(G-8966)*

MACHINE TOOLS, METAL CUTTING: Turret Lathes

Accu-Turn Machine LLC .... G 580 704-8876
  Lawton *(G-3883)*

MACHINE TOOLS, METAL FORMING: Bending

Darby Equipment Co .... E 918 582-2340
  Tulsa *(G-9552)*

MACHINE TOOLS: Metal Cutting

American Swat Solutions LLC .... G 405 568-1413
  Fort Gibson *(G-3172)*
Apache Machine Co Inc .... G 918 834-0022
  Tulsa *(G-9196)*
Bryon K Barrows .... G 918 519-9369
  Skiatook *(G-8534)*
Clicks Machine & Supply .... G 405 273-2497
  Shawnee *(G-8438)*
CMI Terex Corporation .... A 405 787-6020
  Oklahoma City *(G-5792)*
Cool Billet Customs .... G 580 216-0104
  Woodward *(G-11572)*
Crankshaft Service Company .... G 405 685-7553
  Oklahoma City *(G-5851)*
CRC-Evans Pipeline Intl Inc .... C 918 438-2100
  Tulsa *(G-9504)*
Forster & Son Inc .... G 580 332-6020
  Ada *(G-36)*
G C Broach Co .... G 918 369-4320
  Bixby *(G-626)*
Hem Inc .... C 918 825-4821
  Pryor *(G-7966)*
Hem Inc .... D 918 824-0800
  Pryor *(G-7968)*
J & D Gearing & Machining Inc .... G 405 677-7667
  Oklahoma City *(G-6329)*
J&K Machining Inc .... G 918 243-7936
  Cleveland *(G-1725)*
Kennys Machine Shop .... G 918 288-7241
  Skiatook *(G-8556)*
Mills Machine Co .... E 405 273-4900
  Shawnee *(G-8475)*
Wayne Burt Machine .... G 918 786-4415
  Grove *(G-3293)*

MACHINE TOOLS: Metal Forming

Cnc Patterns & Tooling .... G 918 835-2344
  Tulsa *(G-9461)*
Delco LLC .... G 918 527-8058
  Broken Arrow *(G-1122)*
Dentcraft Tools .... F 405 495-0533
  Oklahoma City *(G-5924)*
Expanded Solutions LLC .... E 405 946-6791
  Wewoka *(G-11501)*
H S Boyd Company Inc .... F 918 835-9359
  Tulsa *(G-9876)*
McCaskill Machining & Repair .... G 918 266-5186
  Catoosa *(G-1340)*
Pritchetts Machining LLC .... G 405 567-0183
  Prague *(G-7933)*
Spencer Faith Christn Ctr Inc .... G 812 876-5575
  Spencer *(G-8601)*
Strategic Armory Corps LLC .... G 623 780-1050
  Prague *(G-7936)*

MACHINERY & EQPT, AGRICULTURAL, WHOL: Farm Eqpt Parts/Splys

Hidden Valley Manufacturing .... G 580 343-2303
  Corn *(G-1867)*

MACHINERY & EQPT, AGRICULTURAL, WHOLESALE: Agricultural, NEC

Miami Industrial Supply & Mfg .... E 918 542-6317
  Miami *(G-4415)*

MACHINERY & EQPT, AGRICULTURAL, WHOLESALE: Cultivating

Day In Sun Landscaping .... G 580 768-4986
  Durant *(G-2222)*
Forrest Lawns Landscapes .... G 405 397-4679
  Oklahoma City *(G-6103)*

MACHINERY & EQPT, AGRICULTURAL, WHOLESALE: Farm Implements

Becks Farm Equipment Inc .... G 405 282-1196
  Guthrie *(G-3299)*
Rocky L Emmons & Judy E Sprag .... G 580 305-1940
  Frederick *(G-3199)*

MACHINERY & EQPT, AGRICULTURAL, WHOLESALE: Lawn & Garden

Mower Parts Inc .... E 405 947-6484
  Oklahoma City *(G-6631)*

MACHINERY & EQPT, AGRICULTURAL, WHOLESALE: Livestock Eqpt

Blue Ribbon Show Supply .... G 918 288-7396
  Sperry *(G-8605)*
Built Better Enterprises LLC .... G 580 492-5227
  Fletcher *(G-3161)*
Cattleac Cattle Equipment Inc .... G 580 774-1010
  Weatherford *(G-11398)*
Trojan Livestock Equipment .... G 580 772-1849
  Weatherford *(G-11451)*

MACHINERY & EQPT, INDL, WHOL: Controlling Instruments/Access

Evans Enterprises Inc .... C 405 631-1344
  Norman *(G-4993)*

MACHINERY & EQPT, INDL, WHOL: Environ Pollution Cntrl, Air

AC Systems Integration Inc .... E 918 259-0020
  Tulsa *(G-9084)*

MACHINERY & EQPT, INDL, WHOL: Environ Pollution Cntrl, Water

Midamerica Water Technologies .... G 405 613-0250
  Oklahoma City *(G-6594)*

MACHINERY & EQPT, INDL, WHOL: Indicating Instruments/Access

Paul King Company .... G 918 592-5464
  Tulsa *(G-10475)*

MACHINERY & EQPT, INDL, WHOLESALE: Conveyor Systems

American Automation Inc .... G
  Pryor *(G-7941)*

MACHINERY & EQPT, INDL, WHOLESALE: Drilling Bits

Duncan Bit Service Inc .... F 580 255-9787
  Duncan *(G-2109)*
Prestige Manufacturing Co LLC .... E 405 395-0500
  Shawnee *(G-8485)*

MACHINERY & EQPT, INDL, WHOLESALE: Drilling, Exc Bits

Robert M Cobb Oilfield Eqp Sls .... G 405 840-2902
  Oklahoma City *(G-7035)*
Smith International Inc .... G 580 252-3355
  Duncan *(G-2178)*

MACHINERY & EQPT, INDL, WHOLESALE: Engines & Parts, Diesel

Cummins Southern Plains LLC .... E 405 946-4481
  Oklahoma City *(G-5869)*
Cummins Southern Plains LLC .... E 918 234-3240
  Tulsa *(G-9522)*
Independent Diesel Service .... F 580 234-0435
  Enid *(G-2977)*
Pacific Power Group LLC .... G 405 685-4630
  Oklahoma City *(G-6793)*
United Holdings LLC .... G 405 947-3321
  Oklahoma City *(G-7369)*

MACHINERY & EQPT, INDL, WHOLESALE: Engines, Gasoline

Eastland Lawn Mower Service .... G 580 252-0077
  Duncan *(G-2115)*
Repair Processes Inc .... F 918 758-0863
  Okmulgee *(G-7525)*

Employee Codes: A=Over 500 employees, B=251-500
C=101-250, D=51-100, E=20-50, F=10-19, G=1-9

MACHINERY & EQPT, INDL, WHOLESALE: Hydraulic Systems

Evco Service Co Inc..................E...... 405 381-2172
Tuttle *(G-11198)*
Midwestern Manufacturing Co...........G...... 918 446-1587
Tulsa *(G-10274)*

MACHINERY & EQPT, INDL, WHOLESALE: Indl Machine Parts

A G Equipment Company..................A...... 918 250-7386
Broken Arrow *(G-809)*
Central Parts & Machine Inc............G...... 405 631-5460
Oklahoma City *(G-5725)*
Fd Products LLC.........................G...... 918 698-1644
Vinita *(G-11257)*

MACHINERY & EQPT, INDL, WHOLESALE: Instruments & Cntrl Eqpt

Advantage Controls LLC.................D...... 918 686-6211
Muskogee *(G-4643)*

MACHINERY & EQPT, INDL, WHOLESALE: Machine Tools & Access

D I V C O Inc...........................E...... 918 836-9101
Tulsa *(G-9538)*
Scorpion Pump and Indus LLC.............G...... 785 285-1421
Tecumseh *(G-8927)*

MACHINERY & EQPT, INDL, WHOLESALE: Machine Tools & Metalwork

Eversharp Tool Inc......................F...... 918 250-9400
Tulsa *(G-9711)*
SFM Incorporated........................G...... 405 788-9453
Tecumseh *(G-8928)*

MACHINERY & EQPT, INDL, WHOLESALE: Measure/Test, Electric

Northwest Measurement...................G...... 580 822-3528
Okeene *(G-5260)*
Petrolab LLC............................G...... 918 459-7170
Broken Arrow *(G-1005)*

MACHINERY & EQPT, INDL, WHOLESALE: Petroleum Industry

Archrock Inc............................G...... 918 900-4200
Tulsa *(G-9205)*
Polypipe Hdlg Specialists Inc...........G...... 405 330-4733
Edmond *(G-2573)*
Weststar Oil and Gas Inc................G...... 405 341-2338
Edmond *(G-2685)*

MACHINERY & EQPT, INDL, WHOLESALE: Processing & Packaging

Apergy Artfl Lift Intl LLC..............E...... 405 677-3153
Oklahoma City *(G-5451)*

MACHINERY & EQPT, INDL, WHOLESALE: Trailers, Indl

Diamond T Trailer Mfg Co................E...... 580 587-2432
Rattan *(G-8071)*
Gr Trailers LLC.........................G...... 405 567-0567
Prague *(G-7926)*
Tall Boys Toys..........................G...... 580 323-2765
Clinton *(G-1771)*

MACHINERY & EQPT, INDL, WHOLESALE: Water Pumps

W K Linduff Inc.........................G...... 918 225-6000
Cushing *(G-1968)*

MACHINERY & EQPT, WHOLESALE: Construction & Mining, Pavers

Paving Materials Inc....................G...... 405 799-9880
Moore *(G-4552)*

MACHINERY & EQPT, WHOLESALE: Construction, General

Mels Electric Contracting...............G...... 918 279-6036
Coweta *(G-1891)*

MACHINERY & EQPT, WHOLESALE: Contractors Materials

Dolese Bros Co..........................F...... 580 332-0820
Ada *(G-32)*

MACHINERY & EQPT, WHOLESALE: Oil Field Eqpt

A-1 Sure Shot...........................F...... 405 677-9800
Oklahoma City *(G-5353)*
Adams Affiliates Inc....................F...... 918 582-7713
Tulsa *(G-9101)*
APT Inc.................................G...... 405 354-8438
Yukon *(G-11691)*
Benchmark Completions LLC...............F...... 405 691-5659
Oklahoma City *(G-5550)*
Brown Oil Tools Inc.....................G...... 580 436-0002
Ada *(G-14)*
Calvin Mays Oilfield Svcs Inc...........F...... 405 282-6664
Guthrie *(G-3306)*
Cameron Solutions Inc...................F...... 405 677-8827
Oklahoma City *(G-5680)*
Double Life Corporation.................F...... 405 789-7867
Oklahoma City *(G-5971)*
Duane Waugh.............................G...... 580 596-2485
Cherokee *(G-1416)*
Fox Northeastern Oil Gas Corp...........G...... 918 331-7791
Bartlesville *(G-484)*
Hydro Foam Technology Inc...............F...... 405 547-5800
Perkins *(G-7718)*
Kemper Valve and Fittings...............G...... 580 622-2048
Sulphur *(G-8836)*
King Valve Inc..........................F...... 405 672-0046
Oklahoma City *(G-6421)*
M & D Oilfield Services.................G...... 405 677-5720
Oklahoma City *(G-6505)*
Mason Pipe & Supply Company.............G...... 405 942-6926
Oklahoma City *(G-6536)*
Mayco Inc...............................E...... 405 677-5969
Oklahoma City *(G-6543)*
Oil States Energy Services LLC..........E...... 405 686-1001
Oklahoma City *(G-6720)*
Oilfield Equipment Company..............G...... 405 850-1406
Duncan *(G-2161)*
Panhandle Oilfield Service Com..........D...... 405 608-5330
Oklahoma City *(G-6799)*
Repair Processes Inc....................F...... 918 758-0863
Okmulgee *(G-7525)*
Samson Investment Company...............B...... 918 583-1791
Tulsa *(G-10694)*
Sasco Inc...............................F...... 405 670-3230
Oklahoma City *(G-7085)*
Wood Pipe Service Inc...................G...... 405 672-6097
Oklahoma City *(G-7464)*

MACHINERY & EQPT: Electroplating

Quality Equipment Design Inc............F...... 918 492-4019
Tulsa *(G-10591)*

MACHINERY & EQPT: Farm

Audio Link Inc..........................G...... 405 359-0017
Edmond *(G-2311)*
Bermuda King LLC........................G...... 405 375-5000
Ringwood *(G-8085)*
Blue Ribbon Show Supply.................G...... 918 288-7396
Sperry *(G-8605)*
Blue River Ventures Inc.................G...... 580 798-4810
Overbrook *(G-7538)*
Built Better Enterprises LLC............G...... 580 492-5227
Fletcher *(G-3161)*
Cammond Industries LLC..................F...... 580 332-9300
Ada *(G-18)*
Century Livestock Feeders Inc...........F...... 918 793-3382
Shidler *(G-8524)*
Dale Case Homes Inc.....................G...... 405 755-5055
Oklahoma City *(G-5890)*
Davids Trading Yard.....................G...... 918 432-5671
Kiowa *(G-3837)*
Deans Machine & Welding Inc.............G...... 580 688-3374
Hollis *(G-3564)*
Dover Products Inc......................G...... 918 476-5688
Chouteau *(G-1562)*
Garfield Inc............................E...... 580 242-6411
Enid *(G-2961)*
Gilliam Cattle..........................G...... 405 392-4204
Newcastle *(G-4827)*
Hidden Valley Manufacturing.............G...... 580 343-2303
Corn *(G-1867)*
Johnson Welding.........................G...... 580 569-2231
Mountain Park *(G-4626)*
Mark Armitage...........................G...... 405 279-2372
Meeker *(G-4380)*
Miami Industrial Supply & Mfg...........E...... 918 542-6317
Miami *(G-4415)*
R & R Lawncare & Cleaning...............G...... 580 480-1953
Altus *(G-167)*
Red Fork Mfg LLC........................G...... 405 368-7367
Dover *(G-2044)*
Rocky L Emmons & Judy E Sprag...........G...... 580 305-1940
Frederick *(G-3199)*
Shawnee Milling Company.................G...... 405 352-4336
Minco *(G-4481)*
Southwest Fabricators Inc...............F...... 580 326-3589
Hugo *(G-3621)*
Taylor & Sons Farms Inc.................G...... 405 222-0751
Chickasha *(G-1515)*
Top Secret Case LLC.....................G...... 918 521-0601
Claremore *(G-1693)*
Transfer Cses Cltches Dffrntal..........G...... 405 232-9557
Oklahoma City *(G-7318)*
Trojan Livestock Equipment..............G...... 580 772-1849
Weatherford *(G-11451)*
Walter Shpman Dsblity Ssi Cses..........G...... 580 280-4727
Lawton *(G-4020)*

MACHINERY & EQPT: Gas Producers, Generators/Other Rltd Eqpt

Advance Oil Corporation.................G...... 918 321-9034
Kiefer *(G-3775)*
Kaiser Marketing Northeast LLC..........G...... 918 494-0000
Tulsa *(G-10073)*
Versum Materials Us LLC.................E...... 918 379-7101
Catoosa *(G-1363)*
Wyatts Oil Corp.........................G...... 918 287-4285
Pawhuska *(G-7698)*

MACHINERY & EQPT: Metal Finishing, Plating Etc

US Shotblast Parts & Svc Corp...........G...... 405 842-6766
Oklahoma City *(G-7376)*

MACHINERY & EQPT: Petroleum Refinery

Hollyfrontier Corporation...............B...... 918 581-1800
Tulsa *(G-9942)*
Parfab Field Services LLC...............G...... 918 543-6310
Inola *(G-3671)*

MACHINERY BASES

Cheyenne Products LLC...................G...... 918 639-8583
Owasso *(G-7553)*
Cni Manufacturing LLC...................G...... 580 276-3306
Marietta *(G-4205)*

MACHINERY, COMMERCIAL LAUNDRY: Dryers, Incl Coin-Operated

Hospital Linen Services LLC.............G...... 405 473-0422
Oklahoma City *(G-6265)*

MACHINERY, FOOD PRDTS: Flour Mill

Forster & Son Inc.......................G...... 580 332-6020
Ada *(G-36)*

MACHINERY, FOOD PRDTS: Food Processing, Smokers

Cookshack Inc...........................W-E.... 580 765-3669
Ponca City *(G-7810)*
Midwest Performance Pack Inc............E...... 405 485-3567
Blanchard *(G-723)*

MACHINERY, FOOD PRDTS: Ovens, Bakery

Sophisticated Sweets Inc................G...... 580 704-8038
Cache *(G-1231)*

PRODUCT SECTION

MACHINERY, MAILING: Mailing
Raf Midsouth Technologies LLC..........F....... 918 352-8300
Tulsa *(G-10609)*

MACHINERY, MAILING: Postage Meters
Pitney Bowes Inc ....G....... 405 341-3279
Edmond *(G-2572)*

MACHINERY, METALWORKING: Cutting & Slitting
Cse Bliss Manufacturing LLC ....G....... 580 749-4895
Ponca City *(G-7813)*
Jason and Ricky LLC................................G....... 580 749-4895
Ponca City *(G-7839)*

MACHINERY, OFFICE: Time Clocks & Time Recording Devices
Clock Shop Inc ....G....... 918 583-5835
Tulsa *(G-9455)*

MACHINERY, PAPER INDUSTRY: Converting, Die Cutting & Stampng
Woodward Ind Schl Dst I-1 ....G....... 580 256-5910
Woodward *(G-11656)*

MACHINERY, PRINTING TRADES: Bookbinding Machinery
Fenimore Manufacturing Inc.....................F....... 405 224-2637
Chickasha *(G-1457)*

MACHINERY, PRINTING TRADES: Bronzing Or Dusting
Timothy J and Sharo Flick ....G....... 918 250-2456
Tulsa *(G-10943)*

MACHINERY, PRINTING TRADES: Mats, Advertising & Newspaper
Eagle Marketing ....G....... 580 548-8186
Enid *(G-2948)*

MACHINERY, PRINTING TRADES: Printing Trade Parts & Attchts
Print Finishing Systems Inc......................G....... 405 232-1750
Oklahoma City *(G-6897)*

MACHINERY, PRINTING TRADES: Rules
Thompson Manufacturing Company ....G....... 918 585-1991
Tulsa *(G-10935)*

MACHINERY, SERVICING: Coin-Operated, Exc Dry Clean & Laundry
Hospital Linen Services LLC ....G....... 405 473-0422
Oklahoma City *(G-6265)*
Litta Solutions LLC ....G....... 918 845-4854
Bixby *(G-642)*

MACHINERY, SEWING: Sewing & Hat & Zipper Making
Energy Equip Sales Co.............................G....... 580 276-5900
Burneyville *(G-1216)*

MACHINERY, TEXTILE: Embroidery
B Sew Inn LLC ....G....... 918 687-5762
Muskogee *(G-4652)*
Beckys Embroidery Design ....G....... 918 456-1235
Tahlequah *(G-8852)*
Creative Monogramming EMB..................G....... 580 762-6694
Ponca City *(G-7812)*
Roses Custom ....G....... 580 252-9633
Duncan *(G-2172)*
World Weidner LLC..................................G....... 580 765-9999
Ponca City *(G-7888)*

MACHINERY, TEXTILE: Silk Screens
Gorfam Marketing Inc ....G....... 918 252-3733
Tulsa *(G-9841)*
House T Shirt & Silk Screening ....G....... 405 457-6321
Lookeba *(G-4129)*

MACHINERY, WOODWORKING: Bandsaws
Pine Creek Saw Shop Inc ....G....... 580 933-7376
Valliant *(G-11231)*

MACHINERY, WOODWORKING: Cabinet Makers'
C Easleys Touch ....G....... 918 284-9384
Tulsa *(G-9360)*
Classic Chisel Cabinet Shop ....G....... 405 387-2216
Blanchard *(G-707)*
Custom Drawers and Cabinetry ....G....... 918 322-9819
Glenpool *(G-3232)*

MACHINERY, WOODWORKING: Shapers
Tsdr LLC ....G....... 405 823-1518
Oklahoma City *(G-7346)*

MACHINERY/EQPT, INDL, WHOL: Cleaning, High Press, Sand/Steam
Chase Enterprises Inc ....D....... 405 495-1722
Oklahoma City *(G-5745)*
Hotsy of OK Inc ....G....... 580 234-0608
Enid *(G-2974)*

MACHINERY: Assembly, Exc Metalworking
Alfa Laval Inc..G....... 918 251-7477
Broken Arrow *(G-824)*
Lobito Technology Group Inc ....F....... 918 619-9885
Tulsa *(G-10175)*
Penn Machine Inc.....................................F....... 405 789-0084
Oklahoma City *(G-6824)*

MACHINERY: Automotive Maintenance
Powerhouse Resources Intl Inc................D....... 405 232-7474
Oklahoma City *(G-6870)*

MACHINERY: Automotive Related
Carter Davis Machine Shop Inc ....G....... 918 437-2939
Tulsa *(G-9382)*
Janes Machine Shop LLC ....G....... 580 237-4434
Enid *(G-2980)*
Reputation Services & Mfg LLC ....E....... 918 437-2077
Tulsa *(G-10643)*

MACHINERY: Banking
Integrated Payment Svcs LLC..................G....... 918 492-7094
Tulsa *(G-9995)*
Metavante Holdings LLC..........................G....... 800 554-8095
Oklahoma City *(G-6576)*

MACHINERY: Blasting, Electrical
Buckley Powder Company.......................F....... 580 384-5547
Mill Creek *(G-4467)*

MACHINERY: Centrifugal
Robinson Manufacturing Co......................G....... 918 251-0353
Broken Arrow *(G-1036)*

MACHINERY: Concrete Prdts
Formulated Materials LLC.......................G....... 405 310-1650
Oklahoma City *(G-6102)*

MACHINERY: Construction
A&J Mixing ....G....... 405 946-1461
Oklahoma City *(G-5349)*
Altec Inc..G....... 405 577-6322
Oklahoma City *(G-5426)*
American Castings LLC ....B....... 918 476-4252
Pryor *(G-7942)*
Brown Equipment Corporation ....G....... 405 799-4000
Oklahoma City *(G-5635)*
Cammond Industries LLC ....F....... 580 332-9300
Ada *(G-18)*
Charles Machine Works Inc ....A....... 580 572-2693
Perry *(G-7728)*
Clydes Good Gruel LLC ....G....... 918 323-6143
Tulsa *(G-9458)*
CMI Terex Corporation ....G....... 405 787-6020
Oklahoma City *(G-5793)*
CRC-Evans Pipeline Intl Inc ....C....... 918 438-2100
Tulsa *(G-9504)*

Crosslands A A Rent-All Sls Co................G....... 405 366-8878
Norman *(G-4970)*
Darby Equipment Co ....E....... 918 582-2340
Tulsa *(G-9552)*
Dolese Bros Co ....F....... 580 255-3046
Duncan *(G-2107)*
Double Life Corporation ....F....... 405 789-7867
Oklahoma City *(G-5971)*
E-Z Drill Inc ....G....... 405 372-0121
Perry *(G-7732)*
Four Feathers Transports ....G....... 405 343-9799
Crescent *(G-1915)*
Goff Inc ....F....... 405 278-6200
Seminole *(G-8374)*
Horton World Solutions LLC ....F....... 817 821-8320
Broken Arrow *(G-1133)*
Ideal Crane Corporation ....F....... 800 622-6163
Tulsa *(G-9966)*
Industrial Trctr Parts Co Inc ....G....... 918 258-6580
Broken Arrow *(G-935)*
Ironwolf Manufacturing LLC ....F....... 405 872-1890
Noble *(G-4882)*
J E Shaffer Co ....G....... 918 582-1752
Owasso *(G-7577)*
Kinder Equipment LLC ....G....... 580 335-2363
Frederick *(G-3195)*
Morgan Hauling ....G....... 580 420-3265
Broken Bow *(G-1202)*
N A Blastrac Inc ....D....... 405 478-3440
Oklahoma City *(G-6645)*
Sawyer Manufacturing Company ....E....... 918 834-2550
Tulsa *(G-9034)*
Simmons Tool LLC ....G....... 580 228-2799
Waurika *(G-11364)*
South Central Oilfld Svcs Inc ....G....... 580 465-4498
Wilson *(G-11542)*
Terex Mining ....G....... 918 296-0530
Jenks *(G-3735)*
Terex USA LLC ....F....... 405 787-6020
Oklahoma City *(G-7270)*
Thomas Appraisal Service ....G....... 918 341-5860
Claremore *(G-1692)*
Tribal Consortium Inc ....G....... 580 332-1134
Ada *(G-96)*
Triple C Grading & Excvtg LLC ....G....... 918 605-1848
Sapulpa *(G-8317)*
Western Fibers Inc..................................E....... 509 679-4786
Hollis *(G-3571)*
William L Riggs Company Inc..................G....... 918 437-3245
Tulsa *(G-11125)*

MACHINERY: Cotton Ginning
Farmers Co-Operative Gin Assn ....G....... 580 928-2664
Sayre *(G-8340)*

MACHINERY: Custom
3d Farms & Machine L L C ....G....... 580 772-5543
Weatherford *(G-11386)*
DK Machine Inc ....G....... 918 251-1034
Broken Arrow *(G-890)*
Eversharp Tool Inc ....F....... 918 250-9400
Tulsa *(G-9711)*
Midwest Machine & Comprsr Co ....G....... 405 634-5454
Oklahoma City *(G-6604)*
Northeast Oklahoma Mfg ....G....... 918 663-8805
Tulsa *(G-10361)*
Tote Along Inc ....E....... 918 542-6453
Miami *(G-4433)*

MACHINERY: Dredging
V M I Inc ....F....... 918 225-7000
Cushing *(G-1965)*

MACHINERY: Electrical Discharge Erosion
Rent-A-Crane Inc ....G....... 405 745-2318
Oklahoma City *(G-7007)*
Rent-A-Crane of Okla Inc ....F....... 405 745-2318
Oklahoma City *(G-7008)*
Triangular Silt Dike Co Inc ....G....... 405 277-7015
Luther *(G-4139)*

MACHINERY: Electronic Component Making
Young & New Century LLC ....G....... 281 968-0718
Norman *(G-5205)*

MACHINERY: Electronic Teaching Aids
Simulator Systems Intl Inc ....G....... 800 843-4764
  Tulsa (G-10765)
Simulator Systems Intl Inc ....G....... 918 250-4500
  Tulsa (G-10766)

MACHINERY: Fiber Optics Strand Coating
Trace LLC..F....... 918 510-0210
  Tulsa (G-10964)

MACHINERY: Gas Producers
Crown Midstream LLC...........................G....... 405 753-1955
  Oklahoma City (G-5862)

MACHINERY: General, Industrial, NEC
24 7 Machinery LLC ....G....... 580 762-8965
  Ponca City (G-7789)
Bear Paw Manufacturing ....G....... 918 637-4775
  Wagoner (G-11275)
J&K Machining Inc................................G....... 918 243-7936
  Cleveland (G-1725)
Knowles Performance Engines ....G....... 580 821-4825
  Dill City (G-2036)
Mosley ....G....... 918 407-6619
  Broken Arrow (G-982)
Russells Machine and Fab LLC ....G....... 405 742-6818
  Stillwater (G-8750)
Usfilter..G....... 405 359-7441
  Edmond (G-2663)

MACHINERY: Glassmaking
Pyrotek Incorporated ....E....... 918 224-1937
  Tulsa (G-9030)

MACHINERY: Grinding
Deans Grinding Service ....G....... 918 838-0756
  Tulsa (G-9565)

MACHINERY: Ice Crushers
Lake Ice LLC...G....... 405 882-7227
  Jones (G-3750)

MACHINERY: Industrial, NEC
Affordable Leak Detection ....G....... 405 594-2341
  Oklahoma City (G-5396)
Best Mold Technology LLC..................G....... 405 659-1991
  Cache (G-1224)
Clint Dodson Enterprises LLC.............G....... 580 931-9410
  Durant (G-2216)
J F Machine LLC ....G....... 918 865-5855
  Mannford (G-4183)
Johnny Beard Co ....G....... 918 438-4901
  Tulsa (G-10056)
Kenneth H Knepper ....G....... 918 582-1954
  Tulsa (G-10083)
Mostmachine LLC ....G....... 918 706-0393
  Claremore (G-1658)
Opb Pipe Bending ....G....... 918 583-1566
  Tulsa (G-10432)
Robs Magneto Service ....G....... 918 367-5735
  Tulsa (G-10665)
SBS Industries ....G....... 918 749-8221
  Tulsa (G-10711)
Stewart Tech ....G....... 405 292-8214
  Norman (G-5158)
Twiggs Company ....G....... 405 882-0308
  Yukon (G-11796)
V W Casey Industries LLC ....G....... 918 369-5205
  Bixby (G-669)

MACHINERY: Kilns
Copper Kiln LLC....................................G....... 918 272-5200
  Owasso (G-7555)

MACHINERY: Labeling
A M & A Technical Services ....G....... 918 227-5354
  Sapulpa (G-8245)

MACHINERY: Logging Eqpt
Frontier Logging Corporation................G....... 405 787-3952
  Oklahoma City (G-6122)

MACHINERY: Metalworking
A & W Machine LLC ....G....... 580 927-1188
  Coalgate (G-1774)
Clean Products Inc ....G....... 405 382-1441
  Seminole (G-8364)
Eastern Manufacturing Inc ....G....... 918 482-1544
  Haskell (G-3397)
Emmaus Group LLC ....G....... 918 834-8787
  Tulsa (G-9673)
Master Machine.....................................G....... 918 366-4855
  Bixby (G-643)
Mathey Dearman Inc ....E....... 918 447-1288
  Tulsa (G-10222)
Miami Industrial Supply & Mfg..............E....... 918 542-6317
  Miami (G-4415)
Morton Manufacturing Co Inc...............G....... 918 584-0333
  Tulsa (G-10305)
Rick Leaming Construction LLC ....G....... 580 362-2262
  Newkirk (G-4852)
Rollett Mfg Inc ....G....... 405 427-9707
  Oklahoma City (G-7048)
Safeco Manufacturing Inc ....F....... 918 455-0100
  Broken Arrow (G-1160)
Starlite Welding Supplies ....G....... 580 252-8320
  Duncan (G-2185)

MACHINERY: Milling
Bliss Industries LLC ....D....... 580 765-7787
  Ponca City (G-7800)
Helmco Manufacturing Inc ....G....... 918 336-4757
  Bartlesville (G-492)

MACHINERY: Mining
Century Geophysical Corp....................E....... 918 838-9811
  Tulsa (G-9399)
Cutting Edge Technologies LLC..........G....... 918 284-6069
  Owasso (G-7558)
Enid Drill Systems Inc ....G....... 580 234-5971
  Enid (G-2951)
South Central Machine.........................G....... 580 775-1623
  Durant (G-2258)

MACHINERY: Nuclear Reactor Control Rod & Drive Mechanism
Bolt It Hydraulic Solutions ....F....... 918 296-0202
  Jenks (G-3693)

MACHINERY: Optical Lens
Optical Works Corporation ....F....... 918 682-1806
  Muskogee (G-4726)

MACHINERY: Packaging
Bemis Company Inc..............................C....... 405 207-2200
  Pauls Valley (G-7650)
Clr Enterprises LLC ....G....... 918 298-1943
  Tulsa (G-9457)
Emerald Manufacturing Corp................G....... 405 235-3704
  Oklahoma City (G-6032)
Maxcess Americas Inc.........................G....... 405 755-1600
  Oklahoma City (G-6538)
Maxcess International Corp..................G....... 405 755-1600
  Oklahoma City (G-6539)
Maxcess Intl Holdg Corp ....G....... 405 755-1600
  Oklahoma City (G-6540)
Supplyone Oklahoma City Inc ....C....... 405 947-7373
  Oklahoma City (G-7230)

MACHINERY: Paper Industry Miscellaneous
Magnat-Fairview LLC............................F....... 413 593-5742
  Oklahoma City (G-6517)
Marvel Photo Inc ....G....... 918 836-0741
  Tulsa (G-10218)
Maxcess Americas Inc.........................G....... 405 755-1600
  Oklahoma City (G-6538)
Maxcess International Corp..................G....... 405 755-1600
  Oklahoma City (G-6539)
Maxcess Intl Holdg Corp ....G....... 405 755-1600
  Oklahoma City (G-6540)
Thompson Manufacturing Company ....G....... 918 585-1991
  Tulsa (G-10935)

MACHINERY: Photographic Reproduction
Prophecy In News ....F....... 405 634-1234
  Oklahoma City (G-6917)

MACHINERY: Plastic Working
Bartec Dispensing Tech Inc ....G....... 918 250-6496
  Tulsa (G-9269)

MACHINERY: Recycling
Vintage Plastics Llc.............................F....... 918 439-1016
  Tulsa (G-11078)

MACHINERY: Road Construction & Maintenance
Adair County Commisioners Off ....E....... 918 696-7633
  Stilwell (G-8779)
Combotronics Inc ....E....... 918 543-3300
  Inola (G-3656)
County of Carter ....F....... 580 657-4050
  Lone Grove (G-4116)
Dewey County ....F....... 580 995-3444
  Vici (G-11241)
Dickson Industries Inc.........................E....... 405 598-6547
  Tecumseh (G-8912)
Lincoln County Barn Dist No 3 ....E....... 405 279-3313
  Meeker (G-4379)
Ottawa County District 3 ....F....... 918 676-3227
  Fairland (G-3127)
Swh Construction LLC ....F....... 405 317-0663
  Washington (G-11338)

MACHINERY: Robots, Molding & Forming Plastics
Martin Bionics Innovations LLC ....G....... 405 850-2069
  Oklahoma City (G-6532)

MACHINERY: Saw & Sawing
Dickson Industries Inc.........................E....... 405 598-6547
  Tecumseh (G-8912)
Hem Inc ....D....... 888 729-7787
  Pryor (G-7967)

MACHINERY: Screening Eqpt, Electric
High Country Tek Inc ....E....... 530 265-3236
  Tulsa (G-9928)

MACHINERY: Semiconductor Manufacturing
Lam Research Corporation...................D....... 866 323-1834
  Tulsa (G-10117)

MACHINERY: Service Industry, NEC
Elster Amco Water Inc ....E....... 863 453-5336
  Norman (G-4991)
Fluid Treatment Systems Inc ....G....... 918 933-5678
  Tulsa (G-9763)
SFM Incorporated ....G....... 405 788-9453
  Tecumseh (G-8928)

MACHINERY: Sifting & Screening
Smico Manufacturing Co Inc ....E....... 405 946-1461
  Oklahoma City (G-7153)

MACHINERY: Specialty
Health Engineering System ....G....... 405 329-6810
  Norman (G-5020)
J&K Machining Inc................................G....... 918 243-7936
  Cleveland (G-1725)
Tip Top Prop Shop ....G....... 580 564-3712
  Kingston (G-3831)
US Ferroics LLC ....G....... 601 763-1058
  Ardmore (G-376)

MACHINERY: Tire Shredding
Central Sttes Shrdding Systems ....G....... 405 752-8300
  Oklahoma City (G-5726)

MACHINERY: Woodworking
Marcy A Sharp ....G....... 405 615-9879
  Asher (G-391)
Michael Allan Sharp ....G....... 405 615-3771
  Asher (G-392)

MACHINES: Forming, Sheet Metal
JC Fab LLC ....F....... 580 920-0878
  Durant (G-2240)

PRODUCT SECTION

MANUFACTURING INDUSTRIES, NEC

Mountain Top Machine Inc.............G.......918 787-5510
  Jay *(G-3683)*

MACHINISTS' TOOLS: Measuring, Precision
Hilti of America Inc.............F.......800 879-8000
  Tulsa *(G-9933)*

MACHINISTS' TOOLS: Precision
M&M Precision Components LLC.......D....918 933-6500
  Tulsa *(G-10191)*
Rightway Mfg Solutions LLC.............E.......580 252-2284
  Duncan *(G-2170)*

MAGAZINE STAND
Humps N Horns Bull Riding News.......G.......918 872-9713
  Broken Arrow *(G-932)*

MAGAZINES, WHOLESALE
405 Magazine Inc.............G.......405 604-2623
  Oklahoma City *(G-5332)*
Just Two Publishing Inc.............G.......405 607-2902
  Edmond *(G-2476)*
Riggs Heinrich Media Inc.............E.......918 492-0660
  Tulsa *(G-10652)*

MAGNETIC RESONANCE IMAGING DEVICES: Nonmedical
Evoqua Water Technologies LLC.......C.....978 614-7233
  Tulsa *(G-9712)*
Rose Inc.............G.......918 693-2461
  Sapulpa *(G-8309)*

MAGNETIC TAPE, AUDIO: Prerecorded
Cedar Rdge Rcording Studio LLC.......G.......405 651-5961
  Harrah *(G-3375)*
Computer Solutions + LLC.............G.......405 259-9603
  Choctaw *(G-1534)*
Mark Stevens Industries Inc.............D.......405 948-1077
  Edmond *(G-2504)*

MAGNETS: Ceramic
Midwest Industries Inc.............F.......405 279-2706
  Meeker *(G-4383)*
Tdk Ferrites Corporation.............C.......405 275-2100
  Shawnee *(G-8509)*

MAGNETS: Permanent
Lothrop Technologies Inc.............G.......405 390-3499
  Choctaw *(G-1551)*
Midwest Industries Inc.............G.......405 279-3595
  Meeker *(G-4382)*

MAIL-ORDER HOUSE, NEC
Paia Electronics Inc.............G.......405 340-6300
  Edmond *(G-2559)*

MAIL-ORDER HOUSES: Collectibles & Antiques
Gasoline Alley Classics Inc.............G.......918 806-1000
  Broken Arrow *(G-1128)*

MAIL-ORDER HOUSES: Jewelry
Kathys Kloset Inc.............G.......405 524-9447
  Oklahoma City *(G-6401)*

MAIL-ORDER HOUSES: Tools & Hardware
Native American Capital LLC.............G.......918 289-7489
  Broken Arrow *(G-985)*

MAILBOX RENTAL & RELATED SVCS
Carlsons Rural Mailbox Co.............G.......405 632-7338
  Oklahoma City *(G-5704)*
Hitch N Post LLC.............G.......918 396-9480
  Skiatook *(G-8549)*
UPS Store 6206.............G.......580 248-7800
  Fort Sill *(G-3182)*

MAILING SVCS, NEC
Southwestern Group of Companies.......D.....405 525-9411
  Oklahoma City *(G-7178)*

MANAGEMENT CONSULTING SVCS: Banking & Finance
Jack Henry & Associates Inc.............F.......405 947-6644
  Oklahoma City *(G-6341)*

MANAGEMENT CONSULTING SVCS: Business
Hogan Assessment Systems Inc.......D....918 293-2300
  Tulsa *(G-9937)*
Winfield Solutions LLC.............G.......580 237-2456
  Enid *(G-3082)*

MANAGEMENT CONSULTING SVCS: Business Planning & Organizing
Cbhc Resources Inc.............G.......405 905-9791
  Oklahoma City *(G-5716)*

MANAGEMENT CONSULTING SVCS: Construction Project
Jim Campbell & Associates Rlty.........G....405 372-9225
  Stillwater *(G-8707)*

MANAGEMENT CONSULTING SVCS: Distribution Channels
O Fizz Inc.............F.......918 834-3691
  Tulsa *(G-10370)*

MANAGEMENT CONSULTING SVCS: Industrial
Rocky Mountain Prod Co LLC.............G.......405 720-2000
  Oklahoma City *(G-7046)*

MANAGEMENT CONSULTING SVCS: Industrial & Labor
Wachtman-Schroeder.............G.......918 287-3122
  Pawhuska *(G-7697)*

MANAGEMENT CONSULTING SVCS: Information Systems
Veritris Group Inc.............G.......580 713-4927
  Oklahoma City *(G-7399)*

MANAGEMENT CONSULTING SVCS: Management Engineering
Wombat Labs LLC.............G.......405 355-9662
  Stillwater *(G-8775)*

MANAGEMENT CONSULTING SVCS: Manufacturing
Cutting Edge Technologies LLC.........G....918 284-6069
  Owasso *(G-7558)*

MANAGEMENT CONSULTING SVCS: Planning
Designs By Lex LLC.............G.......580 280-2557
  Lawton *(G-3919)*

MANAGEMENT CONSULTING SVCS: Real Estate
Commercial Property Research.............G.......918 481-8882
  Tulsa *(G-9476)*

MANAGEMENT CONSULTING SVCS: Restaurant & Food
Carlisle Sanitary Maintenance.............G.......405 475-5600
  Oklahoma City *(G-5703)*

MANAGEMENT SERVICES
Patrick Energy Group.............G.......918 477-7755
  Tulsa *(G-10473)*
Petro Speed Inc.............G.......405 364-6785
  Norman *(G-5114)*
Youngman Rock Inc.............F.......918 682-7070
  Muskogee *(G-4759)*

MANAGEMENT SVCS, FACILITIES SUPPORT: Environ Remediation
Energy and Envmtl Svcs Inc.............G.......405 285-8767
  Edmond *(G-2412)*
Mother Earth Eco Entps LLC.............G.......785 250-8706
  Ada *(G-68)*

MANAGEMENT SVCS: Business
Eagle Imaging Management.............G.......405 286-4114
  Oklahoma City *(G-5995)*

MANAGEMENT SVCS: Construction
Advanced Comfort & Energy.............F.......405 329-2237
  Norman *(G-4900)*

MANHOLES COVERS: Concrete
Baray Enterprises Inc.............E.......405 373-1800
  Piedmont *(G-7755)*
GNC Concrete Products Inc.............D.......918 438-1182
  Tulsa *(G-9836)*

MANICURE PREPARATIONS
Allure Salon and Spa LLC.............G.......580 371-9333
  Tishomingo *(G-8961)*
Babe Nail Spa.............G.......918 298-2200
  Tulsa *(G-9250)*
French Nail Spa LLC.............G.......405 843-2080
  Oklahoma City *(G-6117)*
Op Nail.............G.......405 222-1829
  Chickasha *(G-1495)*
Pham Thuy.............G.......918 623-0700
  Okemah *(G-5273)*

MANNEQUINS
Duncan Mannequin Inc.............G.......580 252-5915
  Duncan *(G-2111)*

MANUFACTURED & MOBILE HOME DEALERS
Solitaire Holdings LLC.............G.......580 252-6060
  Duncan *(G-2179)*
Solitaire Homes Inc.............E.......580 252-6060
  Duncan *(G-2180)*

MANUFACTURING INDUSTRIES, NEC
1014 Industries LLC.............G.......405 831-5351
  Guthrie *(G-3295)*
2012 H & H Manufacturing Inc.............G.......918 747-7563
  Tulsa *(G-9057)*
3 D Manufacturing.............G.......918 224-7717
  Sapulpa *(G-8244)*
3I Industries.............G.......580 788-2122
  Elmore City *(G-2893)*
4 B Hunting Industries LLC.............G.......405 823-9100
  Warr Acres *(G-11309)*
4ag Mfg LLC.............G.......580 821-9300
  Elk City *(G-2780)*
A & H Manufacturing.............G.......918 698-0987
  Coweta *(G-1870)*
A-1 Industries LLC.............G.......580 380-2328
  Coleman *(G-1792)*
A-Z Manufacturing LLC.............G.......918 258-2900
  Broken Arrow *(G-811)*
ADC Quality Mfg.............G.......918 808-2329
  Collinsville *(G-1798)*
Adcp Industries LLC.............G.......405 330-4728
  Oklahoma City *(G-5372)*
Aguevent Industries.............G.......580 748-0710
  Cherokee *(G-1413)*
Ala Industries.............G.......405 533-3260
  Stillwater *(G-8653)*
Alan Industries Online.............G.......405 787-1102
  Oklahoma City *(G-5408)*
Alexco Manufacturing LLC.............G.......405 274-4003
  El Reno *(G-2697)*
Allpro Mfg LLC.............G.......580 512-7248
  Tipton *(G-8957)*
American Fiber Industries.............G.......918 335-6100
  Bartlesville *(G-446)*
Ancile Industries.............G.......405 990-5018
  Moore *(G-4489)*
Anderson Rt Industries LLC.............G.......918 607-5150
  Broken Arrow *(G-828)*
Antelope Oil Tool Mfg Co LLC.............G.......405 691-2490
  Oklahoma City *(G-5448)*

Arrow Alliance Industries LLC ... G ... 540 273-1548 Norman *(G-4917)*

Atrue Industries LLC ... G ... 800 782-5440 Lawton *(G-3893)*

Austinn Industries Inc Ncs LLC ... G ... 918 408-2058 Tulsa *(G-9225)*

Auto Way Manufacturing Co LLC ... G ... 405 946-3516 Oklahoma City *(G-5491)*

Axon Industries LLC ... G ... 918 313-8955 Tulsa *(G-9235)*

B & L Industries Inc ... G ... 580 591-1880 Lawton *(G-3895)*

B Brothers Manufacturing LLC ... G ... 918 625-9583 Broken Arrow *(G-840)*

Barnett James ... G ... 405 833-4052 Choctaw *(G-1528)*

Bear Paw Manufacturing ... G ... 918 637-4775 Wagoner *(G-11275)*

Beaver Creek Industries LLC ... G ... 918 469-2779 Kinta *(G-3834)*

Berridge Mfg Dist Ctr ... G ... 405 248-7404 Oklahoma City *(G-5557)*

Bill Jones Mfg ... G ... 405 392-4525 Tuttle *(G-11186)*

Black Star Manufacturing LLC ... G ... 405 315-3336 Chandler *(G-1376)*

Boyer Industries LLC ... G ... 405 310-3015 Norman *(G-4941)*

Bpm LLC ... G ... 405 761-0911 McAlester *(G-4277)*

Bradley Stephen Brown ... G ... 918 639-1853 Oktaha *(G-7530)*

Brier Creek Furn Works LLC ... G ... 903 327-5602 Kingston *(G-3825)*

Brooks Industries LLC ... G ... 405 305-9316 Oklahoma City *(G-5632)*

Broox Creative Industries LLC ... G ... 918 691-8834 Tulsa *(G-8992)*

Budgget Industries Inc ... G ... 918 272-6255 Owasso *(G-7550)*

Buffalo Industries ... G ... 405 720-2324 Oklahoma City *(G-5639)*

By Him Industries LLC ... G ... 918 406-0593 Jenks *(G-3696)*

C R Manufacturing ... G ... 405 780-7368 Stillwater *(G-8664)*

Cairns Manufacturing Inc ... G ... 405 636-4063 Oklahoma City *(G-5669)*

Calico Industries LLC ... G ... 405 732-0638 Midwest City *(G-4437)*

Carters Manufacturing ... G ... 918 437-5428 Tulsa *(G-9384)*

Centermass Industries LLC ... G ... 760 485-7405 Edmond *(G-2342)*

CFM Industries LLC ... G ... 405 213-9557 Edmond *(G-2343)*

Cg Distributors ... G ... 918 336-8882 Bartlesville *(G-460)*

Chemtica USA ... G ... 580 366-6799 Durant *(G-2213)*

Clark Creative Industries Inc ... G ... 405 473-8046 Oklahoma City *(G-5774)*

Clark Seals Ltd ... G ... 918 610-1006 Tulsa *(G-9441)*

Claw Manufacturing LLC ... G ... 918 739-4848 Catoosa *(G-1311)*

Clink Industries ... G ... 918 970-6537 Tulsa *(G-9454)*

Cobo Industries LLC ... G ... 918 574-2123 Tulsa *(G-9463)*

Code Red Industries LLC ... G ... 405 227-1552 Shawnee *(G-8439)*

Colt Ferrell Industries LLC ... G ... 580 439-6106 Comanche *(G-1835)*

Compton Industries LLC ... G ... 405 496-6269 Yukon *(G-11712)*

Conbraco Industries Inc ... G ... 704 841-6000 Westville *(G-11482)*

Continental Industries ... G ... 918 284-9013 Tulsa *(G-9478)*

Copperhead Industries ... G ... 918 712-9927 Tulsa *(G-9485)*

Core Manufacturing LLC ... G ... 405 747-1980 Stillwater *(G-8670)*

Dakk Mfg LLC ... G ... 405 395-2139 Shawnee *(G-8443)*

Dale-Co Industries LLC ... G ... 918 864-2041 Pryor *(G-7958)*

Dashskin LLC ... G ... 918 940-8900 Broken Arrow *(G-887)*

DC Industries ... G ... 405 923-0815 Choctaw *(G-1537)*

Diamond P Machine LLC ... G ... 918 396-7192 Skiatook *(G-8540)*

Divine Thumb Industries Inc ... G ... 405 418-7855 Oklahoma City *(G-5953)*

DMS Terms & Conditions ... G ... 580 303-7500 Duncan *(G-2106)*

Domeck Industries Inc ... G ... 260 833-0917 Tulsa *(G-9593)*

Doodlebugs Etc Inc ... G ... 405 525-1248 Oklahoma City *(G-5968)*

Drake Manufacturing Inc ... G ... 405 760-5336 Shawnee *(G-8445)*

Drake Manufacturing Inc ... G ... 405 799-8157 Oklahoma City *(G-5287)*

Dreyar Industries LLC ... G ... 405 826-2454 Edmond *(G-2396)*

Duct Mate Industries ... G ... 918 340-5122 Wagoner *(G-11279)*

Duke Manufacturing ... G ... 918 653-3404 Heavener *(G-3428)*

Duncan Manufacturing Inc ... G ... 580 251-2137 Duncan *(G-2112)*

Dunlap Manufacturing ... G ... 580 237-3434 Enid *(G-2946)*

Eagle Pump & Mfg LLC ... G ... 918 906-1080 Tulsa *(G-9626)*

Eastern Etching & Mfg ... G ... 918 476-6007 Chouteau *(G-1563)*

Eaves Manufacturing Inc ... G ... 580 889-3530 Atoka *(G-409)*

Eco-Bright Industries LLC ... G ... 918 728-1644 Tulsa *(G-9638)*

Elliott Diversified Inds LLC ... G ... 918 293-2218 Tulsa *(G-9660)*

Elysium Industries ... G ... 405 394-3087 Midwest City *(G-4440)*

Enardo Manufacturing Co ... G ... 918 622-6161 Tulsa *(G-9680)*

Enterprise Manufacturing LLC ... G ... 918 438-4455 Tulsa *(G-9692)*

Et Industries LLC ... G ... 918 485-3374 Wagoner *(G-11283)*

Excel Manufacturing LLC ... G ... 918 418-9589 Vinita *(G-11256)*

F&D Industries LLC ... G ... 918 461-0447 Broken Arrow *(G-904)*

Falcon Mx6 Manufacturing LLC ... G ... 918 647-4433 Poteau *(G-7902)*

Fashion Gear Div ... G ... 405 745-1991 Oklahoma City *(G-6076)*

Fd Products LLC ... G ... 918 698-1644 Vinita *(G-11257)*

Flint Industries ... G ... 918 599-7162 Tulsa *(G-9756)*

Garis Industries LLC ... G ... 405 639-0319 Moore *(G-4525)*

Gold Rule Industries Inc ... G ... 918 682-6500 Muskogee *(G-4681)*

Goodwill Industries of SW ... G ... 580 355-2163 Lawton *(G-3935)*

Gray Eagle Industries LLC ... G ... 918 230-6652 Claremore *(G-1627)*

Green Industries ... G ... 918 825-1044 Pryor *(G-7964)*

Grey Dog Industries LLC ... G ... 405 926-0967 Edmond *(G-2446)*

GTS Industries LLC ... G ... 918 706-2525 Claremore *(G-1630)*

Gwin Industries Inc ... G ... 405 795-4946 Moore *(G-4526)*

H Rockin Industries Inc ... G ... 479 285-1766 Arkoma *(G-385)*

Hacker Industries LLC ... F ... 918 272-6607 Owasso *(G-7573)*

Hadleys Industries ... G ... 405 743-0337 Stillwater *(G-8697)*

Hamilton Industries LLC ... G ... 918 357-3862 Broken Arrow *(G-1130)*

Hannah Industries Inc ... G ... 918 430-0743 Tulsa *(G-9887)*

Harden Metalworks LLC ... G ... 405 812-2812 Norman *(G-5017)*

Hargrove Industries Inc ... G ... 918 231-7290 Sand Springs *(G-8189)*

Hem Mfg ... G ... 918 225-4600 Cushing *(G-1935)*

Hilti Industries Inc ... G ... 918 251-7788 Broken Arrow *(G-929)*

Hix Industries ... G ... 405 640-6980 Wanette *(G-11305)*

Hodges Manufacturing ... G ... 918 629-8723 Sand Springs *(G-8191)*

House Industries LLC ... G ... 405 761-5574 Yukon *(G-11731)*

Hts Manufacturing Corporation ... G ... 918 318-0280 Checotah *(G-1395)*

Hubbard Industries LLC ... G ... 405 388-6798 Oklahoma City *(G-6270)*

Icon Manufacturing LLC ... G ... 903 819-9091 Durant *(G-2237)*

Ikg Industries ... G ... 918 599-8417 Tulsa *(G-9969)*

Inland Manufacturing LLC ... G ... 918 697-4436 Broken Arrow *(G-938)*

Integrated Training & Mfg Tech ... G ... 918 893-2225 Broken Arrow *(G-939)*

Isbell Industries LLC ... G ... 405 828-7228 Dover *(G-2040)*

Issken Industries Inc ... G ... 405 623-2177 Stillwater *(G-8705)*

J T G Industries LLC ... G ... 405 285-6627 Edmond *(G-2466)*

J&C Industries Inc ... G ... 405 473-7834 Piedmont *(G-7764)*

Jacobson Fabrication Inc ... G ... 918 251-1181 Broken Arrow *(G-941)*

Jaf Industries LLC ... G ... 405 834-8362 Oklahoma City *(G-6345)*

Jay Industries LLC ... G ... 405 404-3242 Midwest City *(G-4444)*

Jedd Industries ... G ... 580 339-1500 Hinton *(G-3530)*

Jester Industries Inc ... G ... 405 919-2013 Oklahoma City *(G-6360)*

JM Manufacturing ... G ... 918 261-2816 Broken Arrow *(G-947)*

K & D Manufacturing ... G ... 918 923-6422 Claremore *(G-1648)*

K G Hill Company LLC ... G ... 405 641-4190 Norman *(G-5046)*

K3 Industries LLC ... G ... 205 568-1252 Oklahoma City *(G-5298)*

Kjm Industries LLC ... G ... 405 340-1448 Edmond *(G-2481)*

Kmac Manufacturing LLC ... G ... 918 272-6856 Owasso *(G-7583)*

L&L Manufacturing ... G ... 405 436-8929 Newalla *(G-4811)*

Lakelife Industries LLC ... G ... 918 618-6201 Eufaula *(G-3104)*

Last Ditch Industries LLC ... G ... 405 609-2317 Oklahoma City *(G-6454)*

Laxson Industries LLC ... G ... 918 494-6677 Tulsa *(G-10138)*

Lda Industries LLC ... G ... 918 315-9758 Sallisaw *(G-8147)*

Littrell Industries LLC ... G ... 405 637-8930 Edmond *(G-2489)*

Lkq Remanufacturing Yukon ... G ... 405 494-4908 Yukon *(G-11742)*

Mainstream Manufacturing LLC ... G ... 918 447-1008 Tulsa *(G-10203)*

Manufctring Contract Solutions ... G ... 405 229-7639 Moore *(G-4536)*

Maranatha Industries LLC ... G ... 918 336-1221 Bartlesville *(G-508)*

Mardav Industries Co LLC ... G ... 855 248-2220 Oklahoma City *(G-6522)*

Martinez Industries LLC ... G ... 405 503-4020 Harrah *(G-3380)*

Mbs Manufacturing Inc ... G ... 918 521-6865 Broken Arrow *(G-1142)*

McElroy Manufacturing Inc ... G ... 918 254-7182 Broken Arrow *(G-969)*

Mena Manufacturing ... G ... 918 955-0518 Tulsa *(G-10242)*

Metal Goods Manufacturing ... G ... 918 633-9069 Tulsa *(G-10245)*

Mfg Unlimited LLC ... G ... 405 788-9567 Oklahoma City *(G-6583)*

Mid America Vending Inc ... G ... 405 387-4441 Newcastle *(G-4831)*

Midco Sand Pump Manufacturing ... G ... 405 824-2620 Oklahoma City *(G-6595)*

Military Parts Mfg LLC ... G ... 405 301-2990 Yukon *(G-11755)*

Mimic Manufacturing LLC ... G ... 918 653-7161 Heavener *(G-3430)*

PRODUCT SECTION

MARKING DEVICES: Screens, Textile Printing

Mostly Missiles .... G 405 808-4611
  Edmond *(G-2521)*
Mpl Manufacturing LLC .... G 918 630-9944
  Broken Arrow *(G-983)*
Mr Mfg .... G 918 352-4461
  Drumright *(G-2067)*
Mtm Inc .... G 918 824-3700
  Pryor *(G-7977)*
Mulberry Tree Graphics .... G 580 248-3194
  Lawton *(G-3974)*
Netpro Industries Inc .... G 918 630-3201
  Broken Arrow *(G-987)*
Nickles Industries .... G 580 762-9300
  Ponca City *(G-7859)*
Northfork Marine Manufacturing ... G 918 689-9309
  Eufaula *(G-3107)*
Ohana Manufacturing LLC .... G 918 490-9053
  Eufaula *(G-3108)*
Oil Pro Industries .... G 405 323-6988
  Oklahoma City *(G-6718)*
Oiltech Manufacturing Div LLC .... G 918 534-3568
  Bartlesville *(G-514)*
OK Casting .... G 918 648-5300
  Burbank *(G-1215)*
Ok-1 Manufacturing Co .... G 580 482-0891
  Altus *(G-165)*
Oliver Industries LLC .... G 405 314-4423
  Norman *(G-5102)*
Onpoint Manufacturing .... G 580 284-5431
  Cashion *(G-1292)*
Orcutt Machine .... G 918 629-7930
  Tulsa *(G-10438)*
Oscium .... G 719 695-0600
  Oklahoma City *(G-6786)*
Ottawa Oak Mfg .... G 918 541-8996
  Wyandotte *(G-11661)*
Outlaw Industries LLC .... G 918 569-7555
  Clayton *(G-1710)*
Peak Industries .... G 918 289-0424
  Tulsa *(G-10479)*
Pfl Industries Ltd Co .... G 405 388-0321
  Spencer *(G-8599)*
Pierce Industries Inc .... G 405 923-4201
  Edmond *(G-2569)*
Pj Industries Inc .... G 918 682-8479
  Muskogee *(G-4735)*
Potter Industries .... G 580 775-8580
  Durant *(G-2247)*
Ppm Manufacturing LLC .... G 405 843-4448
  Oklahoma City *(G-6872)*
Precision Industries Ic T .... G 918 833-6072
  Tulsa *(G-10547)*
Project 3810 LLC .... G 405 834-7418
  Oklahoma City *(G-6914)*
Protrac Industries LLC .... G 405 312-5122
  Yukon *(G-11769)*
R K Manufacturing LLC .... G 405 626-8922
  Tuttle *(G-11209)*
R&C Industries LLC .... G 405 640-7239
  Oklahoma City *(G-6964)*
Rank Industries LLC .... G 405 308-0503
  Blanchard *(G-730)*
RCO Fabrication LLC .... G 918 225-0708
  Cushing *(G-1952)*
RDS Manufacturing .... G 918 251-0369
  Broken Arrow *(G-1026)*
Redtail Industries LLC .... G 405 933-6654
  Anadarko *(G-206)*
Rehme Mfg Inc .... F 580 658-2414
  Marlow *(G-4240)*
Rehoboth Robes .... G 918 357-1529
  Broken Arrow *(G-1155)*
Resource Mfg .... G 405 842-0999
  Oklahoma City *(G-7011)*
Rohm-Bolster Mfg Co LLC .... G 405 274-6915
  Oklahoma City *(G-7047)*
Royal Toga Industries LLC .... G 405 641-1643
  Broken Arrow *(G-1158)*
Rt Manufacturing Concepts LLC ..... G 405 388-3999
  Oklahoma City *(G-5314)*
S&F Welding and Mfg LLC .... G 580 341-0790
  Hobart *(G-3545)*
Saber Industries .... G 405 382-3975
  Oklahoma City *(G-7071)*
Sara Smith Inc .... G 918 272-3076
  Owasso *(G-7613)*
Saunders Industries LLC .... G 405 728-3555
  Oklahoma City *(G-7086)*
Scotts Wldg & Fabrication LLC .... G 580 236-2990
  Broken Bow *(G-1204)*

SDS Industries LLC .... G 918 863-3740
  Tulsa *(G-10719)*
Sentient Industries Inc .... G 918 770-0770
  Owasso *(G-7616)*
Short Work Industries Inc .... G 580 774-8563
  Weatherford *(G-11441)*
Skyrock Industries LLC .... G 660 525-7482
  Oklahoma City *(G-7148)*
Slow Hand Manufacturing LLC .... G 580 618-0867
  Afton *(G-122)*
Slow Hand Manufacturing L .... G 918 937-3046
  Norman *(G-5148)*
Sooner Pro Assembly .... G 405 838-2838
  Norman *(G-5150)*
Spiral Waves Industries LLC .... G 405 481-7685
  Shawnee *(G-8503)*
Ssec .... G 405 321-0916
  Norman *(G-5154)*
Starfall Llc .... G 918 269-4364
  Coweta *(G-1898)*
Streater Industries LLC .... G 918 346-3247
  Oologah *(G-7536)*
Stroup Industries LLC .... G 405 737-4170
  Midwest City *(G-4457)*
Sub Industries LLC .... G 918 798-9712
  Elk City *(G-2879)*
Superior Steel Bldg Mfg LLC .... G 918 689-9745
  Eufaula *(G-3116)*
Swift Winds Industries LLC .... G 405 600-9112
  Oklahoma City *(G-7237)*
Taptec Manufacturing LLC .... G 580 467-5142
  Marlow *(G-4244)*
Tefi Tek Industries LLC .... G 918 728-7381
  Tulsa *(G-10917)*
Ten Mfg LLC .... G 405 381-3752
  Tuttle *(G-11215)*
Texas Aluminum Industries .... G 405 677-6767
  Oklahoma City *(G-7277)*
Texoma Mfg LLC .... G 580 920-0878
  Durant *(G-2265)*
Tj Trost LLC .... G 918 269-1582
  Coweta *(G-1900)*
Tom McBride Manufacturing .... G 580 239-9020
  Caney *(G-1264)*
Trb Industries LLC .... G 405 990-4159
  Choctaw *(G-1556)*
Triple H Industries LLC .... G 405 201-8820
  Sulphur *(G-8845)*
Tulsa Industrial Mfg LLC .... G 918 640-3802
  Owasso *(G-7628)*
US Rod Manufacturing LLC .... G 636 359-9447
  Oklahoma City *(G-7375)*
Valor Industries LLC .... G 580 301-3805
  Piedmont *(G-7773)*
Verde Industries LLC .... G 405 413-5599
  Oklahoma City *(G-7398)*
Warrior Industries Inc .... G 918 227-3500
  Sapulpa *(G-8323)*
Weldpro Manufacturing LLC .... G 918 724-3862
  Tulsa *(G-11106)*
Westfall Industries Inc .... G 520 744-2330
  Arcadia *(G-232)*
Whit Industries .... G 405 343-1181
  Ada *(G-106)*
White Shell LLC .... G 918 978-2767
  Broken Arrow *(G-1177)*
Wichita Industries .... G 405 933-2162
  Anadarko *(G-209)*
Wilkinson Mfg Co .... G 918 258-8282
  Broken Arrow *(G-1097)*
Wilsdorf Manufacturing LLC .... G 918 369-5824
  Broken Arrow *(G-1098)*
Withers Manufacturing Inc .... F 918 994-7787
  Tulsa *(G-11142)*
Workhorse Industries LLC .... G 405 884-2023
  Geary *(G-3218)*
Ws Mfg LLC .... G 918 443-2773
  Oologah *(G-7537)*
Yona Mfg Solutions LLC .... G 918 698-9713
  Claremore *(G-1707)*
Zedco LLC .... G 918 521-7587
  Tulsa *(G-11174)*
Zero Hour Industries Inc .... G 918 685-0235
  Gore *(G-3253)*

MAPS

Dynamic Mapping Solutions Inc ..... G 918 446-7803
  Tulsa *(G-9617)*

MARBLE, BUILDING: Cut & Shaped

Allied Stone Inc .... E 580 931-3388
  Durant *(G-2201)*
American Marble .... G 918 812-7940
  Tulsa *(G-9169)*
Classic Marble Design Inc .... G 580 323-4917
  Clinton *(G-1744)*
Conway Custom Marble Co .... G 580 357-3757
  Lawton *(G-3910)*
Crawford Granite Works .... G 918 423-3020
  McAlester *(G-4288)*
Grecian Marble & Granite LLC .... F 405 632-3802
  Oklahoma City *(G-6185)*
Millers Marble and Granite .... G 580 357-1348
  Lawton *(G-3971)*
Professional Marble Company .... G 918 225-5364
  Cushing *(G-1950)*

MARINAS

Bratco Operating Company .... F 918 534-2322
  Dewey *(G-2018)*

MARINE BASIN OPERATIONS

Kole Inc .... G 918 782-3001
  Ketchum *(G-3774)*

MARINE CARGO HANDLING SVCS: Loading

Mt Vernon Coal Transfer Co .... F 918 295-7600
  Tulsa *(G-10311)*

MARINE REPORTING SVCS

Iap Worldwide Services Inc .... F 321 784-7100
  Oklahoma City *(G-6282)*

MARKETS: Meat & fish

Don Regier .... G 580 772-3510
  Weatherford *(G-11405)*
Kilgore Meat Processing Plant .... G 918 967-2613
  Stigler *(G-8635)*
M & M Custom Butchering .... G 918 542-6421
  Miami *(G-4410)*
Thompsons Custom Butcher Barn ... G 918 476-5508
  Chouteau *(G-1572)*

MARKING DEVICES

American Engraving & Trophy .... G 405 360-2744
  Norman *(G-4906)*
Custom Identification Products .... G 405 745-1010
  Oklahoma City *(G-5873)*
Layle Company Corporation .... G 405 329-5143
  Norman *(G-5056)*
Rowmark LLC .... E 405 787-4542
  Oklahoma City *(G-7051)*
Rusco Plastics .... G 580 234-1596
  Enid *(G-3053)*
Trophies n Things .... G 405 247-9771
  Anadarko *(G-207)*
US Fleet Tracking LLC .... E 405 726-9900
  Edmond *(G-2660)*

MARKING DEVICES: Date Stamps, Hand, Rubber Or Metal

Southern Rubber Stamp Co Inc .... G 918 587-3818
  Tulsa *(G-10801)*

MARKING DEVICES: Embossing Seals & Hand Stamps

A-OK Rubber Stamp .... G 580 357-2822
  Lawton *(G-3882)*
Beacon Stamp & Seal Co .... G 918 834-2322
  Tulsa *(G-9276)*
Walker Stamp & Seal Co .... E 405 235-5319
  Oklahoma City *(G-7415)*

MARKING DEVICES: Screens, Textile Printing

Dsignz Custom Screen Printing .... G 405 375-6806
  Kingfisher *(G-3796)*
Texoma Engraving LLC .... G 580 775-7333
  Durant *(G-2264)*

MARKING DEVICES: Seal Presses, Notary & Hand

Aars .... G 918 313-4512
Tulsa (G-9080)

MARKING DEVICES: Time Stamps, Hand, Rubber Or Metal

Robinhood Stamp & Seal Co Inc .... G 918 493-6506
Tulsa (G-10664)

MASSAGE PARLORS

Supercuts Inc .... G 918 775-6389
Sallisaw (G-8154)

MASTIC ROOFING COMPOSITION

Black Thunder Roofing LLC .... G 405 473-8028
Oklahoma City (G-5582)

MATERIAL GRINDING & PULVERIZING SVCS NEC

Ace Grinding .... G 918 439-4113
Tulsa (G-9094)
Tulsa Centerless Bar Proc Inc .... E 918 438-0000
Tulsa (G-10992)

MATERIALS HANDLING EQPT WHOLESALERS

Mid Continent Lift and Eqp LLC .... F 580 255-3867
Duncan (G-2155)

MATTRESS RENOVATING & REPAIR SHOP

Mobility Living Inc .... G 405 672-7237
Oklahoma City (G-6623)

MATTRESS STORES

Montgomery Mattress .... G 580 255-8979
Duncan (G-2156)

MEAT & MEAT PRDTS WHOLESALERS

Kilgore Meat Processing Plant .... G 918 967-2613
Stigler (G-8635)

MEAT CUTTING & PACKING

Alex Rogers .... G 405 677-2306
Oklahoma City (G-5412)
B & B Butlers Custom Process .... G 580 795-2667
Madill (G-4144)
Barnsdall Meat Processors Inc .... G 918 847-2814
Barnsdall (G-436)
Bob Mc Kinney & Sons .... G 918 387-2401
Cushing (G-1924)
Browns Meat Processing .... G 405 379-2979
Holdenville (G-3550)
Butchs Processing Plant Inc .... G 405 382-2833
Seminole (G-8361)
Cable Meat Center Inc .... F 580 658-6646
Marlow (G-4224)
Circle D Meat .... G 580 921-5500
Laverne (G-3876)
Cook Processing .... G 918 542-5796
Miami (G-4392)
Country Home Meat Company .... G 405 341-0267
Edmond (G-2368)
Cuts Custom Butchering LLC .... G 918 534-1382
Dewey (G-2019)
Don Regier .... G 580 772-3510
Weatherford (G-11405)
Double D Foods Inc .... F 405 245-8909
Oklahoma City (G-5970)
Fort Cobb Locker Plant .... G 405 643-2355
Fort Cobb (G-3171)
Four State Meat Processing LLC .... F 918 783-5556
Big Cabin (G-604)
Gage Locker Service .... G 580 923-7661
Gage (G-3210)
Hilltop Custom Processing .... G 405 527-7048
Lexington (G-4035)
Janice Sue Daniel .... G 580 237-2695
Enid (G-2981)
Janice Sue Daniel .... G 580 233-8666
Enid (G-2982)
Kilgore Meat Processing Plant .... G 918 967-2613
Stigler (G-8635)
Lawton Meat Processing .... G 580 353-6448
Lawton (G-3957)
Lopez Foods Inc .... E 405 789-7500
Oklahoma City (G-6494)
M & M Custom Butchering .... G 918 542-6421
Miami (G-4410)
O H S N Inc .... E 580 248-1299
Lawton (G-3977)
Okeen Motel .... G 580 822-4491
Okeene (G-5261)
Prairie Rose Processing Inc .... G 405 224-6429
Chickasha (G-1500)
Ralphs Packing Company .... E 405 547-2464
Perkins (G-7721)
Ray Meat Market .... G 580 256-6031
Woodward (G-11627)
Rowlands Proc & Cattle Co .... F 580 924-2560
Durant (G-2253)
Sallee Meat Processing Inc .... G 405 282-1241
Guthrie (G-3336)
Schones Butcher Shop & Market .... G 580 472-3300
Canute (G-1270)
Seaboard Farms Inc .... G 580 338-4900
Guymon (G-3363)
Sooner Food Group LLC .... G 703 791-9069
Newalla (G-4816)
Stinebrings Custom Processing .... G 405 828-4247
Dover (G-2045)
Temple Custom Slaughter & Proc .... G 580 342-5031
Temple (G-8936)
Tenderette Steak Co Inc .... F 405 634-5655
Oklahoma City (G-7268)
Thompsons Custom Butcher Barn ...... G 918 476-5508
Chouteau (G-1572)
Tonkawa Meat Processing .... G 580 628-4550
Tonkawa (G-8983)
Tyson Foods Inc .... G 918 723-5091
Westville (G-11487)
Tyson Foods Inc .... E 405 379-7241
Holdenville (G-3561)
W R Meat Co .... G 580 622-2494
Sulphur (G-8846)
Walke Brothers Meats Inc .... G 918 341-3236
Claremore (G-1704)
Weavers Meat Processing Inc .... G 918 647-9832
Poteau (G-7917)

MEAT MARKETS

Barnsdall Meat Processors Inc .... G 918 847-2814
Barnsdall (G-436)
Cable Meat Center Inc .... F 580 658-6646
Marlow (G-4224)
Country Home Meat Company .... G 405 341-0267
Edmond (G-2368)
Janice Sue Daniel .... G 580 237-2695
Enid (G-2981)
Janice Sue Daniel .... G 580 233-8666
Enid (G-2982)
Ray Meat Market .... G 580 256-6031
Woodward (G-11627)
Ridleys Butcher Shop Inc .... G 580 255-9330
Duncan (G-2169)
Rowlands Proc & Cattle Co .... F 580 924-2560
Durant (G-2253)
Tonkawa Meat Processing .... G 580 628-4550
Tonkawa (G-8983)
Walke Brothers Meats Inc .... G 918 341-3236
Claremore (G-1704)

MEAT PRDTS: Cooked Meats, From Purchased Meat

Advance Food Company Inc .... C 800 969-2747
Enid (G-2905)
Bruce Packing Company Inc .... G 503 874-3000
Durant (G-2210)

MEAT PRDTS: Cured, From Slaughtered Meat

Robertsons Hams Inc .... F 580 276-3395
Marietta (G-4211)

MEAT PRDTS: Dried Beef, From Purchased Meat

Bulldog Jerky Co .... G 580 479-5542
Grandfield (G-3256)

Davis Morgan International .... G 405 598-2380
Macomb (G-4141)

MEAT PRDTS: Pork, From Slaughtered Meat

Seaboard Corporation .... G 580 468-3790
Guymon (G-3362)
Seaboard Foods LLC .... G 580 338-4900
Guymon (G-3365)

MEAT PRDTS: Prepared Beef Prdts From Purchased Beef

Hardtimes Real Beef Jerky Inc .... E 580 497-7695
El Reno (G-2723)
Kormondy Enterprises Inc .... B 918 274-8787
Owasso (G-7584)
Lopez Foods Inc .... B 405 499-0131
Oklahoma City (G-6493)
Lopez Foods Inc .... E 405 789-7500
Oklahoma City (G-6494)
Lopez Foods Inc .... B 405 789-7500
Oklahoma City (G-6495)

MEAT PRDTS: Sausages, From Purchased Meat

Blue & Gold Sausage Inc .... G 405 399-2954
Jones (G-3742)

MEAT PRDTS: Smoked

B&L Smoked Meats .... G 580 641-1677
Marlow (G-4222)
Robertsons Hams Inc .... F 580 276-3395
Marietta (G-4211)
Slow N Low Smoked Meats .... G 918 946-6894
Tulsa (G-10775)

MEAT PRDTS: Snack Sticks, Incl Jerky, From Purchased Meat

Big Ricks Jerky LLC .... G 405 414-9096
Oklahoma City (G-5565)
Double J Beef Jerky .... G 580 476-2465
Rush Springs (G-8120)
GOAT Beef Jerky Co LLC .... G 405 627-5096
Oklahoma City (G-6164)
Goodtimes Beef Jerky .... G 405 387-5448
Newcastle (G-4829)
Mikes Famous Beef Jerky .... G 405 414-7501
Chickasha (G-1489)
No Mans Land Foods LLC .... D 580 297-5142
Boise City (G-748)
Pine Cove Jerky LLC .... G 918 872-1138
Broken Arrow (G-1007)

MEAT PROCESSED FROM PURCHASED CARCASSES

Advance Food Company Inc .... A 580 237-6656
Enid (G-2906)
Alex Rogers .... G 405 677-2306
Oklahoma City (G-5412)
B & B Butlers Custom Process .... G 580 795-2667
Madill (G-4144)
Bar-S Foods Co .... A 580 331-1628
Clinton (G-1740)
Bar-S Foods Co .... G 405 303-2138
Seminole (G-8357)
Bar-S Foods Co .... C 580 821-5700
Altus (G-144)
Bar-S Foods Co .... B 580 510-3300
Lawton (G-3896)
Barnsdall Meat Processors Inc .... G 918 847-2814
Barnsdall (G-436)
Bob Mc Kinney & Sons .... G 918 387-2401
Cushing (G-1924)
Cable Meat Center Inc .... F 580 658-6646
Marlow (G-4224)
Circle D Meat .... G 580 921-5500
Laverne (G-3876)
Country Home Meat Company .... G 405 341-0267
Edmond (G-2368)
Cuts Custom Butchering LLC .... G 918 534-1382
Dewey (G-2019)
Don Regier .... G 580 772-3510
Weatherford (G-11405)
Dustys Jerky LLC .... G 405 702-8016
Oklahoma City (G-5991)

PRODUCT SECTION

MEDICAL, DENTAL & HOSPITAL EQPT, WHOLESALE: Med Eqpt & Splys

Hilltop Custom Processing .... G....... 405 527-7048
  Lexington *(G-4035)*
Janice Sue Daniel .... G....... 580 233-8666
  Enid *(G-2982)*
Jiggs Smokehouse .... G....... 580 323-5641
  Clinton *(G-1754)*
Kilgore Meat Processing Plant .... G....... 918 967-2613
  Stigler *(G-8635)*
M & M Custom Butchering .... G....... 918 542-6421
  Miami *(G-4410)*
Mc Ferrons Quality Meats Inc .... F....... 918 273-2892
  Nowata *(G-5220)*
McLane Foodservice Dist Inc .... C....... 405 632-0118
  Oklahoma City *(G-6549)*
National Steak Processors LLC .... D....... 918 274-8787
  Owasso *(G-7596)*
OSteen Meat Specialties Inc .... D....... 405 236-1952
  Oklahoma City *(G-6787)*
Prairie Rose Processing Inc .... G....... 405 224-6429
  Chickasha *(G-1500)*
Ray Meat Market .... G....... 580 256-6031
  Woodward *(G-11627)*
Ridleys Butcher Shop Inc .... G....... 580 255-9330
  Duncan *(G-2169)*
Rowlands Proc & Cattle Co .... F....... 580 924-2560
  Durant *(G-2253)*
Sallee Meat Processing Inc .... G....... 405 282-1241
  Guthrie *(G-3336)*
Seaboard Farms Inc .... F....... 580 338-3311
  Guymon *(G-3364)*
Temple Custom Slaughter & Proc .... G....... 580 342-5031
  Temple *(G-8936)*
Thompsons Custom Butcher Barn .... G....... 918 476-5508
  Chouteau *(G-1572)*
Tonkawa Meat Processing .... G....... 580 628-4550
  Tonkawa *(G-8983)*
Unrau Meat Co Inc .... G....... 918 543-8245
  Inola *(G-3676)*
Walke Brothers Meats Inc .... G....... 918 341-3236
  Claremore *(G-1704)*

MEAT PROCESSING MACHINERY

Bar-S Foods Co .... B....... 580 510-3300
  Lawton *(G-3896)*
Schones Butcher Shop & Market .... G....... 580 472-3300
  Canute *(G-1270)*
Swift Eckrich Inc .... G....... 918 258-4565
  Broken Arrow *(G-1069)*

MECHANISMS: Coin-Operated Machines

Crankshaft Service Company .... G....... 405 685-7553
  Oklahoma City *(G-5851)*

MEDIA BUYING AGENCIES

Rbi Advertising .... G....... 918 592-1836
  Tulsa *(G-10624)*

MEDIA: Magnetic & Optical Recording

Andre Anderson .... G....... 405 642-3210
  Moore *(G-4490)*
Benson Sound Inc .... G....... 405 610-7455
  Oklahoma City *(G-5553)*
Broken Arrow Productions Inc .... E....... 405 360-8702
  Norman *(G-4944)*
Indel-Davis Inc .... F....... 918 587-2151
  Tulsa *(G-9976)*

MEDICAL & HOSPITAL EQPT WHOLESALERS

Usut Labs Inc .... G....... 918 459-3844
  Tulsa *(G-11061)*

MEDICAL & SURGICAL SPLYS: Braces, Orthopedic

Brace Place .... G....... 405 858-5200
  Oklahoma City *(G-5623)*
Lux Orthotics & Prosthetics .... G....... 417 624-2332
  Wyandotte *(G-11660)*
Maris Health LLC .... G....... 888 429-1117
  Tulsa *(G-10209)*
Rowdy Hanger .... G....... 918 804-7375
  Broken Arrow *(G-1038)*

MEDICAL & SURGICAL SPLYS: Hydrotherapy

Body Connection LLC .... G....... 580 745-9201
  Durant *(G-2208)*

MEDICAL & SURGICAL SPLYS: Limbs, Artificial

Anthony W Layton Cpo .... G....... 580 353-8885
  Lawton *(G-3890)*
Celerity Prosthetics LLC .... G....... 405 605-3030
  Oklahoma City *(G-5721)*
Hanger Prsthetcs & Ortho Inc .... G....... 479 484-1620
  Enid *(G-2968)*
Hanger Prsthetcs & Ortho Inc .... G....... 918 333-6900
  Bartlesville *(G-489)*
Patriot Prsthtics Orthtics Inc .... G....... 405 577-6778
  Yukon *(G-11764)*
Tim Carlton Prosthetics Inc .... G....... 405 721-7570
  Oklahoma City *(G-7291)*
Total Care Orthtics Prsthtics .... G....... 918 502-5975
  Tulsa *(G-10959)*

MEDICAL & SURGICAL SPLYS: Orthopedic Appliances

Celerity Orthotcs & Prosthetcs .... G....... 405 605-3030
  Oklahoma City *(G-5720)*
Jobri LLC .... F....... 580 925-3500
  Ada *(G-54)*
Lawton Brace & Limb Co Inc .... G....... 580 353-5525
  Lawton *(G-3954)*
Orthotics Pros Inc .... G....... 918 296-3567
  Jenks *(G-3721)*
Pro TEC Orthotics Company .... G....... 405 366-7688
  Norman *(G-5123)*
Progressive Orthotic .... G....... 918 786-7701
  Tulsa *(G-10570)*
Progressive Orthotic & PR .... G....... 918 681-2346
  Tulsa *(G-10571)*
Tgg Prosthetics Orthotics LLC .... G....... 405 285-5499
  Edmond *(G-2639)*

MEDICAL & SURGICAL SPLYS: Personal Safety Eqpt

Hard Hat Safety and Glove LLC .... G....... 405 942-9500
  Oklahoma City *(G-6217)*
Parra World Creations LLC .... G....... 918 938-2278
  Tulsa *(G-10470)*

MEDICAL & SURGICAL SPLYS: Prosthetic Appliances

A X-Ceptional Quality Dntl Lab .... G....... 918 406-1835
  Tulsa *(G-9071)*
Fenner Inc .... G....... 918 832-7768
  Tulsa *(G-9737)*
Hanger Prsthtics Orthotics Inc .... G....... 918 687-1855
  Muskogee *(G-4687)*
Prosthetics By Wade .... G....... 918 850-7544
  Broken Arrow *(G-1012)*
Scott Sabolich Prosthetics & R .... E....... 405 841-6800
  Oklahoma City *(G-7098)*

MEDICAL & SURGICAL SPLYS: Respiratory Protect Eqpt, Personal

Air Inspired Home Medical .... F....... 918 299-3037
  Glenpool *(G-3229)*

MEDICAL & SURGICAL SPLYS: Supports, Abdominal, Ankle, Etc

Texoma Orthtics Prsthtics Pllc .... G....... 580 699-8690
  Lawton *(G-4012)*

MEDICAL & SURGICAL SPLYS: Technical Aids, Handicapped

Bruno Ind Living Aids Inc .... G....... 405 964-5887
  McLoud *(G-4355)*
Work Activity Center Inc .... E....... 405 799-6911
  Moore *(G-4584)*

MEDICAL & SURGICAL SPLYS: Trusses, Orthopedic & Surgical

Applications For Medicine LLC .... G....... 405 330-7910
  Edmond *(G-2306)*

MEDICAL & SURGICAL SPLYS: Walkers

A Walker Electric .... G....... 918 232-6023
  Chelsea *(G-1399)*

MEDICAL & SURGICAL SPLYS: Welders' Hoods

Pemco Inc .... G....... 918 341-7500
  Claremore *(G-1669)*
Steel Systems Plus Inc .... G....... 918 286-7947
  Broken Arrow *(G-1167)*

MEDICAL CENTERS

Eden Clinic Inc .... G....... 405 579-4673
  Norman *(G-4988)*

MEDICAL EQPT: Diagnostic

Advanced Medical Instrs Inc .... C....... 918 250-0566
  Broken Arrow *(G-816)*
Immuno-Mycologics Inc .... F....... 405 360-4669
  Norman *(G-5030)*
Immy Africa LLC .... F....... 405 360-4669
  Norman *(G-5031)*
Sinties Corporation .... E....... 918 359-2000
  Tulsa *(G-10768)*

MEDICAL EQPT: Electrotherapeutic Apparatus

Millennial Technologies LLC .... G....... 405 478-4351
  Oklahoma City *(G-6611)*

MEDICAL EQPT: MRI/Magnetic Resonance Imaging Devs, Nuclear

Advanced Imaging Resources Co .... G....... 918 609-5250
  Broken Arrow *(G-815)*

MEDICAL EQPT: Patient Monitoring

American Intrprtive Monitoring .... G....... 405 841-7826
  Oklahoma City *(G-5437)*

MEDICAL EQPT: Ultrasonic, Exc Cleaning

Usut Labs Inc .... G....... 918 459-3844
  Tulsa *(G-11061)*

MEDICAL EQPT: X-Ray Apparatus & Tubes, Radiographic

Sullins International Inc .... G....... 918 258-5460
  Broken Arrow *(G-1067)*
Wesco Enterprises Inc .... G....... 918 449-1081
  Broken Arrow *(G-1096)*

MEDICAL FIELD ASSOCIATION

Tulsa County Medical Society .... G....... 918 743-6184
  Tulsa *(G-10995)*

MEDICAL, DENTAL & HOSPITAL EQPT, WHOL: Hosptl Eqpt/Furniture

R F Lindgren Enclosures Inc .... G....... 918 299-7572
  Tulsa *(G-10603)*

MEDICAL, DENTAL & HOSPITAL EQPT, WHOLESALE: Hearing Aids

All American Ear Mold Labs .... F....... 405 285-2411
  Edmond *(G-2295)*

MEDICAL, DENTAL & HOSPITAL EQPT, WHOLESALE: Med Eqpt & Splys

Adroit Surgical LLC .... G....... 425 577-2713
  Nichols Hills *(G-4854)*
Cardinal Health 200 LLC .... C....... 918 865-4727
  Mannford *(G-4177)*
Mobility Living Inc .... G....... 405 672-7237
  Oklahoma City *(G-6623)*

Employee Codes: A=Over 500 employees, B=251-500
C=101-250, D=51-100, E=20-50, F=10-19, G=1-9

MEDICAL, DENTAL & HOSPITAL EQPT, WHOLESALE: Med Eqpt & Splys

Smith & Nephew Inc .... C 405 917-8500
  Oklahoma City (G-7154)
Thomas Dist Solutions LLC .... G 580 304-7741
  Ponca City (G-7883)

MEDICAL, DENTAL & HOSPITAL EQPT, WHOLESALE: Oxygen Therapy

O2 Concepts LLC .... E 877 867-4008
  Oklahoma City (G-6706)

MEDICAL, DENTAL & HOSPITAL EQPT, WHOLESALE: Safety

Hard Hat Safety and Glove LLC .... G 405 942-9500
  Oklahoma City (G-6217)

MEDICAL, DENTAL & HOSPITAL EQPT, WHOLESALE: Therapy

B & B Medical Services Inc .... E 919 601-4756
  Oklahoma City (G-5499)

MEMBERSHIP ORGANIZATIONS, BUSINESS: Contractors' Association

Continental Stoneworks Inc .... F 918 835-6725
  Tulsa (G-9479)

MEMBERSHIP ORGANIZATIONS, BUSINESS: Merchants' Association

Oklahoma Restaurant Assn .... F 405 942-8181
  Oklahoma City (G-6761)

MEMBERSHIP ORGANIZATIONS, BUSINESS: Public Utility Assoc

Oklahoma Assn of Elc Coop .... E 405 478-1455
  Oklahoma City (G-6735)

MEMBERSHIP ORGANIZATIONS, NEC: Charitable

J E & L E Mabee Foundation .... F 918 584-4286
  Tulsa (G-10019)

MEMBERSHIP ORGANIZATIONS, PROF: Education/Teacher Assoc

American Choral Directors Assn .... F 405 232-8161
  Oklahoma City (G-5434)

MEMBERSHIP ORGANIZATIONS, RELIGIOUS: Baptist Church

Kingsview Freewill Baptist Ch .... G 405 692-1554
  Oklahoma City (G-5302)

MEN'S & BOYS' CLOTHING ACCESS STORES

Titanium Phoenix Inc .... G 405 305-1304
  Oklahoma City (G-7294)

MEN'S & BOYS' CLOTHING WHOLESALERS, NEC

Emery Bay Corporation .... G 918 494-2988
  Tulsa (G-9671)
Rainbow Spreme Assmbly I O R G .... G 918 423-1328
  McAlester (G-4331)
Speedys TS & More LLC .... G 580 748-0067
  Alva (G-192)

MEN'S & BOYS' SPORTSWEAR CLOTHING STORES

All-Star Trophies & Ribbon Mfg .... G 918 283-2200
  Claremore (G-1581)

MEN'S & BOYS' SPORTSWEAR WHOLESALERS

American Sportswear Inc .... G 918 665-7636
  Tulsa (G-9172)
Hendrie Resources Ltd .... G 405 948-4459
  Oklahoma City (G-6239)
Massive Graphic Screen Prtg .... F 405 364-3594
  Norman (G-5066)

Paul Ziert & Associates Inc .... D 405 364-5344
  Norman (G-5112)

MERCHANDISING MACHINE OPERATORS: Vending

Pinball Doctor .... G 918 582-3130
  Tulsa (G-10515)

METAL & STEEL PRDTS: Abrasive

Albright Steel and Wire Co .... G 580 357-3596
  Lawton (G-3886)

METAL CUTTING SVCS

Baskins Machined Products LLC .... G 918 284-4298
  Collinsville (G-1802)

METAL FABRICATORS: Architechtural

Ace Fence Co .... G 918 682-7895
  Muskogee (G-4641)
American Iron .... G 405 414-2629
  Norman (G-4908)
Angel Ornamental Iron Works .... G 918 584-8726
  Tulsa (G-9191)
B & W Manufacturing Co Ltd .... F 918 248-5201
  Tulsa (G-8989)
Balco Inc .... E 316 945-9328
  Oklahoma City (G-5519)
Beeman Products Co Inc .... G 918 251-1432
  Broken Arrow (G-845)
Berryhill Ornamental Iron LLC .... G 918 258-6531
  Broken Arrow (G-846)
Custom Design By Roberts .... G 918 664-0466
  Tulsa (G-9528)
D & M Steel Manufacturing .... G 405 631-5027
  Oklahoma City (G-5887)
Diw Engineering Fabrication LLC .... E 918 534-0001
  Dewey (G-2020)
Eastpointe Manufacturing Corp .... E 918 683-2169
  Muskogee (G-4671)
Econofab Piping Inc .... F 918 267-5901
  Beggs (G-552)
Ernest Wiemann Iron Works .... G 918 592-1700
  Tulsa (G-9698)
Goodwill Inds Centl Okla Inc .... D 405 236-4451
  Oklahoma City (G-6172)
H & H Ornamental Iron .... G 405 634-0646
  Oklahoma City (G-6196)
Henderson Ornamental Iron .... G 918 341-1089
  Claremore (G-1634)
Iron Horse Metal Works .... G 918 333-8877
  Bartlesville (G-498)
Ironcraft Urban Products LLC .... G 855 601-1647
  Oklahoma City (G-6327)
J&M Stainless Fabricators Ltd .... G 405 517-0875
  Oklahoma City (G-6340)
Kaydawn Manufacturing Co Inc .... G 918 321-5017
  Glenpool (G-3237)
L & M Fabrication .... G 918 825-7145
  Pryor (G-7973)
Liberty Fence Co Inc .... G 918 834-6553
  Tulsa (G-10156)
Longs Excavating .... G 918 782-2235
  Langley (G-3872)
Merrells Welding & Orna Ir .... G 405 321-7733
  Norman (G-5073)
Metal Fab Inc .... G 580 762-2421
  Ponca City (G-7850)
Metallic Works Inc .... G 918 527-6477
  Tulsa (G-10248)
Mikes Welding .... G 918 455-7227
  Broken Arrow (G-975)
Mitchco Fabrication Inc .... G 580 762-0256
  Ponca City (G-7853)
Mitchell Ironworks Inc .... G 580 233-7925
  Enid (G-3014)
Mosley Backhoe Service .... G 405 567-4710
  Prague (G-7931)
Oklahoma Metal Creations LLC .... G 580 917-5434
  Fletcher (G-3165)
Oklahoma Stair Craft Inc .... F 918 446-1456
  Sapulpa (G-8293)
Old World Iron .... G 405 722-0008
  Oklahoma City (G-6771)
Old World Iron Inc .... G 918 445-3063
  Tulsa (G-10411)
Perryton Iron and Metal LLC .... G 580 256-5536
  Woodward (G-11620)

Premiercraft Incorporated .... F 405 600-9339
  Oklahoma City (G-6887)
Pro Stainless & Shtmtl LLC .... G 405 787-4400
  Oklahoma City (G-6906)
Royal Ironworks .... G 580 492-4265
  Edmond (G-2605)
Tulsa Ornamental Iron Works .... G 918 274-7253
  Owasso (G-7629)
Zephyr Southwest Orna LLC .... E 918 251-4133
  Broken Arrow (G-1104)

METAL FABRICATORS: Plate

A R T T Corp .... G 405 681-0749
  Oklahoma City (G-5348)
Air-X-Hemphill LLC .... G 918 283-9220
  Claremore (G-1578)
Aw Specialties LLC .... G 918 798-9272
  Claremore (G-1584)
Balco Inc .... E 316 945-9328
  Oklahoma City (G-5519)
Berry Holdings LP .... G 918 582-3461
  Tulsa (G-9285)
Butner Brothers LLC .... G 405 321-2322
  Norman (G-4949)
Bynum & Company Inc .... F 580 265-7747
  Stonewall (G-8798)
Chart Industries Inc .... G 918 621-5246
  Tulsa (G-9406)
Considilated Fabrications .... G 918 224-3563
  Tulsa (G-8997)
Cundiff Custom Fabrication LLC .... G 405 372-8204
  Stillwater (G-8673)
Custom Seating Incorporated .... C 918 682-4400
  Muskogee (G-4666)
D-K Metal Form Company Inc .... G 580 228-3516
  Waurika (G-11362)
Davco Fab Inc .... E 918 757-2504
  Jennings (G-3739)
Dragon .... G 580 653-2171
  Springer (G-8623)
E-Tech Inc .... E 918 665-1930
  Broken Arrow (G-1124)
Ellen Broach CPA .... G 918 665-7773
  Tulsa (G-9658)
Ellis Construction Spc LLC .... E 405 848-4676
  Oklahoma City (G-6026)
Express Metal Fabricators Inc .... D 918 783-5129
  Big Cabin (G-603)
F C Ziegler Co .... E 918 587-7639
  Tulsa (G-9721)
Fab Seal Industrial Liners Inc .... F 405 878-0166
  Shawnee (G-8449)
G C Broach Company .... D 918 627-9632
  Tulsa (G-9790)
G C Broach Company .... D 918 627-9632
  Tulsa (G-9791)
Genesis Metal Corporation .... F 918 267-5901
  Beggs (G-557)
Harsco Corporation .... E 918 619-8000
  Tulsa (G-9898)
Heartland Tank Services .... G 800 774-3230
  Oklahoma City (G-6234)
Hill Metal Inc .... G 405 375-6284
  Kingfisher (G-3801)
JC Fab LLC .... F 580 920-0878
  Durant (G-2240)
John Crane Inc .... D 918 664-5156
  Tulsa (G-10049)
Johnson Wldg & Fabrication LLC .... G 405 474-3541
  Tuttle (G-11205)
Kelvion Inc .... E 918 416-9058
  Catoosa (G-1326)
Lewis Industries Corp .... E 918 371-2596
  Collinsville (G-1815)
Linde Engineering N Amer LLC .... C 918 477-1424
  Tulsa (G-10164)
Luxfer-GTM Technologies LLC .... F 918 439-4248
  Catoosa (G-1335)
Madden Steel Buildings Lawton .... G 580 357-1699
  Lawton (G-3968)
Metal Fab Inc .... G 580 762-2421
  Ponca City (G-7850)
Metro Mechanical Supply Inc .... F 918 622-2288
  Tulsa (G-10251)
Midco Fabricators Inc .... E 405 282-6667
  Guthrie (G-3324)
Msc Inc .... G 918 425-4996
  Tulsa (G-10309)
Nixon Materials Company .... G 580 621-3297
  Freedom (G-3208)

Old World Iron Inc....G....918 445-3063
Tulsa *(G-10411)*
Phelps Machine & Fabrication....F....580 662-2465
Ringling *(G-8081)*
Pro-Fab Industries Inc....E....918 865-7590
Mannford *(G-4190)*
Reading Equipment & Dist LLC....E....918 283-2999
Claremore *(G-1679)*
Safeco Manufacturing Inc....F....918 455-0100
Broken Arrow *(G-1160)*
Seal Support Systems Inc....F....918 258-6484
Broken Arrow *(G-1046)*
Southwest Filter Company....G....918 835-1179
Tulsa *(G-10808)*
Susan L Chung Chirprtr....G....405 773-8225
Oklahoma City *(G-7233)*
Tank Specialties Inc....F....918 599-8111
Tulsa *(G-10898)*
True Turn of Tulsa LLC....F....918 224-5040
Tulsa *(G-10980)*
Tsi-Enquip Inc....E....918 599-8111
Tulsa *(G-10983)*
Vernon Manufacturing Company....G....918 224-4068
Tulsa *(G-9048)*
Wagner Plate Works LLC....G....918 447-4488
Tulsa *(G-11090)*
Wastequip Manufacturing Co LLC....E....580 924-1575
Durant *(G-2272)*

METAL FABRICATORS: Sheet

4-Star Trailers Inc....C....405 324-7827
Oklahoma City *(G-5331)*
A B Curbs Inc....G....405 427-1222
Oklahoma City *(G-5344)*
A-1 Sheet Metal Inc....F....918 835-6200
Tulsa *(G-9073)*
Acme Manufacturing Corporation....G....800 647-8671
Claremore *(G-1576)*
Advanced Fabrication Svcs LLC....G....405 339-4867
Oklahoma City *(G-5381)*
Adventure Manufacturing Inc....G....405 682-3833
Oklahoma City *(G-5387)*
Agilis Group LLC....E....918 584-3553
Tulsa *(G-9117)*
Airflow Solutions LLC....E....918 574-2748
Tulsa *(G-9129)*
Allstate Sheet Metal Inc....F....405 636-1914
Oklahoma City *(G-5422)*
Andy Anderson Metal Works Inc....F....918 245-2355
Sand Springs *(G-8161)*
Apollo Metal Specialties Inc....F....918 341-7650
Claremore *(G-1583)*
Archer Technologies Intl Inc....G....405 306-3220
Shawnee *(G-8428)*
Awnique....G....405 818-8032
Oklahoma City *(G-5497)*
Axiom Metal Solutions LLC....G....918 361-5982
Okmulgee *(G-7494)*
B & B Sheet Metal Heat & A Inc....G....918 371-1335
Collinsville *(G-1801)*
Ba Manufacturing LLC....G....239 246-3606
Broken Arrow *(G-842)*
Balco Inc....E....316 945-9328
Oklahoma City *(G-5519)*
Big River Sales Inc....G....580 657-4950
Lone Grove *(G-4115)*
Boxel LLC....G....580 239-0819
Atoka *(G-400)*
Braden Shielding Systems Const....E....918 624-2888
Tulsa *(G-9327)*
Breshears Enterprises Inc....F....405 236-4523
Oklahoma City *(G-5624)*
Briggs Rainbow Buildings Inc....C....918 683-3695
Muskogee *(G-4655)*
Butchers Metal Shop....G....580 256-7660
Woodward *(G-11565)*
Bynum & Company Inc....F....580 265-7747
Stonewall *(G-8798)*
Capes Custom Welding & Fabrica....G....918 453-0594
Tahlequah *(G-8855)*
Captive-Aire Systems Inc....D....918 686-6717
Muskogee *(G-4658)*
CCL Acquisition LLC....D....918 739-4400
Catoosa *(G-1309)*
Cherokee Nation Red Wing LLC....E....918 430-3437
Tulsa *(G-9414)*
Choctaw Mfg & Dev Corp....D....580 326-8365
Hugo *(G-3607)*
Choctaw Nation of Oklahoma....D....580 326-8365
Hugo *(G-3610)*

Clinco Mfg LLC....G....580 759-3434
Ada *(G-25)*
CMI Terex Corporation....A....405 787-6020
Oklahoma City *(G-5792)*
Contech Enterprises LLC....F....918 341-6232
Claremore *(G-1609)*
Contech Mfg Inc....G....918 341-6232
Claremore *(G-1610)*
Copper Accents By Jerry....G....918 724-8473
Bixby *(G-618)*
Cundiff Custom Fabrication LLC....G....405 372-8204
Stillwater *(G-8673)*
Custom Storm Shelters LLC....G....405 209-5525
Oklahoma City *(G-5876)*
D & L Enclosures....G....918 396-7355
Skiatook *(G-8538)*
Darrell Monroe....F....405 793-2976
Moore *(G-4513)*
David Muzny....G....405 681-7593
Oklahoma City *(G-5904)*
Diw Engineering Fabrication LLC....E....918 534-0001
Dewey *(G-2020)*
Earl Bannon....G....405 236-8829
Oklahoma City *(G-5998)*
Eastern Sheet Metal Co Inc....G....918 687-6231
Muskogee *(G-4669)*
Elk City Sheet Metal Inc....G....580 225-5844
Elk City *(G-2810)*
Eric Turner....G....918 423-7330
McAlester *(G-4295)*
Ets-Lindgren Inc....E....580 434-7490
Durant *(G-2230)*
Expanded Solutions LLC....E....405 946-6791
Wewoka *(G-11501)*
Fabricating Specialists Inc....F....405 476-1959
Oklahoma City *(G-6068)*
Fabrication Dynamics Inc....G....918 446-1638
Tulsa *(G-9722)*
Fammco Mfg Co Inc....G....918 437-0456
Tulsa *(G-9727)*
Gary Green Cement Construction....G....405 527-5606
Purcell *(G-8008)*
General Plastics Inc....F....405 275-3171
Shawnee *(G-8453)*
Glover Sheet Metal Inc....E....405 619-7117
Edmond *(G-2437)*
Hindman Metal Fabricators....G....918 251-3949
Broken Arrow *(G-930)*
Holman Manufacturing....F....918 479-5861
Locust Grove *(G-4109)*
Honeycutt Contruction Inc....F....918 825-6070
Pryor *(G-7969)*
Ideas Manufacturing Inc....G....405 691-5525
Oklahoma City *(G-5296)*
J C Sheet Metal Fabrication....G....405 787-1902
Oklahoma City *(G-6335)*
Johnson Welding....G....580 569-2231
Mountain Park *(G-4626)*
K and E Fabrication....G....405 635-8552
Oklahoma City *(G-6393)*
Kenneth Petermann....G....405 372-0111
Stillwater *(G-8710)*
Keymiaee Aero-Tech Inc....F....405 235-5010
Oklahoma City *(G-6409)*
Kice Industries Inc....E....580 363-2850
Blackwell *(G-685)*
L & M Fabrication....G....918 825-7145
Pryor *(G-7973)*
Laser Specialities Inc....E....918 760-5690
Tulsa *(G-9016)*
Linde Engineering N Amer LLC....E....918 266-5700
Catoosa *(G-1331)*
Los Angeles Boiler Works Inc....E....580 363-1312
Blackwell *(G-688)*
Love Air Conditioning....G....918 341-0508
Claremore *(G-1651)*
Luther Industries LLC....G....405 819-0346
Blanchard *(G-720)*
M & M Fabrication & Service....G....405 677-1982
Oklahoma City *(G-6506)*
Mac Machine....G....405 238-7280
Pauls Valley *(G-7666)*
Matherly Mechanical Contrs LLC....C....405 737-3488
Midwest City *(G-4446)*
MBI Industrial Inc....F....405 387-4003
Tuttle *(G-11206)*
McCutchen Enterprises Inc....G....918 234-7406
Tulsa *(G-10231)*
McPherson Implement Inc....F....405 321-6292
Norman *(G-5067)*

Metal Fab Inc....G....580 762-2421
Ponca City *(G-7850)*
Metalform Inc....F....918 585-8300
Tulsa *(G-10247)*
Metalspand Inc....F....580 228-2393
Waurika *(G-11363)*
Metro Mechanical Supply Inc....F....918 622-2288
Tulsa *(G-10251)*
Midco Fabricators Inc....E....405 282-6667
Guthrie *(G-3324)*
Mueller Supply Company Inc....G....918 485-2034
Wagoner *(G-11288)*
Old World Iron Inc....G....918 445-3063
Tulsa *(G-10411)*
Paul G Pennington Industries....G....405 392-2317
Blanchard *(G-726)*
Penn Aluminum Inc....G....405 476-5222
Yukon *(G-11765)*
Penny Sheet Metal LLC....F....918 251-6911
Broken Arrow *(G-1002)*
Philip R Eckart....G....580 917-3882
Fletcher *(G-3166)*
Phils Ornamental Iron Inc....G....918 786-2979
Grove *(G-3285)*
Pro Stainless & Shtmtl LLC....G....405 787-4400
Oklahoma City *(G-6906)*
R & J Aluminum Products....G....580 355-1809
Lawton *(G-3987)*
R F Lindgren Enclosures Inc....G....918 299-7572
Tulsa *(G-10603)*
Ross Dub Company Inc....E....405 495-3611
Oklahoma City *(G-7049)*
S-T Magi....G....918 358-2312
Cleveland *(G-1733)*
Sharp Metal Fabricators Inc....F....405 899-4849
Noble *(G-4891)*
Shielding Resources Group....F....918 663-1985
Tulsa *(G-10746)*
Smith Welding Fabg & Repr....G....918 446-2293
Tulsa *(G-10779)*
Sooner Machine & Equipment Co....G....405 794-6833
Moore *(G-4572)*
Southern Specialties Corp....E....918 584-3553
Tulsa *(G-10803)*
SPX Heat Transfer LLC....C....918 234-6000
Tulsa *(G-10827)*
Steel Queen Inc....G....405 949-1664
Oklahoma City *(G-7199)*
T Town Sheet Metal....G....918 437-4756
Tulsa *(G-10893)*
Treat Metal Stamping Inc....G....405 275-3344
Shawnee *(G-8512)*
Trojan Livestock Equipment....G....580 772-1849
Weatherford *(G-11451)*
Tulsa Copper Specialties....G....918 249-4809
Tulsa *(G-10994)*
Valco Inc....E....405 228-0932
Duncan *(G-2191)*
Valco Inc....E....405 228-0932
Oklahoma City *(G-7386)*
Vann Metal Products Inc....G....918 341-0469
Claremore *(G-1701)*
Ventaire LLC....E....918 622-1191
Tulsa *(G-11070)*
Ventaire Corporation....G....918 622-1191
Tulsa *(G-11071)*
Vernon Sheet Metal....G....580 658-6778
Marlow *(G-4246)*
Vogt Sheet Metal....G....580 332-2454
Ada *(G-102)*
W L Walker Co Inc....E....918 583-3109
Tulsa *(G-11089)*
Wagner Plate Works LLC....G....918 447-4488
Tulsa *(G-11090)*
Werco Manufacturing Inc....E....918 251-6880
Broken Arrow *(G-1095)*
Western Seamless Guttering....G....580 225-7983
Elk City *(G-2890)*
Wright Comfort Solutions Inc....G....580 688-3586
Hollis *(G-3572)*
York Metal Fabricators Inc....E....405 528-7495
Oklahoma City *(G-7481)*

METAL FABRICATORS: Structural, Ship

Cnc Metal Shape Cnstr LLC....F....405 605-5500
Oklahoma City *(G-5794)*
Laughing Water Enterprises LLC....G....918 584-2080
Tulsa *(G-10136)*

Employee Codes: A=Over 500 employees, B=251-500
C=101-250, D=51-100, E=20-50, F=10-19, G=1-9
2020 Oklahoma Directory
of Manufacturers & Processors
773

METAL FINISHING SVCS

METAL FINISHING SVCS

Applied Indus Coatings LLC ....E...... 405 692-2249
  Oklahoma City *(G-5455)*
Finishing Technology Inc ....G...... 918 437-3820
  Tulsa *(G-9746)*
Friction Solutions LLC ....G...... 918 622-8989
  Tulsa *(G-9778)*
Northrup Metals LLC ....G...... 918 225-2100
  Cushing *(G-1948)*
Pride Plating Inc ....D...... 918 786-6111
  Grove *(G-3286)*
Topps Powder Coating ....E...... 405 794-2900
  Moore *(G-4578)*
Tulsa Metal Finishers Inc ....G...... 918 241-1290
  Sand Springs *(G-8232)*
Tulsa Metal Finishing Company ....F...... 918 609-5410
  Tulsa *(G-11002)*

METAL MINING SVCS

Buckley Powder Company ....F...... 580 384-5547
  Mill Creek *(G-4467)*
Pontotoc Sands Company LLC ....E...... 580 777-2735
  Stonewall *(G-8802)*

METAL SERVICE CENTERS & OFFICES

Big River Sales Inc ....G...... 580 657-4950
  Lone Grove *(G-4115)*
Desert Moon Enterprises ....G...... 918 540-0333
  Miami *(G-4395)*
Kloeckner Metals Corporation ....E...... 918 660-2050
  Catoosa *(G-1329)*

METAL STAMPING, FOR THE TRADE

Action Spring Company ....E...... 918 836-9000
  Tulsa *(G-9097)*
Avery Barron Industries ....G...... 918 834-6647
  Tulsa *(G-9230)*
Interstate Tool & Mfg Co ....E...... 918 834-6647
  Tulsa *(G-10008)*
Midland Stamping and Fabg Corp ......F...... 918 446-1458
  Tulsa *(G-10263)*
Precision Metal Fab LLC ....E...... 580 762-2421
  Ponca City *(G-7868)*
Precision Tool & Die Ponca Cy ....G...... 580 762-2421
  Ponca City *(G-7869)*
Progressive Stamping LLC ....E...... 405 996-5347
  Oklahoma City *(G-6913)*

METAL STAMPINGS: Ornamental

Hot Stuff Airbrush Inc ....G...... 918 249-0458
  Tulsa *(G-9954)*
Sooner State Spring Mfg Co ....G...... 918 476-5707
  Chouteau *(G-1570)*

METAL STAMPINGS: Patterned

Coman Pattern Works ....D...... 918 270-1775
  Tulsa *(G-9473)*

METALS SVC CENTERS & WHOL: Structural Shapes, Iron Or Steel

Railroad Yard Inc ....E...... 405 377-8763
  Stillwater *(G-8743)*

METALS SVC CENTERS & WHOLESALERS: Pipe & Tubing, Steel

Kingfisher Pipe Sales and Svc ....G...... 405 262-4422
  El Reno *(G-2733)*
Ops Sales Company ....G...... 918 534-3760
  Dewey *(G-2029)*
Taylor & Sons Farms Inc ....G...... 405 222-0751
  Chickasha *(G-1515)*

METALS SVC CENTERS & WHOLESALERS: Reinforcement Mesh, Wire

Oklahoma Post Tension Inc ....F...... 918 627-6013
  Tulsa *(G-10405)*

METALS SVC CENTERS & WHOLESALERS: Rope, Wire, Exc Insulated

Assocted Wire Rope Fabricators ....G...... 918 234-7450
  Tulsa *(G-9219)*

METALS SVC CENTERS & WHOLESALERS: Steel

Accu Cast ....G...... 918 582-3466
  Tulsa *(G-9088)*
Albright Steel and Wire Co ....F...... 405 232-7526
  Oklahoma City *(G-5410)*
Albright Steel and Wire Co ....G...... 580 357-3596
  Lawton *(G-3886)*
Alliance Steel Inc ....C...... 405 745-7500
  Oklahoma City *(G-5420)*
Alro Steel Corporation ....F...... 918 439-1000
  Tulsa *(G-9156)*
Collins Metal Company Inc ....G...... 405 373-3309
  Warr Acres *(G-11316)*
D & B Processing LLC ....F...... 918 619-6452
  Broken Arrow *(G-1119)*
Hill Metal Inc ....G...... 405 375-6284
  Kingfisher *(G-3801)*
Insight Technologies Inc ....F...... 580 933-4109
  Valliant *(G-11226)*
J & I Manufacturing Inc ....E...... 580 795-7377
  Madill *(G-4150)*
Kloeckner Metals Corporation ....E...... 918 266-1666
  Catoosa *(G-1328)*
Metals USA Plates and Shap ....E...... 918 682-7833
  Muskogee *(G-4713)*
Monson Associates Inc ....G...... 918 298-0037
  Tulsa *(G-10300)*
Taylor & Sons Pipe and Stl Inc ....F...... 405 222-0751
  Chickasha *(G-1516)*

METALS SVC CENTERS & WHOLESALERS: Tubing, Metal

J & J Tubulars Inc ....G...... 405 691-2039
  Oklahoma City *(G-6330)*
Webco Industries Inc ....G...... 918 581-0900
  Sand Springs *(G-8236)*
Webco Industries Inc ....G...... 918 836-1188
  Tulsa *(G-11100)*
Webco Industries Inc ....B...... 918 245-2211
  Sand Springs *(G-8237)*

METALS SVC CENTERS/WHOL: Forms, Steel Concrete Construction

Post-Tension Services of Okla ....F...... 405 751-1582
  Oklahoma City *(G-6866)*

METALS SVC CTRS & WHOLESALERS: Aluminum Bars, Rods, Etc

Brown Metals ....G...... 405 321-6866
  Norman *(G-4946)*
Clinco Mfg LLC ....G...... 580 759-3434
  Ada *(G-25)*

METALS: Precious NEC

Heartland Precious Metals ....G...... 405 254-6870
  Edmond *(G-2454)*

METALS: Precious, Secondary

Dastar Inc ....G...... 580 786-8833
  Duncan *(G-2104)*

METALS: Primary Nonferrous, NEC

Allied Manufacturing Tech ....G...... 918 899-9504
  Tulsa *(G-9150)*
Elemetal ....G...... 405 605-2402
  Oklahoma City *(G-6023)*
Magnesium Products Inc ....F...... 918 587-9930
  Tulsa *(G-9018)*

METALWORK: Miscellaneous

Aerostar International Inc ....G...... 918 789-3000
  Chelsea *(G-1401)*
C and C Manufacturing LLC ....G...... 918 288-6558
  Sperry *(G-8606)*
Forbes Enterprises Inc ....G...... 580 564-2599
  Kingston *(G-3828)*
Honeycutt Contruction Inc ....F...... 918 825-6070
  Pryor *(G-7969)*
J&K Machining Inc ....G...... 918 243-7936
  Cleveland *(G-1725)*
J&M Stainless Fabricators Ltd ....G...... 405 517-0875
  Oklahoma City *(G-6340)*
Mayhem Cstm Fbrcation Wldg LLC ....G...... 405 406-5160
  Newalla *(G-4814)*
Premier Business Solutions LLC ....G...... 405 650-3131
  Meeker *(G-4385)*
Premiercraft Incorporated ....F...... 405 600-9339
  Oklahoma City *(G-6887)*
Tms International LLC ....G...... 918 241-0129
  Sand Springs *(G-8230)*
War Metals Inc ....G...... 918 224-2155
  Tulsa *(G-9050)*
War Metals Inc ....G...... 918 629-8057
  Tulsa *(G-11095)*

METALWORK: Ornamental

Apollo Ornamental Iron LLC ....E...... 405 672-5377
  Oklahoma City *(G-5454)*
Osiyo Medals Inc ....F...... 918 258-4717
  Broken Arrow *(G-995)*
Phils Ornamental Iron Inc ....G...... 918 786-2979
  Grove *(G-3285)*
Wassco Corporation ....F...... 918 834-4444
  Tulsa *(G-11097)*
Werco Manufacturing Inc ....E...... 918 251-6880
  Broken Arrow *(G-1095)*

METALWORKING MACHINERY WHOLESALERS

Industrial Enterprise Inc ....G...... 918 476-5907
  Chouteau *(G-1567)*

METERS: Liquid

Weamco Incorporated ....E...... 918 445-1141
  Sapulpa *(G-8324)*

MGMT CONSULTING SVCS: Matls, Incl Purch, Handle & Invntry

Ameracrane and Hoist LLC ....E...... 918 437-4775
  Tulsa *(G-9161)*

MICROPROCESSORS

Legacy Advnced Intllctuals LLC ....G...... 707 358-0332
  Tulsa *(G-10148)*

MICROPUBLISHER

Jamey H Voorhees ....G...... 479 599-9921
  Stillwater *(G-8706)*

MILITARY INSIGNIA, TEXTILE

Ultra Thin Inc ....E...... 405 794-7892
  Moore *(G-4582)*

MILLING: Chemical

Choctaw Nation of Oklahoma ....D...... 580 326-8365
  Hugo *(G-3610)*

MILLING: Grains, Exc Rice

Stockmans Mill & Grain Inc ....G...... 918 762-3459
  Pawnee *(G-7711)*

MILLWORK

12 Acre Woodwork LLC ....G...... 405 328-0655
  Chandler *(G-1372)*
Aaron Custom Creations ....G...... 580 603-0467
  Enid *(G-2902)*
AC Woodworks Inc ....G...... 918 298-6948
  Tulsa *(G-9085)*
AC Woodworks Inc DBA Wood ....G...... 918 384-0111
  Tulsa *(G-9086)*
Ace Hardware ....G...... 580 225-0100
  Elk City *(G-2781)*
All Wood Products Co Inc ....E...... 918 585-9739
  Tulsa *(G-9138)*
American Millwork Company Inc ....E...... 405 681-5347
  Oklahoma City *(G-5440)*
Andrews Woodworking ....G...... 918 664-6722
  Tulsa *(G-9190)*
B & C Custom Woodworks ....G...... 918 830-2416
  Tulsa *(G-9241)*
B&C Custom Woodworks LLC ....G...... 918 639-2416
  Tulsa *(G-9241)*
Bobs Wood Working ....G...... 405 632-4894
  Oklahoma City *(G-5604)*
Cabinet Doors Unlimited ....F...... 918 257-5765
  Afton *(G-114)*

Company	Code	Phone
Caston Architectural Mllwk Inc	E	405 843-6652
Oklahoma City (G-5711)		
Cavanal Woodworks	G	909 649-4346
Poteau (G-7900)		
Centerpiece Custom Wdwkg LLC	G	405 387-9312
Blanchard (G-706)		
Cherokee Woodwork Inc	G	918 798-5037
Tulsa (G-9416)		
Contemporary Cabinets Inc	D	405 330-4592
Edmond (G-2365)		
Copes Woodworking	G	918 698-2104
Tulsa (G-9484)		
Crawson Corporation	F	918 427-8400
Muldrow (G-4633)		
Creekside Woodworks	G	405 528-5432
Oklahoma City (G-5854)		
Croan Custom Woodworks LLC	G	405 227-2067
Edmond (G-2374)		
Crosby Custom Woodwork	G	405 802-9615
Moore (G-4512)		
Custom Cutting Millwork Inc	F	405 942-3196
Oklahoma City (G-5872)		
Custom Seating Incorporated	C	918 682-4400
Muskogee (G-4666)		
Custom Wood Creations	G	580 512-6994
Lawton (G-3915)		
Custom Wood Creations LLC	G	405 517-8689
Crescent (G-1911)		
Custom Wood Works	G	918 279-1333
Coweta (G-1877)		
Cutting Edge Woodwork LLC	G	918 706-1143
Skiatook (G-8537)		
Dale P Jackson	F	580 332-1988
Ada (G-29)		
Die Tech Tool Machine	G	918 683-3422
Okay (G-5257)		
Display With Honor Wdwkg LLC	G	405 659-9894
Oklahoma City (G-5286)		
Egr Construction Inc	E	405 943-0900
Oklahoma City (G-6013)		
Elite Wood Creations LLC	G	580 220-1153
Ardmore (G-284)		
Estey Cabinet Door Co	E	405 771-3004
Spencer (G-8595)		
Eubankswoodworks LLC	G	918 245-7835
Sand Springs (G-8182)		
Extraordinary Woodworks	G	801 995-0906
Enid (G-2956)		
Fadco of Arkansas LLC	G	918 832-1641
Tulsa (G-9726)		
For His Glory Cutting Boards	G	918 633-7233
Tulsa (G-9764)		
Forrest Valentine	G	580 309-2190
Custer City (G-1974)		
Furrs Custom Woodwork	G	918 406-7021
Bixby (G-624)		
Gemini Woodworks	G	405 630-8586
Jones (G-3746)		
Gps Woodworks LLC	G	405 399-2369
Jones (G-3747)		
Grain and Grit Woodworks LLC	G	405 250-6824
Oklahoma City (G-6175)		
Green Cntry Cstm Woodworks LLC	G	918 585-1040
Tulsa (G-9858)		
Gurley Custom Woodwork	G	580 235-3350
Ada (G-46)		
Hansen Millwork & Trim Inc	E	405 239-2564
Oklahoma City (G-6214)		
Hardwood Innovations Inc	F	405 722-5588
Oklahoma City (G-6219)		
Huerecas Woodworking LLC	G	580 302-2687
Weatherford (G-11418)		
Hughes Lumber Company	G	918 266-9100
Catoosa (G-1322)		
Hugo Wyrick Lumber	E	580 326-5569
Hugo (G-3614)		
Integrity Custom Mill Works	G	405 495-9732
Spencer (G-8596)		
J & Js Wdwrk HM Decor & Gifts	G	918 420-9411
McAlester (G-4307)		
J & S Woodworking Inc	G	405 619-9910
Oklahoma City (G-6333)		
J B Woodworking	G	918 760-2399
Bristow (G-781)		
J&Js Woodwork and More	G	918 429-9704
McAlester (G-4308)		
Japa Corp	G	918 893-6763
Broken Arrow (G-943)		
Johnsonwoodworks	G	918 407-7447
Tulsa (G-10057)		
Jts Woodworks LLC	G	918 640-1791
Broken Arrow (G-951)		
Kaonohi Woodworks	G	918 893-4661
Broken Arrow (G-954)		
Kc Woodwork & Fixture Inc	G	918 582-5300
Tulsa (G-10078)		
Kelly L Young	G	918 859-1046
Skiatook (G-8555)		
Knock On Wood Custom	G	918 261-6948
Claremore (G-1650)		
Kohns Doors & Woodworking LLC	G	405 596-8245
Piedmont (G-7766)		
Ksquared Woodworks LLC	G	918 496-3681
Tulsa (G-10104)		
Lakewood Cabinetry Inc	F	918 782-2203
Langley (G-3871)		
Lindsay Woodworks	G	405 370-9712
Choctaw (G-1550)		
M1 Woodworks	G	405 923-4144
Edmond (G-2499)		
Mastercraft Millwork Inc	G	405 895-6050
Moore (G-4537)		
McElyea Custom Woodworking LLC	G	918 332-7651
Bartlesville (G-510)		
McMurtry Cabinet Shop	G	405 627-3275
Oklahoma City (G-6550)		
Mez Woodworks LLC	G	405 589-5408
Edmond (G-2517)		
Mh Woodworking LLC	G	405 799-2661
Moore (G-4540)		
Mill Work Specialties LLC	G	918 639-8385
Tulsa (G-10280)		
Mystik River Woodworks	G	580 606-0071
Comanche (G-1843)		
Naked Wood Works	G	918 864-0229
Broken Arrow (G-984)		
Nicnik Woodworks	G	703 474-7994
Choctaw (G-1552)		
Nolan Custom Woodwork	G	918 576-1158
Tulsa (G-10347)		
Note-Able Workshop LLC	G	918 801-2725
Grove (G-3281)		
Note-Able Workshop LLC	G	918 801-2725
Grove (G-3282)		
Nxt Lvl Woodworking LLC	G	405 613-6637
Norman (G-5096)		
Oconnell Woodworks LLC	G	918 805-7233
Broken Arrow (G-992)		
Oklahoma City Shutter Co Inc	F	405 787-1234
Oklahoma City (G-6742)		
Okrusticwoodworks	G	405 562-0371
Guthrie (G-3331)		
Oro Woodworks	G	405 334-7445
Stillwater (G-8734)		
Paramount Building Pdts LLC	G	405 470-5073
Oklahoma City (G-6804)		
Parker Kustom Woodworking	G	405 414-2820
Del City (G-2005)		
Pawnee Millworks LLC	G	918 767-2565
Pawnee (G-7707)		
Perma-Strong Wood Products Inc	E	405 449-3376
Wayne (G-11369)		
Quality Woodworks Inc	G	918 944-3314
Muskogee (G-4741)		
Rar Wood Works LLC	G	205 233-2920
Broken Arrow (G-1022)		
RC Custom Woodwork	G	405 414-1162
Norman (G-5130)		
Red Dirt Wood Works LLC	G	918 640-5917
Edmond (G-2588)		
Redbird Woodworks	G	918 227-5938
Sapulpa (G-8306)		
Redbud Woodworks	G	316 765-4079
Midwest City (G-4451)		
Rescue Lumber & Wdwkg LLC	G	405 650-4637
Edmond (G-2597)		
Reynolds Custom Woodworks	G	918 595-5988
Claremore (G-1681)		
Rico Woodworking LLC	G	918 743-0741
Tulsa (G-10651)		
Rkb Woodworks	G	405 919-4149
Oklahoma City (G-7030)		
Rockin Wood LLC	G	405 673-5171
Oklahoma City (G-7045)		
S & S Woodworks Inc	G	405 627-8195
Edmond (G-2609)		
S Coker Custom Woodworks	G	918 638-3443
Broken Arrow (G-1042)		
Sanderson Custom Woodworks	G	918 361-1921
Tulsa (G-10704)		
Sandy Creek Millworks Inc	G	405 288-0670
Washington (G-11336)		
Scarab Woodworking LLC	G	405 612-2111
Stillwater (G-8753)		
Shellback Woodworks	G	918 851-3992
Bristow (G-796)		
Shofner Custom Wood	G	405 787-5768
Bethany (G-594)		
Skykae Kreations	G	405 250-4055
Piedmont (G-7770)		
Sooner Cabinet & Trim Inc	E	405 820-2920
Moore (G-4571)		
Sooner Cnc LLC	G	918 261-5231
Tulsa (G-10787)		
Stephens Custom Woodworks	G	405 938-7065
Edmond (G-2632)		
Steveos Custom Wood-Work LLC	G	405 532-1863
Bethany (G-597)		
Sylvan Croft Woodworks	G	405 329-6668
Norman (G-5168)		
Tap Woodworks LLC	G	580 819-0455
Weatherford (G-11445)		
Thomas Millwork Inc	F	405 769-5618
Spencer (G-8602)		
Thompson Woodworks	G	405 269-6480
Stillwater (G-8768)		
Tilman Woodworks LLC	G	405 441-3324
Oklahoma City (G-7290)		
Tracys Wood Shop Inc	G	918 587-4860
Tulsa (G-10966)		
Trim Rite Moldings Inc	G	918 423-2525
McAlester (G-4344)		
Trinity Wood Works	G	918 619-3959
Muskogee (G-4755)		
Trotter Custom Woodworks LLC	G	918 698-5231
Sand Springs (G-8231)		
Unicorn Woodworking	G	580 762-0004
Ponca City (G-7885)		
Unique Wood Works Inc	G	405 249-6615
Maysville (G-4262)		
Urban Okie Custom Woodwork	G	405 420-1176
Edmond (G-2658)		
Urban Okie Custom Woodwork LLC	G	405 635-7800
Edmond (G-2659)		
Urbane Commercial Contrs LLC	G	405 534-1677
Midwest City (G-4460)		
Vanhoose Wood Creations	G	405 443-0454
Blanchard (G-742)		
Wayland Woodworks LLC	G	918 799-6196
Bristow (G-805)		
Wewoka Window Works LLC	F	405 257-3109
Wewoka (G-11514)		
Wfwoodworks LLC	G	405 740-8920
Norman (G-5200)		
White Bffalo Cstm Wdwrk Rnvtio	G	405 387-3278
Blanchard (G-745)		
Wild West Creations	G	405 542-6507
Hinton (G-3540)		
Wndells Woodturning	G	918 775-1124
Sallisaw (G-8155)		
Wood Creations By Rod LLC	G	405 235-2222
Oklahoma City (G-7462)		
Wood Creations By Rod LLC	G	405 912-8099
Moore (G-4583)		
Woodwright Woodworking LLC	G	918 254-6577
Broken Arrow (G-1102)		
Young Construction Supply LLC	G	918 456-3250
Tahlequah (G-8893)		
Yukon Door and Plywood Inc	E	405 354-4861
Yukon (G-11807)		

MINE & QUARRY SVCS: Nonmetallic Minerals

Company	Code	Phone
Kully Chaha Native Stone LLC	G	918 654-3005
Cameron (G-1258)		
Stoney Point Mine	G	580 362-3916
Newkirk (G-4853)		

MINE DEVELOPMENT SVCS: Nonmetallic Minerals

Company	Code	Phone
Trans-Tel Central Inc	C	405 447-5025
Norman (G-5180)		

MINE EXPLORATION SVCS: Nonmetallic Minerals

Company	Code	Phone
Myers & Myers Inc	G	405 341-5861
Edmond (G-2524)		

MINERAL PIGMENT MINING

Ovintiv Exploration Inc .... G 580 243-4101
Elk City *(G-2857)*

MINERAL PRODUCTS

Ppr LLC .... G 574 516-1131
Stillwater *(G-8740)*

MINERAL WOOL

Ets-Lindgren Inc .... E 580 434-7490
Durant *(G-2230)*
Hewlett-Packard Entp Svcs .... G 918 939-4072
Tulsa *(G-9926)*
Johns Manville Corporation .... E 405 552-4115
Oklahoma City *(G-6372)*
Owens Corning Sales LLC .... F 405 235-2491
Oklahoma City *(G-6790)*
Scott Manufacturing LLC .... E 405 949-2728
Oklahoma City *(G-7096)*

MINERAL WOOL INSULATION PRDTS

Western Fibers Inc .... E 509 679-4786
Hollis *(G-3571)*

MINERALS: Ground Or Otherwise Treated

Arysta Life Science Technology ..... G 580 871-2316
Alva *(G-175)*
Mesquite Minerals Inc .... G 405 848-7551
Oklahoma City *(G-6571)*

MINERALS: Ground or Treated

Hewitt Mineral Corporation .... G 580 223-6565
Ardmore *(G-304)*
Iofina Natural Gas .... G 580 871-2316
Alva *(G-183)*
McCabe Industrial Minerals .... G 918 252-5090
Tulsa *(G-10228)*
McCabe Industrial Mnrl Corp .... F 918 252-5090
Tulsa *(G-10229)*
Wildcat Minerals .... G 580 254-0141
Woodward *(G-11653)*

MINIATURES

Gasoline Alley Classics Inc .... G 918 806-1000
Broken Arrow *(G-1128)*
Mystic Rock Miniatures .... G 817 845-1590
El Reno *(G-2741)*

MINING MACHINES & EQPT: Feeders, Ore & Aggregate

Audio Link Inc .... G 405 359-0017
Edmond *(G-2311)*

MINING MACHINES & EQPT: Pellet Mills

Dorssers Usa Inc .... G 918 422-5881
Colcord *(G-1789)*

MINING: Oil Sand

Diamond Oilfield Services Inc .... G 405 243-7113
Yukon *(G-11719)*
Gill X-Stream Investments LLC ...... G 918 743-8379
Tulsa *(G-9826)*

MINING: Oil Shale

Leland Chapman .... G 580 444-2511
Velma *(G-11235)*
Singer Bros .... G 405 236-8596
Oklahoma City *(G-7143)*

MINING: Sand & Shale Oil

Checotah Partners LLC .... G 918 935-2795
Tulsa *(G-9408)*

MISCELLANEOUS FIN INVEST ACTVTS: Mineral Royalty Dealer

Meadowbrook Oil Corp of Okla ...... G 405 672-0240
Del City *(G-2001)*

MISCELLANEOUS FINANCIAL INVEST ACT: Oil/Gas Lease Brokers

Bo Mc Resources Corporation .... G 580 237-2324
Enid *(G-2920)*
Jess Harris Inc .... G 405 840-3271
Oklahoma City *(G-6359)*
Saturn Land Co Inc .... G 405 275-4406
Shawnee *(G-8493)*

MISCELLANEOUS FINANCIAL INVEST ACTIVITIES: Oil Royalties

Gillham Oil & Gas Inc .... G 405 997-8549
Maud *(G-4252)*

MISSILE GUIDANCE SYSTEMS & EQPT

Boeing Company .... A 918 835-3111
Tulsa *(G-9315)*

MIXING EQPT

Jensen Mixers Intl Inc .... E 918 627-5770
Tulsa *(G-10035)*

MIXTURES & BLOCKS: Asphalt Paving

APAC Oklahoma Inc .... E 918 256-8397
Vinita *(G-11247)*
Apac-Central Inc .... F 918 683-1362
Okay *(G-5256)*
Apac-Central Inc .... G 918 256-7853
Vinita *(G-11248)*
CMI Terex Corporation .... A 405 787-6020
Oklahoma City *(G-5792)*
Dunhams Asphalt Services Inc ...... G 918 246-9210
Sand Springs *(G-8180)*
Ergon A E Lawton .... G 580 536-0098
Lawton *(G-3923)*
Ergon Ardmore .... G 580 223-8010
Ardmore *(G-286)*
Ergon Asphalt & Emulsions Inc ..... F 918 683-1732
Muskogee *(G-4673)*
Evans & Associates Cnstr Co .... D 580 765-6693
Ponca City *(G-7827)*
Gem Asset Acquisition LLC .... E 405 200-1992
Oklahoma City *(G-6142)*
Haskell Lemon Construction Co .... C 405 947-6069
Oklahoma City *(G-6223)*
Kline Materials Inc .... F 580 256-2062
Woodward *(G-11603)*
Koch Industries Inc .... G 918 266-7070
Catoosa *(G-1330)*
Majeska & Associates LLC .... F 918 576-6878
Tulsa *(G-10204)*
Oldcastle Materials Inc .... C 918 978-0459
Tulsa *(G-10413)*
Overland Federal LLC .... F 469 269-2303
Ardmore *(G-341)*
Overland Materials and Mfg Inc .... E 580 223-8432
Ardmore *(G-342)*
Paving Materials Inc .... G 405 799-9880
Moore *(G-4552)*
Quapaw Company .... F 918 225-0580
Cushing *(G-1951)*
Quapaw Company Inc .... G 918 352-2533
Drumright *(G-2070)*
Rdnj LLC .... G 405 418-4741
Oklahoma City *(G-6978)*
RLC Holding Co Inc .... E 580 332-3080
Ada *(G-82)*
Road Science LLC .... D 918 960-3800
Tulsa *(G-10661)*
Rose Rock Midstream Field Svcs .. G 918 524-7700
Tulsa *(G-10672)*
Seal Masters Inc .... E 580 369-2393
Davis *(G-1993)*
Semcrude LP .... F 918 524-8100
Tulsa *(G-10727)*
Semgroup Corporation .... B 918 524-8100
Tulsa *(G-10728)*
Semmaterials LP .... G 918 683-1732
Muskogee *(G-4747)*
Semmaterials LP .... G 580 223-8010
Ardmore *(G-353)*
Semmaterials LP .... G 580 536-0098
Lawton *(G-3996)*
Semmaterials LP .... G 918 266-1606
Catoosa *(G-1352)*
Semmaterials LP .... D 918 524-8100
Tulsa *(G-10729)*

MOBILE COMMUNICATIONS EQPT

Josh Leeper .... G 918 618-2215
Eufaula *(G-3103)*

MOBILE HOME PARTS & ACCESS, WHOLESALE

Nupocket LLC .... F 918 850-1903
Broken Arrow *(G-990)*

MOBILE HOMES

Bill Durbins Mobile Home Tra .... G 405 799-3557
Oklahoma City *(G-5280)*
Clayton Homes Inc .... E 918 686-0584
Muskogee *(G-4661)*
Clayton Homes Inc .... G 405 341-4479
Edmond *(G-2356)*
Clayton Homes Inc .... G 580 237-7094
Enid *(G-2931)*
Freedom Homes .... G 918 728-2277
Tulsa *(G-9775)*
Hollands Mobile Homes .... G 918 476-5663
Chouteau *(G-1565)*
Housing USA .... G 405 631-3653
Oklahoma City *(G-6267)*

MOBILE HOMES: Personal Or Private Use

Modernblox LLC .... G 405 673-6215
Tulsa *(G-10292)*

MODELS: General, Exc Toy

Architectural Models .... G 405 360-2828
Norman *(G-4913)*

MODULES: Computer Logic

Accurate By Design .... G 918 445-0292
Tulsa *(G-8986)*

MOLDED RUBBER PRDTS

Da/Pro Rubber Inc .... C 918 258-9386
Broken Arrow *(G-886)*
Da/Pro Rubber Inc .... E 918 272-7799
Tulsa *(G-9544)*
Da/Pro Rubber Inc .... G 918 299-5480
Tulsa *(G-9545)*
Molded Products Incorporated ...... E 918 254-9061
Broken Arrow *(G-1144)*
Rubber Mold Company .... F 405 673-7177
Oklahoma City *(G-7059)*
Skinner Brothers Company Inc ...... F 918 585-5708
Tulsa *(G-10771)*
Texre Inc .... D 918 425-5524
Tulsa *(G-10922)*
Tulsa Rubber Co .... F 918 627-1371
Tulsa *(G-11006)*

MOLDING COMPOUNDS

Grace Fibrgls & Composites LLC .. G 405 233-3203
Harrah *(G-3378)*

MOLDINGS: Picture Frame

D E Ziegler Art Craft Supply .... E 918 584-2217
Tulsa *(G-9537)*
DC Custom Framing .... G 918 549-8754
Skiatook *(G-8539)*
Mitre Box Frame Shop .... G 580 338-2319
Guymon *(G-3356)*

MOLDS: Indl

Edmonds Fnest Mold Dmage Rmval ... G 405 509-9508
Edmond *(G-2406)*
Omg Tooling Inc .... G 405 789-4774
Oklahoma City *(G-6776)*

MOLDS: Plastic Working & Foundry

Encompass Tool & Machine Inc .... E 580 762-5800
Ponca City *(G-7825)*
Samco Polishing Inc .... F 918 789-5541
Chelsea *(G-1412)*
Tech Inc .... F 405 547-8324
Perkins *(G-7724)*

PRODUCT SECTION — MOTOR VEHICLE PARTS & ACCESS: Mufflers, Exhaust

MONUMENTS & GRAVE MARKERS, EXC TERRAZZO
- Gifford Monument Works Inc .... F 580 332-1271
  Ada *(G-42)*
- McLemore Monument Services .... G 405 788-0164
  El Reno *(G-2737)*
- Monumental Rocks .... G 918 240-8398
  Broken Arrow *(G-981)*

MONUMENTS & GRAVE MARKERS, WHOLESALE
- Muskogee Marble & Granite LLC .... E 918 682-0064
  Muskogee *(G-4716)*

MONUMENTS: Concrete
- Skiatook Statuary .... G 918 396-1309
  Skiatook *(G-8570)*
- Williams Monuments .... G 918 225-1344
  Cushing *(G-1971)*

MONUMENTS: Cut Stone, Exc Finishing Or Lettering Only
- Boadie L Anderson Quarries Inc .... E 580 436-2100
  Ada *(G-12)*
- Nicholson Monument Co .... G 580 323-7513
  Clinton *(G-1762)*
- Whm Granite Products Inc .... F 580 535-2184
  Granite *(G-3257)*

MORTAR
- Central Mortar and Grout LLC .... E 918 683-3003
  Muskogee *(G-4659)*

MOTEL
- B Bar Inc .... G 580 824-8338
  Waynoka *(G-11372)*
- Okeen Motel .... G 580 822-4491
  Okeene *(G-5261)*

MOTION PICTURE & VIDEO PRODUCTION SVCS
- Encompass Media LLC .... G 405 823-8081
  Oklahoma City *(G-6035)*
- Treble Services LLC .... G 405 401-1217
  Oklahoma City *(G-7321)*

MOTION PICTURE & VIDEO PRODUCTION SVCS: Cartoon
- Western Cartoons .... G 405 275-1054
  Shawnee *(G-8519)*

MOTOR & GENERATOR PARTS: Electric
- Advanced Indus Dvcs Co LLC .... D 918 445-1254
  Tulsa *(G-9110)*
- Profab .... G 918 486-4464
  Coweta *(G-1894)*
- Union Hill Electric LLC .... G 405 222-1068
  Chickasha *(G-1519)*

MOTOR REBUILDING SVCS, EXC AUTOMOTIVE
- Britton Electric Motor Inc .... G 405 842-8357
  Oklahoma City *(G-5629)*
- S & H Electric Motor Service .... G 580 924-3514
  Durant *(G-2254)*
- Wilson Electric Motor Svc Inc .... F 405 636-1515
  Oklahoma City *(G-7458)*

MOTOR REPAIR SVCS
- Blevins Oilfield Sls & Svc LLC .... F 405 619-9909
  Oklahoma City *(G-5592)*
- Shawns Small Eng Eqp Repr LLC .... G 918 734-1565
  Tulsa *(G-10740)*
- Szabo Szabi .... G 918 697-5441
  Muskogee *(G-4751)*
- Tank & Fuel Solutions LLC .... G 918 960-4361
  Claremore *(G-1691)*

MOTOR VEHICLE ASSEMBLY, COMPLETE: Ambulances
- Heartland Energy Options LLC .... G 405 600-6009
  Piedmont *(G-7763)*

MOTOR VEHICLE ASSEMBLY, COMPLETE: Autos, Incl Specialty
- Accurate Machine Works Inc .... F 405 615-4983
  Blanchard *(G-700)*
- American Street Rod Co .... G 405 373-0376
  Piedmont *(G-7754)*
- Deacon Race Cars .... G 405 348-4419
  Edmond *(G-2387)*
- Dials Race Shop .... G 405 382-4843
  Seminole *(G-8368)*
- Franks Garage Auto Sls & Salv .... G 405 257-6198
  Wewoka *(G-11502)*
- Logistics Management Company .... G 405 633-1201
  Oklahoma City *(G-6490)*
- Patrick Michael Palazzo .... G 918 344-3724
  Tulsa *(G-10474)*
- Ron Shanks Racing Enterprises .... G 918 366-6050
  Bixby *(G-655)*

MOTOR VEHICLE ASSEMBLY, COMPLETE: Fire Department Vehicles
- County of Oklahoma .... G 918 456-3622
  Tahlequah *(G-8859)*

MOTOR VEHICLE ASSEMBLY, COMPLETE: Military Motor Vehicle
- Alpha Omega Mltary/Defence Mfg .... G 918 816-6918
  Muskogee *(G-4647)*

MOTOR VEHICLE ASSEMBLY, COMPLETE: Patrol Wagons
- Oklahoma Dept Public Safety .... E 918 256-3388
  Vinita *(G-11265)*

MOTOR VEHICLE ASSEMBLY, COMPLETE: Truck & Tractor Trucks
- Paccar .... G 918 810-3810
  Broken Arrow *(G-1148)*

MOTOR VEHICLE ASSEMBLY, COMPLETE: Trucks, Pickup
- Elastomer Specialties Inc .... G 918 485-0276
  Wagoner *(G-11282)*
- Performance Plastics Inc .... G 918 627-9621
  Tulsa *(G-10494)*

MOTOR VEHICLE ASSEMBLY, COMPLETE: Universal Carriers, Mil
- Choctaw Defense Mfg LLC .... G 918 426-2871
  McAlester *(G-4283)*
- Choctaw Defense Mfg LLC .... E 580 326-8365
  Hugo *(G-3606)*

MOTOR VEHICLE ASSEMBLY, COMPLETE: Wreckers, Tow Truck
- Paul Wrecker Service .... G 918 333-9685
  Bartlesville *(G-515)*
- Ragsdale Wrecker Service .... G 405 771-5544
  Spencer *(G-8600)*
- Sky Motors LLC .... F 918 321-2800
  Sapulpa *(G-8313)*
- Welchs Wrecker .... G 405 238-6194
  Pauls Valley *(G-7674)*

MOTOR VEHICLE ASSY, COMPLETE: Street Sprinklers & Sweepers
- Broce Manufacturing Co Inc .... G 405 579-4621
  Norman *(G-4943)*

MOTOR VEHICLE DEALERS: Automobiles, New & Used
- Jaguar Meter Service Inc .... G 405 670-2327
  Oklahoma City *(G-6346)*
- James Matthews Ford LLC .... E 918 251-3673
  Broken Arrow *(G-942)*
- Mike Bailey Motors Inc .... F 918 652-9637
  Henryetta *(G-3512)*
- Pfpp LP .... D 405 946-3381
  Oklahoma City *(G-6839)*
- Ronnie Nevitt .... G 918 687-5284
  Muskogee *(G-4745)*
- Rv Station Ltd .... G 888 466-1384
  Colbert *(G-1786)*
- Spess Drilling Company .... F 918 358-5831
  Cleveland *(G-1734)*
- William Pettit .... F 918 297-2564
  Hartshorne *(G-3396)*

MOTOR VEHICLE DEALERS: Cars, Used Only
- Nick & Pauls Quality Car Cornr .... G 918 933-4000
  Tulsa *(G-10341)*

MOTOR VEHICLE DEALERS: Trucks, Tractors/Trailers, New & Used
- Enid Mack Sales Inc .... D 580 234-0043
  Enid *(G-2954)*

MOTOR VEHICLE PARTS & ACCESS: Body Components & Frames
- Advanced Racing Composites LLC .... G 918 760-9990
  Tulsa *(G-9111)*
- Quses .... E 817 829-1086
  Oklahoma City *(G-6956)*

MOTOR VEHICLE PARTS & ACCESS: Cleaners, air
- Odor Control Entps Texas Inc .... F 405 670-5600
  Oklahoma City *(G-6712)*

MOTOR VEHICLE PARTS & ACCESS: Cylinder Heads
- Weingartner Racing LLC .... G 918 520-3480
  Broken Arrow *(G-1176)*

MOTOR VEHICLE PARTS & ACCESS: Engines & Parts
- Econtrols LLC .... F 918 957-1000
  Tulsa *(G-9642)*
- Kelley Repair LLC .... G 918 456-6514
  Tahlequah *(G-8870)*
- Varco Inc .... G 405 732-1637
  Oklahoma City *(G-7395)*
- Wesmar Racing Engines Inc .... G 918 366-7222
  Bixby *(G-672)*

MOTOR VEHICLE PARTS & ACCESS: Engs & Trans, Factory, Rebuilt
- C & C Performance Engines .... G 580 252-4331
  Duncan *(G-2094)*

MOTOR VEHICLE PARTS & ACCESS: Fuel Pipes
- Slw Automotive Inc .... E 918 776-3157
  Sallisaw *(G-8151)*

MOTOR VEHICLE PARTS & ACCESS: Fuel Pumps
- Deatschwerks LLC .... G 405 217-0701
  Oklahoma City *(G-5914)*

MOTOR VEHICLE PARTS & ACCESS: Lifting Mechanisms, Dump Truck
- Gem Dirt LLC .... G 918 298-0299
  Tulsa *(G-9813)*

MOTOR VEHICLE PARTS & ACCESS: Mufflers, Exhaust
- H & H Muffler Whse & Mfg Co .... E 918 371-9633
  Collinsville *(G-1811)*

MOTOR VEHICLE PARTS & ACCESS: Pickup Truck Bed Liners

Line X of Western Oklahoma .... G 580 774-5000
  Weatherford *(G-11425)*

MOTOR VEHICLE PARTS & ACCESS: Pumps, Hydraulic Fluid Power

Slyder Energy Solutions LLC .... G 405 258-3608
  Carney *(G-1280)*

MOTOR VEHICLE PARTS & ACCESS: Tie Rods

Ride Control LLC .... B 800 251-5932
  Chickasha *(G-1502)*

MOTOR VEHICLE PARTS & ACCESS: Transmissions

Atc Technology Corporation .... A 405 577-9901
  Oklahoma City *(G-5483)*
Blumenthal Companies LLc .... G 405 232-9557
  Oklahoma City *(G-5596)*
Blumenthal Companies LLc .... E 405 232-9557
  Oklahoma City *(G-5595)*
Larrys Transmission Service .... G 405 273-3432
  Shawnee *(G-8468)*
Thomas H Scott Western LLC .... G 405 632-6860
  Oklahoma City *(G-7283)*
Transmission Center .... G 405 329-4620
  Norman *(G-5182)*

MOTOR VEHICLE PARTS & ACCESS: Wipers, Windshield

Ron Williams .... G 580 772-3513
  Weatherford *(G-11437)*

MOTOR VEHICLE SPLYS & PARTS WHOLESALERS: New

Bb Machine & Supply Inc .... G 580 237-8686
  Enid *(G-2915)*
Drov LLC .... F 405 463-6562
  Oklahoma City *(G-5984)*
Factor 1 Racing Inc .... G 918 258-7223
  Broken Arrow *(G-905)*
Mac Trailer of Oklahoma Inc .... G 817 900-2006
  Davis *(G-1988)*

MOTOR VEHICLE SPLYS & PARTS WHOLESALERS: Used

D C Ignition Co Inc .... G 580 332-0878
  Ada *(G-28)*
Mac Trailer of Oklahoma Inc .... G 817 900-2006
  Davis *(G-1988)*

MOTOR VEHICLE: Hardware

Shur-Co LLC .... G 405 262-7600
  El Reno *(G-2757)*

MOTOR VEHICLE: Radiators

1 800 Radiator .... G 405 946-9800
  Oklahoma City *(G-5326)*

MOTOR VEHICLES & CAR BODIES

Echota Defense Services .... G 918 384-7409
  Tulsa *(G-9637)*
Fat Alberts Motor Sports .... G 918 647-3069
  Poteau *(G-7903)*
Heartland Locator .... G 580 554-0125
  Pond Creek *(G-7890)*
Ic Bus of Oklahoma LLC .... A 918 833-4000
  Tulsa *(G-9964)*
J J Custom Fire .... G 918 762-2102
  Pawnee *(G-7705)*
James Matthews Ford LLC .... E 918 251-3673
  Broken Arrow *(G-942)*
Major League Sports LLC .... G 918 559-5030
  Nowata *(G-5219)*
Navistar Inc .... D 918 833-4065
  Tulsa *(G-10330)*
Paccar Inc .... E 918 756-4400
  Okmulgee *(G-7521)*
Paccar Inc .... E 405 745-3006
  Oklahoma City *(G-6792)*
Sportschassis LLC .... D 580 323-4100
  Clinton *(G-1770)*
Tuff Troff LLC .... G 918 623-6091
  Okemah *(G-5277)*
Western Okla Powertrain Inc .... G 580 243-4501
  Elk City *(G-2889)*
Wheels of Past .... G 918 225-2250
  Cushing *(G-1969)*

MOTOR VEHICLES, WHOLESALE: Trailers for passenger vehicles

Tall Boys Toys .... G 580 323-2765
  Clinton *(G-1771)*

MOTOR VEHICLES, WHOLESALE: Trailers, Truck, New & Used

Mac Trailer of Oklahoma Inc .... G 817 900-2006
  Davis *(G-1988)*

MOTOR VEHICLES, WHOLESALE: Trucks, commercial

Ramcco Concrete Cnstr LLC .... F 918 266-3838
  Tulsa *(G-10616)*

MOTORCYCLE & BICYCLE PARTS: Frames

Buchanan Bicycles Inc .... G 405 364-5513
  Norman *(G-4948)*

MOTORCYCLE DEALERS

Fat Alberts Motor Sports .... G 918 647-3069
  Poteau *(G-7903)*
Noss Machine .... G 918 358-3804
  Hominy *(G-3593)*

MOTORCYCLE PARTS & ACCESS DEALERS

Cradduck John .... G 405 360-0251
  Norman *(G-4968)*

MOTORCYCLE PARTS: Wholesalers

Pogue Machine Inc .... G 405 677-9397
  Oklahoma City *(G-6860)*

MOTORCYCLES & RELATED PARTS

ABC Choppers LLC .... G 405 990-8641
  Oklahoma City *(G-5358)*
APS of Oklahoma LLC .... G 405 793-8877
  Moore *(G-4492)*
Cave Man Choppers .... G 405 672-8008
  Oklahoma City *(G-5714)*
DC Choppers LLC .... G 918 791-1846
  Coweta *(G-1879)*
Eldon Valley Choppers .... G 918 931-2925
  Tahlequah *(G-8863)*
Passion Racing Engines .... G 918 232-3950
  Owasso *(G-7602)*

MOTORS: Electric

Allied Motion Technologies Inc .... F 918 627-1845
  Tulsa *(G-9151)*
Franklin Electric Co Inc .... B 918 465-2348
  Wilburton *(G-11520)*
Franklin Electric Co Inc .... B 501 455-1234
  Oklahoma City *(G-6113)*

MOTORS: Generators

Adaptive Corporation .... G 440 257-7460
  Tulsa *(G-9103)*
Aei Corp-Okla .... G 405 236-3551
  Oklahoma City *(G-5389)*
Bellofram Corporation .... G 918 965-1964
  Claremore *(G-1595)*
Britton Electric Motor Inc .... G 405 842-8357
  Oklahoma City *(G-5629)*
Buttons Auto Electrical Supply .... G 580 223-3855
  Ardmore *(G-261)*
C & P Catalyst Inc .... G 918 747-8379
  Tulsa *(G-9357)*
Electric Motor Service Company .... G 580 223-8940
  Ardmore *(G-283)*
Emoteq Corporation .... C 918 627-1845
  Tulsa *(G-9674)*
Enerfin Inc .... G 918 258-3571
  Broken Arrow *(G-900)*
Enid Electric Motor Svc Inc .... F 580 234-8622
  Enid *(G-2952)*
Evans Enterprises Inc .... C 405 631-1344
  Norman *(G-4993)*
Fasco Motors Group .... G 405 387-5560
  Norman *(G-4997)*
Interstate Electric Corp .... G 918 245-4508
  Sand Springs *(G-8194)*
L3 Westwood Corporation .... C 918 250-4444
  Tulsa *(G-10108)*
L3 Westwood Corporation .... D 918 250-4444
  Tulsa *(G-10109)*
L3 Westwood Corporation .... C 918 252-0481
  Tulsa *(G-10110)*
Maggie Company Inc .... E 918 438-7800
  Tulsa *(G-10200)*
Petrolab LLC .... G 918 459-7170
  Broken Arrow *(G-1005)*
Pipeline Coating Services LLC .... G 936 494-2919
  Tulsa *(G-10518)*
Southwest Electric Co .... F 918 437-9494
  Tulsa *(G-10805)*

MOTORS: Starting, Automotive & Aircraft

Buttons Auto Electrical Supply .... G 580 223-3855
  Ardmore *(G-261)*

MOVING SVC: Local

Bison Energy Services LLC .... F 405 529-6577
  Oklahoma City *(G-5577)*
Grs Hot Shot Trucking LLC .... G 580 353-9449
  Tuttle *(G-11203)*
Zieglers Bob Portable Bldg Sls .... G 918 486-4462
  Broken Arrow *(G-1181)*

MOWERS & ACCESSORIES

Day In Sun Landscaping .... G 580 768-4986
  Durant *(G-2222)*
Forrest Lawns Landscapes .... G 405 397-4679
  Oklahoma City *(G-6103)*

MUSEUMS & ART GALLERIES

Gretchen Cagle Publications .... G 918 342-1080
  Claremore *(G-1629)*

MUSIC BROADCASTING SVCS

Christy Collins Inc .... G 580 305-0001
  Frederick *(G-3192)*
Versitile Entertainment .... G 812 913-2677
  Seminole *(G-8406)*

MUSIC DISTRIBUTION APPARATUS

Versitile Entertainment .... G 812 913-2677
  Seminole *(G-8406)*

MUSIC RECORDING PRODUCER

Downtown Music Box LLC .... G 405 232-2099
  Oklahoma City *(G-5975)*

MUSICAL ENTERTAINERS

Downtown Music Box LLC .... G 405 232-2099
  Oklahoma City *(G-5975)*
Versitile Entertainment .... G 812 913-2677
  Seminole *(G-8406)*

MUSICAL INSTRUMENT PARTS & ACCESS, WHOLESALE

Downtown Music Box LLC .... G 405 232-2099
  Oklahoma City *(G-5975)*

MUSICAL INSTRUMENT REPAIR

Honest Rons Guitars .... G 405 947-3683
  Oklahoma City *(G-6260)*

MUSICAL INSTRUMENTS & ACCESS: NEC

Clubhouse Trailer Co LLC .... G 405 396-6747
  Edmond *(G-2358)*
Mad Dogs Emporium .... G 918 283-4480
  Claremore *(G-1652)*
Master Works .... G 580 847-2273
  Bennington *(G-564)*

PRODUCT SECTION

Walrus Audio LLC .... F 405 254-4118
  Oklahoma City *(G-7418)*

MUSICAL INSTRUMENTS & SPLYS STORES

Downtown Music Box LLC .... G 405 232-2099
  Oklahoma City *(G-5975)*

MUSICAL INSTRUMENTS WHOLESALERS

Master Works .... G 580 847-2273
  Bennington *(G-564)*

MUSICAL INSTRUMENTS: Guitars & Parts, Electric & Acoustic

Hanson Inc .... G 918 447-0777
  Tulsa *(G-9888)*
Honest Rons Guitars .... G 405 947-3683
  Oklahoma City *(G-6260)*
Synapticgroove LLC .... G 405 205-6094
  Edmond *(G-2635)*

MUSICAL INSTRUMENTS: Violins & Parts

Active Violinist LLC .... G 612 532-1829
  Tulsa *(G-9098)*

NAIL SALONS

Dobbs & Crowder Inc .... G 918 452-3211
  Eufaula *(G-3100)*

NAME PLATES: Engraved Or Etched

Nameplates Inc .... D 918 584-2651
  Tulsa *(G-10324)*

NATIONAL SECURITY FORCES

Dla Document Services .... E 405 734-2177
  Tinker Afb *(G-8953)*

NATIONAL SECURITY, GOVERNMENT: Army

United States Dept of Army .... A 918 420-6642
  McAlester *(G-4348)*

NATURAL BUTANE PRODUCTION

Red Mountain Energy LLC .... F 405 842-4500
  Oklahoma City *(G-6986)*
Red Mountain Operating LLC .... G 405 842-9200
  Oklahoma City *(G-6987)*

NATURAL GAS COMPRESSING SVC, On-Site

Akita Compression Services LLC .... G 405 201-2677
  Edmond *(G-2294)*
Archrock Inc .... G 580 824-0102
  Waynoka *(G-11371)*
Archrock Inc .... F 580 225-2091
  Elk City *(G-2784)*
Archrock Inc .... G 918 558-2216
  Alderson *(G-127)*
Archrock Inc .... G 918 900-4200
  Tulsa *(G-9205)*
Cei Pipeline LLC .... G 405 478-8770
  Oklahoma City *(G-5719)*
El Paso Prod Oil Gas Texas LP .... E 580 994-2171
  Mooreland *(G-4590)*
Lumen Energy Corporation .... F 918 584-0052
  Tulsa *(G-10183)*
Park Energy Services LLC .... G 918 617-4350
  Stigler *(G-8638)*
Sage Natural Resources LLC .... G 940 539-2225
  Tulsa *(G-10689)*
USA Compression .... G 405 790-0300
  Oklahoma City *(G-7377)*
USA Compression Partners LLC .... G 918 742-6548
  Tulsa *(G-11058)*
USA Compression Partners LLC .... G 405 234-3450
  Oklahoma City *(G-7378)*

NATURAL GAS DISTRIBUTION TO CONSUMERS

Centerpint Enrgy Rsources Corp .... G 580 512-5903
  McAlester *(G-4279)*
Cimarex Energy Co .... G 580 330-0188
  Clinton *(G-1743)*
Devon Oei Operating Inc .... A 405 235-3611
  Oklahoma City *(G-5936)*

One Gas Inc .... D 918 947-7000
  Tulsa *(G-10418)*
Oneok Inc .... A 918 588-7000
  Tulsa *(G-10421)*
Oneok Inc .... F 405 878-6267
  Shawnee *(G-8482)*
Oneok Inc .... E 918 588-7000
  Tulsa *(G-10422)*
Sagebrush Pipeline LLC .... G 405 753-5500
  Oklahoma City *(G-7073)*
Samson Natural Gas Company .... B 918 583-1791
  Tulsa *(G-10695)*
Williams Companies Inc .... A 918 573-2000
  Tulsa *(G-11127)*
Xplorer Midstream LLC .... F 918 237-5885
  Oklahoma City *(G-7478)*

NATURAL GAS LIQUID FRACTIONATING SVC

Woodford Express LLC .... F 405 437-0857
  Oklahoma City *(G-7465)*

NATURAL GAS LIQUIDS PRODUCTION

Avalon Exploration Inc .... F 918 523-0600
  Tulsa *(G-9227)*
Bluehawk Energy Inc .... G 405 406-1580
  Edmond *(G-2327)*
Enable Okla Intrstate Trnsm LL .... C 405 525-7788
  Oklahoma City *(G-6033)*
Enable Oklahoma Int Transm LLC .... G 405 356-4060
  Wellston *(G-11469)*
Enable Oklahoma Int Transm LLC .... G 580 323-7450
  Clinton *(G-1750)*
Enogex Services Corporation .... G 405 525-7788
  Oklahoma City *(G-6042)*
Enogex Services Corporation .... E 405 893-2267
  Calumet *(G-1246)*
Frontier Energy Services LLC .... G 918 754-2226
  Tulsa *(G-9780)*
Frontier Energy Services LLC .... F 918 388-8438
  Tulsa *(G-9781)*
G&J Measurement Inc .... G 580 560-3190
  Duncan *(G-2119)*
Hiland Lp LLC .... F 713 369-9000
  Enid *(G-2972)*
J-W Power Company .... G 580 254-5663
  Woodward *(G-11596)*
Oneok Midstream Gas Supply LLC .... F 918 588-7000
  Tulsa *(G-10426)*
Oneok Texas Field Services LP .... D 918 588-7000
  Tulsa *(G-10430)*
Riley Explration - Permian LLC .... G 405 415-8699
  Oklahoma City *(G-7026)*
Sooner Holdings Inc .... F 918 592-7900
  Tulsa *(G-10788)*
Tri Resources Inc .... G 580 363-0243
  Blackwell *(G-694)*

NATURAL GAS LIQUIDS PRODUCTION

BP America Production Company .... F 918 465-2343
  Wilburton *(G-11518)*
Centennial Gas Liquids Ulc .... G 918 481-1119
  Tulsa *(G-9396)*
Dcp Midstream LLC .... F 405 705-7400
  Edmond *(G-2385)*
Deeprock Tank Oper Colo LLC .... E 918 225-7100
  Cushing *(G-1931)*
Eagle Rock Energy Partners LP .... G 281 408-1467
  Tulsa *(G-9629)*
Frontier Midstream LLC .... G 918 388-8438
  Tulsa *(G-9784)*
Mark West Hydrocarbon Inc .... G 800 730-8388
  Tulsa *(G-10212)*
Markwest Hydrocarbon Inc .... E 580 664-5282
  Butler *(G-1221)*
Markwest Pioneer LLC .... G 918 477-8000
  Tulsa *(G-10214)*
Oneok Inc .... F 405 878-6267
  Shawnee *(G-8482)*
Oneok Inc .... A 918 588-7000
  Tulsa *(G-10421)*
Oneok Inc .... E 918 588-7000
  Tulsa *(G-10422)*
Oneok Field Services Co LLC .... B 918 588-7000
  Tulsa *(G-10423)*
Oneok Partners LP .... G 918 588-7000
  Tulsa *(G-10427)*
PTL Prop Solutions LLC .... G 405 848-8000
  Oklahoma City *(G-6920)*

NATURAL GAS PRODUCTION

Pvr Midstreem LLC .... F 580 837-5265
  Beaver *(G-545)*
Range Rsources-Midcontinent LLC ...... C 405 810-7359
  Oklahoma City *(G-6972)*
Spectrum Lng LLC .... F 918 298-6660
  Tulsa *(G-10818)*
Templar Operating LLC .... F 405 548-1200
  Oklahoma City *(G-7267)*
Tom-Stack LLC .... F 405 888-5585
  Edmond *(G-2647)*
Transwestern Pipeline Co LLC .... G 918 492-7272
  Tulsa *(G-10971)*
Tronox Incorporated .... G 580 921-5411
  Woodward *(G-11645)*
Williams Companies Inc .... A 918 573-2000
  Tulsa *(G-11127)*
Williams Energy Resources LLC .... E 918 573-2000
  Tulsa *(G-11128)*

NATURAL GAS PRODUCTION

Atlas Resource Partners LP .... F 918 654-3702
  Cameron *(G-1254)*
Bear Productions Inc .... F 918 768-3364
  Kinta *(G-3833)*
Centurion Resources LLC .... G 918 493-1110
  Tulsa *(G-9398)*
Choctaw Gas Company .... G 918 469-3394
  Quinton *(G-8035)*
Dave Bolton .... G 205 637-1402
  Oklahoma City *(G-5902)*
Devon Energy Corporation .... F 405 235-7798
  Oklahoma City *(G-5928)*
Division Order Beginnings .... G 918 477-4559
  Porter *(G-7892)*
Elkhorn Operating Company .... G 918 492-4418
  Tulsa *(G-9657)*
Energy Financial and Physcl LP .... G 405 702-4700
  Oklahoma City *(G-6039)*
Etx Energy LLC .... D 918 728-3020
  Tulsa *(G-9703)*
Fairway E&P LLC .... G 918 284-5322
  Bixby *(G-622)*
Frontier Gas Services LLC .... G 918 388-8438
  Tulsa *(G-9782)*
Gene Cook Inc .... G 580 256-5335
  Woodward *(G-11587)*
Henry Gungoll Operating Inc .... G 580 234-2302
  Enid *(G-2970)*
Intensity Midstream LLC .... G 918 949-9098
  Tulsa *(G-10002)*
Jacmac Energy Corp .... G 405 224-1284
  Chickasha *(G-1474)*
Jacmor Inc .... G 405 843-0203
  Oklahoma City *(G-6344)*
Jess Harris Inc .... G 405 840-3271
  Oklahoma City *(G-6359)*
Legion Energy LLC .... G 918 895-8785
  Tulsa *(G-10151)*
Mid-America Midstream Gas .... G 405 935-8000
  Oklahoma City *(G-6589)*
Mid-Con Energy II LLC .... G 918 743-7575
  Tulsa *(G-10258)*
Ntu Pipeline LLC .... F 918 392-9255
  Tulsa *(G-10365)*
One Gas Inc .... D 918 947-7000
  Tulsa *(G-10418)*
One Gas Inc .... G 918 831-8218
  Tulsa *(G-10419)*
Pontotoc Gathering LLC .... G 918 742-5835
  Tulsa *(G-10531)*
Rexbo Energy Co .... G 405 359-0458
  Edmond *(G-2598)*
Sagebrush Pipeline LLC .... G 405 753-5500
  Oklahoma City *(G-7073)*
Sooner Holdings Inc .... F 918 592-7900
  Tulsa *(G-10788)*
Targa Resources Corp .... D 580 883-2273
  Ringwood *(G-8095)*
Tridon Oil Inc .... G 918 682-6801
  Muskogee *(G-4754)*
Trinity Gas Corporation .... G 580 233-1155
  Enid *(G-3067)*
United Energy Trading LLC .... G 918 392-8444
  Tulsa *(G-11041)*
Vm Arkoma Stack LLC .... G 405 286-5580
  Oklahoma City *(G-7404)*
Whiting Petroleum Corporation .... C 580 234-5554
  Enid *(G-3079)*
Williams Companies Inc .... A 918 573-2000
  Tulsa *(G-11127)*

Employee Codes: A=Over 500 employees, B=251-500
C=101-250, D=51-100, E=20-50, F=10-19, G=1-9

NATURAL GAS PRODUCTION

Williams Gas Pipeline Co LLC .... G 918 573-2000
  Tulsa *(G-11130)*
Williams Partners LP .... C 918 573-2000
  Tulsa *(G-11132)*

NATURAL GAS TRANSMISSION

Concorde Resource Corporation .... G 918 689-9510
  Eufaula *(G-3099)*
Devon Oei Operating Inc .... A 405 235-3611
  Oklahoma City *(G-5936)*
Enerfin Resources I Ltd Partnr .... E 405 382-3049
  Seminole *(G-8371)*
G&J Measurement Inc .... G 580 560-3190
  Duncan *(G-2119)*
Oneok Partners LP .... E 918 588-7000
  Tulsa *(G-10427)*
Williams Gas Pipeline Co LLC .... G 918 573-2000
  Tulsa *(G-11130)*
Williams Partners LP .... C 918 573-2000
  Tulsa *(G-11132)*

NATURAL GAS TRANSMISSION & DISTRIBUTION

Enable Okla Intrstate Trnsm LL .... C 405 525-7788
  Oklahoma City *(G-6033)*
Mustang Fuel Corporation .... D 405 884-2092
  Oklahoma City *(G-6641)*
Speller Petroleum Corporation .... G 405 942-7869
  Oklahoma City *(G-7183)*

NATURAL GASOLINE PRODUCTION

Wpx Energy Marketing LLC .... G 918 573-0068
  Tulsa *(G-11158)*
Wpx Energy Marketing LLC .... E 918 573-2000
  Tulsa *(G-11159)*

NATURAL LIQUEFIED PETROLEUM GAS PRODUCTION

C & R Olfld Pntg Rustabout Svc .... G 620 272-6699
  Ponca City *(G-7804)*

NATURAL PROPANE PRODUCTION

Bravo Natural Gas LLC .... G 918 712-7008
  Tulsa *(G-9333)*
Oklahoma Propane Gas Assn .... G 405 424-1775
  Oklahoma City *(G-6758)*
Titan Propane LLC .... G 918 838-8804
  Tulsa *(G-10946)*

NAVIGATIONAL SYSTEMS & INSTRUMENTS

Frontier Elctrnic Systems Corp .... C 405 624-7708
  Stillwater *(G-8694)*
Navico Inc .... B 918 437-6881
  Tulsa *(G-10328)*

NEW & USED CAR DEALERS

Sky Motors LLC .... F 918 321-2800
  Sapulpa *(G-8313)*

NEWSPAPERS, WHOLESALE

Lewis County Press LLC .... G 580 363-3370
  Blackwell *(G-687)*

NEWSSTAND

El Nacional News Inc .... G 405 632-4531
  Oklahoma City *(G-6018)*
Latimer County News Tribune .... G 918 465-2321
  Wilburton *(G-11522)*
Valliant Leader Inc .... G 580 933-4570
  Valliant *(G-11233)*

NICKEL ALLOY

Buffalo Nickel Industries LLC .... G 918 287-3899
  Pawhuska *(G-7679)*
Cindy Nickel Aesthetics .... G 405 513-6690
  Edmond *(G-2353)*
Cindy Nickel Inc .... G 405 209-1444
  Edmond *(G-2354)*
Lonnie B Nickels Jr .... G 918 756-3426
  Okmulgee *(G-7514)*
Nickel & Company LLC .... E 918 744-6384
  Tulsa *(G-10342)*
Nickel Creek Photography .... G 918 447-2688
  Tulsa *(G-10343)*

Transtrade LLC .... G 918 521-7271
  Tulsa *(G-10970)*

NONDURABLE GOODS WHOLESALERS, NEC

American Tradition .... G 918 688-7725
  Tulsa *(G-9174)*

NONFERROUS: Rolling & Drawing, NEC

Nickel 8 LLC .... G 405 721-7945
  Oklahoma City *(G-6680)*

NONMETALLIC MINERALS: Support Activities, Exc Fuels

Pats Phase II Hair & Nail Sln .... G 405 232-4746
  Oklahoma City *(G-6811)*

NOTARIES PUBLIC

Aars .... G 918 313-4512
  Tulsa *(G-9080)*
Layle Company Corporation .... G 405 329-5143
  Norman *(G-5056)*

NOTIONS: Pins & Needles

Pins-N-Needles By Sandra .... G 918 270-0204
  Owasso *(G-7603)*

NOVELTIES

Gra Enterprises Inc .... G 405 848-1300
  Oklahoma City *(G-6173)*

NOVELTIES: Plastic

Mark Stevens Industries Inc .... D 405 948-1077
  Edmond *(G-2504)*

NOVELTY SHOPS

Big Red Shop Inc .... G 405 495-5551
  Warr Acres *(G-11313)*
Signature Graphics Corp .... G 918 294-3485
  Bixby *(G-658)*

NOZZLES: Spray, Aerosol, Paint Or Insecticide

Taraco Enterprises LLC .... G 580 679-3956
  Duke *(G-2080)*

NURSERIES & LAWN & GARDEN SPLY STORE, RET: Fountain, Outdoor

Stockmans Supply Company .... G 580 255-7762
  Duncan *(G-2186)*

NURSERIES & LAWN & GARDEN SPLY STORES, RETAIL: Fertilizer

Farmers Co Op .... F 918 456-0557
  Tahlequah *(G-8864)*

NURSERIES & LAWN & GARDEN SPLY STORES, RETAIL: Top Soil

Minick Materials Company .... E 405 789-2068
  Oklahoma City *(G-6616)*

NURSERIES & LAWN/GARDEN SPLY STORE, RET: Lawnmowers/Tractors

Diamond P Forrest Products Co .... F 918 266-2478
  Catoosa *(G-1316)*
Eastland Lawn Mower Service .... G 580 252-0077
  Duncan *(G-2115)*
Green Country Outdoor Eqp .... G 918 396-4250
  Skiatook *(G-8546)*
Lahmeyer Pattern Shop .... G 918 425-6008
  Tulsa *(G-10112)*
Vincent Enterprises Inc .... G 580 252-1322
  Duncan *(G-2194)*

NURSERIES & LAWN/GARDEN SPLY STORES, RET: Garden Splys/Tools

Coalton Road Enterprises LLC .... G 918 652-0474
  Henryetta *(G-3502)*

NURSERIES/LAWN/GRDN SPLY STORE, RET: Nursery Stck, Seed/Bulb

Shawnee Milling Company .... G 405 352-4336
  Minco *(G-4481)*

OFFICE EQPT WHOLESALERS

Kingfisher Office Supply Inc .... G 405 375-3404
  Kingfisher *(G-3806)*
Pioneer Printing Inc .... G 918 542-5521
  Miami *(G-4428)*
Sariel Inc .... G 918 855-1400
  Tulsa *(G-10709)*

OFFICE EQPT, WHOLESALE: Photocopy Machines

Onedoc Managed Print Svcs LLC .... G 405 633-3050
  Oklahoma City *(G-6778)*

OFFICE MACHINES, NEC

Backup Fortress LLC .... G 405 314-2436
  Yukon *(G-11694)*
Pitney Bowes Inc .... G 918 779-7552
  Tulsa *(G-10521)*

OFFICE MANAGEMENT SVCS

Smeac Group International LLC .... G 580 574-4092
  Lawton *(G-3999)*

OFFICE SPLY & STATIONERY STORES

Chaddick & Associates Inc .... F 580 223-1202
  Ardmore *(G-264)*
Fenton Office Supply Co .... E 405 372-5555
  Stillwater *(G-8688)*
Inviting Place .... G 918 488-0525
  Tulsa *(G-10010)*
Memorabilia Corner .... G 405 321-8366
  Norman *(G-5070)*

OFFICE SPLY & STATIONERY STORES: Notary & Corporate Seals

Aars .... G 918 313-4512
  Tulsa *(G-9080)*

OFFICE SPLY & STATIONERY STORES: Office Forms & Splys

262 LLC .... F 918 458-5511
  Tahlequah *(G-8848)*
A & B Printing & Office Supply .... G 580 889-5103
  Atoka *(G-395)*
Abco Printing & Office Supply .... G 580 286-7575
  Idabel *(G-3636)*
Brix Inc .... G 918 584-6484
  Tulsa *(G-9338)*
Chadwick Paper Inc .... G 580 369-2807
  Davis *(G-1979)*
Dps Printing Services Inc .... G 405 285-4614
  Edmond *(G-2394)*
Edmond Printings .... G 405 341-4330
  Edmond *(G-2404)*
Executive Forms & Supplies .... G 817 423-9088
  Oklahoma City *(G-6060)*
Hinkle Printing & Office Sup .... G 405 238-9308
  Pauls Valley *(G-7660)*
Hugo Publishing Company .... G 580 326-3311
  Hugo *(G-3612)*
Kingfisher Office Supply Inc .... G 405 375-3404
  Kingfisher *(G-3806)*
Lewis Printing & Office Supply .... F 405 379-5124
  Holdenville *(G-3557)*
Linderer Printing Co Inc .... F 580 323-2102
  Clinton *(G-1757)*
Offices Etc .... G 918 342-1501
  Claremore *(G-1666)*
Pioneer Printing Inc .... G 918 542-5521
  Miami *(G-4428)*
Shopper News Note .... F 405 756-3169
  Lindsay *(G-4084)*
Snider Printing & Office Sup .... G 405 257-3402
  Wewoka *(G-11511)*
Soltow Business Supply .... G 918 786-4465
  Grove *(G-3289)*
Sooner Industries Inc .... G 918 540-2422
  Miami *(G-4431)*

PRODUCT SECTION

OIL BURNER REPAIR SVCS

Southwest Business Pdts LLC ....G...... 580 765-4401
  Ponca City (G-7878)
Torbett Printing Co & Off Sup ....G...... 918 756-5789
  Okmulgee (G-7528)
Twj Inc ....G...... 405 392-4366
  Tuttle (G-11217)
Vanco Systems ....G...... 405 692-4040
  Oklahoma City (G-5321)
Wallace Printing Company ....G...... 580 326-6323
  Hugo (G-3622)
Watonga Printing & Office Sups ....G...... 580 623-4989
  Watonga (G-11353)
Wilson-Monroe Publishing Co ....G...... 580 933-4579
  Valliant (G-11234)

OFFICE SPLYS, NEC, WHOLESALE

American-Chief Co ....G...... 918 762-2552
  Pawnee (G-7699)
CSC Inc ....G...... 580 938-2533
  Shattuck (G-8420)
Executive Forms & Supplies ....G...... 817 423-9088
  Oklahoma City (G-6060)
Hooker Advance & Office Supply ......G...... 580 652-2476
  Hooker (G-3598)
Warren Products Inc ....F...... 405 947-5676
  Oklahoma City (G-7421)

OFFICES & CLINICS OF HEALTH PRACTITIONERS: Nurse & Med Asst

Eden Clinic Inc ....G...... 405 579-4673
  Norman (G-4988)

OFFICES & CLINICS OF OPTOMETRISTS: Specialist, Contact Lens

Rex Laboratories Inc ....G...... 918 742-9545
  Tulsa (G-10649)

OIL & GAS FIELD EQPT: Drill Rigs

Apollo Oilfield Supply LLC ....G...... 580 254-0164
  Woodward (G-11554)
Seventy Seven Operating LLC ....D...... 405 608-7777
  Oklahoma City (G-7113)

OIL & GAS FIELD MACHINERY

Aceco Valve Inc ....E...... 918 827-3669
  Mounds (G-4608)
Adko Inc ....G...... 405 677-6507
  Oklahoma City (G-5375)
Aether Dbs LLC ....G...... 918 317-2375
  Tulsa (G-8988)
All States Production Eqp Co ....G...... 405 672-2323
  Oklahoma City (G-5414)
American Directional Tech ....G...... 405 449-3362
  Wayne (G-11365)
American Machine & Tool Co ....G...... 405 794-9820
  Wewoka (G-11497)
Apollo Engineering Company ....G...... 918 251-6780
  Broken Arrow (G-830)
Appli-Fab Custom Coating ....G...... 405 235-7039
  Chandler (G-1375)
Atlas Instrument & Mfg Co ....G...... 918 371-1976
  Collinsville (G-1800)
Baker Hughes A GE Company LLC .....G...... 405 227-8471
  Oklahoma City (G-5515)
Baker Hughes Elasto Systems ....F...... 405 670-3354
  Oklahoma City (G-5516)
Baker Hughes Incorporated ....D...... 918 426-6585
  McAlester (G-4272)
Baker Petrolite LLC ....C...... 918 245-2224
  Sand Springs (G-8165)
Bauman Machine Inc ....E...... 405 745-3484
  Oklahoma City (G-5531)
BF Machines Shop Inc ....G...... 580 255-5899
  Duncan (G-2091)
Borets US Inc ....F...... 918 439-7000
  Tulsa (G-9320)
Borets US Inc ....E...... 405 949-0031
  Oklahoma City (G-5621)
Bradshaw Home LLC ....G...... 918 582-5404
  Tulsa (G-9329)
Bri-Chem Supply Corp LLC ....G...... 405 200-5466
  Chickasha (G-1444)
C & H Tool & Machine Inc ....G...... 580 332-1929
  Ada (G-16)
C & H Tool & Machine Inc ....F...... 580 332-1929
  Ada (G-17)

C-Star Mfg Inc ....G...... 405 756-1530
  Lindsay (G-4054)
Callaway Equipment & Mfg ....F...... 405 632-1870
  Oklahoma City (G-5672)
Cameron International Corp ....E...... 405 843-5578
  Oklahoma City (G-5678)
Cameron International Corp ....E...... 405 789-8065
  Oklahoma City (G-5679)
Cameron Technologies Inc ....G...... 405 682-1661
  Moore (G-4503)
Carl Bright Inc ....G...... 405 761-7129
  McLoud (G-4357)
Circle B Msrment Fbrcation LLC ......G...... 918 445-4488
  Tulsa (G-9429)
Cnc Metal Shape Cnstr LLC ....F...... 405 605-5500
  Oklahoma City (G-5794)
Compass Manufacturing LLC ....G...... 405 735-3518
  Oklahoma City (G-5809)
Cougar Drilling Solutions USA ....E...... 405 789-4945
  Oklahoma City (G-5841)
Crowley Oil & Mfg ....G...... 918 744-8129
  Tulsa (G-9514)
Crystaltech Inc ....G...... 580 252-8893
  Duncan (G-2101)
Cyclonic Valve Company ....G...... 918 317-8200
  Broken Arrow (G-883)
D C Jones Machine Co ....G...... 918 786-6855
  Grove (G-3265)
D&L Manufacturing Inc ....G...... 918 587-3504
  Tulsa (G-9542)
Darby Equipment Co ....E...... 918 582-2340
  Tulsa (G-9552)
Electrotech Inc ....G...... 918 224-5869
  Tulsa (G-9002)
Fabricating Specialists Inc ....F...... 405 476-1959
  Oklahoma City (G-6068)
Fammco Mfg Co Inc ....G...... 918 437-0456
  Tulsa (G-9727)
Fhe USA LLC ....G...... 405 350-2544
  Yukon (G-11723)
Fibre Reduction Inc ....G...... 580 223-3401
  Ardmore (G-289)
FMC Technologies Inc ....F...... 405 787-6301
  Oklahoma City (G-6098)
FMC Technologies Inc ....G...... 405 415-9532
  Oklahoma City (G-6100)
Ftdm Investments Llc ....D...... 918 598-3430
  Locust Grove (G-4107)
G & G Quality Services LLC ....G...... 918 961-0288
  Miami (G-4406)
G B E Services Corporation ....G...... 918 428-8665
  Tulsa (G-9788)
Gardner Denver Inc ....D...... 918 664-1151
  Tulsa (G-9800)
Gastech Engineering LLC ....D...... 918 663-8383
  Sapulpa (G-8274)
GE Oil & Gas Pressure Ctrl LP ....E...... 405 273-7660
  Shawnee (G-8451)
H-V Manufacturing Company ....F...... 918 291-2108
  Glenpool (G-3235)
Halliburton Company ....C...... 580 251-3002
  Duncan (G-2122)
Harry H Diamond Inc ....G...... 405 275-5788
  Shawnee (G-8458)
Hoss LLC ....F...... 918 660-7220
  Tulsa (G-9952)
J A Oil Field Mfg Inc ....E...... 405 672-2299
  Oklahoma City (G-6334)
Kerr Machine Co ....G...... 580 622-4207
  Sulphur (G-8837)
Knight Automatics Co Inc ....G...... 918 836-6922
  Tulsa (G-10097)
L M S Products Inc ....G...... 580 336-3555
  Perry (G-7739)
Lahoma Production Inc ....G...... 918 298-2227
  Jenks (G-3715)
Larkin Products LLC ....G...... 918 584-3475
  Tulsa (G-10129)
Lewis Friction Products LLC ....F...... 405 634-5401
  Oklahoma City (G-6470)
Lewis Manufacturing Co LLC ....E...... 405 279-2553
  Meeker (G-4378)
M-I LLC ....G...... 580 225-0104
  Elk City (G-2843)
Machine Parts & Tool ....G...... 580 389-5346
  Ardmore (G-326)
Mark Mullin Co LLC ....G...... 918 245-1426
  Sand Springs (G-8202)
Marple Petroleum LLC ....G...... 405 360-2240
  Norman (G-5064)

Martin-Decker Totco Inc ....F...... 405 350-7408
  Yukon (G-11748)
Mathey Dearman Inc ....E...... 918 447-1288
  Tulsa (G-10222)
Mathey Dearman Inc ....E...... 918 447-1288
  Tulsa (G-10223)
Mayco Inc ....G...... 405 677-5969
  Oklahoma City (G-6543)
N & S Flame Spray LLC ....E...... 918 865-4737
  Mannford (G-4187)
National Oilwell Varco Inc ....D...... 405 745-6850
  Oklahoma City (G-6656)
National Oilwell Varco Inc ....G...... 918 423-8000
  McAlester (G-4322)
National Oilwell Varco Inc ....D...... 405 677-3386
  Oklahoma City (G-6657)
P V Valve ....G...... 580 856-3844
  Ratliff City (G-8061)
Petroleum Instruments Co Inc ....F...... 405 670-6200
  Oklahoma City (G-6837)
Phil Singletary Co Inc ....G...... 918 258-7733
  Broken Arrow (G-1006)
Pipeline Equipment Inc ....E...... 918 224-4144
  Tulsa (G-9024)
Process Products & Service Co ....G...... 918 827-4998
  Mounds (G-4623)
R&R Roustabout Services LLC ....E...... 580 883-4647
  Ringwood (G-8090)
RDS Oilfield Service LLC ....G...... 918 521-9205
  Cushing (G-1953)
Reliance Mfg Solutions LLC ....G...... 405 640-9660
  Oklahoma City (G-7006)
S-T Magi ....G...... 918 358-2312
  Cleveland (G-1733)
Scfm Inc ....E...... 918 663-1309
  Tulsa (G-10713)
Sooner Swage & Coating Co Inc ....G...... 918 689-7142
  Eufaula (G-3114)
SPM Flow Control Inc ....C...... 580 225-1186
  Elk City (G-2875)
Supreme Mch & Stl Fabrication ....F...... 918 387-2036
  Yale (G-11687)
Tam Completion Systems Inc ....G...... 405 601-7564
  Oklahoma City (G-7250)
Testers Inc ....E...... 405 235-9911
  Oklahoma City (G-7273)
Thompson Pump Company ....G...... 918 352-2117
  Drumright (G-2075)
Thompson Pump Company ....F...... 918 756-6164
  Okmulgee (G-7527)
Tokata Oil Recovery Inc ....G...... 405 595-0072
  Stillwater (G-8769)
Tri-Lift Services Inc ....G...... 405 969-2069
  Crescent (G-1921)
Tularosa Inc ....G...... 405 848-0408
  Oklahoma City (G-7349)
U S Weatherford L P ....F...... 580 225-8890
  Elk City (G-2886)
U S Weatherford L P ....F...... 405 756-4331
  Lindsay (G-4095)
United Process Systems Corp ....G...... 918 462-1143
  Wagoner (G-11296)
Wagon Wheel Arklatex LLC ....G...... 918 528-1060
  Jenks (G-3737)
We Buy Scrap LLC ....G...... 580 401-3083
  Ponca City (G-7887)
Weatherford International LLC ....G...... 405 577-5590
  Oklahoma City (G-7432)
Weatherford International LLC ....E...... 940 683-8393
  Oklahoma City (G-7433)
Weatherford International LLC ....G...... 405 350-3357
  Yukon (G-11804)
Weatherford International LLC ....G...... 405 853-7127
  Hennessey (G-3497)
Wenzel Downhole Tools Us Inc ....G...... 405 787-4145
  Oklahoma City (G-7436)
Wilco Machine & Fab Inc ....B...... 580 658-6993
  Marlow (G-4247)
Woolslayer Companies Inc ....C...... 918 523-9191
  Catoosa (G-1368)

OIL BURNER REPAIR SVCS

Action Petroleum Services Corp ......G...... 580 223-6544
  Ardmore (G-237)
Federal Services LLC ....G...... 405 239-7301
  Oklahoma City (G-6080)
Ultimate Chemicals LLC ....G...... 405 703-2771
  Moore (G-4581)

Employee Codes: A=Over 500 employees, B=251-500
C=101-250, D=51-100, E=20-50, F=10-19, G=1-9

OIL FIELD MACHINERY & EQPT

AG Quip Inc .... G 918 536-4325
Ramona *(G-8043)*
Apergy Artfl Lift Intl LLC .... C 432 561-8101
Tulsa *(G-9198)*
APT Inc .... G 405 354-8438
Yukon *(G-11691)*
Bico Drilling Tools Inc .... G 918 872-9983
Broken Arrow *(G-850)*
Big Iron Oilfield Services .... G 580 788-2247
Elmore City *(G-2894)*
Borden Company Inc .... E 918 224-0816
Sapulpa *(G-8258)*
Bronco Manufacturing LLC .... E 918 446-7196
Tulsa *(G-9340)*
Bynum & Company Inc .... F 580 265-7747
Stonewall *(G-8798)*
C & C Equipment Specialist Inc .... E 405 677-3110
Oklahoma City *(G-5655)*
C & H Safety Pin Inc .... G 405 949-5843
Newalla *(G-4806)*
C&H Safety Pin Inc .... G 405 386-3942
McLoud *(G-4356)*
Cameron International Corp .... C 405 745-2715
Oklahoma City *(G-5677)*
Cameron Technologies Inc .... E 580 470-9600
Duncan *(G-2097)*
D Parks Enterprises LLC .... G 405 315-1994
Sand Springs *(G-8177)*
Davco Fab Inc .... E 918 757-2504
Jennings *(G-3739)*
Davis Machine Shop Inc .... F 405 756-3055
Lindsay *(G-4059)*
Deco Development Company Inc .... G 918 747-6366
Tulsa *(G-9566)*
Double Life Corporation .... F 405 789-7867
Oklahoma City *(G-5971)*
Downing Wellhead Equipment LLC .... E 405 486-7858
Oklahoma City *(G-5973)*
Downing Wellhead Equipment LLC .... G 405 789-8182
Oklahoma City *(G-5974)*
Drillers Service Center Inc .... G 405 631-3728
Oklahoma City *(G-5980)*
Enid Mack Sales Inc .... D 580 234-0043
Enid *(G-2954)*
Fabwell Corporation .... E 918 224-9060
Sapulpa *(G-8272)*
FMC Technologies Inc .... F 405 972-1305
Oklahoma City *(G-6099)*
Forum Energy Technologies Inc .... D 405 603-7198
Oklahoma City *(G-6105)*
Forum Energy Technologies Inc .... G 580 622-5058
Davis *(G-1983)*
Forum Production Equipment .... D 580 622-5058
Davis *(G-1984)*
Forum Us Inc .... D 580 788-2333
Elmore City *(G-2896)*
GE Packaged Power LLC .... G 405 395-0400
Shawnee *(G-8452)*
General Manufacturer Inc .... F 918 756-3067
Okmulgee *(G-7504)*
Gordon Bros Supply Inc .... E 918 968-2591
Stroud *(G-8810)*
Halliburton Company .... E 580 251-4614
Duncan *(G-2121)*
Hendershot Tool Company .... E 405 677-3386
Oklahoma City *(G-6238)*
Hunting Titan Inc .... E 405 495-1322
Oklahoma City *(G-6273)*
Hydro Foam Technology Inc .... F 405 547-5800
Perkins *(G-7718)*
Industrial Rubber Inc .... E 405 632-9783
Oklahoma City *(G-6300)*
Industrial Specialties LLC .... G 580 303-9170
Elk City *(G-2826)*
Industrial Vehicles Intl Inc .... E 918 836-6516
Tulsa *(G-9983)*
J E Shaffer Co .... G 918 582-1752
Owasso *(G-7577)*
J P Machine & Tool Co .... F 405 677-3341
Oklahoma City *(G-6337)*
Kimray Inc .... C 405 525-6601
Oklahoma City *(G-6417)*
King Valve Inc .... F 405 672-0046
Oklahoma City *(G-6421)*
Knowles Manufacturing & Mch .... G 405 793-9339
Moore *(G-4532)*
Lewis Manufacturing Co LLC .... G 405 634-5401
Oklahoma City *(G-6471)*
Lowery Well Heads Inc .... G 918 836-1760
Tulsa *(G-10180)*
M & M Fabrication & Service .... G 405 677-1982
Oklahoma City *(G-6506)*
Midco Fabricators Inc .... E 405 282-6667
Guthrie *(G-3324)*
Mingo Manufacturing Inc .... E 918 272-1151
Owasso *(G-7593)*
Morton Grinding Works .... G 918 652-8550
Henryetta *(G-3513)*
Morton Manufacturing Co Inc .... G 918 584-0333
Tulsa *(G-10305)*
Murray Services Inc .... E 405 542-3069
Hinton *(G-3534)*
National Oilwell Varco Inc .... E 918 447-4600
Tulsa *(G-9022)*
National Oilwell Varco LP .... G 405 677-2484
Moore *(G-4544)*
Norriseal-Wellmark Inc .... D 405 672-6660
Oklahoma City *(G-6685)*
Oil States Energy Services LLC .... G 405 702-6536
Oklahoma City *(G-6719)*
Oil States Energy Services LLC .... E 405 686-1001
Oklahoma City *(G-6720)*
Oilfield Equipment & Mfg .... F 405 275-4500
Shawnee *(G-8480)*
Oilfield Improvements Inc .... G 918 250-5584
Broken Arrow *(G-993)*
Ortco Inc .... E 405 670-2803
Oklahoma City *(G-6782)*
Ota Compression LLC .... C 918 623-9922
Okemah *(G-5272)*
Parco Masts & Substructures .... G 918 585-8221
Tulsa *(G-10467)*
Pcs Ferguson Inc .... G 918 967-3236
Stigler *(G-8639)*
Penn Machine Inc .... F 405 789-0084
Oklahoma City *(G-6824)*
Process Manufacturing Co Inc .... C 918 445-0909
Tulsa *(G-9029)*
Psf Services LLC .... G 707 386-8805
Marlow *(G-4239)*
Quality Machine Services Inc .... F 405 495-4962
Oklahoma City *(G-6936)*
R & M Fleet Service Inc .... G 918 367-9326
Cleveland *(G-1732)*
Ralph M Thomas .... G 405 756-4426
Lindsay *(G-4079)*
Sasco Inc .... F 405 670-3230
Oklahoma City *(G-7085)*
Seaboard International Inc .... E 405 619-3099
El Reno *(G-2755)*
Serva Group LLC .... E 918 266-0700
Catoosa *(G-1353)*
Serva Group LLC .... G 580 252-5111
Duncan *(G-2175)*
Sjb Linings LLC .... G 405 225-3829
Oklahoma City *(G-7145)*
Skinner Brothers Company Inc .... F 918 585-5708
Tulsa *(G-10771)*
Solid State Controls Inc .... F 405 273-9292
Shawnee *(G-8501)*
Stream-Flo USA LLC .... G 405 330-5504
Edmond *(G-2634)*
Summit Laydown Services Inc .... E 580 256-5700
Woodward *(G-11636)*
Sydco System Inc .... F 405 350-3161
Foss *(G-3184)*
Tri State Machine & Supply LLC .... G 580 256-6265
Woodward *(G-11644)*
Upco Inc .... D 918 342-1270
Tulsa *(G-11052)*
Valiant Artfl Lift Sltions LLC .... E 405 605-4567
Oklahoma City *(G-7387)*
Valiant Artfl Lift Sltions LLC .... C 405 605-4567
Norman *(G-5191)*
Weatherford International LLC .... F 405 619-7238
Oklahoma City *(G-7434)*
Weatherford International LLC .... E 405 773-1100
Oklahoma City *(G-7430)*
Wenco Energy Corporation .... F 918 252-4511
Tulsa *(G-11108)*
Wildman Manufacturing Inc .... F 405 235-1264
Oklahoma City *(G-7453)*

OIL FIELD SVCS, NEC

007 Operating LLC .... G 580 467-2744
Sulphur *(G-8826)*
300 PSI Inc .... G 918 358-5713
Cleveland *(G-1714)*
66 Oilfield Services LLC .... G 405 735-6666
Oklahoma City *(G-5337)*
A & M Blaylock Cnstr & Parts .... G 918 945-7081
Mc Curtain *(G-4267)*
A-1 Sure Shot .... F 405 677-9800
Oklahoma City *(G-5353)*
ABC Services LLC .... G 580 242-1015
Enid *(G-2903)*
Accelerated Production Svcs .... G 405 603-7492
Oklahoma City *(G-5360)*
Ace Completions OK .... G 580 547-4088
Clinton *(G-1736)*
Ace NDT LLC .... G 580 323-8601
Clinton *(G-1737)*
Action Pipe and Supply Inc .... G 405 853-7170
Hennessey *(G-3443)*
Advanced Pressure Incorporated .... E 405 324-5600
Oklahoma City *(G-5385)*
Advanced Pumping Unit Service .... G 580 658-2050
Marlow *(G-4220)*
Akl Services .... E 918 225-5533
Cushing *(G-1922)*
Alfred N Smith .... G 580 875-3317
Walters *(G-11299)*
Allied Wireline Services LLC .... E 405 445-7135
Moore *(G-4485)*
Altman Engineering Inc .... G 405 368-7889
Kingfisher *(G-3784)*
American Tank Gauge Inc .... F 405 224-7881
Chickasha *(G-1428)*
Anadarko Dozer and Trckg LLC .... G 918 496-4777
Tulsa *(G-9183)*
Anadarko Dozer and Trckg LLC .... G 405 542-3297
Hinton *(G-3521)*
Angel Exploration .... G 405 848-8360
Oklahoma City *(G-5445)*
Apergy Artfl Lift Intl LLC .... E 405 677-3153
Oklahoma City *(G-5451)*
Appli-Fab Custom Coating .... G 405 235-7039
Chandler *(G-1375)*
April Oilfield Services .... G 405 756-5688
Lindsay *(G-4044)*
Arbuckle Wireline LLC .... G 580 226-4001
Ardmore *(G-244)*
Arkoma Tanks LLC .... E 580 622-4794
Wilson *(G-11531)*
Armada Land LC .... G 405 210-7554
Norman *(G-4916)*
Armer & Quillen LLC .... F 405 842-3222
Oklahoma City *(G-5466)*
Asher Oilfield Specialty Inc .... G 405 677-7868
Oklahoma City *(G-5475)*
Asher Oilfield Specialty Inc .... G 405 568-3433
Oklahoma City *(G-5476)*
Aspect Oil Field Servvices LLC .... G 580 774-5006
Weatherford *(G-11391)*
Associated Wire Line Svcs Inc .... F 580 229-0731
Healdton *(G-3407)*
B & B Tool Co Inc .... G 405 756-4530
Lindsay *(G-4045)*
B & R Pump & Equipment Inc .... G 405 632-3051
Oklahoma City *(G-5502)*
Bacas Oilfield Services LLC .... G 580 461-8458
Beaver *(G-539)*
Baker Centrilift Cable Inc .... F 713 439-8600
Claremore *(G-1588)*
Baker Hghes Olfld Oprtions Inc .... G 405 382-0003
Seminole *(G-8356)*
Baker Hghes Olfld Oprtions Inc .... G 405 681-2175
Oklahoma City *(G-5511)*
Baker Hghes Olfld Oprtions LLC .... E 580 256-3333
Oklahoma City *(G-5512)*
Baker Hghes Olfld Oprtions LLC .... C 405 670-3354
Oklahoma City *(G-5513)*
Baker Hghes Olfld Oprtions LLC .... G 918 847-3296
Barnsdall *(G-434)*
Baker Hghes Olfld Oprtions LLC .... B 918 455-3000
Broken Arrow *(G-843)*
Baker Hghes Olfld Oprtions LLC .... G 580 256-7471
Woodward *(G-11559)*
Baker Hghes Olfld Oprtions LLC .... B 918 341-9600
Claremore *(G-1591)*
Baker Hghes Olfld Oprtions LLC .... G 405 756-3384
Lindsay *(G-4046)*
Baker Hughes A GE Company LLC .... D 580 327-2162
Alva *(G-176)*
Baker Hughes A GE Company LLC .... E 806 435-4096
Yukon *(G-11695)*
Baker Hughes A GE Company LLC .... G 580 323-4541
Clinton *(G-1738)*

PRODUCT SECTION — OIL FIELD SVCS, NEC

Company	Code	Phone
Baker Hughes A GE Company LLC	G	918 302-0490
Mcalester (G-4271)		
Baker Hughes A GE Company LLC	E	918 283-1957
Claremore (G-1592)		
Baker Petrolite Inc	G	918 302-0490
Bache (G-429)		
Baker Petrolite LLC	G	918 599-8886
Tulsa (G-9256)		
Baker Petrolite LLC	D	580 323-4541
Clinton (G-1739)		
Baker Well Service Inc	G	405 372-6380
Stillwater (G-8658)		
Baker Wireline	G	405 786-3283
Weleetka (G-11463)		
Balderas LLC	G	580 821-4134
Weatherford (G-11392)		
Baroid Drilling Fluids	G	405 459-6611
Pocasset (G-7774)		
Barrichem Inc	G	580 276-3125
Marietta (G-4199)		
Barry Fennel LLC	G	405 745-7645
Mustang (G-4765)		
Basic Energy Services Inc	E	580 227-3144
Fairview (G-3132)		
Basic Energy Services Inc	G	580 252-6200
Duncan (G-2088)		
Basic Energy Services Inc	G	580 254-3600
Woodward (G-11560)		
Basic Energy Services Inc	G	918 225-0161
Cushing (G-1923)		
Basic Energy Services Inc	G	918 287-3388
Pawhuska (G-7677)		
Basic Energy Services Inc	E	405 756-1820
Lindsay (G-4047)		
Basic Energy Services Inc	G	405 324-0848
Yukon (G-11696)		
Basic Energy Services Inc	F	580 758-1234
Waukomis (G-11359)		
Bayou Oil Field Service & Sup	G	918 398-2166
Tulsa (G-9272)		
Bcrk Limited Partnership	G	405 321-0089
Norman (G-4927)		
Best Oil Field Service Inc	E	405 262-5060
El Reno (G-2701)		
Big Dipper Hot Oil Service	G	580 363-0168
Blackwell (G-674)		
Big League Oil and Gas LLC	G	405 433-9908
Cashion (G-1285)		
Biodynamics Corp	G	405 201-1289
Norman (G-4933)		
BJH Services Inc	G	281 686-3408
Yukon (G-11698)		
Blackhawk Safety LLC	G	580 574-1271
Lawton (G-3898)		
Blackhawk Wireline Services	G	405 238-2929
Pauls Valley (G-7651)		
Blevins Oil Field	G	405 619-9909
Oklahoma City (G-5591)		
Blue Sky Oil Field Svcs LLC	G	580 491-2349
Kaw City (G-3756)		
Blue Star Acid Service Inc	G	918 324-5350
Depew (G-2010)		
BMC Enterprise LLC	G	918 336-4431
Bartlesville (G-457)		
Bob Gene Moore	G	918 371-4381
Collinsville (G-1804)		
BOB Lumber & Grain LLC	F	580 927-3168
Coalgate (G-1775)		
Bobby Joe Cudd Company	G	580 515-3131
Elk City (G-2787)		
BOp Ram-Block Ir Rentals Inc	D	580 772-0250
Weatherford (G-11394)		
Bostick Service Corporation	G	405 969-2198
Crescent (G-1908)		
Bostick Services Corporation	F	405 260-0306
Guthrie (G-3301)		
Brians Hot Oil Service LLC	G	580 778-3549
Turpin (G-11181)		
Brown Oil Tools Inc	G	580 436-0002
Ada (G-14)		
Bruffett Electric	G	918 426-1875
McAlester (G-4278)		
Bulldog Energy Services LLC	G	405 919-9950
Guthrie (G-3302)		
Burton Controls Inc	E	405 692-7278
Oklahoma City (G-5647)		
C 2 Supply Llc	G	918 647-0430
Poteau (G-7898)		
C&J Energy Services Inc	E	405 222-8304
Oklahoma City (G-5664)		
C&J Energy Services Inc	G	580 928-1300
Sayre (G-8337)		
Cactus Wellhead LLC	G	405 708-7200
Oklahoma City (G-5667)		
Calvin Mays Oilfield Svcs Inc	F	405 282-6664
Guthrie (G-3306)		
Camargo Jacks Backhoe Service	G	580 926-3378
Camargo (G-1251)		
Cameron Solutions Inc	F	405 677-8827
Oklahoma City (G-5680)		
Cameron Solutions Inc	G	580 821-0494
Elk City (G-2791)		
Cameron Technologies Inc	E	405 703-8632
Moore (G-4504)		
Can-OK Oil Field Services Inc	E	405 222-2474
Chickasha (G-1446)		
Canadian Pipe & Supply Co	G	405 794-6825
Moore (G-4505)		
Canary LLC	G	405 275-6116
Shawnee (G-8436)		
Cannon Oilfield Services	G	405 387-2644
Newcastle (G-4820)		
Canyon Oilfield Services LLC	E	580 225-7100
Elk City (G-2792)		
Capstone Oil & Gas Inc	G	405 853-7168
Hennessey (G-3449)		
Carbon Economy LLC	G	405 222-9399
Chickasha (G-1448)		
Carnes Oilfield Services LLC	G	580 309-1249
Sayre (G-8338)		
Case Wireline Services Inc	E	580 254-3036
Woodward (G-11567)		
Caseing Crews Inc	G	405 867-1500
Maysville (G-4256)		
Casing Crews Incorporated	D	580 388-4567
Lamont (G-3864)		
Cdl Construction LLC	E	580 323-2847
Clinton (G-1741)		
Cement Specialists LLC	G	432 617-2243
Oklahoma City (G-5722)		
Central Chemical Company	G	580 234-8245
Enid (G-2926)		
Challenger Downhole Tools Inc	G	405 604-0096
Oklahoma City (G-5736)		
Champion Drilling Fluids Inc	G	580 323-0044
Clinton (G-1742)		
Chemical Dynamics Corporation	G	405 392-3505
Tuttle (G-11189)		
Chemoil Energy Inc	B	405 605-5436
Oklahoma City (G-5749)		
Chief Drlg & Foundation Svcs	G	580 302-0124
Weatherford (G-11400)		
Chisholm Oil and Gas Oper LLC	G	918 488-6400
Tulsa (G-9420)		
Cimarron Energy Holding Co LLC	D	405 928-7373
Norman (G-4957)		
Cimarron Energy Inc	G	405 928-2940
Newcastle (G-4822)		
Cimarron Equipment Company	G	918 625-1647
Tulsa (G-9427)		
Clearpoint Chemicals LLC	E	405 320-1719
Pocasset (G-7775)		
Cleveland Lease Service Inc	F	918 358-2791
Cleveland (G-1720)		
Cody Mud Company Inc	G	580 237-5347
Enid (G-2932)		
Coiled Tubing Specialties LLC	G	918 878-7460
Tulsa (G-9466)		
Compass Production Partners LP	E	405 594-4141
Oklahoma City (G-5810)		
Complete Energy LLC	G	405 748-2200
Yukon (G-11710)		
Complete Energy Services Inc	D	405 748-2211
Yukon (G-11711)		
Complete Energy Services Inc	G	580 249-3200
Enid (G-2933)		
Completion Oil Tools LLC	G	580 478-6263
Enid (G-2934)		
Compressco Partners Sub Inc	C	405 677-0221
Oklahoma City (G-5816)		
Cooper Contract Pumping Svc	G	580 487-3552
Forgan (G-3169)		
Copeland Hot Oil Service LLC	G	405 853-2179
Hennessey (G-3452)		
Core Laboratories LP	F	918 834-2337
Tulsa (G-9486)		
Corpo Commission OK	F	580 332-3441
Ada (G-27)		
Corpo Commission OK	F	405 521-4683
Oklahoma City (G-5838)		
Coupling Specialties Inc	F	281 457-2000
Oklahoma City (G-5845)		
CP & C Services	G	918 497-6606
Vinita (G-11251)		
Crescent Services LLC	D	405 603-1200
Oklahoma City (G-5856)		
Cross Roll Inc	G	405 348-9663
Edmond (G-2375)		
Crown Oil Field Services LLC	G	580 363-0269
Blackwell (G-679)		
Cryogas Services LLC	F	580 252-6200
Duncan (G-2100)		
Csi Measurement LLC	G	580 234-4979
Enid (G-2936)		
Cudd Energy Services	G	405 756-4344
Lindsay (G-4057)		
Cudd Operating Corp	G	405 841-1144
Oklahoma City (G-5865)		
Cudd Pressure Control Inc	E	580 243-5890
Elk City (G-2797)		
Cudd Pressure Control Inc	E	405 756-4337
Lindsay (G-4058)		
Cudd Pressure Control Inc	E	580 225-6922
Elk City (G-2798)		
Cudd Pressure Control Inc	D	405 382-2803
Seminole (G-8367)		
Cudd Pressure Control Inc	E	918 423-0160
Krebs (G-3849)		
Cudd Pumping Services	G	580 256-7000
Woodward (G-11575)		
Custom Manufacturing & Maint	G	405 872-1000
Noble (G-4877)		
Cvr Energy	G	405 286-0341
Oklahoma City (G-5882)		
D & B Oil Field Services Inc	D	580 883-2897
Ringwood (G-8087)		
D Wiliams Pipe Insptn Poly LI	G	405 426-7776
Purcell (G-8004)		
D&L Manufacturing Inc	G	918 587-3504
Tulsa (G-9541)		
Danco Inspection Service Inc	G	405 691-5752
Oklahoma City (G-5284)		
Dannys Oilfield Services Inc	G	918 645-1651
Bristow (G-775)		
Davenport Oilfield Services	G	580 465-0314
Ardmore (G-275)		
Db Wireline Services Inc	G	918 389-5038
McAlester (G-4292)		
Deans Casing Service	F	405 379-3495
Holdenville (G-3552)		
Deep Well Tubular Services Inc	F	405 850-5826
Oklahoma City (G-5919)		
Delta Well Logging Svc	G	405 381-2954
Tuttle (G-11195)		
Derrick Hoppes	G	580 667-4373
Tipton (G-8958)		
Devilbiss Coring Service Inc	G	405 392-2515
Blanchard (G-711)		
Deviney Paraffin Scraping	G	405 867-5945
Maysville (G-4259)		
Diamond Energy Services LP	F	918 764-4000
Tulsa (G-9578)		
Diamond Oil Field Services Inc	G	405 863-1052
Yukon (G-11718)		
Diane Oil Co	G	405 528-5100
Oklahoma City (G-5943)		
Direct Oilfield Services LLC	G	405 385-4743
Stillwater (G-8676)		
Dixon Construction Co	E	405 665-5515
Wynnewood (G-11670)		
Don Scott	G	405 969-3649
Crescent (G-1913)		
Don-Nan Pump and Supply Co Inc	G	432 682-7742
Ratliff City (G-8050)		
Donnie Gaines Wldg Fabrication	G	580 668-3249
Wilson (G-11532)		
Double R Oilfield Services LLC	G	580 388-4567
Lamont (G-3868)		
Double R Servcoes Company Inc	E	580 883-4637
Ringwood (G-8088)		
Double S Tank Truck Service	G	580 863-5231
Garber (G-3212)		
Drc Service Co	G	580 661-3300
Thomas (G-8942)		
Drilling Tools Intl Inc	F	405 604-2763
Oklahoma City (G-5981)		
Duane Durkee Pumping Svc	G	405 820-3256
Perry (G-7731)		
Duane Waugh	G	580 596-2485
Cherokee (G-1416)		

Employee Codes: A=Over 500 employees, B=251-500
C=101-250, D=51-100, E=20-50, F=10-19, G=1-9

OIL FIELD SVCS, NEC

Dunlap Oil Tools .... G 918 885-6353
 Hominy *(G-3582)*
Dunlap Well Service Inc .... G 918 367-2660
 Bristow *(G-776)*
E & K Oilfield Services Inc .... G 580 994-2442
 Mooreland *(G-4589)*
E C Carman Casing Gauge Co .... G 918 605-5093
 Tulsa *(G-9620)*
E J R Enterprises LLC .... G 580 623-0051
 Watonga *(G-11346)*
Eagle Oilfield Service LLC .... G 580 774-2240
 Weatherford *(G-11408)*
Earl-Le Dozer Service LLC .... D 918 352-2072
 Drumright *(G-2059)*
Eastern Oil Well Services .... G 405 947-1091
 Oklahoma City *(G-6000)*
Eco-Lift Energy Services Inc .... G 580 772-5157
 Weatherford *(G-11410)*
Eddies Submersible Service Inc ...... F 405 273-9292
 Tecumseh *(G-8913)*
Elk City Forklift Service Inc .... G 580 225-0855
 Elk City *(G-2809)*
Emjo Operations Inc .... G 580 658-6457
 Marlow *(G-4232)*
Energes .... G 580 339-8044
 Elk City *(G-2812)*
Enos Kauk .... G 580 488-3375
 Leedey *(G-4028)*
Entz Ground Sterilant Inc .... G 405 542-3174
 Hinton *(G-3526)*
Envirnmntal Tchncians Okla LLC .... G 580 772-7805
 Weatherford *(G-11411)*
Envirnmntal Tchncians Okla LLC .... G 580 227-2521
 Fairview *(G-3135)*
Enviro Log Operating LLC .... G 405 834-1417
 Piedmont *(G-7761)*
Enviro-Clean Services L L C .... E 405 373-4545
 Oklahoma City *(G-6045)*
Express Energy Svcs Oper LP .... E 405 763-5850
 Oklahoma City *(G-6063)*
Expro Americas LLC .... E 405 378-6762
 Oklahoma City *(G-6065)*
Falcon Field Service Inc .... E 918 885-2244
 Hominy *(G-3583)*
Falcon Flowback Services LLC .... B 405 563-0163
 Oklahoma City *(G-6071)*
Far West Development LLC .... G 405 557-1384
 Oklahoma City *(G-6072)*
Fidgets Oilfield Services LLC .... G 918 473-2765
 Checotah *(G-1393)*
Field Services .... G 580 256-3338
 Woodward *(G-11583)*
Fisher Wireline Services Inc .... G 918 885-6564
 Hominy *(G-3584)*
Five Point Services Inc .... E 580 856-3670
 Ratliff City *(G-8053)*
Flex Chem Corporation .... F 580 772-2386
 Weatherford *(G-11414)*
Flow Testing Inc .... E 918 423-0017
 Krebs *(G-3850)*
Fluid Lift Inc .... G 405 853-6876
 Hennessey *(G-3461)*
Foamtech Inc .... E 580 256-3979
 Woodward *(G-11584)*
Forsythe Oilfield Service Inc .... E 580 668-3371
 Wilson *(G-11533)*
Frac Specialists LLC .... F 432 617-3722
 Oklahoma City *(G-6110)*
Fractalsoft LLC .... G 405 330-3555
 Edmond *(G-2420)*
Fraser Oilfield Service LLC .... G 918 716-0665
 Okemah *(G-5269)*
Freds Rat Hole Service Inc .... F 405 756-4300
 Lindsay *(G-4063)*
Freepoint Pipe & Supply Inc .... G 405 341-1913
 Edmond *(G-2423)*
Frenchs Blue River Cnstr .... F 580 274-3444
 Longdale *(G-4123)*
G&J Enterprises .... G 580 237-2029
 Enid *(G-2960)*
Gambill Oilfield Services LLC .... G 580 471-1451
 Mangum *(G-4171)*
Gaston Services Inc .... G 580 328-5647
 Camargo *(G-1252)*
General Inc .... E 580 921-3365
 Laverne *(G-3878)*
Genesis Oil Tool International .... G 403 298-2430
 Oklahoma City *(G-6143)*
Genie Well Service Inc .... E 405 969-2141
 Crescent *(G-1916)*

Gilliland Fluid Corporation .... G 405 853-7188
 Hennessey *(G-3462)*
Glimp Oil Company LLC .... G 918 352-2978
 Drumright *(G-2060)*
Gonzo LLC .... G 405 373-1715
 Yukon *(G-11727)*
Gore Nitrogen .... G 405 381-4928
 Tuttle *(G-11201)*
Gray Mud Disposal .... G 580 635-2225
 Kremlin *(G-3852)*
Green Country Wireline Inc .... G 918 534-2107
 Dewey *(G-2022)*
Green River Operating Co .... G 405 872-9616
 Noble *(G-4881)*
Greg Tucker Construction .... E 405 756-3958
 Lindsay *(G-4064)*
Grisham Services Incorporated .... F 918 307-7635
 Broken Arrow *(G-924)*
Gryphon Oilfield Solutions .... G 405 446-8065
 Chickasha *(G-1465)*
Guardian Tubular Services Inc .... G 405 262-3800
 El Reno *(G-2721)*
Gyrodata Incorporated .... D 405 677-0200
 Oklahoma City *(G-6195)*
H & J Services .... F 580 237-4613
 Enid *(G-2966)*
H2 Services LLC .... E 405 388-9049
 Guthrie *(G-3317)*
Haken Dozer Service .... G 580 669-2211
 Glencoe *(G-3223)*
Hall & Anderson Services Inc .... E 580 319-5624
 Ardmore *(G-300)*
Hall Energy .... G 405 231-2490
 Oklahoma City *(G-6205)*
Halliburton Company .... E 580 251-3379
 Duncan *(G-2123)*
Halliburton Company .... G 580 251-3420
 Oklahoma City *(G-6206)*
Halliburton Company .... E 918 587-3117
 Tulsa *(G-9881)*
Halliburton Company .... E 405 278-9685
 Duncan *(G-2125)*
Halliburton Company .... G 580 251-4421
 Duncan *(G-2126)*
Halliburton Company .... C 405 231-1800
 Oklahoma City *(G-6207)*
Halliburton Company .... C 806 665-0005
 Duncan *(G-2127)*
Halliburton Company .... E 580 251-3406
 Duncan *(G-2128)*
Halliburton Company .... G 405 459-6611
 Pocasset *(G-7777)*
Halliburton Company .... E 405 552-8520
 Oklahoma City *(G-6208)*
Halliburton Company .... E 405 805-2200
 Oklahoma City *(G-6209)*
Halliburton Company .... D 580 251-3760
 Duncan *(G-2129)*
Halliburton Company .... E 405 231-1800
 Moore *(G-4527)*
Halliburton Company .... G 405 459-6611
 Pocasset *(G-7776)*
Hamm and Phillips Services Co ...... G 580 256-8686
 Woodward *(G-11590)*
Hammer Construction Inc .... C 405 310-3160
 Norman *(G-5014)*
Harvey Kates .... G 918 225-2567
 Cushing *(G-1934)*
Hassler Hot Oil Service LLC .... G 405 756-0448
 Lindsay *(G-4066)*
Hawley Hot Oil LLC .... G 580 839-2416
 Nash *(G-4803)*
Herriman Oilfield Services .... G 580 925-2144
 Konawa *(G-3846)*
High Plains Services Inc .... G 580 225-7388
 Elk City *(G-2822)*
Holden Energy Corp .... E 580 226-3960
 Ardmore *(G-306)*
Holland Services LLC .... G 405 842-9393
 Oklahoma City *(G-6257)*
Homer Rinehart Company .... D 405 756-2785
 Lindsay *(G-4067)*
Homer Rinehart Company .... E 405 756-2785
 Lindsay *(G-4068)*
Horizon Well Servicing LLC .... G 580 482-7500
 Altus *(G-158)*
Horizon Welltesting LLC .... G 918 429-1200
 Mcalester *(G-4304)*
Horton Tool Company .... F 918 885-6941
 Hominy *(G-3588)*

Horton Tool Corporation .... F 918 885-6941
 Hominy *(G-3589)*
Hoskins Wireline LLC .... F 580 303-9101
 Elk City *(G-2824)*
Hoss Consulting Serv .... G 405 324-5543
 Mustang *(G-4776)*
Hot Oil Units Inc .... G 580 256-6461
 Woodward *(G-11592)*
HP Field Services LLC .... G 580 763-1428
 Stillwater *(G-8703)*
Hughes Trucking .... G 580 244-3731
 Smithville *(G-8578)*
Hulls Oilfield LLC .... F 580 668-2619
 Wilson *(G-11536)*
Hutton Inc .... F 580 225-0225
 Elk City *(G-2825)*
Hyperion Energy LP .... F 918 321-3350
 Kiefer *(G-3780)*
Independent Trucking Co Inc .... F 918 352-2539
 Drumright *(G-2063)*
Inman Well Service .... G 918 440-3151
 Bartlesville *(G-497)*
Innovative Oilfield Svcs LLC .... G 918 521-8317
 Red Oak *(G-8078)*
Integrated Fluid Systems .... G 405 418-2897
 Chickasha *(G-1471)*
Integrated Fluid Systems LLC .... G 580 323-8431
 Clinton *(G-1753)*
Integrated Production Services .... G 580 225-5667
 Elk City *(G-2828)*
Integrity Trckg Cnstr Svcs Inc .... E 580 361-2387
 Balko *(G-432)*
Iron Gate Tubular Services .... G 580 303-9046
 Elk City *(G-2829)*
J & A Hot Oilers Inc .... G 405 341-7600
 Edmond *(G-2464)*
J & J Services Inc .... G 580 265-9466
 Stonewall *(G-8801)*
J & J Solutions LLC .... D 580 336-3050
 Perry *(G-7737)*
J & L Oil Field Services LLC .... B 580 938-2205
 Shattuck *(G-8422)*
J & R Service Inc .... G 580 256-6461
 Woodward *(G-11594)*
J B Hot Oil and Steam Co Inc .... G 918 366-3872
 Bixby *(G-636)*
J Scott Inc .... F 405 262-5900
 El Reno *(G-2727)*
J-B Oilfield Services LLC .... F 580 388-4484
 Lamont *(G-3869)*
James A Taylor .... G 918 724-3121
 Pawhuska *(G-7687)*
JB Oil Field Services .... G 580 363-3030
 Blackwell *(G-684)*
Jec Operating LLC .... G 405 235-4454
 Oklahoma City *(G-6352)*
Jeffrey C James .... G 405 728-8145
 Oklahoma City *(G-6355)*
Jeremys Rustabouts Backhoe Inc .. F 580 772-5157
 Weatherford *(G-11421)*
Jerry Dunkin Well Services .... G 580 237-6152
 Enid *(G-2984)*
JM Oilfield Services Inc .... E 501 589-4044
 Enid *(G-2986)*
John L Lewis .... G 405 941-3224
 Sasakwa *(G-8330)*
John W Stone Oil Distributing .... G 918 744-8168
 Tulsa *(G-10053)*
JS Oilfield Services LLC .... G 580 542-7822
 Enid *(G-2989)*
K & W Well Service Inc .... E 918 225-7855
 Cushing *(G-1940)*
K W B Oil Property Management ..... F 918 583-8300
 Tulsa *(G-10070)*
Kathy Tim Lowery .... G 580 925-2171
 Konawa *(G-3847)*
Kautzs Pumping Inc .... G 580 661-3397
 Thomas *(G-8945)*
Kens Hot Oil & Steam Service .... G 405 382-3052
 Earlsboro *(G-2281)*
Key Energy Services Inc .... C 405 262-1231
 Woodward *(G-11600)*
Key Energy Services Inc .... F 405 262-1190
 El Reno *(G-2731)*
Key Energy Services Inc .... F 806 435-5583
 Woodward *(G-11602)*
Key Energy Services Inc .... F 405 756-3347
 Lindsay *(G-4071)*
Kiester Operating Company .... G 580 255-4020
 Duncan *(G-2142)*

PRODUCT SECTION — OIL FIELD SVCS, NEC

Company	Code	Phone
Kings Well Service	F	580 363-3912
Blackwell *(G-686)*		
Kirk Tank Trucks Inc	G	918 733-4503
Morris *(G-4598)*		
L & O Pump and Supply Inc	G	405 756-3877
Lindsay *(G-4072)*		
L Dean Hudgins Inc	G	918 224-6236
Sapulpa *(G-8284)*		
Lamamco Drilling Co	G	580 856-3561
Ratliff City *(G-8056)*		
Landmark Energy LLC	G	405 382-3951
Seminole *(G-8383)*		
Legend Energy Services LLC	E	405 600-1264
Oklahoma City *(G-6464)*		
Liberty Transportation LLC	G	580 225-2784
Elk City *(G-2838)*		
Lightning Services Inc	G	405 853-6669
Hennessey *(G-3472)*		
Litta Solutions LLC	G	918 845-4854
Bixby *(G-642)*		
Logic Energy Solutions LLC	G	405 601-9037
Oklahoma City *(G-6489)*		
Longhorn Service Company LLC	E	405 853-7170
Hennessey *(G-3473)*		
Lost River Oilfield Services L	G	208 670-5787
Edmond *(G-2496)*		
Lubri Flange LLC	G	580 303-9139
Elk City *(G-2840)*		
M & D Oilfield Services	G	405 677-5720
Oklahoma City *(G-6505)*		
M & M Electric	G	580 233-8999
Enid *(G-3002)*		
M & W Oilfield Service LLC	G	580 927-2200
Coalgate *(G-1782)*		
M&M Hot Oil Service LLC	G	580 651-1746
Guymon *(G-3355)*		
M-I LLC	G	580 225-2482
Elk City *(G-2844)*		
M-I LLC	E	405 224-4170
Chickasha *(G-1482)*		
Magnum Energy Inc	G	405 360-2784
Norman *(G-5063)*		
Manford Oilfield Services LLC	G	918 424-3280
McAlester *(G-4314)*		
Marsau	G	580 432-5000
Foster *(G-3186)*		
Marsau Enterprises Inc	A	580 233-3910
Enid *(G-3007)*		
Martin-Decker Totco Inc	G	580 225-8980
Elk City *(G-2847)*		
McCabe Roustabout Service	G	918 534-3131
Dewey *(G-2028)*		
McDonald Safety Anchor Inc	G	405 574-4151
Chickasha *(G-1483)*		
McWI Inc	G	405 360-2277
Norman *(G-5068)*		
Metzger Oil Tools Inc	G	918 885-2456
Hominy *(G-3592)*		
Michael S Azlin	G	405 257-3581
Wewoka *(G-11505)*		
Mid Continent Well Log Svcs	G	405 360-7333
Norman *(G-5075)*		
Mid-States Oilfield Mch LLC	E	405 605-5656
Oklahoma City *(G-6593)*		
Midway Machine & Welding LLC	G	918 968-3316
Stroud *(G-8812)*		
Midway Services LLC	G	405 820-8850
Edmond *(G-2518)*		
Miller Bros Wldg & Roustabout	G	918 968-1611
Stroud *(G-8813)*		
Misson Fluid King Oil Field	G	405 670-8771
Oklahoma City *(G-6619)*		
Mitchells Tank Truck Service	G	580 229-1880
Healdton *(G-3419)*		
Momentum Completion	G	918 364-9444
Tulsa *(G-10297)*		
Mooney Oilfield Services LLC	G	580 660-5203
Weatherford *(G-11429)*		
Moore Contract Pumping	G	918 372-4645
Ripley *(G-8102)*		
Moran Equipment LLC	E	580 225-2575
Elk City *(G-2850)*		
MSI Inspection Service LLC	G	405 265-2121
Oklahoma City *(G-6632)*		
Mt Percussion Drilling LLC	G	918 232-5472
Tulsa *(G-10310)*		
Munoz Oilfield Services LLC	G	580 799-5857
Elk City *(G-2852)*		
Muras Energy Inc	F	405 751-0442
Edmond *(G-2523)*		
Mustang Extreme Environmental	F	405 681-1800
Oklahoma City *(G-6639)*		
Mwd Services LLC	G	918 698-6109
Owasso *(G-7595)*		
Nabors Drilling Tech USA Inc	C	580 243-4000
Elk City *(G-2853)*		
Nabors Well Services Ltd	E	405 262-6262
El Reno *(G-2742)*		
National Oilwell Varco Inc	D	580 251-6900
Duncan *(G-2158)*		
National Oilwell Varco Inc	E	580 225-4136
Elk City *(G-2855)*		
Newpark Drilling Fluids LLC	C	580 323-1612
Clinton *(G-1761)*		
Nexstreem Reclaim Plant	G	580 657-4580
Wilson *(G-11540)*		
Nextier Cmpltion Solutions Inc	E	580 772-3100
Weatherford *(G-11430)*		
Norman Moore	G	405 941-3220
Sasakwa *(G-8333)*		
North Star Well Services Inc	D	580 256-5644
Woodward *(G-11615)*		
Nubs Well Servicing Inc	F	580 856-3887
Ratliff City *(G-8058)*		
Nutech Energy Alliance Ltd	G	405 388-4236
Oklahoma City *(G-5309)*		
O K Plunger Service	G	918 352-4269
Drumright *(G-2068)*		
O K Tank Trucks Inc	F	918 396-3043
Skiatook *(G-8562)*		
Oil Tools Rentals Inc	F	580 242-1140
(G-3024)		
Oilfield Dstrbtons Spclsts LLC	G	580 237-1237
Enid *(G-3025)*		
Oilfield Lease Maintenance	G	405 348-1562
Edmond *(G-2546)*		
Oilfield Technical Svcs LLC	G	405 603-4288
Oklahoma City *(G-6724)*		
Oklahoma Cellulose Inc	G	918 706-5279
Cleveland *(G-1730)*		
Oklahoma Sub Surfc Pump & Sup	G	405 382-7311
Seminole *(G-8392)*		
One Oaks Field Service	D	580 816-4500
Weatherford *(G-11431)*		
Osage Wireline Service Inc	G	918 358-5155
Cleveland *(G-1731)*		
Outsource Group LLC	G	918 307-0110
Tulsa *(G-10446)*		
Owen Oil Tools LP	G	405 495-4441
Oklahoma City *(G-6789)*		
P /Masters C Inc	E	405 293-9777
Guthrie *(G-3332)*		
PAK Oilfield Services LLC	E	580 504-7049
Ardmore *(G-343)*		
Panhandle Construction Svcs	F	580 338-7667
Guymon *(G-3359)*		
Parker Energy Services Co	G	918 626-4982
Pocola *(G-7784)*		
Parks Oil Tools LLC	G	405 485-9515
Blanchard *(G-725)*		
Pat McVicker Oilfield Services	G	580 256-1577
Woodward *(G-11616)*		
Patrick McVicker	G	580 256-1577
Woodward *(G-11617)*		
Payrock II LLC	G	405 608-8077
Oklahoma City *(G-6814)*		
Pcs Ferguson Inc	G	580 256-1317
Woodward *(G-11619)*		
Peak Oilfield Services	G	405 884-2379
Geary *(G-3217)*		
Pearson Pumping Inc	G	918 486-2386
Coweta *(G-1893)*		
Permian Basin Banding	G	432 238-1483
Tulsa *(G-10497)*		
Petra Solutions LLC	G	316 554-6586
Edmond *(G-2567)*		
Petroleum Elastomers	G	405 672-0900
Oklahoma City *(G-6836)*		
Pettitt Wireline Service LLC	G	580 234-0550
Enid *(G-3035)*		
Pinnacle Energy Services LLC	G	405 810-9151
Oklahoma City *(G-6849)*		
Pinson Well Logging	G	405 604-5036
Oklahoma City *(G-6851)*		
Plains Nitrogen LLC	G	405 418-8426
Oklahoma City *(G-6855)*		
Plains Nitrogen LLC	G	918 429-0041
McAlester *(G-4329)*		
Power Rig LLC	F	580 254-3232
Woodward *(G-11622)*		
Premiere Inc	F	405 262-1554
El Reno *(G-2748)*		
Primeenergy Corporation	E	405 375-5203
Oklahoma City *(G-6895)*		
Priority Artificial Lift	G	405 265-1696
Yukon *(G-11768)*		
Pro Directional	G	405 200-1450
Oklahoma City *(G-6903)*		
Pro Ject Chemicals	G	580 445-4345
Weatherford *(G-11434)*		
Pro Oilfield Services LLC	G	405 778-8844
Oklahoma City *(G-6904)*		
Pro Technics International	G	405 680-5560
Oklahoma City *(G-6907)*		
Production String Services	G	580 747-4017
Enid *(G-3039)*		
Protechnics Okc Chemical Off	G	405 601-3078
Oklahoma City *(G-6918)*		
Proven Torque LLC	G	780 982-7597
Mooreland *(G-4593)*		
Qes Pressure Control LLC	D	405 605-2700
Oklahoma City *(G-6930)*		
Qes Pressure Pumping LLC	E	918 338-0808
Bartlesville *(G-519)*		
Qes Pressure Pumping LLC	G	405 483-8000
Union City *(G-11220)*		
Quail Tools LP	G	918 994-4695
Tulsa *(G-10588)*		
Quality Parts Mfg Co Inc	G	918 627-3307
Tulsa *(G-10592)*		
Quality Tank Manufacturing	G	405 756-1188
Lindsay *(G-4078)*		
R & M Packer Inc	G	580 863-2242
Sand Springs *(G-8218)*		
R360 Oklahoma LLC	E	405 262-5900
El Reno *(G-2750)*		
Ram Oilfield Services LLC	G	918 639-2827
Tulsa *(G-10614)*		
Rambler Energy Services Inc	E	580 242-7447
Enid *(G-3042)*		
Rameys Welding & Roustabout	G	918 321-3156
Kiefer *(G-3781)*		
Ranger Rentals LLC	G	580 541-4242
Enid *(G-3043)*		
Rauh Oilfield Services Co	G	580 796-2128
Lahoma *(G-3860)*		
Razor Oilfield Services LLC	F	405 661-0008
Hinton *(G-3535)*		
Recoil Oilfield Services LLC	C	405 227-4198
Blanchard *(G-732)*		
Red Bone Services LLC	F	580 225-1200
Elk City *(G-2865)*		
Red Hills Hot Shot Inc	G	580 225-8686
Sayre *(G-8344)*		
Red River Oilfield Svcs LLC	G	405 802-4280
Edmond *(G-2590)*		
Reddirt Oilfield Services	G	580 665-9321
Elk City *(G-2866)*		
Reliance Ofs	G	303 317-6565
Tulsa *(G-10637)*		
Reliance Oilfield Services LLC	E	918 392-9000
Tulsa *(G-10638)*		
Reliance Pressure Control	G	405 320-5074
Norman *(G-5131)*		
Renegade Services	G	580 254-2828
Woodward *(G-11628)*		
Rifle Tool Company	G	580 856-3030
Ratliff City *(G-8065)*		
Rig Chasers LLC	E	580 254-3830
Woodward *(G-11630)*		
Riley Expiration - Permian LLC	G	405 415-8699
Oklahoma City *(G-7026)*		
Ring Energy Inc	G	918 499-3880
Tulsa *(G-10654)*		
Robert C Brooks Inc	G	405 478-0260
Edmond *(G-2602)*		
Rocking P Sales & Services LLC	G	580 530-0028
Hobart *(G-3544)*		
Rose Rock Midstream Field Svcs	G	918 524-7700
Tulsa *(G-10672)*		
Rpc Inc	E	580 225-0843
Elk City *(G-2871)*		
Rufnex Oilfield Services LLC	G	405 741-8322
Oklahoma City *(G-7061)*		
S & H Tank Service Inc	E	405 756-3121
Lindsay *(G-4081)*		
S & H Tank Service of Oklahoma	F	405 756-3121
Lindsay *(G-4082)*		
Safety Plus USA LLC	E	580 622-4796
Sulphur *(G-8843)*		

Employee Codes: A=Over 500 employees, B=251-500, C=101-250, D=51-100, E=20-50, F=10-19, G=1-9

Samhill LLC ....G.... 580 761-1255
Tonkawa *(G-8981)*
Sampson Brothers Inc....G.... 580 994-2464
Mooreland *(G-4594)*
Sanders Electric....G.... 405 377-1691
Stillwater *(G-8752)*
Schlumberger Technology Corp ....C.... 405 789-1515
Oklahoma City *(G-7089)*
Schlumberger Technology Corp ....C.... 405 422-8700
El Reno *(G-2753)*
Schlumberger Technology Corp ....G.... 580 762-2481
Ponca City *(G-7872)*
Schlumberger Technology Corp ....E.... 405 942-0002
Oklahoma City *(G-7090)*
Schlumberger Technology Corp ....D.... 918 661-2000
Bartlesville *(G-525)*
Schlumberger Technology Corp ....G.... 918 584-6651
Tulsa *(G-10714)*
Schlumberger Technology Corp ....G.... 405 306-8244
Moore *(G-4564)*
Schlumberger Technology Corp ....G.... 580 252-3355
Duncan *(G-2173)*
Schlumberger Technology Corp ....G.... 580 774-7557
Weatherford *(G-11439)*
Schlumberger Technology Corp ....C.... 580 225-0730
El Reno *(G-2754)*
Schlumberger Technology Corp ....E.... 918 247-1300
Kellyville *(G-3767)*
Schlumberger Technology Corp ....G.... 405 682-2284
Yukon *(G-11777)*
Scientific Drilling Intl Inc....D.... 405 787-3663
Yukon *(G-11780)*
Scott Greer Sales Inc....G.... 405 670-4654
Oklahoma City *(G-7095)*
Sean Josephson LLC ....G.... 918 606-9677
Tulsa *(G-9035)*
Select Energy Services LLC ....G.... 405 295-2566
El Reno *(G-2756)*
Select Energy Services LLC ....D.... 918 302-0069
Alderson *(G-128)*
Semgroup Corporation....B.... 918 524-8100
Tulsa *(G-10728)*
Shebester Bechtel Inc ....E.... 405 577-2700
Oklahoma City *(G-7117)*
Shebester Bechtel Inc ....D.... 580 363-4124
Blackwell *(G-691)*
Shebester Bechtel Inc ....E.... 580 242-4876
Enid *(G-3055)*
Sims Electric of Oklahoma Inc ....F.... 580 338-8932
Guymon *(G-3366)*
Sirrah Investments....G.... 405 853-4909
Hennessey *(G-3487)*
Sisk Construction Co ....G.... 405 375-5318
Kingfisher *(G-3815)*
Sjl Oil and Gas Inc ....E.... 405 853-2044
Hennessey *(G-3488)*
Skyline Drctonal Drillling LLC ....E.... 405 429-4050
Moore *(G-4570)*
SM Oil & Gas Inc ....G.... 918 629-2151
Skiatook *(G-8571)*
Smith & Sons Salvage....G.... 580 342-6218
Temple *(G-8935)*
Smith International Inc ....E.... 405 670-7200
Oklahoma City *(G-7155)*
Smith International Inc ....F.... 800 654-6461
Ponca City *(G-7875)*
Smith International Inc ....G.... 580 252-3355
Duncan *(G-2178)*
Smith Pump Supply....G.... 405 258-0834
Chandler *(G-1387)*
Sooner Completions Inc....E.... 405 273-4599
Shawnee *(G-8502)*
Sooner Hot Oil Service....G.... 580 762-2586
Ponca City *(G-7876)*
Sooner Production Services Inc....F.... 580 256-1155
Woodward *(G-11633)*
Southern Plains Enrgy Svcs LLC ....G.... 918 225-3570
Cushing *(G-1960)*
Southstar Energy Corp....G.... 580 223-1553
Ardmore *(G-356)*
Southwest Oilfield Service....G.... 580 302-4069
Weatherford *(G-11444)*
Sparlin Hot Oil Service Inc....G.... 580 795-2513
Madill *(G-4163)*
Spearhead Services....G.... 405 756-8615
Lindsay *(G-4086)*
Spectrum Tracer Services LLC....D.... 405 470-5566
Tulsa *(G-10819)*
Spread Tech LLC....E.... 580 994-2506
Mooreland *(G-4595)*
Spurlock Co Satellite Mapping ....G.... 405 495-8628
Oklahoma City *(G-7189)*
Stacey Oil Services....G.... 918 427-3940
Roland *(G-8114)*
Stallion Oilfield Services Ltd ....E.... 580 225-5800
Elk City *(G-2876)*
Stallion Oilfield Services Ltd ....E.... 580 225-8990
Elk City *(G-2877)*
Star Pipe Service Inc ....F.... 405 672-6688
Oklahoma City *(G-7194)*
Star Well Services Inc....F.... 405 222-4606
Chickasha *(G-1513)*
Steves Construction Company....G.... 580 432-5398
Elmore City *(G-2897)*
Stinger Wllhead Protection Inc....F.... 405 702-6575
Oklahoma City *(G-7205)*
Stinger Wllhead Protection Inc....E.... 405 684-2940
Oklahoma City *(G-7206)*
Stockton Transports Inc....G.... 580 227-3793
Fairview *(G-3152)*
Stride Well Service Inc ....E.... 580 254-2353
Woodward *(G-11635)*
Strong Service LP....G.... 405 756-1716
Lindsay *(G-4089)*
Sum Professionals Inc ....F.... 580 983-2379
Durham *(G-2273)*
Summit Well Servicing LLC ....G.... 580 467-0886
Ratliff City *(G-8068)*
Super Flow Testers Inc....E.... 405 756-8795
Lindsay *(G-4090)*
Super Heaters LLC....F.... 580 225-3196
Elk City *(G-2880)*
Superior Tool Services Inc....G.... 918 640-5503
Bristow *(G-797)*
Sutherland Well Service Inc....D.... 580 229-1338
Healdton *(G-3422)*
Swabbing Johns Inc ....F.... 405 756-8141
Lindsay *(G-4092)*
T D Craighead....G.... 405 329-2229
Norman *(G-5169)*
T K Stanley Inc ....G.... 405 745-3479
Oklahoma City *(G-7246)*
T&T Forklift Service Inc....G.... 405 756-3451
Lindsay *(G-4093)*
T3 Energy LLC....G.... 405 677-8051
Oklahoma City *(G-7247)*
Tamco Plunger & Lift Inc....G.... 405 853-6195
Hennessey *(G-3491)*
Tank Masters ....G.... 580 332-3325
Ada *(G-92)*
Target Completions LLC ....G.... 918 872-6115
Broken Arrow *(G-1071)*
Taylor Rig LLC....D.... 918 266-7301
Tulsa *(G-10906)*
Tcj Oilfield Services LLC ....G.... 580 687-4454
Elmer *(G-2892)*
Ted Smith....G.... 405 677-8402
Oklahoma City *(G-7264)*
Teg Solutions LLC ....F.... 405 354-1951
El Reno *(G-2761)*
Terra Pilot Mwd Tools LLC ....F.... 405 603-2200
Oklahoma City *(G-7271)*
Terraco Production Leasing LLC ....G.... 580 658-3000
Marlow *(G-4245)*
Terry Stutzmann....G.... 405 481-3853
Shawnee *(G-8510)*
Terrys Pump & Supply Inc ....G.... 405 853-6550
Hennessey *(G-3492)*
Testco Inc ....F.... 580 623-4900
Watonga *(G-11350)*
Texas Transco Inc....G.... 903 857-9136
Marietta *(G-4214)*
Three Rivers Corp....G.... 918 492-3239
Tulsa *(G-10938)*
Thru Tubing Solutions Inc....G.... 918 429-7700
McAlester *(G-4341)*
Thru Tubing Solutions Inc....C.... 405 692-1900
Oklahoma City *(G-5320)*
Thru Tubing Solutions Inc....F.... 580 225-6977
Elk City *(G-2882)*
Thurmond-Mcglothlin LLC ....G.... 580 774-2659
Weatherford *(G-11446)*
Tipton Oil Tools LLC....G.... 405 964-3030
Shawnee *(G-8511)*
Tlr Well Services Inc....E.... 580 225-4096
Elk City *(G-2883)*
Tokata Oil Recovery Inc ....G.... 405 595-0072
Stillwater *(G-8769)*
Toms Hot Shot Service....F.... 580 243-4300
Elk City *(G-2884)*
Top O Texas Oilfield Services....G.... 806 662-5206
Atoka *(G-425)*
Total Rod Concepts Inc....G.... 405 677-0585
Oklahoma City *(G-7311)*
Town & Country Hardware....G.... 918 865-2888
Mannford *(G-4192)*
Tpl Southtex Gas Utility Co LP ....E.... 918 574-3500
Tulsa *(G-10963)*
Tri-Co Testing....G.... 580 772-8829
Weatherford *(G-11450)*
Tri-State Industries Inc ....F.... 918 938-6004
Tulsa *(G-10973)*
Triple T Hotshot....G.... 405 745-6698
Mustang *(G-4798)*
Trpr Oilfield Services LLC....G.... 405 853-1988
Weatherford *(G-11452)*
Tucker Energy Services Inc ....F.... 918 806-5647
Tulsa *(G-10984)*
Turney Bros Oilfld Svcs & Pp ....E.... 918 470-6937
McAlester *(G-4345)*
U S Weatherford L P ....F.... 405 756-4389
Lindsay *(G-4096)*
U S Weatherford L P ....E.... 918 465-2311
Oklahoma City *(G-7357)*
Ulterra Drilling Tech LP ....G.... 405 751-6212
Oklahoma City *(G-7358)*
United Services Limited ....F.... 580 256-5335
Woodward *(G-11648)*
US Oil Tools Inc....G.... 580 256-6874
Woodward *(G-11649)*
Valor Energy Services LLC ....G.... 405 513-5043
Edmond *(G-2666)*
Varco LP....G.... 405 677-8889
Oklahoma City *(G-7393)*
Vickers Construction Inc....D.... 405 756-4386
Lindsay *(G-4097)*
Victory Oil Field Services Co ....G.... 405 694-0468
Noble *(G-4893)*
Viking Pipe and Supply LLC ....G.... 405 262-9337
El Reno *(G-2767)*
Vincent Enterprises Inc....G.... 580 252-1322
Duncan *(G-2194)*
Vinces Lease Service ....F.... 405 542-3908
Hinton *(G-3539)*
W A Waterman and Co Inc....G.... 405 632-5631
Oklahoma City *(G-7409)*
W K Linduff Inc....G.... 918 225-6000
Cushing *(G-1968)*
Wajo Chemical Inc ....G.... 580 255-1191
Duncan *(G-2197)*
Wapco Inc ....G.... 405 489-3212
Cement *(G-1370)*
Washita Flow Testers Inc ....D.... 405 756-3397
Lindsay *(G-4099)*
Washita Valley Enterprises ....G.... 405 568-4525
Oklahoma City *(G-7426)*
Washita Valley Enterprises Inc....G.... 580 540-9277
Enid *(G-3075)*
Washita Valley Enterprises Inc....D.... 918 429-0186
McAlester *(G-4349)*
We-Go Perforators Inc....G.... 580 332-1346
Ada *(G-105)*
We-Go Perforators Inc....G.... 405 364-3618
Norman *(G-5197)*
Weatherford Artificia....F.... 405 853-7181
Hennessey *(G-3496)*
Weatherford Artificia....G.... 405 677-2410
Oklahoma City *(G-7429)*
Weatherford International LLC ....F.... 580 225-1237
Elk City *(G-2888)*
Weatherford International LLC ....E.... 405 773-1100
Oklahoma City *(G-7431)*
Welltec Inc ....G.... 918 585-6122
Tulsa *(G-11107)*
Whitetail Well Testing LLC ....F.... 580 225-4200
Lone Wolf *(G-4122)*
Wilson Pinstar Co ....G.... 580 255-5899
Marlow *(G-4248)*
Woods Pumping Service Inc....G.... 405 449-3485
Maysville *(G-4263)*
Wooldridge Oil Co Inc ....G.... 918 465-3073
Wilburton *(G-11529)*
Wooten Pumping Service....G.... 918 642-5312
Fairfax *(G-3122)*
WOW Metallizing & Hard....G.... 918 245-9922
Sand Springs *(G-8243)*
Wtl Oil LLC....D.... 405 608-6007
Oklahoma City *(G-7475)*
Wyoming Casing Service Inc....E.... 580 256-1222
Woodward *(G-11659)*

PRODUCT SECTION

Wyoming Casing Service In .... G 701 456-0136
  Chickasha *(G-1526)*
Xgp LLC .... G 405 584-1444
  Seminole *(G-8408)*
Xtra Oil Field & Cnstr Co .... G 918 352-3722
  Drumright *(G-2077)*
Yandells Well Service .... G 405 756-3407
  Lindsay *(G-4101)*
Young Tool Company LLC .... G 918 352-2213
  Drumright *(G-2078)*

OIL LEASES, BUYING & SELLING ON OWN ACCOUNT

Gulf Exploration LLC .... F 405 840-3381
  Oklahoma City *(G-6193)*
Johnson Otey Properties Inc .... G 580 226-8425
  Ardmore *(G-318)*
T C Craighead & Company .... F 580 223-7470
  Ardmore *(G-365)*
Terraquest Corporation .... E 405 359-0773
  Edmond *(G-2638)*

OIL ROYALTY TRADERS

Lyons & Lyons Inc .... G 918 587-2497
  Tulsa *(G-10186)*
Panhandle Royalty Co .... G 405 945-6100
  Oklahoma City *(G-6800)*
Singer Bros .... G 918 582-6237
  Tulsa *(G-10767)*

OIL TREATING COMPOUNDS

Patriot Chemicals & Svcs LLC .... E 580 856-3114
  Ratliff City *(G-8062)*

OILS & GREASES: Lubricating

Axel Royal LLC .... E 918 584-2671
  Tulsa *(G-9233)*
Legendary Lube and Oil LLC .... G 918 351-5312
  Muskogee *(G-4706)*
Oils Unlimited LLC .... D 918 583-1155
  Tulsa *(G-10389)*
Veterans Eng Group Inc .... G 918 864-6006
  Pryor *(G-7997)*

OILS: Lubricating

Phillips 66 Spectrum Corp .... F 918 977-7909
  Bartlesville *(G-516)*

OILS: Lubricating

Broken Arrow Quality Lube .... G 918 258-5823
  Broken Arrow *(G-858)*
Nu-Tier Brands Inc .... G 918 550-8026
  Tulsa *(G-10366)*
Phillips 66 Spectrum Corp .... F 918 977-7909
  Bartlesville *(G-516)*
Sterling Properties .... G 580 357-6095
  Lawton *(G-4005)*

OILS: Orange

Orange Oil LLC .... G 405 701-3505
  Norman *(G-5103)*

OLEFINS

Excel Paralubes LLC .... G 800 527-3236
  Bartlesville *(G-482)*

ON-LINE DATABASE INFORMATION RETRIEVAL SVCS

Masters Technical Advisors Inc .... G 918 949-1641
  Tulsa *(G-10221)*

OPERATOR: Apartment Buildings

Jim Campbell & Associates Rlty .... G 405 372-9225
  Stillwater *(G-8707)*

OPERATOR: Nonresidential Buildings

Anvil Land and Properties Inc .... G 580 336-4402
  Perry *(G-7726)*
Bob Gene Moore .... G 918 371-4381
  Collinsville *(G-1804)*
Cummins Enterprises Inc .... G 405 232-9022
  Oklahoma City *(G-5867)*

E Lyle Johnson Inc .... G 405 470-2047
  Bethany *(G-577)*
Eddie Brown .... F 580 889-1506
  Atoka *(G-411)*
Eddie Johnsons Wldg & Mch Co .... F 580 856-3418
  Ratliff City *(G-8051)*
Farrier Livingston Technology .... G 580 657-3469
  Ardmore *(G-288)*
Helmerich & Payne Inc .... A 918 742-5531
  Tulsa *(G-9912)*
Jerry Bendorf Trustee .... G 405 840-9900
  Oklahoma City *(G-6357)*
Oklahoma Publishing Co of Okla .... E 405 475-3585
  Oklahoma City *(G-6759)*
Southwestern Sty & Bnk Sup Inc .... D 405 525-9411
  Oklahoma City *(G-7177)*
Watonga Machine & Steel Works .... G 580 623-5830
  Watonga *(G-11352)*

OPHTHALMIC GOODS

Ardmore Optical Co .... G 580 223-8676
  Ardmore *(G-248)*
Dunlaw Optical Labs Inc .... F 580 355-8410
  Lawton *(G-3920)*
Essilor Laboratories Amer Inc .... E 800 568-5367
  (G-9702)
Mustang Optical Inc .... G 405 376-0222
  Mustang *(G-4784)*
Oakley Inc .... G 405 843-5447
  Oklahoma City *(G-6708)*
Ready Reading Glasses Inc .... G 405 840-4440
  Oklahoma City *(G-6979)*
Rva .... G 405 608-0744
  Oklahoma City *(G-7063)*

OPHTHALMIC GOODS WHOLESALERS

Classen Wholesale Optical Inc .... G 405 842-1900
  Oklahoma City *(G-5777)*
Dunlaw Optical Labs Inc .... F 580 355-8410
  Lawton *(G-3920)*
Essilor Laboratories Amer Inc .... E 800 568-5367
  (G-9702)
Omega Optical Co LP .... E 405 703-4133
  Oklahoma City *(G-6775)*

OPHTHALMIC GOODS, NEC, WHOLESALE: Lenses

Accutech Laboratories Inc .... F 405 946-6446
  Warr Acres *(G-11312)*
Doctors Optical Supply Inc .... G 918 256-6416
  Vinita *(G-11255)*

OPHTHALMIC GOODS: Frames, Lenses & Parts, Eyeglasses

Institute Optical Inc .... G 918 747-3937
  Tulsa *(G-9991)*

OPHTHALMIC GOODS: Lenses, Ophthalmic

Empire Optical Inc .... E 918 744-8005
  Tulsa *(G-9676)*

OPTICAL GOODS STORES

Classen Wholesale Optical Inc .... G 405 842-1900
  Oklahoma City *(G-5777)*
Empire Optical Inc .... E 918 744-8005
  Tulsa *(G-9676)*
Institute Optical Inc .... G 918 747-3937
  Tulsa *(G-9991)*
Stonewood Vision Source .... G 918 994-4450
  Broken Arrow *(G-1065)*
Tamatha Holt Od .... G 918 649-0524
  Poteau *(G-7914)*

OPTICAL GOODS STORES: Opticians

Mustang Optical Inc .... G 405 376-0222
  Mustang *(G-4784)*

OPTICAL INSTRUMENTS & APPARATUS

Plx Inc .... G 918 551-6722
  Tulsa *(G-10528)*

OPTICAL INSTRUMENTS & LENSES

Accutech Laboratories .... G 405 603-2956
  Warr Acres *(G-11311)*

Doomsdaytacticalsolutions LLC .... G 580 788-2412
  Elmore City *(G-2895)*
Elens .... G 918 627-5395
  Tulsa *(G-9654)*

OPTOMETRIC EQPT & SPLYS WHOLESALERS

Accutech Laboratories .... G 405 603-2956
  Warr Acres *(G-11311)*

OPTOMETRISTS' OFFICES

Ardmore Optical Co .... G 580 223-8676
  Ardmore *(G-248)*
Institute Optical Inc .... G 918 747-3937
  Tulsa *(G-9991)*

ORDNANCE

Artillery Nation LLC .... G 405 606-5080
  Moore *(G-4495)*
Ducommun Labarge Tech Inc .... C 918 459-2200
  Tulsa *(G-9611)*
Etched Ordnance LLC .... G 918 855-8779
  Coweta *(G-1882)*
Hailey Ordnance Company .... G 405 813-0700
  Oklahoma City *(G-6203)*
Red River Gunsmithing LLC .... G 580 770-1911
  Frederick *(G-3198)*
Redrhino LLC .... G 405 740-5132
  Blanchard *(G-733)*

ORGANIZATIONS: Civic & Social

Oklahoma Soc Prof Engineers .... G 405 528-1435
  Oklahoma City *(G-6763)*

ORGANIZATIONS: Professional

American Assn Petro Geologists .... D 918 584-2555
  Tulsa *(G-9164)*
International Pro Rodeo Assn .... G 405 235-6540
  Oklahoma City *(G-6321)*
Interstate Trucker Ltd .... E 405 948-6576
  Oklahoma City *(G-6323)*
Oklahoma Soc Prof Engineers .... G 405 528-1435
  Oklahoma City *(G-6763)*

ORGANIZATIONS: Religious

Gregory Prizzell P & R M Inc .... G 405 752-0782
  Oklahoma City *(G-6192)*
Ideas Manufacturing Inc .... G 405 691-5525
  Oklahoma City *(G-5296)*
Oral Rbrts Evnglistic Assn Inc .... D 918 591-2000
  Tulsa *(G-10436)*
Tommy Higle Publishers .... G 580 276-5136
  Marietta *(G-4215)*
True North Ministries Inc .... G 405 562-2986
  Edmond *(G-2654)*
Victory House Inc .... G 918 747-5009
  Tulsa *(G-11075)*
Weatherford News Inc .... E 580 772-3301
  Weatherford *(G-11458)*

ORGANIZATIONS: Research Institute

Kihomac Inc .... D 937 429-7744
  Midwest City *(G-4445)*
New X Drives Inc .... F 918 850-4463
  Tulsa *(G-10338)*

ORNAMENTS: Christmas Tree, Exc Electrical & Glass

Karis Gifts .... G 405 330-6428
  Edmond *(G-2478)*

ORTHODONTIST

Carter & Higgins Orthodontics .... G 918 986-9986
  Tulsa *(G-9381)*

OSCILLATORS

Connor-Winfield Corp .... E 405 273-1257
  Shawnee *(G-8440)*

OSICIZERS: Inorganic

MRW Technologies Inc .... E 918 827-6030
  Glenpool *(G-3239)*

OUTBOARD MOTORS & PARTS

Hoss Marine Propulsion Inc.................G....... 918 479-5167
  Locust Grove *(G-4110)*

OUTBOARD MOTORS: Electric

Zebco Corporation.................A....... 918 836-5581
  Tulsa *(G-11172)*

OVENS: Cremating

Crematory Manufacturing & Svc.........E....... 918 446-1475
  Tulsa *(G-9000)*

OVENS: Distillation, Charcoal & Coke

Metro Outdoor Living.................G....... 918 893-2960
  Tulsa *(G-10253)*

PACKAGED FROZEN FOODS WHOLESALERS, NEC

Ralphs Packing Company.................E....... 405 547-2464
  Perkins *(G-7721)*

PACKAGING & LABELING SVCS

Gemini Industries Inc.................D....... 405 262-5710
  El Reno *(G-2719)*
Mohawk Materials Co Inc.................G....... 918 584-2707
  Tulsa *(G-10295)*

PACKAGING MATERIALS, WHOLESALE

Clr Enterprises LLC.................G....... 918 298-1943
  Tulsa *(G-9457)*
Oklahoma Flding Crton Prtg Inc.........F....... 405 352-9920
  Minco *(G-4478)*
Supplyone Oklahoma City Inc.............C....... 405 947-7373
  Oklahoma City *(G-7230)*

PACKAGING MATERIALS: Paper

Beacon Stamp & Seal Co.................G....... 918 834-2322
  Tulsa *(G-9276)*
Berry Global Films LLC.................D....... 918 227-1616
  Tulsa *(G-8990)*
Berry Plastics Corporation.................C....... 918 824-4400
  Pryor *(G-7947)*
International Paper Company.............D....... 580 933-7211
  Valliant *(G-11227)*
Regency Labels Inc.................E....... 405 682-3460
  Oklahoma City *(G-7002)*
Sigma Extruding Corp.................F....... 918 446-6265
  Tulsa *(G-10755)*
Tom Bennett Manufacturing.............F....... 405 528-5671
  Oklahoma City *(G-7302)*

PACKAGING MATERIALS: Paper, Coated Or Laminated

Bemis Company Inc.................C....... 405 207-2200
  Pauls Valley *(G-7650)*
Pregis LLC.................D....... 918 439-9916
  Tulsa *(G-10552)*

PACKAGING MATERIALS: Paperboard Backs For Blister/Skin Pkgs

Media Resources Inc.................E....... 405 682-4400
  Oklahoma City *(G-6555)*

PACKAGING MATERIALS: Polystyrene Foam

Bemis Company Inc.................E....... 918 739-4907
  Catoosa *(G-1301)*
Warner Jwly Box Display Co LLC.......D....... 580 536-8885
  Lawton *(G-4021)*
Western Industries Corporation.........C....... 405 419-3100
  Oklahoma City *(G-7439)*

PACKING & CRATING SVC

Johnson Crating Services LLC.............G....... 405 672-7964
  Oklahoma City *(G-6374)*

PACKING SVCS: Shipping

Mid-Continent Packaging Inc...........D....... 580 234-5200
  Enid *(G-3013)*

PADDING: Foamed Plastics

Environmental Compliance LLC..........F....... 405 949-0103
  Oklahoma City *(G-6046)*

PAGERS: One-way

Microframe Corp.................F....... 918 258-4839
  Broken Arrow *(G-973)*

PAINT STORE

Anchor Paint Mfg Co.................G....... 918 272-0880
  Owasso *(G-7544)*
Ardmore Construction Sup Inc..........G....... 580 223-2322
  Ardmore *(G-245)*
Crown Paint Company.................E....... 405 232-8580
  Oklahoma City *(G-5863)*
Spectrum Paint Company Inc............G....... 405 525-6519
  Oklahoma City *(G-7181)*
Touch Up Unlimited.................G....... 405 527-5609
  Purcell *(G-8023)*

PAINTING SVC: Metal Prdts

Kuykendall Welding LLC.................G....... 405 905-0389
  Chickasha *(G-1480)*
Modern Plating Co Inc.................F....... 918 836-5081
  Tulsa *(G-10291)*

PAINTS & ADDITIVES

Black & Puryear Paint Mfg Co...........G....... 405 348-0447
  Edmond *(G-2324)*
Crown Paint Company.................E....... 405 232-8580
  Oklahoma City *(G-5863)*
Del Technical Coatings Inc.............E....... 405 672-1431
  Oklahoma City *(G-5920)*

PAINTS & ALLIED PRODUCTS

405 Coatings LLC.................G....... 405 822-5095
  Edmond *(G-2284)*
Advanced Aircraft Coatings.............G....... 405 495-7545
  Oklahoma City *(G-5378)*
Anchor Paint Mfg Co.................D....... 918 836-4626
  Tulsa *(G-9185)*
Anchor Paint Mfg Co.................G....... 918 272-0880
  Owasso *(G-7544)*
Appli-Fab Custom Coating..............G....... 405 235-7039
  Chandler *(G-1375)*
Dale P Jackson.................F....... 580 332-1988
  Ada *(G-29)*
Kelly-Moore Paint Company Inc.........G....... 405 350-2375
  Yukon *(G-11739)*
L M R General Contracting LLC.........G....... 405 605-6547
  Oklahoma City *(G-6440)*
Laster/Castor Corporation.............G....... 918 234-7777
  Tulsa *(G-10133)*
Paint Handy LLC.................G....... 918 734-3422
  Bixby *(G-651)*
Paint Pros Inc.................G....... 405 226-8898
  Norman *(G-5108)*
Pixley Coating Inc.................G....... 580 444-2140
  Velma *(G-11236)*
Schmoldt Engineering Services.........F....... 918 336-1221
  Bartlesville *(G-526)*
Spectrum Paint Company Inc............G....... 405 525-6519
  Oklahoma City *(G-7181)*
Touch Up Unlimited.................G....... 405 527-5609
  Purcell *(G-8023)*

PAINTS, VARNISHES & SPLYS WHOLESALERS

Kelly-Moore Paint Company Inc.........G....... 405 350-2375
  Yukon *(G-11739)*

PAINTS, VARNISHES & SPLYS, WHOLESALE: Colors & Pigments

Touch Up Unlimited.................G....... 405 527-5609
  Purcell *(G-8023)*
Tronox US Holdings Inc.................E....... 405 775-5000
  Oklahoma City *(G-7342)*

PAINTS, VARNISHES & SPLYS, WHOLESALE: Lacquers

Mann Solvents Inc.................G....... 918 626-3733
  Arkoma *(G-386)*

PAINTS, VARNISHES & SPLYS, WHOLESALE: Paints

Ardmore Construction Sup Inc..........G....... 580 223-2322
  Ardmore *(G-245)*
George Townsend & Co Inc.............G....... 405 235-1387
  Oklahoma City *(G-6145)*
Spectrum Paint Company Inc............G....... 405 525-6519
  Oklahoma City *(G-7181)*

PAINTS: Oil Or Alkyd Vehicle Or Water Thinned

Capitol Paint Manufacturing.............G....... 405 634-3383
  Oklahoma City *(G-5695)*

PAINTS: Waterproof

H-I-S Paint Mfg Co Inc.................E....... 405 232-2077
  Oklahoma City *(G-6201)*

PALLET REPAIR SVCS

Doug Butler Enterprises Inc.............F....... 918 425-3565
  Tulsa *(G-9599)*

PALLETS

Betty E Jester.................G....... 580 564-9396
  Kingston *(G-3824)*
Chouteau Pallet.................G....... 918 476-6098
  Chouteau *(G-1561)*
Pallet Liquidations Okc LLC............G....... 405 843-0402
  Oklahoma City *(G-6796)*
Pauls Pallet Co.................G....... 918 435-4321
  Eucha *(G-3095)*
Tim E Hutcheson.................G....... 918 313-5710
  Tulsa *(G-10941)*

PALLETS & SKIDS: Wood

Choctaw Mfg Def Contrs Inc............F....... 580 326-8365
  Hugo *(G-3608)*
Choctaw Mfg Def Contrs Inc............G....... 580 298-2203
  Antlers *(G-215)*
Choctaw Mfg Def Contrs Inc............G....... 918 426-2871
  McAlester *(G-4286)*
Duncan Wood Works LLC.................G....... 580 641-1190
  Duncan *(G-2113)*
Fat & Happy Services Inc.............G....... 405 834-5782
  Oklahoma City *(G-6078)*
Frontier Resource Development.........G....... 918 682-6571
  Muskogee *(G-4676)*
Henryetta Pallet Company.............E....... 918 652-9897
  Henryetta *(G-3508)*

PALLETS: Plastic

Berry Plastics Corporation.............C....... 918 824-4400
  Pryor *(G-7947)*
Greystone Logistics Inc.................F....... 918 583-7441
  Tulsa *(G-9863)*
Kratos Unmnned Arial Systems I........G....... 405 248-9545
  Oklahoma City *(G-6435)*

PALLETS: Wooden

AAA Crimstone Operating Co LP........G....... 918 445-5500
  Tulsa *(G-9077)*
Alex Pallets.................G....... 405 414-2710
  Oklahoma City *(G-5411)*
Burgess Manufacturing Okla Inc........E....... 405 282-1913
  Guthrie *(G-3303)*
Cimarron Pallet Mfg Co.................G....... 405 228-0288
  Oklahoma City *(G-5765)*
Doug Butler Enterprises Inc.............F....... 918 425-3565
  Tulsa *(G-9599)*
Hernandez Pallets.................G....... 405 636-0503
  Oklahoma City *(G-6243)*
Ifco Systems.................G....... 405 491-9300
  Oklahoma City *(G-6289)*
Ifco Systems Us LLC.................E....... 405 681-8090
  Oklahoma City *(G-6290)*
Johnson Lumber Company Inc..........E....... 918 253-8786
  Spavinaw *(G-8591)*
Oklahoma AAA Pallet Company..........E....... 405 670-1414
  Oklahoma City *(G-6734)*
Pal-Serv Oklahoma City LLC............E....... 405 672-1155
  Oklahoma City *(G-6794)*
Pallet Logistics of America.............G....... 405 670-1414
  Oklahoma City *(G-6797)*
Pallets Plus LLC.................G....... 580 513-4090
  Davis *(G-1992)*

PRODUCT SECTION

Prime Pallet LLC .... G 918 683-0907
  Muskogee (G-4737)
Pro Pallets .... G 405 679-8076
  Oklahoma City (G-6905)
Propak Logistics Inc .... D 405 694-4441
  Oklahoma City (G-6916)
Simer Pallet Recycling Inc .... F 405 224-8543
  Chickasha (G-1511)
Sooner Pallet Services Inc .... G 918 342-9663
  Claremore (G-1686)
Tasler Pallet Inc .... F 580 276-9800
  Marietta (G-4213)

PANEL & DISTRIBUTION BOARDS & OTHER RELATED APPARATUS

Huber Engineered Woods LLC .... E 580 584-7000
  Broken Bow (G-1192)

PANELS: Building, Metal

Architectural Metal Panels LLC .... G 405 672-7407
  Oklahoma City (G-5462)
Circle K Steel Bldg Cnstr LLC .... F 405 932-4664
  Paden (G-7634)
Metal Panels Inc .... G 918 641-0641
  Tulsa (G-10246)
Terry Building Co Inc .... F 405 634-5777
  Oklahoma City (G-7272)

PANELS: Building, Wood

Shipman Home Improvement Inc .... G 918 514-0049
  Sand Springs (G-8223)
Terry Hall .... E 817 271-4838
  Valliant (G-11232)

PAPER & BOARD: Die-cut

Quik-Print of Oklahoma City .... G 405 840-3275
  Oklahoma City (G-6950)

PAPER CONVERTING

Media Resources Inc .... E 405 682-4400
  Oklahoma City (G-6555)

PAPER MANUFACTURERS: Exc Newsprint

Audrey Parks & Associates Llc .... G 405 328-3186
  Oklahoma City (G-5489)
International Paper Company .... D 580 933-7211
  Valliant (G-11227)

PAPER PRDTS: Facial Tissue

Opp Liquidating Company Inc .... C 918 825-0616
  Pryor (G-7980)

PAPER PRDTS: Infant & Baby Prdts

Kimberly-Clark Corporation .... B 918 366-5000
  Jenks (G-3713)

PAPER PRDTS: Napkins, Sanitary, Made From Purchased Material

Fatutyi Adeshola .... G 785 424-4208
  Lawton (G-3928)

PAPER PRDTS: Sanitary

Cool Baby Inc .... G 405 755-1100
  Edmond (G-2367)
Opp Liquidating Company Inc .... C 918 825-0616
  Pryor (G-7980)

PAPER PRDTS: Sanitary Tissue Paper

Kimberly-Clark Corporation .... B 918 366-5000
  Jenks (G-3713)

PAPER: Absorbent

Hope Minerals International .... G 405 452-3529
  Wetumka (G-11491)

PAPER: Adhesive

Summit Labels Inc .... G 918 936-4950
  Tulsa (G-10868)

PAPER: Cardboard

Cardboard Junkeez LLC .... G 405 990-9443
  Norman (G-4953)
Green Ox Pallet Technology LLC .... G 720 276-8013
  Oklahoma City (G-6187)
International Paper Company .... D 405 745-5800
  Oklahoma City (G-6320)

PAPER: Coated & Laminated, NEC

A-1 Specialties .... G 405 942-1341
  Oklahoma City (G-5352)
Giesecke & Devrient Amer Inc .... D 405 270-8400
  Oklahoma City (G-6154)
Krause Plastics .... G 918 835-4202
  Tulsa (G-10100)
Marpro Label Inc .... G 405 672-3344
  Oklahoma City (G-6530)
Marvel Photo Inc .... G 918 836-0741
  Tulsa (G-10218)
Priority Printworks Inc .... G 918 825-6397
  Pryor (G-7984)
Regency Labels Inc .... E 405 682-3460
  Oklahoma City (G-7002)
Stonehouse Marketing Svcs LLC .... D 405 360-5674
  Norman (G-5160)

PAPER: Packaging

Oklahoma Interpak Inc .... E 918 687-1681
  Muskogee (G-4724)

PAPER: Printer

Midwest City Pub Schools I-52 .... G 405 739-1665
  Oklahoma City (G-6600)

PAPER: Wallpaper

Lechhner Wallcovering .... G 918 744-1742
  Tulsa (G-10145)

PAPER: Wrapping & Packaging

Cascades Holding US Inc .... G 918 825-0616
  Pryor (G-7950)
Online Packaging .... G 580 389-5373
  Ardmore (G-339)
Pechiney Plastic Packaging .... G 918 739-4900
  Catoosa (G-1346)

PAPERBOARD

Oklahoma Interpak Inc .... E 918 687-1681
  Muskogee (G-4724)
Republic Paperboard Co LLC .... C 580 510-2200
  Lawton (G-3993)

PAPERBOARD CONVERTING

Paper Concierge .... G 405 286-3322
  Edmond (G-2561)

PARKING METERS

Southern Specialties Corp .... E 918 584-3553
  Tulsa (G-10803)

PARTITIONS & FIXTURES: Except Wood

Amarillo Cstm Fixs Co Inc Okla .... F 918 266-7752
  Catoosa (G-1296)
Compusign Vinyl Graphics .... G 580 762-4930
  Ponca City (G-7807)
Devon Industries Inc .... E 405 943-3881
  Oklahoma City (G-5935)
Mayco Fixture Co Inc .... F 405 428-5305
  Tulsa (G-10226)
Modular Squad LLC .... G 918 695-0114
  Tulsa (G-10293)
North American Cos .... F 918 592-2000
  Tulsa (G-10360)
Semasys Inc .... E 405 525-2335
  Oklahoma City (G-7107)
Service Pipe & Supply Company .... E 918 336-8433
  Bartlesville (G-527)
Sweeper Metal Fabricators Corp .... E 918 352-9180
  Drumright (G-2073)

PARTITIONS: Wood & Fixtures

Cals Plastics Designs & Fabg .... G 405 670-1690
  Oklahoma City (G-5673)

PERSONAL DOCUMENT & INFORMATION SVCS

Contemporary Cabinets Inc .... D 405 330-4592
  Edmond (G-2365)
E J Higgins Interior Design .... G 405 387-3434
  Newcastle (G-4825)
Holick Family LLC .... G 580 765-3209
  Ponca City (G-7836)
Ketcherside Custom Cabinets .... G 580 254-2672
  Woodward (G-11599)
Majestic Marble & Granite .... E 918 266-1121
  Catoosa (G-1337)
Mastercraft Millwork Inc .... G 405 895-6050
  Moore (G-4537)
North American Cos .... F 918 592-2000
  Tulsa (G-10360)
Perceptions .... G 405 964-7000
  McLoud (G-4362)
Weatherford Cabinets .... G 580 772-7511
  Weatherford (G-11456)

PARTS: Metal

Big River Sales Inc .... G 580 657-4950
  Lone Grove (G-4115)
Harwell Industries .... G 405 948-7775
  Oklahoma City (G-6221)
Mountain Top Machine Inc .... G 918 787-5510
  Jay (G-3683)
Scrap Management Oklahoma Inc ...... F 405 677-7000
  Oklahoma City (G-7100)
Sharp Metal Fabricators Inc .... F 405 899-4849
  Noble (G-4891)

PATTERNS: Indl

Cnc Patterns & Tooling .... G 918 835-2344
  Tulsa (G-9461)
Coman Pattern Works .... D 918 270-1775
  Tulsa (G-9473)
J Bernardoni Pattern Co LLC .... G 520 390-0663
  Quinton (G-8037)
L & M Pattern Mfg Co Inc .... G 918 663-2977
  Tulsa (G-10107)
Liberty Patterns Inc .... G 918 234-1037
  Owasso (G-7586)
Starlite Welding Supplies .... G 580 252-8320
  Duncan (G-2185)

PAVERS

George Townsend & Co Inc .... G 405 235-1387
  Oklahoma City (G-6145)

PAVING MIXTURES

Teeters Asphalt & Materials .... G 918 673-1243
  Picher (G-7751)

PAWN SHOPS

Johnson Bvlle Fine Jwlers Pawn .... G 405 751-1216
  Oklahoma City (G-6373)

PAYROLL SVCS

Paycom Software Inc .... D 405 722-6900
  Oklahoma City (G-6813)

PENS: Meter

Creative Pins .... G 405 390-2038
  Choctaw (G-1535)

PERISCOPES

Periscope Legal .... G 405 418-4155
  Oklahoma City (G-6831)

PERLITE MINING SVCS

Noble Acquisition LLC .... G 405 872-5660
  Noble (G-4887)

PERSONAL & HOUSEHOLD GOODS REPAIR, NEC

Brass Buff .... G 918 592-1717
  Tulsa (G-9332)

PERSONAL DOCUMENT & INFORMATION SVCS

County of Comanche .... G 580 355-3810
  Lawton (G-3911)

PERSONAL INVESTIGATION SVCS

McNally and Associates Inc .... G 918 587-7068
Tulsa *(G-10234)*

PERSONAL ITEM CARE & STORAGE SVCS

Darrell Lewis .... G 405 867-5768
Maysville *(G-4257)*

PERSONAL SVCS, NEC

Beavers High Pressure Wshg LLC .... G 580 512-3530
Apache *(G-218)*

PESTICIDES

Green Horizons LLC .... G 405 364-9921
Norman *(G-5010)*
Helena Agri-Enterprises LLC .... F 580 477-0986
Altus *(G-157)*

PET SPLYS

Blitz USA Inc .... B 918 676-3620
Miami *(G-4391)*
Jumping Bone LLC .... G 918 853-2836
Tulsa *(G-10065)*
Rbs Pet Products .... G 405 373-0235
Piedmont *(G-7769)*
Therapy For Dogs Inc .... G 405 314-7655
Oklahoma City *(G-7278)*
Vision Motorsports .... G 918 260-4981
Tulsa *(G-11081)*

PET SPLYS WHOLESALERS

HALAQ Inc .... G 405 321-7293
Newalla *(G-4810)*
Rbs Pet Products .... G 405 373-0235
Piedmont *(G-7769)*

PETROLEUM & PETROLEUM PRDTS, WHOL Svc Station Splys, Petro

Pump Shop .... G 918 834-8829
Tulsa *(G-10583)*
Tank & Fuel Solutions LLC .... G 918 960-4361
Claremore *(G-1691)*

PETROLEUM & PETROLEUM PRDTS, WHOLESALE Crude Oil

Dark Horse Oil Field Svcs LLC .... G 580 229-0626
Healdton *(G-3412)*
Devon Energy Production Co LP .... A 405 235-3611
Oklahoma City *(G-5932)*
Duncan Oil & Gas Inc .... G 405 360-2183
Norman *(G-4984)*
Mac Oil & Gas .... G 405 375-5619
Kingfisher *(G-3808)*
Tilley Oil & Gas Inc .... G 405 608-4970
Oklahoma City *(G-7289)*

PETROLEUM & PETROLEUM PRDTS, WHOLESALE Diesel Fuel

Wooldridge Oil Co Inc .... G 918 465-3073
Wilburton *(G-11529)*

PETROLEUM & PETROLEUM PRDTS, WHOLESALE Fuel Oil

Hewitt Mineral Corp .... G 580 223-3619
Ardmore *(G-303)*

PETROLEUM & PETROLEUM PRDTS, WHOLESALE Gases

Oneok Inc .... A 918 588-7000
Tulsa *(G-10421)*
Oneok Inc .... E 918 588-7000
Tulsa *(G-10422)*

PETROLEUM & PETROLEUM PRDTS, WHOLESALE Petroleum Brokers

Cornelius Oil Inc .... G 918 247-6743
Kellyville *(G-3762)*
Lema Petroleum Inc .... G 405 379-6678
Holdenville *(G-3556)*

PETROLEUM & PETROLEUM PRDTS, WHOLESALE: Bulk Stations

Texoak Petro Holdings LLC .... G 918 592-1010
Tulsa *(G-10921)*

PETROLEUM BULK STATIONS & TERMINALS

Rose Rock Midstream Field Svcs .... G 918 524-7700
Tulsa *(G-10672)*
Semcrude LP .... F 918 524-8100
Tulsa *(G-10727)*
Semgroup Corporation .... B 918 524-8100
Tulsa *(G-10728)*
Tank & Fuel Solutions LLC .... G 918 960-4361
Claremore *(G-1691)*

PETROLEUM PRDTS WHOLESALERS

Deisenroth Gas Products Inc .... G 918 742-4769
Tulsa *(G-9567)*
Farmers Co-Operative Gin Assn .... G 580 928-2664
Sayre *(G-8340)*
Henke Petroleum Corp .... G 405 878-0909
Shawnee *(G-8460)*
Quiktrip Corporation .... B 918 615-7700
Tulsa *(G-10599)*
Sariel Inc .... G 918 855-1400
Tulsa *(G-10709)*
Sunoco (R&m) LLC .... F 918 586-6246
Tulsa *(G-10873)*
Ward Petroleum Corporation .... G 405 242-4188
Oklahoma City *(G-7419)*

PHARMACEUTICAL PREPARATIONS: Druggists' Preparations

Abbott Laboratories .... A 405 329-5513
Norman *(G-4896)*
Cytovance Biologics Inc .... G 405 319-8310
Oklahoma City *(G-5883)*

PHARMACEUTICAL PREPARATIONS: Emulsions

Dermamedics LLC .... G 405 319-8130
Oklahoma City *(G-5925)*

PHARMACEUTICAL PREPARATIONS: Medicines, Capsule Or Ampule

Rta Systems Incorporated .... G 405 388-6802
Choctaw *(G-1554)*
Winds of Heartland .... G 405 947-8558
Oklahoma City *(G-7460)*

PHARMACEUTICAL PREPARATIONS: Powders

Ultra Botanica LLC .... G 405 694-4175
Oklahoma City *(G-7359)*

PHARMACEUTICAL PREPARATIONS: Proprietary Drug PRDTS

Prescription Care LLC .... G 405 310-9230
Norman *(G-5121)*

PHARMACEUTICAL PREPARATIONS: Solutions

Tcaacp LLC .... G 918 251-6655
Broken Arrow *(G-1072)*

PHARMACEUTICALS

Al Pharma Inc .... G 405 848-3299
Oklahoma City *(G-5406)*
Avara Pharmaceutical Tech Inc .... C 405 217-7670
Norman *(G-4921)*
Barrick Pharmacies Inc .... G 405 273-9417
Shawnee *(G-8431)*
Btg Inc .... G 405 604-9145
Oklahoma City *(G-5638)*
David W and Abbe Belcher .... G 918 376-9816
Owasso *(G-7559)*
Eden Pharmaceuticals .... G 405 455-7200
Midwest City *(G-4439)*
Eli Lilly and Company .... G 918 250-6848
Broken Arrow *(G-896)*
Eli Lilly and Company .... E 918 459-4540
Tulsa *(G-9655)*
Golf Advisors .... G 918 645-6179
Tulsa *(G-9839)*
Hospice Pharmacy Providers LLC ...... G 918 633-6229
Owasso *(G-7574)*
Kmh Enterprises Inc .... G 405 722-4600
Oklahoma City *(G-6430)*
Loud City Pharmaceutical .... G 405 259-9014
Oklahoma City *(G-6497)*
Magnesium Products Inc .... F 918 587-9930
Tulsa *(G-9018)*
Marie Anastasia Labs Inc .... G 405 840-0123
Oklahoma City *(G-6524)*
Medcraft LLC .... G 918 938-0642
Mounds *(G-4620)*
Midwest Med Istpes Nclear Phrm .... G 405 604-4438
Oklahoma City *(G-6605)*
Natural Care Solution LLC .... G 405 919-1982
Mustang *(G-4786)*
Naturalock Solutions LLC .... G 405 812-9058
Norman *(G-5089)*
Novartis Corporation .... G 918 845-0906
Tulsa *(G-10363)*
Okc Allergy Supplies Inc .... D 405 235-1451
Oklahoma City *(G-6726)*
Onesource LLC .... G 580 434-6250
Calera *(G-1242)*
Optionone LLC .... E 405 548-4848
Oklahoma City *(G-6779)*
Phillips & Company .... G 714 663-6324
Millerton *(G-4473)*
Pure Transplant Solutions LLC .... G 512 697-8144
Oklahoma City *(G-6924)*
Qualgen LLC .... E 405 551-8216
Edmond *(G-2578)*
Qualgen LLC .... E 405 551-8216
Edmond *(G-2579)*
Sports & Stress Marketing .... G 580 327-3463
Alva *(G-193)*
Takeda Phrmceuticals N Amer In .... G 405 317-7495
Norman *(G-5170)*
Trimark Labs .... G 405 942-3289
Oklahoma City *(G-7333)*
Willoughby Pharmacy Svcs LLC .... G 580 214-1043
Weatherford *(G-11460)*

PHARMACEUTICALS: Medicinal & Botanical Prdts

Iochem Corporation .... E 580 995-3198
Vici *(G-11243)*
Ocubrite LLC .... G 405 250-2084
Edmond *(G-2544)*
Rtpr LLC .... G 877 787-7180
Edmond *(G-2607)*
Tulsa American Shaman .... G 918 938-0718
Tulsa *(G-10985)*

PHARMACIES & DRUG STORES

Onesource LLC .... G 580 434-6250
Calera *(G-1242)*

PHOTOCONDUCTIVE CELLS

New X Drive Tech Inc .... G 918 850-4463
Tulsa *(G-10337)*

PHOTOCOPY MACHINES

Richard B Collins .... G 405 947-6349
Oklahoma City *(G-7015)*
XCEL Office Solutions LLC .... G 580 595-9235
Lawton *(G-4024)*

PHOTOCOPYING & DUPLICATING SVCS

262 LLC .... F 918 458-5511
Tahlequah *(G-8848)*
AAA Kopy .... G 405 741-5679
Oklahoma City *(G-5354)*
Ajt Enterprises Inc .... F 918 665-7083
Tulsa *(G-9133)*
B & L Printing Inc .... G 918 258-6655
Broken Arrow *(G-839)*
Cooley Enterprises Inc .... G 918 437-6900
Tulsa *(G-9483)*
Copy Write Incorporated .... G 918 224-1148
Sapulpa *(G-8262)*
Cromwells Inc .... G 580 234-6561
Enid *(G-2935)*

PRODUCT SECTION • PIPE SECTIONS, FABRICATED FROM PURCHASED PIPE

Fedex Office & Print Svcs Inc ....F...... 918 492-6701
  Tulsa (G-9732)
Fedex Office & Print Svcs Inc ....E...... 918 252-3757
  Tulsa (G-9733)
Gravley Companies Inc ....G...... 405 842-1404
  Oklahoma City (G-6176)
Holloways Bluprt & Copy Sp Inc ....G...... 918 682-0280
  Muskogee (G-4692)
Kindrick Co Prtg & Copying Svc ....G...... 580 332-1022
  Ada (G-56)
King Kopy LLC ....G...... 405 321-0202
  Norman (G-5052)
Quik-Print of Oklahoma City ....G...... 405 842-1404
  Oklahoma City (G-6946)
Quik-Print of Oklahoma City ....G...... 405 232-7579
  Oklahoma City (G-6948)
Quik-Print of Oklahoma City ....G...... 405 840-3275
  Oklahoma City (G-6950)
Quik-Print of Oklahoma City ....G...... 405 528-7976
  Oklahoma City (G-6951)
Rocket Color Inc ....G...... 405 842-6001
  Oklahoma City (G-7043)
Sooner Press ....G...... 405 382-8351
  Seminole (G-8400)
Two Lees Inc ....G...... 918 663-2390
  Tulsa (G-11027)
Zon Inc ....F...... 918 458-5511
  Tahlequah (G-8894)

PHOTOENGRAVING SVC

B G Specialties Inc ....G...... 918 582-1165
  Tulsa (G-9243)

PHOTOGRAPHIC EQPT & SPLY: Sound Recordg/Reprod Eqpt, Motion

Gypsy Moon Studios ....G...... 918 251-7188
  Broken Arrow (G-925)
Zoe Studios LLC ....G...... 918 258-4073
  Broken Arrow (G-1106)

PHOTOGRAPHIC EQPT & SPLYS

Indel-Davis Inc ....F...... 918 587-2151
  Tulsa (G-9976)
Memorabilia Corner ....G...... 405 321-8366
  Norman (G-5070)
Miraclon Corporation ....F...... 580 772-5502
  Weatherford (G-11428)
Mora Mora Media LLC ....G...... 918 231-6651
  Owasso (G-7594)
Raccoon Technologies Inc ....G...... 580 399-9126
  Ada (G-79)
Techspeedy LLC ....G...... 918 406-0008
  Tulsa (G-10914)
Tulsa Toner Technology ....G...... 918 838-0323
  Tulsa (G-11009)

PHOTOGRAPHIC EQPT & SPLYS: Blueprint Reproduction Mach/Eqpt

Graphic Rsources Reproductions ....F...... 918 461-0303
  Broken Arrow (G-921)

PHOTOGRAPHIC EQPT & SPLYS: Cameras, Aerial

Waylink Systems Corporation ....G...... 405 261-9896
  Stillwater (G-8773)

PHOTOGRAPHIC EQPT & SPLYS: Cameras, Still & Motion Pictures

Marvel Photo Inc ....G...... 918 836-0741
  Tulsa (G-10218)

PHOTOGRAPHIC EQPT & SPLYS: Densitometers

Eseco-Speedmaster ....D...... 918 225-1266
  Cushing (G-1933)
Speedmaster Inc ....D...... 918 225-1266
  Cushing (G-1961)

PHOTOGRAPHIC EQPT & SPLYS: Printing Eqpt

Vanco Systems ....G...... 405 692-4040
  Oklahoma City (G-5321)

PHOTOGRAPHIC EQPT & SPLYS: Toners, Prprd, Not Chem Plnts

Smart Office Stores LLC ....G...... 918 994-5300
  Tulsa (G-10776)

PHOTOGRAPHY SVCS: Commercial

Saan World LLC ....G...... 405 494-1282
  Oklahoma City (G-7070)

PHOTOGRAPHY SVCS: Passport

Marvel Photo Inc ....G...... 918 836-0741
  Tulsa (G-10218)

PHOTOGRAPHY SVCS: Portrait Studios

Encompass Media LLC ....G...... 405 823-8081
  Oklahoma City (G-6035)

PHOTOGRAPHY: Aerial

Encompass Media LLC ....G...... 405 823-8081
  Oklahoma City (G-6035)

PHYSICAL EXAMINATION & TESTING SVCS

Eden Clinic Inc ....G...... 405 579-4673
  Norman (G-4988)

PHYSICIANS' OFFICES & CLINICS: Medical doctors

A-1 Mster Prnta/Hooper Prtg Si ....G...... 518 427-0282
  Oklahoma City (G-5351)
Kenneth E Jones ....G...... 580 832-2227
  Cordell (G-1861)

PICTURE FRAMES: Wood

Southwest Interiors Inc ....G...... 580 323-3050
  Clinton (G-1769)

PIECE GOODS, NOTIONS & DRY GOODS, WHOL: Fabrics Broadwoven

Fabric Factory ....F...... 405 521-1694
  Oklahoma City (G-6067)

PIECE GOODS, NOTIONS & DRY GOODS, WHOLESALE: Tape, Textile

Rainbow Pennant Inc ....E...... 405 524-1577
  Oklahoma City (G-6968)

PIECE GOODS, NOTIONS & OTHER DRY GOODS, WHOL: Flags/Banners

Graphic Rsources Reproductions ....F...... 918 461-0303
  Broken Arrow (G-921)
Wave On Flags and Banners LLC ....G...... 918 782-3330
  Langley (G-3875)

PIECE GOODS, NOTIONS/DRY GOODS, WHOL: Drapery Mtrl, Woven

Interior Designers Supply Inc ....F...... 405 521-1551
  Oklahoma City (G-6318)

PIGMENTS, INORGANIC: Chrome Green, Chrome Yellow, Zinc Yellw

Aircraft Cylinders Amer Iinc ....E...... 918 582-1785
  Tulsa (G-9124)

PIGMENTS, INORGANIC: White

Tronox Worldwide LLC ....F...... 405 775-5000
  Oklahoma City (G-7343)

PILOT SVCS: Aviation

Archein Aerospace LLC ....E...... 682 499-2150
  Ponca City (G-7798)
Kern Valley Industries ....G...... 918 868-3911
  Rose (G-8118)

PINS

Pin Efx LLC ....G...... 405 341-9956
  Edmond (G-2570)

PINS: Cotter

Manufacturing Solutions LLC ....G...... 918 951-0750
  Broken Arrow (G-1141)

PIPE & FITTING: Fabrication

Baker Hughes Elasto Systems ....F...... 405 670-3354
  Oklahoma City (G-5516)
Flatlands Threading Co Inc ....G...... 405 677-7351
  Oklahoma City (G-6089)
Handy & Harman ....E...... 918 258-1566
  Broken Arrow (G-1131)
JM Eagle Co ....G...... 405 273-0900
  Shawnee (G-8464)
Lewis Industries Corp ....E...... 918 371-2596
  Collinsville (G-1815)
Mayco Inc ....E...... 405 677-5969
  Oklahoma City (G-6543)
Mike Cline Inc ....F...... 918 592-3712
  Tulsa (G-10277)
MRC Global (us) Inc ....G...... 918 485-9511
  Wagoner (G-11287)
National Oilwell Varco Inc ....C...... 918 781-4436
  Muskogee (G-4719)
Nortek Air Solutions LLC ....B...... 405 263-7286
  Okarche (G-5247)
Oilfield Equipment Company ....G...... 405 850-1406
  Duncan (G-2161)
Oilfield Improvements Inc ....G...... 918 250-5584
  Broken Arrow (G-993)
Pipeline Equipment Inc ....E...... 918 224-4144
  Tulsa (G-9024)
Pro-Fab Industries Inc ....E...... 918 865-7590
  Mannford (G-4190)
Rise Manufacturing LLC ....E...... 918 994-6240
  Broken Arrow (G-1032)
Safeco Filter Products Inc ....F...... 918 455-0100
  Tulsa (G-9033)
Safeco Manufacturing Inc ....F...... 918 455-0100
  Broken Arrow (G-1160)
Sharp Metal Fabricators Inc ....F...... 405 899-4849
  Noble (G-4891)
Shaw Group Inc ....A...... 918 445-7744
  Tulsa (G-10739)
Sooner Swage & Coating Co Inc ....G...... 918 689-7142
  Eufaula (G-3114)
SUN Engineering Inc ....F...... 918 627-0426
  Tulsa (G-10870)
U S Weatherford L P ....G...... 580 276-5362
  Marietta (G-4216)
Weatherford International LLC ....E...... 405 773-1100
  Oklahoma City (G-7430)
Weatherford International LLC ....E...... 580 490-1476
  Wilson (G-11545)
Wolverine Tube Inc ....A...... 405 275-4850
  Shawnee (G-8522)
Word Inds Fabrication LLC ....E...... 918 382-7704
  Tulsa (G-11152)

PIPE & FITTINGS: Cast Iron

Mayco Inc ....E...... 405 677-5969
  Oklahoma City (G-6543)

PIPE & FITTINGS: Pressure, Cast Iron

Closebend Inc ....F...... 918 445-1131
  Tulsa (G-9456)

PIPE & TUBES: Seamless

Bison Metals Technologies LLC ....G...... 403 395-1405
  Shawnee (G-8433)
Bkw Inc ....G...... 918 836-6767
  Tulsa (G-9299)

PIPE FITTINGS: Plastic

East 74th Street Holdings Inc ....C...... 918 437-3037
  Tulsa (G-9631)
Hackney Ladish Inc ....D...... 580 237-4212
  Enid (G-2967)
J & S Fittings Inc ....G...... 918 324-5777
  Depew (G-2011)

PIPE SECTIONS, FABRICATED FROM PURCHASED PIPE

Ipsco Tubulars Inc ....C...... 918 384-6400
  Catoosa (G-1323)

PIPE, CAST IRON: Wholesalers

Durant Iron & Metal Inc .... E 580 924-0595
  Durant (G-2226)

PIPE, CYLINDER: Concrete, Prestressed Or Pretensioned

Ameron International Corp .... C 918 858-3973
  Tulsa (G-9180)

PIPE, SEWER: Concrete

Cellfill LLC .... G 918 787-2355
  Grove (G-3260)

PIPE: Concrete

Chandler Materials Company .... E 918 836-9151
  Tulsa (G-9403)
Scurlock Industries Miami Inc .... F 918 542-1884
  North Miami (G-5208)

PIPE: Plastic

Advanced Drainage Systems .... G 405 272-1541
  Oklahoma City (G-5380)
Beetle Plastics LLC .... E 580 389-5421
  Ardmore (G-256)
Classic Iron Works Inc .... F 405 577-2877
  Yukon (G-11706)
Dura-Line Corporation .... E 918 302-0330
  Bache (G-430)
Dylans Precision Stainless LLC .... G 918 207-9149
  Hulbert (G-3623)
Prime Conduit Inc .... E 405 670-6132
  Oklahoma City (G-6892)
Silver-Line Plastics Corp .... E 828 252-8755
  Lawton (G-3998)
U S Poly Company .... C 918 446-4471
  Tulsa (G-11029)

PIPE: Sheet Metal

Parfab Industries LLC .... D 918 543-6310
  Inola (G-3672)

PIPE: Water, Cast Iron

United Utlties Specialists LLC .... E 918 342-0840
  Claremore (G-1698)

PIPELINE & POWER LINE INSPECTION SVCS

Cypress Energy Holdings LLC .... F 918 748-3900
  Tulsa (G-9533)
Cypress Energy Holdings II LLC .... G 918 748-3900
  Tulsa (G-9534)
Cypress Energy Partners LP .... G 918 748-3900
  Tulsa (G-9535)
Mid States Technical Svc LLC .... E 918 260-6912
  Skiatook (G-8561)
T Rowe Pipe LLC .... E 580 765-1500
  Ponca City (G-7881)
Tdw Services Inc .... E 918 447-5000
  Tulsa (G-9041)

PIPELINES: Crude Petroleum

Holly Ref & Mktg - Tulsa LLC .... E 918 594-6000
  Tulsa (G-9941)
Hollyfrontier Corporation .... G 918 594-6000
  Tulsa (G-9943)
Rose Rock Midstream Field Svcs .... G 918 524-7700
  Tulsa (G-10672)
Semcrude LP .... F 918 524-8100
  Tulsa (G-10727)
Semgroup Corporation .... B 918 524-8100
  Tulsa (G-10728)

PIPELINES: Natural Gas

Avalon Exploration Inc .... F 918 523-0600
  Tulsa (G-9227)
Enable Okla Intrstate Trnsm LL .... C 405 525-7788
  Oklahoma City (G-6033)
Oneok Inc .... F 405 878-6267
  Shawnee (G-8482)
Oneok Inc .... E 918 588-7000
  Tulsa (G-10422)
Oneok Inc .... A 918 588-7000
  Tulsa (G-10421)

Williams Companies Inc .... A 918 573-2000
  Tulsa (G-11127)

PIPELINES: Refined Petroleum

Devon Oei Operating Inc .... A 405 235-3611
  Oklahoma City (G-5936)

PIPES & TUBES

United Axle .... G 918 344-1157
  Claremore (G-1697)
Vam Usa LLC .... G 405 720-2200
  Oklahoma City (G-7388)

PIPES & TUBES: Steel

Advantage Cnstr Pdts Inc .... G 405 372-3562
  Stillwater (G-8651)
Albright Steel and Wire Co .... F 405 232-7526
  Oklahoma City (G-5410)
Baker Hughes Elasto Systems .... F 405 670-3354
  Oklahoma City (G-5516)
Corrpro Companies Inc .... E 918 245-8791
  Sand Springs (G-8172)
Cutting Edge Machine Inc .... G 580 658-5036
  Marlow (G-4226)
Flow Valve LLC .... E 580 622-2294
  Sulphur (G-8832)
Hunter Steel LLC .... G 918 684-9600
  Muskogee (G-4693)
Innovex Downhole Solutions Inc .... G 405 491-2658
  Oklahoma City (G-6308)
Lps Specialty Products Inc .... G 918 893-5486
  Catoosa (G-1334)
Mid American Stl & Wire Co LLC .... E 580 795-2559
  Madill (G-4157)
MRC Global (us) Inc .... G 918 485-9511
  Wagoner (G-11287)
Oilfield Equipment Company .... G 405 850-1406
  Duncan (G-2161)
Ops Sales Company .... G 918 534-3760
  Dewey (G-2029)
Paragon Industries Inc .... E 918 781-1430
  Muskogee (G-4731)
Paragon Industries Inc .... B 918 291-4459
  Sapulpa (G-8296)
Rolled Alloys Inc .... E 918 594-2600
  Tulsa (G-9031)
Ross Dub Company Inc .... E 405 495-3611
  Oklahoma City (G-7049)
Taylor & Sons Pipe and Stl Inc .... F 405 222-0751
  Chickasha (G-1516)
Webco Industries Inc .... C 918 865-6215
  Mannford (G-4194)
Webco Industries Inc .... E 918 245-9521
  Sand Springs (G-8239)
Webco Industries Inc .... G 918 865-6215
  Kellyville (G-3769)
Webco Industries Inc .... C 918 241-1086
  Sand Springs (G-8238)

PIPES & TUBES: Welded

Cherokee Piping Services LLC .... G 918 931-8593
  Tahlequah (G-8856)

PIPES OR FITTINGS: Sewer, Clay

Ops Sales Company .... G 918 534-3760
  Dewey (G-2029)

PIPES: Steel & Iron

Elite Fabricators LLC .... E 918 824-4528
  Pryor (G-7961)
Karchmer Pipe & Supply Co Inc .... G 405 236-3568
  Oklahoma City (G-6398)
Kingfisher Pipe Sales and Svc .... G 405 262-4422
  El Reno (G-2733)

PLAQUES: Picture, Laminated

Dale Rogers Training Ctr Inc .... E 580 481-6170
  Altus (G-153)
Mart Trophy Co Inc .... G 918 481-3388
  Tulsa (G-10217)

PLASMAPHEROUS CENTER

Vaxart Inc .... G 918 582-4346
  Tulsa (G-11067)

PLASMAS

Octapharma Plasma .... G 405 686-9226
  Oklahoma City (G-6711)
Plasma Bionics LLC .... G 405 564-5333
  Stillwater (G-8738)
Plasma Solutions 1 .... G 918 543-2178
  Inola (G-3673)
Zlb Behring .... G 405 521-9204
  Oklahoma City (G-7487)
Zlb Bio Services .... G 580 248-4851
  Lawton (G-4025)

PLASTER, ACOUSTICAL: Gypsum

Freeman Products Inc .... E 918 258-8861
  Broken Arrow (G-915)

PLASTIC PRDTS

Abmi Inc .... G 405 485-9608
  Blanchard (G-699)
Ashley Cameron Building Prods .... G 405 236-0617
  Oklahoma City (G-5477)
David Logan .... G 918 739-4231
  Catoosa (G-1315)
House of Trophies .... G 918 341-2111
  Claremore (G-1637)
Rusco Plastics .... G 580 234-1596
  Enid (G-3053)
Viking Rain Covers .... G 405 359-1850
  Edmond (G-2671)
Wilson II Geary Wayne .... G 405 330-4888
  Edmond (G-2689)
Wing-It Concepts .... G 405 691-8053
  Oklahoma City (G-5325)

PLASTICS FILM & SHEET

Gooden Studios .... G 405 375-3432
  Kingfisher (G-3799)
Unit Liner Company .... D 405 275-4600
  Shawnee (G-8516)

PLASTICS FILM & SHEET: Polyethylene

Berry Global Films LLC .... D 918 227-1616
  Tulsa (G-8990)
Berry Global Films LLC .... D 918 446-1651
  Tulsa (G-8991)
Berry Plastics Corporation .... C 918 824-4400
  Pryor (G-7947)
Georgia-Pacific LLC .... E 918 687-9800
  Muskogee (G-4678)
Paragon Films Inc .... C 918 250-3456
  Broken Arrow (G-998)

PLASTICS FILM & SHEET: Polyvinyl

F C Witt Associates Ltd .... F 918 342-0083
  Claremore (G-1618)
Vineyard Plating & Sup Co Tx .... F 918 342-0083
  Claremore (G-1702)

PLASTICS MATERIAL & RESINS

AO Inc .... G 918 623-1711
  Okemah (G-5263)
Baker Petrolite LLC .... C 918 847-2522
  Barnsdall (G-435)
Barlow-Hunt Inc .... D 918 250-0828
  Tulsa (G-9265)
Cass Holdings LLC .... E 405 755-8448
  Oklahoma City (G-5707)
Cass Holdings LLC .... G 405 359-5053
  Watonga (G-11343)
Chevron Phillips Chem Co LP .... D 918 825-0364
  Pryor (G-7953)
Chevron Phillips Chem Co LP .... C 918 977-6846
  Bartlesville (G-462)
Chevron Phillips Chem Co LP .... C 918 661-3317
  Bartlesville (G-463)
Elastech Technologies LLC .... G 405 470-1539
  Oklahoma City (G-6021)
Hilti North America Ltd .... G 918 252-6000
  Tulsa (G-9932)
Hobby Supermarket Inc .... E 405 239-6864
  Oklahoma City (G-6256)
Interplastic Corporation .... D 918 825-2755
  Pryor (G-7971)
Interplastic Corporation .... F 918 592-0205
  Tulsa (G-10006)

PRODUCT SECTION

PLATES

Line X of Stillwater..........................G........ 405 743-0911
  Stillwater *(G-8719)*
Nordam Group LLC..........................C........ 918 274-2742
  Tulsa *(G-10356)*
T D Williamson Inc..........................E........ 918 447-5400
  Tulsa *(G-10888)*
Tetrachem Seal Company Inc............F........ 580 924-1717
  Durant *(G-2263)*

PLASTICS MATERIALS, BASIC FORMS & SHAPES WHOLESALERS

Cass Holdings LLC..........................E........ 405 755-8448
  Oklahoma City *(G-5707)*
Cass Holdings LLC..........................G........ 405 359-5053
  Watonga *(G-11343)*
Cope Plastics Inc..........................G........ 405 528-5697
  Oklahoma City *(G-5833)*
Pechiney Plastic Packaging.............G........ 918 739-4900
  Catoosa *(G-1346)*

PLASTICS PROCESSING

Cals Plastics Designs & Fabg...........G........ 405 670-1690
  Oklahoma City *(G-5673)*
Commerce Plastics Inc...................F........ 918 675-4506
  North Miami *(G-5206)*
Cope Plastics Inc..........................G........ 405 528-5697
  Oklahoma City *(G-5833)*
Eaton-Quade Company....................G........ 405 236-4475
  Oklahoma City *(G-6002)*
Fibre Reduction Inc.........................G........ 580 223-3401
  Ardmore *(G-289)*

PLASTICS SHEET: Packing Materials

Emerald Manufacturing Corp............G........ 405 235-3704
  Oklahoma City *(G-6032)*

PLASTICS: Blow Molded

G & H Decoy Inc..............................D........ 918 652-3314
  Henryetta *(G-3507)*

PLASTICS: Cast

Lloyd Freeman Creations LLC..........G........ 918 245-4921
  Sand Springs *(G-8201)*

PLASTICS: Extruded

Cellofoam North America Inc............E........ 918 775-7758
  Sallisaw *(G-8142)*
Georgia-Pacific LLC.........................E........ 918 687-9800
  Muskogee *(G-4678)*

PLASTICS: Finished Injection Molded

D B W Inc..G........ 405 354-6211
  Yukon *(G-11714)*
Devault Enterprises Inc...................G........ 918 249-1595
  Tulsa *(G-9576)*
General Plastics Inc.........................F........ 405 275-3171
  Shawnee *(G-8453)*
Mac Industries Inc...........................G........ 405 631-8553
  Moore *(G-4535)*
Rim Molded Products Co..................F........ 918 438-7070
  Tulsa *(G-10653)*
Sanco Enterprises Inc.....................E........ 405 634-2120
  Oklahoma City *(G-7075)*

PLASTICS: Injection Molded

Aco Inc...G........ 405 239-6863
  Oklahoma City *(G-5368)*
Associated Plastics LLC..................G........ 405 390-0406
  Choctaw *(G-1527)*
Branchcomb Inc...............................E........ 918 224-8094
  Sapulpa *(G-8259)*
Custom Molding Services Inc............G........ 918 333-4872
  Bartlesville *(G-472)*
David Gormley.................................G........ 918 845-0443
  Sapulpa *(G-8265)*
Discovery Plastics LLC....................D........ 918 540-2822
  Miami *(G-4396)*
Durant Plastics & Mfg......................G........ 580 745-9430
  Durant *(G-2227)*
Elastomer Specialties Inc................F........ 800 786-4244
  Wagoner *(G-11280)*
Elastomer Specialties Inc................F........ 918 485-0276
  Wagoner *(G-11281)*
Fiber Pad Inc...................................D........ 918 438-7430
  Tulsa *(G-9739)*

Frontier Plastic Fabricators..............F........ 918 445-5208
  Tulsa *(G-9785)*
H C E Inc..E........ 405 745-2145
  Oklahoma City *(G-6197)*
Imperial Molding LLC.......................F........ 580 362-3412
  Newkirk *(G-4848)*
Imperial Plastics Inc........................F........ 580 362-3412
  Newkirk *(G-4849)*
Jarrt Holdings Inc............................F........ 918 664-0931
  Tulsa *(G-10028)*
K & C Manufacturing Inc..................G........ 580 362-2979
  Ponca City *(G-7842)*
Laska LLC.......................................G........ 405 820-7617
  Edmond *(G-2483)*
M-D Plastics Group.........................G........ 503 981-3726
  Oklahoma City *(G-6511)*
O C & Associates Inc......................G........ 918 251-0971
  Broken Arrow *(G-991)*
Oklahoma Hand Pours....................F........ 580 669-2520
  Glencoe *(G-3225)*
Phil-Good Products Inc...................E........ 405 942-5527
  Oklahoma City *(G-6842)*
Plas-Tech Inc..................................G........ 918 649-0065
  Poteau *(G-7909)*
Plastic Designs Inc.........................G........ 918 224-9187
  Sapulpa *(G-8299)*
Plastic Sup & Fabrication Co...........G........ 918 622-8430
  Tulsa *(G-10526)*
Precision Rotational Molding............G........ 580 362-3262
  Newkirk *(G-4851)*
Rotational Technologies Inc............F........ 918 343-1350
  Claremore *(G-1684)*
Samco Polishing Inc........................F........ 918 789-5541
  Chelsea *(G-1412)*
Sanco Products Inc.........................G........ 405 634-2120
  Oklahoma City *(G-7076)*
Southern Plastics LLC....................G........ 918 274-6767
  Owasso *(G-7618)*
Swan Plastics..................................G........ 405 275-4826
  Shawnee *(G-8506)*
Texre Inc..D........ 918 425-5524
  Tulsa *(G-10922)*
Tgs Plastics Inc..............................E........ 918 252-3636
  Tulsa *(G-10925)*
W J L S Inc.....................................E........ 918 252-3636
  Tulsa *(G-11088)*
Western Plastics LLC.....................F........ 918 235-7272
  Oklahoma City *(G-7441)*

PLASTICS: Molded

Aztec Manufacturing Corp................G........ 405 330-4888
  Edmond *(G-2314)*
Mold Tech Inc..................................G........ 918 247-6275
  Sapulpa *(G-8292)*
Polydyne LLC..................................F........ 918 649-0065
  Poteau *(G-7910)*
RL Hudson & Company....................C........ 918 259-6600
  Broken Arrow *(G-1035)*
Specialty Plastics Inc.....................F........ 580 237-1018
  Enid *(G-3061)*
Tech Inc..F........ 405 547-8324
  Perkins *(G-7724)*

PLASTICS: Polystyrene Foam

Allied Foam Fabricators Inc.............G........ 405 946-0384
  Oklahoma City *(G-5421)*
Armacell LLC..................................G........ 405 494-2800
  Yukon *(G-11693)*
Becky Welch Vacuum Forming..........G........ 918 836-7301
  Tulsa *(G-9278)*
Cellofoam North America Inc............E........ 918 775-7758
  Sallisaw *(G-8142)*
Nomaco Inc.....................................G........ 405 494-2800
  Yukon *(G-11759)*
Scott Manufacturing LLC.................E........ 405 949-2728
  Oklahoma City *(G-7096)*
Tech Inc..F........ 405 547-8324
  Perkins *(G-7724)*
Timber Ridge Spray Foam................G........ 405 608-5995
  Oklahoma City *(G-7292)*
Wise Foamco Inc.............................G........ 918 839-4784
  Poteau *(G-7919)*

PLATE WORK: Metalworking Trade

El Dorado Manufacturing Co LLC......G........ 580 318-2313
  Eldorado *(G-2773)*

PLATEMAKING SVC: Color Separations, For The Printing Trade

Pinecliffe Prtrs of Tecumseh............G........ 405 273-1292
  Shawnee *(G-8483)*

PLATEMAKING SVC: Letterpress

Reflection Foil and Ltr Press............G........ 405 341-8660
  Edmond *(G-2593)*

PLATES

A B Printing.....................................G........ 918 834-2054
  Tulsa *(G-9066)*
A Q Printing....................................G........ 918 438-1161
  Tulsa *(G-9070)*
Advance Graphics & Printing............G........ 405 258-0796
  Chandler *(G-1373)*
Ajt Enterprises Inc..........................F........ 918 665-7083
  Tulsa *(G-9133)*
C & J Printing Co............................G........ 580 355-3099
  Lawton *(G-3902)*
C & R Print Shop Inc.......................G........ 405 224-7921
  Chickasha *(G-1445)*
Carnegie Herald...............................G........ 580 654-1443
  Carnegie *(G-1274)*
Cnhi LLC...F........ 580 338-3355
  Guymon *(G-3346)*
Copy Fast Printing Inc.....................G........ 405 947-7468
  Oklahoma City *(G-5834)*
Countywide News Inc......................F........ 405 598-3793
  Tecumseh *(G-8910)*
CSC Inc..G........ 580 994-6110
  Mooreland *(G-4587)*
Diversified Printing Inc....................F........ 918 665-2275
  Tulsa *(G-9586)*
First Impression Prtg Co Inc............G........ 918 749-5446
  Beggs *(G-553)*
Franklin Graphics Inc......................F........ 918 687-6149
  Muskogee *(G-4675)*
G & S Printing Inc............................G........ 405 789-6813
  Oklahoma City *(G-6129)*
Graphics Universal Inc....................G........ 918 461-0609
  Tulsa *(G-9847)*
Inspired Gifts & Graphics LLC..........G........ 405 295-1669
  El Reno *(G-2725)*
Mattocks Printing Co LLC................G........ 405 794-2307
  Moore *(G-4538)*
MBC Graphics..................................G........ 918 585-2321
  Tulsa *(G-10227)*
Mesa Black Publishing LLC.............G........ 580 544-2222
  Boise City *(G-747)*
Nancy Nelson & Associates............G........ 580 765-0115
  Ponca City *(G-7857)*
North Star Publishing LLC...............D........ 405 415-2400
  Oklahoma City *(G-6688)*
Oklahoma Assn of Elc Coop............E........ 405 478-1455
  Oklahoma City *(G-6735)*
Oklahoma Executive Printing...........G........ 405 948-8136
  Oklahoma City *(G-6748)*
Paperwork Company.........................F........ 918 369-1014
  Bixby *(G-652)*
Peabodys Printing & A Brush Sp......G........ 580 248-8317
  Lawton *(G-3980)*
Pre-Press Graphics Inc...................G........ 918 582-2775
  Tulsa *(G-10541)*
Prices Quality Printing Inc...............G........ 580 924-2271
  Durant *(G-2248)*
Print Shop.......................................G........ 918 342-3993
  Claremore *(G-1674)*
Printed Products Inc........................F........ 918 295-9950
  Tulsa *(G-10561)*
Protype Inc.....................................G........ 918 743-4408
  Tulsa *(G-10576)*
Pryor Printing Inc............................G........ 918 825-2888
  Pryor *(G-7986)*
Quik Print of Tulsa Inc.....................G........ 918 582-1825
  Tulsa *(G-10596)*
Quintella Printing Company Inc........G........ 405 631-6566
  Oklahoma City *(G-6955)*
Signs To Go LLC.............................G........ 405 348-8646
  Edmond *(G-2621)*
Torbett Printing Co & Off Sup..........G........ 918 756-5789
  Okmulgee *(G-7528)*
Transcript Press Inc........................E........ 405 360-7999
  Norman *(G-5181)*
Usher Corporation...........................G........ 405 495-2125
  Oklahoma City *(G-7382)*
Wallis Printing Inc...........................G........ 580 223-7473
  Ardmore *(G-379)*

PLATES

PRODUCT SECTION

Westwood Printing Center ....G....... 405 366-8961
Norman *(G-5199)*

PLATES: Aluminum

Reel Power International Corp.............F....... 405 609-3326
Oklahoma City *(G-6999)*

PLATING & POLISHING SVC

Brass Buff.......................................G....... 918 592-1717
Tulsa *(G-9332)*
Broken Arrow Powdr Coating Inc...........E....... 918 251-2192
Broken Arrow *(G-856)*
Buster Dorsch..................................G....... 918 743-4509
Tulsa *(G-9353)*
Choctaw Mfg & Dev Corp....................D....... 580 326-8365
Hugo *(G-3607)*
Collins Metal Company Inc..................G....... 405 373-3309
Warr Acres *(G-11316)*
H & H Protective Coating Co................G....... 918 582-9187
Tulsa *(G-9871)*
H L Custom Processing......................G....... 580 927-5408
Coalgate *(G-1780)*
LMI Finishing Inc..............................D....... 918 438-1012
Tulsa *(G-10174)*
Metcoat Inc....................................G....... 580 255-6441
Duncan *(G-2154)*
Paysmith Processing LLC....................G....... 918 858-5599
Tulsa *(G-10477)*
Southwest Pickling Inc.......................G....... 580 924-6996
Durant *(G-2259)*
Ted Davis Enterprises Inc...................F....... 405 948-8763
Oklahoma City *(G-7263)*
Ultra Tech Ultra Tech.........................G....... 580 351-1220
Lawton *(G-4016)*

PLATING SVC: Chromium, Metals Or Formed Prdts

Chromium Plating Company..................E....... 918 583-4118
Tulsa *(G-9422)*
Diversified Plating Ltd.......................G....... 405 236-0545
Oklahoma City *(G-5952)*
OK Products of Tulsa Inc....................G....... 918 445-2471
Tulsa *(G-10391)*

PLATING SVC: Electro

C & F Custom Chrome........................G....... 918 587-1110
Tulsa *(G-9356)*
DCI Industries LLC............................E....... 405 947-2863
Oklahoma City *(G-5910)*
Delta Plating Inc..............................G....... 918 664-6880
Tulsa *(G-9570)*
Metal Finishing of Chickasha................F....... 405 224-6703
Chickasha *(G-1485)*
Modern Plating Co Inc........................F....... 918 836-5081
Tulsa *(G-10291)*
Oklahoma Superior Plating LLC.............G....... 580 252-2787
Duncan *(G-2162)*
Precision Anodizing Inc......................F....... 405 631-2079
Oklahoma City *(G-6880)*
Quality Metal Finishing Inc..................F....... 405 236-1155
Oklahoma City *(G-6937)*
Quality Plating Co of Tulsa Inc..............G....... 918 835-2278
Tulsa *(G-10593)*
Ramos Plating Co.............................G....... 405 232-4300
Oklahoma City *(G-6970)*
Sparks Plating Company.....................G....... 918 482-5080
Haskell *(G-3401)*

PLATING SVC: NEC

Classic Custom Plating Company...........G....... 405 787-3075
Bethany *(G-573)*
HB Brackets....................................G....... 405 745-4417
Oklahoma City *(G-6231)*
United Plating Works Inc.....................E....... 918 835-4683
Tulsa *(G-11042)*

PLAYGROUND EQPT

Billiards of Tulsa Inc..........................E....... 918 835-1166
Tulsa *(G-9296)*
Miracle Recreation Eqp Co..................G....... 918 299-1415
Bixby *(G-645)*
Noahs Park & Playgrounds LLC.............F....... 405 607-0714
Edmond *(G-2538)*
Satterlee Teepees............................G....... 405 255-6642
Moore *(G-4563)*

PLEATING & STITCHING FOR THE TRADE: Decorative & Novelty

Baywest Embroidery..........................G....... 580 626-4728
Jet *(G-3741)*

PLEATING & STITCHING SVC

4524 LLC.......................................G....... 405 620-3711
Edmond *(G-2285)*
Big Red Shop Inc..............................G....... 405 495-5551
Warr Acres *(G-11313)*
Cas Monogramming Inc......................G....... 405 350-6556
Yukon *(G-11703)*
Cejco Inc.......................................F....... 405 366-8256
Norman *(G-4954)*
Complete Graphics Inc.......................G....... 405 232-8882
Oklahoma City *(G-5812)*
Cr Stripes Ltd Co..............................G....... 405 946-8577
Oklahoma City *(G-5850)*
Design It.......................................G....... 405 756-3635
Lindsay *(G-4060)*
Genes Customized Tags & EMB.............G....... 580 225-8247
Elk City *(G-2820)*
Green Cntry Trophy Screen Prtg............G....... 918 647-2923
Poteau *(G-7906)*
Inspiration Logos Inc.........................G....... 405 741-5646
Oklahoma City *(G-6310)*
Label Stable Inc...............................G....... 580 223-2037
Ardmore *(G-323)*
Mobile PC Manager LLC......................G....... 574 551-4521
Jenks *(G-3717)*
Pearl District Embroidery LLC...............G....... 918 269-3347
Tulsa *(G-10481)*
S & S Textile Inc..............................F....... 405 632-9928
Oklahoma City *(G-7065)*
Sew Graphics Plus Inc........................G....... 405 364-1707
Norman *(G-5141)*
T S & H EMB & Screen Prtg.................G....... 405 214-7701
Shawnee *(G-8508)*
USA Screen Prtg & EMB Co Inc..............E....... 405 946-3100
Oklahoma City *(G-7380)*

PLUGS: Electric

Mid States Technical Svc LLC...............E....... 918 260-6912
Skiatook *(G-8561)*

PLUMBING & HEATING EQPT & SPLY, WHOL: Htg Eqpt/Panels, Solar

Advanced Power Inc..........................F....... 580 774-2220
Weatherford *(G-11387)*
Electric Green Inc.............................G....... 405 706-1683
Oklahoma City *(G-6022)*

PLUMBING & HEATING EQPT & SPLY, WHOLESALE: Hydronic Htg Eqpt

Pipeline Coating Services LLC..............G....... 936 494-2919
Tulsa *(G-10518)*

PLUMBING & HEATING EQPT & SPLYS WHOLESALERS

Crandall and Sanders Inc....................G....... 405 375-3242
Kingfisher *(G-3794)*
Oklahoma Home Centers Inc................E....... 405 260-7625
Guthrie *(G-3329)*

PLUMBING & HEATING EQPT & SPLYS, WHOL: Plumbing Fitting/Sply

D Vontz LLC....................................F....... 918 622-3600
Tulsa *(G-9540)*
Ferguson Enterprises LLC...................G....... 405 945-0107
Oklahoma City *(G-6082)*
Heatwave Supply Inc.........................G....... 918 333-6363
Bartlesville *(G-491)*

PLUMBING & HEATING EQPT & SPLYS, WHOL: Water Purif Eqpt

T S I L C..G....... 918 357-5992
Broken Arrow *(G-1169)*
Water Bionics Inc.............................G....... 918 446-1988
Tulsa *(G-11098)*

PLUMBING & HEATING EQPT, WHOLESALE: Water Heaters/Purif

Norman Supply Company.....................G....... 405 692-1191
Oklahoma City *(G-5308)*

PLUMBING FIXTURES

D Vontz LLC....................................F....... 918 622-3600
Tulsa *(G-9540)*
Eaton Aeroquip LLC...........................D....... 405 275-5500
Shawnee *(G-8447)*
Ferguson..G....... 918 835-4813
Tulsa *(G-9738)*
Ferguson Enterprises LLC...................G....... 405 945-0107
Oklahoma City *(G-6082)*
H & K Specification & Sls LLC...............F....... 405 844-7456
Edmond *(G-2450)*
Heatwave Supply Inc.........................G....... 918 333-6363
Bartlesville *(G-491)*
Norman Supply Company.....................G....... 405 692-1191
Oklahoma City *(G-5308)*

PLUMBING FIXTURES: Brass, Incl Drain Cocks, Faucets/Spigots

Empire Plumbing Contrs LLC................G....... 918 320-1427
Grove *(G-3267)*

PLUMBING FIXTURES: Plastic

Cimarron Tank Service.......................G....... 405 853-6523
Hennessey *(G-3451)*
Majestic Marble & Granite...................E....... 918 266-1121
Catoosa *(G-1337)*
Pipes Plus LLC.................................G....... 405 942-7473
Oklahoma City *(G-6853)*

PLUMBING FIXTURES: Vitreous

Professional Marble Company...............G....... 918 225-5364
Cushing *(G-1950)*

POINT OF SALE DEVICES

Gibsons Treasures............................G....... 405 835-1109
Oklahoma City *(G-6152)*
Order-Matic Electronics Corp................C....... 405 672-1487
Oklahoma City *(G-6781)*

POLES & POSTS: Concrete

Ameron Pole Products LLC...................E....... 918 585-5611
Tulsa *(G-9181)*

POLISHING SVC: Metals Or Formed Prdts

Central Metal Finishing LLC..................E....... 405 379-5252
Holdenville *(G-3551)*
S&S Professional Polishing LLC.............G....... 405 631-7087
Oklahoma City *(G-7067)*

POLYPROPYLENE RESINS

Bluehawk Energy Inc..........................G....... 405 406-1580
Edmond *(G-2327)*

POLYVINYL CHLORIDE RESINS

J-M Manufacturing Company Inc............D....... 918 446-4471
Tulsa *(G-10025)*
Prime Conduit Inc.............................E....... 405 670-6132
Oklahoma City *(G-6892)*

PORCELAIN ENAMELED PRDTS & UTENSILS

Porcelain Treasure............................G....... 918 230-9618
Tulsa *(G-10534)*

POSTERS

Copy Write Incorporated.....................G....... 918 224-1148
Sapulpa *(G-8262)*

POTTERY

All American Wrought Iron...................G....... 918 213-9949
Bartlesville *(G-445)*
Nell Gavin LLC.................................G....... 972 935-6692
Bartlesville *(G-513)*
Phelps Sculpture Studio......................G....... 405 752-9512
Oklahoma City *(G-6841)*

PRODUCT SECTION

PRINTING, COMMERCIAL: Envelopes, NEC

POULTRY & POULTRY PRDTS WHOLESALERS

O K Foods Inc .... B 918 427-7000
  Muldrow *(G-4635)*

POULTRY & SMALL GAME SLAUGHTERING & PROCESSING

Advance Food Company Inc .... A 580 237-6656
  Enid *(G-2906)*
Bar-S Foods Co .... C 580 821-5700
  Altus *(G-144)*
Kormondy Enterprises Inc .... B 918 274-8787
  Owasso *(G-7584)*
O K Foods Inc .... B 918 427-7000
  Muldrow *(G-4635)*
OSteen Meat Specialties Inc .... D 405 236-1952
  Oklahoma City *(G-6787)*
Simmons Foods Inc .... F 918 676-3285
  Fairland *(G-3130)*
Simmons Foods Inc .... G 918 791-0010
  Grove *(G-3288)*
Tyson Foods Inc .... E 918 723-5494
  Westville *(G-11486)*
Tyson Foods Inc .... E 918 696-4530
  Stilwell *(G-8796)*

POWDER: Metal

Walkers Powder Coating LLC .... G 580 355-5000
  Lawton *(G-4018)*

POWER GENERATORS

Hipower Systems Oklahoma LLC .... G 918 512-6321
  Tulsa *(G-9013)*

POWER HAND TOOLS WHOLESALERS

Jantz Supply Inc .... E 580 369-5503
  Davis *(G-1986)*

POWER SUPPLIES: All Types, Static

Quick Charge Corporation .... E 405 634-2120
  Oklahoma City *(G-6944)*

POWER TOOL REPAIR SVCS

Oak Tree Sales .... G 405 224-9332
  Chickasha *(G-1493)*
Pine Creek Saw Shop Inc .... G 580 933-7376
  Valliant *(G-11231)*

POWER TRANSMISSION EQPT: Mechanical

Bb Machine & Supply Inc .... G 580 237-8686
  Enid *(G-2915)*
Drive Shafts Inc .... G 918 836-0111
  Tulsa *(G-9608)*
H-V Manufacturing Company .... G 918 756-9620
  Okmulgee *(G-7509)*
Imak Industrial Solutions LLC .... G 405 406-9778
  Oklahoma City *(G-6292)*
J & D Gearing & Machining Inc .... G 405 677-7667
  Oklahoma City *(G-6329)*
N & S Flame Spray LLC .... E 918 865-4737
  Mannford *(G-4187)*
Nordam Group LLC .... C 918 274-2742
  Tulsa *(G-10356)*

POWERED GOLF CART DEALERS

Charleys Golf Cars Inc .... G 405 273-6901
  Shawnee *(G-8437)*

PRECAST TERRAZZO OR CONCRETE PRDTS

Precast Solutions LLC .... G 580 819-2455
  Yukon *(G-11767)*
Precast Trtmnt Solutions LLC .... G 405 455-5303
  Oklahoma City *(G-6877)*

PRECIOUS METALS WHOLESALERS

Rings Etc Fine Jewelry .... G 405 359-7464
  Edmond *(G-2601)*

PRECIOUS STONE MINING SVCS, NEC

Greenhill Materials LLC .... F 918 274-6560
  Owasso *(G-7572)*

Tulsa Auto Core .... G 918 584-5899
  Tulsa *(G-10986)*

PRECIOUS STONES & METALS, WHOLESALE

J Thompson Custom Jewelers .... G 405 495-6610
  Warr Acres *(G-11323)*

PRECISION INSTRUMENT REPAIR SVCS

Airico Inc .... G 918 836-2675
  Tulsa *(G-9130)*
Grace Power LLC .... G 512 228-9049
  Lawton *(G-3936)*
William L Riggs Company Inc .... G 918 437-3245
  Tulsa *(G-11125)*

PREFABRICATED BUILDING DEALERS

E & E Construction Company .... G 918 775-6222
  Sallisaw *(G-8144)*
Maddens Portable Buildings .... E 405 799-4989
  Norman *(G-5062)*
Midwest Portable Building .... G 918 245-9335
  Tulsa *(G-10269)*
Vanover Metal Building Sls Inc .... F 918 253-6030
  Spavinaw *(G-8593)*

PRENATAL INSTRUCTION

Eden Clinic Inc .... G 405 579-4673
  Norman *(G-4988)*

PRERECORDED TAPE, COMPACT DISC & RECORD STORES: Compact Disc

C D Connections .... G 580 248-6410
  Lawton *(G-3903)*

PRESTRESSED CONCRETE PRDTS

Tulsa Dynaspan Inc .... C 918 258-8693
  Tulsa *(G-10996)*

PRIMARY METAL PRODUCTS

E E Sewing Inc .... G 918 214-5343
  Bartlesville *(G-476)*
Weldco Mfg .... G 580 296-1585
  Colbert *(G-1788)*

PRINT CARTRIDGES: Laser & Other Computer Printers

Advanced Graphics Technology .... G 405 632-8600
  Oklahoma City *(G-5383)*
Elite Creative Solutions LLC .... E 918 994-5435
  Broken Arrow *(G-897)*
Laser Source LLC .... F 405 843-2528
  Oklahoma City *(G-6450)*
Laser Source LLC .... G 405 330-4442
  Oklahoma City *(G-6451)*

PRINTED CIRCUIT BOARDS

Advance Research & Development .... G 405 321-0550
  Norman *(G-4899)*
Advanced Medical Instrs Inc .... C 918 250-0566
  Broken Arrow *(G-816)*
Beck Illuminations LLC .... E 918 623-2880
  Okemah *(G-5264)*
Goodwill Inds Centl Okla Inc .... D 405 236-4451
  Oklahoma City *(G-6172)*
Newstar Netronics LLC .... G 918 932-8343
  Tulsa *(G-10340)*
Nyikos Inc .... G 918 299-3190
  Tulsa *(G-10368)*

PRINTERS' SVCS: Folding, Collating, Etc

Corner Copy & Printing LLC .... G 405 801-2020
  Norman *(G-4966)*

PRINTERS: Computer

Colorcomm .... G 918 398-7777
  Tulsa *(G-9470)*
Kirklind Global Inc .... G 580 618-2527
  El Reno *(G-2735)*

PRINTING & BINDING: Books

Corner Copy & Printing LLC .... G 405 801-2020
  Norman *(G-4966)*
Qg LLC .... B 405 742-2222
  Stillwater *(G-8741)*
Silver Quill LLC .... G 405 735-9191
  Moore *(G-4569)*

PRINTING & ENGRAVING: Invitation & Stationery

Ardellas Flowers Inc .... F 405 321-6850
  Norman *(G-4915)*
C and H Publishing Co .... G 918 245-9571
  Sand Springs *(G-8169)*
Inviting Place .... G 918 488-0525
  Tulsa *(G-10010)*

PRINTING & ENGRAVING: Plateless

Texoma Engraving LLC .... G 580 775-7333
  Durant *(G-2264)*

PRINTING & ENGRAVING: Poster & Decal

A & B Engraving Inc .... G 918 663-7446
  Tulsa *(G-9061)*
Nameplates Inc .... G 918 561-8732
  Tulsa *(G-10325)*

PRINTING & ENGRAVING: Rolls, Textile Printing

Price Prints Inc .... F 580 832-2492
  Cordell *(G-1862)*

PRINTING & STAMPING: Fabric Articles

Promo Print 4 U LLC .... G 405 259-6721
  Oklahoma City *(G-6915)*

PRINTING & WRITING PAPER WHOLESALERS

Media Technology Incorporated .... E 405 682-4400
  Oklahoma City *(G-6556)*

PRINTING INKS WHOLESALERS

H&H Retail Services LLC .... F 918 369-4055
  Bixby *(G-631)*
Southwestern Process Supply Co .... E 918 582-8211
  Tulsa *(G-10812)*

PRINTING MACHINERY

H S Boyd Company Inc .... F 918 835-9359
  Tulsa *(G-9876)*
Rowmark LLC .... E 405 787-4542
  Oklahoma City *(G-7051)*
Southwestern Process Supply Co .... E 918 582-8211
  Tulsa *(G-10812)*

PRINTING TRADES MACHINERY & EQPT REPAIR SVCS

H&H Retail Services LLC .... F 918 369-4055
  Bixby *(G-631)*

PRINTING, COMMERCIAL: Business Forms, NEC

Capital Business Forms Inc .... F 405 524-2010
  Oklahoma City *(G-5691)*
Liv3design LLC .... G 432 296-1968
  Norman *(G-5060)*

PRINTING, COMMERCIAL: Calendars, NEC

Dbr Publishing Co LLC .... E 918 250-1984
  Owasso *(G-7560)*

PRINTING, COMMERCIAL: Decals, NEC

Nameplates Inc .... D 918 584-2651
  Tulsa *(G-10324)*

PRINTING, COMMERCIAL: Envelopes, NEC

Western Web Envelope Co Inc .... F 405 682-0207
  Oklahoma City *(G-7442)*

PRINTING, COMMERCIAL: Imprinting

S & S Time Corporation..........E....... 918 437-3572
Tulsa *(G-10683)*

PRINTING, COMMERCIAL: Invitations, NEC

Pueblo Motors Inc..........G....... 520 297-3244
Edmond *(G-2577)*

PRINTING, COMMERCIAL: Labels & Seals, NEC

AT&I Resources LLC..........F....... 918 925-0154
Tulsa *(G-9220)*
E C Beights..........G....... 918 674-2773
Miami *(G-4400)*
Marpro Label Inc..........G....... 405 672-3344
Oklahoma City *(G-6530)*

PRINTING, COMMERCIAL: Letterpress & Screen

Corporate Image Inc..........G....... 918 516-8376
Owasso *(G-7556)*
Inklahoma Screen Prtg & EMB..........G....... 405 206-0500
Mustang *(G-4779)*
Leda Grimm..........G....... 918 225-0507
Cushing *(G-1942)*
Skyy Screen Printing..........G....... 405 412-4646
Norman *(G-5147)*
Think Ability Inc..........C....... 580 252-8000
Duncan *(G-2187)*
Tier Lvel Thrads Stuff Screen..........G....... 918 808-7290
Broken Arrow *(G-1074)*
U Big TS Designs Inc..........G....... 405 401-4327
Oklahoma City *(G-7356)*

PRINTING, COMMERCIAL: Literature, Advertising, NEC

Minor Printing Company..........G....... 580 795-3745
Madill *(G-4158)*
Sashay Corporate Services LLC..........E....... 918 664-2507
Tulsa *(G-10710)*

PRINTING, COMMERCIAL: Magazines, NEC

Dps Printing Services Inc..........G....... 405 285-4614
Edmond *(G-2394)*
Marjo Advertising LLC..........G....... 918 500-3108
Sapulpa *(G-8286)*
Stroud Corridor LLC..........G....... 405 823-7561
Stroud *(G-8821)*
Western Cartoons..........G....... 405 275-1054
Shawnee *(G-8519)*
Xposure Inc..........G....... 918 581-8900
Tulsa *(G-11165)*

PRINTING, COMMERCIAL: Promotional

Oklahoma Promo LLC..........G....... 918 248-8145
Jenks *(G-3719)*
Robyn Holdings LLC..........E....... 405 722-4600
Oklahoma City *(G-7041)*
Saan World LLC..........G....... 405 494-1282
Oklahoma City *(G-7070)*
Specialty Advertising Co Inc..........G....... 405 495-3838
Oklahoma City *(G-7180)*
Tourkick LLC..........G....... 918 409-2543
Owasso *(G-7626)*

PRINTING, COMMERCIAL: Publications

American Angler Publications..........G....... 918 364-4210
Catoosa *(G-1297)*
Christian Connections of Okla..........G....... 405 372-2111
Stillwater *(G-8667)*
Civitas Media LLC..........F....... 580 482-1221
Altus *(G-149)*
Cooley Creek Printing..........G....... 918 835-8200
Tulsa *(G-9482)*
Fine Arts Engraving Co Inc..........G....... 918 835-6400
Tulsa *(G-9743)*
Printer Store LLC..........G....... 405 782-0755
Warr Acres *(G-11326)*
Southwstern Group of Companies..........D....... 405 525-9411
Oklahoma City *(G-7178)*
Teeds Up Printing..........G....... 918 279-1018
Coweta *(G-1899)*

PRINTING, COMMERCIAL: Screen

3 Cs Tees LLC..........G....... 405 208-1320
Ada *(G-2)*
A1 Screen Printing..........G....... 405 701-6735
Norman *(G-4895)*
Affinitee Graphics..........G....... 580 861-2253
Lawton *(G-3885)*
All-Star Trophies & Ribbon Mfg..........G....... 918 283-2200
Claremore *(G-1581)*
American Signworx..........G....... 479 650-4562
Pocola *(G-7780)*
American Tradition..........G....... 918 688-7725
Tulsa *(G-9174)*
American Traditions Clothing..........G....... 918 622-8337
Tulsa *(G-9175)*
American TS..........G....... 918 284-7685
Mounds *(G-4609)*
Artistic Apparel..........G....... 918 338-0038
Bartlesville *(G-449)*
B J Printing Inc..........F....... 405 372-7600
Stillwater *(G-8657)*
Bad Boy Signs Graphic..........D....... 405 224-2059
Chickasha *(G-1436)*
Beacon Sign Company Inc..........G....... 405 567-4886
Prague *(G-7921)*
Bees Knees Tees..........G....... 405 370-2132
Choctaw *(G-1530)*
Bentwrench Studios..........G....... 918 406-8070
Sapulpa *(G-8254)*
Black Cat Screen Printing LLC..........G....... 405 895-6635
Moore *(G-4498)*
Board of Trustees of The Teach..........E....... 405 521-2387
Oklahoma City *(G-5597)*
Bob D Berry DBA..........G....... 405 382-3360
Seminole *(G-8360)*
Boley One..........G....... 405 301-7692
Oklahoma City *(G-5616)*
Busy Bee..........G....... 580 661-2946
Thomas *(G-8940)*
Buyers Trading Designs..........G....... 918 592-5477
Tulsa *(G-9355)*
C & H Safety Pin Inc..........G....... 405 949-5843
Newalla *(G-4806)*
Campus Ragz..........G....... 405 329-3300
Norman *(G-4952)*
Cane Advertising LLC..........G....... 918 806-6817
Broken Arrow *(G-863)*
Capitol Hill Graffix LLC..........G....... 405 616-3050
Oklahoma City *(G-5694)*
Causley Productions Inc..........F....... 405 372-0940
Stillwater *(G-8666)*
Cheaper TS Inc..........G....... 918 615-6262
Broken Arrow *(G-867)*
Cimarron Screen Printing..........G....... 405 755-8337
Edmond *(G-2352)*
Cjs Custom Apparel..........G....... 405 340-9677
Edmond *(G-2355)*
Communication Graphics Inc..........D....... 918 258-6502
Broken Arrow *(G-871)*
Corporate To Causal Screen..........G....... 918 686-6688
Muskogee *(G-4662)*
Corporate To Csual Screen Prtg..........G....... 918 686-6688
Muskogee *(G-4663)*
Crafty Manatees LLC..........G....... 405 630-5415
Blanchard *(G-708)*
Custom Graphics..........G....... 580 477-4597
Altus *(G-152)*
D & B Printing Inc..........G....... 405 632-0055
Oklahoma City *(G-5884)*
Daniel P Wollaston..........G....... 580 768-4694
Ardmore *(G-272)*
Daybreak Screen Printing LLC..........G....... 405 919-6386
Oklahoma City *(G-5908)*
Decal Shop..........G....... 918 783-5206
Big Cabin *(G-602)*
Design It..........G....... 405 756-3635
Lindsay *(G-4060)*
Dhs Tees..........G....... 405 397-0274
Edmond *(G-2391)*
Dos Tees LLC..........G....... 405 323-2382
Edmond *(G-2392)*
Dudz and Things Inc..........G....... 918 321-9443
Sapulpa *(G-8269)*
Eagle Imaging Management..........G....... 405 286-4114
Oklahoma City *(G-5995)*
Frog Printing & Awards Ctr LLC..........G....... 580 678-1114
Lawton *(G-3931)*
Game Time Designs LLC..........G....... 405 702-1318
Oklahoma City *(G-6134)*
Gameday Screen Prtg Promotions..........G....... 405 637-8577
Bethany *(G-578)*
Girlinghouse Unlimited LLC..........G....... 405 265-3330
Mustang *(G-4773)*
Gorfam Marketing Inc..........F....... 918 388-9935
Tulsa *(G-9842)*
Great Plins Grphics Shwnee LLC..........G....... 405 273-4263
Shawnee *(G-8455)*
H&A Shirt Cafe Cstm Screen Prt..........G....... 918 357-1115
Broken Arrow *(G-1129)*
Heartbeat Designs LLC..........G....... 918 333-0833
Bartlesville *(G-490)*
Hermann Jermey..........G....... 918 200-2604
Catoosa *(G-1321)*
High Five Graphics..........G....... 918 636-3312
Mannford *(G-4182)*
Hot Rod Shirts & Stuff..........G....... 580 669-2531
Glencoe *(G-3224)*
ID Solutions LLC..........F....... 405 677-8833
Oklahoma City *(G-6287)*
Imaging Concepts..........G....... 918 534-1761
Dewey *(G-2026)*
In His Name Screenprinting LLC..........G....... 405 756-8911
Maysville *(G-4260)*
Infinity Screenprinting LLC..........G....... 405 485-3203
Blanchard *(G-716)*
Inkspot..........G....... 405 793-7200
Moore *(G-4529)*
Integrity Screen Works Inc..........E....... 918 663-8339
Tulsa *(G-9999)*
J W Companies..........G....... 405 789-2460
Bethany *(G-584)*
Jak D Up Tees Inc..........F....... 405 260-0007
Edmond *(G-2467)*
Jeff Mc Kenzie & Co Inc..........G....... 405 236-5848
Oklahoma City *(G-6354)*
Jones Jerseys and Tees LLC..........G....... 405 264-6151
Prague *(G-7928)*
King Screens..........G....... 918 845-0004
Broken Arrow *(G-957)*
Kommunitees LLC..........G....... 405 203-2491
Yukon *(G-11741)*
Lane Victory Screen Printing..........G....... 580 924-3556
Durant *(G-2243)*
Lateesha D Hunter PC..........G....... 405 534-2200
Oklahoma City *(G-6456)*
Lawyer Graphic Screen Process..........G....... 918 438-2725
Tulsa *(G-10137)*
Lighthouse Graphics..........G....... 405 635-0022
Oklahoma City *(G-6476)*
Linder Screen Printing..........G....... 405 558-1275
Moore *(G-4533)*
Loporchio Silk Screen..........G....... 323 258-6459
Ada *(G-61)*
Magic TS..........G....... 580 332-6675
Ada *(G-62)*
Magnum Screen Print Inc..........G....... 918 665-7636
Tulsa *(G-10202)*
Miami Designs..........G....... 918 542-9553
Miami *(G-4414)*
Miller Graphics..........G....... 580 824-2698
Waynoka *(G-11380)*
Misaco Sign & Screen Printing..........G....... 918 542-4188
Miami *(G-4419)*
Mom Hustle Tee Co..........G....... 417 658-6450
Broken Arrow *(G-980)*
Monod Bloc Inc..........G....... 918 622-8132
Tulsa *(G-10299)*
Mountaintop Tees LLC..........G....... 918 508-6208
Sand Springs *(G-8209)*
Mustard Seed Screen Printing..........G....... 918 687-6290
Muskogee *(G-4718)*
My Man Tees LLC..........G....... 580 695-9474
Fletcher *(G-3164)*
Neo Sign Company..........G....... 918 456-1959
Fort Gibson *(G-3177)*
Okie Ink Screenprinting LLC..........G....... 918 681-0736
Muskogee *(G-4723)*
Opportunity Center Inc..........C....... 580 765-6782
Ponca City *(G-7863)*
Panda Screen Printing Entps..........G....... 918 622-3601
Tulsa *(G-10458)*
Peabodys Printing & A Brush Sp..........G....... 580 248-8317
Lawton *(G-3980)*
Performance Screen Printing..........G....... 405 247-9891
Anadarko *(G-205)*
Personali Tees LLC..........G....... 580 759-2188
Stratford *(G-8806)*
Pitezels Ink & Print Inc..........G....... 918 663-2393
Tulsa *(G-10520)*

Play 2 Win Athletics ....G.... 918 341-9500
Claremore (G-1671)
Productive Clutter Inc ....G.... 405 447-3839
Norman (G-5124)
Ps Tees LLC ....G.... 405 694-7979
Oklahoma City (G-6919)
Pyramid Printing ....G.... 918 514-4073
Sand Springs (G-8216)
Ragtops Athletics Inc ....G.... 918 274-3575
Owasso (G-7606)
Reflective Edge Screenprinting ....G.... 405 917-7837
Oklahoma City (G-7001)
Rhinestone Cowgirl ....G.... 405 564-0512
Stillwater (G-8747)
Rhodes Printing ....G.... 918 445-7444
Coweta (G-1896)
Rhodes Printing ....G.... 918 965-1005
Claremore (G-1682)
Rhodes Printing Inc ....G.... 918 457-7801
Tahlequah (G-8880)
Royal Sign & Graphic Inc ....G.... 918 682-6151
Muskogee (G-4746)
S & S Promotions Inc ....E.... 405 631-6516
Oklahoma City (G-7064)
Safetyco LLC ....G.... 405 603-3306
Oklahoma City (G-7072)
Sand Tech Screening and EMB ....G.... 918 458-0312
Tahlequah (G-8882)
Scissortail Tees ....G.... 405 706-6371
Oklahoma City (G-7094)
Shirt Nutz LLC ....G.... 918 900-2362
Owasso (G-7617)
Simply Vintage Tees LLC ....G.... 405 239-0444
Norman (G-5146)
Small Potato Tees LLC ....G.... 405 264-6330
Chickasha (G-1512)
Something Printed ....G.... 918 967-9188
Stigler (G-8646)
Sportees ....G.... 918 618-6201
Eufaula (G-3115)
Stantons Apparel Inc ....G.... 580 353-1777
Lawton (G-4004)
Stitch N Print ....F.... 405 789-8862
Oklahoma City (G-7209)
Sweetandsassytinytees LLC ....G.... 405 470-1170
Yukon (G-11790)
T John Co Inc ....G.... 405 761-3460
Tuttle (G-11214)
T S & H EMB & Screen Prtg ....G.... 405 214-7701
Shawnee (G-8508)
T S & H Shirt Co Inc ....G.... 405 382-3731
Seminole (G-8403)
T-Birds Custom Screenprinting ....G.... 918 521-3996
Tulsa (G-10894)
Tack Designs ....G.... 918 825-1211
Pryor (G-7993)
Tee For Soul ....G.... 405 237-3186
Moore (G-4576)
Tees For Soul ....G.... 405 844-7685
Edmond (G-2637)
Tees Q Usbs Llc ....G.... 405 414-3264
Oklahoma City (G-7265)
TGI Enterprises Inc ....E.... 918 835-4330
Tulsa (G-10924)
Tiger Town Tees ....G.... 918 409-4282
Broken Arrow (G-1075)
Tony Newcomb Sportswear Inc ....G.... 405 232-0022
Oklahoma City (G-7303)
Tornados Screen Printing ....G.... 405 964-5339
McLoud (G-4363)
Trendy Tees ....G.... 405 620-3673
McLoud (G-4364)
Triple Elite LLC ....G.... 405 610-5200
Oklahoma City (G-7337)
Tuna Spot Tees LLC ....G.... 918 931-9586
Stillwater (G-8770)
TWI Industries Inc ....E.... 918 663-6655
Tulsa (G-11022)
Unique Designs Studio More LLC ....G.... 580 237-0034
Enid (G-3070)
Victortees LLC ....G.... 405 889-7763
Norman (G-5196)
Wecktees ....G.... 580 747-5363
Glencoe (G-3227)
Witty Ideas Inc ....G.... 918 367-9528
Bristow (G-806)
Wright Way Screen Printing ....G.... 918 787-7898
Grove (G-3294)
Xzube Tees ....G.... 405 249-9506
Norman (G-5203)

PRINTING, COMMERCIAL: Stamps, Trading, NEC

Kens Advertising ....G.... 405 527-6030
Lexington (G-4036)

PRINTING, LITHOGRAPHIC: Advertising Posters

Ink Images Inc ....G.... 918 828-0300
Tulsa (G-9987)

PRINTING, LITHOGRAPHIC: Decals

Midwest Decals LLC ....G.... 405 787-8747
Oklahoma City (G-6602)
Sign Innovations LLC ....G.... 405 840-1151
Oklahoma City (G-7132)
Tom Bennett Manufacturing ....F.... 405 528-5671
Oklahoma City (G-7302)

PRINTING, LITHOGRAPHIC: Forms, Business

American Bank Systems Inc ....E.... 405 607-7000
Oklahoma City (G-5432)
Capital Business Forms Inc ....F.... 405 524-2010
Oklahoma City (G-5691)
Hipsleys Litho & Prtg Co LLC ....G.... 405 528-2686
Oklahoma City (G-6252)
Print Imaging Group LLC ....E.... 405 235-4888
Oklahoma City (G-6898)

PRINTING, LITHOGRAPHIC: Letters, Circular Or Form

Bakers Printing Co Inc ....G.... 405 842-6944
Oklahoma City (G-5517)
Pioneer Printing Inc ....G.... 918 542-5521
Miami (G-4428)

PRINTING, LITHOGRAPHIC: Offset & photolithographic printing

Qp Broadway EXT ....G.... 405 843-9820
Oklahoma City (G-6931)

PRINTING, LITHOGRAPHIC: On Metal

A & B Printing & Office Supply ....G.... 580 889-5103
Atoka (G-395)
Altus Printing Co Inc ....G.... 580 482-2020
Altus (G-141)
B & L Printing Inc ....G.... 918 258-6655
Broken Arrow (G-839)
C & J Printing Co ....G.... 580 355-3099
Lawton (G-3902)
Carr Graphics Inc ....G.... 918 835-0605
Tulsa (G-9379)
Collins Quality Printing ....G.... 918 744-0077
Tulsa (G-9468)
First Impression Prtg Co Inc ....G.... 918 749-5446
Beggs (G-553)
Hawkeye Printing Co ....G.... 918 744-0158
Tulsa (G-9902)
Imperial Printing Inc ....G.... 918 663-1302
Tulsa (G-9973)
L W Duncan Printing Inc ....G.... 580 355-6229
Lawton (G-3953)
Mattocks Printing Co LLC ....G.... 405 794-2307
Moore (G-4538)
Midwest Publishing Co ....G.... 405 282-1890
Guthrie (G-3325)
Royal Printing Co Inc ....F.... 405 235-8581
Oklahoma City (G-7054)
Tonkawa News ....G.... 580 628-2532
Tonkawa (G-8984)
Tulsa Instant Printing ....G.... 918 627-0730
Tulsa (G-11000)
Vans Printing Service ....G.... 918 786-9496
Grove (G-3291)
Woodcrest Litho Inc ....F.... 918 357-1676
Broken Arrow (G-1178)

PRINTING, LITHOGRAPHIC: Posters & Decals

U Big TS Designs Inc ....G.... 405 401-4327
Oklahoma City (G-7356)

PRINTING, LITHOGRAPHIC: Promotional

Matrix Print & Promo LLC ....G.... 918 994-1943
Bartlesville (G-509)
Sorrels Ventures LLC ....G.... 903 556-2941
Broken Bow (G-1207)

PRINTING, LITHOGRAPHIC: Tickets

Lewis Printing & Office Supply ....F.... 405 379-5124
Holdenville (G-3557)

PRINTING: Books

Sugar Pills Apparel ....G.... 580 277-0231
Ardmore (G-364)
Suggs Orel ....G.... 405 275-6159
Shawnee (G-8505)

PRINTING: Commercial, NEC

A B Printing ....G.... 918 834-2054
Tulsa (G-9066)
A Plus Printing ....G.... 580 765-7752
Ponca City (G-7791)
AAA Kopy ....G.... 405 741-5679
Oklahoma City (G-5354)
Abco Printing & Office Supply ....G.... 580 286-7575
Idabel (G-3636)
Adams Printing ....G.... 580 832-2123
Cordell (G-1853)
Advance Graphics & Printing ....G.... 405 258-0796
Chandler (G-1373)
Advanced Graphic Design ....G.... 918 960-0407
Tulsa (G-9108)
Ajt Enterprises Inc ....F.... 918 665-7083
Tulsa (G-9133)
Anns Quick Print Co Inc ....G.... 405 222-1871
Chickasha (G-1429)
Apache News ....G.... 580 588-3862
Apache (G-217)
ARC Document Solutions LLC ....E.... 918 663-8100
Tulsa (G-9202)
Associated Lithographing Co ....E.... 918 663-9091
Tulsa (G-9217)
Bakers Printing Co Inc ....G.... 405 842-6944
Oklahoma City (G-5517)
Bargain Journal ....G.... 918 426-5500
McAlester (G-4273)
Big House Specialty Prtg Inc ....G.... 918 271-1414
Tulsa (G-9292)
Bill Rathbone ....G.... 918 486-3028
Coweta (G-1872)
Black Gold ....G.... 918 253-3344
Jay (G-3679)
Blankenship Brothers Inc ....G.... 405 943-3278
Oklahoma City (G-5587)
Blue Ribbon Forms Inc ....G.... 918 834-8838
Tulsa (G-9305)
Brix Inc ....G.... 918 584-6484
Tulsa (G-9338)
Broken Arrow Productions Inc ....E.... 405 360-8702
Norman (G-4944)
Brown Printing Co Inc ....G.... 918 652-9611
Henryetta (G-3500)
Burch Printing Co ....G.... 580 225-3270
Elk City (G-2788)
Business Cards & More ....G.... 405 235-9621
Oklahoma City (G-5648)
Cable Printing Co Inc ....F.... 405 756-4045
Lindsay (G-4055)
Charles E Morrison Co ....G.... 405 840-1604
Oklahoma City (G-5742)
Chrome River Wholesale LLC ....G.... 918 610-0810
Tulsa (G-9421)
Clark Printing Inc ....G.... 405 528-5396
Oklahoma City (G-5776)
Collins Quality Printing ....G.... 918 744-0077
Tulsa (G-9468)
Copper Cup Images ....G.... 918 337-2781
Bartlesville (G-469)
CP Solutions Inc ....D.... 918 664-6642
Tulsa (G-9495)
Cplp LLC ....G.... 580 355-5515
Lawton (G-3913)
Cr Stripes Ltd Co ....G.... 405 946-8577
Oklahoma City (G-5850)
Cromwells Inc ....G.... 580 234-6561
Enid (G-2935)
CSC Inc ....G.... 580 994-6110
Mooreland (G-4587)

PRODUCT

Employee Codes: A=Over 500 employees, B=251-500
C=101-250, D=51-100, E=20-50, F=10-19, G=1-9
2020 Oklahoma Directory
of Manufacturers & Processors
797

Dbmac 50 Inc....G.... 918 342-5590
Claremore (G-1613)
Delson Properties Ltd....D.... 405 262-5005
El Reno (G-2711)
Demco Printing Inc....F.... 405 273-8888
Shawnee (G-8444)
Diversified Printing Inc....F.... 918 665-2275
Tulsa (G-9586)
Edmond Printings....G.... 405 341-4330
Edmond (G-2404)
Ellis County Capital....G.... 580 885-7788
Arnett (G-387)
Engatech Inc....F.... 918 599-7500
Tulsa (G-9686)
Engraving Designs LLC....G.... 580 763-4228
Ponca City (G-7826)
Executive Forms & Supplies....G.... 817 423-9088
Oklahoma City (G-6060)
Felkins Enterprises LLC....G.... 918 272-3456
Owasso (G-7568)
First Impression Prtg Co Inc....G.... 918 749-5446
Beggs (G-553)
Fortis Solutions Group....G.... 918 258-8321
Catoosa (G-1320)
Good Printing Co Inc....G.... 405 235-9593
Oklahoma City (G-6171)
Goprints....G.... 918 798-0643
Okmulgee (G-7506)
Graf-X LLC....G.... 405 542-6631
Hinton (G-3529)
Gravley Companies Inc....G.... 918 743-6619
Tulsa (G-9850)
Hipsleys Litho & Prtg Co LLC....G.... 405 528-2686
Oklahoma City (G-6252)
Hoffman Printing LLC....F.... 918 682-8341
Muskogee (G-4691)
Initially Yours Inc....G.... 918 832-9889
Tulsa (G-9986)
Ink Images Inc....G.... 918 828-0300
Tulsa (G-9987)
Inspired Gifts & Graphics LLC....G.... 405 295-1669
El Reno (G-2725)
Jbs Graphic Repair....G.... 918 272-3522
Owasso (G-7579)
Joshua Promotions....G.... 405 590-8894
Harrah (G-3379)
Kelley Printing....G.... 405 238-4848
Pauls Valley (G-7663)
Kindrick Co Prtg & Copying Svc....G.... 580 332-1022
Ada (G-56)
King Kopy LLC....G.... 405 321-0202
Norman (G-5052)
Kinkos Inc....G.... 303 449-9247
Broken Arrow (G-959)
Klassen Enterprises Inc....G.... 918 342-1850
Claremore (G-1649)
Kolb Type Service Incorporated....G.... 405 341-0984
Agra (G-125)
Larry D Hammer....G.... 580 596-3344
Cherokee (G-1418)
Larry D Hammer....F.... 580 227-2100
Fairview (G-3140)
Latimer County News Tribune....G.... 918 465-2321
Wilburton (G-11522)
Lindsey Printing....G.... 580 476-2278
Rush Springs (G-8123)
Mark W McGuffee Inc....G.... 405 603-8113
Oklahoma City (G-6528)
Martin Thomas Enterprises Inc....D.... 918 739-4015
Catoosa (G-1338)
MBC Graphics....G.... 918 585-2321
Tulsa (G-10227)
Mc Clain County Publishing Co....E.... 405 527-2126
Purcell (G-8016)
Mid-West Printing & Pubg Co....F.... 918 224-3666
Sapulpa (G-8291)
Midwest Publishing Co....G.... 405 282-1890
Guthrie (G-3325)
Multiprint Corp....G.... 918 832-0300
Tulsa (G-10315)
Nancy Nelson & Associates....G.... 580 765-0115
Ponca City (G-7857)
Nelson Incorporated....G.... 918 812-5876
Tulsa (G-10332)
Offices Etc....G.... 918 342-1501
Claremore (G-1666)
Ohgoodygoodycom....G.... 315 727-5960
Tulsa (G-10380)
Oklahoma Envelope Company LLC....F.... 405 946-2169
Oklahoma City (G-6746)
Oklahoma Flding Crton Prtg Inc....F.... 405 352-9920
Minco (G-4478)
Oliver & Olivia Apparel....E.... 405 300-8906
Edmond (G-2556)
Onedoc Managed Print Svcs LLC....G.... 405 633-3050
Oklahoma City (G-6778)
Options Inc....F.... 918 473-2614
Checotah (G-1398)
Osborne Design Co....G.... 918 585-3212
Tulsa (G-10444)
Over 60 LLC....G.... 405 224-0711
Chickasha (G-1497)
P M Graphics....G.... 405 525-8789
Oklahoma City (G-5310)
Paul Clinton Hughes....G.... 918 273-1888
Nowata (G-5225)
Pioneer Printing Inc....G.... 918 542-5521
Miami (G-4428)
Pony Express Printing LLC....G.... 405 375-5064
Kingfisher (G-3811)
Premier Printing....G.... 405 632-1132
Oklahoma City (G-6886)
Pressley Press N Prod Fcilty....G.... 405 752-5700
Oklahoma City (G-5311)
Print Imaging Group LLC....E.... 405 235-4888
Oklahoma City (G-6898)
Print Shop....G.... 918 342-3993
Claremore (G-1674)
Printing and Design....G.... 580 871-2396
Dacoma (G-1976)
Printing Solutions Inc....G.... 580 421-6446
Ada (G-76)
Priority Printworks Inc....G.... 918 825-6397
Pryor (G-7984)
Promos Advertising Pdts Inc....G.... 918 343-9675
Claremore (G-1676)
Promotions - Forms Unlimited....G.... 918 627-8800
Tulsa (G-10573)
Pryor Printing Inc....G.... 918 825-2888
Pryor (G-7986)
Put On Your Armor Inc....G.... 918 259-5000
Broken Arrow (G-1015)
Quik Print of Tulsa Inc....E.... 918 665-6246
Tulsa (G-10595)
Quik Print of Tulsa Inc....G.... 918 582-1825
Tulsa (G-10596)
Quik-Print of Oklahoma City....G.... 405 943-3222
Oklahoma City (G-6949)
Quik-Print of Oklahoma City....G.... 405 528-7976
Oklahoma City (G-6951)
Quik-Print of Oklahoma City....G.... 405 842-1404
Oklahoma City (G-6946)
Quik-Print of Oklahoma City....G.... 405 840-3275
Oklahoma City (G-6950)
Reflection Foil and Ltr Press....G.... 405 341-8660
Edmond (G-2593)
Resourceone Communications Inc....G.... 918 295-0112
Tulsa (G-10646)
Royal Printing Co Inc....F.... 405 235-8581
Oklahoma City (G-7054)
Semasys Inc....E.... 405 525-2335
Oklahoma City (G-7107)
Sign Depot....F.... 580 931-9363
Durant (G-2257)
Silsby Media LLC....G.... 405 733-9727
Midwest City (G-4454)
Sooner Industries Inc....G.... 918 540-2422
Miami (G-4431)
Sooner Press....G.... 405 382-8351
Seminole (G-8400)
South Central Golf Inc....G.... 918 280-0787
Tulsa (G-10796)
Spitzer Printing....G.... 580 928-5540
Sayre (G-8346)
Sprekelmeyer Printing Company....G.... 580 223-5100
Ardmore (G-359)
Stuart Beverly &....G.... 580 286-5586
Idabel (G-3648)
Tesprinting LLC....G.... 405 708-7000
Yukon (G-11791)
TO Digital Media LLC....G.... 405 639-8219
Oklahoma City (G-7299)
Toner Express....G.... 405 517-8817
Norman (G-5175)
Torbett Printing Co & Off Sup....G.... 918 756-5789
Okmulgee (G-7528)
Treehouse Embroidery....G.... 580 667-4322
Tipton (G-8960)
UPS Store 6206....G.... 580 248-7800
Fort Sill (G-3182)
Usher Corporation....G.... 405 495-2125
Oklahoma City (G-7382)
Wallace Printing Company....G.... 580 326-6323
Hugo (G-3622)
Wallis Printing Inc....G.... 580 223-7473
Ardmore (G-379)
Watonga Printing & Office Sups....G.... 580 623-4989
Watonga (G-11353)
Worldwide Printing & Dist Inc....C.... 918 295-0112
Tulsa (G-11154)
Zon Inc....F.... 918 458-5511
Tahlequah (G-8894)

PRINTING: Flexographic

Elite Creative Solutions LLC....E.... 918 994-5435
Broken Arrow (G-897)
Keystone Labels LLC....G.... 405 631-2341
Oklahoma City (G-6413)
Regency Labels Inc....E.... 405 682-3460
Oklahoma City (G-7002)
Summit Labels Inc....G.... 918 936-4950
Tulsa (G-10868)

PRINTING: Gravure, Business Form & Card

Deans Typesetting Service....G.... 405 842-7247
Oklahoma City (G-5912)
Hitch N Post LLC....G.... 918 396-9480
Skiatook (G-8549)

PRINTING: Gravure, Job

American-Chief Co....G.... 918 762-2552
Pawnee (G-7699)

PRINTING: Gravure, Rotogravure

Franklin Digital Inc....F.... 918 687-6149
Muskogee (G-4674)
Mojo Sports LLC....F.... 405 390-8935
Midwest City (G-4447)
October Graphics....G.... 580 765-5089
Ponca City (G-7861)
Thomas Digital LLC....G.... 918 836-1540
Tulsa (G-10929)
Wallace Printing Company....G.... 580 326-6323
Hugo (G-3622)

PRINTING: Laser

Hunters Laser Cartridges....G.... 918 740-8164
Tulsa (G-9958)
Rhinestone Cowgirl....F.... 405 387-3111
Newcastle (G-4838)

PRINTING: Letterpress

262 LLC....F.... 918 458-5511
Tahlequah (G-8848)
Britton Printing....G.... 405 840-3291
Oklahoma City (G-5630)
C & J Printing Co....G.... 580 355-3099
Lawton (G-3902)
C & R Print Shop Inc....G.... 580 255-5656
Duncan (G-2095)
C & R Print Shop Inc....G.... 405 224-7921
Chickasha (G-1445)
Davis Printing Company Inc....G.... 580 225-2902
Elk City (G-2800)
Hammer Hoby....G.... 580 227-2100
Fairview (G-3137)
Hardesty Press Inc....F.... 918 582-5306
Tulsa (G-9891)
Heavener Ledger....G.... 918 653-2425
Heavener (G-3429)
Hooper Printing Company Inc....F.... 405 321-4288
Norman (G-5026)
Jet Printing Co Inc....G.... 405 732-1262
Oklahoma City (G-6361)
Lodestone Letterpress LLC....G.... 405 269-9111
Edmond (G-2492)
Mattocks Printing Co LLC....G.... 405 794-2307
Moore (G-4538)
Merrick Printing....G.... 918 876-6264
Bartlesville (G-511)
Mesa Black Publishing LLC....G.... 580 544-2222
Boise City (G-747)
Vinita Printing Co Inc....E.... 918 256-6422
Vinita (G-11271)

PRINTING: Lithographic

30 Cent Print LLC .... G 469 408-8968
Blanchard *(G-698)*
3g Printing .... G 918 284-9433
Coweta *(G-1869)*
3g Printing .... G 918 346-0035
Broken Arrow *(G-1107)*
918 Screen Printers .... G 918 850-9542
Tulsa *(G-9060)*
A Plus Printing .... G 580 765-7752
Ponca City *(G-7791)*
A-1 Mster Prnta/Hooper Prtg Si .... G 518 427-0282
Oklahoma City *(G-5351)*
Adams Printing .... G 580 832-2123
Cordell *(G-1853)*
Affordable Signs & Decals Inc .... G 405 942-7059
Oklahoma City *(G-5397)*
Altus Print Ship .... G 580 482-6855
Altus *(G-140)*
American-Chief Co .... G 918 358-2553
Cleveland *(G-1715)*
Annie Printer .... G 405 670-9640
Oklahoma City *(G-5447)*
Apache News .... G 580 588-3862
Apache *(G-217)*
ARC Document Solutions LLC .... F 405 943-0378
Oklahoma City *(G-5460)*
Avalanche Print Company .... G 405 808-4229
Edmond *(G-2313)*
Awesome Apparel Printing .... G 918 402-3672
Broken Arrow *(G-838)*
B J Printing Products Inc .... G 918 245-6385
Sand Springs *(G-8164)*
B&M Digital Garment Printing .... G 918 954-6994
Tulsa *(G-9248)*
Baywest Embroidery .... G 580 626-4728
Jet *(G-3741)*
Beavers Independent Printe .... G 405 205-5300
Moore *(G-4497)*
Bent Tees Screen Printing .... G 918 734-3996
Tulsa *(G-9283)*
Berkshire Hathaway Inc .... G 918 486-4444
Wagoner *(G-11276)*
Berry Custom Printing LLC .... G 918 266-3732
Catoosa *(G-1302)*
Best Printing Solution LLC .... G 918 794-1771
Tulsa *(G-9287)*
Big Time Designs Screen Prtg .... G 580 658-5000
Marlow *(G-4223)*
Bigfoot Prints LLC .... G 918 805-0543
Collinsville *(G-1803)*
Biz Networks LLC .... G 405 348-6090
Edmond *(G-2323)*
Bluestem Integrated LLC .... E 918 660-0492
Tulsa *(G-9309)*
Bob D Berry DBA .... G 405 382-3360
Seminole *(G-8360)*
Boxing Bear LLC .... G 918 606-9991
Jenks *(G-3694)*
Boxing Bear LLC .... G 918 606-9991
Claremore *(G-1599)*
Braudrick Printery .... G 405 762-2054
Ponca City *(G-7802)*
Brix Inc .... G 918 584-6484
Tulsa *(G-9338)*
Brown Printing Co Inc .... G 918 652-9611
Henryetta *(G-3500)*
Burch Printing Co .... G 580 225-3270
Elk City *(G-2788)*
Business Cards Unlimited .... G 918 810-6265
Tulsa *(G-9350)*
Business Printing Inc 1 .... G 918 481-6078
Tulsa *(G-9351)*
Carnegie Herald .... G 580 654-1443
Carnegie *(G-1274)*
CB Printing and More LLC .... G 405 488-7107
Jenks *(G-3698)*
Cg Printing .... G 405 818-4371
Oklahoma City *(G-5735)*
Charles E Morrison Co .... G 405 840-1604
Oklahoma City *(G-5742)*
Chrome River Wholesale LLC .... G 918 610-0810
Tulsa *(G-9421)*
Cimarron Screen Printing .... G 405 755-8337
Edmond *(G-2352)*
CJ Graphics .... G 405 636-0400
Oklahoma City *(G-5771)*
Classic Design & Print LLC .... G 580 216-0653
Vici *(G-11240)*
CP Solutions Inc .... D 918 664-6642
Tulsa *(G-9495)*
CSC Inc .... G 580 994-6110
Mooreland *(G-4587)*
Cushing Screen Printing LLC .... G 646 267-3513
Cushing *(G-1927)*
Custom Monograms & Lettering .... G 405 495-8586
Bethany *(G-574)*
Dancey-Meador Publishing Co .... G 580 762-9359
Ponca City *(G-7819)*
Dbmac 50 Inc .... G 918 342-5590
Claremore *(G-1613)*
Dbr Publishing Co LLC .... E 918 250-1984
Owasso *(G-7560)*
Demco Printing Inc .... F 405 273-8888
Shawnee *(G-8444)*
Diversified Printing Inc .... F 918 665-2275
Tulsa *(G-9586)*
Dla Document Services .... E 405 734-2177
Tinker Afb *(G-8953)*
Document Centre Inc .... G 405 879-1101
Oklahoma City *(G-5955)*
Dps Printing Services of .... G 918 794-7755
Sperry *(G-8607)*
Dreamers Screen Print and More .... G 580 761-4376
Blackwell *(G-682)*
Drivin Printing By Aaron .... G 405 609-9608
Oklahoma City *(G-5983)*
Education Oklahoma Department .... F 405 743-5531
Stillwater *(G-8682)*
Fenton Office Supply Co .... E 405 372-5555
Stillwater *(G-8688)*
Fifth Quarter Printing LLC .... G 918 471-9390
McAlester *(G-4298)*
Flash Flood Print Studios LLC .... G 918 794-3527
Tulsa *(G-9754)*
French Printing Inc .... G 405 381-4057
Tuttle *(G-11200)*
Gameday Screen Printing .... G 405 570-0176
Oklahoma City *(G-6135)*
Geary Star .... G 405 884-2424
Geary *(G-3216)*
Geiger Printing & Promotion .... G 918 810-2833
Tulsa *(G-9812)*
Globe Marketing Services Inc .... B 800 742-6787
Oklahoma City *(G-6162)*
Go Print USA .... G 405 708-7000
Yukon *(G-11726)*
Go Rowdy Girl Screen Print EMB .... G 580 668-2545
Wilson *(G-11534)*
Graphics Etc .... G 918 274-4744
Owasso *(G-7571)*
Grizzly Grin Printing LLC .... G 918 351-9066
Tulsa *(G-9865)*
Handle It 3d Printing LLC .... G 405 788-9471
Shawnee *(G-8457)*
Hawkeye Signs & Printing .... G 918 864-2035
Tahlequah *(G-8866)*
Heavener Ledger .... G 918 653-2425
Heavener *(G-3429)*
Hendryx Printing Brokerage LLC .... G 405 532-1255
Edmond *(G-2455)*
Herald Publishing Co .... G 580 875-3326
Walters *(G-11302)*
Hg Screen Printing .... G 580 623-3638
Watonga *(G-11347)*
Holloways Bluprt & Copy Sp Inc .... G 918 682-0280
Muskogee *(G-4692)*
Hooker Advance & Office Supply .... G 580 652-2476
Hooker *(G-3598)*
Horsepower Printing Inc .... G 405 631-3800
Oklahoma City *(G-6264)*
House of Trophies .... G 405 452-3524
Wetumka *(G-11492)*
Hugo Publishing Company .... G 580 326-3311
Hugo *(G-3612)*
Image Print & Promo LLC .... G 405 408-6763
Edmond *(G-2459)*
Infocus Print Co LLC .... G 918 465-5572
McAlester *(G-4306)*
Initially Yours Inc .... G 918 832-9889
Tulsa *(G-9986)*
Ink Masters Screen Printing .... G 918 399-5220
Cushing *(G-1938)*
Inkwell Printing .... G 918 508-3634
Tulsa *(G-9988)*
Inspired Gifts & Graphics LLC .... G 405 295-1669
El Reno *(G-2725)*
Its In Print .... G 918 493-4141
Tulsa *(G-10014)*
J Rose Printing LLC .... G 210 875-0947
Yukon *(G-11734)*
Jet Printing Co Inc .... G 405 732-1262
Oklahoma City *(G-6361)*
Jet Set Screen Printing l .... G 918 294-1053
Broken Arrow *(G-944)*
Joans Print Shop Inc .... G 918 624-5858
Tulsa *(G-10047)*
Joe Brent Lansden .... G 580 625-3241
Beaver *(G-541)*
Johnny L Ruth .... G 580 223-3061
Ardmore *(G-316)*
JPS LLC .... G 405 535-5136
Oklahoma City *(G-6389)*
Kdl Print Production Svcs LLC .... G 918 254-8150
Broken Arrow *(G-955)*
Kelley Printing .... G 405 238-4848
Pauls Valley *(G-7663)*
King Design & Printing LLC .... G 580 661-3061
Thomas *(G-8946)*
King Graphics Inc .... G 405 232-2369
Oklahoma City *(G-6420)*
Kingdom Printing .... G 580 512-3789
Lawton *(G-3950)*
Kobe Express LLC .... G 580 920-0444
Durant *(G-2241)*
Larry D Hammer .... F 580 227-2100
Fairview *(G-3140)*
Larry D Hammer .... G 580 596-3344
Cherokee *(G-1418)*
Lawyer Graphic Screen Process .... G 918 438-2725
Tulsa *(G-10137)*
Lbz Prints .... G 405 905-1607
Oklahoma City *(G-6459)*
Leda Grimm .... G 918 225-0507
Cushing *(G-1942)*
Lettering Express .... G 405 260-9022
Oklahoma City *(G-6468)*
Lexso T Shirt Printing .... G 918 861-0772
Tulsa *(G-10155)*
Linderer Printing Co Inc .... F 580 323-2102
Clinton *(G-1757)*
Lindsey Printing .... G 580 476-2278
Rush Springs *(G-8123)*
M2print LLC .... G 505 263-7999
Yukon *(G-11744)*
Makeba Design & Prints LLC .... G 405 719-0104
Yukon *(G-11745)*
Marshall County Publishing Co .... F 580 795-3355
Madill *(G-4155)*
Marshall Printing .... G 405 883-6122
Yukon *(G-11747)*
Mathis Printing Inc .... G 918 682-2999
Muskogee *(G-4708)*
McNally and Associates Inc .... G 918 587-7068
Tulsa *(G-10234)*
Meeks Lithographing Company .... G 918 838-9900
Tulsa *(G-10239)*
Meeks Lithographing Company .... G 918 836-0900
Tulsa *(G-10241)*
Menz Printing Service LLC .... G 405 620-3673
Harrah *(G-3381)*
Merrick Printing .... G 918 876-6264
Bartlesville *(G-511)*
Mid-West Printing & Pubg Co .... F 918 224-3666
Sapulpa *(G-8291)*
Minor Printing Company .... G 580 795-3745
Madill *(G-4158)*
Minuteman Press .... G 405 942-5595
Oklahoma City *(G-6617)*
Mounds Printing .... G 918 827-6573
Mounds *(G-4621)*
Mudd Print & Promo LLC .... G 405 501-6107
Edmond *(G-2522)*
Newspaper Holding Inc .... E 918 456-8833
Tahlequah *(G-8876)*
Newspaper Holding Inc .... D 580 233-6600
Enid *(G-3018)*
Newspaper Holding Inc .... E 580 332-4433
Ada *(G-72)*
Nextstep Custom Printing .... G 580 678-4331
Duncan *(G-2160)*
Nice Printing Co .... G 405 673-9437
Midwest City *(G-4449)*
Okay See Ltd Co .... G 405 562-3154
Edmond *(G-2547)*
Oklahoma City Blazers .... G 405 543-2922
Oklahoma City *(G-6739)*
Ozmo Design and Print LLC .... G 417 655-5615
Tahlequah *(G-8878)*

PRODUCT

Employee Codes: A=Over 500 employees, B=251-500
C=101-250, D=51-100, E=20-50, F=10-19, G=1-9

Panhandle Printing ....G 580 338-1633
Guymon (G-3360)
Paper House Productions LLC ....G 918 835-0172
Tulsa (G-10463)
Paula Gallaher ....G 580 439-6484
Comanche (G-1844)
Ponca City Publishing Co Inc ....E 580 765-3311
Ponca City (G-7866)
Pony Express Printing LLC ....G 405 375-5064
Kingfisher (G-3811)
Premier Printing ....G 405 632-1132
Oklahoma City (G-6886)
Print Happy Fundraising ....G 918 355-4368
Broken Arrow (G-1149)
Print Happy LLC ....G 918 270-1300
Broken Arrow (G-1010)
Print Master General LLC ....G 580 442-2474
Elgin (G-2778)
Print Monkey LLC ....G 405 735-8999
Moore (G-4556)
Print Monkey LLC ....G 405 249-6926
Oklahoma City (G-6899)
Print Party ....G 405 206-2191
Edmond (G-2576)
Print People USA ....G 918 346-2560
Owasso (G-7604)
Print Plus OK LLC ....G 405 371-5365
Blanchard (G-728)
Print Shop ....G 918 342-3993
Claremore (G-1674)
Print This ....G 918 693-5581
Okmulgee (G-7523)
Printed Products Inc ....F 918 295-9950
Tulsa (G-10561)
Priority Printworks Inc ....G 918 825-6397
Pryor (G-7984)
Protype Inc ....G 918 743-4408
Tulsa (G-10576)
Quantum Forms Corporation ....F 918 665-1320
Oklahoma City (G-6940)
Quik-Print of Oklahoma City ....G 405 943-3222
Oklahoma City (G-6949)
R R Donnelley & Sons Company ....G 918 749-6496
Tulsa (G-10606)
Red River Custom Camo & Hydro ....G 580 745-5262
Durant (G-2251)
Robyn Holdings LLC ....E 405 722-4600
Oklahoma City (G-7041)
Sew Graphics Plus Inc ....G 405 364-1707
Norman (G-5141)
Sheryls Print Services ....G 918 724-2452
Tulsa (G-10744)
Silsby Media LLC ....G 405 733-9727
Midwest City (G-4454)
Silverstone LLC ....G 918 371-3622
Sand Springs (G-8225)
Silverstone LLC ....G 918 373-2437
Broken Arrow (G-1051)
Sleeve It Handles ....G 405 250-2419
Shawnee (G-8500)
Soltow Business Supply ....G 918 786-4465
Grove (G-3289)
Sooner Print Imaging ....G 405 272-0600
Oklahoma City (G-7162)
Southwest Cnstr News Svc ....G 405 948-7474
Oklahoma City (G-7173)
Ssi Technologies Inc ....G 918 451-6160
Broken Arrow (G-1059)
Stich This and More ....G 405 207-9922
Pauls Valley (G-7672)
Storehouse Printing ....G 918 286-7222
Tulsa (G-10857)
Sunshine Printing ....G 918 951-6349
Tulsa (G-10874)
Super Signs & Printing LLC ....G 405 842-7070
Oklahoma City (G-7227)
T-Shirts & Hoodies Print Shop ....G 918 861-0772
Tulsa (G-10895)
T-Shirts & Hoodies Print Shop ....G 918 861-0772
Tulsa (G-10896)
Taxes Print Shop ....G 405 521-3165
Oklahoma City (G-7255)
Think Screenprinting LLC ....G 405 590-5131
Edmond (G-2640)
Thompson Manufacturing Company ....G 918 585-1991
Tulsa (G-10935)
Tommy Higle Publishers ....G 580 276-5136
Marietta (G-4215)
Torbett Printing Co & Off Sup ....G 918 756-5789
Okmulgee (G-7528)
Trinity Scrnprntng/Dmond Awrds ....G 580 364-3752
Atoka (G-426)
Tulsa Litho Co Consolidat ....G 918 582-8185
Tulsa (G-11001)
Tulsa Screen Printing ....G 918 488-1331
Broken Arrow (G-1085)
Tuun Leh Zua Printing Services ....G 918 809-7925
Tulsa (G-11020)
Usher Corporation ....G 405 495-2125
Oklahoma City (G-7382)
Vision Print PPG ....G 405 519-4047
Oklahoma City (G-7402)
VITs Screen Printing ....G 405 531-6012
Edmond (G-2675)
Wallace Printing Company ....G 580 326-6323
Hugo (G-3622)
Ward Brothers Printing ....G 918 465-5551
Wilburton (G-11528)
Warrens Screen Prtg EMB L L C ....G 405 422-3900
El Reno (G-2768)
Weatherford News Inc ....E 580 772-3301
Weatherford (G-11458)
What Print Now ....G 580 649-7996
Altus (G-172)
Wild Leaf Screen Prtg & Design ....G 918 440-4945
Ramona (G-8047)
Wilson-Monroe Publishing Co ....G 580 933-4579
Valliant (G-11234)
Woods County Enterprise ....G 580 824-2171
Waynoka (G-11384)

PRINTING: Offset

262 LLC ....F 918 458-5511
Tahlequah (G-8848)
A 1 Master Print Inc ....G 405 787-0505
Bethany (G-571)
A B Printing ....G 918 834-2054
Tulsa (G-9066)
A Plus Printing Inc ....G 918 836-8659
Tulsa (G-9068)
A Plus Printing LLC ....G 580 765-7752
Ponca City (G-7792)
A Q Printing ....G 918 438-1161
Tulsa (G-9070)
A-OK Printing Mill ....G 918 775-6809
Sallisaw (G-8136)
Abco Printing & Office Supply ....G 580 286-7575
Idabel (G-3636)
Ace Information Co ....G 405 677-6747
Oklahoma City (G-5364)
Action Graphics Printing Inc ....G 918 540-3336
Miami (G-4388)
Action Graphics Prtg & Design ....G 918 540-3336
Miami (G-4389)
Action Printing Norman Inc ....E 405 364-3615
Norman (G-4897)
Advance Graphics & Printing ....G 405 258-0796
Chandler (G-1373)
Ajt Enterprises Inc ....F 918 665-7083
Tulsa (G-9133)
Allegra Marketing Print Mail ....G 539 302-2229
Tulsa (G-9140)
Anns Quick Print Co Inc ....G 405 222-1871
Chickasha (G-1429)
Arcadia Printing of Tulsa Inc ....G 918 622-1875
Bixby (G-611)
Archer Printing Inc ....G 405 236-1607
Moore (G-4493)
Associated Lithographing Co ....E 918 663-9091
Tulsa (G-9217)
Bartlesville Print Shop ....G 918 336-6070
Bartlesville (G-452)
Bell Printing and Advertising ....G 405 769-6445
Nicoma Park (G-4866)
Benders ....G 580 256-5656
Woodward (G-11561)
Bill Rathbone ....G 918 486-3028
Coweta (G-1872)
Boomerang Printing LLC ....G 918 747-1844
Tulsa (G-9319)
Britton Printing ....G 405 840-3291
Oklahoma City (G-5630)
C & R Print Shop Inc ....G 580 255-5656
Duncan (G-2095)
C & R Print Shop Inc ....G 405 224-7921
Chickasha (G-1445)
Cable Printing Co Inc ....F 405 756-4045
Lindsay (G-4055)
Century Printing Inc ....G 405 942-7171
Oklahoma City (G-5729)
Cherry Street Print Shop Inc ....G 918 584-0022
Tulsa (G-9417)
Choate Publishing Inc ....F 580 276-3255
Marietta (G-4204)
Clark Printing Inc ....G 405 528-5396
Oklahoma City (G-5776)
Classic Printing Inc ....F 405 524-6889
Oklahoma City (G-5778)
Cnhi Communications ....G 918 723-5445
Westville (G-11481)
Coleman Press ....G 918 437-0000
Tulsa (G-9467)
Color Express ....G 214 384-0887
Mead (G-4365)
Commercial Printing Marketing ....G 918 494-7072
Tulsa (G-9475)
Cooley Enterprises Inc ....G 918 437-6900
Tulsa (G-9483)
Copy Box Inc ....F 918 257-8000
Afton (G-115)
Copy Fast Printing Inc ....F 405 947-7468
Oklahoma City (G-5834)
Cowan Printing & Litho Inc ....F 405 789-1961
Tuttle (G-11191)
Craft Printed Envelopes Inc ....G 918 249-8887
Tulsa (G-9498)
Cromwells Inc ....G 580 234-6561
Enid (G-2935)
CSC Inc ....G 580 256-2409
Mooreland (G-4588)
Davis Printing Company Inc ....G 580 225-2902
Elk City (G-2800)
Dean Printing ....G 580 782-3777
Mangum (G-4170)
Digi Print LLC ....G 405 947-0099
Oklahoma City (G-5945)
Digital Prints Plus Inc ....G 918 520-7630
Collinsville (G-1810)
Durant Printing ....G 580 924-2271
Durant (G-2228)
Edmond Printings ....G 405 341-4330
Edmond (G-2404)
Ellis County Capital ....G 580 885-7788
Arnett (G-387)
Felkins Enterprises LLC ....G 918 272-3456
Owasso (G-7568)
Franklin Graphics Inc ....F 918 687-6149
Muskogee (G-4675)
G & S Printing Inc ....G 405 789-6813
Oklahoma City (G-6129)
Genral Enquries ....G 918 749-1301
Broken Arrow (G-918)
Gh Printing Solutions Inc ....G 405 630-0609
Edmond (G-2435)
Giles Printing Co Inc ....G 918 584-1583
Tulsa (G-9825)
Glo Press ....G 405 275-1038
Shawnee (G-8454)
Good Printing Co Inc ....G 405 235-9593
Oklahoma City (G-6171)
Gravley Companies Inc ....G 405 842-1404
Oklahoma City (G-6176)
Gravley Companies Inc ....G 918 743-6619
Tulsa (G-9850)
Hammer Hoby ....G 580 227-2100
Fairview (G-3137)
Hardesty Press Inc ....F 918 582-5306
Tulsa (G-9891)
Hennessey Clipper ....G 405 853-4888
Hennessey (G-3466)
Hilton Herald Corp Oklahoma ....G 580 229-0132
Healdton (G-3414)
Hinkle Printing & Office Sup ....G 405 238-9308
Pauls Valley (G-7660)
Hoffman Printing LLC ....F 918 682-8341
Muskogee (G-4691)
Holbrook Printing ....G 918 835-5950
Tulsa (G-9938)
Hooper Printing Company Inc ....F 405 321-4288
Norman (G-5026)
Impressions Printing A ....E 405 722-2442
Oklahoma City (G-6293)
Ink Spot Tttoo Bdy Percing LLC ....G 918 637-2897
Broken Arrow (G-1135)
Inked Custom Printing ....G 918 872-6544
Broken Arrow (G-937)
Kimberling City Publishing Co ....G 918 367-2282
Bristow (G-786)
Kindrick Co Prtg & Copying Svc ....G 580 332-1022
Ada (G-56)

PRODUCT SECTION

PRINTING: Screen, Manmade Fiber & Silk, Broadwoven Fabric

Kingfisher Office Supply Inc..................G...... 405 375-3404
  Kingfisher *(G-3806)*
Lakey Printing Co..................................G...... 918 744-0158
  Tulsa *(G-10116)*
Lithaprint Inc.......................................F...... 918 587-7746
  Tulsa *(G-10168)*
Lively Printing....................................G...... 918 582-3668
  Tulsa *(G-10169)*
MBC Graphics....................................G...... 918 585-2321
  Tulsa *(G-10227)*
McCullough Printing..........................G...... 580 286-7681
  Idabel *(G-3641)*
Meeks Lithographing Company...........E...... 918 836-0900
  Tulsa *(G-10240)*
Mesa Black Publishing LLC................G...... 580 544-2222
  Boise City *(G-747)*
Midtown Printing Inc..........................G...... 918 295-0090
  Tulsa *(G-10264)*
Midwest Copy and Printing................G...... 405 737-8311
  Oklahoma City *(G-6601)*
Miller Printing Company Inc..............F...... 918 749-0981
  Tulsa *(G-10281)*
Moe Mark of Excellence LLC.............G...... 405 650-9898
  Oklahoma City *(G-6624)*
Moore Printing Co Inc........................G...... 417 866-6696
  Moore *(G-4543)*
Multiprint Corp..................................G...... 918 832-0300
  Tulsa *(G-10315)*
MWH Enterprises Inc........................G...... 918 665-0944
  Tulsa *(G-10320)*
Newkirk Herald Journal.....................G...... 580 362-2140
  Newkirk *(G-4850)*
North Star Publishing LLC.................D...... 405 415-2400
  Oklahoma City *(G-6688)*
Northwest Printing Inc.......................G...... 580 234-0953
  Enid *(G-3022)*
OK Quality Printing Inc......................G...... 405 624-2925
  Stillwater *(G-8731)*
Oklahoma Executive Printing.............G...... 405 948-8136
  Oklahoma City *(G-6748)*
Oklahoma Offset Veba Inc.................G...... 918 582-0921
  Tulsa *(G-10404)*
Pace Printing Inc...............................G...... 918 585-5664
  Tulsa *(G-10454)*
Paperwork Company.........................F...... 918 369-1014
  Bixby *(G-652)*
Paragon Press Inc.............................G...... 405 681-5757
  Oklahoma City *(G-6803)*
PDQ Printing LLC..............................G...... 580 233-3241
  Enid *(G-3032)*
Phillips Printing Co............................G...... 918 266-3373
  Claremore *(G-1670)*
Pinecliffe Prtrs of Tecumseh...............G...... 405 273-1292
  Shawnee *(G-8483)*
Precision Printing Corporation............G...... 405 794-2500
  Moore *(G-4554)*
Prices Quality Printing Inc.................G...... 580 924-2271
  Durant *(G-2248)*
Print N Copy Inc................................G...... 918 258-8200
  Broken Arrow *(G-1011)*
Printers of Oklahoma LLC..................G...... 405 943-8855
  Oklahoma City *(G-6900)*
Printing Center..................................G...... 405 681-5303
  Oklahoma City *(G-6901)*
Professional Image Inc......................E...... 918 461-0609
  Tulsa *(G-10569)*
Professional Prtg Norman LLC...........G...... 405 823-3383
  Norman *(G-5125)*
Pronto Print Inc.................................G...... 580 223-1612
  Ardmore *(G-347)*
Pryor Printing Inc..............................G...... 918 825-2888
  Pryor *(G-7986)*
Pure Digital Print...............................G...... 918 899-2000
  Tulsa *(G-10584)*
Quad/Graphics Inc............................E...... 405 264-4341
  Oklahoma City *(G-6932)*
Quad/Graphics Inc............................B...... 405 264-4000
  Oklahoma City *(G-6933)*
Quik Print of Tulsa Inc......................G...... 918 250-5466
  Tulsa *(G-10594)*
Quik Print of Tulsa Inc......................E...... 918 665-6246
  Tulsa *(G-10595)*
Quik Print of Tulsa Inc......................G...... 918 582-1825
  Tulsa *(G-10596)*
Quik Print of Tulsa Inc......................G...... 918 491-9292
  Tulsa *(G-10597)*
Quik Print Oklahoma City Inc............E...... 405 840-3275
  Oklahoma City *(G-6945)*
Quik-Print of Oklahoma City..............G...... 405 842-1404
  Oklahoma City *(G-6946)*
Quik-Print of Oklahoma City..............G...... 405 843-9820
  Oklahoma City *(G-6947)*
Quik-Print of Oklahoma City..............G...... 405 232-7579
  Oklahoma City *(G-6948)*
Quik-Print of Oklahoma City..............G...... 405 840-3275
  Oklahoma City *(G-6950)*
Quik-Print of Oklahoma City..............G...... 405 528-7976
  Oklahoma City *(G-6951)*
Quik-Print of Oklahoma City..............G...... 405 751-5315
  Oklahoma City *(G-6952)*
Quintella Printing Company Inc.........G...... 405 631-6566
  Oklahoma City *(G-6955)*
Ra Graphix..G...... 405 703-3599
  Moore *(G-4559)*
RCP Print Solutions...........................G...... 918 341-1950
  Broken Arrow *(G-1024)*
RCP Printing......................................G...... 918 341-1950
  Broken Arrow *(G-1025)*
Red River Printing Corp.....................F...... 405 685-1794
  Oklahoma City *(G-6988)*
Reid Printing Inc...............................G...... 405 348-0066
  Edmond *(G-2596)*
Review Printing Company Inc...........F...... 580 658-6657
  Marlow *(G-4241)*
Richards Printing Co.........................G...... 405 224-8640
  Chickasha *(G-1501)*
Rocket Color Inc................................G...... 405 842-6001
  Oklahoma City *(G-7043)*
Ross Printing LLC.............................G...... 405 947-0099
  Oklahoma City *(G-7050)*
Scissortail Graphics Inc....................G...... 580 255-2914
  Duncan *(G-2174)*
Scotts Printing & Copying Inc...........F...... 405 236-0821
  Oklahoma City *(G-7099)*
Self Printing Inc................................G...... 918 838-2113
  Tulsa *(G-10726)*
Shadowkast Screen Printing LLC.......G...... 405 808-5148
  Edmond *(G-2618)*
Signature Graphics Corp...................G...... 918 294-3485
  Bixby *(G-658)*
Snider Printing & Office Sup..............G...... 405 257-3402
  Wewoka *(G-11511)*
Snyder Printing Inc...........................F...... 405 682-8880
  Oklahoma City *(G-5317)*
Sooner Industries Inc........................G...... 918 540-2422
  Miami *(G-4431)*
Sooner Press.....................................G...... 405 382-8351
  Seminole *(G-8400)*
Southwest Business Pdts LLC...........G...... 580 765-4401
  Ponca City *(G-7878)*
Southwestern Sty & Bnk Sup Inc.......D...... 405 525-9411
  Oklahoma City *(G-7177)*
Spitzer Printing.................................G...... 580 928-5540
  Sayre *(G-8346)*
Sprekelmeyer Printing Company........G...... 580 223-5100
  Ardmore *(G-359)*
Standard Printing Co Inc...................G...... 405 840-0001
  Oklahoma City *(G-7192)*
Steves Bindery Service Inc................G...... 405 946-2183
  Oklahoma City *(G-7204)*
Stigler Digital...................................G...... 918 967-8383
  Stigler *(G-8648)*
Sugarwood Digital Printing...............G...... 918 378-5771
  Jenks *(G-3731)*
Texoma Printing Inc..........................G...... 580 924-1120
  Durant *(G-2267)*
Transcript Press Inc..........................E...... 405 360-7999
  Norman *(G-5181)*
Triple T Printing................................G...... 405 912-1212
  Moore *(G-4579)*
Two Lees Inc....................................G...... 918 663-2390
  Tulsa *(G-11027)*
Unique Printing Inc...........................G...... 405 842-3966
  Oklahoma City *(G-7361)*
Unity Press Inc.................................E...... 405 232-8910
  Tulsa *(G-11045)*
V O Inc..G...... 405 659-0654
  Edmond *(G-2664)*
Vinita Printing Co Inc........................G...... 918 256-6422
  Vinita *(G-11271)*
Vox Printing Incorporated..................D...... 800 654-8437
  Oklahoma City *(G-7406)*
Wallis Printing Inc.............................G...... 580 223-7473
  Ardmore *(G-379)*
Warren Products Inc.........................F...... 405 947-5676
  Oklahoma City *(G-7421)*
Watonga Printing & Office Sups........G...... 580 623-4989
  Watonga *(G-11353)*
Weatherford Press Inc.......................F...... 580 772-5300
  Weatherford *(G-11459)*
Western Prnting Company Inc...........E...... 918 665-2874
  Tulsa *(G-11109)*
Westwood Printing Center.................G...... 405 366-8961
  Norman *(G-5199)*

PRINTING: Overprinting, Man Fiber & Silk, Broadwoven Fabric

Promo Print 4 U LLC.........................G...... 405 259-6721
  Oklahoma City *(G-6915)*

PRINTING: Photolithographic

First Impression Prtg Co Inc..............G...... 918 749-5446
  Beggs *(G-554)*
Pre-Press Graphics Inc......................G...... 918 582-2775
  Tulsa *(G-10541)*

PRINTING: Screen, Broadwoven Fabrics, Cotton

Body Billboards.................................G...... 405 282-9922
  Guthrie *(G-3300)*
Hard Edge Design Inc.......................F...... 405 360-9714
  Norman *(G-5016)*
Massive Graphic Screen Prtg............F...... 405 364-3594
  Norman *(G-5066)*
Misaco Sign and Screen Prtg............G...... 918 542-4188
  Miami *(G-4420)*

PRINTING: Screen, Fabric

A & B Engraving Inc..........................G...... 918 663-7446
  Tulsa *(G-9061)*
American Sportswear Inc...................G...... 918 665-7636
  Tulsa *(G-9172)*
Causley Productions Inc....................F...... 405 372-0940
  Stillwater *(G-8666)*
Clay Serigraphics Inc........................F...... 918 592-2529
  Tulsa *(G-9445)*
Corner Copy & Printing LLC.............G...... 405 801-2020
  Norman *(G-4966)*
Diamond Tees....................................G...... 918 665-0815
  Tulsa *(G-9579)*
Emert Enterprises LLC......................G...... 580 495-5511
  Bennington *(G-563)*
Graphix Xpress..................................G...... 580 765-7324
  Ponca City *(G-7831)*
Initially Yours Inc..............................G...... 918 832-9889
  Tulsa *(G-9986)*
Jan L Jobe..G...... 918 683-0404
  Muskogee *(G-4698)*
King Screen Co.................................G...... 405 258-0416
  Chandler *(G-1383)*
Knl Screenprinting.............................G...... 580 654-5394
  Carnegie *(G-1277)*
Munger and Krout Inc........................F...... 580 237-7060
  Enid *(G-3016)*
Promoz Screen Printing Inc...............G...... 918 439-4030
  Tulsa *(G-10574)*
S & S Textile Inc................................F...... 405 632-9928
  Oklahoma City *(G-7065)*
Shirts & Stuff....................................G...... 918 445-0323
  Tulsa *(G-10749)*
Shops of Standing Rock Inc..............G...... 580 364-0834
  Atoka *(G-423)*
Sides Screenprinting More LLC.........G...... 580 772-8888
  Oklahoma City *(G-7127)*
Speedys TS & More LLC...................G...... 580 748-0067
  Alva *(G-192)*
Tigers Den By Dreamcatcher............G...... 918 478-4873
  Fort Gibson *(G-3180)*
U Big TS Designs Inc........................G...... 405 401-4327
  Oklahoma City *(G-7356)*
USA Screen Prtg & EMB Co Inc.........E...... 405 946-3100
  Oklahoma City *(G-7380)*
Way-Wear LLC...................................G...... 405 410-8367
  Kingfisher *(G-3820)*
Wet Willies Screen Print & CU..........G...... 405 262-6076
  El Reno *(G-2770)*

PRINTING: Screen, Manmade Fiber & Silk, Broadwoven Fabric

Monograms Elite Inc.........................G...... 580 353-1635
  Lawton *(G-3973)*
Semasys Inc.....................................E...... 405 525-2335
  Oklahoma City *(G-7107)*

Employee Codes: A=Over 500 employees, B=251-500
C=101-250, D=51-100, E=20-50, F=10-19, G=1-9

PRINTING: Thermography

Breast & Bdy Thermography Ctr .... G 405 596-8099
Nichols Hills *(G-4855)*

PRODUCT STERILIZATION SVCS

Lemco Enterprises Inc .... G 580 226-7808
Ardmore *(G-324)*

PROFESSIONAL EQPT & SPLYS, WHOLESALE: Optical Goods

Gilmores Sports Concepts Inc .... G 918 250-3910
Tulsa *(G-9827)*
Omega Optical Co LP .... E 405 703-4133
Oklahoma City *(G-6775)*
Optical Works Corporation .... F 918 682-1806
Muskogee *(G-4726)*

PROFESSIONAL EQPT & SPLYS, WHOLESALE: Scientific & Engineerg

Refinery Supply Co Inc .... G 918 621-1700
Tulsa *(G-10635)*

PROFESSIONAL INSTRUMENT REPAIR SVCS

Alberts Auto & Truck Repr Inc .... E 866 772-6065
Weatherford *(G-11389)*
Blevins Oilfield Sls & Svc LLC .... F 405 619-9909
Oklahoma City *(G-5592)*
Iap Worldwide Services Inc .... F 321 784-7100
Oklahoma City *(G-6282)*
Kelley Repair LLC .... G 918 456-6514
Tahlequah *(G-8870)*

PROGRAM ADMIN, GOVT: Air, Water & Solid Waste Mgmt, Cnty

County of Tillman .... G 580 597-3097
Chattanooga *(G-1389)*

PROGRAM ADMIN, GOVT: Air, Water & Solid Waste Mgmt, State

Oklahoma Department of Mines .... G 918 485-3999
Tulsa *(G-10396)*

PROPERTY DAMAGE INSURANCE

Don L Gerbrandt .... G 580 234-3247
Enid *(G-2943)*

PROTECTION EQPT: Lightning

BR Electric .... G 405 354-8994
Yukon *(G-11700)*

PROTECTIVE FOOTWEAR: Rubber Or Plastic

Crackshot Corporation .... G 918 838-1272
Tulsa *(G-9497)*

PUBLIC ADDRESS SYSTEMS

Cns Audio Video Inc .... E 405 256-8546
Oklahoma City *(G-5796)*

PUBLIC ORDER & SAFETY OFFICES, GOVERNMENT: State

Oklahoma Dept Public Safety .... E 918 256-3388
Vinita *(G-11265)*

PUBLIC RELATIONS SVCS

Oklahoma State University .... F 918 253-4332
Jay *(G-3684)*

PUBLISHERS: Book

A Fuller Measure .... G 405 755-5036
Oklahoma City *(G-5346)*
Acp Inc .... G 405 249-8835
Oklahoma City *(G-5369)*
Andrea Koenig .... G 918 745-0828
Tulsa *(G-9189)*
Anvil House Publishers LLC .... G 918 760-8991
Owasso *(G-7545)*
Arista .... G 405 948-1500
Oklahoma City *(G-5464)*
Auryn Creative .... G 918 876-0974
Tulsa *(G-9223)*
Bordon David & Associates LLC .... G 918 495-3508
Broken Arrow *(G-855)*
Camp Chippewa For Boys Inc .... E 218 335-8807
Tulsa *(G-9367)*
Catch 21 .... G 617 227-0730
Oklahoma City *(G-5712)*
Child Heroes LLC .... G 757 286-8181
Oklahoma City *(G-5760)*
Dragonfly Publishing Inc .... G 405 359-6952
Edmond *(G-2395)*
Empowered Life Stores LLC .... G 918 523-5700
Tulsa *(G-9678)*
Freedom Bell Inc .... G 918 671-1089
Tulsa *(G-9774)*
Gateway International Inc .... G 918 747-8393
Tulsa *(G-9807)*
Gretchen Cagle Publications .... G 918 342-1080
Claremore *(G-1629)*
Guy W Logsdon .... G 918 743-2171
Tulsa *(G-9869)*
Hays Publishing .... G 918 456-7717
Tahlequah *(G-8867)*
Hidden Pearls LLC .... G 405 707-0851
Stillwater *(G-8701)*
Hoffman Printing LLC .... F 918 682-8341
Muskogee *(G-4691)*
Independent School .... E 918 245-2622
Sand Springs *(G-8192)*
J Franklin Publishers Inc .... G 628 400-3382
Tulsa *(G-10020)*
Kinda Wilson LLC .... G 405 880-5308
Tulsa *(G-10090)*
Kings Remnant Ministry Inc .... G 918 207-0866
Welling *(G-11467)*
Lloyd Words LLC .... G 918 457-6852
Tulsa *(G-10172)*
Mentorhope LLC .... G 405 752-0940
Oklahoma City *(G-6565)*
Michelangelo Properties LLC .... G 918 341-4771
Claremore *(G-1654)*
Midwest Publishing Co .... G 405 282-1890
Guthrie *(G-3325)*
Nedley Publishing Co .... F 580 223-5980
Ardmore *(G-337)*
Oklahoma Academy Publishing .... G 405 454-6211
Harrah *(G-3383)*
Out On Limb Publishing .... G 918 743-4408
Tulsa *(G-10445)*
Paige 1 Publishing .... G 918 706-4359
Broken Arrow *(G-997)*
Paige Publishing .... G 918 527-3245
Lexington *(G-4039)*
Plan Bible .... G 918 254-6983
Tulsa *(G-10522)*
Rutherford Lterary Group L L C .... G 405 623-9031
Midwest City *(G-4452)*
Trisms Inc .... G 918 585-2778
Tulsa *(G-10977)*
University of Oklahoma .... E 405 325-3189
Norman *(G-5186)*
University of Oklahoma .... E 405 325-3276
Norman *(G-5187)*
West Mattison Publishing Inc .... F 405 842-2266
Edmond *(G-2684)*
Word Among US .... G 918 812-5254
Tulsa *(G-11151)*
Yellow Bird Communication .... G 405 238-6260
Pauls Valley *(G-7675)*
Yorkshire Publishing LLC .... E 918 394-2665
Tulsa *(G-11170)*

PUBLISHERS: Books, No Printing

412 Comics LLC .... G 479 414-0891
Pocola *(G-7779)*
Chastain Enterprises LLC .... G 918 615-9355
Tulsa *(G-9407)*
Cross Shadows Inc .... G 405 262-9777
El Reno *(G-2707)*
Garrett Educational Corp .... E 580 332-6884
Ada *(G-39)*
Hale Publications .... G 405 632-2450
Oklahoma City *(G-6204)*
JB Books Unlimited LLC .... G 918 954-8308
Tulsa *(G-10031)*
Lacebark Inc .... G 405 377-3539
Stillwater *(G-8716)*
Meridian Press Publications .... G 405 751-2342
Oklahoma City *(G-6568)*
New Forums Press Inc .... G 405 372-6158
Stillwater *(G-8727)*
Oklahoma State University .... C 405 744-5723
Stillwater *(G-8733)*
Olam Publishing LLC .... G 918 200-9770
Tulsa *(G-10410)*
Rentpath LLC .... F 918 307-8980
Tulsa *(G-10642)*
Victory House Inc .... G 918 747-5009
Tulsa *(G-11075)*
Wynn Wynn Media .... G 918 283-1834
Claremore *(G-1705)*

PUBLISHERS: Catalogs

Vmebus Intl Trade Assn .... G 480 577-1916
Oklahoma City *(G-7405)*

PUBLISHERS: Directories, NEC

Midwest Publishing Co Inc .... G 918 582-2000
Tulsa *(G-10271)*
Yp LLC .... D 918 835-8600
Tulsa *(G-11171)*

PUBLISHERS: Directories, Telephone

Local Telephone Directory .... G 580 762-9359
Ponca City *(G-7846)*

PUBLISHERS: Guides

Poteau Daily News .... G 918 647-3335
Poteau *(G-7911)*

PUBLISHERS: Magazines, No Printing

AG Youth Magazine .... G 800 599-6884
Sentinel *(G-8409)*
Black Belt Magazine 1000 LLC .... G 405 732-5111
Oklahoma City *(G-5580)*
Dealers Market .... G 405 789-6455
Warr Acres *(G-11318)*
International Gymnast Magazine .... G 405 447-9988
Norman *(G-5035)*
Journal Record Publishing Co .... D 405 278-2848
Oklahoma City *(G-6388)*
Just Two Publishing Inc .... G 405 607-2902
Edmond *(G-2476)*
K9 Media .... E 504 233-2576
Del City *(G-1998)*
Key Magazine .... G 405 602-3300
Oklahoma City *(G-6408)*
Langdon Publishing Co Inc .... F 918 585-9924
Tulsa *(G-10123)*
Lew Graphics Inc .... G 405 743-0890
Stillwater *(G-8717)*
Lost Treasure Inc .... G 918 786-2182
Grove *(G-3279)*
Metro Family Magazine .... G 405 601-2081
Oklahoma City *(G-6579)*
Nightowl Publications Main Off .... G 405 603-8130
Oklahoma City *(G-6681)*
Paul Ziert & Associates Inc .... D 405 364-5344
Norman *(G-5112)*
Phoenix Trade Publication .... G 405 948-6555
Oklahoma City *(G-6846)*
Preview of Green Country Inc .... G 918 745-1190
Tulsa *(G-10556)*
Schuman Publishing Company .... G 918 744-6205
Tulsa *(G-10715)*
T K Publishing Inc .... G 918 582-8504
Tulsa *(G-10891)*
Thunder Road Magazine Oklahoma ...... G 405 612-3844
Oklahoma City *(G-7285)*
Tulsapets Magazine .... G 918 834-1252
Tulsa *(G-11015)*
Vype High School Spt Mag LLC .... F 918 495-1771
Tulsa *(G-11085)*

PUBLISHERS: Miscellaneous

12th Gate Publishing LLC .... G 405 735-7611
Oklahoma City *(G-5327)*
1tr3 Publishing LLC .... G 580 350-9280
Lawton *(G-3880)*
2 Victory Graphics Media .... G 918 394-2665
Tulsa *(G-9054)*
209 LLC .... G 918 584-9944
Tulsa *(G-9058)*

2b Publishing LLC ....G....... 405 209-8465
Edmond *(G-2282)*
405 Magazine Inc ....G....... 405 604-2623
Oklahoma City *(G-5332)*
4rv Publishing LLC ....G....... 405 225-7298
Edmond *(G-2286)*
50th Xpress Mart ....G....... 405 491-7381
Warr Acres *(G-11310)*
A Prior Publishing ....G....... 903 882-5019
Lawton *(G-3881)*
Abundant Grace Companies LLC ....F....... 405 682-2589
Oklahoma City *(G-5359)*
Adventure Publishing LLC ....G....... 918 270-7100
Tulsa *(G-9113)*
Agion Press ....G....... 405 341-7477
Edmond *(G-2293)*
Aj Publishers LLC ....G....... 580 234-0064
Enid *(G-2909)*
Allsbury Marketing & Pubg LLC ....G....... 405 412-0809
Edmond *(G-2297)*
Anatole Publishing LLC ....G....... 405 609-0763
Norman *(G-4909)*
Anvil House Publishers LLC ....G....... 918 760-8991
Owasso *(G-7545)*
Arkansas River Press ....G....... 918 744-1730
Tulsa *(G-9208)*
Art of Manliness LLC ....G....... 405 613-3340
Tulsa *(G-9214)*
Attorney and Legal Publica ....G....... 405 728-0392
Oklahoma City *(G-5487)*
Bennie Publications LLC ....G....... 918 873-0250
Oklahoma City *(G-5552)*
Blackjack Express LLC ....G....... 405 462-7410
Bradley *(G-760)*
Blue Bridge Publishing LLC ....G....... 405 533-2547
Stillwater *(G-8661)*
Blue Sail Publishing Inc ....G....... 630 851-4731
Ardmore *(G-259)*
Bobay Nutrition LLC ....G....... 405 708-0407
Oklahoma City *(G-5602)*
Book Villages LLC ....G....... 719 339-8048
Edmond *(G-2329)*
Books In Sight Inc ....G....... 405 810-9501
Oklahoma City *(G-5617)*
Bridge Creek Publishing Co ....G....... 405 519-6982
Mulhall *(G-4637)*
Buffalo Nickel Press ....G....... 918 287-3899
Pawhuska *(G-7680)*
Bush Publishing ....G....... 901 468-8388
Broken Arrow *(G-1114)*
Bush Publishing & Assoc LLC ....G....... 251 424-7298
Tulsa *(G-9349)*
Capitalist Publishing Co ....G....... 918 808-5665
Tulsa *(G-9371)*
Cattleac Cattle Equipment Inc ....G....... 580 774-1010
Weatherford *(G-11398)*
CCS Publishing LLC ....G....... 405 359-0656
Edmond *(G-2340)*
CD Services ....G....... 918 341-1032
Claremore *(G-1602)*
Cedar Gate LLC ....G....... 405 640-3235
Edmond *(G-2341)*
Chic Galleria Publications ....G....... 918 671-2379
Bartlesville *(G-465)*
Chickasaw Press ....G....... 580 436-7282
Ada *(G-22)*
Choctaw Manufacturing & Dev Co ....G....... 580 310-6021
Ada *(G-23)*
Chumbolly Press LLC ....G....... 918 607-3932
Sand Springs *(G-8170)*
Colt Express ....G....... 918 455-2658
Tulsa *(G-9471)*
Comfort X-Press LLC ....E....... 405 382-5600
Seminole *(G-8366)*
Community Publishers ....E....... 918 273-1040
Nowata *(G-5211)*
Community Publishers Inc ....G....... 918 259-7500
Broken Arrow *(G-872)*
Copypasta Publishing ....G....... 580 236-4071
Broken Bow *(G-1188)*
Counterbattery Press LLC ....G....... 405 794-2885
Moore *(G-4510)*
Countywide News Inc ....F....... 405 598-3793
Tecumseh *(G-8910)*
Dancey-Meador Publishing Co ....G....... 580 762-9359
Ponca City *(G-7819)*
Daniel E and Marl Newport ....G....... 918 445-9129
Tulsa *(G-9550)*
Danny Bowen ....G....... 405 618-3377
Meeker *(G-4377)*

Datebox Inc Okc ....G....... 253 678-1173
Oklahoma City *(G-5901)*
Dbr Publishing Co LLC ....E....... 918 250-1984
Owasso *(G-7560)*
Delphia Publishing LLC ....G....... 918 232-8709
Drumright *(G-2055)*
Don Wilmut ....G....... 405 785-9192
Alex *(G-130)*
Doodle and Peck Publishing ....G....... 405 354-7422
Yukon *(G-11721)*
Draft2digital LLC ....G....... 405 708-7894
Oklahoma City *(G-5979)*
E H Publishing Inc ....G....... 405 258-0877
Chandler *(G-1379)*
Earlywine Press LLC ....G....... 405 820-8208
Oklahoma City *(G-5289)*
Editorial Annex ....G....... 405 474-2114
Edmond *(G-2400)*
Ellis Enterprises Inc ....G....... 405 917-5336
Oklahoma City *(G-6027)*
Endurance Publishing LLC ....G....... 405 332-5273
Stillwater *(G-8683)*
Everhart Publishing LLC ....G....... 405 370-4850
Oklahoma City *(G-6056)*
Ex-Press Vac LLC ....G....... 580 606-0799
Duncan *(G-2117)*
Express Bus Inc ....G....... 918 835-2040
Tulsa *(G-9717)*
Express Home Help ....G....... 405 214-6400
Shawnee *(G-8448)*
Ezekiel Chrles Pblications LLC ....G....... 918 747-8841
Tulsa *(G-9720)*
Featherston Publishing LLC ....G....... 918 289-7877
Owasso *(G-7567)*
Five F Publishing ....G....... 405 732-1050
Oklahoma City *(G-6085)*
Fs & J Music Publishing LLC ....G....... 918 369-6010
Tulsa *(G-9786)*
Ghost Town Press ....G....... 405 396-2166
Arcadia *(G-229)*
Greater Tlsa Rprter Newspapers ....G....... 918 254-1515
Tulsa *(G-9856)*
Gregs Press ....G....... 405 356-4156
Wellston *(G-11471)*
Gypsy Twang Publishing ....G....... 918 398-3116
Bixby *(G-630)*
Hale Publications ....G....... 405 632-2450
Oklahoma City *(G-6204)*
Harrison House Inc ....G....... 918 582-2126
Tulsa *(G-9896)*
Hear My Heart Publishing LLC ....G....... 918 510-1483
Skiatook *(G-8547)*
Highlands Publishing LLC ....G....... 405 596-8391
Norman *(G-5022)*
His Publishing LLC ....G....... 405 390-0518
Choctaw *(G-1544)*
Hmh Publishing ....G....... 405 788-5589
Elk City *(G-2823)*
Hogan Assessment Systems Inc ....D....... 918 293-2300
Tulsa *(G-9937)*
Hoot of Loot ....G....... 918 743-9802
Tulsa *(G-9946)*
Hot Off Press ....G....... 918 492-2313
Tulsa *(G-9953)*
Illbird Press ....G....... 918 859-7789
Tulsa *(G-9970)*
Imoco LLC ....G....... 918 459-8366
Tulsa *(G-9971)*
Indigo Streams Publishing LLC ....G....... 918 293-0247
Tulsa *(G-9978)*
Industrial City Press ....G....... 918 299-2767
Jenks *(G-3707)*
Infinitee By Mars LLC ....G....... 405 474-6505
Oklahoma City *(G-6302)*
Inkana Publishing ....G....... 937 760-8446
Ada *(G-51)*
Inkana Publishing LLC ....G....... 937 725-1296
Moore *(G-4528)*
Insight Publishing Group ....G....... 918 493-1718
Tulsa *(G-9990)*
Janet D Redd ....G....... 580 243-0595
Elk City *(G-2830)*
Jeremy Hart Music Inc ....G....... 918 687-3605
Muskogee *(G-4700)*
Jewell Jordan Publishing LLC ....G....... 405 496-2672
Oklahoma City *(G-6362)*
JM Publications LLC ....G....... 405 639-9472
Oklahoma City *(G-6365)*
JM Publishing LLC ....G....... 405 684-0450
Edmond *(G-2471)*

John Clark ....G....... 918 853-8286
Sperry *(G-8608)*
Just Breathe Publishing LLC ....G....... 405 633-0160
Spencer *(G-8597)*
Kane/Miller Book Publishers ....G....... 918 346-6118
Tulsa *(G-10075)*
Kasm Publishing LLC ....G....... 918 798-8908
Tulsa *(G-10077)*
Kelley Publications LLC ....G....... 405 585-7210
Stratford *(G-8805)*
Kh Publishing LLC ....G....... 405 378-7539
Oklahoma City *(G-5301)*
Kobe Express LLC ....G....... 580 889-2420
Atoka *(G-418)*
Kp Designs LLC ....G....... 865 776-7769
Lawton *(G-3951)*
L S Marann Publishing ....G....... 405 751-9369
Oklahoma City *(G-6441)*
Level Up Publishing LLC ....G....... 405 771-4372
Spencer *(G-8598)*
Life Impact Publishing LLC ....G....... 918 407-9938
Tulsa *(G-10158)*
Lindsey Webb Press ....G....... 405 756-9551
Lindsay *(G-4074)*
Local Hometown Publishing Inc ....G....... 405 273-3838
McLoud *(G-4359)*
Lw Publications ....G....... 405 203-6740
Norman *(G-5061)*
Mac Publishing Company LLC ....G....... 405 964-3576
McLoud *(G-4360)*
Marcelle Publishing LLC ....G....... 405 288-2317
Purcell *(G-8015)*
Marie Thierrey Lucinda ....G....... 405 623-9431
Oklahoma City *(G-6525)*
Mauvaisterre Publishing LLC ....G....... 918 492-3846
Tulsa *(G-10224)*
Meeker Football Press Box ....G....... 405 279-1075
Meeker *(G-4381)*
Mental Note LLC ....G....... 405 301-4182
Edmond *(G-2512)*
Metro Publishing LLC ....G....... 405 593-1335
Yukon *(G-11753)*
Midwest Publication ....G....... 405 948-6506
Oklahoma City *(G-6606)*
MO Publishing LLC ....G....... 580 284-3719
Lawton *(G-3972)*
Mobile Express ....G....... 405 395-9378
Shawnee *(G-8476)*
Mongrel Empire Press LLC ....G....... 405 459-0042
Norman *(G-5078)*
Morning Fax ....G....... 918 357-5245
Broken Arrow *(G-1145)*
Mpress Cards ....G....... 405 590-5393
Norman *(G-5082)*
Musicware Press ....G....... 405 627-1894
Oklahoma City *(G-6637)*
Mythic Press ....G....... 918 516-8255
Tulsa *(G-10321)*
New Forums Press Inc ....G....... 405 372-6158
Stillwater *(G-8727)*
New Plains Review ....G....... 405 974-5613
Edmond *(G-2536)*
Nonovels Press LLC ....G....... 325 721-2577
Oklahoma City *(G-6684)*
Oklahoma Ntry Svc A Div of M- ....G....... 405 948-8900
Oklahoma City *(G-6757)*
Oklahoma Publishing Company ....G....... 405 475-4040
Oklahoma City *(G-6760)*
Okstyle Publishing LLC ....G....... 405 816-3338
Oklahoma City *(G-6768)*
Old Farm Publishing LLC ....G....... 405 237-1153
Moore *(G-4548)*
Oremus Press & Publishing ....G....... 405 368-4645
Dover *(G-2042)*
Original Productions Pubg LLC ....G....... 405 420-9559
Norman *(G-5104)*
Paige Publishing ....G....... 405 527-3245
Lexington *(G-4039)*
Patricia Lyons ....G....... 850 445-4782
Jenks *(G-3722)*
Paxton McMillin Chrisanna ....G....... 918 734-5753
Sapulpa *(G-8297)*
Pegleg Publishing LLC ....G....... 405 618-7740
Oklahoma City *(G-6820)*
Perfect Circle Publishing Inc ....G....... 918 629-0061
Tulsa *(G-10492)*
Philip H Brewer ....G....... 580 657-8029
Ardmore *(G-345)*
Pie In Sky Publishing Co LLC ....G....... 918 762-3310
Pawnee *(G-7709)*

Employee Codes: A=Over 500 employees, B=251-500
C=101-250, D=51-100, E=20-50, F=10-19, G=1-9
2020 Oklahoma Directory
of Manufacturers & Processors
803

Pivot Point Publishing..........G....... 918 347-5415
Sapulpa *(G-8298)*
Press..........G....... 405 464-6181
Oklahoma City *(G-6890)*
Press Go..........G....... 580 889-2399
Atoka *(G-421)*
Princo Press Corp..........G....... 405 760-6064
Edmond *(G-2575)*
Pringle Publications Corp..........G....... 405 848-4859
Oklahoma City *(G-6896)*
Professional Communications..........G....... 580 745-9838
Durant *(G-2249)*
Prometheus Publications LLC..........G....... 717 460-4881
Vinita *(G-11268)*
Purpose Publishing..........G....... 405 808-1332
Oklahoma City *(G-6927)*
Pv Publishing Inc..........G....... 405 409-1799
Oklahoma City *(G-6928)*
Raymond L Weil Pblications LLC..........G....... 580 323-4594
Clinton *(G-1764)*
Red Dog Press LLC..........G....... 405 703-2896
Moore *(G-4560)*
Rigyard Publications LLC..........G....... 405 330-1456
Edmond *(G-2600)*
Rivers Edge Publications..........G....... 918 855-9469
Tulsa *(G-10656)*
Roadrunner Press..........G....... 405 524-6205
Oklahoma City *(G-7031)*
Rwdesign Publishing..........G....... 918 924-8865
Broken Arrow *(G-1041)*
Safetac Publishing LLC..........G....... 559 640-7233
Tulsa *(G-10687)*
Samson Publishing Company LLC..........G....... 918 344-7416
Beggs *(G-560)*
Schatz Publishing Group LLC..........F....... 580 628-4607
Blackwell *(G-690)*
Scout Guide Tulsa LLC..........G....... 918 693-1198
Tulsa *(G-10717)*
Scriptorium..........G....... 405 203-5943
Moore *(G-4566)*
Seminole County Publishing..........G....... 405 382-1125
Seminole *(G-8398)*
Shepherds Heart Music Inc..........G....... 918 781-1200
Muskogee *(G-4749)*
Sooner Publishing Inc..........G....... 580 233-8400
Enid *(G-3058)*
Sound Ink 2 Publishing LLC..........G....... 918 605-6026
Tulsa *(G-9038)*
Spacebar Publishing LLC..........G....... 918 852-6311
Claremore *(G-1687)*
Spangenhelm Publishing..........G....... 405 430-6464
Yukon *(G-11785)*
Sports Fitnes Publications LLC..........G....... 918 587-7223
Tulsa *(G-10824)*
St Bonaventure Press Ltd..........G....... 918 770-8546
Tulsa *(G-10829)*
Starfall Press LLC..........G....... 405 343-2369
Edmond *(G-2630)*
Steeley D Upshaw Pubg LLC..........G....... 405 948-7802
Oklahoma City *(G-7201)*
Stellar Art Publishing Inc..........G....... 918 277-3325
Bixby *(G-665)*
Strawberry Valley Press LLC..........G....... 405 237-1893
Oklahoma City *(G-5318)*
Subtledemon Publishing LLC..........G....... 405 670-3471
Oklahoma City *(G-5319)*
Thomas Tribute Inc..........G....... 580 661-3524
Thomas *(G-8949)*
Tigers Express..........G....... 918 251-0118
Broken Arrow *(G-1076)*
Timothy Publishing Services..........G....... 918 924-6246
Broken Arrow *(G-1077)*
Together Tulsa Publications..........G....... 918 269-1085
Tulsa *(G-10948)*
Towne Publishing LLC..........G....... 405 473-7436
Norman *(G-5178)*
Trenary Publishing LLC..........G....... 918 607-3280
Broken Arrow *(G-1083)*
University of Oklahoma Press..........G....... 405 325-2000
Norman *(G-5189)*
V M Publishing Co..........G....... 405 533-1883
Stillwater *(G-8772)*
Verdavia Press LLC..........G....... 405 254-5030
Edmond *(G-2669)*
Vinson James R Linda F Co..........G....... 405 478-1330
Edmond *(G-2672)*
Western Web Envelope Co Inc..........F....... 405 682-0207
Oklahoma City *(G-7442)*
Wine Press..........G....... 580 540-8913
Enid *(G-3081)*
Wolf Publishing..........G....... 918 500-9921
Tulsa *(G-11145)*
World Arts Press LLC..........G....... 405 314-2578
Nichols Hills *(G-4865)*
World Publishing Company Veba..........G....... 918 582-0921
Tulsa *(G-11153)*
Write Green Light..........G....... 405 722-7823
Yukon *(G-11805)*
Writers Research Group LLC..........F....... 405 682-2589
Oklahoma City *(G-7474)*
You Are Here Curriculum..........G....... 918 650-8586
Henryetta *(G-3519)*
Zeigler Publishing..........G....... 405 771-8754
Spencer *(G-8603)*

PUBLISHERS: Music Book & Sheet Music

Northwood Publishing LLC..........G....... 918 451-9388
Broken Arrow *(G-989)*

PUBLISHERS: Newsletter

5a Enterprises Inc..........G....... 918 260-8909
Drumright *(G-2049)*
Interstate Trucker Ltd..........E....... 405 948-6576
Oklahoma City *(G-6323)*

PUBLISHERS: Newspaper

Bargain Journal..........G....... 918 426-5500
McAlester *(G-4273)*
Berkshire Hathaway Inc..........G....... 918 245-6634
Sand Springs *(G-8166)*
Berkshire Hathaway Inc..........G....... 918 396-1616
Skiatook *(G-8532)*
Berkshire Hathaway Inc..........G....... 918 485-5505
Wagoner *(G-11277)*
Berkshire Hathaway Inc..........G....... 918 486-4444
Wagoner *(G-11276)*
Brently Publishing Intl LLC..........G....... 405 381-9069
Tuttle *(G-11187)*
Cache Times..........G....... 580 429-8200
Cache *(G-1225)*
Cromwells Inc..........G....... 580 234-6561
Enid *(G-2935)*
CSC Inc..........G....... 580 938-2533
Shattuck *(G-8420)*
Daily OCollegian..........D....... 405 744-7371
Stillwater *(G-8674)*
El Nacional News Inc..........G....... 405 632-4531
Oklahoma City *(G-6018)*
Fire Song Publishing..........G....... 405 799-2799
Moore *(G-4524)*
Frost Entertainment..........G....... 405 834-8484
Oklahoma City *(G-6125)*
Fungo Designs..........G....... 405 348-9922
Edmond *(G-2427)*
Grand River Chronicle-Grove..........G....... 918 786-8722
Grove *(G-3272)*
Hooker Advance & Office Supply..........G....... 580 652-2476
Hooker *(G-3598)*
Journal Record Publishing Co..........D....... 405 278-2848
Oklahoma City *(G-6388)*
Latimer County News Tribune..........G....... 918 465-2321
Wilburton *(G-11522)*
Lawrence County Newspapers Inc..........G....... 918 224-5185
Sapulpa *(G-8285)*
Lifes Adult Day Services..........G....... 918 664-9000
Broken Arrow *(G-967)*
Morris Communications Co LLC..........D....... 405 273-4200
Shawnee *(G-8477)*
Newspaper Services..........G....... 918 283-1564
Claremore *(G-1662)*
Oklahoma Assn of Elc Coop..........E....... 405 478-1455
Oklahoma City *(G-6735)*
Oklahoma Bankers..........E....... 405 424-5252
Oklahoma City *(G-6736)*
Oklahoma Eagle LLC..........G....... 918 582-7124
Tulsa *(G-10398)*
Oklahoma Magazine..........F....... 918 744-6205
Tulsa *(G-10402)*
Opubco Development Co..........E....... 405 475-3311
Oklahoma City *(G-6780)*
Owner Value News..........G....... 918 828-9600
Tulsa *(G-10449)*
Paper..........G....... 918 825-2860
Pryor *(G-7981)*
Poteau Daily News..........G....... 918 647-3335
Poteau *(G-7911)*
Rush Springs Gazette..........G....... 580 476-2525
Rush Springs *(G-8125)*
Sherrif..........G....... 918 663-3705
Tulsa *(G-10743)*
Spitzer Printing..........G....... 580 928-5540
Sayre *(G-8346)*
University of Oklahoma..........C....... 405 325-3666
Norman *(G-5188)*
Wanderlust Pen Company..........G....... 918 551-6809
Tulsa *(G-11094)*

PUBLISHERS: Newspapers, No Printing

American-Chief Co..........G....... 918 762-2552
Pawnee *(G-7699)*
Apache News..........G....... 580 588-3862
Apache *(G-217)*
Black Chronicle Inc..........F....... 405 424-4695
Oklahoma City *(G-5581)*
Blanchard News Publishing..........G....... 405 485-2311
Blanchard *(G-702)*
Cable Printing Co Inc..........F....... 405 756-4045
Lindsay *(G-4055)*
Carnegie Herald..........G....... 580 654-1443
Carnegie *(G-1274)*
Chadwick Paper Inc..........G....... 580 369-2807
Davis *(G-1979)*
Cheyenne Star..........G....... 580 497-3324
Cheyenne *(G-1423)*
Choate Publishing Inc..........F....... 580 276-3255
Marietta *(G-4204)*
Civitas Media LLC..........F....... 580 482-1221
Altus *(G-149)*
Cnhi LLC..........F....... 580 338-3355
Guymon *(G-3346)*
Cnhi LLC..........F....... 405 238-6464
Pauls Valley *(G-7654)*
Cnhi LLC..........G....... 918 652-3311
Henryetta *(G-3501)*
Cnhi LLC..........E....... 405 341-2121
Edmond *(G-2359)*
Cnhi LLC..........F....... 918 825-3292
Pryor *(G-7954)*
Cnhi Communications..........G....... 918 723-5445
Westville *(G-11481)*
Coalgate Record Register..........G....... 580 927-2355
Coalgate *(G-1778)*
Countywide News Inc..........F....... 405 598-3793
Tecumseh *(G-8910)*
Dmn Inc..........G....... 405 848-9401
Oklahoma City *(G-5954)*
Drumright Gusher Inc..........G....... 918 352-2284
Drumright *(G-2056)*
Edmond Life & Leisure..........F....... 405 340-3311
Edmond *(G-2403)*
El Nacional..........F....... 405 632-4531
Oklahoma City *(G-6017)*
Ellis County Capital..........G....... 580 885-7788
Arnett *(G-387)*
Gazette Media Inc..........E....... 405 528-6000
Oklahoma City *(G-6139)*
Geary Star..........G....... 405 884-2424
Geary *(G-3216)*
Harper County Journal..........G....... 580 735-2526
Buffalo *(G-1213)*
Heavener Ledger..........G....... 918 653-2425
Heavener *(G-3429)*
Herald Publishing Co..........G....... 580 875-3326
Walters *(G-11302)*
Herald Wakita..........G....... 580 594-2440
Wakita *(G-11298)*
Hughes County Publishing Co..........G....... 405 452-3294
Wetumka *(G-11493)*
Kimberling City Publishing Co..........G....... 918 367-2282
Bristow *(G-786)*
Kingfisher Newspaper Inc..........G....... 405 375-3220
Kingfisher *(G-3805)*
Kiowa County Democrat..........G....... 580 569-2684
Snyder *(G-8581)*
Lake Oologah Leader LLC..........G....... 918 443-2428
Oologah *(G-7534)*
Larry D Hammer..........G....... 580 596-3344
Cherokee *(G-1418)*
Lewis County Press LLC..........G....... 580 363-3370
Blackwell *(G-687)*
Maysville Publishing Co..........G....... 405 867-4457
Maysville *(G-4261)*
McCurtain County News Inc..........F....... 580 286-3321
Idabel *(G-3642)*
McCurtain County News Inc..........F....... 580 584-6210
Broken Bow *(G-1199)*
McIntosh County Democrat..........G....... 918 473-2313
Checotah *(G-1397)*

PRODUCT SECTION

PUBLISHING & PRINTING: Magazines: publishing & printing

Mountain View Printing Company ....G....... 580 347-2231
  Mountain View *(G-4628)*
Mustang Times ....G....... 405 606-1023
  Oklahoma City *(G-6643)*
Navajo County Publishers Inc ....F....... 928 524-6203
  Edmond *(G-2531)*
Nayfa Publications Inc............................G....... 405 373-1616
  Piedmont *(G-7767)*
New ERA ....G....... 918 377-2259
  Davenport *(G-1978)*
Newcastle Pacer Inc ....G....... 405 387-5277
  Newcastle *(G-4833)*
Newkirk Herald Journal ....G....... 580 362-2140
  Newkirk *(G-4850)*
News Enterprises Inc................................G....... 405 376-4571
  Mustang *(G-4787)*
Newspaper Holding Inc ....E....... 918 456-8833
  Tahlequah *(G-8876)*
Newspaper Holding Inc ....D....... 580 233-6600
  Enid *(G-3018)*
Newspaper Holding Inc ....E....... 580 332-4433
  Ada *(G-72)*
Newspaper Holding Inc ....E....... 918 341-1101
  Claremore *(G-1661)*
Newspaper Holding Inc ....E....... 918 297-2544
  Hartshorne *(G-3394)*
Newspaper Holding Inc ....E....... 918 696-2228
  Stilwell *(G-8793)*
Northern Arizona Newspaper ....F....... 928 524-6203
  Edmond *(G-2540)*
Nuestra Comunidad ....G....... 405 685-3822
  Oklahoma City *(G-6703)*
Okemah Leader ....G....... 918 623-0123
  Okemah *(G-5271)*
Oklahoma Eagle Publishing Co ....G....... 918 582-7124
  Tulsa *(G-10399)*
Oklahoma Newspaper ....F....... 405 475-3989
  Oklahoma City *(G-6755)*
Paxton Publishing Co ....G....... 580 782-3321
  Mangum *(G-4173)*
Reid Communications LLC ....G....... 918 285-5555
  Cushing *(G-1955)*
Review News Co ....F....... 405 354-5264
  Yukon *(G-11771)*
Russell Publishing Company ....G....... 405 665-4333
  Wynnewood *(G-11672)*
Sayre Record ....G....... 580 928-5540
  Sayre *(G-8345)*
Southwest Cnstr News Svc ....G....... 405 948-7474
  Oklahoma City *(G-7173)*
Southwest Cnstr News Svc ....G....... 918 493-5066
  Tulsa *(G-10804)*
Spiro Graphic ....G....... 918 962-2075
  Spiro *(G-8618)*
Spitzer Publishing ....G....... 580 928-5540
  Sayre *(G-8347)*
Stroud American Inc ....G....... 918 968-2310
  Stroud *(G-8820)*
Thomas Tribute Inc ....G....... 580 661-3524
  Thomas *(G-8949)*
Tonkawa News ....G....... 580 628-2532
  Tonkawa *(G-8984)*
Tri County Publications Inc ....G....... 918 465-3851
  Wilburton *(G-11526)*
Triple B Media LLC ....G....... 405 732-7577
  Midwest City *(G-4459)*
Watonga Republican Inc ....G....... 580 623-4922
  Watonga *(G-11354)*
Waynoka Pubg Co Woods Cnty ....G....... 580 824-2171
  Waynoka *(G-11381)*
Weekly Leader ....G....... 918 458-8001
  Tahlequah *(G-8892)*
Wesner Publications Company ....F....... 405 789-1962
  Bethany *(G-600)*
Wesner Publications Company ....E....... 580 832-3333
  Cordell *(G-1865)*
Wilson-Monroe Publishing Co ....G....... 580 933-4579
  Valliant *(G-11234)*
Woodward News ....E....... 580 256-2200
  Woodward *(G-11658)*

PUBLISHERS: Pamphlets, No Printing

Vmebus Intl Trade Assn ....G....... 480 577-1916
  Oklahoma City *(G-7405)*

PUBLISHERS: Periodicals, Magazines

Able Engineering Services ....G....... 918 835-3161
  Tulsa *(G-9082)*
AGC Inc ....G....... 913 451-8900
  Oklahoma City *(G-5398)*
American Assn Petro Geologists ....D....... 918 584-2555
  Tulsa *(G-9164)*
C and H Publishing Co ....G....... 918 245-9571
  Sand Springs *(G-8169)*
Chastain Enterprises LLC ....G....... 918 615-9355
  Tulsa *(G-9407)*
Commercial Property Research ....G....... 918 481-8882
  Tulsa *(G-9476)*
Hoffman Printing LLC ....F....... 918 682-8341
  Muskogee *(G-4691)*
International Pro Rodeo Assn ....G....... 918 235-6540
  Oklahoma City *(G-6321)*
Meridian Press Publications ....G....... 405 751-2342
  Oklahoma City *(G-6568)*
Morning Fax ....G....... 918 357-5245
  Broken Arrow *(G-1145)*
Morris Communications Co LLC ....D....... 405 273-4200
  Shawnee *(G-8477)*
Oklahoma Bar Foundation Inc ....E....... 405 416-7000
  Oklahoma City *(G-6737)*
Oklahoma Electric Cooperative ....D....... 405 321-2024
  Norman *(G-5100)*
Oklahoma Grocers Association ....F....... 405 525-9419
  Oklahoma City *(G-6750)*
Oklahoma Magazine ....F....... 918 744-6205
  Tulsa *(G-10402)*
Oklahoma Propane Gas Assn ....G....... 405 424-1775
  Oklahoma City *(G-6758)*
Oklahoma Restaurant Assn ....F....... 405 942-8181
  Oklahoma City *(G-6761)*
Oklahoma Soc Prof Engineers ....G....... 405 528-1435
  Oklahoma City *(G-6763)*
Oklahoma State University ....C....... 405 744-5723
  Stillwater *(G-8733)*
Pigeon Debut ....G....... 405 686-0412
  Oklahoma City *(G-6848)*
Sheet Metal Contractors Assn ....G....... 405 848-3683
  Oklahoma City *(G-7119)*
Tulsa County Medical Society ....G....... 918 743-6184
  Tulsa *(G-10995)*
West Mattison Publishing Inc ....F....... 405 842-2266
  Edmond *(G-2684)*
World Organization China Pntrs ....E....... 405 521-1234
  Oklahoma City *(G-7470)*
Xzeno Productions ....G....... 405 974-4016
  Edmond *(G-2694)*

PUBLISHERS: Periodicals, No Printing

New Forums Press Inc ....G....... 405 372-6158
  Stillwater *(G-8727)*
Oral Rbrts Evnglistic Assn Inc ....D....... 918 591-2000
  Tulsa *(G-10436)*

PUBLISHERS: Racing Forms & Programs

Community Racks LLC ....F....... 405 210-7950
  Yukon *(G-11709)*

PUBLISHERS: Sheet Music

Rocking Chair Enterprises LLC ....G....... 918 455-3744
  Broken Arrow *(G-1037)*

PUBLISHERS: Shopping News

McCurtain County News Inc ....F....... 580 286-3321
  Idabel *(G-3642)*
Shopper News Note ....F....... 405 756-3169
  Lindsay *(G-4084)*
Show and Tell Times Inc ....G....... 918 225-4111
  Cushing *(G-1959)*

PUBLISHERS: Technical Manuals & Papers

Comptech Computer Tech Inc ....E....... 937 228-2667
  Oklahoma City *(G-5817)*
Document Imging Ntwrk Slutions ....G....... 405 818-3888
  Oklahoma City *(G-5956)*

PUBLISHERS: Technical Papers

Educational Concepts LLC ....F....... 918 749-0118
  Tulsa *(G-9644)*

PUBLISHERS: Telephone & Other Directory

User Friendly Phone Book LLC ....F....... 918 384-0224
  Tulsa *(G-11060)*

PUBLISHERS: Television Schedules, No Printing

Farley Redfield ....G....... 405 275-2266
  Tecumseh *(G-8914)*

PUBLISHERS: Textbooks, No Printing

World Energy Resources Inc ....G....... 405 375-6484
  Kingfisher *(G-3823)*

PUBLISHERS: Trade journals, No Printing

American Choral Directors Assn ....F....... 405 232-8161
  Oklahoma City *(G-5434)*

PUBLISHING & BROADCASTING: Internet Only

Ctsa LLC ....G....... 405 478-3501
  Edmond *(G-2377)*
Emerald Quest ....G....... 580 920-5917
  Durant *(G-2229)*
Finity Enterprises Inc ....G....... 580 699-2640
  Lawton *(G-3929)*
Flamingo Media Inc ....G....... 405 620-5889
  Oklahoma City *(G-5291)*
Fronttoback Studio LLC ....G....... 405 788-4400
  Oklahoma City *(G-6124)*
Gust Media LLC ....G....... 641 715-3900
  Edmond *(G-2449)*
N2r Media LLC ....G....... 405 301-0188
  Edmond *(G-2527)*
Osage County Treasurer ....G....... 918 287-3101
  Pawhuska *(G-7691)*
Ram Internet Media ....G....... 405 614-0641
  Stillwater *(G-8744)*

PUBLISHING & PRINTING: Books

Gregath Publishing Company ....G....... 918 542-4148
  Miami *(G-4407)*
Gregory Prizzell P & R M Inc ....G....... 405 752-0782
  Oklahoma City *(G-6192)*
Penielite Ggg Press ....G....... 405 850-5795
  McLoud *(G-4361)*
Tommy Higle Publishers ....G....... 580 276-5136
  Marietta *(G-4215)*

PUBLISHING & PRINTING: Catalogs

Bankers Online ....G....... 888 229-8872
  Edmond *(G-2316)*

PUBLISHING & PRINTING: Comic Books

Loud Graphic Studios LLC ....G....... 405 520-5349
  Edmond *(G-2497)*
Mastermind Comics ....G....... 315 308-0593
  Del City *(G-2000)*

PUBLISHING & PRINTING: Directories, NEC

Brown Publishing Inc ....G....... 405 842-5089
  Nichols Hills *(G-4856)*

PUBLISHING & PRINTING: Directories, Telephone

Souno LLC ....E....... 918 495-1771
  Tulsa *(G-10794)*

PUBLISHING & PRINTING: Magazines: publishing & printing

Clarion Events Inc ....C....... 918 835-3161
  Tulsa *(G-9438)*
Coast To Coast Power Spt LLC ....G....... 918 712-8487
  Tulsa *(G-9462)*
Datapages Inc ....G....... 918 584-2555
  Tulsa *(G-9555)*
Dharma Inc ....G....... 405 366-1336
  Norman *(G-4978)*
DPM Group LLC ....F....... 405 682-3468
  Oklahoma City *(G-5976)*
Editorial Grama Inc ....F....... 918 744-9502
  Tulsa *(G-9643)*
Pdqlipprints LLC ....G....... 580 233-3241
  Enid *(G-3033)*
Souno LLC ....E....... 918 495-1771
  Tulsa *(G-10794)*

Employee Codes: A=Over 500 employees, B=251-500
C=101-250, D=51-100, E=20-50, F=10-19, G=1-9

PUBLISHING & PRINTING: Magazines: publishing & printing

University of Oklahoma .... G 405 325-4531
  Norman *(G-5185)*

PUBLISHING & PRINTING: Newsletters, Business Svc

Ellis Enterprise .... G 405 826-3572
  Purcell *(G-8007)*

PUBLISHING & PRINTING: Newspapers

Aaron Lance Butler .... G 580 220-7715
  Ardmore *(G-235)*
Allen Advocate .... G 580 857-2687
  Allen *(G-132)*
American-Chief Co .... G 918 358-2553
  Cleveland *(G-1715)*
American-Chief Co .... G 918 885-2101
  Hominy *(G-3575)*
Anadarko Publishing Co .... E 405 247-3331
  Anadarko *(G-199)*
Ardmore Inc .... G 405 201-1288
  Ardmore *(G-247)*
Bam Journal LLC .... G 405 307-8220
  Norman *(G-4925)*
Beths Baubles and Bits .... G 405 659-3841
  Luther *(G-4134)*
Biggs Communications Inc .... G 918 523-4425
  Tulsa *(G-9295)*
Blackwell Wind .... G 580 363-0553
  Blackwell *(G-675)*
Buffalo Examiner .... G 580 326-3926
  Hugo *(G-3604)*
Christian Chronicle Inc .... G 405 425-5070
  Edmond *(G-2349)*
Clarence & Lois Parker .... G 580 765-8188
  Ponca City *(G-7806)*
Comanche Nation Pub Info Off .... G 580 492-3381
  Lawton *(G-3909)*
Comanche Sports Group LLC .... G 580 439-5230
  Comanche *(G-1838)*
Comanche Times .... G 580 439-6500
  Comanche *(G-1839)*
Country Connection News Inc .... G 405 797-3648
  Eakly *(G-2278)*
County Democrat .... G 405 273-8888
  Shawnee *(G-8441)*
Daily Dental Solutions Inc .... G 405 373-3299
  Piedmont *(G-7759)*
Daily Perk LLC .... G 405 567-5491
  Prague *(G-7924)*
Daily Stop .... G 405 495-5556
  Oklahoma City *(G-5889)*
Daily Times .... G 918 825-3292
  Pryor *(G-7957)*
Dan Quyen Newspaper .... G 405 691-2522
  Oklahoma City *(G-5283)*
Dartmouth Journal Service .... G 918 286-3513
  Tulsa *(G-9553)*
Deal USA Today LLC .... G 918 825-7835
  Pryor *(G-7959)*
Delaware County Journal Inc .... G 918 253-4322
  Jay *(G-3680)*
Democrat Chief Publishing Co .... G 580 726-3333
  Hobart *(G-3541)*
Driver Examiner Div .... G 580 762-1728
  Ponca City *(G-7824)*
Editorial Grama Inc .... F 918 744-9502
  Tulsa *(G-9643)*
El Latino American Inc .... G 405 632-1934
  Oklahoma City *(G-6016)*
El Reno Tribune .... G 405 262-7231
  El Reno *(G-2715)*
Fairfax Chief .... G 918 642-3814
  Fairfax *(G-3118)*
Ferguson & Ferguson .... G 918 358-2553
  Cleveland *(G-1723)*
Freedom Call LLC .... G 580 621-3578
  Freedom *(G-3206)*
G T R Newspapers Inc .... G 918 254-1515
  Tulsa *(G-9795)*
Gayly .... G 405 496-0011
  Oklahoma City *(G-6138)*
Greater Tlsa Rprter Newspapers .... G 918 743-3458
  Tulsa *(G-9855)*
Greater Tlsa Rprter Newspapers .... G 918 254-1515
  Tulsa *(G-9856)*
Herald James M and Teresa .... G 918 437-7016
  Tulsa *(G-9923)*
High Times Tulsa .... G 918 600-2110
  Tulsa *(G-9929)*
Hilton Herald Corp Oklahoma .... G 580 229-0132
  Healdton *(G-3414)*
Holdenville News .... G 405 379-5411
  Holdenville *(G-3554)*
Hugo Publishing Company .... G 580 326-3311
  Hugo *(G-3612)*
Humps N Horns Bull Riding News .... G 918 872-9713
  Broken Arrow *(G-932)*
Humps N Hrns Bull Rdng Nws LLC .... G 918 476-8213
  Chouteau *(G-1566)*
Imagine Durant Inc .... G 580 380-0743
  Durant *(G-2238)*
Indian Nations Communications .... G 918 696-2228
  Stilwell *(G-8791)*
Jim Roth .... G 405 235-4100
  Oklahoma City *(G-6363)*
Job Paper LLC .... G 405 242-4804
  Yukon *(G-11737)*
Journal Record .... G 405 524-7777
  Oklahoma City *(G-6387)*
Kimberling City Publishing Co .... E 918 756-3600
  Okmulgee *(G-7512)*
Lawton Media Inc .... C 580 355-8920
  Lawton *(G-3958)*
Lawton Newspapers LLC .... D 580 585-5115
  Lawton *(G-3959)*
Leader Tribune .... G 580 921-3391
  Laverne *(G-3879)*
Legal News .... G 918 259-7500
  Tulsa *(G-10150)*
Lincoln County Publishing Co .... F 405 258-1818
  Chandler *(G-1385)*
Lisa Snell .... G 918 708-5838
  Tahlequah *(G-8872)*
Lone Grove Ledger .... G 580 657-6492
  Lone Grove *(G-4118)*
Martin Broadcasting Corp .... E 580 327-1510
  Alva *(G-186)*
Metro Publishing LLC .... G 405 631-5100
  Oklahoma City *(G-6581)*
Miami Newspapers Inc .... E 918 542-5533
  Miami *(G-4417)*
Morris News .... G 918 733-4898
  Morris *(G-4600)*
Newspaper Holding Inc .... E 580 255-5354
  Duncan *(G-2159)*
Newspaper Holding Inc .... D 918 423-1700
  McAlester *(G-4324)*
Newspaper Holding Inc .... F 918 684-2922
  Muskogee *(G-4722)*
Newspaper Sales LLC .... G 918 357-5070
  Broken Arrow *(G-1146)*
Newspress Inc .... F 405 372-5000
  Stillwater *(G-8729)*
Oklahoma Newspaper Foundation .... E 405 499-0020
  Oklahoma City *(G-6756)*
Oklahoma Publishing Co of Okla .... E 405 475-3585
  Oklahoma City *(G-6759)*
Oklahoman Media Company .... F 405 475-3311
  Oklahoma City *(G-6765)*
Omni LLC .... G 405 246-9252
  Oklahoma City *(G-6777)*
Perry Dailey Journal Inc .... G 580 336-2222
  Perry *(G-7741)*
Ponca City Publishing Co Inc .... E 580 765-3311
  Ponca City *(G-7866)*
Prague Times Herald .... G 405 567-3933
  Prague *(G-7932)*
Randy Wyrick .... G 918 848-0117
  Fairland *(G-3128)*
Reporter Publishing Co Inc .... G 918 789-2331
  Chelsea *(G-1411)*
Review Printing Company Inc .... F 580 658-6657
  Marlow *(G-4241)*
Ringling Eagle .... G 580 662-2221
  Ringling *(G-8082)*
Rosemon Martin LLC .... G 918 272-7145
  Owasso *(G-7609)*
Salina Journal .... G 785 822-1470
  Collinsville *(G-1823)*
Sentinel Leader .... G 580 393-4348
  Sentinel *(G-8412)*
Shawnee News-Star .... G 405 273-4200
  Shawnee *(G-8495)*
Southeast Times .... G 580 286-2628
  Idabel *(G-3646)*
Star Nowata .... G 918 273-2446
  Nowata *(G-5230)*
Sun of A Beach .... G 918 938-6219
  Tulsa *(G-10871)*
Taloga Times Advocate .... G 580 328-5619
  Taloga *(G-8908)*
Times Star .... G 918 710-5740
  Collinsville *(G-1827)*
Times-Democrat Company Inc .... G 580 622-2102
  Sulphur *(G-8844)*
Tulsa World .... G 918 664-8683
  Tulsa *(G-11013)*
Tulsa World .... G 918 582-5921
  Tulsa *(G-11014)*
Tulsa World Capitol Bureau .... G 405 528-2465
  Oklahoma City *(G-7350)*
Vinita Printing Co Inc .... E 918 256-6422
  Vinita *(G-11271)*
Washita Valley Weekly .... G 405 224-7467
  Chickasha *(G-1522)*
Wewoka Times .... G 405 257-3341
  Wewoka *(G-11513)*

PUBLISHING & PRINTING: Pamphlets

Jomaga House .... G 918 455-0794
  Broken Arrow *(G-950)*

PUBLISHING & PRINTING: Periodical Statistical Reports

Oklahoma State University .... F 918 253-4332
  Jay *(G-3684)*

PUBLISHING & PRINTING: Trade Journals

International Journal of Ph .... F 405 330-0094
  Edmond *(G-2463)*

PULLEYS: Metal

Campbell Specialty Co Inc .... F 918 756-3640
  Okmulgee *(G-7497)*

PULP MILLS: Kraft Sulfate Pulp

S Kat Embroidery & Quilting .... G 405 200-6283
  Chickasha *(G-1505)*

PULP MILLS: Mechanical & Recycling Processing

Custom Yarmuck Scrap Proc LLC .... G 580 354-9134
  Lawton *(G-3916)*
J and S Trucking Company .... G 580 216-7213
  Woodward *(G-11595)*

PULP MILLS: Soda Pulp

Okc Soda Co LLC .... G 405 628-9543
  Oklahoma City *(G-6730)*

PUMP JACKS & OTHER PUMPING EQPT: Indl

Additive Systems Inc .... F 918 357-3433
  Broken Arrow *(G-814)*
Rod Pump Consulting LLC .... G 918 306-2318
  Cushing *(G-1956)*

PUMPS

Accelated Artfl List Systems .... F 405 207-9449
  Pauls Valley *(G-7649)*
Bartling Pumps & Supplies LLC .... G 580 444-2227
  Duncan *(G-2087)*
Blackhawk Industrial Dist Inc .... C 918 610-4700
  Broken Arrow *(G-853)*
Burleson Pump Company .... G 405 677-6881
  Oklahoma City *(G-5645)*
Climate Control Group Inc .... E 405 745-6858
  Oklahoma City *(G-5786)*
Design Ready Controls Inc .... F 405 605-8234
  Oklahoma City *(G-5926)*
Eddies Submersible Service Inc .... F 405 273-9292
  Tecumseh *(G-8913)*
Excel Products .... G 580 216-0784
  Woodward *(G-11582)*
Fabricating Specialists Inc .... F 405 476-1959
  Oklahoma City *(G-6068)*
Flowserve Corporation .... B 918 627-8400
  Tulsa *(G-9760)*
Flowserve US Inc .... C 918 599-6000
  Tulsa *(G-9761)*
Floyds Machine Shop .... G 918 256-8440
  Vinita *(G-11258)*
Franklin Electric Co Inc .... B 501 455-1234
  Oklahoma City *(G-6113)*

PRODUCT SECTION

Franklin Electric Co Inc .... B 918 465-2348
  Wilburton *(G-11520)*
Fts International Services LLC .... F 405 574-3900
  Chickasha *(G-1460)*
Harley Industries Inc .... G 918 451-2323
  Tulsa *(G-9892)*
HEanderson Company .... F 918 687-4426
  Muskogee *(G-4688)*
Idex Corporation .... D 405 609-1116
  Oklahoma City *(G-6288)*
Industrial Dist Resources LLC .... G 239 591-3777
  Tulsa *(G-9979)*
John Crane Inc .... D 918 664-5156
  Tulsa *(G-10049)*
John Crane Lemco Inc .... E 918 835-7325
  Tulsa *(G-10050)*
K & S Pumping Unit Repair Inc .... F 580 237-7343
  Enid *(G-2991)*
Kimray Inc .... C 405 525-6601
  Oklahoma City *(G-6417)*
Lloyd Edge .... G 580 726-2905
  Hobart *(G-3543)*
O K Plunger Service .... G 918 352-4269
  Drumright *(G-2068)*
Odum Machine & Tool Inc .... G 918 663-6966
  Tulsa *(G-10377)*
Oil States Industries Inc .... D 405 671-2000
  Oklahoma City *(G-6721)*
Oil States Industries Inc .... G 918 250-0828
  Tulsa *(G-10387)*
Perkins South Plains Inc .... E 405 685-4630
  Oklahoma City *(G-6832)*
Philip Lewis .... G 918 850-6195
  Tulsa *(G-10509)*
Pinion Manufacturing & Supply .... F 918 437-5428
  Tulsa *(G-10516)*
Pomco Inc .... F 405 677-8859
  Oklahoma City *(G-6863)*
Practical Sales and Svc Inc .... G 918 446-5515
  Tulsa *(G-10540)*
Pump Shop .... G 918 834-8829
  Tulsa *(G-10583)*
RC Pumps LLC .... G 580 444-2227
  Ratliff City *(G-8064)*
Robbins & Myers Inc .... G 405 672-6793
  Oklahoma City *(G-7033)*
Sentry Pump Units Intl LLC .... G 405 635-1800
  Oklahoma City *(G-7110)*
Sercel-Grc Corp .... C 918 834-9600
  Tulsa *(G-10733)*
Silverback Pump & Anchor LLC .... G 405 756-1148
  Lindsay *(G-4085)*
Solar Power & Pump Company LLC .. F 580 225-1704
  Elk City *(G-2874)*
Special Equipment Mfg Inc .... E 580 252-5111
  Duncan *(G-2183)*
Stanley Filter Company LLC .... G 800 545-9926
  Tulsa *(G-10838)*
Summit Esp LLC .... B 918 392-7820
  Tulsa *(G-10866)*
Total Pump and Supply LLC .... G 405 670-0333
  Oklahoma City *(G-7309)*
Triangle Pump Components Inc .... F 405 672-6900
  Oklahoma City *(G-7327)*
Tulsa Rubber Co .... F 918 627-1371
  Tulsa *(G-11006)*

PUMPS & PARTS: Indl

Bg & S Manufacturing .... E 918 396-3525
  Skiatook *(G-8533)*
Gardner Denver Inc .... D 918 664-1151
  Tulsa *(G-9800)*
Ideas Manufacturing Inc .... G 405 691-5525
  Oklahoma City *(G-5296)*
Montross Tirita .... G 918 241-5637
  Sand Springs *(G-8207)*
Premierflow LLC .... E 918 346-6312
  Tulsa *(G-10554)*
Scorpion Pump and Indus LLC 785 285-1421
  Tecumseh *(G-8927)*

PUMPS & PUMPING EQPT REPAIR SVCS

Ameripump Mfg LLC .... G 405 438-2953
  Tulsa *(G-9178)*
Asher Oilfield Specialty Inc .... G 405 677-7868
  Oklahoma City *(G-5475)*
Bartosh Electric Motor Center .... G 405 567-2840
  Prague *(G-7920)*
Bg & S Manufacturing .... E 918 396-3525
  Skiatook *(G-8533)*

GE Oil & Gas Esp Inc .... C 405 670-1431
  Oklahoma City *(G-6140)*
GE Oil & Gas Esp Inc .... E 405 527-1566
  Purcell *(G-8009)*
Global Oilfield Services LLC .... E 405 741-0163
  Oklahoma City *(G-6161)*
North Central Pump .... G 580 765-9348
  Ponca City *(G-7860)*
Production Engine & Pump Inc .... F 405 672-3644
  Oklahoma City *(G-6910)*
Summit Esp LLC .... B 918 392-7820
  Tulsa *(G-10866)*
T C Whilden Consulting Inc .... F 405 677-6881
  Oklahoma City *(G-7243)*
Thompson Pump Company .... G 918 352-2117
  Drumright *(G-2075)*

PUMPS & PUMPING EQPT WHOLESALERS

Apergy ESP Systems LLC .... D 918 396-0558
  Broken Arrow *(G-1110)*
Bg & S Manufacturing .... E 918 396-3525
  Skiatook *(G-8533)*
Integrity Pump & Supply LLC .... G 405 422-2828
  El Reno *(G-2726)*
Lufkin Industries LLC .... F 405 677-0567
  Oklahoma City *(G-6501)*
Premier Chem & Oilfld Sup LLC .... F 405 893-2321
  Enid *(G-3038)*
Smith Pump Supply .... G 405 258-0834
  Chandler *(G-1387)*
Solar Power & Pump Company LLC .. F 580 225-1704
  Elk City *(G-2874)*
Triangle Pump Components Inc .... F 405 672-6900
  Oklahoma City *(G-7327)*

PUMPS, HEAT: Electric

Climate Master Inc .... A 405 745-6000
  Oklahoma City *(G-5787)*
Summit Esp LLC .... G 918 392-7820
  Enid *(G-3064)*
Summit Esp LLC .... B 405 434-1257
  Norman *(G-5165)*

PUMPS: Domestic, Water Or Sump

C & B Pump Rebuilders .... G 405 789-4808
  Oklahoma City *(G-5654)*
Franklin Electric Co Inc .... G 405 947-2511
  Oklahoma City *(G-6112)*
Global Oilfield Services Inc .... F 918 885-4024
  Hominy *(G-3585)*
Global Oilfield Services LLC .... E 405 741-0163
  Oklahoma City *(G-6161)*
Hfe Process Inc .... G 918 663-9083
  Inola *(G-3661)*
Little Giant Pump Company LLC .... B 405 947-2511
  Oklahoma City *(G-6483)*
Thomas Water Well Service .... G 580 938-2224
  Shattuck *(G-8425)*

PUMPS: Hydraulic Power Transfer

Evco Service Co Inc .... E 405 381-2172
  Tuttle *(G-11198)*
National Oilwell Varco Inc .... G 713 346-7500
  Oklahoma City *(G-6658)*

PUMPS: Measuring & Dispensing

Bartec Dispensing Tech Inc .... G 918 250-6496
  Tulsa *(G-9269)*
HEanderson Company .... F 918 687-4426
  Muskogee *(G-4688)*
Integrity Pump & Supply LLC .... G 405 422-2828
  El Reno *(G-2726)*

PUMPS: Oil Well & Field

Baker Hughes A GE Company LLC ... C 918 828-1600
  Tulsa *(G-9255)*
Blm Equipment & Mfg Co Inc .... F 918 266-5282
  Catoosa *(G-1304)*
Larkin Products LLC .... G 918 584-3475
  Tulsa *(G-10129)*
National Oilwell Varco Inc .... G 918 423-8000
  McAlester *(G-4323)*
Pump & Seal Improvements .... G 918 747-7742
  Tulsa *(G-10582)*
Superior Spling Enrgy Svcs LLC ...... G 405 613-0329
  Purcell *(G-8021)*

RADIO & TELEVISION COMMUNICATIONS EQUIPMENT

T C Whilden Consulting Inc .... F 405 677-6881
  Oklahoma City *(G-7243)*
Thompson Pump Company .... F 918 756-6164
  Okmulgee *(G-7527)*
Tony Gosnell Operating .... G 405 756-8091
  Lindsay *(G-4094)*
Tpl Southtex Gas Utility Co LP .... E 918 574-3500
  Tulsa *(G-10963)*
Whites Welding LLC .... C 580 254-3766
  Woodward *(G-11652)*

PURIFIERS: Centrifugal

Ect Services Inc .... G 918 691-9320
  Sand Springs *(G-8181)*

PURSES: Women's

Sew N Saw .... G 405 282-2241
  Guthrie *(G-3337)*

QUARTZ CRYSTALS: Electronic

Sentry Manufacturing Company .... E 202 262-0225
  Chickasha *(G-1507)*

QUILTING SVC

Adairs Sleep World Inc .... F 405 341-9468
  Edmond *(G-2289)*

QUILTING SVC & SPLYS, FOR THE TRADE

Doris Winford .... G 918 599-8931
  Tulsa *(G-9598)*
Spinning Star Design .... G 405 359-3965
  Edmond *(G-2627)*
Tin Roof Quilting LLC .... G 918 551-7282
  Tulsa *(G-10944)*

QUILTING: Individuals

Christys Quilts .... G 405 853-2155
  Hennessey *(G-3450)*
Debbie Do EMB & Screen Prtg .... G 580 353-2606
  Lawton *(G-3918)*
Doris Winford .... G 918 599-8931
  Tulsa *(G-9598)*

RACEWAYS

405 R/C Raceway & Hobbies LLC ..... G 405 503-0364
  Oklahoma City *(G-5334)*
Lawton RC Raceway LLC .... G 580 595-0814
  Lawton *(G-3960)*
Raceway Electric Inc .... F 918 629-4252
  Catoosa *(G-1348)*
Reynard Promotions LLC .... G 405 793-1049
  Wellston *(G-11476)*
Wichita Raceway Park .... G 580 704-0341
  Lawton *(G-4022)*

RADAR SYSTEMS & EQPT

O & L Resources Inc .... G 918 789-5553
  Chelsea *(G-1408)*
Raytheon Company .... C 580 351-6966
  Lawton *(G-3989)*

RADIATORS, EXC ELECTRIC

Morton Manufacturing Co Inc .... G 918 584-0333
  Tulsa *(G-10305)*
R & R Radiator Co .... G 405 257-3557
  Wewoka *(G-11508)*

RADIO & TELEVISION COMMUNICATIONS EQUIPMENT

Channel One Lighting Systems .... G 918 587-2663
  Tulsa *(G-9404)*
Ducommun Labarge Tech Inc .... C 918 459-2200
  Tulsa *(G-9611)*
Lamar Systems LLC .... G 918 770-0941
  Tulsa *(G-10118)*
Me3 Communications Company LLC . G 405 834-8992
  Oklahoma City *(G-6553)*
Monitron Corp .... F 918 836-6831
  Sand Springs *(G-8206)*
Oklahoma Community TV LLC .... G 405 808-2509
  Oklahoma City *(G-6744)*
Southern Plains Cable LLC .... G 580 529-5000
  Lawton *(G-4000)*

Employee Codes: A=Over 500 employees, B=251-500
C=101-250, D=51-100, E=20-50, F=10-19, G=1-9

RADIO & TELEVISION COMMUNICATIONS EQUIPMENT

Tyler Enterprises ....G....... 405 616-5500
Oklahoma City *(G-7354)*

RADIO BROADCASTING & COMMUNICATIONS EQPT

Carc Inc ....G....... 918 266-1341
Catoosa *(G-1308)*
Louis Systems & Products Inc ....G....... 405 285-0950
Edmond *(G-2498)*

RADIO BROADCASTING STATIONS

Newspress Inc ....F....... 405 372-5000
Stillwater *(G-8729)*

RADIO, TELEVISION & CONSUMER ELECTRONICS STORES: Eqpt, NEC

Instinct Performance LLC ....G....... 405 463-7300
Oklahoma City *(G-6312)*

RADIO, TELEVISION/CONSUMER ELEC STORES: Video Cameras/Access

Dark Peek Technologies LLC ....G....... 405 316-8551
Edmond *(G-2379)*

RADIO, TV & CONSUMER ELEC STORES: Automotive Sound Eqpt

Fred Jones Enterprises LLC ....E....... 800 927-7845
Oklahoma City *(G-6114)*

RADIO, TV & CONSUMER ELEC STORES: High Fidelity Stereo Eqpt

Cambridge Soundworks Inc ....C....... 405 742-6704
Stillwater *(G-8665)*

RAILINGS: Prefabricated, Metal

York Metal Fabricators Inc ....E....... 405 528-7495
Oklahoma City *(G-7481)*

RAILROAD CARGO LOADING & UNLOADING SVCS

Casing Crews Incorporated ....D....... 580 388-4567
Lamont *(G-3864)*

RAILROAD EQPT

Industrial Structures Inc ....E....... 918 341-0300
Tulsa *(G-9982)*
Railroad Sgnling Solutions Inc ....G....... 918 973-1888
Broken Arrow *(G-1020)*
Tag Okc Inc ....G....... 405 685-7728
Oklahoma City *(G-7248)*

RAILROAD EQPT, EXC LOCOMOTIVES

Amerities Holdings LLC ....D....... 405 359-3235
Edmond *(G-2303)*
Amerities South LLC ....F....... 405 359-3235
Edmond *(G-2304)*

RAILROAD EQPT: Cars, Maintenance

Big 3 Woodyard Inc ....G....... 580 298-6123
Antlers *(G-214)*
Freedom Railcar Solutions LLC ....F....... 405 256-6780
Mustang *(G-4772)*

RAILROAD EQPT: Cars, Tank Freight & Eqpt

Trinity Tank Car Inc ....F....... 405 629-1226
Oklahoma City *(G-7335)*

RAILROAD MAINTENANCE & REPAIR SVCS

Harsco Corporation ....E....... 918 619-8000
Tulsa *(G-9899)*

REAL ESTATE AGENCIES & BROKERS

Frank Priegel Co ....G....... 918 756-3161
Okmulgee *(G-7502)*

REAL ESTATE AGENCIES: Leasing & Rentals

H W Allen Co LLC ....E....... 918 747-8700
Tulsa *(G-9877)*

Swiftwater Energy Services LLC ....G....... 405 820-7612
Oklahoma City *(G-7238)*

REAL ESTATE AGENCIES: Residential

Perkins Development Corp ....G....... 918 749-2152
Tulsa *(G-10495)*

REAL ESTATE AGENTS & MANAGERS

J & M Investment ....G....... 405 848-3755
Oklahoma City *(G-6332)*
Jim Campbell & Associates Rlty ....G....... 405 372-9225
Stillwater *(G-8707)*
K W B Inc ....E....... 918 583-8300
Tulsa *(G-10069)*
Rbc Exploration Company ....G....... 918 744-5607
Tulsa *(G-10623)*
Seminole Oilfield Supply ....G....... 918 623-9900
Okemah *(G-5275)*

REAL ESTATE OPERATORS, EXC DEVELOPERS: Commercial/Indl Bldg

Adams Affiliates Inc ....F....... 918 582-7713
Tulsa *(G-9101)*
Colston Corporation ....G....... 580 223-1309
Ardmore *(G-269)*
Nutopia Nuts & More ....G....... 405 663-2330
Hydro *(G-3633)*
Quiktrip Corporation ....B....... 918 615-7700
Tulsa *(G-10599)*
Sitrin Petroleum Corp ....G....... 918 747-1111
Tulsa *(G-10770)*
Stars Restaurants LLC ....E....... 405 947-1396
Edmond *(G-2631)*
Toomey Oil Company Inc ....G....... 918 583-1166
Tulsa *(G-10954)*

RECORDS & TAPES: Prerecorded

Broken Arrow Productions Inc ....E....... 405 360-8702
Norman *(G-4944)*
El Jay Enterprises Inc ....G....... 918 836-8273
Tulsa *(G-9649)*

RECORDS OR TAPES: Masters

Melody House Inc ....G....... 405 840-3383
Oklahoma City *(G-6562)*

RECOVERY OR EXTRACTION SVCS: Explosives

Hman Global Solutions LLC ....G....... 405 338-5348
Morrison *(G-4603)*

RECOVERY SVC: Silver, From Used Photographic Film

Brown Metals ....G....... 405 321-6866
Norman *(G-4946)*
Oklahoma Industrial Silver ....G....... 405 341-6021
Edmond *(G-2551)*

RECREATIONAL VEHICLE DEALERS

Allen Camper Mfg Company Inc ....E....... 580 857-2177
Allen *(G-133)*
Sander Sporting Gds & Atvs LLC ....G....... 580 922-4930
Seiling *(G-8351)*

RECTIFIERS: Electrical Apparatus

Power Cable Solutions LLC ....G....... 405 818-1993
Tuttle *(G-11207)*

RECYCLABLE SCRAP & WASTE MATERIALS WHOLESALERS

Hite Plastics Inc ....E....... 405 297-9818
Oklahoma City *(G-6255)*
We Buy Scrap LLC ....G....... 580 401-3083
Ponca City *(G-7887)*

RECYCLING: Paper

Paper Plus ....G....... 405 948-1120
Oklahoma City *(G-6802)*

REFINERS & SMELTERS: Aluminum

Real Alloy Recycling LLC ....C....... 918 224-4746
Sapulpa *(G-8305)*

REFINERS & SMELTERS: Babbit Metal, Secondary

Identity & Tanning Salon ....G....... 412 269-7879
Tuttle *(G-11204)*

REFINERS & SMELTERS: Germanium, Primary

Umicore Optical Mtls USA Inc ....D....... 918 673-1650
Quapaw *(G-8034)*

REFINERS & SMELTERS: Nonferrous Metal

Borg Compressed Steel Corp ....D....... 918 587-2437
Tulsa *(G-9321)*
Durant Iron & Metal Inc ....E....... 580 924-0595
Durant *(G-2226)*
Metal Check Inc ....F....... 405 636-1916
Oklahoma City *(G-6573)*
Mid America Alloys LLC ....E....... 918 224-3446
Sapulpa *(G-8288)*
Rolled Alloys Inc ....E....... 918 594-2600
Tulsa *(G-9031)*
Tms International LLC ....G....... 918 241-0129
Sand Springs *(G-8230)*

REFINERS & SMELTERS: Silver

Oklahoma Industrial Silver ....G....... 405 341-6021
Edmond *(G-2551)*

REFINERS & SMELTERS: Zinc, Primary, Including Slabs & Dust

American Zinc Recycling Corp ....D....... 918 336-7100
Bartlesville *(G-447)*

REFINING: Petroleum

Airgas Usa LLC ....G....... 405 372-7720
Stillwater *(G-8652)*
Alice Kidd LLC ....G....... 405 401-4391
Hinton *(G-3520)*
Anchor Gasoline Corporation ....D....... 918 584-5291
Tulsa *(G-9184)*
Axel Royal LLC ....E....... 918 584-2671
Tulsa *(G-9233)*
Caulumet Ore Co ....G....... 580 673-2815
Healdton *(G-3409)*
Conoco Inc ....G....... 580 767-3456
Ponca City *(G-7808)*
Conocophillips ....B....... 918 977-6002
Bartlesville *(G-467)*
Cvr Energy Inc ....F....... 913 982-0500
Wynnewood *(G-11666)*
Enable Okla Intrstate Trnsm LL ....C....... 405 525-7788
Oklahoma City *(G-6033)*
Envia Energy Oklahoma City LLC ....G....... 405 427-0790
Oklahoma City *(G-6043)*
Heater Fabricators Tulsa LLC ....E....... 918 430-1127
Tulsa *(G-9908)*
Henke Petroleum Corp ....G....... 405 878-0909
Shawnee *(G-8460)*
Holly Ref & Mktg - Tulsa LLC ....F....... 918 445-0056
Tulsa *(G-9940)*
Hollyfrontier Corporation ....B....... 918 581-1800
Tulsa *(G-9942)*
Liquefied Petro Gas Bd Okla ....F....... 405 521-2458
Oklahoma City *(G-6482)*
Messer LLC ....F....... 580 254-2259
Woodward *(G-11606)*
Mustang Fuel Corporation ....E....... 405 748-9400
Oklahoma City *(G-6640)*
Oxbow Calcining LLC ....F....... 580 874-2201
Kremlin *(G-3854)*
Phillips 66 Company ....G....... 580 767-3456
Ponca City *(G-7865)*
Samson Resources Company ....D....... 918 583-1791
Tulsa *(G-10696)*
Sinclair Companies ....E....... 405 637-8444
Shawnee *(G-8499)*
Sunoco (R&m) LLC ....F....... 918 586-6246
Tulsa *(G-10873)*
Texoak Petro Holdings LLC ....G....... 918 592-1010
Tulsa *(G-10921)*

PRODUCT SECTION — RESEARCH, DEVELOPMENT & TESTING SVCS, COMMERCIAL: Education

Tpi Petroleum Inc .... C 580 221-6288
  Ardmore *(G-373)*
WRB Refining LP .... E 918 977-6600
  Bartlesville *(G-537)*
Wynnewood Refining Company LLC .... E 405 665-6565
  Wynnewood *(G-11677)*

REFRACTORIES: Brick

Commercial Brick Corporation .... C 405 257-6613
  Wewoka *(G-11498)*

REFRACTORIES: Cement, nonclay

Acid Specialists LLC .... G 432 617-2243
  Oklahoma City *(G-5366)*

REFRACTORIES: Clay

Harbisonwalker Intl Inc .... G 918 825-1044
  Pryor *(G-7965)*
Meridian Brick LLC .... G 918 258-7533
  Broken Arrow *(G-971)*
Meridian Brick LLC .... G 405 749-9900
  Oklahoma City *(G-6567)*
Quikrete Companies LLC .... E 405 787-2050
  Oklahoma City *(G-6953)*

REFRACTORIES: Nonclay

Bpi Inc .... G 918 682-5044
  Muskogee *(G-4654)*
Mike Alexander Company Inc .... E 580 765-8085
  Tulsa *(G-10276)*
Quikrete Companies LLC .... E 405 787-2050
  Oklahoma City *(G-6953)*
Refractory Anchors Inc .... E 918 455-8485
  Broken Arrow *(G-1154)*

REFRACTORY MATERIALS WHOLESALERS

Thermal Specialties LLC .... F 918 227-4800
  Tulsa *(G-9044)*

REFRIGERATION & HEATING EQUIPMENT

Alfa Laval Inc .... G 918 251-7477
  Broken Arrow *(G-824)*
Alterntive Gthrmal Sltions Inc .... G 405 948-0410
  Oklahoma City *(G-5427)*
C & B Construction .... G 918 696-4476
  Stilwell *(G-8782)*
Clarios .... A 405 419-5400
  Norman *(G-4959)*
Everest Sciences An S T Co LLC .... F 918 770-7190
  Tulsa *(G-9710)*
International Envmtl Corp .... C 405 605-5024
  Oklahoma City *(G-6319)*
Jack Mangum .... G 580 658-2700
  Marlow *(G-4234)*
Jim Wood Refrigeration Inc .... G 918 426-3283
  McAlester *(G-4309)*
Joshua James Lennox .... G 580 739-1050
  Elk City *(G-2834)*
Lennox Nas .... G 405 370-7001
  Broken Arrow *(G-966)*
Lenox Leasing LLC .... G 405 664-5240
  Oklahoma City *(G-5303)*
National Climate Solutions .... F 844 682-4247
  Tulsa *(G-10326)*
Praxair Distribution Inc .... E 918 266-3210
  Claremore *(G-1673)*
Sierra Technologies Inc .... F 918 445-1090
  Tulsa *(G-10754)*
Specific Systems Ltd .... C 918 663-9321
  Tulsa *(G-10817)*
Trane US Inc .... G 918 250-5522
  Broken Arrow *(G-1079)*
Trane US Inc .... G 855 200-0072
  Broken Arrow *(G-1080)*
Trane US Inc .... G 405 943-6600
  Oklahoma City *(G-7315)*
Trane US Inc .... E 405 787-2237
  Oklahoma City *(G-7316)*
Trane US Inc .... E 405 787-2237
  Broken Arrow *(G-1081)*
Universal Compression Inc .... G 918 742-1801
  Tulsa *(G-11047)*
Washita Refrigeration & Eqp Co .... E 800 235-9476
  Milburn *(G-4464)*
York International Corporation .... D 405 942-9675
  Oklahoma City *(G-7480)*

REFRIGERATION EQPT & SPLYS WHOLESALERS

Washita Refrigeration & Eqp Co .... E 800 235-9476
  Milburn *(G-4464)*

REFRIGERATION EQPT & SPLYS, WHOLESALE: Ice Making Machines

Clinton Ice LLC .... F 580 331-6060
  Clinton *(G-1746)*

REFRIGERATION EQPT: Complete

Rae Corporation .... B 918 825-7222
  Pryor *(G-7988)*

REFRIGERATION REPAIR SVCS

Washita Refrigeration & Eqp Co .... E 800 235-9476
  Milburn *(G-4464)*

REFRIGERATION SVC & REPAIR

Bartosh Electric Motor Center .... G 405 567-2840
  Prague *(G-7920)*
Lahmeyer Pattern Shop .... G 918 425-6008
  Tulsa *(G-10112)*
Tulsa Sheet Metal Inc .... F 918 587-3141
  Tulsa *(G-11007)*

REFUSE SYSTEMS

Henryetta Pallet Company .... E 918 652-9897
  Henryetta *(G-3508)*

REGULATORS: Transmission & Distribution Voltage

Asc Inc .... E 918 445-0260
  Tulsa *(G-9215)*

REMOTE DATABASE INFORMATION RETRIEVAL SVCS

Fjsp Inc .... G 405 306-0735
  Oklahoma City *(G-6087)*

REMOVERS & CLEANERS

Cooper Consulting LLC .... G 918 427-7171
  Muldrow *(G-4632)*
Ultimate Chemicals LLC .... E 405 703-2771
  Moore *(G-4581)*

REMOVERS: Paint

Aerochem Inc .... G 405 440-0380
  Oklahoma City *(G-5391)*
Mann Solvents Inc .... G 918 626-3733
  Arkoma *(G-386)*

RENT-A-CAR SVCS

Jims Truck Center .... G 918 225-1013
  Cushing *(G-1939)*

RENTAL CENTERS: Tools

Hough Oilfield Service Inc .... E 918 225-1851
  Cushing *(G-1936)*
Sooner Tool Company .... G 918 352-4440
  Drumright *(G-2071)*

RENTAL SVCS: Business Machine & Electronic Eqpt

H2 Services LLC .... E 405 388-9049
  Guthrie *(G-3317)*
Onedoc Managed Print Svcs LLC .... G 405 633-3050
  Oklahoma City *(G-6778)*

RENTAL SVCS: Costume

American Entps Whl Dstributers .... G 405 273-4516
  Shawnee *(G-8427)*

RENTAL SVCS: Invalid Splys

Mobility One Transportation .... G 918 437-4488
  Tulsa *(G-10289)*

RENTAL SVCS: Mobile Communication Eqpt

Indian Nations Fiberoptics Inc .... G 580 355-2300
  Lawton *(G-3941)*

RENTAL SVCS: Mobile Home, Exc On Site

Hollands Mobile Homes .... G 918 476-5663
  Chouteau *(G-1565)*

RENTAL SVCS: Office Facilities & Secretarial Svcs

Project 3810 LLC .... G 405 834-7418
  Oklahoma City *(G-6914)*

RENTAL SVCS: Oil Eqpt

BOp Ram-Block Ir Rentals Inc .... D 580 772-0250
  Weatherford *(G-11394)*
Key Energy Services Inc .... F 806 435-5583
  Woodward *(G-11602)*
Special Equipment Mfg Inc .... E 580 252-5111
  Duncan *(G-2183)*

RENTAL SVCS: Photographic Eqpt

Marvel Photo Inc .... G 918 836-0741
  Tulsa *(G-10218)*

RENTAL SVCS: Propane Eqpt

Csi Compressco Sub Inc .... G 918 250-9471
  Tulsa *(G-9518)*

RENTAL SVCS: Trailer

Outlaw Oilfield Supply LLC .... E 580 526-3792
  Erick *(G-3091)*

REPAIR SERVICES, NEC

A-1 Sure Shot .... F 405 677-9800
  Oklahoma City *(G-5353)*
American Drones LLC .... G 405 308-0866
  Moore *(G-4487)*

REPRODUCTION SVCS: Video Tape Or Disk

Big Productions LLC .... G 405 513-6545
  Edmond *(G-2321)*
El Jay Enterprises Inc .... G 918 836-8273
  Tulsa *(G-9649)*
Graphic Rsources Reproductions .... F 918 461-0303
  Broken Arrow *(G-921)*

RESEARCH, DEVELOPMENT & TEST SVCS, COMM: Cmptr Hardware Dev

New X Drive Tech Inc .... G 918 850-4463
  Tulsa *(G-10337)*

RESEARCH, DEVELOPMENT & TEST SVCS, COMM: Research, Exc Lab

Writers Research Group LLC .... F 405 682-2589
  Oklahoma City *(G-7474)*

RESEARCH, DEVELOPMENT & TESTING SVCS, COMM: Agricultural

Flir Detection Inc .... E 405 533-6618
  Stillwater *(G-8689)*

RESEARCH, DEVELOPMENT & TESTING SVCS, COMM: Research Lab

Design Intelligence Inc LLC .... G 405 307-0397
  Noble *(G-4878)*
New X Drives Inc .... F 918 850-4463
  Tulsa *(G-10338)*
Thurmond-Mcglothlin LLC .... G 580 774-2659
  Weatherford *(G-11446)*

RESEARCH, DEVELOPMENT & TESTING SVCS, COMMERCIAL: Education

New X Drives Inc .... F 918 850-4463
  Tulsa *(G-10338)*

Employee Codes: A=Over 500 employees, B=251-500
C=101-250, D=51-100, E=20-50, F=10-19, G=1-9

RESEARCH, DVLPT & TEST SVCS, COMM: Mkt Analysis or Research

Majeska & Associates LLC ....F....... 918 576-6878
Tulsa *(G-10204)*

RESIDENTIAL CARE FOR THE HANDICAPPED

Apex Inc ....E....... 405 247-7377
Anadarko *(G-200)*
Think Ability Inc ....C....... 580 252-8000
Duncan *(G-2187)*

RESIDENTIAL REMODELERS

A P & R Industries Inc ....F....... 405 702-7661
Oklahoma City *(G-5347)*
L & S Seamless Guttering Inc ....G....... 405 392-4487
Blanchard *(G-719)*

RESIDUES

James Land Residual Assets LLC .....G....... 405 842-2828
Oklahoma City *(G-6349)*

RESINS: Custom Compound Purchased

Hite Plastics Inc ....E....... 405 297-9818
Oklahoma City *(G-6255)*
Quikrete Companies LLC ....E....... 405 787-2050
Oklahoma City *(G-6953)*

RESISTORS

Okluma LLC ....G....... 580 716-1343
Oklahoma City *(G-6767)*

RESTAURANT EQPT: Carts

Restaurant Equipment & Sup LLC ....G....... 918 664-1778
Tulsa *(G-10648)*

RESTAURANT EQPT: Food Wagons

Beefys Beastro Food Svc LLC ....G....... 580 491-0325
Broken Arrow *(G-844)*

RESTAURANT EQPT: Sheet Metal

Captive-Aire Systems Inc ....F....... 918 258-0291
Tulsa *(G-9373)*

RESTAURANTS: Delicatessen

Felinis Cookies Inc ....G....... 918 742-3638
Tulsa *(G-9734)*

RESTAURANTS: Full Svc, American

El Reno Bowl Inc ....G....... 405 262-3611
El Reno *(G-2714)*
Nutopia Nuts & More ....G....... 405 663-2330
Hydro *(G-3633)*

RESTAURANTS: Full Svc, Barbecue

Billy Sims Barbeque LLC ....E....... 918 258-1978
Broken Arrow *(G-852)*
Jiggs Smokehouse ....G....... 580 323-5641
Clinton *(G-1754)*
Latimers Barbeque ....G....... 918 425-1242
Tulsa *(G-10134)*

RESTAURANTS: Full Svc, Italian

Pasta Pizzaz Inc ....G....... 405 848-9966
Oklahoma City *(G-6808)*

RESTAURANTS: Full Svc, Steak & Barbecue

Flaming Hope LLC ....G....... 405 924-4380
Noble *(G-4880)*

RESTAURANTS: Limited Svc, Coffee Shop

Viridian Coffee LLC ....G....... 405 795-0773
Duncan *(G-2195)*

RESTAURANTS: Limited Svc, Drive-In

Stars Restaurants LLC ....E....... 405 947-1396
Edmond *(G-2631)*

RESTAURANTS: Limited Svc, Grill

Downtown Pub ....F....... 918 274-8202
Owasso *(G-7563)*

RESTAURANTS: Limited Svc, Soft Drink Stand

Webers Superior Root Beer Inc ....G....... 918 742-1082
Tulsa *(G-11101)*

RETAIL BAKERY: Bread

Tulsa Baking Inc ....E....... 918 747-2301
Tulsa *(G-10989)*

RETAIL BAKERY: Cakes

Tulsa Baking Inc ....D....... 918 712-2918
Tulsa *(G-10988)*

RETAIL BAKERY: Doughnuts

Dandy Donuts ....G....... 580 924-7872
Durant *(G-2220)*
Daylight Donuts ....G....... 918 256-6236
Vinita *(G-11252)*
Daylight Donuts ....G....... 405 598-8707
Tecumseh *(G-8911)*
Daylight Donuts ....G....... 580 279-6560
Ada *(G-31)*
Daylight Donuts Inc ....G....... 405 359-9016
Edmond *(G-2384)*
Krispy Kreme ....G....... 918 294-5293
Tulsa *(G-10103)*
Legend Enterprises Inc ....G....... 405 340-0410
Edmond *(G-2486)*
Paradise Doughnuts ....G....... 405 224-2907
Chickasha *(G-1499)*

RETAIL FIREPLACE STORES

Flame Control Inc ....G....... 405 321-2535
Norman *(G-5001)*
Johnny Beard Co ....G....... 918 438-4901
Tulsa *(G-10056)*

RETAIL LUMBER YARDS

Diamond P Forrest Products Co ....F....... 918 266-2478
Catoosa *(G-1316)*
Doug Butler Enterprises Inc ....F....... 918 425-3565
Tulsa *(G-9599)*
Hughes Lumber Company ....G....... 918 266-9100
Catoosa *(G-1322)*

RETAIL STORES, NEC

David Logan ....G....... 918 739-4231
Catoosa *(G-1315)*
Rehme Mfg Inc ....F....... 580 658-2414
Marlow *(G-4240)*
Rustic Rehab ....G....... 918 314-6647
Grove *(G-3287)*
Solar View LLC ....G....... 918 366-6413
Bixby *(G-660)*
Titanium Phoenix Inc ....G....... 405 305-1304
Oklahoma City *(G-7294)*

RETAIL STORES: Alcoholic Beverage Making Eqpt & Splys

Biotech Products Inc ....G....... 405 235-7575
Oklahoma City *(G-5574)*
C & H Tool & Machine Inc ....F....... 580 332-1929
Ada *(G-17)*
H&H Retail Services LLC ....F....... 918 369-4055
Bixby *(G-631)*
Laster/Castor Corporation ....G....... 918 234-7777
Tulsa *(G-10133)*

RETAIL STORES: Artificial Limbs

Texoma Orthtics Prsthtics Pllc ....G....... 580 699-8690
Lawton *(G-4012)*

RETAIL STORES: Audio-Visual Eqpt & Splys

Resonance Inc ....E....... 405 239-2800
Oklahoma City *(G-7010)*
Walrus Audio LLC ....F....... 405 254-4118
Oklahoma City *(G-7418)*

RETAIL STORES: Banners

American Logo and Sign Inc ....F....... 405 799-1800
Oklahoma City *(G-5438)*
Blankenship Brothers Inc ....G....... 405 943-3278
Oklahoma City *(G-5587)*
Carols Signs ....G....... 405 769-5521
Oklahoma City *(G-5705)*
Hays and Hays Companies Inc ....G....... 405 624-2999
Stillwater *(G-8698)*
Instant Signs Inc ....G....... 405 848-8181
Oklahoma City *(G-6311)*
Miket ADS Inc ....G....... 918 341-2992
Claremore *(G-1655)*
Sign Language ....G....... 405 360-7500
Norman *(G-5145)*
Sign Source ....G....... 580 436-1323
Ada *(G-88)*

RETAIL STORES: Batteries, Non-Automotive

Pro Battery Inc ....G....... 918 437-1920
Tulsa *(G-10564)*

RETAIL STORES: Canvas Prdts

Hays Tent & Awning ....G....... 918 534-1663
Dewey *(G-2023)*
Oklahoma Custom Canvas Pdts ....F....... 918 438-4040
Tulsa *(G-10395)*

RETAIL STORES: Cleaning Eqpt & Splys

3b Industries Inc ....F....... 580 439-8876
Comanche *(G-1832)*
Chase Enterprises Inc ....D....... 405 495-1722
Oklahoma City *(G-5745)*
Coil Chem LLC ....F....... 405 445-5545
Washington *(G-11334)*
Hotsy of OK Inc ....G....... 580 234-0608
Enid *(G-2974)*
Sooner Wiping Rags LLC ....F....... 405 670-3100
Oklahoma City *(G-7168)*

RETAIL STORES: Communication Eqpt

Michael A Phillips ....G....... 918 251-0925
Broken Arrow *(G-972)*

RETAIL STORES: Concrete Prdts, Precast

Decorative Rock & Stone Inc ....G....... 405 672-2564
Oklahoma City *(G-5916)*

RETAIL STORES: Decals

R G Enterprises ....G....... 580 225-2260
Elk City *(G-2864)*
Signs To Go LLC ....G....... 405 348-8646
Edmond *(G-2621)*
Wet Willies Screen Print & CU ....G....... 405 262-6076
El Reno *(G-2770)*

RETAIL STORES: Drafting Eqpt & Splys

Graphic Rsources Reproductions ......F....... 918 461-0303
Broken Arrow *(G-921)*

RETAIL STORES: Educational Aids & Electronic Training Mat

Resource Development Co LLC ....E....... 248 646-2300
Tulsa *(G-10645)*

RETAIL STORES: Electronic Parts & Eqpt

Bartosh Electric Motor Center ....G....... 405 567-2840
Prague *(G-7920)*

RETAIL STORES: Engine & Motor Eqpt & Splys

Evans Enterprises Inc ....G....... 918 825-2200
Tulsa *(G-9707)*
Interstate Electric Corp ....G....... 918 245-4508
Sand Springs *(G-8194)*
Newmans Electric Motor Repair ....G....... 580 310-0151
Ada *(G-71)*

RETAIL STORES: Farm Eqpt & Splys

C & H Ranch ....G....... 918 479-8460
Locust Grove *(G-4105)*

PRODUCT SECTION

RUBBER STAMP, WHOLESALE

C 2 Supply Llc .... G 918 647-0430
  Poteau *(G-7898)*
Jack Mangum .... G 580 658-2700
  Marlow *(G-4234)*
Lanco Services LLC .... E 580 429-6526
  Cache *(G-1229)*

RETAIL STORES: Farm Machinery, NEC

Bob Lowe Farm Machinery Inc .... F 405 224-6500
  Chickasha *(G-1440)*

RETAIL STORES: Foam & Foam Prdts

Jessie Shaw .... G 918 587-6329
  Tulsa *(G-10040)*

RETAIL STORES: Hearing Aids

Clear Tone Hearing Center Inc .... E 918 838-1000
  Tulsa *(G-9449)*

RETAIL STORES: Ice

J Mottos LLC .... G 918 760-3866
  Tulsa *(G-10021)*
K-Dub LLC .... E 580 353-6899
  Lawton *(G-3948)*
Southeastern Ice .... E 918 465-2500
  Wilburton *(G-11524)*

RETAIL STORES: Maps & Charts

American International Ltd .... G 405 364-1776
  Norman *(G-4907)*

RETAIL STORES: Medical Apparatus & Splys

Anthony W Layton Cpo .... G 580 353-8885
  Lawton *(G-3890)*
Maris Health LLC .... G 888 429-1117
  Tulsa *(G-10209)*
Mobility Living Inc .... G 405 672-7237
  Oklahoma City *(G-6623)*
Mother Earth Eco Entps LLC .... G 785 250-8706
  Ada *(G-68)*

RETAIL STORES: Monuments, Finished To Custom Order

Alva Monument Works Inc .... G 580 327-0626
  Alva *(G-174)*
Gifford Monument Works Inc .... F 580 332-1271
  Ada *(G-42)*
Jones Monuments Co .... G 580 255-2276
  Duncan *(G-2138)*
McAlester Monument Co Inc .... G 918 423-1647
  McAlester *(G-4317)*
Morris Monuments .... G 580 924-1323
  Durant *(G-2244)*
Muskogee Marble & Granite LLC .... E 918 682-0064
  Muskogee *(G-4716)*
Nicholson Monument Co .... G 580 323-7513
  Clinton *(G-1762)*
Okmulgee Monuments Inc .... G 918 756-6619
  Okmulgee *(G-7519)*
Williams Monuments .... G 918 225-1344
  Cushing *(G-1971)*

RETAIL STORES: Motors, Electric

Doug Roberson .... G 405 372-2078
  Stillwater *(G-8677)*
Q E M Inc .... G 918 534-2000
  Ochelata *(G-5238)*
S & H Electric Motor Service .... G 580 924-3514
  Durant *(G-2254)*

RETAIL STORES: Orthopedic & Prosthesis Applications

Hanger Prsthetcs & Ortho Inc .... G 918 333-6900
  Bartlesville *(G-489)*
Lawton Brace & Limb Co Inc .... G 580 353-5525
  Lawton *(G-3954)*
Scott Sabolich Prosthetics & R .... E 405 841-8000
  Oklahoma City *(G-7098)*

RETAIL STORES: Perfumes & Colognes

Bath & Body Works LLC .... E 405 748-3197
  Oklahoma City *(G-5529)*
Db Unlimited LLC .... G 855 437-7766
  Tulsa *(G-9563)*

RETAIL STORES: Pet Splys

HALAQ Inc .... G 405 321-7293
  Newalla *(G-4810)*

RETAIL STORES: Picture Frames, Ready Made

Wooden Concepts LLC .... G 405 459-0411
  Weatherford *(G-11461)*

RETAIL STORES: Safety Splys & Eqpt

D & M Steel Manufacturing .... G 405 631-5027
  Oklahoma City *(G-5887)*

RETAIL STORES: Spas & Hot Tubs

Billiards of Tulsa Inc .... E 918 835-1166
  Tulsa *(G-9296)*
Covers Plus Inc .... G 405 670-2221
  Oklahoma City *(G-5846)*
Norman Supply Company .... G 405 692-1191
  Oklahoma City *(G-5308)*

RETAIL STORES: Telephone Eqpt & Systems

Auto Trim Design Signs SE Okla .... G 580 622-3830
  Sulphur *(G-8828)*

RETAIL STORES: Welding Splys

Global Industrial Inc .... D 918 266-5656
  Tulsa *(G-9831)*
Nabors Welding & Supplies Inc .... G 405 756-8198
  Lindsay *(G-4075)*

REUPHOLSTERY & FURNITURE REPAIR

Desert Moon Enterprises .... G 918 540-0333
  Miami *(G-4395)*
Moss Seat Cover Mfg & Sls Co .... F 918 742-3326
  Tulsa *(G-10306)*

REUPHOLSTERY SVCS

Adairs Sleep World Inc .... F 405 341-9468
  Edmond *(G-2289)*
L & L Machine Shop .... G 580 357-3560
  Lawton *(G-3952)*

RIPRAP QUARRYING

Cobble Rock and Stone LLC .... F 405 567-3552
  Prague *(G-7923)*
Souter Limestone and Mnrl LLC .... F 918 489-5589
  Gore *(G-3252)*

ROAD CONSTRUCTION EQUIPMENT WHOLESALERS

Kirby - Smith Machinery Inc .... C 888 861-0219
  Oklahoma City *(G-6425)*

ROBOTS: Assembly Line

Bechtels Heavy Metal Works LLC ...... G 580 251-1412
  Duncan *(G-2089)*

RODS: Plastic

Kt Plastics Inc .... E 580 434-5655
  Calera *(G-1241)*

RODS: Steel & Iron, Made In Steel Mills

Sherrell Steel LLC .... F 580 436-4322
  Ada *(G-87)*

RODS: Welding

Damar Manufacturing Co Inc .... E 918 445-2445
  Tulsa *(G-9549)*

ROLLING MILL EQPT: Galvanizing Lines

Reinforced Earth Company .... E 918 379-0090
  Catoosa *(G-1349)*
Reinforcing Services Inc .... F 918 379-0090
  Catoosa *(G-1350)*
Western Technologies Inc .... F 918 712-2406
  Tulsa *(G-11110)*

ROLLING MILL MACHINERY

CRC-Evans Pipeline Intl Inc .... C 918 438-2100
  Tulsa *(G-9504)*
Dp Manufacturing Inc .... C 918 250-2450
  Jenks *(G-3704)*
G T Bynum Company .... G 918 587-9118
  Tulsa *(G-9794)*

ROLLING MILL ROLLS: Cast Steel

Burrow Construction LLC .... E 800 766-5793
  Fort Gibson *(G-3174)*

ROOF DECKS

Custom Metal Works Inc .... G 918 388-1881
  Tulsa *(G-9529)*
Metal Panels Inc .... G 918 641-0641
  Tulsa *(G-10246)*

ROOFING GRANULES

McCabe Industrial Minerals .... F 580 369-3660
  Davis *(G-1990)*

ROOFING MATERIALS: Asphalt

Atlas Roofing Corporation .... C 580 226-3283
  Ardmore *(G-251)*

ROOFING MATERIALS: Sheet Metal

Cool Green Roofing Supply LLC .... G 918 860-7525
  Broken Arrow *(G-877)*
Nci Group Inc .... E 405 672-7676
  Oklahoma City *(G-6665)*
Storm Roofing & Cnstr LLC .... G 918 688-0165
  Owasso *(G-7620)*
Zoe Homes LLC .... G 405 550-3563
  Oklahoma City *(G-7488)*

RUBBER

Henley Sealants Inc .... G 405 235-7325
  Oklahoma City *(G-6240)*
Southwest Latex LLC .... G 405 420-0018
  Marlow *(G-4243)*

RUBBER PRDTS: Automotive, Mechanical

Joyeaux Inc .... F 918 252-7660
  Tulsa *(G-10060)*
Ranch Acres Car Care .... G 918 742-3902
  Tulsa *(G-10619)*

RUBBER PRDTS: Mechanical

Barlow-Hunt Inc .... D 918 250-0828
  Tulsa *(G-9265)*
Oil States Industries Inc .... E 918 250-0828
  Tulsa *(G-10388)*
Oklahoma Custom Rubber Co .... G 405 634-3943
  Moore *(G-4545)*
Seal Company Enterprises Inc .... G 405 947-3307
  Oklahoma City *(G-7104)*
Thomas Engineering Co Inc .... E 918 587-6649
  Tulsa *(G-10931)*
Tjk Molded Products LLC .... F 409 200-1007
  Ardmore *(G-370)*
Tjk Molded Products LLC .... F 409 200-1007
  Ardmore *(G-371)*
Tulsa Rubber Co .... F 918 627-1371
  Tulsa *(G-11006)*

RUBBER PRDTS: Oil & Gas Field Machinery, Mechanical

Baker Hughes Elasto Systems .... F 405 670-3354
  Oklahoma City *(G-5516)*
Diversified Rubber Pdts Inc .... E 918 241-0193
  Tulsa *(G-9587)*
Oil States Industries Inc .... D 405 671-2000
  Oklahoma City *(G-6721)*
Oil States Industries Inc .... G 918 250-0828
  Tulsa *(G-10387)*

RUBBER STAMP, WHOLESALE

Rowmark LLC .... E 405 787-4542
  Oklahoma City *(G-7051)*

RUGS : Hand & Machine Made

Kinrich .... G 405 842-4307
Oklahoma City *(G-6424)*

SADDLERY STORES

Billy Cook Harn & Saddle Mfg .... D 580 622-5505
Sulphur *(G-8829)*
Custom Lea Sad & Cowboy Decor .... G 918 335-2277
Bartlesville *(G-471)*

SAFES & VAULTS: Metal

Southwest Engineering .... G 405 634-2841
Oklahoma City *(G-7176)*
W E Industries Inc .... G 405 949-0222
Oklahoma City *(G-7410)*

SAFETY EQPT & SPLYS WHOLESALERS

Airgas Usa LLC .... G 405 372-7720
Stillwater *(G-8652)*
H & C Services Inc .... F 580 772-2521
Weatherford *(G-11417)*
Hard Hat Safety and Glove LLC .... G 405 942-9500
Oklahoma City *(G-6217)*
Safetyco LLC .... G 405 603-3306
Oklahoma City *(G-7072)*

SAILS

Kerr Salesmakers & Marine Inc .... G 918 437-0544
Tulsa *(G-10085)*

SALT

Cargill Incorporated .... E 580 621-3246
Freedom *(G-3205)*
Leadership Training Academy .... G 405 551-8059
Edmond *(G-2484)*
Saltfork Service .... G 580 716-1022
Ponca City *(G-7870)*

SAND & GRAVEL

Arkhola Sand & Gravel Co .... G 918 687-4771
Muskogee *(G-4650)*
Arkhola Sand & Gravel Co .... G 918 456-2683
Tahlequah *(G-8850)*
Arkhola Sand & Gravel Co Tahle .... G 918 456-6121
Park Hill *(G-7640)*
B B Sand and Gravel .... G 405 944-1163
Paden *(G-7632)*
Bosendorfer Oil Company .... G 405 604-9025
Oklahoma City *(G-5622)*
Brandon Hyde .... G 405 919-4520
Goldsby *(G-3244)*
Clements Sand Gravel & Excavat .... G 580 465-4191
Ardmore *(G-268)*
Collins Cnstr Fabrications LLC .... G 918 522-4855
Talihina *(G-8906)*
Covia Holdings Corporation .... E 580 456-7772
Roff *(G-8107)*
Dolese Bros Co .... E 405 670-9626
Oklahoma City *(G-5962)*
Double D Sand and Gravel LLC .... G 405 207-8050
Stratford *(G-8804)*
Doug Troxell .... G 405 387-3574
Newcastle *(G-4824)*
Elm Creek Gravel LLC .... E 405 360-7300
Norman *(G-4990)*
Gravel Group LLC .... G 405 359-4932
Edmond *(G-2443)*
Gravel Road LLC .... G 918 766-6368
Bartlesville *(G-488)*
Heady Trucking .... G 580 326-2739
Sawyer *(G-8334)*
Holliday Sand & Gravel Co .... G 918 486-1413
Coweta *(G-1885)*
Holliday Sand Gravel Co LLC .... G 918 369-8850
Bixby *(G-632)*
Jr Sand & Gravel Inc .... G 405 474-8730
Edmond *(G-2474)*
K and G Sand & Gravel LLC .... G 580 369-2244
Davis *(G-1987)*
Keystone Sand & Gravel .... G 918 241-0415
Sand Springs *(G-8198)*
Kline Materials Inc .... F 580 256-2062
Woodward *(G-11603)*
Lattimore Materials Company LP .... F 580 276-4631
Marietta *(G-4208)*

Lawton Transit Mix Inc .... G 580 569-4333
Snyder *(G-8582)*
Lightfoot Ready Mix LLC .... G 405 714-5539
Perkins *(G-7720)*
Mark C Blakley .... G 405 245-3606
Oklahoma City *(G-6526)*
Micheal T Robinson .... G 580 767-9414
Ponca City *(G-7851)*
Minick Materials Company .... E 405 789-2068
Oklahoma City *(G-6616)*
Mohawk Materials Co Inc .... G 918 584-2707
Tulsa *(G-10295)*
Nancy W Gravel .... G 405 348-4409
Edmond *(G-2528)*
Oklahoma Aztec Co Inc .... G 405 784-2475
Asher *(G-393)*
Pryor Sand & Redi-Mix Inc .... G 918 484-2150
Whitefield *(G-11517)*
Rcr Construction .... G 918 682-9033
Muskogee *(G-4742)*
Redline Constructn Sand Dirt .... G 405 380-6994
Wewoka *(G-11509)*
Sand Run LLC .... G 918 296-3205
Tulsa *(G-10703)*
Southern Boys Clay Gravel LLC .... G 580 584-6711
Broken Bow *(G-1208)*
Stanton Sand & Gravel Inc .... G 580 229-3353
Ardmore *(G-363)*
Summit Sand & Gravel LLC .... G 405 256-6029
Mustang *(G-4797)*
Technisand Inc .... D 580 456-7791
Roff *(G-8112)*
TNT Sand & Gravel LLC .... G 580 277-0640
Ardmore *(G-372)*
Two Brothers Sand Grave .... G 405 923-6762
Yukon *(G-11797)*
V5 Contracting LLC .... G 918 720-4675
Claremore *(G-1699)*
Vickers Sand and Gravel .... G 405 573-1989
Norman *(G-5195)*

SAND MINING

Anna Lightle .... G 405 853-4530
Hennessey *(G-3445)*
Cardinal Fg Minerals LLC .... E 580 367-2123
Coleman *(G-1793)*
Dereks Pit LLC .... G 405 485-2562
Blanchard *(G-710)*
Muskie Proppant LLC .... G 405 233-3558
Oklahoma City *(G-6638)*
Muskogee Sand Company Inc .... G 918 683-1766
Porter *(G-7894)*

SAND: Hygrade

Badger Mining Corporation .... G 608 864-1157
Erick *(G-3085)*
Cardinal Industries LLC .... G 918 299-0396
Tulsa *(G-9375)*
Fairmount Minerals .... G 580 303-9160
Elk City *(G-2814)*
Timco Blasting & Coatings .... E 918 367-1700
Bristow *(G-799)*
Timco Blasting & Coatings .... F 918 605-1179
Bristow *(G-800)*
Timco Blasting & Coatings .... G 918 605-1179
Stroud *(G-8823)*
Timco Blasting & Coatings .... G 918 605-1179
Bristow *(G-801)*
Timco Blasting & Coatings .... G 918 608-1179
Stroud *(G-8824)*

SAND: Silica

Taylor Frac LLC .... E 405 293-4208
Oklahoma City *(G-7259)*

SANDBLASTING EQPT

Dickson Industries Inc .... E 405 598-6547
Tecumseh *(G-8912)*
Kuykendall Welding LLC .... G 405 905-0389
Chickasha *(G-1480)*
Memories In Glass Inc .... G 405 878-9688
Shawnee *(G-8473)*

SANDSTONE: Crushed & Broken

Rock Producers Inc .... E 918 969-2100
Bokoshe *(G-754)*

SANITARY SVCS: Environmental Cleanup

Environmate Inc .... G 817 707-5282
Catoosa *(G-1318)*
Tank & Fuel Solutions LLC .... G 918 960-4361
Claremore *(G-1691)*

SANITARY SVCS: Liquid Waste Collection & Disposal

Range Energy Services Company .... F 580 227-3762
Fairview *(G-3148)*

SANITARY SVCS: Rubbish Collection & Disposal

Greg Butcher .... G 918 434-6892
Salina *(G-8134)*

SANITARY SVCS: Waste Materials, Recycling

Bs & W Solutions LLC .... G 918 392-9356
Tulsa *(G-9343)*
Hite Plastics Inc .... E 405 297-9818
Oklahoma City *(G-6255)*
Metal Check Inc .... F 405 636-1916
Oklahoma City *(G-6573)*

SANITARY WARE: Metal

Quarry .... G 918 534-2120
Dewey *(G-2030)*
Stephen Poorboy .... G 918 373-5073
Chouteau *(G-1571)*

SANITATION CHEMICALS & CLEANING AGENTS

Anchor Paint Mfg Co .... D 918 836-4626
Tulsa *(G-9185)*
Baker Petrolite LLC .... C 918 847-2522
Barnsdall *(G-435)*
Bio-Cide International Inc .... G 405 364-1940
Norman *(G-4932)*
Brenntag Southwest Inc .... E 918 266-2951
Catoosa *(G-1306)*
Brenntag Southwest Inc .... E 918 273-2265
Nowata *(G-5209)*
Donald W Cox .... G 918 471-8967
Porum *(G-7895)*
Kar Glo Tuffy .... G 405 631-4091
Oklahoma City *(G-6397)*
Shabby Chicks Smart Clean LLC .... G 405 414-8938
Duncan *(G-2176)*
SMC Technologies Inc .... F 405 737-3740
Midwest City *(G-4455)*
Sooner Energy Services Inc .... G 405 579-3200
Marlow *(G-4242)*

SASHES: Door Or Window, Metal

Hirsch3667 Corp .... D 580 323-6966
Clinton *(G-1752)*

SATELLITE COMMUNICATIONS EQPT

Tulsat Corporation .... D 918 251-2887
Broken Arrow *(G-1087)*

SATELLITES: Communications

His Construction .... G 405 642-4306
Oklahoma City *(G-6253)*
Zephyrus Electronics Ltd .... F 918 437-3333
Tulsa *(G-11177)*

SAW BLADES

H S Boyd Company Inc .... F 918 835-9359
Tulsa *(G-9876)*

SAWING & PLANING MILLS

Diamond P Forrest Products Co .... F 918 266-2478
Catoosa *(G-1316)*
Eastern Red Cedar Products LLC .... G 405 780-7520
Stillwater *(G-8681)*
Gray & Sons Sawmill & Sup LLC .... G 580 924-2941
Durant *(G-2231)*
Hugo Wyrick Lumber .... E 580 326-5569
Hugo *(G-3614)*
International Paper Company .... D 580 933-7211
Valliant *(G-11227)*

PRODUCT SECTION

SECURITY PROTECTIVE DEVICES MAINTENANCE & MONITORING SVCS

Jeffery Mariott .... E 580 320-5474
  Roff (G-8109)
John R Little Jr .... G 405 751-5227
  Oklahoma City (G-6369)
Johnson Lumber Company Inc .... E 918 253-8786
  Spavinaw (G-8591)
Limbsaw Company .... G 580 272-3194
  Noble (G-4885)
Log Cutters .... G 580 371-8349
  Tishomingo (G-8967)
Og Sawmill .... G 918 598-3464
  Hulbert (G-3627)
Sanders Sawmill & Forest Pdts .... G 405 799-0899
  Moore (G-4562)
Shawnee Sawmill LLC .... G 405 788-6186
  Shawnee (G-8496)
T and A Sawmill LLC .... G 580 309-3100
  Thomas (G-8948)
Whitlock Saw Mill .... G 918 652-4410
  Henryetta (G-3518)
Woodstock Sawmill & Timbers Co .... G 405 673-7966
  Oklahoma City (G-7467)

SAWING & PLANING MILLS: Custom

Browns Sawmill .... G 918 617-7935
  Atwood (G-428)
James Bethell .... G 918 677-2328
  Wister (G-11549)

SAWS & SAWING EQPT

Diamond P Forrest Products Co .... F 918 266-2478
  Catoosa (G-1316)
Eastland Lawn Mower Service .... G 580 252-0077
  Duncan (G-2115)
Green Country Outdoor Eqp .... G 918 396-4250
  Skiatook (G-8546)

SCAFFOLDS: Mobile Or Stationary, Metal

Dover Artificial Lift .... G 918 796-1000
  Tulsa (G-9600)

SCALE REPAIR SVCS

Sooner Scale Inc .... F 405 236-3566
  Oklahoma City (G-7165)
Unibridge Scale Systems .... G 580 254-3131
  Woodward (G-11646)

SCALES & BALANCES, EXC LABORATORY

CMI Terex Corporation .... A 405 787-6020
  Oklahoma City (G-5792)
Unibridge Scale Systems .... G 580 254-3131
  Woodward (G-11646)

SCALES: Indl

Sooner Scale Inc .... F 405 236-3566
  Oklahoma City (G-7165)

SCALES: Railroad Track

Unibridge Systems Inc .... E 580 934-3211
  Knowles (G-3841)

SCALES: Truck

Base Scale Company .... G 918 523-9559
  Tulsa (G-9270)
Sooner Scale Inc .... F 580 925-2176
  Konawa (G-3848)

SCHOOLS & EDUCATIONAL SVCS, NEC

Oklahoma School of Welding .... G 405 672-1841
  Del City (G-2004)

SCHOOLS: Vocational, NEC

Dale Rogers Training Ctr Inc .... E 580 481-6170
  Altus (G-153)
Jarvis Inc .... E 918 437-1100
  Tulsa (G-10029)

SCRAP & WASTE MATERIALS, WHOLESALE: Ferrous Metal

Borg Compressed Steel Corp .... D 918 587-2437
  Tulsa (G-9321)
Pruitt Company of Ada Inc .... E 580 332-3523
  Ada (G-78)

SCRAP & WASTE MATERIALS, WHOLESALE: Metal

Scrap Management Oklahoma Inc .... F 405 677-7000
  Oklahoma City (G-7100)

SCRAP & WASTE MATERIALS, WHOLESALE: Paper

Business Records Storage LLC .... E 405 232-7867
  Oklahoma City (G-5649)

SCRAP & WASTE MATERIALS, WHOLESALE: Paper & Cloth Materials

Sooner Wiping Rags LLC .... F 405 670-3100
  Oklahoma City (G-7168)

SCREENS: Window, Metal

Don Young Company Incorporated .... G 405 947-2000
  Oklahoma City (G-5966)
Dynomite Custom Screens LLC .... G 844 396-6648
  Lawton (G-3921)
Lawton Window Co Inc .... G 580 353-4655
  Lawton (G-3962)

SCREENS: Woven Wire

Oklahoma Screen Mfg LLC .... F 918 443-6500
  Oologah (G-7535)

SCREW MACHINE PRDTS

Badgett Corporation .... D 405 224-4138
  Chickasha (G-1437)
Freedom Manufacturing LLC .... G 918 283-1520
  Claremore (G-1623)
Hem Industries .... G 918 534-0579
  Dewey (G-2024)
Kemper Valve and Fittings .... G 580 622-2048
  Sulphur (G-8836)
Kenneth Pace .... E 405 222-1426
  Chickasha (G-1479)
Madewell Machine Works Company .... G 918 543-2904
  Inola (G-3666)
Psf Services LLC .... G 707 386-8805
  Marlow (G-4239)
Rightway Mfg Solutions LLC .... G 580 252-2284
  Duncan (G-2170)
SBS Industries LLC .... C 918 836-7756
  Tulsa (G-10712)
Slim Haney Inc .... E 918 274-1082
  Tulsa (G-10772)
Tape-Matics Inc .... E 580 371-2510
  Tishomingo (G-8969)
Torcsill Foundations LLC .... D 281 825-5200
  Weatherford (G-11448)

SEALANTS

Alliance Sealants & Waterproof .... G 405 627-9474
  Oklahoma City (G-5419)
Flanco Gasket and Mfg Inc .... E 405 672-7893
  Oklahoma City (G-6088)
Red Devil Incorporated .... F 918 585-8111
  Tulsa (G-10629)
Red Devil Incorporated .... D 918 825-5744
  Pryor (G-7989)

SEALS: Oil, Rubber

Clark Seals LLC .... E 918 664-0587
  Tulsa (G-9440)
Global Bearings Inc .... E 918 664-8902
  Tulsa (G-9829)

SEARCH & NAVIGATION SYSTEMS

Aero Dynamics .... F 918 258-0290
  Broken Arrow (G-818)
Aero-TEC Industries Inc .... G 405 382-8501
  Seminole (G-8353)
Aviation Training Devices Inc .... F 918 366-6680
  Bixby (G-613)
Baron Manufacturing Inc .... G 405 947-3362
  Oklahoma City (G-5528)
Barrett Performance Aircraft .... G 918 835-1089
  Tulsa (G-9266)
Critical Infrastructur .... G 918 640-9301
  Jenks (G-3702)
Flightsafety International Inc .... A 918 259-4000
  Broken Arrow (G-910)
Flir Systems Inc .... G 407 810-3634
  Stillwater (G-8691)
Iball Instruments LLC .... F 405 366-6061
  Norman (G-5029)
Kern Valley Industries .... G 918 868-3911
  Rose (G-8118)
L3 Comm AMI Instruments .... G 212 697-1111
  Broken Arrow (G-961)
L3harris Technologies Inc .... D 405 573-2285
  Norman (G-5055)
Lockheed Martin Corporation .... G 580 355-0581
  Lawton (G-3966)
Meta Special Aerospace LLC .... G 405 516-3357
  Bethany (G-589)
Navico Inc .... F 918 437-6881
  Tulsa (G-10329)
Pryer Machine & Tool Company .... C 918 835-8885
  Tulsa (G-10580)
R C Ramsey Co .... F 918 746-4300
  Tulsa (G-10602)
Spirit Aerosystems Inc .... C 918 423-6979
  McAlester (G-4337)
Tech-Aid Products .... G 918 838-8711
  Tulsa (G-10911)
Tgv Rockets Inc .... G 405 366-0779
  Norman (G-5173)

SECURE STORAGE SVC: Document

Business Records Storage LLC .... E 405 232-7867
  Oklahoma City (G-5649)
Mid-Con Data Services Inc .... E 405 478-1234
  Oklahoma City (G-6592)
Print Imaging Group LLC .... E 405 235-4888
  Oklahoma City (G-6898)

SECURITIES DEALING

Baytide Petroleum Inc .... F 918 585-8150
  Tulsa (G-9273)

SECURITY CONTROL EQPT & SYSTEMS

Adams Electronics Inc .... G 918 622-5000
  Tulsa (G-9102)
David Bates .... G 918 457-6169
  Tahlequah (G-8862)
Direct Communications Inc .... E 918 291-0092
  Tulsa (G-9585)
Jarvis Inc .... E 918 437-1100
  Tulsa (G-10029)
Kingdom Alarms Inc .... F 918 627-5454
  Tulsa (G-10091)
Lucas Holdings LLC .... E 405 524-1811
  Oklahoma City (G-6500)
Mathena Inc .... D 405 422-3600
  El Reno (G-2736)
Total Home Controls Inc .... G 405 736-0191
  Oklahoma City (G-7308)
Trinity Technologies LLC .... F 580 475-0900
  Duncan (G-2190)

SECURITY DEVICES

Acquire Cctv Inc .... G 405 324-1300
  Yukon (G-11689)
Alan Beaty .... G 405 664-6768
  El Reno (G-2696)
Baby Bee Safe .... G 918 224-1104
  Sapulpa (G-8251)
Digi Security Systems LLC .... F 918 824-2520
  Tulsa (G-9582)
Jjs Security Cameras Inc .... G 405 408-6096
  Oklahoma City (G-6364)
Lockdown Ltd Co .... F 405 605-6161
  Oklahoma City (G-6485)

SECURITY EQPT STORES

Hughes Gas Measurement Inc .... G 405 227-0904
  Wetumka (G-11494)

SECURITY PROTECTIVE DEVICES MAINTENANCE & MONITORING SVCS

Insight Technologies Inc .... F 580 933-4109
  Valliant (G-11226)
Lynxsystems LLC .... G 918 728-6000
  Tulsa (G-10185)

SECURITY SYSTEMS SERVICES

SECURITY SYSTEMS SERVICES
Digi Security Systems LLC .... F 918 824-2520
 Tulsa *(G-9582)*
Techsico Entp Solutions Inc .... D 918 585-2347
 Tulsa *(G-10913)*
Total Home Controls Inc .... G 405 736-0191
 Oklahoma City *(G-7308)*

SEEDS: Coated Or Treated, From Purchased Seeds
Brad McKinzie .... G 580 355-3810
 Lawton *(G-3900)*

SELF-PROPELLED AIRCRAFT DEALER
Northrop Grumman Systems Corp .... C 405 733-1208
 Oklahoma City *(G-6691)*

SEMICONDUCTOR & RELATED DEVICES: Random Access Memory Or RAM
Kaze LLC .... G 580 857-2707
 Allen *(G-136)*

SEMICONDUCTORS & RELATED DEVICES
Amethyst Research Incorporated .... F 580 657-2575
 Ardmore *(G-238)*
Clayton Macom .... G 918 967-3350
 Stigler *(G-8631)*
Coorstek Inc .... B 405 601-4371
 Oklahoma City *(G-5832)*
Don Tooker .... G 972 742-8515
 Owasso *(G-7562)*
Michael A Phillips .... G 918 251-0925
 Broken Arrow *(G-972)*
Waylolo LLC .... G 405 714-2353
 Stillwater *(G-8774)*

SENSORS: Radiation
Crystaltech Inc .... G 580 252-8893
 Duncan *(G-2101)*

SEPTIC TANK CLEANING SVCS
Carnegie Precast Inc .... F 580 654-1718
 Carnegie *(G-1275)*
Eastside Septic Tank .... G 918 486-2290
 Coweta *(G-1881)*

SEPTIC TANKS: Concrete
Eastside Septic Tank .... G 918 486-2290
 Coweta *(G-1881)*
Foresee Ready-Mix Concrete Inc .... F 918 689-3951
 Eufaula *(G-3101)*
Green Country S Inc .... G 918 224-8244
 Sapulpa *(G-8276)*
Hausners Limited .... F 580 924-6988
 Mead *(G-4366)*
Hausners Precast Con Pdts Inc .... E 918 352-3479
 Drumright *(G-2061)*
Smith Septic Tank Inc .... G 918 456-8741
 Tahlequah *(G-8884)*

SEWAGE & WATER TREATMENT EQPT
Midamerica Water Technologies .... G 405 613-0250
 Oklahoma City *(G-6594)*
Water Bionics Inc .... G 918 446-1988
 Tulsa *(G-11098)*

SEWAGE TREATMENT SYSTEMS & EQPT
Phelps Ra Equipment Co Inc .... G 918 622-2724
 Tulsa *(G-10508)*

SEWING CONTRACTORS
Apex Inc .... E 405 247-7377
 Anadarko *(G-200)*

SEWING MACHINE STORES
B Sew Inn LLC .... G 918 687-5762
 Muskogee *(G-4652)*

SEWING MACHINES & PARTS: Indl
Armed Inc .... G 918 245-1478
 Sand Springs *(G-8162)*

SEWING, NEEDLEWORK & PIECE GOODS STORES: Fabric, Remnants
Rainbow Pennant Inc .... E 405 524-1577
 Oklahoma City *(G-6968)*

SEWING, NEEDLEWORK & PIECE GOODS STORES: Sewing & Needlework
Miami Designs .... G 918 542-9553
 Miami *(G-4414)*

SEWING, NEEDLEWORK & PIECE GOODS STORES: Sewing Splys
Unique Stitches Inc .... G 918 794-5494
 Tulsa *(G-11035)*

SEXTANTS
Sextant Mineral Group LLC .... G 918 299-5115
 Tulsa *(G-10737)*

SHALE: Expanded
Arcosa Acg Inc .... G 405 366-9500
 Norman *(G-4914)*

SHAPES & PILINGS, STRUCTURAL: Steel
C & B Fabricators Inc .... G 918 760-6508
 Bokoshe *(G-752)*
Chickasaw Defense Services Inc .... G 405 203-0144
 Oklahoma City *(G-5759)*

SHAPES: Extruded, Aluminum, NEC
DDB Unlimited Incorporated .... D 405 665-2876
 Wynnewood *(G-11667)*
DDB Unlimited Incorporated .... F 800 753-8459
 Wynnewood *(G-11668)*
DDB Unlimited Incorporated .... E 800 753-8459
 Wynnewood *(G-11669)*

SHAVING PREPARATIONS
Coalton Road Enterprises LLC .... G 918 652-0474
 Henryetta *(G-3502)*
Strop Shoppe LLc .... G 775 557-8767
 Norman *(G-5162)*

SHEET METAL SPECIALTIES, EXC STAMPED
Aeron Group LLC .... F 918 294-1167
 Broken Arrow *(G-819)*
All Sheet Metal Co .... G 405 733-0039
 Del City *(G-1996)*
Allen Sheet Metal Inc .... G 918 834-2279
 Tulsa *(G-9141)*
D & D Design & Mfg Inc .... F 405 745-2126
 Oklahoma City *(G-5885)*
Del Nero Manufacturing Co .... G 405 364-4800
 Norman *(G-4976)*
Dilbeck Mfg Inc .... E 918 836-1555
 Tulsa *(G-9584)*
Don Bateman Shtmtl Fabrication .... G 918 224-0567
 Sapulpa *(G-8267)*
E F L Inc .... D 918 665-7799
 Tulsa *(G-9621)*
Empire Laser & Metal Work LLC .... F 918 584-6232
 Broken Arrow *(G-898)*
Fabrication Dynamics .... D 918 445-6100
 Tulsa *(G-9004)*
Metaltech Inc .... F 405 659-9911
 Oklahoma City *(G-6575)*
Midwest Fabricators LLC .... G 405 755-7799
 Oklahoma City *(G-6603)*
Midwest Precision Inc .... D 918 835-8900
 Tulsa *(G-10270)*
Phoenix Design & Mfg LLC .... G 405 418-4858
 Oklahoma City *(G-6843)*
Redland Sheet Metal Inc .... G 405 673-7107
 Oklahoma City *(G-6997)*
Tulsa Sheet Metal Inc .... F 918 587-3141
 Tulsa *(G-11007)*
Westwind Sheet Metal .... G 918 437-9976
 Tulsa *(G-11112)*

SHEETING: Window, Plastic
Plastic Fabricators Inc .... F 918 836-6611
 Tulsa *(G-10524)*

SHEETS & STRIPS: Aluminum
Clinco Mfg LLC .... G 580 759-3434
 Ada *(G-25)*

SHELLAC
Select Coatings Inc .... F 405 745-9011
 Oklahoma City *(G-7106)*

SHELTERED WORKSHOPS
Apex Inc .... E 405 247-7377
 Anadarko *(G-200)*
Sheltred Work-Activity Program .... E 918 683-8162
 Muskogee *(G-4748)*
Think Ability Inc .... C 580 252-8000
 Duncan *(G-2187)*

SHIP BLDG & RPRG: Drilling & Production Platforms, Oil/Gas
Burrows .... G 918 846-2245
 Hominy *(G-3580)*
Carbon Economy LLC .... F 405 222-4244
 Chickasha *(G-1447)*
Forward Oil and Gas Inc .... G 405 607-2247
 Oklahoma City *(G-6106)*
Heath Technologies LLC .... E 918 342-3222
 Claremore *(G-1631)*
Stiles Services LLC .... G 918 582-7894
 Tulsa *(G-10851)*

SHIP BLDG/RPRG: Submersible Marine Robots, Manned/Unmanned
Submersible Technical Products .... F 405 850-4091
 Pauls Valley *(G-7673)*

SHIP BUILDING & REPAIRING: Lighters, Marine
Custom Upholstery .... G 918 342-3489
 Claremore *(G-1611)*

SHOE MATERIALS: Counters
Bean Counter Inc .... G 918 925-9667
 Claremore *(G-1594)*
Counter Canter Inc .... C 405 321-8326
 Norman *(G-4967)*
Countrstrike Lghtning Prtction .... G 405 863-8480
 Oklahoma City *(G-5844)*
Quality In Counters Inc .... G 405 664-2744
 Guthrie *(G-3333)*

SHOE MATERIALS: Quarters
Lux Grooming Quarters LLC .... G 918 259-9910
 Tulsa *(G-10184)*

SHOE MATERIALS: Rands
Ingersoll-Rand Air Solutio .... G 918 451-9747
 Broken Arrow *(G-936)*
Rand Trans Inc .... G 580 866-3355
 Sharon *(G-8418)*

SHOE MATERIALS: Uppers
Upper Room .... G ......
 Oklahoma City *(G-7374)*

SHOE STORES: Athletic
Play 2 Win Athletics .... G 918 341-9500
 Claremore *(G-1671)*
Tim Dees .... G 918 825-1211
 Pryor *(G-7995)*

SHOE STORES: Men's
C & W Shoes of Georgia Inc .... F 405 755-7112
 Oklahoma City *(G-5658)*

SHOE STORES: Orthopedic
Mobility Living Inc .... G 405 672-7237
 Oklahoma City *(G-6623)*

SHOES: Canvas, Rubber Soled
Vans Inc .... F 405 843-5286
 Oklahoma City *(G-7391)*

PRODUCT SECTION

Vans Inc ....F...... 405 787-9992
  Oklahoma City *(G-7392)*

SHOES: Moccasins

Island Disc Golf Course ....G...... 541 337-8668
  Pawhuska *(G-7686)*
Moccasin Trail Company ....G...... 405 380-8221
  Paden *(G-7636)*
Moccasins of Hope Society ....G...... 605 431-3738
  Ponca City *(G-7854)*

SHOES: Women's, Dress

C & W Shoes of Georgia Inc ....F...... 405 755-7112
  Oklahoma City *(G-5658)*

SHUTTERS, DOOR & WINDOW: Metal

Boomer Blinds & Shutters LLC ....G...... 918 968-2579
  Stroud *(G-8808)*
Classic Shutters ....G...... 918 234-0657
  Tulsa *(G-9442)*
Custom Shutters Inc ....G...... 918 924-3489
  Broken Arrow *(G-882)*
Plantation Shutter Co ....G...... 817 703-1091
  Broken Arrow *(G-1008)*
Southwest Shutter Co ....G...... 405 344-6406
  Purcell *(G-8020)*

SHUTTERS: Door, Wood

Wendell Hicks Construction ....G...... 918 520-9128
  Nowata *(G-5232)*

SHUTTERS: Window, Wood

Leon Kinder ....G...... 580 323-0365
  Clinton *(G-1756)*
Shutters Unlimited Ltd ....F...... 405 843-7762
  Oklahoma City *(G-7126)*

SIDING & STRUCTURAL MATERIALS: Wood

Oklahoma Home Centers Inc ....E...... 405 260-7625
  Guthrie *(G-3329)*
Ufp Shawnee LLC ....G...... 405 273-1533
  Shawnee *(G-8515)*

SIDING, INSULATING: Impregnated, From Purchased Materials

Dryvit Systems Inc ....E...... 918 245-0216
  Sand Springs *(G-8179)*

SIDING: Sheet Metal

Longreach Steel Inc ....F...... 405 598-5691
  Tecumseh *(G-8922)*

SIGN LETTERING & PAINTING SVCS

Htw Inc ....G...... 918 423-4619
  McAlester *(G-4305)*

SIGN PAINTING & LETTERING SHOP

Beacon Sign Company Inc ....G...... 405 567-4886
  Prague *(G-7921)*
Freds Sign Co ....G...... 405 235-8696
  Newalla *(G-4809)*
Klines Signs & Crane ....G...... 580 256-2374
  Woodward *(G-11604)*
Luther Sign Co ....G...... 405 681-6535
  Oklahoma City *(G-6503)*

SIGNALING APPARATUS: Electric

Newstar Netronics LLC ....G...... 918 932-8343
  Tulsa *(G-10340)*

SIGNALING DEVICES: Sound, Electrical

Airelectric Inc ....G...... 918 291-7531
  Tulsa *(G-9127)*

SIGNALS: Railroad, Electric

OK Rail Signals Inc ....G...... 918 378-9520
  Tulsa *(G-10392)*

SIGNALS: Traffic Control, Electric

Econolite Control Products Inc ....G...... 405 485-2230
  Blanchard *(G-713)*

Gades Sales Co ....G...... 405 720-6839
  Oklahoma City *(G-6133)*

SIGNALS: Transportation

Airgo Systems LLC ....F...... 405 346-5807
  Oklahoma City *(G-5404)*
Signaltek Inc ....G...... 918 583-4335
  Tulsa *(G-10758)*

SIGNS & ADVERTISING SPECIALTIES

247 Graphx Studios Inc ....G...... 405 677-7775
  Oklahoma City *(G-5329)*
2911 LLC ....G...... 405 631-2008
  Oklahoma City *(G-5330)*
3g Sign Inc ....G...... 918 630-5976
  Broken Arrow *(G-807)*
4 K Kustomz Designs & Signs ....G...... 580 226-2259
  Ardmore *(G-234)*
405 Sign and Lighting LLC ....G...... 405 445-8888
  Oklahoma City *(G-5335)*
A & B Quick Signs LLC ....G...... 405 789-7446
  Oklahoma City *(G-5342)*
A & S Graphix ....G...... 918 640-1292
  Sulphur *(G-8827)*
A 1 Advertising By L & H ....G...... 918 348-2529
  Muskogee *(G-4639)*
A Finley Sign & Lighting Co ....G...... 405 413-5721
  Oklahoma City *(G-5345)*
A Sign of Surprise ....G...... 918 607-0747
  Broken Arrow *(G-810)*
A-1 Specialties ....G...... 405 942-1341
  Oklahoma City *(G-5352)*
A-Max Signs Co ....E...... 918 622-0651
  Tulsa *(G-9075)*
A1 Vinyl Signs LLC ....G...... 918 392-9905
  Tulsa *(G-9076)*
AAA Sign & Supply Co ....G...... 918 622-7883
  Tulsa *(G-9078)*
Absolute Markings Inc ....F...... 918 660-0600
  Tulsa *(G-9083)*
Accent Displays & Graphics ....G...... 918 437-4338
  Tulsa *(G-9087)*
Advantage Graphics ....G...... 580 363-5734
  Ponca City *(G-7793)*
Advertising Signs & Awngs Inc ....G...... 405 232-7446
  Oklahoma City *(G-5388)*
Al Signs & Wraps LLC ....G...... 405 531-6938
  Del City *(G-1995)*
Alan Thompson Signs ....G...... 918 808-3976
  Broken Arrow *(G-822)*
All-Star Trophies & Ribbon Mfg ....G...... 918 283-2200
  Claremore *(G-1581)*
Allem Sign Co ....G...... 918 241-7206
  Sand Springs *(G-8158)*
Allen Signs ....G...... 580 688-2985
  Hollis *(G-3563)*
Alphagraffix Inc ....G...... 405 354-3000
  Yukon *(G-11690)*
American Logo and Sign Inc ....G...... 405 799-1800
  Moore *(G-4488)*
American Logo and Sign Inc ....F...... 405 799-1800
  Oklahoma City *(G-5438)*
American Signworx ....G...... 479 650-4562
  Pocola *(G-7780)*
Apple Art ....G...... 405 691-4393
  Moore *(G-4491)*
Architectural Sign & Graphics ....G...... 405 354-8829
  Yukon *(G-11692)*
Artworks ....G...... 580 927-9094
  Atoka *(G-396)*
Ask ME About Signs LLC ....G...... 405 317-8157
  Norman *(G-4920)*
Auto Trim Design Signs SE Okla ....G...... 580 622-3830
  Sulphur *(G-8828)*
B Bar Inc ....G...... 580 824-8338
  Waynoka *(G-11372)*
B G Specialties Inc ....G...... 918 582-1165
  Tulsa *(G-9243)*
Bad Boy Signs Graphic ....D...... 405 224-2059
  Chickasha *(G-1436)*
Bakers Sign & Design ....G...... 405 262-5100
  El Reno *(G-2700)*
Banners Signs & Business Cards ....G...... 405 818-4371
  Oklahoma City *(G-5525)*
Beacon Sign Company Inc ....G...... 405 567-4886
  Prague *(G-7921)*
Beacon Stamp & Seal Co ....G...... 918 834-2322
  Tulsa *(G-9276)*
Better Sign Co ....G...... 580 242-9317
  Enid *(G-2916)*

SIGNS & ADVERTISING SPECIALTIES

Bill Koenig ....G...... 405 386-7979
  Newalla *(G-4805)*
Billboards Etc Inc ....G...... 580 326-1660
  Hugo *(G-3603)*
Blankenship Brothers Inc ....G...... 405 943-3278
  Oklahoma City *(G-5586)*
Blankenship Brothers Inc ....G...... 405 943-3278
  Oklahoma City *(G-5587)*
Blankenship Brothers Inc ....G...... 918 627-3278
  Tulsa *(G-9302)*
Blankenship Brothers Inc ....G...... 405 848-7446
  Oklahoma City *(G-5588)*
Bobs Sign Company ....G...... 580 467-3646
  Chickasha *(G-1441)*
Bwb Sign Inc ....F...... 405 292-3534
  Oklahoma City *(G-5651)*
Byrd Signs & Designs ....G...... 918 687-4219
  Muskogee *(G-4656)*
C L and L Inc ....G...... 405 722-9427
  Oklahoma City *(G-5660)*
C M Y K Colour Corp ....G...... 405 270-0060
  Oklahoma City *(G-5661)*
Capstone Music Company Ltd ....G...... 918 273-1888
  Nowata *(G-5210)*
Carols Signs ....G...... 405 769-5521
  Oklahoma City *(G-5705)*
Chambers Signs ....G...... 918 251-6513
  Broken Arrow *(G-865)*
Checotah W T J Shoppe Inc ....G...... 918 473-2819
  Checotah *(G-1391)*
Chris Johnson ....G...... 405 364-3879
  Norman *(G-4956)*
Circle 7 Signs and Wonders ....G...... 918 448-7744
  Wilburton *(G-11519)*
Claremoresigns Com ....G...... 918 965-1233
  Claremore *(G-1608)*
Claude V Sanderson Prop ....G...... 405 232-5878
  Oklahoma City *(G-5780)*
Clear Channel Outdoor Inc ....E...... 405 528-2683
  Oklahoma City *(G-5781)*
Complete Graphics Inc ....G...... 405 232-8882
  Oklahoma City *(G-5812)*
Complete Sign Service LLC ....G...... 405 273-7567
  Tecumseh *(G-8909)*
Compusign Vinyl Graphics ....G...... 580 762-4930
  Ponca City *(G-7807)*
Conyer Signs ....G...... 405 755-0061
  Edmond *(G-2366)*
Corporate Image Inc ....G...... 918 516-8376
  Owasso *(G-7556)*
Corter Enterprises LLC ....G...... 405 326-7001
  Tuttle *(G-11190)*
Crain Displays & Exhibits Inc ....F...... 918 585-9797
  Tulsa *(G-9499)*
Creative Apparel and More Inc ....G...... 918 682-1283
  Muskogee *(G-4664)*
Crown Neon Signs Inc ....G...... 918 437-7446
  Tulsa *(G-9516)*
Custom Expressignz ....G...... 580 252-2868
  Duncan *(G-2102)*
Custom Signs ....G...... 918 225-2749
  Cushing *(G-1928)*
Custom Time & Neon Co Inc ....G...... 405 364-9139
  Norman *(G-4974)*
Custom Vinyl Signs By Chas ....G...... 580 351-4058
  Lawton *(G-3914)*
Cutting Edge Signs ....G...... 918 688-1878
  Edmond *(G-2378)*
D Signs & Wonders LLC ....F...... 405 932-4585
  Paden *(G-7635)*
David Logan ....G...... 918 739-4231
  Catoosa *(G-1315)*
Davis Sign Co ....G...... 580 225-3121
  Elk City *(G-2801)*
Debo Dmnsons Laser Cut Engrave ....G...... 405 843-9098
  Oklahoma City *(G-5915)*
Design My Signs OK LLC ....G...... 918 923-0175
  Claremore *(G-1614)*
Designs and Signs By Jillian ....G...... 405 409-1522
  Jones *(G-3744)*
Digital Theory LLC ....G...... 405 824-6460
  Norman *(G-4980)*
Digital Theory Signs ....G...... 405 438-0222
  Norman *(G-4981)*
Dos Okies Signs & Graphics ....G...... 918 569-7292
  Clayton *(G-1709)*
Doug Strickland ....G...... 580 436-1010
  Ada *(G-33)*
Downing Manufacturing Inc ....F...... 918 224-1116
  Tulsa *(G-9001)*

SIGNS & ADVERTISING SPECIALTIES — PRODUCT SECTION

Company	Location / ID	Section	Phone
Dunbar Event Signs Inc	Owasso (G-7564)	G	918 607-9254
Eagle Graphics	Bartlesville (G-477)	G	918 335-7777
Eaton-Quade Company	Oklahoma City (G-6002)	F	405 236-4475
Elite Media Group LLC	Norman (G-4989)	G	405 928-5800
Elite Sign Brokers	Oklahoma City (G-6025)	G	405 200-6970
Elk Valley Woodworking Inc	Carter (G-1281)	G	580 486-3337
Encinos 3d Custom Products LLC	Tulsa (G-9681)	F	918 286-8535
Estate Sales By Greg Earles	Oklahoma City (G-6052)	G	405 210-8472
Excell Products Inc	Choctaw (G-1542)	E	405 390-4491
Express Ltg & Sign Maint LLC	Oklahoma City (G-6064)	G	405 378-3838
Fairchild Signs	Moore (G-4522)	G	405 439-3100
Fast Signs	Broken Arrow (G-906)	G	918 251-0330
Fastsigns	Owasso (G-7566)	G	918 376-7870
Fastsigns	Norman (G-4999)	G	405 701-2908
Fastsigns of Lawton	Lawton (G-3927)	G	580 595-9101
Fellers Inc	Tulsa (G-9735)	F	918 621-4412
Fellers Inc	Tulsa (G-9736)	C	918 621-4400
Finley Discount Sign Ligh	Moore (G-4523)	G	405 445-8888
First Impressions Inc	Beggs (G-555)	G	918 267-4642
First Thought Inc	Bartlesville (G-483)	G	918 336-3322
Fixtures Express	Edmond (G-2415)	G	405 834-1633
Franks Signs	Bartlesville (G-485)	G	918 335-9715
Frederick Sommers Wstn Sign Co	Tulsa (G-9773)	F	918 587-2300
Freds Sign Co	Newalla (G-4809)	G	405 235-8696
G & S Sign Services LLC	Oklahoma City (G-6130)	G	405 604-3636
Game Changing Image LLC	Beggs (G-556)	G	918 289-3392
George Miller	Edmond (G-2434)	G	405 341-4097
Good Life Concepts Inc	Edmond (G-2439)	G	478 714-9114
Graf-X LLC	Hinton (G-3529)	G	405 542-6631
Graphic Excursions	Watts (G-11356)	G	918 422-5318
Graphix Xpress	Ponca City (G-7831)	G	580 765-7324
Gss Sign & Design LLC	Mounds (G-4617)	F	918 827-6561
H&R Lifting & Bucket Service	Tulsa (G-9878)	G	918 446-5549
Happy Camper Signs	Tulsa (G-9010)	G	918 856-4279
Hays and Hays Companies Inc	Stillwater (G-8698)	G	405 624-2999
Hays Tent & Awning	Dewey (G-2023)	G	918 534-1663
Highway Man Signs	Skiatook (G-8548)	G	918 396-8024
Highway Man Signs LLC	Bartlesville (G-493)	G	918 534-9100
House of Trophies	Claremore (G-1637)	G	918 341-2111
House of Trophies	Wetumka (G-11492)	G	405 452-3524
Howdy Signs	Inola (G-3662)	G	918 543-2854
Htw Inc	McAlester (G-4305)	G	918 423-4619
Integrity Signs	Ramona (G-8046)	G	918 520-2802
Irwin Custom Sign Company LLC	Stillwater (G-8704)	G	405 372-0657
Ixzibit	Jones (G-3748)	G	405 413-2260
Izoom Inc	Tulsa (G-10015)	G	918 836-9666
James P Compton	Muskogee (G-4697)	G	918 682-3700
Jelke Signs	Duncan (G-2134)	G	580 252-2523
Jerry Swanson Sales Co Inc	Tulsa (G-10038)	G	918 712-7446
Jim Did It Signs	Duncan (G-2136)	G	580 255-5533
Jim Ford Sign Co	Ardmore (G-315)	G	580 223-8880
Jim Watkins	Bristow (G-783)	G	918 367-5575
Joe Decker Signs	Norman (G-5044)	G	405 630-8691
Johnson Plastics Plus - Okla	Oklahoma City (G-6376)	G	800 654-4150
Johnson Signs Inc	Arapaho (G-224)	G	580 323-6454
Just-In-Time Signs LLC	Sayre (G-8342)	G	580 821-1140
Kaiser Sign & Graphics Co Inc	Weatherford (G-11423)	G	580 772-3880
Keleher Outdoor Advertising Co	Bartlesville (G-502)	F	918 333-8855
Klines Signs & Crane	Woodward (G-11604)	G	580 256-2374
Krause Plastics	Tulsa (G-10100)	G	918 835-4202
Kustom Graphics	Oklahoma City (G-6436)	G	405 635-8009
Kustom Signs	Oklahoma City (G-6437)	G	405 635-8009
Lake Country Graphics Inc	Muskogee (G-4704)	G	918 682-8849
Le Gravis LLC	Tulsa (G-10142)	G	918 346-6313
Led Signs of Oklahoma	Tulsa (G-10146)	G	918 619-9798
Legacy Signs	Ponca City (G-7844)	G	580 762-2288
Legacy Signs	Tulsa (G-10149)	G	918 409-0835
Lettering Express OK Inc	Oklahoma City (G-6469)	E	405 235-8999
Liberty Signs	Tulsa (G-10157)	G	918 409-4470
Luther Sign Co	Oklahoma City (G-6503)	G	405 681-6535
Lyle S Sign Contractors	Newalla (G-4812)	G	405 386-7443
Marrara Group Inc	Tulsa (G-10216)	G	918 379-0993
Marshall County Publishing Co	Madill (G-4155)	F	580 795-3355
Mart Trophy Co Inc	Tulsa (G-10217)	G	918 481-3388
McCabe Crane & Sign	McAlester (G-4318)	G	918 424-6381
McCurdy and Associates LLC	Oklahoma City (G-6546)	G	405 317-4178
Mercury Sign and Banner	Norman (G-5071)	G	405 360-3303
Mh Signs LLC	Madill (G-4156)	G	580 795-2925
Midwest Decals LLC	Oklahoma City (G-6602)	G	405 787-8747
Midwest Wraps	Tulsa (G-10273)	G	918 624-2111
Miket ADS Inc	Claremore (G-1655)	G	918 341-2992
Miketads Inc	Claremore (G-1656)	G	918 341-2992
ML Sign Service LLC	Newalla (G-4815)	G	405 386-4898
Mltl Enterprises LLC	Norman (G-5077)	G	405 321-2224
Modesto Vinyl Lettering Inc	Ardmore (G-334)	G	580 223-4262
Myprint	Miami (G-4421)	G	918 542-7672
National Sign Market	Edmond (G-2529)	G	405 821-8768
New ERA Signs LLC	Pauls Valley (G-7668)	G	405 926-2050
North American Cos	Tulsa (G-10360)	F	918 592-2000
Oklahoma City Frequency	Oklahoma City (G-6740)	G	405 887-7115
Oklahoma Logo Signs Inc	Oklahoma City (G-6753)	G	405 840-1550
Oklahoma Sign Association	Tulsa (G-10408)	G	918 587-7171
Oklahoma Sign Company	Oklahoma City (G-6762)	G	405 620-6716
Oklahoma Visual Graphics LLC	Oklahoma City (G-6764)	E	405 943-3278
Order-Matic Electronics Corp	Oklahoma City (G-6781)	C	405 672-1487
Osborne Design Co	Tulsa (G-10444)	G	918 585-3212
Paul Clinton Hughes	Nowata (G-5225)	G	918 273-1888
Pg13 Graphics & Design LLC	Oklahoma City (G-6840)	G	405 720-8002
Precision Sign & Design	Tulsa (G-10549)	G	918 430-1102
Prime Signs of Oklahoma Inc	Tulsa (G-10559)	G	918 500-2213
Pro-Feil Mktg Solutions LLC	Lawton (G-3985)	G	580 595-9101
R & R Signs Inc	Durant (G-2250)	G	580 924-4363
R G Enterprises	Elk City (G-2864)	G	580 225-2260
Rainbow Awnings & Signs	Tulsa (G-10610)	G	918 249-0003
Randys Signs Inc	Shawnee (G-8486)	G	405 273-2564
Rbi Advertising	Tulsa (G-10624)	G	918 592-1836
Rebel Sign Company LLC	Oklahoma City (G-6982)	G	405 456-9253
Redwood Country Signs	Newcastle (G-4837)	G	405 596-8737
Reece Supply Company Houston	Tulsa (G-10634)	F	918 556-5000
Rick Knight	Oklahoma City (G-7020)	G	405 232-4954
Robert Smith	Oklahoma City (G-7037)	G	405 722-5188
Robyn Holdings LLC	Oklahoma City (G-7041)	E	405 722-4600
Royal Sign & Graphic Inc	Muskogee (G-4746)	G	918 682-6151
Royal Signs LLC	Hennessey (G-3483)	G	918 507-3303
Rusty Rooster Metal	Stroud (G-8817)	G	918 290-9113
S & S Textile Inc	Oklahoma City (G-7065)	F	405 632-9928
S S Design Co	Roland (G-8113)	G	918 427-3230
Sammys Signs LLC	Chickasha (G-1506)	G	405 320-1156
Semasys Inc	Oklahoma City (G-7107)	E	405 525-2335
Sheehy Signs	Purcell (G-8019)	G	405 623-7777
Sidewinder Signs	Poteau (G-7913)	G	918 647-5306
Sign & Send It LLC	Tulsa (G-10756)	F	918 730-9309
Sign A Rama Inc	Oklahoma City (G-7131)	G	405 631-2008
Sign Depot	Durant (G-2257)	F	580 931-9363
Sign Dezigns	Broken Arrow (G-1050)	G	918 688-3660
Sign Dezigns LLC	Duncan (G-2177)	G	580 656-0621
Sign Factory LLC	Shawnee (G-8498)	G	405 401-9513
Sign Gypsies Ardmore LLC	Ardmore (G-354)	G	512 644-6976
Sign Gypsies Midwest City LLC	Midwest City (G-4453)	G	405 259-9886
Sign Innovations Inc	Bokchito (G-751)	G	214 234-1614
Sign of Lies LLC	Oklahoma City (G-7133)	G	405 618-9695
Sign of Times	Kingfisher (G-3814)	G	405 375-4717
Sign Solutions	Broken Arrow (G-1164)	G	918 449-9439
Sign Source	Ada (G-88)	G	580 436-1323
Sign Up For Emails	Oklahoma City (G-7135)	G	405 236-3100

PRODUCT SECTION
SIGNS: Neon

Sign-A-Rama of Ok Inc ... G ... 405 631-2008
Oklahoma City *(G-7136)*

Signature Graphics Corp ... G ... 918 294-3485
Bixby *(G-658)*

Signco Inc ... G ... 405 615-7572
Yukon *(G-11782)*

Signs 405 LLC ... G ... 405 470-1616
Warr Acres *(G-11329)*

Signs and T-Shirts Oklahoma Cy ... G ... 405 600-7080
Oklahoma City *(G-7137)*

Signs By Dale Inc ... G ... 479 518-3744
Lawton *(G-3997)*

Signs By Jade ... G ... 918 423-0041
McAlester *(G-4335)*

Signs By Sikorski ... G ... 918 257-5164
Afton *(G-121)*

Signs Etc ... G ... 918 447-1065
Tulsa *(G-10760)*

Signs of Times ... G ... 918 512-6747
Sapulpa *(G-8312)*

Signs On A Dime ... G ... 580 237-3078
Enid *(G-3056)*

Signs-N-More ... G ... 918 760-5080
Coweta *(G-1897)*

Skis Tees ... G ... 405 239-7547
Oklahoma City *(G-7146)*

SKM Graphics & Signs ... G ... 405 636-1911
Oklahoma City *(G-7147)*

Skyslate Signs ... F ... 405 818-0838
Oklahoma City *(G-7149)*

Smartsigns LLC ... G ... 405 659-5003
Oklahoma City *(G-7152)*

Son Signs Okc ... G ... 405 830-2536
Oklahoma City *(G-7160)*

Sonburst Graphics LLC ... G ... 918 478-8600
Fort Gibson *(G-3178)*

Sooner Signs ... G ... 405 503-8902
Norman *(G-5151)*

Sooner State Graphics & Signs ... G ... 405 837-5226
Oklahoma City *(G-7166)*

Southland Awards & Signs ... G ... 918 691-9141
Broken Arrow *(G-1056)*

Spraycan Creative LLC ... G ... 405 494-0321
Yukon *(G-11786)*

Srh Lighting LLC ... G ... 405 604-9414
Oklahoma City *(G-7190)*

Stillwater Signs Incorporated ... G ... 405 533-2828
Stillwater *(G-8758)*

Stokely Outdoor Advertising ... E ... 918 664-4724
Tulsa *(G-10852)*

Susan C Willard LLC ... G ... 918 740-4630
Tulsa *(G-10882)*

Tammy Brown ... G ... 918 456-1959
Tahlequah *(G-8887)*

Tcae Enterprises Inc ... G ... 918 664-5977
Tulsa *(G-10908)*

Thinkwerx LLC ... G ... 405 590-3937
Nichols Hills *(G-4864)*

Tom Bennett Manufacturing ... F ... 405 528-5671
Oklahoma City *(G-7302)*

Tornados Screen Printing ... G ... 405 964-5339
McLoud *(G-4363)*

Trade Mark Signs ... G ... 580 242-7446
Enid *(G-3066)*

Tradeshowstuff LLC ... G ... 918 437-4338
Tulsa *(G-10967)*

Trans-Tech LLC ... F ... 405 422-5000
El Reno *(G-2763)*

Trophies n Things ... G ... 405 247-9771
Anadarko *(G-207)*

Tulsa Sign Company ... G ... 918 215-7131
Tulsa *(G-11008)*

Twj Inc ... G ... 405 392-4366
Tuttle *(G-11217)*

Ultra Fast Signs ... G ... 405 269-9468
Tulsa *(G-11033)*

US Safetysign & Decal LLC ... F ... 800 678-2529
Tulsa *(G-11057)*

US Signs & Led LLC ... G ... 405 819-3086
Yukon *(G-11799)*

USA Signs Inc ... G ... 918 392-5544
Tulsa *(G-11059)*

Vinyl Vikings LLC ... G ... 405 260-9022
Edmond *(G-2673)*

Walkers Sign Company ... G ... 580 353-7446
Lawton *(G-4019)*

Warner Jwly Box Display Co LLC ... D ... 580 536-8885
Lawton *(G-4021)*

Waynoka Sign Shop ... G ... 580 824-1717
Waynoka *(G-11382)*

Whimsical Sign and Crafting Co ... G ... 918 315-4715
Roland *(G-8115)*

Whistler Media Group ... G ... 918 605-7446
Tulsa *(G-11117)*

Whistler Sign Co LLC ... F ... 918 491-7446
Tulsa *(G-11118)*

Whitecaps Inc ... G ... 405 610-7007
Midwest City *(G-4461)*

Wyatt Earp Companies ... G ... 918 225-7770
Cushing *(G-1972)*

Yesco ... G ... 918 524-9914
Tulsa *(G-11168)*

SIGNS & ADVERTISING SPECIALTIES: Artwork, Advertising

Multigraphic Design ... G ... 405 672-8201
Oklahoma City *(G-6635)*

SIGNS & ADVERTISING SPECIALTIES: Letters For Signs, Metal

Bigfoot Prints LLC ... G ... 918 805-0543
Collinsville *(G-1803)*

Mt Designs ... G ... 580 317-3921
Fort Towson *(G-3183)*

SIGNS & ADVERTISING SPECIALTIES: Novelties

Barbara Chaple ... G ... 405 721-3758
Oklahoma City *(G-5526)*

Bipo Inc ... E ... 580 262-9640
Oklahoma City *(G-5575)*

Van Horn James ... G ... 405 324-2456
Yukon *(G-11800)*

SIGNS & ADVERTISING SPECIALTIES: Signs

66 Sign and Light LLC ... G ... 405 445-9212
Luther *(G-4131)*

Ace Sign Company Inc ... G ... 918 446-3030
Tulsa *(G-9095)*

Affordable Signs & Decals Inc ... G ... 405 942-7059
Oklahoma City *(G-5397)*

All Signs ... G ... 918 739-3660
Tulsa *(G-9137)*

Anns Quick Print Co Inc ... G ... 405 222-1871
Chickasha *(G-1429)*

Architectural Graphics Inc ... G ... 757 427-1900
Chickasha *(G-1432)*

Arrow Sign Company Inc ... F ... 580 353-2227
Lawton *(G-3891)*

Clark Signs Inc ... G ... 918 291-3411
Kiefer *(G-3777)*

Clay Serigraphics Inc ... F ... 918 592-2529
Tulsa *(G-9445)*

Cutting Edge Signs & Graphics ... G ... 405 262-4300
El Reno *(G-2709)*

Elqui International Ltd Co ... G ... 918 335-5002
Bartlesville *(G-480)*

Emg Graphic Systems Inc ... F ... 918 835-5300
Tulsa *(G-9672)*

Galaxie Sign Co ... G ... 580 226-2944
Ardmore *(G-293)*

Instant Signs Inc ... G ... 405 848-8181
Oklahoma City *(G-6311)*

J & B Graphics Inc ... E ... 405 524-7446
Oklahoma City *(G-6328)*

Jack Pratt Screen-Ad Co ... F ... 405 524-5551
Oklahoma City *(G-6342)*

Jason M Haag ... G ... 918 369-1805
Bixby *(G-638)*

Landmark Design & Sign Corp ... G ... 405 387-3999
Newcastle *(G-4830)*

Lettercrafts ... G ... 918 584-2400
Tulsa *(G-10154)*

Lindsey Printing ... G ... 580 476-2278
Rush Springs *(G-8123)*

Misaco Sign & Screen Printing ... G ... 918 542-4188
Miami *(G-4419)*

Petes Signs ... G ... 580 338-2266
Guymon *(G-3361)*

Precision Image Cnversions LLC ... F ... 918 430-1102
Tulsa *(G-10546)*

Sanford Brothers Co Inc ... F ... 918 665-7358
Tulsa *(G-10706)*

Sign Innovations LLC ... G ... 405 840-1151
Oklahoma City *(G-7132)*

Sign Language ... G ... 405 360-7500
Norman *(G-5145)*

Sign Maker LLC ... G ... 918 728-6060
Tulsa *(G-10757)*

Signs To Go LLC ... G ... 405 348-8646
Edmond *(G-2621)*

Sublime Signs LLC ... G ... 405 364-1700
Norman *(G-5163)*

Tulsa Signs ... G ... 918 251-6262
Broken Arrow *(G-1086)*

Tyler Signs LLC ... G ... 405 631-5174
Oklahoma City *(G-7355)*

Walker Stamp & Seal Co ... E ... 405 235-5319
Oklahoma City *(G-7415)*

Wood Concepts Inc ... G ... 918 836-9481
Tulsa *(G-11147)*

Z Signs Inc ... F ... 405 670-1416
Oklahoma City *(G-7485)*

SIGNS & ADVERTSG SPECIALTIES: Displays/Cutouts Window/Lobby

Tfg In-Store Display LLC ... F ... 918 592-2834
Tulsa *(G-10923)*

SIGNS, EXC ELECTRIC, WHOLESALE

A 1 Advertising By L & H ... G ... 918 348-2529
Muskogee *(G-4639)*

D Signs & Wonders LLC ... F ... 405 932-4585
Paden *(G-7635)*

Fast Signs ... G ... 918 251-0330
Broken Arrow *(G-906)*

Fellers Inc ... C ... 918 621-4400
Tulsa *(G-9736)*

First Thought Inc ... G ... 918 336-3322
Bartlesville *(G-483)*

Neo Sign Company ... G ... 918 456-1959
Fort Gibson *(G-3177)*

R G Enterprises ... G ... 580 225-2260
Elk City *(G-2864)*

Sidewinder Signs ... G ... 918 647-5306
Poteau *(G-7913)*

Sonburst Graphics LLC ... G ... 918 478-8600
Fort Gibson *(G-3178)*

SIGNS: Electrical

Ad Tech Signs Inc ... G ... 405 236-0551
Oklahoma City *(G-5370)*

Allen Sign Studio LLC ... G ... 918 542-1180
Miami *(G-4390)*

Dalmarc Enterprises Inc ... D ... 405 942-8703
Oklahoma City *(G-5893)*

Danny Lee Signs ... G ... 580 832-5256
Cordell *(G-1857)*

Hasco Corporation ... E ... 405 524-6366
Oklahoma City *(G-6222)*

Insignia Signs Inc ... G ... 405 631-5522
Oklahoma City *(G-6309)*

Jack Stout Inc ... G ... 918 781-1000
Muskogee *(G-4696)*

Kay Holding Co ... E ... 580 628-4146
Tonkawa *(G-8977)*

Kennys Sign Graphx-Etchihg In ... G ... 580 477-4250
Altus *(G-160)*

Kline Sign LLC ... G ... 580 237-0732
Enid *(G-2995)*

Ledigital Signs LLC ... G ... 918 504-8506
Tulsa *(G-10147)*

Mullins Sign Shop ... G ... 580 889-4772
Atoka *(G-420)*

Neon Moore and Sign ... G ... 405 672-6277
Oklahoma City *(G-6670)*

Sign Service ... G ... 405 495-0700
Oklahoma City *(G-7134)*

Signs & Stitches ... G ... 918 245-3301
Sand Springs *(G-8224)*

Signtec Signs Distinction Inc ... G ... 405 745-7555
Oklahoma City *(G-7138)*

Technology Licensing Corp ... E ... 918 836-5597
Mounds *(G-4625)*

SIGNS: Neon

Acura Neon Inc ... E ... 918 252-2258
Broken Arrow *(G-813)*

Butner Brothers LLC ... G ... 405 321-2322
Norman *(G-4949)*

Claude Neon Federal Signs Inc ... D ... 918 587-7171
Tulsa *(G-9444)*

Industrial Signs & Neon Inc ... F ... 405 236-5599
Oklahoma City *(G-6301)*

PRODUCT

Employee Codes: A=Over 500 employees, B=251-500
C=101-250, D=51-100, E=20-50, F=10-19, G=1-9

2020 Oklahoma Directory
of Manufacturers & Processors

817

SIGNS: Neon

Oil Capitol Neon Inc ....G........ 918 582-9031
  Tulsa *(G-10386)*
Osage Neon ....G........ 918 583-4430
  Tulsa *(G-10443)*
Premier Signs & Design LLC ....G........ 918 825-6422
  Pryor *(G-7983)*
Reynolds & Sons Neon Studio ....G........ 405 525-6366
  Oklahoma City *(G-7013)*
Stansbury Noble Jr Inc ....G........ 209 847-8408
  Tishomingo *(G-8968)*
Superior Neon Co Inc ....E........ 405 528-5515
  Oklahoma City *(G-7229)*
Triple DS Neon Signs LLC ....G........ 817 447-2830
  Jay *(G-3686)*

SILICA MINING

Covia Holdings Corporation ....E........ 580 456-7772
  Roff *(G-8107)*

SILICON WAFERS: Chemically Doped

Southwest Silicon Tech Corp ....E........ 580 223-5058
  Ardmore *(G-357)*

SILK SCREEN DESIGN SVCS

4524 LLC ....G........ 405 620-3711
  Edmond *(G-2285)*
Body Billboards ....G........ 405 282-9922
  Guthrie *(G-3300)*
Cas Monogramming Inc ....G........ 405 350-6556
  Yukon *(G-11703)*
Cejco Inc ....F........ 405 366-8256
  Norman *(G-4954)*
Complete Graphics Inc ....G........ 405 232-8882
  Oklahoma City *(G-5812)*
Custom Monograms & Lettering ....G........ 405 495-8586
  Bethany *(G-574)*
Design It ....G........ 405 756-3635
  Lindsay *(G-4060)*
Impact Screen Printing ....G........ 918 258-8337
  Broken Arrow *(G-934)*
Inkling Design ....G........ 405 495-5575
  Bethany *(G-583)*
Joys Uniforms Boutique Ltd ....G........ 918 747-4114
  Tulsa *(G-10061)*
Label Stable Inc ....G........ 580 223-2037
  Ardmore *(G-323)*
Sides Screenprinting More LLC ....G........ 580 772-8888
  Oklahoma City *(G-7127)*
Way-Wear LLC ....G........ 405 410-8367
  Kingfisher *(G-3820)*

SILO STAVES: Concrete Or Cast Stone

Cobble Rock and Stone LLC ....F........ 405 567-3552
  Prague *(G-7923)*

SILVER ORES

Inglesrud Corp ....G........ 405 429-7928
  Oklahoma City *(G-6304)*

SILVERWARE & PLATED WARE

Mtm Recognition LLC ....G........ 405 670-4545
  Oklahoma City *(G-6633)*

SIMULATORS: Flight

Cymstar LLC ....G........ 918 251-8100
  Tulsa *(G-9532)*
Cymstar LLC ....C........ 918 251-8100
  Broken Arrow *(G-884)*
L3 Technologies Inc ....G........ 405 601-0874
  Oklahoma City *(G-6442)*
L3 Technologies Inc ....E........ 405 739-3700
  Tinker Afb *(G-8954)*
Safety Training Systems Inc ....E........ 918 665-0125
  Tulsa *(G-10688)*

SIZES

CP Kelco US Inc ....E........ 918 758-2600
  Okmulgee *(G-7498)*
Desired Size ....G........ 405 314-3704
  Oklahoma City *(G-5927)*

SIZES: Rosin

Farrier Livingston Neon Technology ....G........ 580 657-3469
  Ardmore *(G-288)*

SKATING RINKS: Roller

Green Cntry Trophy Screen Prtg ....G........ 918 647-2923
  Poteau *(G-7906)*

SKILL TRAINING CENTER

Alex Arms and Instruction LLC ....G........ 405 351-0806
  Alex *(G-129)*

SKYLIGHTS

Plastic Engrg Co Tulsa Inc ....E........ 918 622-9660
  Tulsa *(G-10523)*

SLAB & TILE: Precast Concrete, Floor

Alpha Concrete Products Inc ....F........ 405 769-7777
  Oklahoma City *(G-5424)*

SLAUGHTERING & MEAT PACKING

Food Svcs Auth of Quapaw Tribe ....F........ 918 542-1853
  Quapaw *(G-8030)*
Mc Ferrons Quality Meats Inc ....F........ 918 273-2892
  Nowata *(G-5220)*
Unrau Meat Co Inc ....G........ 918 543-8245
  Inola *(G-3676)*
Victory Garden Homestead LLC ....G........ 405 306-0308
  Blanchard *(G-744)*

SLINGS: Lifting, Made From Purchased Wire

Byers Products Group Inc ....G........ 405 491-8550
  Oklahoma City *(G-5652)*
Industrial Splicing Sling LLC ....F........ 918 835-4452
  Tulsa *(G-9981)*
United Slings Inc ....G........ 405 598-2616
  Tecumseh *(G-8930)*

SLOT MACHINES

Diamond Game Enterprises ....E........ 405 789-5800
  Oklahoma City *(G-5938)*

SNACK & NONALCOHOLIC BEVERAGE BARS

Wiljackal LLC ....F........ 918 252-2663
  Tulsa *(G-11121)*

SOAPS & DETERGENTS

B & P Industrial Inc ....F........ 918 665-3301
  Tulsa *(G-9242)*
Berkshire Corporation ....G........ 405 677-3391
  Oklahoma City *(G-5556)*
Brenntag Southwest Inc ....E........ 918 266-2951
  Catoosa *(G-1306)*
Cutting Edge Industries Corp ....G........ 918 523-7373
  Tulsa *(G-9530)*
Dermamedics LLC ....G........ 405 319-8130
  Oklahoma City *(G-5925)*
E Environmental LLC ....G........ 405 604-0000
  Oklahoma City *(G-5993)*
Easy Car Wash Systems Inc ....G........ 918 582-4355
  Tulsa *(G-9634)*
Juniper Ridge Inc ....G........ 405 762-2555
  Stillwater *(G-8708)*
Kleen Products Inc ....F........ 405 495-1168
  Oklahoma City *(G-6428)*
NBC Chemical Co Inc ....G........ 580 256-2627
  Woodward *(G-11613)*
Remwood Products Co ....G........ 918 251-8399
  Broken Arrow *(G-1030)*
SMC Technologies Inc ....F........ 405 737-3740
  Midwest City *(G-4455)*
Strop Shoppe LLc ....G........ 775 557-8767
  Norman *(G-5162)*

SOAPS & DETERGENTS: Textile

Schmidt Farms At String Ridge ....G........ 580 919-2111
  Fletcher *(G-3167)*
Shabby Chicks Smart Clean LLC ....G........ 405 414-8938
  Duncan *(G-2176)*

SOCIAL SVCS: Individual & Family

Work Activity Center Inc ....E........ 405 799-6911
  Moore *(G-4584)*

SOFTWARE PUBLISHERS: Application

5 Over Games LLC ....G........ 405 928-5972
  Oklahoma City *(G-5336)*
Adjacent Creations LLC ....G........ 405 819-6507
  Oklahoma City *(G-5374)*
Al Capone Limo Corp ....G........ 405 999-3335
  Oklahoma City *(G-5405)*
Ameriinfovets Inc ....G........ 408 446-4343
  Pryor *(G-7943)*
Canvass LLC ....G........ 580 284-7896
  Blanchard *(G-704)*
Catalog System Inc ....G........ 405 808-1533
  Moore *(G-4507)*
Chorus Labs LLC ....G........ 405 317-2942
  Oklahoma City *(G-5763)*
Christy Collins Inc ....G........ 580 305-0001
  Frederick *(G-3192)*
Cura Telehealth Wellness LLC ....F........ 918 513-1062
  Tulsa *(G-9523)*
Delenda LLC ....G........ 918 409-1313
  Owasso *(G-7561)*
Dick Hall & Associates ....G........ 405 202-4301
  Norman *(G-4979)*
Digii ID LLC ....G........ 405 662-5504
  Oklahoma City *(G-5946)*
Eagle Applctions Solutions Ltd ....G........ 888 511-8720
  Oklahoma City *(G-5994)*
Fjsp Inc ....G........ 405 306-0735
  Oklahoma City *(G-6087)*
Genesis Financial Software ....G........ 580 252-2594
  Duncan *(G-2120)*
Goldtechs Inc ....G........ 918 856-9059
  Bartlesville *(G-487)*
High Rollers Empire LLC ....G........ 405 535-3066
  Oklahoma City *(G-6248)*
Info-Sharp LLC ....G........ 520 204-5093
  Norman *(G-5033)*
Integrated S Mycare ....G........ 405 605-0546
  Oklahoma City *(G-6314)*
Keystone Flex Admnstrators LLC ....G........ 405 285-1144
  Oklahoma City *(G-6412)*
Lightbe Corporation ....G........ 918 760-6968
  Tulsa *(G-10160)*
Masters Technical Advisors Inc ....G........ 918 949-1641
  Tulsa *(G-10221)*
Microsoft Corporation ....D........ 469 775-6864
  Tulsa *(G-10256)*
Monroe Gray LLC ....G........ 918 813-6588
  Bixby *(G-646)*
Quantum Trading Technologies ....G........ 918 876-3921
  Bartlesville *(G-520)*
Quest Loot LLC ....G........ 405 609-4100
  Edmond *(G-2580)*
Rapid Jack Solutions Inc ....G........ 405 203-3131
  Norman *(G-5129)*
S4f Inc ....G........ 888 390-2224
  Broken Arrow *(G-1159)*
Saltus Technologies LLC ....F........ 918 392-3900
  Tulsa *(G-10690)*
Seamless LLC ....G........ 918 743-7935
  Tulsa *(G-10720)*
Shane Lee Duvall ....G........ 918 960-0506
  Broken Arrow *(G-1163)*
Shipzen Inc ....G........ 949 357-2127
  Tulsa *(G-10748)*
Silvertree Solutions LLC ....G........ 405 922-7281
  Yukon *(G-11783)*
Solutionware Ltd ....E........ 405 843-0809
  Oklahoma City *(G-7159)*
True North Ministries Inc ....G........ 405 562-2986
  Edmond *(G-2654)*
Utown LLC ....G........ 918 261-3402
  Tulsa *(G-11062)*

SOFTWARE PUBLISHERS: Business & Professional

Advanced Micro Solutions Inc ....F........ 405 562-0112
  Edmond *(G-2290)*
Arrowhead Software ....G........ 918 744-7239
  Tulsa *(G-9213)*
Bottomline LLC ....G........ 918 261-2354
  Tulsa *(G-9324)*
Businet ....F........ 918 858-4440
  Tulsa *(G-9352)*
Computer Technology Soltn ....G........ 918 607-2136
  Broken Arrow *(G-873)*
Creditpoint Software LLC ....E........ 918 376-9440
  Tulsa *(G-9506)*

PRODUCT SECTION — SPACE VEHICLE EQPT

Company	Code	Phone
Equivaq Software LLC — Stillwater (G-8687)	G	405 742-0598
Genesis Technologies Inc — Tulsa (G-9818)	G	918 307-0098
Idealist Software LLC — Bixby (G-634)	G	918 609-4364
Martek Inc — Inola (G-3667)	G	918 543-6477
Medexperts LLC — Muskogee (G-4711)	F	918 684-4030
Mesh Networks LLC — Oklahoma City (G-6570)	G	832 230-8074
Openlink Financial LLC — Tulsa (G-10433)	D	918 594-7320
PC Net — Pauls Valley (G-7670)	G	405 238-2001
Perk Dynamics LLC — Asher (G-394)	G	405 585-2520
Professional Datasolutions Inc — Tulsa (G-10567)	E	512 218-0463
Ray Computer Services Intl Inc — Jenks (G-3725)	G	918 299-7262
Riggs Heinrich Media Inc — Tulsa (G-10652)	E	918 492-0660
Siemens Industry Software Inc — Tulsa (G-10753)	G	918 505-4220
Tire Soft LLC — Edmond (G-2644)	G	405 341-5070
Tmw Systems Inc — Oklahoma City (G-7298)	G	405 602-6055
Veritris Group Inc — Oklahoma City (G-7399)	G	580 713-4927
Warning Aware LLC — Edmond (G-2681)	G	405 300-8833

SOFTWARE PUBLISHERS: Education

Company	Code	Phone
Corona Technical Services LLC — Tulsa (G-9490)	G	918 398-8052
Jade Fire LLC — El Reno (G-2728)	G	405 295-7734
Northeast Tchnlgy Ctr- Clrmore — Claremore (G-1663)	E	918 342-8066
Resource Development Co LLC — Tulsa (G-10645)	E	248 646-2300
Schoolware Inc — Durant (G-2255)	G	580 745-9100

SOFTWARE PUBLISHERS: NEC

Company	Code	Phone
Actualizing Apps LLC — Tulsa (G-9099)	G	918 627-7450
Adtek Software Company — Oklahoma City (G-5376)	G	815 452-2345
Aloft Software LLC — Oklahoma City (G-5423)	G	405 633-0250
American Bank Systems Inc — Oklahoma City (G-5432)	E	405 607-7000
App-Solute Innovations LLC — Ada (G-10)	G	580 453-0055
At A Glance Software LLC — Oklahoma City (G-5479)	G	405 601-3062
Axiom Automotive Tech Inc — Oklahoma City (G-5498)	G	909 841-8200
Birddog Software Corporation — Oklahoma City (G-5576)	F	405 794-5950
Boolean Inc — Edmond (G-2330)	G	405 341-1499
Buckelew Accnting Slutions LLC — Edmond (G-2334)	G	405 359-5887
Byrum Enterprises Inc — Oklahoma City (G-5653)	G	812 595-4598
Chrysalis Software Inc — Tulsa (G-9423)	E	831 761-1307
Clearbay Software LLC — Norman (G-4960)	G	405 310-9150
Compound Software LLC — Moore (G-4509)	G	405 912-3301
Computer Assistance — Jones (G-3743)	G	405 399-2422
Custom Software Systems Inc — Oklahoma City (G-5875)	G	405 524-1919
Cynergy Software Corp LLC — Warr Acres (G-11317)	G	405 603-2953
Data Systems Consultants — Oklahoma City (G-5899)	G	405 445-0886
DCA Inc — Cushing (G-1929)	E	918 225-0346
Digital Doctor — Oklahoma City (G-5947)	G	405 618-1416
Discoversoft Development LLC — Nichols Hills (G-4859)	G	405 840-1235
Eufrates Com LLC — Tulsa (G-9704)	G	918 280-9270
Global Interface Solutions Inc — Tulsa (G-9832)	G	918 971-1600
Hampton Software Development L — Broken Arrow (G-926)	G	918 607-5307
Hands Down Software — Oklahoma City (G-6212)	G	405 844-6314
IMS Erp Consulting LLC — Tulsa (G-9975)	G	918 508-9544
Innocative Computing Tech — Oklahoma City (G-6306)	G	405 255-4453
Intellevue Ltd — Tulsa (G-10001)	G	918 250-5561
International Sftwr Cons Inc — Durant (G-2239)	G	580 924-1231
Jack Henry & Associates Inc — Oklahoma City (G-6341)	F	405 947-6644
Jansens Software — Oklahoma City (G-5297)	G	405 692-4756
Jbr Software Development LLC — Choctaw (G-1548)	G	405 872-8561
Jireh Software Inc — Broken Arrow (G-945)	G	918 294-8240
Jmz Software LLC — Lawton (G-3945)	G	580 284-9551
Juniper Networks Inc — Tulsa (G-10066)	D	918 877-2642
Lm Software Inc — Edmond (G-2490)	G	405 630-4663
Med-Solve LLC — Muskogee (G-4710)	F	918 684-4030
Medunison LLC — Oklahoma City (G-6560)	E	405 271-9900
Mere Software Inc — Tulsa (G-9020)	G	918 740-5018
New Vision Consulting Group — Edmond (G-2537)	F	405 796-7400
Nextthought LLC — Norman (G-5092)	G	405 673-5588
Norman Computers — Norman (G-5094)	F	405 292-9501
Omni Lighting — Tulsa (G-10417)	G	918 633-7245
Paycom Software Inc — Oklahoma City (G-6813)	D	405 722-6900
Perfecting Software LLC — Tulsa (G-10493)	G	918 250-7610
Permian Software LLC — Norman (G-5113)	G	405 329-6397
Pinnacle Business Systems Inc — Edmond (G-2571)	E	405 359-0121
Pivot Medical Solutions LLC — Muskogee (G-4734)	G	918 684-4030
Point To Point Software — Oklahoma City (G-6861)	G	405 869-9921
Post Software International — Tulsa (G-10535)	G	918 299-2158
Rcs Corporation — Tulsa (G-10625)	G	918 227-7497
Red River Software LLC — Oklahoma City (G-6989)	G	405 728-8102
Red Wind Training — Park Hill (G-7646)	G	918 822-0605
Seaport Software Inc — Broken Arrow (G-1047)	G	918 258-8611
Secureagent Software Inc — Tulsa (G-10722)	E	918 971-1600
Sequoyah Technologies LLC — Sapulpa (G-8310)	F	918 808-7270
Shave Software LLC — Norman (G-5144)	G	405 366-2168
Shi International Corp — Tulsa (G-10745)	G	918 583-4182
Smartmax Software Inc — Tulsa (G-10777)	E	918 388-5900
Software Perfection LLC — Broken Arrow (G-1166)	G	918 266-8883
Srifusion LLC — Lawton (G-4003)	G	774 238-7466
Starling Assoc Inc — Norman (G-5156)	G	405 740-8668
Stonebridge Acquisition Inc — Tulsa (G-10853)	D	918 663-8000
Studylamp Software LLC — Broken Arrow (G-1168)	G	918 357-1946
T A H Software Systems — Oklahoma City (G-7241)	G	405 478-3962
Taylor Accounting Systems — Oklahoma City (G-7256)	G	405 949-9898
Telos Payment Processing LLC — Norman (G-5172)	G	405 321-0474
Top Rim Technology — Delaware (G-2009)	G	918 467-3617
Trackum Inc — Norman (G-5179)	G	405 799-4863
Transelearn — Oklahoma City (G-7317)	G	405 922-4595
Tuxpro Software & Development — Norman (G-5183)	G	405 812-1334
Virtuoso Software LLC — Tulsa (G-11080)	G	918 813-4941
Webready Software Inc — Broken Arrow (G-1093)	G	918 808-8465
Whiteboard Software LLC — Edmond (G-2688)	G	405 408-3326
Wk Winters & Assoc — Edmond (G-2691)	G	405 341-6571
Wolf Software Group Co — Warr Acres (G-11331)	G	405 721-0577
Young Software — Sparks (G-8590)	G	918 290-9876

SOFTWARE PUBLISHERS: Operating Systems

Company	Code	Phone
Ellis Enterprises Inc — Oklahoma City (G-6027)	G	405 917-5336
New X Drives Inc — Tulsa (G-10338)	F	918 850-4463
Phoenix Software Intl Inc — Tulsa (G-10510)	G	918 491-6144

SOFTWARE PUBLISHERS: Publisher's

Company	Code	Phone
Ecapitol LLC — Oklahoma City (G-6003)	G	405 524-2833

SOIL CONDITIONERS

Company	Code	Phone
Goff Associates Inc — Oklahoma City (G-6167)	G	615 750-2900
Hope Minerals International — Wetumka (G-11491)	G	405 452-3529

SOLAR CELLS

Company	Code	Phone
Electric Green Inc — Oklahoma City (G-6022)	G	405 706-1683
Sun Direct Power Inc — Tulsa (G-10869)	G	918 612-4090

SOLAR HEATING EQPT

Company	Code	Phone
Site Distribution LLC — Tulsa (G-10769)	G	918 625-7980

SOLDERING EQPT: Electrical, Handheld

Company	Code	Phone
JJ Perodeau Gunmaker Inc — Sand Springs (G-8195)	G	580 747-1804

SOLVENTS

Company	Code	Phone
Frontier Logistical Svcs LLC — Oklahoma City (G-6123)	G	405 232-4401

SOUND RECORDING STUDIOS

Company	Code	Phone
Benson Sound Inc — Oklahoma City (G-5553)	G	405 610-7455

SOUND REPRODUCING EQPT

Company	Code	Phone
Louis Systems & Products Inc — Edmond (G-2498)	G	405 285-0950

SOYBEAN PRDTS

Company	Code	Phone
Koko-Best Inc — Tulsa (G-10099)	G	918 836-2400
Solae LLC — Pryor (G-7991)	E	918 476-5825

SPACE FLIGHT OPERATIONS, EXC GOVERNMENT

Company	Code	Phone
Flightsafety International Inc — Broken Arrow (G-910)	A	918 259-4000

SPACE VEHICLE EQPT

Company	Code	Phone
Ducommun Labarge Tech Inc — Tulsa (G-9611)	C	918 459-2200

Employee Codes: A=Over 500 employees, B=251-500, C=101-250, D=51-100, E=20-50, F=10-19, G=1-9

SPACE VEHICLE EQPT

Hurst Aerospace Inc .... G 918 543-6527
 Inola *(G-3663)*
Spirit Aerosystems Inc .... C 918 423-6979
 McAlester *(G-4337)*
Stewart Industries Intl LLC .... F 405 260-0990
 Guthrie *(G-3339)*
Valco Inc .... E 405 228-0932
 Oklahoma City *(G-7386)*

SPEAKER SYSTEMS

Rockford Corporation .... C 405 624-6722
 Stillwater *(G-8748)*

SPECIALTY FOOD STORES: Coffee

Minnette Company Ltd .... G 580 226-2929
 Wilson *(G-11538)*
Tulsa Coffee Service Inc .... E 918 836-5570
 Tulsa *(G-10993)*
Wassco Corporation .... F 918 834-4444
 Tulsa *(G-11097)*

SPECIALTY FOOD STORES: Dried Fruit

S & S Foods Inc .... F 405 256-6557
 Mustang *(G-4792)*

SPECIALTY FOOD STORES: Soft Drinks

Sooner Coca-Cola Bottling Co .... G 918 423-0911
 McAlester *(G-4266)*

SPINDLES: Textile

United Axle .... G 918 344-1457
 Claremore *(G-1697)*

SPORTING & ATHLETIC GOODS: Boomerangs

Boomerang .... G 405 250-6597
 Shawnee *(G-8434)*

SPORTING & ATHLETIC GOODS: Bowling Alleys & Access

Dawg Pound .... G 580 622-2695
 Sulphur *(G-8831)*
Duggans Ann Marie Pro Shop .... G 405 715-2695
 Edmond *(G-2397)*
Durant .... G 580 920-2069
 Durant *(G-2225)*
El Reno Bowl Inc .... G 405 262-3611
 El Reno *(G-2714)*
Next Generation .... G 405 606-4455
 Oklahoma City *(G-6673)*

SPORTING & ATHLETIC GOODS: Carts, Golf, Hand

Charleys Golf Cars Inc .... G 405 273-6901
 Shawnee *(G-8437)*

SPORTING & ATHLETIC GOODS: Cases, Gun & Rod

Bedside Gunlock Products .... G 713 443-8172
 Tahlequah *(G-8853)*
Highnoon Tactical LLC .... G 918 801-8737
 Vinita *(G-11259)*

SPORTING & ATHLETIC GOODS: Decoys, Duck & Other Game Birds

G & H Decoy Inc .... D 918 652-3314
 Henryetta *(G-3507)*

SPORTING & ATHLETIC GOODS: Fishing Bait, Artificial

Bills Catfish Bait .... G 918 224-8470
 Sapulpa *(G-8257)*

SPORTING & ATHLETIC GOODS: Fishing Eqpt

Applied Oil Tools LLC .... G 405 670-8665
 Oklahoma City *(G-5458)*
Parrish Enterprises Ltd .... C 580 237-4033
 Enid *(G-3031)*

W C Bradley Co .... D 918 836-5581
 Tulsa *(G-11086)*
Wohali Outdoors LLC .... F 918 343-3800
 Broken Arrow *(G-1100)*
Zebco Sales Company LLC .... G 800 588-9030
 Tulsa *(G-11173)*

SPORTING & ATHLETIC GOODS: Fishing Tackle, General

Anita and Harold Speed .... G 580 838-2297
 Hendrix *(G-3438)*
Newell Manufacturing .... G 918 782-1900
 Langley *(G-3873)*

SPORTING & ATHLETIC GOODS: Football Eqpt & Splys, NEC

Austin Athletic Co Inc .... F 405 273-8681
 Shawnee *(G-8429)*

SPORTING & ATHLETIC GOODS: Game Calls

Steve Harrison Game Calls .... G 918 688-0807
 Tulsa *(G-10849)*

SPORTING & ATHLETIC GOODS: Hunting Eqpt

Britter Creek Hunting Bli .... F 405 392-3588
 Tuttle *(G-11188)*
Out On A Limb Mfg LLC .... G 580 541-3794
 Enid *(G-3027)*
Stealth Mfg .... G 405 843-1954
 Oklahoma City *(G-7198)*

SPORTING & ATHLETIC GOODS: Pools, Swimming, Exc Plastic

Country Leisure Inc .... E 405 799-7745
 Moore *(G-4511)*
Walr Corp .... G 918 253-4773
 Jay *(G-3687)*

SPORTING & ATHLETIC GOODS: Pools, Swimming, Plastic

San Juan Pools of Oklahoma .... G 918 582-8169
 Tulsa *(G-10702)*

SPORTING & ATHLETIC GOODS: Rods & Rod Parts, Fishing

Tight Line Products LLC .... G 918 231-0934
 Tulsa *(G-10940)*
Tridon Composites Inc .... F 918 742-0426
 Kellyville *(G-3768)*
Zebco Corporation .... A 918 836-5581
 Tulsa *(G-11172)*

SPORTING & ATHLETIC GOODS: Shooting Eqpt & Splys, General

2011 Ussa Limited Partnership .... F 918 948-7856
 Tulsa *(G-9055)*

SPORTING & ATHLETIC GOODS: Skateboards

Blaze Skateboards LLC .... G 405 391-3838
 Choctaw *(G-1531)*
Kick16 Skateboards LLC .... G 918 869-6206
 Muskogee *(G-4703)*
Malchus Sktbard Mnistries Assn .... G 405 615-6066
 Edmond *(G-2502)*

SPORTING & ATHLETIC GOODS: Target Shooting Eqpt

Charles Jones .... G 405 348-2187
 Edmond *(G-2345)*

SPORTING & ATHLETIC GOODS: Targets, Archery & Rifle Shooting

Reagent Chemical & RES Inc .... G 580 233-1024
 Enid *(G-3044)*
Reagent Chemical & RES Inc .... F 580 436-4100
 Francis *(G-3191)*

SPORTING & ATHLETIC GOODS: Track & Field Athletic Eqpt

Performance Surfaces LLC .... G 405 463-0505
 Oklahoma City *(G-6830)*

SPORTING & ATHLETIC GOODS: Treadmills

Trilogy Horse Industries Inc .... G 405 248-1010
 Harrah *(G-3388)*

SPORTING & RECREATIONAL GOODS & SPLYS WHOLESALERS

Century LLC .... C 405 732-2226
 Oklahoma City *(G-5728)*

SPORTING & RECREATIONAL GOODS, WHOLESALE: Fishing Tackle

Alluring Lures & Tackle Co LLC .... G 580 832-5177
 Cordell *(G-1854)*
HALAQ Inc .... G 405 321-7293
 Newalla *(G-4810)*

SPORTING & RECREATIONAL GOODS, WHOLESALE: Golf

Golf Car Factory .... G 405 782-0460
 Oklahoma City *(G-6169)*

SPORTING & RECREATIONAL GOODS, WHOLESALE: Gymnasium

Grips Etc Inc .... D 405 447-2559
 Norman *(G-5011)*

SPORTING GOODS

Alluring Lures & Tackle Co LLC .... G 580 832-5177
 Cordell *(G-1854)*
American Iron Sports .... G 580 716-5662
 Tonkawa *(G-8971)*
Big Shot LLC .... G 918 712-7110
 Tulsa *(G-9293)*
Big Shot LLC .... G 918 712-7110
 Tulsa *(G-9294)*
Call .... G 580 789-0074
 Blackwell *(G-677)*
Century LLC .... C 405 732-2226
 Oklahoma City *(G-5728)*
Competitive Action Sports LLC .... G 405 474-7777
 Edmond *(G-2363)*
Covers Plus Inc .... G 405 670-2221
 Oklahoma City *(G-5846)*
Fenix Outfitters .... G 918 259-0099
 Broken Arrow *(G-907)*
Fish Tales Lure Company LLC .... G 918 814-6241
 Claremore *(G-1622)*
Floatingmats LLC .... G 918 504-8586
 Bixby *(G-623)*
Gear Exchange .... G 405 606-3050
 Oklahoma City *(G-6141)*
Greenlure LLC .... G 918 786-9156
 Grove *(G-3273)*
Grips Etc Inc .... D 405 447-2559
 Norman *(G-5011)*
HALAQ Inc .... G 405 321-7293
 Newalla *(G-4810)*
Instinct Performance LLC .... G 405 463-7300
 Oklahoma City *(G-6312)*
Janeway Machine Inc .... E 918 224-0694
 Sapulpa *(G-8282)*
Lure Promo .... G 405 664-3415
 Oklahoma City *(G-6502)*
Majestic Marble & Granite .... E 918 266-1121
 Catoosa *(G-1337)*
McKinley Hardwoods LLC .... G 800 522-3305
 Oklahoma City *(G-6548)*
New Times Technologies Inc .... D 918 872-9600
 Broken Arrow *(G-988)*
Omer Distributors LLC .... G 580 695-3211
 Lawton *(G-3979)*
Paul Ziert & Associates Inc .... D 405 364-5344
 Norman *(G-5112)*
Pistol Wear LLC .... G 918 364-5617
 Tulsa *(G-10519)*
Soccer Wave LLC .... G 405 361-7813
 Edmond *(G-2623)*
SOS Pools .... G 405 471-3792
 Edmond *(G-2624)*

PRODUCT SECTION

Sports Center ....G....... 580 795-2993
  Madill (G-4164)
Sports Vision Inc ....G....... 918 824-7617
  Pryor (G-7992)
Tatur ....G....... 918 244-6918
  Tulsa (G-10902)
Taylor Custom Cues ....G....... 405 317-3298
  Oklahoma City (G-7257)
Tipton Company ....G....... 580 762-0800
  Ponca City (G-7884)
Trilogy Horse Ind ....G....... 405 248-1010
  Oklahoma City (G-7332)
Veteran Bat Company LLC ....G....... 580 439-5230
  Comanche (G-1847)
Wombat Labs LLC ....G....... 405 355-9662
  Stillwater (G-8775)

SPORTING GOODS STORES, NEC

Ragtops Athletics Inc ....G....... 918 274-3575
  Owasso (G-7606)
Sander Sporting Gds & Atvs LLC ...G....... 580 922-4930
  Seiling (G-8351)
Tack Designs ....G....... 918 825-1211
  Pryor (G-7993)

SPORTING GOODS STORES: Firearms

Champlin Firearms Inc ....G....... 580 237-7388
  Enid (G-2929)
Garys Guns ....G....... 405 789-6896
  Bethany (G-579)
Strategic Armory Corps LLC ....G....... 623 780-1050
  Prague (G-7936)

SPORTING GOODS STORES: Playground Eqpt

Noahs Park & Playgrounds LLC ....F....... 405 607-0714
  Edmond (G-2538)
Satterlee Teepees ....G....... 405 255-6642
  Moore (G-4563)

SPORTING GOODS STORES: Pool & Billiard Tables

Billiards of Tulsa Inc ....E....... 918 835-1166
  Tulsa (G-9296)

SPORTING GOODS STORES: Team sports Eqpt

Tim Dees ....G....... 918 825-1211
  Pryor (G-7995)

SPORTING GOODS: Archery

Whitehouse Enterprises ....G....... 918 224-2002
  Sapulpa (G-8325)

SPORTING GOODS: Hammocks & Other Net Prdts

DSA Designs LLC ....G....... 580 493-2723
  Drummond (G-2047)

SPORTS APPAREL STORES

Big Red Shop Inc ....G....... 405 495-5551
  Warr Acres (G-11313)
Fashion Sports By Sia Inc ....F....... 405 524-9990
  Oklahoma City (G-6077)
Magic TS ....G....... 580 332-6675
  Ada (G-62)
Tim Dees ....G....... 918 825-1211
  Pryor (G-7995)

SPORTS CLUBS, MANAGERS & PROMOTERS

Paul Ziert & Associates Inc ....D....... 405 364-5344
  Norman (G-5112)

SPRAYING & DUSTING EQPT

Fisher Products LLC ....D....... 918 582-2204
  Tulsa (G-9750)

SPRINGS: Leaf, Automobile, Locomotive, Etc

Dayton Parts LLC ....D....... 580 931-9350
  Durant (G-2223)

SPRINGS: Precision

A W Bugerman Company ....G....... 580 237-3857
  Enid (G-2901)

SPRINGS: Steel

Action Spring Company ....E....... 918 836-9000
  Tulsa (G-9097)
Cannon & Refermat LLC ....F....... 405 521-0636
  Oklahoma City (G-5688)
Emco LLC ....D....... 918 342-3488
  Claremore (G-1616)
Gardner Industries Inc ....F....... 918 583-0171
  Tulsa (G-9801)
Tulsa Auto Spring Co ....G....... 918 835-6926
  Tulsa (G-10987)

SPRINGS: Wire

Action Spring Company ....E....... 918 836-9000
  Tulsa (G-9097)
Cannon & Refermat LLC ....F....... 405 521-0636
  Oklahoma City (G-5688)
Cannon Racecraft Inc ....G....... 405 524-7223
  Oklahoma City (G-5689)
Ebsco Spring Co Inc ....D....... 918 628-1680
  Tulsa (G-9636)
Emco Industries LLC ....D....... 918 342-3488
  Claremore (G-1617)
Gardner Industries Inc ....F....... 918 583-0171
  Tulsa (G-9801)
Sooner State Spring Mfg Co ....G....... 918 476-5707
  Chouteau (G-1570)

SPRINKLER SYSTEMS: Field

K & S Aluminum Booms ....G....... 580 761-3238
  Tonkawa (G-8976)

SPRINKLING SYSTEMS: Fire Control

All American Fire Systems Inc ....F....... 918 341-6977
  Claremore (G-1579)
Firetech Automatic Sprinklers ....G....... 918 633-3773
  Henryetta (G-3506)
Invictus Engrg Cnstr Svcs ....G....... 405 701-5622
  Norman (G-5037)

STAGE LIGHTING SYSTEMS

Lady Lights & Stage Inc ....G....... 405 376-0076
  Mustang (G-4781)
Trailing Edge Technologies ....G....... 580 536-0559
  Lawton (G-4014)

STAINLESS STEEL

CMC Steel Oklahoma LLC ....G....... 580 634-5092
  Durant (G-2217)
Tubacex Durant Inc ....G....... 724 646-4301
  Durant (G-2270)

STAMPED ART GOODS FOR EMBROIDERING

McSmith Creations LLC ....G....... 405 596-2301
  Bethany (G-588)

STAMPING: Fabric Articles

Townsend Marketing Inc ....G....... 918 496-9222
  Bixby (G-666)

STAMPINGS: Automotive

Tk Aero Inc ....G....... 405 359-8638
  Edmond (G-2645)

STAMPINGS: Metal

Arrow Tool & Gage Co Inc ....F....... 918 438-3600
  Tulsa (G-9212)
Braden Shielding Systems Const ...E....... 918 624-2888
  Tulsa (G-9327)
Braden Shielding Systems LLC ......E....... 918 624-2888
  Tulsa (G-9328)
Component Services LP ....F....... 405 787-7180
  Oklahoma City (G-5813)
Croppinsville ....G....... 405 521-2711
  Owasso (G-7557)
Expanded Solutions LLC ....E....... 405 946-6791
  Wewoka (G-11501)

STEEL FABRICATORS

Flanco Gasket and Mfg Inc ....E....... 405 672-7893
  Oklahoma City (G-6088)
Gardner Industries Inc ....F....... 918 583-0171
  Tulsa (G-9801)
Hunt Jim Sales & Mfg ....G....... 405 670-5663
  Oklahoma City (G-6272)
Industrial Gasket Inc ....E....... 405 376-9393
  Mustang (G-4778)
Metal Fab Inc ....G....... 580 762-2421
  Ponca City (G-7850)
Treat Metal Stamping Inc ....G....... 405 275-3344
  Shawnee (G-8512)
Unified Brands Inc ....G....... 888 994-7636
  Pryor (G-7996)

STARTERS & CONTROLLERS: Motor, Electric

Enovation Controls LLC ....B....... 918 317-4100
  Tulsa (G-9689)

STARTERS: Motor

G P Enterprises ....G....... 405 340-8986
  Edmond (G-2428)
General Auto Supply Inc ....G....... 405 329-0772
  Norman (G-5007)

STATIONERY & OFFICE SPLYS WHOLESALERS

Omni LLC ....G....... 405 246-9252
  Oklahoma City (G-6777)
Paperwork Company ....F....... 918 369-1014
  Bixby (G-652)
Southwestern Sty & Bnk Sup Inc ...D....... 405 525-9411
  Oklahoma City (G-7177)
Usher Corporation ....G....... 405 495-2125
  Oklahoma City (G-7382)

STATIONERY PRDTS

R&D Labs LLC ....G....... 405 875-9937
  Edmond (G-2583)

STATORS REWINDING SVCS

B & B Electric Co ....G....... 918 583-6274
  Tulsa (G-9239)

STEEL FABRICATORS

A & J Fabricators Inc ....E....... 405 352-4120
  Minco (G-4475)
Abco Steel Inc ....F....... 918 322-3435
  Glenpool (G-3228)
Ada Iron and Welding LLC ....G....... 580 332-6694
  Ada (G-6)
Adventure Manufacturing Inc ....G....... 405 682-3833
  Oklahoma City (G-5387)
Air Duct Inc ....F....... 918 445-1196
  Tulsa (G-9119)
Allison Allison Inc ....G....... 918 344-1768
  Bixby (G-610)
American Tank & Cnstr Co ....G....... 918 254-6292
  Tulsa (G-9173)
Amron Enterprises LLC ....F....... 918 224-9222
  Sapulpa (G-8249)
Apollo Metal Specialties Inc ....F....... 918 341-7650
  Claremore (G-1583)
ARC Rvals Wldg Fabrication LLC ...G....... 918 577-5066
  Muskogee (G-4649)
Arcosa Wind Towers Inc ....G....... 918 560-4911
  Tulsa (G-9206)
Asc Inc ....E....... 918 445-0260
  Tulsa (G-9215)
Associated Stl Fabricators Inc ....E....... 405 787-5713
  Oklahoma City (G-5278)
Atlantic Fbrication Design LLC ....G....... 405 619-7607
  Oklahoma City (G-5485)
Avery Barron Industires LLC ....F....... 918 779-6903
  Tulsa (G-9229)
Aviations Simulations Inc ....G....... 918 251-6880
  Broken Arrow (G-837)
B & W Manufacturing Co Ltd ....F....... 918 248-5201
  Tulsa (G-8989)
B&M Metalworks Inc ....G....... 918 266-5103
  Catoosa (G-1300)
Basden Steel-Oklahoma LLC ....E....... 918 341-9468
  Claremore (G-1593)
Bendco Corp ....F....... 918 583-1566
  Tulsa (G-9281)

STEEL FABRICATORS

PRODUCT SECTION

Bennett Steel Inc............................C...... 918 227-2564
  Sapulpa *(G-8252)*
Bethesda Boys Ranch....................F...... 918 827-6409
  Mounds *(G-4610)*
Bixby Fabco Inc..............................F...... 918 366-3446
  Bixby *(G-615)*
Blm Equipment & Mfg Co Inc.........F...... 918 266-5282
  Catoosa *(G-1304)*
Boardman LLC.................................D...... 405 634-5434
  Oklahoma City *(G-5598)*
Bonavista Technologies Inc............G...... 918 250-3435
  Tulsa *(G-9318)*
Brooks Custom Fabrication..............G...... 918 836-2556
  Tulsa *(G-9341)*
Building Concepts Ltd.....................G...... 405 324-5100
  Oklahoma City *(G-5642)*
Butcher & Sons Steel Inds...............G...... 918 434-5276
  Salina *(G-8133)*
By-Weld Industries Inc.....................F...... 918 366-4850
  Bixby *(G-616)*
Bynum & Company Inc....................F...... 580 265-7747
  Stonewall *(G-8798)*
Cairns Manufacturing Inc.................G...... 405 947-1350
  Oklahoma City *(G-5670)*
Cheshire Portable Welding..............G...... 405 373-4669
  Piedmont *(G-7757)*
Cheyenne Innovations Inc...............G...... 918 793-7521
  Shidler *(G-8526)*
Choctaw Mfg & Dev Corp................D...... 580 326-8365
  Hugo *(G-3607)*
Choctaw Mfg & Dev Corp................D...... 580 326-8365
  Atoka *(G-403)*
Choctaw Mfg Def Contrs Inc...........F...... 580 326-8365
  Hugo *(G-3608)*
Choctaw Mfg Def Contrs Inc...........G...... 580 298-2203
  Antlers *(G-215)*
Choctaw Mfg Def Contrs Inc...........G...... 918 426-2871
  McAlester *(G-4286)*
Coanda Company LLC....................G...... 214 601-4972
  Norman *(G-4962)*
Connie Pirple..................................G...... 405 375-4468
  Kingfisher *(G-3792)*
Consoldted Fbrction Cnstructor.......G...... 918 224-3500
  Tulsa *(G-8999)*
Creative Ornamental Inc.................G...... 918 540-1600
  Miami *(G-4393)*
Cushing Truss Manufacturing..........F...... 918 387-2080
  Yale *(G-11683)*
Custom Design Fabrication LLC......G...... 918 773-5691
  Vian *(G-11238)*
Custom Manufacturing Inc..............E...... 405 692-6311
  Oklahoma City *(G-5874)*
D & Z Metal Fabrication..................G...... 918 456-3841
  Welling *(G-11466)*
D and N Fabrication........................G...... 918 224-4400
  Sapulpa *(G-8264)*
D Diamond Enterprises Inc..............G...... 918 827-4727
  Mounds *(G-4612)*
D-K Metal Form Company Inc........G...... 580 228-3516
  Waurika *(G-11362)*
Davco Fab Inc.................................E...... 918 757-2504
  Jennings *(G-3739)*
DC Exteriors & More LLC................G...... 918 231-7303
  Warner *(G-11307)*
Diamondback Steel Company Inc...E...... 918 686-6340
  Muskogee *(G-4667)*
Dmi International Inc......................G...... 918 438-2213
  Tulsa *(G-9589)*
Doug Lee Ingenuity LLC.................G...... 918 542-4686
  Miami *(G-4399)*
Eagleclaw Fabrication....................D...... 918 691-2519
  Tulsa *(G-9630)*
Eastpointe Manufacturing Corp.......E...... 918 683-2169
  Muskogee *(G-4671)*
Eco Incorporated............................G...... 918 258-5002
  Broken Arrow *(G-894)*
Eco 2007 LLC.................................G...... 918 258-5002
  Broken Arrow *(G-895)*
Elite Manufacturing LLC..................G...... 918 266-1077
  Catoosa *(G-1317)*
Enterprise Manufacturing LLC.........G...... 918 438-4455
  Tulsa *(G-9691)*
Equus Metals Inc............................E...... 918 834-9872
  Tulsa *(G-9696)*
Ernest Wiemann Iron Works............E...... 918 592-1700
  Tulsa *(G-9698)*
Express Metal Fabricators LLC......B...... 918 622-1420
  Locust Grove *(G-4106)*
Express Metal Fabricators Inc........D...... 918 783-5129
  Big Cabin *(G-603)*

EZ Carrier LLC................................G...... 918 827-7876
  Mounds *(G-4615)*
Fabricating Specialists Inc.............F...... 405 476-1959
  Oklahoma City *(G-6068)*
Fabrico Inc.....................................G...... 918 274-9329
  Owasso *(G-7565)*
Fammco Mfg Co Inc.........................G...... 918 437-0456
  Tulsa *(G-9727)*
Fat & Happy Services Inc...............G...... 405 834-5782
  Oklahoma City *(G-6078)*
Federal Metals Inc..........................F...... 918 838-1725
  Tulsa *(G-9731)*
Five Star Steel Inc..........................G...... 405 787-7620
  Oklahoma City *(G-6086)*
Forster & Son Inc............................G...... 580 332-6020
  Ada *(G-36)*
Friends Welding..............................G...... 918 482-1544
  Broken Arrow *(G-1127)*
G Highfill..G...... 405 598-5576
  Tecumseh *(G-8915)*
G&E Power LLC...............................E...... 918 396-2899
  Skiatook *(G-8544)*
General Manufacturer Inc..............F...... 918 756-3067
  Okmulgee *(G-7504)*
Gerdau Ameristeel US Inc..............G...... 405 677-9792
  Oklahoma City *(G-6147)*
Grating Company LLC......................G...... 918 834-8100
  Tulsa *(G-9848)*
Great Plains Rebar LLC..................F...... 405 576-3270
  Oklahoma City *(G-6183)*
Greg Butcher..................................G...... 918 434-6892
  Salina *(G-8134)*
H & H Cnstr Met Fbrication Inc......E...... 405 701-1075
  Norman *(G-5013)*
H & H Ornamental Iron....................G...... 405 634-0646
  Oklahoma City *(G-6196)*
Hackney Ladish Inc.........................D...... 580 237-4212
  Enid *(G-2967)*
Honeycutt Contruction Inc.............F...... 918 825-6070
  Pryor *(G-7969)*
Integrated Tower Systems Inc.......E...... 918 749-8535
  Tulsa *(G-9998)*
J & D Fabricators Inc......................F...... 405 356-2243
  Wellston *(G-11473)*
J & G Steel Corporation.................C...... 918 227-3131
  Sapulpa *(G-8280)*
JB Metal Fabrication......................G...... 918 266-3228
  Catoosa *(G-1324)*
Jerrys Dock Construction Inc........F...... 918 256-3390
  Bernice *(G-567)*
Johnston Test Cell Group LLC.......G...... 405 604-2804
  Oklahoma City *(G-6378)*
Kenneth Petermann.......................G...... 405 372-0111
  Stillwater *(G-8710)*
Keymiaee Aero-Tech Inc................F...... 405 235-5010
  Oklahoma City *(G-6409)*
Lbr Smith LLC.................................G...... 405 601-7051
  Oklahoma City *(G-6458)*
Lofland Co......................................G...... 405 631-9555
  Oklahoma City *(G-6488)*
Longreach Steel Inc......................F...... 405 598-5691
  Tecumseh *(G-8922)*
M A C Manufacturing Inc................G...... 405 527-8270
  Purcell *(G-8012)*
Manufacturing Jack LLC Ram.........D...... 580 332-6694
  Ada *(G-63)*
Martin Manufacturing Inc...............G...... 918 583-1191
  Sapulpa *(G-8287)*
Mertz Manufacturing Inc................B...... 580 762-5646
  Ponca City *(G-7849)*
Metal Building Services.................G...... 580 657-3339
  Ardmore *(G-330)*
Metal Fab Inc.................................G...... 580 762-2421
  Ponca City *(G-7850)*
Metalfab LLC..................................G...... 918 718-4040
  Tahlequah *(G-8873)*
Metro Mechanical Supply Inc.........F...... 918 622-2288
  Tulsa *(G-10251)*
Metro Mechanical Supply LLC.......G...... 918 622-2288
  Tulsa *(G-10252)*
Midstate Mfg & Mktg Inc................E...... 405 751-6227
  Oklahoma City *(G-6598)*
Miller Welding & Supply.................G...... 580 492-5464
  Lawton *(G-3970)*
Mitchco Fabrication Inc.................G...... 580 762-0256
  Ponca City *(G-7853)*
Mobile Mini Inc...............................F...... 918 582-5857
  Tulsa *(G-10288)*
Moore Iron & Steel Corp................D...... 918 387-2639
  Yale *(G-11686)*

Morton Buildings Inc.......................E...... 918 683-6668
  Muskogee *(G-4715)*
Neilson Manufacturing Inc.............F...... 918 587-5548
  Tulsa *(G-10331)*
Neisen Family LLC..........................E...... 580 762-2421
  Ponca City *(G-7858)*
OK Fabricators LLC.........................E...... 918 224-3977
  Tulsa *(G-9023)*
OK Machine and Mfg Co Inc...........E...... 918 838-1300
  Tulsa *(G-10390)*
Oklahoma City Steel LLC................G...... 405 235-2300
  Oklahoma City *(G-6743)*
Oklahoma Post Tension Inc...........F...... 918 627-6013
  Tulsa *(G-10405)*
Old World Iron Inc..........................G...... 918 445-3063
  Tulsa *(G-10411)*
Orizon Arstrctures - Grove Inc.......D...... 918 786-9094
  Grove *(G-3284)*
Ozark Steel LLC..............................E...... 918 438-4330
  Tulsa *(G-10450)*
P & M Industries Inc......................E...... 918 660-0055
  Tulsa *(G-10451)*
Pattison Metal Fab Inc...................E...... 918 251-9967
  Broken Arrow *(G-1000)*
Pelco Structural LLC......................D...... 918 283-4004
  Claremore *(G-1668)*
Phoenix Fabworx LLC......................G...... 918 429-8388
  Quinton *(G-8038)*
Powder Coating of Muskogee........G...... 918 681-4494
  Muskogee *(G-4736)*
Power Lift Fndtn RPR OK Inc..........E...... 580 332-8282
  Ada *(G-75)*
Precision Fabricators Inc..............F...... 918 428-7600
  Tulsa *(G-10544)*
Premier Fabricators LLC.................G...... 580 251-9525
  Duncan *(G-2165)*
Premier Plant Services LLC...........F...... 918 227-3131
  Sapulpa *(G-8300)*
Premier Plant Services LLC...........G...... 918 227-1680
  Sapulpa *(G-8301)*
Premier Steel Services LLC...........E...... 918 227-0110
  Glenpool *(G-3241)*
Professional Fabricators Inc.........E...... 918 388-1090
  Tulsa *(G-10568)*
Professional Metal Works Inc........G...... 580 584-7890
  Idabel *(G-3644)*
Pruitt Company of Ada Inc............E...... 580 332-3523
  Ada *(G-78)*
R&R Roustabout Services LLC......E...... 580 883-4647
  Ringwood *(G-8090)*
Railroad Sgnling Solutions Inc......G...... 918 973-1888
  Broken Arrow *(G-1020)*
Railroad Yard Inc...........................E...... 405 377-8763
  Stillwater *(G-8743)*
Rise Manufacturing LLC.................E...... 918 994-6240
  Broken Arrow *(G-1032)*
Robert Mrrson Autocad Svcs LLC..G...... 918 257-4622
  Afton *(G-120)*
Rooks Fabrication LLC...................F...... 918 447-1990
  Tulsa *(G-10669)*
Rt Manufacturing LLC....................F...... 405 222-7180
  Chickasha *(G-1504)*
S & T Mfg Co..................................E...... 918 234-4151
  Tulsa *(G-10684)*
S&S Fabrication.............................G...... 918 447-0447
  Tulsa *(G-9032)*
Safeco Manufacturing Inc.............F...... 918 455-0100
  Broken Arrow *(G-1160)*
Sawyer Manufacturing Company...E...... 918 834-2550
  Tulsa *(G-9034)*
Selman Wldg & Fabrication LLC....G...... 580 330-0887
  Weatherford *(G-11440)*
Shawnee Steel Company...............E...... 405 919-8582
  Shawnee *(G-8497)*
Shelby Steel Service......................E...... 918 234-3098
  Tulsa *(G-10741)*
Sooner Steel and Truss LLC..........E...... 405 232-5542
  Oklahoma City *(G-7167)*
Source Fabrication.........................G...... 580 762-4114
  Ponca City *(G-7877)*
Southwest Fabricators Inc............F...... 580 326-3589
  Hugo *(G-3621)*
Steel Thinking Inc..........................F...... 405 485-2204
  Washington *(G-11337)*
Steelfab Texas Inc.........................E...... 972 562-7720
  Durant *(G-2262)*
Storm SF Ngrnd Trnd Shltrs NC....D...... 405 606-2563
  Oklahoma City *(G-7213)*
Supreme Mch & Stl Fabrication....F...... 918 387-2036
  Yale *(G-11687)*

PRODUCT SECTION

STUDIOS: Sculptor's

T & D Fabrication Inc ....E....... 918 352-8031
  Drumright *(G-2074)*
T Rowe Pipe LLC ....E....... 580 765-1500
  Ponca City *(G-7881)*
Tj Services LLC ....G....... 405 596-5124
  Oklahoma City *(G-7295)*
Tri Red LLC ....E....... 580 476-2551
  Rush Springs *(G-8128)*
Tulsa Metal Fab Inc ....F....... 918 451-7150
  Broken Arrow *(G-1175)*
Tulsa Steel Mfg Company Inc ....E....... 918 227-0110
  Tulsa *(G-9046)*
United Contracting Svcs Inc ......C....... 918 551-7659
  Tulsa *(G-11040)*
United Holdings LLC ....G....... 405 947-3321
  Oklahoma City *(G-7369)*
V&S Schuler Tubular Pdts LLC ...B....... 918 687-7701
  Muskogee *(G-4758)*
Valmont Industries Inc ....D....... 918 266-2800
  Claremore *(G-1700)*
Valmont Industries Inc ....B....... 918 583-5881
  Tulsa *(G-11065)*
Vann Metal Products Inc ....G....... 918 341-0469
  Claremore *(G-1701)*
Vernon Manufacturing Company ...G.... 918 224-4068
  Tulsa *(G-9048)*
W&W Steel Erectors LLC ....G....... 405 235-3621
  Oklahoma City *(G-7412)*
W&W-Afco Steel LLC ....B....... 405 235-3621
  Oklahoma City *(G-7413)*
Wayne Burt Machine ....G....... 918 786-4415
  Grove *(G-3293)*
Wedlake Fabricating Inc ....E....... 918 428-1641
  Tulsa *(G-11103)*
Weldco Mfg ....G....... 580 296-1585
  Colbert *(G-1788)*
Werco Aviation Inc ....G....... 918 251-6880
  Broken Arrow *(G-1094)*
Werco Manufacturing Inc ....E....... 918 251-6880
  Broken Arrow *(G-1095)*
Western Frontier LLC ....E....... 918 760-4977
  Locust Grove *(G-4113)*
Willie Dewayne Brown ....F....... 918 482-1115
  Haskell *(G-3403)*
Wwsc Holdings LLC ....F....... 405 235-3621
  Oklahoma City *(G-7476)*
York Metal Fabricators Inc ....E....... 405 528-7495
  Oklahoma City *(G-7481)*
Zkc Welding ....F....... 580 220-7685
  Ardmore *(G-384)*

STEEL MILLS

3 D Manufacturing ....G....... 918 224-7717
  Sapulpa *(G-8244)*
Abco Steel Inc ....F....... 918 322-3435
  Glenpool *(G-3228)*
Albright Steel and Wire Co ....F....... 405 232-7526
  Oklahoma City *(G-5410)*
Azz Incorporated ....E....... 918 584-6668
  Tulsa *(G-9237)*
Balero ....G....... 580 221-6202
  Ardmore *(G-252)*
Commercial Metals Company .....G....... 580 634-5046
  Durant *(G-2218)*
Cust-O-Bend Inc ....E....... 918 241-0514
  Tulsa *(G-9526)*
Cyber Stitchery ....G....... 405 329-6018
  Norman *(G-4975)*
Gms Lalos Custom Wheels Ltd Co ...G.... 918 622-3616
  Tulsa *(G-9835)*
Ipsco Tubulars Inc ....C....... 918 384-6400
  Catoosa *(G-1323)*
Joco Assembly LLC ....E....... 918 622-5111
  Tulsa *(G-10048)*
Kloeckner Metals Corporation ....E....... 918 266-1666
  Catoosa *(G-1328)*
Metals USA Plates and Shap .....E....... 918 682-7833
  Muskogee *(G-4713)*
Mobile Hightech ....G....... 405 942-4600
  Oklahoma City *(G-6620)*
MRC Global (us) Inc ....G....... 918 485-9511
  Wagoner *(G-11287)*
National Oilwell Varco Inc ....C....... 918 781-4436
  Muskogee *(G-4719)*
Precision Metals LLC ....E....... 918 266-2202
  Tulsa *(G-10548)*
Refractory Anchors Inc ....E....... 918 455-8485
  Broken Arrow *(G-1154)*
Ross Dub Company Inc ....E....... 405 495-3611
  Oklahoma City *(G-7049)*

Tms International LLC ....G....... 918 241-0129
  Sand Springs *(G-8230)*
TRC Rod Services of Oklahoma ..F... 405 677-0585
  Oklahoma City *(G-7320)*

STEEL, COLD-ROLLED: Strip NEC, From Purchased Hot-Rolled

Worthington Industries Inc ....G....... 614 438-3048
  Catoosa *(G-1369)*

STEEL: Cold-Rolled

Albright Steel and Wire Co ....F....... 405 232-7526
  Oklahoma City *(G-5410)*
Carefusion Corporation ....C....... 918 865-4727
  Mannford *(G-4178)*
Carlson Company ....E....... 918 627-4334
  Tulsa *(G-9376)*
Cust-O-Bend Inc ....E....... 918 241-0514
  Tulsa *(G-9526)*
Tmk Ipsco International LLC ......C....... 918 384-6400
  Catoosa *(G-1356)*

STEERING SYSTEMS & COMPONENTS

Enovation Controls LLC ....B....... 918 317-4100
  Tulsa *(G-9689)*

STITCHING SVCS

Monograms Elite Inc ....G....... 580 353-1635
  Lawton *(G-3973)*
Pinpoint Monograms Inc ....F....... 405 228-0600
  Oklahoma City *(G-6850)*

STITCHING SVCS: Custom

Hendrie Resources Ltd ....G....... 405 948-4459
  Oklahoma City *(G-6239)*

STONE: Cast Concrete

Decorative Rock & Stone ....G....... 405 341-8900
  Edmond *(G-2388)*
Precision Stone ....G....... 405 214-2224
  Shawnee *(G-8484)*
Stone Warehouse ....F....... 918 250-0800
  Broken Arrow *(G-1064)*

STONE: Crushed & Broken, NEC

Apac-Central ....G....... 918 534-1741
  Dewey *(G-2016)*
Texoma Materials ....G....... 580 367-2339
  Caddo *(G-1237)*
Third Rock Construction LLC .....G....... 918 429-2011
  McAlester *(G-4340)*

STONE: Dimension, NEC

Cornerstone Quarries Inc ....G....... 918 647-2117
  Cameron *(G-1256)*
Eaves Stones Products ....F....... 580 889-7858
  Atoka *(G-410)*
Hansons Stone & Landscape .....G....... 580 310-0071
  Ada *(G-47)*
Majestic Marble & Granite ....E....... 918 266-1921
  Catoosa *(G-1337)*
Oklahoma Stone ....F....... 405 721-6775
  Yukon *(G-11761)*
Quapaw Company Inc ....E....... 918 767-2985
  Pawnee *(G-7710)*
Sugar Loaf Quarries Inc ....E....... 918 647-4244
  Shady Point *(G-8416)*
Texhoma Limestone ....G....... 580 889-8808
  Caney *(G-1263)*
Whm Granite Products Inc ....F....... 580 535-2184
  Granite *(G-3257)*

STONE: Quarrying & Processing, Own Stone Prdts

Fittstone Inc ....E....... 580 777-2808
  Fittstown *(G-3158)*
V J Stone LLC ....G....... 405 840-2255
  Oklahoma City *(G-7383)*
Valley Stone Inc ....F....... 918 647-2388
  Howe *(G-3600)*

STONEWARE PRDTS: Pottery

CFS Brands LLC ....B....... 405 475-5600
  Oklahoma City *(G-5732)*

CFS Brands LLC ....F....... 405 397-0103
  Oklahoma City *(G-5733)*
Cfsp Acquisition Corp ....G....... 405 475-5600
  Oklahoma City *(G-5734)*

STORE FIXTURES, EXC REFRIGERATED: Wholesalers

Mastercraft Millwork Inc ....G....... 405 895-6050
  Moore *(G-4537)*

STORE FIXTURES: Wood

Days Wood Products Inc ....F....... 405 238-6477
  Pauls Valley *(G-7656)*
Fixtures & Drywall Co Okla Inc ..F....... 918 832-1641
  Tulsa *(G-9751)*

STORES: Auto & Home Supply

C & C Performance Engines ......G....... 580 252-4331
  Duncan *(G-2094)*
Cannon Racecraft Inc ....F....... 405 524-7223
  Oklahoma City *(G-5689)*
D C Ignition Co Inc ....G....... 580 332-0878
  Ada *(G-28)*
Grices Automotive Machine Shop ...G... 580 924-1006
  Durant *(G-2233)*
Hudson Bros Rmanufactured Engs ..G.. 405 598-2260
  Tecumseh *(G-8919)*
Tulsa Auto Spring Co ....E....... 918 835-6926
  Tulsa *(G-10987)*

STORES: Drapery & Upholstery

Springcrest Drapery Center ....G....... 918 258-5644
  Broken Arrow *(G-1058)*

STRAINERS: Line, Piping Systems

Apollo Engineering Company .....G....... 918 251-6780
  Broken Arrow *(G-830)*
Weamco Incorporated ....E....... 918 445-1141
  Sapulpa *(G-8324)*

STRAPPING

Built Better Enterprises LLC ......G....... 580 492-5227
  Fletcher *(G-3161)*

STRAWS: Drinking, Made From Purchased Materials

Solo Cup Operating Corporation ..C..... 580 436-1500
  Ada *(G-90)*

STRUCTURAL SUPPORT & BUILDING MATERIAL: Concrete

Champion Designs & Systems LLC ..G.. 405 888-8370
  Oklahoma City *(G-5737)*
Concrete Products Inc ....E....... 405 427-8686
  Oklahoma City *(G-5819)*
Coreslab Structures Okla Inc .....C....... 405 632-4944
  Oklahoma City *(G-5835)*

STUCCO

Benchmark Stucco ....G....... 918 810-2812
  Sperry *(G-8604)*
Snyders Stucco and Stone ....G....... 580 421-9747
  Ada *(G-89)*
Stucco 2 Stone ....G....... 918 770-2944
  Tulsa *(G-10863)*
Yolanda Olmos ....G....... 918 850-8334
  Tulsa *(G-11169)*

STUDIOS: Artist's

Apple Art ....F....... 405 691-4393
  Moore *(G-4491)*

STUDIOS: Artists & Artists' Studios

Db Unlimited LLC ....G....... 855 437-7766
  Tulsa *(G-9563)*

STUDIOS: Sculptor's

Gooden Studios ....G....... 405 375-3432
  Kingfisher *(G-3799)*

STYLING SVCS: Wigs
Shes Happy Hair Okc LLC .... G 405 328-3464
Oklahoma City *(G-7122)*

SUBDIVIDERS & DEVELOPERS: Real Property, Cemetery Lots Only
Bmi Management Inc .... G 580 762-5659
Ponca City *(G-7801)*

SUNDRIES & RELATED PRDTS: Medical & Laboratory, Rubber
American Phoenix Inc .... C 580 248-1488
Lawton *(G-3887)*

SUPERMARKETS & OTHER GROCERY STORES
Anita and Harold Speed .... G 580 838-2297
Hendrix *(G-3438)*
Bama Foods Limited Partnership ...... C 918 732-2399
Tulsa *(G-9260)*
W H Braum Inc .... E 405 340-9288
Edmond *(G-2678)*

SURFACE ACTIVE AGENTS
Wood Finishers Supply Inc .... C 405 422-1025
El Reno *(G-2772)*

SURGICAL & MEDICAL INSTRUMENTS WHOLESALERS
Espiritu Miki .... G 405 213-5167
Oklahoma City *(G-6051)*

SURGICAL APPLIANCES & SPLYS
Dream Team Prosthetics LLC .... G 580 255-2100
Duncan *(G-2108)*
Evelyn Co Inc .... G 918 665-3952
Tulsa *(G-9708)*
Geronimo Manufacturing Inc .... G 580 336-5707
Perry *(G-7735)*
Hanger Inc .... F 918 742-6464
Tulsa *(G-9885)*
Hanger Prsthetcs & Ortho Inc .... G 580 326-6661
Hugo *(G-3611)*
Hanger Prsthetcs & Ortho Inc .... E 405 525-4000
Oklahoma City *(G-6213)*
Hanger Prsthetcs & Ortho Inc .... G 918 488-0400
Tulsa *(G-9886)*
Hanger Prsthetcs & Ortho Inc .... E 580 226-7900
Ardmore *(G-301)*
Hanger Prsthetcs & Ortho Inc .... G 918 423-1024
McAlester *(G-4303)*
Howmedica Osteonics Corp .... G 918 461-0152
Tulsa *(G-9956)*
Proud Veterans Intl Ltd .... G 316 209-8701
Lawton *(G-3986)*
Steampunk Bnics Innvations LLC ..... G 866 795-6645
Tulsa *(G-10842)*
Wild Olives LLC .... G 580 230-1231
Duncan *(G-2199)*

SURGICAL IMPLANTS
Iq Surgical LLC .... F 918 932-2734
Tulsa *(G-10011)*

SURVEYING & MAPPING: Land Parcels
Frontier Land Surveying LLC .... F 405 285-0433
Edmond *(G-2426)*
Osage Surveying Service .... G 918 287-4029
Pawhuska *(G-7692)*
Scientific Drilling Intl Inc .... D 405 787-3663
Yukon *(G-11780)*
Shafer Kline & Warren Inc .... E 918 499-6000
Tulsa *(G-10738)*

SURVEYING SVCS: Aerial Digital Imaging
Encompass Media LLC .... G 405 823-8081
Oklahoma City *(G-6035)*

SURVEYING SVCS: Photogrammetric Engineering
RMH Survey LLC .... G 918 927-8868
Vinita *(G-11270)*

SVC ESTABLISHMENT EQPT, WHOL: Concrete Burial Vaults & Boxes
Central Burial Vaults Inc .... E 918 224-5701
Tulsa *(G-8996)*

SVC ESTABLISHMENT EQPT, WHOLESALE: Engraving Eqpt & Splys
J & B Graphics Inc .... E 405 524-7446
Oklahoma City *(G-6328)*
Rowmark LLC .... E 405 787-4542
Oklahoma City *(G-7051)*

SVC ESTABLISHMENT EQPT, WHOLESALE: Restaurant Splys
Henderson Coffee Corp .... E 918 682-8751
Muskogee *(G-4690)*

SVC ESTABLISHMENT EQPT, WHOLESALE: Vending Machines & Splys
Galaxy Distributing .... G 918 835-1186
Tulsa *(G-9797)*

SWEEPING COMPOUNDS
John Scoggins Company Inc .... E 918 775-2748
Sallisaw *(G-8146)*

SWIMMING POOL ACCESS: Leaf Skimmers Or Pool Rakes
Zoop-Corp .... G 405 239-8184
Oklahoma City *(G-7489)*

SWIMMING POOL EQPT: Filters & Water Conditioning Systems
Wright Water Corporation .... G 405 224-1839
Chickasha *(G-1525)*

SWITCHES: Electronic
Hermetic Switch Inc .... C 405 224-4046
Chickasha *(G-1470)*

SWITCHGEAR & SWITCHBOARD APPARATUS
Advanced Indus Dvcs Co LLC .... D 918 445-1254
Tulsa *(G-9110)*
Aero Solutions and Services .... G 405 308-6788
Edmond *(G-2291)*
Aero-TEC Industries Inc .... G 405 382-8501
Seminole *(G-8353)*
American Automation Inc .... G
Pryor *(G-7941)*
Design Ready Controls Inc .... F 405 605-8234
Oklahoma City *(G-5926)*
Hermetic Switch Inc .... C 405 224-4046
Chickasha *(G-1470)*
L3 Westwood Corporation .... D 918 250-4444
Tulsa *(G-10109)*
L3 Westwood Corporation .... C 918 252-0481
Tulsa *(G-10110)*
Southwest Electric Co .... F 918 437-9494
Tulsa *(G-10805)*
Tranam Systems Intl Inc .... G 918 488-0007
Tulsa *(G-10968)*
US Pioneer Led Specialists LLC ...... G 918 359-5200
Tulsa *(G-11056)*

SWITCHGEAR & SWITCHGEAR ACCESS, NEC
Russelectric Inc .... D 918 251-7877
Broken Arrow *(G-1040)*
Tactical Power Systems Corp .... E 207 864-5528
Hulbert *(G-3629)*

SYNTHETIC RESIN FINISHED PRDTS, NEC
New Day Creations LLC .... G 918 576-9619
Bixby *(G-648)*

SYRUPS, FLAVORING, EXC DRINK
Springdale Food Co Inc .... G 580 928-2598
Sayre *(G-8348)*

SYSTEMS ENGINEERING: Computer Related
Digital Interface LLC .... G 405 201-5070
Fairland *(G-3124)*
Info-Sharp LLC .... G 520 204-5093
Norman *(G-5033)*

SYSTEMS INTEGRATION SVCS: Local Area Network
Juniper Networks Inc .... D 918 877-2642
Tulsa *(G-10066)*

SYSTEMS INTEGRATION SVCS: Office Computer Automation
Shane Lee Duvall .... G 918 960-0506
Broken Arrow *(G-1163)*
Solid State Controls Inc .... F 405 273-9292
Shawnee *(G-8501)*
Veritris Group Inc .... G 580 713-4927
Oklahoma City *(G-7399)*

TABLE OR COUNTERTOPS, PLASTIC LAMINATED
Brays Cabinet Shop .... G 580 584-6771
Broken Bow *(G-1186)*
Cmg International LLC .... G 918 493-5888
Bixby *(G-617)*

TAGS & LABELS: Paper
Regency Labels Inc .... E 405 682-3460
Oklahoma City *(G-7002)*
Summit Labels Inc .... G 918 936-4950
Tulsa *(G-10868)*

TAGS: Paper, Blank, Made From Purchased Paper
Brenda Riggs .... G 918 543-3530
Inola *(G-3652)*
County of Comanche .... G 580 355-3810
Lawton *(G-3911)*

TANK & BOILER CLEANING SVCS
Bs & W Solutions LLC .... G 918 392-9356
Tulsa *(G-9343)*

TANK COMPONENTS: Military, Specialized
Echota Defense Services .... G 918 384-7409
Tulsa *(G-9637)*

TANK REPAIR & CLEANING SVCS
Line X Prtctive Ctngs Okla LLC .... F 405 232-4994
Oklahoma City *(G-6479)*

TANK REPAIR SVCS
Chris Green Greens Construct .... G 405 207-0690
Pauls Valley *(G-7653)*
Hmt LLC .... G 580 363-8800
Blackwell *(G-683)*

TANK TOWERS: Metal Plate
M J & H Fabrication Inc .... F 580 749-5339
Ponca City *(G-7847)*

TANKS & OTHER TRACKED VEHICLE CMPNTS
Integrated Service Company LLC .... G 918 556-3600
Tulsa *(G-9997)*
Pelagic Tank LLC .... C 580 856-2182
Enid *(G-3034)*

PRODUCT SECTION

TANKS: For Tank Trucks, Metal Plate
Ameripump Mfg LLC .... G 918 438-2953
  Tulsa (G-9178)
Husky Portable Containment Co .... E 918 333-2000
  Bartlesville (G-496)

TANKS: Fuel, Including Oil & Gas, Metal Plate
Harsco Corporation .... E 918 619-8000
  Tulsa (G-9899)
Hmt LLC .... G 580 363-8800
  Blackwell (G-683)
Royalty Fabrication LLC .... G 405 257-6654
  Wewoka (G-11510)
Titan Fuel Systems LLC .... G 405 788-2412
  Norman (G-5174)

TANKS: Lined, Metal
American Tank & Cnstr Co .... G 918 254-6292
  Tulsa (G-9173)
Sufrank Corporation .... E 580 353-4600
  Lawton (G-4006)

TANKS: Plastic & Fiberglass
Beetle Plastics LLC .... E 580 389-5421
  Ardmore (G-256)
Denali Incorporated .... G 713 627-0933
  Tulsa (G-9571)
Fiber Glass Systems LP .... C 918 245-6651
  Sand Springs (G-8183)
Norwesco Inc .... F 405 275-2034
  Shawnee (G-8479)
Reasor Enterprises .... G 918 633-1746
  Broken Arrow (G-1029)

TANKS: Standard Or Custom Fabricated, Metal Plate
Chickasaw Energy Solutions LLC .... E 580 276-3306
  Marietta (G-4202)
Custom Manufacturing Inc .... E 405 692-6311
  Oklahoma City (G-5874)
Los Angeles Boiler Works Inc .... E 580 363-1312
  Blackwell (G-688)
Matrix Service Inc .... E 918 425-3106
  Catoosa (G-1339)
Permian Tank & Mfg Inc .... E 405 295-2525
  El Reno (G-2747)
Rise Manufacturing LLC .... E 918 994-6240
  Broken Arrow (G-1032)
Sawyer Manufacturing Company .... E 918 834-2550
  Tulsa (G-9034)

TANKS: Storage, Farm, Metal Plate
AST Storage LLC .... F 918 208-0100
  Jay (G-3678)

TANKS: Water, Metal Plate
Water Tank Service .... G 918 786-7850
  Grove (G-3292)

TANNING SALONS
Rhinestone Cowgirl .... G 405 564-0512
  Stillwater (G-8747)
Zon Inc .... F 918 458-5511
  Tahlequah (G-8894)

TAR
Drumright Tar .... G 918 352-4000
  Drumright (G-2058)

TARGET DRONES
American Drones LLC .... G 405 308-0866
  Moore (G-4487)

TARPAULINS
Edwards Canvas Inc .... E 405 238-7551
  Pauls Valley (G-7658)
Hays Tent & Awning .... G 918 534-1663
  Dewey (G-2023)

TAX REFUND DISCOUNTING
Aars .... G 918 313-4512
  Tulsa (G-9080)

TAX RETURN PREPARATION SVCS
Aars .... G 918 313-4512
  Tulsa (G-9080)

TECHNICAL MANUAL PREPARATION SVCS
Cutting Edge Robotic Tech LLC .... G 918 247-6012
  Kellyville (G-3764)

TELECOMMUNICATION SYSTEMS & EQPT
Vics Telecommunications .... G 580 512-0313
  Lawton (G-4017)
Zeta .... G 918 664-8200
  Broken Arrow (G-1105)
Zomm LLC .... G 918 995-2233
  Tulsa (G-11179)

TELECOMMUNICATIONS CARRIERS & SVCS: Wireless
Tribalcom Wrless Solutions LLC .... G 405 274-7245
  Oklahoma City (G-7328)

TELEPHONE EQPT INSTALLATION
In-Tele Communication LLC .... G 580 272-0303
  Ada (G-50)

TELEPHONE SVCS
Fenton Office Supply Co .... E 405 372-5555
  Stillwater (G-8688)

TELEPHONE SWITCHING EQPT
Jesse Harbin .... G 918 734-3980
  Tulsa (G-10039)
L3 Westwood Corporation .... G 918 250-4444
  Tulsa (G-10108)
United Sewing Agency Inc .... G 580 924-6936
  Durant (G-2271)

TELEPHONE: Fiber Optic Systems
Catoosa 2 Way .... G 918 234-0055
  Tulsa (G-9389)
Ciena Corporation .... F 918 925-5000
  Tulsa (G-9424)
Indian Nations Fiberoptics Inc .... G 580 355-2300
  Lawton (G-3941)

TELEVISION BROADCASTING & COMMUNICATIONS EQPT
Versatech Industries Inc .... G 918 366-7400
  Bixby (G-670)

TELEVISION SETS
Media Specialists Inc .... G 918 622-0077
  Tulsa (G-10238)

TEMPORARY HELP SVCS
Stand By Personnel .... G 918 582-0522
  Tulsa (G-10834)

TERMITE CONTROL SVCS
Johndrow Home Improvement .... G 580 762-4000
  Ponca City (G-7840)

TEST KITS: Pregnancy
Eden Clinic Inc .... G 405 579-4673
  Norman (G-4988)

TESTERS: Battery
Maccor Inc .... D 918 445-1874
  Tulsa (G-10193)

TESTERS: Liquid, Exc Indl Process
Refinery Supply Co Inc .... G 918 621-1700
  Tulsa (G-10635)

TESTERS: Physical Property
Engius LLC .... G 405 533-3770
  Stillwater (G-8685)

TEXTILE & APPAREL SVCS
Custom Monograms & Lettering .... G 405 495-8586
  Bethany (G-574)
Productive Clutter Inc .... G 405 447-3839
  Norman (G-5124)

TEXTILE FABRICATORS
Chris Johnson .... G 405 364-3879
  Norman (G-4956)

TEXTILE PRDTS: Hand Woven & Crocheted
Crochetangel .... G 918 282-3056
  Broken Arrow (G-879)

TEXTILE: Finishing, Cotton Broadwoven
Fabricut Inc .... F 918 622-7700
  Tulsa (G-9724)

TEXTILES: Jute & Flax Prdts
Mabels Fashion Alteration .... G 405 605-4558
  Oklahoma City (G-6513)

TEXTILES: Linen Fabrics
World Trading Company Inc .... A 405 787-1982
  Oklahoma City (G-7471)

TEXTILES: Mill Waste & Remnant
Sooner Wiping Rags LLC .... F 405 670-3100
  Oklahoma City (G-7168)

THERMITE
East 74th Street Holdings Inc .... C 918 437-3037
  Tulsa (G-9631)

THREAD: Embroidery
Boley One .... G 405 301-7692
  Oklahoma City (G-5616)

TIE SHOPS
Two Guys Bowtie Company LLC .... G 405 612-0116
  Tulsa (G-11026)

TILE: Brick & Structural, Clay
Acme Brick Company .... D 918 834-3384
  Tulsa (G-9096)
Commercial Brick Corporation .... C 405 257-6613
  Wewoka (G-11498)
Mangum Brick .... G 405 410-4478
  Edmond (G-2503)
Meridian Brick LLC .... E 918 687-6734
  Muskogee (G-4712)
Meridian Brick LLC .... G 918 258-7533
  Broken Arrow (G-971)
Meridian Brick LLC .... G 405 749-9900
  Oklahoma City (G-6567)

TILE: Clay, Roof
Heintzelman Cons & Rofing .... G 405 409-8954
  Oklahoma City (G-5294)

TIMBER DRIVING & BOOMING
Rex Ross .... G 580 835-7244
  Eagletown (G-2277)

TIMBER PRDTS WHOLESALERS
Railroad Yard Inc .... E 405 377-8763
  Stillwater (G-8743)

TIMING DEVICES: Electronic
Connor-Winfield Corp .... E 405 273-1257
  Shawnee (G-8440)

TINCTURE OF IODINE
North Amrcn Brine Rsources LLC .... G 405 828-7123
  Enid (G-3021)

Employee Codes: A=Over 500 employees, B=251-500
C=101-250, D=51-100, E=20-50, F=10-19, G=1-9

TINSEL
Kaw Nation Solutions LLC .... G 405 365-8900
Kaw City (G-3759)

TINSMITHING, REPAIR WORK
Eastern Sheet Metal Co Inc .... G 918 687-6231
Muskogee (G-4669)

TIRE DEALERS
Douglas Thompson Auto Inc .... G 405 330-6997
Edmond (G-2393)

TIRE INFLATORS: Hand Or Compressor Operated
Airgo Systems LLC .... F 405 346-5807
Oklahoma City (G-5404)

TIRE SUNDRIES OR REPAIR MATERIALS: Rubber
Setco Inc .... D 580 286-6531
Idabel (G-3645)

TIRES & INNER TUBES
Airgo Systems .... G 877 550-6111
Oklahoma City (G-5403)
Carter BF .... G 918 486-7208
Coweta (G-1874)
Charles Service Station LLC .... G 918 297-3308
Hartshorne (G-3390)

TIRES & TUBES WHOLESALERS
Douglas Thompson Auto Inc .... G 405 330-6997
Edmond (G-2393)

TIRES & TUBES, WHOLESALE: Truck
Auto Trim Design Signs SE Okla .... G 580 622-3830
Sulphur (G-8828)
Shur-Co LLC .... G 405 262-7600
El Reno (G-2757)

TIRES: Auto
Michelin North America Inc .... D 580 226-1200
Ardmore (G-331)

TIRES: Cushion Or Solid Rubber
Southeast Tire Inc .... D 580 286-6531
Idabel (G-3647)

TIRES: Motorcycle, Pneumatic
Nutting Custom Trikes .... G 918 257-8795
Afton (G-119)

TITANIUM MILL PRDTS
Titanium Nutrition LLC .... G 918 697-1012
Broken Arrow (G-1078)

TITLE SEARCH COMPANIES
Frontier Land Co Inc .... G 918 584-2050
Tulsa (G-9783)

TOBACCO STORES & STANDS
Osage Trading Co Inc .... G 918 287-4544
Pawhuska (G-7693)

TOBACCO: Chewing
Treehouse Vapor Co LLC .... G 405 601-6867
Oklahoma City (G-7322)

TOBACCO: Chewing & Snuff
Tall Chief LLC .... G 918 783-8255
Pryor (G-7994)

TOBACCO: Smoking
Handy Mart Inc .... G 580 254-5889
Woodward (G-11591)
Osage Trading Co Inc .... G 918 287-4544
Pawhuska (G-7693)

TOILET PREPARATIONS
Zip ME Up Please LLC .... G 405 614-2778
Stillwater (G-8778)

TOILETS: Portable Chemical, Plastics
A Royal Flush LLC .... G 405 422-2077
Yukon (G-11688)

TOOL & DIE STEEL
Advantage Cnstr Pdts Inc .... G 405 372-3562
Stillwater (G-8651)
Hartco Metal Products Inc .... G 405 471-2784
Edmond (G-2452)
J & L Tool Co Inc .... G 918 835-8484
Tulsa (G-10018)

TOOLS & EQPT: Used With Sporting Arms
Five Star Equipment LLC .... F 918 637-0200
Ramona (G-8045)
Sarduccis Metal Works Inc .... G 918 694-3466
Tulsa (G-10708)

TOOLS: Carpenters', Including Levels & Chisels, Exc Saws
Chiseled In Stone .... G 918 813-5409
Tulsa (G-9419)
Rd Roofing and Carpentry .... G 580 341-0607
Ada (G-80)

TOOLS: Hand
Evans Tool Co Inc .... G 580 889-5770
Atoka (G-412)
Federal Metals Inc .... F 918 838-1725
Tulsa (G-9731)
Helton Custom Knives LLC .... G 918 230-1773
Claremore (G-1633)
J R Lukeman & Associates Inc .... G 405 842-6548
Oklahoma City (G-6338)
M W Bevins Co .... E 918 627-1273
Tulsa (G-10190)
Red Devil Incorporated .... F 918 585-8111
Tulsa (G-10629)
Red Devil Incorporated .... D 918 825-5744
Pryor (G-7989)
William L Riggs Company Inc .... G 918 437-3245
Tulsa (G-11125)
William Reed .... G 405 912-8153
Oklahoma City (G-5324)

TOOLS: Hand, Power
A-1 Sure Shot .... F 405 677-9800
Oklahoma City (G-5353)
Black & Decker (us) Inc .... G 918 249-8641
Tulsa (G-9300)
Charles Machine Works Inc .... A 580 572-2693
Perry (G-7728)
Hilti North America Ltd .... G 918 252-6000
Tulsa (G-9932)
Jantz Supply Inc .... E 580 369-5503
Davis (G-1986)
Subsite LLC .... C 580 572-3700
Perry (G-7748)

TOOLS: Hand, Shovels Or Spades
Hisco Inc .... F 405 524-2700
Oklahoma City (G-6254)

TOOTHBRUSHES: Exc Electric
Oral Health Products Inc .... F 918 622-9412
Tulsa (G-10435)

TOWELS: Fabric & Nonwoven, Made From Purchased Materials
Suntime Products Inc .... G 918 664-8330
Tulsa (G-10875)

TOWERS, SECTIONS: Transmission, Radio & Television
Arbuckle Mountain Tower Corp .... G 580 223-3408
Ardmore (G-243)
High Pointe Construction .... G 405 685-8303
Oklahoma City (G-6247)
Landa Mobile Systems LLC .... G 571 272-3350
Tulsa (G-10121)
Tower Components Inc .... E 918 379-0769
Catoosa (G-1357)

TOYS
Bipo Inc .... E 580 262-9640
Oklahoma City (G-5575)
Dragonslayer Games LLC .... G 918 665-1472
Tulsa (G-9603)
Fresh Monkey Fiction LLC .... G 405 751-3826
Oklahoma City (G-6118)
Sheen Incorporated .... G 405 848-0881
Oklahoma City (G-7118)
Toyko Toys .... G 405 204-7462
Oklahoma City (G-7313)

TOYS & HOBBY GOODS & SPLYS, WHOL: Toy Novelties & Amusements
Wassco Corporation .... F 918 834-4444
Tulsa (G-11097)

TOYS & HOBBY GOODS & SPLYS, WHOLESALE: Board Games
Solidroots LLC .... G 918 770-3549
Tulsa (G-10785)

TOYS, HOBBY GOODS & SPLYS WHOLESALERS
American Drones LLC .... G 405 308-0866
Moore (G-4487)

TOYS: Dolls, Stuffed Animals & Parts
Doodlebugs Etc Inc .... G 405 525-1248
Oklahoma City (G-5968)
Rita S Nicar .... G 580 492-4521
Lawton (G-3995)

TOYS: Kites
Bill Kite Sales .... G 918 806-2958
Broken Arrow (G-851)
Kite Virginia .... G 918 747-9803
Tulsa (G-10094)
Kites In Sky LLC .... G 405 624-6231
Stillwater (G-8714)

TOYS: Video Game Machines
Game King .... G 580 250-0707
Lawton (G-3934)

TRACTOR REPAIR SVCS
Independent Diesel Service .... F 580 234-0435
Enid (G-2977)

TRAILERS & PARTS: Boat
Five A Trailers and Equipment .... G 580 564-2973
Kingston (G-3827)

TRAILERS & PARTS: Horse
Cimarron Trailers Inc .... C 405 222-4800
Chickasha (G-1450)
Hourglass Transport LLC .... G 580 937-4569
Coleman (G-1796)
Tall Boys Toys .... G 580 323-2765
Clinton (G-1771)
W - W Trailer Mfrs Inc .... C 580 795-5571
Madill (G-4166)

TRAILERS & PARTS: Truck & Semi's
Ardmore Dragway .... G 580 226-7811
Ardmore (G-246)
Built Better Enterprises LLC .... G 580 492-5227
Fletcher (G-3161)
C-All Manufacturing Inc .... E 580 889-3351
Atoka (G-401)
Choctaw Global LLC .... G 918 426-2871
McAlester (G-4285)
CMI Terex Corporation .... A 405 787-6020
Oklahoma City (G-5792)
Dickson Industries Inc .... E 405 598-6547
Tecumseh (G-8912)

PRODUCT SECTION

Diw Engneering Fabrication LLC ....E....... 918 534-0001
  Dewey *(G-2020)*
Ebenezer Truck Trailer LL ....G....... 918 289-6669
  Tulsa *(G-9635)*
F & F Automotive Inc ....G....... 580 933-4262
  Valliant *(G-11223)*
Haul Around ....G....... 580 353-0808
  Elgin *(G-2776)*
Hejin Waldran ....G....... 918 408-3500
  Claremore *(G-1632)*
Jbw Ventures LLC ....D....... 580 795-5577
  Madill *(G-4152)*
Kerr-Bilt Trailers Jl Inc ....F....... 580 566-1200
  Boswell *(G-757)*
Kool-Breez LLC ....G....... 918 715-3358
  McAlester *(G-4311)*
Kremlin Welding & Fabrication ....G....... 580 874-2522
  Kremlin *(G-3853)*
Mac Trailer of Oklahoma Inc ....G....... 817 900-2006
  Davis *(G-1988)*
Overbilt Trailer Company ....E....... 918 352-4474
  Drumright *(G-2069)*
Sioux Leasing Company LLC ....G....... 580 772-7100
  Weatherford *(G-11442)*
Spade Leasing Inc ....C....... 580 653-2171
  Springer *(G-8626)*
Tall Boys Toys ....G....... 580 323-2765
  Clinton *(G-1771)*
Tritan Mfg LLC ....G....... 405 375-3332
  Kingfisher *(G-3819)*
Truck Bodies & Eqp Intl Inc ....G....... 918 355-6842
  Broken Arrow *(G-1174)*
Tulsa Trailer LLC ....G....... 918 447-2100
  Tulsa *(G-11010)*
Universal Trlr Holdings Corp ....G....... 405 422-7238
  El Reno *(G-2766)*
V E Enterprises Inc ....E....... 580 653-2171
  Springer *(G-8627)*
W - W Trailer Mfrs Inc ....C....... 580 795-5571
  Madill *(G-4166)*

TRAILERS & TRAILER EQPT

Backwoods Trailers LLC ....G....... 864 237-5906
  Stilwell *(G-8781)*
Best Trailer Products ....G....... 580 931-3534
  Durant *(G-2205)*
Flaming Hcksaw Fabrication LLC ....G....... 479 228-0809
  Westville *(G-11483)*
Holt Trailer Mfg & Sales LLC ....F....... 405 784-2233
  Asher *(G-390)*
Millertime Manufacturing LLC ....G....... 918 273-2040
  Nowata *(G-5221)*
Nickolas Manufacturing Inc ....G....... 918 698-7109
  Tulsa *(G-10344)*
Polypipe Hdlg Specialists Inc ....G....... 405 330-4733
  Edmond *(G-2573)*
Superior Companies Inc ....D....... 918 534-0755
  Dewey *(G-2033)*
Vans Trailer Sales ....G....... 580 323-3999
  Clinton *(G-1772)*

TRAILERS OR VANS: Horse Transportation, Fifth-Wheel Type

4-Star Trailers Inc ....C....... 405 324-7827
  Oklahoma City *(G-5331)*
Cherokee Industries Inc ....D....... 405 691-8222
  Oklahoma City *(G-5750)*
Hart Trailer LLC ....D....... 405 224-3634
  Chickasha *(G-1469)*
R N J Inc ....E....... 918 865-2781
  Mannford *(G-4191)*
Turnbow Trailers Inc ....F....... 918 862-3233
  Oilton *(G-5241)*

TRAILERS: Bodies

Clubhouse Trailer Co LLC ....G....... 405 396-6747
  Edmond *(G-2358)*
J & C Manufacturing Inc. ....F....... 580 476-3217
  Rush Springs *(G-8122)*
Stahl/Scott Fetzer Company ....D....... 580 924-5575
  Durant *(G-2260)*

TRAILERS: Demountable Cargo Containers

Oklahoma Container Corp ....G....... 405 842-8300
  Oklahoma City *(G-6745)*

TRAILERS: House, Exc Permanent Dwellings

Peak Eagles Landing ....G....... 918 636-5152
  Stillwater *(G-8736)*

TRAILERS: Semitrailers, Truck Tractors

Atoka Trailer and Mfg LLC ....E....... 580 889-7270
  Atoka *(G-397)*
C M Trailers ....G....... 580 493-2301
  Drummond *(G-2046)*

TRAILERS: Truck, Chassis

Pfpp LP ....D....... 405 946-3381
  Oklahoma City *(G-6839)*

TRANS PROG REG & ADMIN, GOVT: Motor Vehicle Licensing & Insp

County of Comanche ....G....... 580 355-3810
  Lawton *(G-3911)*

TRANSDUCERS: Electrical Properties

Ashleys Electrical Services ....G....... 918 825-0747
  Pryor *(G-7944)*

TRANSFORMERS: Power Related

Chemco ....G....... 918 481-0537
  Tulsa *(G-9409)*
D & J Enterprises ....G....... 918 906-3951
  Tulsa *(G-9536)*
Fluid Controls Inc ....E....... 918 299-0442
  Tulsa *(G-9762)*
Kimray Inc ....C....... 405 525-6601
  Oklahoma City *(G-6417)*
Lamar Enterprises Inc ....E....... 405 682-5511
  Oklahoma City *(G-6447)*
Northwest Transformer Co Inc ....E....... 405 636-1454
  Oklahoma City *(G-6695)*
Southwest Electric Co ....C....... 405 733-4700
  Oklahoma City *(G-7175)*
Wiley Transformer Co ....G....... 918 225-5772
  Cushing *(G-1970)*

TRANSFORMERS: Specialty

Quick Charge Corporation ....E....... 405 634-2120
  Oklahoma City *(G-6944)*
Quick Start Inc. ....F....... 405 422-3135
  El Reno *(G-2749)*
Southwest Electric Co ....E....... 800 364-4445
  Oklahoma City *(G-7174)*

TRANSMISSIONS: Motor Vehicle

Atc Drivetrain LLC ....A....... 405 577-9901
  Oklahoma City *(G-5480)*
Atc Drivetrain LLC ....B....... 405 350-3600
  Oklahoma City *(G-5481)*
Industrial Axle Company LLC ....D....... 405 273-9315
  Shawnee *(G-8463)*
Liberty Transmission Parts ....G....... 405 634-3450
  Oklahoma City *(G-6473)*
Liberty Transmission Parts ....G....... 405 236-8749
  Oklahoma City *(G-6472)*
Sonny Mac Industries Inc. ....F....... 918 261-8446
  Bixby *(G-661)*

TRANSPORTATION EPQT & SPLYS, WHOL: Aircraft Engs/Eng Parts

Chromalloy Gas Turbine LLC ....C....... 845 359-4700
  Oklahoma City *(G-5764)*

TRANSPORTATION EQPT & SPLYS WHOLESALERS, NEC

A-1 Machine Works Inc ....G....... 918 367-2788
  Bristow *(G-762)*
Aerospace Products SE Inc ....F....... 405 213-1034
  Oklahoma City *(G-5393)*
Cherokee Nation Businesses LLC ....B....... 918 384-7474
  Catoosa *(G-1310)*
EZ Carrier LLC ....G....... 918 827-7876
  Mounds *(G-4615)*
Railroad Sgnling Solutions Inc ....G....... 918 973-1888
  Broken Arrow *(G-1020)*

TRANSPORTATION SVCS, NEC

Railroad Sgnling Solutions Inc ....G....... 918 973-1888
  Broken Arrow *(G-1020)*

TRANSPORTATION: Air, Nonscheduled, NEC

Mission Transportation LLC ....D....... 405 694-4755
  Bethany *(G-591)*

TRANSPORTATION: Local Passenger, NEC

Roger Magerus ....G....... 405 364-7231
  Norman *(G-5134)*

TRAP ROCK: Dimension

Dream Green International LLC ....G....... 814 616-7800
  Norman *(G-4983)*
Keystone Rock & Excavation LLC ....G....... 405 608-7777
  Oklahoma City *(G-6414)*

TRAPS: Animal, Iron Or Steel

P W Manufacturing Company Inc ....G....... 918 652-4981
  Henryetta *(G-3514)*

TRAVEL AGENCIES

Gloria Rae Travel Accessories ....G....... 405 848-1300
  Oklahoma City *(G-6163)*
Southwest Interiors Inc ....G....... 580 323-3050
  Clinton *(G-1769)*

TRAVEL TRAILERS & CAMPERS

Complete Cooling Systems Inc ....G....... 405 272-0453
  Oklahoma City *(G-5811)*
Diamond T Trailer Mfg Co ....E....... 580 587-2432
  Rattan *(G-8071)*
Gr Trailers LLC ....G....... 405 567-0567
  Prague *(G-7926)*
Industrial Axle Company LLC ....D....... 405 273-9315
  Shawnee *(G-8463)*
Resort Rv ....G....... 580 465-4428
  Ardmore *(G-349)*

TROPHIES, NEC

Trophies n Things ....G....... 405 247-9771
  Anadarko *(G-207)*
Yukon Trophy & Awards Inc ....G....... 405 354-5184
  Yukon *(G-11808)*

TROPHIES, SILVER

Dearinger Printing & Trophy ....F....... 405 372-5503
  Stillwater *(G-8675)*

TROPHIES: Metal, Exc Silver

All-Star Trophies & Ribbon Mfg ....G....... 918 283-2200
  Claremore *(G-1581)*
Frog Printing & Awards Ctr LLC ....G 580 678-1114
  Lawton *(G-3931)*
Mart Trophy Co Inc ....G....... 918 481-3388
  Tulsa *(G-10217)*
Mtm Recognition Corporation ....B....... 405 609-6900
  Oklahoma City *(G-6634)*

TROPHY & PLAQUE STORES

All-Star Trophies & Ribbon Mfg ....G....... 918 283-2200
  Claremore *(G-1581)*
American Engraving & Trophy ....G....... 405 360-2744
  Norman *(G-4906)*
Carnegie Herald ....G....... 580 654-1443
  Carnegie *(G-1274)*
Checotah W T J Shoppe Inc ....G....... 918 473-2819
  Checotah *(G-1391)*
Edmond Trophy Co ....G....... 405 341-4631
  Edmond *(G-2405)*
Elk Valley Woodworking Inc ....G....... 580 486-3337
  Carter *(G-1281)*
First Thought Inc. ....G....... 918 336-3322
  Bartlesville *(G-483)*
Green Cntry Trophy Screen Prtg ....G....... 918 647-2923
  Poteau *(G-7906)*
House of Trophies ....G....... 405 452-3524
  Wetumka *(G-11492)*
House of Trophies ....G....... 918 341-2111
  Claremore *(G-1637)*
K & K Wood Products ....G....... 918 396-4004
  Skiatook *(G-8553)*

Employee Codes: A=Over 500 employees, B=251-500
C=101-250, D=51-100, E=20-50, F=10-19, G=1-9

TROPHY & PLAQUE STORES

PRODUCT SECTION

Oklahoma Metal Creations LLC ....G...... 580 917-5434
  Fletcher *(G-3165)*
Promos Advertising Pdts Inc ....G...... 918 343-9675
  Claremore *(G-1676)*
Shine On Designs ....G...... 918 224-7439
  Sapulpa *(G-8311)*
Tack Designs ....G...... 918 825-1211
  Pryor *(G-7993)*
Trophies n Things ....G...... 405 247-9771
  Anadarko *(G-207)*
Yukon Trophy & Awards Inc................G...... 405 354-5184
  Yukon *(G-11808)*

TRUCK & BUS BODIES: Ambulance

Emergency Site Protection LLC ....D...... 580 699-6386
  Medicine Park *(G-4370)*

TRUCK & BUS BODIES: Automobile Wrecker Truck

Cooper Wrecker Service ....G...... 918 639-7381
  Pawnee *(G-7703)*
Givens Wrecker Service ....G...... 580 225-0892
  Elk City *(G-2821)*
Jims Truck Center ....G...... 918 225-1013
  Cushing *(G-1939)*
Robbins Salvage & Auto Sales ....G...... 918 431-1000
  Tahlequah *(G-8881)*

TRUCK & BUS BODIES: Car Carrier

Midwest Clssic Motorsports LLC ....G...... 405 359-0050
  Edmond *(G-2519)*

TRUCK & BUS BODIES: Farm Truck

Rocky L Emmons & Judy E Sprag ....G...... 580 305-1940
  Frederick *(G-3199)*

TRUCK & BUS BODIES: Garbage Or Refuse Truck

Dominion Refuse Inc ....G...... 918 743-8860
  Tulsa *(G-9595)*
Pendpac Incorporated ....D...... 418 831-8250
  Fairview *(G-3145)*

TRUCK & BUS BODIES: Tank Truck

Big J Tank Truck Service Inc ....G...... 580 336-3501
  Perry *(G-7727)*

TRUCK & BUS BODIES: Truck Beds

J & C Manufacturing Inc ....F...... 580 476-3217
  Rush Springs *(G-8122)*
Pfpp LP ....D...... 405 946-3381
  Oklahoma City *(G-6839)*

TRUCK & BUS BODIES: Truck Tops

Miller Mfg Group ....G...... 918 540-1600
  Miami *(G-4418)*

TRUCK & BUS BODIES: Truck, Motor Vehicle

Auto Crane Company ....C...... 918 438-2760
  Tulsa *(G-9226)*
Cadet Manufacturing Inc ....E...... 918 476-8159
  Chouteau *(G-1559)*
Equipment Technology Inc ....F...... 405 748-3841
  Oklahoma City *(G-6049)*
J & I Manufacturing Inc ....E...... 580 795-7377
  Madill *(G-4150)*
Proform Group Inc ....C...... 918 682-8666
  Muskogee *(G-4739)*
Reading Equipment & Dist LLC ....E...... 918 283-2999
  Claremore *(G-1679)*

TRUCK BODIES: Body Parts

Alberts Auto & Truck Repr Inc ....E...... 866 772-6065
  Weatherford *(G-11389)*
B&P Detailing LLC ....G...... 405 684-7730
  Chickasha *(G-1435)*
Boss Seals & Parts LLC ....G...... 918 237-6991
  Tulsa *(G-9323)*
C & S Technical Services LLC ....E...... 918 258-8324
  Tulsa *(G-9358)*
Lafaver Fiberglass Corporation ....G...... 918 258-4845
  Broken Arrow *(G-1137)*
Technical Manufacturing Inc ....F...... 918 485-0380
  Wagoner *(G-11292)*

TRUCK GENERAL REPAIR SVC

Brake Rebuilders Inc ....F...... 918 834-0200
  Tulsa *(G-9331)*
Clyde Welding Service ....G...... 405 222-1364
  Ninnekah *(G-4868)*
R & M Fleet Service Inc ....G...... 918 367-9326
  Cleveland *(G-1732)*
Reputation Services & Mfg LLC ....E...... 918 437-2077
  Tulsa *(G-10643)*
T & E Mobile Service Inc ....G...... 405 990-4022
  Oklahoma City *(G-7240)*

TRUCK PAINTING & LETTERING SVCS

Ace Sign Company Inc ....G...... 918 446-3030
  Tulsa *(G-9095)*
Byrd Signs & Designs ....G...... 918 687-4219
  Muskogee *(G-4656)*
Timco Blasting & Coatings ....E...... 918 367-1700
  Bristow *(G-799)*
Timco Blasting & Coatings ....F...... 918 605-1179
  Bristow *(G-800)*
Timco Blasting & Coatings ....G...... 918 605-1179
  Stroud *(G-8823)*
Timco Blasting & Coatings ....G...... 918 605-1179
  Bristow *(G-801)*
Timco Blasting & Coatings ....G...... 918 608-1179
  Stroud *(G-8824)*

TRUCK PARTS & ACCESSORIES: Wholesalers

Boss Seals & Parts LLC ....G...... 918 237-6991
  Tulsa *(G-9323)*
Line X of Stillwater ....G...... 405 743-0911
  Stillwater *(G-8719)*

TRUCKING & HAULING SVCS: Animal & Farm Prdt

Hoskins Gypsum Company LLC ....F...... 580 274-3446
  Longdale *(G-4124)*

TRUCKING & HAULING SVCS: Building Materials

Commercial Brick Corporation ....C...... 405 257-6613
  Wewoka *(G-11498)*

TRUCKING & HAULING SVCS: Contract Basis

Dobbs & Crowder Inc ....G...... 918 452-3211
  Eufaula *(G-3100)*

TRUCKING & HAULING SVCS: Heavy, NEC

Well Completions Inc ....E...... 918 654-3030
  Cameron *(G-1259)*

TRUCKING & HAULING SVCS: Liquid Petroleum, Exc Local

Brady Welding & Machine Shop ....D...... 580 229-1168
  Healdton *(G-3408)*
Stallion Oilfield Services Ltd ....D...... 580 856-3169
  Ratliff City *(G-8067)*

TRUCKING & HAULING SVCS: Liquid, Local

Martin Tank Trck Csing Pulling ....F...... 918 225-2388
  Cushing *(G-1944)*

TRUCKING & HAULING SVCS: Lumber & Timber

BOB Lumber & Grain LLC ....F...... 580 927-3168
  Coalgate *(G-1775)*

TRUCKING & HAULING SVCS: Petroleum, Local

B & B Tool Co Inc ....G...... 405 756-4530
  Lindsay *(G-4045)*
O K Tank Trucks Inc ....F...... 918 396-3043
  Skiatook *(G-8562)*
Wapco Inc ....G...... 405 489-3212
  Cement *(G-1370)*
Washita Valley Enterprises Inc ....D...... 405 670-5338
  Oklahoma City *(G-7427)*

TRUCKING, AUTOMOBILE CARRIER

Hamil Service LLC ....F...... 405 375-3815
  Kingfisher *(G-3800)*

TRUCKING, DUMP

Heady Trucking ....G...... 580 326-2739
  Sawyer *(G-8334)*
Wadley Bill & Son Drilling Co ....G...... 918 756-4650
  Okmulgee *(G-7529)*
Withers Trucking Co ....G...... 580 668-2320
  Healdton *(G-3424)*

TRUCKING: Except Local

Blackjack Express LLC ....G...... 405 462-7410
  Bradley *(G-760)*
Harrison Gypsum LLC ....F...... 405 366-9500
  Norman *(G-5018)*
Harrison Gypsum LLC ....E...... 580 994-6048
  Mooreland *(G-4591)*
Hart Feeds Inc ....G...... 405 224-0102
  Chickasha *(G-1468)*
Roff Iron & Sales Inc ....E...... 580 456-7850
  Roff *(G-8110)*
T&T Forklift Service Inc ....G...... 405 756-3451
  Lindsay *(G-4093)*

TRUCKING: Local, With Storage

Allens Trucking & Welding Svc ....G...... 405 341-8066
  Arcadia *(G-227)*
Miracle Production Inc ....F...... 405 324-2216
  Oklahoma City *(G-6618)*

TRUCKING: Local, Without Storage

Action Petroleum Services Corp ....G...... 580 223-6544
  Ardmore *(G-237)*
Black Gold Stone Ranch LLC ....G...... 405 590-0700
  Norman *(G-4936)*
Block Sand Co Inc ....E...... 405 391-2919
  McLoud *(G-4352)*
Chesapeake Operating LLC ....A...... 405 848-8000
  Oklahoma City *(G-5757)*
Degges Oil Field Service ....G...... 918 623-1373
  Okemah *(G-5268)*
Dewitt Trucking & Excavation ....G...... 580 669-2534
  Glencoe *(G-3221)*
Dolese Bros Co ....G...... 580 323-1202
  Clinton *(G-1748)*
Dolese Bros Co ....F...... 580 255-3046
  Duncan *(G-2107)*
Eddie Johnsons Wldg & Mch Co ....F...... 580 856-3418
  Ratliff City *(G-8051)*
Independent Trucking Co Inc ....F...... 918 352-2539
  Drumright *(G-2063)*
J and S Trucking Company ....G...... 580 216-7213
  Woodward *(G-11595)*
Jennings Stone Company Inc ....E...... 580 777-2880
  Fittstown *(G-3159)*
Mels Construction Inc ....G...... 405 853-4621
  Hennessey *(G-3477)*
Mid Continent Concrete Company ....E...... 918 647-0550
  Poteau *(G-7908)*
Panhandle Oilfield Service Com ....D...... 405 608-5330
  Oklahoma City *(G-6799)*
S & H Tank Service Inc ....E...... 405 756-3121
  Lindsay *(G-4081)*
S & H Tank Service of Oklahoma .....F...... 405 756-3121
  Lindsay *(G-4082)*
Stallion Oilfield Services Ltd ....D...... 580 856-3169
  Ratliff City *(G-8067)*
T & G Construction Inc ....G...... 580 355-6655
  Lawton *(G-4010)*
W 2 Enterprises LLC ....G...... 918 429-8793
  Tuskahoma *(G-11183)*

TRUCKS & TRACTORS: Industrial

4-Star Trailers Inc ....C...... 405 324-7827
  Oklahoma City *(G-5331)*
Campbell Fbrcation Tooling Inc ....G...... 918 987-0047
  Stroud *(G-8809)*
D & W Cupp Trucking LLC ....G...... 580 821-6844
  Sayre *(G-8339)*
Dickson Industries Inc ....E...... 405 598-6547
  Tecumseh *(G-8912)*
Hawkeye Fleet Services ....E...... 405 495-9939
  Oklahoma City *(G-6226)*
Hejin Waldran ....G...... 918 408-3500
  Claremore *(G-1632)*

PRODUCT SECTION

Industrial Vehicles Intl Inc..............E....... 918 836-6516
  Tulsa *(G-9983)*
Karl Amanns Trucking..............G....... 580 226-2082
  Ardmore *(G-320)*
Kern Valley Industries..............G....... 918 868-3911
  Rose *(G-8118)*
Kremlin Welding & Fabrication..............G....... 580 874-2522
  Kremlin *(G-3853)*
Mobile Mini Inc..............E....... 405 682-9333
  Oklahoma City *(G-6622)*
W - W Trailer Mfrs Inc..............C....... 580 795-5571
  Madill *(G-4166)*

TRUCKS: Forklift

Becks Forklift Svc LLC..............G....... 580 303-8038
  Elk City *(G-2786)*
Darr Lift Main Line..............G....... 580 657-6337
  Ardmore *(G-273)*
Forklift Parts and Service LLC..............G....... 918 251-5119
  Broken Arrow *(G-913)*
Mid Continent Lift and Eqp LLC..............F....... 580 255-3867
  Duncan *(G-2155)*
Walker Forklift Service LLC..............G....... 918 671-0317
  Tulsa *(G-11093)*
Wkd Associates..............G....... 918 336-9865
  Bartlesville *(G-536)*

TRUCKS: Indl

Crandell Salvage Incorporated..............F....... 918 429-0001
  Mcalester *(G-4287)*
Wolfe Heavy Haul and Hotshot..............G....... 918 695-7836
  Tulsa *(G-11146)*

TRUNKS

Dusty Trunk..............G....... 918 446-4203
  Tulsa *(G-9613)*
Junk N Leslies Trunk LLC..............G....... 405 748-6702
  Oklahoma City *(G-6391)*
Nancys Trunk..............G....... 405 413-5037
  Ripley *(G-8103)*

TRUSSES & FRAMING: Prefabricated Metal

Cushing Truss Manufacturing..............F....... 918 387-2080
  Yale *(G-11683)*

TRUSSES: Wood, Floor

Henderson Truss Incorporated..............F....... 918 473-5573
  Checotah *(G-1394)*

TRUSSES: Wood, Roof

Antlers Roof-Truss & Bldrs Sup..............G....... 580 298-3560
  Antlers *(G-213)*
Ardmore Construction Sup Inc..............G....... 580 223-2322
  Ardmore *(G-245)*
Burrow Construction LLC..............E....... 800 766-5793
  Fort Gibson *(G-3174)*
Craco Truss Post Frame Sup LLC..............G....... 918 457-1111
  Park Hill *(G-7641)*
Cushing Truss Manufacturing..............F....... 918 387-2080
  Yale *(G-11683)*
David Kempe..............F....... 580 924-6798
  Durant *(G-2221)*
Do It Best Hardware..............G....... 580 482-8898
  Altus *(G-154)*
En-Fab Corp..............F....... 918 251-9647
  Broken Arrow *(G-1126)*
Harrison Roof Truss Co..............G....... 580 937-4900
  Coleman *(G-1795)*
Higgins & Sons Truss Company..............E....... 405 997-5455
  Tecumseh *(G-8917)*
Higgins & Sons Truss Company..............F....... 405 997-5455
  Tecumseh *(G-8918)*
Mills Enterprises Inc..............G....... 405 236-4470
  Oklahoma City *(G-6613)*
Newell Wood Products..............F....... 918 686-8060
  Muskogee *(G-4721)*
Overstreet Building & Supply..............G....... 580 234-5666
  Enid *(G-3028)*
Quality Line Truss Inc..............G....... 918 783-5227
  Adair *(G-111)*
Quality Truss Co Inc..............G....... 918 543-2077
  Claremore *(G-1677)*
Schultz Roof Truss Inc..............G....... 405 364-6530
  Norman *(G-5138)*
Timberlake Trussworks LLC..............G....... 580 852-3660
  Helena *(G-3437)*

TUB CONTAINERS: Plastic

Scepter Manufacturing LLC..............D....... 918 544-2222
  Miami *(G-4430)*

TUBE & TUBING FABRICATORS

Albright Steel and Wire Co..............G....... 580 357-3596
  Lawton *(G-3886)*
American Pipe Bending Inc..............E....... 918 749-2363
  Tulsa *(G-9171)*
Bendco Corp..............F....... 918 583-1566
  Tulsa *(G-9281)*
Bendmasters Inc..............G....... 918 585-3755
  Tulsa *(G-9282)*
Cust O Bend..............G....... 918 241-0514
  Tulsa *(G-9525)*
Cust-O-Bend Inc..............E....... 918 241-0514
  Tulsa *(G-9526)*
J & J Tubulars Inc..............G....... 405 691-2039
  Oklahoma City *(G-6330)*
Wood Pipe Service Inc..............G....... 405 672-6097
  Oklahoma City *(G-7464)*

TUBES: Boiler, Wrought

Rosa & Unis LLC..............D....... 918 445-4204
  Tulsa *(G-10670)*

TUBES: Finned, For Heat Transfer

Fin Fab Incorporated..............G....... 918 227-1866
  Tulsa *(G-9006)*

TUBES: Fins

Enerfin Inc..............G....... 918 258-3571
  Broken Arrow *(G-900)*
T F T Inc..............E....... 918 834-2366
  Tulsa *(G-10889)*

TUBES: Paper

Capitol Tube Co Inc..............G....... 405 632-9901
  Oklahoma City *(G-5696)*
Sonoco Products Company..............E....... 918 622-3370
  Tulsa *(G-10786)*

TUBES: Steel & Iron

Webco Industries Inc..............B....... 918 245-2211
  Sand Springs *(G-8237)*
Webco Industries Inc..............G....... 865 388-5001
  Catoosa *(G-1364)*
Webco Industries Inc..............G....... 918 581-0900
  Sand Springs *(G-8236)*
Webco Industries Inc..............G....... 918 836-1188
  Tulsa *(G-11100)*

TUBING: Copper

Taylor Forge Engineered..............E....... 918 280-1183
  Tulsa *(G-10904)*
Wolverine Tube Inc..............B....... 405 275-4850
  Shawnee *(G-8521)*
Wolverine Tube Inc..............A....... 405 275-4850
  Shawnee *(G-8522)*

TUBING: Seamless

Mike Alexander Company Inc..............E....... 580 765-8085
  Tulsa *(G-10276)*

TURBINES & TURBINE GENERATOR SET UNITS: Gas, Complete

Caprock Country Entps Inc..............F....... 580 924-1647
  Calera *(G-1239)*
Integrity Power Solutions LLC..............G....... 918 925-9693
  Edmond *(G-2461)*
Schock Manufacturing LLC..............E....... 918 609-3600
  Owasso *(G-7615)*
Vogt Power International Inc..............G....... 502 899-4500
  Sapulpa *(G-8321)*

TURBINES & TURBINE GENERATOR SETS

Bergey Windpower Company Inc..............E....... 405 364-4212
  Norman *(G-4930)*
Dewind Co..............G....... 580 338-3271
  Guymon *(G-3348)*
Next-Gen Wind LLC..............F....... 405 948-1556
  Oklahoma City *(G-6674)*
Ringside Productions..............G....... 818 974-2673
  Tulsa *(G-10655)*
Siemens Energy..............G....... 580 254-7824
  Woodward *(G-11631)*
Solar Turbines Incorporated..............G....... 918 459-5100
  Broken Arrow *(G-1054)*
Suzlon Wind Energy Corporation..............G....... 580 468-2641
  Guymon *(G-3367)*

TURBINES: Hydraulic, Complete

Universal Pressure Pumping Inc..............B....... 405 262-2441
  El Reno *(G-2765)*

TYPESETTING SVC

A & B Printing & Office Supply..............G....... 580 889-5103
  Atoka *(G-395)*
A 1 Master Print Inc..............G....... 405 787-0505
  Bethany *(G-571)*
A B Printing..............G....... 918 834-2054
  Tulsa *(G-9066)*
A Plus Printing..............G....... 580 765-7752
  Ponca City *(G-7791)*
A Q Printing..............G....... 918 438-1161
  Tulsa *(G-9070)*
A-OK Printing Mill..............G....... 918 775-6809
  Sallisaw *(G-8136)*
Abco Printing & Office Supply..............G....... 580 286-7575
  Idabel *(G-3636)*
Ad Type Inc..............G....... 405 942-7951
  Oklahoma City *(G-5371)*
Adams Printing..............G....... 580 832-2123
  Cordell *(G-1853)*
Advance Graphics & Printing..............G....... 405 258-0796
  Chandler *(G-1373)*
Ajt Enterprises Inc..............F....... 918 665-7083
  Tulsa *(G-9133)*
Altus Printing Co Inc..............G....... 580 482-2020
  Altus *(G-141)*
American-Chief Co..............G....... 918 885-2101
  Hominy *(G-3575)*
Anns Quick Print Co Inc..............G....... 405 222-1871
  Chickasha *(G-1429)*
Associated Lithographing Co..............E....... 918 663-9091
  Tulsa *(G-9217)*
B & L Printing Inc..............G....... 918 258-6655
  Broken Arrow *(G-839)*
Bakers Printing Co Inc..............G....... 405 842-6944
  Oklahoma City *(G-5517)*
Bartlesville Print Shop..............G....... 918 336-6070
  Bartlesville *(G-452)*
Bell Printing and Advertising..............G....... 405 769-6445
  Nicoma Park *(G-4866)*
Bill Rathbone..............G....... 918 486-3028
  Coweta *(G-1872)*
Blanchard News Publishing..............G....... 405 485-2311
  Blanchard *(G-702)*
Britton Printing..............G....... 405 840-3291
  Oklahoma City *(G-5630)*
Brix Inc..............G....... 918 584-6484
  Tulsa *(G-9338)*
Brown Printing Co Inc..............G....... 918 652-9611
  Henryetta *(G-3500)*
Burch Printing Co..............G....... 580 225-3270
  Elk City *(G-2788)*
C & J Printing Co..............G....... 580 355-3099
  Lawton *(G-3902)*
C & R Print Shop Inc..............G....... 405 224-7921
  Chickasha *(G-1445)*
Cable Printing Co Inc..............F....... 405 756-4045
  Lindsay *(G-4055)*
Carnegie Herald..............G....... 580 654-1443
  Carnegie *(G-1274)*
Carr Graphics Inc..............G....... 918 835-0605
  Tulsa *(G-9379)*
Cherry Street Print Shop Inc..............G....... 918 584-0022
  Tulsa *(G-9417)*
CJ Graphics..............G....... 405 636-0400
  Oklahoma City *(G-5771)*
Clark Printing Inc..............G....... 405 528-5396
  Oklahoma City *(G-5776)*
Cnhi LLC..............G....... 918 652-3311
  Henryetta *(G-3501)*
Cnhi LLC..............F....... 580 338-3355
  Guymon *(G-3346)*
Collins Quality Printing..............G....... 918 744-0077
  Tulsa *(G-9468)*
Cooley Enterprises Inc..............G....... 918 437-6900
  Tulsa *(G-9483)*
Copy Fast Printing Inc..............F....... 405 947-7468
  Oklahoma City *(G-5834)*

Employee Codes: A=Over 500 employees, B=251-500
C=101-250, D=51-100, E=20-50, F=10-19, G=1-9

TYPESETTING SVC

Company		Phone
Countywide News Inc Tecumseh *(G-8910)*	F	405 598-3793
Cowan Printing & Litho Inc Tuttle *(G-11191)*	F	405 789-1961
Cowboy Copy Center Stillwater *(G-8671)*	F	405 372-8099
Creative Media Sand Springs *(G-8173)*	G	918 245-3779
Cromwells Inc Enid *(G-2935)*	G	580 234-6561
CSC Inc Mooreland *(G-4587)*	G	580 994-6110
Davis Printing Company Inc Elk City *(G-2800)*	G	580 225-2902
Dbmac 50 Inc Claremore *(G-1613)*	G	918 342-5590
Dean Printing Mangum *(G-4170)*	G	580 782-3777
Deans Typesetting Service Oklahoma City *(G-5912)*	G	405 842-7247
Demco Printing Inc Shawnee *(G-8444)*	F	405 273-8888
Digi Print LLC Oklahoma City *(G-5945)*	G	405 947-0099
Diversified Printing Inc Tulsa *(G-9586)*	F	918 665-2275
Edmond Printings Edmond *(G-2404)*	G	405 341-4330
Education Oklahoma Department Stillwater *(G-8682)*	F	405 743-5531
Ellis County Capital Arnett *(G-387)*	G	580 885-7788
Fedex Office & Print Svcs Inc Tulsa *(G-9733)*	E	918 252-3757
Felkins Enterprises LLC Owasso *(G-7568)*	G	918 272-3456
First Impression Prtg Co Inc Beggs *(G-553)*	G	918 749-5446
Franklin Graphics Inc Muskogee *(G-4675)*	F	918 687-6149
French Printing Inc Tuttle *(G-11200)*	G	405 381-4057
G & S Printing Inc Oklahoma City *(G-6129)*	G	405 789-6813
Geary Star Geary *(G-3216)*	G	405 884-2424
Giles Printing Co Inc Tulsa *(G-9825)*	G	918 584-1583
Good Printing Co Inc Oklahoma City *(G-6171)*	G	405 235-9593
Graphics Etc Owasso *(G-7571)*	G	918 274-4744
Gravley Companies Inc Tulsa *(G-9850)*	G	918 743-6619
Gregath Publishing Company Miami *(G-4407)*	G	918 542-4148
Hammer Hoby Fairview *(G-3137)*	G	580 227-2100
Hardesty Press Inc Tulsa *(G-9891)*	F	918 582-5306
Heavener Ledger Heavener *(G-3429)*	G	918 653-2425
Herald Publishing Co Walters *(G-11302)*	G	580 875-3326
Hinkle Printing & Office Sup Pauls Valley *(G-7660)*	G	405 238-9308
Hipsleys Litho & Prtg Co LLC Oklahoma City *(G-6252)*	G	405 528-2686
Hoffman Printing LLC Muskogee *(G-4691)*	F	918 682-8341
Holbrook Printing Tulsa *(G-9938)*	G	918 835-5950
Hooper Printing Company Inc Norman *(G-5026)*	F	405 321-4288
Imperial Printing Inc Tulsa *(G-9973)*	G	918 663-1302
Ink Images Inc Tulsa *(G-9987)*	G	918 828-0300
K D Typesetting Edmond *(G-2477)*	G	405 302-0799
Kelley Printing Pauls Valley *(G-7663)*	G	405 238-4848
Kindrick Co Prtg & Copying Svc Ada *(G-56)*	G	580 332-1022
King Graphics Inc Oklahoma City *(G-6420)*	G	405 232-2369
Kingfisher Office Supply Inc Kingfisher *(G-3806)*	G	405 375-3404
Kolb Type Service Incorporated Agra *(G-125)*		405 341-0984
L W Duncan Printing Inc Lawton *(G-3953)*	G	580 355-6229
Larry D Hammer Fairview *(G-3140)*	F	580 227-2100
Leda Grimm Cushing *(G-1942)*	G	918 225-0507
Lincoln County Publishing Co Chandler *(G-1385)*	F	405 258-1818
Linderer Printing Co Inc Clinton *(G-1757)*	F	580 323-2102
Lithaprint Inc Tulsa *(G-10168)*	F	918 587-7746
Liv3design LLC Norman *(G-5060)*	G	432 296-1968
Mattocks Printing Co LLC Moore *(G-4538)*	G	405 794-2307
Mc Clain County Publishing Co Purcell *(G-8016)*	E	405 527-2126
McCullough Printing Idabel *(G-3641)*	G	580 286-7681
Meeks Lithographing Company Tulsa *(G-10239)*	G	918 838-9900
Meeks Lithographing Company Tulsa *(G-10241)*	G	918 836-0900
Mesa Black Publishing LLC Boise City *(G-747)*	G	580 544-2222
Metro Graphic Systems Tulsa *(G-10249)*	G	918 744-0308
Mid-West Printing & Pubg Co Sapulpa *(G-8291)*	F	918 224-3666
Midtown Printing Inc Tulsa *(G-10264)*	G	918 295-0090
Midwest Publishing Co Guthrie *(G-3325)*	G	405 282-1890
Minor Printing Company Madill *(G-4158)*	G	580 795-3745
Minuteman Press Oklahoma City *(G-6617)*	G	405 942-5595
Mtm Recognition Corporation Oklahoma City *(G-6634)*	B	405 609-6900
Multiprint Corp Tulsa *(G-10315)*	G	918 832-0300
Newcastle Pacer Inc Newcastle *(G-4833)*	G	405 387-5277
Northwest Printing Inc Enid *(G-3022)*	G	580 234-0953
OK Quality Printing Inc Stillwater *(G-8731)*	G	405 624-2925
Oklahoma Assn of Elc Coop Oklahoma City *(G-6735)*	E	405 478-1455
Oklahoma Executive Printing Oklahoma City *(G-6748)*	G	405 948-8136
Peabodys Printing & A Brush Sp Lawton *(G-3980)*	G	580 248-8317
Pinecliffe Prtrs of Tecumseh Shawnee *(G-8483)*	G	405 273-1292
Pony Express Printing LLC Kingfisher *(G-3811)*	G	405 375-5064
Pre-Press Graphics Inc Tulsa *(G-10541)*	G	918 582-2775
Premier Printing Oklahoma City *(G-6886)*	G	405 632-1132
Prices Quality Printing Inc Durant *(G-2248)*	G	580 924-2271
Print N Copy Inc Broken Arrow *(G-1011)*	G	918 258-8200
Print Shop Claremore *(G-1674)*	G	918 342-3993
Printed Products Inc Tulsa *(G-10561)*	F	918 295-9950
Printing Center Oklahoma City *(G-6901)*	G	405 681-5303
Priority Printworks Inc Pryor *(G-7984)*	G	918 825-6397
Pronto Print Inc Ardmore *(G-347)*	G	580 223-1612
Protype Inc Tulsa *(G-10576)*	G	918 743-4408
Pryor Printing Inc Pryor *(G-7986)*	G	918 825-2888
Quik Print of Tulsa Inc Tulsa *(G-10594)*	G	918 250-5466
Quik Print of Tulsa Inc Tulsa *(G-10595)*	E	918 665-6246
Quik-Print of Oklahoma City Oklahoma City *(G-6949)*	G	405 943-3222
Quik-Print of Oklahoma City Oklahoma City *(G-6946)*	G	405 842-1404
Review Printing Company Inc Marlow *(G-4241)*	F	580 658-6657
Russell Publishing Company Wynnewood *(G-11672)*	G	405 665-4333
Self Printing Inc Tulsa *(G-10726)*	G	918 838-2113
Shine On Designs Sapulpa *(G-8311)*	G	918 224-7439
Shopper News Note Lindsay *(G-4084)*	F	405 756-3169
Signature Graphics Corp Bixby *(G-658)*	G	918 294-3485
Snider Printing & Office Sup Wewoka *(G-11511)*	G	405 257-3402
Snyder Printing Inc Oklahoma City *(G-5317)*	F	405 682-8880
Sooner Industries Inc Miami *(G-4431)*	G	918 540-2422
Sooner Press Seminole *(G-8400)*	G	405 382-8351
Spiro Graphic Spiro *(G-8618)*	G	918 962-2075
Spitzer Printing Sayre *(G-8346)*	G	580 928-5540
Sprekelmeyer Printing Company Ardmore *(G-359)*	G	580 223-5100
Standard Printing Co Inc Oklahoma City *(G-7192)*	G	405 840-0001
Star Nowata Nowata *(G-5230)*	G	918 273-2446
Tom Bennett Manufacturing Oklahoma City *(G-7302)*	F	405 528-5671
Tommy Higle Publishers Marietta *(G-4215)*	G	580 276-5136
Torbett Printing Co & Off Sup Okmulgee *(G-7528)*	G	918 756-5789
Transcript Press Inc Norman *(G-5181)*	E	405 360-7999
Tulsa Instant Printing Tulsa *(G-11000)*	G	918 627-0730
Type House Inc Tulsa *(G-11028)*	G	918 492-8513
Unique Printing Inc Oklahoma City *(G-7361)*	G	405 842-3966
Usher Corporation Oklahoma City *(G-7382)*	G	405 495-2125
Vans Printing Service Grove *(G-3291)*	G	918 786-9496
Vinita Printing Co Inc Vinita *(G-11271)*	E	918 256-6422
Vision Type & Design Inc Tulsa *(G-11082)*	G	918 252-3817
Wallace Printing Company Hugo *(G-3622)*	G	580 326-6323
Wallis Printing Inc Ardmore *(G-379)*	G	580 223-7473
Watonga Republican Inc Watonga *(G-11354)*	G	580 623-4922
Weatherford Press Inc Weatherford *(G-11459)*	F	580 772-5300
Westwood Printing Center Norman *(G-5199)*	G	405 366-8961
Wilson-Monroe Publishing Co Valliant *(G-11234)*	G	580 933-4579

UNIFORM STORES

Company		Phone
Barbara J McGinnis Ardmore *(G-253)*	G	580 226-7675
Cas Monogramming Inc Yukon *(G-11703)*	G	405 350-6556

UNISEX HAIR SALONS

Company		Phone
Identity & Tanning Salon Tuttle *(G-11204)*	G	412 269-7879
Super Cuts Sand Springs *(G-8227)*	G	918 245-3320
Supercuts Inc Sallisaw *(G-8154)*	G	918 775-6389

UNIVERSITY

Company		Phone
University of Oklahoma Norman *(G-5186)*	E	405 325-3189
University of Oklahoma Norman *(G-5185)*	G	405 325-4531
University of Oklahoma Norman *(G-5188)*	C	405 325-3666

PRODUCT SECTION

UNSUPPORTED PLASTICS: Floor Or Wall Covering

Hall Painting and Wall Cvg .... G 405 373-2724
  Piedmont *(G-7762)*

UPHOLSTERY WORK SVCS

Custom Upholstery .... G 918 342-3489
  Claremore *(G-1611)*
Custom Upholstery Contracting .... F 405 236-3505
  Oklahoma City *(G-5878)*
Customized Fctry Interiors LLC .... G 405 848-9999
  Oklahoma City *(G-5880)*
E J Higgins Interior Design .... F 405 387-3434
  Newcastle *(G-4825)*

URNS: Cut Stone

Eagle Urns Inc .... G 918 469-3024
  Quinton *(G-8036)*

USED CAR DEALERS

B & W Diesel & Drivetrain Inc .... G 918 427-7918
  Muldrow *(G-4631)*
Banks Motor Co .... G 580 924-8883
  Durant *(G-2204)*
Bob Brooks Motor Company .... C 405 681-2592
  Oklahoma City *(G-5600)*

USED MERCHANDISE STORES

Brass Buff .... G 918 592-1717
  Tulsa *(G-9332)*

UTILITY TRAILER DEALERS

Five A Trailers and Equipment .... G 580 564-2973
  Kingston *(G-3827)*
Holt Trailer Mfg & Sales LLC .... F 405 784-2233
  Asher *(G-390)*
Kerr-Bilt Trailers JI Inc .... F 580 566-1200
  Boswell *(G-757)*
Polypipe Hdlg Specialists Inc .... G 405 330-4733
  Edmond *(G-2573)*
Pruitt Company of Ada Inc .... E 580 332-3523
  Ada *(G-78)*

VACUUM CLEANERS: Household

Als Vacuum Repair .... G 405 550-8599
  Norman *(G-4904)*
Bobs Vacuum Sewing Repair .... G 918 378-1844
  Broken Arrow *(G-854)*

VACUUM CLEANERS: Indl Type

Industrial Commercial Entp .... G 405 681-2991
  Oklahoma City *(G-6298)*
Lindsay Manufacturing Inc .... E 580 762-2457
  Ponca City *(G-7845)*

VALUE-ADDED RESELLERS: Computer Systems

Elvis S Seshie .... G 405 887-3050
  Mustang *(G-4770)*

VALVE REPAIR SVCS, INDL

P V Valve .... G 580 856-3844
  Ratliff City *(G-8061)*

VALVES

Aspen Flow Control LLC .... G 918 933-5617
  Broken Arrow *(G-836)*
Cargill Valve LLC .... G 918 352-2203
  Drumright *(G-2054)*
Central Valve Body .... G 918 341-0266
  Claremore *(G-1605)*
King Valve Co Inc .... G 918 251-0369
  Broken Arrow *(G-958)*
Oklahoma Rep Sales Inc .... G 405 794-5200
  Moore *(G-4547)*
S M T Valve LLC .... G 405 512-4523
  Moore *(G-4561)*
Tim Metz .... G 580 227-2456
  Fairview *(G-3153)*
Wilspec Technologies Inc .... E 405 495-8989
  Oklahoma City *(G-7459)*

VALVES & PIPE FITTINGS

Aceco Valve Inc .... E 918 827-3669
  Mounds *(G-4608)*
Air Power Systems Co LLC .... E 918 622-5600
  Tulsa *(G-9121)*
American Machine & Tool Co .... G 405 794-9820
  Wewoka *(G-11497)*
Badgett Corporation .... D 405 224-4138
  Chickasha *(G-1437)*
Balon Corporation .... A 405 677-3321
  Oklahoma City *(G-5522)*
Barlow-Hunt Inc .... G 918 250-0828
  Tulsa *(G-9265)*
Big Elk Energy Systems LLC .... E 918 947-6800
  Tulsa *(G-9290)*
BS&b Safety Systems LLC .... C 918 622-5950
  Tulsa *(G-9346)*
Carlson Company .... E 918 627-4334
  Tulsa *(G-9376)*
Closebend Inc .... F 918 445-1131
  Tulsa *(G-9456)*
Cust-O-Bend Inc .... E 918 241-0514
  Tulsa *(G-9526)*
Cyclonic Valve Company .... E 918 317-8200
  Broken Arrow *(G-883)*
Eaton Aeroquip LLC .... D 405 275-5500
  Shawnee *(G-8447)*
Ernst Valve & Fittings .... G 918 446-0313
  Tulsa *(G-9003)*
Flowell Corporation .... F 918 224-6969
  Tulsa *(G-9007)*
Fluid Controls Inc .... E 918 299-0442
  Tulsa *(G-9762)*
Gas Products Inc .... G 918 664-5679
  Tulsa *(G-9804)*
GE Oil & Gas Pressure Ctrl LP .... E 405 273-7660
  Shawnee *(G-8451)*
Hackney Ladish Inc .... D 580 237-4212
  Enid *(G-2967)*
J P Machine & Tool Co .... F 405 677-3341
  Oklahoma City *(G-6337)*
King Valve Inc .... F 405 672-0046
  Oklahoma City *(G-6421)*
Lasco Fittings Inc .... G 800 776-2756
  Westville *(G-11484)*
Los Angeles Boiler Works Inc .... E 580 363-1312
  Blackwell *(G-688)*
Mayco Inc .... E 405 677-5969
  Oklahoma City *(G-6543)*
Mercer Valve Co Inc .... E 405 470-5213
  Oklahoma City *(G-6566)*
Metal Goods Manufacturing Co .... F 918 336-4282
  Bartlesville *(G-512)*
Oil Capital Valve Company .... D 918 627-2474
  Tulsa *(G-10385)*
Punch-Lok Co .... E 580 233-4757
  Enid *(G-3040)*
Rotork Valvekits Inc .... F 918 259-8100
  Tulsa *(G-10677)*
Safeco Manufacturing Inc .... F 918 455-0100
  Broken Arrow *(G-1160)*
Strope Manufacturing Inc .... G 918 835-8729
  Tulsa *(G-10861)*
Tdw (us) Inc .... G 918 447-5519
  Tulsa *(G-9040)*
Tmco Inc .... E 405 257-9373
  Wewoka *(G-11512)*
Triangle Pump Components Inc .... F 405 672-6900
  Oklahoma City *(G-7327)*
William L Riggs Company Inc .... G 918 437-3245
  Tulsa *(G-11125)*

VALVES & REGULATORS: Pressure, Indl

BS&b Safety Systems LLC .... G 918 622-5950
  Tulsa *(G-9345)*
Oklahoma Safety Eqp Co Inc .... E 918 258-5626
  Broken Arrow *(G-994)*
Rupture Pin Technology .... E 405 789-1884
  Oklahoma City *(G-7062)*

VALVES: Aerosol, Metal

Oklahoma Safety Eqp Co Inc .... C 918 258-5626
  Broken Arrow *(G-994)*

VALVES: Aircraft, Hydraulic

Crown Products Inc .... E 918 446-4591
  Tulsa *(G-9517)*

VALVES: Fluid Power, Control, Hydraulic & pneumatic

Advent Aircraft Systems Inc .... F 918 388-5940
  Tulsa *(G-9112)*
Devine Industrial Systems Inc .... G 405 627-3448
  Yukon *(G-11717)*
Horton Industries Inc .... E 918 836-3971
  Tulsa *(G-9950)*

VALVES: Indl

Alfa Laval Inc .... G 918 251-7477
  Broken Arrow *(G-824)*
Alfa Lval A Cled Exchngers Inc .... G 918 251-7477
  Broken Arrow *(G-825)*
American Directional Tech .... G 405 449-3362
  Wayne *(G-11365)*
B P S Inc .... G 918 258-7554
  Broken Arrow *(G-841)*
B S & B Safety Systems Inc .... G 918 622-5950
  Tulsa *(G-9245)*
Balon Corporation .... A 405 677-3321
  Oklahoma City *(G-5522)*
Balon Valves .... G 405 670-8300
  Oklahoma City *(G-5523)*
Bellofram .... E 405 677-7222
  Oklahoma City *(G-5545)*
Bgr LLC .... E 405 671-2000
  Oklahoma City *(G-5562)*
BS&b Pressure Safety MGT LLC .... G 918 664-3725
  Tulsa *(G-9344)*
Cameron International Corp .... B 405 631-1321
  Oklahoma City *(G-5676)*
Cameron International Corp .... C 405 745-2715
  Oklahoma City *(G-5677)*
Curtiss-Wright Corporation .... G 405 515-8235
  Norman *(G-4973)*
Cyclonic Valve Company .... E 918 317-8200
  Broken Arrow *(G-883)*
Eichler Valve .... G 405 370-6891
  Edmond *(G-2407)*
Enviro Valve (us) Inc .... G 918 251-6103
  Broken Arrow *(G-902)*
Flow Valve LLC .... E 580 622-2294
  Sulphur *(G-8832)*
Flow-Quip Inc .... E 918 663-3313
  Tulsa *(G-9758)*
Fluid Controls Inc .... E 918 299-0442
  Tulsa *(G-9762)*
Gas Products Inc .... G 918 664-5679
  Tulsa *(G-9804)*
Kimray Inc .... C 405 525-6601
  Oklahoma City *(G-6417)*
King Valve Inc .... F 405 672-0046
  Oklahoma City *(G-6421)*
L6 Inc .... E 918 251-5791
  Broken Arrow *(G-963)*
Mercer Valve Co Inc .... E 405 470-5213
  Oklahoma City *(G-6566)*
Ocv Control Valves LLC .... E 918 627-1942
  Tulsa *(G-10376)*
Omni Valve Company LLC .... E 918 687-6100
  Muskogee *(G-4725)*
Ops Valves LLC .... G 918 273-3300
  Nowata *(G-5224)*
Premier Valve Group .... G 918 519-4309
  Broken Arrow *(G-1009)*
Turbulator Company LLC .... F 405 820-3026
  Oklahoma City *(G-7351)*

VALVES: Plumbing & Heating

Schoeller Bleckman Energy .... G 405 672-4407
  Oklahoma City *(G-7091)*

VAN CONVERSIONS

Heartland Energy Options LLC .... G 405 600-6009
  Piedmont *(G-7763)*

VAN CONVERSIONS

Grand Junction Custom Trucks .... G 918 245-6362
  Tulsa *(G-9844)*
Heartland Energy Options LLC .... G 405 600-6009
  Piedmont *(G-7763)*

VARIETY STORES

B & L Printing Inc .... G 918 258-6655
  Broken Arrow *(G-839)*

Employee Codes: A=Over 500 employees, B=251-500
C=101-250, D=51-100, E=20-50, F=10-19, G=1-9

2020 Oklahoma Directory
of Manufacturers & Processors

VASES: Pottery

Miller Sales Wholesale Distr ....G....... 918 629-4064
Tulsa (G-10282)

VAULTS & SAFES WHOLESALERS

Wilbert Funeral Services Inc..............E....... 405 752-9033
Oklahoma City (G-7451)

VEHICLES: All Terrain

Super Daves Power Sports ....G....... 918 485-9205
Wagoner (G-11291)
Timmy Pickens ....G....... 918 812-5268
Sapulpa (G-8315)
Tommy Biffle Lakeside Polaris ....G....... 918 485-2887
Wagoner (G-11293)

VEHICLES: Recreational

New Vision Manufacturing LLC ....C....... 580 677-9937
Madill (G-4159)
Oasis Rv Center LLC ....G....... 580 233-9400
Enid (G-3023)
Rv Station Ltd..G....... 888 466-1384
Colbert (G-1786)

VENDING MACHINE OPERATORS: Sandwich & Hot Food

Imperial Inc ....F....... 580 357-8300
Lawton (G-3940)
Imperial LLC ....B....... 918 437-1300
Tulsa (G-9972)

VENDING MACHINE REPAIR SVCS

Anytime Propane LLC ....F....... 405 417-0222
Chickasha (G-1430)

VENDING MACHINES & PARTS

Anytime Propane LLC ....F....... 405 417-0222
Chickasha (G-1430)
Ms Enterprises ....G....... 918 627-1824
Tulsa (G-10308)

VENTILATING EQPT: Metal

Bacco Inc..G....... 918 344-3670
Claremore (G-1587)

VENTILATING EQPT: Sheet Metal

Hu Don Manufacturing Co Inc ....F....... 580 223-7333
Ardmore (G-307)

VENTURE CAPITAL COMPANIES

Siegfried Companies Inc ....G....... 918 747-3411
Tulsa (G-10752)

VESSELS: Process, Indl, Metal Plate

Prescor LLC..E....... 918 224-6626
Tulsa (G-9027)

VIDEO & AUDIO EQPT, WHOLESALE

Infinity Home Solutions LLC.................G....... 918 704-8014
Bixby (G-635)
Techsico Entp Solutions Inc ....D....... 918 585-2347
Tulsa (G-10913)

VIDEO CAMERA-AUDIO RECORDERS: Household Use

Camera Guys LLC..................................G....... 405 310-0006
Norman (G-4951)
Tactical Elec Military Sup LLC ....E....... 866 541-7996
Broken Arrow (G-1070)

VIDEO EQPT

Scratchout LLC ....G....... 918 740-8665
Tulsa (G-10718)

VOCATIONAL REHABILITATION AGENCY

Options Inc ....F....... 918 473-2614
Checotah (G-1398)

VOCATIONAL TRAINING AGENCY

Opportunity Center Inc..........................C....... 580 765-6782
Ponca City (G-7863)

WAREHOUSING & STORAGE FACILITIES, NEC

Fake Bake LLC ....E....... 405 843-9660
Oklahoma City (G-6070)

WAREHOUSING & STORAGE, REFRIGERATED: Cold Storage Or Refrig

Red River Cold Storage LLC ....G....... 580 795-9948
Madill (G-4161)

WAREHOUSING & STORAGE, REFRIGERATED: Frozen Or Refrig Goods

Alex Rogers ....G....... 405 677-2306
Oklahoma City (G-5412)
Davis Insulated Building Inc................D....... 918 967-2042
Stigler (G-8632)

WAREHOUSING & STORAGE: Farm Prdts

Rocky L Emmons & Judy E Sprag........G....... 580 305-1940
Frederick (G-3199)

WAREHOUSING & STORAGE: General

Apergy Artfl Lift Intl LLC ....E....... 405 677-3153
Oklahoma City (G-5451)
Helena Agri-Enterprises LLC ....F....... 580 477-0986
Altus (G-157)
Jim Campbell & Associates Rlty ....G....... 405 372-9225
Stillwater (G-8707)

WAREHOUSING & STORAGE: General

Ets-Lindgren Inc....................................E....... 580 434-7490
Durant (G-2230)
Kloeckner Metals Corporation..............E....... 918 660-2050
Catoosa (G-1329)
Mobile Mini Inc ....F....... 918 582-5857
Tulsa (G-10288)
Ndn Enterprises LLC ....G....... 703 772-6635
Pawhuska (G-7690)

WAREHOUSING & STORAGE: Miniwarehouse

Nutopia Nuts & More ....G....... 405 663-2330
Hydro (G-3633)

WAREHOUSING & STORAGE: Oil & Gasoline, Caverns For Hire

Christ Centered Carriers LLC ....E....... 417 850-8137
Canute (G-1267)

WARFARE COUNTER-MEASURE EQPT

Gwacs Defense Inc ....F....... 918 794-5670
Tulsa (G-9870)

WARM AIR HEATING & AC EQPT & SPLYS, WHOLESALE Furnaces

Veterans Eng Group Inc ....G....... 918 864-6006
Pryor (G-7997)

WASHERS

Kennedy Restorations Llc....................G....... 405 761-5303
Oklahoma City (G-5300)
Vortex Parts Washer ....G....... 918 582-4445
Tulsa (G-11084)

WASTE CLEANING SVCS

Phoenix Group Holding Company ....F....... 405 948-7788
Oklahoma City (G-6844)

WATCHES & PARTS, WHOLESALE

S & S Time Corporation........................E....... 918 437-3572
Tulsa (G-10683)
Selco LLC ....E....... 918 622-6100
Tulsa (G-10725)

WATER HEATERS WHOLESALERS EXCEPT ELECTRIC

Lake Tenkiller Hbr Wtr Plant ....G....... 918 457-4811
Park Hill (G-7645)

WATER SOFTENING WHOLESALERS

R W D 9 Mayes County ....G....... 918 434-5000
Salina (G-8135)

WATER SUPPLY

Evoqua Water Technologies LLC ....C....... 978 614-7233
Tulsa (G-9712)
Solar Power & Pump Company LLC ....F....... 580 225-1704
Elk City (G-2874)

WATER TREATMENT EQPT: Indl

Aqua Eco Environmental Svcs ....G....... 952 300-0456
Broken Arrow (G-831)
City of Altus ....F....... 580 481-2270
Altus (G-148)
City of Weatherford ....G....... 580 772-5315
Weatherford (G-11402)
Ecohawk Advnced Wtr Rsrces LLC .....G....... 918 694-6011
Tulsa (G-9639)
Environmental Concepts Inc ....G....... 405 385-0422
Stillwater (G-8686)
Evoqua Water Technologies LLC ....C....... 978 614-7233
Tulsa (G-9712)
Lake Tenkiller Hbr Wtr Plant ....G....... 918 457-4811
Park Hill (G-7645)
Logic Energy Solutions LLC ....G....... 405 601-9037
Oklahoma City (G-6489)
Mid America Hydro Tech ....G....... 405 598-1772
Macomb (G-4143)
Omni Water Consultants Inc ....F....... 918 323-0001
Vinita (G-11266)
T S I L C ....G....... 918 357-5992
Broken Arrow (G-1169)
Veolia Water North America Ope ....G....... 405 354-6245
Yukon (G-11802)
World Water Works Inc........................D....... 405 943-9000
Oklahoma City (G-7472)
World Water Works Holdings Inc ....G....... 800 607-7873
Oklahoma City (G-7473)

WATER: Distilled

O Fizz Inc ....F....... 918 834-3691
Tulsa (G-10370)

WATER: Pasteurized & Mineral, Bottled & Canned

Hometown Bottled Water LLC..............G....... 918 786-4426
Grove (G-3274)
R W D 9 Mayes County ....G....... 918 434-5000
Salina (G-8135)

WATER: Pasteurized, Canned & Bottled, Etc

Minnette Company Ltd ....G....... 580 226-2929
Wilson (G-11538)
Niagara Bottling LLC ....G....... 909 230-5000
Oklahoma City (G-6677)
Round Springs Water Co LLC ....G....... 918 253-8188
Spavinaw (G-8592)
Total Beverage Services LLC................G....... 405 366-1344
Norman (G-5177)

WAVEGUIDE STRUCTURES: Accelerating

Regrid Energy LLC ....G....... 405 837-8707
Edmond (G-2595)

WAX REMOVERS

Super Cuts...G....... 918 245-3320
Sand Springs (G-8227)

WAXES: Mineral, Natural

Baker Petrolite LLC...............................C....... 918 847-2522
Barnsdall (G-435)

WAXES: Petroleum, Not Produced In Petroleum Refineries

Trillium Trnsp Fuels LLC ....F....... 800 920-1166
Oklahoma City (G-7330)

PRODUCT SECTION

Trillium Trnsp Fuels LLC .... G 405 302-6500
  Oklahoma City (G-7331)

WEATHER STRIPS: Metal

M-D Building Products Inc .... B 405 528-4411
  Oklahoma City (G-6510)

WELDING & CUTTING APPARATUS & ACCESS, NEC

A&K Manufacturing Services LLC .... G 918 986-1637
  Tahlequah (G-8849)

WELDING EQPT

Airgas Usa LLC .... F 580 767-1313
  Ponca City (G-7795)
Alltra Corp .... G 918 534-5100
  Dewey (G-2014)
CRC-Evans Pipeline Intl Inc .... C 918 438-2100
  Tulsa (G-9504)
Driskills Welding .... G 580 233-3093
  Enid (G-2944)
Hackney Ladish Inc .... D 580 237-4212
  Enid (G-2967)
Ledets Welding Service Inc .... G 405 760-8935
  Norman (G-5057)
Nabors Welding & Supplies Inc .... G 405 756-8198
  Lindsay (G-4075)
Phelps Machine & Fabrication .... F 580 662-2465
  Ringling (G-8081)
Rieger Hay & Welding .... G 580 985-3608
  Manchester (G-4169)
Wayne Burt Machine .... G 918 786-4415
  Grove (G-3293)
Westair Gas & Equipment LP .... G 580 338-6449
  Guymon (G-3370)

WELDING EQPT & SPLYS WHOLESALERS

A&K Manufacturing Services LLC .... G 918 986-1637
  Tahlequah (G-8849)
Airgas Usa LLC .... G 405 372-7720
  Stillwater (G-8652)
Airgas Usa LLC .... G 405 235-0009
  Oklahoma City (G-5402)
Matheson Tri-Gas Inc .... F 580 536-2965
  Lawton (G-3969)
Mathey Dearman Inc .... E 918 447-1288
  Tulsa (G-10222)
Price Welding and Supply .... G 580 668-3057
  Lone Grove (G-4119)
Sewells Machine & Welding .... G 580 423-7004
  Texhoma (G-8939)

WELDING EQPT & SPLYS: Electrodes

Smith & Smith Construction .... G 918 297-5062
  Hartshorne (G-3395)

WELDING EQPT & SPLYS: Generators, Arc Welding, AC & DC

Barelas Welding .... G 580 497-7485
  Canute (G-1266)
Lincoln Electric Holdings Inc .... G 405 681-0183
  Oklahoma City (G-6478)

WELDING EQPT & SPLYS: Resistance, Electric

Hat Creek Contractors Inc .... G 580 761-6154
  Shidler (G-8527)

WELDING EQPT & SPLYS: Spot, Electric

Blue ARC Metal Specialties .... G 918 341-3903
  Claremore (G-1597)

WELDING EQPT: Electric

Alltra Corporation .... C 918 534-5100
  Dewey (G-2015)
Bluco Inc .... G 800 535-0135
  Dewey (G-2017)

WELDING MACHINES & EQPT: Ultrasonic

Freelance Operations Inc .... G 580 226-7051
  Ardmore (G-292)

WELDING REPAIR SVC

3 Rivers Wldg Fabrication LLC .... G 918 589-2300
  Jay (G-3677)
33 - Welding Company .... G 405 375-4468
  Kingfisher (G-3783)
3r Welding .... G 918 839-8945
  Hartshorne (G-3389)
4 M Welding Services Inc .... G 580 298-9809
  Antlers (G-212)
405 Welding .... G 405 413-5764
  Newcastle (G-4818)
4m Welding Inc .... G 405 484-7293
  Pauls Valley (G-7648)
4v Welding and Dozer LLC .... G 580 371-6524
  Mill Creek (G-4466)
5r Services .... G 580 370-0222
  Perry (G-7725)
7b Custom Welding Fabrication .... G 918 850-1066
  Tulsa (G-9059)
A & A Welding .... G 918 772-0418
  Park Hill (G-7639)
A & Y Enterprises Inc .... G 405 360-0307
  Norman (G-4894)
A and L Welding Services LLC .... G 918 649-7538
  Wister (G-11547)
A T S Welding Service .... G 405 452-5979
  Wetumka (G-11489)
A W Pool Inc .... G 580 323-3454
  Clinton (G-1735)
A-Accurate Welding Inc .... G 918 838-1111
  Tulsa (G-9074)
A1 Quality Welding .... G 405 373-0066
  Piedmont (G-7752)
Able Welding .... G 405 760-1442
  Edmond (G-2288)
Absolute Welding Inc .... G 918 923-7300
  Oologah (G-7532)
Accurate Fence Contruction LLC .... G 580 591-3717
  Lawton (G-3884)
Ace 1 Welding and Insptn LLC .... G 405 408-5370
  Mustang (G-4760)
Ace Welding and Mechanical LLC ...... G 405 219-1490
  Oklahoma City (G-5365)
Acme Custom Welding .... G 405 288-0187
  Washington (G-11332)
Action Machine Shop .... G 918 245-8308
  Sand Springs (G-8157)
Aero Tech Welding .... G 918 764-9675
  Tulsa (G-9115)
Ainsworth Welding .... G 580 512-7874
  Fletcher (G-3160)
Alan Davis .... G 580 651-9961
  Guymon (G-3344)
All Day Welding & Fabrication .... G 405 550-2233
  El Reno (G-2698)
Allens Trucking & Welding Svc .... G 405 341-8066
  Arcadia (G-227)
Allens Welding Service .... G 580 584-2375
  Broken Bow (G-1182)
Always Welding .... G 918 426-9353
  McAlester (G-4269)
Ambrose Welding LLC .... G 580 704-0356
  Elgin (G-2774)
Anchor Auto & Welding Repr LLC ...... G 918 426-7662
  McAlester (G-4270)
Anderson Welding .... G 580 355-9806
  Lawton (G-3888)
Andrews Welding .... G 405 990-7326
  Oklahoma City (G-5444)
Andy Anderson Metal Works Inc .... F 918 245-2355
  Sand Springs (G-8161)
Angel Welding Service LLC .... G 918 706-2237
  Broken Arrow (G-829)
Ansiels Welding & Constructio .... G 580 920-0573
  Durant (G-2202)
API Metallurgical .... G 918 266-4130
  Catoosa (G-1298)
Apollo Metal Specialties Inc .... F 918 341-7650
  Claremore (G-1583)
ARC-Angel Welding .... G 918 838-0047
  Tulsa (G-9203)
Ares West Welding LLC .... G 405 534-6701
  Moore (G-4494)
Arthur Craig .... G 580 488-3398
  Butler (G-1220)
Atoka Welding & Fabrication .... G 580 889-2534
  Atoka (G-398)
Atwood Wldg Cstm Fbrcation LLC ...... G 918 617-7522
  Eufaula (G-3097)

B&T Welding Services LLC .... G 580 326-4760
  Hugo (G-3602)
B-Mac Welding Service .... G 918 370-0921
  Broken Arrow (G-1112)
Bach Welding & Diesel Service .... G 580 593-2599
  Custer City (G-1973)
Backwoods Welding Inc .... G 405 642-5199
  Maysville (G-4254)
Bailey S Mike Welding Inc .... G 405 574-4489
  Ninnekah (G-4867)
Baileys Welding & Machine LLC .... F 405 224-6611
  Chickasha (G-1438)
Baker Welding Mfg Co .... G 405 376-6017
  Mustang (G-4764)
Barnes Welding LLC .... G 580 774-5491
  Watonga (G-11341)
Barrett Performance Aircraft .... G 918 835-1089
  Tulsa (G-9266)
Beaver Fabrication Inc .... G 405 360-0014
  Norman (G-4928)
Benchmark Completions LLC .... F 405 691-5659
  Oklahoma City (G-5550)
Berry Holdings LP .... G 918 582-3461
  Tulsa (G-9285)
Bethel Welding Metal Building .... G 918 367-5776
  Bristow (G-765)
BF Brandt Welding LLC .... G 405 657-4670
  Oklahoma City (G-5561)
Big G Precision Welding .... G 918 406-2876
  Tulsa (G-9291)
Bill Stockton Welding LLC .... G 918 697-7750
  Chelsea (G-1402)
Bills Welding Equipment Repr .... F 405 232-4799
  Oklahoma City (G-5568)
Bison Welding LLC .... G 580 758-3359
  Bison (G-607)
Bluearc Welding LLC .... G 918 341-0629
  Claremore (G-1598)
Boatright Enterprises Inc .... G 405 612-2473
  Vinita (G-11249)
Bob Albauer Portable Welding .... G 405 789-7999
  Oklahoma City (G-5599)
Bob G Welding .... G 918 510-4769
  Pawnee (G-7702)
Bobby L Graham .... G 580 393-2247
  Sentinel (G-8410)
Bost Welding and Fabrication .... G 918 649-1289
  Poteau (G-7897)
Boyd Welding Inc .... G 918 485-3534
  Wagoner (G-11278)
Bradley Welding & Machine .... G 580 223-2250
  Ardmore (G-260)
Brents Welding LLC .... G 918 413-1318
  Pocola (G-7781)
Brian Ringels .... G 580 927-6144
  Coalgate (G-1776)
Brians Welding and Fabrication .... G 405 412-7878
  Norman (G-4942)
Brooks Custom Welding LLC .... G 580 343-2253
  Corn (G-1866)
Brother Built Welding .... G 918 385-1767
  Hodgen (G-3548)
Bruce Burdick Welding .... G 580 774-2906
  Weatherford (G-11395)
Buckys Welding .... G 918 339-4187
  Canadian (G-1260)
Bull Dog Welding .... G 405 412-8199
  Oklahoma City (G-5644)
Burlington Welding LLC .... G 580 596-3381
  Cherokee (G-1415)
Burnam Welding .... G 580 821-0311
  Elk City (G-2789)
Bws Wlding Fabriction Svcs LLC .... G 918 789-3094
  Chelsea (G-1403)
Byfield Welding .... G 918 333-8100
  Bartlesville (G-459)
C & C Welding & Construction .... G 405 769-4924
  Oklahoma City (G-5656)
C & H Safety Pin Inc .... G 405 949-5843
  Newalla (G-4806)
C V West LLC .... G 623 363-3529
  Guthrie (G-3305)
C&S Marine LLC .... G 918 429-2758
  Indianola (G-3651)
C&S Welding & Fabrication Inc .... G 918 282-4122
  Mannford (G-4176)
Caliber Welding Inc .... G 918 486-1388
  Coweta (G-1873)
Canary Customs .... G 405 293-6429
  Guthrie (G-3307)

Employee Codes: A=Over 500 employees, B=251-500
C=101-250, D=51-100, E=20-50, F=10-19, G=1-9

2020 Oklahoma Directory
of Manufacturers & Processors

Canyon Welding Service Inc.................G....... 580 371-8805
Tishomingo *(G-8964)*
Capes Custom Welding & Fabrica........G....... 918 453-0594
Tahlequah *(G-8855)*
Castle Wldg & Fabrication LLC............G....... 580 747-0218
Enid *(G-2925)*
Cerdafied Welding LLC.........................G....... 405 578-8035
Yukon *(G-11704)*
CH Mufflers & Welding LLC...................G....... 405 380-3877
Earlsboro *(G-2279)*
Charles Tigert Welding Sh....................G....... 580 889-3558
Atoka *(G-402)*
Charles Weathers Welding...................G....... 405 341-2413
Edmond *(G-2346)*
Charlies Welding...................................G....... 580 467-2266
Comanche *(G-1834)*
Chc Welding LLC..................................G....... 405 706-3367
Norman *(G-4955)*
Cherokee Welding Industries...............G....... 918 247-6122
Kellyville *(G-3761)*
Chris Green Greens Construct.............G....... 405 207-0690
Pauls Valley *(G-7653)*
Christians Welding Service..................G....... 580 674-3384
Dill City *(G-2034)*
Circle A Welding LLC............................G....... 580 890-9617
Weatherford *(G-11401)*
Cisper Welding......................................G....... 405 665-2599
Wynnewood *(G-11665)*
Cisper Welding Inc................................G....... 918 543-2321
Inola *(G-3654)*
Cisper Welding of Oklahoma................G....... 918 543-7755
Inola *(G-3655)*
Clints Portable Welding.........................G....... 405 834-4517
Oklahoma City *(G-5789)*
Clyde Welding Service..........................G....... 405 222-1364
Ninnekah *(G-4868)*
CMS Welding & Fabrication..................G....... 918 676-3133
Fairland *(G-3123)*
Confederite Welding LLC.......................G....... 918 407-1635
Bristow *(G-773)*
Connie Pirple...G....... 405 375-4468
Kingfisher *(G-3792)*
Cooks Contact Welding Inc...................G....... 405 373-0059
Piedmont *(G-7758)*
Cornerstone Welding.............................G....... 918 387-2538
Yale *(G-11681)*
Crane Machinery Repair........................G....... 918 349-2264
Pawhuska *(G-7683)*
Cris Choate Welding Inc........................G....... 405 853-2792
Hennessey *(G-3455)*
Ctm Welding & Fabrication LLC............G....... 405 408-4628
Yale *(G-11682)*
Custom Metal Works..............................G....... 918 231-4151
Pryor *(G-7956)*
Cwg Welding Services LLC....................G....... 580 819-1045
Weatherford *(G-11403)*
D & D Stud Welding LLC Proj...............G....... 888 965-4155
Cartwright *(G-1282)*
D I V C O Inc...E....... 918 836-9101
Tulsa *(G-9538)*
D J Welding...G....... 405 386-4620
Choctaw *(G-1536)*
D&P Welding Corp.................................G....... 405 624-0170
Glencoe *(G-3220)*
D-A Welding & Fab LLC.........................G....... 580 641-1189
Marlow *(G-4227)*
Daddy Russ Customs & Wldg LLC.........G....... 405 623-9709
Cashion *(G-1287)*
Damar Manufacturing Co Inc................E....... 918 445-2445
Tulsa *(G-9549)*
Dandelion Welding and Fabg LLC.........G....... 405 431-8138
Oklahoma City *(G-5894)*
Darnell Services....................................G....... 918 542-9236
Miami *(G-4394)*
Darrell Lewis..G....... 405 867-5768
Maysville *(G-4257)*
Davenports Welding...............................G....... 918 855-9593
Broken Arrow *(G-1121)*
Daves Welding & Dock Svc LLC............G....... 918 773-5179
Vian *(G-11239)*
Daves Welding LLC...............................G....... 580 938-2707
Shattuck *(G-8421)*
David Adkinson.......................................G....... 580 623-7301
Watonga *(G-11344)*
David D Kuykendall................................G....... 918 223-5055
Ripley *(G-8100)*
David Dollar..G....... 580 965-4155
Cartwright *(G-1283)*
David Kelso Welding..............................G....... 405 630-7108
Edmond *(G-2382)*
David Piatt..G....... 405 542-6974
Lookeba *(G-4128)*
Davis Welding & Fab..............................G....... 405 779-5330
Ninnekah *(G-4869)*
Davis Welding Dock Serv.......................G....... 918 457-4071
Cookson *(G-1849)*
Daytons Trailer Hitch Inc........................G....... 918 744-0341
Tulsa *(G-9562)*
Deans Machine & Welding Inc...............G....... 580 688-3374
Hollis *(G-3564)*
Dennis Roberts Welding........................G....... 405 672-8285
Oklahoma City *(G-5923)*
Dennis Welding.......................................G....... 580 658-5669
Marlow *(G-4228)*
DH Welding LLC.....................................G....... 918 906-6534
Yale *(G-11684)*
Diamond Welding Mfg............................G....... 580 889-7767
Atoka *(G-407)*
Dieco Manufacturing Inc........................D....... 918 438-2193
Tulsa *(G-9581)*
Diversfied Wldg Fbrication LLC............F....... 405 802-5487
Moore *(G-4517)*
Dixon & Sons Inc....................................G....... 918 256-7455
Vinita *(G-11253)*
Dixon Auto Engine Machine Shop.........G....... 918 256-6780
Vinita *(G-11254)*
DK Machine Inc.......................................G....... 918 251-1034
Broken Arrow *(G-890)*
Don Bateman Shtmtl Fabrication..........G....... 918 224-0567
Sapulpa *(G-8267)*
Donerite Welding....................................G....... 918 304-9594
Beggs *(G-551)*
Dosher Kennon.......................................G....... 580 667-5708
Tipton *(G-8959)*
Double Diamnd Wldg Fabrication..........G....... 580 445-4524
Hobart *(G-3542)*
Double H Farms Inc................................G....... 918 486-7635
Coweta *(G-1880)*
Double H Welding...................................G....... 918 653-2289
Heavener *(G-3427)*
Driskills Welding.....................................G....... 580 233-3093
Enid *(G-2944)*
Driver & Son Welding Shop....................G....... 580 323-1714
Clinton *(G-1749)*
Drp Welding Met Buildings LLC..............G....... 405 344-6582
Alex *(G-131)*
Dry Fabrication and Welding..................E....... 580 735-2958
Buffalo *(G-1212)*
DS Welding..G....... 580 623-4104
Fay *(G-3156)*
Dudes Welding & Etc LLC......................G....... 405 510-4786
Spencer *(G-8594)*
Durnal Construction LLC........................G....... 405 413-5458
Perkins *(G-7716)*
Dutton Welding & Construc....................G....... 918 420-5688
Bache *(G-431)*
E & E Construction Company................G....... 918 775-6222
Sallisaw *(G-8144)*
E F L Inc..D....... 918 665-7799
Tulsa *(G-9621)*
E-Saw Wldg & Fabrication LLC..............F....... 580 772-2448
Weatherford *(G-11407)*
Eagles Nest Welding...............................G....... 405 639-8650
Oklahoma City *(G-5997)*
Eastern Okla Fabrication Inc..................G....... 918 654-7344
Cameron *(G-1257)*
Eddie Brown...F....... 580 889-1506
Atoka *(G-411)*
Eddie Johnsons Wldg & Mch Co............F....... 580 856-3418
Ratliff City *(G-8051)*
Eddie Ward..G....... 405 848-3283
Oklahoma City *(G-6009)*
Elliott Precision Products Inc..................E....... 918 234-4001
Tulsa *(G-9661)*
Ellis Welding..G....... 580 856-3907
Ratliff City *(G-8052)*
Eulitt Welding...G....... 918 542-2635
Miami *(G-4402)*
Evans & Assoc Utility Svcs.....................G....... 580 351-1800
Lawton *(G-3924)*
Evans Welding LLC.................................G....... 580 470-8111
Duncan *(G-2116)*
Everetts Welding & Repair......................G....... 580 995-4942
Vici *(G-11242)*
Everything Welding & Safety In..............G....... 405 701-3711
Norman *(G-4994)*
Excalibur Welding Service LLC..............G....... 580 302-2570
Weatherford *(G-11412)*
Fab Tech Welding....................................G....... 405 649-2322
Mulhall *(G-4638)*
Ferguson Welding LLC............................G....... 405 534-1517
Tuttle *(G-11199)*
Fg Welding...G....... 405 863-8210
Oklahoma City *(G-6083)*
Fisher Welding...G....... 580 748-0445
Enid *(G-2958)*
Fitzs Welding LLC....................................G....... 405 371-1167
Mustang *(G-4771)*
Flores Welding Services LLC..................G....... 405 473-5534
Yukon *(G-11725)*
Fm2t Welding LLC...................................G....... 405 837-8495
Norman *(G-5003)*
Foster Jl Welding LLC.............................G....... 405 686-6090
Oklahoma City *(G-6108)*
Four Winds Field Services LLC...............G....... 918 568-1143
Eufaula *(G-3102)*
Friends Welding.......................................G....... 918 482-1544
Broken Arrow *(G-1127)*
Froman Wldg U0026 Fbrction Inc..........G....... 918 798-1050
Claremore *(G-1624)*
G E C Enterprises...................................G....... 405 740-9365
Oklahoma City *(G-6131)*
G T Bynum Company...............................G....... 918 587-9118
Tulsa *(G-9794)*
Garrison Welding.....................................G....... 918 331-6336
Foraker *(G-3168)*
Gary Cobb Welding LLC..........................G....... 580 983-2499
Crawford *(G-1905)*
Garys Welding Inc....................................G....... 918 688-2058
Broken Arrow *(G-916)*
Geralds Welding Fabrication....................F....... 405 222-5510
Chickasha *(G-1462)*
Geralds Welding 2....................................G....... 405 224-8510
Ninnekah *(G-4871)*
Giblet Welding LLC..................................G....... 580 751-0104
Cordell *(G-1860)*
Gilmore Welding & Tractor Svc................G....... 918 479-6224
Locust Grove *(G-4108)*
Glenn Hamil...G....... 918 396-3659
Skiatook *(G-8545)*
Glenn Schlarb Welding.............................G....... 580 327-3832
Alva *(G-182)*
Glenn Tool Inc...D....... 405 787-1400
Oklahoma City *(G-6157)*
Goliath Pipeline and Cnstr LLC................G....... 512 917-9313
Norman *(G-5008)*
Gregs Wldg & Backhoe Svc Inc...............F....... 405 222-1004
Chickasha *(G-1464)*
Grunewald Welding LLC...........................G....... 580 256-2674
Woodward *(G-11589)*
Gs Specialties...G....... 918 230-1295
Inola *(G-3660)*
Gws Welding Inc..G....... 918 527-5776
Coweta *(G-1883)*
H & H Specialty Welding LLC...................G....... 479 322-1125
El Reno *(G-2722)*
H&H Specialty Welding.............................G....... 479 252-1991
Mustang *(G-4774)*
H/H Mobile Welding LLC...........................G....... 405 830-5525
Yukon *(G-11729)*
Harper Welding Design LLC......................G....... 405 396-8558
Arcadia *(G-230)*
Harpers Welding..G....... 580 298-7165
Antlers *(G-216)*
Hart Brothers Welding...............................G....... 918 697-5682
Collinsville *(G-1812)*
Hartins Welding...G....... 580 795-5594
Madill *(G-4149)*
Hathaway & Simpson.................................G....... 580 875-3177
Walters *(G-11301)*
Hayden Betchan Welding LLC...................G....... 580 863-5372
Garber *(G-3214)*
Haynes Welding Service Inc......................G....... 337 380-7126
Bethany *(G-581)*
Hays Welding & Blacksmith.......................G....... 580 287-3458
Willow *(G-11530)*
HCf Welding Services................................G....... 918 907-4274
Tulsa *(G-9906)*
Heirston Welding & Cnstr..........................G....... 580 657-2518
Wilson *(G-11535)*
Henrys Welding and Fab LLC....................G....... 918 535-2264
Ochelata *(G-5235)*
Hickmans Welding.....................................G....... 918 966-3783
Keota *(G-3772)*
Higgins Welding...G....... 580 231-9211
Enid *(G-2971)*
Hnt Welding & Machine..............................G....... 405 348-8249
Edmond *(G-2456)*
Holman Manufacturing................................F....... 918 479-5861
Locust Grove *(G-4109)*

PRODUCT SECTION — WELDING REPAIR SVC

Company	Code	Phone
Hoppers Welding	G	918 885-6978
Hominy (G-3587)		
Hot Rod Welding and Mech LLC	G	918 754-2548
Red Oak (G-8077)		
Hotrod Welding	G	580 229-0888
Healdton (G-3415)		
Hunts Welding Service LLC	G	806 339-4591
Cushing (G-1937)		
Hurley Welding LLC	G	405 224-7332
Amber (G-196)		
Hutson Welding Services LLC	G	918 470-3673
Kiowa (G-3838)		
Hws Hamilton Welding Svc LLC	G	580 889-1725
Atoka (G-413)		
Ideal Machine & Welding Inc	G	918 352-3660
Drumright (G-2062)		
Ideal Specialty Inc	F	918 834-1657
Tulsa (G-9967)		
Ideas Manufacturing Inc	G	405 691-5525
Oklahoma City (G-5296)		
Independence Race Works & Fabg	G	918 489-2353
Gore (G-3250)		
Industrial Enterprise Inc	F	918 476-5907
Chouteau (G-1567)		
Industrial Machine Co Inc	F	405 236-5419
Oklahoma City (G-6299)		
Industrial Pping Companies LLC	D	918 825-0900
Pryor (G-7970)		
Inland Machine & Welding Co	E	405 670-4355
Oklahoma City (G-6305)		
Inman Welding Service	G	918 323-0022
Vinita (G-11262)		
Iron Cowboy Welding LLC	G	580 301-3423
Lawton (G-3942)		
Iron Cowboy Welding LLC	G	580 335-2900
Frederick (G-3194)		
Iron Images	G	918 685-1514
Muskogee (G-4694)		
Ironman Welding & Mfg LLC	G	580 464-3478
Chickasha (G-1472)		
Ironman Welding Machine	G	580 791-3091
Fay (G-3157)		
Ivers Welding and Machine Shop	G	580 765-4882
Ponca City (G-7838)		
J & C Welding Co Inc	G	405 263-4967
Okarche (G-5243)		
J & M Welding	E	918 216-2090
Tulsa (G-9015)		
J B Welding	G	918 574-1806
Bartlesville (G-499)		
J Bs Welding Inc	F	580 332-6194
Ada (G-52)		
J C Sheet Metal	G	580 688-9527
Hollis (G-3566)		
J Fletcher Derrell	G	580 673-2489
Healdton (G-3416)		
J M Welding	G	918 277-4480
Sapulpa (G-8281)		
J Marrs Welding	G	918 396-2221
Skiatook (G-8552)		
J S Welding	G	405 364-1362
Norman (G-5039)		
J T Welding	G	580 504-3862
Ardmore (G-309)		
Jack Chartier Welding LLC	G	918 486-2347
Coweta (G-1888)		
Jackson Welding & Machine	G	580 472-3631
Canute (G-1268)		
Janning Welding and Supply LLC	F	580 225-6554
Elk City (G-2831)		
Jason A Bliss	G	580 304-9432
Shidler (G-8528)		
Jay Hickman Welding Inc	G	405 205-7136
Guthrie (G-3319)		
JB Fabrication	G	580 716-7524
Kaw City (G-3758)		
Jed Welding and Fabrication	G	405 420-9062
Noble (G-4883)		
Jeff Parson Welding	G	405 483-5770
Okarche (G-5244)		
Jerry Ellis	G	580 223-5649
Ardmore (G-314)		
Jerry Woods Portable Welding	G	918 272-6424
Owasso (G-7580)		
JG Welding LLC	G	405 301-3126
Tecumseh (G-8920)		
Jims Welding Service	G	405 853-4522
Hennessey (G-3469)		
Joel Bumpus	G	580 237-5305
Enid (G-2987)		
John Kennedy Welding LLC	G	580 227-2300
Fairview (G-3138)		
John Lankford	G	918 855-4417
Owasso (G-7581)		
John Patrick Raymond	G	580 481-0869
Altus (G-159)		
John Samut-Tagliaferro	G	580 284-6058
Fletcher (G-3163)		
John Ward Welding	G	580 673-2127
Healdton (G-3417)		
Johnny Blaylock	G	918 639-5951
Broken Arrow (G-949)		
Johnson Welding	G	580 569-2231
Mountain Park (G-4626)		
Jones Spclty Wldg Fbrction LLC	G	918 486-7740
Coweta (G-1889)		
Jordan Welding & Fabrication	G	918 346-7243
Claremore (G-1646)		
JP Welding	G	405 714-0232
Morrison (G-4604)		
JP Welding Fabrication	G	580 724-9104
Morrison (G-4605)		
JV Industrial Companies Ltd	G	918 591-5450
Tulsa (G-10068)		
K & J Welding LLC	G	580 541-2200
Enid (G-2990)		
K B Machine & Welding Inc	G	405 375-5888
Kingfisher (G-3803)		
K C Welding & Machine Corp	G	918 336-4560
Bartlesville (G-500)		
K G Machine	G	918 789-2228
Chelsea (G-1407)		
K-H Machine Shop	G	918 273-1058
Nowata (G-5218)		
KCR Welding Inc	G	405 619-0068
Oklahoma City (G-6403)		
Kelley Shepard Welding	G	580 234-3280
Enid (G-2994)		
Kelleys Welding Service Inc	G	405 691-5515
Oklahoma City (G-5299)		
Kelly Blake Welding Inc	G	405 756-0868
Lindsay (G-4070)		
Kenneth Petermann	G	405 372-0111
Stillwater (G-8710)		
Key Welding Inc	G	580 995-4278
Vici (G-11244)		
Kilgore Welding Inc	G	405 872-9677
Lexington (G-4037)		
Kirby - Smith Machinery Inc	C	888 861-0219
Oklahoma City (G-6425)		
Kirkpatrick Welding	G	918 865-2672
Mannford (G-4184)		
Knape Fabrication & Wldg LLC	G	580 564-3107
Kingston (G-3829)		
Koda Welding LLC	G	405 443-9800
Norman (G-5053)		
Koda Welding LLC	G	405 565-1867
Noble (G-4884)		
Kremlin Welding & Fabrication	G	580 874-2522
Kremlin (G-3853)		
Kuykendall Welding LLC	G	405 905-0389
Chickasha (G-1480)		
Kwp Welding & Fabrication LLC	G	580 471-7238
Altus (G-161)		
L & C Ventures LLC	G	405 793-9353
Norman (G-5054)		
L & J Welding & Machine Svc	G	918 885-6666
Hominy (G-3591)		
L & K Seed & Manufacturing Co	G	405 663-2758
Hydro (G-3632)		
L & L Welding Inc	G	405 631-4939
Oklahoma City (G-6438)		
L & M Welding LLC	G	918 534-6864
Dewey (G-2027)		
Laird Welding LLC	G	580 995-4495
Vici (G-11245)		
Lance Easley	G	405 269-1415
Perkins (G-7719)		
Lanes Welding LLC	G	580 302-1279
Elk City (G-2836)		
Larry Bobs Welding LLC	G	405 672-7224
Del City (G-1999)		
Larry Wilcoxson	G	580 327-2110
Alva (G-185)		
Larrys Welding Service	G	918 267-4091
Bristow (G-788)		
Larrys Welding Service	G	918 432-5787
Kiowa (G-3840)		
Lawrence Welding LLC	G	580 272-3294
Ada (G-58)		
Lawton Machine & Welding Works	G	580 355-4678
Lawton (G-3956)		
Lays Custom Welding LLC	G	918 766-5227
Bartlesville (G-505)		
Lazy B Welding and Met Art LLC	G	580 512-8778
Lawton (G-3963)		
Ledets Welding Service Inc	G	405 610-2299
Oklahoma City (G-6463)		
Leviathan Inc	G	580 227-3105
Fairview (G-3141)		
Linley Welding LLC	G	405 420-5968
Elk City (G-2839)		
Lonewlf Welding	G	918 625-9128
Tulsa (G-10178)		
Longbreak Welding Service Inc	G	918 223-5976
Cushing (G-1943)		
Lonnie Williams	G	918 253-4650
Eucha (G-3094)		
Lucas Metal Works Inc	F	918 535-2726
Ochelata (G-5237)		
Luckinbill Inc	D	580 233-2026
Enid (G-3000)		
Lynns Welding LLC	G	580 488-3587
Leedey (G-4029)		
M D Spoonemore Welding	G	580 233-9596
Enid (G-3003)		
M S Welding Fabrication	G	405 368-7451
Hennessey (G-3475)		
M W Machining and Welding Inc	G	918 543-8431
Inola (G-3665)		
M&M Custom Welding	G	918 231-0829
Broken Arrow (G-1139)		
Mac Machine	G	405 238-7280
Pauls Valley (G-7666)		
Mack Smotherman	G	580 526-3089
Erick (G-3088)		
Mader Welding	G	580 658-3593
Marlow (G-4235)		
Madron Welding Service	G	405 257-6161
Wewoka (G-11503)		
Maese Welding Service Llc	G	405 606-4619
Oklahoma City (G-6516)		
Mahurin General Repair LLC	G	918 676-3855
Fairland (G-3126)		
Mainline Industries	G	
Minco (G-4477)		
Mar Welding LLC	G	580 747-9967
Yukon (G-11746)		
Marcum Welding Service	G	405 485-9340
Blanchard (G-721)		
Mark Condit	G	580 656-8028
Duncan (G-2152)		
Mark Hendrix Welding LLC	G	580 657-3716
Ardmore (G-327)		
Martin Jacob Welding LLC	G	580 747-1031
Enid (G-3008)		
Martin Welding Service Inc	G	405 623-5361
Hinton (G-3532)		
Marty Watley	G	580 492-4859
Elgin (G-2777)		
Mc Iron Blacksmithing & Wldg	G	405 613-5215
Stillwater (G-8722)		
McCartney Welding LLC	G	580 542-2564
Lahoma (G-3858)		
McCrary Welding Inc	G	620 200-4733
Weatherford (G-11426)		
McCrays Manufacturing Co	G	918 426-1691
McAlester (G-4319)		
McCutchen Enterprises Inc	G	918 234-7406
Tulsa (G-10231)		
McElroys Welding Services LLC	G	405 354-2019
Yukon (G-11751)		
McKinneys Custom Welding & Fab	G	405 341-6559
Edmond (G-2508)		
McLendon Welding Llc	G	580 304-5187
Enid (G-3011)		
McMillian Welding LLC	G	918 521-6886
Claremore (G-1653)		
Mefford 4 Welding Inc	G	918 773-6326
Sallisaw (G-8148)		
Merrells Welding & Orna Ir	G	405 321-7733
Norman (G-5073)		
Metal Fab Inc	G	580 762-2421
Ponca City (G-7850)		
MG Welding LLC	G	405 365-6416
Norman (G-5074)		
Midway Machine & Welding LLC	G	918 968-3316
Stroud (G-8812)		
Midwest Welders	G	918 456-5981
Tahlequah (G-8874)		

Employee Codes: A=Over 500 employees, B=251-500
C=101-250, D=51-100, E=20-50, F=10-19, G=1-9

Mike Deeds Welding LLC ....G.... 580 863-2339
Garber (G-3215)
Mike Macdowell Welding ....G.... 405 354-1221
Yukon (G-11754)
Mike S Welding ....G.... 918 381-0273
Tulsa (G-10278)
Mikes Welding ....G.... 918 455-7227
Broken Arrow (G-975)
Mikes Welding Service ....G.... 405 387-3782
Blanchard (G-724)
Milton Donaghey ....G.... 580 332-1551
Ada (G-66)
Mitchell T Widler ....G.... 501 860-3738
Burneyville (G-1217)
Mjs Fence Welding ....G.... 580 320-1620
Ada (G-67)
Mlb Portable Welding LLC ....G.... 918 531-2414
Copan (G-1851)
Morris Welding ....G.... 580 486-3474
Chickasha (G-1490)
Morton Grinding Works ....G.... 918 652-8550
Henryetta (G-3513)
Moss Welding LLC ....G.... 580 216-1605
Vici (G-11246)
Musick Welding LLC ....G.... 405 274-1766
Chickasha (G-1491)
Myers Metalkraft LLC ....G.... 405 657-2084
Edmond (G-2525)
Myers Welding LLC ....G.... 405 277-3202
Luther (G-4136)
Myskey Welding ....G.... 918 371-4906
Collinsville (G-1818)
Nabors Welding & Supplies Inc ....G.... 405 756-8198
Lindsay (G-4075)
Nbs Fabrication ....G.... 918 527-5211
Chouteau (G-1568)
Nipps Welding ....G.... 580 668-2915
Wilson (G-11541)
Norman Koehn ....G.... 580 852-3260
Helena (G-3436)
North Welding and Construction ....G.... 580 526-3260
Erick (G-3090)
Northwest Welding Inc ....G.... 405 621-0201
Warr Acres (G-11325)
O K Plunger Service ....G.... 918 352-4269
Drumright (G-2068)
Oakes Wldg & Fabrication LLC ....G.... 918 865-2356
Mannford (G-4189)
OEM Welding LLC ....G.... 918 645-8483
Sand Springs (G-8211)
Ogdens Welding Service ....G.... 405 380-7649
Seminole (G-8390)
OK Machine and Mfg Co Inc ....E.... 918 838-1300
Tulsa (G-10390)
Okie Newts Welding ....G.... 580 564-4724
Kingston (G-3830)
Oklahoma School of Welding ....G.... 405 672-1841
Del City (G-2004)
Old Town Welding Shop ....G.... 918 423-8506
McAlester (G-4326)
On Site Welding & Fabrication ....G.... 918 706-3339
Broken Arrow (G-1147)
Outwest Welding Services LLC ....G.... 918 593-2345
Strang (G-8803)
P & L Welding and Fabrication ....G.... 660 563-1775
Norman (G-5106)
Page Tool & Machine Shop ....G.... 918 775-6766
Sallisaw (G-8150)
Pak Electric Inc ....F.... 580 482-1757
Altus (G-166)
Palin Welding Service LLC ....G.... 405 449-3541
Wayne (G-11368)
Parkers Welding Custom Work ....G.... 405 341-3344
Edmond (G-2564)
Parsons Welding Inc ....G.... 405 263-7495
Okarche (G-5249)
Patriot Wldg & Fabrication LLC ....G.... 918 600-7147
Broken Arrow (G-999)
Patten Equipment & Welding LLC ....G.... 580 334-7035
Woodward (G-11618)
Paul G Pennington Industries ....G.... 405 392-2317
Blanchard (G-726)
Pearce Quinton Weld ....G.... 918 559-3026
Nowata (G-5226)
Pennington Industries ....G.... 405 392-2317
Newcastle (G-4835)
Perks Welding LLC ....G.... 405 853-6848
Hennessey (G-3479)
Phelps Machine & Fabrication ....F.... 580 662-2465
Ringling (G-8081)
Pioneer Metal & Land Svcs LLC ....G.... 405 612-3575
Glencoe (G-3226)
Pioneer Precision Machine Shop ....F.... 580 233-1670
Enid (G-3036)
Piping Enterprise Company Inc ....B.... 918 246-7326
Sand Springs (G-8214)
Platinum Cross Welding Inc ....G.... 918 623-9130
Okemah (G-5274)
Precision Mfg & Design ....E.... 918 782-2723
Langley (G-3874)
Precision Welding Mfg ....G.... 405 872-3530
Noble (G-4888)
Price Welding and Supply ....G.... 580 668-3057
Lone Grove (G-4119)
Pritchards Welding Service ....G.... 405 514-2360
Ninnekah (G-4873)
Pro Fab Welding Inc ....G.... 405 470-8776
Elk City (G-2862)
Profab Welding Inc ....G.... 580 488-2020
Leedey (G-4030)
R & L Mechanics & Welding ....G.... 918 253-4734
Jay (G-3685)
R & W Machine Shop Inc ....G.... 405 632-4020
Oklahoma City (G-6958)
R A D Welding (2) ....G.... 405 206-9434
Meeker (G-4386)
Rafter H Bar Welding Svc LLC ....G.... 918 210-0175
Coweta (G-1895)
Ram Machine Inc ....G.... 918 224-8028
Tulsa (G-10613)
Rate My Welder ....G.... 405 400-0109
Oklahoma City (G-6973)
Rays Portable Welding ....G.... 405 282-3218
Guthrie (G-3335)
RC Welding & Fab LLC ....G.... 580 216-1274
Oklahoma City (G-6977)
Rcw Welding Services LLC ....G.... 918 852-4775
Broken Arrow (G-1153)
Red Line Welding and Services ....G.... 580 591-3162
Lawton (G-3991)
Redding Welding LLC ....G.... 580 883-4683
Ringwood (G-8091)
Richard Vallejos Welding Ser ....G.... 405 688-0804
Oklahoma City (G-7018)
Richard Welding ....G.... 405 459-6717
Pocasset (G-7778)
Richards Welding Service LLC ....G.... 580 584-2831
Hugo (G-3620)
Rick Leaming Construction LLC ....G.... 580 362-2262
Newkirk (G-4852)
Ricks Welding ....G.... 580 470-8111
Duncan (G-2168)
Rjc Welding LLC ....G.... 580 281-0516
Temple (G-8934)
Robinson Welding LLC ....G.... 580 278-9363
Enid (G-3049)
Robs Welding LLC ....G.... 405 596-4906
Yukon (G-11772)
Rocking C Welding LLC ....G.... 405 589-8903
Yukon (G-11773)
Rocking H Welding LLC ....G.... 918 966-3882
Keota (G-3773)
Rod Wiederstein ....G.... 580 938-2998
Shattuck (G-8424)
Rodney Brooks Welding LLC ....G.... 405 663-2256
Hydro (G-3634)
Roff Iron & Sales Inc ....E.... 580 456-7850
Roff (G-8110)
Roger Magerus ....G.... 405 364-7231
Norman (G-5134)
Rohlman Welding Service Inc ....G.... 405 420-4033
Warr Acres (G-11328)
Rons Welding Shop ....G.... 405 352-4331
Minco (G-4479)
Rotert Weld & Fab LLC ....G.... 918 671-2170
Tulsa (G-10674)
Russells Welding Inc ....G.... 918 245-7395
Tulsa (G-10682)
Rustys Welding & Repair ....G.... 580 526-3611
Erick (G-3092)
S & S Welding LLC ....G.... 405 496-1452
Hinton (G-3536)
S&W Welding and Fabrication ....G.... 918 219-2565
Medford (G-4369)
S-T Magi ....G.... 918 358-2312
Cleveland (G-1733)
Sam S Welding ....G.... 580 470-5725
Comanche (G-1845)
Sandra Crow ....G.... 580 588-2321
Apache (G-222)
Sands Weld and Fab Inc ....G.... 918 419-2222
Tulsa (G-10705)
Sasco Inc ....F.... 405 670-3230
Oklahoma City (G-7085)
SE Oklahoma School of Welding ....G.... 918 423-9353
McAlester (G-4334)
Seiger Welding LLC ....G.... 405 853-7237
Hennessey (G-3484)
Seminole Machine Co ....G.... 405 382-0444
Seminole (G-8399)
Sewells Machine & Welding ....G.... 580 423-7004
Texhoma (G-8939)
SF Welding and Boring LLC ....G.... 405 831-8602
Norman (G-5142)
Shane Bralwey Welding LLC ....G.... 936 201-9072
Oklahoma City (G-7114)
Shockey Welding LLC ....G.... 405 473-1783
Moore (G-4567)
Sigman Welding ....G.... 405 596-3035
Tecumseh (G-8929)
Silhouette Shop ....G.... 918 257-6143
Fairland (G-3129)
Silver ARC Welding Inc ....G.... 580 234-2209
Enid (G-3057)
Slavin Welding Services LLC ....G.... 806 217-0429
Woodward (G-11632)
Smith Welding Co ....G.... 580 335-7521
Frederick (G-3201)
Smith Welding Fabg & Repr ....G.... 918 446-2293
Tulsa (G-10779)
Spencer Machine Works LLC ....G.... 580 332-1551
Ada (G-91)
Stand By Personnel ....G.... 918 582-0522
Tulsa (G-10834)
Standard Machine LLC ....G.... 918 423-9430
McAlester (G-4338)
Stansberry Welding Inc ....G.... 580 621-3211
Freedom (G-3209)
Steel Welding Inc ....G.... 405 789-5713
Oklahoma City (G-7200)
Stephen Burns ....G.... 580 657-3237
Wilson (G-11543)
Stout Welding LLC ....G.... 580 254-2139
Woodward (G-11634)
Stouts Welding LLC ....G.... 580 339-8047
Elk City (G-2878)
Strike An ARC Wldg Fbrction LL ....G.... 918 407-7964
Claremore (G-1688)
Sullivan Welding ....G.... 405 301-6034
Oklahoma City (G-7222)
Summer Couch Welding LLC ....G.... 405 408-3675
Moore (G-4575)
Sundance Welding Inc ....G.... 918 627-4065
Tulsa (G-10872)
Superior Companies Inc ....D.... 918 534-0755
Dewey (G-2033)
Superior Welding ....G.... 918 439-9332
Tulsa (G-10879)
Superior Welding & Fabrication ....G.... 580 641-0634
Rush Springs (G-8126)
Swink Welding LLC ....G.... 405 294-0114
Norman (G-5167)
Szabo Szabi ....G.... 918 697-5441
Muskogee (G-4751)
T J Construction ....G.... 580 494-6500
Broken Bow (G-1209)
T&B Welding LLC ....G.... 918 253-4120
Eucha (G-3096)
Taff Welding LLC ....G.... 580 678-8978
Rush Springs (G-8127)
Teals Welding Inc ....G.... 405 756-0615
Blanchard (G-737)
Ted Branham Welding ....G.... 918 275-4431
Nowata (G-5231)
Texoma Millwright and Wldg Inc ....F.... 580 931-9368
Durant (G-2266)
Thomas Welding ....G.... 918 214-7657
Bartlesville (G-532)
Thomass Welding ....G.... 580 821-0843
Hammon (G-3372)
Thompson Services ....E.... 580 256-5005
Woodward (G-11642)
Tonys Welding ....G.... 405 996-6657
Edmond (G-2650)
Toro Welding Inc ....G.... 580 334-8221
Woodward (G-11643)
Town & Country Welding LLC ....G.... 405 664-5361
Harrah (G-3387)
Triple T Welding ....G.... 918 449-0037
Broken Arrow (G-1173)

PRODUCT SECTION

WIRE & WIRE PRDTS

Troutman Enterprises LLC .... G 405 351-0665
  Rush Springs *(G-8129)*
Trunch Bull Service LLC .... F 580 468-1501
  Guymon *(G-3369)*
Tsb Welding LLC .... G 405 485-4274
  Blanchard *(G-740)*
Tsm Industrial Welding .... G 720 290-4431
  Skiatook *(G-8572)*
Turn & Burn Welding Inc .... G 918 543-7224
  Inola *(G-3675)*
Turnair .... G 918 267-3535
  Sand Springs *(G-8233)*
Turner Welding Inc .... F 405 224-3867
  Amber *(G-197)*
Ty Slemp Dakota .... G 405 933-2078
  Gracemont *(G-3254)*
Universal Welding Service .... G 918 455-3241
  Broken Arrow *(G-1088)*
USA Energy Fabrication LLC .... G 918 445-4792
  Tulsa *(G-9047)*
V5 Contracting LLC .... G 918 720-4675
  Claremore *(G-1699)*
Vann Metal Products Inc .... G 918 341-0469
  Claremore *(G-1701)*
VB Welding LLC .... G 918 695-0258
  Tulsa *(G-11068)*
Verser Welding Service .... G 405 352-5048
  Minco *(G-4482)*
Vision Fabrications LLC .... G 580 304-2444
  Ponca City *(G-7886)*
Vm Welding LLC .... G 405 245-2833
  Oklahoma City *(G-5322)*
Von Troutman Timothy .... G 580 583-7004
  Rush Springs *(G-8130)*
W&W Enterprises .... G 580 434-2736
  Colbert *(G-1787)*
Warren West .... G 580 838-2173
  Hendrix *(G-3441)*
Washingtons Welding LLC .... G 918 336-2111
  Bartlesville *(G-534)*
Washita Wldg & Fabrication LLC .... G 405 779-0140
  Chickasha *(G-1523)*
Wasinger Wasinger .... G 580 335-3490
  Frederick *(G-3203)*
Watonga Machine & Steel Works .... G 580 623-5830
  Watonga *(G-11352)*
Wayne Burt Machine .... G 918 786-4415
  Grove *(G-3293)*
Weatherford Machine Works .... G 580 772-5287
  Weatherford *(G-11457)*
Weeks Welding LLC .... G 918 931-1167
  Enid *(G-3077)*
Weins Machine Co Inc .... F 918 865-2187
  Terlton *(G-8938)*
Welding Industry Services LLC .... G 580 479-7068
  Waukomis *(G-11361)*
Welding Shop .... G 580 832-5545
  Cordell *(G-1864)*
Western Welding .... G 580 832-2985
  Rocky *(G-8106)*
Wheelers Welding LLC .... G 918 246-3811
  Sand Springs *(G-8242)*
Whites Welding .... G 405 942-7070
  Oklahoma City *(G-7447)*
Whorton Welding .... G 405 610-6545
  Choctaw *(G-1557)*
Whorton Welding Inc .... G 405 664-7123
  Oklahoma City *(G-7449)*
Wildcat Welding LLC .... G 405 714-2273
  Morrison *(G-4606)*
Williams Ranch Welding LLC .... G 405 509-0289
  Boley *(G-756)*
Willys Fabricating & Wldg LLC .... G 405 250-1250
  Oklahoma City *(G-7456)*
Wilson Welding Works LLC .... F 580 338-7345
  Guymon *(G-3371)*
Wishon Welding LLC .... G 405 808-4673
  Oklahoma City *(G-7461)*
Wj Welding LLC .... G 580 465-4120
  Marietta *(G-4219)*
Woodall Welding .... G 405 736-0599
  Midwest City *(G-4462)*
Wooten Welding .... G 918 655-6981
  Wister *(G-11551)*
Work Horse Welding LLC .... G 918 530-5270
  Pryor *(G-7999)*
Wrights Machine Shop .... G 580 363-1740
  Blackwell *(G-695)*
Wyers Welding .... G 580 854-6277
  Oklahoma City *(G-7477)*

Xs Welding Company LLC .... G 918 346-2550
  Claremore *(G-1706)*
Yt Welding LLC .... G 580 799-1984
  Elk City *(G-2891)*
Zr Welding LLC .... G 405 602-4164
  Lexington *(G-4041)*

WELDING SPLYS, EXC GASES: Wholesalers

Airgas Usa LLC .... G 405 235-0009
  Oklahoma City *(G-5402)*
Pruitt Company of Ada Inc .... E 580 332-3523
  Ada *(G-78)*

WELDMENTS

Metallic Works Inc .... G 918 527-6477
  Tulsa *(G-10248)*
Steel Creek Manufacturing LLC .... G 918 698-3318
  Tulsa *(G-10843)*

WELL LOGGING EQPT

Step Energy Svcs Holdings Ltd .... E 918 423-4300
  McAlester *(G-4339)*
Step Energy Svcs Holdings Ltd .... G 918 252-5416
  Tulsa *(G-10845)*

WESTERN APPAREL STORES

Bob D Berry DBA .... G 405 382-3360
  Seminole *(G-8360)*
Mock Brothers Saddlery Inc .... G 918 245-7259
  Sand Springs *(G-8205)*

WHEELBARROWS

Staton Inc .... G 405 605-3765
  Oklahoma City *(G-7197)*

WHEELCHAIR LIFTS

Mobility Living Inc .... G 405 672-7237
  Oklahoma City *(G-6623)*

WHEELCHAIRS

Get People Moving LLC .... G 405 529-6033
  Oklahoma City *(G-6149)*
Mobility One Transportation .... G 918 437-4488
  Tulsa *(G-10289)*
National Seating Mobility Inc .... G 918 856-3000
  Oklahoma City *(G-6659)*
National Seating Mobility Inc .... G 405 896-3680
  Oklahoma City *(G-6660)*
Texoma Wheelchairs .... G 855 924-2525
  Durant *(G-2268)*

WHEELS: Current Collector, Trolley Rigging

Crosby US Acquisition Corp .... G 918 834-4611
  Tulsa *(G-9511)*

WHEY: Raw, Liquid

Tpl Arkoma Midstream LLC .... G 918 574-3500
  Tulsa *(G-10962)*

WHISTLES

Bells and Whistles .... G 405 470-8400
  Oklahoma City *(G-5546)*

WIGS & HAIRPIECES

Shes Happy Hair Okc LLC .... G 405 328-3464
  Oklahoma City *(G-7122)*

WINCHES

Dp Manufacturing Inc .... C 918 250-2450
  Jenks *(G-3704)*
Paccar Inc .... G 918 251-8511
  Broken Arrow *(G-996)*
Ramsey Industries Inc .... G 918 438-2760
  Tulsa *(G-10617)*
Ramsey Winch Company .... G 918 438-2760
  Tulsa *(G-10618)*
Tulsa Winch Inc .... G 918 298-8300
  Jenks *(G-3736)*

WINDMILLS: Electric Power Generation

Cpv Keenan Renewable Enrgy LLC .... G 580 698-2278
  Woodward *(G-11573)*

Windrunner Energy Inc .... G 580 841-0404
  Duke *(G-2082)*

WINDMILLS: Farm Type

Just Plant It LLC .... G 405 226-3111
  Macomb *(G-4142)*
Mitchell Ironworks Inc .... G 580 233-7925
  Enid *(G-3014)*

WINDOW & DOOR FRAMES

Consolidated Builders Supply .... E 405 631-3033
  Oklahoma City *(G-5821)*
Spade Leasing Inc .... C 580 653-2171
  Springer *(G-8626)*
Wendell Hicks Construction .... G 918 520-9128
  Nowata *(G-5232)*

WINDOW CLEANING SVCS

Clearco Window Cleaning LLC .... G 580 248-9547
  Lawton *(G-3907)*

WINDOW FRAMES & SASHES: Plastic

Champion Opco LLC .... D 405 708-6858
  Oklahoma City *(G-5738)*

WINDOW FRAMES, MOLDING & TRIM: Vinyl

A&B Home Improvement .... G 918 341-7410
  Claremore *(G-1574)*
Lansing Building Products Inc .... G 405 943-2493
  Oklahoma City *(G-6448)*

WINDSHIELDS: Plastic

Dale Kreimeyer Co .... G 405 789-9499
  Bethany *(G-575)*

WINE & DISTILLED ALCOHOLIC BEVERAGES WHOLESALERS

Boardwalk Distribution Co .... F 918 551-6275
  Tulsa *(G-9313)*

WINE CELLARS, BONDED: Wine, Blended

Sand Hill Vineyards LLC .... G 405 760-1268
  Calumet *(G-1248)*
Trio Di Vino LLC .... F 405 494-1954
  Oklahoma City *(G-7336)*

WIRE

Albright Steel and Wire Co .... G 580 357-3596
  Lawton *(G-3886)*
Hanlock-Causeway Company LLC .... F 918 446-1450
  Tulsa *(G-9009)*
M & R Wire Works Inc .... G 580 795-4290
  Madill *(G-4153)*
Pinpoint Wire Technologies LLC .... G 405 447-6900
  Norman *(G-5116)*

WIRE & CABLE: Aluminum

Reel Power Industrial Inc .... D 405 609-3326
  Oklahoma City *(G-6998)*
Reel Power Wire & Cable Inc .... E 918 584-1000
  Oklahoma City *(G-7000)*

WIRE & WIRE PRDTS

Action Spring Company .... E 918 836-9000
  Tulsa *(G-9097)*
Angel Ornamental Iron Works .... G 918 584-8726
  Tulsa *(G-9191)*
Assocted Wire Rope Fabricators .... G 918 234-7450
  Tulsa *(G-9219)*
Continental Wire Cloth LLC .... G 918 794-0334
  Jenks *(G-3701)*
Cooks Fence & Iron Co Inc .... F 405 681-2301
  Oklahoma City *(G-5827)*
Custom Design By Roberts .... G 918 664-0466
  Tulsa *(G-9528)*
D & M Steel Manufacturing .... G 405 631-5027
  Oklahoma City *(G-5887)*
Dodco of Oklahoma LLC .... G 405 314-1757
  Blanchard *(G-712)*
Eastern Okla Fabrication Inc .... G 918 654-7344
  Cameron *(G-1257)*
Gardner Industries Inc .... F 918 583-0171
  Tulsa *(G-9801)*

Employee Codes: A=Over 500 employees, B=251-500
C=101-250, D=51-100, E=20-50, F=10-19, G=1-9

2020 Oklahoma Directory
of Manufacturers & Processors

WIRE & WIRE PRDTS

Givens Manufacturing Inc .... G 888 302-2774
  Mounds *(G-4616)*
Holloway Wire Rope Svcs Inc .... F 918 582-1807
  Tulsa *(G-9939)*
Kaydawn Manufacturing Co Inc .... G 918 321-5017
  Glenpool *(G-3237)*
KG Fab .... G 405 912-9938
  Moore *(G-4531)*
Liberty Fence Co Inc .... G 918 834-6553
  Tulsa *(G-10156)*
M & R Wire Works Inc .... G 580 795-4290
  Madill *(G-4153)*
Mazzella Co .... G 405 423-6283
  Oklahoma City *(G-6544)*
Oklahoma Post Tension Inc .... F 918 627-6013
  Tulsa *(G-10405)*
Oklahoma Screen Mfg LLC .... G 918 443-6500
  Tulsa *(G-10407)*
P W Manufacturing Company Inc ..... G 918 652-4981
  Henryetta *(G-3514)*
Southwestern Wire Inc .... C 405 447-6900
  Norman *(G-5152)*
Swc .... G 918 251-2679
  Broken Arrow *(G-1068)*
Taylor & Sons Farms Inc .... G 405 222-0751
  Chickasha *(G-1515)*
Titan Fence Company .... G 580 237-3412
  Enid *(G-3065)*
Wire Cloth Manufacturers Inc .... G 918 493-9400
  Tulsa *(G-11141)*
Wizard Industries .... G 918 622-5234
  Tulsa *(G-11143)*

WIRE CLOTH & WOVEN WIRE PRDTS, MADE FROM PURCHASED WIRE

Global Wire Cloth LLC .... E 918 836-7211
  Tulsa *(G-9834)*

WIRE MATERIALS: Steel

Dw-Natnal Stndrd-Stllwater LLC .... C 405 377-5050
  Stillwater *(G-8680)*
General Wire & Supply Co Inc .... E 918 245-5961
  Tulsa *(G-9817)*
Givens Manufacturing Inc .... G 888 302-2774
  Mounds *(G-4616)*
Lewis Manufacturing Co LLC .... G 405 634-5401
  Oklahoma City *(G-6471)*
Nomad Defense LLC .... G 405 808-4325
  Yukon *(G-11760)*
Screen Tech Intl Ltd Co .... F 918 234-0010
  Broken Arrow *(G-1161)*
U and S Wire Rope .... G 580 421-1077
  Shawnee *(G-8514)*

WIRE PRDTS: Steel & Iron

Straits Steel and Wire LLC .... G 231 843-3416
  Tulsa *(G-10858)*
Wire Twisters Inc .... G 405 376-0052
  Mustang *(G-4802)*

WOMEN'S & CHILDREN'S CLOTHING WHOLESALERS, NEC

Emery Bay Corporation .... G 918 494-2988
  Tulsa *(G-9671)*
Esb Sales Inc .... G 918 227-0378
  Sapulpa *(G-8270)*
Rainbow Spreme Assmbly I O R G ... G 918 423-1328
  McAlester *(G-4331)*
Sherri Burch .... G 405 720-9021
  Oklahoma City *(G-7121)*
Speedys TS & More LLC .... G 580 748-0067
  Alva *(G-192)*

WOMEN'S & GIRLS' SPORTSWEAR WHOLESALERS

Ajs Tees Inc .... G 918 455-6751
  Broken Arrow *(G-821)*
Apothem .... G 405 447-2345
  Norman *(G-4912)*
Hendrie Resources Ltd .... G 405 948-4459
  Oklahoma City *(G-6239)*
Paul Ziert & Associates Inc .... D 405 364-5344
  Norman *(G-5112)*
Play 2 Win Athletics .... G 918 341-9500
  Claremore *(G-1671)*

WOMEN'S CLOTHING STORES

Artistic Apparel .... G 918 338-0038
  Bartlesville *(G-449)*
Monroe Gray LLC .... G 918 813-6588
  Bixby *(G-646)*
Tumbleweed Creek Cottage .... G 580 242-2767
  Enid *(G-3068)*

WOMEN'S CLOTHING STORES: Ready-To-Wear

Accessories-To-Go .... G 580 467-7408
  Comanche *(G-1833)*
Corporate Image Apparel LLC .... G 405 659-8264
  Oklahoma City *(G-5839)*
Kathys Kloset Inc .... G 405 524-9447
  Oklahoma City *(G-6401)*
Oliver & Olivia Apparel .... E 405 300-8906
  Edmond *(G-2556)*

WOOD CARVINGS, WHOLESALE

Allens Woodcraft .... G 918 224-8796
  Sapulpa *(G-8247)*

WOOD CHIPS, PRODUCED AT THE MILL

Chips Valiant Inc .... F 580 933-5323
  Valliant *(G-11222)*

WOOD PRDTS

Bell Timber Inc .... G 580 584-6902
  Broken Bow *(G-1185)*
Bristow 800 Kelly LLC .... G 248 268-3289
  Bristow *(G-768)*
Clubbs Wood Art .... G 918 569-4401
  Clayton *(G-1708)*
Country Crafts .... G 918 247-6144
  Kellyville *(G-3763)*
Custom WD Fbers Cdar Mulch LLC .. G 405 745-2270
  Oklahoma City *(G-5879)*
Dovetail Enterprises LLC .... G 405 476-3953
  Bethany *(G-576)*
From Heart .... G 405 348-3009
  Edmond *(G-2425)*
Integrity Woodcrafters LLC .... G 918 664-1041
  Tulsa *(G-10000)*
Mjs Crafts .... G 405 598-8105
  Tecumseh *(G-8923)*
Okiewood LLC .... G 405 245-5257
  Oklahoma City *(G-6732)*
PEL Company LLC .... G 405 816-6553
  Oklahoma City *(G-6821)*
Rick Woodten .... G 580 786-5050
  Duncan *(G-2167)*
Smallwood Building LLC .... G 918 424-9378
  McAlester *(G-4336)*
Straight Edge Sawmill .... G 405 401-7798
  Union City *(G-11221)*
Waterwood Parkway LLC .... G 405 341-5077
  Edmond *(G-2682)*
Wynnewood 1500 LLC .... G 248 268-3289
  Wynnewood *(G-11675)*
Wynnewood LLC .... G 248 268-3289
  Wynnewood *(G-11676)*

WOOD PRDTS: Applicators

Woodshed .... E 918 256-9868
  Vinita *(G-11272)*

WOOD PRDTS: Baskets, Fruit & Veg, Round Stave, Till, Etc

Midtown Ventures LLC .... A 918 728-3102
  Tulsa *(G-10265)*

WOOD PRDTS: Flagpoles

American International Ltd .... G 405 364-1776
  Norman *(G-4907)*

WOOD PRDTS: Knobs

Multiples Inc .... G 918 584-7982
  Tulsa *(G-10314)*

WOOD PRDTS: Laundry

Wooden Concepts LLC .... G 405 459-0411
  Weatherford *(G-11461)*

WOOD PRDTS: Moldings, Unfinished & Prefinished

H3 Custom Wood Moldings LLC .... G 918 250-8746
  Tulsa *(G-9879)*
S&S Custom Wood Moldings LLC .... F 214 995-8710
  Bixby *(G-657)*
Wood Systems Inc .... D 918 388-0900
  Tulsa *(G-11148)*
Zara Group Inc .... F 918 782-4473
  Vinita *(G-11273)*

WOOD PRDTS: Panel Work

Fullerton Building Systems Inc .... E 918 246-9995
  Sand Springs *(G-8187)*

WOOD PRDTS: Porch Columns

A R T T Corp .... G 405 681-0749
  Oklahoma City *(G-5348)*

WOOD PRDTS: Porch Work

Winkles Woodworks Ltd .... F 918 486-5022
  Coweta *(G-1902)*

WOOD PRDTS: Saddle Trees

Baties Custom Saddle Tree .... F 918 788-3686
  Welch *(G-11462)*

WOOD PRDTS: Signboards

AS Designs LLC .... G 918 381-2390
  Owasso *(G-7546)*
Marrara Group Inc .... G 918 379-0993
  Tulsa *(G-10216)*

WOOD PRDTS: Trophy Bases

Edmond Trophy Co .... G 405 341-4631
  Edmond *(G-2405)*
K & K Wood Products .... G 918 396-4004
  Skiatook *(G-8553)*
Mtm Recognition Corporation .... B 405 609-6900
  Oklahoma City *(G-6634)*
Rabid .... G 580 234-3632
  Enid *(G-3041)*

WOOD PRODUCTS: Reconstituted

Huber Engineered Woods LLC .... E 580 584-7000
  Broken Bow *(G-1192)*

WOOD SHAVINGS BALES, MULCH TYPE, WHOLESALE

Duncan Wood Works LLC .... G 580 641-1190
  Duncan *(G-2113)*

WOOD TREATING: Structural Lumber & Timber

Cowans Millwork Inc .... G 918 357-3725
  Broken Arrow *(G-1118)*

WOODWORK: Carved & Turned

Allens Woodcraft .... G 918 224-8796
  Sapulpa *(G-8247)*
Yester Year Carousel .... G 405 427-5863
  Oklahoma City *(G-7479)*

WOODWORK: Interior & Ornamental, NEC

Bales Custom Woodwork Inc .... G 918 277-6612
  Beggs *(G-549)*
Cheyenne Woodworks Inc .... G 918 587-3533
  Tulsa *(G-9418)*
Rccs Woodworking LLC .... G 405 694-9680
  Edmond *(G-2587)*

WOODWORK: Ornamental, Cornices, Mantels, Etc.

Elk Valley Woodworking Inc .... G 580 486-3337
  Carter *(G-1281)*
Mike Pung .... G 405 736-6282
  Oklahoma City *(G-6607)*

PRODUCT SECTION

WOVEN WIRE PRDTS, NEC

Unarco Industries LLC .... C 918 485-9531
Wagoner *(G-11295)*

WREATHS: Artificial

Deborah C Montgomery .... G 918 527-9375
Collinsville *(G-1809)*
Hail To Wreath .... G 405 659-2216
Mustang *(G-4775)*
Red Dirt Wreaths & Things .... G 918 809-3973
Oklahoma City *(G-6984)*

Rock Creek Wreaths LLC .... G 405 701-3421
Norman *(G-5133)*
Shawn Wreath .... G 580 571-2598
Sharon *(G-8419)*
Trend To Trend Wreaths .... G 405 503-8992
Blanchard *(G-738)*
Uncommon Touch .... G 580 276-9936
Marietta *(G-4217)*

X-RAY EQPT & TUBES

Desert Industrial X Ray LP .... G 918 650-0018
Henryetta *(G-3504)*

H & H Xray .... G 918 752-0966
Okmulgee *(G-7508)*
South Manufacturing Inc .... G 918 894-5255
Bixby *(G-662)*
Western X-Ray .... E 580 922-3166
Seiling *(G-8352)*
Xit Systems Inc .... G 918 259-9071
Broken Arrow *(G-1103)*

YARN: Embroidery, Spun

Gorfam Marketing Inc .... G 918 252-3733
Tulsa *(G-9841)*